P9-CMF-402

READERS' GUIDE TO PERIODICAL LITERATURE

1987

An Author and Subject Index

Edited by
JEAN M. MARRA

Associate Editor
ROSEMARY STRAMMIELLO

Associate Editor for Production
CYNTHIA PITTSON

Indexers
ANN F. DIETZ
PETER L. DURHAM
OWEN JONES

THE H. W. WILSON COMPANY
NEW YORK   1988

Copyright © 1987, 1988 by The H. W. Wilson Company. All rights reserved. No part of this work may be reproduced or copied in any form or by any means, including but not restricted to graphic, electronic, or mechanical—for example, photocopying, recording, taping, or information storage and retrieval systems—without the express written permission of the Publisher.

International Standard Serial Number 0034-0464

Library of Congress Catalog Card Number 6-8232

PRINTED IN THE UNITED STATES OF AMERICA

ACKNOWLEDGEMENTS

In addition to the staff members whose names appear on the title page, we wish to acknowledge the contributions of Barbara Bristow, Bernie Bayless, and Nina C. Roshon who indexed for this volume.

J.M.

PREFATORY NOTE

The *READERS' GUIDE TO PERIODICAL LITERATURE* is a cumulative author subject index to periodicals of general interest published in the United States.

The main body of the Index consists of subject and author entries to periodical articles arranged in one alphabet. In addition there is a listing of citations to book reviews following the main body of the Index.

The Committee on Wilson Indexes of the American Library Association's Reference and Adult Services Division advises the publisher on indexing and editorial policy by means of in-depth contents studies conducted at intervals of several years.

While the responsibility for all indexing and editorial decisions rests with The H. W. Wilson Company, every effort is made by the Company to follow the recommendations of the Committee and the subscribers to a given periodical index.

Suggestions for addition or deletion of titles should be brought to the attention of The H. W. Wilson Company, 950 University Avenue, Bronx, N.Y. 10452.

This volume includes indexing for periodicals dated January 1, 1987 through December 31, 1987. It supersedes the paper issues of Readers' Guide for March 10, 1987 (Vol. 87 No. 1) through February 1988 (Vol. 87 No. 18).

SUGGESTIONS FOR THE USE OF THE READERS' GUIDE TO PERIODICAL LITERATURE

Arrangement

Authors and subjects are arranged in one alphabet. Under authors and subjects, titles are also arranged in alphabetical order by the first word, initial articles being disregarded. Under personal names titles *by* an author precede those *about* him. Subdivisions of a subject are arranged alphabetically under the subject. Geographical subheads follow the other subdivisions in a separate alphabet.

Author Entries

Articles are indexed under the last name of the author, with the exception that author entries may be omitted for staff writers. The author's name always appears as part of the citation under the subject entry.

Ballet Reviews

Ballet reviews are indexed under the heading "Ballet reviews—Single works" with a *see* reference from the title of the work. Reviews are also indexed under the name of the choreographer.

Book Reviews

For citations to reviews of individual books, see book review section following the main body of the Index.

Cross-References

See references are made from variant forms of subject headings and personal names to the form used in READERS' GUIDE.
See also references are made from a subject to related subjects under which additional material may be found.

Dance Reviews

Modern dance reviews are indexed under the heading "Dance reviews—Single works" with a *see* reference from the title of the work. Reviews are also indexed under the name of the choreographer.

Fiction

Fiction is indexed under the author's name; titles are listed under the headings "Fiction—Single works" and "Science fiction— Single works" with a *see* reference to the author's name.

Motion Picture Reviews

Motion picture reviews are indexed under the heading "Motion picture reviews—Single works" with a *see* reference from the title of the film. Reviews are also indexed under the name of the director.

Musicals, Revues, etc.

Musicals, revues, etc. are indexed under the heading "Musicals, revues, etc.—Reviews—Single works" with a *see* reference from the title of the work.

Opera and Operetta Reviews

Opera and Operetta reviews are indexed under the composer's name with a *see* reference from the title of the opera or operetta; titles are also listed under the headings "Opera reviews—Single works" or "Operetta reviews—Single works."

Phonograph Records

Phonograph record reviews are indexed under the heading "Phonograph records." No title references are made.

Poems

Poems are indexed under the author's name; titles are listed under the headings "Poems—Single works" and "Christmas poems—Single works" with a *see* reference to the author's name.

Radio Program Reviews

Radio program reviews are indexed under the heading "Radio program reviews—Single works" with a *see* reference from the title of the program.

Short Stories

Short stories are indexed under the author's name; titles are listed under the headings "Short stories;" "Children's stories—Single works;" "Christmas stories—Single works;" and "Detective and mystery stories—Single works" with a *see* reference to the author's name.

Television Program Reviews

Television program reviews are indexed under the heading "Television program reviews—Single works" with a *see* reference from the title of the program.

Theater Reviews

Theater reviews are indexed under the dramatist's name with a *see* reference from the title of the work; titles are also listed under the heading "Theater reviews—Single works."

Videodisc and Videotape Reviews

Videodisc and Videotape reviews are indexed under the headings "Videodisc reviews—Single works" and "Videotape reviews—Single works." No title references are made.

For those unfamiliar with forms of reference used in the entries, the following explanation is given.

Sample subject entry:	**Horse racing** A woman of substance [jockey J. Krone] G. Maranto. il pors *Sports Illus* 67:62+ Ag 24 '87
Explanation:	An article on the subject **Horse racing** entitled "A woman of substance," by Gina Maranto, will be found, with illustrations, in the periodical *Sports Illustrated*, volume 67, page 62 (continued on later pages of the same issue) in the August 24, 1987 issue. A title enhancement, "jockey J. Krone," has been added by the indexer to clarify the meaning of the title. Square brackets are used to indicate these editorial interpolations.
Sample name entry:	**Meese, Edwin, III** The law of the Constitution. il *Natl Rev* 39:30-3 Jl 17 '87 *about* The resilient loyalist. E. Shannon. il por *Time* 130:15 Ag 3 '87
Explanation:	An article *by* Edwin Meese will be found in *National Review*, volume 39, pages 30-33, in the July 17, 1987 issue. An article *about* Edwin Meese by Elaine Shannon will be found in *Time*, volume 130, page 15, in the August 3, 1987 issue.

ABBREVIATIONS OF PERIODICALS INDEXED

For full information consult the list of Periodicals Indexed

*50 Plus — 50 Plus

A

Aging — Aging
Am Artist — American Artist
Am Craft — American Craft
*Am Herit — American Heritage
Am Hist Illus — American History Illustrated
Am Sch — The American Scholar
America — America
Americana — Americana
Américas — Américas
Antiques — Antiques
Antiques Collect Hobbies — Antiques & Collecting Hobbies
Archit Dig — Architectural Digest
Archit Rec — Architectural Record
Art Am — Art in America
Art News — Art News
Astronomy — Astronomy
*Atlantic — The Atlantic
Audubon — Audubon
Aviat Week Space Technol — Aviation Week & Space Technology

B

*Better Homes Gard — Better Homes and Gardens
BioScience — BioScience
Black Enterp — Black Enterprise
Bull At Sci — The Bulletin of the Atomic Scientists
Bus Week — Business Week
Byte — Byte

C

Car Driv — Car and Driver
Cent Mag — The Center Magazine
Change — Change
*Changing Times — Changing Times
Channels — Channels (New York, N.Y.: 1986)
Child Today — Children Today
Christ Century — The Christian Century
Christ Today — Christianity Today
Commentary — Commentary
Commonweal — Commonweal
Congr Dig — Congressional Digest
Conservationist — The Conservationist
*Consum Rep — Consumer Reports
*Consum Res Mag — Consumers' Research Magazine
*Courier — The Courier (Unesco)
Ctry J — Country Journal
Curr Health 2 — Current Health 2
Curr Hist — Current History
Current — Current (Washington, D.C.)
Cycle — Cycle

D

Dance Mag — Dance Magazine
Dep State Bull — Department of State Bulletin
Des Arts Educ — Design for Arts in Education
Discover — Discover
Down Beat — Down Beat

E

Earth Sci — Earth Science
*Ebony — Ebony
Educ Dig — The Education Digest
Environment — Environment
Esquire — Esquire
Essence — Essence

F

Fam Handyman — The Family Handyman
FDA Consum — FDA Consumer
Field Stream — Field & Stream
Film Comment — Film Comment
Flower Gard — Flower and Garden
Flying — Flying
Focus — Focus (New York, N.Y.: 1950)
Forbes — Forbes
*Foreign Aff — Foreign Affairs
Foreign Policy — Foreign Policy
*Fortune — Fortune
Futurist — The Futurist

G

Glamour — Glamour
*Good Housekeep — Good Housekeeping
Gourmet — Gourmet

H

*Harpers — Harper's
Harpers Bazaar — Harper's Bazaar
*Health — Health (New York, N.Y.)
*High Fidel — High Fidelity (New York, N.Y.)
Hist Today — History Today
Hobbies — Hobbies
Home Mech — Home Mechanix
*Horizon — Horizon (Tuscaloosa, Ala.)
House Gard — House & Garden
Humanist — The Humanist

I

Int Wildl — International Wildlife

J

Jet — Jet

L

*Ladies Home J — Ladies' Home Journal
Life — Life

M

Macleans — Maclean's
Mademoiselle — Mademoiselle
McCalls — McCall's
Mon Labor Rev — Monthly Labor Review
*Money — Money
Mot Boat Sail — Motor Boating & Sailing
Mot Trend — Motor Trend
Mother Earth News — The Mother Earth News
Ms — Ms.

N

N Y — New York
N Y Rev Books — The New York Review of Books
N Y Times Book Rev — The New York Times Book Review
N Y Times Mag — The New York Times Magazine
*Nat Hist — Natural History
*Nation — The Nation
Nations Bus — Nation's Business
*Natl Geogr — National Geographic
*Natl Geogr World — National Geographic World
Natl Parks — National Parks
*Natl Rev — National Review
Natl Wildl — National Wildlife

New Leader — The New Leader
New Repub — The New Republic
New Yorker — The New Yorker
Newsweek — Newsweek

O

Oceans — Oceans
Omni — Omni (New York, N.Y.)
Opera News — Opera News
*Outdoor Life — Outdoor Life

P

Parents — Parents
People Wkly — People Weekly
Pers Comput — Personal Computing
Petersens Photogr Mag — Petersen's Photographic
    Magazine
Phi Delta Kappan — Phi Delta Kappan
Phys Today — Physics Today
*Pop Mech — Popular Mechanics
Pop Photogr — Popular Photography
Pop Sci — Popular Science
*Prevention — Prevention (Emmaus, Pa.)
Progressive — The Progressive
*Psychol Today — Psychology Today
Publ Wkly — Publishers Weekly

R

Radio-Electron — Radio-Electronics
*Read Dig — Reader's Digest
Redbook — Redbook
Road Track — Road & Track
Rodale's Org Gard — Rodale's Organic Gardening
Roll Stone — Rolling Stone

S

Saturday Evening Post — The Saturday Evening Post
Saturday Rev — Saturday Review
Sch Update — Scholastic Update (Teachers' edition)
*Sci Am — Scientific American
Sci News — Science News
Science — Science

Sea Front — Sea Frontiers
*Seventeen — Seventeen
Sierra — Sierra
Skiing — Skiing
Sky Telesc — Sky and Telescope
Smithsonian — Smithsonian
Society — Society
South Living — Southern Living
Space World — Space World
Sport Mag — Sport Magazine
*Sports Illus — Sports Illustrated
Stereo Rev — Stereo Review
Success Farm — Successful Farming
Sunset — Sunset (Central edition)

T

Technol Rev — Technology Review
Teen — 'Teen
Theatre Crafts — Theatre Crafts
Time — Time
*Travel Holiday — Travel Holiday

U

U S Cathol — U.S. Catholic
*U S News World Rep — U.S. News & World Report
UN Chron — UN Chronicle
USA Today (Periodical) — USA Today (Periodical)

V

Vital Speeches Day — Vital Speeches of the Day
Vogue — Vogue

W

Wash Mon — The Washington Monthly
Weatherwise — Weatherwise
Wilderness — Wilderness
Women's Sports Fitness — Women's Sports & Fitness
Work Woman — Working Woman
Workbench — Workbench
World Health — World Health
World Press Rev — World Press Review
World Tennis — World Tennis
*Writer — The Writer

* Available for the blind and other physically handicapped readers on talking books or in braille. For information address National Library Service for the Blind and Physically Handicapped, Library of Congress, Washington, D.C. 20542

PERIODICALS INDEXED

All data as of latest issue received

*50 Plus. $15. m (ISSN 0163-2027) 50 Plus, 99 Garden St., Marion, OH 43302

A

Aging. $5. q (ISSN 0002-0966) Superintendent of Documents, U.S. Government Printing Office, Washington, DC 20402

America. $28. w (except first Saturday of the year, and alternate Saturdays in Jl and Ag) (ISSN 0002-7049) America Press Inc., 106 W. 56th St., New York, NY 10019

American Artist. $22. m (ISSN 0002-7375) American Artist, 1 Color Court, Marion, OH 43305

American Craft. $40. bi-m (ISSN 0194-8008) Membership Dept., American Craft Council, P.O. Box 1308-CL, Fort Lee, NJ 07024

*American Heritage. $24. 8 times a yr (ISSN 0002-8738) American Heritage Subscription Dept., Forbes Building, 60 Fifth Ave., New York, NY 10011

American History Illustrated. $18. m (except Jl, Ag) (ISSN 0002-8770) American History Illustrated, Box 8200, Harrisburg, PA 17105

The American Scholar. $18. q (ISSN 0003-0937) The American Scholar, Editorial and Circulation Offices, 1811 Q St., N.W., Washington, DC 20009

Americana. $11.90. bi-m (ISSN 0090-9114) Americana Subscription Office, 205 W. Center St., Marion, OH 43302

Américas. $15. bi-m (ISSN 0379-0940) Américas Subscription Service, P.O. Box 973, Farmingdale, NY 11737

Antiques. $38. m (ISSN 0161-9284) The Magazine Antiques, Old Mill Rd., P.O. Box 1975, Marion, OH 43306

Antiques & Collecting Hobbies. $18.50. m (ISSN 0884-6294) Antiques & Collecting Hobbies, Circulation Dept., 1006 S. Michigan Ave., Chicago, IL 60605
  Formerly Hobbies; name changed with March 1985

Architectural Digest. $39.95. m (ISSN 0003-8520) Architectural Digest, P.O. Box 10040, Des Moines, IA 50350

Architectural Record. $39. m (semi-m Ap, S) (ISSN 0003-858X) Architectural Record, P.O. Box 2025, Mahopac, NY 10541

Art in America. $39.95. m (ISSN 0004-3214) Art in America, 542 Pacific Ave., Marion, OH 43306

Art News. $29.95. m (q Je-Ag) (ISSN 0004-3273) Art News, Subscription Service, P.O. Box 969, Farmingdale, NY 11737

Astronomy. $21. m (ISSN 0091-6358) Astronomy, 1027 N. Seventh St., Milwaukee, WI 53233

*The Atlantic. $9.95. m (ISSN 0276-9077) Atlantic Subscription Processing Center, Box 2547, Boulder, CO 80322

Audubon. $16. bi-m (ISSN 0097-7136) National Audubon Society, Membership Data Center, P.O. Box 51000, Boulder, CO 80321-1000

Aviation Week & Space Technology. $70. w (ISSN 0005-2175) Aviation Week & Space Technology, P.O. Box 1505, Neptune, NJ 07754

B

*Better Homes and Gardens. $14. m (ISSN 0006-0151) Better Homes and Gardens, P.O. Box 4536, Des Moines, IA 50336

BioScience. $84. m (bi-m Jl, Ag) (ISSN 0006-3568) BioScience Circulation, AIBS, 730 11th St. N.W., Washington, DC 20001-4584

Black Enterprise. $15. m (ISSN 0006-4165) Black Enterprise, Circulation Service Center, P.O. Box 3009, Harlan, IA 51537

The Bulletin of the Atomic Scientists. $29.50. m (except F, Ag) (ISSN 0096-3402) Bulletin of the Atomic Scientists, Circulation Dept., 6042 S. Kimbark Ave., Chicago, IL 60637

Business Week. $39.95. w (except 1 issue in Ja) (ISSN 0007-7135) Business Week, P.O. Box 430, Hightstown, NJ 08520

Byte. $22. m (except 2 issues in Je and O) (ISSN 0360-5280) Byte Subscriber Service, P.O. Box 7643, Teaneck, NJ 07666-9866

C

Car and Driver. $16.98. m (ISSN 0008-6002) Car and Driver, P.O. Box 2770, Boulder, CO 80302

The Center Magazine. $25. bi-m (ISSN 0008-9125) Center Magazine, Box 4068, Santa Barbara, CA 93103

Change. $40. bi-m (ISSN 0009-1383) Heldref Publications, 4000 Albemarle St., N.W., Washington, DC 20016

*Changing Times. $15. m (ISSN 0009-143X) Changing Times, The Kiplinger Magazine, Editors Park, MD 20782

Channels (New York, N.Y.: 1986). $65. m (bi-m Jl/Ag) (ISSN 0276-1572) Channels, Subscription Service Dept., Box 2001, Mahopac, NY 10541
  Formerly Channels of Communications; name changed with September 1986

Children Today. $16. bi-m (ISSN 0361-4336) Superintendent of Documents, U.S. Government Printing Office, Washington, DC 20402

The Christian Century. $28. w (occasional bi-w issues) (ISSN 0009-5281) Christian Century, Subscription Service Dept., 5615 W. Cermak Rd., Cicero, IL 60650

Christianity Today. $24.95. semi-m (m Ja, My, Je, Jl, Ag, D) (ISSN 0009-5753) Christianity Today Subscription Services, 465 Gundersen Dr., Carol Stream, IL 60188

Commentary. $36. m (ISSN 0010-2601) American Jewish Committee, 165 E. 56th St., New York, NY 10022

Commonweal. $28. bi-w (m Christmas-New Year's and Jl, Ag) (ISSN 0010-3330) Commonweal Foundation, 15 Dutch St., New York, NY 10038

Congressional Digest. $24. m (bi-m Je-Jl, Ag-S) (ISSN 0010-5899) Congressional Digest Corp., 3231 P St., N.W., Washington, DC 20007

The Conservationist. $5. bi-m (ISSN 0010-650X) Conservationist Circulation Office, P.O. Box 1500, Latham, NY 12110

*Consumer Reports. $18. m (ISSN 0010-7174) Subscription Director, Consumer Reports, P.O. Box 53029, Boulder, CO 80322

*Consumers' Research Magazine. $18. m (ISSN 0095-2222) Circulation Dept., Consumers' Research Magazine, P.O. Box 642, Holmes, PA 19043

Country Journal. $16.95. m (ISSN 0094-0526) Country Journal, P.O. Box 392, Mt. Morris, IL 61054
  Formerly Blair & Ketchum's Country Journal; name changed with October 1986

*The Courier (Unesco). $7.55 (9 French francs). m (ISSN 0041-5278) Bernan Associates, Unipub, Periodicals Dept., 10033-F King Highway, Lanham, MD 20706

Current Health 2. $5.25. m (S-My) (ISSN 0163-156X) General Learning Corporation, 60 Revere Rd., Northbrook, IL 60062

Current History. $27. m (except Je, Jl, Ag) (ISSN 0011-3530) Current History, 4225 Main St., Philadelphia, PA 19127

Current (Washington, D.C.). $37. m (bi-m Mr-Ap, Jl-Ag) (ISSN 0011-3131) Current, 4000 Albemarle St., N.W., Washington, DC 20016

Cycle. $15.94. m (ISSN 0574-8135) Cycle Circulation Dept., P.O. Box 2776, Boulder, CO 80302

D

Dance Magazine. $23.95. m (ISSN 0011-6009) Dance Magazine, P.O. Box 960, Farmingdale, NY 11737

Department of State Bulletin. $25. m (ISSN 0041-7610) Superintendent of Documents, U.S. Government Printing Office, Washington, DC 20402

Design for Arts in Education. $35. 6 times a yr (ISSN 0011-9253) Design for Arts in Education, 4000 Albemarle St., N.W., Washington, DC 20016

Discover. $27. m (ISSN 0274-7529) Time Inc., Time & Life Building, Rockefeller Center, New York, NY 10020-1393

Down Beat. $18. m (ISSN 0012-5768) Down Beat, 222 W. Adams St., Chicago, IL 60606

E

Earth Science. $10. q (ISSN 0012-8228) Earth Science, 4220 King St., Alexandria, VA 22302

*****Ebony.** $16. m (ISSN 0012-9011) Ebony, 820 S. Michigan Ave., Chicago, IL 60605

The Education Digest. $21. m (S-My) (ISSN 0013-127X) Prakken Publications, Inc., 416 Longshore Dr., P.O. Box 8623, Ann Arbor, MI 48107

Environment. $43. m (bi-m Ja-F, Jl-Ag) (ISSN 0013-9157) Environment, 4000 Albemarle St., N.W., Washington, DC 20016

Esquire. $17.94. m (ISSN 0194-9535) Esquire Subscriptions, 1225 Portland Pl., Boulder, CO 80323

Essence. $12. m (ISSN 0014-0880) Essence, P.O. Box 53400, Boulder, CO 80322

F

The Family Handyman. $11.97. m (bi-m My-Je, Jl-Ag) (ISSN 0014-7230) Family Handyman, Subscriber Service Dept., 52 Woodhaven Rd., Marion, OH 43302

FDA Consumer. $9.50. m (bi-m Jl-Ag, D-Ja) (ISSN 0362-1332) Superintendent of Documents, U.S. Government Printing Office, Washington, DC 20402

Field & Stream. $15.94. m (ISSN 0015-0673) Field & Stream, P.O. Box 2822, Boulder, CO 80302

Film Comment. $14.95. bi-m (ISSN 0015-120X) Film Comment, 140 W. 65th St., New York, NY 10023

Flower and Garden. $8. bi-m (ISSN 0162-3249) Circulation Dept., Flower and Garden Magazine, 4251 Pennsylvania Ave., Kansas City, MO 64111

Flying. $18.98. m (ISSN 0015-4806) Flying, Circulation Dept., P.O. Box 2772, Boulder, CO 80302

Focus (New York, N.Y.: 1950). $10. q (ISSN 0015-5004) Focus/AGS, Suite 600, 156 Fifth Ave., New York, NY 10010

Forbes. $45. bi-w (except w 2 weeks in Ap and 2 weeks in O) (ISSN 0015-6914) Forbes Subscription Service, 60 Fifth Ave., New York, NY 10011

*****Foreign Affairs.** $28. 5 times a yr (ISSN 0015-7120) Foreign Affairs, P.O. Box 2615, Boulder, CO 80322

Foreign Policy. $21. q (ISSN 0015-7228) Foreign Policy Association, 729 Seventh Ave., New York, NY 10019

*****Fortune.** $47.97. bi-w (3 issues in O) (ISSN 0015-8259) Fortune, P.O. Box 30604, Tampa, FL 33630-0604

The Futurist. $30. bi-m (ISSN 0016-3317) World Future Society Headquarters, 4916 St. Elmo Ave., Bethesda, MD 20814

G

Glamour. $15. m (ISSN 0017-0747) Glamour, Box 5203, Boulder, CO 80322

*****Good Housekeeping.** $15.97. m (ISSN 0017-209X) Good Housekeeping, P.O. Box 10055, Des Moines, IA 50350

Gourmet. $18. m (ISSN 0017-2553) Gourmet, P.O. Box 2980, Boulder, CO 80302

H

*****Harper's.** $18. m (ISSN 0017-789X) Harper's Magazine, P.O. Box 1937, Marion, OH 43305

Harper's Bazaar. $16.97. m (ISSN 0017-7873) Harper's Bazaar, P.O. Box 10055, Des Moines, IA 50350

*****Health (New York, N.Y.).** $22. m (ISSN 0014-7249) Health Subscription Dept., P.O. Box 6030, Palm Coast, FL 32037-6030

*****High Fidelity (New York, N.Y.).** $13.95. m (ISSN 0018-1455) High Fidelity, P.O. Box 10759, Des Moines, IA 50340

History Today. $42. m (ISSN 0018-2753) Expeditors of the Printed Word, Ltd., 527 Madison Ave., New York, NY 10022

Hobbies. $18.50. m (ISSN 0018-2907) Hobbies, Circulation Dept., 1006 S. Michigan Ave., Chicago, IL 60605
    Name changed to Antiques & Collecting Hobbies with March 1985

Holiday. See Travel Holiday

Home Mechanix. $13.94. m (ISSN 8755-0423) Home Mechanix, Subscription Dept., P.O. Box 2830, Boulder, CO 80322

*****Horizon (Tuscaloosa, Ala.).** $21.95. m (bi-m Ja-F, Jl-Ag) (ISSN 0018-4977) Horizon Subscription Service, P.O. Box 37104, Washington, DC 20013

House & Garden. $24. m (ISSN 0018-6406) House & Garden, Box 5202, Boulder, CO 80322

The Humanist. $18. bi-m (ISSN 0018-7399) Humanist, 7 Harwood Dr., Amherst, NY 14226

I

International Wildlife. $15. bi-m (ISSN 0020-9112) National Wildlife Membership Services, 8925 Leesburg Pike, Vienna, VA 22184

J

Jet. $36. w (ISSN 0021-5996) Johnson Publishing Co. Inc., 820 S. Michigan Ave., Chicago, IL 60605

L

*****Ladies' Home Journal.** $19.95. m (ISSN 0023-7124) Ladies' Home Journal, P.O. Box 10895, Des Moines, IA 50336-0895

Life. $32.50. m (ISSN 0024-3019) Time Inc., Time & Life Building, Rockefeller Center, New York, NY 10020-1393

M

Maclean's. $60.50. w (ISSN 0024-9262) Subscription Dept., Maclean's, P.O. Box 1600, Postal Station A, Toronto, Ont. M5W 2B8, Canada

Mademoiselle. $15. m (ISSN 0024-9394) Mademoiselle, Box 5204, Boulder, CO 80322

The Magazine Antiques. See Antiques

McCall's. $12.95. m (ISSN 0024-8908) McCall's Customer Relations Manager, Box 56093, Boulder, CO 80322

*****Money.** $31.95. 13 times a yr (ISSN 0149-4953) Money, P.O. Box 54429, Boulder, CO 80322

Monthly Labor Review. $16. m (ISSN 0098-0818) Superintendent of Documents, U.S. Government Printing Office, Washington, DC 20402

The Mother Earth News. $18. bi-m (ISSN 0027-1535) Mother Earth News Subscription Office, P.O. Box 3015, Harlan, IA 51593-4255

Motor Boating & Sailing. $15.97. m (ISSN 0027-1799) Motor Boating & Sailing, P.O. Box 10075, Des Moines, IA 50350

Motor Trend. $18.94. m (ISSN 0027-2094) Petersen Publishing Co., 8490 Sunset Blvd., Los Angeles, CA 90069

Ms. $16. m (ISSN 0047-8318) Ms. Magazine, P.O. Box 57131, Boulder, CO 80322-7131

N

*****The Nation.** $36. w (except for the first week in Ja and bi-w Jl, Ag) (ISSN 0027-8378) Nation, Subscription Services, P.O. Box 1953, Marion, OH 43305

*****National Geographic.** $18. m (ISSN 0027-9358) National Geographic Society, 17th and M Sts., N.W., Washington, DC 20036

*****National Geographic World.** $10.95. m (ISSN 0361-5499) National Geographic World, 17th and M Sts., N.W., Washington, DC 20036

National Parks. $22. bi-m (ISSN 0027-9870) National Parks & Conservation Association, 1701 18th St., N.W., Washington, DC 20009

*****National Review.** $36. bi-w (48p issue only, pub. in alternate weeks) (ISSN 0028-0038) National Review, Circulation Dept., 150 E. 35th St., New York, NY 10016

National Wildlife. $15. bi-m (ISSN 0028-0402) National Wildlife Membership Services, 1412 16th St., N.W., Washington, DC 20036

Nation's Business. $22. m (ISSN 0028-047X) Chamber of Commerce of the U.S., 1615 H St., N.W., Washington, DC 20062

*Natural History.** $20. m (ISSN 0028-0712) Natural History, Box 5000, Harlan, IA 51537

The New Leader. $24. bi-w (except occasional combined issues) (ISSN 0028-6044) New Leader, 275 Seventh Ave., New York, NY 10001

The New Republic. $56. w (except 4 bi-w issues) (ISSN 0028-6583) Subscription Service Dept., New Republic, P.O. Box 56515, Boulder, CO 80322

New York. $35. w (bi-w year-end issue and first 2 weeks in Jl) (ISSN 0028-7369) New York Magazine Subscription Dept., Box 2979, Boulder, CO 80322

The New York Review of Books. $34. bi-w (m Jl, Ag, S) (ISSN 0028-7504) New York Review, Subscription Service Dept., P.O. Box 940, Farmingdale, NY 11737

The New York Times Book Review. $26. w (ISSN 0028-7806) New York Times Co., Times Sq., New York, NY 10036

The New York Times Magazine. $94 (complete Sunday ed; not sold separately). w New York Times, Times Bldg., 229 W. 43rd St., New York, NY 10036

The New Yorker. $32. w (ISSN 0028-792X) New Yorker Magazine, 25 W. 43rd St., New York, NY 10036

Newsweek. $41.08. w (ISSN 0028-9604) Newsweek, The Newsweek Bldg., Livingston, NJ 07039

O

Oceans. $19.95. bi-m (ISSN 0029-8174) Oceanic Society, P.O. Box 10167, Des Moines, IA 50340

Omni (New York, N.Y.). $24. m (ISSN 0149-8711) Omni Publications International Ltd., 1965 Broadway, New York, NY 10023-5965

Opera News. $30. m (My-N) (bi-w during Metropolitan Opera broadcasting season) (ISSN 0030-3607) Opera News Circulation Dept., 1865 Broadway, New York, NY 10023

Organic Gardening. See Rodale's Organic Gardening

*Outdoor Life.** $13.94. m (ISSN 0030-7076) Outdoor Life, Subscription Dept., Box 54733, Boulder, CO 80322-4733

P

Parents. $18. m (ISSN 0195-0967) Parents, P.O. Box 3042, Harlan, IA 51537

People Weekly. $61.88. w (bi-w year end issue) (ISSN 0093-7673) People Weekly, Time & Life Bldg., Chicago, IL 60611

Personal Computing. $18. m (ISSN 0192-5490) Personal Computing, P.O. Box 2941, Boulder, CO 80321

Petersen's Photographic Magazine. $15.94. m (ISSN 0199-4913) Petersen Publishing Co., 8490 Sunset Blvd., Los Angeles, CA 90069

Phi Delta Kappan. $25. m (S-Je) (ISSN 0031-7217) Phi Delta Kappa, Inc., 8th & Union, P.O. Box 789, Bloomington, IN 47402

Physics Today. $85. m (ISSN 0031-9228) AIP S/F Division, 500 Sunnyside Blvd., Woodbury, NY 11797

*Popular Mechanics.** $13.97. m (ISSN 0032-4558) Popular Mechanics, P.O. Box 10064, Des Moines, IA 50350

Popular Photography. $11.97. m (ISSN 0032-4582) Popular Photography Subscription Service, P.O. Box 2775, Boulder, CO 80302

Popular Science. $13.94. m (ISSN 0032-4647) Popular Science Subscription Dept., Box 54965, Boulder, CO 80322-4965

*Prevention (Emmaus, Pa.).** $13.97. m (ISSN 0032-8006) Rodale Press, Inc., 33 E. Minor St., Emmaus, PA 18049

The Progressive. $23.50. m (ISSN 0033-0736) The Progressive, P.O. Box 54615, Boulder, CO 80321-4615

*Psychology Today.** $15.99. m (ISSN 0033-3107) Customer Service Dept., Psychology Today, P.O. Box 2563, Boulder, CO 80322

Publishers Weekly. $91. w (bi-w year end issue) (ISSN 0000-0019) Publishers Weekly, P.O. Box 1979, Marion, OH 43302

R

Radio-Electronics. $16.97. m (ISSN 0033-7862) Radio-Electronics Subscription Dept., Box 55115, Boulder, CO 80321-5115

*Reader's Digest.** $13.97 (plus .96 for postage) Available in a special Large-Type Edition at $8.95. m (ISSN 0034-0375) Reader's Digest Association, Pleasantville, NY 10570

Redbook. $11.97. m (ISSN 0034-2106) Redbook Consumer Relations Manager, Box 5242, Des Moines, IA 50340

Road & Track. $19.94. m (ISSN 0035-7189) Road & Track, P.O. Box 5331, 1255 Portland Pl., Boulder, CO 80321

Rodale's Organic Gardening. $12.97. m (ISSN 0884-3252) Rodale Press, Inc., 33 E. Minor St., Emmaus, PA 18049

Formerly Organic Gardening; name changed with August 1985

Rolling Stone. $23.95. bi-w (except combined issues in Jl and at year end) (ISSN 0035-791X) Straight Arrow Publishers, Inc., 745 Fifth Ave., New York, NY 10151

S

The Saturday Evening Post. $12.97. m (bi-m Ja-F, My-Je, Jl-Ag) (ISSN 0048-9239) Saturday Evening Post Subscription Offices, P.O. Box 10675, Des Moines, IA 50336

Saturday Review. $16. bi-m (ISSN 0361-1655) Saturday Review, Subscription Dept., P.O. Box 10010, Des Moines, IA 50340

Publication suspended with August/September 1986

Scholastic Update (Teachers' edition). $19. bi-w during the school year (ISSN 0037-2242) Scholastic Update, P.O. Box 644, Lyndhurst, NJ 07071-9985

Formerly Senior Scholastic; name changed with April 1, 1983

Science. $98. w (except for last week in December; extra issue in February) (ISSN 0036-8075) American Association for the Advancement of Science, 1333 H St., N.W., Washington, DC 20005

Science News. $34.50. w (bi-w year end issue) (ISSN 0036-8423) Science News, Subscription Dept., 231 W. Center St., Marion, OH 43305

*Scientific American.** $24. m (ISSN 0036-8733) Scientific American, P.O. Box 965, Farmingdale, NY 11737-9665

Sea Frontiers. $22. bi-m (ISSN 0036-9993) International Oceanographic Foundation, 3979 Rickenbacker Causeway, Virginia Key, Miami, FL 33149

Incorporating: Sea Secrets

Sea Secrets. See Sea Frontiers

Senior Scholastic. See Scholastic Update (Teachers' edition)

*Seventeen.** $13.95. m (ISSN 0037-301X) Seventeen Subscription Dept., Radnor, PA 19088

Sierra. $12. bi-m (ISSN 0161-7362) Sierra Club, 730 Polk St., San Francisco, CA 94109

Skiing. $11.94. 7 times a yr (S-Mr) (ISSN 0037-6264) Skiing, P.O. Box 2777, Boulder, CO 80302

Sky and Telescope. $21.95. m (ISSN 0037-6604) Sky Publishing Corp., 49 Bay State Rd., Cambridge, MA 02238-1290

Smithsonian. $20. m (ISSN 0037-7333) Smithsonian, P.O. Box 55593, Boulder, CO 80322

Society. $50. bi-m (ISSN 0147-2011) Society, Box A, Rutgers–The State University, New Brunswick, NJ 08903

Southern Living. $21.95 in 17 Southern States and District of Columbia. $24 in other states. m (ISSN 0038-4305) Southern Living, Box 523, Birmingham, AL 35201

Space World. $18. m (ISSN 0038-6332) Palmer Publications, Inc., Amherst, WI 54406

Sport Magazine. $12. m (ISSN 0038-7797) Sport, P.O. Box 5016, Des Moines, IA 50306

*Sports Illustrated.** $64.26. w (except semi-w issue in S and N and bi-w year end issue) (ISSN 0038-822X) Sports Illustrated, 541 N. Fairbanks Court, Chicago, IL 60811

Stereo Review. $11.97. m (ISSN 0039-1220) Stereo Review, Circulation Dept., P.O. Box 2771, Boulder, CO 80302

Successful Farming. $10. m (semi-m Ja, F, Mr, Ap, bi-m My-Je, Jl-Ag) (ISSN 0039-4432) Successful Farming, Customer Service, P.O. Box 4536, Des Moines, IA 50336

Iowa edition indexed with January 1987

Sunset (Central edition). $14 in Alaska, Ariz., Calif., Colo., Hawaii, Idaho, Mont., Nev., N.Mex., Ore., Utah, Wash., Wyo. $18 in other states. m (ISSN 0039-5404) Sunset Magazine, 80 Willow Rd., Menlo Park, CA 94025

T

Technology Review. $27. 8 times a yr (Ja, F/Mr, Ap, My/Je, Jl, Ag/S, O, N/D) (ISSN 0040-1692) Technology Review, Building W59, Room 10-140, MIT, Cambridge, MA 02139

'Teen. $14.95. m (ISSN 0040-2001) Petersen Publishing Co., 8490 Sunset Blvd., Los Angeles, CA 90069

Theatre Crafts. $30. m (bi-m Je-Jl, Ag-S) (ISSN 0040-5469) Subscription Dept., Theatre Crafts, P.O. Box 470, Mt. Morris, IL 61054-0470

Time. $58.24. w (ISSN 0040-781X) Time, 541 N. Fairbanks Court, Chicago, IL 60611

*Travel Holiday. $11. m (ISSN 0161-7184) Travel Subscription Office, Travel Bldg., Floral Park, NY 11001

U

U.S. Catholic. $15. m (ISSN 0041-7548) U.S. Catholic, 205 W. Monroe St., Chicago, IL 60606

*U.S. News & World Report. $34.50. w (except 2 issues combined at year end) (ISSN 0041-5537) U.S. News & World Report, Subscription Dept., P.O. Box 55929, Boulder, CO 80323-5929

UN Chronicle. $14. q (ISSN 0251-7329) United Nations Publications, Room DC2-0853, United Nations, New York, NY 10017

The Unesco Courier. See The Courier (Unesco)

Update. See Scholastic Update (Teachers' edition)

USA Today (Periodical). $150. m (ISSN 0161-7389) The Society for the Advancement of Education, 99 W. Hawthorne Ave., Valley Stream, NY 11580

V

Vital Speeches of the Day. $27.50. semi-m (ISSN 0042-742X) City News Publishing Co., 389 Highway 17 By-Pass, Mount Pleasant, SC 29464

Vogue. $28. m (ISSN 0042-8000) Vogue, Box 5201, Boulder, CO 80322

W

The Washington Monthly. $33. m (bi-m Jl-Ag) (ISSN 0043-0633) Washington Monthly, 1711 Connecticut Ave., N.W., Washington, DC 20009

Weatherwise. $38. bi-m (ISSN 0043-1672) Weatherwise, Circulation Office, 4000 Albemarle St., N.W., Washington, DC 20016

Wilderness. $20. q (ISSN 0736-6477) The Wilderness Society, 1400 Eye St., N.W., Washington, DC 20005

Women's Sports & Fitness. $12.95. 10 times a yr (ISSN 8750-653X) Women's Sports & Fitness, P.O. Box 472, Mt. Morris, IL 61054
        Formerly Women's Sports; name changed with May 1984

Workbench. $6. bi-m (ISSN 0043-8057) Workbench Circulation Dept., 4251 Pennsylvania, Kansas City, MO 64111

Working Woman. $18. m (ISSN 0145-5761) Working Woman, P.O. Box 10132, Des Moines, IA 50340

World Health. $14. 10 times a yr (ISSN 0043-8502) World Health, WHO, Avenue Appia, 1211 Geneva 27, Switzerland

World Press Review. $24.97. m (ISSN 0195-8895) World Press Review, Subscription Dept., Box 915, Farmingdale, NY 11737

World Tennis. $15.94. m (ISSN 0043-910X) World Tennis Magazine, Subscription Dept., P.O. Box 6042, Palm Coast, FL 32037

*The Writer. $20. m (ISSN 0043-9517) The Writer, Inc., 120 Boylston St., Boston, MA 21116

* Available for the blind and other physically handicapped readers on talking books or in braille. For information address National Library Service for the Blind and Physically Handicapped, Library of Congress, Washington, D.C. 20542

ABBREVIATIONS

+	continued on later pages of same issue		m	monthly
			Mr	March
			My	May
abr	abridged			
Ag	August		N	November
ann	annual		no	number
Ap	April			
Assn	Association		O	October
Aut	Autumn			
Ave	Avenue		por	portrait
			pseud	pseudonym
Bart	Baronet		pt	part
bi-m	bimonthly		pub	published, publisher, publishing
bi-w	biweekly			
bibl	bibliography			
bibl f	bibliographical footnotes		q	quarterly
bldg	building			
			rev	revised
Co	Company			
comp	compiled, compiler		S	September
cont	continued		sec	section
Corp	Corporation		semi-m	semimonthly
			Soc	Society
D	December		Sp	Special
Dept	Department		Spr	Spring
			Sq	Square
			Sr	Senior
ed	edited, edition, editor		St	Street
			Summ	Summer
F	February		supp	supplement
			supt	superintendent
il	illustration,-s			
Inc	Incorporated			
int	interviewer		tr	translated, translation, translator
introd	introduction, introductory			
Ja	January		v	volume
Je	June			
Jl	July			
Jr	Junior		w	weekly
jt auth	joint author		Wint	Winter
Ltd	Limited		yr	year

Readers' Guide to Periodical Literature
1987

3-D computer graphics *See* Computer graphics
3-D television *See* Television, Stereoscopic
3Com Corp.
It's high noon for the little guys. J. W. Wilson. il *Bus Week* p111 Ap 27 '87
3D Distribution Systems, Inc.
One business owner tells her story [C. Draper] H. Waldrop. il por *Work Woman* 12:40-1 Ap '87
3M Company *See* Minnesota Mining & Mfg. Co.
4-D *See* Hyperspace
4D (New York, N.Y.: Nightclub) *See* New York (N.Y.)—Restaurants, nightclubs, bars, etc.
4mm video cameras *See* Video cameras
4W (Firm)
With repossession you get egg rolls. P. M. Fielding. il pors *Nations Bus* 75:60 Mr '87
7-Eleven Stores *See* Southland Corp.
8mm video cameras *See* Video cameras
20th Century Insurance Company
If you own a Porsche, don't bother applying. T. Carson. il por *Bus Week* p61 Ag 10 '87
21 Club (New York, N.Y.: Restaurant) *See* New York (N.Y.)—Restaurants, nightclubs, bars, etc.
24 Hours of Daytona (Race) *See* Automobile racing
29th Street Saxophone Quartet
29th Street Saxophone Quartet. P. Bloom. il *Down Beat* 54:26-8 F '87
35mm cameras *See* Cameras
35mm single-lens reflex cameras *See* Cameras, Single-lens reflex
50 plus (Periodical)
News you can use. B. Lindeman. il *50 Plus* 27:4 S '87
60 minutes [television program] See Television program reviews—Single works
72 Market St. Oyster Bar & Grill (Venice, Calif.) *See* Venice (Calif.)—Restaurants, nightclubs, bars, etc.
84 Charing Cross Road [film] See Motion picture reviews—Single works
92nd Street Y (New York, N.Y.)
The care-giver [Parkbench playgroup] E. Hopkins. il *N Y* 20:26 Je 15 '87
227 [television program] See Television program reviews—Single works
401(k) plan
A question of money. *50 Plus* 27:42 Je '87
Retirement money can help you out now [loans] I. Pave. *Bus Week* p150 O 19 '87
737 airplanes *See* Airplanes, Jet
747 airplanes *See* Airplanes, Jet
800 telephone numbers *See* Toll-free telephone service
911 telephone numbers *See* Telephone—Emergency use
1984 [drama] See Kohout, Pavel

A

A-10 airplanes *See* Airplanes, Military
A.B. Tompane & Company
Blown away by Black Monday. A. Feinberg. il por *N Y Times Mag* p38-9+ D 20 '87
A. C. Nielsen Co.
Nielsen boosts its ratings [acquisition of Information Resources Inc.] A. Dunkin. il *Bus Week* p40 S 14 '87
No go. TV networks nix new high-tech rating system. K. R. Sheets. *U S News World Rep* 103:39 Jl 20 '87
Ratings brawl [CBS and ABC allow contracts with Nielsen to expire] *Time* 130:57 Jl 20 '87
A.D. Players
Beyond bathrobe drama. J. Duin. il *Christ Today* 31:49-50 Ap 3 '87
A G B Research plc
People meters arrive. A. A. Lappen. il *Forbes* 140:8 S 21 '87

A. G. Gaston Enterprises
Full speed ahead at 94 [A. G. Gaston] F. White, III. il pors *Ebony* 42:52-4+ Je '87
A. H. Robins Company, Inc.
Buying into Chapter 11: the method in Rorer's madness [bid for A. H. Robins] C. S. Eklund. il *Bus Week* p73-4 Jl 20 '87
The sad legacy of the Dalkon Shield. G. Kolata. *N Y Times Mag* p120 D 6 '87
A-Mark Precious Metals Inc.
Got the postcrash blues? A bullion dealer may have the cure [B. L. Kaplan] T. Segal. il por *Bus Week* p180-1 D 28 '87-Ja 4 '88
A stars
White Sirian stars: class A. J. B. Kaler. il *Sky Telesc* 73:491-4 My '87
A.T. & E. Corp.
The shorts in AT&E: caught with their pants down? G. G. Marcial. il *Bus Week* p94 Mr 9 '87
A. T. Cross Co.
Playing a 'Ronald Reagan market' [views of Harold A. Mackinney] G. G. Marcial. il *Bus Week* p122 Mr 16 '87
A&M Records (Firm)
Gil Friesen [interview] S. Pond. il por *Roll Stone* p103-4+ D 17-31 '87
John McClain creates solid gold money-makers. A. Edmond, Jr. il por *Black Enterp* 18:54-7+ N '87
Music business charts future for minorities. *Jet* 72:62 S 7 '87
A&P Company *See* Great Atlantic & Pacific Tea Company, Inc.
A&W Brands Inc.
High on root beer? Believe it. G. G. Marcial. *Bus Week* p112 O 19 '87
AAAS *See* American Association for the Advancement of Science
AAFLI *See* Asian American Free Labor Institute
AAP *See* Association of American Publishers
AAPT *See* American Association of Physics Teachers
Aaron, David
Verification: will it work? [cover story] il *N Y Times Mag* p36-40+ O 11 '87
> *about*
How many fingers on the button? B. Van Voorst. il por *Time* 129:32 Ap 20 '87
Aaron, Hank, 1934-
> *about*
Aaron bearing up under pressure with the Braves. por *Jet* 71:47 F 23 '87
Aaron says Ruth chase was unforgettable hell. por *Jet* 72:48 S 14 '87
Hank Aaron turned down offers to manage team. por *Jet* 73:50 S 28 '87
Aaron, Hervé
> *about*
Follow the dealer: New York's Hervé Aaron . . . B. Plumb. il *Vogue* 177:486 S '87
AARP *See* American Association of Retired Persons
AAUP *See* Association of American University Presses
AAUP Book Show *See* Book exhibits
ABA *See* American Booksellers Association
Abaco Island (Bahamas) *See* Great Abaco Island (Bahamas)
Abakanowicz, Magdalena
> *about*
Magdalena Abakanowicz. E. Beck. il *Art News* 86:202 O '87
Abalkin, Leonid
> *about*
"The Soviet economy is in a grave state" [interview] P. Fuhrman. il pors *Forbes* 140:106+ O 19 '87
Abandonment of property
> *See also*
> Massachusetts. Dept. of the State Treasurer. Abandoned Property Division
Abatemarco, Fred
Editor's note. See issues of Personal Computing beginning November 1986

Abbado, Claudio
about
Abbado's Verdi: newly minted on CD. T. Eckert, Jr.
il por *High Fidel* 37:63-5 Ap '87
Abbeville Press Inc.
Abbeville announces joint publishing program with the
Soviets. *Publ Wkly* 232:24 S 4 '87
Abbey, Edward, 1927-
Reading Updike. *Nation* 244:409-10 Mr 28 '87
When spring paints the desert [condensed from Beyond
the wall] il *Read Dig* 130:164-7 Ap '87
Abbotsford International Air Show *See* Aviation—Ex-
hibitions
Abbott, Carl, and Starker, Joan
Great places to live: the ten best cities for active women.
il map *Women's Sports Fitness* 9:42-6 My '87
Abbott, George
about
Broadway [drama] Reviews
N Y 20:63 Jl 13 '87. J. Simon
New Yorker 63:57-8 Jl 6 '87. M. Kramer
Broadway birthday. G. Clarke. il pors *Time* 129:75 Je
15 '87
Marking his first century, George Abbott once again
brings Broadway to Broadway. R. Arias. por *People
Wkly* 28:36-7 Jl 6 '87
Three men on a horse [drama] Reviews
Macleans 100:50 S 21 '87. J. Bemrose
Abbott, Gregory
about
Gregory Abbott quit Wall St. to Shake you down. il
por *People Wkly* 27:80 F 23 '87
Gregory Abbott shakes down fame and fortune. J. A.
Baggett. por *Sch Update* 119:32 My 18 '87
'Shake down' artist. P. Tyre. por *N Y* 20:14 Ja 12
'87
Abbott, Jim
about
That great Abbott switch. H. Hersch. il pors *Sports
Illus* 66:28-9 My 25 '87
Abbott, Ken
about
Rosenberg and Abbott: giant steps in desktop publishing.
P. Finch. il pors *Bus Week* p81 F 9 '87
Abbott, Lee K.
Revolutionaries [story] il *Atlantic* 259:62-8 F '87
Abbott, Shirley
The Charleston inheritance. il *Am Herit* 38:62-9 Ap
'87
Abbott Laboratories/Diagnostics Division
In medical testing, Abbott is the name of the game.
K. Deveny. il *Bus Week* p90-1 Je 1 '87
Abboud, A. Robert, 1929-
about
A billion-dollar bailout, Texas style. K. R. Sheets. il
por *U S News World Rep* 103:54 S 21 '87
Bob Abboud is back in banking—but what a bank.
T. Vogel. il por *Bus Week* p30 S 21 '87
Here comes the cavalry. G. Bock. il por *Time* 130:52
S 21 '87
A new Abboud? N. J. Perry. il por *Fortune* 116:192
O 12 '87
ABC *See* American Broadcasting Companies, Inc.
ABC-CLIO (Firm)
Large-print for children: ABC-CLIO's two new lines.
D. E. Roback. il *Publ Wkly* 232:23 S 25 '87
Abdallah, Georges Ibrahim
about
France's turnabout on terror. H. Anderson. il por
Newsweek 109:42 Mr 9 '87
In France, when a terrorist needs a lawyer, Jacques
Vergès usually gets the call. P. Andriotakis. il pors
People Wkly 27:109-10 Mr 9 '87
A Paris court stands firm. K. Brady. il por *Time* 129:53
Mr 9 '87
Terrorism on trial. A. Bilski. il *Macleans* 100:31 Mr
9 '87
Abdic, Fikret
about
Corruption and scandal. T. Fennell. il por *Macleans*
100:38 S 21 '87
Abdominal exercises *See* Exercise
Abdul, Paula
about
Showstopper: Paula Abdul. C. Rogers. por *Essence* 17:23
F '87
Video's dandiest dance-maker is ex-cheerleader Paula
Abdul. J. Friedman. il pors *People Wkly* 27:101-2+
Mr 23 '87

Abdul-Jabbar, Kareem, 1947-
about
Kareem denies romance with 'Hill Street' star; builds
on record career. il por *Jet* 71:32-3 Mr 16 '87
Kareem fights English's suit with one of his own. *Jet*
72:48 Ap 6 '87
Kareem to keep house, sells his L.A. business. *Jet* 72:48
Ap 20 '87
A Laker presses anew. L. Green. il por *Sport Mag*
78:88 Mr '87
Lakers show gratitude, $5 mil. pact for Kareem. *Jet*
72:46 Jl 6 '87
A lot of hurt: inaction got Kareem creamed. J. Papanek.
il pors *Sports Illus* 67:89-92+ O 19 '87
Abdussalam, M.
Ignorance means risk. il *World Health* p5-7 Mr '87
Abé, Kobo
The red cocoon [story]; tr. by Lane Dunlop. *Harpers*
274:34-5 Ja '87
Abe, Shintaro
about
A talk with Shintaro Abe: the U.S. is 'going too far'.
R. J. Dowling and L. Armstrong. por *Bus Week* p37
Ap 20 '87
Abeel, Erica
Bedroom eyes: erotic movies come home. il *Mademoiselle*
93:194-5+ O '87
Magnificent obsession: a house in the country [cover
story] il *N Y Times Mag* p20-6+ Ap 19 '87
Abel, Ernest L., 1943-
"The most-hated man in America". bibl il pors *Am
Hist Illus* 22:10-15+ D '87
Abel, Gene G.
The child abuser: how can you spot him?; ed. by Nora
Harlow. il *Redbook* 169:98-100+ Ag '87
Abel, Kathleen
Could you be better organized? [quiz] *Redbook* 169:27-8
My '87
Abel-Smith, Brian
Counting the cost. il *World Health* p18-19 Ap '87
Abeles, Sigmund, 1934-
about
Sigmund Abeles: the Max drawings. T. Bolt. il *Am
Artist* 51:50-5 O '87
Abell, Sam
about
Travel photographer Sam Abell seeks out "solemn
beauty". H. Chapnick. il por *Pop Photogr* 94:30 S
'87
Abelman, Robert
Television literacy programs for gifted children. *Educ
Dig* 52:30-2 My '87
Abelson, Philip H.
about
Abelson receives National Medal of Science. J. L.
Teramani. il por *Science* 237:661 Ag 7 '87
Abelson, Philip H., and Rowe, James W.
A new agricultural frontier. bibl f *Science* 235:1450-1
Mr 20 '87
Abercrombie, Josephine
about
Fighting lady. D. Remnick. il pors *Sports Illus* 66:62-6+
F 2 '87
Riding high. W. P. Rayner. il pors *Vogue* 177:200-3+
Ja '87
Abercrombie & Fitch Company
Endangered species? E. Paris. il por *Forbes* 139:136-7
Mr 9 '87
Abernethy, Y., and Turner, R. E.
US forested wetlands: 1940-1980. bibl il maps *BioScience*
37:721-7 N '87
Ability
See also
Creativity
Learning, Psychology of
Mathematical ability
Motor ability
Success
Exceptional abilities [conference sponsored by the Institute
of Noetic Sciences] A. Hornaday. *Omni* 10:14 O '87
Ability grouping in education
In defense of tracking. C. Nevi. *Educ Dig* 53:50-2 S
'87
Should kids be grouped by ability? F. Roberts. il *Parents*
62:59 Je '87
The social impact of ability grouping [research by Linda
Grant and James Rothenberg] G. W. Bracey. il *Phi
Delta Kappan* 68:701-2 My '87
Ability tests *See* Aptitude tests
ABM (Anti-ballistic missile) system *See* Guided missiles—
Defenses

ABM (Anti-Ballistic Missile) Treaty *See* Disarmament

Abnormalities

> *See also*
> Birth defects
> Chromosome abnormalities
> Dwarfs and dwarfism

Abolitionists

> *See also*
> Underground railroad

Aborigines, Australian *See* Australian aborigines

Abortifacients

> *See also*
> RU-486 (Drug)

Abortion

Discarding the females. il *World Press Rev* 34:5 Mr '87

A matter of choice. J. Simmons. *Essence* 18:55+ O '87

We do abortions here: a nurse's story. S. Tisdale. *Harpers* 275:66-70 O '87

When life begins: embryo research. *Current* 292:9-10 My '87

Laws and regulations

> *See also*
> United States. Supreme Court—Decisions—Abortion decisions

Abortion, ethics and the law. C. Wallis. il *Time* 130:82-3 Jl 6 '87

Abortion law complications [parental notification argument before the Supreme Court] *Christ Today* 31:47+ D 11 '87

Abortion: once more to the fore. M. Satchell. il *U S News World Rep* 103:16-17 S 7 '87

Abortion: the Democrats shift to the right. *Newsweek* 109:21 My 25 '87

Can states restrict a minor's access to abortion? [upcoming Supreme Court decision] *Christ Today* 31:44+ Ap 3 '87

Clinical procedures [guidelines that would limit ability of federally funded family planning clinics to counsel pregnant women] *Nation* 245:217 S 12 '87

The future of federal family-planning programs [interview with N. Cabaniss] il por *Christ Today* 31:42-3 O 16 '87

"I had no choice" [decision to have an illegal abortion in 1954 after being raped] S. Matulis. il por *Redbook* 168:38+ Mr '87

One step forward . . . [enforcing a 1970 law that prohibits organizations that promote abortions from receiving federal funds] M. Gallagher. *Natl Rev* 39:29-30 Mr 13 '87

Prolifers say civil rights measure could expand the practice of abortion [Civil Rights Restoration Act] *Christ Today* 31:46 Ap 17 '87

Proposed prolife bill goes for the jugular. B. Spring. *Christ Today* 31:48-9 Je 12 '87

Reagan moves to redirect family-planning policy. K. A. Lawton. il *Christ Today* 31:56+ S 4 '87

Reagan's backdoor war on abortion. M. Kramer. il *U S News World Rep* 103:14 Ag 17 '87

Teenagers and abortion [parental consent] B. Kantrowitz. *Newsweek* 110:81 O 12 '87

Trouble in Grove City [Civil Rights Restoration Act and abortion concerns] M. Gallagher. *Natl Rev* 39:40 Jl 17 '87

International aspects

Mary Ann Glendon: "We have let our love of individual liberty trump everything else, such as our sense of community" [interview] M. Asnes. il por *Vogue* 177:238+ N '87

China

A mother's ordeal. S. Mosher. il *Read Dig* 130:49-55 F '87

Moral and religious aspects

> *See also*
> Black Americans for Life

Abortion, ethics and the law. C. Wallis. il *Time* 130:82-3 Jl 6 '87

Abortion more precious than $20 mil. grant: Wattleton [Planned Parenthood grant from U.S. Agency for International Development] *Jet* 72:36 My 11 '87

Abortion: the life you destroy may be your own [Catholic Church; interview with J. T. Burtchaell] por *U S Cathol* 52:20-7 Jl '87

Attracting clients and controversy [centers that counsel women against abortion] P. P. Wong. il *Christ Today* 31:32-3 S 18 '87

Bringing up baby [Reagan administration's new anti-abortion initiatives] F. Barnes. *New Repub* 197:10-12 Ag '24 '87

The Catholic legacy & abortion: a debate [transcript of debate at University of Notre Dame, February 9, 1987; with editorial comment] D. C. Maguire; J. T. Burtchaell. il *Commonweal* 114:657-63+ N 20 '87

Conscience over duty [Toronto policeman D. Packer refuses to guard abortion clinic] C. Barrett. *Macleans* 100:24 S 21 '87

The fear of doing nothing [jailed anti-abortionist J. Andrews] C. W. Colson. il *Christ Today* 31:72 My 15 '87

The flesh peddlers [fetal tissue transplants] *Progressive* 51:9-10 O '87

Help from the unborn [cell implants from aborted fetuses] J. Levine. il *Time* 129:62 Ja 12 '87

How to keep the pro-life movement small. J. Thomas-Bailey. *Commonweal* 114:308-9 My 22 '87

In a family way [adaptation of address] J. T. Burtchaell. il por *Christ Today* 31:24-7 Je 12 '87

A just-war theory for abortion. F. F. Church. *Christ Century* 104:733-4 Ag 26-S 2 '87

Legal attack by bishops [National Conference of Catholic Bishops has asked the Supreme Court to overturn an order demanding that the bishops relinquish church files to critics of their stand on abortion] *Christ Century* 104:881-2 O 14 '87

The mind of an anti-abortionist. K. Pollitt. il *Nation* 244:65+ Ja 24 '87

New questions—same old debate [Catholic view] J. Cavanaugh-O'Keefe. *America* 156:334-5 Ap 25 '87

Prolife and prochoice activists renew the battle. B. Spring. il *Christ Today* 31:48-50 F 20 '87

Quiet, please! B. D. Colen. il *Health* 19:6+ N '87

Real prolifers defend women, too [with readers' comments] J. Ball. *U S Cathol* 52:16-21 Ag '87

Sarabeth Eason [interview with 11 year old expelled from Toledo Catholic school for supporting free choice] C. Grant. il pors *Ms* 15:60-1+ Ja '87

Should medicine use the unborn? [fetal tissue implants] M. Clark. il *Newsweek* 110:62-3 S 14 '87

Single-issue politics and the Church [Catholic Church] K. R. Himes. *America* 156:377-81 My 9 '87

Spying on Henry Hyde at Mass. C. W. Colson. il *Christ Today* 31:80 N 6 '87

U.S. antiabortion policy may increase abortions. C. Holden. *Science* 238:1222 N 27 '87

Wattleton raps Reagan's cut of overseas abortion funds. por *Jet* 72:9 Ag 17 '87

Psychological aspects

Abortion and his responsibility. C. L. Mithers. *Glamour* 85:180 Jl '87

Abortion, Spontaneous *See* Miscarriage

Abortion clinics

Abort/adopt [Nova Health Services runs joint operation] *Time* 130:60 N 2 '87

We do abortions here: a nurse's story. S. Tisdale. *Harpers* 275:66-70 O '87

California

When picketing pays [Adopt-a-Picket program run by NOW to raise money for abortions in Concord, Calif.] D. G. Albrecht. il *Ms* 16:91 N '87

Florida

The fear of doing nothing [jailed anti-abortionist J. Andrews] C. W. Colson. il *Christ Today* 31:72 My 15 '87

Illinois

A day in the life of an abortion clinic [Planned Parenthood's Midwest Center in Chicago] R. Distelheim. il *Glamour* 85:238-9+ F '87

Missouri

Domestic terrorism: on the front line at an abortion clinic [work of clinic director J. Widdicombe in St. Louis] M. Kort. il por *Ms* 15:48-51+ My '87

Ontario

Conscience over duty [Toronto policeman D. Packer refuses to guard abortion clinic] C. Barrett. *Macleans* 100:24 S 21 '87

Abortion decisions *See* United States. Supreme Court—Decisions—Abortion decisions

Abortion in motion pictures

A new attack on abortion [Eclipse of reason] D. Gelman. il *Newsweek* 109:32 F 2 '87

Abraham, A. S.

Rage and rebellion against Beijing. il *World Press Rev* 34:19-20 D '87

Abraham, George, and Abraham, Katy

Garden uses for old tires. il *Flower Gard* 31:32 Je/Jl '87

Will the real Vidalia please stand up? il *Flower Gard* 31:64+ F/Mr '87

Abraham, Jesse M.
Taking it on the chin: what tax reform means to the construction industry and you. il *Archit Rec* 175:39+ F '87
Whither housing in the next decade? il *Archit Rec* 175:33 Ap '87

Abraham, Katy
(jt. auth) See Abraham, George, and Abraham, Katy

Abraham, Lorraine A.
about
"I had to protect Baby M" [interview] J. Liebmann-Smith. il por *Redbook* 169:130-1+ O '87

Abraham & Straus
Into the valley of death? [opens in Herald Square] J. Flint. il *Forbes* 140:160 O 19 '87

Abrahams, Edward, 1949-
'Let them all be damned—I'll do as I please' [cover story] *Am Herit* 38:44-57 S/O '87

Abrahamson, James A.
about
Abrahamson asks contractors to gear up for mass production of SDI components. T. M. Foley. *Aviat Week Space Technol* 126:22-3 Ja 26 '87

Abramov, Valery
And toxic flows the Rhine! il *World Health* p24-6 Mr '87
Family planning research [interview] il *World Health* p2-5 N '87
Silkworm for starters. il *World Health* p24 N '87

Abramovitz, Mimi
The bottom line is society loses. il *Nation* 245:410-12 O 17 '87

Abrams, Elliott
Central America: what are the alternatives? [address, April 21, 1987] *Dep State Bull* 87:83-7 Jl '87
Costa Rican initiative [statement, March 6, 1987] *Dep State Bull* 87:90-1 My '87
Development of U.S.-Nicaragua policy [statements, February 5, 1987] *Dep State Bull* 87:75-9 My '87
Expanding freedom: a formula for growth in the Americas. il *Dep State Bull* 87:79-84 F '87
FY 1988 assistance requests for Latin America and the Caribbean [statement, March 25, 1987] il *Dep State Bull* 87:84-90 My '87
Latin America and the Caribbean: the paths to democracy [address, June 30, 1987] *Dep State Bull* 87:81-5 S '87
Proposed sale of F-5s to Honduras [statement, May 19, 1987] *Dep State Bull* 87:87-9 Jl '87
Situation in Chile. *Dep State Bull* 87:63-6 O '87
The spirit behind the Monroe Doctrine [address, April 28, 1987] *Dep State Bull* 87:80-3 Jl '87
about
Abrams on the hot seat. T. Jacoby. il por *Newsweek* 109:18-19 Je 8 '87
By a thread. F. Barnes. *New Repub* 197:11-13 Jl 13-20 '87
Elliott Abrams must now face the music on Nicaragua, and Congress is calling the tune. W. Plummer. por *People Wkly* 27:44-5 Je 8 '87
Elliott Abrams: the teflon Assistant Secretary. E. Alterman. por *Wash Mon* 19:19-22+ My '87
Lying in State. *Nation* 244:835 Je 20 '87
Some trouble for an ideologue. T. Jacoby. il por *Newsweek* 109:33 Mr 2 '87
Week 4: the other figures emerge. J. P. Shapiro. il por *U S News World Rep* 102:21 Je 8 '87

Abrams, Herbert L.
Human instability and nuclear weapons. bibl f il *Bull At Sci* 43:34-9 Ja/F '87

Abrams, Isabel S.
Caretakers of the Environment. il *Curr Health 2* 14:10-11 D '87
The drug trip: a rough detour. il *Curr Health 2* 14:11-13 O '87

Abrams, Joan D.
How superintendents can work better with others. *Educ Dig* 53:26-8 O '87

Abrams, Maxine
(ed) See Kaye, Donald. Infectious diseases

Abrams, Roger
about
The arbitrator's game. M. Chass. il por *Sport Mag* 78:29 Je '87

Abrams, Steven
about
Made in the U.S.A. R. Koselka. il pors *Forbes* 139:80-1+ Je 15 '87

Abrams (Harry N.), Inc. *See* Harry N. Abrams, Inc.

Abrasives
See also
Sandpaper

Absence from school *See* School attendance

Absenteeism
See also
Sick leave
The great escape. G. Johns. bibl (p62) il *Psychol Today* 21:30-1+ O '87

Absenteeism, Student *See* School attendance

Absher, Tom
August poem [poem] *Nation* 245:168 Ag 29 '87

Abshire, David M., 1926-
about
Iranscam: will Reagan's answer man be allowed to answer? B. Javetski and others. *Bus Week* p55 Ja 12 '87

Absolute
Absolutes and my grandfather's Aunt Sarah [discussion of September 7, 1987 article, A talk with Leszek Kolakowski] M. Mihajlov. *New Leader* 70:19-20 D 14 '87
A talk with Leszek Kolakowski [cover story; interview] M. Mihajlov. *New Leader* 70:10-12 S 7 '87

Absorptiometry
Detecting osteoporosis early [use of dual photon absorptiometry] il *USA Today (Periodical)* 115:15 F '87
Scanning your bones: can these tests do any good? [computerized tomography or dual photon absorptiometry] S. Festa. il *Women's Sports Fitness* 9:18 Jl '87

Absorption (Physiology)
Absence of significant cellular dilution during ADH-stimulated water reabsorption. K. Strange and K. R. Spring. bibl f il *Science* 235:1068-70 F 27 '87
Close encounters with an osteoclast [bone resorption] D. M. Barnes. bibl il *Science* 236:914-16 My 22 '87

Absorption (Plants)
See also
Plants—Water requirements

Absorption of light
Intracellular topography of rhodopsin bleaching [toads] C. L. Makino and others. bibl f il *Science* 238:1716-17 D 18 '87

Abstinence *See* Fasting; Self denial
Abstract art *See* Art, Abstract
Abstract expressionism
Exhibitions
The interpretive link. H. Drohojowska. il *Art News* 86:29+ F '87
Toddling toward modernism [Interpretive link exhibit] J. Perl. il *Vogue* 177:106 Mr '87

ABT *See* American Ballet Theatre
Abu Hureyra excavations *See* Syria—Antiquities
Abu-Lughod, Lila
Bedouin blues. il *Nat Hist* 96:24-33 Jl '87

Abu-Mostafa, Yaser S., and Psaltis, Demetri
Optical neural computers. bibl (p128) il *Sci Am* 256:88-95 Mr '87

Abu Nidal
about
Who is Abu Nidal? J. Miller. pors *N Y Times Mag* p47 Ja 4 '87

Abu Zalaf, Mahmud
about
'Israelis cannot impose their will' [interview] J. R. Moskin. il por *World Press Rev* 34:20-1 Jl '87

Abuko Nature Reserve (Gambia) *See* National parks and reserves—Gambia

Abuladze, Tengiz
about
Repentance [film] Reviews
Christ Century 104:676-7 Ag 12-19 '87. J. Forest
Newsweek il 109:20-1 Ja 5 '87
Time il 130:54 D 14 '87. T. A. Sancton

Aburdene, Patricia
(jt. auth) See Naisbitt, John, and Aburdene, Patricia

Aca Joe (Firm)
The dog ate his homework [president H. Kraatz] J. R. Hayes. il por *Forbes* 140:186 O 19 '87

Academic achievements *See* Student achievements
Academic degrees *See* Degrees, Academic
Academic freedom
See also
Tennessee evolution controversy
Authority and academic freedom. R. Kirtland. *America* 156:348-9 Ap 25 '87
Catholics and their colleges. *America* 156:225 Mr 21 '87

Academic freedom—*cont.*

The CIA-Harvard controversy over secrecy. T. A. Idinopulos. il *USA Today (Periodical)* 115:38-40 My '87

One, holy, Catholic and somewhat infallible [Catholic college's allegiance to academic freedom] D. O'Brien. *America* 156:276-8 Ap 4 '87

Religiously affiliated colleges and American freedom. K. D. Whitehead. *America* 156:96-8+ F 7 '87

Academic research *See* Colleges and universities—Research

Academic tenure *See* College teachers—Tenure

Academy Awards

The annual lullaby of Hollywood. il *Newsweek* 109:84 Ap 13 '87

Dexter Gordon, Hancock win Oscar nominations. il pors *Jet* 71:63 Mr 2 '87

Dressing for Oscar [excerpt from Oscar dearest] P. H. Brown and J. Pinkston. il *Life* 10:89-92 Ap '87

Entertaining [S. Lazar's Oscar Awards party] W. P. Rayner and C. Rayner. il pors *Vogue* 177:120+ Jl '87

For glamour and good food on Oscar night, Hollywood's top drawer opts for Swifty's. il *People Wkly* 27:42-3 Ap 13 '87

Looney Platoons and Marlee maladies [critics' predictions] R. Corliss. il *Film Comment* 23:2 Mr/Ap '87

Orion can't wait to hear 'The envelope, please'. R. Grover. il *Bus Week* p98 Mr 30 '87

Oscar: little statue of dreams. J. Culhane. il *Read Dig* 130:53-8 Mr '87

Oscar steps out. T. O'Brien. *Commonweal* 114:147-9 Mr 13 '87

Oscar 'tout sheet'. A. Thompson. il *Film Comment* 23:52-5 Ja/F '87

Oscar was a 'stunning' award for Herbie Hancock. il por *Jet* 72:58-9 Ap 20 '87

Oscar's firsts, mosts, and onlys. H. Haun. il *Horizon* 30:11-12 Ap '87

Paul Newman, no longer a loser, finally hustles up that Oscar for The color of money. il pors *People Wkly* 27:122-3 Ap 13 '87

People. G. D. Garcia. il *Time* 129:72-3 Ap 13 '87

Academy Chicago Publishers

Academy Chicago makes the grade. M. Berkley. il *Publ Wkly* 232:19-22 Ag 28 '87

Academy of Sciences of the USSR

Gorbachev tackles the Academy. R. Cornwell. *World Press Rev* 34:53 Ag '87

Marchuk is president of Soviet Academy. W. Sweet. *Phys Today* 40:71-2 Ja '87

Shake-up announced for Soviet Academy. D. Dickson. *Science* 235:1565 Mr 27 '87

Acadians

Louisiana

A country called Cajun. M. Burton. il *Saturday Evening Post* 259:82-4 S '87

Do we have a swamp for you! [Louisiana Cajun country] B. Keating. il *50 Plus* 27:55-9+ Jl '87

Passing a good time on the bayou [Atchafalaya Basin] C. Maddox. il map *South Living* 22:108-15 Mr '87

Acanthamoeba keratitis *See* Eye—Diseases and defects

Acapulco (Mexico)

Housing

Where the dollar still buys a hot property [Acapulco] A. Bard. il *Bus Week* p180 My 25 '87

ACC *See* American Craft Council

Accelerated Christian Education

Ace Virtueson meets Pastor Alltruth. P. F. Parsons. *Christ Today* 31:22 S 4 '87

The world as seen by students in Accelerated Christian Education schools [with reply by Ronald E. Johnson] D. B. Fleming and T. C. Hunt. bibl f il *Phi Delta Kappan* 68:518-23 Mr '87

Acceleration (Mechanics)

See also

Automobiles, Foreign—Acceleration

Accelerator mass spectrometry *See* Spectrum analysis

Accelerators (Electrons, etc.)

See also

Superconducting Super Collider

Abragam and Rubbia reports chart future for CERN. W. Sweet. il *Phys Today* 40:71-5 S '87

Bright synchrotron sources evolve. A. L. Robinson. il *Science* 235:841-2 F 20 '87

CERN panel backs new accelerator. D. Dickson. *Science* 235:1567 Mr 21 '87

Collision at 1.8 TeV [Tevatron experiment] *Sci News* 131:87 F 7 '87

Free electron laser success explained. A. L. Robinson. il *Science* 235:27-9 Ja 2 '87

Key decision nears on proposed Argonne photon source. W. Sweet. *Phys Today* 40:71 Ja '87

Los Alamos begins work on NPB test accelerator [Neutral Particle Beam Ground Test Accelerator] T. M. Foley. il *Aviat Week Space Technol* 127:93-4+ O 19 '87

Neutral B mesons show surprisingly large flavor mixing [observed at the DORIS electron-positron storage ring] B. M. Schwarzschild. bibl il *Phys Today* 40 pt1:17-20 Ag '87

Soviet physicists map collider strategy. M. Crawford. il *Science* 238:1036-7 N 20 '87

Soviets plan huge linear collider. M. Crawford. *Science* 238:16-17 O 2 '87

Stanford/TRW team demonstrates potential lethality increase of space-based free-electron lasers. *Aviat Week Space Technol* 126:23 Mr 16 '87

Surfing on a plasma wave [plasma wake-field acceleration] il *Sci Am* 256:66-7 Ap '87

Through a peephole tantalizingly [hadrons produced along single muon at DESY-PETRA laboratory] *Sci News* 132:219 O 3 '87

Tristan e+ e− collider in Japan yields 50 GeV center of mass. G. B. Lubkin. il *Phys Today* 40:21-3 Ja '87

UNK: the accelerator that couldn't shoot straight. R. P. Crease and C. C. Mann. il *Omni* 9:63-6+ Je '87

Yale accelerator to be dedicated. A. L. Robinson. *Science* 237:592 Ag 7 '87

Magnets

See Magnets

Accents

Uzing fo-netix, Robert Easton tranes moovey grates inn most evry axsent there iz. K. Hubbard. il pors *People Wkly* 28:69-70+ S 21 '87

Accessions, Museum *See* Art galleries and museums—Acquisitions

Accessories, Dress *See* Dress accessories

Accessories, Household *See* Household furnishings

Accessory tables (Machine work) *See* Machinery—Stands, tables, etc.

Accident law

See also

Damages

Liability (Law)

Accidents

See also

Amusement parks—Accidents

Artificial satellites—Accidents

Aviation—Accidents

Burns and scalds

Drowning

Fireworks—Accidents

First aid in illness and injury

Mountaineering—Accidents

Railroads—Accidents

Rescue work

Shipwrecks

Space flight—Accidents

Traffic accidents

Traumatism

If you live alone: 9 ways to deal with emergencies. il *Glamour* 85:99 Ap '87

Anecdotes, facetiae, satire, etc.

Emergency! Is your partner a help or a hindrance in a crisis? B.-J. Raphael. *Glamour* 85:68 My '87

Prevention

See also

Safety education

The ABC's of safe parenting. J. Gillis and M. E. R. Fise. il *Good Housekeep* 205:90+ S '87

Baby-proofing. il *Sunset* 178:54-5 Ja '87

Checklist for a happy—and safe—holiday. A. Arnott. il *McCalls* 114:100 Ja '87

Childproof your home. G. Branson. il *Fam Handyman* 37:57 F '87

Guard against falls, and buckle up. J. Carey and J. Silberner. il *U S News World Rep* 103:62-3 Ag 17 '87

Maurice Scales—brother of invention [7 year old inventor of Baby-No-Mash] il pors *Ebony* 42:51-2+ O '87

A safe-child checklist [Christmas safety] A. Arnott. il *McCalls* 115:61 D '87

Summer safety & first aid. C. L. Carney. il *Parents* 62:96-8+ Jl '87

Toddler-proofing your home. J. T. Gibson. il *Parents* 62:184 Mr '87

Accidents, Industrial *See* Industrial accidents

ACCION International

Do-gooders who really do good. P. Duggan. il *Forbes* 140:117-18 N 30 '87

Acclimatization

See also

Altitude, Influence of

Acclimatization—See also—*cont.*
    Animal introduction
Accompaniment, Musical *See* Musical accompaniment
The accomplish'd maid [opera] See Piccinni, Niccolò, 1728-1800
Accordion
    Accordions [A. Carozza comments on the resurgence of accordions] *New Yorker* 63:37-8+ D 14 '87
Accordion music
    Pumping out the new sound of rock. N. Jennings. il *Macleans* 100:50 Ag 10 '87
    What's wrong with this instrument? J. Morthland. il *High Fidel* 37:71-2 Ag '87
Accountability (Education)
    Who is accountable for 'thoughtfulness'? R. Brown. bibl f il *Phi Delta Kappan* 69:49-52 S '87
Accountants
    See also
    American Institute of Certified Public Accountants
    Controllers
    Taking off by the numbers. M. Leepson. il *Nations Bus* 75:48-50 Ag '87
        Anecdotes, facetiae, satire, etc.
    Raw meat for the accountant. B. Staples. il *N Y Times Mag* p38-9 Mr 15 '87
Accounting
    See also
    Agriculture—Accounting
    American Institute of Certified Public Accountants
    Auditing
    Automobile industry—Accounting
    Cash flow
    Computer service industries—Accounting
    Computers—Accounting use
    Corporations—Accounting
    Cost accounting
    Deferred taxation—Accounting
    Financial statements
    Goodwill in business—Accounting
    Government accounting
    Insurance—Self insurance—Accounting
    Intangible assets
    Investment banking—Accounting
    Mortgage banks—Accounting
    Real estate agencies and agents—Accounting
    Retirement benefits—Accounting
    Savings and loan associations—Accounting
    Small business—Accounting
    Stock purchase options—Accounting
    Telephone companies—Accounting
    Television industry—Accounting
        Laws and regulations
    You've come a long way, shareholder. L. Jereski. il *Forbes* 140:282+ Jl 13 '87
        Standards
    See also
    Financial Accounting Standards Board
        Japan
    On thin ice [accounting procedures of Japanese banks] L. Jereski. il *Forbes* 140:152 S 21 '87
Accounting ethics
    Blood on the ledger. R. Greene. il *Forbes* 139:202+ My 18 '87
    Blood on the ledger. A. A. Lappen. il *Forbes* 140:8 N 2 '87
    Imagine a cutthroat CPA. G. Weiss. il *Bus Week* p96 S 28 '87
    Numbers game. See issues of Forbes
    You've come a long way, shareholder. L. Jereski. il *Forbes* 140:282+ Jl 13 '87
Accounting firms
    See also
    Arthur Young & Company
    Coopers & Lybrand
    Laventhol & Horwath
    Taking off by the numbers. M. Leepson. il *Nations Bus* 75:48-50 Ag '87
        Consulting services
    Blood on the ledger. R. Greene. il *Forbes* 139:202+ My 18 '87
    Blood on the ledger. A. A. Lappen. il *Forbes* 140:8 N 2 '87
Accounts, Bank *See* Bank accounts
Accounts, Collecting of *See* Collecting of accounts
Accounts, Escrow *See* Escrow accounts
Accounts receivable
    See also
    Factoring (Finance)
Acculturation
    See also
    East and West

Accuracy
    Taking better aim [training for accuracy in sports] R. Brody. il *Sport Mag* 78:91+ Ag '87
ACDA *See* United States. Arms Control and Disarmament Agency
Acesulfame K *See* Sugar substitutes
Acetaminophen
        Contamination
    See also
    Tylenol poisoning case, 1982
Acetates
    Natural abundances of carbon isotopes in acetate from a coastal marine sediment. N. E. Blair and others. bibl f il *Science* 236:66-8 Ap 3 '87
Acetylcholine receptors *See* Chemoreceptors
Acetylenes
    See also
    Polyacetylene
Acetylsalicylic acid *See* Aspirin
Acevedo, Guillermo Soberón *See* Soberón Acevedo, Guillermo
Achenback, Anne Donlon
    Prime-time conversation. *America* 156:475-6 Je 13 '87
Achievement *See* Success
Achievement tests *See* Educational tests and measurements
Achievements, Student *See* Student achievements
Achilles tendon *See* Tendons
Acid-base equilibrium
    Acid-base balance: an educational computer game. J. Boyle and G. Robinson. il *BioScience* 37:511-13 Jl/Ag '87
Acid dew
    Acid dew: what it does [research by William L. Chameides] R. Monastersky. *Sci News* 132:247 O 17 '87
Acid lakes *See* Lakes
Acid rain
    A $2.5-billion acid rain plan [coal-burning power plants] M. Crawford. *Science* 235:1567 Mr 27 '87
    100 trillion ants drop acid [research by Thomas Graedel] il *Discover* 8:8 S '87
    Acid rain: China, United States, and a remote area. J. N. Galloway and others. bibl f il maps *Science* 236:1559-62 Je 19 '87
    Acid rain in Europe [cover story; special section; with editorial comment by Leen Hordijk] bibl f il maps *Environment* 29:inside cover, 4-15+ N '87
    Acid rain monitor. W. D. Scott. il *Radio-Electron* 58:48-9+ Ap '87
    The acid rain question. F. W. Woods. il por *Futurist* 21:34-7 Ja/F '87
    Acid showers and damage to plants [crops] *Sci News* 132:158 S 5 '87
    Air pollution by particles. R. W. Shaw. bibl (p116) il *Sci Am* 257:96-103 Ag '87
    Ants and the atmosphere: no picnic [research by Thomas Graedel] R. Monastersky. *Sci News* 131:345 My 30 '87
    Biogenic sulfur and the acidity of rainfall in remote areas of Canada. J. O. Nriagu and others. bibl f il *Science* 237:1189-92 S 4 '87
    Black duck decline: an acid rain link. J. R. Luoma. il map *Audubon* 89:18-20+ My '87
    Changing perspectives on air-pollution stress. F. H. Bormann and G. E. Likens. *BioScience* 37:370 Je '87
    A deadly rain [effect of acid rain on wild ducks] L. Williamson. il *Outdoor Life* 179:46+ Je '87
    The death of Ducktown [desert created in Tennessee 100 years ago when copper smelter fumes killed vegetation] W. Barnhardt. il map *Discover* 8:34-6+ O '87
    Déjà vu: acid rain in China. I. Peterson. *Sci News* 131:406 Je 27 '87
    Discounting the threat of acid rain [National Acid Precipitation Assessment Program] I. Peterson. *Sci News* 132:197 S 26 '87
    Disulfate ion as an intermediate to sulfuric acid in acid rain formation. S. G. Chang and others. bibl f il *Science* 237:756-8 Ag 14 '87
    Federal report on acid rain draws criticism [National Acid Precipitation Assessment Program] L. Roberts. il *Science* 237:1404-6 S 18 '87
    Fighting acid rain with gold [use as catalyst to reduce nitrogen oxide after coal is burned for fuel; work of Arun Someshwar] *USA Today (Periodical)* 115:5-6 Je '87
    Forests are dying but is acid rain really to blame? J. R. Luoma. il map *Audubon* 89:36-8+ Mr '87
    The grade-schoolers unraveling acid rain's mysteries [National Geographic Kids Network] M. Bluestone. *Bus Week* p116 O 19 '87

Acid rain—*cont.*
Green devolution [West Germany] il map *Natl Parks* 61:17 S/O '87
Monumental corrosion [effect of acid rain on sculptures; views of Robert Baboian] K. Rosenberg. il *Technol Rev* 90:11-12 O '87
NPCA report reveals state of acid rain in parks. il *Natl Parks* 61:38 S/O '87
On the trail of acid rain. S. Begley. il map *Natl Wildl* 25:6-13 F/Mr '87
Ozone and acid rain. P. H. Abelson. *Science* 238:141 O 9 '87
Sounding taps for the sugar maple. J. W. Edwards. il *Natl Wildl* 25:20 O/N '87
Spending more for cleaner coal. I. Peterson. *Sci News* 131:199 Mr 28 '87
Sulfur that doesn't stay put [Canadian study by Jerome O. Nriagu and others] *Sci News* 132:204 S 26 '87
Watch on acid rain: a midterm report. I. Peterson. *Sci News* 132:36 Jl 18 '87

Laws and regulations
See also
Citizens for Sensible Control of Acid Rain
Acid rain [statement, March 18, 1987] R. Reagan. *Dep State Bull* 87:8 Je '87
The acid test. *Commonweal* 114:100-1 F 27 '87
April fooling. D. Seligman. *Fortune* 115:153 My 11 '87
Attempts to clear the air [United States and Canada] I. Austen. il *Macleans* 100:18-19 Mr 30 '87
Canada's view on acid rain. M. Mardon. il *Sierra* 72:20-2 Jl/Ag '87
Downfall of 'The Acid Rainmaker' [M. K. Deaver indicted on perjury counts] M. McDonald. il por *Macleans* 100:22-3 Mr 30 '87
The Missouri standard [U.S. failure to curb acid rain and chlorofluorocarbons] H. Evans. il *U S News World Rep* 103:90 O 12 '87
Some states won't wait on acid rain. J. F. King. il map *Sierra* 72:18-19 My/Je '87
Turning off the maples. P. A. A. Berle. *Audubon* 89:6 S '87
What can be done about acid rain? [with editorial comment by Duncan Barnes] G. Reiger. *Field Stream* 91:7, 15-16+ Ap '87
Acid soils *See* Soil acidity
Acids, Fatty
See also
ALD (Disease)
Arachidonic acid
Erucic acid
Lipids
Myristic acid
Prostaglandins
Dietary fats: a primer [omega-3 fatty acids] H. Fisher. il *Prevention* 39:98-100+ Mr '87
Acids, Organic
See also
Formic acid
Lactic acid
Salicylic acid
Sialic acid
Acis and Galatea [oratorio] *See* Handel, George Frideric, 1685-1759
Acker, C. Edward
about
This shareholder uprising may give Pan Am a tailwind. G. G. Marcial. por *Bus Week* p130 My 25 '87
Acker, Michael A., and others
Skeletal muscle as the potential power source for a cardiovascular pump: assessment in vivo. bibl f il *Science* 236:324-7 Ap 17 '87
Ackerman, Diane
Mass meeting on the Coast. il *Life* 10:21+ My '87
Travel and adventure. il *N Y Times Book Rev* 92:17 D 6 '87
Ackerman, Forrest J.
about
Monster trash. B. Arbinger. il *Omni* 10:28+ D '87
Ackerman Institute for Family Therapy
What comforts AIDS families [AIDS Family Therapy Project; cover story] L. A. Walker. il *N Y Times Mag* p16-22+ Je 21 '87
Ackroyd, Peter
Oscar Wilde: comedy as tragedy. il *N Y Times Book Rev* 92:14 N 1 '87
about
PW interviews. A. Smith. por *Publ Wkly* 232:59-60 D 25 '87

ACLU *See* American Civil Liberties Union
ACMAT Corp.
Life after death [after asbestos claims litigation scares off insurers, Acmat Corp. forms own company to write liability policies] B. Leonard. il por *Forbes* 139:132-3 My 4 '87
Acne
Acne alert: beating the breakouts. *Harpers Bazaar* 120:108 Je '87
Acne and me. B. C. Brown. il *Seventeen* 46:112+ My '87
Adult acne. D. Longstreet. il *Harpers Bazaar* 120:130+ Ag '87
Blemish busters. il *Teen* 31:72-3 Jl '87
A clear solution [adult acne] J. Torrey. il *Health* 19:42-4+ Ja '87
Put the brakes on breakouts. il *Mademoiselle* 93:16 Ag '87
Rx for healthy skin. il *Redbook* 169:108-11 O '87
Acocella, Joan Ross
American Ballet Theatre at the Met: armies of angels. il *Dance Mag* 61:48-53 S '87
Ashton and anniversaries. il *Dance Mag* 61:56-9 Mr '87
The Bolshoi hedges its bets. il *Art Am* 75:30-1+ N '87
Cinderella in America. il *Art Am* 75:43-5 S '87
In search of Sacre. il *Dance Mag* 61:44-8 N '87
Sixties in the eighties: programming the revolution. il pors *Dance Mag* 61:70-3 F '87
Aconcagua (Argentine) climbs *See* Mountaineering
ACORN (Organization)
Take it from the bank. M. Ruoff. il *Progressive* 51:13 D '87
Acosta, Luis Alberto
A color television [story] il *Américas* 39:47-9 Jl/Ag '87
Acoustic levitation
Materials get a lift from sound. *Sci News* 132:349 N 28 '87
Acoustic phenomena in nature
See also
Thunderstorms
Acoustical engineering *See* Audio engineering
Acoustical Society of America
Acoustical Society appoints Strasberg new secretary. por *Phys Today* 40:59 Je '87
Acoustical Society of America 1986 awards. il *Phys Today* 40:99-101 Ap '87
Ward is president-elect of Acoustical Society of America. *Phys Today* 40:75-6 S '87
Acoustics *See* Music—Acoustics and physics
Acoustics, Architectural
Musical events:
Critique of acoustics in renovated Carnegie Hall. A. Porter. *New Yorker* 63:76-9 Ap 20 '87
Retrofitting the sixties: retuning the sound of your house. R. Long. *Theatre Crafts* 21:28+ D '87
Acquired immunodeficiency syndrome *See* AIDS (Disease)
Acquisitions, Library *See* Libraries—Acquisitions
Acquisitions, Museum *See* Art galleries and museums—Acquisitions
Acrobats and acrobatism
See also
Children as acrobats
High wire walking
Tumbling
Human high-rise [human castle builders in Catalonia, Spain] il map *Natl Geogr World* 147:21-3 N '87
Acropolis (Athens, Greece)
The Parthenon at dusk [excerpt from The journey to the East]; tr. by Ivan Zaknic and Nicola Pertuiset. Le Corbusier. *Harpers* 275:27-8+ Jl '87
Acrosomal membrane *See* Spermatozoa
ACS *See* American College of Surgeons
ACT *See* Action for Children's Television; American College Testing Program
ACTH
Highs and woes of runners' hormones [elevated ACTH and cortisol levels] D. D. Edwards. *Sci News* 131:325 My 23 '87
Interleukin-1's secret message to ACTH. D. D. Edwards. *Sci News* 132:277 O 31 '87
The regulation of ACTH secretion by IL-1. M. D. Lumpkin. bibl f *Science* 238:452-4 O 23 '87
Virus-induced increases in plasma corticosterone [with reply by J. Edwin Blalock] il *Science* 238:1423-5 D 4 '87
Actin
Actin polymerization and ATP hydrolysis. E. D. Korn and others. bibl f il *Science* 238:638-44 O 30 '87

Actin—*cont.*
F-actin and microtubule suspensions as indeterminate fluids. R. E. Buxbaum and others. bibl f il *Science* 235:1511-14 Mr 20 '87
Acting
See also
Dramatization in education
Impersonation
Study and teaching
See also
League of Professional Theatre Training Programs
Lights, camera . . . briefcase: act for success [Acting for Businesspeople courses] P. Kripke. il *Work Woman* 12:122 S '87
They may seem driven, but pupils of commercial king Randy Kirby would settle for 30 seconds of work. K. Hubbard. il pors *People Wkly* 28:173-6 N 30 '87
Uzing fo-netix, Robert Easton tranes moovey grates inn most evry axsent there iz. K. Hubbard. il pors *People Wkly* 28:69-70+ S 21 '87
Action for Children's Television
ACT promotes TV-smart viewing, bicentennial participation. il *Child Today* 16:4-5 Mr/Ap '87
Action photography *See* Photography of moving objects
Action Technologies (Firm)
From prison to a software fortune. il por *Fortune* 115:132 Je 8 '87
Actions and defenses
See also
Air traffic control—Suits and claims
Airlines—Suits and claims
Airplane industry—Suits and claims
Asbestos industry—Suits and claims
Banks and banking—Suits and claims
Challenger (Space shuttle) explosion, 1986—Suits and claims
Chemical industries—Suits and claims
Computer service industries—Suits and claims
Damages
Drug industry—Suits and claims
Electronic industries—Suits and claims
Estoppel
Farmers—Suits and claims
Helicopter industry—Suits and claims
Libel and slander
Manufacturers' agents—Suits and claims
Medical equipment industry—Suits and claims
Nuclear industry—Suits and claims
Servicemen—Suits and claims
Summary proceedings
Telephone companies—Suits and claims
Television industry—Suits and claims
Textile machinery industry—Suits and claims
Theatrical agencies and agents—Suits and claims
Tobacco industry—Suits and claims
Torts
Travel agencies and agents—Suits and claims
Trusts and trustees—Suits and claims
Order in the court—and weirdness, too. T. Gest. il *U S News World Rep* 102:24 Mr 2 '87
See you in court. S. Vetzner. il *Changing Times* 41:65+ Mr '87
Too many lawyers? J. G. Kester. il *Read Dig* 130:153-4+ Ap '87
Tort reform. M. B. Zuckerman. il *U S News World Rep* 103:68 S 7 '87
Anecdotes, facetiae, satire, etc.
I'll sue—that's what I'll do! [frivolous suits] T. Simmons. *Read Dig* 131:17-18 Ag '87
Activated carbon *See* Carbon, Activated
Actmedia Inc.
An upstart is upsetting Actmedia's shopping carts [Cooperative Marketing Co.] R. Mitchell. il *Bus Week* p28-9 S 7 '87
Actor (Computer language)
Actor 1.0. L. Moskowitz. *Byte* 12:266-9 S '87
Actors and actresses
See also
Acting
Actors' Equity Association
Black actors and actresses
Children as actors and actresses
Homeless as actors and actresses
Motion picture actors and actresses
Parents of actors and actresses
Television performers
Youth as actors and actresses
See also names of actors and actresses
20 newest hairdos [modeled by actresses] il *Good Housekeep* 205:112-19+ Jl '87

Eye on . . . scene-stealers [supporting actresses] il *Harpers Bazaar* 120:158-61 Ag '87
On a role: stars on the stage. D. Shewey. il *Harpers Bazaar* 120:310-13 Mr '87
Theater and the individual talent [Actors Equity prohibition on foreign actors] R. Brustein. *New Repub* 197:28-9 Ag 3 '87
Agencies and agents
See Theatrical agencies and agents
Political activities
The performing liberal. D. K. Mano. *Natl Rev* 39:69-70 S 11 '87
Salaries, pensions, etc.
Enter worried [parents footing the bills of child's acting career] D. Machan. il *Forbes* 139:246+ Je 15 '87
Training
See Acting—Study and teaching
Actors and actresses, Handicapped
See also
National Theater Workshop of the Handicapped
After years of lying, actress Madlyn Rhue reveals the truth about her multiple sclerosis [interview] L. Armstrong. il pors *People Wkly* 28:105+ N 16 '87
Against all odds: Suzy Gilstrap. M. Altman. il por *Seventeen* 46:214 Ag '87
"Are all cripples bad guys?". B. Davidson. *McCalls* 114:67-8 S '87
Actors' Equity Association
Theater and the individual talent [prohibition on foreign actors] R. Brustein. *New Repub* 197:28-9 Ag 3 '87
Actresses *See* Actors and actresses; Black actors and actresses; Motion picture actors and actresses
Acts (Advanced Communications Technology Satellite) *See* Communications satellites—Data transmission use
Actualization, Self *See* Self realization
Acuña, Cristóbal de, 1597-1676?
In search of the Amazons [excerpt from New discovery of the great river of the Amazons] il *Courier* 40:9 Ap '87
Acupuncture
Acupuncture and me [knee injury] S. R. Brady. il por *Good Housekeep* 205:58+ Ag '87
Acura (Automobile) *See* Automobiles, Foreign
Acuson Corporation
Image conscious. T. Jaffe. il *Forbes* 140:246 N 2 '87
Acylation
Acylation of proteins with myristic acid occurs cotranslationally. C. Wilcox and others. bibl f il *Science* 238:1275-8 N 27 '87
Ad hominem argument *See* Argument
Ada, Gordon L., and Nossal, G. J. V. (Gustav Joseph Victor), 1931-
The clonal-selection theory. bibl (p116) il *Sci Am* 257:62-9 Ag '87
Ada (Computer language)
Ada moves to micros [compilers] N. C. Shammas. il *Byte* 12:239-43 Jl '87
Black runs company that develops computer ware for Defense Department [W. A. Rolling of AdaSoft] *Jet* 72:23 My 4 '87
Government agencies promote business, industry access to Ada. B. D. Nordwall. il *Aviat Week Space Technol* 127:91+ N 16 '87
Name, rank and computer log-on. K. Healy. il *Forbes* 139:87+ Ap 20 '87
Adam, Robert, 1728-1792
about
British architecture. S. B. Sherrill. il *Antiques* 131:1170+ Je '87
Museum accessions. E. H. Gustafson. il *Antiques* 131:1228-9 Je '87
Robert Adam's "artificers". G. W. Beard. bibl f il *Antiques* 131:1292-303 Je '87
Adam Opel AG
What's making Opel GM's diamond in the rough [luxury Omega] J. E. Pluenneke. il *Bus Week* p87-8 Jl 20 '87
Adamadama, Randy
about
Give Randy Adamadama 40 minutes—he'll have you seeing the light. il por *People Wkly* 28:134-5 D 14 '87
Adaman and Nicobar Islands
See also
Port Blair (India)
Adamantius *See* Origen
Adams, Alice, 1926-
The drinking club [story] *New Yorker* 63:28-34 Ag 31 '87

Adams, Ansel, 1902-1984
about
Ansel Adams: one with beauty. C. D. Long. il *USA Today (Periodical)* 116:56-65 S '87
The spirit of photography. M. Wade. il *Horizon* 30:61 Jl/Ag '87

Adams, Arlin M.
The problem of punitive damages [address, April 8, 1987] *Vital Speeches Day* 53:509-12 Je 1 '87

Adams, Brock
Should the Byrd-Warner Amendment be adopted? [excerpts from debate, October 16, 1987] *Congr Dig* 66:309+ D '87

Adams, Brooks
Clothed in magic. il *Harpers Bazaar* 120:240-1 O '87
Miró: conjurer of earthy magic. il *Harpers Bazaar* 120:184-5+ My '87

Adams, Bryan
about
The life of Bryan. S. Pond. il pors *Roll Stone* p42-4+ S 10 '87
The mass appeal of Bryan Adams. S. Hochman. il por *Roll Stone* p93-4 My 21 '87
The superstar [cover story; special section] il pors *Macleans* 100:32-8 Jl 6 '87
What's so special about Bryan Adams? K. Miller. por *Seventeen* 46:51+ Ag '87

Adams, Bud
about
This Bud's not for you. F. Deford. il pors *Sports Illus* 67:67-8+ N 2 '87

Adams, Cecil
about
He's the wisest of wise guys. E. Dolnick. il por *Discover* 8:82-4+ Ja '87
Is a yawn really contagious? E. Dolnick. il *Read Dig* 131:99-102 Jl '87

Adams, Christie
Walk on! il *Essence* 18:116 Jl '87

Adams, Cindy
Angela Lansbury. il por *Ladies Home J* 104:38+ F '87
Bob Hope: thanks for the memories. il por *Ladies Home J* 104:40+ D '87

Adams, Gordon
(jt. auth) See Cain, Stephen Alexis, and Adams, Gordon

Adams, Harold L.
Technology [address, September 9, 1987] *Vital Speeches Day* 54:83-5 N 15 '87

Adams, Henry
First 'a marvel,' then out of fashion, a fine artist returns [cover story] bibl (p146) il *Smithsonian* 18:46-59 Jl '87

Adams, James Ring
Reba McEntire: country singer of the year. il pors *McCalls* 114:51-2 Ja '87

Adams, John
about
John Adams puts Dick, Pat and Mao back onstage in his opera extravaganza, Nixon in China. S. K. Reed. il pors *People Wkly* 28:127-8+ D 14 '87
A John Adams sampler. R. Freed. por *Stereo Rev* 52:190 N '87
The minimalist with the mostest. K. R. Schwarz. il pors *High Fidel* 37:57-9 Ag '87
Nixon in China [opera] Reviews
N Y il 20:102+ N 9 '87. P. G. Davis
N Y Times Mag il p126 O 11 '87. B. Weber
New Yorker 63:124+ N 30 '87. A. Porter
Opera News il 52:24+ O '87. S. Von Buchau
Time il 130:110 N 9 '87. M. Walsh
A talented Yank in Chairman Mao's court. M. Horn. il por *U S News World Rep* 103:64-5 D 14 '87

Adams, John, 1735-1826
Homes
Adamses at home [cover story] P. C. Nagel. il por *Americana* 15:28-32 S/O '87

Adams, Joseph
about
The contras' little list. A. Nairn. il *Progressive* 51:24-6 Mr '87

Adams, Junius
Have you declared your independence? *Essence* 18:95+ S '87

Adams, Lloyd
about
Homemade. *New Yorker* 63:26-9 Mr 9 '87

Adams, Mac, 1943-
about
Malice aforethought. P. Stimson. il *Art Am* 75:114-17 Ja '87

Adams, Pamela J.
Can you afford to keep that pet? il *Essence* 18:95-6 Je '87

Adams, Patricia
All in the name of aid. il *Sierra* 72:45-50 Ja/F '87

Adams, Phoebe-Lou
Brief reviews. See issues of The Atlantic

Adams, Robert Martin, 1915-
The bard of Wichita Falls. il *N Y Rev Books* 34:39-41 Ag 13 '87
Folies de grandeur. il map *House Gard* 159:48+ Ja '87
Natives and others. il *N Y Rev Books* 34:32-6 Mr 26 '87
On the trail of Santa Fe. il *N Y Rev Books* 34:28-31 Mr 12 '87

Adams, Robert McCormick, 1926-
Smithsonian horizons. See issues of Smithsonian beginning October 1984

Adams, Simon
A patriot for whom? Stanley, York and Elizabeth's Catholics. bibl il *Hist Today* 37:46-50 Jl '87

Adams, Tom
about
Texas producer puts dance at top of his list. E. Elam. *Dance Mag* 61:16-17 Mr '87

Adams, William Howard
Old Westbury Gardens, Old Westbury, New York. bibl f il *Antiques* 132:304-15 Ag '87
What makes a garden? il *House Gard* 159:32+ Mr '87

Adams, Zoleka
about
A new light on love [interview] J. Simmons. il por *Essence* 18:83-4+ My '87
Taking care of you [interview] J. Simmons. pors *Essence* 18:77+ Je '87

The Adams chronicles [television program] See Television program reviews—Single works

Adams County (Colo.)
Parks and playgrounds
Outdoor play . . . one Head Start program's approach [cover story] F. Wardle. il *Child Today* 16:16-19 Mr/Ap '87

Adams National Historic Site
Adamses at home [cover story] P. C. Nagel. il por *Americana* 15:28-32 S/O '87

Adamson, Jeffrey K.
A view from the shop floor. por *Newsweek* 109:8-9 F 9 '87

Adamson, Rebecca L.
about
America's new entrepreneurs [cover story] R. J. Margolis. por *New Leader* 70:11-12 N 30 '87

Adaptation (Biology)
Blockade of "NMDA" receptors disrupts experience-dependent plasticity of kitten striate cortex. A. Kleinschmidt and others. bibl f il *Science* 238:355-8 O 16 '87
Climbing adaptations in the early Eocene mammal Chriacus and the origin of Artiodactyla. K. D. Rose. bibl f il *Science* 236:314-16 Ap 17 '87
Diving adaptations of the Weddell seal. W. M. Zapol. bibl (p136) il *Sci Am* 256:100-5 Je '87
Survival: human adaptation to extreme conditions. F. Z. Meerson. il *Courier* 40:4-7 Je '87

Adaptations, Ballet *See* Ballet adaptations
Adaptations, Motion picture *See* Motion picture adaptations
Adaptations, Television *See* Television adaptations

Adaptec Inc.
Man the pumps. M. Beauchamp. il por *Forbes* 140:400+ Jl 13 '87

Adarkwa, Kwasi
Where eight share one room. il *World Health* p20-1 Jl '87

AdaSoft Inc.
Black runs company that develops computer ware for Defense Department [W. A. Rolling] *Jet* 72:23 My 4 '87

Adcroft, Patrice G.
Omni. *Writer* 100:22 My '87

Adderholdt-Elliott, Miriam, 1957-
Too hard on yourself? [excerpt from Perfectionism] *Teen* 31:40+ S '87

Addictive behavior
The addictive personality: are you a creature of habits? L. F. McCarthy. il *Mademoiselle* 93:184 S '87
"Boy, could I use a . . ." (a) drink, (b) pill, (c) joint. If you filled in the blank you could be a preaddict. W. Gallagher. *Mademoiselle* 93:210-11+ O '87
Patterns of addiction [cover story; special section; with list of treatment resources] il *Ms* 15:35-9+, 63-6 F '87

Addicts, Drug *See* Drug abuse
Addison, Calvin, Jr.
about
Minn. Bible College jock says he was expelled for dating white girl there. il por *Jet* 72:14 My 11 '87
Addison, David R.
about
The lopsided technology company. A. A. Lappen. il por *Forbes* 140:64+ N 30 '87
Addison, Rita
about
A crusader who helps offices go smoke-free. P. Finch. il por *Bus Week* p105 Mr 23 '87
Addison-Wesley Publishing Co.
A-W's technical book program launched its DTP involvement [desktop publishing] il *Publ Wkly* 232:37-8 N 13 '87
Additions, House *See* Houses, Remodeled
Additives, Food *See* Food additives
Addor, Catherine Confino- *See* Confino-Addor, Catherine
Address, Forms of *See* Forms of address
Ade, George, 1866-1944
about
Hoosier humorist, three letters. A. Ashforth. *Am Sch* 56:565-73 Aut '87
Adekunle, Ope
CAMAS: born amid turmoil. il *World Health* p24-6 Je '87
Adelman, John P., and others
Two mammalian genes transcribed from opposite strands of the same DNA locus. bibl f il *Science* 235:1514-17 Mr 20 '87
Adelman, Kenneth L.
Arms control [address, December 10, 1986] *Vital Speeches Day* 53:226-9 F 1 '87
Arms control and openness [address, February 5, 1987] *Dep State Bull* 87:19-22 My '87
Ballistic missiles and SDI [address, November 13, 1986] *Vital Speeches Day* 53:181-4 Ja 1 '87
My cousin, the gambler. *Read Dig* 131:84-8 D '87
Verification in an age of mobile missiles [address, June 26, 1987] *Dep State Bull* 87:27-31 S '87
Why an INF agreement makes sense [address, May 1, 1987] *Vital Speeches Day* 53:514-18 Je 15 '87
A world without nuclear weapons [address, November 13, 1986] *Dep State Bull* 87:35-8 Ja '87
Adelsen, Charles E.
Turkey's ancient treasures. il map *Travel Holiday* 168:56-9 O '87
Adelson, Merv
about
A local kid makes good in Hollywood. M. Rogers. il por *Fortune* 115:100 Ja 5 '87
Adenosine
Bitter jitters [panic attack patients exhibit sensitivity to coffee's bitter taste] M. O'Brian. il *Health* 19:22 N '87
Adenosine monophosphate
Cyclic AMP-modulated potassium channels in murine B cells and their precursors. D. Choquet and others. bibl f il *Science* 235:1211-14 Mr 6 '87
Recombinant fragment of protein kinase inhibitor blocks cyclic AMP-dependent gene transcription. J. R. Grove and others. bibl f il *Science* 238:530-3 O 23 '87
Structure of the nucleotide activation switch in glycogen phosphorylase a. S. Sprang and others. bibl f il *Science* 237:1012-19 Ag 28 '87
Adenosine triphosphatase
Ouabain resistance conferred by expression of the cDNA for a murine Na⁺,K⁺-ATPase α subunit. R. B. Kent and others. bibl f il *Science* 237:901-3 Ag 21 '87
Adenosine triphosphate
Actin polymerization and ATP hydrolysis. E. D. Korn and others. bibl f il *Science* 238:638-44 O 30 '87
Microtubule gelation-contraction: essential components and relation to slow axonal transport. R. C. Weisenberg and others. bibl f il *Science* 238:1119-22 N 20 '87
Structure of the nucleotide activation switch in glycogen phosphorylase a. S. Sprang and others. bibl f il *Science* 237:1012-19 Ag 28 '87
Adenoviruses *See* Oncogenic viruses; Viruses
Adenylate cyclase *See* Enzymes
Adenylyl cyclase *See* Enzymes
Aderans Corporation of America
Rug merchant. E. F. Cone. il por *Forbes* 140:57+ Ag 24 '87
Adey, Walter H.
Food production in low-nutrient seas. bibl f il *BioScience* 37:340-8 My '87
Adgate, Cary
'We do it our way'. il *Skiing* 39:58-60 Spr '87

ADH (Antidiuretic hormone) *See* Vasopressin
Adhami, Ali Naji al- *See* Al-Adhami, Ali Naji
Adhesion
Biomaterial-centered infection: microbial adhesion versus tissue integration. A. G. Gristina. bibl f il *Science* 237:1588-95 S 25 '87
Making contacts in the developing embryo [research by Masatoshi Takeichi and others] J. L. Marx. il *Science* 236:30-1 Ap 3 '87
Neural cell adhesion molecule: structure, immunoglobulin-like domains, cell surface modulation, and alternative RNA splicing. B. A. Cunningham and others. bibl f il *Science* 236:799-806 My 15 '87
New perspectives in cell adhesion: RGD and integrins. E. Ruoslahti and M. D. Pierschbacher. bibl f il *Science* 238:491-7 O 23 '87
Thrombospondin promotes cell-substratum adhesion. G. P. Tuszynski and others. bibl f il *Science* 236:1570-3 Je 19 '87
Adhesive tape
How to capture on film the faint glow emitted when sticky tape is peeled off a surface. J. Walker. il *Sci Am* 257:138-41 D '87
Adhesives
See also
Loctite Corp.
Conductive inks and adhesives. F. M. Mims. il *Radio-Electron* 58:81-4 N '87
How glue works. J. Truini and L. Green. il *Pop Mech* 164:100-3 N '87
Medical use
Stuck like glue [adhesive Carbopol in time release drugs] L. Lang. *Health* 19:21 D '87
Surgery without sutures. S. Weisburd. il *Sci News* 131:234-5 Ap 11 '87
Adipose tissues
See also
Cellulite
Adipsin: a circulating serine protease homolog secreted by adipose tissue and sciatic nerve. K. S. Cook and others. bibl f il *Science* 237:402-5 Jl 24 '87
A chemical thermostat for fat? [adipsin] D. D. Edwards. *Sci News* 132:70-1 Ag 1 '87
Adipsin *See* Proteases
Adirondack chairs *See* Chairs
Adirondack lakes *See* Lakes—New York (State)
Adirondack Mountains (N.Y.)
Caulked boots and white water [Adirondack logging in the 19th and early 20th centuries] D. Wharton. il *Conservationist* 41:38-43 Mr/Ap '87
Adirondack Park (N.Y.) *See* New York (State)—Parks and reserves
Adjustable rate mortgages *See* Mortgages
Adjustment (Psychology)
See also
High school students—Adjustment
Maturity
School children—Adjustment
Security and insecurity (Psychology)
Are you "driven crazy" by things you can't control? Learn how to accept . . . B. L. Stern. *Vogue* 177:477 O '87
Adkins, Bobby Joe
about
Black Miss. sheriff seeks recount, despite cross burning in front yard. *Jet* 72:5 Ag 31 '87
Adkins, Vincent
The road to Damascus [poem] *Christ Century* 104:331 Ap 8 '87
Adkisson, Perry L.
about
Adkisson wins 1987 AIBS Distinguished Service Award. por *BioScience* 37:526 Jl/Ag '87
Adler, Allan
Is the administration approach to federal employee drug testing sound? [excerpts from testimony, September 25, 1986] *Congr Dig* 66:141+ My '87
Adler, Bill, 1929-
What is a cat? [excerpts] il *Good Housekeep* 204:166 Je '87
What is a perfect child? il *Good Housekeep* 205:104 S '87
What is a perfect vacation? il *Good Housekeep* 205:44 Ag '87
Adler, Frederick R.
about
Weathering the slump with Fred Adler. D. Machan. il pors *Forbes* 140:228+ N 30 '87
Adler, James B.
Beyond the big time. por *Publ Wkly* 232:67 S 11 '87

Adler, Jerry
Father of the bride. il pors *Esquire* 107:170-2+ Je '87
Adler, Mortimer Jerome, 1902-
"Critical thinking" programs: why they won't work. *Educ Dig* 52:9-11 Mr '87
We hold these truths [excerpts; with editorial comment by Bruce M. Smith] il *Phi Delta Kappan* 69:250, 269-74 D '87
about
"The last great Aristotelian". E. Bowen. il pors *Time* 129:84-5 My 4 '87
Adler, Renata
Coup at the Court. il *New Repub* 197:37+ S 14-21 '87
about
The press on trial. R. M. Dworkin. bibl f il *N Y Rev Books* 34:27-37 F 26 '87
Adler, Richard
News meltdown hits L.A. il *Channels* 7:70-1 F '87
Adler & Adler Publishers Inc.
Adler & Adler, lacking backlist, to fold after fall 1988 season. H. Fields. *Publ Wkly* 232:12 N 13 '87
Adler & Company
Weathering the slump with Fred Adler. D. Machan. il pors *Forbes* 140:228+ N 30 '87
Adler Planetarium
Adler Planetarium introduces 20-inch telescope. il *Astronomy* 15:64-5 Ag '87
Adlon, Percy
about
Midnacht at the oasis. B. Walker. il por *Film Comment* 23:4+ Jl/Ag '87
Administration, Military *See* Military administration
Administrative assistants
Executive assistants—is there power behind the throne? A. Hornaday. il *Ms* 16:28+ O '87
Administrative law
See also
Regulatory agencies
Administrators, College *See* College officials
Admiraal, Pieter
about
Death by choice. G. Ferrieri. *World Press Rev* 34:51 D '87
Admission to business school *See* Business schools and colleges—Admission
Admission to college *See* Colleges and universities—Admission
Admission to private schools *See* Private schools—Admission
Adobe building *See* Building, Adobe
Adobe Systems Inc.
How two pioneers brought publishing to the desktop [J. E. Warnock and P. Brainerd] K. M. Hafner. il pors *Bus Week* p61-2 O 5 '87
Adolescence
See also
Black youth
High school students
Peer groups
Problem children
Puberty
Young men
Young women
Youth
Adolescence: challenges of the teen years [cover story] N. Gallo. il *Curr Health 2* 14:3-9 O '87
Are you trapped by your image? C. Jakobson. il *Seventeen* 46:204-5+ Ap '87
As they grow/11 through 13. J. P. Comer. See issues of *Parents*
As they grow/14 through 18. D. Elkind. See issues of *Parents* beginning January 1987
Bound to bicker [adolescents and parents] L. D. Steinberg. il *Psychol Today* 21:36-9 S '87
Bummer blues. A. Bell. il *Teen* 31:100-1 Ap '87
Collectible adolescence [nostalgia for 1950s youth] A. M. Dershowitz. il *N Y Times Mag* p46 My 31 '87
Girl to woman: a growing-up guide. A. Bell. il *Teen* 31:50+ N '87
Never a right age [divorce of parents is hardest on adolescents] E. Collins. *Sci Am* 257:32 S '87
Old at seventeen. D. Vecsey. il *N Y Times Mag* p50 D 20 '87
Relating. A. Wood. See issues of *Seventeen*
Teen rage. D. Salvatore. il *Ladies Home J* 104:95-7+ F '87
Those gangly years [cover story] A. C. Petersen. il *Psychol Today* 21:28-34 S '87
Tough times for teens [views of Cynthia Baum] il *USA Today (Periodical)* 116:9-10 S '87
The unhappy years. *Sci Am* 256:60 Ja '87

The ups and downs of teenage life [views of M. Csikszentmihalyi and R. Larson] J. Fischman. il *Psychol Today* 21:56-7 My '87
Adolescent drinking *See* Alcohol and youth
Adolescent literature *See* Young adults' literature
Adolescent obesity *See* Obesity
Adolescent prostitution *See* Prostitution
Adolescent suicide *See* Suicide
Adolph Coors Co.
A long-brewing boycott ends at Coors [AFL-CIO wins right to try to organize workers] *Newsweek* 110:46 Ag 31 '87
Will labor's Joe Sixpack come back to Coors? [union boycott ends as AFL-CIO wins right to organize] S. D. Atchison. il *Bus Week* p29 S 7 '87
Woman bites dog [J. Smith, brand director of Coors Light] E. Giltenan. il por *Forbes* 140:198 S 21 '87
Adonis *See* Adūnīs, 1930-
Adopt-A-Cow (Firm)
Looking for that significant udder? Try calling the Panagakos family and their new agency, Adopt-A-Cow. il por *People Wkly* 28:89 Jl 20 '87
Adoption and adopted children
See also
Steinberg, Elizabeth, d. 1987—Child abuse case
Abort/adopt [Nova Health Services runs joint operation] *Time* 130:60 N 2 '87
Adopted children. L. G. Katz. il *Parents* 62:116 Ja '87
Adoption by blacks in Illinois at record high. *Jet* 71:29 Mr 16 '87
At last—it's a boy! [couple witnesses birth of child they hope to adopt] M. Grant. il *Life* 10:28-34 Je '87
Black family adoption: making homes for our own. D. A. Williams. il *Essence* 18:87+ My '87
"The children I could never forget" [C. Smith adopts a child from a Japanese orphanage]; ed. by Maria Karagianis. C. Smith. il pors *Redbook* 170:30+ N '87
Christianity today talks to Steve Standiford [adopting refugee children] *Christ Today* 31:35 F 20 '87
A desperate search for a second life [adoptee A. Sferrino gets kidney from natural mother] M. Jacobbi and R. Wright. il pors *McCalls* 114:127-9 Je '87
Don't forget them after Christmas [children in need all year-round] H. Smith. por *U S News World Rep* 103:5 D 21 '87
The emigration of innocents [adoption of Latin American children] C. J. Carney. *Commonweal* 114:79-82 F 13 '87
'The Father Clements story' dramatizes fight of Chicago priest to adopt a son. C. Waldron. il por *Jet* 73:30-2 D 14 '87
How can government encourage adoption? *Christ Today* 31:53-4 O 2 '87
"If we don't take them, who will?" [N. Claypool raising six handicapped children] A. Steinbach. il por *McCalls* 115:135-7 D '87
Is private adoption too private? E. Ehrlich. il *Bus Week* p106 D 14 '87
It's time to notice our invisible children [special needs adoption] R. Laws. por *U S News World Rep* 103:4 Ag 10 '87
Miss. kids finding homes thanks to preacher's wife [efforts of L. West] il por *Jet* 71:32 Ja 19 '87
New York businessman Jonathan Blount searches for his natural mother. J. C. Mathews. por *Jet* 73:14-15 O 26 '87
No place to call home: special report on America's adoption scandal. C. Berman. il *Redbook* 170:100-1+ D '87
Out of Africa with Diane Sawyer [starving Malian boy Mohammed Ag Albakaye adopted by C. Carter-Shotts] M. G. Stoddard. il pors *Saturday Evening Post* 259:52-4+ Ap '87
Should whites adopt black children? W. Leavy. il *Ebony* 42:76+ S '87
Taking a chance on love [adoption of handicapped children] P. Caporale. il por *Ladies Home J* 104:22+ My '87
A tale of two Minnesota mothers: one seeks the truth behind their son's death, the other stands accused [investigation into death of Dennis Jurgens] D. Chu. il pors *People Wkly* 27:28-31 Mr 2 '87
Two mothers for Laura [open adoption] R. Distelheim. il pors *McCalls* 114:135-7 S '87
"We have a problem" [adoption of older child] J. Marks. il *Parents* 62:62+ O '87
What it's like to adopt. P. Schneider. il por *Parents* 62:167-70+ N '87

Adoption and adopted children—*cont.*
"Where are my children?" [Walters family of Marshall County, Ky. reunited after fifty years] S. Kelly. il *Read Dig* 130:151-2+ Je '87
Whites adopting black kids works out well, study says. *Jet* 71:22 Mr 23 '87
Adrenal glands

Transplantation
Adrenal medulla grafts enhance recovery of striatal dopaminergic fibers. M. C. Bohn and others. bibl f il *Science* 237:913-16 Ag 21 '87
The amazing new brain surgery for Parkinson's disease. E. Kiester. il *50 Plus* 27:24-6+ O '87
Back to normal [cells from adrenal glands transplanted into brain to treat Parkinson's disease] C. Wallis. il *Time* 129:57 Ap 13 '87
Brain grafts benefit Parkinson's patients [work of Ignacio Madrazo and others] R. Lewin. *Science* 236:149 Ap 10 '87
Breakthrough for Parkinson's disease? [cells from adrenal glands transplanted into brain] B. Wallace. il *Macleans* 100:46-7 My 18 '87
Dramatic results with brain grafts [treatment of Parkinson's disease] R. Lewin. il *Science* 237:245-7 Jl 17 '87
The edge of knife [adrenal glands grafted to brain] J. Carpi. *Health* 19:25 Jl '87
Hole in the head [uncertainties surrounding adrenal cell transplants into the brain as cure for Parkinson's] R. Bazell. *New Repub* 197:13-14 Ag 10-17 '87
New Parkinson's surgery [adrenal glands transplanted into brain] *Sci News* 131:244 Ap 18 '87
Parkinson's: is this the cure? [adrenal cell transplants into the brain] K. McAuliffe. il *U S News World Rep* 102:12-13 Ap 13 '87
Progress in Parkinsonism [transferring adrenal gland cells into the brain] *Time* 129:59 Ap 20 '87
Steps toward a brave new world [treating neural disorders with brain implants of fetal nerve tissue and adrenal gland tissue] L. Jaroff. il *Time* 130:56-7 Jl 13 '87
Therapy by transplant [adrenal cells transplanted into brains of Parkinson's victims; work of Ignacio Madrazo and others] *Sci Am* 256:29-30 Je '87
Transplants in the brain [adrenal grafts for Parkinson's victims] S. Begley. il *Newsweek* 109:64 Ap 13 '87
Adrenal medulla *See* Adrenal glands
Adrenergic blocking agents
See also
Guanethidine
Propranolol
High-speed pork [use of porcine somatotropin and beta adrenergic agonists] K. Coble. il *Success Farm* 85:42 N '87
The SAT pill. *Newsweek* 110:103 N 16 '87
Adrenergic receptors *See* Chemoreceptors
Adrenocorticotropic hormone *See* ACTH
Adrenocorticotropin *See* ACTH
Adrenoleukodystrophy *See* ALD (Disease)
Adrian, Jane *See* Leach, Penelope
Adriatic Sea region

Description and travel
The Adriatic connection. R. W. Cox. il map *Travel Holiday* 167:46-51+ Je '87
ADRs *See* American depositary receipts
Ads *See* Advertising
Adsorption
See also
Carbon, Activated
Desorption
ADT, Inc.
The British raider who sneaked up on ADT [M. Ashcroft] M. Maremont. il por *Bus Week* p33+ Ag 31 '87
Adult-child relationship *See* Child-adult relationship
Adult children and parents *See* Parent-child relationship
Adult education
See also
Aged—Education
Labor—Education
Literacy education
Police—Education
United States. Office of Vocational and Adult Education
University extension
Adult education: classes of '87 [New York City] L. Dyett. il *N Y* 20:38-42+ Ag 17 '87
Back to school full-time: should you go for it? G. Hechinger. *Glamour* 85:248+ Je '87
I thought I was a terrific teacher until one day . . . [dealing with older women returning to college] M. Yudkin. il *Ms* 16:66-7 O '87

Roads scholar Stephen James quits life in the bus lane to shoot for a Harvard Ph.D. [34 year old Bronx bus driver graduates from college] M. Brower. il pors *People Wkly* 27:87-8 Je 22 '87
Would it pay you to go back to school? D. S. Johnson. il *Better Homes Gard* 65:34+ Ap '87
Adultery
Are all sins created equal? D. Neff. il *Christ Today* 31:20-1 N 20 '87
The current state of affairs [single women and married men] E. B. Fein. *Mademoiselle* 93:247+ Ag '87
Diary of a divorce. I. Miller. il por *Ladies Home J* 104:67-70+ Ja '87
Gordon MacDonald leaves the helm of InterVarsity. il por *Christ Today* 31:38-9 Jl 10 '87
My husband is cheating on me. N. J. White. il *Ladies Home J* 104:14+ Ap '87
Preaching & practice [cases of G. Hart and J. Bakker] D. R. Carlin, Jr. *Commonweal* 114:342-3 Je 5 '87
A thoroughly modern mistress. K. Samon. il *Mademoiselle* 93:246-7+ Ag '87
Why men cheat. R. Masello. il *Glamour* 85:146-7+ Jl '87
Why women cheat. P. Grant. il *Glamour* 85:148-9+ Jl '87

Anecdotes, facetiae, satire, etc.
Extraterrestrial congress: the case of the bed-hopping aliens. Crypton, Dr. il *Discover* 8:104 O '87
Adultery in motion pictures
Homebody heat: the family triumphs over the libido. M. Haskell. *Vogue* 177:74 D '87
Killer! Fatal attraction strikes gold as a parable of sexual guilt [cover story] R. Corliss. il *Time* 130:72-6+ N 16 '87
Sex and the psychopath factor [Fatal attraction] F. Bruning. por *Macleans* 100:7 N 23 '87
Adulthood *See* Maturity
Adults and children *See* Child-adult relationship
Adūnis, 1930-
about
The silence in Arab culture. F. Ajami. *New Repub* 196:27-33 Ap 6 '87
Advanced medium-range air-to-air missiles *See* Guided missiles—Launching from airplanes
Advanced Micro Devices, Inc.
Silicon Valley's vale of tears [battle with Japanese semiconductor makers] P. Dworkin. il por *U S News World Rep* 102:47 Mr 2 '87
Advent
See also
Second Advent
Advent: is there someone worth waiting for? M. Scheiber. *U S Cathol* 52:34-5 D '87
Advent meditation:
Conceiving Christ first within one's heart. E. J. Bush. *Christ Century* 104:1054-5 N 25 '87
The Mary in us all. R. Goetz. *Christ Century* 104:1108-9 D 9 '87
'Messy Christmas'. J. R. Wimmer. *Christ Century* 104:1132-3 D 16 '87
Causes for rejoicing; Master of the household. P. J. Ryan. *America* 157:439 D 5 '87
Future challenges. P. J. Ryan. il *America* 157:391 N 21 '87
Interior road work. P. J. Ryan. il *America* 157:415 N 28 '87
Advent International
Foreign affairs of a venture capitalist [P. Brooke] A. Ramirez. il pors *Fortune* 115:84-6+ F 2 '87
Adventure and adventurers
See also
Society of Woman Geographers
Voyages
Voyages around the world

Bibliography
Travel and adventure. D. Ackerman. il *N Y Times Book Rev* 92:17 D 6 '87
Adventure stories
See also
Detective and mystery stories
Western stories
Adventure vacations *See* Vacations
Adventure video games *See* Video games
Adventures in babysitting [film] *See* Motion picture reviews—Single works
Advertisements *See* Advertising
Advertising
See also
Animals in advertising
Banks and banking—Advertising
Baseball, Professional—Advertising

Advertising—See also—*cont.*
  Books—Advertising
  Camps—Advertising
  Cereal foods—Advertising
  Cigarette industry—Advertising
  Clothing industry—Advertising
  Computer industry—Advertising
  Condoms—Advertising
  Contraceptives—Advertising
  Cosmetics industry—Advertising
  Credit cards—Advertising
  Current events in advertising
  Display of merchandise
  Electric industries—Advertising
  Executives in advertising
  Fast food restaurants—Advertising
  Football, College—Advertising
  Hair care products industry—Advertising
  Hospitals—Advertising
  Individual retirement accounts—Advertising
  Insurance companies—Advertising
  Investment trusts—Advertising
  Labor in advertising
  Lawyers—Advertising
  Light bulbs—Advertising
  Meat industry—Advertising
  Motion picture industry—Advertising
  Music in advertising
  Nudity in advertising
  Peanut butter—Advertising
  Penguins in advertising
  Pet industries—Advertising
  Pizza—Advertising
  Poultry industry—Advertising
  Premiums
  Public relations
  Radio advertising
  Raisins—Advertising
  Real estate business—Advertising
  Realism in advertising
  Salami—Advertising
  Samples (Merchandising)
  Service industries—Advertising
  Sex discrimination in advertising
  Sex in advertising
  Shampoos—Advertising
  Shoe industry—Advertising
  Shopping carts in advertising
  Sin in advertising
  Soap industry—Advertising
  Soft drink industry—Advertising
  Tax consultants—Advertising
  Telephone companies—Advertising
  Television advertising
  Television industry—Advertising
  Theater—Advertising
  Toy and game industry—Advertising
  Vacuum cleaner industry—Advertising
  Voiceovers (Advertising)
  Wine industry—Advertising
  Women in advertising
  Word-of-mouth advertising
Confronting the negatives. E. Giltenan. il *Forbes* 139
  Ann Directory:83-4 Ap 27 '87
Image and reality. E. F. Cone. il *Forbes* 140:226+ D
  14 '87
Is it time for an ad agency? S. McGlashan and J. Clausen.
  il *Nations Bus* 75:74+ O '87
Madison Avenue's big Latin beat. S. Brown. il *Time*
  130:57 Jl 20 '87
On Madison Avenue. B. Kanner. See issues of New
  York
Selling it. See issues of Consumer Reports
          Anecdotes, facetiae, satire, etc.
Great ad copy in American poetry: an anthology. D.
  Penrice. il *Atlantic* 260:40-1 O '87
The joys of Ad Land. R. Baker. il *N Y Times Mag*
  p16 Jl 19 '87
                    Awards
    See also
    Television industry—Advertising—Awards
The winning edge [Best Business Advertising Competition]
  M. I. Finney. il *Nations Bus* 75:41-4 Ap '87
You tell us [Best Business Advertising Competition] il
  Nations Bus 75:43-8 F '87
          Anecdotes, facetiae, satire, etc.
Winners and sinners: on Madison Avenue [1987] B.
  Kanner. il *N Y* 20:30-2 D 21-28 '87
                    History
Enticing the customer. N. L. Croft. il *Nations Bus* 75:64-5
  Jl '87

                    Laws and regulations
Advertising pleads the First. M. L. Wulf. *Commonweal*
  114:75-9 F 13 '87
              Moral and religious aspects
    See also
    Religious advertising
                    Prize contests
    See Prize contests
                Psychological aspects
Beyond the hidden persuaders. J. A. Trachtenberg. il
  Forbes 139:134-5+ Mr 23 '87
                    Taxation
Down on the levy [ad tax dampens Orlando TV market
  boom] M. Clary. il *Channels* 7:53-5 N '87
Florida's service tax sparks a revolt. G. DeGeorge. il
  Bus Week p49 Je 22 '87
Taxing patience on Madison Ave. [advertisers' opposition
  to sales tax on service industries in Fla.] R. Hornik.
  il *Time* 129:52 Je 1 '87
Why Florida faces tax rebellion. A. L. Taylor, III. il
  Fortune 116:82-3 Jl 6 '87
                    Terminology
A word from our sponsor. P. Volk. il *N Y Times Mag*
  p12+ Ag 23 '87
                    Testimonials
Cosby ranks highest in TV ad 'believability,' too. *Jet*
  71:28 Mr 9 '87
Endorsements: John Madden's career year? B. Condor.
  il pors *Sport Mag* 78:34-5 Je '87
"It seemed like a good idea at the time" [wrong spokes-
  men] C. Marshall. il *Forbes* 140:98-9 D 28 '87
Jordan's Wilson deal nets him $1 million [M. Jordan]
  por *Jet* 73:50 O 26 '87
Lori McNeil accepts an apparel endorsement deal. por
  Jet 73:48 N 2 '87
Smooth sailing up Madison Ave. [D. Conner's endorse-
  ments] A. Miller. il por *Newsweek* 109:53 Mr 30 '87
Star turns that can turn star-crossed [celebrity advertising]
  A. Gabor. il *U S News World Rep* 103:57 D 7 '87
This little tennis star goes to market [S. Graf] P. R.
  Range. il pors *U S News World Rep* 103:46 S 7
  '87
Who cares what Eszter Balint drinks? B. Kallen. il *Forbes*
  140:192-3 N 2 '87
                    Want ads
    See Advertising, Classified
Advertising, Classified
    See also
    Personals
The doomsday book [ads for used cars] A. Girdler.
  il *Road Track* 39:22 D '87
How to answer a want ad and make them want you.
  il *Glamour* 85:112 D '87
Sifting and winnowing [classified ads for used cars] P.
  Egan. il *Road Track* 39:18 S '87
Advertising, Direct mail
    See also
    Advertising, Political
    Advo-System, Inc.
    Catalogs, Commercial
    Mailing lists
Direct-mail audio line due from Prentice Hall. il *Publ*
  Wkly 232:70 O 9 '87
TV goes postal. R. Buck. *Channels* 7:59 Je '87
              Anecdotes, facetiae, satire, etc.
Uncivil liberties. C. Trillin. *Nation* 245:42 Jl 18-25 '87
Advertising, Government *See* Government publicity
Advertising, Magazine
    See also
    Cigarette industry—Advertising
    Personals
Attention-grabbing ads. M. Gray. il *Macleans* 100:54
  D 14 '87
Can Time's new deal bring the ads back? D. Lieberman
  and M. N. Vamos. il *Bus Week* p30 S 28 '87
The escalating ads race. A. Miller. il *Newsweek* 110:65
  D 7 '87
From the publisher [cost of advertising in Antiques
  & collecting hobbies] D. K. Graham. *Antiques Collect*
  Hobbies 92:6+ Ap '87
In just 20 years, so many felt the sting [Forbes advertising]
  M. S. Forbes. il *Forbes* 140:35 Jl 13 '87
Leer campaign [nudity in ads for Lear's magazine] N.
  J. Perry. il *Fortune* 116:159 N 9 '87
Making the scene [advertising in avant garde magazines
  to reach yuppie market] B. Kallen. il *Forbes* 140:230
  D 14 '87
Print ads that make you stop, look—and listen. A.
  Dunkin. il *Bus Week* p38 N 23 '87
Sex and salesmanship [nudity in ads for Lear's magazine]
  A. Steacy. il *Macleans* 100:64 O 5 '87

Advertising, Newspaper
   See also
   Advertising, Classified
   Books—Advertising
   Personals
Local TV stalks print clients. C. Hall. il *Channels* 7:46-8 N '87
What's free, full of ads, and read all over? [antitrust suit against New York Times Co. by direct mailer Advo-System] C. Welles. il *Bus Week* p122+ N 2 '87

Advertising, Outdoor
   See also
   Billboards

Advertising, Political
Campaign '88 makes a cable connection. R. Fly and F. Seghers. il *Bus Week* p74 N 23 '87
Free speech and free air [candidates should be given free TV time] H. Evans. il *U S News World Rep* 102:82 My 11 '87
Getting the black vote [Nathan Group targets radio commercials in the South] M. Eaton. il por *Black Enterp* 17:20 F '87
The gold mine is playing out [Republican Party direct mail fund raising] J. Novack. il *Forbes* 139:146+ Ap 6 '87
Kirk's cant [P. Kirk's proposal to arrest the decline of voter participation in elections] T. Ferguson. *Nation* 244:385 Mr 28 '87
Republican dirty tricks [anti-Kemp mailing traced to G. Bush operatives] F. Barnes. *New Repub* 197:18+ Jl 27 '87
The selling of the president in '88. P. Sellers. il *Fortune* 116:131-2+ D 21 '87

Advertising, Public service
AIDS and PSAs: broadcasters are seizing the initiative locally. P. Hersch. il *Channels* 7:6 N '87
Hype in a good cause [work of J. Wishnow and M. Umansky] L. Brown. il por *Channels* 7:26 Jl/Ag '87
Media & the message [government information campaign against AIDS] *Commonweal* 114:612-13 N 6 '87
One more for the road [anti-drunk driving ads] il *Read Dig* 130:113-15 Je '87
Poster girls [ads celebrating benefits of women's participation in sports] *Women's Sports Fitness* 9:62 Ag '87
Public service and the bottom line [National Association of Broadcasters antidrug public service announcements] J. L. Swerdlow. il *Channels* 7:66 Ja '87
   Canada
A different way of saying it [Telecaster Committee of Canada's rejection of AIDS-prevention ads mentioning condoms] S. MacLeod. por *Macleans* 100:64 Mr 30 '87

Advertising, Religious *See* Religious advertising

Advertising agencies
   See also
   Backer Spielvogel Bates Worldwide
   Beber Silverstein & Partners
   Campbell-Ewald Co.
   Campbell Mithun Inc.
   Charnas, Inc.
   Chiat/Day Inc. Advertising
   Della Femina, Travisano & Partners
   DFS Dorland Worldwide
   Doyle Graf Mabley (Firm)
   Emmons Advertising (Firm)
   Grace & Rothschild
   Hal Riney & Partners
   J. Walter Thompson Company
   Kirshenbaum & Bond
   Lotas Minard Patton McIver Inc.
   Margeotes/Fertitta & Weiss
   N. W. Ayer & Son, Inc.
   Ogilvy & Mather
   Scali, McCabe, Sloves, Inc.
   Sosa & Associates
   Ted Bates Worldwide, Inc.
   William Esty Company
   Young & Rubicam Inc.
Do your ads need a superagency? [integrated marketing] A. Ramirez. il *Fortune* 115:81-2+ Ap 27 '87
Is it time for an ad agency? [small firms] S. McGlashan and J. Clausen. il *Nations Bus* 75:74+ O '87
   Acquisitions and mergers
Not all the news is bad. J. A. Trachtenberg. il *Forbes* 139:280-1 Ja 12 '87
   International aspects
And Madison Avenue thought, 'it can't happen here' [J. Walter Thompson gets bid from WPP Group] M. N. Vamos and R. A. Melcher. il *Bus Week* p48 Je 22 '87

Bare knuckles on Madison Avenue [Saatchi & Saatchi takeover of Ted Bates] A. Kleiner. il por *N Y Times Mag* p34-9+ N 8 '87
Buying American [British invasion of U.S. advertising industry] B. Kanner. il *N Y* 20:20-1 Ag 10 '87
Hang on, Madison Avenue, Martin Sorrell isn't finished [WPP Group acquires J. Walter Thompson] R. A. Melcher and M. N. Vamos. il por *Bus Week* p80-1 Jl 13 '87
   Finance
A case of the shakes on Madison Avenue [effects of stock crash] M. N. Vamos. *Bus Week* p65-6 N 16 '87
   Canada
Death sentences from America [Ford of Canada ordered to drop Canadian advertising agencies] P. C. Newman. il *Macleans* 100:39 O 5 '87
   Great Britain
   See also
   Saatchi & Saatchi Company plc
Buying American [British invasion of U.S. advertising industry] B. Kanner. il *N Y* 20:20-1 Ag 10 '87
   Japan
   See also
   Dentsu Inc.

Advertising as a profession
How to survive in advertising [R. Joseph] D. Machan. il por *Forbes* 140:446+ Jl 13 '87

Advertising awards *See* Advertising—Awards

Advertising cards
The business of dating: it's in the cards [use of business cards] S. Mernit. il *Work Woman* 12:91 Ap '87
SMT project: a business-card tone generator [surface mount technology] F. M. Mims. il *Radio-Electron* 58:85-6+ N '87

Advertising characters
   See also
   Marlboro Man (Advertising character)
   Spuds MacKenzie (Advertising character)

Advertising displays *See* Display of merchandise

Advertising ethics
   See also
   Mail fraud
How to market good works [Save the Children Federation] J. A. Conway. il *Forbes* 139:10 Mr 23 '87
Tell us it's new and improved—but keep health out of it. Z. Schiller and R. Rhein, Jr. il *Bus Week* p47 Ag 10 '87
Warning: manipulation ahead [rebuke of TV guide for using author's picture in full page N.Y. times ad] W. F. Buckley. *Natl Rev* 39:63 F 27 '87

Advertising jingles
   See also
   Radio Kings (Firm)
Despite their jingular success, Buskin and Batteau insist they'd rather be just folks. M. Neill. il pors *People Wkly* 28:109-10 D 21 '87
Swan song for a jingle singer. R. Ragaini. por *Newsweek* 109:13 Ja 12 '87

Advertising mediums
Ads where you least expect them. J. Reed. il *U S News World Rep* 102:46 Mr 9 '87
   Automobiles
   See Automobiles in advertising
   Purchasing
   See also
   Television advertising—Time purchasing
   Shopping carts
   See Shopping carts in advertising
   Trucks
   See Trucks in advertising
   Videotapes
A word from our sponsor. B. Kanner. il *N Y* 20:22-3 My 25 '87

Advertising posters *See* Posters

Advertising premiums *See* Premiums

Advertising research
The people's choice [Video Storyboard Tests] B. Kanner. il *N Y* 20:21-2 Ap 20 '87

Advertising signs *See* Billboards

Advertising slogans *See* Slogans

Advertising tokens *See* Tokens

Advice
Answers [J.-P. Fenyo, the Free Advice Man of Greenwich Village] *New Yorker* 63:18-19 Ag 17 '87
"The best advice I can give you" [symposium] il *Redbook* 169:68-71 Ag '87
Driven crazy by advice? L. Felder. il *Parents* 62:94-6+ My '87
"If you ask me . . .". K. Karlsrud and D. Schultz. il *Parents* 62:146 Jl '87

Advice—*cont.*

When not to give advice. il *Glamour* 85:59 Je '87

Who should you trust? Advice on taking advice. J. Stone. *Glamour* 85:227 S '87

Words that give us strength. C. T. Rowan. il pors *Read Dig* 130:49-50+ Ap '87

Anecdotes, facetiae, satire, etc.

Welcome to the real world! [excerpt] W. Smith. il *Read Dig* 131:15-16 O '87

Advice columns *See* Newspapers—Advice columns

Advisers, Business *See* Business consultants

Advisers, Investment *See* Investment advisers

Advisers, Political *See* Political consultants

Advisory Commission on Textbook Specifications

Textbook 'spec' changes temporary but significant. J. P. Frank. il *Publ Wkly* 232:29-30 Ag 21 '87

Advo-System, Inc.

What's free, full of ads, and read all over? [antitrust suit against New York Times Co.] C. Welles. il *Bus Week* p122+ N 2 '87

Advocacy, Political *See* Lobbyists and lobbying

Advocacy Institute

What every lobbyist should know [views of M. Pertschuk] J. L. Swerdlow. il por *Channels* 7:76 F '87

AdvSys (Computer language)

An adventure authoring system [using AdvSys for writing text adventure games] D. Betz. il *Byte* 12:125-6+ My '87

Adzuki beans *See* Beans

AEBCU *See* Ampere/Essex Business Credit Union

Aebi, Tania

about

Around the world in 29 months, Tania Aebi blows into New York with a record Guinness may not validate. T. Cunneff. il pors *People Wkly* 28:128-9 N 23 '87

Aegean Islands

See also

Thera (Greece: Island)

Description and travel

Two on the isles. J. Traub. il *Vogue* 177:234+ Ap '87

Aegean Sea

See also

Petroleum—Aegean Sea

AEL Industries Inc.

Buried treasure. T. Jaffe. *Forbes* 139:122 Je 29 '87

Aerial bombing *See* Bombing, Aerial

Aerial photography *See* Photography, Aerial

Aerial reconnaissance

See also

Artificial satellites—Military use

Technical survey: tactical airborne reconnaissance [cover story; special section] il *Aviat Week Space Technol* 127:68-9+ S 7 '87

USAF pursues standardized allied reconnaissance data. *Aviat Week Space Technol* 127:25 S 21 '87

Aeritalia SpA

Aeritalia will develop microgravity facility for use on Spacelab [bubble drop and particle unit] *Aviat Week Space Technol* 127:54 Jl 20 '87

Airlines place eight year-end orders for ATR42 transport. J. M. Lenorovitz. il *Aviat Week Space Technol* 126:44+ Ja 12 '87

Continental upgrades commuter fleet with purchase of ATR42 aircraft. D. M. North. il *Aviat Week Space Technol* 127:40-1 N 16 '87

Europeans will enter ATR42 in U.S. STOL competition [military cargo version] il *Aviat Week Space Technol* 126:28-9 F 23 '87

Italy proposes building, operating Columbus mission control center. *Aviat Week Space Technol* 127:135 Jl 13 '87

Aerobatics *See* Aviation—Stunt flying

Aerobic race walking *See* Race walking

Aerobics

See also

Aerobikata

Aerobics videos: the top 30. K. Allard. il *Women's Sports Fitness* 9:30-3 Jl '87

Are you ready for Rambo aerobics? H. Leitch. il *Women's Sports Fitness* 9:60-1 Jl '87

Choosing your workout. H. Edleson. il *Changing Times* 41:41-4+ Ag '87

Easy-does-it exercise: non-impact aerobics. C. Straley. il *Parents* 62:30 Ag '87

Is there too much sex in aerobics? [videos] K. Andes. il *Women's Sports Fitness* 9:60 Ja '87

It doesn't have to hurt [study by Peter and Lorna Francis] L. Kleinmann. il *Health* 19:18 S '87

Jazz up your warm-up routine. C. Straley. il *Parents* 62:28 F '87

Lining up for FIRM form [aerobic workout with weights] G. Bakoulis. il *Health* 19:62-4 Je '87

The low stress, high energy workout [yogaerobics] il *Mademoiselle* 93:280-3 Mr '87

The lowdown on low-impact aerobics. A. Kott. il *Mademoiselle* 93:84 Ja '87

The lowdown on low-impact exercise. C. Winters. il *Work Woman* 12:151+ N '87

The man in the mirror [Real Men Do Aerobics program] L. Kleinmann. il *Health* 19:16 O '87

Mellow moves. K. McCleary and A. G. Britton. il *Good Housekeep* 204:110+ My '87

Softer, safer, saner. J. Rosenbaum. il *Women's Sports Fitness* 9:60-1 Ag '87

Subtle power: low-impact exercise is gaining popularity. S. R. Gregg. il *Black Enterp* 17:334 Je '87

Top aerobics rated. il *Vogue* 177:245 Je '87

The training effect: enough is just right. T. Monahan. il *Work Woman* 12:117-18+ Je '87

Video shopping. il *Women's Sports Fitness* 9:94 Mr '87

Videos you won't find in stores. il *Women's Sports Fitness* 9:66 F '87

Competitions

How to enter—and win—a competition. H. Leitch. il *Women's Sports Fitness* 9:64 Ap '87

Kickoff of a craze: aerobics get competitive with beach-front bouts [A. Miller and M. Mylrea] M. A. Fischer. il pors *Life* 10:53-4+ Ag '87

Equipment

Aerobics and fitness [footwear] M. Kort. il *Women's Sports Fitness* 9:38-40+ Mr '87

Psychological aspects

You can visualize a new body. E. Rogers. il *Women's Sports Fitness* 9:58-9 Je '87

Aerobics shoes *See* Aerobics—Equipment

Aerobikata

Take it to the limit! il *Seventeen* 46:168-71 N '87

Aerodynamics

See also

Ballistics

Hypersonics

Motorcycles—Aerodynamics

Trajectories

Turbulence

Vortex generators

Vortex motion

Wind tunnels

Advanced computing for manufacturing. A. M. Erisman and K. W. Neves. bibl (p184) il *Sci Am* 257:162-9 O '87

Aerodynamics of wind pollination. K. J. Niklas. bibl (p116) il *Sci Am* 257:90-5 Jl '87

Eidetics proposes upgrades to improve F-16 performance. M. A. Dornheim. il *Aviat Week Space Technol* 127:59+ S 28 '87

How to fly like a fish [work of Cornelis P. van Dam] S. Budiansky. il *U S News World Rep* 102:64 Je 1 '87

The physics of aerobatic flight [cover story] C. R. O'Dell. il *Phys Today* 40:24-30 N '87

Spins and sweep [secrets of low speed and high speed] J. M. McClellan. il *Flying* 114:24+ O '87

USAF, Eidetics plan vortex flow, high-angle-of-attack studies. *Aviat Week Space Technol* 126:31 Ja 19 '87

Water wings [work of Cornelis P. van Dam] il *Sci Am* 256:74 Ap '87

Aeroformation (Firm)

Aeroformation plans brisk training pace for A320 flight crews. il *Aviat Week Space Technol* 127:48-9 N 30 '87

Aerojet-General Corp.

Aerojet completes tests of engine for adaptable space propulsion system [Transtar] R. G. O'Lone. il *Aviat Week Space Technol* 127:130-1 Ag 10 '87

Aerojet develops missile radome cooling technique for SDIO. *Aviat Week Space Technol* 127:76 Ag 17 '87

USAF, Aerojet revive concept of integrated rocket stages. R. G. O'Lone. il *Aviat Week Space Technol* 126:37-8 Ap 27 '87

Aeronautic instruments *See* Aviation equipment

Aeronautic records *See* Aviation records

Aeronautic research *See* Aviation research

Aeronautics *See* Aviation

Aeronautics, Military *See* Aviation, Military

Aerosols

Air pollution by particles. R. W. Shaw. bibl (p116) il *Sci Am* 257:96-103 Ag '87

Effect of ship-stack effluents on cloud reflectivity. J. A. Coakley, Jr. and others. bibl f il *Science* 237:1020-2 Ag 28 '87

Aerosols—cont.

Frozen fire [study of volcanic aerosols in Greenland ice cores] il *Earth Sci* 40:14-16 Spr '87

Going star-crazy [aerosols resulting from sulfurous materials ejected by El Chichon believed to cause cloudy airliner windows] R. Gannon. il *Earth Sci* 40:16-17 Fall '87

Volcanic residue cited as possible source of misleading ozone data [Antarctic ozone hole] R. G. O'Lone. *Aviat Week Space Technol* 126:91-2 Ja 12 '87

Volcanic winter [study of volcanic aerosols from Mt. Etna eruption] il *Sci Am* 256:83-4 F '87

Aerospace industries

See also

Aerojet-General Corp.
Airplane industry
Avco Corp.
Avionics industry
Ball Corporation
Boeing Co.
Collective labor agreements—Aerospace industries
E-Prime Aerospace Corporation
Electrospace Systems, Inc.
External Tanks Corporation
Fairchild Industries Inc.
Ford Aerospace & Communications Corp.
General Dynamics Corp.
Globesat, Inc.
Goodyear Aerospace Corp.
Grumman Corp.
Guided missile industries
Hercules Aerospace Company
Hughes Aircraft Co.
Lockheed Corp.
LTV Aerospace & Defense Co.
Martin Marietta Corp.
Rocketdyne (Firm)
Rockwell International Corp.
Singer Company
Textron Inc.
UNC Inc.
United Technologies Corp. Hamilton Standard Division

Aerospace/defense executives must put their own shops in order [discussion of November 23, 1987 article, The aerospace leadership void] P. Mann. por *Aviat Week Space Technol* 127:61-3 D 21 '87

The aerospace leadership void [address, November 13, 1987] P. Mann. *Aviat Week Space Technol* 127:15 N 23 '87

Industry observer. See issues of Aviation Week & Space Technology

Rocky Mountain high-tech [Colorado] E. Truitt. il *Space World* X-1-277:22-4 Ja '87

Acquisitions and mergers

Chrysler's aerospace involvement grows with takeover of Texas firm [Electrospace Systems, Inc.] C. A. Shifrin. *Aviat Week Space Technol* 127:66-7 Jl 20 '87

Is Textron in Ford's future? The pros think so. G. G. Marcial. il *Bus Week* p61 Jl 27 '87

Loral to acquire Goodyear Aerospace for $640 million in cash transaction. *Aviat Week Space Technol* 126:30 Ja 19 '87

Merci, Jimmy [Loral's acquisition of Goodyear Aerospace] S. N. Chakravarty. il por *Forbes* 139:114+ Je 15 '87

International aspects

Europeans increase acquisition of U.S. firms. *Aviat Week Space Technol* 127:30-1 Ag 10 '87

Employees

See also

International Association of Machinists and Aerospace Workers

Ethical aspects

Industry grapples with challenges posed by contract compliance. W. H. Gregory. *Aviat Week Space Technol* 126:84-5+ F 2 '87

Exhibitions

See Aviation—Exhibitions

Export-import trade

The aerospace challenge. D. E. Fink. *Aviat Week Space Technol* 126:53 Je 15 '87

Britain expects exports to continue record growth. *Aviat Week Space Technol* 126:91 Mr 9 '87

Congress readies trade bill to ease export controls [Trade and International Policy Reform Act of 1987] M. Mecham. il *Aviat Week Space Technol* 126:315-16+ Je 15 '87

European industry evolves to challenge U.S. leadership. D. A. Brown. *Aviat Week Space Technol* 126:88-9+ Mr 9 '87

French aerospace companies report downturn in export orders for 1986. *Aviat Week Space Technol* 127:69 Ag 17 '87

French companies face increased competition in export sales. J. M. Lenorovitz. il *Aviat Week Space Technol* 126:92-3 Mr 9 '87

Record U.S. turnout to offset lack of key firms [1987 Paris Air Show] M. Mecham. *Aviat Week Space Technol* 126:71-2 Ap 27 '87

U.S. military exports continue slow growth. *Aviat Week Space Technol* 126:87-8 Mr 9 '87

Federal aid

Procurement reform [special section] *Aviat Week Space Technol* 126:98-9+ Ap 13 '87

The space station launching a thousand contracts. S. Payne. il *Bus Week* p126-7+ N 23 '87

Star Wars fell on Alabama [Huntsville profits from Strategic Defense Initiative] D. Charles. il *Nation* 245:748-50 D 19 '87

Why we mustn't create an "industrial policy" in space. A. Crawford. il *USA Today (Periodical)* 115:21-5 Ja '87

Finance

Aerospace and defense. H. Banks. il *Forbes* 139:64-5 Ja 12 '87

AIAA forecasts sales rate will slow to 5% in 1987. il *Aviat Week Space Technol* 126:85 F 2 '87

The challenges ahead. D. E. Fink. *Aviat Week Space Technol* 126:13 Mr 9 '87

Firms report losses or lower profits for fourth quarter. *Aviat Week Space Technol* 126:24-5 F 9 '87

Growth trends: U.S. aerospace industry [chart] il *Aviat Week Space Technol* 126:22-3 Mr 9 '87

U.S. aerospace sales hit record $112 billion in 1987. *Aviat Week Space Technol* 127:32 D 21 '87

International aspects

See also

United Aerospace Defense Systems

Aerospace forecast & inventory [special issue; with editorial comment by Donald E. Fink] il *Aviat Week Space Technol* 126:13-23+ Mr 9 '87

International aerospace strategies [cover story; special section] il *Aviat Week Space Technol* 126:107-11+ Je 15 '87

Laurels 1987. D. E. Fink. *Aviat Week Space Technol* 127:13 D 21 '87

Laurels for 1986. D. E. Fink. *Aviat Week Space Technol* 126:11 Ja 12 '87

Martin evaluates bids on Titan launch adapter [Titan 3 dual satellite adapter] *Aviat Week Space Technol* 126:62-3 Je 22 '87

Management

Wall Street and aerospace: restructuring ahead? J. R. Stodden. il *Aviat Week Space Technol* 127:64-6 Ag 31 '87

Securities

Aerospace industry joins tumble in erratic Wall Street trading. *Aviat Week Space Technol* 127:33 O 26 '87

Market focus. J. R. Stodden. See issues of Aviation Week & Space Technology beginning December 1, 1986

Pickens picks: a Boone for investors? J. P. Newport, Jr. il *Fortune* 116:126+ S 14 '87

The turmoil in aerospace could boost Honeywell. G. G. Marcial. il *Bus Week* p62 Ag 10 '87

Wall Street and aerospace: disenchantment sets in. J. R. Stodden. il *Aviat Week Space Technol* 127:64-5+ Ag 17 '87

Wall Street and aerospace: financial pressures build. J. R. Stodden. il *Aviat Week Space Technol* 127:81+ Ag 24 '87

Wall Street and aerospace: restructuring ahead? J. R. Stodden. il *Aviat Week Space Technol* 127:64-6 Ag 31 '87

Argentina

See also

Fabrica Argentina de Material Aerospacial

Australia

See also

AUSSAT Pty. Ltd.

Brazil

See also

Avibras Industria Aeroespacial SA

Orbita Aerospace Systems (Firm)

Brazil's goal of self-sufficiency in arms impeded by inflation, record high indebtedness. il *Aviat Week Space Technol* 127:40+ Ag 24 '87

Canada

See also

Canadair Ltd.

MacDonald Dettwiler and Associates

Aerospace industries—Canada—*cont.*
Canadian aerospace industry predicts solid short term. *Aviat Week Space Technol* 126:73+ Mr 9 '87
Chile
See also
Empresa Nacional de Aeronautica
China
China tailors exhibit to pursue military, commuter aircraft markets [Paris Air Show] il *Aviat Week Space Technol* 126:25-6 Je 22 '87
France
See also
Aerospatiale
Matra SA
French aerospace companies report downturn in export orders for 1986. *Aviat Week Space Technol* 127:69 Ag 17 '87
French companies face increased competition in export sales. J. M. Lenorovitz. il *Aviat Week Space Technol* 126:92-3 Mr 9 '87
French seek competitive edge through international efforts. J. M. Lenorovitz. il *Aviat Week Space Technol* 126:140-1+ Je 15 '87
Germany (West)
See also
Dornier GmbH
Messerschmitt-Bölkow-Blohm GmbH
Need for key aerospace decisions puts West Germany at crossroads. K. F. Mordoff. il *Aviat Week Space Technol* 126:163-4+ Je 15 '87
Great Britain
See also
British Aerospace plc
Plessey Co. plc
Britain expects exports to continue record growth. *Aviat Week Space Technol* 126:91 Mr 9 '87
British industry scrutinizes worth of collaborative projects. D. A. Brown. il *Aviat Week Space Technol* 126:147+ Je 15 '87
Israel
See also
Israel Aircraft Industries Ltd.
Israel seeking broad range of collaborative programs. il *Aviat Week Space Technol* 126:174-5 Je 15 '87
Israeli aerospace industry faces critical decisions. il *Aviat Week Space Technol* 126:95 Mr 9 '87
Italy
Italy hopes current international efforts will lead to new joint programs. il *Aviat Week Space Technol* 126:169+ Je 15 '87
Japan
Japan, the armsmaker. P. Genet. *World Press Rev* 34:52-3 O '87
Latin America
Aerospace in South America: industry [cover story; special section] il *Aviat Week Space Technol* 127:40-3+ Ag 17 '87
Aerospace in South America: military and space [cover story; special section] il *Aviat Week Space Technol* 127:40-1+ Ag 24 '87
South American aerospace programs press ahead despite weak economies. E. H. Kolcum. il *Aviat Week Space Technol* 126:182-4+ Je 15 '87
Pacific region
Third Chinese launch pad signals aerospace growth in Pacific Basin [Pacific Basin international symposium on space] C. Covault. *Aviat Week Space Technol* 126:66-7 Je 15 '87
Spain
See also
Construcciones Aeronauticas SA
Sweden
See also
Saab-Scania AB
Switzerland
See also
Contraves AG
Turkey
See also
Tusas Aerospace Industries, Inc.
United States
See Aerospace industries
Western Europe
See also
Arianespace
European groups seek mutual weapons development programs. *Aviat Week Space Technol* 126:82+ Mr 9 '87
European industry evolves to challenge U.S. leadership. D. A. Brown. *Aviat Week Space Technol* 126:88-9+ Mr 9 '87

Europe's aerospace companies are in seventh heaven. T. Peterson. il *Bus Week* p54 N 23 '87
Partnerships reflect growing role of European firms in spacecraft bids. *Aviat Week Space Technol* 127:48 N 16 '87
Aerospace Training and Research Center *See* University of North Dakota. Aerospace Training and Research Center
Aerospaceplane *See* Spaceplane
Aerospatiale
Aerospatiale proposes modifying A300B4s for strategic support. *Aviat Week Space Technol* 126:31 F 23 '87
Aerospatiale's Toulouse data center helps speed A320 certification program [use of French Telecom 1 communications satellite] map *Aviat Week Space Technol* 126:44-5 My 18 '87
Airlines place eight year-end orders for ATR42 transport. J. M. Lenorovitz. il *Aviat Week Space Technol* 126:44+ Ja 12 '87
Continental upgrades commuter fleet with purchase of ATR42 aircraft. D. M. North. il *Aviat Week Space Technol* 127:40-1 N 16 '87
Europeans will enter ATR42 in U.S. STOL competition [military cargo version] il *Aviat Week Space Technol* 126:28-9 F 23 '87
France keeps option open on missile contractor choice. *Aviat Week Space Technol* 126:107 F 9 '87
Aerospatiale. Helicopter Division
Aerospatiale adding rotor, avionics improvements to its product line. il *Aviat Week Space Technol* 126:101+ Ja 19 '87
Aerospatiale Helicopter plans to diversify U.S. facility. *Aviat Week Space Technol* 126:78 Mr 16 '87
Aerospatiale testing modified version of AS 332 Super Puma. *Aviat Week Space Technol* 126:27 Mr 16 '87
Conflicting requirements stymie German/French PAH-2 project. *Aviat Week Space Technol* 126:80-1 Ja 19 '87
France, Germany agree on common specifications for combat helicopter [PAH-2 program] il *Aviat Week Space Technol* 126:61-2 Ap 6 '87
Two firms vie for new Canadian helicopter program [E. H. Industries' EH101 and Aerospatiale's AS332 Mk. 2 Super Puma] il *Aviat Week Space Technol* 126:28-9 Je 22 '87
Aerovias Venezolanas SA
AVENSA braces to meet challenges. il *Aviat Week Space Technol* 127:54-5 Ag 31 '87
AES *See* Audio Engineering Society
Aesthetic movement *See* Arts and crafts movement
Aesthetics
See also
Avant-garde (Aesthetics)
Kitsch
Modernism (Aesthetics)
Nature (Aesthetics)
Neoclassicism
Romanticism
Style, Artistic
The artist in us all [chimp drawings; research by Sarah T. Boysen] A. H. Rosenfeld. il *Psychol Today* 21:20 S '87
Escape into esthetics. J. J. Pelikan. *Cent Mag* 20:57-8 Ja/F '87
Goodness knows nothing of beauty: on the distance between morality and art. W. H. Gass. il *Harpers* 274:37-44 Ap '87
AFDC (Aid to Families with Dependent Children) program *See* Public welfare
Affection
See also
Embracing
Intimacy
Kissing
Affiliate Artists, Inc.
What it's all about. C. Mobley. il *Opera News* 52:32-5 Jl '87
Affiliates, Television *See* Television stations
Affinity cards
An affinity for flying [cards cosponsored by airlines and banks] G. Eichler. il *Esquire* 108:82 O '87
Comes the virtuous credit card. B. Bauer. il *U S News World Rep* 103:82 O 5 '87
Credit cards for special causes. E. Card. il *Ms* 15:82 Ap '87
Affirmative action *See* Discrimination
Affirmative action in college and university admission *See* Colleges and universities—Admission

Affirmative action in employment *See* Blacks—Employment; Discrimination in employment; Women—Employment
Affliction *See* Suffering
AFG Industries, Inc.
GenCorp feels the pincers [Wagner & Brown-AFG team] T. Carson and Z. Schiller. *Bus Week* p33-4 Mr 30 '87
What makes Dee Hubbard run after companies. T. Carson. il por *Bus Week* p56 Ap 27 '87
Afghan refugees *See* Refugees, Afghan
Afghanistan
See also
Afghans
Military assistance, American—Afghanistan
United Nations—Afghanistan
Foreign relations
Pakistan
Gap on time-frame for withdrawal of troops narrowed to less than a year. il *UN Chron* 24:42 My '87
The great game. S. R. Weisman. *New Repub* 197:20-3 Ag 10-17 '87
Pakistanis want an Afghan peace. A. Rashid. il *Nation* 244:110-12+ Ja 31 '87
Search for political solution on two tracks—Geneva process and intra-Afghan discussion. *UN Chron* 24:32 Ag '87
Talks held in Geneva on situation relating to Afghanistan; Under-Secretary-General to continue efforts. *UN Chron* 23:76 N '86
Zia's Afghan dilemma [cease fire collapse] N. Cooper. il por *Newsweek* 109:42 F 16 '87
United States
See United States—Foreign relations—Afghanistan
Politics and government
See also
Afghanistan—Russian invasion, 1979-
Religious institutions and affairs
See also
Muslims—Afghanistan
Russian invasion, 1979-
See also
Afghanistan Day
1987: year eight. *Natl Rev* 39:23 Ja 30 '87
The Afghan bunker. R. D. Kaplan. *New Repub* 197:18-19 D 28 '87
Afghanistan: seven years of Soviet occupation. C. Karp. il maps *Dep State Bull* 87:1-21 F '87
The alchemy of turning guns into luxury villas [diversion of U.S. aid] E. Girardet. il *U S News World Rep* 103:36 N 30 '87
The catastrophe [visiting places related to the Afghan resistance] D. M. Lessing. *New Yorker* 63:74-90+ Mr 16 '87
Caught in the cross fire [Afghan refugees in Pakistan] K. Gannon. il *Progressive* 51:14 Ja '87
The great game. S. R. Weisman. *New Repub* 197:20-3 Ag 10-17 '87
Hemming in the Kremlin. il *U S News World Rep* 103:25 D 21 '87
Hot pursuit [Soviet-backed Afghan air force strikes at Pakistan] *Time* 129:42 Ap 6 '87
Inside an unlovely war. W. Burger. il *Newsweek* 110:46-8 O 12 '87
Insurgencies: two of a kind [U.S.-backed rebels in Afghanistan] R. Watson. il *Newsweek* 109:32-3 Mr 23 '87
Lost in Afghanistan [C.I.A.-run aid program] D. Corn and J. Morley. *Nation* 245:43 Jl 18-25 '87
On the receiving end. B. Crozier. *Natl Rev* 39:26+ Jl 17 '87
Situation in Afghanistan [statement, November 4, 1986] H. S. Okun. *Dep State Bull* 87:84-6 Ja '87
The Soviet Union and Afghanistan in 1987. L. Dupree. bibl f *Curr Hist* 86:333-5 O '87
Soviets' Afghan agony worsens. J. P. Shapiro. il *U S News World Rep* 103:12 Ag 24 '87
Stalemate in Kabul. G. Barendson. il *World Press Rev* 34:28-30 S '87
War of a thousand skirmishes. R. Schultheis and K. Olsen. il *Time* 129:50-1 My 18 '87
Winning the war for Afghanistan. A. Bennigsen. *Natl Rev* 39:36-8 My 8 '87
Aerial operations
U.S. credits Afghan resistance with thwarting Soviet air power. M. Mecham. *Aviat Week Space Technol* 127:26-7 Jl 13 '87
Desertions
Cherishing new freedom [Soviet Army deserters from Afghanistan now living in Canada] S. Aikenhead. il *Macleans* 100:10 Ag 24 '87

Moral and religious aspects
Afghan refugees find help at the border [World Vision outreach program in Pakistan] il *Christ Today* 31:40-1 Ap 3 '87
Peace and mediation
The Afghan 'peace' prospect. B. Crozier. *Natl Rev* 39:26 F 27 '87
Afghanistan: cease-fire? R. Watson. il *Newsweek* 109:31 Ja 12 '87
Arrangements for implementing settlement relating to Afghanistan completed, issue of withdrawal time-frame remains. *UN Chron* 24:72 F '87
Assembly urges political solution for situation relating to Afghanistan. il *UN Chron* 24:69-72 F '87
Bear in a briarpatch: prospects for a Soviet pullout. G. Perkovich. il *Commonweal* 114:725-6 D 18 '87
Gap on time-frame for withdrawal of troops narrowed to less than a year. il *UN Chron* 24:42 My '87
Gap on time-frame for withdrawal of troops shortened but not bridged. *UN Chron* 24:54 N '87
Is Moscow ready to cut its losses? R. A. Manning. il map *U S News World Rep* 102:30-1 Ja 19 '87
Maneuvering toward a pullout from Afghanistan. R. E. Farrell and others. il *Bus Week* p63 Ja 26 '87
Messengers from Moscow. E. W. Desmond. il *Time* 129:43 Ja 19 '87
The once and future king? [former king, Mohammed Zahir Shah] F. Willey. por *Newsweek* 109:39 Je 1 '87
Pakistanis want an Afghan peace. A. Rashid. il *Nation* 244:110-12+ Ja 31 '87
Peace offerings. A. Bilski. il *Macleans* 100:23 Ja 26 '87
Political solution urged by Assembly for situation relating to Afghanistan. map *UN Chron* 23:12-14 Ja '86
Search for political solution on two tracks—Geneva process and intra-Afghan discussion. *UN Chron* 24:32 Ag '87
Show 'em the way to go home [possible pullout of Soviet troops] M. S. Serrill. il *Time* 130:52-3 D 14 '87
Soviet withdrawal deception. *Dep State Bull* 87:12 F '87
The sting [Reagan administration could spoil peace process by stepping up arms to Afghan guerrillas] A. Rashid. *Nation* 244:241-2 F 28 '87
Strategy for peace. A. Bilski. il *Macleans* 100:32 Ja 19 '87
Survival without Soviets a remote hope in Kabul. J. Trimble and R. A. Manning. il map *U S News World Rep* 102:32-3 Mr 2 '87
Talks held in Geneva on situation relating to Afghanistan; Under-Secretary-General to continue efforts. *UN Chron* 23:76 N '86
Treaties of guarantee. J. H. Wolfe. il *USA Today (Periodical)* 116:63 Jl '87
War's backlash steps up Kremlin's hunt for way out. J. Trimble. il *U S News World Rep* 102:39 Mr 16 '87
Zia's Afghan dilemma [cease fire collapse] N. Cooper. il por *Newsweek* 109:42 F 16 '87
Reporters and reporting
Caught in the crossfire [excerpt] J. Goodwin. il por *Ladies Home J* 104:22+ Ap '87
J-school for Afghan rebels [Boston University project in Pakistan] E. Salholz. il *Newsweek* 109:75-6 Mr 30 '87
Afghanistan and Iran *See* Iran and Afghanistan
Afghanistan Day
Afghanistan Day, 1987 [proclamation, March 20, 1987] R. Reagan. *Dep State Bull* 87:87-8 Je '87
Afghans
Italy
The once and future king? [former king, Mohammed Zahir Shah] F. Willey. por *Newsweek* 109:39 Je 1 '87
AFL-CIO
The AFL-CIO: a tougher team with the Teamsters. A. Bernstein and S. B. Garland. il *Bus Week* p110 N 9 '87
AFL-CIO's strange bedfellows [Teamsters seek readmission] *U S News World Rep* 103:13 N 2 '87
A century of struggle [cover story; special section] bibl f il *Mon Labor Rev* 110:32-40 Ag '87
Labor & Nicaragua [urging condemnation of aid to the contras] *Nation* 245:472-3 O 31 '87
Labor's best candidate may be no candidate at all. R. Fly and S. B. Garland. il *Bus Week* p59 My 11 '87

AFL-CIO—*cont.*
A long-brewing boycott ends at Coors [AFL-CIO wins right to try to organize workers] *Newsweek* 110:46 Ag 31 '87
Long haul to democracy [Teamsters back in AFL-CIO] *Nation* 245:505 N 7 '87
Mobbed [Teamsters readmitted to the AFL-CIO] T. Geoghegan. *New Repub* 197:11-12 N 16 '87
Perks for the rank and file. B. Cohn. *Newsweek* 109:42 Ap 6 '87
Politics: a change of Hart [G. Hart courts union support] C. O'Connor. il por *Newsweek* 109:27 F 23 '87
The tragic impact of joblessness. R. A. Oswald. il *USA Today (Periodical)* 115:28-30 Mr '87
Will labor's Joe Sixpack come back to Coors? [union boycott ends as AFL-CIO wins right to organize] S. D. Atchison. il *Bus Week* p29 S 7 '87
AFL-CIO. American Institute for Free Labor Development
See American Institute for Free Labor Development
Africa
See also
Africans
Agriculture—Africa
AIDS (Disease)—Africa
Birth control—Africa
Birth rate—Africa
Child welfare—Africa
Civil rights—Africa
Congo River
Deserts—Africa
East Africa
Eating—Africa
Economic assistance, American—Africa
Food supply—Africa
Hunting—Africa
Medical care—Africa
Military assistance, Cuban—Africa
Paleontology—Africa
Public health—Africa
Relief work—Africa
Sahel
Southern Africa
Sports—Africa
Television broadcasting—Africa
United Nations—Africa
Veterinary medicine—Africa
West Africa
Regional report: Africa. B. Shelby. See issues of World Press Review beginning June 1986
Bibliography
Book reviews. *Curr Hist* 86:221+ My '87
Climate
See also
Droughts—Africa
Economic conditions
See also
United Nations. Economic Commission for Africa
Africa's population growth erodes living standards, World Bank study says. *UN Chron* 23:107 N '86
Economic policy
African development: an administration perspective [address, May 7, 1987] J. C. Whitehead. *Dep State Bull* 87:15-17 Jl '87
Secretary-General establishes Steering Committee to help implement African recovery programme. il *UN Chron* 23:94 N '86
Foreign relations
United States
See United States—Foreign relations—Africa
Industries
See also
Wine industry—Africa
Politics and government
See also
Organization of African Unity
Africa, 1987 [special issue] bibl f map (inside back cover) *Curr Hist* 86:193-234 My '87
Population
Africa's population growth erodes living standards, World Bank study says. *UN Chron* 23:107 N '86
Religious institutions and affairs
See also
Missions—Africa
Spirituality: an African view [interview with C. E. Glover, Jr.] J. D. Simmons. por *Essence* 18:61+ D '87
African art *See* Art, African
African Development Bank
Out of Africa [B. N'Diaye] E. A. Finn, Jr. il por *Forbes* 140:246 D 14 '87

African jewelry *See* Jewelry, African
African literature
The emergence of African voices. G. Weisser. *World Press Rev* 34:62 Mr '87
African locusts *See* Grasshoppers
African Methodist Episcopal Church
AME Church bicentennial. W. J. Dawkins. il *Black Enterp* 17:22 Jl '87
Bicentennial of the A.M.E. tradition. D. C. Lyons. il *Ebony* 43:108+ N '87
Church files $40 million damage suit; A.M.E. bishops announce their support [Metropolitan A.M.E. Church in Washington, D.C.] *Jet* 72:29 Ap 20 '87
Georgia leader urges AME delegates to fight crime [views of C. Smyre] *Jet* 73:32 S 28 '87
Historic D.C. church closed; blame nearby construction [Metropolitan African Methodist Episcopal Church] il *Jet* 71:37-8 Ja 26 '87
This far by faith [C. Williams-Bryant, black woman minister at Bethel AME Church, Baltimore] H. Cole and A. Edwards. il pors *Essence* 18:107-8+ S '87
African music *See* Music, African
African National Congress
ANC leader Mbeki freed after 23 years in jail. il *Jet* 73:28 N 23 '87
ANC turns 75. J. M. Woods. il *Black Enterp* 17:18 Ap '87
Freedom's friend or freedom's foe? [O. Tambo visits the U.S.] S. Powell. il por *U S News World Rep* 102:12 F 9 '87
The future of South Africa [address, November 24, 1986] G. M. Buthelezi. *Vital Speeches Day* 53:194-6 Ja 15 '87
'The government smashes our hope' [restrictions placed on G. Mbeki] il por *Newsweek* 110:49 D 21 '87
Hit squads in Africa? [attacks on officials] L. Howard. il *Newsweek* 110:6 Jl 27 '87
Mandela's ANC fights for a foothold. J. Jones. il *U S News World Rep* 103:36 S 7 '87
Oliver Tambo's war cry [visit to Canada] H. Mackenzie. il por *Macleans* 100:25 S 7 '87
Out of jail and on his feet [release of African National Congress leader G. Mbeki] R. Nordland. il por *Newsweek* 110:81 N 16 '87
The Red and the black [role of Communist Party member J. Slovo] W. R. Doerner. il por *Time* 129:36 Mr 2 '87
The return of a rebel [release of G. Mbeki] il por *U S News World Rep* 103:16-17 N 16 '87
The right books [Keith Campbell's ANC: a Soviet task force?] C. Williamson. *Natl Rev* 39:56 Mr 13 '87
Secretary meets with ANC leader Tambo [State Dept. statement, January 28, 1987] il pors *Dep State Bull* 87:28 Mr '87
South Africa: it takes two to Tambo [O. Tambo's visit to the U.S.] il por *Newsweek* 109:43 F 9 '87
Stiff challenge, swift reaction. W. Svoboda. il *Time* 129:38 Ja 19 '87
Talking with Tambo. H. Anderson. il *Newsweek* 109:26 Ja 19 '87
Tambo on tour [U.S. visit] *Nation* 244:167-8 F 14 '87
Tambo visit centers U.S. focus on S. Africa fight. il pors *Jet* 71:7 F 16 '87
Tambo's risky game [talks between African National Congress and Washington] M. Whitaker. il por *Newsweek* 109:34-5 F 2 '87
Tango with Tambo. *Natl Rev* 39:19 F 27 '87
Two questions about South Africa [efficacy of sanctions and Communist domination of African National Congress] D. Seligman. *Fortune* 115:122+ Mr 2 '87
Uncle Joe [J. Slovo] S. Mufson. *New Repub* 197:20-3 S 28 '87
Why free Mbeki? S. Mufson. *Nation* 245:670-1 D 5 '87
The African Queen [film] *See* Motion picture reviews—Single works
African refugees *See* Refugees, African
Africanized honey bees *See* Bees
Africano, Nicholas
about
Nicholas Africano at Holly Solomon. H. Cotter. *Art Am* 75:138-9 Mr '87
Africans
Foreign countries
AIDS: fear of foreigners. R. Nordland. il *Newsweek* 109:36 Ap 6 '87
Afrikaners
An Afrikaans insider questions the system [industrialist J. Rupert] S. Mufson. il por *Bus Week* p80+ My 18 '87

Afrikaners—*cont.*

South Africa: the Afrikaner angst. P. H. Baker. *Foreign Policy* 69:61-79 Wint '87/'88

United no more [Afrikaners opposed to apartheid] O. Friedrich. il *Time* 129:28-35+ My 4 '87

Afro-American (Black) History Month *See* Black History Month

Afro-Americans *See* Blacks

Afterlife *See* Future life

Afternoon teas *See* Teas

Aga Khan, Sadruddin, Prince, 1933-

about

"What a legacy for our children!" [interview] P. Gupte. il por *Forbes* 139:100+ Je 15 '87

Aga Khan, Yasmin *See* Khan, Yasmin

Aga Khan Award for Architecture *See* Architecture—Awards

Aga Khan University Hospital and Medical College

Indigenous high-tech [cover story] M. F. Schmertz. il *Archit Rec* 175:136-49 My '87

Agapanthus

Petite, midsize, or full-size? Time to choose agapanthus in bloom. il *Sunset* 178:254 My '87

Agar, Eunice

Audrey Ushenko. il *Am Artist* 51:42-5+ Mr '87

Monhegan: an artist's island. il map *Am Artist* 51:46-51+ My '87

Tom Orlando. il por *Am Artist* 51:40-3+ S '87

Agar, Michael

Sailors of the Fourth Coast try to look ahead. il *Smithsonian* 18:116-20+ S '87

Agassi, Andre

Diary of a rookie tour. il pors *World Tennis* 35:32-6+ D '87

Agassiz, Louis, 1807-1873

about

Hatracks and theories. S. J. Gould. il *Nat Hist* 96:12+ Mr '87

Agatha Christie's Miss Marple [television program] *See* Television program reviews—Single works

AGB Research plc *See* A G B Research plc

Age

See also

Aging

Air pilots—Age

Athletes—Age

Brokers—Age

Executives—Age

Longevity

Middle age

Reagan, Ronald, 1911-—Age

School age

Stars—Age

The aging of immunity [research by Steven J. Schleifer and others] J. Greenberg and B. Bower. *Sci News* 131:328 My 23 '87

Childbearing and age. M. Konner. il *N Y Times Mag* p22-3 D 27 '87

Animals

The age of the nautilus [work of Neil H. Landman] *Oceans* 20:5-6 N/D '87

Insects

Itching to know why man ages? Mosquitoes may help us find out [work of John P. Richie Jr. with nordihydroguaiaretic acid] il *Discover* 8:13-14 Ja '87

Psychology

All eyes on her [younger woman-older man] E. Harper. il *N Y Times Mag* p40 My 24 '87

Breaking the age taboo [loving a man younger than you] B. M. Campbell. il *Essence* 17:50-2+ F '87

It's about your heart [teenage boy and older woman] B. Greene. il *Esquire* 108:59-60+ S '87

Life flow [cover story; special section; with editorial comment] il *Psychol Today* 21:24-6+, 29-30+ My '87

Memory: age or practice? [prose recall; study by Hilary Horn Ratner] E. Stark. *Psychol Today* 21:24 O '87

Say, brother [relationship with older woman] L. Smith. por *Essence* 18:10+ Jl '87

Season of autumn-summer love [older women marrying younger men] A. Toufexis. il *Time* 130:75 N 30 '87

Turning 30 and going nowhere? [special section] il *Harpers Bazaar* 120:160+ O '87

Why women lie about their age. M. Hodge. il *50 Plus* 27:40-2 F '87

Reptiles

Why do turtles live so long? [cover story] J. W. Gibbons. bibl f il *BioScience* 37:262-9 Ap '87

AGE (Organization) *See* Americans for Generational Equity

Age and crime *See* Crime and age

Age and employment

See also

Aged—Employment

Children—Employment

Retirement

Youth—Employment

An aging work force puts a drag on the economy . . . and has a hand in squelching big wage gains. G. Koretz. il *Bus Week* p17 Jl 27 '87

Age and intelligence

Older and wiser? [Everyday Problem-Solving Inventory intelligence test; research by Steven W. Cornelius and Avshalom Caspi] A. H. Rosenfeld. *Psychol Today* 21:20 N '87

Age determination by radioactivity *See* Radioactive dating

Age Discrimination in Employment Act *See* Discrimination in employment

Aged

See also

Ageism

Aging

Alcohol and the aged

Centenarians

Dance and the aged

Drugs and the aged

Gerontology

Industry—Elderly services programs

Information storage and retrieval systems—Aged

Nursing home patients

Retirement

Telephone in service to the aged

Theater and the aged

United States. Administration on Aging

Between issues. *New Leader* 70:2 O 5 '87

The elders among us. A. McCarthy. *Commonweal* 114:138-9 Mr 13 '87

Experience exchange. See issues of Aging

News notes. See issues of Aging

The oldest old: the years after 85. J. Meer. map *Psychol Today* 21:82 My '87

P-s-s-t. See issues of 50 Plus

State and community news. See issues of Aging

The Ten Commandments of an aging society [address, November 6, 1987] R. D. Lamm. *Vital Speeches Day* 54:133-9 D 15 '87

Activities

See also

Aged—Political activities

Aged—Travel

Experience exchange. See issues of Aging

The smartest thing I did in my 60s. M. Reiter. il *50 Plus* 27:24-7+ F '87

Bibliography

Publications. See issues of Aging

Care and hygiene

See also

Aged—Housing

Aged—Medical care

Day care for the aged

Foster home care for the aged

Home care services

Life care communities

Nursing homes

Senior Companion Program (U.S.)

United States. Congress. House. Select Committee on Aging. Subcommittee on Health and Long-Term Care

$2.4 million for projects focusing on family caregivers. J. Steen. il *Aging* no356:38-9 '87

AARP caregiver pubs for employers, local groups and individuals. *Aging* no355:26-7 '87

Age-proofing the home. C. Simon. il *Psychol Today* 21:52-3 D '87

Business helps the elderly [Gatekeeper Program] il *Futurist* 21:53 Mr/Ap '87

The Chinese and the Eskimos. P. Chance. *Psychol Today* 21:47 Jl '87

Commissioner's corner [booklet entitled Where to turn for help for older persons] C. F. Fisk. il *Aging* no355:inside cover '87

Diabetics and the elderly—special care for vulnerable feet. il *Prevention* 39:125-6+ Mr '87

Ethical guidelines for assisting the elderly. D. Christiansen. il *America* 156:72-5 Ja 31 '87

A grand old age. E. Beregi. il *Courier* 40:25-7 Ag '87

The graying of America spawns a new crisis. S. B. Garland. il *Bus Week* p60+ Ag 17 '87

Health styles of the rich and famous. D. Ragan. il *50 Plus* 27:92-4 Mr '87

A healthy future for older Americans [study by Lois Verbrugge] il *USA Today (Periodical)* 115:6 My '87

Healthy New Year! [special section] il *50 Plus* 27:29-32+ Ja '87

Aged—Care and hygiene—*cont.*

How you gonna keep 'em down on the (fat) farm after they've seen George Lawroski's workout video? [exercises for aged based on farm chore movement] il *People Wkly* 28:179 N 30 '87

Hypothermia and the elderly. *FDA Consum* 21:34-5 F '87

Keep it simple [cover story; excerpt from Always beautiful] K. Pickford. il por *50 Plus* 27:26-30 Ag '87

New options for the aging. M. Loeb. il *Saturday Evening Post* 259:112 O '87

Planning ahead together [adult children caring for their parents] K. Leishman. bibl il *McCalls* 114:65-7 Jl '87

A tale of two regeneration people [Laurie Spicer and Leah O'Toole] M. Golin. il *Prevention* 39:70+ F '87

True stories of regeneration. R. Rodale. il *Prevention* 39:17-18+ Jl '87

The use of community services. D. Fowles. il *Aging* no355:36-inside back cover '87

A walker in the city [95 yr. old G. Clark of New York City] B. Kevles. il por *N Y* 20:32 S 28 '87

"We have a problem" [aged parent living with son's family] J. Marks. il *Parents* 62:82+ Ap '87

Clubs and societies
See also
Senior centers

Crimes against
See also
Aged—Mistreatment

Economic conditions
See also
Retirement income

Aging in America: wealth and the elderly. R. England. *Current* 294:26-9 Jl/Ag '87

Life planning for old age, focus of AoA projects. J. H. Wehling. *Aging* no356:37-8 '87

Poverty key to troubles of nation's black seniors. il *Jet* 72:51 S 7 '87

Poverty linked with living alone. M. Hodge. il *50 Plus* 27:17-18 Mr '87

Twilight self-sufficiency. A. McGrath. il *U S News World Rep* 103:60 Ag 3 '87

Education
See also
Elderhostel

Expanding the domain of arts education. P. Greenberg. bibl f *Des Arts Educ* 88:39-40 Ja/F '87

The last diploma he got was in high school, but Ed Gorman, 69, is setting his cap on a masters from Oxford [American student] il por *People Wkly* 27:58 Ap 20 '87

Employment
See also
Aged and business

Adjusting to an aging population. C. Holden. il *Science* 236:772-3 My 15 '87

Age bias: the uphill battle. J. Mitchell. *50 Plus* 27:32+ Mr '87

Age bias: the uphill battle [interview with C. G. Mackaronis] F. Greve. il por *50 Plus* 27:33-6 Mr '87

The back-to-work handbook [excerpt from Making more money] J. S. Mitchell. il *50 Plus* 27:36+ Jl '87

Courts v. EEOC on over-65 pension rights. A. J. Sheinman. *50 Plus* 27:19-20 My '87

EEOC defines "age harassment". A. J. Sheinman. *50 Plus* 27:14+ Ag '87

The "graying" of America [address, May 15, 1987] R. B. Maxwell. *Vital Speeches Day* 53:710-12 S 15 '87

How to win on social security [repeal earnings penalty] M. S. Forbes, Jr. il *Forbes* 140:27 D 28 '87

Let's get serious about age bias. B. Lindeman. il *50 Plus* 27:4-5 O '87

Older worker project delivers jobs to Oklahoma seniors. H. Atkins. il *Aging* no356:26-7 '87

Workers rejecting incentives to stay on the job [views of Carolyn E. Paul on early retirement] il *USA Today (Periodical)* 115:16+ Ap '87

Working after you retire. *Black Enterp* 18:42 S '87

Family relationships
$2.4 million for projects focusing on family caregivers. J. Steen. il *Aging* no356:38-9 '87

AARP caregiver pubs for employers, local groups and individuals. *Aging* no355:26-7 '87

The aged mother. R. Rosenblatt. il *Time* 129:78 Je 1 '87

Are you taking care of someone who is sick or elderly? Help may be ahead for you. M. Engel. il *Glamour* 85:50+ My '87

A calendar of feasts [mother's growing frailty] R. A. Blake. il *America* 156:321-3 Ap 18 '87

Caring for nana [women over 50 caring for an aging parent] M. Opsata. il *50 Plus* 27:54-9 Ja '87

Elders abused by their loved ones [study by Karl Pillemer and David Finkelhor] il *USA Today (Periodical)* 116:8-9 S '87

Ethical guidelines for assisting the elderly. D. Christiansen. il *America* 156:72-5 Ja 31 '87

The graying of America spawns a new crisis. S. B. Garland. il *Bus Week* p60+ Ag 17 '87

The nursing home dilemma. T. Stafford. il *Christ Today* 31:22 N 6 '87

Planning ahead together [adult children caring for their parents] K. Leishman. bibl il *McCalls* 114:65-7 Jl '87

Son, behold your mother. T. Unsworth. *U S Cathol* 52:28-30 Jl '87

Talking more easily with older people. il *Glamour* 85:100 N '87

"We have a problem" [aged parent living with son's family] J. Marks. il *Parents* 62:82+ Ap '87

Federal aid
See Old age assistance

Gardens and gardening
Tough guys grow petunias. S. Brewer. il *50 Plus* 27:28-31 My '87

Turning your green thumb into a new career [cover story] S. Brewer. il *50 Plus* 27:27-31 O '87

Health and hygiene
See Aged—Care and hygiene

Housing
See also
Foster home care for the aged
Halfway houses for the aged
Life care communities
Nursing homes

Adaptive reuse for elderly housing [report] *Aging* no355:26 '87

Age-proofing the home. C. Simon. il *Psychol Today* 21:52-3 D '87

The Commissioner's corner. C. F. Fisk. *Aging* no356:inside cover '87

Congregate housing development guide for small communities. *Aging* no356:31 '87

Here's a win-win deal: buy your folks' house. G. Weiss. il *Bus Week* p110-11 Je 15 '87

Housing options for seniors today. P. B. Pollak. il *Aging* no356:2-5 '87

Old buildings come alive [reuse for elderly housing] L. McNickle and B. Deacon. il *Aging* no356:6-12 '87

An old woman's victory garden [independence at home] M. K. Blakely. il por *Ms* 16:94+ S '87

Recycled schools [conversion into housing] M. Sinclair. *50 Plus* 27:17-18 Jl '87

Reverse mortgages: the new way to use home equity. M. Hodge. il *50 Plus* 27:32-5 Jl '87

The right mix [R. Millican's mixed-use building provides housing for the elderly in New York City] G. Wen. il por *N Y* 20:42 S 21 '87

Rose finally unpacked her belongings [Wallace H. Campbell & Co. and Jewish Family Services team up to run high-rise apartment for the elderly in Baltimore, Md.] J. B. Kurland and G. E. J. Lipsitz. il *Aging* no355:6-9 '87

Surplus schools can serve the community. K. Noyes. il *Aging* no356:13-16 '87

The trade-down: your golden home. G. Anrig, Jr. il *Money* 16:103-4+ Je '87

International aspects
Our aging world. G. Canal Ramírez. *World Press Rev* 34:28 Ag '87

Legal status, laws, etc.
See also
Coalition of Advocates for the Rights of the Infirm Elderly
Legal assistance to the aged
National Senior Citizens Law Center (U.S.)

It's still full speed ahead for Ralph Nader. I. Wolfman. il por *50 Plus* 27:24-7 N '87

Who's guarding the guardians? M. Sinclair. il *50 Plus* 27:12+ D '87

Medical care
See also
Home care services
Medicaid
Medicare
United States. Congress. House. Select Committee on Aging. Subcommittee on Health and Long-Term Care

Aged—Medical care—*cont.*

Ageism is bad medicine [doctors' attitudes] B. Lindeman. il *50 Plus* 27:4 Ja '87

Aging in America: wealth and the elderly. R. England. *Current* 294:26-9 Jl/Ag '87

A bridge between hospital and home [Halfway to Health housing program] L. A. Poppleton and R. Cornman. il *Aging* no355:12-13 [14-15] '87

The crisis in health benefits. S. B. Garland. il *Bus Week* p36 Je 15 '87

Employer-sponsored health insurance for retirees: the need and the cost. *Mon Labor Rev* 110:38 My '87

Examining the limits of life [views of D. Callahan] B. Angelo. il por *Time* 130:76-7 N 2 '87

The eyes have it [National Eye Care Project] *50 Plus* 27:18 Ag '87

Letters [discussion of August 15-22, 1987 article, Limiting health care for the old] D. Callahan. *Nation* 245:362+ O 10 '87

Limiting health care for the old [cover story] D. Callahan. *Nation* 245:109+ Ag 15-22 '87

The medicine vendors. E. Kiester. il *50 Plus* 27:36-40+ Ja '87

Meeting the elderly's growing health needs [Office of Technology Assessment report] il *Futurist* 21:54 My/Je '87

No patience for elder patients [ageism among physicians; study by Michele G. Greene] M. Schanback. il *Psychol Today* 21:22 F '87

Panel urges dementia be diagnosed with care. G. Kolata. *Science* 237:725 Ag 14 '87

The rising cost of health care: what it means to the nation, the elderly, and you [cover story; special issue] il *Sch Update* 119:2-12+ Ap 20 '87

Senior Center becomes medical satellite to hospital in Pittsburgh [Vintage Senior Adult Center and West Penn Hospital] il *Aging* no355:29-30 '87

Shouldn't you get immunized? P. Spencer. il *50 Plus* 27:16+ O '87

Sick retirees could kill your company. J. Nielsen. il *Fortune* 115:98-9 Mr 2 '87

Unfunded, nonregulated, miscalculated [retiree health benefits] C. Murphy. il *50 Plus* 27:14+ O '87

Memory

See Memory

Mental health

See Aged—Psychology

Mistreatment

Attacking elderly abuse [Texas] P. Chance. il *Psychol Today* 21:24-5 S '87

Elders abused by their loved ones [study by Karl Pillemer and David Finkelhor] il *USA Today (Periodical)* 116:8-9 S '87

Nutrition

Eat it, we're paying you! [nutrition study at Tufts University] E. Kiester. il *50 Plus* 27:24-5+ Ag '87

The feel like a million diet. S. C. Finn. il *50 Plus* 27:32-6+ My '87

Hospital offers senior suppers [Anna Jaques Hospital in Newburyport, Mass.] il *Aging* no356:29 '87

A Meals on Wheels program adds liquid nutrient supplements. *Aging* no355:31-2 '87

Old friends [New York City's Meals on Wheels program] G. Greene. il *N Y* 20:10-11 Ja 12 '87

Test your nutrition IQ. S. C. Finn. il *50 Plus* 27:56+ F '87

Turn over a new leaf. F. Ferretti. il *50 Plus* 27:74-7 Mr '87

USDA bulletins tell Americans how to apply the dietary guidelines. *Aging* no355:27 '87

Occupations

Get paid for your advice! R. Brody. il *50 Plus* 27:67+ N '87

Turning your green thumb into a new career [cover story] S. Brewer. il *50 Plus* 27:27-31 O '87

Pensions

See Pensions

Political activities

The Peace March presses on. L. Lindeman. il *50 Plus* 27:22+ F '87

Still on the road for peace [veterans of the Great Peace March continue to be involved] L. Lindeman. il *50 Plus* 27:20-2 Je '87

Taking the long road to peace [Americans join Soviets in peace march through Russia] L. Lindeman. il *50 Plus* 27:50-5 O '87

Psychology

50-plussers are conservatives at heart! [mellowness of maturity] W. F. Buckley. il pors *50 Plus* 27:56-60 Mr '87

Old memories [work of Elisabeth Koss and others] *Sci Am* 256:26+ Je '87

An old woman's victory garden [independence at home] M. K. Blakely. il por *Ms* 16:94+ S '87

A quicker response [improving video game response time; research by Jane E. Clark] P. McCarthy. *Psychol Today* 21:23 O '87

Reading between the lines [role of age in interpreting emotional expression; study by Carol Zander Malatesta] A. H. Rosenfeld. *Psychol Today* 21:16 O '87

The vintage years. J. C. Horn and J. Meer. bibl (p95) il *Psychol Today* 21:76-7+ My '87

Weakened, memories, but sound minds [views of Elizabeth Zelinski] *USA Today (Periodical)* 116:5-6 Ag '87

What does a sixty-year-old man see when he looks in the mirror? T. B. Morgan. il *Esquire* 107:161-4+ My '87

You're as young as you think. H. H. Broun. il *50 Plus* 27:100 Mr '87

Recreation

See also

Aged—Travel

Elderhostel

Getting the homebound out of the house [National Council of Jewish Women recreation program at senior center in Brooklyn, N.Y.] il *Aging* no355:22 '87

Tailgating: nobody does it better than seniors! L. Wheeler. il *50 Plus* 27:68-70 S '87

Religious life

See also

Church work with the aged

The gift of aging. C. E. Simcox. *Christ Century* 104:1090-2 D 2 '87

Retirement

See Retirement

Social security

See Social security

Sports

See also

Senior Olympics

The 7th annual All-America Team [aged athletes] H. Higdon. il *50 Plus* 27:58-64 N '87

Advantage: Gardnar Mulloy [tennis player] L. Lindeman. il pors *50 Plus* 27:68-70+ Ja '87

Aging gracefully. N. Kuscsik. il *Women's Sports Fitness* 9:16-21 O '87

A celebration of life [senior tennis] S. Stevenson. il *World Tennis* 35:38-42 O '87

My first jump [skydiving at age 70] D. Fitzpatrick. il *Read Dig* 130:29-30+ Mr '87

Of tykes and patriarchs [skiing] A. H. Greenberg. *Skiing* 40:40-1 D '87

Older athletes: ice and fire. H. H. Broun. il *50 Plus* 27:80 N '87

Snow job [H. Higdon promotes skiing for older people] B. Lindeman. il *50 Plus* 27:6 F '87

Take a dive [scuba diving] G. Norman. il *50 Plus* 27:32-6 S '87

Anecdotes, facetiae, satire, etc.

Exit laughing [only men and women aged sixty-five and over should be permitted to hunt and fish] E. Zern. il *Field Stream* 91:150 Mr '87

State aid

See Old age assistance

Statistics

Captain's log. D. Fowles. il *Aging* no356:44-inside back cover '87

Suicide

See Suicide

Taxation

Good news, bad news for 50-plussers. R. Rosenblatt. il *50 Plus* 27:17-18 F '87

How to win on social security [repeal earnings penalty] M. S. Forbes, Jr. il *Forbes* 140:27 D 28 '87

Nasty surprise for older taxpayers? *50 Plus* 27:22 N '87

Survival of the smartest. M. Hodge. il *50 Plus* 27:75-7 Ja '87

Working after you retire. *Black Enterp* 18:42 S '87

Terminology

A classic case [suggestions for the perfect alternative to "senior citizen"] G. G. Hotchkiss. il *50 Plus* 27:10 Je '87

Travel

Don't let your travel agent take you for a ride. A. Keefe. il *50 Plus* 27:56-7 O '87

Hooked on cruising. J. Clarke. il *50 Plus* 27:44-5+ My '87

Aged—Travel—*cont.*
Jet-sitters [globetrotting contest among C. D. Buckley, J. Clouse, and P. Thompson] il pors *Life* 10:91-4 My '87
Kings of the road [J. Clouse and P. Thompson] B. Rice. il pors *50 Plus* 27:22-5+ Mr '87
On the road again [Airstream trailer couple Lueen and Howard Miller] R. Micheli. il *Money* 16:140-4 S '87
The race to visit every country on earth [competition between J. Clouse and P. Thompson] B. Rice. il *50 Plus* 27:17 Ap '87
Snowbirds [migratory retirees descend on the Rio Grande Valley each winter] L. M. Keefe. il *Forbes* 139:117-18 Mr 23 '87
Ten trusty tips for packing light. A. Keefe. il *50 Plus* 27:78+ Mr '87

Canada
Today's baby-boomers, tomorrow's elderly. L. Hurst. *World Press Rev* 34:26-8 Ag '87

China
The Chinese and the Eskimos. P. Chance. *Psychol Today* 21:47 Jl '87

Greece
History
Greek geriatrics [ancient Greece] R. Garland. bibl il *Hist Today* 37:12-18 S '87

Japan
Adjusting to an aging population. C. Holden. il *Science* 236:772-3 My 15 '87

United States
See Aged
Aged and business
Business helps the elderly [Gatekeeper Program] il *Futurist* 21:53 Mr/Ap '87
Aged and children *See* Child-adult relationship
Aged and dance *See* Dance and the aged
Aged and drugs *See* Drugs and the aged
Aged and mass media
Aging America campaign to publicize the aging network. *Aging* no355:25-6 '87
Distorted images: the elderly and the media. L.-M. Delloff. il *Christ Century* 104:12-16 Ja 7-14 '87
Aged and the press
Why seven magazines pretend you don't exist [women's magazines] D. Heyn. il *50 Plus* 27:38-41 Mr '87
Aged and theater *See* Theater and the aged
Aged as artists
Elizabeth Layton: portrait of the artist as an old woman. A. Fadiman. il pors *Life* 10:21-2 Mr '87
Aged as authors
When I retire . . . D. M. Murray. *Writer* 100:5-6 F '87
Aged as consumers *See* Aged market
Aged as musicians
See also
Senior Citizens' Orchestra of Miami Beach
Aged athletes *See* Athletes
Aged in cable television
TV goes gray at the grass roots. A. J. Sheinman. il *50 Plus* 27:24-7+ S '87
Aged in television
How gray is network TV? *50 Plus* 27:54-5 S '87
It's take two for former teacher Leona Morris as she starts another career on Baltimore TV. il por *People Wkly* 27:84 Ap 27 '87
What makes The golden girls so hot? J. Porcino. il *50 Plus* 27:28-30 S '87
Aged market
Packaging for the older consumer [address, March 6, 1987] M. Bender. *Vital Speeches Day* 53:490-2 Je 1 '87

Japan
The rush is on to mine the 'silver generation'. M. Berger. il *Bus Week* p52-3 Je 15 '87
Aged prisoners *See* Prisoners
Aged volunteers in education *See* Volunteer workers in education
Ageism
Ageism is bad medicine [doctors' attitudes] B. Lindeman. il *50 Plus* 27:4 Ja '87
No patience for elder patients [ageism among physicians; study by Michele G. Greene] M. Schanback. il *Psychol Today* 21:22 F '87
Agencies, Advertising *See* Advertising agencies
Agencies, Employment *See* Employment agencies
Agencies, Federal *See* United States—Executive departments
Agencies, Literary *See* Literary agencies and agents
Agencies, Regulatory *See* Regulatory agencies
Agencies, Travel *See* Travel agencies and agents
Agency for International Development (U.S.) *See* United States. Agency for International Development

Agent Orange
Agent Orange study hits brick wall [Vietnam veterans] W. Booth. il *Science* 237:1285-6 S 11 '87
Answers at last? [research] J. Gardner. il *Nation* 244:460-2 Ap 11 '87
A piece of the action [litigation and lawyer compensation] D. Fanning. il *Forbes* 140:68 O 19 '87
A war with hope [Vietnam vet's battle with Agent Orange-induced cancer]; ed. by John Grossmann. E. Zumwalt, III. il por *Health* 19:86+ Je '87
Agents, Literary *See* Literary agencies and agents
Agents, Real estate *See* Real estate agencies and agents
Agents, Sports *See* Sports agencies and agents
Agents, Talent *See* Theatrical agencies and agents
Agents of foreign principals *See* Foreign propagandists
Aggression (International law)
See also
United Nations. Special Committee on Enhancing the Effectiveness of the Principle of the Non-Use of Force in International Relations
Aggressive behavior in animals *See* Animals—Habits and behavior
Aggressiveness (Psychology)
See also
Assertiveness (Psychology)
Hostility (Psychology)
Violence
How aggressive can you be with a man? P. Grant. *Glamour* 85:254 F '87
Aggressiveness in children
See also
Bullying
Aghion, Dany Simon
New life for a medieval castle: architect Roger Anger reclaims a Provençal ruin. il *Archit Dig* 44:184-9+ Mr '87
Agility *See* Motor ability
Aging
See also
Gerontology
Aging gracefully. N. Kuscsik. il *Women's Sports Fitness* 9:16-21 O '87
Anti-aging beauty: the myths, the facts. S. Sommers. il *Ladies Home J* 104:68+ N '87
Beat the clock! G. Witkin-Lanoil. il *Health* 19:8 Mr '87
Can you stop the aging clock? E. Kiester. il *50 Plus* 27:20-3 Ag '87
Extended culture of mouse embryo cells without senescence: inhibition by serum. D. T. Loo and others. bibl f il *Science* 236:200-2 Ap 10 '87
Glucose and aging. A. C. Cerami and others. bibl (p128) il *Sci Am* 256:90-6 My '87
How old is your body? Beat-the-clock strategies. J. Kaplan. il *Mademoiselle* 93:92+ Je '87
Human aging: usual and successful. J. W. Rowe and R. L. Kahn. bibl f *Science* 237:143-9 Jl 10 '87
Lowering pressure as a fountain of youth? [research by Aram V. Chobanian] J. Silberner. *Sci News* 131:89 F 7 '87
The molecular biology of aging. J. P. Cohn. il *BioScience* 37:99-102 F '87
The riddle of aging. A. H. Becker. il *Christ Today* 31:18-19 N 6 '87
Sensory underload [aging and sensory loss] R. Sekuler and R. Blake. il *Psychol Today* 21:48-51 D '87

Anecdotes, facetiae, satire, etc.
Cosby comes of age [condensed from Time flies] B. Cosby. il *Read Dig* 131:111-14 N '87
Son of 'Fatherhood' [B. Cosby's Time flies] H. F. Waters. il pors *Newsweek* 110:78-9 S 14 '87
Time flies [excerpt] B. Cosby. il por *Good Housekeep* 205:60+ S '87

Conferences
See Gerontology—Conferences

Nutritional aspects
Your diet: anti-aging eating? J. S. Stern. *Vogue* 177:372 Ag '87

Psychology
See Aged—Psychology

Research
See Gerontology
Aging Administration (U.S.) *See* United States. Administration on Aging
Agins, Neuma
about
One woman's smart formula: don't only tend to your knitting. J. Alexander. il por *Money* 16:41-2+ N '87
Agnelli, Marella
Villar Perosa. il *House Gard* 159:144-53+ S '87

Agnes, the indomitable de Mille [television program] See Television program reviews—Single works
Agnes von Hohenstaufen [opera] See Spontini, Gasparo, 1774-1851
Agnos, Art
about
An upstart mayor, a shaky future. P. A. Witteman. il por *Time* 130:29-30 D 21 '87
Agranoff, Ann
(jt. auth) See Anderes, Fred, and Agranoff, Ann
Agrarian reform See Land reform
Agreements See Contracts
Agreements, Collective labor See Collective labor agreements
Agribusiness See Agricultural industries
Agricultural accidents See Agriculture—Accidents
Agricultural administration
See also
Land reform
United States. Dept. of Agriculture
Anatomy of a rip-off [Archer-Daniels-Midland profiting from government agricultural subsidies and gasohol program] J. A. Barnes. *New Repub* 197:20-1 N 2 '87
Barter system has little potential, says Lyng [field hearing of the Senate Agriculture Committee in Burlington, Vt.] *Success Farm* 85:62J O '87
Can we put U.S. agriculture on the road to recovery? D. Amstutz. il *USA Today (Periodical)* 116:18-20 N '87
Cattlemen: don't dismiss the 50/92 option. B. Eftink. il *Success Farm* 85 no5:26Q Mr '87
Congress to mull mandatory crop controls. *Success Farm* 85 no1:14A Ja '87
Court: accused farmers deserve due process, too [farm program payments] *Success Farm* 85:46 S '87
Dairy buyout ends. J. R. Borcherding. il *Success Farm* 85:44+ O '87
The farm opportunity [conservation easements] P. A. A. Berle. *Audubon* 89:4 Ja '87
Farmers continue court battles with lenders; Lenders gut Nebraska debt law. *Success Farm* 85 no4:18AM F '87
Farmers: 'Get lost, Uncle Sam'. *Success Farm* 85:62F-62G O '87
Farmers will reap a bumper crop of supports. M. A. Pollock. *Bus Week* p83 Ja 12 '87
Government farm programs yield higher prices. C. Warden. il *Consum Res Mag* 70:26-9 N '87
Green thumbs: the PIK and Roll and other scams from the farm belt. J. L. Pasley. il *Wash Mon* 19:11-14+ S '87
Harkin bill will turn heads this spring [Harkin-Gephardt Save the Family Farm bill] *Success Farm* 85 no4:6 F '87
Harvest '87: making hay [subsidies as campaign issue] D. Gates. il *Newsweek* 110:6 Ag 24 '87
The heretics of the heartland [farmers that want off the public dole] J. McCormick. il por *Newsweek* 109:46-7 Mr 30 '87
Hold down weeds on idle acres. J. Walter and B. Freese. il *Success Farm* 85 no1:24-5 Ja '87
Hold milk output in line to avoid 1988 support cut. J. R. Borcherding. *Success Farm* 85:D1 Je '87
In the farm belt, the worst is over. T. Smart. il *Bus Week* p46-7 My 18 '87
Income cap is only farm program surprise. T. White. il *Success Farm* 85 no1:6 Ja '87
New life on the farm. K. R. Sheets. il *U S News World Rep* 103:18-20 Ag 31 '87
One good subsidy merits another [U.S. subsidizes wheat sale to Soviet Union] *Newsweek* 109:61 My 11 '87
Options afloat to chop farm program costs. *Success Farm* 85:5 My '87
PIK and Roll: you sell, buy; then sell again. *Success Farm* 85:62F O '87
Proposed changes threaten big farms [$50,000 payment rules] D. Allen and P. Smith. il *Success Farm* 85:42-4 Ag '87
Seeds of recovery in the Farmbelt. G. Bock. il *Time* 130:44 D 7 '87
Some dare call them . . . robber barons [government agricultural subsidies and gasohol program] M. Fumento. il *Natl Rev* 39:32-3+ Mr 13 '87
Sowing a revolution in farm policy. T. Smart. il *Bus Week* p84-5 O 26 '87
Time to retrain the American farmer. L. C. Thurow. il *Technol Rev* 90:22-3 My/Je '87
Trade frictions and farm subsidies. H. Banks. *Forbes* 139:27 Ja 26 '87
U.S. foreign agricultural policy and the sugar program [address, February 24, 1987] D. W. McMinn. *Dep State Bull* 87:40-3 My '87

The unsweetened truth about sugar subsidies. T. K. Billington. *Read Dig* 131:51-4 Ag '87
Use it or lose it. C. Siler. il *Forbes* 140:80+ D 14 '87
Washington report. P. Smith. See issues of Successful Farming beginning April 1987
What do Cory Aquino, cocaine addicts, and American consumers have in common? They are all victims of the U.S. sugar program. R. Karaim. *Wash Mon* 19:17-21 N '87
What's known now about next year's farm program. *Success Farm* 85:10 S '87
Who's getting federal payments? *Success Farm* 85:18AN Ap '87
Why big feedlots feel 'PIKed' on. B. Eftink. il *Success Farm* 85 no2:B4+ Ja '87
Why farm subsidies have come a cropper. W. Tucker. il *Read Dig* 130:81-6 Ja '87
International aspects
Attacking farm subsidies. D. Jenish. il *Macleans* 100:30 Jl 20 '87
International agricultural trade reform [statement, July 6, 1987] R. Reagan. *Dep State Bull* 87:33 S '87
Pleading for the farmers [western Canadian leaders call for increased federal aid and end to global subsidies] J. Howse. *Macleans* 100:15 Je 8 '87
Subsidies, science more powerful than demand [views of Dennis Avery] *Success Farm* 85 no1:27 Ja '87
The war over subsidies [Canada's campaign to end international agricultural support payments] M. Janigan. il *Macleans* 100:14 Je 1 '87
While his attack on farm subsidies seems doomed [global campaign launched by R. Reagan] T. Smart. *Bus Week* p83 Jl 20 '87
A worldwide glut of food. M. Drohan. il *Macleans* 100:37-8 N 9 '87
Canada
Down and out on the farm [Ottawa sets grain prices] M. Janigan. il *Macleans* 100:8-10 My 4 '87
Down times on the farm. M. McIver. *Macleans* 100:64 S 28 '87
Pleading for the farmers [western Canadian leaders call for increased federal aid and end to global subsidies] J. Howse. *Macleans* 100:15 Je 8 '87
The war over subsidies [Canada's campaign to end international agricultural support payments] M. Janigan. il *Macleans* 100:14 Je 1 '87
China
China lights a 'Spark'. K. Forestier-Walker. il *World Press Rev* 34:46-7 Ag '87
China's food policy and population. K.-I. Chen. bibl f *Curr Hist* 86:257-60+ S '87
Cuba
Marx's carbuncles. J. Beatty. il *Atlantic* 259:20+ Ja '87
Japan
Rebel with a cause [Lion Petroleum's T. Sato's campaign against rice subsidies] A. Tanzer. il por *Forbes* 139:84+ Mr 23 '87
The rice plot [rice subsidies] J. M. Fallows. il *Atlantic* 259:22-6 Ja '87
Mexico
Mexico's agricultural policy. S. W. Sanderson. bibl f *Curr Hist* 86:109-12+ Mr '87
United States
See Agricultural administration
Agricultural airplanes See Airplanes in agriculture
Agricultural banks See Agricultural credit
Agricultural chemicals
See also
Herbicides
Pesticides
Computers can simplify chemical buying choices. *Success Farm* 85 no5:26F Mr '87
Handling
Pneumatics enjoy whirlwind success. D. Mowitz. il *Success Farm* 85 no4:22-5 F '87
Wind tunnel measures drift [dry granule agricultural chemicals displaced by wind] R. Fee. il *Success Farm* 85 no5:26AN Mr '87
Laws and regulations
Food that can save your life. R. Rodale. il *Prevention* 39:17-18+ Ag '87
You can help turn the toxic tide (I). R. Rodale. il *Rodale's Org Gard* 34:20-2 Jl '87
You can help turn the toxic tide (II). R. Rodale. il *Rodale's Org Gard* 34:18-20 Ag '87
Safety devices and measures
Industry comes alive on chemical safety. B. Freese. il *Success Farm* 85:18AV Ap '87

Agricultural contracts *See* Contracts, Agricultural
Agricultural cooperation *See* Agriculture, Cooperative
Agricultural cooperatives *See* Agriculture, Cooperative
Agricultural credit
    See also
    Farm Credit System (U.S.)
    United States. Farmers Home Administration
Dealers becoming hard-liners on credit [fertilizer dealers]
    R. Fee. *Success Farm* 85 no5:21 Mr '87
Fighting to stave off foreclosure, farmer Garth Conlan
    ends up taking his bank to the cleaners. D. Grogan.
    il por *People Wkly* 28:50-2 Ag 10 '87
Restructuring lowered breakeven costs. D. Allen. il *Success
    Farm* 85:62T O '87
Some banks expand ag loans. *Success Farm* 85:40 Ag
    '87
Laws and regulations
    See Agricultural administration
Agricultural diversification *See* Diversification in agriculture
Agricultural ecology
Concentrate your garden's greening power. R. Rodale.
    il *Rodale's Org Gard* 34:16-18 Ap '87
Conservation of traditional agroecosystems. M. L. Oldfield
    and J. B. Alcorn. bibl f il *BioScience* 37:199-208 Mr
    '87
Down on the farm: genetic engineering meets ecology.
    D. Pimentel. il *Technol Rev* 90:24-30 Ja '87
Farmer of the future: a conservationist [excerpt from
    1939 essay] A. Leopold. il *Success Farm* 85 no6:22-3
    Mr '87
Farming with a future: the passing of the plow [permacul-
    ture; interview with B. Mollison, W. Jackson, and
    M. Fukuoka] P. Stone. bibl il pors *Mother Earth
    News* 104:110-14+ Mr/Ap '87
The healing garden [regeneration gardening] R. Rodale.
    il *Rodale's Org Gard* 34:24-6 F '87
Monoculture. J. F. Power and R. F. Follett. il *Sci Am*
    256:78-86 Mr '87
Observing the fruits of research on low-input agriculture
    [visit of government officials to Rodale Institute's
    Experimental Farms] N. Bell. *BioScience* 37:548 S
    '87
Conferences
International Permaculture Conference. J. Cox. *Rodale's
    Org Gard* 34:30-1 F '87
Agricultural economics *See* Agriculture—Economic aspects
Agricultural education
    See also
    Gasconade Farm
Learning to homestead [Malachite Small Farm School,
    Colo.] S. Voynick. il *Ctry J* 14:60 Ja '87
What schools teach kids about agriculture. C. Tevis.
    il *Success Farm* 85 no3:M6 F '87
Agricultural equipment
    See also
    All terrain vehicles—Agricultural use
    Baling machinery
    Cultivators
    Dairy equipment
    Grain dryers
    Grain handling
    Harvesting machinery
    Hoes
    Irrigation equipment
    Mowing machines
    Planters (Farm machines)
    Spraying equipment
Farm ideas from around the world. G. Vincent and
    D. Mowitz. il *Success Farm* 85 no6:14-17 Mr '87
Machinery. See issues of Successful Farming
Anecdotes, facetiae, satire, etc.
Read for fun: farmer-humorist's 'machinery guide'. J.
    Cordova. *Success Farm* 85 no3:18 F '87
Cost of operation
Bold buying decisions. D. Allen and C. Finck. il *Success
    Farm* 85:24-7 O '87
Farmers who machine themselves to the times [joint
    ownership of equipment] C. Finck. il *Success Farm*
    85:18BA Ap '87
Leasing and renting
Bold buying decisions. D. Allen and C. Finck. il *Success
    Farm* 85:24-7 O '87
Lease loophole preserves investment tax credit. C. Finck.
    il *Success Farm* 85:18T My '87
Maintenance and repair
Dealers brew up more incentives for off-season service.
    C. Finck. il *Success Farm* 85 no5:26D Mr '87
Wrenches and welders take to the fields [field service
    trucks] D. Mowitz. il *Success Farm* 85 no6:18V Mr
    '87

Prices
Good deals still exist. C. Finck. il *Success Farm* 85:29
    Je '87
Standards
The importance and impact of standards [address, Decem-
    ber 17, 1986] J. D. Michaels. *Vital Speeches Day*
    53:441-4 My 1 '87
Agricultural equipment dealers
Dealers brew up more incentives for off-season service.
    C. Finck. il *Success Farm* 85 no5:26D Mr '87
Agricultural equipment industry
    See also
    Caterpillar Inc.
    Collective labor agreements—Agricultural equipment
      industry
    Deere & Company
    J. I. Case Company
    Tenneco Inc.
Finance
Machinery sales upturn positive for ag economy. *Success
    Farm* 85 no4:18AP F '87
Agricultural exhibitions
    See also
    Livestock shows
Agricultural extension work
    See also
    United States. Extension Service
Agricultural forecasting
America's agricultural future. O. L. Freeman. il por
    Futurist 21:15-17 S/O '87
Computer predicts $1/pound feeders in three years [beef
    industry predictions] *Success Farm* 85 no4:B12 F '87
Agricultural industries
    See also
    Archer-Daniels-Midland Co.
    ConAgra, Inc.
    Gold Kist Inc.
Bringing new agricultural technology to the market [ad-
    dress, January 29, 1987] W. D. Carpenter. *Vital
    Speeches Day* 53:350-2 Mr 15 '87
Export-import trade
Agriculture on the high seas. J. C. Webster. il *Nations
    Bus* 75:49-50 D '87
Finance
The 400 largest farms in the U.S. P. Smith. il map
    Success Farm 85 no2:7-14 Ja '87
Food processors. J. Novack. il *Forbes* 139:134-5+ Ja
    12 '87
Japan
Tomatomation: Japan's high-tech food factories. K.
    Hiroshi. il *Courier* 40:17-19 Mr '87
United States
    See Agricultural industries
Agricultural innovations
Bringing new agricultural technology to the market [ad-
    dress, January 29, 1987] W. D. Carpenter. *Vital
    Speeches Day* 53:350-2 Mr 15 '87
Technology. See occasional issues of Successful Farming
Agricultural land utilization *See* Land utilization
Agricultural laws and regulations *See* Agricultural
    administration
Agricultural machinery *See* Agricultural equipment
Agricultural machinery industry *See* Agricultural equipment
    industry
Agricultural marketing *See* Farm produce—Marketing;
    Produce trade
Agricultural museums
    See also
    Ardenwood Historic Farm
Everyman's farm . . . one man's struggle [fight to turn
    Overhome into a museum] T. Krautwurst. il pors
    Mother Earth News 108:114-17 N/D '87
Teaching history—alive and well [Lincoln Log Cabin
    project in Illinois] H. Malehorn. il *Phi Delta Kappan*
    69:166-8 O '87
Agricultural options *See* Commodity options
Agricultural pests *See* Insects
Agricultural planning *See* Farm management
Agricultural policy *See* Agricultural administration
Agricultural produce trade *See* Produce trade
Agricultural production *See* Production, Agricultural
Agricultural products *See* Farm produce
Agricultural research
    See also
    Educational Concerns for Hunger Organization
    Field experiments (Agriculture)
    Food supply—New sources
    Ortho Research Center
    Plant genetics
    Plants—Breeding
    Rodale Research Center

Agricultural research—cont.

Agricultural R&D [discussion of September 18, 1987 article, A competitive R&D strategy for U.S. agriculture] D. A. Holt. *Science* 238:1493-5 D 11 '87

Another plea for agricultural R&D. M. Crawford. *Science* 236:1180 Je 5 '87

A competitive R&D strategy for U.S. agriculture. D. A. Holt. bibl f *Science* 237:1401-2 S 18 '87

Awards

See also

General Foods World Food Prize

Federal aid

Agricultural biotechnology: strategies for competitiveness [report by the National Research Council] L. Tangley. *BioScience* 37:463 Jl/Ag '87

Balancing basic and applied science: the case of agricultural research. G. Fox and others. bibl f il *BioScience* 37:507-9 Jl/Ag '87

Observing the fruits of research on low-input agriculture [visit of government officials to Rodale Institute's Experimental Farms] N. Bell. *BioScience* 37:548 S '87

Plant science grant program nears approval. M. Crawford. *Science* 236:1620 Je 26 '87

UC told to review impact of research [ruling primarily benefits small farmers] M. Sun. *Science* 238:1221 N 27 '87

International aspects

See also

Consultative Group on International Agricultural Research

Beyond the green revolution [report by the Worldwatch Institute] L. Tangley. il *BioScience* 37:176-80 Mr '87

Central America

See also

Centro Agronómico Tropical de Investigación y Enseñanza

Agricultural societies

See also

Community-Supported Agriculture (Organization)
International Federation of Organic Agriculture Movements

Agricultural Stabilization and Conservation Service (U.S.)

See United States. Agricultural Stabilization and Conservation Service

Agricultural subsidies *See* Agricultural administration

Agricultural surplus products *See* Surplus products, Agricultural

Agricultural workers *See* Farm labor

Agriculture

See also

Airplanes in agriculture
All terrain vehicles—Agricultural use
Aquaculture
Burning of land
Cable television—Agricultural programs
Companion crops
Computers—Agricultural use
Contour farming
Dairying
Direct broadcast satellite services—Agricultural programs
Diversification in agriculture
Electronics in agriculture
Farm labor
Farm life
Farm management
Farmers
Food supply
Homesteads
Hydroponics
Indians of North America—Agriculture
Irrigation
Livestock
Mayas—Agriculture
National Agriculture Day
Organic farming
Poultry industry
Radiotelephone in agriculture
Religion and agriculture
Robots—Agricultural use
Rotation of crops
Seeding
Seeds
Shifting cultivation
Strip cropping
Terraces (Agriculture)
Tillage
Tomography—Agricultural use
Truck farming
Viticulture

Monoculture. J. F. Power and R. F. Follett. il *Sci Am* 256:78-86 Mr '87

Accidents

Burning alive! [C. Marsh saves S. Moses from farm accident electrocution] S. Kelly. il *Read Dig* 131:95-9 S '87

Grain-bin 'lifeguards'. C. Tevis. il *Success Farm* 85:62R-62S O '87

Maimed in a terrible accident, Minnesota farm boy David Virnig boldly faces life without arms. D. Chu. il pors *People Wkly* 28:67-8 O 19 '87

Nightmare in the hayfield [T. Argrave run over by tractor and drags himself out of field] P. Michelmore. il *Read Dig* 130:64-9 Je '87

Accounting

The terrible truth about farm accounting. R. Ferguson. il *Success Farm* 85 no1:W1+ Ja '87

Conferences

Across the editor's desk [ADAPT 100 conference] R. Krumme. il *Success Farm* 85 no1:4 Ja '87

'Dear sir: I've got an idea for your conference' [ADAPT 2] il *Success Farm* 85:18 N '87

Ostriches, okra, oyster mushrooms at ADAPT 2. *Success Farm* 85:62B-62C O '87

Economic aspects

See also

Agricultural administration
Agricultural credit
Agricultural industries
Agriculture—Accounting
Contracts, Agricultural
Farm Aid (Organization)
Farm rents
Farms—Size
Land reform
Land values
Organic farming—Economic aspects
Produce trade
Production, Agricultural

Better news from the farms. H. Banks. il *Forbes* 140:27 O 19 '87

Beyond the farming crisis. D. Ehrenfeld. il *Technol Rev* 90:46-56 Jl '87

Broken heartland [farm crisis in Iowa] D. Bauer. il *Esquire* 107:68-77 Ja '87

Chapter 12 offers new option to family farmers. C. Tevis. il *Success Farm* 85 no4:18V-18W F '87

Down on the farm near Coon Rapids [Soviet view] V. Lishchenko. il *World Press Rev* 34:36-7 F '87

Facing up to the farm crisis [Interreligious Conference on Rural Life; cover story] V. Rebeck. *Christ Century* 104:381-3 Ap 22 '87

Farms without farmers. O. Davidson. il *Progressive* 51:25-7 Ag '87

Hands reach out to a hungry heartland. C. Tevis. il *Success Farm* 85 no3:M1 F '87

Hot air—and hope—for Iowa. H. Sidey. il *Time* 130:14 Ag 10 '87

In Nebraska, persistence pays off [E. Krajicek and family] C. Kenney. il por *50 Plus* 27:14+ D '87

In the farm belt, the worst is over. T. Smart. il *Bus Week* p46-7 My 18 '87

An Iowa farm family's effort to stay on the land amid the worst farm crisis in 50 years [Loren and Ruth Book] D. Miller. il *Sch Update* 119:8 Mr 23 '87

Is farming on the mend? R. Pottorff and H. F. Breimyer. *Success Farm* 85:11 S '87

The John Denver '87 farm program. *Success Farm* 85:62K O '87

Learning to survive on the land [farm wives] M. Bosc. il *U S News World Rep* 102:30 F 2 '87

Look quickly and you'll see farmers smiling! D. Allen and G. Johnston. il *Success Farm* 85:18N My '87

Money. See issues of *Successful Farming*

New life on the farm. K. R. Sheets. il *U S News World Rep* 103:18-20 Ag 31 '87

A New York businessman settles an old score (and his conscience) by paying a 1966 debt to 80 farmers [W. P. Carey reimburses farmers for losses incurred by liquidation of sugar refinery] L. Aitken. il por *People Wkly* 27:74+ F 23 '87

Not so down on the farm. T. Young. il *Fortune* 116:52 S 14 '87

Plowed under. S. Broder. il *Progressive* 51:35-40 My '87

Profit. See occasional issues of *Successful Farming*

Profit up, debt down, leaves many farmers in better financial position [Successful Farming Index] D. Allen. il *Success Farm* 85:27-8 Je '87

Seeds of discontent [Prairie Provinces, Canada] A. Walmsley. il *Macleans* 100:30-1 Ap 6 '87

Agriculture—Economic aspects—cont.

Seeds of recovery in the Farmbelt. G. Bock. il *Time* 130:44 D 7 '87

Sugar City goes sour [Colorado] A. A. Rooney. il *Saturday Evening Post* 259:26 Ja/F '87

This land is their land [struggle of farmers' wives] M. Vold. il *Ms* 16:76+ N '87

Time to retrain the American farmer. L. C. Thurow. il *Technol Rev* 90:22-3 My/Je '87

Waiting for recovery is like watching corn grow. P. Houston. il *Bus Week* p82-3 Ja 12 '87

"We will never, ever give up!" [D. and E. Paulsen face loss of Iowa farm; with editorial comment by Elizabeth Sloan] B. Raymond. il pors *McCalls* 145:10, 66+ Mr '87

What role does the church play in agriculture? P. Smith. il *Success Farm* 85:19 Ap '87

A yield against the odds: harvest time on a Missouri farm. R. Rhodes. il *Harpers* 274:53-7 Ap '87

Energy usage

EPA tests confirm lack of lead in gas damages engines. *Success Farm* 85:37 Ag '87

Food or fuel: the ultimate choice? J. Chapline. il *Ctry J* 14:11 Mr '87

Fuel refund of $80 waiting for users who file forms. *Success Farm* 85:66C S '87

'Low-tech' farmers still farming [Small Farm Energy Project] *Success Farm* 85:18AN Ap '87

Environmental aspects

See Agricultural ecology

Federal aid

See Agricultural administration

History

See also

Agriculture, Prehistoric

International aspects

See also

Food and Agriculture Organization of the United Nations

First word [feeding the world] L. Ruppe. il *Omni* 9:6 Je '87

How U.S. farmers rate in world competition. D. Ohrtman. il *Success Farm* 85:10-13 Ap '87

World agriculture and soil erosion. D. Pimentel and others. bibl f il *BioScience* 37:277-83 Ap '87

World food. P. H. Abelson. *Science* 236:9 Ap 3 '87

Moral and religious aspects

See Religion and agriculture

Periodicals

See also

Successful farming (Periodical)

Research

See Agricultural research

Study and teaching

See Agricultural education

Taxation

See also

Farmers—Taxation

Africa

Drought in Africa. M. H. Glantz. il maps *Sci Am* 256:34-40 Je '87

FAO 'food summit' adopts four-prong strategy for African agricultural recovery. *UN Chron* 23:94 N '86

FAO heads international campaign to avert locust and grasshopper outbreaks and save Africa's crops. il *UN Chron* 23:92-3 N '86

FAO reports locust infestations continue, harvests better in Africa. il *UN Chron* 24:74 My '87

Managing the soils of Sub-Saharan Africa. R. Lal. bibl f il maps *Science* 236:1069-76 My 29 '87

The rediscovery of traditional agriculture. il *Courier* 40:24-5 Mr '87

Report on reports: Continuing the commitment: agricultural development in the Sahel [Office of Technology Assessment report] L. Olsson. il *Environment* 29:25-7 Mr '87

Alabama

Their numbers said change crops [Debbie and Thomas Kirkland] D. Allen and G. Johnston. il *Success Farm* 85:16-17 Je '87

Brazil

A new agricultural frontier [Cerrado region] P. H. Abelson and J. W. Rowe. bibl f *Science* 235:1450-1 Mr 20 '87

California

Designer tomatoes [crop innovations] E. Paris. il *Forbes* 139:98-100 Je 1 '87

Farm fresh [Bay Area] il *Sunset* 179:10-11+ S '87

Fighting to stave off foreclosure, farmer Garth Conlan ends up taking his bank to the cleaners. D. Grogan. il por *People Wkly* 28:50-2 Ag 10 '87

The invasion of the avocado snatchers [Medfly] J. Flynn. il *Bus Week* p42 S 14 '87

West Coast petal pushers Jay and Pamela North foster a flowering culinary fad. N. Geeslin. il pors *People Wkly* 28:95+ Ag 17 '87

Canada

Seeds of discontent [Prairie Provinces] A. Walmsley. il *Macleans* 100:30-1 Ap 6 '87

China

See also

Agricultural administration—China

The ancient cultured citrus ant: a tropical ant is used to control insect pests in southern China. H. T. Huang and P. Yang. bibl il map *BioScience* 37:665-71 O '87

Setting a full table [improvement in farm production chronicled by S. H. Witter and others] G. Garelik. il *Time* 130:55 O 12 '87

Colorado

Sugar City goes sour. A. A. Rooney. il *Saturday Evening Post* 259:26 Ja/F '87

Developing countries

See also

Food and Agriculture Organization of the United Nations

World Food Council

Beyond the green revolution [report by the Worldwatch Institute] L. Tangley. il *BioScience* 37:176-80 Mr '87

Biotechnology, agriculture and development [cover story; special issue; with editorial comment by Edouard Glissant] il *Courier* 40:3-34 Mr '87

Low-cost irrigation project interests other developing countries [drip irrigation] Wan Qinghua. il *UN Chron* 24:65 Ag '87

Low-tech food development. J. Millman. il *Technol Rev* 90:12-13 Jl '87

Ethiopia

Saving Ethiopia from itself. D. MacKenzie. il *World Press Rev* 34:52 D '87

Illinois

They profit from corn and beans [Loren and Ann Wiese] D. Allen and G. Johnston. il *Success Farm* 85:17+ Je '87

Tofu-quality beans earn 40¢ premium for Illinois growers. *Success Farm* 85 no2:18 Ja '87

Indiana

See also

Arrowhead Country Forage Council

The best forage grower in Indiana [David Forgey] J. R. Borcherding. il *Success Farm* 85:56-7 Ag '87

Iowa

Broken heartland [farm crisis] D. Bauer. il *Esquire* 107:68-77 Ja '87

Chores don't end in hog house for Iowa brothers [Steve and Don Hanson] D. Allen and G. Johnston. il *Success Farm* 85:12-13 Je '87

Co-op expands choices for these farmer-feeders [cattle] D. Ohrtman. il *Success Farm* 85 no6:B10+ Mr '87

Down on the farm near Coon Rapids [Soviet view] V. Lishchenko. il *World Press Rev* 34:36-7 F '87

Farmers plow up Pentagon's budget [movement to transfer funding from the military budget to Iowa's FmHA program] M. Helmberger. *Progressive* 51:15-16 Mr '87

An Iowa farm family's effort to stay on the land amid the worst farm crisis in 50 years [Loren and Ruth Book] D. Miller. il *Sch Update* 119:8 Mr 23 '87

Old and new meet on 25,000-head hog farm [cover story] G. Johnston. il *Success Farm* 85:H6-H7 My '87

"We will never, ever give up!" [D. and E. Paulsen face loss of farm; with editorial comment by Elizabeth Sloan] B. Raymond. il pors *McCalls* 145:10, 66+ Mr '87

Israel

Israel's miracle food from the desert. J. D. Auerbach. il *Saturday Evening Post* 259:48-9+ S '87

Italy

Agriturismo [vacationing on Italian farms] D. Morneau. il *Ctry J* 14:14-15 Ja '87

Jamaica

Jamaica's new agriculture. J. M. Weiss. il *Américas* 39:52-3 Mr/Ap '87

Mexico

See also

Agricultural administration—Mexico

Middle Western States

Corn Belt states organizing to lure feedlot customers. *Success Farm* 85 no6:B20 Mr '87

The Corn Belt: waning in importance? M. D. Winsberg. il *Focus* 37:32 Summ '87

Agriculture—Middle Western States—cont.
Plowed under. S. Broder. il *Progressive* 51:35-40 My '87

Minnesota
Bottom-line tillage trials [demonstration plots] R. Fee. il *Success Farm* 85 no4:18P F '87

Missouri
See also
Gasconade Farm
The sporting life 'ADAPTs' their farm [John and Mary Jo Rouse farm] J. Walter. il *Success Farm* 85 no4:27 F '87
A yield against the odds: harvest time on a Missouri farm. R. Rhodes. il *Harpers* 274:53-7 Ap '87

Nebraska
In Nebraska, persistence pays off [E. Krajicek and family] C. Kenney. il por *50 Plus* 27:14+ D '87

New Hampshire
Thrifty cow feeding, New England style [Knoxland Farm, Weare] il *Success Farm* 85 no5:D2-D3 Mr '87

New Zealand
The friendly farms of New Zealand [accommodations for tourists] il *Sunset* 178:46 Ap '87
Kiwi gothic: Grant Wood farmstays in New Zealand [farmers who invite travelers into their homes] D. P. Marshall. il map *Travel Holiday* 168:42-7 N '87

North Dakota
He's diversified in 6 cattle enterprises [Jeff Breker] R. Watkins. il *Success Farm* 85 no4:B14 F '87
North Dakota: tough times on the prairie. B. Hodgson. il map *Natl Geogr* 171:320-47 Mr '87

Saudi Arabia
Joan Wallace probes Saudi problems in agriculture. por *Jet* 71:6 Mr 2 '87

South America
Rethinking continuous cultivation in Amazonia. P. M. Fearnside. bibl f il *BioScience* 37:209-14 Mr '87
A supergrain for the future [quinoa] P. E. Rogers. il *Américas* 39:36-8 My/Je '87
Yurimaguas technology [discussion of March 1987 article, Rethinking continuous cultivation in Amazonia] P. M. Fearnside. *BioScience* 37:638-40 O '87

South Dakota
Tillage cuts found in new crop survey. *Success Farm* 85:70J Ag '87

Soviet Union
See also
Food supply—Soviet Union
An apple a day keeps *perestroika* rolling along. P. Galuszka. il *Bus Week* p41-2 Ag 31 '87
For Moscow, a harvest of good news. D. Stanglin and J. Trimble. il *U S News World Rep* 103:79 S 28 '87
New directions in Soviet agriculture. F. Dovring. bibl f il *Curr Hist* 86:329-32+ O '87
On the farm, Ma and Pa Pyatayev are raising some cash cows. P. Galuszka. il *Bus Week* p80 D 7 '87

Tanzania
Fertilizing with rocks [work of Ward Chesworth] S. Strauss. il *Technol Rev* 90:11-12 Ap '87

Thailand
Thailand: a booming nation of farmers moves to democracy. L. Hopping. il *Sch Update* 119:12-13 Ap 6 '87

Tropics
Low-input cropping for acid soils of the humid tropics. P. A. Sanchez and J. R. Benites. bibl f il *Science* 238:1521-7 D 11 '87

United States
See Agriculture

Wisconsin
Green forage to white milk to green $$$ [Koepke dairy] D. Allen and G. Johnston. il *Success Farm* 85:13 Je '87
How they protect their groundwater. B. Freese. il *Success Farm* 85:12-13 S '87
Wisconsin Dairy Task Force has new long-range strategy. J. R. Borcherding. il *Success Farm* 85 no3:D1 F '87

Agriculture, Cooperative
See also
Better Beef Marketing
Gold Kist Inc.
Sunkist Growers, Inc.
Co-op expands choices for these farmer-feeders [cattle] D. Ohrtman. il *Success Farm* 85 no6:B10+ Mr '87
Grain pools help beat red tape. G. Johnston. *Success Farm* 85:5 Ag '87

Agriculture, Prehistoric
Early farming in northwestern Europe [Neolithic period] J. M. Howell. il map *Sci Am* 257:118-24+ N '87

Gazelle killing in Stone Age Syria [emergence of agriculture at Tell Abu Hureyra] A. J. Legge and P. A. Rowley-Conwy. il map *Sci Am* 257:88-95 Ag '87
Letters [discussion of August 1987 article, Gazelle killing in Stone Age Syria] A. J. Legge and P. A. Rowley-Conwy. *Sci Am* 257:8+ N '87
The worst mistake in the history of the human race. J. M. Diamond. il *Discover* 8:64-6 My '87

Agriculture and religion *See* Religion and agriculture
Agriculture and state *See* Agricultural administration
Agriculture Dept. (U.S.) *See* United States. Dept. of Agriculture

Agriculture in art
He paints the dignity of farming [R. Burgess; cover story] il pors *Success Farm* 85:13-15 O '87

Agrobacterium
Gene transfer in corn. D. D. Edwards. *Sci News* 131:37 Ja 17 '87
Ingrained genes. *Sci Am* 256:68 Mr '87
Site-specific nick in the T-DNA border sequence as a result of Agrobacterium vir gene expression. K. Wang and others. bibl f il *Science* 235:587-91 Ja 30 '87
Strange bedfellows. P. B. Moses. il *BioScience* 37:6-10 Ja '87
Transgenic plants as tools to study the molecular organization of plant genes. J. St. Schell. bibl f *Science* 237:1176-83 S 4 '87

Agrokomerc (Firm)
All the party chief's men. K. W. Banta. il *Time* 130:40 S 28 '87
Corruption and scandal [F. Abdic scandal's effect on Yugoslavia's economic system] T. Fennell. il por *Macleans* 100:38 S 21 '87

Agua Caliente Indians *See* Cahuilla Indians
Aguilar Zinser, Adolfo
Mexico: the presidential problem. bibl f *Foreign Policy* 69:40-60 Wint '87/'88

Agusta SpA
Agusta A129 marks European entry into 1990s combat helicopter design. R. R. Ropelewski. il *Aviat Week Space Technol* 126:50-1+ Je 8 '87

Agustini, Delmira, 1886-1914
about
Amorous fantasies. L. Fox-Lockert. por *Américas* 39:38-41 Ja/F '87

Agutter, Jenny, 1952-
about
A movie star goes to Watts to make sure the Bard gets a good rap. K. Hubbard. il pors *People Wkly* 27:83-4 Je 29 '87

Ahearn, John, 1951-
about
John Ahearn with Rigoberto Torres at Brooke Alexander. P. Smith. *Art Am* 75:153 F '87

Ahearne, John F.
Nuclear power after Chernobyl. bibl f il *Science* 236:673-9 My 8 '87

Ahmad, Humma
China's silken success. il *World Press Rev* 34:49 D '87

Ahmad, Jameel
about
A civil engineer declares holey war on the city's mean streets. il por *People Wkly* 27:63 Ja 12 '87

Aho, C. Michael, and Levinson, Marc
A Canadian opportunity. *Foreign Policy* 66:143-55 Spr '87

Ahola, Terry
Real life on the pro tour. il pors *Skiing* 40:153+ D '87

AI *See* Artificial intelligence
AIA *See* American Institute of Architects
AIBS *See* American Institute of Biological Sciences
AID *See* United States. Agency for International Development
AID (Artificial insemination with donor) *See* Artificial insemination, Human
Aid to Families with Dependent Children (Program) *See* Public welfare
Aida [opera] *See* Verdi, Giuseppe, 1813-1901
AIDS (Disease)
See also
United States. Presidential Commission on AIDS
7,000 cases of heterosexual AIDS predicted in next four years. il *Glamour* 85:110+ Ja '87
'AIDS: a bad way to die' [prison problems] A. Press. il *Newsweek* 109:30 Mr 23 '87
AIDS: a diary of the plague in America [cover story] J. Friedman and D. Van Biema. il pors *People Wkly* 28:61-4+ Ag 3 '87

AIDS (Disease)—*cont.*

AIDS and Eros; tr. by Leon Roudiez. J. Kristeva. *Harpers* 275:24-5 O '87

AIDS and 'straights': unsettling questions. K. McAuliffe. il *U S News World Rep* 103:34 Ag 17 '87

AIDS and the sexual counter-revolution. *Natl Rev* 39:19 Jl 3 '87

AIDS: and then, what? W. F. Buckley. *Natl Rev* 39:56 My 22 '87

AIDS: are heterosexuals at risk? M. Fumento. *Commentary* 84:21-7 N '87

AIDS: at the dawn of fear [special section; with editorial comment by Morton B. Zuckerman] bibl il *U S News World Rep* 102:60-70, 76 Ja 12 '87

AIDS: attacking the brain. E. E. Goode and J. Silberner. il *U S News World Rep* 103:48-9 S 7 '87

AIDS: balancing the concerns [cover story; special section] il *Humanist* 47:10-25+ Jl/Ag '87

AIDS becomes a political issue [conservative cause] A. Stanley. il *Time* 129:24 Mr 23 '87

AIDS behind bars—a prisoner's concern. H. Rowe. il *U S News World Rep* 102:7 F 2 '87

AIDS: breaking out? *Sci Am* 256:70+ Ap '87

AIDS: CDC report card . . . and lesbian transmission? *Sci News* 131:8 Ja 3 '87

AIDS commission bills proliferate. D. M. Barnes. *Science* 235:1136 Mr 6 '87

AIDS debate: round two [discussion of September 1986 article, AIDS update: still no reason for hysteria] J. Langone. *Discover* 8:104+ Ja '87

AIDS: education, testing continued. *Sci News* 132:236 O 10 '87

The AIDS epidemic: looking into the 1990s. J. E. Harris. il *Technol Rev* 90:58-64 Jl '87

AIDS: everything you must know [special issue] E. M. Whelan. bibl il por map *USA Today (Periodical)* 116:1-16 O '87

AIDS fear leads many singles to marriage. *Jet* 71:31 F 23 '87

AIDS: hope . . . and warnings. *Sci Am* 256:86-8 F '87

AIDS in '88. J. McLaughlin. *Natl Rev* 39:24 My 8 '87

AIDS may affect course of syphilis [research by Donna Felsenstein and others] R. Weiss. *Sci News* 131:391 Je 20 '87

The AIDS pandemic. *Sci Am* 256:58-9 Ja '87

The AIDS scare: answers to frightening questions. A. G. Fettner. *Redbook* 168:28-30+ Ap '87

AIDS: today's most deadly challenge. J. A. Baggett. il *Sch Update* 119:19 Ap 20 '87

AIDS: what must be done now. A. M. Rosenthal. *Read Dig* 131:91-2 S '87

AIDS: what we know now. *McCalls* 114:143-7 Ap '87

AIDS: what you should know! What you should tell your children! D. Sobel. il *Good Housekeep* 204:71-5 Je '87

At last, the battle is joined [policy debates] J. D. Reed. il *Time* 129:56-8 Je 15 '87

Backlash? W. F. Buckley. *Natl Rev* 39:66-7 N 20 '87

The big chill: fear of AIDS [special section] il *Time* 129:50-6+ F 16 '87

Brain damage by AIDS under active study. D. M. Barnes. bibl il *Science* 235:1574-7 Mr 27 '87

Calculating the odds [uncircumcised men more likely to be infected after exposure to AIDS] *Time* 130:40 O 19 '87

The changing face of AIDS [black and Hispanic victims] R. Stengel. il *Time* 130:12-14 Ag 17 '87

'Competition' cause of AIDS dementia? [work of Mark E. Gurney and others] D. D. Edwards. *Sci News* 132:150-1 S 5 '87

Don't get around much anymore. A. Edwards. *Essence* 18:77+ S '87

Dual infection of the central nervous system by AIDS viruses with distinct cellular tropisms. Y. Koyanagi and others. bibl f il *Science* 236:819-22 My 15 '87

The elders among us. A. McCarthy. *Commonweal* 114:138-9 Mr 13 '87

Epidemics and civil rights. D. E. Koshland, Jr. *Science* 235:729 F 13 '87

Experts fault leadership on AIDS [General Accounting Office survey] W. Booth. *Science* 237:838 Ag 21 '87

Exploring the kingdom of AIDS [heterosexual community] P. Davis. il *N Y Times Mag* p32-6+ My 31 '87

Facing life in the AIDies. M. Kramer. il *U S News World Rep* 102:13 Je 15 '87

A fall from grace on the right [views of Surgeon-General C. E. Koop] D. deF. Whitman. il por *U S News World Rep* 102:27-8 My 25 '87

Fear of AIDS chills sex industry [Nevada and Japan] W. L. Chaze. il *U S News World Rep* 102:25 F 16 '87

Federal officials take aim at AIDS. *Sci News* 132:95 Ag 8 '87

Fighting AIDS. J. H. Tanne. il *N Y* 20:22-31 Ja 12 '87

Functional interaction and partial homology between human immunodeficiency virus and neuroleukin [cause of dementia] M. R. Lee and others. bibl f il *Science* 237:1047-51 Ag 28 '87

Hazardous to your health [Surgeon General's report] W. Lutton. *Natl Rev* 39:54-6 Ja 30 '87

Heterosexuals and AIDS. K. Leishman. il *Atlantic* 259:39-49+ F '87

Heterosexuals and AIDS: mixed messages. D. D. Edwards. il map *Sci News* 132:60-1 Jl 25 '87

High-risk sex studied in women, men. D. D. Edwards. *Sci News* 132:116 Ag 22 '87

How AIDS affects us all. D. Salvatore. il *Ladies Home J* 104:119-21+ O '87

'I want him crucified' [pediatrician R. J. Huse loses his practice after testing positive for AIDS] G. Hackett. il por *Newsweek* 110:36 O 5 '87

Is there a man in your man's life? What every girl should know about the bisexual guy. A. C. Heller. *Mademoiselle* 93:134-5+ Jl '87

Killer cells, MHC: factors in AIDS? D. D. Edwards. *Sci News* 132:52 Jl 25 '87

A 'Manhattan Project' to vanquish the AIDS virus? S. Findlay. il *U S News World Rep* 103:30 S 21 '87

Mathilde Krim: "Across the U.S., one man in thirty is infected . . . one never knows with any man" [interview] M. Orth. il por *Vogue* 177:246+ O '87

More couples live together; fear catching AIDS. *Jet* 72:37 S 14 '87

Myths and facts about AIDS. il *Glamour* 85:88 O '87

Never love a stranger. L. Darling. *Mademoiselle* 93:214 S '87

New database for AIDS research. D. M. Barnes. *Science* 235:634 F 6 '87

The new foreplay: how do you ask about AIDS? B. Weber. *Mademoiselle* 93:141 O '87

The new sexual morality. il *Ebony* 43:52+ N '87

NMA leader warns of blacks being scapegoat for AIDS scare in U.S. [views of Dr. John O. Brown] *Jet* 71:53 Mr 2 '87

Notes from the expanding AIDS front. *Sci News* 131:312 My 16 '87

The odyssey of a brochure on AIDS. W. Booth. *Science* 237:1410 S 18 '87

A perilous double love life [bisexuals and AIDS] D. Gelman. il *Newsweek* 110:44-6 Jl 13 '87

Presidential AIDS [lack of government policy] F. Barnes. *New Repub* 196:10+ Ap 27 '87

A progress report on AIDS research. M. Segal. il *FDA Consum* 21:8-12 O '87

Q and A on AIDS. M. Stone. il *N Y* 20:34-43 Mr 23 '87

The 'small health problem' of AIDS [pooh-poohing of epidemic] M. Kaus. il *Newsweek* 110:46 Jl 13 '87

Surgeon General C. Everett Koop forecasts the death toll from AIDS: 170,000 Americans in just four years [interview] M. Dubrow. il por *People Wkly* 27:43-4+ Mr 16 '87

The terrifying normalcy of AIDS. S. J. Gould. il *N Y Times Mag* p32-3 Ap 19 '87

Time from infection to AIDS computed; Revised AIDS definition released. *Sci News* 132:136 Ag 29 '87

Time's up [American attention span] *New Repub* 197:4+ Jl 27 '87

The truth about AIDS. L. Norment. il *Ebony* 42:126+ Ap '87

The uneven odds: minorities are afflicted with AIDS in significantly disproportionate numbers. A. Levine. il *U S News World Rep* 103:31-3 Ag 17 '87

What older Americans need to know about A.I.D.S. K. B. Taylor. *50 Plus* 27:45-50 N '87

What you must know about AIDS. *Read Dig* 130:59-60 Je '87

What you need to know: the latest AIDS information. E. Ward. il *Sch Update* 120:18-19 O 16 '87

Why you won't get AIDS. B. D. Colen. il *Health* 19:6+ S '87

Will AIDS make the Black Death look pale? il *Discover* 8:4 Ap '87

Bibliography

Conquering disease through knowledge [with checklist] W. Goldstein. *Publ Wkly* 231:41-8 My 1 '87

AIDS (Disease)—*cont.*

Causes

See also
HIV viruses

AIDS and insects. W. Booth. il *Science* 237:355-6 Jl 24 '87

AIDS and insects. K. Leishman. il *Atlantic* 260:56-66+ S '87

AIDS infects health workers. *Sci News* 131:326 My 23 '87

Blood donation under the AIDS regime [assessing danger of being infected] D. D. Edwards. *Sci News* 131:376 Je 13 '87

Calculated risk factor. *Natl Rev* 39:19-20 N 20 '87

Changing the rules [contraction of AIDS by three health workers] *Time* 129:59 Je 1 '87

Critical condition [conflicts in AIDS research lab at the Centers for Disease Control] R. Blow. il por *Roll Stone* p67-8+ Mr 26 '87

Dangerous leaks in AIDS lab [laboratory workers infected] *Discover* 8:14+ D '87

Drug addicts with dirty needles. W. A. Schwartz. il *Nation* 244:843-6 Je 20 '87

Fear of tainted transfusions triggers a boom in the bank-your-own-blood business. *People Wkly* 27:47 Mr 16 '87

Freeing hemophiliacs from the risk of AIDS [synthetic clotting factor offers hope] R. Rhein, Jr. and L. Therrien. il *Bus Week* p38 Ap 13 '87

Immunization: the drive must continue [fear of AIDS] il *World Health* p30 Ap '87

Misplaced fears over new AIDS cases [health workers] K. McAuliffe. il *U S News World Rep* 102:58 Je 1 '87

The mosquito AIDS scare. M. Clark. il *Newsweek* 110:47 Jl 13 '87

New clues about AIDS. *Time* 129:60 My 25 '87

The new panic in Needle Park: AIDS [heroin addicts] T. Morganthau. il *Newsweek* 109:63 Ap 13 '87

A new worry for health-care workers [contact with AIDS-contaminated blood] J. Seligmann. il *Newsweek* 109:55 Je 1 '87

Seeing red [Daxor Corp.'s entry into autologous blood transfusion in wake of AIDS scare] S. N. Chakravarty. il por *Forbes* 139:76+ Je 1 '87

Slapping down the mosquito. il *Time* 130:56 Jl 13 '87

An unexplained AIDS infection [medical laboratory worker infected] *Newsweek* 110:63 S 14 '87

What do you know about AIDS? [quiz] *Jet* 72:22+ Je 22 '87

What triggers AIDS? [cover story] J. Silberner. *Sci News* 131:220-1 Ap 4 '87

Winning and losing in the AIDS fight. D. D. Edwards. *Sci News* 131:262 Ap 25 '87

Workers and blood: call for caution. S. Weisburd. *Sci News* 131:341 My 30 '87

Conferences

AIDS: statistics but few answers. D. M. Barnes. il *Science* 236:1423-5 Je 12 '87

Confrontation and concern about AIDS. J. Barber. il *Macleans* 100:40-1 Je 15 '87

Crowded sessions, long lines-and few answers. J. Silberner. il *U S News World Rep* 102:18 Je 15 '87

Politics, science, people . . . and AIDS. D. D. Edwards. *Sci News* 131:356 Je 6 '87

Probing the AIDS virus and its relatives [special section] J. L. Marx. il *Science* 236:1523-5 Je 19 '87

Costs

A burden too heavy to bear. G. Bock. il *Time* 130:39 Ag 31 '87

The global costs of AIDS. R. Sabatier. il *Futurist* 21:19-21 N/D '87

Health care economics and AIDS. A. Myatt. il por *Humanist* 47:18-20+ Jl/Ag '87

One couple's finances: paying AIDS' cruel cost [Rick Atkins and Phil Hastings] S. Seixas. il *Money* 16:89-90+ Jl '87

Risk and reality: the AIDS crisis and insurance [address, July 14, 1987] D. R. Ross. *Vital Speeches Day* 53:681-4 S 1 '87

The staggering price of AIDS. L. J. Lord. il *U S News World Rep* 102:16-18 Je 15 '87

Throwing money at AIDS. L. Smith. il *Fortune* 116:64-7 Ag 31 '87

What you don't know about AIDS but should [special section] il *Money* 16:90-4+ N '87

Who will pay the high cost of AIDS? P. M. Jones. il *Sch Update* 120:28-9 O 16 '87

Diagnosis

AIDS: a time of testing [cover story; special section] il *U S News World Rep* 102:56-9+ Ap 20 '87

AIDS: fear of foreigners [testing Africans abroad] R. Nordland. il *Newsweek* 109:36 Ap 6 '87

An AIDS plan touches a nerve [expanding testing to include more groups] *U S News World Rep* 102:11 F 16 '87

AIDS: testing insurance. J. B. Quinn. il *Newsweek* 109:55 Je 8 '87

AIDS tests for teachers [teacher V. Chalk fights to regain position in Orange County, Calif.] J. N. Baker. por *Newsweek* 110:81 O 19 '87

AIDS: to test or not to test? J. H. Tanne. il *N Y* 20:40-6 S 28 '87

The AIDS virus: "Does my husband have it? . . . If yes, do I, too? . . . I had to know". K. Winston. il *Glamour* 85:292-3+ O '87

AIDS: who should be tested? [views of Secretary of Education W. J. Bennett] T. Monmaney. il por *Newsweek* 109:64-5 My 11 '87

Baker's recipe [H. Baker's input into AIDS testing policy] F. Barnes. *New Repub* 196:9-10 Je 29 '87

Bavaria requires AIDS testing. D. Dickson. *Science* 236:1057 My 29 '87

A better test for AIDS [AIDS Viral Test] N. Underwood. il *Macleans* 100:48 Je 1 '87

China and AIDS [blood testing] *Newsweek* 109:55 My 18 '87

Cowboys start AIDS tests; entire team disease free. il *Jet* 72:46 Ag 17 '87

Devastating findings [inaccurate test results] *U S News World Rep* 103:68 N 23 '87

Eye, skin disorders may mean HIV infection. S. Eisenberg. *Sci News* 132:308 N 14 '87

A fever lurking in the blood [virus can go undetected by conventional testing] J. Silberner. *U S News World Rep* 103:14-15 O 12 '87

How not to control the AIDS epidemic [adaptation of address, June 1987] M. Krim. il por *Humanist* 47:14-15+ N/D '87

If you're really worried: how to get tested for AIDS. I. Pave. il *Bus Week* p112 Je 15 '87

Is it Alzheimer's or AIDS? C. SerVaas. il *Saturday Evening Post* 259:92-4 O '87

Mandatory testing for AIDS? J. Seligmann. il *Newsweek* 109:22 F 16 '87

Mandatory tests for AIDS? [interviews with B. Primm and M. Silverman] pors *U S News World Rep* 102:62 Mr 9 '87

Meese and AIDS [compulsory testing policy] *Nation* 244:837-8 Je 20 '87

A new panic over AIDS [testing of blood recipients] L. Martz. il *Newsweek* 109:18-19 Mr 30 '87

New questions about AIDS test accuracy. D. M. Barnes. il *Science* 238:884-5 N 13 '87

A new romance. M. Kramer. il *N Y Times Mag* p71 Ag 16 '87

Paying for peace of mind [dating services offer screening tests] J. Castro. il *Time* 129:26 My 11 '87

The problem with testing. B. Kantrowitz. il *Newsweek* 109:60-2 Je 15 '87

Profile of a New-Age date [dating services requiring screening tests for AIDS] G. Sikes. *Mademoiselle* 93:187+ Ag '87

The pros and cons of compulsory tests for AIDS. L. Norment. il *Ebony* 42:118+ S '87

Putting AIDS to the test [merits of mass screening] A. Wilentz. il *Time* 129:60 Mr 2 '87

The quest for an AIDS cure is igniting stocks. K. Deveny. il *Bus Week* p82-3 Je 29 '87

Reagan booed, Taylor cheered at AIDS benefit [routine testing advocated] *Jet* 72:7 Je 15 '87

Redefining the deadly enemy. il *Newsweek* 109:65 My 11 '87

Secondary infection [blood testing for AIDS] *Nation* 244:165 F 14 '87

She took the AIDS test. D. Kleiman. il *N Y Times Mag* p22-3+ Jl 5 '87

Single and free—of AIDS [Peace of Mind dating service offers screening tests] T. Gallant-Stokes. por *Black Enterp* 18:24 Ag '87

The states start wading into the AIDS-test thicket. S. Findlay. il *U S News World Rep* 103:14 O 5 '87

Strictly speaking, watch your mouth [oral leukoplakia as precursor to AIDS; research by John S. Greenspan] *Sci News* 131:135 F 28 '87

Surgeon General Koop asks for more voluntary AIDS testing [cover story] H. G. Miller. il pors *Saturday Evening Post* 259:58-61+ N '87

Synthetic peptide immunoassay distinguishes HIV type 1 and HIV type 2 infections. J. W. Gnann, Jr. and others. bibl f il *Science* 237:1346-9 S 11 '87

AIDS (Disease)—Diagnosis—*cont.*

Teen Challenge: conquering drugs and AIDS [Teen Challenge groups voluntarily take AIDS tests] D. Manuel. il *Saturday Evening Post* 259:52-5+ D '87

Test balloon for testing [AIDS policy] *Sci Am* 257:30 Ag '87

Testing dilemma [Washington prepares controversial new policy] R. Stengel. il *Time* 129:20-2 Je 8 '87

Testing for AIDS [address, June 26, 1987] R. E. Windom. *Vital Speeches Day* 53:676-9 S 1 '87

Testing for AIDS [Reagan administration proposals] *Commonweal* 114:403-5 Jl 17 '87

Then have an anonymous, free AIDS test. C. SerVaas. il *Saturday Evening Post* 259:56-61+ S '87

This is what you thought: 50% say AIDS tests should be mandatory [results of survey] *Glamour* 85:99 Ag '87

Tough new rules for life insurance [tests for AIDS in Canada] C. Wood. il *Macleans* 100:45 My 18 '87

A transfusion of fear [blood recipients tested] A. Wilentz. il *Time* 129:24-5 Mr 30 '87

Update on AIDS testing. C. Schaeffer. *Changing Times* 41:16+ O '87

What the AIDS MOBILE has taught us [free tests offered] C. SerVaas. il *Saturday Evening Post* 259:54-5+ O '87

Who should take the test for HIV and why? [interviews with G. L. Bauer and N. Hunter] L. Kravitz. il pors *Sch Update* 120:21 O 16 '87

Fund raising

See also
Art Against AIDS

Dionne Warwick organizing AIDS fund-raiser in D.C.; cited by Reagan and Barry. il pors *Jet* 73:22+ O 12 '87

Elizabeth Taylor's crusade against AIDS [cover story; interview] H. G. Miller. il pors *Saturday Evening Post* 259:52-3+ S '87

The fashionable charity. J. Conant. il *Newsweek* 110:54-5 D 28 '87

The fight against AIDS [work of E. Taylor] E. Sherman. il por *Ladies Home J* 104:90+ S '87

New frontiers [AIDS benefit program Dancing for life] T. Tobias. il *N Y* 20:119-20 O 26 '87

To fight AIDS, American troupes will dance for life. il *Dance Mag* 61:6 S '87

Genetic aspects

Hereditary factor in AIDS? *Sci News* 131:311 My 16 '87

History

The appalling saga of Patient Zero [R. Shilts traces epidemic to G. Dugas] W. A. Henry. il pors *Time* 130:40+ O 19 '87

A boy who died in 1969 may have been America's first AIDS victim [research by M. Elvin-Lewis] D. Chu. il pors *People Wkly* 28:179-80 N 16 '87

The Columbus of AIDS [G. Dugas named Patient Zero] *Natl Rev* 39:19 N 6 '87

The making of an epidemic [research by R. Shilts] J. Miller. il por *Newsweek* 110:91+ O 19 '87

A new clue in the AIDS mystery [evidence that teenage boy died of the disease in 1969] M. Clark. il *Newsweek* 110:62 N 9 '87

Patient Zero [G. Dugas] por *People Wkly* 28:47 D 28 '87-Ja 4 '88

'Patient Zero' and the AIDS virus [R. Shilts traces epidemic to G. Dugas] A. Steacy. il por *Macleans* 100:53 O 19 '87

Strange trip back to the future [1969 death of Robert R.] C. Gorman. il *Time* 130:83 N 9 '87

The sudden spread of the AIDS epidemic. T. Hanneman. il *Sch Update* 120:32-3 O 16 '87

International aspects

AIDS and sex [cover story; special section; with editorial comment by Kevin Doyle] il *Macleans* 100:2, 30-8 Ag 31 '87

AIDS and the year 2000 [cover story; special section; with editorial comment by Edward Cornish] il *Futurist* 21:2+ 9-21 N/D '87

The AIDS bomb is ticking. N. Stensgaard. *World Press Rev* 34:50 S '87

AIDS: the plague that knows no boundaries [with editorial comment] J. Pekkanen. *Read Dig* 130:9-11, 49-58 Je '87

And now, a worldwide war against AIDS [World Health Organization program] J. Carey. il map *U S News World Rep* 102:13 Ap 6 '87

The challenge of AIDS. *Courier* 40:30 Ag '87

The global AIDS situation. J. M. Mann. il *World Health* p6-8 Je '87

How other nations cope with AIDS. C. McHugh. il *Sch Update* 120:30-1 O 16 '87

WHO launches world-wide AIDS 'awareness' campaign. il *UN Chron* 24:74 Ag '87

Legal aspects

AIDS & the law [discussion of October 1986 article, Sodomy and the Supreme Court] D. Robinson. *Commentary* 83:2+ F '87

AIDS and democracy. E. Fallot. map *World Press Rev* 34:51-2 S '87

The AIDS debate: call it a draw [conflict between French and U.S. researchers resolved] *Newsweek* 109:64 Ap 13 '87

AIDS patent dispute settled. D. M. Barnes. *Science* 236:17 Ap 3 '87

AIDS victims bequeath legal problems [views of Rev. Raymond C. O'Brien] *USA Today (Periodical)* 115:5 Ap '87

Assault with a deadly virus [willful transmission of AIDS virus] R. Lacayo. il *Time* 130:63 Jl 20 '87

Black man's teeth a deadly weapon, jury rules [case of J. V. Moore] il por *Jet* 72:24 Jl 13 '87

Carson's son claims AIDS to make girlfriend abort baby: judge nixes test [child support suit against C. Carson] il por *Jet* 72:13-14 Ag 3 '87

The charge: AIDS assault. A. Press. il por *Newsweek* 109:24 Je 22 '87

Congress heads for an ugly battle over AIDS. D. Harbrecht. il *Bus Week* p53 O 12 '87

Cops fear AIDS after bites from alleged prostitutes [New York City] il *Jet* 72:8 Je 29 '87

The cost of kissing and not telling [negligence suits] D. Brand. il *Time* 129:78 Je 8 '87

Cracking down on the victims: as AIDS spreads, civil liberties may also be at risk. A. Toufexis. il *Time* 130:82-3 Jl 6 '87

Crewmember with AIDS barred at Gatwick [Delta Air Lines steward] *Aviat Week Space Technol* 126:36 F 23 '87

Drugs, AIDS and the threat to privacy. Y. Kamisar. il *N Y Times Mag* p108-10+ S 13 '87

The states start wading into the AIDS-test thicket. S. Findlay. il *U S News World Rep* 103:14 O 5 '87

Yalta of AIDS [agreement between French and American researchers] *Time* 129:57 Ap 13 '87

Mathematical models

Mathematical model predicts AIDS spread [work of Robert May and Roy Anderson] G. Kolata. il *Science* 235:1464-5 Mr 20 '87

Modeling calamity. *Sci Am* 257:26 Jl '87

Mortality

AIDS: how wide the cover-up? il *U S News World Rep* 102:8 F 23 '87

Counting the AIDS victims. T. Monmaney. il *Newsweek* 109:65 F 23 '87

The face of AIDS [cover story] P. L. Goldman. il *Newsweek* 110:22-31+ Ag 10 '87

First word [attributing AIDS-related deaths to other causes] R. C. Gallo. por *Omni* 10:10 D '87

Forecasts for AIDS cases and deaths. il *Futurist* 21:11 N/D '87

Some encouraging news about AIDS [longer survival patterns] *Newsweek* 110:62 N 30 '87

The toll: bad news for women and I.V. users. *Newsweek* 110:85 N 2 '87

Prevention

Ads that shatter an old taboo; Campaigns round the world [TV commercials for condoms] A. Toufexis. il *Time* 129:63 F 2 '87

AIDS [special section] il *Saturday Evening Post* 259:52-61+ S '87

AIDS [special section] il *Saturday Evening Post* 259:52-9+ O '87

AIDS and education: the front line of prevention. D. D. Lenaghan and M. J. Lenaghan. il pors *Futurist* 21:17-19 N/D '87

AIDS and PSAs: broadcasters are seizing the initiative locally. P. Hersch. il *Channels* 7:6 N '87

AIDS and the traveler. E. S. Orzac. *Travel Holiday* 168:32 D '87

AIDS education [cover story] M. Segal. il *FDA Consum* 21:26-30 S '87

AIDS scare changes way stars make love on TV. il *Jet* 73:58-9 S 28 '87

AIDS, sexual oppression, and violence: a call for prevention. J. W. Prescott. il por *Humanist* 47:15-17+ Jl/Ag '87

The AIDS tracers [contact tracing program in Colo.] R. Healy. il *Life* 10:52-5 O '87

AIDS: working together to meet the crisis [cover story; special issue] il *Sch Update* 120:3-10+ O 16 '87

AIDS (Disease)—Prevention—cont.

Another muzzle for AIDS education? [Congress attacks comic book aimed at homosexuals] W. Booth. *Science* 238:1036 N 20 '87

Black morticians take precautions against AIDS. *Jet* 72:51 S 7 '87

Catching up to AIDS [contact tracing] R. Bazell. *New Repub* 196:12-13 F 23 '87

Chaste out of town? [Hollywood is preaching a new morality] M. Brower. il *People Wkly* 27:102-3+ My 11 '87

Citizens join government in addressing the AIDS crisis. K. A. Lawton. il *Christ Today* 31:38-9 O 16 '87

Condom sense. K. Freifeld. il *Health* 19:92 Je '87

Condoms may not stop AIDS. J. Carey. il *U S News World Rep* 103:83 O 19 '87

Confrontation and concern about AIDS. J. Barber. il *Macleans* 100:40-1 Je 15 '87

A dangerous silence [sex education; views of E. C. Koop] A. C. Lewis. il *Phi Delta Kappan* 68:348-9 Ja '87

The days of the condom. B. Kanner. il *N Y* 20:10-12 Ja 5 '87

A different way of saying it [Telecaster Committee of Canada's rejection of AIDS-prevention ads mentioning condoms] S. MacLeod. por *Macleans* 100:64 Mr 30 '87

Disowning the Surgeon General [C. E. Koop excoriated] P. Schlafly and P. Weyrich. *Harpers* 275:16-17 Ag '87

Facing the AIDS crisis [Reagan administration] T. Morganthau. il *Newsweek* 109:16-18 Je 8 '87

A fact of life: AIDS & explicit education. J. Garvey. il *Commonweal* 114:694-5 D 4 '87

The hot new politics of AIDS [public education plans] J. Reed. il *U S News World Rep* 102:30-1 Mr 30 '87

If papa won't preach it, young Ron Reagan will, with a TV pitch promoting safe sex. S. Haller. il pors *People Wkly* 28:38-40 Jl 13 '87

Is preventing AIDS the responsibility of women? The media seem to think so [excerpt from Advice for life] C. Norwood. il *Glamour* 85:18 Jl '87

Kids and contraceptives. B. Kantrowitz. il *Newsweek* 109:54-8+ F 16 '87

Koop makes waves in his war on AIDS. C. O'Connor. por *Newsweek* 109:31 Mr 2 '87

Married N.Y. inmates get condoms to battle AIDS. *Jet* 71:38 Ja 26 '87

Media & the message [government information campaign against AIDS] *Commonweal* 114:612-13 N 6 '87

Medicine today and tomorrow [address, April 13, 1987] J. Coury. *Vital Speeches Day* 53:621-4 Ag 1 '87

More gay-bashing [congressional amendment to appropriations bill that will hamstring safer sex education programs aimed at gays] *Nation* 245:473 O 31 '87

A necessary offense [various New York groups objecting to advertising of condoms] H. Evans. il *U S News World Rep* 102:80 My 25 '87

Not by condoms alone. D. R. Carlin, Jr. *Commonweal* 114:137-8 Mr 13 '87

Our cure for AIDS [sketch of a national program] il *New Repub* 197:7-9 Ag 31 '87

Playing safe: the new sexual landscape [condoms] il *Vogue* 177:226-7+ Je '87

The president talks about AIDS. *America* 156:493-4 Je 20-27 '87

Responding to the AIDS crisis [advertising condoms on television and broadening sex education efforts] K. A. Lawton. il *Christ Today* 31:34-6 Ap 3 '87

Safe sex 1987: how to make love this year. E. Kunes. il *Mademoiselle* 93:106+ Ag '87

'Safe sex' and the presence of the absence [Dartmouth College's safe sex kit] J. Hart. *Natl Rev* 39:43+ My 8 '87

Safer sex: no more talk about birds and bees. M. Horosko. il *Dance Mag* 61:52-3 Jl '87

Should schools offer sex education? J. Leo. *Read Dig* 130:138-42 Mr '87

Special AIDS report. il *Saturday Evening Post* 259:50-61+ N '87

Special help urged to halt black AIDS cases [views of Beny J. Primm] il *Jet* 73:33 O 12 '87

Spreading the news about AIDS. J. Barber. il *Macleans* 100:50+ Mr 23 '87

Talking to kids about AIDS. C. Schaeffer. bibl *Changing Times* 41:23+ D '87

Teach the children well [Catholic response to pending California legislation requiring AIDS prevention education] W. J. Wood. il *America* 156:397-400 My 16 '87

Telling '80s kids about sex. E. E. Goode. bibl il *U S News World Rep* 103:83-4 N 16 '87

Tracing a killer [contact tracing to prevent spread of disease] A. Toufexis. il *Time* 129:56 F 16 '87

An unflinching AIDS campaign [condom ads in New York City] T. E. Johnson. il *Newsweek* 109:24 My 25 '87

Young Reagan makes a pitch for condoms [TV documentary] il por *Newsweek* 109:24 Je 22 '87

Psychological aspects

The AIDS epidemic hits home [results of survey of parents of homosexuals] B. E. Robinson and others. bibl (p65) il *Psychol Today* 21:48-52 Ap '87

AIDS hysteria. C. Krauthammer. *New Repub* 197:18+ O 5 '87

ARC: life in limbo [AIDS-related complex; studies by Susan Tross and Jeffrey S. Mandel] P. Knight. *Psychol Today* 21:18 Mr '87

California fever. T. A. Bass. *Omni* 10:43 N '87

The paranoia of a modern plague. L. Wainwright. il *Life* 10:11 Ag '87

Public opinion

Americans react to AIDS. *Society* 25:2+ N/D '87

This is what you thought: 98 percent say it should be a crime to knowingly spread AIDS [results of survey] *Glamour* 85:81 D '87

Religious aspects

See also
AIDS (Disease) and priests
Church work with AIDS patients

AIDS and the death penalty as consistency tests for the prolife movement. J. R. Kelly. *America* 157:151-5 S 26 '87

AIDS education: the moral substance [statement issued by United States Catholic Conference] D. Hollenbach. *America* 157:493-4 D 26 '87

America's bishops rule on condoms. *Newsweek* 110:57 D 21 '87

The bishops' split on AIDS [controversy over condoms divides the Catholic hierarchy] R. N. Ostling. il *Time* 130:64 D 28 '87

The bishops' statement on AIDS. *America* 157:491-2 D 26 '87

Catholics, AIDS and condoms [statement by bishops] *Time* 130:60 D 21 '87

Choices in plague time. D. L. Schiedermayer. il por *Christ Today* 31:20-2 Ag 7 '87

The condom conundrum: a sermon on AIDS to raise the conscience of our times. C. Thitchener. il pors *Humanist* 47:11-14+ Jl/Ag '87

The condom preacher—and his pantless past [Rev. C. F. Thitchener] il por *Newsweek* 109:69 Mr 2 '87

Deceiving ourselves about 'safe sex'. A. B. Robinson. *Christ Century* 104:550 Je 17-24 '87

Jerry Falwell's anti-AIDS dollar drive. M. Doan. il por *U S News World Rep* 102:12-13 My 4 '87

The judgment mentality. B. Patterson. il *Christ Today* 31:16-17 Mr 20 '87

Media & the message [government information campaign against AIDS] *Commonweal* 114:612-13 N 6 '87

Minister gives condoms to stop AIDS, starts a controversy on subject [C. Thitchener] il por *Jet* 71:10 F 23 '87

A plague, not a war: the religious press confronts itself through AIDS. G. G. Seibert. *America* 157:260-1 O 24 '87

Responding to the AIDS crisis. K. A. Lawton. il *Christ Today* 31:34-6 Ap 3 '87

Teach the children well [Catholic response to pending California legislation requiring AIDS prevention education] W. J. Wood. il *America* 156:397-400 My 16 '87

Statistics

A frustrating glimpse of the true AIDS epidemic. W. Booth. *Science* 238:747 N 6 '87

Tracking the spread of AIDS. N. Underwood. *Macleans* 100:32 Ag 31 '87

Testing

See AIDS (Disease)—Diagnosis

Therapy

See also
Institute for Immunological Disorders

AIDS drug approval recommended [AZT] J. Silberner. *Sci News* 131:56 Ja 24 '87

AIDS drug approved, vaccine tested. D. D. Edwards. *Sci News* 131:198 Mr 28 '87

AIDS research: where the battle stands. S. Siwolop. il *Bus Week* p128+ Mr 23 '87

AIDS stocks worth the gamble. M. McFadden. il *Fortune* 115:113-14 Ap 13 '87

AIDS stresses health care in San Francisco. D. M. Barnes. *Science* 235:964 F 27 '87

AIDS (Disease)—Therapy—*cont.*
Beefing up the defenses [use of GM-CSF in fighting infection in AIDS patients] il *Time* 130:69 S 14 '87
Blocking of HIV-1 infectivity by a soluble, secreted form of the CD4 antigen. D. H. Smith and others. bibl f il *Science* 238:1704-7 D 18 '87
Boosting cell numbers in AIDS [use of GM-CSF] D. D. Edwards. *Sci News* 132:165 S 12 '87
Breaking the F.D.A. drugjam. A.-C. D'Adesky. il *Nation* 245:405-6+ O 17 '87
Changing the rules [FDA allows use of experimental drugs] *Time* 129:59 Je 1 '87
Clinical trials planned for new AIDS drug [peptide T] G. Kolata. il *Science* 235:1138-9 Mr 6 '87
Compassion vs. control: FDA investigational drug regulation. D. H. Gieringer. il *USA Today (Periodical)* 115:69-73 Mr '87
Counting on a cure [AIDS-related stocks] D. R. Katz. il *Esquire* 108:71-2 N '87
Debate over potential AIDS drug [peptide T] D. M. Barnes. il *Science* 237:128-30 Jl 10 '87
Defrauding the desperate: quackery and AIDS. M. Segal. il *FDA Consum* 21:16-19 O '87
Enzyme blockers slay AIDS 'giants' [castanospermine and dNM] D. D. Edwards. *Sci News* 132:294 N 7 '87
Extending AIDS patients' lives [two-drug combination used to attack Pneumocystis carinii pneumonia] M. Clark. il *Newsweek* 110:85 N 2 '87
Fast-tracking the first AIDS drug [zidovudine; interview with E. Cooper and J. Bilstad] B. Stone. pors *FDA Consum* 21:13-15 O '87
Fateful decisions on treating AIDS. E. Bowen. il *Time* 129:62 F 2 '87
Fighting a killer virus [Pneumocystis carinii pneumonia] N. Underwood. il *Macleans* 100:68 N 9 '87
First AIDS drug approved [azidothymidine] *FDA Consum* 21:4-5 Je '87
The frustrating fight against AIDS. J. Schecter. il *Technol Rev* 90:65 Jl '87
Imminent marketing of AZT raises problems. G. Kolata. il *Science* 235:1462-3 Mr 20 '87
Medicine's race for a cure. D. O. Relin. il *Sch Update* 120:22 O 16 '87
Meeting on AIDS drugs turns into open forum. D. M. Barnes. il *Science* 237:1287-8 S 11 '87
"On the shelf" AIDS drug in clinical trial [fusidic acid] D. M. Barnes. *Science* 238:276 O 16 '87
Peptide T: future AIDS treatment? D. D. Edwards. *Sci News* 131:376 Je 13 '87
Preying on AIDS patients [quacks] T. Monmaney. il *Newsweek* 109:52-4 Je 1 '87
The quest for an AIDS cure is igniting stocks. K. Deveny. il *Bus Week* p82-3 Je 29 '87
Questions raised about peptide T's action. J. L. Marx. *Science* 236:1523 Je 19 '87
Retroviruses and mouse embryos: a rapid model for neurovirulence and transplacental antiviral therapy. A. H. Sharpe and others. bibl f il *Science* 236:1671-4 Je 26 '87
Ribavirin antagonizes the effect of azidothymidine on HIV replication. M. W. Vogt and others. bibl f il *Science* 235:1376-9 Mr 13 '87
Risky business on AIDS [ICN's experience with ribavirin] J. Crudele. il *N Y* 20:16+ Ap 27 '87
Search for a drug to fight AIDS. T. Jackson. il *World Press Rev* 34:52-3 Mr '87
Transfer factor and AIDS. J. Silberner. *Sci News* 131:153 Mr 7 '87
The unhealthy profits of AZT. T. Kingston. il *Nation* 245:408-9 O 17 '87
Uproar over AIDS drugs. M. Clark. il *Newsweek* 109:24 Ap 6 '87
Whither go the AIDS treatments? D. D. Edwards. *Sci News* 131:372 Je 13 '87

Vaccines and vaccination
After 1986, nowhere to go but up. *World Press Rev* 34:56 F '87
AIDS drug approved, vaccine tested. D. D. Edwards. *Sci News* 131:198 Mr 28 '87
AIDS: the search for a vaccine [D. Zagury serves as his own guinea pig] M. Clark. il por *Newsweek* 109:79 Mr 30 '87
AIDS vaccine: a sliver of hope? [FDA picks MicroGeneSys to begin tests] R. Rhein, Jr. *Bus Week* p30-1 Ag 31 '87
AIDS vaccine? Now, tests on humans. J. Silberner. il *U S News World Rep* 103:10 Ag 31 '87
AIDS vaccine: research on target. R. Weiss. *Sci News* 132:84 Ag 8 '87

AIDS vaccine: time for human tests? S. Weisburd. *Sci News* 131:213 Ap 4 '87
AIDS vaccine trial OKed. D. M. Barnes. *Science* 237:973 Ag 28 '87
AIDS vaccines: the problems of human testing. S. Weisburd. *Sci News* 131:329-32 My 23 '87
Broad issues debated at AIDS vaccine workshop. D. M. Barnes. il *Science* 236:255-7 Ap 17 '87
Candidate AIDS vaccine [recombinant vaccinia virus; work of Daniel Zagury] D. M. Barnes. *Science* 235:1575 Mr 27 '87
Critical steps in war on AIDS. N. Underwood. il *Macleans* 100:38 Ag 31 '87
Giving potential AIDS vaccines a 'boost' [work of Daniel Zagury] D. D. Edwards. *Sci News* 132:391 D 19-26 '87
Human test of AIDS vaccine approved. D. D. Edwards. *Sci News* 132:116 Ag 22 '87
Hybrid particle mimics AIDS virus [retrotransposons] D. D. Edwards. *Sci News* 132:151 S 5 '87
Inching toward a vaccine. J. Carey. *U S News World Rep* 102:31 Mr 30 '87
Medicine's race for a cure. D. O. Relin. il *Sch Update* 120:22 O 16 '87
No progress, no panic. D. Brand. il *Time* 129:58 Je 15 '87
The race for an AIDS vaccine. S. Gannes. il *Fortune* 116:115+ D 21 '87
Second AIDS vaccine approved for testing. S. Eisenberg. *Sci News* 132:357 D 5 '87
Taking his own medicine [D. Zagury innoculates himself] E. Magnuson. il por *Time* 129:25 Mr 30 '87
A tough old soldier joins the fight against AIDS [J. Salk] S. Siwolop and R. Rhein, Jr. il por *Bus Week* p69-70 Jl 27 '87
Will there be an AIDS vaccine? S. Weisburd. il *Sci News* 131:297-9 My 9 '87
"You first" [human tests of VaxSyn] *Time* 130:56 Ag 31 '87

Africa
Africa begins to face up to AIDS. D. Dickson. il *Science* 238:605-7 O 30 '87
AIDS: the plague that knows no boundaries [with editorial comment] J. Pekkanen. *Read Dig* 130:9-11, 49-58 Je '87
For fear of blood. C. Fenyvesi. *U S News World Rep* 102:64 Ja 12 '87
In the grip of the scourge. M. S. Serrill. il map *Time* 129:58-9 F 16 '87
The march of AIDS. R. Klingholz. *World Press Rev* 34:56-7 F '87
The plague. R. Bazell. *New Repub* 196:14-15 Je 1 '87
A plague in the tropics. C. Wood. il *Macleans* 100:36-7 Ag 31 '87
Stunting progress in Africa. V. Mallet. il *World Press Rev* 34:53 S '87

Brazil
'An epidemic like Africa's'. S. Seibert. il *Newsweek* 110:38 Jl 27 '87

Canada
AIDS and sex [cover story; special section; with editorial comment by Kevin Doyle] il *Macleans* 100:2, 30-8 Ag 31 '87
Dentistry and AIDS. M. McIver. *Macleans* 100:66 N 16 '87
Ethical issues of AIDS. A. Steacy. *Macleans* 100:46 S 7 '87
Fear of death and disease. A. Finlayson. il *Macleans* 100:34-5 Ja 12 '87
A grim milestone on P.E.I [first recorded death] B. MacAndrew. *Macleans* 100:52 O 5 '87
Threats stalk the victims of a plague [perceived danger of AIDS in the classroom] N. Underwood. il *Macleans* 100:50+ O 5 '87
Tough new rules for life insurance. C. Wood. il *Macleans* 100:45 My 18 '87

China
China and AIDS [blood testing] *Newsweek* 109:55 My 18 '87

France
France, Britain boost AIDS funds. D. Dickson. *Science* 235:1136 Mr 6 '87

Great Britain
France, Britain boost AIDS funds. D. Dickson. *Science* 235:1136 Mr 6 '87

Haiti
A mask on the face of death. R. Selzer. il por *Life* 10:58-64 Ag '87
The plague. R. Bazell. *New Repub* 196:14-15 Je 1 '87
A plague in the tropics. C. Wood. il *Macleans* 100:36-7 Ag 31 '87

AIDS (Disease)—*cont.*

Philippines

AIDS near U.S. bases. *Christ Century* 104:11 Ja 7-14 '87

U.S. bases spread AIDS virus. C. D. Brubaker. il *Progressive* 51:14 F '87

Soviet Union

AIDS and punishment. *Time* 130:32 S 7 '87

'Those who endanger the people'. il *Newsweek* 110:41 S 7 '87

Zambia

Zambia president reveals cause of son's death: AIDS. por *Jet* 73:14 N 2 '87

AIDS (Disease) and artists

AIDS: the creative response [cover story; with editorial comment by Gray D. Boone] D. Kaufman. il *Horizon* 30:2, 13-20 N '87

The artist and AIDS. E. White. *Harpers* 274:22+ My '87

How artists respond to AIDS. R. Corliss. il *Time* 130:62-3 Jl 27 '87

AIDS (Disease) and children

AIDS: how teenagers are meeting the crisis. M. Christopher. il *Sch Update* 120:17 O 16 '87

AIDS instruction: a troubling test for educators. K. McCormick. *Educ Dig* 53:56-9 S '87

An AIDS patient's fight for life [R. White] M. Nichols. il por *Sch Update* 119:4 Ap 20 '87

Anatomy of a hate campaign [Ray family burned out of home because of fear of AIDS in Arcadia, Fla.] W. Plummer. il *People Wkly* 28:32-7 S 14 '87

An artist throws the book at misinformation [picture book on AIDS created by N. de Saint Phalle] il *Newsweek* 109:61 Je 15 '87

The castaways: fears about AIDS drive three boys from home [Ray family burned out of home in Arcadia, Fla.] M. Voboril. il *Life* 10:98-100 O '87

Diver Greg Louganis returns to dancing, his first love, before the eyes of his pal Ryan White. W. Plummer. il pors *People Wkly* 28:44-5 N 9 '87

Do AIDS teens have a right to school? D. Sussman. il *Sch Update* 120:27 O 16 '87

Four teens on the frontlines. il *Sch Update* 120:15-16 O 16 '87

Immunization: the drive must continue [fear of AIDS] il *World Health* p30 Ap '87

Kids ask about AIDS. P. Krantz. *Better Homes Gard* 65:96+ O '87

Kids with AIDS [cover story; special section] il *Newsweek* 110:50-4+ S 7 '87

Talking to kids about AIDS. C. Schaeffer. bibl *Changing Times* 41:23+ D '87

Teen Challenge: conquering drugs and AIDS [Teen Challenge groups voluntarily take AIDS tests] D. Manuel. il *Saturday Evening Post* 259:52-5+ D '87

Teens & AIDS: what you should know. L. Stambler. *Teen* 31:92-3+ Je '87

Threats stalk the victims of a plague [perceived danger of AIDS in the classroom] N. Underwood. il *Macleans* 100:50+ O 5 '87

AIDS (Disease) and congressmen

AIDS makes another chilling advance, claiming the life of a congressman [S. B. McKinney] il por *People Wkly* 27:53 My 25 '87

AIDS strikes down a congressman [S. B. McKinney] por *Newsweek* 109:47 My 18 '87

AIDS (Disease) and dentists

Dentistry and AIDS. M. McIver. *Macleans* 100:66 N 16 '87

Dentists begin to take precautions. il *Newsweek* 110:59 Ag 3 '87

Nat. Dental Assn. staff to ask members to take precautions for AIDS. *Jet* 72:6 Ag 10 '87

AIDS (Disease) and employment

AIDS: a corporate attitude [address, October 14, 1987] A. V. Smith. *Vital Speeches Day* 54:113-15 D 1 '87

AIDS: a job-rights victory [Supreme Court decision] G. Witkin. il *U S News World Rep* 102:10-11 Mr 16 '87

The AIDS epidemic and business [special section] il *Bus Week* p122-8+ Mr 23 '87

AIDS in the workplace. I. D. Singer. il *Nations Bus* 75:36-9 Ag '87

AIDS tests for teachers [teacher V. Chalk fights to regain position in Orange County, Calif.] J. N. Baker. por *Newsweek* 110:81 O 19 '87

Handicap rights [Supreme Court extends rights to those with contagious diseases] R. Lacayo. il *Time* 129:66 Mr 16 '87

On unwarranted fears [Supreme Court confers privileged victim status on individuals with contagious diseases] *America* 156:266-7 Ap 4 '87

Preparing for the worst. M. Pollick. il *Nations Bus* 75:28+ O '87

Supreme Court holds that contagious diseases are handicaps. T. J. Flygare. *Phi Delta Kappan* 68:705-6 My '87

A victory for AIDS victims [Supreme Court decision] A. Press. il *Newsweek* 109:33 Mr 16 '87

Where 'boss' stops and 'friend' begins. L. Booth. il *Work Woman* 12:70-4+ F '87

Your Constitution: is disease a legal handicap? D. Pawelek. *Sch Update* 119:12 Ap 20 '87

AIDS (Disease) and physicians

Black health professionals urge AIDS precautions. *Jet* 73:33 O 12 '87

Denounce doctors who shun AIDS patients [views of C. Everett Koop] *Jet* 73:29 S 28 '87

Doctors fear AIDS, too. M. Clark. il *Newsweek* 110:58-9 Ag 3 '87

AIDS (Disease) and priests

AIDS and the priesthood. M. Gray. il *Macleans* 100:43 F 23 '87

As Father Michael Peterson lay dying of AIDS, his Catholic Church showed it cared deeply for one of its own. D. Chu. il por *People Wkly* 27:131-2 My 11 '87

AIDS (Disease) and servicemen

AIDS more prevalent in black military recruits. *Jet* 72:37 Ag 3 '87

AIDS near U.S. bases [Philippines] *Christ Century* 104:11 Ja 7-14 '87

The charge: AIDS assault [case of Army Pfc. A. G. Morris] A. Press. il por *Newsweek* 109:24 Je 22 '87

U.S. bases spread AIDS virus [Philippines] C. D. Brubaker. il *Progressive* 51:14 F '87

AIDS (Disease) and sports

Boxing groups join fight to score KO over AIDS. *Jet* 72:37 Ag 3 '87

Cowboys start AIDS tests; entire team disease free. il *Jet* 72:46 Ag 17 '87

The death of an athlete [Gay Games organizer, T. Waddell, dies of AIDS] D. Schaap. il *Sports Illus* 67:26-8+ Jl 27 '87

Putting on the gloves to fight AIDS [boxing referees ordered to wear rubber gloves] il *Newsweek* 110:49 Jl 27 '87

AIDS (Disease) and the press

Celebrity AIDS. E. Diamond. il *N Y* 20:16+ Mr 2 '87

A plague, not a war: the religious press confronts itself through AIDS. G. G. Seibert. *America* 157:260-1 O 24 '87

Sexual hysteria. E. Diamond. il *N Y* 20:14-16 Je 22 '87

Villains, and victims of AIDS [A. Waugh's pieces in The spectator] G. Bain. il *Macleans* 100:44 Ap 20 '87

AIDS (Disease) and veterans

Report from the front. P. Morrisroe. il *N Y* 20:58-70 N 30 '87

AIDS (Disease) and women

AIDS. L. Van Gelder. il *Ms* 15:64+ Ap '87

AIDS and women. *Time* 129:66 Ap 27 '87

AIDS epidemiology: women and drugs [study by Mary Guinan and Ann Hardy] il *Discover* 8:12 Jl '87

Facing the fear: help for women with AIDS [work of S. Gage, director of the Women's AIDS Project in Los Angeles] R. L. Bray. il por *Ms* 15:31 My '87

Is preventing AIDS the responsibility of women? The media seem to think so [excerpt from Advice for life] C. Norwood. il *Glamour* 85:18 Jl '87

Nobody's safe [threat to black women] L. Villarosa and J. Roberts. *Essence* 18:73-4+ Je '87

Sex, AIDS and pillow talk. S. Nelson. il *Glamour* 85:350-1+ S '87

She took the AIDS test. D. Kleiman. il *N Y Times Mag* p22-3+ Jl 5 '87

The toll: bad news for women and I.V. users. *Newsweek* 110:85 N 2 '87

Two women battle AIDS [Canadian women] A. Walmsley. il *Macleans* 100:34-5 Ag 31 '87

A warning to women on AIDS [views of H. S. Kaplan] J. Seligmann. il por *Newsweek* 110:72 Ag 31 '87

AIDS (Disease) and youth *See* AIDS (Disease) and children

AIDS (Disease) in drama

Theater. T. M. Disch. *Nation* 244:656+ My 16 '87

AIDS (Disease) in mass media

AIDS: the creative response [cover story; with editorial comment by Gray D. Boone] D. Kaufman. il *Horizon* 30:2, 13-20 N '87

AIDS (Disease) in television
If papa won't preach it, young Ron Reagan will, with a TV pitch promoting safe sex. S. Haller. il pors *People Wkly* 28:38-40 Jl 13 '87
Young Reagan makes a pitch for condoms [TV documentary] il por *Newsweek* 109:24 Je 22 '87

AIDS (Disease) literature
  See also
  AIDS (Disease)—Bibliography
An artist throws the book at misinformation [picture book on AIDS created by N. de Saint Phalle] il *Newsweek* 109:61 Je 15 '87
The need to self-publish AIDS books [work of B. Moffatt] L. See. *Publ Wkly* 232:56 Ag 28 '87
A worthy cause [S. Alyson's efforts to get the publishing community to produce a free book about fighting AIDS] L. Fleischer. *Publ Wkly* 232:40 Ag 21 '87

AIDS (Disease) viruses *See* HIV viruses

AIDS patients
  See also
  Church work with AIDS patients
AIDS: treating it, fearing it [survey of nurses] *Sci News* 131:89 F 7 '87
AIDS volunteers. J. Stone. il *Glamour* 85:288-9+ Mr '87
AIDS: when fear takes charge [victim driven out of Williamson, W. Va.; cover story] L. Rosellini and E. E. Goode. il map *U S News World Rep* 103:62-5+ O 12 '87
Black health professionals urge AIDS precautions. *Jet* 73:33 O 12 '87
Courage, Doc [C. E. Koop reprimands health professionals who refuse to treat AIDS patients] por *Time* 130:57 S 21 '87
Death of a conservative [T. Dolan] J. Alter. il *Newsweek* 109:23 Ja 12 '87
Denounce doctors who shun AIDS patients [views of C. Everett Koop] *Jet* 73:29 S 28 '87
Doctors fear AIDS, too. M. Clark. il *Newsweek* 110:58-9 Ag 3 '87
Fighting AIDS, the quiet way. B. Kantrowitz. il *Newsweek* 109:64-6 Ap 27 '87
The human impact of AIDS: four cases of altered lives. il *Sch Update* 120:6-7 O 16 '87
'I'm dying—AIDS is your problem now'. J. Hurley. por *Newsweek* 110:38-9 Ag 10 '87
Notes and comment [C. Jones initiates AIDS memorial quilt] *New Yorker* 63:31-2 O 5 '87
On tour with Rock Hudson [promoting Rock Hudson, his story] S. Davidson. il *N Y Times Mag* p54+ My 3 '87
The secret that could not be kept. W. Schwartz. il *Progressive* 51:34 O '87
Taking up needles and thread to honor the dead helps AIDS survivors patch up their lives [C. Jones organizes memorial quilt] C. Ruskin. il por *People Wkly* 28:42-4+ O 12 '87
When a friend has AIDS. P. Bissonette. por *U S News World Rep* 103:9 Jl 6 '87

Dental care
Dentistry and AIDS. M. McIver. *Macleans* 100:66 N 16 '87
Dentists begin to take precautions. il *Newsweek* 110:59 Ag 3 '87
Nat. Dental Assn. staff to ask members to take precautions for AIDS. *Jet* 72:6 Ag 10 '87

Employment
  See AIDS (Disease) and employment

Family relationships
AIDS is a human disease [victim E. S. Loeb] J. Norberg. il pors *Saturday Evening Post* 259:52-3 O '87
Carol Lynn Pearson pens a moving memoir on her gay husband's death from AIDS. K. McMurran. il pors *People Wkly* 27:91+ F 2 '87
For better, for worse [AIDS and marriage of T. and K. Jones] K. Casey. il *Ladies Home J* 104:89-91+ My '87
The long agony of Shirley Fish [mother of sufferer Lauren Burk] G. Bennett. il por *McCalls* 114:148-50 Ap '87
What comforts AIDS families [AIDS Family Therapy Project at the Ackerman Institute; cover story] L. A. Walker. il *N Y Times Mag* p16-22+ Je 21 '87

Legal status, laws, etc.
  See AIDS (Disease)—Legal aspects

Photographs and photography
Facing AIDS. J. Rosett and G. Ray. il *Ms* 16:64-9 S '87

Psychology
  See AIDS (Disease)—Psychological aspects

Aigen, Betsy
  about
"I just got tired of not having a baby in my arms": Betsy Aigen's own story. *McCalls* 114:57-8 Je '87
Searching for a very special woman. L. Arking. *McCalls* 114:55-6 Je '87

Aiken, Joan, 1924-
Using imagination in plotting. *Writer* 100:7-10+ D '87

Aiken (S.C.)
  Police
James Brown says he was mistreated by police, after alleged accident. por *Jet* 73:54 N 30 '87

Aikman, David, 1944-
  about
Secular journalism: a ripe opportunity for Christians [interview] il por *Christ Today* 31:58 Mr 6 '87

Ailments *See* Diseases

Aioli *See* Mayonnaise

AIP *See* American Institute of Physics

Air
  See also
  Atmosphere
  Analysis
  See also
  Air pollution—Measurement
Amber yields samples of ancient air [work of Robert A. Berner and Gary P. Landis] R. Monastersky. *Sci News* 132:293 N 7 '87
Ancient air analyzed in dinosaur-age amber [research by Robert Berner and Gary Landis] R. A. Kerr. *Science* 238:890 N 13 '87
Heirs to ancient air [plan to study sealed Egyptian crypt; cover story] R. Monastersky. il *Sci News* 132:172-3 S 12 '87
Putting on ancient airs [ancient atmosphere trapped in amber found to contain 50% more oxygen] il *Time* 130:82 N 9 '87
A quest for ancient Egyptian air [use of remote sensing in archeological investigation] C. Holden. il *Science* 236:1419-20 Je 12 '87

Air agreements *See* Aviation—International aspects

Air Atlanta
The $90 million dream: the rise and fall of Michael Hollis. C. Whitaker. il pors *Ebony* 43:188-90+ N '87
Cosby helps save black-owned airline; brokers a $3.5 million loan from E. F. Hutton Group Inc. il *Jet* 71:28 Mr 9 '87
The crash of Air Atlanta. R. Witherspoon. il por *Black Enterp* 17:59-60 Je '87

Air B.C.
AirBC-Air Canada alliance demonstrates upheaval in Canadian airline business. J. Ott. il *Aviat Week Space Technol* 126:47+ My 11 '87

Air bags, Automobile *See* Automobiles—Air bags

Air bases
  See also
  Guided missile bases
All talk [Ellington Air Base used as service stop for military pilots] G. Baxter. il *Flying* 114:106-7 Ag '87
CF-18 revolutionizes Cold Lake test data, software operations [Canada] il *Aviat Week Space Technol* 127:128-9+ S 28 '87
Cold Lake matures into strategic base. P. Mann. il map *Aviat Week Space Technol* 127:124-8 S 28 '87
Construction of new orbiter at Vandenberg assessed. *Aviat Week Space Technol* 126:61 Mr 23 '87
The day of the sparrow [U.S. airmen murdered near Clark Air Base, Philippines] H. Anderson. il *Newsweek* 110:54 N 9 '87
Goose Bay modernizes, prepares for air defense role with CF-18. P. Mann. il map *Aviat Week Space Technol* 127:82-3+ O 5 '87
The message from Madrid [U.S. asked to remove F-16s from Torrejón Air Base, Spain] H. Anderson. il *Newsweek* 110:83 N 16 '87
Oil rigs near Vandenberg concern USAF. *Aviat Week Space Technol* 126:110 My 11 '87
Swedish Air Force declares two Base 90 facilities operational. il *Aviat Week Space Technol* 126:56-7 My 11 '87
Three European Air Forces step up training at Goose Bay. *Aviat Week Space Technol* 127:86 O 5 '87
Washington could get burned by putting the heat on Madrid. J. Patterson and others. il *Bus Week* p58 N 23 '87
When the stepping stones of world power are rocky bases [Spain-U.S. dispute over Torrejón Air Base] J. Wallace. il *U S News World Rep* 103:30-1 N 23 '87

Air bases—cont.
Environmental aspects
Jets to invade a national park [Fuji-Hakone-Izu National Park] J. Hamilton. il *Sierra* 72:132-3 Ja/F '87
USAF to the rescue [Atlantic loggerhead turtle nest sites at Eglin Air Force Base] *Oceans* 20:4-5 N/D '87
Runways
Air Force RFP opens bidding on aircraft to calibrate navigation, approach aids [business jets] *Aviat Week Space Technol* 126:150 Ap 27 '87

Air Canada
Air Canada resumes flights after reaching pact with union. *Aviat Week Space Technol* 127:38 D 21 '87
AirBC-Air Canada alliance demonstrates upheaval in Canadian airline business. J. Ott. il *Aviat Week Space Technol* 126:47+ My 11 '87
Canada reallocates world service to improve efficiency, planning. *Aviat Week Space Technol* 127:36-7 O 12 '87
Grounding Air Canada [strike] C. Barrett. il *Macleans* 100:15 D 7 '87
Not-so-friendly skies [strike] D. Jenish. il *Macleans* 100:31 D 21 '87
Private plans for Air Canada. A. Shortell. il *Macleans* 100:24-5 Jl 6 '87
Returning to the air [strike ends] L. Van Dusen. il *Macleans* 100:49 D 28 '87
Strike forces Air Canada to halt flight operations. *Aviat Week Space Technol* 127:35 D 7 '87
Turbulence in the skies [British-Canadian dispute over airline routes] T. Tedesco. il *Macleans* 100:27 Ag 31 '87

Air cleaners *See* Air filters
Air conditioning
See also
Automobiles—Air conditioning
Boats and boating—Air conditioning
Hvac systems: in pursuit of comfort. I. Peterson. *Archit Rec* 175:150-3 My '87
Air conditioning equipment
See also
Dehumidifiers
Heat pumps
Humidifiers
Air-conditioners. il *Consum Rep* 52:427-31 Jl '87
Air-conditioners. il *Consum Rep* 52:246-50 D '87
Conditioning yourself for a cool summer. J. Rachlin. il *U S News World Rep* 102:53 Je 1 '87
Keeping cool. L. Green. il map *Pop Mech* 164:138-40 Je '87
When your furnace or central air conditioner or water heater needs replacement. L. Green. il *Good Housekeep* 204:218+ Ap '87
Energy usage
Cool savings for muggy climates [heat pipe enhanced air conditioner] V. E. Gilmore. il *Pop Sci* 231:30 N '87
Top of the line cooling choices. J. Seisler. il *Consum Res Mag* 70:11-13+ My '87
Air cushion vehicles
Cushioned [M. Lass's hovercraft built from mail order plans] *New Yorker* 62:21-2 Ja 26 '87
Air defenses
See also
Airplanes, Military
Guided missiles
Guns, Anti-aircraft
New York (State). Air National Guard
Radar defense networks
Air Force altering budget priorities for Project Forecast 2. J. D. Morrocco. il *Aviat Week Space Technol* 126:22-3 Ap 13 '87
Air Force defines milestones for Project Forecast 2 initiatives. J. D. Morrocco. *Aviat Week Space Technol* 126:139+ My 11 '87
Army air combat [special section] il *Aviat Week Space Technol* 127:18-22 O 19 '87
Army proposes changing strategy to acquire new air defense system. *Aviat Week Space Technol* 126:22 Mr 2 '87
Army tests line-of-sight air defense systems [forward area air defense system] C. A. Shifrin. *Aviat Week Space Technol* 127:20-2 Jl 6 '87
The Army's new air defense [forward area air defense] il *Pop Mech* 164:118 O '87
Boeing Aerospace wins contract to provide LOS-R Stinger system [line of sight-rear component of the Army's forward area air defense system] C. A. Shifrin. il *Aviat Week Space Technol* 127:25-6 Ag 31 '87
The door SDI won't shut [inadequate air defenses] C. Hammer. il *Wash Mon* 19:21-4 Mr '87

Expendable defenses [special section] il *Aviat Week Space Technol* 127:22-5 S 21 '87
France, USAF discuss joint efforts on Project Forecast 2 technologies. *Aviat Week Space Technol* 126:78-9 Je 1 '87
GE cannot meet Army air defense test deadline [forward-area air defense system] *Aviat Week Space Technol* 126:30 Ja 19 '87
Joint venture to bid on LOS-F-H portion of FAADs [line of sight-forward heavy portion of the Army's forward area air defense system] *Aviat Week Space Technol* 126:29 Ap 20 '87

Air Europe Ltd.
Air Europe to use Sabre system as marketing tool. *Aviat Week Space Technol* 126:49 Ap 20 '87
Air filters
Air cleaners for your home. *Better Homes Gard* 65:81 Mr '87
Air cleaners: the inside story. J. Hayes. il *Saturday Evening Post* 259:30-1 Ja/F '87
Air flow
See also
Vortex generators
Bedform alignment in directionally varying flows [cover story] D. M. Rubin and R. E. Hunter. bibl f il *Science* 237:276-8 Jl 17 '87
Toxic wind. M. H. Brown. il map *Discover* 8:42-9 N '87
Air Force Academy (U.S.) *See* United States Air Force Academy
Air Force Avionics Laboratory (U.S.)
AFAL programs constrained by budget cuts. *Aviat Week Space Technol* 126:65 F 9 '87
Air Force Flight Dynamics Laboratory (U.S.)
USAF, Eidetics plan vortex flow, high-angle-of-attack studies. *Aviat Week Space Technol* 126:31 Ja 19 '87
Air Force Flight Test Center (U.S.)
Integrated systems drive increased USAF flight testing. *Aviat Week Space Technol* 126:58-60 Ap 20 '87
Air Force Logistics Command (U.S.) *See* United States. Air Force Logistics Command
Air Force One (Airplane) *See* Airplanes, Government
Air Force Space Technology Center (U.S.)
Air Force labs concentrate on SDI research. *Aviat Week Space Technol* 127:50 N 2 '87
USAF Center develops lightweight projectiles for SDI applications [Lightweight Exoatmospheric Projectile program] T. M. Foley. il *Aviat Week Space Technol* 127:46-7 N 2 '87
Air Force Survival School (U.S.)
Crash course. M. Rozek. il *Natl Wildl* 25:20-3 F/Mr '87
Air Force Systems Command (U.S.) *See* United States. Air Force Systems Command
Air France
Air France shows strong gains in first-half traffic growth. *Aviat Week Space Technol* 127:54 Ag 3 '87
Air freight service
See also
3D Distribution Systems, Inc.
Airborne Freight Corp.
Airplanes, Freight
Federal Express Corp.
There's still time to get it there [Christmas gifts] D. Moreau. il *Changing Times* 41:113-14 D '87
International aspects
See also
DHL Worldwide Courier Express
Rates
Federal Express delivers a price shock. D. Foust. il *Bus Week* p31-2 Mr 30 '87
Routes
Western Europe
Overnight mail: who will rule the routes? J. Heard. il *Bus Week* p78 My 25 '87
Traffic
Air express growth creates night rush at Midwest center [Indianapolis] J. Ott. il *Aviat Week Space Technol* 126:37+ F 23 '87
Courier companies pursue growth to meet demand for global service. C. Preble. il *Aviat Week Space Technol* 127:50+ Jl 6 '87
Small-package carriers lead U.S. air cargo growth. il *Aviat Week Space Technol* 126:221-2 Mr 9 '87
Air guns
On target! J. Bashline. il *Pop Mech* 164:68-71 Ja '87
Reborn Model 70 and some great new shooting gear. J. Carmichel. il *Outdoor Life* 179:36+ Ap '87
Shooting for tomorrow. P. W. Johnston. il *Field Stream* 91:59-60 Ap '87

Air India

Air-India considers MD-11 for key role in fleet rejuvenation. *Aviat Week Space Technol* 126:30 My 25 '87

Air Line Pilots Association

Air pockets around United [pilots propose employee buyout] G. M. Bock. il *Time* 129:52-3 Ap 20 '87

Eastern refuses to deal with ALPA until pilots end safety campaign. E. H. Kolcum. *Aviat Week Space Technol* 127:37+ N 9 '87

Friendly guy, unfriendly skies [United's pilots choose W. R. Howard as the executive to help them buy the company] N. J. Perry. il por *Fortune* 116:122 S 14 '87

Pilots' offer to buy United meets company, union opposition. J. Ott. *Aviat Week Space Technol* 126:32-3 Ap 20 '87

TWA pilots extend current contract. *Mon Labor Rev* 110:42 Mr '87

UAL's pilots may put the airline into play [employee ownership offer] J. E. Ellis. il *Bus Week* p25 Ap 20 '87

United's pilots are inching closer to a coup [employee ownership] J. E. Ellis. il por *Bus Week* p32-3 Ag 31 '87

United's pilots get a captain and cash [mounting a buyout] *Newsweek* 110:32 Ag 24 '87

What it's like to work for Frank Lorenzo [Continental Airlines] J. E. Davis. il por *Bus Week* p76+ My 18 '87

Air mail service

See also

Pigeon postal service

Air National Guard (N.Y.) *See* New York (State). Air National Guard

Air National Guard (U.S.) *See* United States. Air National Guard

Air navigation

Routine emergency [Beech 99 crew wanders astray] P. Garrison. *Flying* 114:14+ Ap '87

Aids and devices

See also

Artificial satellites—Navigational use

Aviation charts

Calculators—Aviation use

Computers—Aviation use

Inertial guidance systems

Loran

Micronav Ltd.

Microwave landing systems

Radio in aviation

Bendix, Israeli firm demonstrate high-accuracy helmet sight. il *Aviat Week Space Technol* 127:148 Ag 10 '87

Flight Dynamics prepares to test wind shear guidance with HUD [holographic head-up display] il *Aviat Week Space Technol* 126:107+ Ja 12 '87

Single-engine aircraft tests polar navigation [Arctic Tern] map *Aviat Week Space Technol* 126:76 F 2 '87

Air pilots

See also

Air Line Pilots Association

Airplanes—Piloting

Airplanes, Light—Piloting

Airplanes, Military transport—Piloting

Airships—Piloting

Alcohol and air pilots

Black air pilots

Celebrities as air pilots

Drugs and air pilots

Helicopter pilots

International Federation of Airline Pilots Associations

Prisoners as air pilots

Turner, David L.

Women air pilots

Yeager, Chuck, 1923-

Check six, George. M. Trahan. *Flying* 114:104 F '87

Fighter, helicopter test pilots challenge cockpit design concepts. W. B. Scott. *Aviat Week Space Technol* 127:65+ N 16 '87

The lowdown. L. Morgan. il *Flying* 114:8-9 Ag '87

Too green to fly? [crash at Denver's Stapleton Airport raises doubts about pilots] B. Kantrowitz. il *Newsweek* 110:32+ N 30 '87

Where is Bill? [World War II] L. Morgan. il *Flying* 114:10+ Je '87

The wrong airport blues [landing at the wrong field] L. Morgan. il *Flying* 114:8-9 N '87

X-men [X-29 test pilots at Dryden Research Center] E. Weiner. il *Flying* 114:38-40+ Ja '87

Age

Old dogs, new tricks. L. Morgan. il *Flying* 114:10-11 O '87

Health and hygiene

Canadians investigate pilot's loss of consciousness prior to F-20A crash [May 14, 1985] *Aviat Week Space Technol* 126:75+ Mr 23 '87

Ready to drop [pilot fatigue] P. Bradley. il *Flying* 114:54-7 Ja '87

Safety Board urges pilot training in G-induced loss of consciousness [crash of F-20A prototype at Goose Bay, Labrador, May 14, 1985] il *Aviat Week Space Technol* 126:103-4 Mr 30 '87

What do you suppose B-forces make? [high ratio of daughters to sons in fighter pilots exposed to high G-forces; research by Bertis Little] *Sci News* 132:377 D 12 '87

Language

Watch your language. G. Baxter. il *Flying* 114:95+ N '87

Legal status, laws, etc.

Free-for-all: what deregulation means to the airline pilot. P. Scott. il *Flying* 114:40-2+ Jl '87

Psychology

How to teach judgment [pilot personality factor; study by Lewis Lester] J. Munson. *Flying* 114:98 Ja '87

Stress test. P. Garrison. il *Flying* 114:54-7 Je '87

Rating

FAA developing new policy for pilot type ratings. J. Ott. *Aviat Week Space Technol* 126:30-1 Mr 30 '87

Salaries, pensions, etc.

See also

Collective bargaining—Airlines

El Al proposes two-tier pay scale for pilots. D. A. Brown. *Aviat Week Space Technol* 127:36-7 S 14 '87

What it's like to work for Frank Lorenzo [Continental Airlines] J. E. Davis. il por *Bus Week* p76+ My 18 '87

Supply and demand

Airline hiring shrinks supply of well-qualified corporate pilots. *Aviat Week Space Technol* 127:113 S 28 '87

Eastern begins replacing hundreds of pilots who quit in midst of dispute. C. Preble. *Aviat Week Space Technol* 127:36 Ag 10 '87

Flight crew requirements through 1999 spur Lufthansa to bolster pilot corps. il *Aviat Week Space Technol* 127:38-9 Ag 10 '87

Japanese defense, transport agencies agree to transfer military pilots to offset aircrew shortage among airlines. *Aviat Week Space Technol* 127:40 D 7 '87

NWA funds training center for zero-time pilot candidates [Northwest Airlines] il *Aviat Week Space Technol* 127:69+ Jl 6 '87

Professional pilot shortage [special section] il *Aviat Week Space Technol* 127:93-7 O 5 '87

Wanted: a lot of good pilots [airline recruitment] W. J. Cook. il *U S News World Rep* 103:83-4 N 9 '87

Training

See Aviation—Study and teaching

Air pilots as authors

Once a Navy bomber pilot, Stephen Coonts soars again with a supersonic first novel. R. Arias. il pors *People Wkly* 27:51-2 Ja 19 '87

Air pilots' headphones *See* Headphones

Air plants

From the jungle to your front door: "air plants" in wreaths. il *Sunset* 179:190-1 D '87

Air pollution

See also

Acid dew

Acid rain

Automobiles—Environmental aspects

Electric plants—Environmental aspects

Plants, Effect of air pollution on

Radon pollution

Smelters—Environmental aspects

Smog

Smoke

Trees, Effect of air pollution on

Airborne toxic releases: are communities prepared? S. L. Cutter. bibl f il map *Environment* 29:12-17+ Jl/Ag '87

Exercise may worsen NO_2 toxicity. J. Raloff. *Sci News* 131:169 Mr 14 '87

Health hazard from copier exhaust [air pollution from wet process copiers; research by Yoshio Tsuchiya] S. Weisburd. *Sci News* 132:166 S 12 '87

How safe is the air inside your home? M. Lipske. il *Natl Wildl* 25:34-9 Ap/My '87

Indoor air effects. S. M. Sims. il *Vogue* 177:158-9+ Ja '87

Air pollution—*cont.*

Indoor air quality under the microscope. D. Eaton. il *Pop Mech* 164:103-6 Ag '87

Is your house making you sick? J. Bailey. il *Redbook* 168:116-19 Mr '87

Is your house making you sick? [views of Gary Cook] *USA Today (Periodical)* 116:3 D '87

Is your office toxic? H. Manley. il *Good Housekeep* 205:268 S '87

Living in the shadow of poisonous air [toxic chemicals] S. Q. Stranahan. il *Natl Wildl* 25:30-3 Ag/S '87

Pollution in your home. C. Loomis. il *Parents* 62:15 S '87

Rate your home: how safe is it? [excerpt from House dangerous] E. J. Greenfield. *Redbook* 168:117-18 Mr '87

Scenic sites under siege [air pollution in national parks] C. Peterson. il *Natl Wildl* 25:44-5 Je/Jl '87

Should you jog in smog? P. McCarthy. il *Women's Sports Fitness* 9:15 N '87

Shower shudders [breathing toxins; research by Julian Andelman] G. Woolley. il *Sierra* 72:13-14 Jl/Ag '87

Toxic hazards in the home: sometimes the best thing to do is nothing. il *Money* 16:47 Mr '87

Toxic wind. M. H. Brown. il map *Discover* 8:42-9 N '87

Control

See also
Automobiles—Pollution control devices
Diesel engines, Automotive—Pollution control devices
Dust collectors
Industry and the environment
Motorcycles—Pollution control devices
Odors—Control

Air [Environmental Quality Index] il *Natl Wildl* 25:35 F/Mr '87

Cleaning the air [rapid removal of nitrogen oxides process; work of Robert A. Perry] *Sci Am* 256:75 Mr '87

Cleaning up with a smokestack's siren song [use of acoustic agglomeration to control particle emissions from coal-fired power plants] I. Peterson. *Sci News* 131:342 My 30 '87

Fighting acid rain with gold [use as catalyst to reduce nitrogen oxide after coal is burned for fuel; work of Arun Someshwar] *USA Today (Periodical)* 115:5-6 Je '87

The pollution within [use of heat recovery ventilator] P. V. Fossel. il *Ctry J* 14:44-9 S '87

Staving off dirty air. H. R. Kennedy. *U S News World Rep* 103:107 S 28 '87

Your house may be hazardous to your health. D. Noyes. il *Parents* 62:180-2+ N '87

International aspects

See also
Vienna Convention for the Protection of the Ozone Layer (1985)

Air: an atmosphere of uncertainty. N. Grove. il map *Natl Geogr* 171:502-37 Ap '87

It could be your office that is 'sick' [sick building syndrome] E. Verdecchia. *World Press Rev* 34:50 My '87

What a difference the lead makes [use of lead isotope ratios to differentiate between U.S. and Canadian emissions; work of L. A. Barrie and W. T. Sturges] *Sci News* 132:204 S 26 '87

Laws and regulations

See also
Clean Air Act
Emission reduction credits

A clean-air bill won't be such a breeze. T. Smart. *Bus Week* p57 F 23 '87

Smog, the EPA, and cans of paint yanked off the shelf. *Sunset* 179:86 S '87

Measurement

Air pollution by particles. R. W. Shaw. bibl (p116) il *Sci Am* 257:96-103 Ag '87

Thunderstorms: an important mechanism in the transport of air pollutants. R. R. Dickerson and others. bibl f il *Science* 235:460-5 Ja 23 '87

What a difference the lead makes [use of lead isotope ratios to differentiate between U.S. and Canadian emissions; work of L. A. Barrie and W. T. Sturges] *Sci News* 132:204 S 26 '87

California

See also
California. Air Resources Board
Los Angeles (Calif.)—Air pollution

You only choke twice [southern Calif. forest fire smoke contains automobile exhaust] il *Discover* 8:6+ O '87

China

Acid rain: China, United States, and a remote area. J. N. Galloway and others. bibl f il maps *Science* 236:1559-62 Je 19 '87

Déjà vu: acid rain in China. I. Peterson. *Sci News* 131:406 Je 27 '87

Lung cancer and indoor air pollution in Xuan Wei, China [burning of smoky coal] J. L. Mumford and others. bibl f il map *Science* 235:217-20 Ja 9 '87

Colorado

See also
Denver (Colo.)—Air pollution

Europe

Acid rain in Europe [cover story; special section; with editorial comment by Leen Hordijk] bibl f il maps *Environment* 29:inside cover, 4-15+ N '87

Great Lakes region

A double dose of danger for the lakes [airborne toxic chemicals] M. Griffin. il *Sierra* 72:47 N/D '87

Mexico

See also
Mexico City (Mexico)—Air pollution

Poland

See also
Krakow (Poland)—Air pollution

Switzerland

Avalanche! S. Cashen. il *Int Wildl* 17:36-7 My/Je '87

United States

See Air pollution

Western States

Deadlines for Clean Air. il *Sunset* 179:207 D '87

Air pressure *See* Atmospheric pressure

Air purifiers *See* Air filters

Air races *See* Airplane racing

Air Resources Board (California) *See* California. Air Resources Board

Air rights *See* Airspace (Law)

Air routes *See* Airlines—Routes

Air safety *See* Aviation—Safety devices and measures

Air-sea interaction *See* Ocean-atmosphere interaction

Air ships *See* Airships

Air shows *See* Aviation—Exhibitions

Air shuttle service *See* Airlines—Shuttle service; Helicopter airlines—Shuttle service

Air space (International law) *See* Airspace (International law)

Air speeds *See* Airplanes—Speed

Air stewardesses *See* Airlines—Flight attendants

Air taxi service
See also
Helicopter airlines

Air-to-surface missiles *See* Guided missiles—Launching from airplanes

Air traffic *See* Airlines—Traffic

Air traffic control
See also
Airplanes—Collision avoidance systems
Computers—Aviation use
Radar in aviation

Air express growth creates night rush at Midwest center [Indianapolis] J. Ott. il *Aviat Week Space Technol* 126:37+ F 23 '87

Air safety: erosion of confidence [special section; with editorial comment by Donald E. Fink] il *Aviat Week Space Technol* 127:11, 18-25 Ag 24 '87

Air traffic control [address, November 14, 1986] W. F. Bolger. *Vital Speeches Day* 53:251-3 F 1 '87

Airlines vs. private pilots. il *U S News World Rep* 103:56 D 7 '87

The answer to intolerable congestion at America's airports [getting the FAA out of air traffic control] M. S. Forbes, Jr. il *Forbes* 140:29 Jl 27 '87

ATC's long hot summer. D. E. Fink. *Aviat Week Space Technol* 126:11 My 18 '87

"Be careful out there" [growing concerns about safety] E. Magnuson. il *Time* 129:24-32 Ja 12 '87

Bum rap. R. L. Collins. *Flying* 114:28 N '87

Cerritos inquiry reviews separation, collision avoidance procedures [August 1986 collision of DC-9 and Piper aircraft] *Aviat Week Space Technol* 127:67-70 D 21 '87

Changes in East Coast routes offer potential to reduce delays. *Aviat Week Space Technol* 126:36 F 23 '87

Collisions [cover story; special section] il *Flying* 114:66-9+ Je '87

Conferees urge establishment of national airspace, airport development program. W. B. Scott. *Aviat Week Space Technol* 127:41-2 D 14 '87

Confusion, collision [collision of Falcon and Cherokee Archer over Fairview, N.J.] P. Garrison. *Flying* 114:23-4 D '87

Air traffic control—*cont.*

Corporate control [privatization] R. L. Collins. *Flying* 114:28-9 O '87

Crandall proposes commission empowered to limit flights. J. Ott. *Aviat Week Space Technol* 126:32-3 Je 29 '87

Crandall seeks Congress' support for restrictions on general aviation. *Aviat Week Space Technol* 127:41 S 14 '87

Dole proposes upgrade of nine radar service areas to TCA status [airport terminal control areas] *Aviat Week Space Technol* 127:33 Ag 31 '87

Easing airport congestion. M. S. Forbes, Jr. il *Forbes* 139:25 Ja 26 '87

East Side story [FAA's East Coast Plan] R. L. Collins. il *Flying* 114:14 Je '87

Executives debate new structure for FAA. *Aviat Week Space Technol* 126:40 Ja 26 '87

FAA disputes recommendations for summer traffic reductions. *Aviat Week Space Technol* 126:36 Je 1 '87

FAA investigators seek pattern in near-midair collisions. P. Proctor. il *Aviat Week Space Technol* 126:63-4 Ap 27 '87

FAA prepares for second phase of expanded East Coast Plan. K. J. Stein. *Aviat Week Space Technol* 127:115+ Jl 6 '87

Fear of flying frequently. P. S. Dempsey. por *Newsweek* 110:12 O 5 '87

Flight delays. R. Coorsh. il *Consum Res Mag* 70:4 Je '87

Flying's safer than ever, but stress is increasing. il *Nations Bus* 75:24 N '87

The great communicator. R. L. Collins. il *Flying* 114:20 F '87

Hang 'em High [FAA's new stance on TCA airspace] J. M. McClellan. *Flying* 114:28-9 F '87

Heliport planning, development gain from pressures of fixed-wing traffic. P. Proctor. map *Aviat Week Space Technol* 126:59+ Mr 2 '87

High anxiety and rage. S. Koepp. il *Time* 130:52-4 Jl 20 '87

How not to eliminate flight delays. J. Ott. *Aviat Week Space Technol* 126:11 Ap 6 '87

How safe is the air traffic control system? [cover story] G. V. Molinari. il *USA Today (Periodical)* 116:12-14 N '87

How to end airport gridlock. T. Jacoby. il *Newsweek* 109:28 My 11 '87

IFR/VFR mix and match. M. Brenlove. *Flying* 114:96 D '87

Industry foresees wide-bodies as aid to congested system. J. Ott. il *Aviat Week Space Technol* 127:36-7 S 28 '87

The late show. B. Kallen. il *Forbes* 139:166+ Je 1 '87

NTSB blames ATC system for midair crash [Aug. 31, 1986 collision of Aeromexico DC-9-30 and Piper PA-28-181] *Aviat Week Space Technol* 127:34 Jl 13 '87

NTSB recommends limits to ease summer air traffic congestion. C. Preble. il *Aviat Week Space Technol* 126:32-3 My 4 '87

NTSB urges traffic reductions in congested control zones. *Aviat Week Space Technol* 126:31 My 18 '87

'Playing chicken' aloft. J. B. Copeland. il *Newsweek* 109:54 Je 8 '87

Production of ATC modernization equipment moves into high gear [National Airspace System Plan] J. Ott. *Aviat Week Space Technol* 126:31-2 Mr 23 '87

Red for La Guardia, brown for J.F.K. [FAA's new computer system] P. Elmer-Dewitt. il *Time* 129:60-1 Je 1 '87

Report endorses shifting ATC responsibility to local airports [prepared for the National Council on Public Works Improvement] *Aviat Week Space Technol* 126:40 Je 29 '87

Safe air and hot air [FAA and need to improve system] M. B. Zuckerman. il *U S News World Rep* 103:84 S 21 '87

Safety record. R. L. Collins. *Flying* 114:22 Ap '87

Skirting the issue. P. Bradley. il *Flying* 114:10-11 N '87

Slow role [rescue the FAA from the DOT] R. L. Collins. *Flying* 114:32 Je '87

Solving the crisis in the skies. R. L. Crandall. il por *Fortune* 116:203-4 S 28 '87

Stage 2 cutoff dates recommended by U.S. Task Force [Aircraft Noise/Airport Capacity] *Aviat Week Space Technol* 127:37 S 28 '87

Straight talk. R. L. Collins. il *Flying* 114:58-60+ Ag '87

TCA trauma [cover story; special section] il *Flying* 114:28-34+ D '87

Traffic advisory limits. M. Brenlove. *Flying* 114:108 N '87

Traffic reduction plan results in hundreds of airline delays. J. Ott. *Aviat Week Space Technol* 126:79 Je 15 '87

U.S. needs comprehensive plan to restore air traffic control. P. J. Foltz. por *Aviat Week Space Technol* 127:81 O 5 '87

The volatile airline industry [address, February 23, 1987] R. L. Crandall. *Vital Speeches Day* 53:468-72 My 15 '87

Why air traffic is a mess. K. Labich. il *Fortune* 116:54-6+ Ag 17 '87

Worries in busy skies. W. J. Cook. il *U S News World Rep* 103:18-19 Ag 24 '87

History

Grand Canyon collision [June 30, 1956 crash ushers in modern air traffic control] R. L. Collins. *Flying* 114:22+ S '87

International aspects

See also
International Civil Airports Association

International air transport: building for traffic growth [cover story; special section; with editorial comment by James Ott] il *Aviat Week Space Technol* 127:15, 49-51+ N 9 '87

Suits and claims

Engen warns against local challenges to national airspace system. *Aviat Week Space Technol* 126:50 Ap 13 '87

For safety's sake: indemnify air traffic control manufacturers. R. H. Jones. *Aviat Week Space Technol* 127:11 Jl 20 '87

China

China's air traffic control system hampered by poor coordination. *Aviat Week Space Technol* 127:58-9 O 12 '87

Japan

Japan accelerates controller hiring, training programs. *Aviat Week Space Technol* 127:137 N 9 '87

Korea (South)

South Korea activates automated civil air traffic control system. il *Aviat Week Space Technol* 126:157 My 11 '87

Soviet Union

Transsiberian flights conducted routinely. *Aviat Week Space Technol* 126:32 Je 8 '87

Western Europe

Eurocontrol investigating traffic control changes to handle projected growth in commercial flights. *Aviat Week Space Technol* 127:126 N 9 '87

Europe heads toward an air safety crisis of its own. M. Maremont. il *Bus Week* p44-5 S 21 '87

Air traffic controllers (Persons)

See also
Black air traffic controllers (Persons)
National Air Traffic Controllers Association
National Association of Air Traffic Specialists
Strikes—Air traffic controllers (Persons)

Budget cuts could cause shortages in air traffic system personnel. *Aviat Week Space Technol* 127:45 D 14 '87

Positive control: two TCAs, and the controllers in the ATC shuffle. P. Scott. il *Flying* 114:30-2 D '87

Rough chop ahead for the FAA. P. Cary. il *U S News World Rep* 103:62-3+ Jl 6 '87

To rehire or not to rehire? B. Cohn. il *Newsweek* 110:55 N 23 '87

Air Transport Association of America

Air traffic control [address, November 14, 1986] W. F. Bolger. *Vital Speeches Day* 53:251-3 F 1 '87

ATA proposes easing rules on foreign repair stations. *Aviat Week Space Technol* 126:53 Ja 26 '87

Air travel

See also
Airlines
Business travel
Computers and air travel
Fear of flying
Frequent flier programs
Jet lag
Private flying

Air travelers' gripes climb into the clouds. C. P. Work. il *U S News World Rep* 103:8 Jl 27 '87

Airline bonuses: not just for the jet set. J. E. Ellis. il *Bus Week* p116-17 S 28 '87

Airline hassles: how to hassle back. M. Schiffres. il *Changing Times* 41:64-6 Jl '87

Airline officials split on usefulness of expanded consumer reports [issued by Transportation Dept.] J. Ott. il *Aviat Week Space Technol* 127:31+ N 16 '87

Air travel—*cont.*

Concorde crossing. R. L. Collins. il *Flying* 114:14+ O '87

Delays, service problems prompt strong congressional reaction [airlines] J. Ott. *Aviat Week Space Technol* 127:33-5 Ag 10 '87

Fares, bumping, baggage: what an air traveler needs to know. il *Sunset* 179:37 N '87

Flight delays. R. Coorsh. il *Consum Res Mag* 70:4 Je '87

Flying complaints. J. W. Merline. il *Consum Res Mag* 70:38 Ja '87

How to avoid air travel hassles. E. McGowan. il *Good Housekeep* 205:241 N '87

Hub, spoke, turmoil. L. Morgan. il *Flying* 114:10-11 D '87

Is airline deregulation working? S. Shane. *Travel Holiday* 168:6 Ag '87

The late show. B. Kallen. il *Forbes* 139:166+ Je 1 '87

New hype over service in the skies [Dept. of Transportation report] B. Bauer. il *U S News World Rep* 103:47 N 23 '87

Northwest, TWA and Continental targets of most service complaints. *Aviat Week Space Technol* 127:41 S 14 '87

Passenger complaints fell in September. *Aviat Week Space Technol* 127:36 O 19 '87

Pay now, fly later. A. Holzinger. il *Nations Bus* 75:22-4 N '87

Queasy riders [first time passengers] N. Moll. *Flying* 114:67 My '87

The sky isn't falling [cover story] G. Easterbrook. *New Repub* 197:18+ N 30 '87

Tips for fliers in the hands of the fearsome five. M. Wellemeyer. il *Fortune* 115:71 My 11 '87

Two over the pond [flying to Paris on Boeing 767] *Pop Mech* 164:17 O '87

U.S. airline service draws increased federal scrutiny. *Aviat Week Space Technol* 126:30-1 Je 1 '87

Was man meant to fly? M. M. Hunt. il *N Y Times Mag* p42-4+ N 1 '87

What troubles airline passengers. il *Consum Res Mag* 70:17-20 Je '87

What you can and can't do about airline snafus. il *Glamour* 85:91 O '87

Year of the near miss [cover story; special section] il *Newsweek* 110:20-7 Jl 27 '87

The youngest jet-setters [children] B. Kantrowitz. il *Newsweek* 109:52-3 Je 29 '87

Anecdotes, facetiae, satire, etc.

Three daze in the life. J. Dinkel. il *Road Track* 39:39-42 D '87

Physiological aspects

See Aviation—Physiological aspects

Security measures

Terror-proof tourism [excerpt from The terrorism survival guide] A. Lightbody. *Harpers* 275:24 Jl '87

Taxation

Welcome to the U.S.: let's have your wallet. G. Eichler. il *Esquire* 108:40 Ag '87

Air warfare

See also
Airplanes, Military
Bombing, Aerial
Close air support
Guns, Anti-aircraft

Multipilot air-to-air combat evaluated in Northrop simulator. M. A. Dornheim. il *Aviat Week Space Technol* 127:64-5+ N 30 '87

Was 1945 a break in history? M. S. Sherry. bibl f il *Bull At Sci* 43:12-15 Jl/Ag '87

Maneuvers

See Military maneuvers

Airborne Freight Corp.

Flying harder. M. Beauchamp. il *Forbes* 140:65 S 7 '87

Airborne warning and control system *See* Airplanes, Military—Radar equipment

Airbrush art

Airbrushing your photos. M. Bright and D. Bright. il *Petersens Photogr Mag* 15:38-41 Ap '87

Airbus Industrie

A320 fly-by-wire controls pass basic flight testing. J. M. Lenorovitz. il *Aviat Week Space Technol* 126:41+ My 18 '87

A330/A340 launch decision awaits completion of partner financing. J. M. Lenorovitz. il *Aviat Week Space Technol* 126:34 Mr 23 '87

Airbus A320 begins 1,200-hour flight test program. il *Aviat Week Space Technol* 126:30-1 Mr 2 '87

Airbus announces new orders for wide-body transports. il *Aviat Week Space Technol* 127:35 O 26 '87

Airbus charts long-term plan for civil aircraft product line. J. M. Lenorovitz. il *Aviat Week Space Technol* 126:40-1 Je 1 '87

Airbus comes of age. H. Banks. il *Forbes* 139:36-7 F 23 '87

Airbus defines new A340 to use CFM56 turbofans. J. M. Lenorovitz. *Aviat Week Space Technol* 126:36-8 Ap 13 '87

Airbus expands transport family to meet airlines' changing needs. J. M. Lenorovitz. il *Aviat Week Space Technol* 127:67-8 N 9 '87

Airbus expecting delivery delays for A320s powered by V2500 engine. J. M. Lenorovitz. *Aviat Week Space Technol* 127:32-3 D 14 '87

Airbus increases A330/A340 wingspan. *Aviat Week Space Technol* 126:32 Ap 20 '87

Airbus Industrie faces decision of whether to launch A330/A340. il *Aviat Week Space Technol* 126:215+ Mr 9 '87

Airbus Industrie to offer International Aero Engines SuperFan on proposed A340. J. M. Lenorovitz. *Aviat Week Space Technol* 126:33 Ja 5 '87

Airbus makes sales bid to MD-11 customers with Super-Fan version of A340. M. Feazel. *Aviat Week Space Technol* 126:33 Ja 26 '87

Airbus seeking joint efforts with U.S. companies. *Aviat Week Space Technol* 127:32 Jl 20 '87

All's fair in the airliner war. A. Faujas. *World Press Rev* 34:49-50 Je '87

American wields leverage in aircraft lease arrangement [leasing order divided between Airbus Industrie and Boeing] J. Ott. il *Aviat Week Space Technol* 126:258-9 Mr 9 '87

Bids in a jumbo gamble [MD-11 vs. A-340] J. Barber. il *Macleans* 100:46-7 Ja 19 '87

British Aerospace rejects A330/A340 aid proposal. *Aviat Week Space Technol* 126:36 Mr 30 '87

British agree on launch aid for A330/A340. *Aviat Week Space Technol* 126:33 My 18 '87

The dogfight to control the skies. C. P. Work. il *U S News World Rep* 102:42-3 Ap 20 '87

Emirates plans Airbus A310-300 service to Europe this summer. il *Aviat Week Space Technol* 126:44 Je 1 '87

Europeans criticize U.S. subsidy charges at Airbus A320 rollout. J. M. Lenorovitz. il *Aviat Week Space Technol* 126:30-1 F 23 '87

Exim Bank backs 767 sale to All Nippon to foil Airbus bid. *Aviat Week Space Technol* 126:31 Je 29 '87

Fly-by-wire, digital avionics ease A320 transition training [evaluation flight] D. M. North. il *Aviat Week Space Technol* 127:40-1+ N 30 '87

German government commits funds to Airbus A330/A340 development. *Aviat Week Space Technol* 126:35 Je 8 '87

Industry officials see obstacles to Airbus' drive to share risks [special section; with editorial comment by Donald E. Fink] *Aviat Week Space Technol* 127:15, 34-7 Ag 3 '87

International carriers weigh A340, MD-11 acquisition options. J. M. Lenorovitz. *Aviat Week Space Technol* 126:53+ Ap 6 '87

Lufthansa orders 15 A340s with V2500 SuperFan engines. *Aviat Week Space Technol* 126:34-5 Ja 26 '87

Manufacturers discuss cooperation despite aircraft subsidy dispute [U.S. and Europe] D. A. Brown. *Aviat Week Space Technol* 126:30-1 Je 29 '87

McDonnell Douglas to launch Airbus A330 competitor. *Aviat Week Space Technol* 126:40 Je 22 '87

McDonnell executives question target date of SuperFan engine. R. G. O'Lone. *Aviat Week Space Technol* 126:30-1 F 16 '87

MD-11, A340 competition gains momentum at Thai International. R. G. O'Lone. *Aviat Week Space Technol* 126:30-1 Mr 16 '87

New-generation Airbus A320 transport demonstrates fly-by-wire technology. il *Aviat Week Space Technol* 126:284-5 Je 15 '87

New international initiatives [Airbus Industrie and its European partner companies; special section] il *Aviat Week Space Technol* 127:16-19 Jl 27 '87

Northwest's A330/A340 choice fuels aircraft subsidy debate. J. Ott. il *Aviat Week Space Technol* 126:38-9 Ap 13 '87

Sky wars over Airbus [U.S. threatening to slap duties on its U.S. sales] F. J. Comes. *Bus Week* p48 F 16 '87

Airbus Industrie—*cont.*
A time for cool heads [dispute over subsidies to Europe's Airbus Industrie civil transport programs] D. E. Fink. *Aviat Week Space Technol* 126:11 F 23 '87
Trouble on the horizon. B. Rudolph. il *Time* 129:50-1 My 11 '87
U.S., Europe agree on agenda for aircraft financing talks. D. A. Brown. *Aviat Week Space Technol* 127:36 N 2 '87
U.S., Europe seek rapid cure in Airbus subsidy dispute. M. Mecham. *Aviat Week Space Technol* 127:35+ O 26 '87
U.S., Europeans clash over Airbus subsidies. D. A. Brown. il *Aviat Week Space Technol* 126:18-20 F 9 '87
Widebody wars: Airbus decides 'to go for the kill' [fierce battle with McDonnell Douglas] F. J. Comes. il *Bus Week* p80-1 Jl 6 '87

AirCal
AirCal line maintenance crews to join American workforce. *Aviat Week Space Technol* 126:46 Je 29 '87
AirCal will begin service as American on July 1. M. A. Dornheim. map *Aviat Week Space Technol* 126:53 My 11 '87

Aircraft
See also
Airplanes
Airships
Balloons
Helicopters
Microwave aircraft
Rotor aircraft

Aircraft carriers
See also
Airplanes, Military—Landing on carriers
Sneak attack [C. Weinberger requests funding for aircraft carriers] por *Time* 129:32 Ap 27 '87

History
See also
Sable (Aircraft carrier)
Wolverine (Aircraft carrier)

Aircraft carriers, Atomic powered *See* Nuclear aircraft carriers

Aircraft carriers, Japanese
See also
Shinano (Aircraft carrier)

Aircraft industry *See* Airplane industry

Aircraft Sales Company
Aircraft Sales Co. gains FAA approval of L-1011 freighter. *Aviat Week Space Technol* 126:97 Je 1 '87

Airfoils
See also
Airplanes—Wings

Airframe industry *See* Airplane industry

Airframes
See also
Airplanes, Military—Frames
Helicopters—Frames
NASA, Army testing composite airframe crashworthiness. E. H. Phillips. il *Aviat Week Space Technol* 127:61+ S 28 '87

Failure
Geriatric airframes. J. M. McClellan. il *Flying* 114:20+ D '87

Airgas, Inc.
Life is a gas. R. Simon. il por *Forbes* 140:114+ D 14 '87

Airline flight attendants *See* Airlines—Flight attendants
Airline passenger clubs *See* Airlines—Passenger service
Airline passenger head taxes *See* Air travel—Taxation
Airline passengers *See* Air travel
Airline schedules *See* Airlines—Schedules
Airline stocks *See* Airlines—Securities
Airlines
See also
Air Atlanta
Air Transport Association of America
Allegis Corporation
American Airlines, Inc.
Atlantic Southeast Airlines Inc.
Braniff, Inc.
Collective bargaining—Airlines
Collective labor agreements—Airlines
Continental Air Lines, Inc.
Delta Air Lines, Inc.
Eastern Air Lines, Inc.
Jet America Airlines Inc.
McClain Airlines Inc.
MGM Grand Air Inc.
Northwest Airlines, Inc.
Pacific Southwest Airlines
Pan American World Airways, Inc.

People Express Inc.
Texas Air Corp.
Trans World Airlines Inc.
UAL Inc.
United Air Lines, Inc.
US Air, Inc.
Western Air Lines, Inc.
World Airways, Inc.
Airline observer. See issues of Aviation Week & Space Technology
Airline officials split on usefulness of expanded consumer reports [issued by Transportation Dept.] J. Ott. il *Aviat Week Space Technol* 127:31+ N 16 '87
New hype over service in the skies [Dept. of Transportation report] B. Bauer. il *U S News World Rep* 103:47 N 23 '87
Shortlines. See issues of Aviation Week & Space Technology

Acquisitions and mergers
AirCal line maintenance crews to join American workforce. *Aviat Week Space Technol* 126:46 Je 29 '87
AirCal will begin service as American on July 1. M. A. Dornheim. map *Aviat Week Space Technol* 126:53 My 11 '87
Boeing financing of United orders reflects stiffening competition. *Aviat Week Space Technol* 126:29-30 My 18 '87
Boeing had good reason to take Allegis under its wing. J. E. Ellis. il *Bus Week* p64+ My 25 '87
Carl Icahn is at it again [bid for USAir] C. Hawkins. *Bus Week* p42+ Mr 16 '87
Carrier consolidation may intensify competition among regional airlines. C. Preble. il *Aviat Week Space Technol* 126:195+ Mr 9 '87
Carrier realignment emerges as key 1987 business issue. J. Ott. *Aviat Week Space Technol* 126:32-3 Ja 5 '87
Closer ties between regional, major airlines predicted. R. G. O'Lone. *Aviat Week Space Technol* 127:40+ D 7 '87
Exchange of stock signals Pan Am, Braniff merger. *Aviat Week Space Technol* 127:36 D 14 '87
For Carl Icahn, the flight path never ends [takeover bid for USAir] por *Newsweek* 109:50 Mr 16 '87
Frank Lorenzo. J. E. Davis. il por *Bus Week* Sp Issue:228 Ap 17 '87
A high roller moves in on Pan Am [bid by K. Kerkorian] R. Grover. il por *Bus Week* p30-3 N 23 '87
House approves labor protection for employees of merged airlines. *Aviat Week Space Technol* 126:33-4 Je 29 '87
How USAir cut Icahn out [plan to buy Piedmont] S. Payne. il por *Bus Week* p35 Mr 23 '87
Law judge rejects USAir/Piedmont merger on regional antitrust grounds. M. Mecham. *Aviat Week Space Technol* 127:41+ S 28 '87
Long-term effects of airline consolidation still uncertain. C. A. Shifrin. il *Aviat Week Space Technol* 126:198-9+ Mr 9 '87
The new master of the skies [F. Lorenzo] K. Labich. il por *Fortune* 115:72-3 Ja 5 '87
Pan Am seeks partner/buyer following $400-million loss. J. Ott. *Aviat Week Space Technol* 126:30-1 Mr 2 '87
Pan Am union coalition attempts buyout. *Aviat Week Space Technol* 127:32 Jl 27 '87
Pan American council examines takeover, restructure plan [K. Kerkorian plan] J. Ott. *Aviat Week Space Technol* 127:34 O 19 '87
People Express, New York Air merging under Continental umbrella. C. Preble. *Aviat Week Space Technol* 126:32-3 Ja 19 '87
Piedmont delays acquisition decision, invites new bids. il *Aviat Week Space Technol* 126:34 F 23 '87
Reports of Pan Am's sale may not be greatly exaggerated. C. Hawkins. il *Bus Week* p33 F 2 '87
Shareholders fail to block Texas Air's Continental buy. *Aviat Week Space Technol* 126:32 F 16 '87
Supreme Court overturns injunction blocking Delta-Western merger. C. Preble. map *Aviat Week Space Technol* 126:32-3 Ap 6 '87
Teamsters' vote clears path for USAir's acquisition of PSA. C. Preble. il *Aviat Week Space Technol* 126:41 My 25 '87
Texas Air will maintain Eastern's identity. *Aviat Week Space Technol* 126:32 Ja 19 '87
Transportation Dept. approves proposed USAir/Piedmont merger. J. Ott. *Aviat Week Space Technol* 127:44 N 9 '87
United finds a new friend [Allegis' deal with Boeing] J. B. Copeland. il *Newsweek* 109:38 My 25 '87

Airlines—Acquisitions and mergers—*cont.*

USAir, Piedmont ask administration to overturn decision against merger. *Aviat Week Space Technol* 127:44 O 12 '87

USAir-Piedmont merger pending government, shareholder approval. C. Preble. map *Aviat Week Space Technol* 126:34-6 Mr 16 '87

What's standing between USAir and Piedmont. S. Payne. il *Bus Week* p40 O 5 '87

Will it be Kerkorian to the rescue at Pan Am? C. Hawkins and R. Grover. il *Bus Week* p57-8 O 19 '87

You'll buy tickets, airlines will buy each other. C. Hawkins. il *Bus Week* p98-9 Ja 12 '87

International aspects

Airlines poised for global consolidation. *Aviat Week Space Technol* 126:45 My 18 '87

Ansett's stock purchase will place foreign stake in America West at 20%. M. A. Dornheim. il map *Aviat Week Space Technol* 127:41-2+ Jl 20 '87

Canada

AirBC-Air Canada alliance demonstrates upheaval in Canadian airline business. J. Ott. il *Aviat Week Space Technol* 126:47+ My 11 '87

Great Britain

British Caledonian threatens to scuttle merger with British Airways. D. A. Brown. *Aviat Week Space Technol* 127:38 Ag 3 '87

British government approves British Airways merger proposal [British Caledonian] *Aviat Week Space Technol* 127:36 N 16 '87

CAA chief backs move by small carriers to prevent British Airways/BCal merger; British Caledonian downplays impact of merger on competitors. D. A. Brown. *Aviat Week Space Technol* 127:56-7 Ag 3 '87

Caledonian board accepts offer to merge with British Airways. D. A. Brown. *Aviat Week Space Technol* 127:36 Jl 20 '87

SAS bid for British Caledonian cleared by British government. *Aviat Week Space Technol* 127:36 D 21 '87

SAS, British Airways boost bids for stake in British Caledonian. *Aviat Week Space Technol* 127:34 D 14 '87

SAS seeks British Caledonian tie to boost international traffic. D. A. Brown. *Aviat Week Space Technol* 127:30-1 N 30 '87

Western Europe

European deregulation expected to lead to airline mergers [proposed SAS-Sabena merger] *Aviat Week Space Technol* 126:203+ Mr 9 '87

European skies are freer but no friendlier. J. Heard. il *Bus Week* p54 D 21 '87

Europe's skies may be full of mergers [SAS and Sabena] J. Kapstein and others. il *Bus Week* p62 My 11 '87

SAS bid for British Caledonian cleared by British government. *Aviat Week Space Technol* 127:36 D 21 '87

SAS board authorizes merger talks with Sabena. *Aviat Week Space Technol* 126:34 My 4 '87

SAS, British Airways boost bids for stake in British Caledonian. *Aviat Week Space Technol* 127:34 D 14 '87

SAS seeks British Caledonian tie to boost international traffic. D. A. Brown. *Aviat Week Space Technol* 127:30-1 N 30 '87

Agreements

See Airlines—Cooperation

Antitrust cases

Texas Air unit charges American with restraining CRS business [computer reservation systems] C. A. Shifrin. *Aviat Week Space Technol* 127:51 D 7 '87

Automation

Air Europe to use Sabre system as marketing tool. *Aviat Week Space Technol* 126:49 Ap 20 '87

Alitalia joins new European computer reservation system [Galileo Distribution Systems] *Aviat Week Space Technol* 127:66 Ag 31 '87

Amadeus and Galileo boost efforts to add airlines to European CRS networks [computer reservation and travel systems] *Aviat Week Space Technol* 127:47 D 21 '87

American Airlines offers Europeans choice of CRS assistance [computerized passenger reservations system] *Aviat Week Space Technol* 127:34 Jl 20 '87

American begins operations at secure computer center [underground center in Tulsa, Okla.] *Aviat Week Space Technol* 126:43+ Ap 20 '87

AMR, Pan Am end pact on Sabre system use [computer reservations system] C. A. Shifrin. *Aviat Week Space Technol* 127:33-4 Ag 24 '87

European airline groups will develop two competing reservation systems. *Aviat Week Space Technol* 127:33-4 Jl 20 '87

European CRS consortium bids for new members [Amadeus computer reservation system] K. F. Mordoff. *Aviat Week Space Technol* 127:37 Ag 3 '87

Feeders, computer systems key to North Atlantic competition. il *Aviat Week Space Technol* 126:208-9+ Mr 9 '87

PS/2's United Airline [automated reservation system] S. Makrias. il *Pers Comput* 11:34 N '87

Secret formula [automation at American Airlines] E. Dyson. il *Forbes* 140:242 O 5 '87

A shoving match in the travel agency [competition in reservations systems] C. L. Harris. il *Bus Week* p116-18 Je 22 '87

Texas Air unit charges American with restraining CRS business [computer reservation systems] C. A. Shifrin. *Aviat Week Space Technol* 127:51 D 7 '87

Texas Instruments targets airlines for its AI products. *Aviat Week Space Technol* 127:43 O 19 '87

Varig upgrades computerized passenger information system. *Aviat Week Space Technol* 127:45 Ag 31 '87

Baggage handling

See Airlines—Luggage handling

Beverage service

High and mighty [prices of alcoholic drinks] W. G. Flanagan. il *Forbes* 140:104+ Ag 24 '87

Cooperation

Closer ties between regional, major airlines predicted. R. G. O'Lone. *Aviat Week Space Technol* 127:40+ D 7 '87

Israeli airline seeks partners to survive deregulated era. *Aviat Week Space Technol* 127:37 S 14 '87

United names Wolf, shares CRS codes with British Airways. *Aviat Week Space Technol* 127:35 D 14 '87

Employees

See also

Air pilots

Airlines—Flight attendants

Airplane crews

Airplane mechanics (Persons)

International Association of Machinists and Aerospace Workers

Strikes—Airline employees

Trade unions—Airline employees

Cocaine arrests prompt efforts to investigate airline employee records [smuggling rings uncovered at Kennedy Airport] *Aviat Week Space Technol* 126:36 Mr 16 '87

Salaries, pensions, etc.

American vs. its unions: double trouble [two-tier pay scales for pilots and flight attendants] T. Mason. il por *Bus Week* p45 F 23 '87

Eastern will slash labor costs by $490 million this year. E. H. Kolcum. *Aviat Week Space Technol* 126:35+ Ja 26 '87

House approves labor protection for employees of merged airlines. *Aviat Week Space Technol* 126:33-4 Je 29 '87

Judge blocks transfer of Eastern workers. *Aviat Week Space Technol* 127:31 Jl 13 '87

Lorenzo starts his attack [cost cutting at Eastern] D. Pauly. il por *Newsweek* 109:49 F 2 '87

What it's like to work for Frank Lorenzo [Continental Airlines] J. E. Davis. il por *Bus Week* p76+ My 18 '87

Energy usage

Jet A fuel price increase erodes airline cost advantage. J. Ott. il *Aviat Week Space Technol* 126:33+ Je 8 '87

Midway's option on MD-91/92X represents gamble on fuel prices. J. Ott. il *Aviat Week Space Technol* 127:43+ Jl 6 '87

Fares

See also

Frequent flier programs

Air fare arbitrage [cancellation insurance] M. Fritz. il *Forbes* 139:152 Mr 23 '87

Air fares you won't believe—until you hear the catch [Texas Air's MaxSaver] K. R. Sheets. *U S News World Rep* 102:46 F 9 '87

Airline yield managers foresee clashes in 1987. J. Ott. il *Aviat Week Space Technol* 126:192-3 Mr 9 '87

Airlines expect higher fall fares will cap off strong traffic year. J. Ott. il *Aviat Week Space Technol* 127:33-4 S 21 '87

Airlines follow Continental's lead in setting fares, ticket restrictions. C. A. Shifrin. *Aviat Week Space Technol* 127:32-3 Ag 17 '87

Airlines—Fares—cont.

American Airlines plans to raise domestic fares. C. Preble. *Aviat Week Space Technol* 126:32-3 F 23 '87

Bargain flights for summer nights. il *Fortune* 115:10 Je 8 '87

Best buys in Europe [ski trips] C. Walter. il *Skiing* 40:196 S '87

Can United afford Texas Air's low fares? J. E. Ellis. il *Bus Week* p34 F 16 '87

Cheap fares: come fly with me. C. P. Work. il *U S News World Rep* 102:43-4 F 23 '87

Continental: full planes may not mean full coffers. J. E. Davis. il *Bus Week* p37 Mr 16 '87

Continental's Maxsaver becomes a minisaver. C. Hawkins and J. E. Davis. il *Bus Week* p37 My 4 '87

Cost of flying: how to beat the scariest part—the fares. il *Money* 16:26 N '87

ECAC, U.S. renew North Atlantic pact [European Civil Aviation Conference] *Aviat Week Space Technol* 126:32 F 23 '87

A fare fight over on-time flights. il *U S News World Rep* 103:10 S 14 '87

Flying high at low cost. H. Gieseking. *Travel Holiday* 167:92-3 Mr '87

Getting less for less [discount agents and fares] G. Eichler. il *Esquire* 107:62 Ap '87

Has Lorenzo fired the first salvo in a fare war? C. Hawkins and J. E. Ellis. *Bus Week* p37-8 S 14 '87

The high price of bargain fares [nonrefundable fares] *Consum Rep* 52:308 My '87

No-frills travel agents. R. Simon. il *Forbes* 139:140+ My 4 '87

Refunds for stormy weather? B. Bauer. il *U S News World Rep* 103:12 N 30 '87

Stalking bargain air travel: four steps to getting there the cheapest way. R. Micheli. il *Money* 16:207-8 Je '87

Texas Air Corp. fare initiatives spur summer traffic demand. J. Ott. il *Aviat Week Space Technol* 126:30-1 Je 1 '87

U.S. airlines raise fares, restrict discount tickets. C. Preble. il *Aviat Week Space Technol* 126:32-3 F 2 '87

U.S. carriers match new fare cuts; Dutch, Danish decisions spark fare wars. *Aviat Week Space Technol* 126:36 F 9 '87

U.S. denies British Airways ticket offer to continental Europe. J. Ott. *Aviat Week Space Technol* 126:34-5 Ap 6 '87

Who will be Sky King? [fare wars between Texas Air and American Airlines] A. Miller. il pors *Newsweek* 109:54 Mr 2 '87

Federal aid

USAF weighs methods to boost strategic cargo airlift capacity [Civil Reserve Air Fleet] *Aviat Week Space Technol* 127:49+ S 7 '87

Finance

Air transport. H. Banks. il *Forbes* 139:66-7 Ja 12 '87

Airline income and expense: first quarter 1987. il *Aviat Week Space Technol* 127:39 Ag 31 '87

Airline income and expense: full year 1986. il *Aviat Week Space Technol* 126:99 Je 15 '87

Airline income and expense: third quarter 1986. il *Aviat Week Space Technol* 126:41 F 9 '87

Airline income and expense: third quarter 1986. il *Aviat Week Space Technol* 126:47 F 16 '87

Airline yield managers foresee clashes in 1987. J. Ott. il *Aviat Week Space Technol* 126:192-3 Mr 9 '87

Carrier realignment emerges as key 1987 business issue. J. Ott. *Aviat Week Space Technol* 126:32-3 Ja 5 '87

Long-term effects of airline consolidation still uncertain. C. A. Shifrin. il *Aviat Week Space Technol* 126:198-9+ Mr 9 '87

Market collapse will increase operating pressures on airlines. P. Proctor. *Aviat Week Space Technol* 127:42 O 26 '87

The volatile airline industry [address, February 23, 1987] R. L. Crandall. *Vital Speeches Day* 53:468-72 My 15 '87

Winners in the air wars. K. Labich. il *Fortune* 115:68-70+ My 11 '87

You'll buy tickets, airlines will buy each other. C. Hawkins. il *Bus Week* p98-9 Ja 12 '87

Flight attendants

See also
Association of Flight Attendants International
Independent Federation of Flight Attendants
Strikes—Airline employees

Gathering no dust, Kate Linder sweeps up on TV and in the skies. J. Callan. il pors *People Wkly* 27:73-4 Je 15 '87

Health and hygiene

Crewmember with AIDS barred at Gatwick [Delta Air Lines steward] *Aviat Week Space Technol* 126:36 F 23 '87

Food service

Adventures in bad eating. L. Morgan. il *Flying* 114:8-9 Ap '87

Better airline fare. K. Freifeld. il *Health* 19:59-61 Jl '87

A choice of menus at 30,000 feet. I. Pave. il *Bus Week* p117 S 7 '87

In search of the perfect (okay, decent) airline meal. G. Eichler. il *Esquire* 108:68 D '87

Freight service

See Air freight service

Fuel requirements

See Airlines—Energy usage

History

Beginner's pluck. L. Morgan. il *Flying* 114:56-60+ S '87

International aspects

See also
International Air Transport Association

Laws and regulations

See Aviation—Laws and regulations

Local service

See also
AirCal
America West Airlines, Inc.
Brockway Air, Inc. (Vt.)
Chalk's International Airlines
Comair, Inc.
Jetstream International Airlines
Midway Airlines, Inc.
New York Air
NPA (Firm)
Piedmont Aviation, Inc.
Princeton Air Link
Southwest Airlines Co.
Wings West Airlines

Airline president predicts demise of independent U.S. commuters [views of K. G. Morse] il *Aviat Week Space Technol* 126:53 Je 29 '87

Carrier consolidation may intensify competition among regional airlines. C. Preble. il *Aviat Week Space Technol* 126:195+ Mr 9 '87

Closer ties between regional, major airlines predicted. R. G. O'Lone. *Aviat Week Space Technol* 127:40+ D 7 '87

Direct flights to ski country. S. Russell. *Skiing* 40:46-7 D '87

Economics, code sharing threaten survival of commuter airlines. il *Aviat Week Space Technol* 126:57-8+ Ap 27 '87

FAA predicts expansion for regionals, commuters. C. Preble. il *Aviat Week Space Technol* 126:54-6 Mr 16 '87

Operators attack plan to stem New England commuter service [plan to divert traffic from Boston's Logan Airport to reliever airports] *Aviat Week Space Technol* 127:41+ S 7 '87

Texas Air buys commuter aircraft for affiliates' use. *Aviat Week Space Technol* 127:43 S 14 '87

Top 50 U.S. regional airlines in 1986 and their code-sharing partners. il *Aviat Week Space Technol* 127:154 N 9 '87

Traffic growth spurs move by commuters to larger aircraft. P. Proctor. il *Aviat Week Space Technol* 127:153-4 N 9 '87

Luggage handling

Airlines ordered to regulate carry-on bags. *Aviat Week Space Technol* 127:34 Jl 13 '87

Carry-on bags: sky no longer the limit. il *U S News World Rep* 103:14 D 28 '87-Ja 4 '88

Carry-on luggage. H. Gieseking. *Travel Holiday* 168:79-80 N '87

To check or not to check [women executives] B. G. Kempton. il *Work Woman* 12:45-6 Mr '87

Maintenance

See Airplanes, Jet—Maintenance and repair

Management

Lost com. L. Morgan. il *Flying* 114:12-13 Jl '87

Pilot ownership concept takes several forms at world carriers. *Aviat Week Space Technol* 126:49+ My 11 '87

Profiting from deregulation. M. Rowland. il *Work Woman* 12:49-50+ Mr '87

The sky isn't falling [cover story] G. Easterbrook. *New Repub* 197:18+ N 30 '87

Airlines—*cont.*

Marketing

See also

Frequent flier programs

Airline bonuses: not just for the jet set. J. E. Ellis. il *Bus Week* p116-17 S 28 '87

Winners in the air wars. K. Labich. il *Fortune* 115:68-70+ My 11 '87

Military use

GAO study cites safety improvements in defense charters. *Aviat Week Space Technol* 126:43 Ap 20 '87

Non-scheduled operations

See also

Executive Air Fleet

Passenger entertainment

Flying in 1995—and beyond [Boeing 7J7 inflight entertainment and cabin management system] il *Pop Mech* 164:68 N '87

Passenger service

Do you speak the same language as your airline? il *Glamour* 85:61 F '87

Getting into first class. G. Eichler. il *Esquire* 107:56 Mr '87

Learning to love layovers [clubs run by the airlines] P. Plawin. il *Changing Times* 41:87-9 Je '87

MGM Grand Air begins all-first-class transcontinental service with 727-100s. B. A. Smith. il *Aviat Week Space Technol* 127:41 S 21 '87

The nuts & bolts of hubs & spokes. S. Shane. *Travel Holiday* 167:18 Ap '87

Welcome aboard. The champagne is on ice [all frills McClain Airlines and MGM Grand Air] S. Toy. il por *Bus Week* p61-2 Ja 19 '87

Passenger traffic

See Airlines—Traffic

Passengers

See Air travel

Rates

See Air freight service—Rates; Airlines—Fares

Regional service

See Airlines—Local service

Regulation

See Aviation—Laws and regulations

Reservation systems

Anecdotes, facetiae, satire, etc.

Reservations. J. Crane. il *Atlantic* 260:32 Jl '87

Automation

See Airlines—Automation

Routes

Argentina

LADE pioneers air routes to southern Argentina. il *Aviat Week Space Technol* 127:62-3 Ag 31 '87

Siberia (Soviet Union)

British carriers boost service to Far Eastern destinations [transsiberian route] D. A. Brown. *Aviat Week Space Technol* 126:32-3 Je 8 '87

Soviets grant British carriers right to overfly Siberia. *Aviat Week Space Technol* 126:36 Ap 6 '87

Transsiberian flights conducted routinely. *Aviat Week Space Technol* 126:32 Je 8 '87

Tibet

Tibetan air operations. C. Covault. il map *Aviat Week Space Technol* 127:54-5+ O 12 '87

Transatlantic

ECAC, U.S. renew North Atlantic pact [European Civil Aviation Conference] *Aviat Week Space Technol* 126:32 F 23 '87

Feeders, computer systems key to North Atlantic competition. il *Aviat Week Space Technol* 126:208-9+ Mr 9 '87

KLM gains Orlando gateway over U.S. carriers' protests. *Aviat Week Space Technol* 127:44 Ag 3 '87

North Atlantic summer traffic offsets last year's slump. J. M. Lenorovitz. *Aviat Week Space Technol* 127:40 Ag 3 '87

Two over the pond [flying to Paris on Boeing 767] *Pop Mech* 164:17 O '87

U.S. airlines oppose KLM service to Orlando. *Aviat Week Space Technol* 126:42 My 11 '87

Transpacific

Competitors vie for position in growing Pacific market. *Aviat Week Space Technol* 126:209 Mr 9 '87

U.S., Australian officials deadlock over Continental Airlines schedule. *Aviat Week Space Technol* 126:41 Je 1 '87

United States

America West continues expansion with transcontinental 757 service. B. A. Smith. il *Aviat Week Space Technol* 126:42-3 Mr 2 '87

Changes in East Coast routes offer potential to reduce delays. *Aviat Week Space Technol* 126:36 F 23 '87

Western Europe

Emirates plans Airbus A310-300 service to Europe this summer. il *Aviat Week Space Technol* 126:44 Je 1 '87

Storm disrupts airline traffic in Western Europe [snowstorm] *Aviat Week Space Technol* 126:34 Ja 19 '87

U.S. denies British Airways ticket offer to continental Europe. J. Ott. *Aviat Week Space Technol* 126:34-5 Ap 6 '87

Safety devices and measures

See Aviation—Safety devices and measures

Schedules

Airline delays. H. Gieseking. il *Travel Holiday* 168:67-8 D '87

Airlines view flight adjustments as trend toward reregulation. J. Ott. *Aviat Week Space Technol* 126:32-4 F 9 '87

Carriers discuss schedule changes in response to Transportation order. il *Aviat Week Space Technol* 126:33 Mr 23 '87

Carriers, FAA continue talks on Atlanta Hartsfield schedule. *Aviat Week Space Technol* 126:36 Ap 20 '87

Crandall proposes commission empowered to limit flights. J. Ott. *Aviat Week Space Technol* 126:32-3 Je 29 '87

Crandall proposes filing of on-time reports. *Aviat Week Space Technol* 126:39 Mr 30 '87

Easing airport congestion. M. S. Forbes, Jr. il *Forbes* 139:25 Ja 26 '87

Fear of flying frequently. P. S. Dempsey. por *Newsweek* 110:12 O 5 '87

Flight delays. R. Coorsh. il *Consum Res Mag* 70:4 Je '87

How not to eliminate flight delays. J. Ott. *Aviat Week Space Technol* 126:11 Ap 6 '87

How to end airport gridlock. T. Jacoby. il *Newsweek* 109:28 My 11 '87

It's time to bring truth in scheduling to airlines. E. E. Bailey and D. M. Kirstein. il *USA Today (Periodical)* 116:15-17 N '87

The late show. B. Kallen. il *Forbes* 139:166+ Je 1 '87

New travel rules. R. Coorsh. il *Consum Res Mag* 70:4 O '87

NTSB recommends limits to ease summer air traffic congestion. C. Preble. il *Aviat Week Space Technol* 126:32-3 My 4 '87

The nuts & bolts of hubs & spokes. S. Shane. *Travel Holiday* 167:18 Ap '87

Policing air delays [Dept. of Transportation actions] *Newsweek* 110:57 S 14 '87

Race against time [Mooney 252 vs. the airlines for business trips] G. Baxter. il *Flying* 114:78-81 Ag '87

Senate panel approves bill requiring airlines to reveal on-time data. *Aviat Week Space Technol* 127:34 Jl 20 '87

Traffic reduction plan results in hundreds of airline delays. J. Ott. *Aviat Week Space Technol* 126:79 Je 15 '87

Transportation Dept. imposes standards for on-time performance. J. Ott. *Aviat Week Space Technol* 127:36-7 S 7 '87

U.S. airline service draws increased federal scrutiny. *Aviat Week Space Technol* 126:30-1 Je 1 '87

Securities

Market focus. J. R. Stodden. See issues of Aviation Week & Space Technology beginning December 1, 1986

Shuttle service

Brazilian air shuttle boarding record passengers attracted by low fares, airport convenience [Rio-Sao Paulo-Rio air shuttle] il *Aviat Week Space Technol* 127:52-3 Ag 31 '87

Pan Am Shuttle aims for half share of Northeast market. *Aviat Week Space Technol* 126:56 Mr 16 '87

Smoking problem

See Smoking on airplanes

Statistics

Narrow-body aircraft direct expenses: first quarter 1987. il *Aviat Week Space Technol* 127:50-1 D 21 '87

Narrow-body aircraft direct expenses: fourth quarter 1986. il *Aviat Week Space Technol* 126:42-3 My 25 '87

Narrow-body aircraft direct expenses: third quarter 1986. il *Aviat Week Space Technol* 126:42-3 F 9 '87

Wide-body aircraft operating costs: first quarter 1987. il *Aviat Week Space Technol* 127:52-3 D 21 '87

Wide-body aircraft operating costs: fourth quarter 1986. il *Aviat Week Space Technol* 126:42-3 Je 1 '87

Wide-body aircraft operating costs: third quarter 1986. il *Aviat Week Space Technol* 126:50-1 Ja 26 '87

Airlines—cont.

Suits and claims

A lawyers' rush for judgments [Northwest Airlines crash in Detroit] T. Gest. il *U S News World Rep* 103:23 Ag 31 '87

Taxation

See also
Air travel—Taxation
New tax laws increase cost of leasing, buying aircraft. M. Feazel. *Aviat Week Space Technol* 126:47+ Ap 13 '87

Traffic

Airline traffic: December 1986. il *Aviat Week Space Technol* 126:44 My 25 '87

Airline traffic: February 1987. il *Aviat Week Space Technol* 126:48 Je 22 '87

Airline traffic: first nine months, 1987. il *Aviat Week Space Technol* 127:39 D 21 '87

Airline traffic: January 1987. il *Aviat Week Space Technol* 126:101 Je 15 '87

Airline traffic: March 1987. il *Aviat Week Space Technol* 126:48 Je 29 '87

Airline traffic: November 1986. il *Aviat Week Space Technol* 126:48 My 4 '87

Airline traffic: October 1986. il *Aviat Week Space Technol* 126:41 Mr 2 '87

Airline traffic: September 1986. il *Aviat Week Space Technol* 126:41 Ja 19 '87

Holiday traffic surge refutes fears of economic slowdown. P. Proctor. *Aviat Week Space Technol* 127:32 N 30 '87

Industry foresees wide-bodies as aid to congested system. J. Ott. il *Aviat Week Space Technol* 127:36-7 S 28 '87

International air transport: building for traffic growth [cover story; special section; with editorial comment by James Ott] il *Aviat Week Space Technol* 127:15, 49-51+ N 9 '87

International bookings promise strong summer travel activity. C. Preble. *Aviat Week Space Technol* 126:32 Je 1 '87

North Atlantic summer traffic offsets last year's slump. J. M. Lenorovitz. *Aviat Week Space Technol* 127:40 Ag 3 '87

Argentina

See also
Lineas Aereas del Estado (Argentina)

Australia

See also
Ansett Airlines of Australia
Australian Boeing order exploits greater domestic competition. J. Ott. *Aviat Week Space Technol* 127:36-7 O 12 '87

Belgium

See also
Sabena Belgian World Airlines

Brazil

See also
Cruzeiro do Sul SA
Transbrasil SA-Linhas Aéreas
Varig SA Viação Aérea Rio-Grandense
Viacao Aerea Sao Paolo SA
Brazilian air shuttle boarding record passengers attracted by low fares, airport convenience [Rio-Sao Paulo-Rio air shuttle] il *Aviat Week Space Technol* 127:52-3 Ag 31 '87

Regional carriers mark gains in Brazil following down years. il *Aviat Week Space Technol* 127:53-4 Ag 31 '87

Canada

See also
Air Canada
Canadian Airlines International
Wardair Inc.
Midair clashes. D. Jenish. il *Macleans* 100:26-7 N 23 '87

Chile

See also
Ladeco (Firm)

China

China making slow progress in improving airline service. R. G. O'Lone. il *Aviat Week Space Technol* 127:39+ N 23 '87

China reshapes airlines to meet demand surge [cover story] R. G. O'Lone. il *Aviat Week Space Technol* 127:37-9 N 30 '87

China reshaping industry to meet extensive needs [cover story; with editorial comment by Donald E. Fink] R. G. O'Lone. il map *Aviat Week Space Technol* 127:9, 16-21 N 16 '87

Tibetan air operations. C. Covault. il map *Aviat Week Space Technol* 127:54-5+ O 12 '87

France

See also
Air France

Germany (West)

See also
DLT German Domestic Airlines
Lufthansa

Great Britain

See also
Air Europe Ltd.
British Airways
British Caledonian Airways Ltd.
London European Airways
Privatization sparks scramble for competitive edge in England. il *Aviat Week Space Technol* 127:128+ N 9 '87

Hong Kong

See also
Dragon Airlines Ltd.

India

See also
Air India

Israel

See also
El Al Israel Airlines Ltd.

Italy

See also
Alitalia SpA

Japan

See also
All Nippon Airways Co. Ltd.
Japan Air Lines Co. Ltd.
Competitors vie for position in growing Pacific market. *Aviat Week Space Technol* 126:209 Mr 9 '87

Japanese defense, transport agencies agree to transfer military pilots to offset aircrew shortage among airlines. *Aviat Week Space Technol* 127:40 D 7 '87

Latin America

Aerospace in South America: airlines [cover story; special section] il *Aviat Week Space Technol* 127:40-1+ Ag 31 '87

Commercial air transport gains as dollar earner in South America. E. H. Kolcum. *Aviat Week Space Technol* 127:133+ N 9 '87

Netherlands

See also
KLM Royal Dutch Airlines

Scandinavia

See also
SAS

Switzerland

See also
Crossair AG
Swissair AG

Thailand

See also
Thai Airways International Ltd.

United Arab Emirates

See also
Emirates (Firm)

United States

See Airlines

Venezuela

See also
Aerovias Venezolanas SA
Venezolana Internacional de Aviacion SA

Western Europe

Alitalia joins new European computer reservation system [Galileo Distribution Systems] *Aviat Week Space Technol* 127:66 Ag 31 '87

Amadeus and Galileo boost efforts to add airlines to European CRS networks [computer reservation and travel systems] *Aviat Week Space Technol* 127:47 D 21 '87

American Airlines offers Europeans choice of CRS assistance [computerized passenger reservations system] *Aviat Week Space Technol* 127:34 Jl 20 '87

Common Market threats force carriers toward liberalization. *Aviat Week Space Technol* 127:146+ N 9 '87

European airline groups will develop two competing reservation systems. *Aviat Week Space Technol* 127:33-4 Jl 20 '87

European CRS consortium bids for new members [Amadeus computer reservation system] K. F. Mordoff. *Aviat Week Space Technol* 127:37 Ag 3 '87

Lufthansa rejects airline consolidation. *Aviat Week Space Technol* 126:47 F 9 '87

Airlines, Local service *See* Airlines—Local service

Airplane accidents *See* Aviation—Accidents

Airplane batteries *See* Storage batteries

Airplane brakes *See* Brakes, Airplane

Airplane brokers
   See also
   International Lease Finance Corporation

Airplane carriers *See* Aircraft carriers

Airplane crews
   Crew miscue [September 1985 crash of Midwest Express DC-9] P. Garrison. *Flying* 114:22+ Ag '87
   FAA urges use of standard procedures, more discipline in Delta cockpits. E. H. Phillips. *Aviat Week Space Technol* 127:44 S 28 '87
   NTSB focuses on cockpit communication, inspection methods in Milwaukee crash [September 1985 crash of a Midwest Express DC-9] P. Proctor. *Aviat Week Space Technol* 126:41 F 16 '87

   Psychology
   Routine emergency [Beech 99 crew wanders astray] P. Garrison. *Flying* 114:14+ Ap '87

   Training
   See Aviation—Study and teaching

Airplane engines
   See also
   Airplane engines, Jet
   Helicopter engines
   Remotely piloted vehicle engines

   Cooling
   New power to the props [rotary designs and liquid cooling] F. Mackerodt. il *Pop Mech* 164:14 Ap '87

   Design
   Dyna-Cam. J. M. McClellan. *Flying* 114:68+ N '87
   Flying Porsche [light aircraft engine] B. Kocivar. il *Pop Sci* 230:39 My '87
   New power to the props [rotary designs and liquid cooling] F. Mackerodt. il *Pop Mech* 164:14 Ap '87

   Energy usage
   See also
   Airlines—Energy usage
   Fuel crisis [Cessna 150 runs out of gas on approach] B. Lloyd. il *Flying* 114:102 Ja '87

   Failure
   A-7D crash accents different USAF, Navy emergency rules [attempted flameout approach] il *Aviat Week Space Technol* 127:31 N 2 '87
   High explosives [Cessna 206 floatplane with leaky fuel lines] W. Haines. il *Flying* 114:108-9 Jl '87

   Fuel
   Contamination
   Tiny bubbles [water contaminated avgas on Cessna 150 flight] R. Wanttaja. il *Flying* 114:100 My '87

   Fuel consumption
   See Airplane engines—Energy usage

   Fuel feeding
   High explosives [Cessna 206 floatplane with leaky fuel lines] W. Haines. il *Flying* 114:108-9 Jl '87

   History
   Piston packin' mamas. L. Morgan. il *Flying* 114:70-4+ S '87
   Powerful memories. L. Morgan. il *Flying* 114:10-11 My '87

   Noise
   See Airplanes—Noise

   Specifications
   U.S. reciprocating engines [tables] il *Aviat Week Space Technol* 126:162-3 Mr 9 '87

   Superchargers
   Mooney tunes [252] G. Baxter. il *Flying* 114:114 F '87
   Splash & dash [Lake Turbo Renegade; cover story] N. Moll. il *Flying* 114:68-75 Jl '87

   Testing
   Body by Cessna, power by Porsche. R. L. Collins. il *Flying* 114:38-44+ N '87

Airplane engines, Jet
   See also
   Allison Gas Turbine Operations
   Garrett Corporation
   General Electric Co.
   International Aero Engines
   Japan Aero Engines Corporation
   Pratt & Whitney Aircraft Group
   Rohr Industries, Inc.
   Rolls-Royce Ltd.

   Blades
   Defects
   Canada's suspension of CF-18 deliveries viewed as repair-cost negotiating tactic. P. Mann. *Aviat Week Space Technol* 127:26-7 N 16 '87

   Certification
   See Airplane engines, Jet—Standards

   Control
   Hidec tests show potential for thrust, fuel improvements through propulsion, flight control link [highly integrated digital engine control] W. B. Scott. *Aviat Week Space Technol* 126:62+ Ap 6 '87

   Defects
   Garrett tests new ATF-3 seal to correct oil leak problems. *Aviat Week Space Technol* 126:26-7 Je 22 '87
   MD-80 modified to reduce foreign object damage. il *Aviat Week Space Technol* 126:33 My 4 '87

   Design
   7J7 delay could erode GE's position in ultrahigh bypass development. il *Aviat Week Space Technol* 127:28-9 Ag 31 '87
   Afterburning TF41 assessed for A-7D upgrade. *Aviat Week Space Technol* 126:28 F 16 '87
   Airbus defines new A340 to use CFM56 turbofans. J. M. Lenorovitz. *Aviat Week Space Technol* 126:36-8 Ap 13 '87
   Airbus expecting delivery delays for A320s powered by V2500 engine. J. M. Lenorovitz. *Aviat Week Space Technol* 127:32-3 D 14 '87
   Airbus Industrie to offer International Aero Engines SuperFan on proposed A340. J. M. Lenorovitz. *Aviat Week Space Technol* 126:33 Ja 5 '87
   Airbus makes sales bid to MD-11 customers with Super-Fan version of A340. M. Feazel. *Aviat Week Space Technol* 126:33 Ja 26 '87
   Boeing expects next transport to resemble 7J7 design, but powerplant may vary. *Aviat Week Space Technol* 127:34-5 D 21 '87
   Boeing will consider alternative to unducted fan for twin-aisle 7J7 [IAE V2500 SuperFan] R. G. O'Lone. il *Aviat Week Space Technol* 126:31-2 Ja 26 '87
   CFM plans no ultrahigh bypass competitor to IAE's SuperFan. J. M. Lenorovitz. il *Aviat Week Space Technol* 126:28-30 F 2 '87
   Decision near in West Germany on EFA interim engine [European fighter aircraft] *Aviat Week Space Technol* 127:27 S 28 '87
   Douglas advances MD-91X target launch date by half-year. *Aviat Week Space Technol* 126:33 My 25 '87
   Douglas plans UHB-powered MD-91X as successor to turbofan transports. M. A. Dornheim. il *Aviat Week Space Technol* 126:90-3 Ap 13 '87
   Engine makers examine IAE to avoid pitfalls in collaborative efforts [V2500 SuperFan development problems] S. W. Kandebo. *Aviat Week Space Technol* 126:245-6 Je 15 '87
   Eurojet stresses thrust, maintainability in design of EJ200 engine for EFA [European fighter aircraft] il *Aviat Week Space Technol* 126:94 Je 29 '87
   Evolving requirements shape military engine development. S. W. Kandebo. il *Aviat Week Space Technol* 126:59+ Mr 9 '87
   First F110-powered F-16Cs join wing at Ramstein Air Base. il *Aviat Week Space Technol* 126:212-13 Je 15 '87
   Garrett ATF3: outgrowing its growing pains. J. M. McClellan. il *Flying* 114:38+ Ap '87
   GE boosting CF6-80C2 production to meet order backlog. il *Aviat Week Space Technol* 126:56 Ap 6 '87
   GE examines technical challenges to ducted UHB engine development [ultrahigh bypass turbine engine concepts] *Aviat Week Space Technol* 126:31-2 F 2 '87
   GE, Turbo-Union allowed to rebid on EFA interim engine [European fighter aircraft program] *Aviat Week Space Technol* 126:24 F 23 '87
   General Electric will expand collaborative engine programs. il *Aviat Week Space Technol* 126:30-1 Je 22 '87
   IAE board cancels development of V2500 SuperFan version; International Aero Engines' decision on V2500 SuperFan raises questions, controversy. D. A. Brown. *Aviat Week Space Technol* 126:34-6 Ap 13 '87
   International Aero Engines seeks solutions to V2500 development problems; IAE details V2500 turbofan test program. S. W. Kandebo. il *Aviat Week Space Technol* 126:88-9 Ap 13 '87
   Leasing company selects CFM56-5 to power A320s [International Lease Finance Corp.] *Aviat Week Space Technol* 126:33 Ap 6 '87
   Lufthansa delays decision on retaining IAE V2500. il *Aviat Week Space Technol* 127:36 N 9 '87
   Lufthansa reevaluates V2500 as powerplant for A320 fleet. *Aviat Week Space Technol* 126:30 My 25 '87
   McDonnell executives question target date of SuperFan engine. R. G. O'Lone. *Aviat Week Space Technol* 126:30-1 F 16 '87

Airplane engines, Jet—Design—*cont.*

Pratt & Whitney expands role in V2500 compressor work; Rolls-Royce retains lead in IAE V2500 cold-section development. *Aviat Week Space Technol* 126:32-3 Mr 16 '87

Pratt & Whitney expects to regain market share with PW2000, PW4000. S. W. Kandebo. il *Aviat Week Space Technol* 127:70-1 Ag 31 '87

Pratt, Allison team for P-3 follow-on engine candidate. *Aviat Week Space Technol* 127:32 D 21 '87

Rolls, GE propose engine versions to power A330. *Aviat Week Space Technol* 126:36 Mr 30 '87

Rolls-Royce and Allison unite to pursue U.S. military market. *Aviat Week Space Technol* 127:34 O 12 '87

Small engine manufacturers join forces in developing new powerplants. P. Proctor. il *Aviat Week Space Technol* 126:248+ Je 15 '87

A spanner in the works [privatization of Rolls-Royce endangered by V2500 setbacks] H. Banks. il *Forbes* 139:36-7 Je 1 '87

Strong demand prompts increase in CF6, CFM56 engine production. J. M. Lenorovitz. *Aviat Week Space Technol* 127:35-6 N 9 '87

Technical survey: ultrahigh bypass ratio engines [special section] il *Aviat Week Space Technol* 126:52-8+ Ap 13 '87

Turbine primer. P. Garrison. il *Flying* 114:20+ N '87

Ultrahigh bypass engines will enter commercial service by late 1990s. il *Aviat Week Space Technol* 126:189+ Mr 9 '87

Uncertainty prompts manufacturers to link business jet engine efforts. il *Aviat Week Space Technol* 127:111-13 S 28 '87

Why Pratt & Whitney is sputtering [investment in International Aero Engines] R. W. King and F. J. Comes. il *Bus Week* p24 Ap 20 '87

Energy usage

See also

Airlines—Energy usage

Orion, the hunter [low on fuel and hunting for a runway] K. Welch. il *Flying* 114:102-4 O '87

Failure

Crew miscue [September 1985 crash of Midwest Express DC-9] P. Garrison. *Flying* 114:22+ Ag '87

Investigators cite engine failure in Polish Ilyushin Il-62M crash [May 9, 1987 crash] *Aviat Week Space Technol* 127:57 Ag 3 '87

Manufacturing error cited in stator failure of V2500 test version. *Aviat Week Space Technol* 126:34 Ja 26 '87

Fuel

Advanced fuel systems crucial to high-speed transport progress. P. Proctor. il *Aviat Week Space Technol* 126:45+ F 9 '87

Jet A fuel price increase erodes airline cost advantage. J. Ott. il *Aviat Week Space Technol* 126:33+ Je 8 '87

Midway's option on MD-91/92X represents gamble on fuel prices. J. Ott. il *Aviat Week Space Technol* 127:43+ Jl 6 '87

Proposed EPA rules on petroleum storage may boost fuel costs [underground fuel tanks] *Aviat Week Space Technol* 127:33 Jl 6 '87

Fuel consumption

See Airplane engines, Jet—Energy usage

Fuel feeding

Engine shutdown prompts FAA directive [accidental shutdown caused by hitting fuel control switches] *Aviat Week Space Technol* 127:36 Jl 6 '87

History

The inventions that change our lives often meet with indifference, even active resistance—as did the jet engine. R. M. Adams. *Smithsonian* 18:12 Jl '87

Jet engine milestone [50th anniversary of the Whittle Unit] *Aviat Week Space Technol* 126:15 Ap 13 '87

More power on high. P. Garrison. il *Flying* 114:116-21 S '87

They created the Jet Age [F. Whittle and H. von Ohain] N. Vietmeyer. il *Read Dig* 130:162-6 My '87

Inspection

GE suspends engine shipments to correct inspection failure. *Aviat Week Space Technol* 126:32 Ap 13 '87

NTSB focuses on cockpit communication, inspection methods in Milwaukee crash [September 1985 crash of a Midwest Express DC-9] P. Proctor. *Aviat Week Space Technol* 126:41 F 16 '87

Lubrication and lubricants

See Airplanes, Jet—Lubrication and lubricants

Maintenance and repair

See also

Airplane engines, Jet—Inspection

Pratt & Whitney plans expanded operations to pursue growth in overhaul, repair work. *Aviat Week Space Technol* 127:66 Jl 20 '87

Noise

See Airplanes—Noise

Refueling

McDonnell Douglas will develop expanded aerial refueling system for USAF KC-10s. il *Aviat Week Space Technol* 126:72 Je 22 '87

Specifications

International gas turbine engines [tables] il *Aviat Week Space Technol* 126:167-9 Mr 9 '87

Multinational gas turbine engines [tables] il *Aviat Week Space Technol* 126:162-3 Mr 9 '87

U.S. gas turbine engines [tables] il *Aviat Week Space Technol* 126:164-6 Mr 9 '87

Standards

A310-300 nears certification with Pratt & Whitney PW4000. il *Aviat Week Space Technol* 126:40 My 18 '87

Engine reliability prompts bid for unlimited overwater flights [twinjets] J. Ott. il *Aviat Week Space Technol* 126:36-8 My 11 '87

IAE delays V2500 certification to develop new components. *Aviat Week Space Technol* 126:31 My 25 '87

Large engine manufacturers discount effect of EROPS rules on sales [twin-engine extended-range operations] S. W. Kandebo. il *Aviat Week Space Technol* 127:76+ N 9 '87

Testing

Component deliveries delay PW-Allison propfan first flight. S. W. Kandebo. *Aviat Week Space Technol* 127:28-9 N 30 '87

Flight test validations near for Hamilton Standard propfans. il *Aviat Week Space Technol* 126:78-9 Ap 13 '87

GE will build UDF production version, nears end of demonstrator test program [GE36 unducted fan engine] K. F. Mordoff. il *Aviat Week Space Technol* 126:28-9 F 2 '87

General Electric and Boeing analyze data following initial UDF flight tests [unducted fan] *Aviat Week Space Technol* 126:67 Ap 13 '87

IAE V2500 engine enters critical development period. S. W. Kandebo. il *Aviat Week Space Technol* 127:33-4 D 14 '87

International Aero Engines seeks solutions to V2500 development problems; IAE details V2500 turbofan test program. S. W. Kandebo. il *Aviat Week Space Technol* 126:88-9 Ap 13 '87

Lockheed, GE run ultrahigh bypass engine prototypes in ground tests. il *Aviat Week Space Technol* 126:46-7 Ap 27 '87

Lockheed, NASA will begin propfan test assessment flights; NASA continues UHB development role [ultrahigh bypass engines] il *Aviat Week Space Technol* 126:56-8 Ap 13 '87

McDonnell Douglas resumes flight tests with GE UDF engine [unducted fan engine] *Aviat Week Space Technol* 127:35 N 2 '87

McDonnell Douglas UHB demonstrator flies with GE unducted fan engine [ultrahigh bypass ratio engine] M. A. Dornheim. il *Aviat Week Space Technol* 126:32-4 My 25 '87

No. 2 UDF engine prototype will fly on MD-80 by June [GE unducted fan ultrahigh bypass engine] il *Aviat Week Space Technol* 126:58+ Ap 13 '87

Pratt testing increased-thrust F100 engine. il *Aviat Week Space Technol* 126:55 F 23 '87

Rolls-Royce tests XG-40 engine fuel system, afterburner design. il *Aviat Week Space Technol* 126:63 Mr 2 '87

UHB demonstrator aircraft continues unducted fan tests [GE UDF engine] il *Aviat Week Space Technol* 127:81 O 26 '87

Thrust

CFM56-5C1 to receive thrust improvements for operation on the Airbus A340 transport. il *Aviat Week Space Technol* 126:44 My 4 '87

Pratt testing increased-thrust F100 engine. il *Aviat Week Space Technol* 126:55 F 23 '87

Rolls developing increased-thrust RB211 versions for future transports. S. W. Kandebo. il *Aviat Week Space Technol* 127:81-2 Ag 3 '87

Rolls examines development of RB211-700 engine for future twinjet aircraft. *Aviat Week Space Technol* 127:23 Jl 20 '87

Rolls-Royce commits to developing increased-thrust RB211-524 version. *Aviat Week Space Technol* 127:36 Ag 24 '87

Airplane engines, Jet—Thrust—*cont.*
Volvo/GE developing higher thrust engine to enhance combat capability of JAS-39 [Gripen aircraft] il *Aviat Week Space Technol* 126:20-1 My 4 '87

Airplane equipment industry *See* Airplane industry

Airplane evacuation
Emergency evacuation report criticized [FAA report] *Aviat Week Space Technol* 126:40 Ja 26 '87

Airplane factories

Location
Lycoming reverses LTS101 decision. *Aviat Week Space Technol* 126:71 F 23 '87

Shutdowns
T-46 termination will force closure of Fairchild facility on Long Island. *Aviat Week Space Technol* 126:27 Mr 23 '87

Airplane fares *See* Airlines—Fares

Airplane hijacking
See also
Beirut airplane hijacking, 1985
The long shadow of Tehran [Shiite terrorists hijack Iraqi jet] W. E. Smith. il map *Time* 129:56 Ja 5 '87
A sting on the Mediterranean [FBI traps hijacker F. Yunis] S. Seibert. il por *Newsweek* 110:36 S 28 '87

Prevention
See also
Airports—Security measures
International aviation group discusses sanctions on supporters of terrorism. *Aviat Week Space Technol* 126:41 F 23 '87

Airplane industry
See also
Aircraft Sales Company
Airplane factories
Allison Gas Turbine Operations
Avtek Corporation
Beech Aircraft Corp.
Boeing Co.
Bromon Aircraft Company
Cessna Aircraft Company
Classic Aircraft Corporation
Commuter Air Transports (Firm)
Eidetics International (Firm)
Fairchild Aircraft Corporation
Fairchild Industries Inc.
Garrett Corporation
Gates Learjet Corp.
General Aviation Manufacturers Association
General Dynamics Corp.
Grumman Corp.
Gulfstream Aerospace Corp.
Helicopter industry
Hughes Aircraft Co.
Lockheed Corp.
Marsh Aviation
McDonnell Douglas Corp.
Mod Squad (Firm)
Mooney Aircraft Corporation
National Business Aircraft Association
Northrop Corp.
Piper Aircraft Corp.
Pratt & Whitney Aircraft Group
Rockwell International Corp.
Rohr Industries, Inc.
Ryder System, Inc.
Schweizer Aircraft Corp.
Skytrader Corporation
Valsan Inc.
Industry observer. See issues of Aviation Week & Space Technology

Acquisitions and mergers
Blitz on Boeing [targeted for takeover by T. B. Pickens] por *Time* 130:35 Ag 10 '87
Boone buys a bunch of Boeing. il por *Newsweek* 110:50 Ag 10 '87
Is Boone bluffing? [buying into Boeing] K. M. Hafner. il por *Bus Week* p22-3 Ag 10 '87
Mesa purchase of Boeing stock highlights industry pressures. R. G. O'Lone. *Aviat Week Space Technol* 127:24-5 Ag 3 '87
Sale will enable Fairchild Aircraft to end uncertainty, pursue growth. C. A. Shifrin. il *Aviat Week Space Technol* 127:105+ D 14 '87

International aspects
Americanization of a high-flyer [DeHavilland Aircraft of Canada since the Boeing takeover] P. C. Newman. il *Macleans* 100:42 F 23 '87

Customer relations
Beech nears Starship production, develops customer training. E. H. Phillips. il *Aviat Week Space Technol* 127:78-9+ N 16 '87

Ethical aspects
The hidden threat to air safety [bogus parts] A. C. Isgrò. il *Fortune* 115:81-2+ Ap 13 '87

Exhibitions
See Aviation—Exhibitions

Export-import trade
Air-India considers MD-11 for key role in fleet rejuvenation. *Aviat Week Space Technol* 126:30 My 25 '87
Airbus announces new orders for wide-body transports. il *Aviat Week Space Technol* 127:35 O 26 '87
Airbus expecting delivery delays for A320s powered by V2500 engine. J. M. Lenorovitz. *Aviat Week Space Technol* 127:32-3 D 14 '87
Airbus Industrie to offer International Aero Engines SuperFan on proposed A340. J. M. Lenorovitz. *Aviat Week Space Technol* 126:33 Ja 5 '87
Airbus makes sales bid to MD-11 customers with SuperFan version of A340. M. Feazel. *Aviat Week Space Technol* 126:33 Ja 26 '87
Airlines place eight year-end orders for ATR42 transport. J. M. Lenorovitz. il *Aviat Week Space Technol* 126:44+ Ja 12 '87
All's fair in the airliner war. A. Faujas. *World Press Rev* 34:49-50 Je '87
Ansett Airlines prepares Fokker 50 for start of service in November. K. F. Mordoff. il *Aviat Week Space Technol* 127:49-50 S 28 '87
Australian Boeing order exploits greater domestic competition. J. Ott. *Aviat Week Space Technol* 127:36-7 O 12 '87
Beech, Piaggio weigh market for new business aircraft sales [Beech Starship 1 and Rinaldo Piaggio PD. 180 Avanti] D. A. Brown. il *Aviat Week Space Technol* 126:68-9+ Je 29 '87
Bids in a jumbo gamble [MD-11 vs. A-340] J. Barber. il *Macleans* 100:46-7 Ja 19 '87
Britain-U.S. export pact protects AWACS technology. *Aviat Week Space Technol* 126:263 Mr 9 '87
British Airways places orders for 14 Boeing transports. *Aviat Week Space Technol* 127:36 Ag 24 '87
China mounts effort to boost military aircraft sales. il *Aviat Week Space Technol* 127:112 Jl 13 '87
Continental upgrades commuter fleet with purchase of ATR42 aircraft. D. M. North. il *Aviat Week Space Technol* 127:40-1 N 16 '87
Debate over F-15 derivative clouds selection of Japanese FS-X fighter. il *Aviat Week Space Technol* 126:178+ Je 15 '87
Delivery of C-130s expands French military airlift capability. il *Aviat Week Space Technol* 127:29 D 14 '87
The dogfight to control the skies. C. P. Work. il *U S News World Rep* 102:42-3 Ap 20 '87
E-3 offsets expected to reach $2 billion [Boeing's agreement with Britain] *Aviat Week Space Technol* 127:25 O 26 '87
Eurofighter bidding rules may bar U.S. companies. M. Feazel. *Aviat Week Space Technol* 126:18-19 Ja 19 '87
Europeans criticize U.S. subsidy charges at Airbus A320 rollout. J. M. Lenorovitz. il *Aviat Week Space Technol* 126:30-1 F 23 '87
Europeans will enter ATR42 in U.S. STOL competition [military cargo version] il *Aviat Week Space Technol* 126:28-9 F 23 '87
Exim Bank backs 767 sale to All Nippon to foil Airbus bid. *Aviat Week Space Technol* 126:31 Je 29 '87
Expanded Exim credit could aid Douglas aircraft negotiations. *Aviat Week Space Technol* 126:31 My 11 '87
Fairchild delivers Metro 3 AEW testbed to Sweden [airborne early warning] C. A. Shifrin. il *Aviat Week Space Technol* 127:127+ O 19 '87
France orders Boeing E-3s; Britain signs formal contract. *Aviat Week Space Technol* 126:27 Mr 2 '87
International carriers weigh A340, MD-11 acquisition options. J. M. Lenorovitz. *Aviat Week Space Technol* 126:53+ Ap 6 '87
Japan's defense agency selects F-16 as basis for FS-X aircraft [General Dynamics chosen] *Aviat Week Space Technol* 127:22-3 O 26 '87
Leasing company selects CFM56-5 to power A320s [International Lease Finance Corp.] *Aviat Week Space Technol* 126:33 Ap 6 '87
Lufthansa delays decision on retaining IAE V2500. il *Aviat Week Space Technol* 127:36 N 9 '87
Lufthansa orders 15 A340s with V2500 SuperFan engines. *Aviat Week Space Technol* 126:34-5 Ja 26 '87
Lufthansa reevaluates V2500 as powerplant for A320 fleet. *Aviat Week Space Technol* 126:30 My 25 '87

Airplane industry—Export-import trade—*cont.*

McDonnell Douglas offers F/A-18 for French Navy's carrier air fleet. J. D. Morrocco. *Aviat Week Space Technol* 127:33-5 S 7 '87

McDonnell Douglas to launch Airbus A330 competitor. *Aviat Week Space Technol* 126:40 Je 22 '87

McDonnell executives question target date of SuperFan engine. R. G. O'Lone. *Aviat Week Space Technol* 126:30-1 F 16 '87

MD-11, A340 competition gains momentum at Thai International. R. G. O'Lone. *Aviat Week Space Technol* 126:30-1 Mr 16 '87

MD-11 continues to add orders despite A340 SuperFan sales effort. B. A. Smith. *Aviat Week Space Technol* 126:32-3 Mr 16 '87

NATO pushes the 'eject' button on U.S. contractors [replacement program for F-16 fighters] J. Kapstein. *Bus Week* p50 F 2 '87

Northwest's A330/A340 choice fuels aircraft subsidy debate. J. Ott. il *Aviat Week Space Technol* 126:38-9 Ap 13 '87

One thing after another [Pratt & Whitney] H. Banks. *Forbes* 140:184 N 16 '87

Proposed sale of F-5s to Honduras [statement, May 19, 1987] E. Abrams. *Dep State Bull* 87:87-9 Jl '87

Reduced value of dollar abroad aids general aviation sales [views of James S. Walsh] C. A. Shifrin. *Aviat Week Space Technol* 126:28 Mr 16 '87

Sales results cause Embraer to hike Brasilia delivery rates [30-40-passenger aircraft class] *Aviat Week Space Technol* 127:78 N 9 '87

SAS considers Boeing 767 to replace DC-10. *Aviat Week Space Technol* 126:34 My 4 '87

Sky wars over Airbus [U.S. threatening to slap duties on its U.S. sales] F. J. Comes. *Bus Week* p48 F 16 '87

Soviet Union seeks to renew industry relations with China [Aviation Expo/China] *Aviat Week Space Technol* 127:29 O 26 '87

Strong demand prompts increase in CF6, CFM56 engine production. J. M. Lenorovitz. *Aviat Week Space Technol* 127:35-6 N 9 '87

Thirteen new orders placed for British Aerospace 146s; second production line planned. *Aviat Week Space Technol* 126:267 Mr 9 '87

A time for cool heads [dispute over subsidies to Europe's Airbus Industrie civil transport programs] D. E. Fink. *Aviat Week Space Technol* 126:11 F 23 '87

Trouble on the horizon [success of Airbus Industrie] B. Rudolph. il *Time* 129:50-1 My 11 '87

U.S., Europe agree on agenda for aircraft financing talks. D. A. Brown. *Aviat Week Space Technol* 127:36 N 2 '87

U.S., Europe seek rapid cure in Airbus subsidy dispute. M. Mecham. *Aviat Week Space Technol* 127:35+ O 26 '87

U.S., Europeans clash over Airbus subsidies. D. A. Brown. il *Aviat Week Space Technol* 126:18-20 F 9 '87

U.S. parts embargo grounds Chilean Air Force F-5 fleet. il *Aviat Week Space Technol* 127:73+ Ag 24 '87

U.S. transport sales continue domination of world market. *Aviat Week Space Technol* 126:69 Je 15 '87

Widebody wars: Airbus decides 'to go for the kill' [fierce battle with McDonnell Douglas] F. J. Comes. il *Bus Week* p80-1 Jl 6 '87

Wings West commuter orders 10 British Advanced Turboprops. *Aviat Week Space Technol* 127:31 S 28 '87

Wings West orders 15 Jetstream 31 commuters. *Aviat Week Space Technol* 127:36 O 19 '87

Federal aid

Congress approves air show deductions, cuts Exim funding. *Aviat Week Space Technol* 127:23 Jl 13 '87

Finance

Birthday blues [general aviation industry] R. L. Collins. il *Flying* 114:17-18 Jl '87

Budget constraints heighten military trainer competition. il *Aviat Week Space Technol* 127:97+ Jl 6 '87

Cost pressures on airframe makers prompt rise in risk-sharing ventures. il *Aviat Week Space Technol* 127:157+ N 9 '87

General aviation billings rise despite drop in unit shipments. P. Proctor. *Aviat Week Space Technol* 126:147-8 Ap 27 '87

Reduced value of dollar abroad aids general aviation sales [views of James S. Walsh] C. A. Shifrin. *Aviat Week Space Technol* 126:28 Mr 16 '87

Steady economy will spur business flying through 1990. P. Proctor. il *Aviat Week Space Technol* 126:247-9 Mr 9 '87

U.S. general aviation aircraft manufacturing slump deepens. P. Proctor. il *Aviat Week Space Technol* 126:26-7 Ja 19 '87

International aspects

See also

CFM International

GPA Airbus A320 (Firm)

International Aero Engines

Agile Falcon draws interest of potential European partners. J. D. Morrocco. *Aviat Week Space Technol* 127:33 N 9 '87

Airbus seeking joint efforts with U.S. companies. *Aviat Week Space Technol* 127:32 Jl 20 '87

Airframe makers express views on collaboration. *Aviat Week Space Technol* 126:47 Je 22 '87

Airframe manufacturers near landmark UHB decisions [ultrahigh bypass ratio engine] il *Aviat Week Space Technol* 126:52-5 Ap 13 '87

British Aerospace, McDonnell Douglas will propose new Harrier version [AV-8B/GR. 5 Advanced Harrier] *Aviat Week Space Technol* 126:24 Je 22 '87

British seek risk-sharing partners for high-agility aircraft project [Small Agile Battlefield Aircraft] D. A. Brown. il *Aviat Week Space Technol* 127:61 D 14 '87

Builders of the future. N. Moll. il *Flying* 114:142-5 S '87

Business aircraft sales slump forces breach in international partnerships. il *Aviat Week Space Technol* 126:256+ Je 15 '87

Business flying [cover story; special section; with editorial comment by Donald E. Fink] il *Aviat Week Space Technol* 127:15, 68-73+ S 28 '87

Chinese join wing, fuselage of second coproduced MD-82. W. B. Scott. *Aviat Week Space Technol* 127:38-9 Ag 17 '87

Crowded skies [military planes] H. Banks. il *Forbes* 140:48+ Ag 24 '87

FAA officials visit MD-82 facilities in China [inspect controls and procedures for coproduction of MD-82 transports in Shanghai] *Aviat Week Space Technol* 126:42 Ap 6 '87

FIMA consortium designing two airlifter versions [Future International Military/Civil Airlifter] il *Aviat Week Space Technol* 127:52 Ag 10 '87

First Chinese-assembled MD-82 nears completion in SAIC facilities. il *Aviat Week Space Technol* 126:34-5 Je 1 '87

General Dynamics proposes F-16 upgrade for 1990s [Agile Falcon] J. D. Morrocco. il *Aviat Week Space Technol* 127:22-3 Ag 3 '87

Industry officials see obstacles to Airbus' drive to share risks [special section; with editorial comment by Donald E. Fink] *Aviat Week Space Technol* 127:15, 34-7 Ag 3 '87

International aerospace strategies [cover story; special section] il *Aviat Week Space Technol* 126:107-11+ Je 15 '87

International air transport: building for traffic growth [cover story; special section; with editorial comment by James Ott] il *Aviat Week Space Technol* 127:15, 49-51+ N 9 '87

International groups strive for mid-1990s UHB production [ultrahigh bypass ratio engines] il *Aviat Week Space Technol* 126:85-6 Ap 13 '87

Japanese to codevelop U.S. aircraft derivative for FS-X. *Aviat Week Space Technol* 127:34 O 12 '87

Manufacturers discuss cooperation despite aircraft subsidy dispute [U.S. and Europe] D. A. Brown. *Aviat Week Space Technol* 126:30-1 Je 29 '87

MBB seeks members for consortium to develop medium-size transport. il *Aviat Week Space Technol* 126:53-4 Mr 16 '87

McDonnell Douglas/European talks include larger version of MD-11. B. A. Smith. *Aviat Week Space Technol* 126:42 Ap 13 '87

McDonnell Douglas grabs a piece of China's sky. D. J. Yang. il *Bus Week* p35 Ag 17 '87

McDonnell Douglas signing partners in MD-11 development program. *Aviat Week Space Technol* 126:34-5 Ja 26 '87

MD-82 coproduction could aid in forming U.S.-China bilateral. B. A. Smith. il *Aviat Week Space Technol* 126:43+ Ap 6 '87

MPC-75 consortium may include suppliers, engine manufacturers. il *Aviat Week Space Technol* 126:69 Je 22 '87

New international initiatives [Airbus Industrie and its European partner companies; special section] il *Aviat Week Space Technol* 127:16-19 Jl 27 '87

Pentagon endorses USAF Agile Falcon codevelopment plan. *Aviat Week Space Technol* 127:21-2 O 19 '87

Airplane industry—International aspects—*cont.*

Pentagon initiative triggers new interest in joint ventures [aircraft upgrade projects] *Aviat Week Space Technol* 127:23 Ag 3 '87

Rolls-Royce and Allison unite to pursue U.S. military market. *Aviat Week Space Technol* 127:34 O 12 '87

Spanish/Indonesian CN-235 transport nears initial commercial operations [pilot report; cover story] R. R. Ropelewski. il *Aviat Week Space Technol* 126:102-3+ Ap 27 '87

Three international teams compete for USAF contract to provide flight inspection aircraft. *Aviat Week Space Technol* 127:25 Ag 17 '87

U.S. will discuss codevelopment of updated F/A-18 with allies [Hornet 2000] J. D. Morrocco. il *Aviat Week Space Technol* 127:20-1 D 21 '87

USAF may develop Agile Falcon without allied participation. J. D. Morrocco. *Aviat Week Space Technol* 127:23-4 O 26 '87

Marketing

Airline commitments prompt Boeing to launch 737-500. R. G. O'Lone. il *Aviat Week Space Technol* 126:28-9 My 25 '87

Boeing financing of United orders reflects stiffening competition. *Aviat Week Space Technol* 126:29-30 My 18 '87

Boeing had good reason to take Allegis under its wing. J. E. Ellis. il *Bus Week* p64+ My 25 '87

General aviation manufacturers focus on technology advances to spur sales. P. Proctor. *Aviat Week Space Technol* 126:108-9+ My 18 '87

McDonnell Douglas discussing MD-11 with potential customers. B. A. Smith. il *Aviat Week Space Technol* 126:40+ Ja 12 '87

MD-80 delivery delays force some airlines to curb expansion. B. A. Smith. il *Aviat Week Space Technol* 127:34-6 Jl 6 '87

NBAA Show [special section] il *Aviat Week Space Technol* 127:18-21 O 5 '87

Orders spur McDonnell to launch MD-11 program. *Aviat Week Space Technol* 126:35 Ja 5 '87

Product liability costs cited as key factor in delivery slump [general aviation] P. Proctor. il *Aviat Week Space Technol* 127:55 Jl 27 '87

The widebody wars are about to flare up again [McDonnell Douglas' MD-11s] J. E. Ellis. il *Bus Week* p41-2 Ja 12 '87

Quality control

McArtor cites quality control in call for inspection program. E. H. Phillips. *Aviat Week Space Technol* 127:41 O 5 '87

Statistics

Business/utility aircraft shipments: first quarter 1987. il *Aviat Week Space Technol* 126:153 Ap 27 '87

Business/utility aircraft shipments: fourth quarter 1986. il *Aviat Week Space Technol* 126:83 F 2 '87

Suits and claims

Product liability costs cited as key factor in delivery slump [general aviation] P. Proctor. il *Aviat Week Space Technol* 127:55 Jl 27 '87

Argentina

See also
Fabrica Argentina de Material Aerospacial

Brazil

See also
Embraer Empresa Brasileira de Aeronautica SA

Canada

See also
Canadair Ltd.
DeHavilland Aircraft of Canada, Limited

China

See also
Xian Aircraft Corp.

China reshaping industry to meet extensive needs [cover story; with editorial comment by Donald E. Fink] R. G. O'Lone. il map *Aviat Week Space Technol* 127:9, 16-21 N 16 '87

China tailors exhibit to pursue military, commuter aircraft markets [Paris Air Show] il *Aviat Week Space Technol* 126:25-6 Je 22 '87

Chinese developing Y-12 export version. R. G. O'Lone. il *Aviat Week Space Technol* 127:97-8+ D 14 '87

Chinese exhibition underscores aviation modernization efforts [Aviation Expo/China; with editorial comment by Donald E. Fink] R. G. O'Lone. *Aviat Week Space Technol* 127:13, 28-9 O 26 '87

Chinese join wing, fuselage of second coproduced MD-82. W. B. Scott. *Aviat Week Space Technol* 127:38-9 Ag 17 '87

Chinese plan to display aircraft at Paris Air Show. il *Aviat Week Space Technol* 126:21 Ja 19 '87

FAA officials visit MD-82 facilities in China [inspect controls and procedures for coproduction of MD-82 transports in Shanghai] *Aviat Week Space Technol* 126:42 Ap 6 '87

First Chinese-assembled MD-82 nears completion in SAIC facilities. il *Aviat Week Space Technol* 126:34-5 Je 1 '87

International involvement highlights Chinese show. il *Aviat Week Space Technol* 127:30-1 O 19 '87

McDonnell Douglas grabs a piece of China's sky. D. J. Yang. il *Bus Week* p35 Ag 17 '87

MD-82 coproduction could aid in forming U.S.-China bilateral. B. A. Smith. il *Aviat Week Space Technol* 126:43+ Ap 6 '87

France

See also
Aerospatiale
Dassault Breguet Aviation (Avions Marcel)
SOCATA

Germany (West)

See also
Deutsche Airbus
MTU Motoren-und-Turbinen-Union

Great Britain

See also
Airship Industries, Ltd.

Indonesia

Spanish/Indonesian CN-235 transport nears initial commercial operations [pilot report; cover story] R. R. Ropelewski. il *Aviat Week Space Technol* 126:102-3+ Ap 27 '87

Italy

See also
Aeritalia SpA
Agusta SpA
Rinaldo Piaggio (Firm)

Japan

See also
Japan Aero Engines Corporation

Japanese industry urges FS-X fighter development despite U.S. opposition. D. A. Brown. *Aviat Week Space Technol* 127:47-9 S 21 '87

Netherlands

See also
Fokker BV

Northern Ireland

See also
Short Brothers Ltd.

Soviet Union

Soviet Union displays advanced transport designs [Paris Air Show] il *Aviat Week Space Technol* 126:64-5 Je 15 '87

Soviets developing advanced aircraft to upgrade civil, military air fleets [Paris Air Show] il *Aviat Week Space Technol* 126:20-2 Je 22 '87

Spain

See also
Construcciones Aeronauticas SA

Western Europe

See also
Airbus Industrie
Eurojet (Firm)
Panavia Aircraft GmbH
Turbo-Union, Ltd.

European business aircraft forecast mixed. *Aviat Week Space Technol* 126:251-2 Mr 9 '87

European transport programs prepare for growth in demand. K. F. Mordoff. il *Aviat Week Space Technol* 127:71-2+ N 9 '87

European transport strategy geared to new technology. J. M. Lenorovitz. il *Aviat Week Space Technol* 126:286+ Je 15 '87

Airplane inspection *See* Airplanes, Military—Inspection

Airplane instruments *See* Aviation equipment

Airplane junkyards
Partifacts. M. Phelps. il *Flying* 114:44-8 Ap '87

Airplane mechanics (Persons)
Did the mechanics say too much? [Eastern disciplines mechanics who talked to press] il *U S News World Rep* 103:8 Ag 10 '87

Supply and demand

Airlines foresee shortage of qualified technicians. E. H. Phillips. *Aviat Week Space Technol* 127:145-6 N 9 '87

Airplane models
Now, Voyager [paper model] il *Omni* 9 Omni Exper:14-16 Ap '87

Airplane ownership *See* Airplanes—Private ownership

Airplane parts
See also
Airplane junkyards

Airplane parts—*cont.*

The hidden threat to air safety [bogus parts] A. C. Isgrò. il *Fortune* 115:81-2+ Ap 13 '87

Parts shortages crippling U.S. general aviation operators. *Aviat Week Space Technol* 126:94 Ap 13 '87

Export-import trade

See Airplane industry—Export-import trade

Airplane pilots *See* Air pilots

Airplane propellers *See* Airplanes—Propellers

Airplane racing

Dead heat [Mooney 252 and Piper Malibu] E. Weiner. il *Flying* 114:38-41+ O '87

Airplane service stations

See also

United States. Federal Aviation Administration—Flight service stations

All talk [Ellington Air Base used as service stop for military pilots] G. Baxter. il *Flying* 114:106-7 Ag '87

FBOs expand services to boost survivability [fixed base operations] il *Aviat Week Space Technol* 127:89-90+ S 28 '87

International aspects

ATA proposes easing rules on foreign repair stations. *Aviat Week Space Technol* 126:53 Ja 26 '87

FAA will ease regulations on foreign repair stations. C. Preble. *Aviat Week Space Technol* 126:34 Ap 20 '87

Israel

Israelis petition FAA for repair station rule exemption. *Aviat Week Space Technol* 126:31 Mr 30 '87

Switzerland

See also

Jet Aviation (Firm)

Venezuela

Demand for aircraft servicing grows in Venezuela. il *Aviat Week Space Technol* 127:61 Ag 17 '87

Airplane simulators *See* Flight simulators

Airplane speed records

Breaking the sound barrier [Air Force X-1] C. Yeager. il pors *Pop Mech* 164:90-2+ N '87

Airplane tails *See* Airplanes, Light—Tails

Airplane travel *See* Air travel

Airplanes

See also

Airplanes, Amphibious

Airplanes, Antique

Airplanes, Business

Airplanes, Freight

Airplanes, Government

Airplanes, Home-built

Airplanes, Jet

Airplanes, Light

Airplanes, Military

Airplanes, Remodeled

Airplanes, Restored

Airplanes, Short take-off and landing

Airplanes, Supersonic

Airplanes, Training

Airplanes, Used

Aviation

Fund raising on airplanes

Helicopters

Human powered aircraft

Microwave aircraft

Remotely piloted vehicles

Seaplanes

Tank airplanes

Accidents

See Aviation—Accidents

Aerodynamics

See Aerodynamics

Batteries

See Storage batteries

Bird collisions

See Aviation—Bird hazards

Brakes

See Brakes, Airplane

Charts

See Aviation charts

Collision avoidance systems

Carriers question U.S. timetable for mandatory T/CAS operation. P. J. Klass. *Aviat Week Space Technol* 127:42+ D 21 '87

FAA receives general support for plan to mandate T/CAS [traffic alert/collision avoidance system] P. J. Klass. *Aviat Week Space Technol* 127:44 S 14 '87

Flying with TCAS II. il *Time* 129:32 Ja 12 '87

Navy, Air Force test ground collision avoidance system. *Aviat Week Space Technol* 127:62 N 30 '87

New warning systems: about to come aboard? [traffic alert and collision avoidance systems] *Newsweek* 109:54 Je 8 '87

Piedmont to spend $4 million for T/CAS fleet installation [traffic alert/collision avoidance system] *Aviat Week Space Technol* 127:37 N 23 '87

Proposed rulemaking sets mandatory T/CAS timetable [airborne traffic alert/collision avoidance system] P. J. Klass. *Aviat Week Space Technol* 127:145+ Ag 10 '87

TCAS [traffic alert/collision avoidance system] J. M. McClellan. il *Flying* 114:82+ Je '87

Control

See also

Automatic pilot (Airplanes)

Design

Builders of the future. N. Moll. il *Flying* 114:142-5 S '87

Electronic equipment

See also

Air navigation—Aids and devices

Airplanes—Collision avoidance systems

Automatic pilot (Airplanes)

Airlines zigzag on in-seat computing. M. Antonoff. *Pers Comput* 11:141 Jl '87

EFIS expectations [electronic flight instrument systems] P. Garrison. il *Flying* 114:12-13 Ja '87

Electroluminescent thin-film panels developed for aircraft [by Sigmatron Nova, Inc.] K. J. Stein. *Aviat Week Space Technol* 126:83+ Ap 6 '87

Fear no EFIS [electronic flight instrument systems] J. M. McClellan. *Flying* 114:103 Mr '87

Golden age of radio. J. M. McClellan. il *Flying* 114:110-12+ S '87

Wisdom of the gauges [future of avionics] J. M. McClellan. il *Flying* 114:146-7 S '87

Energy usage

See Airplane engines—Energy usage

Engines

See Airplane engines

Equipment

See also

Aviation equipment

Flight recorders

Exhibitions

See Aviation—Exhibitions

Fires and fire prevention

Halon provides extinguishing gains. il *Aviat Week Space Technol* 126:137 F 9 '87

Fuel

See Airplane engines—Fuel

Fuel consumption

See Airplane engines—Energy usage

Hijacking

See Airplane hijacking

History

See Aviation—History

Instrument panels

Electroluminescent thin-film panels developed for aircraft [by Sigmatron Nova, Inc.] K. J. Stein. *Aviat Week Space Technol* 126:83+ Ap 6 '87

Instruments

See Aviation equipment

Landing

See also

Microwave landing systems

Cat's eyes [Category II landing; cover story] J. M. McClellan. il *Flying* 114:48-50+ N '87

Initial approaches [instrument flying] P. Garrison. il *Flying* 114:76-8+ Ap '87

New policy backs acquisition, use of traditional ILSs [instrument landing system] *Aviat Week Space Technol* 126:36 Mr 23 '87

Side-by-side in the soup [simultaneous ILS approaches] M. Brenlove. *Flying* 114:98 Je '87

Laws and regulations

See Aviation—Laws and regulations

Leasing and renting

Wing ding [airplane rental insurance] P. Bradley. il *Flying* 114:10 Mr '87

Maintenance and repair

See also

Airplane mechanics (Persons)

Airplane service stations

Fault line [fault analysis] R. L. Collins. *Flying* 114:85-7 My '87

Manufacture

See Airplane industry

Materials

Precious metal [aluminum] P. Garrison. il *Flying* 114:12-13 Mr '87

Airplanes—cont.

Noise

See also
Airplanes, Jet—Nacelles
Airports—Noise

Airframe makers face challenge of characterizing propfan noise. il *Aviat Week Space Technol* 126:83-4 Ap 13 '87

Congress examines aircraft noise issue [national parks] *Aviat Week Space Technol* 126:112 My 18 '87

FAA solicits information on en route noise levels. *Aviat Week Space Technol* 126:40 Mr 23 '87

Inaction on noise standards raises industry concern over Stage 2 fleet. C. Preble. *Aviat Week Space Technol* 127:38 Jl 6 '87

Industry group urges Stage 2 phase-out, halt to noise limits. C. Preble. *Aviat Week Space Technol* 127:30-1 Jl 13 '87

NASA/Lockheed-Georgia Program continues to explore propfan noise. S. W. Kandebo. *Aviat Week Space Technol* 127:91 O 5 '87

Quiet Nacelle Corp. cleared to install hush kits on DC-8s. E. H. Kolcum. il *Aviat Week Space Technol* 126:96-7 Je 1 '87

Stage 2 cutoff dates recommended by U.S. Task Force [Aircraft Noise/Airport Capacity] *Aviat Week Space Technol* 127:37 S 28 '87

UPS introduces 757 freighters to expand service, constrain noise. M. Mecham. il *Aviat Week Space Technol* 127:49+ S 14 '87

Valsan reengining 727-200s to meet noise regulations. *Aviat Week Space Technol* 126:121 F 16 '87

Valsan's 727-200 reengining program enters final design engineering phase [cockpit, fuselage and engine modifications] S. W. Kandebo. il *Aviat Week Space Technol* 127:137+ S 7 '87

Parts

See Airplane parts

Passenger service

See Airlines—Passenger service

Patrol work

See Airplanes in patrol work

Piloting

See also
Air navigation
Aviation—Instrument flying
Aviation—Overwater flying

All the right moves [VFR flying] P. Garrison. il *Flying* 114:40-2+ Ag '87

I learned about flying from that. See issues of Flying

The sport of it [cover story; special section] il *Flying* 114:54-62+ My '87

Vectors. L. Morgan. See issues of Flying

Pitot tubes

See Pitot tubes

Pneumatic equipment

Rapco's stronger standby. J. M. McClellan. *Flying* 114:91 Ja '87

Power supply

Wing-tip dynamos spin out extra power. D. Stover. il *Pop Sci* 231:65+ S '87

Private ownership

See also
Airplanes, Used—Purchasing

MiG's over America [surplus Soviet-designed fighters] il *Discover* 8:12+ S '87

Propellers

Spin-offs. P. Garrison. il *Flying* 114:60-4 F '87

Pumps, Vacuum

See Vacuum pumps

Radar equipment

See also
Airplanes—Collision avoidance systems
Radar meteorology

Radio equipment

See also
Radiotelephone on airplanes

Prime line [Honeywell Primus II SRZ-850] J. M. McClellan. il *Flying* 114:48-51 Ag '87

Talk is cheap [PS Engineering's Aerocom] M. Phelps. il *Flying* 114:98 Ap '87

Recovery

This parachute keeps the whole plane aloft. P. Houston. il *Bus Week* p86 N 2 '87

Safety devices and measures

Crunch time [survivable airplane crashes] M. Phelps. il *Flying* 114:72-5 N '87

Sales

See Airplane industry—Marketing

Specifications

International aircraft [tables] il *Aviat Week Space Technol* 126:148-51 Mr 9 '87

Multinational aircraft [tables] il *Aviat Week Space Technol* 126:154-5 Mr 9 '87

Soviet aircraft [tables] il *Aviat Week Space Technol* 126:139 Mr 9 '87

Turbine-powered business aircraft [tables] il *Aviat Week Space Technol* 126:147 Mr 9 '87

U.S. commercial cargo transports [tables] il *Aviat Week Space Technol* 126:146 Mr 9 '87

U.S. commercial passenger transports [tables] il *Aviat Week Space Technol* 126:145 Mr 9 '87

U. S. military aircraft [tables] il *Aviat Week Space Technol* 126:140-3 Mr 9 '87

Speed

Spins and sweep [secrets of low speed and high speed] J. M. McClellan. il *Flying* 114:24+ O '87

Records

See Airplane speed records

Spinning

Spin training: kill or cure? E. Collins. il *Flying* 114:60-2 O '87

Spins and sweep [secrets of low speed and high speed] J. M. McClellan. il *Flying* 114:24+ O '87

"A staggering comparison" [discussion of October 1987 article, Spin training: kill or cure?] E. Collins. il *Flying* 114:6+ D '87

Stability and stabilizers

Low-profile vortex generators provide aerodynamic improvements through boundary layer control. il *Aviat Week Space Technol* 126:88+ Je 1 '87

Out of control. J. M. McClellan. il *Flying* 114:48-50+ Jl '87

Stopping

Late braking news [runway friction and airplane weight] B. Newell. *Flying* 114:98 Mr '87

Theft

See also
Airplane hijacking

Vacuum pumps

See Vacuum pumps

Wings

How to fly like a fish [work of Cornelis P. van Dam] S. Budiansky. il *U S News World Rep* 102:64 Je 1 '87

Joint resolution [joined wings] P. Garrison. il *Flying* 114:12-13 My '87

Water wings [work of Cornelis P. van Dam] il *Sci Am* 256:74 Ap '87

Wing-tip dynamos spin out extra power. D. Stover. il *Pop Sci* 231:65+ S '87

Airplanes, Amphibious

Testing

Dornier readies Seastar CD2 for Paris flight demonstrations. K. F. Mordoff. il *Aviat Week Space Technol* 126:125 My 11 '87

Splash & dash [Lake Turbo Renegade; cover story] N. Moll. il *Flying* 114:68-75 Jl '87

Airplanes, Antique

Airplanes unearthed. L. Morgan. il *Flying* 114:8-9 Mr '87

The flying Bugatti [R-100] W. Weith. il *Car Driv* 32:31-2 Je '87

Airplanes, Business

See also
Airplanes in business
National Business Aircraft Association

Certification

See Airplanes, Business—Standards

Cost of operation

Aircraft pool arrangements offer companies convenient scheduling, cost savings. *Aviat Week Space Technol* 127:94-5 S 28 '87

Design

Avtek modifies 400A design to improve comfort, performance. il *Aviat Week Space Technol* 127:111 D 14 '87

Bargain-basement Fanjet [Swearingen Fanjet] J. M. McClellan. il *Flying* 114:88 Ja '87

Beech nears Starship production, develops customer training. E. H. Phillips. il *Aviat Week Space Technol* 127:78-9+ N 16 '87

Beech, Piaggio weigh market for new business aircraft sales [Beech Starship 1 and Rinaldo Piaggio PD. 180 Avanti] D. A. Brown. il *Aviat Week Space Technol* 126:68-9+ Je 29 '87

Citation 5 debut promises altitude performance gains. il *Aviat Week Space Technol* 127:20 O 5 '87

Airplanes, Business—Design—*cont.*

Corporate plans [British Aerospace designs] J. M. McClellan. il *Flying* 114:12-13 Ap '87

Deltas get you there [new Learjet models] M. McDonnell. il *Flying* 114:93 D '87

Former Gates Learjet employees are assembling Avanti sections. il *Aviat Week Space Technol* 127:78 S 28 '87

French accelerate Falcon production. *Aviat Week Space Technol* 126:26-7 F 16 '87

Gates Learjet unveils Model 31, Model 55C jets. *Aviat Week Space Technol* 127:21 O 5 '87

Unusual twins: Starship and Avanti. J. M. McClellan. *Flying* 114:63 D '87

Electronic equipment

Avionics companies emphasize integrated displays, electronics. il *Aviat Week Space Technol* 127:116-17+ S 28 '87

Engines

See Airplane engines, Jet

History

Baby bizjet boom. P. Garrison. il *Flying* 114:122-6 S '87

Boardroom bombers [WWII bombers remodeled for corporate use] R. Munson. il *Flying* 114:94-9 S '87

Gray flannel fliers. R. L. Collins. il *Flying* 114:36-42 S '87

Leasing and renting

Aircraft pool arrangements offer companies convenient scheduling, cost savings. *Aviat Week Space Technol* 127:94-5 S 28 '87

Ohio group offers shared ownership of business jets [EJA Group] *Aviat Week Space Technol* 127:102+ S 28 '87

Maintenance and repair

Operators extending service life by use of overhauls. il *Aviat Week Space Technol* 127:71-3 S 28 '87

Manufacture

See Airplane industry

Purchasing

Air Force RFP opens bidding on aircraft to calibrate navigation, approach aids [business jets] *Aviat Week Space Technol* 126:150 Ap 27 '87

Three international teams compete for USAF contract to provide flight inspection aircraft. *Aviat Week Space Technol* 127:25 Ag 17 '87

Remodeled airplanes

See Airplanes, Remodeled

Security measures

Corporate concern about terrorism spurs sales of security systems. P. Proctor. il *Aviat Week Space Technol* 126:80-1 F 2 '87

Terrorism issues lead firms to increase flight security. *Aviat Week Space Technol* 127:99+ S 28 '87

Specifications

See Airplanes—Specifications

Standards

Beech Starship advances to final phase of testing needed for flight certification. *Aviat Week Space Technol* 127:82 N 16 '87

Testing

Advantage, Avanti. J. M. McClellan. il *Flying* 114:54-63 D '87

Beech Starship advances to final phase of testing needed for flight certification. *Aviat Week Space Technol* 127:82 N 16 '87

French bred [Dassault Falcon 200] J. M. McClellan. il *Flying* 114:30-6 Ap '87

Gee-IV [Gulfstream IV] J. M. McClellan. il *Flying* 114:58-64 Ja '87

Old faithful [Beech King Air C90A; cover story] R. L. Collins. il *Flying* 114:30-4+ Ag '87

Piaggio's Avanti combines jet-like handling with turboprop efficiency [cover story] B. M. Greeley, Jr. il *Aviat Week Space Technol* 127:118-20+ Ag 10 '87

Used airplanes

See Airplanes, Used

Airplanes, Commuter *See* Airplanes, Jet

Airplanes, Drone *See* Remotely piloted vehicles

Airplanes, Experimental

See also

Experimental Aircraft Association
Spaceplane
Voyager (Airplane)

Airplanes, Freight

See also

Air freight service

Design

UPS introduces 757 freighters to expand service, constrain noise. M. Mecham. il *Aviat Week Space Technol* 127:49+ S 14 '87

Standards

Aircraft Sales Co. gains FAA approval of L-1011 freighter. *Aviat Week Space Technol* 126:97 Je 1 '87

Testing

Stretch runner [Cessna Caravans of Federal Express] R. L. Collins. il *Flying* 114:32-7 Jl '87

Airplanes, Government

Air Force exploits speed, range of Gulfstream C-20 in VIP role. P. Proctor. il *Aviat Week Space Technol* 126:74-5 Je 8 '87

New wings for the president [Boeing 747-200B] il *Pop Mech* 164:65 N '87

Airplanes, Home-built

Design

M2: son of Melmoth. P. Garrison. il *Flying* 114:62-6+ Ap '87

The whole kit and caboodle [Questair Venture kit] R. L. Collins. il *Flying* 114:12+ N '87

Testing

A touch of glass [Stoddard-Hamilton Glasair] M. Phelps. il *Flying* 114:36-42 F '87

Wing ding [Davis Flying Wing] J. Campbell. il *Pop Mech* 164:53-6 Ja '87

Airplanes, Jet

See also

Airplanes, Business
Airplanes, Military
Airplanes, Supersonic

Boeing faces major decisions on 737. R. G. O'Lone. *Aviat Week Space Technol* 127:36 Ag 17 '87

Boeing plans to end 737-200 production. *Aviat Week Space Technol* 127:36 O 5 '87

Accidents

See Aviation—Accidents

Bulkheads

Defects

Japanese cite faulty bulkhead repair as cause of JAL 747 crash in 1985. *Aviat Week Space Technol* 126:34 Je 29 '87

Cabins

American configures 747SPs to serve Tokyo first/business-class market. il *Aviat Week Space Technol* 126:54 My 11 '87

Boeing 747-400 to offer flight crew rest area, advanced two-man cockpit. R. G. O'Lone. il *Aviat Week Space Technol* 127:47+ O 26 '87

Cabin interior layouts highlighted at Le Bourget. il *Aviat Week Space Technol* 127:75 Jl 6 '87

Cabin section of 7J7 transport prepared for display at Paris. il *Aviat Week Space Technol* 126:45 Je 1 '87

Dornier designs DO. 328 cabin for comfort, reduced sound levels. il *Aviat Week Space Technol* 126:43 Je 22 '87

Flying in 1995—and beyond [Boeing 7J7 inflight entertainment and cabin management system] il *Pop Mech* 164:68 N '87

Northwest configures 747-400 as model for rest of aircraft. il *Aviat Week Space Technol* 127:64+ Jl 6 '87

Certification

See Airplanes, Jet—Standards

Cockpits

Automated flight engineer functions ease crew workload in MD-11 cockpit. M. A. Dornheim. il *Aviat Week Space Technol* 126:147+ My 11 '87

Boeing 747-400 to offer flight crew rest area, advanced two-man cockpit. R. G. O'Lone. il *Aviat Week Space Technol* 127:47+ O 26 '87

Customer input aids development of advanced Fokker 100 cockpit. M. Feazel. il *Aviat Week Space Technol* 126:43-4+ F 23 '87

Page Avjet, Kollsman completing design for Boeing 727 flight deck conversion. E. H. Kolcum. *Aviat Week Space Technol* 127:52+ S 28 '87

Soviet Tu-204 transport will incorporate advanced cockpit. il *Aviat Week Space Technol* 126:20-1 Je 22 '87

Control

See also

Airplanes, Jet—Stability and stabilizers

Boeing evaluating new control laws in 7J7 advanced-technology simulator. B. D. Nordwall. il *Aviat Week Space Technol* 126:54-6+ Je 29 '87

Cost of operation

Narrow-body aircraft direct expenses: first quarter 1987. il *Aviat Week Space Technol* 127:50-1 D 21 '87

Narrow-body aircraft direct expenses: fourth quarter 1986. il *Aviat Week Space Technol* 126:42-3 My 25 '87

Narrow-body aircraft direct expenses: third quarter 1986. il *Aviat Week Space Technol* 126:42-3 F 9 '87

Wide-body aircraft operating costs: first quarter 1987. il *Aviat Week Space Technol* 127:52-3 D 21 '87

Airplanes, Jet—Cost of operation—*cont.*

Wide-body aircraft operating costs: fourth quarter 1986. il *Aviat Week Space Technol* 126:42-3 Je 1 '87

Wide-body aircraft operating costs: third quarter 1986. il *Aviat Week Space Technol* 126:50-1 Ja 26 '87

Design

7J7. N. Moll. il *Flying* 114:37+ My '87

A330/A340 launch decision awaits completion of partner financing. J. M. Lenorovitz. il *Aviat Week Space Technol* 126:34 Mr 23 '87

Air-India considers MD-11 for key role in fleet rejuvenation. *Aviat Week Space Technol* 126:30 My 25 '87

Airbus expands transport family to meet airlines' changing needs. J. M. Lenorovitz. il *Aviat Week Space Technol* 127:67-8 N 9 '87

Airbus Industrie faces decision of whether to launch A330/A340. il *Aviat Week Space Technol* 126:215+ Mr 9 '87

Airbus seeking joint efforts with U.S. companies. *Aviat Week Space Technol* 127:32 Jl 20 '87

Airframe makers near key technology decisions. R. G. O'Lone. il *Aviat Week Space Technol* 126:183-5+ Mr 9 '87

Airline commitments prompt Boeing to launch 737-500. R. G. O'Lone. il *Aviat Week Space Technol* 126:28-9 My 25 '87

Airlines place eight year-end orders for ATR42 transport. J. M. Lenorovitz. il *Aviat Week Space Technol* 126:44+ Ja 12 '87

Ansett Airlines prepares Fokker 50 for start of service in November. K. F. Mordoff. il *Aviat Week Space Technol* 127:49-50 S 28 '87

Bids in a jumbo gamble [MD-11 vs. A-340] J. Barber. il *Macleans* 100:46-7 Ja 19 '87

Boeing delays 7J7 program; mid-1993 certification expected [special section] il *Aviat Week Space Technol* 127:28-31 Ag 31 '87

Boeing evolves 7J7 design, prepares specification details. R. G. O'Lone. il *Aviat Week Space Technol* 126:34-6 My 18 '87

British Aerospace rejects A330/A340 aid proposal. *Aviat Week Space Technol* 126:36 Mr 30 '87

Bromon plans first flight for late 1988. S. W. Kandebo. il *Aviat Week Space Technol* 126:329-30 Je 15 '87

But is there legroom? il *U S News World Rep* 102:43 Ap 20 '87

Canadair will limit redesign, costs of Challenger upgrade [upgrade from business jet to commuter transport] il *Aviat Week Space Technol* 127:42 D 7 '87

Continental upgrades commuter fleet with purchase of ATR42 aircraft. D. M. North. il *Aviat Week Space Technol* 127:40-1 N 16 '87

De Havilland rolls out stretched Dash 8-300. P. Proctor. il *Aviat Week Space Technol* 126:32-3 Mr 30 '87

Displays of new transports highlight Chinese exhibition [Aviation Expo/China] il *Aviat Week Space Technol* 127:72-3 N 2 '87

Dornier begins full-scale development of 30-passenger DO. 328 commuter. K. F. Mordoff. il *Aviat Week Space Technol* 126:36 My 25 '87

Douglas advances MD-91X target launch date by half-year. *Aviat Week Space Technol* 126:33 My 25 '87

Douglas approaches airlines with stretched MD-11 concept. il *Aviat Week Space Technol* 127:41 O 19 '87

Douglas begins building long-lead MD-11 components. il *Aviat Week Space Technol* 126:50+ Ap 6 '87

Douglas plans UHB-powered MD-91X as successor to turbofan transports. M. A. Dornheim. il *Aviat Week Space Technol* 126:90-3 Ap 13 '87

Engineering tomorrow's airliners [cover story] J. Schefter. il *Pop Sci* 230:49-52+ Ap '87

Fairchild seeks launch orders for new Metro 3 versions [Metro 5 and 6] *Aviat Week Space Technol* 126:46 Ap 13 '87

First Chinese-assembled MD-82 nears completion in SAIC facilities. il *Aviat Week Space Technol* 126:34-5 Je 1 '87

Industry foresees wide-bodies as aid to congested system. J. Ott. il *Aviat Week Space Technol* 127:36-7 S 28 '87

International carriers weigh A340, MD-11 acquisition options. J. M. Lenorovitz. *Aviat Week Space Technol* 126:53+ Ap 6 '87

Lavi cancellation sets back Pratt's PW1120 engine program. *Aviat Week Space Technol* 127:24-5 S 7 '87

Lufthansa advances fleet modernization with A300-600 introduction. il *Aviat Week Space Technol* 126:35 Mr 23 '87

Manufacturer preparing to deliver first Fokker 50 to Ansett. il *Aviat Week Space Technol* 126:299 Je 15 '87

Manufacturers discuss cooperation despite aircraft subsidy dispute [U.S. and Europe] D. A. Brown. *Aviat Week Space Technol* 126:30-1 Je 29 '87

MBB seeks members for consortium to develop medium-size transport. il *Aviat Week Space Technol* 126:53-4 Mr 16 '87

McDonnell Douglas/European talks include larger version of MD-11. B. A. Smith. *Aviat Week Space Technol* 126:42 Ap 13 '87

McDonnell Douglas discussing MD-11 with potential customers. B. A. Smith. il *Aviat Week Space Technol* 126:40+ Ja 12 '87

McDonnell Douglas focusing resources on MD-90, MD-11 transport programs. B. A. Smith. il *Aviat Week Space Technol* 127:59+ N 9 '87

McDonnell Douglas to launch Airbus A330 competitor. *Aviat Week Space Technol* 126:40 Je 22 '87

MD-11, A340 competition gains momentum at Thai International. R. G. O'Lone. *Aviat Week Space Technol* 126:30-1 Mr 16 '87

MD-11 continues to add orders despite A340 SuperFan sales effort. B. A. Smith. *Aviat Week Space Technol* 126:32-3 Mr 16 '87

MPC-75 consortium may include suppliers, engine manufacturers. il *Aviat Week Space Technol* 126:69 Je 22 '87

New short-haul transports displayed at Paris Show. *Aviat Week Space Technol* 126:38-9 Je 22 '87

Orders spur McDonnell to launch MD-11 program. *Aviat Week Space Technol* 126:35 Ja 5 '87

Predicted traffic surge drives Boeing's transport planning. R. G. O'Lone. il *Aviat Week Space Technol* 127:53-4 N 9 '87

Sales results cause Embraer to hike Brasilia delivery rates [30-40-passenger aircraft class] *Aviat Week Space Technol* 127:78 N 9 '87

Soviet Union displays advanced transport designs [Paris Air Show] il *Aviat Week Space Technol* 126:64-5 Je 15 '87

Sutter's lucky sevens [J. Sutter's designs for Boeing] N. Moll. por *Flying* 114:35 My '87

Switzerland's Crossair considers purchase of stretched Saab SF340. J. M. Lenorovitz. il *Aviat Week Space Technol* 126:42-3 Je 8 '87

Texas Air buys commuter aircraft for affiliates' use. *Aviat Week Space Technol* 127:43 S 14 '87

Traffic growth spurs move by commuters to larger aircraft. P. Proctor. il *Aviat Week Space Technol* 127:153-4 N 9 '87

Widebody wars: Airbus decides 'to go for the kill' [fierce battle with McDonnell Douglas] F. J. Comes. il *Bus Week* p80-1 Jl 6 '87

The widebody wars are about to flare up again [McDonnell Douglas' MD-11s] J. E. Ellis. il *Bus Week* p41-2 Ja 12 '87

Electronic equipment

See also

Air navigation—Aids and devices

Computers—Aviation use

Y-7-100 instrument panel houses displays for U.S.-built systems [Chinese passenger aircraft] il *Aviat Week Space Technol* 127:58-9 D 21 '87

Energy usage

See Airplane engines, Jet—Energy usage

Engines

See Airplane engines, Jet

Export-import trade

See Airplane industry—Export-import trade

Fires and fire prevention

Airline safety: a shocking truth. D. Nolan. il *Read Dig* 130:125-30 Ja '87

God has a good idea for airplane seats [X-Ogen flame-resistant seats] *Discover* 8:7-8 Jl '87

Seat fire standards frustrate operators. il *Aviat Week Space Technol* 127:72-3 S 28 '87

Flaps

Langley develops new airflow visualization system [analysis and evaluation of vortex flap effectiveness] *Aviat Week Space Technol* 127:76-7 N 16 '87

Northwest wreckage confirms flaps retracted on takeoff [Detroit crash] J. Ott. *Aviat Week Space Technol* 127:32-3 Ag 31 '87

Fuel consumption

See Airplane engines, Jet—Energy usage

History

Boeing [jetliner development] N. Moll. il *Flying* 114:28-39 My '87

Airplanes, Jet—History—*cont.*
The quantum leap. J. Slocum. il *Flying* 114:78-82+ S
'87

Landing
East-west misunderstanding [Samantha Smith Beech 99
accident] J. M. McClellan. il *Flying* 114:20-2 My '87
The wrong airport blues [landing at the wrong field]
L. Morgan. il *Flying* 114:8-9 N '87

Landing gear
MD-80 modified to reduce foreign object damage. il
Aviat Week Space Technol 126:33 My 4 '87

Leasing and renting
See also
International Lease Finance Corporation
American wields leverage in aircraft lease arrangement
[leasing order divided between Airbus Industrie and
Boeing] J. Ott. il *Aviat Week Space Technol* 126:258-9
Mr 9 '87
International companies unite in A320 leasing venture.
Aviat Week Space Technol 126:36 Ja 19 '87
New tax laws increase cost of leasing, buying aircraft.
M. Feazel. *Aviat Week Space Technol* 126:47+ Ap
13 '87

Lubrication and lubricants
Garrett tests new ATF-3 seal to correct oil leak problems.
Aviat Week Space Technol 126:26-7 Je 22 '87

Maintenance and repair
American commits $225 million to upgrade maintenance
operations. C. A. Shifrin. il *Aviat Week Space Technol*
126:44-6 Je 29 '87
FAA faults Eastern's maintenance procedures; airline
disputes findings. P. Proctor. *Aviat Week Space Technol*
127:34 D 7 '87
Questions about Eastern [maintenance procedures] J.
Castro. il *Time* 130:41 Ag 24 '87

Marketing
See Airplane industry—Marketing

Nacelles
Quiet Nacelle Corp. cleared to install hush kits on DC-8s.
E. H. Kolcum. il *Aviat Week Space Technol* 126:96-7
Je 1 '87

Piloting
See also
Air navigation

Propellers
7J7 delay could erode GE's position in ultrahigh bypass
development. il *Aviat Week Space Technol* 127:28-9
Ag 31 '87
Airframe makers face challenge of characterizing propfan
noise. il *Aviat Week Space Technol* 126:83-4 Ap 13
'87
Allison, Pratt & Whitney team for propfan engine market.
il *Aviat Week Space Technol* 126:32-3 Mr 2 '87
Back to the future [unducted fan engine] T. Beardsley.
Sci Am 257:46 O '87
Boeing will consider alternative to unducted fan for
twin-aisle 7J7 [IAE V2500 SuperFan] R. G. O'Lone.
il *Aviat Week Space Technol* 126:31-2 Ja 26 '87
Component deliveries delay PW-Allison propfan first
flight. S. W. Kandebo. *Aviat Week Space Technol*
127:28-9 N 30 '87
Flight test validations near for Hamilton Standard prop-
fans. il *Aviat Week Space Technol* 126:78-9 Ap 13
'87
GE will build UDF production version, nears end of
demonstrator test program. K. F. Mordoff. il *Aviat
Week Space Technol* 126:28-9 F 2 '87
General Electric and Boeing analyze data following initial
UDF flight tests. *Aviat Week Space Technol* 126:67
Ap 13 '87
General Electric develops quieter UDF propeller blade
configuration; production engine work under way [un-
ducted fan] *Aviat Week Space Technol* 126:34-5 My
25 '87
Lockheed, GE run ultrahigh bypass engine prototypes
in ground tests. il *Aviat Week Space Technol* 126:46-7
Ap 27 '87
Lockheed, NASA will begin propfan test assessment
flights; NASA continues UHB development role [ul-
trahigh bypass engines] il *Aviat Week Space Technol*
126:56-8 Ap 13 '87
McDonnell Douglas resumes flight tests with GE UDF
engine [unducted fan engine] *Aviat Week Space Technol*
127:35 N 2 '87
McDonnell Douglas UHB demonstrator flies with GE
unducted fan engine [ultrahigh bypass ratio engine]
M. A. Dornheim. il *Aviat Week Space Technol* 126:32-4
My 25 '87
MTU plans key shrouded propfan tests for 1988. K.
F. Mordoff. *Aviat Week Space Technol* 127:88-9 Jl
6 '87

NASA/Lockheed-Georgia Program continues to explore
propfan noise. S. W. Kandebo. *Aviat Week Space
Technol* 127:91 O 5 '87
No. 2 UDF engine prototype will fly on MD-80 by
June [GE unducted fan ultrahigh bypass engine] il
Aviat Week Space Technol 126:58+ Ap 13 '87
Rolls skeptical about early propfan service introduction.
il *Aviat Week Space Technol* 126:68-70 Ap 13 '87
Technical survey: ultrahigh bypass ratio engines [special
section] il *Aviat Week Space Technol* 126:52-8+ Ap
13 '87
UHB demonstrator aircraft continues unducted fan tests
[GE UDF engine] il *Aviat Week Space Technol* 127:81
O 26 '87

Seats
Airline safety: a shocking truth. D. Nolan. il *Read Dig*
130:125-30 Ja '87
Airline seats, and why they're like that. G. Eichler.
il *Esquire* 108:46 Jl '87
Boeing 7J7 cabin layout features six-abreast seating. il
Aviat Week Space Technol 127:77 Jl 6 '87
God has a good idea for airplane seats [X-Ogen flame-
resistant seats] *Discover* 8:7-8 Jl '87
Seat fire standards frustrate operators. il *Aviat Week
Space Technol* 127:72-3 S 28 '87

Speed records
See Airplane speed records

Stability and stabilizers
Structural failure [1985 crash of an Embraer Bandeirante
in Florida] P. Garrison. *Flying* 114:17+ F '87

Stalling
Crew miscue [September 1985 crash of Midwest Express
DC-9] P. Garrison. *Flying* 114:22+ Ag '87

Standards
Aerospatiale's Toulouse data center helps speed A320
certification program [use of French Telecom 1
communications satellite] map *Aviat Week Space
Technol* 126:44-5 My 18 '87
Boeing delays 7J7 program; mid-1993 certification expect-
ed [special section] il *Aviat Week Space Technol*
127:28-31 Ag 31 '87
European nations press to establish common airworthiness
regulations [European Joint Airworthiness Regulations]
Aviat Week Space Technol 126:312-13 Je 15 '87
FAA adopting new certification strategies for foreign
aircraft, parts [airworthiness bilaterals] J. Ott. il *Aviat
Week Space Technol* 126:307-8+ Je 15 '87
FAA urges China to clear path to bilateral airworthiness
pact. *Aviat Week Space Technol* 127:38-9 Ag 17 '87
MD-82 coproduction could aid in forming U.S.-China
bilateral. B. A. Smith. il *Aviat Week Space Technol*
126:43+ Ap 6 '87

Tails
Defects
Structural failure [1985 crash of an Embraer Bandeirante
in Florida] P. Garrison. *Flying* 114:17+ F '87

Take-off
Northwest wreckage confirms flaps retracted on takeoff
[Detroit crash] J. Ott. *Aviat Week Space Technol*
127:32-3 Ag 31 '87

Testing
146-300 debuts at Le Bourget [Paris Air Show] il *Aviat
Week Space Technol* 127:105 Jl 6 '87
A320 fly-by-wire controls pass basic flight testing. J.
M. Lenorovitz. il *Aviat Week Space Technol* 126:41+
My 18 '87
Airbus A320 begins 1,200-hour flight test program. il
Aviat Week Space Technol 126:30-1 Mr 2 '87
Fly-by-wire, digital avionics ease A320 transition training
[evaluation flight] D. M. North. il *Aviat Week Space
Technol* 127:40-1+ N 30 '87
New-generation Airbus A320 transport demonstrates fly-
by-wire technology. il *Aviat Week Space Technol*
126:284-5 Je 15 '87
Spanish/Indonesian CN-235 transport nears initial
commercial operations [pilot report; cover story] R.
R. Ropelewski. il *Aviat Week Space Technol* 126:102-3+
Ap 27 '87

Windows
Going star-crazy [aerosols resulting from sulfurous
materials ejected by El Chichon believed to cause
cloudy airliner windows] R. Gannon. il *Earth Sci*
40:16-17 Fall '87

Wings
Airbus increases A330/A340 wingspan. *Aviat Week Space
Technol* 126:32 Ap 20 '87
Chinese join wing, fuselage of second coproduced MD-82.
W. B. Scott. *Aviat Week Space Technol* 127:38-9 Ag
17 '87
MD-80 modified to reduce foreign object damage. il
Aviat Week Space Technol 126:33 My 4 '87

Airplanes, Light

See also
Airplanes, Business
Airplanes, Home-built
Human powered aircraft

Design

1990 Cessna? [Cessna 210 update by DrDesign] il *Flying* 114:66-70 F '87

Wings for tomorrow [designing the Popular Mechanics Scorpion; cover story] B. Davisson. il *Pop Mech* 164:70-5+ Ag '87

Electronic equipment

Panel game. R. L. Collins. *Flying* 114:59 My '87

History

Personal effects [V-tail Bonanza] J. M. McClellan. il *Flying* 114:106-9 S '87

Piper then and now [J-3 Cub and Malibu] F. Mackerodt. il *Pop Mech* 164:12+ Ag '87

Seeing the light. N. Moll. il *Flying* 114:46-50 S '87

Instrument flying

See Aviation—Instrument flying

Landing

Approach. R. L. Collins. *Flying* 114:18 O '87

The art of dropping in [short-field landing] P. Bradley. il *Flying* 114:10 Ap '87

A Cessna to the rescue [helping Cherokee pilot land in stationary cold front] F. Anders. *Flying* 114:101 Jl '87

Fuel crisis [Cessna 150 runs out of gas on approach] B. Lloyd. il *Flying* 114:102 Ja '87

Maintenance and repair

Parts shortages crippling U.S. general aviation operators. *Aviat Week Space Technol* 126:94 Ap 13 '87

Piloting

Bread-and-butter airplane [Cessna 172] G. Baxter. il *Flying* 114:104+ Mr '87

Fergie wins her wings and Andy's a backseat pilot. il por *People Wkly* 27:36 Mr 2 '87

Hoodwinked over Oklahoma [flying in the clouds] M. Coan. il *Flying* 114:104-5 Ap '87

The lowdown. L. Morgan. il *Flying* 114:8-9 Ag '87

Malibu U. [Piper Malibu training center in Vero Beach, Fla.] E. Weiner. il *Flying* 114:82-5+ Jl '87

Mooney tunes [252] G. Baxter. il *Flying* 114:114 F '87

Queasy riders [first time passengers] N. Moll. *Flying* 114:67 My '87

Thirty years aloft [first solo flight] G. Baxter. il *Flying* 114:104 Ja '87

Tiny bubbles [water contaminated avgas on Cessna 150 flight] R. Wanttaja. il *Flying* 114:100 My '87

Propellers

Porsche develops torque-shaft system for light aircraft. *Aviat Week Space Technol* 126:97 Je 29 '87

Remodeled airplanes

See Airplanes, Remodeled

Safety devices and measures

Prime movers [accident records of the Cessna Skyhawk, Mooney 201 and Bonanza A36] J. M. McClellan. il *Flying* 114:50-2+ Mr '87

Speed

V-tail Bonanza: a twisted tale? [speed restrictions] J. M. McClellan. il *Flying* 114:66-8+ Ja '87

Tails

Beech will modify V-tail Bonanzas built from 1951-82. il *Aviat Week Space Technol* 126:108-9 My 18 '87

Defects

V-tail Bonanza: a twisted tale? [speed restrictions] J. M. McClellan. il *Flying* 114:66-8+ Ja '87

V-tail tale: the epilogue [Bonanza controversy] J. M. McClellan. il *Flying* 114:10-11+ Ag '87

Take-off

Takeoff traps. R. L. Collins. il *Flying* 114:76-8+ Jl '87

Testing

Body by Cessna, power by Porsche. R. L. Collins. il *Flying* 114:38-44+ N '87

Bonanza F33A. N. Moll. il *Flying* 114:66-70 Ag '87

Dead heat [Mooney 252 and Piper Malibu] E. Weiner. il *Flying* 114:38-41+ O '87

From the pilot's seat [Mooney 252] R. L. Collins. *Flying* 114:82 Ag '87

Portrait of a survivor: personal twin Beech Baron 58. J. M. McClellan. il *Flying* 114:76-7+ My '87

Race against time [Mooney 252 vs. the airlines for business trips] G. Baxter. il *Flying* 114:78-81 Ag '87

Reborn Roundy [Waco Classic YMF-5] R. L. Collins. il *Flying* 114:28-35 Ja '87

Wings

Defects

FAA uncovers additional PA-28s with cracked wing spars. *Aviat Week Space Technol* 127:53 Ag 10 '87

Airplanes, Microwave See Microwave aircraft

Airplanes, Military

See also
Airplanes, Training
Remotely piloted vehicles
Spaceplane

Naval Air Reserve will add A-6Es as part of modernization effort. D. M. North. il *Aviat Week Space Technol* 126:64-5+ Mr 2 '87

Accidents

See Aviation—Accidents

Armaments

See also
Guided missiles—Launching from airplanes

AC-130 gunship upgrades will improve combat lethality. il *Aviat Week Space Technol* 127:51-2+ D 14 '87

AFTI F-16 testbed to evaluate sensors for close air support. il *Aviat Week Space Technol* 127:76 N 2 '87

British Aerospace Hawk 200 displays variety of weapons. il *Aviat Week Space Technol* 126:70-1 Je 22 '87

The case against the Air Force [developing planes designed to deliver smart bombs behind enemy lines at the expense of providing close air support] R. Coram. il *Wash Mon* 19:17-24 Jl/Ag '87

Defense Dept. asks USAF to broaden design options for new CAS aircraft [close air support] il *Aviat Week Space Technol* 127:28-9 N 23 '87

Expendable defenses [special section] il *Aviat Week Space Technol* 127:22-5 S 21 '87

Let the Army fly its own close air support. B. M. Greeley, Jr. *Aviat Week Space Technol* 126:11 F 9 '87

Speed, stealth, maneuverability sought for survivable close air support. B. M. Greeley, Jr. *Aviat Week Space Technol* 126:143+ Ap 27 '87

Study supports call for design of new close air support aircraft [Institute for Defense Analysis] J. D. Morrocco. il *Aviat Week Space Technol* 127:29-30 S 28 '87

Teams ready bids for EFA contracts [external stores carrying units/weapon release systems] *Aviat Week Space Technol* 127:101 Jl 6 '87

U.S. and Soviet nuclear-capable aircraft (1987). il *Bull At Sci* 43:56 N '87

USAF, Army grapple with key issues of close air support mission. B. M. Greeley, Jr. *Aviat Week Space Technol* 126:50-1+ Mr 23 '87

USAF, Defense Dept. reach compromise on new CAS aircraft [close air support] *Aviat Week Space Technol* 127:33 D 7 '87

USAF panel urges separate CAS, interdiction aircraft [close air support] *Aviat Week Space Technol* 127:22-3 Jl 27 '87

USAF seeks designs for close air support successor to A-10. *Aviat Week Space Technol* 126:37 Je 22 '87

Cockpits

Advanced cockpit development effort signals wide industry involvement. B. D. Nordwall. il *Aviat Week Space Technol* 126:72-3+ Ap 20 '87

Crew systems lab offers rapid feedback on cockpit concepts [Northrop Corp.] il *Aviat Week Space Technol* 127:98-9+ N 23 '87

Fighter, helicopter test pilots challenge cockpit design concepts. W. B. Scott. *Aviat Week Space Technol* 127:65+ N 16 '87

Virtual Prototyping System speeds evaluation of cockpit configurations. il *Aviat Week Space Technol* 127:81+ D 7 '87

Control

See also
Airplanes, Military—Stability and stabilizers
Computers—Aviation use

General Dynamics considers ways to advance F-16 agility. C. A. Shifrin. *Aviat Week Space Technol* 126:120-1+ F 16 '87

Costs

The $40 billion dogfight [Advanced Tactical Fighter] H. Banks. il *Forbes* 139:35-8 My 4 '87

B-1B bomber inquiry triggers Aspin probes of Stealth weapons [House Armed Services Committee] P. Mann. *Aviat Week Space Technol* 126:18-20 Mr 23 '87

The B-1B: haste is making waste. D. Griffiths. *Bus Week* p29 F 9 '87

Congress questions cost of B-1B recovery program. *Aviat Week Space Technol* 126:28-9 Mr 2 '87

Congressional, Navy leaders back Grumman A-6F at roll-out. il *Aviat Week Space Technol* 127:31 Ag 10 '87

Crowded skies. H. Banks. il *Forbes* 140:48+ Ag 24 '87

Airplanes, Military—Costs—_cont._

Defense Dept. seeks funds to continue P-3C production. J. D. Morrocco. _Aviat Week Space Technol_ 127:26 Ag 31 '87

Funding cut would halt AV-8B attack squadron upgrade [Marine Corps modernization] il _Aviat Week Space Technol_ 127:25-6 Jl 6 '87

GAO report on Lavi indicates spending will exceed cap. J. D. Morrocco. _Aviat Week Space Technol_ 126:20-2 Mr 2 '87

Grumman gets a slap in the face from the Navy [F-14 contract] D. Griffiths. _Bus Week_ p45 Ap 13 '87

High cost of aircraft avionics threatens U.S. defense capability. B. D. Nordwall. _Aviat Week Space Technol_ 126:79+ Je 8 '87

House panel warns of future risks in B-1B program costs and schedule [Armed Services Committee] _Aviat Week Space Technol_ 126:20-1 Ap 6 '87

House weighs major cuts for combat aircraft, missiles. _Aviat Week Space Technol_ 127:32-3 O 19 '87

Israel at the crossroads [Lavi fighter program] D. E. Fink. _Aviat Week Space Technol_ 126:11 Je 8 '87

Israel wins U.S. financial concessions to cover possible cancellation of Lavi. _Aviat Week Space Technol_ 127:25 Jl 13 '87

Military aircraft: how much high tech is enough? D. Griffiths. il _Bus Week_ p76+ My 11 '87

National pride vs. economics [Lavi airplane issue] R. Rosenberg. il _U S News World Rep_ 103:36 Ag 31 '87

Navy opts to cut F-14D buy, will compete F-14A update. D. M. North. _Aviat Week Space Technol_ 126:18-20 Mr 30 '87

Navy seeks 125 maritime patrol aircraft. _Aviat Week Space Technol_ 126:19 F 23 '87

Navy's emphasis on ATA threatens A-6F funding. D. M. North. _Aviat Week Space Technol_ 127:20-1 O 26 '87

Pentagon initiative triggers new interest in joint ventures [aircraft upgrade projects] _Aviat Week Space Technol_ 127:23 Ag 3 '87

Real money, 'sham' mountains [B-1B bombers] M. E. Marty. _Christ Century_ 104:255 Mr 11 '87

Rockwell sneaks up on the Stealth bomber [challenging Northrop] D. Griffiths. il _Bus Week_ p96 Je 29 '87

U.S. increases pressure on Israel to abandon Lavi. M. Mecham. _Aviat Week Space Technol_ 127:21 Ag 17 '87

USAF expects fully operational B-1B by 1988 within spending limits. il _Aviat Week Space Technol_ 126:24-5 Ja 26 '87

The wages of Stealth [Northrop's Stealth bomber] _Commonweal_ 114:644 N 20 '87

What price sky-high glory? [Lavi warplane] J. Greenwald. il _Time_ 130:48 Jl 20 '87

Defects

Air Force crews cite progress of B-1B in initial operations. C. A. Shifrin. il _Aviat Week Space Technol_ 126:21-3 Mr 30 '87

"Bail out, Tommy! Eject!" [T. Goyette's successful landing of defective A7 jet] P. Michelmore. il _Read Dig_ 130:106-11 F '87

The Pentagon's "Flying Edsel" [B-1B bomber] B. Van Voorst. il _Time_ 129:21 Ja 19 '87

Rockwell International investigates production line damage on B-1Bs. W. B. Scott. _Aviat Week Space Technol_ 127:29 Ag 17 '87

Rockwell probe determines causes of B-1B production line damage. _Aviat Week Space Technol_ 127:24 S 7 '87

Design

Agile Falcon draws interest of potential European partners. J. D. Morrocco. _Aviat Week Space Technol_ 127:33 N 9 '87

Air power 2000. T. H. Cole and J. Eppinger. il _Pop Mech_ 164:70-82 D '87

B-1B: a timely lesson in risk management. L. A. Skantze. _Aviat Week Space Technol_ 126:11 Mr 23 '87

Battle brews over follow-on close air support aircraft [successor to A-10 Thunderbolt] _Aviat Week Space Technol_ 126:19 F 2 '87

Boeing designs ASW version of De Havilland Dash 8-100 [antisubmarine warfare version] il _Aviat Week Space Technol_ 127:22-3 Jl 20 '87

Boeing withdraws from bidding to replace Navy ASW aircraft. _Aviat Week Space Technol_ 127:25 N 16 '87

British Aerospace, McDonnell Douglas will propose new Harrier version [AV-8B/GR. 5 Advanced Harrier] _Aviat Week Space Technol_ 126:24 Je 22 '87

Defense Dept. asks USAF to broaden design options for new CAS aircraft [close air support] il _Aviat Week Space Technol_ 127:28-9 N 23 '87

Eidetics proposes upgrades to improve F-16 performance. M. A. Dornheim. il _Aviat Week Space Technol_ 127:59+ S 28 '87

Four contenders vie for Navy maritime patrol aircraft contract [P-3 successor] P. Proctor. il _Aviat Week Space Technol_ 127:24-5 Jl 27 '87

General Dynamics proposes F-16 upgrade for 1990s [Agile Falcon] J. D. Morrocco. il _Aviat Week Space Technol_ 127:22-3 Ag 3 '87

Grumman A-6F design stresses aircraft maintenance, survivability. il _Aviat Week Space Technol_ 127:74-5 N 16 '87

Lockheed ATF team splits responsibilities [advanced tactical fighter] _Aviat Week Space Technol_ 126:29 Mr 23 '87

Lockheed reorganizes advanced tactical fighter effort. _Aviat Week Space Technol_ 127:29 D 21 '87

LTV receives Air Force contract to modernize, reengine A-7Ds. C. A. Shifrin. il _Aviat Week Space Technol_ 126:85+ Je 1 '87

Manufacturer investigating modified Gulfstream 4s as Navy P-3 follow-on. P. Proctor. il _Aviat Week Space Technol_ 126:94-5 Ap 13 '87

Marines would swap A-6Es for all-weather F/A-18Ds. il _Aviat Week Space Technol_ 127:21-2 O 26 '87

Navy expanding competition for follow-on patrol aircraft [P-3C successor] D. M. North. il _Aviat Week Space Technol_ 126:21-2 Mr 23 '87

Navy solicits proposals for P-3C ASW successor [antisubmarine warfare aircraft] B. D. Nordwall. _Aviat Week Space Technol_ 127:30-2 S 28 '87

Navy will request information on ATF concepts this spring [advanced tactical fighter] _Aviat Week Space Technol_ 126:20 Ap 6 '87

Pentagon endorses USAF Agile Falcon codevelopment plan. _Aviat Week Space Technol_ 127:21-2 O 19 '87

Program review team seeks to freeze X-31A aircraft design. il _Aviat Week Space Technol_ 127:26-7 N 30 '87

Study supports call for design of new close air support aircraft [Institute for Defense Analysis] J. D. Morrocco. il _Aviat Week Space Technol_ 127:29-30 S 28 '87

Three international teams compete for USAF contract to provide flight inspection aircraft. _Aviat Week Space Technol_ 127:25 Ag 17 '87

U.S. will discuss codevelopment of updated F/A-18 with allies [Hornet 2000] J. D. Morrocco. il _Aviat Week Space Technol_ 127:20-1 D 21 '87

USAF, Defense Dept. reach compromise on new CAS aircraft [close air support] _Aviat Week Space Technol_ 127:33 D 7 '87

USAF, Eidetics plan vortex flow, high-angle-of-attack studies. _Aviat Week Space Technol_ 126:31 Ja 19 '87

USAF may develop Agile Falcon without allied participation. J. D. Morrocco. _Aviat Week Space Technol_ 127:23-4 O 26 '87

USAF plans to introduce A-10s into forward air control fleet. J. D. Morrocco. _Aviat Week Space Technol_ 126:23 F 9 '87

Electronic equipment

See also

Air navigation—Aids and devices
Airplanes, Military—Radar equipment
Airplanes, Military—Radio equipment
Computers—Aviation use

Air Force issues RFPs for Chinese F-8-2 avionic upgrade kits. _Aviat Week Space Technol_ 126:19 Mr 23 '87

Airborne Optical Adjunct [infrared system mounted in aircraft for missile tracking as part of SDI] il _Aviat Week Space Technol_ 127:69+ N 23 '87

Boeing selected over Lockheed for P-3 avionics update award. B. M. Greeley, Jr. _Aviat Week Space Technol_ 127:22-3 Jl 20 '87

Cessna offers modified Caravan for low-cost reconnaissance. B. D. Nordwall. il _Aviat Week Space Technol_ 127:153 O 12 '87

Defensive systems to undergo full flight test in 1988 [B-1B avionics] il _Aviat Week Space Technol_ 127:69+ S 14 '87

French Air Force modifies C. 160s for Elint/ESM mission [electronic intelligence/electronic support measures] il _Aviat Week Space Technol_ 126:90 F 16 '87

GE/Martin selected to provide ATF electro-optic sensor [YF-22A advanced tactical fighter] _Aviat Week Space Technol_ 126:73 Je 15 '87

High cost of aircraft avionics threatens U.S. defense capability. B. D. Nordwall. _Aviat Week Space Technol_ 126:79+ Je 8 '87

Airplanes, Military—Electronic equipment—*cont.*

Martin develops simplified Flir for night-vision attack capability. *Aviat Week Space Technol* 127:101 S 21 '87

Military aircraft: how much high tech is enough? D. Griffiths. il *Bus Week* p76+ My 11 '87

New Grumman facility advances F-14D avionics integration. K. J. Stein. il *Aviat Week Space Technol* 127:141+ S 7 '87

New Zealand's modernized Skyhawks readied for initial flight tests. K. J. Stein. il *Aviat Week Space Technol* 127:69+ N 30 '87

Northrop developing tactical infrared focal plane array. il *Aviat Week Space Technol* 127:82-3 N 2 '87

Off-the-shelf civil components improve nontactical avionics [commercial equipment in military aircraft] K. J. Stein. il *Aviat Week Space Technol* 126:87+ My 4 '87

Special report: electronic warfare—the operational challenge. il *Aviat Week Space Technol* 126:49-51+ F 9 '87

Special report: electronic warfare—the technological response. il *Aviat Week Space Technol* 126:48-9+ F 16 '87

Technical survey: tactical airborne reconnaissance [cover story; special section] il *Aviat Week Space Technol* 127:68-9+ S 7 '87

USAF demonstrates electro-optical reconnaissance system on RF-4C. J. D. Morrocco. *Aviat Week Space Technol* 126:123+ My 18 '87

Defects

The B-1B: haste is making waste. D. Griffiths. *Bus Week* p29 F 9 '87

Congress questions cost of B-1B recovery program. *Aviat Week Space Technol* 126:28-9 Mr 2 '87

Real money, 'sham' mountains [B-1B bombers] M. E. Marty. *Christ Century* 104:255 Mr 11 '87

Maintenance and repair

New automated testing system aids SAC FB-111 maintenance. K. J. Stein. il *Aviat Week Space Technol* 126:91+ Mr 2 '87

Engines

See Airplane engines, Jet

Escape devices

Crest seat tested in wind tunnel up to Mach 3. *Aviat Week Space Technol* 127:34 N 9 '87

Export-import trade

See Airplane industry—Export-import trade

Fires and fire prevention

Navy grounds F/A-18 aircraft following engine fire incidents. *Aviat Week Space Technol* 127:31 N 23 '87

Flaps

F-106 aids vortex flow study to improve fighter performance [advanced-technology fighters] E. H. Phillips. il *Aviat Week Space Technol* 127:51-2 S 21 '87

Frames

Airframe designs hamper EW advances [electronic warfare] *Aviat Week Space Technol* 126:65 F 16 '87

History

Grasshoppers and flitfires [early liaison airplanes flown during World War II] G. Baxter. il *Flying* 114:98-9 O '87

UFO update [1945 disappearance of TBM Avenger bombers] S. Baker. il *Omni* 9:91 S '87

Inspection

Rockwell International investigates production line damage on B-1Bs. W. B. Scott. *Aviat Week Space Technol* 127:29 Ag 17 '87

Rockwell probe determines causes of B-1B production line damage. *Aviat Week Space Technol* 127:24 S 7 '87

Landing

A-7D crash accents different USAF, Navy emergency rules [attempted flameout approach] il *Aviat Week Space Technol* 127:31 N 2 '87

Air Force RFP opens bidding on aircraft to calibrate navigation, approach aids [business jets] *Aviat Week Space Technol* 126:150 Ap 27 '87

"Bail out, Tommy! Eject!" [T. Goyette's successful landing of defective A7 jet] P. Michelmore. il *Read Dig* 130:106-11 F '87

Orion, the hunter [low on fuel and hunting for a runway] K. Welch. il *Flying* 114:102-4 O '87

Landing on carriers

Rafale completes initial aircraft carrier approach tests. il *Aviat Week Space Technol* 126:20 My 18 '87

Leasing and renting

Administration expected to back lease of E-2Cs to Pakistan. M. Mecham. *Aviat Week Space Technol* 126:27-8 My 4 '87

Maintenance and repair

See also
Airplanes, Military—Inspection

Argentines cut overhaul/maintenance capacity [Taller Aeronaval Central] *Aviat Week Space Technol* 127:50 Ag 24 '87

Reliability of B-1B improves as line crews gain experience. B. D. Nordwall. il *Aviat Week Space Technol* 127:63-4 S 14 '87

Repairs for an image [controversy over awarding CF-18 jet fighter maintenance contract to Canadair] M. Clark. il *Macleans* 100:7 Ja 5 '87

Manufacture

See Airplane industry

Materials

Boeing to begin tests on A-6E/F composite wing. B. M. Greeley, Jr. il *Aviat Week Space Technol* 127:121-2 O 12 '87

New materials promise low radar reflectance [retinyl Schiff base salts] il *Aviat Week Space Technol* 126:22-3 My 18 '87

Rockwell team demonstrates automatic construction of large composite wings. il *Aviat Week Space Technol* 126:333+ Je 15 '87

Visions of an invisible aircraft [retinyl Schiff base salts; work of Robert R. Birge and others] il *Sci News* 132:137 Ag 29 '87

Noise

Strategic Air Command bombs out [Minnesota residents block low-altitude bomber training flights] M. Helmberger. il *Progressive* 51:11-12 Ag '87

Photographs and photography

Our spy on high [SR-71] C. Cole. il *N Y Times Mag* p30-4 My 10 '87

Radar equipment

Administration expected to back lease of E-2Cs to Pakistan. M. Mecham. *Aviat Week Space Technol* 126:27-8 My 4 '87

Army/USAF use diverse technologies to validate Joint STARS concepts. il *Aviat Week Space Technol* 126:84-5+ Mr 2 '87

Army's R&D plan stresses development of passive interferometry detectors. *Aviat Week Space Technol* 126:113 F 9 '87

Britain-U.S. export pact protects AWACS technology. *Aviat Week Space Technol* 126:263 Mr 9 '87

British Aerospace offers Terprom navigation system to U.S. military. il *Aviat Week Space Technol* 126:85 My 4 '87

British set date to change Tornado radar contract. *Aviat Week Space Technol* 126:26 Ap 6 '87

E-3 offsets expected to reach $2 billion [Boeing's agreement with Britain] *Aviat Week Space Technol* 127:25 O 26 '87

European fighter programs spur development of advanced radars. W. B. Scott. il *Aviat Week Space Technol* 127:145+ Jl 13 '87

Fairchild delivers Metro 3 AEW testbed to Sweden [airborne early warning] C. A. Shifrin. il *Aviat Week Space Technol* 127:127+ O 19 '87

Flying into a tight corner [U.S. promise to supply AWACs to Pakistan] E. W. Desmond. il *Time* 129:41 Je 22 '87

France orders Boeing E-3s; Britain signs formal contract. *Aviat Week Space Technol* 126:27 Mr 2 '87

GAO renews criticism of services for lack of radar warning receiver commonality. *Aviat Week Space Technol* 127:93 Ag 24 '87

GAO tells House Security Subcommittee Defense Dept. fails to follow guideline on common radar warning receiver. B. D. Nordwall. *Aviat Week Space Technol* 126:33 My 11 '87

General Dynamics begins tests in new anechoic chamber [cover story] C. A. Shifrin. *Aviat Week Space Technol* 127:51-2 O 19 '87

Guardians for the Far North [Canadian AWACS] P. C. Newman. il *Macleans* 100:30 My 25 '87

Hughes APG-70 radar provides enhanced F-15 combat capabilities. W. B. Scott. il *Aviat Week Space Technol* 126:95+ My 25 '87

Hughes group wins ATF avionics contract [advanced tactical fighter] *Aviat Week Space Technol* 127:32 Ag 3 '87

Hughes hybrid radar will improve F-14D tracking/shootdown capability. W. B. Scott. il *Aviat Week Space Technol* 127:85+ N 16 '87

Inauguration of NATO E-3A force boosts Norway's mountain defenses [airborne warning and control system] *Aviat Week Space Technol* 126:88 My 25 '87

Airplanes, Military—Radar equipment—*cont.*

An invisible eye to stand a watch [infrared sensors instead of radar] S. Budiansky. il *U S News World Rep* 103:61-2 Jl 20 '87

Israel developing 707-based surveillance platform [Phalcon] il *Aviat Week Space Technol* 126:175 Je 15 '87

Japan's Navy weighs E-3, additional E-2Cs for AEW mission [airborne early warning mission] *Aviat Week Space Technol* 126:59 My 11 '87

Joint STARS intensifies reliance on software in development phase. E. H. Kolcum. il *Aviat Week Space Technol* 126:81-2+ F 23 '87

Litton, Loral to deliver F-16 warning systems. *Aviat Week Space Technol* 126:104 F 9 '87

Litton using new technologies to upgrade radar warning receivers. il *Aviat Week Space Technol* 126:91+ F 16 '87

Navy/USAF begin flight testing airborne self-protection jammer. *Aviat Week Space Technol* 126:91 F 9 '87

Northrop leads U.S. production of airborne jamming equipment. il *Aviat Week Space Technol* 126:83+ F 16 '87

Pentagon task force to develop model for radar technology transfer. J. D. Morrocco. *Aviat Week Space Technol* 127:30 Ag 24 '87

Radar designed for intense EW environment [Swedish airborne phased-array early warning radar under development by Ericsson Radio Systems] *Aviat Week Space Technol* 127:130 O 19 '87

Siemens testing new RWRs, Elint equipment for multinational aircraft [radar warning receivers, electronic intelligence equipment and jam-resistant communications systems] il *Aviat Week Space Technol* 126:71+ F 16 '87

Smokey snooping at 40,000 feet [Navy's use of Whistler radar detectors] S. Wilkinson. il *Car Driv* 33:29 S '87

Technical survey: tactical airborne reconnaissance [cover story; special section] il *Aviat Week Space Technol* 127:68-9+ S 7 '87

UTL is ready to equip those AWACS. G. G. Marcial. *Bus Week* p130 My 25 '87

Radio equipment

First production GPS receiver delivered ahead of schedule [Global Positioning System/Navstar] P. J. Klass. il *Aviat Week Space Technol* 127:93+ S 21 '87

Remodeled airplanes

See Airplanes, Remodeled

Safety devices and measures

See also

Airplanes, Military—Escape devices

Specifications

See Airplanes—Specifications

Speed records

See Airplane speed records

Stability and stabilizers

Ames-Dryden to study airflow around fighter aircraft at high angles of attack. *Aviat Week Space Technol* 126:20 Mr 30 '87

Yaw vanes improve performance of F-14A in initial test flights. il *Aviat Week Space Technol* 126:50-1 My 4 '87

Testing

See also

Air Force Flight Test Center (U.S.)

Military maneuvers

Naval Air Test Center (U.S.)

AFTI/F-111 testbed will evaluate mission adaptive wing control modes. *Aviat Week Space Technol* 126:133+ Ap 27 '87

AFTI F-16 testbed to evaluate sensors for close air support. *Aviat Week Space Technol* 127:76 N 2 '87

Air Force crews cite progress of B-1B in initial operations. C. A. Shifrin. il *Aviat Week Space Technol* 126:21-3 Mr 30 '87

B-1B combines brisk low-altitude handling, more capable avionics. D. M. North. il *Aviat Week Space Technol* 127:54-5+ S 14 '87

CF-18 revolutionizes Cold Lake test data, software operations [Canada] il *Aviat Week Space Technol* 127:128-9+ S 28 '87

Combined Test Force evaluates upgrades for U.S., foreign F-16s. W. B. Scott. il *Aviat Week Space Technol* 126:93+ My 18 '87

First F-15E fighter begins supersonic handling tests. il *Aviat Week Space Technol* 126:53 My 4 '87

First X-29A aircraft to begin performance investigation flights. *Aviat Week Space Technol* 126:60 Ap 20 '87

Flight program emphasizes weapons delivery, stall tests [B-1B flight test program] W. B. Scott. *Aviat Week Space Technol* 127:77 S 14 '87

Funds sought for AV-8B live-fire testing [wing box design] *Aviat Week Space Technol* 126:25 Je 8 '87

General Dynamics begins tests in new anechoic chamber [cover story] C. A. Shifrin. *Aviat Week Space Technol* 127:51-2 O 19 '87

Lavi multirole combat aircraft begins flight testing in Israel. il *Aviat Week Space Technol* 126:18-19 Ja 12 '87

New CF-18 fatigue tests raise more doubts about service life [Canadian fighter] P. Mann. il *Aviat Week Space Technol* 127:18-20 Ag 17 '87

The next generation: can we pull it off? T. Scanlan. por *Aviat Week Space Technol* 126:111+ Je 1 '87

Schweizer demonstrates SA 2-37A low-cost surveillance aircraft. P. Proctor. *Aviat Week Space Technol* 126:100-1 Je 1 '87

Schweizer's super snooper [SA2-37A] N. Moll. il *Flying* 114:54-8 O '87

Trading places [piloting the F-18 Hornet] B. Rahal. il *Car Driv* 32:153+ Ap '87

X-31A highly maneuverable fighter design tested in wind tunnel. il *Aviat Week Space Technol* 126:18-19 Mr 30 '87

X-men [X-29 test pilots at Dryden Research Center] E. Weiner. il *Flying* 114:38-40+ Ja '87

Yaw vanes improve performance of F-14A in initial test flights. il *Aviat Week Space Technol* 126:50-1 My 4 '87

Wings

AFTI/F-111 testbed will evaluate mission adaptive wing control modes. *Aviat Week Space Technol* 126:133+ Ap 27 '87

Avco group eyes tactical missile work. il *Aviat Week Space Technol* 126:135-6 My 11 '87

Boeing to begin tests on A-6E/F composite wing. B. M. Greeley, Jr. il *Aviat Week Space Technol* 127:121-2 O 12 '87

Funds sought for AV-8B live-fire testing [wing box design] *Aviat Week Space Technol* 126:25 Je 8 '87

Rockwell team demonstrates automatic construction of large composite wings. il *Aviat Week Space Technol* 126:333+ Je 15 '87

Defects

Navy imposes A-6 flight restrictions. *Aviat Week Space Technol* 126:29 Ja 26 '87

Wing section fatigue restricts operations of C-2A, E-2C aircraft. *Aviat Week Space Technol* 126:28-9 Je 29 '87

Argentina

Superpowers, stagnant economy influence Argentine Navy's recovery strategy. il *Aviat Week Space Technol* 127:49-50+ Ag 24 '87

Australia

Australia drafts 25-year plan to upgrade Air Force fleet. P. Proctor. il *Aviat Week Space Technol* 127:121-2 S 7 '87

New Australian defense strategy prompts early warning, aerial buildup. *Aviat Week Space Technol* 126:139+ Ap 27 '87

Brazil

Brazil's goal of self-sufficiency in arms impeded by inflation, record high indebtedness. il *Aviat Week Space Technol* 127:40+ Ag 24 '87

Canada

Canada's suspension of CF-18 deliveries viewed as repair-cost negotiating tactic. P. Mann. *Aviat Week Space Technol* 127:26-7 N 16 '87

CF-18 revolutionizes Cold Lake test data, software operations. il *Aviat Week Space Technol* 127:128-9+ S 28 '87

Cold Lake matures into strategic base. P. Mann. il map *Aviat Week Space Technol* 127:124-8 S 28 '87

Goose Bay modernizes, prepares for air defense role with CF-18. P. Mann. il map *Aviat Week Space Technol* 127:82-3+ O 5 '87

Guardians for the Far North [Canadian AWACS] P. C. Newman. il *Macleans* 100:30 My 25 '87

New CF-18 fatigue tests raise more doubts about service life. P. Mann. il *Aviat Week Space Technol* 127:18-20 Ag 17 '87

Old age of Air Force fleet complicates modernization. il *Aviat Week Space Technol* 127:69+ S 21 '87

Repairs for an image [controversy over awarding CF-18 jet fighter maintenance contract to Canadair] M. Clark. il *Macleans* 100:7 Ja 5 '87

Chile

Chile focuses on future fighter project. *Aviat Week Space Technol* 127:62-3 Ag 17 '87

Airplanes, Military—Chile—*cont.*

U.S. parts embargo grounds Chilean Air Force F-5 fleet. il *Aviat Week Space Technol* 127:73+ Ag 24 '87

China

Air Force issues RFPs for Chinese F-8-2 avionic upgrade kits. *Aviat Week Space Technol* 126:19 Mr 23 '87

China mounts effort to boost military aircraft sales. il *Aviat Week Space Technol* 127:112 Jl 13 '87

Chinese Air Force developing few new aircraft designs. R. G. O'Lone. il *Aviat Week Space Technol* 127:55+ D 7 '87

Chinese display trainer, ground attack aircraft [Paris Air Show] il *Aviat Week Space Technol* 126:63 Je 15 '87

Chinese F-8-2 fighter configured for all-weather, day/night missions. il *Aviat Week Space Technol* 126:42-3 Ja 19 '87

France

Dassault proposes Rafale program with 1996 service introduction. *Aviat Week Space Technol* 126:25 Ap 20 '87

French Air Force will receive improved Mirage 2000 fighters. *Aviat Week Space Technol* 126:71 Mr 16 '87

French approve Rafale follow-on. *Aviat Week Space Technol* 126:25 F 23 '87

McDonnell Douglas offers F/A-18 for French Navy's carrier air fleet. J. D. Morrocco. *Aviat Week Space Technol* 127:33-5 S 7 '87

Rafale completes initial aircraft carrier approach tests. il *Aviat Week Space Technol* 126:20 My 18 '87

Germany (West)

Decision near in West Germany on EFA interim engine [European fighter aircraft] *Aviat Week Space Technol* 127:27 S 28 '87

First F110-powered F-16Cs join wing at Ramstein Air Base. il *Aviat Week Space Technol* 126:212-13 Je 15 '87

Great Britain

Britain-U.S. export pact protects AWACS technology. *Aviat Week Space Technol* 126:263 Mr 9 '87

British Aerospace defines military aircraft versions. il *Aviat Week Space Technol* 126:97 Je 29 '87

British Aerospace Hawk 200 displays variety of weapons. il *Aviat Week Space Technol* 126:70-1 Je 22 '87

British Aerospace seeks projects for EAP aircraft [Experimental Aircraft Program] *Aviat Week Space Technol* 127:69 D 7 '87

British seek risk-sharing partners for high-agility aircraft project [Small Agile Battlefield Aircraft] D. A. Brown. il *Aviat Week Space Technol* 127:61 D 14 '87

British set date to change Tornado radar contract. *Aviat Week Space Technol* 126:26 Ap 6 '87

E-3 offsets expected to reach $2 billion [Boeing's agreement with Britain] *Aviat Week Space Technol* 127:25 O 26 '87

Probe of Harrier crash focuses on emergency parachute system. D. A. Brown. il *Aviat Week Space Technol* 127:30-1 N 2 '87

Honduras

Proposed sale of F-5s to Honduras [statement, May 19, 1987] E. Abrams. *Dep State Bull* 87:87-9 Jl '87

Israel

Fallen state [implications of the Lavi fiasco] A. Kenan. *Nation* 245:293 S 26 '87

GAO report on Lavi indicates spending will exceed cap. J. D. Morrocco. *Aviat Week Space Technol* 126:20-2 Mr 2 '87

Israel Aircraft Industries displays F-4E Super Phantom conversion [Paris Air Show] il *Aviat Week Space Technol* 126:92-3 Je 29 '87

Israel at the crossroads [Lavi fighter program] D. E. Fink. *Aviat Week Space Technol* 126:11 Je 8 '87

Israel developing 707-based surveillance platform [Phalcon] il *Aviat Week Space Technol* 126:175 Je 15 '87

Israel plans to complete third Lavi prototype. *Aviat Week Space Technol* 127:27-8 S 28 '87

Israel renews debate on Lavi development. D. E. Fink. *Aviat Week Space Technol* 126:18-19 Je 1 '87

Israel wins U.S. financial concessions to cover possible cancellation of Lavi. *Aviat Week Space Technol* 127:25 Jl 13 '87

Israeli aerospace industry faces critical decisions [Lavi aircraft] il *Aviat Week Space Technol* 126:95 Mr 9 '87

Israeli Air Force to decide on F-4 conversion by next year [Super Phantom] D. A. Brown. il *Aviat Week Space Technol* 126:65-6 Je 22 '87

Israelis review decisions that led to Lavi cancellation; International partners sought to complete Lavi. D. A. Brown. *Aviat Week Space Technol* 127:22-4 S 14 '87

Lavi multirole combat aircraft begins flight testing in Israel. il *Aviat Week Space Technol* 126:18-19 Ja 12 '87

Lavi termination [special section; with editorial comment by Donald E. Fink] il *Aviat Week Space Technol* 127:15, 22-5 S 7 '87

National pride vs. economics [Lavi airplane issue] R. Rosenberg. il *U S News World Rep* 103:36 Ag 31 '87

U.S. increases pressure on Israel to abandon Lavi. M. Mecham. *Aviat Week Space Technol* 127:21 Ag 17 '87

What price sky-high glory? [Lavi warplane] J. Greenwald. il *Time* 130:48 Jl 20 '87

Japan

Debate over F-15 derivative clouds selection of Japanese FS-X fighter. il *Aviat Week Space Technol* 126:178+ Je 15 '87

Japanese industry urges FS-X fighter development despite U.S. opposition. D. A. Brown. *Aviat Week Space Technol* 127:47-9 S 21 '87

Japanese to codevelop U.S. aircraft derivative for FS-X. *Aviat Week Space Technol* 127:34 O 12 '87

Japan's defense agency selects F-16 as basis for FS-X aircraft [General Dynamics chosen] *Aviat Week Space Technol* 127:22-3 O 26 '87

Japan's Navy weighs E-3, additional E-2Cs for AEW mission [airborne early warning mission] *Aviat Week Space Technol* 126:59 My 11 '87

Latin America

Aerospace in South America: military and space [cover story; special section] il *Aviat Week Space Technol* 127:40-1+ Ag 24 '87

New Zealand

New Zealand's modernized Skyhawks readied for initial flight tests. K. J. Stein. il *Aviat Week Space Technol* 127:69+ N 30 '87

Norway

Norwegian Air Force to weigh replacing F-16 fighter force. D. A. Brown. *Aviat Week Space Technol* 126:81+ My 25 '87

Pakistan

Flying into a tight corner [U.S. promise to supply AWACs to Pakistan] E. W. Desmond. il *Time* 129:41 Je 22 '87

Soviet Union

See also

Spaceplane, Russian

MiG's over America [private ownership of surplus Soviet-designed fighters] il *Discover* 8:12+ S '87

Soviets upgrading MiG-25s into Foxbat-E version. il *Aviat Week Space Technol* 126:125 Ap 27 '87

U.S. and Soviet nuclear-capable aircraft (1987). il *Bull At Sci* 43:56 N '87

USAF, Navy track four Bear bombers in twin intercept over Alaska. il *Aviat Week Space Technol* 126:79 Je 22 '87

Sweden

Fairchild delivers Metro 3 AEW testbed to Sweden [airborne early warning] C. A. Shifrin. il *Aviat Week Space Technol* 127:127+ O 19 '87

Radar designed for intense EW environment [airborne phased-array early warning radar under development by Ericsson Radio Systems] *Aviat Week Space Technol* 127:130 O 19 '87

Sweden schedules first flights of JAS-39 Gripen prototypes. il *Aviat Week Space Technol* 126:136 Je 15 '87

Sweden's Gripen rolls out. D. E. Fink. *Aviat Week Space Technol* 126:11 My 4 '87

Swedish Air Force seeks backing for increased Gripen production. D. A. Brown. il *Aviat Week Space Technol* 126:18-20 My 4 '87

Swedish firm develops lightweight airborne system for sea surveillance. *Aviat Week Space Technol* 127:101 S 21 '87

Swedish Gripen's first flight delayed by software problems [fly-by-wire flight control system] D. A. Brown. *Aviat Week Space Technol* 127:25 O 5 '87

Thailand

Thai Air Force upgrades fleet to meet Vietnamese threat. R. G. O'Lone. il *Aviat Week Space Technol* 126:92-3 Mr 30 '87

Tibet

Chinese deploy J-7 fighters in Tibet to counter Indian threat. C. Covault. il *Aviat Week Space Technol* 127:103-4 O 19 '87

Airplanes, Military—*cont.*

Turkey

Joint venture to build aircraft modernization installation in Turkey [Tusas Aerospace facility in Murted] J. D. Morrocco. il *Aviat Week Space Technol* 126:70-1 Ap 6 '87

United States

See Airplanes, Military

Venezuela

F-16s give Venezuelan Air Force realistic combat capability. il *Aviat Week Space Technol* 127:67-8 Ag 24 '87

Western Europe

Agile Falcon draws interest of potential European partners. J. D. Morrocco. *Aviat Week Space Technol* 127:33 N 9 '87

Decision near in West Germany on EFA interim engine [European fighter aircraft] *Aviat Week Space Technol* 127:27 S 28 '87

Eurofighter bidding rules may bar U.S. companies. M. Feazel. *Aviat Week Space Technol* 126:18-19 Ja 19 '87

Eurofighter, Panavia explore restructuring of EFA program [European fighter aircraft] il *Aviat Week Space Technol* 126:65 Je 29 '87

Eurojet stresses thrust, maintainability in design of EJ200 engine for EFA [European fighter aircraft] il *Aviat Week Space Technol* 126:94 Je 29 '87

European coproducers study F-16 upgrades, replacements. K. F. Mordoff. il *Aviat Week Space Technol* 126:214+ Je 15 '87

European fighter programs spur development of advanced radars. W. B. Scott. il *Aviat Week Space Technol* 127:145+ Jl 13 '87

European groups seek mutual weapons development programs. *Aviat Week Space Technol* 126:82+ Mr 9 '87

France orders Boeing E-3s; Britain signs formal contract. *Aviat Week Space Technol* 126:27 Mr 2 '87

Funding delays continue to plague EFA development [European fighter aircraft] K. F. Mordoff. *Aviat Week Space Technol* 127:29 Ag 24 '87

GE, Turbo-Union allowed to rebid on EFA interim engine [European fighter aircraft program] *Aviat Week Space Technol* 126:24 F 23 '87

General Dynamics proposes F-16 upgrade for 1990s [Agile Falcon] J. D. Morrocco. il *Aviat Week Space Technol* 127:22-3 Ag 3 '87

Inauguration of NATO E-3A force boosts Norway's mountain defenses [airborne warning and control system] *Aviat Week Space Technol* 126:88 My 25 '87

NATO pushes the 'eject' button on U.S. contractors [replacement program for F-16 fighters] J. Kapstein. *Bus Week* p50 F 2 '87

Pentagon endorses USAF Agile Falcon codevelopment plan. *Aviat Week Space Technol* 127:21-2 O 19 '87

Teams ready bids for EFA contracts [external stores carrying units/weapon release systems] *Aviat Week Space Technol* 127:101 Jl 6 '87

U.S. will discuss codevelopment of updated F/A-18 with allies [Hornet 2000] J. D. Morrocco. il *Aviat Week Space Technol* 127:20-1 D 21 '87

USAF may develop Agile Falcon without allied participation. J. D. Morrocco. *Aviat Week Space Technol* 127:23-4 O 26 '87

West Germany releases funds for EFA component development [European fighter aircraft] K. F. Mordoff. il *Aviat Week Space Technol* 127:26-7 S 28 '87

Airplanes, Military transport

See also

United States. Civil Reserve Air Fleet

Costs

Air Force seeks funding for new STOL transports. *Aviat Week Space Technol* 126:24 Ja 19 '87

Defense keeps tightening the screws on contractors [Lockheed reduces price of Air Force C-5B] D. Griffiths. il *Bus Week* p34 F 2 '87

Lockheed trims $273-million from C-5B price. *Aviat Week Space Technol* 126:30 Ja 26 '87

Design

The C-17 abuilding. il *Pop Mech* 164:117 O '87

FIMA consortium designing two airlifter versions [Future International Military/Civil Airlifter] il *Aviat Week Space Technol* 127:52 Ag 10 '87

NASA evaluates transportation of large space station payloads [C-5A modifications] B. A. Smith. il *Aviat Week Space Technol* 127:47+ Ag 10 '87

Skytrader develops light utility STOL transport for military use. *Aviat Week Space Technol* 126:27 Ap 6 '87

Super STOL takes big loads to small fields. B. Kocivar. il *Pop Sci* 230:65+ Ja '87

History

The whale's tale [C-46] L. Morgan. il *Flying* 114:64-70 D '87

Maintenance and repair

Douglas stresses reliability early in C-17 development. B. A. Smith. il *Aviat Week Space Technol* 127:61-2 Jl 20 '87

Piloting

Latter-day Load Star [C-5 Galaxy] R. L. Collins. il *Flying* 114:17-18 Mr '87

Weekend warriors [New York Air National Guards C-5 Galaxies] P. Scott. il *Flying* 114:60-4 Je '87

Purchasing

Air Force exploits speed, range of Gulfstream C-20 in VIP role. P. Proctor. il *Aviat Week Space Technol* 126:74-5 Je 8 '87

Radar equipment

Air Force, Marine Corps study C-130 missile defense systems. D. Hughes. il *Aviat Week Space Technol* 127:89+ Ag 24 '87

Lockheed-Georgia seeking major role in ADI development [C-130 phased array antennas] E. H. Kolcum. il *Aviat Week Space Technol* 126:126-7 My 18 '87

France

Aerospatiale proposes modifying A300B4s for strategic support. *Aviat Week Space Technol* 126:31 F 23 '87

Delivery of C-130s expands French military airlift capability. il *Aviat Week Space Technol* 127:29 D 14 '87

French Air Force modifies C. 160s for Elint/ESM mission [electronic intelligence/electronic support measures] il *Aviat Week Space Technol* 126:90 F 16 '87

Western Europe

Airbus Industrie forms office to sell transports tailored for military use. il *Aviat Week Space Technol* 127:18-19 Jl 27 '87

European air forces interested in Socata/Mooney TBM 700 [single-engine business turboprop as transport aircraft for military officials] *Aviat Week Space Technol* 127:147 O 12 '87

Europeans will enter ATR42 in U.S. STOL competition [military cargo version] il *Aviat Week Space Technol* 126:28-9 F 23 '87

U.S. firms seek links to European airlifter program. *Aviat Week Space Technol* 127:18 Jl 27 '87

Airplanes, Model *See* Airplane models

Airplanes, Private

See also

Airplanes—Private ownership

Private flying

Airplanes, Reconnaissance *See* Airplanes, Military

Airplanes, Remodeled

Beech King Air turboprops modified to regional airline configuration. P. Proctor. il *Aviat Week Space Technol* 126:71 Ap 20 '87

Canadair will limit redesign, costs of Challenger upgrade [upgrade from business jet to commuter transport] il *Aviat Week Space Technol* 127:42 D 7 '87

Cessna offers modified Caravan for low-cost reconnaissance. B. D. Nordwall. il *Aviat Week Space Technol* 127:153 O 12 '87

LTV receives Air Force contract to modernize, reengine A-7Ds. C. A. Shifrin. il *Aviat Week Space Technol* 126:85+ Je 1 '87

Manufacturer investigating modified Gulfstream 4s as Navy P-3 follow-on. P. Proctor. il *Aviat Week Space Technol* 126:94-5 Ap 13 '87

Valsan's 727-200 reengining program enters final design engineering phase [cockpit, fuselage and engine modifications] S. W. Kandebo. il *Aviat Week Space Technol* 127:137+ S 7 '87

History

Boardroom bombers [WWII bombers remodeled for corporate use] R. Munson. il *Flying* 114:94-9 S '87

Testing

Flight certification tests continue on S-2 modified by Marsh Aviation. il *Aviat Week Space Technol* 126:119 F 16 '87

The high Chaparral [Mod Squad Mooney] R. L. Collins. il *Flying* 114:40-5 Je '87

Rocket ride [Riley Rocket P210; cover story] R. L. Collins. il por *Flying* 114:32-6 O '87

Superstar [Machen modified Piper Aerostar 602P] R. L. Collins. il *Flying* 114:50-4+ F '87

Airplanes, Restored

Airplanes unearthed. L. Morgan. il *Flying* 114:8-9 Mr '87

Piper then and now [J-3 Cub and Malibu] F. Mackerodt. il *Pop Mech* 164:12+ Ag '87

Airplanes, Short take-off and landing
See also
Airplanes, Amphibious
Design
Skytrader develops light utility STOL transport for military use. *Aviat Week Space Technol* 126:27 Ap 6 '87
Airplanes, Supersonic
See also
Airplanes, Military
Concorde crossing. R. L. Collins. il *Flying* 114:14+ O '87
Studies confirm viability of Mach 2-5 transport. il *Aviat Week Space Technol* 127:33-5 Ag 17 '87
Design
International interest grows in advanced high-speed aircraft. il *Aviat Week Space Technol* 126:62-3 Je 22 '87
Maching birds. N. Moll. il *Flying* 114:148+ S '87
Noise
See also
Sonic boom
Airplanes, Tank *See* Tank airplanes
Airplanes, Toy *See* Toys
Airplanes, Training
Costs
T-46 requiem. D. E. Fink. *Aviat Week Space Technol* 127:9 Ag 31 '87
T-46 termination will force closure of Fairchild facility on Long Island. *Aviat Week Space Technol* 126:27 Mr 23 '87
USAF seeks initial funding for new multiengine trainer. P. Proctor. il *Aviat Week Space Technol* 127:142+ O 12 '87
Design
Budget constraints heighten military trainer competition. il *Aviat Week Space Technol* 127:97+ Jl 6 '87
First F-16N delivered to Navy for combat training [cover story] il *Aviat Week Space Technol* 126:60 My 4 '87
Electronic equipment
Contractor expands inventory for airborne threat training [Flight International] B. M. Greeley, Jr. il *Aviat Week Space Technol* 127:139+ O 12 '87
Flight International will provide USAF electronic warfare training [use of corporate jets] *Aviat Week Space Technol* 126:101 Je 1 '87
History
Bear country [fly-in celebrating 50th anniversary of the Piper Cub] R. Munson. il *Flying* 114:64-9 O '87
Good Vultee vibes [BT-13 Vultee Valiant World War II trainer] L. Hester. il *Flying* 114:92 Ap '87
Testing
1987 Model T-33 Skyfox. P. Garrison. il *Flying* 114:46-8 Je '87
Fanstar. E. Weiner. il *Flying* 114:52-4 Ag '87
Improved VTOL performance of TAV-8B adds realism to attack force training. B. M. Greeley, Jr. il *Aviat Week Space Technol* 127:68-70+ Ag 3 '87
The last trainer? [Piper Warrior] R. L. Collins. il *Flying* 114:86-8+ F '87
T-45A trainer will be built, tested at Palmdale. *Aviat Week Space Technol* 127:136 O 12 '87
Trainers make strong showing in Le Bourget flight program [Paris Air Show] il *Aviat Week Space Technol* 127:57 Jl 27 '87
Wings
Defects
F-16 wing buckles in static test, forcing USAF to restrict training. M. Mecham. *Aviat Week Space Technol* 127:32-3 N 9 '87
Chile
Pillan's progress. J. M. McClellan. il *Flying* 114:66+ N '87
Airplanes, Used
Age before beauty [flying time] R. L. Collins. il *Flying* 114:14 Ja '87
Purchasing
Kerosene Alley [used Learjets] J. M. McClellan. il *Flying* 114:44-8+ O '87
Airplanes in agriculture
U.S. agricultural aircraft [tables] il *Aviat Week Space Technol* 126:146 Mr 9 '87
Airplanes in astronomy
Eight miles high: a breathtaking view [flight in Kuiper Airborne Observatory] R. Spangenburg and D. Moser. il *Space World* X-11-287:14-18 N '87
Observing Halley from 41,000 feet [Kuiper Airborne Observatory and Lear Jet Observatory] H. Campins and H. A. Weaver. *Sky Telesc* 73:251 Mr '87

To catch a child's imagination [Halley's comet project aboard the Kuiper Airborne Observatory] J. H. Nicholson. il *Sky Telesc* 74:303-5 S '87
Airplanes in business
See also
Airplanes, Business
Executive Air Fleet
Helicopters in business
National Business Aircraft Association
Air-minded enterprise [Phillips Petroleum] J. M. McClellan. il *Flying* 114:90+ S '87
Business flying [cover story; special section; with editorial comment by Donald E. Fink] il *Aviat Week Space Technol* 127:15, 68-73+ S 28 '87
Single minded [National Healthcare's fleet of Cessna 210s] R. L. Collins. il *Flying* 114:34-8 Je '87
Taxation
State effort to tax transient business aircraft raises concern [Ohio] *Aviat Week Space Technol* 127:56 Jl 27 '87
Airplanes in hunting and fishing
Fishing in God's country [God's Lake, Manitoba] P. Barrett. il *Field Stream* 91:86+ Ap '87
Airplanes in insect control
Beetle patrol [pine beetles] G. Baxter. il *Flying* 114:88+ D '87
Airplanes in medical care
Aeromedical aircraft accidents register sharp increase in 1987. P. Proctor. *Aviat Week Space Technol* 127:55+ Jl 13 '87
"Two saves, partial panel" [medevac mission in Alaska] T. Olden. il *Flying* 114:110-11 Ag '87
Airplanes in meteorology
Flying high—and hairy [missions through the Antarctic ozone hole in the ER-2 research plane] il *Time* 130:60-1 O 19 '87
Flying into an ozone hole [Airborne Antarctic Ozone Experiment] *Sci News* 132:95 Ag 8 '87
Flying into the eye of a hurricane [cover story] J. M. Masters. il *Weatherwise* 40:128-33 Je '87
Airplanes in narcotics regulation
Lockheed to supply P-3 AEW aircraft to Customs Service. B. A. Smith. *Aviat Week Space Technol* 126:29-30 Je 8 '87
Airplanes in narcotics trade
Cocaine arrests prompt efforts to investigate airline employee records [smuggling rings uncovered at Kennedy Airport] *Aviat Week Space Technol* 126:36 Mr 16 '87
Airplanes in patrol work
Swedish firm develops lightweight airborne system for sea surveillance. *Aviat Week Space Technol* 127:101 S 21 '87
Airplanes in photography *See* Photography, Aerial
Airplanes in sightseeing
NTSB cites air tour rules in canyon crash [airliner-helicopter crash, June 18, 1986] *Aviat Week Space Technol* 126:40 Mr 30 '87
Overflight bill includes flight-free zones. *Natl Parks* 61:38 My/Je '87
Overflight rules not tough enough [Grand Canyon] *Natl Parks* 61:46-8 Mr/Ap '87
Airplanes in the petroleum industry
Venezuelan oil firms maintain fleets to service remote sites. il *Aviat Week Space Technol* 127:55+ Ag 31 '87
Airport and Airway Trust Fund *See* Airports—Federal aid
Airport buildings
The temple of marketing [H. Jahn's United Airlines terminal at Chicago's O'Hare Airport] H. Muschamp. il *New Repub* 197:25-8 O 26 '87
Lighting
Lighting the way [United Airlines Terminal at O'Hare Airport] S. R. Shemitz. il *Archit Rec* 175:148-55 N '87
Airports
See also
Air bases
Airplane service stations
Air traffic control
See Air traffic control
Automobile rental services
See Automobiles—Leasing and renting
Bird hazards
See Aviation—Bird hazards
Buildings
See Airport buildings
Concessions (Food, etc.)
Adventures in bad eating. L. Morgan. il *Flying* 114:8-9 Ap '87
Airport concessions: new opportunities for black business. il *Ebony* 42:54-6+ Ap '87

Airports—Concessions (Food, etc.)—*cont.*

Blacks fly with Marriott [concessionary business at Tampa International Airport] R. Baker. il *Black Enterp* 17:22 Ap '87

John Lewis amends bill to aid black businesses. *Jet* 72:8 Je 22 '87

Federal aid

Airport groups propose $1.8-billion improvement plan. il *Aviat Week Space Technol* 126:33 F 9 '87

Conferees urge establishment of national airspace, airport development program. W. B. Scott. *Aviat Week Space Technol* 127:41-2 D 14 '87

Congressional battle shapes up over Aviation Trust Fund use. J. Ott. il *Aviat Week Space Technol* 126:32-3 My 18 '87

Corporate control [privatization of air traffic control system] R. L. Collins. *Flying* 114:28-9 O '87

House approves $28.5-billion Trust Fund [Aviation Trust Fund] *Aviat Week Space Technol* 127:34 O 5 '87

Only new airports can break the airborne gridlock. S. Payne. il *Bus Week* p174 My 25 '87

Pay now, fly later. A. Holzinger. il *Nations Bus* 75:22-4 N '87

Reagan submits legislation to improve airports, airways. *Aviat Week Space Technol* 126:33 F 23 '87

Senate passes $15.6-billion Trust Fund spending bill [Aviation Trust Fund] *Aviat Week Space Technol* 127:44 N 2 '87

Fees

Carriers dispute British airport fees [U.S. airlines] D. A. Brown. *Aviat Week Space Technol* 126:39 F 16 '87

General aviation fights Midway fee hike. *Aviat Week Space Technol* 127:52 O 26 '87

National groups prepare to fight plan to restrict access at Logan. D. Hughes. il *Aviat Week Space Technol* 127:34-5 D 21 '87

Opposition grows to plan for fee increase at Logan. D. Hughes. *Aviat Week Space Technol* 127:52+ O 26 '87

Finance

See also
Airports—Federal aid

What's keeping new airports from getting off the ground. M. Ivey. il *Bus Week* p32 Jl 27 '87

Health clubs

See Health clubs

History

Field day. P. Scott. il *Flying* 114:64-5 S '87

International aspects

See also
International Civil Airports Association

Future airports. *World Press Rev* 34:58 O '87

International air transport: building for traffic growth [cover story; special section; with editorial comment by James Ott] il *Aviat Week Space Technol* 127:15, 49-51+ N 9 '87

Laws and regulations

See also
Air traffic control

Luggage handling

See Airlines—Luggage handling

Management

"We enterprised it" [Miami International's manager R. Judy] J. Parr. il por *Forbes* 140:298+ N 16 '87

Noise

FAA assessing impact of regulation setting airline noise budget at Denver's Stapleton Airport. *Aviat Week Space Technol* 126:33 Mr 30 '87

Industry group urges Stage 2 phase-out, halt to noise limits. C. Preble. *Aviat Week Space Technol* 127:30-1 Jl 13 '87

Runways

Late braking news [runway friction and airplane weight] B. Newell. *Flying* 114:98 Mr '87

Safety devices and measures

See also
Radar in aviation

Security measures

Airline crackdown. il *Newsweek* 110:5 D 14 '87

FAA defends domestic airport security measures. C. Preble. *Aviat Week Space Technol* 126:36 Je 29 '87

From smoking gun to smoking dog: a 'Beat the devil' investigation [killing of dogs at Topeka's Forbes Field Airport before arrival of R. Reagan] A. Cockburn. map *Nation* 245:332-3 O 3 '87

New technology bomb detectors will improve airport security. J. Ott. il *Aviat Week Space Technol* 127:43-4 Ag 3 '87

Toward safer flying. D. E. Petzal. il *Field Stream* 92:22 N '87

Travel-protect your film [getting film through airport security] W. Hampton. il *Petersens Photogr Mag* 16:24+ O '87

Shutdowns

Vanishing act [general aviation airports] E. Weiner. il *Flying* 114:70-2+ Ap '87

Stores

Airport shopping. D. P. Marshall. *Travel Holiday* 167:28-31 F '87

Those airport deals aren't always a steal [duty free stores] B. Bauer. il *U S News World Rep* 102:48-9 Ap 20 '87

Traffic control

See Air traffic control

Transportation

Carless in America [airport owner lends author a car to get into town] P. Egan. il *Road Track* 39:20 N '87

California

See also
Los Angeles (Calif.)—Airports

Aviation heaven [Mojave Airport] F. Mackerodt. il *Pop Mech* 164:39 Je '87

Voyager is home for a while in Mojave's Hangar 77. il *Sunset* 178:18 My '87

Colorado

See also
Denver (Colo.)—Airports

Dubai (United Arab Emirates: Emirate)

A great place, for an hour [duty free shop] J. Barnes. il *U S News World Rep* 102:49 Ap 20 '87

Easter Island

Shuttle contingency landing site built by Chile on Easter Island. *Aviat Week Space Technol* 127:77 Ag 24 '87

Florida

See also
Miami (Fla.)—Airports
Orlando (Fla.)—Airports
Tampa (Fla.)—Airports

Georgia

See also
Atlanta (Ga.)—Airports

Great Britain

See also
London (England)—Airports

Carriers dispute British airport fees [U.S. airlines] D. A. Brown. *Aviat Week Space Technol* 126:39 F 16 '87

Illinois

See also
Chicago (Ill.)—Airports

Indiana

See also
Indianapolis (Ind.)—Airports

Japan

See also
Osaka (Japan)—Airports

Increasing Japanese traffic spurs airport construction. *Aviat Week Space Technol* 127:137 N 9 '87

Kansas

See also
Topeka (Kan.)—Airports

Massachusetts

See also
Boston (Mass.)—Airports

Morocco

New shuttle site [Trans Atlantic Abort site at Ben Gurir] *Space World* X-9-285:7 S '87

New England

Massport to cut Logan traffic, foster use of reliever airports. *Aviat Week Space Technol* 127:44 S 7 '87

Operators attack plan to stem New England commuter service [plan to divert traffic from Boston's Logan Airport to reliever airports] *Aviat Week Space Technol* 127:41+ S 7 '87

New Jersey

See also
Newark (N.J.)—Airports

New York (State)

See also
New York (N.Y.)—Airports

North Carolina

See also
Charlotte (N.C.)—Airports
Raleigh (N.C.)—Airports

Québec (Province)

See also
Montreal (Québec)—Airports

Texas

See also
Dallas (Tex.)—Airports

Airports—*cont.*
United States
See Airports
Washington (D.C.)
See Washington (D.C.)—Airports
Airship Industries, Ltd.
Airship's fortunes are suddenly afloat [contract with the U.S. Navy] M. Maremont. il *Bus Week* p52 Je 22 '87
Westinghouse-Airship joint venture wins Navy aerial surveillance contract. *Aviat Week Space Technol* 126:69 Je 15 '87
Airships
Gasbags are back. E. Weiner. *Flying* 114:78 Mr '87
Relaunching the airship. J. Barber. il *Macleans* 100:36-9 Jl 20 '87
History
See also
Hindenburg (Airship)
Piloting
Fat & happy [Airship International blimp] E. Weiner. il *Flying* 114:70-6 Mr '87
Airships in patrol work
Airship's fortunes are suddenly afloat [contract with the U.S. Navy] M. Maremont. il *Bus Week* p52 Je 22 '87
Navy may buy larger airship as surveillance platform. *Aviat Week Space Technol* 126:28 Je 29 '87
Westinghouse-Airship joint venture wins Navy aerial surveillance contract. *Aviat Week Space Technol* 126:69 Je 15 '87
Airsickness *See* Motion sickness
Airspace (International law)
See also
Korean Air Lines Flight 007 disaster, 1983
Audacious airman [M. Rust lands in Red Square] il pors map *Life* 10:66-9 Ag '87
Destination Red Square [German pilot, M. Rust, lands small plane] B. Levin. il *Macleans* 100:24 Je 8 '87
A folk hero in the slammer [M. Rust arrested after landing small plane in Red Square] N. Cooper. il por *Newsweek* 109:36 Je 15 '87
Four years for a "fun" flight [sentencing of German pilot, M. Rust, for landing plane in Moscow] W. R. Doerner. il por *Time* 130:42 S 14 '87
Gaps in Soviet defenses? [West German, M. Rust, lands plane in Moscow] R. Kaylor. il *U S News World Rep* 102:30 Je 15 '87
A hard landing in Moscow [M. Rust sentenced to 4 yrs. in Soviet labor camp] C. Redden. il por *Macleans* 100:22 S 14 '87
Joyride [M. Rust's flight to Moscow] W. F. Buckley. *Natl Rev* 39:56 Jl 17 '87
Kremlin prop wash [West German, M. Rust, lands Cessna in Red Square] W. R. Doerner. il por *Time* 129:30-2 Je 15 '87
Red faces in Red Square [West German, M. Rust, lands small plane in Moscow] N. Cooper. il por *Newsweek* 109:36 Je 8 '87
Rust's unhappy landing [sentenced to a labor camp for flying small plane into Red Square] S. Seibert. il *Newsweek* 110:49 S 14 '87
USAF, Navy track four Bear bombers in twin intercept over Alaska. il *Aviat Week Space Technol* 126:79 Je 22 '87
Welcome to Moscow [German pilot, M. Rust, lands plane in Red Square] J. Greenwald. il por *Time* 129:34-5 Je 8 '87
Airspace (Law)
FAA reports frequent violations of airspace over Reagan's ranch [near midair collision, August 13, 1987] map *Aviat Week Space Technol* 127:24-5 Ag 24 '87
Airspeeds *See* Airplanes—Speed; Airplanes, Light—Speed
Airstream trailers *See* Automobile trailers
Airways
See also
Airlines—Routes
Traffic control
See Air traffic control
Airworthiness certification of airplanes *See* Airplanes, Jet—Standards
AISC *See* American Institute of Steel Construction
Aiwa Co. Ltd.
DAT finally released [Aiwa's XD-001 DAT deck] B. Harrell. il *Stereo Rev* 52:18+ Ap '87
Aiyangar, Srinivasa Ramanujan *See* Ramanujan Aiyangar, Srinivasa, 1887-1920
Ajami, Fouad
The silence in Arab culture. *New Repub* 196:27-33 Ap 6 '87

Akers, John
Spring training at home. il *Sport Mag* 78:79-80 My '87
Akers, John F., 1934-
about
John Akers. R. Mitchell. il por *Bus Week* Sp Issue:210 Ap 17 '87
Letting the sun shine in. N. J. Perry. por *Fortune* 116:29 Ag 3 '87
Akhavi, Shahrough
Institutionalizing the new order in Iran. bibl f *Curr Hist* 86:53-6+ F '87
Akili, John-Michael
Women are the superstars [poem] *Essence* 18:122 D '87
Akinkugbe, Oladipo O.
A third world perspective. il *World Health* p24-5 Ap '87
Akira, Shizuo, and others
Two pairs of recombination signals are sufficient to cause immunoglobulin V-(D)-J joining. bibl f il *Science* 238:1134-8 N 20 '87
Akron (Ohio)
Stores
See also
West Point Market
Aksenov, Vasiliĭ Pavlovich, 1932-
Beatniks and Bolsheviks; tr. by Bess Powell. *New Repub* 197:28-30+ N 30 '87
A Soviet emigre takes the 'A' Train. il *N Y Times Mag* p60+ My 3 '87
Through the *glasnost*, darkly. *Harpers* 274:65-7 Ap '87
"We're Stateniks!" The cult of America in the U.S.S.R. [condensed from In search of melancholy baby] il *Read Dig* 131:171-2+ Ag '87
about
From Russia—with real love. J. Podhoretz. il por *U S News World Rep* 103:49-50 Ag 17 '87
Aksyonov, Vassily *See* Aksenov, Vasiliĭ Pavlovich, 1932-
Al-Adhami, Ali Naji
about
Obituary
New Repub 197:10 S 28 '87
Al-Awadi, Abdul Rahman
Meeting health needs. il *World Health* p28-9 Ag/S '87
Al-Khalifa, Ali al-Sabah *See* Al-Sabah, Ali al-Khalifa
Al-Kūfah (Iraq)
History
The city-builders of Islam. M. A. Sinaceur. bibl f il *Courier* 40:20-4 Jl '87
Al-Qaddafi, Muammar *See* Qaddafi, Muammar al-, 1942-
Al-Sabah, Ali al-Khalifa
about
Dealmaker for a dynasty. S. Tully. por *Fortune* 116:64 Ag 3 '87
Al-Sabah, Saud Nasir
about
Kuwait shies away from confronting Iran [interview] L. Lief. il *U S News World Rep* 103:40 N 2 '87
Alabama
See also
Agriculture—Alabama
Art—Alabama
Cemeteries—Alabama
Colleges and universities—Alabama
Criminal justice, Administration of—Alabama
Educational laws and regulations—Alabama
Flower gardens and gardening—Alabama
Medical care—Alabama
Police—Alabama
Antiquities
Digging for the past [excavations at Cahawba] il map *Natl Geogr World* 144:19-23 Ag '87
Race relations
Ala. cabinet member and governor apologize for racial, ethnic slurs [remarks directed against A. Holmes] por *Jet* 72:32 Jl 20 '87
Alabama Shakespeare Festival
A home for Shakespeare in Alabama. J. T. Black. il *South Living* 22:164-9 Ap '87
Alaïa, Azzedine
about
The defiant ones. D. Drier. il pors *Art Am* 75:47-9+ S '87
Alamo (San Antonio, Tex.)
Empty tomb honors Alamo heroes [Alamo Cenotaph] il *South Living* 22:20-1 Je '87

Alamo (San Antonio, Tex.) in art
Exhibitions
Eleven artists paint the same location [exhibit at the San Antonio Museum of Art] M. S. Doherty. il *Am Artist* 51:30-41 F '87
Alan, Ray
Down among the backwoodsmen. *New Leader* 70:8-9 O 5 '87
The long march of the Prince of Wales. il por *New Leader* 70:10-12 Ja 12-26 '87
Mining the spy world. il *New Leader* 70:9-11 N 16 '87
Niceness (seasonally adjusted) is all. *New Leader* 70:8-9 Ap 6 '87
Alanine
α₂-antiplasmin Enschede: alanine insertion and abolition of plasmin inhibitory activity. W. E. Holmes and others. bibl f il *Science* 238:209-11 O 9 '87
D-alanine in the frog skin peptide dermorphin is derived from L-alanine in the precursor. K. Richter and others. bibl f il *Science* 238:200-2 O 9 '87
Alar (Chemical) *See* Daminozide
Alarm air launched antiradiation missiles *See* Guided missiles—Launching from airplanes
Alarm industry *See* Electronic industries
Alarms
See also
ADT, Inc.
Automobiles—Alarms
Freezers—Alarms
Burglarproofing. *Changing Times* 41:12-13 My '87
Cop in a box—and other clever ways to chase away crooks. G. B. Latamore. il *Pop Sci* 230:68-70 Ap '87
Digital arming switch [remote alarm system switch] D. Petraglia. il *Pop Sci* 230:127 F '87
High-tech, low-cost electronic home security: three systems, each less than $350. D. S. Johnson. il *Better Homes Gard* 65:89 Mr '87
Notes and comment [buying a burglar alarm after moving out of Mafia-protected neighborhood in New York City] *New Yorker* 63:21-2 Ag 31 '87
Protect your home with an alarm system. G. S. Burdick. il *Consum Res Mag* 70:22-5 Ag '87
Smart security systems: matching wits with burglars. G. Williams. bibl il *Home Mech* 83:28-30+ N '87
To catch a thief. E. Paris. il *Forbes* 140:92-3 Ag 24 '87
Alaska
See also
Aleutian Islands (Alaska)
Augustine Volcano (Augustine Island, Alaska)
Aviation—Alaska
Bering Sea
Copper mines and mining—Alaska
Denali National Park and Preserve (Alaska)
Eskimos
Fishing—Alaska
Gas pipelines—Alaska
Haines (Alaska)
Hunting—Alaska
Indians of North America—Alaska
Kennecott (Alaska)
Ketchikan (Alaska)
Paleontology—Alaska
Petroleum—Alaska
Railroads—Alaska
Sitka region (Alaska)
Water pollution—Alaska
Wildlife—Alaska
Wildlife sanctuaries—Alaska
Wrangell Island (Alaska)
Yukon Territory
Climate
Alaskan weather. D. M. Ludlum. See issues of *Weatherwise*
Economic conditions
In Alaska: boom times yield to a bitter bust. P. A. Witteman. il *Time* 129:18 Mr 30 '87
Industries
See also
Gold mines and mining—Alaska
Zinc mines and mining—Alaska
Alaska Air Group Inc.
Alaska Air Group breaks up Jet America. *Aviat Week Space Technol* 127:34 Ag 24 '87
Alaska Air: is it California dreamin'? J. B. Levine. il por *Bus Week* p150 N 30 '87
Alaska Airlines, Inc.
See also
Alaska Air Group Inc.

Alaskan brown bear hunting *See* Bear hunting
Alastair Little (London, England: Restaurant) *See* London (England)—Restaurants, nightclubs, bars, etc.
Alaton, Kalef
about
Virtues of nuance. M. Ennis. il *Archit Dig* 44:62-9 F '87
Albacore
See also
Cooking—Fish
Albakaye, Mohammed Ag
about
Out of Africa with Diane Sawyer. M. G. Stoddard. il pors *Saturday Evening Post* 259:52-4+ Ap '87
Albania
See also
Albanians
Politics and government
Albania peeks out, never forgetting 'life is earnest'. R. Knight. il map *U S News World Rep* 102:36 My 11 '87
Religious institutions and affairs
Where religion has disappeared. S. Mumper. il por *Christ Today* 31:50+ S 4 '87
Albanians
Yugoslavia
Yugoslavia's national question. J. H. Wolfe. il *USA Today (Periodical)* 116:51 S '87
Albany (N.Y.)
Galleries and museums
See also
New York State Museum
Albany State College (Ga.)
White professor wins reverse bias law suit against black college [D. Voiku wins case] *Jet* 72:32 Ap 20 '87
Albarelli, Dean
Midnight mass. il *Seventeen* 46:100-1 D '87
Albatrosses
Paint chips and albatross chicks [Laysan albatrosses poisoned from eating paint chips] G. S. Grant. il *Sea Front* 33:270-2 Jl/Ag '87
Restarting the wandering gooneys [Laysan albatrosses returned to Midway Island after resting at Oakland Rotary Wildlife Center, San Francisco, Calif.] R. Carino. il *Sea Front* 33:42-5 Ja/F '87
Albee, George W.
A country wok; ed. by Margaret Tong. il *Ctry J* 14:26-31 F '87
Alben, Alexander
The Indian ordeal. il *N Y Times Mag* p78 Mr 8 '87
Albero d'Oro (New York, N.Y.: Restaurant) *See* New York (N.Y.)—Restaurants, nightclubs, bars, etc.
Alberola, Jean-Michel, 1953-
about
Jean Michel Alberola: Daniel Templon. R. T. Bellido. il *Art News* 86:172 D '87
Albers, Hans
about
Clean desk on the Rhine. L. S. Richman. il por *Fortune* 116:50-1 Ag 3 '87
Albers, Harold
about
This doctor is for the birds [cover story] E. Boddie. il pors *50 Plus* 27:20-4 Jl '87
Albert, Laura
What do you do with a baby? il *Parents* 62:156-7 N '87
Albert, Morris
about
More than Feelings. il por *Time* 130:37 Ag 10 '87
Albert and Mary Lasker Foundation
Behavioral, DNA workers win Laskers. D. D. Edwards. il *Sci News* 132:198 S 26 '87
Albert Nipon, Inc.
Pearl picks up the pieces. M. Rowland. il pors *Work Woman* 12:114-17 My '87
Albert Schweitzer Music Award
Magical maestro [L. Bernstein] G. D. Boone. il por *Horizon* 30:2 Je '87
Alberta
See also
Bassano Dam (Alta.)
Calgary (Alta.)
Edmonton (Alta.)
Environmental movement—Alberta
Irrigation—Alberta
Jasper National Park (Alta.)
Paleontology—Alberta
Resorts—Alberta
Skis and skiing—Alberta
Trials—Alberta

Alberta—See also—*cont.*
Waterton-Glacier International Peace Park (Alta. and Mont.)

Description and travel
In the tracks of the Olympians. il map *Sunset* 179:50+ D '87

Politics and government
Alberta's part-time premier [D. Getty] J. Howse. il por *Macleans* 100:12 Mr 9 '87
Blitzing the West [visit by Brian Mulroney and Cabinet] M. Clark. il *Macleans* 100:12 Jl 20 '87
A dissident is shut out [Alberta Tory MP D. Kilgour disciplined for comments about lack of party commitment to the West] por *Macleans* 100:13 Ap 20 '87

Alberta Ballet Company
Alberta Ballet is 20. M. Crabb. *Dance Mag* 61:10-11 Mr '87

Alberto-Culver Co.
An acid test for antitakeover laws [Minnesota law could help Alberto-Culver land Lamaur] M. J. Pitzer. il *Bus Week* p31 S 28 '87
Alberto's A's and B's [stock price] T. Jaffe. *Forbes* 140:218 O 19 '87

Albrecht, Donna G.
When picketing pays. il *Ms* 16:91 N '87

Albrecht, Ulrich
Revive the Reykjavik dynamism. il *Bull At Sci* 43:40-1 Mr '87

Albright, David
Pakistan's bomb-making capacity. bibl f il *Bull At Sci* 43:30-3 Je '87

Albright, David, and Feiveson, Harold A.
Plutonium recycling [discussion of March 27, 1987 article, Why recycle plutonium?] *Science* 237:707-8 Ag 14 '87
Why recycle plutonium? bibl f il *Science* 235:1555-6 Mr 27 '87

Albright, Horace Marden
Horace M. Albright: in memoriam [excerpt from The National Park Service] il *Natl Parks* 61:46-7 Jl/Ag '87
about
Obituary
Natl Parks 61:5 My/Je '87. S. M. McPherson

Albright, Robert L.
The clarion call [address, January 7-8, 1987] *Vital Speeches Day* 53:297-305 Mr 1 '87

Albright, Tenley
about
Guts and gold. W. Bingham. il pors *Sports Illus* 67:57+ O 19 '87

Album covers, Phonograph record *See* Phonograph record covers

Albumins
Yeast KEX2 protease has the properties of a human proalbumin converting enzyme. I. C. Bathurst and others. bibl f il *Science* 235:348-50 Ja 16 '87

Albums
See also
Photograph albums

Albuquerque (N.M.)
Arts
Albuquerque [special section] il *Horizon* 30:25-38+ O '87

Bookstores
See Booksellers and bookselling—New Mexico

Description
Albuquerque [special section] il *Horizon* 30:25-38+ O '87

Employees
Black 'over qualified' for job sues Albuquerque, N.M. [H. Bailey] *Jet* 72:39 Mr 30 '87

Galleries and museums
See also
Albuquerque Museum

Music
See also
Albuquerque Civic Light Opera Association
Opera SouthWest

Theater
See also
La Compañia de Teatro de Albuquerque

Albuquerque Civic Light Opera Association
The hum of success. G. Chow. il *Horizon* 30:28 O '87

Albuquerque Museum
A policy of progress. N. D'Ambrosio. il *Horizon* 30:30 O '87

ALC Communications Corporation
This merger has a long way to go. K. Dreyfack. il *Bus Week* p153 Mr 23 '87

Alcalay, Glenn
Connecting the dots on the map. il *Nation* 245:84-7 Ag 1-8 '87

Alcatraz Island (Calif.)
See also
Birds—Alcatraz Island (Calif.)

Alceste [opera] See Gluck, Christoph Willibald, Ritter von, 1714-1787

Alcibiades, ca. 450-404 B.C.
about
A patriot for whom? Alcibiades of Athens. P. Cartledge. bibl il por *Hist Today* 37:15-19 O '87

Alcina [opera] See Handel, George Frideric, 1685-1759

Alcindor, Lew See Abdul-Jabbar, Kareem, 1947-

Alcoa See Aluminum Co. of America

Alcohol
See also
Drinking customs
Prohibition

Physiological effects
See also
Alcohol antagonists
Blood—Alcohol content
Alcohol and disease. il *World Health* p30 Je '87
Body heat boosts alcohol's effects. il *Prevention* 39:6 Ja '87
Hangovers: tips before you toast. D. Webb. *McCalls* 114:105 Ja '87
Lipid takes a stand against alcohol [phosphatidylinositol; research by Theodore F. Taraschi and others] D. D. Edwards. *Sci News* 131:38-9 Ja 17 '87
Make mine OJ [alcohol consumption and vitamin C; research by Vincent G. Zannoni and Robert Susick] il *Prevention* 39:10 D '87
Small molecule, large effects. K. McAuliffe. il *U S News World Rep* 103:60-1 N 30 '87
Stewed to the eyeballs [eyelyzer alcohol measurement test invented by Gwynne Giles] il *Discover* 8:14 D '87
To drink, or not to drink? H. Fisher. il *Prevention* 39:99+ N '87
Understanding alcohol [cover story] S. Goodman. bibl il *Curr Health 2* 14:3-9 N '87

Psychological effects
Alcohol use and great expectations [research by G. Alan Marlatt] *Sci News* 132:218 O 3 '87
Facing up to booze [drinking impairs ability to interpret facial expressions; research by J. Borrill] G. Lowe. *Psychol Today* 21:23 S '87

Alcohol and air pilots
Bottle to throttle. *Sci Am* 256:86 F '87
Hung over. R. L. Collins. il *Flying* 114:20 Ap '87

Alcohol and authors
F. Scott Fitzgerald's little drinking problem. J. M. Irwin. *Am Sch* 56:415+ Summ '87

Alcohol and automobile drivers
See also
Mothers Against Drunk Driving
Curbing teens' number one killer. il *Curr Health 2* 14:24-6 O '87
Every 27 minutes . . . L. Weltner. il *Read Dig* 130:136-8 F '87
Gordon detained by French police on 1967 DUI charge [D. Gordon] por *Jet* 72:57 Jl 20 '87
Has the backlash had a sobering effect? A. Heil. il *Seventeen* 46:162-3+ My '87
The menace on the roads. A. Press. il *Newsweek* 110:42-3 D 21 '87
Michael Spinks wrecks car, faces DUI charge. *Jet* 72:46 Ap 6 '87
One more for the road [anti-drunk driving ads] il *Read Dig* 130:113-15 Je '87
Passing up one for the road [intoxication tests] E. Henry. *Changing Times* 41:112-13 My '87
Pennsylvania gothic [death of K. Umstadter in alcohol-related traffic accident results in her brother's murdering of driver in Honesdale] G. Hackett. il por *Newsweek* 110:27 Ag 17 '87
Primed to kill, an angry young man shoots his dead sister's boyfriend, leaving two families in ruins [T. Umstadter kills G. Evans] J. Hammer. il *People Wkly* 28:159-60+ N 16 '87
Putting the brakes on drunk driving. W. White. il *Teen* 31:22+ Mr '87
What should we do with drunk drivers? J. R. Nerad. *Mot Trend* 39:166 My '87
Why I defend guilty clients. B. Winston. il *Read Dig* 130:81-4 My '87
"You can't do this to me . . ." [weak drunk driving laws in Texas] G. Baxter. il *Car Driv* 33:28 D '87

Alcohol and boating
A few too many on the water. E. Williams. il *Newsweek* 110:22 Ag 3 '87

Alcohol and congressmen
The presence of malice [rumors concerning Senator D. P. Moynihan] G. F. Will. il *Newsweek* 110:106 D 7 '87

Alcohol and employment
A promise of renewal [film industry worker] D. B. Smith. il *N Y Times Mag* p52 F 15 '87
Walking the fine line at holiday office parties [employer liability for alcohol-related damages] L. J. Moore. il *U S News World Rep* 103:75 D 21 '87

Alcohol and Indians (American)
A girl's anger rouses her kinfolk from an alcoholic daze [work of Shuswap Indians A. and P. Chelsea in Alkali Lake, B.C.] M. Green. il pors *People Wkly* 27:83-4 Ja 26 '87

Alcohol and sports
The NHL's alcohol problem. R. Friedman. il *Sport Mag* 78:13 N '87

Alcohol and the aged
Alcohol: how much is too much? W. A. Nolen. il *50 Plus* 27:82+ Mr '87

Alcohol and women
See also
Women for Sobriety
Alcohol alert. *Vogue* 177:368 Ag '87
Alcohol-breast cancer link. D. D. Edwards. *Sci News* 131:292 My 9 '87
Betty Ford's brave mission. E. Sherman. il pors *Ladies Home J* 104:80+ Je '87
"Boy, could I use a . . ." (a) drink, (b) pill, (c) joint. If you filled in the blank you could be a preaddict. W. Gallagher. *Mademoiselle* 93:210-11+ O '87
Breast cancer & alcohol. B. Weinhouse. *Ladies Home J* 104:58+ Ag '87
The day my family saved my life [excerpt from Betty]; ed. by Chris Chase. B. Ford. il pors *Good Housekeep* 204:132-3+ F '87
Does alcohol increase risk of breast cancer? . . . J. Kaplan. *Vogue* 177:174 N '87
Drinker's dilemma [alcohol may raise risk of breast cancer] J. D. Schwartz. il *Health* 19:24 O '87
Drinking. L. Van Gelder. il *Ms* 15:38 F '87
Drinking and breast cancer. *Newsweek* 109:73 My 18 '87
Female trouble [alcohol-breast cancer link] *Sci Am* 257:24+ Jl '87
Frank as ever, former First Lady Betty Ford describes her harrowing years of addiction. A. Chambers. il pors *People Wkly* 27:88-9+ Mr 9 '87
From only one drink a week? [alcohol may trigger breast cancer] J. Silberner. il *U S News World Rep* 102:64-5 My 18 '87
How strong is the alcohol/breast cancer link? il *Glamour* 85:86 O '87
'I'm one drink away from a drunk' [interview with N. Robertson] B. Brophy. il por *U S News World Rep* 103:63 N 30 '87
"My husband wouldn't give up on me" [J. Breckenridge's story] L. Crane. il pors *Good Housekeep* 205:74+ Ag '87
The new breast-cancer scare—should you say no to alcohol? E. R. Shell. il *Mademoiselle* 93:112 Ag '87
Should women drink less? [alcohol consumption linked to breast cancer] M. D. Lemonick. il *Time* 129:66 My 18 '87
You can't drink like a man—the latest word on women and alcohol. J. M. Toal. il *Mademoiselle* 93:104+ My '87

Alcohol and youth
See also
Project 714 (Organization)
Alcoholism: yes, it can happen to you. D. Hymes. il *Curr Health 2* 13:18-21 F '87
Are wine coolers leading kids to drink? E. Ehrlich. il *Bus Week* p38 O 26 '87
Campus report: is there a drinker in the house? [Wellesley's Alcohol Informational Theater] K. FitzGerald. il *Ms* 15:30 F '87
Curbing teens' number one killer. il *Curr Health 2* 14:24-6 O '87
Drinking, drugs and kids: what to say. L. Salk. il *McCalls* 115:65 O '87
Drug abuse: who says it can't happen to your kid? M. O'Connell-Cahill. il *U S Cathol* 52:20-5 O '87
Frothing anti-drink forces set out to nip Spuds in the Bud [objections to Spuds MacKenzie's appeal to children] il *People Wkly* 28:87 O 26 '87

Has the backlash had a sobering effect? A. Heil. il *Seventeen* 46:162-3+ My '87
Kids can be drink and drug free. il *Parents* 62:22 O '87
The law and youth substance abuse [American Bar Association report] il *Child Today* 16:4 Ja/F '87
My brother is an alcoholic. D. Madison. il *Seventeen* 46:174-5 Mr '87
One more for the road [anti-drunk driving ads] il *Read Dig* 130:113-15 Je '87
Pennsylvania gothic [death of K. Umstadter in alcohol-related traffic accident results in her brother's murdering of driver in Honesdale] G. Hackett. il por *Newsweek* 110:27 Ag 17 '87
Primed to kill, an angry young man shoots his dead sister's boyfriend, leaving two families in ruins [T. Umstadter kills G. Evans] J. Hammer. il *People Wkly* 28:159-60+ N 16 '87
Putting the brakes on drunk driving. W. White. il *Teen* 31:22+ Mr '87
Understanding alcohol [cover story] S. Goodman. bibl il *Curr Health 2* 14:3-9 N '87

Alcohol antagonists
Booze blocker [Ro15-4513; research by Steven M. Paul and others] G. Lowe. *Psychol Today* 21:12 Je '87
Seizures in drug-treated animals [discussion of December 5, 1986 article, A selective imidazobenzodiazepine antagonist of ethanol in the rat (Ro15-4513)] P. D. Suzdak and others. bibl f *Science* 235:1127-8 Mr 6 '87

Alcohol as fuel
Alcohol fuels move off the back burner. M. Ivey. il *Bus Week* p100-1 Je 29 '87
Anatomy of a rip-off [Archer-Daniels-Midland profiting from government agricultural subsidies and gasohol program] J. A. Barnes. *New Repub* 197:20-1 N 2 '87
Gas pains [boats] B. Stearns. il *Field Stream* 92:89-90 O '87
Some dare call them . . . robber barons [government agricultural subsidies and gasohol program] M. Fumento. il *Natl Rev* 39:32-3+ Mr 13 '87
Test for alcohol in gasoline? il *Consum Rep* 52:194 Ap '87

Alcohol in chocolate *See* Chocolate
Alcohol use by animals *See* Animals—Habits and behavior
Alcoholic beverages
See also
Beer
Cocktails
Liqueurs
Wine
Wine coolers
Creating a lavish holiday party. E. Fried. il *Black Enterp* 18:106-8+ D '87
Here's to the private reserve. il *Esquire* 108:194-5 D '87
The hot and cold of it. J. F. Mariani. il *Mot Boat Sail* 159:30 F '87
Party hearty without getting drunk. J. Friedrich. il *Mademoiselle* 93:296 Mr '87
The thinking woman's drinking guide. il *Glamour* 85:200-3 Ja '87

Contamination
Water, water everywhere, but . . . [urethane] S. Weiss. *Sci News* 132:390-1 D 19-26 '87
Prices
High and mighty [prices of drinks on airlines] W. G. Flanagan. il *Forbes* 140:104+ Ag 24 '87

Alcoholics and alcoholism
See also
Alcohol—Physiological effects
Alcohol—Psychological effects
Children of alcoholics
Alcohol and free will. R. Wright. *New Repub* 197:14-16 D 14 '87
Coming to grips with alcoholism [cover story; special section] il *U S News World Rep* 103:56-63 N 30 '87
How much do you know about alcohol? [quiz] H. Manley. *Good Housekeep* 205:185 Ag '87
Out in the open [cover story] E. W. Desmond. il *Time* 130:80-6+ N 30 '87

Genetic aspects
Neurogenetic adaptive mechanisms in alcoholism. C. R. Cloninger. bibl f il *Science* 236:410-16 Ap 24 '87
Reactions to alcohol: cortisol clues [research by Marc A. Schuckit] B. Bower. *Sci News* 132:324 N 21 '87
History
The geography of drinking. C. J. Smith. il map *Focus* 36:16-23 Wint '86

Alcoholics and alcoholism—*cont.*
Legal aspects
The Deaver defense: the drink made me do it. D. Baer. il *por U S News World Rep* 103:60 N 2 '87
Is alcoholism a disease? [case of Eugene Traynor and James P. McKelvey vs. the Veterans Administration] C. Holden. *Science* 238:1647 D 18 '87
Pondering a high-proof defense [M. Deaver's alcoholism used as legal defense] A. Wilentz. il *por Time* 130:60 N 2 '87
Rehabilitation
See Alcoholics and alcoholism—Therapy
Research
It's about time. G. Bronson. il *Forbes* 140:92-3 Jl 27 '87
Therapy
See also
> Alcohol antagonists
> Alcoholics Anonymous
> Health Concepts IV Inc.
> Women for Sobriety

Alcoholism and the medical cost crunch. C. Holden. il *Science* 235:1132-3 Mr 6 '87
Alcoholism treatment [discussion of April 3, 1987 article, Is alcoholism treatment effective?] C. Holden. *Science* 237:1094 S 4 '87
Antidepressants may curb addictions. *Prevention* 39:60 O '87
Is alcoholism treatment effective? C. Holden. il *Science* 236:20-2 Ap 3 '87
The long road back. S. Begley. il *Newsweek* 109:66 My 11 '87
Sobering facts on rehab. R. Phalon. il *Forbes* 139:140+ Mr 9 '87
Soviet Union
War on Soviet alcoholism. N. Morris. il *Macleans* 100:48 Ja 19 '87
Alcoholics Anonymous
A humanist alternative to A.A.'s twelve steps. B. F. Skinner. *Humanist* 47:5 Jl/Ag '87
'I'm one drink away from a drunk' [interview with N. Robertson] B. Brophy. il *por U S News World Rep* 103:63 N 30 '87
Alcoholics' families
Alcoholics: there's no place like home [difference between marriages of in-home and out-of-home drinkers; research by Nancy Jo Dunn] B. L. Benderly. *Psychol Today* 21:22 O '87
'The hand that rocks the cradle . . . '. G. G. Seibert. *America* 157:343 N 7 '87
"My husband wouldn't give up on me" [J. Breckenridge's story] L. Crane. il *pors Good Housekeep* 205:74+ Ag '87
"We have a problem". J. Marks. il *Parents* 62:78+ Mr '87
Alcoholism *See* Alcoholics and alcoholism
Alcohols
See also
> Glycerol
> Glycols
> Mannitol

Alcorn, Janis B.
(jt. auth) *See* Oldfield, Margery L., and Alcorn, Janis B.
Alcorn, Sam
On safari in New Jersey. il *Travel Holiday* 167:34-5 F '87
Pigeon Island. il *Travel Holiday* 167:14+ Je '87
Where Edison brought good things to life. il *Travel Holiday* 168:32-4 Ag '87
Alcoves
Alcove built-ins. A. Hontoir. il *Workbench* 43:77-80 N/D '87
Elegant alcove built-ins. A. W. Lees. il *Pop Sci* 231:88-90 S '87
Fireplace seating and storage. il *Sunset* 178:146 My '87
ALD (Disease)
Nutritional aspects
They won't let their son die [Odone family] J. Adler. il *Newsweek* 110:98-100 N 16 '87
Aldersey-Williams, Hugh
Exhibition report: New architecture: Foster, Rogers, Stirling. *Archit Rec* 175:73+ Mr '87
Aldrich Museum of Contemporary Art (Ridgefield, Conn.)
Started on a whim. C. Giuliano. il *Art News* 86:32+ S '87
Aldridge, Edward C.
Space and national strategy [address, May 15, 1987] *Vital Speeches Day* 53:614-16 Ag 1 '87

Aldrin, Buzz *See* Aldrin, Edwin E.
Aldrin, Edwin E.
(jt. auth) *See* Armstrong, Neil, 1930-, and Aldrin, Edwin E.
about
The Martian Metro. F. Braun and O. Davies. il *Omni* 10:52-4+ N '87
Aldus Corporation
Desktop publishing challenges. R. A. Shaffer. il *Pers Comput* 11:59 D '87
How two pioneers brought publishing to the desktop [J. E. Warnock and P. Brainerd] K. M. Hafner. il *pors Bus Week* p61-2 O 5 '87
Alechinsky, Pierre, 1927-
about
Alechinsky's realm: the artist's house and studios near Paris. D. Sylvester. il *pors Archit Dig* 44:138-43+ Mr '87
Heir heads. K. Larson. il *N Y* 20:94-5 Mr 30 '87
Alecto Historical Editions
High-tech printing techniques create an 'elaborately forged' Domesday book. S. D. Bell. il *Publ Wkly* 231:50-2 Ap 17 '87
Alegre family
about
That California rumble is no quake: it's only the Alegre family, all tanked up and out for a drive. il *People Wkly* 27:43 Ja 26 '87
Alejandro, Leandro, d. 1987
about
Leandro Alejandro: victim of militarism. D. Friesen. *Christ Century* 104:877-8 O 14 '87
Alertness *See* Attention
Aleshire, Joan
Marcus Aurelius [poem] *Am Sch* 56:330 Summ '87
To Charlotte Brontë [poem] *Am Sch* 56:576 Aut '87
Alessandra, Anthony J.
(jt. auth) *See* Hunsaker, Phillip L., and Alessandra, Anthony J.
Aletti, Vince
Chuck Berry tells all—sort of. il *pors Roll Stone* p71-2+ D 3 '87
Aleutian Islands (Alaska)
See also
> Lighthouses—Aleutian Islands (Alaska)
> Volcanoes—Aleutian Islands (Alaska)
Exploring expeditions
A Russian on the coast of Alaska [excerpt from Peregrinations of the Russian merchant Grigori Shelikhov from Okhotsk to the coasts of America by the Eastern Ocean] G. I. Shelekhov. il *Courier* 40:13-14 Ap '87
Alex (Fictional character)
Alex on today's youth: creeching goloses and filthy toofles! A. Burgess. il *N Y Times Book Rev* 92:7+ My 31 '87
Alexander, Benjamin H.
Before you lambast this generation [address, October 19, 1987] *Vital Speeches Day* 54:70-2 N 15 '87
Why be ugly when you can be beautiful [address, December 7, 1986] *Vital Speeches Day* 53:202-4 Ja 15 '87
Alexander, Brooks
Theology from the Twilight Zone. il *por Christ Today* 31:22-6 S 18 '87
Alexander, Bryan
A beast for all seasons [photographs] il *map Int Wildl* 17:44-51 My/Je '87
Alexander, Caroline
The North Borneo Expedition of 1981. *map New Yorker* 63:39-44+ S 14 '87
Alexander, Christopher, and others
Toward a personal workplace. il *Archit Rec* 175:130-41 mid-S '87
Alexander, Clifford
about
Ex-Army boss to examine baseball's plan for action. *por Jet* 72:46 Je 29 '87
Former Army Secretary and woman scientist try to change baseball image. il *pors Jet* 73:50-1 N 9 '87
Alexander, Cyrus
about
S.C. State, UAPB name new men's basketball coaches. *Jet* 72:51 Ap 27 '87
Alexander, David
Rajesh Bedi's indelible India. il *por Int Wildl* 17:52-9 Mr/Ap '87
Alexander, Dorothy, 1904-1986
about
Obituary
> *Dance Mag por* 61:98-100 Mr '87. D. Hering

Alexander, E. Porter
With Lee at Appomattox [cover story] il pors map *Am Hist Illus* 22:40-5+ S '87
Alexander, Erika
about
A star is bored. J. Sherman. il por *Vogue* 177:72 D '87
Alexander, Franklin
Painting skin the color of life. il *Am Artist* 51:66-70 Mr '87
Alexander, Jeffrey C.
Constructing scandal. *New Repub* 196:18+ Je 8 '87
Personal politics. *New Repub* 196:12-13 Ap 6 '87
Alexander, Jonathan
The making of the Age of Chivalry. il *Hist Today* 37:3-11 N '87
Alexander, Lamar
National Governors' Association report on education reform. *Educ Dig* 52:2-5 Ap '87
Alexander, Mary, and others
Nailing the consumer. il *Consum Res Mag* 70:26-9 Mr '87
Alexander, Pamela, 1948-
Acuity [poem] il *Atlantic* 260:42 Ag '87
Alexander, Roberta
about
Roberta Alexander. J. W. Freeman. por *Stereo Rev* 52:113 My '87
Alexander, Sherry
The dream that grew in our garden. il *Good Housekeep* 204:58 Mr '87
Alexander, Stanford J., 1928-
about
Real estate profits in Houston? Yes, in Houston. J. E. Davis. il por *Bus Week* p178 D 28 '87-Ja 4 '88
Alexander & Alexander Services Inc.
Follow the leader. J. Andresky. il *Forbes* 139:40-1 Je 29 '87
Alexander & Baldwin, Inc.
A Hawaiian stock's eternal summer. G. G. Marcial. *Bus Week* p148 S 14 '87
Alexander Doll Company
A doll's house. K. Healy. il por *Forbes* 140:120 D 28 '87
Alexandre, Laurien
Inciting the Libyans. *Nation* 244:850 Je 20 '87
Alexandria (La.)
Architecture
Acadian in spirit. L. Hallam. il *South Living* 22:182-4 N '87
A sense of home in Louisiana. L. Hallam. il *South Living* 22:72-5 F '87
Alexandria (Va.)
Education
Teachers fight for control of their own profession [School Improvement Project] P. Welsh. *Educ Dig* 53:18-21 S '87
Monuments, statues, etc.
Readymade ruins [Promenade classique, A. and P. Poirier's outdoor sculpture installation] A. Thorson. il *Art News* 86:32-3 F '87
Alexis, Kim
about
Here comes Kim! H. Herman. por *Health* 19:37+ O '87
ALF (Fictional character)
Most marketable monster. N. Gunther. il *Channels* 7:15-16 N '87
ALF [television program] See Television program reviews—Single works
Alfa Romeo (Automobile) See Automobiles, Foreign
Alfa Romeo SpA
Ford bids again, Fiat gets the nod [Fiat outbids Ford for Alfa Romeo] P. Lienert. *Road Track* 38:100 F '87
New vroom [Alfa Romeo tackles U.S. market] P. Berman. il *Forbes* 139:79 Ja 26 '87
Alfano, Franco, 1876-1954
about
The man Turandot finished. P. G. Davis. il por *Opera News* 51:14-17 Mr 28 '87
Alfaro, Luis Felipe Neri de
about
Splendid sanctuary. J. Richardson. il *House Gard* 159:104-7+ D '87
Alfin Fragrances, Inc.
Think twice before turning up your nose at Alfin [stock price] G. G. Marcial. il *Bus Week* p98 S 28 '87
Was Alfin's beauty only skin-deep? [Glycel skin care line] C. Power. il *Bus Week* p62-3 Ja 19 '87

Alfonsín, Raúl
about
Aftershock of the dirty war. H. Anderson. il por *Newsweek* 109:38-9 Ap 27 '87
Argentina's mixed blessing. H. Anderson. il por *Newsweek* 109:36 My 4 '87
Argentine democracy: sign of contradiction. *America* 156:374-5 My 9 '87
"Democracy is not negotiable". J. Smolowe. il por *Time* 129:39 Ap 27 '87
The dirty war's dirty laundry. F. Willey. il por *Newsweek* 109:40 F 23 '87
Facing down the army. A. McLeod. il por *Macleans* 100:31-2 My 4 '87
Fallout after a military mutiny. J. Greenwald. il *Time* 129:40 My 4 '87
Familiar tune. il por *Time* 130:114 O 26 '87
Fitting justice to reality. J. De Onis. il *U S News World Rep* 102:38 Ja 26 '87
Out of victory, defeat; or How to satisfy the generals. C. A. Robbins. il por *U S News World Rep* 102:33 Je 15 '87
Readjusting to democracy in Argentina. G. W. Wynia. bibl f *Curr Hist* 86:5-8+ Ja '87
A talk with Alfonsin: 'the debt cannot be paid'. J. Ryser and R. A. Kessler. por *Bus Week* p66 Je 22 '87
Time out or time's up. P. Lacefield. *Commonweal* 114:375-7 Je 19 '87
Torturers saved by the bell, almost. D. L. Boroughs. il *Progressive* 51:13 Ap '87
Alford, Steve
about
That championship touch. A. Wolff. il pors *Sports Illus* 66:36-8 Ap 13 '87
Alfred A. Knopf, Inc.
Album of the Knopfs. S. Kauffmann. *Am Sch* 56:371-81 Summ '87
Gottlieb to leave Knopf for New Yorker. por *Publ Wkly* 231:20 Ja 23 '87
The heart of the Mehta [A. S. Mehta appointed editor and president] R. Koenig. il *N Y* 20:23 Mr 2 '87
Masson loses libel suit against 'New Yorker,' Malcolm and Knopf. M. Colin. *Publ Wkly* 232:11 S 4 '87
Sonny Mehta named president of Knopf. M. Reuter. por *Publ Wkly* 231:289 Ja 30 '87
Alfvén waves
The Jupiter-Io connection: an Alfvén engine in space. J. W. Belcher. bibl f il *Science* 238:170-6 O 9 '87
A new light on auroras [cause of long-duration auroras; research by Bruce T. Tsurutani and Walter D. Gonzalez] il *Sky Telesc* 74:344-5 O '87
A new source of power to drive the aurora [research by Bruce Tsurutani and Walter Gonzalez] R. A. Kerr. il *Science* 237:974 Ag 28 '87
Algae
See also
Dinoflagellates
Kelp
Lichens
Plankton
Red tide
Seaweed
Stromatolites
Water bloom
Coralline algae: pink plants of the seafloor. H. W. Johansen. il *Sea Front* 33:438-43 N/D '87
Food production in low-nutrient seas. W. H. Adey. bibl f il *BioScience* 37:340-8 My '87
Not-so-naked ancestors [electron microscope study of naked algae] G. McFadden. il *Sea Front* 33:46-51 Ja/F '87
Valonia. P. V. Chetirkin. il *Sea Front* 33:256-8 Jl/Ag '87
Algae, Fossil
See also
Stromatolites
Algal bloom See Water bloom
Algañaraz, Julio
The Italian miracle begins underground. *World Press Rev* 34:50-1 Je '87
Algebra
See also
Algorithms
Equations
Permutations
Algebra and the differential gear. A. Bass. il *Technol Rev* 90:56 Ap '87
Alger, Frederick Moulton
about
Fred Alger is high on the 'one-world' economy. G. G. Marcial. il por *Bus Week* p83 Ja 19 '87

Alger, Frederick Moulton—about—cont.
Live and learn. D. Machan. il por *Forbes* 140:135 S
7 '87

Alger, Horatio, 1832-1899
about
Horatio Alger: creator of the American success story.
J. Gustaitis. por *Am Hist Illus* 22:36-7 O '87

Alger (Fred) Management Inc. *See* Fred Alger Management
Inc.

Algeria
See also
Medical care—Algeria
Description and travel
See also
Automobile touring—Algeria
Foreign relations
Morocco
See also
Western Sahara conflict, 1975-

Algonquin (New York, N.Y.: Hotel) *See* New York (N.Y.)—
Hotels, motels, etc.

Algorithms
See also
Linear programming
Algopuzzles: wherein trains of thought follow algorithmic
tracks to solutions. A. K. Dewdney. il *Sci Am*
256:128-31 Je '87
Computer-aided routing of printed circuit boards [Lee's
Algorithm] S. E. Belter. bibl il *Byte* 12:199-200+ Je
'87
A fast CRC [XMODEM cyclic redundancy check al-
gorithm] J. LeVan. bibl il *Byte* 12:339-41 N '87
Focus on algorithms. D. Pountain. See issues of Byte
beginning June 1987
Fourier transformation. *Sci Am* 257:26+ Jl '87
Heuristic algorithms [special section] il *Byte* 12:147-52+
O '87
Introduction to image processing algorithms. B. M.
Dawson. bibl il *Byte* 12:169-70+ Mr '87
Netting a better sales route [elastic net algorithm; work
of Richard Durbin and David Willshaw] I. Peterson.
Sci News 131:262 Ap 25 '87
Observation of phase transitions in spreading activation
networks. J. Shrager and others. bibl f il *Science*
236:1092-4 My 29 '87
Once more through the Sieve [Sieve of Eratosthenes
prime number generator] S. Ciarcia. il *Byte* 12:36+
D '87
Vector-to-raster algorithms. D. Pountain. *Byte* 12:177-8+
S '87

Alhambra (Granada, Spain)
Gardens
Poetry in water. R. Lane Fox. il *House Gard* 159:104-15+
Ja '87

Alhambra National Water Company
Old-time seltzer in new-fangled bottles [plastic squirt
container] J. O. Hamilton. il por *Bus Week* p164
S 14 '87

Ali, Iqbal Unnisa, and others
Reduction to homozygosity of genes on chromosome
11 in human breast neoplasia. bibl f il *Science* 238:185-8
O 9 '87

Ali, Masarrat, and Vedeckis, Wayne V.
The glucocorticoid receptor protein binds to transfer
RNA. bibl f il *Science* 235:467-70 Ja 23 '87

Ali, Muhammad, 1942-
about
Ali denies seeking cure for Parkinson's disease. por *Jet*
72:53 Jl 27 '87
Ali is 'greatest' to people around world. por *Jet* 73:48
N 2 '87
Ali makes new friends during Detroit jail visit. *Jet* 72:28
Je 22 '87
Ali: on the ropes. J. B. Copeland. il por *Newsweek*
109:40-1 Je 22 '87
Ali shows he's sharp enough to say 'no' to brain surgery.
il pors *Jet* 72:47 Ag 3 '87
Ali's car in demand before plant is built. il por *Jet*
71:46 Ja 19 '87
Muhammad Ali inducted to Ring's Hall of Fame. por
Jet 72:50 S 14 '87
Will the Ali car ever come out of its corner? M. E.
Recio. il por *Bus Week* p133 Ja 12 '87

Ali, Zine el Abidine ben *See* Ben Ali, Zine el Abidine
Ali (Sports car) *See* Sports cars
Ali Ahmad Said *See* Adūnis, 1930-
Ali al-Khalifa al-Sabah *See* Al-Sabah, Ali al-Khalifa
Ali Motors Inc.
Ali's car in demand before plant is built. il por *Jet*
71:46 Ja 19 '87

Will the Ali car ever come out of its corner? M. E.
Recio. il por *Bus Week* p133 Ja 12 '87

Ali Triana, Jorge
about
A time to die [film] Reviews
Américas 39:60-1 Ja/F '87. J. Mosier
Alice [ballet] *See* Ballet reviews—Single works
Alice Austen House (Staten Island, N.Y.) *See* Staten Island
(New York, N.Y.)—Historic houses, sites, etc.
Alice Busch Opera Theatre (Cooperstown, N.Y.) *See* Opera
houses
Alice Springs (Australia)
Race relations
A sidelong look at The Alice. R. Symanski. il map
Focus 37:22-7 Summ '87
Alice Tully Hall (New York, N.Y.)
Alice Tully. *New Yorker* 63:32-4 O 5 '87
Alien animals *See* Animal introduction
Alien insects *See* Insect introduction
Alien labor
See also
Migrant labor
Coming soon: crackdown on hiring illegal aliens [Immigra-
tion Reform and Control Act of 1986] R. Thompson.
il *Nations Bus* 75:32-4+ Ap '87
Confusion on both sides of the border [amnesty and
illegal aliens] A. Bernstein and others. il *Bus Week*
p68-9 Jl 20 '87
Engineers and immigration. S. Shulman. il *Technol Rev*
90:15 Ja '87
Immigration: bordering on the absurd [new law and
hiring of illegal aliens] D. Whitman. il *U S News
World Rep* 103:25-6 S 14 '87
Immigration law: when the best minds in Washington
. . . [regulations for companies] K. R. Sheets. *U S
News World Rep* 102:39 Mr 9 '87
No aliens, lots of paperwork [Immigration Reform and
Control Act] H. Bacas. il *Nations Bus* 75:26+ N '87
Now that illegal aliens are out, au pairs are in. D.
B. Moskowitz. il *Bus Week* p148 Ja 12 '87
Out of the shadows [Immigration Reform and Control
Act of 1986] R. Stengel. il *Time* 129:14-17 My 4
'87
Reform breeds its own crisis: how the new immigration
law affects employers. M. E. Recio. il *Bus Week* p26-7
Mr 30 '87
What every manager must know about the new immigra-
tion law. J. Sherman. *Work Woman* 12:17-18+ Jl
'87
Your papers, please [instructions for employer compliance
with Immigration Reform Act] E. Knoll. *Progressive*
51:4 My '87
Alien plants *See* Plant introduction
Alienated Catholics Anonymous
Alienated Catholics Anonymous [interview with T. P.
Cahalane] *America* 156:477-81 Je 13 '87
Alienation (Social psychology)
What the market will bear. T. A. Shannon. il
Commonweal 114:234-5 Ap 24 '87
Alienation (Social psychology) in motion pictures
Alienation of affections. K. R. Hey. *USA Today
(Periodical)* 115:90 My '87
Aliens
See also
Alien labor
Citizenship
United States. Immigration and Naturalization Ser-
vice
A boxcar horror in Sierra Blanca [death of illegal Mexican
aliens] il *U S News World Rep* 103:15 Jl 13 '87
The boxcar that became a coffin [Mexican aliens suffocate
in Texas] E. Magnuson. il *Time* 130:21 Jl 13 '87
Can the trek to El Norte be curbed? [enforcing new
immigration law; special section] il *U S News World
Rep* 102:22-6 Ja 19 '87
The challenge of immigration. F. Peña. il *USA Today
(Periodical)* 115:60-2 Ja '87
A chance to leave the sweatshop behind [program to
legalize undocumented aliens begins] D. deF. Whitman.
il *U S News World Rep* 102:18 My 11 '87
Death ride to the American Dream [Mexican aliens
suffocate in boxcar] F. Bruning. por *Macleans* 100:7
Ag 3 '87
Doors and walls [Immigration and Naturalization Service
rules for processing applications for amnesty for aliens]
America 156:294 Ap 11 '87
Immigration reform II. *New Repub* 196:7-8 Mr 30 '87
The jittery 'other illegals' [European-born aliens] T. Mor-
ganthau. il *Newsweek* 110:35-6 O 5 '87
Moral borders. M. Kondracke. *New Repub* 197:12-15
N 23 '87

Aliens—*cont.*

New law won't stop illegals' influx [immigration reform law; views of David Heer] *USA Today (Periodical)* 115:7 Ap '87

A new statute of liberty. T. Bethell. *Natl Rev* 39:38+ D 18 '87

Quietly keeping them out: the dark side of immigration reform. A. J. Estrada. il *Harpers* 275:42-3 Ag '87

Ripping off immigrants: amnesty breeds abuses. G. Hackett. il *Newsweek* 110:21-2 S 7 '87

Sad return of the prodigal sons [Mexicans returning to Huandacareo as result of new immigration law] J. Moody. il *Time* 129:52 My 18 '87

Tragedy in Texas [Mexican aliens suffocate in boxcar] A. Bilski. il *Macleans* 100:19 Jl 13 '87

U.S. should consider open borders [views of Annelise Anderson] il *USA Today (Periodical)* 115:7 Ap '87

The uneasy amnesty. *America* 156:413 My 23 '87

Canada

Saying no [cover story; special section] il map *Macleans* 100:8-17 Ag 24 '87

Aliens and the church *See* Church and social problems

Alignment of planets *See* Conjunctions (Astronomy)

Alimony

Divorce settlements: lump sum versus alimony. T. Hauser. il *McCalls* 114:75 Jl '87

U.S. Rep. Major Owens fights ex-wife on charges of race bias, back alimony. il pors *Jet* 73:16-17 N 2 '87

Aline, Countess of Romanones

The spy wore red [excerpt] il pors *Saturday Evening Post* 259:46-9 N '87

about

Dressed to kill. C. Cox. il por *Vogue* 177:196 My '87

Alireza, Marianne

Women of Saudi Arabia [cover story] il *Natl Geogr* 172:422-53 O '87

Alitalia SpA

Alitalia joins new European computer reservation system [Galileo Distribution Systems] *Aviat Week Space Technol* 127:66 Ag 31 '87

Alive Films (Firm)

The moviemaker [producer C. Pfeiffer] A. P. Sanoff. il por *U S News World Rep* 102:61 Ja 26 '87

Alkaloids

See also

Colchicine

Potato eaters [glycoalkaloid dangers] E. Collins. *Sci Am* 257:31 S '87

Warning: peel potatoes before cooking [glycoalkaloid dangers] *Sci News* 132:8 Jl 4 '87

Alkenes *See* Olefins

Alkylation

Isolation and structure of a covalent cross-link adduct between mitomycin C and DNA. M. Tomasz and others. bibl f il *Science* 235:1204-8 Mr 6 '87

Alkylbenzoates *See* Benzoates

All-America Selections (Plants) *See* Plants—All-America Selections

All-American football players *See* Football players

All-American Girl Contest

All-American-Girl talk [finalist H. Margolis] por *Teen* 31:14 S '87

All-American Girl-talk [finalist K. Schick] il por *Teen* 31:68 N '87

All-American Girl talk [finalist S. L. Christy] por *Teen* 31:72 Ag '87

All-American-Girl talk [finalist T. Moy] il por *Teen* 31:77 O '87

All-American Girl-talk [winner T. Hunnicutt] il pors *Teen* 31:46 Jl '87

All-American good looks [makeovers for finalists] il *Teen* 31:80-5 Jl '87

All-American Soap Box Derby *See* Soap box derbies

All American SportsClub Inc.

Robert McNulty: back on discounting's fast track. K. Kelly. il por *Bus Week* p91 N 9 '87

All my sons [drama] See Miller, Arthur, 1915-

All Nippon Airways Co. Ltd.

All Nippon seeks new routes to U.S., Australia and Europe. D. A. Brown. il *Aviat Week Space Technol* 126:45-6 Je 22 '87

Exim Bank backs 767 sale to All Nippon to foil Airbus bid. *Aviat Week Space Technol* 126:31 Je 29 '87

Hostile skies [effects of airline deregulation] H. Katayama. il *Forbes* 140:60 O 5 '87

All Saints' Day

Saints alive! G. G. Seibert. *America* 157:279 O 24 '87

Saints of common place. B. L. Rohrig. *Christ Century* 104:934-5 O 28 '87

All-star games *See* Baseball, Professional—All-star games; Basketball, Professional—All-star games

All terrain bicycles *See* Bicycles

All terrain vehicles

Agricultural use

ATVs continue their march on agriculture. C. Finck. il *Success Farm* 85:30-1 Je '87

ATVs go to work. M. Ferrara. il *Home Mech* 83:28 Jl '87

Environmental aspects

Hot roadsters are breaking the peace [river riding on the Black River] il *Newsweek* 109:27 Je 29 '87

Of turbo boots and rooster tails: the ORV and the public lands. R. Reinhardt. il *Wilderness* 50:28-36 Summ '87

Laws and regulations

Will the government corral all-terrain vehicles? il *Consum Rep* 52:270 My '87

Safety devices and measures

ATV safety debate: statistics show young people at risk. *Success Farm* 85:56A N '87

ATV warning. J. W. Merline. *Consum Res Mag* 70:38 D '87

The controversial ATV. T. Opre. il *Outdoor Life* 179:38+ Mr '87

Kids and ATVs. W. Shipman. il *Ctry J* 14:8 S '87

Rough rides [ATV injuries to children] il *Time* 129:64 Ja 12 '87

Three-wheelers likely to be history in a few years. *Success Farm* 85:18BD Ap '87

Trouble on three wheels [injuries to B. Vance] W. Plummer. il pors *People Wkly* 27:30-3 F 23 '87

Why ATVs could land in a heap of trouble. D. B. Moskowitz. il *Bus Week* p38 N 30 '87

Testing

All-terrain FatCat. N. Mayersohn. il *Pop Mech* 164:52 F '87

Tour de FourTrax [Honda Foreman FourTrax] J. Skorupa. il *Pop Mech* 164:37 S '87

All the king's men [drama] See Hall, Adrian

All weather cameras *See* Cameras

Alladice, Darryl

Fettuccine [poem] *Essence* 18:137 O '87

Allamandola, L. J., and others

Interstellar polycyclic aromatic hydrocarbons and carbon in interplanetary dust particles and meteorites. bibl f il *Science* 237:56-9 Jl 3 '87

Allan, Donald

Room for expansion. il *World Health* p8-9 Ja/F '87

Allan, Doug

Encounter under the ice. il *Int Wildl* 17:48-51 Mr/Ap '87

Allard, Charles

about

A news junkie's national dream. P. C. Newman. il por *Macleans* 100:34 Jl 20 '87

Allard, Kevyn

Aerobics videos: the top 30. il *Women's Sports Fitness* 9:30-3 D '87

Water workout: cool in the pool. bibl il *Women's Sports Fitness* 9:43 Ag '87

Alldredge, Alice L., and Cohen, Yehuda

Can microscale chemical patches persist in the sea? Microelectrode study of marine snow, fecal pellets. bibl f il *Science* 235:689-91 F 6 '87

Alleghany Corp.

St. Paul may be doing too well. M. J. Pitzer. il *Bus Week* p41-2 D 21 '87

Allegheny Airlines, Inc. *See* US Air, Inc.

Allegheny Beverage Corp.

Out of his depth [M. Lapides] M. Kuntz. il por *Forbes* 139:56-7 F 23 '87

Allegheny International Inc.

A deal that would get Allegheny out of the spotlight [leveraged buyout] M. Rothman and G. L. Miles. il *Bus Week* p34 Mr 23 '87

Allegheny Observatory (Pittsburgh, Pa.) *See* Astronomical observatories

Allegis Corporation

The Allegis experiment turns into a bonanza. J. E. Ellis. *Bus Week* p123+ N 9 '87

Allegis flies into debt [fending off Coniston Partners] il *Fortune* 115:8 Je 22 '87

Allegis: is a name change enough for UAL? J. E. Ellis. il por *Bus Week* p54-5+ Mr 2 '87

Allegis will live on—in the nightmares of CEOs. J. H. Dobrzynski. il *Bus Week* p29 Je 29 '87

Allegis will sell Canadian hotels to thwart takeover attempt. *Aviat Week Space Technol* 126:38 Je 8 '87

Allegis Corporation—*cont.*

Boeing financing of United orders reflects stiffening competition. *Aviat Week Space Technol* 126:29-30 My 18 '87

Boeing had good reason to take Allegis under its wing. J. E. Ellis. il *Bus Week* p64+ My 25 '87

Coniston stalks Allegis. J. E. Ellis. il *Bus Week* p37 Je 8 '87

Even if Allegis wins, the victory could be pyrrhic [fending off Coniston Partners] J. E. Ellis. por *Bus Week* p37 Je 15 '87

How Dick Ferris blew it. K. Labich. il por *Fortune* 116:42-4+ Jl 6 '87

Investors' breakup of Allegis prompts Ferris resignation. *Aviat Week Space Technol* 126:82 Je 15 '87

One man's dream comes down to earth [R. Ferris' failed strategy] C. P. Work and H. Wells. il por *U S News World Rep* 102:44-5 Je 22 '87

Stopping a Ferris wheel. D. Pauly. il por *Newsweek* 109:42-3 Je 22 '87

The trio that humbled Allegis [Coniston Partners] S. P. Sherman. il pors *Fortune* 116:52-4+ Jl 20 '87

United finds a new friend [Allegis' deal with Boeing] J. B. Copeland. il *Newsweek* 109:38 My 25 '87

United once more. J. Castro. il *Time* 129:46-7 Je 22 '87

The unraveling of an idea [R. J. Ferris ousted] J. E. Ellis and C. Hawkins. il por *Bus Week* p42-3 Je 22 '87

Alleman, Richard

Travel now. See issues of Vogue

Allen, Armin B.
> *about*

An eye for complexity. O. Bernier. il *House Gard* 159:172-7+ Mr '87

Allen, Bonnie

The best and the worst of the fall TV lineup. il *Ms* 16:36+ O '87

God's great gift, Aretha. il por *Ms* 16:77-8 D '87

Me and my bed [cover story] il pors *Ms* 16:20+ D '87

Victor Love. il pors *Essence* 17:40-2+ Ap '87

Allen, David A.

Laying bare Venus' dark secrets. il *Sky Telesc* 74:350-3 O '87

Star formation and IRAS galaxies. il *Sky Telesc* 73:372-4 Ap '87

Allen, Debbie
> *about*

Debbie Allen and Phylicia Rashad's mother Vivian Ayers talks about their fame [cover story] il pors *Jet* 72:54-5 My 18 '87

Debbie Allen looks ahead after final 'Fame' episode. por *Jet* 72:55 Mr 30 '87

Fosse leaves legacy of helping blacks, Allen says. il por *Jet* 73:18 O 12 '87

Sisters: Debbie Allen and Phylicia Rashad. S. Flatow. il pors *McCalls* 114:90-5 Jl '87

Allen, Dick, 1939-

Lost love [poem] *New Yorker* 63:34 Je 29 '87

Allen, F. M., and others

Direct observation of dissociated dislocations in garnet. bibl f il *Science* 238:1695-7 D 18 '87

Allen, Fred, 1894-1956
> *about*

Unforgettable Fred Allen. M. Zolotow. il *Read Dig* 131:55-6+ O '87

Allen, George

Why we need the new U.S. Fitness Academy. il por *Prevention* 39:94-6 Ap '87

Allen, Jennifer

The apostle of angst. il pors *Esquire* 107:210-12+ Je '87

Architectural digest visits: Robert Wagner. il pors *Archit Dig* 44:124-31+ My '87

Cottage by the sea: Maria Tallchief and Henry D. Paschen on Martha's Vineyard. il *Archit Dig* 44:170-5+ O '87

Past perfect: Bernard and Barbara Bergreen on Fifth Avenue. il por *Archit Dig* 44:190-9 N '87

Allen, Jim
> *about*

Perdition [drama] Reviews

Nation 245:187 S 5 '87. A. Cockburn

New Repub 196:15-17 Mr 2 '87. D. Pryce-Jones

Allen, Jo Harvey
> *about*

Woman of parts [interview] M. Small. il pors *People Wkly* 28:97-8+ O 12 '87

Allen, Mary

Benefits, buffet style. il *Nations Bus* 75:45-7 Ja '87

Allen, Pamela Payne

The blessing and the burden. *Christ Century* 104:1169-70 D 23-30 '87

Creativity and the challenge of worship. il *Christ Century* 104:756-8 S 9-16 '87

Feasting on herbs in the midst of love: a conversation with Jeff Smith. por *Christ Century* 104:1087-90 D 2 '87

Allen, Paul
> *about*

The next chapter. E. F. Cone. il por *Forbes* 139:168 Ap 6 '87

Allen, Paul M.

(jt. auth) See Unanue, Emil R., and Allen, Paul M.

Allen, Phylicia Ayers- See Rashad, Phylicia

Allen, Richard

A Carol Christmas [story] il *Teen* 31:32+ D '87

Allen, Robert Day

The microtubule as an intracellular engine. il *Sci Am* 256:42-9 F '87

Allen, Samuel N.

Pinstripe pug: a Wall Street lawyer turns to boxing. il pors *N Y* 20:34-9 F 23 '87

Allen, Walter R.

Black colleges vs. white colleges: the fork in the road for black students. il *Change* 19:28-31+ My/Je '87

Allen, William H.

Jacobean lily. il *Flower Gard* 31:60 O/N '87

Allen, Woody

True colors. il *N Y Rev Books* 34:38 Ag 13 '87
> *about*

Beauty in a world of schlock. M. Burkhart. il *Commonweal* 114:294-6 My 8 '87

Class clowns. A. White. il *Film Comment* 23:11-14 Mr/Ap '87

Looking north at a world of self. M. Gallagher. *America* 157:82-3 Ag 15-22 '87

M.O.B. rule. M. Mancini. il por *Film Comment* 23:76-7 Jl/Ag '87

The oeuvre de Woody (a short, uptight quiz). D. Wild. il pors *Esquire* 107:91 Ap '87

Radio days [film] Reviews

America 156:237+ Mr 21 '87. R. A. Blake

Commonweal il 114:111-12 F 27 '87. T. O'Brien

Glamour il 85:225 Mr '87. J. G. Boyum

Macleans il 100:47 F 9 '87. L. O'Toole

Mademoiselle il 93:76+ My '87. R. Rosenbaum

Ms 15:17+ Mr '87. L. Stone

N Y il 20:95-6 F 9 '87. D. Denby

Nation 244:229-31 F 21 '87. T. Rafferty

Natl Rev 39:57-9 Mr 27 '87. J. Simon

New Leader il 70:19-20 F 9-23 '87. J. Gardner

New Repub 196:24 Mr 9 '87. S. Kauffmann

New Yorker 63:96+ Mr 9 '87. P. Kael

Newsweek il 109:71 F 2 '87. D. Ansen

People Wkly il 27:10 F 16 '87. P. Travers

Time il 129:73 F 2 '87. R. Schickel

Vogue il 177:90+ Mr '87. M. Haskell

The Rolling stone interview: Woody Allen [cover story] W. Geist. il pors *Roll Stone* p38-40+ Ap 9 '87

September [film] Reviews

Macleans 100:61 D 21 '87. B. D. Johnson

People Wkly il 28:10 D 21 '87. R. Novak

Time il 130:74 D 21 '87. R. Schickel

Woody: the first fifty years [cover story] T. Shales. il pors *Esquire* 107:88-95 Ap '87

Allen-Edmonds Shoe Corp.

Shoe wars: an angry American takes on Japan [J. Stollenwerk] *Newsweek* 109:38 Ja 26 '87

Allen University

Allen University: the best choice for the best future. *Jet* 72:9 Ap 27 '87

Allender, David

William Steig at 80. il por *Publ Wkly* 232:116-18 Jl 24 '87

Allentini, Georgio
> *about*

His last $500 gambled on a sexy tape, princely Georgio Allentini signs on to make millions with Motown. il por *People Wkly* 27:109 Je 29 '87

Allergic bronchial asthma See Asthma

Allergic contact dermatitis See Skin—Diseases

Allergy

> See also
> Food allergy
> Hay fever
> Pet allergy
> Poison ivy

Allergies? There's no reason why you can't garden. K. Wilson. il *Rodale's Org Gard* 34:21-4 Ag '87

Allergy—*cont.*
Allergy alert [immunoglobulin E blood test for children] C. Bushnell. il *Health* 19:15 Ja '87
Best-bet relief from allergy season. il *Prevention* 39:34-6+ My '87
Detecting allergy-prone children [immunoglobulin E blood test] *USA Today (Periodical)* 115:12 F '87
"I'm allergic to my family"; ed. by Barbara Yost. B. Jorgensen. il por *Redbook* 168:42+ Ap '87
Infant allergies. K. Karlsrud and D. Schultz. il *Parents* 62:182 Mr '87
It's just an ah, ah, a-llergy! M. McFadden. *Work Woman* 12:144 Ap '87
Molds, mites & pollen particles. M. Castleman. il *Redbook* 169:24+ S '87
Taking the sneeze out of spring. I. Pave. il *Bus Week* p106 Mr 30 '87
When you're allergic to your home. H. J. Lehman. *Changing Times* 41:14 Ja '87
Allerød (Denmark)
Buildings
Danish modern [IBM Software and Publications Center] P. M. Sachner. il *Archit Rec* 175:134-41 O '87
Alley, Kirstie
about
A great mixer, Kirstie Alley is the toast of Cheers—where nobody gives a dram about her predecessor. J. Kaufman. il pors *People Wkly* 28:122-4+ N 30 '87
Kirstie Alley: "I'm nobody's fluff" [cover story; interview] A. W. Petrucelli. il pors *Redbook* 169:10+ O '87
Alleyne, George A. O.
Health problems old and new. il *World Health* p9-10 O '87
Alliance for Progress
Letters [discussion of Winter 1986-1987 article, Misreading Latin America—again] H. J. Wiarda. *Foreign Policy* 67:177-80 Summ '87
Alliance Technology Fund
High tech: big returns from small stocks [interview with R. Coons] J. Mendes. il por *Fortune* 116:128 S 28 '87
High-tech's durable performer. *Money* 16:27 Je '87
Alliance to Save Energy
Alliance to Save Energy. J. L. Wolf. *Environment* 29:3-4 Ap '87
Alliances
See also
ANZUS Council
ASEAN
North Atlantic Treaty Organization
Warsaw Treaty Organization
Hidden commitments. T. L. Deibel. *Foreign Policy* 67:46-63 Summ '87
New Zealand and an interdependent world [address, March 13, 1987] P. M. Cleveland. map *Dep State Bull* 87:80-3 Je '87
Allied Corp.
See also
Allied-Signal Inc.
Allied-Lyons plc
The $1.2-million sales pitch [corporate junket sponsored by Allied-Lyons to highlight stake in Hiram Walker] D. Francis. por *Macleans* 100:9 Je 29 '87
The expansive Reichmanns. D. Jenish. il *Macleans* 100:36 D 7 '87
Allied-Signal Inc.
Small payoffs from big deals. P. Nulty. il por *Fortune* 116:139+ D 7 '87
Will all that restructuring ever pay off for Ed Hennessy's Allied? J. H. Dobrzynski. il por *Bus Week* p78-80 F 2 '87
Allied Stores Corp.
Campeau's cash squeeze [R. Campeau's takeover of Allied Stores] T. Fennell. il por *Macleans* 100:26 Mr 2 '87
Is Campeau in over his head at Allied Stores? D. Cook. il *Bus Week* p52-3 F 9 '87
A top law firm feels the heat [Sullivan & Cromwell's G. C. Kern charged by SEC with violating disclosure rules during Campeau's bid on Allied Stores] C. Friday. *Newsweek* 110:40-1 Jl 13 '87
When companies talk turkey, investors should be told [SEC charges against G. C. Kern and Allied Stores over inadequate disclosure in Campeau hostile takeover] V. Cahan. il *Bus Week* p100 Jl 13 '87
Alligator Records (Firm)
Our blues. J. W. Poses. il *High Fidel* 37:84-5 D '87
Alligators
Alligators are back, breeding like crazy and making a big splash. D. D. Jackson. bibl (p131) il *Smithsonian* 17:36-44+ Ja '87

Coming back from the brink [removal from endangered species list] M. D. Lemonick. il *Time* 130:70 Jl 20 '87
From the jaws of death [M. Morgret saved from alligator attack] H. Hurt. il *Read Dig* 130:116-20 Ap '87
Gators are snapping back. il *U S News World Rep* 103:14 Jl 13 '87
No more alligator tears? [removal from endangered species list] *Sci News* 132:24 Jl 11 '87
Searching for truth in alligator country. T. A. Lewis. il *Natl Wildl* 25:12-19 O/N '87
The unendangered alligator's rapid fall from grace. G. Laycock. il *Audubon* 89:38-43 S '87
Allison, Eric W. (Eric William), and Allison, Mary Ann
How to work without a secretary. *Work Woman* 12:22 Ag '87
Allison, Mary Ann
(jt. auth) See Allison, Eric W. (Eric William), and Allison, Mary Ann
Allison Gas Turbine Operations
Afterburning TF41 assessed for A-7D upgrade. *Aviat Week Space Technol* 126:28 F 16 '87
Allison, Pratt & Whitney team for propfan engine market. il *Aviat Week Space Technol* 126:32-3 Mr 2 '87
Component deliveries delay PW-Allison propfan first flight. S. W. Kandebo. *Aviat Week Space Technol* 127:28-9 N 30 '87
Italy, West Germany examine upgrading Allison engines [helicopters] *Aviat Week Space Technol* 126:72 F 23 '87
Pratt, Allison team for P-3 follow-on engine candidate. *Aviat Week Space Technol* 127:32 D 21 '87
Rolls-Royce and Allison unite to pursue U.S. military market. *Aviat Week Space Technol* 127:34 O 12 '87
Allium
About alliums. S. Pacher. il *Mother Earth News* 108:32-4+ N/D '87
Onions that produce flowers, beautiful to bizarre, fresh or dried. il *Sunset* 179:233 N '87
Allman, William F.
Designing computers that think the way we do. il *Technol Rev* 90:58-65 My/Je '87
Allman Brothers Band
The Allman Brothers Band: The Fillmore East, New York City, March 11th-13th, 1971. D. Fricke. il *Roll Stone* p79-80+ Je 4 '87
Allmon, Charles
about
Famous artists. R. Phalon. il pors *Forbes* 139:102+ Je 1 '87
Allnet Communication Services, Inc.
See also
ALC Communications Corporation
Alloys
See also
Aluminum alloys
Nitinol
Quasicrystals
Shape memory alloys
Alltel Corp.
Most improved. il *Forbes* 139:213 Ja 12 '87
Allusions
Going gentle on my mind. W. Safire. il *N Y Times Mag* p6+ Je 7 '87
The PAWs that refresh [poetic allusion watch] W. Safire. il *N Y Times Mag* p10+ Ap 26 '87
Poetic allusion watch. W. Safire. il *N Y Times Mag* p12+ Mr 1 '87
Allwaste Inc.
Allwaste: turning garbage into gold. G. G. Marcial. *Bus Week* p100 S 7 '87
Alma-Ata (Soviet Union)
Riots
The 'glasnost' test. R. Pipes. *New Repub* 196:16-17 F 2 '87
Meanwhile, back in the Kazakh SSR . . . A. J. Motyl. *New Leader* 70:9 F 9-23 '87
What really happened in Alma-Ata [minority riots] J. O. Jackson. il map *Time* 129:25 Mr 2 '87
Almanacs
See also
Astronomy—Almanacs
All about almanacs. N. Bubel. il *Ctry J* 14:26-8 Ja '87
Almendros, Nestor
I am a camera. il *Film Comment* 23:18-21 Jl/Ag '87
Almodóvar, Pedro
about
Law of desire [film] Reviews
New Yorker 63:80-1 Ap 20 '87. P. Kael
People Wkly 28:12 Ag 3 '87. P. Travers

Almond cake *See* Cake

Almonds
See also
Marzipan

Almost by chance a woman: Elizabeth [drama] *See* Fo, Dario

Almy, Kathleen
Reading the rocks. il *Sierra* 72:92-4 N/D '87

Aloe
For winter bloom or year-round drama . . . the aloes. il *Sunset* 178:184-5 F '87

Aloff, Mindy
Cossacks of classicism. il *Dance Mag* 61:36-9 D '87
Dance. See occasional issues of The Nation

Alomar, Carlos
about
Carlos Alomar: generating electric dreams. G. Santoro. il pors *Down Beat* 11:20-2 N '87

Alovert, Nina
The Soviet dance theater of Yuri Grigorovich. il por *Dance Mag* 61:39-42 D '87
Yuri Grigorovich: an appreciation. il por *Dance Mag* 61:44-7 Jl '87

Alpacas *See* Llamas

Alpenhorn
Horn of plenty. B. Bachmann-Geiser. il *Courier* 40:29-31 F '87

Alper, Joseph
Tax reform and the part-time farmer. il *Ctry J* 14:73-9 F '87

Alpert, Richard *See* Ram Dass

Alpha fetoprotein *See* Fetoprotein

Alpha Phi Alpha Fraternity *See* College fraternities

Alphabet in art
The Omni alphabestiary. M. Wilks. il *Omni* 9:75-9 Ag '87

Alphorn *See* Alpenhorn

Alpine climbing *See* Mountaineering

Alpine flora
Between a rock and a cold place. R. Wolkomir and J. Wolkomir. il *Natl Wildl* 25:46-51 Je/Jl '87
Global flora: new research links alpine wildflowers around the world. L. Tejada-Flores. il *Natl Parks* 61:26-9 S/O '87

Alpine ibex *See* Ibex

Alpine strawberries *See* Strawberries

Alps
Alpine Europe [cover story; special issue; with editorial comment by Edouard Glissant] il maps *Courier* 40:3-38 F '87
Cracks appear in the magic mountain [Switzerland's policy of shortchanging the mountains while favoring tourism] E. Beck. il *Sierra* 72:116-19 Ja/F '87
'Green death' in the Alps. E. Brunner. *World Press Rev* 34:53 D '87
Six-wheeling the Alps [BMW K75 and BMW325i in the Tyrolean Alps] T. West. il *Road Track* 38:132-4+ F '87
With lots of help, alpine ibex return to their mountains. C. Grodinsky and M. Stüwe. il *Smithsonian* 18:68-72+ D '87
Climate
The ALPEX experiment. R. Newson. il *Courier* 40:34-6 F '87
Passes
The great transalpine routes. B. Parisi. il *Courier* 40:11-13 F '87

ALS *See* Amyotrophic lateral sclerosis

Alston, Douglas Banes
about
Atlanta mayor's daughter weds before 500 guests. il pors *Jet* 72:33 Jl 27 '87

Alston, Lisa Young
about
Atlanta mayor's daughter weds before 500 guests. il pors *Jet* 72:33 Jl 27 '87

Alt, Carol
about
Carol and her big lug. E. M. Swift. il pors *Sports Illus* 66:88-91+ F 9 '87

Alt, Frederick W., and others
Development of the primary antibody repertoire. bibl f il *Science* 238:1079-87 N 20 '87

Alt, Gary
about
A bear of America. C. Fergus. il *Ctry J* 14:43-7+ O '87

Altable, Juan
'A golden childhood'. *World Press Rev* 34:30 Ap '87

Altar girls
Barred from the church altar [S. Bernier prohibited from serving as altar girl in Toronto] M. McIver. por *Macleans* 100:45 Jl 6 '87

Altarpieces
Conservation and restoration
A canary in an aquarium [Adoration of the mystic lamb altarpiece by J. and H. van Eyck now hung in Saint Bavon Cathedral, Ghent] B. Grauman. il *Art News* 86:101-2 Ja '87

Altbach, Philip G.
Politics and the university. il *Change* 19:56-9 Jl/Ag '87
Toward a worldwide copyright era. il *Publ Wkly* 232:44 D 11 '87

Alter, Catherine Foster
Preventing family dependency. *Society* 24:12-16 Mr/Ap '87

Alter, Robert
Defenders of the faith. *Commentary* 84:52-5 Jl '87

Alteration of clothing *See* Tailoring

Alterman, Eric
Elliott Abrams: the teflon Assistant Secretary. por *Wash Mon* 19:19-22+ My '87
Glasnost TV-guide. *New Repub* 197:12-13 D 21 '87
Inside Ollie's mind. il *New Repub* 196:12-15 F 16 '87
On the outside, cashing in. *Harpers* 275:48-9 Jl '87
Scandal sheet. *New Repub* 196:17-18+ Ap 20 '87

Alternative life styles *See* Counterculture

Alternative medicine *See* Holistic medicine

Alternative minimum tax *See* Income tax

Alternative pregnancy centers
Attracting clients and controversy. P. P. Wong. il *Christ Today* 31:32-3 S 18 '87

Alternative schools *See* Education, Experimental

Alternative sentences (Criminal justice) *See* Criminal justice, Administration of

Altes, Stephen Korthals- *See* Korthals-Altes, Stephen

Althorp, Charles Edward Maurice Spencer, Viscount
about
Di's brother: new man on the beat. D. Waggoner. il pors *People Wkly* 27:22-5 Mr 2 '87

Altitude, Influence of
See also
Mountain sickness
It's tough at the top. G. Antesena and others. il *Courier* 40:8-11 Je '87

Altman, Julius
about
A violinist's deathbed confession solves the 51-year riddle of a stolen Stradivarius. R. Arias. il pors *People Wkly* 27:36-8 Je 1 '87

Altman, Mara
Against all odds: Suzy Gilstrap. il por *Seventeen* 46:214 Ag '87
The spirit of Esprit! il *Seventeen* 46:83-4+ Je '87

Altman, Robert, 1925-
about
Beyond therapy [film] Reviews
Commonweal 114:183-4 Mr 27 '87. T. O'Brien
Macleans il 100:57 Mr 9 '87. L. O'Toole
New Repub 196:25 Mr 23 '87. S. Kauffmann
Time il 129:74+ Mr 2 '87. R. Corliss

Altman, Steven
Presidential perspectives on university writing requirements [address, March 7, 1987] *Vital Speeches Day* 53:494-6 Je 1 '87

Altman (B.) & Co. *See* B. Altman & Co.

Altmeyer, Jeannine, 1948-
about
The Altmeyer story. M. Mayer. il pors *Opera News* 51:8-10 F 28 '87

Altruism
See also
Assistance in emergencies
Helping behavior
No greater love [willingness of Vietnamese boy to give up his life for another during wartime] J. W. Mansur. il *Read Dig* 131:49-50 Ag '87
Teaching selflessness in a selfish society. T. J. Lasley. bibl f il *Phi Delta Kappan* 68:674-8 My '87

Aluminum airplanes *See* Airplanes—Materials

Aluminum alloys
Disorder in Al-Li-Cu and Al-Mn-Si icosahedral alloys. P. A. Heiney and others. bibl f il *Science* 238:660-3 O 30 '87

Aluminum bicycles *See* Bicycles—Materials

Aluminum Co. of America
Alcoa: recycling itself to become a pioneer in new materials. G. L. Miles and M. Rothman. il por *Bus Week* p56-8 F 9 '87

Aluminum Co. of America—*cont.*
Alcoa restructures to enter value-added product market. S. W. Kandebo. il *Aviat Week Space Technol* 126:65-7 F 23 '87
Aluminum electric wiring *See* Electric wire and wiring
Aluminum in the body
Acid rain, aluminum, and Alzheimer's disease. *Futurist* 21:36 Ja/F '87
Aluminum: a high price for a surrogate? [research by Timothy L. MacDonald and others] D. D. Edwards. il *Sci News* 131:245 Ap 18 '87
Promotion of tubulin assembly by aluminum ion in vitro. T. L. MacDonald and others. bibl f il *Science* 236:183-6 Ap 10 '87
Aluminum industry
See also
Aluminum Co. of America
Reynolds Metals Co.
Aluminum nails *See* Nails
Aluminum wheels, Automobile *See* Automobiles—Wheels
Alumni, College *See* College graduates
Alvarez, A. (Alfred), 1929-
Spa Italian style. il *House Gard* 159:74+ O '87
Where stars don't matter. il *House Gard* 159:30+ F '87
(tr) *See* Levi, Primo, 1919-1987. Two poems
Alvarez, Alfred *See* Alvarez, A. (Alfred), 1929-
Alvarez, Elizabeth, and Fuchs, Sharon
Bouncing back from surgery. il *Health* 19:49-50+ Mr '87
Alvarez, Luis W.
Mass extinctions caused by large bolide impacts [adaptation of address, December 11, 1986; cover story] bibl f il *Phys Today* 40:24-33 Jl '87
about
Where have all the dinos gone? il *U S News World Rep* 103:67 Jl 6 '87
Alvarez, Richard A.
(jt. auth) *See* Bridges, C. David, and Alvarez, Richard A.
Alvarez Bravo, Manuel, 1902-
about
Mexico's poet of the commonplace. D. Roberts. il por *Archit Dig* 44:38+ My '87
Alvergue, Pablo Mauricio
The Central American crisis and the Contadora process. *USA Today (Periodical)* 115:29-30 Ja '87
Alves, Maria Adelaide Moreira de Morais
Breaking down the barriers for visually handicapped children. il *Courier* 40:30-2 Jl '87
Alvin (Submarine) *See* Oceanographic submersibles
Alvin Ailey American Dance Theater
Ailey launches a Katherine Dunham renaissance: Miss D's day. R. Philp. il pors *Dance Mag* 61:50-5 D '87
Dancing:
Program of K. Dunham dances. A. Croce. *New Yorker* 63:102 D 21 '87
Reviews:
Performances at City Center, New York City. S. Sommer. *Dance Mag* 61:21-2 Jl '87
Wanted: a choreographer [performances at City Center] T. Tobias. il *N Y* 20:47-8 Ja 5 '87
ALVs *See* Autonomous land vehicles
Alwang, Jennifer
A voice for the frail elderly. il *Aging* no355:10-13 '87
Alwin Nikolais Dance Theatre *See* Nikolais Dance Theatre
Alyson, Sasha
about
A worthy cause. L. Fleischer. *Publ Wkly* 232:40 Ag 21 '87
Alyssum, Sweet *See* Sweet alyssum
Alzheimer's disease
Alzheimer's: a cancer-like mechanism? [work of Peter Davies] R. Weiss. *Sci News* 132:348 N 28 '87
Alzheimer's protein is also in infant brains [research by Peter Davies and others] D. M. Barnes. *Science* 238:1652 D 18 '87
Alzheimer's quiz. il *Psychol Today* 21:89+ My '87
Conservation of brain amyloid proteins in aged mammals and humans with Alzheimer's disease [cover story] D. J. Selkoe and others. bibl f il *Science* 235:873-7 F 20 '87
An expert says doctors still have no cure but are closing in on the causes of Alzheimer's [interview with D. Selkoe] G. Verner. il por *People Wkly* 27:83-4 Je 1 '87
Honoring her stricken mother, Rita Hayworth, Yasmin Khan stages a dazzling benefit. il pors *People Wkly* 27:36-7 My 25 '87

Long-term neuropathological and neurochemical effects of nucleus basalis lesions in the rat. G. W. Arendash and others. bibl f il *Science* 238:952-6 N 13 '87
Piano playing preserved in dementia [research by William W. Beatty and others] S. Weisburd. *Sci News* 132:286 O 31 '87
Ubiquitin is a component of paired helical filaments in Alzheimer's disease. H. Mori and others. bibl f il *Science* 235:1641-4 Mr 27 '87
Update on Alzheimer's disease: the progress, the hope. A. Dowden. *McCalls* 114:144+ My '87
Costs
OTA cites financial disaster of Alzheimer's. C. Holden. *Science* 236:253 Ap 17 '87
Diagnosis
Is it Alzheimer's or AIDS? C. SerVaas. il *Saturday Evening Post* 259:92-4 O '87
Genetic aspects
Absence of duplication of chromosome 21 genes in familial and sporadic Alzheimer's disease. P. H. St George-Hyslop and others. bibl f il *Science* 238:664-6 O 30 '87
Alzheimer/Down syndrome bond tightens. *Sci News* 131:188 Mr 21 '87
Alzheimer's: new clues [isolation of a gene and genetic markers] J. Seligmann. il *Newsweek* 109:65-6 Mr 2 '87
Amyloid β protein gene: cDNA, mRNA distribution, and genetic linkage near the Alzheimer locus. R. E. Tanzi and others. bibl f il *Science* 235:880-4 F 20 '87
The amyloid β protein gene is not duplicated in brains from patients with Alzheimer's disease. R. E. Tanzi and others. bibl f il *Science* 238:666-9 O 30 '87
β amyloid gene duplication in Alzheimer's disease and karyotypically normal Down syndrome. J.-M. Delabar and others. bibl f il *Science* 235:1390-2 Mr 13 '87
Characterization and chromosomal localization of a cDNA encoding brain amyloid of Alzheimer's disease. D. Goldgaber and others. bibl f il *Science* 235:877-80 F 20 '87
Closing in on Alzheimer's. N. Underwood. *Macleans* 100:44 Mr 2 '87
Defect in Alzheimer's is on chromosome 21. D. M. Barnes. *Science* 235:846-7 F 20 '87
A dread disease yields a clue [genetic markers found] il *U S News World Rep* 102:13 Mr 2 '87
Family study of platelet membrane fluidity in Alzheimer's disease. G. S. Zubenko and others. bibl f il *Science* 238:539-42 O 23 '87
Gene dosage of the amyloid β precursor protein in Alzheimer's disease. M. B. Podlisny and others. bibl f il *Science* 238:669-71 O 30 '87
Genetic clues [isolation of gene and genetic markers] *Time* 129:63 Mr 2 '87
The genetic defect causing familial Alzheimer's disease maps on chromosome 21. P. H. St George-Hyslop and others. bibl f il *Science* 235:885-90 F 20 '87
Inherited membranes predict Alzheimer's? [fluidity of platelet membranes] *Sci News* 132:301 N 7 '87
Key to Alzheimer's? [defect tracked to chromosome 21] *Sci Am* 256:68 Ap '87
Localization of amyloid β protein messenger RNA in brains from patients with Alzheimer's disease. S. Bahmanyar and others. bibl f il *Science* 237:77-80 Jl 3 '87
Role of Alzheimer's protein is tangled. J. L. Marx. bibl il *Science* 238:1352-3 D 4 '87
Nutritional aspects
Acid rain, aluminum, and Alzheimer's disease. *Futurist* 21:36 Ja/F '87
Therapy
Alzheimer's drug trial put on hold. J. L. Marx. il *Science* 238:1041-2 N 20 '87
Bringing back fading memories [work of Anders Björklund and others with nerve growth factor] D. D. Edwards. *Sci News* 132:149-50 S 5 '87
No cure soon for Alzheimer's disease. *Futurist* 21:54 S/O '87
Palliative [THA; work of William Summers] *Sci Am* 256:72 Ja '87
THA trials suspended, research probed. R. Weiss. *Sci News* 132:292 N 7 '87
Variety, the spice of memory [improving memory; study by Curt Sandman] C. Simon. il *Psychol Today* 21:20 N '87
Alzheimer's disease patients
Lost together in paradise [R. Bing, former head of the Metropolitan Opera] J. Kelly. il pors *Time* 129:73 F 23 '87

Alzheimer's disease patients—*cont.*
Remembering Rita [cover story] il pors *People Wkly* 27:72-6+ Je 1 '87
Yasmin Khan: my mother, Rita Hayworth. C. Ford. il pors *McCalls* 114:138-9+ My '87
Family relationships
Easing the burden on Alzheimer's families [New York City] L. B. Cheek. il *Aging* no355:16-19 '87
Putting their caring on the line [telephone support network for families caring for Alzheimer's patients] C. C. Goodman. il *Aging* no355:20-1 '87
Taking care of immunity [lowered immune function in families caring for Alzheimer's patients; research by Janice K. Kiecolt-Glaser and others] B. Bower. *Sci News* 132:168 S 12 '87
Training respite workers for Alzheimer's families. L. Middleton. il *Aging* no356:24-6 '87
AMA *See* American Medical Association
Amabile, Teresa
about
Art for art's sake. A. Kohn. il pors *Psychol Today* 21:52-7 S '87
AMACOM Book Division
Touch it, feel it, reach out and grab it [J. Lyons handling the ad campaign for his book Guts] L. Fleischer. *Publ Wkly* 232:46 Jl 3 '87
Amalgam dental fillings *See* Dental materials
Amalgamated Beverage Industries Pty. Ltd.
If Coke has its way, blacks will soon own 'the real thing'. S. Mufson. il *Bus Week* p56 Mr 23 '87
Amalric, Jacques
Erosion of U.S. power. il *World Press Rev* 34:12-13 F '87
Amana Society
Manna from Amana. W. Mueller. il *Saturday Evening Post* 259:84-5+ Jl/Ag '87
Manna from Amana. D. Swift. il *Mother Earth News* 107:54-7 S/O '87
Amanda the Panda, Inc.
Amanda the Panda [program helps children with cancer] M. Conroy. il *Better Homes Gard* 65:81-2+ D '87
Amaral, Suzana
about
The hour of the star [film] Reviews
Américas 39:62-3 My/Je '87. J. Mosier
New Yorker 63:110-11 F 23 '87. P. Kael
Vogue il 177:32+ Ja '87. M. Haskell
Amaranth
Amaranth: the color of soy sauce. *Prevention* 39:53-4 O '87
Amaretto (Ship)
The round haul [Penobscot Bay herring fishery; excerpt from Amaretto] J. Upton. il *Oceans* 20:8-17 Ja/F '87
Amarillo (Tex.)
Social life and customs
The present and the apocalypse. C. Widmann. *World Press Rev* 34:51 Mr '87
Amartya Kumar Sen *See* Sen, Amartya Kumar
AMAS Repertory Theatre, Inc.
Essence woman [founder R. LeNoire] P. A. Carter. il *Essence* 18:30 My '87
Amateur art *See* Art, Amateur
Amateur astronomers *See* Astronomers, Amateur
Amateur musicians *See* Musicians, Amateur
Amateur photography *See* Photography
Amateur scientists *See* Scientists, Amateur
Amateur tape recordings *See* Tape recordings—Amateur recordings
Amateur videotape recordings *See* Videotapes—Amateur recordings
Amateurism (Sports)
Barred from track again, Gault settles on football. por *Jet* 72:48 Ap 20 '87
Cheap labor on campus. D. Glasner. por *Newsweek* 110:12 N 9 '87
The good life of the new amateurs. M. Kort. il *Women's Sports Fitness* 9:23-6+ Ja '87
Amato Opera Theatre
Musical events:
A. C. Gomes' Salvator Rosa. A. Porter. *New Yorker* 63:93 My 25 '87
Natural wonder [production of Salvator Rosa] P. G. Davis. il *N Y* 20:114-15 My 25 '87
AMAX Inc.
Al Born digs AMAX out of a hole. C. Leinster. il pors *Fortune* 115:205-6+ Ap 27 '87
Amax finds a way out of the abyss. J. R. Norman. il por *Bus Week* p82-3 O 26 '87
Diary of a decision: a week in the life of Amax [A. Born's struggle to buoy his company's stock] J. R. Norman. il por *Bus Week* p118+ N 9 '87

Amaya, Mary
about
Battling the IQ-test ban. J. N. Baker. il por *Newsweek* 110:53 Jl 27 '87
Amazing Events, Inc.
Prankster Jeff Pinsker profits profoundly from improbable practical jokes. S. Dougherty. il por *People Wkly* 27:58-9 Je 15 '87
Amazing Grace and Chuck [film] See Motion picture reviews—Single works
Amazing Randi *See* Randi, James
Amazon River
Adrift on the Amazon. W. Hamilton. il *House Gard* 159:64+ F '87
Attacking the Amazon. R. Blount. il pors *Sports Illus* 66:60-4+ Ap 13 '87
The great Amazonian expedition [M. S. Forbes and friends] C. T. Buckley. il pors map *Forbes* 140:193-8+ O 19 '87
Kayaking the Amazon. P. Chmielinski. il pors map *Natl Geogr* 171:460-73 Ap '87
A land of contrasts [waters of the Amazon contrasted with drought-stricken Northeast Brazil] T. de Mello. il map *Courier* 39:4-10 D '86
Taming the Amazon [cruise on 148-ft. yacht Calliope] P. Whittell. il *Mot Boat Sail* 159:36-43+ My '87
Amazon River Valley
See also
Geology—Amazon River Valley
Postal service—Amazon River Valley
An imperilled people [Brazil's Yanoama endangered by Amazonian development] B. Levin. il map *Macleans* 100:26-7 Je 29 '87
The last frontier [Brazil's Amazon policy] B. Levin. il *Macleans* 100:28 Ja 19 '87
Rethinking continuous cultivation in Amazonia. P. M. Fearnside. bibl f il *BioScience* 37:209-14 Mr '87
Risky business [Peruvian Amazon markets] C. Padoch. il *Nat Hist* 96:56-65 O '87
Rubber and Amazon alliances. S. Schwartzman. il map *Technol Rev* 90:15-16 Ap '87
Yurimaguas technology [discussion of March 1987 article, Rethinking continuous cultivation in Amazonia] P. M. Fearnside. *BioScience* 37:638-40 O '87
Description and travel
The call of the Amazon. C. Langevin. il map *Travel Holiday* 168:60-5+ Jl '87
Ways to go. R. O'Hanlon. *Harpers* 274:23 Je '87
Discovery and exploration
In search of the Amazons [1639 expedition; excerpt from New discovery of the great river of the Amazons] C. de Acuña. il *Courier* 40:9 Ap '87
Amazon women on the moon [film] See Motion picture reviews—Single works
Amazonia *See* Amazon River Valley
Amazons
In search of the Amazons [1639 expedition; excerpt from New discovery of the great river of the Amazons] C. de Acuña. il *Courier* 40:9 Ap '87
Ambassadors
See also
Lauder, Ronald S., 1944-
Instructions to ambassadors on chain of command. G. P. Shultz; R. Reagan. *Dep State Bull* 87:40-1 Mr '87
Amber
Amber yields samples of ancient air [work of Robert A. Berner and Gary P. Landis] R. Monastersky. *Sci News* 132:293 N 7 '87
Ancient air analyzed in dinosaur-age amber [research by Robert Berner and Gary Landis] R. A. Kerr. *Science* 238:890 N 13 '87
Putting on ancient airs [ancient atmosphere trapped in amber found to contain 50% more oxygen] il *Time* 130:82 N 9 '87
An upper Eocene frog from the Dominican Republic and its implication for Caribbean biogeography. G. O. Poinar and D. C. Cannatella. bibl f il *Science* 237:1215-16 S 4 '87
Ambition
Something in the way he works . . . why we have an eye for the driven guy. B. G. Harrison. il *Mademoiselle* 93:262-3+ S '87
You get ahead, she gets mad. G. Blair. *Mademoiselle* 93:219 S '87
Anecdotes, facetiae, satire, etc.
Youthful ambitions. R. Baker. il *N Y Times Mag* p16 Je 14 '87
Amblyopia *See* Eye—Diseases and defects
Amboseli National Park (Kenya) *See* National parks and reserves—Kenya

Ambrose, Stephen E.
about
'The best and worst of presidents' [interview] A. P. Sanoff. il pors *U S News World Rep* 102:67-8 My 4 '87
Ambrus, Katherine
A sense of scents. il *Conservationist* 42:42-7 Jl/Ag '87
Ambulance service
Ambulance emergencies and how to get help fast. *Better Homes Gard* 65:53 Je '87
Ambulatory surgery See Surgery
Ambulatory surgical centers See Health facilities
Ambush bugs
Guerrillas of the goldenrod [cover story] L. G. Mason. il *Nat Hist* 96:34-9 Ag '87
AMC See American Motors Corp.
Amdahl Corporation
Learning from disaster. M. Beauchamp. il *Forbes* 140:96 O 19 '87
Amdur, Neil
Editor's page. See issues of World Tennis beginning June 1984
Amelia goes to the ball [opera] See Menotti, Gian Carlo, 1911-
Amemiya, Yoshiyuki, and others
Laser-stimulated luminescence used to measure X-ray diffraction of a contracting striated muscle. bibl f il *Science* 237:164-8 Jl 10 '87
Amen [television program] See Television program reviews—Single works
Amendments to the Constitution See United States. Constitution—Amendments; United States. Constitution. 1st-10th amendments
Amenorrhea See Menstruation—Disorders
Amerada Hess Corp.
Leon Hess: can the bottom-of-the-barrel oil baron get back on top? J. R. Norman. il por *Bus Week* p50-1+ Je 29 '87
America
See also
Canada
Latin America
United States

Antiquities
See also
Paleo-Indians
Discovery and exploration
See also
Canada—Discovery and exploration
Santa Maria (Ship)
United States—Exploring expeditions
Basques in the Age of Exploration. C. S. Campbell. il map *Focus* 36:24-9 Wint '86
Columbus's biggest discovery. R. Sokolov. il *Nat Hist* 96:66-7 Ag '87
Retracing the path of Christopher Columbus. il *Sea Front* 33:307 Jl/Ag '87
Searching for Columbus's lost colony [La Navidad in Haiti] K. A. Deagan. il *Natl Geogr* 172:672-5 N '87
History
The Americas: enlightenment and enterprise [excerpt from Memory of fire]; tr. by Cedric Belfrage. E. H. Galeano. *Harpers* 274:24+ F '87
America (Periodical)
America and theological education [Catholic theology; address] G. W. Hunt. *America* 157:6-8 Jl 4-11 '87
Of many things. G. W. Hunt. *America* 157:2 Jl 4-11 '87
Of many things. G. W. Hunt. *America* 156:inside cover Ap 11 '87
America by design [television program] See Television program reviews—Single works
America the Beautiful Fund
Seeds that grow hope. H. Hurt. il *Read Dig* 130:19-22+ Mr '87
America West Airlines, Inc.
America West continues expansion with transcontinental 757 service. B. A. Smith. il *Aviat Week Space Technol* 126:42-3 Mr 2 '87
Ansett's stock purchase will place foreign stake in America West at 20%. M. A. Dornheim. il map *Aviat Week Space Technol* 127:41-2+ Jl 20 '87
Deregulation's latest darling. J. Schwartz. il por *Newsweek* 110:68 D 7 '87
This upstart could be flying a bit too high. S. Toy. il *Bus Week* p76 Je 15 '87
American Academy and Institute of Arts and Letters
American portraits [National Portrait Gallery exhibition entitled Portraits from the American Academy and Institute of Arts and Letters] S. B. Sherrill. il *Antiques* 131:1186 Je '87

American Academy in Rome
An academic presence in Rome. R. Lynes. il *Archit Dig* 44:27+ My '87
American Airlines, Inc.
AirCal will begin service as American on July 1. M. A. Dornheim. map *Aviat Week Space Technol* 126:53 My 11 '87
American Airlines offers Europeans choice of CRS assistance [computerized passenger reservations system] *Aviat Week Space Technol* 127:34 Jl 20 '87
American Airlines plans to raise domestic fares. C. Preble. *Aviat Week Space Technol* 126:32-3 F 23 '87
American Airlines seeks simpler long-term fleet composition. C. A. Shifrin. il *Aviat Week Space Technol* 126:37 Mr 30 '87
American begins operations at new Raleigh hub complex [Raleigh/Durham Airport] C. A. Shifrin. il *Aviat Week Space Technol* 127:54+ Jl 6 '87
American begins operations at secure computer center [underground center in Tulsa, Okla.] *Aviat Week Space Technol* 126:43+ Ap 20 '87
American commits $225 million to upgrade maintenance operations. C. A. Shifrin. il *Aviat Week Space Technol* 126:44-6 Je 29 '87
American configures 747SPs to serve Tokyo first/business-class market. il *Aviat Week Space Technol* 126:54 My 11 '87
American diversifies operations based on airline-related skills. C. A. Shifrin. il *Aviat Week Space Technol* 126:38-40 Ap 20 '87
American, pilots sign agreement on retroactive pay, work rule changes. *Aviat Week Space Technol* 126:40 Mr 30 '87
American vs. its unions: double trouble [two-tier pay scales for pilots and flight attendants] T. Mason. il por *Bus Week* p45 F 23 '87
American wields leverage in aircraft lease arrangement [leasing order divided between Airbus Industrie and Boeing] J. Ott. il *Aviat Week Space Technol* 126:258-9 Mr 9 '87
Americans' flight attendants union to merge with AFL-CIO group. *Aviat Week Space Technol* 127:33 Ag 24 '87
AMR, Pan Am end pact on Sabre system use [computer reservations system] C. A. Shifrin. *Aviat Week Space Technol* 127:33-4 Ag 24 '87
Crandall proposes commission empowered to limit flights. J. Ott. *Aviat Week Space Technol* 126:32-3 Je 29 '87
Federal mediator joins American, pilot talks. *Aviat Week Space Technol* 126:31 F 16 '87
Pan Am, American continue negotiations [joint frequent-flier program] *Aviat Week Space Technol* 127:54 Ag 3 '87
Secret formula [automation] E. Dyson. il *Forbes* 140:242 O 5 '87
Texas Air unit charges American with restraining CRS business [computer reservation systems] C. A. Shifrin. *Aviat Week Space Technol* 127:51 D 7 '87
The volatile airline industry [address, February 23, 1987] R. L. Crandall. *Vital Speeches Day* 53:468-72 My 15 '87
Who will be Sky King? [fare wars between Texas Air and American Airlines] A. Miller. il pors *Newsweek* 109:54 Mr 2 '87
American antelope hunting See Pronghorn hunting
American antelopes See Pronghorns
American Antiquarian Society
A good home for old words. G. Avery. il *Am Herit* 38:104-6 Jl/Ag '87
Top 1987 APHA awards to Tanselle, Antiquarian Society. por *Publ Wkly* 231:76 F 6 '87
American-Arab Anti-Discrimination Committee
Cure, Arab group reach accord on song [objections to song titled Killing an Arab] A. DeCurtis. *Roll Stone* p30 F 26 '87
American architecture See Architecture, American
American art See Art, American
American artist (Periodical)
Anniversary events and issues [fiftieth anniversary] M. S. Doherty. il *Am Artist* 51:12 Ja '87
American artists See Artists, American
American Association for the Advancement of Science
AAAS news. See occasional issues of Science
Alvin Trivelpiece of DOE is named new executive officer of AAAS. B. J. Culliton. por *Science* 235:840 F 20 '87
Alvin W. Trivelpiece: AAAS Executive Officer. C. M. Susskind. il por *Science* 236:377 Ap 24 '87
Annual report of the executive officer. W. D. Carey. *Science* 235:638-41 F 6 '87

American Association for the Advancement of Science
—cont.

Walter E. Massey: president-elect of AAAS. N. M. Bradburn and D. Rosen. bibl f por *Science* 238:1657-8 D 18 '87

William D. Carey [retirement as executive officer] D. E. Koshland, Jr. *Science* 235:1553 Mr 27 '87

Meetings

AAAS annual meeting [1988 preliminary program] il *Science* 238:817-28 N 6 '87

AAAS Council meeting, 1987. *Science* 236:95-8 Ap 3 '87

Soviet science and technology at the Boston meeting. A. W. Trivelpiece. *Science* 238:1631 D 18 '87

American Association for the Advancement of Slavic Studies

Gorbachev's profs. J. Rupnik. *New Repub* 197:10+ D 7 '87

American Association of Community Theatres

AACT/Fest. M. LaRue. il *Theatre Crafts* 21:20 O '87

American Association of Individual Investors

The "nonprofit" with the fat profit margin. R. Simon. il por *Forbes* 140:37-8 N 2 '87

American Association of Physics Teachers

AAPT and APS meet in San Francisco. M. Marynowski. il *Phys Today* 40:65-6 Ja '87

AAPT elects Wheeler to be its new president in 1988. por *Phys Today* 40:72 Ap '87

American Association of Retired Persons

AARP caregiver pubs for employers, local groups and individuals. *Aging* no355:26-7 '87

Against maturity. D. Seligman. il *Fortune* 116:170 D 21 '87

Brickfield to go. Who will follow his act? R. Rosenblatt. *50 Plus* 27:15+ Je '87

Let's get serious about age bias. B. Lindeman. il *50 Plus* 27:4-5 O '87

Lobbies rock the retirement boat [American Assoc. of Retired Persons vs. C. Pepper] C. Murphy. il *50 Plus* 27:13-14 Ja '87

Protecting the golden goose [lobbying power] A. Plattner. il *U S News World Rep* 103:20 N 30 '87

Under new management. C. McLaughlin. *50 Plus* 27:20-1 N '87

American Astronomical Society

The 169th meeting of the American Astronomical Society. il *Astronomy* 15:76-80 Ap '87

AAS adopts resolution on space science. W. Sweet. *Phys Today* 40:70-1 Ap '87

AAS involves teachers in meetings. *Phys Today* 40:101-2 F '87

Halley in Heidelberg, planets in Paris. R. Berry. il *Astronomy* 15:24+ Mr '87

Meeting in Pasadena, astronomers report the latest on the deaths of stars and the births of solar systems and galaxies. J. P. Wiley, Jr. il *Smithsonian* 17:34+ Mr '87

American authors *See* Authors, American

American Ballet Theatre

American Ballet Theatre at the Met: armies of angels. J. R. Acocella. il *Dance Mag* 61:48-53 S '87

Argentina's golden boy Julio Bocca. M. Hunt. il pors *Dance Mag* 61:60-1 Mr '87

The big Sleep [performances of The sleeping beauty] T. Tobias. il *N Y* 20:76-7 My 11 '87

Blossom time in New York. L. A. Jacobs. il *New Leader* 70:22-3 Jl 1-15 '87

Dancing:

Legacy of A. Tudor and staging of works by P. Taylor and C. Tippet. A. Croce. *New Yorker* 63:70+ Jl 6 '87

The sleeping beauty and Giselle. A. Croce. *New Yorker* 63:88-90 My 25 '87

A glimpse into fairyland [production of Sleeping beauty] M. Duffy. il *Time* 129:86 Ap 20 '87

Second sight [J. Bocca] T. Tobias. por *N Y* 20:111-12 My 25 '87

Too stark a 'Beauty' [performance of Sleeping beauty] L. A. Jacobs. *New Leader* 70:22 Ap 20 '87

Trials by Fire [revival of Pillar of fire with K. Moore and E. Brown] M. Hunt. il pors *Dance Mag* 61:42-5 My '87

Photographs and photography

American Ballet Theatre's early years: the way it was. W. Como. il *Dance Mag* 61:100-21 Je '87

American Ballroom Theater

Dancing:

Performances at the Joyce Theater. A. Croce. *New Yorker* 63:103 D 21 '87

Signs of the times [performance of Presley pieces at the Joyce Theater] T. Tobias. il *N Y* 20:155-6 D 7 '87

American Bell Association

Bells. *New Yorker* 63:21-3 Je 29 '87

American bison *See* Bison, American

American Black Achievement Awards

American Black Achievement Awards. il *Ebony* 42:128-30+ Ja '87

Natalie Cole, George Benson: hosts of TV's American Black Achievement Awards. il *Jet* 71:54-9 Ja 12 '87

American Book Awards

See also

National Book Awards

American Booksellers Association

See also

Booksellers Order Service

1987 ABA: success on many levels [special section] A. Symons and S. Bolle. il *Publ Wkly* 231:71-94 Je 19 '87

ABA 1987 [special section] il maps *Publ Wkly* 231:139-61+ My 15 '87

ABA to be exclusive distributor of 'Chronicle of 20th century' [distribution handled through BOS] *Publ Wkly* 231:14 Ap 3 '87

ABA's Rath addresses bookselling issues [interview] A. Symons. il por *Publ Wkly* 231:49-50 My 22 '87

Audio and video at ABA. T. Spain. il *Publ Wkly* 231:96+ Je 19 '87

Audio and video: the bookseller's perspective. J. Tangorra. *Publ Wkly* 231:102-3 Je 19 '87

Children's books at ABA: a vibrant atmosphere [symposium] il *Publ Wkly* 231:43-5+ Je 26 '87

Looking ahead to ABA: no video ghetto in D.C. il *Publ Wkly* 231:49-50 Mr 20 '87

Merchandising gift books. W. Goldstein. *Publ Wkly* 232:30-1 S 11 '87

Record-breaking ABA: 'overwhelming' in numbers, bustle, business. il *Publ Wkly* 231:12 Je 5 '87

Waldenbooks intends to resign from ABA. A. Symons. *Publ Wkly* 231:12 Mr 27 '87

Waldenbooks officially withdraws from Booksellers Association. il *Publ Wkly* 231:10 Ap 3 '87

American Brands, Inc.

American Brands is breaking its cigarette habit. R. W. King. il *Bus Week* p86+ S 14 '87

Caveat fumator [rulings in favor of Liggett & Myers and American Brands in product liability cases] J. Castro. il *Time* 130:43 S 7 '87

American Broadcasting Companies, Inc.

ABC's Amerikan dream. H. F. Waters. il *Newsweek* 109:21-2 F 16 '87

Amerika: it can't happen here. A. Kopkind. *Nation* 244:165+ F 14 '87

Amerika the controversial. R. Zoglin. il *Time* 129:72-3 F 9 '87

Better red than dud [miniseries Amerika] N. Atkins. il *Roll Stone* p29-30 F 12 '87

The big money battle [ABC wins TV broadcast rights to Calgary Winter Olympics] P. Young. il *Macleans* 100:36-7 Mr 23 '87

Black cameramen lose their $3.5 mil. suit against ABC. *Jet* 72:22 Ag 24 '87

An exception to Murphy's Law? [Capital Cities/ABC] S. N. Chakravarty. il por *Forbes* 140:36-8 Ag 10 '87

A golden boy gets axed [sportscaster J. Lampley] W. Taaffe. il *Sports Illus* 67:67 Jl 13 '87

Loyal Amerikans [Amerika] *Natl Rev* 39:18 Mr 13 '87

Made in Amerika [UN protests] J. Vitale. *Channels* 7:18 F '87

A new miniseries imagines Amerika's future—if the Soviets won World War III. D. Scheuer. il *Sch Update* 119:23 Ja 26 '87

Not ready for prime time? [Capital Cities/ABC] G. Fabrikant. il pors *N Y Times Mag* p30+ Ap 12 '87

Only in 'Amerika': the mini-series everyone loves to hate. P. Hoban. il *N Y* 20:36-41 Ja 26 '87

A relish for risks [R. Arledge] H. F. Waters. il por *Newsweek* 109:59 Je 15 '87

Remember, it's only a movie [ABC's Amerika] M. Bosc. il *U S News World Rep* 102:15 Ja 19 '87

Situation Commie [Amerika] J. Maslin. *New Repub* 196:25-7 F 23 '87

A TV man views the storm [Amerika broadcast] V. G. Sauter. il *U S News World Rep* 102:68 F 16 '87

Twin ads: a case of mistaken identity [Michelob and ABC Sports run commercials using song Everybody have fun tonight by Wang Chung] *Newsweek* 110:37 Ag 24 '87

Up from 'Club Thirteen': the rise and rise of Peter Jennings. D. Blum. il pors *N Y* 20:50-6 N 30 '87

American Broadcasting Companies, Inc.—*cont.*
Will bad Russians make good ratings? [Amerika] A. P. Sanoff. il *U S News World Rep* 102:66-7 F 16 '87
Will temptation undo the tie that binds [networks questioning affiliate compensation] S. Behrens. il *Channels* 7:41-3 My '87

American Business Network
Rising above trade rivalry [BizNet teleconference on U.S.-Japanese trade] il *Nations Bus* 75:45-6 Ap '87

American businesswomen in foreign countries *See* Americans—Foreign countries

American Can Company
See also
Primerica Corp.

American cheese *See* Cheese

American cheese cooking *See* Cooking—Cheese

American Cinema Awards
Sophia Loren and Kirk Douglas waltz through their latest roles as Hollywood honorees. il pors *People Wkly* 27:72-3 Ja 26 '87

American citizenship *See* Citizenship

American City Business Journals, Inc.
Demand-side journalism. R. McGough. il pors *Forbes* 139:68+ F 23 '87
What's black and white—and in the red? M. Ivey. il pors *Bus Week* p60 F 16 '87

American Civil Liberties Union
ACLU sues to end school bd. appointments in Va. [black discrimination cited] *Jet* 73:37 N 2 '87
Who are the 'moderates'? [ACLU objects to Detroit Tigers' attempt to curb fans' vulgarity] G. F. Will. il *Newsweek* 110:100 O 12 '87

American College of Surgeons
Miller named 1st black pres. of the American College of Surgeons S. Calif. chapter [R. M. Miller] por *Jet* 72:26 Ap 27 '87

American College Testing Program
Cramming for college [coaching courses to boost SAT and ACT scores] K. McCormick. il *Changing Times* 41:61+ S '87

American conservatism *See* Conservatism

American Continental Corp.
Charles Keating: feeling the heat in Phoenix. K. Kelly. il por *Bus Week* p80 Ag 31 '87

American cooking *See* Cooking, American

American correspondents in foreign countries *See* Foreign correspondents

American Council for the Arts
A national network of leadership [National Patrons of the American Council for the Arts] M. Rhodes. il *Horizon* 30:4 Ap '87

American Craft Council
Council awards gold medals, inducts 12 fellows. il *Am Craft* 47:6+ Ag/S '87
New faces at ACC. *Am Craft* 47:9 O/N '87
Three join American Craft Council board. il *Am Craft* 47:6 Je/Jl '87

American Craft Enterprises, Inc.
American Craft Enterprises, Inc. scores record year. il *Am Craft* 47:6+ D '87/Ja '88

American Craft Museum (New York, N.Y.)
American Craft Museum to host young talent showcase in 1988. il *Am Craft* 47:6+ O/N '87
American craft: poetry of the physical. P. J. Smith. il *USA Today (Periodical)* 116:74-85 S '87
Consummate connoisseur [P. J. Smith leaving position as director] R. Kehlmann. il por *Am Craft* 47:50-5 O/N '87
A fine American hand. D. Brenner. il *Archit Rec* 175:122-7 Mr '87
Museum Associates host benefit auction at Sotheby's. L. Moran. il *Am Craft* 47:8+ D '87/Ja '88
A new presence for craft. P. Goldberger. il *Am Craft* 47:30-2 F/Mr '87
Off press [reviews of inaugural exhibit Craft today: poetry of the physical] *Am Craft* 47:11-12 F/Mr '87
Paul Smith named director emeritus of museum. *Am Craft* 47:6 Je/Jl '87
Skill full [architecture] J. Lebensohn. il *Am Craft* 47:33-5 F/Mr '87

American Crystallographic Association
Templetons honored for work in crystallography. il pors *Phys Today* 40:83 Jl '87

American culture *See* United States—Civilization

American Cut Glass Association
American Cut Glass Association's convention in Washington, D.C. *Antiques Collect Hobbies* 92:32 Jl '87

American Cyanamid Co.
Cyanamid is bullish on a cure for sick cows [acquiring stake in Applied Microbiology's protein for mastitis] G. G. Marcial. il *Bus Week* p136 My 11 '87

American dance *See* Dance

American decorative arts *See* Decoration and ornament

American defectors *See* Defectors, Political

American depositary receipts
The ABCs of ADRs. A. A. Lappen. il *Forbes* 139:244 Je 15 '87
Best ways to buy foreign stocks. R. Micheli. il *Money* 16:75+ My '87
The cheapest stocks in the world. J. Edgerton and J. E. Goodman. il *Money* 16:7 N '87
An easy way to send your portfolio overseas. D. Zigas. il *Bus Week* p128-9 O 5 '87
How to buy foreign stocks. P. Sherrid. il *U S News World Rep* 102:54+ My 11 '87
Sour notes for Hard Rock Cafe. G. G. Marcial. *Bus Week* p72 Ap 6 '87

American dramatists *See* Dramatists, American

American dream (Philosophy)
Alternative universes: literature, ethics and the American dream. C. A. Rubino. *America* 157:332+ N 7 '87
The American dream: the family's tie. K. Zinsmeister. *Current* 290:9-13 F '87
American dreamer. A. Fadiman. See issues of Life beginning February 1986 through October 1987
My American dream [desire to emigrate to America from the Soviet Union] V. V. Tokarev. il *Newsweek* 110:49 D 14 '87

American economic assistance *See* Economic assistance, American

American Economic Association
The newest name in economics: John Maynard Keynes. N. Jonas and J. Berger. *Bus Week* p42 Ja 12 '87

American embassy buildings *See* Embassies (Buildings)

American Express Co.
American Express may be a sleeper. G. G. Marcial. *Bus Week* p88 Je 29 '87
Career makeover: from ticket agent to advertising director [L. Lockman-Brooks] il por *Glamour* 85:134 Ag '87
Charge of the plastic brigade [Optima card] J. Castro. il *Time* 129:52 Mr 23 '87
Credit cards: hey, big spender, the Optima is for you [variable-rate card] il *Money* 16:26 My '87
From American Express—revolving credit [Optima card] J. B. Levine and C. Farrell. *Bus Week* p146 Mr 23 '87
A green light for the Green Card. il *Money* 16:8 Je '87
Service starts with the man at the top. B. Saporito and M. J. Williams. il pors *Fortune* 116:108 D 7 '87
Synergy works at American Express. M. J. Williams. il *Fortune* 115:79-80 F 16 '87
You must know me [credit card ads] A. Miller. il *Newsweek* 110:64 Ag 17 '87
Your humble servant [Authorizer's Assistant AI-based system] E. Dyson. il *Forbes* 140:204 N 2 '87

American fashion designers *See* Fashion designers

American Federation of Labor and Congress of Industrial Organizations *See* AFL-CIO

American fiction
See also
Western stories
American classics [recipes inspired by meals in American literature] il *Ladies Home J* 104:106-9+ Jl '87
Esquire summer reading [cover story; special section] il *Esquire* 108:62-4+ Ag '87
The fiction we deserve. C. Iannone. *Commentary* 83:60-2 Je '87
The fictions of America. E. Hardwick. il *N Y Rev Books* 34:12+ Je 25 '87
Minimalist fiction [discussion of June 1987 article, The fiction we deserve] C. Iannone. *Commentary* 84:14-15+ O '87
What's left out of literature. C. H. Newman. il *N Y Times Book Rev* 92:1+ Jl 12 '87
Wheatland Conference: American writers carp at the state of U.S. literature. H. Fields. *Publ Wkly* 231:10 My 8 '87
Yuppie lit: publicize or perish. R. Z. Sheppard. il *Time* 130:77-9 O 19 '87

American Financial Corp.
How Lindner keeps his troops and investments in line. D. Cook. il por *Bus Week* p81 Ap 20 '87

American folk art *See* Folk art
American furniture *See* Furniture, American
American General Corp.
Harold Hook's magnificent machine. W. P. Barrett. il por *Forbes* 140:48+ O 19 '87
American Geophysical Union
American Geophysical Union honored eight in 1986. il *Phys Today* 40:83-4+ Je '87
American glass *See* Glassware
American Health and Beauty Aids Institute
The battle of the curls [objects to Revlon racist statement about black consumers and black hair care manufacturers] K. Smikle. *Black Enterp* 17:18 Ja '87
Black beauty industry fetes Chicago's Mayor Washington. il *Jet* 71:12 Mr 2 '87
Soft Sheen president-CEO elected new AHBAI chair [G. Gardner] por *Jet* 73:25 O 12 '87
American heritage (Periodical)
Letter from the editor. B. Dobell. See issues of American Heritage
American historians *See* Historians, American
American history *See* United States—History
American Home Economics Association
Special "cooking friends" add spice to Head Start nutrition programs [Volunteer Nutrition Consultant Project] S. A. Koblinsky and M. G. Phillips. il *Child Today* 16:26-9 Jl/Ag '87
American Home Products Corp.
Slumbering giant [stock price] T. Jaffe. *Forbes* 140:138 Ag 24 '87
American house decoration *See* House decoration, American
American humor *See* Humor, American
American Indians *See* Indians (American)
American Institute for Free Labor Development
AFL-CIO is Spanish for union busting [U.S. efforts to destroy independent labor movement in El Salvador] F. Smyth. *Wash Mon* 19:24-7 S '87
Duarte's secret friends [U.S. efforts to divide and destroy new independent labor movement in El Salvador] F. Smyth. il *Nation* 244:316-18 Mr 14 '87
Which side are they on? The AFL-CIO tames Guatemala's unions. J. Slaughter. il *Progressive* 51:32-5 Ja '87
American Institute of Architects
Design awards/competitions. See issues of Architectural Record

Meetings
AIA convention forums on professional development anticipated a startling period of far-reaching change. C. K. Hoyt. il *Archit Rec* 175:35 Ag '87
AIA convention news: fact and fantasy under the Florida sun. D. Dietsch and P. M. Sachner. il *Archit Rec* 175:37+ Ag '87
Can there ever be too many architects? M. F. Schmertz. *Archit Rec* 175:9 Ag '87
Conference report: the AIA takes a new look at 'America's Sunporch' [conference sponsored by design committee that investigated The fantasy architecture of Miami] P. M. Sachner. il *Archit Rec* 175:39 Ja '87
Monterey 1987: glamour out, humanism back in [Monterey Design Conference] P. M. Sachner. il *Archit Rec* 175:57-8 Je '87
American Institute of Biological Sciences
AIBS news. E. G. Sorohan. See occasional issues of BioScience
Annual AIBS meeting. See issues of BioScience
American Institute of Certified Public Accountants
Imagine a cutthroat CPA. G. Weiss. il *Bus Week* p96 S 28 '87
American Institute of Physics
AIP in 1986: an annual report. il *Phys Today* 40:49-56 Jl '87
AIP publishes profile of member society membership. il *Phys Today* 40:57 Je '87
AIP will start a new magazine, Computers in physics, in 1988. il *Phys Today* 40:71-2 Ap '87
Governing bodies consider moving AIP headquarters or units to DC area. W. Sweet. il *Phys Today* 40:75-6 D '87
H. William Koch and AIP. F. Seitz and others. *Phys Today* 40:144 Ap '87
IUPAP and Corporate Associates meet in Washington. W. Sweet. il *Phys Today* 40:76-7 D '87
Rigden is new physics director at AIP. por *Phys Today* 40:61-2 Jl '87
Watkins starts work as AIP senior education fellow. por *Phys Today* 40:85 N '87
American Institute of Steel Construction
American Institute of Steel Construction 1987 Architectural Awards of Excellence. il *Archit Rec* 175:66-9 S '87

American International Toy Fair *See* Toys—Exhibitions
American investments *See* Investments, American
American Israel Public Affairs Committee
The lobby with a lock on Congress. J. Weisberg. il *Newsweek* 110:46+ O 19 '87
American Jazz Orchestra
Benny Carter/American Jazz Orchestra. M. Bourne. il por *Down Beat* 54:56-7 Je '87
Jazz. G. Santoro. *Nation* 244:374-6 Mr 21 '87
American liberalism *See* Liberalism
American List Corp.
Addressing the student market [M. Lerner] M. Gill. il por *Esquire* 108:76 D '87
American literature
See also
Black literature
The Civil War and American destiny. T. J. Fleming. il *Natl Rev* 39:48+ N 6 '87
Esquire's guide to the literary universe [with introd. by Rust Hills] il *Esquire* 108:51-3+ Ag '87
Collectors and collecting
A passion for history [J. Engelhard's collections] J. Fleming. il *House Gard* 159:122-5+ Mr '87
Voluminous obsession. C. Burden. il *House Gard* 159:126-31+ Mr '87
Jewish authors
Defenders of the faith [P. Roth's The counterlife and C. Ozick's The messiah of Stockholm] R. Alter. *Commentary* 84:52-5 Jl '87
American loyalists
The prodigal son [B. Franklin's son William] J. M. Taylor. il pors *Am Hist Illus* 22:10-21 Mr '87
American Lubrication Company
Old-fashioned service. J. C. Johnson. il por *Nations Bus* 75:48-9 Je '87
American Management Association
In Chicago: seminars everywhere. R. Conniff. il *Time* 130:12 O 12 '87
American manuscripts *See* Manuscripts, American
American Medical Association
Medical assistance [mutual fund interests] R. Phalon. il *Forbes* 139:114 Ap 20 '87
American Medical International, Inc.
On the mend. T. Jaffe. *Forbes* 139:202 Je 1 '87
American Metal Climax, Inc. *See* AMAX Inc.
American military assistance *See* Military assistance, American
American minorities *See* Minorities
American Motors Corp.
Chrysler courts AMC. P. Lienert. il *Road Track* 38:110+ Mr '87
A daredevil wheel deal [Chrysler buys AMC] G. Russell. il *Time* 129:40-1 Mr 23 '87
How bright is the future for AMC? M. Keller. il *Mot Trend* 39:174 Je '87
Jeep/Eagle: preview of an evolution [Chrysler's acquisition of AMC] M. Keller. il *Mot Trend* 39:150 N '87
Moving upscale. W. J. Mitchell. il *Time* 129:68 F 23 '87
Now, for Chrysler's next trick . . . [acquisition of American Motors Corp.] W. J. Hampton. il *Bus Week* p32-3 Mr 23 '87
The payoff to customers from Chrysler-AMC merger. J. A. Seamonds. il *U S News World Rep* 102:58-9 Mr 23 '87
Survival of the fleetest [Chrysler's acquisition of AMC and Lamborghini] J. Lamm. il *Road Track* 39:118+ O '87
'Zip, overnight': a Chrysler Jeep [Chrysler's bid for AMC] B. Powell. il *Newsweek* 109:38-9 Mr 23 '87
American Movie Classics (Firm)
Manna from Turner. A. B. Block. il *Forbes* 139:126+ My 18 '87
American Museum of Natural History
At the American Museum. See issues of Natural History
The living museum. See issues of Natural History
Making prehistory [dinosaur models at Reproductions Shop] C. Rubin. il *Vogue* 177:58 Jl '87
American music *See* Music, American
American Music Awards
Janet Jackson leading American Music nominations. il por *Jet* 71:57 Ja 19 '87
Janet pleased with wins; Run D.M.C. shocked with loss at Music Awards show. il por *Jet* 71:60-1 F 16 '87
American Music Theater Festival *See* Music festivals—Pennsylvania
American Natural Beverage Corporation
Soda war [American National Beverage fights trademark dispute with Anheuser-Busch] R. L. Stern. il *Forbes* 139:82-3 My 4 '87

American Natural Beverage Corporation—*cont.*
SoHo skirmish [wins trademark dispute with Anheuser-Busch] J. A. Conway. il *Forbes* 139:8 Je 29 '87
A splashy soda upstart pours it on. J. Schwartz. il *Newsweek* 109:52 Je 8 '87
American Natural Foods, Inc.
A sorcerer's sauce [Wizard Baldour's Hot Stuff] M. Oberlaender. il por *Nations Bus* 75:70 Ja '87
American Newspaper Publishers Association
Hire more minorities in nation's newsrooms: ANPA. *Jet* 72:22 Je 8 '87
American Nobel Fellowships *See* Scholarships and fellowships
American novelists *See* Novelists, American
American Numismatic Association
American Numismatic Association offering counterfeit detection and coin grading seminars. *Antiques Collect Hobbies* 92:82+ My '87
American Opera Center *See* Juilliard American Opera Center
American painting *See* Painting, American
American Paper Institute
Richard Storat succeeds Norman Pace at API. por *Publ Wkly* 232:45 S 4 '87
American patriotism *See* Patriotism
American Physical Society
The APS Council and the DEW study [letters] *Phys Today* 40:9+ O '87
APS on SDI: too soon to decide. D. E. Thomsen. *Sci News* 131:276 My 2 '87
APS panel disowns council statement [statement that argued against early deployment of Strategic Defense Initiative] C. Norman. *Science* 238:155 O 9 '87
APS releases report on directed-energy weapons [special section] bibl f il *Phys Today* 40:S1-S16 My '87
APS report on SDI [discussion of May 1, 1987 article, Doubt cast on laser weapons] C. Norman. *Science* 236:1411-12 Je 12 '87
APS Star Wars study given prominent coverage in US press. W. Sweet. *Phys Today* 40:55-6 Je '87
Arthur Gordon Webster, founder of the APS. M. Phillips. il pors *Phys Today* 40:48-52 Je '87
Debate on APS directed-energy weapons study. G. H. Canavan and others. bibl f pors *Phys Today* 40:48-53 N '87
Doubt cast on laser weapons. C. Norman. il *Science* 236:509-10 My 1 '87
How eminent physicists have lent their names to a politicized report on strategic defense. A. M. Codevilla. *Commentary* 84:21-6 S '87
Mightier than the SDI. *Commonweal* 114:261-2 My 8 '87
News from APS. See occasional issues of Physics Today
Panel disputes SDI timetable. *Aviat Week Space Technol* 126:37 Ap 27 '87
The people deceived. *Natl Rev* 39:16 N 20 '87
Physicists assess laser lethality for ballistic missile defense role. P. J. Klass. *Aviat Week Space Technol* 126:104-5 My 18 '87
Scientists shoot down Star Wars. W. Sweet. *Bull At Sci* 43:7-9 Jl/Ag '87
SDI attempts to zap APS directed-energy weapons report. I. Goodwin. il *Phys Today* 40:43-6 Je '87
SDI: paper pile grows on APS study. K. Hartley. *Sci News* 132:38 Jl 18 '87
SDI watch. *Natl Rev* 39:16-17 My 22 '87
SDI watch. *Natl Rev* 39:16 Jl 17 '87
SDI watch. *Natl Rev* 39:16 Ag 14 '87
SDI zapped. *Sci Am* 256:18 Je '87
Thoughts of a retiring APS president. S. D. Drell. il *Phys Today* 40 pt1:56-62 Ag '87
Three receive APS plasma physics awards. il *Phys Today* 40:85-6 Mr '87
Weapons designers challenge SDI report. W. Booth. *Science* 237:127 Jl 10 '87

Meetings
AAPT and APS meet in San Francisco. M. Marynowski. il *Phys Today* 40:65-6 Ja '87
APS holds March meeting in New York. M. Marynowski. il *Phys Today* 40:81-5 F '87
American Physical Society. International Physics Group
International Physics Group is increasingly active. il *Phys Today* 40:105 My '87
American poetry

Anecdotes, facetiae, satire, etc.
Great ad copy in American poetry: an anthology. D. Penrice. il *Atlantic* 260:40-1 O '87

American poets laureate *See* Poets laureate, American
American portraits *See* Portraits, American
American posters *See* Posters
American pottery *See* Pottery, American
American President Companies Ltd.
Train, ahoy! J. Cook. il por *Forbes* 139:60+ My 18 '87
American Printing History Association
Top 1987 APHA awards to Tanselle, Antiquarian Society. por *Publ Wkly* 231:76 F 6 '87
American propaganda *See* Propaganda
American Psychiatric Association
The parable of the cheek-turners and the cheek-smiters [feminist opposition to proposed revision of the Diagnostic and statistical manual of mental disorders] S. Boxer. il *Discover* 8:80-3 Ag '87
The politics of masochism [feminists challenge proposed revisions to Diagnostic and statistical manual of mental disorders] D. Franklin. il *Psychol Today* 21:52-7 Ja '87
American public opinion *See* Public opinion
American Quasar Petroleum Co.
See also
Wolverine Exploration Company
American Repertory Theatre *See* Harvard University. American Repertory Theatre
American Revolution *See* United States—History—Revolution, 1775-1783
American Rocket Company
American Rocket negotiating for suborbital test flight of hybrid launch vehicle. M. A. Dornheim. il *Aviat Week Space Technol* 126:67-8 Mr 16 '87
Amroc official cites resistance to space commercialization [views of William R. Claybaugh] *Aviat Week Space Technol* 126:79 My 4 '87
Amroc pursues SDI as first paying customer. il *Aviat Week Space Technol* 127:24-5 O 19 '87
Slow progress may delay decision on antitactical missile. J. D. Morrocco. *Aviat Week Space Technol* 127:26-7 N 23 '87
American Scientific Affiliation
Evolution and creation: one missed opportunity. F. J. Ayala. *BioScience* 37:450 Jl/Ag '87
American sculpture *See* Sculpture, American
American Society for the Prevention of Cruelty to Animals
Bernstein for the defenseless [lawyer enforces New York's animal protection laws] K. Pritzker. il por *McCalls* 114:62 Jl '87
American Society of Composers, Authors and Publishers
Lena Horne receives ASCAP's top award. il por *Jet* 72:62 Ap 6 '87
American splendor [drama] See Rose, Lloyd
American Spoon Foods (Firm)
For forager Justin Rashid, the woods are lovely, dark and deep—and filled with things that he can eat. M. Neill. il pors *People Wkly* 28:125-7 O 19 '87
American State Bank (Lubbock, Tex.)
Behind the times—and glad of it. T. Mack. il *Forbes* 140:36 N 2 '87
American Stock Exchange *See* Stock exchanges—American exchange
American students in Great Britain *See* Foreign students—Great Britain
American studies
The American studies of Henry Nash Smith. R. Bridgman. *Am Sch* 56:259-68 Spr '87
Exhuming the corpse [in the Soviet Union] S. Strasser. il *Newsweek* 110:44 D 14 '87
American tables *See* Tables
American Telephone & Telegraph Co.
AT&T is eating 'em alive. J. J. Keller. il *Bus Week* p28-9 F 16 '87
AT&T may be ready to cut its losses in computers [Olivetti to join in a spinoff] J. J. Keller. il *Bus Week* p30 Jl 6 '87
AT&T's epic push in computers. P. Petre. il por *Fortune* 115:42-4+ My 25 '87
Broad shoulders to bear the burden [J. Olson] P. Petre. il por *Fortune* 116:31+ Ag 3 '87
Can't anyone out there repair this phone? B. Willis. por *U S News World Rep* 103:12 N 9 '87
Childbearing: the dangers of high tech [AT&T policy regarding pregnant semiconductor workers] il *U S News World Rep* 102:12 Ja 26 '87
Cooperative training in telecommunications: case studies [Communications Workers of America and American Telephone and Telegraph] M. Hilton and R. Straw. bibl f *Mon Labor Rev* 110:32-6 My '87
Danger in the clean room [semiconductor workers have increased risk of miscarriage] il *Time* 129:48 Ja 26 '87

American Telephone & Telegraph Co.—*cont.*

Info gridlock [U.S. lagging in videotex due to breakup of AT&T] *New Repub* 196:4 Ja 26 '87

The long-distance wars get hotter. J. J. Keller. il *Bus Week* p150-4+ Mr 23 '87

Moms-to-be banned from 'chip room'. *Sci News* 131:73 Ja 31 '87

More rabbits, please, Signor De Benedetti [Olivetti's linkup with AT&T] S. Solomon. por *Forbes* 139:114+ Mr 9 '87

Some modest proposals [survival in the computer business] K. K. Wiegner. il *Forbes* 139:38+ Ap 20 '87

The Swedes give AT&T, and the U.S., painful black eyes [L. M. Ericsson captures piece of Compagnie Générale de Constructions Téléphoniques] T. Peterson and F. J. Comes. il *Bus Week* p44-5 My 4 '87

Telephone talk [realism in TV advertising for small business phone systems] B. Kanner. il *N Y* 20:22+ Ap 27 '87

Why the FCC wants to cap rates instead of profits. F. Seghers. il *Bus Week* p88 Ag 17 '87

American tennis players *See* Tennis players

American Toxxic Control (Firm)

"Sailing was boring" [president L. Purmort] B. Leonard. il por *Forbes* 140:50-1 Jl 27 '87

American toys *See* Toys

American University (Washington, D.C.)

Big man on campus [A. Khashoggi's pledge to contribute $5 million] C. McCarthy. *Nation* 244:252-4 F 28 '87

American University of Beirut

The fantasy world of Gunpoint U. B. Dorler. il *World Press Rev* 34:60 Mr '87

American Vacuum Society

Coburn elected 1988 president in Vacuum Society balloting. por *Phys Today* 40:72 Ap '87

Vacuum Society meets in Anaheim. R. Hart and M. Marynowski. il *Phys Today* 40:75-7 O '87

American Warranty Company

New protection for goods in the gray market. il *Consum Rep* 52:525 S '87

American Wing *See* Metropolitan Museum of Art (New York, N.Y.). American Wing

American Woman's Economic Development Corporation

Polishing women entrepreneurs. S. Nelton. il *Nations Bus* 75:61-3 Jl '87

American youth *See* Youth

Americana

American historical flasks: glassware symbolic of a growing nation. K. McConnell. il *Antiques Collect Hobbies* 92:40-2 O '87

Americana in calendars—1988. J. O'Dwyer. il *Americana* 15:24-5 N/D '87

Americana in miniature [quiz] V. Nash. il *Americana* 15:21 N/D '87

Cabin fever. il *Redbook* 169:98-105 Jl '87

[Special issue on State Dept. Building] *Antiques* 132:118-87 Jl '87

Americana (Brazil)

In Brazil: echoes from the Confederacy [descendants of Americans who fled the South after the Civil War] M. Kepp. il *Time* 130:14 N 16 '87

Americana (Periodical)

Note from the editor [crossword puzzler W. Lutwiniak] S. Wilmot. il por *Americana* 15:3 My/Je '87

Americans

See also

　Arab Americans

　Bostonians

　Californians

　Chinese Americans

　Cuban Americans

　Greek Americans

　Horatio Alger Association of Distinguished Americans

　Irish Americans

　Italian Americans

　Japanese Americans

　Korean Americans

　Mexican Americans

　Morale, National

　Nebraskans

　Southerners

　Texans

　Vermonters

　Westerners

The 1987 Esquire register [special section] il *Esquire* 108:95+ D '87

American dreamer. A. Fadiman. See issues of Life beginning February 1986 through October 1987

Notes and comment [American character defined by being an automobile driver] *New Yorker* 63:29-30 N 30 '87

Who lives there? R. Rosenblatt. il *Time* 130:98 Jl 6 '87

Austria

An American in Vienna: Aerin Lauder. C. Hanauer. pors *Seventeen* 46:118+ S '87

History

An American's attempt to rescue Lafayette [rescue attempt by F. Huger; cover story] A. L. Levin. il por *Am Hist Illus* 22:16-20+ O '87

Belize

Peace Corps follies. S. Donziger. il *Progressive* 51:28-31 Mr '87

Brazil

See also

　Fraternidade Descendencia Americana

A bizarre escape from Brazil [mercenary T. Carmody] por *Newsweek* 109:35 Ja 5 '87

History

Whistling Dixie in Brazil [disillusioned southerners settle in Brazil, 1865-79] J. H. Kennedy. il *Américas* 39:26-31 Ja/F '87

Central America

Vacation at Club Dead. S. L. Wisenberg. il *Progressive* 51:34 Jl '87

China

One question. M. Salzman. *Harpers* 275:24+ N '87

Dominican Republic

History

How the Peace Corps exports friendship. H. Browne. il *Sch Update* 119:27 F 23 '87

Ethiopia

Bootstrap time in a luckless land [D. Carlson and B. Downing working in Ethiopia for Save the Children Federation] J. Buckley. il pors map *U S News World Rep* 103:88-90+ D 28 '87-Ja 4 '88

A state of permanent revolution. M. Thomas. il *Harpers* 274:53-6+ Ja '87

Tourists in hell [excerpt from Breakfast in hell] M. Harris. *Harpers* 274:28-31 F '87

Europe

See also

　United States—Armed Forces—Forces in Europe

Foreign countries

See also

　United States—Armed Forces—Forces in foreign countries

Travel advisories [nonpolitical service offered by the Bureau of Consular Affairs] *Dep State Bull* 87:19 O '87

What if you break your leg in Karachi? [travel assistance services] F. S. Chapman. il *U S News World Rep* 102:51-2 Je 15 '87

When Americans land in foreign jails. G. Breitstein. il *Sch Update* 119:14 F 9 '87

Employment

Making big bucks from the Big Bang [A. Berkowitch working for Booz, Allen & Hamilton in London] S. Seixas. il pors *Money* 16:161-2+ My '87

Taxation

Good reasons for that overseas post. P. Philipps. il *Bus Week* p108 Ja 26 '87

What if you just happen to be 'far away' on Apr. 15? G. Weiss. il *Bus Week* p111 Ap 13 '87

France

Americans in Paris [blacks] S. S. Oliver. il *Essence* 18:97-9 O '87

Architectural digest visits: James Baldwin. J. Baldwin. il pors *Archit Dig* 44:122-5 Ag '87

Buying a second house in Paris [experience of B. and C. Haber] C. Styles-McLeod. il pors *Archit Dig* 44 Archit Dig Travels:10+ O '87

Gordon detained by French police on 1967 DUI charge [D. Gordon] por *Jet* 72:57 Jl 20 '87

Why Paris? [blacks; cover story] B. Chase-Riboud. il *Essence* 18:65-6 O '87

History—Bibliography

Pilgrims in Paris. J. E. Seigel. *New Repub* 197:30-4 S 28 '87

Germany (West)

See also

　United States. Air Force—Forces in Germany (West)

　United States. Army—Forces in Germany (West)

Great Britain

Making big bucks from the Big Bang [A. Berkowitch working for Booz, Allen & Hamilton in London] S. Seixas. il pors *Money* 16:161-2+ My '87

Americans—Great Britain—_cont._
History
America in London. B. Dunning. il *Am Herit* 38:76-9+ Ap '87
Edmund Wilson among the 'despicable English' [1954 visit] Sir I. Berlin. il por *N Y Times Book Rev* 92:1+ Ap 12 '87
India
The poor break through. J. McGowan. il *Commonweal* 114:383-6 Je 19 '87
Iran
See also
Iranian seizure of United States embassy, 1979-1981
Not without my daughter [escape of American woman trapped by husband in Iran; excerpt]; ed. by William Hoffer. B. Mahmoody. il por *Ladies Home J* 104:20+ Ag '87
Italy
Living with fallout [effect of Chernobyl disaster] M. J. Salter. il *Atlantic* 259:30-2+ Ja '87
The return of a 'native' brings cheers in Italy from everyone but Madonna's family elders. il pors *People Wkly* 28:36-7 S 21 '87
Young tells Italians he can be businessman and pastor [Mayor A. Young] il *Jet* 72:40 Je 29 '87
Japan
An American in Tokyo shows the Japanese he's got it at Go [M. Redmond] il por *People Wkly* 28:63 Ag 24 '87
Do you have the yen to travel? H. Katayama. il *Forbes* 139:222+ My 18 '87
The hottest American import in Japan [baseball player R. Bass] C. Neff. il pors *Sports Illus* 66:72-6+ Mr 23 '87
A new kind of Orient Express [baseball player B. Horner] A. Wolff. il por *Sports Illus* 66:28-9 My 18 '87
Korea
See also
Korean War, 1950-1953—American participation
Laos
Looking for the mysterious 'Mr. Roly' [possible identification of MIA C. S. Rowley] il pors *Life* 10:119-20+ N '87
Lebanon
See also
Beirut airplane hijacking, 1985
Lebanon hostage cases, 1984-
U.S. policy, not militia gunfire, drives missionary teacher Nancie Wingo out of Lebanon. M. Avrech. il pors *People Wkly* 27:32-4+ Mr 16 '87
Why are any Americans left in Beirut? R. Nordland. *Newsweek* 109:21 F 2 '87
Malaysia
Modern times [use of pay phones in Kuala Lumpur to connect with MCI Mail via Singapore] J. M. Fallows. il *Atlantic* 259:24+ F '87
Mexico
Paradise, down Mexico way [residents of towns surrounding Lake Chapala] J. Moody. il *Time* 130:63 Ag 24 '87
Psst, you wanna plastic surgeon? [Americans seeking health care services] J. Borrell. il *Time* 129:60 Je 15 '87
Nicaragua
Beat the devil [reporting on death of B. E. Linder] A. Cockburn. *Nation* 244:636-7 My 16 '87
Caught in the cross fire [death of American engineer B. Linder] il *Newsweek* 109:47 My 11 '87
The execution of Ben Linder. A. Cockburn. *Nation* 245:402-3 O 17 '87
Mrs. Kirkpatrick visits Managua. W. F. Buckley. *Natl Rev* 39:67 N 20 '87
Notes and comment [death of B. E. Linder and letter from friend Mira Brown] *New Yorker* 63:21-2 Je 8 '87
The sad saga of a Sandalista [American volunteer worker B. Linder killed by contras] J. Smolowe. il por *Time* 129:34 My 11 '87
Sightseeing in Sandinistaland. P. J. O'Rourke. il *Roll Stone* p37-8 D 3 '87
History
My Vanderbilt movie [C. Vanderbilt] P. Baida. il *Am Herit* 38:20+ N '87
Panama
The color of money. C. Lane. il *Newsweek* 110:27 Ag 24 '87
In the Zone: the end of an American enclave. J. Borrell. il *Time* 130:8-9 Jl 20 '87
Peru
Busted [false arrest for cocaine possession] J. Jameson. *New Repub* 196:9-10 My 25 '87

Philippines
See also
United States. Air Force—Forces in the Philippines
Letter from Manila. R. E. Huke. *Focus* 37:33 Summ '87
The Philippines: a land in shadow [visit in preparation for 1988 solar eclipse expedition] S. J. O'Meara. il *Sky Telesc* 73:432-3 Ap '87
Singlaub's new mission. B. Levin. il por *Macleans* 100:20 Mr 2 '87
Romania
The erotic stripped bare. L. Mizejewski. il *Harpers* 274:57-62 Mr '87
Saba (Netherlands Antilles)
Dive bums [American skin divers] R. Rothenberg and S. Roy. il *Oceans* 20:38-45 Ja/F '87
Saudi Arabia
Anguish and languishing in Saudi Arabia [case of American businessman S. Bamieh] por *Newsweek* 109:32 Ja 12 '87
Soviet Union
For Scotty and Lida Sclocchini, a unique superpower detente begins at home in Irkutsk. J. W. Seymore. il pors *People Wkly* 27:42+ Ap 6 '87
From L.A. to Russia with love: promoter Joanna Stingray says 'Da' to her Soviet rocker [Y. Kasparyan] il pors *People Wkly* 28:68-70 N 30 '87
From Moscow to the Bering Sea [T. Watson retraces WWII flights] S. Talbott. il pors *Time* 130:34 Ag 3 '87
From Russia with *glasnost*. K. Rodeghier. il *Travel Holiday* 168:60-6 Ag '87
A Moscow mystery [Lockshin family from Houston defects to Moscow] J. Fayard. il *Life* 10:42-3+ Mr '87
Notes and comment [visit of M. Cuomo] *New Yorker* 63:36 O 12 '87
Pierce takes U.S. group on tour of Soviet Union. por *Jet* 73:4 O 26 '87
Stirring up the comrades [P. Donahue's broadcasts] R. Zoglin. il por *Time* 129:79 F 16 '87
Taking the long road to peace [Americans join Soviets in peace march through Russia] L. Lindeman. il *50 Plus* 27:50-5 O '87
Trailblazers of the US/USSR dance exchange. H. Breazeale. il *Dance Mag* 61:70-2 Ap '87
Travelers to a changing land [delegation from the Council on Foreign Relations] J. Greenwald. il *Time* 129:34-5 F 16 '87
White nights, Red faces [U.S. anglers in Soviet Union] C. Gammon. il *Sports Illus* 67:76-8+ O 26 '87
History
Black man returns home after 47 years in Russia [R. Robinson] S. Booker. il pors *Ebony* 42:67+ Je '87
A kinswoman of famed journalist John Reed finds that Ten days still shakes the Soviet Union. S. K. Reed. il pors *People Wkly* 27:114+ Ap 6 '87
Spain
See also
United States. Air Force—Forces in Spain
Vietnam
At home in Vietnam. G. C. Clifford. il *Life* 10:58-61+ D '87
History
See also
Vietnamese War, 1957-1975—American participation
Western Europe
Destination: Europe. J. Castro. il *Time* 129:42-3 Je 29 '87
Europe welcomes a peaceful invasion. M. Gray. il *Macleans* 100:40 Jl 27 '87
This summer, Paris should sizzle. W. C. Symonds. il *Bus Week* p66 My 18 '87
The time has come for American travelers to return to Europe. M. Mercouri. il *USA Today (Periodical)* 115:70-3 My '87
Americans abroad *See* Americans—Foreign countries
Americans for Generational Equity
A lobby's lonely mission: rescue the kid. il *Fortune* 116:82 Jl 20 '87
Americares Foundation
This Connecticut Yankee cares [work of R. Macauley] T. Armbrister. il pors *Read Dig* 130:131-5 F '87
Americas *See* America
America's Cup races
America's car to America's Cup (I) [driving a Corvette from Melbourne to Perth] J. R. Nerad. il *Mot Trend* 39:34-7+ Mr '87
America's car to America's Cup (II) [driving a Corvette from Melbourne to Perth] J. R. Nerad. il map *Mot Trend* 39:86-92 Ap '87

America's Cup races—*cont.*

The America's Cup. il *Sport Mag* 78:58-9 F '87

The America's Cup goes home again. R. L. Miller. il por *Macleans* 100:50 F 16 '87

The America's Cup: may the best technology win. O. Port. il *Bus Week* p74-5 F 2 '87

Auld mug's game [crews of Stars & Stripes and Kookaburra III] J. D. Reed. il *Time* 129:46-7 F 9 '87

Boat warrior [D. Conner guides Stars & Stripes to victory] B. Lewis. il pors *Sport Mag* 78:43-4+ D '87

Captains and kangaroos. P. J. O'Rourke. il *Roll Stone* p60-2+ Ap 9 '87

The Cup comes back [Stars & Stripes' victory] T. Gibbs. il *New Yorker* 63:86-90+ Mr 2 '87

Cup tech continued. il *Pop Mech* 164:68 Je '87

Dennis Conner clobbers the Kiwis [challenge races] D. Wallace. il por *Mot Boat Sail* 159:36-41+ Mr '87

Dennis Conner's crusade. P. A. Janssen. il *Mot Boat Sail* 159:9+ Mr '87

Does K stand for killjoy? [challenge by New Zealand banker M. Fay] E. Bowen. il *Time* 130:84 D 14 '87

Dragster in the danger zone [D. Conner's Stars & Stripes leading New Zealand in challenge races] J. D. Reed. il por *Time* 129:75 Ja 26 '87

The final days [challenge races] T. Chamberlain. il *Mot Boat Sail* 159:34-41+ Ja '87

Fremantle says good on yer, mates [D. Conner's Stars & Stripes wins] T. Callahan. il por *Time* 129:66 F 16 '87

Going for the Cup [D. Conner's Stars & Stripes] T. Callahan. il pors *Time* 129:42-5 F 9 '87

Gone with the wind [success of challenger New Zealand] D. Wallace. il *Mot Boat Sail* 159:58-62+ F '87

The holy war [Golden Gate Challenge syndicate's USA] P. Lyons. il *Car Driv* 32:102-4+ F '87

How we won the Cup. T. Whidden. il por *Mot Boat Sail* 159:30+ Ap '87

Light air off Perth. P. A. Janssen. *Mot Boat Sail* 159:11 F '87

Look lively, lubbers, it's the America's Cup [to be broadcast on ESPN] W. O. Johnson. il *Sports Illus* 66:74 Ja 19 '87

Master on a mission [Stars & Stripes vs. Kookaburra III] S. Ballard. il por *Sports Illus* 66:66-71 F 9 '87

Mission accomplished. D. Conner. il por *Sports Illus* 66:18-19 F 16 '87

Of brains, brawn and boats [D. Conner and Stars & Stripes] W. D. Marbach. il por *Newsweek* 109:79 F 2 '87

Polishing up the old Cup: the Australians have brought new luster to a sailing classic. W. O. Johnson. por *Sports Illus* 66:80 F 2 '87

The quest for the Cup. A. Finlayson. il *Macleans* 100:27 F 2 '87

Return of the wave warrior [D. Conner] il por *People Wkly* 27:88-9+ F 9 '87

Sailing back to the future [New Zealand challenge to race supermaxis] S. Ballard. il *Sports Illus* 67:28-30+ D 7 '87

Sails & science. T. H. Cole. il *Pop Mech* 164:67-70 F '87

A sea dog primes his guns [D. Conner in the challenge races] C. Neff. il pors *Sports Illus* 66:56-62 Ja 5 '87

Socking it to the Kiwis [Stars & Stripes wins right to race for the Cup] S. Ballard. il *Sports Illus* 66:10-15 Ja 26 '87

Stars & Stripes [cover story] J. S. Letcher, Jr. and others. il *Sci Am* 257:34-40+ Ag '87

Stars & Stripes [New York City parade for D. Conner and victorious crew] *New Yorker* 63:26-7 F 23 '87

Stars & Stripes . . . forever? C. Leerhsen. il por *Newsweek* 109:23 F 16 '87

Stars & Stripes—forever. D. Wallace. il *Mot Boat Sail* 159:42-7+ Ap '87

Still upbeat Down Under [Australia's loss] R. Yallop. il por *Sports Illus* 66:90 F 16 '87

Sunk by a slam dunk [challenge series] S. Ballard. il *Sports Illus* 66:86-7 Ja 12 '87

Techno-yachts. H. Aldersey-Williams. il *Pop Sci* 230:84-7+ F '87

Two hours before the mast [USA vs. Stars & Stripes in challenge round] B. Lewis. il *Sport Mag* 78:68-9+ F '87

Victory at sea [Stars & Stripes] S. Ballard. il por *Sports Illus* 66:10-17 F 16 '87

Bibliography

Sports books due in wake of America's Cup and Super Bowl. *Publ Wkly* 231:82-3 Mr 6 '87

Economic aspects

America's challenge [M. Kobayashi] H. Katayama. il por *Forbes* 140:452+ Jl 13 '87

The America's Cup: just racing means winning [Australia and New Zealand interests] R. L. Miller and C. Debes. il *Bus Week* p100 Ja 19 '87

ESPN is finding the sailing smoother. R. W. King. il *Bus Week* p96 F 9 '87

Rough sailing [M. Burnham of Sail America Foundation] G. Buchalter. il por *Forbes* 140:452 Jl 13 '87

Smooth sailing up Madison Ave. [D. Conner's endorsements] A. Miller. il por *Newsweek* 109:53 Mr 30 '87

They're already racing to host the next America's Cup [vying for 1990 site] C. Debes and E. Anderson. il *Bus Week* p52 F 23 '87

History

The first America's Cup race [1851] P. Sinz. *Mot Trend* 39:92 Ap '87

The great Cup race [1851 race] J. Dyson. il *Read Dig* 130:90-5 F '87

Sailing on Shamrock [experience as helmsman of America's Cup challenger in 1983] J. Rousmaniere. *Mot Boat Sail* 159:150+ F '87

Photographs and photography

The wet and windy way to the Cup. il *Sports Illus* 66:46-55 Ja 5 '87

Américas Photography Contest *See* Photography—Competitions

America's Stonehenge (North Salem, N.H.)

America's Stonehenge. L. Millman. il *Travel Holiday* 168:28-9 Jl '87

Americus Shareowner Service Corporation

Choosing dividends or price. L. Wiener. il *U S News World Rep* 103:60-1 S 7 '87

'Primes' and 'Scores' can soup up your portfolio. J. M. Laderman. *Bus Week* p86 Ag 31 '87

Amerika [television program] *See* Television program reviews—Single works

Amery, Colin

A pastoral pavilion. il *House Gard* 159:182-9+ My '87

Villa civility. il *House Gard* 159:184-9+ S '87

Ames, Anthony

about

New style in the Old South. E. Greene. il *House Gard* 159:140-5+ Jl '87

Ames, Bruce N., and others

Paleolithic diet, evolution, and carcinogens [discussion of April 17, 1987 article, Ranking possible carcinogenic hazards] *Science* 238:1633-4 D 18 '87

Ranking possible carcinogenic hazards. bibl f il *Science* 236:271-80 Ap 17 '87

Ames, Frank

The paisley shawl: anecdotes and facts [cover story] il *Antiques Collect Hobbies* 92:32-6 S '87

Ames, Robert S.

U.S. must understand the link between R&D and the economy. por *Aviat Week Space Technol* 127:149-50 O 12 '87

Ames (Iowa)

Education

A gathering of legends [students arrange reunion of Eddie Rickenbacker's WW2 flight crew] J. Fincher. il *Read Dig* 131:49-53 Jl '87

Ames Department Stores, Inc.

Gremlins are eating up the profits at Ames. J. R. Norman. il por *Bus Week* p132-3 O 19 '87

Ames Research Center

Ames-Dryden to study airflow around fighter aircraft at high angles of attack. *Aviat Week Space Technol* 126:20 Mr 30 '87

Ames wind tunnel to reopen after seven-year shutdown. R. G. O'Lone. il *Aviat Week Space Technol* 126:26-7 Je 29 '87

Into the wind tunnel . . . and the future. il *Sunset* 178:80 Je '87

NASA/Army upgrading simulation facilities at Ames [helicopters] il *Aviat Week Space Technol* 126:57 Ja 19 '87

NASA tests electro-expulsive deicer that could protect F/A-18 engines. B. D. Nordwall. il *Aviat Week Space Technol* 127:89+ Ag 3 '87

NASA uses supercomputer for aerodynamic simulation [Numerical Aerodynamic Simulator] il *Aviat Week Space Technol* 126:264-5 Mr 9 '87

Silicosms [Numerical Aerodynamic Simulator] R. Schultz. il *Omni* 9:52-7 Ag '87

A super-supercomputer [Numerical Aerodynamic Simulator] *Sci News* 131:166 Mr 14 '87

Amex *See* Stock exchanges—American exchange

Amfac, Inc.

A boardroom drama as time ran out for Amfac's CEO [R. R. Sloan loses to chairman H. A. Walker] J. B. Levine. il pors *Bus Week* p59 D 7 '87

Amfac, Inc.—*cont.*
A palmy idea from Amfac. G. G. Marcial. *Bus Week* p94 Mr 9 '87
Amgen (Firm)
The hormone that's making Amgen grow [erythropoietin] J. Flynn. il *Bus Week* p96+ Mr 16 '87
Amherst (Mass.)
Bookstores
See Booksellers and bookselling—Massachusetts
AMI *See* American Medical International, Inc.
AMI Investment Corporation
Fear and salvation [church bond underwriter W. May] R. Koselka. por *Forbes* 139:38-9 Je 1 '87
Amicus curiae
Can the Court be swayed? [amicus briefs before the Supreme Court; study by Karen O'Connor] *USA Today (Periodical)* 116:11-12 Ag '87
Amidei, Nancy
Rethinking hunger in America: adapting the Sullivan principles. il *Christ Century* 104:51-4 Ja 21 '87
Amiel, Barbara
Column. See occasional issues of Maclean's
Amiga (Computer) *See* Computers
Amines
See also
Ethylamines
Nitrosamines
Amino acid sequence
Cloning, sequencing, and expression of the gene coding for the human platelet α_2-adrenergic receptor. B. K. Kobilka and others. bibl f il *Science* 238:650-6 O 30 '87
Conservation of the Duchenne muscular dystrophy gene in mice and humans. E. P. Hoffman and others. bibl f il *Science* 238:347-50 O 16 '87
D-alanine in the frog skin peptide dermorphin is derived from L-alanine in the precursor. K. Richter and others. bibl f il *Science* 238:200-2 O 9 '87
Evidence for dispensable sequences inserted into a nucleotide fold. R. M. Starzyk and others. bibl f il *Science* 237:1614-18 S 25 '87
Genomic organization and deduced amino acid sequence of a putative sodium channel gene in Drosophila. L. Salkoff and others. bibl f il *Science* 237:744-9 Ag 14 '87
HLA is factor in diabetes [human leukocyte antigen; research by John A. Todd and others] *Sci News* 132:247 O 17 '87
Many random sequences functionally replace the secretion signal sequence of yeast invertase. C. A. Kaiser and others. bibl f il *Science* 235:312-17 Ja 16 '87
Neural cell adhesion molecule: structure, immunoglobulin-like domains, cell surface modulation, and alternative RNA splicing. B. A. Cunningham and others. bibl f il *Science* 236:799-806 My 15 '87
Neuronal pp60$^{c\text{-}src}$ contains a six-amino acid insertion relative to its non-neuronal counterpart. R. Martinez and others. bibl f il *Science* 237:411-15 Jl 24 '87
Primary structure and biochemical properties of an M_2 muscarinic receptor. E. G. Peralta and others. bibl f il *Science* 236:600-5 My 1 '87
Proteolytic self-cleavage of hepatitis B virus core protein may generate serum e antigen. R. H. Miller. bibl f il *Science* 236:722-5 My 8 '87
Receptor families reunited [neurotransmitters] *Sci News* 132:37 Jl 18 '87
Self-examination [major histocompatibility complex protein and T cell recognition of foreign molecules; work of Malcolm L. Gefter and others] *Sci Am* 256:65-6+ My '87
Sequence analysis on microcomputers. G. C. Cannon. bibl f il *Science* 238:97-103 O 2 '87
A synaptic vesicle protein with a novel cytoplasmic domain and four transmembrane regions. T. C. Südhof and others. bibl f il *Science* 238:1142-4 N 20 '87
Amino acids
See also
Alanine
Arginine
Aspartic acid
Cysteine
Methionine
Peptides
Phenylalanine
Taurine
Tryptophan
Amino acids from space [Murchison meteorite] *Astronomy* 15:95-6 D '87
Epitope mapping by chemical modification of free and antibody-bound protein antigen. A. Burnens and others. bibl f il *Science* 235:780-3 F 13 '87

Interstellar ooze? [study of Murchison meteorite; work of Samuel Epstein and others] il *Sky Telesc* 74:233-4 S '87
Synthesis
Multiple global regulators control HIS4 transcription in yeast. K. T. Arndt and others. bibl f il *Science* 237:874-80 Ag 21 '87
Aminobutyric acid
Delayed transneuronal death of substantia nigra neurons prevented by γ-aminobutyric acid agonist. M. Saji and D. J. Reis. bibl f il *Science* 235:66-9 Ja 2 '87
Depolarization without calcium can release γ-aminobutyric acid from a retinal neuron. E. A. Schwartz. bibl f il *Science* 238:350-5 O 16 '87
Aminolevulinic acid
Killing weeds with daylight. *Success Farm* 85 no3:20 F '87
Amirav, Moshe
about
The strange bedfellows. M. J. Kubic. il por *Newsweek* 110:42 O 5 '87
Amis, Martin
Nuke City: wake up, America, to another sunny doomsday in Washington, District of Catastrophe. il *Esquire* 108:97-100+ O '87
about
Britain's brat of letters. C. Michener. por *Esquire* 107:108-11 Ja '87
Amis, Suzy
about
About to be famous Amis. A. Engeler. por *Vogue* 177:132 S '87
Who's that girl? T. Minsky. por *Roll Stone* p40-2+ My 21 '87
Amish
Everybody in this picture is named Miller or Yoder except for one poor guy [postmaster T. Hagedorn's problem with family names in town of Kalona, Iowa] D. Van Biema. il por *People Wkly* 27:46-8 Mr 30 '87
Amish quilts *See* Quilts and quilting
Ammeters
Fluke LCA-10 line current test adapter [multimeter accessory] il *Radio-Electron* 58:28+ Mr '87
Ammonia
Does ammonia hydrogen bond? D. D. Nelson, Jr. and others. bibl f il *Science* 238:1670-4 D 18 '87
Ammonium
Rotation and solvation of ammonium ion. C. L. Perrin and R. K. Gipe. bibl f il *Science* 238:1393-4 D 4 '87
Ammons, A. R., 1926-
Fall's end [poem] *Harpers* 275:32 D '87
Ammunition
See also
Cartridges
Projectiles
Amnesia
The anatomy of memory. M. Mishkin and T. Appenzeller. bibl (p136) il *Sci Am* 256:80-9 Je '87
The husband who vanished [J. McDonnell] J. P. Blank. il pors *Read Dig* 130:131-5 Ja '87
Thanks for the memory [anterograde amnesia; research by Larry Squire and others] D. M. Barnes. il *Science* 238:1651-2 D 18 '87
Therapy
Uncovering amnesiacs' hidden memories [work of Daniel L. Schacter] J. Greenberg. *Sci News* 131:118 F 21 '87
Amnesty
Amnesty for the opposition [South Korea] il *Macleans* 100:24 Jl 20 '87
Churches band together to help register undocumented aliens. R. Frame. il *Christ Today* 31:34-5 Jl 10 '87
Confusion on both sides of the border [amnesty and illegal aliens] A. Bernstein and others. il *Bus Week* p68-9 Jl 20 '87
Doors and walls [Immigration and Naturalization Service rules for processing applications for amnesty for aliens] *America* 156:294 Ap 11 '87
The growing enemies of a Managua cease-fire [Sandinista's program] C. A. Robbins. il *U S News World Rep* 103:37-8 O 26 '87
Ripping off immigrants: amnesty breeds abuses. G. Hackett. il *Newsweek* 110:21-2 S 7 '87
The uneasy amnesty. *America* 156:413 My 23 '87
Wooing the migrant farmer [growers' campaign to explain Immigration Reform and Control Act] J. B. Copeland. il *Newsweek* 109:47 Je 29 '87

Amnesty International

Amnesty membership up; tour cited. A. DeCurtis. *Roll Stone* p25 Ap 23 '87

Group cites racism in death penalty sentence. *Jet* 72:38 Ap 13 '87

Voices of freedom rock London [benefit] il *Roll Stone* p6-7 My 7 '87

Amnion

Human amnion membrane serves as a substratum for growing axons in vitro and in vivo. G. E. Davis and others. bibl f il *Science* 236:1106-9 My 29 '87

Amniotic liquid

Amniotic fluid. P. A. Hillard. il *Parents* 62:184+ Ag '87

Amoco Canada Petroleum Company Ltd.

Amoco becomes bolder [bid for Dome] C. Siler. il *Forbes* 140:88 N 2 '87

Dome's day of reckoning [creditors disappointed with Amoco Canada bid] T. Tedesco. il *Macleans* 100:29 My 25 '87

Dome's deepening saga [proposed sale of Dome to Amoco Canada Petroleum Co. Ltd.] D. Jenish. il *Macleans* 100:26 Jl 6 '87

Dome's last deal [bid by Amoco Canada; cover story; special section; with editorial comment by Kevin Doyle] il *Macleans* 100:2, 34-42 My 4 '87

Dome's light at the end of the tunnel [Amoco raises its takeover offer] D. Jenish. il *Macleans* 100:50 N 30 '87

Dome's lingering drama [agreement with Amoco Canada Petroleum] T. Tedesco. il *Macleans* 100:40 My 18 '87

A threat to the public interest [loss to Canada of Dome to Amoco] P. C. Newman. il *Macleans* 100:31 Jl 6 '87

Amoco Corporation

Amoco becomes bolder. C. Siler. il *Forbes* 140:88 N 2 '87

Is there oil in Iowa? [prospecting in Halbur] C. O'Connor. il *Newsweek* 109:26 Je 22 '87

One cautious gambler [R. M. Morrow] C. Knowlton. por *Fortune* 116:51 Ag 3 '87

Amok (Los Angeles, Calif.: Bookstore) *See* Booksellers and bookselling—California

Amor, Bernardo Sepúlveda *See* Sepúlveda Amor, Bernardo

Amor Artis Chorale and Orchestra

Musical events:
Handel's Esther performed in Alice Tully Hall. A. Porter. *New Yorker* 63:72 Mr 16 '87

Amorphous solids *See* Solids

Amory, Cleveland

The Stork Club. il *N Y* 20:78-9 D 21-28 '87

Amory, Jean

about

Sylvan cider mill: Jean and Harcourt Amory's Westchester Hills restoration. S. M. L. Aronson. il *Archit Dig* 44:204-8+ Je '87

Amos, Gregory Wallace

Say, brother. por *Essence* 17:9 Ap '87

Amos, Wally

about

Famous Amos among ten rags-to-riches inductees. por *Jet* 72:6 Mr 30 '87

Amos 'n' Andy (Fictional characters)

Judge blocks production of 'Amos 'n' Andy' musical [copyright owned by CBS] *Jet* 72:56 S 14 '87

Amoskeag Co.

Frederic Dumaine: upstreaming the profits. D. A. Saunders. il por *Forbes* 140:258-9+ Jl 13 '87

AMP *See* Adenosine monophosphate

Ampere/Essex Business Credit Union

AEBCU means business. W. M. Woodard. *Black Enterp* 17:66 Je '87

Ampex Corporation

Little Orphan Ampex looks for Daddy Warbucks. J. B. Levine. *Bus Week* p39-40 Ap 13 '87

Amphetamines

A mild dose of candor [K. Dukakis reveals former amphetamine dependency] W. Shapiro. il pors *Time* 130:34 Jl 20 '87

Amphibia

See also
Embryology—Amphibia
Eye—Amphibia
Frogs
Salamanders
Sexual behavior—Amphibia
Skin—Amphibia
Toads

Amphibious airplanes *See* Airplanes, Amphibious

Amphoras

The Madrague de Giens wreck [Roman freighter off coast of France] A. Tchernia. il *Courier* 40:11 N '87

Amplifiers

Amplifiers. il *Stereo Rev* 52:83-4+ F '87

Digital dexterity. F. Vizard. il *Pop Mech* 164:51 My '87

Tunable IF. H. Friedman. il *Radio-Electron* 58:86 Ja '87

Design

Broadcast-band RF amplifier. D. J. Housley. il *Radio-Electron* 58:42 Mr '87

The driving force. D. Lander. il *Pop Mech* 164:100-2 D '87

Instrumentation amplifiers. R. F. Scott. il *Radio-Electron* 58:87-8 Je '87

Micropower op-amp. R. F. Scott. il *Radio-Electron* 58:94 S '87

Miniature wideband amplifier. J. Clawson. il *Radio-Electron* 58:45-6+ My '87

Transistor amplifier design. J. Cunkelman. il *Radio-Electron* 58:55-6+ Ag '87

Energy usage

MAXimum headroom. L. Klein. *High Fidel* 37:52-3 Jl '87

Optical equipment

Light music [fiber optic beam connects Kenwood CD player to amplifiers] W. J. Hawkins. il *Pop Sci* 230:14 My '87

Testing

Acoustic Research A-06 integrated amp. il *High Fidel* 37:21-2 My '87

Do all amplifiers sound the same? [listening test conducted by David L. Clark; with editorial comment by William Livingstone] I. Masters. il *Stereo Rev* 52:8, 78-84 Ja '87

Hafler XL-280 power amplifier. il *High Fidel* 37:36+ Ap '87

Harman Kardon Citation 21 preamplifier. il *High Fidel* 37:38+ D '87

Harman Kardon Citation Twenty-Two power amplifier. J. D. Hirsch. il *Stereo Rev* 52:37-8+ Jl '87

Harman Kardon PM-635 integrated amplifier. il *High Fidel* 37:61-2 Ja '87

Kenwood KA-3300D integrated amplifier. J. D. Hirsch. il *Stereo Rev* 52:41-2+ S '87

Luxman LV-105 audio-video integrated amplifier. il *High Fidel* 37:56-7 Ja '87

Nakamichi CA-7A preamplifier. il *High Fidel* 37:31-2+ Ap '87

Parasound D/AS-1000 power amplifier. il *High Fidel* 37:36+ S '87

Perreaux PMF-3150 power amplifier. il *High Fidel* 37:57-8+ Ja '87

Perreaux SM3 preamplifier. J. D. Hirsch. il *Stereo Rev* 52:75-6 N '87

Pioneer C-90 preamplifier. J. D. Hirsch. il *Stereo Rev* 52:35-6+ Ap '87

PS Audio 4.5 preamplifier. J. D. Hirsch. il *Stereo Rev* 52:47-8 Je '87

SAE P102 preamplifier. J. D. Hirsch. il *Stereo Rev* 52:46+ F '87

Shure AVC 20 Power Station. J. D. Hirsch. il *Stereo Rev* 52:33-4+ My '87

Sleuthing sonic differences [differential-signal testing] R. Hodges. il *Stereo Rev* 52:124 Ap '87

Sony TA-F700ES integrated amplifier. il *High Fidel* 37:27+ Jl '87

Soundcraftsmen Pro-Power 4 power amplifier. il *High Fidel* 37:32+ Jl '87

Tandberg TPA-3016A power amplifier. il *High Fidel* 37:28-9 Mr '87

Technics SU-A200 preamplifier. il *High Fidel* 37:35+ Ja '87

Testing semiconductors (VI) [op amps] T. J. Byers. il *Radio-Electron* 58:61-3 S '87

Testing semiconductors (VII) [op amps] T. J. Byers. il *Radio-Electron* 58:115-17+ N '87

Yamaha AVC-50 integrated audio/video amplifier. J. D. Hirsch. il *Stereo Rev* 52:43-4+ Ja '87

Zapco S-80 car power amplifier. il *High Fidel* 37:53-4 My '87

Amplitude interferometry *See* Interferometers and interferometry

Amputees

Gardening saved his life [J. G. Wilson] P. H. Johnson. il por *Rodale's Org Gard* 34:60-4 My '87

The heart of Canton, Ohio [amputee C. Torrence] H. Hurt. *Read Dig* 130:49-52 Mr '87

Amputees—cont.

Sports

Golden Girl [D. Golden, amputee ski racer] P. Miller. il pors *Skiing* 40:44+ N '87

Setbacks along the way [one legged runner S. Fonyo] R. Laver. il por *Macleans* 100:42 Mr 30 '87

A triumph of will/Barbara Shook. J. Kaplan. il por *Vogue* 177:454-5+ Mr '87

AMR Corp.

AMR, Pan Am end pact on Sabre system use [computer reservations system] C. A. Shifrin. *Aviat Week Space Technol* 127:33-4 Ag 24 '87

AMRAAM (Advanced medium-range air-to-air missiles) *See* Guided missiles—Launching from airplanes

Amritraj, Vijay

about

India's giver. R. Jacob. il por *World Tennis* 35:56+ D '87

Amsterdam, Jane

about

Editorial freedom vs. the red suspenders. *Newsweek* 109:47 Ap 6 '87

Lipson, Inc. E. Diamond. il por *N Y* 20:28+ Ap 27 '87

Amsterdam (Netherlands)

Churches (Buildings)

Bones of contention [Rembrandt] A. Steacy. por *Macleans* 100:66-7 D 7 '87

Galleries and museums

See also

Jewish Historical Museum (Amsterdam, Netherlands)

Monuments, statues, etc.

Dutch tribute to gay pride [monument to homosexuals killed during Nazi regime] K. Golden. *Ms* 15:32 Je '87

Music

See also

Opera—Netherlands

Amstutz, Daniel

Can we put U.S. agriculture on the road to recovery? il *USA Today (Periodical)* 116:18-20 N '87

Amtrak *See* National Railroad Passenger Corp.

Amundsen, Roald, 1872-1928

about

Frozen in time. M. Loke. il *N Y Times Mag* p46-9 O 4 '87

Amusement parks

See also

Boardwalk and Baseball (Amusement park)

Bumper cars

Coney Island (New York, N.Y.)

Disneyland (Anaheim, Calif.)

EPCOT (Fla.)

Heritage USA (N.C.)

Sea Life Park (Waimanalo, Hawaii)

Walt Disney World (Fla.)

On safari in New Jersey [Great Adventure in Jackson] S. Alcorn. il *Travel Holiday* 167:34-5 F '87

Theme parks: this slugfest is no fantasy [Disney vs. MCA] R. Grover. il *Bus Week* p38 Mr 23 '87

Accidents

Killer coasters. T. H. Cole. il *Pop Mech* 164:56-9+ S '87

"We are forever on the hook". K. Hannon. il *Forbes* 140:98 Ag 10 '87

Equipment

See also

Roller coasters

France

See also

Euro Disneyland

Germany (West)

See also

Luna Luna (Hamburg, Germany)

Japan

See also

Disneyland (Tokyo, Japan)

Western Europe

It's King Kong vs. the 'ravenous rat' [MCA and Disney compete for theme park market] K. Kelly. il *Bus Week* p54 O 5 '87

Amuzegar, Jahangir

Dealing with debt. *Foreign Policy* 68:140-58 Fall '87

Amyloid

Alzheimer/Down syndrome bond tightens. *Sci News* 131:188 Mr 21 '87

Amyloid β protein gene: cDNA, mRNA distribution, and genetic linkage near the Alzheimer locus. R. E. Tanzi and others. bibl f il *Science* 235:880-4 F 20 '87

The amyloid β protein gene is not duplicated in brains from patients with Alzheimer's disease. R. E. Tanzi and others. bibl f il *Science* 238:666-9 O 30 '87

β amyloid gene duplication in Alzheimer's disease and karyotypically normal Down syndrome. J.-M. Delabar and others. bibl f il *Science* 235:1390-2 Mr 13 '87

Characterization and chromosomal localization of a cDNA encoding brain amyloid of Alzheimer's disease. D. Goldgaber and others. bibl f il *Science* 235:877-80 F 20 '87

Conservation of brain amyloid proteins in aged mammals and humans with Alzheimer's disease [cover story] D. J. Selkoe and others. bibl f il *Science* 235:873-7 F 20 '87

Gene dosage of the amyloid β precursor protein in Alzheimer's disease. M. B. Podlisny and others. bibl f il *Science* 238:669-71 O 30 '87

Localization of amyloid β protein messenger RNA in brains from patients with Alzheimer's disease. S. Bahmanyar and others. bibl f il *Science* 237:77-80 Jl 3 '87

Role of Alzheimer's protein is tangled. J. L. Marx. bibl il *Science* 238:1352-3 D 4 '87

Amyloses

An amylose antiparallel double helix at atomic resolution. W. Hinrichs and others. bibl f il *Science* 238:205-8 O 9 '87

Amyotrophic lateral sclerosis

The battle of his life [Lou Gehrig's disease hits B. Waters and other former San Francisco 49ers] R. Fimrite. il pors *Sports Illus* 67:72-80 Ag 24 '87

Genius unbound [S. W. Hawking] R. Morais. il por *Forbes* 139:142 Mr 23 '87

'He loves life' [story behind S. W. Hawking's A brief history of time] L. Fleischer. *Publ Wkly* 232:56 O 16 '87

An incurable killer strikes three ex-49ers, and an anguished victim doubts it's a coincidence [B. Waters, victim of Lou Gehrig's disease] D. Grogan. il por *People Wkly* 27:94-5 F 9 '87

My father's last year. L. Cherry. il *Glamour* 85:300-1+ O '87

New treatment approach [thyrotropin releasing hormone therapy for neuromuscular diseases; work of W. King Engel] il *USA Today (Periodical)* 115:8 F '87

Probing a mysterious "cluster" [three former San Francisco football players] C. Wallis. il *Time* 129:70 F 23 '87

ANA *See* American Numismatic Association

Anabolic steroids *See* Steroids

Anacomp, Inc.

Hard times may be over for the high techs. G. G. Marcial. il *Bus Week* p120 My 18 '87

Anacostia Neighborhood Museum (Washington, D.C.)

Powerful vision at Anacostia [Contemporary visual expressions exhibit] C. Bond. il *Smithsonian* 18:188 My '87

Anagrams

Recursion + data structures = anagrams. M. Morton. bibl il *Byte* 12:325-8+ N '87

Anaheim (Calif.)

Restaurants, nightclubs, bars, etc.

Where to eat in . . . Anaheim. C. Beason. il *Work Woman* 12:106 Mr '87

Analemmas (Celestial motion) *See* Solar system—Motion in space

Analgesia and analgesics

See also

Acupuncture

Aspirin

Heroin

Good news about drugs. A. Hornaday. *Ms* 15:66 F '87

It only hurts when I don't laugh [laughter as a pain killer; research by Rosemary Cogan] E. Grant. *Psychol Today* 21:21 S '87

Music as medicine [use in pain treatment] J. R. Goldberg. *McCalls* 114:105 Ja '87

A new route to comprehending pain. J. Silberner. il *U S News World Rep* 102:52 Je 29 '87

Relieving cancer pain. J. Dahl and D. Joranson. il *World Health* p28-9 N '87

The search for the right pain reliever. il *Consum Rep* 52:82-5 F '87

Self-administered pain-killer. B. Bialick. il *McCalls* 114:144 Jl '87

Analgesics *See* Analgesia and analgesics

Analog to digital converters *See* Digital electronics

Analysis, Conformational *See* Conformational analysis

Anarchism and anarchists

See also

Terrorism

Anasazi culture *See* Pueblo Indians
Anastas, Lila
(jt. auth) See Michaud, Ellen, and Anastas, Lila
Anatolia (New York, N.Y.: Restaurant) *See* New York (N.Y.)—Restaurants, nightclubs, bars, etc.
Anatomy
See also
Body, Human
Dissection
Homology (Biology)
Physiology
Women—Anatomy and physiology
Anatomy, Artistic
Study and teaching
'This incredible machine' [cadaver studied in New York Academy of Art anatomy class] R. Bass. il *Art News* 86:182 Mr '87
Anatomy, Comparative
Distribution of cones in human and monkey retina: individual variability and radial asymmetry [cover story] C. A. Curcio and others. bibl f il *Science* 236:579-82 My 1 '87
Hominoid lineages and keystone clues [Robert B. Eckhardt's challenge to Todd R. Olson's nasal bone theory] B. Bower. il *Sci News* 132:71 Ag 1 '87
Robust hominids: tooth and consequences [australopithecines] B. Bower. il *Sci News* 131:229 Ap 11 '87
Anaya, Herbert Ernesto
about
Anaya's murder. A. Cockburn. *Nation* 245:546-7 N 14 '87
'The same old assassins'. *Commonweal* 114:646 N 20 '87
Ancestry *See* Genealogy
Anchor Glass Container Corp.
What keeps Anchor Glass steady: buying shaky rivals [acquisition of Diamond-Bathurst] G. DeGeorge. il por *Bus Week* p72-3 Jl 27 '87
Anchor Hocking Corp.
Still expanding [Newell Co. acquisition of Anchor Hocking] A. A. Lappen. il *Forbes* 140:8 O 19 '87
Anchorage
See also
Condominiums (Boat docking)
Anchorages away [anchoring away from marinas] H. Halsted. il *Mot Boat Sail* 159:28 Mr '87
Boatkeeper's guide to anchors and anchoring. B. Gladstone. il *Mot Boat Sail* 160:65-7 Jl '87
Coping with crowded anchorages. H. Halsted. il *Mot Boat Sail* 159:26 Je '87
Anchorage (Alaska)
Race relations
Anchorage's King snub may imperil Olympic bid. *Jet* 73:48 O 26 '87
Anchoring *See* Anchorage
Anchors
Boatkeeper's guide to anchors and anchoring. B. Gladstone. il *Mot Boat Sail* 160:65-7 Jl '87
Anchors (Newscasters) *See* Television broadcasting—News
Anchovies
Larvae
See Larvae
Ancient art *See* Art, Ancient
Ancient astronomy *See* Astronomy, Ancient
Ancient Rome *See* Rome
Ancient ships *See* Ships, Ancient
Ancient tablets *See* Tablets, Ancient
Andacht, Sandra
Joe Franklin's show biz memorabilia. il por *Antiques Collect Hobbies* 91:78-81 Ja '87
Anderes, Fred, and Agranoff, Ann
The magic chill of ice palaces still beckons us. bibl (p131) il *Smithsonian* 17:62-9 Ja '87
Anders, Jaroslaw
(tr) See Herbert, Zbigniew. Mass for the imprisoned
Andersen, Christopher P.
Meet the presidents: Donna Steigerwaldt. il por *Good Housekeep* 205:64+ Ag '87
Meet the presidents: Orville Redenbacher. il por *Good Housekeep* 204:164+ My '87
Andersen, D. R.
Conflict: the heartbeat of a play. *Writer* 100:14-17+ S '87
Andersen, Martin
Kissinger and the 'dirty war'. il *Nation* 245:477-80 O 31 '87
Andersen, Morten
about
Great Dane in town. J. Lieber. il pors *Sports Illus* 67:73-4+ D 21 '87

Andersen, Tom
The Kemp's ridley puzzle. il *Oceans* 20:42-9 My/Je '87
Anderson, Alastair
Governments—beware! il *World Health* p8-10 Ap '87
Anderson, Anne S.
about
Making a place for finding the past. D. Young. il *South Living* 22:78 Ja '87
Anderson, Barbara
Solo fathers. il *Essence* 18:108+ N '87
Anderson, Bernard E.
Education: key to minorities gaining jobs. il *Black Enterp* 17:45 F '87
Anderson, Bruce
America's new golden girl. il pors *Sports Illus* 67:28-30+ Ag 10 '87
A bargain at any price. il por *Sports Illus* 66:36-7 Je 15 '87
Catch a rising star. il *Sports Illus* 66:46 Mr 30 '87
Just a Pipp of a legend. il pors *Sports Illus* 66:78-82+ Je 29 '87
The Kings' crown princes. il pors *Sports Illus* 66:58+ Ja 26 '87
What's foul is fair game. il por *Sports Illus* 67:98 Jl 6 '87
With Ozzie, it was easy. il por *Sports Illus* 66:87+ My 11 '87
Anderson, Carl
about
Does it damage children to deceive them about Santa Claus? Ho, ho, no, says Dr. Carl Anderson [interview] L. Armstrong. il pors *People Wkly* 28:45+ D 21 '87
Anderson, Craig V.
Pruning time for Shirley MacLaine? *Christ Century* 104:182-3 F 25 '87
Anderson, Denton L.
(jt. auth) See Sheldon, Jeffrey G., and Anderson, Denton L.
Anderson, Doug, 1954?-
about
Doug Anderson. G. Henry. il *Art News* 86:153+ Mr '87
Anderson, Gary
about
Lightning strikes back. J. D. Miller. il por *Sport Mag* 78:34-7+ Ja '87
Anderson, Gary R.
Ethics and feasibility. *Society* 24:16-19 Mr/Ap '87
Anderson, Gene
about
Seattle's Gene Anderson throws the book at white-collar coke users who once knew no fear. M. Green. il por *People Wkly* 27:111-12 F 2 '87
Anderson, George M.
Dying young: infant mortality in the United States. il *America* 157:498-500+ D 26 '87
Anderson, Ian, 1947-
about
Tull test: resorting to knavery. J. Rosenbluth. il por *Roll Stone* p16 N 19 '87
Anderson, Jack, 1922-
about
Mellowing of a muckraker [cover story] D. Corn. il *Nation* 245:541+ N 14 '87
Anderson, James N.
The role of music research in teacher training programs. bibl f *Des Arts Educ* 88:42-4 My/Je '87
Anderson, Jane V.
about
Any resemblance . . . *Nation* 244:132-3 F 7 '87
Closing accounts on Plath's 'Bell jar'. *Newsweek* 109:58 F 9 '87
From book to film: a novel case of libel. A. Press. il por *Newsweek* 109:63 F 2 '87
Libel in fiction to be tested in Bell jar suit. M. Yen. *Publ Wkly* 231:290 Ja 30 '87
Of whom the Bell told. R. Lacayo. il por *Time* 129:60-1 F 9 '87
Parties settle Bell jar suit out of court. *Publ Wkly* 231:19 F 13 '87
Salinger and 'The bell jar': what do they mean to publishers? C. E. Rinzler. il *Publ Wkly* 231:20-2 Ap 24 '87
Anderson, Jay
Prospects for the March 1988 total solar eclipse [cover story] il maps *Astronomy* 15:38-42 Ag '87
Anderson, Joan B., and Lee, Dwight R.
The political economy of military waste. il *USA Today (Periodical)* 115:30-3 My '87

Anderson, John
about
Pen & ink: John Anderson. M. S. Doherty. il *Am Artist* 51:64-7 Ag '87
Anderson, Judith
Gardening by mail. il por *Flower Gard* 31:40+ F/Mr '87
Anderson, Karen, 1945-
Small wonders [condensed from Full house: the story of the Anderson quintuplets]; ed. by Jo Robinson. il *Read Dig* 131:120-4 S '87
Anderson, Lee B.
about
A Gothic tale. E. Lebow. il *House Gard* 159:190-7+ My '87
Anderson, Lindsay, 1923-
about
The whales of August [film] Reviews
  America 157:384 N 21 '87. R. A. Blake
  Film Comment il 23:2+ Ja/F '87. J. Ney
  New Repub 197:28 N 2 '87. S. Kauffmann
  People Wkly il 28:70-2+ D 14 '87. B. Darrach
  People Wkly il 28:14 O 26 '87. P. Travers
Anderson, Lisa, 1950-
Libya's Qaddafi: still in command? bibl f *Curr Hist* 86:65-8+ F '87
Anderson, Loni
about
Loni Anderson: matters of the heart. N. Gittelson. il pors *McCalls* 114:12-14+ My '87
Loni Anderson: "Why are people so cruel to us?". L. Eisenberg. il pors *Redbook* 168:82+ Mr '87
Anderson, Lorna
about
A late indictment may close the case behind TV's Murder ordained. J. Calio. il pors *People Wkly* 27:107-8+ Je 8 '87
Anderson, Louie
about
He's getting laughs all over TV, and Louie Anderson has only just begun to throw his weight around. il pors *People Wkly* 28:82+ S 7 '87
Anderson, Michael, and Gehrke, Craig
The degradation factor. il *Wilderness* 51:38-40 Fall '87
Anderson, Michael, 1920-
about
The jeweller's shop [film] Reviews
  Macleans il 100:50 Ag 31 '87. P. Young
Anderson, Norman G.
Electrophoresis and large-scale databases. bibl f *Science* 235 pt2:G65 F 27 '87
Anderson, Pamela K.
about
Corporate partners in a maxi-marriage. C. Hutton. il pors *Fortune* 115:46 Ja 5 '87
Anderson, Pearl
about
Oaklander wins $1 mil. on Reno slot machine. il por *Jet* 72:52 S 21 '87
Anderson, Peter R.
about
Sticking with big-company stocks [interview] A. E. Serwer. por *Fortune* 116:200 O 12 '87
Anderson, Philip Warren, 1923-
Advice on applying for a postdoc. por *Phys Today* 40:7+ S '87
The resonating valence bond state in La$_2$CuO$_4$ and superconductivity. bibl f il *Science* 235:1196-8 Mr 6 '87
Anderson, Ray Sherman
God bless the children—and the childless. il *Christ Today* 31:28 Ag 7 '87
Anderson, Richard Dean
about
In a fix? Call MacGyver, not the average Joe who plays him. S. Stevens. il pors *People Wkly* 27:57-8 Ja 19 '87
MacGyver's Richard Dean Anderson: TV's gentle daredevil. R. Meryman. il por *McCalls* 114:35-6+ F '87
Anderson, Richard E., 1943-
Tuition prepurchase plans. il *Change* 19:36-41 Mr/Ap '87
Anderson, Robert Bernerd, 1910-
about
Stain on a shining record. por *Time* 129:52 Ap 6 '87
Anderson, Robert Orville, 1917-
about
Robert Anderson is shaking up the oil patch again. J. Flynn. il por *Bus Week* p39 Ag 17 '87

Anderson, Roland C., and Vanderwerff, Joyce E.
Stars with thousands of feet [cover story] bibl il *Sea Front* 33:422-6 N/D '87
Anderson, Ronald Kinloch, d. 1984
about
Memories of his master's voice [interview] E. E. Swenson. il por *High Fidel* 37:56-9 My '87
Anderson, Stanley
In the Casbah: transforming a labyrinthine Moroccan residence. il *Archit Dig* 44:198-204 O '87
Anderson, Walter Inglis, 1903-1965
about
Walter Inglis Anderson at Luise Ross. L. Campbell. *Art Am* 75:227 Ap '87
Anderson, William T., 1952-
Holland, Michigan. il *Saturday Evening Post* 259:82-4 My/Je '87
Anderson (L.W.) Genealogical Library *See* L.W. Anderson Genealogical Library
Anderson quintuplets *See* Quintuplets
Andes, Karen
Is there too much sex in aerobics? il *Women's Sports Fitness* 9:60 Ja '87
Andes
The High Andes: South America's islands in the sky. L. McIntyre. il maps *Natl Geogr* 171:422-59 Ap '87
Andes climbs *See* Mountaineering
Andō, Hiroshige *See* Hiroshige (Andō Hiroshige), 1797-1858
André the Giant
about
As The princess bride's champion, wrestler Andre the Giant takes to the movies in a big way. T. Kahn. il pors *People Wkly* 28:169-70 N 30 '87
Andreas, Dwayne O.
about
Gorbachev's prairie pals. T. Jacoby. il pors *Newsweek* 109:31 Ap 6 '87
Profiles. E. J. Kahn. por *New Yorker* 62:41-2+ F 16 '87
Andrée's Restaurant (New York, N.Y.) *See* New York (N.Y.)—Restaurants, nightclubs, bars, etc.
Andreev, Aleksander F.
(jt. auth) See Maris, Humphrey J., and Andreev, Aleksander F.
Andrew, Prince, Duke of York, 1960-
about
Andrew and "Fergie": royalty's happiest, most unusual marriage [cover story] D. Keay. il pors *Good Housekeep* 204:130-1+ Ap '87
Connecticut Yankees court the Yorks [cover story] L. Rozen. il pors *People Wkly* 28:96-7+ S 21 '87
'Fabulous Fergie' [cover story; special section; with editorial comment by Kevin Doyle] il pors *Macleans* 100:2, 26-30+ Jl 27 '87
Fergie and Andrew do Niagara, and Canada falls. il pors *People Wkly* 28:36-7 Ag 3 '87
Jobs too frantic? City living just too much? Rent a cozy rural hideway like Andy and Fergie did. il por *People Wkly* 27:101 F 16 '87
Roughing it in the bush. M. McIver. il pors *Macleans* 100:46 Ag 10 '87
Royal welcome in the West. M. Gray. il pors *Macleans* 100:36-7 Ag 3 '87
A triumphant transformation: Fergie's first year. J. Whitaker. il pors *McCalls* 114:32-4+ Je '87
Andrews, Colman
Real Mexican, at last. il *Harpers Bazaar* 120:108+ F '87
Andrews, Joan
about
The fear of doing nothing. C. W. Colson. il *Christ Today* 31:72 My 15 '87
Andrews, Lynn V.
about
Andrews's sisters. R. M. Staubs. il por *Omni* 10:28 O '87
Andrews, Peter, 1931-
The defense of Wake. bibl il map *Am Herit* 38:65-80 Jl/Ag '87
Andrews, Roy Chapman, 1884-1960
about
A daring gamble in the Gobi Desert took the jackpot. D. J. Preston. il pors *Smithsonian* 18:94-8+ D '87
Andrews, Stuart
Classicism and the American Revolution. bibl f il *Hist Today* 37:37-42 Ja '87
Andrews, T. Coleman, III
about
The prodigy who came to World's rescue. P. Finch. il por *Bus Week* p58 Ap 27 '87

Andrews, William
about
NFL Falcons' star sues Ga. police for $400,000. *Jet* 72:50 Jl 27 '87

Andreyev, Leonid, 1871-1919
about
My grandfather, Leonid Andreyev: heard again, loud and clear. O. A. Carlisle. il por *N Y Times Book Rev* 92:15-16 O 4 '87

Androgens
See also
Testosterone

Androgyny (Psychology)
Early feminist fashion [views of designer E. Hawes] B. Berch. il por *Ms* 15:26 Mr '87
Mergers & acquisitions: manstyle for women. il *Harpers Bazaar* 120:154-63 F '87
The short life of the androgynous person. il *Christ Today* 31:35 O 2 '87

Androids *See* Robots

Andrus (Ethel Percy) Gerontology Center *See* Ethel Percy Andrus Gerontology Center

Anechoic chambers *See* Sound laboratories

Anély, Max *See* Segalen, Victor, 1878-1919

Anemia
See also
Sickle cell anemia
Anemia—are you at risk? [iron deficiency anemia] E. Coleman. il *Women's Sports Fitness* 9:12 Mr '87
For weary women only—how to get energy to go. J. Cohen. il *Mademoiselle* 93:128 Mr '87

Anencephaly
A death, a life [anencephalic baby kept alive to keep organs healthy for transplantation] il *Time* 130:76 N 2 '87
First word [rejection of anencephalic newborn as organ donor] G. Marell. il *Omni* 9:8 My '87
A life-giving death [anencephalic baby kept alive to serve as organ donor] N. Underwood. il *Macleans* 100:45 N 2 '87
Suffering and joy [anencephalic baby as heart donor] A. Steacy. il *Macleans* 100:40-1 N 23 '87

Anenden, H.
Zimbabwe: from supermarket to cafeteria. il *World Health* p21-3 Je '87

Anesthesia and anesthetics
See also
Chloroform
Fentanyl
Halothane
Babies in pain [surgery without painkillers] A. Fischer. il *Redbook* 169:124-5+ O '87
Circumcision: why no pain relief? *Redbook* 169:185 O '87
A different kind of oral sensation [electronic dental anesthesia] *Sci News* 132:268 O 24 '87
Pain-free dentistry? [electronic anesthesia] L. S. Senz. *Health* 19:20 D '87

Anesthetics *See* Anesthesia and anesthetics

Aneutronic fusion *See* Nuclear fusion

Angel, Roger
about
The mirror maker. M. M. Waldrop. il pors *Discover* 8:78-84+ D '87
Spinning scopes. A. Fisher. il pors *Pop Sci* 231:76-9+ O '87

Angel heart [film] *See* Motion picture reviews—Single works

Angell, Roger
The arms talks. *New Yorker* 63:103-12+ My 4 '87
Get out your handkerchiefs. *New Yorker* 63:51-2+ D 7 '87
Greetings, friends! [poem] il *New Yorker* 63:39 D 28 '87
Up at the Hall. il *New Yorker* 63:35-8+ Ag 31 '87

Angelo, Richard
about
Long Island's 'angel of death'. D. Gates. il por *Newsweek* 110:35 N 30 '87

Angelou, Maya
A brother's love. por *N Y Times Book Rev* 92:29-30 D 20 '87

Angels of Swedenborg [dance] *See* Dance reviews—Single works

Angelyne
about
Here's a new way to fame: just paint yourself into a big corner. il pors *People Wkly* 27:73 Je 22 '87

Anger, Roger
about
New life for a medieval castle: architect Roger Anger reclaims a Provençal ruin. D. S. Aghion. il *Archit Dig* 44:184-9+ Mr '87

Anger
See also
Peeves
Temper
Anger: let me call you @#&*! J. Garvey. il *U S Cathol* 52:14-15 Ag '87
Don't get angry [study by Gary Emery] *USA Today (Periodical)* 116:11 N '87
Eight great anger-busters. B. Walters and E. Glass. il *Seventeen* 46:80+ Mr '87
My husband is always angry. S. F. Enos. il *Ladies Home J* 104:12+ O '87
Say it well, say it loud! H. H. Broun. il *50 Plus* 27:112 Ap '87
Shame and rage—the emotional chain reaction. C. Tavris. *Vogue* 177:198 Ap '87
Suppressing anger a fatal flaw [work of Mara Julius] *Prevention* 39:16 My '87
Teen rage. D. Salvatore. il *Ladies Home J* 104:95-7+ F '87
"You make me so mad!" [parents and children]; ed. by Martha Moraghan Jablow. N. Samalin. il *Parents* 62:53-7 Ja '87

Anger in children
Dealing with your child's anger. J. Segal and Z. Segal. il *Parents* 62:190 Mr '87

Anger of God *See* God—Wrath

Angevin, Susan
about
Riverside Drive. A. Jolles. il por *N Y* 20:30 Ag 24 '87

Angier, Natalie
Light cast on a darkling gene. il *Discover* 8:84-96 Mr '87

Angina pectoris *See* Heart—Diseases

Angiogenesis *See* Blood vessels

Angiogenin
Tissue distribution and developmental expression of the messenger RNA encoding angiogenin. H. L. Weiner and others. bibl f il *Science* 237:280-2 Jl 17 '87

Angiography *See* Radiography, Medical

Angioplasty, Arterial *See* Arteries—Diseases—Therapy

Angles
Gauging angles in the 17th century. A. Chapman. il *Sky Telesc* 73:362-4 Ap '87

Angleton, James
about
Obituary
U S News World Rep por 102:16 My 25 '87. J. L. Galloway

Anglican Church *See* Church of England

Angling *See* Fishing

Anglo American Corp. of South Africa, Ltd.
Anglo-American faces life. S. Mufson. *New Repub* 197:26+ S 14-21 '87
The Anglo Empire shows its other face. W. L. Chaze. il *U S News World Rep* 103:32-3 S 7 '87

Angola
See also
Military assistance, American—Angola
Military assistance, Cuban—Angola
Military assistance, Saudi Arabian—Angola
Foreign relations
South Africa
See South Africa—Foreign relations—Angola
Soviet Union
See Soviet Union—Foreign relations—Angola
United States
See United States—Foreign relations—Angola
History
Slave trade to insurgency. G. Sandford. il *U S News World Rep* 102:31 F 16 '87
Politics and government
See also
Press and politics—Angola
Angola: trapped in the cross fire. R. Knight. il map *U S News World Rep* 102:30-1 F 16 '87
Birth of a Soviet satellite. B. Amiel. il *Macleans* 100:9 Ag 17 '87
Can this man save Africa? [UNITA's J. Savimbi] D. Reed. il por *Read Dig* 130:221-2+ My '87
The Canadian connection [South Africa using Canadian-designed weaponry in Angola] A. Bilski. il map *Macleans* 100:36 O 19 '87
Cuba in Africa. P. S. Falk. map *Foreign Aff* 65:1077-96 Summ '87

Angola—Politics and government—*cont.*
Cuba's strange mission in Angola. J. Brooke. il *N Y Times Mag* p24+ F 1 '87
Ideological contradictions in U.S. policy toward Angola. R. A. Fangmeier. il *Christ Century* 104:1061-3 N 25 '87
A remote-control war. A. Bilski. il map *Macleans* 100:33 O 12 '87
Angrist, Stanley W.
Commodities. See issues of Forbes
Anguilla
Description and travel
Gourmet holidays. D. Beal. il map *Gourmet* 47:42-7+ Ja '87
Angus, Michael
about
Pulling together a two-part company. R. I. Kirkland, Jr. il pors *Fortune* 116:40 Ag 3 '87
Angus Wilkie Antiques (Firm)
Gemütlich grandeur. M. Boodro. il por *House Gard* 159:20+ F '87
Anheuser-Busch, Inc.
Anheuser-Busch: the scandal may be small beer after all [kickback charges] M. D. Oneal. il *Bus Week* p72-3 My 11 '87
Break out the suds for Spuds: contrary to rumors, he's alive—and not only that, he's a she! il *People Wkly* 28:62-4 S 14 '87
Frothing anti-drink forces set out to nip Spuds in the Bud [objections to Spuds MacKenzie's appeal to children] il *People Wkly* 28:87 O 26 '87
How Busch wins in a doggy market. P. Sellers. il por *Fortune* 115:99-100+ Je 22 '87
Pow! Bam! A one-two punch from Bob Arum and Budweiser [Hagler-Leonard fight] M. D. Oneal. il *Bus Week* p44 Ap 6 '87
Soda war [American National Beverage fights trademark dispute with Anheuser-Busch] R. L. Stern. il *Forbes* 139:82-3 My 4 '87
SoHo skirmish [American Natural Beverage wins trademark dispute with Anheuser-Busch] J. A. Conway. il *Forbes* 139:8 Je 29 '87
Top dog [Bud Light's Spuds MacKenzie] B. Kanner. il *N Y* 20:20+ S 28 '87
Anikulapo-Kuti, Fela *See* Fela, 1938-
Animal and Plant Health Inspection Service (U.S.) *See* United States. Animal and Plant Health Inspection Service
Animal behavior *See* Animals—Habits and behavior
Animal breeding *See* Breeding
Animal calling
See also
Bird calling
All about rattling [antlers used as deer calls] K. Etling. il *Outdoor Life* 179:58-9+ Ap '87
Deer calling secrets [whitetails] B. McGuire. il *Outdoor Life* 179:48-9+ F '87
Don't bugle up a grizzly bear [bowhunting bugling bull elk] B. McRae. il *Outdoor Life* 179:54-5+ Ap '87
Hunt with a grunt [calls for whitetailed deer; cover story] K. Etling. il *Outdoor Life* 180:65-7+ Jl '87
Animal camouflage *See* Mimicry (Biology)
Animal communication
See also
Bird communication
Insect communication
Be hep to your pet [body language] H. E. Whiteley. il *Saturday Evening Post* 259:70-1 S '87
Dolphin talk [interview with D. Reiss] G. Hartwell. *Oceans* 20:62-3 Mr/Ap '87
His howl is a lot worse than his bite [research by Fred Harrington] il *Discover* 8:10+ Jl '87
The man who cries wolf. F. H. Harrington. il *Nat Hist* 96:22+ F '87
The smell of fear [rats; research by Michael Fanselow] P. Chance. *Psychol Today* 21:16 Jl '87
Strange encounter on Coho Creek [timber wolves in Alaska] M. H. Erwin. il *Read Dig* 130:11-16 My '87
Animal defenses *See* Defense mechanisms (Biology)
Animal drugs *See* Veterinary drugs
Animal ecology
See also
Animal introduction
Animal populations
Wildlife management
Life and death in the fast lane [highway dividers trap crossing animals] M. Kantor. il *Sierra* 72:14 S/O '87
The longest meadow [effect of roads] P. Schullery. il *Ctry J* 14:83-6 Ap '87
Social life: a question of costs and benefits [special section] R. Lewin. il *Science* 236:775-7 My 15 '87

When you hear a splat, reach for Roger Knutson's Flattened fauna. il por *People Wkly* 28:105 Ag 17 '87
Animal experimentation
See also
Dissection
Xenografts
Animal passions [National Research Council study] T. Beardsley. *Sci Am* 257:30 O '87
Animals, cages, and handling equipment. *Science* 235 pt2:G23+ F 27 '87
Do house pets belong in research labs? M. Engel. il *Glamour* 85:252 S '87
Earth station, can you read me? [monkey onboard Soviet space vehicle frees arm from restraints] il *Time* 130:36 O 19 '87
Gauging the value of carcinogen assays. J. Raloff. *Sci News* 131:343 My 30 '87
Industry toxicologists keen on reducing animal use. C. Holden. il *Science* 236:252 Ap 17 '87
Prediction of chemical carcinogenicity in rodents from in vitro genetic toxicity assays. R. W. Tennant and others. bibl f il *Science* 236:933-41 My 22 '87
Anecdotes, facetiae, satire, etc.
My beef about micro pig, and your stake—or chop—in it. J. Gorman. il *Discover* 8:24+ Ja '87
Laws and regulations
Animal regulations: so far, so good. C. Holden. il *Science* 238:880-2 N 13 '87
Animal welfare. *Sci Am* 256:60 F '87
A frog's day in court [animal rights movement] M. Chinnici. il *Discover* 8:42-3 D '87
Protests, demonstrations, etc.
Animal rightists raid USDA lab [interruption of toxoplasmosis research at Animal Parasitology Institute] C. Holden. *Science* 237:1099 S 4 '87
Letting cats out of the lab: a cautionary tale [animal activists' interruption of toxoplasmosis research at the Animal Parasitology Institute] P. Gadsby. il *Discover* 8:22 N '87
Winning through intimidation? S. Budiansky. il *U S News World Rep* 103:48-9 Ag 31 '87
Great Britain
'All heaven in a rage'. M. Daly. il *Hist Today* 37:7-9 My '87
Animal extinction *See* Animals, Extinct
Animal genetics
Animal patent debate heats up. R. Weiss. *Sci News* 132:69-70 Ag 1 '87
Animals can now be patented. L. Tangley. *BioScience* 37:461-2 Jl/Ag '87
Controversy over animal patents. A. L. Spitler. *BioScience* 37:652 O '87
Here come the bionic piglets. G. Bylinsky. il *Fortune* 116:74-6+ O 26 '87
If it moves, patent it [animals produced by biotechnology] *Sci News* 131:263 Ap 25 '87
Lab-built plants, animals mean change. G. Vincent. il *Success Farm* 85:B-C My '87
Man-beast: patent pending. il *U S News World Rep* 102:18 Ap 27 '87
Patenting animals. G. Vincent. il *Success Farm* 85:64 Ag '87
Religious groups join animal patent battle. M. Crawford. *Science* 237:480-1 Jl 31 '87
Should animals be patented? C. Wallis. il *Time* 129:110 My 4 '87
Should man make beast? T. Monmaney. il *Newsweek* 109:64 My 4 '87
Animal habitat *See* Animal ecology
Animal hospitals *See* Veterinary hospitals
Animal instinct *See* Instinct
Animal intelligence
See also
Psychology, Comparative
Are cats smart? Yes, at being cats. P. W. Moser. il *Discover* 8:76-7+ My '87
Calculating apes [cover story] B. Bower. il *Sci News* 131:334-5 My 23 '87
The elephant as artist [work of D. Gucwa with Siri] J. Ehmann. il *Natl Wildl* 25:26-8 F/Mr '87
An elephant who draws pictures [work of D. Gucwa with Siri] J. Ehmann. il por *Read Dig* 131:96-9 O '87
The smartest family of birds? [corvids] L. Barash. il *Natl Wildl* 26:45 D '87/Ja '88
Think like a dolphin [role models for managers learning strategic thinking skills] *Futurist* 21:52 Mr/Ap '87

Animal introduction

Ecological invasions offer opportunities [Hawaii as a research area] R. Lewin. il *Science* 238:752-3 N 6 '87

The ecology of biological invasions. H. A. Mooney and J. A. Drake. bibl f il maps *Environment* 29:10-15+ Je '87

Joe and Rosie go for it [captive dolphins retrained and released] E. Linden. il *Time* 130:72 Ag 17 '87

Outward bound for chimps [reintroduction to the wild at Abuko Nature Reserve, Gambia] B. McBride. il map *Int Wildl* 17:18-21 S/O '87

When aliens take over [feral animals in the Galapagos] T. De Roy. il *Int Wildl* 17:34-7 Ja/F '87

With lots of help, alpine ibex return to their mountains. C. Grodinsky and M. Stüwe. il *Smithsonian* 18:68-72+ D '87

Animal language *See* Animal communication

Animal learning

The cerebellum and memory storage [discussion of August 29, 1986 article, The neurobiology of learning and memory] R. F. Thompson. *Science* 238:1728-30 D 18 '87

Dissecting learning in Aplysia [research by Thomas J. Carew and others] S. Weisburd. *Sci News* 132:286 O 31 '87

Japanese quail can learn phonetic categories. K. R. Kluender and others. bibl f il *Science* 237:1195-7 S 4 '87

Learning by instinct. J. L. Gould and P. Marler. il *Sci Am* 256:74-85 Ja '87

Long-term sensitization in Aplysia: biophysical correlates in tail sensory neurons. K. P. Scholz and J. H. Byrne. bibl f il *Science* 235:685-7 F 6 '87

Neural models yield data on learning [special section] D. M. Barnes. *Science* 236:1628-9 Je 26 '87

New connections may be memorable [Aplysia learning associated circuit formation; research by Craig Bailey and others] R. Weiss. *Sci News* 132:342 N 28 '87

Animal locomotion

The by-the-wind sailor: a masterpiece of natural design. S. Brownlee. il *Discover* 8:46 Ag '87

Climbing adaptations in the early Eocene mammal Chriacus and the origin of Artiodactyla. K. D. Rose. bibl f il *Science* 236:314-16 Ap 17 '87

Diving adaptations of the Weddell seal. W. M. Zapol. bibl (p136) il *Sci Am* 256:100-5 Je '87

Leatherback deep dives [turtles] il *Sea Front* 33:304-5 Jl/Ag '87

Newly identified 'glutamate interneurons' and their role in locomotion in the lamprey spinal cord. J. T. Buchanan and S. Grillner. bibl f il *Science* 236:312-14 Ap 17 '87

Pterosaurs waddled when they walked? [theory of David M. Unwin] *Sci News* 131:344 My 30 '87

Test tank for fast fish [researching body temperature regulation and swimming dynamics of warm-blooded albacore tuna] *Oceans* 20:5 My/Je '87

Yertle: 1; Orca: 0 [deep diving by leatherback turtles; research by Scott A. Eckert] il *Discover* 8:14 S '87

Photographs and photography

Jumping blues [frogs] S. Dalton. il *Nat Hist* 96:96-7 Mr '87

Animal lore

See also

Wolves in religion, folklore, etc.

Animal models of human diseases *See* Diseases—Animal models

Animal Parasitology Institute (U.S.)

Animal rightists raid USDA lab [interruption of toxoplasmosis research] C. Holden. *Science* 237:1099 S 4 '87

Letting cats out of the lab: a cautionary tale [animal activists' interruption of toxoplasmosis research] P. Gadsby. il *Discover* 8:22 N '87

Animal populations

See also

Fish populations

Population genetics—Animals

Abundance. P. Steinhart. il *Audubon* 89:8+ Ja '87

Control

See also

Wildlife management

Animal print fabrics *See* Textile fabrics

Animal products

She sells springboks by the seashore [A. De Geer's shop, Africa in Hawaii] T. Ryan. il por *Sierra* 72:17 Ja/F '87

Want to save endangered animals? Shop smart. M. Engel. il *Glamour* 85:214 Mr '87

Animal shelters

See also

American Society for the Prevention of Cruelty to Animals

Great Britain

See also

Donkey Sanctuary (Devonshire, England)

Animal societies *See* Animals—Habits and behavior

Animal sounds

See also

Animal communication

Birds—Song

Fish sounds

Frog went a-courtin' [gray tree frog; work of Georg M. Klump and H. Carl Gerhardt] il *Sci Am* 256:28 Je '87

Sonic punch: dolphins and whales generate "bangs" that may stun prey [research by Kenneth Marten and Kenneth S. Norris] T. Beardsley. *Sci Am* 257:36 O '87

Animal temperature *See* Temperature, Animal and human

Animal toys *See* Toys

Animal tracks and trails

The oldest writing [snow trails] J. Madson. il *Audubon* 89:62-3 Ja '87

The tracking snow. C. Fergus. il *Ctry J* 14:32-7 F '87

Watch a trail to take a trophy [deer] W. L. Prothero. il *Outdoor Life* 180:72-3+ Jl '87

Who did what? Studying animals through their tracks. R. Schuessler. il *Conservationist* 41:18-23 Ja/F '87

Animal traps *See* Traps

The animal trilogy [dance] *See* Dance reviews—Single works

Animals

See also

Domestic animals

Eye—Animals

Feces—Animals

Game

Hearing—Animals

Horns—Animals

Livestock

Perfumes for animals

Pets

Pheromones—Animals

Rare animals

Reproductive organs—Animals

Teeth—Animals

Ungulates

Vision—Animals

Wildlife

See also names of animals

Accidents and hazards

See also

Automobile driving—Animal hazards

Animal accidents and deaths [game species] J. J. Jonkel. il *Outdoor Life* 179:56-7+ Ja '87

Breeding

See Breeding

Civil rights

See Animals—Treatment

Collisions with automobiles

See Automobile driving—Animal hazards

Diseases and pests

See also

Rabies

Veterinary medicine

First aid

See First aid for animals

Food and feeding

See also

Grazing

Herbivores

Optimal foraging theory

Pet food

Salt licks

Habits and behavior

See also

Animal intelligence

Defense mechanisms (Biology)

Hibernation

Instinct

Kin recognition

Mimicry (Biology)

Parental behavior in animals

Psychology, Comparative

Sex differences—Animals

Sexual behavior—Animals

Suckling

Territoriality (Zoology)

Tracking and trailing

Animals—Habits and behavior—*cont.*

All together, now [schooling, herding, and flocking behavior] P. Schullery. il *Ctry J* 14:30-1 Je '87·

Common pet myths: sorting fact from fiction. C. Lamb. il *Better Homes Gard* 65:182+ O '87

Do animals read minds, tell lies? [deceptive behavior] R. Lewin. il *Science* 238:1350-1 D 4 '87

High-cadmium diet: recipe for stress? [increased alcohol consumption in rats; research by Jack R. Nation and others] B. Bower. *Sci News* 132:101-2 Ag 15 '87

Interview [K. Lorenz] B. Lawren. por *Omni* 9:84-6+ Ap '87

Social life: a question of costs and benefits [special section] R. Lewin. il *Science* 236:775-7 My 15 '87

War among the chimps [cover story] M. P. Ghiglieri. il *Discover* 8:66-70+ N '87

What are friends for? [East African olive baboons] B. Smuts. il *Nat Hist* 96:36-45 F '87

Why the deer and the antelope play [ungulates] J. A. Byers. il *Nat Hist* 96:54-61 My '87

Intelligence

See Animal intelligence

Language

See Animal communication

Miscellanea

If I were an animal, I'd be a . . . [excerpts] F. Cowles. il *Redbook* 168:78+ Mr '87

Navigation

See Orientation

Photographs and photography

A different breed of mom. W. Chandoha. il *Good Housekeep* 204:157 My '87

Protection

See Game laws; Wildlife conservation; Wildlife sanctuaries

Temperature

See Temperature, Animal and human

Tracks

See Animal tracks and trails

Training

See also

Bears—Training

Marine mammals—Training

Treatment

See also

American Society for the Prevention of Cruelty to Animals

Animal experimentation

Chimpanzees—Treatment

Donkeys—Treatment

Food Animal Concerns Trust

Horses—Treatment

Hunting—Ethical aspects

All animal rights activists are not the same. B. Eftink. *Success Farm* 85 no2:B1 Ja '87

Animal abuse: a difficult problem [pets] R. H. Pitcairn. *Prevention* 39:65-7 Je '87

Ban on dog training? [Anti-Live Animal Lure Act of 1987] R. Herzberg. *Outdoor Life* 180:152 S '87

Dominion over the earth [cover story] G. Moran. bibl il *Commonweal* 114:697-701 D 4 '87

Animals, Cruelty to *See* Animals—Treatment

Animals, Extinct

See also

Dinosaurs

Mass extinction of species

As an exterminating agency, humans are comparable with any natural form of violence that has ever come along. R. M. Adams. il *Smithsonian* 18:10 S '87

Environmental trends in extinction during the Paleozoic. J. J. Sepkoski, Jr. bibl f il *Science* 235:64-6 Ja 2 '87

Solving the extinction paradox [work of J. J. Sepkoski] *USA Today (Periodical)* 115:9-10 Je '87

Animals, Fossil *See* Paleontology

Animals, Geographical distribution of *See* Geographical distribution of animals and plants

Animals, Infancy of

See also

Parental behavior in animals

Spring's renewal: a small portfolio of new life. il *Conservationist* 41:29-32 My/Je '87

Young wildlife: look—don't touch! S. H. Clarke. il *Conservationist* 41:26-8 My/Je '87

Animals, Mechanical

Kong is back . . . [construction of mechanical King Kong for Universal Studios tour] il *Natl Geogr World* 137:9-15 Ja '87

Animals, Mythical

See also

Jackalopes

Loch Ness monster

Sasquatch

Sea monsters

Animals, Predatory

See also

Baboons

Coyotes

Foxes

Wolves

Animals, Rare *See* Rare animals

Animals, Treatment of *See* Animals—Treatment

Animals and children *See* Children and animals

Animals and civilization

Phenomena, comment and notes [how zoo visitors perceive animals] M. Robinson. il *Smithsonian* 17:30+ F '87

Bibliography

Animals and us. S. J. Gould. il *N Y Rev Books* 34:20-5 Je 25 '87

Animals and music

Lobster lovers should thank Philly's Morty Krouse—he's singing for their supper. il por *People Wkly* 27:71 Je 1 '87

Animals and the handicapped *See* Handicapped and animals

Animals as actors

See also

Chimpanzees as actors

Dogs as actors

Animals as artists

See also

Chimpanzees as artists

Elephants as artists

Animals as carriers of infection

Ecology of a new disease. J. A. Miller. il *BioScience* 37:11-15 Ja '87

Poker players, pneumonia and cat tales [Q fever rickettsia transmitted by cat] D. D. Edwards. *Sci News* 132:255 O 17 '87

Risky shell game: pet turtles can infect kids. C. Lecos. il *FDA Consum* 21:19-21 D '87/Ja '88

Animals in advertising

Anecdotes, facetiae, satire, etc.

The wild side of television advertising. J. Maas. il *Saturday Evening Post* 259:50-1+ S '87

Animals in art

See also

Birds in art

Dinosaurs in art

Horses in art

Sharks in art

Art for the outdoorsman [work of A. Hughes] H. Middleton. il por *South Living* 22:100+ Je '87

Art from the heart of nature [work of K. Carlson] M. Wexler. il por *Natl Wildl* 25:34-9 Ag/S '87

Art: woodland prints. H. H. Broun. il *Archit Dig* 44:178-83 Je '87

A canvas of steel [wildlife gun engravings] R. L. Wilson and E. R. Ricciuti. il *Audubon* 89:100-9 N '87

Fish, frogs and furniture [designs of F. Saunders] il por *Workbench* 43:96 N/D '87

Guy Coheleach—artist and hunter [cover story] A. Fornora. il *Conservationist* 42:26-33 N/D '87

Itty Bitty monster hits [animal figurines from United Design Corporation] J. Culpepper and S. Dark. il pors *Nations Bus* 75:58 Jl '87

Kent Ullberg's monumental sculptures [cover story] M. S. Doherty. il pors *Am Artist* 51:48-53 N '87

A sporting tradition [cover story] J. Madson. il *Natl Wildl* 25:48-57 O/N '87

Terry Shortt: a life's journey into nature. R. M. Peck. il por *Int Wildl* 17:4-11 Jl/Ag '87

Urban animals [building ornaments] K. C. Bloomer. il *Audubon* 89:68-75 Ja '87

Collectors and collecting

Popularity of the animal-motif banks. M. Jailer. il *Antiques Collect Hobbies* 92:42-4 S '87

A practiced eye: J. Garvin Mecking in Greenwich Village. S. M. L. Aronson. il *Archit Dig* 44:156-63+ Ap '87

Exhibitions

Animal magnetism [selection of display pieces by T. Lawton for the Arthur M. Sackler Gallery in Washington, D.C.] D. Kazanjian. il *House Gard* 159:166-71+ S '87

Computer-part art [exhibition at the Computer Museum, Boston] il *Natl Geogr World* 145:3-5 S '87

Poetry in porcelain [animal sculptures of E. M. Boehm at Bellingrath Gardens] il por *South Living* 22:26 Ja '87

Robert Bateman's incisive eye [Portraits of nature exhibit at the National Museum of Natural History] C. Bond. il *Smithsonian* 17:136-7 Ja '87

Animals in captivity *See* Zoos
Animals in literature
    See also
    Peter Rabbit (Fictional character)
The truth about Black Beauty [unrealistic portrayal of
    animals in children's literature; views of H. N.
    Christensen] D. Sobel. *Omni* 9:27 Mr '87
Animals in motion pictures
    See also
    Dogs in motion pictures
Animals in music
    See also
    PetSong (Firm)
Animals in television
    See also
    Cats in television
    Dogs in television
    Swine in television
Animals in television advertising *See* Animals in advertising
Animated cartoons *See* Television broadcasting—Cartoons
Animated films *See* Motion pictures—Animated films;
    Videotapes—Animated films
Anions *See* Ions
Anjard, Ronald P.
    Fascinating bricks. il *Antiques Collect Hobbies* 92:72-5
    S '87
Ankerberg, John
                    about
    Ankerberg discusses the part he played. il por *Christ
    Today* 31:52 Je 12 '87
Ann Arbor (Mich.)
                    Buildings
    In the Middle West [Industrial Technology Institute]
    G. Anderson. il *Archit Rec* 175:96-9 Jl '87
                    Charities
    Notes and comment [donation of garbage truck to sister
    city Juigalpa, Nicaragua] *New Yorker* 63:15-16 Ag 17
    '87
Ann Arbor (Mich.). University of Michigan *See* University
    of Michigan
Anna [film] *See* Motion picture reviews—Single works
Annan, Gabriele
    Changeling. il *N Y Rev Books* 34:3-4 S 24 '87
Annapolis Tidal Power Plant (Nova Scotia) *See* Dams—
    Canada
Annaud, Jean-Jacques
                    about
    The name of the rose [film] Reviews
    Humanist il 47:39-40 Mr/Ap '87. H. M. Geduld
    USA Today (Periodical) il 115:95-6 Ja '87. K. R.
    Hey
**Anne, Princess, daughter of Elizabeth II, Queen of Great
    Britain, 1950-**
                    about
    Anne, the princess who pulls her own weight, comes
    to Nashville for a little horseplay and charity. M.
    Niel. il pors *People Wkly* 28:106-7+ O 26 '87
    Princess Anne clears a new hurdle: the steeplechase.
    J. Cooper. il pors *People Wkly* 27:36-7 Mr 30 '87
Anne of Green Gables—the sequel [television program]
    See Television program reviews—Single works
Annecy (France)
                    Description and travel
    Gourmet holidays. N. Stancioff. il maps *Gourmet* 47:64-9+
    My '87
Annelids
    See also
    Leeches
    Nervous system—Annelids
    Fans of the worms [Myxicola worms raised for axon
    research by David Dean] P. A. Erickson. il *Oceans*
    20:62-3 S/O '87
Annenberg, Walter H., 1908-
                    about
    Why huge fortunes roll off the presses. B. Dumaine.
    il por *Fortune* 116:156-7 O 12 '87
Annenberg Library and Communications Center (Mass.)
    Richardsonian recalls. H. L. Smith, Jr. il *Archit Rec*
    175:104-9 Ap '87
Annihilationism (Theology)
    Everlasting punishment. D. F. Wells. il por *Christ Today*
    31:41-2 Mr 20 '87
    Fire, then nothing. C. H. Pinnock. por *Christ Today*
    31:40-2 Mr 20 '87
Anniversaries
    See also
    Wedding anniversaries
    Happy anniversary, writers! J. Yolen. *Writer* 100:7-8
    Ja '87

Annual reports, Corporate *See* Corporation reports
Annuities
    Locking up safe returns in annuities or insurance. M.
    Harris. il *Money* 16:124-5 D '87
    Some nest eggs aren't all they're cracked up to be.
    P. Martin. il *50 Plus* 27:34-6+ N '87
    What's under the rock? [high-yield insurance products
    financed with junk bonds] B. Kallen. il *Forbes* 139:134-5
    F 23 '87
                    Taxation
    Annuities: shelters' last stand. K. McCormally. il
    Changing Times 41:80-2+ Je '87
    The annuity alternative. *Consum Rep* 52:13 Ja '87
Annular solar eclipses *See* Eclipses, Solar
Annunziata, Lucia
    Another useful tool [discussion of April 18, 1987 article,
    Democrats and the Arias plan] *Nation* 244:565 My
    2 '87
    Democrats and the Arias plan [cover story] il *Nation*
    244:489+ Ap 18 '87
Anopheles *See* Mosquitoes
Anorexia nervosa
    Anorexia and bulimia: causes and cures. K. Lehrman.
    il *Consum Res Mag* 70:29-32 S '87
    Diabetes and eating disorders [study by Randi Birk
    and Martha Spencer] K. Ullman. *Psychol Today* 21:23
    N '87
    A thinly disguised message [link between image of women
    in advertisements and anorexia nervosa] D. Marquardt.
    il *Ms* 15:33 My '87
Anoxemia
    See also
    Mountain sickness
Ansari, Hamied
    Egypt: repression and liberalization. *Curr Hist* 86:77-80+
    F '87
Anschutz, Philip
                    about
    Denver's quiet billionaire comes out fighting. M. Ivey.
    il por *Bus Week* p70-1 Jl 27 '87
    A dogfight in Denver. M. Ivey. il por *Bus Week* p38
    Ap 27 '87
Anschutz Corporation
    Denver's quiet billionaire comes out fighting [P. Anschutz]
    M. Ivey. il por *Bus Week* p70-1 Jl 27 '87
Anscombe, Roderick
    Stranger than fiction. por *Newsweek* 109:8-9 My 4 '87
Anselmo, René
                    about
    The feud that toppled a TV empire. G. Critser. il pors
    Channels 7:24-31 Ja '87
Anselmo, Tony
                    about
    If it quacks like this odd duck, it must be Tony Anselmo.
    il por *People Wkly* 27:127 My 18 '87
Ansett Airlines of Australia
    Ansett Airlines prepares Fokker 50 for start of service
    in November. K. F. Mordoff. il *Aviat Week Space
    Technol* 127:49-50 S 28 '87
Ansett Transport Industries, Ltd.
    Ansett's stock purchase will place foreign stake in America
    West at 20%. M. A. Dornheim. il map *Aviat Week
    Space Technol* 127:41-2+ Jl 20 '87
Anson, Mike
    Starting grid. See issues of Motor Trend beginning October
    1986
Anson, Robert Sam, 1945-
    Best intentions: Edmund Perry's path from Harlem to
    Exeter to death on a street in Morningside Heights
    [excerpt] il pors map *N Y* 20:30-45 My 11 '87
Anspaugh, David
                    about
    Hoosiers [film] Reviews
    Commonweal 114:215-16 Ap 10 '87. T. O'Brien
    Macleans il 100:46 Mr 2 '87. L. O'Toole
    New Repub 196:26-7 Ap 6 '87. S. Kauffmann
    Newsweek il 109:73 F 9 '87. D. Ansen
    People Wkly il 27:34-5 Mr 30 '87. L. Aitken
    People Wkly il 27:12 F 23 '87. S. Haller
    Time il 129:74 F 9 '87. R. Schickel
Antacids
    Six months and half a million dollars, all for 15 seconds
    [Young & Rubicam does a television commercial for
    Warner-Lambert's Rolaids] J. E. Pfeiffer. il *Smithsonian*
    18:134-8+ O '87
Antarctic exploration
    The Antarctic challenge [R. F. Scott's journey to the
    South Pole] P. M. Scott. il pors *Natl Geogr* 171:538-43
    Ap '87

Antarctic exploration—*cont.*
In the footsteps of Scott [retracing R. Scott's route to South Pole] R. Swan. il pors map *Natl Geogr* 171:544-55 Ap '87
Trying to cap Antarctic daredevilry [M. Kristensen's failed attempt to retrace Roald Amundsen's race to the South Pole] M. Satchell. il por map *U S News World Rep* 102:75 F 16 '87

Photographs and photography
Frozen in time [R. Amundsen's 1910 expedition] M. Loke. il *N Y Times Mag* p46-9 O 4 '87

Antarctic regions
See also
Antarctic exploration
Birds—Antarctic regions
Fish—Antarctic regions
Ice—Polar regions
Natural resources—Antarctic regions
Paleobotany—Antarctic regions
Shellfish fisheries—Antarctic regions
Skis and skiing—Antarctic regions
United Nations—Antarctic regions

Caricatures and cartoons
Opus goes home: Bloom County's penguin returns to his roots in Antarctica. B. Breathed. il *Life* 10:42-7+ My '87

Climate
Antarctic ozone reaches lowest levels. R. Monastersky. *Sci News* 132:230 O 10 '87
Antarctic ozone: the plot thickens. R. Monastersky. *Sci News* 131:326 My 23 '87
Antarctic stratospheric chemistry of chlorine nitrate, hydrogen chloride, and ice: release of active chlorine. M. J. Molina and others. bibl f il *Science* 238:1253-7 N 27 '87
Can we close the ozone hole? F. S. Rowland. il *Technol Rev* 90:50-8 Ag/S '87
Culprits of the stratosphere [study by Crofton Farmer on the Antarctic ozone hole] M. D. Lemonick. il *Time* 130:57 S 21 '87
The endangered ozone layer [cover story; with editorial comment by Gilbert F. White] G. Brasseur. bibl il *Environment* 29:inside cover, 6-11+ Ja/F '87
Flying high—and hairy [missions through the ozone hole in the ER-2 research plane] il *Time* 130:60-1 O 19 '87
Flying into an ozone hole [Airborne Antarctic Ozone Experiment] *Sci News* 132:95 Ag 8 '87
Forecasting for the frigid desert of Antarctica [cover story] D. P. Mullen. il map *Weatherwise* 40:304-11 D '87
Halocarbons linked to ozone hole [research by Philip Solomon and others] R. A. Kerr. il *Science* 236:1182-3 Je 5 '87
Layers of complexity in ozone hole. J. Silberner. *Sci News* 131:164 Mr 14 '87
Made in the shade? No way [ozone hole] G. Taubes. il *Discover* 8:62-71 Ag '87
More clues to the mysterious ozone hole. R. Monastersky. *Sci News* 132:182 S 19 '87
New threats to the sky [depletion in Antarctic ozone layer] A. Steacy. il *Macleans* 100:44-5 S 14 '87
The ozone hole. *Sci Am* 257:19-20 Ag '87
Ozone hole updates. *Sci News* 132:302 N 7 '87
Ozone watch. T. Beardsley. *Sci Am* 257:18 N '87
Reaction of chlorine nitrate with hydrogen chloride and water at Antarctic stratospheric temperatures. M. A. Tolbert and others. bibl f il *Science* 238:1258-60 N 27 '87
U.S., Soviets to study Antarctic ozone. R. Monastersky. *Sci News* 131:408 Je 27 '87
Volcanic residue cited as possible source of misleading ozone data. R. G. O'Lone. *Aviat Week Space Technol* 126:91-2 Ja 12 '87
Watch this space [ozone hole] E. R. Shell. il *Omni* 9:36-8+ Ag '87
Weather versus chemicals [controversy over chlorofluorocarbons and ozone hole] E. R. Shell. il *Atlantic* 259:27-31 My '87
Winds, pollutants drive ozone hole. R. A. Kerr. il map *Science* 238:156-8 O 9 '87

Territorial claims
A cold war: Britain, Argentina and Antarctica. P. J. Beck. bibl il maps *Hist Today* 37:16-23 Je '87

Antarctic research
Antarctica. P. J. Vesilind. il map *Natl Geogr* 171:556-60 Ap '87
Laboratory Antarctica: research contributions to global problems. G. Weller and others. bibl f il maps *Science* 238:1361-8 D 4 '87

Lateral isotopic discontinuity in the lower crust: an example from Antarctica. R. I. Kalamarides and others. bibl f il maps *Science* 237:1192-5 S 4 '87
Leg 113: drilling into Antarctica's past. S. Weisburd. map *Sci News* 131:278-9 My 2 '87
Microbial trace-fossil formation, biogenous, and abiotic weathering in the Antarctic cold desert. E. I. Friedmann and R. Weed. bibl f il *Science* 236:703-5 My 8 '87
Ocean drilling details steps to an icy world. R. A. Kerr. il map *Science* 236:912-13 My 22 '87
Resources of Antarctica. il *Oceans* 20:69 S/O '87
Winter in Antarctica: health despite discomfort [positive stress; study by Lawrence A. Palinkas] E. Smith. il *Psychol Today* 21:60-1 Mr '87

International aspects
U.S., Soviets to study Antarctic ozone. R. Monastersky. *Sci News* 131:408 Je 27 '87

Antarctic Treaty (1959)
Antarctica. P. J. Vesilind. il map *Natl Geogr* 171:556-60 Ap '87
Question of Antarctica reviewed for fourth time; Assembly adopts three texts. il *UN Chron* 24:94 F '87
Resources of Antarctica. il *Oceans* 20:69 S/O '87
The success of the Antarctic Treaty [address, March 27, 1987] J. Negroponte. *Dep State Bull* 87:29-30 Je '87

Anteaters, Fossil
First record of giant anteater (Xenarthra, Myrmecophagidae) in North America. C. A. Shaw and H. G. McDonald. bibl f il map *Science* 236:186-8 Ap 10 '87
Have land bridge, will travel [research by H. Gregory McDonald and others] *Sci News* 131:296 My 9 '87

Antelope hunting
See also
Pronghorn hunting

Antelopes
See also
Pronghorns

Antennas (Electronics)
See also
Radar—Antennas
Radio antennas

Anterograde amnesia *See* Amnesia

Antesena, Gerardo, and others
It's tough at the top. il *Courier* 40:8-11 Je '87

Anthes, Richard A.
(jt. auth) See Tribbia, Joseph J., and Anthes, Richard A.

Anthimos, Bishop of Denver
about
A black prince of the church. G. Clifford. il pors *People Wkly* 28:30-5 S 28 '87

Anthologies
See also
Science fiction—Anthologies
Sweet are the uses of anthology. A. Manguel. il *N Y Times Book Rev* 92:1+ Ag 23 '87

Anthony, Carolyn T.
Remaindering now. il *Publ Wkly* 231:29-31+ Ap 17 '87

Anthony, Joseph
Home equity credit: banking on your home [cover story] il *Consum Res Mag* 70:11-14 Ag '87
Life insurance as investment. *Consum Res Mag* 70:22-4 N '87

Anthony, Michael, 1932-
about
The puzzle for Caribbean writers. N. Faria. *World Press Rev* 34:62 Ja '87

Anthony, Mitch
about
Mitch Anthony's war. D. Eble. por *Christ Today* 31:20 Mr 20 '87

Anthony, Pat
about
Motherly love works a miracle [cover story] E. Levin. il pors *People Wkly* 28:38-43 O 19 '87

Anthony, Susan Brownell, 1820-1906
about
Letter to the past. C. McHugh. il por *Sch Update* 119:12-14 My 18 '87

Anthrax
Churchill's anthrax bombs: a debate [discussion of January/February 1987 article, Churchill's secret biological weapons] B. J. Bernstein. *Bull At Sci* 43:42-5 N '87

Anthropic principle *See* Anthropocentrism

Anthropocentrism
A 'what you see is what you beget' theory [cover story] T. Rothman. il *Discover* 8:90-6+ My '87

Anthropologists
    See also
    Good, Ken
    Women anthropologists
Anthropology
    See also
    Archeology
    Evolution
    Forensic anthropology
    Intercultural research
    Man
    Man, Prehistoric
    Philosophical anthropology
       Ethical aspects
Anthropologists turn advocates for the Brazilian Indians. G. Kolata. il *Science* 236:1183-7 Je 5 '87
Recent discussions with Indian leaders have raised questions about repatriation of skeletal remains and sacred objects. R. M. Adams. il *Smithsonian* 18:12 N '87
We have an obligation to return the Indian skeletal remains in our collections to tribal descendants. R. M. Adams. *Smithsonian* 18:12 My '87
Anthropometry
    See also
    Craniometry
Anti-aging skin care cosmetics *See* Cosmetics
Anti-aging skin care drugs *See* Skin—Care and hygiene
Anti-aircraft guns *See* Guns, Anti-aircraft
Anti-ballistic missile system *See* Guided missiles—Defenses
Anti-Ballistic Missile Treaty *See* Disarmament
Anti-Catholicism
       History
Papal visit recalls America's "Catholic note"! [1869 dollar] E. Rochette. il *Antiques Collect Hobbies* 92:76-7 S '87
Anti-Communist movements
    See also
    United States—Foreign relations—Anti-Communist measures
Minority report [Second Thoughts Conference] C. Hitchens. *Nation* 245:511+ N 7 '87
Scoundrel time again. E. Knoll. *Progressive* 51:4 D '87
What is to be done? J. Muravchik. *New Repub* 197:16-17 N 30 '87
       History
And what about those red hills she painted? [FBI's investigation of G. O'Keeffe at height of McCarthyism] J. Herzfeld. il *Art News* 86:198 Ap '87
The defiling of writers [FBI files on American authors; cover story] N. S. Robins. il *Nation* 245:367-70+ O 10 '87
Policing America's writers [FBI files on great American writers] H. Mitgang. *New Yorker* 63:47-8+ O 5 '87
Security risk. J. B. Montague, Jr. il *Progressive* 51:34 S '87
A southern ex-Communist remembers [J. I. Scales' memoir Cause at heart] B. Summer. *Publ Wkly* 231:55 My 29 '87
Three lives [discussion of October 10, 1987 article, The defiling of writers] N. S. Robins. *Nation* 245:666 D 5 '87
Two writers probe FBI surveillance of American authors [H. Mitgang and N. S. Robins] W. Goldstein. *Publ Wkly* 232:38 O 30 '87
       Great Britain
    See also
    Great Britain—Foreign relations—Anti-Communist measures
       Philippines
Resistance on the right. M. Liu. il *Newsweek* 110:44 Ag 10 '87
Rise of the vigilantes. M. S. Serrill. il *Time* 129:40 My 11 '87
Singlaub's new mission. B. Levin. il por *Macleans* 100:20 Mr 2 '87
Vigilantes for Aquino. F. Willey. il por *Newsweek* 109:34+ Mr 30 '87
Vigilantes resurgent [right wing Alsa Masa movement] D. Friesen. il *Progressive* 51:21-3 N '87
A war of vigilantes. B. Levin. il *Macleans* 100:26 Mr 30 '87
Anti-helicopter weapons
All stuck up, no way to go [soft kill weapons; views of S. A. Hoenig] S. Budiansky. il *U S News World Rep* 103:62 Jl 20 '87
Anti-lock braking system *See* Brakes, Automobile; Brakes, Motorcycle
Anti-nuclear movement
    See also
    Citizens' Action for Safe Energy
    Great Peace March, 1986

    Nuclear-free zones
    SANE/FREEZE (Organization)
    Union of Concerned Scientists
About face [interview with physicist T. B. Taylor] D. Sheff. il por *Roll Stone* p59+ S 24 '87
Be your own peacemaker [views of A. Ayvazian and M. T. Klare] S. H. Day, Jr. il *Progressive* 51:17-18 Ap '87
Bonded by love and conscience, the Gumps of Morton Grove accept prison. D. Chu. il pors *People Wkly* 28:163-4+ D 14 '87
Does a protester have a right to damage a missile site? D. O. Relin. il *Sch Update* 120:32 N 20 '87
Getting involved. E. Berg. il *Parents* 62:100-2 My '87
Medium gains. *Nation* 245:327-8 O 3 '87
Moscow "radicals" stop a nuclear plant [Zimmer Ohio Nuclear Power Station] J. Lawless. il por *Sierra* 72:125-30 Ja/F '87
Nuclear war as an environmental issue. J. Salzman. *Environment* 29:4-5+ Ja/F '87
One night in the Beatty lockup. L. R. Peattie. il *Commonweal* 114:140-3 Mr 13 '87
A plea to close defense reactors [plutonium manufacturing] E. Marshall. *Science* 238:886-7 N 13 '87
Still on the road for peace [elderly veterans of the Great Peace March continue to be involved] L. Lindeman. il *50 Plus* 27:20-2 Je '87
Summer of our discontent. H. Wasserman. *Nation* 245:233-4 S 12 '87
The task for a new peace movement. V. F. Weisskopf. il *Bull At Sci* 43:26-32 Ja/F '87
Torpedoing free speech [ordinance to regulate anti-nuclear protests in Groton, Conn.] S. Burkholder. il *Progressive* 51:15-16 My '87
Witnessing for peace [update on Silo Pruning Hooks case] R. Pollak. *Nation* 244:567-8 My 2 '87
       History
Science and scientists in the public arena [atomic scientists since WW II] E. A. Shils. *Am Sch* 56:185-202 Spr '87
Voyage of a peace activist [E. Reynolds] S. A. Wittman. il por *Progressive* 51:16 F '87
       International aspects
    See also
    International Forum for a Nuclear-Free World
    International Physicians for the Prevention of Nuclear War
Good vibrations: the new peace offensive. D. Brooks. il *Natl Rev* 39:36-9 N 6 '87
Independent initiatives: an alternative peace process. M. Sommer and G. Feller. *Current* 292:36-9 My '87
       Europe
    See also
    European Nuclear Disarmament (Organization)
To win the peace [Russian offer on Euromissiles sets stage for peace movement] *Nation* 244:561-2 My 2 '87
       France
The churches and the peace movement in France. M. B. Davis. il *Christ Century* 104:826-8 S 30 '87
       Great Britain
The women of Greenham Common. O. Ward. il *World Press Rev* 34:32-4 Ap '87
Zapped? [women at Greenham Common peace camp fear they are victims of non-ionizing electromagnetic radiation] L. Slesin. *Nation* 244:313 Mr 14 '87
       Japan
Reflections of a Japanese physicist. M. Kimura. il pors *Bull At Sci* 43:7-10 N '87
       New Zealand
Beyond California. R. Sandall. *Commentary* 83:56-60 Je '87
The genesis of New Zealand's ban. J. Salzman. il *Bull At Sci* 43:45-6+ Jl/Ag '87
Kiwis just say 'no'. J. Salzman. *Sierra* 72:32+ My/Je '87
Minority report. C. Hitchens. *Nation* 244:600 My 9 '87
New Zealand paying for nuclear ban. K. P. Clements. bibl f il *Bull At Sci* 43:41-4 Jl/Ag '87
New Zealand's antinuclear stand. K. P. Clements. il *Bull At Sci* 43:32-4 Mr '87
       Soviet Union
Taking the long road to peace [Americans join Soviets in peace march through Russia] L. Lindeman. il *50 Plus* 27:50-5 O '87
       United States
    See Anti-nuclear movement
       Western Europe
Peaceniks packing up. P. Sherrid. il *U S News World Rep* 103:40 D 7 '87

Anti-nuclear movement—*cont.*

Yugoslavia

Hard rain falls on Yugoslavia [effects of Chernobyl] S. Drakulich. il *Nation* 244:177-8+ F 14 '87

Anti-pollution devices (Diesel engines) *See* Diesel engines, Automotive—Pollution control devices

Anti-satellite weapons

See also

Railguns

DOD wants to boost ASAT program. *Sci News* 131:201 Mr 28 '87

Soviet ground lasers threaten U.S. geosynchronous satellites. J. D. Morrocco. *Aviat Week Space Technol* 127:27 N 2 '87

Soviet strategic defense technology. E. Stubbs. bibl f il map *Bull At Sci* 43:14-19 Ap '87

Space and national strategy [address, May 15, 1987] E. C. Aldridge. *Vital Speeches Day* 53:614-16 Ag 1 '87

Year of decision for ASAT program. D. C. Morrison. il *Science* 236:1512-14 Je 19 '87

Testing

Defense Dept. unveils $1.2-billion ASAT restructuring plan. *Aviat Week Space Technol* 126:19-21 Mr 16 '87

SDI testing may ignite antisatellite race. M. Crawford. *Science* 237:482 Jl 31 '87

Anti-Semitism

See also

Neo-Nazis

Anti-Semitism, left & right [discussion of November 1986 article, The hate that dare not speak its name] N. Podhoretz. *Commentary* 83:2+ Mr '87

Arabs anonymous [National Association of Arab Americans sponsorship of essay contest on America's Middle East policy] J. L. Pasley. *New Repub* 197:17-18 Ag 10-17 '87

White Protestants polled on Jews. *Society* 24:2 Mr/Ap '87

History

See also

Holocaust, Jewish (1939-1945)

National socialism

Wagner as anti-Semite [J. Katz's The darker side of genius] S. Lipman. *Commentary* 83:57-60 Ja '87

Canada

Canada's Nazi presence [war criminals] M. Drohan. il *Macleans* 100:38-9 My 25 '87

One teacher's prejudice [J. Israeli urges New Brunswick to take action against anti-Semitic school teacher M. Ross] K. Harley. il pors *Macleans* 100:17 Ap 27 '87

France

Exhibitions

The Dreyfus affair: Jewish Museum. M. Moorman. il *Art News* 86:152+ D '87

The other fin de siècle [The Dreyfus affair and Art nouveau Bing] K. Silver. bibl f il *Art Am* 75:104-11+ D '87

Great Britain

History

Among the anti-Semites: memoirs of a British Zionist. H. Fairlie. *New Repub* 196:24 Je 8 '87

Japan

Japan's money woes: blaming it on the Jews. *Newsweek* 109:40 Mr 23 '87

Portnoy-san's complaints [F. Kometani's book Passover stirs controversy] J. Adler. il por *Newsweek* 109:72+ My 25 '87

Nicaragua

Sandinista anti-Semitism [discussion of September 1986 article, Sandinista anti-Semitism and its apologists] J. Muravchik and others. *Commentary* 83:2+ Ja '87

Poland

History

Poland's Jewish ghosts. R. R. Wisse. *Commentary* 83:25-33 Ja '87

Poles and Jews [discussion of January 1987 article, Poland's Jewish ghosts] R. R. Wisse. *Commentary* 83:2+ My '87

Soviet Union

Will *'glasnost'* reach the Jews? N. Levin. *Commonweal* 114:596-9 O 23 '87

Anti-Semitism in drama

British traditions [controversy surrounding J. Allen's play Perdition] A. Cockburn. *Nation* 245:187 S 5 '87

Foul play [controversy surrounding production of J. Allen's Perdition by the Royal Court Theatre] D. Pryce-Jones. *New Repub* 196:15-17 Mr 2 '87

Anti-Semitism in literature

Portnoy-san's complaints [F. Kometani's book Passover stirs controversy] J. Adler. il por *Newsweek* 109:72+ My 25 '87

Anti-ship missiles *See* Guided missiles

Anti-smoking campaigns *See* Smoking

Anti-smoking laws and regulations *See* Smoking—Laws and regulations

Anti-submarine helicopters *See* Helicopters—Military use

Anti-submarine warfare

Antisubmarine warfare [address, May 20, 1987] C. A. H. Trost. *Vital Speeches Day* 53:551-3 Jl 1 '87

Boeing designs ASW version of De Havilland Dash 8-100. il *Aviat Week Space Technol* 127:22-3 Jl 20 '87

Boeing selected over Lockheed for P-3 avionics update award. B. M. Greeley, Jr. *Aviat Week Space Technol* 127:22-3 Jl 20 '87

Boeing withdraws from bidding to replace Navy ASW aircraft. *Aviat Week Space Technol* 127:25 N 16 '87

Deadly game of hide-and-seek [cover story; special section] il *U S News World Rep* 102:36-43 Je 15 '87

Defense Dept. seeks funds to continue P-3C production. J. D. Morrocco. *Aviat Week Space Technol* 127:26 Ag 31 '87

Navy master plan emphasizes airborne ASW systems. J. D. Morrocco. *Aviat Week Space Technol* 127:111-12+ Jl 13 '87

Navy solicits proposals for P-3C ASW successor [antisubmarine warfare aircraft] B. D. Nordwall. *Aviat Week Space Technol* 127:30-2 S 28 '87

Navy to exploit V-22's VTOL, range in hunting Arctic subs. B. M. Greeley, Jr. *Aviat Week Space Technol* 126:30-1 Je 8 '87

The ritual of the sub hunt [Sikorsky SH-3H Sea King] D. Powers. il *Flying* 114:56-8+ Ap '87

Waging submarine warfare. J. Handler. bibl f il *Bull At Sci* 43:40-3 S '87

Anti-tank helicopters *See* Helicopters—Military use

Anti-tank weapons

All stuck up, no way to go [soft kill weapons; views of S. A. Hoenig] S. Budiansky. il *U S News World Rep* 103:62 Jl 20 '87

Army modifies TOW missile to counter recent advances in Soviet reactive armor. *Aviat Week Space Technol* 127:23 Jl 27 '87

Martin Marietta ADATS wins Army air defense competition [Anti-Tank Air Defense System] J. D. Morrocco. il *Aviat Week Space Technol* 127:26-7 D 7 '87

Testing

Air defense leaders emerge from live-fire trials; Contenders for Army mobile air defense system near completion of tests at White Sands Range. il *Aviat Week Space Technol* 127:18-19 O 19 '87

Army will begin ADATS field testing in 1989. *Aviat Week Space Technol* 127:24 D 21 '87

Antibacterial agents *See* Antibiotics

Antibiotic feed supplements

Dangers of "miracle" drugs. *Futurist* 21:51-2 Mr/Ap '87

New cattle feed additives on the way. *Success Farm* 85:B1 My '87

Antibiotics

See also

Bacteria—Resistance and sensitivity

Fusidic acid

Mitomycin

Quinolones

Spectinomycin

Bacterial resistance to β-lactam antibiotics: crystal structure of β-lactamase from Staphylococcus aureus PC1 at 2.5 Å resolution. O. Herzberg and J. Moult. bibl f il *Science* 236:694-701 My 8 '87

Bespoke bactericide [for gram-negative bacteria; work of Stephen M. Hammond] J. Benditt. *Sci Am* 257:32+ S '87

The case of the frog that healed leads Dr. Michael Zasloff to a medical leap ahead. M. Brower. il por *People Wkly* 28:34-5 Ag 17 '87

Firing squad [antibiotic pump implant developed by Clayton R. Perry] W. Barnhill. *Health* 19:24 Jl '87

Frogs get the jump on microbes [research by Michael Zasloff] S. Weisburd. *Sci News* 132:85 Ag 8 '87

Frog's gift to man [Michael Zasloff discovers natural antibiotic in frog skin] il *U S News World Rep* 103:6 Ag 10 '87

New approach to treating gum disease. *Sci News* 132:268 O 24 '87

New class of antibiotics confirmed [effective against gram-negative bacteria; work of Robert Goldman and others] R. Weiss. *Sci News* 132:180-1 S 19 '87

Antibiotics—*cont.*

Ribbiting evidence [anti-infection peptides in skin of African clawed frog; work of Michael Zasloff] il *Time* 130:31 Ag 10 '87

Skin of frog . . . [natural antibiotic found by Michael Zasloff] T. Beardsley. il *Sci Am* 257:36+ O '87

You can mix probiotics with certain antibiotics. *Success Farm* 85:58 S '87

Antibodies *See* Antigens and antibodies

Anticoagulants

See also
Aspirin
Heparin
TPA (Drug)

The regulation of natural anticoagulant pathways [protein C] C. T. Esmon. bibl f il *Science* 235:1348-52 Mr 13 '87

Thin your blood and live longer. G. Maleskey. *Prevention* 39:89-91+ My '87

Anticonvulsants

See also
Valproic acid

Drug may protect brains of heart attack victims [use of MK-801 to limit neuronal injury after ischemia] D. M. Barnes. il *Science* 235:632-3 F 6 '87

New drug controls seizures [McN-4853] *USA Today (Periodical)* 115:8-9 F '87

Antidepressants

See also
Wellbutrin

Antidepressants may curb addictions. *Prevention* 39:60 O '87

Breakthrough against cocaine. P. Mann. *Read Dig* 130:185-6+ Ap '87

Antidiuretic hormone *See* Vasopressin

Antiemetics

See also
Bendectin

Antiferromagnetism *See* Magnetism

Antifouling paint *See* Paint, Protective

Antigens and antibodies

See also
Complements (Immunity)
Immunoassay
Immunogenetics
Immunoglobulins
Immunologic diseases
Immunological tolerance
Major histocompatibility complex
Monoclonal antibodies
Rh factor

Antibodies, monoclonal antibodies, immunologics, and antigens. *Science* 235 pt2:G26-G29 F 27 '87

Antigenicity of myohemerythrin [discussion of March 6, 1987 article, Chemistry of antibody binding to a protein] H. M. Geysen and others. *Science* 238:1584-6 D 11 '87

Blocking of HIV-1 infectivity by a soluble, secreted form of the CD4 antigen. D. H. Smith and others. bibl f il *Science* 238:1704-7 D 18 '87

Chemistry of antibody binding to a protein [myohemerythrin] H. M. Geysen and others. bibl f il *Science* 235:1184-90 Mr 6 '87

The clonal-selection theory. G. L. Ada and G. J. V. Nossal. bibl (p116) il *Sci Am* 257:62-9 Ag '87

Cloned gene of rickettsia rickettsii surface antigen: candidate vaccine for Rocky Mountain spotted fever. G. A. McDonald and others. bibl f il *Science* 235:83-5 Ja 2 '87

Early restriction of the human antibody repertoire. H. W. Schroeder, Jr. and others. bibl f il *Science* 238:791-3 N 6 '87

Encystation and expression of cyst antigens by Giardia lamblia in vitro. F. D. Gillin and others. bibl f il *Science* 235:1040-3 F 27 '87

Epitope mapping by chemical modification of free and antibody-bound protein antigen. A. Burnens and others. bibl f il *Science* 235:780-3 F 13 '87

Evolutionary and somatic selection of the antibody repertoire in the mouse. K. Rajewsky and others. bibl f il *Science* 238:1088-94 N 20 '87

Glucocorticoid receptor-like antigen in lymphoma cell membranes: correlation to cell lysis. B. Gametchu. bibl f il *Science* 236:456-61 Ap 24 '87

Histocompatibility restriction explained. J. L. Marx. il *Science* 235:843-4 F 20 '87

HLA is factor in diabetes [human leukocyte antigen; research by John A. Todd and others] *Sci News* 132:247 O 17 '87

Human lymphocytes making rheumatoid factor and antibody to ssDNA belong to Leu-1+ B-cell subset. P. Casali and others. bibl f il *Science* 236:77-81 Ap 3 '87

Identification and isolation of a variant surface glycoprotein from Trypanosoma vivax. P. R. Gardiner and others. bibl f il *Science* 235:774-7 F 13 '87

Immune molecule's 3-D structure revealed [X ray crystallography of human leukocyte antigen; work of Donald C. Wiley and others] R. Weiss. il *Sci News* 132:228 O 10 '87

An in vitro neurite-promoting antigen functions in axonal regeneration in vivo. A. W. Sandrock, Jr. and W. D. Matthew. bibl f il *Science* 237:1605-8 S 25 '87

Mapping the main immunogenic region and toxin-binding site of the nicotinic acetylcholine receptor. T. Barkas and others. bibl f il *Science* 235:77-80 Ja 2 '87

Mechanisms of antibody binding to a protein [myohemerythrin] E. D. Getzoff and others. bibl f il *Science* 235:1191-6 Mr 6 '87

Megabase-scale mapping of the HLA gene complex by pulsed field gel electrophoresis [major histocompatibility complex] S. K. Lawrance and others. bibl f il *Science* 235:1387-90 Mr 13 '87

Naturally acquired antibodies to sporozoites do not prevent malaria: vaccine development implications. S. L. Hoffman and others. bibl f il *Science* 237:639-42 Ag 7 '87

New insights into antigen recognition. P. Marrack. *Science* 235:1311-13 Mr 13 '87

New transplant findings fit like a glove [research by Elaine Reed and others] R. Weiss. *Sci News* 131:375 Je 13 '87

Programmed gene rearrangements altering gene expression. P. Borst and D. R. Greaves. bibl f il *Science* 235:658-67 F 6 '87

Proteolytic self-cleavage of hepatitis B virus core protein may generate serum e antigen. R. H. Miller. bibl f il *Science* 236:722-5 My 8 '87

Stopping sperm may block AIDS [virus penetration of HLA-DR tagged cells; research by Ellyn Ashida and Virginia Scofield] *Discover* 8:11+ O '87

A subset of yeast snRNA's contains functional binding sites for the highly conserved Sm antigen. N. Riedel and others. bibl f il *Science* 235:328-31 Ja 16 '87

Unwinding of duplex DNA from the SV40 origin of replication by T antigen. M. Dodson and others. bibl f il *Science* 238:964-7 N 13 '87

Antigua (Antigua and Barbuda)

See also
Resorts—Antigua (Antigua and Barbuda)

Antigua (Guatemala)

Historic houses, sites, etc.

Casa de las Mil Flores: Harold and Matilda Stream in Guatemala. C. T. Buckley. il *Archit Dig* 44:108-15 Ag '87

Antihistamines

Awake at the wheel [nonsedating drugs] F. Lunzer. *Forbes* 139:102 Je 29 '87

Antihypertensive agents

See also
Guanethidine
Propranolol

Antimacassars

Overlays for quick color accent. il *South Living* 22:136 F '87

Antimalarials

See also
Chloroquine

Antimatter

Antimatter, antichemistry [using Bogdan Maglich's migma device] D. E. Thomsen. *Sci News* 132:205 S 26 '87

Fast Forward: a conversation with Robert L. Forward. R. M. Powers. il por *Space World* X-1-277:30-6 Ja '87

Antin, Amy

(tr) See Ivo, Lêdo. The poor in the bus depot

Antioxidants

Antiarthritic gold compounds effectively quench electronically excited singlet oxygen. E. J. Corey and others. bibl f il *Science* 236:68-9 Ap 3 '87

Bilirubin: bad, yet good? *Sci News* 131:169 Mr 14 '87

Bilirubin is an antioxidant of possible physiological importance. R. Stocker and others. bibl f il *Science* 235:1043-6 F 27 '87

Promising sulfite alternatives [research by Gerald M. Sapers] *Sci News* 132:63 Jl 25 '87

Vitamins for your inner youth. H. Rodale. *Prevention* 39:27-31 Ap '87

Antiplasmin *See* Fibrinolysin
Antiprotons
  Anti-proton fishing [balloon experiment] S. J. Nadis. il *Technol Rev* 90:15-16 Jl '87
  A negative way to get positive results. *Discover* 8:7 F '87
Antique airplanes *See* Airplanes, Antique
Antique Auto and Music Museum (Stone Mountain, Ga.)
  Behind the wheel in Georgia. il *South Living* 22:31 F '87
Antique automobiles *See* Automobiles, Antique
Antique boats *See* Boats, Antique
Antique chairs *See* Chairs
Antique dealers
    See also
    Angus Wilkie Antiques (Firm)
    Galerie 360
    Hyde Park Antiques Ltd.
    Kentshire Galleries Ltd.
    Place des Antiquaires (New York, N.Y.)
  The antique tradition of Marshall Field's [cover story] il *Antiques Collect Hobbies* 92:28-33 N '87
  Antiques' travel guide. *Antiques* 132:1330-7 D '87
  Antiques' travel guide. il *Antiques* 132:564-71 S '87
  Antiques' travel guide. il *Antiques* 131:1330-7 Je '87
  Antiques' travel guide. *Antiques* 131:662-9 Mr '87
            France
    See also
    Hôtel Drouot (Paris, France)
  An antiques dealer's secret sources: Bruce Newman in Paris and England. J. Kornbluth. il pors *Archit Dig* 44 Archit Dig Travels:20-31+ O '87
          Great Britain
    See also
    Christie's (London, England)
    Sotheby's (Firm)
  An antiques dealer's secret sources: Bruce Newman in Paris and England. J. Kornbluth. il pors *Archit Dig* 44 Archit Dig Travels:20-31+ O '87
  An eye for complexity [American A. B. Allen sets up shop in London] O. Bernier. il *House Gard* 159:172-7+ Mr '87
Antique furniture *See* Furniture
Antique jewelry *See* Jewelry
Antique motorcycles *See* Motorcycles, Antique
Antique radio receivers *See* Radio receivers
Antique tables *See* Tables
Antique valentines *See* Valentines
Antiques
    See also
    Americana
    Display of antiques, art objects, etc.
  Living with antiques. V. Hahn. il *Parents* 62:134-6+ F '87
  The sampler: a selection of previews, reviews, sundries, and suggestions. See issues of Americana
          Bibliography
  Books about antiques. A. M. Eckardt. See issues of Antiques
     Collectors and collecting
  Buying antiques. D. P. Marshall. *Travel Holiday* 168:22-4 O '87
  Global treasure trove [Paris apartment of A. Dandois] C. Vogel. il por *N Y Times Mag* p62-6 Mr 1 '87
  Living with antiques:
    A collection of American neoclassical furnishings on the East Coast. A. M. Eckardt. il *Antiques* 131:858-63 Ap '87
    A collection of early Delaware River Valley furnishings. E. D. Garrett. il *Antiques* 131:282-7 Ja '87
    Melrose in Natchez, Mississippi. W. N. Banks. bibl f il *Antiques* 131:650-7 Mr '87
    Mount Cuba in Delaware. M. H. Heckscher. il *Antiques* 131:1078-87 My '87
  Long-time collectors' secret unveiled [F. and E. Billingsley] *Antiques Collect Hobbies* 92:78 My '87
          Exhibitions
    See also
    Metropolitan Museum of Art (New York, N.Y.). American Wing
  Calendar of shows. See issues of Antiques
  Calendar of shows. See issues of Antiques & Collecting Hobbies beginning March 1985
  Current and coming. S. B. Sherrill. See issues of Antiques
  Mr. Peepers's nights: the Versailles squeak [receptions prior to the Winter Antiques Show in New York City] il *N Y* 20:21-2 Ja 26 '87
  On exhibit. See issues of Americana
  A summit for collectors [Winter Antiques Show] C. Vogel. il *N Y Times Mag* p62-7 Ja 18 '87

  What's where when. S. B. Sherrill. See issues of Antiques beginning August 1984
           Prices
  Price guides. F. Donegan. il *Americana* 15:13-14+ Mr/Ap '87
  What's new in antiques? F. Donegan. il *Americana* 15:18-20 Jl/Ag '87
         Valuation
  Find out what it's worth. M. Halperin. il *Americana* 15:14+ S/O '87
  From the publisher. D. K. Graham. *Antiques Collect Hobbies* 92:6 Ag '87
Antiques & collecting hobbies (Periodical)
  From the publisher [cost of advertising] D. K. Graham. *Antiques Collect Hobbies* 92:6+ Ap '87
Antiquities
    See also subhead Antiquities under names of continents, countries, states, cities, etc.
    Photographs and photography
  New view of old rocks. M. Grimm and T. Grimm. il *Travel Holiday* 168:38-41 S '87
         Pillaging
    See Pillage
         Protection
    See Cultural property—Protection
Antisatellite weapons *See* Anti-satellite weapons
Antithrombin
  Heparin promotes the inactivation of antithrombin by neutrophil elastase. R. E. Jordan and others. bibl f il *Science* 237:777-9 Ag 14 '87
Antitrust Division (Dept. of Justice) *See* United States. Dept. of Justice. Antitrust Division
Antitrust law
    See also
    Airlines—Antitrust cases
    Booksellers and bookselling—Antitrust cases
    Cable television—Antitrust cases
    Corporations—Acquisitions and mergers—Laws and regulations
    Football, Professional—Antitrust cases
    Freight forwarders—Antitrust cases
    Ice cream industry—Antitrust cases
    Insurance companies—Antitrust cases
    Newspaper publishers and publishing—Antitrust cases
    Petroleum industry—Antitrust cases
    Publishers and publishing—Antitrust cases
    Telecommunication—Antitrust cases
    Telephone companies—Antitrust cases
    United States. Dept. of Justice. Antitrust Division
  Antitrust's only proper quarry: collusion. G. S. Becker. il *Bus Week* p22 O 12 '87
  The rhetoric of antitrust. T. J. DiLorenzo. bibl *Society* 24:43-6 S/O '87
Antitrypsin
  Clonal gene therapy: transplanted mouse fibroblast clones express human α1-antitrypsin gene in vivo. R. I. Garver, Jr. and others. bibl f il *Science* 237:762-4 Ag 14 '87
  Interaction of a liver-specific nuclear factor with the fibrinogen and α_1-antitrypsin promoters. G. Courtois and others. bibl f il *Science* 238:688-92 O 30 '87
  Mending a torn screen in the lung. D. D. Edwards. il *Sci News* 131:277 My 2 '87
Antitumor substances *See* Cancer inhibiting substances
Antiviral agents *See* Viruses—Inactivation
Antiviral proteins *See* Interferon
Antlers
  All about rattling [antlers used as deer calls] K. Etling. il *Outdoor Life* 179:58-9+ Ap '87
  At the drop of a rack [shedding of elk antlers] G. J. Lamarre. il *Outdoor Life* 179:32-3 Ap '87
  Non-typical, near mythical [deer; photographs] M. Biggs. il *Field Stream* 92:50-1 Ag '87
Antley, Corinne M.
  I was too young for skin cancer. por *Ladies Home J* 104:22+ Je '87
Antoinette Perry Awards *See* Tony Awards
Antolini, Anthony
        about
  Rachmaninoff's lost chords. D. Neff. il pors *Christ Today* 31:63-4 D 11 '87
Antonio, José
        about
  Jose Antonio leads Spain's National Ballet back to the United States. L. Kumin. il *Dance Mag* 61:6 D '87
Antony Tudor [television program] *See* Television program reviews—Single works
Ants
  100 trillion ants drop acid [research by Thomas Graedel] il *Discover* 8:8 S '87

Ants—cont.

The ancient cultured citrus ant: a tropical ant is used to control insect pests in southern China. H. T. Huang and P. Yang. bibl il map *BioScience* 37:665-71 O '87

Ant wars. H. Topoff. il *Nat Hist* 96:62-6+ Ja '87

Ants and the atmosphere: no picnic [research by Thomas Graedel] R. Monastersky. *Sci News* 131:345 My 30 '87

The body snatchers [western slave-making ants] H. Topoff. il *Natl Wildl* 25:33 O/N '87

Antwerp (Belgium)

Galleries and museums

See also

Museum of Contemporary Art (Antwerp, Belgium)

Anxiety

See also

Fear

Stage fright

Worry

Actions speak louder than fears [views of Gary Emery] *USA Today (Periodical)* 115:12 Ap '87

Attacks real, not imaginary [panic attacks verified by increased heart rates; Stanford University School of Medicine study] il *USA Today (Periodical)* 115:12-13 Ap '87

Bitter jitters [panic attack patients exhibit sensitivity to coffee's bitter taste] M. O'Brian. il *Health* 19:22 N '87

Does love make you anxious? C. Tavris. *Vogue* 177:154 Ag '87

Don't panic, you're pregnant [work of David T. George and others] *Sci News* 132:120 Ag 22 '87

The effects of exam anxiety on grandma's health. J. J. Chiodo. *Educ Dig* 52:45-7 Ja '87

The SAT pill [beta blockers quell anxiety] *Newsweek* 110:103 N 16 '87

Tips on conquering paralyzing anxiety: fearing the worst [panic attacks and social phobias] J. H. Tanne and E. Rapp. il *N Y* 20:44-9 F 9 '87

What is your body trying to tell you? [panic attacks] A. Fischer. *Redbook* 168:89-91+ Mr '87

"You bet I'm scared" [anxiety in business] S. Blotnick. il *Forbes* 139:124 Ap 20 '87

Anything goes [musical] See Musicals, revues, etc.—Reviews—Single works

Anza-Borrego Desert State Park (Calif.) See California—Parks and reserves

Anza Observatory (Calif.) See Astronomical observatories

ANZAC See Great Britain. Army. Australian and New Zealand Army Corps

ANZUS Council

Administration supports New Zealand Preference Elimination Act [statements, September 22, 1987] J. S. Roy. *Dep State Bull* 87:46-7 N '87

The genesis of New Zealand's ban. J. Salzman. il *Bull At Sci* 43:45-6+ Jl/Ag '87

Kiwis just say 'no' [anti-nuclear stand by New Zealand] J. Salzman. *Sierra* 72:32+ My/Je '87

New Zealand and an interdependent world [address, March 13, 1987] P. M. Cleveland. map *Dep State Bull* 87:80-3 Je '87

New Zealand paying for nuclear ban. K. P. Clements. bibl f il *Bull At Sci* 43:41-4 Jl/Ag '87

AOA See United States. Administration on Aging

Aoi, Joichi

about

After the scandal. F. H. Katayama. por *Fortune* 116:60 Ag 3 '87

Aoi, Tadao

about

James Baker, meet the dokushin kizoku. A. Tanzer. il por *Forbes* 139:46-8 Ap 20 '87

AP See Associated Press

APA See American Psychiatric Association

Apartheid

See also

Church and race relations—South Africa

Day of Solidarity with South African Political Prisoners

International Day of Solidarity with the Struggle of Women of South Africa and Namibia

International Day of Solidarity with the Struggling Peoples of South Africa

United Nations. Special Committee against Apartheid

306 solutions to a baffling problem [views of L. Louw and F. Kendall] B. W. Nelan. il pors *Time* 129:36 Mr 23 '87

AAUP opposes embargo on sales of books to South Africa. C. Reid. *Publ Wkly* 232:12 D 11 '87

An Afrikaans insider questions the system [industrialist J. Rupert] S. Mufson. il por *Bus Week* p80+ My 18 '87

Amy Carter gets probation for Brown apartheid protest. *Jet* 72:22 Mr 30 '87

ANC leader Mbeki freed after 23 years in jail. il *Jet* 73:28 N 23 '87

ANC turns 75 [African National Congress] J. M. Woods. il *Black Enterp* 17:18 Ap '87

Anglo-American faces life. S. Mufson. *New Repub* 197:26+ S 14-21 '87

The Anglo Empire shows its other face. W. L. Chaze. il *U S News World Rep* 103:32-3 S 7 '87

Apartheid: 'a slippery slope' [interview with H. Oppenheimer] S. Reiss. il *Newsweek* 110:53 S 14 '87

Apartheid: a study in black and white [role of transnational corporations] il *UN Chron* 22:26-8 N/D '85

Apartheid and diplomacy [J. Clark's visit] C. Wood. il por *Macleans* 100:22-3 Ag 24 '87

Apartheid fighters zero in on presidential race [TransAfrica] *Jet* 71:14 Mr 23 '87

Apartheid's troubled children. A. Getz. *World Press Rev* 34:34-5 D '87

Arch foe of apartheid [H. Suzman] V. Butler. por *Read Dig* 130:157-62 Mr '87

Assembly urges Security Council to impose mandatory oil embargo against South Africa: thirteen texts adopted on apartheid, Namibia issues. il *UN Chron* 24:40-4 F '87

Bashing heads before balloting. W. E. Smith. il *Time* 129:38 My 11 '87

Bishop Tutu calls for dismantling of apartheid system, beginning of dialogue with blacks. por *UN Chron* 22:17 N/D '85

Black actor stars in S. African 'Othello' [J. Kani] il por *Jet* 73:22 O 5 '87

Black labor power [strike of black miners] *Nation* 245:183-4 S 5 '87

A bloody campaign trail. A. Bilski. il *Macleans* 100:26-7 My 4 '87

Botha defies the tides, gets tougher. J. Jones. il por *U S News World Rep* 102:32-3 F 16 '87

Botha in the lions' den [visit to Sharpeville] S. Reiss. il por *Newsweek* 109:43 Je 15 '87

Botha's triumph: South Africa's tragedy? [election results] J. Jones. il *U S News World Rep* 102:12-13 My 18 '87

Boxer wins award for his fight vs. apartheid [L. Honeyghan] por *Jet* 72:48 Je 8 '87

Britain's assault on the Commonwealth [Britain refuses to agree to wider sanctions against South Africa] H. Mackenzie. il *Macleans* 100:24-5 O 26 '87

The business of fighting apartheid. M. Massing. il *Atlantic* 259:26-32 F '87

Campaign of the iron fist [crackdown on protesters backfires] W. E. Smith. il *Time* 129:36-7 Ap 27 '87

CBC pushes for new African agenda [Congressional Black Caucus] G. McKinney. il *Black Enterp* 17:19 My '87

Champ refuses to fight South African, junks belt [L. Honeyghan] il por *Jet* 71:46 Ja 26 '87

The chief [G. Buthelezi] M. Massing. bibl f il por *N Y Rev Books* 34:15-22 F 12 '87

Children on the front line. S. Reiss. il *Newsweek* 110:39 Jl 27 '87

Citicorp pulls out. A. Edmond, Jr. *Black Enterp* 18:22 S '87

Clark's compromise offer [Canadian efforts to combat apartheid] H. Mackenzie. il por *Macleans* 100:24 S 21 '87

Commandments without Moses [L. Sullivan, author of Sullivan principles, demands withdrawal of U.S. firms] W. E. Smith. il por *Time* 129:34 Je 15 '87

A correspondent's farewell to Johannesburg. S. Mufson. il *Bus Week* p56 Je 8 '87

Cosby heads 'Unlock Apartheid Jails' drive; hits reporter's insult. il por *Jet* 73:56 O 19 '87

A crazy game of musical chairs. il *Time* 129:54 Mr 9 '87

Crockett heads drive for a day honoring Mandela. pors *Jet* 73:4 N 9 '87

Cutting ties to a troubled land [impact of U.S. corporate pullout] B. Rudolph. il *Time* 129:44-5 Je 29 '87

Dealing from strength [call for a general election] S. Reiss. il *Newsweek* 109:32 Ja 12 '87

Democracy in South Africa. R. Brookhiser. *Natl Rev* 39:34-6 Jl 31 '87

The democratic future of South Africa [address, September 29, 1987] G. P. Shultz. *Dep State Bull* 87:9-12 N '87

Apartheid—*cont.*

Digging out to avoid a cave-in [miners' strike settled] B. W. Nelan. il *Time* 130:32 S 7 '87

Dow and South Africa [address, April 11, 1987] R. K. Long. *Vital Speeches Day* 53:520-4 Je 15 '87

Economic sanctions against South Africa [messages and letter to Congress, September 25-29, 1986] R. Reagan. *Dep State Bull* 86:35-7 D '86

'End apartheid by 1 January 1987', Panel of Eminent Persons asks; details world programme for action by TNCs. il *UN Chron* 22:18-20 N/D '85

Execution of ANC member deplored and condemned [B. Moloise] por *UN Chron* 22:14 N/D '85

Exxon becomes 87th U.S. firm to quit S. Africa. *Jet* 71:4 Ja 19 '87

Exxon pulls the plug [sale of South African holdings] T. Fennell. il *Macleans* 100:27 Ja 12 '87

The fall of the Front [United Democratic Front] S. Mufson. *New Repub* 196:17-19 Mr 23 '87

Fantasies about South Africa. P. L. Berger and B. Godsell. *Commentary* 84:35-40 Jl '87

A farewell to South Africa. A. Cowell. il *N Y Times Mag* p36-9+ Ja 25 '87

Fifty-two witnesses present testimony during four days of hearings [role of transnational corporations] il *UN Chron* 22:21-5 N/D '85

Fugitives from apartheid. L. Arditi. il *Progressive* 51:32-4 Ap '87

The future of South Africa [address, November 24, 1986] G. M. Buthelezi. *Vital Speeches Day* 53:194-6 Ja 15 '87

Getting the story (I) [J. Qwelane, black reporter on the Johannesburg Star] W. Finnegan. *New Yorker* 63:31-4+ Jl 13 '87

Getting the story (II) [J. Qwelane, black reporter on the Johannesburg Star] W. Finnegan. *New Yorker* 63:40-2+ Jl 20 '87

'The government smashes our hope' [restrictions placed on G. Mbeki] il por *Newsweek* 110:49 D 21 '87

'Graceland' in Africa [controversy surrounding P. Simon's album] N. Cooper. il por *Newsweek* 109:45 F 23 '87

Gray calls on Reagan to help S. African detainees. por *Jet* 72:12 Ag 31 '87

The "graying" of a nation [integration of neighborhoods] W. R. Doerner. il *Time* 130:38 N 30 '87

Harvard to the rescue [divestiture of portfolio in South Africa; candidates for overseer] W. F. Buckley. *Natl Rev* 39:58 Jl 3 '87

The high cost of non-nationhood [homelands policy] W. R. Doerner. il map *Time* 130:39 O 12 '87

The Horatio Algers of South Africa. J. Jones. il *U S News World Rep* 103:41-2 Jl 20 '87

Ignoring both carrot and stick [effect of sanctions on South Africa] W. R. Doerner. il *Time* 130:36 O 5 '87

In South Africa, white makes right. K. Owen. il *World Press Rev* 34:43 Jl '87

Is South Africa invulnerable? J. Keegan. il map *U S News World Rep* 102:30-3 Mr 23 '87

Jockeying for the right corner. B. W. Nelan. il *Time* 129:38 Je 1 '87

Labor: now it's showdown time. S. Mufson. il *Bus Week* p48 My 4 '87

A lurch to the right [election results] W. E. Smith. il *Time* 129:42-3 My 18 '87

Mandela: 25 years later, still a force in South Africa. *Jet* 72:6 Ag 24 '87

Mandela's ANC fights for a foothold. J. Jones. il *U S News World Rep* 103:36 S 7 '87

Mary Frances Berry. J. Barthel. por *Ms* 15:68-70+ Ja '87

McGraw-Hill to sell South Africa branch. *Publ Wkly* 231:10 Mr 13 '87

Nephew of S. African envoy weds 'colored' [nephew of Piet Koornhof] por *Jet* 72:12 Jl 6 '87

New man in the townships [black U.S. ambassador E. Perkins] B. W. Nelan. il por *Time* 129:58 F 23 '87

New rules for black schools [South Africa] W. R. Doerner. *Time* 129:48 Ja 12 '87

Oliver Tambo's war cry [visit to Canada] H. Mackenzie. il por *Macleans* 100:25 S 7 '87

On death row in Pretoria Central [capital punishment] D. Bruck. *New Repub* 197:18-21+ Jl 13-20 '87

Out of Africa [Comprehensive Anti-Apartheid Act] J. M. Woods. il *Black Enterp* 17:15 Ja '87

Out of jail and on his feet [release of African National Congress leader G. Mbeki] R. Nordland. il por *Newsweek* 110:81 N 16 '87

Out of South Africa [American investments] J. M. Woods. *Essence* 17:30 Mr '87

Out of South Africa [black exchange student, Mvelase] J. Levine. il pors *N Y Times Mag* p81+ S 20 '87

Out of South Africa: divestment hits a snag [Baltimore ordinance requiring public pension funds to sell stocks challenged] E. Weiner and L. J. Tell. il *Bus Week* p53 Jl 6 '87

Paul Simon goes on tour with black South Africans. *Jet* 71:17 Mr 2 '87

Paul Simon's amazing Graceland tour [cover story] D. Fricke. il pors *Roll Stone* p42-4+ Jl 2 '87

Perkins makes 1st public protest against S. Africa [U.S. ambassador E. J. Perkins] por *Jet* 72:24 My 11 '87

Pretoria's 'New Nats'. S. Reiss. il *Newsweek* 109:44 Mr 9 '87

Pro and con [Secretary of State's Advisory Committee on South Africa urges sanctions] *Time* 129:58 F 23 '87

Probing for an Africa policy. P. R. Range. il por map *U S News World Rep* 102:32-3 Ja 19 '87

Profiles [House of Assembly member H. Suzman] E. J. Kahn. por *New Yorker* 63:50-1+ Ap 20 '87

Pull out of S. Africa in 9 months, Sullivan urges. por *Jet* 72:4 Je 22 '87

PW interviews [N. Gordimer] M. Berkley. por *Publ Wkly* 231:80-1 Ap 10 '87

Quiet sting [views of U.S. Ambassador E. J. Perkins] W. R. Doerner. il por *Time* 130:50 D 21 '87

The return of a rebel [release of G. Mbeki] il por *U S News World Rep* 103:16-17 N 16 '87

Robert Brown oversees the enrollment of Mandela's daughter at Boston Univ. il por *Jet* 72:28 Je 8 '87

Running against America. B. W. Nelan. il *Time* 129:40 F 16 '87

S. African mines hit hard with 'big' strike. il *Jet* 72:4 Ag 24 '87

Sanctions and survival [South Africa and the 1986 nonaligned nations conference] R. Shaplen. il *New Yorker* 62:74-80+ F 2 '87

Security Council does not adopt text calling for selective mandatory sanctions against South Africa. il *UN Chron* 24:22-5 My '87

Singer Paul Simon strikes sour chord with students at Howard U. over album [Graceland] *Jet* 71:59 F 2 '87

South Africa. S. Mufson. *Bus Week* p65 My 11 '87

South Africa [discussion of July 1987 article, Fantasies about South Africa] P. L. Berger and B. Godsell. *Commentary* 84:11-12+ O '87

South Africa: a clash of wills [mine strike] S. Reiss. il *Newsweek* 110:28-9 Ag 24 '87

South Africa: coercion and demands for change. K. W. Grundy. bibl f *Curr Hist* 86:197-200+ My '87

South Africa embattled. J. De St. Jorre. bibl f *Foreign Aff* 65 Sp Issue:538-63 ['87]

South Africa: glimmers of hope? D. Reed. il *Read Dig* 131:131-6 Ag '87

South Africa hemorrhages. F. J. Parker. *America* 156:10-12 Ja 3-10 '87

South Africa: lessons of a bitter strike [miners] S. Reiss. il *Newsweek* 110:35 S 7 '87

South Africa: subtle stakes. J. Jones. il *U S News World Rep* 102:29-30 My 11 '87

South Africa: the Afrikaner angst. P. H. Baker. *Foreign Policy* 69:61-79 Wint '87/'88

South Africa: toward peace and stability [address, December 1, 1986] C. A. Crocker. *Dep State Bull* 87:40-2 F '87

South Africa: why Leon Sullivan gave up his 'principles'. R. A. Manning. il por *U S News World Rep* 102:10-11 Je 15 '87

South African author tells of horrors of racism in new book [M. Mathabane] il pors *Jet* 72:8-9 Ag 3 '87

South African countdown [novelist N. Gordimer] W. Clemons. por *Newsweek* 109:78 My 4 '87

South African disinvestment: social responsibility for the long haul. K. Bean. il por *Humanist* 47:28-9+ S/O '87

South African journal [with interview with C. S. King] J. Goodwin. il por *Ladies Home J* 104:74+ Ja '87

South African miners test political clout. M. August. il *Black Enterp* 18:19-20 N '87

South Africa's fault lines. S. Reiss. il *Newsweek* 109:42 My 11 '87

South Africa's Jonathan Butler finds a new home in pop music. S. Dougherty. il pors *People Wkly* 28:97-8+ N 23 '87

South Africa's medical front [Alexandra Health Center and University Clinic aids black patients] M. McNamara. il *Ms* 16:76 D '87

South Africa's sports isolation. G. Behrens. *World Press Rev* 34:57 Ap '87

Apartheid—*cont.*

South Africa's war on children. R. A. Falk. il *Nation* 245:516-17 N 7 '87

South Africa's whites face a new reality [striking black miners] J. Jones. il *U S News World Rep* 103:29 Ag 24 '87

South Africa's Zulu chief [G. Buthelezi] G. Behrens. il pors *World Press Rev* 34:34-5 Ja '87

Southern Africa: American hopes for the future [address, December 4, 1986] G. P. Shultz. *Dep State Bull* 87:36-40 F '87

Stiff challenge, swift reaction. W. Svoboda. il *Time* 129:38 Ja 19 '87

Stop the torture! [South African youth] B. F. Chavis. por *Essence* 18:146 O '87

A strike at a nation's heart [miners] il *Macleans* 100:23 Ag 24 '87

Struggle for Southern Africa. R. G. Mugabe. *Foreign Aff* 66:311-27 Wint '87/'88

A study in disinvestment [Barclays Bank leaves South Africa] C. Wolman. *World Press Rev* 34:54 O '87

A stunning roar for apartheid [election results] S. Reiss. il *Newsweek* 109:52 My 18 '87

Subtle changes in South Africa? M. Dönhoff, Gräfin. il *World Press Rev* 34:26-8 My '87

'Sullivan principles' deadline draws near. por *Jet* 71:14 Ja 12 '87

Sullivan says divest [Rev. L. Sullivan] F. D. Brown and D. C. Ruffin. il por *Black Enterp* 18:17 Ag '87

Sullivan's principles [call for disinvestment] L. Waldorf. *New Repub* 197:14-16 S 7 '87

A sweeping shift to the right [election results] A. Bilski. il *Macleans* 100:22 My 18 '87

Tainted money: the ethics and rhetoric of divestment [colleges and business] R. L. Payton. il *Change* 19:55-60 My/Je '87

Talking with Tambo. H. Anderson. il *Newsweek* 109:26 Ja 19 '87

Tambo on tour [U.S. visit] *Nation* 244:167-8 F 14 '87

Tambo visit centers U.S. focus on S. Africa fight. il pors *Jet* 71:7 F 16 '87

Tambo's risky game [talks between African National Congress and Washington] M. Whitaker. il por *Newsweek* 109:34-5 F 2 '87

Tango with Tambo. *Natl Rev* 39:19 F 27 '87

Tapping pop music's African roots [P. Simon's Graceland album and tour] N. Jennings. il por *Macleans* 100:52-3 My 4 '87

Text calling for mandatory selective sanctions against South Africa vetoed in Security Council. il *UN Chron* 23:3-5 Ja '86

This miners' strike may hit political pay dirt. A. Fine. il *Bus Week* p35 Ag 24 '87

Trouble from belowground [miners' strike] W. E. Smith. il *Time* 130:33 Ag 24 '87

The truth about sanctions. J. H. Wolfe. *USA Today (Periodical)* 115:9 Mr '87

Two questions about South Africa [efficacy of sanctions and Communist domination of African National Congress] D. Seligman. *Fortune* 115:122+ Mr 2 '87

Two voices that will not be stilled [N. and W. Mandela] B. W. Nelan. il pors *Time* 129:37 Ja 5 '87

The U.S. and apartheid. L. H. Sullivan; P. Duignan. *Current* 297:11-17 N '87

U.S. policy toward Southern Africa [address, December 1, 1986] C. A. Crocker. *Vital Speeches Day* 53:197-9 Ja 15 '87

UN forgives Paul Simon for 'Graceland' album. *Jet* 71:30 F 23 '87

United no more [Afrikaners opposed to apartheid] O. Friedrich. il *Time* 129:28-35+ My 4 '87

Universities and apartheid. A. Pifer. *Cent Mag* 20:61-2 Mr/Ap '87

Useful Zulu phrases [managing servants in South Africa] L. Freed. il *Harpers* 274:26-8 My '87

A vote under siege. A. Bilski. il *Macleans* 100:34 My 11 '87

Voting in South Africa. D. L. Lewis. il *Nation* 244:534+ Ap 25 '87

The war of blacks against blacks. J. Greenwald. il *Time* 129:30-1 Ja 26 '87

When freedom to read suffers [implications of decisions of McGraw-Hill and other publishing firms to terminate their South African operations] I. L. Horowitz. por *Publ Wkly* 232:38 Jl 17 '87

Why black workers may say 'thanks, but no thanks' to Ford [partial worker ownership of Samcor] S. Mufson. il *Bus Week* p47 Jl 6 '87

Why deny the children? [effects of American publishers' boycott of South Africa] G. Miklowitz. por *Publ Wkly* 232:66 O 9 '87

Why free Mbeki? S. Mufson. *Nation* 245:670-1 D 5 '87

Why sanctions are a failure. S. Jenkins. il *U S News World Rep* 103:40 S 21 '87

Why South Africa shrugs at sanctions. P. Brimelow. il *Forbes* 139:100-4 Mr 9 '87

Winnie Mandela [interview] A. Frense. il por *Ms* 15:82-3+ Ja '87

Women battling apartheid [black women from Southern Africa on lecture tour of U.S.] M. Oshin. il *Essence* 17:24 Ja '87

Won't someone listen? [G. Buthelezi's views] *Natl Rev* 39:22 Ja 30 '87

Yale anti-apartheid protest. il *Jet* 72:15 Je 15 '87

Zambia president Kaunda urges Reagan to support efforts to end apartheid. il pors *Jet* 73:4 N 2 '87

Apartheid [television program] See Television program reviews—Single works

Apartheid in literature

Before the revolution. L. M. Thompson. il *N Y Rev Books* 34:20+ Je 11 '87

Conscious of time and place [N. Gordimer] P. Schwartz. il por *World Press Rev* 34:61 O '87

Nadine Gordimer: choosing to be a white African. C. Sternhell. il pors *Ms* 16:28+ S '87

Apartheid in motion pictures

Apartheid chic [Cry freedom] A. White. il *Film Comment* 23:11-12+ N/D '87

Black and white [Cry freedom] M. Peretz. *New Repub* 197:42 D 21 '87

A black Gandhi [Cry freedom depicts life of S. Biko] G. Stern. il *Horizon* 30:37-8 N '87

Cry freedom [story of S. Biko] C. Tyson. il pors *Ebony* 43:60-2+ D '87

Donald and Wendy Woods talk about the real-life drama behind Cry freedom [interview] C. Krupp. il pors *Glamour* 85:166+ D '87

Girls apart [documentary by C. Sheppard and C. Sauvageot] M. Gevisser. *Nation* 245:463-4 O 24 '87

Movies [D. Washington portrays S. Biko in Cry freedom] D. Denby. il por *N Y* 20:54-5 S 21 '87

Newsman Donald Woods still seeks justice for Stephen Biko in the film Cry freedom. W. Plummer. il pors *People Wkly* 28:64+ N 23 '87

"One star in a huge black sky". D. Worrell. il *Time* 130:80 S 21 '87

Richard Attenborough's 'Biko'. L. Shaw. il *World Press Rev* 34:60 Je '87

What's wrong with this picture? [Cry freedom] E. Mitchell. il *Roll Stone* p31-2 D 3 '87

Apartheid in television

Apartheid chic [Mandela] A. White. il *Film Comment* 23:11-12+ N/D '87

Danny Glover stars in 'Mandela' movie that tugs at heart, shocks senses [cover story] il pors *Jet* 73:58-60 O 5 '87

Apartment houses
See also
Seattle (Wash.)—Housing

Apartments
See also
Art in the home

1 plus 1 [decorating ideas for newlyweds] il *Seventeen* 46:92-4 F '87

1 room living. il *Glamour* 85:394-6 S '87

Allure in the grand manner [J. T. de la Chaume's French-style apartment in Manhattan] J. Kornbluth. il por *House Gard* 159:152-9+ D '87

Architectural digest visits: Beverly Sills. J. Gruen. il pors *Archit Dig* 44:184-9 N '87

Architectural digest visits: Sophia Loren [Williams Island apartment] M. Peppiatt. il pors *Archit Dig* 44:116-23 Mr '87

Artful tradition [East Side apartment decorated by Renny B. Saltzman] C. D. B. Bryan. il *Archit Dig* 44:200-5 N '87

An author's maison de plume: Dominick Dunne in his New York penthouse [decorated by Chester Cleaver] D. Dunne. il por *Archit Dig* 44:146-9+ S '87

Bennison style [London rooms of decorator G. Bennison] C. Gibbs. il *House Gard* 159:170-7+ Ap '87

Boston uncommon [W. Hodgins' Back Bay flat] D. Roberts. il *Archit Dig* 44:156-9 S '87

A change of space [Manhattan apartment designed by Gwathmey Siegel Architects] C. Vogel. il *N Y Times Mag* p32-5 D 27 '87

Chelsea chaste [minimalist London apartment designed by John Pawson and Claudio Silvestrin] M. Filler. il *House Gard* 159:156-61+ N '87

Apartments—*cont.*

Classical collage [J. Saladino's decoration of New York duplex] S. Stephens. il *House Gard* 159:138-45+ D '87

Coloratura: old world living in a New York apartment [decorated by Rubén de Saavedra] J. Gruen. il *Archit Dig* 44:166-9 O '87

Composition for two: Robert Fizdale and Arthur Gold's city residence [New York City] M. M. Thomas. il pors *Archit Dig* 44:212-15+ N '87

A connoisseur's esprit: Princess Jeanne-Marie de Broglie's apartment in France. C. Aillaud. il por *Archit Dig* 44:192-5 Ap '87

The door to his heart: how he reads your apartment. B. Weber. *Mademoiselle* 93:216 S '87

Dramatic license: an author's Park Avenue residence [decorated by Robert Bray and Michael Schaible] J. Kornbluth. il *Archit Dig* 44:164-9 N '87

East Side story [Manhattan apartment decorated by Dale Montgomery and Luis Rey] J. Gruen. il *Archit Dig* 44:92-5 Jl '87

An elemental attraction [Sutton Place apartment decorated by Bob Patino and Vicente Wolf] S. M. L. Aronson. il *Archit Dig* 44:216-21 N '87

English transfer [decoration of Manhattan apartment by C. Cleaver] T. Brown. il *House Gard* 159:196-203 N '87

An eye for detail: the Paris apartment of Michel and Noémi Ermelin. B. D. Colen. il *Archit Dig* 44:132-42 Ja '87

Fin de siècle fantasy [New York duplex of P. de Malleray] O. Bernier. il por *House Gard* 159:146-51 Jl '87

For ever England [H. Nye's Manhattan duplex] E. Greene. il por *House Gard* 159:198-203 My '87

Formal details [Manhattan apartment designed for D. and J. Carter by Michael de Santis] J. Gruen. il *Archit Dig* 44:186-92 D '87

Frames of reference: varied palette for a New York apartment. P. Carlsen. il *Archit Dig* 44:120-7 D '87

French ensemble: the Paris apartment of Rena Dumas and Jean-Louis Dumas-Hermès. C. Aillaud. il por *Archit Dig* 44:132-6 Jl '87

Great greenhouse add-ons. il *McCalls* 114:90-3+ Ag '87

Handily done [Manhattan apartment designed by Mark Simon] C. Vogel. il *N Y Times Mag* p59-61 F 8 '87

In a glass house [Seattle apartment] M. Schafer. il *House Gard* 159:112-21 F '87

Inside stories: author Judith Green's Park Avenue residence [decorated by Ann Downey] J. Kornbluth. il por *Archit Dig* 44:134-9+ D '87

An intimate grandeur [Manhattan apartment decorated by Robert Metzger] R. Conniff. il *Archit Dig* 44:80-5 Ag '87

Less is Moorish [New York City apartment with prominent stained glass window] M. Bethany. il *N Y* 20:82-4 N 16 '87

A living scrapbook [M. Buatta's rendition of English country style in apartment designed for Cathy Hardwick] C. Vogel. il *N Y Times Mag* p34-7 S 6 '87

Love at first sight [artist D. Love's Upper East Side apartment] M. Bethany. il *N Y* 20:50-3 F 9 '87

Luminous close-ups [Manhattan apartment of decorators Bob Patino and Vicente Wolf] G. Winkel. il *House Gard* 159:210-17 Ap '87

Lyn Revson's beaux-arts address [Upper East Side, New York City] Suzy. il por *Archit Dig* 44:130-9+ N '87

Man about town at home [J. Zipkin's apartment] C. T. Buckley. il por *House Gard* 159:190-3+ O '87

Manhattan mood [apartment decorated by Juan Montoya] A. Berman. il *Archit Dig* 44:132-7 My '87

Manhattan still life [C. Fisher's East Side apartment] J. Giovannini. il *House Gard* 159:178-83+ Je '87

A matter of symmetry [Manhattan apartment decorated by John Saladino] J. Taylor. il *Archit Dig* 44:182-90 S '87

Mix master [New York City apartment of Mark Golderman] M. Bethany. il *N Y* 20:44-7 Ja 12 '87

Moroccan in Manhattan [apartment of Leon Amar] O. Bernier. il *House Gard* 159:164-7+ F '87

A New York of one's own: Mario Buatta furnishes a pied-à-terre on Fifth Avenue. E. Greene. il *House Gard* 159:204-9 Ap '87

A nice place to visit [New York City pied-à-terres] L. J. Gallagher. il *Esquire* 107:42 Ja '87

Objects of affection [B. Fouret's Paris apartment] J. J. Buck. il pors *Vogue* 177:400-7+ N '87

Odyssey by the bay: the San Francisco peregrinations of Herb Caen. H. Caen. il por *Archit Dig* 44:68-71+ Jl '87

On Gramercy Park: the New York apartment of Sharon and James Hoge. S. K. Hoge. il por *Archit Dig* 44:56-61+ Jl '87

On Russian Hill: transforming a 1920s San Francisco residence [decorated by Robert Hutchinson] J. D. Houston. il *Archit Dig* 44:116-21 S '87

Parisian exotic [Left Bank apartment of F. and C. Rochas] J.-M. Baron. il por *House Gard* 159:130-9+ Jl '87

Penthouse poise [Manhattan apartment decorated by Juan Pablo Molyneux] M. Morse. il *House Gard* 159:126-33 Ja '87

A place for roses: the inimitable world of Ned and Marlo Phillips. M. Peppiatt. il por *Archit Dig* 44:206-11 N '87

Reflections of my many lives. il *House Gard* 159:66-77+ Ja '87

Return to romance: Linda and Steve Horn's Manhattan penthouse. S. M. L. Aronson. il por *Archit Dig* 44:122-7+ O '87

Romantic modernism: a New York apartment to refresh the senses [decorated by Bob Patino and Vicente Wolf] J. Taylor. il *Archit Dig* 44:132-5 Ag '87

Stress-relief decorating. il *Glamour* 85:314-16 Mr '87

Thomas and Nan Kempner in New York: evolution of a Park Avenue apartment [decorated by Michael Taylor] B. Hayward. il por *Archit Dig* 44:166-71+ My '87

Venice-on-the-Hudson [West Village penthouse designed and owned by A. E. Smith] P. Warner. il por *Archit Dig* 44:140-7+ N '87

A versatile retreat: designer's Lake Tahoe apartment [R. Crosetti] H. Junker. il *Archit Dig* 44:132-7 Mr '87

Visual intrigue [Beekman Place apartment of P. Marino and J. Trapnell] S. M. L. Aronson. il pors *Archit Dig* 44:228-32+ N '87

What works: priceless tips from the super-decorators [cover story] M. Bethany. il *N Y* 20:36-58+ Ap 13 '87

Anecdotes, facetiae, satire, etc.

World Expo Larry 'n' Dot '87: an appraisal. B. McCall. il *New Yorker* 63:32-3 F 23 '87

Leasing and renting

See also

Landlord and tenant

Rent laws

House conversion reaps cash rewards [rental apartment] H. Porter. *Fam Handyman* 37:18+ My/Je '87

How to find an apartment (seriously) [New York City; cover story] J. Goldman. il *N Y* 20:30-8 Je 22 '87

Lords, serfs, psychics, apples [tour of Rutherford Place in New York City, newly remodeled into rental units] *New Yorker* 63:23-5 Mr 30 '87

A separate space [creating an apartment in your home] R. Barnhart. il *Home Mech* 83:38-42 Ja '87

Apartments, Remodeled

Where opposites attract [Tribeca, N.Y. loft remodeled by Siris/Coombs] E. Greene. il *House Gard* 159:144-9+ Ja '87

APBA Pro League Baseball Game

Strat-O-Matic vs. APBA: a tough call. A. Kim. *Sport Mag* 78:84+ S '87

Apes

See also

Chimpanzees

Gorillas

Orangutans

Why is ape tool use so confusing? [research by William McGrew] R. Lewin. *Science* 236:776-7 My 15 '87

Apes, Fossil

Empire of the apes [Lake Turkana fossils; work of Richard Leakey] S. J. Gould. il *Nat Hist* 96:20+ My '87

Hominoid lineages and keystone clues [Robert B. Eckhardt's challenge to Todd R. Olson's nasal bone theory] B. Bower. il *Sci News* 132:71 Ag 1 '87

Apfelbaum, Jonathan

Vacuum failure. il *Flying* 114:112 N '87

Aphids *See* Plant lice

APHIS *See* United States. Animal and Plant Health Inspection Service

Aphrodisiacs

Sensuous side effect [antidepressant Wellbutrin increases sexual desire] *Time* 129:86 My 4 '87

Apianus, Petrus, 1495-1552

about

An early star mapper. G. Lovi. il *Sky Telesc* 74:391-2 O '87

Apiculture *See* Bee culture

Apios americana *See* Groundnuts

Apker Award *See* Physics—Awards

APL Corporation
Every man for himself [V. Posner buys controlling block of APL Corp. from NVF Co.] A. Sloan. il por *Forbes* 139:37-8 Je 29 '87

Aplex Corporation
Women are lining up for Lore Harp's Le Funelle. P. Finch. il por *Bus Week* p80 Je 8 '87

Aplysia learning behavior *See* Animal learning

Aplysia nervous system *See* Nervous system—Mollusks

Apnea
The darker side of snoring [sleep apnea] *Consum Rep* 52:137 Mr '87
New mouthpiece stops apnea [sleep apnea] *Prevention* 39:15 O '87

Apocalyptic literature
Survival in the apocalyptic era. G. A. Larue. il *Humanist* 47:11-17 S/O '87

Apocalyptic thought *See* Eschatology

Apochromatic lenses *See* Lenses, Photographic

Apogee Acoustics (Firm)
Ribbons of sound. G. Burks. il *Forbes* 140:224 N 30 '87

Apolipoproteins *See* Lipoproteins

Apollo [ballet] *See* Ballet reviews—Single works

Apollo 11 flight *See* Space flight to the moon—Apollo 11 flight

Apollo Theatre (New York, N.Y.)
Headlining the Apollo; ed. by Steven Dougherty. R. Cooper. il pors *People Wkly* 28:71+ O 19 '87

Apollonia
about
Prince's intriguing women [cover story] L. Norment. il pors *Ebony* 43:162-3+ N '87

Apollonia (Libya: Ancient city)
Apollonia, a model port of antiquity. *Courier* 40:38 N '87

Apologies
How to say you're sorry. D. Hales. *McCalls* 115:22+ O '87
"I'm sorry!" [parents' apologies] J. Vedral. il *Parents* 62:91-4 Ap '87
The indispensable art of apology. S. Jacoby. il *Read Dig* 130:133-5 Mr '87
Regrets only: the ABCs of apology. D. Heyn. *Mademoiselle* 93:98 F '87

Aponte, Christopher
about
Aponte makes Spokane's dream come true. S. English. por *Dance Mag* 61:8-9 Ap '87

Aponte, José
about
In the wake of a tragic hotel fire, disaster attorneys seek compensation for the victims—and for themselves. J. S. Kunen. il pors *People Wkly* 27:36-8 Ja 26 '87

Apostrophes [television program] *See* Television program reviews—Single works

Appalachian region
See also
Arts and crafts—Appalachian region
Description and travel
The southern Appalachians. G. S. Bush. il map *Better Homes Gard* 65:132+ Ag '87

Appalachian Trail
Showdown in the Saddleback [proposal to enlarge the Saddleback Mountain ski area] il *Wilderness* 50:7+ Summ '87
Trail among the clouds. H. Middleton. il *South Living* 22:42+ S '87
A tunnel through time. N. Grove. il supp (folded map) maps *Natl Geogr* 171:216-43 F '87

Appalled (Term)
I am appalled. W. Safire. il *N Y Times Mag* p20+ D 20 '87

Apparel industry *See* Clothing industry

Apparitions
See also
Jesus Christ—Apparitions and miracles
Mary, Blessed Virgin, Saint—Apparitions and miracles

Appel, Karel, 1921-
about
Optimism and apocalypse. C. Ratcliff. il por *Archit Dig* 44:44+ Ap '87

Appelbaum, Paul S.
Crazy in the streets. *Commentary* 83:34-9 My '87
Crazy in the streets: the policy of deinstitutionalization. *Current* 296:4-10 O '87

Street people [discussion of May 1987 article, Crazy in the streets] *Commentary* 84:14-16+ S '87

Appellate courts
See also
United States. Court of Appeals (District of Columbia Circuit)

Appenzeller, Tim
(jt. auth) *See* Mishkin, Mortimer, and Appenzeller, Tim

Appetite
See also
Anorexia nervosa
Bulimia
Hunger
Pica (Pathology)
Making weight loss even sweeter [xylitol sweetener reduces appetite] *Prevention* 39:52 O '87

Appetite suppressing drugs *See* Weight reducing preparations

Appetizers
See also
Dim sum
Tapas
Appetizers and salads for two. il *South Living* 22:214-15 Ap '87
Appetizers from the sea. il *South Living* 22:198-9 My '87
Appetizers: the microwave is the great entertainer! il *Better Homes Gard* 65:146+ Ap '87
Celebrate with appetizers that are easy on the cook and on the waistline. il *Sunset* 178:90-1 Ja '87
Do-ahead hors d'oeuvres [microwaving] il *Good Housekeep* 205:128+ N '87
Easy holiday hors d'oeuvres. il *McCalls* 115:52 D '87
Feasting on healthy appetizers. J. B. Hurley. il *Prevention* 39:40+ Ap '87
Fry this appetizer [Tex-Mex wontons] il *South Living* 22:166 S '87
Have fun with phyllo appetizers. il *South Living* 22:207 Mr '87
An hors d'oeuvres buffet. il *Gourmet* 48:76-8+ Je '87
Micro-way cooking. il *McCalls* 114:113-14 Ap '87
The nacho experience. K. Haedrich. il *Ctry J* 14:22-5 F '87
Party appetizers. il *Good Housekeep* 205:214 D '87
Party hits! il *Redbook* 168:109-14 Ja '87
Recipe of the week [party egg salad appetizer] il *Jet* 73:38 D 21 '87
Recipe of the week [salmon spread and crackers] il *Jet* 73:28 D 28 '87-Ja 4 '88
Recipe of the week [sesame chicken nuggets] il *Jet* 73:38 D 14 '87
Snow peas stuffed with dollar bills: hauts hors d'oeuvres. J. Adler. il *Newsweek* 109:49 Ja 5 '87
Stocking up on quick appetizers. il *Sunset* 179:148 D '87
Sweet and tart fruit aïoli. il *Sunset* 178:212 Ap '87
Tom's four star finger salads [fresh vegetables and dips] T. Ney. il *Rodale's Org Gard* 34:65-6+ My '87
Warm greetings for the holidays [hot drinks and finger foods] J. R. Nyenhuis. il *Saturday Evening Post* 259:76-8 D '87

Applause
What is the sound of two hands clapping? il *Discover* 8:9-10 Ag '87

Apple, Max
Research [story] il *Harpers* 274:66-71 Ja '87
Ripening desire and the muse of middle age [excerpt from Voicelust] il *N Y Times Book Rev* 92:1+ Mr 1 '87
Roommates. il *N Y Times Mag* p68 My 3 '87

Apple, Michael W.
Hidden effects of computers on teachers and students. *Educ Dig* 53:2-6 O '87

Apple (Computer) *See* Computers

Apple butter
Dutch treat: making Pennsylvania apple butter. L. Furgatch. il *Ctry J* 14:31-2 O '87

Apple Computer Inc.
After a long diet, Apple bites back. P. Dworkin. il *U S News World Rep* 102:47-8 Ja 26 '87
Apple Computer's Debi Coleman. M. Dowie. il por *Ms* 15:60-2+ My '87
Apple cracks the business market. il *Fortune* 116:10 Ag 17 '87
Apple finally invades the office. B. O'Reilly. il *Fortune* 116:52-3+ N 9 '87
Apple goes for a bigger bite of corporate America. K. M. Hafner. il *Bus Week* p74-5 Ag 24 '87
Apple's big Mac attack [Macintosh SE and Macintosh II] J. Schwartz. il *Newsweek* 109:48 Mr 9 '87

Apple Computer Inc.—*cont.*

Apple's comeback [concentrating on Macintosh sales to business] K. M. Hafner. il por *Bus Week* p84-9 Ja 19 '87

Apples, frogs, and animal rights [Apple Computer television commercial] C. Holden. *Science* 238:1345 D 4 '87

Good, better, best [D. Coleman] F. M. Henley. il pors *Work Woman* 12:86-9 D '87

Hyper-excitement at Apple [HyperCard] M. Rogers. il *Newsweek* 110:45 Ag 31 '87

In the study of John Sculley [chairman] il por *Esquire* 107:86-7 Ap '87

A look at Apple's Cray simulation engine. *Byte* 12:37-8 S '87

The Mac is back [cover story; special section; with editorial comment by Fred Abatemarco] A. C. Hixson. il *Pers Comput* 11:5, 102-7+ Ap '87

Most improved. il *Forbes* 139:105 Ja 12 '87

Odyssey: John Sculley and the saga of the Macintosh (I) [excerpt from Odyssey] J. Sculley. il *Pers Comput* 11:182-5+ N '87

Odyssey: John Sculley and the saga of the Macintosh (II) [excerpt from Odyssey] J. Sculley. il *Pers Comput* 11:201-3+ D '87

The passion is back at Apple Computer. il *Fortune* 115:8 Ja 19 '87

Pied Piper of the computer [A. Kay] F. Rose. il por *N Y Times Mag* p56+ N 8 '87

Planting seeds at Apple [HyperCard for the Macintosh] R. A. Shaffer. il *Pers Comput* 11:55 N '87

The power of pizzazz [Macintosh II] R. A. Shaffer. il *Pers Comput* 11:61 Je '87

Professionals and their computers. J. Sculley. por *Pers Comput* 11:236 O '87

Sculley's lessons from inside Apple [ousting S. Jobs; excerpt from Odyssey] J. Sculley. il pors *Fortune* 116:108-11+ S 14 '87

Software plays hardball [Apple's proposed programming company and IBM's deal with Lotus] *Time* 129:52 My 11 '87

The wall comes tumbling down [IBM and Apple personal computers] P. Elmer-Dewitt. il *Time* 129:68 F 2 '87

The world according to John Sculley. K. M. Hafner. il por *Bus Week* p71+ S 28 '87

Apple desserts *See* Desserts

Apple juice

See also

New England Apple Products Company Inc.

Labeling

Beech-Nut indicted over phony juice. il *FDA Consum* 21:4 F '87

Apple pastry *See* Pastry

Apple pie *See* Pie

Apple trees

Training new apple trees. J. Ruttle. il *Rodale's Org Gard* 34:48-9 D '87

Applebaum, Irwyn

about

Realizing the potential at Pocket Books. J. Davis. il pors *Publ Wkly* 231:45-8 Ja 23 '87

Applebee, Arthur N., and others

Learning to be literate: reading, writing, reasoning. *Educ Dig* 53:6-8 D '87

National writing assessments: trends across 10 years [excerpt from Writing] *Educ Dig* 52:24-6 F '87

Applebome, Peter

Is there life after football? il *N Y Times Mag* p73-4+ O 4 '87

Applegate, Jeffrey

about

A time to be cautious, not bearish [interview] por *U S News World Rep* 102:56 My 4 '87

Applegate, Judith

about

Judith's place. M. Bethany. il por *N Y* 20:30 N 30 '87

Apples, Jonathon

about

Reviews:

Performances at the Bessie Schönberg Theater, New York City. C. Hardy. *Dance Mag* 61:20 Ja '87

Apples

See also

Apple trees

Cooking—Fruit

A is for apple. il *Good Housekeep* 205:220 N '87

The Duchess of Oldenburg and other edible antiques. M. Hofferber. il *Ctry J* 14:68-71 O '87

Old-fashioned apples, new-fangled ideas. il *Sunset* 179:204-6 S '87

Quest for flavor [work of T. and J. Vorbeck] J. Ruttle. il *Rodale's Org Gard* 34:42-4+ D '87

Contamination

An apple a day is O.K.—for now [food processing industry rejects apples treated with growth regulator Alar] il *Consum Rep* 52:594 O '87

Diseases and pests

Better apples the low-spray way [use of botanical insecticides] J. Ruttle. il *Rodale's Org Gard* 34:48-52 Ag '87

Picking

Apple picking time. D. J. Williamson. il *Americana* 15:54-7+ S/O '87

Apples (Jonathon) Plus Company *See* Jonathon Apples Plus Company

Apples in decoration *See* Fruits, vegetables, etc. in decoration

Applesauce

Scorch-free applesauce . . . in 10 minutes [microwaved] J. B. Hurley. il *Rodale's Org Gard* 34:87-8 D '87

Appleton, Bonnie Lee

Landscape renovation. il *Flower Gard* 31:64-5 Je/Jl '87

Applewhite, E. J.

A Buckminster Fuller dictionary. il pors *Futurist* 21:24-8 S/O '87

Appliances, Household *See* Household appliances

Appliances, Personal care *See* Personal care appliances

Applications for positions *See* Job applications

Applied Microbiology Inc.

Cyanamid is bullish on a cure for sick cows [acquiring stake in Applied Microbiology's protein for mastitis] G. G. Marcial. il *Bus Week* p136 My 11 '87

Applied science *See* Technology

Applin, Stephen

First frost [poem] *America* 157:402 N 28 '87

Appliqué work

Quick! Appliqué a designer sweater. il *Redbook* 169:43-4+ S '87

Wood appliqué art [ornaments created by Lillian Renko Bledow] J. Williams. il *Better Homes Gard* 65:58-60+ O '87

Appomattox Campaign, 1865

With Lee at Appomattox [cover story] E. P. Alexander. il pors map *Am Hist Illus* 22:40-5+ S '87

Appomattox Court House National Historical Park (Va.)

Appomattox today. il *Am Hist Illus* 22:55 S '87

Apportionment (Election law)

See also

Gerrymander

Proportional representation

Beware of Republicans bearing voting rights suits. M. Cooper. *Wash Mon* 19:11-15 F '87

Appraisal *See* Assessment

Appraisal, Antiques *See* Antiques—Valuation

Appraisal, Business *See* Corporations—Valuation

Appraisal, Real property *See* Real property—Valuation

Appraisal of employees *See* Employees—Rating

Appraisers

Find out what it's worth. M. Halperin. il *Americana* 15:14+ S/O '87

Ethical aspects

Business appraising: beware of amateur hour. S. Weiss. il *Bus Week* p74 F 9 '87

Appreciation of art *See* Art—Appreciation

Approach plate books *See* Aviation charts

Appropriations Committee (House) *See* United States. Congress. House. Committee on Appropriations

Appropriations Committee (Senate) *See* United States. Congress. Senate. Committee on Appropriations

Approximation theory

See also

Relaxation methods (Mathematics)

Apricots

See also

Cooking—Fruit

April

The April almanac. il *Atlantic* 259:14 Ap '87

April snow [drama] See Linney, Romulus, 1930-

Aprill, Dennis

Everyone needs a quiet place. il *Conservationist* 42:56 Jl/Ag '87

APS *See* American Physical Society

Apted, Michael

about

Critical condition [film] Reviews

Jet il 71:58-9 F 9 '87

Macleans 100:54 Ja 26 '87. M. Jackson

People Wkly il 27:16 F 2 '87. T. Cunneff

Aptitude tests

See also

Scholastic Aptitude Test

Aptitude tests—*cont.*
This test may tell you to switch careers [Exploring career options] J. A. Byrne. il *Bus Week* p125 S 21 '87
Aquacises *See* Water exercises
Aquaculture
See also
Fish culture
Shellfish culture
Aquaculture: food for thought [special issue] il *BioScience* 37:308-12+ My '87
Aquaphobia
One with water [program for aquaphobes by Paul Lennon] D. Groves. il *Health* 19:16 Ja '87
Water, water everywhere . . . but not for me, thanks! L. Dormen. il *Health* 19:43 My '87
Aquarium (Musical group)
Aquarium's leader rises to the surface [B. Grebenschikov] N. Traver. il por *People Wkly* 27:51 Ap 6 '87
Aquariums
See also
Dolphins Plus (Key Largo, Fla.)
Monterey Bay Aquarium
New England Aquarium
New York Aquarium
Oklahoma City Zoo. Aquaticus
Sea Life Park (Waimanalo, Hawaii)
Sealand Aquarium (West Brewster, Mass.)
Waikiki Aquarium
Aquariums. See issues of Oceans beginning January/February 1987
Aquatic biology
See also
Fresh water ecology
Marine biology
Marine fauna
Aquatic insects *See* Insects, Aquatic
Aquatic plants
See also
Algae
Duckweeds
Water hyacinths
Aquatic sports
See also
Boats and boating
Diving
Rowing
Sailing
Skin diving
Surfing
Swimming
Water skis and skiing
Splash! The fitness plunge. il *Harpers Bazaar* 120:136-9+ My '87
Summer champions [women] C. Davis. il *Mot Boat Sail* 159:52-7+ Je '87
Accidents and injuries
Getting an earful [swimmer's ear and surfer's ear] S. Berne. il *Women's Sports Fitness* 9:20 Je '87
Equipment
Fun in the sun [new wave riders] D. Hoover. il *Mot Boat Sail* 160:50-1 Ag '87
Sit down and hang on for a wet, wild ride [boat-towable water toys] il *Sunset* 179:78-9 Jl '87
Aquatic weed control
Weed-proofing hooks and lures. N. Strung. il *Field Stream* 92:116 Jl '87
Aquatic weeds
Salad days [bass fishing through weedbeds] J. Doggett. il *Field Stream* 92:42-3+ Ag '87
Weed-beating bass [largemouth bass fishing] L. Larsen. il *Outdoor Life* 179:68-9+ Je '87
Aquino, Corazon
Visit of Philippines' President Aquino [remarks, September 17, 1986] il por map *Dep State Bull* 86:55-7 D '86
about
'After Aquino'. A. Doronila. *World Press Rev* 34:41 D '87
Aquino: an end to innocence. N. Cooper. il *Newsweek* 109:37 F 2 '87
Aquino hands over power and problems. W. A. Taylor. il por *U S News World Rep* 103:31-2 Ag 3 '87
Aquino in the corner. H. Anderson. il por *Newsweek* 110:46+ S 14 '87
Aquino needs a new miracle. L. Kraar. il por *Fortune* 116:90-2+ S 14 '87
Aquino under fire. T. Jacoby. il *Newsweek* 110:40 O 5 '87
Aquino wins a victory—but can she govern? H. Anderson. il por *Newsweek* 109:38-9 F 16 '87

Aquino's close call. B. Levin. il *Macleans* 100:26-7 S 7 '87
Aquino's first year. P. Tarr. il *Nation* 244:353-7 Mr 21 '87
Aquino's mandate won't make the tightrope any less shaky. D. J. Yang. il *Bus Week* p51 F 16 '87
Aquino's muddle in Manila. R. Vokey. il por *Newsweek* 110:35 S 28 '87
Aquino's Philippines: the center holds. S. Burton. *Foreign Aff* 65 Sp Issue:524-37 ['87]
Aquino's troubled win. L. Neumann. il por *Macleans* 100:24 F 16 '87
Are church groups backing opponents of Corazon Aquino? K. A. Lawton. *Christ Today* 31:46-7 Ja 16 '87
The Army can't back up Aquino's tough talk. R. Gourlay. *Bus Week* p57 Ap 6 '87
'Bloody Thursday'. L. Neumann. il *Macleans* 100:55 F 2 '87
A brave woman's fight to heal a troubled U.S. ally. J. Martin. il pors *Sch Update* 119:14-15 Ap 6 '87
Bungled coup, foiled return. J. Smolowe. il *Time* 129:34-5 F 9 '87
Can Aquino break the grip of crony corruption? A. Paul. il pors *Read Dig* 131:83-7 Jl '87
Can Aquino take charge? H. Anderson. il por *Newsweek* 109:40-1 F 9 '87
The center holds in the Philippines. *America* 156:145 F 21 '87
Chiller in Manila. *Nation* 245:219-20 S 12 '87
Cory [special section] il pors *Time* 129:18-27+ Ja 5 '87
Cory Aquino and the psychology of bubbles. M. Singer. il *Natl Rev* 39:34-8 Ag 14 '87
Cory hallelujah. *New Repub* 196:7-9 Mr 2 '87
The Cory myth. A. Cockburn. *Nation* 245:258-9 S 19 '87
Cory's broken promise. J. Collins. il *Nation* 245:549-50+ N 14 '87
The coup that failed. H. G. Chua-Eoan and E. W. Desmond. il por *Time* 130:24-7 S 7 '87
Death in Manila. E. W. Desmond. il por *Time* 129:34-6 F 2 '87
Defense vs. Cory. L. Howard. il *Newsweek* 109:5 My 4 '87
Divine guidance? Aquino may need it. J. M. Fallows. il por *U S News World Rep* 102:41-2 Mr 16 '87
Divisions in the ranks. A. Bilski. il *Macleans* 100:22 F 9 '87
Embattled Aquino gets a new mandate. B. D. Williams and D. Cunningham. *Christ Century* 104:157-8 F 18 '87
The embattled Mrs. Aquino. S. Mydans. il pors *N Y Times Mag* p42-3+ N 15 '87
For Aquino, another thriller in Manila. W. L. Chaze. il por *U S News World Rep* 103:10-11 S 7 '87
For Aquino, crisis is a way of life. W. A. Taylor. il *U S News World Rep* 102:42 F 9 '87
Foreign money runs scared. L. Reaves. *Bus Week* p54 O 5 '87
Giant step for democracy. T. A. Sancton. il por *Time* 129:48 My 25 '87
The ground is crumbling under Aquino. W. A. Taylor. il por *U S News World Rep* 103:51 N 2 '87
Has Aquino used up last of miracles? W. A. Taylor. il por *U S News World Rep* 103:49 S 14 '87
How Aquino can recoup [cover story] R. J. Kessler. il *New Leader* 70:3-5 O 5 '87
"I know you still love me". J. D. Reed. il *Time* 129:44 Ja 19 '87
Inside the rebel camp. M. Liu. il pors *Newsweek* 110:40-2 S 21 '87
The Joker was not laughing. H. G. Chua-Eoan. il por *Time* 130:37 S 21 '87
King Peace Prize goes to Corazon Aquino. il por *Jet* 71:8 F 2 '87
Land reform: Aquino passes the buck. il *Newsweek* 110:33 Ag 3 '87
Last call for Cory? *Commonweal* 114:643-4 N 20 '87
The last days of Aquino? H. Anderson. il *Newsweek* 110:50 O 12 '87
Making the Constitution work [cover story] R. J. Kessler. por *New Leader* 70:8-10 Mr 9 '87
Mean momma. H. G. Chua-Eoan. il por *Time* 130:68 N 2 '87
Mutiny in Manila. H. Anderson. il pors map *Newsweek* 110:26-9 S 7 '87
New troubles for Aquino. W. A. Taylor. il por *U S News World Rep* 102:33-4 F 2 '87
Peace in the Philippines. D. Murphy. *America* 156:406-8 My 16 '87

Aquino, Corazon—about—*cont.*

The Philippine revolution: a year later. F. F. Claver. *America* 156:232-5 Mr 21 '87

Philippines. L. Reaves. *Bus Week* p81 My 25 '87

The Philippines: Aquino's first year. D. A. Rosenberg. bibl f *Curr Hist* 86:160-3+ Ap '87

Philippines: danger signs. H. Anderson. il por *Newsweek* 109:36-8 My 11 '87

Praying for time. H. G. Chua-Eoan. il por *Time* 130:36-7 N 23 '87

Putting Corypower to the test. J. Clad. il *World Press Rev* 34:24-6 Ja '87

Save Cory. *New Repub* 197:7-9 N 2 '87

Seizing a most wanted man. M. Liu. il por *Newsweek* 110:48 D 21 '87

Slowly turning the corner. W. Stewart. il *Time* 129:59 Ap 27 '87

Snapping at the revolution. *New Repub* 196:5-6 F 16 '87

The sweet, sweet taste of victory. W. R. Doerner. il por *Time* 129:36 F 16 '87

Testing an ally's resolve. W. L. Chaze. il por map *U S News World Rep* 103:73-5 S 28 '87

The thin edge (I). R. Shaplen. *New Yorker* 63:43-6+ S 21 '87

The thin edge (II). R. Shaplen. *New Yorker* 63:63-74+ S 28 '87

Things fall apart. H. G. Chua-Eoan. il por *Time* 130:32-3 S 28 '87

Tough words from the top. W. Svoboda. il por *Time* 129:41 Ap 6 '87

Vigilantes for Aquino. F. Willey. il por *Newsweek* 109:34+ Mr 30 '87

When the cheering stopped. H. G. Chua-Eoan. il por *Time* 130:40-1 S 14 '87

Will a sudden show of spine save Cory Aquino? W. L. Chaze. il por *U S News World Rep* 103:12 S 21 '87

Will Aquino finally trade velvet glove for iron fist? M. Shao and L. Reaves. il *Bus Week* p51 S 14 '87

Religion

Cory Aquino: religious newsmaker no. 1. D. Peerman. *Christ Century* 104:3-4 Ja 7-14 '87

Visit to the United States, 1986

Visit of Philippines' President Aquino [remarks, September 17, 1986] R. Reagan; C. Aquino. il por map *Dep State Bull* 86:55-7 D '86

Aquino, Michael A.

about

'The Second Beast of Revelation'. J. Adler. il por *Newsweek* 110:73 N 16 '87

Arab Americans

See also

American-Arab Anti-Discrimination Committee

Political activities

See also

National Association of Arab Americans

The untouchables [harassment by Immigration and Naturalization Service] *Nation* 244:348-9 Mr 21 '87

Arab civilization *See* Civilization, Arab

Arab countries

See also

Cities and towns—Arab countries

Investments, Arab

Kuwait

Oman

Commerce

Israel

See Israel—Commerce—Arab countries

Foreign relations

Israel

See Jewish-Arab relations

United States

See United States—Foreign relations—Arab countries

Israeli occupation, 1967-

See Israel-Arab Wars, 1967- —Territorial questions

Politics and government

See also

Arab League

Arab vs. Arab over Palestine. D. Pipes. *Commentary* 84:17-25 Jl '87

Arab-Israel Wars, 1967- *See* Israel-Arab Wars, 1967-

Arab-Jewish relations *See* Jewish-Arab relations

Arab League

Meeting with Arab League delegation [remarks, May 7, 1987] G. P. Shultz. il por *Dep State Bull* 87:63 Jl '87

A radical returns to the ranks [Jordan summit] M. S. Serrill. il *Time* 130:35 N 23 '87

A 'sea change' in Arab attitudes? [Jordan summit] J. Barnes. il *U S News World Rep* 103:36 N 23 '87

A show of Arab unity. A. Bilski. il *Macleans* 100:23 N 23 '87

The summit of brotherly love. C. Dickey. il *Newsweek* 110:41 N 23 '87

Arab terrorists *See* Terrorists, Arab

Arabian Investment Banking Corporation

The boys from Bahrain. R. Morais. il por *Forbes* 140:181 O 5 '87

Arabic poetry

See also

Folk poetry, Arabic

Arabs

See also

Bedouins

Jewish-Arab relations

Palestinian Arabs

Philippines

History

The obedience due to princesses [visit with Ordoudjã in the 14th century; excerpt from Rihla] Ibn Battuta. il *Courier* 40:34-5 Ap '87

United States

See also

Arab Americans

Arachidonic acid

See also

Lipoxins

New bearers of nerve tidings? [effect of eicosanoids on Aplysia neurons; research by Daniele Piomelli and others] D. D. Edwards. *Sci News* 132:5 Jl 4 '87

Arachnids

See also

Mites

Spiders

Ticks

Vision—Arachnids

Food and feeding

On display: the stars of the stripes [fruit fly mimicry of jumping spider territorial display; research by Erick Greene and others] il *Discover* 8:9-10 My '87

A sheep in wolf's clothing: tephritid flies mimic spider predators. M. H. Mather and B. D. Roitberg. bibl f il *Science* 236:308-10 Ap 17 '87

A tephritid fly mimics the territorial displays of its jumping spider predators. E. Greene and others. bibl f il *Science* 236:310-12 Ap 17 '87

Why the spider did not eat the fly [jumping spider mimicry among fruit flies] S. Weisburd. il *Sci News* 131:261 Ap 25 '87

Arader, W. Graham. III

about

Profiles. M. Singer. il *New Yorker* 63:44-6+ N 30 '87

Arafat, Yasir, 1929-

about

Arafat makes another comeback. S. Reed. il *Nation* 244:137-41 F 7 '87

Arafat: still first among equals. F. Willey. il por *Newsweek* 109:42 Ap 27 '87

Arafat's answer. *New Repub* 196:9 My 4 '87

Arafat's back, reshaping outlook for Mideast talks. W. L. Chaze. il por *U S News World Rep* 102:40 My 4 '87

An interview with Yasser Arafat (I). S. MacLeod. bibl f il *N Y Rev Books* 34:36-40 Je 11 '87

An interview with [Yasser] Arafat (II). S. MacLeod. bibl f il pors *N Y Rev Books* 34:41-5 Je 25 '87

A show of PLO unity. J. Bierman. il por *Macleans* 100:27 My 4 '87

Show of unity. il por *Time* 129:40 My 4 '87

Aragon, Vicky

about

Battling for her place. P. Dexter. il pors *Sports Illus* 66:48-52 F 23 '87

Woman to watch: Vicky Aragon. O. Young. il por *Women's Sports Fitness* 9:54 Je '87

Aralia ivy *See* Fatshedera

Arana-Ward, Marie

(tr) *See* Voinovich, Vladimir, 1932- and Zalygin, Sergei. Where glasnost has its limits

Araskog, Rand V.

Award of honor. il *N Y Times Mag* p54 S 6 '87

about

How cleaning house may help ITT clean up. C. Power. il por *Bus Week* p64+ Mr 23 '87

Arbatov, Georgi A.

Is the real aim the status quo? il *World Press Rev* 34:14-15 N '87

Arbeiter, Solomon
Black enrollments: the case of the missing students.
il *Change* 19:14-19 My/Je '87
Arbetter, Sandra R.
Body language: your body's silent movie. il *Curr Health
2* 13:11-13 F '87
By their own hands. il *Curr Health 2* 14:18-21 S '87
Psychological disorders: turbulence of the mind. il *Curr
Health 2* 14:10-12 N '87
Recognizing the signs of suicide. il *Curr Health 2* 13:12-13
Mr '87
Arbinger, Blythe
Monster trash. il *Omni* 10:28+ D '87
Arbit, Harold
             about
Money men, California style. il por *Fortune* 116:34 Jl
20 '87
Arbitrage
          See also
     M. D. Sass Institutional Arbitrage Partners
Asher the arb [A. Edelman] R. L. Stern. por *Forbes*
139:35 F 23 '87
Be your own arb. T. Jaffe. il *Forbes* 139:290 Ja 12
'87
A big crack in the 'Chinese wall' [arbitrage coexisting
with investment banking] C. Welles. il *Bus Week*
p33 Mr 2 '87
Easy pickings? [market crash and arbitrage stocks] A.
Sloan. il *Forbes* 140:36 N 30 '87
An extra slice of the pie [Drexel Burnham Lambert's
special investment in I. Boesky's arbitrage fund] A.
Sloan. il *Forbes* 139:32-3 F 9 '87
The paranoid life of arbitragers. J. Fierman. il *Fortune*
116:97+ N 9 '87
Arbitration, Commercial
Battling your broker gets harder [Supreme Court upholds
arbitration] D. P. Wiener. il *U S News World Rep*
102:51 Je 22 '87
Can't sue your broker? It's no big loss [Supreme Court
decision upholds arbitration] D. Zigas. il *Bus Week*
p128 Je 22 '87
Did you agree not to sue? [use of arbitration to settle
broker-stockholder disputes] *U S News World Rep*
103:45 N 9 '87
How to settle a beef with your broker. *Money* 16:13
Ap '87
Low-cost mediation settles disputes out of court. H.
Porter. *Fam Handyman* 37:16+ My/Je '87
Remodeling woes? Don't get mad, get arbitration. D.
Stover. *Pop Sci* 230:83 Ap '87
Sue your stockbroker? You can't, you know [upcoming
Supreme Court ruling] S. Weiss. il *Bus Week* p75-6
Mr 2 '87
We wuz robbed [arbitration in broker-customer cases]
R. L. Stern. il *Forbes* 140:60-1 D 28 '87
When you're burned by your broker. il *Changing Times*
41:77-80+ Ap '87
Why stockbrokers sleep at night [Supreme Court upholds
binding arbitration] M. Meyer. il *Money* 16:105-8+
Jl '87
Arbitration, Industrial
          See also
     Collective bargaining
     United States. National Labor Relations Board
Arbitration, Sports
The arbitrator's game [baseball salary arbitrator R.
Abrams] M. Chass. il por *Sport Mag* 78:29 Je '87
Arbitration and award
          See also
     Doggy Court
Participatory justice. G. Stephens. *Futurist* 21:22-3 Ja/F
'87
Solutions, not winners [community mediators] D. G.
Pruitt. bibl (p63) il *Psychol Today* 21:58-62 D '87
Arbor House Publishing Company, Inc.
Arbor House to become imprint of Morrow. *Publ Wkly*
231:16 Je 19 '87
Arboretums
          See also
     National Arboretum (U.S.)
Arbors
Enjoy an arbor this summer. D. Hastings. il *South Living*
22:174 My '87
Vines and arbors: a superb combination. T. A. Steadman.
il *South Living* 22:38-9 Jl '87
Arboviruses
A novel mode of arbovirus transmission involving a
nonviremic host. L. D. Jones and others. bibl f il
Science 237:775-7 Ag 14 '87

Arby's Inc.
Three sparkling turnarounds: can this really be Victor
Posner? P. Engardio. il por *Bus Week* p56-7 Jl 27
'87
Arcade, Penny
             about
Penny Arcade's sideshow. L. Robinson. por *Vogue* 177:102
Ap '87
Arcades
Cleveland's splendor under glass [shopping arcade] il
Am Herit 38:90-1 Jl/Ag '87
Arcadia (Fla.)
                 Crime
Anatomy of a hate campaign [Ray family burned out
of home because of fear of AIDS] W. Plummer. il
People Wkly 28:32-7 S 14 '87
The castaways: fears about AIDS drive three boys from
home [Ray family burned out of home] M. Voboril.
il *Life* 10:98-100 O '87
Arcand, Denys
             about
The decline of the American empire [film] Reviews
Natl Rev 39:61-3 Ja 30 '87. J. Simon
Time il 129:70+ Ja 19 '87. R. Schickel
Arcata (Calif.)
              Sanitary affairs
The marsh that Arcata built. J. W. Price. il *Sierra*
72:51-3 My/Je '87
Arcata Marsh and Wildlife Sanctuary (Calif.) See Wildlife
sanctuaries—California
Archaebacteria
Isolation of extremely thermophilic sulfate reducers:
evidence for a novel branch of archaebacteria. K.
O. Stetter and others. bibl f il *Science* 236:822-4 My
15 '87
Archaeology *See* Archeology
Archaeopteryx *See* Birds, Fossil
Archambault, Florence
Eighteenth-century teapots. bibl il *Antiques Collect
Hobbies* 91:27-9 Ja '87
Archean period *See* Paleontology—Archean
Archeological pillage *See* Pillage
Archeologists
          See also
     Barkay, Gabriel
     Malcom, Corey
     Soren, David
     Youth as archeologists
     Zarins, Juris, 1945-
Archeology
          See also
     Alabama—Antiquities
     Anthropology
     Antiquities
     Assyria—Antiquities
     Bible—Antiquities
     Bone implements and weapons
     Brazil—Antiquities
     Bronze Age
     Caesarea (Ancient city)
     Canada—Antiquities
     Cave drawings and paintings
     Chile—Antiquities
     China—Antiquities
     Cities and towns, Ruined, extinct, etc.
     Colombia—Antiquities
     Costa Rica—Antiquities
     Easter Island—Antiquities
     Egypt—Antiquities
     Eskimos—Antiquities
     France—Antiquities
     Great Britain—Antiquities
     Greece—Antiquities
     Jerusalem—Antiquities
     Jordan—Antiquities, Roman
     Kenya—Antiquities
     Kyŏngju (Korea)—Antiquities
     Lincolnshire (England)—Antiquities
     London (England)—Antiquities
     London (England)—Antiquities, Roman
     Man, Prehistoric
     Mayas—Antiquities
     Mediterranean region—Antiquities
     Middle East—Antiquities
     Mummies
     New York (State)—Antiquities
     Pacific Northwest—Antiquities
     Pompeii (Ancient city)
     Saint Matthias Islands (Papua New Guinea)—Anti-
        quities
     Santa Rosa Island (Calif.)—Antiquities

Archeology—See also—*cont.*
   Sri Lanka—Antiquities
   Stone Age
   Stone implements and weapons
   Syria—Antiquities
   Tomography—Archeological use
   Venezuela—Antiquities
   Whithorn (Scotland)—Antiquities
   Yukon Territory—Antiquities
          Methodology
   See also
   Artificial satellites—Archeological use
   Parapsychology and archeology
Archeology's dating game. S. Strauss. il *Technol Rev* 90:8+ O '87
Heirs to ancient air [plan to study sealed Egyptian crypt; cover story] R. Monastersky. il *Sci News* 132:172-3 S 12 '87
New tools for an ancient dig [pharaoh's wooden bark observed in sealed chamber at Great Pyramid at Giza] W. D. Marbach. il *Newsweek* 110:80-1 N 2 '87
Pharaoh's boat found in ancient pit [use of remote sensing] R. Monastersky. *Sci News* 132:295 N 7 '87
Probing the chambers of Cheops [video camera reveals wooden boat inside Great Pyramid] D. S. Jackson. il *Time* 130:75 N 2 '87
A quest for ancient Egyptian air [use of remote sensing] C. Holden. il *Science* 236:1419-20 Je 12 '87
They didn't carry out the trash [use of remote sensing to locate hut remains in Valley Forge National Historical Park; work of Jay Parrish] R. Monastersky. *Sci News* 132:319 N 14 '87
Archeology, Astronomical *See* Astronomy, Ancient
Archeology, Submarine
   See also
   Central America (Steamship)
   Commodore (Ship)
   Geldermalsen (Ship)
   Kronan (Ship)
   Mary Rose (Ship)
   Monitor (Ironclad)
   Nuestra Señora de Atocha (Ship)
   Regina (Ship)
   Republic (Steamship)
   Titanic (Steamship)
   Treasure trove
   Vasa (Warship)
   Whidah (Ship)
Archaeology under water [cover story; special issue] il maps *Courier* 40:3-38 N '87
Digging for Bronze Age treasures [Earthwatch's Lake Neuchâtel project] S. Ocko. il *Technol Rev* 90:70-1 F/Mr '87
Diving for dollars [special section] il *Macleans* 100:36-42 Ag 10 '87
How Carthage lost the sea [reconstruction of Punic warship] H. Frost. il maps *Nat Hist* 96:58-67 D '87
Oldest known shipwreck reveals splendors of the Bronze Age [cover story] G. F. Bass. il map *Natl Geogr* 172:692-733 D '87
Resurrector of wrecks [J. R. Steffy] M. Geannette. il pors *Oceans* 20:36-41 N/D '87
          Methodology
Technology and the marine archaeologist. C. Mazel. il *Courier* 40:15-21 N '87
Archer, Anne
         about
Once a washout, Anne Archer now bubbles up in Fatal attraction. J. Jerome. il pors *People Wkly* 28:53-4 O 19 '87
Archer, Dane
         about
Murder in mind. J. Wilkes. il pors *Psychol Today* 21:26-8+ Je '87
Archer, Jeffrey, 1940-
         about
Author's life imitates his art. A. Deming. il por *Newsweek* 110:62 Ag 3 '87
Spare pennies. W. R. Doerner. il por *Time* 130:31-2 Ag 3 '87
Archer, Mike
         about
A bull's-eye for a new Archer. H. Hersch. il *Sports Illus* 67:26-8+ S 14 '87
Archer, Robyn, 1948-
         about
Robyn Archer sings Brecht. E. Salzman. il por *Stereo Rev* 52:116 My '87

Archer-Daniels-Midland Co.
Anatomy of a rip-off [profiting from government agricultural subsidies and gasohol program] J. A. Barnes. *New Repub* 197:20-1 N 2 '87
Profiles [D. O. Andreas, chief executive officer] E. J. Kahn. por *New Yorker* 62:41-2+ F 16 '87
Some dare call them . . . robber barons [government agricultural subsidies and gasohol program] M. Fumento. il *Natl Rev* 39:32-3+ Mr 13 '87
Archery
   See also
   Hunting with bow and arrow
Arches
   See also
   Vaults (Architecture)
Arches and vaults in the ancient Near East [cover story] G. W. Van Beek. il map *Sci Am* 257:96-103 Jl '87
Archibald, Nolan D.
         about
How Black & Decker got back in the black. C. S. Eklund. il por *Bus Week* p86+ Jl 13 '87
Architects
   See also
   Adam, Robert, 1728-1792
   Ames, Anthony
   Anger, Roger
   Architectural firms
   Athfield, Ian, 1940-
   Aubry, Eugene
   Badanes, Steve
   Barba, F. Javier
   Bellini, Mario, 1935-
   Bill, Max, 1908-
   Bofill, Ricardo, 1939-
   Botta, Mario
   Buchsbaum, Alan, 1936-1987
   Bulfinch, Charles, 1763-1844
   Cardinal, Douglas
   Coleman, David
   Crépain, Jo
   Currie, Leonard J.
   Delano, William Adams, 1874-1960
   Ferri, Roger C., 1949-
   Fort-Brescia, Bernardo
   Foster, Norman, 1935-
   Gehry, Frank
   Graves, Michael, 1934-
   Greenberg, Allan
   Harris, William
   Howard, Coy
   Hunt, Richard Morris, 1827-1895
   Isozaki, Arata
   Jacobsen, Hugh Newell
   Jahn, Helmut
   Johnson, Ralph
   Jones, Edward Vason, 1909-1980
   Landscape architects
   Le Corbusier, 1887-1965
   MacDonald, Donald W.
   Maki, Fumihiko, 1928-
   May, Clifford, 1908-
   Meier, Richard, 1934-
   Moore, Arthur Cotton
   Moore, Charles Willard
   Moss, Eric Owen
   Murphy, Brian Alfred
   Neeley, Dennis J.
   Olbrich, Josef Maria, 1867-1908
   Pedersen, William
   Phelps, Barton
   Portman, John Calvin
   Predock, Antoine
   Puppo, Giancarlo
   Quigley, Robert Wellington, 1946-
   Rogers, Richard, 1933-
   Sellers, David
   Soane, Sir John, 1753-1837
   Stern, Robert A. M., 1939-
   Stirling, James Frazer
   Sullivan, Louis H., 1856-1924
   Tange, Kenzo
   Vandenhove, Charles
   Venturi, Robert
   Wright, Frank Lloyd, 1867-1959
   Wright, Lloyd
The architect as facility manager—fiction and fact. M. C. P. McElroy. il *Archit Rec* 175:42-3 O '87
Architects for the 1990s. B. Dumaine. il *Fortune* 115:152-5+ Je 22 '87
Architecture for the birds [birdhouses designed by architects] il *House Gard* 159:106-9 Jl '87

Architects—*cont.*
Legal status, laws, etc.
Architects' responsibility versus the liability crisis. *Archit Rec* 175:35+ Mr '87
Computers: changing the legal rules. P. M. Lurie and B. D. Weiss. *Archit Rec* 175:35+ Ap '87
Here's one way to deal with clients' unpaid bills [architects' rights provided in mechanics' lien statutes] S. A. Glazer. *Archit Rec* 175:39 Mr '87
Integration of law and practice into the curriculum. B. Greenstreet. il por *Archit Rec* 175:43 Mr '87
Liability insurance: is the time right for captives? J. Trewhitt. il *Archit Rec* 175:47 Ag '87
Tort reform scores significant victories. C. K. Hoyt. il *Archit Rec* 175:35 N '87
Licenses and registration
See also
National Council of Architectural Registration Boards
Selection and appointment
Furor over embassy security points to tighter screening of architects. P. Hoffmann. il *Archit Rec* 175:39 Je '87
Supply and demand
Can there ever be too many architects? [AIA convention discussion] M. F. Schmertz. *Archit Rec* 175:9 Ag '87
Training
See Architecture—Study and teaching
Architects' offices
Architects on the move. H. L. Smith, Jr. il *Archit Rec* 175:101-17 Je '87
Architectural acoustics *See* Acoustics, Architectural
Architectural competitions *See* Architecture—Competitions
Architectural conferences *See* Architecture—Conferences
Architectural design
See also
Architectural drawing
Design news. See issues of Architectural Record
In the public interest: design guidelines. J. Barnett. il *Archit Rec* 175:114-25 Jl '87
Architectural drawing
Architectural education: drawing the line—graphics should clearly communicate design. T. Porter and G. Dombek. pors *Archit Rec* 175:45 My '87
Beyond the Peak [work of Z. M. Hadid] D. Dietsch. il *Archit Rec* 175:118-29 Je '87
Exhibitions
Zaha Hadid at Max Protetch. J. Merkel. il *Art Am* 75:184-5 O '87
Architectural education *See* Architecture—Study and teaching
Architectural engineering *See* Structural engineering
Architectural firms
See also
Arquitectonica International Corporation
Art In Construction (Firm)
Clark Tribble Harris & Li, Architects
CRS Sirrine, Inc.
Gwathmey Siegel Architects
Jersey Devil (Firm)
Kohn Pedersen Fox Associates, PC
Neeley/Lofrano Inc.
Robert A. M. Stern Architects
Swanke, Hayden, Connell Architects
Cooperation
Joint ventures or associations; do they work? J. Falick. il *Archit Rec* 175:29 Ja '87
Management
Making the architect-engineer relationship work. S. M. Sessler. *Archit Rec* 175:43 F '87
Public relations
Build an image for your firm. R. Pollock. *Archit Rec* 175:44-5 O '87
Change in the blink of an eye [roundtable of the Society for Marketing Professional Services] J. Capelin. il *Archit Rec* 175:45+ F '87
Marketing: base public relations on content, not form. R. L. Miller. il *Archit Rec* 175:39 Jl '87
Mastering polished audiovisual presentations. W. Salisbury. il *Archit Rec* 175:29+ Ap '87
Pro bono architecture in Appalachia and elsewhere [L. J. Currie and his staff provide free architectural services to the poor] M. F. Schmertz. *Archit Rec* 175:9 Mr '87
Canada
See also
IKOY Partnership
France
See also
Architecture Studio (Firm)

Architectural fittings *See* Building fittings
Architectural literature
See also
Booksellers and bookselling—Architectural literature
Architectural models
See also
Castle models
House models
The National Gallery model: a miniature with a purpose. A. Bahar. il *Antiques Collect Hobbies* 92:55-7 My '87
Architectural photography *See* Photography, Architectural
Architectural record (Periodical)
Record Houses 1987 [with introd. by Douglas Brenner] il *Archit Rec* 175:69-147 mid-Ap '87
Record Interiors 1987 [cover story; special issue; with introd. by Charles K. Gandee] il *Archit Rec* 175:83-161 mid-S '87
Architectural rendering *See* Architectural drawing
Architectural schools
See also
Harvard University. Graduate School of Design
University of Miami. School of Architecture
University of Wisconsin—Milwaukee. Dept. of Architecture
Accreditation
See also
National Architectural Accrediting Board (U.S.)
Architectural space *See* Space (Architecture)
Architecture
See also
Airport buildings
Arcades
Arches
Architects
Architectural drawing
Art galleries and museums—Architecture
Atriums
Beach architecture
Building materials
Buildings
Carpentry
Castles
Ceilings
Centers for the performing arts
Churches (Buildings)
City planning
Classicism in architecture
College architecture
Computers—Architectural use
Concert halls
Concrete construction
Courthouses
Courtyards
Desert architecture
Environmental design
Environmental engineering (Buildings)
Façades
Follies (Architecture)
Garden houses, shelters, etc.
Glass construction
Greenhouses
Gymnasiums
Health facilities—Architecture
Hillside architecture
Hospitals—Architecture
Hotels, motels, etc.—Architecture
Information storage and retrieval systems—Architectural use
Laboratories—Architecture
Lakeside architecture
Landscape architecture
Library architecture
Lodges
Metal construction
Office buildings—Architecture
Palaces
Pavilions
Plywood construction
Porticoes
Post office buildings
Prisons—Architecture
Pyramids
Roofs and roofing
School buildings
Stone construction
Tension structures
Terminals (Transportation)
Theater buildings
Towers
Vaults (Architecture)

Architecture—See also—*cont.*
    Visitor centers—Architecture
    Walls
    Wood construction
    Zoos—Buildings
Awards
See also
Pritzker Architecture Prize
Western Home Awards
The Aga Khan Award for Architecture 1986: "third-world myths and first-world fashions": a critical view. W. J. R. Curtis. il *Archit Rec* 175:104-5 Ja '87
A call for affirmative action: the 1986 winners of the Aga Khan Award for Architecture. il *Archit Rec* 175:94-103 Ja '87
Design awards/competitions. See issues of Architectural Record
House & Garden Design Awards [special section] il *House Gard* 159:140-61+ O '87
Record Houses 1987 [with introd. by Douglas Brenner] il *Archit Rec* 175:69-147 mid-Ap '87
Bibliography
Architecture. *Antiques* 131:170+ Ja '87
Architecture. P. Goldberger. il *N Y Times Book Rev* 92:22+ D 6 '87
Competitions
Design awards/competitions. See issues of Architectural Record
Conferences
Calendar. See issues of Architectural Record
Conservation and restoration
See also
    Barns and stables—Conservation and restoration
    Churches (Buildings)—Conservation and restoration
    Concert halls—Conservation and restoration
    Cottages, Restored
    Georgian Group
    Great American Salvage Company
    Historic houses, sites, etc.
    Hospitals—Conservation and restoration
    Houses, Restored
    Lighthouses—Conservation and restoration
    Railroads—Stations—Conservation and restoration
    Subway stations—Conservation and restoration
    Temples—Conservation and restoration
    Theater buildings—Conservation and restoration
    Villages, Restored
Eugene Viollet-le-Duc: restorer of France's architectural legacy. C. Styles-McLeod. il por *Archit Dig* 44:172+ Ag '87
Preservation and postmodernism: a common cause? M. F. Schmertz. *Archit Rec* 175:9 Je '87
To save the world we built [interview with J. M. Fitch] S. Rattner. il *Am Herit* 38:84-91 Ap '87
Designs and plans
See also
    Architectural drawing
    Architecture, Domestic—Designs and plans
Exhibitions
See also
    Architectural drawing—Exhibitions
    Architecture, Modern—Exhibitions
Calendar. See issues of Architectural Record
History
PW interviews [architectural historian M. Girouard] A. Smith. por *Publ Wkly* 232:55-6 D 4 '87
International aspects
Do you speak architecture? R. Lynes. il *Archit Dig* 44:30+ Ja '87
Periodicals
See also
    Architectural record (Periodical)
    Builder (Periodical)
Photographs and photography
See Photography, Architectural
Social aspects
See also
    Architecture and the handicapped
In the public interest: design guidelines. J. Barnett. il *Archit Rec* 175:114-25 Jl '87
Pro bono architecture in Appalachia and elsewhere [L. J. Currie and his staff provide free architectural services to the poor] M. F. Schmertz. *Archit Rec* 175:9 Mr '87
Study and teaching
See also
    Bauhaus
    National Institute for Architectural Education
The apprentice system: should it make a comeback? [views of J. F. Hartray] M. F. Schmertz. *Archit Rec* 175:9 N '87

Architectural education: drawing the line—graphics should clearly communicate design. T. Porter and G. Dombek. pors *Archit Rec* 175:45 My '87
The possibilities for research on architecture teaching. S. M. Dinham. bibl f por *Archit Rec* 175:41+ Ap '87
Alabama
See also
    Mobile (Ala.)—Architecture
Argentina
See also
    Buenos Aires (Argentina)—Architecture
Belgium
See also
    Brussels (Belgium)—Architecture
California
See also
    Beverly Hills (Calif.)—Architecture
    Del Mar (Calif.)—Architecture
    Hollywood (Calif.)—Architecture
    Los Angeles (Calif.)—Architecture
    Marina del Rey (Calif.)—Architecture
    Oakland (Calif.)—Architecture
    Saint Helena (Calif.)—Architecture
    Venice (Calif.)—Architecture
California Council 1987 Design Awards. il *Archit Rec* 175:60-3 Jl '87
Eric Owen Moss: watching his garden grow. K. D. Stein. il *Archit Rec* 175:51 Je '87
The Graves of wrath [M. Graves' design of Clos Pegase Winery in Napa Valley] D. Ketcham. il *Vogue* 177:110 Ap '87
A man who made architecture an art of the unexpected [F. Gehry] M. Webb. bibl (p162) il por *Smithsonian* 18:48-54+ Ap '87
Monterey 1987: glamour out, humanism back in [Monterey Design Conference] P. M. Sachner. il *Archit Rec* 175:57-8 Je '87
A shrine to wine [Clos Pegase, a Napa Valley winery designed by M. Graves] M. Filler. il *House Gard* 159:154-7+ S '87
Canada
Heavy metal [three buildings designed by IKOY Partnership] P. M. Sachner. il *Archit Rec* 175:126-35 My '87
Connecticut
See also
    Greenwich (Conn.)—Architecture
Connecticut Society of Architects 1986 Design Awards. il *Archit Rec* 175:74-5 My '87
Florida
See also
    Miami (Fla.)—Architecture
    Winter Park (Fla.)—Architecture
France
See also
    Saint-Paul-de-Vence (France)—Architecture
An architect's impressions of France. R. A. M. Stern. il por *Archit Dig* 44:234+ Je '87
Eugene Viollet-le-Duc: restorer of France's architectural legacy. C. Styles-McLeod. il por *Archit Dig* 44:172+ Ag '87
Germany (West)
See also
    Berlin (Germany: West)—Architecture
Great Britain
See also
    Headington (England)—Architecture
    London (England)—Architecture
Building bridges: George Godwin and architectural journalism. R. Thorne. bibl il por *Hist Today* 37:11-17 Ag '87
Hong Kong
How to keep the dragons happy [use of feng shui] H. G. Chua-Eoan. il *Time* 129:44 Je 22 '87
Illinois
See also
    Chicago (Ill.)—Architecture
    Wilmette (Ill.)—Architecture
India
See also
    Chandigarh (India)—Architecture
Japan
Japan is on the go. K. Andersen. il *Time* 130:68-70+ S 21 '87
The Japanese are coming (again). K.-H. Krüger. il *World Press Rev* 34:59 Ap '87
Kentucky
See also
    Lexington (Ky.)—Architecture

Architecture—*cont.*
Louisiana
See also
Alexandria (La.)—Architecture
Baton Rouge (La.)—Architecture
New Orleans (La.)—Architecture
Massachusetts
See also
Mattapoisett (Mass.)—Architecture
West Stockbridge (Mass.)—Architecture
Mexico
See also
San Miguel de Allende (Mexico)—Architecture
Xilitla (Mexico)—Architecture
Zihuatanejo (Mexico)—Architecture
Mississippi
See also
Jackson (Miss.)—Architecture
New England
New England Regional Council/AIA 1986 Awards for Design Excellence. il *Archit Rec* 175:68-9 F '87
New Mexico
See also
Santa Fe (N.M.)—Architecture
Taos (N.M.)—Architecture
New York (State)
See also
New York (N.Y.)—Architecture
Pennsylvania
See also
Ligonier (Pa.)—Architecture
Southern States
Bibliography
Books about the South. il *South Living* 22:140 S '87
Spain
See also
Barcelona (Spain)—Architecture
Tennessee
See also
Chattanooga (Tenn.)—Architecture
Texas
See also
Galveston (Tex.)—Architecture
Houston (Tex.)—Architecture
La Porte (Tex.)—Architecture
Ticino (Switzerland)
Architects of the Ticino [with editorial comment by Mildred F. Schmertz] D. Rastorfer. il *Archit Rec* 175:9, 110-27 Ap '87
Virginia
See also
Virginia Beach (Va.)—Architecture
Waterford (Va.)—Architecture
Architecture, American
Architects for the 1990s. B. Dumaine. il *Fortune* 115:152-5+ Je 22 '87
Exhibitions
Report from Paris: no small plans [exhibit entitled Chicago architecture, 1872-1922 at the Musée d'Orsay] K. D. Stein. il *Archit Rec* 175:69 N '87
Architecture, Baroque
The baroque [cover story; special issue] bibl il *Courier* 40:3-46+ S '87
Architecture, British
From old England to New England. J. Richardson. il *House Gard* 159:214-21+ N '87
Architecture, Classical
See also
Classicism in architecture
Neoclassicism (Architecture)
Architecture, Computer network *See* Computer network architecture
Architecture, Domestic
See also
Apartments
Architects
Beach architecture
Building, Adobe
Cabins
City houses
Condominiums
Cottages
Country estates
Decks, patios, terraces, etc.
Farmhouses
Garages
Guest houses
Halls
Hardware
Hillside architecture
House construction

Houses
Houses, Earth sheltered
Houses, Prefabricated
Houses, Remodeled
Houses, Round
Housing
Lakeside architecture
Lodges
Log cabins, houses, etc.
Model houses
Pergolas
Ranch houses
Row houses
Solar houses
Stone houses
Swimming pools, Home
Tea houses
Two family houses
Vacation houses
Today's architectural details. M. Walsh. il *Better Homes Gard* 65:54+ Ap '87
Designs and plans
8 prizewinning new houses. J. McCloskey and B. A. Lewis. il *Better Homes Gard* 65:41-50 F '87
Build our contemporary classic. il *South Living* 22:120 Jl '87
Canned house plans: well, what did you expect for $100? D. Moreau. il *Changing Times* 41:63+ Je '87
Carolina cottage. il *South Living* 22:142 F '87
The comforts of a colonial [cottage] il *South Living* 22:182 Ap '87
A cottage of sticks and stones [reprint from February 1982 issue] il *South Living* 22:124 Je '87
Country comforts in a brand-new American barn. il *Good Housekeep* 204:126-31 Mr '87
Garden view cottage. il *South Living* 22:88 Ja '87
Greek revival, vernacular style. il *South Living* 22:190 N '87
House of the month. See issues of Home Mechanix beginning July 1986
Innovation house. B. A. Lewis. il *Better Homes Gard* 65:29-36 Ag '87
Louisiana country house. il *South Living* 22:156 My '87
Record Houses 1987 [with introd. by Douglas Brenner] il *Archit Rec* 175:69-147 mid-Ap '87
Saddlebrook House. il *South Living* 22:148 S '87
A shingle-style cottage. il *South Living* 22:96 Ag '87
Simply southern. il *South Living* 22:106 D '87
A Texas-style farmhouse. il *South Living* 22:157 O '87
Environmental engineering
See Environmental engineering (Buildings)
Alabama
See also
Birmingham (Ala.)—Architecture
Mobile (Ala.)—Architecture
Barbados
Life at Heron Bay: Palladian pavilion on the island of Barbados [cover story] M. Tree. il *Archit Dig* 44:54-9+ Ag '87
Mango Bay: Pamela Harriman's residence on Barbados [designed and built by Oliver Messel] W. Walton. il *por Archit Dig* 44:84-9 Ja '87
A weekend with Claudette [home of C. Colbert] W. Walton. il *House Gard* 159:156-9+ Je '87
Belgium
See also
Brussels (Belgium)—Architecture
Villa civility [J. Crepain creates modern classical house for De Wachter family] C. Amery. il *House Gard* 159:184-9+ S '87
California
See also
Beverly Hills (Calif.)—Architecture
Del Mar (Calif.)—Architecture
Hollywood (Calif.)—Architecture
Los Angeles (Calif.)—Architecture
Malibu (Calif.)—Architecture
Marina del Rey (Calif.)—Architecture
Saint Helena (Calif.)—Architecture
San Diego (Calif.)—Architecture
Venice (Calif.)—Architecture
After Arcadia [three houses by R. W. Quigley] P. M. Sachner. il *Archit Rec* 175:138-49 Je '87
Architecture: Johannes Van Tilburg [home of Dr. and Mrs. William C. Janss, Jr. in the Santa Monica Mountains] J. Giovannini. il *Archit Dig* 44:136-42 F '87
Beaux arts in southern California [Resnick home] il *House Gard* 159:174-9+ D '87

Architecture, Domestic—California—*cont.*
Conquering a California hillside [work of architect Paul Gray, landscape architect Isabelle Greene, and owner] W. B. Logan. il *House Gard* 159:90-9+ Jl '87
Farmhouse for the 80s: open but energy-efficient. il *Sunset* 178:164-5 Ap '87
The next generation of "solar" houses. il *Sunset* 179:98-101 N '87
Wide open. il *Sunset* 178:82-5 Mr '87

Catskill Mountains region (N.Y.)
Little house in the mountains [architect M. Hann's hideaway] A. Gordon. il *House Gard* 159:100-3+ Ja '87

Colorado
See also
Aspen (Colo.)—Architecture
American heritage: Yankee art, western vistas [home of E. and L. Lauder] F. Stanfill. il pors *Vogue* 177:340-7+ Ap '87
By showing consumers how to save energy, Amory and Hunter Lovins put the (solar) heat on high-cost power. M. Small. il pors *People Wkly* 28:119-20+ O 19 '87

Connecticut
See also
Greenwich (Conn.)—Architecture
Brillig on the wave: island aerie of Nancy and Henry Luce III [summer house off Connecticut shore] C. T. Buckley. il pors *Archit Dig* 44:180-3+ My '87
Edwardian evocation [private residence] H. L. Smith, Jr. il *Archit Rec* 175:128-33 mid-Ap '87

Costa Brava (Spain)
Earth sheltered: blending with nature on the Costa Brava [home designed by F. J. Barba] N. Shrady. il *Archit Dig* 44:90-5 Ja '87

Dominican Republic
Pavilions in the sun [work of H. N. Jacobsen] W. Walton. il *House Gard* 159:118-25 D '87

Eleuthera Island (Bahamas)
Out-island builder [stone house] J. B. Gans. il map *Mother Earth News* 104:48-55 Mr/Ap '87

Fire Island (N.Y.)
Tree house retreat: a designer's Fire Island aerie [M. Dwork's house] P. Carlsen. il *Archit Dig* 44:60-5 Ag '87

Florida
See also
Winter Park (Fla.)—Architecture

France
See also
Saint-Paul-de-Vence (France)—Architecture
Building on the past [remodeled Provençal farmhouse of C. Confino-Addor] C. de Liagre. il *House Gard* 159:124-31+ Ag '87

Fripp Island (S.C.)
Lighthearted at the beach [cover story] L. Hallam. il *South Living* 22:70-2 Ag '87

Georgia
See also
Atlanta (Ga.)—Architecture
Saddlebrook House. il *South Living* 22:148 S '87

Great Britain
See also
Headington (England)—Architecture
London (England)—Architecture

Greece
Classical allusions: a hillside pavilion in Greece [designed by Hugh Newell Jacobsen] C. Aillaud. il *Archit Dig* 44:72-7 Jl '87

Illinois
See also
Wilmette (Ill.)—Architecture

Italy
A tower in Tuscany [home of G. and B. von Rezzori] B. Chatwin. il *House Gard* 159:78-85+ Ja '87

Japan
Builders of promise: seven Japanese architects worth watching. A. Isozaki. il *House Gard* 159:28+ Ja '87

Jordan
Architectural digest visits: King Hussein and Queen Noor of Jordan [beach house on Gulf of Aqaba] G. Y. Dryansky. il pors *Archit Dig* 44:68-77+ Ja '87

Kentucky
See also
Lexington (Ky.)—Architecture

Long Island (N.Y.)
Architectural digest visits: Paul Simon [summer home designed by Paul Krause] J. Thurman. il por *Archit Dig* 44:108-115 S '87
Architectural vigor of the summer enclave [the Hamptons] P. Goldberger. il *Archit Dig* 44:74+ Je '87

Hamptons homestead: the D. Ronald Daniels' converted barn. D. Harris. il *Archit Dig* 44:158-63 Je '87
Homes: an artless Victorian makes a perfect refuge [summer home of Chuck and Martha Baker] M. Bethany. il *N Y* 20:84-8 Je 29-Jl 6 '87

Louisiana
See also
Alexandria (La.)—Architecture
Baton Rouge (La.)—Architecture
New Orleans (La.)—Architecture
Louisiana country house. il *South Living* 22:156 My '87

Martha's Vineyard (Mass.)
Cottage by the sea: Maria Tallchief and Henry D. Paschen on Martha's Vineyard [home decorated by Bruce Gregga] J. Allen. il *Archit Dig* 44:170-5+ O '87
In the dunes [K. Cornell's summer home] C. Vogel. il *N Y Times Mag* p70-4 My 31 '87

Massachusetts
See also
Mattapoisett (Mass.)—Architecture
West Stockbridge (Mass.)—Architecture

Mexico
See also
Mexico City (Mexico)—Architecture
San Miguel de Allende (Mexico)—Architecture
Zihuatanejo (Mexico)—Architecture

Minnesota
Dean Brady: a house built in the north woods. P. S. Gelfman. il *Fam Handyman* 37:49 Ja '87
The house as art [F. Gehry's Winton guesthouse; cover story] M. Filler. il por *House Gard* 159:152-61+ O '87

Mississippi
See also
Jackson (Miss.)—Architecture
Three generations under one roof [lake house] il *South Living* 22:122-3 Jl '87

Montana
Cabin in the sky: a designer's retreat in the Montana Rockies [home of M. London] B. D. Colen. il por *Archit Dig* 44:132-9+ Je '87

New England
From old England to New England. J. Richardson. il *House Gard* 159:214-21+ N '87

New Hampshire
Architecture: David Sellers [design of rustic log house on Lake Winnipesaukee] V. J. Scully. il por *Archit Dig* 44:146-51+ Je '87

New Jersey
Architecture: Michael Graves [home of Thomas and Ingrid Plocek] C. Jencks. il por *Archit Dig* 44:138-45+ My '87

New Mexico
See also
Santa Fe (N.M.)—Architecture
Taos (N.M.)—Architecture

New York (State)
See also
East Hampton (N.Y.)—Architecture
Southampton (N.Y.)—Architecture
Staten Island (New York, N.Y.)—Architecture
Choice not chance [home designed and built for Ira Friedlander by Hadi Clements] il *Mother Earth News* 106:50-3 Jl/Ag '87
Classic modern [Westchester County home designed by R. Meier] C. Vogel. il *N Y Times Mag* p60-4 F 1 '87
The country set [William Diamond revives shingle style for Westchester house] E. Greene. il *House Gard* 159:162-9 D '87
Eminent domain [work of architect R. Meier] M. Filler. il *House Gard* 159:162-9+ Ap '87
A road less traveled: New York country haven of Marilynn and Ivan Karp. J. Kornbluth. il *Archit Dig* 44:196-203+ Je '87

New Zealand
Architecture: Ian Athfield: a residence for vintners in Hawkes Bay, New Zealand. F. FitzGerald. il por *Archit Dig* 44:78-83 Ja '87

Pennsylvania
See also
Ligonier (Pa.)—Architecture
A pastoral pavilion [work of R. Ferri] C. Amery. il *House Gard* 159:182-9+ My '87

Sea Island (Ga.)
Architecture: John C. Portman, Jr. [beach house; cover story] P. Goldberger. il por *Archit Dig* 44:98-111 D '87

Architecture, Domestic—*cont.*
Southern States
Build our contemporary classic. il *South Living* 22:120 Jl '87
Simply southern. il *South Living* 22:106 D '87
Switzerland
Chalet Balthus. J. Leymarie. il por *House Gard* 159:108-17 D '87
Tennessee
See also
Chattanooga (Tenn.)—Architecture
Texas
See also
Galveston (Tex.)—Architecture
Houston (Tex.)—Architecture
La Porte (Tex.)—Architecture
Together in the country [Foster family compound in the Texas Hill Country] E. Wood. il *South Living* 22:80-2 Ag '87
United States
See Architecture, Domestic
Vermont
North star: a shining presence in woodland Vermont [home designed by D. Coleman for Zeke and Emily Church] L. Atwill. il *Archit Dig* 44:154-7 Mr '87
Virginia
See also
Charlottesville (Va.)—Architecture
Virginia Beach (Va.)—Architecture
In Virginia: homes with gusto [built by architectural firm Jersey Devil] T. Brewster. il por *Time* 129:15+ Ap 27 '87
Kluckhuhns: a house built on a mountain lakeshore [Lake Anna] P. S. Gelfman. il *Fam Handyman* 37:47 Ja '87
Washington (State)
See also
Seattle (Wash.)—Architecture
Cushmans: a house built to overlook the ocean [Hat Island] P. S. Gelfman. il *Fam Handyman* 37:45 Ja '87
Western States
See also
Western Home Awards
Bibliography
What's different about a Western house? Three books show us. il *Sunset* 178:136-7 My '87
Architecture, Ecclesiastical *See* Churches (Buildings)
Architecture, French
French flavor in Napa: Provence style for a California house and winery [home of Lloyd and Elaine Cunningham in St. Helena] J. Chatfield-Taylor. il *Archit Dig* 44:140-5+ Je '87
Architecture, Georgian
See also
Georgian Group
Architecture, Gothic revival
Pugin & the medieval dream. N. Yates. bibl il *Hist Today* 37:33-40 S '87
Architecture, Greek revival
Greek revival, vernacular style. il *South Living* 22:190 N '87
Architecture, Islamic
The Aga Khan Award for Architecture 1986: "third-world myths and first-world fashions": a critical view. W. J. R. Curtis. il *Archit Rec* 175:104-5 Ja '87
A call for affirmative action: the 1986 winners of the Aga Khan Award for Architecture. il *Archit Rec* 175:94-103 Ja '87
Indigenous high-tech [Aga Khan University Hospital and Medical College, Karachi, Pakistan; cover story] M. F. Schmertz. il *Archit Rec* 175:136-49 My '87
Architecture, Mexican
Architecture: Ricardo Legorreta: the Los Angeles residence of Georgiana and Ricardo Montalban. C. Fuentes. il por *Archit Dig* 44:164-71+ Mr '87
Architecture, Modern
See also
Bauhaus
Neoclassicism (Architecture)
Late postmodern: the end of style. D. Davis. bibl f il *Art Am* 75:14-19+ Je '87
A man who made architecture an art of the unexpected [F. Gehry] M. Webb. bibl (p162) il por *Smithsonian* 18:48-54+ Ap '87
Preservation and postmodernism: a common cause? M. F. Schmertz. *Archit Rec* 175:9 Je '87
What's modern now [cover story] M. Bethany. il *N Y* 20:48-73 S 28 '87

Exhibitions
"Die Revision der Moderne": postmodernism on display at Williams College. J. V. Iovine. il *Archit Rec* 175:91 Je '87
Architecture, Portuguese
The stately heritage of Portuguese baroque. J.-A. França. il *Courier* 40:27-9 S '87
Architecture, Russian
A Russian teahouse: memories of St. Petersburg in Germany [built in Russia and moved to Kronberg over a century ago] J. Rykwert. il *Archit Dig* 44:164-7 Je '87
Architecture, Spanish American
Configuration for a canyon [B. Phelps's Arroyo House] T. S. Hines. il *Archit Dig* 44:166-9+ S '87
Architecture, Victorian
Blue Ridge variation: augmenting a house in the Virginia horse country [Queen Anne farmhouse addition by O'Neil & Manion] J. S. Wamsley. il *Archit Dig* 44:176-9 Ap '87
Galveston revival: Victorian gems amid castles of sand. C. Barrington. il *Travel Holiday* 168:54-9 D '87
Homes: an artless Victorian makes a perfect refuge [Long Island summer home of Chuck and Martha Baker] M. Bethany. il *N Y* 20:84-8 Je 29-Jl 6 '87
More gaudy ladies. J. O'Dwyer. il *Americana* 15:44-5 S/O '87
The new Victorians. L. J. Gallagher. il *Esquire* 108:42+ Ag '87
Social graces in Georgetown: Polly and Clayton Fritchey's Victorian enclave. S. M. Alsop. il pors *Archit Dig* 44:188-91 O '87
Architecture and climate
See also
Winter cities
Architecture and religion
Acts of faith [with introd. by Douglas Brenner] il *Archit Rec* 175:93-109 F '87
Architecture and the handicapped
Simple changes with a wheelchair in mind [kitchen] il *Sunset* 179:150 S '87
Architecture in art
The architecture of Charles Bulfinch on historical blue Staffordshire (II). H. Goldberg. bibl f il *Antiques* 131:434-43 F '87
Pen & ink: John Anderson. M. S. Doherty. il *Am Artist* 51:64-7 Ag '87
Architecture Studio (Firm)
A discourse of symbols: the recent work of Architecture Studio. T. Matthews. il *Archit Rec* 175:41 Ja '87
ARChive of Contemporary Music
One of each, please. B. Barol. il pors *Newsweek* 109:54-5 Ap 6 '87
Archives
See also
Ellington, Duke, 1899-1974—Archives
Farmer, James—Archives
King, Martin Luther, 1929-1968—Archives
National Security Archive
United States. National Archives and Records Administration
Williams, John Alfred, 1925——Archives
Archive [anniversary of the idea of linking archival training with humanities training] *New Yorker* 63:37 N 2 '87
Great Britain
A tale of two Cliffords. R. Hutton. il por *Hist Today* 37:8-9 Jl '87
Archives of American Art
Around the Mall and beyond. E. Park. *Smithsonian* 17:26+ Mr '87
Boxes full of art history. D. Grant. *Am Artist* 51:10+ S '87
Arcimboldo, Giuseppe, ca. 1527-1593
about
A man for each season. E. P. Williams. il *Vogue* 177:86 My '87
Sight gags. C. Hope. il *N Y Rev Books* 34:41-4 S 24 '87
ARCO *See* Atlantic Richfield Co.
Arcs (Astronomy)
Arcs, birth and a disk in the sky [arcs of light curving around clusters of galaxies] M. D. Lemonick. il *Time* 129:59 Ja 19 '87
The biggest mystery in the cosmos [luminous arcs between galaxies; work of Roger Lynds] B. Weber. il *N Y Times Mag* p70 Jl 19 '87
Birth announcements [disk of particles around Beta Pictoris; possible new radio galaxy 3C 326.1; luminous arcs encircling distant galaxies] *Sci Am* 256:60+ Mr '87

Arcs (Astronomy)—*cont.*
The giant arcs are gravitational mirages [theory of Roger Lynds and Vahe Petrosian] M. M. Waldrop. il *Science* 238:1351-2 D 4 '87
Giant galactic arcs [research by Roger Lynds and Vahe Petrosian] L. J. Robinson. il *Sky Telesc* 73:379 Ap '87
Luminous arcs discovered between galaxies [galactic clusters; research by Roger Lynds and Vahe Petrosian] D. E. Thomsen. il *Sci News* 131:36 Ja 17 '87
Luminous arcs dwarf the galaxies [research by Roger Lynds and Vahe Petrosian] M. M. Waldrop. il *Science* 235:631-2 F 6 '87
Ring around a gravitational lens [luminous arcs between galaxies; work of Vahe Petrosian and Roger Lynds] D. E. Thomsen. *Sci News* 132:326 N 21 '87
Arctic char fishing *See* Char fishing
Arctic exploration
 See also
  Franklin Expedition (1845)
  Peary Expeditions (1886-1909)
Ann Bancroft [first woman to reach North Pole by dogsled] S. Margolis. il pors *Ms* 15:71-2+ Ja '87
The Arctic adventures of Ann Bancroft. M. Specktor. il pors *McCalls* 114:101 Ja '87
Dog-sledder goes it alone [P. Flowers attempts solo trek from Ellsmere Island, Canada to North Pole] N. Klouda. il por *Women's Sports Fitness* 9:20 Mr '87
An epic Arctic journey [expedition retracing Inuit migration and demonstrating Canadian Arctic sovereignty; special section; with editorial comment by Kevin Doyle] il map *Macleans* 100:2, 20-8+ My 11 '87
Everything is North/Ann Bancroft [first woman to reach North Pole by dogsled] J. Kaplan. il por *Vogue* 177:452-3+ Mr '87
Over the Arctic ice cap [D. Shparo proposes Soviet-Canadian ski expedition] A. Steacy. il por *Macleans* 100:46-7 Ap 6 '87
Solo to the Pole [interview with J.-L. Etienne] il pors *Courier* 40:30-2 Je '87
Arctic National Wildlife Refuge (Alaska) *See* Wildlife sanctuaries—Alaska
Arctic Ocean
 See also
  Norwegian Sea
Arctic peoples
 See also
  Eskimos
  Lapps
Circumpolar contrasts. M. Nichols. il *Macleans* 100:30 My 11 '87
Arctic regions
 See also
  Alaska
  Birds—Arctic regions
  Northwest Passage
  Northwest Territories
  Paleontology—Arctic regions
  Skis and skiing—Arctic regions
  Yukon Territory
    Climate
Cloud conundrums [possible methane plumes in Soviet Arctic; cover story] S. Weisburd. il map *Sci News* 131:204-6 Mr 28 '87
Life upon the permafrost. F. Bruemmer. il *Nat Hist* 96:30-9 Ap '87
Probing the permafrost [work of Arthur H. Lachenbruch and B. Vaughn Marshall] il *Sci Am* 256:62 F '87
    Defenses
 See also
  Soviet Union—Navy—Forces in the Arctic
  United States. Air Force. Alaskan Air Command
Canada sees nuclear subs as key to Arctic defenses. il *Aviat Week Space Technol* 127:85+ S 21 '87
The Canadian Arctic is a new U.S.-Soviet hot spot. W. J. Holstein. il *Bus Week* p41 Ag 10 '87
    Industries
 See also
  Tourist trade—Arctic regions
Arden, Harvey
"The fire that never dies". il map *Natl Geogr* 172:370-403 S '87
Arden (Elizabeth) Inc. *See* Elizabeth Arden, Inc.
Ardennes, Battle of the, 1944-1945
Old castles and Old Glory: Luxembourg pays tribute to America. C. Males. il map *Travel Holiday* 168:34-41 D '87
Ardenwood Historic Farm
Antique chuggers at Fremont's farm. il *Sunset* 178:76 Ap '87

Arditi, Lynn
Fugitives from apartheid. il *Progressive* 51:32-4 Ap '87
Ardmore, Jane
"The sister I never knew I had saved my life". il por *Good Housekeep* 205:180+ S '87
Ardolino, Emile
    about
Dirty dancing [film] Reviews
 Dance Mag il 61:64 O '87. D. Towers
 Glamour 85:297-8 S '87. J. G. Boyum
 Macleans 100:50 Ag 24 '87. L. O'Toole
 N Y il 20:60-1 S 7 '87. D. Denby
 New Yorker il 63:79-80 Ag 24 '87. P. Kael
 People Wkly il 28:8 Ag 31 '87. T. Cunneff
 Time il 130:77 S 14 '87. R. Schickel
 Vogue il 177:64 Ag '87. M. Haskell
Are you lonesome tonight? [drama] *See* Bleasdale, Alan
Area measurement
 See also
  Surfaces—Areas and volumes
Area studies
 See also
  American studies
  Asian studies
  European studies
  Irish studies
  Latin American studies
  Soviet studies
Arecibo Observatory *See* Astronomical observatories—Puerto Rico
Arena football
New football league tabs black head coach for D.C. [B. Harrison] *Jet* 72:51 Je 8 '87
Reader's digest football. D. S. Looney. il *Sports Illus* 67:22-4 Jl 20 '87
    Economic aspects
A summertime fix for football fans. L. Therrien. il *Bus Week* p50 Ag 3 '87
Arenas, Sports *See* Stadiums
Arendash, Gary W., and others
Long-term neuropathological and neurochemical effects of nucleus basalis lesions in the rat. bibl f il *Science* 238:952-6 N 13 '87
Arens, W., 1940-
    about
Are the horrors of cannibalism fact—or fiction? G. Kolata. il por *Smithsonian* 17:150-2+ Mr '87
Areton, Lana
    about
How can Lana lose? An overweight teen and her family reach for help. J. Mason. il pors *Life* 10:34-8+ F '87
Aretsky, Ken
    about
Once it was Jack and Charlie's and now it's Ken and Anne's, but is it still the 21 Club? A. Richman. il pors *People Wkly* 27:49-50 My 25 '87
Arévalo, Vinicio Cerezo *See* Cerezo Arévalo, Vinicio
Argan, Giulio Carlo, 1909-
Three great domes. il *Courier* 40:10 S '87
Argenteuil (New York, N.Y.: Restaurant) *See* New York (N.Y.)—Restaurants, nightclubs, bars, etc.
Argentina
 See also
  Airlines—Routes—Argentina
  Argentines
  Astronomical observatories—Argentina
  Body snatching—Argentina
  Buenos Aires (Argentina)
  Civil rights—Argentina
  Eating—Argentina
  Genetic research—Argentina
  Investments, Argentine
  Loans, Bank—Argentina
  Missing children—Argentina
  Opera—Argentina
  Patagonia (Argentina and Chile)
  Resorts—Argentina
  San Carlos de Bariloche (Argentina)
  Skis and skiing—Argentina
  Trials—Argentina
    Air Force
Argentine Air Force drafts master plan for year 2000. il *Aviat Week Space Technol* 127:61 Ag 24 '87
    Army
Aftershock of the dirty war [military rebellion put down] H. Anderson. il por *Newsweek* 109:38-9 Ap 27 '87
Argentina: a test for Latin democracy. R. A. Kessler and others. *Bus Week* p49 My 4 '87
Argentina's mixed blessing. H. Anderson. il por *Newsweek* 109:36 My 4 '87

Argentina—Army—cont.

Argentine democracy: sign of contradiction. *America* 156:374-5 My 9 '87

Church and insurrection in Argentina. R. K. DeHainaut. *Christ Century* 104:582-3 Jl 1-8 '87

Facing down the army [failed coup attempt] A. McLeod. il por *Macleans* 100:31-2 My 4 '87

Fallout after a military mutiny. J. Greenwald. il *Time* 129:40 My 4 '87

Out of victory, defeat; or How to satisfy the generals [R. Alfonsín and army] C. A. Robbins. il por *U S News World Rep* 102:33 Je 15 '87

Commerce

United States

See United States—Commerce—Argentina

Defenses

See also

Airplanes, Military—Argentina

Description and travel

The new Argentina. L. Valenzuela. il *Vogue* 177:248+ Ap '87

¡Viva Argentina! L. B. Martin. il map *Travel Holiday* 167:50-5 Mr '87

Economic policy

Familiar tune [R. Alfonsín's austerity plan] il por *Time* 130:114 O 26 '87

A talk with Alfonsín: 'the debt cannot be paid'. J. Ryser and R. A. Kessler. por *Bus Week* p66 Je 22 '87

Foreign relations

Great Britain

See Great Britain—Foreign relations—Argentina

United States

See United States—Foreign relations—Argentina

Industries

See also

Fabrica Argentina de Material Aerospacial

Lineas Aereas del Estado (Argentina)

Tea industry—Argentina

Navy

Superpowers, stagnant economy influence Argentine Navy's recovery strategy. il *Aviat Week Space Technol* 127:49-50+ Ag 24 '87

Politics and government

See also

Elections—Argentina

Aftershock of the dirty war [military rebellion put down] H. Anderson. il por *Newsweek* 109:38-9 Ap 27 '87

Argentina: a test for Latin democracy. R. A. Kessler and others. *Bus Week* p49 My 4 '87

Argentina's mixed blessing. H. Anderson. il por *Newsweek* 109:36 My 4 '87

Argentine democracy: sign of contradiction. *America* 156:374-5 My 9 '87

Church and insurrection in Argentina. R. K. DeHainaut. *Christ Century* 104:582-3 Jl 1-8 '87

Closing the book. *Nation* 244:239-40 F 28 '87

"Democracy is not negotiable" [R. Alfonsín quells military rebellion] J. Smolowe. il por *Time* 129:39 Ap 27 '87

The dirty war's dirty laundry [human rights trials] F. Willey. il por *Newsweek* 109:40 F 23 '87

Facing down the army [failed coup attempt] A. McLeod. il por *Macleans* 100:31-2 My 4 '87

Fallout after a military mutiny. J. Greenwald. il *Time* 129:40 My 4 '87

Fitting justice to reality [prosecution of human rights violators] J. De Onis. il *U S News World Rep* 102:38 Ja 26 '87

Out of victory, defeat; or How to satisfy the generals [R. Alfonsín and army] C. A. Robbins. il por *U S News World Rep* 102:33 Je 15 '87

Readjusting to democracy in Argentina. G. W. Wynia. bibl f *Curr Hist* 86:5-8+ Ja '87

A talk with Alfonsín: 'the debt cannot be paid'. J. Ryser and R. A. Kessler. por *Bus Week* p66 Je 22 '87

Time out or time's up [R. Alfonsín's request for legislation that would free most of the military officers currently up on charges of human rights abuse] P. Lacefield. *Commonweal* 114:375-7 Je 19 '87

Torturers saved by the bell, almost [R. Alfonsin signs bill stopping the initiation of human rights abuse cases] D. L. Boroughs. il *Progressive* 51:13 Ap '87

Undue obedience [military officers convicted of human rights abuses granted amnesty] W. E. Smith. il *Time* 130:17 Jl 6 '87

Religious institutions and affairs

See also

Catholic Church—Argentina

Evangelical churches—Argentina

Argentine cooking *See* Cooking, Argentine

Argentines

France

History

Dance-floor democracy [1846; excerpt from Travels] D. F. Sarmiento. il *Courier* 40:30 Ap '87

Argento, Dominick

about

Christopher Sly [opera] Reviews

N Y il 20:89-90 F 9 '87. P. G. Davis

Arginine

On the mend with arginine. H. Fisher. *Prevention* 39:98+ O '87

Arginine deiminase *See* Hydrolases

Argiope spiders *See* Spiders

Argo Communications Corporation

Francesco Galesi isn't used to losing. P. Finch. il por *Bus Week* p114 My 4 '87

Argo-Jason (Submarine) *See* Oceanographic submersibles

Argon-potassium dating *See* Radioactive dating

Argonne National Laboratory

Key decision nears on proposed Argonne photon source. W. Sweet. *Phys Today* 40:71 Ja '87

Argrave, Truvy

about

Nightmare in the hayfield. P. Michelmore. il *Read Dig* 130:64-9 Je '87

Arguedas, José María

about

José María Arguedas: godfather of liberationism. S. B. Wall-Smith. *Christ Century* 104:1034-9 N 18 '87

Arguello, Maryam

about

A young Sandinista's effort to serve her nation. J. Lantigua. il por *Sch Update* 119:17 Mr 9 '87

Argument

Le nouveau canard [accusations of bigotry used as ad hominem argument by liberals] J. Sobran. *Natl Rev* 39:44-5+ F 13 '87

Argument (Psychology) *See* Quarrels

Argyros, George L.

about

A winning gambit on a losing team. J. Flynn. il por *Bus Week* p102 My 4 '87

Ariadne Australia Ltd.

Bruce Judge: Simon's kindred spirit from Down Under. C. Debes. por *Bus Week* p86 Mr 9 '87

Ariail, Jacqueline

The mother next door [story] il *Redbook* 168:46-8+ F '87

Ariane (Launch vehicle) *See* Space vehicles—Propulsion systems

Arianespace

Ariane launch teams complete training. il *Aviat Week Space Technol* 127:67 N 2 '87

Arianespace moves to cut costs, improve management of boosters. J. M. Lenorovitz. il *Aviat Week Space Technol* 127:63-4 O 12 '87

Arias, Juan

Recovering Michelangelo's true colors. *World Press Rev* 34:60 Ap '87

Arias, Susana

about

The primitive intuitive being. V. G. Stoddart. il por *Américas* 39:55-7 S/O '87

Arias

See also

Compact discs—Arias

Phonograph records—Arias

Arias Calderón, Ricardo

Panama: disaster or democracy. bibl f *Foreign Aff* 66:328-47 Wint '87/'88

Arias Sanchez, Oscar

Visit of Costa Rican president [remarks, December 4, 1986] il por map *Dep State Bull* 87:56-7 Mr '87

about

Blessed are the peacemakers. *America* 157:283-4 O 31 '87

Costa Rica's Arias at midterm. L. Gudmundson. bibl f *Curr Hist* 86:417-20+ D '87

Golden opportunity for Don Oscar. J. Smolowe. il por *Time* 130:44+ O 26 '87

The hole in the summit agenda. M. Kramer. il *U S News World Rep* 103:40 D 21 '87

Leaning on Arias. M. Honey and T. Avirgan. *Nation* 245:220-1 S 12 '87

More than a peacemaker. J. S. Fuerst. il *Commonweal* 114:701-3 D 4 '87

The Nobel difference. H. Anderson. il por *Newsweek* 110:44+ O 26 '87

Arias Sanchez, Oscar—about—*cont.*
Nobel winner Oscar Arias makes Costa Rica the mouse that roars for peace in Central America. M. Brower. il pors *People Wkly* 28:57-8+ N 9 '87
Oscar's Nobel. M. Kondracke. *New Repub* 197:14-16 N 9 '87
Potholes on the road to peace [with interview] J. Smolowe. il por *Time* 129:34+ Je 29 '87
Whose peace plan is it anyway? J. Smolowe. por *Time* 130:34 S 28 '87
        Visit to the United States, 1986
Visit of Costa Rican president [remarks, December 4, 1986] R. Reagan; O. Arias Sanchez. il por map *Dep State Bull* 87:56-7 Mr '87
        Visit to the United States, 1987
Speaking his peace. J. Smolowe. il por *Time* 130:34-5 O 5 '87
Arid regions
        See also
        Deserts
Arid and semi-arid zones. il *Courier* 40:15 O '87
Beating the odds in arid Africa [Turkana of Kenya] J. T. McCabe and J. E. Ellis. il map *Nat Hist* 96:32-41 Ja '87
Ariel Capital Management Inc.
A jock shows how to scout for small stocks that can score [J. Rogers] D. M. Topolnicki. il por *Money* 16:224 My '87
Aries (Constellation) *See* Constellations
Arikha, Avigdor, 1929-
        about
Profiles. D. Hofstadter. il *New Yorker* 63:37-40+ Je 1 '87
Arinc Inc.
Arinc files request to deploy AvSat communications system. P. J. Klass. map *Aviat Week Space Technol* 126:50+ Ap 27 '87
Arinc to initiate space service with leased satellites. *Aviat Week Space Technol* 127:47 D 7 '87
FCC rejects Arinc proposal to form global aviation satellite system. P. J. Klass. *Aviat Week Space Technol* 127:27 S 21 '87
Aristech Chemical Corporation
Good chemistry. J. Flint. *Forbes* 139:274 Je 15 '87
Aristide, Jean-Bertrand
        about
The priest who fights the regime [cover story] A. Wilentz. *Nation* 245:217+ S 12 '87
Aristides *See* Epstein, Joseph
The aristocats [film] *See* Motion picture reviews—Single works
Aristocracy
        See also
        Elite (Social sciences)
        Nobility
Arita, Isao
Progress in the right direction. il *World Health* p12-13 Ag/S '87
Arithmetic
        See also
        Floating-point arithmetic
        Fractions
        Study and teaching
        Aids and devices
Fractions as fun [board games] il *Sunset* 179:125-6 O '87
Arithmetic ability *See* Mathematical ability
Ariyoshi, Rita
Kauai in bloom. il map *Travel Holiday* 168:42-9 S '87
Arizona
        See also
        Birds—Arizona
        Booksellers and bookselling—Arizona
        Camps—Arizona
        Colorado Plateau
        Colorado River (Colo.-Mexico)
        Education—Arizona
        Geology—Arizona
        Grand Canyon (Ariz.)
        Grand Canyon National Park (Ariz.)
        Hunting—Arizona
        Lake Powell (Utah and Ariz.)
        Lakes—Arizona
        Mount Graham (Ariz.)
        Paleontology—Arizona
        Public lands—Arizona
        Resorts—Arizona
        Sonoran Desert
        Sycamore Canyon (Ariz.)
        Vegetable gardens and gardening—Arizona

        Verde River (Ariz.)
        Wilderness areas—Arizona
        Wildlife—Arizona
        Wildlife sanctuaries—Arizona
        Yavapai County (Ariz.)
        Description and travel
Amazing canyon country. G. S. Bush. il map *Better Homes Gard* 65:128+ Je '87
On the 300-year-old trail of Father Kino. il map *Sunset* 179:52+ O '87
Wandering along Arizona's copper trail. il map *Sunset* 178:58+ Mr '87
        Politics and government
Arizona airhead [Gov. E. Mecham] P. Goudinoff and S. Tobias. *New Repub* 197:15-16 O 26 '87
Arizona's outspoken new governor, Evan Mecham, seems to enjoy diving straight into political hot water. D. Chu. il por *People Wkly* 28:39-40 Ag 24 '87
At odds in Arizona [Gov. E. Mecham] S. L. Hawkins. il por *U S News World Rep* 102:26 Mr 23 '87
Evan Mecham, please go home [recall campaign] J. D. Hull. il por *Time* 130:61 N 9 '87
A land rush—or the bum's rush? [Gov. E. Mecham faces recall] D. Gates. il por *Newsweek* 110:10 O 12 '87
No rebates [growing effort to recall Gov. E. Mecham] por *Time* 129:42 Mr 9 '87
Shooting from the lip [Governor E. Mecham] C. O'Connor. il por *Newsweek* 109:31 F 9 '87
Up in arms in Arizona [Gov. E. Mecham] A. Weisman. il por *N Y Times Mag* p50-1+ N 1 '87
When Evan Mecham talks, Arizona shudders. R. Grover. il por *Bus Week* p110+ S 28 '87
        Caricatures and cartoons
'Doonesbury' in Arizona [depiction of Governor E. Mecham] il *Newsweek* 110:41 S 14 '87
        Race relations
Ariz. gov. nixes King Day; Wonder snubs the state. *Jet* 71:60 F 9 '87
Arizona gov. stirs rift by denying racial slur [E. Mecham] *Jet* 72:29 Ap 13 '87
Arizona gov. vows to repeal King holiday [E. Mecham] *Jet* 71:37 Ja 19 '87
Arizona gov's stance on King holiday may cost state $18 million loss. *Jet* 72:36 Je 22 '87
Arizona house passes King Day legislation. *Jet* 71:4 Mr 9 '87
Arizona loses NBNA confab [National Black Nurses Association] A. Edmond, Jr. il *Black Enterp* 17:62 Je '87
Arizona observes King holiday despite repeal of state bill by governor. *Jet* 71:12 F 2 '87
Black publishers pull out of Arizona confab [protest against repeal of Martin Luther King Day] *Jet* 71:8 F 9 '87
Critics: Mecham's offer to honor Martin Luther King is unacceptable. *Jet* 72:12 Jl 6 '87
Foreman nixes Arizona for heavyweight bout. il por *Jet* 73:51 N 16 '87
Governor's stance on King holiday stirs controversy in Arizona: tempers flare. W. Wofford, Jr. il por *Jet* 73:24-6 N 2 '87
Group wants recall of Arizona Gov. Mecham; NBA cancels meeting. *Jet* 72:14 Jl 27 '87
Vandross cancels Phoenix concerts to protest Ariz. snubbing of King holiday. por *Jet* 72:53 Je 15 '87
Arizona 206 (New York, N.Y.: Restaurant) *See* New York (N.Y.)—Restaurants, nightclubs, bars, etc.
Arizona Opera Company
Ringleader for opera [G. Ross] K. Milam. il por *Horizon* 30:48 My '87
Arizona Theatre Company
Focus on excellence. G. Chow. il *Horizon* 30:44 My '87
Arkansas
        See also
        Black River (Ark. and Mo.)
        Blacks—Arkansas
        Botany—Arkansas
        Crowley's Ridge (Ark. and Mo.)
        Norfork Lake (Ark.)
        Ozark Mountains region
        Saint Francis National Forest (Ark.)
Arkansas. State Highway Commission
Black appointed to Ark. Highway Commission, hired by Arkansas State Univ. [R. Slater] *Jet* 72:15 Ap 13 '87
Rodney Slater, 32, Ark. gov's ex-staffer, gets university post. por *Jet* 72:30 My 18 '87
Arkansas Best Corp.
Most improved. il *Forbes* 139:211 Ja 12 '87

Arkansas Racing Commission
  Black appointed racing commissioner in Arkansas [G. Hammons] *Jet* 71:17 F 16 '87
Arkansas State University
  Black appointed to Ark. Highway Commission, hired by Arkansas State Univ. [R. Slater] *Jet* 72:15 Ap 13 '87
  Rodney Slater, 32, Ark. gov's ex-staffer, gets university post. por *Jet* 72:30 My 18 '87
Arkes, Hadley
about
  John XXIII and the hand grenade. R. J. Neuhaus. *Natl Rev* 39:51 S 25 '87
Arkin, William M.
  General Nutting and the invaders. *Bull At Sci* 43:6-7 Ja/F '87
  Greece's balancing act. *Bull At Sci* 43:11-12 Mr '87
  Happy birthday, flexible response. *Bull At Sci* 43:5-6 D '87
  Long on data, short on intelligence. il *Bull At Sci* 43:5-6 Je '87
  Navy autonomy thwarts arms control. bibl f il *Bull At Sci* 43:14-18 S '87
  Pentagon banking on Castro phobia. *Bull At Sci* 43:4-5 My '87
  Red herring in the Pacific. *Bull At Sci* 43:6-7 Ap '87
Arking, Linda
  Searching for a very special woman. *McCalls* 114:55-6 Je '87
Arledge, Roone
about
  Friends in high places. B. Yagoda. il pors *Channels* 7:54-61 Ja '87
  A relish for risks. H. F. Waters. il por *Newsweek* 109:59 Je 15 '87
Arline, Gene
about
  Black TB victim in Fla. wins fight for her job. *Jet* 72:39 Mr 30 '87
Arlington National Cemetery (Va.)
  Matthew Henson will be reburied in Arlington. por *Jet* 73:26 N 23 '87
Arm, Artificial
  Maimed in a terrible accident, Minnesota farm boy David Virnig boldly faces life without arms. D. Chu. il pors *People Wkly* 28:67-8 O 19 '87
Arm exercises *See* Exercise
Arm wrestling
  In Florida: "Lock up!" and the pulse pounds [Southern States International Arm Wrestling Council championships] P. Jordan. il *Time* 130:14+ N 2 '87
Armacost, Michael H.
  The Philippines and the United States [address, October 6, 1986] *Dep State Bull* 86:52-5 D '86
  Refugee situation in Southern Africa [statement, February 5, 1987] map *Dep State Bull* 87:65-7 My '87
  South Asia and the United States: an evolving partnership [address, April 29, 1987] map *Dep State Bull* 87:75-80 Jl '87
  The U.S. and Southern Africa: a current appraisal [address, June 15, 1987] *Dep State Bull* 87:47-50 Ag '87
  U.S. foreign policy achievements and challenges [address, October 18, 1986] *Dep State Bull* 87:61-4 Ja '87
  The U.S., Japan, and Asian Pacific security in perspective [address, May 29, 1987] *Dep State Bull* 87:51-6 Ag '87
  U.S. national interest and the budget crisis [address, May 7, 1987] *Dep State Bull* 87:43-5 S '87
  U.S. policy in the Persian Gulf and Kuwaiti reflagging [statement, June 16, 1987] *Dep State Bull* 87:78-81 Ag '87
  U.S. policy toward the third world [address, October 17, 1986] *Dep State Bull* 87:56-60 Ja '87
  U.S.-Soviet relations: coping with conflicts in the third world [address, September 26, 1986] *Dep State Bull* 86:57-61 D '86
  U.S.-Soviet relations: testing Gorbachev's "new thinking" [address, July 1, 1987] *Dep State Bull* 87:36-41 S '87
about
  Under Secretary Armacost's interview on "Meet the press" [transcript of program, August 30, 1987] *Dep State Bull* 87:32-4 O '87
Armacost, Samuel H., 1939-
about
  The most beleaguered banker. G. Hector. il por *Fortune* 115:86 Ja 5 '87

Armament industries *See* Munitions
Armaments
See also
  Airplanes, Military—Armaments
  Disarmament
  Militarism
  Munitions
Armandt, Lynn
about
  Chronicle of a ruinous affair. M. Green. il pors *People Wkly* 27:104-8 Je 15 '87
Armbrister, Trevor
  This Connecticut Yankee cares. il pors *Read Dig* 130:131-5 F '87
  We can conquer cocaine. il *Read Dig* 130:63-8 F '87
Armed Forces
See also
  Canada—Armed Forces
  Germany (West)—Armed Forces
  Great Britain—Armed Forces
  Israel—Armed Forces
  Japan—Armed Forces
  Mercenary troops
  National service
  Philippines—Armed Forces
  Soviet Union—Armed Forces
  Syria—Armed Forces
  United States—Armed Forces
Appropriations and expenditures
  A stark tally of defense spending run rampant. G. Koretz. il *Bus Week* p30 D 21 '87
Armed Forces Radio and Television Service (U.S.) *See* United States. Armed Forces Radio and Television Service
Armed Services Committee (House) *See* United States. Congress. House. Committee on Armed Services
Armed Services Committee (Senate) *See* United States. Congress. Senate. Committee on Armed Services
Armgard, Beatrix Wilhelmina *See* Beatrix, Queen of the Netherlands, 1938-
Armies
See also
  Argentina—Army
  Brazil—Army
  France—Army
  India—Army
  Nicaragua—Army
  Philippines—Army
  Soviet Union—Army
  United States. Army
Armitage, Karole
about
  Armitage's brazen classicism. L. A. Jacobs. *New Leader* 70:21-2 F 9-23 '87
  Artsmart. il *Harpers Bazaar* 120:164+ Ja '87
Dancing:
  Performances of The tarnished angels and The Elizabethan phrasing. A. Croce. *New Yorker* 63:104-5 D 21 '87
  Karole Armitage & David Salle. S. Allison. il pors *Life* 10:104-6+ N '87
  Postmodernism on its toes. E. Kendall. il pors *Vogue* 177:42 Ja '87
Reviews:
  Performances at the Joyce Theater, New York City. O. Stuart. *Dance Mag* 61:189-91 Je '87
  Signs of the times. T. Tobias. il *N Y* 20:155-6 D 7 '87
Armitage Ballet
  Armitage's brazen classicism. L. A. Jacobs. *New Leader* 70:21-2 F 9-23 '87
Dancing:
  Performances of The tarnished angels and The Elizabethan phrasing. A. Croce. *New Yorker* 63:104-5 D 21 '87
Reviews:
  Performances at the Joyce Theater, New York City. O. Stuart. *Dance Mag* 61:189-91 Je '87
  Signs of the times [performances at the Brooklyn Academy of Music] T. Tobias. il *N Y* 20:155-6 D 7 '87
Armoires
  A gentleman's wardrobe. N. Barrett, Jr. il *Pop Mech* 164:86-90 Mr '87
  Low-cost armoire. D. R. Berger. il *Workbench* 43:92-5 Mr/Ap '87
Armored tanks, Military *See* Tanks, Military
Arms, Robotic *See* Manipulators (Mechanism)
ARMs (Adjustable rate mortgages) *See* Mortgages
Arms and armor
See also
  Slingshots and slingshooting

Arms and armor—*cont.*
Create armour from junkyard scrap [theater costumes]
P. McCrory. il *Theatre Crafts* 21:66 F '87
One-way armor. N. J. Freundlich. il *Pop Sci* 231:38
S '87
Arms control *See* Disarmament
Arms Control and Disarmament Agency (U.S.) *See* United
States. Arms Control and Disarmament Agency
Arms race *See* Nuclear weapons
Arms smuggling *See* Smuggling
Arms trade *See* Munitions—Export-import trade
Armstrong, Clay M., and Lopez-Barneo, Jose
External calcium ions are required for potassium channel
gating in squid neurons. bibl f il *Science* 236:712-14
My 8 '87
Armstrong, Jeffrey *See* Saint Silicon
Armstrong, Neil, 1930-, and Aldrin, Edwin E.
The first men on the moon [remarks made after setting
foot on moon, July 1969] il *Courier* 40:10 Ap '87
Armstrong, Scott
about
Must reading. il por *Time* 129:29 Je 1 '87
Armstrong-Jones, Tony *See* Snowdon, Antony Armstrong-
Jones, Earl of, 1930-
Army Air Forces (U.S.) *See* United States. Army Air
Forces
Army Aviation Systems Command (U.S.) *See* United States.
Army Aviation Systems Command
Army Engineer Corps *See* United States. Army. Corps
of Engineers
Army Reserve (U.S.) *See* United States. Army Reserve
Armyworms
Control
Flies to the rescue [maggots of Archytas marmoratus
feed on corn earworms and fall armyworms; work
of Robert D. Jackson] il *USA Today (Periodical)* 115:7-8
Je '87
Arn, Win
Is TV appropriate for mass evangelism? por *Christ Today*
31:50 O 16 '87
Arnault, Bernard
about
The marriage of high finance and high fashion. F. J.
Comes. il por *Bus Week* p59 F 23 '87
Arnaz, Desi, Jr.
about
A TV child grows up. M. Cooper. il por *Macleans*
100:8 Ja 19 '87
Arndt, Kim T., and others
Multiple global regulators control HIS4 transcription in
yeast. bibl f il *Science* 237:874-80 Ag 21 '87
Arneson, Robert, 1930-
about
Robert Arneson. C. Santiago. il *Art News* 86:55+ My
'87
Arnhem, Battle of, 1944
The last disaster of the war [Operation Market Garden]
B. E. Urquhart. il *N Y Rev Books* 34:27-30 S 24
'87
Arnold, Benedict, 1741-1801
about
Could Canada have ever been our Fourteenth Colony?
[cover story] E. Park. bibl (p204) il map *Smithsonian*
18:40-9 D '87
Arnold, Duane W. H.
The significance of Augustine. il por *Christ Today* 31:22
D 11 '87
Arnold, Eve
I remember Norma Jean [excerpt from Marilyn Monroe]
il pors *People Wkly* 28:72-4+ Ag 10 '87
Arnold, Genevieve H., and Biggers, Vicki
One community's response to the dropout problem. *Phi
Delta Kappan* 68:708-9 My '87
Arnold, Matthew, 1822-1888
about
The good, the true, the beautiful. J. Hart. *Natl Rev*
39:46 Mr 27 '87
Arnold, Patrick M.
The rise of Catholic fundamentalism. il *America*
156:297-302 Ap 11 '87
Arnold, Terrell E.
The king is hostage. il *Natl Rev* 39:34-6+ Ap 10 '87
Arnosky, Jim
about
Watching the artist watch nature. K. O. Fakih. il por
Publ Wkly 231:43-4 My 29 '87
Arnott, Ann
Home news. See issues of McCall's beginning March
1986
Timesavers, funmakers: star-quality kitchen toys for
cooks. il *Work Woman* 12:172+ My '87

Arnout, Susan
What makes love last. il pors *McCalls* 114:166+ F '87
**Arnove, Robert F. (Robert Frederick), and Graff, Harvey
J.**
National literacy campaigns: historical and comparative
lessons. bibl f il *Phi Delta Kappan* 69:202-6 N '87
Arns, Paulo Evaristo, Cardinal
about
A miracle, a universe (I). L. Weschler. *New Yorker*
63:69-84+ My 25 '87
A miracle, a universe (II). L. Weschler. *New Yorker*
63:72-80+ Je 1 '87
Aroma therapy
Aromatherapy: the new tension prevention. il
Mademoiselle 93:34 O '87
What kind of therapy smells? J. Adler. il *Newsweek*
109:62 Mr 2 '87
Aromas *See* Odors
Aromatic compounds
See also
Benzoates
Aromatic cross-links in insect cuticle: detection by solid-
state ^{13}C and ^{15}N NMR. J. Schaefer and others. bibl
f il *Science* 235:1200-4 Mr 6 '87
Assemblage of ortho cleavage route for simultaneous
degradation of chloro- and methylaromatics. F. Rojo
and others. bibl f il *Science* 238:1395-8 D 4 '87
Aromatic hydrocarbons *See* Hydrocarbons
Aron, Laurie Joan
An unexpected gift. il *McCalls* 115:70 N '87
Aron (Jane Baerwald) Art Center *See* Jane Baerwald Aron
Art Center
Aronoff, Stanley J.
State and local arts agencies: doing what they do best.
Des Arts Educ 88:23-4 N/D '86
Aronow, Donald Joel
about
Don Aronow's murder leaves Miami wondering: were
'Cigarettes' hazardous to his health? J. Hammer. il
por *People Wkly* 27:75-6+ Mr 30 '87
Obituary
Mot Boat Sail il por 159:11+ Ap '87. P. A. Janssen
Aronsfeld, C. C.
Ernst Lissauer and the Hymn of hate. bibl il por *Hist
Today* 37:48-50 D '87
Spain's returning Jews. bibl il *Hist Today* 37:38-43 Je
'87
Aronson, Boris
about
He made the stage come alive. F. Rich and L. Aronson.
il por *N Y Times Mag* p52-4+ O 11 '87
Aronson, Lisa
(jt. auth) See Rich, Frank, and Aronson, Lisa
Aronson, Steven M. L.
Back country Greenwich. il *House Gard* 159:132-9+ Ag
'87
Classical cool. il por *House Gard* 159:100-11+ Mr '87
The collectors: a rare aesthetic: Stuart Pivar's cornucopia
of art in Manhattan. il *Archit Dig* 44:124-31+ Mr
'87
An elemental attraction. il *Archit Dig* 44:216-21 N '87
Golden threads. il por *House Gard* 159:20+ O '87
Night lights. il *House Gard* 159:56+ F '87
Possession obsession. il por *House Gard* 159:186-96 D
'87
A practiced eye: J. Garvin Mecking in Greenwich Village.
il *Archit Dig* 44:156-63+ Ap '87
Return to romance: Linda and Steve Horn's Manhattan
penthouse. il por *Archit Dig* 44:122-7+ O '87
Sylvan cider mill: Jean and Harcourt Amory's Westchester
Hills restoration. il *Archit Dig* 44:204-8+ Je '87
Visual intrigue. il pors *Archit Dig* 44:228-32+ N '87
Around the world flights *See* Aviation—World flights
Around the world voyages *See* Voyages around the world
Around the world yacht races *See* Yacht racing
Arp, Hans *See* Arp, Jean, 1887-1966
Arp, Jean, 1887-1966
about
Modern Arp: the Boston Museum shows a playful Dada.
J. Perl. il *Vogue* 177:52 Jl '87
The world according to Arp. M. Stevens. il *Newsweek*
110:64 Ag 24 '87
Arpino, Gerald
about
Clowns [ballet] Reviews
Dance Mag 61:26+ N '87. A. Barzel
Arquette, Patricia
about
A new Arquette is Daddy's pregnant little girl. il por
People Wkly 27:115 Ap 13 '87

Arquitectonica International Corporation
Bernardo Fort-Brescia and Laurinda Spear: the iconoclasts. B. Dumaine. il pors *Fortune* 115:152-3 Je 22 '87

Arra, Ron
about
Surfcasting with a home-run swing. J. Skorupa. il por *Pop Mech* 164:59 N '87

Arrandale, Tom
No peace on the Pueblo. il *Sierra* 72:30-3 Mr/Ap '87

Arrangement of flowers See Flower arrangement

Arrest
See also
Preventive detention
Spouse beaters—the handcuff cure. *U S News World Rep* 102:12 Mr 2 '87

Arrest records See Criminal records

Arrhythmia
Therapy
See also
Defibrillators

Arriza, Jeffrey L., and others
Cloning of human mineralocorticoid receptor complementary DNA: structural and functional kinship with the glucocorticoid receptor. bibl f il *Science* 237:268-75 Jl 17 '87

Arrow Dynamics, Inc.
All aboard! K. Hannon. il por *Forbes* 140:96-8 Ag 10 '87

Arrowhead Country Forage Council
Indiana's Arrowhead Country Forage Council on fast track. il *Success Farm* 85:D1 My '87

Arrowhead Drinking Water Company
Perrier's unquenchable U.S. thirst. J. Rossant. *Bus Week* p46 Je 29 '87

Arroyo, Joker
about
The Joker was not laughing. H. G. Chua-Eoan. il por *Time* 130:37 S 21 '87

Arruza, Tony
Less is more. il *Pop Photogr* 94:38-43 Ap '87

Arscott, Caroline
(jt. auth) See Wolff, Janet, and Arscott, Caroline

Arsenides
See also
Gallium arsenide

Arson
See also
Insurance, Fire
Anatomy of a hate campaign [Ray family burned out of home because of fear of AIDS in Arcadia, Fla.] W. Plummer. il *People Wkly* 28:32-7 S 14 '87
Arson: a chemical fire? [arsonists' lower levels of serotonin; research by Matti Virkkunen and Markku Linnoila] J. Fischman. *Psychol Today* 21:18 Jl '87
The castaways: fears about AIDS drive three boys from home [Ray family burned out of home in Arcadia, Fla.] M. Voboril. il *Life* 10:98-100 O '87
D.C. mayor's mother-in-law pleads guilty to arson [P. L. Harris] *Jet* 72:8 Jl 13 '87
Death in a towering inferno [Dupont Plaza hotel in San Juan, Puerto Rico] B. Levin. il *Macleans* 100:16-19 Ja 12 '87
"A New Year we'll never forget" [fire at Dupont Plaza, San Juan] A. Wilentz. il map *Time* 129:19-20 Ja 12 '87
San Juan's towering inferno [Dupont Plaza hotel] G. Hackett. il *Newsweek* 109:24 Ja 12 '87
Search for a firebug [Charlottetown, P.E.I.] A. Steacy. *Macleans* 100:46 Ag 10 '87
Trial by fire [University of Michigan law student J. Picozzi accused of arson] T. Senger. il *Roll Stone* p111-12+ S 24 '87
White man gets 6 years for arson to blacks' home [K. Falk of Chicago] *Jet* 72:33 Ap 27 '87

Art
See also
Aesthetics
Anatomy, Artistic
Art deco
Art nouveau
Artists
Arts
Arts and crafts
Arts and crafts movement
Bronzes
Caricatures and cartoons
Children's art
Christian art and symbolism
Classicism in art
Computers—Art use

Copyright—Art
Costume
Cubism
Decoration and ornament
Design
Drawing
Figurative art
Folk art
Frescoes
Graffiti
Illumination of books and manuscripts
Illustration
Image processing—Art use
Impressionism (Art)
Inflatable art
Information storage and retrieval systems—Art use
Landscape drawing
Landscape painting
Light in art
Mannerism (Art)
Miniature painting
Mural painting and decoration
National socialism and art
Painting
Pastel drawing
Pen drawing
Photocopying—Art use
Photography, Artistic
Posters
Pottery
Public art
Publishers and publishing—Art
Realism in art
Robots—Art use
Santos (Art)
Sculpture
Style, Artistic
Television broadcasting—Art programs
Underwater art
Video art
Videodiscs—Art
Videotapes—Art use
Watercolor painting
The art world. C. Tomkins. See occasional issues of The New Yorker
The Vasari diary. Vasari. See issues of Art News
Appreciation
See also
Art critics and criticism
Is there recognition after death? D. Grant. *Am Artist* 51:70-3 Jl '87
Moonlight in the Brooklyn Museum [painting by R. A. Blakelock] P. Auster. il *Art News* 86:104-5 S '87
Archives
See also
Archives of American Art
Bibliography
Art. J. Russell. il *N Y Times Book Rev* 92:11-12 My 31 '87
Art. J. Russell. il *N Y Times Book Rev* 92:11+ D 6 '87
Art books. See issues of American Artist
Books. See issues of Art News
Pretty pages [art books for Christmas] K. Larson. il *N Y* 20:89-90 D 14 '87
Review of books. See issues of Art in America
Censorship
China's odd couple [exhibit cancelled after Chinese refuse to include portraits of Douglas MacArthur and Golda Meir] il *U S News World Rep* 103:10 Jl 27 '87
Politically incorrect [Beijing exhibit of American portraits canceled after Chinese insisted that paintings of Golda Meir and General Douglas MacArthur be removed] D. Lanchner. il *Art News* 86:71 O '87
Collaboration
The unknown soldiers of the art world. D. Grant. *Am Artist* 51:12+ D '87
Collections
See Art—Collectors and collecting
Collectors and collecting
See also
Art as an investment
Art in the home
Art discoveries and resurrections. C. K. Firmage. See issues of Antiques & Collecting Hobbies beginning July 1987
Art fever: the passion and frenzy of the ultimate rich man's sport [cover story] D. Smith. il *N Y* 20:34-43 Ap 20 '87

Art—Collectors and collecting—*cont.*

An art-filled villa finds a special setting in Texas [donation by W. R. Reves of Villa La Pausa Collection to Dallas Museum of Art] H. Dudar. il pors *Smithsonian* 17:50-9 Ja '87

The baron thinks twice [uncertainty as to where the Thyssen-Bornemisza Collection will be housed] E. Beck. il por *Art News* 86:45 N '87

Buchheim vs. Duisburg: another round. J. Dornberg. il por *Art News* 86:45+ N '87

The collectors: a rare aesthetic: Stuart Pivar's cornucopia of art in Manhattan. S. M. L. Aronson. il *Archit Dig* 44:124-31+ Mr '87

Denis Mahon and his 'old friends' [collector of 17th-century Italian paintings] I. Shenker. il por *Art News* 86:121-7 Mr '87

Douglas Cramer: passionate perfectionist. P. Clothier. il por *Art News* 86:146-50 Summ '87

The Italian baroque paintings of Morton and Mary Jane Harris. C. Ratcliff. il por *Archit Dig* 44:50+ My '87

Jan Mitchell—the varied tastes of a New York connoisseur. C. Ratcliff. il por *Archit Dig* 44:298+ N '87

Joseph Moure's California impressionist paintings. I. Borger. il por *Archit Dig* 44:86+ Mr '87

Last of a breed [collection of H. P. McIlhenny] D. Solomon. il *Harpers Bazaar* 121:88+ D '87

Lessons of a judicious couple who won big collecting art [W. and M. Norris] M. Willens. il pors *Money* 16:152 Ja '87

MOCA-Panza dispute settled [dispute over possible sale of Panza Collection] R. W. Walker. *Art News* 86:21-2 Mr '87

Philadelphia's pride [McIlhenny collection up for auction] C. Vogel. il *N Y Times Mag* p70-2 My 10 '87

A private passion for art [collectors opening their own museums] C. McGuigan. il *Newsweek* 109:68-9 Je 15 '87

Real and fake in the 'Zagreb Louvre' [A. T. Mimara Collection] A. Decker. il pors *Art News* 86:151-8 Summ '87

Rediscovering an early modern vision [S. Thayer's Dial Collection of art in the Lila Acheson Wallace Wing of the Metropolitan Museum] J. Richardson. il por *House Gard* 159:158-63+ F '87

The Rene Di Rosas in Napa Valley. J. Chatfield-Taylor. il por *Archit Dig* 44:258+ Je '87

The Saatchi factor [tycoon C. Saatchi, major player in contemporary art marketplace] R. W. Walker. il por *Art News* 86:117-21 Ja '87

Sidney and Frances Lewis—the quest for the best in art. J. Tully. il pors *Smithsonian* 18:84-8+ N '87

Sidney Janis waiting a year for the blue. J. James. il por *Art News* 86:85-6 D '87

Spirited composition on Chester Square: the London house of Baron and Baroness Thyssen-Bornemisza. J. J. Norwich. il por *Archit Dig* 44:104-11 O '87

Turn of the century: America's imperial collectors. R. W. Walker. il *Art News* 86:157-9 N '87

Why collectors buy contemporary art [interview with E. Broad] M. S. Doherty. por *Am Artist* 51:10-11 Ap '87

Williams College coup [G. Panza di Biumo Collection to be housed in North Adams, Mass.] C. Giuliano. *Art News* 86:58+ Summ '87

Competitions

See also

Children's art—Competitions

Art contest winners [Seventeen contest] il *Seventeen* 46:48+ Ap '87

The Golden Anniversary National Art Competition: prize winners announced. il *Am Artist* 51:1 S '87

Introducing the artists whose work was selected in the American Artist Golden Anniversary National Art Competition [cover story; special issue] il *Am Artist* 51:32-75 Je '87

Conferences

Art and Design in Action: Detroit show guide [special section] il *Am Artist* 51:S1-S2+ N '87

Art and Design in Action: San Francisco show guide [special section] il *Am Artist* 51:S1-S2+ Ja '87

Sculptors strengthen ties at landmark conference [National Sculpture Conference: Works by Women] F. Grossen. *Am Craft* 47:13 O/N '87

Conservation and restoration

See also

Altarpieces—Conservation and restoration

Painting—Conservation and restoration

Smithsonian Institution. Museum Support Center

Art's grime and place [excerpt from address, May 1987] A. C. Danto. *Harpers* 275:13-14 S '87

Behind the scenes at the Smithsonian. D. Young. il *South Living* 22:173-4+ N '87

High tech and old masters. W. D. Marbach. il *Newsweek* 109:70-1 Mr 30 '87

Critics and criticism

See Art critics and criticism

Exhibitions

See also

Art deco—Exhibitions

Art galleries and museums

Arts and crafts—Exhibitions

Drawing—Exhibitions

Illustration—Exhibitions

Photography—Exhibitions

Around the galleries. See issues of Americana beginning May/June 1984

Art. A. C. Danto. See issues of The Nation beginning October 20, 1984

Art. K. Larson. See issues of New York

Art [New York City; fall preview] K. Larson and E. Newhall. il *N Y* 20:66+ S 21 '87

Artsmart. See issues of Harper's Bazaar beginning December 1986

Bulletin board. See issues of American Artist

Current and coming. S. B. Sherrill. See issues of Antiques

Exhibits. S. Kirby. See issues of American Artist

International exhibition calendar. See issues of Art News beginning Summer 1985

The nation. See issues of Art News

On exhibit. See issues of Americana

On view. See issues of House & Garden beginning October 1986

Review of exhibitions. See issues of Art in America

What's where when. S. B. Sherrill. See issues of Antiques beginning August 1984

The world. See issues of Art News

Expertising

Art discoveries and resurrections. C. K. Firmage. See issues of Antiques & Collecting Hobbies beginning July 1987

But is it art? J. Horgan. il *Sci Am* 257:48-9+ O '87

A morbid curiosity [deathbed portrait of man wrongly assumed to be the Duke of Monmouth] J. Prendergast. il *Hist Today* 37:62 My '87

Next time, ask [drawings sold as Piranesis at Sotheby's returned due to questionable authenticity] R. W. Walker. *Art News* 86:25-6 O '87

Rembrandt: the unvarnished truth? [attributions by the Rembrandt Research Project; cover story] S. Hochfield. il pors *Art News* 86:102-11 D '87

Federal aid

See Art and state

Forgeries

See also

Art—Expertising

The eye of the beholder [work of A. Dossena] R. Lynes. il por *Archit Dig* 44:26+ Ap '87

Fake masks [African art market] N. Lemann. il *Atlantic* 260:24+ N '87

Real and fake in the 'Zagreb Louvre' [A. T. Mimara Collection] A. Decker. il pors *Art News* 86:151-8 Summ '87

Exhibitions

The Walters Art Gallery [exhibit entitled Artful deception: the craft of the forger] il *Antiques Collect Hobbies* 92:54 S '87

Galleries and museums

See Art galleries and museums

History

Study and teaching

Editorial. W. Garrett. *Antiques* 131:811 Ap '87

For collectors and students. S. B. Sherrill. See issues of Antiques

Profiles [R. Bernier] C. Tomkins. por *New Yorker* 62:38-40+ Ja 19 '87

Information services

A study in art investment. D. Grant. il *Consum Res Mag* 70:23-5 Ja '87

Insurance

See Insurance, Art

Laws and regulations

See also

Artists' rights

Art laws: a handshake, yes, but what are my rights? D. Grant. *Am Artist* 51:16+ My '87

Missing and found works

Fortunes in missing masterpieces. J. Lee and M. Horn. il *U S News World Rep* 103:52-3 Ag 10 '87

A woeful gallery of the world's lost masterpieces. B. Conrad. bibl (p271) il *Smithsonian* 18:239-40+ N '87

Art—cont.

Mutilation, defacement, etc.
Art vandals: why do they do it? [views of D. Gamboni]
J. Dornberg. il por *Art News* 86:102-9 Mr '87

Periodicals
See also
American artist (Periodical)
Art news (Periodical)
Artsreview

Philosophy
The third parent [excerpt from address, March 25, 1987]
G. W. S. Trow. *Harpers* 275:34-5 Jl '87

Prices
See also
Art as an investment

$40 million van Gogh brings back mixed and vivid memories. M. S. Forbes. il *Forbes* 139:20+ Je 1 '87

Art for money's sake. il *Fortune* 116:9 O 12 '87

Art for the pensioners' sake [prices of Japanese print collection of British Rail Pension Fund] L. Scheer. il *Forbes* 140:117-18 D 28 '87

An artful dodger? [speculation about A. Bond as buyer of van Gogh's Irises] E. C. Baig. il por *Fortune* 116:166 D 21 '87

Blue Irises and blue chips [record price for van Gogh's painting] il *Newsweek* 110:85 N 23 '87

British Rail: on track [sale of old master prints from the collection of the British Rail Pension Fund] G. Barker. il *Art News* 86:25 O '87

Conspicuous consumer [Y. Goto buys van Gogh's Sunflowers] H. Katayama. il por *Forbes* 139:252 Je 15 '87

Da Vinci drawing tops 'triumphant' Gaines sale [J. R. Gaines Collection] R. W. Walker. *Art News* 86:16 Ja '87

F-111 flies high [contemporary art sold at November auctions in New York City] R. W. Walker. il *Art News* 86:15-16 Ja '87

Five-figure estimates, six-figure prices. R. W. Walker. *Art News* 86:32 My '87

Flower power [Van Gogh's Sunflowers sold at Christie's for $39.9 million] R. W. Walker. il *Art News* 86:31 My '87

Fortunes in missing masterpieces. J. Lee and M. Horn. il *U S News World Rep* 103:52-3 Ag 10 '87

'Irises' [van Gogh painting sold] *America* 157:396-7 N 28 '87

Is there recognition after death? D. Grant. *Am Artist* 51:70-3 Jl '87

Klee: for discerning buyers only. R. W. Walker. *Art News* 86:22 Ap '87

The museum without walls [sale of van Gogh's Sunflowers for $40 million] W. F. Buckley. *Natl Rev* 39:60-1 My 8 '87

A mystery buyer plucks van Gogh's buds for a record sum [interview with R. Feigen] M. Small. il por *People Wkly* 27:55-7 Ap 20 '87

The picture is still pretty in the art world—so far. J. H. Dobrzynski. il *Bus Week* p184-5 D 28 '87-Ja 4 '88

Sotheby's art market trends. See issues of Forbes beginning November 2, 1987

Stella stars at auction. R. W. Walker. *Art News* 86:17-18 F '87

Van Gogh's Irises: how much? R. W. Walker. il *Art News* 86:25 N '87

'A wonderful, haunting picture' [sale of Rembrandt's Portrait of a young girl, wearing a gold-trimmed cloak] R. W. Walker. il *Art News* 86:17 F '87

Private collections
See Art—Collectors and collecting

Reproductions
Expanding your market with multiples [posters, prints, and reproductions based on paintings] M. S. Doherty. il *Am Artist* 51:52-9 My '87

Social aspects
See also
Art Against AIDS

Tell us your story and we will know who you are. J. R. May. *Am Craft* 47:22+ Je/Jl '87

Study and teaching
See also
Art—Appreciation
Art—History—Study and teaching
Art schools
Artists as teachers
Drawing—Study and teaching
Grand Central Art Galleries Educational Association
Painting—Study and teaching
Whitney Museum of American Art. Independent Study Program

Discipline-based art education: not if, but where? [college education] C. H. Welter. bibl f *Des Arts Educ* 89:22-8 N/D '87

A report on discipline-based art education. D. C. Hines. *Am Artist* 51:68-9+ Ag '87

Spotlight on schools. il *Teen* 31:96 D '87

Aids and devices
Videocassette tapes: a source directory. K. J. Thomas. *Am Artist* 51:62+ Jl '87

Directories
1987 directory of art schools and workshops. il *Am Artist* 51:D1-D16+ Mr '87

Taxation
See Taxation of works of art

Technique
See also
Painting—Technique

Terminology
Anecdotes, facetiae, satire, etc.
Talking good art talk. D. Perlberg. *Art News* 86:81 O '87

Themes
See also
Agriculture in art
Alamo (San Antonio, Tex.) in art
Alphabet in art
Animals in art
Architecture in art
Artists in art
Astronomical observatories in art
Australia in art
Automobiles in art
Baseball in art
Bees in art
Bicycles in art
Biology in art
Birds in art
Blacks in art
Buddhas in art
California in art
Children in art
Churches (Buildings) in art
Computers in art
Confederate States of America in art
Dance in art
Dinosaurs in art
Ducks in art
Edo (Japan) in art
Elections in art
Eskimos in art
Fish in art
Flowers in art
Food in art
Games in art
Gardens and gardening in art
Grasshoppers in art
History in art
Holocaust, Jewish (1939-1945), in art
Homosexuality in art
Horses in art
Human figure in art
Hunting in art
Indians (American) in art
Industry in art
Infants, Premature, in art
Insects in art
Jews in art
Leaves in art
Light in art
Livingston Manor (N.Y.: Estate) in art
Maine in art
Marine fauna in art
Meteors in art
Nature in art
New York (N.Y.) in art
New York (State) in art
Nude in art
Paper money in art
Paris (France) in art
Plants in art
Politics in art
Pottery—Themes
Primitivism in art
Rooms in art
Sharks in art
Shinnecock Hills (N.Y.) in art
Sierra Nevada Mountains (Calif. and Nev.) in art
Sound in art
Southern States in art
Southwestern States in art
Space flight in art

Art—Themes—See also—*cont.*
   Stations of the Cross in art
   Summer in art
   Sunlight in art
   Taos (N.M.) in art
   Tarot in art
   Traffic accidents in art
   Unicorns in art
   Vermont in art
   Virginia in art
   Volcanoes in art
   Weather in art
   Western States in art
   Wildflowers in art
   Windows in art
   Women in art
   Words in art

Alabama
Anecdotes, facetiae, satire, etc.
Vickie Lou's letters from Long Island. il *Am Artist* 51:24+ Je '87

Alaska
   See also
   Haines (Alaska)—Art

Belgium
   See also
   Brussels (Belgium)—Art

California
   See also
   Los Angeles (Calif.)—Art
   Sacramento (Calif.)—Art
   San Francisco (Calif.)—Art
The California school of watercolor. J. Lovoos. il por *Am Artist* 51:62-9+ Ap '87
The Rene Di Rosas in Napa Valley. J. Chatfield-Taylor. il por *Archit Dig* 44:258+ Je '87

Canada
Missing the message in billboard art [Art on billboards program in 8 Canadian cities] G. James. il *Macleans* 100:54+ F 9 '87

France
   See also
   Paris (France)—Art

Germany (West)
   See also
   Berlin (Germany: West)—Art
   Frankfurt am Main (Germany)—Art
   Hamburg (Germany)—Art
Report from Germany. D. Galloway. il *Art Am* 75:31-5+ Je '87

Great Britain
   See also
   Leeds (England)—Art
   London (England)—Art
   Manchester (England)—Art
Brushstrokes of genius. S. Billen. il *Horizon* 30:22-6 N '87
Site reading: British art in public spaces [TSWA 3D show] R. Cork. il *Art Am* 75:144-51 S '87

Haiti
Hunting art in Haiti. J. B. Harris. il *Black Enterp* 17:36 My '87

Illinois
   See also
   Chicago (Ill.)—Art

Indiana
   See also
   Indianapolis (Ind.)—Art

Italy
   See also
   Milan (Italy)—Art

Jamaica
Jamaican designs. E. M. Gomez. il map *Travel Holiday* 167:48-51 Ja '87

Japan
   See also
   Tokyo (Japan)—Art

Latvia
Comrade artist [D. Skulme, head of Latvian Artists League] A. Stille. il por *Art News* 86:10+ Ja '87

Massachusetts
   See also
   Nantucket (Mass.)—Art

Mexico
   See also
   Mexico City (Mexico)—Art

New Mexico
Neon lights the desert. K. Rosenberg. il *Technol Rev* 90:14-15 F/Mr '87
Visions of magic [New Mexican artists] N. D'Ambrosio. il *Horizon* 30:46-52 O '87

New York (State)
   See also
   New York (N.Y.)—Art

Palestine
Opposite page [Treasures of the Holy Land: ancient art from the Israel Museum] J. D. Flam. il *Am Craft* 47:104-inside back cover Je/Jl '87
Treasures of the Holy Land. il *USA Today (Periodical)* 115:78-87 My '87

Pennsylvania
   See also
   Philadelphia (Pa.)—Art

Portugal
   See also
   Lisbon (Portugal)—Art

Soviet Union
   See also
   Soviet Cultural Foundation

Spain
Art in post-Franco Spain. B. P. Solomon. il *Art News* 86:120-4 O '87

Texas
   See also
   Houston (Tex.)—Art
Texas: state of the art. J. Gambrell. il *Art Am* 75:114-31+ Mr '87

United States
   See Art

Washington (State)
   See also
   Olympia (Wash.)—Art
   Seattle (Wash.)—Art

Art, Abstract
   See also
   Abstract expressionism
   Constructivism
The artist as cynic [views of P. Halley] J. Masheck. *New Leader* 70:22-3 Je 29 '87
Talking abstract (I) [cover story; interviews with eight American painters] L. Wei. il *Art Am* 75:80-97 Jl '87
Talking abstract (II) [cover story; interviews with nine American painters] L. Wei. il *Art Am* 75:112-29+ D '87

Exhibitions
Astrazione [young Italian artists at Bockley Gallery and Studio School, New York] M. E. Haus. il *Art News* 86:159-60 Mr '87
Comedy of mannerism [Post-abstract abstraction at the Aldrich Museum of Contemporary Art, Ridgefield, Conn.] K. Larson. il *N Y* 20:114-15 Ag 24 '87
Medium cool: new Chicago abstraction [The non-spiritual in art: abstract painting 1985-????] M. Bonesteel. il *Art Am* 75:138-47 D '87
Pyramid power in paint [The spiritual in art: abstract painting 1890-1985 at the Los Angeles County Museum] R. Hughes. il *Time* 129:81 Ja 12 '87
Spirituality in abstract art [The spiritual in art: abstract painting 1890-1985; cover story] P. Schaeffer. il *Christ Century* 104:819-22 S 30 '87

Art, African
   See also
   Smithsonian Institution. Center for African, Near Eastern and Asian Cultures
Fake masks [African art market] N. Lemann. il *Atlantic* 260:24+ N '87

Exhibitions
   See also
   National Museum of African Art (U.S.)

Art, Amateur
Art: schoolgirl paintings: nineteenth-century works by American amateur artists. J. R. Mellow. il *Archit Dig* 44:140-5+ D '87

Art, American
   See also
   Americana
   Archives of American Art
   Art, Black
   Artists, American
   Arts and crafts
   Indians of North America—Art
   Painting, American
   Pottery, American
   Sculpture, American
1902. R. Lynes. il *Art News* 86:154-6 N '87
A plain, exalted vision: for the young republic in search of a style, antiquity was destiny. R. Hughes. il *Time* 130:74-7 Jl 6 '87
Pleasure in creation [Arts and crafts movement in America] F. Strebeigh. bibl il *Am Herit* 38:82-9 Jl/Ag '87

Art, American—*cont.*

Exhibitions

See also

Metropolitan Museum of Art (New York, N.Y.). American Wing

National Museum of American Art (U.S.)

R.H. Love Galleries, Inc.

Terra Museum of American Art (Chicago, Ill.)

Whitney Museum of American Art

Aestheticism then and now [Metropolitan Museum's In pursuit of beauty] C. Ratcliff. il *Art Am* 75:90-103 F '87

The American arts and crafts movement [The art that is life: the arts and crafts movement in America, 1875-1920] S. B. Sherrill. il *Antiques* 131:508+ Mr '87

American women artists, 1830-1930 [exhibition at National Museum of Women in the Arts] M. Moorman. il *Art News* 86:57-8 Summ '87

The art that is life [Arts and crafts movement in America, 1875-1920] D. Welebit. il *Americana* 14:32-4 Ja/F '87

The elegance of line: back to basics with the eloquent masters of the arts and crafts movement [The art that is life: the arts and crafts movement in America, 1875-1920] B. Plumb. il *Vogue* 177:332 Mr '87

The embodiment of ingenuity [Craft today; In pursuit of beauty: Americans and the aesthetic movement; The Machine Age in America: 1918-1941] M. Kangas. bibl f il *Am Craft* 47:46-53 Ag/S '87

Generic genius [After Matisse] J. Perl. *Vogue* 177:36 Je '87

The Golden Anniversary National Art Competition: prize winners announced. il *Am Artist* 51:1 S '87

Introducing the artists whose work was selected in the American Artist Golden Anniversary National Art Competition [cover story; special issue] il *Am Artist* 51:32-75 Je '87

Reforming America: Boston's Museum of Fine Arts offers a fresh interpretation of the Arts and crafts movement in America, 1875-1920. C. Lynn. il *Am Craft* 47:40-9+ Je/Jl '87

Too much too soon? [proliferation of retrospective exhibits of young artists' work] C. Coulson. il *Art News* 86:115-19 S '87

A woman's place [American women artists, 1830-1930 exhibit at the National Museum of Women in the Arts] A. Schwartz. il *Americana* 15:30-2+ Mr/Ap '87

Art, Ancient

Exhibitions

Opposite page [Treasures of the Holy Land: ancient art from the Israel Museum] J. D. Flam. il *Am Craft* 47:104-inside back cover Je/Jl '87

Treasures of the Holy Land. il *USA Today (Periodical)* 115:78-87 My '87

Art, Asian

See also

Art, Oriental

Smithsonian Institution. Center for African, Near Eastern and Asian Cultures

An Asian mystique: Dale and Patricia Keller's New York apartment. L. Bernikow. il pors *Archit Dig* 44:94-101 S '87

Exhibitions

See also

Arthur M. Sackler Gallery (Washington, D.C.)

Art, Baroque

See also

Painting, Baroque

Sculpture, Baroque

The baroque [cover story; special issue] bibl il *Courier* 40:3-46+ S '87

Splendid sanctuary [decoration in Atotonilco, Mexico church built by L. F. N. de Alfaro] J. Richardson. il *House Gard* 159:104-7+ D '87

Art, Black

See also

Harlem renaissance

Exhibitions

Color-blind art history [exhibition entitled Masters and pupils: the education of the black artist in New York, 1900-1980] S. Staggs. *Art News* 86:15+ Ap '87

Powerful vision at Anacostia [Contemporary visual expressions exhibit] C. Bond. il *Smithsonian* 18:188 My '87

Art, Brazilian

The Week of Modern Art, 1922. il *Courier* 39:38-9 D '86

Art, British

See also

Art, English

Sculpture, British

Brushstrokes of genius. S. Billen. il *Horizon* 30:22-6 N '87

Exhibitions

The British accent in 20th-century art [Royal Academy of Arts exhibition] W. Feaver. il *Art News* 86:114-19 Ap '87

Image in line [exhibit of drawings, lithographs and etchings by British figurative artists at Bernard Jacobson Gallery, New York City] J. Higgins. il *Art News* 86:166+ My '87

Singular and grand Britons [British art in the 20th century at the Royal Academy in London] R. Hughes. il *Time* 129:82-3 Ap 6 '87

Terminal culture? "The British Edge" [exhibition at Boston's Institute of Contemporary Art] P. H. Smith. il *Art Am* 75:36-9+ S '87

Art, Buddhist

Introduction to Buddhist collectibles. J. R. Cooner. il *Antiques Collect Hobbies* 92:28-32 Mr '87

Art, Canadian

Exhibitions

An official guide to the periphery [From sea to shining sea exhibit at the Power Plant gallery in Toronto] G. James. il *Macleans* 100:45-6 Ag 3 '87

Art, Chinese

See also

Pottery, Chinese

Eskenazi's early Chinese art. E. Lambert. il por *Archit Dig* 44:156+ Ja '87

Exhibitions

China studies [The Chinese scholar's studio: artistic life in the late Ming period at the Asia Society] K. Larson. il *N Y* 20:108-9 N 2 '87

Museum piece: the Chinese Collections, Royal Ontario Museum. P. Johnston. il *Hist Today* 37:60-2 Ap '87

Art, Christian *See* Christian art and symbolism

Art, Classical

See also

Classicism in art

Neoclassicism (Art)

Art, Commercial

See also

Illustration

Art, Decorative *See* Decoration and ornament

Art, Dutch

See also

Painting, Dutch

Art, Egyptian

Exhibitions

Rameses the Great [traveling exhibition] il *USA Today (Periodical)* 115:8-9 Ap '87

Art, English

See also

Painting, English

Pottery, English

Exhibitions

An Age of Chivalry [Age of Chivalry: art in Plantagenet England 1200-1400 at the Royal Academy; cover story; special issue] il *Hist Today* 37:2-57 N '87

Blazing exceptions to nature [English Gothic art in The Age of Chivalry at the Royal Academy in London] R. Hughes. il *Time* 130:94+ N 30 '87

"Force of circumstance" at P.P.O.W. E. Heartney. *Art Am* 75:151-2 F '87

Sharing the poet's obsession [William Wordsworth and the age of English Romanticism at the New York Public Library] R. Hughes. il *Time* 130:95 D 14 '87

Words' worth [William Wordsworth and the age of English Romanticism at the New York Public Library] K. Larson. il *N Y* 20:140+ D 7 '87

Art, Erotic *See* Erotic art

Art, European

See also

Painting, European

Pottery, European

Exhibitions

European decorative arts [exhibition entitled J. Pierpont Morgan, collector: European decorative arts from the Wadsworth Atheneum] S. B. Sherrill. il *Antiques* 131:48+ Ja '87

The magic of Medusa: European mannerisms [exhibit at Künstlerhaus in Vienna] A. Hunt. il *Art News* 86:161 S '87

Tycoon taste [exhibition entitled J. Pierpont Morgan, collector: European decorative arts from the Wadsworth Atheneum] J. Strouse. il por *House Gard* 159:94+ My '87

Art, Fantastic

Brigazoon [work of P. LaCombe] T. M. Disch. il *Omni* 9:74-7 S '87

Art, Fantastic—*cont.*
Thirteenth night [paintings of G. Williams] K. McKinney. il *Omni* 10:102-7 O '87

Exhibitions
The art of the fantastic [Latin America, 1920-1987] V. G. Stoddart. il *Américas* 39:56-8 N/D '87
Devotees of the fantastic [Hispanic art in the United States and Art of the fantastic: Latin America, 1920-1987] M. Stevens. il *Newsweek* 110:66-8 S 7 '87
Fantastic festival! [Art of the fantastic: Latin America, 1920-1987] B. Golightly. il *Horizon* 30:33 Jl/Ag '87

Art, French
See also
Pottery, French

Exhibitions
The post-Beaubourg generation [New York shows featuring new French work] A. Rochette. il *Art Am* 75:41-7+ Je '87

Art, German
See also
Pottery, German
Sculpture, German

Exhibitions
Art from the Exiled City [Berlinart 1961-1987 at the Museum of Modern Art] H. Cotter. il *Art Am* 75:43-5+ O '87
Art up against the wall [Berlinart 1961-1987 at the Museum of Modern Art] J. Perl. il *Vogue* 177:50 Jl '87
Berlin: a place for painting [Berlinart 1961-1987 at Museum of Modern Art] K. Ottman. il *Harpers Bazaar* 120:136-7+ Je '87
Berlinart 1961-1987 [exhibit at Museum of Modern Art] A. C. Danto. *Nation* 245:28-9 Jl 4-11 '87
Divide and conquer [Berlinart 1961-1987 at the Museum of Modern Art] K. Larson. il *N Y* 20:74-5 Je 22 '87
Out of the wall's shadow [Berlinart 1961-1987 at the Museum of Modern Art] R. Hughes. il *Time* 130:64-5 Ag 24 '87
Report from Germany. D. Galloway. il *Art Am* 75:31-5+ Je '87

Art, Gothic

Exhibitions
An Age of Chivalry [Age of Chivalry: art in Plantagenet England 1200-1400 at the Royal Academy; cover story; special issue] il *Hist Today* 37:2-57 N '87
Blazing exceptions to nature [English Gothic art in The Age of Chivalry at the Royal Academy in London] R. Hughes. il *Time* 130:94+ N 30 '87

Art, Haitian
See also
Painting, Haitian

Art, Hispanic American
The Spanish influence: a visual legacy [cover story] C. Kuhl. il *Horizon* 30:17-30+ D '87

Exhibitions
See also
Millicent Rogers Museum (Taos, N.M.)
Devotees of the fantastic [Hispanic art in the United States and Art of the fantastic: Latin America, 1920-1987] M. Stevens. il *Newsweek* 110:66-8 S 7 '87

Art, Indian (American) *See* Indians of North America—Art

Art, Indian (East Indian)
The birth of the classics. V. Gladstone. il *Horizon* 30:18-19 Mr '87
Visions of a modern age. V. Gladstone. il *Horizon* 30:20-1 Mr '87

Exhibitions
A passage from India [Clive Museum at Powis Castle, Wales] K. Nurse. il *Hist Today* 37:2-3 S '87

Art, Islamic

Exhibitions
See also
Museum of Islamic Art (Marrakesh, Morocco)

Art, Italian
See also
Painting, Italian
The great illusionists [Italian baroque] A. B. D. Lavergnee. il *Courier* 40:30-3 S '87

Exhibitions
Astrazione [young Italian artists at Bockley Gallery and Studio School, New York] M. E. Haus. il *Art News* 86:159-60 Mr '87

Art, Japanese
See also
Japonesque (Firm)

Exhibitions
A confusion of realms [Tokyo: form and spirit at the IBM Gallery] K. Larson. il *N Y* 20:55+ Ja 12 '87

East meets West, postmodern style [traveling exhibit entitled Tokyo: form and spirit] R. Silberman. il *Art Am* 75:13-15+ My '87
Empire of the sun [Arts of Japan galleries at the Metropolitan Museum of Art] J. Spayde. il *Art News* 86:155 D '87
Haiku to high tech [Tokyo: form and spirit exhibit] il *Sunset* 178:50 Mr '87
New trends: Setagaya Museum. P. Mollenkof. il *Art News* 86:172+ D '87
A visual wisdom [new portion of Metropolitan Museum's Sackler Galleries] M. Filler. il *House Gard* 159:174-7+ Je '87
Zen and the art of museum installation [Arts of Japan galleries at the Metropolitan Museum of Art] K. Larson. il *N Y* 20:58-9 Ag 31 '87

Art, Latin American
See also
Art, Pre-Columbian
The angel with the arquebus. M. Rojas-Mix. il *Courier* 40:36-8 S '87
Art. V. G. Stoddart. See issues of *Américas*
'A new form of self-expression' [Latin American baroque] L. Zea. il *Courier* 40:34-5 S '87
The Spanish influence: a visual legacy [cover story] C. Kuhl. il *Horizon* 30:17-30+ D '87

Exhibitions
The art of the fantastic [Latin America, 1920-1987] V. G. Stoddart. il *Américas* 39:56-8 N/D '87
Devotees of the fantastic [Hispanic art in the United States and Art of the fantastic: Latin America, 1920-1987] M. Stevens. il *Newsweek* 110:66-8 S 7 '87
Fantastic festival! [Art of the fantastic: Latin America, 1920-1987] B. Golightly. il *Horizon* 30:33 Jl/Ag '87

Art, Maya *See* Mayas—Art

Art, Mexican

Exhibitions
Splendors of the Golden Age: three centuries of Spanish colonial art [cover story; catalog of exhibit at EPCOT] il *Horizon* 30:41-56 Jl/Ag '87

Art, Mexican American
See also
Border Art Workshop. Taller de Arte Fronterizo

Art, Middle Eastern
See also
Smithsonian Institution. Center for African, Near Eastern and Asian Cultures
Frenchy and the Persians [N. Sakhai and H. Mahboubian mastermind New York City theft of Near Eastern antiquities for insurance recovery] C. Trillin. *New Yorker* 63:44+ Je 29 '87

Exhibitions
See also
Arthur M. Sackler Gallery (Washington, D.C.)

Art, Modern
See also
Abstract expressionism
Art, Abstract
Art deco
Body art
Boston school of painting
Conceptual art
Constructivism
Cubism
Dadaism
Environment (Art)
Fauvism
Impressionism (Art)
Neo-expressionism (Art)
Neo-geo (Art)
Performance art
Photo-realism
Pop art
Surrealism
Wearable art
Clement Greenberg—the critic and his artists. S. Schwartz. *Am Sch* 56:535-45 Aut '87
Criticism and culture, or Greenberg's doubt [views of C. Greenberg] S. Tillim. *Art Am* 75:122-7+ My '87
The hot new cool art: simulationism [New York movement] E. Heartney. il *Art News* 86:130-7 Ja '87
Museums buying contemporary art. D. Grant. *Am Artist* 51:10+ Je '87
The Saatchi factor [tycoon C. Saatchi, major player in contemporary art marketplace] R. W. Walker. il por *Art News* 86:117-21 Ja '87
The Week of Modern Art, 1922 [Brazil] il *Courier* 39:38-9 D '86
Why collectors buy contemporary art [interview with E. Broad] M. S. Doherty. por *Am Artist* 51:10-11 Ap '87

Art, Modern—cont.

Exhibitions

See also

Aldrich Museum of Contemporary Art (Ridgefield, Conn.)

Centre National d'Art Contemporain (Grenoble, France)

Corcoran Gallery of Art. Biennial Exhibition of Contemporary American Painting

Documenta

Havana Biennial

Leo Castelli Gallery

Los Angeles County Museum of Art

Massachusetts Museum of Contemporary Art and Architecture

Metropolitan Museum of Art (New York, N.Y.). Lila Acheson Wallace Wing

Museum of Contemporary Art (Antwerp, Belgium)

Museum of Contemporary Art (Los Angeles, Calif.)

Museum of Modern Art (New York, N.Y.)

National Museum of Modern Art (Kyoto, Japan)

National Museum of Modern Art (Seoul, Korea)

San Francisco Museum of Modern Art

Whitney Museum of American Art. Biennial Exhibition

The antique future [exhibition at the Massimo Audiello Gallery in New York City] D. Rubey. il *Art News* 86:188+ O '87

Art from the Exiled City [Berlinart 1961-1987 at the Museum of Modern Art] H. Cotter. il *Art Am* 75:43-5+ O '87

Art up against the wall [Berlinart 1961-1987 at the Museum of Modern Art] J. Perl. il *Vogue* 177:50 Jl '87

Berlin: a place for painting [Berlinart 1961-1987 at Museum of Modern Art] K. Ottman. il *Harpers Bazaar* 120:136-7+ Je '87

Berlinart 1961-1987 [exhibit at Museum of Modern Art] A. C. Danto. *Nation* 245:28-9 Jl 4-11 '87

Border lines [Juxtapositions: recent sculpture from England and Germany at P.S. 1] K. Larson. il *N Y* 20:66+ My 25 '87

The British accent in 20th-century art [Royal Academy of Arts exhibition] W. Feaver. il *Art News* 86:114-19 Ap '87

A century of modern sculpture [Selections from the Patsy and Raymond Nasher Collection at the National Gallery of Art] il *USA Today (Periodical)* 116:8-9 Ag '87

Devotees of the fantastic [Hispanic art in the United States and Art of the fantastic: Latin America, 1920-1987] M. Stevens. il *Newsweek* 110:66-8 S 7 '87

Divide and conquer [Berlinart 1961-1987 at the Museum of Modern Art] K. Larson. il *N Y* 20:74-5 Je 22 '87

Generic genius [After Matisse] J. Perl. *Vogue* 177:36 Je '87

Heir heads [Peggy Guggenheim's other legacy at the Guggenheim] K. Larson. il *N Y* 20:94-5 Mr 30 '87

Juxtapositions at P.S.1. E. Heartney. il *Art Am* 75:177 N '87

"Liars" at State of Illinois Art Gallery. S. Taylor. il *Art Am* 75:187+ S '87

The masters behind the masterpieces. M. Horn. il *U S News World Rep* 102:70-1 Mr 2 '87

Modern times [L'epoque, la mode, la morale, la passion at the Pompidou Center and Warhol/Beuys/Polke at Milwaukee Art Museum] J. Perl. il *Vogue* 177:90+ Ag '87

"Modern times" at Hirschl & Adler. J. Weinberg. *Art Am* 75:144-5 F '87

Monte Carlo sculpture '87. C. Mosley. il *Art News* 86:201 O '87

New trends: Setagaya Museum. P. Mollenkof. il *Art News* 86:172+ D '87

"Northwest impressions" at Henry Art Gallery. M. Kangas. *Art Am* 75:191+ My '87

An official guide to the periphery [From sea to shining sea exhibit at the Power Plant gallery in Toronto] G. James. il *Macleans* 100:45-6 Ag 3 '87

Out of the wall's shadow [Berlinart 1961-1987 at the Museum of Modern Art] R. Hughes. il *Time* 130:64-5 Ag 24 '87

The post-Beaubourg generation [New York shows featuring new French work] A. Rochette. il *Art Am* 75:41-7+ Je '87

Report from Leningrad [Paintings and decorative art from the reserves of the State Russian Museum] C. Douglas. il *Art Am* 75:25+ Ap '87

Russian and Soviet political art, 1900-1986 [exhibit at Baruch College] E. Heartney. il *Art News* 86:188 O '87

Shrinking history [Morality tales: history painting in the 1980s at NYU's Grey Art Gallery] K. Larson. il *N Y* 20:101-2 O 5 '87

Sidney and Frances Lewis—the quest for the best in art. J. Tully. il pors *Smithsonian* 18:84-8+ N '87

Singular and grand Britons [British art in the 20th century at the Royal Academy in London] R. Hughes. il *Time* 129:82-3 Ap 6 '87

Symbols of the sacred [Montreal exhibition of contemporary art entitled Stations] G. James. il *Macleans* 100:49 Ag 31 '87

Texas: state of the art. J. Gambrell. il *Art Am* 75:114-31+ Mr '87

Too much too soon? [proliferation of retrospective exhibits of young artists' work] C. Coulson. il *Art News* 86:115-19 S '87

Trading passion for boredom at the Pompidou [L'époque, la mode, la morale, la passion] A. Hunt. il *Art News* 86:199 O '87

What isn't modern sculpture? [What is modern sculpture? at the Pompidou Center, Paris] A. E. Elsen. il *Art News* 86:144-7 Ja '87

Anecdotes, facetiae, satire, etc.

Vickie Lou's letters from Long Island. il *Am Artist* 51:24+ Je '87

Art, Neoclassical *See* Neoclassicism (Art)

Art, Oriental

See also

Art, Chinese

Art, Japanese

Global treasure trove [Paris apartment of A. Dandois] C. Vogel. il por *N Y Times Mag* p62-6 Mr 1 '87

Exhibitions

See also

Metropolitan Museum of Art (New York, N.Y.). Sackler Galleries for Asian Art

Art, Pre-Columbian

Pre-Columbian priority: rare treasures in a Manhattan apartment. D. Rosenthal. il *Archit Dig* 44:140-4+ Ag '87

Art, Primitive

See also

Art, Pre-Columbian

Cave drawings and paintings

Art, Roman

See also

Sculpture, Roman

Art, Russian

See also

Icons

Painting, Russian

Soviet art: new freedom, new directions. S. Hochfield. il *Art News* 86:102-7 O '87

Exhibitions

Report from Leningrad [Paintings and decorative art from the reserves of the State Russian Museum] C. Douglas. il *Art Am* 75:25+ Ap '87

Russian and Soviet political art, 1900-1986 [exhibit at Baruch College] E. Heartney. il *Art News* 86:188 O '87

Art, Shaker

Shaker village views. R. P. Emlen. il *Nat Hist* 96:48-57 S '87

Exhibitions

Back by popular demand: Shaker design. N. A. Ruhling. il *Antiques Collect Hobbies* 92:12-16 Mr '87

Art, Slavic

Baroque in the Slav countries. G. D. Gatchev. il *Courier* 40:46 S '87

Art, Spanish

Art in post-Franco Spain. B. P. Solomon. il *Art News* 86:120-4 O '87

An art of gilt and pathos [Spanish baroque] J. Gallego. il *Courier* 40:14-17 S '87

The Spanish influence: a visual legacy [cover story] C. Kuhl. il *Horizon* 30:17-30+ D '87

Art, Turkish

Exhibitions

The Age of Sultan Suleyman the Magnificent. E. Atil. il *USA Today (Periodical)* 116:78-86 Jl '87

A golden trove fit for a sultan [The Age of Sultan Süleyman the Magnificent] C. McGuigan. il *Newsweek* 109:66-7 F 2 '87

His sultanic majesty's bequest [The Age of Sultan Süleyman the Magnificent] J. Perl. il *Vogue* 177:74 Ap '87

Sultan Suleyman courts America. M. Horn and C. Fenyvesi. il *U S News World Rep* 102:72 F 9 '87

Art, Turkish—Exhibitions—*cont.*

A sultan's collection [The Age of Sultan Süleyman the Magnificent] E. Stein. *Horizon* 30:68 Ja/F '87

Topkapi treasures [The Age of Sultan Süleyman the Magnificent] O. Bernier. il *House Gard* 159:186-94 F '87

Art, Victorian

Editorial [Victorian classicism] W, Garrett. il *Antiques* 131:223 Ja '87

Art Against AIDS

Art Against AIDS. J. Tully. *Art News* 86:54+ Summ '87

The art world goes all-out against AIDS. il *N Y Times Mag* p35 My 31 '87

Top artists draw the beautiful people to a big bash to boost the battle against AIDS. M. Small. il *People Wkly* 27:109-10 Je 22 '87

Art and architecture

See also
Architecture in art

Art and children

See also
Children in art
Children's art

Living with antiques. V. Hahn. il *Parents* 62:134-6+ F '87

Art and fashion See Fashion and art

Art and industry

See also
Industry in art

The $2 million man [Chase Manhattan art consultant J. L. Boulton] A. Virshup. il por *Art News* 86:112-14 S '87

Art & business in the 80's: the billion-dollar merger. V. F. Brooks. il *Art News* 86:19+ Ja '87

Art for the pensioners' sake [prices of Japanese print collection of British Rail Pension Fund] L. Scheer. il *Forbes* 140:117-18 D 28 '87

The big payoff in corporate art. F. Rice. il *Fortune* 115:106-12 My 25 '87

British Rail: on track [sale of old master prints from the collection of the British Rail Pension Fund] G. Barker. il *Art News* 86:25 O '87

Conspicuous consumer [Y. Goto buys van Gogh's Sunflowers] H. Katayama. il por *Forbes* 139:252 Je 15 '87

Take this art and . . . [visual arts program at First Bank System, Minn.] J. Herzfeld. il *Art News* 86:12+ Ap '87

Today's Medicis wear suits and ties [corporate patrons] M. Horn. il *U S News World Rep* 103:71-3 O 19 '87

Will British Rail sell all? [art and antiques collection amassed by British Rail Pension Fund expected to go on market] T. Trucco. il *Art News* 86:99-103 My '87

Art and literature

Hemingway's Miró. S. Staggs. il *Art News* 86:12 D '87

Art and mental illness

The wretched life and death of an 'American van Gogh' [R. A. Blakelock] A. A. Davidson. il por *Smithsonian* 18:80-6+ D '87

Art and morals

Goodness knows nothing of beauty: on the distance between morality and art. W. H. Gass. il *Harpers* 274:37-44 Ap '87

Art and nature See Nature (Aesthetics)

Art and photography

See also
Photography, Artistic

Playful plagiarism: imitating art with Alan Bergman. B. Hurter. il por *Petersens Photogr Mag* 15:44-9 F '87

Roger Winter. B. D. Stroud. il *Am Artist* 51:52-5 Jl '87

Exhibitions

Barbara Noah. L. Smallwood. *Art News* 86:57 My '87

Photography becomes art [Photography and art: interactions since 1946] R. Atkins. il *Horizon* 30:38-40 Je '87

San Francisco exhibits exceed photography's boundaries. L. Lufkin. il *Pop Photogr* 94:26+ Ja '87

Art and poetry

Exhibitions

Sharing the poet's obsession [William Wordsworth and the age of English Romanticism at the New York Public Library] R. Hughes. il *Time* 130:95 D 14 '87

Words' worth [William Wordsworth and the age of English Romanticism at the New York Public Library] K. Larson. il *N Y* 20:140+ D 7 '87

Art and politics

Keep politics out of art. R. Kimball. *Art News* 86:174 S '87

Wall painting [American politics as conceptual art] L. H. Lapham. *Harpers* 275:12+ O '87

Art and psychoanalysis See Psychoanalysis and art

Art and religion

See also
Christian art and symbolism
Stations of the Cross in art
Wesley Theological Seminary. Center for the Arts and Religion

Spirituality in abstract art [The spiritual in art: abstract painting 1890-1985; cover story] P. Schaeffer. il *Christ Century* 104:819-22 S 30 '87

Tell us your story and we will know who you are. J. R. May. *Am Craft* 47:22+ Je/Jl '87

Art and science

See also
Art and technology

Art and society See Art—Social aspects

Art and state

See also
National Endowment for the Arts
Public art

Public support for artists through percent for art. J. Jevnikar. il *Am Artist* 51:12+ Mr '87

Austria

A $124 million band-aid [financing package allows Kunsthistorisches Museum to install climate control equipment] F. Protzman. il *Art News* 86:39+ D '87

Austria reviews claims on looted art [artworks confiscated under the Nazi regime] A. Decker. *Art News* 86:37-8 F '87

A slow process [claims proceedings for Austrian-held artworks confiscated under the Nazi regime] A. Decker. il *Art News* 86:71-2 O '87

Cuba

See also
Havana Biennial

France

Le Big Bang [auction market] R. Morais. il *Forbes* 140:46+ Jl 27 '87

Germany (West)

The perils of public sculpture. D. Galloway. il *Art Am* 75:37-9+ D '87

Netherlands

The Dutch dam art subsidies [closure of the Visual Arts Arrangement] J. Turner. *Art News* 86:72 O '87

Soviet Union

See also
Soviet Cultural Foundation

Report from Leningrad [Paintings and decorative art from the reserves of the State Russian Museum] C. Douglas. il *Art Am* 75:25+ Ap '87

Soviet art for export. P. Bonet. *World Press Rev* 34:60 D '87

Soviet art: new freedom, new directions. S. Hochfield. il *Art News* 86:102-7 O '87

A surprise at the Pushkin [M. Chagall exhibit] S. Strasser. il por *Newsweek* 110:87 S 14 '87

Art and technology

Exhibitions

P.U.L.S.E. at 420 West Broadway. E. Heartney. *Art Am* 75:122 Jl '87

Art and the press See Art news

Art and war

See also
United States—History—Civil War, 1861-1865—Art and the war
Vietnamese War, 1957-1975—Art and the war

Art appreciation See Art—Appreciation

Art as a profession

1987 business supplement [special section] il *Am Artist* 51:58-62+ Jl '87

Twenty-six artists describe a crystallizing experience [decision to become an artist or to redirect career] M. C. Nelson. il *Am Artist* 51:74-6+ F '87

What becomes an artist most. G. Danto. il *Art News* 86:149-53 N '87

Art as an investment

Art fever: the passion and frenzy of the ultimate rich man's sport [cover story] D. Smith. il *N Y* 20:34-43 Ap 20 '87

Lessons of a judicious couple who won big collecting art [W. and M. Norris] M. Willens. il pors *Money* 16:152 Ja '87

The picture is still pretty in the art world—so far. J. H. Dobrzynski. il *Bus Week* p184-5 D 28 '87-Ja 4 '88

Art as an investment—*cont.*

Plenty of money—for big spenders only. R. W. Walker. il *Art News* 86:29-30 Summ '87

A study in art investment. D. Grant. il *Consum Res Mag* 70:23-5 Ja '87

To win big on a print, bet on the artist. R. W. King. il *Bus Week* p178-9 My 25 '87

Will British Rail sell all? [art and antiques collection amassed by British Rail Pension Fund expected to go on market] T. Trucco. il *Art News* 86:99-103 My '87

Art auctions *See* Art trade

Art books *See* Art literature

Art Center (Europe) *See* Art Center College of Design (Pasadena, Calif.). European campus

Art Center College of Design (Pasadena, Calif.). European campus

Art Center (Europe). R. Hutton. il *Car Driv* 33:29 Ag '87

Art centers

See also

Centers for the performing arts

California

See also

Jane Baerwald Aron Art Center

Kansas

See also

Lawrence Arts Center (Kan.)

Michigan

See also

Interlochen Center for the Arts

Art clubs and societies

See also

American Craft Council

Foundation for the Community of Artists

Glass Art Society

Grand Central Art Galleries Educational Association

Surface Design Association (U.S.)

Art collectors and collecting *See* Art—Collectors and collecting

Art Commission of the City of New York *See* New York (N.Y.). Art Commission

Art competitions *See* Art—Competitions

Art conferences *See* Art—Conferences

Art consultants

See also

Boulton, Jack L.

Art critics and criticism

See also

Cortissoz, Royal, 1869-1948

Greenberg, Clement, 1909-

Hughes, Robert

Schapiro, Meyer, 1904-

Stella, Frank

The envelope, please . . . Who deserves more time in the spotlight? Who should be hooked off the stage? The experts cast their votes. P. Gardner. il *Art News* 86:167-71 N '87

Off press [reviews of American Craft Museum's inaugural exhibit Craft today: poetry of the physical] *Am Craft* 47:11-12 F/Mr '87

Art deco

Antiques: art deco rugs. C. Bricker. il *Archit Dig* 44:160-5 S '87

Art deco [bedroom] il *Fam Handyman* 37:68+ My/Je '87

Art deco tour of downtown Los Angeles. il *Sunset* 179:50 S '87

Deco doyen [R. Buthaud] A. Duncan. il por *House Gard* 159:36B+ Ja '87

Collectors and collecting

Art deco bronze and ivory figures [cover story] S. Jones. il *Antiques Collect Hobbies* 92:24-8 Ag '87

Collectors' finds in Paris: discoveries in painting, wallpaper and posters [papier peint wallpapers and art deco advertising posters] J. A. Cuadrado. il *Archit Dig* 44:210+ D '87

A deco discovery [collection of H. P. Rothberg] A. Duncan. il *House Gard* 159:156-9+ My '87

Exhibitions

See also

Musée van Buuren (Brussels, Belgium)

Art deco rooms at the Musée des Arts Décoratifs. O. Bernier. il *Antiques* 132:776-81 O '87

Twentieth-century American decorative arts and sculpture [American art deco at the Renwick Gallery] S. B. Sherrill. il *Antiques* 131:734+ Ap '87

Art donations as tax deductions *See* Income tax—Deductions

Art education *See* Art—Study and teaching

Art exhibitions *See* Art—Exhibitions

Art fairs *See* Art—Exhibitions; Arts and crafts—Exhibitions

Art galleries and museums

See also

National Gallery of Art (U.S.)

Sculpture gardens and parks

A private passion for art [collectors opening their own museums] C. McGuigan. il *Newsweek* 109:68-9 Je 15 '87

Quilt havens: new showcases [museums dedicated to quilts] J. Tognini. il *Am Craft* 47:50-1 D '87/Ja '88

Acquisitions

Museum accessions. E. H. Gustafson. See occasional issues of Antiques

Museums buying contemporary art. D. Grant. *Am Artist* 51:10+ Je '87

Air conditioning

A $124 million band-aid [financing package allows Kunsthistorisches Museum to install climate control equipment] F. Protzman. il *Art News* 86:39+ D '87

Dirty Dürers, empty coffers [fundraising efforts to purchase climate control system for Kunsthistorisches Museum, Vienna] F. Protzman. il *Art News* 86:58 S '87

Architecture

An architectural kaleidoscope: Sir John Soane's Museum in London. P. Thornton. bibl f il *Antiques* 131:264-77 Ja '87

Assessing the museum boom. R. Lynes. il *Archit Dig* 44:28+ F '87

The Aulenti uproar. C. Vogel. il por *N Y Times Mag* p26-32+ N 22 '87

Balladur's last stand [Louvre] B. Grauman. il *Art News* 86:39 D '87

Bastion of culture [National Museum of Modern Art, Seoul, South Korea] D. Dietsch. il *Archit Rec* 175:138-47 N '87

Brooklyn Museum master plan design competition. il *Archit Rec* 175:45 Ja '87

The buildings in close-up [architecture of the Los Angeles County Museum of Art and the Museum of Contemporary Art] S. Stephens. il *Art Am* 75:152-5 My '87

Charles Moore at Williams [Williams College Museum of Art] V. J. Scully. il por *Archit Dig* 44:66+ D '87

Do we need another hero? [J. Stirling's design for the Clore Wing of the Tate Gallery] S. Jones. il *Hist Today* 37:3-4 My '87

Eastern diplomacy [F. Maki's design for the National Museum of Modern Art, Kyoto, Japan; cover story] D. Dietsch. il *Archit Rec* 175:116-27 O '87

A far, far better thing: the Guggenheim and Whitney redesign their expansion schemes. il *Archit Rec* 175:45+ Ap '87

A fine American hand [American Craft Museum, New York City] D. Brenner. il *Archit Rec* 175:122-7 Mr '87

A gathering of fragments [Robert O. Anderson Building, L.A. County Museum of Art] M. F. Schmertz. il *Archit Rec* 175:110-19 F '87

The geology of art: Cleveland Museum of Art has walls and sculptures made of rock, and sidewalks made of skeletons [cover story] J. T. Hannibal and M. T. Schmidt. il *Earth Sci* 40:12-15 Summ '87

Good neighbors [architect C. Moore's projects at Hood Museum of Art and Williams College Museum of Art] K. Norment and C. Giuliano. il *Art News* 86:51-2 Ja '87

Growing pains [new expansion plans for the Whitney and the Guggenheim] M. Filler. il *Art Am* 75:14-19 Jl '87

Heir heads [proposed additions to the Guggenheim and the Whitney] K. Larson. il *N Y* 20:94-5 Mr 30 '87

The homecoming [J. F. Stirling's design for the Clore Wing of the Tate Gallery; cover story] D. Dietsch. il *Archit Rec* 175:104-13 Jl '87

In the neighborhood of art [De Menil Collection, Houston, Tex.] R. Banham. il *Art Am* 75:124-9 Je '87

L.A. elevation [Museum of Contemporary Art designed by A. Isozaki] M. Filler. il *House Gard* 159:86-9+ Ja '87

The L.A. Museum of Contemporary Art: what's in a name? H. Muschamp. il *Archit Rec* 175:83+ My '87

Missed connections [G. Aulenti's design for the Musée d'Orsay, Paris] C. K. Gandee. il por *Archit Rec* 175:128-39 Mr '87

A new presence for craft [American Craft Museum] P. Goldberger. il *Am Craft* 47:30-2 F/Mr '87

Art galleries and museums—Architecture—*cont.*
New treasures on the Mall [National Museum of African Art and Arthur M. Sackler Gallery] H. Dudar. il *Smithsonian* 18:44-63 S '87
Order out of hodgepodge [Chrysler Museum] J. Meyer. il *Art News* 86:28+ D '87
A quiet place for art [De Menil Collection, Houston, Tex.] M. Filler. il *House Gard* 159:74+ Jl '87
Rating the new American museums. S. Stephens. il *House Gard* 159:62+ O '87
The Sainsbury Wing: an extension to the National Gallery in London. K. D. Stein. il *Archit Rec* 175:65 My '87
Skill full [architecture of the American Craft Museum] J. Lebensohn. il *Am Craft* 47:33-5 F/Mr '87
The sky line [design of Guggenheim Museum by F. L. Wright] B. Gill. *New Yorker* 63:49-50+ Je 8 '87
Soft sell [Terra Museum of American Art, Chicago] P. M. Sachner. il *Archit Rec* 175:112-15 N '87
Winging it: does adding on add up? D. Davis. il *Newsweek* 109:70-3 F 23 '87

Directories
Guide to galleries, museums, artists [special issue] il *Art Am* 75:37-43+ Ag '87

Directors
See Museum directors

History
The artist and the museum. F. Haskell. il *N Y Rev Books* 34:38-42 D 3 '87

Management
See also
Museum directors
How not to run a museum. M. Esterow. *Art News* 86:238 Summ '87

Membership
All the fine young connoisseurs: museums tap new patrons. C. McGuigan. il *Newsweek* 109:67 Je 1 '87

Thefts
See Art thefts

Tours
See Art tours

Arizona
See also
Tucson Museum of Art

Austria
See also
Kunsthistorisches Museum (Vienna, Austria)

Belgium
See also
Musée van Buuren (Brussels, Belgium)
Museum of Contemporary Art (Antwerp, Belgium)

Benelux countries
High art in the Low Countries. H. Minetree. il *Harpers Bazaar* 120:78+ Ag '87

California
See also
Frederick R. Weisman Museum
J. Paul Getty Museum
Laguna Art Museum
Los Angeles County Museum of Art
Monterey Peninsula Museum of Art
Museum of Contemporary Art (Los Angeles, Calif.)
Newport Harbor Art Museum (Balboa, Calif.)
Oakland Museum
San Francisco Museum of Modern Art
Santa Monica (Calif.)—Galleries and museums
Triton Museum of Art
Venice (Calif.)—Galleries and museums

Connecticut
See also
Aldrich Museum of Contemporary Art (Ridgefield, Conn.)
Wadsworth Atheneum

Ecuador
See also
Chordeleg (Ecuador)—Galleries and museums

Florida
See also
Cummer Gallery of Art
Jacksonville Art Museum (Fla.)

France
See also
Centre National d'Art Contemporain (Grenoble, France)
Musée des Arts Décoratifs (Paris, France)
Musée d'Orsay (Paris, France)
Musée du Louvre

Germany (West)
See also
Franz Marc Museum (Kochel, Germany)
Wilhelm-Lehmbruck-Museum der Stadt Duisburg

Great Britain
See also
Bowes Museum (Barnard Castle, England)
Dulwich Picture Gallery (London, England)
National Gallery (Great Britain)

Illinois
See also
Art Institute of Chicago
R.H. Love Galleries, Inc.
Struve Gallery
Terra Museum of American Art (Chicago, Ill.)

Indiana
See also
Indianapolis Museum of Art

Japan
See also
National Museum of Modern Art (Kyoto, Japan)

Korea (South)
See also
National Museum of Modern Art (Seoul, Korea)

Maryland
See also
Baltimore Museum of Art

Massachusetts
See also
Massachusetts Museum of Contemporary Art and Architecture
Mount Holyoke College. Art Museum
Smith College. Museum of Art
Sterling and Francine Clark Art Institute
University of Massachusetts at Amherst. Fine Arts Center
Williams College. Museum of Art
Worcester Art Museum

Minnesota
See also
Tweed Museum of Art (Duluth, Minn.)

Mississippi
See also
Kate Freeman Clark Art Gallery

Morocco
See also
Museum of Islamic Art (Marrakesh, Morocco)

New England
The New England montage. C. Bowden. il *Art News* 86:87-8+ Summ '87

New Hampshire
See also
Hood Museum of Art

New Mexico
See also
Albuquerque Museum
Millicent Rogers Museum (Taos, N.M.)

New York (State)
See also
Metropolitan Museum of Art (New York, N.Y.)
Paula Cooper Gallery
Queens Museum
Solomon R. Guggenheim Museum
Whitney Museum of American Art

North Carolina
See also
North Carolina Museum of Art

Pennsylvania
See also
Brandywine River Museum

Peru
See also
Museo Oro del Peru

Soviet Union
See also
Pushkin Museum of Fine Arts (Moscow, Soviet Union)

Spain
See also
Palacio Nacional de Montjuich (Barcelona, Spain)

Switzerland
The baron thinks twice [uncertainty as to where the Thyssen-Bornemisza Collection will be housed] E. Beck. il por *Art News* 86:45 N '87

Tennessee
See also
Museum of Appalachia

Texas
See also
Dallas Museum of Art
De Menil Collection (Houston, Tex.)
Museum of Fine Arts (Houston, Tex.)
San Antonio Museum of Art

Art galleries and museums—*cont.*
United States
See Art galleries and museums
Vermont
See also
Shelburne Museum
Virginia
See also
Chrysler Museum
Virginia Museum of Fine Arts
Wales
See also
Clive Museum (Wales)
Washington (State)
See also
Seattle Art Museum
Yugoslavia
See also
Zagreb (Yugoslavia)—Galleries and museums
Art historians
See also
Schapiro, Meyer, 1904-
Art history *See* Art—History
Art In Construction (Firm)
Pigments of imagination. K. D. Stein. il *Archit Rec* 175:18-19 D '87
Art in discotheques
Art wanes in clubland. G. Danto. il *Art News* 86:16 O '87
Art in hotels, motels, etc.
Hotels as galleries. L. Kundell. il *Travel Holiday* 167:56-61 Ja '87
Want a room with a view? This hotel has one of hell [paintings on walls of Carlton Arms Hotel] M. Small. il por *People Wkly* 28:175-7 N 16 '87
Art in motion pictures
Extraterrestrials in Alphabetland [work of J. Davis to be used in Batteries not included] G. Henry. il por *Art News* 86:17 My '87
Love story [Caravaggio] L. Tillman. il *Art Am* 75:21-3 Ja '87
Art in prisons
Paradise lost [M. Schwartz's sculptural environment in main entry plaza of new Seattle jail] L. Smallwood. il *Art News* 86:57 O '87
Art in public buildings *See* Public art
Art in restaurants
Manhattan in Madrid [New Yorker restaurant] J.-P. Hayden, Jr. il *Horizon* 30:33-4 D '87
Art in the home
See also
Antiques
An aesthetic concern: the Los Angeles apartment of Walter and Helga Oppenheimer [decorated by Leonard Stanley] I. Borger. il *Archit Dig* 44:180-5 D '87
Architectural digest visits: Andy Williams [New York apartment; cover story] C. Ratcliff. il por *Archit Dig* 44:40-7+ Jl '87
An Asian mystique: Dale and Patricia Keller's New York apartment. L. Bernikow. il pors *Archit Dig* 44:94-101 S '87
Beaux arts in southern California [Resnick home] il *House Gard* 159:174-9+ D '87
The collectors: a rare aesthetic: Stuart Pivar's cornucopia of art in Manhattan. S. M. L. Aronson. il *Archit Dig* 44:124-31+ Mr '87
Douglas Cramer: passionate perfectionist. P. Clothier. il por *Art News* 86:146-50 Summ '87
An eye for the best [G. Lois' Greenwich Village apartment] E. G. Carter. il *House Gard* 159:218-21+ O '87
Folk tales: of baseballs and weathervanes in Washington, D.C. [J. and J. Wallach's collection of American folk art] C. T. Buckley. il pors *Archit Dig* 44:62-7+ Jl '87
Frames of reference: varied palette for a New York apartment. P. Carlsen. il *Archit Dig* 44:120-7 D '87
A gift of vision [Houston home of D. de Menil] R. Bernier. il por *House Gard* 159:120-9+ Jl '87
Global treasure trove [Paris apartment of A. Dandois] C. Vogel. il por *N Y Times Mag* p62-6 Mr 1 '87
Hacienda La Trinidad: artists' retreat near Guanajuato, Mexico [home and studio of C. and J. W. Summers] S. Cadwallader. il *Archit Dig* 44:126-31 Ja '87
International style: Oriental touch for Mexico City [interior design by Jay Spectre] P. Warner. il *Archit Dig* 44:84-91 Jl '87
Jan Mitchell—the varied tastes of a New York connoisseur. C. Ratcliff. il por *Archit Dig* 44:298+ N '87
Living with antiques:
A New England folk art collection. S. Klein and S. Rotenstreich. il *Antiques* 132:538-45 S '87

Memoir through objects. L. Kirstein. il *House Gard* 159:116-21+ Ja '87
Metropolitan life [Trump Tower apartment designed by Michael de Santis] M. Weber. il *Archit Dig* 44:100-7 Mr '87
An oasis in Bangkok: abstract art defines a penthouse apartment [decorated by Sally Sirkin Lewis for T. Takahashi] L. Bernikow. il *Archit Dig* 44:60-7 Ja '87
Paintings of the table [art considered suitable for the dining room] L. Blanch. il *Archit Dig* 44:24+ Mr '87
Past perfect: Bernard and Barbara Bergreen on Fifth Avenue. J. Allen. il por *Archit Dig* 44:190-9 N '87
Possession obsession [A. Warhol's collection] S. M. L. Aronson. il por *House Gard* 159:186-96 D '87
A practiced eye: J. Garvin Mecking in Greenwich Village. S. M. L. Aronson. il *Archit Dig* 44:156-63+ Ap '87
Pre-Columbian priority: rare treasures in a Manhattan apartment. D. Rosenthal. il *Archit Dig* 44:140-4+ Ag '87
La Quinta Norte: Douglas S. Cramer's ranch in the Santa Ynez Valley [decorated by Michael Taylor] L. Bernikow. il por *Archit Dig* 44:136-47 Ap '87
Rancho La Vista: western themes in California's Ojai Valley [western art collector V. Milner] M. Webb. il pors *Archit Dig* 44:112-19 D '87
The Rene Di Rosas in Napa Valley. J. Chatfield-Taylor. il por *Archit Dig* 44:258+ Je '87
Rooms for art [P. Naggar decorates Manhattan apartment to highlight collection] J. Plumb. il por *House Gard* 159:142-51+ O '87
Sculptural strengths: the B. Gerald Cantors in Manhattan [apartment decorated by Bebe Winkler] M. M. Thomas. il *Archit Dig* 44:118-23+ My '87
Shock of the past: ancient objects accent a visionary San Francisco design [R. Hutchinson's apartment] J. Chatfield-Taylor. il *Archit Dig* 44:116-27 Ap '87
Sleight of hand [Los Angeles studio of A. Machado] J. Chatfield-Taylor. il por *Archit Dig* 44:146-51+ My '87
Spirited composition on Chester Square: the London house of Baron and Baroness Thyssen-Bornemisza. J. J. Norwich. il por *Archit Dig* 44:104-11 O '87
Stained glass for the home. C. Zusy. bibl f il *Antiques* 131:848-57 Ap '87
View from Malibu: Michael and Kim McCarty in California. B. D. Colen. il pors *Archit Dig* 44:96-101+ Jl '87
A vitrine for art [Juan Montoya's apartment design for a Manhattan collector] S. Stephens. il *House Gard* 159:172-5 S '87
Art Institute of Chicago
Art times two. M. Wade. il *Horizon* 30:58-61 My '87
Art insurance *See* Insurance, Art
Art literature
See also
Art—Bibliography
Publishers and publishing—Art literature
Art talk: a few words on the relationship of reference books to art collecting. A. S. Bamberger. *Antiques Collect Hobbies* 92:31 D '87
Art market *See* Art trade
Art materials *See* Artists' materials
Art metal work
See also
Brass work
Goldsmithing
Jewelry
Mounts (Decorative arts)
Ormolu
Pewter
Art Moving Center (Firm)
Making it in a man's world [C. Terada] P. Sherrid. il por *U S News World Rep* 103:41 Jl 27 '87
Art museums *See* Art galleries and museums
Art news
Artworld. See issues of Art in America
News coverage of arts and arts education. B. Hall. *Des Arts Educ* 88:10-12 Jl/Ag '87
Off press. il *Am Craft* 47:71-2 Ap/My '87
The sampler: a selection of previews, reviews, sundries, and suggestions. See issues of Americana
Art news (Periodical)
Art circles: portrait photographs from ARTnews, 1905-1986 [exhibit at the International Center of Photography] A. H. Hoy. il *Art News* 86:93-100 F '87
The first 85 years [cover story; special issue] il *Art News* 86:143-8+ N '87
Art nouveau
See also
Art deco

Art nouveau—*cont.*

Art nouveau Meissen emerges from long neglect. S. Jones. il *Antiques Collect Hobbies* 91:11-14 F '87

Historic architecture: Joseph Maria Olbrich: a jugendstil design at the Mathildenhöhe artists' colony. J. Rykwert. il por *Archit Dig* 44:180-5+ Ap '87

Exhibitions

Cooper-Hewitt Museum [Art nouveau Bing: Paris style 1900 exhibition; cover story] il *Antiques Collect Hobbies* 92:49+ Jl '87

The other fin de siècle [The Dreyfus affair and Art nouveau Bing] K. Silver. bibl f il *Art Am* 75:104-11+ D '87

Art objects

See also
Art in the home
Display of antiques, art objects, etc.
Jade art objects

Conservation and restoration

See Art—Conservation and restoration

Insurance

See Insurance, Art

Reproductions

See Art—Reproductions

Taxation

See Taxation of works of art

Art of living See Conduct of life

Art on ocean liners

Seaworthy exhibits. H. Basch and S. Slater. il *Travel Holiday* 167:52-5+ Ja '87

Art patronage

See also
Art and industry
Arts and industry
Dia Art Foundation

All the fine young connoisseurs: museums tap new patrons. C. McGuigan. il *Newsweek* 109:67 Je 1 '87

The artist and the museum. F. Haskell. il *N Y Rev Books* 34:38-42 D 3 '87

'Cultivated capital' [culture and patronage of the arts in nineteenth-century Manchester and Leeds] J. Wolff and C. Arscott. bibl il *Hist Today* 37:22-8 Mr '87

Forget-me-nots: patronage in Gothic England. N. Saul. bibl il *Hist Today* 37:18-24 N '87

A national network of leadership [National Patrons of the American Council for the Arts] M. Rhodes. il *Horizon* 30:4 Ap '87

Painting Petworth [tradition of artists portraying stately English home] M. Egremont. il *House Gard* 159:116+ N '87

Professional page [getting sponsorship of painting trips abroad] W. Mangum. il *Am Artist* 51:10+ Ag '87

Art publishing See Publishers and publishing—Art

Art sales See Art trade

Art schools

See also
Black Mountain College (N.C.)
California College of Arts and Crafts
New York Academy of Art
School of Visual Arts (New York, N.Y.)
Whitney Museum of American Art. Independent Study Program

Directories

1987 directory of art schools and workshops. il *Am Artist* 51:D1-D16+ Mr '87

Switzerland

See also
Art Center College of Design (Pasadena, Calif.). European campus

Art shows See Art—Exhibitions

Art studios See Artists' studios

Art teachers

Education

Learning to teach art: an integrative process. D. J. Reeves. *Des Arts Educ* 89:41-4 S/O '87

Art thefts

See also
United States. Federal Bureau of Investigation. National Stolen Art File

Art cop [Detective T. Moscardini tracks art theft in New York City] H. Polskin. il por *N Y* 20:28+ O 26 '87

Going undercover for art's sake [Italy's special police unit] R. Suro. il *N Y Times Mag* p42-3+ D 13 '87

Whose Chagall is it, anyway? [Solomon R. Guggenheim Museum suit against R. Lubell for recovery of a purportedly stolen Marc Chagall gouache] A. Decker. *Art News* 86:21 D '87

Art tours

Star tours [Metropolitan Museum of Art] il *Art News* 86:11 D '87

Art trade

See also
American Craft Enterprises, Inc.
Antiques—Valuation
Art Against AIDS
Art galleries and museums
Barry Friedman Ltd.
Hanzel Galleries
Indian Market (Santa Fe, N.M.)
Kuromatsu (Firm)
Leo Castelli Gallery
Photographs—Marketing
Sidney Janis Gallery
Street art and artists

1987 business supplement [special section] il *Am Artist* 51:58-62+ Jl '87

Art for barter: a cultural currency. D. Grant. *Am Artist* 51:S12+ N '87

The art market. See issues of Art News

The artist as cynic [views of P. Halley] J. Masheck. *New Leader* 70:22-3 Je 29 '87

Auction fever runs high. il *Macleans* 100:30 Ap 13 '87

Auction signals: how to bid like an insider. P. Gardner. il *Art News* 86:101-5 F '87

Collectors cotton to Texas bargains [auctions] B. Kallen. il *Forbes* 139:144+ Mr 9 '87

Fame and fortune in the art world. H. Brown. bibl f il *Am Artist* 51:46-51+ Mr '87

From the gavel. See issues of Antiques & Collecting Hobbies beginning January 1987 through May 1987

Of Vincent and Eanum Pig [auctions of van Gogh's Sunflowers and the Duchess of Windsor's jewelry] R. Hughes. il *Time* 129:80-1 Ap 13 '87

Philadelphia's pride [McIlhenny collection up for auction] C. Vogel. il *N Y Times Mag* p70-2 My 10 '87

Profiles [dealer W. G. Arader] M. Singer. il *New Yorker* 63:44-6+ N 30 '87

S.R.O. at Hanzel Galleries April art & antique auction. il *Antiques Collect Hobbies* 92:50-1 Je '87

The Saatchi factor [tycoon C. Saatchi, major player in contemporary art marketplace] R. W. Walker. il por *Art News* 86:117-21 Ja '87

Sublime views [market for American romantic landscapes] F. Donegan. il *Americana* 15:62-4 N/D '87

Talk about lines! A guy paid $26,400 for this drawing—and then they demolished it [auction of conceptual art by S. LeWitt] M. Small. il por *People Wkly* 27:43-4 My 25 '87

Anecdotes, facetiae, satire, etc.

How to buy the Louvre. R. Buchwald. *Art News* 86:238 Summ '87

Ethical aspects

Christie's and Cristallina settle [fraud and negligent misrepresentation suit against Christie's] R. W. Walker. il *Art News* 86:21-2 Ap '87

Fake masks [African art market] N. Lemann. il *Atlantic* 260:24+ N '87

Frenchy and the Persians [N. Sakhai and H. Mahboubian mastermind New York City theft of Near Eastern antiquities for insurance recovery] C. Trillin. *New Yorker* 63:44+ Je 29 '87

Next time, ask [drawings sold as Piranesis at Sotheby's returned due to questionable authenticity] R. W. Walker. *Art News* 86:25-6 O '87

Warrant for Lee's arrest dropped [dispute between French government and former Cleveland Museum of Art director S. E. Lee over the export of a N. Poussin painting] R. W. Walker. *Art News* 86:30 Summ '87

France

See also
Hôtel Drouot (Paris, France)

Le Big Bang [auction market] R. Morais. il *Forbes* 140:46+ Jl 27 '87

Great Britain

See also
Christie's (London, England)
Sotheby's (Firm)

Of horse and hound [G. Nevill, dealer in hunting art] C. Gibbs. il por *House Gard* 159:76+ N '87

India

Delhi's cuisine and craftsmen. L. Nicholson. il *Gourmet* 47:66-71+ S '87

Shamianas, anyone? [S. Pennathur's linkup with Indian artisans] P. Gupte. il pors *Forbes* 140:190+ O 5 '87

Italy

Artisans of Florence. A. M. Zwack. il *Gourmet* 47:50-5+ Jl '87

Japan

The power of the yen. R. W. Walker. il *Art News* 86:25 S '87

Art trade—Japan—*cont.*

A yen for Western art. il *U S News World Rep* 102:14 Ap 20 '87

Panama

See also

Cristallina SA

Soviet Union

Soviet art for export. P. Bonet. *World Press Rev* 34:60 D '87

Art treasures, Protection of *See* Cultural property—Protection

Arteries

Diseases

See also

Arteriosclerosis

Kawasaki syndrome

Plaque hemorrhage linked to stroke [use of computer tomography to scan carotid arteries; research by Antonio Culebras and others] S. Weisburd. il *Sci News* 131:167 Mr 14 '87

Therapy

See also

Blood vessels—Surgery

Cardiac catheterization

Ballooning-out gets mostly good marks [angioplasty] D. D. Edwards. il *Sci News* 131:311 My 16 '87

Clogged arteries take the laser's heat—painlessly. J. Carey. il *U S News World Rep* 102:69 F 16 '87

Drugs for heart attacks [FDA ruling on streptokinase] *FDA Consum* 21:7 S '87

Help's arrived for heart-attack victims [angioplasty] S. Findlay. il *U S News World Rep* 103:109-11 D 28 '87-Ja 4 '88

Lasers and tips and drills, oh my!; Implanting 'stents' with staying power. D. D. Edwards. *Sci News* 132:376 D 12 '87

Steel strands for the clogged heart [stents] il *U S News World Rep* 103:10-11 N 30 '87

Unclogging arteries [use of lasers and balloons] P. Gadsby and L. J. Brown. il *Good Housekeep* 204:213 Je '87

Surgery

See Blood vessels—Surgery

Arteriosclerosis

Atherosclerosis KOs anti-spasm fighter [endothelium-derived relaxing factor; research by Donald D. Heistad and others] D. D. Edwards. *Sci News* 132:342 N 28 '87

Causes

Artery clogging and apo-B. J. Silberner. il *Sci News* 131:90-1 F 7 '87

Lipoprotein findings may solve one riddle . . . and pose another [apolipoprotein(a)'s influence] D. D. Edwards. *Sci News* 132:311 N 14 '87

Type A and coronary artery disease [research by Jeffrey P. Kahn and others] S. Eisenberg. *Sci News* 132:293 N 7 '87

Nutritional aspects

See also

Cholesterol

Vitamin C goes with the flow. *Prevention* 39:8 Mr '87

Vitamins patrol artery walls. *Prevention* 39:54 O '87

Therapy

Bypass breakthrough [University of Southern California study on lowering cholesterol through diet and drugs] il *Time* 129:52 Je 29 '87

Diet, drugs slow heart-felt 'insults' [lowering cholesterol; University of Southern California study] D. D. Edwards. il *Sci News* 131:407 Je 27 '87

Killer cholesterol: the news is good [study by University of Southern California] il *U S News World Rep* 102:11 Je 29 '87

One for the heart [University of Southern California study on lowering cholesterol through diet and drugs] T. Monmaney. il *Newsweek* 109:56-7 Je 29 '87

Study bolsters case against cholesterol [University of Southern California research] L. Roberts. il *Science* 237:28-9 Jl 3 '87

Arthritis

See also

Gout

Lyme disease

National Institute of Arthritis, Musculoskeletal, and Skin Diseases (U.S.)

When arthritis strikes. M. Callahan. il *Parents* 62:273-5 N '87

Causes

Are you running into arthritis? *Prevention* 39:64 Mr '87

Substance P activation of rheumatoid synoviocytes: neural pathway in pathogenesis of arthritis. M. Lotz and others. bibl f il *Science* 235:893-5 F 20 '87

Nutritional aspects

Does meatless equal painless for arthritics? [work of Lars Sköldstam] *Prevention* 39:100 Ap '87

Fish oil: a new arthritis tamer? M. Mihalik. *Prevention* 39:30-2 Mr '87

New evidence for arthritis diet? *Prevention* 39:100 Jl '87

Therapy

Antiarthritic gold compounds effectively quench electronically excited singlet oxygen. E. J. Corey and others. bibl f il *Science* 236:68-9 Ap 3 '87

Arthritis: looking for immunotherapy [rheumatoid arthritis] D. D. Edwards. *Sci News* 131:228 Ap 11 '87

Be fit and well—even with arthritis. il *Prevention* 39:34-6+ Je '87

The bender mender [knee replacement surgery; work of C. S. Ranawat] S. Shapiro. il *Discover* 8:22-3 O '87

An 'F' for fake: wonder-drug science project gets bad grade from FDA [Dio-Hemo-2000 developed by 16 yr. old boy] A. Hecht. il *FDA Consum* 21:41-2 F '87

The gold standard [guanethidine to treat rheumatoid arthritis] J. R. Goldberg. *Health* 19:26-7 Je '87

Her joints are jumping [artificial hip recipient B. Benson] P. Spencer. il pors *50 Plus* 27:44-50 Ja '87

Risking all for a cure [rheumatoid arthritis] K. K. Goldstein. il *50 Plus* 27:51-2 Ja '87

Survey results: how readers cope with arthritis. *Prevention* 39:18+ My '87

Why does gold help arthritics? [research by Elias J. Corey and others] *Sci News* 131:264 Ap 25 '87

Arthropods

See also

Horseshoe crabs

Arthroscopes and arthroscopy

Joint venture [arthroscopy to treat TMJ syndrome] J. Carpi. *Health* 19:26 Je '87

Mending knees. P. Gadsby and L. J. Brown. il *Good Housekeep* 204:212 Je '87

Arthur, King

about

In search of Camelot. A. J. S. Rayl. il *Omni* 9:24+ Mr '87

Tomb

Morte d'Arthur. F. Barker. il map *Hist Today* 37:3-4 F '87

Arthur D. Little, Inc.

Can this canary swallow a cat? [Plenum wants Arthur D. Little] K. H. Hammonds. *Bus Week* p30-1 Jl 27 '87

Your problem is solved. P. Baida. il *Am Herit* 38:20-1 F/Mr '87

Arthur Guinness & Sons plc

See also

Guinness plc

Arthur M. Sackler Gallery (Washington, D.C.)

Animal magnetism [selection of display pieces by T. Lawton] D. Kazanjian. il *House Gard* 159:166-71+ S '87

Cavern fever. B. Forgey. il *Art News* 86:27 D '87

Dr. Arthur M. Sackler, for whom our new gallery is named, sought to link the arts and sciences with the humanities. R. M. Adams. il *Smithsonian* 18:10 O '87

New treasures on the Mall. H. Dudar. il *Smithsonian* 18:44-63 S '87

Peering into a people's soul. M. Horn. il *U S News World Rep* 103:67-8 O 5 '87

Smithsonian opens new museum complex on National Mall. il *Am Craft* 47:12 O/N '87

Arthur Young & Company

An eye on the bottom line [Arthur Young/Audit Smarter, Quicker package] D. Garfinkel. il *Pers Comput* 11:69-70 Je '87

Arthurian romances

Models of kingship: Arthur in medieval romance. B. Stone. il *Hist Today* 37:32-8 N '87

Artichokes

See also

Cooking—Vegetables

Articles for periodicals *See* Periodical articles

Artifacts, Indian (American) *See* Indians of North America—Antiquities

Artifacts, Protection of See Cultural property—Protection
Artificial arm See Arm, Artificial
Artificial body parts See Prosthesis
Artificial chromosomes See Chromosomes, Artificial
Artificial ear See Ear, Artificial
Artificial fertilization in vitro See Fertilization in vitro
Artificial flowers See Flowers, Artificial
Artificial fog See Fog, Artificial
Artificial heart See Heart, Artificial
Artificial heart valves See Heart, Artificial
Artificial hip joint See Hip joint, Artificial
Artificial insemination
> See also
> Ova—Transplantation

Artificial insemination, Human
> See also
> Ova—Transplantation
> Surrogate mothers

Gay gothic [two homosexual couples jointly raise a child]
L. Van Gelder. il *Ms* 16:146-7+ Jl/Ag '87
New option for infertile couples [sperm washing] il *USA
Today (Periodical)* 115:11-12 F '87
Washing away infertility [sperm washing]. J. Pratt. il
Health 19:21 Ap '87

Moral and religious aspects
Unnatural acts and other papal indiscretions [Catholic
Church's views] K. R. Lawrence. il *Ms* 16:118 S '87
What is sex for? [Vatican statement on human reproduc-
tion] S. Grenz. il por *Christ Today* 31:22-3 Je 12
'87

Artificial intelligence
> See also
> Expert systems (Computers)
> Heuristic programming
> Hypertext
> Machine translating
> Natural language processing
> Neural network computers

AI 'fair' demonstrates application of expert systems to
C³I operations. K. J. Stein. *Aviat Week Space Technol*
126:104-5+ Je 1 '87
Artificial intelligence. J. J. Kroger. il por *Futurist* 21:38-40
Jl/Ag '87
Artificial intelligence and natural resource management.
R. N. Coulson and others. bibl f il *Science* 237:262-7
Jl 17 '87
Artificial intelligence moves into mainstream. M. M.
Waldrop. il *Science* 237:484-5 Jl 31 '87
Artificial intelligence: the rational optimist [H. A. Simon]
C. Holden. *Current* 293:36-40 Je '87
Associations or rules in learning language? G. Kolata.
il *Science* 237:133-4 Jl 10 '87
Causality, structure, and common sense. M. M. Waldrop.
il *Science* 237:1297-9 S 11 '87
Chinese food by computer [CHEF program expands AI;
work of Kristan Hammond] il *USA Today (Periodical)*
115:12-13 Je '87
The chip behind TI's smart weapons [Lisp chip] T.
Mason. il *Bus Week* p104-6 Mr 9 '87
Computerizing with confidence (VI). K. Berney. il *Nations
Bus* 75:22-4 Ap '87
Do-it-yourself chips get easier [circuit design machines]
O. Port. *Bus Week* p92 Mr 30 '87
Facing reality: computer scientists aid war efforts. J.
Weizenbaum. il *Technol Rev* 90:22-3 Ja '87
The future of artificial intelligence. G. Heilmeier. il
Radio-Electron 58:85-90 My '87
Moving toward AI. E. Shapiro. *Byte* 12:263-4+ Ag '87
The new world of artificial intelligence. D. De Gregorio.
il *Courier* 40:14-15 Jl '87
Novel developments in artificial intelligence. il
Radio-Electron 58:6 D '87
Pied Piper of the computer [A. Kay] F. Rose. il por
N Y Times Mag p56+ N 8 '87
The power of artificial intelligence. S. Bentley. *Black
Enterp* 17:33 Ap '87
The search for a thinking computer. N. Doi and others.
il *Courier* 40:16-19 Jl '87
Some researchers concerned with Defense funding of
AI projects [Strategic Computing Initiative] *Byte* 12:40
O '87
Texas Instruments targets airlines for its AI products.
Aviat Week Space Technol 127:43 O 19 '87
The Turing point: is it real or is it silicon? F. Kendig.
il *Omni* 9 Omni Exper:6-9 Ap '87
Your humble servant [American Express' Authorizer's
Assistant AI-based system] E. Dyson. il *Forbes* 140:204
N 2 '87
Your mindless brain [views of M. L. Minsky] P. Hoffman.
il *Discover* 8:84-5+ S '87

Artificial islands
Who says no man is an island? Builder Forbes Kiddoo
is surrounded on all sides by water and curiosity.
M. Dougherty. il por *People Wkly* 28:50-2 Ag 31
'87
Artificial joints See Joints, Artificial
Artificial knee See Knee, Artificial
Artificial ligaments See Ligaments, Artificial
Artificial lighting See Lighting
Artificial pacemaker (Heart) See Pacemaker, Artificial
(Heart)
Artificial rain and rainfall See Rain and rainfall, Artificial
Artificial reefs See Reefs, Artificial
Artificial rumen See Rumen, Artificial
Artificial satellites
> See also
> Eosat (Firm)

The Perseus flasher: mystery solved! [momentary reflec-
tions of sunlight by rotating satellites] *Sky Telesc* 73:604
Je '87
Perseus flasher: satellite glints [momentary reflections
of sunlight by rotating satellites] *Sci News* 131:397
Je 20 '87

Accidents
Soviet Proton booster fails; reconnaissance satellite explodes. C. Covault. il *Aviat Week Space Technol*
126:26-7 F 9 '87

Archeological use
Archaeology from above. N. McAleer. il map *Space
World* X-2-278:21-5 F '87
New findings on ancient Maya. map *USA Today
(Periodical)* 115:11-12 Je '87
Satellites help in study of ancient civilization [Mayan
civilization] *Astronomy* 15:64 Ag '87

Astronomical use
The best little telescope in the solar system [International
Ultraviolet Explorer] A. Stern. il *Space World*
X-1-277:18-20 Ja '87
Beyond the rainbow. J. Rhea. il *Space World*
X-2-278:17-19 F '87
COBE's missing mass [Cosmic Background Explorer]
G. Freiherr. il *Space World* X-2-278:15 F '87
Color this quasar infrared [IRAS 13349+2438] *Astronomy*
15:79-80 Mr '87
Continuing the tradition: amateur astronomers and the
Space Telescope [address, August 7, 1986] R. Giacconi.
il por *Astronomy* 15:24+ Ja '87
Cosmic collisions [IRAS data] S. P. Maran. *Nat Hist*
96:22+ Ag '87
The extreme ultraviolet: a promising new window on
the universe. J. K. Davies. il *Astronomy* 15:82-7 Jl
'87
Frosty the . . . nebula? [IRAS 09371 + 1212; work
of Thierry Forveille and others] il *Sky Telesc* 74:346
O '87
Hubble trouble? [possibility of damage from collisions
with other satellites and space debris] il *Sky Telesc*
73:31 Ja '87
Infrared cirrus [Infrared Astronomical Satellite] il *Sky
Telesc* 73:601-2 Je '87
Infrared eyes on the universe: a conversation with Nancy
Boggess [Infrared Astronomical Satellite] T. Reichhardt
and J. Rhea. il por *Space World* X-2-278:12-16 F
'87
IRAS and the quasars. R. Tresch-Fienberg. il *Sky Telesc*
73:13 Ja '87
IRAS asteroid catalogue. il *Sky Telesc* 73:599 Je '87
IRAS puts astronomers out of (one) business. R. A.
Kerr. *Science* 235:30-1 Ja 2 '87
IRAS serendipitous survey observations of Pluto and
Charon. M. V. Sykes and others. bibl f il *Science*
237:1336-40 S 11 '87
IUE: nine years of astronomy [International Ultraviolet
Explorer] L. A. Shore. il *Astronomy* 15:14-22 Ap '87
IUE satellite observes supernova in ultraviolet [Inter-
national Ultraviolet Explorer] il *Aviat Week Space
Technol* 126:260-1 Mr 9 '87
Leaving the shuttle can be a hard trip [Cosmic Background
Explorer] J. Eberhart. *Sci News* 132:166 S 12 '87
New satellite would extend VLBI into space [QUASAT]
il *Astronomy* 15:76 F '87
Observing the energetic universe. D. H. Smith. il *Technol
Rev* 90:66-73 My/Je '87
Results from X-ray satellites [Japanese satellites] *Sky
Telesc* 73:11 Ja '87
Star formation and IRAS galaxies. D. A. Allen. il *Sky
Telesc* 73:372-4 Ap '87
Waiting to look at the edge of the universe [Hubble
Space Telescope] il *Newsweek* 110:52-3 Ag 17 '87
Will Space Telescope be ready? J. K. Beatty. il *Sky
Telesc* 73:146-8 F '87

Artificial satellites—*cont.*
Biological use
See also
    Artificial satellites—Cosmos missions
Lives of the cell [Lifesat] A. R. Oberg. il *Omni* 9:20+ Ag '87
Soviets target launch of large biomedical satellite for 1990. *Aviat Week Space Technol* 127:48 N 16 '87
Spying from on high [satellite wildlife telemetry] M. Bowker. il *Int Wildl* 17:22-3 S/O '87
U.S., Soviets to cooperate on September launch of biosatellite [Vostok biological satellite] il *Aviat Week Space Technol* 127:18-19 Jl 13 '87
Communication use
See Communications satellites
Cosmos missions
Soviet Proton booster fails; reconnaissance satellite explodes. C. Covault. il *Aviat Week Space Technol* 126:26-7 F 9 '87
Soviets conduct unusual manned, unmanned activities. C. Covault. *Aviat Week Space Technol* 127:29-30 S 7 '87
Soviets lose Proton booster, payload in launch failure. *Aviat Week Space Technol* 126:24 My 4 '87
Atmospheric entry
Cosmos 1402's uranium remains. J. Eberhart. *Sci News* 132:278-9 O 31 '87
Detection of uranium from Cosmos-1402 in the stratosphere [from nuclear reactor power supply] R. Leifer and others. bibl f il *Science* 238:512-14 O 23 '87
Soviet biological satellite misses target by 2,000 miles [Cosmos 1,887] C. Covault. *Aviat Week Space Technol* 127:32-3 O 19 '87
Costs
"Cheapsats". A. Stern. *Space World* X-9-285:9-10 S '87
Earth sciences use
See also
    Artificial satellites—Meteorological use
    Artificial satellites—Oceanographic use
Canada approves development of scaled-back Radarsat. T. M. Foley. il *Aviat Week Space Technol* 127:51+ Jl 13 '87
China evaluates benefits, intelligence value of Landsat [cover story] C. Covault. il *Aviat Week Space Technol* 127:42-5 O 5 '87
Commerce urged to divert weather satellite funding to save Landsat. *Aviat Week Space Technol* 126:62-3 Mr 23 '87
Congress to provide $62.5 million for Landsat follow-on program, pending compromise with administration. T. M. Foley. *Aviat Week Space Technol* 127:29-30 Jl 6 '87
Detection of Rift Valley fever viral activity in Kenya by satellite remote sensing imagery [vegetation measurement linked to flood conditions that produce mosquitoes] K. J. Linthicum and others. bibl f il maps *Science* 235:1656-9 Mr 27 '87
Eosat to mount challenge to Landsat restrictions [use by news media] *Aviat Week Space Technol* 127:26-7 N 2 '87
Eosat will market Landsat data from Chinese ground stations. il *Aviat Week Space Technol* 127:52-3 Jl 20 '87
Europe's Spot changes top management following data production problems. J. M. Lenorovitz. il *Aviat Week Space Technol* 126:64-5 Ap 20 '87
French Spot satellite shows Soviet Northern Fleet facilities. il *Aviat Week Space Technol* 126:44-5 Mr 2 '87
Government reins on private satellites [coping with press use of photos from space] J. Eberhart. *Sci News* 132:87 Ag 8 '87
Landsat commercialization stumbles again. M. M. Waldrop. *Science* 235:155 Ja 9 '87
Making of a desert [Landsat images help study effects of 20-year drought on the Inland Niger Delta in Mali; work of Patricia Jacobberger] J. Dall'Acqua. il map *Earth Sci* 40:19-21 Spr '87
Monitoring earth and sun by satellite [special section] R. A. Kerr. il *Science* 236:1624-5 Je 26 '87
New Landsat plans could terminate Eosat contract. *Aviat Week Space Technol* 127:139-40 S 28 '87
Pentagon, State Dept. granted veto over U.S. remote sensing satellites. T. M. Foley. *Aviat Week Space Technol* 127:20-1 Jl 20 '87
Plain sense [satellite image comparison study conducted on Kansas plains] J. Horgan. *Sci Am* 257:27-8 S '87
Reagan asked to intercede to save Landsat program. T. M. Foley. *Aviat Week Space Technol* 126:29-30 Ap 6 '87

Ride panel will urge lunar base, earth science as new space goals. C. Covault. il *Aviat Week Space Technol* 127:16-18 Jl 13 '87
Rift Valley fever: long-distance diagnosis [vegetation measurement linked to floods and mosquitoes; study by Kenneth J. Linthicum and others] J. Silberner. *Sci News* 131:199 Mr 28 '87
Satellites to forecast malaria hazard. il *USA Today (Periodical)* 115:6 Je '87
Soviet strategic laser sites imaged by French Spot satellite. C. Covault. il *Aviat Week Space Technol* 127:26-7 O 26 '87
Spot-ing earth from space. J. Schefter. il *Pop Sci* 230:78-81 F '87
Spot photographs secret base for USSR nuclear submarines [Barents Sea] C. Covault. il *Aviat Week Space Technol* 127:18-19 Jl 20 '87
A spy satellite for the press? E. Marshall. il *Science* 238:1346-8 D 4 '87
Unique satellite image shows geology of Cape Cod. il *Earth Sci* 39:7-8 Wint '86
History
President's message [construction of Vanguard satellite in 1957] B. Bova. il *Space World* X-10-286 Space Advocate:A8 O '87
Sputnik: the little sphere that changed the world. G. Williams. il *Pop Mech* 164:59-61+ O '87
Insurance
See Insurance, Space flight
Launching
Are the profits really there? [satellite launching business] W. W. Crook, III. il *Space World* X-7-283:34 Jl '87
Blast-off for profits [satellite-launching business] J. Castro. il *Time* 129:44-5 Mr 2 '87
British offer Ariane deployment system for use on Titan 3 [Spelda dual satellite deployment system] il *Aviat Week Space Technol* 126:32-3 Ja 12 '87
Computer simulates multi-spacecraft deployment from Ariane 4 launcher. il *Aviat Week Space Technol* 126:70-1 F 2 '87
General Dynamics cites launch candidates for Atlas G/Centaur. il *Aviat Week Space Technol* 126:25 Mr 23 '87
Getting into orbit—the non-NASA way. J. Eberhart. *Sci News* 131:326 My 23 '87
Leaving the shuttle can be a hard trip [Cosmic Background Explorer] J. Eberhart. *Sci News* 132:166 S 12 '87
Martin evaluates bids on Titan launch adapter [Titan 3 dual satellite adapter] *Aviat Week Space Technol* 126:62-3 Je 22 '87
NASA assigns launch dates to shuttle science missions. il *Astronomy* 15:82-3 Ja '87
Private launch prospects improve. M. M. Waldrop. il *Science* 236:766-8 My 15 '87
Starship enterprise: chasing NASA's unfinished business. S. Payne. il *Bus Week* p98-9+ N 9 '87
U.S. Air Force Titan launch restarts heavy booster flights [KH-11 imaging reconnaissance satellite launched] C. Covault. il *Aviat Week Space Technol* 127:24-5 N 2 '87
USAF plans launch of KH-11 replacement [imaging reconnaissance satellites] *Aviat Week Space Technol* 126:22 F 2 '87
USAF Titan 34D launches missile warning satellite. E. H. Kolcum. il *Aviat Week Space Technol* 127:30-1 D 7 '87
Meteorological use
Above and beyond and auroras. il *Nat Hist* 96:6+ S '87
Chinese building geosynchronous weather spacecraft; prepare polar-orbit satellite for launch. *Aviat Week Space Technol* 126:23 Je 29 '87
Commerce Dept. will buy ELVs from private sector [National Oceanic and Atmospheric Administration] *Aviat Week Space Technol* 126:24-5 Mr 23 '87
Commerce urged to divert weather satellite funding to save Landsat. *Aviat Week Space Technol* 126:62-3 Mr 23 '87
GOES-7: rebuilding the weather watch. J. Eberhart. *Sci News* 131:150 Mr 7 '87
GOES will provide full U.S. weather monitoring capability. *Aviat Week Space Technol* 126:68+ Mr 16 '87
Haynes offers PC-based weather, flight plan system [WeatherStar satellite information system] *Aviat Week Space Technol* 126:100 My 25 '87
Lab for the universe [International Solar-Terrestrial Physics Program] T. Kiely. il *Technol Rev* 90:8+ N/D '87

Artificial satellites—Meteorological use—*cont.*

Langley develops optical technique for storing satellite data [Earth Radiation Budget Experiment satellites] *Aviat Week Space Technol* 127:145 Ag 10 '87

NASA solves problems, corrects GOES-H orbit. B. D. Nordwall. *Aviat Week Space Technol* 126:266-7 Mr 9 '87

NOAA, FAA consider volcano monitoring system. il *Aviat Week Space Technol* 127:30-1 Jl 6 '87

NOAA to hold competition to buy GOES launchers [Geostationary Operational Environmental Satellites] *Aviat Week Space Technol* 126:24 Ja 19 '87

Ready, set, GOES: weather eyes for the 21st century. J. Heckman. il maps *Space World* X-7-283:23-6 Jl '87

U.S., Japan present plans for joint spacecraft mission [Tropical Rainfall Measuring Mission] il *Aviat Week Space Technol* 127:69+ O 26 '87

Volcanic residue cited as possible source of misleading ozone data [Antarctic ozone hole] R. G. O'Lone. *Aviat Week Space Technol* 126:91-2 Ja 12 '87

Voyager crew uses satellite weather data. *Aviat Week Space Technol* 126:27 Ja 5 '87

Military use
See also
> Anti-satellite weapons
> Artificial satellites—Cosmos missions
> Strategic Defense Initiative

Antisubmarine warfare [address, May 20, 1987] C. A. H. Trost. *Vital Speeches Day* 53:551-3 Jl 1 '87

Arms control pacts can be verified. K. Tsipis. il maps *Discover* 8:79-93 Ap '87

Canada regards space-based radar as follow-on to North Warning System. il *Aviat Week Space Technol* 127:135+ S 28 '87

The challenge of space surveillance. J. A. Howell. il *Sky Telesc* 73:584-6+ Je '87

Congressman urges public disclosure of spy satellite data [views of George Brown] il *Aviat Week Space Technol* 126:30-1 Ap 6 '87

Defense Dept. official cites need for early decision on space-based radars as part of ADI surveillance network [Air Defense Initiative] *Aviat Week Space Technol* 126:25-6 Ap 13 '87

Defense officials express concern over Soviet military space work. *Aviat Week Space Technol* 127:28 Jl 27 '87

Dueling satellites. B. Van Voorst. il *Time* 130:73 O 5 '87

Easing of shuttle weight limits key to new USAF upper stage [Adaptable Space Propulsion System] B. A. Smith. *Aviat Week Space Technol* 126:25 Ja 19 '87

French Spot satellite shows Soviet Northern Fleet facilities. il *Aviat Week Space Technol* 126:44-5 Mr 2 '87

Long on data, short on intelligence [spy satellites] W. M. Arkin. il *Bull At Sci* 43:5-6 Je '87

Martin converts USAF Titan 2 to launch vehicle for placing defense payloads into polar orbit. il *Aviat Week Space Technol* 127:18-19 Ag 10 '87

Martin Marietta hosts Reagan SDI visit [Zenith Star laser spacecraft project] T. M. Foley. il *Aviat Week Space Technol* 127:21-2 N 30 '87

The media's new spies in the sky. C. R. Mohan. il *World Press Rev* 34:55-6 Je '87

NORAD, Space Command request system for surveillance of Soviet weapons. C. Covault. *Aviat Week Space Technol* 126:73+ Ap 6 '87

Pentagon, State Dept. granted veto over U.S. remote sensing satellites. T. M. Foley. *Aviat Week Space Technol* 127:20-1 Jl 20 '87

Recent DSP satellite version uses graphite epoxy struts. il *Aviat Week Space Technol* 126:57 Mr 2 '87

SDI considers cluster booster to launch Zenith Star spacecraft. C. Covault. il *Aviat Week Space Technol* 127:20-1 N 30 '87

Several U.S. military spacecraft operating on final backup systems. *Aviat Week Space Technol* 126:22-3 Mr 30 '87

Soviet spacecraft improve naval targeting. *Aviat Week Space Technol* 126:34 Ap 27 '87

Soviet strategic laser sites imaged by French Spot satellite. C. Covault. il *Aviat Week Space Technol* 127:26-7 O 26 '87

Space-based radar [Air Defense Initiative] G. N. Tsandoulas. bibl f il map *Science* 237:257-62 Jl 17 '87

Spot photographs secret base for USSR nuclear submarines [Barents Sea] C. Covault. il *Aviat Week Space Technol* 127:18-19 Jl 20 '87

Static firing of solid rocket motor clears USAF Titan 34Ds for launch. W. B. Scott. il *Aviat Week Space Technol* 127:26-7 Jl 20 '87

U.S./Canadian radar research questioned. *Aviat Week Space Technol* 126:22 Ap 20 '87

U.S. Air Force Titan launch restarts heavy booster flights [KH-11 imaging reconnaissance satellite launched] C. Covault. il *Aviat Week Space Technol* 127:24-5 N 2 '87

U.S. planning new emphasis on lightweight satellite systems. R. G. O'Lone. il *Aviat Week Space Technol* 127:22-3 Ag 10 '87

USAF narrows contractors for new upper stage. *Aviat Week Space Technol* 126:25 My 4 '87

USAF plans launch of KH-11 replacement [imaging reconnaissance satellites] *Aviat Week Space Technol* 126:22 F 2 '87

USAF seeks technology to cut heavy-lift launch costs; USAF prepares program to procure heavy-lift vehicles. *Aviat Week Space Technol* 126:24-5 Ja 26 '87

USAF Titan 34D launches missile warning satellite. E. H. Kolcum. il *Aviat Week Space Technol* 127:30-1 D 7 '87

Navigational use

1988 buyer's guide: Lorans, radars, sat navs, plotters. G. West. il *Mot Boat Sail* 160:67+ D '87

After all is said and done, will Everest still be number one? [Navstar satellite altitude measurement; work of George Wallerstein] J. Krakauer. bibl (p231) il map *Smithsonian* 18:176-8+ O '87

British scientists reveal signal format of Soviet Navsat [Global Navigation Satellite System] P. J. Klass. il *Aviat Week Space Technol* 126:109+ Ap 13 '87

Defense Dept. will seek funds to expand Navstar constellation. P. J. Klass. map *Aviat Week Space Technol* 127:30-2 O 5 '87

Everest toppled [Navstar satellite altitude measurement; work of George Wallerstein] il *Sky Telesc* 74:121 Ag '87

First production GPS receiver delivered ahead of schedule [Global Positioning System/Navstar] P. J. Klass. il *Aviat Week Space Technol* 127:93+ S 21 '87

GPS, Glonass and *glasnost* [Navstar/Global Positioning System] P. J. Klass. *Aviat Week Space Technol* 127:11 O 5 '87

Industry devising GPS receivers with hybrid navigation aids [Global Positioning System] P. J. Klass. il *Aviat Week Space Technol* 127:121-3 D 14 '87

Japan to test Navsat system after ETS-5 launch. *Aviat Week Space Technol* 126:142 My 11 '87

King of the mountains [Navstar satellite measurements prove Everest is higher than K2] il *Time* 130:75 N 2 '87

New automated factory to produce GPS equipment at significant savings [Global Positioning System/Navstar] P. J. Klass. il *Aviat Week Space Technol* 127:102-3+ O 5 '87

Pique over peaks: K2 versus Everest [use of Navstar satellite to determine height] J. Kluger. il *Discover* 8:16 O '87

Precision of Global Positioning increases [monitoring changes in the earth's crust] R. A. Kerr. *Science* 236:1625 Je 26 '87

Soviets' silence on Glonass leaves its availability in doubt. P. J. Klass. *Aviat Week Space Technol* 127:38-9 Jl 27 '87

Soviets to suggest scheme for global satellite system. *Aviat Week Space Technol* 127:125 D 14 '87

Washout at the GPS shootout? [Global Positioning System] S. Weisburd. *Sci News* 131:9 Ja 3 '87

Nuclear power plants
See Artificial satellites—Power supply

Oceanographic use

Japan set to launch satellite for ocean remote sensing [Marine Observation Satellite] il *Aviat Week Space Technol* 126:21-2 F 16 '87

New generation of ocean-observation satellites [N-ROSS and Topex] il *Sea Front* 33:59-60 Ja/F '87

Remote sensing: adding to our knowledge of oceans—and earth. J. McClintock. il *Sea Front* 33:105-13 Mr/Ap '87

U.S./French satellite to map the world's oceans [Topex/Poseidon] il *Earth Sci* 39:8-10 Wint '86

Orbits
NASA solves problems, corrects GOES-H orbit. B. D. Nordwall. *Aviat Week Space Technol* 126:266-7 Mr 9 '87

Power supply
Cosmos 1402's uranium remains. J. Eberhart. *Sci News* 132:278-9 O 31 '87

Artificial satellites—Power supply—*cont.*

Detection of uranium from Cosmos-1402 in the stratosphere [from nuclear reactor power supply] R. Leifer and others. bibl f il *Science* 238:512-14 O 23 '87

Rocketdyne selected to build SDI nuclear power demonstration units. *Aviat Week Space Technol* 127:28 D 21 '87

SDI experts clash on nuclear satellites [views of Lowell Wood] C. Norman. il *Science* 238:883-4 N 13 '87

Refueling

Last gas for 22,000 miles. B. Nolley. il *Space World* X-2-278:26-8 F '87

Rescue work use

A chirping 'bird' helps rescuers find planes that vanish [emergency locator transmitters] G. Williams. bibl (p183) il map *Smithsonian* 17:136-40+ Mr '87

EPIRBs: which ones can save your life? [Emergency Position Indicating Radio Beacon] D. Fales. il *Mot Boat Sail* 160:74+ Jl '87

The Starduster's last flight [M. Ryan rescued after plane crash with use of emergency locator transmitter] P. O. D'Aulaire and E. D'Aulaire. il *Read Dig* 131:75-80 Jl '87

Shielding (Heat)

China to launch satellite with wooden heat shield. *Aviat Week Space Technol* 127:52-3 Jl 27 '87

Solar energy use

In the glare of the moon. P. Ceravolo. il *Astronomy* 15:24+ My '87

Solar power satellites: still in the dark. M. Weiss. il *Space World* X-11-287:21-5 N '87

Surveillance use, Military

See Artificial satellites—Military use

Tethered satellites

Satellites on a string. R. G. Nichols. il *Sky Telesc* 73:383-5 Ap '87

Weight

COBE's missing mass [Cosmic Background Explorer] G. Freiherr. il *Space World* X-2-278:15 F '87

U.S. planning new emphasis on lightweight satellite systems. R. G. O'Lone. il *Aviat Week Space Technol* 127:22-3 Ag 10 '87

Artificial satellites, Australian

See also

AUSSAT Pty. Ltd.

Artificial satellites, Canadian

Canada approves development of scaled-back Radarsat. T. M. Foley. il *Aviat Week Space Technol* 127:51+ Jl 13 '87

Canada regards space-based radar as follow-on to North Warning System. il *Aviat Week Space Technol* 127:135+ S 28 '87

Artificial satellites, Chinese

China to launch satellite with wooden heat shield. *Aviat Week Space Technol* 127:52-3 Jl 27 '87

Chinese building geosynchronous weather spacecraft; prepare polar-orbit satellite for launch. *Aviat Week Space Technol* 126:23 Je 29 '87

Chinese will launch French payload [Matra piggyback microgravity payload carried on board a Chinese satellite to be launched by a Long March 2] *Aviat Week Space Technol* 126:23 My 4 '87

Artificial satellites, French

Chinese will launch French payload [Matra piggyback microgravity payload carried on board a Chinese satellite to be launched by a Long March 2] *Aviat Week Space Technol* 126:23 My 4 '87

Europe's Spot changes top management following data production problems. J. M. Lenorovitz. il *Aviat Week Space Technol* 126:64-5 Ap 20 '87

For the City of Light, a Ring of Light that's out of this world [space structure to mark the 100th anniversary of the Eiffel Tower] il *Discover* 8:6 F '87

France's Ring of Light [space structure to mark 100th anniversary of the Eiffel Tower] P. Lewis. il *Macleans* 100:22 Ja 5 '87

French Spot satellite shows Soviet Northern Fleet facilities. il *Aviat Week Space Technol* 126:44-5 Mr 2 '87

Soviet strategic laser sites imaged by French Spot satellite. C. Covault. il *Aviat Week Space Technol* 127:26-7 O 26 '87

Spot-ing earth from space. J. Schefter. il *Pop Sci* 230:78-81 F '87

Spot photographs secret base for USSR nuclear submarines [Barents Sea] C. Covault. il *Aviat Week Space Technol* 127:18-19 Jl 20 '87

Twinkle, twinkle, great big bauble [proposed Ring of Light to mark 100th anniversary of the Eiffel Tower] G. Taubes. il *Discover* 8:60-2+ N '87

A "yes" for the French space ring. C. Raymo. *Sky Telesc* 74:5 Jl '87

Artificial satellites, Japanese

Japan set to launch satellite for ocean remote sensing [Marine Observation Satellite] il *Aviat Week Space Technol* 126:21-2 F 16 '87

Japan to develop three advanced spacecraft. *Aviat Week Space Technol* 127:21 Ag 10 '87

Japan to test Navsat system after ETS-5 launch. *Aviat Week Space Technol* 126:142 My 11 '87

Japan's blossoming space science. M. Oda and Y. Tanaka. il map *Sky Telesc* 73:7-11 Ja '87

Artificial satellites, Russian

See also

Artificial satellites—Cosmos missions

British scientists reveal signal format of Soviet Navsat [Global Navigation Satellite System] P. J. Klass. il *Aviat Week Space Technol* 126:109+ Ap 13 '87

Defense officials express concern over Soviet military space work. *Aviat Week Space Technol* 127:28 Jl 27 '87

GPS, Glonass and *glasnost* [Navstar/Global Positioning System] P. J. Klass. *Aviat Week Space Technol* 127:11 O 5 '87

The legacy of Sputnik [cover story; special issue; with editorial comment by John Rhea] il *Space World* X-10-286:3, 7-32+ O '87

Soviet spacecraft improve naval targeting. *Aviat Week Space Technol* 126:34 Ap 27 '87

Soviets' silence on Glonass leaves its availability in doubt. P. J. Klass. *Aviat Week Space Technol* 127:38-9 Jl 27 '87

Soviets target launch of large biomedical satellite for 1990. *Aviat Week Space Technol* 127:48 N 16 '87

Soviets to suggest scheme for global satellite system. *Aviat Week Space Technol* 127:125 D 14 '87

Sputnik 1 plus 30 years: the long and the short of it. J. Eberhart. *Sci News* 132:231 O 10 '87

Sputnik: the little sphere that changed the world. G. Williams. il *Pop Mech* 164:59-61+ O '87

U.S., Soviets to cooperate on September launch of biosatellite [Vostok biological satellite] il *Aviat Week Space Technol* 127:18-19 Jl 13 '87

Artificial seeds *See* Seeds, Artificial

Artificial skin *See* Skin, Artificial

Artificial sweeteners *See* Sugar substitutes

Artificial teeth *See* Dentures

Artillery

See also

Projectiles

Artis, Kenneth J.

Coping with the new tax law. il *Saturday Evening Post* 259:112 Ap '87

Artisans

Artisans of Florence. A. M. Zwack. il *Gourmet* 47:50-5+ Jl '87

Artistic Ambassador Program (U.S.)

Major-league talents. T. W. Libbey, Jr. il *High Fidel* 37:56 Ag '87

Artistic anatomy *See* Anatomy, Artistic

Artistic License (Organization)

A clearing-house for Victorian crafts [cover story] N. R. Day. il *Americana* 15:36-41 Mr/Ap '87

Artistic Lighting Inc.

Night lights. S. M. L. Aronson. il *House Gard* 159:56+ F '87

Artistic photography *See* Photography, Artistic

Artists

See also

Aged as artists

Art as a profession

Chimpanzees as artists

Drugs and artists

Elephants as artists

Physicians as artists

Street art and artists

Women artists

The envelope, please . . . Who deserves more time in the spotlight? Who should be hooked off the stage? The experts cast their votes. P. Gardner. il *Art News* 86:167-71 N '87

Learning to become a nation of artists [developing an appreciation of materials] M. Flannery. *Educ Dig* 52:24-6 My '87

Correspondence, reminiscences, etc.

See also

Archives of American Art

Directories

Guide to galleries, museums, artists [special issue] il *Art Am* 75:37-43+ Ag '87

Artists—cont.

Economic conditions

Families: the ultimate support system for artists. D. Grant. *Am Artist* 51:70+ O '87

Health and hygiene

See also

AIDS (Disease) and artists

Medical care

See also

Doctors for Artists (Organization)

Photographs and photography

Art circles: portrait photographs from ARTnews, 1905-1986 [exhibit at the International Center of Photography] A. H. Hoy. il *Art News* 86:93-100 F '87

Newman's people [work of A. Newman] S. Weiley. il por *Art News* 86:128-34 D '87

Psychology

The psychology of art. J. Croghan. See issues of American Artist beginning November 1986

Twenty-six artists describe a crystallizing experience [decision to become an artist or to redirect career] M. C. Nelson. il *Am Artist* 51:74-6+ F '87

Salaries, pensions, etc.

See also

Artists—Taxation

Taxation

Tax law: a pox on artists. D. Grant. *Am Artist* 51:13+ N '87

Travel

Professional page [getting sponsorship of painting trips abroad] W. Mangum. il *Am Artist* 51:10+ Ag '87

Artists, American

See also

Africano, Nicholas
Anderson, John
Arneson, Robert, 1930-
Berry, William A., 1933-
Black artists
Blair, Dike
Boggs, J. S. G.
Borofsky, Jonathan
Buck, John E., 1946-
Calder, Alexander, 1898-1976
Carlson, Cynthia
Conal, Robbie
Conner, Bruce, 1933-
Cornell, Joseph, 1903-1972
Daw, Leila
Farley, Lee, 1955-
Gerson, Barry
Goldin, Nan
Graham, Dan, 1942-
Grooms, Red
Holland, Tom, 1936-
Jess
Kane, Mitchell, 1946-
Kaplowitz, Jane
Kottler, Howard, 1930-
Kozloff, Joyce
Kruger, Barbara
La Farge, John, 1835-1910
Ladda, Justen
LeWitt, Sol, 1928-
Longo, Robert
Machado, Anthony
Martin, Eddie Owens, 1908-1986
Muldavin, Phyllis Smirle
Mullican, Matt, 1951-
Nagy, Peter
Noah, Barbara
Page, Ann Takayoshi
Paha, Michael
Rankin, Aimee
Ringgold, Faith
Saunders, Raymond, 1934-
Siler, Todd
Solien, T. L.
Spitzmiller, Walt
Staller, Eric
Stankard, Paul J.
Toynton, Norman, 1939-
Turrell, James, 1943-
Young, Purvis

Artists and their families [cover story; special issue; with editorial comment by M. Stephen Doherty] il *Am Artist* 51:10-11+ O '87

Eight artists interviewed [Los Angeles artists] H. Cotter. il *Art Am* 75:162-79+ My '87

Fame and fortune in the art world. H. Brown. bibl f il *Am Artist* 51:46-51+ Mr '87

Individual aesthetics [Indianapolis artists] il *Horizon* 30:20-1 Je '87

Introducing the artists whose work was selected in the American Artist Golden Anniversary National Art Competition [cover story; special issue] il *Am Artist* 51:32-75 Je '87

Los Angeles: the new Mecca. B. Conrad, III. il *Horizon* 30:17-30 Ja/F '87

To be rich, famous, and an artist. J. Reed. il *U S News World Rep* 102:56-7 Mr 9 '87

Too much too soon? [proliferation of retrospective exhibits of young artists' work] C. Coulson. il *Art News* 86:115-19 S '87

Visions of magic [New Mexican artists] N. D'Ambrosio. il *Horizon* 30:46-52 O '87

Photographs and photography

Eye of the beholder [work of T. Greenfield-Sanders] S. Edelson. il por *N Y* 20:36 Ap 27 '87

Artists, Australian

See also

Parr, Mike

Artists, Austrian

See also

Olbrich, Josef Maria, 1867-1908
Rainer, Arnulf, 1929-

Artists, Canadian

See also

Hebert, Pierre

Artists, Chinese

See also

Wang Lan
Xu Donglin

Artists, English

See also

Leonard, Michael

Artists, French

See also

Buthaud, René, b. 1886
Heller, André

Artists, German

See also

Merz, Gerhard, 1947-
Penck, A. R., 1939-
Richter, Gerhard

Artists, Handicapped

The case of the colorblind painter. O. W. Sacks and R. Wasserman. bibl f il *N Y Rev Books* 34:25-34 N 19 '87

Artists, Irish

See also

Ireland, Patrick

Artists, Italian

See also

Michelangelo Buonarroti, 1475-1564
Parmiggiani, Claudio

Artists, Mentally ill *See* Art and mental illness

Artists, Russian

See also

Fechin, Nicolai, 1881-1955

Artists, Spanish

See also

Miralda, Antoni, 1942-
Picasso, Pablo, 1881-1973

Artists, Swedish

See also

Håfström, Jan, 1937-

Artists, Swiss

See also

Bill, Max, 1908-
Grossen, Françoise, 1943-
Weiss, David, 1946-

Artists, Welsh

See also

Adams, Mac, 1943-

Artists' and authors' colonies

See also

Artpark (Lewiston, N.Y.)
Monhegan Island (Me.)

Alaska

See also

Haines (Alaska)

Germany

Historic architecture: Joseph Maria Olbrich: a jugendstil design at the Mathildenhöhe artists' colony. J. Rykwert. il por *Archit Dig* 44:180-5+ Ap '87

Artists as teachers

The artists-in-schools concept and curriculum-based instruction: what relationship? B. Hall. *Des Arts Educ* 88:40-1 N/D '86

Artists as teachers—*cont.*

A challenge and an opportunity for arts educators [artists-in-schools programs] R. Bell. il *Des Arts Educ* 89:41-3 N/D '87

A practicing artist-in-residence looks at the view from back stage. J. Eis. *Des Arts Educ* 88:34-9 N/D '86

Artists' families

See also

Children of artists

Artists and their families [cover story; special issue; with editorial comment by M. Stephen Doherty] il *Am Artist* 51:10-11+ O '87

Artists in art

Exhibitions

Portraits of the artists [R. Grooms's parodic drawings of New York School artist-heroes] H. Cotter. il *Art Am* 75:154-7 N '87

Artists' materials

See also

Rice paper

Art mart. See issues of American Artist

Artists' materials. B. B. Stretch. il *Art News* 86:147+ O '87

Holiday shopping guide [gifts for artists] il *Am Artist* 51:46-7 N '87

New materials. See issues of Art News

New products [Art and Design in Action Show] il *Am Artist* 51:S16+ N '87

New products [Art and Design in Action Show] il *Am Artist* 51:S10+ Ja '87

Starting with a clean slate, old masters of Etch A Sketch make marketable art in a new medium. M. Small. il *People Wkly* 27:93+ Ja 19 '87

Technical page [questions and answers] C. T. Chieffo. See issues of American Artist

Artists' rights

Art for whose sake? [Visual Artists Rights Act of 1987] R. Bailey. il *Forbes* 140:36 D 14 '87

Art laws: a handshake, yes, but what are my rights? D. Grant. *Am Artist* 51:16+ My '87

L.L. Bean vs. the preppified pooch [artist W. Spitzmiller's suit against L. L. Bean's doctoring of hunting scene on catalog cover] il por *Newsweek* 109:53 Mr 16 '87

Artists' studios

Alechinsky's realm: the artist's house and studios near Paris. D. Sylvester. il pors *Archit Dig* 44:138-43+ Mr '87

Eight artists open their studios. M. S. Doherty. il *Am Artist* 51:48-57 F '87

Hacienda La Trinidad: artists' retreat near Guanajuato, Mexico [home and studio of C. and J. W. Summers] S. Cadwallader. il *Archit Dig* 44:126-31 Ja '87

Her life for art [Bjornson House/Studio, Venice, Calif.] C. K. Gandee. il *Archit Rec* 175:140-7 mid-Ap '87

An imaginative kingdom: sculptor Bernard Langlais' Maine legacy. A. Berman. il *Archit Dig* 44:174-7+ Je '87

Sleight of hand [Los Angeles studio of A. Machado] J. Chatfield-Taylor. il por *Archit Dig* 44:146-51+ My '87

Studio visits. J. Croghan. il *Am Artist* 51:18+ Ja '87

Artnews (Periodical) *See* Art news (Periodical)

Artpark (Lewiston, N.Y.)

Lewiston, N.Y. [opera performances] E. T. Glasow. *Opera News* 52:53-4 D 5 '87

Arts

See also

Art

Mass media and the arts

Performing arts

Socialism and the arts

Television broadcasting—Arts programs

Video art

Artsmart. See issues of Harper's Bazaar beginning December 1986

Cross country. See issues of Horizon (Tuscaloosa, Ala.)

Raising the curtain on a new breed of talent. M. Horn. il *U S News World Rep* 103:96+ D 28 '87-Ja 4 '88

Administration

See Arts—Management

Appreciation

Applause for the audience. M. Rhodes. il *Horizon* 30:9 S '87

Awards

See also

National Medal of Arts

Economic aspects

USArts: strategies for the 80's. See issues of Horizon (Tuscaloosa, Ala.)

Federal aid

See Arts and state

Management

From 1965 to 1987 and counting. M. Rhodes. il *Horizon* 30:4 Ja/F '87

Periodicals

See also

Arts Georgia (Periodical)

Philosophy

See also

Avant-garde (Aesthetics)

Study and teaching

See also

Art schools

Arts teachers

Getty Center for Education in the Arts

Interlochen Center for the Arts

Kaleidoscope (Program)

Arts education, the board of education, and you. W. B. Newman. *Des Arts Educ* 89:34-7 N/D '87

The arts in education: a search for balance. J. I. Bundra. bibl f *Des Arts Educ* 89:25-30 S/O '87

A challenge and an opportunity for arts educators [artists-in-schools programs] R. Bell. il *Des Arts Educ* 89:41-3 N/D '87

Degrees of art [Mills College, Oakland, Calif.] il *Horizon* 30:37 Ja/F '87

Demographic changes: what meaning for arts education? [effect of growing minorities] D. Funes. *Des Arts Educ* 89:29-33 N/D '87

Higher education: innovator or inhibitor? [special issue] bibl f *Des Arts Educ* 88:2-40 Jl/Ag '87

Learning to become a nation of artists [developing an appreciation of materials] M. Flannery. *Educ Dig* 52:24-6 My '87

Lessons to be learned [symposium at Interlochen, Mich.] M. Rhodes. il *Horizon* 30:9 N '87

Media: what strategy? [cover story; special issue] *Des Arts Educ* 88:2-4+ Jl/Ag '87

Philanthropy: blessing or barrier? [patronage of arts education; special issue] *Des Arts Educ* 88:2-32+ Mr/Ap '87

Quo vadis arts education: a national agenda. J. Remer. *Des Arts Educ* 89:38-40 N/D '87

Research: who cares? [special issue] bibl f il *Des Arts Educ* 88:2-44 My/Je '87

The richer language. M. Rhodes. il *Horizon* 30:4 Mr '87

State and local arts councils: what role? [special issue] bibl f *Des Arts Educ* 88:2-48 N/D '86

Toward an integrated study of cultural and educational policy. D. B. Pankratz. bibl f *Des Arts Educ* 89:12-21 N/D '87

Why arts are basic. E. W. Eisner. *Educ Dig* 53:20-2 D '87

Alabama

See also

Impressions (Periodical)

Arizona

See also

Tucson (Ariz.)—Arts

California

See also

Monterey County (Calif.)—Arts

Oakland (Calif.)—Arts

Orange County (Calif.)—Arts

Valley arts (Periodical)

Exploring California [special issue; with editorial comment by Gray D. Boone] il *Horizon* 30:2, 17-46+ Ja/F '87

Caribbean region

Highbrow nightlife. J. B. Harris. il *Black Enterp* 17:39-40 My '87

Florida

See also

Jacksonville (Fla.)—Arts

Solid support for the arts. M. Rhodes. il *Horizon* 30:9 Jl/Ag '87

France

See also

Paris (France)—Arts

Georgia

See also

Arts Georgia (Periodical)

Savannah (Ga.)—Arts

Great Britain

Great Britain: the state of the arts [special section] il *Horizon* 30:21-34+ N '87

India

Reflections of India [special section] il *Horizon* 30:17-30+ Mr '87

Arts—*cont.*

Indiana

See also
Indianapolis (Ind.)—Arts

Kansas

See also
Lawrence (Kan.)—Arts

Massachusetts

See also
Springfield (Mass.)—Arts
Worcester County (Mass.)—Arts

Minnesota

See also
Duluth (Minn.)—Arts

New Mexico

See also
Albuquerque (N.M.)—Arts
Santa Fe (N.M.)—Arts
Taos (N.M.)—Arts

New York (State)

See also
New York (N.Y.)—Arts

South Africa

Optimistic tragedies [special issue of TriQuarterly entitled
From South Africa] R. Nixon. *Nation* 245:453-4 O
24 '87

United States

See Arts

Virginia

See also
Fairfax County (Va.)—Arts

Arts, Black

See also
Harlem renaissance
From tube to theater: some art du jour. H. Als. il
Essence 17:26 Ap '87

Arts, Brazilian

Return ticket [Brazilian arts in Portugal] F. A. Cristóvão.
il *Courier* 39:37+ D '86

Arts administration See Arts—Management

Arts and children

You can lead a kid to culture . . . L. Schnurnberger.
il *Parents* 62:122-4+ D '87

Arts and Christianity See Arts and religion

Arts and crafts

See also
Appliqué work
Artisans
Arts and crafts movement
Baskets
Braiding
Christmas projects
Dough craft
Eggs, Decorated
Folk art
Glass blowing and working
Jewelry
Lacquer and lacquering
Needlework
Paper work (Art)
Papier-mâché
Plaques and plaquettes
Pottery
Shellwork
Spatter work (Craft)
Stencil work
Tapestry
Textile crafts
Weaving
Wood carving
Woodworking

Country crafts: 25 great gifts from snippets and scraps.
J. Williams and J. Severson. il *Better Homes Gard*
65:59-63+ S '87
Objects of affection: 5 loving gifts to craft [Valentine's
Day gifts] J. Williams and J. Severson. il *Better Homes
Gard* 65:98-9+ F '87
Portfolio. See issues of American Craft

Awards

Council awards gold medals, inducts 12 fellows [American
Craft Council] il *Am Craft* 47:6+ Ag/S '87

Bibliography

Books. See issues of American Craft

Competitions

American Craft Museum to host young talent showcase
in 1988. il *Am Craft* 47:6+ O/N '87

Conferences

School leaders meet at Museum [conference on Sharing
Resources at the American Craft Museum] M. J.
Edwards. il *Am Craft* 47:6 Ap/My '87

Critics and criticism

See Art critics and criticism

Exhibitions

See also
Contemporary Crafts Association (Portland, Or.)
Detroit Gallery of Contemporary Crafts
American craft: poetry of the physical [American Craft
Museum touring exhibition] P. J. Smith. il *USA Today
(Periodical)* 116:74-85 S '87
Calendar. See issues of American Craft
A celebration of American crafts [Craft today traveling
exhibit] il *Sunset* 178:88 My '87
Comment [F. Yoshimura's Three bicycles included in
the exhibition Craft today: poetry of the physical]
A. Palinkas. il *Am Craft* 47:20+ D '87/Ja '88
Contemporary craft at the Met [Lila Acheson Wallace
Wing] J. Tognini. il *Am Craft* 47:50-5 Ap/My '87
The contemporary crafts movement has come of age,
and at the Renwick Gallery its prospects have never
been brighter. R. M. Adams. *Smithsonian* 17:12 Ja
'87
Crafts [American craft at the Armory show] *New Yorker*
63:34-5 My 18 '87
The embodiment of ingenuity [Craft today; In pursuit
of beauty: Americans and the aesthetic movement;
The Machine Age in America: 1918-1941] M. Kangas.
bibl f il *Am Craft* 47:46-53 Ag/S '87
Fall brings craft fairs [North Carolina] il *South Living*
22:34-5 S '87
Gallery. See issues of American Craft
Off press [reviews of American Craft Museum's inaugural
exhibit Craft today: poetry of the physical] *Am Craft*
47:11-12 F/Mr '87
Second New Art Forms Expo draws crowds to Navy
Pier [Chicago International New Art Forms Exposition]
J. Tognini. il *Am Craft* 47:16-17 D '87/Ja '88

Galleries and museums

See Art galleries and museums

Marketing

See Art trade

Photographs and photography

Collecting artwork on film. M. Grimm and T. Grimm.
il *Travel Holiday* 167:16-19 Ja '87

Study and teaching

See also
California College of Arts and Crafts
School leaders meet at Museum [conference on Sharing
Resources at the American Craft Museum] M. J.
Edwards. il *Am Craft* 47:6 Ap/My '87

Appalachian region

See also
Museum of Appalachia
Appalachia's art of the useful. C. E. Martin. il *Nat
Hist* 96:50-9 Jl '87

Baltic States

Baltic crafts. W. D. Romey. il map *Focus* 37:24-8 Fall
'87

Ecuador

Saving cultural assets [OAS-backed Community Museum
project in Chordeleg] G. Urriolagoitia V. il *Américas*
39:56 Ja/F '87

Hawaii

Hawaii's prized quilts. A. Satterfield. il *Travel Holiday*
167:12-13 Ja '87

Hong Kong

Weaves of grass [craftsman Chan Chong Chi makes
grasshopper figures out of grass] B. B. Ryan. il pors
Travel Holiday 167:34-6 Mr '87

India

Crafted by Indian hands. J. B. Harris. il *Horizon* 30:22-3
Mr '87

Japan

See also
Kuromatsu (Firm)

Massachusetts

Handmade in Massachusetts: Pioneer Valley crafts. D.
D. Meehan. il *Travel Holiday* 167:44-7 Ja '87

Arts and crafts movement

Art: paintings from the Arts and crafts period. T. Pelzel.
il *Archit Dig* 44:78-83+ Jl '87
Attic attitudes: Leighton and aesthetic philosophy. S.
Jones. bibl il *Hist Today* 37:31-7 Je '87
Before remodeling, they dug back into the house's roots
[Craftsman era house in Piedmont, Calif.] il *Sunset*
179:118+ O '87
Pleasure in creation [in America] F. Strebeigh. bibl il
Am Herit 38:82-9 Jl/Ag '87

Exhibitions

Aestheticism then and now [Metropolitan Museum's In
pursuit of beauty] C. Ratcliff. il *Art Am* 75:90-103
F '87

Arts and crafts movement—Exhibitions—*cont.*

The American arts and crafts movement [The art that is life: the arts and crafts movement in America, 1875-1920] S. B. Sherrill. il *Antiques* 131:508+ Mr '87

The art that is life [Arts and crafts movement in America, 1875-1920] D. Welebit. il *Americana* 14:32-4 Ja/F '87

The elegance of line: back to basics with the eloquent masters of the arts and crafts movement [The art that is life: the arts and crafts movement in America, 1875-1920] B. Plumb. il *Vogue* 177:332 Mr '87

The embodiment of ingenuity [Craft today; In pursuit of beauty: Americans and the aesthetic movement; The Machine Age in America: 1918-1941] M. Kangas. bibl f il *Am Craft* 47:46-53 Ag/S '87

Reforming America: Boston's Museum of Fine Arts offers a fresh interpretation of the Arts and crafts movement in America, 1875-1920. C. Lynn. il *Am Craft* 47:40-9+ Je/Jl '87

Arts and crafts trade *See* Art trade

Arts and industry
See also
Art and industry

Arts exchange. See issues of Horizon (Tuscaloosa, Ala.) beginning May 1986

Blending arts with wine [Monterey County, Calif.] M. Wade. il *Horizon* 30:60-1 Jl/Ag '87

A guide for fundraisers [corporate giving programs] M. Rhodes. il *Horizon* 30:8 O '87

Philanthropy: blessing or barrier? [patronage of arts education; special issue] *Des Arts Educ* 88:2-32+ Mr/Ap '87

A tradition of support. G. D. Boone. *Horizon* 30:2 D '87

USArts: strategies for the 80's. See issues of Horizon (Tuscaloosa, Ala.)

Viewpoint [corporate sponsorship of opera] J. L. Poole. *Opera News* 52:6 D 5 '87

Arts and mass media *See* Mass media and the arts

Arts and religion
See also
Wesley Theological Seminary. Center for the Arts and Religion

Creativity and the challenge of worship [Languages of Worship Workshop at Boston U. School of Theology] P. P. Allen. il *Christ Century* 104:756-8 S 9-16 '87

Arts and socialism *See* Socialism and the arts

Arts and state
See also
American Council for the Arts

Learning about the arts from the sciences. M. Rhodes. il *Horizon* 30:9 My '87

State and local arts councils: what role? [special issue] bibl f *Des Arts Educ* 88:2-48 N/D '86

Toward an integrated study of cultural and educational policy. D. B. Pankratz. bibl f *Des Arts Educ* 89:12-21 N/D '87

Czechoslovakia

Human rights and all that jazz [crackdown on Jazz Section members] *Newsweek* 109:36 Mr 23 '87

Jazz leaders face trial in Czechoslovakia. J. A. Glusman. *Roll Stone* p16 Ap 9 '87

Notes and comment [arrests of members of the Jazz Section of the Union of Musicians] *New Yorker* 63:25-6 Mr 23 '87

Prague & the perils of jazz [persecution of Czechoslovak Union of Musicians' Jazz Section] K. Roth. il *Commonweal* 114:351-4 Je 5 '87

Hungary

The dialectics of dissent [excerpt from The velvet prison] M. Haraszti. *Harpers* 275:28+ D '87

The seduction of censorship. M. Haraszti. *New Repub* 197:32-4+ N 23 '87

Soviet Union

Glasnost: between hope and history. S. Schmemann. il *N Y Times Book Rev* 92:12-13 Ap 26 '87

The pas de *perestroika*. J. Kroll. il *Newsweek* 110:42-3 D 14 '87

A poet's view of *glasnost*; tr. by Antonina W. Bouis. A. Voznesenskii. *Nation* 244:810-12 Je 13 '87

A rebirth of Soviet arts. Y. A. Yevtushenko. il por *World Press Rev* 34:26-8 F '87

A Soviet poet's praise for freedom [A. Voznesenskii] W. French. il *World Press Rev* 34:61 Je '87

Arts and the handicapped
See also
Hope University

Arts Assembly of Jacksonville, Inc.

Advocating the arts. M. Wade. il *Horizon* 30:56 D '87

Arts education *See* Arts—Study and teaching

Les Arts Florissants (Chamber orchestra)

The real thing [New York City performances] P. G. Davis. il *N Y* 20:146+ D 7 '87

Arts Georgia (Periodical)

Arts Georgia on the stands. M. Wade. il *Horizon* 30:15-16 S '87

Georgia: the arts state. G. D. Boone. *Horizon* 30:2 Jl/Ag '87

Arts management *See* Arts—Management

Arts teachers

Education

The Holmes Group: implications for arts education. J. Ross. bibl *Des Arts Educ* 89:19-24 S/O '87

A look at field experiences for preservice teachers in the arts. B. L. Bennett. *Des Arts Educ* 89:12-13 S/O '87

Mythologies in arts teacher education. L. V. Castiglione. *Des Arts Educ* 89:14-18 S/O '87

Artsreview

Waiting lists and hand biting. il *Art News* 86:16 S '87

Artweave Textile Gallery

Stuffs from the steppes. D. M. Lisi. il pors *House Gard* 159:58+ D '87

Aruba

Description and travel

Aruba! [cover story] il pors *Essence* 17:52-9 Ap '87

Collage of cultures. R. J. Christmas. il *Travel Holiday* 168:22-4 D '87

Arum, Bob, 1931-

about

And in both corners . . . G. Buchalter. il por *Forbes* 139:170+ Ap 6 '87

Pow! Bam! A one-two punch from Bob Arum and Budweiser. M. D. Oneal. il *Bus Week* p44 Ap 6 '87

Arzhak, Nikolai *See* Daniel', Ĭŭliĭ, 1925-

As is [drama] *See* Hoffman, William M.

As it is in heaven [drama] *See* Sutton, Joe

Asa Wright Nature Center (Trinidad and Tobago) *See* Nature centers—Trinidad and Tobago

Asahi Mutual Life Insurance Company

In Japan, using 'logic and emotion' [investment specialist S. Kaneko] B. Buell. il por *Bus Week* p155 D 28 '87-Ja 4 '88

ASARCO Inc.

Lean, mean and prosperous. J. Cook. il por *Forbes* 140:48-9 D 28 '87

ASATs *See* Anti-satellite weapons

Asbestos

Asbestos: hindsight is 20/20. S. C. Florman. il *Technol Rev* 90:20-1 Jl '87

Asbestos subpoena quashed [request by the R. J. Reynolds Tobacco Co.] J. Raloff. *Sci News* 132:55 Jl 25 '87

Deadly dust: how to find asbestos in your home and what—if anything—you should do about it. N. Cooper. il *Home Mech* 83:58-62 My '87

I saved my family from asbestos contamination. J. A. Mazoué. il por *Good Housekeep* 204:108 Ap '87

Living with asbestos. J. Knudsen. *Changing Times* 41:20 N '87

Disposal

How to get rid of asbestos. M. Strange. il *Consum Res Mag* 70:29-32 Ap '87

Laws and regulations

Asbestos: a back-to-school hazard. J. L. Sheler. *U S News World Rep* 103:33 S 14 '87

Asbestos industry
See also
Raymark Corporation

Suits and claims

An asbestos decision that's hazardous to insurers' health [California court sticks them with $2 billion tab for claims] R. Brandt. *Bus Week* p33-4 Je 15 '87

How Raytech means to sidestep Manville's fate [fear of asbestos suits] J. R. Norman. il *Bus Week* p56+ Ag 24 '87

Life after death [after asbestos claims litigation scares off insurers, Acmat Corp. forms own company to write liability policies] B. Leonard. il por *Forbes* 139:132-3 My 4 '87

Asbestos workers

Health and hygiene

How Raytech means to sidestep Manville's fate [fear of asbestos suits] J. R. Norman. il *Bus Week* p56+ Ag 24 '87

ASCAP *See* American Society of Composers, Authors and Publishers

Asceticism

Asceticism & the evil one. J. Garvey. *Commonweal* 114:311-12 My 22 '87

Asch, Moses, d. 1986
about
This man captured the true sounds of a whole world.
T. Scherman. il pors *Smithsonian* 18:110-12+ Ag '87
Ascher, Barbara Lazear
How to write the perfect love letter. il *Seventeen* 46:38+
F '87
Ascher, Nancy
about
Nancy Ascher, M.D.: on the frontiers of medicine. M.
Dowie. il por *Ms* 16:86+ N '87
Ascher, Rebecca
Colorizing black-and-white films is a crime against art!
por *Seventeen* 46:78-9 N '87
Ascherson, Neal
The death doctors. il *N Y Rev Books* 34:29-34 My
28 '87
Poland's 20th-century struggles [cover story] il *Hist Today*
37:44-9 Je '87
Ascorbic acid *See* Vitamins—Vitamin C
Ascots
The ascot. J. Berendt. il *Esquire* 108:42+ O '87
Ascutney Mountain Resort (Vt.) *See* Resorts—Vermont
ASEA AB
See also
ASEA Brown Boveri (Firm)
ASEA Brown Boveri (Firm)
Power surge in Scandinavia. B. Childs and T. Peterson.
il *Bus Week* p36 Ag 24 '87
ASEAN
ASEAN: a model for regional cooperation [remarks, May
27, 1987] G. P. Shultz. *Dep State Bull* 87:10-13 Jl
'87
Secretary's visit to Asia and the Pacific [statements and
texts of press conferences, June 13-22, 1987] G. P.
Shultz. *Dep State Bull* 87:29-37 Ag '87
United States policy in Southeast Asia. E. Colbert. bibl
f *Curr Hist* 86:145-7+ Ap '87
Asekoff, L. S.
Two poems [poem] *New Yorker* 62:34 Ja 19 '87
Ash, Agnes
Palm Beach game plan. il *Harpers Bazaar* 120:122-33+
Je '87
Ash, Jennifer
Starstruck. il *Life* 10:107-8+ Ap '87
Ash, Timothy Garton *See* Garton Ash, Timothy
Ash, Volcanic *See* Volcanic ash, tuff, etc.
Ash Creek Wildlife Area (Calif.) *See* Wildlife sanctuaries—
California
Ash Lawn-Highland (Va.: Historic house)
James Monroe's Highland home. il *South Living* 22:22
My '87
Ash Meadows National Wildlife Refuge (Nev.) *See* Wildlife
sanctuaries—Nevada
Ash Wednesday
The acceptable time. M. K. Hellwig. *America* 156:inside
back cover F 28 '87
The most uncomfortable day of the year. B. L. Rohrig.
il *Christ Century* 104:180-1 F 25 '87
Ashbery, John
April galleons [poem] *New Yorker* 63:34 Ap 20
'87
Art songs [poem] *New Repub* 197:32 O 26 '87
Drab shutters [poem] *Harpers* 275:26 O '87
Fantastic voyages. il *Art Am* 75:148-9+ D '87
Frost [poem] *New Yorker* 63:36 My 4 '87
A mood of quiet beauty [poem] *N Y Rev Books*
34:8 Mr 12 '87
Mystery mansion. il por *House Gard* 159:148-53+ Mr
'87
Never to get it really right [poem] *N Y Rev Books*
34:4 F 12 '87
Sighs and inhibitions [poem] *New Yorker* 63:30
Je 29 '87
about
How good is John Ashbery? R. McDowell. *Am Sch*
56:275-8+ Spr '87
Ashcroft, Michael
about
The British raider who sneaked up on ADT. M.
Maremont. il por *Bus Week* p33+ Ag 31 '87
Cleaning up. A. A. Lappen. il por *Forbes* 139:118 Je
15 '87
Ashe, Arthur
about
12 who mattered: Arthur Ashe. S. Flink. il por *World
Tennis* 35:46 Je '87
Arthur Ashe and wife Jeanne Moutoussamy-Ashe are
parents of baby girl. il pors *Jet* 71:22 F 9 '87
Arthur Ashe raps role sports plays in society. por *Jet*
72:29 Ap 27 '87

Arthur Ashe seeks cure for U.S. tennis malaise. por
Jet 72:49 Ag 31 '87
Ashe, Gibson raise funds for tennis, UNCF on yacht.
il pors *Jet* 72:8 Ag 10 '87
Ashe hopes tennis clinic will erase lazy players. por
Jet 72:51 S 21 '87
Can Arthur Ashe put this idea over the net? B. Welling.
il por *Bus Week* p120 S 21 '87
Ashe, Jeanne Moutoussamy- *See* Moutoussamy-Ashe,
Jeanne, 1951-
Ashenfelter, Orley, 1942-
about
Buying wine before its time. S. W. Angrist. il por *Forbes*
140:222+ N 30 '87
Asher, Don
Ice-cream music. il *Harpers* 274:68-71 Je '87
Asher, Elise
about
Elise Asher at Ingber. C. Little. il *Art Am* 75:158-9
Je '87
Asher, Gerald
Houston. il *Gourmet* 47:66-73+ O '87
San Francisco shopping. il *Gourmet* 48:60-5+ Je '87
Wine journal. See occasional issues of Gourmet
Asher, Jules
Born to be shy? bibl (p65) il *Psychol Today* 21:56-9+
Ap '87
Ashes
Model studies of polychlorinated dibenzo-*p*-dioxin forma-
tion during municipal refuse incineration [fly ash] F.
W. Karasek and L. C. Dickson. bibl f il *Science*
237:754-6 Ag 14 '87
Asheville (N.C.)
Description
Asheville: a cool salute to summer. C. Griffith. il map
South Living 22:92-6 Je '87
Historic houses, sites, etc.
Christmas elegance in Asheville. il *South Living* 22:14+
D '87
Ashforth, Albert
Hoosier humorist, three letters. *Am Sch* 56:565-73 Aut
'87
Ashkenazi, Avi, and others
An M2 muscarinic receptor subtype coupled to both
adenylyl cyclase and phosphoinositide turnover. bibl
f il *Science* 238:672-5 O 30 '87
Ashkenazy, Daniella
History and the body politic in Israel. il *Christ Century*
104:822-3 S 30 '87
Ashkenazy, Vladimir
about
Music. E. W. Said. *Nation* 244:336-8 Mr 14 '87
Ashkin, A., and Dziedzic, J. M.
Optical trapping and manipulation of viruses and bacteria.
bibl f il *Science* 235:1517-20 Mr 20 '87
Ashland (Or.)
Description
Ashland without Shakespeare. il *Sunset* 179:41-2 N '87
Ashland Management Inc.
Giving stocks a 'rational value' [views of Charles C.
Hickox and Parry v. S. Jones] G. G. Marcial. *Bus
Week* p136 My 11 '87
Ashley, Bernard
about
Forever Ashley. H. Montgomery-Massingberd. il *House
Gard* 159:158-65+ S '87
Ashley, Laura
about
Forever Ashley. H. Montgomery-Massingberd. il *House
Gard* 159:158-65+ S '87
A welcoming home [excerpt from Laura Ashley style]
I. Gale and S. Irvine. il *Redbook* 170:83-9 N '87
Ashley, Merrill
about
Ashley's "all-American" Aurora bemuses British bal-
letomanes. M. E. Willis. il por *Dance Mag* 61:102
S '87
Dance Magazine Awards 1987. il pors *Dance Mag* 61:44-6
F '87
Ashley, Steven
What's new in home improvement. See issues of Popular
Science beginning May 1986
Ashman, Charles R., and Trescott, Pamela
When diplomatic immunity is a crime [condensed from
Diplomatic crime] *Read Dig* 131:129-32 D '87
Ashton, Alan
Not everyone needs everything in OS/2. por *Pers Comput*
11:230 O '87

Ashton, Sir Frederick, 1906-
about
La fille mal gardée [ballet] Reviews
Dance Mag il 61:56-9 Mr '87. J. R. Acocella
Ashton-Tate, Inc.
Ashton-Tate: a high hurdle for a front-runner [creating new software for 80386 machines] R. Neff. il *Bus Week* p85-6 Ja 26 '87
Ashwell, Jonathan D., and others
T-cell tumor elimination as a result of T-cell receptor-mediated activation. bibl f il *Science* 237:61-4 Jl 3 '87
Ashworth, William
The great & fragile lakes [cover story] il *Sierra* 72:42-50 N/D '87
Asia
See also
Asians
Birth control—Asia
Central Asia
East and West
East Asia
Geology—Asia
Southeast Asia
Regional report: Asia/Pacific. A. Giarelli. See issues of World Press Review beginning October 1986
Economic conditions
See also
United Nations. Economic and Social Commission for Asia and the Pacific
Economic relations
Japan
See Japan—Economic relations—Asia
Languages
See Oriental languages
Politics and government
Asia's future. R. A. Scalapino. *Foreign Aff* 66:77-108 Fall '87
Race relations
Asia: nobody wants a melting pot. J. M. Fallows. il *U S News World Rep* 102:39 Je 22 '87
Social conditions
See also
United Nations. Economic and Social Commission for Asia and the Pacific
Asia-Pacific International Trade Fair
ASPAT '85 held in Beijing in November. il *UN Chron* 23:86 Ja '86
Asian American Free Labor Institute
What's it all about, AAFLI? [discussion of August 15-22, 1987 article, Was the U.S. behind it?] J. Wypijewski. *Nation* 245:666+ D 5 '87
Asian American market
Tapping into a blossoming Asian market. J. Schwartz and D. Wang. il *Newsweek* 110:47-8 S 7 '87
Asian Americans
Crimes against
Prejudice against Asians: anxiety and acceptance. K. Zinsmeister. *Current* 297:37-40 N '87
Education
Are Asian-American kids really smarter? F. Butterfield. il *Read Dig* 130:87-90 Ja '87
Do colleges set Asian quotas? E. Salholz. il *Newsweek* 109:60 F 9 '87
The new whiz kids [cover story] D. Brand. il *Time* 130:42-6+ Ag 31 '87
Employment
A 'superminority' tops out [job discrimination] J. Schwartz. il *Newsweek* 109:48-9 My 11 '87
Asian art *See* Art, Asian
Asian cockroaches *See* Cockroaches
Asian cooking *See* Cooking, Asian
Asian languages *See* Oriental languages
Asian studies
The Pacific century. D. P. Gardner. *Science* 237:233 Jl 17 '87
Asians
United States
Immigration challenge. *Society* 24:2 My/Je '87
Asimov, Isaac, 1920-
The robot in the 21st century. il *Radio-Electron* 58:99-101 My '87
Science fiction today. il *Writer* 100:7-10 F '87
Asinamali! [drama] See Ngema, Mbongeni
Askew, Essie
about
Becoming an entrepreneur—overnight. L. Sorenson. il pors *Work Woman* 12:37+ Jl '87
Askew Distributing Company
Becoming an entrepreneur—overnight [E. Askew] L. Sorenson. il pors *Work Woman* 12:37+ Jl '87

Aslet, Clive, 1955-
Master of plaster. il *House Gard* 159:204-5+ N '87
Regency redux. il por *House Gard* 159:106+ N '87
Asparagus
See also
Cooking—Vegetables
Asparagus. P. G. McWilliams. il *Ctry J* 14:47-50 My '87
Asparagus adventures. il *Sunset* 178:114-15 Ja '87
Better asparagus . . . is on the way. W. E. Wooldridge. il *Flower Gard* 31:38-9 Ap/My '87
Asparagus peas *See* Winged peas
Asparagus salads *See* Salads
Aspartame *See* Sugar substitutes
Aspartate *See* Aspartic acid
Aspartate receptors *See* Chemoreceptors
Aspartic acid
The catalytic role of the active site aspartic acid in serine proteases. C. S. Craik and others. bibl f il *Science* 237:909-13 Ag 21 '87
Zinc: moderator in brain cell chatter? [research by D. Choi and others] *Sci News* 131:313 My 16 '87
Zinc selectively blocks the action of N-methyl-D-aspartate on cortical neurons. S. Peters and others. bibl f il *Science* 236:589-93 My 1 '87
ASPAT *See* Asia-Pacific International Trade Fair
ASPCA *See* American Society for the Prevention of Cruelty to Animals
Aspen
Aspens. M. P. Gadomski. il *Conservationist* 41:24-6 Ja/F '87
Aspen (Colo.)
Architecture
Castle in the air: a family lodge above Aspen [architecture by Michael Mahaffey; decorated by Steve Chase] G. Greene. il *Archit Dig* 44:136-9+ Ag '87
Description
True West [summer pleasures] G. Greene. il *N Y* 20:44-6+ Jl 27 '87
Restaurants, nightclubs, bars, etc.
True West [summer pleasures] G. Greene. il *N Y* 20:44-6+ Jl 27 '87
Aspen Music Festival *See* Music festivals—Colorado
Asphalt driveways *See* Driveways
Asphyxia
A boxcar horror in Sierra Blanca [death of illegal Mexican aliens] il *U S News World Rep* 103:15 Jl 13 '87
The boxcar that became a coffin [Mexican aliens suffocate in Texas] E. Magnuson. il *Time* 130:21 Jl 13 '87
Death ride to the American Dream [Mexican aliens suffocate in boxcar] F. Bruning. por *Macleans* 100:7 Ag 3 '87
Tragedy in Texas [Mexican aliens suffocate in boxcar] A. Bilski. il *Macleans* 100:19 Jl 13 '87
Aspidistra
Adopt an aspidistra. B. Gould. il *Flower Gard* 31:74 Ap/My '87
Aspillaga Lombard, Florentino
about
Spilled beans. K. M. Pierce. il *Time* 130:17 Ag 24 '87
Aspin, Les
Conventional defense must be strengthened. *Aviat Week Space Technol* 127:15 N 2 '87
Unilateral moves for stability. il *Bull At Sci* 43:12-15 D '87
about
Aspin believes INF unworkable without SALT 2 compliance. M. Mecham. *Aviat Week Space Technol* 127:135 O 12 '87
Aspin's scalp. *New Repub* 196:7 F 2 '87
B-1B bomber inquiry triggers Aspin probes of Stealth weapons. P. Mann. *Aviat Week Space Technol* 126:18-20 Mr 23 '87
The fall and rise of Les Aspin. J. D. Isaacs. il por *Bull At Sci* 43:4-5 Ap '87
In the House, an abrasive defender of defense. D. Griffiths. por *Bus Week* p53 Ag 24 '87
Jess and Les. por *Time* 129:25 F 2 '87
'Never double-cross your friends'. G. Borger. il por *U S News World Rep* 102:21 Ja 19 '87
The Old Breed strikes back. C. J. Matthews. il *New Repub* 196:21-3 Mr 2 '87
Aspinall, John
about
Wild gaming. B. Masters. il por *House Gard* 159:222-5+ N '87
Aspirin
As use of kids' aspirin drops, so do cases of Reye syndrome. D. Stehlin. il *FDA Consum* 21:20-1 O '87

Aspirin—cont.

Aspirin: when it helps, how it hurts. il *Glamour* 85:340 N '87

Assad, Hafez

about

Assad and his allies: irreconcilable differences? C. Dickey. bibl f *Foreign Aff* 66:58-76 Fall '87

Assad's Lebanese quagmire. R. Nordland. il *Newsweek* 109:34 Mr 2 '87

Can Syria clean up Lebanon? N. Cooper. il *Newsweek* 109:40-1 Mr 9 '87

Can Syria's Assad keep his footing? J. P. Tarpey and B. Javetski. *Bus Week* p161 N 2 '87

Opening the road to Damascus. H. G. Chua-Eoan. il por *Time* 130:46 Jl 20 '87

An overture from Assad [with interview] C. Dickey. il por *Newsweek* 110:32-3 S 28 '87

Syrian bullets impose Beirut peace—for now. P. R. Range. il pors *U S News World Rep* 102:32-3 Mr 9 '87

Assael, Shaun

The future of the compact disc—interactive. *Roll Stone* p77 S 10 '87

Assassination

See also

Bishop, Maurice—Assassination

Karami, Rashid—Assassination

Letelier, Orlando—Assassination

Palme, Olof, 1927-1986—Assassination

Reagan, Ronald, 1911—Assassination attempt, March 30, 1981

Romero, Oscar A. (Oscar Arnulfo), 1917-1980—Assassination

Roosevelt, Theodore, 1858-1919—Assassination attempt, October 14, 1912

Sadat, Anwar, 1918-1981—Assassination

Sankara, Thomas—Assassination

Washington, George, 1732-1799—Assassination plot, 1776

Anaya's murder. A. Cockburn. *Nation* 245:546-7 N 14 '87

Assassination in South Lebanon [French Jesuit A. Masse] H. Madelin. *America* 157:397-8 N 28 '87

The contras' little list [American mercenary J. Adams discloses assassination plots against Nicaraguan leaders by the contras] A. Nairn. il *Progressive* 51:24-6 Mr '87

Leandro Alejandro: victim of militarism [Philippines] D. Friesen. *Christ Century* 104:877-8 O 14 '87

'The same old assassins' [slaying of Salvadoran human-rights activist H. Anaya] *Commonweal* 114:646 N 20 '87

Assassination [film] See Motion picture reviews—Single works

Assateague Island National Seashore (Md. and Va.)

A barrier island interlude. C. Fergus. il maps *Ctry J* 14:21-5 Je '87

Photographs and photography

An Assateague album. il *Ctry J* 14:26-9 Je '87

The assault [film] See Motion picture reviews—Single works

Assault and battery

Alice Bond, Carmen Butler meet before magistrate to argue battery charge [Mrs. J. Bond's accusations of cocaine abuse directed against husband Julian] il por *Jet* 72:6 My 11 '87

As Hollywood's fastest fists fly again, a prosecutor plans to give Sean Pennance. E. Levin. il pors *People Wkly* 27:38-9 My 18 '87

Assault charges dropped against Harvard's Loury. pors *Jet* 72:25 S 7 '87

First he lost his temper, now he's lost his freedom: Sean Penn is going to jail. il por *People Wkly* 28:38 Jl 6 '87

Harvard prof charged with beating up live-in lover [charges against G. C. Loury] il pors *Jet* 72:24-5 Je 29 '87

Mike Tyson faces assault and battery rap; tried to kiss girl, hit her boss. il por *Jet* 72:51 Jl 27 '87

Tyson cleared in assault of LA parking employee. por *Jet* 73:48 O 19 '87

"We have a problem" [mugging of a 10 yr. old] J. Marks. il *Parents* 62:61-4 S '87

Assay, Biological See Biological assay

Asselstine, James K.

about

The case of the dissenting commissioner. A. Stine. il pors *Sierra* 72:46-50 My/Je '87

Assembler language (Computer language)

386ІASM/LINK 1.1e. M. Trask. *Byte* 12:224-7 Ag '87

Atari 520ST projects: an interface board for the Atari ST cartridge port. T. G. Hunkler. il *Byte* 12:161-2+ Je '87

Better batch files through assembly language. W. J. Claff. bibl il *Byte* 12 no12 Sp Issue:159-60+ '87

Reviewer's notebook [MetaWare's High C compiler and Phar Lap Software's assembler package for 80386 machines] R. Grehan. *Byte* 12:201 Ap '87

Shareware assembler/debugger, Eric Isaacson. il *Radio-Electron* 58 ComputerDigest:94 N '87

Assemblies of God

Divided Pentecostals: Bakker vs. Swaggart. E. L. Blumhofer. *Christ Century* 104:430-1 My 6 '87

Ousting two from the clergy [J. Bakker and R. Dortch fired] R. N. Ostling. il por *Time* 129:65 My 18 '87

Untold story of black founder of Pentecostal church body rocked by sex scandal of whites [W. J. Seymour of the Assemblies of God and reaction to J. Bakker scandal] S. Booker. il pors *Jet* 72:12-14+ My 18 '87

Assembly language (Computer language) See Assembler language (Computer language)

Assembly line methods

See also

Automobile factories

Team work in industry

Automation and microsurgery [Moscow Scientific Research Institute of Eye Microsurgery] S. Fedorov. il *Courier* 40:33-4 Ag '87

Assertiveness (Psychology)

Assertiveness breeds contempt [male vs. female evaluations of assertive female managers; study by David L. Mathison] V. Bozzi. *Psychol Today* 21:15 S '87

Groupthink, rethink: speaking up—even against the majority. B. L. Stern. *Vogue* 177:360-1 D '87

Why can't a woman say no like a man? B. Weber. *Mademoiselle* 93:112 Je '87

Bibliography

Assertiveness training: getting your own way. J. Zinsser. il *50 Plus* 27:32-3 Ag '87

Asses, Domestic See Donkeys

Assessment

See also

Appraisers

Challenging your property tax assessment. S. Carmichael. il *Home Mech* 83:30-1 Ag '87

Assessment of colleges and universities See Colleges and universities—Evaluation

Assessment of education See Education—Evaluation

Asset-backed financing

See also

Financial Security Assurance

Fight for survival [proposed reform of Glass-Steagall to allow securitization by banks] S. Koepp. il *Time* 129:72-3 My 4 '87

Making more debt do double duty [securitization] C. Farrell. il *Bus Week* p67-8 Mr 30 '87

Assignments, Teaching See Teaching assignments

Assistance in emergencies

See also

Ambulance service

First aid in illness and injury

Helping Hands (Organization)

Red Cross

Relief work

Rescue work

Help on the highway. P. McCarthy. il *Psychol Today* 21:12+ Jl '87

Screams from somewhere else. R. Rosenblatt. il *Time* 130:98 N 16 '87

Associated Black Charities

Associated Black Charities. F. Simon. il *Essence* 17:28 Ap '87

Associated Book Publishers plc

Octopus to acquire ABP's trade publishing lines. V. Menkes. *Publ Wkly* 232:12 D 18 '87

Simon & Schuster bids on stake in Britain's ABP. V. Menkes. *Publ Wkly* 231:10 Je 26 '87

Thomson to sell general publishing units of ABP conglomerate. V. Menkes. *Publ Wkly* 232:16 O 2 '87

Associated Dry Goods Corp.

David Farrell [acquisition of Associated Dry Goods by May Department Stores] M. D. Oneal. il por *Bus Week* Sp Issue:236 Ap 17 '87

Powerhouse potential [May Department Stores buys Associated Dry Goods] T. Jaffe. il *Forbes* 139:110 Ja 26 '87

Associated Press

Hal Buell leads the Associated Press into the future. H. Chapnick. il por *Pop Photogr* 94:40 Jl '87

Association (Biology) See Symbiosis

Association for European Astronauts

Panel calls for interim manned capsule. *Aviat Week Space Technol* 127:48-9 Jl 27 '87

Association for the Rights of Catholics in the Church
Human rights & Catholic rights. L. Swidler. *Commonweal* 114:485-6 S 11 '87

Association of American Publishers
AAP: a concerned member speaks. R. Benjamin. por *Publ Wkly* 231:54 My 22 '87
AAP and seven authors ask to join Random House in Salinger appeal [blocked publication of I. Hamilton's biography of J. D. Salinger] H. Fields. *Publ Wkly* 232:11 S 25 '87
AAP files amicus brief for Random House in appeal of Salinger decision [appeals court decision to bar publication of I. Hamilton's biography of J. D. Salinger] M. Yen. *Publ Wkly* 231:90 F 27 '87
AAP protests to U.S. Customs Service over 'user fee' on imported books. H. Fields. *Publ Wkly* 231:87 F 27 '87
AAP will admit affiliate members to boost income. H. Fields. *Publ Wkly* 232:10 N 27 '87
Korea says piracy accord can't be enforced. H. Fields. il *Publ Wkly* 232:11 N 20 '87
A new broom at the AAP. T. Weyr. il pors *Publ Wkly* 232:16-20 N 6 '87

Meetings
AAP meeting to hear Bale and Kastenmeier. H. Fields. *Publ Wkly* 231:16 Ja 16 '87
AAP's Florida meeting. M. Reuter. il *Publ Wkly* 231:16-19 Ap 17 '87

Association of American Universities
A halt to earmarking. *Sci News* 131:341 My 30 '87

Association of American University Presses
AAUP in Tucson: some burning issues. J. F. Baker and C. B. Grannis. il *Publ Wkly* 232:21-6 Jl 10 '87
AAUP opposes embargo on sales of books to South Africa. C. Reid. *Publ Wkly* 232:12 D 11 '87
AAUP's half century. C. B. Grannis. il *Publ Wkly* 231:26-30 Je 5 '87
Phillips named AAUP director. por *Publ Wkly* 232:32 O 9 '87

Association of American University Presses Book Show
See Book exhibits

Association of Booksellers for Children
Association of Booksellers for Children [annual meeting] D. E. Roback and S. Bolle. il *Publ Wkly* 231:43 Je 26 '87

Association of Catholic Colleges and Universities
The uses of spectacle [Pope meets Catholic educators] A. McCarthy. il *Commonweal* 114:472-3 S 11 '87

Association of Community Organizations for Reform Now
See ACORN (Organization)

Association of Flight Attendants International
Americans' flight attendants union to merge with AFL-CIO group. *Aviat Week Space Technol* 127:33 Ag 24 '87

Association of Old Crows
Old Crows cite contractor optimism, program instability for EW problems. *Aviat Week Space Technol* 126:107-8 F 9 '87

Association of Sicilian Women Against the Mafia
Jailed Mafia men face the wrath of Sicilian widows. il pors *People Wkly* 27:40-2+ My 18 '87

Association of Southeast Asian Nations *See* ASEAN

Associations, institutions, etc.
See also
Environmental associations
A sense of belonging. W. McGowan. il *N Y Times Mag* p46-8 Ag 23 '87

Assured Enterprises
Risky business. A. A. Lappen. il por *Forbes* 140:106 Jl 27 '87

Assyria

Antiquities
Business, B.C. [work of Assyriologist I. Spar] B. Weber. il por *N Y Times Mag* p114 N 22 '87

Astaire, Fred
about
The Astaire illusion. J. E. Mueller. *Dance Mag* 61:34 N '87
First encounters. E. Sorel and N. C. Sorel. il *Atlantic* 259:61 Ja '87
Obituary
Dance Mag il por 61:35 N '87. J. E. Mueller
Film Comment il 23:91-2+ S/O '87. H. Meyerson
Macleans il por 100:54 Jl 6 '87. L. O'Toole
Natl Rev 39:20-1 Jl 17 '87
New Repub 197:26 Ag 3 '87. S. Kauffmann
New Yorker 63:21 Jl 6 '87
Newsweek il por 110:48 Jl 6 '87. J. Kroll
People Wkly il pors 28:96-106 Jl 6 '87. B. Darrach
Time il por 130:19 Jl 6 '87. R. Schickel

U S News World Rep il por 103:68 Jl 6 '87. M. McLoughlin

Asteroids
See also
Space flight—Asteroid missions
And then there were three . . . *Sky Telesc* 73:366-7 Ap '87
An appulse of asteroids [Hebe and Iris] il *Sky Telesc* 74:172 Ag '87
The asteroid Astraea. il *Sky Telesc* 73:180 F '87
Asteroid impact gets more support [research by Bruce Bohor and others] R. A. Kerr. bibl il *Science* 236:666-8 My 8 '87
Astraea in M44. il *Sky Telesc* 74:109 Jl '87
A big splash in the Pacific [work of Frank Kyte and others] map *Sky Telesc* 74:12 Jl '87
Ceres sails by the Lagoon. il *Sky Telesc* 73:639 Je '87
The comet-asteroid connection [research by William K. Hartmann and others] *Sky Telesc* 74:343 O '87
Dark time [E. M. and C. Shoemaker's observations] R. Preston. *New Yorker* 63:64+ O 26 '87
Do asteroid impacts trigger geomagnetic reversals? [theory of Richard Muller and Donald Morris] B. M. Schwarzschild. bibl f il *Phys Today* 40:17-20 F '87
Extinction upon impact? [research by Bruce F. Bohor and others] R. Monastersky. il *Sci News* 131:309-10 My 16 '87
IRAS asteroid catalogue. il *Sky Telesc* 73:599 Je '87
IRAS puts astronomers out of (one) business. R. A. Kerr. *Science* 235:30-1 Ja 2 '87
Mass extinctions caused by large bolide impacts [adaptation of address, December 11, 1986; cover story] L. W. Alvarez. bibl f il *Phys Today* 40:24-33 Jl '87
More than just a spot: facing an asteroid at last [speckle interferometer images of Vesta; work of Jack Drummond and others] J. Eberhart. il *Sci News* 132:343 N 28 '87
Pallas this spring and summer. il *Sky Telesc* 73:526-7 My '87
Shock of impact [shocked quartz as evidence of asteroid impact with earth; work of Bruce F. Bohor and others] *Sci Am* 257:22-3 Jl '87
Shocked quartz in the Cretaceous-Tertiary boundary clays: evidence for a global distribution. B. F. Bohor and others. bibl f il map *Science* 236:705-9 My 8 '87
Speckled Vesta [use of speckle interferometer] il *Sky Telesc* 73:598 Je '87
Trillion-dollar asteroids? *Sky Telesc* 74:11-12 Jl '87
What killed the dinosaurs? [asteroid impact theory; work of Eric Essene and Daniel Fisher] il *USA Today (Periodical)* 115:9 Je '87
Where have all the dinos gone? [work of L. Alvarez] il *U S News World Rep* 103:67 Jl 6 '87
Who killed the dinosaurs? [impact-generated extinction theory] *Space World* X-8-284:9 Ag '87

Orbits
More clues to asteroid-dead comet connections. R. A. Kerr. *Science* 235:29-30 Ja 2 '87

Satellites
No satellites of asteroids. R. A. Kerr. *Science* 237:250 Jl 17 '87

Spectra and spectroscopy
Organic matter on asteroid 130 Elektra. D. P. Cruikshank and R. H. Brown. bibl f il *Science* 238:183-4 O 9 '87
Pinpointing near-earth asteroids [radar studies; work of Donald Yeomans, Steven Ostro, and Paul Chodas] *Sky Telesc* 74:576 D '87

Asthma
Child asthma alert. S. Berkman. il *Good Housekeep* 205:187 Ag '87
Childhood asthma: what you should know. C. Loomis. il *Parents* 62:227-8+ My '87

Therapy
A biobehavioral approach to managing childhood asthma. D. P. Kohen. bibl f il *Child Today* 16:6-10 Mr/Ap '87
Wheezer in the E.R.: musings on a cookbook admission [asthmatic children] P. Klass. il *Discover* 8:18+ Ap '87

Astin, Alexander W.
Competition or cooperation? [address, March 1987] il *Change* 19:12-19 S/O '87

Astin, Mackenzie
about
Prime time profiles. pors *Teen* 31:66 Je '87

Aston-Jones, Gary, and others
Asymmetry of neural feedback in the organization of behavioral states [discussion of November 7, 1986 article, The brain nucleus locus coeruleus: restricted afferent control of a broad efferent network] *Science* 237:537-8 Jl 31 '87

Aston Martin (Automobile) *See* Sports cars

Aston Martin Lagonda Ltd.
Cash flow in the fast lane [Ford buys Aston Martin] T. Tedesco. il *Macleans* 100:39 S 21 '87
Have you driven an Aston Martin lately? [Ford agrees to buy Aston Martin Lagonda] il *Newsweek* 110:64 S 21 '87

Astor, Brooke
Dogs' best friends. il *House Gard* 159:134-7 D '87

Astor, John Jacob, 1763-1848
about
"Poor Jacob!". P. Baida. il por *Forbes* 140 Sp Issue:345+ O 26 '87

Astraea (Asteroid) *See* Asteroids

Astroarcheology *See* Astronomy, Ancient

Astroblemes *See* Craters

Astrochemistry
See also
Matter, Interstellar
Nucleosynthesis
Deuterium, dust, and infant stars [study of Kleinmann-Low nebula; work of Malcolm Walmsley and others] *Sky Telesc* 74:236 S '87
E.T. may look like us [research by Cyril Ponnamperuma] il *USA Today (Periodical)* 115:16 Je '87

Astrocytes *See* Nerve cells

Astrology
See also
Zodiac
Fashion and the stars [views of Adolfo] M. Luther. il *Good Housekeep* 204:210 F '87
Fashion and the stars [views of Carolyne Roehm] M. Luther. il *Good Housekeep* 204:21 My '87
Fashion and the stars [views of Givenchy] M. Luther. il *Good Housekeep* 204:48 Mr '87
Fashion and the stars [views of Louis Dell'Olio] M. Luther. il *Good Housekeep* 205:80 Ag '87
Fashion and the stars [views of Nolan Miller] M. Luther. il *Good Housekeep* 204:36 Ja '87
Fashion and the stars [views of Norma Kamali] M. Luther. il *Good Housekeep* 205:19 Jl '87
Fashion and the stars [views of Sonia Rykiel] M. Luther. il *Good Housekeep* 204:21 Je '87
Fashion and the stars [views of William Travilla] M. Luther. il *Good Housekeep* 204:54 Ap '87
Horoscope. See issues of 'Teen
Horoscope. R. Gardiner. See issues of Vogue beginning July 1984
Horoscope. D. Kempton-Smith. See issues of Seventeen beginning March 1985
Horoscopes. Aurora. See issues of Harper's Bazaar
Inkblots and star charts—astrology and therapy. C. Tavris. *Vogue* 177:96 Jl '87
Mane man Anthony Morrocco works on moon time to deliver the kindest cut of all. il por *People Wkly* 28:113 Jl 13 '87
Misreading the stars. N. Henbest. il *World Press Rev* 34:55 S '87
Overloaded [astrologer D. Hayes] *New Yorker* 62:28-31 F 9 '87
Sign time. A. J. Grice. See issues of Essence
Star man [astrologer P. Walker] E. Newhall. il por *N Y* 20:20 F 23 '87
Starcast. M. L. Fiel. See issues of Mademoiselle
Stars in our eyes. P. Glick. il *Psychol Today* 21:6-7 Ag '87
Your horoscope. Chiron. See issues of McCall's beginning August 1986

Anecdotes, facetiae, satire, etc.
Who can serve better, Crabs or Scorpios? D. D. Jackson. il *Smithsonian* 18:162 Je '87

Astronautics *See* Space flight

Astronauts
See also
Association for European Astronauts
Chang-Diaz, Franklin R., 1950-
Grissom, Gus, 1926-1967
Leonov, Aleksei
Vasyutin, Vladimir
The astronauts after Challenger. J. Reston. il *N Y Times Mag* p46-7+ Ja 25 '87
Beyond the Challenger era [proposed space program from the astronauts] R. Wolkomir. il *Omni* 9:62-4+ Mr '87

European countries begin expanding astronaut ranks. *Aviat Week Space Technol* 127:98-9 O 26 '87
NASA urged to broaden astronaut base. *Aviat Week Space Technol* 127:48-9 Jl 27 '87
Space station crew time extended to cut dependence on shuttle. T. M. Foley. *Aviat Week Space Technol* 127:30-1 Ag 3 '87
The story of the century [NASA's Journalist in Space program] C. Wise. il *Space World* X-4-280:22-5 Ap '87

Attitudes
How to make space livable. il *Futurist* 21:56 Mr/Ap '87

Food
See Space flight—Food problems

Health and hygiene
See also
Weightlessness
Asleep in the cosmos. S. J. Nadis. il *Omni* 9:26+ Je '87
Medical hazards of Mars mission [views of William DeCampli] il *USA Today (Periodical)* 115:4 Je '87

Training
See also
Weightlessness simulators
Young Astronaut Council
The class of '87 [cover story] L. L. Kofler. il *Space World* X-11-287:9-13 N '87
Foreign cosmonauts train for flights on Mir space station. *Aviat Week Space Technol* 126:105 My 11 '87

Astronomers
See also
Angel, Roger
Apianus, Petrus, 1495-1552
Barnard, Edward Emerson, 1857-1923
Boss, Lewis
Fiedler, Ralph
Houston, Walter Scott
Messier, Charles, 1730-1817
Roberts, Isaac
Shelton, Ian
Shoemaker, Eugene Merle, 1928-
Tombaugh, Clyde, 1906-
Tucker, Richard H.

Astronomers, Amateur
See also
Children as astronomers
Amateur astronomers. S. J. O'Meara. See issues of Sky and Telescope
Amateurs triumph in Paris [colloquium celebrating the 100th anniversary of the Société Astronomique de France] S. J. O'Meara. il *Sky Telesc* 74:481-3 N '87
Astronomy on the open road. B. Aiken. il *Astronomy* 15:26+ Je '87
Continuing the tradition: amateur astronomers and the Space Telescope [address, August 7, 1986] R. Giacconi. il por *Astronomy* 15:24+ Ja '87
Eight ways to combat astronomy burnout. H. Jandorf. *Astronomy* 15:36 D '87
Gleanings for ATM's. R. W. Sinnott. See issues of Sky and Telescope
Globetrotting observer Paul Maley: chasing the fleeting moment [interview] R. Reeves. il por *Astronomy* 15:40+ N '87
Inside the IHW: the amateurs [interview with S. J. Edberg of International Halley Watch] A. MacRobert. il por *Sky Telesc* 73:264-5 Mr '87
Moonlighting [Greenwich Village astronomer T. Hoffman offers passersby a look through a telescope] J. Stone. il *Discover* 8:93-5 O '87
Observing an amateur astronomer: his wife's view. R. Critchley. il *Astronomy* 15:28 Ag '87
A super stargazer [supernovas discovered by R. Evans] il por *Time* 129:66 Mr 23 '87

Anecdotes, facetiae, satire, etc.
Hot tub astronomy: a fire on the moon [bright light in sky over California caused by missile misfiring] B. Mosier. il *Astronomy* 15:26+ Ap '87

Astronomical clocks
Adding the moon to a real-time clock. R. W. Sinnott. il *Sky Telesc* 73:536-7 My '87

Astronomical distances
See also
Stars—Distances
Sun—Distance
Extragalactic gamma-ray bursters? [views of Bohdan Paczynski] *Sky Telesc* 74:9-10 Jl '87
Gamma-ray bursters might be as distant as quasars [views of Bohdan Paczynski] *Astronomy* 15:83-4 Ja '87

Astronomical distances—*cont.*

Radio images and planetaries' distances [observations by Very Large Array] Y. Terzian. il *Sky Telesc* 73:128 F '87

Redshift theory may alter cosmic distances [research by Emil Wolf] il *Astronomy* 15:97-8 D '87

Were Titius and Bode right? il *Sky Telesc* 73:371 Ap '87

Astronomical equipment

   See also

   Binoculars

   Chronograph

   Image processing—Astronomical use

   Interferometers and interferometry

   Radio telescopes

   Spectrograph

   Telescopes

Astronomy reviews. See issues of Astronomy

Backyard astronomy. T. H. Cole. il *Pop Mech* 164:27 O '87

Equipment atlas. See issues of Astronomy

Gauging angles in the 17th century. A. Chapman. il *Sky Telesc* 73:362-4 Ap '87

Gearing up for summer deep-sky observing. D. J. Eicher. il *Astronomy* 15:64-70 Mr '87

Halbach's "astroflash" [gravity-operated flashlight] E. A. Halbach. il *Sky Telesc* 74:90-1 Jl '87

Directories

Astronomy equipment directory 1987. il *Astronomy* 15:60A-60P O '87

Dealers and manufacturers. il *Sky Telesc* 74 Sky Telesc Handb:22-9 S '87

Astronomical interferometry See Interferometers and interferometry

Astronomical literature

The education of Mary Somerville. K. Weitzenhoffer. por *Sky Telesc* 73:138-9 F '87

Authorship

How to teach (and learn) astronomy? Write a column! M. S. Smith. il *Astronomy* 15:26+ F '87

Astronomical measurements

Getting small [measurement of Pluto and its satellite] *Sci Am* 256:68 Ap '87

Astronomical models

   See also

   Planispheres

Birth of a quasar [supercomputer model developed by Stuart Shapiro and Saul Teukolsky] A. Fisher. il *Pop Sci* 231:10 S '87

Birth of the moon [giant impact theory] A. Fisher. il *Pop Sci* 230:60-4+ Ja '87

Do-it-yourself universes [research by Alan H. Guth and others] M. M. Waldrop. *Science* 235:845-6 F 20 '87

Simulating clusters on your computer. T. B. Woods. il *Astronomy* 15:63-7 S '87

Stonehenge in Missouri [half-scale model at Univ. of Missouri-Rolla] il *Sky Telesc* 74:83 Jl '87

Astronomical names See Astronomy—Nomenclature

Astronomical observations See Astronomy—Observations

Astronomical observatories

Astronomy under Texas skies [McDonald Observatory] S. Preston. il *Sky Telesc* 74:81-2 Jl '87

A garage-roof observatory. B. Wingate. il *Sky Telesc* 74:202-3 Ag '87

A new California observatory [Anza Observatory] J. Sanford. il *Sky Telesc* 73:546 My '87

A night on historic Mount Wilson. D. W. Green. il *Sky Telesc* 74:438-41 O '87

Observatories. il *Sky Telesc* 74 Sky Telesc Handb:9-10 S '87

A portable observatory, you say? D. Clapp. il *Sky Telesc* 74:87-9 Jl '87

Saving Mt. Wilson. *Sci News* 132:294 N 7 '87

Science at McDonald Observatory [study of O-type stars] R. Reeves. il pors *Astronomy* 15:6-17 Jl '87

The scientific and cultural heritage of Allegheny Observatory [restoration of Fitz/Clark 13-inch refractor] T. R. Jones. *Astronomy* 15:28+ Ap '87

Two new major observatories: Powell Observatory's 30-inch reflector. T. J. Martinez. il *Sky Telesc* 73:545 My '87

The wandering stars of Allegheny [addition of Multichannel Astrometric Photometer to 30-inch Thaw refractor; cover story] R. W. Sinnott. il *Sky Telesc* 74:360-3 O '87

Argentina

Charting the southern sky [work at San Luis, 1908-10] J. Lankford. il pors *Sky Telesc* 74:243-6 S '87

Australia

Japanese data center in Australia [NEC Halley's Comet Observation Center] S. J. O'Meara. il *Sky Telesc* 73:201-3 F '87

Laying bare Venus' dark secrets [infrared observations with the Anglo-Australian Telescope] D. A. Allen. il *Sky Telesc* 74:350-3 O '87

Chile

A boatbuilder's dome in Chile. W. Liller. il *Sky Telesc* 74:664-5 D '87

Great Britain

In search of historic observatories [watercolors by D. K. Northrop] S. J. O'Meara. il *Sky Telesc* 73:315-16 Mr '87

Hawaii

Bugs versus stars? [Mauna Kea observatories] S. Wong. il *Technol Rev* 90:13-14 N/D '87

Hawaii's radio eyes [Caltech Submillimeter Observatory on Mauna Kea] il *Sky Telesc* 73:152-3 F '87

India

Kavalur's stellar hermitage [Vainu Bappu Observatory's 2.3-meter reflector] D. M. Salwi. il *Sky Telesc* 73:375-6 Ap '87

Italy

Astronomy for the Italian public [Giorgio Abetti Observatory] G. G. C. Palumbo and R. Serra. il *Sky Telesc* 74:656-8 D '87

Japan

Japan's largest public observatory [Nichihara Observatory] T. Sato. il *Sky Telesc* 73:201-2 F '87

Netherlands

Variable star day at Leiden. J. A. Mattei. il *Sky Telesc* 74:535-6 N '87

North America

Focal points: observatories, planetariums, and museums for astronomy enthusiasts to visit throughout the United States and Canada. il *Astronomy* 15:42-53 Je '87

Puerto Rico

Overcoming radio noise at the Arecibo dish. il *Astronomy* 15:77 Mr '87

Astronomical observatories, Airborne See Airplanes in astronomy

Astronomical observatories in art

In search of historic observatories [watercolors by D. K. Northrop] S. J. O'Meara. il *Sky Telesc* 73:315-16 Mr '87

Astronomical photography

   See also

   Comets—Photographs and photography

   Earth—Photographs and photography

   Eclipses, Lunar—Photographs and photography

   Eclipses, Solar—Photographs and photography

   Galaxies—Photographs and photography

   Jupiter (Planet)—Photographs and photography

   Mars (Planet)—Photographs and photography

   Mercury (Planet)—Transits—Photographs and photography

   Milky Way—Photographs and photography

   Moon—Photographs and photography

   Nebulae—Photographs and photography

   Sky—Photographs and photography

   Sun—Photographs and photography

Big eye on the sky [Palomar Sky Survey] T. Dickinson. il *Pop Mech* 164:60-3+ S '87

Improving astrophotos by copying. T. B. Hunter. il *Sky Telesc* 74:326-8 S '87

Photography in astronomy. See issues of Astronomy

Surveying the northern sky [new Palomar Sky Survey] J. Schombert. il *Sky Telesc* 74:128-31 Ag '87

Equipment

Adventures in gas hypering. B. Iburg. il *Sky Telesc* 73:110-12 Ja '87

A camera that tracks comets. R. Arbour. il *Sky Telesc* 74:428-30 O '87

Experiments with a toothless sector. D. A. Harbour. il *Sky Telesc* 74:546-8 N '87

Gaining confidence with piggyback astrophotography. R. Dilsizian. il *Astronomy* 15:39-46 Ap '87

Hassle-free astrophotography [precision sidereal-rate clock drive kit] R. Berry. il *Astronomy* 15:38-9 O '87

How to build and use an all-sky camera. J. Charles and others. il *Astronomy* 15:64-70 Ap '87

A portable photographic platform. W. G. Pursell. il *Astronomy* 15:91-3 Jl '87

Possibilities of a "tetrapod" [tetrahedral tripod] D. Trott. il *Sky Telesc* 74:426-8 O '87

Regulating the voltage of a DC motor [with comments by Roger W. Sinnott] A. Kremers. il *Sky Telesc* 74:198-201 Ag '87

Skyshooting with the fastest color film [Konica SR-V3200] D. Di Cicco. il *Sky Telesc* 74:558-61 N '87

Astronomical photography—Equipment—*cont.*
SR-V 3200: the superfilm from Konica. R. Berry. il *Astronomy* 15:78-83 N '87
Taming the Schmidt camera. R. Reeves and M. Hooley. il *Astronomy* 15:82-7 D '87
A wire micrometer for photographs. L. Balbi. il *Sky Telesc* 74:310-11+ S '87

History
The legacy of E. E. Barnard. G. S. Mumford. il por *Sky Telesc* 74:30-4 Jl '87
Astronomical photometry *See* Photometry, Astronomical
Astronomical research
See also
Balloons—Research use

Federal aid
Astronomy, Challenger, and budget cuts. P. B. Boyce. il *Sky Telesc* 73:468 My '87
Observing the energetic universe. D. H. Smith. il *Technol Rev* 90:66-73 My/Je '87
Astronomical societies
See also
American Astronomical Society
Astronomical Society of the Pacific
British Astronomical Association
International Halley Watch
Société Astronomique de France
Societies; Astronomy clubs. il *Sky Telesc* 74 Sky Telesc Handb:11-18 S '87
Staying up nights. il *Astronomy* 15:64-71 Je '87
Astronomical Society of the Pacific
ASP 1987 Bruce Medal to Salpeter; 1986 medal to Whipple. il *Phys Today* 40:83-5 Jl '87
Astronomical spectroscopy
See also
Asteroids—Spectra and spectroscopy
Comets—Spectra and spectroscopy
Galaxies—Spectra and spectroscopy
Halley's comet—Spectra and spectroscopy
Infrared astronomy
Nebulae—Spectra and spectroscopy
Pluto (Planet)—Spectra and spectroscopy
Quasars—Spectra and spectroscopy
Stars—Spectra and spectroscopy
Sun—Spectra and spectroscopy
Ultraviolet astronomy
Astronomy
See also
Airplanes in astronomy
Arcs (Astronomy)
Artificial satellites—Astronomical use
Asteroids
Astrophysics
Black holes (Astronomy)
Comets
Computers—Astronomical use
Conjunctions (Astronomy)
Constellations
Dark matter (Astronomy)
Eclipses, Lunar
Eclipses, Solar
Electronic astronomy
Galaxies
Gamma ray astronomy
Herbig-Haro objects
Image processing—Astronomical use
Information storage and retrieval systems—Astronomical use
Infrared astronomy
Lasers—Astronomical use
Life on other planets
Lunar bases—Astronomical use
Magellanic clouds
Mechanics, Celestial
Meteorites
Meteors
Milky Way
Nebulae
Occultations
Olbers' paradox
Orbits
Parallax
Planetariums
Planetesimal hypothesis
Planets
Precession
Quasars
Radar in astronomy
Radio astronomy
Radio broadcasting—Science programs
Ring systems (Astronomy)
Sky

Solar system
Space and time
Space astronomy
Stars
Sun
Telephone in astronomy
Telescopes
Ultraviolet astronomy
Universe
X ray astronomy
Zodiac
Zodiacal light
Astronews. See issues of Astronomy
Astronomy forum. See issues of Astronomy
Astronomy's 1987 summer travel guide [special section] il *Astronomy* 15:40-59+ Je '87
News notes. See issues of Sky and Telescope
Sky reporter. S. P. Maran. See occasional issues of Natural History

Almanacs
Floppy Almanac [computer program] J. E. Mosley. *Sky Telesc* 73:85 Ja '87
Floppy Almanac is a real deal. B. L. Gotwols. *Astronomy* 15:47-8+ D '87
Sky-gazer's almanac 1987. il *Sky Telesc* 73:59-62 Ja '87

Awards
ASP 1987 Bruce Medal to Salpeter; 1986 medal to Whipple. il *Phys Today* 40:83-5 Jl '87
Bibliography
Astronomy reviews. See issues of Astronomy
Books and the sky. M. D. Boring. See issues of Sky and Telescope
Charts, diagrams, etc.
See also
Planispheres
Stars—Atlases
Beeping the faith [Prayer Times Clock and international lunar date line calculations for Moslem travelers] map *Sci Am* 256:74 Mr '87
Celestial events. T. D. Nicholson. See issues of Natural History
Charting the southern sky [work at San Luis, Argentina, 1908-10] J. Lankford. il pors *Sky Telesc* 74:243-6 S '87
An early star mapper [P. Apianus] G. Lovi. il *Sky Telesc* 74:391-2 O '87
Fun with stereographic projections [computer program] R. A. Mulford. il *Sky Telesc* 74:407-8 O '87
Southern stars. See alternate issues of Sky and Telescope
Stars for [the month] See issues of Sky and Telescope
Conferences
See also
Planets—Conferences
Amateur telescope makers have come a long way, but the goal remains the same: a way to see the rest of the universe [Stellafane Convention] J. P. Wiley, Jr. il *Smithsonian* 18:36+ O '87
Astrocalendar. See issues of Astronomy
The children of Stellafane. S. J. O'Meara. il *Sky Telesc* 74:417-19 O '87
Riverside Telescope Maker's Conference. R. Berry. il *Astronomy* 15:34-6 S '87
Star Party in the Lone Star State [Texas Star Party] D. J. Eicher and J. Kanipe. il *Astronomy* 15:36-40 S '87
Staying up nights. il *Astronomy* 15:64-71 Je '87
Thunderbolts can't short-circuit Texas Star Party. J. Kanipe. il *Astronomy* 15:26+ S '87
The top 10 telescope ideas of 1987 [Stellafane, Riverside and the Texas Star Party] il *Sky Telesc* 74:590-4 D '87
The universe from British Columbia [1985 Mount Kobau Star Party] G. C. Knight. il *Astronomy* 15:30+ Ja '87
Directories
Popular astronomy handbook. il *Sky Telesc* 74 Sky Telesc Handb:1-31 S '87
History
Charting the southern sky [work at San Luis, Argentina, 1908-10] J. Lankford. il pors *Sky Telesc* 74:243-6 S '87
An early star mapper [P. Apianus] G. Lovi. il *Sky Telesc* 74:391-2 O '87
The education of Mary Somerville. K. Weitzenhoffer. por *Sky Telesc* 73:138-9 F '87
Gauging angles in the 17th century. A. Chapman. il *Sky Telesc* 73:362-4 Ap '87
Guest stars are always welcome. F. R. Stephenson. *Nat Hist* 96:72+ S '87

Astronomy—History—cont.

Newton's Principia: a retrospective. G. E. Christianson. il por *Sky Telesc* 74:18-20 Jl '87

A revisit to the guest star of A.D. 185. Y.-L. Huang and G. H. Moriarty-Schieven. bibl f il *Science* 235:59-60 Ja 2 '87

International aspects

See also
Global Oscillation Network Group

Astronomy in West Germany goes supernational. D. E. Thomsen. *Sci News* 132:332-3 N 21 '87

International news. See issues of Sky and Telescope beginning December 1986

Nomenclature

Naming names [work of H. Masursky] G. Freiherr. il por *Space World* X-8-284:31-3 Ag '87

Observations

Backyard astronomy. A. MacRobert. See occasional issues of Sky and Telescope beginning August 1983

Celestial calendar. A. MacRobert. See issues of Sky and Telescope beginning October 1984

Gazer's gazette. See issues of Astronomy

Gearing up for summer deep-sky observing. D. J. Eicher. il *Astronomy* 15:64-70 Mr '87

Globetrotting observer Paul Maley: chasing the fleeting moment [interview] R. Reeves. il por *Astronomy* 15:40+ N '87

In the glare of the moon. P. Ceravolo. il *Astronomy* 15:24+ My '87

Moonlighting [Greenwich Village astronomer T. Hoffman offers passersby a look through a telescope] J. Stone. il *Discover* 8:93-5 O '87

Nature [Samuel Storch's lecture on Messier objects] *New Yorker* 62:26 F 2 '87

A night on historic Mount Wilson. D. W. Green. il *Sky Telesc* 74:438-41 O '87

An observer's midsummer night's dream. D. L. Graham. il *Astronomy* 15:26+ My '87

Observer's page. D. Di Cicco. See issues of Sky and Telescope

Observing from the city. A. MacRobert. il *Sky Telesc* 74:35-7 Jl '87

Anecdotes, facetiae, satire, etc.

Stunned. J. Handey. *New Yorker* 63:33 Ap 27 '87

Periodicals

See also
Sky and telescope (Periodical)

Research

See Astronomical research

Study and teaching

See also
Project STAR

AAS involves teachers in meetings. *Phys Today* 40:101-2 F '87

Astronomy 101: alone against the universe. H. M. Steinberg. *Astronomy* 15:24+ O '87

Creationism in Ontario [threat to astronomy curriculum] D. E. Thomsen. *Sci News* 132:24 Jl 11 '87

The pride of Globe, Arizona [K. Zeigler's high school astronomy program] J. K. Beatty. il por *Sky Telesc* 74:192-3 Ag '87

Projects

To catch a child's imagination [Halley's comet project aboard the Kuiper Airborne Observatory] J. H. Nicholson. il *Sky Telesc* 74:303-5 S '87

Textbooks

Astronomy texts from Abell to Zeilik. H. P. Coyle. il *Sky Telesc* 74:487-93 N '87

Canada

The universe from British Columbia [1985 Mount Kobau Star Party] G. C. Knight. il *Astronomy* 15:30+ Ja '87

Germany (West)

Astronomy in West Germany goes supernational. D. E. Thomsen. *Sci News* 132:332-3 N 21 '87

Great Britain

British plan for the year 2000. D. H. Smith. il *Sky Telesc* 73:497 My '87

Japan

Observational neutrino astrophysics. M.-T. Koshiba. bibl il map *Phys Today* 40:38-42 D '87

Spotlight on Japan [special section] il *Sky Telesc* 73:200-3 F '87

What do we learn from space? Space science in Japan. M. Oda. bibl il *Phys Today* 40:26-33 D '87

Philippines

The Philippines: a land in shadow [visit in preparation for 1988 solar eclipse expedition] S. J. O'Meara. il *Sky Telesc* 73:432-3 Ap '87

Astronomy, Ancient

Computer dating [astronomical dating] F. R. Stephenson. il *Nat Hist* 96:24+ Ja '87

Extinction angles and megaliths [computer program] B. E. Schaefer. il *Sky Telesc* 73:426 Ap '87

The old and the ethnic in astronomy [cover story] D. E. Thomsen. il *Sci News* 131:170-1 Mr 14 '87

Two gamma-ray sources and ancient guest stars. Z.-R. Wang. bibl f il *Science* 235:1485-6 Mr 20 '87

Astronomy, Chinese

A revisit to the guest star of A.D. 185. Y.-L. Huang and G. H. Moriarty-Schieven. bibl f il *Science* 235:59-60 Ja 2 '87

Two gamma-ray sources and ancient guest stars. Z.-R. Wang. bibl f il *Science* 235:1485-6 Mr 20 '87

Astronomy, Spherical and practical

See also
Equinoxes

Astronomy (Periodical)

Behind the scenes. R. Berry. See issues of Astronomy

Astrophotography *See* Astronomical photography

Astrophysics

See also
Black holes (Astronomy)
Canadian Institute for Theoretical Astrophysics
Cosmic rays
Neutron stars
Pulsars
Quasars
Red shift
Solar wind
Space stations—Physics use
Stars—Evolution
Universe

Astrophysics. *Phys Today* 40:S4-S11 Ja '87

A bold agenda for Soviet astrophysics. il *Sky Telesc* 74:601 D '87

Why astronomers need the SSC [Superconducting Super Collider] D. N. Schramm. il *Sky Telesc* 74:588 D '87

Conferences

The Texas Symposium on Relativistic Astrophysics [special section] M. M. Waldrop. il *Science* 235:283-5 Ja 16 '87

Astroporpa *See* Echinoderms

Asunción (Paraguay)

Social life and customs

Leaving yesterday behind. D. Pardo de Carugati. il *World Press Rev* 34:28 D '87

ASW *See* Anti-submarine warfare

Asylum, Right of

El Norte's sheltering arms [Supreme Court ruling] il *U S News World Rep* 102:13 Mr 23 '87

Gimme shelter [Supreme Court requires INS to use more lenient standards in asylum cases] R. Lacayo. il *Time* 129:70 Mr 23 '87

No refugees need apply. C. Dreifus. il *Atlantic* 259:32-5 F '87

Supreme Court eases rules on political asylum. R. Frame. *Christ Today* 31:45 Ap 17 '87

Asymetrix Corporation

The next chapter [founder P. Allen] E. F. Cone. il por *Forbes* 139:168 Ap 6 '87

Asyst (Computer program) *See* Computers—Scientific use—Programming

At mother's request [television program] See Television program reviews—Single works

AT&T *See* American Telephone & Telegraph Co.

AT&T Bell Labs

New developments in computer and communications technologies [address, March 31, 1987] J. S. Mayo. *Vital Speeches Day* 53:499-503 Je 1 '87

The startling discovery Bell Labs kept in the shadows [N. Karmarkar's linear programming algorithm] W. G. Wild, Jr. and O. Port. por *Bus Week* p69+ S 21 '87

Atalanta Sosnoff Capital Corp.

My wife, the Comtesse [M. Sosnoff] D. Machan. il por *Forbes* 139 Ann Directory:119-20 Ap 27 '87

Atanasoff, John V.

about

The 'first computer' controversy [discussion of March 1987 article, The first electronic computer] A. R. Mackintosh. *Phys Today* 40:13+ D '87

The first electronic computer. A. R. Mackintosh. bibl f il pors *Phys Today* 40:25-32 Mr '87

Ataxia

A walking example of B$_6$ deficiency [research by Monica C. Schaeffer] *Prevention* 39:104-5 Ag '87

ATC *See* Aviation Training Center
ATC *See* Air traffic control
Atchafalaya River (La.)
Regulation
Atchafalaya [Army Corps of Engineers' Old River Control operation] J. A. McPhee. *New Yorker* 63:39-44+ F 23 '87
Atelier Brocard
Regal needles. S. De Rochambeau. il *House Gard* 159:88+ S '87
Atema, Jelle
about
Getting to the heart of lobster love. D. Q. Haney. il por *Natl Wildl* 25:18-21 Ap/My '87
Lobster lust: Don Juans of the deep [with editorial comment by Paul Hoffman] W. Ravven. il por *Discover* 8:4, 34-40 D '87
Atencio, Benjamin
An enthusiasm to learn through video. *Phi Delta Kappan* 68:632-3 Ap '87
Athalia [oratorio] *See* Handel, George Frideric, 1685-1759
Atheism
Religion and atheism in the Soviet Union [special section] *Humanist* 47:5-24+ Ja/F '87
Athens (Greece)
Antiquities
See also
Acropolis (Athens, Greece)
Parthenon (Athens, Greece)
History
A patriot for whom? Alcibiades of Athens. P. Cartledge. bibl il por *Hist Today* 37:15-19 O '87
Hotels, motels, etc.
Royal Grande Bretagne. E. Lynne. il *Saturday Evening Post* 259:91-2 Mr '87
Athens (Tex.)
Hospitals
Healing waters [Lakeland Medical Center] M. Gaskie. il *Archit Rec* 175:102-7 O '87
Athens, Ga. [film] *See* Motion picture reviews—Single works
Atherosclerosis *See* Arteriosclerosis
Athfield, Ian, 1940-
about
Architecture: Ian Athfield: a residence for vintners in Hawkes Bay, New Zealand. F. FitzGerald. il por *Archit Dig* 44:78-83 Ja '87
Athlete product endorsements *See* Advertising—Testimonials
Athletes
See also
Automobile racing drivers
Baseball players
Basketball players
Black athletes
Boxers
Discrimination in sports
Football players
Golfers
Hockey players
Motorcyclists
Skiers
Tennis players
Women athletes
See also names of athletes
The 7th annual All-America Team [aged athletes] H. Higdon. il *50 Plus* 27:58-64 N '87
Athletes or role models? Demanding higher standards from players is unrealistic. J. Papanek. por *Sports Illus* 66:84 Je 15 '87
Faces in the crowd. See issues of Sports Illustrated
The good hands people [athletes' mastery of catching a ball] G. Legwold. il *Sport Mag* 78:81+ N '87
A lineup of stars [stars to watch at the Olympic Winter Games in Calgary] il *Macleans* 100:38-9 Mr 23 '87
Ms. Right and Mr. Wrong [women athletes score higher than male athletes in tests of moral reasoning] L. Howard. il *Women's Sports Fitness* 9:45 O '87
Newly at a loss for worlds [American athletes in a slump] T. Callahan. il *Time* 130:43 S 28 '87
Older athletes: ice and fire. H. H. Broun. il *50 Plus* 27:80 N '87
The reach for athletic gold [American Olympic contenders] il *U S News World Rep* 103:70-3 D 28 '87-Ja 4 '88
Ready, set . . . win! [young Olympic hopefuls] il map *Natl Geogr World* 148:9-15 D '87
When negative is positive [effect of negative ions on athletic performance] J. Venturino. il *Women's Sports Fitness* 9:55 Ap '87

Age
The comeback trail [returning to a sport] S. Hanks. il *Esquire* 107:35-6 Ja '87
Awards
See Sports—Awards
Crime
Police blotter. *Sport Mag* 78:101-2 D '87
Education
The best and the brightest [unsung college football players who are also good students] E. M. Swift. il *Sports Illus* 67:40-5 Ag 31 '87
Big-time college athletics: academic eligibility rules are elitist. G. R. Roberts. il *USA Today (Periodical)* 116:68-70 Jl '87
Big-time college athletics: commercialization and corruption. T. A. Luken. il *USA Today (Periodical)* 116:64-7 Jl '87
The graduates [four collegiate student-athletes] il *Sports Illus* 66:60-4 Je 8 '87
Jan Kemp [professor's stand against college athletes' low academic standards at the Univ. of Georgia] C. Reece. il por *Ms* 15:44+ Ja '87
School and the student racer [public high schoolers who are ski racers] C. Cooper. il *Skiing* 39:22-3 Ja '87
What I learned in school today [sitting in on a class taken by football players at the University of Michigan] S. Shuger. il *Sport Mag* 78:60-1 O '87
Anecdotes, facetiae, satire, etc.
Setting things right in school. G. V. Griffith. por *Newsweek* 110:16-17 S 21 '87
Ethics
See Sports—Ethical aspects
Health and hygiene
See also
AIDS (Disease) and sports
Alcohol and sports
Blood boosting
Drugs and sports
The sleepless sportsman. J. Poppy. il *Esquire* 108:71-2 O '87
The truth about DMSO. S. Festa. il *Women's Sports Fitness* 9:62 My '87
Nutrition
The active gourmet [recipes devised by triathlete E. Burt] J. Myers. il pors *Women's Sports Fitness* 9:37-9 N '87
Choosing the right energy drink. S. Krasnow. il *Sport Mag* 78:93 Jl '87
Diet vs. exercise. *Vogue* 177:170 Ag '87
Get a daily carbo boost [glycogen burning] G. Sloan. il *Women's Sports Fitness* 9:16 Ag '87
Hiking light: meal in a capsule [Sustain SP] J. Venturino. il *Women's Sports Fitness* 9:59 My '87
Nutrition and the athlete [cover story] D. Henderson. il *FDA Consum* 21:18-21 My '87
The portable breakfast. E. Hackman. il *Women's Sports Fitness* 9:56 Ap '87
Six of one, 2.5 of another [sports drinks] *Women's Sports Fitness* 9:59 F '87
Soda loading [use of sodium bicarbonate to improve athletic performance] D. Groves. il *Women's Sports Fitness* 9:68 D '87
Psychology
See Sports—Psychological aspects
Salaries, pensions, etc.
See also
Amateurism (Sports)
Cheap labor on campus. D. Glasner. por *Newsweek* 110:12 N 9 '87
Free the professional 2,900! F. S. Worthy. il *Fortune* 116:95 O 26 '87
NCAA union: no pay, no play? [compensating major college athletes; views of Dick DeVenzio] D. Whitford. il *Sport Mag* 78:14 Ja '87
Sport 100 salary survey [cover story] C. Pesmen. *Sport Mag* 78:23-9+ Je '87
Training
See also
Plyometrics
The abdominal showmen. J. Hanc. il *Sport Mag* 78:81+ O '87
Big-league machines for the home. D. Groves. il *Sport Mag* 78:80 Je '87
The comeback trail [returning to a sport] S. Hanks. il *Esquire* 107:35-6 Ja '87
Gaining good weight [weight training] C. Pesmen. il *Sport Mag* 78:87-8 Mr '87
Spinal tip: building a sport-safe back. S. Beitler. il *Sport Mag* 78:79-80 F '87
Sprinting to find your stride and joy. C. Pesmen. il *Sport Mag* 78:75+ Ja '87

Athletes—Training—cont.

Taking better aim [accuracy in sports] R. Brody. il *Sport Mag* 78:91+ Ag '87

Ultimate fitness [cover story; special section] il *Esquire* 107:113-16+ My '87

When athletes and machines meet. T. Osborne. il *Curr Health 2* 13:16-17 F '87

When less is more [tapering before a competition] J. Venturino. *Women's Sports Fitness* 9:88 Mr '87

Workout wizardry: how to turn your personal computer into a personal coach. S. Reeder. il *Women's Sports Fitness* 9:52-5 F '87

Vision

See Vision

Volunteer service

See Volunteer service

Athletes' agents *See* Sports agencies and agents

Athletes and drugs *See* Drugs and sports

Athletes as authors

Jock lit [books by and about sports personalities] J. McCallum. il *Sports Illus* 67:80-4+ S 21 '87

Athlete's foot (Disease)

Athlete's foot: watch your step. il *Bus Week* p179 Jl 20 '87

Athletes in restaurant management

A room of one's own. B. L. Ladson. il *Sport Mag* 78:85+ N '87

Athletic buildings *See* Gymnasiums

Athletic clubs *See* Sports clubs

Athletic locker rooms *See* Locker rooms

Athletic scholarships *See* Scholarships and fellowships

Athletic shoes *See* Footwear

Athletics

See also

Athletes
Coaches (Athletics)
College athletics
Gymnastics
Olympic Games
Pan American Games
School athletics
Track and field athletics

Atil, Esin

The Age of Sultan Suleyman the Magnificent. il *USA Today (Periodical)* 116:78-86 Jl '87

Atkeson, Timothy, and Dower, Roger C.

The unrealized potential of SARA: mobilizing new protection for natural resources [with editorial comment by Alan McGowan] bibl f *Environment* 29:2, 6-8+ My '87

Atkins, Charles Agee

about

Pied Piper to the truly rich. F. Ungeheuer. il por *Time* 129:52 Ap 6 '87

Sidney Poitier and others linked to tax shelter scam. *Jet* 72:14 Ap 13 '87

So you thought you'd seen the last of tax straddles. D. Zigas. il por *Bus Week* p90 Je 15 '87

Wall Street's prime-time crime drama. D. Pauly. il por *Newsweek* 109:44 Ap 6 '87

Atkins, David *See* Sinbad

Atkins, Norman

Better red than dud. il *Roll Stone* p29-30 F 12 '87

Fast food for thought. il por *Roll Stone* p110-12+ Mr 26 '87

Oliver's twists. il *Roll Stone* p65-6+ Jl 16-30 '87

Atkins, Ralph

Thatcher—past, present, and future? *World Press Rev* 34:16 My '87

Atkins, Robert

American sublime. il *Horizon* 30:36-9 S '87

Anselm Kiefer. il *Horizon* 30:12-16 D '87

The modern Met. il *Horizon* 30:33-6 Mr '87

Photography becomes art. il *Horizon* 30:38-40 Je '87

Two years on. il *Horizon* 30:29-32 Ap '87

Atkins (Nancy), Inc. *See* Nancy Atkins, Inc.

Atkinson, A. B. (Anthony Barnes)

Original Sen. il *N Y Rev Books* 34:41-4 O 22 '87

Atkinson, Anthony Barnes *See* Atkinson, A. B. (Anthony Barnes)

Atkinson, Melissa

No heartbeat. *Parents* 62:134-5 Ap '87

Atkinson, Rick

about

HM spends $600G for book on West Pt. Class of '66. *Publ Wkly* 231:37 My 8 '87

Atlanta (Ga.)

Airports

Carriers, FAA continue talks on Atlanta Hartsfield schedule. *Aviat Week Space Technol* 126:36 Ap 20 '87

Swiss, U.S. exchange access to Atlanta for check-in rights. *Aviat Week Space Technol* 127:34 Jl 27 '87

Top two U.S. airports headed by black execs [C. Carter of Hartsfield] pors *Jet* 72:8 Je 22 '87

Architecture

New style in the Old South [A. Ames designs home for Frank Hulse] E. Greene. il *House Gard* 159:140-5+ Jl '87

Vintage design travels to Atlanta. C. Engle. il *South Living* 22:108-9 Je '87

Auditoriums, convention facilities, etc.

All booked up [facilities for the Democratic National Convention] il *Newsweek* 109:7 Mr 2 '87

Blacks

Atlanta blacks make biggest income, educational gains. *Jet* 73:33 S 28 '87

Atlanta: the city of the next generation. N. McCall. il *Black Enterp* 17:56-8 My '87

City hall

Atlanta City Hall to get facelift; black firm helps build new addition. il *Jet* 72:33 S 21 '87

Crime

Atlanta probes murder mystery of black wife of white millionaire [murder of L. M. Sullivan] D. M. Cheers. il pors *Jet* 72:24-7 My 25 '87

Jewelry valued at $25,000 is stolen from Alice Bond. por *Jet* 72:36 Ag 10 '87

Description

A neighborly look at Atlanta [Virginia-Highland area] C. Griffith. il map *South Living* 22:74-6 Ja '87

Reading the face of Atlanta [Fairlie-Poplar walking tour] il *South Living* 22:85 Ap '87

Education

Atlanta, Chicago schools among the most segregated. *Jet* 72:12 Ag 10 '87

Memphis educator named Atlanta superintendent [W. W. Herenton] por *Jet* 73:22 N 9 '87

Schools are my business [Rich's department store program for high school students] J. M. Zimmerman. por *Newsweek* 109:6-7 My 11 '87

Gardens and gardening

Gardening with Eve [garden of Eve Davis] il *South Living* 22:53 Je '87

Hospitals

Visible improvement [Northside Hospital] M. Gaskie. il *Archit Rec* 175:112-15 O '87

Housing

Bloody house puzzles Atlanta couple, cops [seeping blood mystery in home of W. Winston] il por *Jet* 73:29 O 12 '87

Industries

A tale of two cities [new segregation as businesses move to white suburbs leaving black workers behind] D. Beers and D. Hembree. il *Nation* 244:357-60 Mr 21 '87

Young tells Italians he can be businessman and pastor [Mayor A. Young] il *Jet* 72:40 Je 29 '87

Politics and government

Alice Bond, Carmen Butler meet before magistrate to argue battery charge [Mrs. J. Bond's accusations of cocaine abuse directed against husband Julian] il por *Jet* 72:6 My 11 '87

Andrew Young's ill-timed call [A. Bond's accusations of cocaine use] il por *Time* 129:34 My 25 '87

Atlanta grand jury not questioning Julian Bond in city's drug scandal. *Jet* 72:4 Je 15 '87

Atlanta mayor testifies in drug probe; says his family shaken by slurs [A. Young] il pors *Jet* 72:4 Je 1 '87

Atlanta mayor Young to testify before grand jury in city's drug scandal. por *Jet* 72:4 My 25 '87

Atlanta's coke controversy [charges against J. Bond] il por *Newsweek* 109:36 Ap 27 '87

Georgia woman tied to Julian Bond in drug probe gets 22-year sentence [C. Butler] por *Jet* 72:52 S 21 '87

Julian Bond denies using cocaine and lashes media; Mayor Young implicated. pors *Jet* 72:8 My 4 '87

A scandal scars Atlanta [cocaine charges against A. Young and J. Bond] T. E. Johnson. il pors *Newsweek* 109:28 Je 1 '87

Young clear in drug probe, fellow Democrats cheer; ponders bid for governor. il pors *Jet* 72:24 Jl 6 '87

Poor

Atlanta mayor wears disguise and feels hurt of the homeless [A. Young] T. S. Moore. il pors *Jet* 71:22-4 Mr 16 '87

Prisons and reformatories

Excludable from justice [Cuban detainees at U.S. penitentiary] G. Galbaugh. *America* 156:315-16 Ap 18 '87

Atlanta (Ga.)—*cont.*

Race relations

Atlanta NAACP is fuming over white talk show host's calling Lewis 'Buckwheat' [E. Tyll's remarks concerning Congressman J. Lewis] il pors *Jet* 72:22 Ag 10 '87

A tale of two cities [new segregation as businesses move to white suburbs leaving black workers behind] D. Beers and D. Hembree. il *Nation* 244:357-60 Mr 21 '87

Restaurants, nightclubs, bars, etc.

Atlanta's new southern hospitality. R. L. Balzer. il *Travel Holiday* 168:36+ Jl '87

Atlanta Ballet

Reviews:

Performances of Coppelia in Atlanta. O. Stuart. *Dance Mag* 61:27-9 Mr '87

Atlanta University

Dorcas Bowles named prexy of Atlanta University. *Jet* 72:12 Ag 17 '87

Atlantic and Pacific Tea Company *See* Great Atlantic & Pacific Tea Company, Inc.

Atlantic Canada Opportunities Agency

An Atlantic beginning? M. Gee. il *Macleans* 100:10-11 Je 22 '87

New money, old refrains. S. MacLeod. por *Macleans* 100:52 Ag 31 '87

Atlantic City (N.J.)

Economic conditions

Battle royal on the old boardwalk. J. Reed. il *U S News World Rep* 102:60-1 Ap 27 '87

Hotels, motels, etc.

See also

Casinos

Trump's Castle Hotel and Casino

Poor

Under the boardwalk. B. Jacobs. il *Progressive* 51:20-2 O '87

Atlantic coast

See also

Cruising—Atlantic coast

East Coast redux [ports] E. A. Finn, Jr. il *Forbes* 139:162 My 18 '87

Atlantic flights *See* Aviation—Transatlantic flights

Atlantic Monthly Press

Atlantic launches two series at ABA convention. *Publ Wkly* 231:59-60 Je 12 '87

Atlantic Ocean

Underwater canyons [Atlantic trip in submarine Alvin] R. Gannon. il *Pop Sci* 231:60-4+ Jl '87

Atlantic Records (Firm)

Atlantic at 40 [N. Ertegun] G. Santoro. por *Down Beat* 54:63 Ag '87

In the listening room of Ahmet Ertegun. il por *Esquire* 108:156-7 S '87

Atlantic Richfield Co.

Dancing into the limelight [L. M. Cook] B. O'Reilly. por *Fortune* 116:62 Ag 3 '87

How Arco is priming the pump. R. Grover. il por *Bus Week* p80+ Je 1 '87

One office the Mac has conquered [Atlantic Richfield uses Apple Macintosh in exploration strategy] il por *Fortune* 116:60 N 9 '87

Atlantic salmon *See* Salmon

Atlantic Southeast Airlines Inc.

Atlantic Southeast expects to double service at Dallas/Ft. Worth hub. C. Preble. il *Aviat Week Space Technol* 126:41+ My 4 '87

Big brother. T. Jaffe. il *Forbes* 139:274 Je 15 '87

Atlantic States

See also

Automobile touring—Atlantic States

Colleges and universities—Atlantic States

Express highways—Atlantic States

Forests and forestry—Atlantic States

Hotels, motels, etc.—Atlantic States

Housing—Atlantic States

Restaurants—Atlantic States

Fisheries

See Fisheries

Atlas, James

Dr. Johnson's open house. il por *House Gard* 159:12+ D '87

A magazine junkie. il *N Y Times Mag* p22 N 1 '87

MIA at the MLA. *New Repub* 196:12-13 Ja 26 '87

Putting one letter after another. il *N Y Times Book Rev* 92:1+ Mr 15 '87

Atlas (Launch vehicle) *See* Space vehicles—Propulsion systems

Atlas Fund

A world investor's favorite markets [interview with N. Fachler] J. Mendes. il por *Fortune* 116:130 S 14 '87

Atlases

See also

Stars—Atlases

Atlee, Champ

Max Planck and the squirrel [poem] *America* 157:65 Ag 1-8 '87

Atmosphere

See also

Biosphere

Carbon dioxide

Haze

Jupiter (Planet)—Atmosphere

Jupiter (Planet)—Satellites—Atmosphere

Ozone

Uranus (Planet)—Atmosphere

Venus (Planet)—Atmosphere

Winds

Atmospheric trends in methylchloroform and the global average for the hydroxyl radical. R. G. Prinn and others. bibl f il *Science* 238:945-50 N 13 '87

Simple experiments in atmospheric physics. C. F. Bohren. See issues of Weatherwise

Atmosphere, Upper

See also

Jet stream

Noctilucent clouds

Ozone

Energetic electrons: an ozone killer? *Sci News* 131:377 Je 13 '87

Spacelab-2 plasma depletion experiments for ionospheric and radio astronomical studies. M. Mendillo and others. bibl f il *Science* 238:1260-4 N 27 '87

Atmosphere-ocean interaction *See* Ocean-atmosphere interaction

Atmospheric aerosols *See* Aerosols

Atmospheric circulation

Windfalls of dust [determining ancient wind patterns from core samples of wind sediments] D. K. Rea. il map *Nat Hist* 96:28+ F '87

Atmospheric electricity

See also

Auroras

Lightning

Thunderstorms

Atmospheric methane *See* Methane

Atmospheric models *See* Meteorological models

Atmospheric nucleation

See also

Condensation (Meteorology)

Atmospheric pollution *See* Air pollution

Atmospheric pressure

See also

Southern Oscillation

Rapid pressure changes near thunderstorms, directional lightning. T. Schlatter. il *Weatherwise* 40:99-100 Ap '87

Physiological effects

See also

Decompression (Physiology)

Atmospheric research

See also

Artificial satellites—Meteorological use

Balloons—Research use

Computers—Meteorological use

International Geosphere-Biosphere Program

Lasers—Meteorological use

Meteorology

Ocean-atmosphere interaction

Atmospheric temperature

See also

Degree days

Greenhouse effect

Summer simmer index

Windchill index

Measuring and predicting the minimum temperature. T. Schlatter. il *Weatherwise* 40:275-7 O '87

Temperature extremes [1986] D. H. Hickcox. il *Weatherwise* 40:38-40 F '87

ATMs *See* Automated teller machines

Atocha (Ship) *See* Nuestra Señora de Atocha (Ship)

Atomic beams

Cooling and trapping atoms. W. D. Phillips and H. J. Metcalf. bibl (p128) il *Sci Am* 256:50-6 Mr '87

Four groups build more efficient atom traps. A. L. Robinson. il *Science* 237:26-8 Jl 3 '87

Laser spectroscopy of trapped atomic ions. W. M. Itano and others. bibl f il *Science* 237:612-17 Ag 7 '87

Atomic bomb shelters

Nuclear war? Head for the basement [research by Robert Ehrlich and James Ring] *Sci News* 131:233 Ap 11 '87

Atomic bombs
Back with a vengeance [B53 H-bomb] J. Horgan. il *Sci Am* 257:26+ O '87
Ethical aspects
See Nuclear warfare—Ethical aspects
History
See also
Hiroshima (Japan)—Bombardment, 1945
Nagasaki (Japan)—Bombardment, 1945
The conscientious spy [K. Fuchs] S. E. Toulmin. bibl f il *N Y Rev Books* 34:54-60 N 19 '87
The making of the Soviet bomb [excerpt from How it began]; tr. by John Crowfoot. V. S. Yemelyanov. *Bull At Sci* 43:39-41 D '87
Was 1945 a break in history? M. S. Sherry. bibl f il *Bull At Sci* 43:12-15 Jl/Ag '87
Physiological effects
See Radiation—Physiological effects
Radioactive pollution
See Radioactive pollution
Testing
See Nuclear weapons—Testing
Atomic bombs in literature *See* Nuclear warfare in literature
Atomic energy *See* Nuclear energy
Atomic Energy Agency *See* International Atomic Energy Agency
Atomic Energy of Canada Ltd.
Nuclear deal-making. M. Drohan. il *Macleans* 100:28+ N 23 '87
Nuclear slowdown. C. Wood. il *Macleans* 100:24 Ag 10 '87
Atomic facilities *See* Nuclear facilities
Atomic insurance *See* Insurance, Nuclear hazards
Atomic medicine *See* Nuclear medicine
Atomic nuclei
Energy levels
See Energy levels (Quantum mechanics)
Spin
See Nuclear spin
Atomic physics *See* Nuclear physics
Atomic power *See* Nuclear energy
Atomic power industry *See* Nuclear industry
Atomic power plants *See* Nuclear power plants
Atomic power workers *See* Nuclear power workers
Atomic powered aircraft carriers *See* Nuclear aircraft carriers
Atomic powered artificial satellites *See* Artificial satellites—Power supply
Atomic powered space vehicles *See* Space vehicles—Power supply
Atomic powered submarines *See* Nuclear submarines
Atomic research *See* Nuclear research
Atomic research laboratories *See* Nuclear research laboratories
Atomic warfare *See* Nuclear warfare
Atomic warfare in literature *See* Nuclear warfare in literature
Atomic weapons *See* Nuclear weapons
Atoms
See also
Electrons
Neutrinos
Protons
Altering atomic structures [use of scanning tunneling microscope] T. H. Cole. il *Pop Mech* 164:10 S '87
Covalent group IV atomic clusters. W. L. Brown and others. bibl f il *Science* 235:860-5 F 20 '87
Playing with atoms, one at a time [use of the scanning tunneling microscope] S. Budiansky. il *U S News World Rep* 102:72 F 16 '87
Beams
See Atomic beams
Atonality
Atonal music and its limits. N. M. Ribe. *Commentary* 84:49-54 N '87
Atotonilco (Mexico)
Churches (Buildings)
Splendid sanctuary [baroque decoration in church built by L. F. N. de Alfaro] J. Richardson. il *House Gard* 159:104-7+ D '87
ATP *See* Adenosine triphosphate
ATPase *See* Adenosine triphosphatase
ATR-42 airplanes *See* Airplanes, Jet
Atrial natriuretic factor
Brain barrier tissues: end organs for atriopeptins. L. Steardo and J. A. Nathanson. bibl f il *Science* 235:470-3 Ja 23 '87
Coexistence of guanylate cyclase and atrial natriuretic factor receptor in a 180-kD protein. A. K. Paul and others. bibl f il *Science* 235:1224-6 Mr 6 '87
Heart peptide goes to the head [research by James A. Nathanson and Luca Steardo] D. D. Edwards. *Sci News* 131:68 Ja 31 '87

Physiological role of silent receptors of atrial natriuretic factor. T. Maack and others. bibl f il *Science* 238:675-8 O 30 '87
Atrium (Heart) *See* Heart
Atriums
The apotheosis of the atrium [architecture of the State of Illinois Center in Chicago] M. F. Schmertz. *Archit Rec* 175:9 My '87
Greenery and a weeping wall in the middle of their house. il *Sunset* 178:168 Ap '87
Heating and ventilation
Tempering a landscape [hvac system of Cascades atrium, Opryland Hotel, Nashville] D. Rastorfer. il *Archit Rec* 175:154-7 My '87
Attaché cases *See* Briefcases
Attached houses *See* Row houses
'Attār, Farid al-Dīn, d. ca. 1230
The mystic way [excerpt from Book of affliction] il *Courier* 40:26 Ap '87
Attenborough, David, 1926-
about
Sir David Attenborough. L. J. Fisher. il por map *Earth Sci* 40:11-12 Fall '87
Attenborough, Richard
Sir Richard Attenborough on Thomas Paine. *Humanist* 47:22 My/Je '87
about
Cry freedom [film] Reviews
America 157:482+ D 19 '87. R. A. Blake
Commonweal 114:655 N 20 '87. T. O'Brien
Ebony il pors 43:60-2+ D '87. C. Tyson
Film Comment il 23:11-12+ N/D '87. A. White
Glamour 85:159-60 D '87. J. G. Boyum
Horizon il 30:37-8 N '87. G. Stern
Macleans il 100:59 N 23 '87. L. O'Toole
Mademoiselle il 93:108 N '87. L. Morice
N Y il 20:54-5 S 21 '87. D. Denby
N Y il 20:113-15 N 16 '87. D. Denby
New Repub 197:42 D 21 '87. M. Peretz
New Repub 197:26 D 7 '87. S. Kauffmann
New Yorker 63:101-4 N 30 '87. P. Kael
Newsweek il 110:79+ N 9 '87. J. Kroll
People Wkly il 28:64+ N 23 '87. W. Plummer
People Wkly il 28:18 N 30 '87. P. Travers
Roll Stone il p31-2 D 3 '87. E. Mitchell
Time il 130:91 N 9 '87. R. Corliss
Vogue il 177:82 N '87. M. Haskell
Richard Attenborough's 'Biko'. L. Shaw. il *World Press Rev* 34:60 Je '87
Attention
See also
Listening
The art (and science) of concentration. J. E. Cohn. il *Seventeen* 46:50 Ap '87
Big success from little signs [alertness when fishing] B. Stearns. il *Field Stream* 92:115-16 My '87
Dynamics of automatic and controlled visual attention. E. Weichselgartner and G. Sperling. bibl f il *Science* 238:778-80 N 6 '87
The early bird makes the grade [students and teachers who are most alert in the morning perform better; study by Julian Biggers] P. Chance. *Psychol Today* 21:22 O '87
Food for thought [drop in concentration after meals; research by Andrew Smith and Christopher Miles] G. Lowe. *Psychol Today* 21:14 F '87
Marijuana use may cause mental problems: study. *Jet* 73:28 S 28 '87
Attention deficit disorder
Out of a darkness. F. Wolkenberg. il *N Y Times Mag* p62+ O 11 '87
Attic ventilators *See* Ventilators
Attics, Remodeled
Cash in on overhead space. A. W. Lees. il *Pop Sci* 230:92-3+ Mr '87
A decision maker's guide to attic remodeling. il *Mother Earth News* 103:80-4+ Ja/F '87
Housetop hideaways: master suites in the attic [cover story] S. Ross. il *Fam Handyman* 37:25-8+ Jl/Ag '87
Attitude heading reference systems (Airplanes) *See* Gyroscopic equipment
Attitudes
See also
Optimism
Political attitudes
Public opinion
Stereotype (Psychology)
Attorney, Power of *See* Power of attorney
Attorney General's Commission on Pornography (U.S.) *See* United States. Attorney General's Commission on Pornography

Attorneys *See* Lawyers
Attracting of birds *See* Birds, Attracting of
Attracting of butterflies *See* Butterflies, Attracting of
Attracting of wildlife *See* Wildlife, Attracting of
Attraction, Interpersonal *See* Interpersonal attraction
Attwood, James A.
    about
 Stodgy no more. J. A. Conway. il por *Forbes* 139:8
  My 4 '87
ATVs *See* All terrain vehicles
Atwan, Robert
 Great moments in literary baseball. il *Atlantic* 259:34
  My '87
Atwater, Brian F.
 Evidence for great Holocene earthquakes along the outer
  coast of Washington State. bibl f il maps *Science*
  236:942-4 My 22 '87
Atwater, Harvey Leroy *See* Atwater, Lee, 1951-
Atwater, James D.
 Echoes and voices summoned from a half-hour in hell.
  bibl (p271) il map *Smithsonian* 18:196-200+ N '87
Atwater, Lee, 1951-
    about
 Republican dirty tricks. F. Barnes. *New Repub* 197:18+
  Jl 27 '87
Atwill, Lionel
 Antiques: ship models. il *Archit Dig* 44:178-9 Mr '87
 North star: a shining presence in woodland Vermont.
  il *Archit Dig* 44:154-7 Mr '87
Atwood, Margaret, 1939-
 Great unexpectations. il *Ms* 16:78-9+ Jl/Ag '87
 Happy endings [story] il *Ms* 15:58+ F '87
 Margaret Atwood [address] il *Humanist* 47:5-7+ S/O
  '87
 Margaret Drabble: the magic of the ordinary. il *Ms*
  16:62+ N '87
 Two Margarets on Maggie [interview with M. Drabble]
  por *Ms* 16:65-6 N '87
    about
 Margaret Atwood. L. Van Gelder. il por *Ms* 15:48-50+
  Ja '87
 Margaret Atwood's testaments: resisting the Gilead within.
  J. K. Larson. *Christ Century* 104:496-8 My 20-27
  '87
Atwood Richards, Inc.
 To Moreton Binn, Sultan of Swap, cash is nice, but
  barter is better. A. Abrahams. il pors *People Wkly*
  28:105-6 N 30 '87
Atys [opera] *See* Lully, Jean Baptiste, 1632-1687
Au pair employees *See* Household employees
Aubrey G. Lanston & Company
 Bearish on stocks, bullish on bonds [interview with R.
  Kelly] B. Weberman. *Forbes* 140:54+ N 16 '87
Aubry, Eugene
    about
 Architect Eugene Aubry: Wortham Theater Center's
  master builder. G. Schmidgall. il por *Opera News*
  52:16 O '87
Aubut, Marcel
    about
 A tenacious will for winning. il por *Macleans* 100:30-1
  D 28 '87
Auchincloss, Mrs. Douglas
    about
 Maine light: the summer house of Mr. and Mrs. Douglas
  Auchincloss. S. M. Alsop. il *Archit Dig* 44:188-95
  Je '87
Auchincloss, Louis
 Recognizing Gaddis. il por *N Y Times Mag* p36+ N
  15 '87
 Reflections on Wall Street. il por *Archit Dig* 44:254+
  N '87
Auclair, Deni
    about
 One of the boys. D. J. Higdon. il por *N Y* 20:42 N
  16 '87
AuClaire, Philip, and Schwartz, Ira M.
 Are home based services effective? A public child welfare
  agency's experiment. il *Child Today* 16:6-9 My/Je '87
Auctions
  See also
  Art trade
 The $5.7 million secret [auctioning of thoroughbred Lady's
  Secret] W. F. Reed. il *Sports Illus* 67:82 N 23 '87
 Auctioning an empire [PTL Network] M. Green. il pors
  People Wkly 27:40-3 Je 8 '87
 Auto auctions [government auctions] P. L. Spencer. il
  Consum Res Mag 70:2 Jl '87
 Bake sale [auction of the equipment from out-of-business
  Lichtman's bakery in Manhattan] *New Yorker* 63:23-4
  Jl 20 '87

Bargain condos: going once, going twice . . . A. Fins.
 il *Bus Week* p163 Je 22 '87
Betting too big on the blood [catalog entry for thorough-
 bred horse at Keeneland Selected Yearling Sale] C.
 Flake. *Harpers* 274:58-9 My '87
Carting your upscale items to the auction block. L.
 Zinn. il *Bus Week* p162 N 30 '87
Filling Uncle Sam's auction house [government auctions
 of confiscated property] R. N. Ostling. il *Time* 130:73
 D 14 '87
Getting a car bargain at auction. il *Money* 16:13 Jl
 '87
How to solve the trade problem [auctionable quota plan]
 R. Thomas. il *Newsweek* 109:40 Ja 12 '87
Josephine Baker's adopted children sell her last valuables
 at public auction. il pors *Jet* 72:26-8 Je 15 '87
Men for sale [bachelor auctions for charity] L. Darling.
 Mademoiselle 93:138 O '87
Monster trash [auction of duplicates from F. J. Acker-
 man's collection] B. Arbinger. il *Omni* 10:28+ D '87
Of Vincent and Eanum Pig [auctions of van Gogh's
 Sunflowers and the Duchess of Windsor's jewelry]
 R. Hughes. il *Time* 129:80-1 Ap 13 '87
Post time? [investing in thoroughbred horses] K. Hannon.
 il *Forbes* 140:74+ O 5 '87
Queen of diamonds [E. Taylor's purchase at auction
 of the Duchess of Windsor's gems] B. Darrach. il
 pors *People Wkly* 27:28-33 Ap 27 '87
The quickest way to sell real estate. I. Ross. il *Fortune*
 116:85+ O 12 '87
Selling your heirloom gems. J. H. Dobrzynski. il *Bus
 Week* p141 My 4 '87
"Sold! to the young man in shorts" [bicycle bought
 at Kansas City, Mo. police auction] P. Harvey. il
 Read Dig 131:265-6 N '87
This car for sale [Southern California Auto Auction]
 R. Titus. il *Mot Trend* 39:94-8 Ag '87
U.S. import rights: going once, going twice . . . [auctioning
 quotas] A. S. Blinder. il *Bus Week* p27 Mr 9 '87
What am I bid for this fine quota? [proposal to auction
 off import rights] S. Koepp. il *Time* 129:59 Mr 16
 '87
Audi (Automobile) *See* Automobiles, Foreign
Audi AG
 Audi agonistes [unintended acceleration in the 5000s]
  C. Csere. il *Car Driv* 32:51-7 Je '87
 Audi takes the gloves off [cases of unintended acceleration
  in the 5000s] T. Orme. il *Mot Trend* 39:34 My '87
 In for repairs [unintended acceleration in the Audi 5000
  and Audi's new ad campaign] B. Kanner. il *N Y*
  20:32+ O 19 '87
Audiences
  See also
  Applause
  Motion picture audiences
  Television audiences
 Applause for the audience. M. Rhodes. il *Horizon* 30:9
  S '87
Audio amplifiers *See* Amplifiers
Audio disc players *See* Compact disc players
Audio discs *See* Compact discs
Audio distortion *See* Audio systems—Noise
Audio engineering
  See also
  Sound—Recording and reproducing
  Sound laboratories
  Theater—Electronic sound control
 Is American audio technology dead? J. D. Hirsch. il
  Stereo Rev 52:24+ Je '87
 The rational audiophile. M. Riggs. il *High Fidel* 37:5
  N '87
Audio Engineering Society
 AES report [annual convention] S. Pollock. *Theatre Crafts*
  21:31-4 Mr '87
Audio equipment industry
  See also
  Ampex Corporation
  Apogee Acoustics (Firm)
  Audio Services Company
  Bose Corp.
  Carver Corp.
  Chace Productions, Inc.
  Dolby Laboratories Inc.
  Koss Corp.
  Marantz Co., Inc.
  Polk Audio, Inc.
 American audio [cover story] S. Birchall. il *Stereo Rev*
  52:66-75 Je '87
 Is American audio technology dead? J. D. Hirsch. il
  Stereo Rev 52:24+ Je '87

Audio equipment industry—*cont.*
Directories
American audio companies. W. Burton. il *Stereo Rev* 52:76-8 Je '87
Car stereo manufacturers. il *Stereo Rev* 52:65-6 My '87
Directory of manufacturers. *Stereo Rev* 52:167 F '87
Export-import trade
Sight and sound: buyer beware! [gray market equipment] H. Fantel. *Opera News* 51:44 Je '87
Canada
Canadian audio companies. il *Stereo Rev* 52:78 Je '87
Japan
See also
　Aiwa Co. Ltd.
FX vs. high-tech. M. Riggs. il *High Fidel* 37:2 Jl '87
Japanese audio [cover story] B. Harrell. il *Stereo Rev* 52:48-57 Jl '87
United States
See Audio equipment industry
Western Europe
European audio [cover story] I. Masters. il *Stereo Rev* 52:56-62 Ag '87

Audio equipment stores
Strategies for equipment shopping. C. Curtis. il *Stereo Rev* 52:68-71 My '87
Ethical aspects
"I can make you an awesome deal": real-life devious speaker selling practices. K. L. Kantor. il *High Fidel* 37:42-4+ Je '87

Audio Renaissance Tapes (Firm)
Walden, WPS just say 'no' to condoms [refusal to carry cassette packaged with condoms] il *Publ Wkly* 232:48 O 30 '87

Audio Services Company
An audible impact [black woman president M. Topham] S. Moore. il por *Essence* 18:118 O '87

Audio systems
See also
　Amplifiers
　Automobiles—Audio systems
　Automobiles, Foreign—Audio systems
　Karaokes
　Loudspeakers
　Phonograph
　Radio receivers
　Tape recorders and recording
1987 equipment buying guide [special section] W. Burton and others. il *Stereo Rev* 52:71-2+ F '87
American audio [cover story] S. Birchall. il *Stereo Rev* 52:66-75 Je '87
Audio. F. Vizard. See issues of Popular Mechanics beginning October 1986
Audio Q&A. I. Masters. See issues of Stereo Review beginning October 1986
Audio update. L. Klein. See issues of Radio-Electronics beginning January 1987
Good listening. C. Begole. See occasional issues of Glamour
The new separates. M. Smolen. il *Stereo Rev* 52:86-92 N '87
Sound advice [choosing a stereo system] D. Moreau. il *Changing Times* 41:80-2+ O '87
Stereo '88 [special section] il *Pop Mech* 164:93-8+ D '87
Strategies for equipment shopping. C. Curtis. il *Stereo Rev* 52:68-71 My '87
Technology special [special section] il *Roll Stone* p69-70+ Je 18 '87
Upgrading to hear the sonic boom. L. Wiener. il *U S News World Rep* 103:96+ N 9 '87
Caricatures and cartoons
The winner of the Rodrigues Caption Contest. W. Livingstone. il *Stereo Rev* 52:14 Jl '87
Compatibility
System compatibility. J. D. Hirsch. il *Stereo Rev* 52:22+ F '87
Design
The high end. R. Hodges. See issues of Stereo Review beginning June 1984
Equipment
See also
　Headphones
ADC Sound Shaper SS-525X equalizer/analyzer. il *High Fidel* 37:27-8+ S '87
Electronic musical chairs [Yamaha digital sound field processor and graphic equalizers] F. Vizard. il *Pop Mech* 164:44+ S '87
EQ'ing [equalizers] R. Hodges. il *Stereo Rev* 52:104 Ag '87
The great equalizers. C. J. Esse. il *High Fidel* 37:14+ N '87

Hi-fi holiday gifts [with editorial comment by Louise Boundas] il *Stereo Rev* 52:8, 79-83 D '87
The joys of equalization. L. Klein. il *Radio-Electron* 58:85-7 F '87
The joys of equalization. L. Klein. il *High Fidel* 37:62-5+ N '87
New products: latest audio equipment and accessories. See issues of Stereo Review
The resurgence of surround sound [DSP-1 Digital Sound Field Processor] L. Klein. il *Radio-Electron* 58:74-5+ My '87
Exhibitions
1987 Japan Audio Fair. B. Harrell. il *Stereo Rev* 52:89-92+ D '87
Berlin International Audio and Video Fair. M. Smolen. il *Stereo Rev* 52:99-103 D '87
CES show stoppers. W. Burton. il *Stereo Rev* 52:66-70 Ap '87
CES show stoppers. W. Burton. il *Stereo Rev* 52:12-16 S '87
Japan Audio Fair. C. J. Esse. il *High Fidel* 37:18-19 Ja '87
Japan Audio Fair. B. Harrell. il *Stereo Rev* 52:96-100+ Ja '87
Pieces of '88 [Summer Consumer Electronics Show] R. Long and E. B. Meyer. il *High Fidel* 37:40-1+ S '87
Products at an exhibition [Winter Consumer Electronics Show; cover story] R. Long and E. B. Meyer. il *High Fidel* 37:44-55 Ap '87
Sight and sound: DAT's what it's all about [Consumer Electronics Show] H. Fantel. il *Opera News* 52:48+ N '87
Installation
Heard but not seen. F. Vizard. il *Pop Mech* 164:34 Mr '87
In the listening room of Ahmet Ertegun. il por *Esquire* 108:156-7 S '87
Systems. W. Burton. il *Stereo Rev* 52:118-21 N '87
Wired. I. Masters. il *Stereo Rev* 52:100-4 N '87
Noise
Detecting distortion. J. D. Hirsch. il *Stereo Rev* 52:18+ Jl '87
Dolby. R. Hodges. il *Stereo Rev* 52:168 Ja '87
Prices
Going for broke [most expensive components] *U S News World Rep* 103:102 N 9 '87
Luxuries and bargains. L. G. Boundas. il *Stereo Rev* 52:8 S '87
The rational audiophile. M. Riggs. il *High Fidel* 37:5 N '87
Sound to satisfy the superrich. D. H. Dunn. il *Bus Week* p114 Ap 13 '87
Specifications
What the specs won't tell you. J. D. Hirsch. il *Stereo Rev* 52:27-8 D '87
Terminology
Wine, words, & song [wine and audiophile jargon] R. Warren. il *High Fidel* 37:53-5 Mr '87
Testing
Equipment test reports. J. D. Hirsch and C. Stark. See issues of Stereo Review
Hitachi MXW-50 slimline system. J. D. Hirsch. il *Stereo Rev* 52:31+ D '87
Midpriced audio dynamite. H. Fantel. il *Roll Stone* p107-8 My 21 '87
Product of the Year Award. D. Ranada. il *High Fidel* 37:50-4 D '87
Rack stereo systems. il *Consum Rep* 52:692-7 N '87
Stereo components. il *Consum Rep* 52:698-9 N '87
Technical talk. J. D. Hirsch. See issues of Stereo Review
Test reports. See issues of High Fidelity (New York, N.Y.)
Who tests? R. Hodges. il *Stereo Rev* 52:136 Je '87
Why test? R. Hodges. il *Stereo Rev* 52:124 Mr '87
Volume control
Sound isolation. R. Hodges. il *Stereo Rev* 52:116 Jl '87

Audio/Video Affiliates, Inc.
From street kid to superstar? [bid for Cyclops by S. Rose] D. Cook. il por *Bus Week* p33 F 16 '87
Audio-video receivers
Innocence lost. C. J. Esse. il *High Fidel* 37:12+ Jl '87
Testing
NEC AVR-1000 receiver. J. D. Hirsch. il *Stereo Rev* 52:59-60+ Je '87
NEC AVR-700 AM/FM audio-video receiver. il *High Fidel* 37:32-5 S '87
Onkyo TX-84M AM/FM audio-video receiver. il *High Fidel* 37:27+ D '87

Audio-visual equipment
See also
Business presentations—Aids and devices
Compact disc interactive
Compact disc players
Compact discs
Television equipment
Videodiscs
Videotape recorders and recording
Videotapes
Currents. See issues of High Fidelity (New York, N.Y.)
Control
Magic wand [RC-AV1 Unifier] S. A. Booth. il *Pop Mech* 164:46 Jl '87
Multivision 1.1 Digital Video Controller. il *High Fidel* 37:46-7 N '87
The new unified remote controls. J. Cohen. il *Consum Res Mag* 70:29-30 D '87
Remote possibilities [all-in-one wireless remote controls] J. B. Meigs. il *Roll Stone* p155 Ap 23 '87
Shure AVC 20 Power Station. J. D. Hirsch. il *Stereo Rev* 52:33-4+ My '87
Testing
Product of the Year Award. D. Ranada. il *High Fidel* 37:50-4 D '87
Audio-visual instruction
See also
Educational technology
Motion pictures in education
Tape recordings—Educational use
Television in education
Videotapes—Educational use
Electronic media—can they really support the arts? J. A. C. Baird. *Des Arts Educ* 88:37-40 Jl/Ag '87
Audiocassette books See Talking books
Audiocassette recordings See Tape recordings
Audiocassette tape See Tape, Magnetic
Auditing
Internal control
Cracks in the foundation. K. Murray. il *Forbes* 140:65 N 16 '87
Auditing, Environmental See Environmental auditing
Auditing, Tax See Tax auditing
Auditor General's Office (Canada) See Canada. Office of the Auditor General
Auditoriums
See also
Concert halls
Auditory pattern recognition See Sound pattern recognition
Auditory system See Hearing
Audubon, John James, 1785-1851
about
Twins Scott and Stuart Gentling sell off a high-priced Audubon and give wing to their own bird book. M. Vespa. il pors *People Wkly* 27:117-18 Je 15 '87
Audubon (Periodical)
Audubon essay winners. A. Hogge and G. Musick. il *Audubon* 89:104-5 S '87
Illuminating manuscripts [photographs used in July 1987 issue] L. Line. il *Audubon* 89:4 Jl '87
Milestones. L. Line. il *Audubon* 89:6-7 Mr '87
Audubon bird sanctuaries See Bird sanctuaries
Audubon Park and Zoological Garden (New Orleans, La.)
Audubon Zoo has special place for kids. il *South Living* 22:28 Ap '87
Audubon societies
Showing the colors: classy patches from National Audubon Society chapters [portfolio] il *Audubon* 89:68-73 Mr '87
Audubon Society See National Audubon Society
Auel, Jean M.
"Commercial" vs. "literary"—the artificial debate. il *Writer* 100:9-12+ O '87
about
Life with Ayla and her friends: Jean Auel and the new phenomenon of Ice Age fiction. B. M. Fagan. *Sci Am* 256:132-5 Je '87
Auerbach, Jerold S.
Liberalism & the Hebrew prophets. *Commentary* 84:58-60 Ag '87
Auerbach, Jonathan D.
Israel's miracle food from the desert. il *Saturday Evening Post* 259:48-9+ S '87
Aufderheide, Pat
Black magic. il *Progressive* 51:26-7 S '87
A map upside down: third world artists explore their territory. il *Progressive* 51:36-8 Mr '87
Oriental insurgents. *Film Comment* 23:73-6 N/D '87
Augsburger, David
The private lives of public leaders. il por *Christ Today* 31:23-4 N 20 '87

August, Bonnie
about
Taking creative control. P. Kripke. il por *Work Woman* 12:50-1 Ag '87
August
The August almanac. il *Atlantic* 260:12 Ag '87
August House Inc.
August House starts American folklore series this fall. *Publ Wkly* 231:60+ Je 12 '87
Augusta National (Ga.: Golf course) See Golf courses
Augustine, Saint, Bishop of Hippo
about
The good life. R. J. Foster. il por *Christ Today* 31:20-4 D 11 '87
The significance of Augustine. D. W. H. Arnold. il por *Christ Today* 31:22 D 11 '87
Augustine Volcano (Augustine Island, Alaska)
Tsunamis generated by eruptions from Mount St. Augustine volcano, Alaska [cover story] J. Kienle and others. il maps *Science* 236:1442-7 Je 12 '87
Aulenti, Gae
about
Aulenti assoluta. M. Filler. il pors *House Gard* 159:134-41+ Je '87
The Aulenti uproar. C. Vogel. il por *N Y Times Mag* p26-32+ N 22 '87
Missed connections. C. K. Gandee. il por *Archit Rec* 175:128-39 Mr '87
Ault, Bob
Music memorabilia. See issues of Antiques & Collecting Hobbies beginning May 1986
Aunts
My Aunt Rosie. J. Kelman. il por *Good Housekeep* 204:120 Ap '87
Auping, Michael
Songs of innocence. il *Art Am* 75:118-27+ Ja '87
Aurandt, Paul
(ed) See Harvey, Paul, 1918-. More of Paul Harvey's Rest of the story
Aurangzeb, Emperor of Hindustan, 1618-1707
about
The East India Company and the Emperor Aurangzeb. B. Lenman. bibl il map *Hist Today* 37:23-9 F '87
Auras
Aura watching. D. K. Mano. *Natl Rev* 39:66-7 O 23 '87
Auriculin See Atrial natriuretic factor
Aurora
Horoscopes. See issues of Harper's Bazaar
Aurora (Ill.)
Religious institutions and affairs
Upstairs, downstairs in a house of peace [Resurrection Life, home for unwed mothers] R. Clapp. il *Christ Today* 31:16-17 Ja 16 '87
Aurora (New York, N.Y.: Restaurant) See New York (N.Y.)—Restaurants, nightclubs, bars, etc.
Auroras
Above and beyond and auroras. il *Nat Hist* 96:6+ S '87
The awesome aurora [cover story] A. J. Sadar. il *Weatherwise* 40:76-7 Ap '87
Curtains of light, horsemen of night. W. Sullivan. il map *Audubon* 89:40-51 Ja '87
A new light on auroras [long-duration auroras caused by Alfven waves; research by Bruce T. Tsurutani and Walter D. Gonzalez] il *Sky Telesc* 74:344-5 O '87
A new source of power to drive the aurora [Alfvén waves; research by Bruce Tsurutani and Walter Gonzalez] R. A. Kerr. il *Science* 237:974 Ag 28 '87
Those mysterious lights in the sky. il map *Natl Geogr World* 148:18-23 D '87
Auschwitz (Poland: Concentration camp) See Concentration camps—Poland
Ause, John
about
A creative approach to learning. C. Orange. por *Progressive* 51:12 N '87
AUSSAT Pty. Ltd.
Aussat considering proposals for next-generation satellite. *Aviat Week Space Technol* 127:22 D 21 '87
Aussat orbital delivery plan confirms satellite user trend. M. A. Dornheim. il *Aviat Week Space Technol* 127:59+ S 7 '87
Aussat tender requires orbital delivery. *Aviat Week Space Technol* 127:19 S 21 '87
Australia will use satellite purchase to foster domestic space industry. T. M. Foley. *Aviat Week Space Technol* 126:78-9 Ap 6 '87

Austen, Alice
about
The high summer of Alice Austen. O. Jensen. il pors *House Gard* 159:94-9+ Ag '87
Austen, Francis
about
Jane's fighting ships. P. Honan. bibl il pors *Hist Today* 37:40-6 Ag '87
Austen, Jane, 1775-1817
about
Jane's fighting ships. P. Honan. bibl il pors *Hist Today* 37:40-6 Ag '87
Austen (Alice) House (Staten Island, N.Y.) *See* Staten Island (New York, N.Y.)—Historic houses, sites, etc.
Auster, Paul, 1947-
Moonlight in the Brooklyn Museum. il *Art News* 86:104-5 S '87
Austin, Arthur Everett, 1900-1957
about
The Austin phenomenon. R. Lynes. il pors *Archit Dig* 44:51+ O '87
Austin, Denise
One-minute exercises [excerpts from Denise Austin's 1-minute exercises] il pors *Good Housekeep* 204:82+ F '87
One-minute exercises for busy bodies. il *Redbook* 169:97-100 O '87
Austin, Doris Jean
about
Word star. B. Guy-Sheftall. por *Essence* 18:28 O '87
Austin, Jesse
about
Collecting pot lids: Staffordshire Pratt ware painted by Jesse Austin. M. Ginaven. il *Antiques Collect Hobbies* 92:22-4 D '87
Austin, Penelope
Going back [poem] *New Repub* 197:52 S 14-21 '87
Modernism [poem] *New Repub* 196:38 Je 29 '87
Austin, Teri
about
Live wire Teri Austin turns a Knots plot into a real-life romance. K. Hubbard. por *People Wkly* 27:135-6 My 4 '87
Austin (Tex.)
City planning
Tex mess. K. Northcott. il *Progressive* 51:36-9 Ap '87
Economic conditions
Tex mess. K. Northcott. il *Progressive* 51:36-9 Ap '87
Welcome to the capital of Texas. W. P. Barrett. il *Forbes* 140:188+ D 14 '87
Festivals
ChildFest. K. Cummins. il *Child Today* 16:12-13 Ja/F '87
Galleries and museums
Silver lining, Texas-style. K. Gregor. il *Art News* 86:18 O '87
Music
Hot debut for Austin music conference [South By Southwest Regional Music and Media Conference] B. Beuttler. il *Down Beat* 54:12 Je '87
Music festivals
See Music festivals—Texas
Austin Rover Cars of North America
Can this born salesman launch a luxury car? [N. Braman stresses Sterling's price] G. DeGeorge. il por *Bus Week* p107 My 4 '87
Norman Braman—megadealer making megabucks. J. R. Nerad. por *Mot Trend* 39:70-1 F '87
Australia
See also
Alice Springs (Australia)
Astronomical observatories—Australia
Australians
Automobile racing—Australia
Birds—Australia
Blacks—Australia
Canberra (Australia)
Dance festivals—Australia
Education—Australia
Fisheries—Australia
Fremantle (Australia)
Geology—Australia
Great Barrier Reef (Australia)
Hamilton Island (Australia)
Investments, American—Australia
Investments, Australian
Kangaroo Island (Australia)
Money—Australia
Natural history—Australia

Opera—Australia
Paleontology—Australia
Prisons—Australia
Queensland (Australia)
Radioactive pollution—Australia
Railroads—Australia
Securities—Australia
Shark Bay (Australia)
South Australia (Australia)
Space centers—Australia
Taxation—Australia
Treasury bills and notes—Australia
Centennial celebrations, etc.
Australian bicentenary: 1988. A. Lyons. il *America* 157:451-4 D 12 '87
Commerce
United States
See United States—Commerce—Australia
Defenses
See also
Airplanes, Military—Australia
New Australian defense strategy prompts early warning, aerial buildup. *Aviat Week Space Technol* 126:139+ Ap 27 '87
Description and travel
See also
Automobile touring—Australia
Cycling—Australia
From Melbourne meat pies . . . to Brisbane mud crabs. F. Ferretti. il *Gourmet* 47:42+ S '87
Thumbs up for Down Under. P. Plawin. il *Changing Times* 41:138-42+ Ja '87
Foreign relations
Great Britain
See Great Britain—Foreign relations—Australia
Libya
Washing Libya out of their hair. H. G. Chua-Eoan. il por *Time* 129:45 Je 1 '87
Pacific region
Australia's new role. *World Press Rev* 34:36 Mr '87
United States
See United States—Foreign relations—Australia
Industries
See also
Airlines—Australia
Ansett Airlines of Australia
Ansett Transport Industries, Ltd.
Ariadne Australia Ltd.
Bell Group Ltd.
Bond Group
Brewing industry—Australia
Corporations—Acquisitions and mergers—Australia
Elders IXL Limited
Gold mines and mining—Australia
Mass media industry—Acquisitions and mergers—Australia
Orbital Engine Company
Underwater Systems Australia Ltd.
Westfield Group
Wine industry—Australia
Worsley Alumina Trust
Native peoples
See also
Australian aborigines
Politics and government
See also
Elections—Australia
Religious institutions and affairs
See also
Church and race relations—Australia
Social conditions
Australia's cup. *New Repub* 196:4 F 9 '87
The laid-back and lucky land. T. Clifton. il *Newsweek* 109:38-9 F 2 '87
Australia. Royal Australian Air Force
Australia drafts 25-year plan to upgrade Air Force fleet. P. Proctor. il *Aviat Week Space Technol* 127:121-2 S 7 '87
Australia in art
The vivid imagery of Australia's artists. P. Fuller. il *Archit Dig* 44:204+ S '87
Australia in literature
Robert Hughes: the art of bushwhacking the bourgeoisie [interview] M. Blonsky. por *Vogue* 177:212-13+ Ja '87
Australia-United States air agreements *See* Aviation—International aspects
Australian aborigines
Interview [E. Willmot] K. Keeton. il por *Omni* 9:80-2+ Je '87

Australian aborigines—*cont.*
A sidelong look at The Alice. R. Symanski. il map *Focus* 37:22-7 Summ '87

Civil rights
Rough justice in Australia? [jail deaths of aborigines] S. Seibert. il *Newsweek* 110:34 Ag 31 '87
Two hundred years later . . . [government-proposed treaty] H. G. Chua-Eoan. il *Time* 130:48 S 21 '87

Land tenure
Australian bicentenary: 1988. A. Lyons. il *America* 157:451-4 D 12 '87

Religion and mythology
Daydream believers. S. Cuyler. il *Omni* 9:16+ Je '87
The Lizard Man. B. Chatwin. il *N Y Rev Books* 34:47-8 Ag 13 '87

Australian and New Zealand Army Corps (Great Britain)
See Great Britain. Army. Australian and New Zealand Army Corps

Australian Ballet
Australian troupe bids "G'day" to Tetley and the Far East. P. Laughlin. il *Dance Mag* 61:37+ Je '87

Australian communications satellites *See* Communications satellites, Australian

Australian cooking *See* Cooking, Australian

Australian Grand Prix *See* Automobile racing—Australia

Australian painting *See* Painting, Australian

Australians

United States
Walkabout [Australian visitor T. Dunlap attends a boomerang competition] *New Yorker* 63:23-4 Jl 27 '87

Australopithecus *See* Man, Prehistoric

Austria
See also
Alps
Americans—Austria
Art and state—Austria
Automobile racing—Austria
Ballet—Austria
Burgenland (Austria)
Catholic Church—Relations (Diplomatic)—Austria
Jews—Austria
Music festivals—Austria
Opera—Austria
Skis and skiing—Austria
United States—Diplomatic and consular service—Austria
Vienna (Austria)

Foreign relations
United States
See United States—Foreign relations—Austria

Politics and government
Waldheim must resign. L.-M. Delloff. *Christ Century* 104:1167-8 D 23-30 '87
Waldheim's end game? [problems of a Nazi past] F. Willey. il por *Newsweek* 110:29 D 28 '87

Austrian cooking *See* Cooking, Austrian

Austrian Grand Prix *See* Automobile racing—Austria

Authoritarianism
See also
Fascism
Totalitarianism

Authority
Patients. M. L. Magie. *Commentary* 83:48-52 F '87

Authority (Religion)
See also
Bible—Evidence, authority, etc.
Catholic Church—Authority

Authors
See also
Aged as authors
Air pilots as authors
Alcohol and authors
Athletes as authors
Authorship
Black authors
Copyright
Executives as authors
Lawyers as authors
Literary agencies and agents
Literature
Nuns as authors
Royalties
Women authors
Writers Guild of America
Youth as authors
Pages '87. il *People Wkly* 27:60-1 Ja 5 '87
PW interviews. See issues of Publishers Weekly

Anecdotes, facetiae, satire, etc.
Great moments in literary baseball. R. Atwan. il *Atlantic* 259:34 My '87

Attitudes
30 wise men: eleven literary lights reveal their modern Magi. il *Esquire* 108:291 D '87
Twisting the tale at the end: a symposium [changes to literary endings] il *N Y Times Book Rev* 92:52-3 D 6 '87
Who created whom? Characters that talk back. il *N Y Times Book Rev* 92:36-7 My 31 '87

Conferences
See Authors' conferences

Correspondence, reminiscences, etc.
Putting one letter after another [biographers' use of authors' letters] J. Atlas. il *N Y Times Book Rev* 92:1+ Mr 15 '87

Anecdotes, facetiae, satire, etc.
Wackos and other strangers. J. G. Dunne. il *Esquire* 107:105-6 Ja '87

Homes and haunts
See Historic houses, sites, etc.

Information services
See also
Poets & Writers, Inc.

Political activities
The bankers' hero [M. Vargas Llosa leads opposition to A. García Perez's efforts to nationalize financial institutions] A. Cockburn. *Nation* 245:402 O 17 '87
The defiling of writers [FBI files on American authors; cover story] N. S. Robins. il *Nation* 245:367-70+ O 10 '87
Fighting words: the myth of the 'hereditary enemy'. J. Blot. il *Courier* 40:25-8 Jl '87
Policing America's writers [FBI files on great American writers] H. Mitgang. *New Yorker* 63:47-8+ O 5 '87
Three lives [discussion of October 10, 1987 article, The defiling of writers] N. S. Robins. *Nation* 245:666 D 5 '87
Two writers probe FBI surveillance of American authors [H. Mitgang and N. S. Robins] W. Goldstein. *Publ Wkly* 232:38 O 30 '87

Promotion tours
See Books—Advertising

Psychology
Acceptance. A. Z. Leventhal. *Writer* 100:7-8 Ag '87
Be reasonable—unless you're a writer. W. Kennedy. il *N Y Times Book Rev* 92:3 Ja 25 '87
Hearing voices. J. G. Dunne. il *Esquire* 107:55+ My '87
The hidden censor. D. Lefer. *Writer* 100:7-10 My '87
Inspiring story ideas: a baker's dozen. C. Kyle and L. A. Walker. *Writer* 100:5-6 N '87
Postwritum depression, false stagnancy and other ills caused by writing books. C. Salzberg. il *N Y Times Book Rev* 92:3 Mr 8 '87
Remembering how it was [using childhood memories in writing for children] L. Lowry. il *Writer* 100:16-19 Jl '87
What writers live on. K. Reed. por *Publ Wkly* 232:55 Ag 28 '87
The world's worst critics [self criticism] J. C. Oates. il *N Y Times Book Rev* 92:1+ Ja 18 '87
The writer's compass. W. E. Stafford. *Writer* 100:5-6 S '87

Public relations
See Authors and readers

Reading
Writers reading. J. Parini. il *Horizon* 30:63 O '87

Salaries, pensions, etc.
See also
Authors—Taxation

Taxation
Authors hail tax decision allowing them to deduct expenses currently. *Publ Wkly* 231:31 Je 12 '87
Book 'em. *New Repub* 197:4 S 14-21 '87
IRS and expenses: good news and bad news for publishers, authors. H. Fields; R. G. Stern. *Publ Wkly* 232:12 N 6 '87
Only the rich will write. K. Kelley. por *Newsweek* 110:7 Ag 24 '87
Senators appear sympathetic to change in tax capitalization. H. Fields. *Publ Wkly* 232:18-19 Ag 14 '87
A taxing issue [taxes imposed on money paid to American authors by foreign publishers] R. Curtis. por *Publ Wkly* 231:52 Mr 20 '87

Anecdotes, facetiae, satire, etc.
Writer write-off. *Nation* 245:255-6 S 19 '87

Travel
Anecdotes, facetiae, satire, etc.
Snap books [books by big-name authors about their brief experiences in foreign countries] M. Massing. *New Repub* 196:21+ My 4 '87

Authors, American
  See also
  Beattie, Ann
  Bellamy, Edward, 1850-1898
  Black authors
  Bradley, Marion Zimmer
  Brown, Margaret Wise, 1910-1952
  Brown, Mary Ward
  Campbell, Joseph, 1904-1987
  Canin, Ethan
  Capote, Truman, 1924-1984
  Carver, Raymond
  Dickey, James
  Didion, Joan
  Donald, David Herbert, 1920-
  Dunne, John Gregory, 1932-
  Emerson, Ralph Waldo, 1803-1882
  Foote, Shelby
  Hellman, Lillian, 1906-1984
  Holley, Marietta, 1836-1926
  Hurd, Thacher
  James, Henry, 1843-1916
  Keillor, Garrison
  Kennedy, William, 1928-
  Mailer, Norman
  Mencken, H. L. (Henry Louis), 1880-1956
  Neill, Robert H.
  Nichols, John Treadwell, 1940-
  O'Connor, Flannery
  Ozick, Cynthia
  Poe, Edgar Allan, 1809-1849
  Seuss, Dr.
  Thoreau, Henry David, 1817-1862
  Twain, Mark, 1835-1910
  Vidal, Gore, 1925-
  Wangerin, Walter
  Welty, Eudora, 1909-
  Wolfe, Tom
  Wright, Richard, 1908-1960
The defiling of writers [FBI files on American authors; cover story] N. S. Robins. il *Nation* 245:367-70+ O 10 '87
Esquire's guide to the literary universe [with introd. by Rust Hills] il *Esquire* 108:51-3+ Ag '87
Policing America's writers [FBI files on great American writers] H. Mitgang. *New Yorker* 63:47-8+ O 5 '87
Three lives [discussion of October 10, 1987 article, The defiling of writers] N. S. Robins. *Nation* 245:666 D 5 '87
Tracking New York's literary ghosts [writers' and publishers' burial places] J. Culbertson and T. Randall. il *Publ Wkly* 232:27-9 Jl 17 '87
Treasured places [favorite wilderness areas of 8 American writers; cover story] il *Life* 10:35-42+ Jl '87
Two writers probe FBI surveillance of American authors [H. Mitgang and N. S. Robins] W. Goldstein. *Publ Wkly* 232:38 O 30 '87
Washington: a city of letters . . . [favorite places of writers living in the capital; symposium] il *Publ Wkly* 231:140-2 My 15 '87
What next? B. Levine. il *Publ Wkly* 231:61-3 Ja 9 '87
Writers remember: American authors look back on their favorite cars. P. Egan. il *Road Track* 38:108+ Je '87
Authors, Argentine
  See also
  Borges, Jorge Luis, 1899-1986
Authors, Black See Black authors
Authors, British
The literary impulse. J. Parini. il *Horizon* 30:27-8 N '87
Authors, Canadian
  See also
  Mowat, Farley
Authors, English
  See also
  Ackroyd, Peter
  Austen, Jane, 1775-1817
  Dickens, Charles, 1812-1870
  Doyle, Sir Arthur Conan, 1859-1930
  Johnson, Samuel, 1709-1784
  Kingsley, Mary Henrietta, 1862-1900
  Lawrence, D. H. (David Herbert), 1885-1930
  Potter, Beatrix, 1866-1943
  Raban, Jonathan
  Wilson, A. N., 1950-
Authors, French
  See also
  Mérimée, Prosper, 1803-1870
  Sartre, Jean Paul, 1905-1980

Authors, German
  See also
  Benjamin, Walter, 1892-1940
Authors, Irish
  See also
  Beckett, Samuel, 1906-
  Joyce, James, 1882-1941
  Wilde, Oscar, 1854-1900
Authors, Israeli
What's new in Jerusalem. H. R. Lottman. il *Publ Wkly* 231:26-35 F 20 '87
Authors, Italian
  See also
  Levi, Primo, 1919-1987
Authors, Jewish
  See also
  Authors, Israeli
  Sevela, Efraim
  Wiesel, Elie, 1928-
Authors, Nicaraguan
  See also
  Ramírez Mercado, Sergio, 1942-
Authors, Nigerian
  See also
  Soyinka, Wole
Authors, Russian
  See also
  Andreyev, Leonid, 1871-1919
  Brodsky, Joseph, 1940-
  Sevela, Efraim
  Solzhenitsyn, Aleksandr, 1918-
Beatniks and Bolsheviks; tr. by Bess Powell. V. P. Aksenov. *New Repub* 197:28-30+ N 30 '87
Authors, Women See Women authors
Authors, Yugoslav
  See also
  Karadžić, Vuk Stefanović, 1787-1864
Authors and editors
As they said in the Writer in 1887 . . . [reprint of April 1887 article] C. M. Hammond. *Writer* 100:1 S '87
Beating the rejection blues. J. Harayda. *Writer* 100:21-3 S '87
Editor to writer. J. Kahn. *Writer* 100:12-13+ Ap '87
Erasing the blue-pencil blues. D. Petersen. *Writer* 100:14-16 F '87
Lunches with writers can be a succession of doors opening on new worlds; the best are as stimulating as a week's vacation. J. P. Wiley, Jr. *Smithsonian* 18:32+ Je '87
Multiple queries and submissions: what editors think: the pros and the cons. *Writer* 100:22-4 F '87
Special to the Writer. See issues of The Writer beginning February 1987
Writing for Celestial Arts. P. Reed and D. Hinds. *Writer* 100:26-7 Ja '87
  Anecdotes, facetiae, satire, etc.
Bret, like, brainstorms [excerpt from Vanna Karenina] F. Gannon. *Harpers* 275:35-6 D '87
Getting assignments. M. E. Marty. *Christ Century* 104:175 F 18 '87
Authors and publishers
  See also
  Copyright
  Literary agencies and agents
  Royalties
Acceptance. A. Z. Leventhal. *Writer* 100:7-8 Ag '87
Contracts: panel attempts new look at old conflicts. C. Reid. *Publ Wkly* 232:14 N 20 '87
A double perspective: publishers & authors. L. Felder. il *Publ Wkly* 232:23-4 Ag 28 '87
Double your sales power. S. S. Baker. *Writer* 100:11-13+ N '87
Facts on File offers database that contains author contracts. *Publ Wkly* 232:12 S 11 '87
Fayard and Holt settle dispute over world rights to Walesa autobio. W. Goldstein. il pors *Publ Wkly* 232:23-4 Jl 31 '87
Give them what they want [magazine article submissions] R. A. Caras. *Writer* 100:7-8 Je '87
The growing market for juvenile books. *Writer* 100:28-30 O '87
HM spends $600G for book on West Pt. Class of '66 [R. Atkinson's The long gray line] *Publ Wkly* 231:37 My 8 '87
How to make writing pay [reprint of October 1887 article] C. M. Hammond. *Writer* 100:18 O '87
An inviting market for free lancers . . . Sunday magazines [directory] *Writer* 100:25-9 Ap '87
Is it art yet? [story behind K. Gibbons' Ellen Foster] L. Fleischer. *Publ Wkly* 231:34 My 8 '87

Authors and publishers—*cont.*

Juvenile articles that sell. M. Johnston. *Writer* 100:28-9 S '87

Lawyer's first novel goes to Warner for $750,000 floor [G. Bernau's Promises to keep] W. Goldstein. *Publ Wkly* 232:78 Ag 14 '87

Making a name in poetry, or, How did Emily Dickinson do it? X. J. Kennedy. *Writer* 100:18-21+ N '87

Market newsletter. See issues of The Writer

Morrow pays $155,000 for first novel by 23-year-old author [M. Chabon's The mysteries of Pittsburgh] W. Goldstein. por *Publ Wkly* 231:73-4 Ap 10 '87

Multiple queries and submissions: what editors think: the pros and the cons. *Writer* 100:22-4 F '87

A new lease on life for old books [permitting authors and heirs to terminate contracts before the end of their book's copyright term] C. E. Rinzler. il *Publ Wkly* 232:27-9 Jl 10 '87

Offbeat auction [L. Erdich's dissatisfaction with Bantam leads to acquisition of rights to Tracks by Harper & Row] P. S. Nathan. *Publ Wkly* 232:40 N 13 '87

Rag time [small press literary magazines] J. Queenan. *New Repub* 196:13-14 Ap 6 '87

Sen. Cochran again introduces writers' work-for-hire bill. H. Fields. *Publ Wkly* 231:16 Je 19 '87

Special to the Writer. *Writer* 100:24-5 Jl '87

This month's special market lists. See issues of The Writer

Tips for DTP users [desktop publishing] J. Woodman. *Publ Wkly* 232:28 N 13 '87

Waiting for the book: storms before the calm. P. Lopate. il *N Y Times Book Rev* 92:1+ My 24 '87

Where to sell manuscripts. See issues of The Writer

Who is Roseanne Barr, and why is she worth a quarter of a mil? [bidding for comedienne's forthcoming book] L. Fleischer. *Publ Wkly* 232:38 O 23 '87

Authors and readers

Literacy wars: a modest proposal [program to get writers involved in literacy problems] P. Balla. por *Publ Wkly* 231:376 Ja 30 '87

The reader as partner. T. Hillerman. *Writer* 100:14-16 O '87

Readers & writers: reflecting the demands upon women. A. McCarthy. *Commonweal* 114:6-7 Ja 16 '87

Where art and commerce coexist [public readings] J. Eidus. por *Publ Wkly* 232:43 D 18 '87

Anecdotes, facetiae, satire, etc.

'Ever et raw meat?' and other weird questions. S. King. il *N Y Times Book Rev* 92:7 D 6 '87

Your book saved my life, Mister. G. Keillor. *New Yorker* 63:40-1 D 28 '87

Authors as photographers

Eudora Welty's eye for the story [cover story] P. H. Samway. il *America* 156:417-20 My 23 '87

Authors' clubs and societies

See also

International Association of Crime Writers

PEN

Society of Children's Book Writers

Authors' conferences

See also

Bread Loaf Writers' Conference of Middlebury College

Benefits of a writers' conference [with list of 1987 conferences] M. G. Wirth. il *Writer* 100:23-33 My '87

A map upside down: third world artists explore their territory [conference at Duke University's Center for International Studies] P. Aufderheide. il *Progressive* 51:36-8 Mr '87

Wheatland Conference: American writers carp at the state of U.S. literature. H. Fields. *Publ Wkly* 231:10 My 8 '87

Writers conferences. *Writer* 100:27 Jl '87

Writers conferences. *Writer* 100:33-4 Ap '87

Writers conferences. *Writer* 100:33 S '87

Writers conferences. *Writer* 100:32-3 Ag '87

Soviet Union

Crime: a new East-West dialogue [meeting in Yalta of the International Association of Crime Writers] L. See. il *Publ Wkly* 232:25 O 16 '87

My week with Oleg 1: writers, detectives and the caviar Mafia [executive committee meeting of the International Association of Crime Writers] R. L. Simon. il *N Y Times Book Rev* 92:11 S 13 '87

Authors' contracts *See* Authors and publishers

Authors' diaries *See* Diaries

Authors' markets *See* Authors and publishers

Authors' rights

See also

Copyright

Royalties

Authorship

See also

Astronomical literature—Authorship

Authors

Autobiography

Baseball literature—Authorship

Biography

Business writing

Children's literature—Authorship

Christian literature—Authorship

Computers—Authors' use

Cookbooks—Authorship

Creative writing

Dedications (in books)

Detective and mystery stories—Authorship

Drama—Technique

Educational literature—Authorship

Fiction—Authorship

Fiction—Technique

Food literature—Authorship

Garden literature—Authorship

Historical fiction—Authorship

Horror tales—Authorship

Humor—Authorship

Journalism

Literary research

Literature—Technique

Medical literature—Authorship

Motion picture authorship

New Age literature—Authorship

Outlines (Authorship)

Periodical articles

Plagiarism

Plots (Drama, novel, etc.)

Poetry—Authorship

Science fiction—Authorship

Scientific literature—Authorship

Shakespeare, William, 1564-1616—Authorship

Short story

Spy stories—Authorship

Television authorship

Textbooks—Authorship

Travel literature—Authorship

Western stories—Authorship

Word processors and processing—Authors' use

Young adults' literature—Authorship

Youth as authors

As they said in the Writer in 1887 . . . [reprint of June 1887 article] H. Holt. *Writer* 100:1 Je '87

Making the most of time. S. A. Keller. *Writer* 100:22-3 Jl '87

Off the cuff. See issues of The Writer

On writing. J. G. Dunne. See issues of Esquire beginning October 1986 through May 1987

To be a writer: what does it take? J. Jakes. *Writer* 100:9-11 Ja '87

Bibliography

The writer's library. See occasional issues of The Writer

Collaboration

A case of bigamy [partnership of author and J. Falsey] J. Brand. il *N Y Times Mag* p100 My 17 '87

Pros and cons of a writing partnership. K. A. Goldner and C. G. Vogel. *Writer* 100:24-5 S '87

Competitions

See Literature—Competitions

Copy preparation

Revision and life: take it from the top—again. N. Ephron. *Writer* 100:7-8 Ap '87

Psychological aspects

See Authors—Psychology

Autism

A child's prison [excerpt from The children at Santa Clara] E. Marek. *Harpers* 274:32-4 Mr '87

Fighting for Tony [excerpt] M. Callahan. il por *Ladies Home J* 104:66+ O '87

The "perfect" student: being alert to autism. M. A. Coppola. *Educ Dig* 52:33-5 My '87

Therapy

Are autistic children high on themselves? [Barbara Herman's work with opioid-blocking drug naltrexone] *Discover* 8:6-7 F '87

Autism: a chemical excess? [naltrexone used to treat children with abnormal opioid levels; research by Barbara Herman] S. Vandershaf. *Psychol Today* 21:15-16 Mr '87

Chad's dad [D. Brandon uses toys to treat son's autism]; ed. by John Grossmann. D. Brandon. il *Health* 19:79-80 Ap '87

Autism—Therapy—*cont.*

Child of silence: retrieved from the shadow-world of autism, Katy finds her voice [K. Haigh responds to holding therapy] J. Mason. il pors *Life* 10:84-9 S '87

A drug that lets the real world in [naltrexone; work of Barbara Herman and Kathryn Hammock] K. McAuliffe. il *U S News World Rep* 102:66 F 2 '87

Healthy addiction [use of opioid receptor blocking agent naltrexone] J. R. Goldberg. il *Health* 19:18 Ag '87

Saving grace [intensive therapy; work of O. I. Lovaas] P. Chance. il *Psychol Today* 21:42-4 D '87

Auto-Shade, Inc.

A shady business. il *Newsweek* 109:61 My 11 '87

Autobiography

See also

Publishers and publishing—Autobiography

Audio reviews: celebrity autobiographies. *Publ Wkly* 231:58-9 My 29 '87

The best of all stories. J. E. Birren. *Psychol Today* 21:91-2 My '87

Celebrity autobiographies on audio. A. Postman. il *Publ Wkly* 231:56-7 My 29 '87

The importance of being remembered [responses from readers of memoirs who were acquaintances of author] S. A. Toth. il *N Y Times Book Rev* 92:1+ Je 28 '87

Autodesk Inc.

The pack leader still acts 'like a hungry rat'. J. B. Levine. il por *Bus Week* p84 My 25 '87

Autofocus cameras *See* Cameras

Autofocus cameras, Single-lens reflex *See* Cameras, Single-lens reflex

Autofocus lenses *See* Lenses, Photographic

Autographs

Collectors and collecting

A baseball for dad [ball autographed by S. Musial] P. Thomson. il *Read Dig* 130:13-14+ Mr '87

Getting a taste for the scribbles of history. S. Woolley. il *Bus Week* p117 S 28 '87

Autoimmune diseases *See* Immunologic diseases

AutoInfo Inc.

The high margins in heavy metal. F. Meeks. il *Forbes* 140:82+ O 19 '87

Autologous blood transfusion *See* Blood—Transfusion

Autologous Systems Inc.

A battle over blood. L. Van Dusen. il *Macleans* 100:58 N 16 '87

Automata, Cellular *See* Cellular automata

Automated teller machines

Cash-machine magician [R. Post's use of magnetic encoding machine in robberies] *Time* 129:61 Je 1 '87

Don't go abroad without your trusty cash card. D. Zigas. il *Bus Week* p179 Jl 20 '87

Emergency funds: getting money around the world. L. Hazelton. il *Black Enterp* 17:38 Mr '87

Notes and comment. *New Yorker* 63:21-2 Je 15 '87

Soon, Citicorp 'branches' could be all over Japan [sharing machines with Dai-Ichi Kangyo] J. B. Treece. *Bus Week* p82 Ja 19 '87

Teller machine robberies [study by Bank Administration Institute] il *USA Today (Periodical)* 116:6 D '87

Security measures

How randomness protects you and your banker during an automated transaction. il *Discover* 8:76-7 Ja '87

Service charges

ATMs bite the hand that feeds them. il *Money* 16:13 S '87

Automatic cameras *See* Cameras

Automatic exposure cameras *See* Cameras

Automatic exposure cameras, Single-lens reflex *See* Cameras, Single-lens reflex

Automatic film winders *See* Photography—Equipment

Automatic pilot (Airplanes)

Autopilot by piece [Century 2000 autopilot] J. M. McClellan. il *Flying* 114:94 Ja '87

Autopilot rules to live by. J. M. McClellan. *Flying* 114:99-101 D '87

Loyalist or anarchist? J. M. McClellan. il *Flying* 114:10+ F '87

Automatic sprinklers *See* Sprinklers

Automatic transmission *See* Automobiles—Transmission

Automation

See also

Airlines—Automation

Automobile factories—Automation

Automobile junkyards—Automation

Avionics industry—Automation

Credit—Rating—Automation

Electronic industries—Automation

Facility management—Automation

Flexible manufacturing systems

Honeywell Inc.

Lotteries—Automation

Munitions—Automation

Nuclear power plants—Automation

Offices—Automation

Robots—Industrial use

Vision systems (Machines)

Word processors and processing

A century of struggle [trade unions and technology] bibl f il *Mon Labor Rev* 110:41-7 Ag '87

Factories automate—but slowly [computer integrated manufacturing] il *Futurist* 21:55 Jl/Ag '87

The high tech race: computers and chips. G. Bylinsky. *Current* 291:17-20 Mr/Ap '87

Jobs without people and people without jobs: the coming mismatch in the information society. W. H. Kolberg. il *USA Today (Periodical)* 116:18-20 Jl '87

Successful worker training programs help ease impact of technology. S. Deutsch. bibl f *Mon Labor Rev* 110:14-20 N '87

Technological change and employment: some results from BLS research. J. A. Mark. il *Mon Labor Rev* 110:26-9 Ap '87

Wait 'til next year [interview with H. Shaiken] J. Flint. *Forbes* 139:112 Je 15 '87

China

Don't discount China's potential to succeed as industrial power. L. Bertain. por *Aviat Week Space Technol* 127:61-2 D 7 '87

The factory that made a great leap forward [Shanghai Metallurgical & Mining Machinery Mfg.] D. J. Yang. il *Bus Week* p145 N 2 '87

Japan

How are Japanese unions responding to microelectronics-based automation? W. E. Klay. bibl f *Mon Labor Rev* 110:39-40 Mr '87

Automatons *See* Robots

Automats (Cafeterias) *See* Cafeterias

Automobile accidents *See* Traffic accidents

Automobile alarms *See* Automobiles—Alarms

Automobile assembly plants *See* Automobile factories

Automobile auctions *See* Auctions

Automobile batteries *See* Storage batteries

Automobile boat trailers

Improving the boat trailer. J. Pektas. il *Mot Boat Sail* 159:102 F '87

Practical fishing trailer. W. Morse. il *Field Stream* 92:134 Jl '87

Automobile bodies *See* Automobiles—Bodies

Automobile bodies, Remodeled *See* Automobiles, Remodeled

Automobile brakes *See* Brakes, Automobile

Automobile buying *See* Automobiles—Purchasing

Automobile clubs

See also

Midwestern Council of Sports Car Clubs

Sports Car Club of America

An auto club can smooth that bumpy ride. W. Zellner. il *Bus Week* p81 Jl 27 '87

Why you should shop for an auto service club. M. Stern. il *Home Mech* 83:88+ F '87

Automobile covers *See* Automobiles—Equipment

Automobile dealers

See also

Black automobile dealers

Grand Motors (Firm)

Chain and franchise operations

Does GM rate shelf space? [views of J. D. Power on superdealers] M. Beauchamp. il por *Forbes* 139:144 F 23 '87

Automobile decoration

Removing and replacing trim. M. Thompson. il *Fam Handyman* 37:96+ S '87

Automobile demolition derbies

The dukes of destruction [Sudden Impact team] J. R. Nerad. il *Mot Trend* 39:96-9+ Je '87

Automobile drivers

See also

Alcohol and automobile drivers

Taxicab drivers

Women automobile drivers

Auto focus [teenage drivers; special section] il *Seventeen* 46:84-5 F '87

Notes and comment [American character defined by being an automobile driver] *New Yorker* 63:29-30 N 30 '87

Responsibility. M. Anson. il *Mot Trend* 39:8 Mr '87

Turning highway rights into wrongs [young drivers injured in accidents] D. Hochberg. por *U S News World Rep* 103:6 N 30 '87

Automobile drivers—*cont.*
Health and hygiene
Sunshine: every little bit hurts. il *Prevention* 39:8+ Je '87
Licenses
The high-schooler's informational IQ test [proposal for test as requirement for teenage driver's license] W. F. Buckley. *Natl Rev* 39:57 Jl 17 '87
Psychology
Driving passion [cover story] P. E. Marsh and P. Collett. il *Psychol Today* 21:16-18+ Je '87

How to handle on-the-road hostility. D. McCluggage. il *Glamour* 85:120+ N '87

Keeping cool when traffic heats up. B. Brophy. il *U S News World Rep* 103:26-7 S 7 '87

Mayhem on the freeways [drivers' responses to congestion] A. Lobue. por *U S News World Rep* 103:9 S 28 '87

Romancing the road: the all-American drive to nowhere. il *Glamour* 85:100 S '87
Testing
Acing your driver's test. L. St. James. il *Seventeen* 46:84 F '87

The g-analyst: the driver's lie detector. R. Titus. il *Mot Trend* 39:114 O '87

Automobile driving
See also
    Automobile drivers
    Automobile touring
    Automobiles—Speed
    Traffic accidents

Alone on the highway. K. Kelly. il *Parents* 62:66+ Ag '87

The car in front of you breaks down . . . what should you do? D. Chaikin. il *Home Mech* 83:26 Ag '87

Car smarts: how to handle any emergency. J. Kaufman. il *Seventeen* 46:120+ Mr '87

Don't overlook the fun factor. M. Anson. il *Mot Trend* 39:6 My '87

Drive defensively—and live. S. L. Englebardt. il *Read Dig* 131:81-2+ N '87

Driver's notebook. See issues of Motor Trend beginning January 1987

Hidden driveway ahead . . . what should you do? D. Chaikin. il *Home Mech* 83:22 Jl '87

How to handle summer's special driving conditions. D. McCluggage. il *Glamour* 85:96+ Jl '87

If you're forced off the road. D. Chaikin. il *Home Mech* 83:22 Ja '87

Making a left turn across traffic. D. Chaikin. il *Home Mech* 83:32 Mr '87

Miscellaneous ramblings. J. Dinkel. il *Road Track* 39:39 D '87

A motorcar is a terrible thing to waste. B. W. Yates. il *Car Driv* 33:24 N '87

Safe driving quiz. D. Chaikin. il *Home Mech* 83:81-3 Ja '87

Surviving 18-wheelers. D. Chaikin. il *Home Mech* 83:36 Ap '87

The technique of cornering [excerpt from The g-analyst guide to expert driving] P. Bedard. il *Car Driv* 33:105-6+ D '87

What to do when you suddenly can't see. D. McCluggage. il *Glamour* 85:106+ Ja '87

When everyone else is speeding . . . D. Chaikin. il *Home Mech* 83:22 S '87

When someone is going the wrong way . . . D. Chaikin. il *Home Mech* 83:34 My '87

When you have a back-seat driver . . . what should you do? D. Chaikin. il *Home Mech* 83:12 D '87

When you're driving alone [women] D. McCluggage. il *Essence* 18:112 S '87

You just missed your exit . . . what should you do? D. Chaikin. il *Home Mech* 83:26 N '87
Animal hazards
Animal crossing—driver, beware. L. St. James. il *Seventeen* 46:96-7 O '87

Life and death in the fast lane [highway dividers trap crossing animals] M. Kantor. il *Sierra* 72:14 S/O '87

The longest meadow. P. Schullery. il *Ctry J* 14:83-6 Ap '87

What to do if your car hits an animal. D. McCluggage. il *Glamour* 85:198+ My '87

When you hear a splat, reach for Roger Knutson's Flattened fauna. il por *People Wkly* 28:105 Ag 17 '87
Mud hazards
Getting unstuck. S. L. White. il *Field Stream* 92:82+ O '87

Storm hazards
Car smarts [driving in rain] L. St. James. *Seventeen* 46:20 Ap '87

You see an accident about to happen . . . [safe driving in the rain] D. Chaikin. il *Home Mech* 83:16 O '87
Study and teaching
See also
    Automobile racing—Study and teaching

"Behind the wheel with Jackie Stewart". M. Anson. il pors *Mot Trend* 39:130+ My '87

Bob Bondurant School of High-Performance Driving. G. Brown. il *Mot Trend* 39:84 Ja '87

Drive & Survive [school run by former British policeman P. Catlin in the U.S. and Great Britain] P. Bingham. il por *Mot Trend* 39:137+ Je '87

Driving on ice [Ford Ice Driving School, Steamboat Springs, Colo.] L. Tejada-Flores. il *Skiing* 40:214+ D '87

Driving with the pros. E. Henry. *Changing Times* 41:106+ S '87

Freedom [Freedom Place, where student drivers can practice in Manhattan] *New Yorker* 63:22-3 Ag 24 '87

Learning how to drive on ice [Ford Ice Driving School, Steamboat Springs, Colo.] M. Thompson. il *Fam Handyman* 37:67 N '87

Why Johnny can't drive. G. Witzenburg. il *Home Mech* 83:78-81+ S '87
Winter driving
Beetles on ice [VW Beetle as winter car] P. Egan. il *Road Track* 38:16 Ap '87

Driving on ice [Ford Ice Driving School, Steamboat Springs, Colo.] L. Tejada-Flores. il *Skiing* 40:214+ D '87

Four-wheel steering on snow and ice [Honda Prelude] il *Road Track* 38:104+ Jl '87

Learning how to drive on ice [Ford Ice Driving School, Steamboat Springs, Colo.] M. Thompson. il *Fam Handyman* 37:67 N '87

Stranded: could you survive? C. Loomis. il *Parents* 62:17 Ja '87
California
See also
    California. Dept. of Motor Vehicles
Maryland
See also
    Maryland. Motor Vehicle Administration
Western Europe
Run to the sun [Callaway Turbo Corvette vs. Koenig Twin-Turbo Porsche 911 in Europe; cover story] J. Rusz. il *Road Track* 38:46-52 Ag '87

Automobile driving with children See Travel with children
Automobile engineering
Cars of 1990's [University of Michigan's forecast] il *USA Today (Periodical)* 116:12 Ag '87

Cars of the 90's [cover story; special section] il *U S News World Rep* 103:38-45 Ag 10 '87

Detroit '88—reengineering the family car. D. McCosh. il *Pop Sci* 231:82-5+ O '87

Does racing relate? [transfer of technology from racing cars to street-driven cars] M. Anson. il *Mot Trend* 39:8 Ja '87

Engineering the new cars. il *Pop Mech* 164:135-42 O '87

High-tech times. M. Anson. il *Mot Trend* 39:6 O '87

Miscellaneous ramblings [open letter to Ford CEO D. Petersen] J. Dinkel. il *Road Track* 39:37-9 O '87

Technical highlights [1988 cars] N. Bissoon Dath. il *Car Driv* 33:57-60 O '87

Technical tidbits. D. Simanaitis. See issues of Road & Track beginning January 1985

Technologue. R. Grable. See issues of Motor Trend

Technology meets the road [Ford Motor Co.] R. Voegelin. il *Mot Trend* 39 no12 Sp Issue:26-31 '87

Trickle-down technology. T. Swan. il *Home Mech* 83:80-4 Ap '87
Automobile engines
See also
    Automobiles, Racing—Engines
    Carburetors
    Diesel engines, Automotive
    Gas turbines, Automotive
    Tachometers

Pick the engine that's right for you. D. Chaikin. il *Home Mech* 83:60-3 Ag '87

Powerful urges [memorable engines] P. Bedard. il *Car Driv* 32:120 F '87

Requiem for a flathead. P. Egan. il *Road Track* 39:16 O '87

Automobile engines—*cont.*

Air supply

See also
Automobile engines—Superchargers

Belts

Check your belts now: timing is everything. M. J. Schultz. il *Pop Mech* 164:155-8　F '87

Cleaning

Underhood cleanup. M. Ferrara. il *Home Mech* 83:28 Ag '87

Cooling

Coolant recovery: stage two [HYDRO-FILL system] R. Titus. il *Mot Trend* 39:144　My '87
When your engine overheats. L. St. James. il *Seventeen* 46:206　Ag '87
When your engine overheats. P. Weissler. il *Home Mech* 83:72-5　Jl '87

Cylinders

Smooth that rough idle. P. Stenquist. il *Pop Mech* 164:177-80　Ap '87

Design

The advanced Jaguar six advances further [AJ6] P. Bedard. il *Car Driv* 32:111　Ja '87
Can the two-stroke make it this time? [Orbital engine] D. Scott. il *Pop Sci* 230:74-6　F '87
General Motors' little engine that could [Quad 4] W. J. Hampton. il *Bus Week* p88-9　Ag 3 '87
A high-tech V-6 for the 300ZX [Nissan 300ZR] J. K. Yamaguchi. il *Road Track* 38:92+　F '87
Of technical interest [Honda Civic] K. Reynolds. il *Road Track* 39:60-1　N '87
A stirring variation on a Thema [Ferrari-engined Lancia Thema 8.32] P. Frère. il *Road Track* 38:70+　My '87
Technical highlights [1988 cars] N. Bissoon Dath. il *Car Driv* 33:57-60　O '87
Technical highlights [Merkur Scorpio V-6] C. Csere. il *Car Driv* 32:72　Je '87
Technical highlights [Subaru Justy three-cylinder engine] C. Csere. il *Car Driv* 32:77　Ap '87
To Vee or not to Vee; and is 8 enough? [Japanese carmakers] J. K. Yamaguchi. il *Road Track* 38:103-4 Ap '87
Two strokes revisited [Orbital Combustion Process] P. L. Albrecht. il *Road Track* 38:64+　Ap '87
Yamaha to build Ford V6. D. McCosh. il *Pop Sci* 231:14　S '87

Detonation

Knock, knock. M. S. Dolan. il *Consum Res Mag* 70:2 N '87

Energy usage

See also
Diesel engines, Automotive—Energy usage
The 1988 EPA mileage estimates. il *Consum Res Mag* 70:18-21+　N '87
Dropping the fuel economy standards [Corporate Average Fuel Economy standard] il *Consum Rep* 52:134　Mr '87
A gallon of gas, 121 miles and thou [Renault Vesta II research vehicle] P. Frère. il *Road Track* 39:96 D '87

Environmental aspects

See Automobiles—Environmental aspects

Exhaust

See also
Automobiles—Environmental aspects
Automobiles—Pollution control devices
Repairing your exhaust system. P. Stenquist. il *Pop Mech* 164:151-4　Je '87
When you smell your car's exhaust. P. Weissler. il *Home Mech* 83:90+　N '87
You only choke twice [southern Calif. forest fire smoke contains automobile exhaust] il *Discover* 8:6+　O '87

Failure

The car in front of you breaks down . . . what should you do? D. Chaikin. il *Home Mech* 83:26　Ag '87
Fear of walking. P. Egan. il *Road Track* 38:16　Ja '87

Fan belts

Miscellaneous ramblings [Gates aftermarket fan belts] J. Dinkel. il *Road Track* 39:31　S '87

Filters

Do-it-yourself guide [change your own oil and oil filter] il *Consum Rep* 52:102　F '87
Fuel filter basics. M. Ferrara. il *Home Mech* 83:26　Jl '87
An oil change for the better. M. Ferrara. il *Home Mech* 83:34　Mr '87
Oil-filter wrenches. il *Consum Rep* 52:90-4　D '87
Oil-filter wrenches. il *Consum Rep* 52:99-101　F '87
Oil filters. il *Consum Rep* 52:86-90　D '87
Oil filters. il *Consum Rep* 52:95-8　F '87

Fuel

See also
Alcohol as fuel
Gasoline

Fuel consumption

See Automobile engines—Energy usage

Fuel feeding

Performance sentinels [oxygen sensors] K. Zino. il *Pop Sci* 230:25-6+　My '87

History

Early automotive engines: how it used to be. R. Grable. il *Mot Trend* 39:110-11　Ag '87

Hoses

Replacing a hose. M. Thompson. il *Fam Handyman* 37:70　N '87

Ignition

See also
Spark plugs

Lubrication and lubricants

See Automobiles—Lubrication and lubricants

Maintenance and repair

Car-care quiz. S. Mercaldo. il *Pop Sci* 231:48+　S '87
Smooth that rough idle. P. Stenquist. il *Pop Mech* 164:177-80　Ap '87
Tune up your engine. il *Pop Mech* 164:108-10+　My '87
When your tune-up goes off key. P. Weissler. il *Home Mech* 83:98-101　F '87

Materials

See also
Diesel engines, Automotive—Materials
Déjà vu—yet again [ceramic auto engines] J. Zweig. il *Forbes* 140:282+　N 16 '87

Repairing

See Automobile engines—Maintenance and repair

Starting

See Automobiles—Starting

Superchargers

See also
Automobiles, Racing—Engines—Superchargers
300ZX Turbo [Nissan] R. Grable. il *Mot Trend* 39:83-4+ Je '87
1939 Graham Series 97 Supercharger. H. Rasmussen. il *Mot Trend* 39:93-6+　Ja '87
1988 Mazda 626. D. C. Ross. il *Mot Trend* 39:102-4+ D '87
1988 Porsche 944 Turbo. R. Titus. il *Mot Trend* 39:86-7+ D '87
1988 Subaru XT. il *Road Track* 39:58　O '87
Bentley Turbo R. I. Ireland. il *Road Track* 38:53-5 Ja '87
Bondurant Thunderbird 5.0. il por *Road Track* 39:62-4 O '87
Buick GNX. T. Assenza. il *Car Driv* 32:135+　My '87
A car for all seasons [Subaru RX] E. Henry. il *Changing Times* 41:120　Mr '87
Chevrolet Sprint Turbo. T. Assenza. il *Car Driv* 32:117-19 Ap '87
Chrysler LeBaron Turbo. R. Ceppos. il *Car Driv* 32:121-3+ My '87
Decisions, decisions . . . [Porsche 924S, 944, 944S and 944 Turbo; cover story] il *Road Track* 39:44-53　N '87
Detroit's flashy coupes [Chevrolet Beretta GT, Ford Thunderbird Turbo Coupe, and Chrysler Le Baron Turbo Coupe; cover story] il *Consum Rep* 52:486-92 Ag '87
Dodge Daytona Shelby Z. D. C. Ross. il *Mot Trend* 39:96-8　Jl '87
Dodge Shelby Charger GLHS. T. Assenza. il *Car Driv* 32:93　F '87
Domestic dynamite [Buick Regal Grand National, Chevy Camaro IROC 350 Z, Corvette, Dodge Daytona Turbo, Ford Mustang GT and Thunderbird Turbo Coupe and Pontiac Firebird GTA; cover story] R. Grable. il *Mot Trend* 39:44-51　Ag '87
Dream machines [Ruf Porsche Turbo and Autokraft AC Mk IV; cover story] il *Road Track* 38:40-7　My '87
The econohunks [Ford Escort GT, Isuzu I-Mark Turbo, Dodge Shadow ES, Renault GTA, Chevrolet 224, Toyota Corolla FX16, Mitsubishi Mirage Turbo, Pontiac Sunbird Turbo GT, VW GTI 16V and Acura Integra LS] P. Bedard. il *Car Driv* 32:42-9+　Mr '87
Europe's fastest of the fast [Ferrari Testarossa, Lamborghini Countach, Lotus Esprit Turbo and Porsche 928S 4] R. Grable. il *Mot Trend* 39:28-35　Ja '87
Fast Frenchies [Peugeot 405, Citroën BX GTI 16 and Renault 21 Turbo] P. Frère. il *Road Track* 39:108+ N '87

Automobile engines—Superchargers—*cont.*

Ferrari F40 [cover story] D. Sherman. il *Car Driv* 33:40-3+ N '87

Ferrari F40 [cover story] D. Simanaitis. il *Road Track* 39:44-9 O '87

Ferrari Testarossa Quad Turbo. R. Grable. il *Mot Trend* 39:57-9+ Je '87

Ferrari's F40 tops them all! M. Cotton. il *Mot Trend* 39:16-17 O '87

Fiero Formula vs MR2 Supercharged [Pontiac vs. Toyota] il *Road Track* 39:50-7 O '87

Flat out on the flats [Aerotech with Quad 4 engine] P. Bedard. il *Car Driv* 33:167 O '87

Ford Sierra RS Cosworth [European production model] L. Griffin. il *Car Driv* 33:103-4+ O '87

Ford Thunderbird Turbo Coupe. il *Road Track* 38:66-8+ Ag '87

Four European sports sedans [Volvo 760 Turbo, Saab 9000 Turbo, BMW 325i and Sterling 825-SL] il *Consum Rep* 52:556-63 S '87

Gambling with a convertible, gambolling with a convertible [Saab 9000 Turbo] R. Homan. il *Road Track* 38:80+ Ag '87

A gathering of eagles [AMG Hammer, Callaway Corvettes, Ferrari Testarossa, Keith Black Camaro, Motorsport Design Porsche 911 Turbo and Norwood Ferrari-Chevrolet GTO; cover story] R. Ceppos. il *Car Driv* 33:42-51 D '87

Hartge Grand National [Buick] C. Csere. il *Car Driv* 33:110-11 Ag '87

Hot coupes [Toyota MR2 and Celica All-Trac Turbo] D. McCosh. il *Pop Sci* 231:71 D '87

Isuzu I-Mark Turbo. J. R. Nerad. il *Mot Trend* 39:86-90 Ag '87

Isuzu Impulse Turbo RS. T. Assenza. il *Car Driv* 32:137-9 Je '87

Isuzu Impulse Turbo RS. B. Nagy. il *Mot Trend* 39:70-2+ Ap '87

Just in time—American-style [Garrett turbochargers made in Japan] G. Bronson. il *Forbes* 139:132+ Mr 9 '87

Life with 5000 [Audi Quattro long term test] A. St. Antoine. il *Car Driv* 33:65-7+ Jl '87

Maserati Biturbo i Spyder. R. Grable. il *Mot Trend* 39:49-50 O '87

Maserati Biturbo i Spyder. L. Griffin. il *Car Driv* 33:51-3+ S '87

Matchmaker, matchmaker, make me a turbo [improved designs] H. Halverson. il *Road Track* 39:78 D '87

Mazda Luce. Y. Ishiwatari. il *Car Driv* 32:38 Mr '87

Mazda MX-6 GT Turbo. T. Assenza. il *Car Driv* 33:63-5+ S '87

Mazda RX-7 Turbo II. R. Titus. il *Mot Trend* 39:88-9+ S '87

Merkur XR4Ti [owners report] M. Lamm. il *Pop Mech* 164:71+ Mr '87

Mitsubishi Tredia Turbo at 50,000 miles. il *Road Track* 38:136+ Ap '87

More power to the Japanese [Mazda RX-7 Cabriolet and Nissan Skyline GTS-R] J. K. Yamaguchi. il *Road Track* 39:112+ D '87

More sting for the Mazda 323 [Infini] J. K. Yamaguchi. il *Road Track* 38:162+ Je '87

Nissan's quest for execu-tech [Cedric/Gloria] J. K. Yamaguchi. il *Road Track* 39:95-6 O '87

Peugeot 505 Turbo Wagon [long term test] R. Titus. il *Mot Trend* 39:124+ My '87

PM comparison test: daily drivers. il *Pop Mech* 164:71-4+ My '87

PM long-term car tests: Dodge Shadow Turbo, Tempo 4WD, Corvette Convertible. M. Allen and J. Oldham. il *Pop Mech* 164:120-1+ D '87

PM's long-term test reports [Corvette Roadster, Dodge Shadow Turbo, Ford Tempo 4WD] il *Pop Mech* 164:53-5+ Ag '87

Pontiac Grand Am SE Turbo. D. C. Ross. il *Mot Trend* 39:91-2+ Ag '87

Porsche 911 Turbo Cabriolet. B. W. Yates. il *Car Driv* 33:32-7+ S '87

Porsche 959. C. Csere. il *Car Driv* 33:116-18+ N '87

Power to the fore! [turbo Buick Riviera] W. Hoyt. il *Pop Mech* 164:47 Je '87

The Quattro quandary [Audi 5000 CS Turbo and Quattro] C. Csere. il *Car Driv* 32:79+ F '87

Record-shattering trio? [Aerotech project using modified Quad 4 turbo engine] P. Lienert. il *Road Track* 38:50-2 Ja '87

Reliant Scimitar 1800Ti. R. Hutton. il *Car Driv* 33:25 S '87

Rotary rocket [Mazda RX-7 Turbo] T. Wilkinson. il *Pop Sci* 230:32+ Ja '87

RS 200/Sierra RS Cosworth [European Ford production models of rally cars] M. Cotton. il *Mot Trend* 39:98+ Mr '87

Run to the sun [Callaway Turbo Corvette vs. Koenig Twin-Turbo Porsche 911 in Europe; cover story] J. Rusz. il *Road Track* 38:46-52 Ag '87

Saab 900 Turbo Convertible. J. R. Nerad. il *Mot Trend* 39:67+ Ja '87

Saab 9000S. il *Road Track* 38:97-8 Jl '87

Shelby Charger GLH-S. il *Road Track* 38:96-7 Jl '87

Shelby Charger GLH-S. R. Titus. il *Mot Trend* 39:78+ Mr '87

Shelby CSX. N. Bissoon Dath. il *Car Driv* 33:125-7 N '87

Shelby Lancer. R. Titus. il *Mot Trend* 39:59-61+ Ap '87

Speed thrills [Chevrolet's Callaway Corvette and Buick's Regal GNX] M. Allen. il *Pop Mech* 164:63-6+ Mr '87

Subaru's 4WD Turbo Wagon. B. Kilpatrick. il *Field Stream* 91:93-4 F '87

Supercar showdown [Aston Martin Vantage Zagato vs. Ferrari 288 GTO; cover story] P. Bingham. il *Mot Trend* 39:46-51+ D '87

Supercharging is back! D. McCosh. il *Pop Sci* 230:66-9+ Ja '87

This sportin' life [Acura Legend, Alfa Romeo Milano Gold, Mercury Sable, Pontiac Bonneville, Saab 9000 Turbo, Sterling 825S and Toyota Cressida] il *Pop Mech* 164:60-4+ Ja '87

Thunderbird Turbo Coupe. D. Fuller. il *Mot Trend* 39 no12 Sp Issue:48-53 '87

Toyota Celica All-Trac Turbo. P. Bedard. il *Car Driv* 33:59-62+ N '87

Toyota Celica All-Trac Turbo & MR2 Supercharged. D. Fuller. il *Mot Trend* 39:82-3+ N '87

Toyota Celica GT-Four. Y. Ishiwatari. il *Car Driv* 32:29 Ap '87

Toyota MR2 1600G-Limited. Y. Ishiwatari. il *Car Driv* 32:27 Ap '87

Toyota MR2 Supercharged. N. Bissoon Dath. il *Car Driv* 33:55-8+ D '87

Toyota Supra Turbo. il *Road Track* 38:85 F '87

Toyota Supra Turbo. A. St. Antoine. il *Car Driv* 32:43-6+ Ap '87

Update: long-term tests [Acura Legend Coupe L, Ford Taurus and Porsche 944 Turbo] il *Road Track* 39:64 D '87

Update: long-term tests [Chevrolet Corvette, Saab 9000 and Ford Taurus] il *Road Track* 38:130 Ap '87

Update: long-term tests [Chevrolet Corvette, Saab 9000 and Toyota MR2] il *Road Track* 38:134 Je '87

Update: long-term tests [Porsche 944 Turbo, Ford Taurus and Toyota MR2] il *Road Track* 39:62 N '87

The world's fastest cars [AMG Hammer, Ferrari GTO and Testarossa, Isdera Imperator 108i, Koenig/RS, Lamborghini Countach, Porsche 959 and Ruf Twin-Turbo; cover story] P. Egan. il *Road Track* 38:50-61 Jl '87

Valves

Fast-track valve trains. B. Hartford. il *Pop Mech* 164:12 My '87

Heavy metal [V12-powered German luxury cars] D. McCosh. il *Pop Sci* 230:18+ Ja '87

How to give your engine a valve job. P. Stenquist. il *Pop Mech* 164:145-8 Mr '87

Automobile equipment *See* Automobiles—Equipment

Automobile equipment industry

See also

Auto-Shade, Inc.

Eaton Corporation

Echlin Inc.

Genuine Parts Company

Standard Products Company (Ohio)

Turtle Wax (Firm)

Finance

Automotive. J. Flint. il *Forbes* 139:71-3 Ja 12 '87

Quality control

U.S. parts makers just won't say 'Uncle'. J. B. Treece. il *Bus Week* p76+ Ag 10 '87

Securities

Geriatric autos. L. Ehrenkrantz. por *Forbes* 140:136 Ag 24 '87

Australia

See also

Orbital Engine Company

Japan

Just in time—American-style [Garrett turbochargers made in Japan] G. Bronson. il *Forbes* 139:132+ Mr 9 '87

U.S. parts makers just won't say 'Uncle'. J. B. Treece. il *Bus Week* p76+ Ag 10 '87

Automobile factories

Chrysler's conundrum [no factory available to produce Omni/Horizon] S. Flack. il por *Forbes* 139:104 Ap 20 '87

GM's bootstrap battle: the factory-floor view [E. Schaefer brings team management to Van Nuys plant] A. Gabor. il por *U S News World Rep* 103:52-3 S 21 '87

Automation

The automotive world of the 21st century. D. E. Petersen. il *Radio-Electron* 58:91-5 My '87

Linden [GM assembly plant for Chevrolet Beretta and Corsica in N.J.] R. Ceppos. il *Car Driv* 32:37 F '87

Robot auto inspector [VICTER (Vision Inspection and Calibration Test by Robot)] D. Scott. il *Pop Sci* 230:66 F '87

Employees

See Automobile industry workers

Location

Carmakers are doing their dreaming in California [American and Japanese design studios in California] S. Toy. il *Bus Week* p50+ Mr 30 '87

Shutdowns

Detroit is bracing for a one-two punch. J. B. Treece. il *Bus Week* p136-7+ N 16 '87

In Flint, tough times last [General Motors pulls out] M. Moore. il *Nation* 244:753-6 Je 6 '87

What ended VW's American dream [closing plant in Westmoreland County, Pa.] J. Templeman. il *Bus Week* p63 D 7 '87

A 'wise' decision backfires on Volkswagen [closing plant in New Stanton, Pa.] il *Newsweek* 110:62 D 7 '87

Canada

Keeping the assembly line rolling [government aid keeps GM plant in Boisbriand, Que. open] il *Macleans* 100:10 Ap 13 '87

Italy

Maranello revisited [Ferrari] L. C. Crane. il *Road Track* 39:114+ S '87

Red cars rising [Ferrari factories in Modena and Maranello] D. Sherman. il *Car Driv* 33:93-5+ Ag '87

Mexico

The Mexican connection [U.S. auto factories] P. Lyons. *Car Driv* 32:69 Mr '87

Automobile filters *See* Automobile engines—Filters

Automobile headlights *See* Automobiles—Lighting

Automobile horns

How to fix a stuck or mute horn. M. Thompson. il *Fam Handyman* 37:110 My/Je '87

Automobile ice racing *See* Automobile racing

Automobile industry

See also

> Ali Motors Inc.
> American Motors Corp.
> Austin Rover Cars of North America
> Automobile dealers
> Automobile factories
> Black automobile dealers
> Buick Motor Division
> Cadillac Motor Car Division
> Chevrolet Motor Division
> Chrysler Corp.
> Collective bargaining—Automobile industry
> Collective labor agreements—Automobile industry
> Ford Motor Co.
> General Motors Corp.
> New Avanti Motor Corp.
> Saturn Corporation
> Subaru of America, Inc.
> Unique Mobility (Firm)
> Volkswagen of America Inc.
> Yugo America Inc.
> Zimmer Corp.

But in Detroit, beware of 'the glut'. J. A. Seamonds. il *U S News World Rep* 103:47 N 30 '87

Carmakers are doing their dreaming in California [American and Japanese design studios in California] S. Toy. il *Bus Week* p50+ Mr 30 '87

Detroit report. D. C. Ross. See issues of Motor Trend

For your information. A. St. Antoine. See issues of Car and Driver

Inside Detroit. J. Dunne. See issues of Popular Mechanics beginning January 1986

Putting the brakes on the Orient Express [views of D. Halberstam in The reckoning] J. M. Fallows. *Wash Mon* 19:39-45 Ap '87

Accounting

Fiddling with figures while sales drop [General Motors] J. Flint and L. Jereski. il *Forbes* 140:32-5 Ag 24 '87

Acquisitions and mergers

Chrysler courts AMC. P. Lienert. il *Road Track* 38:110+ Mr '87

A daredevil wheel deal [Chrysler buys AMC] G. Russell. il *Time* 129:40-1 Mr 23 '87

Jeep/Eagle: preview of an evolution [Chrysler's acquisition of AMC] M. Keller. il *Mot Trend* 39:150 N '87

Now, for Chrysler's next trick . . . [acquisition of American Motors Corp.] W. J. Hampton. il *Bus Week* p32-3 Mr 23 '87

The payoff to customers from Chrysler-AMC merger. J. A. Seamonds. il *U S News World Rep* 102:58-9 Mr 23 '87

Survival of the fleetest [Chrysler's acquisition of AMC and Lamborghini] J. Lamm. il *Road Track* 39:118+ O '87

'Zip, overnight': a Chrysler Jeep [Chrysler's bid for AMC] B. Powell. il *Newsweek* 109:38-9 Mr 23 '87

International aspects

Cash flow in the fast lane [Ford buys Aston Martin] T. Tedesco. il *Macleans* 100:39 S 21 '87

Have you driven an Aston Martin lately? [Ford agrees to buy Aston Martin Lagonda] il *Newsweek* 110:64 S 21 '87

Lotus: living with the General. P. Bingham. il *Mot Trend* 39:48-51 F '87

Tooling into the luxury market in a Lamborghini [Chrysler's deal] W. C. Symonds. il *Bus Week* p45+ My 4 '87

Western Europe

Ford bids again, Fiat gets the nod [Fiat outbids Ford for Alfa Romeo] P. Lienert. *Road Track* 38:100 F '87

Advertising

The auto, love & advertising [collecting] D. Stewart. il *Antiques Collect Hobbies* 92:75-9 Ap '87

Buy two, they're cheap [advertising the Suzuki Samurai] J. Flint. il *Forbes* 140:193+ N 2 '87

Death sentences from America [Ford of Canada ordered to drop Canadian advertising agencies] P. C. Newman. il *Macleans* 100:39 O 5 '87

How to buy a Rolls: follow your nose [scent strip ads] il *Newsweek* 109:46 Je 22 '87

In for repairs [unintended acceleration in the Audi 5000 and Audi's new ad campaign] B. Kanner. il *N Y* 20:32+ O 19 '87

Jaguar revs up. B. Kanner. il *N Y* 20:23+ Ag 31 '87

The Lone Driver rides again [TV car commercial symbolic of Reagan era fantasy] T. Gitlin. il *Progressive* 51:36-40 F '87

Shoot-out in Los Angeles: how Chiat/Day captured Nissan. J. Flynn and R. Grover. il *Bus Week* p70+ Ag 17 '87

Those heartbeat ads are a hit in the heartland [Chevrolet] C. Dugas. il *Bus Week* p107 F 23 '87

To be continued [GM's serial television ads] B. Kanner. il *N Y* 20:14+ F 2 '87

Awards

See also

> Motor Trend Awards

Customer relations

Today's buyers have high expectations. M. Anson. il *Mot Trend* 39:6 Ag '87

Employees

See Automobile industry workers

Ethical aspects

A free ride at Chrysler [odometer scandal] G. Carroll and J. B. Copeland. il *Newsweek* 110:37 Jl 6 '87

Iacocca: 'Did we screw up? You bet' [odometer scandal] *Newsweek* 110:42 Jl 13 '87

Would you buy a used Chrysler from this man? [disconnected odometers] C. P. Work. *U S News World Rep* 103:44 Jl 6 '87

Export-import trade

See Automobiles—Export-import trade

Finance

Automotive. J. Flint. il *Forbes* 139:71-3 Ja 12 '87

Detroit has little choice but to downshift. W. Zellner and J. B. Treece. il *Bus Week* p62-3 D 7 '87

Detroit is bracing for a one-two punch. J. B. Treece. il *Bus Week* p136-7+ N 16 '87

Detroit is stuck in low gear. W. Zellner. il *Bus Week* p72 Jl 20 '87

Detroit's share keeps getting smaller. W. J. Hampton. il *Bus Week* p71 Ja 12 '87

U.S. auto sales hit record high in 1986. il *Mot Trend* 39:26 Ap '87

Who's ahead in the world auto war. A. L. Taylor, III. il *Fortune* 116:74-8+ N 9 '87

Automobile industry—*cont.*

History

What's good for America. J. Flint. il *Forbes* 140:173-6+ Jl 13 '87

International aspects

See also

New United Motor Mfg., Inc.

GNP will take a hit from lagging auto output . . . and even the Japanese are feeling the crunch. G. Koretz. il *Bus Week* p14 Je 29 '87

International report. See issues of Motor Trend

Who's ahead in the world auto war. A. L. Taylor, III. il *Fortune* 116:74-8+ N 9 '87

Laws and regulations

See Automobiles—Laws and regulations

Management

1988: a year of reckoning for Detroit [address, September 8, 1987] H. K. Sperlich. *Vital Speeches Day* 54:92-5 N 15 '87

Can Roy Roberts rebuild the GM machine? [cover story] K. D. Thompson. il pors *Black Enterp* 18:57-60+ D '87

Can we make U.S. industry competitive again? H. A. Poling. il *USA Today (Periodical)* 116:22-4 N '87

Detroit vs. the UAW: at odds over teamwork. A. Bernstein and W. Zellner. il *Bus Week* p54-5 Ag 24 '87

Detroit—lean and mean or fat and foolish? T. D. Kane. il *USA Today (Periodical)* 116:37 S '87

Lee Iacocca's production whiz [R. E. Dauch] A. L. Taylor, III. il pors *Fortune* 115:36-8+ Je 22 '87

Nissan, Tennessee [poor treatment of workers at Smyrna plant; cover story] J. Junkerman. il *Progressive* 51:16-18+ Je '87

Rocketing into '88. D. Sherman. il *Car Driv* 33:9 O '87

Roy Roberts gets top personnel post at GM. por *Jet* 72:27 Ap 27 '87

Thought for food. D. Sherman. il *Car Driv* 32:9 My '87

Marketing

See also

Automobile dealers

Allanté: slow off the mark. J. Flint. il *Forbes* 140:204 N 30 '87

America über alles [luxury sedan market] B. W. Yates. il *Car Driv* 32:20 Ja '87

America's favorite cars for the road. J. A. Seamonds. il *U S News World Rep* 102:52-3 Ja 19 '87

Cars women want: a driving force. M. Knepper. *Harpers Bazaar* 120:174+ S '87

Detroit drives faster just to stay in place. W. Zellner. il *Bus Week* p26-7 Ap 20 '87

Detroit vs. new upscale imports. A. L. Taylor, III. il *Fortune* 115:69-70+ Ap 27 '87

Detroit's balm for sticker shock. J. A. Seamonds. il *U S News World Rep* 102:58-9 Mr 16 '87

Detroit's share keeps getting smaller. W. J. Hampton. il *Bus Week* p71 Ja 12 '87

GM's new luxury cars: why they're not selling. R. Mitchell. il *Bus Week* p94+ Ja 19 '87

Is anybody out there listening? [Ford's market research techniques] R. Ceppos. il *Car Driv* 33:24-5 O '87

It's clearance time again [incentives] *Fortune* 115:8 Mr 2 '87

Maybe this time . . . [Detroit hangs on against imports and immigrant autos] J. Flint. il *Forbes* 140:34 S 7 '87

The new Chevys aren't driving away with the market. W. Zellner. il *Bus Week* p34-5 Je 15 '87

Soft sell [women car buyers] E. Henry. il *Changing Times* 41:82 Jl '87

Thinking big [Cadillac] D. Seligman. il *Fortune* 115:115+ My 25 '87

Warranty warfare. B. Bauer. il *U S News World Rep* 102:46 F 16 '87

Quality control

The Boz, the UAW, and your new Chevy [B. Bosworth's comments on assembly line workers] D. Fuller. il *Mot Trend* 39:116-17 Ja '87

Detroit is trying, but its image lags. W. J. Hampton. il *Bus Week* p138-9 Je 8 '87

Detroit's cars really are getting better. J. Main. il *Fortune* 115:90-8 F 2 '87

Somebody does it better [Ford and GM cars made in Europe] M. Keller. il *Mot Trend* 39:102 Ja '87

Securities

Auto stocks get ready to go . . . vroom, vroom. B. Hager and W. L. Updegrave. il *Money* 16:7 S '87

Bargains in luxury car stocks? P. Duggan. il *Forbes* 140:146 D 28 '87

How Wall Street views the Detroit auto makers. C. P. Work. il *U S News World Rep* 102:59 Mr 23 '87

Brazil

The land of pistol-packing car poachers. D. Sherman. il *Car Driv* 32:5 Ap '87

Canada

See also

Chrysler Canada Ltd.

Ford Motor Co. of Canada Limited

General Motors of Canada Ltd.

Egypt

See also

General Motors Egypt S.A.E.

Nasr Automotive Manufacturing Company

France

See also

Peugeot SA

Renault (Regie Nationale des Usines Renault)

Germany (West)

See also

Adam Opel AG

Audi AG

Bayerische Motoren Werke AG

Daimler-Benz AG

Porsche AG

Volkswagen AG

Heavy traffic in the fast lane [German styling] D. Pauly. il *Newsweek* 109:56-7 My 18 '87

Great Britain

See also

Aston Martin Lagonda Ltd.

Fleur de Lys Automobile Manufacturing, Ltd.

Group Lotus Car Companies Ltd.

Jaguar plc

Rolls-Royce Motors Ltd.

Rover Group plc

Italy

See also

Alfa Romeo SpA

Ferrari SpA Esercizio Fabbriche Automobili e Corse

Fiat SpA

Lamborghini (Firm)

Zagato (Firm)

Japan

See also

Daihatsu Motor Co. Ltd.

Honda Motor Co., Ltd

Mitsubishi Motors Corp.

Nissan Motor Co. Ltd.

Suzuki Motor Company Ltd.

Toyota Motor Corporation

Carmakers are doing their dreaming in California [American and Japanese design studios in California] S. Toy. il *Bus Week* p50+ Mr 30 '87

End run [Japanese automakers in Taiwan] A. Tanzer. il *Forbes* 139:52 My 4 '87

Japan is winning friends in the Rust Belt [midwesterners becoming less protectionist as a result of Japanese auto plant locations] W. J. Holstein. il *Bus Week* p54 O 19 '87

Made in America: the Japanese auto cartel. A. T. Denzau. *Society* 24:30-5 S/O '87

Maybe this time . . . [Detroit hangs on against imports and immigrant autos] J. Flint. il *Forbes* 140:34 S 7 '87

Putting the brakes on the Orient Express [views of D. Halberstam on The reckoning] J. M. Fallows. *Wash Mon* 19:39-45 Ap '87

The rites of spring [Japanese autos in U.S. market] M. Keller. il *Mot Trend* 39:110 F '87

Korea (South)

See also

Daewoo Corporation

Hyundai Motor Co. Ltd.

The top of the wish list [appeal of low-priced Korean cars] M. Keller. il *Mot Trend* 39:130 Ap '87

Mexico

See also

Automobile factories—Mexico

Volkswagen de Mexico SA de CV

South Africa

See also

Samcor (Firm)

Sweden

See also

Saab-Scania AB

Taiwan

End run [Japanese automakers in Taiwan] A. Tanzer. il *Forbes* 139:52 My 4 '87

Automobile industry—*cont.*
United States
See Automobile industry
Western Europe
See also
Ford International Automotive Operations. Ford of Europe Inc.
Bargains in luxury car stocks? P. Duggan. il *Forbes* 140:146 D 28 '87
Somebody does it better [Ford and GM cars made in Europe] M. Keller. il *Mot Trend* 39:102 Ja '87
Automobile industry workers
See also
Automobile mechanics (Persons)
Strikes—Automobile industry workers
United Automobile, Aerospace and Agricultural Implement Workers of America
Women automobile industry workers
The Boz, the UAW, and your new Chevy [B. Bosworth's comments on assembly line workers] D. Fuller. il *Mot Trend* 39:116-17 Ja '87
Nissan, Tennessee [poor treatment of workers at Smyrna plant; cover story] J. Junkerman. il *Progressive* 51:16-18+ Je '87
A view from the shop floor [GM worker] J. K. Adamson. por *Newsweek* 109:8-9 F 9 '87
Salaries, pensions, etc.
A pension breakthrough [Chrysler Canada agrees to index pensions against inflation] D. Jenish. il *Macleans* 100:32-3 S 28 '87
A U-turn for Chrysler's fund [pension fund sells bonds to buy stocks] S. Weiss. *Bus Week* p146 Mr 23 '87
Why Chrysler's cash handles like a dream [treasurer of pension fund F. W. Zuckerman] S. Weiss. il por *Bus Week* p116 Je 8 '87
Training
Continuing education for blue-collar workers [UAW-Ford Employee Development and Training Program] P. H. Abelson. *Science* 238:875 N 13 '87
Automobile insurance *See* Insurance, Automobile
Automobile junkyards
Confessions of a junkyard junkie. M. Lamm. il *Pop Mech* 164:72-5 Mr '87
Automation
The high margins in heavy metal [AutoInfo] F. Meeks. il *Forbes* 140:82+ O 19 '87
Automobile laws and regulations *See* Automobiles—Laws and regulations
Automobile lighting *See* Automobiles—Lighting
Automobile locks and keys
Putting the skids on car theft [Quadra Lock system] R. Titus. il *Mot Trend* 39:116 Jl '87
Automobile lore
We call it autolore. M. T. Marsden. il *Mot Trend* 39:144 D '87
Automobile manuals *See* Automobiles—Handbooks, manuals, etc.
Automobile mechanics (Persons)
Car repairs: where can you go? Whom can you trust? T. Swan. il *Better Homes Gard* 65:98-9+ My '87
Driven to perfection [Porsche mechanic J. Howe] P. Bedard. il pors *Esquire* 107:109-10 Je '87
Smart strategies for car repair. il *Glamour* 85:96 S '87
Anecdotes, facetiae, satire, etc.
Tom Sawyer's garage. T. West. il *Road Track* 38:28 Je '87
Professional ethics
Highway robbery: the scandal of auto repair in America. R. Sikorsky. il por map *Read Dig* 130:90-9 My '87
Knock, knock. Who's there? A. Girdler. il *Road Track* 39:20 S '87
'Thieves' at the auto shop. E. Hofmann. por *Newsweek* 110:10-11 S 28 '87
Automobile models
1932 Rolls Royce Sedanca Coupe [wooden scale model] B. Couch. il *Workbench* 43:82-6 Ja/F '87
1935 Mercedes-Benz 500/AK [wooden replica] B. Couch. il *Workbench* 43:68-73 S/O '87
Cars in scale. G. Parrill. See occasional issues of Road & Track
Control
Radio racers. T. Assenza. il *Car Driv* 33:155-6+ Jl '87
Automobile museums
See also
Antique Auto and Music Museum (Stone Mountain, Ga.)
Vida's Vintage Vehicles Antique Car Museum
Automobile oil filters *See* Automobile engines—Filters
Automobile ownership
See also
Automobiles—Purchasing

Automobiles, Used—Selling
'227' star fills man void with pricey toy [A. Reed's autos] il por *Jet* 73:35 N 16 '87
The big wheels' wheels. E. Henry. il *Changing Times* 41:40-2+ Mr '87
The cars the customers love. S. J. Madden. il *Fortune* 116:78-9 N 9 '87
Celebrities and their favorite cars [black celebrities] il *Ebony* 43:27-8+ N '87
Musician cars. P. Egan. il *Road Track* 38:18 F '87
Staff cars [Popular mechanics] W. Hoyt. il *Pop Mech* 164:41 My '87
Writers remember: American authors look back on their favorite cars. P. Egan. il *Road Track* 38:108+ Je '87
Automobile painting *See* Automobiles—Painting
Automobile parking
See also
Garages
Garages, Municipal
Private parking. M. Myers. il *Rodale's Org Gard* 34:52-4 D '87
Automobile parts
See also
Automobile junkyards
Buying car parts. J. Koblenz. il *Home Mech* 83:83-4 Mr '87
Endangered species [demise of various auto parts] P. Bedard. il *Car Driv* 32:199 My '87
Miscellaneous ramblings. J. Dinkel. il *Road Track* 38:43-6 Jl '87
Automobile parts industry *See* Automobile equipment industry
Automobile race tracks *See* Speedways
Automobile racing
See also
Automobile racing drivers
Automobile rallies
Automobiles, Racing
Drag racing
Go-karting
Midwestern Council of Sports Car Clubs
National Association for Stock Car Auto Racing
Penske Corporation
Speedways
Truck racing
A $20 driving lesson [Solo II, autocross or slalom racing] M. Anson. *Mot Trend* 39:6 D '87
About the sport. J. Rusz. See issues of Road & Track
Blast from the past [vintage road racing] R. Taylor. il *Pop Mech* 164:78-81 Je '87
Chevy wins one for the gyppers! [Manufacturers Challenge Cup] J. Dinkel. il *Road Track* 39:38-40 N '87
Close company [Winston Cup series] A. Girdler. il *Road Track* 39:120-2+ D '87
Confessions of a vintage-racing junkie. R. Taylor. il *Car Driv* 33:149 D '87
Daytona do [A. Holbert's team wins 24 Hours of Daytona] J. Rusz. il *Road Track* 38:118-20+ My '87
Good to the last drop [B. Elliott wins the Daytona 500] S. Moses. il *Sports Illus* 66:32-3 F 23 '87
GTO spotter's guide. D. Sherman. il *Car Driv* 32:183-4+ Je '87
Have helmet, will travel [A. Unser, Sr. wins Indianapolis 500] S. Moses. il por *Sports Illus* 66:30-3 Je 1 '87
Holler-day on ice [race on Lake Superior] D. Knowles. il *Road Track* 38:114+ Mr '87
Indy 1987. T. West. il *Road Track* 39:142-6+ S '87
Indy air show [run for the Indianapolis 500 pole] S. Moses. il *Sports Illus* 66:22-7 My 18 '87
The Longest Day of Nelson 1987. J. Dinkel. il *Road Track* 39:126-8 O '87
Monterey histrionics [Monterey Historic Races honoring Chevrolet] D. Sherman. il *Car Driv* 33:138-9+ D '87
Motorsport. P. Bingham. See issues of Motor Trend
NASCAR '87: Winston Cup preview. B. Nagy. il *Mot Trend* 39:111-12+ My '87
Paul Newman and Tom Cruise spend a so-so day at the races, but fans lap it up anyway [Road Atlanta series] il pors *People Wkly* 28:36-7 Jl 13 '87
Perfection on Pikes Peak [hillclimb won by W. Röhrl] L. Griffin. il pors *Car Driv* 33:146-8+ N '87
Post-500 depression. B. W. Yates. il *Car Driv* 33:16 S '87
Racing isn't always racing [Showroom Stock racing] L. Frank. il *Mot Trend* 39:138 Mr '87
A revelation in Pittsburgh [Pittsburgh Vintage Grand Prix] D. Simanaitis. il *Road Track* 39:140+ N '87
Revival [sports car racing] P. Egan. il *Road Track* 39:18 D '87

Automobile racing—*cont.*

Rising to greatness [R. Dreyfus in the Mt. Equinox Hillclimb] T. West. il pors *Road Track* 38:56-60 Mr '87

Rubber match [Indianapolis 500] L. Griffin. il *Car Driv* 33:136-8+ S '87

Speed thrills [Indy 500] il *Sport Mag* 78:70-1 Je '87

Sport. L. Griffin. See issues of Car and Driver

Street smart in Motown [A. Senna and A. Prost in the Detroit Grand Prix] R. F. Jones. il pors *Sports Illus* 66:68-9 Je 29 '87

Summer stock [SCCA Showroom Stock racing] R. Titus. il *Mot Trend* 39:108-13+ Mr '87

Taking an active role [A. Senna wins Detroit Grand Prix] R. Walker. il *Road Track* 39:130-4 O '87

They burned up the track [A. Holbert's team in the 24 Hours of Daytona] S. Moses. il *Sports Illus* 66:72-3 F 9 '87

Time & place. See issues of Road & Track

Win on Sunday, sell on Monday [Nelson Ledges] M. Allen. il *Pop Mech* 164:149 O '87

Accidents and injuries

When Jim Fitzgerald was killed, racing lost its grand old man, and Paul Newman lost a friend. il pors *People Wkly* 28:122-3 N 23 '87

Anecdotes, facetiae, satire, etc.

Winter racing. P. Egan. il *Road Track* 38:16 Mr '87

Economic aspects

A candid interview with Mickey Matus, Ford SVO marketing manager. J. Asher. il por *Mot Trend* 39 no12 Sp Issue:90-3+ '87

Chrysler to go Grand Prix racing! N. Wollheim and others. *Mot Trend* 39:18 Ag '87

Jaguar's racing renaissance. M. Cotton. il *Mot Trend* 39:105-8 O '87

The Monaco of the Midwest [Grand Prix racing in Detroit] K. Springen. il *Newsweek* 110:42 Jl 13 '87

A new way to reach America's good ol' girls [corporate sponsors trying to attract women stock car fans] B. Bauer. il *U S News World Rep* 102:41 Je 29 '87

The price of victory. P. Bingham. il *Mot Trend* 39:163-4+ Je '87

History

The dawn of speed [origins of auto racing at Daytona] B. R. Kimes. il *Am Herit* 38:92-4+ N '87

John Surtees [seven-time world motorcycling champion and winner of the 1964 World Grand Prix Championship] C. Fox. il pors *Cycle* 38:68-71+ My '87

Monterey histrionics [Monterey Historic Races honoring Chevrolet] D. Sherman. il *Car Driv* 33:138-9+ D '87

Riverside Records [phonograph records from the 1950s] C. Farran. il *Road Track* 38:70-2 Ja '87

Rosemeyer revisited [discussion of July 1987 article, The Silver Comet] L. S. Riggs. *Car Driv* 33:16 N '87

The Silver Comet [Grand Prix driver B. Rosemeyer] L. S. Riggs. il pors *Car Driv* 33:141-2+ Jl '87

Sultan of the Smith Corona [auto relation L. S. Riggs] D. Sherman. il *Car Driv* 33:9 Jl '87

Ten best races of all time. B. W. Yates. il *Car Driv* 32:43-7 Ja '87

To race for love or money [1967 Daytona 500] I. Ireland. il *Road Track* 38:136-8+ My '87

Varzi's honor [A. Varzi] L. S. Riggs. il pors *Car Driv* 32:143-4+ Mr '87

Years ago. See issues of Road & Track

Anecdotes, facetiae, satire, etc.

Even fungus has them . . . [sneaking into Los Angeles County Fairgrounds in 1960] T. West. il *Road Track* 38:18 Ap '87

The Indy book of weird records. D. Davidson. il *Mot Trend* 39:118-23+ Je '87

Photographs and photography

Images that linger: forty years of racing in Road & track. J. T. Crow. il *Road Track* 38:98-102+ Je '87

On these hallowed venues [excerpt from With flying colours] il *Car Driv* 33:145-8+ O '87

International aspects

The 1986 Grand Prix season [A. Prost wins World Driving Championship] J. Thompson. il *Road Track* 38:148-50+ Mr '87

Alain Prost: world champion. P. Windsor. il pors *Car Driv* 32:111-16+ F '87

Has Formula One gotten too fast? [changes in regulations to reduce power of F1 engines] B. Cahier and P. Bingham. il *Mot Trend* 39:149-50+ My '87

King Honda reigns in the F1 title joust. B. Cahier and B. Nagy. il *Mot Trend* 39:133-6 D '87

Niki Lauda: meine story [excerpt] N. Lauda. il pors *Mot Trend* 39:105-8 Ja '87

Racing's record-breaker [A. Prost] S. McBride. il pors *N Y Times Mag* p42+ N 8 '87

Unsung hero [world champion D. Bell resigns from Porsche team to race in the U.S.] R. Bulgin. il pors *Mot Trend* 39:115-17 F '87

Rules

F1 technical regs, all change, yet again. A. Henry. *Road Track* 38:122 F '87

Has Formula One gotten too fast? [changes in regulations to reduce power of F1 engines] B. Cahier and P. Bingham. il *Mot Trend* 39:149-50+ My '87

Summer stock (some are not) [SCCA and IMSA pro showroom stock] J. Rusz. il *Road Track* 38:112+ Ag '87

Study and teaching

Buck Baker Driving School. M. Anson. il *Mot Trend* 39:78 F '87

Anecdotes, facetiae, satire, etc.

Upon the fyne arte of flying the coupe [racing lessons from J. Stewart] T. West. il *Road Track* 38:22 F '87

Australia

Nigel's championship hopes go flat [A. Prost wins Australian Grand Prix] I. Ireland. il *Road Track* 38:126-8+ F '87

Racing with the sun [5M Sunraycer] il *Sci News* 132:219 O 3 '87

Racing with the sun [Pentax Solar Challenge: cover story] D. McCosh. il map *Pop Sci* 231:84-7 N '87

Solar-powered cars to race across Australia. il *Radio-Electron* 58:4 N '87

Winning a race in the sun [Sunraycer] *Sci News* 132:349 N 28 '87

Austria

Now Nelson, now Nigel [N. Piquet wins Hungarian Grand Prix; N. Mansell wins Austrian Grand Prix] I. Ireland. il *Road Track* 39:134-8+ D '87

Baja California (Mexico: Peninsula)

A thousand miles of bad road [Baja 1000] D. Granger. il *Sport Mag* 78:90 F '87

Belgium

Prost claims the magic 27 [Belgian Grand Prix] I. Ireland. il *Road Track* 39:128-30+ S '87

Brazil

The champ, like a champ [A. Prost wins Brazilian Grand Prix] I. Ireland. il *Road Track* 38:140-2+ Jl '87

A day in the life of the world's best race driver [A. Senna at the Brazilian Grand Prix] R. Bulgin. il pors *Mot Trend* 39:115-18 Ag '87

France

See also

Automobile rallies—France

24 Heures du Mans 1987. P. L. Albrecht. il *Road Track* 39:160-4+ N '87

Williamsville [N. Mansell wins French Grand Prix] I. Ireland. il *Road Track* 39:136-8 O '87

Germany (West)

Williams again [N. Piquet wins German Grand Prix] I. Ireland. il *Road Track* 39:152-4+ N '87

Great Britain

Minute Man(sell) [N. Mansell wins British Grand Prix] R. Walker. il *Road Track* 39:144-6+ N '87

Hungary

Now Nelson, now Nigel [N. Piquet wins Hungarian Grand Prix; N. Mansell wins Austrian Grand Prix] I. Ireland. il *Road Track* 39:134-8+ D '87

Italy

Black flag, black mood for Prost [N. Piquet wins Italian Grand Prix] I. Ireland. il pors *Road Track* 38:128-30 Ja '87

Mille Miglia 1987. il *Road Track* 39:80+ O '87

The Mille Miglia lives! L. Griffin. il map *Car Driv* 33:134-5+ O '87

Mostly Mansell [N. Mansell wins San Marino Grand Prix] R. Walker. il *Road Track* 38:144-6+ Ag '87

Anecdotes, facetiae, satire, etc.

Having fun while getting even [inexpensive tour of Mille Miglia course] T. C. Browne. map *Mot Trend* 39:144-5 Ap '87

History

1930 Mille Miglia. J. T. Crow. il *Road Track* 38:72 Ag '87

The Monza 500 races [1957 and 1958 races between Indy car drivers and Grand Prix drivers] D. Davidson. il *Road Track* 38:202-4+ Je '87

Mexico

Berger king [G. Berger wins the Mexican Grand Prix] R. Walker. il por *Road Track* 38:120-2+ F '87

La Carrera Classic II. T. Assenza. il *Car Driv* 33:135-6+ Ag '87

Automobile racing—*cont.*
Monaco
Senna savvy [Monaco Grand Prix] R. Walker. il *Road Track* 39:136-8 S '87
Portugal
More Mansell magic [N. Mansell wins Portuguese Grand Prix] R. Walker. il por *Road Track* 38:132-4 Ja '87
Soviet Union
USSRRRC. M. Kuuse. il *Road Track* 39:138+ N '87
United States
See Automobile racing
Western Europe
All crossed up [rallycross] W. Hoyt. il *Pop Mech* 164:32 Ja '87
Automobile racing drivers
See also
Bell, Derek
Berger, Gerhard
Bernstein, Kenny
Dreyfus, René
Earnhardt, Dale
Elliott, Bill
Holbert, Al
Mansell, Nigel
Millen, Steve
Piquet, Nelson
Prost, Alain
Rahal, Bobby
Richmond, Tim
Röhrl, Walter
Rosemeyer, Bernd
Senna, Ayrton
St. James, Lyn
Sullivan, Danny
Surtees, John
Unser, Al, 1939-
Varzi, Achille, 1904-1948
1986 Formula 1 annual drivers' ratings: four above the rest. R. Walker. il *Road Track* 38:144-7 Mr '87
1987 Grand Prix spotter's guide. il *Road Track* 38:134-8 Jl '87
Motorsport. P. Bingham. See issues of Motor Trend
Six of the best: the human beings behind the helmets. P. Bingham. il *Mot Trend* 39:139-42 Ap '87
Who goes where [F1 drivers and teams] il *Mot Trend* 39:152 My '87
Health and hygiene
Fit to win [McGill University's Motor Sport Research Group] T. West. il *Road Track* 38:126-8+ Je '87
Automobile racing fans
A new way to reach America's good ol' girls [corporate sponsors trying to attract women stock car fans] B. Bauer. il *U S News World Rep* 102:41 Je 29 '87
Automobile radios *See* Automobiles—Radio equipment
Automobile rallies
Death of the killer Bs [Olympus Rally for Group B rally cars] L. Griffin. il *Car Driv* 32:165-73+ Ap '87
From sea to shining sea [Plymouth Pride in America Road Rally in which participants depend on the generosity of strangers] M. Neill. il map *People Wkly* 28:28-33 S 21 '87
Rally 'round the pace car, boys [Toyota Olympus Rally] P. King. il *Mot Trend* 39:139-42+ N '87
Seven days in April [One Lap of America] B. W. Yates. il *Car Driv* 33:21 Ag '87
International aspects
Eight thousand miles of bad road [Paris-Dakar Rally] E. A. McCabe. il pors map *Esquire* 108:96-104 Jl '87
France
Night without end [racing across France to bring Beaujolais nouveau back to England] P. Bingham. il *Mot Trend* 39:55-6+ My '87
Automobile renting *See* Automobiles—Leasing and renting
Automobile research
See also
Automobiles, Experimental
Automobile sales personnel
See also
Automobile dealers
Professional ethics
The customer's right to be wrong [study by Peter J. DePaulo] J. C. Horn. il *Psychol Today* 21:12 Ja '87
Automobile service stations
See also
American Lubrication Company
John Howe West Inc.
The 9 to 5 Garage [Bronx Volvo garage owned by Vietnam veterans] W. Weith. il *Car Driv* 32:25-6 Mr '87

Grease job [Grease Pro ten-minute oil change place in Panama City, Fla.] P. Bedard. il *Car Driv* 33:158 N '87
Now, the McLube. *Newsweek* 109:48 Je 15 '87
Sushi and an oil change [auto repair malls] J. Parr. il *Forbes* 140:93-4 Ag 24 '87
Japan
See also
Lions Petroleum Company
Automobile shows *See* Automobiles—Exhibitions
Automobile speed records
Flat out [endurance speed record set in Saab 9000 Turbo] B. Warner. il *Road Track* 38:124+ Ap '87
Automobile styling *See* Automobiles—Design
Automobile supplies *See* Automobiles—Equipment
Automobile supply industry *See* Automobile equipment industry
Automobile telephones *See* Cellular radio in automobiles
Automobile test equipment *See* Testing equipment
Automobile tires *See* Tires, Automobile
Automobile tools *See* Tools
Automobile touring
Eating out . . . when you're on the road. il *Glamour* 85:192 Jl '87
The heartland highway [traveling U.S. 50 from Ocean City, Md. to Sacramento, Calif. in Porsche 911 Cabriolet] L. Griffin. il map *Car Driv* 32:84-7+ Ap '87
Merkur Scorpio [driving cross country] D. C. Ross and others. il *Mot Trend* 39:78-80+ My '87
Romancing the road: the all-American drive to nowhere. il *Glamour* 85:100 S '87
Sea to Sterling sea [driving a Sterling 825S across the U.S.] J. R. Nerad. *Mot Trend* 39:66-7 F '87
Summer driving guide. E. Janicki and J. C. McAdams. il *Essence* 18:107-8 Jl '87
Ten best and worst things to eat in the car. P. Bedard. il *Car Driv* 32:69 Ja '87
Anecdotes, facetiae, satire, etc.
Trekking in America [driving cross country in an English car] T. West. il *Road Track* 38:36 Ag '87
Algeria
Into Africa [testing Audis in the Algerian Sahara] P. Bingham. il map *Mot Trend* 39:118-23+ D '87
Just desert [driving Audis through the Sahara] J. Rusz. il *Road Track* 39:54-6 N '87
Atlantic States
A separate reality on I-95. J. O'Reilly. il *Time* 130:10 N 30 '87
Australia
America's car to America's Cup (I) [driving a Corvette from Melbourne to Perth] J. R. Nerad. il *Mot Trend* 39:34-7+ Mr '87
America's car to America's Cup (II) [driving a Corvette from Melbourne to Perth] J. R. Nerad. il map *Mot Trend* 39:86-92 Ap '87
Brazil
Tally-ho, Carioca! [driving a VW Fox] D. Clendenin. il *Road Track* 38:186-8+ My '87
California
California gold rush country. I. Ireland. il map *Road Track* 38:52-6 F '87
Maturity with taste: a visit to northern California wine country in a Mitsubishi Galant. il *Mot Trend* 39:101+ Jl '87
Where the Gold Rush began . . . an autumn drive [Georgetown Divide] il map *Sunset* 179:12-13+ O '87
Where the tasting never stops [Sonoma Valley wineries] J. Hooper. il *Esquire* 108:51+ S '87
France
Paris isn't bad, but have you seen Amboise? I. Pave. il *Bus Week* p109 Je 29 '87
Morocco
Morocco's mystique. D. Brown. il por *Essence* 18:20+ N '87
Pennsylvania
The case of the kidnapped couple [practice of stopping cars from out of town to show off West Chester, Pa. as part of Boost Pennsylvania Week] B. Greene. il *Esquire* 107:45-6 Mr '87
Romania
Multi ani, Romania! E. Serotta. il *Road Track* 38:102-4 Ja '87
Southern Africa
Landscapes open and closed. B. Lopez. il map *Harpers* 275:51-8 Jl '87
Southwestern States
Southwestward: the great American space. A. Kazin. il map *Am Herit* 38:52-61 Ap '87

Automobile touring—*cont.*
United States
See Automobile touring
Western Europe
Six-wheeling the Alps [BMW K75 and BMW325i in the Tyrolean Alps] T. West. il *Road Track* 38:132-4+ F '87
Yugoslavia
Wherever Yugo, there you are [driving a Yugo GVL from Belgrade to Dubrovnik] J. R. Nerad. il *Mot Trend* 39:72-8+ Ag '87
Automobile touring with children *See* Travel with children
Automobile traffic *See* City traffic
Automobile trailers
> *See also*
> Automobile boat trailers

A buyer's guide to vacation vehicles. M. Thompson and D. Prestly. il *Fam Handyman* 37:97-100+ Ap '87
The countryman's trailer. E. N. Robinson. il *Ctry J* 14:25-7 My '87
On the road again [Airstream trailer couple Lueen and Howard Miller] R. Micheli. il *Money* 16:140-4 S '87
Tenting camping trailers. T. Opre. il *Outdoor Life* 180:58+ Jl '87
Towing
How to handle summer's special driving conditions. D. McCluggage. il *Glamour* 85:96+ Jl '87
Pullin' its weight [trailer towing capabilities of Ford's F-Series trucks] il *Mot Trend* 39 no12 Sp Issue:89 '87
Wiring adapter for a trailer hitch. H. F. Williamson. il *Pop Sci* 230:110 Ap '87
Automobile trips *See* Automobile touring
Automobile vacuum cleaners *See* Vacuum cleaners
Automobile warranty *See* Warranty
Automobile wheels *See* Automobiles—Wheels
Automobile workers *See* Automobile industry workers; Automobile mechanics (Persons)
Automobiles
> *See also*
> Convertibles (Automobiles)
> Jeep automobiles
> Sports cars
> Station wagons
> Trucks

5 million smiles [PM owners report on Chevy Nova, Saab 9000, Pontiac Bonneville] M. Lamm. il *Pop Mech* 164:76-8+ N '87
The 1987 cars [cover story; special issue] il *Consum Rep* 52:195-202+ Ap '87
1988 Detroit model review. R. Huntington. il *Consum Res Mag* 70:11-13 N '87
The 1988s are here. D. Chaikin and M. Ferrara. il *Home Mech* 83:82-5 N '87
AMC 1988. il *Mot Trend* 39:72-5 O '87
Ask the man who owns one [Buick Riviera, Dodge Shadow/Plymouth Sundance, Acura Legend] M. Lamm. il *Pop Mech* 164:59-62+ Ag '87
Automotive newsfront. D. McCosh. See issues of Popular Science beginning January 1986
Black enterprise auto guide: new faces of 1988 [special section] J. Koblenz. il *Black Enterp* 18:75+ N '87
Cars for 1988. il *Ebony* 43:170-1+ N '87
Chrysler 1988. il *Mot Trend* 39:77-8+ O '87
Chrysler, Ford and Premier of 1988. P. Lienert. il *Road Track* 39:106+ O '87
Chrysler LeBaron GTS and Dodge Lancer [owners report] M. Lamm. il *Pop Mech* 164:67+ Mr '87
Detroit report. D. C. Ross. See issues of Motor Trend
For your information. A. St. Antoine. See issues of Car and Driver
Ford 1988. il *Mot Trend* 39:83-5 O '87
Ford Taurus/Mercury Sable [owners report] M. Lamm. il *Pop Mech* 164:137-8+ F '87
Freewheeling. W. Hoyt. See issues of Popular Mechanics beginning January 1986
GM 1988. il *Mot Trend* 39:86-91+ O '87
GM flexes its 1988 muscle. P. Lienert. il *Road Track* 39:126+ N '87
Here come the '88s. *U S News World Rep* 103:75 O 12 '87
Letter from Detroit. P. Lienert. See issues of Road & Track through December 1987
A look at the '88s. E. Henry. il *Changing Times* 41:106 S '87
The new Family handyman garage. M. Thompson. See issues of The Family Handyman beginning July/August 1987
Owner survey: Ford Thunderbird. D. C. Ross. il *Mot Trend* 39:89-90 Mr '87

Sneak peeks—new cars from around the globe. D. McCosh. il *Pop Sci* 230:70-1 Ja '87
Ten best [special section] il *Car Driv* 32:35-41+ Ja '87
USA '88: new car preview. D. C. Ross. il *Mot Trend* 39:99-100+ S '87
Women and cars. L. J. Nonkin. See issues of Vogue beginning January 1986
Women and their cars. See issues of McCall's beginning April 1986
Accessories
See Automobiles—Equipment
Accidents
See Traffic accidents
Advertising
See Automobile industry—Advertising
Aerodynamics
New shape, new image [work of Ford designer J. Telnack] R. Voegelin. il pors *Mot Trend* 39 no12 Sp Issue:22-5 '87
The shape of Ford's success [designer J. Telnack; cover story] P. Patton. il pors *N Y Times Mag* p18-22+ My 24 '87
Air bags
TRW's air-bag business looks ready to balloon. S. Phillips. il *Bus Week* p74+ N 2 '87
Air conditioning
Auto air conditioning. il *Mother Earth News* 106:110+ Jl/Ag '87
Alarms
Auto alarm systems. il *Consum Rep* 52:97-101 D '87
Car alarms are getting smarter all the time. S. Woolley. il *Bus Week* p150 O 19 '87
Headlight alarm. C. Lowell. il *Radio-Electron* 58:67 Ap '87
How alarms compare. E. Henry. il *Changing Times* 41:34 Ag '87
Audio systems
> *See also*
> Automobiles—Radio equipment

Alpine 7902 car tuner/CD player. il *High Fidel* 37:37-8+ Jl '87
Auto sound [cover story; special section] F. Vizard. il *Radio-Electron* 58:31-3+ Jl '87
Auto sound goes truckin'. F. Vizard. il *Roll Stone* p69-70 Je 18 '87
The autophile. J. C. Taylor. See occasional issues of High Fidelity (New York, N.Y.) beginning February 1985
Autosound [special section] il *Pop Mech* 164:103-8+ Je '87
B&W MASS car speakers. C. Greenleaf. il *Stereo Rev* 52:162+ Ja '87
The best sound on wheels [car CD players] A. Eisenberg. il *Stereo Rev* 52:59-63 My '87
Big Three autosound update. C. J. Esse. il *High Fidel* 37:11-12 My '87
Blaupunkt TQR-07 Berlin car tuner/tape deck. il *High Fidel* 37:35+ O '87
Car CD players: big sound, big price, big problem. N. Henderson. il *Changing Times* 41:93-6 Ap '87
Car stereo. C. Greenleaf and J. D. Hirsch. See alternate issues of Stereo Review
Car stereo [special report] il *High Fidel* 37:35-8+ My '87
Car stereo manufacturers. il *Stereo Rev* 52:65-6 My '87
Car tunes. F. Vizard. il *Pop Mech* 164:81-3+ My '87
Clarion Audia 200 car front end. il *High Fidel* 37:44+ Mr '87
Compact disc for your car [CD adapters] M. Thompson. il *Fam Handyman* 37:92-3 S '87
DAT: going mobile. F. Vizard. il *Pop Mech* 164:36 Jl '87
Geared for sound. J. C. Taylor. il *High Fidel* 37:54-7 O '87
Gearing up for car stereo. I. Masters. il *Stereo Rev* 52:52-6 My '87
The great equalizers. C. J. Esse. il *High Fidel* 37:14+ N '87
Jensen JS-6400 car stereo receiver/tape deck. il *High Fidel* 37:43-4 O '87
Sherwood CRD-350 car front end. il *High Fidel* 37:42-4 Mr '87
Testing car stereo. J. D. Hirsch. il *Stereo Rev* 52:30-1 Mr '87
Turning your car into a concert hall. W. J. Hampton. il *Bus Week* p85 Ag 31 '87
Versatile autosound [Blaupunkt system] F. Vizard. il *Pop Mech* 164:42 N '87
Competitions
Crank 'em ups. R. Hodges. il *Stereo Rev* 52:132 My '87

Automobiles—Audio systems—Competitions—*cont.*
In search of excellence [Car Audio Nationals] C. J. Esse. il *High Fidel* 37:16-17 D '87
Thunder road: the sound and the fury at the first Car Audio Nationals. F. Vizard. il *Roll Stone* p123-4 N 19 '87

Maintenance and repair
Keeping the music clear. M. Ferrara. il *Home Mech* 83:38 Ap '87

Security measures
Antisocial security. J. C. Taylor. *High Fidel* 37:43 My '87
Stop, thief! I. Berger. il *Road Track* 38:122-4 Mr '87

Awards
See also
Motor Trend Awards
Anecdotes, facetiae, satire, etc.
Ten best winners and losers, 1986. T. Azzenza. il *Car Driv* 32:81-3 Ja '87

Batteries
See Storage batteries

Bibliography
Reviews. See issues of Road & Track

Bodies
Body dimensions. il *Consum Rep* 52:254-6 Ap '87
Tune up your body. il *Pop Mech* 164:146-8 My '87

Bodies, Remodeled
See Automobiles, Remodeled

Brakes
See Brakes, Automobile

Braking
See Automobiles—Stopping

Business use
See Automobiles in business

Camping equipment
See also
Automobile trailers

Carburetors
See Carburetors

Care
See Automobiles—Maintenance and repair

Chassis
Tune up your chassis. il *Pop Mech* 164:128-30+ My '87

Cleaning
See also
Turtle Wax (Firm)
Do power washers really work? M. Thompson. il *Fam Handyman* 37:81-2 Jl/Ag '87
Doin' the neutron buff [cleaning a Ford Escort at Steve's Detailing] T. Assenza. il *Car Driv* 32:23 My '87
For a sparkling interior. M. Ferrara. il *Home Mech* 83:16 My '87
Tune up your body. il *Pop Mech* 164:146-8 My '87
Tune up your interior. il *Pop Mech* 164:140-1+ My '87
WallWalker wizard's washup wonder [Turbo-Wash creator F. Reinstein] G. Buchalter. il por *Forbes* 139:240 My 18 '87

Clubs
See Automobile clubs

Clutches
Viscosity for sale [Ferguson viscous coupling] C. Csere. il *Car Driv* 32:116 Mr '87

Collectors and collecting
Automotive shrining. M. T. Marsden. il *Mot Trend* 39:160 Je '87
Fins and chrome in a classic comeback. J. A. Seamonds. il *U S News World Rep* 103:78 S 21 '87
Got a '56 Chevy? You'll find a buyer in Japan. il *Newsweek* 110:63 O 26 '87
Rancho Cadillac [E. Cholakian's collection] T. Assenza. il pors *Car Driv* 32:101+ Mr '87

Collisions with animals
See Automobile driving—Animal hazards

Communication systems
Taking communications to the road. M. T. Marsden. il *Mot Trend* 39:128 Mr '87

Control
Preaching to the converted [automatic ride control system] M. Anson. *Mot Trend* 39:8 F '87

Cost of operation
Car costs. M. S. Dolan. *Consum Res Mag* 70:2 Ag '87

Costs
How much does your car really cost? M. Ferrara. il *Home Mech* 83:77-8 Ja '87

Dashboards
The dashboard as mantelpiece. M. T. Marsden. il *Mot Trend* 39:112 F '87

Miscellaneous ramblings [improper placement of switches and controls] J. Dinkel. il *Road Track* 38:31-2 Ap '87

Decoration
See Automobile decoration

Defects
See also
Automobiles—Recall
Danger: defects. E. Henry. *Changing Times* 41:47-9 Ap '87
Miscellaneous ramblings [origins of lemon laws] J. Dinkel. il *Road Track* 38:35 Mr '87

Demolition derbies
See Automobile demolition derbies

Design
See also
Automobiles—Safety devices and measures
Automobiles, Foreign—Design
Automobiles, Racing—Design
Convertibles (Automobiles)—Design
Industrie Pininfarina SpA
Sports cars—Design
America the beautiful [designer cars from American studios] J. Dunne. il *Pop Mech* 164:79-81 Ap '87
An auto designer at home [J. Schinella] M. Ferrara. il pors *Home Mech* 83:68-9 Jl '87
Beguiling Berettas. J. Lamm. il *Road Track* 39:74 D '87
A Caprice for the '90s [Chevrolet] D. C. Ross. il *Mot Trend* 39:17 S '87
Carmakers are doing their dreaming in California [American and Japanese design studios in California] S. Toy. il *Bus Week* p50+ Mr 30 '87
Cars of 1990's [University of Michigan's forecast] il *USA Today (Periodical)* 116:12 Ag '87
Cars of the 90's [cover story; special section] il *U S News World Rep* 103:38-45 Ag 10 '87
Charting the changes [1988 cars] A. St. Antoine. il *Car Driv* 33:49-51+ O '87
The Chrysler guidebook to creative packaging [spinning new models from old designs] il *Fortune* 115:39 Je 22 '87
Chrysler's crystal ball. P. Lienert. *Road Track* 38:98 My '87
Detroit sneak preview. J. Dunne. il *Pop Mech* 164:76-7+ Je '87
Engineering the new cars. il *Pop Mech* 164:135-42 O '87
Foreign bodies [European styling] M. Knepper. il *Harpers Bazaar* 120:132+ F '87
Future Daytona [1990 Dodge Daytona] D. McCosh. il *Pop Sci* 230:18 My '87
GM's new cars for the nineties. P. Lienert. il *Road Track* 39:94+ S '87
New-car designs hot off the press. D. Sherman. il *Car Driv* 33:11 D '87
New shape, new image [work of Ford designer J. Telnack] R. Voegelin. il pors *Mot Trend* 39 no12 Sp Issue:22-5 '87
Now we're getting somewhere [drawings of Saturn cars] D. C. Ross. il *Mot Trend* 39:18-19 Mr '87
The priority is design [1988 models] J. Dunne. il *Pop Mech* 164:51-8 O '87
The shape of Ford's success [designer J. Telnack; cover story] P. Patton. il pors *N Y Times Mag* p18-22+ My 24 '87
The stylist who put Ford out in front [J. Telnack] A. L. Taylor, III. il por *Fortune* 115:78+ Ja 5 '87
Ten best designers. M. Jordan. il pors *Car Driv* 32:58-62 Ja '87
Ten ugliest cars. L. Griffin. il *Car Driv* 32:62 Ja '87

Driving
See Automobile driving

Economic aspects
See also
Automobiles—Cost of operation
Automobiles—Purchasing

Electric equipment
Connection cleaning. M. Thompson. il *Fam Handyman* 37:85 O '87

Electric wiring
Preventing battery brownouts. P. Stenquist. il *Pop Mech* 164:111-14 Ag '87
Repairing/replacing battery cables. M. Thompson. il *Fam Handyman* 37:66 F '87
Short circuits. B. Cerullo. il *Pop Sci* 230:106+ F '87
Smart circuits revolutionize auto wiring. D. McCosh. il *Pop Sci* 230:71-4+ Je '87

Electronic equipment
See also
Radar detectors

Automobiles—Electronic equipment—*cont.*

The automotive world of the 21st century. D. E. Petersen. il *Radio-Electron* 58:91-5 My '87

Computerized anvils and torches [1988 Lincoln Continental's computer controlled air suspension] P. Bedard. il *Car Driv* 33:152 O '87

Computerized oil-change reminder. D. McCosh. il *Pop Sci* 231:132 O '87

Driving by the glow of a screen [Etak Navigator and DriverGuide] P. Elmer-Dewitt. il *Time* 129:63 Ap 20 '87

Gee, Mr. Wizard! [electronic gadgets] D. Sherman. il *Car Driv* 33:111+ Jl '87

Pocket-size dragstrip [Vericom VC-200 Performance Computer] R. Titus. il *Mot Trend* 39:124 Mr '87

Environmental aspects

Alcohol fuels move off the back burner. M. Ivey. il *Bus Week* p100-1 Je 29 '87

Equipment

See also
Automobile equipment industry
Automobile horns
Automobiles—Audio systems
Automobiles—Radio equipment
Automobiles—Safety devices and measures
Speedometers
Tires, Automobile

All the sights, sounds and comforts of home. L. Wiener. il *U S News World Rep* 103:45 Ag 10 '87

A buyer's guide to ski racks. P. Oliver. il *Skiing* 40:220+ D '87

Car comforts to make driving more fun. D. McCluggage. il *Glamour* 85:208+ Mr '87

Freedom of choice vs. a good deal. M. Keller. il *Mot Trend* 39:146 D '87

GM's 1988 prices are lower—in a way. J. B. Treece. il *Bus Week* p41-2 O 12 '87

How to protect your car from the sun [use of shades and covers] M. Thompson. il *Fam Handyman* 37:109-15 My/Je '87

Make your car even better. M. Anson. il *Mot Trend* 39:8 N '87

New/auto. See issues of Popular Mechanics beginning January 1986

The new modular cartop racks . . . what can they really carry? il *Sunset* 178:124-5+ Ap '87

Options you can add—after you've bought the car. D. Chaikin. il *Home Mech* 83:80-2 Mr '87

A shady business [selling advertising on auto screens by Auto-Shade] il *Newsweek* 109:61 My 11 '87

What's new? il *Pop Mech* 164:168+ My '87

What's new for your car. J. Keebler. See issues of Popular Science

Which options to choose? il *Consum Rep* 52:204-5 Ap '87

Exhibitions

See also
Henry Ford Museum and Greenfield Village

1986 British Motor Show. R. Hutton. il *Car Driv* 32:24 F '87

1987 Frankfurt Auto Show. il *Car Driv* 33:34-5 D '87

An American in Geneva. J. Rusz and P. Frère. il *Road Track* 38:102+ Jl '87

Chicago Auto Show. P. Lienert. il *Road Track* 38:94+ My '87

Corvette Mecca [Bloomington, Ill.] C. Gromer. il *Pop Mech* 164:16-17 D '87

Geneva '87. M. Cotton. il *Mot Trend* 39:81-3+ Jl '87

Henry Ford Museum & Greenfield Village [The automobile in American life exhibit] il *Antiques Collect Hobbies* 92:47-8 Jl '87

Paris Auto Show. il *Car Driv* 32:31 Ja '87

Paris Salon 1987. M. Cotton. il *Mot Trend* 39:52-4+ F '87

Road shows [vintage car shows] E. Henry and J. Yonan. il *Changing Times* 41:88-90+ S '87

Souvenirs de Paris. il *Road Track* 38:112+ Ja '87

Time & place. See issues of Road & Track

Export-import trade

The 3,000-pound European souvenir [buying a car in Europe to be shipped to the U.S.] M. Opsata. il *50 Plus* 27:68-75 Je '87

Can Chrysler make a comeback in Europe, too? J. B. Treece. il *Bus Week* p168-9 N 16 '87

Clobbering car buyers [U.S. auto industry calls for new limits on Japanese imports] R. J. Samuelson. il *Newsweek* 110:69 D 14 '87

Detroit vs. new upscale imports. A. L. Taylor, III. il *Fortune* 115:69-70+ Ap 27 '87

A hot American car may hit Japan: the Honda [strong yen could prompt Japanese carmakers to reexport from the U.S.] W. J. Hampton and others. il *Bus Week* p50 Ja 26 '87

It's tough, but it isn't doomsday [Japanese import share of U.S. new car market] R. Phalon. il *Forbes* 139:53+ My 4 '87

Just what the U.S. needs: an even smaller car from Japan [Daihatsu's Charade] S. Toy. il *Bus Week* p26 Ap 20 '87

Made in America: the Japanese auto cartel. A. T. Denzau. *Society* 24:30-5 S/O '87

Maybe this time . . . [Detroit hangs on against imports and immigrant autos] J. Flint. il *Forbes* 140:34 S 7 '87

More Chevys may be cruising the Autobahn. J. E. Pluenneke. il *Bus Week* p55 Mr 16 '87

New vroom [Alfa Romeo tackles U.S. market] P. Berman. il *Forbes* 139:79 Ja 26 '87

The rites of spring [Japanese autos in U.S. market] M. Keller. il *Mot Trend* 39:110 F '87

The road most traveled [Hyundai] S. B. Weiner. il *Forbes* 140:60+ O 19 '87

Saying hello to BMW-san [BMW's success in exporting cars to Japan] B. Hillenbrand. il *Time* 129:56-7 My 25 '87

Shh! Please don't call this car a Rover [Sterling] M. Maremont. il *Bus Week* p59 Ja 12 '87

The top of the wish list [appeal of low-priced Korean cars] M. Keller. il *Mot Trend* 39:130 Ap '87

What Ford can afford [argument for cutting car prices to fight imports] P. A. London. *New Repub* 196:16+ Je 8 '87

You've come a long way, baby [U.S. foreign car market] M. Anson. il *Mot Trend* 39:6 Ap '87

Fires and fire prevention

What to do if your car catches fire. D. McCluggage. il *Glamour* 85:216+ Ap '87

Four wheel drive

See also
Automobiles, Foreign—Four wheel drive
Automobiles, Remodeled—Four wheel drive
Jeep automobiles
Sports cars—Four wheel drive
Station wagons—Four wheel drive

1987 Ford Tempo All Wheel Drive. D. C. Ross. il *Mot Trend* 39:58-60 My '87

Driving on all fours. W. D. Marbach. il *Newsweek* 109:69 Mr 16 '87

Family cars that go in snow, mud and rain. D. Chaikin. il *Home Mech* 83:44-6+ My '87

Ford Tempo All Wheel Drive. A. St. Antoine. il *Car Driv* 33:103+ S '87

Four-wheeling into your future. J. Rettie. il *Pop Mech* 164:56-8+ Ag '87

PM long-term car tests: Dodge Shadow Turbo, Tempo 4WD, Corvette Convertible. M. Allen and J. Oldham. il *Pop Mech* 164:120-1+ D '87

PM's long-term test reports [Corvette Roadster, Dodge Shadow Turbo, Ford Tempo 4WD] il *Pop Mech* 164:53-5+ Ag '87

Traction for sale [history of four wheel drive] C. Csere. il *Car Driv* 32:113+ Mr '87

Front wheel drive

See also
Automobiles, Foreign—Front wheel drive

Designed to be different [GM10 cars] T. Assenza. il *Car Driv* 33:44-5 O '87

GM's future may ride on two new Chevys [Beretta and Corsica] W. Zellner. il *Bus Week* p41 Ap 6 '87

Revealed! '90 Chevrolet GM 10. D. C. Ross. il *Mot Trend* 39:28-9 N '87

Tracking GM's Taurus beaters [GM10 project] P. Lienert. il *Road Track* 38:106+ Ag '87

Fuel systems

See Automobile engines—Fuel feeding

Gas mileage

See Automobile engines—Energy usage; Diesel engines, Automotive—Energy usage

Gearing

See also
Automobiles—Steering gear
Automobiles—Transmission

Handbooks, manuals, etc.

Tools of the trade [auto tools and service manuals] il *Pop Mech* 164:150-1+ My '87

Heating and ventilation

Winter car comfort. M. Ferrara. il *Home Mech* 83:22 D '87

Automobiles—*cont.*

History

See also

Automobiles, Antique
Automobiles, Racing—History
Convertibles (Automobiles)—History
Sports cars—History

1939 Graham Series 97 Supercharger. H. Rasmussen. il *Mot Trend* 39:93-6+ Ja '87
1950 Mercury Sport Coupe. H. Rasmussen. il *Mot Trend* 39:147-52+ Je '87
1951 Nash Ambassador Super. T. C. Browne. il *Mot Trend* 39:109-14+ S '87
1955 Ford Thunderbird. S. Tyson. il *Mot Trend* 39 no12 Sp Issue:78-83 '87
De Soto Adventurer II [1954] P. Bedard. il *Car Driv* 33:58-61 S '87
Déjà vroom [1987 Mustang LX and Firebird Formula vs. 1970 Mustang Boss 302 and 1969 Trans Am] il *Road Track* 39:44-52 S '87
Faded glory [American luxury cars] W. Hoyt. il *Pop Mech* 164:16 Jl '87
Road & track 40th anniversary [special section; with editorial comment by Peter Egan] il *Road Track* 38:20, 72+ Je '87
Ten best cars that changed the world. R. Ceppos. il *Car Driv* 32:70-4 Ja '87
Years ago. See issues of Road & Track

Photographs and photography

California Cadillacs [work of S. Banks] L. Griffin. il *Car Driv* 33:108-12 N '87

Horns

See Automobile horns

Instrument panels

See Automobiles—Dashboards

Insurance

See Insurance, Automobile

Laws and regulations

See also

Automobiles—Environmental aspects
Traffic regulations

Miscellaneous ramblings [origins of lemon laws] J. Dinkel. il *Road Track* 38:35 Mr '87

Leakage

How to identify leaks. M. Thompson. il *Fam Handyman* 37:62 Ja '87

Leasing and renting

See also

Avis, Inc.
National Car Rental System, Inc.
PHH Group Inc.

Buy or lease? R. McNatt. il *Essence* 18:104 N '87
Car rentals: airports take their cut. *Consum Rep* 52:595 O '87
Getting more car for less cash. W. J. Mitchell. il *Time* 129:57 My 18 '87
Is leasing a car cheaper than buying one? T. Tilling. il *Parents* 62:50 Jl '87
Leasing vs. buying: how the numbers add up. W. J. Hampton. il *Bus Week* p120-1 Mr 9 '87
Look before you lease. J. Clements. il *Forbes* 140:99-100 Jl 27 '87
Rent-a-Rolls—great cars to drive for a day. L. J. Nonkin. il *Vogue* 177:152 D '87
Renting a dream machine. G. Eichler. il *Esquire* 107:62 My '87
Should you lease your next car? il *Consum Res Mag* 70:18-22 My '87
Small fry start nipping at the whales of auto rental. J. E. Ellis. il *Bus Week* p81 Ag 31 '87
When leasing a car makes sense. K. McCormally. il *Changing Times* 41:39-40+ S '87
Who says a rental car has to be boring? J. B. McDaniel. il *Bus Week* p90 F 2 '87
Why car rentals drive you nuts. A. L. Taylor, III. il *Fortune* 116:74-6+ Ag 31 '87

Ethical aspects

Cracking down on a costly car-rental option [collision waivers] C. Brown. il *Bus Week* p135 N 30 '87
Rental-car insurance: don't get taken for a ride. T. Segal. *Bus Week* p106 Ja 19 '87

License plates

GR8 PL8S: the sequel [vanity plates] L. Griffin. il *Car Driv* 33:87-9+ Jl '87
It's a dirty job, but California's special DMV unit has to make sure that motorists clean their plates [offensive vanity plates] il *People Wkly* 28:69 Jl 13 '87
Lobster tales: the plate debate [controversial Maine plate] il *U S News World Rep* 102:26 Ap 6 '87
Ten best vanity plates. L. Griffin. il *Car Driv* 32:56-7 Ja '87

Vanity of vanities [allowing GOD on license plates in Maryland] H. H. Morris. *Christ Century* 104:932 O 28 '87

Lighting

A bright idea? [laws in Canada and Sweden requiring driving with headlights on] J. Dinkel. *Road Track* 38:34-6 Ja '87
Bring back the light. P. Weissler. il *Home Mech* 83:117-18+ O '87
Daytime headlights could save your life. *Prevention* 39:10 O '87
Flash a friend today [flashing headlights to warn other drivers of radar traps] B. W. Yates. il *Car Driv* 33:24 D '87
For safer night driving [headlight maintenance] M. Ferrara. il *Home Mech* 83:20 Ja '87
Headlight alarm. C. Lowell. il *Radio-Electron* 58:67 Ap '87
Rear-window brake lights: install one to make your car safer. D. Stokes. *Better Homes Gard* 65:38 O '87

Locks

See Automobile locks and keys

Lubrication and lubricants

See also

American Lubrication Company

Computerized oil-change reminder. D. McCosh. il *Pop Sci* 231:132 O '87
Do-it-yourself guide [change your own oil and oil filter] il *Consum Rep* 52:102 F '87
Grease job [Grease Pro ten-minute oil change place in Panama City, Fla.] P. Bedard. il *Car Driv* 33:158 N '87
If your oil turns black too quickly. P. Weissler. il *Home Mech* 83:80+ My '87
Motor oils. il *Consum Rep* 52:88-94 F '87
Neater, easier ways to change oil. P. Weissler. il *Home Mech* 83:82 Je '87
Now, the McLube. *Newsweek* 109:48 Je 15 '87
An oil change for the better. M. Ferrara. il *Home Mech* 83:34 Mr '87
Pre-lubrication [Lubrication Research Inc.'s Preluber] R. Titus. il *Mot Trend* 39:128 Ap '87

Maintenance and repair

See also

Automobile engines—Maintenance and repair
Automobile mechanics (Persons)
Automobile service stations
Radio broadcasting—Automobile repair programs

Alone on the highway. K. Kelly. il *Parents* 62:66+ Ag '87
Auto Q&A. P. Weissler. See issues of Home Mechanix beginning January 1985
Autohypochondria [women] W. Shipman. il *Ctry J* 14:10 N '87
An automotive "summerization". il *Mother Earth News* 105:102+ My/Je '87
Can your car go the distance? W. W. Watt. il *Consum Res Mag* 70:25-8 Je '87
Car care: how to tune up your whole car [cover story; special section] il *Pop Mech* 164:101+ My '87
Car-care quiz. S. Mercaldo. il *Pop Sci* 230:100-2+ Mr '87
Car-care quiz. S. Mercaldo. il *Pop Sci* 231:74+ N '87
Car clinic. M. J. Schultz. See issues of Popular Mechanics
Car repair. P. Weissler. See issues of Home Mechanix beginning January 1985
Do-it-yourself car repair. M. Corwell. il *Essence* 17:91-2 Mr '87
Fast fixes. M. Thompson. See issues of The Family Handyman beginning July/August 1986
Frequency-of-repair records, 1981-1986. *Consum Rep* 52:134-67 D '87
Frequency-of-repair records, 1981-1986. il *Consum Rep* 52:232-46 Ap '87
Help on the highway [studies of Good Samaritanism] P. McCarthy. il *Psychol Today* 21:12+ Jl '87
Home mechanix Easy-Maintenance Car of the Year: 1988 Chevrolet Corsica/Beretta. il *Home Mech* 83:39+ My '87
Maintenance—cheap insurance. M. Anson. *Mot Trend* 39:8 S '87
Microchip mechanic [Buick's Computerized Automotive Maintenance System] T. Swan. il *Pop Sci* 231:73-4+ Jl '87
Prepping your car for winter. W. W. Watt. il *Consum Res Mag* 70:25-8 D '87
Pretrip checklist. D. Chaikin. il *Home Mech* 83:76-8 Jl '87
Preventive maintenance. M. Ferrara. See issues of Home Mechanix beginning November 1985

Automobiles—Maintenance and repair—*cont.*

Say, Smokey. S. Yunick. See issues of Popular Science
Smart strategies for car repair. il *Glamour* 85:96 S '87
Taking care of your car. S. Mercaldo. See issues of Popular Science
Technologue. R. Grable. See issues of Motor Trend
What's best for your car [special section] il *Consum Rep* 52:88-109 F '87

Caricatures and cartoons

Modern mechanics. S. Mott. il *Road Track* 38:105-8 Ja '87

Materials

See also
Automobile engines—Materials
Automobiles, Foreign—Materials
Convertibles (Automobiles)—Materials

Mirrors

Clean glass for a clear view. M. Ferrara. il *Home Mech* 83:24 N '87

Noise

For your ears only. A. Girdler. il *Road Track* 38:18 My '87

Options

See Automobiles—Equipment

Ownership

See Automobile ownership

Painting

How to buy a new paint job. M. J. Schultz. il *Fam Handyman* 37:64-9 F '87
Richie the striper [painting pinstripes on cars] P. Bedard. il *Car Driv* 32:176 Ja '87

Parts

See Automobile parts

Periodicals

See also
Car and driver (Periodical)
Road & track (Periodical)

Photographs and photography

Goin' fishin' with Jim [J. Dunne's photographs of prototype cars] R. Ceppos. il por *Car Driv* 32:96-7 My '87
Location car shoot. P. Stergiopoulos. il *Petersens Photogr Mag* 15:48-9 Ap '87
The spy who loves cars [H. G. Lehmann's photographs of prototype cars] R. Hutton. il pors *Car Driv* 32:90-1+ My '87
Ten best wild things. A. St. Antoine. il *Car Driv* 32:52-7 Ja '87

Pollution control devices

See also
Diesel engines, Automotive—Pollution control devices
Another antismog device? [controlling ozone by trapping vapors from gasoline refueling] il *U S News World Rep* 103:8 Ag 3 '87
EPA attacks vapor villain [reducing ozone pollution by trapping gasoline vapors emitted during refueling] *Mot Trend* 39:44 N '87
Performance sentinels [oxygen sensors] K. Zino. il *Pop Sci* 230:25-6+ My '87
Troubleshooting your EGR system. M. J. Schultz. il *Pop Mech* 164:149-52 Jl '87

Prices

Basic transportation: HM's guide to buying a car for under $6,000 [Ford Festiva, Subaru Justy, Mitsubishi Precis, VW Fox, Chevy Sprint, Yugo GV] M. Ferrara. il *Home Mech* 83:54-6+ Ag '87
Clobbering car buyers [U.S. auto industry calls for new limits on Japanese imports] R. J. Samuelson. il *Newsweek* 110:69 D 14 '87
Conjuring up today's sticker prices. M. Keller. il *Mot Trend* 39:130 S '87
Entry-level cars: the used-car alternative? M. Anson. *Mot Trend* 39:6 Jl '87
Freedom of choice vs. a good deal. M. Keller. il *Mot Trend* 39:146 D '87
GM's 1988 prices are lower—in a way. J. B. Treece. il *Bus Week* p41-2 O 12 '87
The price you pay for a new car. M. Keller. il *Mot Trend* 39:126 Ag '87
The right car at the right price [cover story; special section] il *Changing Times* 41:29-42+ D '87
What Ford can afford [argument for cutting car prices to fight imports] P. A. London. *New Repub* 196:16+ Je 8 '87

Purchasing

See also
Automobiles, Foreign—Purchasing
Automobiles, Used—Purchasing

Car buying without fear [interview with R. Sutton] J. Thornton. il por *U S News World Rep* 103:74-6 O 12 '87
Cars women want: a driving force. M. Knepper. *Harpers Bazaar* 120:174+ S '87
Ford chasing women. il *Mot Trend* 39:38 Ag '87
How to get the best deal. il *Consum Rep* 52:195-8 Ap '87
Match or mismatch? [matching car you buy to use and technical acumen] M. Anson. il *Mot Trend* 39:10 Je '87
New car shopping's not so bad! Just trust your instincts! il *Fam Handyman* 37:8 D '87
The new math of car ownership. M. Thompson. il *Fam Handyman* 37:58+ Ja '87
The right car at the right price [cover story; special section] il *Changing Times* 41:29-42+ D '87
Soft sell [women car buyers] E. Henry. il *Changing Times* 41:82 Jl '87
Today's buyers have high expectations. M. Anson. il *Mot Trend* 39:6 Ag '87

Radar detectors

See Radar detectors

Radio antennas

See Radio antennas

Radio equipment

See also
Cellular radio in automobiles
Eliminating radio noise. M. Thompson. il *Fam Handyman* 37:94 Mr '87
New life for old car radios (I) [conversion to home receiver] G. McClellan. il *Radio-Electron* 58:42-4 My '87
New life for old car radios (II) [deluxe shortwave converter] G. McClellan. il *Radio-Electron* 58:50-2 Je '87

Recall

Danger: defects. E. Henry. *Changing Times* 41:47-9 Ap '87

Repairing

See Automobiles—Maintenance and repair

Restoration

See Automobiles, Restored

Safety belts

Blatant busybodyism [seat belt laws] P. Bedard. il *Car Driv* 32:154 Mr '87
The case for safety belts. L. J. Brown. il *Good Housekeep* 204:280 My '87
The controversy over rear-seat lap belts. J. Tomerlin. il *Road Track* 38:63-4+ Ja '87
Facing seat belt facts head-on. il *Curr Health 2* 13:26-7 Mr '87
Miscellaneous ramblings [passive seat belt systems] J. Dinkel. il *Road Track* 38:39-42 Ag '87
Now, the 'seat belt defense' [Michigan case] *Newsweek* 109:69 F 16 '87
Safer rear seats. D. Chaikin. il *Home Mech* 83:70 Jl '87
Slack thinking in Detroit [poorly designed seatbelts] P. Bedard. il *Car Driv* 32:190-1 Je '87

Safety devices and measures

See also
Automobiles—Air bags
Automobiles—Safety belts
High-style safety seat [Bobob] M. Ferrara. il *Home Mech* 83:11 My '87
In a crash, bigger is better [report by the Highway Loss Data Institute] il *U S News World Rep* 103:106 S 28 '87
A new auto sales pitch: safety. il *Fortune* 115:8-9 My 11 '87
Passive restraints: hits and misses. il *Consum Rep* 52:202 Ap '87
Protecting children in cars [car seats; views of Kathleen Weber and John W. Melvin] il *USA Today (Periodical)* 116:13-14 Ag '87
Safer driving. E. Giltenan. il *Forbes* 139:116-17 F 9 '87
The safest cars, the least costly cars [report by the Highway Loss Data Institute] il *Consum Res Mag* 70:14-17 N '87
Safety: going for it. il *Natl Geogr World* 147:26-31 N '87
Why some new cars will be safer [passive restraints] H. Manley. il *Good Housekeep* 205:181 Ag '87

Security measures

See also
Automobiles—Alarms
Add-on devices car thieves hate! D. Chaikin. il *Home Mech* 83:38+ N '87
In quest of the burglar proof buggy. R. McNatt. il *Money* 16:171-2+ F '87

Automobiles—Security measures—*cont.*
Outsmart the car thieves. E. Henry. il *Changing Times* 41:32-7 Ag '87
Warning: car clouters ahead. B. Keil. il *Outdoor Life* 179:112-13 Je '87

Selling
See also
Automobiles, Used—Selling

Service stations
See Automobile service stations

Shock absorbers
Don't hit bottom on your vacation. P. Weissler. il *Home Mech* 83:76-8 Ag '87
Simple shocks [Varlo] D. Scott. il *Pop Sci* 231:24 N '87

Shows
See Automobiles—Exhibitions

Skidding
Keeping a grip on slippery roads. M. Daly. il *Better Homes Gard* 65:142-3 F '87

Social aspects
Auto postures. M. T. Marsden. il *Mot Trend* 39:132 Ap '87
Carless in America [airport owner lends author a car to get into town] P. Egan. il *Road Track* 39:20 N '87
The dashboard as mantelpiece. M. T. Marsden. il *Mot Trend* 39:112 F '87
Finding the Fury [search for 1956 Plymouth Fury] B. Boggs. il *N Y Times Mag* p37 Ag 2 '87
The open or closed road? M. T. Marsden. il *Mot Trend* 39:104 Ja '87
Thanks, Mike. D. C. Ross. *Mot Trend* 39:118 Jl '87
Wheels! The thrill of going mobile. J. R. Nerad. il *Mot Trend* 39:122 F '87

Specifications
See also
Automobiles, Foreign—Specifications
Mechanical specifications. il *Consum Rep* 52:248-53 Ap '87
Road & track specifications 1987. il *Road Track* 38:128-33 Mr '87

Speed
See also
Automobiles, Racing—Speed
Speedometers
Domestic dynamite [Buick Regal Grand National, Chevy Camaro IROC 350 Z, Corvette, Dodge Daytona Turbo, Ford Mustang GT and Thunderbird Turbo Coupe and Pontiac Firebird GTA; cover story] R. Grable. il *Mot Trend* 39:44-51 Ag '87

Speed control
"Audiocruise: this is your driver speaking". N. J. Freundlich. il *Pop Sci* 230:86-7 Ja '87

Speed limits
See Traffic regulations

Springs and suspension
See also
Automobiles—Shock absorbers
Automobiles, Foreign—Springs and suspension
Sports cars—Springs and suspension
Active suspension. R. Grable. il *Mot Trend* 39:100-1 Ja '87
Computerized anvils and torches [1988 Lincoln Continental's computer controlled air suspension] P. Bedard. il *Car Driv* 33:152 O '87
Don't hit bottom on your vacation. P. Weissler. il *Home Mech* 83:76-8 Ag '87
. . . or bumps [active suspension] il *U S News World Rep* 103:42 Ag 10 '87

Starting
Cold-weather starting tips. il *Mother Earth News* 103:96+ Ja/F '87
What to do when your car won't crank. P. Stenquist. il *Pop Mech* 164:135-8 N '87
When a warm engine won't restart. P. Weissler. il *Home Mech* 83:84+ Je '87
When your car won't start. P. Stenquist. il *Pop Mech* 164:131-4 Ja '87

Steering gear
See also
Automobiles, Foreign—Steering gear
4-wheel steering. R. Grable. il *Mot Trend* 39:108 F '87
Steering clear of trouble [preventive maintenance] M. Ferrara. il *Home Mech* 83:34 F '87
Steering into a new era [four wheel steering] E. Henry. *Changing Times* 41:108-9 S '87
Steering into a storm of controversy [four wheel steering] D. Sherman. il *Car Driv* 32:9 Je '87

Steering into the future [four wheel steering] il *U S News World Rep* 103:40-1 Ag 10 '87
Tightening up u-ees and lou-ees: steering with all fours. T. Dworetzky. il *Discover* 8:20+ D '87

Stereo systems
See Automobiles—Audio systems

Stopping
Slippin' and slidin' [traction and braking of different types of tires] D. Simanaitis. il *Road Track* 39:172-3 D '87

Styling
See Automobiles—Design

Testing
See also
Automobiles, Experimental—Testing
Automobiles, Foreign—Testing
Automobiles, Remodeled—Testing
Automobiles, Three wheel—Testing
Automobiles, Used—Testing
Convertibles (Automobiles)—Testing
Sports cars—Testing
1987 Buick Riviera T-Type. J. R. Nerad. il *Mot Trend* 39:92-3+ Mr '87
1987 Car of the Year [Ford Thunderbird Turbo Coupe] il *Mot Trend* 39:27-32+ F '87
1987 Chevrolet Beretta GT. D. C. Ross. il *Mot Trend* 39:38-42 Ja '87
1987 Chevrolet Corsica: the family car refocused. D. C. Ross. il *Mot Trend* 39:40 Ja '87
1987 Pontiac LeMans. P. Bingham. il *Mot Trend* 39:57+ F '87
1988 Buick Regal. il *Mot Trend* 39:68-70 O '87
1988 Cadillac Eldorado. D. C. Ross. il *Mot Trend* 39:93-4+ D '87
1988 Chevrolet Beretta GT. R. Ceppos. il *Car Driv* 32:32-6+ F '87
1988 Dodge Dynasty. il *Mot Trend* 39:58-60+ O '87
1988 Lincoln Continental. il *Mot Trend* 39:62-3+ O '87
1988 Pontiac LeMans. J. Thompson. il *Road Track* 38:84 F '87
1988 Pontiac LeMans SE. L. Griffin. il *Car Driv* 32:85-7+ F '87
1988 Renault Medallion LX [renamed Eagle Medallion] R. Ceppos. il *Car Driv* 32:64-5+ Ap '87
1988 Renault Premier [American Motors Premier] il *Mot Trend* 39:52-4+ O '87
AMC Premier. R. Ceppos. il *Car Driv* 33:67 O '87
Basic transportation: HM's guide to buying a car for under $6,000 [Ford Festiva, Subaru Justy, Mitsubishi Precis, VW Fox, Chevy Sprint, Yugo GV] M. Ferrara. il *Home Mech* 83:54-6+ Ag '87
Battle for the basics [Volkswagen Fox and Pontiac LeMans] D. McCosh and R. Stepler. il *Pop Sci* 230:38-9 F '87
Battle of the behemoths [Cadillac Brougham vs. Lincoln Town Car] il *Pop Mech* 164:53-5+ S '87
The best American GT [Camaro vs. Mustang vs. Firebird] R. Ceppos. il *Car Driv* 32:40-5+ Je '87
The best and worst 1987 cars [excerpts from The 1987 car book] J. Gillis. il *Good Housekeep* 205:265 S '87
Best of the '88 auto buys! M. Corwell. il *Essence* 18:103-4 N '87
The big wheels' wheels. E. Henry. il *Changing Times* 41:40-2+ Mr '87
Bondurant Thunderbird 5.0. il por *Road Track* 39:62-4 O '87
The British are coming! [Sterling 825SL vs. Cadillac Seville and Mercedes-Benz 300E] T. Wilkinson. il *Pop Sci* 230:28-30+ Ap '87
Buick GNX. T. Assenza. il *Car Driv* 32:135+ My '87
Buick Grand National GNX. J. Lamm. il *Road Track* 38:138-40+ Je '87
Buick LeSabre T Type. R. Ceppos. il *Car Driv* 33:119-21 Ag '87
Buick Regal Limited. R. Ceppos. il *Car Driv* 33:43-7 S '87
Buick Riviera T Type. R. Ceppos. il *Car Driv* 32:117-19 Ja '87
Cadillac Touring Sedan. J. R. Nerad. il *Mot Trend* 39:116-17+ Je '87
Chevrolet Beretta. D. Chaikin. il *Home Mech* 83:22-3 Ap '87
Chevrolet Beretta GT. il *Road Track* 38:52-5 Ap '87
Chevrolet Camaro RS. M. Brockman. il *Mot Trend* 39:51-2 My '87
Chevrolet Celebrity Eurosport VR. R. Ceppos. il *Car Driv* 33:95-7+ O '87
Chevrolet Celebrity Eurosport VR. D. C. Ross. il *Mot Trend* 39:92-4 S '87

Automobiles—Testing—*cont.*

Chevrolet Corsica/Beretta. M. Allen. il *Pop Mech* 164:160-1 F '87

Chevrolet Corsica [5,000 mile test] T. Wilkinson. il *Pop Sci* 230:76 My '87

Chevrolet Corsica CL. B. Nagy. il *Mot Trend* 39:67-8+ Jl '87

Chevrolet Corsica LT. L. Griffin. il *Car Driv* 33:119-20 O '87

Chevrolet Nova. D. Chaikin. il *Home Mech* 83:28-9 Ja '87

Chevrolet Sprint Turbo. T. Assenza. il *Car Driv* 32:117-19 Ap '87

Chrysler LeBaron Coupe. il *Road Track* 38:62-6 Jl '87

Chrysler LeBaron Turbo. R. Ceppos. il *Car Driv* 32:121-3+ My '87

Corsica [Chevrolet] R. Ceppos. il *Car Driv* 32:36 F '87

Crash course in crash tests. E. Henry. il *Changing Times* 41:117-19+ N '87

Crash tests for small cars. il *Consum Res Mag* 70:23 My '87

Déjà vroom [1987 Mustang LX and Firebird Formula vs. 1970 Mustang Boss 302 and 1969 Trans Am] il *Road Track* 39:44-52 S '87

Detroit's flashy coupes [Chevrolet Beretta GT, Ford Thunderbird Turbo Coupe, and Chrysler Le Baron Turbo Coupe; cover story] il *Consum Rep* 52:486-92 Ag '87

Dodge Daytona Shelby Z. D. C. Ross. il *Mot Trend* 39:96-8 Jl '87

Dodge Dynasty. T. Assenza. il *Car Driv* 33:65 O '87

Dodge Shelby Charger GLHS. T. Assenza. il *Car Driv* 32:93 F '87

Domestic dynamite [Buick Regal Grand National, Chevy Camaro IROC 350 Z, Corvette, Dodge Daytona Turbo, Ford Mustang GT and Thunderbird Turbo Coupe and Pontiac Firebird GTA; cover story] R. Grable. il *Mot Trend* 39:44-51 Ag '87

The econohunks [Ford Escort GT, Isuzu I-Mark Turbo, Dodge Shadow ES, Renault GTA, Chevrolet 224, Toyota Corolla FX16, Mitsubishi Mirage Turbo, Pontiac Sunbird Turbo GT, VW GTI 16V and Acura Integra LS] P. Bedard. il *Car Driv* 32:42-9+ Mr '87

Escort GT. S. Tyson. il *Mot Trend* 39 no12 Sp Issue:42-5 '87

Exotic Yankeeland [Daihatsu and Ford Festiva] J. K. Yamaguchi. il *Road Track* 38:106+ Mr '87

Festiva LX. D. Fuller. il *Mot Trend* 39 no12 Sp Issue:68-71 '87

Ford Festiva. J. R. Nerad. il *Mot Trend* 39:74-6 My '87

Ford Festiva L. il *Road Track* 38:76-8+ Jl '87

Ford Festiva LX. C. Csere. il *Car Driv* 32:47-9+ My '87

Ford Thunderbird Turbo Coupe. il *Road Track* 38:66-8+ Ag '87

Four cheap little runabouts [Honda Civic, Dodge Colt, Volkswagen Fox, and Subaru Justy] il *Consum Rep* 52:615-22 O '87

Four factory hot rods [Chevrolet Camaro IROC-Z and Pontiac Firebird Trans Am GTA vs Toyota Supra and Nissan 300ZX 2 + 2] il *Road Track* 38:158-64+ Ap '87

Four small family sedans [Nissan Sentra, Chevrolet Cavalier, Ford Tempo, Plymouth Sundance] il *Consum Rep* 52:53-9 Ja '87

GM's come back cars [Chevrolet Beretta and Pontiac Bonneville] J. Keebler and T. Wilkinson. il *Pop Sci* 230:22-4+ F '87

How CU tests and rates cars. il *Consum Rep* 52:207-9 Ap '87

How to test drive a new car. M. Knepper. il *Better Homes Gard* 65:180-1 Ap '87

Import flair at domestic prices [Chevrolet Corsica and Beretta] E. Henry. il *Changing Times* 41:146 Ja '87

In this corner, the Toyota Camry [Mitsubishi Galant, Nissan Stanza, Pontiac Grand Am] il *Consum Rep* 52:110-17 F '87

An international Pontiac [LeMans] M. Ferrara. il *Home Mech* 83:83 Jl '87

Life with Lancer [long term tests] P. Bedard. il *Car Driv* 32:99-100 My '87

Lincoln Continental. P. Bedard. il *Car Driv* 33:63 O '87

Lincoln Continental Signature Series. A. St. Antoine. il *Car Driv* 33:65-8+ D '87

Lincoln Mark VII LSC. C. Csere. il *Car Driv* 33:43-6+ Jl '87

Lincoln Town Car. C. Csere. il *Car Driv* 32:99+ Ap '87

Living with the Mercedes, the Taurus, the Astro Van. il *Consum Rep* 52:194 Ap '87

A lot of cars. See occasional issues of Road & Track beginning June 1986

Mercury Cougar. B. Nagy. il *Mot Trend* 39:48-51 S '87

Mercury Tracer. il *Road Track* 38:50-3 Mr '87

Mercury Tracer. T. Assenza. il *Car Driv* 32:67-9+ Mr '87

Mercury Tracer. D. C. Ross. il *Mot Trend* 39:45+ Mr '87

Mercury's Mexican Mazda [Tracer] D. Chaikin. il *Home Mech* 83:101 My '87

Minicar invasion [Hyundai Excel, Yugo GV, Subaru Justy, Pontiac LeMans, VW Fox and Ford Festiva; cover story] J. Keebler and others. il *Pop Sci* 230:42-6+ My '87

Mustang GT. D. Fuller. il *Mot Trend* 39 no12 Sp Issue:34-7 '87

The New-Age family cars [Volkswagen Fox GL, Chevrolet Corsica, Ford Taurus, Dodge Dynasty, Pontiac Bonneville, Buick Electra] M. Knepper. il *Better Homes Gard* 65:48+ N '87

Oldsmobile Calais GT Quad 4. P. Bingham. il *Mot Trend* 39:67-70 Ag '87

Oldsmobile Calais Supreme. P. Bedard. il *Car Driv* 32:131 My '87

Oldsmobile Cutlass Supreme. T. Assenza. il *Car Driv* 33:69 O '87

Oldsmobile Delta 88. D. Fuller. il *Mot Trend* 39:101-2+ Ap '87

Oldsmobile Ninety Eight Touring Sedan. C. Csere. il *Car Driv* 32:127+ Mr '87

PM comparison test: daily drivers. il *Pop Mech* 164:71-4+ My '87

PM long-term car tests: Dodge Shadow Turbo, Tempo 4WD, Corvette Convertible. M. Allen and J. Oldham. il *Pop Mech* 164:120-1+ D '87

PM long-term car tests: Nissan SE Pickup, Ford Taurus LX, Oldsmobile Delta 88. W. Hoyt and M. Allen. il *Pop Mech* 164:78+ Jl '87

PM's long-term test reports [Corvette Roadster, Dodge Shadow Turbo, Ford Tempo 4WD] il *Pop Mech* 164:53-5+ Ag '87

Pontiac Bonneville. D. Chaikin. il *Home Mech* 83:22-3 My '87

Pontiac Bonneville SE. il *Road Track* 38:68-71 F '87

Pontiac Bonneville SE. L. Griffin. il *Car Driv* 32:56-8+ Mr '87

Pontiac Firebird GTA. M. Brockman. il *Mot Trend* 39:126-8+ Je '87

Pontiac Grand Am SE revisited. J. Oldham. il *Pop Mech* 164:47 N '87

Pontiac Grand Am SE Turbo. D. C. Ross. il *Mot Trend* 39:91-2+ Ag '87

Pontiac Grand Prix SE [cover story] C. Csere. il *Car Driv* 33:40-6 O '87

Pontiac LeMans. il *Road Track* 38:61-3 My '87

Pontiac LeMans SE. M. Thompson. il *Fam Handyman* 37:88-9 O '87

Pontiac LeMans vs. Mercury Tracer. J. R. Nerad. il *Mot Trend* 39:81-5 Ag '87

Power to the fore! [turbo Buick Riviera] W. Hoyt. il *Pop Mech* 164:47 Je '87

Regal GNX [Buick] R. Grable. il *Mot Trend* 39:55-8 Ap '87

Regal vs. Cougar and LeBaron. D. McCosh. il *Pop Sci* 231:24-5+ D '87

Renault Medallion [renamed Eagle Medallion] D. Chaikin. il *Home Mech* 83:12-13 N '87

Renault Medallion LX [renamed Eagle Medallion] P. Bingham. il *Mot Trend* 39:61-2+ Mr '87

Road & track's 10 best cars by value and passion [cover story] il *Road Track* 39:46-57 D '87

Road tests: Eagle Medallion, Chevrolet Corsica. il *Consum Rep* 52:708-11 N '87

Shelby Charger GLH-S. il *Road Track* 38:96-7 Jl '87

Shelby Charger GLH-S. R. Titus. il *Mot Trend* 39:78+ Mr '87

Shelby CSX. N. Bissoon Dath. il *Car Driv* 33:125-7 N '87

Shelby Lancer. R. Titus. il *Mot Trend* 39:59-61+ Ap '87

Son of E²F² attacks Newport Beach [1986 fun factor rating] D. Simanaitis. il *Road Track* 38:150 Ja '87

Speed, style, and a sticker that won't drive you away [Chrysler's LeBaron] W. J. Hampton. il *Bus Week* p95 Ap 20 '87

Speed thrills [Chevrolet's Callaway Corvette and Buick's Regal GNX] M. Allen. il *Pop Mech* 164:63-6+ Mr '87

Automobiles—Testing—*cont.*

Sport coupe for the '90s [Buick Regal] D. McCosh. il *Pop Sci* 231:66-7 S '87

Summary judgments of the 1987 cars. il *Consum Rep* 52:210-29 Ap '87

Taurus LX. D. Fuller. il *Mot Trend* 39 no12 Sp Issue:56-9 '87

Tempo GLS. S. Tyson. il *Mot Trend* 39 no12 Sp Issue:64-7 '87

Ten best cars. D. Sherman. il *Car Driv* 32:36-41 Ja '87

Ten best performers. C. Csere. il *Car Driv* 32:48-50 Ja '87

This sportin' life [Acura Legend, Alfa Romeo Milano Gold, Mercury Sable, Pontiac Bonneville, Saab 9000 Turbo, Sterling 825S and Toyota Cressida] il *Pop Mech* 164:60-4+ Ja '87

Those crash-test ratings for cars. C. Kitch. il *Good Housekeep* 204:150 Ja '87

Thunderbird Turbo Coupe. D. Fuller. il *Mot Trend* 39 no12 Sp Issue:48-53 '87

Touring coupes [Acura Legend Coupe, Ford Thunderbird and Buick LeSabre T-Type] T. Wilkinson. il *Pop Sci* 231:26-8+ S '87

Update: long-term tests [Acura Legend Coupe L, Ford Taurus and Porsche 944 Turbo] il *Road Track* 39:64 D '87

Update: long-term tests [Chevrolet Corvette, Saab 9000 and Ford Taurus] il *Road Track* 38:130 Ap '87

Update: long-term tests [Chevrolet Corvette, Toyota MR2 and Ford Taurus] il *Road Track* 38:74 F '87

Update: long-term tests [Ford Taurus, Saab 9000 and Toyota MR2] il *Road Track* 39:53 S '87

Update: long-term tests [Porsche 944 Turbo, Ford Taurus and Toyota MR2] il *Road Track* 39:62 N '87

Upscale family sedans [Mercury Sable LS, Pontiac Bonneville SE, and Chrysler New Yorker] il *Consum Rep* 52:296-302 My '87

Which car for under $6500? [Toyota Tercel, Chevrolet Sprint, Hyundai Excel and Dodge Omni America] il *Consum Rep* 52:155-61 Mr '87

Which cars do better in a crash? il *Consum Rep* 52:199-201 Ap '87

Zimmer QuickSilver [cover story] P. Bedard. il *Car Driv* 32:36-40 Ap '87

Theft

See also
Automobiles—Security measures

Lost and found [1969 Barracuda 340-S] A. Girdler. il *Road Track* 39:20 O '87

What to do if your car is stolen—and to prevent it from happening. D. McCluggage. il *Glamour* 85:124+ F '87

Tires

See Tires, Automobile

Towing

How to avoid problems when you're towed. M. Thompson. il *Fam Handyman* 37:90+ Mr '87

Traction

Chain-free traction [Spikes-Spider] M. Ferrara. il *Home Mech* 83:94 Ja '87

The g-analyst: the driver's lie detector. R. Titus. il *Mot Trend* 39:114 O '87

Slippin' and slidin' [traction and braking of different types of tires] D. Simanaitis. il *Road Track* 39:172-3 D '87

Trailers

See Automobile trailers

Transmission

See also
Automobiles, Foreign—Transmission

The CVT has arrived [continuously variable transmission] R. Hutton and Y. Ishiwatari. il *Car Driv* 33:30-1 Ag '87

Finally—CVT. D. McCosh. il *Pop Sci* 231:56-9 S '87

Gambling on going gearless [continuously variable transmissions] S. B. Weiner. il *Forbes* 139:236-7 Je 15 '87

Keeping your manual transmission trouble-free. M. Ferrara. il *Home Mech* 83:14 O '87

When your automatic transmission acts up. P. Weissler. il *Home Mech* 83:74-6 Ja '87

Defects

A new auto sales pitch: safety. il *Fortune* 115:8-9 My 11 '87

Warranty

See Warranty

Washing

See Automobiles—Cleaning

Wheels

This wheelmaker is on a roll [Philips Industries aluminum wheel] G. G. Marcial. *Bus Week* p94 Mr 9 '87

Windows

When a window won't work. P. Weissler. il *Home Mech* 83:86+ Mr '87

Windshield defrosters

Keeping your rear vision clear. M. Ferrara. il *Home Mech* 83:20 S '87

Winter car comfort. M. Ferrara. il *Home Mech* 83:22 D '87

Windshield wipers

Ways to beat the rain. M. Thompson. il *Fam Handyman* 37:82+ O '87

When your wipers don't do their job. P. Weissler. il *Home Mech* 83:88+ Ap '87

Windshields

Clean glass for a clear view. M. Ferrara. il *Home Mech* 83:24 N '87

What your windshield shows about the clouds [origin of clouds and dew] R. Williams. il *Weatherwise* 40:260-1 O '87

Automobiles, Antique

1926 Rickenbacker Super Sport. B. R. Kimes. il *Road Track* 38:76-82 Ja '87

1927 AC Montlhéry [racer] C. Posthumus. il *Road Track* 38:136-42 Ag '87

1929 Cord L-29 Special Coupe. H. Rasmussen. il *Mot Trend* 39:101-4+ Ag '87

1930 Alfa Romeo 6C 1750 Gran Sport. J. Ethridge. il *Mot Trend* 39:107-10+ Jl '87

1933 Lagonda M45 Tourer. J. Ethridge. il *Mot Trend* 39:99-103 O '87

1934 Packard Twelve Speedster. T. C. Browne. il *Mot Trend* 39:137-40+ My '87

1935 Hispano-Suiza J12. T. C. Browne. il *Mot Trend* 39:101-7 F '87

1937 Bugatti 57G. P. Hill. il *Road Track* 38:126-32 Jl '87

Caldwell's curious contraptions [E. P. Caldwell's 1907-1908 horseless carriages] J. A. Wren. il *Road Track* 38:144 My '87

Manhattan or bust [R. Harding and K. Hill drive Model T in Great American Race] J. Paris. il pors *Read Dig* 131:5-6+ Jl '87

La Royale [1931 Bugatti Type 41] A. St. Antoine. il *Car Driv* 33:70-4 Ag '87

Collectors and collecting

Australian classic: the Robin and Peter Briggs house near Perth [decorated by Annalaura Angeletti] C. Aillaud. il por *Archit Dig* 44:116-23 F '87

Exhibitions

See Automobiles—Exhibitions

Automobiles, Electric

Is Newman's car for real? il *Pop Mech* 164:82 Jl '87

Pumped-up batteries [experimental car developed by Saied Motaei] T. A. Heppenheimer. *Pop Sci* 230:48 F '87

Unique Mobility. R. Grable. il *Mot Trend* 39:90-5 My '87

Automobiles, Experimental

American dreams [Pontiac Pursuit, Dodge Daytona Concept, Chevrolet Express, Lincoln by Vignale and Oldsmobile Aerotech; cover story] R. Ceppos. il *Car Driv* 32:36-43 My '87

Dodge Daytona X91 [cover story] il *Mot Trend* 39:28-30 Ap '87

Dreamcars. P. Bingham. il *Mot Trend* 39:92-4 O '87

Dreamer's dozen. D. Sherman. il *Car Driv* 33:71-4 O '87

Expressly yours from Chevrolet [Express showcase car] D. C. Ross. il *Mot Trend* 39:18-19+ Mr '87

A gallon of gas, 121 miles and thou [Renault Vesta II research vehicle] P. Frère. il *Road Track* 39:96 D '87

Hot Pursuit [Pontiac show car] D. McCosh. il *Pop Sci* 231:40-1 Ag '87

Lamborghini Portofino takes the stand. M. Cotton. il *Mot Trend* 39:17 D '87

Thoughts down the road [Chevrolet Express] P. Lienert. il *Road Track* 38:106+ Ap '87

Turbine turn-on [Chevrolet Express] D. McCosh. il *Pop Sci* 230:38-40 Ap '87

Materials

Technoid of the year [Lancia Experimental Composite Vehicle] W. Hoyt. il *Pop Mech* 164:41 My '87

Automobiles, Experimental—*cont.*

Speed

Beyond the Brougham [Oldsmobile Aerotech project] D. Sherman. il *Car Driv* 32:7 Ja '87

Flat out on the flats [Aerotech with Quad 4 engine] P. Bedard. il *Car Driv* 33:167 D '87

Record-shattering trio? [Aerotech project using modified Quad 4 turbo engine] P. Lienert. il *Road Track* 38:50-2 Ja '87

Testing

Pontiac Pursuit. P. Bingham. il *Mot Trend* 39:60-4 S '87

Pontiac Pursuit. C. Csere. il *Car Driv* 33:83+ S '87

Automobiles, Foreign

See also
  Convertibles (Automobiles)
  Sports cars
  Station wagons, Foreign

5 million smiles [PM owners report on Chevy Nova, Saab 9000, Pontiac Bonneville] M. Lamm. il *Pop Mech* 164:76-8+ N '87

The 1987 cars [cover story; special issue] il *Consum Rep* 52:195-202+ Ap '87

Asia '88. B. Nagy and J. R. Nerad. il *Mot Trend* 39:115-16+ N '87

Ask the man who owns one [Buick Riviera, Dodge Shadow/Plymouth Sundance, Acura Legend] M. Lamm. il *Pop Mech* 164:59-62+ Ag '87

Audi to replace U.S. models. M. Cotton. il *Mot Trend* 39:26 S '87

Beetles on ice [VW Beetle as winter car] P. Egan. il *Road Track* 38:16 Ap '87

Black enterprise auto guide: new faces of 1988 [special section] J. Koblenz. il *Black Enterp* 18:75+ N '87

BMW roundup '87. T. West. il *Road Track* 38:94-6 Ja '87

Cars for 1988. il *Ebony* 43:170-1+ N '87

Chasing the tail of the Jag [Austin-Rover Sterling and Acura Legend] il *U S News World Rep* 102:47 Mr 9 '87

Europe '88. M. Cotton. il *Mot Trend* 39:127-31 N '87

For your information. A. St. Antoine. See issues of Car and Driver

A hit in Europe, but a miss in the states [Merkur] J. B. Treece. il *Bus Week* p81 S 28 '87

Hyundai Excel [PM owners report] M. Lamm. il *Pop Mech* 164:186+ My '87

Imports. B. Hartford. See issues of Popular Mechanics

Imports '87 [special section] il *Pop Mech* 164:95+ F '87

International report. See issues of Motor Trend

Italian body, Swedish guts [Volvo 780] D. Chaikin. il *Home Mech* 83:32 Je '87

Just what the U.S. needs: an even smaller car from Japan [Daihatsu's Charade] S. Toy. il *Bus Week* p26 Ap 20 '87

Letter from Europe. P. Frère. See issues of Road & Track through December 1987

Letter from Japan. J. K. Yamaguchi. See issues of Road & Track through December 1987

Luxury never sleeps [Jaguar, Lotus and BMW] il *Road Track* 39:102+ O '87

The M-cars are coming [BMWs] A. St. Antoine. il *Car Driv* 32:103 Ja '87

The man, the myth, the mileage! Californian Albert Klein motors his 1963 Beetle one million miles. N. Geeslin. il pors *People Wkly* 28:40+ Ag 3 '87

Merkur XR4Ti [owners report] M. Lamm. il *Pop Mech* 164:71+ Mr '87

Mitsubishi Starion/Chrysler Conquest, Nissan 300ZX and Toyota Supra [owner surveys] P. Bohr. il *Road Track* 38:154-8+ My '87

Sneak peeks—new cars from around the globe. D. McCosh. il *Pop Sci* 230:70-1 Ja '87

What's making Opel GM's diamond in the rough [luxury Omega] J. E. Pluenneke. il *Bus Week* p87-8 Jl 20 '87

You've come a long way, baby [U.S. foreign car market] M. Anson. il *Mot Trend* 39:6 Ap '87

Yugo GV [owners report] M. Lamm. il *Pop Mech* 164:146-8 Je '87

Acceleration

Audi agonistes [unintended acceleration in the 5000s] C. Csere. il *Car Driv* 32:51-7 Je '87

Audi takes the gloves off [cases of unintended acceleration in the 5000s] T. Orme. il *Mot Trend* 39:34 My '87

Felony baloney [cases of unintended acceleration alleged to be the fault of the driver and not the car] P. Bedard. il *Car Driv* 32:179 Ap '87

In for repairs [unintended acceleration in the Audi 5000 and Audi's new ad campaign] B. Kanner. il *N Y* 20:32+ O 19 '87

Is half a recall better than none? [Audi 5000s] il *Consum Rep* 52:193 Ap '87

Sudden acceleration stumps NHTSA [Audi 5000S] T. Orme. *Mot Trend* 39:48+ Je '87

Anecdotes, facetiae, satire, etc.

Trekking in America [driving cross country in an English car] T. West. il *Road Track* 38:36 Ag '87

Audio systems

Japanese connections [Acura/Bose system] C. J. Esse. il *High Fidel* 37:12 Ag '87

Awards

See also
  Motor Trend Awards

Japanese Car of the Year [Nissan Pulsar] J. K. Yamaguchi. il *Road Track* 38:98+ Ap '87

Opel wins again [Omega wins European Car of the Year Award] P. Frère. il *Road Track* 38:98+ Mr '87

Defects

See also
  Automobiles, Foreign—Recall

Design

See also
  Nissan Design International

Alfa's fresh-faced sedan and 150-mph sportster. P. Bingham. il *Mot Trend* 39:40 Je '87

Charting the changes [1988 cars] R. Ceppos. il *Car Driv* 33:101-4 N '87

Dutch treat [Volvo 480ES] D. Scott. il *Pop Sci* 230:122 F '87

Faster and more luxurious Audis to come [Audi 80 and 90] P. Frère. *Road Track* 38:90+ Ap '87

Foray into the fourth dimension [updated Mazda 626 series] J. K. Yamaguchi. il *Road Track* 38:98+ Ag '87

Heavy traffic in the fast lane [German styling] D. Pauly. il *Newsweek* 109:56-7 My 18 '87

Jaguar's new sedan [XJ6] B. Hartford. il *Pop Mech* 164:12 Ja '87

Radical supercar, Coupe, and V-8 from Audi. P. Bingham. il *Mot Trend* 39:19 N '87

Electronic equipment

"Car of the future" obeys voice commands [Votan system] il *Radio-Electron* 58:4 F '87

The hacker-rodders [decoding and reprogramming BMW's Bosch Motronic system] C. Csere. il *Car Driv* 33:50-1 Ag '87

Engines

See Automobile engines

Four wheel drive

1988 Subaru XT. il *Road Track* 39:58 O '87

Audi 5000S Quattro. R. Ceppos. il *Car Driv* 33:123 O '87

Audi 90 Quattro. il *Road Track* 39:148-52 D '87

Audi 90 Quattro. P. Bingham. il *Mot Trend* 39:76-9+ D '87

BMW 325ix. M. Scarlett. il *Mot Trend* 39:54+ Mr '87

Ford Sierra 4x4 at 34,000 miles [European Ford] I. Ireland. il *Road Track* 38:90-1 Ja '87

Hot coupes [Toyota MR2 and Celica All-Trac Turbo] D. McCosh. il *Pop Sci* 231:71 D '87

Life with 5000 [Audi Quattro long term test] A. St. Antoine. il *Car Driv* 33:65-7+ Jl '87

The Quattro quandary [Audi 5000 CS Turbo and Quattro] C. Csere. il *Car Driv* 32:79+ F '87

RS 200/Sierra RS Cosworth [European Ford production models of rally cars] M. Cotton. il *Mot Trend* 39:98+ Mr '87

Subaru Alcyone. Y. Ishiwatari. il *Car Driv* 33:31 O '87

Subaru goes six [VX coupe] J. K. Yamaguchi. il *Road Track* 39:96+ O '87

Toyota Celica All-Trac Turbo. P. Bedard. il *Car Driv* 33:59-62+ N '87

Toyota Celica All-Trac Turbo & MR2 Supercharged. D. Fuller. il *Mot Trend* 39:82-3+ N '87

Toyota Celica GT-Four. Y. Ishiwatari. il *Car Driv* 32:29 Ap '87

Front wheel drive

Toyota-san's Shinjucoupes. J. K. Yamaguchi. il *Road Track* 39:100+ S '87

History

See also
  Automobiles, Antique

1939 Talbot T150C. R. Thursby. il *Road Track* 39:120-4+ S '87

1939 Tatra 87. R. Thursby. il *Road Track* 38:56-62 Ap '87

Automobiles, Foreign—History—*cont.*

The orphan as big as the Ritz [VW Beetle] A. Girdler. il *Road Track* 38:218 Je '87

Materials

Midas Gold [plastic composite monocoque] M. Cotton. il *Mot Trend* 39:63-4 Ja '87

Prices

1987 import car prices. il *Pop Mech* 164:106 F '87

Anatomy of a sticker price [Aston Martin Lagonda vs. Subaru Justy DL] J. Hooper. il *Esquire* 108:167-71 O '87

Basic transportation: HM's guide to buying a car for under $6,000 [Ford Festiva, Subaru Justy, Mitsubishi Precis, VW Fox, Chevy Sprint, Yugo GV] M. Ferrara. il *Home Mech* 83:54-6+ Ag '87

Can this born salesman launch a luxury car? [N. Braman stresses Sterling's price] G. DeGeorge. il por *Bus Week* p107 My 4 '87

Purchasing

The 3,000-pound European souvenir [buying a car in Europe to be shipped to the U.S.] M. Opsata. il *50 Plus* 27:68-75 Je '87

The right car at the right price [cover story; special section] il *Changing Times* 41:29-42+ D '87

Recall

A risky little lunge forward [Audi 5000 recall] il *U S News World Rep* 102:13 Ja 26 '87

Remodeled automobiles

See Automobiles, Remodeled

Specifications

Road & track specifications 1987. il *Road Track* 38:128-33 Mr '87

Springs and suspension

Of technical interest [Honda Civic] K. Reynolds. il *Road Track* 39:60-1 N '87

Sonar suspension [Nissan system] J. Schefter. il *Pop Sci* 231:62+ D '87

Steering gear

The 4-wheel steer age [Honda Prelude] J. K. Yamaguchi. il *Road Track* 38:118+ Jl '87

4-wheel-steering showdown [Honda Prelude vs. Mazda 627] D. McCosh and T. Wilkinson. il *Pop Sci* 231:50-3 Ag '87

4ws: will it stick? [1988 Honda Prelude] W. Hoyt. il *Pop Mech* 164:20+ S '87

1988 Honda Prelude Si 4ws. B. Nagy. il *Mot Trend* 39:55-6+ Ag '87

Four-wheel steering: boon or folly? [Honda and Mazda] D. Chaikin. il *Home Mech* 83:72-3+ N '87

Four-wheel steering on snow and ice [Honda Prelude] il *Road Track* 38:104+ Jl '87

Hanging out at the corner [4-wheel steering] D. Simanaitis. il *Road Track* 39:66-8+ S '87

Honda four-wheel steering. D. McCosh. il *Pop Sci* 230:18 F '87

Honda gets there first [Prelude with 4-wheel steering] J. Bird. il *Mot Trend* 39:32 Jl '87

Honda Prelude 2.0 Si [four wheel steering] il *Road Track* 38:54-8 Ag '87

Honda Prelude Si 4ws [cover story] R. Ceppos. il *Car Driv* 33:40-5 Ag '87

How to turn on a dime [four wheel steering on Japanese cars] P. Elmer-Dewitt. il *Time* 130:56-7 D 7 '87

Just ahead: four-wheel steering [Japanese cars] W. J. Hampton. il *Bus Week* p160-1+ S 14 '87

Mazda leads 4-wheel-steering race. J. Bird. il *Mot Trend* 39:44 Je '87

Technical highlights [Mazda's four wheel steering system] D. Sherman. il *Car Driv* 33:64-5 S '87

Turning points [four-wheel steering by Honda and Mazda] C. Csere. il *Car Driv* 33:75-7+ D '87

Stereo systems

See Automobiles, Foreign—Audio systems

Testing

'88 Honda Civic: a bench mark gets better. D. McCosh. il *Pop Sci* 231:101+ N '87

1987 Audi 4000. R. Hutton. il *Car Driv* 32:28 Ja '87

1987 Nissan Pulsar NX. R. Titus. il *Mot Trend* 39:44-5 Ja '87

1987 Peugeot 505 STX. J. R. Nerad. il *Mot Trend* 39:51-3 Ja '87

1987 Toyota Tercel. R. Titus. il *Mot Trend* 39:49+ Mr '87

1988 BMW 735i. B. Nagy. il *Mot Trend* 39:86-9 Ja '87

1988 Honda Prelude Si 4ws. B. Nagy. il *Mot Trend* 39:55-6+ Ag '87

1988 Mazda 626. D. C. Ross. il *Mot Trend* 39:102-4+ D '87

1988 Mitsubishi Galant Sigma. T. C. Browne. il *Mot Trend* 39:70-3 D '87

Acura fine tunes its image [Legend Coupe] M. Ferrara. il *Home Mech* 83:20 Ag '87

Acura Legend [long term test] M. Anson. il *Mot Trend* 39:66+ Jl '87

Acura Legend [long term test] G. Brown. il *Mot Trend* 39:72+ Mr '87

Acura Legend Coupe. il *Road Track* 38:128-30+ My '87

Acura Legend Coupe. L. Griffin. il *Car Driv* 32:57-60 My '87

Acura Legend Coupe. B. Nagy. il *Mot Trend* 39:105-8 My '87

Adventures in travel. T. Assenza. il *Car Driv* 33:27 N '87

Alfa Romeo 164. R. Hutton. il *Car Driv* 33:32 N '87

Alfa Romeo Milano. D. Fuller. il *Mot Trend* 39:80-3+ F '87

Alfa Romeo Milano Verde. R. Ceppos. il *Car Driv* 33:99-100 S '87

Alfa Romeo Milano Verde. J. R. Nerad. il *Mot Trend* 39:94-5+ N '87

Alfa Romeo Milano Verde 3.0. il *Road Track* 39:54-6+ S '87

Asian invasion! il *Pop Mech* 164:90-4+ Jl '87

Audi 80/90. R. Ceppos. il *Car Driv* 33:77-8 N '87

Austin Rover Sterling. D. Chaikin. il *Home Mech* 83:14-15 Mr '87

Autobahn burners [BMW 735i and Merkur Scorpio] H. Shuldiner. il *Pop Sci* 231:62-3 Ag '87

Basic transportation: HM's guide to buying a car for under $6,000 [Ford Festiva, Subaru Justy, Mitsubishi Precis, VW Fox, Chevy Sprint, Yugo GV] M. Ferrara. il *Home Mech* 83:54-6+ Ag '87

Battle for the basics [Volkswagen Fox and Pontiac LeMans] D. McCosh and R. Stepler. il *Pop Sci* 230:38-9 F '87

Bentley Eight. D. Sherman. il *Car Driv* 33:71-3+ S '87

Bentley Turbo R. I. Ireland. il *Road Track* 38:53-5 Ja '87

The best and worst 1987 cars [excerpts from The 1987 car book] J. Gillis. il *Good Housekeep* 205:265 S '87

BMW 325is. C. Csere. il *Car Driv* 33:49-52+ Ag '87

BMW 735i. il *Road Track* 38:148-52 Jl '87

BMW 735i. L. Griffin. il *Car Driv* 32:59-62+ Je '87

BMW 735i. J. R. Nerad. il *Mot Trend* 39:74-9 Jl '87

BMW 735i. A. St. Antoine. il *Car Driv* 32:100-1+ Ja '87

The BMW 750iL. il *Road Track* 39:73+ N '87

BMW 750iL. C. Csere. il *Car Driv* 33:87+ N '87

BMW 750iL V-12. B. Nagy. il *Mot Trend* 39:74-6+ N '87

BMW M3. M. Brockman. il *Mot Trend* 39:63-4+ D '87

BMW M3. A. St. Antoine. il *Car Driv* 33:49-52 N '87

BMW M5. L. Griffin. il *Car Driv* 33:87-9+ D '87

BMW M6. P. Bingham. il *Mot Trend* 39:52-4+ S '87

BMW M6 [cover story] R. Ceppos. il *Car Driv* 33:36-41 Jl '87

Bread-and-butter Bentley [Bentley Eight] B. Hartford. il *Pop Mech* 164:22 Mr '87

The British are coming! [Sterling 825SL vs. Cadillac Seville and Mercedes-Benz 300E] T. Wilkinson. il *Pop Sci* 230:28-30+ Ap '87

Can Japan win back the cheap car market? [Subaru Justy] M. Ferrara. il *Home Mech* 83:33 Je '87

A car for all seasons [Subaru RX] E. Henry. il *Changing Times* 41:120 Mr '87

Citroën AX. P. Frère. il *Road Track* 38:122+ Ja '87

Citroën CX25 GTi. C. Csere. il *Car Driv* 32:57-9+ F '87

Civic pride [Honda] D. Clendenin. il *Road Track* 39:57-61 N '87

Compact challenge [Honda Accord, Nissan Stanza, Toyota Camry and Renault Medallion] T. Wilkinson. il *Pop Sci* 231:24-6+ Jl '87

Crash tests for small cars. il *Consum Res Mag* 70:23 My '87

Daihatsu Charade TX. Y. Ishiwatari. il *Car Driv* 32:35 Je '87

Daihatsu Leeza. Y. Ishiwatari. il *Car Driv* 33:26 S '87

Dueling Renaults: Alliance vs. GTA. M. Brockman. il *Mot Trend* 39:58-61 Ja '87

The econohunks [Ford Escort GT, Isuzu I-Mark Turbo, Dodge Shadow ES, Renault GTA, Chevrolet 224, Toyota Corolla FX16, Mitsubishi Mirage Turbo, Pontiac Sunbird Turbo GT, VW GTI 16V and Acura Integra LS] P. Bedard. il *Car Driv* 32:42-9+ Mr '87

Exotic Yankeeland [Daihatsu and Ford Festiva] J. K. Yamaguchi. il *Road Track* 38:106+ Mr '87

Automobiles, Foreign—Testing—*cont.*

Fast Frenchies [Peugeot 405, Citroën BX GTI 16 and Renault 21 Turbo] P. Frère. il *Road Track* 39:108+ N '87

Feistier flagship [Mitsubishi Galant] J. Keebler. il *Pop Sci* 231:32 N '87

Ford Sierra RS Cosworth [European production model] L. Griffin. il *Car Driv* 33:103-4+ O '87

Four cheap little runabouts [Honda Civic, Dodge Colt, Volkswagen Fox, and Subaru Justy] il *Consum Rep* 52:615-22 O '87

Four European sports sedans [Volvo 760 Turbo, Saab 9000 Turbo, BMW 325i and Sterling 825-SL] il *Consum Rep* 52:556-63 S '87

Four factory hot rods [Chevrolet Camaro IROC-Z and Pontiac Firebird Trans Am GTA vs Toyota Supra and Nissan 300ZX 2 + 2] il *Road Track* 38:158-64+ Ap '87

Four small family sedans [Nissan Sentra, Chevrolet Cavalier, Ford Tempo, Plymouth Sundance] il *Consum Rep* 52:53-9 Ja '87

Four sporty cars [Acura Integra, Toyota Corolla FX16, Nissan Pulsar NX, Renault GTA] il *Consum Rep* 52:448-55 Jl '87

A Foxy car [Volkswagen Fox] E. Henry. il *Changing Times* 41:110 My '87

Good news travels fast [Audi 80 series] P. Frère. il *Road Track* 38:120-2 Ja '87

Heavy metal [V12-powered German luxury cars] D. McCosh. il *Pop Sci* 230:18+ Ja '87

Honda City. Y. Ishiwatari. il *Car Driv* 32:31 My '87

Honda Civic Si. M. Brockman. il *Mot Trend* 39:74-5 Ja '87

Honda Prelude 2.0 Si [four wheel steering] il *Road Track* 38:54-8 Ag '87

Honda Prelude Si 4ws [cover story] R. Ceppos. il *Car Driv* 33:40-5 Ag '87

Honda's Civic pride. B. Nagy. il *Mot Trend* 39:62-6+ N '87

How CU tests and rates cars. il *Consum Rep* 52:207-9 Ap '87

Hyundai Excel GL. R. Titus. il *Mot Trend* 39:107-8+ Je '87

In this corner, the Toyota Camry [Mitsubishi Galant, Nissan Stanza, Pontiac Grand Am] il *Consum Rep* 52:110-17 F '87

Into Africa [testing Audis in the Algerian Sahara] P. Bingham. il map *Mot Trend* 39:118-23+ D '87

Isuzu I-Mark Turbo. J. R. Nerad. il *Mot Trend* 39:86-90 Ag '87

Isuzu Impulse Turbo RS. T. Assenza. il *Car Driv* 32:137-9 Je '87

Isuzu Impulse Turbo RS. B. Nagy. il *Mot Trend* 39:70-2+ Ap '87

Jaguar XJ6. il *Road Track* 38:62-6+ Je '87

Jaguar XJ6. P. Egan. il *Road Track* 38:136-8 Ja '87

Jaguar XJ6. L. Griffin. il *Car Driv* 32:117+ Je '87

Jaguar XJ6. R. Hutton. il *Car Driv* 32:109-12+ Ja '87

Jaguar XJ6 3.6. M. Anson. il *Mot Trend* 39:81-6 S '87

Jaguar—state-of-the-art sensuality [XJ6] D. Davis. *Vogue* 177:160 N '87

Just desert [driving Audis through the Sahara in Algeria] J. Rusz. il *Road Track* 39:54-6 N '87

Lancia Thema 8.32. M. Cotton. il *Mot Trend* 39:112-15 Ap '87

Lancia Thema 8.32. R. Hutton. il *Car Driv* 33:31 Jl '87

Late bloomers [VW Fox, Acura Legend Coupe, AMG Hammer, Merkur Scorpio] S. Parker. il *Pop Mech* 164:63-5 Ag '87

Legendary performer [Acura Legend Coupe] T. Wilkinson. il *Pop Sci* 230:83 Je '87

Living with the Mercedes, the Taurus, the Astro Van. il *Consum Rep* 52:194 Ap '87

A lot of cars. See occasional issues of Road & Track beginning June 1986

Maturity with taste: a visit to northern California wine country in a Mitsubishi Galant. il *Mot Trend* 39:101+ Jl '87

Mazda 626/MX-6. M. Allen. il *Pop Mech* 164:120+ O '87

Mazda 929. T. Assenza. il *Car Driv* 33:93-4 N '87

Mazda 929. R. Titus. il *Mot Trend* 39:99-101 N '87

Mazda Luce. Y. Ishiwatari. il *Car Driv* 32:38 Mr '87

Mazda MX-6. il *Road Track* 39:142-5 D '87

Mazda MX-6 GT Turbo. T. Assenza. il *Car Driv* 33:63-5+ S '87

Mercedes: a sedan with a sports-car soul [300E and 260E] W. J. Hampton. il *Bus Week* p103 Mr 2 '87

Mercedes-Benz 190E 2.3. T. Assenza. il *Car Driv* 33:123+ D '87

Mercedes-Benz 190E 2.6. R. Ceppos. il *Car Driv* 32:111-13 Ap '87

Mercedes-Benz 300CE. T. Assenza. il *Car Driv* 33:99 N '87

Mercedes-Benz 420SEL. il *Road Track* 39:60-2 S '87

Mercedes-Benz 560SEL. R. Ceppos. il *Car Driv* 33:121+ Jl '87

Mercedes swings the hammer [Mercedes-Benz 190 2.6] P. Frère. il *Road Track* 38:104+ F '87

Merkur Scorpio. il *Road Track* 38:226-30 Je '87

Merkur Scorpio. P. Bedard. il *Car Driv* 32:68-9+ Je '87

Merkur Scorpio [driving cross country] D. C. Ross and others. il *Mot Trend* 39:78-80+ My '87

Midas Gold [plastic composite monocoque] M. Cotton. il *Mot Trend* 39:63-4 Ja '87

Minicar invasion [Hyundai Excel, Yugo GV, Subaru Justy, Pontiac LeMans, VW Fox and Ford Festiva; cover story] J. Keebler and others. il *Pop Sci* 230:42-6+ My '87

Mirage and Mirage L [Mitsubishi] il *Road Track* 38:95 Mr '87

Mitsubishi Galant. P. Bingham. il *Mot Trend* 39:85-7 Mr '87

Mitsubishi Galant Σ. C. Csere. il *Car Driv* 33:69-71+ N '87

Mitsubishi Tredia Turbo at 50,000 miles. il *Road Track* 38:136+ Ap '87

More power to the Japanese [Mazda RX-7 Cabriolet and Nissan Skyline GTS-R] J. K. Yamaguchi. il *Road Track* 39:112+ D '87

More power to you [Alfa Romeo 6V 3.0 America] P. Frère. il *Road Track* 38:148+ Je '87

More sting for the Mazda 323 [Infini] J. K. Yamaguchi. il *Road Track* 38:162+ Je '87

Motor Trend's 1987 Import Car of the Year [Acura Legend Coupe] J. R. Nerad. il *Mot Trend* 39:35-9+ Ap '87

The New-Age family cars [Volkswagen Fox GL, Chevrolet Corsica, Ford Taurus, Dodge Dynasty, Pontiac Bonneville, Buick Electra] M. Knepper. il *Better Homes Gard* 65:48+ N '87

New looks and engine for old favorite [Toyota Camry] D. Chaikin. il *Home Mech* 83:79 Ja '87

Nissan 200 SX SE. D. Fuller. il *Mot Trend* 39:58+ Jl '87

Nissan Be-1. Y. Ishiwatari. il *Car Driv* 33:32-3 Jl '87

Nissan Pulsar NX SE. il *Road Track* 38:98-101 Ja '87

Nissan Pulsar NX SE. il *Mot Trend* 39:70-2+ S '87

Nissan Pulsar NX SE. T. Assenza. il *Car Driv* 32:41-5 F '87

Nissan Sentra. D. Chaikin. il *Home Mech* 83:20-1 F '87

Nissan Skyline GTS. M. T. Hotta. il *Mot Trend* 39:46-7 F '87

Nissan's quest for execu-tech [Cedric/Gloria] J. K. Yamaguchi. il *Road Track* 39:95-6 O '87

Nissan's wagon-notchback-hatchback [Pulsar] T. Swan. il *Home Mech* 83:103 Mr '87

Opel Omega. R. Hutton. il *Car Driv* 32:26 F '87

Peugeot 205 GTI 1.9 dazzles. P. Frère. *Road Track* 38:124 Ja '87

Peugeot 309GTI. R. Hutton. il *Car Driv* 32:36-7 Je '87

Peugeot 405. R. Hutton. il *Car Driv* 33:32 O '87

Peugeot 505 STX. il *Road Track* 38:76-8 Ag '87

Peugeot 505STX. A. St. Antoine. il *Car Driv* 32:115 Ap '87

PM comparison test: daily drivers. il *Pop Mech* 164:71-4+ My '87

The Quattro quandary [Audi 5000 CS Turbo and Quattro] C. Csere. il *Car Driv* 32:79+ F '87

Road & track's 10 best cars by value and passion [cover story] il *Road Track* 39:46-57 D '87

RS 200/Sierra RS Cosworth [European Ford production models of rally cars] M. Cotton. il *Mot Trend* 39:98+ Mr '87

Saab 9000S. il *Road Track* 38:97-8 Jl '87

Saab 9000S. L. Griffin. il *Car Driv* 32:141+ My '87

Saab 9000S. B. Nagy. il *Mot Trend* 39:91-2+ Je '87

Say "fun-to-drive," in Japanese [Mazda 626] D. Simanaitis. il *Road Track* 39:90+ O '87

Simple, sturdy, Brazilian-built [Volkswagen Fox] M. Ferrara. il *Home Mech* 83:31 Mr '87

Six-wheeling the Alps [BMW K75 and BMW325i in the Tyrolean Alps] T. West. il *Road Track* 38:132-4+ F '87

Son of E²F² attacks Newport Beach [1986 fun factor rating] D. Simanaitis. il *Road Track* 38:150 Ja '87

Automobiles, Foreign—Testing—*cont.*

Soon to be built in the USA [Mazda 626/MX-6] D. Chaikin. il *Home Mech* 83:96 O '87

Stargazing [1988 Mercedes-Benzes] J. Rusz. il *Road Track* 39:78+ N '87

Sterling 825 SL. il *Road Track* 38:56-9 My '87

Sterling 825S. J. R. Nerad. il *Mot Trend* 39:64-7+ F '87

Sterling 825SL. T. Assenza. il *Car Driv* 32:91-4 Ja '87

A stirring variation on a Thema [Ferrari-engined Lancia Thema 8.32] P. Frère. il *Road Track* 38:70+ My '87

Stopping and going [Mazda RX-7 with anti-lock brakes and Mercedes-Benz 190 2.6] il *Road Track* 38:88-9 F '87

Subaru Justy GL. T. Assenza. il *Car Driv* 32:75-7+ Ap '87

Subaru Justy GL. R. Homan. il *Road Track* 38:64+ My '87

Subaru's Justy. B. Kilpatrick. il *Field Stream* 92:106 Jl '87

Summary judgments of the 1987 cars. il *Consum Rep* 52:210-29 Ap '87

Tally-ho, Carioca! [driving a VW Fox in Brazil] D. Clendenin. il *Road Track* 38:186-8+ My '87

Ten best cars. D. Sherman. il *Car Driv* 32:36-41 Ja '87

Ten best performers. C. Csere. il *Car Driv* 32:48-50 Ja '87

This BMW has a gorgeous engine, too [M6 coupe] R. Mitchell. il *Bus Week* p92 Ag 24 '87

This sportin' life [Acura Legend, Alfa Romeo Milano Gold, Mercury Sable, Pontiac Bonneville, Saab 9000 Turbo, Sterling 825S and Toyota Cressida] il *Pop Mech* 164:60-4+ Ja '87

Those crash-test ratings for cars. C. Kitch. il *Good Housekeep* 204:150 Ja '87

Touring coupes [Acura Legend Coupe, Ford Thunderbird and Buick LeSabre T-Type] T. Wilkinson. il *Pop Sci* 231:26-8+ S '87

Toyota Camry. A. St. Antoine. il *Car Driv* 32:91-3+ Je '87

Toyota Camry LE. R. Titus. il *Mot Trend* 39:65+ My '87

Toyota Corolla. D. Sherman. il *Car Driv* 33:97 N '87

Toyota Corolla GT-S. B. Nagy. il *Mot Trend* 39:80-3+ D '87

Toyota FX16 GT-S. il *Road Track* 38:46-9 Ja '87

Toyota-san's Shinjucoupes. J. K. Yamaguchi. il *Road Track* 39:100+ S '87

Toyota Supra Turbo. il *Road Track* 38:85 F '87

Toyota Supra Turbo. A. St. Antoine. il *Car Driv* 32:43-6+ Ap '87

Toyota Tercel. L. Griffin. il *Car Driv* 33:99+ Jl '87

Update: long-term tests [Acura Legend Coupe L, Ford Taurus and Porsche 944 Turbo] il *Road Track* 39:64 D '87

Update: long-term tests [Chevrolet Corvette, Saab 9000 and Ford Taurus] il *Road Track* 38:130 Ap '87

Update: long-term tests [Chevrolet Corvette, Saab 9000 and Toyota MR2] il *Road Track* 38:134 Je '87

Update: long-term tests [Ford Taurus, Saab 9000 and Toyota MR2] il *Road Track* 39:53 S '87

Volkswagen Fox. D. Chaikin. il *Home Mech* 83:14-15 Jl '87

Volkswagen Fox. J. R. Nerad. il *Mot Trend* 39:87+ F '87

Volkswagen Fox GL. il *Road Track* 38:47-51 F '87

Volkswagen Fox GL. D. Sherman. il *Car Driv* 32:49-53 F '87

Volkswagen GTI [long term test] B. Nagy. il *Mot Trend* 39:124-5 Je '87

Volkswagen GTI 16V. il *Road Track* 38:214-16+ Je '87

Volkswagen GTI 16V. R. Ceppos. il *Car Driv* 33:83+ Ag '87

Volkswagen GTI 16V. J. R. Nerad. il *Mot Trend* 39:65-7 Ap '87

Volkswagen Jetta GLI 16V. A. St. Antoine. il *Car Driv* 33:129+ N '87

Volvo 780. A. St. Antoine. il *Car Driv* 32:79+ My '87

Volvo 780 Coupe. F. M. H. Gregory. il *Mot Trend* 39:92-5 F '87

Volvo 780 Coupe. J. Thompson. il *Road Track* 38:88 Ja '87

VW Jetta GLI 16V. B. Nagy. il *Mot Trend* 39:96-7 O '87

VW, Toyota, & Renault: made in the U.S.A. J. Keebler. il *Pop Sci* 230:20-2+ Mr '87

Wherever Yugo, there you are [driving a Yugo GVL from Belgrade to Dubrovnik] J. R. Nerad. il *Mot Trend* 39:72-8+ Ag '87

Which car for under $6500? [Toyota Tercel, Chevrolet Sprint, Hyundai Excel and Dodge Omni America] il *Consum Rep* 52:155-61 Mr '87

Which cars do better in a crash? il *Consum Rep* 52:199-201 Ap '87

Transmission

Fiat Uno goes CVT. P. Frère. il *Road Track* 38:94-5 Ag '87

History in the making . . . but not at GM [Subaru Justy available with continuously variable transmission] il *Mot Trend* 39:26 My '87

Automobiles, Government

Testing

Cadillac presidential limousine. L. Griffin. il *Car Driv* 33:116-17+ D '87

Automobiles, Home-built

Rolling your own. P. Bedard. il *Car Driv* 33:158 S '87

Automobiles, Miniature *See* Automobile models

Automobiles, Racing

1987 Grand Prix spotter's guide. il *Road Track* 38:134-8 Jl '87

About the sport. J. Rusz. See issues of Road & Track

Death of the killer Bs [Olympus Rally for Group B rally cars] L. Griffin. il *Car Driv* 32:165-73+ Ap '87

GTO spotter's guide. D. Sherman. il *Car Driv* 32:183-4+ Je '87

Motorsport. P. Bingham. See issues of Motor Trend

Sport. L. Griffin. See issues of Car and Driver

Design

See also

Penske Corporation

Adventures of the red LeBaron [Chrysler Indy 500 pace car] P. Lienert. il *Road Track* 38:104+ Ag '87

Does racing relate? [transfer of technology from racing cars to street-driven cars] M. Anson. il *Mot Trend* 39:8 Ja '87

GT-O my gosh [Porsche 961 modified for IMSA GTO racing] J. Rusz. il *Road Track* 38:111-12+ F '87

It has 400 HP, costs $40,000—and comes from Toyota? [Turbo Supra race car] J. O. Hamilton. il *Bus Week* p39 Ap 27 '87

Project Salt Shaker [land speed record set at Bonneville in Pontiac Aero Trans Am] S. Parker. il *Pop Mech* 164:78-81+ F '87

Engines

The Cosworth letters. J. Rusz. il *Road Track* 39:80+ S '87

Has Formula One gotten too fast? [changes in regulations to reduce power of F1 engines] B. Cahier and P. Bingham. il *Mot Trend* 39:149-50+ My '87

Indy engine spotter's guide. J. Rettie. il *Pop Mech* 164:75-7 My '87

Superchargers

Benetton-BMW B186 Formula 1 [cover story] I. Ireland. il *Road Track* 38:42-9 Mr '87

Camel GTP Corps [Mustang GTP Probe, Corvette GTP, Nissan GTP ZX, Porsche 962, Group 44 Jaguar XJR-7 and BMW GTP] J. Rusz. il *Road Track* 38:72-4+ Ap '87

Changing horses [Chevrolet-Ilmor V-8] J. Rusz. il *Road Track* 38:84+ Jl '87

Fiat ECV [rally car] R. Hutton. il *Car Driv* 32:32-3 Ap '87

Green flag and a green car for Porsche's Indy program. J. Rusz. il *Road Track* 38:122+ My '87

The Ilmor-Chevrolet arrives. P. Van Valkenburgh. il *Mot Trend* 39:121-2+ Jl '87

It has 400 HP, costs $40,000—and comes from Toyota? [Turbo Supra race car] J. O. Hamilton. il *Bus Week* p39 Ap 27 '87

King Honda reigns in the F1 title joust. B. Cahier and B. Nagy. il *Mot Trend* 39:133-6 D '87

Power plays [challengers to Cosworth DFX V-8 engine] C. Csere. il *Car Driv* 33:149-50+ S '87

Top-speed trapshoot [NASCAR Chevy Monte Carlo and IMSA Porsche 962] J. Rusz. il *Road Track* 38:40-5 Ja '87

History

See also

Automobiles, Antique

1948 Blue Crown Special. R. Busenkell. il *Road Track* 38:232-8 Je '87

1951 Barlow Simca Special. D. Batchelor. il *Road Track* 39:82-8 D '87

1951 Ferrari 340 America Vignale. P. Hill. il *Road Track* 39:72-8 O '87

1955 OSCA MT4. R. T. Devlin and M. T. Lynch. il *Road Track* 38:134-40 Mr '87

1957 Cooper Climax F2. I. Ireland. il *Road Track* 38:76-82 F '87

Automobiles, Racing—History—*cont.*

1958 Vanwall. P. Hill. il *Road Track* 38:166-72+ My '87

1963 Saab 96. R. Thursby. il *Road Track* 39:94-100 N '87

It's okay, we're with the car [Ford Talladega] A. Girdler. il *Road Track* 39:130-1 D '87

Old and new [Pirelli race cars] D. Sherman. il *Car Driv* 33:9 N '87

Sliding pillars, hemi heads and other old-fashioned action. D. Simanaitis. il *Road Track* 39:182-3 N '87

Models
See Automobile models

Speed
Speed thrills [Indy 500] il *Sport Mag* 78:70-1 Je '87

Testing
Benetton-BMW B186 Formula 1 [cover story] I. Ireland. il *Road Track* 38:42-9 Mr '87

Camel GTP Corps [Mustang GTP Probe, Corvette GTP, Nissan GTP ZX, Porsche 962, Group 44 Jaguar XJR-7 and BMW GTP] J. Rusz. il *Road Track* 38:72-4+ Ap '87

Cavalier attitude [IMSA RS Chevy] D. Knowles. il *Road Track* 38:114-16+ Ap '87

Fiat ECV [rally car] R. Hutton. il *Car Driv* 32:32-3 Ap '87

Fiero vs. Fiero at the Glen [racing GTP car vs. production GT] R. Grable. il *Mot Trend* 39:76-83 Ja '87

If I had my life to live over, I'd live over a Formula 1 garage [technicalities encountered in testing Benetton B186 F1] D. Simanaitis. il *Road Track* 38:164 Mr '87

Lap and learn [Morrison-Cook Motorsports' IMSA GTO Corvette] R. Ceppos. il *Car Driv* 32:171-3+ Je '87

Lotus Elan Autocrosser. il *Road Track* 38:57-9 F '87

This Bud's for Bear [fighter pilot W. Pickavance drives B. Rahal's March-Cosworth Indy car] P. Lyons. il pors *Car Driv* 32:158 Ap '87

Top-speed trapshoot [NASCAR Chevy Monte Carlo and IMSA Porsche 962] J. Rusz. il *Road Track* 38:40-5 Ja '87

Transmission
Porsche's gearbox gamble [Porsche 962C with PDK transmission] P. Frère. il *Road Track* 38:106+ F '87

Automobiles, Rebodied *See* Automobiles, Remodeled

Automobiles, Remodeled

Exotic, erotic Corvettes [cover story] J. R. Nerad. il *Mot Trend* 39:40-6 S '87

Making your auto into you. J. A. Seamonds. il *U S News World Rep* 103:62 S 7 '87

Nauti-mobile [1968 Buick Le Sabre with flying bridge] P. Garner. il *Road Track* 38:224 Je '87

Four wheel drive
The new Outdoorsman conversions [customized hunting and fishing Suburbans] T. Opre. il *Outdoor Life* 179:70-2+ Ap '87

Waterfowl wagon [GMC Suburban becomes Duck Truck] T. Opre. il *Outdoor Life* 180:32+ S '87

Testing
AMG Hammer [remodeled Mercedes] J. Rusz. il *Road Track* 38:124-6+ Ag '87

Dream machines [Ruf Porsche Turbo and Autokraft AC Mk IV; cover story] il *Road Track* 38:40-7 My '87

Ferrari Testarossa double-header [Straman and Agnelli convertibles; cover story] J. Thompson and G. Rogliatti. il *Road Track* 39:38-43 S '87

A gathering of eagles [AMG Hammer, Callaway Corvettes, Ferrari Testarossa, Keith Black Camaro, Motorsport Design Porsche 911 Turbo and Norwood Ferrari-Chevrolet GTO; cover story] R. Ceppos. il *Car Driv* 33:42-51 D '87

Hartge Grand National [Buick] C. Csere. il *Car Driv* 33:110-11 Ag '87

JMX Taurus. A. St. Antoine. il *Car Driv* 32:120+ Ap '87

Lister-Jaguar XJ-S NAS. T. West. il *Road Track* 39:82+ N '87

Mera [Fiero remodeled as Ferrari replica] T. Assenza. il *Car Driv* 32:127 Je '87

Mercedes-Benz 560SEC AMG. M. Brockman. il *Mot Trend* 39:65-6 Ag '87

Run to the sun [Callaway Turbo Corvette vs. Koenig Twin-Turbo Porsche 911 in Europe; cover story] J. Rusz. il *Road Track* 38:46-52 Ag '87

Saleen Mustang. C. Csere. il *Car Driv* 33:87+ O '87

Testarossa Targa [Ferrari] T. Madigan. il *Mot Trend* 39:67+ Je '87

Toyota MR2 Convertible. J. R. Nerad. il *Mot Trend* 39:135 Je '87

Automobiles, Restored

Cars that don't run [1920's Nash] J. R. Nerad. il *Mot Trend* 39:112 Ag '87

Automobiles, Solar

Racing with the sun [GM Sunraycer] il *Sci News* 132:219 O 3 '87

Racing with the sun [Pentax Solar Challenge: cover story] D. McCosh. il map *Pop Sci* 231:84-7 N '87

Solar-powered cars to race across Australia. il *Radio-Electron* 58:4 N '87

Winning a race in the sun [Sunraycer] *Sci News* 132:349 N 28 '87

Automobiles, Three wheel

Testing
Messerschmitt Kabinenroller. P. Lyons. il *Cycle* 38:67-70+ F '87

Automobiles, Toy *See* Toys

Automobiles, Used

The Beach Boys go heavy metal [1967 Pontiac GTO] R. Titus. il *Mot Trend* 39:132 Je '87

Finding the Fury [search for 1956 Plymouth Fury] B. Boggs. il *N Y Times Mag* p37 Ag 2 '87

Prices
Blue book. P. L. Spencer. *Consum Res Mag* 70:2 Je '87

Car values down the road. E. Henry. il *Changing Times* 41:87-9 F '87

Entry-level cars: the used-car alternative? M. Anson. *Mot Trend* 39:6 Jl '87

Purchasing
1987 models as used cars. *Consum Rep* 52:102-33 D '87

How to buy a used car. L. F. McCarthy. il *Seventeen* 46:90 My '87

How to buy a used car and separate the dogs from the deals. D. McCluggage. il *Glamour* 85:108+ Ag '87

How to find a good used car. il *Consum Rep* 52:257-9 Ap '87

Odometer fraud: it's worse than you think. D. B. Zukowski. il *Changing Times* 41:55-6+ S '87

Selling
The doomsday book [ads for used cars] A. Girdler. il *Road Track* 39:22 D '87

Gone . . . but not forgotten [1969 musclecar] A. Girdler. il *Road Track* 38:20 Mr '87

Sifting and winnowing [classified ads] P. Egan. il *Road Track* 39:18 S '87

Testing
Falling apart and falling in love [1973 Alfa Romeo GTV and 1968 MGB] il *Road Track* 39:107 N '87

Old crocks and Englishmen (and Italians) go out in the noon-day sun [1973 Alfa Romeo 2000 GTV and 1968 MGB Tourer] P. Bohr and P. Egan. il *Road Track* 38:60-2+ Ag '87

Triumph TR6. P. Bohr. il *Road Track* 38:82-4+ Mr '87

Automobiles in advertising

Oscar Mayer Wienermobile. J. R. Nerad. il *Mot Trend* 39:108-13 D '87

A shady business [selling advertising on auto screens by Auto-Shade] il *Newsweek* 109:61 My 11 '87

Automobiles in art

Art and the automobile [work by Héctor Luis Bergandi, Ken Dallison, Dennis Brown and Mark Stehrenberger] J. Thompson. il *Road Track* 38:74-81 Je '87

Exhibitions
See also
L'Art et L'Automobile Gallery

Automobiles in business

A Chicago sting: CEO scofflaws, beware [company cars ticketed] *Newsweek* 109:52 F 9 '87

Fleet management. J. Candler. il *Nations Bus* 75:61-2+ My '87

Small fry start nipping at the whales of auto rental. J. E. Ellis. il *Bus Week* p81 Ag 31 '87

Automobiles in literature

Ten best novels of the road. M. B. Lewis. il *Car Driv* 32:77-8 Ja '87

Automobiles in television

The cars of Miami Vice [cover story] C. Gromer. il *Pop Mech* 164:85-9+ Jl '87

Automotive diesel engines *See* Diesel engines, Automotive

Automotive electronics *See* Automobiles—Electronic equipment; Automobiles, Foreign—Electronic equipment

Automotive engineering *See* Automobile engineering

Automotive gas turbines *See* Gas turbines, Automotive

Automotive industries

See also
Automobile equipment industry
Automobile industry

Automotive industries—See also—*cont.*
Truck industry
Management
Performance of multifactor productivity in the steel and
motor vehicles industries. M. K. Sherwood. bibl f
il *Mon Labor Rev* 110:22-31 Ag '87
Automotive journalism *See* Journalism, Automotive
Autonomous land vehicles
"Unmanned" warfare due in the future? il *Radio-Electron*
58:4 Ap '87
Autonomous University of Guadalajara *See* Universidad
Autónoma de Guadalajara
Autonomy
See also
National liberation movements
United Nations. Decolonization Committee
United Nations. Special Committee on the Situation
with Regard to the Implementation of the Declara-
tion on the Granting of Independence to Colonial
Countries and Peoples
Autopilots *See* Automatic pilot (Airplanes)
Autoradiography
Three-dimensional representation and analysis of brain
energy metabolism [glucose] L. S. Hibbard and others.
bibl f il *Science* 236:1641-6 Je 26 '87
Autotype U.S.A. (Firm)
Paul Bunyan dons a giant T-shirt—are tall tails next?
[statue in Bemidji, Minn.] il *People Wkly* 28:97 Ag
3 '87
Autowinders (Photography) *See* Photography—Equipment
Autumn
See also
November
October
1987's stars of the fall [special section] il *People Wkly*
28:63-6+ Ag 31 '87
An Old West autumn. D. Young. il *South Living* 22:38+
O '87
Urban autumn. *America* 157:204-5 O 10 '87
Photographs and photography
Moods of autumn [cover story] il *Ctry J* 14:40-7 N
'87
Autumn leaves, Color of *See* Color of leaves
Autumn vacations *See* Vacations
Auxiliary equipment on boats *See* Boats and boating—Equip-
ment
AV-8B airplanes *See* Airplanes, Military
Av Paul, Annette *See* Paul, Annette av
Available-light photography *See* Photography—Light and
lighting
Avalanches
See also
Landslides
Avalanche! [Switzerland] S. Cashen. il *Int Wildl* 17:36-7
My/Je '87
Collapsing volcanoes. P. Francis and S. Self. bibl (p136)
il *Sci Am* 256:90-7 Je '87
The limits of '*glasnost*' [attitudes of ski areas towards
publicizing avalanche dangers] A. H. Greenberg. *Skiing*
40:64-5+ N '87
Avalon, Frankie
about
Frankie and Annette: back to the beach. E. Sherman.
il pors *Ladies Home J* 104:48+ Jl '87
Once more unto the beach. R. Wolmuth. il pors *People
Wkly* 28:24-7 Ag 10 '87
Avant-garde (Aesthetics)
The avant-garde: moving into middle America. M. Horn.
il *U S News World Rep* 102:68-9 My 18 '87
The terrorist aesthetic; tr. by John Satriano. A. Moravia.
Harpers 274:37-9+ Je '87
Utopia revisited [Black Mountain College] M. Wade.
il *Horizon* 30:13-16 Je '87
Avant-garde art *See* Art, Modern
Avant-garde films *See* Motion pictures—Experimental films
Avant-garde music *See* Music, Experimental
Avant-garde phonograph records *See* Phonograph records—
Experimental music
Avanti Motor Corp.
See also
New Avanti Motor Corp.
Avarice
All hail the new greed. L. Wainwright. il *Life* 10:12
Je '87
Covetousness: the one who dies with the most toys
wins. D. Morris. il *U S Cathol* 52:13-14 Ag '87
Don't believe all the epitaphs. M. Greenfield. il *Newsweek*
110:124 N 16 '87
Good greed. D. Seligman. il *Fortune* 115:119 Mr 2
'87

Greed that starts at the top. A. Fotheringham. il *Macleans*
100:52 Mr 2 '87
Paying for a good squeeze. C. Gordon. por *Macleans*
100:7 Mr 9 '87
Avco Corp.
Avco group eyes tactical missile work. il *Aviat Week
Space Technol* 126:135-6 My 11 '87
Avco Lycoming business plan stresses quality and service.
S. W. Kandebo. il *Aviat Week Space Technol* 126:79+
Je 1 '87
Avco Lycoming seeks solutions to LT101 reliability
problems. P. Proctor. *Aviat Week Space Technol*
126:61-2 My 25 '87
Avco pleads guilty to $1.5-million overcharge. *Aviat Week
Space Technol* 126:21 Je 29 '87
Lycoming reverses LTS101 decision. *Aviat Week Space
Technol* 126:71 F 23 '87
Avebury, Eric Reginald Lubbock, 4th Baron of, 1928-
about
A British lord wants to go to the dogs . . . literally!
il por *People Wkly* 27:94 F 23 '87
Avedon, Richard
about
Through Eastern eyes. M. Kozloff. il *Art Am* 75:90-7
Ja '87
AVENSA *See* Aerovias Venezolanas SA
Averages, Stock *See* Stocks—Price indexes and averages
Averill, Ric
about
The imagination express. M. Wade. il por *Horizon*
30:19-20 S '87
Avermectins
See also
Ivermectin
Avery, Gillian, 1926-
A good home for old words. il *Am Herit* 38:104-6
Jl/Ag '87
Avery International Corporation
A sticky business. M. Beauchamp. il por *Forbes* 139:61
Ja 26 '87
Avgas *See* Airplane engines—Fuel
Avian erythroblastosis virus *See* Leukemia viruses
Avian leukosis viruses *See* Oncogenic viruses
Aviation
See also
Air navigation
Air travel
Airlines
Airplanes
Airports
Airships
Balloon ascensions
Calculators—Aviation use
Computers—Aviation use
Gliding and soaring
Image processing—Aviation use
Information storage and retrieval systems—Aviation
use
Private flying
Radar in aviation
Radio in aviation
Superconductors and superconductivity—Aviation
use
Videodiscs—Aviation use
Videotapes—Aviation use
Aviation. D. Eskow. See issues of Popular Mechanics
beginning January 1986 through January 1987
News digest. See issues of Aviation Week & Space
Technology
Reporting points. See issues of Flying
The sport of it [cover story; special section] il *Flying*
114:54-62+ My '87
Accident prevention
See Aviation—Safety devices and measures
Accidents
See also
Airplanes—Collision avoidance systems
Airplanes, Jet—Fires and fire prevention
Airplanes, Military—Fires and fire prevention
Drugs and airplane accidents
Helicopters—Accidents
United States. National Transportation Safety Board
A-7D crash accents different USAF, Navy emergency
rules [attempted flameout approach] il *Aviat Week
Space Technol* 127:31 N 2 '87
Actor, athlete and dashing pilot, Dean Paul Martin dies
when his jet crashes on a mountainside. R. Arias.
il *People Wkly* 27:128-30 Ap 13 '87
Aeromedical aircraft accidents register sharp increase
in 1987. P. Proctor. *Aviat Week Space Technol* 127:55+
Jl 13 '87

Aviation—Accidents—*cont.*

Aftermath. P. Garrison. See issues of Flying

Air safety: erosion of confidence [special section; with editorial comment by Donald E. Fink] il *Aviat Week Space Technol* 127:11, 18-25 Ag 24 '87

Alone in the shark-filled sea [W. Wyatt adrift after small plane crashes] P. Michelmore. il *Read Dig* 131:116-21 O '87

Australian panel investigates 1985 crash of IAI Westwind [report on October 10 accident off the South Head of Botany Bay, New South Wales] il *Aviat Week Space Technol* 126:357-8+ Je 15 '87

Bird strike suspected as cause of B-1B crash that killed three. W. B. Scott. *Aviat Week Space Technol* 127:21 O 5 '87

Board examines radar's role in Cerritos midair collision [August 31, 1986 collision in California] *Aviat Week Space Technol* 127:127-8+ D 14 '87

British L-1011 accident report raises questions on braking data [1985 British Airtours accident] D. A. Brown. *Aviat Week Space Technol* 127:52 O 12 '87

Canadian Safety Board assesses crash of F-20A prototype [May 14, 1985] il *Aviat Week Space Technol* 126:89+ Mr 16 '87

Canadians investigate pilot's loss of consciousness prior to F-20A crash [May 14, 1985] *Aviat Week Space Technol* 126:75+ Mr 23 '87

A case of Delta blues [near disasters] il *Time* 130:53 Jl 27 '87

Cerritos inquiry reviews separation, collision avoidance procedures [August 1986 collision of DC-9 and Piper aircraft] *Aviat Week Space Technol* 127:67-70 D 21 '87

Cold weather, pilot training focus of DC-9 crash inquiry [Continental Airlines crash in Denver, November 15, 1987] il *Aviat Week Space Technol* 127:34-6 N 23 '87

Collisions [cover story; special section] il *Flying* 114:66-9+ Je '87

Crunch time [survivable airplane crashes] M. Phelps. il *Flying* 114:72-5 N '87

Dangers in a crowded sky [Northwest Airlines Flight 255] B. Wallace. il *Macleans* 100:44 Ag 31 '87

Dark clouds over Delta [four near misses] il *Newsweek* 110:41 Jl 20 '87

David Burke's deadly revenge [fired USAir employee causes PSA jet to crash] E. Magnuson. il por *Time* 130:30 D 21 '87

Delta Air Lines officials baffled by series of unrelated mishaps. C. Preble. il *Aviat Week Space Technol* 127:31-2 Jl 20 '87

Disaster in the skies [bomb suspected in downing of Korean Air Lines Flight 858] A. Bilski. il *Macleans* 100:24 D 14 '87

Disasters waiting to happen. G. Bock. il *Time* 130:43-4 Ag 3 '87

FAA investigation focuses on Delta operations, training. C. Preble. il *Aviat Week Space Technol* 127:31 Jl 27 '87

FAA investigators seek pattern in near-midair collisions. P. Proctor. il *Aviat Week Space Technol* 126:63-4 Ap 27 '87

FAA urges use of standard procedures, more discipline in Delta cockpits. E. H. Phillips. *Aviat Week Space Technol* 127:44 S 28 '87

Glacier greaser [Twin Comanche gets lost and crashes in Greenland] J. Justis. il map *Flying* 114:109-10 F '87

Grand Canyon collision [June 30, 1956 crash ushers in modern air traffic control] R. L. Collins. *Flying* 114:22+ S '87

The gremlins in the sky [near misses] C. P. Work. il *U S News World Rep* 103:12-13 Jl 20 '87

Gunman seen as key to crash of PSA flight that killed 43 [D. A. Burke] M. A. Dornheim. il *Aviat Week Space Technol* 127:31 D 14 '87

High anxiety and rage. S. Koepp. il *Time* 130:52-4 Jl 20 '87

Investigators assess pilots' ability to sight aircraft on collision course [August 1986 collision of Aeromexico DC-9 and Piper Cherokee over Cerritos, Calif.] *Aviat Week Space Technol* 127:91+ D 7 '87

Investigators cite engine failure in Polish Ilyushin Il-62M crash [May 9, 1987 crash] *Aviat Week Space Technol* 127:57 Ag 3 '87

Japanese cite faulty bulkhead repair as cause of JAL 747 crash in 1985. *Aviat Week Space Technol* 126:34 Je 29 '87

A lawyers' rush for judgments [Northwest Airlines crash in Detroit] T. Gest. il *U S News World Rep* 103:23 Ag 31 '87

Lost at sea [surviving a plane crash off Haiti] F. B. Randall. il pors map *N Y* 20:36-43 Ag 10 '87

Mass murder in the clouds [D. A. Burke and crash of PSA Flight 1771] M. Satchell. il por *U S News World Rep* 103:14-15 D 21 '87

Mastering the microburst [cover story] R. Monastersky. il *Sci News* 131:185-7 Mr 21 '87

Midair collision builds pressure for CVRs in commuter aircraft [cockpit voice recorders] *Aviat Week Space Technol* 126:32 Ja 26 '87

Military air accident rates parallel 1986's low levels. D. M. North. il *Aviat Week Space Technol* 126:66-7+ Je 8 '87

The mystery of Flight 858 [North Koreans suspected of planting bomb on Korean Air Lines plane] *Time* 130:46 D 14 '87

Northwest wreckage confirms flaps retracted on takeoff [Detroit crash] J. Ott. *Aviat Week Space Technol* 127:32-3 Ag 31 '87

NTSB analyzes factors leading to California midair collision of DC-9, Piper aircraft. *Aviat Week Space Technol* 127:59-60+ N 30 '87

NTSB blames ATC system for midair crash [Aug. 31, 1986 collision of Aeromexico DC-9-30 and Piper PA-28-181] *Aviat Week Space Technol* 127:34 Jl 13 '87

NTSB cites air tour rules in canyon crash [airliner-helicopter crash, June 18, 1986] *Aviat Week Space Technol* 126:40 Mr 30 '87

NTSB cites erroneous transponder code in near collision [two American Airlines Boeing 727s near O'Hare International Airport] *Aviat Week Space Technol* 126:82 Je 15 '87

NTSB determines probable causes of Delta accident [Dallas/Ft. Worth Delta airline crash, August 2, 1985] *Aviat Week Space Technol* 126:95+ Ja 26 '87

NTSB focuses on cockpit communication, inspection methods in Milwaukee crash [September 1985 crash of a Midwest Express DC-9] P. Proctor. *Aviat Week Space Technol* 126:41 F 16 '87

NTSB recommends upgraded training, reporting to avoid wind shear [August 2, 1985 Delta Flight 191 crash at Dallas/Ft. Worth] *Aviat Week Space Technol* 126:93+ F 2 '87

On the record. M. Phelps. See issues of Flying

Our troubled skies (contd.) [succession of near disasters] J. Horowitz. il *Time* 130:35 Ag 10 '87

Out of control. J. M. McClellan. il *Flying* 114:48-50+ Jl '87

The poisoned flight of KAL [possible North Korean involvement in bombing of Flight 858] il *U S News World Rep* 103:12 D 14 '87

Prime movers [accident records of the Cessna Skyhawk, Mooney 201 and Bonanza A36] J. M. McClellan. il *Flying* 114:50-2+ Mr '87

Probe of Harrier crash focuses on emergency parachute system. D. A. Brown. il *Aviat Week Space Technol* 127:30-1 N 2 '87

The riddle of Flight 255 [Northwest crash in Detroit] W. D. Marbach. il *Newsweek* 110:20 Ag 31 '87

Safer flying? R. L. Collins. *Flying* 114:17 N '87

Safety Board cites 1986 as one of safest years ever. *Aviat Week Space Technol* 126:36 Ja 19 '87

Safety Board cites limitations of airport weather surveillance [August 2, 1985 Delta Flight 191 crash at Dallas/Ft. Worth] *Aviat Week Space Technol* 126:113-14+ Ja 12 '87

Safety Board urges pilot training in G-induced loss of consciousness [crash of F-20A prototype at Goose Bay, Labrador, May 14, 1985] il *Aviat Week Space Technol* 126:103-4 Mr 30 '87

Settling a score [murders aboard PSA airliner linked to USAir ex-employee D. Burke] G. Hackett. il por *Newsweek* 110:43 D 21 '87

A shattered dream [excerpt from The sorrow and the terror: the haunting legacy of the Air India tragedy] C. Blaise and B. Mukherjee. il pors *Macleans* 100:42-5 My 25 '87

Sifting through the wreckage [crash of Northwest Airlines Flight 255 in Detroit] R. Stengel. il *Time* 130:15-16 Ag 31 '87

The Starduster's last flight [M. Ryan rescued after plane crash with use of emergency locator transmitter] P. O. D'Aulaire and E. D'Aulaire. il *Read Dig* 131:75-80 Jl '87

Survival at sea [plane crash off Haiti] A. Randall. il por map *Seventeen* 46:108-9+ D '87

There's more choppiness ahead for Delta. S. Ticer. il *Bus Week* p30-1 Ag 3 '87

'This is a miracle!' came the cry of disbelief—'My God, we're alive!' [K. Engelhart, stewardess on Continental Flight 1713] il por *People Wkly* 28:103 D 21 '87

Aviation—Accidents—*cont.*

Too green to fly? [crash at Denver's Stapleton Airport raises doubts about pilots] B. Kantrowitz. il *Newsweek* 110:32+ N 30 '87

A tragic repeat [private plane collides with commuter airline over Utah] E. Magnuson. il *Time* 129:22 Ja 26 '87

Trapped in the wreckage of Flight 1713, Robert Linck survives to fly home again. A. Richman. il pors *People Wkly* 28:98-102 D 21 '87

USAF, Rockwell strengthen B-1B against bird strikes. D. M. North. *Aviat Week Space Technol* 127:30 D 21 '87

Who destroyed Korean Air 858? M. Liu. il *Newsweek* 110:61 D 14 '87

Wind shear and airplane crashes [microbursts; research by T. T. Fujita] il *USA Today (Periodical)* 115:5 Je '87

Worries in busy skies. W. J. Cook. il *U S News World Rep* 103:18-19 Ag 24 '87

Wrong track [near misses and sloppy safety procedures] E. Magnuson. il *Time* 130:29+ S 14 '87

Year of the near miss [cover story; special section] il *Newsweek* 110:20-7 Jl 27 '87

Altitude flying

Altitude alert. J. M. McClellan. il *Flying* 114:44-6+ F '87

Bibliography

Books. M. Phelps. *Flying* 114:96 Ag '87

Bird hazards

Bird strike suspected as cause of B-1B crash that killed three. W. B. Scott. *Aviat Week Space Technol* 127:21 O 5 '87

These eyes high in the Japanese sky are strictly for the birds [All Nippon Airways painting eyes on turbines to discourage birds] il *Discover* 8:8-9 Ja '87

USAF, Rockwell strengthen B-1B against bird strikes. D. M. North. *Aviat Week Space Technol* 127:30 D 21 '87

Charts

See Aviation charts

Cold weather conditions

See Aviation—Winter flying

Communication systems

See also

Arinc Inc.

Communications satellites—Aviation use

Crouzet, Bendix will develop voice command system [military aircraft] *Aviat Week Space Technol* 127:77 Jl 20 '87

Defense Dept., NASA aid Voyager communications. il *Aviat Week Space Technol* 126:26-7 Ja 5 '87

Straight talk. R. L. Collins. il *Flying* 114:58-60+ Ag '87

Competitions

See also

Airplane racing

Clued up to fly [aerial treasure hunt] J. Wynbrandt. *Flying* 114:100-1 Ap '87

Conferences

See also

European Civil Aviation Conference

Aerospace calendar. See issues of Aviation Week & Space Technology

Calendar. See issues of Flying beginning August 1985

Economic aspects

See also

Airlines—Fares

Energy usage

See also

Airlines—Energy usage

Exhibitions

37th Paris Air Show to emphasize space, subcontracting, propulsion. J. M. Lenorovitz. il *Aviat Week Space Technol* 126:66-9 Ap 27 '87

Ascot of the air [Paris Air Show] A. Cockburn. il *House Gard* 159:34+ My '87

Aviation's twin meccas [Sun 'n' Fun and Oshkosh] F. Mackerodt. *Pop Mech* 164:40 Je '87

Bear country [fly-in celebrating 50th anniversary of the Piper Cub] R. Munson. il *Flying* 114:64-9 O '87

Calendar. See issues of Flying beginning August 1985

Chinese exhibition underscores aviation modernization efforts [Aviation Expo/China; with editorial comment by Donald E. Fink] R. G. O'Lone. *Aviat Week Space Technol* 127:13, 28-9 O 26 '87

Chinese plan to display aircraft at Paris Air Show. il *Aviat Week Space Technol* 126:21 Ja 19 '87

Congress approves air show deductions, cuts Exim funding. *Aviat Week Space Technol* 127:23 Jl 13 '87

Displays of new transports highlight Chinese exhibition [Aviation Expo/China] il *Aviat Week Space Technol* 127:72-3 N 2 '87

Exhibition space sold out for 1988 Farnborough show. *Aviat Week Space Technol* 127:147 D 14 '87

Exhibitors' list falling short for planned U.S. air show [Air/Space America 88] B. A. Smith. *Aviat Week Space Technol* 127:57 N 30 '87

Hardcore Oshkosh. P. Scott. il *Flying* 114:42-7+ D '87

Helicopter show reflects slow worldwide sales [Helicopter Assn. International meeting and industry exposition] P. Proctor. il *Aviat Week Space Technol* 126:76-7 Mr 16 '87

High-flying Oshkosh. M. G. Davidson. *Travel Holiday* 167:34+ Je '87

How to steal the Paris Air Show [Soviet exhibit outshines U.S. exhibit] E. M. Reingold. il *Time* 130:49 Jl 13 '87

International involvement highlights Chinese show [Aviation Expo/China] il *Aviat Week Space Technol* 127:30-1 O 19 '87

Letter from Paris [Paris Air Show] S. Butler-Hannifin. il *Space World* X-9-285:30-3 S '87

O Canada [Abbotsford Air Show] N. Moll. il *Flying* 114:44-50 Ja '87

Paris 87: the rain reigned. N. Moll. *Flying* 114:86 O '87

Paris Air Show [cover story; special issue] il *Aviat Week Space Technol* 126:60-5+ Je 15 '87

Paris Air Show [cover story; special section] il *Aviat Week Space Technol* 127:75+ Jl 6 '87

Paris Air Show [cover story; special section; with editorial comment by Donald E. Fink] il *Aviat Week Space Technol* 126:13, 20-31, 38-40, 62-3+ Je 22 '87

Paris Air Show [cover story; special section; with editorial comment by Donald E. Fink] il *Aviat Week Space Technol* 126:11, 65+ Je 29 '87

Record U.S. turnout to offset lack of key firms [1987 Paris Air Show] M. Mecham. *Aviat Week Space Technol* 126:71-2 Ap 27 '87

Report from Paris. F. Mackerodt. il *Pop Mech* 164:16-17 O '87

Soviet Union seeks to renew industry relations with China [Aviation Expo/China] *Aviat Week Space Technol* 127:29 O 26 '87

Soviets exhibit full-scale model of Mir complex at Paris Air Show. il *Aviat Week Space Technol* 127:58-60 Jl 20 '87

Trainers make strong showing in Le Bourget flight program [Paris Air Show] il *Aviat Week Space Technol* 127:57 Jl 27 '87

Fees

A question of fees [fees on international airline tickets to cover the rising costs of inspections] S. Shane. *Travel Holiday* 167:39 F '87

Fog hazards

Hopeless optimism [fatal crash of a VFR-only Mooney 201 pilot departing San Antonio in low IFR conditions] J. M. McClellan. *Flying* 114:24+ Jl '87

Out of character [crash of Cessna T210 in snow and fog] P. Garrison. *Flying* 114:20+ O '87

Handbooks, manuals, etc.

See also

Aviation charts

History

See also

Airlines—History

Airplanes, Antique

Airports—History

Aviation—Transatlantic flights—History

Aviation—World flights—History

60th anniversary issue [cover story; special issue; with editorial comment by Richard L. Collins] il *Flying* 114:2+ S '87

Curvaceous Connie [Lockheed Constellation] G. Baxter. il *Flying* 114:105-6 Jl '87

Fascinating aviation forecasts made 75 years ago. il *Forbes* 139:18 Mr 23 '87

On the numbers. L. Morgan. il *Flying* 114:8-9 F '87

On the wings of yesterday [K. Kellett] D. Young. il pors *South Living* 22:125-6 F '87

Retracing Lindy's victorious trip across the country. M. Parfit. bibl (p231) il pors map *Smithsonian* 18:200-2+ O '87

Ice hazards

Airframe icing has posed problems for DC-9-10 aircraft. *Aviat Week Space Technol* 127:36 N 23 '87

Deicing for the Bonanza [TKS anti-ice system] J. M. McClellan. il *Flying* 114:100 Jl '87

Frost bitten [Cessna Cardinal has icing problem on approach] T. Owings. il *Flying* 114:110 Mr '87

Aviation—Ice hazards—*cont.*

Heavy burden [ice brings down a Saratoga] P. Garrison. *Flying* 114:24+ Je '87

Icy connotations. R. L. Collins. il *Flying* 114:20+ Ap '87

NASA tests electro-expulsive deicer that could protect F/A-18 engines. B. D. Nordwall. il *Aviat Week Space Technol* 127:89+ Ag 3 '87

Out of character [crash of Cessna T210 in snow and fog] P. Garrison. *Flying* 114:20+ O '87

Insect hazards

Bugged pitot. J. Holloway. il *Flying* 114:104 D '87

Instrument flying

Canceling VFR. P. Scott. *Flying* 114:75 F '87

Cat's eyes [Category II landing; cover story] J. M. McClellan. il *Flying* 114:48-50+ N '87

East-west misunderstanding [Samantha Smith Beech 99 accident] J. M. McClellan. il *Flying* 114:20-2 My '87

Hardball IFR [cover story] R. L. Collins. il *Flying* 114:58-62 Mr '87

High school [National Intercollegiate Flying Association] R. L. Collins. il *Flying* 114:17-18 Ag '87

Hopeless optimism [fatal crash of a VFR-only Mooney 201 pilot departing San Antonio in low IFR conditions] J. M. McClellan. *Flying* 114:24+ Jl '87

IFR/VFR mix and match. M. Brenlove. *Flying* 114:96 D '87

IFR tactics [changes due to new traffic control rules] R. L. Collins. il *Flying* 114:33 D '87

Initial approaches [instrument flying] P. Garrison. il *Flying* 114:76-8+ Ap '87

Mile high memories. R. L. Collins. il *Flying* 114:17-18+ S '87

New policy backs acquisition, use of traditional ILSs [instrument landing system] *Aviat Week Space Technol* 126:36 Mr 23 '87

Out of character [crash of Cessna T210 in snow and fog] P. Garrison. *Flying* 114:20+ O '87

Side-by-side in the soup [simultaneous ILS approaches] M. Brenlove. *Flying* 114:98 Je '87

"Two saves, partial panel" [medevac mission in Alaska] T. Olden. il *Flying* 114:110-11 Ag '87

International aspects

See also
Airspace (International law)
Helicopter Association International
International Air Transport Association
International Civil Airports Association
International Civil Aviation Organization

Canada, Britain agree on air services pact. *Aviat Week Space Technol* 127:36 O 5 '87

Carriers dispute British airport fees [U.S. airlines] D. A. Brown. *Aviat Week Space Technol* 126:39 F 16 '87

ECAC, U.S. renew North Atlantic pact [European Civil Aviation Conference] *Aviat Week Space Technol* 126:32 F 23 '87

FAA adopting new certification strategies for foreign aircraft, parts [airworthiness bilaterals] J. Ott. il *Aviat Week Space Technol* 126:307-8+ Je 15 '87

FAA urges China to clear path to bilateral airworthiness pact. *Aviat Week Space Technol* 127:38-9 Ag 17 '87

Foreign airlines switching tactics in seeking rights to U.S. market. J. Ott. *Aviat Week Space Technol* 126:227+ Je 15 '87

KLM gains Orlando gateway over U.S. carriers' protests. *Aviat Week Space Technol* 127:44 Ag 3 '87

MD-82 coproduction could aid in forming U.S.-China bilateral. B. A. Smith. il *Aviat Week Space Technol* 126:43+ Ap 6 '87

Soviets grant British carriers right to overfly Siberia. *Aviat Week Space Technol* 126:36 Ap 6 '87

Swiss, U.S. exchange access to Atlanta for check-in rights. *Aviat Week Space Technol* 127:34 Jl 27 '87

Turbulence in the skies [British-Canadian dispute over airline routes] T. Tedesco. il *Macleans* 100:27 Ag 31 '87

U.S. airlines oppose KLM service to Orlando. *Aviat Week Space Technol* 126:42 My 11 '87

U.S., Australian officials deadlock over Continental Airlines schedule. *Aviat Week Space Technol* 126:41 Je 1 '87

U.S. denies British Airways ticket offer to continental Europe. J. Ott. *Aviat Week Space Technol* 126:34-5 Ap 6 '87

Laws and regulations

See also
Air pilots—Legal status, laws, etc.
Air traffic control
Airspace (International law)
United States. Federal Aviation Administration

The airlines counterattack on Capitol Hill. S. Payne. il *Bus Week* p58 O 19 '87

Aviation safety: fact or fiction [effects of deregulation; cover story] R. R. Gray. il *Technol Rev* 90:32-40 Ag/S '87

Crandall seeks Congress' support for restrictions on general aviation. *Aviat Week Space Technol* 127:41 S 14 '87

Delays, service problems prompt strong congressional reaction [airlines] J. Ott. *Aviat Week Space Technol* 127:33-5 Ag 10 '87

The docket. P. Bradley. See issues of Flying beginning July 1986 through August 1987

Free-for-all: what deregulation means to the airline pilot. P. Scott. il *Flying* 114:40-2+ Jl '87

House approves labor protection for employees of merged airlines. *Aviat Week Space Technol* 126:33-4 Je 29 '87

House panel considers reregulation of airlines. C. Preble. *Aviat Week Space Technol* 126:74-5 Je 15 '87

Is airline deregulation working? S. Shane. *Travel Holiday* 168:6 Ag '87

The legacy of airline deregulation: public benefits, but new problems. M. Levine. por *Aviat Week Space Technol* 127:161+ N 9 '87

Legislation may set capacity levels to control airport congestion. *Aviat Week Space Technol* 127:34+ N 16 '87

Overflight bill includes flight-free zones. *Natl Parks* 61:38 My/Je '87

Overflight rules not tough enough. *Natl Parks* 61:46-8 Mr/Ap '87

Profiting from deregulation. M. Rowland. il *Work Woman* 12:49-50+ Mr '87

Rule models. E. Weiner. *Flying* 114:154-5 S '87

The sky isn't falling [summing up deregulation; cover story] G. Easterbrook. *New Repub* 197:18+ N 30 '87

The straight and narrow [enforcing FARs] R. L. Collins. *Flying* 114:14+ Ja '87

The volatile airline industry [address, February 23, 1987] R. L. Crandall. *Vital Speeches Day* 53:468-72 My 15 '87

Meteorological aspects

See Meteorology, Aviation

Mountain flying

Mountains and storms [thunderstorms] R. L. Collins. *Flying* 114:17-18 N '87

Option play [Cessna T210 crashes into Sierra Nevadas after pilot ignores severe turbulence warnings] J. M. McClellan. *Flying* 114:20+ Mr '87

Peak primer. E. Weiner. il *Flying* 114:44-6+ Mr '87

Night flying

Expanded night-fighting capability shapes Army flight training needs [helicopters] il *Aviat Week Space Technol* 126:115+ Ja 19 '87

In the dark. P. Bradley. il *Flying* 114:20-1 Je '87

Overwater flying

Engine reliability prompts bid for unlimited overwater flights [twinjets] J. Ott. il *Aviat Week Space Technol* 126:36-8 My 11 '87

Physiological aspects

See also
Jet lag

Flying with a cold: save your ears. G. Weiss. il *Bus Week* p148 Ja 12 '87

Sound savers [ear care, sinusitis and air travel] E. S. Orzac. il *Travel Holiday* 168:30 Ag '87

Polar flights

Arctic Tern flight planned for completion this summer. il *Aviat Week Space Technol* 126:153 Mr 9 '87

Single-engine aircraft tests polar navigation [Arctic Tern] map *Aviat Week Space Technol* 126:76 F 2 '87

Records

See Aviation records

Safety devices and measures

See also
Air traffic control
Airplane engines, Jet—Inspection
Airplane evacuation
Airplanes—Collision avoidance systems
Airplanes—Safety devices and measures
Airplanes, Military—Escape devices
Parachutes
Radar in aviation
United States. Federal Aviation Administration—Flight service stations
United States. National Transportation Safety Board

Air safety: erosion of confidence [special section; with editorial comment by Donald E. Fink] il *Aviat Week Space Technol* 127:11, 18-25 Ag 24 '87

Aviation—Safety devices and measures—*cont.*
Airline safety: a shocking truth. D. Nolan. il *Read Dig* 130:125-30 Ja '87
Aviation safety: fact or fiction [effects of deregulation; cover story] R. R. Gray. il *Technol Rev* 90:32-40 Ag/S '87
Avoidance tactics. R. L. Collins. il *Flying* 114:76-7+ Je '87
"Be careful out there" [growing concerns about safety] E. Magnuson. il *Time* 129:24-32 Ja 12 '87
Disasters waiting to happen. G. Bock. il *Time* 130:43-4 Ag 3 '87
Eastern Airlines agrees to pay fine of $9.5 million for safety violations. *Aviat Week Space Technol* 126:34 F 16 '87
Eastern refuses to deal with ALPA until pilots end safety campaign. E. H. Kolcum. *Aviat Week Space Technol* 127:37+ N 9 '87
Fault line [fault analysis] R. L. Collins. *Flying* 114:85-7 My '87
Flying the safer skies [women pilots; research by Gayle Vail] K. Burkett. il *Ms* 15:33 Je '87
GAO study cites safety improvements in defense charters. *Aviat Week Space Technol* 126:43 Ap 20 '87
High anxiety and rage. S. Koepp. il *Time* 130:52-4 Jl 20 '87
How to cut the risk of your number coming up. C. P. Work. il *U S News World Rep* 103:65 Jl 6 '87
Listening to the heartbeat [American public's perceptions of aviation] R. L. Collins. *Flying* 114:24+ My '87
McArtor presses for safety gains, airport construction in 1988 plan. P. Proctor. *Aviat Week Space Technol* 127:36 S 21 '87
New FAA chief will require airline safety audit. *Aviat Week Space Technol* 127:38 Ag 3 '87
Our troubled skies (contd.) [succession of near disasters] J. Horowitz. il *Time* 130:35 Ag 10 '87
Pacific growth could lead to expanded FAA safety duties. J. Ott. *Aviat Week Space Technol* 126:40+ Ap 6 '87
Practice imperfect. P. Bradley. il *Flying* 114:10 Jl '87
Questions about Eastern [maintenance procedures] J. Castro. il *Time* 130:41 Ag 24 '87
Safety experts cite need for increased monitoring [conference at Northwestern University] J. Ott. il *Aviat Week Space Technol* 127:45-6+ Jl 13 '87
Shape up or ship out [general aviation] R. L. Collins. *Flying* 114:24 Ja '87
Solving the crisis in the skies. R. L. Crandall. il por *Fortune* 116:203-4 S 28 '87
Warning signs. R. L. Collins. *Flying* 114:27 Ag '87
Worries in busy skies. W. J. Cook. il *U S News World Rep* 103:18-19 Ag 24 '87
Wrong track [near misses and sloppy safety procedures] E. Magnuson. il *Time* 130:29+ S 14 '87
Year of the near miss [cover story; special section] il *Newsweek* 110:20-7 Jl 27 '87

Social aspects
Listening to the heartbeat [American public's perceptions of aviation] R. L. Collins. *Flying* 114:24+ My '87

Storm hazards
See also
Wind shear
A Cessna to the rescue [helping Cherokee pilot land in stationary cold front] F. Anders. *Flying* 114:101 Jl '87
Hardball IFR [instrument flight rules; cover story] R. L. Collins. il *Flying* 114:58-62 Mr '87
Mountains and storms [thunderstorms] R. L. Collins. *Flying* 114:17-18 N '87
Option play [Cessna T210 crashes into Sierra Nevadas after pilot ignores severe turbulence warnings] J. M. McClellan. *Flying* 114:20+ Mr '87
Orion, the hunter [low on fuel and hunting for a runway] K. Welch. il *Flying* 114:102-4 O '87
Refunds for stormy weather? B. Bauer. il *U S News World Rep* 103:12 N 30 '87
Storm disrupts airline traffic in Western Europe [snowstorm] *Aviat Week Space Technol* 126:34 Ja 19 '87
Storm window [Stormscope] R. L. Collins. il *Flying* 114:76-8+ N '87
Stormbusters [Sperry's LSZ-850 lightning sensor and Primus 870 turbulence-detecting radar] J. M. McClellan. il *Flying* 114:64-6+ Mr '87
Stormy weather. R. L. Collins. il *Flying* 114:17-18 My '87
Thunder blunder. G. Baxter. il *Flying* 114:100 Je '87

Study and teaching
See also
Aeroformation (Firm)
Air Force Flight Test Center (U.S.)

Airplanes, Training
Aviation Training Center
Flight International Group, Inc.
Flight simulators
FlightSafety International, Inc.
National Test Pilot School
SimuFlite Training International, Inc.
University of North Dakota. Aerospace Training and Research Center
Airlines move swiftly to expand, improve pilot training programs. D. Hughes. il *Aviat Week Space Technol* 127:141+ N 9 '87
Airplane specific: training the pilot to suit the airplane. E. Weiner. *Flying* 114:30 Jl '87
Eastern to enroll 4,000 a year in college-based pilot training. *Aviat Week Space Technol* 127:94 O 5 '87
Expanded night-fighting capability shapes Army flight training needs [helicopters] il *Aviat Week Space Technol* 126:115+ Ja 19 '87
FAA urges use of standard procedures, more discipline in Delta cockpits. E. H. Phillips. *Aviat Week Space Technol* 127:44 S 28 '87
Getting into training [special section] il *Flying* 114:72-8+ F '87
How to teach judgment [pilot personality factor; study by Lewis Lester] J. Munson. *Flying* 114:98 Ja '87
Human factors research key element of LHX design. il *Aviat Week Space Technol* 126:118-19+ Ja 19 '87
Insurance companies spur increase in pilot training. P. Proctor. *Aviat Week Space Technol* 126:82-3 My 4 '87
Lufthansa, Swissair introduce full-simulator pilot training [Futura] K. F. Mordoff. il *Aviat Week Space Technol* 127:38-9+ Ag 10 '87
Malibu U. [Piper Malibu training center in Vero Beach, Fla.] E. Weiner. il *Flying* 114:82-5+ Jl '87
Management skill courses devised for key flight department personnel. *Aviat Week Space Technol* 127:114-15 S 28 '87
McArtor orders industry-wide assessment of pilot training. *Aviat Week Space Technol* 127:20-1 Ag 24 '87
Military Airlift Command will transition to C-130 flight crew training system. K. J. Stein. il *Aviat Week Space Technol* 127:109-10 Jl 6 '87
Model pilots [British Airways pilot training program] R. L. Collins. *Flying* 114:90+ N '87
NWA funds training center for zero-time pilot candidates [Northwest Airlines] il *Aviat Week Space Technol* 127:69+ Jl 6 '87
Regional airlines play key role in Continental's pilot development. *Aviat Week Space Technol* 127:40-1 N 16 '87
Rising cost of aerospace systems shapes military, civil pilot training. W. B. Scott. il *Aviat Week Space Technol* 126:194+ Je 15 '87
SAC stresses air crew training to defeat Soviet defenses. B. M. Greeley, Jr. il *Aviat Week Space Technol* 126:72-3+ F 9 '87
Safer flying? R. L. Collins. *Flying* 114:17 N '87
Spin training: kill or cure? E. Collins. il *Flying* 114:60-2 O '87
"A staggering comparison" [discussion of October 1987 article, Spin training: kill or cure?] E. Collins. il *Flying* 114:6+ D '87
Tailored training [personal flying] R. L. Collins. *Flying* 114:27 D '87
Three European Air Forces step up training at Goose Bay. *Aviat Week Space Technol* 127:86 O 5 '87
Tough guy [simulated failure of attitude indicators causes crash of Australian business jet] J. M. McClellan. *Flying* 114:24+ N '87
Training stresses flight deck management, coordination. *Aviat Week Space Technol* 127:104+ S 28 '87
United conducts total training of MAC C-5 crews. il *Aviat Week Space Technol* 127:112 Jl 6 '87
United, SIU Carbondale seek more black pilots. *Jet* 72:16 Ag 3 '87

Aids and devices
New videos from ATC [Aviation Training Center] J. M. McClellan. *Flying* 114:99-100 Ag '87
Updater videos from King. J. M. McClellan. *Flying* 114:95 D '87

Stunt flying
See also
Patrouille de France (Flight squadron)
Snowbirds (Flight squadron)
United States. Air Force. Thunderbirds
Administrator's admission [stunt in Culver Cadet nearly ends in disaster] D. D. Engen. il *Flying* 114:176 S '87
Air show and tell. P. Scott. il *Flying* 114:72-7 Ag '87

Aviation—Stunt flying—*cont.*

Cheryl Rae fell head over heels for stunt pilot Gene Littlefield, and look where it landed her [wingwalking stunts] S. K. Reed. il pors *People Wkly* 28:62-4 N 9 '87

High roller. L. Loudenslager. il *Pop Mech* 164:66-8 O '87

The physics of aerobatic flight [cover story] C. R. O'Dell. il *Phys Today* 40:24-30 N '87

Study and teaching

Flip side [learning with D. Cole] J. M. McClellan. il por *Flying* 114:56-9 My '87

Taxation

See also

Air travel—Taxation

Terminology

Speaking our language. P. Scott. *Flying* 114:94 D '87

Transatlantic flights

History

Lindbergh's Spirit. P. Garrison. il por *Flying* 114:30-4 S '87

Visual flight rules

See Airplanes—Piloting

Volcano hazards

NOAA, FAA consider volcano monitoring system. il *Aviat Week Space Technol* 127:30-1 Jl 6 '87

Wind hazards

See Aviation—Storm hazards

Winter flying

See also

Aviation—Ice hazards

Cold facts. R. L. Collins. il *Flying* 114:72-6 Ja '87

World flights

See also

Voyager (Airplane)

History

1937 [A. Earhart mystery] K. Ide. por *Am Herit* 38:108-9 Jl/Ag '87

The enduring mystery of Amelia Earhart. G. Bruder. bibl il pors map *Am Hist Illus* 22:10-19+ My '87

Alaska

"Two saves, partial panel" [medevac mission] T. Olden. il *Flying* 114:110-11 Ag '87

Brazil

The doyenne of Brazilian skies [A. Pinheiro Machado] A. Fernández. il por *Américas* 39:54-5 Ja/F '87

California

Coast to coast. R. L. Collins. *Flying* 114:18+ Ag '87

Greenland

Glacier greaser [Twin Comanche gets lost and crashes in Greenland] J. Justis. il map *Flying* 114:109-10 F '87

Pacific region

Pacific growth could lead to expanded FAA safety duties. J. Ott. *Aviat Week Space Technol* 126:40+ Ap 6 '87

Soviet Union

Audacious airman [M. Rust lands in Red Square] il pors map *Life* 10:66-9 Ag '87

Destination Red Square [German pilot, M. Rust, lands small plane] B. Levin. il *Macleans* 100:24 Je 8 '87

A folk hero in the slammer [M. Rust arrested after landing small plane in Red Square] N. Cooper. il por *Newsweek* 109:36 Je 15 '87

Four years for a "fun" flight [sentencing of German pilot, M. Rust, for landing plane in Moscow] W. R. Doerner. il por *Time* 130:42 S 14 '87

From Moscow to the Bering Sea [T. Watson retraces WWII flights] S. Talbott. il pors *Time* 130:34 Ag 3 '87

Gaps in Soviet defenses? [West German, M. Rust, lands plane in Moscow] R. Kaylor. il *U S News World Rep* 102:30 Je 15 '87

A hard landing in Moscow [M. Rust sentenced to 4 yrs. in Soviet labor camp] C. Redden. il por *Macleans* 100:22 S 14 '87

Joyride [M. Rust's flight to Moscow] W. F. Buckley. *Natl Rev* 39:56 Jl 17 '87

Kremlin prop wash [West German, M. Rust, lands Cessna in Red Square] W. R. Doerner. il por *Time* 129:30-2 Je 15 '87

Red faces in Red Square [West German, M. Rust, lands small plane in Moscow] N. Cooper. il por *Newsweek* 109:36 Je 8 '87

Rust's unhappy landing [sentenced to a labor camp for flying small plane into Red Square] S. Seibert. il *Newsweek* 110:49 S 14 '87

Soviet aircraft [tables] il *Aviat Week Space Technol* 126:139 Mr 9 '87

Welcome to Moscow [German pilot, M. Rust, lands plane in Red Square] J. Greenwald. il por *Time* 129:34-5 Je 8 '87

Aviation, Military

See also

Afghanistan—Russian invasion, 1979- —Aerial operations

Air bases

Aircraft carriers

Airplanes, Military

Bombing, Aerial

Close air support

Helicopters—Military use

Iranian-Iraqi War, 1980- —Aerial operations

United States. Air Force

Military [special section] il *Aviat Week Space Technol* 126:27+ Mr 9 '87

History

See also

Airplanes, Military—History

World War, 1939-1945—Aerial operations

Brazil

Brazilian Army to buy 260 helicopters for airmobile battalions. *Aviat Week Space Technol* 127:47 Ag 17 '87

Canada

See also

Snowbirds (Flight squadron)

EH 101 helicopter favored in Canadian bid. il *Aviat Week Space Technol* 127:28-9 Ag 10 '87

Two firms vie for new Canadian helicopter program [E. H. Industries' EH101 and Aerospatiale's AS332 Mk. 2 Super Puma] il *Aviat Week Space Technol* 126:28-9 Je 22 '87

France

See also

Patrouille de France (Flight squadron)

Great Britain

See also

Great Britain. Royal Air Force

Soviet Union

Soviet weapons exports increase battlefield threat worldwide. il *Aviat Week Space Technol* 126:49 Ja 19 '87

Tibet

Tibetan air operations [special section] il *Aviat Week Space Technol* 127:103-4+ O 19 '87

Western Europe

Europeans seek interoperable battle reconnaissance systems. J. M. Lenorovitz and K. F. Mordoff. il *Aviat Week Space Technol* 127:77+ S 7 '87

Aviation and health *See* Aviation—Physiological aspects

Aviation and state

See also

United States. Federal Aviation Administration

U.S. airline service draws increased federal scrutiny. *Aviat Week Space Technol* 126:30-1 Je 1 '87

Washington roundup. See issues of Aviation Week & Space Technology

Whose aviation policy is this? S. C. Keiter. por *Aviat Week Space Technol* 126:117+ My 18 '87

Canada

Private plans for Air Canada. A. Shortell. il *Macleans* 100:24-5 Jl 6 '87

China

China reshapes airlines to meet demand surge [cover story] R. G. O'Lone. il *Aviat Week Space Technol* 127:37-9 N 30 '87

China reshaping industry to meet extensive needs [cover story; with editorial comment by Donald E. Fink] R. G. O'Lone. il map *Aviat Week Space Technol* 127:9, 16-21 N 16 '87

Chinese exhibition underscores aviation modernization efforts [Aviation Expo/China; with editorial comment by Donald E. Fink] R. G. O'Lone. *Aviat Week Space Technol* 127:13, 28-9 O 26 '87

FAA urges China to clear path to bilateral airworthiness pact. *Aviat Week Space Technol* 127:38-9 Ag 17 '87

France

Conflicting requirements stymie German/French PAH-2 project. *Aviat Week Space Technol* 126:80-1 Ja 19 '87

France, Germany agree on common specifications for combat helicopter [PAH-2 program] il *Aviat Week Space Technol* 126:61-2 Ap 6 '87

France, Germany authorize combat helicopter development [PAH-2/HAP/HAC-3G] J. M. Lenorovitz and K. F. Mordoff. il *Aviat Week Space Technol* 127:20-2 Jl 27 '87

French, West Germans consider combining helicopter versions. *Aviat Week Space Technol* 126:27 F 23 '87

Germany (West)

Conflicting requirements stymie German/French PAH-2 project. *Aviat Week Space Technol* 126:80-1 Ja 19 '87

Aviation and state—Germany (West)—*cont.*

France, Germany agree on common specifications for combat helicopter [PAH-2 program] il *Aviat Week Space Technol* 126:61-2 Ap 6 '87

France, Germany authorize combat helicopter development [PAH-2/HAP/HAC-3G] J. M. Lenorovitz and K. F. Mordoff. il *Aviat Week Space Technol* 127:20-2 Jl 27 '87

French, West Germans consider combining helicopter versions. *Aviat Week Space Technol* 126:27 F 23 '87

Funding delays continue to plague EFA development [European fighter aircraft] K. F. Mordoff. *Aviat Week Space Technol* 127:29 Ag 24 '87

German government commits funds to Airbus A330/A340 development. *Aviat Week Space Technol* 126:35 Je 8 '87

Germany backs development of PAH-2 combat helicopter. K. F. Mordoff. *Aviat Week Space Technol* 127:28-9 N 16 '87

Need for key aerospace decisions puts West Germany at crossroads. K. F. Mordoff. il *Aviat Week Space Technol* 126:163-4+ Je 15 '87

West Germany releases funds for EFA component development [European fighter aircraft] K. F. Mordoff. il *Aviat Week Space Technol* 127:26-7 S 28 '87

Great Britain
See also
    Great Britain. Civil Aviation Authority

British Aerospace rejects A330/A340 aid proposal. *Aviat Week Space Technol* 126:36 Mr 30 '87

British agree on launch aid for A330/A340. *Aviat Week Space Technol* 126:33 My 18 '87

British research funding method hampers rotary-wing developments. il *Aviat Week Space Technol* 126:105-7+ Ja 19 '87

EH101 helicopter rolled out; British to order utility version. D. A. Brown. il *Aviat Week Space Technol* 126:30 Ap 13 '87

Rolls will request government aid for V2500 SuperFan development. D. A. Brown. *Aviat Week Space Technol* 126:36 Mr 2 '87

Israel
Fallen state [implications of the Lavi fiasco] A. Kenan. *Nation* 245:293 S 26 '87

Israel plans to complete third Lavi prototype. *Aviat Week Space Technol* 127:27-8 S 28 '87

Israel renews debate on Lavi development. D. E. Fink. *Aviat Week Space Technol* 126:18-19 Je 1 '87

Israelis review decisions that led to Lavi cancellation; International partners sought to complete Lavi. D. A. Brown. *Aviat Week Space Technol* 127:22-4 S 14 '87

Lavi termination [special section; with editorial comment by Donald E. Fink] il *Aviat Week Space Technol* 127:15, 22-5 S 7 '87

Japan
Hostile skies [effects of airline deregulation on All Nippon] H. Katayama. il *Forbes* 140:60 O 5 '87

Western Europe
All's fair in the airliner war. A. Faujas. *World Press Rev* 34:49-50 Je '87

Common Market threats force carriers toward liberalization. *Aviat Week Space Technol* 127:146+ N 9 '87

ECAC approves liberalizing fare, capacity regulations. *Aviat Week Space Technol* 126:36 Ja 12 '87

European coproducers study F-16 upgrades, replacements. K. F. Mordoff. il *Aviat Week Space Technol* 126:214+ Je 15 '87

European groups seek mutual weapons development programs. *Aviat Week Space Technol* 126:82+ Mr 9 '87

European industry evolves to challenge U.S. leadership. D. A. Brown. *Aviat Week Space Technol* 126:88-9+ Mr 9 '87

European nations press to establish common airworthiness regulations [European Joint Airworthiness Regulations] *Aviat Week Space Technol* 126:312-13 Je 15 '87

European skies are freer but no friendlier. J. Heard. il *Bus Week* p54 D 21 '87

Europeans criticize U.S. subsidy charges at Airbus A320 rollout. J. M. Lenorovitz. il *Aviat Week Space Technol* 126:30-1 F 23 '87

Manufacturers discuss cooperation despite aircraft subsidy dispute [U.S. and Europe] D. A. Brown. *Aviat Week Space Technol* 126:30-1 Je 29 '87

McDonnell Douglas/European talks include larger version of MD-11. B. A. Smith. *Aviat Week Space Technol* 126:42 Ap 13 '87

A time for cool heads [dispute over subsidies to Europe's Airbus Industrie civil transport programs] D. E. Fink. *Aviat Week Space Technol* 126:11 F 23 '87

U.S., Europe agree on agenda for aircraft financing talks. D. A. Brown. *Aviat Week Space Technol* 127:36 N 2 '87

U.S., Europe seek rapid cure in Airbus subsidy dispute. M. Mecham. *Aviat Week Space Technol* 127:35+ O 26 '87

U.S., Europeans clash over Airbus subsidies. D. A. Brown. il *Aviat Week Space Technol* 126:18-20 F 9 '87

Aviation associations
See also
    Air Transport Association of America
    Experimental Aircraft Association
    General Aviation Manufacturers Association
    Helicopter Association International
    International Air Transport Association
    National Business Aircraft Association
    Short-Wing Piper Club

Aerospace calendar. See issues of Aviation Week & Space Technology

Calendar. See issues of Flying beginning August 1985

Aviation charts
Harris Corp. offering digital map generator for airborne operations. E. H. Kolcum. il *Aviat Week Space Technol* 126:84-5+ Mr 16 '87

Jeppesen charts by laser [Lasertrak FP100] J. M. McClellan. il *Flying* 114:107 N '87

Aviation communications *See* Aviation—Communication systems

Aviation education *See* Aviation—Study and teaching

Aviation engineering
See also
    Computers—Aviation use
    Eidetics International (Firm)

Aviation equipment
See also
    Air navigation—Aids and devices
    Airplanes—Electronic equipment
    Airplanes—Instrument panels
    Airplanes—Radio equipment
    Airplanes, Business—Electronic equipment
    Airplanes, Jet—Electronic equipment
    Airplanes, Light—Electronic equipment
    Airplanes, Military—Electronic equipment
    Airplanes, Training—Electronic equipment
    Automatic pilot (Airplanes)
    Flight recorders
    Image processing—Aviation use
    Inertial guidance systems

For the complete pilot. il *Flying* 114:72-7 D '87

Aviation fuel *See* Airplane engines—Fuel

Aviation landing areas
See also
    Air bases—Runways

Aviation meteorology *See* Meteorology, Aviation

Aviation museums
See also
    Kansas Cosmosphere and Space Center
    Museum of Flight (Seattle, Wash.)

Aviation policy *See* Aviation and state

Aviation records
See also
    Airplane speed records

Record players. P. Scott. il *Flying* 114:52-4 S '87

Aviation research
See also
    Air Force Flight Dynamics Laboratory (U.S.)
    Eidetics International (Firm)
    Langley Research Center (U.S.)
    United States. Army Aviation Systems Command
    United States. National Aeronautics and Space Administration

Engineering tomorrow's airliners [cover story] J. Schefter. il *Pop Sci* 230:49-52+ Ap '87

General aviation manufacturers focus on technology advances to spur sales. P. Proctor. *Aviat Week Space Technol* 126:108-9+ My 18 '87

Laurels 1987. D. E. Fink. *Aviat Week Space Technol* 127:13 D 21 '87

Laurels for 1986. D. E. Fink. *Aviat Week Space Technol* 126:11 Ja 12 '87

U.S. must understand the link between R&D and the economy. R. S. Ames. por *Aviat Week Space Technol* 127:149-50 O 12 '87

Aviation schools *See* Aviation—Study and teaching

Aviation Training Center
New videos from ATC. J. M. McClellan. *Flying* 114:99-100 Ag '87

Aviation workers
See also
    Air pilots
    Air traffic controllers (Persons)

Aviation workers—See also—*cont.*
   Airlines—Employees
   Airplane mechanics (Persons)
Avibras Industria Aeroespacial SA
   Avibras emerges as major exporter for Brazilian aerospace industry. il *Aviat Week Space Technol* 127:49+ Ag 17 '87
Avins, Carol
   (tr) See Ratushinskaya, Irina. Give me a nickname, prison
Avionics
   See also
      Air Force Avionics Laboratory (U.S.)
      Airplanes—Electronic equipment
      Airplanes, Business—Electronic equipment
      Airplanes, Jet—Electronic equipment
      Airplanes, Light—Electronic equipment
      Airplanes, Military—Electronic equipment
      Airplanes, Training—Electronic equipment
      Computers—Aviation use
      Helicopters—Electronic equipment
   Avionics. See issues of Aviation Week & Space Technology
Avionics industry
   See also
      Bendix Corp.
      Flight Dynamics, Inc.
      Kollsman Instrument Co.
      Loral Corp.
      Sigma Tek, Inc.
      Singer Company
      Sperry Flight Systems
         Acquisitions and mergers
   Honeywell's Sperry Group sells ARC product line. *Aviat Week Space Technol* 127:32 S 14 '87
   Paul Bilzerian still don't get no respect [bid for Singer] P. Engardio. il por *Bus Week* p62+ N 23 '87
   Ripe enough for Pickens [T. B. Pickens stalks Singer] R. Mitchell. il *Bus Week* p23 Ag 24 '87
         International aspects
   GEC completes purchase of Lear Siegler units. *Aviat Week Space Technol* 127:125 O 12 '87
   Lear Siegler sells subsidiary companies to Smiths Industries. *Aviat Week Space Technol* 127:32 Ag 3 '87
         Automation
   Automated military avionics factory reducing flaws in workmanship [Rockwell/Collins] il *Aviat Week Space Technol* 127:89-90+ O 26 '87
   New automated factory to produce GPS equipment at significant savings [Global Positioning System/Navstar] P. J. Klass. il *Aviat Week Space Technol* 127:102-3+ O 5 '87
         Ethical aspects
   USAF suspends AIL from new contracts pending billing inquiry. *Aviat Week Space Technol* 127:30 N 16 '87
         Export-import trade
   Air Force issues RFPs for Chinese F-8-2 avionic upgrade kits. *Aviat Week Space Technol* 126:19 Mr 23 '87
   Avionics field marked by dwindling dependence on U.S. production. K. J. Stein. il *Aviat Week Space Technol* 126:233+ Je 15 '87
   Pentagon task force to develop model for radar technology transfer. J. D. Morrocco. *Aviat Week Space Technol* 127:30 Ag 24 '87
   Y-7-100 instrument panel houses displays for U.S.-built systems [Chinese passenger aircraft] il *Aviat Week Space Technol* 127:58-9 D 21 '87
         International aspects
   Avionics companies seek greater collaboration. *Aviat Week Space Technol* 126:28-30 Je 22 '87
         Canada
   See also
      Virtual Prototypes, Inc.
         France
   See also
      Crouzet (Firm)
         Great Britain
   See also
      Smiths Industries plc
         United States
   See Avionics industry
Avions Marcel Dassault Breguet Aviation *See* Dassault Breguet Aviation (Avions Marcel)
Avirgan, Tony
   (jt. auth) See Honey, Martha, and Avirgan, Tony
Avirgan, Tony, and Honey, Martha
   The C.I.A.'s war in Costa Rica. *Nation* 244:105-7 Ja 31 '87
Avis, Inc.
   Sans Simon, Wesray cleans up on Avis. il *Fortune* 116:8-9 O 26 '87

When you own the company, you try harder [employee buyout] E. Spragins. *Bus Week* p32-3 S 28 '87
Avocados
   See also
      Cooking—Fruit
Avoidance (Psychology)
   Avoiding the hard part. M. Greenfield. il *Newsweek* 110:76 S 7 '87
Avol, Milton
                  about
   Rx for the 'Ratlord': live in your own slums. por *Newsweek* 110:54 Jl 27 '87
   Trials of a landlord. D. Seligman. il *Fortune* 116:95-6 Ag 17 '87
Avon, Anthony Eden, Earl of *See* Eden, Anthony, Earl of Avon, 1897-1977
Avon Books (Firm)
   Giving no ground, Avon and NCBA settle suit. M. Colin. *Publ Wkly* 232:9 N 13 '87
   Lighter-weight paper for mass market 'Whirlwind' saves Avon some heavy cost. J. P. Frank. il *Publ Wkly* 232:59-63 O 16 '87
Avon Products, Inc.
   Anyhow, it was nice while it lasted. G. Morgenson. il por *Forbes* 139:50+ Ja 12 '87
   Avon calling! [100 years of collectibles] il *Antiques Collect Hobbies* 92:77-9 Jl '87
   Avon calling—at the Tokyo Exchange [selling 40% of Japanese subsidiary to the Japanese] T. Holden. il *Bus Week* p116 D 14 '87
   Avon picks UniWorld [advertising agency] K. Smikle. il *Black Enterp* 17:24 F '87
   Big names are opening doors for Avon [moving into department stores] A. Dunkin. il *Bus Week* p96-7 Je 1 '87
   Brainy is beautiful [successful salespersons] il *McCalls* 114:118-21 Ja '87
   Cam Starrett [cover story] S. McHenry. *Ms* 16:52 N '87
   For Avon, Rodeo Drive is no easy street [upscale perfume marketing] W. Konrad. il *Bus Week* p78 D 28 '87-Ja 4 '88
AVS *See* American Vacuum Society
Avtek Corporation
   Avtek modifies 400A design to improve comfort, performance. il *Aviat Week Space Technol* 127:111 D 14 '87
AWACS (Airborne warning and control system) *See* Airplanes, Military—Radar equipment
Awad, Mubarak E.
                  about
   Seeking justice through nonviolent resistance. W. G. Pippert. *Christ Today* 31:53-4 Mr 20 '87
Awadi, Abdul Rahman al- *See* Al-Awadi, Abdul Rahman
Awards *See* Rewards, prizes, etc.
Awards of merit *See* Certificates of merit
Awkwardness
   Are you a klutz? E. Goldson. il *Teen* 31:56 S '87
Awnings
   Made in the shade. D. Kassler. il *Workbench* 43:74-6 S/O '87
Awosting, Lake (N.Y.) *See* Lake Awosting (N.Y.)
Axelgard, Frederick W.
   Iraq and the war with Iran. bibl f *Curr Hist* 86:57-60+ F '87
Axelrod, Daniel
   (jt. auth) See Kaku, Michio, and Axelrod, Daniel
Axelrod, Joan
                  about
   Decorating scruples. J. Krantz. il por *House Gard* 159:208-17+ O '87
Axions *See* Particles (Nuclear physics)
Axon regeneration *See* Regeneration (Biology)
Axonal transport *See* Biological transport
Axons *See* Nerve cells
Axthelm, Pete
   [Column] See occasional issues of Newsweek
Ayala, Francisco J., 1934-
   Evolution and creation: one missed opportunity. *BioScience* 37:450 Jl/Ag '87
Ayala, G. F.
   (jt. auth) See Dichter, Marc A., and Ayala, G. F.
Ayer (N. W.) & Son, Inc. *See* N. W. Ayer & Son, Inc.
Ayeroff, Jeff
                  about
   Virgin's odd couple. S. Pond. pors *Roll Stone* p22+ Ap 9 '87

Ayers, Vivian

about

Debbie Allen and Phylicia Rashad's mother Vivian Ayers talks about their fame [cover story] il pors *Jet* 72:54-5 My 18 '87

Ayers, William

How a male teacher sees early childhood education. *Educ Dig* 52:27-9 Ap '87

Ayers-Allen, Phylicia *See* Rashad, Phylicia

Ayler, Ethel

about

Ethel Ayler's second career. L. Barrett. por *Essence* 17:44 Ja '87

Aymara language

Ancient language as tool for computer age [Aymara for computerized translation; work of Ivan Guzman de Rojas] il *Futurist* 21:55 Mr/Ap '87

Ayres, Linda, 1947-

Frontier life: portrayals of the American West. il *USA Today (Periodical)* 116:76-83 N '87

Ayres, Richard E.

(jt. auth) See Strait, Donald S., and Ayres, Richard E.

Ayvazian, Andrea

about

Be your own peacemaker. S. H. Day, Jr. il *Progressive* 51:17-18 Ap '87

Azalea Festival (Norfolk, Va.) *See* Norfolk (Va.)—Festivals

Azaleas

A blooming azalea column . . . train your own. il *Sunset* 178:273 My '87

Azcona Hoyo, José

about

Odd man out. J. Eldridge. *America* 157:348-9 N 14 '87

Azel, José

Anyone seen a blue ox? [photographs] il *Sports Illus* 67:54-9 Ag 10 '87

Azevedo, Mario

The post-Ahidjo era in Cameroon. bibl f *Curr Hist* 86:217-20+ My '87

Azidothymidine

AIDS drug approval recommended. J. Silberner. *Sci News* 131:56 Ja 24 '87

AIDS drug approved, vaccine tested. D. D. Edwards. *Sci News* 131:198 Mr 28 '87

Fast-tracking the first AIDS drug [zidovudine; interview with E. Cooper and J. Bilstad] B. Stone. pors *FDA Consum* 21:13-15 O '87

Fateful decisions on treating AIDS. E. Bowen. il *Time* 129:62 F 2 '87

First AIDS drug approved. *FDA Consum* 21:4-5 Je '87

The government bends to AIDS victims' pleas [FDA approval of AZT] D. S. Greenberg. il *U S News World Rep* 102:76 Mr 23 '87

Imminent marketing of AZT raises problems. G. Kolata. il *Science* 235:1462-3 Mr 20 '87

Retroviruses and mouse embryos: a rapid model for neurovirulence and transplacental antiviral therapy. A. H. Sharpe and others. bibl f il *Science* 236:1671-4 Je 26 '87

Ribavirin antagonizes the effect of azidothymidine on HIV replication. M. W. Vogt and others. bibl f il *Science* 235:1376-9 Mr 13 '87

Uproar over AIDS drugs. M. Clark. il *Newsweek* 109:24 Ap 6 '87

Prices

The unhealthy profits of AZT. T. Kingston. il *Nation* 245:408-9 O 17 '87

An uproar over AIDS drugs [Burroughs Wellcome accused of overcharging for Retrovir] J. Branegan. il *Time* 129:58 Ap 6 '87

Azinger, Paul

about

Simply 'Amazinger'. R. Reilly. il por *Sports Illus* 67:10 Jl 20 '87

Very British Open. R. Reilly. il pors *Sports Illus* 67:18-23 Jl 27 '87

Azinhal (Portugal: Country estate) *See* Country estates—Portugal

Azores

See also
Festivals—Azores

Industries

See also
Shellfish fisheries—Azores
Whaling—Azores

AZT *See* Azidothymidine

Aztec lilies *See* Jacobean lilies

Aztecs

Why were the Aztecs and Mayas stuck in the Stone Age? Obsidian, a kind of volcanic glass, may be the answer. T. Stocker. *Earth Sci* 40:32 Summ '87

Azymuth (Musical group)

Hot sounds from a cool group. M. Holston. il *Américas* 39:56-8 Mr/Ap '87

B

B-1B airplanes *See* Airplanes, Military

B. Altman & Co.

Updating a classic [new owners P. C. Semprevivo and A. Conti] B. Kanner. il pors *N Y* 20:19-20 Jl 13 '87

B cells *See* Lymphocytes

B. Dalton Booksellers

Dalton drops troubled video program in back-to-basics push. T. Spain. *Publ Wkly* 231:39-40+ Ap 3 '87

Dalton re-examining video program. *Publ Wkly* 231:52 F 20 '87

Will publishers resist Dalton's costly new television ads? A. Symons. *Publ Wkly* 231:25 Je 12 '87

B E T plc

The flack who came in from the cold [C. Walton] L. Minard. il por *Forbes* 140:120+ D 28 '87

B.F. Goodrich Co.

See also
Uniroyal Goodrich Tire Co.

B mesons *See* Particles (Nuclear physics)

B stars

The B stars: beacons of the skies. J. B. Kaler. il *Sky Telesc* 74:147-50 Ag '87

B3R Country Meat, Inc.

'It's our beef from ranch to retail'. B. Eftink. il *Success Farm* 85 no4:B10 F '87

Baba, Akira, 1935-

about

Brooks Brothers, beware! H. Katayama. por *Forbes* 139:173 Ap 6 '87

Baba Ram Dass *See* Ram Dass

Babangida, Ibrahim

about

Nigeria between dictatorship and democracy. L. Diamond. bibl f *Curr Hist* 86:201-4+ My '87

Babb, Glenn

about

An awkward visit. D. Smith. il por *Macleans* 100:20 Mr 23 '87

Babbitt, Bruce E.

about

Declaring their intentions. K. Gross. il por *People Wkly* 27:36-7 Ap 13 '87

"I can't take another day". M. Riley. il por *Time* 130:27 N 23 '87

Throwing the 'long bomb'. M. Kaus. pors *Newsweek* 109:20 Je 8 '87

What two of the darkest horses are running on: ideas. P. Magnusson. il pors *Bus Week* p126+ D 21 '87

Will reform work? Two experts debate [interview] M. Christopher. pors *Sch Update* 119:20 Mr 23 '87

Babcock, Richard

about

The barn builder. B. Trebilcock. il pors *Ctry J* 14:34-40 Mr '87

Babenco, Hector, 1945?-

about

Ironweed [film] Reviews

Horizon il 30:35-6 D '87. J. Parini

Newsweek il 110:68 D 21 '87. D. Ansen

Time il 130:74 D 21 '87. R. Corliss

Babesiosis

Ecology of a new disease. J. A. Miller. il *BioScience* 37:11-15 Ja '87

Babies *See* Infants

Baboons

Changing of the guard [aging gelada baboon loses his harem to a younger male] R. I. M. Dunbar. il *Int Wildl* 17:30-3 Ja/F '87

The "Gang" moves to a strange new land [Pumphouse Gang of olive baboons translocated to new habitat in Kenya] S. Strum. il por map *Natl Geogr* 172:676-90 N '87

What are friends for? [East African olive baboons] B. Smuts. il *Nat Hist* 96:36-45 F '87

Baboons—*cont.*
What happens when the boss is a baboon [study by Anthony Coelho] il *Discover* 8:12-13 Je '87
Baby animals *See* Animals, Infancy of
Baby Bells *See* Telephone companies
Baby boom [film] See Motion picture reviews—Single works
Baby boom generation
See also
Americans for Generational Equity
Baby boomers face hearing aid future. il *USA Today (Periodical)* 115:5 F '87
The baby boomers take to the waves [powerboat industry] R. McGough. il *Forbes* 139:72-3 Ap 20 '87
Deathbed politics: Medicare and the baby boom generation. P. Longman. *New Repub* 196:18-20 Mr 30 '87
Fox's new network goes after the baby boomers. R. Grover. *Bus Week* p41+ Ap 6 '87
The growing claims of the aged. D. Cohen. por *Macleans* 100:7 Mr 2 '87
Middle-aged America. R. J. Samuelson. il *Newsweek* 110:45 Jl 27 '87
The patrimony society [cover story] R. Kuttner. *New Repub* 196:18-21 My 11 '87
So you're 40, baby boomer [advice of Morris Spier] il *USA Today (Periodical)* 116:8-9 N '87
Suicide: a future boom for baby boomers? [study by Dan G. Blazer] J. Folkenberg. *Psychol Today* 21:22 S '87
Thirty-fourth winter. C. F. Wall. il *South Living* 22:80 Ja '87
Those big-spending middle-aged baby boomers. G. Koretz. il *Bus Week* p20 O 19 '87
Today's baby-boomers, tomorrow's elderly. L. Hurst. *World Press Rev* 34:26-8 Ag '87
The war between the generations. L. Smith. il *Fortune* 116:78-80+ Jl 20 '87
What baby boomers really think, fear, care about [excerpts from 100 predictions for the baby boom and Not like our parents] C. Russell and D. Q. Mills. il *Glamour* 85:288-91 N '87

Anecdotes, facetiae, satire, etc.
Golden oldies in the year 2017. C. Gordon. por *Macleans* 100:9 Ja 12 '87

Political activities
Al Gore's generation gap. E. Calonius. il por *Newsweek* 110:44 D 21 '87
Baby-boomerang: why the Democrats can't count on generational politics. F. F. Siegel. *Commonweal* 114:442-5 Ag 14 '87
Playing politics by the numbers [Democratic candidates figuring how to win baby boomers' votes] G. Borger and D. Baer. il *U S News World Rep* 102:28-9 Je 22 '87

Religious life
Bull market for religion. R. Clapp. *Christ Today* 31:15 Ap 3 '87
Baby bottles
Head Start combats baby bottle tooth decay [American Indians] M. G. Phillips and P. E. Stubbs. il *Child Today* 16:25-8 S/O '87
Baby bust generation
Investing in a baby bust. J. B. Quinn. il *Newsweek* 110:57 N 23 '87
Welcome, America, to the baby bust. J. S. DeMott. il *Time* 129:28-9 F 23 '87
Baby care *See* Infants—Care and hygiene
Baby carriages
See also
Racing Strollers (Firm)
Baby cribs *See* Cribs (Beds)
Baby dishes *See* Pottery
Baby Doe rules
Bibliography
The legacy of Baby Doe. J. B. Ciulla. il *Psychol Today* 21:70-1+ Ja '87
Baby food *See* Infants—Nutrition
Baby Jane Doe case, 1983
See also
Baby Doe rules
Baby M case
After the Baby M case. B. Kantrowitz. il *Newsweek* 109:22-3 Ap 13 '87
All for love of a baby [surrogate mother M. B. Whitehead sues for custody] M. Shaughnessy. il por *People Wkly* 27:50-2 Mr 23 '87
"Baby M". M. Gordon. il *Ms* 15:25-6+ Je '87
The Baby M case: pregnancy and M.S. il *Discover* 8:13 Je '87
Baby M.—emotions for sale. R. Rosenblatt. il *Time* 129:88 Ap 6 '87

Baby M winner [surrogate matchmaker N. P. Keane] M. Gladwell and R. Sharpe. *New Repub* 196:15-16+ F 16 '87
A battle of ethics, money and blood. M. Gray. il *Macleans* 100:44 Ja 26 '87
The battle over Baby M. J. M. Wall. *Christ Century* 104:99-100 F 4-11 '87
Bringing up Baby M. B. D. Colen. il *Health* 19:9 Jl '87
Buying & selling babies. M. Novak. il *Commonweal* 114:406-7 Jl 17 '87
Calling King Solomon. *New Repub* 196:9-10 F 23 '87
Childless couples seeking surrogate mothers call Michigan lawyer Noel Keane—he delivers. J. S. Kunen. il pors *People Wkly* 27:93+ Mr 30 '87
The contract for 'Baby M'. M. Kempton. il *N Y Rev Books* 34:44 Ap 9 '87
Contracting anguish. J. Garvey. il *Commonweal* 114:232 Ap 24 '87
Dilemma in swaddling clothes [surrogate parenting agreement] J. Levine. *Harpers* 274:47-8 Ap '87
Finally, a ruling—'M' is for Melissa. T. Gest. il *U S News World Rep* 102:60-1 Ap 13 '87
Hard questions about the Baby M case: McCall's asks the experts. V. Cadden. *McCalls* 114:58+ Je '87
"I had to protect Baby M" [interview with court-appointed guardian A. Abraham] J. Liebmann-Smith. il por *Redbook* 169:130-1+ O '87
In the best interests of a child [custody given to W. Stern] R. Lacayo. il *Time* 129:71 Ap 13 '87
Letters [discussion of May 23, 1987 article, The strange case of Baby M] K. Pollitt. *Nation* 245:38+ Jl 18-25 '87
The life and custody of Baby M. il *Macleans* 100:34 Ap 13 '87
Natural instincts under contract. B. Amiel. il *Macleans* 100:13 Mr 23 '87
Our fascination with Baby M. A. T. Fleming. il por *N Y Times Mag* p32-6+ Mr 29 '87
Questions raised by Baby M. *America* 156:313-14 Ap 18 '87
The rent-a womb dilemma. C. Kocol. il por *Humanist* 47:37 Jl/Ag '87
The strange case of Baby M [cover story] K. Pollitt. *Nation* 244:667+ My 23 '87
Surrogate-gate. *Commonweal* 114:35-6 Ja 30 '87
Surrogate mothers: no way to treat a baby [case of M. B. Whitehead] B. G. Harrison. *Mademoiselle* 93:96 Ja '87
What Baby M is telling us. *America* 156:90-1 F 7 '87
Who keeps 'Baby M'? [surrogate mother M. B. Whitehead sues for custody] B. Kantrow. il por *Newsweek* 109:44-9 Ja 19 '87
Whose baby is 'Baby M'? [surrogate motherhood dispute] T. Gest. il por *U S News World Rep* 102:15 Ja 19 '87
Whose child is this? [surrogate mother M. B. Whitehead sues for custody] R. Lacayo. il por *Time* 129:56-8 Ja 19 '87
Womb to let. M. Gallagher. il *Natl Rev* 39:27-30 Ap 24 '87
Baby products *See* Infants—Equipment
Baby sitters
Baby-sitter's survival guide. il *Teen* 31:64 Mr '87
Baby-sitting emergencies. G. Sikes. *Seventeen* 46:246-7 Ag '87
Baby-sitting the brat. G. Sikes. il *Seventeen* 46:184+ Mr '87
Can you get a sitter? B. Kantrowitz. il *Newsweek* 109:84 My 18 '87
Emergency advice for your babysitter. *Parents* 62:40+ Jl '87
Babylon (Ancient city)
The view from the Mustansiriyah. M. Viorst. map *New Yorker* 63:76-96 O 19 '87
Baby's-tears (Plant)
How to propagate baby's-tears. E. Waltner. il *Flower Gard* 31:60 Ap/My '87
Baca Grande (Colo.)
Maurice Strong: reviving a valley with beer and religion. S. D. Atchison. il por *Bus Week* p146 D 7 '87
Bacard, André
Sparking life into our youth. il *Humanist* 47:46 Jl/Ag '87
Bacardi Corp.
Rum deal in an old family firm. R. Hornik. il *Time* 129:56 My 25 '87
Baccalaureate, International *See* International baccalaureate
Baccalaureate addresses
Cosby to speak at Wesleyan for daughter's graduation. *Jet* 72:58 My 18 '87

Baccalaureate addresses—*cont.*
Now, a few words from the wise. il *Time* 129:69-70 Je 22 '87
The Bacchae [drama] *See* Euripides, ca. 485-ca. 406 B.C.
Bacerra, Ralph, 1938-
about
Deliberately decorative: the ceramics of Ralph Bacerra. M. McCloud. il por *Am Craft* 47:50-5 Je/Jl '87
Bach, Caleb
Gopher baroque. il por *Américas* 39:2-7+ S/O '87
Bach, Elvira
about
Elvira Bach. N. Grimes. il *Art News* 86:148 S '87
Bach and broccoli [film] *See* Motion picture reviews—Single works
Bacharach, Burt, 1928-
about
Architectural digest visits: Burt Bacharach and Carole Bayer Sager. B. Gooch. il pors *Archit Dig* 44:128-33+ O '87
Bache, Ellyn
The baby-sitter [story] il por *McCalls* 145:147-9 Mr '87
Running from love [story] il *McCalls* 115:178+ O '87
Bachelder, Robert S.
Have ethics disappeared from Wall Street? il *Christ Century* 104:628-30 Jl 15-22 '87
Japan and the U.S.: the economics of equity. *Christ Century* 104:719-23 Ag 26-S 2 '87
Bachelors *See* Single men
Bachman, Jerald G.
An eye on the future. il *Psychol Today* 21:6+ Jl '87
Bachman, Richard *See* King, Stephen, 1947-
Bachmann-Geiser, Brigitte
Horn of plenty. il *Courier* 40:29-31 F '87
Bacik, James
Lust: it can be wrong when it feels so right. il *U S Cathol* 52:10-11 Ag '87
Bacillus
New roles for an old-trouper vaccine? [bacillus Calmette-Guérin mycobacteria used as a multipurpose vaccine] *Sci News* 131:396 Je 20 '87
Bacillus thuringiensis
Bt's beneficial spray. B. Pleasant. il *Rodale's Org Gard* 34:34-7 D '87
State wants to spray pesticide on New River [use of Bti to exterminate breeding grounds of the black fly] *Natl Parks* 61:43 Mr/Ap '87
Back exercises *See* Exercise
Back muscle *See* Muscle
Back packs *See* Backpacks and backpacking
Back to the beach [film] *See* Motion picture reviews—Single works
Backache
Aching back? Arthur Jones says he has the answer. M. Frons. il por *Bus Week* p59+ D 14 '87
Ah, my non-aching back: a longtime sufferer finds it's all in the mind [work of J. Sarno] T. Schwartz. il por *N Y* 20:44-8+ Mr 16 '87
Backaches of pregnancy. P. A. Hillard. il *Parents* 62:194+ My '87
Bad backs: pains in the wallet. R. J. Chapel. il *Nations Bus* 75:43-4 Ja '87
Coping with an aching back. W. A. Nolen. il *50 Plus* 27:68-72 F '87
Electricity may have the potential to heal injured back muscles. *Prevention* 39:63 O '87
Gut strength [abdominal exercises] J. Poppy. il *Esquire* 108:71+ S '87
Help for your aching back: how to avoid spending an arm and a leg for the wrong products. M. Willens. il *Money* 16:128-32+ Mr '87
Hubert Rosomoff only hurts the back-pain patients he loves. D. Van Biema. il pors *People Wkly* 27:73-4+ My 18 '87
Lower back pain: coping with a common problem. J. R. Denton. por *McCalls* 114:84 Ag '87
Relax your back. P. Rudolf. il *Redbook* 168:92-3 Mr '87
The saga of a bad back. M. Teich. il *Health* 19:11-12+ O '87
Spinal tip: building a sport-safe back. S. Beitler. il *Sport Mag* 78:79-80 F '87
Take care of your working back. K. McCleary. il *Work Woman* 12:154+ Ap '87
Two days' bed rest could be all that's needed to ease the pain of a bum lower back. il *Prevention* 39:32 Jl '87
'A walk a day keeps my back pain away'. P. McNabb. il *Prevention* 39:45-6+ Ag '87

What to do for your aching back. il *Consum Rep* 52:379-83 Je '87
Backer, Dorothy
Rootless. *Am Sch* 56:269-74 Spr '87
Backer, Terry
about
An oysterman's battle to keep 'black mayonnaise' at bay. R. Mitchell. il *Bus Week* p98 O 12 '87
Backer & Spielvogel, Inc.
See also
Backer Spielvogel Bates Worldwide
Backer Spielvogel Bates Worldwide
Nice guy finishes first [C. Spielvogel] B. Kanner. il por *N Y* 20:29-31 S 14 '87
Background in photography *See* Photography—Setting and scenery
Backhouse, Janet
Devotions & delights: the illuminated books of Gothic England. bibl il *Hist Today* 37:25-31 N '87
Backlist books *See* Booksellers and bookselling—Backlist books; Publishers and publishing—Backlist books
Backmann, René
Remember El Salvador? *World Press Rev* 34:24-5 Ag '87
Backpacks and backpacking
A twenty-pound weekend. E. A. Bauer. il *Outdoor Life* 179:40+ My '87
Backward running *See* Running
Backyard playgrounds *See* Playgrounds, Home
Backyards *See* Home grounds
Bacon, Francis, 1909-
about
Francis Bacon. N. Grimes. il *Art News* 86:167 O '87
Bacon, Kevin
about
Making the big screen scene. il pors *Teen* 31:77 Ag '87
Bacon
Curing
A safer strip [Cure-trol avoids use of sodium nitrite] P. McCarthy. il *Health* 19:11 F '87
Bacteria
See also
Agrobacterium
Archaebacteria
Bacillus
Bacillus thuringiensis
Campylobacter
Escherichia coli
Legionella
Mutation—Bacteria
Pseudomonas
Resistance and sensitivity
Antibiotic-resistant VD on increase. *Sci News* 131:200 Mr 28 '87
Bacterial resistance to β-lactam antibiotics: crystal structure of β-lactamase from Staphylococcus aureus PC1 at 2.5 Å resolution. O. Herzberg and J. Moult. bibl f il *Science* 236:694-701 My 8 '87
Belligerent bug makes Korean debut [spectinomycin-resistant Neisseria gonorrhoeae; research by John W. Boslego and others] *Sci News* 132:94 Ag 8 '87
Dangers of "miracle" drugs [antibiotic feed supplements] *Futurist* 21:51-2 Mr/Ap '87
A new venereal threat [penicillin-resistant gonorrhea] N. Underwood. il *Macleans* 100:51 S 21 '87
Bacteria, Effect of antibiotics on *See* Bacteria—Resistance and sensitivity
Bacteria, Fossil *See* Micropaleontology
Bacteria, Marine
Stimulation of heterotrophic microplankton production by resuspended marine sediments. S. C. Wainright. bibl f il *Science* 238:1710-12 D 18 '87
Swept away: resuspension of bacterial mats regulates benthic-pelagic exchange of sulfur. J. Grant and U. V. Bathmann. bibl f il *Science* 236:1472-4 Je 12 '87
Bacteria, Methanogenic
Bacterial methanogenesis and growth from CO_2 with elemental iron as the sole source of electrons. L. Daniels and others. bibl f il *Science* 237:509-11 Jl 31 '87
Making a meal of iron [role of methanogens in biocorrosion; work of Lacy Daniels and others] *Sci News* 132:104 Ag 15 '87
Mussels munch methane [research by James Childress] il *Technol Rev* 90:18 F/Mr '87
Bacteria, Nitrogen fixing
See also
Rhizobium
Bacteria, Pathogenic
See also
Borrelia

Bacteria, Pathogenic—See also—*cont.*
  Neisseria
  Salmonella
  Staphylococci
  Streptococcus
  Yersinia
Bacteria, Photosynthetic
  See also
  Rhodopseudomonas
Bacteria, Sulfate reducing
  Isolation of extremely thermophilic sulfate reducers: evidence for a novel branch of archaebacteria. K. O. Stetter and others. bibl f il *Science* 236:822-4 My 15 '87
Bacteria, Sulfur oxidizing
  Swept away: resuspension of bacterial mats regulates benthic-pelagic exchange of sulfur. J. Grant and U. V. Bathmann. bibl f il *Science* 236:1472-4 Je 12 '87
  Symbiosis in the deep sea [sulfide based ecosystem at hydrothermal vents] J. J. Childress and others. il *Sci Am* 256:114-20 My '87
Bacteria, Thermophilic
  Isolation of extremely thermophilic sulfate reducers: evidence for a novel branch of archaebacteria. K. O. Stetter and others. bibl f il *Science* 236:822-4 My 15 '87
Bacterial degradation *See* Biodegradation
Bacterial diseases
  See also
  Anthrax
  Legionnaires' disease
  Toxic shock syndrome
  Typhoid fever
Bacterial genetics *See* Microbial genetics
Bacterial membranes *See* Membranes (Biology)
Bacterial plasmids *See* Plasmids
Bacterial proteins
  Protein plays Trojan horse [invasin] *Sci News* 132:204 S 26 '87
Bacterial viruses *See* Bacteriophages
Bacteriology
  See also
  Toxins and antitoxins
    Equipment
  See also
  Petri dishes
  Bacterial analysis and chemicals. *Science* 235 pt2:G30-G31 F 27 '87
Bacteriophages
  Bacteriophage M13 procoat protein inserts into the plasma membrane as a loop structure. A. Kuhn. bibl f il *Science* 238:1413-15 D 4 '87
  A sequence in M13 phage detects hypervariable minisatellites in human and animal DNA. G. Vassart and others. bibl f il *Science* 235:683-4 F 6 '87
  A small viral RNA is required for in vitro packaging of bacteriophage φ29 DNA. P. Guo and others. bibl f il *Science* 236:690-4 My 8 '87
  Variable occurrence of the *nrd*B intron in the T-even phages suggests intron mobility. J. Pedersen-Lane and M. Belfort. bibl f il *Science* 237:182-4 Jl 10 '87
Bacteriorhodopsin *See* Pigments (Biology)
Baculoviruses *See* Viruses, Insect
Bad habits *See* Habits
Bad moods *See* Moods
Badalyan, Levon
    about
  Some thought on bioethics [interview] Y. Samoilov. *World Press Rev* 34:52 Ag '87
Badanes, Steve
    about
  In Virginia: homes with gusto. T. Brewster. il por *Time* 129:15+ Ap 27 '87
Baden-Baden (Germany)
  Gourmet holidays: cross-country skiing from Baden-Baden. P. J. Wade. il map *Gourmet* 47:48-53+ F '87
Baden-Wurttemberg (Germany)
    Industries
  See also
  Textile machinery industry—Germany (West)
Badenweiler (Germany)
  A spa in Germany. R. Gay. *Am Sch* 56:549-56 Aut '87
Bader, Scott E.
  The watercolor page. il por *Am Artist* 51:58-63 F '87
Badgers
  The old couple [coyotes and badgers hunting together] P. Schullery. il *Ctry J* 14:86-8 O '87

Badham, John
    about
  Stakeout [film] Reviews
    Macleans il 100:51 Ag 17 '87. L. O'Toole
    New Yorker il 63:80-1 Ag 24 '87. P. Kael
    Newsweek il 110:56-7 Ag 10 '87. D. Ansen
    People Wkly il 28:10 Ag 17 '87. R. Novak
    Time il 130:62 Ag 17 '87. R. Schickel
Badia a Coltibuono (Cooking school)
  A cooking school in Chianti. Z. E. Zakroff. il pors *Gourmet* 47:70-5+ My '87
Badminton House (Avon, England) *See* Historic houses, sites, etc.—Great Britain
Badr, Ihsan
  Saving sight in Saudi Arabia. il *World Health* p23-4 My '87
Baechler, Mary
    about
  Merrily they roll along. R. Orr. il pors *Nations Bus* 75:65 N '87
Baechler, Phil
    about
  Merrily they roll along. R. Orr. il pors *Nations Bus* 75:65 N '87
Baer, Eric, and others
  Hierarchical structure in polymeric materials. bibl f il *Science* 235:1015-22 F 27 '87
Baer, Michelle L.
  Let's hear it from the boys. il *Teen* 31:30+ Ap '87
  Teen tycoons. il *Teen* 31:60-1 Mr '87
Baerwald, David
    about
  David and David, a couple of musical moralists who look at L.A. from down the up staircase. il pors *People Wkly* 27:71 Ja 12 '87
Baez, Joan
    about
  The enduring queen of folk. C. McGuigan. il pors *Newsweek* 110:62 Jl 20 '87
  How the times they are a-changin' [interview] A. P. Sanoff. il por *U S News World Rep* 102:60 Je 29 '87
  Joan Baez [interview] M. Sager. por *Roll Stone* p163-4 N 5-D 10 '87
Bag ladies *See* Homeless women
Bag Lady dolls *See* Dolls
Bagatti Valsecchi, Pier Fausto, baron
    about
  Gardens: plotting an alpine cliffhanger: the Bagatti Valsecchi villa above Lake Como. M. Spark. il por *Archit Dig* 44:124-9+ F '87
Bagaza, Jean-Baptiste
    about
  Catching the early plane. por *Macleans* 100:9 S 14 '87
Bagdad (Iraq) *See* Baghdad (Iraq)
Bagdade, Al
  (jt. auth) See Bagdade, Susan, and Bagdade, Al
Bagdade, Susan, and Bagdade, Al
  Childhood memories are preserved in radio premiums. il *Antiques Collect Hobbies* 92:76-9 Mr '87
  Classics in china. See issues of Antiques & Collecting Hobbies beginning March 1985
  Classics in china. See issues of Hobbies beginning May 1984 through February 1985
Baget, Andre
  Those dreaded utility lines. il *Petersens Photogr Mag* 16:34-5 Ag '87
Baggage *See* Luggage
Baggett, James A.
  How to talk to your parents. il *Sch Update* 119:21 Mr 23 '87
Baghdad (Iraq)
    Description
  The view from the Mustansiriyah. M. Viorst. map *New Yorker* 63:92+ O 12 '87
Bagley, Bruce Michael
  Colombian politics: crisis or continuity? bibl f *Curr Hist* 86:21-4+ Ja '87
Bagnall, Philip M.
  The quadrantids: bright prospects for 1987. il *Astronomy* 15:39-42 Ja '87
Bagne, Paul
  Forbidden facts. il *Omni* 9:18+ F '87
Bagni de Lucca (Italy: Spa) *See* Health resorts, watering places, etc.—Italy
Bagpipe
  Philadelphia piping [Irish bagpiper T. Britton and the convention of the National Irish Pipers Club] M. D. Lemonick. il por *Time* 129:12+ Mr 16 '87

Bags
See also
Camera bags, cases, etc.
Handbags
Sacks
Brown-bagging it [tote bags] C. Donovan. il *N Y Times Mag* p64-5 Ap 19 '87
It's in the bag: toting to the office in style. il *Mademoiselle* 93:62 O '87

Bahaism
Holy terror [persecution of Bahais in Iran] F. M. Bordewich. il *Atlantic* 259:26+ Ap '87

Bahamas
See also
Bird sanctuaries—Bahamas
Fishing—Bahamas
Geology—Bahamas
Great Abaco Island (Bahamas)
Marine caves—Bahamas
Nassau (Bahamas)
Resorts—Bahamas
Samana Cay (Bahamas)
Description and travel
Discover the Bahamas [special section] T. W. Traska. il *Travel Holiday* 168:67-8+ Ag '87
Politics and government
See also
Elections—Bahamas

Bahar, Ann
The icons of old Russia. il *Antiques Collect Hobbies* 92:24-8 My '87
Jean-Henri Riesener: furniture maker to royalty. il por *Antiques Collect Hobbies* 92:39-42 N '87
Miniatures. See issues of Antiques & Collecting Hobbies beginning March 1985
Miniatures. See issues of Hobbies through February 1985

Bahia (Brazil) See Salvador (Brazil)

Bahmanyar, Sina, and others
Localization of amyloid β protein messenger RNA in brains from patients with Alzheimer's disease. bibl f il *Science* 237:77-80 Jl 3 '87

Bahr, Howard L.
Beside the still waters. il *South Living* 22:140 My '87

Baida, Peter
Eli Whitney's other talent. il *Am Herit* 38:22-3 My/Je '87
The fear of getting caught. il *Am Herit* 38:22+ S/O '87
Harvard's capitalist experiment. il *Am Herit* 38:20-1 D '87
A legendary chairman. il *Am Herit* 38:16+ Jl/Ag '87
My Vanderbilt movie. il *Am Herit* 38:20+ N '87
Your problem is solved. il *Am Herit* 38:20-1 F/Mr '87

Baikal, Lake (Soviet Union) See Lake Baikal (Soviet Union)

Bailard, Biehl & Kaiser
REITs are looking rosy again . . . and gold is panning out. G. G. Marcial. *Bus Week* p88 Ap 13 '87
Sitting tight in Japan [interview with L. Biehl] A. E. Serwer. il por *Fortune* 115:306 Ap 27 '87
The watchword after Bloody Monday: diversify. D. Zigas. *Bus Week* p142 N 9 '87

Bailey, Anthony
Outer Banks. *New Yorker* 63:94-104+ My 25 '87

Bailey, Elizabeth E., and Kirstein, David M.
It's time to bring truth in scheduling to airlines. il *USA Today (Periodical)* 116:15-17 N '87

Bailey, F. Lee (Francis Lee), 1933-
First word. il *Omni* 9:4 Ap '87

Bailey, Francis Lee See Bailey, F. Lee (Francis Lee), 1933-

Bailey, Harold
about
Black 'over qualified' for job sues Albuquerque, N.M. *Jet* 72:39 Mr 30 '87

Bailey, Herbert Smith
about
Herbert Bailey wins 'Ben' Award. il por *Publ Wkly* 231:18 Ap 17 '87

Bailey, Johnny
about
A young man in a rush. J. Garrity. il por *Sports Illus* 67:72-3 N 23 '87

Bailey, Julie
The fine art of leading a meeting. il *Work Woman* 12:68-70+ Ag '87
Is your house making you sick? il *Redbook* 168:116-19 Mr '87

Bailey, Lee
The last of the belles. il *Vogue* 177:536+ S '87
New-Age cocktails. il *Vogue* 177:212 D '87

Bailey, Paul, 1937-
about
PW interviews. A. Smith. por *Publ Wkly* 231:55-6 Je 26 '87

Bain, George
Media watch. See occasional issues of Maclean's

Bain, Geri
The Philadelphia story. il *Travel Holiday* 167:44-8 Ap '87

Bain & Company
A consulting firm too hot to handle? N. J. Perry. il *Fortune* 115:91-2+ Ap 27 '87

Bain Capital Fund Limited Partners
Putting it on the line. L. Jereski. il por *Forbes* 140:240 N 30 '87

Bainbridge, John
London journal. See occasional issues of Gourmet

Baird, Dugald Euan, 1937-
about
Euan Baird. J. Rossant. il por *Bus Week* Sp Issue:264 Ap 17 '87

Baird, Euan See Baird, Dugald Euan, 1937-

Baird, Jo Ann C.
Electronic media—can they really support the arts? *Des Arts Educ* 88:37-40 Jl/Ag '87

Bait
See also
Crayfish
Earthworms
Shiners (Fish)
Live baits & lures. A. H. Putnam. il *Field Stream* 92:97+ My '87
Anecdotes, facetiae, satire, etc.
What to do with leftover bait. A. H. Putnam. il *Field Stream* 91:34+ Ap '87

Bait, Artificial See Fishing lures, flies, etc.

Baja California (Mexico: Peninsula)
See also
Automobile racing—Baja California (Mexico: Peninsula)
Cabo San Lucas (Mexico)
Motorcycle racing—Baja California (Mexico: Peninsula)
Wildlife—Baja California (Mexico: Peninsula)
Description and travel
See also
Cruising—Baja California (Mexico: Peninsula)
State of Baja California Sur: San José del Cabo. T. Harrison. il map *Saturday Evening Post* 259:68-9+ O '87

Bajan cooking See Cooking, Barbadian

Bake sales See Fund raising

Baker, Anita
about
Anita Baker [cover story] W. Brown. pors *Essence* 18:48-50+ D '87
Anita Baker: at home with newest music crossover queen. C. Waldron. il pors *Jet* 71:56-8 Mr 9 '87
Anita Baker benefit raises $135,032.50 for Chicago's LaRabida Children's Hospital. il por *Jet* 72:58 My 4 '87
Anita Baker leads parade of black Grammy winners. il por *Jet* 71:55-6 Mr 16 '87
Anita Baker's gift of song. C. McGuigan. il pors *Newsweek* 109:56-7 Ja 19 '87
Nightlife. A. Virshup. il por *N Y* 20:124-5 S 21 '87
Who's the greatest? [cover story] W. Leavy. il pors *Ebony* 42:140+ O '87

Baker, David
about
35th annual International Critics Poll [with editorial comment by Art Lange] J. McDonough. il pors *Down Beat* 54:5, 20-4 Ag '87

Baker, DeWitt C., and Hileman, Jim
College publishers and used books. il *Publ Wkly* 232:18-21 D 11 '87

Baker, Donald S.
Say, brother. por *Essence* 17:9 F '87

Baker, Ella, 1903-1986
about
Obituary
Jet por 71:18 Ja 19 '87

Baker, George
about
Bringing down the House. M. Drohan. por *Macleans* 100:8+ N 30 '87

Baker, Houston A.
What Charles knew: homage to an English teacher [excerpt from An apple for my teacher] pors *N Y Times Book Rev* 92:3+ Mr 22 '87

Baker, Howard H. (Howard Henry), 1925-
about
Baker breaks the fever. E. Magnuson. il por *Time* 129:24+ Mr 16 '87
Baker in '88: 'not inconceivable'. E. Clift. il por *Newsweek* 109:5 Mr 16 '87
The Baker regency. *Nation* 244:311-12 Mr 14 '87
Baker's half-dozen. F. Barnes. *New Repub* 196:10-12 Mr 30 '87
Baker's mission. W. F. Buckley. *Natl Rev* 39:61 Ap 10 '87
Baker's recipe. F. Barnes. *New Repub* 196:9-10 Je 29 '87
Can he rescue Reagan? G. Borger and K. T. Walsh. por *U S News World Rep* 102:23 Mr 9 '87
Changing the guard. K. Scanlon. il por *Macleans* 100:22 Mr 9 '87
Giving normalcy a good name. H. Sidey. il por *Time* 129:22 My 11 '87
Gunning for Baker. L. Howard. il por *Newsweek* 110:4 Jl 20 '87
The hard road ahead on the comeback trail [special section; with editorial comment by Mortimer B. Zuckerman] il pors *U S News World Rep* 102:16-20, 88 Mr 16 '87
"The Heifer" takes some hits. B. Seaman. il pors *Time* 130:16 O 19 '87
How the new right is undermining Howard Baker. R. Fly. il por *Bus Week* p43 S 21 '87
Howard Baker: fighting the president's final battles [cover story] D. Eisenhower. il pors *N Y Times Mag* p18-21+ S 6 '87
Howard Baker gets serious. L. Howard. por *Newsweek* 109:6 Ja 12 '87
Howard Baker's long, hot summer. L. Walczak and others. il por *Bus Week* p24-5 Ag 3 '87
Letter from Washington. Cato. *Natl Rev* 39:14 Mr 27 '87
Letter from Washington. Cato. *Natl Rev* 39:14 N 6 '87
One for the Gipper: Baker signs on. B. Barol. il pors *Newsweek* 109:22 Mr 9 '87
The president's new men. W. Shapiro. il por *Time* 129:24 Ap 6 '87
Putting the president out front. G. Borger. il pors *U S News World Rep* 102:21-2 Ap 13 '87
Reagan breaks his fall. R. Fly and others. il pors *Bus Week* p34-5 Mr 16 '87
Reagan's kingpin. T. Jacoby. il pors *Newsweek* 110:15 Ag 24 '87
The right man at the right time. J. V. Lamar, Jr. il pors *Time* 129:27 Mr 9 '87
The "turn-to" scenarios. L. I. Barrett. il pors *Time* 129:26 Ap 13 '87
Watch Baker. J. McLaughlin. *Natl Rev* 39:24 Ap 10 '87
Why business is bananas over Baker. il por *Fortune* 115:8 Mr 30 '87
Baker, James
Whose power to which people? il *Sierra* 72:22-4 Ja/F '87
Baker, James A., III
about
Baker to Bush: no. il por *Newsweek* 110:7 O 19 '87
Baker: "Wait and see" [interview] C. Redman. por *Time* 130:24-5 N 2 '87
Baker's plan: no glitter. M. McNamee. por *Bus Week* p56 O 19 '87
The buck stops where? *New Repub* 196:6-8 F 16 '87
Challenge for a great persuader. J. Castro. il por *Time* 129:61 Je 8 '87
Did Baker call the right play? B. Powell. il por *Newsweek* 109:22 My 4 '87
Economic amnesia? R. J. Samuelson. il *Newsweek* 110:58 N 16 '87
Golden promise. il *Natl Rev* 39:17-18 N 6 '87
Investors should rejoice. M. S. Forbes, Jr. il por *Forbes* 140 Sp Issue:29 O 26 '87
The Jim and Alan show: will the markets buy it? T. Morganthau. il pors *Newsweek* 110:18-19 N 2 '87
Jim Baker shakes up a little gold dust. *Newsweek* 110:66 O 12 '87
The man and the myth. M. B. Zuckerman. il *U S News World Rep* 102:68 Je 15 '87
The president's budget battler. L. Smith. il por *Fortune* 116:58 N 23 '87
Testing time for Jim Baker. E. Mervosh. il por *U S News World Rep* 102:43-4 Ja 19 '87
Baker, James Thomas
Revisiting 'The Farm': from commune to suburb. il *Christ Century* 104:918-20 O 21 '87

Baker, Josephine, 1906-1975
about
Josephine Baker's adopted children sell her last valuables at public auction. il pors *Jet* 72:26-8 Je 15 '87
Baker, Lillian
about
In praise of pins. D. Reed. il por *Americana* 15:30-4 My/Je '87
Baker, M. T.
The cigar-store Indian. il *Antiques Collect Hobbies* 92:52-4+ Je '87
Baker, Pauline H.
South Africa: the Afrikaner angst. *Foreign Policy* 69:61-79 Wint '87/'88
United States policy in Southern Africa. bibl f *Curr Hist* 86:193-6+ My '87
Baker, Ralph
about
A net plus for safety, Ralph Baker's Life Chute may save lives in high-rise fires. J. Calio. il por *People Wkly* 28:107-8 Jl 13 '87
Baker, Russell, 1925-
Sunday observer. See issues of The New York Times Magazine through March 13, 1988
Baker, Samm Sinclair
Double your sales power. *Writer* 100:11-13+ N '87
Baker, Sherry
Forbidden foods. il *Health* 19:55-6 My '87
Mighty mouth. il *Health* 19:55-6 Ja '87
Baker, Thomas C.
(jt. auth) See Phelan, P. Larry, and Baker, Thomas C.
Baker International Corp.
Why the Baker-Hughes merger almost didn't happen. C. S. Eklund and T. Vogel. il pors *Bus Week* p110-11 My 11 '87
Bakers and bakeries
See also
Beeler's Meat Market and Bakery
Dunkin' Donuts Incorporated
Giordano's Bakery
Interstate Bakeries Corporation
Lloyd's Carrot Cake (Firm)
Mrs. Fields Cookies
Nabisco Brands, Inc.
Bake sale [auction of the equipment from out-of-business Lichtman's bakery in Manhattan] *New Yorker* 63:23-4 Jl 20 '87
Young chefs' full-baked ideas. J. J. Famularo. il *N Y Times Mag* p71-2 Mr 29 '87
Marketing
Soggy cookie monster. J. A. Trachtenberg. il *Forbes* 140:156+ O 19 '87
France
Let them eat pastry [Paris patisserie Xavier Gourmet] K. Hom. il *N Y Times Mag* p55-6 D 20 '87
Bakeware *See* Kitchen utensils and appliances
Bakhash, Shaul
The riddle of terrorism. il *N Y Rev Books* 34:12-16 S 24 '87
Baking
See also
Bread
Cake
Cookies
Gingerbread
Pastry
Pie
Bake sale best-sellers [excerpt from Blue ribbon winners] C. Hanley. il *Ladies Home J* 104:134-5+ O '87
Holiday baking in minutes [microwaved] il *South Living* 22:216 N '87
Holiday baking spices the air [cover story] S. Payne. il *South Living* 22:118-19+ D '87
Young chefs' full-baked ideas. J. J. Famularo. il *N Y Times Mag* p71-2 Mr 29 '87
Baking pans *See* Kitchen utensils and appliances
Baking soda *See* Sodium bicarbonate
Bakke, Timothy O.
What's new for your lawn and garden. See occasional issues of Popular Science beginning June 1986
Bakker, Jim
about
Ankerberg discusses the part he played. il por *Christ Today* 31:52 Je 12 '87
As the spiritual soap opera plays on, an expert assesses how Jim Bakker's fall could change television preaching [interview with J. K. Hadden] J. S. Podesta. il pors *People Wkly* 27:44-6 Ap 13 '87
Auctioning an empire. M. Green. il pors *People Wkly* 27:40-3 Je 8 '87

Bakker, Jim—about—*cont.*

Bakker quits. *Christ Century* 104:328 Ap 8 '87

The Bakker tragedy. T. C. Muck. il por *Christ Today* 31:14-15 My 15 '87

The Bakkers vs. the hired gun. G. Carroll. il por *Newsweek* 110:61-2 S 7 '87

Baring body and soul. il pors *People Wkly* 28:32-7 O 5 '87

Beyond Bakker. W. F. Buckley. *Natl Rev* 39:59 Jl 3 '87

Breaking faith, two TV idols fall. J. Wadler. il pors *People Wkly* 27:80-2+ My 18 '87

Can Jim and Tammy make a comeback? G. Witkin. il por *U S News World Rep* 103:21 O 19 '87

A crackdown at PTL. il por *Christ Today* 31:51+ Je 12 '87

Divided Pentecostals: Bakker vs. Swaggart. E. L. Blumhofer. *Christ Century* 104:430-1 My 6 '87

Evangelists in Babylon. H. Fairlie. *New Repub* 196:22-4 Ap 27 '87

The fall of the House of Bakker. J. M. Wall. *Christ Century* 104:323-4 Ap 8 '87

False profits. T. McNichol. *New Repub* 196:11-12 Ap 13 '87

Fresh out of miracles. R. Watson. il por *Newsweek* 109:70-2 My 11 '87

God and money [cover story; special section] il pors *Newsweek* 109:16-23 Ap 6 '87

God and money [cover story; special section] il pors *Time* 130:48-55 Ag 3 '87

The gospel according to the free market. T. Mason and S. Ticer. il por *Bus Week* p43-4 Ap 6 '87

Gospelgate II: target Falwell. L. Martz. il pors *Newsweek* 109:56-7+ Je 1 '87

Hahn bares her soul, etc. G. Hackett. il pors *Newsweek* 110:43 O 12 '87

Heaven can wait [cover story; special section] il pors *Newsweek* 109:58-62+ Je 8 '87

Heaven in 15 minutes or less. A. Fotheringham. il *Macleans* 100:56 Ap 20 '87

Hellfire, brimstone—and a TV scandal. B. Levin. il pors *Macleans* 100:42-3 Ap 6 '87

How much money did Jim and Tammy need? il por *Newsweek* 110:60-1 Ag 3 '87

Jim and Tammy rise again. J. Adler. il por *Newsweek* 110:77 O 19 '87

The Jim Bakker affair. il pors *Christ Today* 31:36-7 Ap 17 '87

Jim Bakker made me do it. P. Yancey. il *Christ Today* 31:64 O 16 '87

Jim Bakker's lost America. A. Kopkind. il pors *Esquire* 108:174-8+ D '87

New Bakker charge. K. L. Woodward. il por *Newsweek* 109:6 Ap 13 '87

Of God and greed. R. N. Ostling. il pors *Time* 129:70-2+ Je 8 '87

On having fun with fundamentalists. W. F. Buckley. *Natl Rev* 39:60 My 8 '87

Ousting two from the clergy. R. N. Ostling. il por *Time* 129:65 My 18 '87

An "outrageous" ministry. D. Brand. il por *Time* 129:82 My 4 '87

Paying the wages of sin. G. Hackett. il por *Newsweek* 109:28 Mr 30 '87

Pearlygate satires are weak on substance. L. I. Sweet. *Christ Century* 104:644-5 Jl 29-Ag 5 '87

Preacher-bashing and the public life. J. M. Wall. *Christ Century* 104:347-8 Ap 15 '87

Preaching & practice. D. R. Carlin, Jr. *Commonweal* 114:342-3 Je 5 '87

PTL: a battle of words in the holy war. il pors *Newsweek* 110:25 Jl 6 '87

A really bad day at Fort Mill. R. N. Ostling. il por *Time* 129:70 Mr 30 '87

Religious distraction. K. Burris. *Commonweal* 114:310-11 My 22 '87

Spring cleaning at Jim Bakker's PTL. J. L. Sheler and J. Thornton. il *U S News World Rep* 102:8-9 My 11 '87

Stones fly in the TV temple. G. Witkin. il pors *U S News World Rep* 102:10-11 Je 8 '87

Taking command at Fort Mill. R. N. Ostling. il pors *Time* 129:60 My 11 '87

The televangelist fiasco: top '87 religion story. *Christ Century* 104:1163-5 D 23-30 '87

Thou shalt not smirk. *Natl Rev* 39:17 Ap 24 '87

A troubled homecoming. L. Martz. il pors *Newsweek* 109:21+ Je 22 '87

TV's endless holy wars. M. Gray. *Macleans* 100:45 Jl 6 '87

TV's raging holy wars. L. Black. il por *Macleans* 100:54 My 11 '87

TV's unholy row [cover story] R. N. Ostling. il pors *Time* 129:60-4+ Ap 6 '87

Untold story of black founder of Pentecostal church body rocked by sex scandal of whites. S. Booker. il pors *Jet* 72:12-14+ My 18 '87

The value of preacher-bashing [discussion of April 15, 1987 article, Preacher-bashing and the public life] J. M. Wall. *Christ Century* 104:532-4 Je 3-10 '87

War of the evangelists: unfunny reflections. T. H. Stahel. *America* 156:293 Ap 11 '87

What profits a preacher? K. L. Woodward. il *Newsweek* 109:68 My 4 '87

Anecdotes, facetiae, satire, etc.

Hostile takeovers. M. E. Marty. *Christ Century* 104:343 Ap 8 '87

Bakker, Robert T.

about

How dumb was the dinosaur, anyway? S. Budiansky. il por *U S News World Rep* 103:66-7 Jl 6 '87

Bakker, Tammy

about

As the spiritual soap opera plays on, an expert assesses how Jim Bakker's fall could change television preaching [interview with J. K. Hadden] J. S. Podesta. il pors *People Wkly* 27:44-6 Ap 13 '87

Auctioning an empire. M. Green. il pors *People Wkly* 27:40-3 Je 8 '87

Breaking faith, two TV idols fall. J. Wadler. il pors *People Wkly* 27:80-2+ My 18 '87

God and money [cover story; special section] il pors *Time* 130:48-55 Ag 3 '87

Heaven can wait [cover story; special section] il pors *Newsweek* 109:58-62+ Je 8 '87

Jim Bakker's lost America. A. Kopkind. il pors *Esquire* 108:174-8+ D '87

Tammy Faye Bakker. il *People Wkly* 28:86-7 D 28 '87-Ja 4 '88

A troubled homecoming. L. Martz. il pors *Newsweek* 109:21+ Je 22 '87

Anecdotes, facetiae, satire, etc.

Tammymania! il por *People Wkly* 27:113-15 Je 22 '87

Bakoulis, Gordon

Bottled bonanza. il *Health* 19:34+ Mr '87

Can you go the distance? il *Health* 19:34-6+ O '87

Lining up for FIRM form. il *Health* 19:62-4 Je '87

Mix-and-match fitness selector. il *Work Woman* 12:125-6 Je '87

Playing it cool: the inside story on beating the heat. il *Work Woman* 12:120+ Je '87

Prime choices. il *Health* 19:49-51 Je '87

Summer skin care: staying safe in the danger zone. *Work Woman* 12:128 Je '87

Bakshi, Ralph

about

His X-rated Fritz (and L.A.) behind him, cartoonist Ralph Bakshi tries to make the grade as a painter. R. Arias. il pors *People Wkly* 28:91-2+ D 7 '87

Bakshian, Aram

A patriot for whom? Yusuf Khan: conflicts of loyalty in eighteenth-century India. il map *Hist Today* 37:40-4 Ap '87

Balance of nature *See* Ecology

Balance of payments

See also

Balance of trade

Capital movements

And now the bill comes due [U.S. foreign debt] B. Nussbaum. il *Bus Week* p160-1+ N 16 '87

The growing foreign role in U.S. policy. K. N. Johnson. il por *Fortune* 116:36-8 Jl 6 '87

International financial reform [address, May 18, 1987] A. T. Lambert. *Vital Speeches Day* 53:689-91 S 1 '87

It's time to put an end to the borrowing binge. A. S. Blinder. il *Bus Week* p22 My 4 '87

Learning to love stocks and bonds [U.S. as a debtor nation] G. Bock. il *Time* 130:56 S 14 '87

The scariest deficit of them all? G. Koretz. il *Bus Week* p24 N 9 '87

The U.S. gets foreign aid [Treasury bond sale] J. B. Copeland. il *Newsweek* 109:58 My 18 '87

Whose debt crisis is it anyway? [U.S. as debtor compared to Latin America] P. Davidson. il *New Leader* 70:14-15 Ag 10-24 '87

Why the dollar could head south again . . . and send the economy into recession next year [U.S. as debtor nation] G. Koretz. il *Bus Week* p20 Jl 13 '87

Why the dollar will fall. L. C. Thurow. il *Technol Rev* 90:24-5 N/D '87

Balance of payments—*cont.*

Japan

Japan's expanding role [address, September 25, 1987] Y. Kashiwagi. *Vital Speeches Day* 54:79-83 N 15 '87

Balance of power

Faltering America, or Russia? B. Crozier. *Natl Rev* 39:22 D 31 '87

Is America going to the dogs? J. McLaughlin. *Natl Rev* 39:22 Jl 31 '87

Of many things [views of P. M. Kennedy on the decline of America] G. W. Hunt. *America* 157:98 Ag 29-S 5 '87

The (relative) decline of America [cover story] P. M. Kennedy. il *Atlantic* 260:29-34+ Ag '87

The shifting balance of world power. M. I. Goldman. il por *Technol Rev* 90:20-1 Ap '87

The Soviet threat: Western schizophrenia. E. V. Rostow. *Current* 295:25-9 S '87

The U.S. as world leader: the (relative) decline of America. P. M. Kennedy. il *Current* 298:30-8 D '87

The U.S.-Soviet conflict: concert through decompression. G. Liska. *Current* 289:32-40 Ja '87

Balance of trade

See also
   Mercantile system

American competitiveness is healthier than it looks. P. C. Roberts. il *Bus Week* p18 Jl 13 '87

Another U.S. account heads for the red [invisible trade account] H. Banks. *Forbes* 140:45 Jl 13 '87

A better trade balance won't work miracles. V. Brownstein. il *Fortune* 115:43+ Ap 13 '87

Beware the deadly endive [decline of dollar and trade deficits] L. H. Lapham. *Harpers* 274:8-10 Ap '87

The bishops' letter, world debt and the U.S. trade deficit [pastoral letter on the economy] J. A. Gylys. il *America* 157:86-7 Ag 15-22 '87

The buck stops where? *New Repub* 196:6-8 F 16 '87

Can the shifting economy keep on an even keel? K. Pennar. il *Bus Week* p27-8 Jl 27 '87

A clear warning to Washington. D. Francis. il *Macleans* 100:9 N 16 '87

Competitiveness in America: is protectionism the answer? [address, May 27, 1987] D. W. McMinn. *Dep State Bull* 87:56-9 Ag '87

Correcting the trade deficit. M. S. Feldstein. bibl f *Foreign Aff* 65:795-806 Spr '87

Crawling out of the trade tunnel. V. Brownstein. il *Fortune* 116:43-4 D 21 '87

Dangerous drift. M. S. Forbes, Jr. il *Forbes* 139:25 My 4 '87

A declining dollar is just one piece in the puzzle. A. M. Solomon. il *Bus Week* p20 Ap 13 '87

Did Baker call the right play? [dollar bashing] B. Powell. il por *Newsweek* 109:22 My 4 '87

The dollar and the deficits: what to do [cover story; special section] il *Fortune* 116:36-40+ D 7 '87

The dollar: should we worry? *Natl Rev* 39:20 F 27 '87

Don't let the Grinch steal Christmas. G. F. Gilder. il *Natl Rev* 39:40-4 Ap 24 '87

Double-talk on the dollar [plunging dollar] R. Thomas. il *Newsweek* 109:45 F 2 '87

The economic black hole [U.S. trade deficit and foreign debt] L. C. Thurow and L. D. Tyson. bibl f *Foreign Policy* 67:3-21 Summ '87

Economic imbalances and world politics. C. F. Bergsten. bibl f *Foreign Aff* 65:770-94 Spr '87

The economy draws power from spending for equipment. . . but some of the benefits seem headed overseas. G. Koretz. il *Bus Week* p38 D 28 '87-Ja 4 '88

The falling dollar has thrown the trade deficit a curve. J. Berger. il *Bus Week* p68 My 11 '87

The falling dollar is improving the trade picture. W. B. Franklin and J. C. Cooper. il *Bus Week* p39-40 Je 1 '87

The Fed sees trouble if the deficits diverge. K. Pennar. il *Bus Week* p80 Mr 30 '87

Federal and trade deficits. P. H. Abelson. *Science* 238:1211 N 27 '87

Finance: improvement in trade renews our real growth. P. E. Kidd. il *Archit Rec* 175:44 Ag '87

Finance ministers meet on exchange rates [statement, February 22, 1987] *Dep State Bull* 87:31-2 Ap '87

Foreign trade policy. *Congr Dig* 66:163-92 Je/Jl '87

A game of chicken [drop in value of dollar fails to help trade deficit] G. Russell. il *Time* 129:44-6 Ja 26 '87

Guess who's stuck with the check [U.S. trade deficit results in higher prices for imported goods] B. Bauer. il *U S News World Rep* 102:52-3 F 2 '87

Hard times. R. L. Heilbroner. *New Yorker* 63:96-8+ S 14 '87

Harris chief warns of economic chaos if manufacturing continues overseas move [views of J. A. Boyd] E. H. Kolcum. *Aviat Week Space Technol* 127:89 S 14 '87

How Volcker sabotaged the president's agenda. P. C. Roberts. il *Bus Week* p18 Je 15 '87

Imposing order on a global economy [Group of 7 meeting in Washington] il *Macleans* 100:30 Ap 20 '87

An improving trade picture. J. C. Szabo. il *Nations Bus* 75:9 N '87

In the shadows of the Twin Towers [budget and trade deficits] S. Koepp. il *Time* 130:46-8 N 2 '87

In this corner, Uncle Sam [lower dollar helps American industry] D. Pauly. il *Newsweek* 110:61-2 D 7 '87

Interest rates have nowhere to go but up [dollar decline] S. Bartlett. il *Bus Week* p142-3 S 14 '87

International financial reform [address, May 18, 1987] A. T. Lambert. *Vital Speeches Day* 53:689-91 S 1 '87

Is the dollar doomed? [economic conference in Venice] A. Smith. il *Esquire* 107:51-2 Ja '87

It may look volatile, but the trade gap is stubborn. W. B. Franklin and J. C. Cooper. il *Bus Week* p31-2 Mr 16 '87

It's up to Germany and Japan to ease the trade trauma . . . but emerging economies could be the wild card. G. Koretz. il *Bus Week* p24+ My 4 '87

New lows ahead for the incredible diving dollar. B. Riemer and W. Glasgall. il *Bus Week* p30 Ja 19 '87

"No more Mr. Nice Guy". H. Banks. il *Forbes* 139:84-7 F 9 '87

The Paris pact may not buoy the dollar for long [February 1987 meeting] B. Riemer and others. il *Bus Week* p40-1 Mr 9 '87

The Reagan Fed can put a Democrat in the White House. P. C. Roberts. il *Bus Week* p21 O 5 '87

Real trade relief is coming . . . slowly. H. Banks. *Forbes* 140:27 Ag 24 '87

Revisions wiped out the good news on trade. W. B. Franklin and J. C. Cooper. il *Bus Week* p25-6 Ja 19 '87

The risks of a free-fall [plunging dollar] B. Riemer and W. Glasgall. il *Bus Week* p28-9 F 2 '87

Socking it to imports [proposals to deal with the trade deficit] G. Russell. il *Time* 129:48-9 F 9 '87

Some trade numbers are looking good—for now. J. C. Cooper. il *Bus Week* p25-6 F 16 '87

Spurious worries and real cares. H. Banks. *Forbes* 139:27 Ap 20 '87

Sunrise, sunset. *Nation* 244:455-6 Ap 11 '87

Supply and demand have rarely been so out of sync. J. C. Cooper. il *Bus Week* p23-4 Ag 31 '87

Supporting the dollar [Group of Five meeting in Paris] A. Finlayson. *Macleans* 100:38 Mr 9 '87

Taming the wild buck [Group of Five intervention] M. R. Meyer. il *Newsweek* 109:53 Mr 2 '87

Testing time for Jim Baker [dollar and trade deficit policies] E. Mervosh. il por *U S News World Rep* 102:43-4 Ja 19 '87

There's no panacea for six years of bad policy. R. Kuttner. il *Bus Week* p28 My 11 '87

Too many hopes are riding on a falling dollar. J. Berger. il *Bus Week* p92 D 7 '87

Trade: debate over protection. H. Eason. il *Nations Bus* 75:30+ Ja '87

The trade deficit. P. H. Abelson. *Science* 236:653 My 8 '87

Trade fetish. il *Natl Rev* 39:19-20 O 23 '87

The trade gap is a symptom. Low growth is the disease. N. Jonas. il *Bus Week* p40 Ja 26 '87

The trade gap is still hammering the dollar. W. B. Franklin and J. C. Cooper. *Bus Week* p25-6 O 26 '87

The trade gap may finally have set its last record; How imports and exports color the U.S. job picture. G. Koretz. il *Bus Week* p24 O 5 '87

The trade numbers are better than they look. W. B. Franklin and J. C. Cooper. il *Bus Week* p24 S 28 '87

The trade picture is no prettier. W. B. Franklin and J. C. Cooper. il *Bus Week* p27-8 Ap 27 '87

Trade progress may face its biggest obstacle in Asia [U.S. trade balance and exploding imports from the Asian Tigers] G. Koretz. il *Bus Week* p26 N 23 '87

Trade winds blow more ill than ever. M. W. Karmin. il *U S News World Rep* 103:14-15 D 21 '87

Tradeamok [cutting federal budget deficit] *New Repub* 196:7-9 Ap 27 '87

Balance of trade—*cont.*

The turn in trade is under way—for now. C. F. Bergsten. il *Fortune* 115:16-17 Ja 5 '87

Twin deficits and the G-7 [Paris accord] il *Natl Rev* 39:19-20 Ap 24 '87

U.S. trade policy and the trade deficit [statement, February 10, 1987; with appendix] C. K. Yeutter. il *Dep State Bull* 87:22-30 Ap '87

Uncle Sam's supermoney. R. J. Samuelson. il *Newsweek* 109:50 Mr 9 '87

Where the dollar is headed—with luck [down] V. Brownstein. il *Fortune* 115:39-40 F 16 '87

Where will the buck stop? B. Powell. il *Newsweek* 109:37 Ja 26 '87

Why the trade gap won't go away [surge of imports] K. Pennar. il *Bus Week* p26-7 Ag 31 '87

Statistics

Of apples, oranges and Toyotas [quarterly figures more reliable than monthly figures] E. A. Finn, Jr. il *Forbes* 139:34-5 Ja 26 '87

One month of trade: a sampler of U.S. exports and imports. il *Fortune* 115:220-1+ Ap 27 '87

Rise and fall of the dollar. R. Thompson. il *Nations Bus* 75:9-10 F '87

Germany (West)

The mark puts a stranglehold on exporters. F. A. Miller. il *Bus Week* p60 F 23 '87

Japan

The ballad of Ron and Yasu [effects of high yen; cover story] M. Sayle. *New Repub* 196:18-21 Je 15 '87

Damn the dollar, full speed ahead. M. Tharp. il *U S News World Rep* 103:50-1 D 14 '87

Economic imbalances and world politics. C. F. Bergsten. bibl f *Foreign Aff* 65:770-94 Spr '87

Harnessing the 'yen monster'. M. R. Meyer. il *Newsweek* 110:60 S 21 '87

Japan to purchase foreign aircraft to ease balance of trade [helicopter imports] *Aviat Week Space Technol* 127:22 Jl 6 '87

Japan's case of malaise. R. J. Samuelson. il *Newsweek* 109:47 My 4 '87

Japan's pump-priming won't do much for U.S. exports. B. Buell. il *Bus Week* p49 Ap 27 '87

Playing by different rules. J. M. Fallows. il *Atlantic* 260:22+ S '87

The swollen yen is weighing heavily on Japan. M. Berger. il *Bus Week* p34 My 4 '87

Tokyo's end run around its 'trade problem'. N. Gross. il *Bus Week* p54-5 Jl 13 '87

Waiting for the yen to stop pummeling profits. L. Armstrong. il *Bus Week* p58-9 Je 1 '87

Taiwan

Liquidity trap. A. Tanzer. il *Forbes* 139:37-8 Ap 6 '87

Taiwan's wealth crisis. M. Shao. il *Bus Week* p46-7 Ap 13 '87

United States

See Balance of trade

Balance sheets *See* Financial statements

Balances (Scales)

$18 darkroom chemical balance. T. F. Fuller. il *Petersens Photogr Mag* 16:66-7 Ag '87

Balances and gravimetric equipment. *Science* 235 pt2:G31-G33 F 27 '87

A ternary state of affairs. R. T. Kurosaka. il *Byte* 12:319-20+ F '87

Balanchine, George, 1904-1983

about

Apollo [ballet] Reviews

Dance Mag il 61:156-65 Je '87. J. Gruen

The ballet without Balanchine. M. Horn. il *U S News World Rep* 103:60 Jl 13 '87

Bournonville divertissements [ballet] Reviews

N Y 20:64-5 Je 22 '87. T. Tobias

Mozart violin concerto [ballet] Reviews

N Y 20:60-1 F 9 '87. T. Tobias

La sonnambula [ballet] Reviews

N Y il 20:64 Je 22 '87. T. Tobias

N Y il 20:84-5 D 14 '87. T. Tobias

New Yorker 63:72-4 Je 22 '87. A. Croce

Swan Lake [ballet] Reviews

New Yorker 63:71-2 Je 22 '87. A. Croce

Le tombeau de Couperin [ballet] Reviews

N Y il 20:100-1 My 18 '87. T. Tobias

Valse fantaisie [ballet] Reviews

Dance Mag 61:176-7 Je '87. L. Horn

Variations pour une porte et un soupir [ballet] Reviews

N Y il 20:60 F 9 '87. T. Tobias

New Leader il 70:22-3 Jl 1-15 '87. L. A. Jacobs

Balboa (Calif.)

Galleries and museums

See also

Newport Harbor Art Museum (Balboa, Calif.)

Balch, Stephen H., and London, Herbert Ira

The academy [discussion of October 1986 article, The tenured left] *Commentary* 83:11-12 Ja '87

Bald-Headed Men of America

None but the bald. R. P. Crease. il *50 Plus* 27:74+ F '87

Baldness

See also

Bald-Headed Men of America

Hair problems: too much, too little. P. Gadsby and H. Twidale. il *Good Housekeep* 204:216 Je '87

"Why is my hair falling out?". P. Von Nostitz. il *Parents* 62:167-70 F '87

Baldness remedies

Anti-baldness drug linked with sexual staying power [minoxidil] *Jet* 71:38 F 23 '87

Baldness drug gets a boost [minoxidil combined with tretinoin] il *Prevention* 39:14 S '87

Hair-loss help? *Vogue* 177:360 My '87

Hair-raising news [minoxidil] il *Time* 129:62 Mr 30 '87

A hairy problem [minoxidil as hair restorative not yet proven] il *FDA Consum* 21:37-8 Ap '87

Pumping hair. il *Esquire* 108:231-2 S '87

Putting the brakes on the baldness-cure bandwagon [Minox-a-gro] il *FDA Consum* 21:34-5 S '87

Baldrige, Letitia

about

You call this a party? J. Adler. il por *Newsweek* 110:90 O 5 '87

Baldrige, Malcolm

Space: the next business sector. por *Aviat Week Space Technol* 126:111 Je 1 '87

about

Obituary

Bus Week p35 Ag 10 '87. S. J. Dryden

Natl Rev 39:20 Ag 28 '87

Newsweek il por 110:20 Ag 3 '87

U S News World Rep il por 103:7 Ag 10 '87

Baldwin, B. A.

(jt. auth) See Kendrick, K. M., and Baldwin, B. A.

Baldwin, Billy, 1903-1983

about

In the Baldwin tradition. C. Vogel. il por *N Y Times Mag* p89-91 My 3 '87

Baldwin, Bruce A.

Take a real vacation! il *Read Dig* 130:89-91 Ap '87

Baldwin, James, 1924-1987

Architectural digest visits: James Baldwin. il pors *Archit Dig* 44:122-5 Ag '87

about

Notes and comment. *New Yorker* 63:31 D 21 '87

Obituary

Jet il por 73:14-15 D 28 '87-Ja 4 '88

Jet por 73:18 D 21 '87

Macleans il 100:13 D 21 '87. F. Bruning

N Y Times Book Rev il pors 92:1+ D 20 '87

Nation 245:740 D 19 '87

Natl Rev 39:17 D 31 '87. J. Hart

Newsweek il por 110:86 D 14 '87. P. S. Prescott

People Wkly il por 28:89 D 21 '87. B. Darrach

Time il por 130:80-1 D 14 '87. O. Friedrich

Baldwin, Kenneth

about

On its 50th birthday, a survivor celebrates his victory over the Golden Gate Bridge. W. Plummer. il pors *People Wkly* 27:110-12 My 25 '87

Baldwin, Malcolm F.

Wetlands: fortifying federal and regional cooperation. bibl f il *Environment* 29:16-20+ S '87

Baldwin, Mark

Barnyard diplomacy. il *Opera News* 52:38-9 Jl '87

Baldwin, Mike

about

Mike Baldwin. K. Cameron. il pors *Cycle* 38:76-80+ Mr '87

Baldwin, Steve

about

One is not enough. C. Davis. il pors *Mot Boat Sail* 160:38-41 Jl '87

Baldwin, Tom

about

Rich list candidate: 1995. S. W. Angrist. il *Forbes* 140 Sp Issue:401 O 26 '87

Baldwin-United Corp.

See also

PHLCorp Inc.

Baldwin-United Corp.—*cont.*
A fight over Baldwin's ghost [Leucadia goes after PHLCorp] C. S. Eklund. il *Bus Week* p72 Mr 30 '87
Balf, Todd
The mourning after. il pors *Sport Mag* 78:32-4 Mr '87
Balick, Bruce
The shaping of planetary nebulae. il *Sky Telesc* 73:125-7+ F '87
Baling machinery
From field to feedlot with bale buses. D. Mowitz. il *Success Farm* 85:B5 My '87
Balk, Christianne
Elegy [poem] *Harpers* 274:37-8 Mr '87
John Muir remembers Eliza Hendricks [poem] *New Yorker* 63:46 D 7 '87
Balkan Peninsula
See also
Albania
Ball, Aimee Lee
A cook's fantasy comes true. il *Work Woman* 12:164 N '87
Money, honey! The six-figure kids of Wall Street. il *Mademoiselle* 93:236-7+ Ag '87
Romancing the phone. il *Mademoiselle* 93:132-3+ Je '87
Ball, Judy
Real prolifers defend women, too [with readers' comments] *U S Cathol* 52:16-21 Ag '87
Ball catching
The good hands people [athletes' mastery] G. Legwold. il *Sport Mag* 78:81+ N '87
Ball Corporation
Ball Aerospace will test ground-based laser element [Relay Mirror Experiment] B. A. Smith. il *Aviat Week Space Technol* 127:99+ O 19 '87
A passion for fine-tuning. R. McGough. il por *Forbes* 139:44 My 4 '87
Ball throwing
See also
Pitching (Baseball)
Guide to a good arm. G. Legwold. il *Sport Mag* 78:73-4 Je '87
Balla, Philip
Literacy wars: a modest proposal. por *Publ Wkly* 231:376 Ja 30 '87
Ballantine Books, Inc.
Book-smart style [office of S. Petersen, president] P. Kripke. il por *Work Woman* 12:118-19 N '87
Ballard, J. G., 1930-
about
The strange visions of J.G. Ballard [interview] J. Cott. il por *Roll Stone* p76+ N 19 '87
Ballard, Jerry
about
An American Christian's view of Castro's Cuba. R. Frame. il pors *Christ Today* 31:49+ N 6 '87
Ballard, Jimmy
about
School for swingers. G. Waggoner. il *Esquire* 108:31-2 N '87
Ballard, Robert D.
Epilogue for Titanic. il *Natl Geogr* 172:454-63 O '87
about
A man with Titanic vision. F. Golden. il pors *Discover* 8:50-3+ Ja '87
Ballard, Sarah
Golf and glory. il *Sports Illus* 67:54-9 Jl 13 '87
He knows whereof he speaks. il pors *Sports Illus* 67:30-1 D 21 '87
Master on a mission. il por *Sports Illus* 66:66-71 F 9 '87
My, oh Mize. il pors *Sports Illus* 66:36-43 Ap 20 '87
Sailing back to the future. il *Sports Illus* 67:28-30+ D 7 '87
Socking it to the Kiwis. il *Sports Illus* 66:10-15 Ja 26 '87
Sumptuous sea fare. il por *Sports Illus* 66:81 Je 15 '87
Sunk by a slam dunk. il *Sports Illus* 66:86-7 Ja 12 '87
Taming a toothless tiger. il *Sports Illus* 66:128-30 Ap 6 '87
Victory at sea. il por *Sports Illus* 66:10-17 F 16 '87
Ballare [dance] See Dance reviews—Single works
Ballentine, Carol, and Maifarth, Shelly
Luring consumers down the primrose path. il *FDA Consum* 21:34-5 N '87
Ballet
See also
American Ballet Theatre

Armitage Ballet
Atlanta Ballet
Ballet/Aspen
Ballet Michigan
Ballet Oklahoma
Ballet West of New Mexico
Boston Ballet
Cleveland Ballet
Dallas Ballet
Dance Theatre of Harlem
Dayton Ballet Company
Feld Ballet
Hartford Ballet
Joffrey Ballet
Miami City Ballet
Motion pictures—Dance films
New York City Ballet
New York Theatre Ballet
Nikolais Dance Theatre
Oakland Ballet
Pacific Northwest Ballet
Pennsylvania Ballet
Pittsburgh Ballet Theatre
San Francisco Ballet
Spokane Ballet
State Ballet of Missouri
Tampa Ballet
Trockadero Gloxinia Ballet Company
Tulsa Ballet Theatre
Videotapes—Ballet
Washington Ballet
Westport Ballet Theater
The ballet without Balanchine. M. Horn. il *U S News World Rep* 103:60 Jl 13 '87
Changes in ballet and modern dance techniques: crossovers/fallouts. M. Horosko. il *Dance Mag* 61:168-71 Je '87
Dance magazine summer dance calendar '87 [special section] il *Dance Mag* 61:SC1-SC8+ My '87
Dancing:
Twyla Tharp Dance Company's appearance at the Brooklyn Academy occasions thoughts on relationship of modern dance and ballet. A. Croce. *New Yorker* 63:118-20 F 23 '87
Editors log. W. Como. See issues of Dance Magazine
Looking back: divertimento 1986. W. Como. il *Dance Mag* 61:56-63+ Ja '87
Nutcracker and holiday performance calendar [special section] il *Dance Mag* 61:HC1-HC2+ D '87
Performance calendar. See issues of Dance Magazine
Presstime news. See issues of Dance Magazine
Bibliography
Dancebooks. See issues of Dance Magazine
Competitions
New York's own ballet competition: fighting for glitter and gold in NYC. D. Cox. il *Dance Mag* 61:62-3 O '87
NY tourney announces judges [New York International Ballet Competition] il *Dance Mag* 61:26 Je '87
Swiss Prix is 15 [Prix de Lausanne] il *Dance Mag* 61:16-17 My '87
Yugoslav tourney unites young dancers. L. A. Lawrence. il *Dance Mag* 61:16-17 My '87
Directories
Dance directory. See issues of Dance Magazine
History
The ascent of Apollo: mounting Olympus. J. Gruen. il *Dance Mag* 61:156-65 Je '87
Dancing:
M. Hodson's reconstruction of Le sacre du printemps. A. Croce. *New Yorker* 63:140-2+ N 23 '87
Exploding a favored myth: ballet and its booms. C. Barnes. il *Dance Mag* 61:88-95 Je '87
In search of Sacre [work of M. Hodson] J. R. Acocella. il *Dance Mag* 61:44-8 N '87
A wishbook of danceworks we'd like to see again: revivals. R. Philp. il *Dance Mag* 61:136-49 Je '87
Stage setting and scenery
Dancing:
Swan Lake and La sonnambula. A. Croce. *New Yorker* 63:71-4 Je 22 '87
Jens-Jacob Worsaae sets a sparkling stage: designing the light fantastic. M. Hunt. il por *Dance Mag* 61:48-52 Ap '87
Study and teaching
See also
Dance schools
School of American Ballet
Education. M. Horosko. See issues of Dance Magazine

Ballet—Study and teaching—*cont.*

Emigré teaching—mystique or method? [Russian teachers and coaches] M. Horosko. il *Dance Mag* 61:76-7 Mr '87

The indomitable Sulamith Messerer: the eyes have it. J. K. Nelson. il pors *Dance Mag* 61:70-3 Mr '87

Technique: Plisetskaya teaches. M. Horosko. il pors *Dance Mag* 61:54-6 O '87

Australia

See also

Australian Ballet

Austria

In Vienna, Brunner has driven dance into the 1980s [artistic director of the Vienna State Opera Ballet] il *Dance Mag* 61:99 Ap '87

Belgium

See also

Maurice Bejart Ballet of the Twentieth Century

Canada

See also

Alberta Ballet Company
Ballet British Columbia
Ballet de Montréal
Les Ballets Jazz de Montréal
Les Grands Ballets Canadiens
National Ballet of Canada
Royal Winnipeg Ballet

Chile

See also

Ballet de Santiago

China

See also

Beijing Dance Conservatory

Denmark

See also

Royal Danish Ballet

France

See also

Ballet du Nord
Ballet National de Marseille
Lyon Opera Ballet
Paris Opera Ballet

Germany (West)

See also

Berlin Ballet
Stuttgart Ballet

Great Britain

See also

Ballet Rambert
London Festival Ballet
Royal Ballet
Sadler's Wells Royal Ballet

Israel

See also

Israel Ballet

Italy

See also

La Scala Ballet

Mexico

See also

Ballet Nacional de México

Monaco

See also

Ballet de Monte Carlo

Netherlands

See also

Dutch National Ballet
Netherlands Dance Theater

New York (State)

Dance [1987 performances] T. Tobias. il *N Y* 20:124-5 D 21-28 '87

Dance [New York City; fall preview] R. Gilbert. il *N Y* 20:100+ S 21 '87

Poland

See also

Warsaw Ballet

Soviet Union

See also

Bolshoi Ballet
Kirov Ballet
Moscow Ballet

Spain

See also

Royal Spanish National Ballet

Sweden

See also

Royal Swedish Ballet

Switzerland

See also

Basel Ballet
Zurich Ballet

United States

See Ballet

Yugoslavia

Yugoslav tourney unites young dancers. L. A. Lawrence. il *Dance Mag* 61:16-17 My '87

Ballet adaptations

The Gatsby gamble [A. Prokovsky adapts F. S. Fitzgerald's Gatsby for Pittsburgh Ballet Theatre] S. Flatow. il *Horizon* 30:60-2 O '87

Ballet/Aspen

At Ballet/Aspen, a director plans for the future [J. Bentley] L. Daily. por *Dance Mag* 61:16-18 F '87

Ballet British Columbia

Vancouver's Ballet British Columbia: staking a claim. O. Stuart. il *Dance Mag* 61:50-1 Ag '87

Ballet companies *See* Ballet

Ballet costume *See* Costume, Theatrical

Ballet de Monte Carlo

Editor's log. W. Como. il *Dance Mag* 61:32 Mr '87

Ballet de Montréal

Reviews:

Performances at Place des Arts. L. Howe-Beck. *Dance Mag* 61:35+ Ja '87

Performances of Symphonie du nouveau monde. L. Howe-Beck. *Dance Mag* 61:181-3 Je '87

Ballet de Santiago

Reviews:

Performance of Coppélia at the Teatro Municipal in Santiago. C. Hardy. *Dance Mag* 61:69+ D '87

Ballet du Nord

Catá and his Ballet du Nord: France's northern lights. M. E. Willis. il *Dance Mag* 61:50-3 O '87

Reviews:

Performance at the American Festival, Roubaix, France. S. Ueno. il *Dance Mag* 61:20+ Mr '87

Ballet Español de Yoko Komatsubara

Reviews:

Goya: luz y sombra at the Teatro Español in Madrid. L. Kumin. *Dance Mag* 61:75+ Ap '87

Ballet festivals *See* Dance festivals

Ballet Makers, Inc.

Capezio centenary: family affairs. N. V. Dalva. il pors *Dance Mag* 61:90-4 My '87

Ballet Michigan

Reviews:

Twelfth season at the University of Michigan-Flint theater. M. D. Rudnicki. il *Dance Mag* 61:18 S '87

Ballet music

See also

Compact discs—Ballet music
Phonograph records—Ballet music

Ballet Nacional de México

Reviews:

Ballet Nacional de Mexico and other groups at the San Antonio Festival. J. Neal. *Dance Mag* 61:25+ Ja '87

Ballet National de Marseille

Reviews:

Performances of The Blue Angel in Paris. M. E. Willis. il *Dance Mag* 61:20-1+ Ag '87

Ballet of the 20th Century *See* Maurice Bejart Ballet of the Twentieth Century

Ballet Oklahoma

New life for Ballet Oklahoma. L. C. Livingston. *Dance Mag* 61:16-17 F '87

Ballet Rambert

Ballet Rambert returns [scheduled performances in New York City] il *Dance Mag* 61:5 F '87

Fighting-mad [performances at City Center, New York City] T. Tobias. il *N Y* 20:123-4 F 23 '87

Reviews:

Performances at City Center, New York City. A. Smith. *Dance Mag* 61:27+ S '87

Ballet reviews

Dancing. A. Croce. See occasional issues of The New Yorker

Reviews. See issues of Dance Magazine

Single works

Alice

Dance Mag 61:36-8 F '87. C. Hardy

Macleans il 100:44 Jl 13 '87. M. Crabb

Apollo

Dance Mag il 61:156-65 Je '87. J. Gruen

Les biches

Atlantic il 259:86-8 F '87. H. Brubach

The Blue Angel

Dance Mag il 61:20-1+ Ag '87. M. E. Willis

Blue snake

Dance Mag 61:74 Ja '87. J. Gruen

Ballet reviews—Single works—*cont.*
Bournonville divertissements
  N Y 20:64-5 Je 22 '87. T. Tobias
Cinderella
  Art Am il 75:43-5 S '87. J. R. Acocella
  Art Am il 75:43-5 S '87. J. R. Acocella
  Dance Mag il 61:58-63 F '87. M. E. Willis
  Dance Mag il 61:28-9 My '87. C. Hardy
  Dance Mag il 61:32 S '87. W. Como
  Dance Mag 61:76-7 D '87. A. Smith
  N Y 20:57-8 Jl 13 '87. T. Tobias
  New Leader 70:21-2 Jl 13-27 '87. L. A. Jacobs
Clowns
  Dance Mag 61:26+ N '87. A. Barzel
Coppélia
  Dance Mag il 61:52-3 F '87. T. Tobias
  Dance Mag 61:27-9 Mr '87. O. Stuart
  Dance Mag 61:69+ D '87. C. Hardy
Ecstatic orange
  N Y 20:58 F 2 '87. T. Tobias
Embraced waltzes
  N Y 20:108 O 19 '87. T. Tobias
Enough said
  New Yorker 63:75-6 Jl 6 '87. A. Croce
Fancy free
  N Y il 20:92 Mr 30 '87. T. Tobias
La fille mal gardée
  Dance Mag il 61:56-9 Mr '87. J. R. Acocella
Les gentilhommes
  N Y il 20:64 Je 1 '87. T. Tobias
  New Yorker 63:82-3 Je 8 '87. A. Croce
Giselle
  N Y il 20:50-1 Ag 3 '87. T. Tobias
  New Yorker 63:90 My 25 '87. A. Croce
The golden age
  Art Am il 75:30-1+ N '87. J. R. Acocella
  N Y 20:52 Jl 20 '87. T. Tobias
  New Leader 70:22-3 Ag 10-24 '87. L. A. Jacobs
  New Yorker 63:61 Jl 27 '87. A. Croce
The great Gatsby
  Horizon il 30:60-2 O '87. S. Flatow
In memory of . . .
  Dance Mag 61:83 My '87. J. Gruen
The Kabuki
  Dance Mag il 61:84-9 My '87. W. Como
Malraux
  Dance Mag il por 61:12 Jl '87
  Dance Mag il 61:20 My '87. L. Moffett
  Dance Mag il 61:84-9 My '87. W. Como
The merry widow
  Dance Mag il 61:62-7 Mr '87. M. Crabb
Mozart violin concerto
  N Y 20:60-1 F 9 '87. T. Tobias
Napoli
  Dance Mag 61:34+ My '87. L. Svedin
Les noces
  Atlantic il 259:86-8 F '87. H. Brubach
The Nutcracker
  Dance Mag il 61:HC1-HC2+ D '87
Les petits riens
  N Y 20:58 F 2 '87. T. Tobias
Phaedra
  Dance Mag 61:25 O '87. J. Neal
Pillar of fire
  Dance Mag il por 61:54-9 S '87
Raymonda
  N Y il 20:50-1 Ag 3 '87. T. Tobias
  New Yorker 63:61-2 Jl 27 '87. A. Croce
Rite of spring
  Dance Mag il 61:6 O '87. L. Garafola
Romeo and Juliet
  Dance Mag 61:20-1 My '87. H. Koegler
La ronde
  Macleans il 100:65 N 30 '87. P. Hluchy
Le sacre du printemps
  Dance Mag il 61:44-8 N '87. J. R. Acocella
  Dance Mag il 61:49-51 N '87. R. Philp
  N Y il 20:100 N 16 '87. T. Tobias
  New Leader il por 70:22-3 N 30 '87. L. A. Jacobs
  New Yorker il 63:140-2+ N 23 '87. A. Croce
  Newsweek il 110:109 N 16 '87. L. Shapiro
  Theatre Crafts il 21:15 D '87. B. Howard
  Time il 130:97 N 16 '87. M. Duffy
  Vogue il 177:114 N '87. L. Friedman
The sleeping beauty
  Dance Mag il 61:20 Ag '87. H. Koegler
  N Y il 20:76 My 11 '87. T. Tobias
  New Leader 70:22 Ap 20 '87. L. A. Jacobs
  New Yorker 63:88-90 My 25 '87. A. Croce
  Time il 129:86 Ap 20 '87. M. Duffy

La sonnambula
  N Y il 20:64 Je 22 '87. T. Tobias
  N Y il 20:84-5 D 14 '87. T. Tobias
  New Yorker 63:72-4 Je 22 '87. A. Croce
Swan Lake
  Dance Mag 61:178-9 Je '87. M. E. Willis
  Dance Mag 61:29+ Mr '87. J. Neal
  Dance Mag il 61:74-5 Mr '87. I. Wydler-Roth
  Dance Mag il 61:19+ S '87. W. Salisbury
  Dance Mag il 61:18 D '87. M. Crabb
  New Yorker 63:71-2 Je 22 '87. A. Croce
Symphonie du nouveau monde
  Dance Mag 61:181-3 Je '87. L. Howe-Beck
Tales of Hans Christian Andersen
  Dance Mag il 61:52-4 N '87. I. M. Fanger
Terpsicore
  Nation 244:624-6 My 9 '87. M. Aloff
Le tombeau de Couperin
  N Y il 20:100-1 My 18 '87. T. Tobias
Trois etudes pour Alexandre
  Dance Mag 61:21+ O '87. L. Moffett
Valse fantaisie
  Dance Mag 61:176-7 Je '87. L. Horn
Variations pour une porte et un soupir
  N Y il 20:60 F 9 '87. T. Tobias
  New Leader il 70:22-3 Jl 1-15 '87. L. A. Jacobs
Winter dreams
  Dance Mag 61:28-9 N '87. C. Hardy
Ballet schools *See* Dance schools
Ballet shoes
    See also
    Ballet Makers, Inc.
Ballet West of New Mexico
  Go west, young dancer. E. Gwinn. il *Horizon* 30:32
  O '87
Balletfore
    See also
    New York Theatre Ballet
Les Ballets Jazz de Montréal
  Montreal troupes light birthday candles at 15 and 30.
  K. Greenaway. il *Dance Mag* 61:14 N '87
Balliett, Whitney
  Jazz. See occasional issues of The New Yorker
  Profiles [C. Sloane and J. Wilson] pors *New Yorker*
  63:72-4+ Ap 6 '87
  Profiles [J. La Rosa] por *New Yorker* 63:57-8+ S 28
  '87
  Profiles [M. Powell] por *New Yorker* 63:37-43 My 25
  '87
Balling, Robert C., Jr.
  (jt. auth) See Norman, Royal, Jr., and Balling, Robert
  C., Jr.
Ballistic Recovery Systems Inc.
  This parachute keeps the whole plane aloft. P. Houston.
  il *Bus Week* p86 N 2 '87
Ballistic transistors *See* Transistors
Ballistics
  Time the speeding bullet. J. Carmichel. il *Outdoor Life*
  179:38+ Ja '87
  The wayward wind. J. Carmichel. il *Outdoor Life*
  179:18-19+ F '87
  When the bullet gets there. J. Carmichel. il *Outdoor
  Life* 179:42+ Je '87
Un ballo in maschera [opera] See Verdi, Giuseppe,
  1813-1901
Ballonzoli, Joelle
                              about
  News watch. T. Tobias. il *N Y* 20:80-1 Ap 6 '87
Balloon ascensions
  Balloonatic Richard Branson puts his faith in hot air
  [proposed Atlantic crossing] R. Arias. il pors *People
  Wkly* 27:91-2 Je 15 '87
  The big splashdown [R. Branson and P. Lindstrand
  bail out short of Britain] N. Cooper. il pors *Newsweek*
  110:37 Jl 13 '87
  Hot air. P. Scott. il *Flying* 114:68+ My '87
  Ich bin ein ballooner [M. Forbes' motorcycle and hot
  air balloon trip through Germany] B. Conrad, III.
  il map *Forbes* 140:116-20+ Ag 24 '87
Balloon dilatation, Arterial *See* Arteries—Diseases—Therapy
Balloons
    See also
    Balloon ascensions
  Aiming high, André Heller floats the U.S. a fantastic
  loan. K. Hubbard. il por *People Wkly* 28:90-1 S 28
  '87
  Balloons [Greenwich Village School participates in the
  Triangle Coalition National Balloon Launch] *New
  Yorker* 63:26-8 Ap 20 '87
  Giving parades a lift [cover story] il *Natl Geogr World*
  140:6-9 Ap '87

Balloons—*cont.*

Medical use

Stomach 'bubble': diet device not without risks. E. Zamula. il *FDA Consum* 21:28-31 Ap '87

Research use

See also

National Scientific Balloon Facility

Anti-proton fishing. S. J. Nadis. il *Technol Rev* 90:15-16 Jl '87

Balloon flights view sun and gather cosmic rays. *Sky Telesc* 73:481-2 My '87

Balloons launch National Science & Technology Week. *Earth Sci* 40:6 Summ '87

The canopy raft [balloons in forest ecology research] il *Courier* 40:25-6 O '87

Down to the treetops by balloon [exploring the tropical forest canopy; work of Francis Halle and others] il map *Natl Geogr World* 146:13-19 O '87

French offer balloon platform for use on Soviet Mars mission. J. M. Lenorovitz. il *Aviat Week Space Technol* 127:63+ Ag 3 '87

Out on a limb [exploring the tropical forest canopy by hot air balloon; work of Francis Halle and others] K. Brower. il *Omni* 9:56-64+ Ap '87

Up, up, and away: students will launch thousands of helium-filled balloons in nationwide experiment to learn about wind and weather [cover story] A. H. Livermore. il map *Earth Sci* 40:12-13 Spr '87

Balloons, Toy

Build a balloon dog. il *Natl Geogr World* 140:22 Ap '87

Ballou, Hosea, 1771-1852

about

Hosea Ballou. C. E. White. il *Christ Today* 31:35 Mr 20 '87

Ballparks *See* Stadiums

Ballroom dancing

See also

American Ballroom Theater

Having a ball. G. Heymont. il *Saturday Evening Post* 259:38-9+ N '87

Balls

See also

Ball catching

Ball throwing

Baseballs

Tennis balls

Balls (Parties)

High hats & coronets: nothing succeeds like excess. J. Etra. il *Harpers Bazaar* 121:70+ D '87

Mrs. Eunice W. Johnson, Warren Bacon reign at regal Carnaval [charity ball for DuSable Museum] il pors *Jet* 72:33 S 7 '87

Rio on a plate [M. O'Donoghue's Bal Existential] *New Yorker* 63:25-6 Je 15 '87

Ballweg, Mary Lou

about

Endometriosis: one woman's struggle. J. Coudert. *McCalls* 114:86-8 S '87

Bally Manufacturing Corp.

For Bally, dumping Trump raises the ante [purchase of Golden Nugget in Atlantic City] M. D. Oneal. il *Bus Week* p45 Mr 9 '87

Is Bally going private—or going into play? G. G. Marcial. il *Bus Week* p78 Ag 3 '87

Zero-sum game [Bally buys Golden Nugget's Atlantic City casino] R. Phalon. il pors *Forbes* 139:110-12 Mr 23 '87

Balmain (Pierre) (Firm) *See* Pierre Balmain (Firm)

Baloyra, Enrique A., 1942-

The seven plagues of El Salvador. *Curr Hist* 86:413-16+ D '87

Balter, Lawrence

Understanding kids. See issues of Ladies' Home Journal beginning February 1984

(jt. auth) See Samuels, Jonathan, and Balter, Lawrence

Balter, Michael S.

Pritikin gets respect. il *Health* 19:67-8+ Je '87

Balthus, 1908-

about

Chalet Balthus. J. Leymarie. il por *House Gard* 159:108-17 D '87

Baltic Freedom Day

Baltic Freedom Day, 1987 [proclamation, June 13, 1987] R. Reagan. *Dep State Bull* 87:38 S '87

Baltic States

See also

Arts and crafts—Baltic States

Baltimore, David, 1938-

about

'Quarantining will help no one' [interview] por *U S News World Rep* 102:70 Ja 12 '87

Baltimore (Md.)

Education

Kids and parents at a Baltimore grade school are uniformly opposed to costly kid fashions [uniforms at Cherry Hill public school] il *People Wkly* 28:133 O 12 '87

Galleries and museums

See also

Baltimore Museum of Art

Lillie Carroll Jackson Museum

Gardens and gardening

A yard for all seasons [home of Eric and Jacqueline Gratz] W. Oehme. il *Rodale's Org Gard* 34:48-50 O '87

Historic houses, sites, etc.

At home with H. L. Mencken. il por *South Living* 22:30 S '87

Urban living at its finest [1797 row house] C. Engle. il *South Living* 22:170-2 Ap '87

Housing

Rose finally unpacked her belongings [Wallace H. Campbell & Co. and Jewish Family Services team up to run high-rise apartment for the elderly] J. B. Kurland and G. E. J. Lipsitz. il *Aging* no355:6-9 '87

Ordinances

Out of South Africa: divestment hits a snag [ordinance requiring public pension funds to sell stocks challenged] E. Weiner and L. J. Tell. il *Bus Week* p53 Jl 6 '87

Politics and government

Baltimore may elect first black mayor, 37-year-old atty. Kurt L. Schmoke. il por *Jet* 73:4 O 5 '87

First black mayor of Baltimore begins building coalition [C. H. Burns] il por *Jet* 71:54 F 9 '87

Holy Schmoke! [black mayoral candidate K. Schmoke] il por *Time* 130:25 S 28 '87

Kurt Schmoke takes oath as first black elected mayor of Baltimore, Md. il por *Jet* 73:12 D 28 '87-Ja 4 '88

Religious institutions and affairs

This far by faith [C. Williams-Bryant, black woman minister at Bethel AME Church] H. Cole and A. Edwards. il pors *Essence* 18:107-8+ S '87

Social history

The phantom amendment & the Duchess of Baltimore [E. P. Bonaparte] W. H. Earle. il pors *Am Hist Illus* 22:32-9 N '87

Baltimore (Md.). World Trade Center *See* World Trade Center (Baltimore, Md.)

Baltimore Museum of Art

Singles mingle [Singles Sunday] M. Giuliano. il *Art News* 86:21 My '87

Baltimore Publishers Association

Baltimore publishers hold fifth annual show. H. Fields. il *Publ Wkly* 231:18 Ja 16 '87

Baltimore Zoo

His life is a zoo [head veterinarian M. Cranfield] D. Young. il por *South Living* 22:145 Mr '87

Baltistan (Pakistan)

Description and travel

Baltistan. G. A. Rowell. il map *Natl Geogr* 172:526-50 O '87

Baltzell, E. Digby (Edward Digby), 1915-

about

The benefits of elitism. E. F. Cone. il por *Forbes* 140 Sp Issue:380 O 26 '87

Baltzell, Edward Digby *See* Baltzell, E. Digby (Edward Digby), 1915-

Balukas, Jean

about

The best woman in the hall. R. Starr. il por *N Y Times Mag* p30+ O 18 '87

Balzac, Honoré de, 1799-1850

about

The gastronomic world of Balzac. N. Barry. il *Gourmet* 47:48-53+ S '87

Balzer, Robert Lawrence

1988 Travel/Holiday guide to fine dining: United States, Canada, Mexico [cover story] il *Travel Holiday* 168:83-116 D '87

Concerning food and wine. See alternate issues of Travel Holiday

Balzhiser, Richard E., and Yeager, Kurt E.

Coal-fired power plants for the future. il *Sci Am* 257:100-7 S '87

BAM *See* Brooklyn Academy of Music

La bamba [film] See Motion picture reviews—Single works

Bamberger, Alan S.
Art talk: a few words on the relationship of reference books to art collecting. *Antiques Collect Hobbies* 92:31 D '87

Bamboo
Dwarf bamboo for ground cover that's different. J. W. Waddick. il *Flower Gard* 31:34+ F/Mr '87

Bamboo fishing rods *See* Fishing tackle

Bamford, James, 1946-
Carlucci and the N.S.C. il *N Y Times Mag* p16-19+ Ja 18 '87

about
An expert says tear down our bugged embassy in Moscow [interview] M. Ryan. il por *People Wkly* 27:91+ Ap 27 '87

Bamieh, Sam

about
Anguish and languishing in Saudi Arabia. por *Newsweek* 109:32 Ja 12 '87
Yet another Saudi connection. E. Magnuson. il *Time* 129:16 Je 29 '87

Banana slugs *See* Slugs

Bananarama (Musical group)
Britain's Bananarama, ripe with success, insist they're more than a bunch of cute Chiquitas. D. Hutchings. il *People Wkly* 28:90-1 O 19 '87

Bananas

Diseases and pests
Can a banana splice save the banana split? [breeding against black sigatoka disease; work of Phillip Rowe] il *Discover* 8:7-8 Ag '87

Banc One Corp.
A dazzling bank's drooping multiple. A. E. Serwer. il *Fortune* 115:131-2 Mr 2 '87

Banco Ambrosiano, SpA
Did corruption soil Vatican's inner sanctum? J. P. Shapiro. il por *U S News World Rep* 102:10 Mr 9 '87
Following the money. J. Howse. il por *Macleans* 100:11 Jl 27 '87
Hiding behind the walls [arrest warrant issued for P. Marcinkus in Vatican] S. Allis. il por *Time* 129:54 Mr 9 '87
Vatican bank scandal. *Christ Century* 104:265 Mr 18-25 '87
Vatican horror: a banking scandal widens. por *Newsweek* 109:48 Mr 9 '87

Banco do Brasil SA
View from the middle [interview with A. M. da Silva] E. A. Finn, Jr. il por *Forbes* 140:60+ N 16 '87

Bancorp Hawaii Inc.
Banks may get a lei from Hawaii. G. G. Marcial. *Bus Week* p76 F 9 '87

Bancroft, Ann

about
Ann Bancroft. S. Margolis. il pors *Ms* 15:71-2+ Ja '87
The Arctic adventures of Ann Bancroft. M. Specktor. il pors *McCalls* 114:101 Ja '87
Everything is North/Ann Bancroft. J. Kaplan. il por *Vogue* 177:452-3+ Mr '87

Bancroft, Anne, 1931-

about
The private side of Anne Bancroft. J. Goodman. il pors *Ladies Home J* 104:72+ O '87

Bancroft, Carter
(jt. auth) *See* Lufkin, Thomas, and Bancroft, Carter

Bancroft, Tom

about
Keeping a key pigeon in the Keys. G. Laycock. il por *Audubon* 89:76-80 Mr '87

Bancroft Convertible Fund, Inc.
$11 for a $10 bill? [M. B. Javett's bid] R. Phalon. il *Forbes* 139:99 Ja 26 '87

BancTexas Group Inc.
A 'rescue finance' team takes on banking [Hallwood Group takes on BancTexas Group] D. Cook. il por *Bus Week* p120 Mr 16 '87

Band, Hamid, and others
Immunochemical proof that a novel rearranging gene encodes the T cell receptor δ subunit. bibl f il *Science* 238:682-4 O 30 '87

Band (Musical group)
Bob Dylan and The Band: U.S. tour, January-February 1974. D. Fricke. il pors *Roll Stone* p85-7+ Je 4 '87
Robbie Robertson [interview] M. Goldberg. por *Roll Stone* p187-9 N 5-D 10 '87

Bandannas *See* Scarves

Banding, Bird *See* Bird banding

Bandler, Michael J.
Christopher Reeve: it isn't easy being Superman! il pors *McCalls* 114:53-4 S '87

The Farrah Fawcett/Barbara Hutton connection [interview with F. Fawcett and L. Persky] il pors *McCalls* 115:186-8 N '87
Farrah Fawcett: happy as can be [interview] il por *McCalls* 115:12-16+ O '87
The good enough parent's parent. il pors *Parents* 62:189-90+ N '87
Seuss on the loose. il pors *Parents* 62:116-18+ S '87

Bandow, Doug
Inefficient at best [with reply by B. Gants] il *Consum Res Mag* 70:14-17 My '87
Mercenary morality. *New Repub* 197:20-2 O 19 '87

Bands (Music)
See also
Lester Lanin Orchestras
Rock groups
St. Johns River City Band
Steel bands (Music)
Band on the run [Stanford University's marching band] J. B. Meigs. il *Roll Stone* p86-9+ S 24 '87
Music, military style [outdoor concerts in Washington, D.C.] K. Lingo. il *South Living* 22:10-12 Jl '87

Bandsaws *See* Saws and sawing

Bangkok (Thailand)

Stores
Far-Eastern finds. D. G. Salter. il *Essence* 18:27-9+ S '87

Bangkok House (New York, N.Y.: Restaurant) *See* New York (N.Y.)—Restaurants, nightclubs, bars, etc.

Bangladesh
See also
Birth control—Bangladesh
Dams—Bangladesh
Technical assistance, Dutch—Bangladesh

Politics and government
A revolt against poverty. C. Wood. il *Macleans* 100:28-9 D 14 '87

Bangles (Musical group)
The Bangles. M. Ehrman. il *Teen* 31:76-7 S '87
The Bangles. A. Ferrar. il *Stereo Rev* 52:85-7 Ja '87
California girls. S. Orlean. il *Roll Stone* p62-4+ Mr 26 '87
Meet the Bangles. D. Goldman. il *Sch Update* 120:14 S 18 '87

Bangs (Hairstyling) *See* Hairstyling

Banham, Reyner
In the neighborhood of art. il *Art Am* 75:124-9 Je '87

Banishment *See* Exiles

Banister, Debra

about
Family business: murder would settle it, and Debra Banister knew who to ask. J. Wadler. il pors *People Wkly* 28:57-8+ Jl 6 '87

Bank accounting *See* Banks and banking—Accounting

Bank accounts
See also
Cash management accounts
Certificates of deposit
Escrow accounts

Brokered deposits
"We're the lifeblood" [regulators turn to money brokers for help with weak thrifts] M. Schifrin. il *Forbes* 140:43-4 Jl 27 '87

Insurance
See also
Federal Deposit Insurance Corporation
Federal Savings and Loan Insurance Corporation
What the S&L crisis means to you. il *Money* 16:11 Je '87

Interest (Economics)
Fine print: bank-deposit shenanigans [overstating rates] *Money* 16:13 Ag '87
In the CD wars, the customers are winning. S. Weiss. il *Bus Week* p151 Je 8 '87
Job growth explains why consumers keep on spending . . . and interest income may give them more to burn. K. Pennar. il *Bus Week* p24 O 26 '87
Places for investors to park their profits [money market deposit accounts and money market mutual funds] M. J. Williams. il *Fortune* 116:127 S 28 '87
Saving: float like a butterfly before you sock away your cash. il *Money* 16:40 Je '87
Savings: good riddance to '86, a year when yields plunged 25%. il *Money* 16:39 Ja '87
Savings: how to hang loose with your loose change [money-market account] il *Money* 16:27 D '87
Savings: how you can catch rising rates at their peak. il *Money* 16:29 Jl '87
Savings: the highs of Texas are nearly behind you. il *Money* 16:27 S '87

Bank accounts—Interest (Economics)—*cont.*
Savings: wait for a great rate on a late-spring date. il *Money* 16:35 Ap '87
Savings: why interest rates are headed thataway. il *Money* 16:35 Mr '87
Savings: why the days of ultrahigh rates are numbered. il *Money* 16:25 Ag '87
Will the real yield please stand up. J. Bodnar. il *Changing Times* 41:125-6+ Ja '87

Bank consultants
See also
Sheshunoff & Company
Bank credit cards *See* Credit cards
Bank debit cards *See* Debit cards
Bank deposits *See* Bank accounts
Bank employees
Salaries, pensions, etc.
Axed in an acquisition [finances of laid-off bank manager Mike Garbutt] S. Seixas. il *Money* 16:104-8 Mr '87
Training
Going to investment banking 'boot camp' with Midland's Marines. A. Beam. *Bus Week* p82 Ap 6 '87
Bank ethics *See* Banks and banking—Ethical aspects
Bank failures
Another great year—for defaults. S. Bartlett. il *Bus Week* p108-9 Ja 12 '87
Are worries about bank failures justified? G. G. Kaufman. il *USA Today (Periodical)* 115:43-6 Ja '87
Closely watched banks: one that got away [Central National Bank of New York] F. A. Miller and R. A. Kessler. il por *Bus Week* p108 O 19 '87
Feuding among the ruins of failed thrifts. J. B. Levine. il *Bus Week* p116 My 18 '87
"Nobody thought it would be us" [FDIC liquidates Unitedbank-Houston] R. Woodbury. il *Time* 129:53 My 11 '87
A wave of defaults capsizes black banks. il *Black Enterp* 17:187-8+ Je '87
A wave of embezzlement hits banking. G. DeGeorge. il *Bus Week* p49 My 18 '87
Bank fees *See* Banks and banking—Service charges; Investment banking—Service charges
Bank holding companies
See also
Banc One Corp.
BancTexas Group Inc.
BankAmerica Corp.
Bessemer Group, Inc.
Citicorp
CityFed Financial Corp.
Continental Illinois National Bank & Trust Co. of Chicago
Equimark Corp.
Financial Corp. of America
First Bank System Inc.
First City Bancorporation of Texas, Inc.
First Interstate Bancorp
First Pennsylvania Corp.
First Union Corp.
H. F. Holdings
Hawkeye Bancorporation
Manufacturers Hanover Corp.
Norwest Corporation
Seafirst Corporation
U.S. Bancorp
Wells Fargo & Co.
Acquisitions and mergers
Buy or be bought [U.S. Bancorp] J. Heins. il por *Forbes* 139:48 My 18 '87
The man who would be boss at BankAmerica [J. Pinola of First Interstate Bancorp] R. E. Norton. il pors *Fortune* 115:88-90+ F 16 '87
Texas banks: who wants 'em? T. Vogel. il *Bus Week* p120 Je 8 '87
Who needs BankAmerica? Not Joe Pinola [First Interstate bows out] T. Carson. il por *Bus Week* p46 F 23 '87
Bank Julius Baer & Co. AG
A Swiss banker's goal: just don't lose money [H. Looser] B. Riemer. il por *Bus Week* p154 D 28 '87-Ja 4 '88
Bank Leu AG
Bank Leu's new brouhaha [Guinness spillover] J. Templeman. il *Bus Week* p50 F 2 '87
Bank loans *See* Loans, Bank
Bank notes
A note from Santa Claus! [bank notes depicting Santa Claus] E. Rochette. il *Antiques Collect Hobbies* 92:80-1 D '87

Bank of America National Trust & Savings Assn.
See also
BankAmerica Corp.
Bank of British Columbia
High adventure in the bank trade. P. C. Newman. il por *Macleans* 100:38 Ja 26 '87
Bank of Canton of California
The bank of what? P. Fuhrman. il *Forbes* 139:38+ Ap 6 '87
Bank of China
Banking on China. D. Fong. por *Forbes* 140:304 N 16 '87
Bank of England
A crash diet for an overweight economy [hikes interest rates] R. A. Melcher. il *Bus Week* p34-5 Ag 24 '87
Bank of New York
Is Irving worth the wait? [Bank of New York bids for Irving Trust] F. A. Miller. il *Bus Week* p162 O 12 '87
Bank One, Cleveland, NA
Peripatetic banker [K. Horn] D. Machan. il por *Forbes* 139:170+ Je 1 '87
Bank planting *See* Hillside gardens and gardening
Bank premiums *See* Premiums
Bank rates *See* Interest (Economics)
Bank reserves *See* Banks and banking—Reserves
Bank robberies
Cash-machine magician [R. Post's use of magnetic encoding machine to rob automated bank teller machines] *Time* 129:61 Je 1 '87
The gang that couldn't rob straight [robberies in Kansas] il *Newsweek* 110:30 S 28 '87
Guard hailed by police fired by bank; gets a better job and pay raise [J. Massey of Wells Fargo Bank, San Francisco] *Jet* 72:12 Mr 30 '87
Teller machine robberies [study by Bank Administration Institute] il *USA Today (Periodical)* 116:6 D '87
Bank secrecy *See* Confidential communications—Banking
Bank stocks *See* Banks and banking—Securities
Bank Street Writer (Word processor program) *See* Word processors and processing—Programming
Bank swallows *See* Swallows
BankAmerica Corp.
Bank of America's blueprint for a policy on AIDS. N. L. Merritt. por *Bus Week* p127 Mr 23 '87
BankAmerica's new tight spot [reserve set aside against third world debt] J. B. Levine and S. Bartlett. il *Bus Week* p50 Je 22 '87
Deja vu at BankAmerica [management style of A. W. Clausen] J. B. Levine. il por *Bus Week* p59 My 25 '87
The man who would be boss at BankAmerica [J. Pinola of First Interstate Bancorp] R. E. Norton. il pors *Fortune* 115:88-90+ F 16 '87
Monarch buys its own insurance policy [acquisition of BankAmerica's investment management subsidiaries] K. H. Hammonds. il *Bus Week* p93+ S 7 '87
The most beleaguered banker [S. Armacost] G. Hector. il por *Fortune* 115:86 Ja 5 '87
Tom Clausen. J. B. Levine. il por *Bus Week* Sp Issue:216 Ap 17 '87
Who needs BankAmerica? Not Joe Pinola [First Interstate bows out] T. Carson. il por *Bus Week* p46 F 23 '87
Bankers
See also
Women bankers
Bankers Life & Casualty Co.
Damage control [Supreme Court to decide on damages awarded in suit against Bankers Life] D. Fanning. il *Forbes* 139:84 Je 29 '87
Bankers Trust Company
Managing the needs of others [R. Schnitzer controls direction of computer users in the corporate finance department] P. Honan. il por *Pers Comput* 11:164-5 O '87
Bankhead, Tallulah, 1902-1968
about
Three neighbors. T. Capote. il pors *Esquire* 108:223-4 D '87
Banking *See* Banks and banking
Banking ethics *See* Banks and banking—Ethical aspects
Banking, Housing, and Urban Affairs Committee *See* United States. Congress. Senate. Committee on Banking, Housing and Urban Affairs
Banknotes *See* Bank notes
Bankowski, Zbigniew
"A wasteful mockery". il *World Health* p3-4 Ap '87
Bankowski, Zbigniew, and Gutteridge, Frank
Health, ethics and human values. il *World Health* p9-11 Je '87

Bankruptcy
> *See also*
> Bank failures
> Business failures

Chapter 12 offers new option to family farmers. C. Tevis. il *Success Farm* 85 no4:18V-18W F '87

John Connally goes belly up after betting big on a Texas oil economy that ran out of gas [personal and partnership bankruptcy] W. Plummer. il pors *People Wkly* 28:36-7 Ag 17 '87

Singer Barbara McNair files for bankruptcy. il por *Jet* 72:22 S 14 '87

Banks, Allan R., 1948-
> *about*

Allan R. Banks [cover story] M. E. Stegmaier. il por *Am Artist* 51:42-7+ Ag '87

Banks, Ann
Mother love. il *Parents* 62:114-15 Ag '87

Banks, C. Tillery
Inside [poem] *Essence* 17:110 Ap '87
So [poem] *Essence* 18:147 S '87

Banks, Dean
An alternative to alternative education. *Educ Dig* 53:33-5 D '87

Banks, Gene
> *about*

Injury may end career of Bulls' Gene Banks. *Jet* 72:46 Jl 20 '87

Banks, Howard
What's ahead for business. See issues of Forbes beginning January 16, 1984

Banks, Leo
Arizona's atomic attraction. il *Travel Holiday* 168:92 Ag '87
The Santa Fe blend. il *Travel Holiday* 168:64-8 S '87

Banks, Peter A.
Inflammatory bowel disease: recognizing the symptoms. por *McCalls* 114:108 Ja '87

Banks, Peter M., and Black, David C.
The future of science in space. bibl f *Science* 236:244-5 Ap 17 '87

Banks, Steve
> *about*

California Cadillacs. L. Griffin. il *Car Driv* 33:108-12 N '87

Banks, William Nathaniel
History in towns: Edgartown, Martha's Vineyard. il *Antiques* 132:1302-17 D '87
Melrose in Natchez, Mississippi. bibl f il *Antiques* 131:650-7 Mr '87
> *about*

American grandeur. B. Gill. il por *House Gard* 159:112-23+ S '87
American simplicity. B. Gill. il *House Gard* 159:162-73+ O '87

Banks, Coin
Money in the bank [piggy banks] K. Vogel and C. Vogel. il *Workbench* 43:38 N/D '87
> **Collectors and collecting**

Nonsense-theme mechanical banks. M. Jailer. il *Antiques Collect Hobbies* 92:42-4 My '87
Popularity of the animal-motif banks. M. Jailer. il *Antiques Collect Hobbies* 92:42-4 S '87

Banks and banking
> *See also*
> Agricultural credit
> Bank holding companies
> Bank of New York
> Bankers Trust Company
> Black banks and banking
> Chase Manhattan Bank, N. A.
> Chemical Bank
> Citibank N.A.
> Clearinghouse (Banking)
> Computers—Banking use
> Confidential communications—Banking
> Credit
> Development banks
> Federal Reserve banks
> Federal Reserve System (U.S.)
> Information storage and retrieval systems—Banking use
> Interest (Economics)
> Investment banking
> Loans, Bank
> Marine Midland Bank, N.A.
> Mortgage banks
> Savings and loan associations
> Savings banks
> Thrift institutions
> U.S. Trust Co. of New York

Banking in the 80s [address, November 5, 1986] R. M. Rosenberg. *Vital Speeches Day* 53:232-5 F 1 '87
Money & banking. See issues of Business Week
> **Accounting**

Biting half a bullet [further write-offs of foreign loan losses by big banks] A. Sloan. il *Forbes* 140:38-9 Jl 27 '87
Judgment? Or foot-dragging? [accounting rules for reserves against loss] L. Jereski. il *Forbes* 139:88 Je 29 '87
On thin ice [accounting procedures of Japanese banks] L. Jereski. il *Forbes* 140:152 S 21 '87
> **Acquisitions and mergers**

Battling bankers. il *Fortune* 116:9+ O 26 '87
Is Irving worth the wait? [Bank of New York bids for Irving Trust] F. A. Miller. il *Bus Week* p162 O 12 '87
Leaning on banks to lend to the poor [activists citing redlining are holding up mergers] D. Foust. *Bus Week* p76 Mr 2 '87
> *International aspects*

Banking on greatness [Canadian operations of Hongkong and Shanghai Banking Corporation] P. C. Newman. il por *Macleans* 100:32 Ap 13 '87
> *Great Britain*

And now, the Saatchi & Saatchi bank? [attempt to merge with Midland Bank] M. Maremont. il *Bus Week* p92 S 28 '87
> **Advertising**

The selling of home equity, 1987. *Consum Rep* 52:654 N '87
> **Automated teller machines**
> *See* Automated teller machines
> **Branch banking**
> *See also*
> Banks and banking, International

Bank hype [Illinois ban on interstate banking about to fall] J. Parr. il *Forbes* 139:121-2 My 4 '87
Banking across state lines. J. D. Lord. il map *Focus* 37:10-15 Spr '87
In interstate banking, don't tread on New Hampshire. A. Beam. il *Bus Week* p35 Ja 19 '87
> **Customer relations**

Citibank wows the consumer. R. E. Norton. il *Fortune* 115:48-50+ Je 8 '87
> **Debit cards**
> *See* Debit cards
> **Employees**
> *See* Bank employees
> **Ethical aspects**

The biggest drug bust. J. A. Conway. il *Forbes* 139:8 Je 1 '87
Closely watched banks: one that got away [Central National Bank of New York] F. A. Miller and R. A. Kessler. il por *Bus Week* p108 O 19 '87
Did corruption soil Vatican's inner sanctum? [Banco Ambrosiano scandal] J. P. Shapiro. il por *U S News World Rep* 102:10 Mr 9 '87
Fine print: bank-deposit shenanigans [overstating rates] *Money* 16:13 Ag '87
Following the money [Banco Ambrosiano scandal aftermath] J. Howse. il por *Macleans* 100:11 Jl 27 '87
Hiding behind the walls [arrest warrant issued for P. Marcinkus in Vatican] S. Allis. il por *Time* 129:54 Mr 9 '87
Stain on a shining record [R. Anderson pleads guilty to illegal banking operations] por *Time* 129:52 Ap 6 '87
Vatican bank scandal. *Christ Century* 104:265 Mr 18-25 '87
Vatican horror: a banking scandal widens. por *Newsweek* 109:48 Mr 9 '87
A wave of embezzlement hits banking. G. DeGeorge. il *Bus Week* p49 My 18 '87
> **Finance**
> *See also*
> Bank failures
> Banks and banking, International—Finance

Another great year—for defaults. S. Bartlett. il *Bus Week* p108-9 Ja 12 '87
Are banks obsolete? S. Bartlett. il *Bus Week* p74-6+ Ap 6 '87
Banks and thrifts. T. Pouschine. il *Forbes* 139:74-7 Ja 12 '87
Bleak year for the banks. G. Bock. il *Time* 130:60-1 D 28 '87
Credit cards: more combat, more casualties [bank cards] F. A. Miller. il *Bus Week* p104+ D 21 '87
Down-home banks are busting out all over. D. Foust. il *Bus Week* p60 Ag 31 '87
More is less [squeeze on bank credit card profits] B. Weberman. il *Forbes* 139:60-1 Je 29 '87

Banks and banking—Finance—*cont.*

Savings: five ways to look for Mr. Good Bank. il *Money* 16:23 N '87

Why bankers must say no. A. Sheshunoff. il por *Fortune* 115:177-8+ Je 22 '87

Statistics

Bank scoreboard. il *Bus Week* p83-9+ Ap 6 '87

Float

Finders, keepers. B. Weberman. il *Forbes* 139:90 Mr 23 '87

Less bounce in your checks [Federal Reserve's second chance check clearing plan] il *Consum Rep* 52:593 O '87

Foreign branches

See Banks and banking, International

Foreign business

See Banks and banking, International

Holding companies

See Bank holding companies

Insurance of accounts

See Bank accounts—Insurance

Laws and regulations

See also

Community Reinvestment Act of 1977

Federal Deposit Insurance Corporation

United States. Congress. Senate. Committee on Banking, Housing and Urban Affairs

United States. Federal Home Loan Bank Board

Are banks obsolete? S. Bartlett. il *Bus Week* p74-6+ Ap 6 '87

Bank hype [Illinois ban on interstate banking about to fall] J. Parr. il *Forbes* 139:121-2 My 4 '87

Banking across state lines. J. D. Lord. il map *Focus* 37:10-15 Spr '87

Banking on deregulation. J. McLaughlin. *Natl Rev* 39:24 O 23 '87

Banking on Texas [bank commissioner K. Littlefield] L. M. Keefe. il por *Forbes* 139:254+ Je 15 '87

Banking reform has two chances: slim and none. V. Cahan. *Bus Week* p45 Ap 13 '87

Banks may get reform—but they may not like it. V. Cahan. il *Bus Week* p174 N 2 '87

Control of the purse strings [Canadian inspector general of banks M. Mackenzie] M. Drohan. il por *Macleans* 100:38 Mr 16 '87

Fight for survival [proposed reform of Glass-Steagall to allow securitization by banks] S. Koepp. il *Time* 129:72-3 My 4 '87

"I don't trust regulators" [interview with R. E. Litan] J. Novack. il por *Forbes* 140:92+ N 2 '87

In interstate banking, don't tread on New Hampshire. A. Beam. il *Bus Week* p35 Ja 19 '87

Is bigger better in banking? [banks need deregulation to compete internationally] C. P. Work. il *U S News World Rep* 103:52-4 O 12 '87

More problems with protectionism [effect on major banks] il *Fortune* 116:10 S 28 '87

Oil Patch thrifts are deep in gloom [guidelines for revaluing assets issued by Federal Home Loan Bank Board] T. Vogel. il *Bus Week* p47-8 F 23 '87

Owning a bank isn't for just anybody [letting nonfinancial companies own commercial banks] S. Bartlett. *Bus Week* p123 Je 22 '87

A radical approach to banking reform [address, February 12, 1987] T. G. Labrecque. *Vital Speeches Day* 53:354-7 Ap 1 '87

Rewriting the banking rules: maybe this time . . . V. Cahan. il *Bus Week* p115-16 Ja 12 '87

Set us free [Glass-Steagall] D. Fanning. il *Forbes* 139:94+ F 23 '87

Shortening the tether on bankers. R. Hornik. il *Time* 130:50 Ag 17 '87

Volcker tries wrestling a bear called bank reform. B. Riemer and V. Cahan. por *Bus Week* p51 Mr 16 '87

Why banks fear Congress' help [trade bill restrictions on Japanese banks and brokers in the U.S.] M. McNamee. il *Bus Week* p35 S 14 '87

Premiums

See Premiums

Public relations

Leaning on banks to lend to the poor [activists citing redlining are holding up mergers] D. Foust. *Bus Week* p76 Mr 2 '87

Real estate operations

Chemical Bank finds a home in real estate. S. Bartlett. il *Bus Week* p89 Je 15 '87

Reserves

Judgment? Or foot-dragging? [accounting rules for reserves against loss] L. Jereski. il *Forbes* 139:88 Je 29 '87

Preparing for the worst [Canadian banks and third world loans] T. Tedesco. il *Macleans* 100:32-3 Ag 3 '87

Securities

See also

Decision/Capital Fund Inc.

Are big-bank shares a bargain? [market reaction to Brazil's suspension of interest payments] J. Egan. *U S News World Rep* 102:68 Mr 30 '87

Bank stocks and the Brazil factor. M. McFadden. il *Fortune* 115:103-5 Mr 30 '87

The banks head for the Street. S. Bartlett. il *Bus Week* p98 Jl 13 '87

Best buys among banks [value adjusted for Latin debt] J. Edgerton and others. il *Money* 16:7 Jl '87

A cloud lifts on Wall Street. A. McGrath. *U S News World Rep* 102:46-7 Je 1 '87

Giant regional banks with stunted stocks. J. Mendes. il *Fortune* 115:115 Ap 13 '87

Hidden riches in regional banks. J. P. Newport, Jr. il *Fortune* 116:195-6 O 12 '87

Requiem for a heavyweight [bank broker C. H. Howard for Thomson McKinnon] L. Jereski. il *Forbes* 140:152 N 30 '87

A surprise welcome for bank issues [new issues] F. A. Miller. il *Bus Week* p93 S 28 '87

Securities handling

See also

Cash management accounts

Are banks obsolete? S. Bartlett. il *Bus Week* p74-6+ Ap 6 '87

Bank introduces indexed investing [Chase Manhattan's Market Investment Index] R. Brady. il *Nations Bus* 75:85-6 My '87

Banks may get reform—but they may not like it. V. Cahan. il *Bus Week* p174 N 2 '87

CDs that play the market [S&P CDs] *Money* 16:13 O '87

Chase chases the stock runup—and big investors [Market Index Investment] G. Weiss. il *Bus Week* p115 Je 8 '87

Fight for survival [proposed reform of Glass-Steagall to allow securitization by banks] S. Koepp. il *Time* 129:72-3 My 4 '87

First join 'em, then beat 'em [J. P. Morgan] B. Weberman. il *Forbes* 139:152 F 23 '87

How the shocker at VW could undo a buddy system [banks go public with criticism of management in West Germany] J. E. Pluenneke. il *Bus Week* p61 Je 22 '87

Look who's charging into the merger business [big banks] S. Bartlett. il *Bus Week* p44 Mr 9 '87

Need a quick billion or two? Just ask your banker [lending for mergers and LBOs] S. Bartlett. il *Bus Week* p98-9 O 26 '87

Savings: a new insured account chases the stock market [Chase Market Index Investment] il *Money* 16:25 My '87

Service charges

Bank fees still going up. il *Consum Rep* 52:5 Ja '87

Services

See also

Bank accounts

Credit cards

Debit cards

Retail trade—Banking services

Once you've arrived, why wait in line? S. Bartlett. il *Bus Week* p130-1 Ap 27 '87

Suits and claims

Battling a billion-dollar debt [Hunt brothers; cover story] J. A. Jenkins. il *N Y Times Mag* p24-9+ S 27 '87

Credit where credit is due [L. Carlin sues Southeast Banking Corp. over credit rating dispute] il por *50 Plus* 27:16+ S '87

It's white-knuckle time for the Hunts [bankruptcy court to decide fate of Placid Oil Gulf drilling project] T. Mason. il *Bus Week* p29 Mr 30 '87

Trust departments

Putting his money where the trends are [interview with N. Miller of Chase Manhattan's Intermediate Cap Growth Fund] A. E. Serwer. il por *Fortune* 115:174 Je 22 '87

Riding the rate curve [Provident National Bank] B. Weberman. il *Forbes* 140 Sp Issue:395 O 26 '87

Africa

See also

African Development Bank

Brazil

See also

Banco do Brasil SA

Banks and banking—*cont.*
British Columbia
See also
Vancouver (B.C.)—Banks
California
See also
Bank of Canton of California
City National Bank (Beverly Hills, Calif.)
National Bank of Catalina
Wells Fargo Bank, National Association
Canada
See also
Bank of British Columbia
Royal Bank of Canada
Banking on new business. D. Jenish. il *Macleans* 100:24-5 Ag 31 '87
The banks get tough [third world debt] D. Jenish. il *Macleans* 100:28 Je 8 '87
Control of the purse strings [inspector general of banks M. Mackenzie] M. Drohan. il por *Macleans* 100:38 Mr 16 '87
Dominoes in a grim game of debt [Canadian banks' reaction to Brazil's decision to suspend interest payments] P. C. Newman. il *Macleans* 100:40 Mr 16 '87
Preparing for the worst [Canadian banks and third world loans] T. Tedesco. il *Macleans* 100:32-3 Ag 3 '87
Settling Brazil's account. C. Wood. il *Macleans* 100:36 N 16 '87
Stakes in metropolitan power [proposal to make Canadian cities international banking centers overlooks Toronto] S. Aikenhead. il *Macleans* 100:34 Ja 26 '87
China
See also
Bank of China
Colorado
See also
Colorado National Bank
Connecticut
See also
Citytrust
Florida
See also
First American Bank & Trust (North Palm Beach, Fla.)
France
See also
Paris (France)—Banks
Rothschild & Associates Bank
Germany (West)
See also
Bundesbank
Deutsche Bank AG
How the shocker at VW could undo a buddy system [banks go public with criticism of management] J. E. Pluenneke. il *Bus Week* p61 Je 22 '87
Great Britain
See also
Bank of England
Barclays Bank plc
London (England)—Banks
Midland Bank plc
National Westminster Bank plc
Hawaii
See also
Bancorp Hawaii Inc.
Hong Kong
See also
Hongkong and Shanghai Banking Corporation
Illinois
See also
Continental Illinois National Bank & Trust Co. of Chicago
Exchange National Bank of Chicago
First National Bank of Chicago
Bank hype [ban on interstate banking about to fall] J. Parr. il *Forbes* 139:121-2 My 4 '87
Iowa
See also
Hawkeye Bancorporation
Italy
See also
Banco Ambrosiano, SpA
Japan
See also
Dai-Ichi Kangyo Bank, Ltd.
Industrial Bank of Japan, Ltd.
Sumitomo Bank, Ltd.
The hesitant money machine. J. Dreyfuss. il *Fortune* 115:38-9+ Mr 30 '87

On thin ice [accounting procedures] L. Jereski. il *Forbes* 140:152 S 21 '87
The tidal wave that's sweeping international finance. B. Buell and others. il *Bus Week* p56-7 Jl 13 '87
Why banks fear Congress' help [trade bill restrictions on Japanese banks and brokers in the U.S.] M. McNamee. il *Bus Week* p35 S 14 '87
Luxembourg
Luxembourg: color it green [cover story] E. A. Finn, Jr. il *Forbes* 139:42-5 Ap 20 '87
Massachusetts
See also
Boston Safe Deposit & Trust Co.
ComFed Savings Bank
New England
Cracks in the plaster. J. Willoughby. il *Forbes* 140:46+ S 7 '87
Requiem for a heavyweight [bank broker C. H. Howard for Thomson McKinnon] L. Jereski. il *Forbes* 140:152 N 30 '87
New Hampshire
In interstate banking, don't tread on New Hampshire. A. Beam. il *Bus Week* p35 Ja 19 '87
North Carolina
See also
Mechanics & Farmers Bank
Ohio
See also
Banc One Corp.
Bank One, Cleveland, NA
Ontario
See also
Toronto Dominion Bank
Pennsylvania
See also
Mellon Bank NA
Switzerland
See also
Bank Leu AG
Union Bank of Switzerland
Opening a Swiss account is no big secret. S. Woolley. il *Bus Week* p95 Ag 3 '87
Swiss secrecy: don't bank on it. G. Bock. il *Time* 130:49 D 7 '87
The world as seen from the vantage point of a Swiss banker [address, June 17, 1987] R. E. Gut. *Vital Speeches Day* 53:668-71 Ag 15 '87
Texas
See also
American State Bank (Lubbock, Tex.)
Mason Best Company
Unitedbank-Houston
Banking on Texas [bank commissioner K. Littlefield] L. M. Keefe. il por *Forbes* 139:254+ Je 15 '87
Texas banks: who wants 'em? T. Vogel. il *Bus Week* p120 Je 8 '87
The unloved ones. T. Mack. il *Forbes* 140:34-6 N 2 '87
United States
See Banks and banking
Banks and banking, International
See also
Barclays Bank plc
Chase Manhattan Bank, N. A.
Citibank N.A.
Citicorp
Development banks
Eurobond market
Export-Import Bank of the United States
Money—International aspects
Royal Bank of Canada
World Bank
A global new deal. G. Soros. il *N Y Rev Books* 34:52-3 Ag 13 '87
The hesitant money machine [Japan] J. Dreyfuss. il *Fortune* 115:38-9+ Mr 30 '87
Hookers, Jaguars, and lots of stupid loans [views of S. C. Gwynne] C. Lane. *Wash Mon* 18:55-7 Ja '87
Is bigger better in banking? [banks need deregulation to compete internationally] C. P. Work. il *U S News World Rep* 103:52-4 O 12 '87
The safety of the world's funds [address, September 10, 1987] W. D. Mulholland. *Vital Speeches Day* 54:86-8 N 15 '87
Set us free [Glass-Steagall] D. Fanning. il *Forbes* 139:94+ F 23 '87
Stakes in metropolitan power [proposal to make Canadian cities international banking centers overlooks Toronto] S. Aikenhead. il *Macleans* 100:34 Ja 26 '87

Banks and banking, International—*cont.*

The tidal wave that's sweeping international finance [Japan] B. Buell and others. il *Bus Week* p56-7 Jl 13 '87

U.S. exporters need first-rate global banking networks. H. R. Heller. il *Bus Week* p20 Je 8 '87

The world as seen from the vantage point of a Swiss banker [address, June 17, 1987] R. E. Gut. *Vital Speeches Day* 53:668-71 Ag 15 '87

Finance

The biggest banks outside the U.S. [with introd. by Leslie Brody] il *Fortune* 116:242-6 Ag 3 '87

Bannan, Patricia

about

A successful balancing act [interview] A. E. Serwer. il por *Fortune* 116:180 D 7 '87

Banner Industries, Inc.

The next takeover artist you meet could be Jeff Steiner [Banner Industries takeover of Rexnord Inc.] Z. Schiller. il por *Bus Week* p33+ F 9 '87

Bannister, Alan

about

High hopes for a great Briton. F. Lidz. il por *Sports Illus* 67 Sp Issue:75 N 18 '87

Bannister, Anthony

A real drag [photograph] il *Nat Hist* 96:86-7 Jl '87

Banse, Tim

Engine room. See issues of Motor Boating & Sailing

Banta (George) Company, Inc. *See* George Banta Company, Inc.

Bantam Audio Publishing

Bantam, General Mills schedule audio promotion. il *Publ Wkly* 232:69-70 O 9 '87

Bantam mixed-media promotions feature audio, paperbacks. il *Publ Wkly* 231:31-2 Mr 27 '87

Bantam Books, Inc.

Bantam launching Shakespeare series. il *Publ Wkly* 232:24 N 6 '87

The blockbustering of Lee Iacocca. P. Wyden. il *N Y Times Book Rev* 92:1+ S 13 '87

'He loves life' [story behind S. W. Hawking's A brief history of time] L. Fleischer. *Publ Wkly* 232:56 O 16 '87

Offbeat auction [L. Erdich's dissatisfaction with Bantam leads to acquisition of rights to Tracks by Harper & Row] P. S. Nathan. *Publ Wkly* 232:40 N 13 '87

Bantam chickens *See* Poultry

Bantam, Doubleday, Dell Publishing Group

Bantam Group launches incentive plan for retailers. *Publ Wkly* 232:71 S 18 '87

Bantam marketing people move to Dell. *Publ Wkly* 231:11 Mr 20 '87

Nancy Evans heads Doubleday, Carole Baron heads Dell. il *Publ Wkly* 231:288 Ja 30 '87

Playing marriage counselor to Doubleday and Bantam [A. Vitale] C. Power. il por *Bus Week* p73 Ag 10 '87

Bantry (Ireland)

Description

When Irish skies are frowning. R. J. Margolis. il *New Leader* 70:15-16 S 7 '87

Baptism

See also

Jesus Christ—Baptism

At the river: thoughts on baptism. B. J. Leonard. *Christ Century* 104:813-15 S 30 '87

The new baptism: you can't get the water and run [Catholic sacrament; cover story] J. Deedy. il *U S Cathol* 52:6-13 F '87

The R.C.I.A. misunderstood? [Catholic Church's Rite of Christian Initiation of Adults] R. A. Duffy. il *America* 156:385+ My 9 '87

Baptists

United States

At the river: thoughts on baptism. B. J. Leonard. *Christ Century* 104:813-15 S 30 '87

Baptist Convention urges fortifying black family. *Jet* 73:32 S 28 '87

Baptist groups gear up for annual conventions. *Jet* 72:38 Jl 27 '87

Battle on the Bible [Southern Baptists seek help outside their ranks in effort to settle the issue of inerrancy] R. Frame. il *Christ Today* 31:44-6 Je 12 '87

Going topless and other sins [row over Mercer University] B. Kantrowitz and A. Murr. il *Newsweek* 110:79-80 O 26 '87

Moderates and minicoups [Southern Baptist Convention] J. Carey. il *U S News World Rep* 103:16 N 23 '87

More ferment among Southern Baptists. K. A. Lawton. il *Christ Today* 31:46-7+ N 20 '87

New policies on divorce and speaking in tongues [Southern Baptists] *Christ Today* 31:51+ S 18 '87

Nine wins in a row [Southern Baptist Convention reelects A. Rogers] il por *Time* 129:57 Je 29 '87

Rumors of peace [Southern Baptists] R. Frame. il *Christ Today* 31:37-8 Ag 7 '87

SBC battles. *Christ Century* 104:992-3 N 11 '87

SBC moderates win a few rounds. J. M. Wall. *Christ Century* 104:1075-6 D 2 '87

Southeastern Seminary: fundamentalists move in. W. H. Willimon. *Christ Century* 104:1020-1 N 18 '87

Southern Baptists: calm, or new storms? [St. Louis convention] S. Hastey. *Christ Century* 104:612-14 Jl 15-22 '87

Swordplay in Sunday school [Southern Baptist indoctrination] R. R. Smith. por *Newsweek* 110:9 D 21 '87

Vice President Bush worships at black church, boosts families [Shiloh Baptist Church in Washington, D.C.] il pors *Jet* 71:24-5 Ja 19 '87

Bar Association of the District of Columbia

Marshall shows for D.C. Bar tribute to Wiley Branton. il pors *Jet* 71:6-7 Ja 12 '87

Bar associations

See also

Bar Association of the District of Columbia

Chicago Bar Association

National Bar Association

State Bar of Michigan

Bar coding

See also

Bookland EAN system

How Levi Strauss is getting the lead out of its pipeline. J. O. Hamilton. il *Bus Week* p92 D 21 '87

Bar cookies *See* Cookies

Baraka, Amiri *See* Baraka, Imamu Amiri, 1934-

Baraka, Imamu Amiri, 1934-

We carry him as us. il por *N Y Times Book Rev* 92:27+ D 20 '87

Baranov, Alexander

about

That new word *'glasnost'* [interview] B. Shelby. *World Press Rev* 34:16-17 Ap '87

Baranyi, Joe

about

Museum. *New Yorker* 63:34-6 N 23 '87

Baratz-Snowden, Joan

Good news, bad news: black performance on standardized tests. il *Change* 19:50-4 My/Je '87

Barba, F. Javier

about

Earth sheltered: blending with nature on the Costa Brava. N. Shrady. il *Archit Dig* 44:90-5 Ja '87

Barbadian cooking *See* Cooking, Barbadian

Barbados

See also

Architecture, Domestic—Barbados

Bridgetown (Barbados)

Festivals—Barbados

Investments, American—Barbados

Marijuana—Laws and regulations—Barbados

Description and travel

Down and out in the Caribbean. W. G. Flanagan. il *Forbes* 139:272-3+ Ja 12 '87

Industries

See also

Electronic industries—Barbados

Barbara Cook: a concert for the theatre [musical] *See* Musicals, revues, etc.—Reviews—Single works

Barbary States

Barbary Coast. il *Dep State Bull* 87:3 S '87

Barbash, Steven

about

Steven Barbash. J. C. Oresman. il por *Am Artist* 51:26 F '87

Barbato, Joseph

Independent publishing. See occasional issues of Publishers Weekly beginning October 23, 1987

Barbecue carts *See* Carts

Barbecue cooking

A 30-minute barbecue. il *Glamour* 85:292 Ag '87

All-out cookouts. L. Hoppe. il *Better Homes Gard* 65:86-92+ Je '87

Assertive seasoning pastes for barbecued seafood or meat. il *Sunset* 179:134 Ag '87

Barbecue! B. Greenwood. il *Better Homes Gard* 65:20-1 Jl '87

Barbecue island style. il *Ladies Home J* 104:96-7+ Ag '87

Barbecue time! M. Langan. il *McCalls* 114:99-105+ Je '87

Barbecue cooking—*cont.*
The big grill: a do-it-yourself barbecue for eight. il *Mademoiselle* 93:158-9+ Je '87
A choice of barbecue herbs. il *Sunset* 178:206 Ap '87
Cooking for a family reunion. P. A. Toussaint. il *Essence* 18:92-4+ Jl '87
Deep in the heart of Texas [HK Ranch barbecues] J. Nathan. il *Mother Earth News* 106:54-9 Jl/Ag '87
A different barbecue [Chinese influences] K. Lee and A. Branyon. il *N Y Times Mag* p59-60 Jl 12 '87
Gastronomie sans argent [grilling] il *Gourmet* 47:60-1+ Jl '87
The great indoor venison barbecue. A. D. Livingston. il *Outdoor Life* 179:76-7+ Mr '87
Grilling. K. Haedrich. il *Ctry J* 14:46-50 Je '87
High on the hog [barbecued spareribs and sauce] il *Esquire* 108:70-1 Jl '87
It was inevitable, pizza on the barbecue [cover story] il *Sunset* 179:70-1 Jl '87
Look what's sizzling on the grill. D. G. Lowery. il *South Living* 22:122-3 Ap '87
Microwave before you grill [with tangy barbecue sauce] J. B. Hurley. il *Prevention* 39:52 Je '87
Nothing like a Thai grill. E. Sahatjian. il *Esquire* 107:52+ Je '87
Outdoor entertaining. C. Lyons. il *Ebony* 42:108-14 Je '87
Recipe of the week [island barbecued chicken and ribs] il *Jet* 72:37 Je 22 '87
Santa Maria invites you for a rancher's barbecue. il *Sunset* 178:40 Je '87
Spareribs in a hot-sweet sauce. il *Sunset* 179:124 Ag '87

Equipment
Hutch holds everything the barbecuer needs. il *Sunset* 179:113 Jl '87
Barbecue grills
Gas barbecue grills. il *Consum Rep* 52:21-4 D '87
Queue up for summer cookouts. J. Seisler. il *Consum Res Mag* 70:15-16 Je '87
Barbecue sauces See Sauces
Barber, Elinor G., and Morgan, Robert P., 1934-
The impact of foreign graduate students on engineering education in the United States. bibl f il *Science* 236:33-7 Ap 3 '87
Barber, James David
The fight to stop torture. il *USA Today (Periodical)* 116:29-31 N '87
about
A critic's view of Reagan's tussles with the truth [interview] D. Grogan. il *People Wkly* 27:40-2 Mr 9 '87
Barber, Jill
The private lives of star moms [excerpt from Starring mothers] il pors *McCalls* 114:57+ My '87
Barber, Larry W., and McClellan, Mary C.
Looking at America's dropouts: who are they? il *Phi Delta Kappan* 69:264-7 D '87
Barber-Colman Co.
Record $3.8 million awarded S.C. black in liability case [award to Clarence Barnwell] il *Jet* 72:28 Jl 6 '87
The barber of Seville [opera] See Rossini, Gioacchino, 1792-1868
Barbera, Joe, 1911-
about
Joe Barbera. D. Diehl. il pors *People Wkly* 27:69+ Mr 16 '87
Somebody say hallelujah! G. Buchalter. il por *Forbes* 139:160 Mr 23 '87
Barbera-Hogan, Mary
Pregnant teens: no easy answers. il *Teen* 31:28+ F '87
Sibling sins: when you're punished too. il *Teen* 31:34+ Mr '87
Teen fathers: the other side of the story. *Teen* 31:32+ Jl '87
Teen sex for sale: who pays the price? il *Teen* 31:20+ Ja '87
Barberries
Bright, varied, berried barberries pep up your landscape. P. Byers. il *Flower Gard* 31:16+ F/Mr '87
Barbie, Klaus
about
Barbie and the children. *Newsweek* 109:44 Je 15 '87
The Barbie file [cover story] T. Morgan. il pors *N Y Times Mag* p18-24+ My 10 '87
Barbie on trial. M. Ophuls. *Nation* 244:634-5 My 16 '87
The Barbie trial: J'accuse. F. Coleman. il pors *Newsweek* 109:41 My 11 '87
Barbie's mockery of justice. M. S. Serrill. il por *Time* 129:51 My 25 '87

Breaking the silence. K. McCaffrey. il *Commonweal* 114:418-20 Jl 17 '87
The "Butcher of Lyons" in the dock. W. R. Doerner. il por *Time* 129:49 My 18 '87
Europe faces its Nazi past. S. Sullivan. il pors *Newsweek* 109:34-6 Ap 20 '87
Final verdict for the Butcher of Lyons. P. Lewis. il por *Macleans* 100:20 Jl 13 '87
France brings Barbie—and itself—to trial [interview] R. Z. Chesnoff. il pors *U S News World Rep* 102:35-6 My 18 '87
Judgment at Lyons: the prisoner is guilty. F. Coleman. il pors *Newsweek* 110:29 Jl 13 '87
Klaus Barbie's circus of evil. M. Ophuls. il *Nation* 244:884-7 Je 27 '87
Letter from Europe. J. Kramer. *New Yorker* 63:130-6+ O 12 '87
The Nazi hunt [cover story; special section] il pors *Macleans* 100:34-41 My 25 '87
Remembering Liane, age six. G. F. Will. il por *Newsweek* 109:80 My 25 '87
A rush from judgment. F. Coleman. il por *Newsweek* 109:28 My 25 '87
Shame and punishment. J. J. Buck. il pors *Vogue* 177:392-3+ N '87
The threat of Klaus Barbie. H. Evans. il *U S News World Rep* 102:74 Ap 13 '87
A verdict on the Butcher. F. Painton. il por *Time* 130:40 Jl 13 '87
Voices from the Barbie trial [cover story] T. Morgan. il pors *N Y Times Mag* p20-5+ Ag 2 '87
Was he normal? Human? Poor humanity. E. Wiesel. il pors *Time* 129:93-4 My 11 '87
Barbieri, Richard
Perfecting the body count. il *Channels* 7:15 Je '87
Barbiturates
See also
Phenobarbital
Barbosa-Lima, Carlos
about
A gentle genius of the guitar. H. M. Holstein. il pors *Américas* 39:50-3 Jl/Ag '87
Barbour, Alan G., and Garon, Claude F.
Linear plasmids of the bacterium Borrelia burgdorferi have covalently closed ends. bibl f il *Science* 237:409-11 Jl 24 '87
Barceló, Miquel, 1957-
about
Five from Spain. J. Gambrell. il pors *Art Am* 75:160-71 S '87
Barcelona (Spain)
Architecture
Architecture: Ricardo Bofill. N. Shrady. il *Archit Dig* 44:124-31+ Jl '87
Description
Gourmet holidays: Barcelona. P. T. Mitchell. il *Gourmet* 48:48-53+ Je '87
Galleries and museums
See also
Palacio Nacional de Montjuich (Barcelona, Spain)
Industries
See also
Publishers and publishing—Spain
Music
See also
Opera—Spain
Plazas
Plaza to plaza in Barcelona. il maps *Sunset* 179:41-2 D '87
Barcenas-Ruiz, L., and others
Sodium-calcium exchange in heart: membrane currents and changes in [Ca^{2+}]i. bibl f il *Science* 238:1720-2 D 18 '87
Barclays Bank plc
A study in disinvestment [leaves South Africa] C. Wolman. *World Press Rev* 34:54 O '87
Barco Vargas, Virgilio
about
Colombian politics: crisis or continuity? B. M. Bagley. bibl f *Curr Hist* 86:21-4+ Ja '87
Bard, Mitchell, and Lenhoff, Howard M.
The humanitarian side of the Reagan administration: the rescue of Ethiopian Jews. *Humanist* 47:25-6+ N/D '87
Bardach, John E.
Aquaculture. il *BioScience* 37:318-19 My '87
Barden, Don
about
Cable for Motor City. M. Walker. il por *Black Enterp* 17:18 Ja '87

Barden Cablevision
Cable for Motor City. M. Walker. il por *Black Enterp* 17:18 Ja '87
Bardia Wildlife Reserve (Nepal) *See* Wildlife sanctuaries—Nepal
Bardstown (Ky.)
    Historic houses, sites, etc.
Jim Cantrell. B. S. Goldman. il por *Am Artist* 51:32-7 Jl '87
Bardwick, Judith M., 1933-
    about
Career plateaus: how to handle the inevitable [interview] L. Mosedale. *Glamour* 85:218 F '87
Bare, Charles W.
A VFW post with a spiritual vision. *Christ Century* 104:193-4 F 25 '87
Bareboat chartering *See* Yachts and yachting—Leasing and renting
Barefoot water skiing *See* Water skis and skiing
Barendson, Guido
Stalemate in Kabul. il *World Press Rev* 34:28-30 S '87
Barfly [film] See Motion picture reviews—Single works
Bargaining (Environmental) *See* Environmental mediation
Bargaining (Industrial) *See* Collective bargaining
Bargaining (Shopping) *See* Haggling (Shopping)
Bargains
April best buys. J. Jameson. il *Good Housekeep* 204:249 Ap '87
I can get it for you retail [lessening allure of bargains] G. Morgenson. il *Forbes* 139 Ann Directory:84 Ap 27 '87
I love a bargain! il *Ladies Home J* 104:98-103 Mr '87
January best buys. J. Hershey. il *Good Housekeep* 204:149 Ja '87
Sales & bargains. L. Fleischer. See issues of New York
Barger, Brian
    about
The real heroes of contra-gate. J. Morley and T. Rosenberg. il pors *Roll Stone* p48-50+ S 10 '87
Barger, M. Susan
(jt. auth) See Herman, Jan K., and Barger, M. Susan
Barges
Don't be a litterbarge [various cities turn away barge filled with garbage from Islip, N.Y.] J. V. Lamar, Jr. il map *Time* 129:26 My 4 '87
The good news barge [garbage barge Mobro] M. W. Robbins. il *Oceans* 20:2 Jl/Ag '87
Barich, Bill
Chasers. *New Yorker* 63:78-83 Mr 23 '87
Dublin for the stout of heart. il *Esquire* 107 Summ Traveler:T12-T16+ Ap '87
Profiles [L. and K. Looper] il *New Yorker* 63:51-2+ O 12 '87
Barilla, Pietro
    about
Mangia, mangia. T. Pouschine. il por *Forbes* 140:232 N 30 '87
Barilla Group
Mangia, mangia [chief executive P. Barilla] T. Pouschine. il por *Forbes* 140:232 N 30 '87
Bariteau, Corinne Adria
A mother's Christams Eve wish [poem] *Redbook* 170:174 D '87
Seasonal blooms [poem] *Good Housekeep* 204:153 Ja '87
Bark
Bark takes center stage. il *South Living* 22:56 Ja '87
Barkas, T., and others
Mapping the main immunogenic region and toxin-binding site of the nicotinic acetylcholine receptor. bibl f il *Science* 235:77-80 Ja 2 '87
Barkay, Gabriel
    about
Mystery of the buried amulet. C. Safran. il *Read Dig* 130:95-9 Je '87
Barker, Clive
Babel's children [story] il *Omni* 9:48-50+ Mr '87
    about
Meet the new (Stephen) King of horror, Briton Clive Barker. A. Chambers. il pors *People Wkly* 27:87-8 Je 15 '87
Barker, D., and others
Gene for von Recklinghausen neurofibromatosis is in the pericentromeric region of chromosome 17. bibl f il *Science* 236:1100-2 My 29 '87
Barker, Dan
Feathered friends. il por *Mother Earth News* 103:29 Ja/F '87

Barker, Dan
    about
Gardening for self-respect. P. H. Johnson. il por *Rodale's Org Gard* 34:59-62 Jl '87
Barker, Lucius J.
Dialogue on a new dilemma. *Society* 24:29-37 Ja/F '87
Barker, Maggie
The training of Nell. il *Mother Earth News* 107:32-4+ S/O '87
Barkin, Ellen
    about
Barkin's bite. D. Edelstein. il por *Roll Stone* p23-5+ Ag 13 '87
Barkley, Charles
    about
Call him 'Round Mound' at your peril; Charles Barkley's bite is worse than his woof. A. Richman. il pors *People Wkly* 27:76-8+ Ap 27 '87
Millionaire dropout going back to school for degree because 'grandma' told him. por *Jet* 72:48 My 25 '87
Barletta, Cosimo, and others
Relationship between the *c-myb* locus and the 6q-chromosomal aberration in leukemias and lymphomas. bibl f il *Science* 235:1064-7 F 27 '87
Barley, Betsy Gregg
Stress & disease. *Ladies Home J* 104:38+ My '87
Barlow, Christopher R.
    about
They've got one-stop shopping for vacation homes. P. Houston. il pors *Bus Week* p75 Ag 10 '87
Barlow, Hank
Winter Park. il *Skiing* 39:46-52 Ja '87
Barnaby, Frank, 1927-
The nuclear arsenal in the Middle East. il map *Technol Rev* 90:27-34 My/Je '87
Barnacles
    Larvae
  See Larvae
Barnard, Charles N.
Ah, Fuji! il *Int Wildl* 17:24-7 S/O '87
". . . and then I heard the chain saws". il *Natl Wildl* 26:46-9 D '87/Ja '88
Barnard, Edward Emerson, 1857-1923
    about
The legacy of E. E. Barnard. G. S. Mumford. il por *Sky Telesc* 74:30-4 Jl '87
Barnard Castle Museum *See* Bowes Museum (Barnard Castle, England)
Barneo, Jose Lopez- *See* Lopez-Barneo, Jose
Barnes, Barbara
    about
Baba says ta ta to Wills and Harry—the question is, did Charles and Di get the nanny's goat? B. Johnson. il pors *People Wkly* 27:44+ F 2 '87
Barnes, C. B.
    about
Prime time profiles. pors *Teen* 31:66 Je '87
Barnes, Clive, 1927-
Exploding a favored myth: ballet and its booms. il *Dance Mag* 61:88-95 Je '87
Barnes, Duncan
Editorial. See issues of Field & Stream
Barnes, Edward, and Shebar, William
Quitting the Mafia. il pors *Life* 10:108-9+ D '87
Barnes, Fred
All smiles [cover story] il *New Repub* 196:17-20 My 18 '87
Britain's cheesy campaign [cover story] il *New Repub* 196:22-5 Je 22 '87
Charade on Main Street. *New Repub* 196:15-17 Je 15 '87
Jesse goes country [cover story] *New Repub* 197:15-20 Ag 3 '87
Pee-Wee's big adventure [cover story] il *New Repub* 197:25-7 O 5 '87
Raising kids in an X-rated society. *Des Arts Educ* 89:47-8 N/D '87
Ronald Biden. il *New Repub* 196:18-19 Je 1 '87
Westy's revenge [cover story] *New Repub* 196:21+ Ap 6 '87
Barnes, J. David, 1929-
    about
Mellon Bank looks for a repairman. M. Rothman. il por *Bus Week* p97 Ap 27 '87
Mellon muscle. *Time* 129:54 Ap 27 '87
Once-mighty Mellon is busy 'plugging holes'. M. Rothman. il por *Bus Week* p68 F 2 '87

Barnes, James E., 1934-
about
Right side of the table. R. McGough. por *Forbes* 139:56 Ja 26 '87
Barnes, John A.
Anatomy of a rip-off. *New Repub* 197:20-1 N 2 '87
Barnes, Kate
The horses' water [poem] *Ctry J* 14:53 Je '87
The stairs [poem] *Ctry J* 14:64 S '87
Barnes, Kenneth
about
Road-shows toward a bonanza. P. C. Newman. il por *Macleans* 100:40 S 21 '87
Barnes, Peter, 1931-
about
Red noses [drama] Reviews
   America 157:411 N 28 '87. G. G. Seibert
Barnes, Robert, and Smith, Terry M.
Motion light traces. il *Petersens Photogr Mag* 15:36-7 Mr '87
Barnes, S. Brandi
Gentlemen at the barber shop [poem] *Essence* 18:124-5 N '87
A jazz festival [poem] *Essence* 18:149 S '87
Mourning song [poem] *Essence* 18:134 O '87
We got stuff [poem] *Essence* 18:156 S '87
Barnes, Taylor
about
The couple with the hippest greeting cards in town. P. Finch. il pors *Bus Week* p80 Je 8 '87
Their season to be jolly. M. Barrier. il pors *Nations Bus* 75:75 D '87
Barnes, Thomas
about
Former campaign manager of Richard Hatcher ousts him as mayor of Gary, Ind. il por *Jet* 72:15 My 25 '87
Barnes & Noble
Judge limits trade books in Marin college stores [Marin County Community College] M. Colin. *Publ Wkly* 232:10 O 30 '87
Barnes-Connally Partnership
John Connally goes belly up after betting big on a Texas oil economy that ran out of gas. W. Plummer. il pors *People Wkly* 28:36-7 Ag 17 '87
Barnes Investor Relations Ltd.
Road-shows toward a bonanza [K. Barnes] P. C. Newman. il por *Macleans* 100:40 S 21 '87
Barnes-Svarney, Patricia
A greater Salt Lake. il map *Earth Sci* 39:22-3 Wint '86
Hubbard glacier. il *Earth Sci* 40:20 Fall '87
In search of ancient shores. il *Earth Sci* 40:22-3 Spr '87
Living near a glacial oddity. il *Conservationist* 41:22-5 Mr/Ap '87
Barnet, Richard J.
The four pillars. *New Yorker* 63:76-84+ Mr 9 '87
Barnett, Charles R.
Intrepid filmmaker braves Greenland ice cap with an expedition searching for mysterious fifth force of the universe. il *Smithsonian* 18:40+ N '87
Barnett, Jonathan, 1937-
In the public interest: design guidelines. il *Archit Rec* 175:114-25 Jl '87
Barnett, Roger W.
U.S. maritime strategy: sound and safe. *Bull At Sci* 43:30-3 S '87
Barnett, T. P.
(jt. auth) See Graham, N. E., and Barnett, T. P.
Barnett, Tracy L.
Tibetan society bridges the future. il por *Progressive* 51:15 Ap '87
Barney, Joanne, and Koford, Judy
Schools and single parents. *Educ Dig* 53:40-3 O '87
Barney, Joshua, 1759-1818
about
Pint-sized ship of state. B. B. Ryan. il por *Am Hist Illus* 22:36-7+ S '87
Barnhardt, Wilton
The death of Ducktown. il map *Discover* 8:34-6+ O '87
Barnhill, William
A child for Christmas. il pors *Good Housekeep* 205:66+ D '87
Barnitt, John
about
Who was that mast man? C. Neff. il *Sports Illus* 66:17 F 16 '87

Barns, Converted See Houses, Remodeled
Barns and stables
See also
   Calf pens and sheds
   Swine houses
Architecture
Equine expectations [broodmare barn and turnout ring at Catoctin Stud, Waterford, Va.] M. Gaskie. il *Archit Rec* 175:122-5 My '87
The thoroughbred way of life: houses fit for the world's noblest horses. A. Gordon. il *House Gard* 159:148-61+ Ap '87
Conservation and restoration
Barn Again! J. Walter. il *Success Farm* 85:11-13 My '87
Barn Again! is a buildin'. *Success Farm* 85:22 N '87
Barn Again! revives a glorious past. il *Success Farm* 85:68 S '87
The barn builder [R. Babcock] B. Trebilcock. il pors *Ctry J* 14:34-40 Mr '87
How your barn can make history. M. Humstone and J. Walter. il *Success Farm* 85:34 Je '87
A well-rounded barn. M. Hofferber. il *Ctry J* 14:42-6 F '87
Barnum [musical] See Musicals, revues, etc.—Reviews—Single works
Barocco (New York, N.Y.: Restaurant) See New York (N.Y.)—Restaurants, nightclubs, bars, etc.
Barometer rising [drama] See Ouzounian, Richard
Barometers
Making a barometer that works with water in place of mercury. J. Walker. il *Sci Am* 256:122-7 Ap '87
Baron, Jean-Marie
Parisian exotic. il por *House Gard* 159:130-9+ Jl '87
Baron, Larry
Immoral, inviolate or inconclusive? bibl *Society* 24:6-12 Jl/Ag '87
Baronas, Robin E.
Copper Canyon high adventure. il map *Travel Holiday* 168:58-63 S '87
Switzerland by gypsy wagon: a one-horsepower Jura tour. il *Travel Holiday* 167:52-5+ My '87
Baroody, Elizabeth
Cast iron: heavy metal for collectors. il *Antiques Collect Hobbies* 92:28-32 Jl '87
Godey and Hale: a fashionable alliance. il *Antiques Collect Hobbies* 92:34-8 N '87
Baroque architecture See Architecture, Baroque
Baroque art See Art, Baroque
Baroque civilization See Civilization, Baroque
Baroque painting See Painting, Baroque
Baroque sculpture See Sculpture, Baroque
Barr, Donald J.
Letter from the publisher. See issues of Sports Illustrated beginning December 9, 1985
Barr, Nancy Verde
Biscotti. il *Gourmet* 47:108-9+ N '87
Barr, Roseanne
about
Roseanne Barr. S. Dworkin. il pors *Ms* 16:106-8+ Jl/Ag '87
Roseanne Barr: domestic goddess. T. Young. il por *Vogue* 177:334-6 Ap '87
Who is Roseanne Barr, and why is she worth a quarter of a mil? L. Fleischer. *Publ Wkly* 232:38 O 23 '87
Barra Island (Scotland)
The outermost Hebride. A. F. Burghardt. il map *Focus* 37:34-5 Summ '87
Barranca de Cobre (Mexico)
Copper Canyon high adventure. R. E. Baronas. il map *Travel Holiday* 168:58-63 S '87
Barrel racing See Rodeos
Barreto-Morales, Ernesto
about
Escape from a Dutch jail. D. Burke. por *Macleans* 100:44 Je 15 '87
Barrett, Katherine, and Greene, Richard
Money news. See issues of Ladies' Home Journal beginning March 1983
Barrett, Lezli-An
about
A young filmmaker with a sense of purpose. J. M. Wall. *Christ Century* 104:739-40 S 9-16 '87
Barrett, Majel
about
Gene Roddenberry and Majel Barrett's most successful Enterprise isn't a starship; it's their 17-year marriage. N. Geeslin. il pors *People Wkly* 27:111-12+ Mr 16 '87

Barrett, Marvin
A kind of dying [story] *New Yorker* 63:40-3 O 12 '87
Barrett, Nancy
How to complain and make it count. il *Ladies Home J* 104:38+ O '87
Barrett, Neal, Jr.
Diner [fiction] il *Omni* 10:92-4+ N '87
Barrett, Nina
Brent springs eternal. il por *Publ Wkly* 232:60-2 S 11 '87
Women & Children First: the evolution of a specialty market. il *Publ Wkly* 231:26-7 Mr 27 '87
Barrett, Peter
Fishing. See issues of Field & Stream beginning February 1984
Barrett, Spencer C. H.
Mimicry in plants. bibl (p120) il *Sci Am* 257:76-83 S '87
Barrick Resources Corp.
Munk's glittering gamble [purchase of Consolidated Gold Fields stock by Barrick Resources] D. Jenish. il por *Macleans* 100:22-3 Ja 12 '87
Barrie, J. M. (James Matthew), 1860-1937
about
Peter Pan [drama] Reviews
Macleans il 100:51 Ag 31 '87. J. Bemrose
Barrie, Jack A.
Beating wings [photographs] il *Audubon* 89:62-9 N '87
Barrie, James Matthew *See* Barrie, J. M. (James Matthew), 1860-1937
Barrier, Phyllis M.
Murmurs of the heart. il *Nations Bus* 75:82 D '87
Barrier contraceptives *See* Contraceptives
Barrier islands
Beaches and barrier islands. R. Dolan and H. F. Lins. il map *Sci Am* 257:68-73+ Jl '87
The enchanted land [Georgia coast] H. Middleton. il map *South Living* 22:76-81 F '87
Barrier Reef, Great (Australia) *See* Great Barrier Reef (Australia)
Barrilleaux, Doris
Confessions of a steroid user [interview with anonymous female body builder] il *Women's Sports Fitness* 9:84 N '87
about
Doris Barrilleaux, 56. M. Kort. por *Women's Sports Fitness* 9:19 O '87
Barrington, Byron L.
Curriculum-based programs for the gifted. *Educ Dig* 52:48-51 Ja '87
Barrington, Carol
Galveston revival: Victorian gems amid castles of sand. il *Travel Holiday* 168:54-9 D '87
Portugal's manor houses. il map *Travel Holiday* 168:48-53 N '87
Barrio, Constance García- *See* García-Barrio, Constance
Barris (Chuck) Productions Inc. *See* Chuck Barris Productions Inc.
Barro, Robert J.
about
And you thought Harvard was only keen on Keynes. N. Jonas. il por *Bus Week* p78+ S 7 '87
Barron, John, 1930-
Our new Moscow embassy—bungled and bugged. *Read Dig* 130:100-4 Je '87
The spy family that imperiled America [condensed from Breaking the ring] il *Read Dig* 130:62-70+ Ap '87
Barron, Slater
about
In California: a palette of lint. G. Jaynes. il por *Time* 129:14 Je 1 '87
Barrot, Olivier
South Korea: anticipating visitors. il *World Press Rev* 34:62 Jl '87
Barrows, Sydney Biddle
about
The wages of sin. *Time* 129:77 Mr 23 '87
Barry, Dave
A few words about public speaking. il *Saturday Evening Post* 259:28 Ja/F '87
How to talk to new parents. il *Glamour* 85:30+ My '87
Miami to New York: drop dead. *Harpers* 275:36+ D '87
Barry, David
The Teacher and the Crows. il *Car Driv* 32:109+ My '87
Barry, Ellen
Settings of a lifetime: Ellen and Philip Barry's moveable feast. il pors *Archit Dig* 44:160+ Ag '87

Barry, Lynda
about
In Lynda Barry's world, poodles are tough and the weasels drink daiquiries. K. Hubbard. il pors *People Wkly* 27:109-10 Mr 30 '87
Barry, Marion, 1936-
about
Barry promises youth jobs, training at start of term 3. il por *Jet* 71:9 Ja 26 '87
Black politicos condemn U.S. probe of Marion Barry. *Jet* 72:31 Jl 27 '87
D.C. mayor Barry sues U.S. Atty. over 'leak a week'. *Jet* 72:5 Jl 13 '87
D.C. mayor Marion Barry denies cocaine usage. il por *Jet* 72:4 Jl 6 '87
The imperial mayor. J. Williams. *New Repub* 197:21-3 O 26 '87
The trials of Marion Barry. G. Hackett. il por *Newsweek* 110:21 Ag 31 '87
Barry, Naomi
Chefs of influence. il pors *Gourmet* 47:82-3+ D '87
The gastronomic world of Balzac. il *Gourmet* 47:48-53+ S '87
Music, art and country pleasures. il *House Gard* 159:140-7+ Mr '87
Paris' haute chocolaterie. il *Gourmet* 47:58-63+ Mr '87
Barry, Pat
All for the love of trains. il *Petersens Photogr Mag* 15:32-7 Ja '87
Barry, Philip, 1896-1949
about
Settings of a lifetime: Ellen and Philip Barry's moveable feast. E. Barry. il pors *Archit Dig* 44:160+ Ag '87
Barry, Rick
My love affair with tennis. il *World Tennis* 34:88 My '87
Barry, William A.
The Kingdom of God and discernment. *America* 157:156-9 S 26 '87
A meditation on death and life. *America* 157:409-10 N 28 '87
Barry Friedman Ltd.
Imprints of the avant-garde—Barry Friedman. A. Berman. il por *Archit Dig* 44:114+ N '87
Bars and barrooms
See also
Sports bars
Water bars
The best new bars and restaurants of 1987. J. F. Mariani. il *Esquire* 108:169-72+ N '87
A new thirst for 'brewpubs'. G. C. Lubenow. il *Newsweek* 109:49 F 9 '87
Working girl by day/party animal by night. S. Orlean. il *Mademoiselle* 93:132-3+ F '87
Mississippi
Photographs and photography
Delta blues [Mississippi juke joints photographed by B. Imes] S. Piperato. il *Pop Photogr* 94:60-5 O '87
Bars for the home
The bar-none bar. N. Malkin. il *Mademoiselle* 93:252 My '87
Mirrors reflect glass shelves [built-in bar and serving counter] il *South Living* 22:157 Mr '87
Barschall, H. H. (Henry Hermann), 1915-
Reminiscences of the early days of fission. bibl f il *Phys Today* 40:27-32 Je '87
Barschall, Henry Hermann *See* Barschall, H. H. (Henry Hermann), 1915-
Barschel, Uwe, d. 1987
about
A deadly game of dirty tricks. S. Seibert. il *Newsweek* 110:49 O 26 '87
Barstow, Anne
Witch hunts: the sex factor. il *Ms* 16:85 N '87
Barstow, Daniel
The world's cheapest weather recording instruments. il *Weatherwise* 40:146-8 Je '87
Barta, Russell
Toward a civilization of work. *America* 156:187-8 Mr 7 '87
Bartel, Pauline C.
Will you get a cold this month? il *Mademoiselle* 93:152 N '87
Bartell, Lawrence S., and others
A new method for analyzing powder diffraction patterns: confirmation of a predicted phase of SF_6. bibl f il *Science* 236:1463-5 Je 12 '87
Bartender magazine
"Any jerk can publish a magazine". F. Meeks. il por *Forbes* 140:394+ Jl 13 '87

Barter, Christie, and Burton, William
Bulletin. See issues of Stereo Review beginning September 1986

Barter, Christie, and Simels, Steve
Record makers. See issues of Stereo Review beginning March 1984

Barter, Phil
about
A Pacific future for the taking. P. C. Newman. il por *Macleans* 100:37 Ap 6 '87

Barter
See also
Atwood Richards, Inc.
Service Credit Volunteer Program
Art for barter: a cultural currency. D. Grant. *Am Artist* 51:S12+ N '87
Barter system has little potential, says Lyng [field hearing of the Senate Agriculture Committee in Burlington, Vt.] *Success Farm* 85:62J O '87
Confessions of a gun swapper. J. Bashline. il *Field Stream* 92:74+ Jl '87

Barth, Jack
Praising 'Arizona'. il por *Film Comment* 23:18-20+ Mr/Ap '87
(jt. auth) See Wilkins, Mike, and Barth, Jack

Barth, Jack, and Wilkins, Mike
Roadside rock. il *Roll Stone* p104-5+ Jl 16-30 '87

Barth, John
The point [fiction] il *Esquire* 107:128-30 F '87
Talk about teachers! il *Read Dig* 130:61-6 Mr '87
about
The Scheherazade factor [interview] A. P. Sanoff. il por *U S News World Rep* 103:55 Ag 31 '87

Barth, Shelly Rosenberg
about
Talk about teachers! J. Barth. il *Read Dig* 130:61-6 Mr '87

Barthel, Joan
Mary Frances Berry. por *Ms* 15:68-70+ Ja '87

Barthelemy, Robert R.
about
Aero-Space Plane project chief named. *Aviat Week Space Technol* 127:28 O 5 '87

Barthelemy, Sidney
about
Black mayors of Atlanta, New Orleans will host 1988 political conventions. il pors *Jet* 71:5 Mr 2 '87

Barthelme, Donald
The author. *New Yorker* 63:27 Je 15 '87
January [story] *New Yorker* 63:40-4 Ap 6 '87
Jaws [story] *New Yorker* 63:20-1 Ag 17 '87
On the deck [story] *New Yorker* 62:27 Ja 12 '87

Barthelme, Frederick
Cooker [story] *New Yorker* 63:22-8 Ag 10 '87
Law of averages [story] *New Yorker* 63:36-9 O 5 '87

Barthos, Gordon
A look at the record. il *World Press Rev* 34:12-13 Ja '87

Bartizan Corporation
An impression on business. P. M. Fielding. il por *Nations Bus* 75:66 F '87

Bartky, Ian R.
The bygone era of time balls. il *Sky Telesc* 73:32-5 Ja '87

Bartlett, Jennifer, 1941-
about
Boat, fence and house. B. Weber. il por *N Y Times Mag* p94 O 18 '87
Leader of the pack. K. Larson. il *N Y* 20:110+ Mr 9 '87

Bartlett, Joseph W., 1933-
Beware of state takeover laws. il *Fortune* 116:179+ N 9 '87

Bartlett, Marie
Once upon a time . . . il *Good Housekeep* 204:78 Ap '87

Bartlett, Paul A., and Marlowe, Charles K.
Evaluation of intrinsic binding energy from a hydrogen bonding group in an enzyme inhibitor. bibl f il *Science* 235:569-71 Ja 30 '87

Bartlett, R. J., and others
A new probe for the diagnosis of myotonic muscular dystrophy. bibl f il *Science* 235:1648-50 Mr 27 '87

Bartlett, Sarah
Should you hock your house? il *Read Dig* 130:86-8 Je '87

Bartocci, Barbara
Golden scrapbooks of the mind. il *Read Dig* 131:137-40 D '87

Bartolomé, Fernando, and Laurent, André
The role of the manager: the use of power. *Current* 291:12-16 Mr/Ap '87

Barton, Barbara J.
about
Gardening by mail. J. Anderson. il por *Flower Gard* 31:40+ F/Mr '87

Barton, Gerald Gaylord, 1931-
about
Just so much popcorn. E. Paris. il por *Forbes* 139:44+ Je 1 '87

Barton, Laurie
The grammar/glamour connection. bibl f *Des Arts Educ* 88:15-18 Mr/Ap '87

Bartusiak, Marcia, 1950-
Heavenly drifters. il *Omni* 9:22 My '87
Long day's journey. il *Omni* 10:40 D '87

Baruch, Jacques, 1922-1986
about
Obituary
Am Craft il por 47:71 Je/Jl '87. F. Grossen

Bary-Cooper, Allene
The watercolor page. il por *Am Artist* 51:58 Je '87

Baryshnikov, Mikhail, 1948-
about
Abiding passions. T. Tobias. il *N Y* 20:108-9 O 19 '87
Baryshnikov a strong but silent Man of the Year. D. Cox. por *Dance Mag* 61:7 My '87
Baryshnikov: no time for conflicts. M. Pally. por *Film Comment* 23:81 S/O '87
A dance for détente. P. Young. il por *Macleans* 100:74 F 2 '87
For the birds. B. Rowes. il pors *Life* 10:86-9 O '87
Lovers leap: behind the scenes with Baryshnikov. H. Brubach. il pors *Vogue* 177:220-3+ Jl '87
Malicious Misha [excerpt from Dancing on my grave]; ed. by Greg Lawrence. G. Kirkland. il pors *Ladies Home J* 104:74+ Jl '87
Mikhail Baryshnikov [interview] N. Collins. pors *Roll Stone* p56-60+ O 8 '87
Misha in motion. il pors *Newsweek* 110:69 O 19 '87
Mother Russia's new Red carpet. por *U S News World Rep* 102:10 F 2 '87
Siren songs from Moscow. M. S. Serrill. il por *Time* 129:46 F 2 '87

Barzelatto, José
about
Family planning research [interview] V. Abramov. il *World Health* p2-5 N '87

Barzun, Jacques, 1907-
A little matter of sense. il *N Y Times Book Rev* 92:1+ Je 21 '87
Thoreau the thorough impressionist [excerpt from address, July 12, 1986] *Am Sch* 56:250-8 Spr '87

Basal readers (Books) *See* Readers (Books)

Basch, Harry, and Slater, Shirley
Seaworthy exhibits. il *Travel Holiday* 167:52-5+ Ja '87

Base three numeration *See* Ternary system

Baseball
See also
Baseball players
Batting (Baseball)
Boardwalk and Baseball (Amusement park)
Home runs (Baseball)
Pitching (Baseball)
Softball

Equipment
See also
Baseball bats
Baseball gloves
Baseballs

Terminology
Brush up on the fine points of baseball. il *Glamour* 85:97 Ap '87

Tournaments
No cigar for Cuba [Pan Am Games] C. Neff. il *Sports Illus* 67:22-3 Ag 24 '87

Dominican Republic
From Michigan, with love [baseball gloves sent to Dominican Republic] N. Shine. il por *Read Dig* 130:134-8 My '87
Standing tall at short [shortstops from the Dominican Republic in organized ball] S. Wulf. il *Sports Illus* 66:132-5+ F 9 '87

Soviet Union
Mighty Ivan at the bat. il *Newsweek* 110:36 Jl 27 '87
Anecdotes, facetiae, satire, etc.
Evil umpires? Not in Soviet baseball. J. Leo. il *Time* 130:56 Ag 10 '87

Baseball, Children's

From Michigan, with love [baseball gloves sent to Dominican Republic] N. Shine. il por *Read Dig* 130:134-8 My '87

A modern coach [Little League] J. Holusha. il *N Y Times Mag* p46 My 10 '87

Photographs and photography

Little League action! B. Hurter. il *Petersens Photogr Mag* 16:40-1 Je '87

Tournaments

Out of their (Little) League [Taiwan's victory in World Series] il *Sports Illus* 67:12 S 7 '87

Taiwan

Taiwan 11, USA 4 [Little League success] M. Shapiro. il *Sport Mag* 78:65-7 S '87

Baseball, College

Tournaments

The Cardinal rules [Stanford wins College World Series] H. Hersch. il *Sports Illus* 66:60-1 Je 15 '87

Baseball, Professional

See also
    Baseball fans
    Baseball managers
    Baseball Network
    Baseball players
    Batting (Baseball)
    Home runs (Baseball)
    National Baseball Hall of Fame and Museum
    Pitching (Baseball)

Baseball 1987 [cover story; special section] il *Sports Illus* 66:36-40+ Ap 6 '87

Baseball finally comes back to town. H. Quinn. il *Macleans* 100:38+ Ap 6 '87

Baseball preview '87 [special section] il *Sport Mag* 78:30-6+ Ap 6 '87

Baseball: spring training special [cover story] il map *Sport Mag* 78:22-4+ Mr '87

Batters are up in Florida [spring training] D. Young. il *South Living* 22:8-10+ Mr '87

Beers with [interview with Texas Rangers manager B. Valentine] B. Shapiro. il por *Sport Mag* 78:23-4 Ag '87

Billy the Kid rides again [positive effect of second baseman B. Ripken on Baltimore Orioles] P. Gammons. il pors *Sports Illus* 67:18-19 Ag 3 '87

Birds on the wing [Toronto-Detroit series; cover story] P. Gammons. il *Sports Illus* 67:22-7 O 5 '87

Black managers face off first for pro baseball [Boise Hawks meet Bend Bucks] *Jet* 72:49 Jl 20 '87

The Bucs don't stop here [resurgent Pittsburgh Pirates] P. Gammons. il *Sports Illus* 67:22-4 S 28 '87

Carved down to a play-off few [division playoffs] T. Callahan. il *Time* 130:75 O 12 '87

Close to a clincher [San Francisco Giants defeat Cincinnati Reds] P. Gammons. il *Sports Illus* 67:22-5 S 21 '87

Don't take me out to the football game [football vs. baseball] B. G. Harrison. *Mademoiselle* 93:108 F '87

The Erie sensation [Cleveland Indians] G. Macnow. il por *Sport Mag* 78:37-43 My '87

The Expos sont là, again. D. Burke. il *Macleans* 100:38 Ag 17 '87

Get out your handkerchiefs. R. Angell. *New Yorker* 63:51-2+ D 7 '87

Heading for a photo finish [AL West] S. Wulf. il *Sports Illus* 67:34-6+ S 14 '87

A heady start [Milwaukee Brewers' record season-opening victory streak] B. Newman. il *Sports Illus* 66:18-23 Ap 27 '87

How 'bout those Expos? A. Wolff. il *Sports Illus* 67:28-9 O 5 '87

Humm-dinger of a playoff [Giants vs. Cardinals] S. Wulf. il *Sports Illus* 67:30-4+ O 19 '87

Inside baseball. P. Gammons. See issues of Sports Illustrated published during the baseball season beginning April 14, 1986

It won't be an Indian summer [Cleveland's slow start] R. Fimrite. il *Sports Illus* 66:28-30+ Je 29 '87

Let's just play ball. R. Fimrite. por *Sports Illus* 66:154 Ap 6 '87

Midseason baseball report with statistical analysis by Bill James. P. Gammons. il *Sports Illus* 67:26-34 Jl 20 '87

More bang for more bucks [T. Raines returns to Expos and helps to defeat Mets] S. Wulf. il pors *Sports Illus* 66:32-3 My 11 '87

A new set of Twins [Minnesota holds first place in the American League West] A. Murphy. il *Sports Illus* 67:36-8+ Jl 27 '87

Oh, the woes of the O's [Baltimore Orioles] F. Deford. por *Sports Illus* 67:102 S 21 '87

On the grapefruit circuit [visiting spring training camps] J. Rachlin. il *U S News World Rep* 102:48 Mr 9 '87

One day in baseball [special section] il *Sports Illus* 67:24-44+ Jl 6 '87

One rip-roaring family affair [Ripken family and the Baltimore Orioles] H. Hersch. il pors *Sports Illus* 66:26-8+ Mr 9 '87

Out! [Detroit vs. Toronto for AL East title] P. Gammons. il *Sports Illus* 67:20-5 O 12 '87

Padre with a passion [manager L. Bowa] R. Fimrite. il pors *Sports Illus* 66:52-4+ My 4 '87

Pete has 'em seeing Red [Cincinnati team] H. Hersch. il *Sports Illus* 67:24-7 Ag 10 '87

Pow! Pow! Pow! [Orioles' home run barrage] E. M. Swift. il *Sports Illus* 66:42-4+ Je 1 '87

A raging pennant fever. H. Quinn. il *Macleans* 100:48 O 5 '87

Replete with Bronx cheer [New York Yankees] P. Gammons. il *Sports Illus* 67:24-5 Jl 13 '87

Revving up in Motown [Tigers-Yankees series; cover story] J. Garrity. il *Sports Illus* 67:22-5 Ag 17 '87

A season to remember. H. Quinn. il por *Macleans* 100:37 Ag 24 '87

Showdown in the Bronx [Yankees-Blue Jays series] H. Quinn. il *Macleans* 100:45-6 Je 15 '87

Take that! [Cardinals vs. Mets] S. Wulf. il *Sports Illus* 67:18-21 S 21 '87

Taking the rap [New York Mets] S. Wulf. il pors *Sports Illus* 67:20-3 Jl 13 '87

Ten wins and therefore no ties [Milwaukee Brewers] T. Callahan. il *Time* 129:66 Ap 27 '87

To know 'em is to fear 'em [Blue Jays sweep series with Yankees and take over first place] P. Gammons. il *Sports Illus* 66:24-6+ Je 22 '87

What a win for the Twins [Minnesota beats Detroit in American League playoffs; cover story] P. Gammons. il *Sports Illus* 67:40-2+ O 19 '87

The World Series, eh? [chances of a Jay-Expos Series] H. Quinn. il *Macleans* 100:48-9 S 21 '87

Accidents and injuries

Battered Birds flying high [St. Louis Cardinals] R. Fimrite. il *Sports Illus* 66:38-41 My 18 '87

Advertising

The Bucs start here [Pirates Winter Caravan '87] D. Levine. il *Sport Mag* 78:90 My '87

All-star games

An All-star campaign [Canadian fans vote for Canadian players] H. Quinn. il por *Macleans* 100:28 Jl 20 '87

The crowd roars: end the All-star vote. N. Cohen. *Sport Mag* 78:6 Je '87

Raines, Smith resemble black gold as N.L. stars. pors *Jet* 72:50 Ag 3 '87

Anecdotes, facetiae, satire, etc.

The closing of the American game. E. Levin. *Nation* 245:437-8+ O 24 '87

Great moments in literary baseball. R. Atwan. il *Atlantic* 259:34 My '87

Awards

Bell, Dawson, capture baseball's MVP Awards. pors *Jet* 73:17 D 7 '87

An MVP (boo) and lights (sigh) for the Cubs [A. Dawson selected National League MVP] P. Gammons. il por *Sports Illus* 67:18 N 30 '87

Benefit games

Owens fouls with Edwards; now pitches to Ueberroth [M. Owens wants benefit game in honor of Jackie Robinson] por *Jet* 73:49 N 2 '87

Collectibles

One fan's tribute to baseball greats—and almost-greats [collection of B. Halper; cover story] R. W. Creamer. il por *Smithsonian* 18:102-6+ Ap '87

Economic aspects

See also
    Baseball players—Salaries, pensions, etc.

Hamming it up [Japan] H. Katayama. il *Forbes* 139:150 Ap 6 '87

Take that, Peter Ueberroth [minor league teams] R. Behar. il *Forbes* 139:36-8 F 9 '87

The Twins have clinched stardom for Carl Pohlad. P. Houston. il por *Bus Week* p79-80 O 26 '87

A winning gambit on a losing team [G. Argyros must sell the Seattle Mariners] J. Flynn. il por *Bus Week* p102 My 4 '87

Ethical aspects

Astros' Hatcher uses bat of teammate; later ejected because it was corked. por *Jet* 72:46 S 21 '87

Batty balls [corked bats and scuffed balls] T. Callahan. *Time* 130:45 Ag 24 '87

Baseball, Professional—Ethical aspects—*cont.*

The case for the defence [lawyer's account of baseball player F. Jenkins' narcotics case; excerpt from Greenspan] E. L. Greenspan and G. Jonas. il pors *Macleans* 100:48-50+ O 19 '87

Coke and a pitching ace [D. Gooden case] il por *Macleans* 100:26 Ap 13 '87

A crash landing for an ace [D. Gooden enters clinic for cocaine abuse treatment] S. Wulf. il pors *Sports Illus* 66:32-4 Ap 13 '87

Dr. K strikes out [D. Gooden enters drug rehabilitation] por *Time* 129:67 Ap 13 '87

Drug tests may explain why Vida Blue retired. por *Jet* 71:50 Mr 23 '87

Expos' Youmans enters drug treatment clinic. *Jet* 73:50 N 2 '87

Going to bat against the fear of failure [D. Gooden cocaine case] J. M. Wall. *Christ Century* 104:371-2 Ap 22 '87

Gooden sheds light on his problem with cocaine. *Jet* 72:52 Jl 13 '87

Gooden to start working back into Mets rotation. il por *Jet* 72:48 My 18 '87

It's war out there! [pitchers throwing at batters followed by bench-clearing brawls; cover story] H. Hersch. il *Sports Illus* 67:14-17 Jl 20 '87

Maury Wills favors drug testing for all players. il por *Jet* 71:46 Mr 2 '87

Mets moral support may speed up Gooden's return after drug rehabilitation. il pors *Jet* 72:50 Ap 20 '87

Mets provide protection while 'Dr. K' heals himself [D. Gooden] por *Jet* 72:46 My 25 '87

Milner quietly beat drugs, but he's talking about it [E. Milner] *Jet* 72:46 S 7 '87

O.K., drop that emery board [crackdown on cheating] P. Gammons. il *Sports Illus* 67:34-7 Ag 17 '87

Off to a troubled start [D. Gooden case] P. Axthelm. il pors *Newsweek* 109:66-7 Ap 13 '87

Say it ain't snow, Doc! Baseball hero Dwight Gooden is knocked out of the box by cocaine. J. S. Kunen. il por *People Wkly* 27:123-4 Ap 20 '87

The truth about bean-ball wars. P. Axthelm. il *Newsweek* 110:49 Jl 20 '87

History

40 years after Jackie Robinson, baseball still has no black managers. N. O. Unger. il pors *Jet* 72:48-51 My 4 '87

40th anniversary: biggest breakthrough in sports [J. Robinson; excerpt from Negro firsts in sports] A. S. Young. il pors *Ebony* 42:66-8+ My '87

Doby honored by Indians as 1st black AL player. por *Jet* 72:50 S 21 '87

The fuse that lit the fire [J. Robinson] G. F. Will. il *Newsweek* 109:88 Ap 13 '87

Getting to first base [All-American Girls Professional Baseball League to be commemorated in exhibit at Baseball Hall of Fame] J. Rodewald. il *Women's Sports Fitness* 9:48-9 O '87

Happy days [former commissioner H. Chandler reaches 90th birthday] F. Deford. il pors *Sports Illus* 67:56-60+ Jl 20 '87

Just a Pipp of a legend [Yankee benched in favor of L. Gehrig in 1925] B. Anderson. il pors *Sports Illus* 66:78-82+ Je 29 '87

Kid K [pitcher R. Necciai's no hit, 27 strike out game for the minor league Bristol Twins in 1952] P. Jordan. il pors *Sports Illus* 66:82-6+ Je 1 '87

Memoirs of a Moose; ed. by Bill Shaw. B. Skowron. il pors *People Wkly* 28:103-4+ S 14 '87

Once upon a time in Cleveland . . . [1954 championship season] R. W. Creamer. il *Sports Illus* 66:78 Ap 6 '87

Remembering . . . Jackie Robinson. S. A. Robinson. il pors *Essence* 17:49 Ap '87

Septembers to remember. P. Gammons. il *Sports Illus* 67:40-3+ S 14 '87

This mother could hit [defunct All-American Girls Professional Baseball League]; ed. by Todd Gold. H. St. Aubin. il pors *People Wkly* 28:77-8+ Ag 17 '87

Where are the black fans? [cover story] B. Staples. il *N Y Times Mag* p26-32+ My 17 '87

Old-timers games

A little sales pitch and a lot of slow pitches [Equitable's sponsorship] B. Welling. il *Bus Week* p114-15 Je 22 '87

Organization and administration

Aaron bearing up under pressure with the Braves. por *Jet* 71:47 F 23 '87

'Actions' aren't racist Yankee boss tells NAACP [G. Steinbrenner's comments] *Jet* 73:48 O 12 '87

Atlanta NAACP targets Turner's Hawks, Braves. *Jet* 73:48 D 14 '87

Baseball exec defended after 'blackface' remark. *Jet* 72:13 Jl 6 '87

Baseball takes steps [attempting to end racial discrimination] il *Sports Illus* 66:11 Je 22 '87

A big winner, in two leagues [N. Doubleday] N. J. Perry. il por *Fortune* 115:32-5 Ja 5 '87

Black baseball owners sell Savannah Cardinals. il por *Jet* 73:50 D 7 '87

Black NY group seeks Harry Edwards' ouster [Black United Fund of New York] il por *Jet* 72:46 S 14 '87

Black youth from ghetto to Giants' front office [J. Wallace] *Jet* 72:46 Ag 31 '87

Edwards and Ueberroth, classmates now teammates [racism in baseball] pors *Jet* 72:51 Je 29 '87

Edwards hires Campanis to assist baseball job. il por *Jet* 72:48 S 14 '87

Ex-Army boss to examine baseball's plan for action [C. Alexander to review affirmative action plans] por *Jet* 72:46 Je 29 '87

Ex-manager Martin tells Jesse: stick to politics [views of B. Martin] por *Jet* 72:46 Jl 13 '87

Ex-NFL star Hill joins Orioles bd. of directors [C. Hill] por *Jet* 72:48 Ag 10 '87

Former Army Secretary and woman scientist try to change baseball image [C. Alexander and J. Hill] il pors *Jet* 73:50-1 N 9 '87

Gussied up for the game [club owners during World Series] R. Fimrite. il por *Sports Illus* 67:116 N 2 '87

How about it, Mr. Pete? Ten good reasons Denver deserves a major league team. R. Reilly. por *Sports Illus* 67:90 Ag 24 '87

Minorities in his office a priority, Ueberroth says. *Jet* 72:50 S 7 '87

Of Spenser, the Red Sox, and drinking in the stands [A. B. Giamatti, president of the National League] B. Welling. il por *Bus Week* p66 Ag 17 '87

Oh, for those glory days of yesteryear [L.A. Dodgers] P. Gammons. il *Sports Illus* 67:42-4+ Ag 10 '87

The only baseball boss who's young, female and black, Tracy Lewis holds the cards in Savannah. P. Jordan. il pors *People Wkly* 27:108-10 My 18 '87

Peter principles [work of P. Ueberroth] por *Sports Illus* 66:72-3 Ap 27 '87

Tigers hire black exec, answer civil rights call [comptroller M. Wilson] *Jet* 72:52 Je 22 '87

Ueberroth vows baseball will lead in hiring. *Jet* 72:47 Ag 17 '87

Yankees owner points to 'black boy' in office as affirmative action [remarks by G. Steinbrenner] *Jet* 72:52 Jl 20 '87

Photographs and photography

Baseball's little acre [minor league ball in the Sally League] D. Burnett. il *Sport Mag* 78:50-7 My '87

Scene at the ballpark [minor leagues] J. Kennard. il *Americana* 15:45-9 My/Je '87

Player trades

Look what Santa brought [trades at winter meetings] P. Gammons. il *Sports Illus* 67:64-5 D 21 '87

Psychological aspects

'In my mind I know I'm going to be a star' [work of J. Johnson, sports psychologist for the Houston Astros] L. Rosellini. il pors *U S News World Rep* 102:58-9 Je 15 '87

Public opinion

Results: the Sport baseball poll. il *Sport Mag* 78:14 Je '87

Radio broadcasting

See Radio broadcasting—Sports

Records

See Baseball records

Social aspects

A resonant moment at the ballpark. J. M. Wall. *Christ Century* 104:547-8 Je 17-24 '87

Take a kid to the ball game. R. A. Mazer. por *Newsweek* 109:8 Ap 6 '87

Statistics

See also
APBA Pro League Baseball Game
Rotisserie League Baseball
Strat-O-Matic Baseball (Game)

Square root, root, root for the home team. B. Cipher. il *Discover* 8:87-8+ O '87

Strange news from the diamond market [computer program comparing baseball player salaries to performance] D. Seligman. il *Fortune* 115:118 My 25 '87

Baseball, Professional—*cont.*
Television broadcasting
See Cable television—Sports; Television broadcasting—Sports
Umpiring
All umps alike? You make the call. L. Lynn. il *Sport Mag* 78:14 Je '87
Bob's job is his calling [B. Engel] B. Newman. il pors *Sports Illus* 67:86-7 Jl 6 '87
What ever happened to the strike zone? P. Gammons. il *Sports Illus* 66:36-40+ Ap 6 '87
Uniforms
Baseball flannels are hot [reproductions of classic jerseys] D. Butwin. il por *Sports Illus* 67:105 Jl 6 '87
World Series
Game 6 [Mets vs. Red Sox in 1986] P. Gammons. il *Sports Illus* 66:110-14+ Ap 6 '87
Gussied up for the game [club owners during World Series] R. Fimrite. il por *Sports Illus* 67:116 N 2 '87
Home team [ex-Minnesotan in New York rooting for the Twins] *New Yorker* 63:34-7 N 2 '87
Internal strife at the World Series [Cardinals vs. Twins] T. Callahan. il *Time* 130:140 O 26 '87
No-names and the lame at the Dome [Twins vs. Cardinals] H. Quinn. il *Macleans* 100:44-5 O 26 '87
An oddly appropriate end [Twins vs. Cardinals] H. Quinn. il *Macleans* 100:47 N 2 '87
Series heroes require introductions [Minnesota Twins vs. St. Louis Cardinals] T. Callahan. il *Time* 130:98 N 2 '87
Sight for sore ears [behavior of Minnesota Twins fans] il *Time* 130:86 N 9 '87
Sweet music [Twins defeat Cardinals; cover story] S. Wulf. il *Sports Illus* 67:26-36+ N 2 '87
Twin wins [Twins vs. Cardinals; cover story] P. Gammons. il *Sports Illus* 67:46-53 O 26 '87
Twins take World Series by thumping Cardinals. il *Jet* 73:52 N 9 '87
History
Catchers and pitchers [Cardinals vs. Yankees in 1964; excerpt from Oh, baby, I love it!] T. McCarver. il *Sport Mag* 78:56 Jl '87
The lucky sevens [eight Series played in years ending with the number seven] B. Shapiro. il *Sport Mag* 78:61+ N '87
World Series comebacks. W. Bingham. il *Sports Illus* 67:55+ O 12 '87
Television broadcasting
See Television broadcasting—Sports
Canada
See also
Canadian Baseball Hall of Fame
Japan
Baseball at ground zero [Hiroshima Stadium built near epicenter of nuclear explosion] G. Mitchell. il *Progressive* 51:20-1 Ag '87
Hamming it up. H. Katayama. il *Forbes* 139:150 Ap 6 '87
The hottest American import in Japan [R. Bass] C. Neff. il pors *Sports Illus* 66:72-6+ Mr 23 '87
A new kind of Orient Express [American player B. Horner] A. Wolff. il por *Sports Illus* 66:28-9 My 18 '87
Baseball bats
Buying the perfect piece of wood. J. Schuster. il *Sport Mag* 78:91 Ap '87
Baseball camps *See* Camps
Baseball cards
Baseball is a hobby for this Jackson [collector E. Jackson of the Pittsburgh Steelers] J. Reynolds. il por *Sports Illus* 67:12 N 23 '87
The boychiks of summer [collecting Jewish ballplayers' cards] N. Karlen. il *N Y* 20:29 Ap 20 '87
Buy Pete Rose, trade Johnny Bench. D. Seideman. il *Time* 129:53 Je 1 '87
Newly-discovered baseball card rarity sells for $10,000 [1909 T206 Joe Doyle baseball card] il *Antiques Collect Hobbies* 92:25 Jl '87
Baseball coaches
See also
Ripken, Cal, Sr.
A modern coach [Little League] J. Holusha. il *N Y Times Mag* p46 My 10 '87
Baseball commissioner *See* Baseball, Professional—Organization and administration
Baseball fans
An All-star campaign [Canadian fans vote for Canadian players] H. Quinn. il por *Macleans* 100:28 Jl 20 '87

Baseball camps: where big league dreams come true [adult camps] L. Kaufman. il *Travel Holiday* 167:48-51 My '87
A baseball for dad [ball autographed by S. Musial] P. Thomson. il *Read Dig* 130:13-14+ Mr '87
Baseball missing black fans for many reasons. *Jet* 72:48 Jl 6 '87
Batters are up in Florida [spring training] D. Young. il *South Living* 22:8-10+ Mr '87
The crowd roars: end the All-star vote. N. Cohen. *Sport Mag* 78:6 Je '87
Home team [ex-Minnesotan in New York rooting for the Twins] *New Yorker* 63:34-7 N 2 '87
Keeping the Cardinals in stitches [baseball quilts by F. Claas and C. Rothmeier] J. E. Vader. il pors *Sports Illus* 67:44 O 26 '87
On the grapefruit circuit [visiting spring training camps] J. Rachlin. il *U S News World Rep* 102:48 Mr 9 '87
A resonant moment at the ballpark. J. M. Wall. *Christ Century* 104:547-8 Je 17-24 '87
A roof-raising ruckus [Minnesota fans] R. Fimrite. il *Sports Illus* 67:51 O 26 '87
Rootin' from the roofs [Chicago Cubs fans] R. Telander. il *Sports Illus* 67:82-4 Jl 6 '87
Sight for sore ears [behavior of Minnesota Twins fans] il *Time* 130:86 N 9 '87
Take a kid to the ball game. R. A. Mazer. por *Newsweek* 109:8 Ap 6 '87
What's foul is fair game [L. Miller catches foul ball at Oakland A's game] B. Anderson. il por *Sports Illus* 67:98 Jl 6 '87
Where are the black fans? [cover story] B. Staples. il *N Y Times Mag* p26-32+ My 17 '87
Anecdotes, facetiae, satire, etc.
A civilized pastime. R. Baker. il *N Y Times Mag* p16 Ap 5 '87
Civil rights
Free speech and the 'bleacher creatures' [Tiger Stadium's efforts to curb fans' bad behavior] il *Newsweek* 110:38 S 21 '87
Who are the 'moderates'? [ACLU objects to Detroit Tigers' attempt to curb fans' vulgarity] G. F. Will. il *Newsweek* 110:100 O 12 '87
Baseball gloves
Buying the perfect piece of leather. D. Whitford. il *Sport Mag* 78:91+ Ap '87
From Michigan, with love [baseball gloves sent to Dominican Republic] N. Shine. il por *Read Dig* 130:134-8 My '87
Baseball in art
Exhibitions
Baseball through the artist's eyes [traveling exhibit called Diamonds are forever: artists and writers on baseball] D. Levine. il *Sport Mag* 78:88 O '87
The magical game [Diamonds are forever: artists and writers on baseball] R. Bongartz. il *Americana* 15:24-6+ S/O '87
Seventh-inning sketch. M. Moorman. il *Art News* 86:15+ Summ '87
Baseball in literature
Exhibitions
Baseball through the artist's eyes [traveling exhibit called Diamonds are forever: artists and writers on baseball] D. Levine. il *Sport Mag* 78:88 O '87
The magical game [Diamonds are forever: artists and writers on baseball] R. Bongartz. il *Americana* 15:24-6+ S/O '87
Baseball literature
Authorship
Striking out. J. G. Dunne. il *Esquire* 107:53-4 Ap '87
Bibliography
Play book! [books by the New York Mets] C. Bayer. il *Publ Wkly* 231:28 My 1 '87
Baseball managers
See also
Berra, Yogi, 1925-
Bowa, Larry
Durocher, Leo, 1905-
Herzog, Whitey
Howser, Dick, 1936-1987
Lasorda, Tom
Martin, Billy, 1928-
Roberts, Mel
Robinson, Frank
Rose, Pete, 1941-
Thomas, Derrel
Trebelhorn, Tom
40 years after Jackie Robinson, baseball still has no black managers. N. O. Unger. il pors *Jet* 72:48-51 My 4 '87

Baseball managers—*cont.*

Al Campanis [loss of job with Dodgers after remarks about lack of black baseball managers] F. C. Klein. il por *Sport Mag* 78:97-8 D '87

Baseball: a crisis in black and white [furor over remarks of A. Campanis regarding black managers] P. Axthelm. *Newsweek* 109:71 Ap 20 '87

Baseball manager candidates seeking a try with control [blacks] il *Jet* 72:46 Je 8 '87

Black managers far off, say Williams, Roseboro. il por *Jet* 73:46 O 19 '87

Bob Gibson fears baseball will fail to promote blacks. por *Jet* 72:50 Jl 27 '87

Bowie Kuhn: Campanis did blacks a favor. por *Jet* 72:46 Jl 27 '87

The Campanis affair [Los Angeles Dodgers VP's remarks on dearth of black managers] P. Gammons. il por *Sports Illus* 66:31 Ap 20 '87

Ex-Dodger Joe Black hurls pitch to owners on how to strike out baseball bias. il pors *Jet* 72:50 My 18 '87

The foul ball that shook baseball's front office [Dodgers VP, A. Campanis, reveals bias against blacks as managers] A. P. Sanoff. il por *U S News World Rep* 102:12-13 Ap 20 '87

Hank Aaron turned down offers to manage team. por *Jet* 73:50 S 28 '87

In America's national pastime, says Frank Robinson, white is the color of the game off the field [interview] il pors *People Wkly* 27:46+ Ap 27 '87

Morgan says he'd manage only with the right team [J. Morgan] por *Jet* 72:46 Jl 27 '87

Phils boss ignored blacks when hiring new manager. il *Jet* 72:47 Jl 6 '87

Racism at bat [A. Campanis forced to resign from Dodger organization after remarks on lack of black baseball managers] T. Callahan. por *Time* 129:63 Ap 20 '87

Racist remarks spark push for black execs [remarks concerning black baseball managers by A. Campanis] il por *Jet* 72:46 Ap 27 '87

Reggie picks Winfield to go to bat for blacks. pors *Jet* 72:50 Je 15 '87

"We have a serious problem that isn't going away" [discrimination against blacks; cover story]; ed. by Peter Gammons. R. Jackson. il pors *Sports Illus* 66:40-2+ My 11 '87

Dismissal

Derrel Thomas fired as minor league manager. por *Jet* 72:50 Ag 17 '87

Retirement

Facing the sad truth [D. Howser too ill to manage the Kansas City Royals] R. Fimrite. il por *Sports Illus* 66:96 Mr 9 '87

Baseball Network

Baseball Network formed to aid minority hiring. il *Jet* 73:46 N 30 '87

Baseball players

See also

Aaron, Hank, 1934-
Abbott, Jim
Bass, Randy, 1954-
Baylor, Don, 1949-
Bell, George
Bernazard, Tony
Blue, Vida
Boggs, Wade
Bowa, Larry
Boyd, Dennis
Bunning, Jim
Burks, Ellis
Carlton, Steve
Carpenter, Cris
Carter, Gary
Carter, Joe
Clark, Jack, 1955-
Clemens, Roger
Clemente, Roberto, 1934-1972
Concepcion, Dave
Dandridge, Ray
Darling, Ron
Davis, Eric
Dawson, Andre
Doby, Larry
Durocher, Leo, 1905-
Eisenreich, Jim
Garvey, Steve
Gehrig, Lou, 1903-1941
Gibson, Bob, 1935-
Gooden, Dwight
Griffey, Ken, Jr.
Hatcher, Billy

Hempen, Hal
Hernandez, Keith, 1953-
Horner, Bob
Jackson, Bo
Jackson, Reggie
Jenkins, Ferguson, 1943-
Johnson, Howard, 1960-
Johnson, Joe
Leach, Rick
Leonard, Jeffrey
Maddox, Garry, 1949-
Madlock, Bill
Magrane, Joe
Major League Baseball Players Association
Maris, Roger, 1934-1985
Mattingly, Don
McGwire, Mark
McLain, Denny, 1944-
McMahon, Don, d. 1987
McRae, Hal
Milner, Eddie
Molitor, Paul
Morgan, Joe
Murphy, Dale
Necciai, Ron
Nieves, Juan
Nokes, Matt
Odom, John
Parker, Dave, 1951-
Pipp, Wally
Puckett, Kirby
Raines, Tim
Rawley, Shane
Rice, Jim
Ripken, Billy
Ripken, Cal, Jr.
Robinson, Jackie, 1919-1972
Rose, Pete, 1941-
Saberhagen, Bret
Santiago, Benito
Schmidt, Mike, 1949-
Scott, Mike, 1955-
Seaver, Tom
Seitzer, Kevin
Simmons, Ted, 1949-
Smith, Dave, 1955-
Smith, Lonnie
Smith, Ozzie
Snyder, Cory
Stanley, Bob
Stewart, Dave
Strawberry, Darryl
Sullivan, Marc
Surhoff, B. J.
Terry, Ralph, 1936-
Valentine, Bobby
Viola, Frank, 1960-
White, Devon
Williams, Billy
Wills, Maury
Winfield, Dave, 1951-
Youmans, Floyd

Another phenom-enal freshman class [rookies] P. Gammons. il *Sports Illus* 66:106 Ap 6 '87

Black players, pitchers numbers are decreasing. *Jet* 73:47 S 28 '87

The boychiks of summer [collecting Jewish ballplayers' cards] N. Karlen. il *N Y* 20:29 Ap 20 '87

Here come the young lions [rookies; special section] il *Sports Illus* 67:40-2+ Jl 13 '87

How they spent their winter vacation. il *Sport Mag* 78:27+ Mr '87

Major league nightmares [bad dreams] H. Hewes. il *Sport Mag* 78:79-81 Ag '87

Standing tall at short [shortstops from the Dominican Republic in organized ball] S. Wulf. il *Sports Illus* 66:132-5+ F 9 '87

Strangers in a strange land (Miami), four Japanese baseball players find it tough getting to first base [playing for the Marlins in the minor leagues] P. Jordan. il *People Wkly* 28:46-8 Jl 13 '87

Where are the black fans? [cover story] B. Staples. il *N Y Times Mag* p26-32+ My 17 '87

Accidents and injuries

See Baseball, Professional—Accidents and injuries

Awards

See Baseball, Professional—Awards

Nutrition

The spring training diet. S. Krasnow. il *Sport Mag* 78:93 Mr '87

Baseball players—*cont.*

Photographs and photography

The character is back! F. Scavullo. il *Esquire* 107:97-101 Ap '87

Doc [102 foot Duratrans mural of D. Gooden that hangs in Penn Station] *New Yorker* 63:29-30+ Mr 23 '87

Fathers & sons. il *Sports Illus* 66:62-73 Ap 6 '87

Press relations

Mets provide protection while 'Dr. K' heals himself [D. Gooden] por *Jet* 72:46 My 25 '87

Psychology

See Baseball, Professional—Psychological aspects

Retirement

Vida Blue pulls a switch, retires despite new pact. il por *Jet* 71:50 Mr 9 '87

Salaries, pensions, etc.

The arbitrator's game [salary arbitrator R. Abrams] M. Chass. il por *Sport Mag* 78:29 Je '87

'At times you flat cry': how LaRue Harcourt's baseball player clients were driven to tears. A. Keteyian. il *Sports Illus* 67:90-1 O 19 '87

Baseball finally comes back to town. H. Quinn. il *Macleans* 100:38+ Ap 6 '87

Baseball is big bucks business for black stars. il *Jet* 72:46 My 11 '87

Baseball salaries '87 [cover story] il *Sports Illus* 66:54-8+ Ap 20 '87

Baseball's black millionaires. N. O. Unger. il *Ebony* 42:92+ My '87

Benching the best to save a buck. A. P. Sanoff. il *U S News World Rep* 102:70-1 Ap 13 '87

The best money can buy [free agents] P. Gammons. il *Sports Illus* 67:30-2+ D 14 '87

The cloud over baseball's new season. H. Quinn. il *Macleans* 100:40-1 Mr 2 '87

Collusion course: the verdict. J. Millman. il *Sport Mag* 78:13 Je '87

Divided they fell [views of M. Miller] D. Whitford. il por *Sport Mag* 78:84-5 Jl '87

The Expos face a season without stars [free agents] H. Quinn. il *Macleans* 100:48+ Mr 16 '87

Is collusion the name of the game? [halt of bidding war has led players to charge owners with conspiracy] B. Spitz. il *N Y Times Mag* p22-3+ Jl 12 '87

Last picture show [free agents] il *Sports Illus* 66:32-5 Ja 19 '87

National pastime: capital vs. labor [free agency] il *Fortune* 116:9 S 28 '87

The penalties for delay of game [free agency issue] T. Callahan. il *Time* 130:59-60 O 5 '87

Playing hardball [owners hold the line on signing free agents] P. Gammons. por *Sports Illus* 66:108 Ja 12 '87

Springing for the check [owners and players clash over salaries] T. Callahan. il *Time* 129:78-9 Mr 23 '87

Strange news from the diamond market [computer program comparing baseball player salaries to performance] D. Seligman. il *Fortune* 115:118 My 25 '87

Why the owners can't scuttle free agents. J. Hoerr. il *Bus Week* p42 O 5 '87

Trades

See Baseball, Professional—Player trades

Training

Guide to a good arm. G. Legwold. il *Sport Mag* 78:73-4 Je '87

Master of swat [M. Schmidt; cover story] G. Waggoner. il pors *Esquire* 107:139-40+ My '87

Spring training at home [off-season conditioning] J. Akers. il *Sport Mag* 78:79-80 My '87

Baseball players' wives

Playing by her own rules [M. Simmons] A. Wolff. il por *Sports Illus* 67:38-9 Jl 6 '87

Baseball records

Aaron says Ruth chase was unforgettable hell. por *Jet* 72:48 S 14 '87

Kid K [pitcher R. Necciai's no hit, 27 strike out game for the minor league Bristol Twins in 1952] P. Jordan. il pors *Sports Illus* 66:82-6+ Je 1 '87

A Murderers' Row of one [D. Mattingly ties record for homers in consecutive games] C. Neff. il pors *Sports Illus* 67:24-5 Jl 27 '87

Pow! Pow! Pow! [Orioles' home run barrage] E. M. Swift. il *Sports Illus* 66:42-4+ Je 1 '87

Streak City [minor league Salt Lake Trappers win 28 straight games] J. Garrity. il *Sports Illus* 67:14-17 Ag 3 '87

Three for the record books [D. Mattingly's feats] il por *Time* 130:62 Ag 3 '87

Baseball stadiums *See* Stadiums

Baseballs

Is it all in the ball? [home run explosion in the majors] T. N. Dawidoff. il *Sports Illus* 66:44 Je 1 '87

It's a routine . . . home run. T. Callahan. il *Time* 130:72 Jl 13 '87

Rabbit ball: whodunit? F. Deford. por *Sports Illus* 67:94 Jl 27 '87

Basel (Switzerland)

Stores

See also

Johann Wanner (Firm)

Basel Ballet

Editor's log [Taormina Music and Ballet Festival] W. Como. il *Dance Mag* 61:30 N '87

Stirring up Swan Lake in Basel. I. Wydler-Roth. il *Dance Mag* 61:74-5 Mr '87

Basements

See also

Root cellars

Wine cellars

Nuclear war? Head for the basement [research by Robert Ehrlich and James Ring] *Sci News* 131:233 Ap 11 '87

Waterproofing

See Waterproofing

Basements, Remodeled

Good times that are built in [cover story] J. R. Provey. il *Home Mech* 83:40-5 Ap '87

Bases (Chemistry)

See also

Schiff base salts

Bases (Military) *See* Military bases

Bases (Missile) *See* Guided missile bases

Bases (Nitrogenous) *See* Nitrogenous bases

BASF AG

Clean desk on the Rhine [H. Albers] L. S. Richman. il por *Fortune* 116:50-1 Ag 3 '87

Bash, Paul A., and others

Calculation of the relative change in binding free energy of a protein-inhibitor complex. bibl f il *Science* 235:574-6 Ja 30 '87

Free energy calculations by computer simulation. bibl f il *Science* 236:564-8 My 1 '87

Bashfulness

Born to be shy? [studies of infants and monkeys by Jerome Kagan and Stephen Suomi] J. Asher. bibl (p65) il *Psychol Today* 21:56-9+ Ap '87

Children who are shy. J. Segal and Z. Segal. il *Parents* 62:196 Ag '87

The shy guy tells all (finally!). L. Stambler. il *Teen* 31:18+ N '87

Shy twos. B. Weissbourd. il *Parents* 62:151 F '87

The shyness chemical [low dopamine levels] *Time* 129:78 Mr 16 '87

Bashline, Jim

[Column] *See* issues of Field & Stream

Bashline, Sylvia

Bounty. *See* issues of Field & Stream

Basic (Computer language)

Another approach to data compression [Basic programs explore the Nyquist sampling theorem] R. J. Sciamanda. il *Byte* 12:137-8+ F '87

Basic compilers for the Macintosh. S. L. Norman. il *Byte* 12:241-4+ My '87

A contouring subroutine. P. D. Bourke. il *Byte* 12:143-6+ Je '87

Faster, bigger, better [Turbo Basic and QuickBasic] J. Pournelle. il *Byte* 12:243-4+ Ag '87

Microsoft QuickBasic 2.0. D. P. Dykstra. il *Byte* 12:247-50 F '87

MTBASIC. F. D. Davis. il *Byte* 12:336-9 Ja '87

Polynomial curve fitter. W. G. Hood. il *Byte* 12:155-6+ Je '87

QuickBasic 4.0. G. M. Vose. il *Byte* 12:111-12+ N '87

Reviewer's notebook [Turbo Basic vs. QuickBasic] C. Baskin and G. A. Stewart. il *Byte* 12:227 Je '87

Turbo Basic. G. A. Stewart. il *Byte* 12:101-6+ Mr '87

Windows for Basic. J. W. Ross. il *Byte* 12 no12 Sp Issue:201-4+ '87

Basie, Count, 1904-1984

about

The common law of Count Basie. J. McDonough. il por *Down Beat* 54:61 My '87

First encounters. E. Sorel and N. C. Sorel. il *Atlantic* 259:61 Ja '87

Yessir, that's Count Basie. C. Albertson. por *Stereo Rev* 52:180 N '87

Basie, William *See* Basie, Count, 1904-1984
Basie (Count) Orchestra *See* Count Basie Orchestra
Basinger, Kim
about
It's a match: this time around, Basinger gets Bridges. il pors *Life* 10:61-4 Jl '87
Kim Basinger: the sexiest thing on screen. C. Krupp. pors *Glamour* 85:304+ S '87
Photographs and photography
Kim Basinger [cover story] M. Rolston. il pors *Esquire* 108:203-9 D '87
Basket making *See* Baskets
Basketball
See also
Basketball players
Korfball
Good show, comrades [Soviet junior team defeats Indiana high school all stars] A. Wolff. il *Sports Illus* 66:79-80 Je 1 '87
Shooting baskets & flying without wings. T. Osborne. il *Curr Health 2* 14:22-3 D '87
"You were great, Dad" [son admires father's skills] B. Cohen. il *Read Dig* 131:124-6 D '87
Equipment
The pursuit of hoopiness [driveway backboards and goals] A. Kim. il *Sport Mag* 78:87-8 N '87
Study and teaching
A guide to the summer hoop camps. M. George. il *Sport Mag* 78:93-4 Jl '87
The hot way to turn up the heat [pressure defense] A. Wolff. il *Sports Illus* 67 Sp Issue:46-50 N 18 '87
Aids and devices
Bank shot [CBS-Fox Video's line of NBA basketball tapes] A. D. Frank. il *Forbes* 139:252+ Je 15 '87
Tournaments
In your face, comrades! [Milwaukee Bucks vs. Soviet team in McDonald's Basketball Open] J. McCallum. il *Sports Illus* 67:50-2+ N 2 '87
Basketball, Children's
Lots of toddlers dribble, but not like this big, burly hoop star, supertot Hank Martin. il pors *People Wkly* 28:120-1 S 21 '87
Basketball, College
See also
Basketball coaches
Big East Conference Television Network
Another case of the South Bends [Notre Dame defeats DePaul] A. Murphy. il *Sports Illus* 66:32-4 Mr 9 '87
Back from the brink [coach B. Knight's behavior during 1987-1988 Indiana season] J. Feinstein. il pors *Sport Mag* 78:29-30+ D '87
Beers with . . . [interview with North Carolina State coach J. Valvano] B. Jacobs. il por *Sport Mag* 78:25-6 Ap '87
Best krewe in the bayou [University of New Orleans] H. Hersch. il *Sports Illus* 66:59 Mr 9 '87
Black-and-blue division [Big Ten] P. Axthelm. il *Newsweek* 109:60+ Mr 2 '87
Black college basketball conference standings. See issues of Jet published during the college basketball season
Can't anybody coach these guys? [University of Pittsburgh coach P. Evans] T. Kertes. il pors *Sport Mag* 78:53-4+ F '87
College basketball. See issues of Sports Illustrated published during the college basketball season beginning December 8, 1986
College basketball '87-88. il *Sports Illus* 67 Sp Issue:6-16+ N 18 '87
Female coach takes over men's summer cage team [Y. Laney] *Jet* 72:48 Jl 27 '87
A ferocious game of family feud [Big Ten] C. Kirkpatrick. il *Sports Illus* 66:74-6+ F 9 '87
How the Tide has turned [coach W. Sanderson and the Alabama team] R. Wiley. il *Sports Illus* 66:32-4 F 2 '87
Jackie Joyner-Kersee to coach UCLA female cagers. il por *Jet* 73:48 O 19 '87
Making its points, the hard way [University of Nevada, Las Vegas] T. Callahan. il *Time* 129:59 Mr 2 '87
Maybe Pitt is it. C. Kirkpatrick. il por *Sports Illus* 66:20-2+ F 16 '87
Oh, what a sorry state [Louisville and Kentucky suffering through painful seasons] A. Wolff. il *Sports Illus* 66:44-5 Mr 2 '87
Raising the roof [Kentucky beats Indiana] C. Kirkpatrick. il *Sports Illus* 67:16-19 D 14 '87
S.C. State, UAPB name new men's basketball coaches. *Jet* 72:51 Ap 27 '87
Seems like everyone has a shot this year [NCAA title up for grabs] C. Kirkpatrick. il *Sports Illus* 66:36-8+ Mr 2 '87

She's stealing the heart of Texas [J. Conradt, coach of University of Texas women's team] S. Hollandsworth. il pors *Women's Sports Fitness* 9:49-51+ F '87
A slip on poll mountain [UNLV defeated by Oklahoma] C. Kirkpatrick. il *Sports Illus* 66:18-20 Ja 26 '87
Temple's Chaney wins coach of year honors. por *Jet* 72:46 Ap 6 '87
Texas by an eyelash [women's basketball preseason picks] J. Jennings. il *Sports Illus* 67 Sp Issue:104 N 18 '87
A Texas waltz in Tennessee [Lady Longhorns defeat Vols] H. Hersch. il *Sports Illus* 67:44-6+ D 21 '87
A time for heeling [North Carolina upsets Syracuse in Tip-Off Classic] A. Wolff. il *Sports Illus* 67:50-1+ N 30 '87
Whoo? Yes, it's the Owls [Temple team] A. Murphy. il *Sports Illus* 66:42-3 Ja 19 '87
A wild new Cats' meow [play of R. Chapman in Kentucky-Louisville game] C. Kirkpatrick. il pors *Sports Illus* 66:18-19 Ja 5 '87
The Wildcats' great hope [Northwestern University coach B. Foster] A. H. Malcolm. il por *N Y Times Mag* p38-9+ Mr 1 '87
Anecdotes, facetiae, satire, etc.
Back from the future. C. Kirkpatrick. por *Sports Illus* 67 Sp Issue:116 N 18 '87
Ethical aspects
Bias' friend Tribble glad 'system did not fail me'. pors *Jet* 72:48 Je 22 '87
Charge two in drug probe of U-Texas cager's death [case of H. Jackson] *Jet* 72:52 Je 1 '87
The downfall of a champion [cocaine use during career at Villanova and afterwards]; ed. by Jeffrey Marx. G. McLain. il pors *Sports Illus* 66:42-6+ Mr 16 '87
Driesell denies saying cocaine helps athletes. *Jet* 72:50 Jl 6 '87
Indiana coach Knight has no sympathy for Bias; 'He was so cool'. *Jet* 72:46 Ag 3 '87
'Life is like basketball' [story of D. Cochran] R. L. Mahon. por *Newsweek* 109:10 F 23 '87
Not first class, coach: Rick Pitino deserted Providence, and so his players suffer. J. McCallum. por *Sports Illus* 67:86 Ag 3 '87
Photographs and photography
Anatomy of the game. J. McDonough. il *Sports Illus* 67 Sp Issue:34-43 N 18 '87
Before the ball is tipped [University of Louisville's locker room] B. Luster. il *Sport Mag* 78:60-6+ Mr '87
Polls
Please don't pick us no. 1. C. Kirkpatrick. il *Sports Illus* 67 Sp Issue:54-6+ N 18 '87
Recruiting
The juco express [junior college transfers] A. Wolff. il *Sports Illus* 67 Sp Issue:6-13 N 18 '87
Signed, sealed and sorry [case of S. Higgins] A. Keteyian and A. Wolff. il por *Sports Illus* 66:24-6 F 23 '87
Rules
The three-point uproar. J. McCallum. il *Sports Illus* 66:40-3 Ja 5 '87
Television broadcasting
See Cable television—Sports; Television broadcasting—Sports
Tournaments
Bigger but not better [NCAAs] F. Deford. por *Sports Illus* 66:86 Mr 30 '87
College basketball's Knight-errant [Indiana wins NCAA tournament] T. Callahan. pors *Time* 129:67-8 Ap 13 '87
Coming to the four with more [NCAA tournament] T. Callahan. il *Time* 129:84 Mr 30 '87
Flood Tide in the SEC. A. Wolff. il *Sports Illus* 66:18-19 Mr 16 '87
Four on the floor [NCAA tournament; special section] il *Sports Illus* 66:14-23 Mr 30 '87
The heat is on [conference tournaments] C. Kirkpatrick. il *Sports Illus* 66:14-17 Mr 16 '87
Smart and super [Indiana defeats Syracuse in NCAA championship game] C. Kirkpatrick. il *Sports Illus* 66:30-5 Ap 6 '87
Smart shot [winning Indiana shot in NCAA championships] S. Krasnow. il por *Sport Mag* 78:9 D '87
Strutting their stuff [NCAA early rounds] A. Wolff. il *Sports Illus* 66:26-30+ Mr 23 '87
A Tennessee waltz [NCAA women's championship] J. Diaz. il *Sports Illus* 66:124+ Ap 6 '87
A terrible omission [defending champion Louisville not extended an NCAA invitation] C. Kirkpatrick. por *Sports Illus* 66:74 Mr 16 '87
V is for Final IV. T. Kertes. il *Sport Mag* 78:84-5+ Ap '87

Basketball, College—Tournaments—*cont.*
Va. Union captures 42nd CIAA basketball tourney. il *Jet* 72:50 Mr 30 '87

History
It was more than just a game [1963 NCAA championship game between Loyola and Cincinnati] R. Fimrite. il *Sports Illus* 67 Sp Issue:106-10+ N 18 '87

Basketball, High school
His love is like a ball and chain [disciplinary measures of Crown Point (Ind.) High School coach Tom May] il *Women's Sports Fitness* 9:50 Jl '87
The Lady Bobcats [junior high game in rural Maine] *New Yorker* 62:27-8 Ja 19 '87
Miles from nowhere [Virginia's Oak Hill Academy] H. Hersch. il *Sports Illus* 66:78-82+ F 16 '87
Rebound for glory [St. Mary's basketball team in Trenton, N.J.] B. Doyle. il *U S Cathol* 52:26-33 O '87

Ethical aspects
Ga. team turns in trophy to win universal respect [Bulldogs of Rockdale County High] *Jet* 72:49 Je 29 '87

History
Hoosiermania [Milan High School's championship in 1954] H. Nuwer. il *Saturday Evening Post* 259:52-3+ Mr '87
Milan, Indiana still weeps for joy over its 1954 championship team that inspired Hoosiers. L. Aitken. il *People Wkly* 27:34-5 Mr 30 '87

Basketball, Professional
See also
   Basketball fans
   Basketball players
   Harlem Globetrotters
   International Basketball Association
   Naismith Memorial Basketball Hall of Fame
   National Basketball Association
   Strikes—Basketball players
The 1987-88 NBA preview [cover story] J. Capouya. il *Sport Mag* 78:23-5+ N '87
Atop the Pacific Rim [Portland Trail Blazers] J. McCallum. il *Sports Illus* 67:22-3 D 14 '87
Barnstorming, NBA style [Utah Jazz road trip] J. Coplon. il map *Sport Mag* 78:65-6+ Ap '87
The battle of the band-aids [Lakers defeat Celtics] J. McCallum. il *Sports Illus* 67:32-4+ D 21 '87
Beers with [interview with Los Angeles Lakers coach P. Riley] J. Capouya. il por *Sport Mag* 78:19-21 Je '87
Big birds on the wing [Atlanta Hawks] J. McCallum. il *Sports Illus* 66:44-6+ Ap 20 '87
Bloody time in Boston [Celtics defeat Detroit Pistons in Eastern Conference championship] P. Axthelm. il *Newsweek* 109:88 Je 8 '87
Crunch time [Los Angeles leading Boston in NBA finals; cover story] J. McCallum. il *Sports Illus* 66:18-23 Je 15 '87
Dallas does LA—in seven. J. Sullivan. il *Sport Mag* 78:33 My '87
Empty bucket [Sacramento Kings' inept quarter of play against the Los Angeles Lakers] T. Balf. il *Sport Mag* 78:10+ D '87
The fourth estate gets its day in court [sportswriter acts as assistant coach of the Albany Patroons in the Continental Basketball Association] J. Capouya. il *Sport Mag* 78:98 Ap '87
Give the NBA a break [attractions worth noting] J. McCallum. por *Sports Illus* 67:116 N 9 '87
Green and mean [Celtics vs. Bucks in Eastern Conference semifinals] J. McCallum. il *Sports Illus* 66:22-7 My 25 '87
The joy of getting even [outstanding play of Seattle guard D. Ellis in playoffs against Dallas] J. McCallum. il por *Sports Illus* 66:28-30 My 4 '87
The king at his new court [Sacramento Kings coach B. Russell] J. McCallum. il pors *Sports Illus* 67:36-9+ N 16 '87
Laying down the L.A. law [victory over Boston] J. McCallum. il *Sports Illus* 66:20-3 F 23 '87
The mystique goes on [Celtics beat Detroit to reach the NBA finals; cover story] J. McCallum. il *Sports Illus* 66:30-2+ Je 8 '87
One on one [women in men's pro basketball; interview with W. Reed and N. Lieberman] L. Villarosa. pors *Health* 19:30 Jl '87
Playing it tough in the East [Celtics-Pistons playoff series] J. McCallum. il *Sports Illus* 66:34-6+ Je 1 '87
Pro basketball 1987-88 [NBA preview; special section] il *Sports Illus* 67:46-54+ N 9 '87
The road to nowhere [Los Angeles Clippers] B. Newman. il *Sports Illus* 66:56-60 Mr 23 '87

Russell to coach Kings then become pres., owner. por *Jet* 72:48 My 18 '87
Sexism in "men-only" sports: why I'm not a victim. N. Lieberman. il por *Glamour* 85:64 Ag '87
Sonic boom gone bust [loss to Lakers in Western Conference finals] R. Wiley. il *Sports Illus* 66:41 Je 1 '87
The stuff dreams are made of [L. Bird and M. Johnson clash in NBA finals] D. Halberstam. il pors *Sports Illus* 66:38-40+ Je 29 '87
There's just no doubting Thomas [Detroit Pistons vs. Atlanta Hawks in playoffs; cover story] J. McCallum. il pors *Sports Illus* 66:30-2+ My 18 '87
They can't get off the ground [Houston Rockets] J. McCallum. il *Sports Illus* 66:54+ Ja 19 '87
They might be giants [Atlanta Hawks; cover story] J. Capouya. il *Sport Mag* 78:28-30+ My '87
They're front and Central [rugged divisional play] J. McCallum. il *Sports Illus* 66:14-17 Mr 2 '87
Your ball, L.A. [Los Angeles beats Boston for the NBA championship; cover story] J. McCallum. il *Sports Illus* 66:14-21 Je 22 '87

Accidents and injuries
Clippers star agrees to surgery after pay stops [M. Johnson] por *Jet* 72:46 Ap 13 '87
A King eyes a court comeback [New York Knicks player B. King] B. Newman. il por *Sports Illus* 66:32-3 Mr 30 '87
The pain that won't go away [epidemic of stress fractures] R. Demak. il *Sports Illus* 66:60-2+ Ap 27 '87
Sampson missed All-star game, may sit out season. *Jet* 71:47 F 23 '87

All-star games
The NBA All-star game [special section] il *Sport Mag* 78:45-7+ Mr '87

Anecdotes, facetiae, satire, etc.
Me and my good friends [celebrities at the Los Angeles Lakers games] C. Kirkpatrick. il *Sports Illus* 66:24-5 Je 15 '87

Awards
'Dr. J,' 'Magic' honored at NBA players dinner. il por *Jet* 73:48 O 5 '87

Draft
Black college stars look forward to NBA's draft. il *Jet* 72:46-7 Ap 20 '87
NBA draft a pleasant change for black colleges. il *Jet* 72:46 Jl 13 '87
NBA players sue league over draft, salary cap. *Jet* 73:49 O 19 '87
What's on draft [preview] T. Kertes. il *Sport Mag* 78:77-8+ Jl '87

Economic aspects
Build an arena now, get a team later—maybe. M. E. Recio. il *Bus Week* p90 Ap 20 '87
Embodiment of the dream [G. Shinn] E. F. Cone. il por *Forbes* 140:72-3 N 30 '87

Ethical aspects
Banned NBAer files suit over his '86 drug relapse [M. R. Richardson] *Jet* 72:50 My 25 '87
Dark clouds over Sun country [drug bust implicating present and former members of the Phoenix Suns] A. Keteyian. il *Sports Illus* 66:24-5 Ap 27 '87
Drug charges lose steam as Suns' trio pass tests [Phoenix Suns] il *Jet* 72:47 My 11 '87
Drug scandal witness dies, Phoenix case loses steam. por *Jet* 72:47 Jl 6 '87
Getting fooled by drugs: the perils of taking NBA cocaine users at their word. J. McCallum. il por *Sports Illus* 66:70 Ja 26 '87
New NBA trio implicated in Phoenix drug probe. il *Jet* 72:49 Je 1 '87
Rockets' pair bombed out of NBA for cocaine use [M. Wiggins and L. Lloyd] pors *Jet* 71:50 F 2 '87
Three strikes and he's . . . back [cocaine abuser J. Lucas playing for the Milwaukee Bucks] B. Newman. il pors *Sports Illus* 66:18-19 Mr 2 '87
Time to rise and shine [drug charges against Phoenix Suns players] C. Neff. il *Sports Illus* 67:30-2+ N 23 '87

History
Sweetwater [excerpt from From set shot to slam dunk] C. Salzberg. il por *Sport Mag* 78:63 Jl '87

Organization and administration
See also
   International Basketball Association
   National Basketball Association
Atlanta NAACP targets Turner's Hawks, Braves. *Jet* 73:48 D 14 '87
Bulls 1st black executive: 'I've got a lot to learn' [B. McKinney] por *Jet* 72:46 Je 29 '87

Basketball, Professional — Organization and administration—*cont.*

Ex-Celtic Tom Sanders joins NBA front office. por *Jet* 72:50 Ag 24 '87

Full court mess [New York Knicks] M. Lupica. il *Esquire* 108:63-4 N '87

NBA leading pro sports in hiring of minorities. *Jet* 73:46 N 9 '87

Refereeing

Where fouls are fair. L. Montville. il *Sports Illus* 67:66-9 N 9 '87

Television broadcasting

See Cable television—Sports; Television broadcasting—Sports

Italy

McAdoo a driving force in Italy. por *Jet* 73:50 N 2 '87

McAdoo does it right for Italian league hoop team. por *Jet* 72:50 Je 1 '87

Basketball camps *See* Camps

Basketball coaches

See also

Alexander, Cyrus
Chaney, John
Conradt, Jody
Dees, Benny
Driesell, Lefty
Evans, Paul
Knight, Bobby
Laney, Yolanda
Pitino, Rick
Ramsay, Jack
Reed, Willis
Riley, Pat
Russell, Bill
Sanderson, Wimp
Smith, Steve
Summitt, Pat Head
Unseld, Wes
Valvano, Jim

Dynasty! [University of Tennessee program's production of women basketball coaches] P. L. Hudson. *Women's Sports Fitness* 9:26 My '87

The fourth estate gets its day in court [sportswriter acts as assistant coach of the Albany Patroons in the Continental Basketball Association] J. Capouya. il *Sport Mag* 78:98 Ap '87

Dismissal

Wrong chemistry brings end for coach Van Lier. por *Jet* 71:46 F 16 '87

Basketball fans

Magic offers his fans membership in a family [M. Johnson] por *Jet* 72:51 Ap 6 '87

Basketball Hall of Fame *See* Naismith Memorial Basketball Hall of Fame

Basketball players

See also

Abdul-Jabbar, Kareem, 1947-
Alford, Steve
Bannister, Alan
Barkley, Charles
Bias, Len, 1963-1986
Bird, Larry
Bogues, Muggsy
Bol, Manute
Chamberlain, Wilt, 1936-
Chambers, Tom
Chapman, Rex
Chievous, Derrick
Cochran, David
Cooper, Michael
Cousy, Bob, 1928-
Dantley, Adrian
Davis, Walter
Dawkins, Darryl
Dembo, Fennis
Drew, John, 1954-
Eaton, Mark
Ellis, Dale
English, Alex
Erving, Julius
Frazier, Walt, 1945-
Free, World B.
Gillom, Jennifer
Grant, Harvey
Grant, Horace
Grayer, Jeff
Haskins, Clemette
Hawkins, Hersey
High, Johnny, d. 1987
Hopson, Dennis

Horford, Tito
Houston, Kevin
Jackson, Hernell, d. 1987
Johnson, Earvin, 1959-
Johnson, Gus
Johnson, Marques, 1956-
Jordan, Michael
Kerr, Steve
Keys, Randolph
King, Bernard
Lemon, Meadowlark
Lichti, Todd
Lieberman, Nancy, 1958-
Lloyd, Lewis
Lorenzen, Lynne
Lucas, John
Malone, Moses
Mann, Terri
McAdoo, Bob, 1951-
McFadden, Kenny
McMillen, Tom, 1952-
Mills, Terry
National Basketball Players Association
Owens, Carlton
Parish, Robert, 1953-
Person, Chuck
Pippen, Scott
Reed, Willis
Reid, J. R.
Richardson, Micheal Ray
Robinson, David
Robinson, Rumeal
Russell, Bill
Sampson, Ralph
Sanders, Tom
Scallion, Mark
Schintzius, Dwayne
Smart, Keith
Smith, Michael
Sparrow, Rory
Stevens, Trisha
Strikes—Basketball players
Thomas, Isiah
Unseld, Wes
Vandeweghe, Kiki
Walker, Chet
Washburn, Chris
Washington, Kermit
Webb, Spud
White, Jackie
Wicks, Sue
Wiggins, Mitchell
Williams, Reggie
Woodard, Lynette

Clash of the titans [shotblockers in the pros] R. Goldberg. il *Sport Mag* 78:56-8+ Ja '87

The NBA's unsung heroes [All-underrated team] J. McCallum. il *Sports Illus* 66:42-4+ Mr 9 '87

One for the books [student-athletes of the University Athletic Association conference] A. Murphy. il *Sports Illus* 67 Sp Issue:96-9 N 18 '87

Accidents and injuries

See Basketball, Professional—Accidents and injuries

Awards

See Basketball, Professional—Awards

Salaries, pensions, etc.

5 blacks are highest earners in basketball. il *Jet* 73:48 N 30 '87

The free-agency fandango. il *Sports Illus* 67:15 O 12 '87

NBA players sue league over draft, salary cap. *Jet* 73:49 O 19 '87

Sampson soon to settle lifelong Rockets' pact [R. Sampson] por *Jet* 72:50 Je 1 '87

Study says black cagers are paid less than whites. *Jet* 72:51 Je 22 '87

Training

Let's get physical [NBA premium on size and physicality] B. Newman. il *Sports Illus* 67:46-54+ N 9 '87

Baskets

Breakfast baskets. il *Sunset* 178:110-11 Ap '87

Exhibitions

John McQueen/Bellas artes. E. Lebow. il *Am Craft* 47:88-9 O/N '87

Baskin, Cathryn

Reviewer's notebook. See issues of Byte beginning March 1987 through October 1987

Basque Nation and Liberty See ETA (Organization)
Basques
See also
ETA (Organization)
Basques in the Age of Exploration. C. S. Campbell.
il map *Focus* 36:24-9 Wint '86
Basra (Iraq)
Life among the smoldering ruins. D. Fischer. il map
Time 129:47 Mr 30 '87
Bass, George Fletcher, 1932-
Oldest known shipwreck reveals splendors of the Bronze
Age [cover story] il map *Natl Geogr* 172:692-733 D
'87
Bass, Herbert
about
What do Live from the Met and Family ties have
in common? il pors *Bus Week* p71 Ag 31 '87
Bass, Judy
In defense of book critics. por *Publ Wkly* 231:48 My
8 '87
Bass, Randy, 1954-
about
The hottest American import in Japan. C. Neff. il pors
Sports Illus 66:72-6+ Mr 23 '87
Bass, Robert M.
about
Taft Broadcasting may become a Carl Lindner production.
D. Cook. il por *Bus Week* p37-8 Ap 27 '87
Bass, Ruth
Minimalism made human [cover story] il pors *Art News*
86:94-101 Mr '87
A new view of Kokoschka. il por *Art News* 86:106-11
F '87
Bass
See also
Cooking—Fish
Sexual behavior
See Sexual behavior—Fish
Bass Brothers Enterprises Inc.
The Bass brothers fish in new waters. J. Reed. il *U
S News World Rep* 102:48-9 F 9 '87
Bass culture *See* Fish culture
Bass fishing
Against the grain. J. Doggett. il *Field Stream* 91:62-3+
Mr '87
Are walleyes better than bass? J. Murray. il *Outdoor
Life* 179:60-1+ Ap '87
The art of finding bass cover. S. Price. il *Field Stream*
91:80-1+ Ap '87
Back to bugging bass. J. Dean. il *Outdoor Life* 179:87-9+
My '87
Bass at point-blank range. J. Doggett. il *Field Stream*
91:50-1+ F '87
Bass fishing the old way [B. Plummer's techniques] J.
Gibbs. il por *Outdoor Life* 180:74-5+ O '87
Bass in the brrrrrrrr. L. Stout. il *Outdoor Life* 180:88-9+
N '87
Bass in the clear. L. Larsen. il *Outdoor Life* 179:54-5+
F '87
Beat bass at their own game [suggestions from BASS
Masters Classic competitors] L. Cribb. il *Outdoor Life*
179:64-5+ Mr '87
Big event, small fish [1987 BASS Masters Classic] J.
Skorupa. il *Pop Mech* 164:25+ D '87
Blessed are the weak [use of floating/shallow-diving plug]
C. Hauptman. il *Field Stream* 92:56-7 S '87
Bring bass bugs, just in case [smallmouth bass in Maine]
P. Barrett. il *Field Stream* 92:107-8+ My '87
Cranking in the cold [crankbait for bass] L. Larsen.
il *Outdoor Life* 179:52-3+ Ja '87
Cross Creek. K. McCafferty. il *Field Stream* 91:60-1+
Mr '87
A fall bass dividend. P. Barrett. il *Field Stream* 92:73-4+
O '87
Fishing in the fast lanes [largemouth bass fishing] J.
Doggett. il *Field Stream* 92:60-1+ Je '87
Floating worms for finicky bass [largemouth] J. Arrington.
il *Outdoor Life* 180:52-3+ D '87
Getting the edge on bass. C. Hauptman. il *Field Stream*
92:88-90 My '87
Going with the gold [golden shiners as bait for largemouth
bass] J. Gibbs. il *Outdoor Life* 179:92-3+ My '87
The greatest smallmouth catcher of all [crayfish as bass
bait] J. Bashline. il *Field Stream* 92:52+ Ag '87
Home by dark-thirty [Ozark smallmouth bass] P.
Kaminsky. il *Field Stream* 91:58-9+ Ja '87
Landlubber largemouths [technique of J. Burkett] D.
Bartholomew. il por *Outdoor Life* 180:70-1+ Jl '87
A lesson from the great teacher. C. Hauptman. il *Field
Stream* 92:66-7 Jl '87

The minis: big medicine for bass [fishing jigs] J. Gibbs.
il *Outdoor Life* 179:24+ Ap '87
Nail 'em in neutral [neutrally buoyant crankbaits] J.
Murray. il *Outdoor Life* 180:62-3+ Ag '87
Nature's signposts to better bass fishing. L. Larsen. il
Outdoor Life 179:58-9+ Je '87
Nighttime smallmouths. M. Hicks. il por *Outdoor Life*
180:78-9+ Jl '87
The promised land [largemouth bass fishing in the
Everglades] P. Kaminsky. il *Field Stream* 92:62-3+
N '87
Quarry bass. M. McCray. il *Field Stream* 92:86-8 Ag
'87
Salad days [bass fishing through weedbeds] J. Doggett.
il *Field Stream* 92:42-3+ Ag '87
Salty snacks for sweet bass [saltwater lures] J. Gibbs.
il *Outdoor Life* 180:46+ O '87
Siren song of the slim minnow. J. Doggett. il *Field
Stream* 91:69+ Ap '87
Small-water bass. K. Schultz. il *Field Stream* 92:48+
Jl '87
Smallies in the swelter [small mouth bass fishing] K.
Etling. il *Outdoor Life* 179:60-1+ Je '87
Stripers on top. J. Gibbs. il *Outdoor Life* 179:78+ My
'87
Ten tips for better bass fishing. J. Doggett. *Field Stream*
92:100 My '87
Thin-water bass. B. W. Dalrymple. il *Field Stream*
91:60-1+ Ja '87
Think like a fish [reprint from July 1970 issue] T.
Trueblood. il *Field Stream* 91:37-8+ Ja '87
Trolling for bass. K. Schultz. il *Field Stream* 92:73+
My '87
Trouble-shooting problem bass [largemouth bass] D.
Oster. il *Outdoor Life* 179:51-3+ Ap '87
Weed-beating bass [largemouth bass fishing] L. Larsen.
il *Outdoor Life* 179:68-9+ Je '87
Why not try a dragonfly? C. Hauptman. il *Field Stream*
92:64-5+ Je '87

Competitions
See Fishing—Competitions
Bass tournaments *See* Fishing—Competitions
Bassano Dam (Alta.)
From desert to oasis. J. Howse. il *Macleans* 100:9-10
S 21 '87
Bassett, W. A., and Huang, E.
Mechanism of the body-centered cubic-hexagonal close-
packed phase transition in iron. bibl f il *Science*
238:780-3 N 6 '87
Basso, Alberto
The musical offering. il *Courier* 40:11-13 S '87
Bastogne, Battle of the, 1944-1945 *See* Ardennes, Battle
of the, 1944-1945
Bat Conservation International
Bat guano can make a man come face-to-face with his
values. J. Gorman. il *Discover* 8:32+ S '87
Bat houses
A place to hang your bat. J. F. King. il *Sierra* 72:16
Mr/Ap '87
Tuttle's bat house. W. Shipman. il *Ctry J* 14:64-5 My
'87
Batchan, Alexander
Mad Russian [interview with V. Dyomin] il por *Film
Comment* 23:48-51 My/Je '87
Batchler, Amelia
Amelia Batchler: for 51 years she's carried the torch
for Columbia. il por *People Wkly* 27:48-9 F 9 '87
Bateman, Justine
about
Let's get metaphysical. B. Goodwin. por *Roll Stone*
p34-5 Ja 29 '87
Warm-weather style on Justine Bateman: most attractive
of TV faces. il *Vogue* 177:260 My '87
Bateman, Richard La Trobe- *See* La Trobe-Bateman,
Richard
Bateman, Robert, 1930-
The spotted owl: a diptych. il *Audubon* 89:74-5 Mr
'87
about
Robert Bateman's incisive eye. C. Bond. il *Smithsonian*
17:136-7 Ja '87
Bateman, Tommie Faye
about
Black student 'outraged' after she is fired from white
pharmacy in Georgia. il por *Jet* 72:30 Ag 31 '87
Bates, Caroline
Limu: a Hawaiian delicacy. il *Gourmet* 47:72-3+ S '87
Spécialités de la maison. See issues of Gourmet

Bates, Daisy
about
Scholarships given in honor of Daisy Bates and her late husband. *Jet* 72:23 Ag 3 '87
School named for Daisy Bates in Little Rock. il por *Jet* 72:22 S 21 '87
Bates, Lincoln S.
Standoff at Oregon Inlet. il *Oceans* 20:5-6 Mr/Ap '87
Bates, Robert Latimer, 1912-
Salt of the earth. il *Earth Sci* 40:23-4 Wint '87
Bates (Ted) Worldwide, Inc. *See* Ted Bates Worldwide, Inc.
Bateson, Gregory, 1904-1980
about
Ghosts to believe in: recalling Bateson and Mead. M. C. Bateson. *N Y Times Book Rev* 92:49 N 15 '87
Bateson, Mary Catherine, 1939-
Ghosts to believe in: recalling Bateson and Mead. *N Y Times Book Rev* 92:49 N 15 '87
Batey, Brian
about
His fundamentalist mother and his father's gay lover square off over custody of young Brian Batey. M. Brower. il pors *People Wkly* 28:112-14 N 9 '87
Bath (England)
Chapels
Lady Huntingdon's chapel. T. Aldous. il por *Hist Today* 37:2-3 Ag '87
Bath products
Bathing botanicals [herbal cleaning] il *Health* 19:56-8+ N '87
Bath tubs *See* Bathtubs
Bathgate, Lawrence E., II
about
Raising bucks for Bush. R. Brownstein. il pors *N Y Times Mag* p42-4+ My 17 '87
Bathing *See* Baths
Bathing customs
Japan
Steamy Oriental splash. il *Health* 19:40-1 D '87
Bathing suits
See also
H₂O Swimwear Ltd.
16 super suits from every body. Z. Lovén and K. Repinski. il *McCalls* 114:24-7 My '87
Choosing the swimwear that suits your figure [men] T. Segal. il *Bus Week* p163 My 11 '87
In the swim. L. Lippincott. il *Women's Sports Fitness* 9:64 My '87
Instant swimsuit makeovers. il *Glamour* 85:186-93 Je '87
Look, Mao—no pajamas! [female body builders in China permitted to compete in bikinis] O. Schell. il *Women's Sports Fitness* 9:68+ Ag '87
My first sexy bathing suit. M. K. Blakely. il *Glamour* 85:176-7+ Jl '87
Ocean views. il *Teen* 31:108-9 My '87
Rubber rides the tide. il *Harpers Bazaar* 120:140-5 My '87
Suing over a transparent bikini, Cheri Ikerd made the judge see right through her argument. il por *People Wkly* 28:113 Ag 24 '87
Swimwear: new thinking, new answers. K. Beckett. *Vogue* 177:144+ My '87
Tropical oasis. E. W. Johnson. il *Ebony* 42:80-1+ Ja '87
What suit's you? il *Redbook* 169:114-17 My '87
Your body is showing. il *Mademoiselle* 93:26+ Je '87
Anecdotes, facetiae, satire, etc.
Mommie barest [mother-son relationship tested by search for sexy swimsuit] R. Rothenstein. il *50 Plus* 27:84+ Je '87
Care
Swimsuit savvy: care for your waterwear. il *Teen* 31:112 My '87
Photographs and photography
Bathing beauties on the beach & in the studio [cover story] J. Britt. il *Petersens Photogr Mag* 16:16-19+ Jl '87
Bathmann, Ulrich V.
(jt. auth) See Grant, Jonathan, and Bathmann, Ulrich V.
Bathrobes
The greatest of ease [men's robes and pajamas] il *N Y Times Mag* p42 Mr 15 '87
Bathroom cleaners *See* Cleaning compositions
Bathroom fixtures
See also
Plumbing
Toilet seats
Toilets

Towel racks, rings, etc.
Bathroom vanities (Furniture) *See* Vanities (Furniture)
Bathroom ventilators *See* Ventilators
Bathrooms
See also
Public comfort stations
5 foolproof fixes [common bathroom repairs] M. Henkenius. il *Pop Mech* 164:132-4+ Ap '87
All-wood bathroom. A. W. Lees. il *Pop Sci* 231:74-5 D '87
Enlarged . . . without adding an inch. il *Sunset* 179:111 O '87
Fanciful tile counter updates a 1950s bathroom. il *Sunset* 178:74 Ja '87
For a bright new bathroom, they pushed a wall out 5 feet. il *Sunset* 178:114 Je '87
Master suites: the hottest new remodeling trend: bedroom/bath retreats. G. G. Butler. il *Better Homes Gard* 65:64-71+ Ja '87
Mastering the bath. A. J. Hand. il *Pop Sci* 230:82-4+ Ja '87
Mirror surround and vanity wrap. N. Cooper. il *Home Mech* 83:50 D '87
Remodel small spaces. P. Pederson. il *Workbench* 43:8-9+ My/Je '87
Remodel with tile. B. Sanders. il *Workbench* 43:80-4 Mr/Ap '87
Shelf, storage, toilet . . . all in tight corner. il *Sunset* 178:152 Je '87
Small-bath remodeling. G. D. Cook. il *Better Homes Gard* 65:42-5 O '87
Smart bathroom makeover. S. Ross. il *Fam Handyman* 37:31-4 O '87
Stacked-on master bath. T. O. Bakke. il *Pop Sci* 231:89-91 O '87
Under the eaves, they found room for a big bath. il *Sunset* 179:144-5 O '87
Wide-open bathroom in the master suite. il *Sunset* 179:161 S '87
Baths
See also
Bathing customs
Sauna
Shower baths
Steam baths
Bubble, bubble—good-bye, trouble. J. Ramsey. il *Work Woman* 12:156 Ap '87
Splendor in the bath. C. Morris. il *Essence* 18:47+ My '87
Baths, Vapor *See* Steam baths
Baths, Whirlpool
See also
Hot tubs
Bathtubs
Make a splash in a high-tech bathtub. J. Hurlock. il *Bus Week* p168 Mr 23 '87
Bathurst, Ian C., and others
Yeast KEX2 protease has the properties of a human proalbumin converting enzyme. bibl f il *Science* 235:348-50 Ja 16 '87
Batis maritima *See* Saltwort
Batist, Gerald
about
Doctor with a mission. L. Van Dusen. il por *Macleans* 100:49-50 My 18 '87
Baton Rouge (La.)
Architecture
The memories are built in [Georgian Revival house] il *South Living* 22:78-80 S '87
Gardens and gardening
Part open, part woodland, all wonderful! B. McDougald. il *South Living* 22:64-5 Jl '87
A touch of Britain in Baton Rouge. il *South Living* 22:89+ My '87
Newspapers
See also
Baton Rouge advocate
Social life and customs
The unmaking of a southern belle. R. F. Dew. il pors *Ms* 16:92+ O '87
Baton Rouge advocate
Swaggart column nixed [charges of plagiarism] *Christ Century* 104:552 Je 17-24 '87
Batra, Raveendra N.
about
From boom to doom? por *Time* 130:38 Ag 24 '87
If Dr. Ravi Batra's theories hold water, man the lifeboats for the great depression of 1990. E. Levin. il pors *People Wkly* 28:59-60+ O 12 '87
Ravi Batra's phony baloney. P. Brimelow. il por *Forbes* 140:100+ S 7 '87

Batra, Raveendra N.—about—cont.
There's no depression in Ravi Batra's royalties. J. Weber, Jr. il por *Bus Week* p128 N 30 '87
Writing to sell in the MTV era. A. Smith. il *Esquire* 108:87+ D '87
Batra, Ravi See Batra, Raveendra N.
Batra, Suzanne W. T.
Deceit and corruption in the blueberry patch. il *Nat Hist* 96:56-9 Ag '87
Bats
See also
Bat Conservation International
Bat houses
Applauding the beleaguered bat. J. P. Cohn. il *Américas* 39:14-17+ N/D '87
Batmom's daily nightmare [Mexican free-tailed bat maternity colonies] G. F. McCracken and M. K. Gustin. il map *Nat Hist* 96:66-73 O '87
Britain goes batty over bats. H. Gibson. il *Int Wildl* 17:42-4 N/D '87
In search of wintering bats [annual survey in New York State] A. Hicks. *Conservationist* 41:14-17+ Ja/F '87
Anecdotes, facetiae, satire, etc.
Bat guano can make a man come face-to-face with his values. J. Gorman. il *Discover* 8:32+ S '87
Brain
See Brain
Food and feeding
Bat predation and its influence on calling behavior in neotropical katydids. J. J. Belwood and G. Morris. bibl f il *Science* 238:64-7 O 2 '87
Driven batty, katydids change tune [influence of predator bats; research by J. J. Belwood and G. Morris] R. Weiss. *Sci News* 132:231 O 10 '87
Hearing
See Hearing—Animals
Bats, Baseball See Baseball bats
Battaglia, Carl
In quest of Rossini. il *Opera News* 52:30-1+ Ag '87
A joyful noise [with editorial comment by Jane L. Poole] il *Opera News* 51:4, 10-15 Ja 3 '87
Keepers of the flame. il pors *Opera News* 52:28-30+ N '87
Staged by Scotto [with editorial comment by Jane L. Poole] il pors *Opera News* 51:4, 10-13 Ja 17 '87
Battan, Louis J.
about
Obituary
Weatherwise por 40:100 Ap '87
Batteau, Robin
about
Despite their jingular success, Buskin and Batteau insist they'd rather be just folks. M. Neill. il pors *People Wkly* 28:109-10 D 21 '87
Battelle, Phyllis
Kate [cover story] il pors *Ladies Home J* 104:124-5+ O '87
On the road with Kenny Rogers. il por *Ladies Home J* 104:42+ Ja '87
Batten, David C.
about
Trying to patch up a family quarrel in banking. R. A. Melcher. il por *Bus Week* p66 F 2 '87
Batterberry, Ariane
Nostalgia food: the diner updated and fond memories of forties and fifties fare. il por *House Gard* 159:54+ Mr '87
Battered wives See Wife abuse
Batteries, Automobile See Storage batteries
Batteries, Electric See Electric batteries
Batteries, Storage See Storage batteries
Battery charging See Electric batteries—Charging; Storage batteries—Charging
Battery Park City (New York, N.Y.)
On the waterfront [N. Smyth's installation on the esplanade] N. Princenthal. il *Art Am* 75:210-11+ Ap '87
A vision with a message. C. Wiseman. il *Archit Rec* 175:112-21 Mr '87
Batterymarch Financial Management
Is Dean LeBaron worried? A little. A. Beam. il por *Bus Week* p128 My 25 '87
Batting (Baseball)
The anatomy of an at-bat [Houston pitcher M. Scott vs. Cincinnati batter D. Parker; cover story] D. Granger. il pors *Sport Mag* 78:26-9 Jl '87
Getting to first base [tips for softball players] R. Schuessler. il *Women's Sports Fitness* 9:58 Ap '87
The triple. J. Kaplan. il *Sport Mag* 78:52-5+ S '87

Battistini, Mattia, 1856-1928
about
Mattia Battistini: the king of baritones. S. M. Stroff. il pors *Antiques Collect Hobbies* 91:70-4 Ja '87
Twin glories (I). W. Crutchfield. il pors *Opera News* 52:10-13 D 19 '87
Battle, Kathleen
about
The enchanting Kathleen Battle. R. Freed. il *Stereo Rev* 52:88 Ap '87
Battle, Rudy
about
A few rounds with the third man in the ring. J. Millman. il *Sport Mag* 78:98 Jl '87
Battle, William
about
Be true to your school. C. Meherani and R. Orr. il pors *Nations Bus* 75:46+ Je '87
Battle of the sexes in literature See Women and men in literature
Battle of Waterloo See Waterloo, Battle of, 1815
Battlefields
See also
Gettysburg National Military Park (Pa.)
Saratoga National Historical Park (N.Y.)
Blue and Gray Virginia: commemorating battles of a nation divided. C. B. Hayes. il map *Travel Holiday* 167:52-5+ Je '87
Battles
See also
War
World War, 1939-1945—Campaigns and battles
Battleships See Warships
Batts, Sharon
about
Dear Mr. Jesus. il por *Time* 130:61 D 21 '87
Batzdorff, Susanne M.
A martyr of Auschwitz. por *N Y Times Mag* p52-5+ Ap 12 '87
Baudelaire, Charles, 1821-1867
Anecdotes, facetiae, satire, etc.
Flowers of evil: ask Charles Baudelaire. F. Gannon. il por *Atlantic* 260:44 S '87
Baudrillard, Jean, 1929-
Ads for ourselves; tr. by Barry Schwabsky. *Harpers* 275:32 O '87
'A perverse logic'. il *Courier* 40:7-9 Jl '87
about
Reluctant prophet. E. Heartney. por *Art News* 86:18 S '87
Bauer, Douglas
Broken heartland. il *Esquire* 107:68-77 Ja '87
Bauer, Gary L.
Nothing less will do. por *Saturday Evening Post* 259:14+ N '87
Teaching morality in the classroom. *Educ Dig* 52:2-5 Mr '87
What we must teach our children about freedom. il *Read Dig* 130:102-4 My '87
about
How the new right is undermining Howard Baker. R. Fly. il por *Bus Week* p43 S 21 '87
The mouse that roars. J. B. Judis. *New Repub* 197:23-5 Ag 3 '87
Who should take the test for HIV and why? [interview] L. Kravitz. il pors *Sch Update* 120:21 O 16 '87
Bauer, P. T. (Péter Tamás)
Accounts receivable. *New Repub* 196:10-12 Je 15 '87
Population scares. *Commentary* 84:39-42 N '87
Bauer, Péter Tamás See Bauer, P. T. (Péter Tamás)
Bauer, Patricia E.
Hollywood Inc. See issues of Channels (New York, N.Y.: 1986) beginning September 1986
Bauer, Robert S., and Margaritondo, Giorgio, 1946-
Probing semiconductor-semiconductor interfaces. bibl f il *Phys Today* 40:26-34 Ja '87
Bauer, Wolf
about
Wolf Bauer's mission. K. Brueckmann and D. Brueckmann. il pors *Oceans* 20:48-53 Mr/Ap '87
Bauer-Stuchly, Judy
The man he used to be [story] il *Redbook* 168:36+ F '87
Bauhaus
Perpetuating the Bauhaus ideal [M. Bill] M. Peppiatt. il por *Archit Dig* 44:48+ Ag '87
Bauhofer, Valerie
Prison parenting: a challenge for children's advocates. il *Child Today* 16:15-16 Ja/F '87

Baumann-Hudson, Edith
about
Edith Baumann-Hudson at Newspace. F. Colpitt. il *Art Am* 75:163 Je '87
Baumel, Judith
Ginestra [poem] *New Yorker* 63:26 Ag 10 '87
Baumgaertner, Jill P.
'The meaning is in you': Flannery O'Connor in her letters. *Christ Century* 104:1172-6 D 23-30 '87
Baumgardt, James
Astrophotography without a telescope. il *Astronomy* 15:46-51 Ja '87
Baumgardt, John P.
In our own back yard. See issues of Flower and Garden
Baumgold, Julie
Dancing on the lip of the volcano: Christian Lacroix's crash chic [cover story] il pors *N Y* 20:36-49 N 30 '87
Schrafft's. il *N Y* 20:72-3 D 21-28 '87
Baum's, Inc.
Baum's celebrates 100 years. L. M. Brooks. il *Dance Mag* 61:25 Je '87
Bausch, Richard, 1945-
The man who knew Belle Starr [story] il *Atlantic* 259:61-9 Ap '87
Police dreams [story] il *Atlantic* 259:54-60 My '87
Bausch & Lomb Inc.
Bausch & Lomb is correcting its vision of research. L. Therrien. il *Bus Week* p91 Mr 30 '87
A tale of mice and lens. C. Leinster. *Fortune* 116:126-7 S 28 '87
Bavadra, Timoci
about
Was the U.S. behind it? J. Wypijewski. il *Nation* 245:117-18+ Ag 15-22 '87
Bavaria (Germany)
See also
Medical policy—Bavaria (Germany)
Bavaro, Mark
about
Legend in the making [cover story] P. Zimmerman. il pors *Sports Illus* 67 Sp Issue:50-4+ S 9 '87
Bavasi, Peter
about
A whole new ballgame. E. F. Cone. il por *Forbes* 139:162 My 4 '87
Bavendam, Fred
The anomalous Galápagos [cover story] il *Oceans* 20:26-35 N/D '87
Baxter, Diane
Chlordane's health threat. *Rodale's Org Gard* 34:83+ D '87
Baxter, Gordon
about
Cock-a-leekie. R. Morais. il por *Forbes* 140:68+ S 7 '87
Baxter, Gordon, 1923-
Bax seat. See issues of Flying
[Column] See alternate issues of Car and Driver
Baxter, Meredith *See* Birney, Meredith Baxter
Baxter Travenol Laboratories Inc.
A booster shot for Baxter Labs [acquisition of Caremark Inc.] K. Deveny. il *Bus Week* p63 My 25 '87
Baxters of Speyside Ltd.
Cock-a-leekie. R. Morais. il por *Forbes* 140:68+ S 7 '87
Bay Area (Calif.) *See* San Francisco Bay region (Calif.)
Bay Area Discovery Museum
Discovering the Bay in Marin. il *Sunset* 179:17 D '87
Bay Island Hotel (Port Blair, India) *See* Port Blair (India)—Hotels, motels, etc.
Bay of Fundy
Modeling tidal power [tidal power dam in the Bay of Fundy would raise tide levels in the Gulf of Maine] D. A. Greenberg. il maps *Sci Am* 257:128-128C+ N '87
Bay of Fundy dam *See* Dams—Canada
Bay of Pigs invasion *See* Cuba—History—Invasion, 1961
Bay windows *See* Windows
Bayer, Ann
Shhh . . . my romance with libraries. il *Seventeen* 46:48+ F '87
Bayer, Cary
Play book! il *Publ Wkly* 231:28 My 1 '87
Bayer, Walter
John Paul: the view from home; ed. by Linda Marx. il pors *People Wkly* 28:118-20 S 14 '87
Bayer AG
The breadth of a salesman [H.-J. Strenger] L. S. Richman. il por *Fortune* 116:50 Ag 3 '87

Bayerische Motoren Werke AG
BMW's head-on challenge to Mercedes for prestige. il *Fortune* 115:78 Ap 27 '87
The M doctrine [Motorsport Division] D. Sherman. il *Car Driv* 33:40 Jl '87
Saying hello to BMW-san [BMW's success in exporting cars to Japan] B. Hillenbrand. il *Time* 129:56-7 My 25 '87
Why BMW could burn rubber. G. G. Marcial. *Bus Week* p122 D 14 '87
Bayfront Center (Saint Petersburg, Fla.)
Bayfront Center. M. Loeffler. il *Theatre Crafts* 21:50-1+ D '87
Bayless, Skip
Backstage at Wimbledon. il *Sport Mag* 78:33-6+ Jl '87
SMU. il *Sport Mag* 78:98 D '87
Bayley, John, 1925-
Poet of the air. il *N Y Rev Books* 34:20+ O 8 '87
Riding the bronze horse. il *N Y Rev Books* 34:9-10 O 22 '87
Baylis, Thomas A.
East Germany's economic model. bibl f *Curr Hist* 86:377-81+ N '87
Baylor, Denis A.
(jt. auth) See Schnapf, Julie L., and Baylor, Denis A.
Baylor, Don, 1949-
about
For Don Baylor, baseball is a hit or be hit proposition. J. Friedman. il por *People Wkly* 28:89-90 Ag 24 '87
Bayly, Joanne
The mother lobby. il *Ms* 16:75 D '87
Bayonets
Enter the 'smart' bayonet [M-9] T. H. Cole. il *Pop Mech* 164:92 Ap '87
The new bayonet stabs, slices and even dices, thanks to Mickey Finn [M-9 Multi-Purpose Bayonet] il por *People Wkly* 27:79 Ja 5 '87
Bayou Steel (Firm)
How's Bayou? R. Greene. *Forbes* 140:160 N 16 '87
Bayous
Louisiana's bayou blues. F. Gibney. il map *Newsweek* 109:54-5 Je 22 '87
Bays, Karl
about
Why IC is uncoupling itself from the past. K. Deveny. il por *Bus Week* p120+ O 12 '87
Bays and gulfs
See also
Chesapeake Bay (Md. and Va.)
Delaware Bay (Del. and N.J.)
Fjords
Monterey Bay (Calif.)
Padilla Bay (Wash.)
Puerto Mosquito (Vieques Island, Puerto Rico)
Salt River Bay (Virgin Islands of the U.S.)
Shark Bay (Australia)
Baysa, Fred O.
Rapture: a dream of dying [poem] *Nation* 244:545 Ap 25 '87
Bazell, Robert
Bees did it. *New Repub* 196:9-10 F 2 '87
Catching up to AIDS. *New Repub* 196:12-13 F 23 '87
Dying for drugs. *New Repub* 197:17-19 N 9 '87
Gene of the week. *New Repub* 196:13-14 Mr 23 '87
Hole in the head. *New Repub* 197:13-14 Ag 10-17 '87
The plague. *New Repub* 196:14-15 Je 1 '87
Quark barrel politics. *New Repub* 196:9-10 Je 22 '87
Sins and twins. *New Repub* 197:17-18 D 21 '87
Space scuttle. *New Repub* 197:11-12 O 12 '87
Yuppie plague. *New Repub* 196:13-14 Ap 27 '87
Bazin, Jean
about
A new senator's troubled debut. M. Gee. il por *Macleans* 100:14 F 16 '87
Bazzaz, Fakhri A., and others
Allocating resources to reproduction and defense. bibl f il *BioScience* 37:58-67 Ja '87
BBC
BBC says, 'No, prime minister'. R. Laver. il *Macleans* 100:45 F 16 '87
The blowup over the BBC. *Newsweek* 109:43 F 16 '87
British television's Catholic pioneer [mime H. Pepler] M. E. Evans. il *America* 157:501-3 D 26 '87
New statesman downed by law [government harassment] C. Hitchens. il *Nation* 244:217-19 F 21 '87
BBC Brown, Boveri & Company, Ltd.
See also
ASEA Brown Boveri (Firm)

BCG vaccine *See* Tuberculosis—Vaccines and vaccination
BCI Holdings Corporation
Getting top dollar for Beatrice's leftovers. L. Therrien. il por *Bus Week* p50-1 Jl 6 '87
Me too, me too [Drexel Burnham Lambert's killing in the leveraged buyout and breakup of the old Beatrice Cos.] L. Jereski. *Forbes* 140:38 S 21 '87
BCI International Food Company
Buying into the big time [R. Lewis's TLC Group purchase BCI International Food Company] J. M. Horowitz. il por *Time* 130:42 Ag 24 '87
Reg Lewis hits the big time—and takes it in stride [acquisition] P. Finch. il por *Bus Week* p27+ Ag 24 '87
Reginald Lewis cuts the big deal [cover story; with editorial comment by Earl G. Graves] A. Edmond, Jr. il pors *Black Enterp* 18:9, 42-6 N '87
TLC deal signals new era for black business [acquisition of Beatrice International] K. D. Thompson. por *Black Enterp* 18:21-2 O '87
Beach, Barbara Kres
Invading the heart of the problem [interview with N. Freedlander Gibans] bibl f *Des Arts Educ* 88:45-8 N/D '86
Beach architecture
Architectural digest visits: Dinah Shore [Malibu beach house decorated by Val Arnold] B. D. Colen. il por *Archit Dig* 44:158-63+ D '87
Architectural digest visits: King Hussein and Queen Noor of Jordan [beach house on Gulf of Aqaba] G. Y. Dryansky. il pors *Archit Dig* 44:68-77+ Ja '87
Architectural vigor of the summer enclave [the Hamptons] P. Goldberger. il *Archit Dig* 44:74+ Je '87
Architecture: John C. Portman, Jr. [beach house on Sea Island, Ga.; cover story] P. Goldberger. il por *Archit Dig* 44:98-111 D '87
Architecture: Richard Meier [Malibu home of Norman and Lisette Ackerberg; cover story] R. Hughes. il *Archit Dig* 44:152-9+ O '87
Brillig on the wave: island aerie of Nancy and Henry Luce III [summer house off Connecticut shore] C. T. Buckley. il pors *Archit Dig* 44:180-3+ My '87
Caribbean folly: Lord Glenconner's villa on Mustique. Suzy. il *Archit Dig* 44:132-9 S '87
A coastal contradiction in terms [Del Mar, Calif. beach house designed for Bill and Lila Jaeger by R. W. Quigley] P. M. Sachner. il *Archit Rec* 175:146-9 Je '87
Cottage by the sea: Maria Tallchief and Henry D. Paschen on Martha's Vineyard [home decorated by Bruce Gregga] J. Allen. il *Archit Dig* 44:170-5+ O '87
Cushmans: a house built to overlook the ocean [Hat Island, Wash.] P. S. Gelfman. il *Fam Handyman* 37:45 Ja '87
In the dunes [K. Cornell's summer home in Martha's Vineyard] C. Vogel. il *N Y Times Mag* p70-4 My 31 '87
Jamaican cadence: Rose Marie Bogley's cottage above Montego Bay. J. S. Wamsley. il *Archit Dig* 44:202-7 My '87
Life at Heron Bay: Palladian pavilion on the island of Barbados [cover story] M. Tree. il *Archit Dig* 44:54-9+ Ag '87
Lighthearted at the beach [Fripp Island house; cover story] L. Hallam. il *South Living* 22:70-2 Ag '87
The past lives at the bay [home overlooking Galveston Bay] il *South Living* 22:114-15 Je '87
Sea-struck living [Malibu home] B. Moore. il por *House Gard* 159:78+ S '87
Tree house retreat: a designer's Fire Island aerie [M. Dwork's house] P. Carlsen. il *Archit Dig* 44:60-5 Ag '87
Beach Boys (Musical group)
Brian Wilson [interview] S. Pond. il por *Roll Stone* p174-6 N 5-D 10 '87
Beach erosion *See* Coast changes
Beach towels *See* Towels
Beacham, Stephanie
about
Spoofing it: the TV rich are very different from the real rich. L. Robinson. por *Vogue* 177:207 Ja '87
Beaches
See also
Bathing customs
At the beach [toddlers] J. T. Gibson. il *Parents* 62:156 Je '87
Our troubled coasts [cover story; special issue; with editorial comment by Michael W. Robbins] il *Oceans* 20:2, 8-53+ Mr/Ap '87

Anecdotes, facetiae, satire, etc.
How to be a totally awesome beach babe. B. Stepko. il *Seventeen* 46:59 Jl '87
International aspects
A perfect 10: the world's best beaches. G. Kingdom. il *Travel Holiday* 167:40-5+ F '87
Photographs and photography
See Marine photography
Sanitation
Our befouled beaches. J. Adler. il *Newsweek* 110:50-1 Jl 27 '87
California
The September-glorious Mendocino-Sonoma coast. il map *Sunset* 179:60-5 S '87
Cape Cod (Mass.)
The case of Cape Cod [beach erosion] B. Sargent. *Oceans* 20:47 Mr/Ap '87
Swept away at Chatham [breach in sand barrier at Nauset Beach] D. Thompson. il *Time* 130:43 Ag 10 '87
Florida
On the sugar sands of Florida's panhandle [cover story] D. Young. il map *South Living* 22:54-61 Jl '87
Hawaii
Oahu's other beaches. il map *Sunset* 178:72-7 Mr '87
Long Island (N.Y.)
On the beach [erosion in Westhampton] S. Weinstein. il *N Y* 20:21 Jl 20 '87
Maui (Hawaii)
Maui's southwest coast: 10 miles of mostly hidden beaches. il map *Sunset* 178:67+ Je '87
New York (State)
See also
Coney Island (New York, N.Y.)
Pacific Northwest
Wolf Bauer's mission. K. Brueckmann and D. Brueckmann. il pors *Oceans* 20:48-53 Mr/Ap '87
Rhode Island
On the beach: plovers vs. nudists. il *Newsweek* 110:63 Ag 3 '87
Texas
What's up when the surf's up [Galveston] C. Barrington. *Travel Holiday* 168:59 D '87
Beacons
See also
Lighthouses
Lightships
Radio beacons
Beadle, J. Grant, 1932-
about
A stitch in time. J. Parr. il por *Forbes* 140:172+ N 16 '87
Beagle, Peter S.
Authors in search of a universe. il *Omni* 10:40+ N '87
Beagles (Dogs)
A clinically doggone beagle, medical miracle Miles is a former chilly dog back from the beyond [work of P. Segall] il *People Wkly* 27:85 Ap 20 '87
Today a frozen dog, tomorrow the iceman [beagle named Miles brought back from the dead; work of Hal Sternberg] il *Discover* 8:9 Je '87
Beahm, George
Graphic novels: comics, magazines, or books? por *Publ Wkly* 232:22 N 6 '87
Beaks (Birds) *See* Bills (Birds)
Beal, Doone
Gourmet holidays. il map *Gourmet* 47:42-7+ Ja '87
Gourmet holidays. il maps *Gourmet* 47:46-51+ Mr '87
Gourmet holidays: France's Atlantic islands. il map *Gourmet* 47:50-5+ Ag '87
Beale, Thomas Jefferson
about
Ciphernauts. P. Hoffman. il *Omni* 9:26+ My '87
Beale Street (Memphis, Tenn.)
The blues are over for Beale Street. il *South Living* 22:30-1 N '87
The words of Beale Street. il *South Living* 22:28 D '87
Beall, Pamela Conn
about
Take a gander at Mother Goose's newest champions, Pam Beall and Susan Nipp of Wee Sing. A. Chambers. il pors *People Wkly* 28:66+ S 14 '87
Beals, Vaughn
about
Harley back in gear. J. A. Conway. il *Forbes* 139:8 Ap 20 '87
Beam (James B.) Distilling Co. *See* James B. Beam Distilling Co.

Beamish, Richard
The Adirondack Park—a 2020 vision. il map *Conservationist* 42:22-5 Jl/Ag '87
Beamon, Bob
about
Giants on the earth. K. Moore. il pors *Sports Illus* 66:48-50+ Je 29 '87
Beams, Atomic *See* Atomic beams
Beams, Electron *See* Electron beams
Beams, Molecular *See* Molecular beams
Beams Award *See* Physics—Awards
Bean, Karen E.
'If Americans knew . . .'. il *Progressive* 51:24 Ag '87
Bean, Kevin
South African disinvestment: social responsibility for the long haul. il por *Humanist* 47:28-9+ S/O '87
Bean (L. L.), Inc. *See* L. L. Bean, Inc.
Bean salads *See* Salads
Bean soups *See* Soups
Beanbag weapons *See* Weapons
Beans
See also
Cooking—Vegetables
Soybeans
Beneficial beans? [fava bean consumption in the Mediterranean region] *Courier* 40:13 My '87
Better beans [protection from stressful temperature swings] D. Bilderback. il *Rodale's Org Gard* 34:25-9 Ag '87
A Eugene gardener may have designed the perfect bean trellis. il *Sunset* 178:240+ Ap '87
Oriental beans [mung and adzuki beans] J. H. Sanchez. il *Rodale's Org Gard* 34:54+ Ja '87
Diseases and pests
Fungi feel their way to feast [bean rust fungi; research by Harvey C. Hoch and others] S. Weisburd. il *Sci News* 131:214 Ap 4 '87
Signaling for growth orientation and cell differentiation by surface topography in Uromyces. H. C. Hoch and others. bibl f il *Science* 235:1659-62 Mr 27 '87
Bear, Greg, 1951-
The visitation [fiction] il *Omni* 9:54-6 Je '87
Bear, John, 1938-
(jt. auth) *See* Bear, Marina, and Bear, John, 1938-
Bear, Marina, and Bear, John, 1938-
Food first-aid [excerpt from How to repair food] il *Ladies Home J* 104:82+ Jl '87
Bear, Mark F., and others
A physiological basis for a theory of synapse modification. bibl f il *Science* 237:42-8 Jl 3 '87
Bear baits and repellents
A defensive solution [grizzly repellent] G. Turbak. il *Field Stream* 92:59+ Je '87
Bear hunting
Bear facts [black bear; cover story] B. Bell. il *Field Stream* 92:53+ O '87
Black bears across America [cover story] T. Huggler. il map *Outdoor Life* 180:53-5+ Ag '87
Dangerous game, dangerous country [Kodiak brown bear; cover story] T. Dawson. il *Field Stream* 92:39-41+ Ag '87
Hound music and a very big bear [record black bear in Arizona] F. Peters. il *Outdoor Life* 179:94-5+ My '87
Bear, Stearns & Co. Inc.
The $4.50 window [introduces currency exchange warrants] E. A. Finn, Jr. il *Forbes* 140:345-6 Jl 13 '87
Ace may be the Street's top card [A. C. Greenberg] B. Hetzer. il por *Fortune* 115:94 Ja 5 '87
Bear Stearns: hitting its stride while others trip [computerized mortgage securities trading] D. Zigas. il por *Bus Week* p59-60 Ag 31 '87
Jardine's giant step from Hong Kong to Wall Street [stake in Bear Stearns] D. J. Yang and others. il por *Bus Week* p39-40 O 12 '87
"Just a simple customers' man from Oklahoma" [chairman A. Greenberg] D. Machan. il por *Forbes* 140:118+ S 7 '87
Beard, Geoffrey W.
Robert Adam's "artificers". bibl f il *Antiques* 131:1292-303 Je '87
Bearden, Joyce Alvin, 1903-1986
about
Obituary
Phys Today 40:88-90 Mr '87. R. D. Deslattes
Bearden, Romare, 1914-1988
about
Fitzgerald, Bearden get president's Medal of Arts. il por *Jet* 72:52 Jl 6 '87
Romare Bearden at Cordier & Ekstrom. N. Princenthal. il *Art Am* 75:149 F '87

Beards
The battle for Beirut: a close shave [Syria's war on beards] C. Dickey and S. Issa. il *Newsweek* 109:47 Mr 16 '87
The macho man behind the beard [self perception; study by Douglas Wood] V. Bozzi. il *Psychol Today* 21:20 My '87
My beard and I. W. P. Hogue. il *Glamour* 85:230 Je '87
Beardtongues *See* Penstemons
Bearings (Machinery)
Friction-free magnetic bearings. D. Scott and J. Free. il *Pop Sci* 230:70-1 Mr '87
Béarnaise sauce *See* Sauces
Bears
See also
Pandas
Polar bears
A bear in camp [Alaskan brown bear]; ed. by Larry Mueller. B. Herron. il *Outdoor Life* 180:80-1+ N '87
A bear of America [Pocono Mountain black bears; work of G. Alt] C. Fergus. il *Ctry J* 14:43-7+ O '87
"The beast that walks on sacred paws" [Yellowstone grizzlies] B. Pettinga. il *Wilderness* 51:29 Wint '87
Don't bugle up a grizzly bear [bowhunting bugling bull elk] B. McRae. il *Outdoor Life* 179:54-5+ Ap '87
Get back to your manzanita berries! [new black bear policies at Yosemite, Kings Canyon, and Sequoia national parks] il *Sunset* 179:42 Ag '87
The grizzly attacked! [attack on Montana warden Louis Kis] R. P. Smith. il *Outdoor Life* 180:82-4 O '87
How to be safe in bear country [survival course taught by B. Brown] M. Reiss. il *Outdoor Life* 179:50-1+ Ja '87
Last stronghold of the grizzly [Alaska] J. W. Schoen and others. il map *Nat Hist* 96:50-61 Ja '87
The photographer who got too close [W. J. Tesinsky killed by grizzly bear in Yellowstone National Park] J. G. Mitchell. il *Audubon* 89:28+ Mr '87
A "turrible" animal [grizzlies in the Old West] J. Merritt. il *Field Stream* 91:52-3+ F '87
Anecdotes, facetiae, satire, etc.
The night the bear ate goombaw. P. F. McManus. il *Outdoor Life* 180:110+ D '87
Photographs and photography
The last picture by a man who loved bears [photographer C. Gibbs killed by grizzly in Glacier National Park] il por *Audubon* 89:16-17 Jl '87
Training
Making bad bears into good bears could spare bears [retraining bad bears; work of C. Jonkel] G. Laycock. il *Audubon* 89:22-4+ Mr '87
Bears, Fossil
Bad news bear [prehistoric syphilis] il *Discover* 8:8 D '87
Prehistoric syphilis [found in bear bones] *Sci News* 132:205 S 26 '87
Who spread syphilis? [Indiana bear fossil found to have had disease] *Newsweek* 110:73 S 21 '87
Bears, Toy *See* Teddy bears
Bears (Musical group)
East meets Midwest. M. McCormick. il por *Roll Stone* p22-3 Je 4 '87
Béart, Emmanuelle
about
French kiss. E. White. por *Vogue* 177:76 N '87
New star style! il pors *Harpers Bazaar* 121:178-97 N '87
Beasley, Allyce
about
"Ms. Dipesto, you look fabulous!" [interview] K. Henderson. il pors *Redbook* 168:18+ Mr '87
Beasley, Mitch
about
Chicago model gets role in hit movie 'Big shots' after gracing cover of Ebony. il pors *Jet* 73:60 N 9 '87
Beasley, William Howard, III
about
Lone Star's Howard Beasley likes trouble—but not this much trouble. T. Mason. il por *Bus Week* p54+ F 2 '87
Beastie Boys (Musical group)
The Beastie Boys: getting a bum rap? M. L. Baer. il *Teen* 31:54 Jl '87
The Beastie Boys—rap's Three Stooges—fight for the right to be rude. L. Russell. il *People Wkly* 27:92-3 F 9 '87
Hymning the joys of girls, gunplay and getting high. J. Miller. il *Newsweek* 109:70-1 F 2 '87
The kings of rap, together. B. Barol. il *Newsweek* 109:71 Je 29 '87

Beastie Boys (Musical group)—*cont.*
Rude boys. D. Handelman. il *Roll Stone* p15-16+ Ap 23 '87
Young, loud and snotty. A. DeCurtis. il *Roll Stone* p18 F 12 '87

Beat generation *See* Beatniks

Beatification
Blessed Edith Stein. *America* 156:354-5 My 2 '87
Edith Stein's early years. J. W. Donohue. *America* 156:7-9+ Ja 3-10 '87
A martyr of Auschwitz [E. Stein] S. M. Batzdorff. por *N Y Times Mag* p52-5+ Ap 12 '87
Saintly passions [Jews protest beatification of E. Stein, also known as Teresa Benedicta of the Cross] D. Brand. por *Time* 129:82-3 My 4 '87

Beatles
Beatles buy-out [Beatles song Revolution used in Nike TV ad] J. Wiener. *New Repub* 196:13-14 My 11 '87
Beatles CDs generate strong sales. D. Wild. il *Roll Stone* p13+ Ap 9 '87
The Beatles on compact disc. S. Simels. il *Stereo Rev* 52:122 Je '87
Beatles sue over Nike commercial. A. DeCurtis. *Roll Stone* p15 S 10 '87
The Beatles: the roof of Apple Records, London, January 30th, 1969. D. Fricke. il *Roll Stone* p58-60+ Je 4 '87
Capitol to release Beatles CD's. D. Fricke. *Roll Stone* p25+ F 26 '87
Controversy surrounds Beatles CDs. M. Walker and D. Handelman. *Roll Stone* p25+ Ap 23 '87
A cruel cut for Sergeant Pepper [losing copyright in Japan] N. Gross. il *Bus Week* p62 Je 22 '87
The digital Fab Four [Beatles CD's] S. Pond. il *Roll Stone* p129+ Jl 16-30 '87
George Harrison [interview] A. DeCurtis. por *Roll Stone* p47-8+ N 5-D 10 '87
Glimpse the truth [Help!; Rubber soul; Revolver; Sgt. Pepper's Lonely Hearts Club Band] il *High Fidel* 37:94-9+ N '87
Goals of 'Sgt. Pepper' yet to materialize: McCartney. por *Jet* 72:59 Je 22 '87
Here come the CD Beatles. il *U S News World Rep* 102:42 F 23 '87
It was twenty years ago today . . . [making of Sgt. Pepper] K. Loder. il *Roll Stone* p51-2+ Je 18 '87
Lost Beatles script to emerge [musical based on unfinished screenplay by J. Orton to be composed by T. Rundgren] M. Jenkins. *Roll Stone* p14 Mr 12 '87
Mop-top pop. G. Santoro. *Down Beat* 54:44-5 S '87
One, two, three, four! [CD and video] il *High Fidel* 37:70-2+ Je '87
Paul McCartney [interview] A. DeCurtis. por *Roll Stone* p39-40+ N 5-D 10 '87
Rock's most influential album? [reaction to Sgt. Pepper] M. Goldberg. *Roll Stone* p57+ Je 18 '87
Running on recall [song Revolution used in Nike commercial] A. White. il *Film Comment* 23:72+ Jl/Ag '87
The Sarge at 20 [photographing cover of Sgt. Pepper album twenty years ago] il *People Wkly* 27:159-61 Je 8 '87
'Sgt. Pepper' TV show planned. *Roll Stone* p11 Mr 12 '87
Wanna buy a Revolution? [Beatles song in Nike commercial] J. Cocks. il *Time* 129:78 My 18 '87
When stereo isn't stereo [releasing early non-stereo Beatles albums on stereo compact discs] M. Riggs. il *High Fidel* 37:5 D '87

Beatniks
Beatniks and Bolsheviks; tr. by Bess Powell. V. P. Aksenov. *New Repub* 197:28-30+ N 30 '87

Beaton, Sir Cecil, 1904-1980
Bibliography
The chic lens. D. Bourdon. il *Art Am* 75:15-17+ Ja '87

Beatrice Companies Inc.
Getting top dollar for Beatrice's leftovers. L. Therrien. il por *Bus Week* p50-1 Jl 6 '87
How Beatrice lost at its own game [football prize contest] L. Baum. il *Bus Week* p66 Mr 2 '87
Me too, me too [Drexel Burnham Lambert's killing in the leveraged buyout and breakup of the old Beatrice Cos.] L. Jereski. *Forbes* 140:38 S 21 '87

Beatrice Foods Co.
See also
Beatrice Companies Inc.

Beatrix, Queen of the Netherlands, 1938-
about
The house of Orange-Nassau's modest queen. P. Dragadze. il pors *Forbes* 140 Sp Issue:66-7 O 26 '87

Shrewd managers of regal riches. T. Paré. il pors *Fortune* 116:134-5 O 12 '87

Beattie, Ann
Horatio's trick [story] *New Yorker* 63:42-50 D 28 '87
Imagine a day at the end of your life [story] il *Harpers* 275:70-2 D '87
about
Psyching out Katz. G. Henry. il pors *Art News* 86:23 Summ '87

Beatty, Jack
In harm's way [cover story] il map *Atlantic* 259:37-46+ My '87

Beatty, Perrin
about
About-face in defence strategy. P. C. Newman. il por *Macleans* 100:28 Ja 12 '87
A defence plan for Canada. H. Mackenzie and M. Clark. il por *Macleans* 100:18+ Je 15 '87

Beatty, Warren, 1937-
about
Dustin on Warren [cover story] S. Allison. il pors *Life* 10:62-5+ My '87
On the road to Ishtar [cover story] B. Darrach. il pors *People Wkly* 27:102-4+ My 25 '87
The road to 'Ishtar'. D. Blum. il pors *N Y* 20:34-43 Mr 16 '87

Beaujolais (Wine) *See* Wine

Beauman, Sally
about
Hot scenes and a cool million make Sally Beauman's first novel a diamond in the buff. S. Healy. il pors *People Wkly* 27:63-4 Ap 27 '87

Beaumarchais, Pierre Augustin Caron de, 1732-1799
about
The marriage of Figaro [drama] Reviews
Opera News il 51:28+ Ja 31 '87. G. R. Marek

Beaumont, Michael, Seigneur of Sark
about
The Lord of Sark may not have serfs, but his pigeon rights are heir-tight. J. Cooper. il pors *People Wkly* 28:89-91 Jl 27 '87

Beauregard-Keyes House (New Orleans, La.) *See* New Orleans (La.)—Historic houses, sites, etc.

Beauticians
See also
Hairstylists

Beautiful city [drama] See Walker, George F.

Beauty *See* Aesthetics

Beauty, Personal
See also
Baths
Beauty shops
Body image
Cosmetics
Exercise
Hair
Hairstyling
Hand—Care
Leg—Care
Lips
Makeup
Manicuring
Powder (Face, toilet, etc.)
Skin—Care and hygiene
8 great high-school-reunion makeovers. il *McCalls* 114:27-30 Je '87
9 to 5 glamor for the working woman [black women] il *Ebony* 42:32+ Jl '87
12 beauty highs for midwinter lows. il *Glamour* 85:210-15 F '87
16 matchless makeovers [eight sets of identical twins] il *Good Housekeep* 205:118-23+ Ag '87
25 tips for good health and great looks [condensed from How to become a healthier, prettier you] M. E. Pinkham. il *Read Dig* 130:112-14 Ja '87
All-American good looks [makeovers for finalists] il *Teen* 31:80-5 Jl '87
All-star black beauty. il *Harpers Bazaar* 120:104-7+ Jl '87
Altered egos [imaginary makeovers of celebrities] il *Seventeen* 46:116-21 Jl '87
America's 10 most beautiful women [cover story] il *Harpers Bazaar* 120:340-71+ S '87
America's 10 most beautiful women reveal their beauty secrets [special section] il *Harpers Bazaar* 120:30+ S '87
Are your looks up-to-date? [quiz] *Teen* 31:28 Ag '87
Basic black. il *Seventeen* 46:192-5 S '87
Be a snob! Uptown—the new beauty direction. il *Mademoiselle* 93:226-9 Ap '87

Beauty, Personal—*cont.*

Beauty & health report. S. Young. See issues of Glamour

Beauty at the beach: 20 terrific tips. il *McCalls* 114:25+ Je '87

Beauty Bazaar. il *Harpers Bazaar* 120:78+ S '87

Beauty Bazaar. il *Harpers Bazaar* 120:30+ O '87

Beauty bonanza. M. Clarke. il *McCalls* 114:22-5 Jl '87

Beauty boosts. M. Fox. il *Health* 19:38-40+ O '87

The beauty buddy system: a supermodel (Ashley) shares her secrets. il pors *Mademoiselle* 93:232-7 N '87

Beauty building: a three-dimensional approach. P. Boyer. *Prevention* 39:55-6 D '87

Beauty confidence: how to get it. il *Teen* 31:112 Ap '87

Beauty exposé: Teen models tell all. il *Teen* 31:70-2 Mr '87

Beauty first aid. L. J. Johnson. il *Ladies Home J* 104:154-9 N '87

Beauty, health and fitness! C. Morris. il *Essence* 18:64-5 Je '87

Beauty hotline: person to person. il *Harpers Bazaar* 120:82-7 Je '87

Beauty journal. See issues of Ladies' Home Journal

The beauty network. See issues of Prevention (Emmaus, Pa.) through March 1987

Beauty notebook. See issues of Good Housekeeping

Beauty Q & A. See issues of Mademoiselle

Beauty Q & A. See issues of Vogue

Beauty Q and A. See issues of Seventeen beginning October 1987

Beauty questions. See issues of Glamour

Beauty talk. See issues of Mademoiselle

Beauty view. See issues of McCall's beginning October 1986

Beauty workshop. See issues of Mademoiselle

Beautystyle. A. Robinson and D. Schefer. See issues of Vogue beginning July 1985

Best beauty bets. See issues of Harper's Bazaar

Best beauty boosts: 12 ways to save time & 8 luxurious ways to spend it. il *Glamour* 85:210-15 D '87

Between friends. il *Seventeen* 46:276 Ag '87

Black beauty basics. il *Teen* 31:82-3 Ap '87

Body be beautiful (I) [special section] il *Good Housekeep* 204:79+ My '87

Body be beautiful (II) [special section] il *Good Housekeep* 205:79-80+ O '87

Boys' eye view of beauty. il *Teen* 31:76-7 Ap '87

Brooke Shields post-grad beauty book. il pors *Harpers Bazaar* 120:96-9+ Je '87

A busy mother's beauty time-savers. C. Straley. il *Parents* 62:153-6 My '87

"Can this be me?". il *Mademoiselle* 93:148-53 F '87

Catch the wave [summer beauty] il *Seventeen* 46:110-19 Je '87

Coming attractions. il *Redbook* 169:94-7 Ag '87

Cut & color makeovers. il *Redbook* 168:84-7 F '87

Dear beauty editor. See issues of Seventeen through September 1987

Dear beauty editor. See issues of 'Teen

The defenders: stop the invasion of the beauty snatchers. il *Mademoiselle* 93:222-5 Ag '87

Detox! The big beauty cleanup. il *Mademoiselle* 93:250-5 Mr '87

Do a number on your looks: 50 super how-to's. il *Teen* 31:52-5 Ja '87

Don't be in the dark about your looks [tips for brunettes] il *Teen* 31:90-1 N '87

Double up for beauty. il *Teen* 31:70-3 D '87

Dress to dazzle during the holidays: best advice from some top professionals. il *Glamour* 85:55 D '87

Even if you look like the Pentagon, make-over man David Kibbe claims he can bring out the beauty within. K. Hubbard. il pors *People Wkly* 28:113+ O 26 '87

Five hot summer looks and how to make them work for you. B. Livermore. il *Health* 19:38-40 Je '87

From drab to dazzling hair and beauty makeovers; ed. by Maureen Lynch. L. Blanchard. il *Good Housekeep* 204:102-5+ Ja '87

Get-ahead good looks: 8 insider beauty tips. il *Mademoiselle* 93:182-5 O '87

Get organized! C. Straley. il *Parents* 62:213-16 N '87

Good looks. See issues of McCall's through July 1986

Great looks: a day in the life of a model [L. Valentine] il pors *Harpers Bazaar* 120:278-83 Mr '87

Heartland U.S.A. makeovers. il *Glamour* 85:290-7 Mr '87

Holiday '87: hits and misses. il *McCalls* 115:25-30 D '87

Holiday makeovers to make you shine. il *Glamour* 85:194-9 D '87

"I can't believe it's me!". C. Straley. il *Parents* 62:155-8 S '87

"I deserve a change" [stories of A. Diehl and C. Orlaskey] S. Schneider. il pors *Redbook* 168:82-5 Ja '87

Images/beauty now. See issues of Vogue beginning November 1987

In style. il *Ladies Home J* 104:55-6+ My '87

Indulge [featuring A. MacDowell; cover story; special section] K. W. Wiley. il pors *Health* 19:37-48+ D '87

Indulge! Take a beauty rest. il *Glamour* 85:314-17 Ap '87

Is your diet sabotaging your looks? il *Glamour* 85:280-3 Mr '87

Look like a natural. il *Redbook* 170:104-7 N '87

Looking better than ever! [makeovers] il *Redbook* 168:100-3 Mr '87

Looks count! il *Teen* 31:102-5 S '87

Magnificent makeovers! [black women] il *Essence* 18:68-71 Ag '87

Makeover magic. L. J. Johnson. il *Ladies Home J* 104:90-3 Je '87

Makeover of the month. See issues of Good Housekeeping

Makeovers=grade-A looks. il *Teen* 31:97-9 Ag '87

Making the stars shine [work of hair and makeup expert Jeff Jones] S. Lee. il *Redbook* 170:10 D '87

McCall's makeover: new look for Karen Long! M. Clarke. il *McCalls* 145:49 Mr '87

Mid-summer beauty & health boosters. L. J. Johnson. il *Ladies Home J* 104:106-12 Ag '87

"Ms. Dipesto, you look fabulous!" [interview with A. Beasley] K. Henderson. il pors *Redbook* 168:18+ Mr '87

Natural beauty [special section] il *Harpers Bazaar* 120:210-27+ O '87

The new come-on: 6 steps get you fit to flirt. il *Mademoiselle* 93:222-5 N '87

On the beach: the bad and the beautiful. il *Mademoiselle* 93:130-3 Jl '87

On the cheat. il *Teen* 31:92-5 O '87

One-hour beauty getaway. il *Redbook* 169:176-9 S '87

Over-40 & young! [special section] il *Harpers Bazaar* 120:124-37+ Ag '87

Party makeovers. C. Straley. il *Parents* 62:145-8 D '87

The perfect vacation: a first-class beauty and fashion guide. L. J. Johnson. il *Ladies Home J* 104:110-17 Jl '87

Personal style: the new moods of beauty. L. Hirschberg. il *Harpers Bazaar* 120:147+ F '87

Please fake me over! Beauty tricks of the stars. L. Rozen. il *Mademoiselle* 93:64 Ja '87

Please make me over! See occasional issues of Glamour

Post-grad beauty by degree [special section] il *Harpers Bazaar* 120:106-9+ Je '87

Priscilla Presley just gets more gorgeous [interview] E. Byron. il pors *Redbook* 168:8+ Ja '87

Prom pizazz! il *Teen* 31:57-8+ Ap '87

Reader of the Year: beauty. il *McCalls* 115:46+ O '87

Right at first sight. il *Mademoiselle* 93:112-15 Ja '87

Salt Lake City makeovers. il *Glamour* 85:296-9 O '87

School day diary: sign up for first-class looks. il *Teen* 31:90-5 Ag '87

Seriously, smile! Laughter—the new beauty attitude. il *Mademoiselle* 93:256-61 S '87

Sexy looks: celebrity secrets. il pors *Harpers Bazaar* 120:146-57 My '87

Soft, softer softest; the new beauty appeal. il *Glamour* 85:244-9 Ag '87

Splashdown to summer! [Malibu U.; cover story; special section] il *Teen* 31:98-111 My '87

Star beauty attractions [Hollywood's hottest stars] il *Teen* 31:98-9 O '87

Star-studded! [holiday looks for black women] il *Essence* 18:71-4+ D '87

The ten most beautiful black women in America [cover story] il *Ebony* 42:130-2+ Jl '87

There's a little bit of Marilyn in all of us [recreating the M. Monroe look] il pors *Ladies Home J* 104:93-5 Ag '87

Three women, three life styles, one aim: looking my best. il *Good Housekeep* 205:156-61 O '87

To catch a beauty thief. il *Mademoiselle* 93:248-51 Ap '87

Wedding day beauty blunders. il *Essence* 17:62-6+ F '87

Will the real president please stand up? il *Mademoiselle* 93:146-9 Je '87

Winning at beauty [teenage athletes L. Harwood, L. Blasko, I. Rubinshtein, and S. Rehe] il pors *Teen* 31:74-7 Jl '87

Beauty, Personal—*cont.*

Work up a beauty sweat. il *Mademoiselle* 93:154-9 Ja '87

Your beauty I.D.: face up to it. il *Teen* 31:78-9 Mr '87

Exhibitions

See also

International Beauty Show

See also **Men**

Skin

The masculine presence. S. Lord. *Vogue* 177:187-8+ Je '87

The outer man. il *Esquire* 108:231-4 S '87

What guys really think about their own looks. B. Serlen. il *Seventeen* 46:164-6 Ap '87

Psychological aspects

Baby face-off: the roots of attraction [study by Judith H. Langlois and others] B. Bower. *Sci News* 131:310 My 16 '87

Beauty is in the eye of the baby [infants prefer attractive faces; research by Judith H. Langlois] H. Hall. il *Psychol Today* 21:12 Ag '87

Do men always fall for beauties? B. Weber. *Mademoiselle* 93:178 Ap '87

Eating healthfully: for appearance' sake [study by Diane Hayes and Catherine E. Ross] S. Walton. *Psychol Today* 21:18 D '87

In the eye of the beholder [adolescence] D. Elkind. il *Parents* 62:212 My '87

The sneaky signs of stress. S. Young. il *Glamour* 85:336 Mr '87

Stress: the no.1 beauty enemy. D. Blumenthal. il *Ladies Home J* 104:92-5 Ja '87

When beauty blooms: do friends fade? il *Teen* 31:30 Ja '87

When you're born a 2.5. A. Russell. il *Glamour* 85:58+ O '87

Beauty and the beast [opera] See Oliver, Stephen, 1950-

Beauty and the beast [television program] See Television program reviews—Single works

Beauty contests

See also

Miss America Pageant

Miss Rheingold (Beauty contest)

Miss Teenage America Pageant

Miss USA Pageant

Campus queens at black colleges. il *Ebony* 42:70-2+ Ap '87

Can the beauty pageant be saved? [Ms. Santa Monica Pageant] K. S. Seal. il *Ms* 15:32 My '87

W. Va. Univ. elects first black homecoming queen [T. L. Cunningham] *Jet* 71:27 Ja 19 '87

Anecdotes, facetiae, satire, etc.

We were number one [1905 beauty contest winner Della Carson of Chicago Divinity School] M. E. Marty. il *Christ Century* 104:151 F 4-11 '87

Beauty preparations See Cosmetics

Beauty queens See Beauty contests

Beauty resorts See Health resorts, watering places, etc.

Beauty shops

See also

Turning Heads (Firm)

Coast-to-coast pros: the best in beauty. A. G. Britton. il *Harpers Bazaar* 120:46+ S '87

Earlybird hairstyle [early openings] il *Harpers Bazaar* 120:16 Ja '87

The hair fixers: a cross-country guide. il *Mademoiselle* 93:74 S '87

Lunchtime lifts [hairstyling salons] il *Harpers Bazaar* 120:126 Mr '87

Nails [nail salons] *New Yorker* 63:23-4 S 7 '87

Slim chance! New-season shapeup. S. F. Buckmaster. il *Harpers Bazaar* 120:186-7 F '87

Beauvais, Edward R.

about

Deregulation's latest darling. J. Schwartz. il por *Newsweek* 110:68 D 7 '87

Beaver Creek (Colo.: Resort) See Resorts—Colorado

Beavers

Beaver-pond trout. P. Barrett. il *Field Stream* 92:121-2+ S '87

An inside story [beaver lodge] R. J. McNamara. il *Conservationist* 41:27-9 Ja/F '87

Beber Silverstein & Partners

Did success spoil Beber Silverstein? P. Engardio. il *Bus Week* p98 Je 1 '87

Bechet, Sidney

about

Great & imperishable. R. De Toledano. *Natl Rev* 39:56-7 Je 19 '87

Beck, Bernard

Inglorious color. *Society* 24:4-12 My/Je '87

Beck, Clifford Keith, 1913-1986

about

Obituary

Phys Today 40:86+ Mr '87. W. G. Pollard

Beck, Elizabeth

Duluth [special section] il *Horizon* 30:13-26+ Ap '87

Beck, Ernest

Botta buildings for all time. il por *Horizon* 30:66-8 O '87

Cracks appear in the magic mountain. il *Sierra* 72:116-19 Ja/F '87

Beck, James, 1930-

about

Art historian James Beck urges the Vatican to clean up its act, not Michelangelo's frescoes [interview] H. Shapiro. il por *People Wkly* 27:69+ Mr 30 '87

Beck, Norman

about

Buying and servicing outdoor power equipment [interview] M. Ferrara. il por *Home Mech* 83:24-5 Ja '87

Beck, Peter J.

A cold war: Britain, Argentina and Antarctica. bibl il maps *Hist Today* 37:16-23 Je '87

Beck (Martin) Theatre (New York, N.Y.) See Martin Beck Theatre (New York, N.Y.)

Becker, Arthur H.

The riddle of aging. il *Christ Today* 31:18-19 N 6 '87

Becker, Boris

about

Boris's blunder. C. Kirkpatrick. il pors *Sports Illus* 67:21 Jl 6 '87

Class on grass [cover story] K. Cunningham. il pors *World Tennis* 35:40-4 Jl '87

Germany shows a pair of aces. T. Callahan. il pors *Time* 129:58-60 Je 29 '87

The trials of a phenom. J. Diaz. il por *Sports Illus* 66:50-1 Mr 2 '87

Woes of the wunderkind. R. Sullivan. il pors *Sports Illus* 67:38-9 D 14 '87

Yankee flameout in Hartford. F. Lidz. il pors *Sports Illus* 67:20-1 Ag 3 '87

Becker, Craig

Taking the Fifth. *Nation* 244:101 Ja 31 '87

Becker, Elizabeth

Stalemate in Cambodia. bibl f *Curr Hist* 86:156-9+ Ap '87

Becker, Gary S.

Antitrust's only proper quarry: collusion. il *Bus Week* p22 O 12 '87

Let's not use mirrors to balance the budget. por *Bus Week* p22 D 7 '87

The NCAA: a cartel in sheepskin clothing. il *Bus Week* p24 S 14 '87

Productivity is the best affirmative action plan. il *Bus Week* p18 Ap 27 '87

The results are in: overregulation kills growth. il *Bus Week* p24 Je 22 '87

Seeing through the rhetoric on 'fair' trade. il *Bus Week* p22 Jl 20 '87

Should drug use be legalized? il *Bus Week* p22 Ag 17 '87

Taiwan and Korea should be praised, not punished. il *Bus Week* p22 My 25 '87

Why a depression isn't in the cards. por *Bus Week* p22 N 9 '87

Why not let immigrants pay for speedy entry? il *Bus Week* p20 Mr 2 '87

Why we can't live without economists. il *Bus Week* p20 F 2 '87

Becker, Helmut

Hyundai tries to pass the Japanese. *World Press Rev* 34:47+ My '87

New worries in South Korea. *World Press Rev* 34:47 S '87

Becker, Lisa

What not to say to a widow. il *U S Cathol* 52:28-30 F '87

Becker, Michael

Credit card caps curtail consumer choices. il *Consum Res Mag* 70:24-7 S '87

Becker, Norman

Homeowners' clinic. See issues of Popular Mechanics beginning June 1984

Becker, Vivienne, 1953-

King's Road ransom. il pors *House Gard* 159:76+ My '87

Beckerdite, Luke

Philadelphia carving shops: Hercules Courtenay and his school. bibl f il *Antiques* 131:1044-63 My '87

Beckett, Samuel, 1906-
about
Ed the collector, Jake the dentist and Beckett: a tale that ends in Texas. C. Lake. il *N Y Times Book Rev* 92:2 S 6 '87
Happy days [drama] Reviews
N Y il 20:133-4 S 28 '87. J. Simon
Nation 245:348-9 O 3 '87. T. M. Disch
Bibliography
The Nayman of Noland. M. H. Levenson. il *New Repub* 197:34-7 Jl 6 '87
Beckman, Ericka, 1951-
about
A feminist fairy tale. V. Dika. il *Art Am* 75:31-3 Ap '87
Beckmann, Mathilde, 1904?-1986
about
Beckmann will challenged. A. Decker. *Art News* 86:21 Mr '87
Beckmann, Max, 1884-1950
about
Beckmann will challenged. A. Decker. *Art News* 86:21 Mr '87
Beckurts, Karl Heinz, 1930-1986
about
Obituary
Phys Today 40:86+ Jl '87. W. Gläser
Beckwith, Barbara
Finding the children. il *Ms* 16:88 S '87
Becton, Dickinson & Co.
An inside look at a LAN data archive system. M. W. Perry. il *Byte* 12:169-70+ Jl '87
Most improved. il *Forbes* 139:140 Ja 12 '87
Bed and breakfast accommodations
The B&B boom. H. Gieseking. *Travel Holiday* 167:111-12 Ap '87
Drawing a bead on a new dream: having helped two sons to become world-class biathletes, a couple now address their own future [Jim and Betty Schreiner to run a bed-and-breakfast business] S. Seixas. il *Money* 16:182-4 F '87
Pennsylvania's inn places: Bucks County bed & breakfast. M. M. Mason. il *Travel Holiday* 168:54-9 N '87
Room at the inn [Deborah and Tim Sakach's guide to historic inns] L. See. *Publ Wkly* 232:51 D 25 '87
So you want to be an innkeeper . . . L. J. Gallagher. il *Esquire* 108:74 N '87
Bed canopies *See* Canopies
Bed rest
Two days' bed rest could be all that's needed to ease the pain of a bum lower back. il *Prevention* 39:32 Jl '87
Bed trays *See* Trays
Bed wetting *See* Urine—Incontinence
Bedard, Patrick
[Column] See issues of Car and Driver
Driven to perfection. il pors *Esquire* 107:109-10 Je '87
The technique of cornering [excerpt from The g-analyst guide to expert driving] il *Car Driv* 33:105-6+ D '87
Two for the road. il *Esquire* 107:31-2 Ap '87
Bedding
See also
Quilts and quilting
Sheets
Bedding plants (Perennials) *See* Perennials (Plants)
Bedford (Tex.)
Ordinances
Bedford, Texas runs the flag out of town, causing a flap. K. Demaret. il por *People Wkly* 27:53-4 My 11 '87
Bedi, Rajesh
about
Rajesh Bedi's indelible India. D. Alexander. il por *Int Wildl* 17:52-9 Mr/Ap '87
Bednorz, J. Georg
(jt. auth) See Müller, K. Alex, 1927-, and Bednorz, J. Georg
about
The 1987 Nobel Prize for Physics. M. M. Waldrop. il pors *Science* 238:481-2 O 23 '87
Bednorz and Müller win Nobel Prize for new superconducting materials. A. Khurana. il pors *Phys Today* 40:17-19 D '87
Nobel prizes: physics. J. Horgan. *Sci Am* 257:46 D '87
Bednorz, J. Georg, and others
Superconductivity in alkaline earth-substituted La_2CuO_{4-y}. bibl f il *Science* 236:73-5 Ap 3 '87

Bedouins
Egypt
Bedouin blues [poetry] L. Abu-Lughod. il *Nat Hist* 96:24-33 Jl '87
Bedquilts *See* Quilts and quilting
Bedroom furniture
See also
Beds
The bedroom window [film] See Motion picture reviews—Single works
Bedrooms
See also
Children's rooms
Guest rooms
White House (Washington, D.C.). Lincoln Bedroom
Addition uses existing space. il *South Living* 22:186-7 N '87
Art deco. il *Fam Handyman* 37:68+ My/Je '87
Bedrooms with a country air. il *Good Housekeep* 205:120-3 Jl '87
Built-ins organize this master suite. il *South Living* 22:137 F '87
The details add up. il *South Living* 22:162-3 My '87
French dressing [use of sheets in bedroom decoration] il *Seventeen* 46:272-3 Mr '87
From bland to grand: how to dress up a boxy bedroom. il *Better Homes Gard* 65:115 N '87
Low-rise, high-style bedroom. L. M. Dalsgaard. il *Home Mech* 83:56-8+ Mr '87
Making a small room special. il *South Living* 22:92 Ag '87
Master suites: the hottest new remodeling trend: bedroom/bath retreats. G. G. Butler. il *Better Homes Gard* 65:64-71+ Ja '87
Nordic lights. il *Seventeen* 46:114-15+ Ja '87
Private space. il *Glamour* 85:256-8 F '87
Room for two. il *Seventeen* 46:342-5 Ag '87
They cut into the roof for a new top-floor bedroom. il *Sunset* 178:102 F '87
Beds
See also
Cradles
Cribs (Beds)
Waterbeds
Bedtime story [arched-headboard bed] N. Barrett, Jr. il *Pop Mech* 164:72-5+ O '87
Build a stick bed. G. Campbell. il *Home Mech* 83:32 Ja '87
Custom-made bed with an antique look [iron-and-brass bed] il *South Living* 22:174 Mr '87
Headboard illusion. N. Cooper. il *Home Mech* 83:51 D '87
How to make a padded headboard. il *Fam Handyman* 37:72-3+ My/Je '87
It's a jumping-horse bed. il *Sunset* 178:112 Mr '87
Metal beds. R. E. Jaffin and J. D. Johnson. il *Better Homes Gard* 65:96-7 F '87
Restore iron and brass beds. C. Seibels. il *Americana* 15:63-6 Mr/Ap '87
Sheraton Field Bed [kit] K. Childers. il *Fam Handyman* 37:44 Ap '87
Anecdotes, facetiae, satire, etc.
Me and my bed [used for sleeping and working; cover story] B. Allen. il pors *Ms* 16:20+ D '87
Beds, Vegetable garden *See* Vegetable gardens and gardening
Bee culture
Backyard superbees [blue orchard bees and horn-faced bees] G. Dickman. il *Rodale's Org Gard* 34:69-71 N '87
Bee fever. R. A. Morse. bibl il *Conservationist* 41:33-5 My/Je '87
The hobby that challenges you to think like a bee. J. Doherty. bibl (p146-7) il *Smithsonian* 18:62-70+ Jl '87
Beeba's Creations Inc.
A big deal for little Beeba's [J. C. Penney's investment] G. G. Marcial. *Bus Week* p61 Jl 27 '87
Keeping teens decked out in whatever's hot. il por *Bus Week* p88 My 25 '87
Beech
Trees of the trembling earth [southern beech forest of Chile] T. T. Veblen. il *Nat Hist* 96:42-7 S '87
Beech Aircraft Corp.
Beech nears Starship production, develops customer training. E. H. Phillips. il *Aviat Week Space Technol* 127:78-9+ N 16 '87
Beech, Piaggio weigh market for new business aircraft sales [Beech Starship 1 and Rinaldo Piaggio PD. 180 Avanti] D. A. Brown. il *Aviat Week Space Technol* 126:68-9+ Je 29 '87

Beech Aircraft Corp.—*cont.*
Beech will modify V-tail Bonanzas built from 1951-82. il *Aviat Week Space Technol* 126:108-9 My 18 '87
Cessna, Beech trim operations as jet, turboprop sales improve. il *Aviat Week Space Technol* 127:82 S 28 '87

Beech-Nut Nutrition Corp.
Beech-Nut indicted over phony juice. il *FDA Consum* 21:4 F '87

Beecham Products Division
A case of malpractice—in market research? [Beecham sues Yankelovich over research on new detergent] M. Rothman. *Bus Week* p28-9 Ag 10 '87

Beef
See also
Cooking—Meat
For cattle, the svelte look is in [lower fat beef] S. D. Atchison. il *Bus Week* p154-5 N 30 '87
The granddaddy of branded beef [Certified Angus Beef] B. Eftink. *Success Farm* 85:32 S '87
Ground beef. B. T. Hunter. il *Consum Res Mag* 70:8-9 F '87
How now to sell a cow? E. Zuckerman. il *N Y Times Mag* p68-70+ N 29 '87
Of maize and meat: culinary traditions and cultural identity in Mexico and Argentina. P. Petrich. il *Courier* 40:10-13 My '87
Prime choices [eating red meat] G. Bakoulis. il *Health* 19:49-51 Je '87
Surf 'n turf [cattle injected with fish oil to produce meat with less saturated fat] M. Mintzer. il *Health* 19:15 S '87

Advertising
See Meat industry—Advertising
Packaging
See Meat—Packaging
Prices
See Meat—Prices
Beef cattle See Cattle
Beef cattle industry See Cattle industry
Beef grading See Meat—Grading
Beef industry See Cattle industry
Beef processing industry See Meat industry
Beef stew See Stew
Beekeeping See Bee culture
Beeler's Meat Market and Bakery
All-natural pork. K. Coble. il *Success Farm* 85:38 O '87
Beeman, William W., d. 1987
about
Obituary
Phys Today 40:92-3 Jl '87. H. H. Barschall
Beene, Geoffrey
about
Geoffrey Beene: the winning edge. il *Harpers Bazaar* 120:210-13 Ap '87
The world of Geoffrey Beene. il *Vogue* 177:688-97 S '87
Beeper pagers See Paging devices
Beer, William R., 1943-
Resolute ignorance: social science and affirmative action. *Society* 24:63-9 My/Je '87
The wages of discrimination: comparing salaries. *Current* 297:33-6 N '87
Beer
See also
Brewing industry
Cooking—Beer
All-American brews. J. F. Mariani. il *Mot Boat Sail* 160:26 D '87
A barroom brawl with Mexico [Canada vs. Mexico over Corona's impact] W. J. Holstein. *Bus Week* p38 Ag 10 '87
Calories and alcohol in wine and beer coolers. il *Consum Res Mag* 70:30-2 Mr '87
Canadian draft picks. W. Grimes. il *Esquire* 107:34 Ap '87
A glass of handmade [beer from local breweries] W. Least Heat Moon. il *Atlantic* 260:75-9+ N '87
No bad hops with Wally [W. McNeil, top beer seller at Metrodome baseball games] F. Lidz. il pors *Sports Illus* 67:54+ Jl 6 '87

History
History with gusto [beer and prehistoric man; theory of S. Katz] il *Time* 129:57 Ap 6 '87
Beer, Nonalcoholic
Calories and alcohol in wine and beer coolers. il *Consum Res Mag* 70:30-2 Mr '87
Liquor without the alcohol kicker. A. Robbins. il *Mademoiselle* 93:332 S '87

When is a cocktail a mocktail? J. Venturino. il *Women's Sports Fitness* 9:8-9 Ag '87
Beer making See Brewing
Beers, David, and Hembree, Diana
A tale of two cities. il *Nation* 244:357-60 Mr 21 '87
Bees
See also
Bee culture
Feces—Bees
Bee-coming beards [beekeepers wearing bee beards] L. Barash. il *Natl Wildl* 25:12-13 Ag/S '87
Beeboppers [stopping Africanized bees] J. Horgan. il *Sci Am* 257:31-2 S '87
Fingerprinting the mean bees [Africanized bees; research by Dave Carlson and Barry Lavine] *Sci News* 131:218 Ap 4 '87
Here come the killer bees [Africanized honeybees] D. Lessem. il *Int Wildl* 17:12-15 My/Je '87
Invasion of the killer bees! [Africanized honey bees] S. Begley. il map *Newsweek* 109:62 Ap 6 '87
Killer bees advancing on U.S. [views of Thomas Rinderer] il *USA Today (Periodical)* 116:12-13 Ag '87
Nature's dynamo, the bumblebee. H. Middleton. il *South Living* 22:72+ Ap '87

Reproduction
See Insects—Reproduction
Temperature
See Temperature, Animal and human
Bees, Spelling See Spelling—Competitions
Bees in art
Exhibitions
Breaking out in hives [work of G. Puett at the Curt Marcus Gallery in SoHo] G. Henry. il *Art News* 86:174 F '87
Garnett Puett at Dart. S. Taylor. il *Art Am* 75:142-3 Mr '87
Beesley, H. Brent
about
The Farm Credit System slouches toward recovery. P. Houston. il por *Bus Week* p114 N 23 '87
Beethoven, Ludwig van, 1770-1827
about
Edward Rothstein on music. *New Repub* 197:26-8 Ag 10-17 '87
Small world. P. G. Davis. il *N Y* 20:92+ Mr 23 '87
The 'tramp of a giant'. A. Rich. il *Newsweek* 109:69 Mr 9 '87
The Vienna Philharmonic: the complete Beethoven symphonies and concertos. E. W. Said. *Nation* 244:619-20+ My 9 '87
Beetles
See also
Dung beetles
Control
Beetle patrol [pine beetles] G. Baxter. il *Flying* 114:88+ D '87
Begging and beggars
Talk about gelt trips! With only a tin cup, Sylvia Orzoff, 77, has begged $2 million for charity [collecting for the Jewish National Fund in Los Angeles] il por *People Wkly* 27:91 Je 1 '87
Beggs, James Montgomery, 1926-
about
Beggs and General Dynamics cleared of fraud. I. Goodwin. *Phys Today* 40 pt1:53 Ag '87
General Dynamics, Beggs cleared of fraud charges. *Aviat Week Space Technol* 126:25-6 Je 29 '87
Indictment of Beggs dropped. E. Marshall. *Science* 237:21 Jl 3 '87
Justice Dept.'s broadax. D. E. Fink. *Aviat Week Space Technol* 127:9 Jl 13 '87
Begley, Sharon
On the trail of acid rain. il map *Natl Wildl* 25:6-13 F/Mr '87
The way we were—20,000 years ago; ed. by Louise Lief. il *Read Dig* 130:167-72 Mr '87
Begole, Christine
Good listening. See occasional issues of Glamour
New tech. See occasional issues of Glamour
The new video camcorders. il *Better Homes Gard* 65:200+ N '87
Putting the byte on computer software. il *Seventeen* 46:124+ S '87
Take better pictures. See issues of Glamour
The well-equipped home office. il *Better Homes Gard* 65:37-9 Ap '87
Begonias
Blast them with begonias. il *Sunset* 178:78-9 F '87

Begun, Iosif
about
A day in the depths of the gulag. J. O. Jackson. il por *Time* 129:52 Mr 9 '87
Freedom for a refusenik [interview] il por *Macleans* 100:6+ Ap 27 '87
Behan, Kathy P.
For your eyes only: how to protect those baby blues, browns, grays . . . *Mademoiselle* 93:114 My '87
Those lips, those eyes . . . what your looks reveal about your health. il *Mademoiselle* 93:76+ Ja '87
Behavior, Animal *See* Animals—Habits and behavior
Behavior, Organizational *See* Organizational behavior
Behavior (Psychology)
See also
Addictive behavior
Conditioned responses
Helping behavior
Obsessive-compulsive behavior
Psychology, Comparative
Type A behavior
Type E behavior
Type T behavior
Interview [K. Lorenz] B. Lawren. por *Omni* 9:84-6+ Ap '87
Mood foods to raise your energy or lower your stress [excerpt from Managing your mind and mood through food]; ed. by Margaret Danbrot. J. J. Wurtman. il *Redbook* 168:106-9+ F '87
Behavior control, Electronic *See* Electronic behavior control
Behavior modification
How to break your man's bad habits. D. Hales. *McCalls* 114:56-7 Ja '87
Mind control [visuo-motor behavior rehearsal technique of R. M. Suinn] M. Teich and G. Dodeles. il *Omni* 10:53-60 O '87
Smile your way to a longer life [work of Meyer Friedman] L. Vaughn. il *Prevention* 39:87-90+ Ag '87
Behavior problems (Children) *See* Problem children
Behavioral genetics
Nature, nurture, and behavior. D. E. Koshland, Jr. *Science* 235:1445 Mr 20 '87
Behavioral medicine *See* Medicine, Psychosomatic
Behavioral pharmacology *See* Psychopharmacology
Behavioral research *See* Psychological research
Behrens, Gerd
South Africa's sports isolation. *World Press Rev* 34:57 Ap '87
South Africa's Zulu chief. il pors *World Press Rev* 34:34-5 Ja '87
Behrman, Bertha
about
A doll's house. K. Healy. il por *Forbes* 140:120 D 28 '87
Behrman, Dan
The sea within us. il *Courier* 40:23-6 Je '87
Beijing (China)
Description
Letter from Beijing. F. C. Shapiro. *New Yorker* 63:96-103 D 28 '87
Youth
Beijing's popcorn entrepreneur [excerpt from Chinese lives] Zhang Xinxin. *Harpers* 275:35-6+ N '87
Beijing Dance Conservatory
Where East meets East: Chinese are busy in Japan. S. Ueno. il *Dance Mag* 61:18 Ja '87
Beineix, Jean-Jacques
about
Beineix blue. M. Pally. il pors *Film Comment* 23:21-4 Ja/F '87
Beineix wages cinematic 'war'. M. Fraser. por *World Press Rev* 34:61 Mr '87
Betty Blue [film] Reviews
New Leader 70:22 Ja 12-26 '87. J. Gardner
Time il 129:72-3 Ja 19 '87. R. Schickel
Beinhorn, George
Desktop publishing for independent presses. il *Publ Wkly* 232:30+ N 13 '87
Beirut (Lebanon)
Beirut's fragile peace. J. Muir. il *Macleans* 100:22 Mr 23 '87
Living the good life in Beirut [relatively tranquil East Beirut] J. Barnes. il *U S News World Rep* 102:33 Mr 9 '87
Terrorism
See Terrorism—Lebanon
Beirut [drama] See Bowne, Alan
Beirut airplane hijacking, 1985
The big fish and the rule of law [M. A. Hamadei arrested in West Germany] il por *Newsweek* 109:34 Ja 26 '87

A hero pilot's new flight plan [J. Testrake] D. Gates. il por *Newsweek* 110:6 N 23 '87
No deals [West Germany refuses to extradite M. A. Hamadei to the U.S.] por *Time* 130:17 Jl 6 '87
A triumph over terror [interview with J. Testrake] il pors *Christ Today* 31:46-7 Je 12 '87
Wanted for murder and air piracy [M. A. Hamadei arrested in Frankfurt] W. Svoboda. il *Time* 129:29 Ja 26 '87
West Germany to prosecute terrorist [White House statement, June 24, 1987] *Dep State Bull* 87:85 Ag '87
The West reels in 'a big fish' at last [capture of M. A. Hamadei in Frankfurt] il *U S News World Rep* 102:14 Ja 26 '87
Beiswinger, George L., 1924-
Protecting your credit cards. il *McCalls* 114:127 S '87
Beitler, Stephen
Spinal tip: building a sport-safe back. il *Sport Mag* 78:79-80 F '87
Béjart, Maurice
about
Béjart mounts Malraux and The Kabuki. W. Como. il *Dance Mag* 61:84-9 My '87
Béjart's bye-bye to Brussels. L. Moffett. por *Dance Mag* 61:62 S '87
Malraux [ballet] Reviews
Dance Mag il 61:20 My '87. L. Moffett
Dance Mag il por 61:12 Jl '87
Trois etudes pour Alexandre [ballet] Reviews
Dance Mag 61:21+ O '87. L. Moffett
Bekaert, Geert
An unexpected surprise [tr. by Herbert L. Smith] il *Archit Rec* 175:126-35 Jl '87
Bel Canto Opera (Company)
Musical events:
Leonora by W. H. Fry. A. Porter. *New Yorker* 63:94-5 Mr 9 '87
Reich's progress [performance of I. Pizzetti's Murder in the cathedral] P. G. Davis. il por *N Y* 20:110-11 N 23 '87
Belafonte, Harry
about
Belafonte succeeds Kaye as UNICEF ambassador. pors *Jet* 71:30 Mr 23 '87
Belafonte testifies on behalf of UNICEF. *Jet* 72:59 Ap 27 '87
Belanger, Diana
3 children who needed a medical miracle; ed. by Sara Nelson. il *Redbook* 168:111+ F '87
Belau *See* Palau
Belcher, John W.
The Jupiter-Io connection: an Alfvén engine in space. bibl f il *Science* 238:170-6 O 9 '87
Belcher, Nancy Hoyt
The other side of paradise. il maps *Travel Holiday* 168:54-9+ Ag '87
Passage to Bangkok: rail adventures through Southeast Asia. il map *Travel Holiday* 168:42-7 D '87
Belew, Adrian
about
East meets Midwest. M. McCormick. il por *Roll Stone* p22-3 Je 4 '87
Belfast (Northern Ireland)
Social conditions
Belfast: the allure of the 'troubles' [excerpt from Living with war] S. Belfrage. *Harpers* 275:27+ O '87
In Belfast, war is a way of life [excerpt from Living with war] S. Belfrage. il *Nation* 245:156-8 Ag 29 '87
Belfort, Marlene
(jt. auth) See Pedersen-Lane, Joan, and Belfort, Marlene
Belfrage, Cedric
(tr) See Galeano, Eduardo H., 1940-. The Americas: enlightenment and enterprise
Belfrage, Sally, 1936-
Belfast: the allure of the 'troubles' [excerpt from Living with war] *Harpers* 275:27+ O '87
In Belfast, war is a way of life [excerpt from Living with war] il *Nation* 245:156-8 Ag 29 '87
Belgian Grand Prix *See* Automobile racing—Belgium
Belgium
See also
Architecture, Domestic—Belgium
Automobile racing—Belgium
Brussels (Belgium)
Motorcycle racing—Belgium
Music festivals—Belgium
Opera—Belgium
Shopping and shoppers—Belgium
Trials—Belgium

Belgium—*cont.*

Industries

See also

Sabena Belgian World Airlines

Belief and doubt

See also

Faith

Irreligion

Truth

Easter meditation:

Believing Thomas. B. L. Rohrig. il *Christ Century* 104:350-1 Ap 15 '87

Gray matters. R. T. Habermas. il por *Christ Today* 31:23-5 Ag 7 '87

Belief in God *See* Faith

Believercise (Firm)

Run in place and Praise the Lord. il *Newsweek* 109:63 Je 1 '87

The believers [film] *See* Motion picture reviews—Single works

Belitsky, Ellen Frey

I'm just a girl who can't say no. il *Ms* 15:48+ F '87

Belize

See also

Americans—Belize

Cable television—Belize

Industry and the environment—Belize

Investments, American—Belize

Lighthouse Reef (Belize)

Rain forests—Belize

Real estate investment—Belize

Wildlife conservation—Belize

Politics and government

Belize. L. Martin. *Sch Update* 119:15 Mr 9 '87

Belkin, Lisa

The make-over at Estee Lauder. il pors *N Y Times Mag* p32-3+ N 29 '87

The prisoner of Seventh Avenue: how Halston lost the right to his own name. il pors *N Y Times Mag* p16-22+ Mr 15 '87

Bell, Alexa

Girl to woman: a growing-up guide. il *Teen* 31:50+ N '87

Bell, Alison

Breaking up: how to know when you should. il *Teen* 31:22+ Jl '87

Bummer blues. il *Teen* 31:100-1 Ap '87

Crushes: why you fall so hard. il *Teen* 31:36+ Ag '87

Hijacked heart [story] il *Teen* 31:62+ Ag '87

The late show: curfew crisis. il *Teen* 31:20+ N '87

Mothers & daughters: talent x two. il *Teen* 31:52+ D '87

Nnnerves: how to overcome them. il *Teen* 31:84+ My '87

Bell, C. Gordon

about

SURA gets new president from DOE: NSF loses two computer chiefs. I. Goodwin. *Phys Today* 40:60-1 D '87

Bell, Derek

about

Unsung hero. R. Bulgin. il pors *Mot Trend* 39:115-17 F '87

Bell, Derrick A.

To make a nation whole. il *N Y Times Mag* p42-4+ S 13 '87

about

Black Harvard professor protests tenure policy. *Jet* 72:28 Je 29 '87

Bell, George

about

An All-star campaign. H. Quinn. il por *Macleans* 100:28 Jl 20 '87

Bell, Dawson, capture baseball's MVP Awards. pors *Jet* 73:17 D 7 '87

Toronto's big brass Bell. R. Fimrite. il pors *Sports Illus* 67:24-6+ S 7 '87

Bell, Janice L.

Down under a sand dollar: world of the tiniest crab. il *Sea Front* 33:210-15 My/Je '87

Bell, Judith

Sun dancing. il *Omni* 10:34+ D '87

Bell, Leland, 1922-

about

Leland Bell. L. Fleming. il *Art News* 86:49-50 My '87

Leland Bell: gesture and trope. J. Hollander. il *Art Am* 75:112-19 Jl '87

Bell, Madison Smartt

about

PW interviews. B. Summer. por *Publ Wkly* 232:45-6 D 11 '87

Bell, Nancy

Congress considers global climate change. *BioScience* 37:258 Ap '87

Observing the fruits of research on low-input agriculture. *BioScience* 37:548 S '87

Bell, Richard

A challenge and an opportunity for arts educators. il *Des Arts Educ* 89:41-3 N/D '87

Bell, Robert

about

Lotto winner keeps cool after winning $4 million. il por *Jet* 72:40 Jl 6 '87

Bell, Robert H.

Minutes of the parents' meeting. *Commonweal* 114:582-3 O 23 '87

A rose by any other name. *Commonweal* 114:470-1 S 11 '87

Singing the cordon bleus. *Commonweal* 114:70-1 F 13 '87

Your audit: a guide for the perplexed. il *Commonweal* 114:196-7 Ap 10 '87

Bell, Robert Maurice, 1944-

(jt. auth) See Hannun, Yusuf A., and Bell, Robert Maurice, 1944-

Bell, S. D.

High-tech printing techniques create an 'elaborately forged' Domesday book. il *Publ Wkly* 231:50-2 Ap 17 '87

Bell, Terrel Howard

about

Ex-Education chief cites racism in Reagan staff. por *Jet* 73:38 N 9 '87

Bell, Tiffany

Baroque expansions. bibl f il *Art Am* 75:126-9+ F '87

Magasin: new life for an old building. il *Art Am* 75:53-5 S '87

Bell, Tom

about

Saga of a High country newsman. G. O'Gara. por *Sierra* 72:72-7 Mr/Ap '87

Bell, Trudy E.

Lost wilderness. por *Space World* X-9-285:40 S '87

Bell & Howell Co.

B&H: the new belle of the ball. L. Therrien. il *Bus Week* p32 S 28 '87

Bell Atlantic Corp.

Astride the bounciest Baby Bell [T. E. Bolger] D. P. Wiener. il por *Fortune* 115:87 Ja 5 '87

Bell Canada Enterprises Inc.

A giant charts its future [Bell Canada Enterprises buys stake in Memotec Data] B. Wallace. il *Macleans* 100:26-7 My 25 '87

Bell Group Ltd.

Holmes a Court's fortunes are sinking Down Under. C. Debes. il por *Bus Week* p142-4 D 7 '87

Stalker of wounded game [R. Holmes à Court's interest in Texaco stock] T. Jaffe. il por *Forbes* 139:38+ Je 15 '87

Bell Helicopter Textron Inc.

Bell/Boeing team developing tilt-rotor Pointer RPV. B. M. Greeley, Jr. il *Aviat Week Space Technol* 126:58-9 Mr 9 '87

Bell/McDonnell team reviews design of Army LHX entry. *Aviat Week Space Technol* 126:85-6 Ja 19 '87

Bell-Boeing schedules first flight of Pointer tilt-rotor demonstrator. S. W. Kandebo. il *Aviat Week Space Technol* 127:56 Ag 10 '87

Bell, Boeing study specialized missions for V-22 Osprey. *Aviat Week Space Technol* 126:88-9 Ja 19 '87

Bell Helicopter flying second-generation version of model 680 research rotor. il *Aviat Week Space Technol* 126:81+ Ja 19 '87

Bell pushes for broader application of composites to helicopter structures. il *Aviat Week Space Technol* 126:95-6 Ja 19 '87

Bell shifts assembly of light helicopters to Canadian facility. il *Aviat Week Space Technol* 126:77-8 Mr 16 '87

Workers strike at Bell Helicopter, De Havilland plants. *Aviat Week Space Technol* 126:27 Je 29 '87

The bell jar [film] *See* Motion picture reviews—Single works

Bell Laboratories *See* AT&T Bell Labs

Bell miners (Birds) *See* Bellbirds

Bell-Northern Research Ltd.

A revolution in chip power. il *Macleans* 100:42 Ap 20 '87

Bell Telephone Laboratories, Incorporated

See also

AT&T Bell Labs

Bellagio (Italy)
Gardens and gardening
Gardens: Villa Melzi: Count Gallarati Scotti's flowering hills on Lake Como. N. Shrady. il *Archit Dig* 44:126-31 Ag '87
Bellah, Robert Neelly, 1927-
Resurrecting the common good. il *Commonweal* 114:736-41 D 18 '87
about
Decadence American style. K. S. Kantzer. il *Christ Today* 31:12-13 Ag 7 '87
Bellamy, Edward, 1850-1898
about
Looking back at Edward Bellamy. por *Futurist* 21:52 N/D '87
Bellamy, Ralph, 1904-
Unforgettable Jimmy Cagney. il por *Read Dig* 130:107-11 My '87
Belland AG
Wash-away plastics. S. Ashley. il *Pop Sci* 230:45+ Je '87
Bellbirds
The bird that farms the dell [relationship between bell miners, psyllids, and eucalyptus dieback] R. H. Loyn. il *Nat Hist* 96:54-60 Je '87
Belle, Regina
about
Sensuous soul sensation. J. Miller. por *Newsweek* 109:77 Je 22 '87
Belle of Louisville (Steamboat)
Riding the river with a Kentucky Belle. J. T. Black. il *South Living* 22:22+ Je '87
Belleek ware
An Irish Belleek fruit basket. S. Bagdade and A. Bagdade. il *Antiques Collect Hobbies* 92:63 N '87
Belleview Biltmore Resort and Spa (Clearwater, Fla.) *See* Resorts—Florida
Belleville, Bill
Commodore wreck: prototype "Open boat". *Oceans* 20:58-9 My/Je '87
Bellevue Hospital
Bellevue: no one was ever turned away [250th anniversary] W. A. Nolen. il *Am Herit* 38:36-43 F/Mr '87
Bellflowers *See* Campanulas
Bellhops
Sam Cascio, nonagenarian bellhop, refuses to bag it [Chicago Hilton & Towers employee] il por *People Wkly* 28:119 S 21 '87
Belli, Melvin M., 1907-
about
PTL: a battle of words in the holy war. il pors *Newsweek* 110:25 Jl 6 '87
Bellingrath Gardens
Poetry in porcelain [animal sculptures of E. M. Boehm] il por *South Living* 22:26 Ja '87
Bellini, Giovanni, ca. 1426-1516
about
True colors of a classic canvas. il *N Y Times Mag* p54 Jl 26 '87
Bellini, Mario, 1935-
about
Mario Bellini: designer on view at the Museum of Modern Art. il por *Archit Rec* 175:59 Ag '87
Bellini (Cocktail) *See* Cocktails
Bellini by Cipriani (New York, N.Y.: Restaurant) *See* New York (N.Y.)—Restaurants, nightclubs, bars, etc.
Bellini-Gergley, Lisa
Get shrewd about food: five nutrition updates. il *Mademoiselle* 93:114 Ag '87
The great snack exchange. *Mademoiselle* 93:144 Ap '87
The pizza diet. il *Harpers Bazaar* 120:107+ Je '87
Slim & trim: the pineapple diet. il *Harpers Bazaar* 120:172-3+ My '87
Slim and fit. il *Harpers Bazaar* 120:128+ Ag '87
Bellocchio, Marco
about
Devil in the flesh [film] Reviews
Commonweal 114:387 Je 19 '87. T. O'Brien
N Y 20:69 Je 8 '87. D. Denby
Natl Rev 39:52-3 Jl 3 '87. J. Simon
New Repub 196:24-5 Je 15 '87. S. Kauffmann
Bellow, Saul
The civilized barbarian reader. il *N Y Times Book Rev* 92:1+ Mr 8 '87
The leaden road to ruin [excerpt from The Dean's December] il *Discover* 8:76-7 D '87
about
Bellow: 'the quest never stops'. W. Clemons. por *Newsweek* 109:79 Je 8 '87
The reigning king of literature [interview] A. P. Sanoff. il por *U S News World Rep* 103:52-3 S 7 '87

Bells
Acoustics of ancient Chinese bells. S. Shen. il map *Sci Am* 256:104-10 Ap '87
Collectors and collecting
See also
American Bell Association
Belly button *See* Umbilical cord
Belly dancing
The official wiggle jiggle bump & grind program [belly dancing by Farouché] E. Kiester. il pors *50 Plus* 27:46-9 O '87
Belmont, Vera
about
Red kiss [film] Reviews
Ms 15:16 F '87. L. Stone
Belmont Stakes *See* Horse racing
Belser, Nancy
about
Something about Nancy Belser rubs animals the right way. il por *People Wkly* 27:121 My 18 '87
Belsky, Jay, 1952-, and Draper, Patricia
Reproductive strategies and radical solutions. *Society* 24:20-4 Mr/Ap '87
Belson, Eve
A TV studio guide. il *Travel Holiday* 168:27-9 Ag '87
Belson, Jerry
about
Surrender [film] Reviews
People Wkly il 28:14 N 9 '87. R. Novak
Belt sanders *See* Sanding and sanding equipment
Belter, John Henry, 1804-1863
about
Belter style. R. Christian. il pors *Americana* 15:46-50 S/O '87
Belter furniture *See* Furniture, Rococo
Belting
See also
Automobile engines—Belts
Belts
See also
Automobile engines—Fan belts
Beltsville Agricultural Research Center. Animal Parasitology Institute *See* Animal Parasitology Institute (U.S.)
Belwood, Jacqueline J., and Morris, Glenn
Bat predation and its influence on calling behavior in neotropical katydids. bibl f il *Science* 238:64-7 O 2 '87
Belz, Herman
Equality before the law: the Civil War amendments [cover story; with discussion] il por *Cent Mag* 20:4-19 N/D '87
Belzberg family
about
Belzbergs on the prowl. T. Fennell. il *Macleans* 100:32 Je 29 '87
The greenmail factor. L. Black. il *Macleans* 100:67 F 2 '87
Beman, Deane
about
Spreading the wealth [cover story] R. Behar. il pors *Forbes* 140:74-7+ Ag 10 '87
Bembenek, Lawrencia
about
Ex-cop Lawrencia Bembenek claims she was wrongly convicted of murder in the case of the unsmoking gun. J. S. Kunen. il pors *People Wkly* 28:116-18+ D 7 '87
Bemberg, Maria Luisa
about
An Argentinian Edith Wharton. W. Gimbel. il por *Vogue* 177:78 My '87
Miss Mary [film] Reviews
Commonweal 114:16 Ja 16 '87. T. O'Brien
Glamour 85:175+ F '87. J. G. Boyum
Time il 129:70 Ja 19 '87. R. Corliss
The woman behind Argentina's new film hit [interview] L. Stone. *Ms* 15:14+ F '87
Bemidji (Minn.)
Monuments, statues, etc.
Paul Bunyan dons a giant T-shirt—are tall tails next? [Autotype U.S.A. dresses statue] il *People Wkly* 28:97 Ag 3 '87
Ben & Jerry's Homemade Inc.
Cold comfort. D. C. Craig. il pors *Life* 10:58-9 S '87
Is Haagen-Dazs trying to freeze out Ben & Jerry's? K. H. Hammonds. il *Bus Week* p65 D 7 '87
Ben Ali, Zine el Abidine
about
Defeat of the supreme combatant. M. S. Serrill. por *Time* 130:48 N 16 '87
Sidelining of a legend. *Macleans* 100:24 N 16 '87

Ben-Gurion, David, 1886-1973
about
Israel's providential men. P. Johnson. *Commentary* 84:60-3 O '87
Ben-Shlomo, Yoseph
about
In defense of West Bank settlement [interview] *Harpers* 275:18-20 S '87
Benair, Jonathan
Funny man Frank. il por *Film Comment* 23:58-61 Mr/Ap '87
Benbrook, Doris, and Pfahl, Magnus
A novel thyroid hormone receptor encoded by a cDNA clone from a human testis library. bibl f il *Science* 238:788-91 N 6 '87
Bence, Evelyn, 1952-
Two kinds of thanks. il por *Christ Today* 31:34 Ja 16 '87
Benches
See also
Workbenches
2 pine benches. C. Wedlake and R. Englert. il *Workbench* 43:42-5 My/Je '87
Build a deck bench. il *Workbench* 43:47-9 Jl/Ag '87
For storage or a bench. il *Sunset* 178:146 Je '87
A smart solution for a stark deck. il *South Living* 22:45 Jl '87
Sturdy table/bench yard set. M. Landis. il *Workbench* 43:40-1 Jl/Ag '87
Benchley, Robert, 1889-1945
How to travel in peace [excerpt from Chips off the old Benchley] il *50 Plus* 27:59-61 Je '87
Benchmark testing (Computers) *See* Computers—Testing
Bendectin
Deformed D.C. boy gets $95 million award in product liability suit [award to S. Ealy in Bendectin case] por *Jet* 72:26 Ag 3 '87
Bendel, Mary-Ann
A different Dolly. il por *Ladies Home J* 104:118+ N '87
Bendel (Henri) Inc. *See* Henri Bendel Inc.
Bender, Bruce G.
(jt. auth) *See* Berch, Daniel B., and Bender, Bruce G.
Bender, May
Packaging for the older consumer [address, March 6, 1987] *Vital Speeches Day* 53:490-2 Je 1 '87
Bender, Timothy P., and others
Differential expression of c-*myb* mRNA in murine B lymphomas by a block to transcription elongation. bibl f il *Science* 237:1473-6 S 18 '87
Bendix, Reinhard
The intellectual's dilemma in the modern world. *Society* 25:63-4+ N/D '87
Bendix Corp.
Bendix, Israeli firm demonstrate high-accuracy helmet sight. il *Aviat Week Space Technol* 127:148 Ag 10 '87
Crouzet, Bendix will develop voice command system [military aircraft] *Aviat Week Space Technol* 127:77 Jl 20 '87
Bends *See* Decompression (Physiology)
Benedick, Richard Elliot
The environmental agenda and foreign policy [address, April 16, 1987] *Dep State Bull* 87:54-5 Jl '87
Bénédictine SA
Hundred-year wonder. P. Fuhrman. il por *Forbes* 139:152 Mr 9 '87
Benedictines
Lives of heart and soul [Benedictine Priory in Montreal] G. Ferzoco. il *Macleans* 100:42 S 14 '87
The monks of St. Peters [abbey in Muenster, Sask.] il *Macleans* 100:6+ Je 29 '87
Benefit auctions *See* Auctions
Benefit funds (Trade unions) *See* Trade unions—Benefit funds
Benefit performances
See also
Baseball, Professional—Benefit games
Bishop Tutu Peace Concert, 1987
Dance—Benefit performances
Ice shows—Benefit performances
Rock concerts—Benefit performances
Welcome Home concert, 1987
How artists respond to AIDS. R. Corliss. il *Time* 130:62-3 Jl 27 '87
Sammy brings Broadway to Newark for fundraiser [S. Davis Jr.] il pors *Jet* 72:53 Je 8 '87
Benefits, Employee *See* Fringe benefits
Benelux countries
See also
Art galleries and museums—Benelux countries

Benequity Holdings, a California Limited Partnership
A drum, a drum, Renouf doth come. H. Rudnitsky. il *Forbes* 139:146+ My 18 '87
Benét, Stephen Vincent, 1898-1943
Johnny Pye and the Fool-killer [story] il *Saturday Evening Post* 259:42-5+ O '87
Johnny Pye and the Fool-killer [story] il *Saturday Evening Post* 259:34-8+ S '87
Bénéteau (Firm)
Can Beneteau fill its sails in the U.S. boat market? M. Resener. il por *Bus Week* p75 Ag 17 '87
Benetton SpA
Benetton is betting on more of everything. W. C. Symonds and A. Dunkin. il *Bus Week* p93 Mr 23 '87
Folding [art of folding sweaters at a store in Manhattan] *New Yorker* 63:30-1 My 25 '87
Benge, Michael D.
about
Mike Benge and his marvelous tree. J. G. Hubbell. il por *Read Dig* 131:103-7 Ag '87
Benglis, Lynda, 1941-
about
Lynda Benglis at Paula Cooper. H. Cotter. *Art Am* 75:124 Jl '87
Benites, Jose R.
(jt. auth) *See* Sanchez, Pedro A., and Benites, Jose R.
Benjamin, George
about
Musical events:
Performances of Ringed by the flat horizon and A mind of winter. A. Porter. *New Yorker* 63:110-11 D 21 '87
Benjamin, Roy
AAP: a concerned member speaks. por *Publ Wkly* 231:54 My 22 '87
Benjamin, Walter, 1892-1940
about
A fateful intellectual friendship. E. Rothstein. *Commentary* 84:41-9 D '87
Benjamin (Curtis) Award *See* Publishers and publishing—Awards
Benjamin Banneker Honors College *See* Prairie View A & M University. Benjamin Banneker Honors College
Benjamin E. Mays Academy of Scholars
Benjamin E. Mays Program at I.U.P. seeks scholars. *Jet* 71:33 Mr 23 '87
Benji (Dog) *See* Dogs in motion pictures
Benji the hunted [film] *See* Motion picture reviews—Single works
Benn, Tony, 1925-
Writing our own history. il pors *Hist Today* 37:9-12 Ap '87
Bennack, Frank A., Jr.
about
Citizens rich [cover story] W. P. Barrett. il pors *Forbes* 140:141-3+ D 14 '87
Benner, Richard
about
Too outrageous! [film] Reviews
Macleans 100:58 O 5 '87. L. O'Toole
Bennett, Barbara Lee
A look at field experiences for preservice teachers in the arts. *Des Arts Educ* 89:12-13 S/O '87
Bennett, Charles H.
Demons, engines and the second law. bibl (p150-1) il *Sci Am* 257:108-16 N '87
Bennett, Gareth V., 1929-1987
about
Anglicans in turmoil. K. L. Woodward. il pors *Newsweek* 110:57 D 21 '87
Death and the archbishop. R. N. Ostling. il pors *Time* 130:60 D 21 '87
Bennett, Gary L.
Return to Jupiter. il *Astronomy* 15:6-15 Ja '87
Voyage into the third dimension. il *Astronomy* 15:14-22 My '87
Bennett, Georgette
The long agony of Shirley Fish. il por *McCalls* 114:148-50 Ap '87
Bennett, John C.
about
John Bennett on Oxford '37. D. McCreary. il por *Christ Century* 104:942-4 O 28 '87
Bennett, Lerone, 1928-
Founders of the black press. il pors *Ebony* 42:96+ F '87
Passing the baton of black history. il *Jet* 71:36 Mr 2 '87
Three major gifts blacks gave to America. *Jet* 71:50+ F 23 '87

Bennett, Lerone, 1928-—*cont.*
about
Black History Month commemorates one of greatest stories in history of the world. il por *Jet* 71:22+ F 16 '87
Lerone Bennett Jr. named executive editor of Ebony; two others also promoted. il por *Jet* 73:19 D 28 '87-Ja 4 '88

Bennett, Michael
about
Obituary
Dance Mag por 61:32 O '87. C. Barnes
Dance Mag 61:33 O '87. O. Stuart
Jet il por 72:58 Jl 20 '87
N Y 20:49 Jl 20 '87. J. Simon
Newsweek por 110:66 Jl 13 '87
People Wkly il por 28:92-3 Jl 20 '87
Time il por 130:66 Jl 13 '87. W. A. Henry

Bennett, Michael J., and Kline, Charles H.
Chemicals: an industry sheds its smokestack image. il *Technol Rev* 90:36-45 Jl '87

Bennett, Paul
Coyote [poem] *America* 156:405 My 16 '87
In the shadow of the pine [poem] *America* 156:54 Ja 24 '87

Bennett, Ralph Kinney
The closing of the American mind. *Read Dig* 131:81-4 O '87
Expelled! How we ousted 80 Soviet spies. il *Read Dig* 130:47-52 Ja '87
The Toshiba scandal: anatomy of a betrayal. *Read Dig* 131:95-100 D '87
Triumph at Pad 17. il *Read Dig* 131:59-64 Jl '87

Bennett, William Ira
Monitoring drugs for the aged. il *N Y Times Mag* p73-4 D 13 '87

Bennett, William John, 1943-
In defense of our common culture. il por *USA Today (Periodical)* 115:45-7 Mr '87
The quality of the university today: an exchange at Harvard [address, October 1986] *Current* 291:4-9 Mr/Ap '87
Remarks [arts education; address, November 24, 1986] *Des Arts Educ* 88:43-5 Mr/Ap '87
Sex and the education of our children [address, January 22, 1987] *America* 156:120-5 F 14 '87
Should Congress enact the Quayle amendments to the Bilingual Education Act? [excerpts from testimony, June 5, 1986] *Congr Dig* 66:76+ Mr '87
What we must teach our children about character. il *Read Dig* 130:100-2 My '87
Why Johnny can't abstain. *Natl Rev* 39:36-8+ Jl 3 '87
about
AIDS: who should be tested? T. Monmaney. il por *Newsweek* 109:64-5 My 11 '87
Better grades for Bill Bennett. E. Bowen. il por *Time* 129:60-1 Ja 19 '87
Bill Bennett's dilemma. D. Wagner. il *Natl Rev* 39:28-31+ Je 19 '87
Koop and Bennett agree to disagree. B. Barol. il pors *Newsweek* 109:64 F 16 '87
Mister Ed. J. B. Judis. *New Repub* 196:16-19 Ap 27 '87
Mister Ed: William Bennett. J. B. Judis. *Educ Dig* 53:36-8 D '87
Mr. Bennett warns lotus eaters. J. W. Donohue. *America* 156:373-4 My 9 '87
Taking on Secretary Bennett. M. P. McPherson and P. Korshin. pors *U S News World Rep* 102:6 Je 29 '87
Which system is the worst? por *Time* 130:69 N 23 '87

Bennice, Donn A.
about
White charges Lincoln U. violated his civil rights. *Jet* 72:23 Ag 31 '87

Bennigsen, Alexander
Winning the war for Afghanistan. *Natl Rev* 39:36-8 My 8 '87

Bennink, Han
about
Han Bennink/Peter Brotzmann: first entrances and last exits [interview] B. Shoemaker. il pors *Down Beat* 54:24-6 Ja '87

Bennison, Geoffrey
about
Bennison style. C. Gibbs. il *House Gard* 159:170-7+ Ap '87

Benoit, Robert, and others
A new prosomatostatin-derived peptide reveals a pattern for prohormone cleavage at monobasic sites. bibl f il *Science* 238:1126-9 N 20 '87

Bensman, David, 1949-
Back to work. *Nation* 244:875 Je 27 '87

Benson, Betty
about
Her joints are jumping. P. Spencer. il pors *50 Plus* 27:44-50 Ja '87

Benson, E. F.
about
The rivals. L. Fleischer. *Publ Wkly* 231:130 My 15 '87

Benson, George
about
George Benson: strike up the band [cover story; interview] H. Mandel. il pors *Down Beat* 54:16-19 My '87

Benson, Michael R.
Back in the U.S.S.R. *Nation* 244:824-6 Je 13 '87
Rock in Russia. il *Roll Stone* p15-16+ Mr 26 '87

Benson, Nancy C.
Santos by Roybal. il por *Americana* 15:45-8 Mr/Ap '87

Benson, Olive Lee
about
Hair care now! [interview] M. Garth-Taylor. por *Essence* 18:50 S '87

Bentkowski, Tom
Music. See occasional issues of New York

Bentley (Automobile) See Automobiles, Foreign

Benton, Robert
about
Nadine [film] Reviews
Commonweal 114:499 S 11 '87. T. O'Brien
Macleans 100:51 Ag 17 '87. L. O'Toole
New Yorker 63:81-2 Ag 24 '87. P. Kael
Newsweek 110:58 Ag 10 '87. J. Kroll
People Wkly il 28:8 Ag 10 '87. P. Travers
Time il 130:62 Ag 17 '87. R. Corliss
Vogue il 177:132+ S '87. M. Haskell

Benton, Tim
Historic houses: Le Corbusier's cabanon. il *Archit Dig* 44:146-51+ D '87

Benton (Ky.)
Music festivals
See Music festivals—Kentucky

Bentsen, Lloyd
about
Guess who's not coming to brunch. il por *Newsweek* 109:19 F 16 '87

Bentwood furniture
Bentwood chair and lamp. K. Meyers. il *Workbench* 43:54-9 S/O '87

Benvenisti, Meron
about
A visionary's Mideast peace plan. J. M. Wall. *Christ Century* 104:459-60 My 13 '87

Benxi (China)
Stores
Cabbages and capitalists [storeowner Guan Guangmei] D. Elliott. il por *Newsweek* 110:37 Jl 20 '87

Benzoates
Redesigning metabolic routes: manipulation of TOL plasmid pathway for catabolism of alkylbenzoates. J. L. Ramos and others. bibl f il *Science* 235:593-6 Ja 30 '87

Benzodiazepines See Tranquilizing drugs

Bequests See Wills

Berbick, Trevor
about
Ex-champ Berbick OKs deflated fight purse. *Jet* 72:52 Mr 30 '87

Berch, Bettina
Early feminist fashion. il por *Ms* 15:26 Mr '87

Berch, Daniel B., and Bender, Bruce G.
Margins of sexuality. bibl (p63) il *Psychol Today* 21:54-7 D '87

Beré, James F.
Shaping America's future competitiveness [address, September 30, 1986] *Vital Speeches Day* 53:208-10 Ja 15 '87

Bereaved, Church work with the See Church work with the bereaved

Bereavement See Grief

Beregi, Edit
A grand old age. il *Courier* 40:25-7 Ag '87

Berendt, John
The ascot. il *Esquire* 108:42+ O '87
The baseball cap. il *Esquire* 108:19-20 Jl '87
Boxer shorts. il *Esquire* 108:44+ S '87

Berendt, John—*cont.*
The cowboy hat. il *Esquire* 107:16+ F '87
The Fair Isle sweater. il *Esquire* 107:30 Mr '87
The Hawaiian shirt. il *Esquire* 108:22+ Ag '87
The homburg. il *Esquire* 107:32+ Ap '87
The motorcycle jacket. il *Esquire* 108:36 D '87
The muffler. *Esquire* 107:18+ Ja '87
The pea coat. il *Esquire* 108:32 N '87
The sneaker. il *Esquire* 107:26+ My '87
Suspenders. il *Esquire* 107:42+ Je '87
Berenger, Tom
about
Oliver's army. F. Schruers. il por *Roll Stone* p24 Ja
29 '87
Tom Berenger: satanic Sergeant Barnes. R. LaBrecque.
il por *People Wkly* 27:56 Mr 9 '87
Berenson, Margaret Mathews- *See* Mathews-Berenson, Margaret
Berenson, Robert A.
In a doctor's wallet. *New Repub* 196:11-13 My 18 '87
Berenstain, Jan, 1923-
(jt. auth) See Berenstain, Stan, 1923-, and Berenstain,
Jan, 1923-
Berenstain, Stan, 1923-, and Berenstain, Jan, 1923-
It's all in the family. See occasional issues of Good
Housekeeping
Beresford, Bruce
about
Crimes of the heart [film] Reviews
Christ Century 104:60 Ja 21 '87. J. M. Wall
Commonweal 114:55 Ja 30 '87. T. O'Brien
Glamour 85:176 F '87. J. G. Boyum
Glamour il 85:134 Ja '87. C. Krupp
Ms il 15:12+ F '87. M. Rochlin
Natl Rev 39:56 F 13 '87. J. Simon
New Repub 196:26-7 F 2 '87. S. Kauffmann
USA Today (Periodical) il 115:95 Mr '87. K. R.
Hey
Vogue il 177:82+ F '87. M. Haskell
The fringe dwellers [film] Reviews
Ms 15:20-1 Mr '87. L. Stone
Bereuter, Douglas K.
Should Congress adopt the House-passed "Gephardt
Amendment"? [excerpts from debate, April 29, 1987]
Congr Dig 66:187+ Je/Jl '87
Berg, Alban, 1885-1935
about
Lulu [opera] Reviews
Atlantic il 260:93-6 S '87. W. H. Youngren
Berg, Barbara J.
The guilt that drives working mothers crazy. il *Ms*
15:56-9+ My '87
Berg, Elizabeth
The best birthday presents ever. il *Parents* 62:102-4+
Ag '87
"Christmas in November is okay with me". il *Parents*
62:136-7 N '87
Getting involved. il *Parents* 62:100-2 My '87
My hotel weekend. il *Parents* 62:48+ F '87
Night & day. il *Parents* 62:100-1 Ag '87
Small moments. il *Parents* 62:108-10+ D '87
Why I'm at home. il *Parents* 62:122-3 Ap '87
Bergamo (Italy)
Description
An excursion from Milan: Bergamo. D. L. Parker. il
Gourmet 47:60-5+ S '87
Bergant, Dianne
about
Holy Moses! The New Testament is only half the story
[interview] por *U S Cathol* 52:20-7 F '87
Bergé, Pierre
about
Gardens: Château Gabriel: Yves Saint Laurent and Pierre
Bergé at Deauville [cover story] C. Aillaud. il *Archit
Dig* 44:172-9+ My '87
Gardens: Majorelle remembered: Yves Saint Laurent
and Pierre Bergé in Marrakesh. C. Aillaud. il pors
Archit Dig 44:160-5 O '87
Bergelin, Lennart
Studying the Swedes. il *World Tennis* 34:80 Ap '87
Bergen, Candice
about
Candice Bergen. J. Etra. pors *Harpers Bazaar* 120:204,
354-7 S '87
Bergen County (N.J.)
See also
KIDS of Bergen County (Program)
Bergenfield (N.J.)
Youth
Bergenfield's tragic foursome [teen suicides] il *U S News
World Rep* 102:11 Mr 23 '87

The copycat suicides [teenagers] L. Martz. il *Newsweek*
109:28-9 Mr 23 '87
Teen suicide. A. Wilentz. il *Time* 129:12-13 Mr 23
'87
Berger, Arthur Asa, 1933-
Film technology's latest Frankenstein. *Society* 24:12-13
My/Je '87
Berger, Brigitte
Limits of doing good. *Society* 24:25-7 Mr/Ap '87
Berger, Brigitte, and Berger, Peter L.
Conservatism [discussion of October 1986 article, Our
conservatism and theirs] *Commentary* 83:6-8+ F '87
Berger, Gerhard
about
Berger king. R. Walker. il por *Road Track* 38:120-2+
F '87
Berger, Harlan
Hearing where the bullet will hit. il *Outdoor Life* 180:126+
N '87
Berger, John, 1926-
Imagine Paris. il *Harpers* 274:72-4 Ja '87
To take paper, to draw. il *Harpers* 275:57-60 S '87
about
Living and writing the peasant life. G. Marzorati. il
pors *N Y Times Mag* p38-9+ N 29 '87
Berger, Joseph
Being Catholic in America [cover story] il *N Y Times
Mag* p22-7+ Ag 23 '87
Berger, Oscar
U.S. presidents on war and peace. il *Saturday Evening
Post* 259:36+ Ja/F '87
Berger, Paula S.
Teaching about teen suicide using young-adult novels.
Educ Dig 52:48-9 Ap '87
Berger, Peter L.
Moral judgment and political action [address, October
26, 1987] *Vital Speeches Day* 54:115-22 D 1 '87
(jt. auth) See Berger, Brigitte, and Berger, Peter L.
Berger, Peter L., and Godsell, Bobby
Fantasies about South Africa. *Commentary* 84:35-40 Jl
'87
South Africa [discussion of July 1987 article, Fantasies
about South Africa] *Commentary* 84:11-12+ O '87
Berger, Phil
Boxing's angry man. il pors *N Y Times Mag* p34-6+
Mr 22 '87
On cooling a beef. il *Sport Mag* 78:79-80 S '87
Berger, Philip A.
about
Stanford psychiatrist resigns under a cloud. C. Holden.
por *Science* 237:479-80 Jl 31 '87
Berger, Stuart
What to do when your doctor says there's nothing wrong
with you and you still feel awful. *Good Housekeep*
204:129+ Ap '87
about
Medical disputes you should know about. G. Williams.
Ladies Home J 104:56+ Mr '87
Bergesen, Albert
Oh, well. il *Atlantic* 260:16+ Jl '87
Bergin, Thomas Goddard, 1904-1987
about
Obituary
Natl Rev 39:20 D 18 '87
Berglie, Carole, and Geffen, Alice M.
At the Kutztown Fair [with editorial comment by Sandra
Wilmot] il map *Americana* 15:2, 33-7 Jl/Ag '87
Bergman, Alan
Characters: sparking the joy and finding the eccentricity.
il *Petersens Photogr Mag* 15:44-6 Ja '87
about
Playful plagiarism: imitating art with Alan Bergman.
B. Hurter. il por *Petersens Photogr Mag* 15:44-9 F
'87
Bergman, Carol, and Nussbaum, Muriel
Nellie Bly. il pors *Am Hist Illus* 22:22-6+ Mr '87
Bergman, Susan
Talking drums and juju joy. il pors *Christ Today* 31:10-11
Ag 7 '87
Bergmann, Sherrel
Teaching middle-schoolers decision-making skills. *Educ
Dig* 52:48-50 Mr '87
Bergreen, Barbara
about
Past perfect: Bernard and Barbara Bergreen on Fifth
Avenue. J. Allen. il por *Archit Dig* 44:190-9 N '87
Bergreen, Bernard
about
Past perfect: Bernard and Barbara Bergreen on Fifth
Avenue. J. Allen. il por *Archit Dig* 44:190-9 N '87

Bergstein, Barry
Miles Davis' solo on Tutu—a trumpet transcription. il *Down Beat* 54:51 My '87
Bergsten, C. Fred, 1941-
Crisis and reform [address, November 13, 1986] *Vital Speeches Day* 53:281-8 F 15 '87
Economic imbalances and world politics. bibl f *Foreign Aff* 65:770-94 Spr '87
Bergues (Geneva, Switzerland: Hotel) *See* Geneva (Switzerland)—Hotels, motels, etc.
Bering Land Bridge
Beringia. N. N. Dikov. il map *Courier* 40:32-4 N '87
Blood test. S. L. Zegura. il *Nat Hist* 96:8+ Jl '87
Bering Sea
Whales and walruses as tillers of the sea floor [side-scan sonar studies of the Bering Sea] C. H. Nelson and K. R. Johnson. il maps *Sci Am* 256:112-17 F '87
Bering Strait
See also
Bering Land Bridge
Bering Strait swims *See* Swimming
Beringia *See* Bering Land Bridge
Berk, Sally Ann
Anatomy of a national tour. il *Publ Wkly* 232:46-8 O 16 '87
Berkeley, Bill
Zimbabwe's tortured path. *New Repub* 196:21-3 F 16 '87
Berkeley (Calif.)
Restaurants, nightclubs, bars, etc.
Spécialités de la maison:
Café Pastoral. C. Bates. *Gourmet* 47:20+ Jl '87
Dakota Grill & Bar. C. Bates. il *Gourmet* 47:48+ O '87
Stores
When you're truly in dire knead, line up at the Cheese Board with Berkeley's well-bread upper crust. il *People Wkly* 27:78-9 F 23 '87
Theater
See also
Berkeley Repertory Theatre
Berkeley Repertory Theatre
James LeBrecht [sound designer] A. M. Hale. il por *Theatre Crafts* 21:34-5+ F '87
Berkenbosch, Frank, and others
Corticotropin-releasing factor-producing neurons in the rat activated by interleukin-1. bibl f il *Science* 238:524-6 O 23 '87
Berkley, George
Getting along with your boss [condensed from How to manage your boss] il *Read Dig* 131:13-16 Jl '87
Berkley, Miriam
Academy Chicago makes the grade. il *Publ Wkly* 232:19-22 Ag 28 '87
Prometheus unbound. il por *Publ Wkly* 231:32-4 Ja 16 '87
Russia's big bestseller: a talk with Julian Semyonov. il pors *Publ Wkly* 232:34-5 O 16 '87
Berkley (W. R.) Corp. *See* W. R. Berkley Corp.
Berkley Publishing Group
Berkley makes a move [distribution deal with Warner Publisher Services] A. Symons. il *Publ Wkly* 231:50-2 My 8 '87
Berkowitch, Anne
about
Making big bucks from the Big Bang. S. Seixas. il pors *Money* 16:161-2+ My '87
Berkowitz, Natalie
Weekends European-style. il *Harpers Bazaar* 120:42+ Je '87
Berkshire Hills (Mass.)
Description and travel
Bach and knolls in the Berkshires. P. Harris and D. Lyon. il *Travel Holiday* 167:38+ My '87
The Berkshires: hills of heaven. J. Colihan. il *Am Herit* 38:26+ My/Je '87
Berkshire Museum (Pittsfield, Mass.)
Some said Mary Mace had bats in her belfry, until she proved who made the toys in the basement [discovery of painted wooden toys created by A. Calder] il por *People Wkly* 27:53 Ja 26 '87
Berkson, Bill
David Park: facing Eden. bibl f il *Art Am* 75:164-71+ O '87
The sweet singer of modernism. il *Art Am* 75:138-43 Je '87
Berkson, Jerrold, and Griggs, Shirley A.
Intergenerational understanding in the middle school. *Educ Dig* 52:30-2 Ap '87

Berle, Milton
Bill Cosby: "My wife helped me become a better person" [interview] il pors *Redbook* 169:72+ Je '87
Closing night at the Zebra Lounge [story] il por *Redbook* 168:62+ Mr '87
A new act [story] il *Ladies Home J* 104:112+ N '87
Berle, Peter A. A.
The Audubon view. See issues of Audubon beginning November 1985
Berleant, Arnold, 1932-
(jt. auth) See Berleant-Schiller, Riva, and Berleant, Arnold, 1932-
Berleant-Schiller, Riva, and Berleant, Arnold, 1932-
Charlestown, Nevis. il map *Focus* 37:32-3 Fall '87
Berlin, Ira, 1941-, and others
Family and freedom: black families in the American Civil War. bibl f il *Hist Today* 37:8-15 Ja '87
Berlin, Sir Isaiah
Edmund Wilson among the 'despicable English'. il por *N Y Times Book Rev* 92:1+ Ap 12 '87
Berlin, Jeff
about
Jeff Berlin: beyond the bas(s)ics. B. Milkowski. il pors *Down Beat* 54:22-4 Ap '87
Berlin (Germany)
Anniversaries, etc.
750th anniversary of Berlin [proclamation, June 8, 1987] R. Reagan. *Dep State Bull* 87:25 Ag '87
Music
See also
Opera—Germany
Berlin (Germany: East)
The battle for Berlin. G. Martin. il *Esquire* 108:204-13 N '87
Description
The other Berlin. R. Kostelanetz. il *House Gard* 159:50+ Je '87
Galleries and museums
See also
Museum für Deutsche Geschichte (Berlin, Germany: East)
Municipal improvement
East Berlin gets a new face. R. Giardina. il *World Press Rev* 34:59 F '87
Music
See also
Opera—Germany (East)
Youth
Meanwhile, in East Berlin [youths clash with police while attempting to listen to concert in West Berlin] il *Time* 129:20 Je 22 '87
Berlin (Germany: West)
The battle for Berlin. G. Martin. il *Esquire* 108:204-13 N '87
Architecture
Beyond the Peak [work of Z. M. Hadid] D. Dietsch. il *Archit Rec* 175:118-29 Je '87
Rebuilding Berlin—yet again [program undertaken by the International Building Exhibition] K. Andersen. il *Time* 129:66-8 Je 15 '87
Art
750th birthday blast. A. Hunt. *Art News* 86:57-8 S '87
Art from the Exiled City [Berlinart 1961-1987 at the Museum of Modern Art] H. Cotter. il *Art Am* 75:43-5+ O '87
Art up against the wall [Berlinart 1961-1987 at the Museum of Modern Art] J. Perl. il *Vogue* 177:50 Jl '87
Berlin: a place for painting [Berlinart 1961-1987 at Museum of Modern Art] K. Ottman. il *Harpers Bazaar* 120:136-7+ Je '87
Berlinart 1961-1987 [exhibit at Museum of Modern Art] A. C. Danto. *Nation* 245:28-9 Jl 4-11 '87
Divide and conquer [Berlinart 1961-1987 at the Museum of Modern Art] K. Larson. il *N Y* 20:74-5 Je 22 '87
Out of the wall's shadow [Berlinart 1961-1987 at the Museum of Modern Art] R. Hughes. il *Time* 130:64-5 Ag 24 '87
Dance
At 750, Berlin kicks up its heels. D. Teal. il *Dance Mag* 61:34-5 Je '87
Description
Ich bin ein ballooner [M. Forbes' motorcycle and hot air balloon trip] B. Conrad, III. il map *Forbes* 140:116-20+ Ag 24 '87
In the capital of modern cruelty. A. Valiunas. *Commentary* 83:45-56 Ja '87

Berlin (Germany: West)—*cont.*

Galleries and museums

See also

Reichstag (Berlin, Germany: West)

Music

See also

Opera—Germany (West)

Stores

Berlin bazaar. A. Rand. il *Harpers Bazaar* 120:60 Jl '87

Berlin Ballet

Reviews:

Performance of Romeo and Juliet in West Berlin. H. Koegler. *Dance Mag* 61:20-1 My '87

Berlin Film Festival *See* Motion picture festivals—Germany (West)

Berlin Jazz Festival *See* Music festivals—Germany (West)

Berlin question, 1945-

Anomalous Berlin. N. Gelb. il *New Leader* 70:8-9 Ja 12-26 '87

In the capital of modern cruelty. A. Valiunas. *Commentary* 83:45-56 Ja '87

Berliner, Henry A., Jr.

about

A good niche is hard to find. J. Wynn. il por *Forbes* 139:90 Ja 26 '87

Berlioz, Hector, 1803-1869

about

Enthusiastic response. P. G. Davis. il por *N Y* 20:114-15 O 5 '87

Berlioz, Louis Hector *See* Berlioz, Hector, 1803-1869

Berlusconi, Silvio

about

Outfoxing the establishment. P. Sherrid. il por *U S News World Rep* 103:40-1 Jl 27 '87

Berman, Avis

Antiques: papier-mâché. il *Archit Dig* 44:108-13+ Jl '87

Art: Taos landscapes. il *Archit Dig* 44:158-63 Mr '87

Edith Wharton: on her 125th anniversary. il por *Archit Dig* 44:310+ N '87

Eileen Gray: in the vanguard of twentieth-century design. il por *Archit Dig* 44:62+ My '87

An imaginative kingdom: sculptor Bernard Langlais' Maine legacy. il *Archit Dig* 44:174-7+ Je '87

Imprints of the avant-garde—Barry Friedman. il por *Archit Dig* 44:114+ N '87

Manhattan mood. il *Archit Dig* 44:132-7 My '87

Berman, Claire

Bridging the distance between office and home. il *Work Woman* 12:128 D '87

A grandmother too soon! il *McCalls* 114:84-6 My '87

How many friends are enough? il *Parents* 62:64-6+ Ja '87

Learning to live with a sloppy kid. il *Parents* 62:128-30+ N '87

No place to call home: special report on America's adoption scandal. il *Redbook* 170:100-1+ D '87

Raising a responsible child. il *Parents* 62:110-12+ O '87

Berman, Irving S.

Macmillan's music series set new DTP standards. il *Publ Wkly* 232:38-9 N 13 '87

Berman, Joel C.

A case of colic. il *N Y Times Mag* p64 N 29 '87

Berman, Paul, 1949-

Don't follow leaders [cover story] il *New Repub* 197:28-35 Ag 10-17 '87

Bermel, Joyce

A matter of neglect. il *Parents* 62:335-6+ N '87

Bermuda

See also

Hotels, motels, etc.—Bermuda

Traffic accidents—Bermuda

Description and travel

A pink, white and azure paradise. A. Fotheringham. il *Macleans* 100:60 N 23 '87

Try the Bermuda angle. M. T. O'Keefe. il *Saturday Evening Post* 259:82-4 Ap '87

Bernadotte, Lennart, graf

about

Profiles: Count and Countess Lennart Bernadotte. D. H. Minassian. il pors *Archit Dig* 44:174-9+ D '87

Bernadotte, Sonja

about

Profiles: Count and Countess Lennart Bernadotte. D. H. Minassian. il pors *Archit Dig* 44:174-9+ D '87

Bernard, Bruce

A critic's complaints. *World Press Rev* 34:62 F '87

Bernard, Duke

Poor man's storage scope. il *Radio-Electron* 58:113-14 N '87

Bernard, Jami

The stupid things we do. il *Seventeen* 46:60 Mr '87

Bernard, Josef

High definition TV. il *Radio-Electron* 58:48-51 Ag '87

Inside cellular telephone. il *Radio-Electron* 58:53-5+ S '87

Bernard, Philippe

German companies serve as schools. *World Press Rev* 34:47 Ap '87

Le Bernardin (New York, N.Y.: Restaurant) *See* New York (N.Y.)—Restaurants, nightclubs, bars, etc.

Bernau, George

about

Lawyer's first novel goes to Warner for $750,000 floor. W. Goldstein. *Publ Wkly* 232:78 Ag 14 '87

Bernazard, Tony

about

Like father, like sons. J. McCallum. il por *Sports Illus* 67:32-3 Jl 6 '87

Berne, Tim

about

Tim Berne: beyond the five-year plan. K. Whitehead. il pors *Down Beat* 54:23-5 Jl '87

Berne Convention for the Protection of Literary and Artistic Works

10 publishers say adherence would not affect moral rights issue. H. Fields. *Publ Wkly* 232:13 O 16 '87

Berne hearings: witnesses argue question of joining or not. H. Fields. *Publ Wkly* 232:29 O 9 '87

Coalition is formed to fight U.S. joining Berne convention. H. Fields. *Publ Wkly* 232:13 S 11 '87

International protection of U.S. copyrights [statement, July 23, 1987] W. A. Wallis. *Dep State Bull* 87:26-8 O '87

'Moral rights' provision is now moot for joining Berne Convention, officials say. H. Fields. *Publ Wkly* 232:309 Ag 7 '87

New coalition of 47 joins battle over Berne. H. Fields. *Publ Wkly* 232:10 S 25 '87

Bernier, Olivier

Art deco rooms at the Musée des Arts Décoratifs. il *Antiques* 132:776-81 O '87

An eye for complexity. il *House Gard* 159:172-7+ Mr '87

Fin de siècle fantasy. il por *House Gard* 159:146-51 Jl '87

The kerosene lamp. il *Am Herit* 38:24-5 N '87

Moroccan in Manhattan. il *House Gard* 159:164-7+ F '87

Napoleon's grand designs. il *House Gard* 159:146-51+ D '87

The silver punch bowl. il *Am Herit* 38:24-5 D '87

Topkapi treasures. il *House Gard* 159:186-94 F '87

Bernier, Rosamond

A gift of vision. il por *House Gard* 159:120-9+ Jl '87

about

Profiles. C. Tomkins. por *New Yorker* 62:38-40+ Ja 19 '87

Bernier, Sandra

about

Barred from the church altar. M. McIver. por *Macleans* 100:45 Jl 6 '87

Bernikow, Louise, 1940-

An Asian mystique: Dale and Patricia Keller's New York apartment. il pors *Archit Dig* 44:94-101 S '87

Don't spend a night without armor: the condom. il *Mademoiselle* 93:116-18+ Ja '87

The joy—no kidding—of sex. il *Mademoiselle* 93:248-9+ N '87

An oasis in Bangkok: abstract art defines a penthouse apartment. il *Archit Dig* 44:60-7 Ja '87

Opposite attractions. il *Archit Dig* 44:176-81 O '87

La Quinta Norte: Douglas S. Cramer's ranch in the Santa Ynez Valley. il por *Archit Dig* 44:136-47 Ap '87

Second wind for a sassy band [excerpt from Alone in America] il *50 Plus* 27:72-5+ My '87

Southwest rhythms: restoring a Sante Fe adobe. il por *Archit Dig* 44:130-5 F '87

Traditional comforts on the Sound: a welcoming Connecticut residence. il *Archit Dig* 44:70-5 F '87

Bernini, Gian Lorenzo, 1598-1680

about

Sculpture, theatre of the sublime. F. Souchal. il *Courier* 40:20-2 S '87

Berns, Walter, 1919-

Government by lawyers & judges. *Commentary* 83:17-24 Je '87

Judicial review [discussion of June 1987 article, Government by lawyers & judges] *Commentary* 84:6+ N '87

Bernsen, Corbin
about
Good-bye swinging bachelor, hello calculated commitment seeker. C. Krupp. il pors *Glamour* 85:234+ O '87
Networking class hero. G. Kilday. il por *Roll Stone* p37-9+ Je 4 '87
Bernsen, Randy
about
Randy Bernsen. B. Milkowski. il por *Down Beat* 54:54-5 Ap '87
Bernstam, Mikhail S.
The collapse of the Soviet welfare state. *Natl Rev* 39:40-1 N 6 '87
Bernstein, Armyan
about
Cross my heart [film] Reviews
  Macleans il 100:66-7 N 30 '87. L. O'Toole
  People Wkly il 28:12 D 7 '87. T. Cunneff
Bernstein, Barton J.
The birth of the U.S. biological-warfare program. bibl (p136) il *Sci Am* 256:116-21 Je '87
Churchill's anthrax bombs: a debate [discussion of January/February 1987 article, Churchill's secret biological weapons] *Bull At Sci* 43:42-5 N '87
Churchill's secret biological weapons. bibl f *Bull At Sci* 43:46-50 Ja/F '87
Leo Szilard: giving peace a chance in the nuclear age. il pors *Phys Today* 40:40-7 S '87
Bernstein, Burton
Laughter in the Balkans. *New Yorker* 63:98-101+ O 26 '87
Bernstein, Dennis
(jt. auth) See Connie, Blitt, and Bernstein, Dennis
Bernstein, Gary
Pro talk. See issues of Petersen's Photographic Magazine
about
Taylor by Bernstein [interview] F. Cameron. il por *Petersens Photogr Mag* 15:20-2 Ja '87
Bernstein, George L.
The entrepreneurial family and its future [address, December 9, 1986] *Vital Speeches Day* 53:205-7 Ja 15 '87
Bernstein, Jeremy, 1929-
Au flair. Am Sch 56:167-70+ Spr '87
A journey to Lhasa. map *New Yorker* 63:47-50+ D 14 '87
The life it brings (I). *New Yorker* 62:35-8+ Ja 26 '87
The life it brings (II). *New Yorker* 62:39-42+ F 2 '87
Some things I didn't write. *Am Sch* 56:455-8+ Aut '87
Bernstein, Kenny
about
Expanding on a fast track. S. Gatty. il por *Nations Bus* 75:78 O '87
Bernstein, Leonard, 1918-
about
Age of gold. P. G. Davis. il *N Y* 20:80+ O 12 '87
Bernstein's greatest hits. D. Denby. il *Vogue* 177:102 Ap '87
A frank biography finds that Leonard Bernstein's passions, like his talents, are boundless [interview with J. Peyser] E. Levin. il pors *People Wkly* 27:48-50 My 4 '87
Magical maestro. G. D. Boone. il por *Horizon* 30:2 Je '87
The music man. E. Rothstein. il *New Repub* 196:27-9 Je 22 '87
Portrait of the artist, with smudges. M. Walsh. il por *Time* 129:87 My 18 '87
PW interviews [biographer J. Peyser] J. F. Baker. por *Publ Wkly* 231:63-4 Je 5 '87
Bernstein, Madeline
about
Bernstein for the defenseless. K. Pritzker. il por *McCalls* 114:62 Jl '87
Bernstein, Paula, 1933-
Dream jobs: the big switch. *Harpers Bazaar* 120:299+ Mr '87
Bernstein, R. E., and others
Acantharian fluxes and strontium to chlorinity ratios in the North Pacific Ocean. bibl f il *Science* 237:1490-4 S 18 '87
Bernstein, Richard
Fanning French fears. il por *N Y Times Mag* p50+ O 4 '87
Bernstein, Robert L., 1923-
about
After the un-Random showdown. M. Reuter. il pors *Publ Wkly* 232:11 O 30 '87
The rumble at Random House. J. Alter. il pors *Newsweek* 110:62 O 26 '87

Bernstein, Ted S.
about
Risky business. A. A. Lappen. il por *Forbes* 140:106 Jl 27 '87
Bernton, Edward W., and others
Release of multiple hormones by a direct action of interleukin-1 on pituitary cells. bibl f il *Science* 238:519-21 O 23 '87
Berntsen, Bredo
Marathon man. il por *Courier* 40:33-4 Je '87
Berquist, Kenneth
about
A small war. il *Newsweek* 109:7 Je 1 '87
Berra, Yogi, 1925-
about
Cinema Berraté: Yogi at the movies. T. N. Dawidoff. il por *Sports Illus* 67:10 D 21 '87
Berri, Claude
about
Jean de Florette [film] Reviews
  Commonweal 114:420-1 Jl 17 '87. T. O'Brien
  Glamour 85:102 Jl '87. J. G. Boyum
  N Y il 20:50-1 Jl 20 '87. D. Denby
  New Repub 197:26-7 Jl 6 '87. S. Kauffmann
  New Yorker 63:76-7 Jl 13 '87. P. Kael
  Newsweek il 110:61 Jl 13 '87. J. Kroll
  Time il 130:75 Jl 20 '87. R. Schickel
Manon of the spring [film] Reviews
  N Y 20:115 N 16 '87. D. Denby
  Natl Rev 39:57 D 18 '87. J. Simon
  New Repub il 197:24-5 N 23 '87. S. Kauffmann
  Newsweek il 110:77 N 9 '87. D. Ansen
Berrie (Russ) & Co., Inc. See Russ Berrie & Co., Inc.
Berries
See also
Blackberries
Blueberries
Cooking—Fruit
Mulberries
Raspberries
Strawberries
Cane and bush fruits. D. A. Jimerson and J. A. McKeon. il *Better Homes Gard* 65:32 Mr '87
Diseases and pests
See also
Mummy berry fungus
Berry, Anthony G.
about
A whiz kid bids for Manpower. M. D. Oneal and R. A. Melcher. il por *Bus Week* p37-8 Ag 17 '87
Berry, Chuck, 1926-
Maybellene and other high notes [excerpt from Chuck Berry] il pors *People Wkly* 28:71-2+ N 2 '87
about
Chuck Berry tells all—sort of. V. Aletti. il pors *Roll Stone* p71-2+ D 3 '87
'Hail! Hail! Rock 'n' roll' honors Chuck Berry. S. Rogers. il por *Roll Stone* p9 N 19 '87
Rock 'n' roller Berry gets Hollywood star. *Jet* 73:53 O 26 '87
Rocker, lover, duck walker. C. McGuigan. il pors *Newsweek* 110:90 O 26 '87
Rock's growly grandpa. R. Wolmuth. il pors *People Wkly* 28:92+ N 2 '87
Still reelin', still rockin'. R. Corliss. il por *Time* 130:84 O 19 '87
Berry, Edwin C., 1910-1987
about
Obituary
  Jet il por 72:16 Je 1 '87
Berry, Henry W., d. 1987
about
Obituary
  Jet 71:15 Mr 16 '87
Berry, John F. (John Francis), 1935-
The schizoid life of the media analyst. il *Channels* 7:62-8 F '87
Berry, Karen
. . . about women. il *Ms* 16:164-5 Jl/Ag '87
Berry, Mary Frances
How hard it is to change. il *N Y Times Mag* p93-4+ S 13 '87
about
Mary Frances Berry. J. Barthel. por *Ms* 15:68-70+ Ja '87
The powers that shouldn't be: five Washington insiders the next Democratic president shouldn't hire [cover story] P. Glastris. pors *Wash Mon* 19:39-46+ O '87
Study of race violence a 'ploy,' Berry says. por *Jet* 71:31 F 23 '87

Berry, Richard, 1946-
Behind the scenes. See issues of Astronomy
Berry, Tommy Lee
about
'Root doctor' held in murder of his former wife. *Jet* 72:29 Je 1 '87
Berry, Wendell, 1934-
Four poems [poem] *Ctry J* 14:30-1 N '87
Preserving wildness. il *Wilderness* 50:39-40+ Spr '87
Berry, William A., 1933-
about
William A. Berry. B. S. Goldman. il por *Am Artist* 51:68-73+ F '87
Berry desserts *See* Desserts
Berst, Jesse
The latest word in desktop publishing. il *Publ Wkly* 232:26+ N 13 '87
Bertain, Leonard
Don't discount China's potential to succeed as industrial power. por *Aviat Week Space Technol* 127:61-2 D 7 '87
Bertell, Rosalie
about
Rosalie Bertell. B. Lawren. *Omni* 9:96-7 S '87
Bertelsmann AG
Bantam's Vitale to head Doubleday-Dell trade group [changes in wake of Bertelsmann takeover] *Publ Wkly* 231:24 Ja 9 '87
Bertelsmann's U.S. invasion may be just beginning. J. E. Pluenneke. il *Bus Week* p72-3 Ag 10 '87
D'day Manufacturing reorganized with Bertelsmann. J. P. Frank. *Publ Wkly* 232:71 O 2 '87
Bertinelli, Valerie, 1960?-
about
"He is my life". N. Gittelson. il pors *McCalls* 114:14-15+ F '87
Valerie Bertinelli gets her sexiest role yet, but she'd rather be a mom. F. A. Bernstein. il pors *People Wkly* 27:94-5+ Mr 9 '87
BERTL (Computer language)
Programming in BERTL. il *Byte* 12:115-17 My '87
Bertolucci, Bernardo
Billions of emperors. il por *Film Comment* 23:34 N/D '87
about
The last emperor [film] Reviews
　Commonweal 114:747-8 D 18 '87. T. O'Brien
　Life il 10:36-40 Ap '87. D. Leigh-Kile
　Macleans il 100:66 D 14 '87. L. O'Toole
　N Y il 20:76-8 N 30 '87. D. Denby
　Natl Rev 39:54-7 D 18 '87. J. Simon
　New Repub 197:22-3 D 14 '87. S. Kauffmann
　New Yorker 63:98-101 N 30 '87. P. Kael
　Newsweek 1 110:81-2 N 23 '87. D. Ansen
　People Wkly il 28:12 D 7 '87. P. Travers
　Time il 130:100 N 23 '87. R. Schickel
Model citizen: Bernardo Bertolucci on location in China [cover story] T. Rayns. il por *Film Comment* 23:31-2+ N/D '87
Bertram, Christoph, 1937-
Europe's security dilemmas. *Foreign Aff* 65:942-57 Summ '87
Beryllium
The cosmic synthesis of lithium, beryllium and boron. V. E. Viola and G. J. Mathews. il *Sci Am* 256:38-45 My '87
Besançon, Alain
Modern ideologies & the Jews. *Commentary* 83:41-5 Mr '87
Bespaloff, Alexis
Wine. See occasional issues of New York
Besse, Jean
(jt. auth) See Courtillot, Vincent, and Besse, Jean
Bessemer Group, Inc.
A family office. B. Weberman. il *Forbes* 139:218-20 Je 15 '87
Bessette, Ernie
about
Pioneer. *New Yorker* 63:27-8 F 23 '87
Bessie, Simon Michael
about
Mikhail Gorbachev, author [interview] A. P. Sanoff. il por *U S News World Rep* 103:73 O 12 '87
Besson, Paul
How to keep the tax man out of your nest egg. il *Black Enterp* 17:65-6+ Mr '87
Bessone, Lisa Twyman
Winning at life. il *Women's Sports Fitness* 9:46-50 S '87

Best, Tony
Crop Over: more than a big party [cover story] il *Américas* 39:16-21 Jl/Ag '87
Best books *See* Books and reading—Best books
Best Business Advertising Contest *See* Advertising—Awards
Best Products Co., Inc.
Best Products: trying to put pizzazz back in the showroom. T. Smart. il por *Bus Week* p39-40 Mr 16 '87
Best seller [film] See Motion picture reviews—Single works
Best sellers
25 years of university press best sellers. *N Y Times Book Rev* 92:58 O 11 '87
Audio preview: bestsellers on the way. il *Publ Wkly* 232:53-5 Jl 31 '87
Best sellers. See issues of The New York Times Book Review
Bestselling UP backlist. *Publ Wkly* 231:39-41 Je 5 '87
The blockbustering of Lee Iacocca. P. Wyden. il *N Y Times Book Rev* 92:1+ S 13 '87
Current religious bestsellers. *Publ Wkly* 231:28 Je 26 '87
Current religious bestsellers. *Publ Wkly* 231:24 Ap 17 '87
Hardcover bestsellers. D. Maryles. il *Publ Wkly* 231:20-3 Mr 13 '87
Longest-running hardcover bestsellers for 1986; Longest-running paperback bestsellers for 1986. il *Publ Wkly* 231:54-5 Ja 9 '87
A look at the issues in Blatty's appeal to the Supreme Court [best seller list dispute with N.Y. times] C. E. Rinzler. *Publ Wkly* 232:16-17 Ag 28 '87
Paperback best sellers. See issues of The New York Times Book Review
Paperback top sellers. J. Mutter. *Publ Wkly* 231:24-8 Mr 13 '87
Publishers weekly hardcover bestsellers. See issues of Publishers Weekly
Publishers weekly paperback bestsellers. See issues of Publishers Weekly
Religious bestsellers. *Publ Wkly* 231:43 Mr 6 '87
'A season on the brink' is the season's surprise #1 bestseller. D. Masello. il pors *Publ Wkly* 231:28-30 Mr 27 '87
Story behind the bestseller: Allan Bloom's 'The closing of the American mind'. W. Goldstein. il por *Publ Wkly* 232:25-7 Jl 3 '87
The top of the charts; The mega hardcover sellers. *Publ Wkly* 231:53 Ja 9 '87
Beta blockers (Drugs) *See* Adrenergic blocking agents
Beta-carotene *See* Carotene
Beta decay
Double-beta decay [work of Michael K. Moe and others] J. Horgan. *Sci Am* 257:22+ N '87
Double-beta decay caught in the act [work of Michael K. Moe and others] S. Weisburd. *Sci News* 132:148 S 5 '87
Possible first hints of double beta decay [work of Frank T. Avignone III and others] M. M. Waldrop. *Science* 235:534 Ja 30 '87
Two-neutrino double β-decay seen; neutrinoless decay sought [work of Steven Elliott and others] B. G. Levi. bibl il *Phys Today* 40:19-22 D '87
Beta-lactam antibiotics *See* Antibiotics
Beta Lyrae (Star) *See* Stars, Eclipsing binary
Beta Pictoris solar system *See* Solar system
Beta rays
See also
　Beta decay
Betamax case *See* Videotapes—Unauthorized use
Betcher, William
How to keep your love alive: playing for keeps [excerpts from Intimate play] il *Glamour* 85:250-2+ F '87
Betelgeuse (Star) *See* Stars, Giant
Bethany, Marilyn
Design. See issues of New York beginning February 20, 1984
What works: priceless tips from the super-decorators [cover story] il *N Y* 20:36-58+ Ap 13 '87
What's modern now [cover story] il *N Y* 20:48-73 S 28 '87
Bethea, Elvin Lamonte
about
Ex-football all-star Elvin Bethea planned for life after NFL. il pors *Jet* 71:48-9 Mr 9 '87
Bethea, Larry
about
A Cowboy's long way home. G. Norman. il pors *Sport Mag* 78:79-80+ D '87
Guilty of theft, Bethea awaits sentencing in Va. *Jet* 71:49 Ja 19 '87

Bethell, Tom
California, here I come. il *Natl Rev* 39:33-6 F 27 '87
A new statute of liberty. *Natl Rev* 39:38+ D 18 '87
Totem and taboo at Stanford. *Natl Rev* 39:42+ O 9 '87

Bethesda (Md.)
Religious institutions and affairs
Major Maryland Presbyterian Church switches its affiliation [Fourth Presbyterian Church to join Evangelical Presbyterian Church] *Christ Today* 31:59 Ja 16 '87

Bethlehem
Politics and government
Bitterness in Bethlehem [West Bank violence] J. Bierman. il *Macleans* 100:10+ Ja 5 '87

Bethlehem, Star of *See* Star of Bethlehem
Bethlehem (Pa.)
Description
Christmas in Bethlehem. S. Ferrell. il *Saturday Evening Post* 259:66-70 D '87
Pennsylvania's own Star of Bethlehem. C. La VO. *Travel Holiday* 168:14-15 D '87

Bethlehem Steel Corp.
Walter Williams. G. L. Miles. il por *Bus Week* Sp Issue:250 Ap 17 '87

Bethune, John
That cozy bookstore café. il *Publ Wkly* 231:46-8 Ap 24 '87

Bethune, Norman, d. 1939
about
Making a legend [cover story; special section; with editorial comment by Kevin Doyle] il pors *Macleans* 100:2, 26-34 Ag 10 '87

Betsch, Madeline
about
Advertising success in Minneapolis. J. Giambanco. il pors *Work Woman* 12:117-18+ O '87

Bettelheim, Bruno
The importance of play [cover story] il *Atlantic* 259:35-46 Mr '87
about
The good enough parent's parent. M. J. Bandler. il pors *Parents* 62:189-90+ N '87
Parents, use your heads. B. Kantrowitz. il por *Newsweek* 109:78-9 Je 22 '87

Bettenhausen, Elizabeth
about
Contract not renewed. *Christ Century* 104:936 O 28 '87

Better Beef Marketing
New cattlemen's co-op hits the road. B. Eftink. il *Success Farm* 85:28-9 N '87

Better homes and gardens (Periodical)
Anniversary almanac [with editorial comment by David Jordan] il *Better Homes Gard* 65:10, 17-18 Jl '87
Editor's letter. D. Jordan. See issues of Better Homes and Gardens beginning November 1984

Betterway Publications Inc.
Betterway: publishing for a profitable retirement. B. Summer. *Publ Wkly* 232:38 N 20 '87

Betting *See* Gambling; Horse race betting

Betts, Judi
The watercolor page. il por *Am Artist* 51:60-3+ N '87

Betty (Musical group)
In 1988 Washington's dream ticket may be a 'rockapella' trio named Betty. il *People Wkly* 28:125 O 5 '87

Betty Blue [film] See Motion picture reviews—Single works

Beuttler, Bill
Billy Cobham: on the attack [interview] il pors *Down Beat* 54:19-21 Ap '87
The Charlie Watts interview. il pors *Down Beat* 54:16-19+ F '87
Dave Weckl: new drumslinger in town [cover story] il por *Down Beat* 54:16-18 D '87
The Jack DeJohnette interview [cover story] il pors *Down Beat* 54:16-19 S '87
Musicfest U.S.A./Chicago! il *Down Beat* 54:26-31 Jl '87
On the beat. See alternate issues of Down Beat beginning June 1985 through December 1987

Beuys, Joseph, 1921-1986
about
Modern times. J. Perl. il *Vogue* 177:90+ Ag '87

Bevan, Aneurin, 1897-1960
about
Demythologising Nye Bevan. J. Campbell. bibl il pors *Hist Today* 37:13-18 Ap '87

Bevan, Laurie
(jt. auth) See Strickland, Richard M., 1950-, and Bevan, Laurie

Bevan, Tim
about
The Brit pack. R. Nicolson. il pors *Vogue* 177:80 D '87

Beväringen Company
Fattening up the Nobel Prize [Nobel Foundation going public] J. Kapstein. *Bus Week* p48 O 26 '87

Bevel squares *See* Carpenters' squares

Beverage containers
See also
Drinking vessels
The big chill [M. Zolp's self-cooling can scam] J. Crudele. il *N Y* 20:19+ Ag 24 '87
Old-time seltzer in new-fangled bottles [plastic squirt container] J. O. Hamilton. il por *Bus Week* p164 S 14 '87
Self-cooling cans. G. Davis. il *Pop Sci* 230:53 Ap '87
Veryfine: oh, what a difference packaging makes [New England Apple Products Co.] K. H. Hammonds. il por *Bus Week* p71 Ag 31 '87
Recycling
See Recycling (Waste, etc.)

Beverage industry
See also
American Natural Beverage Corporation
Brewing industry
Liquor industry
Soft drink industry
Wine industry
Finance
Beverages and tobacco. H. Seneker. il *Forbes* 139:78+ Ja 12 '87

Beverage mixes
Creating your own hot chocolate mix. il *Sunset* 179:155 D '87
Labeling
Wrong whey [false claims for Rockland Corporation beverage mix] il *FDA Consum* 21:38 D '87/Ja '88

Beverages
See also
Airlines—Beverage service
Alcoholic beverages
Beer, Nonalcoholic
Bottled water
Coffee
Fruit juices
Milkshakes
Punch (Beverage)
Tea (Beverage)
Wine, Nonalcoholic
After-dinner drinks. il *Essence* 18:84+ D '87
Choosing the right energy drink. S. Krasnow. il *Sport Mag* 78:93 Jl '87
Italian coolers . . . they're sparkling fruit fizzes. il *Sunset* 179:128-9 Ag '87
Making steamed milk . . . plain or flavored, for cappuccino or for sipping by itself. il *Sunset* 178:234 My '87
Refreshers [fruit drinks] A. C. Boe. il *Good Housekeep* 204:126 My '87
Six of one, 2.5 of another [sports drinks] *Women's Sports Fitness* 9:59 F '87
Summer coolers: tall, tasty, and quick! A. Bailey. il *Parents* 62:134+ Jl '87
Warm greetings for the holidays [hot drinks and finger foods] J. R. Nyenhuis. il *Saturday Evening Post* 259:76-8 D '87

Beverley, Ted
about
Hot ice. M. R. Enright. il por *Nations Bus* 75:57 Jl '87

Beverley Ice Company
Hot ice. M. R. Enright. il por *Nations Bus* 75:57 Jl '87

Beverly, Gary
Chino Valley changes. il por *Mother Earth News* 103:64-5 Ja/F '87

Beverly Hills (Calif.)
Architecture
California crafted [architect C. Howard transforms M. Palevsky's house] il *House Gard* 159:182-9 Ap '87
Banks
See also
City National Bank (Beverly Hills, Calif.)
Bookstores
See Booksellers and bookselling—California
Education
Fun and profits at Beverly Hills High [deal with Twentieth Century-Fox Film Corp.] il *Newsweek* 110:45 Ag 31 '87

Beverly Hills (Calif.)—*cont.*
Galleries and museums
See also
Frederick R. Weisman Museum
Historic houses, sites, etc.
Paean to glamour: dramatic formality for an Italianate villa in Beverly Hills [decorated by Illya Hendrix and Thomas Allardyce] J. Gruen. il *Archit Dig* 44:102-7 S '87
Restaurants, nightclubs, bars, etc.
A Beverly Hills bar has water, water from everywhere, and that's all there is to drink [Ixi:z owned by S. Mills] il *People Wkly* 27:109-10 F 9 '87
A Beverly Hills diner-saur named Ed Debevic's takes customers back to the Stone Age of rock 'n' roll. M. Neill. il por *People Wkly* 28:180-1 N 30 '87
Hands up and butts out! [ban on smoking] M. Smilgis. il *Time* 129:78 Ap 27 '87
Savings and loan associations
See also
Columbia Savings & Loan Assoc.
Stores
Christmas shopping on the Drive [Rodeo Drive] D. P. Marshall. il *Travel Holiday* 168:20-1+ D '87
Streets
See also
Rodeo Drive (Beverly Hills, Calif.)
Beverly Hills cop II [film] See Motion picture reviews—Single works
Bevins, William C., Jr.
about
At Ted's right hand. C. Capuzzi. por *Channels* 7:54 Je '87
Beyda & Associates Inc.
Beyda & Associates: selling children's books wholesale. A. Symons. il *Publ Wkly* 231:138-9 F 27 '87
Beyer, Troy
about
Troy Beyer explains why she once rebelled and ran away from home. por *Jet* 73:37 D 7 '87
Troy Beyer: more than meets the eye. il pors *Ebony* 43:102+ D '87
Troy Beyer's career soaring after 'Dynasty'. por *Jet* 73:53 O 26 '87
Beyond therapy [film] See Motion picture reviews—Single works
Beza-Mahafaly (Madagascar) *See* National parks and reserves—Madagascar
Bezoars
A bizarre bezoar tale [research by Eckard W. Hellmuth] S. Weisburd. *Sci News* 132:190 S 19 '87
Bhaktipada
about
Dial om for murder. J. Hubner and L. Gruson. il pors *Roll Stone* p53-4+ Ap 9 '87
Bharathan, Desikan
(jt. auth) See Penney, Terry R., and Bharathan, Desikan
Bhat, Ramesh V.
Moulds that can kill. il *World Health* p20-2 Mr '87
Bhoge, Leakh
about
I spy: how a Queens College student helped catch a KGB agent and set off a superpower showdown. M. Daly. il pors *N Y* 20:34-47 Ap 6 '87
Bhonslay, Marianne
Get the perfect fit. il *Women's Sports Fitness* 9:23-4+ N '87
Bhopal (India)
See also
Bhopal poisonous gas disaster, India, 1984
Bhopal poisonous gas disaster, India, 1984
The Bhopal syndrome [excerpt] D. Weir. il *Omni* 10:38+ N '87
The legacies of two disasters. il *World Press Rev* 34:55-6 Mr '87
The lessons of Bhopal. F. M. Bordewich. il *Atlantic* 259:30-3 Mr '87
Twice poisoned [views of D. Kurzman] M. Isikoff. *Wash Mon* 19:49-50 D '87
Bhutto, Benazir
about
Getting to know you. il pors *Time* 130:23 Ag 10 '87
A match made in Pakistan. R. Nordland. il pors *Newsweek* 110:47 Ag 10 '87
Something old, something new. il pors *Newsweek* 110:31 D 28 '87
Biafra, Jello
about
Biafra trial ends in hung jury. J. Ressner. il por *Roll Stone* p22 O 8 '87

Dead Kennedys break up; Jello Biafra's legal problems persist. D. Fricke. *Roll Stone* p14 Ja 29 '87
Rockin' with the First Amendment. S. Wishnia. il *Nation* 245:444-6 O 24 '87
Biaggi, Mario, 1917-
about
Charges of bribery. B. Levin. il por *Macleans* 100:30 Je 15 '87
Biagiotti, Laura
about
The cool retreat in Venice. il por *Vogue* 177:766-73 S '87
Bialer, Seweryn
The curtain rises on Gorbachev's Act II. il *U S News World Rep* 103:36-7 Jl 13 '87
Gorbachev: risking all for reform [with editorial comment by Mortimer B. Zuckerman] il por *U S News World Rep* 102:50-1, 79-80 Ap 27 '87
Gorbachev's move. *Foreign Policy* 68:59-87 Fall '87
Marx had it wrong. Does Gorbachev? il *U S News World Rep* 103:41-2 O 19 '87
Perestroika means mountains to move. il *U S News World Rep* 103:80-1 N 9 '87
about
The latest myths about the Soviet Union. N. Eberstadt. *Commentary* 83:17-27 My '87
Bianco, Frank, and Schemmel, William
Southern sampler. il *Travel Holiday* 167:79-88 Mr '87
Bianculli, David
The Roots of the problem. il *Channels* 7:32-3 Ja '87
Bias, Len, 1963-1986
about
Bias' friend Tribble glad 'system did not fail me'. pors *Jet* 72:48 Je 22 '87
Indiana coach Knight has no sympathy for Bias; 'He was so cool'. *Jet* 72:46 Ag 3 '87
One mother's crusade against drug abuse [interview] pors *Christ Today* 31:50+ My 15 '87
Bias, Lonise
about
One mother's crusade against drug abuse [interview] pors *Christ Today* 31:50+ My 15 '87
Biathlon
Jump, shoot, ski . . . win [Nordic World Ski Championships silver medalists K. Lynch and J. Thompson] B. Koch. il por *Skiing* 40:42+ S '87
Ready, aim . . . medal! [American J. Thompson takes a silver in the World Championships] J. Lieber. il por *Sports Illus* 66:54-5 F 23 '87
Economic aspects
Drawing a bead on a new dream: having helped two sons to become world-class biathletes, a couple now address their own future [Jim and Betty Schreiner to run a bed-and-breakfast business] S. Seixas. il *Money* 16:182-4 F '87
Biayenda, Emile, Cardinal
about
A cardinal who spoke truth to power. R. Fegley. *Christ Century* 104:325-6 Ap 8 '87
Bible
See also
Change in the Bible
Dinners and dining in the Bible
Light and darkness in the Bible
National Bible Week
Prophets
Suicide in the Bible
Water in the Bible
Publish bad tidings. T. Stafford. il *Christ Today* 31:30 F 20 '87
Anecdotes, facetiae, satire, etc.
Giving the Word [gift of the Bible to Iran's "moderates"] W. Goodman. *New Leader* 70:7 Ja 12-26 '87
Last word [Middle Testament] J. Carlson and J. Trueson. il *Omni* 9:122 S '87
Antiquities
The hunt for a lost holy past. S. Begley. il *Newsweek* 109:56+ Je 22 '87
Bibliography
Books on the Bible [cover story] D. J. Harrington. *America* 157:431-7 D 5 '87
Criticism, interpretation, etc.
Scriptural scholarship [cover story; special section] il *America* 157:286-303+ O 31 '87
The Word. M. K. Hellwig. See issues of America beginning June 23-30, 1984 through June 20-27, 1987
The Word. P. J. Ryan. See issues of America beginning November 21, 1987
The Word. G. G. Seibert. See issues of America beginning July 4-11, 1987 through November 14, 1987

Bible—*cont.*

Evidence, authority, etc.

Battle on the Bible [Southern Baptists seek help outside their ranks in effort to settle the issue of inerrancy] R. Frame. il *Christ Today* 31:44-6 Je 12 '87

Anecdotes, facetiae, satire, etc.

Jessica who? M. E. Marty. *Christ Century* 104:839 S 30 '87

Geography

A book of revelations [Harper atlas of the Bible] G. Hill. *World Press Rev* 34:55 D '87

Inerrancy

See Bible—Evidence, authority, etc.

Language, style

Speaking of postliberalism [G. A. Lindbeck on biblical language] M. E. Marty. *Christ Century* 104:391 Ap 22 '87

Literary character

The literary study of the Bible. J. S. Kselman. *America* 157:297-9+ O 31 '87

Reading the Bible like a book. T. Longman, III. il por *Christ Today* 31:27-8 Mr 6 '87

Manuscripts, Hebrew

Mystery of the buried amulet [G. Barkay discovers ancient biblical manuscripts in Jerusalem] C. Safran. il *Read Dig* 130:95-9 Je '87

Publication and distribution

The boss was a hustler or, How I got my Bible [Bibles of Yore secondhand business] E. M. Halliday. *N Y Times Book Rev* 92:20 D 13 '87

The Good Book can be good for you [bookstore sales] F. Couch and K. Stephens. il *Publ Wkly* 232:67-8 O 9 '87

Jeremiad on Bible manufacture in the United States [Thomas Nelson turning to foreign manufacturing] W. Griffin. *Publ Wkly* 232:24 Ag 21 '87

Quotations

If Luther were sitting in the end zone. D. H. Hopper. *Christ Century* 104:781-2 S 23 '87

Study and teaching

Anecdotes, facetiae, satire, etc.

BSAT [Biblical Scholastic Aptitude Test] D. Halberstein. *New Repub* 197:12 S 14-21 '87

Translations

See Bible—Versions

Versions

Christian missions and the Western guilt complex [cover story] L. O. Sanneh. il *Christ Century* 104:330-4 Ap 8 '87

The classics. M. E. Marty. *Christ Century* 104:951 O 28 '87

The good news on 'man' [New American Bible dumps generic use of word 'man' when the Greek meaning is inclusive of both sexes] *Commonweal* 114:228-9 Ap 24 '87

In the beginning was the word [M. Morris' Kwikscan reading system] W. G. Flanagan. il por *Forbes* 139:100-1 Ap 20 '87

New reading system promises to increase data retention [Kwikscan New Testament] J. P. Frank. il *Publ Wkly* 232:64-5 O 16 '87

Once more, the sound of music [new Roman Catholic version] R. N. Ostling. il *Time* 129:64 Ap 20 '87

Bible. N.T.

The good news on 'man' [New American Bible dumps generic use of word 'man' when the Greek meaning is inclusive of both sexes] *Commonweal* 114:228-9 Ap 24 '87

Once more, the sound of music [new Roman Catholic version] R. N. Ostling. il *Time* 129:64 Ap 20 '87

Criticism, interpretation, etc.

Believe it or not:

New Testament perspectives on faith (I). G. McCauley. il *America* 156:200 Mr 7 '87

New Testament perspectives on faith (II). G. McCauley. *America* 156:217 Mr 14 '87

New Testament perspectives on faith (III). G. McCauley. *America* 156:236 Mr 21 '87

Scripture and dogma today [Catholic doctrine] R. E. Brown. *America* 157:286-9 O 31 '87

Bible. N.T. Epistles of Paul

Cosmic groanings. R. Goetz. il *Christ Century* 104:1083-7 D 2 '87

A new paradigm for Paul. D. J. Harrington. il *America* 157:290-3 O 31 '87

Bible. N.T. Paul, Epistles of *See* Bible. N.T. Epistles of Paul

Bible. New Testament *See* Bible. N.T.

Bible. O.T.

Criticism, interpretation, etc.

Believe it or not:

Old Testament forms of faith. G. McCauley. *America* 156:177 F 28 '87

Holy Moses! The New Testament is only half the story [interview with D. Bergant] por *U S Cathol* 52:20-7 F '87

Bible. O.T. Exodus

Moses [discussion of June 1987 article, The uses of Exodus] F. Eberstadt. *Commentary* 84:8+ O '87

The uses of Exodus [interpretations] F. Eberstadt. *Commentary* 83:25-33 Je '87

Bible. O.T. Hosea

Submitting to freedom. P. Yancey. il *Christ Today* 31:64 Je 12 '87

Bible. O.T. Pentateuch

Who wrote the first five books of the Bible? [views of R. E. Friedman] A. P. Sanoff. il por *U S News World Rep* 103:52-3 Ag 24 '87

Bible. Old Testament *See* Bible. O.T.

Bible as literature *See* Bible—Literary character

Bible in motion pictures

A motion picture Bible according to Mormonism [edited version of the New Media Bible] R. Frame. il *Christ Today* 31:44+ S 18 '87

Anecdotes, facetiae, satire, etc.

The gospel according to Joe Bob. J. B. Briggs. il *Film Comment* 23:51-2+ Mr/Ap '87

Bible societies

See also

International Council on Biblical Inerrancy

Bible Speaks (Church)

An heiress vs. a pastor [E. Dovydenas vs. C. Stevens and his Bible Speaks church] G. Hackett. por *Newsweek* 109:33 Ap 20 '87

Bible stories

See also

Videotapes—Bible stories

Bibliographic data bases *See* Information storage and retrieval systems

Biblioteca Apostolica Vaticana

The Vatican goes to Hell [ancient texts recreated by computer imaging] E. Stone. il *Omni* 9:24 S '87

Bicak, Charles J.

(jt. auth) See Horton, James C., and Bicak, Charles J.

Bicarbonate of soda *See* Sodium bicarbonate

Bice (New York, N.Y.: Restaurant) *See* New York (N.Y.)—Restaurants, nightclubs, bars, etc.

Les biches [ballet] *See* Ballet reviews—Single works

Bichevskaya, Janna

about

Janna Bichevskaya is Russia's most popular balladeer—and sounds just like Joan Baez. S. K. Reed. il pors *People Wkly* 27:76+ Ap 6 '87

Bickley, Cary

Why solo vacations are my secret salvation. il *Glamour* 85:28+ Ag '87

Bicycle accidents *See* Cycling—Accidents and injuries

Bicycle industry

See also

Huffy Corporation

Murray Ohio Mfg. Co.

Bicycle messengers

Wild in the streets [woman messenger M. Sprizzo in New York City] D. Frost. il pors *Women's Sports Fitness* 9:33-6 My '87

Bicycle racing

BMX racer: beating the boys at their own game [H. McKenzie] K. Dickerson. il *Teen* 31:67 S '87

High on the mountain [woman racer J. Phelan] S. Rubin. il pors *Women's Sports Fitness* 9:29-32 My '87

Highway to glory [Ore-Ida Women's Challenge] J. Mills and H. Delehanty. il *Women's Sports Fitness* 9:48-53 N '87

Woman to watch: Janie Eickhoff. H. R. Madison. por *Women's Sports Fitness* 9:25 Ap '87

France

Bright wheels rolling [Tour de France] A. Wolff. il *Sports Illus* 67:54-5 Jl 20 '87

Score a big one for the Irish [S. Roche wins Tour de France] A. Wolff. il por *Sports Illus* 67:22-3 Ag 3 '87

A wheeler, but no dealer [A. Hampsten, America's hope in upcoming Tour de France] A. Wolff. il pors *Sports Illus* 66:58+ Je 29 '87

Bicycles

See also

Cycling

Bicycles—See also—*cont.*
Mopeds
Bikes that can cope with mean streets [city bikes] P. Angiolillo. il *Bus Week* p184 O 12 '87
Buying bicycles: making the best choice for each family member. M. Conroy. il *Better Homes Gard* 65:90+ My '87
Cycles. N. Mayersohn. See issues of Popular Mechanics beginning January 1986
In search of the perfect bike. R. McNatt. il *Money* 16:56-8+ Ag '87
Rad wheels. N. Mayersohn. il *Pop Mech* 164:84-7 My '87
Two-wheel terrors [mountain bikes] J. Foote. il *Newsweek* 110:72 S 28 '87
Two-wheeling in the urban jungle [use of mountain bikes] R. McManus. il *Sierra* 72:107-8 N/D '87

Collectors and collecting
The two-wheeled time machine [balloon tire bikes] K. M. Miller. il *Esquire* 107:17-18 Ja '87

Equipment
Boost your pedal power. A. Klein. il *Women's Sports Fitness* 9:56 Ag '87

Laws and regulations
See Cycling—Laws and regulations

Maintenance and repair
10 tips for keeping your bike rolling. il *Teen* 31:95 Je '87
Be your own bike mechanic. K. Delhagen. bibl il *Women's Sports Fitness* 9:68-9 My '87

Materials
Aluminum bikes. S. F. Brown. il *Pop Sci* 230:86-7+ Mr '87

Police use
Recycled as cyclists, Seattle's posse of bike-riding crime fighters put their mettle to the pedal. D. Chu. il *People Wkly* 28:53-4 N 9 '87

Testing
Women on wheels: a buyer's guide to bicycles, clothing, and accessories. S. Weaver. il *Women's Sports Fitness* 9:33+ F '87
Bicycles, Exercise *See* Exercising equipment
Bicycles, Recumbent *See* Human powered vehicles
Bicycles in art

Exhibitions
Comment [F. Yoshimura's Three bicycles included in the exhibition Craft today: poetry of the physical] A. Palinkas. il *Am Craft* 47:20+ D '87/Ja '88
Bicycling *See* Cycling
Bicycling clothes *See* Clothing and dress—Sports clothes
Bidar (India)

History
Reflections on solitude [encounters with Muslims in 15th century] A. Nikitin. il *Courier* 40:15 Ap '87
Biddick (Durham, England: Historic house) *See* Historic houses, sites, etc.—Great Britain
Biddle, Wayne
Who's counting? *Nation* 245:148-9 Ag 29 '87
Biden, Joseph R.

about
And then there were six. G. J. Church. il por *Time* 130:24-5 O 5 '87
Biden Star Chamber? M. Fumento. *Natl Rev* 39:30 Mr 13 '87
Bidenquiddick. *Natl Rev* 39:15+ Ag 28 '87
Biden's belly flop. M. Kaus. il pors *Newsweek* 110:23-4 S 28 '87
Biden's familiar quotations. W. Shapiro. il por *Time* 130:17 S 28 '87
Biden's main chance. T. Morganthau. il por *Newsweek* 110:35-6 S 21 '87
Biden's truth. *Nation* 245:328-9 O 3 '87
Caddell's defeat. il por *Newsweek* 110:9 O 5 '87
A candidate's character in question. M. McDonald. il por *Macleans* 100:24+ S 28 '87
A case of plagiarized passion? *Newsweek* 110:35 S 21 '87
A caveat for candidates. B. McBarton. por *Newsweek* 110:14 O 19 '87
Crucible for a candidate. D. Baer. il pors *U S News World Rep* 103:24-5 S 21 '87
Debacle for the Duke. J. Klein. il por *N Y* 20:26+ O 12 '87
Duke of piety. S. Lehigh and F. J. Connolly. *New Repub* 197:13-15 O 26 '87
The dwarfs in disarray. G. J. Church. il pors *Time* 130:22+ O 12 '87
The fall of a contender. M. McDonald. il por *Macleans* 100:30 O 5 '87
The fall of Joe Biden. J. Alter and H. Fineman. il por *Newsweek* 110:28 O 5 '87

Gary Hart and Joe Biden: a surfeit of behavior. *America* 157:203 O 10 '87
'The hottest fight in a decade'. N. Cooper. il pors *Newsweek* 110:30 Jl 20 '87
In praise of winging it. G. F. Will. il *Newsweek* 110:80 Jl 6 '87
Is Joe Biden more than 'just a speech'? D. Harbrecht. il por *Bus Week* p59-60 Mr 30 '87
Joe Biden in the crunch. G. Smith. il pors *Life* 10:78-80+ O '87
No heavy lifting. W. Safire. il *N Y Times Mag* p12+ S 27 '87
Now, a Dukakis fiasco. M. Kaus. il por *Newsweek* 110:40 O 12 '87
Of many things. G. W. Hunt. *America* 157:202 O 10 '87
On trial: character. G. Borger. il pors *U S News World Rep* 103:26-7 S 28 '87
Orator for the next generation. L. I. Barrett. il pors *Time* 129:24+ Je 22 '87
Peccadillos and presidents. A. Fotheringham. il *Macleans* 100:68 S 28 '87
A populist message hits home [cover story] A. Kopkind. il *Nation* 245:37+ Jl 18-25 '87
The price of deception. J. Bierman. *Macleans* 100:32 O 12 '87
The reduction of Joe Biden. J. Klein. por *N Y* 20:26+ O 5 '87
Ronald Biden. F. Barnes. il *New Repub* 196:18-19 Je 1 '87

Anecdotes, facetiae, satire, etc.
Talking head. A. Z. Posner. *New Repub* 197:8+ O 12 '87
Bidinotto, Robert James
The invincible voice of Cape Ann. il por *Read Dig* 131:201-2+ O '87
Bidwill, Bill

about
Why the football Cardinals are singing the St. Louis blues. J. E. Ellis. il *Bus Week* p44 D 21 '87
Biederman, James

about
James Biederman at John Weber. S. Ellis. il *Art Am* 75:177-8 O '87
Biedermeier furniture
Biedermeier chairs. A. Wilkie. il *Antiques* 132:798-807 O '87

Exhibitions
See also
Angus Wilkie Antiques (Firm)
Biedermeier glassware

Collectors and collecting
Biedermeier keepsakes. N. F. Weber. il *House Gard* 159:120-3+ Ag '87
Biehl, David L.

about
The watchword after Bloody Monday: diversify. D. Zigas. *Bus Week* p142 N 9 '87
Biehl, Larry

about
Sitting tight in Japan [interview] A. E. Serwer. il por *Fortune* 115:306 Ap 27 '87
Bielski, Vince, and others
The death squads hit home: which side is the FBI on? il *Progressive* 51:15-19 O '87
Bielsky, Tuvia, d. 1987

about
Obituary
New Repub 197:43 Ag 3 '87. L. Wieseltier
Biemann, Klaus, and Scoble, Hubert A.
Characterization by tandem mass spectrometry of structural modifications in proteins. bibl f il *Science* 237:992-8 Ag 28 '87
Bienal International do Livro (Brazil) *See* Book fairs
Bienefeld, Herbert

about
King's Road ransom. V. Becker. il pors *House Gard* 159:76+ My '87
Bienewitz, Peter *See* Apianus, Petrus, 1495-1552
Biennials (Plants)
Biennial flowers for easy care. B. Pleasant. il *Rodale's Org Gard* 34:54-6+ Je '87
Bierds, Linda
Erebus [poem] *New Yorker* 63:42 O 5 '87
Strike [poem] *New Yorker* 63:46 My 11 '87
Biesenkamp, Jack

about
Gathering moss. K. Whiteside. il *House Gard* 159:144-9+ My '87

Bifocal sunglasses *See* Sunglasses
Big Audio Dynamite (Musical group)
Big Audio Dynamite [performance in Chicago] D. Brogan. il *Roll Stone* p14 Ja 29 '87
Big Bang theory *See* Universe
Big Bear, Inc.
Are hunters after Big Bear Inc.? G. G. Marcial. *Bus Week* p124 Je 8 '87
Big business
See also
Competition
Trusts, Industrial
Big is beautiful. T. Jaffe. il *Forbes* 139 Ann Directory:330 Ap 27 '87
Tapping a growth market [cooperation between small and large firms; views of David Birch] il *Nations Bus* 75:14 Jl '87
Big East Conference Television Network
Free throw. R. Koselka. il por *Forbes* 139:162+ My 4 '87
The Big Easy [film] *See* Motion picture reviews—Single works
Big game hunting *See* Hunting
Big Oak Boys Ranch (Ala.)
John Croyle's speck of heaven. R. Exum. il *Read Dig* 130:85-9 My '87
Big screen television *See* Television projection
Big Singing (Festival) *See* Music festivals—Kentucky
Big South Fork National River and Recreation Area (Tenn. and Ky.)
Big South Fork. C. Males. il *Travel Holiday* 167:12+ My '87
Big Thicket National Preserve (Tex.)
Lost! (but not for long) [survival instruction course] M. W. Perin. il *Parents* 62:92-4+ Jl '87
Bigfoot *See* Sasquatch
Biggar, Joanna
A meeting of the twain. bibl (p65) il *Psychol Today* 21:46-50+ N '87
Biggers, Vicki
(jt. auth) See Arnold, Genevieve H., and Biggers, Vicki
Biggs, Michael
Non-typical, near mythical [photographs] il *Field Stream* 92:50-1 Ag '87
Biggs, Tyrell
about
Mike Tyson wins fight; KO's Biggs in the 7th. il pors *Jet* 73:51 N 2 '87
Very tough night at the office. W. Nack. il pors *Sports Illus* 67:64+ O 26 '87
Bigham, Barbara J.
Prospecting in the home. il *Nations Bus* 75:55-6 N '87
Bigham, Jim
about
"We may never go home". B. Spring. il pors *Christ Today* 31:14-15 Mr 20 '87
Bigham, June
about
"We may never go home". B. Spring. il pors *Christ Today* 31:14-15 Mr 20 '87
Bighorn sheep *See* Mountain sheep
Bign, Stanley
Bye bye, so long. il *Esquire* 108:78 N '87
Bigotry *See* Prejudice
Bihova, Diana, and Schrader, Constance, 1933-
Pretty, sexy, kissable [excerpt from Beauty from the inside out] il *Ladies Home J* 104:100-3 F '87
Bik Bok Gruppen
A couple of Norwegian dogs. T. Jaffe. il *Forbes* 139:109 My 4 '87
Bikales, Gerda
(jt. auth) See Imhoff, Gary, and Bikales, Gerda
Biking *See* Cycling
Bikinis *See* Bathing suits
Biko, Stephen, 1946-1977
about
Apartheid chic. A. White. il *Film Comment* 23:11-12+ N/D '87
Black and white. M. Peretz. *New Repub* 197:42 D 21 '87
Cry freedom. C. Tyson. il pors *Ebony* 43:60-2+ D '87
Donald and Wendy Woods talk about the real-life drama behind Cry freedom [interview] C. Krupp. il pors *Glamour* 85:166+ D '87
Movies. D. Denby. il por *N Y* 20:54-5 S 21 '87
Newsman Donald Woods still seeks justice for Stephen Biko in the film Cry freedom. W. Plummer. il pors *People Wkly* 28:64+ N 23 '87
Richard Attenborough's 'Biko'. L. Shaw. il *World Press Rev* 34:60 Je '87

What's wrong with this picture? E. Mitchell. il *Roll Stone* p31-2 D 3 '87
Bilateral air agreements *See* Aviation—International aspects
Bilderback, Diane
Better beans. il *Rodale's Org Gard* 34:25-9 Ag '87
Bildner, James L.
about
The price of quick riches. R. Simon. il por *Forbes* 140:112+ S 21 '87
Bildner (J.) & Sons *See* J. Bildner & Sons
Bile acids and salts
Why carrots may reduce cholesterol. *Sci News* 131:409 Je 27 '87
Bile pigments
See also
Bilirubin
Biliary calculi *See* Gallstones
Bilingual education
Bilingual education: a barrier to achievement. N. Sanchez. *Educ Dig* 53:42-3 D '87
Bilingual education and politics. J. Cummins. *Educ Dig* 53:30-3 N '87
Federal aid
Bilingual education. *Congr Dig* 66:68-96 Mr '87
Bilingualism
Angry words in the East [decision to appoint a francophone postmaster ignites protest in New Brunswick] M. Gee. *Macleans* 100:13 Ag 31 '87
Backlash over language [Ontario] S. Aikenhead. il *Macleans* 100:12-13 Ag 17 '87
The battle over preserving the English language [English Language Amendment] G. Imhoff and G. Bikales. il *USA Today (Periodical)* 115:63-5 Ja '87
A cautionary case of bilingualism [French language in Canada] P. Brimelow. *Commentary* 84:63-5 N '87
Dr. Jekyll, Señor Hyde [personality and coordinate bilinguals; study by Philip V. Hull] C. Simon. il *Psychol Today* 21:16 D '87
An echo of past battles [Quebec Court of Appeal decision declaring mandatory French-only signs illegal sparks vandalism] B. Wallace. il *Macleans* 100:14 Ja 12 '87
Language on trial [Quebec Court of Appeal rules against language charter requiring French-only commercial signs] B. Wallace. *Macleans* 100:8 Ja 5 '87
New fury over language [Quebec] B. Wallace. il *Macleans* 100:16-17 N 9 '87
A tougher language bill [bilingualism requirements in Canada] P. Gessell. il *Macleans* 100:15 Jl 6 '87
U.S. language debate rages. E. Branch. *Black Enterp* 17:20+ Jl '87
Why English should be our official language. S. I. Hayakawa. *Educ Dig* 52:36-7 My '87
Bilirubin
Bilirubin: bad, yet good? *Sci News* 131:169 Mr 14 '87
Bilirubin is an antioxidant of possible physiological importance. R. Stocker and others. bibl f il *Science* 235:1043-6 F 27 '87
Bill, Max, 1908-
about
Perpetuating the Bauhaus ideal. M. Peppiatt. il por *Archit Dig* 44:48+ Ag '87
Bill collecting *See* Collecting of accounts
Bill of rights (U.S.) *See* United States. Constitution. 1st-10th amendments
Bill T. Jones/Arnie Zane & Company
Reviews:
Performances of The animal trilogy at the Brooklyn Academy of Music. C. Hardy. *Dance Mag* 61:23-4 Jl '87
Wanted: a choreographer [performances of The animal trilogy at the Brooklyn Academy of Music] T. Tobias. il *N Y* 20:47-8 Ja 5 '87
Billard, Annick
A roof for refugees . . . il *World Health* p12-15 Jl '87
Billboards
Missing the message in billboard art [Art on billboards program in 8 Canadian cities] G. James. il *Macleans* 100:54+ F 9 '87
Billen, Stephanie
Brushstrokes of genius. il *Horizon* 30:22-6 N '87
Billes family
about
Battle to control a retail institution. T. Tedesco. il *Macleans* 100:38 Ja 19 '87
Canadian Tire showdown. T. Tedesco. il *Macleans* 100:36 Je 22 '87
The epic struggle [special section] il *Macleans* 100:26-33 Ja 26 '87

Billfish

Where have all the billfish gone? B. Waitzkin. il *Mot Boat Sail* 160:44-5+ O '87

Billfish fishing

Viva Venezuela. J. Clemans. il *Mot Boat Sail* 159:42-5+ Ja '87

Where have all the billfish gone? B. Waitzkin. il *Mot Boat Sail* 160:44-5+ O '87

Billfish tournaments *See* Fishing—Competitions

Billiards

The best woman in the hall [J. Balukas] R. Starr. il por *N Y Times Mag* p30+ O 18 '87

Billig, Amy

about

The hitchhiker [excerpt from The corpse had a familiar face] E. Buchanan. il por *Glamour* 85:140+ O '87

Billings, Henry

Writing textbooks isn't child's play. por *U S News World Rep* 103:6 Jl 27 '87

Billingsley, Eunice

about

Long-time collectors' secret unveiled. *Antiques Collect Hobbies* 92:78 My '87

Billingsley, Floyd

about

Long-time collectors' secret unveiled. *Antiques Collect Hobbies* 92:78 My '87

Billington, James H., 1929-

Realism and vision in American foreign policy. *Foreign Aff* 65 Sp Issue:630-52 ['87]

about

New Librarian of Congress looks at books vs. technologies. H. Fields. il por *Publ Wkly* 232:16 O 16 '87

Billington, Rachel

50 rooms with a view. il pors *Vogue* 177:314-21+ My '87

Billington, Thomas K.

The unsweetened truth about sugar subsidies. *Read Dig* 131:51-4 Ag '87

Billionaire Boys Club

The Billionaire Boy—and the missing body [trial of J. Hunt] por *Newsweek* 109:61 My 4 '87

Murder and intrigue California-style. M. Gray. por *Macleans* 100:44 F 16 '87

Billionaire Boys Club [television program] See Television program reviews—Single works

Billionaires

See also

Khashoggi, Adnan

The billionaires: the world's richest people [cover story; special section] il *Fortune* 116:115-17+ O 12 '87

Deepest pockets. il *U S News World Rep* 103:12 O 5 '87

The world's billionaires [cover story; special section] il map *Forbes* 140:81-5+ O 5 '87

Anecdotes, facetiae, satire, etc.

Filthy rich—and tightfisted [Canadian billionaires on Fortune's and Forbes' lists] A. Fotheringham. il *Macleans* 100:72 O 5 '87

Japan

Land of the Rising Billionaires [cover story] A. Tanzer. il *Forbes* 140:66-9+ Jl 27 '87

Bills (Birds)

Natural selection: bird seeds of change [research by Peter R. Grant and H. Lisle Gibbs] R. Monastersky. il *Sci News* 131:373-4 Je 13 '87

Where would a bird be without its bill? J. K. Terres. il *Natl Wildl* 25:42-51 Ag/S '87

Billy Galvin [film] See Motion picture reviews—Single works

Bilodeau Gingras, Christiane

about

A second chance. L. Van Dusen. il por *Macleans* 100:44 N 23 '87

Bilodeaux, Caitlin

about

Getting her point across. D. Stathoplos. il pors *Sports Illus* 66:54-6 Mr 9 '87

Biloxi (Miss.)

Galleries and museums

See also

Seafood Industry Museum (Biloxi, Miss.)

Bilozir, Will

Introducing zunkins. il por *Rodale's Org Gard* 34:88-9 O '87

Bilski, John R.

Anecdotes, facetiae, satire, etc.

One man, one vote [J. R. Bilski receives one vote in mayoral primary] M. E. Marty. *Christ Century* 104:319 Ap 1 '87

Bilstad, James

about

Fast-tracking the first AIDS drug [interview] B. Stone. pors *FDA Consum* 21:13-15 O '87

Bilton, Peter

(tr) See Halbo, Sverre. Our lives are here and now

Bilz, H. (Heinz), 1926-1986

about

Obituary

Phys Today por 40:88+ Jl '87. M. Cardona

Bilz, Heinz See Bilz, H. (Heinz), 1926-1986

Bilzerian, Paul A.

about

Paul Bilzerian still don't get no respect. P. Engardio. il por *Bus Week* p62+ N 23 '87

The Street is fretting over 'Street sweeps'. A. Bianco. il por *Bus Week* p71-2 Ag 3 '87

Bimota (Firm)

A better Bimota: db1 SR. B. De Prato. il *Cycle* 38:84-5+ Jl '87

Binary stars See Stars, Double

Binder twins See Siamese twins

Bindernagel, Lutz

Birthplace of the conquerors. il *World Press Rev* 34:63 Mr '87

Binding sites (Biochemistry)

See also

Chemoreceptors

Drug receptors

Hormone receptors

Protein receptors

Antigenicity of myohemerythrin [discussion of March 6, 1987 article, Chemistry of antibody binding to a protein] H. M. Geysen and others. *Science* 238:1584-6 D 11 '87

Calculation of the relative change in binding free energy of a protein-inhibitor complex. P. A. Bash and others. bibl f il *Science* 235:574-6 Ja 30 '87

The catalytic role of the active site aspartic acid in serine proteases. C. S. Craik and others. bibl f il *Science* 237:909-13 Ag 21 '87

Chemical conversion of a DNA-binding protein into a site-specific nuclease. C.-H. B. Chen and D. S. Sigman. bibl f il *Science* 237:1197-1201 S 4 '87

Chemistry of antibody binding to a protein [myohemerythrin] H. M. Geysen and others. bibl f il *Science* 235:1184-90 Mr 6 '87

Computer simulations of the diffusion of a substrate to an active site of an enzyme. K. Sharp and others. bibl f il *Science* 236:1460-3 Je 12 '87

Direct evidence for DNA bending at the lambda replication origin. K. Zahn and F. R. Blattner. bibl f il *Science* 236:416-22 Ap 24 '87

Evaluation of intrinsic binding energy from a hydrogen bonding group in an enzyme inhibitor. P. A. Bartlett and C. K. Marlowe. bibl f il *Science* 235:569-71 Ja 30 '87

Fluorescence properties of calmodulin-binding peptides reflect alpha-helical periodicity. K. T. O'Neil and others. bibl f il *Science* 236:1454-6 Je 12 '87

Global flexibility in a sensory receptor: a site-directed cross-linking approach. J. J. Falke and D. E. Koshland, Jr. bibl f il *Science* 237:1596-600 S 25 '87

Mechanisms of antibody binding to a protein [myohemerythrin] E. D. Getzoff and others. bibl f il *Science* 235:1191-6 Mr 6 '87

Model studies in molecular recognition [cover story] J. Rebek, Jr. il *Science* 235:1478-84 Mr 20 '87

The relation between major histocompatibility complex (MHC) restriction and the capacity of Ia to bind immunogenic peptides. S. Buus and others. bibl f il *Science* 235:1353-8 Mr 13 '87

Structure of the nucleotide activation switch in glycogen phosphorylase a. S. Sprang and others. bibl f il *Science* 237:1012-19 Ag 28 '87

Structures of two thermolysin-inhibitor complexes that differ by a single hydrogen bond. D. E. Tronrud and others. bibl f il *Science* 235:571-4 Ja 30 '87

A subset of yeast snRNA's contains functional binding sites for the highly conserved Sm antigen. N. Riedel and others. bibl f il *Science* 235:328-31 Ja 16 '87

Synthesis of a site-specific DNA-binding peptide. M. F. Bruist and others. bibl f il *Science* 235:777-80 F 13 '87

The three-dimensional structure of Asn[102] mutant of trypsin: role of Asp[102] in serine protease catalysis. S. Sprang and others. bibl f il *Science* 237:905-9 Ag 21 '87

Tinkering with enzymes: what are we learning? J. R. Knowles. bibl f il *Science* 236:1252-8 Je 5 '87

Bindings, Ski *See* Skis and skiing—Equipment
Bing, Sir Rudolf, 1902-
about
Lost together in paradise. J. Kelly. il pors *Time* 129:73 F 23 '87
Bing, Siegfried, 1838-1905
about
Cooper-Hewitt Museum [cover story] il *Antiques Collect Hobbies* 92:49+ Jl '87
The other fin de siècle. K. Silver. bibl f il *Art Am* 75:104-11+ D '87
Binge buying *See* Compulsive shopping
Binge-purge syndrome *See* Bulimia
Bingham, Alfred M.
Raiders of the lost city. il pors map *Am Herit* 38:54-64 Jl/Ag '87
Bingham, Hiram, 1875-1956
about
Raiders of the lost city. A. M. Bingham. il pors map *Am Herit* 38:54-64 Jl/Ag '87
Bingham, Phillip
Motorsport. See issues of Motor Trend
Bingham, Sallie
about
After a woman is scorned, a publishing family cashes out. J. Nielsen. il por *Fortune* 115:93 Ja 5 '87
Bingham, Walter
Bobsleigh, luge and speed skating. il *Sports Illus* 67:51+ D 14 '87
Guts and gold. il pors *Sports Illus* 67:57+ O 19 '87
The miracle upsets. il *Sports Illus* 67:47+ S 21 '87
The Pan American Games: stepping stone to the Olympics. il *Sports Illus* 67:39+ Jl 27 '87
The race for gold. il *Sports Illus* 67:41+ N 23 '87
World Series comebacks. il *Sports Illus* 67:55+ O 12 '87
You must remember this. por *Sports Illus* 66:94 Ap 27 '87
Bingham family
about
After a woman is scorned, a publishing family cashes out. J. Nielsen. il por *Fortune* 115:93 Ja 5 '87
Macmillan cancels Bingham book after challenge by family patriarch. *Publ Wkly* 232:310-11 Ag 7 '87
Binghamton (N.Y.)
Prisons and reformatories
Pregnant woman found hanged in N.Y. jail cell; angry blacks ask probe [case of S. A. Harris-Smith] *Jet* 72:8 Jl 13 '87
Bingo
Bingo! W. Ecenbarger. il *Read Dig* 131:155-6+ Jl '87
Moral and religious aspects
Who says bingo is for losers? W. Flaherty. *U S Cathol* 52:40 Ja '87
Binn, Moreton I.
about
To Moreton Binn, Sultan of Swap, cash is nice, but barter is better. A. Abrahams. il pors *People Wkly* 28:105-6 N 30 '87
Binnig, Gerd
about
Physics Nobel Prize. P. F. Schewe. bibl f *Phys Today* 40:S70 Ja '87
Physics Nobel Prize awarded for microscopies old and new. B. M. Schwarzschild. il pors *Phys Today* 40:17-21 Ja '87
Binns, Tom
about
Artful jewels. il por *Vogue* 177:280 Ap '87
Binoculars
A buyers' guide to binoculars. B. Schwalberg. il *Pop Photogr* 94:66-71 Je '87
High-class glass. D. E. Petzal. il *Field Stream* 92:82+ Jl '87
Observing spring galaxies with binoculars. C. Crossen. il *Astronomy* 15:62-7 My '87
Bins
Derzinski's sandbox. R. N. Hoffman. il *Workbench* 43:82 S/O '87
Extra grain storage. il *Success Farm* 85:56 N '87
Grain-bin 'lifeguards' [farm accidents] C. Tevis. il *Success Farm* 85:62R-62S O '87
No-bug bins. il *Success Farm* 85:34 S '87
Binyon, Michael, 1944-
Still the 'Evil Empire'? il *World Press Rev* 34:15 Ap '87
Bio-Technology General Corp.
A quick cure for Bio-Technology? [stock price] G. G. Marcial. *Bus Week* p78 Ag 17 '87

Bioassay *See* Biological assay
Biochemistry
See also
Binding sites (Biochemistry)
Biogeochemistry
Chemotaxis
Immunochemistry
Isoelectric focusing
Neurochemistry
Pigments (Biology)
Porphyrins
Synthesis
Biodegradation
Assemblage of ortho cleavage route for simultaneous degradation of chloro- and methylaromatics. F. Rojo and others. bibl f il *Science* 238:1395-8 D 4 '87
Biology's answer to toxic dumps [microbes] J. J. Holbrook. *Sierra* 72:24-5+ Ja/F '87
Discovering microbes with a taste for PCBs. L. Roberts. il *Science* 237:975-7 Ag 28 '87
Polychlorinated biphenyl dechlorination in aquatic sediments [river sediments] J. F. Brown and others. bibl f il *Science* 236:709-12 My 8 '87
Redesigning metabolic routes: manipulation of TOL plasmid pathway for catabolism of alkylbenzoates. J. L. Ramos and others. bibl f il *Science* 235:593-6 Ja 30 '87
Toxic wastes? A little fungus may help. S. Budiansky. il *U S News World Rep* 103:85 N 9 '87
Bioelectricity *See* Electrophysiology
Bioenergetics
See also
Muscle strength
Chemical energy fuels ecosystems. il *Sea Front* 33:62-4 Ja/F '87
Bioethics
See also
Animal experimentation
Gene therapy—Ethical aspects
Genetic research—Ethical aspects
Medical ethics
Reproduction—Moral and religious aspects
Bioethical shock. R. J. White. il *America* 156:174-6 F 28 '87
Some thought on bioethics [interview with L. Badalyan] Y. Samoilov. *World Press Rev* 34:52 Ag '87
The war against reason. R. J. Neuhaus. *Natl Rev* 39:45 D 18 '87
Biofeedback *See* Biological control systems
Biofeedback training
The biofeedback way to starve stress. M. Golin. *Prevention* 39:30-2 Je '87
I learned to "think" stress away—and so can you. M. F. Hoyt. il pors *Good Housekeep* 204:50+ Je '87
Psychic log on [biofeedback videos by Bodylog, Inc.] D. Groves. il *Health* 19:18 Ja '87
Biogeochemical cycles
See also
Carbon cycle (Biogeochemistry)
Nitrogen cycle (Biogeochemistry)
Has the biosphere done a flip-flop? [changes from the Archean; views of James C. G. Walker] S. Eisenberg. *Sci News* 132:278 O 31 '87
Biogeochemistry
Prospecting with plants. F. R. Siegel. il *Earth Sci* 40:18-19 Fall '87
Biogeography *See* Geographical distribution of animals and plants
Biographical dictionaries
See also
Who's who in America
Biography
See also
Autobiography
Epitaphs
Executives—Biography
Obituaries
Public officers—Biography
The golden age of biography. A. P. Sanoff. il *U S News World Rep* 103:49-51 Ag 3 '87
In pursuit of the ultimate fiction. J. Kaplan. il *N Y Times Book Rev* 92:1+ Ap 19 '87
Putting one letter after another [biographers' use of authors' letters] J. Atlas. il *N Y Times Book Rev* 92:1+ Mr 15 '87
Reflections of a biographer. E. H. P. Longford, Countess of. *Writer* 100:20-1+ Jl '87
What makes life worth writing? D. Donoghue. il *N Y Times Book Rev* 92:11-12 Mr 29 '87

Biography—*cont.*

Where orphans can still become heiresses [relationship between the novel and biography] C. Ozick. il *N Y Times Book Rev* 92:13 Mr 8 '87

Writing biographies for children. G. Kamen. *Writer* 100:19-21 Mr '87

Writing great-grandfather's biography [S. M. Jones, Toledo's turn of the century mayor] M. Jones. *Am Sch* 56:519-34 Aut '87

Anecdotes, facetiae, satire, etc.

"Negative biography": a Who's who for who's not. J. Skow. il *Smithsonian* 18:172 Ap '87

Bibliography

Lives of the rich and famous [biographies for children] C. C. Epstein. il *Parents* 62:71-3+ Ap '87

Biological and chemical weapons *See* Chemical and biological weapons

Biological assay

See also

Immunoassay

Gauging the value of carcinogen assays. J. Raloff. *Sci News* 131:343 My 30 '87

Identification and localization of mutations at the Lesch-Nyhan locus by ribonuclease A cleavage. R. A. Gibbs and C. T. Caskey. bibl f il *Science* 236:303-5 Ap 17 '87

Prediction of chemical carcinogenicity in rodents from in vitro genetic toxicity assays. R. W. Tennant and others. bibl f il *Science* 236:933-41 My 22 '87

Biological clocks *See* Biological rhythms

Biological control of insects *See* Insect control

Biological control systems

See also

Biofeedback training

Cellular control mechanisms

The inversion of sensory processing by feedback pathways: a model of visual cognitive functions. E. Harth and others. bibl f il *Science* 237:184-7 Jl 10 '87

Biological cycles *See* Biological rhythms

Biological equipment

See also

Centrifuges

Microscopes and microscopy

1987 guide to biotechnology products and instruments [with editorial comment] S. S. Roberts. *Science* 235 pt2:G4, G23+ F 27 '87

The biologist's toolbox. See issues of BioScience beginning February 1985

Instrumentation and equipment [special issue; with editorial comment by Philip H. Abelson] il *Science* 238:257, 305-41 O 16 '87

Biological literature

See also

Information storage and retrieval systems—Biological use

Biological luminescence *See* Bioluminescence

Biological materials

Biomaterial-centered infection: microbial adhesion versus tissue integration. A. G. Gristina. bibl f il *Science* 237:1588-95 S 25 '87

Imaging unaltered cell structures with X-rays [scanning microscope] A. L. Robinson. il *Science* 237:723-4 Ag 14 '87

Time-resolved X-ray diffraction of biological materials. S. M. Gruner. bibl f il *Science* 238:305-12 O 16 '87

The use of a charge-coupled device for quantitative optical microscopy of biological structures. Y. Hiraoka and others. bibl f il *Science* 238:36-41 O 2 '87

Biological models

Modeling for biologists. J. C. Horton and C. J. Bicak. bibl il *BioScience* 37:808-9 D '87

Biological productivity *See* Productivity, Biological

Biological research

See also

Fluorescent indicators in biological research

Genetic research

Medical research

BioBriefs. See issues of BioScience

International aspects

Human frontiers at the economic summit. D. Dickson. *Science* 236:1518 Je 19 '87

Biological resources *See* Natural resources

Biological rhythms

See also

Jet lag

Photoperiodism

Antidepressant and circadian phase-shifting effects of light. A. J. Lewy and others. bibl f il *Science* 235:352-4 Ja 16 '87

Avoiding the morning danger zone [work of Stefan N. Willich] il *Prevention* 39:16 Ag '87

Borrowed time [transplantation of suprachiasmatic nuclei restores circadian rhythm in hamsters] *Sci Am* 256:84 F '87

Circadian variation in ozone tolerance [research by Leendert van Bree and others] J. Raloff. *Sci News* 131:169 Mr 14 '87

Deadly blooms and curious clocks [Gonyaulax; research by Donald M. Anderson and Bruce A. Keafer] *Sci News* 131:122 F 21 '87

Diurnal expression of transducin mRNA and translocation of transducin in rods of rat retina. M. R. Brann and L. V. Cohen. bibl f il *Science* 235:585-7 Ja 30 '87

The early bird makes the grade [students and teachers who are most alert in the morning perform better; study by Julian Biggers] P. Chance. *Psychol Today* 21:22 O '87

Fatigue: are you fighting your internal clock? L. C. Cool. il *McCalls* 115:144+ D '87

Food for thought [drop in concentration after meals; research by Andrew Smith and Christopher Miles] G. Lowe. *Psychol Today* 21:14 F '87

For too many, life is just a snore. S. N. Wellborn. il *U S News World Rep* 102:56-7 Je 15 '87

Lag time [participation in study testing effectiveness of triazolam in treating jet lag] K. Lautman. il *Omni* 9:16 Ja '87

The light: fantastic! D. E. Zimmer. *World Press Rev* 34:55 Ap '87

A light in time [light exposure to reset biological clock; study by Charles Czeisler] M. Roberts. il *Psychol Today* 21:22 Ja '87

Mathematics of sleep [interaction between circadian rhythm and the sleep-wake cycle; work of Steven Strogatz and others] S. J. Nadis. il *Technol Rev* 90:13-14 F/Mr '87

One more reason to stay in bed [morning heart attacks and blood platelet aggregation; research by Geoffrey Tofler and others] *Discover* 8:6+ O '87

Safe supinity [platelet aggregation and morning heart attacks; research by Geoffrey H. Tofler and others] *Sci News* 131:409 Je 27 '87

The time of our lives: subterranean experiments on the rhythms imposed by the solar day [experiments in Midnight Cave, Tex.] M. Siffre. il *Courier* 40:14-15 Je '87

Using body rhythms to boost productivity. L. Washer. *Work Woman* 12:19-20 Ag '87

Winter depression: day for night [correction of melatonin production timing; research by Alfred J. Lewy and others] J. Meer. il *Psychol Today* 21:12 Je '87

Your body clock and what makes it tick. L. Lamberg. il *Better Homes Gard* 65:57 Ag '87

Biological societies

See also

American Institute of Biological Sciences

Biological transport

See also

Blood-brain barrier

Cloning of genomic and complementary DNA from Shaker, a putative potassium channel gene from Drosophila. D. M. Papazian and others. bibl f il *Science* 237:749-53 Ag 14 '87

Direct activation of mammalian atrial muscarinic potassium channels by GTP regulatory protein G_k. A. Yatani and others. bibl f il *Science* 235:207-11 Ja 9 '87

Elevated levels of glucose transport and transporter messenger RNA are induced by *ras* or *src* oncogenes. J. S. Flier and others. bibl f il *Science* 235:1492-5 Mr 20 '87

External calcium ions are required for potassium channel gating in squid neurons. C. M. Armstrong and J. Lopez-Barneo. bibl f il *Science* 236:712-14 My 8 '87

Genomic organization and deduced amino acid sequence of a putative sodium channel gene in Drosophila. L. Salkoff and others. bibl f il *Science* 237:744-9 Ag 14 '87

Glycolysis preferentially inhibits ATP-sensitive K^+ channels in isolated guinea pig cardiac myocytes. J. N. Weiss and S. T. Lamp. bibl f il *Science* 238:67-9 O 2 '87

Increased numbers of ion channels promoted by an intracellular second messenger. R. Gunning. bibl il *Science* 235:80-2 Ja 2 '87

The microtubule as an intracellular engine. R. D. Allen. il *Sci Am* 256:42-9 F '87

Microtubule gelation-contraction: essential components and relation to slow axonal transport. R. C. Weisenberg and others. bibl f il *Science* 238:1119-22 N 20 '87

Biological transport—*cont.*

Mitogens and oncogenes can block the induction of specific voltage-gated ion channels. J. M. Caffrey and others. bibl f il *Science* 236:570-3 My 1 '87

Multiple calcium channels and neuronal function. R. J. Miller. bibl f il *Science* 235:46-52 Ja 2 '87

Preferred microtubules for vesicle transport in lobster axons. R. H. Miller and others. bibl f il *Science* 235:220-2 Ja 9 '87

Sequence of a probable potassium channel component encoded at Shaker locus of Drosophila. B. L. Tempel and others. bibl f il *Science* 237:770-5 Ag 14 '87

Single-channel and genetic analyses reveal two distinct A-type potassium channels in Drosophila. C. K. Solc and others. bibl f il *Science* 236:1094-8 My 29 '87

Slow transport of tubulin in the neurites of differentiated PC 12 cells. C. H. Keith. bibl f il *Science* 235:337-9 Ja 16 '87

Transformation of rat fibroblasts by FSV rapidly increases glucose transporter gene transcription [Fujinami sarcoma virus] M. J. Birnbaum and others. bibl f il *Science* 235:1495-8 Mr 20 '87

Biological warfare *See* Chemical and biological weapons

Biologists

Is the organismic biologist an endangered species? H. M. Lenhoff. *BioScience* 37:244 Ap '87

People and places. See issues of BioScience

Biology

See also
Adaptation (Biology)
Artificial satellites—Biological use
Cells
Clones (Biology)
Competition (Biology)
Computers—Biological use
Cryobiology
Cytology
Death (Biology)
Developmental biology
Ecology
Electrophysiology
Embryology
Environment
Evolution
Growth
Homology (Biology)
Hybridization
Information storage and retrieval systems—Biological use
Lasers—Biological use
Life (Biology)
Marine biology
Membranes (Biology)
Molecular biology
Morphogenesis
Mutation
Natural history
Neurobiology
Parthenogenesis
Phylogeny
Polarity (Biology)
Polymorphism (Biology)
Population biology
Predation (Biology)
Regeneration (Biology)
Reproduction
Sex (Biology)
Space biology
Symbiosis

Awards

Adkisson wins 1987 AIBS Distinguished Service Award. por *BioScience* 37:526 Jl/Ag '87

Bibliography

Books. See occasional issues of BioScience

Classification

See also
Cladistic analysis
Species

The value of research collections. R. B. Finley, Jr. *BioScience* 37:92 F '87

Conferences

Calendar. See occasional issues of BioScience

Periodicals

See also
Conservation biology (Periodical)

Periodicity

See Biological rhythms

Philosophy

The storehouse of the possible. P. Caws. *Wilderness* 51:64 Fall '87

Study and teaching

Modeling for biologists. J. C. Horton and C. J. Bicak. bibl il *BioScience* 37:808-9 D '87

Mythology in introductory biology. S. Vogel. bibl *BioScience* 37:611-14 S '87

A teen fights for frog rights, and bio may never be the same [J. Graham refuses to dissect frog in biology class in Victorville, Calif.] il por *People Wkly* 27:109 My 25 '87

Aids and devices

Apples, frogs, and animal rights [Apple Computer television commercial] C. Holden. *Science* 238:1345 D 4 '87

Terminology

Mythology in introductory biology. S. Vogel. bibl *BioScience* 37:611-14 S '87

When does homology mean something else? R. Lewin. *Science* 237:1570 S 25 '87

Biology in art

Exhibitions

There's a protozoan in that painting [Art and science exhibition in Venice, Italy] L. Green. il *BioScience* 37:181-5 Mr '87

Bioluminescence

See also
Electric organs in fish
Fireflies

Glowing tobacco [gene tagging with luciferase] A. Fisher. il *Pop Sci* 230:8 Ap '87

Lighting up [gene tagging with luciferase] il *Sci Am* 256:60-2 Ja '87

Marine firefleas. il *Sea Front* 33:386 S/O '87

A million stars caught in the sea [Puerto Mosquito, phosphorescent bay on Vieques] W. C. Rice. *Sierra* 72:75-6 S/O '87

Wheels of light, sea of fire. P. Huyghe. il *Oceans* 20:20-5 N/D '87

You light up my life, Vargula [firefleas] il *Sci News* 131:282 My 2 '87

Biomagnetics *See* Magnetic fields—Physiological effects

Biomass energy

See also
Wood as fuel

Bioenergy can meet global needs [report from World Resources Institute] *Futurist* 21:44 Ja/F '87

Food security: a technological alternative: biotechnology can convert biomass into a stable food supply. M. H. Rogoff and S. L. Rawlins. bibl il *BioScience* 37:800-7 D '87

Tanking up on biomass gas [research at the Solar Energy Research Institute] J. Raloff. *Sci News* 131:265 Ap 25 '87

Biomechanics

See also
Flexibility (Physiology)
Stretch (Physiology)

When athletes and machines meet. T. Osborne. il *Curr Health 2* 13:16-17 F '87

Therapeutic use

See also
Dance therapy

The personal you: the inner circle [Pilates exercises for the inner thighs] M. Horosko. il *Dance Mag* 61:74-5 O '87

Pilates power—all over warm-up exercises (III). M. Horosko. il *Dance Mag* 61:84-5 Ja '87

Pilates power—all over warm-up exercises (IV). M. Horosko. il *Dance Mag* 61:82-3+ F '87

Biomedical engineering

See also
Medical electronics

Biomedical ethics *See* Medical ethics

Biomedical research *See* Medical research

Biomet, Inc.

Biomet should boom as baby boomers get older. J. E. Ellis. il *Bus Week* p77 Jl 27 '87

Biondi, Frank Joseph, Jr.

about

Planting for Coke's harvest. M. Brown and C. Capuzzi. il pors *Channels* 7:78-9 Je '87

Biondi, Matt

about

Graduating with honors. C. Neff. il pors *Sports Illus* 66:52+ Ap 13 '87

Biophysics

See also
Medical physics

Biopsy

Speaking of biopsies. J. Cassidy. il *Curr Health 2* 14:24-5 D '87

Bioregionalism

The great, green deep-ecology revolution. A. Chase. il *Roll Stone* p61-2+ Ap 23 '87

Living there. S. Zuckerman. il *Sierra* 72:61-6 Mr/Ap '87

Bioresources *See* Natural resources

Biorhythms *See* Biological rhythms

Biosensors

Biotrodes: food for thought. I. Amato. il *Sci News* 131:92-3 F 7 '87

Closing the biosensor gap [molecular-based transistor; work of Mark S. Wrighton] S. Weisburd. *Sci News* 132:214 O 3 '87

Biosphere

See also

Gaia hypothesis

International Geosphere-Biosphere Program

Exchange of materials between terrestrial ecosystems and the atmosphere. H. A. Mooney and others. bibl f il *Science* 238:926-32 N 13 '87

Has the biosphere done a flip-flop? [changes from the Archean; views of James C. G. Walker] S. Eisenberg. *Sci News* 132:278 O 31 '87

Report on reports: Sustainable development of the biosphere. G. R. Conway. *Environment* 29:25-7 N '87

Biosphere II

Bioshelters. D. Sagan. il *Omni* 9:54-9 Mr '87

Earth's first visitors to Mars. G. Maranto. il *Discover* 8:28-31+ My '87

Mars colony grows in Arizona. R. A. Lewis. il *Technol Rev* 90:12-13 My/Je '87

Not your average terrarium. S. Begley. il *Newsweek* 109:60+ Je 1 '87

Biosphere reserves

France

See also

Cévennes Biosphere Reserve and National Park (France)

Biosynthesis *See* Synthesis

Biotechnica International Inc.

BioTechnica tests EPA review process [field test of Rhizobium bacteria] M. Crawford. *Science* 235:840 F 20 '87

Coming from RJR: high-tech vegetables. il *Bus Week* p44 O 5 '87

"No—Bug Lite" [BioTechnica's high tech beer made with recombinant yeast] *Sci Am* 256:89 F '87

Biotechnology research *See* Genetic research

Biotechnology research (Plants) *See* Plant genetics

Biotechnology Science Coordinating Council (U.S.)

Wyngaarden to chair Biotech Council. M. Crawford. *Science* 238:1504-5 D 11 '87

Biotelemetry

See also

Monitoring (Medical care)

Dashboards for humans [lifesign detectors; work of Charles Lessard] D. Lampe. *Pop Sci* 231:33 S '87

Debate around the collar [collaring Florida panthers] B. Latoof. il *Sierra* 72:18+ Mr/Ap '87

Junk jewelry [collars and tags] G. Hill. il *Field Stream* 92:24 O '87

Of whales and weather [biotelemetry tracking of whales in deep water; work of Bruce Mate] S. Strauss. il *Technol Rev* 90:11 Jl '87

Spying from on high [satellite wildlife telemetry] M. Bowker. il *Int Wildl* 17:22-3 S/O '87

Whale tracking is all up in the air [work of Bruce R. Mate] K. Hartley. il *Sci News* 132:118 Ag 22 '87

Biotherapeutics

Medicines from the body. C. P. Weinstock. il *FDA Consum* 21:6-10 Ap '87

Biotherapeutics Inc.

The anticancer company expands. G. Bylinsky. il *Fortune* 116:121+ N 23 '87

Pay-your-own-way research. M. Clark. il *Newsweek* 109:61 F 9 '87

Biotrodes *See* Biosensors

Biphenyl compounds

See also

Polychlorinated biphenyls

Birchall, Steve

Digital audio tape. il *Stereo Rev* 52:56-9 Mr '87

Birchglen (Steamship)

S.S. Birchglen. H. W. Serig, Jr. il map *Oceans* 20:46-55+ S/O '87

Bird, Larry

about

Beers with . . . [interview] P. Vecsey. por *Sport Mag* 78:19-20 Mr '87

Detroit's Thomas sees Bird in black & white. pors *Jet* 72:50 Je 22 '87

The stuff dreams are made of. D. Halberstam. il pors *Sports Illus* 66:38-40+ Je 29 '87

Bird, Rose Elizabeth

about

Bork and Bird. H. Meyerson. *New Repub* 197:21+ S 14-21 '87

The 'Onion Field' parole: Rose Bird's parting shot. por *Newsweek* 109:26 Ja 12 '87

Bird, Sarah

The art of lite dating. il *Mademoiselle* 93:340+ S '87

Bird, Tom

about

A late indictment may close the case behind TV's Murder ordained. J. Calio. il pors *People Wkly* 27:107-8+ Je 8 '87

Bird attracting *See* Birds, Attracting of

Bird banding

Junk jewelry [collars and tags] G. Hill. il *Field Stream* 92:24 O '87

Bird beaks *See* Bills (Birds)

Bird cages

A better bird cage. J. Wigdabl. il *Home Mech* 83:122 O '87

Collectors and collecting

Antiques: birdcages. J. R. Mellow. il *Archit Dig* 44:116-21 Ag '87

Bird calling

Phool a pheasant. D. Zutz. il *Outdoor Life* 180:92-3+ N '87

Seven faces of old Tom [gobblers] J. Trout, Jr. il *Outdoor Life* 179:45-7+ F '87

Bird calls *See* Birds—Song

Bird communication

Flocking together: it may help ospreys to fish more efficiently [research by Erick Greene] J. Horgan. il *Sci Am* 257:40 D '87

Bird control

See also

Ducks, Wild—Control

Russia is for the birds. J. Boswall. il *Discover* 8:78-83 Mr '87

Bird dogs *See* Hunting dogs

Bird feeders

Capturing the birds on film. S. R. Swinburne. il *Ctry J* 14:47-9 F '87

Easy-to-make bird feeder. W. Gustafson. il *Workbench* 43:28-31 Mr/Ap '87

No soggy seeds with a bird feeder he built with hardware-store parts. il *Sunset* 178:72 Ja '87

Squirrel-proof your bird feeder. K. Childers. il *Fam Handyman* 37:32-3 D '87

Bird houses *See* Birdhouses

Bird hunting *See* Game bird shooting; Water bird shooting

Bird introduction

An African bird makes its move around the world [cattle egret] J. H. Heminway. bibl (p183) il map *Smithsonian* 18:60-6+ My '87

Seized parrots could restore a lost species [thick-billed parrot] il *Audubon* 89:22 Jl '87

Bird populations

See also

Population genetics—Birds

Control

See Bird control

Bird sanctuaries

Birdland, U.S.A. [photographs] M. Melford. il *Life* 10:48-52+ Jl '87

Bahamas

Keeping flamingos under his wing [work of J. Nixon on Great Inagua] B. Krist. il por *Int Wildl* 17:46-51 Ja/F '87

North Carolina

Wing Haven [garden and bird sanctuary of E. Clarkson] K. Whiteside. il *House Gard* 159:166-73+ Je '87

Trinidad and Tobago

Asa Wright and her tropical forest ark. F. Graham. il maps *Audubon* 89:82-95 My '87

Bird shooting *See* Game bird shooting; Water bird shooting

Bird songs *See* Birds—Song

Bird study

See also

Bird banding

National Audubon Society

Videotapes—Bird study

All that jizz. J. Leo. il *Time* 129:72-3+ My 25 '87

Bird-watching basics. P. Hodgins. bibl il *Better Homes Gard* 65:222+ N '87

Bird study—*cont.*

Birding's fledgling phenoms [Victor Emanuel Nature Tours birding camp in Arizona desert] F. Graham. il por *Audubon* 89:38-40+ My '87

Birdland. F. Graham. See issues of Audubon

The hobby that lifts your heart. J. Culhane. il *Read Dig* 130:56-60 F '87

'The most vivid expression of life'. R. T. Peterson. il por *Life* 10:56 Jl '87

Pterodactyl eats two in park [bird watching in Central Park] J. Adler. il *Newsweek* 109:86 My 18 '87

Bird tagging *See* Bird banding

Bird watching *See* Bird study

Birdcages *See* Bird cages

Birdhouses

Architecture for the birds [birdhouses designed by architects] il *House Gard* 159:106-9 Jl '87

Bluebird bungalows. M. Matthews. il por *Mother Earth News* 104:40+ Mr/Ap '87

Birding *See* Bird study

Birdland (New York, N.Y.: Jazz club) *See* New York (N.Y.)—Restaurants, nightclubs, bars, etc.

Birds

See also
Birdhouses
Ear—Birds
Embryology—Birds
Shore birds
Water birds
See also names of birds

Birdland. F. Graham. See issues of Audubon

Feathered friends are good for us. il *Prevention* 39:12 Mr '87

Fine feathered friends [choosing a pet] M. Ingebretsen. il *Better Homes Gard* 65:226 N '87

The importance of "tweety birds". S. Cook. il *Natl Wildl* 25:46-7 O/N '87

Accidents and hazards

See also
Aviation—Bird hazards

Anatomy

See also
Bills (Birds)

Banding

See Bird banding

Breeding

Adventures of a birder [New York Breeding Bird Atlas project] W. E. Cook. il *Conservationist* 41:36-41 My/Je '87

Collisions with airplanes

See Aviation—Bird hazards

Coloration

See Color of birds

Control

See Bird control

Diseases and pests

Looking for Mr. Goodbird [relationship between garish plumage and parasite resistance; research by Andrew Read] il *Discover* 8:8 O '87

Ecology

Firewood gathering hits a snag [endangering bird habitats in national forests] M. Kantor. il *Sierra* 72:24+ Mr/Ap '87

Food and feeding

See also
Bird feeders

A bird in the hand [joys and pitfalls of winter feeding] R. Holland. il *Natl Wildl* 25:42-3 F/Mr '87

The bird that farms the dell [relationship between bell miners, psyllids, and eucalyptus dieback] R. H. Loyn. il *Nat Hist* 96:54-60 Je '87

Birds of a feather feed together [feeding on horseshoe crab eggs by migrating shore birds at Delaware Bay] W. P. Carty. il *Américas* 39:28-33+ S/O '87

Cast master [bait fishing by green-backed herons of Suizenji Park, Kumamoto, Japan] H. Higuchi. il *Nat Hist* 96:40-3 Ag '87

A favor returned [winter feeding] R. K. Collett. il *Flower Gard* 32:56-7 D '87/Ja '88

Flocking together: it may help ospreys to fish more efficiently [research by Erick Greene] J. Horgan. il *Sci Am* 257:40 D '87

Hard times on mussel beach [oystercatcher competition for food on the Exe estuary, England] J. Goss-Custard. il *Nat Hist* 96:64-71 Mr '87

The small-water factor [ducks] B. W. Dalrymple. il *Field Stream* 92:60-1+ O '87

Smart bird gets the moth! [jays learn to find camouflaged moths] il *Natl Geogr World* 143:30-1 Jl '87

Habits and behavior

See also
Parental behavior in birds
Sexual behavior—Birds
Territoriality (Zoology)

Indefatigable watcher of nesting birds [A. F. Skutch] il *Audubon* 89:128+ N '87

The neighborly great gray owl [cover story] E. L. Bull and M. G. Henjum. il *Nat Hist* 96:32-41 S '87

Handbooks, manuals, etc.

See also
Videotapes—Bird study

Identification

See Bird study

Intelligence

See Animal intelligence

Memory

See Memory

Migration

See also
Bird banding
Cranes (Birds)—Migration
Shore birds—Migration
Water birds—Migration

Hitchhikers in the sky. J. K. Terres. il *Natl Wildl* 25:38-40 O/N '87

Nests

Building a better home. J. K. Terres. il *Natl Wildl* 25:42-9 Ap/My '87

Photographs and photography

Green mansion [house sparrow nest in traffic light, Tucson, Ariz.] C. A. Morgan. il *Nat Hist* 96:108-9 N '87

Periodicals

See also
Audubon (Periodical)

Photographs and photography

Birding: shooting blind. S. K. Sneddon; D. Braud. il *Petersens Photogr Mag* 16:44-7 Ag '87

Birdland, U.S.A. M. Melford. il *Life* 10:48-52+ Jl '87

Capturing the birds on film. S. R. Swinburne. il *Ctry J* 14:47-9 F '87

Protection

See also
Audubon societies
Bird sanctuaries
Birds, Attracting of
National Audubon Society

Song

In Brazil, bird songs aren't just cheap trills. M. Levinson. il *Int Wildl* 17:48-53 S/O '87

Listening in on the loons' tunes [work of William Barklow] S. Morton. il *Sierra* 72:14-15 My/Je '87

Mockingbird song aimed at mates, not rivals [research by Randall Breitwisch and George Whitesides] R. Lewin. il *Science* 236:1521-2 Je 19 '87

Russia is for the birds. J. Boswall. il *Discover* 8:78-83 Mr '87

Sopranos of the skies [work of Stephen Nowicki] *Sci Am* 256:70-1 Mr '87

Tuning in to songbirds and their songs. S. Weisburd. *Sci News* 131:182-3 Mr 21 '87

Treatment

See also
Geese, Wild—Treatment
Pelicans—Treatment

Alcatraz Island (Calif.)

The real birdman of Alcatraz [R. Pierotti] K. Schafer. il pors *Natl Wildl* 25:18-21 Ag/S '87

Antarctic regions

See also
Penguins

Icy realm of Antarctic birds. K. Shackleton. il *Int Wildl* 17:54-9 S/O '87

Arctic regions

Seabird citadels of the Arctic [thick-billed murres] A. J. Gaston. il *Nat Hist* 96:54-9 Ap '87

Arizona

Birding's fledgling phenoms [Victor Emanuel Nature Tours birding camp in Arizona desert] F. Graham. il por *Audubon* 89:38-40+ My '87

Australia

See also
Kookaburras

The bird that farms the dell [relationship between bell miners, psyllids, and eucalyptus dieback] R. H. Loyn. il *Nat Hist* 96:54-60 Je '87

The royal spoonbill. M. P. Kahl. il map *Natl Geogr* 171:280-4 F '87

Birds—*cont.*

Brazil

In Brazil, bird songs aren't just cheap trills. M. Levinson. il *Int Wildl* 17:48-53 S/O '87

California

Biking and birding around southern San Francisco Bay. il *Sunset* 178:10-11 Ja '87

Empty the skies [loss of wetland habitat for migrating water birds] P. Steinhart. il maps *Audubon* 89:70-97 N '87

Cape Cod (Mass.)

Bank swallows. R. Finch. il *Ctry J* 14:76-80 My '87

Chile

Birds of a poet's native land [poems]; tr. by Jack Schmitt. P. Neruda. il *Int Wildl* 17:16-17 My/Je '87

Connecticut

Too many mallards [Storrs] R. Holland. il *Audubon* 89:64-7 Ja '87

Cuba

"I saw it!" [ivory-billed woodpecker] L. L. Short and J. F. M. Horne. il *Int Wildl* 17:22-3 Mr/Ap '87

Florida

Endangered species? Load the shotgun! [K. Ghumman accused of shooting red cockaded woodpeckers] R. L. Di Silvestro. il *Audubon* 89:12 S '87

This doctor is for the birds [H. Albers; cover story] E. Boddie. il pors *50 Plus* 27:20-4 Jl '87

Florida Keys (Fla.)

Keeping a key pigeon in the Keys [work of T. Bancroft with white-crowned pigeons] G. Laycock. il por *Audubon* 89:76-80 Mr '87

Galapagos Islands

Natural selection: bird seeds of change [research by Peter R. Grant and H. Lisle Gibbs] R. Monastersky. il *Sci News* 131:373-4 Je 13 '87

Great Britain

Hard times on mussel beach [oystercatcher competition for food on the Exe estuary] J. Goss-Custard. il *Nat Hist* 96:64-71 Mr '87

Hawaii

Hand of man seen in birds [tandem particle accelerator mass spectrometry used in dating; research by Storrs Olson and others] R. Lewin. *Science* 236:1522 Je 19 '87

Heimaey (Iceland)

Huffin' for puffins [rescuing young puffins on Heimaey, Iceland] il map *Natl Geogr World* 144:12-15 Ag '87

India

Photographs and photography

Some birds of Corbett Park. il *Audubon* 89:56-7 Jl '87

Japan

Cast master [bait fishing by green-backed herons of Suizenji Park, Kumamoto] H. Higuchi. il *Nat Hist* 96:40-3 Ag '87

Jenny Lind Island (N.W.T.)

Photographs and photography

Brooding on the tundra [sanderlings] B. Lyon. il *Nat Hist* 96:84-7 D '87

Kauai (Hawaii)

Suburbs close in on a seabird colony [proposed expansion of Kilauea National Wildlife Refuge] J. Yoshimoto and C. Proczka. il *Sierra* 72:69-70 My/Je '87

Manitoba

Grouse and spouse [willow ptarmigan] K. Martin. il *Nat Hist* 96:62-9 F '87

Maryland

Tales of two rails [Maryland's black rail and Michigan's yellow rail] W. G. Burt, III; R. McKee. il *Audubon* 89:78-87 S '87

Mexico

Back from oblivion [work of A. J. Grayson] F. Graham. il map *Audubon* 89:20-4+ S '87

Michigan

Tales of two rails [Maryland's black rail and Michigan's yellow rail] W. G. Burt, III; R. McKee. il *Audubon* 89:78-87 S '87

Midway Islands

Paint chips and albatross chicks [Laysan albatrosses poisoned from eating paint chips] G. S. Grant. il *Sea Front* 33:270-2 Jl/Ag '87

New York (State)

Adventures of a birder [New York Breeding Bird Atlas project] W. E. Cook. il *Conservationist* 41:36-41 My/Je '87

From beyond the horizon [snowy owls] D. Harding. il *Conservationist* 41:20-1 Mr/Ap '87

Pterodactyl eats two in park [bird watching in Central Park] J. Adler. il *Newsweek* 109:86 My 18 '87

Spirit of the northern waters [status of common loon in upstate New York] K. E. Parker. il *Conservationist* 42:16-21 Jl/Ag '87

The wings of spring [return of migrating ducks; cover story] G. Lemmo. il *Conservationist* 41:26-31 Mr/Ap '87

New Zealand

No room for a hermit [yellow-eyed penguin] A. Vernon. il *Int Wildl* 17:22-4 N/D '87

Prince Leopold Island (N.W.T.)

Murre mysteries. F. Graham. il map *Audubon* 89:16+ Ja '87

Soviet Union

Russia is for the birds. J. Boswall. il *Discover* 8:78-83 Mr '87

Western Europe

Europe's vanishing storks. D. Seward. il *Int Wildl* 17:4-11 My/Je '87

Western States

Back from oblivion [work of A. J. Grayson] F. Graham. il map *Audubon* 89:20-4+ S '87

Birds, Attracting of

See also

Bird feeders

A bird in the hand [joys and pitfalls of winter feeding] R. Holland. il *Natl Wildl* 25:42-3 F/Mr '87

Gardening for the birds. W. Shipman. il *Ctry J* 14:12 My '87

A tree for the birds. il *South Living* 22:54 D '87

Birds, Effect of temperature on

Chickadee down. P. Schullery. il *Ctry J* 14:78-80 Mr '87

Birds, Fossil

Age and diet of fossil California condors in Grand Canyon, Arizona. S. D. Emslie. bibl f il *Science* 237:768-70 Ag 14 '87

Ancient death and modern survival [California condor; work of Steven D. Emslie] *Sci News* 132:136 Ag 29 '87

As an exterminating agency, humans are comparable with any natural form of violence that has ever come along. R. M. Adams. il *Smithsonian* 18:10 S '87

Bird hoax [Archaeopteryx] I. Smullen. il *Omni* 9:100 My '87

Feathers still fly in row over fossil bird [Archaeopteryx debate] D. Dickson. il *Science* 238:475-6 O 23 '87

Fossils extend condor's range, pose questions [discovery in upstate New York of three fossil California condor bones] il *Audubon* 89:14 Jl '87

Fossils of ancient bird unearthed in west Texas [Protoavis discovered by Sankar Chatterjee] il *Earth Sci* 40:7 Spr '87

Hand of man seen in birds [tandem particle accelerator mass spectrometry used in dating; research by Storrs Olson and others] R. Lewin. *Science* 236:1522 Je 19 '87

Birds in art

See also

Ducks in art

Owls in art

Art: woodland prints. H. H. Broun. il *Archit Dig* 44:178-83 Je '87

Back from oblivion [work of A. J. Grayson] F. Graham. il map *Audubon* 89:20-4+ S '87

Guy Coheleach—artist and hunter [cover story] A. Fornora. il *Conservationist* 42:26-33 N/D '87

Icy realm of Antarctic birds. K. Shackleton. il *Int Wildl* 17:54-9 S/O '87

Terry Shortt: a life's journey into nature. R. M. Peck. il por *Int Wildl* 17:4-11 Jl/Ag '87

Twins Scott and Stuart Gentling sell off a high-priced Audubon and give wing to their own bird book. M. Vespa. il pors *People Wkly* 27:117-18 Je 15 '87

Birds of paradise [musical] See Musicals, revues, etc.—Reviews—Single works

Birds of prey

See also

Condors

Hawks

Ospreys

Owls

Turkey vultures

Birdwatching See Bird study

Birkerts, Gunnar

about

Formed to light: thirteen projects by Gunnar Birkerts. D. Rastorfer. il *Archit Rec* 175:141-9 Mr '87

Birkett, Deborah

West Africa's Mary Kingsley. bibl il pors *Hist Today* 37:10-16 My '87

Birmingham, Stephen

Antiques: transformation tables: ingenious designs with multiple uses. il *Archit Dig* 44:160-5 My '87

Birmingham (Ala.)
Architecture
Timeless design lives big. il *South Living* 22:78-9 D '87
Blacks
Full speed ahead at 94 [A. G. Gaston] F. White, III. il pors *Ebony* 42:52-4+ Je '87
Buildings
Southern comfort [YMCA facility] D. Dietsch. il *Archit Rec* 175:96-9 Ag '87
Description
Birmingham Turf Club. W. Schemmel. il *Travel Holiday* 168:8-10 Jl '87
Birmingham (England)
Cemeteries
A British town's cemeteries begin charging extra for oversize clients, and the plot thickens. il *People Wkly* 27:129 My 18 '87
History
Joseph Chamberlain and the municipal ideal. D. Fraser. bibl il por *Hist Today* 37:33-9 Ap '87
Religious institutions and affairs
Choosing new Anglican bishops. K. Slack. *Christ Century* 104:460-1 My 13 '87
Birmingham Steel Corp.
Help wanted: Stakhanovites only. J. Flint. il por *Forbes* 140:82+ S 7 '87
Birnbaum, Jeffrey H., 1956-
about
Inside tax reform. P. Glastris. *Wash Mon* 19:52-6 Je '87
Birnbaum, Morris J., and others
Transformation of rat fibroblasts by FSV rapidly increases glucose transporter gene transcription. bibl f il *Science* 235:1495-8 Mr 20 '87
Birnbaum, Norman
The politics of empire. il *Nation* 244:9-12 Ja 10 '87
Birnbaum, Stephen
Travel news. See issues of Good Housekeeping
Birney, Meredith Baxter
about
A real-life supermom: Meredith Baxter Birney. L. Fissinger. il pors *McCalls* 114:75-7 Ag '87
Birren, James E.
The best of all stories. *Psychol Today* 21:91-2 My '87
Birsh, Andy
Spécialités de la maison. See issues of Gourmet beginning May 1986
Birth *See* Childbirth
Birth, Multiple
See also
Quadruplets
Quintuplets
Sextuplets
Triplets
Twins
Clarifying cause of multiple pregnancy [fertility drugs; work of Oscar A. Kletzky] il *USA Today (Periodical)* 115:10 F '87
Birth certificates *See* Registers of births, etc.
Birth control
See also
Abortion
Contraceptives
Planned Parenthood Federation of America
Sterilization, Sexual
The practical facts about birth control [teenagers] K. McCoy. *Seventeen* 46:56+ Ap '87
Reproductive strategies and radical solutions. J. Belsky and P. Draper. *Society* 24:20-4 Mr/Ap '87
The rocky courtship of teens and birth control. H.-J. P. Mullins. il *Ms* 15:25 Mr '87
International aspects
See also
Family Planning International Assistance
United Nations Fund for Population Activities
Sex, love and the family [cover story; special issue] il *World Health* p2-27 N '87
The threat of population growth. il *World Press Rev* 34:58-9 Ag '87
Moral and religious aspects
Catholics and natural family planning: tradition or innovation? R. Kambic. *America* 157:244-6+ O 17 '87
Church-based clinic gives contraceptives to teens [Fairlington United Methodist Church, Va.] S. P. Wissler. il *Christ Today* 31:50+ F 20 '87
The last thing teens need is birth control [with readers' comments] M. Finley. *U S Cathol* 52:14-19 Ap '87
Student clinics: a sexy issue [Catholic bishops condemn high school birth control clinics] D. Whitman. il *U S News World Rep* 103:12 N 30 '87

Africa
The demographic trap. M. Morain. *Humanist* 47:31 Jl/Ag '87
In Africa, hope and difficulties. il *UN Chron* 24:45 N '87
Asia
Asia: reaching maturity. il *UN Chron* 24:44 N '87
Bangladesh
In the shadow of Uncle Sam [effect of USAID cutoff of funds to Family Planning International Assistance] A. Boggan. il *Ms* 16:69 N '87
China
China's controversial policy: 'one couple, one child'. L. Kravitz. il *Sch Update* 120:22-3 S 18 '87
China's food policy and population. K.-I. Chen. bibl f *Curr Hist* 86:257-60+ S '87
China's population program [discussion of March 6, 1987 article, Fertility policy in China: future options] S. Greenhalgh and J. Bongaarts. *Science* 238:1025-6 N 20 '87
The Chinese experience. F. T. G. Webb. il *World Health* p22-3 N '87
Fertility policy in China: future options. S. Greenhalgh and J. Bongaarts. bibl f il *Science* 235:1167-72 Mr 6 '87
Developing countries
Abortion more precious than $20 mil. grant: Wattleton [Planned Parenthood grant from U.S. Agency for International Development] *Jet* 72:36 My 11 '87
The moral implications of our population policy. W. Fornos. il por *Humanist* 47:30-2 Ja/F '87
Sex, love and the family [cover story; special issue] il *World Health* p2-27 N '87
U.S. antiabortion policy may increase abortions. C. Holden. *Science* 238:1222 N 27 '87
Wattleton raps Reagan's cut of overseas abortion funds. por *Jet* 72:9 Ag 17 '87
Kenya
Kenya uses soap opera to stem high birth rate. *Jet* 72:62 Ag 31 '87
Working together in the third world [soap opera promotes family planning] M. Morain. il por *Humanist* 47:33-4 S/O '87
Latin America
Lack of political commitment hampering population progress in Latin America. il *UN Chron* 24:47 N '87
Middle East
Middle Eastern countries try to strike a balance. il *UN Chron* 24:46 N '87
United States
See Birth control
Birth control clinics
Beyond sex ed: school clinics tackle the teen-pregnancy epidemic. L. Van Gelder and P. Brandt. il *McCalls* 114:89+ My '87
Clinical examination [case for school-based clinics] A. P. Weisman. *New Repub* 196:15-16 Mr 16 '87
The last thing teens need is birth control [with readers' comments] M. Finley. *U S Cathol* 52:14-19 Ap '87
Student clinics: a sexy issue [Catholic bishops condemn high school birth control clinics] D. Whitman. il *U S News World Rep* 103:12 N 30 '87
Teens back birth control clinics, Reagan against it. *Jet* 71:28 Ja 19 '87
This is what you thought: 85% say school clinics should provide contraceptives [results of survey] *Glamour* 85:77 Je '87
Federal aid
Clinical procedures [guidelines that would limit ability of federally funded family planning clinics to counsel pregnant women] *Nation* 245:217 S 12 '87
The future of federal family-planning programs [interview with N. Cabaniss] il por *Christ Today* 31:42-3 O 16 '87
One step forward . . . [enforcing a 1970 law that prohibits organizations that promote abortions from receiving federal funds] M. Gallagher. *Natl Rev* 39:29-30 Mr 13 '87
Reagan moves to redirect family-planning policy. K. A. Lawton. il *Christ Today* 31:56+ S 4 '87
Florida
A challenge to school clinics [decision to cut funding] J. Seligmann. il *Newsweek* 110:54 Ag 10 '87
Virginia
Church-based clinic gives contraceptives to teens [Fairlington United Methodist Church] S. P. Wissler. il *Christ Today* 31:50+ F 20 '87
Birth defects
See also
Anencephaly

Birth defects—See also—*cont.*
    Baby Doe rules
    Fetus—Diseases
    Neural tube—Diseases
    Spina bifida
Cause for concern—and optimism. J. Adler. il *Newsweek* 109:63-4+ Mr 16 '87
Deformed D.C. boy gets $95 million award in product liability suit [award to S. Ealy in Bendectin case] por *Jet* 72:26 Ag 3 '87
Every parent's nightmare. J. Adler. il *Newsweek* 109:56-61+ Mr 16 '87
The genetic effect. C. Marshall. *Vogue* 177:404+ O '87
Heaven sent? [priests test vaccine for pregnant women that could prevent cytomegalovirus] D. Tonnessen. il *Health* 19:18 D '87
The poisoned womb [views of John Elkington] *Futurist* 21:55 My/Je '87
San Antonio: putting family first [Mayor H. Cisneros declines race for governor; chooses to care for new son ailing from birth defects] D. Pedersen. il por *Newsweek* 110:8 S 14 '87
The thalidomide tragedy—25 years ago. W. Grigg. il *FDA Consum* 21:14-17 F '87

Birth order
And baby makes four [second child] V. E. Pomeranz and D. Schultz. il *Parents* 62:108 Ja '87
Middle child: caught in the squeeze? il *Teen* 31:76 My '87
Oldest, youngest, middle, or only: what your birth order says about you. C. Hanauer. il *Seventeen* 46:106-7+ Ja '87
The second child. A. Quindlen. il *Ladies Home J* 104:60+ S '87
What your birth order explains about you. C. Jabs. *McCalls* 114:25+ F '87

Birth rate
    See also
    Baby boom generation
    Baby bust generation
    Birth control
    Population
Battling over birth policy [views of B. J. Wattenberg] E. Bowen. il *Time* 130:58 Ag 24 '87
The birth dearth. T. Kaye. *New Repub* 196:20-3 Ja 19 '87
The birth dearth: dangers ahead? [excerpts; cover story] B. J. Wattenberg. il por *U S News World Rep* 102:56-62+ Je 22 '87
The birth dearth debate [criticism of B. J. Wattenberg's arguments] A. Levine. il *U S News World Rep* 102:64-5 Je 22 '87
Depleting asset? [views of Ben Wattenberg] M. S. Forbes, Jr. il *Forbes* 140:41 Jl 13 '87
Motherhood's sad loss of social esteem: one couple's reaction to America's birth dearth. S. Jacob and G. Jacob. pors *U S News World Rep* 103:6 Ag 17 '87
The notion that we've entered a second baby boom is a bust [views of Charles F. Westoff] il *Discover* 8:8 Ja '87

    International aspects
Birth rates sharply divide the world. *Sci News* 131:25 Ja 10 '87

    Africa
Burgeoning birthrate. B. Shelby. *World Press Rev* 34:43 N '87

    Canada
Facing a future with fewer people. M. Rose. il *Macleans* 100:16-17 Ag 24 '87

    Singapore
The government as a matchmaker. A. Peters. il *World Press Rev* 34:58 F '87

    United States
    See Birth rate

Birth technology *See* Reproduction

Birth weight
A boost for low-weight babies. *Sci News* 132:46 Jl 18 '87

Birthday gifts for children *See* Gifts for children

Birthday parties
100% successful birthday parties. J. Gaylin. il *Parents* 62:70-2 Ja '87
Happy birthday, Dr. Spock! B. Spock. il *Redbook* 169:19-20 My '87

Birthdays
It was a big day for 'Big Jule'—and me [birthdate newspapers] J. Kastner. il *Smithsonian* 18:154 Jl '87

Birthmarks
About birthmarks. K. Karlsrud and D. Schultz. il *Parents* 62:154 Je '87

Birthmarks and moles: what they are, what you can do about them. L. Rosch. *Glamour* 85:30 N '87

Birtwistle, Harrison
    about
Musical events:
American premieres of works by Kurtág, Ruders and Birtwistle. A. Porter. *New Yorker* 62:96+ F 9 '87

Biryukov, Dmitri
A Soviet assessment; tr. by Gretchen Trimble. il por *U S News World Rep* 103:54 O 19 '87

Birzeit University
The Palestinian campus. L. Wolfe. il *N Y Times Mag* p67-8+ Ap 19 '87

Biscoe, Gillian
Too few nurses? il *World Health* p14-15 Ap '87

Biscotti *See* Cookies

Biscuit joints *See* Joints (Carpentry)

Biscuits *See* Bread

Bisexuality
Is there a man in your man's life? What every girl should know about the bisexual guy. A. C. Heller. *Mademoiselle* 93:134-5+ Jl '87
A perilous double love life [bisexuals and AIDS] D. Gelman. il *Newsweek* 110:44-6 Jl 13 '87

BISG *See* Book Industry Study Group

Bishop, J. Michael, 1936-
The molecular genetics of cancer. bibl f il *Science* 235:305-11 Ja 16 '87

Bishop, John, 1929-
    about
The musical comedy murders of 1940 [drama] Reviews *N Y* 20:63-4 Ja 26 '87. J. Simon

Bishop, John
Winter shooting. il *Pop Photogr* 94:60-1 F '87

Bishop, Maurice
    Assassination
Some fell slow and some fell fast. G. Wagner. *Natl Rev* 39:32-3 Je 5 '87
Yesterday's revolution. B. Shacochis. il *Harpers* 275:41-4+ O '87

Bishop, Michael, 1945-
God's hour [fiction] *Omni* 9:58-60 Je '87

Bishop, Morin
The big D stands for destiny. il *Sports Illus* 66:75-6 Je 29 '87
More than halfway there. il pors *Sports Illus* 67:26-7 Ag 24 '87
Sports around the clock. il *Sports Illus* 67:91 Jl 27 '87
Whistling a new tune. il pors *Sports Illus* 67:72-4+ N 30 '87

Bishop, Randa
Haiti's majestic monuments. il *Américas* 39:2-7+ Ja/F '87

Bishop, Raymond F., and Kümmel, H. (Hermann), 1922-
The coupled-cluster method. bibl f il *Phys Today* 40:52-60 Mr '87

Bishop College
Bishop College's loss of its accreditation upheld. *Jet* 72:22 My 4 '87
UNCF approves withdrawal of $600,000 by Bishop. *Jet* 72:12 Ag 10 '87

Bishop Tutu Peace Concert, 1987
Tutu Peace Concert slated for L.A. in fall. *Jet* 72:60 Ag 24 '87

Bishops
    See also
    Black bishops
    Boy bishops
    Catholic Church. National Conference of Catholic Bishops
    Synod of Bishops (1987)
    Synods of bishops
    United States Catholic Conference
The Pope and the bishops: 'telling it like it is'. *America* 157:179-80 O 3 '87
    Appointment, call and election
Choosing new Anglican bishops [Birmingham, England] K. Slack. *Christ Century* 104:460-1 My 13 '87
    Sexual behavior
A black prince of the church [Greek Orthodox Bishop A. Draconakis seduces D. Gallas] G. Clifford. il pors *People Wkly* 28:30-5 S 28 '87

Bisiach & Carrù SpA
Entrepreneurial capitalism. H. Banks. il *Forbes* 140:228 Jl 13 '87

Bismuth
A bug, not what's bugging you, may cause ulcers [development of bacteria fighting drugs] Z. Schiller and S. Siwolop. il *Bus Week* p90 Ag 3 '87

Bison, American
See also
Buffalo hunting
Buffalo industry
Burdensome bison [Yellowstone] J. Robbins. il *Audubon* 89:24+ Ja '87
Bisque dolls *See* Dolls
Bisques (Cooking)
Extra-oystery oyster bisque. il *Sunset* 178:132 F '87
Red chili and green cilantro color and flavor this corn bisque. il *Sunset* 179:174 O '87
Bissell, Frances
The new English cooking. il *Harpers Bazaar* 120:104+ Ap '87
Bisset, Jacqueline
about
Bewitched, bothered and Bisset. M. Green. por *Harpers Bazaar* 120:205+ Ap '87
Do men make good pals? L. Kleinmann. por *Health* 19:42 N '87
Bissonette, Pete
When a friend has AIDS. por *U S News World Rep* 103:9 Jl 6 '87
Bissonnette, André
about
The police and the MP. M. Rose. *Macleans* 100:9 Ag 31 '87
A political minefield [special section; with editorial comment by Kevin Doyle] il pors *Macleans* 100:2, 8-9+ F 2 '87
The Tories strike back. M. Gee. il por *Macleans* 100:10-11 F 9 '87
Bites, Dog *See* Dog bites
Bites, Human
Black man's teeth a deadly weapon, jury rules [case of J. V. Moore] il por *Jet* 72:24 Jl 13 '87
Bites, Insect *See* Insect bites and stings
Bits (Drilling and boring)
A bit more. M. Morris. il *Home Mech* 83:7 Ja '87
Router bits. il *Fam Handyman* 37:11 O '87
Bitstream Inc.
A personal type. A. Ward. il pors *N Y Times Mag* p146 S 20 '87
Bittle, Camilla R.
Her secret [story] il *Redbook* 169:22-4 Ag '87
Biumo, Guiseppe Panza di *See* Panza di Biumo, Giuseppe
Biva, Paul *See* Biya, Paul, 1933-
Bivalves *See* Mollusks
BIX (Byte Information Exchange) *See* Computer networks
Biya, Paul, 1933-
about
The post-Ahidjo era in Cameroon. M. Azevedo. bibl f *Curr Hist* 86:217-20+ My '87
Bizet, Georges, 1838-1875
about
Carmen [opera] Reviews
Art Am il 75:180-5+ Ap '87. K. Kertess
N Y 20:104-6 Mr 2 '87. P. G. Davis
New Yorker 63:60-1 Jl 6 '87. A. Porter
Opera News il 51:42-3 Ap 11 '87. N. Goodwin
Opera News il 51:26, 28-30 Mr 14 '87
Opera News il 51:36-7+ Mr 14 '87. L. Halévy
Biznet *See* American Business Network
Bjorke, Clark
about
Self-reliance grows in their garden. J. Ruttle. il por *Rodale's Org Gard* 34:66-8 Je '87
Bjorke, Pat
about
Self-reliance grows in their garden. J. Ruttle. il por *Rodale's Org Gard* 34:66-8 Je '87
Bjorken, James D.
Generalizing the SSC decision. *Phys Today* 40:136 Mr '87
Bjorklund, Barbara
(jt. auth) See Bjorklund, David F., and Bjorklund, Barbara
Bjorklund, David F., and Bjorklund, Barbara
As they grow/7 through 10. See issues of Parents beginning January 1987
Bjornson, Teresa
about
Her life for art. C. K. Gandee. il *Archit Rec* 175:140-7 mid-Ap '87
BL Lacertae objects *See* Radio sources (Astronomy)
BL plc
See also
Rover Group plc
Black, Barbara Aronstein
about
Columbia Law School gets its first housewife-scholar-dean. C. M. Eckhardt. il por *Ms* 16:62-5+ O '87

Black, Conrad M.
about
Black and white and read all over. T. Fennell. il por *Macleans* 100:32-3 Je 15 '87
Partners for the Post. P. Best. por *Macleans* 100:40 O 19 '87
Saturday night fever. P. Young. por *Macleans* 100:55 Je 29 '87
Black, David, 1945-
Endless summer of love. il *Harpers* 274:47-52 My '87
Black, David C.
(jt. auth) See Banks, Peter M., and Black, David C.
Black, George
Delle Chiaie: from Bologna to Bolivia [cover story] il *Nation* 244:525+ Ap 25 '87
Black, George
about
The last brickmaker in America. C. Kuralt. il *Read Dig* 130:53-6 My '87
Black, Ira B., and others
Biochemistry of information storage in the nervous system. bibl f il *Science* 236:1263-8 Je 5 '87
Black, Jeremy
Edmund Burke: history, politics and polemic. bibl il por *Hist Today* 37:42-7 D '87
Black, Joe
about
Ex-Dodger Joe Black hurls pitch to owners on how to strike out baseball bias. il pors *Jet* 72:50 My 18 '87
Black, Mary C.
Ammi Phillips portraits rediscovered. bibl f il *Antiques* 132:558-9 S '87
Black, Richard B., 1933-
about
Richard Black is back—this time as a startup star. P. Finch. il por *Bus Week* p118-19 Ap 6 '87
Black, Scott M.
about
Stocks even a skeptic can love. C. Farrell. *Bus Week* p69 F 2 '87
Black, Shane
about
Lethal weapon gives writer Shane Black a shot at fame. il por *People Wkly* 27:121 Je 15 '87
Black & Decker Corp.
How Black & Decker got back in the black. C. S. Eklund. il por *Bus Week* p86+ Jl 13 '87
Black & Decker Mfg. Co.
See also
Black & Decker Corp.
Black actors and actresses
See also
Blacks in motion pictures
Blacks in television
See also names of black actors and actresses
Image Awards omits actress category citing few roles. *Jet* 73:18 N 16 '87
Black advertising agencies
See also
Creative Resources Management Inc.
Mingo-Jones Advertising Inc.
Muse-Cordero-Chen & Baca Advertising
UniWorld Group
Black aged *See* Aged
Black air pilots
Collins: United Airlines must hire more blacks. *Jet* 71:8 Mr 23 '87
Drug testing OK with most black pilots, execs say. *Jet* 71:32 F 23 '87
United, SIU Carbondale seek more black pilots. *Jet* 72:16 Ag 3 '87
Black air traffic controllers (Persons)
Air pair [B. and H. Williams at the Cleveland Air Route Traffic Control Center] il pors *Ebony* 42:36+ Ap '87
Black ambassadors
See also
Perkins, Edward J.
Black Americans for Life
Enlisting blacks in the battle against abortion [interview with K. James] por *Christ Today* 31:63+ O 2 '87
Black and white [dance] *See* Dance reviews—Single works
Black and white films *See* Photography—Films
Black and white photography *See* Photography
Black and white processing (Photography) *See* Photography—Processing
Black architectural firms
See also
Cruz-Stark Associates PA

Black art See Art, Black
Black artists
    See also
    Bearden, Romare, 1914-1988
    Johnson, Joshua, 1765-1830
    Lawrence, Jacob
    Puryear, Martin, 1941-
    Tanner, James, 1941-
    Williamson, Philemona
Artists, persevere! C. Young-Johnson. por *Essence* 17:140 Ap '87
Black arts See Arts, Black
Black astronauts
    See also
    Jemison, Mae C.
Black athletes
    See also names of black athletes
Best black athletes of all time [results of Ebony poll] il *Ebony* 42:134+ O '87
Blacks dominate for U.S. in track championships [World Championships in Rome] il *Jet* 73:46-7 S 28 '87
The complexities of complexions. T. Callahan. il *Time* 129:80 Je 22 '87
Doctor of sports and sociology [H. Edwards] A. Collier. il pors *Ebony* 42:101-2+ O '87
Ex-pros plan conference, as bias talks continue. *Jet* 72:28 My 25 '87
A sporting chance . . . N. O. Unger. See issues of Jet beginning December 31, 1984-January 7, 1985 through January 26, 1987
Sports. See issues of Jet
Stars turn little goals into big success. il *Jet* 72:26-8 Ag 24 '87
Strike one and you're out [racism in sports] L. Rosellini. il *U S News World Rep* 103:52-7 Jl 27 '87
Education
    See also
    National Organization on the Status of Minorities in Sports
Campbell back in school; assists student-athletes [University of Texas] *Jet* 71:49 Ja 26 '87
A failed game plan [college sports and black youth] M. Naison. il *Commonweal* 114:199-200 Ap 10 '87
Millionaire dropout going back to school for degree because 'grandma' told him [C. Barkley] por *Jet* 72:48 My 25 '87
Salaries, pensions, etc.
$1.1 mil. suit filed by athletes in Fla. land deal [legal malpractice against Holland & Knight] *Jet* 72:50 Je 8 '87
Blacks lead the way for best-paid 100 athletes. il *Jet* 72:52 My 18 '87
How athletes handle their money. W. Leavy. il *Ebony* 42:76+ Je '87
Black authors
    See also
    Austin, Doris Jean
    Baldwin, James, 1924-1987
    Haley, Alex
    Morrison, Toni, 1931-
    Walker, Alice, 1944-
    Wright, Richard, 1908-1960
Blacks find jobs scarce for writers in Hollywood. *Jet* 71:25 Mr 23 '87
Black automobile dealers
    See also
    Ray Sykes Buick
Auto dealers shift into maximum overdrive. J. Koblenz. il *Black Enterp* 17:245-6+ Je '87
Car slide hits black dealers. G. S. Johnson. il *Black Enterp* 18:36 D '87
Jackson buys California automobile dealership [R. Jackson] por *Jet* 73:48 N 9 '87
Reggie purchases stake in Nissan dealership [R. Jackson] *Jet* 73:50 O 26 '87
Black bachelors See Single men
Black banks and banking
    See also
    Black investment banking
    Black savings and loan associations
    Freedom National Bank of New York
    Mechanics & Farmers Bank
Black banks: high risks and slow growth. A. F. Brimmer. il *Black Enterp* 17:31 Mr '87
Hot careers in banking. C. Mitchell. il *Black Enterp* 17:62-4+ F '87
A wave of defaults capsizes black banks. il *Black Enterp* 17:187-8+ Je '87

Black baseball fans See Baseball fans
Black baseball leagues See Baseball, Professional—History
Black baseball managers See Baseball managers
Black baseball players See Baseball players
Black basketball players See Basketball players
Black bear hunting See Bear hunting
Black bears See Bears
Black bishops
    See also
    Fisher, Carl A.
Pope John-Paul's historic meeting with black bishops. il por *Jet* 73:24 N 9 '87
Black brokers
    See also
    National Association of Securities Professionals
Making fast money in high finance. N. McCall. il *Black Enterp* 17:52-6 F '87
Black bus drivers
Roads scholar Stephen James quits life in the bus lane to shoot for a Harvard Ph.D. [34 year old Bronx bus driver graduates from college] M. Brower. il pors *People Wkly* 27:87-8 Je 22 '87
Black business enterprises
    See also
    American Health and Beauty Aids Institute
    Black entrepreneurs
    Minority Business Enterprise Legal Defense and Education Fund Inc.
    National Business League
15th annual report on black business [cover story; special issue; with editorial comment by Earl G. Graves] il *Black Enterp* 17:13-14, 109+ Je '87
Airport concessions: new opportunities for black business. il *Ebony* 42:54-6+ Ap '87
Black businesses: growth and diversification. A. F. Brimmer. il *Black Enterp* 18:37 N '87
Black-owned businesses: 1982. il *Black Enterp* 18:39 Ag '87
Blacks fly with Marriott [concessionary business at Tampa International Airport] R. Baker. il *Black Enterp* 17:22 Ap '87
Economics [address, February 20, 1987] T. Brown. *Vital Speeches Day* 53:400-4 Ap 15 '87
John H. Johnson named 'Entrepreneur of Decade,' JPC top black business. il pors *Jet* 72:6-9+ My 25 '87
Making it. See issues of Black Enterprise
A trailblazer's trip to the top [J. B. Llewellyn] F. McCoy. il por *Bus Week* p129+ N 16 '87
When Wall Street began to take blacks seriously. R. H. Bork, Jr. il por *U S News World Rep* 103:44 Ag 31 '87
Directories
Philadelphia In the black [directory of black-owned business] W. J. Dawkins. il pors *Black Enterp* 17:66 Je '87
Federal aid
    See also
    United States. Minority Business Development Agency
Black businessman charges conspiracy behind losses [J. N. Grayson of Univox California, Inc.] il por *Jet* 71:15 Mr 23 '87
Desperately seeking defense contracts. D. C. Ruffin. il *Black Enterp* 18:43 D '87
HUD grants $4.3 billion to black business under Pierce. il por *Jet* 72:12 Ap 20 '87
John Lewis amends bill to aid black businesses. *Jet* 72:8 Je 22 '87
Minority business: old players, new agenda. D. C. Ruffin. il *Black Enterp* 17:77-8 Je '87
Minority business with gov. hit record level in 1986. *Jet* 72:26 Ap 27 '87
Mitchell rigs 'hot line' for black firm contracts. *Jet* 73:38 O 12 '87
Neal stays as lone black SBA policymaker in D.C. [E. C. Neal] *Jet* 72:12 Ag 24 '87
History
Black entrepreneurship in America. W. Hoffer. il *Nations Bus* 75:56-7 Je '87
International aspects
Congressman Merv Dymally leads trade mission to Japan and Seoul, Korea. il por *Jet* 72:37 My 18 '87
Japan: hopes, but no gains [better relationship between Japan and black American consumers] D. C. Ruffin. il *Black Enterp* 18:22 Ag '87
Looking toward international markets. M. Simms. il *Black Enterp* 18:39-40 O '87
Location
Sun Belt best spot for black businesses: study. *Jet* 72:4 Ag 17 '87

Black business enterprises—*cont.*
Caribbean region
See also
Caribbean American Chamber of Commerce and Industry
South Africa
The Horatio Algers of South Africa. J. Jones. il *U S News World Rep* 103:41-2 Jl 20 '87
If Coke has its way, blacks will soon own 'the real thing' [bid to sell off stake in South African bottler] S. Mufson. il *Bus Week* p56 Mr 23 '87
Black businessmen
See also
Black business enterprises
Black entrepreneurs
Black executives
National Business League
On the move. See issues of Black Enterprise
Black cadets
S.C. panel tells Citadel to stop playing 'Dixie!'. *Jet* 71:33 Mr 23 '87
U.S. Military Academy seeks minority candidates. *Jet* 71:22 Jl 6 '87
Black candidates, Political *See* Black political candidates
Black Caucus *See* Congressional Black Caucus
Black celebrities
Celebrities and their favorite cars. il *Ebony* 43:27-8+ N '87
Celebrities express their thoughts at Christmastime. il *Jet* 73:56 D 28 '87-Ja 4 '88
Celebrities salute their mothers on 'Mother's Day'. il *Jet* 72:58 My 11 '87
Celebrities tell why they can never forget that first love. il *Jet* 71:22-4 Mr 2 '87
Do celebrities make best role models for blacks? il *Jet* 72:54-5 Jl 20 '87
Does a famous name help or hurt? [children] il *Ebony* 43:60+ N '87
Does success spoil marriage? il *Jet* 72:54-6 Ag 3 '87
Father's Day: celebrity dads talk about their children. il *Jet* 72:14-16 Je 22 '87
How children of celebrities cope with privilege and prejudice. il *Jet* 72:58-9+ Jl 27 '87
How stars make time for their children. il *Jet* 73:58-60 O 26 '87
'My best Christmas ever'. il *Ebony* 43:34+ D '87
'My most embarrassing moment'. il *Ebony* 42:110+ S '87
People. See issues of Jet
People are talking about . . . See issues of Jet
Siblings without rivalry. il *Jet* 72:54-6 Jl 6 '87
Stars talk about marriage proposals. il *Jet* 71:56-8 F 23 '87
The ten most beautiful black women in America [cover story] il *Ebony* 42:130-2+ Jl '87
Photographs and photography
The best photos of 1987. il *Jet* 73:33+ D 28 '87-Ja 4 '88
Memorable photos from the Ebony files. See issues of Ebony beginning June 1984
Psychology
Famous people tell what they fear most. il *Jet* 72:54+ Je 8 '87
Sports
Stars shined for Sugar but most bet on Hagler. il *Jet* 72:49 Ap 27 '87
Black children
Feeling of inferiority disappears when black kids given positive images [study by Darlene Powell-Hopson] il *Jet* 72:36 S 21 '87
Poussaint: money, play keeps black kids slimmer than fat white kids. il *Jet* 72:36 Jl 13 '87
A question of black pride: studies show little improvement in black youths' self image. A. Toufexis. il *Time* 130:74 S 14 '87
Adoption
See Adoption and adopted children
Crimes against
See Blacks—Crimes against
Education
See Blacks—Education
Black churches
See also
African Methodist Episcopal Church
Church businesses spread the gospel of self help [community development and black churches] il *Ebony* 42:61-2+ F '87
Vice President Bush worships at black church, boosts families [Shiloh Baptist Church in Washington, D.C.] il pors *Jet* 71:24-5 Ja 19 '87

Black churches and politics *See* Religion and politics
Black clergy
See also
Black missionaries
13-year-old conducts wedding like veteran [W. Hudson of Chicago] il por *Jet* 71:29 Mr 16 '87
13-year-old preacher talks about love, sex, sin and forgiveness [W. Hudson] T. S. Moore. il pors *Jet* 72:14-16 Je 29 '87
In Chicago, God's word often comes out of the mouth of a mere babe—the Rev. William Hudson III, 13. D. Grogan. il pors *People Wkly* 28:102+ Ag 24 '87
Crime
Convicted Va. minister quits council, churches [case of C. Johnson] por *Jet* 72:6 Ag 24 '87
Daughter alleges father sired his own grandkids [case of Rev. L. Elliott] il por *Jet* 72:16+ Ag 31 '87
Miami preacher convicted for selling heroin [case of C. Scott] *Jet* 72:10 Je 15 '87
Minister/councilman's rape conviction still stuns his church, city [Rev. C. Johnson] D. M. Cheers. il por *Jet* 72:16-17 Jl 13 '87
Minister/lawmaker may get 161 years in prison for rape, sexual battery [case of C. Johnson] il por *Jet* 72:4-6 Je 29 '87
Petersburg, Va. pastor charged with alleged sexual abuse of 6 girls [case of C. L. Johnson] *Jet* 72:10 Je 15 '87
Texas preacher guilty of siring 12 of his grandkids [L. Elliott] il por *Jet* 73:16 D 7 '87
Va. minister convicted of sex crimes gets 120 years [case of C. L. Johnson] por *Jet* 73:51 O 5 '87
Political activities
Black ministers: a new force in U.S. politics. S. Booker. il *Jet* 71:14-16 F 2 '87
This congressman preaches in church every Sunday [interview with F. H. Flake] por *Christ Today* 31:58-9 Mr 20 '87
Black coaches *See* Coaches (Athletics)
Black collectibles
See also
Black music—Collectibles
Collecting black memorabilia. T. Bolden Davis. il *Black Enterp* 17:49+ Je '87
Black college graduates
The class of 1987 [graduates of Florida A & M] il *Ebony* 42:116-18+ Ag '87
Roads scholar Stephen James quits life in the bus lane to shoot for a Harvard Ph.D. [34 year old Bronx bus driver graduates from college] M. Brower. il pors *People Wkly* 27:87-8 Je 22 '87
Why fewer blacks are graduating. R. A. Taylor. il *U S News World Rep* 102:75-6 Je 8 '87
Employment
Leroy Nunery: working for a bigger crop of minority MBAs. M. Mallory. por *Bus Week* p76 O 26 '87
Wanted: black M.B.A.s. M. Mallory. il *Black Enterp* 18:28 O '87
Black college presidents
See also
Blake, J. Herman
Cole, Johnnetta B.
Gloster, Hugh M.
Kappner, Augusta Souza
Keith, Leroy
Smith, Albert E.
Sudarkasa, Niara
Black college students *See* Black students
Black college teachers
Business is his business [black professor J. I. Cash] il pors *Ebony* 42:31-3+ O '87
An ebony view of the ivory power: memories of a black faculty member. W. B. Harvey. *Change* 19:46-9 My/Je '87
Psychology
Stress hits black profs harder than whites, study. *Jet* 72:5 Mr 30 '87
Black colleges and universities
See also
Albany State College (Ga.)
Allen University
Bishop College
Central State University (Ohio)
Dillard University
Fisk University
Florida A & M University
Grambling State University
Hampton University
Howard University
Jackson State University
Lincoln University (Pa.)

Black colleges and universities—See also—*cont.*
　Meharry Medical College
　Morehouse College
　Prairie View A & M University
　Savannah State College
　Spelman College
　St. Augustine's College
　Talladega College
　Texas Southern University
　Tuskegee University
Black colleges vs. white colleges: the fork in the road for black students. W. R. Allen. il *Change* 19:28-31+ My/Je '87
The clarion call [address, January 7-8, 1987] R. L. Albright. *Vital Speeches Day* 53:297-305 Mr 1 '87

Accreditation
Bishop College's loss of its accreditation upheld. *Jet* 72:22 My 4 '87

Federal aid
Black colleges get EEOC settlement of $3.6 million. il *Jet* 71:4 Mr 23 '87
Critics wary of Reagan wooing black colleges. *Jet* 73:38 O 5 '87
Howard, Grambling get fed. funds for anti drug plans. *Jet* 73:32 N 2 '87
Reagan orders feds to support black colleges. *Jet* 72:4 Ag 24 '87
Schools want to cash in on $50 million set aside as aid for black colleges. *Jet* 72:30 My 18 '87
Student-loan rules may hurt black schools. il *Jet* 73:4 D 7 '87

Finance
　See also
　Black colleges and universities—Gifts, legacies, etc.
　Dr. Lacey Kirk Williams Educational Trust
　United Negro College Fund
10 richest black colleges. il *Jet* 72:14-15 Je 15 '87

Gifts, legacies, etc.
Bill and Camille Cosby make $1.3 million gift to aid Fisk University. *Jet* 71:52 Ja 12 '87
Fisk president tells meaning of the Cosbys' gift of $1.3 million. il por *Jet* 71:16 Ja 19 '87
Jackson State, Meharry get $100,000 each from grads. *Jet* 72:25 Je 22 '87
Prairie View gets $109,500 in funds. *Jet* 73:22 O 19 '87
Sugar Ray Leonard, an Eddie Robinson fan, gifts $250G's to Grambling. il pors *Jet* 72:50 Jl 13 '87
Untold story—real reason the Cosbys gave Fisk $1.3 million. il por *Jet* 71:14-15 F 9 '87

Student recruiting
Recruitment drives seek to attract black students [special section] *Jet* 72:8-10+ Ap 27 '87

Black comedians
　See also
　Hall, Arsenio
　Just June
　Murphy, Eddie
　Stickney, Phyllis
Gleason remembered for helping black comedians. il *Jet* 72:60-1 Jl 13 '87

Black computer personnel *See* Computer personnel

Black congressmen
　See also
　Congressional Black Caucus
　Crockett, George W., Jr.
　Dymally, Mervyn M.
　Ford, Harold, 1945-
　Gray, William H., III
　Lewis, John Robert
　Mitchell, Parren J.
　Owens, Major
　Savage, Gus
　Stokes, Louis
Black reps cheered as they take on 100th U.S. Congress. il *Jet* 71:4-5 Ja 26 '87
Legislators develop a new agenda. F. D. Brown. il *Black Enterp* 17:27-8 F '87
A step foreward in black congressional power. il map *Ebony* 42:87+ F '87

Black consumers
The battle of the curls [American Health and Beauty Aids Institute objects to Revlon racist statement about black consumers and black hair care manufacturers] K. Smikle. *Black Enterp* 17:18 Ja '87
Can Revlon repair its image? [black boycott] P. Wang and M. Malone. il *Newsweek* 109:53 F 23 '87
Economics [address, February 20, 1987] T. Brown. *Vital Speeches Day* 53:400-4 Ap 15 '87

A gaffe at Revlon has the black community seething [disparaging black-owned hair-care companies] C. Dugas and K. Dreyfack. il *Bus Week* p36-7 F 9 '87
Japan: hopes, but no gains [better relationship between Japan and black American consumers] D. C. Ruffin. il *Black Enterp* 18:22 Ag '87
Operation PUSH continues boycott of Revlon products. *Jet* 71:17 Ja 12 '87
The push for economic parity. E. G. Graves. il *Black Enterp* 18:9 O '87
Urban black consumers. il *Black Enterp* 18:39 N '87

Black contractors
　See also
　H. J. Russell Construction Co., Inc.
EPA rule change threatens black contractors' jobs. *Jet* 72:5 Ag 31 '87
Hospital gets facelift [North General Hospital, Harlem] M. Scott. *Black Enterp* 18:20 N '87
King helps create new minority contract office in Fulton County, Ga. [M. L. King III] por *Jet* 72:31 Jl 27 '87
Minority claims in state contracts being probed [road construction in Illinois] *Jet* 73:32 N 2 '87

Black cooking *See* Cooking, Black
Black corporation directors *See* Corporations—Directors
Black credit unions
　See also
　Ampere/Essex Business Credit Union
Black criminals *See* Blacks—Crime
Black dance *See* Dance, Black
Black diplomats
　See also
　Keyes, Alan
　Sadler, Charles A.
Black divorcees *See* Divorcees
Black drama
August Wilson. B. Staples. por *Essence* 18:50-1+ Ag '87
A voice from the streets [work of A. Wilson] S. G. Freedman. il pors *N Y Times Mag* p36+ Mr 15 '87
Black ducks, Wild *See* Ducks, Wild
Black economists
　See also
　Loury, Glenn C.
　Sowell, Thomas, 1930-
Black education *See* Blacks—Education
Black educators
　See also
　Black college teachers
　Burton, Michael
　Dorsett, Beryl
　Wesley, Charles Harris, 1891-1987
Black engineers
　See also
　National Council of Black Engineers and Scientists
Black-English dialects
　See also
　Gullah dialect
Black enterprise (Periodical)
Networking update [Black Enterprise Professional Exchange] il *Black Enterp* 18:25 Ag '87
Networking update [Black Enterprise Professional Exchange] C. Bullock. il *Black Enterp* 18:26 S '87
Power networking Black enterprise style. S. R. King. il *Black Enterp* 18:70-3 N '87
Black entertainers
Fosse leaves legacy of helping blacks, Allen says. il por *Jet* 73:18 O 12 '87
The Harlem Opera House. *New Yorker* 63:20-1 Je 29 '87
Headlining the Apollo; ed. by Steven Dougherty. R. Cooper. il pors *People Wkly* 28:71+ O 19 '87
Stars who have black managers. C. Waldron. il *Jet* 73:54-6 O 12 '87

Health and hygiene
How the stars keep in shape. il *Ebony* 42:138+ My '87
Black Entertainment Television
Essence woman [views of TV producer J. Brown on black women in video] L. B. Randolph. il por *Essence* 17:24 Ja '87
Black entrepreneurs
Finding capital in the tax reform era. M. King. il *Black Enterp* 17:60-5 Ap '87
Finding the franchise formula for success [Black enterprise Franchise 50; cover story; special section; with editorial comment by Earl G. Graves] il *Black Enterp* 18:9, 50-2+ S '87
How to start your own business. il *Ebony* 43:44+ N '87

Black entrepreneurs—*cont.*
A quest for excellence [special section] B. Robson. il *Black Enterp* 17:273-4+ Je '87
Rewards and recognition. E. G. Graves. il *Black Enterp* 17:9 F '87
Venturing out on your own. T. Gallant-Stokes. il *Black Enterp* 17:49-52 Ja '87

History
Black entrepreneurship in America. W. Hoffer. il *Nations Bus* 75:56-7 Je '87

Black executives
Getting organized for 1987. K. V. Brailsford. il *Black Enterp* 17:54-6 Ja '87
How to succeed in corporate America. L. Norment. il *Ebony* 42:51-2+ Ag '87
The new corporate environment [cover story; special section; with editorial comment by Earl G. Graves] il *Black Enterp* 18:9, 40-2+ Ag '87

Dismissal
Will black managers survive corporate downsizing? [special section; with editorial comment by Earl G. Graves] il *Black Enterp* 17:7, 49-52+ Mr '87

Promotion
Breaking stride in the corporate marathon. W. Whitmore. il *Black Enterp* 17:56-8+ Mr '87
Waiting for the right phone call [W. S. Norman of Amtrak] D. Machan. il por *Forbes* 140:110-11 Ag 10 '87

Psychology
Power. D. Wickham. bibl il *Black Enterp* 17:52-4+ Ap '87

Recruiting
How to tap top talent. B. Robson. il *Black Enterp* 17:278 Je '87

Salaries, pensions, etc.
What to do with your severance package. F. McCoy. il *Black Enterp* 17:63-4 Mr '87

Travel
See Business travel
Black eye *See* Eye—Wounds and injuries
Black-eyed pea cooking *See* Cooking—Vegetables
Black family
Baby Faith [black family's involvement with language and creativity] M. Wallace. il por *Ms* 16:154+ Jl/Ag '87
Baptist Convention urges fortifying black family. *Jet* 73:32 S 28 '87
'Don't you talk about my mama!' [adaptation of address, 1987] J. Jordan. *Essence* 18:53+ D '87
Families that work [two career black couples] P. V. Pressley. il *Essence* 17:75-7+ Mr '87
Family reunions helping blacks face unsure future. il *Jet* 73:20+ O 5 '87
Keeping our families strong. L. Gite. il *Essence* 18:51-2+ Jl '87
Md. Sen. blasts negative reports on black family [views of B. Mikulski] *Jet* 72:8 Mr 30 '87
Say, brother. G. Powell. por *Essence* 17:10 Mr '87
A show of strength: celebrating the black family with 'reunions'. B. Kantrowitz. il *Newsweek* 110:73 Ag 17 '87

History
Family and freedom: black families in the American Civil War. I. Berlin and others. bibl f il *Hist Today* 37:8-15 Ja '87
Black family in drama
'Raisin' doesn't typify black family life: Rolle. il por *Jet* 72:59 Ap 27 '87
Black farmers
See also
United Farmers Organization
A harvest of struggle. Y. Moore. il *Black Enterp* 17:64 Je '87
Lean years for black farmers. O. Davidson. il *Progressive* 51:27 Ag '87
Black FBI agents *See* United States. Federal Bureau of Investigation
Black fiction
The last days of Richard Wright. O. Harrington. il pors *Ebony* 42:58-60+ Mr '87
Black Filmmakers Hall of Fame
MUMM V.S.O.P. Cognac presents black filmfest [Chicago] il *Jet* 72:60-3 Je 29 '87
Sammy Davis Jr. saluted at Black Filmmakers' weekend. il pors *Jet* 71:12-13 Mr 16 '87
Black flies *See* Blackflies
Black football coaches *See* Football coaches
Black football owners *See* Football, Professional—Organization and administration

Black football players *See* Football players
Black-footed ferrets *See* Ferrets
Black Foreign Service officers *See* United States. Dept. of State. Foreign Service
Black golfers *See* Golfers
Black government employees
Bias suit wins $2.4 mil. for 362 black GPO workers. *Jet* 72:17 S 7 '87
Black GPO workers awarded $2.4 million in bias case. *Jet* 72:22 Je 8 '87
Commerce Dept. black cites job bias and is demoted [R. Nichols] por *Jet* 73:17 N 30 '87
Dotson transferred to save pension in alleged mishap [case of B. L. Dotson] *Jet* 72:18 Ap 20 '87
EEOC's Thomas wants blacks in high-paying fed. jobs. por *Jet* 73:38 O 12 '87
Faces of middle class America: Bonnie Jenkins is single and living in Washington D.C. [FBI translator] il pors *Ebony* 42:146+ Ag '87
Getting ahead in government [B. Crawford, IRS employee] L. Gite. il por *Black Enterp* 17:93-4+ F '87

Health and hygiene
Black federal workers oppose drug testing. *Jet* 72:23 Je 22 '87
Black hair care *See* Hair—Care
Black hair care products industry *See* Hair care products industry
Black hairstyling *See* Hairstyling
Black Hills (S.D. and Wyo.)
See also
Hell Canyon (S.D.)
Give it back to the Indians? [P. Stevens leads Sioux claim] T. Jacoby. il pors *Newsweek* 110:47 D 7 '87
The heart of everything that is [Sioux Indians battle for return of the Black Hills] W. Greider. il *Roll Stone* p37-8+ My 7 '87
More precious than gold [opposition to open pit gold mining] J. W. Wilson. il *Progressive* 51:11 N '87
Black history *See* Blacks—History
Black History Month
Black History Month commemorates one of greatest stories in history of the world. il por *Jet* 71:22+ F 16 '87
Coca-Cola USA awards seven scholarships in Black History sweepstakes [Black History Month "Share the Dream" sweepstakes] il *Jet* 72:26-7 Jl 6 '87
Black holes (Astronomy)
Birth of a quasar [supercomputer model developed by Stuart Shapiro and Saul Teukolsky] A. Fisher. il *Pop Sci* 231:10 S '87
The birth of neutron stars and black holes [cover story] A. Burrows. bibl f il *Phys Today* 40:28-37 S '87
Black holes: coming to a galaxy near you. il *Discover* 8:10 O '87
Black holes: the ultimate in space-time curvature. *Astronomy* 15:19 O '87
Hearts of darkness: evidence grows that black holes lurk at the center of galaxies. J. Horgan. il *Sci Am* 257:30+ O '87
Massive objects in galactic nuclei may be black holes. P. H. Andersen. bibl il *Phys Today* 40:22 O '87
Quasars: the movie [work of Stuart Shapiro and Saul Teukolsky] il *Sky Telesc* 74:457 N '87
Signs of black holes [work of Douglas Richstone and Alan Dressler] A. Fisher. il *Pop Sci* 231:14+ N '87
Black hospital patient representatives
Advocates for patients. C. Bullock. *Black Enterp* 18:24 O '87
Black infant mortality *See* Infant mortality
Black insurance companies
See also
Supreme Life Insurance Company
Universal Life Insurance Company
Meeting the demand for comprehensive coverage. S. Kennedy. il *Black Enterp* 17:223-4+ Je '87
Black investment banking
Conrail sale aids bankers. M. A. Fortune. *Black Enterp* 17:22 Ap '87
Making fast money in high finance. N. McCall. il *Black Enterp* 17:52-6 F '87
Black journalism *See* Black press
Black journalists
See also
Hunter-Gault, Charlayne
Johnson, Ben
Johnson, Bill
National Association of Black Journalists
Qwelane, Jon
Blacks file bias suit against N.Y. Daily news. *Jet* 71:15 Mr 2 '87

Black journalists—*cont.*

Blacks win lawsuit filed against N.Y. Daily news. *Jet* 72:24 My 4 '87

Daily news makes $3.1 mil. settlement in job bias case. *Jet* 72:22 Jl 6 '87

Guilty of race bias [New York Daily news] *Newsweek* 109:63 Ap 27 '87

Hire more minorities in nation's newsrooms: ANPA. *Jet* 72:22 Je 8 '87

Journalists win bias suit [black journalists vs. N.Y. Daily news] Y. Rice. il *Black Enterp* 17:15-16 Jl '87

Tabloid pays a big tab [settlement in discrimination case against the New York Daily news] *Time* 129:65 Je 22 '87

Black judges

See also

Brown, Harry C.
Clemon, U. W.
Harris, Jesse
Hastings, Alcee L.
Keith, Damon
McCree, Wade H., 1920-1987
Parker, Barrington D.
Stokes, Carl
Thomas, Maxine F.
Williams, Marcus D.

Picking federal judges: color-blind or blind to blacks. D. C. Ruffin. il *Black Enterp* 17:25 Ap '87

Black jurors *See* Jury

Black labor *See* Blacks—Employment

Black law firms

Making a case for choosing a black law firm. M. King. il *Black Enterp* 17:133-6+ F '87

Black lawyers

See also

Blair, Chester L.
Branton, Wiley A., 1923-
Cornwell, David
Davis, Hardge, Jr.
Espy, Michael
Figures, Michael A.
Gary, Willie
Girton, Brenda M.
Joyner, Gail Tusan
Joyner, Gordon L.
Maddox, Alton H.
Mason, C. Vernon
McKee, Clarence
National Bar Association
Simmons, Althea
Sutton, Walter L., Jr.
Wells, Ted

Black leadership

30 leaders of the future. il *Ebony* 42:38-9+ Je '87

The 100 most influential black Americans. il *Ebony* 42:52+ My '87

126 VIPs chosen for historic White House dinner during summit. S. Booker. il *Jet* 73:4-6+ D 28 '87-Ja 4 '88

American blacks [discussion of January 1987 article, Who speaks for American blacks?] G. C. Loury. *Commentary* 83:2+ Ap '87

Black leaders in uproar over new surge of racism. il *Jet* 71:6-8 Ja 26 '87

Who speaks for American blacks? G. C. Loury. *Commentary* 83:34-8 Ja '87

Black legislators

See also

Maryland Legislative Black Caucus
National Black Caucus of State Legislators

Health and hygiene

Ohio's most powerful black lawmaker reveals fight to conquer cancer [C. J. McLin] il por *Jet* 73:29 S 28 '87

Black light photography *See* Ultraviolet photography

Black literature

See also

Black authors
Black drama
Black fiction
Blacks in literature
Harlem renaissance
Publishers and publishing—Black literature

Bibliography

Ebony book shelf. See issues of Ebony

A roundup of notable titles. T. Bolden Davis. il *Black Enterp* 18:21-2+ D '87

Collectors and collecting

See also

Schomburg Center for Research in Black Culture

Black lobbyists and lobbying

See also

TransAfrica (Organization)

Black marketing managers

Can this man keep Team Xerox no. 1? [A. B. Rand] A. Edmond, Jr. il *Black Enterp* 18:58-60+ Ag '87

These guys don't blink [C. Ware and C. Morrison of Coca-Cola] A. Edmond, Jr. il pors *Black Enterp* 17:310-12+ Je '87

Xerox moves Rand to top [A. B. Rand] M. A. Fortune. por *Black Enterp* 17:17 My '87

Black markets

In defense of the black market [work of H. de Soto]; tr. by Alfred J. MacAdam. M. Vargas Llosa. il *N Y Times Mag* p28-31+ F 22 '87

Black married couples *See* Married couples

Black mayors

See also

Barry, Marion, 1936-
Barthelemy, Sidney
Burns, Clarence H.
Dixon, Richard Clay
Gantt, Harvey
Goode, W. Wilson
Holley, James G., III
Milner, Thirman L.
Officer, Carl
Perkins, Helen
Rochelle, Wilbert D.
Sawyer, Eugene
Schmoke, Kurt
Shackelford, Lottie
Smith, John H.
Washington, Harold
Young, Andrew, 1932-
Young, Coleman

5 top metros for black professionals [cover story; with editorial comment by Earl G. Graves] il *Black Enterp* 17:7, 55-8+ My '87

Black mayors rap funding for U.S. war on drugs. *Jet* 73:6 N 16 '87

Prichard, Ala.'s Smith is black mayors' leader [J. H. Smith] por *Jet* 72:24 My 18 '87

Attitudes

Black mayors put money, jobs above racism concerns. *Jet* 72:12 My 11 '87

Black medical colleges

See also

Morehouse School of Medicine

Federal aid

Reagan OKs $10 mil. act to aid black health colleges. *Jet* 72:14 S 14 '87

Gifts, legacies, etc.

$4 mil. loan set to aid minority medical students. il *Jet* 73:12 N 16 '87

Black medical students

$4 mil. loan set to aid minority medical students. il *Jet* 73:12 N 16 '87

Black memorabilia *See* Black collectibles

Black men and women *See* Women and men

Black middle class *See* Middle classes

Black militants

See also

Black Panther Party

The fire this time: two tough lawyers spur a new black activism [A. H. Maddox and C. V. Mason] P. Blauner. il pors *N Y* 20:42-7 Ap 27 '87

Black ministers *See* Black clergy

Black missionaries

Black Christians find unity in missions and evangelism. J. W. Reapsome. il *Christ Today* 31:54+ My 15 '87

The call of Destiny [black Christians to play major role in world evangelization] R. Frame. il *Christ Today* 31:64 S 4 '87

Black models (Persons) *See* Models (Persons)

Black Monday *See* Stock market crash, 1987

Black motion picture directors

See also

Lee, Spike
Townsend, Robert

Black Mountain College (N.C.)

Utopia revisited. M. Wade. il *Horizon* 30:13-16 Je '87

Black music

See also

Black Rock Coalition
Blues music
Compact discs—Black music
Gospel music
Phonograph records—Black music
Rap music
Slavery—Songs and music

Black music—*cont.*

Bibliography

New books on black music. D. L. Smith. il *Black Enterp* 18:37 Ag '87

Collectibles

Black American musical collectibles. D. E. Reno. il *Antiques Collect Hobbies* 92:63-5 D '87

Black musicians

See also names of black musicians

Critics dispute Elvis as king of rock 'n' roll. il por *Jet* 72:53 Ag 31 '87

John Hammond, discoverer of black stars, dies at 76. il *Jet* 72:55 Jl 27 '87

Political activities

See also

Black Rock Coalition

From ballads to ballots [J. Butler elected county commissioner in Chicago] il pors *Ebony* 42:152+ F '87

The Iceman cometh back [J. Butler, entertainer and Cook County Commissioner] B. Barol. il pors *Newsweek* 110:65 N 9 '87

Black Muslims

Islam's new entrepreneur [L. Farrakhan] S. Monroe and J. Schwartz. il por *Newsweek* 110:38-9 Jl 13 '87

Black nationalism *See* Blacks—Nationalism

Black newspapers *See* Black press

Black organizations

See also

Baseball Network

Black Women's Agenda

Congress of Racial Equality

Links (Organization)

National Association for the Advancement of Colored People

National Black Nurses Association

National Coalition of Black Voter Participation

National Council of Black Engineers and Scientists

National Forum of State Leaders

National Rainbow Coalition

People United to Serve Humanity (Organization)

Universal Negro Improvement Association

Black groups miss out on boom in donations spurred by tax reform. *Jet* 71:33 Ja 26 '87

Black Panther Party

Danny Glover says he was never a member of the Black Panther Party. por *Jet* 72:59 Ap 20 '87

Black periodicals

See also

Black enterprise (Periodical)

Ebony (Periodical)

Jet (Periodical)

Johnson Publishing Company, Inc.

Black pharmacists

Henry Cade named new Pharmacy Board prexy. por *Jet* 72:14 Jl 13 '87

Black photographers

See also

McLemore, Lamonte

Moutoussamy-Ashe, Jeanne, 1951-

Roberts, Richard Samuel, 1880-1936

Sleet, Moneta

Tomlin, Elaine

Black physicians

See also

Green, Frederick C.

Holmes, Richard

Jones, Edith Irby

National Medical Association

Doctors find a prescription for profits. B. Robinson. il *Black Enterp* 17:70-2+ Mr '87

Health and hygiene

Black doctors have higher rate of heart disease. *Jet* 72:36 Ap 13 '87

Black poets

See also

Brooks, Gwendolyn

Dove, Rita

Black police

See also

National Organization of Black Law Enforcement Executives

Black N.Y. police officer turns down a promotion; says he's no 'quota cop' [S. Brown] *Jet* 71:25 Mr 23 '87

Black police applicants seek millions in Louisville protest. *Jet* 71:8 Mr 16 '87

Black wins case against Pennsylvania state police; will receive $485,000 [case of black policeman R. Clanagan] *Jet* 72:38 My 11 '87

Blacks, state police in Alabama reach agreement in $2.5 million suit. *Jet* 72:8 S 7 '87

Boston police may get 1st minority lieutenants. *Jet* 72:40 Ag 3 '87

Court upholds racial quota [blacks in the Alabama state trooper force; Supreme Court decision] D. Camper. il *Black Enterp* 17:15 My '87

A one-white, one-black quota for promotions [Supreme Court decision in Alabama state trooper case] T. Gest. il *U S News World Rep* 102:8 Mr 9 '87

A racial quota for Alabama [state trooper hirings; Supreme Court decision] A. Press. il *Newsweek* 109:55 Mr 9 '87

Replying in the affirmative [Supreme Court approves promotion quotas for black state troopers in Alabama] R. Lacayo. il *Time* 129:66 Mr 9 '87

Supreme Court approves quotas for promotions [Alabama state troopers case] *Jet* 71:8 Mr 16 '87

Supreme Court upholds promotion quotas [Alabama state troopers case] *Mon Labor Rev* 110:41 My '87

Black police chiefs

See also

National Organization of Black Law Enforcement Executives

Baltimore police chief is new top cop for Maryland [B. Robinson] *Jet* 71:4 Mr 9 '87

Chicago mayor names city's second black police chief [L. Martin] il por *Jet* 73:5 N 16 '87

First black police chief hired in Greenville, Miss. [M. Wynn] por *Jet* 72:10 Ag 31 '87

First black police chief in Greensboro, N.C. is used to being a first [S. Daughtry] por *Jet* 72:12 Ap 13 '87

Pennsylvania gets first black state police major [R. M. Sharpe] por *Jet* 71:32 Mr 23 '87

Pittsburgh's black police chief quits over authority [W. Moore] *Jet* 72:8 Je 1 '87

Sharpe is 1st black tabbed to head Pa. state police. por *Jet* 72:8 Ag 31 '87

Sharpe is first black Pa. state police chief. por *Jet* 73:47 N 2 '87

Town manager fired, mayor quits in row over new black police chief in N.C. [Chadbourn, N.C.] por *Jet* 72:8 Ap 6 '87

Black political candidates

Pittsburgh voters approve new system; ups chances for black candidates. *Jet* 72:12 Je 8 '87

Politics. See issues of Jet

Black postal employees

Reinstates San Francisco postmaster 'forced' to quit [case of J. Wilson] *Jet* 73:35 N 30 '87

Black power

See also

Blacks—Political activities

The color of power. C. Riley. por *Essence* 18:148 N '87

Black press

See also

Black journalists

Milwaukee community journal

Black press is vital, says Detroit mayor Young. por *Jet* 72:40 Jl 13 '87

History

Founders of the black press [Freedom's journal founders S. Cornish and J. Russwurm] L. Bennett. il pors *Ebony* 42:96+ F '87

Black Press Hall of Fame

John H. Johnson among honorees inducted into Black Press Hall of Fame. il por *Jet* 73:14-15 N 23 '87

Black priests

'The Father Clements story' dramatizes fight of Chicago priest to adopt a son. C. Waldron. il por *Jet* 73:30-2 D 14 '87

Black prisoners

Redd Foxx does prison benefits in memory of his ex-con brother. il pors *Jet* 72:56-7 Mr 30 '87

Say, brother. D. K. Shipman. por *Essence* 18:10 Je '87

Black prisoners, Women *See* Women prisoners

Black professionals

5 top metros for black professionals [cover story; with editorial comment by Earl G. Graves] il *Black Enterp* 17:7, 55-8+ My '87

Blacks at the top: torn between two worlds. E. Hopkins. il *N Y* 20:20-31 Ja 19 '87

Ebony examines new black middle class. il *Jet* 72:40 Ag 17 '87

Network to network. D. Wickham. il *Black Enterp* 17:123-4+ F '87

Networking news. See issues of Black Enterprise beginning November 1987

Networking update [Black Enterprise Professional Exchange] il *Black Enterp* 18:25 Ag '87

Black professionals—*cont.*
Networking update [Black Enterprise Professional Exchange] C. Bullock. il *Black Enterp* 18:26 S '87
The new black middle class [cover story; special issue] il *Ebony* 42:22+ Ag '87
Power networking Black enterprise style. S. R. King. il *Black Enterp* 18:70-3 N '87
Reagan tells Tuskegee grads to choose black role models in sciences and professions. il pors *Jet* 72:13 My 25 '87
Salary roundup: who earns what. il *Black Enterp* 17:71-2 F '87
We're black yuppies. Which world do we belong in? C. King. il *Glamour* 85:78 My '87

Black promoters and promoting
See also
Haymon, Alan
King, Don, 1929-

Black psychiatrists
Black psychiatrists tell how racism hurts whites, too. il *Jet* 72:16-17 Jl 20 '87

Black public officers
See also
National Forum of State Leaders
Black appointed to USDA office; fourth director; Massie, Davenport get high level Energy Dept. posts. *Jet* 72:22 Je 15 '87
Black elected officials. *Society* 25:6-7 N/D '87
A black history celebration: pathfinders in public service. il *Ebony* 42:29-30+ F '87
Black leaders' roles [views of Michael B. Preston] il *USA Today (Periodical)* 116:13 D '87
Blacks slated for key posts in U.S. Dept. of Education. il *Jet* 72:27 Je 1 '87
Blacks win major offices; black voters show power. il *Jet* 73:4+ N 23 '87
Elected black officials off the beaten path. il *Ebony* 42:52+ Mr '87

Black radio stations *See* Radio stations, Black
Black railroad workers
Blacks win 15-year-old suit against L.I. Railroad. *Jet* 72:36 Ag 17 '87

Black real estate agencies and agents
See also
National Association of Real Estate Brokers
Real estate agents and brokers. il *Black Enterp* 18:43 O '87
Selling the home advantage [R. and E. Trass] S. Herbert. il pors *Black Enterp* 18:90-2 O '87

Black River (Ark. and Mo.)
Hot roadsters are breaking the peace [river riding] il *Newsweek* 109:27 Je 29 '87

Black Rock Coalition
Back in black: a group of musicians unites to reclaim the right to rock. D. Fricke. il pors *Roll Stone* p64+ S 24 '87
Black Rock against racism. M. Johnson. il *Essence* 17:28 Mr '87

Black savings and loan associations
See also
Carver Federal Savings Bank
Making the tough transition to financial independence. A. Kimbrough. il *Black Enterp* 17:203-4+ Je '87
Black school board members *See* School boards
Black school superintendents and principals
Selection and appointment
Memphis educator named Atlanta superintendent [W. W. Herenton] por *Jet* 73:22 N 9 '87
Student boycott ends in Senatobia, Miss. [hiring of black assistant superintendent] *Jet* 72:22 Ap 6 '87

Black scientists
See also
National Council of Black Engineers and Scientists
Black Sea follies [musical] *See* Musicals, revues, etc.—Reviews—Single works
Black sheriffs
Black Miss. sheriff seeks recount, despite cross burning in front yard [B. J. Adkins] *Jet* 72:5 Ag 31 '87
Calif.'s first black-elected sheriff: humble and proud [C. Byrd] por *Jet* 71:30 F 23 '87
First black sheriff is elected in McCormick, S.C. [G. Reid] por *Jet* 71:17 F 2 '87
Willie Jones becomes second black sheriff in Georgia. *Jet* 71:31 Mr 23 '87

Black sigatoka disease *See* Bananas—Diseases and pests
Black singers
See also
Phonograph records—Black music

Black single mothers *See* Single mothers
Black Sparrow Press
Black Sparrow: the house a poet helped to build [C. Bukowski] J. Barbato. il pors *Publ Wkly* 232:26-7 O 23 '87

Black state officers
NAACP criticizes Florida Gov. Martinez on hiring. *Jet* 72:29 Ap 13 '87
Black stockholders
How high the bull? R. D. Hylton. il *Black Enterp* 18:49-50+ N '87
NASP: blacks should buy part of American economy. il *Jet* 72:33 S 21 '87

Black students
See also
Black medical students
Colleges and universities—Desegregation
Colleges and universities—Segregation
Public schools—Segregation
The alarming decline in the number of black college students. M. Marshall. il *Ebony* 42:44+ S '87
Are more blacks bound for college? [rising SAT scores] il *U S News World Rep* 103:13 O 5 '87
Blacks follow trend in pursuing business degree. *Jet* 71:39 F 23 '87
Blacks in higher education: the climb toward equality [cover story; special issue] *Change* 19:6-7+ My/Je '87
Blacks more likely to be suspended, punished in nation's public schools. *Jet* 72:32 Ap 20 '87
Blacks protest campus racism. B. Kantrowitz. il *Newsweek* 109:30 Ap 6 '87
Blacks push Md. colleges' enrollment to record high. *Jet* 73:22 N 9 '87
Blacks' scores still lag despite big rise, Stewart [views of Donald M. Stewart] il *Jet* 73:36 O 12 '87
College board prexy says Reagan's ed. policy hurts minority students most [views of D. M. Stewart] por *Jet* 72:8 Ap 27 '87
Cuts in aid has drastic effect on black students. *Jet* 72:32 Ap 20 '87
Racism on campus. E. T. Louis. *Essence* 18:53+ Ag '87
SAT scores rise for black students. *Newsweek* 110:92 O 5 '87
Ticker tape scholars selected for '87-'88 [students having financial trouble] il *Jet* 72:23-4 Jl 27 '87
Two blacks among 32 U.S. Rhodes scholarship winners. il *Jet* 71:22 Ja 26 '87
University of Michigan agrees to blacks' demands; Jesse Jackson assists. *Jet* 72:5 Ap 13 '87
Why fewer blacks are graduating [college students] R. A. Taylor. il *U S News World Rep* 102:75-6 Je 8 '87
Wrong message from academe [racist incidents] E. Bowen. il *Time* 129:57-8 Ap 6 '87
Scholarships and fellowships
See Scholarships and fellowships
Black students, Women *See* Women college students
Black studies
Scholarships and fellowships
See also
Benjamin E. Mays Academy of Scholars
Black suffrage
Beware of Republicans bearing voting rights suits. M. Cooper. *Wash Mon* 19:11-15 F '87
Blacks in Springfield, Ill. win voting rights case. *Jet* 71:17 F 2 '87
Crusader Charles Melton gets last wish; new vote system for Westchester, Pa. il por *Jet* 73:6-7 S 28 '87
Judge in Springfield, Ill. to decide on voting issue. *Jet* 72:12 Je 8 '87
Judge orders Springfield, Ill. to vote on new government. *Jet* 72:4 Ap 20 '87
NAACP hits Tulsa with voting rights suit. *Jet* 72:29 Ag 10 '87
New challenges to voting rights. D. C. Ruffin. il *Black Enterp* 18:27 N '87
Pact reached in voting issue at Springfield, Ill. *Jet* 72:30 Jl 13 '87
What went wrong with the Voting Rights Act [views of A. M. Thernstrom] P. H. Schuck. *Wash Mon* 19:51-5 N '87

Black surgeons
See also
Carson, Benjamin
Joyner, John E.
Miller, Ross M., Jr.
Organ, Claude, Jr.
Black teachers
See also
Black college teachers

Black women in newspaper publishing *See* Women in newspaper publishing

Black women in publishing *See* Women in publishing

Black women in restaurant management *See* Women in restaurant management

Black women in the radio industry *See* Women in the radio industry

Black women in the television industry *See* Women in the television industry

Black women in trade unions *See* Trade unions—Women

Black women in videotapes *See* Women in videotapes

Black women legislators *See* Women legislators

Black women lobbyists and lobbying *See* Women lobbyists and lobbying

Black women ministers *See* Women clergy

Black women municipal officers *See* Women municipal officers

Black women physicians *See* Women physicians

Black women prisoners *See* Women prisoners

Black women real estate agents *See* Women real estate agents

Black women school superintendents and principals *See* Women school superintendents and principals

Black women singers *See* Women singers

Black women telephone workers *See* Telephone workers

Black Women's Agenda
Black women leaders view needed reforms in welfare. *Jet* 73:15 O 26 '87

Black women's cosmetics *See* Cosmetics

Black workers *See* Blacks—Employment

Black youth
See also
Black students
30 leaders of the future. il *Ebony* 42:38-9+ Je '87
A black American youth torn between cultures [cover story] R. J. Rousseve. il por *Humanist* 47:5-8 Mr/Ap '87
Eugene Cain: black men must help black youth. *Jet* 73:24 O 26 '87

Crime
See Juvenile delinquents and delinquency

Employment
Make strides to help minority youths: N.Y. gov. [views of M. Cuomo] *Jet* 72:30 My 25 '87
Urban youth lose jobs to suburbs. A. F. Brimmer. il *Black Enterp* 18:45 S '87

Health and hygiene
Drew U. medical study focuses on 75 twins [heart research] il *Jet* 72:36 Ap 13 '87

Unemployment
See Unemployment

Blackadar, Alfred
Using your computer. See issues of Weatherwise beginning June 1984

Blackberries
Brambles: berries of the brier patch. L. B. Trigg. il *South Living* 22:68-71 F '87
Knee-deep in blackberries. E. Sahatjian. il *Esquire* 108:20 Jl '87
'Olallie' blackberries. J. Cox. il *Rodale's Org Gard* 34:80 Ja '87

Blackberry pie *See* Pie

Blackbody radiation
See also
Cosmic background radiation

Blackfeet Indians *See* Siksika Indians

Blackflies
See also
Onchocerciasis

Control
State wants to spray pesticide on New River [use of Bti to exterminate breeding grounds of the black fly] *Natl Parks* 61:43 Mr/Ap '87

Blackford, John
Technology. See issues of Personal Computing beginning July 1987

Blackhawk (Calif.)

Housing
For sale: the rich look. J. Adler. il *Newsweek* 109:80 Je 22 '87

Blacklisting
Memories of HUAC. P. Bosworth. *Nation* 245:436-7 O 24 '87
Not necessarily the First Lady [complications stemming from Hollywood blacklisting of actress named Nancy Davis] J. Wiener. *Nation* 245:337 O 3 '87
Notes on the . . . blacklist [Hollywood blacklisting period; special section] il *Film Comment* 23:37-9+ N/D '87
The return of the blacklist [Justice Department's use of suspension orders against government contractors] D. Fanning. il *Forbes* 139:84 Ap 6 '87

Security risk. J. B. Montague, Jr. il *Progressive* 51:34 S '87

Vindication for a blacklist victim [case of P. Kimball] D. Gates. il por *Newsweek* 110:8 S 28 '87

Blackouts (Electric power) *See* Electric power failures

Blacks
See also
Black Muslims
Intelligence—Blacks
Museums and blacks
National Research Council (U.S.). Committee on the Status of Black Americans
Smoking and blacks
Trade unions—Blacks
Vietnamese War, 1957-1975—Blacks
The 100 most influential black Americans. il *Ebony* 42:52+ My '87
Is it true what they say about black men? B. M. Campbell. il *Ebony* 42:116+ Jl '87
Toward the 21st century. L. Rhoades. por *Essence* 17:114 Ja '87

Attitudes
The black middle class: moving up at last? *Current* 293:9-15 Je '87
Majority of blacks have been insulted due to race [telephone poll] *Jet* 71:31 F 23 '87
Moving up at last? [black middle class; Harper's forum] il *Harpers* 274:35-9+ F '87
Why blacks are reluctant to donate organs for transplants. il *Jet* 73:52-3 N 2 '87

Awards
See also
American Black Achievement Awards
Calif. Links group lauds superstar Ray Charles. il pors *Jet* 71:29 Mr 2 '87
Don King gets Dr. King Award in Jamaica fete. il pors *Jet* 71:36-7 F 9 '87
Image Awards omits actress category citing few roles. *Jet* 73:18 N 16 '87
Urban pioneers receive KOOL Achiever Awards. il *Jet* 73:6-7 O 12 '87

Caricatures and cartoons
Strictly for laughs. See issues of Ebony

Charities
See also
Associated Black Charities

Civil rights
See also
Alabama—Race relations
Anchorage (Alaska)—Race relations
Arizona—Race relations
Atlanta (Ga.)—Race relations
Boston (Mass.)—Race relations
Chicago (Ill.)—Race relations
Civil rights demonstrations
Cumming (Ga.)—Race relations
Flint (Mich.)—Race relations
Gage Park (Ill.)—Race relations
Gaithersburg (Md.)—Race relations
Glendale (Calif.)—Race relations
Greenwood (Miss.)—Race relations
Howard Beach case
Indianapolis (Ind.)—Race relations
Isola (Miss.)—Race relations
Keysville (Ga.)—Race relations
Long Branch (N.J.)—Race relations
Los Angeles (Calif.)—Race relations
Louisville (Ky.)—Race relations
Martin Luther King, Jr. Center for Nonviolent Social Change
Miami (Fla.)—Race relations
Mobile (Ala.)—Race relations
Moody (Ala.)—Race relations
Nashville (Tenn.)—Race relations
New Hampshire—Race relations
New York (N.Y.)—Race relations
North Carolina—Race relations
Portsmouth (Va.)—Race relations
Richmond (Va.)—Race relations
Rome (Ga.)—Race relations
Rumford (Me.)—Race relations
San Diego (Calif.)—Race relations
San Jose (Calif.)—Race relations
Shaker Heights (Ohio)—Race relations
Tampa (Fla.)—Race relations
Tifton (Ga.)—Race relations
United States—Race relations
Virginia—Race relations
Warren (Mich.)—Race relations
Washington (D.C.)—Race relations

Blacks—Civil rights—*cont.*

Affirmative action: cure or contradiction? [discussion] il *Cent Mag* 20:20-8 N/D '87

The appointment of death [Supreme Court rejects view that death penalty is racially biased] M. Kempton. il *N Y Rev Books* 34:40 My 28 '87

The bench and the chair [Supreme Court's ruling that death penalty doesn't discriminate against blacks] *Natl Rev* 39:15 My 22 '87

Bush's covenants [G. Bush's stand on civil rights and restrictive housing covenants] D. Robb. *Nation* 245:616-17 N 28 '87

Civil rights setbacks [actions of E. Meese] F. D. Brown. *Essence* 18:30 Jl '87

Civil rights supporters plea for defeat of Bork. il *Jet* 73:8 O 12 '87

Clearing a path to the chair [Supreme Court rejects argument that the death penalty discriminates against blacks] R. Lacayo. il *Time* 129:80 My 4 '87

Do conservatives discriminate against blacks? *Society* 25:4+ N/D '87

Fingerprinting only black males in town sparks tension, fear [Homestead, Pa.] L. Ransom. il *Jet* 72:12-14+ S 21 '87

Georgia murder conviction overturned: black jurors struck for racial reasons [case of W. Gamble] *Jet* 72:40 Ag 3 '87

Gridlock on death row [Supreme Court rejects view that death penalty is racist] A. Press. il *Newsweek* 109:60-1 My 4 '87

Group cites racism in death penalty sentence [views of Amnesty International] *Jet* 72:38 Ap 13 '87

Homestead NAACP chided on fingerprint support. il *Jet* 73:7 S 28 '87

Jury selection series cited by Marshall wins an award [Dallas morning news series on jury discrimination] *Jet* 72:23 Jl 20 '87

Making a resolution to gain equality. E. G. Graves. il *Black Enterp* 17:9 Ja '87

Mary Frances Berry. J. Barthel. por *Ms* 15:68-70+ Ja '87

Open door to the execution chamber? [Supreme Court ruling that death penalty does not discriminate against blacks] T. Gest. il *U S News World Rep* 102:25 My 4 '87

Reagan puts black progress on hold, Alex Haley says. por *Jet* 72:29 Ap 27 '87

Rewards and recognition. E. G. Graves. il *Black Enterp* 17:9 F '87

The search for a rapist [blacks asked to submit to fingerprinting in Homestead, Pa.] il *Newsweek* 110:42 S 14 '87

A shared fate [Supreme Court ruling that death penalty is not racially biased] M. O. Finkelstein. *Nation* 244:599 My 9 '87

Simmons, Jones mastermind move to dump Robert Bork. pors *Jet* 73:12 O 26 '87

Supreme Court rule may give new trials to blacks [blacks convicted by all white juries] *Jet* 71:6 F 2 '87

Thinking about the death penalty [Supreme Court rules death penalty not racially biased] *America* 156:393 My 16 '87

Trying to trace a rapist [fingerprinting of blacks in Homestead, Pa.] F. Trippett. il *Time* 130:28 S 14 '87

An uneasy festival for Martin Luther King. il *Newsweek* 109:24-5 Ja 26 '87

The unending nightmare of racism. L. Wainwright. il *Life* 10:13 F '87

We need a movement. J. Richardson. por *Essence* 17:135 Mr '87

History

See also
Civil rights demonstrations—History

The black and the red [W.E.B. Du Bois] C. V. Woodward. por *New Repub* 196:32-6 Mr 16 '87

Civil wrongs [television program Eyes on the prize] C. Schine. il *Vogue* 177:44+ Ja '87

Equality before the law: the Civil War amendments [cover story; with discussion] H. Belz. il por *Cent Mag* 20:4-19 N/D '87

Eyes on the prize [civil rights movement series produced by H. Hampton] J. Rosen. il por *Channels* 7:48-50 O '87

A farewell to civil rights. J. Nuechterlein. *Commentary* 84:25-36 Ag '87

Fighting back [TV series Eyes on the prize] F. Powledge. *Nation* 244:120-2 Ja 31 '87

Grading the presidents [civil rights records; views of T. Marshall] por *Newsweek* 110:33 S 21 '87

Happy Juneteenth! It's time to celebrate [blacks and the Constitution's bicentennial] E. Walton. por *U S News World Rep* 102:9 My 25 '87

Images of glory [TV documentary Eyes on the prize] R. Zoglin. il *Time* 129:24 Ja 19 '87

A journey to another time and, to many, another world [television documentary Eyes on the prize] L. J. Lord. il *U S News World Rep* 102:58-9 Mr 9 '87

The King to come [M. L. King; adaptation of address, January 19, 1987] B. Rustin. *New Repub* 196:19-21 Mr 9 '87

Lent: with our Eyes on the prize. *America* 156:165-6 F 28 '87

PBS flashes back to the civil rights era [television program Eyes on the prize] A. White. il *Essence* 17:22 Ja '87

Skinner chides youths' ignorance of King legacy [views of T. Skinner] il pors *Jet* 71:16 F 9 '87

They had a dream [TV series Eyes on the prize] J. Leonard. il *N Y* 20:68 Ja 26 '87

Thurgood Marshall ranks Reagan last among U.S. presidents he observed. il por *Jet* 73:12-13 S 28 '87

To form a more perfect union [black America and the Constitution; cover story; special section; with editorial comment by Earl G. Graves] il *Black Enterp* 17:11, 51+ Jl '87

To make a nation whole [14th Amendment and racial reform] D. A. Bell. il *N Y Times Mag* p42-4+ S 13 '87

Crime

Georgia leader urges AME delegates to fight crime [views of C. Smyre] *Jet* 73:32 S 28 '87

Why our children are killing one another. A. Poinsett. il *Ebony* 43:88+ D '87

Crimes against

Why our children are killing one another. A. Poinsett. il *Ebony* 43:88+ D '87

Culture

See also
Schomburg Center for Research in Black Culture

Economic conditions

See also
Blacks—Employment

Black enterprise annual money management issue [special issue; with editorial comment by Earl G. Graves] il *Black Enterp* 18:9, 48-50+ O '87

The black middle class: moving up at last? *Current* 293:9-15 Je '87

Black philanthropy. il *Black Enterp* 18:55 D '87

Blacks and poverty. J. E. Jacob. *Cent Mag* 20:55-6 Ja/F '87

Blacks made few economic gains in '70s: Census. *Jet* 72:24 Ap 20 '87

Breaking out of the ghetto: the origins of the underclass. N. Lemann. *Current* 289:4-15 Ja '87

Charity begins with a budget. L. Brown. il *Black Enterp* 18:77-8+ D '87

Ebony examines new black middle class. il *Jet* 72:40 Ag 17 '87

Economic perspectives. A. F. Brimmer. See issues of Black Enterprise

Economics [address, February 20, 1987] T. Brown. *Vital Speeches Day* 53:400-4 Ap 15 '87

Economics and race. J. A. Schnepper. il *USA Today (Periodical)* 115:19 Mr '87

Facts and figures. See issues of Black Enterprise

Finding a prescription for black wealth [Black enterprise Board of Economists] D. T. Dingle. il *Black Enterp* 17:38-40+ Ja '87

A man alone [T. Sowell] P. Brimelow. il por *Forbes* 140:40-1+ Ag 24 '87

Meeting the challenges of family finances [cover story] D. W. Hairston. il *Black Enterp* 17:40-4+ Jl '87

Money moves for a financially healthier 1987. *Black Enterp* 17:26 Ja '87

Moving up at last? [black middle class; Harper's forum] il *Harpers* 274:35-9+ F '87

The new black middle class [cover story; special issue] il *Ebony* 42:22+ Ag '87

Personal finance. D. Lamaute. See issues of Black Enterprise beginning March 1986

Racism, depression peril black America, Jacob says [J. E. Jacob of National Urban League] por *Jet* 71:4 F 2 '87

Rescuing the urban poor. T. H. Kean. il *USA Today (Periodical)* 116:72-5 N '87

The resegregation of America. J. Sleeper. il *Commonweal* 114:619-23 N 6 '87

Say, brother [change in economic status affects relationships with women] R. Clements. por *Essence* 18:6 O '87

Blacks—Economic conditions—*cont.*

A society that is just and fair [address, July 19, 1987] J. E. Jacob. *Vital Speeches Day* 53:733-6 S 15 '87

Task force offers answers for problems facing blacks [sponsored by Joint Center for Political Studies] *Jet* 72:9 Mr 30 '87

Two for a fresh start [newlyweds Lis and George Crawford] L. Gite. il *Black Enterp* 17:31-2+ Ja '87

Winning the loan game: how to score points with your banker. L. Marsa. il *Black Enterp* 18:63-4+ N '87

Education

See also

Benjamin E. Mays Academy of Scholars

Black athletes—Education

Black colleges and universities

Black students

Colleges and universities—Desegregation

Colleges and universities—Segregation

Public schools—Desegregation

Public schools—Segregation

Thurgood Marshall Black Education Fund

Black critics blast bias of SAT, ACT college test. *Jet* 71:40 Mr 9 '87

Blacks boycott schools in Coffeeville, Miss. [protest over transfer of black teacher, Gwendolyn English] *Jet* 72:12 S 7 '87

Blacks in higher education: the climb toward equality [cover story; special issue] *Change* 19:6-7+ My/Je '87

Business leaders urge more aid for poor kids. K. D. Thompson. il *Black Enterp* 18:30 D '87

A call for Comer [J. P. Comer hired as consultant by Norfolk Public School System] S. S. Harrison. por *Black Enterp* 17:20 Ap '87

"Demanding families" and black student achievement. C. R. Wharton. *Educ Dig* 52:18-20 My '87

Education is the way out and up. J. P. Comer. il pors *Ebony* 42:61-2+ Ag '87

Escape to freedom [independent schools; address, March 6, 1987] J. D. Ratteray. *Vital Speeches Day* 53:497-8 Je 1 '87

High schools that work [inner-city schools] R. E. McKinney. il *Ebony* 43:34+ N '87

Is protest losing steam? [new curriculum for black students in South Africa] il *U S News World Rep* 102:32-3 Ja 19 '87

Man poses as 14-year-old for chance at education [R. Turner of Milpitas, Calif.] il por *Jet* 72:8 Je 1 '87

Marva Collins may teach in Chicago and Compton. por *Jet* 72:12 Ag 17 '87

Md. Caucus to submit plan to aid black collegians. *Jet* 73:22 S 28 '87

The miseducation of our children. R. L. Bray. il *Essence* 18:79-80+ S '87

New rules for black schools [South Africa] W. R. Doerner. *Time* 129:48 Ja 12 '87

Positive primary education for young black males. S. H. Holland. *Educ Dig* 53:56-8 N '87

Self-help at its best. D. L. Evans. por *Newsweek* 109:8 Mr 16 '87

Teen sues for being denied love role opposite white [J. L. Mosley's suit over role in school musical in Oxford, Miss.] *Jet* 72:22 Mr 30 '87

Top-grade perks for teens [program at DuSable High School, Chicago] M. Oshin. il *Essence* 18:38 Je '87

Up from poverty [M. Burton, teacher and dean at The Harvard School, Chicago] C. Whitaker. il pors *Ebony* 42:110-11+ Ag '87

Why preferential admission? G. C. Loury. *Current* 296:27-9 O '87

Why preferential admission is not enough for blacks. G. C. Loury. *Educ Dig* 53:42-5 S '87

Employment

See also

Black business enterprises

Black businessmen

Black college graduates—Employment

Black entrepreneurs

Black executives

Black youth—Employment

Blacks—Occupations

Bias suit wins $2.4 mil. for 362 black GPO workers. *Jet* 72:17 S 7 '87

Black cameramen lose their $3.5 mil. suit against ABC. *Jet* 72:22 Ag 24 '87

Black FBI agent sues bureau for harassment; white wife threatened [D. Rochon] il por *Jet* 73:16 N 23 '87

Black GPO workers awarded $2.4 million in bias case. *Jet* 72:22 Je 8 '87

Black N.Y. police officer turns down a promotion; says he's no 'quota cop' [S. Brown] *Jet* 71:25 Mr 23 '87

Black 'over qualified' for job sues Albuquerque, N.M. [H. Bailey] *Jet* 72:39 Mr 30 '87

Black police applicants seek millions in Louisville protest. *Jet* 71:8 Mr 16 '87

Blacks file bias suit against N.Y. Daily news. *Jet* 71:15 Mr 2 '87

Blacks, state police in Alabama reach agreement in $2.5 million suit. *Jet* 72:8 S 7 '87

Blacks win 15-year-old suit against L.I. Railroad. *Jet* 72:36 Ag 17 '87

Blacks win lawsuit filed against N.Y. Daily news. *Jet* 72:24 My 4 '87

Cicero case prompts bias charges against Detroit suburbs: Justice Dept. *Jet* 71:7 Ja 19 '87

Close to home [telecommuting program for blacks in Watts] J. Koblenz. il *Black Enterp* 17:22 F '87

Collins: United Airlines must hire more blacks. *Jet* 71:8 Mr 23 '87

Commerce Dept. black cites job bias and is demoted [R. Nichols] por *Jet* 73:17 N 30 '87

Conyers hits plan to open the FBI's arrest records [impact on black employment] *Jet* 73:12 N 9 '87

Court upholds racial quota [blacks in the Alabama state trooper force; Supreme Court decision] D. Camper. il *Black Enterp* 17:15 My '87

Daily news makes $3.1 mil. settlement in job bias case. *Jet* 72:22 Jl 6 '87

Diplomat wins $150,000 for job discrimination [C. A. Sadler] *Jet* 72:16 Jl 6 '87

Education: key to minorities gaining jobs. B. E. Anderson. il *Black Enterp* 17:45 F '87

Guilty of race bias [New York Daily news] *Newsweek* 109:63 Ap 27 '87

Journalists win bias suit [black journalists vs. N.Y. Daily news] Y. Rice. il *Black Enterp* 17:15-16 Jl '87

Making human resources more competitive. M. Simms. il *Black Enterp* 17:37 Jl '87

NAACP criticizes Florida Gov. Martinez on hiring. *Jet* 72:29 Ap 13 '87

NBA pres. urges High Court to uphold affirm. action [views of T. J. Broome] por *Jet* 71:26 Ja 12 '87

The new corporate environment [cover story; special section; with editorial comment by Earl G. Graves] il *Black Enterp* 18:9, 40-2+ Ag '87

A one-white, one-black quota for promotions [Supreme Court decision in Alabama state trooper case] T. Gest. il *U S News World Rep* 102:8 Mr 9 '87

A racial quota for Alabama [state trooper hirings; Supreme Court decision] A. Press. il *Newsweek* 109:55 Mr 9 '87

Reinstates San Francisco postmaster 'forced' to quit [case of J. Wilson] *Jet* 73:35 N 30 '87

Replying in the affirmative [Supreme Court approves promotion quotas for black state troopers in Alabama] R. Lacayo. il *Time* 129:66 Mr 9 '87

Supreme Court approves quotas for promotions [Alabama state troopers case] *Jet* 71:8 Mr 16 '87

Supreme Court upholds promotion quotas [Alabama state troopers case] *Mon Labor Rev* 110:41 My '87

Tabloid pays a big tab [settlement in discrimination case against the New York Daily news] *Time* 129:65 Je 22 '87

A tale of two cities [new segregation in Atlanta as businesses move to white suburbs leaving black workers behind] D. Beers and D. Hembree. il *Nation* 244:357-60 Mr 21 '87

Tenn. reps urge their gov. to hire more blacks. *Jet* 72:13 Jl 6 '87

What every manager should know about discrimination. J. Sherman. *Work Woman* 12:31+ N '87

When a pay cut may be your best bet. L. Bethel. il *Black Enterp* 18:76-8 S '87

Photographs and photography

Working for the B.E. 100 [Black enterprise 100] il *Black Enterp* 17:252-7 Je '87

Hairstyling

See Hairstyling

Health and hygiene

See also

Blacks—Medical care

Sickle cell anemia

10 easy steps to a healthier you. il *Ebony* 42:152+ Mr '87

A black health crisis. T. Monmaney. il *Newsweek* 110:53-4 Jl 13 '87

Black M.D.'s convene in Atlanta on hypertension. il *Jet* 72:16 Ap 13 '87

The changing face of AIDS. R. Stengel. il *Time* 130:12-14 Ag 17 '87

Five-year, $4 million cancer control program set for Chicago blacks. *Jet* 71:24 F 23 '87

Blacks—Health and hygiene—*cont.*

Hypertension, hostility, and race [study by Neil Schneiderman] *USA Today (Periodical)* 115:9 My '87

NMA leader warns of blacks being scapegoat for AIDS scare in U.S. [views of Dr. John O. Brown] *Jet* 71:53 Mr 2 '87

The pros and cons of compulsory tests for AIDS. L. Norment. il *Ebony* 42:118+ S '87

Special help urged to halt black AIDS cases [views of Beny J. Primm] il *Jet* 73:33 O 12 '87

The truth about AIDS. L. Norment. il *Ebony* 42:126+ Ap '87

The uneven odds: minorities are afflicted with AIDS in significantly disproportionate numbers. A. Levine. il *U S News World Rep* 103:31-3 Ag 17 '87

History
See also
> United States—History—Civil War, 1861-1865—Blacks
> Black family—History
> Black History Month
> Harlem renaissance
> Slavery
> Underground railroad

Passing the baton of black history. L. Bennett. il *Jet* 71:36 Mr 2 '87

This week in black history. See issues of Jet

Three major gifts blacks gave to America. L. Bennett. *Jet* 71:50+ F 23 '87

Collectibles
See Black collectibles

Photographs and photography
From the Ebony files. il *Ebony* 42:160-2 Mr '87

Richard Samuel Roberts [exhibit of photographs at Columbia Museum, Columbia, S.C.] J. Meyer. il *Art News* 86:35+ Mr '87

Housing
The black middle class: where it lives. il *Ebony* 42:34-6+ Ag '87

Breaking ground [P. Noel builds his dream house] L. Brown. il por *Black Enterp* 18:76-8+ O '87

Creating a dream home. L. Gite. il *Black Enterp* 18:66-8+ O '87

Demolition dilemma [West Dallas housing projects] L. Gite. il *Black Enterp* 18:26 O '87

Home economics. S. Kennedy. il *Black Enterp* 18:55-6+ O '87

Interracial couple in N.Y. get damages from landlord. *Jet* 72:29 My 4 '87

Major breakup of Dallas housing project planned. *Jet* 72:22 Je 1 '87

San Francisco housing complex ordered to pay black for discrimination [case of Robert Cannon] *Jet* 72:18 My 25 '87

Income
See Blacks—Economic conditions

Legal status, laws, etc.
Legislators develop a new agenda. F. D. Brown. il *Black Enterp* 17:27-8 F '87

Medical care
Health care and black communities. C. Patton. *Cent Mag* 20:61-2 Jl/Ag '87

Migration
Black flight to the South [study by James Johnson] *Society* 24:2 Jl/Ag '87

The Great Migration of Afro-Americans, 1915-40 [cover story] S. R. Crew. il *Mon Labor Rev* 110:34-6 Mr '87

Exhibitions
'Gone up north, gone out west, gone!' [Field to factory: Afro-American migration, 1915-1940] J. Cohen. il *Smithsonian* 18:72-6+ My '87

Two recent events raise the question of how Smithsonian museums should deal with artifacts of our own time [Field to factory: Afro-American migration 1915-1940] R. M. Adams. il *Smithsonian* 17:12 Mr '87

Museums
See also
> DuSable Museum of African American History, Inc.
> Lillie Carroll Jackson Museum
> Old Slave Mart Museum

Nationalism
See also
> Ras Tafari movement
> Universal Negro Improvement Association

November issue of Ebony remembers Marcus Garvey. il por *Jet* 73:37 N 16 '87

Remembering Marcus Garvey. il pors *Ebony* 43:138+ N '87

Rousing [Marcus Garvey: the centennial exhibition at the Schomburg Center in Harlem] *New Yorker* 63:22-4 Ag 31 '87

Occupations
Careers and opportunities 1987. E. Newton. il *Black Enterp* 17:75-6+ F '87

Degrees of success. L. Gite. il *Black Enterp* 17:92-4+ F '87

Speaking of people. See issues of Ebony

Photographs and photography
Free lance photog who worked for Jet has her life's work stolen [E. Tomlin] *Jet* 72:22 S 14 '87

Memorable photos from the Ebony files. See issues of Ebony beginning June 1984

Political activities
See also
> Black clergy—Political activities
> Black congressmen
> Black political candidates
> Black public officers
> Communism and blacks
> Joint Center for Political Studies (U.S.)
> National Coalition of Black Voter Participation

American blacks [discussion of January 1987 article, Who speaks for American blacks?] G. C. Loury. *Commentary* 83:2+ Ap '87

Black Americans need their own agenda [with discussion] S. Fisher. il por *Cent Mag* 20:25-36 My/Je '87

Black leaders' roles [views of Michael B. Preston] il *USA Today (Periodical)* 116:13 D '87

Black mayors of Atlanta, New Orleans will host 1988 political conventions. il pors *Jet* 71:5 Mr 2 '87

Black politicos condemn U.S. probe of Marion Barry. *Jet* 72:31 Jl 27 '87

Black politics in crisis. M. Marable. il *Progressive* 51:18-23 Ja '87

Black solons camp out in D.C. streets for needy. il *Jet* 71:32 Mr 23 '87

Blacks win major offices; black voters show power. il *Jet* 73:4+ N 23 '87

Contra-gate: a black issue. R. Knight. por *Essence* 18:144 Je '87

Ethnic politics American style. P. Greene. *America* 157:28+ Jl 18-25 '87

Getting the black vote [Nathan Group targets radio commercials in the South] M. Eaton. il por *Black Enterp* 17:20 F '87

The GOP's black eye [ballot integrity program backfires on Republican National Committee] H. Klingeman. *Natl Rev* 39:31 Ja 30 '87

Jackson, Reagan confab suggests open door policy. il pors *Jet* 71:5-6 Mr 16 '87

A new form of black politics [leader J. Jackson] W. L. Chaze. il por *U S News World Rep* 102:20-1 My 25 '87

OAU leader meets with black politicos in D.C. to cement U.S. African ties [I. Oumarou] il por *Jet* 72:14 Je 1 '87

Politics. See issues of Jet

Putting a shine on the Big Apple [New York City blacks] R. Howell. *Black Enterp* 17:308 Je '87

Ticker tape U.S.A. S. Booker. See issues of Jet

Washington page. D. C. Ruffin. See issues of Black Enterprise beginning April 1984

Who speaks for American blacks? G. C. Loury. *Commentary* 83:34-8 Ja '87

Psychology
The Ebony advisor. See issues of Ebony

Hypertension, hostility, and race [study by Neil Schneiderman] *USA Today (Periodical)* 115:9 My '87

My greatest challenge: thirteen men discuss the obstacles they seek to surmount. P. Johnson and C. James. il *Essence* 18:58-60+ N '87

Say, brother [lack of communication between black men] C. Marberry. por *Essence* 18:9 My '87

Talk is not cheap [communication among blacks] C. James. por *Essence* 18:130 Ag '87

Race identity
See also
> Blacks—Nationalism
> Negritude

Between two worlds. M. Southgate. por *Essence* 18:54-5+ Ag '87

A black American youth torn between cultures [cover story] R. J. Rousseve. il por *Humanist* 47:5-8 Mr/Ap '87

Blacks at the top: torn between two worlds. E. Hopkins. il *N Y* 20:20-31 Ja 19 '87

A conversation with . . . Dr. Frances Cress Welsing about her theory of skin color and oppression. K. J. Halliburton. pors *Essence* 18:32 My '87

Blacks—Race identity—cont.

Crossover dreams [black women in a white corporate world] A. Edwards. *Essence* 17:45+ Mr '87

Feeling of inferiority disappears when black kids given positive images [study by Darlene Powell-Hopson] il *Jet* 72:36 S 21 '87

Louisiana woman losing her bid to be categorized white [S. Phipps] por *Jet* 71:36 Ja 12 '87

The price of success. A. F. Poussaint. il por *Ebony* 42:76+ Ag '87

Pride and prejudice [self image studies questioned] D. Seligman. il *Fortune* 116:192 S 28 '87

A question of black pride: studies show little improvement in black youths' self image. A. Toufexis. il *Time* 130:74 S 14 '87

Recreation

A look at some fun and games. il *Ebony* 42:123-4+ Ag '87

Religious life

See also

Black churches
Black theology
Catholic Church—Blacks
Church and race relations

Blacks more frequent churchgoers than whites. *Jet* 71:36 Ja 26 '87

Scholarships and fellowships

See Scholarships and fellowships

Segregation

See also

Apartheid
Church and race relations
Colleges and universities—Segregation
Public schools—Desegregation
Public schools—Segregation

Segregation: still alive and thriving [views of Reynolds Farley] il *USA Today (Periodical)* 115:8 My '87

Segregation, Resistance to

See Civil rights demonstrations

Sexual behavior

See Sexual behavior

Social conditions

See also

Blacks—Segregation

American dilemmas and black responses [work of the Committee on the Status of Black Americans; special section] bibl *Society* 24:3-38 Ja/F '87

Black Americans need their own agenda [with discussion] S. Fisher. il por *Cent Mag* 20:25-36 My/Je '87

Blacks and poverty. J. E. Jacob. *Cent Mag* 20:55-6 Ja/F '87

Brothers [cover story; special section] il *Newsweek* 109:54-66+ Mr 23 '87

Do celebrities make best role models for blacks? il *Jet* 72:54-5 Jl 20 '87

The empty shoes of a native son [J. Baldwin] F. Bruning. por *Macleans* 100:13 D 21 '87

The ghetto: from bad to worse [20 years after 1967 riots; special section] il *Time* 130:18-22 Ag 24 '87

A man alone [T. Sowell] P. Brimelow. il por *Forbes* 140:40-1+ Ag 24 '87

Re-examining America's underclass [views of W. J. Wilson] J. E. White. il por *Time* 129:28 My 11 '87

The resegregation of America. J. Sleeper. il *Commonweal* 114:619-23 N 6 '87

A society that is just and fair [address, July 19, 1987] J. E. Jacob. *Vital Speeches Day* 53:733-6 S 15 '87

Bibliography

American apartheid. A. Hacker. bibl f il *N Y Rev Books* 34:26-33 D 3 '87

Statistics

Big-city mayors want blacks counted accurately in 1990 census report. il *Jet* 72:8 Ag 17 '87

Black population: present and future. il *Black Enterp* 17:39 Jl '87

Dymally pushing for fair black count in 1990 census. por *Jet* 73:34 N 30 '87

Taxation

Blacks fall short in taxes—and income. A. F. Brimmer. il *Black Enterp* 17:35-6 Ap '87

Finding help before the tax man comes. D. Lamaute. il *Black Enterp* 17:29-30 Ap '87

The new tax facts. J. Malveaux. il *Essence* 17:94+ Ja '87

Travel

A vacation to remember [Disney World] il *Ebony* 42:136+ Ag '87

Unemployment

See Unemployment

Vocational-technical education

Education: key to minorities gaining jobs. B. E. Anderson. il *Black Enterp* 17:45 F '87

Making human resources more competitive. M. Simms. il *Black Enterp* 17:37 Jl '87

Voter registration

See Voter registration

Alabama

See also

Birmingham (Ala.)—Blacks

Arkansas

History

Traveling exhibit salutes black Arkansans during black history month. il *Jet* 71:6-7 F 23 '87

Australia

History

Billy Blue: a legend of early Sydney. I. Duffield. bibl il *Hist Today* 37:43-8 F '87

Brazil

Black theatre, black consciousness. A. V.-B. da Mota. *Courier* 39:18 D '86

California

See also

Los Angeles (Calif.)—Blacks
Oakland (Calif.)—Blacks
Watts (Los Angeles, Calif.)

Florida

History

Holding the fort [Fort Mose excavations] il map *Sci Am* 257:18-19 Ag '87

Scientists explore site of first free U.S. blacks [Fort Mose] *Jet* 71:25 F 16 '87

France

See also

France—Race relations
Paris (France)—Blacks

History

The last days of Richard Wright. O. Harrington. il pors *Ebony* 42:58-60+ Mr '87

Georgia

See also

Atlanta (Ga.)—Blacks

Great Britain

Blacks in Parliament. D. J. Dent. il *Black Enterp* 18:22 S '87

First 3 blacks elected to British Parliament. il *Jet* 72:36 Jl 6 '87

Illinois

See also

Chicago (Ill.)—Blacks
Lake Forest (Ill.)—Blacks

Indiana

See also

Indianapolis (Ind.)—Blacks

Jamaica

See also

Ras Tafari movement

Massachusetts

See also

Boston (Mass.)—Blacks

New Jersey

See also

Newark (N.J.)—Blacks

New York (State)

See also

Harlem (New York, N.Y.)
New York (N.Y.)—Blacks

Pennsylvania

See also

Philadelphia (Pa.)—Blacks

Sea Islands

"Nowhere to lay down weary head". C. L. Blockson. il maps *Natl Geogr* 172:734-43+ D '87

South Africa

See also

Apartheid

Botha in the lions' den [visit to Sharpeville] S. Reiss. il por *Newsweek* 109:43 Je 15 '87

Getting the story (I) [J. Qwelane, black reporter on the Johannesburg Star] W. Finnegan. *New Yorker* 63:31-4+ Jl 13 '87

Getting the story (II) [J. Qwelane, black reporter on the Johannesburg Star] W. Finnegan. *New Yorker* 63:40-2+ Jl 20 '87

The war of blacks against blacks. J. Greenwald. il *Time* 129:30-1 Ja 26 '87

South Carolina

See also

Columbia (S.C.)—Blacks

Blacks—cont.

Southern States
Black flight to the South [study by James Johnson] *Society* 24:2 Jl/Ag '87

Soviet Union
History
Black man returns home after 47 years in Russia [R. Robinson] S. Booker. il pors *Ebony* 42:67+ Je '87

Tennessee
Tenn. reps urge their gov. to hire more blacks. *Jet* 72:13 Jl 6 '87

Vermont
How blacks fare in the whitest state. L. B. Randolph. il *Ebony* 43:44+ D '87
Revealing report on how blacks cope in whitest state in U.S. il *Jet* 73:26 D 7 '87

Washington (D.C.)
See Washington (D.C.)—Blacks
Blacks, Famous *See* Black celebrities
Blacks and communism *See* Communism and blacks
Blacks and Jews *See* Jews and blacks
Blacks and politics *See* Blacks—Political activities
Blacks and radio
Atlanta NAACP is fuming over white talk show host's calling Lewis 'Buckwheat' [E. Tyll's remarks concerning Congressman J. Lewis] il pors *Jet* 72:22 Ag 10 '87
Racial jokes bring end of campus radio station [University of Michigan] *Jet* 71:33 Mr 23 '87
Blacks and smoking *See* Smoking and blacks
Blacks and television
Black viewers turn to NBC. il *Channels* 7:64 N '87
Blacks help keep some TV shows on the air. *Jet* 72:12 Ap 13 '87
'Different world' to be a hit with blacks; study. *Jet* 73:61 O 26 '87
Philip Michael Thomas and Olivia Brown: how blacks are influencing TV network shows [cover story] il *Jet* 72:54-6 My 25 '87
TV survey reveals blacks turned-off by racism, sex and violence. il *Jet* 73:60-1 D 7 '87
Blacks and the environment
Black areas often used for toxic waste dumps. *Jet* 72:36 My 11 '87
Blacks and the press
N.Y. sax player labeled criminal in Daily news in case of mistaken identity [case of D. Foster] il por *Jet* 72:38 My 11 '87
Newsman Mike Wallace apologizes at UM for past racist remark. *Jet* 72:31 My 25 '87
Pulling punches [Washington post's coverage of blacks] C. Coulson. *New Repub* 196:10-12 My 25 '87
Blacks and trade unions *See* Trade unions—Blacks
Blacks in art

Exhibitions
Jacob Lawrence: art as seen through a people's history. R. Wernick. bibl (p153) il por *Smithsonian* 18:56-64+ Je '87
Blacks in baseball management *See* Baseball, Professional—Organization and administration
Blacks in basketball management *See* Basketball, Professional—Organization and administration
Blacks in business *See* Black businessmen
Blacks in campaign management *See* Campaign management
Blacks in fast food restaurant management *See* Fast food restaurant management
Blacks in football management *See* Football, Professional—Organization and administration
Blacks in highway engineering *See* Highway engineering
Blacks in literature
Black victims, black villains [The color purple and Reckless eyeballing] D. Pinckney. bibl f il *N Y Rev Books* 34:17-20 Ja 29 '87
Maxine Waters blocks controversial text in California legislature [racist charges levelled against The making of America] *Jet* 72:5 Ap 6 '87
Racism charge by Brown prompts Calif. gov. to probe new history text. *Jet* 71:28 Mr 23 '87

Bibliography
Ebony book shelf. See issues of Ebony
Blacks in motion pictures
See also
Black Filmmakers Hall of Fame
Black magic. P. Aufderheide. il *Progressive* 51:26-7 S '87
Black victims, black villains [The color purple and Reckless eyeballing] D. Pinckney. bibl f il *N Y Rev Books* 34:17-20 Ja 29 '87
Class clowns [W. Allen's Radio days and R. Townsend's Hollywood shuffle] A. White. il *Film Comment* 23:11-14 Mr/Ap '87

'Fatal beauty' love scene cut; Goldberg cites racism. por *Jet* 73:63 O 5 '87
Robert Townsend: Hollywood 'shuffling' to the top. M. Marshall. il pors *Ebony* 42:54D Jl '87
Spike Lee filming banned at alma mater in Atlanta [Morehouse College] *Jet* 72:55 My 11 '87
Whoopi's blue eyes [The color purple; interview with S. Lee] M. Glicksman. *Harpers* 274:29 Ja '87
Blacks in newspaper publishing
See also
National Newspaper Publishers Association
Group urges more minority managers in newsrooms [Institute for Journalism Education] *Jet* 72:24 My 4 '87
Blacks in politics *See* Blacks—Political activities
Blacks in publishing
See also
Johnson Publishing Company, Inc.
Writers & Readers Publishing Inc.
Blacks in retail trade
Making it on Main Street. M. Russell. il *Black Enterp* 18:66-8+ D '87
Blacks in sports management *See* Sports—Organization and administration
Blacks in television
See also
Blacks in the television industry
Black like Mich [making of A gathering of old men] A. Horton. il por *Film Comment* 23:8-9 Mr/Ap '87
Blacks better portrayed on TV than Hispanics: study. *Jet* 72:23 Jl 20 '87
Cosby raps network execs for not hiring more blacks. *Jet* 72:59 Je 22 '87
New faces for TV's new season. il *Ebony* 42:155-6+ O '87
'Roots' cast reunites for show's 10th anniversary. il *Jet* 71:36-7 F 16 '87
Television. See issues of Jet
TV's disappearing color line. A. P. Sanoff. il *U S News World Rep* 103:56-7 Jl 13 '87
What TV stars are doing on their vacations. il *Jet* 72:58-9 Je 8 '87
Blacks in the Air Force *See* United States. Air Force—Blacks
Blacks in the Armed Forces *See* United States—Armed Forces—Blacks
Blacks in the Army *See* United States. Army—Blacks
Blacks in the automobile industry *See* Automobile industry
Blacks in the mass media industry
See also
World Institute of Black Communications
Blacks in the motion picture industry
See also
Black Filmmakers Hall of Fame
Blacks in the Navy *See* United States. Navy—Blacks
Blacks in the phonograph record industry
Introducing: producer/songwriter Narada Michael Walden. il pors *Ebony* 43:68+ D '87
Introducing: 'Producers of the Year' Jimmy (Jam) Harris and Terry Lewis. pors *Ebony* 42:126 Jl '87
Jam and Lewis take control. M. Goldberg. il pors *Roll Stone* p30+ Ap 23 '87
John McClain creates solid gold money-makers [A&M Records] A. Edmond, Jr. il por *Black Enterp* 18:54-7+ N '87
Music business charts future for minorities. *Jet* 72:62 S 7 '87
NAACP blasts record biz. A. DeCurtis. *Roll Stone* p15+ My 21 '87
Blacks in the radio industry
See also
Radio stations, Black
Blacks in the television industry
See also
Television stations, Black
Blacks at the top in TV. il *Ebony* 42:82-4+ Ap '87
Bob Jordan: tops in news and health. il pors *Ebony* 42:145-6+ F '87
Carew "Busts loose" [T. Carew] S. Herbert. por *Black Enterp* 18:25 S '87
Engineering his way to success [broadcast engineer, M. Noble] L. Gite. il por *Black Enterp* 17:92-3 F '87
Eyes on the prize [civil rights movement series produced by H. Hampton] J. Rosen. il por *Channels* 7:48-50 O '87
Johnson: network TV is still white man's club [views of J. Johnson] *Jet* 72:23 Ag 10 '87
L.A.'s major TV stations dominated by white men. *Jet* 72:22 Jl 20 '87
Blacks in the toy and game industry
See also
International Black Toy Manufacturers Association

Blacks in the toy and game industry—*cont.*
Black toymakers. il *Ebony* 43:144+ D '87
Blacks in videotapes
Video's best. D. Mills. il *Essence* 17:32+ Mr '87
Blackstone Group
Meet Pete Peterson, the new merchant banker on the block. S. Bartlett. il por *Bus Week* p108-9 N 23 '87
Blackwelder, Brent, and Campbell, David
Tax reform as environmental policy. *Sierra* 72:33-6 Mr/Ap '87
Blackwell, Chris
about
Chris Blackwell's Island life. J. Milward. il por *N Y* 20:43 D 7 '87
Bladder

Cancer
Causes
Your bladder: use it or lose it? [dangers of postponing urination] *Sci News* 131:200 Mr 28 '87
Diseases
See also
Cystitis
Urine—Incontinence
Bladder stones
Fighting stones with seeds [pumpkin seeds] il *Prevention* 39:53 O '87
Bladen, Ashby
Observations. See occasional issues of Forbes
Bladen, Barbara
about
Columnist Barbara Bladen sees her love story with a convict flower onscreen in Weeds. J. Stark. il pors *People Wkly* 28:83-4+ D 7 '87
Bladen, Ronald, 1918-1988
about
Expanded pictograms. S. Ellis. bibl f il *Art Am* 75:204-9 Ap '87
Blades, Rubén
about
Ruben Blades: up from salsa. A. DePalma. il pors *N Y Times Mag* p24+ Je 21 '87
Rubén Blades's Latin revolution. D. Fricke. por *Roll Stone* p36+ Ap 23 '87
Blades, Airplane engine *See* Airplane engines, Jet—Blades
Blair, Alistair
about
Alistair Blair has designs on the Duchess. il por *People Wkly* 28:29 Jl 20 '87
Blair, Billie
about
Self-renewal: Billie Blair's story. M. Whigham. por *Essence* 17:47+ Ja '87
Blair, Charles E.
about
A concerned Christian goes the Second Mile. *Christ Today* 31:47-8 F 6 '87
Blair, Chester L.
about
Black attorney in line to head Chicago Bar Assn. por *Jet* 72:29 Ap 13 '87
Blair, Dike
about
Dike Blair at Cash/Newhouse. J. Rian. *Art Am* 75:221 Ap '87
Blair, Erica
The regime within [interview with V. Havel]; tr. by A. G. Brain. *Harpers* 274:24+ Je '87
Search for the human dimension [interview with V. Havel] il por *World Press Rev* 34:24-5 My '87
Blair, Gwenda
Am I blue! il *Mademoiselle* 93:270-1+ S '87
What every single girl should know. See issues of Mademoiselle beginning September 1987
Blair, Gwenda, and Mann, Charles C.
Media savvy. *Ms* 16:40+ Jl/Ag '87
Blair, Neal E., and others
Natural abundances of carbon isotopes in acetate from a coastal marine sediment. bibl f il *Science* 236:66-8 Ap 3 '87
Blair, Scott
about
A Wall Street broker's story. D. O. Relin. il por *Sch Update* 120:5 D 18 '87
Blair (D. H.) & Co., Inc. *See* D. H. Blair & Co., Inc.
Blair (John) & Company *See* John Blair & Company
Blaisdell, Harold F.
A deer to believe in. il *Read Dig* 131:25-6+ N '87

Blaise, Clark, and Mukherjee, Bharati
A shattered dream [excerpt from The sorrow and the terror: the haunting legacy of the Air India tragedy] il pors *Macleans* 100:42-5 My 25 '87
Blake, Daniel B.
Spiny sea dwellers. il *Earth Sci* 40:17-19 Wint '87
Blake, David
Why oil prices could rise again. *World Press Rev* 34:48+ Jl '87
Blake, Elias
Equality for blacks. *Change* 19:10-13 My/Je '87
Blake, J. Herman
about
J. Herman Blake, Tougaloo College president, resigns. por *Jet* 72:22 Ap 6 '87
Blake, Randolph
(jt. auth) See Sekuler, Robert, and Blake, Randolph
Blake, Richard A.
A calendar of feasts. il *America* 156:321-3 Ap 18 '87
Blakelock, Ralph Albert, 1847-1919
about
Moonlight in the Brooklyn Museum. P. Auster. il *Art News* 86:104-5 S '87
The wretched life and death of an 'American van Gogh'. A. A. Davidson. il por *Smithsonian* 18:80-6+ D '87
Blakely, Mary Kay
The great baby sit-in for peace. il por *Ms* 16:83-5 D '87
Growing girls and grandmothers. il por *Ms* 15:12+ Ja '87
My first sexy bathing suit. il *Glamour* 85:176-7+ Jl '87
My son the man. por *Ms* 15:28-9 Mr '87
An old woman's victory garden. il por *Ms* 16:94+ S '87
Postnuclear family. il por *Ms* 16:134+ Jl/Ag '87
Blakely (Ga.)

Crime
'Root doctor' held in murder of his former wife [T. L. Berry] *Jet* 72:29 Je 1 '87
Blakemore, Steven
(tr) See Chamorro, Jaime. How "La prensa" was silenced
(tr) See Chamorro, Jaime. "Our people cannot be silenced"
Blakey, William A., 1943-
about
Take a leaf from Joe Paterno . . . [interview] R. Edgerton. il pors *Change* 19:40-3 My/Je '87
Blame *See* Fault finding
Blame, Self *See* Self blame
Blanch, Lesley
Paintings of the table. il *Archit Dig* 44:24+ Mr '87
Blanchard, Duncan C.
(jt. auth) See Iacono, Michael J., and Blanchard, Duncan C.
Blanchard, Hattie
about
She cares. por *Essence* 18:12 Ag '87
Blanchard, Leslie
From drab to dazzling hair and beauty makeovers; ed. by Maureen Lynch. il *Good Housekeep* 204:102-5+ Ja '87
Blanchard, Melinda
about
Family affair. S. W. Angrist. il pors *Forbes* 140:184+ O 5 '87
Blanchard, Robert
about
Family affair. S. W. Angrist. il pors *Forbes* 140:184+ O 5 '87
Blanchard & Blanchard & Son Ltd.
Family affair. S. W. Angrist. il pors *Forbes* 140:184+ O 5 '87
Blandford, Linda
Places in the heart. il pors *Vogue* 177:326-33+ Ag '87
Blank, Joseph P.
The husband who vanished. il pors *Read Dig* 130:131-5 Ja '87
Lieutenant Holguin's final mission. il *Read Dig* 130:83-8 Ap '87
Blanket chests *See* Chests
Blankets
See also
Indian blankets, rugs, etc. (American)
Blaschka, Leopold
about
Forever flowers of glass and magic. L. Ware. il *Audubon* 89:96-109 My '87
Blaschka, Rudolph
about
Forever flowers of glass and magic. L. Ware. il *Audubon* 89:96-109 My '87

Blask, Ann Sabatini
The Bermuda Collection. *Travel Holiday* 168:30-3 N '87
Easy visas. *Travel Holiday* 168:41+ Jl '87
Traveling safely. il *Travel Holiday* 168:88-90+ S '87

Blasko, Lori
about
Winning at beauty. il pors *Teen* 31:74-7 Jl '87

Blass, Bill
about
Blass country. C. T. Buckley. il *House Gard* 159:132-43+ My '87
Playing to a full house. C. Vogel. il *N Y Times Mag* p51-3 Ag 9 '87

Blasting, Submarine
Divers' dilemma [offshore rig removal vs. endangered marine species] J. S. McKinna. il *Oceans* 20:10 N/D '87
Not the best way to save turtles [proposed experiment to study the impact of underwater explosions on endangered sea turtles] il *Oceans* 20:69 N/D '87

Blattner, Frederick R.
(jt. auth) See Zahn, Kenneth, and Blattner, Frederick R.

Blatty, William Peter
about
A look at the issues in Blatty's appeal to the Supreme Court. C. E. Rinzler. *Publ Wkly* 232:16-17 Ag 28 '87

Blau, Theodore H.
about
Psychologist with a badge. R. J. Trotter. il pors *Psychol Today* 21:26+ N '87

Blaue Reiter (Group)
Murnau and Kochel: where the Blue Rider was born. J. Dornberg. il pors *Art News* 86:77-8+ D '87

Blaun, Randi
Dealing with impotence. il *N Y* 20:50-8 Mr 30 '87

Blauner, Peter
Back to the future: Columbia replays the battles of '68. il *N Y* 20:30-3 My 18 '87
Dressed to kill. il pors *N Y* 20:50-4 Mr 9 '87
'Fat Cat' and the crack wars: brash young dealers muscle the drug establishment. il por *N Y* 20:46-54 S 7 '87
The fire this time: two tough lawyers spur a new black activism. il pors *N Y* 20:42-7 Ap 27 '87
Out of Africa: the Senegalese peddlers of New York. il *N Y* 20:42-6 F 16 '87
Sugar Hill: a citadel of style and echoes of an earlier America. il map *N Y* 20:90-2 My 4 '87
The unplugged city: the story of New York cable is a model municipal mess. il map *N Y* 20:36-42 Jl 20 '87
(jt. auth) See Renfrew, Nita M., and Blauner, Peter

Blaustein, Albert P., 1921-
about
Custom framer. il por *Life* 10:92 Fall '87

Blauvelt, Peter
Educators and police working together. *Educ Dig* 53:26-9 N '87

Blaylock, Kenneth T.
Is the administration approach to federal employee drug testing sound? [excerpts from testimony, March 18, 1986] *Congr Dig* 66:149+ My '87

Blazers *See* Coats
Bleaches *See* Bleaching materials
Bleaching materials
How to renew weathered wood siding. G. Branson. il *Fam Handyman* 37:66+ S '87

Bleasdale, Alan
about
Are you lonesome tonight? [drama] Reviews
Macleans il 100:49 Jl 13 '87. A. Thurlow

Blechman, Fred
Using the Polapulse battery. il *Radio-Electron* 58:61-3+ F '87

Blecker, Robert
A verdict by their peers. il *Nation* 245:334-6 O 3 '87

Bleckner, Ross, 1949-
about
Signs and symbols. K. Larson. il *N Y* 20:96+ Mr 2 '87

Bledsoe, Tempestt
about
Growing up on T.V.: Tempestt Bledsoe. por *Teen* 31:64 N '87
Waking up rich and famous. il pors *Ebony* 42:36+ S '87

Bleeck, Oliver *See* Thomas, Ross, 1926-
Bleecker, Samuel E.
Rethinking how we work: the office of the future. il por *Futurist* 21:15-21 Jl/Ag '87
Bleeding *See* Hemorrhage
Bleeker, Diana
When bad things happen to rich people. *New Repub* 197:17-18 N 23 '87
Blenders (Appliances)
Skinny-shake maker. il *McCalls* 114:118-19 Jl '87
Blessing, Lee
about
A walk in the woods [drama] Reviews
Time il 129:88 Mr 9 '87. W. A. Henry
Bley, Carla
about
Carla Bley. F. Bouchard. il por *Down Beat* 54:14 Ja '87
Blickling Hall (Norfolk, England: Historic house) *See* Historic houses, sites, etc.—Great Britain
Blight, James G., and others
The Cuban Missile Crisis revisited. bibl f *Foreign Aff* 66:170-88 Fall '87
Blind
See also
Guide dogs
Museums and the blind
Music and the blind
Theater and the blind
A bus melee provides grim insight into the life of the blind [M. Collinsworth] D. Chu. il pors *People Wkly* 27:105-6 Je 29 '87
"If we don't take them, who will?" [N. Claypool raising six handicapped children] A. Steinbach. il por *McCalls* 115:135-7 D '87
Education
Among the seven pillars of wisdom [blind East Indian student at Pomona College] V. Mehta. *New Yorker* 63:34-6+ Ag 24 '87
At the gates of California [blind student applies for college admission in 1952] V. Mehta. *New Yorker* 63:82-97 My 11 '87
Equipment
See also
Computers and the blind
Sports
On eye opening [blind sailor J. Dickson attempts to sail across the Atlantic alone] W. F. Buckley. *Natl Rev* 39:73 S 11 '87
Blind as consumers *See* Blind market
Blind date [film] *See* Motion picture reviews—Single works
Blind market
Denny Daughters, teenage shopkeeper, is a soft touch when it comes to helping blind customers [proprietor of Please Touch in Castro Valley, Calif.] il por *People Wkly* 28:120 O 12 '87
Blind pools (Securities)
Don't dive into a 'blank-check' blind pool. B. Hitchings. *Bus Week* p180 My 25 '87
Investment pools: blind faith. M. C. Paulson. il *Changing Times* 41:73-5 S '87
Smoke signals [brokers promote American Indian tax free municipals] M. Schifrin. il *Forbes* 139:42+ Je 15 '87
Blinder, Alan S.
Balance the budget—but not with an amendment. il *Bus Week* p16 Jl 27 '87
Cents are nonsense. il *Read Dig* 131:79-80 Ag '87
A handicapper's guide to Reaganomics. il *Bus Week* p18 F 9 '87
How to cut pollution and the deficit at the same time. il *Bus Week* p10 Ag 24 '87
How to read Wall Street's scrambled messages. por *Bus Week* p28 N 16 '87
Improving the chances of our weakest underdogs—poor children. por *Bus Week* p20 D 14 '87
It's time to put an end to the borrowing binge. il *Bus Week* p22 My 4 '87
The market wants the dollar to fall. Let it happen. por *Bus Week* p18 O 19 '87
Mr. Volcker: higher interest is the last thing we need. il *Bus Week* p30 Je 1 '87
Paul Volcker was the Babe Ruth of central banking. il *Bus Week* p12 Je 29 '87
Plain talk about the dreaded 'T' word. il *Bus Week* p20 S 21 '87
Tight money and loose fiscal policy. bibl *Society* 24:80-3 Jl/Ag '87
Yes, inflation could hit 5%. No, it's not cause for panic. il *Bus Week* p22 Ap 6 '87

Blinder, Meyer
about
Blind 'em and rob 'em. M. Schifrin. il por *Forbes* 140:8 N 2 '87
Blinder, Robinson—blind 'em and rob 'em. M. Schifrin. il *Forbes* 139:33-8 Ap 20 '87
Meet the prince of penny stocks: Meyer Blinder. D. R. Katz. il por *Fortune* 115:108-10+ Ja 19 '87
Blinder, Robinson & Company
Blind 'em and rob 'em. M. Schifrin. il por *Forbes* 140:8 N 2 '87
Blinder, Robinson—blind 'em and rob 'em. M. Schifrin. il *Forbes* 139:33-8 Ap 20 '87
Meet the prince of penny stocks: Meyer Blinder. D. R. Katz. il por *Fortune* 115:108-10+ Ja 19 '87
Blindness
See also
Blind
Color blindness
Onchocerciasis
Snowblindness
Xerophthalmia
Prevention
Save sight [cover story; special issue] il *World Health* p3-15+ My '87
Blinds
See also
Shutters
For places where you want a wall but you don't. il *Sunset* 178:70-1 Ja '87
Blinds (Camouflage)
Birding: shooting blind. S. K. Sneddon; D. Braud. il *Petersens Photogr Mag* 16:44-7 Ag '87
Camouflex: a sensible stalking aid [for photographers] K. Geller-Shinn. il *Petersens Photogr Mag* 15:72-3 Ap '87
Shooting from a mobile blind [wildlife photos] D. Spier. il *Conservationist* 41:44-7 Mr/Ap '87
Anecdotes, facetiae, satire, etc.
Testaments from the blind. K. Cowgill. il *Field Stream* 92:33-4 N '87
Bliss, Corinne Demas, 1947-
The dream broker [story] il *Redbook* 169:52+ Jl '87
Bliss, John William Michael See Bliss, Michael, 1941-
Bliss, Michael, 1941-
The lessons of history. il *Macleans* 100:23 O 19 '87
Blithe spirit [drama] See Coward, Noel
Blitzer, Wolf
I spy, you spy. *New Repub* 196:15-16 Ap 13 '87
Bliven, Naomi
Searching for Kaaterskill Falls. il *New Yorker* 63:43-58 Ag 3 '87
Blizzards See Snowstorms
Bloating (Physiology) See Swelling (Physiology)
Bloch, Bradley W.
The stamina to succeed. il *Work Woman* 12:130+ O '87
Bloch, Erich
NSF's budget and economic competitiveness. *Science* 235:621 F 6 '87
Bloch, Henry Wollman, 1922-
about
Bloch that IRS return. W. Hoffer. il pors *Nations Bus* 75:69-70 Mr '87
Block, Jean Libman
"I am Bryan, your brother". il por *Good Housekeep* 204:82+ Mr '87
We got our son back for Christmas. il por *Good Housekeep* 205:111-13 D '87
Block, Judy
about
How two owners handled the tax changes. D. Shilling. il pors *Work Woman* 12:40-1 Mr '87
Block grants See Grants-in-aid
Block Island (R.I.)
Description and travel
Isle of light. B. M. Boyd. il *Vogue* 177:218+ Ag '87
Block printing
See also
Wood engraving
Blockbuster Entertainment Corp.
A video stock on fast-forward. J. M. Laderman. il *Bus Week* p98 Je 15 '87
Blocker, Robert L.
Weaving the cultural fabric of society. *Des Arts Educ* 88:34-5 Mr/Ap '87
Blocker Energy Corp.
Creating value [R. Rainwater's petroleum plays] J. Merwin. il *Forbes* 139 Ann Directory:57 Ap 27 '87

Blocking (Meteorology)
Blocking highs. D. M. Ludlum. il *Ctry J* 14:80-2 Ap '87
Blockson, Charles L.
"Nowhere to lay down weary head". il maps *Natl Geogr* 172:734-43+ D '87
The underground railroad. il *Essence* 17:43+ F '87
Blodgett, Richard
Money talks. See issues of McCall's
Our wild, weird world of coincidence. il *Read Dig* 131:125-8 S '87
Bloembergen, Nicolaas, 1920-
(jt. auth) See Patel, C. Kumar N., and Bloembergen, Nicolaas, 1920-
Blohm, Bernhard
Japan's problems with exports [interview with K. Miyazawa] *World Press Rev* 34:51 Ja '87
Blomstedt, Kaisa
about
Northern light [cover story] P. M. Sachner. il *Archit Rec* 175:120-5 Ag '87
Blond hair See Hair
Blondet, Maurizio
Talk—and fear—of a recession. il *World Press Rev* 34:24-5 N '87
Blonsky, Marshall
Robert Hughes: the art of bushwhacking the bourgeoisie [interview] por *Vogue* 177:212-13+ Ja '87
Blood
See also
Hemorrhage
Blood: the river of life [cover story] P. Skalka. bibl il *Curr Health 2* 14:3-9 D '87
Bloody house puzzles Atlanta couple, cops [seeping blood mystery in home of W. Winston] il por *Jet* 73:29 O 12 '87
Alcohol content
Passing up one for the road [intoxication tests] E. Henry. *Changing Times* 41:112-13 My '87
Calcium content
See also
Hypercalcemia
Circulation
See also
Blood-brain barrier
Blood flow
Blood pressure
Blushing
Snakes under pressure [circulatory system adapts to the demands of gravity; cover story] H. B. Lillywhite. il *Nat Hist* 96:58-67 N '87
Visualization of viral clearance in the living animal. E. M. Verdin and others. bibl f il *Science* 236:439-42 Ap 24 '87
Circulation, Disorders of
See also
Hypertension
Coagulation
See also
Anticoagulants
Antithrombin
Fibrinolysin
Thromboplastin
Freeing hemophiliacs from the risk of AIDS [synthetic clotting factor offers hope] R. Rhein, Jr. and L. Therrien. il *Bus Week* p38 Ap 13 '87
Collection and preservation
See also
Blood banks
Diseases
See also
Anemia
Hemophilia
Leukemia
Sickle cell anemia
Fats
See Blood—Lipids
Flow
See Blood flow
Formation
See Blood cells—Growth
Lipids
See also
Cholesterol
Glycerides
No fat advantage in meatless meals? [research by Bonnie Worthington-Roberts] il *Prevention* 39:8 N '87
Parasites
See also
Plasmodium (Parasite)
Trypanosomes

Blood—*cont.*

Pigments

See also
Hemoglobin

Plasma

See also
Blood substitutes

Pressure

See Blood pressure

Proteins

See also
Angiogenin
Fibrinogen
Glycophorin
Haptoglobins
Hemerythrin
Hemoglobin
Immunoglobulins
Myoglobin
Thrombospondin
Transferrin

Serum

See Serums

Testing

See also
Drug abuse—Testing

AIDS: a time of testing [cover story; special section] il *U S News World Rep* 102:56-9+ Ap 20 '87

An AIDS plan touches a nerve [expanding testing to include more groups] *U S News World Rep* 102:11 F 16 '87

AIDS: testing insurance. J. B. Quinn. il *Newsweek* 109:55 Je 8 '87

AIDS: to test or not to test? J. H. Tanne. il *N Y* 20:40-6 S 28 '87

The AIDS virus: "Does my husband have it? . . . If yes, do I, too? . . . I had to know". K. Winston. il *Glamour* 85:292-3+ O '87

AIDS: who should be tested? [views of Secretary of Education W. J. Bennett] T. Monmaney. il por *Newsweek* 109:64-5 My 11 '87

Allergy alert [immunoglobulin E blood test for children] C. Bushnell. il *Health* 19:15 Ja '87

Baker's recipe [H. Baker's input into AIDS testing policy] F. Barnes. *New Repub* 196:9-10 Je 29 '87

Bavaria requires AIDS testing. D. Dickson. *Science* 236:1057 My 29 '87

A better test for AIDS [AIDS Viral Test] N. Underwood. il *Macleans* 100:48 Je 1 '87

Blood donation under the AIDS regime [assessing danger of being infected] D. D. Edwards. *Sci News* 131:376 Je 13 '87

China and AIDS. *Newsweek* 109:55 My 18 '87

Detecting allergy-prone children [immunoglobulin E blood test] *USA Today (Periodical)* 115:12 F '87

Devastating findings [inaccurate test results] *U S News World Rep* 103:68 N 23 '87

Doctors' do-it-yourself lab tests: how reliable? J. P. Cohn. il *FDA Consum* 21:36-9 F '87

A fever lurking in the blood [virus can go undetected by conventional testing] J. Silberner. *U S News World Rep* 103:14-15 O 12 '87

Finding the children [identifying Argentine missing children through genetic testing] B. Beckwith. il *Ms* 16:88 S '87

Hospital vampires? [ordering excessive blood tests] *Prevention* 39:8+ Ag '87

How not to control the AIDS epidemic [adaptation of address, June 1987] M. Krim. il por *Humanist* 47:14-15+ N/D '87

If you're really worried: how to get tested for AIDS. I. Pave. il *Bus Week* p112 Je 15 '87

Mandatory testing for AIDS? J. Seligmann. il *Newsweek* 109:22 F 16 '87

Meese and AIDS [compulsory testing policy] *Nation* 244:837-8 Je 20 '87

A new panic over AIDS [testing of blood recipients] L. Martz. il *Newsweek* 109:18-19 Mr 30 '87

New questions about AIDS test accuracy. D. M. Barnes. il *Science* 238:884-5 N 13 '87

A new romance [getting tested for AIDS] M. Kramer. il *N Y Times Mag* p71 Ag 16 '87

The problem with testing [AIDS] B. Kantrowitz. il *Newsweek* 109:60-2 Je 15 '87

The pros and cons of compulsory tests for AIDS. L. Norment. il *Ebony* 42:118+ S '87

Putting AIDS to the test [merits of mass screening] A. Wilentz. il *Time* 129:60 Mr 2 '87

Reagan booed, Taylor cheered at AIDS benefit [routine testing advocated] *Jet* 72:7 Je 15 '87

Secondary infection [blood testing for AIDS] *Nation* 244:165 F 14 '87

She took the AIDS test. D. Kleiman. il *N Y Times Mag* p22-3+ Jl 5 '87

The states start wading into the AIDS-test thicket. S. Findlay. il *U S News World Rep* 103:14 O 5 '87

Surgeon General Koop asks for more voluntary AIDS testing [cover story] H. G. Miller. il pors *Saturday Evening Post* 259:58-61+ N '87

Test balloon for testing [AIDS policy] *Sci Am* 257:30 Ag '87

Testing dilemma [Washington prepares controversial new policy] R. Stengel. il *Time* 129:20-2 Je 8 '87

Testing for AIDS [address, June 26, 1987] R. E. Windom. *Vital Speeches Day* 53:676-9 S 1 '87

Testing for AIDS [Reagan administration proposals] *Commonweal* 114:403-5 Jl 17 '87

Then have an anonymous, free AIDS test. C. SerVaas. il *Saturday Evening Post* 259:56-61+ S '87

This is what you thought: 50% say AIDS tests should be mandatory [results of survey] *Glamour* 85:99 Ag '87

Tough new rules for life insurance [tests for AIDS in Canada] C. Wood. il *Macleans* 100:45 My 18 '87

A transfusion of fear [blood recipients tested for AIDS] A. Wilentz. il *Time* 129:24-5 Mr 30 '87

Ultra-sensitive blood test is a new anti-crime weapon [isoelectric focusing] R. Layne. *Pop Sci* 230:104 Ap '87

Update on AIDS testing. C. Schaeffer. *Changing Times* 41:16+ O '87

Watching cholesterol. J. W. Merline. il *Consum Res Mag* 70:38 Ap '87

What the AIDS MOBILE has taught us [free tests offered] C. SerVaas. il *Saturday Evening Post* 259:54-5+ O '87

Who should take the test for HIV and why? [interviews with G. L. Bauer and N. Hunter] L. Kravitz. il pors *Sch Update* 120:21 O 16 '87

Your cholesterol, more or less. *U S News World Rep* 103:64 N 23 '87

Patents

The AIDS debate: call it a draw [conflict between French and U.S. researchers resolved] *Newsweek* 109:64 Ap 13 '87

AIDS patent dispute settled. D. M. Barnes. *Science* 236:17 Ap 3 '87

Yalta of AIDS [agreement between French and American researchers] *Time* 129:57 Ap 13 '87

Transfusion

See also
Blood boosting

Blood donation under the AIDS regime [assessing danger of being infected] D. D. Edwards. *Sci News* 131:376 Je 13 '87

Donate your blood now, get it back later [autologous transfusions] C. Schaeffer. *Changing Times* 41:14+ My '87

Donating blood for yourself. K. Donnan. il *McCalls* 114:149 S '87

Fear of tainted transfusions triggers a boom in the bank-your-own-blood business. *People Wkly* 27:47 Mr 16 '87

Freeing hemophiliacs from the risk of AIDS [synthetic clotting factor offers hope] R. Rhein, Jr. and L. Therrien. il *Bus Week* p38 Ap 13 '87

How to donate blood to yourself [autologous transfusions] J. Carey. il *U S News World Rep* 102:59 Je 1 '87

Husbands for safe blood [transfusions in the OB/GYN departments] C. SerVaas. il *Saturday Evening Post* 259:82+ N '87

Is the blood supply safe? il *Consum Rep* 52:596-8 O '87

Need major surgery? Donate your own blood [autologous transfusions] C. SerVaas. *Saturday Evening Post* 259:100+ Jl/Ag '87

A new panic over AIDS [testing of blood recipients] L. Martz. il *Newsweek* 109:18-19 Mr 30 '87

Seeing red [Daxor Corp.'s entry into autologous blood transfusion in wake of AIDS scare] S. N. Chakravarty. il por *Forbes* 139:76+ Je 1 '87

Should you store your own blood? What to consider. il *Glamour* 85:92+ F '87

Stand up to AIDS [D. C. Wade and P. Gann, victims through transfusion] M. G. Stoddard. il pors *Saturday Evening Post* 259:54-5 S '87

A transfusion of fear [blood recipients tested for AIDS] A. Wilentz. il *Time* 129:24-5 Mr 30 '87

Blood, Artificial *See* Blood substitutes
Blood banks
See also
Daxor Corporation
Blood bank errors [closing down Augusta Plasma Center, Inc. in Augusta, Ga.] il *FDA Consum* 21:30-1 My '87
Put your blood in a private bank? *Consum Rep* 52:597 O '87

Canada
See also
Autologous Systems Inc.
Blood boosting
Controversial 'blood doping' revisited. *Sci News* 131:344 My 30 '87
Endurance by the pint. D. Pine. il *Women's Sports Fitness* 9:56 Jl '87
Intravenous aerobics [blood doping] *Time* 129:60 Je 15 '87
Blood-brain barrier
Brain barrier tissues: end organs for atriopeptins. L. Steardo and J. A. Nathanson. bibl f il *Science* 235:470-3 Ja 23 '87
Brainy ties that bind [astrocytes; research by Robert C. Janzer and Martin C. Raff] D. D. Edwards. il *Sci News* 131:68 Ja 31 '87
Heart peptide goes to the head [research by James A. Nathanson and Luca Steardo] D. D. Edwards. *Sci News* 131:68 Ja 31 '87
Neocortical transplants in the mammalian brain lack a blood-brain barrier to macromolecules. J. M. Rosenstein. bibl f il *Science* 235:772-4 F 13 '87
Nerve transplant: proceed with caution. D. D. Edwards. *Sci News* 131:135 F 28 '87
Blood cell aggregation
One more reason to stay in bed [morning heart attacks and blood platelet aggregation; research by Geoffrey Tofler and others] *Discover* 8:6+ O '87
Safe supinity [platelet aggregation and morning heart attacks; research by Geoffrey H. Tofler and others] *Sci News* 131:409 Je 27 '87
Thrombospondin promotes cell-substratum adhesion. G. P. Tuszynski and others. bibl f il *Science* 236:1570-3 Je 19 '87
Blood cells
See also
Leukocytes
Lymphocytes
Cloning, sequencing, and expression of the gene coding for the human platelet α_2-adrenergic receptor. B. K. Kobilka and others. bibl f il *Science* 238:650-6 O 30 '87
Family study of platelet membrane fluidity in Alzheimer's disease. G. S. Zubenko and others. bibl f il *Science* 238:539-42 O 23 '87
Inherited membranes predict Alzheimer's? [fluidity of platelet membranes] *Sci News* 132:301 N 7 '87
Cancer
Genetic aspects
Avian v-*myc* replaces chromosomal translocation in murine plasmacytomagenesis. M. Potter and others. bibl f il *Science* 235:787-9 F 13 '87
Growth
See also
Colony-stimulating factors
Erythropoietin
G-CSF
GM-CSF
Clinical promise with new hormones [hematologic growth factors] G. Kolata. il *Science* 236:517-19 My 1 '87
Immune boosters [hematologic growth factors; cover story] G. Kolata. il *Discover* 8:68-72+ S '87
The molecular control of blood cell development. L. Sachs. bibl f il *Science* 238:1374-9 D 4 '87
Blood clot anticoagulants *See* Anticoagulants
Blood clotting *See* Blood—Coagulation
Blood doping *See* Blood boosting
Blood feuds *See* Feuds
Blood flow
Does the release of potassium from astrocyte endfeet regulate cerebral blood flow? O. B. Paulson and E. A. Newman. bibl f il *Science* 237:896-8 Ag 21 '87
Blood groups
See also
Rh factor
Blood pressure
See also
Hypertension
Score another one for the Mediterranean diet. *Prevention* 39:57 My '87

Measurement
See also
Sphygmomanometers
High blood pressure: once is not enough. *Prevention* 39:8 S '87
Blood substitutes
Sanguine substitutes [cover story] R. Weiss. il *Sci News* 132:200-2 S 26 '87
Blood tests *See* Blood—Testing
Blood transfusions *See* Blood—Transfusion
Blood vessels
See also
Angiogenin
Arteries
Cardiovascular system
Angiogenesis research comes of age. J. L. Marx. il *Science* 237:23-4 Jl 3 '87
Angiogenic factors. J. Folkman and M. Klagsbrun. bibl f il *Science* 235:442-7 Ja 23 '87
Lowering pressure as a fountain of youth? [research by Aram V. Chobanian] J. Silberner. *Sci News* 131:89 F 7 '87
Diseases
Smooth muscle-mediated connective tissue remodeling in pulmonary hypertension. R. P. Mecham and others. bibl f il *Science* 237:423-6 Jl 24 '87
Radiography
See Radiography, Medical
Surgery
See also
Cardiac catheterization
A laser to lighten the heart [vaporizing cholesterol] M. Nichols. il *Macleans* 100:45 Ag 31 '87
Lasers and heart disease [work of James M. Seeger and others in treating arteries] R. Anthony. il *Technol Rev* 90:14-15 Ap '87
Bloodletting
See also
Leeches—Medical use
Bloody poetry [drama] *See* Brenton, Howard, 1942-
Bloom, Allan David
'A book can transform a life'. il por *U S News World Rep* 103:95 S 28 '87
Liberty, equality, sexuality. *Commentary* 83:24-30 Ap '87
Today's university: where democracy is anarchy. *Current* 297:22-7 N '87
about
Are student heads full of emptiness? E. Bowen. il *Time* 130:56-7 Ag 17 '87
A best-seller's puzzling sizzle. F. Bruning. por *Macleans* 100:7 Ag 31 '87
Bloom and doom. W. Greider. il *Roll Stone* p39-40 O 8 '87
Campus 1987 [cover story; special section; with editorial comment by Richard Vigilante] *Natl Rev* 39:34-8+ O 9 '87
Chicago philosophy professor Allan Bloom warns that America's universities are crumbling [interview] S. K. Reed. il por *People Wkly* 28:141-2+ S 14 '87
The closing of the American mind. R. K. Bennett. *Read Dig* 131:81-4 O '87
A dunce cap for America. D. Gates. il pors *Newsweek* 109:72-4 Ap 20 '87
A nation that has lost its intellectual bearings [interview] A. P. Sanoff. il por *U S News World Rep* 102:78 My 11 '87
Nietzsche by another name. E. Bowen. por *Time* 129:79 Ap 13 '87
Sex and drugs and Heidegger. J. Weisberg. *Wash Mon* 19:49-53 S '87
Story behind the bestseller: Allan Bloom's 'The closing of the American mind'. W. Goldstein. il por *Publ Wkly* 232:25-7 Jl 3 '87
Undemocratic vistas. M. C. Nussbaum. bibl f il *N Y Rev Books* 34:20-6 N 5 '87
Writing to sell in the MTV era. A. Smith. il *Esquire* 108:87+ D '87
Bloom, Barbara
about
Barbara Bloom at Nature Morte. J. Rian. il *Art Am* 75:127-8 Jl '87
Bloom, Benjamin S.
about
Master of mastery. P. Chance. bibl (p65) il pors *Psychol Today* 21:42-6 Ap '87
Bloom, John *See* Briggs, Joe Bob
Bloom, Ken
Cokin creative filter system. il *Petersens Photogr Mag* 16:48-50 Je '87

Bloom, Lloyd
about
Agents of turmoil. C. Neff. il pors *Sports Illus* 67:34-40+ Ag 3 '87
Agents of violence? B. Selcraig. il por *Sports Illus* 66:25 Ap 6 '87
Bloom, Marc, 1947-
Shake, rattle, and roll. il *N Y* 20:72-87 N 23 '87
Bloom, Mark
Cancer M.D.'s clash over interleukin therapy. il por *Science* 235:154-5 Ja 9 '87
Bloom, Naomi
Training in the commuter lane. il *Women's Sports Fitness* 9:66-7 Ap '87
Bloom, Pamela
29th Street Saxophone Quartet. il *Down Beat* 54:26-8 F '87
Bloom, Patrice
Risks of love [fiction] il por *Good Housekeep* 204:143-6+ Je '87
Bloomer, Kent C., 1935-
Urban animals. il *Audubon* 89:68-75 Ja '87
Bloomfield, Maureen
Lotto [poem] *New Repub* 196:32 My 18 '87
Bloomingdale's
No holiday blues at Bloomingdale's. A. Dunkin. il *Bus Week* p61-2 D 7 '87
Window-dressing. B. Kanner. il *N Y* 20:12-13 Ag 17 '87
Bloomington (Minn.)
Stores
On time in Bloomington [Ghermezian brothers complete deal to build Fashion Mall of America] D. Jenish. il *Macleans* 100:36 Ja 19 '87
Bloom's syndrome
Bloom's enzyme identified [DNA ligase] *Sci News* 131:72 Ja 31 '87
Bloomsbury group
Bloomsbury revisited. A. Bayer. il *Life* 10:76-84 Mr '87
A style of one's own: a new home furnishings collection inspired by the work of the Bloomsbury group. B. Plumb. il *Vogue* 177:278 F '87
Bloomsbury Publishing Ltd.
Win one, lose one. L. Fleischer. *Publ Wkly* 231:38 Ap 3 '87
Blooston, George
Editor Katrina Kenison of Ticknor & Fields. il por *Publ Wkly* 231:64+ F 13 '87
A talk with Erroll McDonald, editor of the 1986 Nobel laureate for literature. por *Publ Wkly* 231:86+ Mr 6 '87
Blot, Jean
Fighting words: the myth of the 'hereditary enemy'. il *Courier* 40:25-8 Jl '87
Blotnick, Srully
Insights. See issues of Forbes beginning July 28, 1986
about
Secret of a success. por *Time* 130:61 Ag 3 '87
Blouke, Morley
(jt. auth) See Janesick, James, and Blouke, Morley
Blount, Jonathan Dunn Sebastian
about
New York businessman Jonathan Blount searches for his natural mother. J. C. Mathews. por *Jet* 73:14-15 O 26 '87
Blount, Roy
Attacking the Amazon. il pors *Sports Illus* 66:60-4+ Ap 13 '87
The incongruous 'We'. il *N Y Times Mag* p14+ S 13 '87
Making love is not aerobic—so what? il *N Y Times Book Rev* 92:27-8 Ap 5 '87
My geophagy problem—and yours. il *Atlantic* 260:46-7 N '87
What guys hate! [poem] il *Esquire* 107:234 Je '87
Yet another true study of mankind. il *Atlantic* 259:34 Ap '87
Blow, Richard
Critical condition. il por *Roll Stone* p67-8+ Mr 26 '87
Blow, Simon
The Maltese connection. il *House Gard* 159:56+ Ag '87
Blow dryers *See* Hair dryers
Blowers, Leaf *See* Lawn equipment
Blue, Billy, d. 1834
about
Billy Blue: a legend of early Sydney. I. Duffield. bibl il *Hist Today* 37:43-8 F '87

Blue, Vida
about
Drug tests may explain why Vida Blue retired. por *Jet* 71:50 Mr 23 '87
Vida Blue pulls a switch, retires despite new pact. il por *Jet* 71:50 Mr 9 '87
The Blue Angel [ballet] See Ballet reviews—Single works
Blue Arrow Group *See* Blue Arrow plc
Blue Arrow plc
A whiz kid bids for Manpower. M. D. Oneal and R. A. Melcher. il por *Bus Week* p37-8 Ag 17 '87
Blue Chip Electronics (Firm)
Blue Chip chips away. W. J. Hawkins. il *Pop Sci* 230:28+ F '87
Blue collar workers *See* Labor
Blue jays *See* Jays
Blue Moon Mexican Cafe (New York, N.Y.) *See* New York (N.Y.)—Restaurants, nightclubs, bars, etc.
Blue Ridge Folklife Festival *See* Festivals—Virginia
Blue Ridge Institute
Preserving mountain ways. il *South Living* 22:20 O '87
Blue snake [ballet] See Ballet reviews—Single works
Blue snake [film] See Motion picture reviews—Single works
Blue velvet [film] See Motion picture reviews—Single works
Bluebell [television program] See Television program reviews—Single works
Blueberries
Don't wait until spring to plant blueberries. il *South Living* 22:74 N '87
Managing the unmanageable berries . . . in pots. il *Sunset* 178:52-3 Ja '87
Blueberry cake *See* Cake
Bluebird houses *See* Birdhouses
Bluebirds
See also
North American Blue-Bird Society
Bluefish
See also
Cooking—Fish
Bluefish: the most vicious fish in the sea? [photographs] B. Krist. il *Natl Wildl* 25:22-4 Je/Jl '87
Bluegrass music festivals *See* Music festivals
Bluehead wrasses *See* Wrasses
Blues *See* Depression, Mental
Blues concerts
Blues breaker [L. Brooks] S. G. Freedman. il pors *Roll Stone* p91-2+ S 24 '87
Music [Blues from the Delta to the Piedmont & Chicago] G. Santoro. *Nation* 244:481-2 Ap 11 '87
Blues music
See also
Cable television—Blues music
Compact discs—Blues music
Phonograph records—Blues music
Radio broadcasting—Blues music
History
Cafe au Go Go [New York City] P. Herbst. il *N Y* 20:81 D 21-28 '87
Illinois
See also
Chicago (Ill.)—Music
Blues music festivals *See* Music festivals
Bluhm, Neil G.
about
The Second City duo building a first-class colossus. J. N. Frank. il pors *Bus Week* p100 O 5 '87
Blum, Albert A.
Fallowships: fertilizing the groves of academe. il *Phi Delta Kappan* 69:71-2 S '87
Blum, Arlene, 1945-
about
Arlene Blum: from molecules to mountains. M. Nelson. il pors *Ms* 16:106+ S '87
Blum, David
Couch potatoes: the new nightlife. il *N Y* 20:24-30 Jl 20 '87
Emotion pictures. *New Repub* 196:13-15 F 9 '87
From Russia without love: Aina Robertovna's dream and how she got it. il pors *N Y* 20:46-50+ My 11 '87
One block: a tale of two cities on West 80th Street. il *N Y* 20:24-32 F 9 '87
The road to 'Ishtar'. il pors *N Y* 20:34-43 Mr 16 '87
The song of Mandy Patinkin. il pors *N Y* 20:52-61 S 14 '87
Up from 'Club Thirteen': the rise and rise of Peter Jennings. il pors *N Y* 20:50-6 N 30 '87
Where have you gone, Woody Allen? il *N Y* 20:48-53 O 12 '87
Where tough guys go to get tougher: Fort Liddy. il por *N Y* 20:64-71 Ap 13 '87

Blum, Howard, 1948-
The spy who came in from the mall. il pors *Roll Stone* p71-2+ O 8 '87
Blumberg, Arthur, 1923-, and Jonas, R. Stevan
Permitting access: teachers controlling supervision. *Educ Dig* 53:22-5 N '87
Blumenthal, Deborah
Stress: the no.1 beauty enemy. il *Ladies Home J* 104:92-5 Ja '87
Blumenthal, Michael
Looking homeward. il *N Y Times Mag* p78 Je 14 '87
The word "love" [poem] *Nation* 244:26 Ja 10 '87
Blumenthal, Sidney, 1948-
Dateline Washington: the conservative crackup. *Foreign Policy* 69:166-88 Wint '87/'88
The lightweight philosopher. *Wash Mon* 19:53-7 O '87
Blumenthal, W. Michael
about
Unisys: so far, so good—but the real test is yet to come. R. Mitchell. il por *Bus Week* p84+ Mr 2 '87
Blumer, Herbert, 1900-1987
about
Obituary
Society por 24:79 S/O '87. I. L. Horowitz
Blumstein, Alfred, and Cohen, Jacqueline
Characterizing criminal careers. bibl f il *Science* 237:985-91 Ag 28 '87
Blunders *See* Errors
Blunt, Russell
about
An old hand at winning, N.C. coach retires on top. il por *Jet* 72:50 Je 29 '87
Blurbs, Book *See* Books—Advertising
Blush wines *See* Wine
Blusher application *See* Makeup
Blushing
Branded! The red-hot tales of a chronic blusher. J. Crichton. il *Seventeen* 46:54 My '87
The truth about blushing. R. Roberts. il *Teen* 31:46-7 N '87
Bly, Nellie *See* Cochrane, Elizabeth, 1867-1922
Blyskal, Jeff
The fickle ways of Ginnie Mae. il *50 Plus* 27:78-83 F '87
(jt. auth) See Hodge, Marie, and Blyskal, Jeff
Blyskal, Jeff, and Hodge, Marie
Why your mail is so slow [cover story] il *N Y* 20:42-52+ N 9 '87
Blyskal, Marie Hodge *See* Hodge, Marie
Blyth, Myrna
Editor's journal. See issues of Ladies' Home Journal
Blyth Summer Festival (Ont.) *See* Drama festivals—Ontario
Blythe, Arthur
about
Arthur Blythe's creative challenge. J. Levenson. il pors *Down Beat* 54:23-5 O '87
Blythe, Bruce L.
about
Ford's Bruce Blythe has a big blank check—and a mission. J. B. Treece. il por *Bus Week* p79+ D 21 '87
BMC Industries Inc.
Surviving the cure. J. Parr. il por *Forbes* 140:52-3 Jl 27 '87
BMI *See* Broadcast Music, Inc.
BMW *See* Bayerische Motoren Werke AG
BMW (Automobile) *See* Automobile, Foreign
BMX racing (Bicycle) *See* Bicycle racing
Bo Ky (New York, N.Y.: Restaurant) *See* New York (N.Y.)—Restaurants, nightclubs, bars, etc.
Boa constrictors
Snakes in the bathroom [Hamilton, Ont.] N. Underwood. *Macleans* 100:42 Ag 24 '87
Board games *See* Educational games
Boarding schools *See* Private schools
Boards of directors *See* Corporations—Directors
Boards of education *See* School boards
Boardsailing
See also
Ice surfing
A boardhead's paradise [Hood River, Or.] J. N. Baker. il *Newsweek* 110:59 Ag 24 '87
Who owns the water? *Women's Sports Fitness* 9:20 Mr '87
Windjamming. J. Poppy. il *Esquire* 108:39+ Jl '87
Accidents and injuries
Taking the splinters out of board sailing. C. Schaeffer. il *Changing Times* 41:16 Jl '87
Study and teaching
Boom and board [U.S. Boardsailing Team offers clinics in Melbourne, Fla.] il *Women's Sports Fitness* 9:60 F '87

Boardwalk and Baseball (Amusement park)
Take me out to the amusement park. L. Lynn. il *Sport Mag* 78:84 S '87
Boat accessories *See* Boats and boating—Equipment
Boat building *See* Boatbuilding
Boat buying *See* Boats and boating—Purchasing
Boat clubs
See also
Yacht clubs
Boat covers *See* Boats and boating—Equipment
Boat decoration
The Breakaway: a seagoing scenario for George Hamilton. I. Borger. il por *Archit Dig* 44:86-9 Ag '87
The Highlander: aboard Malcolm Forbes' remarkable yacht [decorated by Jon Bannenberg] C. T. Buckley. il por *Archit Dig* 44:100-9+ Ja '87
Boat engines *See* Marine engines; Motor boat engines
Boat gages *See* Gages
Boat handling *See* Boats and boating—Handling
Boat living
In Florida: everyman's dream [Couvreux family] G. Jaynes. il *Time* 129:16-17 Mr 9 '87
Boat loans
Good news from Uncle Sam. S. Bernardo. il *Mot Boat Sail* 159:60-2 Ja '87
Have your boat and a tax break, too. S. Bernardo. il *Mot Boat Sail* 159:82-4 F '87
Boat models *See* Ship and boat models
Boat ownership
See also
Boats and boating—Purchasing
Confessions: what yacht captains really think of owners. C. Davis. il *Mot Boat Sail* 160:48-9+ N '87
Family fun. D. Wallace. il *Mot Boat Sail* 159:34-43 Je '87
Getting there [boat owners who commute via boat] C. Davis. il *Mot Boat Sail* 159:56-9+ Ap '87
Multiple ownership. B. Stearns. il *Field Stream* 92:141-2 S '87
On board with Ed McMahon. S. Duke. il por *Mot Boat Sail* 160:54-5+ Jl '87
The optimum boat. R. Florence. See issues of Motor Boating & Sailing beginning June 1986
Boat paint, Antifouling *See* Paint, Protective
Boat parts
Repair parts: the name-brand game [counterfeit boat parts] T. Banse. il *Mot Boat Sail* 159:104 F '87
Boat propellers *See* Boats and boating—Propellers
Boat racing
See also
Boat rallies
Catamaran racing
Motor boat racing
Rowing
Sailboat racing
Yacht racing
Ready, set . . . Whatever! [Great Kennebec River Whatever Race, Me.] il *Natl Geogr World* 143:24-9 Jl '87
Boat radar *See* Radar in navigation
Boat rallies
Great Britain
Dinking around London [Carlsberg 'Round London Boat Marathon for inflatable dinghies] D. Wallace. il *Mot Boat Sail* 159:44-7+ Je '87
Boat repairing *See* Boats and boating—Maintenance and repair
Boat searches *See* Searches and seizures
Boat shows *See* Boats and boating—Exhibitions
Boat speed records
Around the world in 80 days [attempt to break powerboat record in boat built by Certified Marine] B. Duke and S. Duke. il map *Mot Boat Sail* 159:48-51+ Ap '87
On board with Philippe Monnet [holds record for around-the-world solo sailing] M. Pennybaker. il por *Mot Boat Sail* 160:54-5+ N '87
Boat toilets *See* Boats and boating—Toilet facilities
Boat tools *See* Tools
Boat towing *See* Boats and boating—Towing
Boat trade *See* Boating industry
Boat trailers *See* Automobile boat trailers
Boatbuilding
See also
Boats and boating—Materials
Burger Boat Company, Inc.
Family boating fun can start with a kit. H. Wicks. il *Home Mech* 83:80-1 F '87
Put yourself afloat [plans to order] il *Home Mech* 83:76+ F '87

Boatbuilding—*cont.*
Sliding-seat dory. P. Butler and M. Butler. il *Pop Sci* 230:84-6 Je '87

Acquisitions and mergers
The booming boating business. P. A. Janssen. *Mot Boat Sail* 159:11 F '87

Finance
The baby boomers take to the waves [powerboat industry] R. McGough. il *Forbes* 139:72-3 Ap 20 '87
Dollars ahoy! [cover story] H. Rudnitsky and R. L. Stern. il *Forbes* 140:131-6+ N 2 '87

France
See also
Bénéteau (Firm)
Boating clothes *See* Clothing and dress—Sports clothes
Boating industry
Dollars ahoy! [cover story] H. Rudnitsky and R. L. Stern. il *Forbes* 140:131-6+ N 2 '87

Marketing
Down to the sea in dreams. J. A. Trachtenberg. il *Forbes* 140 Sp Issue:362-4 O 26 '87
A pastrami and Hatteras, to go. P. A. Janssen. il *Mot Boat Sail* 160:15 S '87
Boatman, Edwin S., and others
Today's microscopy [cover story] bibl f il *BioScience* 37:384-94 Je '87
Boats, Antique
The unsinkable allure of 'antique' boats [wooden boats] il *Bus Week* p108-9 Je 29 '87
Boats, Used

Testing
Evaluating a used boat. T. Banse. il *Mot Boat Sail* 159:79 Je '87
Boats and boating
See also
Alcohol and boating
Boat living
Boat speed records
Boatbuilding
Boating industry
Canoes and canoeing
Condominiums (Boat docking)
Cruisers (Pleasure boats)
Cruising
Ferries
Fishing boats
Gondolas
Hydrofoils
Information storage and retrieval systems—Boating use
Jet boats
Kayaks and kayaking
Motor boats
Navigation
Patrol boats
Praus (Boats)
River trips
Running rapids
Sailboats
Sailing
Seamanship
Sightseeing boats
Tugboats
Women in sailing
Yachts and yachting
The beauty of boats. N. Strung. il *Field Stream* 92:69-71 My '87
Boating. B. McKeown. See issues of Outdoor Life beginning May 1983
Boating. B. Stearns. See alternate issues of Field & Stream
Boating '87 [special section] il *Pop Mech* 164:91+ Mr '87
Boats to go [portable boats] R. McManus. il *Sierra* 72:51-6 Jl/Ag '87
Down to the sea again. L. Wainwright. il *Life* 10:11 My '87
Getting there [boat owners who commute via boat] C. Davis. il *Mot Boat Sail* 159:56-9+ Ap '87
New boat 1987 directory [special section] T. Bottomley. *Mot Boat Sail* 159:79-118 Ja '87
New boats. See issues of Motor Boating & Sailing
The new fastest way to get through the water [Flying Fish II, human powered boat] S. Morris. il *Omni* 9:111-12 Ja '87
Scenes. See issues of Motor Boating & Sailing
Trends '88 [cover story; special section] il *Mot Boat Sail* 160:42-55 S '87
Up front. See issues of Motor Boating & Sailing

Air conditioning
Air conditioning for every boat. B. Gladstone. il *Mot Boat Sail* 160:89-91 Ag '87

Anchoring
See Anchorage

Cabins
See also
Boats and boating—Galleys

Carburetors
See Carburetors

Cleaning
How to make an old boat look new. B. Gladstone. il *Mot Boat Sail* 159:65-7 My '87

Design
Design board. See issues of Motor Boating & Sailing

Electric equipment
Maintenance and repair
Give your boat an electrical checkup. B. Gladstone. il *Mot Boat Sail* 159:99-101 F '87

Electronic equipment
See also
Computers—Navigational use
Loran
Radar in navigation
Radiotelephone on ships, boats, etc.
Sonar
Complete electronics [excerpt from The optimum sailboat] R. Florence. *Mot Boat Sail* 159:109-10+ My '87
Electronics Q&A. G. West. See issues of Motor Boating & Sailing
Gadgets that make boating more of a pleasure. B. Hitchings. il *Bus Week* p103 Mr 30 '87
New electronics. See issues of Motor Boating & Sailing

Engines
See Marine engines; Motor boat engines

Equipment
See also
Anchors
Marine canvas work
The art of poling. B. Stearns. il *Field Stream* 92:69-70 D '87
Chandlery. See issues of Motor Boating & Sailing
Christmas gift shop. B. Gladstone and others. il *Mot Boat Sail* 160:59-66 D '87
Christmas kicks [cover story] D. Hoover. il *Mot Boat Sail* 160:50-3 D '87
Easy-on, easy-off boat-cover rack. E. F. Lindsley. il *Pop Sci* 230:120 Je '87
Great gear. T. H. Cole. il *Pop Mech* 164:104-6+ Mr '87
Make a CPVC support frame for your boat cover. E. Morrissey. il *Home Mech* 83:98-100 O '87
What's new. See issues of Outdoor Life
Whole sea catalog [special section] il *Mot Boat Sail* 159:35-42 F '87

Exhibitions
Handling boat shows. H. Halsted. il *Mot Boat Sail* 160:20 S '87
How to get to both Miami boat shows. map *Mot Boat Sail* 159:84-5 F '87
New York Boat Show '87 [special section] il map *Mot Boat Sail* 159:57-62+ Ja '87

Fires and fire prevention
Fire aboard! H. Halsted. il *Mot Boat Sail* 160:90 O '87

Food problems
See also
Cooking, Marine

Galleys
The complete galley [excerpt from The optimum sailboat] R. Florence. *Mot Boat Sail* 159:126-9 Je '87

Handling
Boat handling. H. Halsted. See issues of Motor Boating & Sailing
Heavy weather docking. S. Stapleton. il *Mot Boat Sail* 159:28 Je '87

History
Whole sea catalog [special section] il *Mot Boat Sail* 159:35-42 F '87

Interior decoration
See Boat decoration

Laws and regulations
The licensing labyrinth. P. A. Janssen. il *Mot Boat Sail* 160:13 Ag '87
Notices to boatmen. E. S. Maloney. See issues of Motor Boating & Sailing

Maintenance and repair
30 tips for spring commissionings. B. Gladstone and others. il *Mot Boat Sail* 159:81-8 Ap '87
Boatkeeper. B. Gladstone. See issues of Motor Boating & Sailing
Boatyard. B. Gladstone. See issues of Motor Boating & Sailing

Boats and boating—Maintenance and repair—*cont.*
Caring for inflatables. J. W. Going. il *Mot Boat Sail* 160:68 Jl '87
Getting back into the water. B. Stearns. il *Home Mech* 83:74-8 Mr '87
When your boat looks like a lawn ornament. H. Halsted. il *Mot Boat Sail* 159:28 Ap '87

Materials
The good old boats [traditional wooden boats] O. Cecil. il *Field Stream* 92:56-7+ N '87
Repairing holes and dents in fiberglass. B. Gladstone. il *Mot Boat Sail* 160:81-3 N '87
Toughing it [fiberglass] C. Caswell. il *Pop Mech* 164:96-9 Mr '87

Medical aspects
Medical emergencies at sea. S. Stapleton. il *Mot Boat Sail* 159:30 Mr '87

Mooring
See Anchorage

Options
See Boats and boating—Equipment

Parts
See Boat parts

Photographs and photography
Boating! R. Ermshar. il *Petersens Photogr Mag* 16:14-19+ Ag '87
Camera on deck [work of G. Gurney] B. London. il por *Pop Photogr* 94:70-6 Jl '87
Picture-perfect boating. B. McKeown. il *Outdoor Life* 180:32+ Ag '87

Prices
10 new boats for under $20,000. J. A. Fishman. il *Mot Boat Sail* 160:36-41 D '87
Family fun [boats under $50,000] D. Wallace. il *Mot Boat Sail* 159:34-43 Je '87
You don't need a fortune to own a boat. B. Hitchings. il *Bus Week* p102-3 Mr 30 '87

Propellers
The mystery of single-screw reversing. H. Halsted. il *Mot Boat Sail* 160:26 Ag '87

Purchasing
Boat buyer's checklist. J. Wooldridge. *Mot Boat Sail* 159:86-7+ F '87
Dreams for sale. J. Wooldridge. il *Mot Boat Sail* 159:57-8+ Ja '87
Starting over. P. A. Janssen. il *Mot Boat Sail* 160:11 N '87

Radio equipment
See also
Cellular radio on ships, boats, etc.
Radio direction finders
Radiotelephone on ships, boats, etc.

Safety devices and measures
See also
Life preservers
Lighthouses
Lightships
Radio beacons
The safety checklist. H. Halsted. il *Mot Boat Sail* 159:28+ My '87

Sanitation
See also
Boats and boating—Toilet facilities

Security measures
Boating security. S. Stapleton. il *Mot Boat Sail* 160:28 Ag '87

Solar energy use
A solar genset. T. Banse. il *Mot Boat Sail* 159:71-2 Mr '87

Steering gear
Tiller extension for electrics. B. Stearns. il *Field Stream* 92:133 My '87

Storm hazards
The end of the season [fishing excursion in bad weather] P. A. Janssen. il *Mot Boat Sail* 160:9 D '87
Storm warnings. B. McKeown. il *Outdoor Life* 180:32+ N '87
Stormy (summer) weather. S. Stapleton. il *Mot Boat Sail* 160:26 Jl '87

Study and teaching
Learning the ropes [Chapman School of Seamanship] J. Clemans. il *Mot Boat Sail* 159:60-2+ Mr '87
The licensing labyrinth. P. A. Janssen. il *Mot Boat Sail* 160:13 Ag '87

Taxation
Cheap shots at fat cats. P. A. Janssen. il *Mot Boat Sail* 159:11 Je '87
Good news from Uncle Sam. S. Bernardo. il *Mot Boat Sail* 159:60-2 Ja '87
Have your boat and a tax break, too. S. Bernardo. il *Mot Boat Sail* 159:82-4 F '87

Take my yacht. Please! [charitable deduction] W. G. Flanagan and L. Scheer. il *Forbes* 140:114-15 D 28 '87

Testing
Boat Show '87: editors' reports [10 new boats] il *Mot Boat Sail* 159:67-72 Ja '87
Fun inflatable sport boats. D. Fales. il *Mot Boat Sail* 159:48-53+ My '87
Riding on air [new inflatables] T. H. Cole. il *Pop Mech* 164:94-7 Ap '87

Theft
See also
Boats and boating—Security measures
The sleuth who snoops for sloops [B. Schachter] B. Rice. il por *50 Plus* 27:76-8+ Je '87

Toilet facilities
The optimum boat [excerpt from The optimum sailboat] R. Florence. *Mot Boat Sail* 160:127-8+ S '87

Towing
Tender tugs [towing yachts with dinghies] H. Halsted. il *Mot Boat Sail* 160:24 Jl '87

Transportation
See also
Automobile boat trailers

Water supply
Adding a fresh or salt water washdown. B. Gladstone. il *Mot Boat Sail* 159:65-7 Mr '87

Boats in business
Commodore for a night. W. G. Flanagan. il *Forbes* 140:112+ S 7 '87

Boats in motion pictures
"But I had the right of way . . . " [filming of Russkies] J. Clemans. il *Mot Boat Sail* 159:60-1 Ap '87

Boats in narcotics regulation
Night patrol in the drug war [Coast Guard patrol in the Gulf Stream off Miami] C. Davis. il *Mot Boat Sail* 159:46-9+ Mr '87

Boats in narcotics trade
The boat that wouldn't sink [Coyote racer, scuttled by drug smugglers off Florida coast, floats to England] P. A. Janssen. il *Mot Boat Sail* 160:60-1 Jl '87
Don Aronow's murder leaves Miami wondering: were 'Cigarettes' hazardous to his health? J. Hammer. il por *People Wkly* 27:75-6+ Mr 30 '87

Bob, Paul
The Machine Age on display. il *Esquire* 107:132 F '87

Bob Bondurant School of High Performance Driving *See* Automobile driving—Study and teaching

Bobbers (Fishing) *See* Fishing tackle

Bobbsey Twins (Literary characters)
Updated Bobbsey Twins series follows Nancy Drew, Hardy Boys. il *Publ Wkly* 232:32 Ag 28 '87

Bobcat hunting
Attack of the midnight screamer. W. J. Buchanan. il *Read Dig* 130:169-70+ Ap '87

Bobcats
Shy survivor. G. Turbak. il *Natl Wildl* 26:12-16 D '87/Ja '88

Bobet Biarritz (France: Resort) *See* Health resorts, watering places, etc.—France

Bobolinks
The song of Bob O'Lincoln. J. Balfoort. il *Conservationist* 41:56 My/Je '87

Bobsled racing
Slip-slidin' away to '88 [U.S. team led by M. Roy] W. Nack. il por *Sports Illus* 66:64-5 Mr 9 '87
Willie Gault adds speed to his swift lifestyle. *Jet* 71:51 F 16 '87

History
Bobsleigh, luge and speed skating [U.S. Olympic competitors] W. Bingham. il *Sports Illus* 67:51+ D 14 '87

Bobwhite shooting *See* Quail shooting

BOC Challenge *See* Yacht racing

Bocca, Julio
about
Argentina's golden boy Julio Bocca. M. Hunt. il pors *Dance Mag* 61:60-1 Mr '87
Second sight. T. Tobias. por *N Y* 20:111-12 My 25 '87

Bodanis, David
Hidden wonders of your house [condensed from The secret house] *Read Dig* 130:126-8 F '87
about
They say a man's home is his castle, but David Bodanis' Secret house reveals the creepy truth. il pors *People Wkly* 27:133-5 Ap 20 '87

Boddie, Ellen
Great Scott! il pors *50 Plus* 27:30-1+ D '87
This doctor is for the birds [cover story] il pors *50 Plus* 27:20-4 Jl '87

Bode, Janet
Sex for shelter: when your landlord wants more than the rent. il *Glamour* 85:318-19+ N '87
Bode, Richard
I stopped my daughter's wedding. il pors *Good Housekeep* 204:106+ Mr '87
Bodega Marine Laboratory
A day at Bodega Bay. J. Lowenstein. *Oceans* 20:72 My/Je '87
Bodies, rest, and motion [drama] *See* Hedden, Roger
Bodrug, S. E., and others
Molecular analysis of a constitutional X-autosome translocation in a female with muscular dystrophy. bibl f il *Science* 237:1620-4 S 25 '87
Bodrum (Turkey)
Description
Turkey's ancient treasures. C. E. Adelsen. il map *Travel Holiday* 168:56-9 O '87
Body, Human
See also
Mind and body
Physiology
Symmetry (Biology)
Women—Anatomy and physiology
Exhibitions
Ride through the human body [new Body Wars attraction at EPCOT] il *Pop Mech* 164:53 D '87
Body and mind *See* Mind and body
Body art
Her bold looks made her a standout in the '60s, but now Veruschka paints herself into the background. M. Small. il pors *People Wkly* 27:88-90 F 16 '87
Body building
Body by design [regimen of R. Petty] M. Kort. il pors *Women's Sports Fitness* 9:34-8 S '87
Confessions of a steroid user [interview with anonymous female body builder] D. Barrilleaux. il *Women's Sports Fitness* 9:84 N '87
Doris Barrilleaux, 56. M. Kort. por *Women's Sports Fitness* 9:19 O '87
Eight ways to total-body fitness. D. Groves. il *Work Woman* 12:134+ Je '87
How I spent my summer vacation: one woman's journey to fantasy bodybuilding camp [Pro Muscle Bodybuilding and Fitness Training Camp] D. Frost. il *Women's Sports Fitness* 9:38-41 Je '87
A tale of two regeneration people [Laurie Spicer and Leah O'Toole] M. Golin. il *Prevention* 39:70+ F '87
Competitions
Look, Mao—no pajamas! [female body builders in China permitted to compete in bikinis] O. Schell. il *Women's Sports Fitness* 9:68+ Ag '87
Psychological aspects
Of muscles and mania [steroid induced psychosis; study by Harrison G. Pope Jr. and David L. Katz] E. Grant. il *Psychol Today* 21:12 S '87
Body building camps *See* Camps
Body by Jake (Firm)
Jake Steinfeld: master of motivation. L. Kleinmann. por *Health* 19:60 F '87
Body fat *See* Fat
Body fluids
See also
Amniotic liquid
Blood
Perspiration
Saliva
Urine
Water in the body
Body heat *See* Temperature, Animal and human
Body image
Body image and self-esteem. *Society* 25:7 N/D '87
Build a better body image. L. Rogers. il *McCalls* 114:16 Ag '87
Do you really want to be thin? N. Malkin. il *Mademoiselle* 93:190 F '87
"Honey, do I look fat?". D. Heyn. *Mademoiselle* 93:110 Je '87
How do men feel about their bodies? P. Richmond. il *Glamour* 85:312-13+ Ap '87
How's your body vision? When thin women see fat. D. Heyn. il *Mademoiselle* 93:212-13+ Ap '87
Looking good: the double standard [excerpt from Beauty bound] R. J. Freedman. *Vogue* 177:357+ Ap '87
Overweight or underconfident? Coming to terms with your body. K. McCoy. *Seventeen* 46:32+ F '87

Body language *See* Communication, Nonverbal
Body odors *See* Odors
Body parts, Artificial *See* Prosthesis
Body rhythms *See* Biological rhythms
Body size
How big can a species be? [research by John Eadie and others] R. Lewin. *Science* 237:1117 S 4 '87
Body snatching
Argentina
Holding (Peron's) hands in Argentina. A. M. Shapiro. il *New Leader* 70:5-7 Ag 10-24 '87
Body temperature *See* Temperature, Animal and human
Body therapy *See* Biomechanics—Therapeutic use
Body types, Human *See* Somatotypes
Body weight *See* Weight (Physiology)
Boehm, Edward Marshall
about
Poetry in porcelain. il por *South Living* 22:26 Ja '87
Boehmer, Linda Sue
Travels with my computer. il por *Work Woman* 12:62 Ap '87
Boehmig, Stuart
about
Happy hour at Mr. C's. R. Frame. il por *Christ Today* 31:12-13 O 16 '87
Boeing Co.
Airframe makers near key technology decisions. R. G. O'Lone. il *Aviat Week Space Technol* 126:183-5+ Mr 9 '87
Airline commitments prompt Boeing to launch 737-500. R. G. O'Lone. il *Aviat Week Space Technol* 126:28-9 My 25 '87
American wields leverage in aircraft lease arrangement [leasing order divided between Airbus Industrie and Boeing] J. Ott. il *Aviat Week Space Technol* 126:258-9 Mr 9 '87
Americanization of a high-flyer [DeHavilland Aircraft of Canada since the Boeing takeover] P. C. Newman. il *Macleans* 100:42 F 23 '87
Australian Boeing order exploits greater domestic competition. J. Ott. *Aviat Week Space Technol* 127:36-7 O 12 '87
Blitz on Boeing [targeted for takeover by T. B. Pickens] por *Time* 130:35 Ag 10 '87
Boeing [jetliner development] N. Moll. il *Flying* 114:28-39 My '87
Boeing 747-400 to offer flight crew rest area, advanced two-man cockpit. R. G. O'Lone. il *Aviat Week Space Technol* 127:47+ O 26 '87
Boeing Aerospace wins contract to provide LOS-R Stinger system [line of sight-rear component of the Army's forward area air defense system] C. A. Shifrin. il *Aviat Week Space Technol* 127:25-6 Ag 31 '87
Boeing battles to stay on top. K. Labich. il *Fortune* 116:64-6+ S 28 '87
Boeing braces for dip in 1987 sales despite 1986 growth. *Aviat Week Space Technol* 126:36 F 2 '87
Boeing delays 7J7 program; mid-1993 certification expected [special section] il *Aviat Week Space Technol* 127:28-31 Ag 31 '87
Boeing designs ASW version of De Havilland Dash 8-100 [antisubmarine warfare version] il *Aviat Week Space Technol* 127:22-3 Jl 20 '87
Boeing evaluating new control laws in 7J7 advanced-technology simulator [fly-by-wire control system] B. D. Nordwall. il *Aviat Week Space Technol* 126:54-6+ Je 29 '87
Boeing evolves 7J7 design, prepares specification details. R. G. O'Lone. il *Aviat Week Space Technol* 126:34-6 My 18 '87
Boeing expects next transport to resemble 7J7 design, but powerplant may vary. *Aviat Week Space Technol* 127:34-5 D 21 '87
Boeing faces major decisions on 737. R. G. O'Lone. *Aviat Week Space Technol* 127:36 Ag 17 '87
Boeing financing of United orders reflects stiffening competition. *Aviat Week Space Technol* 126:29-30 My 18 '87
Boeing had good reason to take Allegis under its wing. J. E. Ellis. il *Bus Week* p64+ My 25 '87
Boeing, McDonnell Douglas programs reflect need for collaborative efforts. R. G. O'Lone. il *Aviat Week Space Technol* 126:301-2+ Je 15 '87
Boeing plans to end 737-200 production. *Aviat Week Space Technol* 127:36 O 5 '87
Boeing selected over Lockheed for P-3 avionics update award. B. M. Greeley, Jr. *Aviat Week Space Technol* 127:22-3 Jl 20 '87
Boeing to begin tests on A-6E/F composite wing. B. M. Greeley, Jr. il *Aviat Week Space Technol* 127:121-2 O 12 '87

Boeing Co.—*cont.*

Boeing to build space station modules under $750-million award. il *Aviat Week Space Technol* 127:20-1 D 7 '87

Boeing will consider alternative to unducted fan for twin-aisle 7J7 [IAE V2500 SuperFan] R. G. O'Lone. il *Aviat Week Space Technol* 126:31-2 Ja 26 '87

Boeing wins contract to design MX rail-garrison basing system. B. A. Smith. *Aviat Week Space Technol* 127:21 S 21 '87

Boeing withdraws from bidding to replace Navy ASW aircraft. *Aviat Week Space Technol* 127:25 N 16 '87

Boeing's first-quarter earnings fall 20% as DHC-8 deliveries lag. *Aviat Week Space Technol* 126:129 My 11 '87

British Airways places orders for 14 Boeing transports. *Aviat Week Space Technol* 127:36 Ag 24 '87

Cool, calm, and lawyerly [F. Shrontz] A. Ramirez. il por *Fortune* 116:54 Ag 3 '87

E-3 offsets expected to reach $2 billion [agreement with Britain] *Aviat Week Space Technol* 127:25 O 26 '87

Efficient thin-film solar cells revive interest in space uses. B. D. Nordwall. *Aviat Week Space Technol* 126:105+ Je 29 '87

Exim Bank backs 767 sale to All Nippon to foil Airbus bid. *Aviat Week Space Technol* 126:31 Je 29 '87

France orders Boeing E-3s; Britain signs formal contract. *Aviat Week Space Technol* 126:27 Mr 2 '87

General Electric and Boeing analyze data following initial UDF flight tests [unducted fan] *Aviat Week Space Technol* 126:67 Ap 13 '87

Is Boone bluffing? [buying into Boeing] K. M. Hafner. il por *Bus Week* p22-3 Ag 10 '87

Japanese cite faulty bulkhead repair as cause of JAL 747 crash in 1985. *Aviat Week Space Technol* 126:34 Je 29 '87

Mesa purchase of Boeing stock highlights industry pressures. R. G. O'Lone. *Aviat Week Space Technol* 127:24-5 Ag 3 '87

New Boeing facility will play key role in ATF competition [advanced tactical fighter] *Aviat Week Space Technol* 126:89+ Ja 26 '87

Predicted traffic surge drives Boeing's transport planning. R. G. O'Lone. il *Aviat Week Space Technol* 127:53-4 N 9 '87

SAS considers Boeing 767 to replace DC-10. *Aviat Week Space Technol* 126:34 My 4 '87

TWA discussing aircraft order with McDonnell Douglas, Boeing. C. Preble. *Aviat Week Space Technol* 126:38-9 Mr 30 '87

United finds a new friend [Allegis' deal with Boeing] J. B. Copeland. il *Newsweek* 109:38 My 25 '87

Boeing Co. Boeing Vertol Company (Div.)

Army developing helicopter derivatives for special operations missions. S. W. Kandebo. il *Aviat Week Space Technol* 127:47+ D 14 '87

Bell/Boeing team developing tilt-rotor Pointer RPV. B. M. Greeley, Jr. il *Aviat Week Space Technol* 126:58-9 Mr 9 '87

Bell-Boeing schedules first flight of Pointer tilt-rotor demonstrator. S. W. Kandebo. il *Aviat Week Space Technol* 127:56 Ag 10 '87

Bell, Boeing study specialized missions for V-22 Osprey. *Aviat Week Space Technol* 126:88-9 Ja 19 '87

Boeing Vertol Model 360 helicopter to undergo performance, stability tests [cover story] il *Aviat Week Space Technol* 127:143 Jl 13 '87

Boeing Vertol Company (Div.) *See* Boeing Co. Boeing Vertol Company (Div.)

Boers *See* Afrikaners

Boesky, Ivan F.

about

Back in the spotlight. F. Ungeheuer. il por *Time* 130:55 D 21 '87

The Boesky scandal. il *World Press Rev* 34:22 Ja '87

Boesky's sentence: who will be next? il por *Newsweek* 110:36 D 28 '87

Crime and punishment. T. Tedesco. *Macleans* 100:43 D 28 '87

Crook of the year. G. Kinkead. il por *Fortune* 115:48-9 Ja 5 '87

Distressed merchandise. R. Phalon. por *Forbes* 139:180 Ap 6 '87

An extra slice of the pie. A. Sloan. il *Forbes* 139:32-3 F 9 '87

The grin is gone, but arbitrageur Boesky still sings. K. R. Sheets. il por *U S News World Rep* 102:45 My 4 '87

Ivan Boesky's final deal. il por *U S News World Rep* 103:13 D 28 '87-Ja 4 '88

Ivan Boesky's latest deal: a guilty plea. il por *Newsweek* 109:45 My 4 '87

Ivan Boesky's secret 'parking lots'. C. Welles. il por *Bus Week* p130 Je 22 '87

Minority report. C. Hitchens. *Nation* 244:39 Ja 17 '87

The price of Ivan Boesky's greed. C. Friday. il por *Newsweek* 110:51 D 21 '87

Tracing Ivan's deals, Ivan's money. P. Sherrid; A. Gabor. por *U S News World Rep* 102:47 F 2 '87

Trading places. por *Time* 130:63 D 28 '87

Were Drexel and Boesky in cahoots? J. Egan and D. Baer. il por *U S News World Rep* 102:45 F 16 '87

What the Boesky scandal means to you and your money. J. Edgerton. il *Money* 16:64-7 Ja '87

Boetig, Donna

Dentists polish up their image. il *Saturday Evening Post* 259:28-9+ N '87

Boff, Shannon

about

And baby makes four: for the first time a surrogate bears a child genetically not her own. B. Johnson. il por *People Wkly* 27:95-6+ My 4 '87

Boffey, Philip M.

Dr. Marks' crusade: shaking up Sloan-Kettering for a new assault on cancer [cover story] il pors *N Y Times Mag* p26-31+ Ap 26 '87

Bofill, Ricardo, 1939-

about

Architecture: Ricardo Bofill. N. Shrady. il *Archit Dig* 44:124-31+ Jl '87

Bofors Nobel AB

As Stockholm lays siege to Nobel . . . [arms smuggling charges] J. Kapstein. il *Bus Week* p46 S 21 '87

Bogan, Kathleen

Snow shelters. il *Sierra* 72:143-5 Ja/F '87

Bogarde, Dirk, 1921-

An Englishman's house in France. il por *Archit Dig* 44:22+ F '87

Bogayevicz, Yurek

about

Anna [film] Reviews

N Y 20:116 N 9 '87. D. Denby

Vogue il 177:82 O '87. M. Haskell

Bogdanov, Michael

about

Turned-on Shakespeare. J. Bemrose. il *Macleans* 100:54 Je 1 '87

Boggan, Ann

In the shadow of Uncle Sam. il *Ms* 16:69 N '87

Boggess, Bill, and Boggess, Louise

Charles Tuthill: a legend in cut and intaglio glass. il *Antiques Collect Hobbies* 92:14-18 Ap '87

Boggess, Louise

(jt. auth) See Boggess, Bill, and Boggess, Louise

Boggess, Nancy W.

about

Infrared eyes on the universe: a conversation with Nancy Boggess. T. Reichhardt and J. Rhea. il por *Space World* X-2-278:12-16 F '87

Boggs, Bill

Finding the Fury. il *N Y Times Mag* p37 Ag 2 '87

Boggs, Billie *See* Brown, Joyce

Boggs, J. S. G.

about

The Monet of money paints himself into a corner. il por *People Wkly* 27:77 Mr 2 '87

Boggs, Stephen *See* Boggs, J. S. G.

Boggs, Wade

about

The secret of my new success. J. Coplon. il pors *Sport Mag* 78:50-1+ N '87

Bogle, John C.

about

These funds want to tie the averages. C. S. Eklund. il por *Bus Week* p80 Ja 19 '87

Bogley, Rose Marie

about

Jamaican cadence: Rose Marie Bogley's cottage above Montego Bay. J. S. Wamsley. il *Archit Dig* 44:202-7 My '87

Bogosian, Eric

Strange air [excerpt from Talk radio] il *Harpers* 274:34-6 Je '87

about

Bogosian's voices. S. Holden. il por *N Y Times Mag* p34-5+ My 24 '87

By turns hilarious and bizarre, Talk radio's Eric Bogosian finds the real voice of America. M. Small. il pors *People Wkly* 28:99-100 Ag 17 '87

Talk radio [drama] Reviews

N Y il 20:74 Je 8 '87. J. Simon

Bogosian, Eric—about—Talk radio—*cont.*
　New Repub 197:28-30 Jl 6 '87. R. Brustein
　New Yorker 63:69 Je 8 '87. E. Oliver
Bogotá (Colombia)
　　　　　Description
Bogotá: echoes of the past. E. Durand. il *Américas*
　39:24-30 N/D '87
Bogs
Mysteries of the bog. L. E. Levathes. il *Natl Geogr*
　171:396-420 Mr '87
Bogues, Muggsy
　　　　　about
Biggest little man. F. Lidz. il pors *Sports Illus* 66:72-3
　F 16 '87
College basketball's little man seeks big NBA break.
　il por *Jet* 72:47 Mr 30 '87
A short (but sweet) story. H. Hersch. il pors *Sports
　Illus* 67:20-1 Jl 20 '87
Bohan, Marc
　　　　　about
Bohan: the power behind Dior. P. McColl. il pors *Harpers
　Bazaar* 120:162+ S '87
La Bohème (New York, N.Y.: Restaurant) *See* New York
　(N.Y.)—Restaurants, nightclubs, bars, etc.
La bohème [opera] *See* Puccini, Giacomo, 1858-1924
Bohemia Inc.
Almost out of the woods. M. Beauchamp. il *Forbes*
　140:198-9 O 5 '87
Bohemianism
　　See also
　　　Beatniks
　　　Hippies
Bohlen, Janet Trowbridge
Jaguars: why protect a killer? [cover story] il map *Int
　Wildl* 17:4-11 Mr/Ap '87
Bohm, David
　　　　　about
Interview. J. Briggs and F. D. Peat. por *Omni* 9:68-70+
　Ja '87
Bohmann, Dirk, and others
Human proto-oncogene c-*jun* encodes a DNA binding
　protein with structural and functional properties of
　transcription factor AP-1. bibl f il *Science* 238:1386-92
　D 4 '87
Bohn, Martha C., and others
Adrenal medulla grafts enhance recovery of striatal
　dopaminergic fibers. bibl f il *Science* 237:913-16 Ag
　21 '87
Bohor, Bruce F., and others
Shocked quartz in the Cretaceous-Tertiary boundary clays:
　evidence for a global distribution. bibl f il map *Science*
　236:705-9 My 8 '87
Bohren, Craig F., 1940-
Simple experiments in atmospheric physics. See issues
　of Weatherwise
Boies, David
　　　　　about
David Boies: the ace litigator playing Texaco's hand.
　L. J. Tell. il por *Bus Week* p79 Ap 20 '87
Boikov, Vyacheslav
A Soviet view. *World Press Rev* 34:14 Je '87
Boiler room scams *See* Fraud
Boilers
　　　　　Energy usage
Home heating: high-efficiency furnaces and boilers. M.
　Fillon. il *Workbench* 43:18+ N/D '87
Boisbriand (Québec)
　　　　　Industries
Keeping the assembly line rolling [government aid keeps
　GM plant open] il *Macleans* 100:10 Ap 13 '87
Boise State University
Financial exigency is alive and well in Idaho [justification
　for dismissal of tenured faculty members] T. J. Flygare.
　Phi Delta Kappan 68:550-1 Mr '87
Boito, Arrigo, 1842-1918
　　　　　about
Mefistofele [opera] Reviews
　Opera News 52:44 Ag '87. S. Modi
Bojangles' of America Inc.
Why didn't they pay him to stay home? [Horn & Hardart's
　Bojangles' stores mismanaged by B. Florescue] B.
　Leonard. il por *Forbes* 139:120-1 Je 15 '87
Bok, Derek Curtis
The quality of the university today: an exchange at
　Harvard [address, October 1986] *Current* 291:9-11
　Mr/Ap '87
Bok globules *See* Nebulae
Bokassa I, Emperor of the Central African Empire, 1921-
　　　　　about
Former emperor Bokassa is sentenced to death. *Jet* 72:9
　Je 29 '87

Bol, Manute
　　　　　about
Clash of the titans. R. Goldberg. il *Sport Mag* 78:56-8+
　Ja '87
Boland, Eavan
The black lace fan my mother gave me [poem] *New
　Yorker* 63:40 O 19 '87
Boland, Edward P.
　　　　　about
Boland, NASA at odds over launch of Mars Observer.
　M. M. Waldrop. por *Science* 235:743 F 13 '87
Bolar Pharmaceutical Co.
The little drug company that could. J. Merwin. il por
　Forbes 139:72-3 Ja 26 '87
Bolcom, William
　　　　　about
Forces of nature. P. G. Davis. il *N Y* 20:71-2 Ja 26
　'87
Music, every which way. J. Rockwell. il pors *N Y Times
　Mag* p32-3+ Ag 16 '87
Musical events:
　Songs of innocence and of experience by W. Bolcom.
　　A. Porter. il *New Yorker* 62:70-3 F 2 '87
Tiger, tiger daring, bright. A. Rich. il por *Newsweek*
　109:58 Ja 19 '87
Bolger, Ray, 1904-1987
　　　　　about
Obituary
　Natl Rev 39:22 F 13 '87
　People Wkly il 27:98 F 2 '87
Bolger, Thomas E.
　　　　　about
Astride the bounciest Baby Bell. D. P. Wiener. il por
　Fortune 115:87 Ja 5 '87
Bolger, William F.
Air traffic control [address, November 14, 1986] *Vital
　Speeches Day* 53:251-3 F 1 '87
Bolivar County (Miss.)
　　　　　Politics and government
Bolivar County, Miss. gets black as circuit clerk [R.
　S. Simmons] por *Jet* 72:6 S 14 '87
Bolivia
　　See also
　　　Christmas—Bolivia
　　　Loans, Bank—Bolivia
　　　Narcotics laws and regulations—Bolivia
　　　Narcotics trade—Bolivia
　　　Rain forests—Bolivia
　　　　　Description and travel
Discovering Bolivia's spirit. R. Falcão. il *World Press
　Rev* 34:61 D '87
　　　　　Economic policy
Bolivia beats 5-digit inflation. A. Nader. il *World Press
　Rev* 34:44-5 S '87
Bolivia's economic crisis. J. Malloy. *Curr Hist* 86:9-12+
　Ja '87
　　　　　Foreign relations
　　　　　United States
　See United States—Foreign relations—Bolivia
　　　　　Native peoples
　See Indians of South America—Bolivia
　　　　　Politics and government
Bolivia's economic crisis. J. Malloy. *Curr Hist* 86:9-12+
　Ja '87
　　　　　Religious institutions and affairs
　　See also
　　Catholic Church—Bolivia
Bolkiah, Muda Hassanal *See* Hassanal Bolkiah, Sultan
　of Brunei, 1946-
Bollag, Brenda
Klimov & Co. il *Film Comment* 23:40+ My/Je '87
Bolle, Sonja
　(jt. auth) *See* Symons, Allene, and Bolle, Sonja
Bollettieri, Nick
The Baltic basher. il por *World Tennis* 34:12 Mr '87
Motivation. il *World Tennis* 34:35 Ap '87
Raise the level of your workout. il *World Tennis* 35:32-4
　Ag '87
Traveling men. il *World Tennis* 34:24+ My '87
Underdog. il *World Tennis* 35:88+ S '87
Bollettieri (Nick) Tennis Academy (Bradenton, Fla.) *See*
　Nick Bollettieri Tennis Academy (Bradenton, Fla.)
Bollier, David
A fight for time on the air. il *Sierra* 72:18-20 S/O
　'87
Bolling, Bill
　　　　　about
Bill Bolling: boarded, bothered and busted. P. Whittell.
　il pors *Mot Boat Sail* 159:66-9+ F '87

Bolling, Claude
about
Claude Bolling/Slim Gaillard. F. Bouchard. il por *Down Beat* 54:51 Ja '87
Bollworms
Control
Flies to the rescue [maggots of Archytas marmoratus feed on corn earworms and fall armyworms; work of Robert D. Jackson] il *USA Today (Periodical)* 115:7-8 Je '87
Bologna Children's Book Fair *See* Book fairs
Bolometers and bolometry
Limits on sensitivity of large silicon bolometers for solar neutrino detection. C. J. Martoff. bibl f il *Science* 237:507-9 Jl 31 '87
Bolotin, Norm, 1951-
Klondike scrapbook. il *Am Hist Illus* 22:26-35 O '87
Bolsa (Stock exchange) *See* Stock exchanges—Mexico exchange
Bolshoi Ballet
Back from the USSR: Bolshoi blockbuster [cover story] M. E. Willis. il *Dance Mag* 61:34-8 Jl '87
The Bolshoi hedges its bets [production of The golden age] J. R. Acocella. il *Art Am* 75:30-1+ N '87
Bolshoi intrigue. L. Shapiro. il *Newsweek* 110:47 Jl 6 '87
Bolshoi lords aleaping [American tour] M. Duffy. il *Time* 130:74-5 Jl 27 '87
The Bolshoi's big news: Irek Mukhamedov, superstar. M. E. Willis. il pors *Dance Mag* 61:58-63 Ap '87
Brought to you by . . . [videotaped performances] il *Dance Mag* 61:76-7 O '87
Cossacks of classicism [performances at the Metropolitan Opera House, New York City] M. Aloff. il *Dance Mag* 61:36-9 D '87
Dancing:
Metropolitan Opera House performances. A. Croce. *New Yorker* 63:60-2 Jl 27 '87
Extracts from a Bolshoi diary: on the road again [touring the United Kingdom] M. E. Willis. il *Dance Mag* 61:39-44 Jl '87
Fool's gold [performances of Raymonda and Giselle at the Metropolitan Opera House] T. Tobias. il *N Y* 20:50-1 Ag 3 '87
The next great leap: measuring the Bolshoi. D. McDonagh. *Commonweal* 114:499-500 S 11 '87
Skirting controversy at home, the Bolshoi's Yuri Grigorovich brings his dancers to the U.S. il por *People Wkly* 28:40-2 Jl 27 '87
So big [performances of The golden age and Highlights programs at the Metropolitan Opera House] T. Tobias. il *N Y* 20:52-3 Jl 20 '87
The Soviet dance theater of Yuri Grigorovich. N. Alovert. il por *Dance Mag* 61:39-42 D '87
Stumbling at the Bolshoi [New York engagement] L. A. Jacobs. *New Leader* 70:22-3 Ag 10-24 '87
Yuri Grigorovich: an appreciation. N. Alovert. il por *Dance Mag* 61:44-7 Jl '87
Bolt, Robert
about
A man for all seasons [drama] Reviews
N Y 20:52-3 Ja 19 '87. J. Simon
Bolt, Thomas
Daniel Dallmann. il *Am Artist* 51:56-61 Mr '87
Four objects, four interpretations. il *Am Artist* 51:28-31 Jl '87
Sigmund Abeles: the Max drawings. il *Am Artist* 51:50-5 O '87
Bolton, David W.
Underground frontiers. il *Earth Sci* 40:16-18 Summ '87
Bolton Landing (N.Y.)
Hotels, motels, etc.
The Sagamore Hotel. R. Hartman. il *Black Enterp* 17:333 Je '87
Bolts and nuts
Keep nuts tight. D. Richmond. il *Pop Sci* 231:138+ N '87
Bomb detectors
The chemical nose [Thermedics sniffers] W. Baldwin. il *Forbes* 140:278 N 16 '87
New technology bomb detectors will improve airport security. J. Ott. il *Aviat Week Space Technol* 127:43-4 Ag 3 '87
Bomb shelters *See* Atomic bomb shelters
Bombardier, Denise
Islamic terrorism: a growing peril [interview with A. Taheri] il *World Press Rev* 34:17-19 My '87
Bombay (India)
Child welfare
Bombay's 'red-light' children. B. Sadasivam. *World Press Rev* 34:54 Jl '87

Social life and customs
Entertaining [hostess S. Pitember] W. P. Rayner and C. Rayner. il por *Vogue* 177:128 Je '87
Bombay Company
The big money in Raffles tables. E. F. Cone. il *Forbes* 140:68-9+ D 28 '87
Bombay Palace Restaurants Inc.
Adding spice to the food chain. G. G. Marcial. *Bus Week* p113 My 4 '87
"Inner patience". P. Gupte. por *Forbes* 139:74-5 Ja 26 '87
Bombeck, Erma
Christmas at my house [excerpt from Family] il por *Ladies Home J* 104:160-1+ D '87
Family: the ties that bind . . . and gag! [excerpt] il *Redbook* 169:186-8+ S '87
The high cost of raising a daughter. por *Teen* 31:64 D '87
Bomber jackets *See* Jackets
Bombers (Airplanes) *See* Airplanes, Military
Bombing, Aerial
See also
Afghanistan—Russian invasion, 1979- —Aerial operations
World War, 1939-1945—Aerial operations
Was 1945 a break in history? M. S. Sherry. bibl f il *Bull At Sci* 43:12-15 Jl/Ag '87
Bombings, Terrorist *See* Terrorism
Bombs
See also
Atomic bombs
Bon Jovi, Jon
about
Jon Bon Jovi: no longer livin' on a prayer. M. L. Baer. por *Teen* 31:75 S '87
The kids are all right. S. Orlean. il por *Roll Stone* p34-5+ My 21 '87
Bon Jovi (Musical group)
Bon Jovi hits the big time. D. Goldman. il *Sch Update* 120:28 S 4 '87
The kids are all right. S. Orlean. il por *Roll Stone* p34-5+ My 21 '87
Rock wrap up. il por *Teen* 31:58 Mr '87
Bonaparte, Elizabeth Patterson, 1785-1879
about
The phantom amendment & the Duchess of Baltimore. W. H. Earle. il por *Am Hist Illus* 22:32-9 N '87
Bonaparte, Jérôme, 1784-1860
about
The phantom amendment & the Duchess of Baltimore. W. H. Earle. il pors *Am Hist Illus* 22:32-9 N '87
Bonaparte, Napoleon *See* Napoleon I, Emperor of the French, 1769-1821
Bonatti, Enrico
The rifting of continents. bibl (p128) il maps *Sci Am* 256:96-103 Mr '87
Bonavoglia, Angela
The ordeal of Pamela Rae Stewart. il pors *Ms* 16:92-5+ Jl/Ag '87
Bond, Alan
about
An artful dodger? E. C. Baig. il por *Fortune* 116:166 D 21 '87
Is Carling Black Label worth a trip from Australia? M. D. Oneal. il por *Bus Week* p33-4 S 21 '87
The raiders Down Under may be down and out. C. Debes. il por *Bus Week* p55 N 9 '87
Two Australian beer barons take their brawl abroad. C. Debes and P. Finch. il pors *Bus Week* p138+ O 19 '87
Bond, Alice
about
Alice Bond, Carmen Butler meet before magistrate to argue battery charge. il por *Jet* 72:6 My 11 '87
Andrew Young's ill-timed call. il por *Time* 129:34 My 25 '87
Jewelry valued at $25,000 is stolen from Alice Bond. por *Jet* 72:36 Ag 10 '87
Bond, Jean Faulkner
That special teacher. il *South Living* 22:128 F '87
Bond, Julian
about
Alice Bond, Carmen Butler meet before magistrate to argue battery charge. il por *Jet* 72:6 My 11 '87
Atlanta grand jury not questioning Julian Bond in city's drug scandal. *Jet* 72:4 Je 15 '87
Atlanta mayor testifies in drug probe; says his family shaken by slurs. il pors *Jet* 72:4 Je 1 '87
Atlanta mayor Young to testify before grand jury in city's drug scandal. por *Jet* 72:4 My 25 '87

Bond, Julian—about—*cont.*

Atlanta's coke controversy. il por *Newsweek* 109:36 Ap 27 '87

Bond criticizes media on personal life prying. por *Jet* 72:22 Jl 6 '87

Georgia woman tied to Julian Bond in drug probe gets 22-year sentence. por *Jet* 72:52 S 21 '87

Julian Bond denies using cocaine and lashes media; Mayor Young implicated. pors *Jet* 72:8 My 4 '87

Julian Bond hired to promote Paul Simon tour. il por *Jet* 72:55 Je 1 '87

Julian Bond's wife accuses him of using drugs daily; she later recants story. il por *Jet* 72:54 Ap 27 '87

A scandal scars Atlanta. T. E. Johnson. il pors *Newsweek* 109:28 Je 1 '87

Young clear in drug probe, fellow Democrats cheer; ponders bid for governor. il pors *Jet* 72:24 Jl 6 '87

Bond, James (Fictional character) *See* James Bond (Fictional character)

Bond funds *See* Investment trusts

Bond Group

Is Carling Black Label worth a trip from Australia? [A. Bond's bid for G. Heileman Brewing] M. D. Oneal. il por *Bus Week* p33-4 S 21 '87

Bond index funds *See* Index funds

Bond market *See* Bonds

Bonderoff, Jason

Sally Field, superstar [excerpt] il pors *McCalls* 115:96-8+ O '87

Bondholders

A bondholder's revenge [investor S. Licht] M. Schifrin. il por *Forbes* 140:111 Ag 24 '87

Bonding, Parental-infant *See* Parent-child relationship

Bonding (Dentistry) *See* Dentistry

Bonds

See also

Banks and banking—Securities handling
Bondholders
Brokers
Convertible bonds
Eurobond market
Junk bonds
Mortgage bonds and notes
Municipal bonds
Zero coupon bonds

All eyes are again on bonds. J. Edgerton. il *Money* 16:105-6+ D '87

Capital markets. B. Weberman. See issues of Forbes

The chaotic world of bonds. D. Pauly. il *Newsweek* 110:36 Jl 6 '87

Gentlemen—and women—no longer prefer bonds [with interview with J. Applegate] J. Rachlin. il *U S News World Rep* 102:54-6 My 4 '87

The long and short of it? Take the short. D. Zigas. il *Bus Week* p162-3 D 28 '87-Ja 4 '88

Ways to jump aboard the bond wagon. J. P. Newport, Jr. il *Fortune* 116:210 N 23 '87

Default

Cuba sí, WPPSS no. M. Schifrin. il *Forbes* 140:42+ N 2 '87

Duration

Is that bond a good buy? Here's how the pros decide. J. M. Laderman. il *Bus Week* p82 Jl 27 '87

Prices

A $100-billion bath in bonds. K. Labich. il *Fortune* 115:34-5 My 25 '87

After the shocks of April, the bond market is mellowing out. C. Farrell. il *Bus Week* p68+ Jl 6 '87

April showers. B. Weberman. il *Forbes* 139:255 My 18 '87

Are bonds calling a turn? J. Crudele. il *N Y* 20:16+ My 11 '87

Bargains in battered bonds. J. J. Curran. il *Fortune* 115:121-2 My 25 '87

The bears may be taking the wrong trail. J. M. Laderman. il *Bus Week* p100-1+ O 19 '87

The bright side of the crash [surge in bonds] il *Fortune* 116:8 N 23 '87

The bust in bonds. D. P. Wiener. il *U S News World Rep* 103:50 S 21 '87

Half the picture [bond market predictions] M. Hulbert. il *Forbes* 140:140 D 28 '87

How the bond market is forcing the Fed's hand. S. Bartlett. il *Bus Week* p42 My 11 '87

The market wants the dollar to fall. Let it happen. A. S. Blinder. por *Bus Week* p18 O 19 '87

Swap a bond, save a buck. L. Wiener. il *U S News World Rep* 103:79 O 5 '87

Swapping bonds: the best revenge for paper losses. D. Zigas. *Bus Week* p164 Je 22 '87

What to do when bond funds fall. J. M. Laderman. il *Bus Week* p140-1 My 4 '87

Redemption

Dirty tricks [electric utility bonds and call protection] B. Weberman. il *Forbes* 139:173 My 4 '87

Zero coupon bombs. B. Weberman. il *Forbes* 139:103 Ja 26 '87

Refunding

Bad calls [use of preferred stock] B. Weberman. il *Forbes* 140:129 Ag 24 '87

Yields

Another way of looking at today's battered bond market. C. Farrell. il *Bus Week* p101 O 19 '87

Bond mutual funds. il *Consum Rep* 52:280-90 D '87

Bonds away! Getting off the canvas after the market's shocking KO [bond funds] B. Hager and others. il *Money* 16:26-7 Je '87

Bonds look good. B. Weberman. il *Forbes* 139:167 Mr 9 '87

Chasing yield [closed-end bond funds] D. Henry. il *Forbes* 139:262 Je 15 '87

Double damned. K. L. Fisher. il *Forbes* 140:238 O 5 '87

Fixed-income mutual funds. il *Consum Rep* 52:570-9 S '87

The honor system. B. Weberman. il *Forbes* 140:255 D 14 '87

How risky are bonds? M. Kuntz and D. Pardee. il *Forbes* 139:168 Mr 23 '87

Mutual fund ads: only the hype is '100% guaranteed!' [bond funds] T. Segal. *Bus Week* p92 Ag 24 '87

No place to hide [hyping of bond fund yields] J. B. Quinn. il *Newsweek* 109:62 My 11 '87

Patience, sir [closed-end bond funds] B. Weberman. il *Forbes* 140:235 N 2 '87

Placing your bets in '87. J. B. Quinn. il *Newsweek* 109:44 Ja 5 '87

Time to hang tough in bonds. J. J. Curran. il *Fortune* 116 Sp Issue:20 Fall '87

What to do about the bond bust: timely answers to help mutual fund investors rethink their strategies. il *Money* 16:68-9 Je '87

Bonds, Chemical *See* Chemical bonds

Bonds, Church *See* Church securities

Bonds, Government

See also

Bonds, Housing authority
Municipal bonds
Treasury bills and notes

Bonds away at the Bank Board [new issues from The Financing Corp.] V. Cahan. *Bus Week* p102 O 5 '87

Investing in government savings bonds. T. Tilling. *Parents* 62:54 Ap '87

Playing politics [FSLIC bailout bonds] B. Weberman. il *Forbes* 140:209 S 21 '87

International aspects

A bond voyage to high yields [foreign bond mutual funds] G. Anrig, Jr. il *Money* 16:129-30+ My '87

Playing for a fall [investment outlook in light of falling dollar] E. A. Finn, Jr. il *Forbes* 139:98-101 F 23 '87

Great Britain

New glitter for sterling. G. Slutsker. il *Forbes* 139:37 Je 1 '87

Indonesia

The Assad connection [Eurobond frauds masterminded by H. Zubaidi] R. Morais. il *Forbes* 139:32-3 Je 15 '87

Japan

Japan writes a new definition of zaitech: 'investor beware' [problems of Tateho Chemical Industries] B. Buell. *Bus Week* p45 S 21 '87

United States

See Bonds, Government

Bonds, Housing *See* Mortgage bonds and notes

Bonds, Housing authority

Three notches down [Tarrant County Housing bonds] B. Weberman. il *Forbes* 140:171 Jl 27 '87

Bonds, Industrial development

See also

Massachusetts. Industrial Finance Agency

A new bond for small business [Citytrust Capital Market industrial development bonds] R. W. King. *Bus Week* p109 Je 1 '87

The safe Whoopses [projects 1, 2 and 3] B. Weberman. il *Forbes* 139:297 Ja 12 '87

When tax reform clobbers small business [interest rates may soar on industrial development bond loans] L. Helm. il *Bus Week* p41 My 4 '87

Bonds, Industrial development—*cont.*
Wonders never cease [comeback in bonds of Washington Public Power Supply System] B. Weberman. il *Forbes* 140:213 O 19 '87

Default
The jury's still out on 'WHOOPS'—way out [Washington Public Power Supply System] H. Gleckman. il *Bus Week* p168 N 2 '87
WHOOPS haunts the Street [SEC investigation] C. Farrell. *Bus Week* p122 Mr 16 '87

Rating
How E. F. Hutton is trying to clean its slate [industrial revenue bond imbroglio] G. Weiss. il *Bus Week* p79 Ja 26 '87

Bonds, Industrial revenue *See* Bonds, Industrial development
Bonds, Mortgage *See* Mortgage bonds and notes
Bonds, Revenue
See also
Bonds, Industrial development
Bondurant, Bob, 1933-
about
Bondurant Thunderbird 5.0. il *por Road Track* 39:62-4 O '87
Bondurant (Bob) School of High Performance Driving *See* Automobile driving—Study and teaching
Bone, Robert W.
Sheer beauty. il *Travel Holiday* 167:13-17 Mr '87
Bone
See also
Fractures
Heel bone
Ligaments
Maxilla & Mandible (Firm)
Skeleton
Skull
Swimming builds stronger bones [study by Eric S. Orwoll] il *Prevention* 39:6 S '87
Well-rounded exercise may build more bone [work of Jon E. Block] il *Prevention* 39:12 Ag '87

Diseases
See also
Osteomyelitis
Osteoporosis
Avascular necrosis: occurrence in diving Cretaceous mosasaurs. B. Rothschild and L. D. Martin. bibl f il *Science* 236:75-7 Ap 3 '87
Bone implements and weapons
The Ginsberg experiment [Clovis and pre-Clovis artifacts] D. J. Stanford. il *Nat Hist* 96:10+ S '87
New dates from old bones [Old Crow site in Yukon Territory] W. N. Irving. map *Nat Hist* 96:8+ F '87
Bone marrow *See* Marrow
Bone resorption *See* Absorption (Physiology)
Boneau, Chris
The press release. il *Theatre Crafts* 21:92+ N '87
Bonefish fishing
Big success from little signs [alertness when fishing] B. Stearns. il *Field Stream* 92:115-16 My '87
Bonelli, Staci
about
Girl, 12, rescued from freezing Philly sand pit. il *por Jet* 71:18 Mr 23 '87
Boner, Bill
about
The battle of Nashville. T. E. Johnson. il *por Newsweek* 110:38 S 21 '87
Bones, Fossil *See* Paleontology
Bonesteel, Michael
Medium cool: new Chicago abstraction. il *Art Am* 75:138-47 D '87
Bonestell, Chesley
about
Lunar fantasies. R. Miller and F. C. Durant. il *Omni* 9:50-5 F '87
Bonet, Lisa
about
Aruba! [cover story] il *pors Essence* 17:52-9 Ap '87
Bill Cosby: 'I did not read the script . . . Lisa made the decision'. *pors Jet* 71:62 Mr 23 '87
Film group to reconsider Bonet's 'Angel heart' film. il *por Jet* 71:16 Mr 2 '87
Lisa Bonet. il *pors Harpers Bazaar* 120:30, 340-3 S '87
Lisa Bonet: a very private person. E. Miller. il *pors Seventeen* 46:79-80+ Ap '87
Lisa Bonet debuts in 'Angel heart' film of sex and violence. C. Waldron. il *pors Jet* 71:60-1 Mr 23 '87
Lisa Bonet finds new success in 'A different world' [cover story] il *pors Jet* 73:54-5 O 26 '87

Lisa Bonet marries musician Lenny "Romeo" Kravitz, son of 'The Jeffersons' TV star. il *pors Jet* 73:6 D 7 '87
Lisa Bonet: on her own. E. Sherman. il *pors Ladies Home J* 104:60+ N '87
Lisa Bonet: the growing pains of a rising star [cover story] L. Norment. il *pors Ebony* 43:150+ D '87
Lisa Bonet's double image. B. Barol. il *pors Newsweek* 109:49 Mr 23 '87
Why Lisa Bonet of 'Cosby' fame made X-rated film. il *pors Jet* 71:60-1 Mr 16 '87
Bonet, Pilar
Soviet art for export. *World Press Rev* 34:60 D '87
Bongaarts, John, 1945-
(jt. auth) *See* Greenhalgh, Susan, and Bongaarts, John, 1945-
Bongartz, Roy
A guide to the guides. il *Publ Wkly* 231:46-8+ F 13 '87
The magical game. il *Americana* 15:24-6+ S/O '87
South End Press: the long march continues. il *Publ Wkly* 232:17+ Jl 17 '87
Bongo, Omar
Visit of Gabon president [remarks, July 31, 1987] il *por Dep State Bull* 87:14-15 O '87
Visit to the United States, 1987
Reagan, Gabon's Bongo meet on African issues. il *por Jet* 72:4 Ag 17 '87
Visit of Gabon president [remarks, July 31, 1987] R. Reagan; O. Bongo. il *por Dep State Bull* 87:14-15 O '87
Bonino, Susan B.
How do you grow your dusty millers? As annuals, or perennials? il *Flower Gard* 31:81-2 F/Mr '87
Bonkovsky, Frederick O.
West Germany chooses a chancellor. il *Commonweal* 114:14-16 Ja 16 '87
Bonn (Germany)

Music
See also
Opera—Germany (West)
Bonne Bell Inc.
Make up, stand up and cheer [Team Colors makeup kits] il *Sports Illus* 67:16 S 21 '87
Bonnell, Kimberly
Love and hate on one leg. il *por Glamour* 85:73-4 O '87
Bonner, Elena
about
Glasnost: 'There's no turning back' [interview] M. B. Zuckerman. il *pors U S News World Rep* 102:31 Ap 20 '87
A hard bargain [special section] il *pors Newsweek* 109:12-23 Ja 5 '87
Bonner, Raymond
about
Manila fudge. J. M. Fallows. *Wash Mon* 19:53-6 S '87
Bonner, T. I., and others
Identification of a family of muscarinic acetylcholine receptor genes. bibl f il *Science* 237:527-32 Jl 31 '87
Bonneville land speed records *See* Land speed records
Bonneville Media Communications
Bonneville: a new player aims high. T. Spain. il *Publ Wkly* 232:53-4 N 13 '87
Bonnot, Daniel
about
A well-traveled bistro brings an Eiffel-utin air to New Orleans. J. Greene. il *pors People Wkly* 28:83-4 O 26 '87
Bonny Doon Vineyard
Identified flying object [Cigare Volant wine] F. J. Prial. il *por N Y Times Mag* p30 Ja 4 '87
Bono
about
Band on the run [cover story] J. Cocks. il *pors Time* 129:72-7 Ap 27 '87
Bono. il *por People Wkly* 28:66-7 D 28 '87-Ja 4 '88
Bono [cover story; interview] D. Breskin. il *pors Roll Stone* p42-5+ O 8 '87
Bono [interview] D. Breskin. *por Roll Stone* p282-4 N 5-D 10 '87
On the road with U2. S. Pond. il *por Roll Stone* p15-16+ My 21 '87
Truths and consequences [cover story] A. DeCurtis. il *pors Roll Stone* p26-8+ My 7 '87
U2: finding what they're looking for. il *por Teen* 31:86 S '87
Bonomi, Patricia U.
about
Another look at colonial religion. M. E. Marty. *Christ Century* 104:314-15 Ap 1 '87

Bonsai
Bedroom view is his bonsai garden. il *Sunset* 178:102+ Mr '87
Bonta, David
Planting with nature. il *Rodale's Org Gard* 34:65-6 F '87
Bonta, Marcia
A jungle haven in Peru. il *Américas* 39:8-13 Ja/F '87
Bonus system
Bonuses for steelworkers? [National Intergroup] S. W. Angrist. il por *Forbes* 139 Ann Directory:126 Ap 27 '87
GM: the bonus days are over [scrapping bonuses in favor of stock option plan] J. Schwartz. il *Newsweek* 109:53 Ap 27 '87
Radical way to save more [big year-end bonus; views of F. Thomas Juster] *USA Today (Periodical)* 116:10 Jl '87
'Thanks for the bonus, but where's my raise?'. B. Brophy and M. Walsh. il *U S News World Rep* 103:43-4 Jl 20 '87
Boodro, Michael
Gemütlich grandeur. il por *House Gard* 159:20+ F '87
Booher, Dianna Daniels
Ten ways to cut paperwork and do your job better [excerpt from Cutting paperwork in the corporate culture] *Work Woman* 12:136-7 S '87
Book advertising *See* Books—Advertising
Book awards *See* Literary prizes
Book binding *See* Bookbinding
Book blurbs *See* Books—Advertising
Book buying
Book buying up among younger readers [Gallup survey] L. A. Wood. il *Publ Wkly* 232:64 S 11 '87
Book censorship *See* Censorship
Book clubs
See also
Doubleday Book & Music Clubs
Limited Editions Club
Book collecting *See* Books—Collectors and collecting
Book contracts *See* Authors and publishers
Book covers
Cover art: heating up. J. P. Frank. il *Publ Wkly* 232:70-1 O 2 '87
Cross-cultural covers [British and American cover design] P. Chevannes and L. Garrard. il *Publ Wkly* 232:37-40 N 27 '87
Defeating cover warp. *Publ Wkly* 232:43-4 S 4 '87
Holograms for books—a hit and a miss. il *Publ Wkly* 231:58-60 Je 5 '87
The new book jackets. J. P. Frank. il *Publ Wkly* 231:46+ Ap 3 '87
Tale of a cover: casebound to paperback [Perfume by Patrick Suskind] il *Publ Wkly* 232:44 Jl 3 '87
A unique jacket snows on 'Red snow' [novel by Edward Topol] il *Publ Wkly* 232:31-2 Ag 21 '87
The YA cover story. D. Evans. il *Publ Wkly* 232:112-15 Jl 24 '87
Book critics and criticism *See* Book reviews and reviewing
Book design
See also
Book covers
Illustration
Book design & manufacturing. J. P. Frank. See first issue of every month of Publishers Weekly
Claire Van Vliet's Janus Press. W. T. Taylor. il por *Am Craft* 47:52-9+ F/Mr '87
Awards
Juvenile books win judges' plaudits in PIA competition [Printing Industries Association Graphic Arts Awards Competition] il *Publ Wkly* 231:51-2 Ap 3 '87
Exhibitions
See Book exhibits
Book discussion groups
Club Lit: reading groups of the rich and famous [New York City] E. Hopkins. il *N Y* 20:32-5 Jl 20 '87
Book distributors *See* Book wholesalers and distributors
Book exhibits
See also
Book fairs
1987 regional trade show schedule. il *Publ Wkly* 232:30-2 Jl 17 '87
University press book quality admired, but juror Zapf sees tendency to 'overdo' [AAUP Book Show] C. B. Grannis. il *Publ Wkly* 232:409-10 Ag 7 '87
Book fairs
Americans in Frankfurt: mixed reviews. il *Publ Wkly* 232:24-5 O 30 '87
Bologna '87 [Children's Book Fair; special section] il *Publ Wkly* 231:19-20+ Mr 20 '87

Books come alive at Miami International Book Fair. A. Symons. il *Publ Wkly* 232:52-3 D 25 '87
Business, but not as usual: first Small Press Expo. M. Yen. *Publ Wkly* 231:12 Mr 20 '87
A bustling Bologna [Children's Book Fair] D. E. Roback. il *Publ Wkly* 231:20-4 My 8 '87
Frankfurt '87. H. R. Lottman. *Publ Wkly* 232:12-13 O 23 '87
Frankfurt '87: fair guide for rights buyers & sellers. il *Publ Wkly* 232:77-121 S 18 '87
Frankfurt '87: riding the merger wave. H. R. Lottman. il *Publ Wkly* 232:19-23 O 30 '87
French April fair moves to bigger venue, offers British titles [Salon du Livre] H. R. Lottman. *Publ Wkly* 232:16 D 18 '87
International book fairs 1988. *Publ Wkly* 232:133 S 18 '87
International front [Salón Internacional del Libro] H. R. Lottman. *Publ Wkly* 232:31 N 6 '87
Jerusalem's fair. *Publ Wkly* 231:30-1 F 20 '87
London's new look [London Book Fair] V. Menkes. il *Publ Wkly* 231:30-2 My 8 '87
Managua's first book fair. H. Rohmer. il *Publ Wkly* 232:19-21 S 4 '87
Moscow '87: the *glasnost* fair [special section] il *Publ Wkly* 232:21-3+ O 16 '87
The Moscow Book Fair: *glasnost* has its limits. J. Laber. il *N Y Times Book Rev* 92:13-14 O 11 '87
The new Jerusalem [Jerusalem Book Fair] H. R. Lottman. il *Publ Wkly* 231:25-9 My 8 '87
Paris's book fair turns international [Salon du Livre] H. R. Lottman. il *Publ Wkly* 231:25 Ap 24 '87
Rio's book fair [Bienal Internacional do Livro] H. R. Lottman. il *Publ Wkly* 232:18-20 O 23 '87
Small presses gather for the 12th—and last—New York Book Fair. M. Yen. il *Publ Wkly* 231:21 My 1 '87
The small time [Small Press Expo '87] S. Klawans. *Nation* 244:407-9 Mr 28 '87
The way we were [New York Book Fair] S. O. Zavrian. por *Publ Wkly* 231:41 Ap 24 '87
Why I went to Jerusalem [Jerusalem International Book Fair] J. F. Glusman. por *Publ Wkly* 231:61 My 29 '87
Book Gallery (Charlottesville, Va.: Bookstore) *See* Booksellers and bookselling—Virginia
Book illustration *See* Illustration
Book indexing programs *See* Computers—Indexing use—Programming
Book industries
See also
Book Industry Study Group
Book wholesalers and distributors
Bookbinding
Books—Marketing
Books—Prices
Books by Wire (Firm)
Booksellers and bookselling
Computers—Book industries use
Crane Duplicating Service Inc.
Interstate Book Manufacturers Inc.
Literary agencies and agents
Printing industry
Publishers and publishing
AAP will admit affiliate members to boost income. H. Fields. *Publ Wkly* 232:10 N 27 '87
Book design & manufacturing. J. P. Frank. See first issue of every month of Publishers Weekly
Doing business with printers: the unwritten rules [Bookbinders Guild panel] il *Publ Wkly* 231:78-9 Mr 6 '87
Making reader-friendly books [fine bookmaking] K. Fitz-Gerald. il *Ms* 15:34 Je '87
Smoothing the buyer-vendor relationship [Bookbinders Guild panel] il *Publ Wkly* 231:73-5 F 6 '87
U.S. book manufacturing: the new dynamics [special section] J. P. Frank. il *Publ Wkly* 232:S1+ D 18 '87
Acquisitions and mergers
Krueger buys Nelson's Interstate Book Mfrs. *Publ Wkly* 231:54 Je 19 '87
International aspects
Krueger signs intent to buy 50% of Koon Wah. *Publ Wkly* 232:44 Jl 3 '87
Quebecor acquires Semline; names John Collins president. *Publ Wkly* 231:68 Ja 9 '87
Conferences
Book manufacturing: a changing world [Publishers weekly seminar] J. P. Frank. il *Publ Wkly* 231:47-50+ Je 19 '87

Book industries—Conferences—*cont.*

New manufacturing ideas—how to keep more jobs at home [Publishers weekly seminar] J. P. Frank. il *Publ Wkly* 232:39-41 Jl 3 '87

Publishers weekly to sponsor first ever book manufacturing seminar. *Publ Wkly* 231:13 Mr 13 '87

International aspects

Jeremiad on Bible manufacture in the United States [Thomas Nelson turning to foreign manufacturing] W. Griffin. *Publ Wkly* 232:24 Ag 21 '87

Laws and regulations

See also

Copyright

Canada

Canada lifts tariff on books; publishing industry rejoices. B. Slopen. *Publ Wkly* 231:29 Mr 6 '87

Colombia

See also

Carvajal SA

United States

See Book industries

Book Industry Study Group

BISG assays publishing's international context. D. Maryles and E. Mangin. il *Publ Wkly* 232:103-5 Jl 24 '87

Book jackets *See* Book covers

Book manufacturing industry *See* Book industries

Book marks *See* Bookmarks

Book match covers *See* Matchcovers

Book orders, Library *See* Libraries—Acquisitions

Book prices *See* Books—Prices

Book prizes *See* Literary prizes

Book promotion *See* Books—Advertising

Book rarities *See* Rare books

Book restoration *See* Books—Conservation and restoration

Book reviews and reviewing

See also

Five owls (Periodical)

Los Angeles times book review

New York review of books

Breaking into print with book reviews. J. Yanofsky. *Writer* 100:28-9 Ja '87

The great L.A. poetry battle [brouhaha over poetry policy of the Los Angeles times book review] L. See. *Publ Wkly* 231:52 My 29 '87

In defense of book critics. J. Bass. por *Publ Wkly* 231:48 My 8 '87

Keep your compassion, give me your madness. A. Broyard. il *N Y Times Book Rev* 92:12 Je 21 '87

'Philadephia inquirer' changes format, editor of book coverage. *Publ Wkly* 232:13 D 18 '87

The 'San Francisco chronicle' focuses on children's books. M. Colin. il *Publ Wkly* 231:39-40 My 29 '87

Slings and arrows. J. G. Dunne. *Esquire* 107:125-6 F '87

So many books so little space: what makes a book review editor pick up a book? H. Eisenberg. il *Publ Wkly* 231:25-30 Ap 10 '87

Tuning out the inner critic [remarks, May 1987] J. Updike. *N Y Times Book Rev* 92:29 Je 21 '87

Who reads book reviews anyway? A. M. Greeley. por *Publ Wkly* 231:78 Ap 10 '87

Book shelves *See* Bookcases

Book shows *See* Book exhibits

Book stands

Look it up [oak dictionary stand] il *Pop Mech* 164:162+ F '87

Book thefts

See also

Booksellers and bookselling—Security measures

Book titles *See* Titles of books, stories, etc.

Book wholesalers and distributors

See also

Beyda & Associates Inc.

Books by Wire (Firm)

Ingram Book Company

Mendenhall Enterprises

Quality Books Inc.

Riverside Book and Bible House Inc.

Warner Publishers Services, Inc.

A holiday guide to wholesaler services. *Publ Wkly* 232:36 N 20 '87

Bookbinding

Textbook 'spec' changes temporary but significant. J. P. Frank. il *Publ Wkly* 232:29-30 Ag 21 '87

Equipment

Binderies are going high-tech. il *Publ Wkly* 231:64+ Ja 9 '87

Bookcases

Book keeper [solid oak barrister's bookcase with lift-up, slide-back doors] N. Barrett, Jr. il *Pop Mech* 164:74-8 Ja '87

Built-in bookcases with hidden storage. R. McQuilkin. il *Workbench* 43:74-7 N/D '87

Her bookcase has some hidden storage. il *Sunset* 178:130 Mr '87

Little space, lots of books. il *South Living* 22:86 Ag '87

Stacking bookcases. il *Workbench* 43:90-1 Ja/F '87

Storage and work space built of interlocking custom-milled maple. il *Sunset* 179:107 Ag '87

Bookends and bookracks

See also

Book stands

Booker, Simeon

Black man returns home after 47 years in Russia. il pors *Ebony* 42:67+ Je '87

Ticker tape U.S.A. See issues of Jet

Bookland EAN system

The progress of Bookland EAN. G. Goldberg and J. Goldberg. il *Publ Wkly* 232:51-5 O 16 '87

Booklets *See* Pamphlets

Bookmarks

Collectors and collecting

Stevengraph bookmarkers. K. M. McClinton. il *Antiques Collect Hobbies* 91:51-4 Ja '87

Books

See also

Best sellers

Manuscripts

Paperback books

Picture books

Pop-up books

Printing

Rare books

Royalties

Talking books

Textbooks

University of Iowa. Iowa Center for the Book

Polonius and the book loan [suggestions on lending and borrowing books] A. Landi. por *Publ Wkly* 231:90 F 6 '87

Advertising

Anatomy of a national tour [author tours] S. A. Berk. il *Publ Wkly* 232:46-8 O 16 '87

The best kind of advertising [word of mouth makes M. S. Peck's The road less traveled into best seller] J. A. Trachtenberg. il por *Forbes* 139:91-2 Ap 20 '87

Bookselling & merchandising. A. Symons and S. Bolle. See issues of Publishers Weekly

The breakfast circuit: rising in style [book and author breakfasts at ABA convention] il *Publ Wkly* 231:74-5 Je 19 '87

Carrying the torch for children's books in California [advertising efforts of regional booksellers associations] L. See. il *Publ Wkly* 231:104 F 27 '87

Collins autobio inspires sound track. S. Bolle. *Publ Wkly* 232:50 O 16 '87

Drive in U.K. to push children's books. J. Taylor. *Publ Wkly* 231:38 Mr 20 '87

The great flap copy letdown. W. P. Kinsella. por *Publ Wkly* 231:54 Ap 3 '87

Ingram launches retail print ad campaign [project with Gannett newspapers] A. Symons. *Publ Wkly* 232:35 Jl 10 '87

Lights! Camera! Action! [promotability of authors] J. Harayda. por *Publ Wkly* 231:78 Ja 16 '87

Literary agents challenge publicity at PPA meeting. A. Symons. il *Publ Wkly* 232:36 D 18 '87

New solutions to old problems [use of desktop publishing] B. Slone. il *Publ Wkly* 232:36 N 13 '87

On tour with Rock Hudson [promoting Rock Hudson, his story] S. Davidson. il *N Y Times Mag* p54+ My 3 '87

The one-minute publicist. L. Zigman. por *Publ Wkly* 232:57 S 25 '87

A publicist's-eye view of the Chicago market. T. Unsworth. *Publ Wkly* 232:38 D 11 '87

Radio reviews to help the bookseller [Tom Carney, manager of Hatch's #7 bookstore in Denver, previews new titles on radio] B. List. il *Publ Wkly* 231:47 Ja 16 '87

Record turnout for children's book breakfast [book and author breakfast at ABA convention] K. O. Fakih. il *Publ Wkly* 231:50 Je 26 '87

'So you want your author on the radio . . . ' [views of an interviewer] B. Thompson. il por *Publ Wkly* 232:42 O 30 '87

Touch it, feel it, reach out and grab it [J. Lyons handling the ad campaign for his book Guts] L. Fleischer. *Publ Wkly* 232:46 Jl 3 '87

Books—Advertising—*cont.*

Turning the tables on tours. C. Kuppig. por *Publ Wkly* 231:90 F 13 '87

Wedding fair at Bookworks [Albuquerque retailers hold promotion featuring author M. Stewart] B. List. il *Publ Wkly* 232:45-6 Ag 21 '87

What's wrong with co-op and three ways to make it better [bookseller and publisher cooperative advertising] W. Cassell. *Publ Wkly* 232:62+ O 2 '87

Where art and commerce coexist [public readings by authors] J. Eidus. por *Publ Wkly* 232:43 D 18 '87

Will publishers resist Dalton's costly new television ads? A. Symons. *Publ Wkly* 231:25 Je 12 '87

Anecdotes, facetiae, satire, etc.

A writer's 'TV block'. R. Baker. il *N Y Times Mag* p12 Ja 11 '87

Care
See Books—Conservation and restoration

Censorship
See Censorship

Collectors and collecting
See also
Libraries, Private
Manuscripts—Collectors and collecting
Rare books

Confessions of a bibliophile. J. Griswold. *Writer* 100:5-6 My '87

Gin, sin, and floozies [paperbacks] N. Karlen. il *Esquire* 108:46 S '87

"The Samantha stories". D. E. Matter and R. M. Matter. il *Antiques Collect Hobbies* 91:48-50 Ja '87

Conservation and restoration
Brittle books and journals. P. H. Abelson. *Science* 238:595 O 30 '87

Mass deacidification beckons, perhaps. E. Stange. il *N Y Times Book Rev* 92:3 Mr 29 '87

Millions of books are turning to dust—can they be saved? E. Stange. il *N Y Times Book Rev* 92:3+ Mr 29 '87

Dedications
See Dedications (in books)

Design
See Book design

Exhibitions
See Book exhibits

Export-import trade
AAP protests to U.S. Customs Service over 'user fee' on imported books. H. Fields. *Publ Wkly* 231:87 F 27 '87

AAUP opposes embargo on sales of books to South Africa. C. Reid. *Publ Wkly* 232:12 D 11 '87

Canada lifts tariff on books; publishing industry rejoices. B. Slopen. *Publ Wkly* 231:29 Mr 6 '87

Quebec's French connection. J. Poulin. il *Publ Wkly* 232:24 N 13 '87

Trade bill addresses 'dumping' and Canada's bar to investment. H. Fields. *Publ Wkly* 232:19 Ag 14 '87

U.S. exports, imports, UNESCO reports: 1986 figures. C. B. Grannis. il *Publ Wkly* 232:123-5 S 18 '87

Why deny the children? [effects of American publishers' boycott of South Africa] G. Miklowitz. por *Publ Wkly* 232:66 O 9 '87

First editions
See Rare books

Illustration
See Illustration

Manufacture
See Book industries

Marketing
See also
Book wholesalers and distributors
Bookland EAN system
Booksellers and bookselling
Catalogs, Publishers'
Paperback books—Marketing

Book coupon launch elicits low consumer response. A. Symons. *Publ Wkly* 231:68+ F 6 '87

Bookselling & merchandising. A. Symons and S. Bolle. See issues of Publishers Weekly

The changing foreign rights market [children's books] L. E. Owen. il *Publ Wkly* 231:28-30+ Mr 20 '87

Direct marketing success stories [publishers] L. Shanley. il *Publ Wkly* 232:48-50 N 13 '87

A double perspective: publishers & authors. L. Felder. il *Publ Wkly* 232:23-4 Ag 28 '87

Frankfurt '87: fair guide for rights buyers & sellers. il *Publ Wkly* 232:77-121 S 18 '87

Legally bound [publishers in France dismayed by red tape involved in selling rights to Americans] H. R. Lottman. *Publ Wkly* 231:34 Je 12 '87

Marketing. A. Symons. See occasional issues of Publishers Weekly beginning October 16, 1987

Marketing on two fronts [children's literature] A. Meeker. *Publ Wkly* 232:44-7 N 27 '87

Reaching the top markets. A. Symons. *Publ Wkly* 232:45 O 16 '87

Yuppie lit: publicize or perish. R. Z. Sheppard. il *Time* 130:77-9 O 19 '87

Preservation
See Books—Conservation and restoration

Prices
Discounting: history of a strategy. S. Bolle. *Publ Wkly* 231:56-7 Ja 9 '87

Title output level, prices stabilized. C. B. Grannis. il *Publ Wkly* 231:16-19 Mr 13 '87

Turning off youthful readers [high prices, shoddy production, and poor editorial quality of books] C. R. Larson. por *Publ Wkly* 232:49 N 20 '87

U.S. book title output and average prices, final 1986 figures. C. B. Grannis. il *Publ Wkly* 232:45+ O 2 '87

Warehouse clubs: an expanding market. J. Crichton. il *Publ Wkly* 231:56-8+ F 13 '87

Statistics
See Publishers and publishing—Statistics

Books, Filmed *See* Motion picture adaptations

Books, Televised *See* Television adaptations

Books & Books (Coral Gables, Fla.: Bookstore) *See* Booksellers and bookselling—Florida

Books & Co. (Dayton, Ohio: Bookstore) *See* Booksellers and bookselling—Ohio

Books and reading
See also
Authors—Reading
Biography
Book buying
Book reviews and reviewing
Books as gifts
Children's reading
Detective and mystery stories
Executives—Reading
Fiction
Libraries
Libraries, Private
Literary clubs and societies
Literature
Lost books
Marginalia
Presidential candidates—Reading
Reading aloud
Religious literature
Television and reading
Women—Reading
Year of the Reader, 1987
Young adults' reading

About books. A. Broyard. See occasional issues of The New York Times Book Review beginning November 11, 1984

Amnesia in litteris. P. Süskind. il *Harpers* 274:71-3 Mr '87

The civilized barbarian reader. S. Bellow. il *N Y Times Book Rev* 92:1+ Mr 8 '87

Confessions of a bibliophile. J. Griswold. *Writer* 100:5-6 My '87

The future of the printed word [symposium] il *USA Today (Periodical)* 115:88-90 Mr '87

The Gallup survey. L. A. Wood. See occasional issues of Publishers Weekly

Quest for a proper place to read. J. Russell. *Writer* 100:5-6 Mr '87

Where one reads. M. E. Marty. il *Christ Century* 104:511 My 20-27 '87

Anecdotes, facetiae, satire, etc.
Literary fantasies: summer reading that could really wise him up. B.-J. Raphael. il *Glamour* 85:114 Ag '87

'Wafted to Mars, he fights four-armed green Tharks'. R. Wolkomir. il *Smithsonian* 18:192 My '87

Best books
See also
Best sellers
Books as gifts

Advice without platitudes. S. Blotnick. il *Forbes* 139:119 Je 29 '87

Best of '86. il *Time* 129:81 Ja 5 '87

Booked up! Undercover attractions. J. DeLynn. il *Harpers Bazaar* 120:30+ Jl '87

Books [1987] R. Koenig. il *N Y* 20:125-6+ D 21-28 '87

Books [fall preview] R. Koenig. il *N Y* 20:112+ S 21 '87

Books and reading—Best books—*cont.*

Books for vacation reading. il *N Y Times Book Rev* 92:38-42 My 31 '87

Classic tales of captains and castles . . . and corporations. B. G. Kempton. il *Work Woman* 12:102-5+ O '87

Classics revisited. P. S. Green. il *Forbes* 140:171+ O 19 '87

Editors' choice: the best books of 1987. il *N Y Times Book Rev* 92:3+ D 6 '87

Einstein on the beach. il *Vogue* 177:114 Jl '87

Lazy, hazy summer fare. D. James. il *Macleans* 100:50-1 Jl 20 '87

The luxury of summer reading. R. L. Bray and K. FitzGerald. il *Ms* 15:16+ Je '87

Notable books of the year. il *N Y Times Book Rev* 92:54+ D 6 '87

PW's choice: the year's best books. *Publ Wkly* 231:51-3 Ja 9 '87

Reads: picking through the paperbacks. C. McGee. il *N Y* 20:140+ Je 29-Jl 6 '87

Summer reading. il *Time* 130:64-6 Jl 27 '87

Bibliography
See also
> Best sellers
> Books and reading—Best books

1987 fall announcements. il *Publ Wkly* 232:317-83+ Ag 7 '87; Addendum. 232:136 S 18 '87

1987 spring books. J. Davis and W. Goldstein. *Publ Wkly* 231:297-357 Ja 30 '87

Bestsellers revisited? [fall preview] il *Publ Wkly* 231:57-64+ Je 19 '87

Book reviews. See issues of The Humanist

Books. See issues of The American Scholar

Books. See issues of Américas

Books. See issues of Business Week

Books. See issues of The Christian Century

Books. See issues of Maclean's

Books. See issues of Ms.

Books. See issues of The New Yorker

Books. See alternate issues of USA Today (Periodical)

Books. L. Mathews. See issues of Glamour

Books. J. Maynard. See issues of Mademoiselle beginning January 1985

Books in brief. See issues of National Review

Brief reviews. P.-L. Adams. See issues of The Atlantic

[Column] G. M. Costello. See issues of U.S. Catholic beginning January 1985

Forecasts. See issues of Publishers Weekly

Hot hardcovers for summer. il *Publ Wkly* 231:36-40 Ap 24 '87; Addendum. 231:252 My 15 '87

Looking ahead to 1988. il *Publ Wkly* 232:24-8+ D 11 '87

The New Yorker lists at this season some books by its contributors published during the year. *New Yorker* 63:100-1 D 21 '87

Noted with pleasure. See issues of The New York Times Book Review beginning January 1, 1984

People picks & pans. See issues of People Weekly

Recent arrivals. See issues of The Christian Century

The right books. C. Williamson. See issues of National Review

Ripe for reading: dreams that came true. D. B. Moskowitz. il *Bus Week* p108 Ja 19 '87

Roundup of 1987 boxed book sets. il *Publ Wkly* 232:70+ Ag 14 '87

Spring reading: from time travel to Gucci. D. B. Moskowitz. il *Bus Week* p134 Ap 27 '87

Talking about books. See issues of Vogue beginning March 1985

Writers & writing. B. Gewen. See occasional issues of The New Leader

The writer's library. See occasional issues of The Writer

Study and teaching
See Literature—Study and teaching

Great Britain
Drive in U.K. to push children's books. J. Taylor. *Publ Wkly* 231:38 Mr 20 '87

Soviet Union
An open book. I. Petryanov-Sokolov. il *Courier* 40:28-9 Ja '87

Books as gifts

The 10 best new picturebooks. W. Lamb. il *Redbook* 170:24+ D '87

. . . and to all a good book [children's books for Christmas] C. Loomis. il *Parents* 62:92+ N '87

Artful presents. A. Cockburn. il *House Gard* 159:22+ D '87

Booking for Christmas. W. Clemons. il *Newsweek* 110:64-7 D 21 '87

Books for gardeners. il *Flower Gard* 31:64-6 O/N '87

Children's books for Christmas. F. McNulty. *New Yorker* 63:132+ N 30 '87

Christmas book roundup and video cassettes too [woodworking] R. N. Hoffman. il *Workbench* 43:26 N/D '87

Critics' choices for Christmas. il *Commonweal* 114:706-15 D 4 '87

For giving: a 'read to me' wrap-up. L. Shapiro. il *Newsweek* 110:51-2 D 28 '87

Gold, frankincense, and books. L. Sibley. il *Christ Today* 31:58-60 D 11 '87

Holiday gift books. *Christ Century* 104:1097-8 D 2 '87

Illustrated books for Christmas. il *Hist Today* 37:52-3 D '87

Illustrated books for Christmas: give the big picture. il *N Y Times Book Rev* 92:26-9 D 13 '87

Illustrated gift books. il *Publ Wkly* 232:32+ S 11 '87

It's Christmas books '87 time [special issue] il *N Y Times Book Rev* 92:3+ D 6 '87

Joys for young readers. P. Young. il *Macleans* 100:54+ D 7 '87

Know ye by these presents [English dictionaries] W. Safire. il *N Y Times Mag* p14+ D 13 '87

Liberating youthful spirits [Christmas gifts for children] S. Kanfer. il *Time* 130:78-9 D 14 '87

Literary tidings of comfort and joy. il *Macleans* 100:56-7 D 14 '87

Merchandising gift books [ABA panel] W. Goldstein. *Publ Wkly* 232:30-1 S 11 '87

Our holiday lists. *Nation* 245:793-804 D 26 '87-Ja 2 '88

Pretty pages [art books for Christmas] K. Larson. il *N Y* 20:89-90 D 14 '87

A roundup of notable titles. T. Bolden Davis. il *Black Enterp* 18:21-2+ D '87

A shelf of holiday treats and treasures [Christmas gifts] il *Time* 130:64-6 D 21 '87

A vacation trip for young readers around the world of science. P. Morrison and P. Morrison. *Sci Am* 257:148-57 D '87

Books by Wire (Firm)

Books by Wire gift program begins test phase. S. Bolle. *Publ Wkly* 232:35 Jl 10 '87

Forget flowers: an FTD for book fanciers. *Newsweek* 110:37 Jl 6 '87

Books for Cooks (London, England: Bookstore) *See* Booksellers and bookselling—Great Britain

Books from motion pictures *See* Motion pictures and literature

Books on cassette *See* Talking books

Booksellers and bookselling
See also
> American Booksellers Association
> Book fairs
> Books—Marketing
> Books—Prices
> College bookstores
> Olsson's Books · Records (Firm)
> Supermarkets—Book departments
> Videotapes—Bookselling use

Another kind of censorship [reluctance of publishers and booksellers to deal with report of Pornography Commission] M. J. McManus. por *Publ Wkly* 231:70 Ja 23 '87

Bantam Group launches incentive plan for retailers. *Publ Wkly* 232:71 S 18 '87

Bookselling & merchandising. A. Symons and S. Bolle. See issues of Publishers Weekly

Christmas 1986: customers bought across the board. S. Bolle. *Publ Wkly* 231:364-5 Ja 30 '87

The Gallup survey. L. A. Wood. See occasional issues of Publishers Weekly

Market crash makes minor impact on bookstore sales. *Publ Wkly* 232:44 N 13 '87

PW business survey: a suspenseful and scholarly summer. S. Bolle. il *Publ Wkly* 232:39-43 Ag 28 '87

PW business survey: plunging stocks boost books. S. Bolle and others. il *Publ Wkly* 232:24+ D 18 '87

Stocking up on Shakespeare [booksellers' ratings of various editions] W. Goldstein and B. Levine. *Publ Wkly* 232:26 N 6 '87

That cozy bookstore café. J. Bethune. il *Publ Wkly* 231:46-8 Ap 24 '87

Tube power [miniseries based on books and their influence on bookstore sales] L. See. il *Publ Wkly* 231:49-50+ Je 12 '87

Advertising
See Books—Advertising

Antitrust cases
Crown to countersue NCBA and individual booksellers. M. Reuter. *Publ Wkly* 231:19 F 13 '87

Booksellers and bookselling—Antitrust cases—*cont.*
Judge dismisses suits between NCBA, chains. M. Colin. *Publ Wkly* 232:13 O 23 '87
Judge freezes NCBA-chain lawsuit until September. M. Colin. *Publ Wkly* 231:15 My 1 '87
NCBA sues three chains for 'inducing' unfair discounts. M. Reuter. *Publ Wkly* 231:16 F 6 '87

Architectural literature
Peter Miller Books: where design professionals go to shop [Seattle bookstore] K. Harmon. il pors *Publ Wkly* 231:56-8 F 20 '87

Backlist books
Panel offers backlist tips by age category [ABA convention] D. E. Roback. *Publ Wkly* 231:45 Je 26 '87
Wrap-up: a look to the future [children's books] K. O. Fakih. il *Publ Wkly* 231:49 Je 26 '87

Chain and franchise operations
See also
B. Dalton Booksellers
Barnes & Noble
Bookstop (Firm)
Crown Books Corporation
Waldenbooks
Waldenkids (Firm)

Children's literature
See also
Association of Booksellers for Children
Waldenkids (Firm)
Children in the New Age bookstore. S. Little. *Publ Wkly* 232:72 S 25 '87
Children's books: a junior high [ABA convention] D. E. Roback. il *Publ Wkly* 231:83-5 Je 19 '87
Children's books at ABA: a vibrant atmosphere [symposium] il *Publ Wkly* 231:43-5+ Je 26 '87
Foreign language makes a comeback. S. Bolle. il *Publ Wkly* 232:163 Jl 24 '87
Marketing on two fronts. A. Meeker. *Publ Wkly* 232:44-7 N 27 '87
Music to their ears [audio and video in children's bookstores] J. Wallace. il *Publ Wkly* 231:140+ F 27 '87
Selling children's foreign-language books. S. Bolle. il *Publ Wkly* 232:160-2 Jl 24 '87
Women & Children First: the evolution of a specialty market [Chicago bookstore] N. Barrett. il *Publ Wkly* 231:26-7 Mr 27 '87

Cookbooks
London journal [Books for Cooks, London bookstore] J. Bainbridge. il *Gourmet* 47:20+ F '87

Employees
Writing the book on staff training [method used at Books & Co. bookstore, Dayton, Ohio] S. Bolle. il *Publ Wkly* 232:140-2 S 18 '87

Feminist literature
Busman's holiday in Rome [Al Tempo Ritrovato] M. Herring. il *Publ Wkly* 232:47 Ag 21 '87
Women & Children First: the evolution of a specialty market [Chicago bookstore] N. Barrett. il *Publ Wkly* 231:26-7 Mr 27 '87

Foreign language books
Foreign language makes a comeback. S. Bolle. il *Publ Wkly* 232:163 Jl 24 '87
Selling children's foreign-language books. S. Bolle. il *Publ Wkly* 232:160-2 Jl 24 '87

Gambling literature
A book store for the betting man [Gambler's Book Shop in Las Vegas] B. Condor. il *Sport Mag* 78:94 Mr '87

Guidebooks
The widening world of travel books. G. Feldman. il *Publ Wkly* 231:31-2+ F 13 '87

Homosexual literature
Toronto book shop wins suit against customs over 'Joy of gay sex' [Glad Day Bookshop wins obscenity suit] B. Slopen. *Publ Wkly* 231:20 Ap 17 '87

Horror tales
Horror spreads across the country. S. Sherman. il *Publ Wkly* 232:26-8 D 4 '87

Illustrated books
Merchandising gift books [ABA panel] W. Goldstein. *Publ Wkly* 232:30-1 S 11 '87

International aspects
Looking for the great bookstore. J. Perry. por *Publ Wkly* 232:58 D 25 '87

Music
Music to buy books by [New Age music sold in bookstores] J. Zinsser. il *Publ Wkly* 231:40+ Ap 17 '87

Nature literature
See also
Nature Company

New Age materials
Children in the New Age bookstore. S. Little. *Publ Wkly* 232:72 S 25 '87
New Age. D. Tuller. il *Publ Wkly* 232:29-33 S 25 '87
New Age causes growing pains in general bookstores. A. Symons. *Publ Wkly* 232:73 S 25 '87
New media for a New Age. il *Publ Wkly* 232:60-1 S 25 '87
Selling New Age at Sunsight [Minneapolis bookstore] A. Symons. il *Publ Wkly* 232:70-2 S 25 '87

Order processing
See also
Booksellers Order Service

Paperback books
See also
Paperback books—Marketing

Photographic literature
See also
Museum of Photographic Arts (San Diego, Calif.). Bookstore

Photographs and photography
Rep photographer makes camera his marketing tool [Doubleday sales rep R. Williams takes photographs of bookstore displays] B. List. il *Publ Wkly* 231:53-4 My 29 '87

Religious literature
See also
Christian Booksellers Association
Zondervan Corp.
The Good Book can be good for you. F. Couch and K. Stephens. il *Publ Wkly* 232:67-8 O 9 '87

Remainders
Remaindering now. C. T. Anthony. il *Publ Wkly* 231:29-31+ Ap 17 '87

Returns to publishers
See Publishers and publishing—Returns policy

Secondhand books
College publishers and used books. D. C. Baker and J. Hileman. il *Publ Wkly* 232:18-21 D 11 '87
It was a lovely year for a bookstore [owning a secondhand bookstore in post World War II Greenwich Village] A. Broyard. il *N Y Times Book Rev* 92:12 My 17 '87

Security measures
ABA panel discusses staff pilferage and shoplifting. S. Bolle. *Publ Wkly* 231:65 Je 12 '87
To catch a thief: what some booksellers do. S. Sherman. il *Publ Wkly* 231:63-5 Je 12 '87

Sidelines
1988 calendar update. il *Publ Wkly* 232:34 O 23 '87
1988 calendar update. il *Publ Wkly* 232:36-7 Jl 10 '87
1988 calendars. il *Publ Wkly* 231:35-6+ Ap 10 '87
Bookstore sidelines for the holidays. il *Publ Wkly* 232:62-9 Ag 14 '87
Stocking children's sidelines. A. Symons. *Publ Wkly* 231:48 Je 26 '87

Stationery
Stationery sidelines spring 1987. il *Publ Wkly* 231:62-3+ Mr 6 '87

Statistics
First quarter sales: vigorous. J. P. Dessauer. il *Publ Wkly* 232:426 Ag 7 '87
Second quarter sales: solid. J. P. Dessauer. il *Publ Wkly* 232:40 O 16 '87
Slow finish to lackluster 1986. J. P. Dessauer. il *Publ Wkly* 231:24 Ap 3 '87

Study and teaching
Together in Venice [Mauri Booksellers School] H. R. Lottman. il *Publ Wkly* 231:25-7 My 1 '87

Talking books
Audio at Olsson's [Olsson's Books・Records in Washington, D.C. area] T. Spain. il *Publ Wkly* 231:153 My 15 '87
Audio: back to the books [B. Dalton's policy] *Publ Wkly* 231:40 Ap 3 '87

Tape recordings
Audio and video at ABA. T. Spain. il *Publ Wkly* 231:96+ Je 19 '87
Audio and video expand beyond national chains. il *Publ Wkly* 231:58+ Ja 9 '87
Audio and video: the bookseller's perspective [ABA convention] J. Tangorra. *Publ Wkly* 231:102-3 Je 19 '87
AV products on the move. il *Publ Wkly* 231:66-7 Je 12 '87
Good news for the holidays. il *Publ Wkly* 232:29-30 D 18 '87
Music to their ears [audio and video in children's bookstores] J. Wallace. il *Publ Wkly* 231:140+ F 27 '87

Booksellers and bookselling—*cont.*
Videotapes
Audio and video at ABA. T. Spain. il *Publ Wkly* 231:96+ Je 19 '87

Audio and video expand beyond national chains. il *Publ Wkly* 231:58+ Ja 9 '87

Audio and video: the bookseller's perspective [ABA convention] J. Tangorra. *Publ Wkly* 231:102-3 Je 19 '87

AV products on the move. il *Publ Wkly* 231:66-7 Je 12 '87

Dalton drops troubled video program in back-to-basics push. T. Spain. *Publ Wkly* 231:39-40+ Ap 3 '87

Dalton re-examining video program. *Publ Wkly* 231:52 F 20 '87

Movies for Christmas. il *Publ Wkly* 232:37-8 Ag 21 '87

Music to their ears [audio and video in children's bookstores] J. Wallace. il *Publ Wkly* 231:140+ F 27 '87

Arizona
In Arizona: a rancher's bookstore [W. Bundy's Singing Wind Bookshop] G. Jaynes. il por *Time* 129:12 My 18 '87

Atlantic States
See also
Mid-Atlantic Booksellers Association
California
See also
Museum of Photographic Arts (San Diego, Calif.). Bookstore
Northern California Booksellers Association
Southern California Booksellers Association

40 to lose jobs when Hunters in Westwood, Beverly Hills close. L. See. *Publ Wkly* 232:23 D 25 '87

Amok: books on the dark side, for a 'dark time' [Los Angeles bookstore] L. See. *Publ Wkly* 232:84 S 25 '87

City Lights: still doing things its own way [San Francisco] L. See. *Publ Wkly* 231:34 Je 26 '87

Canada
See also
Canadian Booksellers Association
Colorado
Radio reviews to help the bookseller [Tom Carney, manager of Hatch's #7 bookstore in Denver, previews new titles on radio] B. List. il *Publ Wkly* 231:47 Ja 16 '87

Florida
Books & Books in Miami [Coral Gables bookstore] A. Symons. il *Publ Wkly* 231:43-5 Ap 17 '87

Great Britain
London journal [Books for Cooks, London bookstore] J. Bainbridge. il *Gourmet* 47:20+ F '87

Pentos to expand Dillons. C. T. Anthony. il *Publ Wkly* 232:28-9 N 27 '87

Illinois
Brent springs eternal [Stuart Brent Books in Chicago] N. Barrett. il por *Publ Wkly* 232:60-2 S 11 '87

Obscenity test challenged in U.S. Supreme Court [intent of Miller test questioned in Pope v. Illinois] H. Fields. *Publ Wkly* 231:10 Mr 13 '87

Supreme Court fine-tunes third part of 'Miller' test [Pope v. Illinois] *Publ Wkly* 231:20 My 22 '87

Women & Children First: the evolution of a specialty market [Chicago bookstore] N. Barrett. il *Publ Wkly* 231:26-7 Mr 27 '87

Indiana
High Court asked to rule on RICO bookstore case [adult bookstore] *Publ Wkly* 232:10 N 13 '87

Italy
Busman's holiday in Rome [Al Tempo Ritrovato, bookstore featuring feminist literature] M. Herring. il *Publ Wkly* 232:47 Ag 21 '87

Massachusetts
Getting your WordsWorth [Cambridge bookstore] J. Rosen. il *Publ Wkly* 232:419-22 Ag 7 '87

The Jeffery Amherst Bookshop: cultivating a narrow specialty [Amherst store specializing in E. Dickinson] K. McCune. il pors *Publ Wkly* 232:29-31 Jl 3 '87

Middle Western States
See also
Upper Midwest Booksellers Association
Minnesota
A literary repast for a Hungry Mind [bookstore in Saint Paul] S. Little. il por *Publ Wkly* 232:41-3 N 13 '87

Selling New Age at Sunsight [Minneapolis bookstore] A. Symons. il *Publ Wkly* 232:70-2 S 25 '87

Nevada
A book store for the betting man [Gambler's Book Shop in Las Vegas] B. Condor. il *Sport Mag* 78:94 Mr '87

New England
See also
New England Booksellers Association
New Mexico
Wedding fair at Bookworks [Albuquerque retailers hold promotion featuring author M. Stewart] B. List. il *Publ Wkly* 232:45-6 Ag 21 '87

New York (State)
See also
New York Regional Booksellers Association
The boss was a hustler or, How I got my Bible [Bibles of Yore secondhand business] E. M. Halliday. *N Y Times Book Rev* 92:20 D 13 '87

It was a lovely year for a bookstore [owning a secondhand bookstore in post World War II Greenwich Village] A. Broyard. il *N Y Times Book Rev* 92:12 My 17 '87

One for the books [Gotham Book Mart in Manhattan]; ed. by Bobbie Stein. F. Steloff. il pors *People Wkly* 27:87-8+ Ja 26 '87

Ohio
Writing the book on staff training [method used at Books & Co. bookstore, Dayton] S. Bolle. il *Publ Wkly* 232:140-2 S 18 '87

Ontario
Toronto book shop wins suit against customs over 'Joy of gay sex' [Glad Day Bookshop wins obscenity suit] B. Slopen. *Publ Wkly* 231:20 Ap 17 '87

Oregon
Expanding in Portland [Powell's Books] K. K. Rusch. il *Publ Wkly* 231:40-1+ Ja 23 '87

Southeastern States
See also
Southeastern Booksellers Association
Southern States
See also
South-Central Booksellers Association
Tennessee
Success and succession at R. M. Mills [Nashville bookstores] A. Symons. il *Publ Wkly* 232:34-7 D 11 '87

Texas
See also
Bookstop (Firm)
United States
See Booksellers and bookselling
Virginia
Charlottesville Book Gallery. A. Symons. il *Publ Wkly* 232:35-7 S 4 '87

Washington (D.C.)
The bookstore scene: a shop for every interest. il *Publ Wkly* 231:149-50 My 15 '87

Washington (State)
Peter Miller Books: where design professionals go to shop [Seattle bookstore] K. Harmon. il pors *Publ Wkly* 231:56-8 F 20 '87

Western States
See also
Mountains and Plains Booksellers Association
Booksellers Order Service
ABA to be exclusive distributor of 'Chronicle of 20th century' [distribution handled through BOS] *Publ Wkly* 231:14 Ap 3 '87

Bookshelves *See* Bookcases
Bookstop (Firm)
Selling books, Texas style. J. Schwartz. il por *Newsweek* 110:63 O 26 '87

Bookstores *See* Booksellers and bookselling
Bookstores, College *See* College bookstores
Bookworks (Albuquerque, N.M.: Bookstore) *See* Booksellers and bookselling—New Mexico
Boomerangs
Boomerangs: you can't throw them away. il *Natl Geogr World* 147:12-15 N '87

Prehistoric tusk: early boomerang? [mammoth tusk found in Polish cave; research by Pawel Valde-Nowak and others] B. Bower. *Sci News* 132:215 O 3 '87

Walkabout [Australian visitor T. Dunlap attends a boomerang competition] *New Yorker* 63:23-4 Jl 27 '87

Boone, Debby
about
The private lives of star moms [excerpt from Starring mothers] J. Barber. il pors *McCalls* 114:57+ My '87

Boone, Pat, 1934-
about
One man's family. L. Feldman. il pors *McCalls* 115:18-22
D '87
Boorman, John
about
Hope and glory [film] Reviews
  Commonweal 114:704-6 D 4 '87. T. O'Brien
  Glamour il 85:249 N '87. J. G. Boyum
  Macleans 100:52 N 2 '87. L. O'Toole
  N Y 20:115-16 O 26 '87. D. Denby
  New Repub 197:28-9 N 2 '87. S. Kauffmann
  New Yorker 63:91-2 O 5 '87. P. Kael
  Newsweek il 110:84 O 19 '87. D. Ansen
  People Wkly il 28:14 N 2 '87. P. Travers
  Time il 130:76 O 19 '87. R. Corliss
Boorstin, Daniel J. (Daniel Joseph), 1914-
The historian: 'a wrestler with the angel'. il *N Y Times
  Book Rev* 92:1+ S 20 '87
'The image' and publishing: 1962 [excerpt from The
  image] *Publ Wkly* 232:24 D 4 '87
about
Boorstin joins Doubleday as editor-at-large. por *Publ
  Wkly* 232:33 O 9 '87
The joy of reading, the joy of writing: Daniel Boorstin's
  career among books. W. Goldstein. il por *Publ Wkly*
  232:23-5 D 4 '87
The odyssey of Daniel Boorstin [cover story] J. Wiener.
  il *Nation* 245:289+ S 26 '87
Summer reading for candidates. H. Sidey. bibl il por
  Time 130:21 Ag 3 '87
Boorstin, Jon
Facing a flop. il *N Y Times Mag* p102 O 11 '87
Boose, David L.
Needed: a Clean Soil Act. il *Technol Rev* 90:22-3 O
  '87
Boosler, Elayne, 1952?-
about
Cable and movies calling, comic Elayne Boosler finds
  her place in the fun. L. Rozen. il pors *People Wkly*
  28:114-16 O 12 '87
Boosters for guided missiles *See* Guided missiles—
  Propulsion systems
Boosters for space vehicles *See* Space vehicles—Propulsion
  systems
Bootes (Constellation) *See* Constellations
Booth, Leah
Where 'boss' stops and 'friend' begins. il *Work Woman*
  12:70-4+ F '87
Booth, Pat
A divorce alternative. il *Harpers Bazaar* 120:141+ Ag
  '87
Booth, Philip E.
United States [poem] *America* 157:272 O 24 '87
Booth, Stephen A.
Electronics. See issues of Popular Mechanics beginning
  February 1985
Photography. See issues of Popular Mechanics beginning
  January 1986
Boothe, Clare *See* Luce, Clare Boothe, 1903-1987
Booths, Dressing *See* Dressing booths
Boots, Wilson T.
Moment of decision arrives in Haiti. *Christ Century*
  104:1077-8 D 2 '87
Boots *See* Footwear
Boots, Ski *See* Skis and skiing—Equipment
Booz, Allen & Hamilton Inc.
Is Booz Allen having a mid-life crisis? L. Baum. il
  por *Bus Week* p76+ Mr 9 '87
Making big bucks from the Big Bang [American A.
  Berkowitch working in London] S. Seixas. il pors *Money*
  16:161-2+ My '87
Boozer, Melvin, d. 1987
about
Obituary
  Jet 72:13 Mr 30 '87
Borawski, John
U.S.-Soviet move toward risk reduction. bibl f *Bull
  At Sci* 43:16-18 Jl/Ag '87
Borcherding, James R.
Dairy. See occasional issues of Successful Farming through
  June 1987
Borchers, Robert R.
about
Editor of new AIP magazine-journal discusses computers
  in physics [interview] por *Phys Today* 40:109 O '87
Bordan, Phillip
Peaceful toy soldiers. il *Antiques Collect Hobbies* 92:40-2
  Jl '87

Bordeaux (France)
A delightful tour of Bordeaux and Cognac. F. E. Ruffin.
  il *Black Enterp* 18:109-10 O '87
  Wine industry
  See Wine industry—France
Bordeaux wines *See* Wine
Borden, Lizzie
about
Working girls [film] Reviews
  Macleans 100:55 Je 1 '87. L. O'Toole
  Ms il 15:20-1 My '87. A. B. Snitow
  Nation 244:482-4 Ap 11 '87. M. Pally
  New Repub 196:26 Mr 16 '87. S. Kauffmann
  Time il 129:79 Ap 27 '87. R. Schickel
  Vogue il por 177:218-19+ Jl '87. M. Kramer
Borden, Inc.
How Borden milks packaged goods. B. Saporito. il *Fortune*
  116:139-40+ D 21 '87
Border Art Workshop. Taller de Arte Fronterizo
Erasing the line. L. Goldman. il *Art News* 86:63 O
  '87
Border Cafe (New York, N.Y.) *See* New York (N.Y.)—
  Restaurants, nightclubs, bars, etc.
Borderline personalities *See* Personality—Disorders
Borders, Garden *See* Garden borders
Bordewich, Fergus M.
Holy terror. il *Atlantic* 259:26+ Ap '87
The lessons of Bhopal. il *Atlantic* 259:30-3 Mr '87
Bordowitz, Hank
Adventures in Fusionland. il por *High Fidel* 37:87-8+
  Ja '87
Boredom
Are you (no! not me!) boring? B. Levine. il *Seventeen*
  46:82+ My '87
Feeling bored and restless? How to stay fresh on the
  job. M. M. Kennedy. il *Glamour* 85:216-18+ F '87
Of many things. G. W. Hunt. *America* 156:inside cover
  Mr 7 '87
Stuck in a rut? 6 ways to dig out [on the job] M.
  M. Kennedy. il *Glamour* 85:62 Jl '87
Boren, David L.
Should the Boren Amendment approach to curtailing
  PAC's be adopted? [excerpts from debate, August 11,
  1986] *Congr Dig* 66:44+ F '87
Borer, Jeffrey S.
about
NIH finally resolves 7-year dispute. C. Holden. *Science*
  238:151 O 9 '87
Borers (Insects)
Corn borers, beware the chips [computer model] D.
  D. Edwards. il *Sci News* 131:20 Ja 10 '87
  Control
  They'll bug you this summer [European corn borer]
  B. Freese. il *Success Farm* 85:34C Je '87
Borey, Susan
Aural Fixation. il por *Theatre Crafts* 21:42+ O '87
Borg, Björn, 1956-
about
Bjorn again! [cover story] S. Stevenson. il pors *World
  Tennis* 35:18-24 D '87
Hall of Fame deserves the best. S. Flink. il por *World
  Tennis* 35:22+ Jl '87
Borg, James C.
Birth of an island. il map *Oceans* 20:26-33 Jl/Ag '87
Borg, Marcus
Jesus and the Kingdom of God. *Christ Century* 104:378-80
  Ap 22 '87
Borg-Warner Corp.
Cornering Borg-Warner [GAF's offer] J. E. Ellis. il por
  Bus Week p39 Ap 13 '87
Will GAF cash in its Borg-Warner chips—or up the
  ante? [leveraged buyout led by Merrill Lynch] J. E.
  Ellis. *Bus Week* p34-5 Ap 27 '87
Borgens, Richard B., and others
Behavioral recovery induced by applied electric fields
  after spinal cord hemisection in guinea pig. bibl f
  il *Science* 238:366-9 O 16 '87
Borger, Irene
An aesthetic concern: the Los Angeles apartment of
  Walter and Helga Oppenheimer. il *Archit Dig* 44:180-5
  D '87
The Breakaway: a seagoing scenario for George Hamilton.
  il por *Archit Dig* 44:86-9 Ag '87
Fitness now. il *Vogue* 177:302+ S '87
Joseph Moure's California impressionist paintings. il por
  Archit Dig 44:86+ Mr '87
Present primeval. il por *Archit Dig* 44:56+ S '87
True grit. il *Vogue* 177:356-7+ Ag '87

Borges, Jacobo, 1932-
about
Jacobo Borges at C.D.S. L. Campbell. *Art Am* 75:222 Ap '87
Borges, Jorge Luis, 1899-1986
about
The other Borges: a precursor from the future. E. Sacerio-Garí. il por *Christ Century* 104:1026-9 N 18 '87
Señor Borges's portico. J. Epstein. *Commentary* 83:55-62 Ap '87
Borgeson, Bet
Further techniques for using colored pencils [cover story] il por *Am Artist* 51:52-7 Ap '87
Borget, Lou
about
A trader runs amok. T. Mack. por *Forbes* 140:8 N 16 '87
Borgman, Ruth Elizabeth
Lone dangers. il *Omni* 9:24 My '87
Borguss family
about
Contact with dolphins. P. Curtis. il *Oceans* 20:18-23 Ja/F '87
Bori, Lucrezia, 1887-1960
about
Viewpoint. G. Fitzgerald. por *Opera News* 52:4 D 19 '87
Boric acid
Boric-acid poisoning. il *Parents* 62:20 D '87
Borin, Elliot
Indian: on the road again. il pors *Cycle* 38:68-72+ S '87
Boring, Mollie D.
Books and the sky. See issues of Sky and Telescope
Boring *See* Drilling and boring (Earth and rocks)
Boring machinery *See* Drilling and boring machinery
Boris Godunov [opera] *See* Mussorgsky, Modest Petrovich, 1839-1881
Boritt, G. S., 1940-
Looking for Lincoln in the 1980's. bibl il pors *N Y Times Book Rev* 92:1+ F 8 '87
Borjas, George J., and Tienda, Marta
The economic consequences of immigration. bibl f il *Science* 235:645-51 F 6 '87
Bork, Robert H., 1927-
about
286 editors sign letter against Bork nomination. *Publ Wkly* 232:13 O 16 '87
1787 and all that. *Nation* 245:37 Jl 18-25 '87
Abortion: the battle heats up again. M. Engel. il por *Glamour* 85:192+ O '87
Advise and dissent [cover story; special section] il pors *Time* 130:12-18+ S 21 '87
All eyes on the undecideds. T. Jacoby. il por *Newsweek* 110:30 O 5 '87
Area Man. M. McGough. *New Repub* 197:17 S 14-21 '87
The battle against Bork will be long, bitter—and likely to fail. P. Dwyer and D. Harbrecht. por *Bus Week* p45 Jl 13 '87
The battle begins. R. Lacayo. il por *Time* 130:10-12 Jl 13 '87
The battle of Bork. M. Laurino. il por *Ms* 16:111-12 S '87
The battle of Judge Bork. M. McDonald. il por *Macleans* 100:30-1 O 19 '87
Battle of the Bork. *Commonweal* 114:547-8 O 9 '87
The battle over Bork. L. Martz. il por *Newsweek* 110:12-14 Ag 24 '87
Believing in Judge Bork. T. Gest. il *U S News World Rep* 103:29 S 28 '87
Bidenquiddick. *Natl Rev* 39:15+ Ag 28 '87
Biden's main chance. T. Morganthau. il por *Newsweek* 110:35-6 S 21 '87
The bitter legacy of the battle over Bork. P. Dwyer. por *Bus Week* p67 O 19 '87
Black thought, black talk. W. F. Buckley. *Natl Rev* 39:54-5 Ag 14 '87
Blacks get group of state legislators to dump Bork. *Jet* 72:29 S 21 '87
Bork and Bird. H. Meyerson. *New Repub* 197:21+ S 14-21 '87
The Bork appointment. *Natl Rev* 39:14-15 Jl 31 '87
Bork bashers beware. M. S. Forbes, Jr. il *Forbes* 140:25 Ag 10 '87
The Bork battle. *Natl Rev* 39:17-18 S 11 '87
The Bork battle [cover story; special section] il pors *Newsweek* 110:22-6+ S 14 '87
The Bork disaster. *Natl Rev* 39:16 N 6 '87
The Bork fight. *Natl Rev* 39:17-18 O 9 '87

Bork in the balance. A. Press. il por *Newsweek* 110:38+ O 12 '87
The Bork nomination. *America* 157:99-100 Ag 29-S 5 '87
The Bork nomination. R. M. Dworkin. bibl f il *N Y Rev Books* 34:3+ Ag 13 '87
'The Bork nomination': an exchange [discussion of August 13, 1987 article] R. M. Dworkin. il *N Y Rev Books* 34:59-61 O 8 '87
The Bork nomination and the political game. J. M. Wall. *Christ Century* 104:707-8 Ag 26-S 2 '87
Bork nomination threatens basic liberties. E. Doerr. il *Humanist* 47:41 S/O '87
Bork of the month. J. Klein. il *N Y* 20:28+ S 21 '87
The Bork screw. A. Sullivan. *New Repub* 197:14+ O 19 '87
Bork talk. F. Barnes. *New Repub* 197:9-11 S 7 '87
Bork v. Senate. *Natl Rev* 39:16-18 O 23 '87
Bork v. the First. J. Kalven. *Nation* 245:269-70 S 19 '87
A Bork without the bite. J. V. Lamar, Jr. il por *Time* 130:18-19 S 28 '87
Bork's bite. *New Repub* 197:7-9 Jl 27 '87
Bork's last stand. A. Press. il por *Newsweek* 110:26-7 O 19 '87
Bork's progress. M. Lerner. *New Repub* 197:18+ S 14-21 '87
Bound by the Constitution. D. A. Degnan. *Commonweal* 114:481-3 S 11 '87
A brief against Bork. il *Progressive* 51:7-8 S '87
The brief on Judge Bork [cover story] M. Kramer. il pors *U S News World Rep* 103:18-24 S 14 '87
The case against Bork. *New Repub* 197:7-10 O 5 '87
Catching the last train to the Court. F. Trippett. il pors *Time* 130:13 Jl 13 '87
Civil rights supporters plea for defeat of Bork. il *Jet* 73:8 O 12 '87
Coup at the Court. R. Adler. il *New Repub* 197:37+ S 14-21 '87
Defining the real Robert Bork. J. V. Lamar, Jr. il por *Time* 130:16 Ag 24 '87
Democratic majority. *Nation* 245:397 O 17 '87
The Democrats' glass chin. G. F. Will. il *Newsweek* 110:66 Jl 20 '87
Did Robert Bork bend the rules in a 1984 case? T. Gest. il por *U S News World Rep* 103:12 Jl 20 '87
The effort to intimidate Reagan. W. F. Buckley. *Natl Rev* 39:57 Jl 31 '87
A fight for one man, one vote. J. V. Lamar, Jr. il *Time* 130:25 O 5 '87
For all the marbles. G. Borger. il por *U S News World Rep* 103:20-3 S 21 '87
For want of a nail. M. Gallagher. il *Natl Rev* 39:32+ N 20 '87
The frantic reflagging of Bork [cover story] H. Schwartz. il *Nation* 245:253+ S 19 '87
From Bork to Kennedy. R. M. Dworkin. bibl f il *N Y Rev Books* 34:36+ D 17 '87
Going . . . going . . . G. Borger. il pors *U S News World Rep* 103:20-2 O 12 '87
Gone with the wind. J. V. Lamar, Jr. il por *Time* 130:18-20 O 12 '87
The great debate inside Robert Bork. P. Dwyer. il por *Bus Week* p34-5 S 14 '87
The grilling of Judge Bork. A. Press. il por *Newsweek* 110:27+ S 28 '87
The higher law: Bork, Burke, & moral relativism. D. R. Carlin, Jr. *Commonweal* 114:729-30 D 18 '87
'The hottest fight in a decade'. N. Cooper. il pors *Newsweek* 110:30 Jl 20 '87
How we shred the past. M. Greenfield. il *Newsweek* 110:98 O 5 '87
Into the trenches over Bork. T. Gest. il por *U S News World Rep* 103:39 Ag 17 '87
The Judge Bork blues. il *Commonweal* 114:579-80 O 23 '87
Judging Robert Bork. M. McDonald. il por *Macleans* 100:26 S 28 '87
A judicial shift to the right. por *Macleans* 100:18 Jl 13 '87
The last hurrahs. *Nation* 245:291-2 S 26 '87
Letter from Washington. E. Drew. *New Yorker* 63:150-4+ N 2 '87
Letter from Washington. Cato. *Natl Rev* 39:14 N 6 '87
The line on Bork. D. Seligman. *Fortune* 116:96 Ag 17 '87
A look at Robert Bork and rulings affecting the church. K. A. Lawton. il por *Christ Today* 31:42-3 Ag 7 '87

Bork, Robert H., 1927——*about—cont.*
NAACP, NEA opposing Reagan's pick for Court. il *Jet* 72:8 Jl 20 '87
A new majority moves to the right. T. Gest. il por *U S News World Rep* 103:28-9 Jl 13 '87
Nice try; If you have tears . . . W. F. Buckley. *Natl Rev* 39:70-1 O 23 '87
Notes and comment. *New Yorker* 63:17-20 Ag 3 '87
The old frontier. J. Klein. il por *N Y* 20:26+ O 19 '87
On the Bork front. D. Schorr. *New Leader* 70:5-6 O 19 '87
On trial: character. G. Borger. il pors *U S News World Rep* 103:26-7 S 28 '87
Open and shut. *New Repub* 197:4 Ag 24 '87
Privacy and the undressed. M. Greenfield. il *Newsweek* 110:100 O 19 '87
A record that speaks for itself. F. J. Flaherty. il *Commonweal* 114:477-80 S 11 '87
The road to Bork's last stand. J. V. Lamar, Jr. il por *Time* 130:15-16 O 19 '87
Second thoughts on Bork. *Natl Rev* 39:18-19 S 25 '87
Shifting odds in the fight over Bork. T. Gest. il por *U S News World Rep* 103:25 O 5 '87
Simmons, Jones mastermind move to dump Robert Bork. pors *Jet* 73:12 O 26 '87
The skirmishing begins again. A. Press. por *Newsweek* 110:32 O 26 '87
A sophist's theory of free speech. G. Marzorati. *Harpers* 275:62-3 S '87
The struggle for the uncommitted. T. Gest. il *U S News World Rep* 103:24 Ag 24 '87
A 'tempest in a teapot' (pace Cicero). M. Kramer. il *U S News World Rep* 103:20 S 28 '87
This smoking gun won't shoot. M. Kramer. il por *U S News World Rep* 103:16 S 21 '87
To the bitter end [with interview with E. Meese] G. Borger. il por *U S News World Rep* 103:18-20 O 19 '87
Trying to leave a conservative legacy. A. Press. il por *Newsweek* 110:22-3 Jl 13 '87
Who's afraid of Robert Bork? [cover story] R. Vigilante. il *Natl Rev* 39:25-30 Ag 28 '87
Why roast Bork? C. W. Colson. il *Christ Today* 31:80 O 2 '87
Will a new justice tip the Court's delicate balance? L. Kravitz. por *Sch Update* 120:13 S 4 '87
Winning one from the Gipper. A. R. Dowd. il pors *Fortune* 116:125+ N 9 '87
With Bork out, Reagan starts over. A. Press. il por *Newsweek* 110:56 N 2 '87

Anecdotes, facetiae, satire, etc.
Cool with Coolidge. M. Meltsner. *Nation* 245:365 O 10 '87

Borkoski, Joanne
Fruitful endings. il *Ladies Home J* 104:104-5+ Ag '87

Borland, Hal, 1900-1978
Deliberate September [excerpt from Hal Borland's Twelve moons of the year] il *Audubon* 89:45 S '87
The dog who came to stay [condensation] il *Read Dig* 130:123-30+ Je '87
The elusive gentians [excerpt from Hal Borland's Twelve moons of the year] il *Audubon* 89:51 N '87
June-becoming-July [excerpt from Hal Borland's Twelve moons of the year] il *Audubon* 89:43 Jl '87

Borland International
The maverick [P. Kahn] D. Garfinkel. il pors *Pers Comput* 11:118-21+ Mr '87

Borletti, Ferdinando
about
'Irangate' unfolds in Italy. W. C. Symonds. *Bus Week* p46 S 21 '87

Bormann, F. H., and Likens, Gene E., 1935-
Changing perspectives on air-pollution stress. *BioScience* 37:370 Je '87

Born, C. Allen
about
Al Born digs AMAX out of a hole. C. Leinster. il pors *Fortune* 115:205-6+ Ap 27 '87
Amax finds a way out of the abyss. J. R. Norman. il por *Bus Week* p82-3 O 26 '87
Diary of a decision: a week in the life of Amax. J. R. Norman. il por *Bus Week* p118+ N 9 '87

Born, David
Baffled by brushes. il *Saturday Evening Post* 259:18-19+ My/Je '87
Dentistry: forecasting the future. il *Saturday Evening Post* 259:30-1+ S '87
How safe is your dentist? il *Saturday Evening Post* 259:28-9+ Jl/Ag '87

Super solutions for tooth decay. il *Saturday Evening Post* 259:16+ Ja/F '87
TMJ—jawbone pain that's all too common. il *Saturday Evening Post* 259:26-7 D '87
Tooth or consequences: what to do in a dental emergency. il *Saturday Evening Post* 259:26-7 Ap '87

Born in East L.A. [film] See Motion picture reviews—Single works

Bornemisza, Hans Heinrich Thyssen- See Thyssen-Bornemisza, Hans Heinrich, Baron, 1921-

Bornemisza, Tita Thyssen- See Thyssen-Bornemisza, Tita, Baroness

Borneo
See also
Brunei
Wildlife—Borneo

Description and travel
Hanging around in Borneo. C. Raffaele. il map *Natl Geogr World* 140:30-5 Ap '87
The North Borneo Expedition of 1981 [college students collect samples of agricultural pests] C. Alexander. map *New Yorker* 63:39-44+ S 14 '87

Borofsky, Jonathan
about
Big fish, big pond. S. Staggs. il *Art News* 86:17-18 My '87

Boron
The cosmic synthesis of lithium, beryllium and boron. V. E. Viola and G. J. Mathews. il *Sci Am* 256:38-45 My '87

Boron compounds
Icosahedral boron-rich solids. D. Emin. bibl f il *Phys Today* 40:55-62 Ja '87

Boron nitrides
High-temperature cubic boron nitride P-N junction diode made at high pressure. O. Mishima and others. bibl f il *Science* 238:181-3 O 9 '87
Putting the heat on new semiconductors [cubic boron nitride diode; work of Osamu Mishima and others] I. Peterson. *Sci News* 132:247 O 17 '87

Boroughs, Don L.
Torturers saved by the bell, almost. il *Progressive* 51:13 Ap '87

Borowitz, Eugene B.
Between anarchy and fanaticism: religious freedom's challenge. il *Christ Century* 104:619-22 Jl 15-22 '87

Borregaard, N., and others
Chemoattractant-regulated mobilization of a novel intracellular compartment in human neutrophils. bibl f il *Science* 237:1204-6 S 4 '87

Borrelia
Linear plasmids of the bacterium Borrelia burgdorferi have covalently closed ends. A. G. Barbour and C. F. Garon. bibl f il *Science* 237:409-11 Jl 24 '87

Borrow, George, 1803-1881
Scholar Gypsy [excerpt from The Bible in Spain] il *Courier* 40:16 Ap '87

Borrowing of money See Credit; Loans, Personal

Borst, Piet, and Greaves, D. R.
Programmed gene rearrangements altering gene expression. bibl f il *Science* 235:658-67 F 6 '87

Bortle, John E.
Comet digest. See issues of Sky and Telescope

Borts, Rhona H., and Haber, James E.
Meiotic recombination in yeast: alteration by multiple heterozygosities. bibl f il *Science* 237:1459-65 S 18 '87

Bortz, Cindy
about
Woman to watch: Cindy Bortz. M. Friedlander. il por *Women's Sports Fitness* 9:18 F '87

Bortz, Jeffrey
The dilemma of Mexican labor. *Curr Hist* 86:105-8+ Mr '87

Bortz, Paul, 1941-
about
The importance of being patient. M. Brown. il *Channels* 7:22 O '87

Boruch, Marianne
Napping in trees [poem] *Nation* 244:622 My 9 '87
November garden with moon [poem] *Nation* 245:384 O 10 '87

Borysenko, Joan
Six mind traps to avoid. il *Health* 19:74-8 Jl '87

BOS See Booksellers Order Service

Bosch, Daniel
Robert Bly quelling riots in Miami [poem] *New Repub* 197:38 Ag 31 '87

Bosch, William J.
Books on World War II. *America* 156:256-8+ Mr 28 '87

Boschwitz, Rudy
Should the Boren Amendment approach to curtailing PAC's be adopted? [excerpts from debate, August 11, 1986] *Congr Dig* 66:41+ F '87

Bose, Amar
about
Beating Japan loud and clear. J. D. Reed. il por *Fortune* 116:65+ O 26 '87

Bose Corp.
Beating Japan loud and clear. J. D. Reed. il por *Fortune* 116:65+ O 26 '87

Boskin, Michael J.
The coming social security surplus. il *Fortune* 115:111+ Mr 30 '87

Boss, Lewis
about
Charting the southern sky. J. Lankford. il pors *Sky Telesc* 74:243-6 S '87

Boss-employee relations *See* Psychology, Industrial

Boss rule (Politics)
Boss [F. Hague, mayor and political boss of Jersey City] *New Yorker* 63:22-4 Je 15 '87

Boss Tweed *See* Tweed, William Marcy, 1823-1878

Bosson, Barbara
about
In the market for bitter fruit? Hooperman's Barbara Bosson seems always to harvest a bumper crop. J. Kaufman. il pors *People Wkly* 28:83-4 N 16 '87

Boston (Mass.)

Airports
Massport to cut Logan traffic, foster use of reliever airports. *Aviat Week Space Technol* 127:44 S 7 '87
National groups prepare to fight plan to restrict access at Logan. D. Hughes. il *Aviat Week Space Technol* 127:34-5 D 21 '87
Operators attack plan to stem New England commuter service [plan to divert traffic from Boston's Logan Airport to reliever airports] *Aviat Week Space Technol* 127:41+ S 7 '87
Opposition grows to plan for fee increase at Logan. D. Hughes. *Aviat Week Space Technol* 127:52+ O 26 '87

Art
See also
Boston (Mass.)—Monuments, statues, etc.

Banks
See also
Boston Safe Deposit & Trust Co.

Blacks
Secession move defeated [Mandela] J. Ball. *Black Enterp* 17:16 Ja '87

History
The Boston Four Hundred: 1940 [excerpt from The autobiography of Malcolm X] Malcolm X. *Harpers* 274:43 F '87

City planning
No little plans: an ambitious mixed-use scheme for Boston [Fan Pier] R. Strickland. il *Archit Rec* 175:60-1 F '87

Crime
Assault charges dropped against Harvard's Loury. pors *Jet* 72:25 S 7 '87
Harvard prof charged with beating up live-in lover [charges against G. C. Loury] il pors *Jet* 72:24-5 Je 29 '87
The rise and fall of Glenn Loury [drug possession charges] il por *Newsweek* 110:53 D 14 '87

Economic conditions
Down and out in the midst of Boston's boom. K. H. Hammonds. il *Bus Week* p53 Ag 10 '87

Education
Computers in the classroom [Project Headlight at Hennigan Elementary School, Roxbury] A. Bass. il por *Technol Rev* 90:52-62+ Ap '87

Galleries and museums
Art in Boston: an overview. N. Stapen. il *Art News* 86:75+ Summ '87

Gardens and gardening
See also
Boston Public Garden

Harbor
Breaking the dumping habit. M. James. il *Sierra* 72:80-1 Mr/Ap '87
Toward a cleaner harbor [exhibit at the New England Aquarium] *Oceans* 20:57 My/Je '87

Historic houses, sites, etc.
Beacon Hill spirit [Honora Haley Hillier redecorates Beacon Hill row house] E. Greene. il *House Gard* 159:154-61 Mr '87

History
See also
Boston Tea Party, 1773

Intellectual life
First encounters [W. D. Howells' first meeting with J.R. Lowell and the Boston brahmins] E. Sorel and N. C. Sorel. il *Atlantic* 260:101 N '87

Monuments, statues, etc.
Boston makes way for ducklings: the Mallard family in bronze [N. Schön's sculpture of R. McCloskey's children's book characters in the Boston Public Garden] A. Meeker. il *Publ Wkly* 232:27 O 30 '87
Sculpture in the subways? Is there a better place for it? R. Wolkomir. il *Smithsonian* 18:114-18+ Ap '87

Music
See also
Boston Symphony Orchestra
Opera Company of Boston

Police
Boston police may get 1st minority lieutenants. *Jet* 72:40 Ag 3 '87

Poor
Death of a homeless man. S. R. Sanders. il *Progressive* 51:50 Mr '87
Facing eviction from his Boston hovel, hermit Bill Britt pleads there's no place like home. C. Neuhaus. il pors *People Wkly* 27:61-2 Ap 13 '87

Protests, demonstrations, etc.
Haitian sets self afire in protest of nation's strife [A. Thurel] *Jet* 72:4 S 21 '87

Race relations
Rowers snub South Boston club race that bans blacks. *Jet* 72:16 Je 8 '87
South Boston club ends it's ban against blacks [rowing club] *Jet* 72:4 Je 15 '87
Up against the wall in Beantown [racial problems and pro sports] A. P. Sanoff. il *U S News World Rep* 103:54-5 Jl 27 '87

Schools
See Boston (Mass.)—Education

Social history
Federal Bostonians and their London jeweler, Stephen Twycross. M. G. Fales. bibl f il *Antiques* 131:642-9 Mr '87

Sports
To Boston with love [people who live and toil along the Marathon course] L. Montville. il *Sports Illus* 66:94-8+ Ap 20 '87
Up against the wall in Beantown [racial problems and pro sports] A. P. Sanoff. il *U S News World Rep* 103:54-5 Jl 27 '87

Stations
Sculpture in the subways? Is there a better place for it? R. Wolkomir. il *Smithsonian* 18:114-18+ Ap '87
A transparent fortress [Suffolk Downs Station] G. Anderson. il *Archit Rec* 175:76-9 Ja '87

Water pollution
Breaking the dumping habit. M. James. il *Sierra* 72:80-1 Mr/Ap '87
Toward a cleaner harbor [exhibit at the New England Aquarium] *Oceans* 20:57 My/Je '87

Boston (Mass.) in television
'Spenser: for hire': Boston plugs its hero. il *Newsweek* 109:54 Ap 13 '87

Boston (Musical group)
Boston [concert in Philadelphia] D. Wild. il *Roll Stone* p12 Ag 13 '87
Boston: out of the studio and onto the road. il *Roll Stone* p18 Je 18 '87

Boston Ballet
Celebration! [production of Tales of Hans Christian Andersen] I. M. Fanger. il *Dance Mag* 61:52-5 N '87
Reviews:
1987 Discovery Festival in Boston. I. M. Fanger. *Dance Mag* 61:73-4 S '87
Travels with Coppélia. T. Tobias. il *Dance Mag* 61:52-3 F '87

Boston Beer Company
Brewing American [Samuel Adams beer] S. W. Angrist. il por *Forbes* 139:172 Ap 6 '87

Boston CitiNet
Boston CitiNet is boffo. K. H. Hammonds. il por *Bus Week* p92+ O 19 '87

Boston Computer Society
A different kind of computer whiz kid [J. Rotenberg] A. Beam. il por *Bus Week* p97-8 Mr 9 '87

Boston Early Music Festival Orchestra
Musical events:
F. Geminiani's The enchanted forest. A. Porter. *New Yorker* 63:92 My 25 '87

Boston Garden (Mass.: Arena)
Home field advantage [J. Hynes' plans for development]
B. Leonard. il por *Forbes* 139:91-2 Ja 26 '87
Boston Light *See* Lighthouses
Boston Marathon *See* Marathon running
Boston Public Garden
Boston makes way for ducklings: the Mallard family
in bronze [N. Schön's sculpture of R. McCloskey's
children's book characters] A. Meeker. il *Publ Wkly*
232:27 O 30 '87
Boston Safe Deposit & Trust Co.
High-octane banking. J. Willoughby. il por *Forbes* 140:58+
S 21 '87
Boston school of painting
Art: the Boston school of painters. R. Rosenblum. il
Archit Dig 44:188-93 My '87
Boston Symphony Orchestra
The clearing of Vanessa Redgrave. M. Heins. il *Nation*
245:713-15 D 12 '87
Musical events:
Boston Symphony performs D. Martino's The white
island. A. Porter. *New Yorker* 63:98+ My 11 '87
H. W. Henze's Seventh symphony. A. Porter. *New
Yorker* 63:134+ N 23 '87
Boston Tea Party, 1773
How dark was the night of the Boston Tea Party? S.
W. Schultz. il *Astronomy* 15:24 Ag '87
Boston University
Robert Brown oversees the enrollment of Mandela's
daughter at Boston Univ. il por *Jet* 72:28 Je 8 '87
Boston University. College of Communication
J-school for Afghan rebels [project in Pakistan] E. Salholz.
il *Newsweek* 109:75-6 Mr 30 '87
Boston University. School of Theology
Contract not renewed [faculty member E. Bettenhausen
charges sexism] *Christ Century* 104:936 O 28 '87
Boston Ventures Management Inc.
The Hollywood superstar no one's ever heard of [W.
F. Thompson] G. Geipel. il por *Bus Week* p98-9
Ja 26 '87
Bostonians
Anecdotes, facetiae, satire, etc.
Cold roast Boston. il *Mother Earth News* 106:128 Jl/Ag
'87
Boswall, Jeffery
Russia is for the birds. il *Discover* 8:78-83 Mr '87
Boswell, Thomas, 1948-
Temper fugit [excerpt from Strokes of genius] il *Sport
Mag* 78:59-60 Jl '87
Bosworth, Brian
about
Bosworth faces the music. C. Neff. il pors *Sports Illus*
66:20-2+ Ja 5 '87
The Boz, the UAW, and your new Chevy. D. Fuller.
il *Mot Trend* 39:116-17 Ja '87
A star flunks his test. P. Axthelm. il por *Newsweek*
109:48-9 Ja 5 '87
Bosworth, Patricia
480 Lex. por *N Y* 20:100 D 21-28 '87
Memories of HUAC. *Nation* 245:436-7 O 24 '87
Botanical chemistry *See* Plants—Analysis and chemistry
Botanical gardens
Georgia
Georgia's new garden showplace [State Botanical Garden]
il *South Living* 22:46 Ag '87
Kentucky
She planted Kentucky's gardens [M. J. Carter] D. Young.
il por *South Living* 22:134+ S '87
Botanical illustration *See* Flowers in art
Botanical museums
See also
Harvard University. Botanical Museum
Botanical research
See also
Computers—Botanical use
Federal aid
Botany bids for the "big science" league [Flora of North
America project] M. Sun. il *Science* 237:967-8 Ag
28 '87
Botanicals *See* Botany, Medical
Botanists
See also
Burbank, Luther, 1849-1926
Botany
See also
Alpine flora
Chromosomes (Botany)
Clones (Botany)
Ethnobotany
Fungi
Hybridization

Information storage and retrieval systems—Botanical
use
Leaves
Lichens
Molds (Botany)
Morphogenesis
Paleobotany
Plants
Roots
Seeds
Anatomy
See also
Plant cells and tissues
Classification
Botany bids for the "big science" league [Flora of North
America project] M. Sun. il *Science* 237:967-8 Ag
28 '87
Global flora: new research links alpine wildflowers around
the world. L. Tejada-Flores. il *Natl Parks* 61:26-9
S/O '87
Ecology
See also
Forest ecology
Plant competition
Plant introduction
Large herbivore foraging and ecological hierarchies. R.
L. Senft and others. bibl il *BioScience* 37:789-95+
D '87
On the benefits of being eaten [herbivory benefits plants;
research by Ken Paige and Thomas Whitham] R.
Lewin. il *Science* 236:519-20 My 1 '87
Plant physiological ecology today [special issue] il
BioScience 37:18-67 Ja '87
Physiology
See also
Chloroplasts
Photosynthesis
Plants—Reproduction
Plant physiological ecology today [special issue] il
BioScience 37:18-67 Ja '87
Arkansas
Alum Cove, Arkansas [French's shooting stars in Ozark
National Forest] R. H. Mohlenbrock. il map *Nat Hist*
96:60-2 Ap '87
North America
Botany bids for the "big science" league [Flora of North
America project] M. Sun. il *Science* 237:967-8 Ag
28 '87
Philippines
The curse of cadang-cadang [Philippine coconut palm
disease] K. Maramorosch. il *Nat Hist* 96:20-2 Jl '87
Botany, Economic
See also
Rubber producing plants
Botany, Medical
See also
Aloe
Acupuncture and me [knee injury treated with Chinese
herbal tea and acupuncture] S. R. Brady. il por *Good
Housekeep* 205:58+ Ag '87
Bathing botanicals [herbal cleaning] il *Health* 19:56-8+
N '87
Can herbs really heal? R. W. Miller. il *FDA Consum*
21:32-4 Je '87
Chinese folk remedy may promote cancer [plants con-
taining phorbal esters linked to nasopharyngeal cancer;
research by L. David Tomei and others] R. Weiss.
Sci News 132:148 S 5 '87
Combing the earth for cures to cancer, AIDS. W. Booth.
il *Science* 237:969-70 Ag 28 '87
Dr. Plotkin's jungle pharmacy: an ethnobotanist goes
native for science [work among the Tirió tribe in
Suriname] A. Fadiman. il pors *Life* 10:15-17 Je '87
Plant therapy in the fight against cancer [Chinese
medicine] Xing Sishao. il *Courier* 40:20 Ag '87
Readers' survey: healing with herbs. il *Prevention* 39:22+
Je '87
Saved by the Indians [scurvy antidote given to French
explorers; excerpt from Voyages au Canada] J. Cartier.
il *Courier* 40:12 Ap '87
Scouring the globe for natural cures for cancer. *FDA
Consum* 21:35 Je '87
A side order of sea slugs [Chinese herbal cookery at
Emperor Herbal Restaurant, San Francisco] L. Shapiro.
il *Newsweek* 110:77 S 14 '87
Useless yew aids cancer fight [drug from Pacific yew
bark] il *Audubon* 89:14 S '87
Botelho, Antonio José J.
Brazil's independent computer strategy [cover story] il
maps *Technol Rev* 90:36-45 My/Je '87

Botha, Pieter W.
about
Botha defies the tides, gets tougher. J. Jones. il por *U S News World Rep* 102:32-3 F 16 '87
Botha in the lions' den. S. Reiss. il por *Newsweek* 109:43 Je 15 '87
Botha's defiant show of force. S. Reiss. il *Newsweek* 109:34 My 4 '87

Botham, Ian
about
Black Botham. M. Weiss. il pors *Esquire* 107:82-6 Ja '87

Botsford, Keith, 1928-
The Pollini sound. il pors *N Y Times Mag* p30-1+ Mr 1 '87

Botstein, David
(jt. auth) See Lander, Eric S., and Botstein, David

Botswana
See also
Hunting—Botswana
Wildlife—Botswana
Description and travel
Botswana: beauty and the beasts [Okavango delta] A. Faujas. il *World Press Rev* 34:62 Ap '87

Botta, Mario
about
Botta buildings for all time. E. Beck. il por *Horizon* 30:66-8 O '87
A little bit timeless. P. M. Sachner. il *Archit Rec* 175:124-9 mid-S '87
The return of humanism: Mario Botta at MOMA. R. Kimball. il *Archit Rec* 175:41+ Ja '87

Botting, Ingrid
'Most of us are scared'. il por *Macleans* 100:45 S 7 '87

Bottled messages See Drift bottles
Bottled water
See also
Seltzer
Bottled bonanza. G. Bakoulis. il *Health* 19:34+ Mr '87
New wave at work. A. Oshins. il *Work Woman* 12:92 Ap '87
Rating
Water. il *Consum Rep* 52:372-6 D '87
Water, water everywhere. il *Consum Rep* 52:42-7 Ja '87

Bottled water industry
See also
Alhambra National Water Company
Arrowhead Drinking Water Company
Acquisitions and mergers
Perrier's unquenchable U.S. thirst [acquiring Arrowhead Drinking Water Co.] J. Rossant. *Bus Week* p46 Je 29 '87
Marketing
See also
Water bars
France
See also
Source Perrier SA

Bottles
See also
Baby bottles
Beverage containers
Drift bottles
Collectors and collecting
American historical flasks: glassware symbolic of a growing nation. K. McConnell. il *Antiques Collect Hobbies* 92:40-2 O '87
Collecting patented medicine bottles. L. C. May. il *Antiques Collect Hobbies* 91:22-4 Ja '87

Bottomley, Tom, 1924-
New boat 1987 directory [special section] *Mot Boat Sail* 159:79-118 Ja '87

Botwin, Carol, and Parsons, Edward L.
Good women, bad marriages. *Redbook* 168:94-5+ F '87

Bouatchidzé, Gaston, and Glissant, Edouard, 1928-
The poetry of Ilya Chavchavadze. il *Courier* 40:31-2 O '87

Bouchard, Benoît
about
Ottawa's refugee dilemma. H. Mackenzie. por *Macleans* 100:10 Jl 27 '87

Boucher, Gaetan
about
The price of glory. J. Howse. il por *Macleans* 100:40-2 D 14 '87

Boucher, Laurence
about
Man the pumps. M. Beauchamp. il por *Forbes* 140:400+ Jl 13 '87

Bouchier, David
Universities and the government: a lesson from Britain. *Educ Dig* 52:50-2 My '87

Boudoir photography See Erotic photography
Bouillon See Soups

Bouis, Antonina W.
(tr) See Voznesenskiĭ, Andreĭ, 1933-. A poet's view of glasnost
(tr) See Yevtushenko, Yevgeny Aleksandrovich, 1933-. First word

Boulanger, Daniel
Short stories: weapons of pessimists; tr. by Penny Million Pucelik and Marijo Despréaux Schneider. *Harpers* 275:40-1 N '87

Bouley (New York, N.Y.: Restaurant) See New York (N.Y.)—Restaurants, nightclubs, bars, etc.

Boulez, Pierre, 1925-
about
Musical events:
Performances of works in New York and Los Angeles. A. Porter. *New Yorker* 63:97-9 Je 1 '87

Boulton, Alexander Ormond
Good fences. il *Am Herit* 38:90-5 F/Mr '87

Boulton, Jack L.
about
The $2 million man. A. Virshup. il por *Art News* 86:112-14 S '87

Boulud, Daniel
about
Breezing along. C. Claiborne and P. Franey. il *N Y Times Mag* p43-5 Jl 26 '87

Bouncers [drama] See Godber, John
Bouncing of checks See Checks, Fraudulent

Boundaries
See also
Territorial waters

Boundary layer
See also
Laminar flow

Boundas, Louise Gooch
Speaking my piece. See issues of Stereo Review beginning May 1987

Bounty Mutiny, 1789
Pitcairn lives. W. F. Buckley. *Natl Rev* 39:63 D 18 '87

Bouquet, Carole
about
New Chanel scent star: Carole Bouquet. il pors *Vogue* 177:134 D '87

Bouquets
See also
Tussie mussies

Bourassa, Robert, 1933-
about
'A great step for Quebec' [interview] A. Wilson-Smith. il por *Macleans* 100:12 My 11 '87
What Bourassa won. M. Rose. il *Macleans* 100:11 My 11 '87

Bourdin, Michel
about
Chefs of influence. N. Barry. il pors *Gourmet* 47:82-3+ D '87

Bourgeois, Louise
about
Sex, rage & Louise Bourgeois. B. Rose. il por *Vogue* 177:764-5+ S '87

Bourguiba, Habib, 1903-
about
Defeat of the supreme combatant. M. S. Serrill. por *Time* 130:48 N 16 '87
Punishing the pious. M. S. Serrill. il por *Time* 130:42 O 12 '87
Sidelining of a legend. *Macleans* 100:24 N 16 '87
'The worst has been avoided'. S. Seibert. il por *Newsweek* 110:52 O 12 '87

Bourjaily, Vance, 1922-
In and out of Storyville: jazz and fiction. il *N Y Times Book Rev* 92:1+ D 13 '87

Bourke, Walter, and Furniss, Ronnie D.
After-school discussion helps problem students. il *Phi Delta Kappan* 69:241-2 N '87

Bourne, Bob
about
A burden gallantly borne. A. Murphy. il pors *Sports Illus* 67:26-7 D 21 '87

Bourne, Michael
Kevin Eubanks: a new breed of guitarist. il pors *Down Beat* 54:20-2 Jl '87
Lew Soloff: big band brass man. il pors *Down Beat* 54:24-6 S '87

Bourne, Michael—*cont.*
Steve Turré: trombone straight from the hip. il pors *Down Beat* 54:28-30 D '87
Bourne, Russell
When the First Lady speaks her mind. il *Am Herit* 38:108-9 S/O '87
Bournonville, August, 1805-1879
about
Bournonville lives in oral memoirs. por *Dance Mag* 61:108-9 Mr '87
Napoli [ballet] Reviews
   Dance Mag 61:34+ My '87. L. Svedin
Bournonville divertissements [ballet] See Ballet reviews—Single works
Bourque, Ray, 1960-
about
Bulwark of the Bruins. F. Lidz. il pors *Sports Illus* 66:36-8+ Mr 9 '87
Bourride *See* Stew
Bourse (Paris) *See* Stock exchanges—Paris exchange
Bouton, Katherine
Fertility and family. *Ms* 15:92 Ap '87
Marian Wright Edelman. por *Ms* 16:98-100+ Jl/Ag '87
Bouvier, Virginia Marie, 1958-
Business as usual: life after the Pope's visit. il *Commonweal* 114:373-5 Je 19 '87
Bova, Ben, 1932-
President's message. See issues of Space World beginning January 1986
Bova, Jeff
about
Jeff Bova. B. Milkowski. il por *Down Beat* 11:47-9 N '87
Bovard, James
The failure of federal job training programs. il *USA Today (Periodical)* 116:12-17 Jl '87
Bovine papilloma virus *See* Papilloma viruses
Bow and arrow
See also
   Crossbow
Bow hunting *See* Hunting with bow and arrow
Bow Valley Industries Ltd.
Educating the managers [shareholder challenges] A. Shortell. il *Macleans* 100:28-9 S 28 '87
An oil-patch marriage [British Gas buys major stake in Bow Valley Industries] J. Howse. il *Macleans* 100:33 Ag 17 '87
Bowa, Larry
about
Padre with a passion. R. Fimrite. il pors *Sports Illus* 66:52-4+ My 4 '87
Bowden, Christopher
The New England montage. il *Art News* 86:87-8+ Summ '87
Bowden, Suella
Sweet inspiration. il *World Tennis* 34:22-3 Ap '87
Bowe, Frank
Making computers accessible to disabled people. il *Technol Rev* 90:52-9+ Ja '87
Bowen, Ezra
Constitutional Convention, Philadelphia, 1787. bibl (p146) il map *Smithsonian* 18:32-43 Jl '87
Bowen, Gordon L.
Four candles in the wind. il *Commonweal* 114:726-7 D 18 '87
Bowen, Harry
about
Economic power. S. R. Reed. *Pers Comput* 11:71 Mr '87
Bowen, Otis R.
about
An Rx for catastrophe. O. Friedrich. il por *Time* 129:38-9 Ja 5 '87
Bowen, William G.
about
Great university presidents have to be miracle men. M. S. Forbes. por *Forbes* 139:26 My 18 '87
Bowery Savings Bank
Sweet charity. A. A. Lappen. il *Forbes* 140:8 N 2 '87
Why the Bowery deal wasn't a ripoff. S. Bartlett. il *Bus Week* p105 O 19 '87
Bowes, Frances
about
San Francisco style from Frances Bowes: city skirt-and-sweater dressing. il pors *Vogue* 177:328 F '87
Bowes, Watson A., Jr.
about
A new program offers important advice to couples just thinking of having a baby. G. Williams. *McCalls* 115:62-3 O '87

Bowes-Lyon, John
The sweet smell of Sussex. il por *House Gard* 159:188-95 N '87
Bowes-Lyon family
about
All in the family. il *Time* 129:45 Ap 20 '87
A royal family secret. il *Macleans* 100:24 Ap 20 '87
The royal family's gothic shocker. N. Cooper. il *Newsweek* 109:49 Ap 20 '87
Bowes Museum (Barnard Castle, England)
Durham's hidden gems. D. Byrne. il *Hist Today* 37:5-6 Jl '87
Bowhead whales *See* Whales
Bowie, David
about
David Bowie [Giants Stadium concert] A. DeCurtis. il por *Roll Stone* p26 S 24 '87
David Bowie and The Spiders from Mars: U.S. tour, September-December 1972. D. Fricke. il por *Roll Stone* p83+ Je 4 '87
David Bowie ch-ch-ch-changes his tune. J. Pareles. il pors *Mademoiselle* 93:44 Jl '87
The Glass Spider tour: designer remedies for Bowie's theatre bug. M. Loeffler. il pors *Theatre Crafts* 21:38-41+ N '87
Never say never. S. Pond. il *Roll Stone* p129-30 Je 4 '87
Rockers: then & now. il pors *Teen* 31:62-3 O '87
Stardust memories [interview] K. Loder. il pors *Roll Stone* p74-7+ Ap 23 '87
Bowker, Michael
Spying from on high. il *Int Wildl* 17:22-3 S/O '87
Bowl football games *See* Football, College
Bowler, K. C., and others
Exploiting highly concurrent computers for physics. bibl f il *Phys Today* 40:40-8 O '87
Bowles, Dorcas
about
Dorcas Bowles named prexy of Atlanta University. *Jet* 72:12 Ag 17 '87
Bowling
See also
   Ladies Touring Players Association
Breakthrough in bowling [black bowler G. Branham] il pors *Ebony* 42:142+ Mr '87
Lady in a fast lane [L. Wagner] G. Maranto. il pors *Sports Illus* 67:44-7 S 28 '87
Thank you, Pete Weber [victory in the Firestone] D. S. Looney. il pors *Sports Illus* 66:26-7 My 4 '87
Woman to watch: Leila Wagner. B. Cooper. il por *Women's Sports Fitness* 9:62 N '87
Equipment
Look what's going high fashion. il *U S News World Rep* 102:48-9 F 16 '87
Social aspects
A clean, well-lighted alley [bowling and yuppies] B. Barol. il *Newsweek* 109:63 Mr 2 '87
Television broadcasting
See Television broadcasting—Sports
Tournaments
Amateur bowlers on a roll. W. Roessing. il *Saturday Evening Post* 259:38-9+ O '87
Bowling alleys
Finding big bucks in the alleys. C. Skrzycki. il *U S News World Rep* 102:48-9 F 16 '87
Bowls
See also
   Punch bowls
World-class turner [wooden bowls of B. Stocksdale] R. La Trobe-Bateman. il *Am Craft* 47:30-5 D '87/Ja '88
Bowls in house decoration
Holiday accents by the bowlful. J. Williams and J. Severson. il *Better Homes Gard* 65:144-5 N '87
A touch of the Orient [porcelain bowls] il *South Living* 22:94-5 N '87
Bowne, Alan
about
Beirut [drama] Reviews
   N Y il 20:55 Jl 27 '87. J. Simon
   Nation 245:134 Ag 15-22 '87. T. M. Disch
   New Yorker 63:69 Je 22 '87. E. Oliver
Bows (Ribbon) *See* Ribbons
Box, Cloyce K., 1924-
about
Shootout at the OKC Corral. E. F. Cone. por *Forbes* 140:86+ D 14 '87
Box joints *See* Joints (Carpentry)
Box lacrosse (Professional) *See* Lacrosse, Professional
Box Tree Hotel (New York, N.Y.) *See* New York (N.Y.)—Hotels, motels, etc.

Box turtles *See* Turtles
Boxer, C. R. (Charles Ralph), 1904-
The shipwrecked remainders of Europe's china boom.
il *Hist Today* 37:45-8 Ap '87
Boxer, Charles Ralph *See* Boxer, C. R. (Charles Ralph),
1904-
Boxer, Sarah
Will creationism rise again? il *Discover* 8:80-5 O '87
Boxer shorts *See* Underwear
Boxers
See also
Ali, Muhammad, 1942-
Berbick, Trevor
Biggs, Tyrell
Breland, Mark
Bugner, Joe
Camacho, Hector
Chávez, Julio César
Cobb, Randall
Cooney, Gerry
Cruz, Stevie
Curry, Donald
Czyz, Bobby
Davis, Howard
Foreman, George
Grandchamp, Gail
Greb, Harry, 1894-1926
Hagler, Marvin
Harris, Tracy
Haugen, Greg
Hearns, Thomas
Hilton, Matthew
Hitzelburger, Bobby
Holmes, Larry
Holyfield, Evander
Honeyghan, Lloyd
Lawyers as boxers
Leonard, Sugar Ray
Louis, Joe, 1914-1981
McCallum, Mike, 1957?-
McGuigan, Barry
Ocasio, Ossie
Olajide, Michael
Patterson, Floyd
Pazienza, Vinny
Pryor, Aaron
Qawi, Dwight Muhammad
Robinson, Sugar Ray
Roldan, Juan Domingo
Rosario, Edwin
Smith, James
Spinks, Leon
Spinks, Michael
Starling, Marlon
Tate, Frank
Terrell, Ernie
Thomas, Pinklon
Tonawanda, Jackie
Tucker, Tony
Tyson, Mike
Witherspoon, Tim
Young, Bobby Joe
Ranking boxing's best punches. J. Ryan. il *Sport Mag*
78:15 O '87
Weavers of boxing dreams [triplet boxers] F. Lidz. il
Sports Illus 67:83 Ag 3 '87
Accidents and injuries
See Boxing—Accidents and injuries
Health and hygiene
Boxing groups join fight to score KO over AIDS. *Jet*
72:37 Ag 3 '87
Putting on the gloves to fight AIDS [referees ordered
to wear rubber gloves] il *Newsweek* 110:49 Jl 27 '87
Photographs and photography
Boxers, Leicas, and available light. B. Witkowski. il
Petersens Photogr Mag 16:50-3 D '87
Retirement
Ray Leonard retires but won't close the door. il por
Jet 72:46 Je 15 '87
Sugar Ray retires to promote Garden bouts. por *Jet*
72:46 S 7 '87
Training
Ex-champ Ernie Terrell training Foreman's foe [B. Hitzel-
burger] *Jet* 71:50 Mr 2 '87
Boxes, cases, etc.
See also
Bread boxes
Briefcases
Jewelry boxes, cases, etc.
Light boxes
Mailboxes

Recipe boxes, files, etc.
Toy chests
Building a better box [Automatic Loc-Bottom corrugated
cardboard boxes] E. R. C. Capulong. il *Pop Sci* 231:120
O '87
Small storage box. E. Waltner. il *Workbench* 43:60-1
Mr/Ap '87
When only the best will do [L. Maxym's imports of
handpainted Russian lacquer boxes] R. Hotch. il por
Nations Bus 75:78+ My '87
Boxing
Breland knocked out of boxing unbeaten ranks [M.
Starling wins bout] il pors *Jet* 72:52 S 14 '87
Clash of the opposites [M. Hagler vs. S. R. Leonard]
P. Axthelm. pors *Newsweek* 109:52 Ap 6 '87
Comeback for the ages [S. R. Leonard defeats M. Hagler
for middleweight title] W. Nack. il pors *Sports Illus*
66:18-25 Ap 13 '87
The corner man [manager A. Dundee] G. Smith. il
pors *Sports Illus* 67:92-6+ N 2 '87
'Everything I did worked' [S. R. Leonard's thoughts
after defeating M. Hagler] W. Nack. il pors *Sports
Illus* 66:50-2+ Ap 20 '87
Fateful date against Tate [F. Tate defeats M. Olajide
for IBF middleweight crown] P. Putnam. pors *Sports
Illus* 67:48-9 O 19 '87
The fiesta in the town of ghosts [ritual fistfight in Bolivian
Andes] G. Smith. il *Sports Illus* 67:76-80+ O 5 '87
Foreman nixes Arizona for heavyweight bout. il por
Jet 73:51 N 16 '87
Fourth title for Thomas [T. Hearns defeats J. Roldan
for WBC middleweight title] R. Wiley. il pors *Sports
Illus* 67:34-6 N 9 '87
Hagler vs. Leonard: the seniors tour. M. Katz. il pors
Sport Mag 78:76-82 Ap '87
'Hit Man' Hearns ready to make boxing history [upcoming
match with Juan Roldan] por *Jet* 72:48 S 21 '87
Holyfield stops Ocasio, setting up Qawi rematch. *Jet*
72:46 S 7 '87
Iron Mike passes a test [M. Tyson-P. Thomas heavyweight
bout] R. Wiley. il pors *Sports Illus* 66:26-7 Je 8 '87
Killer instinct [excerpt from On boxing] J. C. Oates.
il *Sport Mag* 78:57 Jl '87
Larry Holmes agrees to fight Mike Tyson in '88. *Jet*
73:48 O 26 '87
Leonard adds new tactic in preparing for Hagler. il
por *Jet* 71:46 F 23 '87
Leonard banks on a decision while Hagler mulls a murder
and Hearns wants a double KO. pors *Jet* 72:50 Ap
6 '87
Local boy makes good [V. Pazienza defeats G. Haugen
in IBF lightweight championship] P. Putnam. il pors
Sports Illus 66:59 Je 15 '87
Loud left from a quiet champ [M. McCallum-D. Curry
middleweight bout] P. Putnam. il pors *Sports Illus*
67:34-5 Jl 27 '87
Mike Tyson wins fight; KO's Biggs in the 7th. il pors
Jet 73:51 N 2 '87
New champs' date with destiny promises action; Loss
least of woes for Tim Witherspoon. il pors *Jet* 71:48
Ja 12 '87
Notes and comment [watching the Leonard-Hagler fight
on closed circuit TV in Town Hall, New York City]
New Yorker 63:25-6 Ap 20 '87
Off the mark [M. Breland loses WBA welterweight title
to M. Starling] il por *Sports Illus* 67:13 Ag 31 '87
On cooling a beef [recommendation that pro athletes
use the body punch in arguments during games] P.
Berger. il *Sport Mag* 78:79-80 S '87
One will be made whole [upcoming M. Hagler-S. R.
Leonard fight] R. Reilly. il pors *Sports Illus* 66:58-64+
Mr 30 '87
Only one no. 1 [M. Tyson defeats T. Tucker for IBF
heavyweight crown; cover story] P. Putnam. il pors
Sports Illus 67:20-3 Ag 10 '87
Prediction [upcoming M. Hagler-S. R. Leonard fight]
W. Nack. il pors *Sports Illus* 66:70-2+ Mr 30 '87
Pryor's comeback KO'd, now faces court fight. il por
Jet 72:49 Ag 31 '87
A real nobody did it better [S. Cruz vs. B. McGuigan
in WBA featherweight title bout] R. Wiley. il pors
Sports Illus 66:32-4+ Ja 12 '87
Record fourth title win sets Hearns atop boxing [knockout
of J. D. Roldan] il pors *Jet* 73:46 N 16 '87
Say good night, Gerry [M. Spinks defeats G. Cooney
in heavyweight bout] W. Nack. il pors *Sports Illus*
66:22-3 Je 22 '87
Spinks cleared to fight, but Cooney camp is quiet. por
Jet 72:47 Ap 13 '87
Spinks-Cooney 'title' fight boasts equal opportunity. *Jet*
72:46 Je 1 '87

Boxing—*cont.*

Spinks loses round one in bid to fight Cooney. por *Jet* 71:48 Ja 19 '87

Spinks says victory tells little guys to stand tall [knockout of G. Cooney] il por *Jet* 72:48 Jl 6 '87

Stars shined for Sugar but most bet on Hagler. il *Jet* 72:49 Ap 27 '87

Sugar Ray Leonard says he has a plan for Hagler. il pors *Jet* 71:47 Ja 12 '87

Sugar Ray Leonard scores upset, joins history's greatest [victory over M. Hagler] il pors *Jet* 72:51 Ap 20 '87

Sugar Ray Leonard: why I am fighting again [upcoming fight with M. Hagler; cover story] N. O. Unger. il *Ebony* 42:92-4+ Ap '87

Sugar's sweet comeback. il pors *People Wkly* 27:40-1 Ap 20 '87

Sugar's sweetest confection [S. R. Leonard beats M. Hagler] P. Axthelm. il pors *Newsweek* 109:71 Ap 20 '87

Sunset in Sunrise for the Hawk [A. Pryor loses comeback fight to B. J. Young] P. Putnam. il por *Sports Illus* 67:16 Ag 17 '87

A super finish to a SuperFight [S. R. Leonard beats M. Hagler for middleweight title] il pors *Macleans* 100:46 Ap 20 '87

Too good for his own good [J. C. Chavez defeats E. Rosario for WBA lightweight title] P. Putnam. il pors *Sports Illus* 67:89-90 N 30 '87

Too moving to be mayhem [S. R. Leonard beats M. Hagler] T. Callahan. il pors *Time* 129:62 Ap 20 '87

Tuning up for Tyson [E. Holyfield defeats D. Qawi to retain IBF cruiserweight title] C. Gammon. il pors *Sports Illus* 67:48-50+ D 14 '87

Tyson crowned champ during a $1/4 million coronation ceremony. R. E. Johnson. il pors *Jet* 72:51+ Ag 17 '87

Tyson lives up to billing, stars help him celebrate. il pors *Jet* 72:52 Je 15 '87

Tyson schedule so full Spinks may wait a year. pors *Jet* 72:48 Jl 20 '87

Tyson taps ex-champ Thomas as his next foe. *Jet* 72:48 Ap 13 '87

Tyson wins 2nd crown, works harder at party. il pors *Jet* 71:52-4 Mr 23 '87

Very tough night at the office [M. Tyson defeats T. Biggs to retain heavyweight title] W. Nack. il pors *Sports Illus* 67:64+ O 26 '87

Why Cooney can't win . . . [preview of Spinks fight in Atlantic City] J. Ryan. il pors *Sport Mag* 78:13 Jl '87

You ready, Boom Boom? [H. Camacho defeats H. Davis] P. Putnam. il por *Sports Illus* 66:96 My 11 '87

Accidents and injuries

Tip from Ali helped Smith survive onslaught of Tyson, who cracked his ribs. il pors *Jet* 72:48 Mr 30 '87

Awards

Second boxing award impresses even Tyson. por *Jet* 71:49 F 16 '87

Economic aspects

And in both corners . . . [B. Arum] G. Buchalter. il por *Forbes* 139:170+ Ap 6 '87

Ex-champ Berbick OKs deflated fight purse. *Jet* 72:52 Mr 30 '87

Fighters sue Don King for $35 million in damages. *Jet* 72:40 Je 1 '87

Fighting lady [manager and promoter J. Abercrombie] D. Remnick. il pors *Sports Illus* 66:62-6+ F 2 '87

Pow! Bam! A one-two punch from Bob Arum and Budweiser [Hagler-Leonard fight] M. D. Oneal. il *Bus Week* p44 Ap 6 '87

Ethical aspects

Boxing slips the drug punch. J. Ryan. il *Sport Mag* 78:19 Ag '87

Let's count boxing out. F. Deford. il por *Sports Illus* 66:222 F 9 '87

History

Bittersweet twilight for Sugar [S. R. Robinson] R. Wiley. il pors *Sports Illus* 67:68-72+ Jl 13 '87

The Sugar Ray of his day [middleweight H. Greb fought with detached retina in the 1920's] J. Harvey. il por *Sports Illus* 66:83 Mr 30 '87

Twin boxers: it wasn't twice the fun [Stolley twins boxing in Pekin, Ill. in the late 1930's] R. B. Stolley. il *Sports Illus* 66:77 F 2 '87

Judging

Fight judge files a suit against ex-champ Holmes [F. Brunette] por *Jet* 72:50 Je 8 '87

The illusion of victory: another view of the Leonard-Hagler decision. H. McIlvanney. il por *Sports Illus* 66:120 Ap 20 '87

One of the boys [woman boxing judge D. Auclair] D. J. Higdon. il por *N Y* 20:42 N 16 '87

Qawi's loss is a win when decision comes in. por *Jet* 72:51 Je 8 '87

Periodicals

See also

Ring (Periodical)

Photographs and photography

Dream fight [S. R. Leonard vs. M. Hagler] J. McDonough. il pors *Sport Mag* 78:56-63 D '87

They could have danced all night . . . [M. Tyson vs. J. Smith for WBA heavyweight championship] il pors *Sports Illus* 66:20-1 Mr 16 '87

Refereeing

A few rounds with the third man in the ring [views of referee R. Battle] J. Millman. il *Sport Mag* 78:98 Jl '87

Putting on the gloves to fight AIDS [referees ordered to wear rubber gloves] il *Newsweek* 110:49 Jl 27 '87

Training

See Boxers—Training

South Africa

Boxer wins award for his fight vs. apartheid [L. Honeyghan] por *Jet* 72:48 Je 8 '87

Champ refuses to fight South African, junks belt [L. Honeyghan] il por *Jet* 71:46 Ja 26 '87

Boxing in literature

Ifs, ands, butts. A. Krystal. il *Harpers* 274:63-7 Je '87

Boxing judges *See* Boxing—Judging

Boxwood

Forever boxwood. S. Bender. il *South Living* 22:88-91 N '87

Boy bishops

Boy into bishop: a festive role-reversal. N. Mackenzie. bibl il *Hist Today* 37:10-16 D '87

Boy George

about

Boy George comes clean—and tries to come back—after heroin addiction and his pals' drug deaths. L. S. Healy. il pors *People Wkly* 28:92-3+ Ag 24 '87

More problems for Boy George. M. Goldberg. *Roll Stone* p13 Ja 15 '87

Mr. Clean: Boy George straightens up his act. M. Goldberg. il pors *Roll Stone* p87-8+ O 8 '87

Boy Scouts of America

Humanists versus religiosity in the Boy Scouts. D. Carroll. por *Humanist* 47:37 N/D '87

Boyanton, Janet Shafer

Brainstorming alone. *Writer* 100:29-30 Ag '87

Boyce, Peter B.

Astronomy, Challenger, and budget cuts. il *Sky Telesc* 73:468 My '87

Boycott

See also

Olympic Games—1988—Summer Olympics—Boycott

Blacklisting

Can Revlon repair its image? [black boycott] P. Wang and M. Malone. il *Newsweek* 109:53 F 23 '87

Farmworkers out on the line again [proposed UFW grape boycott] A. Stine. il *Sierra* 72:14+ Jl/Ag '87

Hamburgers are killing trees [boycott of fast-food outlets until they stop using Central American beef] il *Newsweek* 110:74 S 14 '87

Japan's Israel problem [Japan's compliance with Arab economic boycott of Israel] H. Stanislawski. *New Repub* 196:11-12 Mr 9 '87

A long-brewing boycott ends at Coors [AFL-CIO wins right to try to organize workers] *Newsweek* 110:46 Ag 31 '87

Operation PUSH continues boycott of Revlon products. *Jet* 71:17 Ja 12 '87

Racial mishap sparks buy boycott in Isola, Miss. [treatment of B. Greenwood by police sparks boycott] *Jet* 73:32 N 2 '87

Student boycott ends in Senatobia, Miss. [hiring of black assistant superintendent] *Jet* 72:22 Ap 6 '87

UN forgives Paul Simon for 'Graceland' album. *Jet* 71:30 F 23 '87

UN group attacks Paul Simon: says 'Graceland' broke cultural boycott of South Africa. R. Tannenbaum. *Roll Stone* p11+ F 12 '87

Will labor's Joe Sixpack come back to Coors? [union boycott ends as AFL-CIO wins right to organize] S. D. Atchison. il *Bus Week* p29 S 7 '87

Boyd, Blanche M., 1945-

Isle of light. il *Vogue* 177:218+ Ag '87

Boyd, Dennis

about

'Oil Can' Boyd slides back into action for Red Sox. il por *Jet* 72:48 Jl 13 '87

Boyd, Joseph A., 1921-
about
Harris chief warns of economic chaos if manufacturing continues overseas move. E. H. Kolcum. *Aviat Week Space Technol* 127:89 S 14 '87

Boyd, Liona
about
Liona Boyd. A. Nash. por *Stereo Rev* 52:82 Mr '87

Boyd, Oil Can *See* Boyd, Dennis

Boyd, William, 1952-
Cockney charisma. il pors *N Y Times Mag* p52+ D 6 '87

Boyer, David S.
Pride of two nations. il maps *Natl Geogr* 171:796-823 Je '87

Boyer, Ernest L.
Discover yourself [address, May 10, 1987] *Vital Speeches Day* 53:686-8 S 1 '87
How to grade a college [excerpt from College: the undergraduate experience in America] *Money* 16:112-13 S '87
Improving urban schools. *Educ Dig* 53:6-9 S '87
Smoothing the transition from high school to college. *Educ Dig* 52:2-5 My '87

Boyer, G. Bruce
Passing through customs. il *Esquire* 108:218-20+ S '87
The shape of suits to come. il *Esquire* 108:130-5 O '87

Boyer, Paul S.
How S.D.I. will change our culture. il *Nation* 244:1+ Ja 10 '87

Boyfriends and girlfriends *See* Women and men

Boyle, James
Voyeurism in politics. por *Newsweek* 109:8 My 25 '87

Boyle, Joseph, and Robinson, Gloria
Acid-base balance: an educational computer game. il *BioScience* 37:511-13 Jl/Ag '87

Boyle, Lara Flynn
about
Catch some rising stars. pors *Teen* 31:58 My '87

Boyle, M. B., and others
Xenopus oocytes injected with rat uterine RNA express very slowly activating potassium currents. bibl f il *Science* 235:1221-4 Mr 6 '87

Boyle, Robert H.
Autumn's hidden harvest. il *Natl Wildl* 25:4-9 O/N '87
Forecast for disaster. il *Sports Illus* 67:78-84+ N 16 '87

Boyle, T. Coraghessan
Hard sell. *Harpers* 275:17-20 D '87
Sorry fugu [story] il *Harpers* 275:50-7 O '87
about
PW interviews. W. Brisick. il por *Publ Wkly* 232:71-2 O 9 '87

Boyle family
about
Beyond the image [exhibit in London] W. Feaver. il *Art News* 86:99+ Ja '87

Boynton, Sandra
Getting ready for the holidays [excerpt from Christmastime] il *Ladies Home J* 104:126+ D '87

Boys
See also
Sex differences
Boys, toys . . . joys. J. Kelman. il *McCalls* 115:63-4 D '87
Anecdotes, facetiae, satire, etc.
The secret life of boys. L. Dormen and M. Zussman. il *Seventeen* 46:222-4 Ap '87

Boys' clubs
See also
Boy Scouts of America

Boys Town (Neb.)
Boys Town: new ways but respect for the past. M. Bosc. il *U S News World Rep* 102:38-9 Mr 30 '87

Boyum, Joy Gould, 1934-
Movies. See issues of Glamour

Bozic, Michael
about
Can Sears get sexier but keep the common touch? M. D. Oneal. il por *Bus Week* p93-5 Jl 6 '87

Bozzone, Bill
about
House arrest [drama] Reviews
New Yorker 63:122-3 N 30 '87. M. Kramer

Bracelets
Cuffs: decorative arm-ory. il *Harpers Bazaar* 120:102-7 Jl '87

Braces, Orthodontic *See* Orthodontics

Bracey, Gerald W.
Measurement-driven instruction: catchy phrase, dangerous practice. bibl f il *Phi Delta Kappan* 68:683-6, 688-9 My '87
Research. See alternate issues of Phi Delta Kappan beginning March 1984

Brach, Paul, 1924-
John Graham: brilliant amateur? il *Art Am* 75:130-7 D '87

Brackeen, JoAnne
about
Blindfold test. F. Bouchard. por *Down Beat* 54:46 Ag '87

Bracken, Candace
about
"The sister I never knew I had saved my life". J. Ardmore. il por *Good Housekeep* 205:180+ S '87

Brackmann, Albert, 1871-1952
about
Albert Brackmann & the Nazi adjustment of history. M. Burleigh. bibl il por *Hist Today* 37:42-6 Mr '87

Bracy, Arnold
about
Black Marine's parents cry their son is a 'scapegoat' in sex for secrets case. il por *Jet* 72:5 Ap 20 '87
From Russia with love and espionage. il pors *Macleans* 100:18-19 Ap 13 '87
Holes in a spy scandal. S. W. Cloud. il por *Time* 130:31 Jl 20 '87
The honey-trap spy case widens. il pors *U S News World Rep* 102:12 Ap 6 '87
Innocent man. por *Time* 129:23 Je 22 '87
The Marine case falls apart. M. Kaus. il por *Newsweek* 109:23 Je 22 '87
The Marine spy scandal: "It's a biggie". A. Wilentz. il pors *Time* 129:21-2 Ap 6 '87
The Marine traitors. *Natl Rev* 39:18 Ap 24 '87
Military justice comes to attention. R. Lacayo. il por *Time* 129:62 My 18 '87
Moonlighting in Moscow? R. Watson. il pors *Newsweek* 109:32-3 Ap 6 '87
Spy charges against black Marine dropped. por *Jet* 72:9 Je 29 '87

Bradburn, Norman M., and Rosen, David
Walter E. Massey: president-elect of AAAS. bibl f por *Science* 238:1657-8 D 18 '87

Bradburn, Norman M., and others
Answering autobiographical questions: the impact of memory and inference on surveys. bibl f il *Science* 236:157-61 Ap 10 '87

Bradbury, Malcolm, 1932-
The comic bad men of English letters. il *N Y Times Book Rev* 92:15 Mr 22 '87

Braddy, Sonja
about
Richie rewards Miami student as 1st 'Scholar'. il pors *Jet* 72:56 Jl 20 '87

Braden, Joan
about
A Rocky horror shower scene looms large in the lusty memoir Joan Braden wants to forget. W. Plummer. il pors *People Wkly* 28:38-40 S 28 '87

Bradford, Michael J.
(jt. auth) See Peterman, Randall M., and Bradford, Michael J.

Bradley, Bill
about
The best possible way for Cuomo and Bradley to run. M. S. Forbes. *Forbes* 140:17 D 14 '87
Bill Bradley [interview] il pors *Life* 10:17-18+ D '87
Black Monday and beyond: a talk with Bill Bradley. L. Weymouth. il pors *N Y* 20:56-9 D 14 '87
Born-again Bradley? R. Brookhiser. il *Natl Rev* 39:44-6 S 25 '87
Cuomo and Bradley: second thoughts? J. Alter. il pors *Newsweek* 110:28 N 9 '87
Down and out in L.A. A. Kopkind. il *Nation* 244:309+ Mr 14 '87
Jump shots and free throws. L. I. Barrett. il por *Time* 130:13 Jl 6 '87
Overdue Bill. J. Klein. il por *N Y* 20:22-3 N 23 '87
President Bradley? J. McLaughlin. *Natl Rev* 39:26 F 13 '87
Shrinking violets. *New Repub* 196:4+ Je 22 '87
Why Bradley isn't running. R. Rothenberg. il pors *N Y Times Mag* p28-31+ Ag 2 '87
Anecdotes, facetiae, satire, etc.
On to the White House. C. Neff. il por *Sports Illus* 67:102 N 16 '87

Bradley, Ian C.
'Having and holding': the Highland land war of the 1880s. bibl il *Hist Today* 37:23-8 D '87
Titus Salt: enlightened entrepreneur. bibl il por *Hist Today* 37:30-6 My '87

Bradley, Jacqui
about
Building an empire. P. F. Stewart. il por *Ladies Home J* 104:158 O '87

Bradley, John Ed
Whiskey Land, USA, Booker Noe, Prop. il pors *Esquire* 108:204-8+ S '87

Bradley, Marion Zimmer
about
PW interviews. L. See. il por *Publ Wkly* 232:49-50 O 30 '87

Bradley, Omar Nelson, 1893-1981
about
Unforgettable Omar Bradley. C. B. Hansen. il por *Read Dig* 131:118-24 Ag '87

Bradley, Pat
about
Finished with life as an also-ran, go-for-it golfer Pat Bradley climbs the stare way to victory. A. Abrahams. il pors *People Wkly* 27:119-20 My 25 '87
Time for the Pat and Nancy show. J. Diaz. il pors *Sports Illus* 66:84+ F 9 '87

Bradley, Patrick
The docket. See issues of Flying beginning July 1986 through August 1987
Leading edge. See issues of Flying beginning February 1985

Bradley, R. S., and others
Precipitation fluctuations over Northern Hemisphere land areas since the mid-19th century. bibl f il maps *Science* 237:171-5 Jl 10 '87

Bradshaw, James
about
Jailed. il *FDA Consum* 21:31 My '87

Bradt, William
about
A hot commodity. S. W. Angrist. il por *Forbes* 139:256 Je 15 '87

Brady, Charles
And a light shines in darkness [poem] il *America* 157:488 D 19 '87

Brady, Holly
Software for learning. il *Parents* 62:296+ N '87

Brady, Kathleen
The executive superstar of the opera. il pors *Work Woman* 12:62-3+ Je '87
The power of positive stress. il pors *Work Woman* 12:74-7 Jl '87

Brady, Lois Smith
A labor of wanderlust. il pors *Esquire* 107:48 Ja '87
A ruin with a view. il *Esquire* 108:23-4 Jl '87
Where the grizzlies go. il *Esquire* 107:33-4 Mr '87
You oughta be in paintings. il *Esquire* 108:54 O '87

Brady, Ray
It's your money. See issues of Nation's Business beginning September 1983

Brady, Sally Ryder
Acupuncture and me. il por *Good Housekeep* 205:58+ Ag '87

Braendle, Charles
Negative vision: staying on the reverse side of Vericolor slide film. il *Petersens Photogr Mag* 16:20-2 O '87

Braff, David
The forgotten Founding Father: the impact of Thomas Paine [address, January 29, 1987] il pors *Humanist* 47:21-3+ My/Je '87
about
Dessert. *New Yorker* 63:21-3 Jl 27 '87

Bragg, George Lee, 1932-
about
How to compete with IBM. S. W. Angrist. il por *Forbes* 139:145 F 23 '87

Bragga, Laurence
Camp diary: blistered are the weak. il *World Tennis* 34:38-9 Ja '87

Brahman cattle *See* Cattle

Braiding
Braiding: prettier than ever. il *Good Housekeep* 204:194-7 My '87
Exhibitions
Interlacing: the elemental fabric [exhibit at the American Craft Museum] B. Freudenheim. il *Am Craft* 47:42-9 Ap/My '87

Braiker, Harriet B., 1948-
Who is the right man for a woman like you? [excerpt from The Type E woman] il *Work Woman* 12:72-4+ Ja '87
Why depression is different for high-achieving women. il *Work Woman* 12:79-83 D '87

Brailsford, Karen V.
Getting organized for 1987. il *Black Enterp* 17:54-6 Ja '87

Brain, A. G.
(tr) See Blair, Erica. The regime within

Brain
See also
Consciousness
Cybernetics
Electroencephalography
Human information processing
Hypothalamus
Intelligence
Laterality
Magnetoencephalography
Memory
Mind
Mind and body
Nervous system
Neurobiology
Neuropsychology
Sleep
Abnormalities
See also
Anencephaly
Analysis and chemistry
See also
Chemoreceptors
Drug receptors
Endorphins
Hormone receptors
Protein receptors
Alzheimer's protein is also in infant brains [research by Peter Davies and others] D. M. Barnes. *Science* 238:1652 D 18 '87
Functional analysis of a complementary DNA for the 50-kilodalton subunit of calmodulin kinase II. R. M. Hanley and others. bibl f il *Science* 237:293-7 Jl 17 '87
Identification of an α subunit of dihydropyridine-sensitive brain calcium channels. M. Takahashi and W. A. Catterall. bibl f il *Science* 236:88-91 Ap 3 '87
A mab to a unique cerebellar neuron generated by immunosuppression and rapid immunization. S. Hockfield. bibl f il *Science* 237:67-70 Jl 3 '87
Memory: learning how it works [cover story] G. Johnson. il por *N Y Times Mag* p16-21+ Ag 9 '87
Monoclonal antibodies as phylogenetic labels [discussion of July 3, 1987 article, A mab to a unique cerebellar neuron generated by immunosuppression and rapid immunization] S. Hockfield. *Science* 238:1730-1 D 18 '87
Neurosteroids: cytochrome P-450$_{scc}$ in rat brain. C. Le Goascogne and others. bibl f il *Science* 237:1212-15 S 4 '87
Patterns and processes mark brain activity. D. M. Barnes. il *Science* 238:892-3 N 13 '87
A synaptic vesicle protein with a novel cytoplasmic domain and four transmembrane regions. T. C. Südhof and others. bibl f il *Science* 238:1142-4 N 20 '87
Cancer
Brain cancer claims NBA Bullets' star Gus Johnson. il *Jet* 72:47 My 18 '87
Facing the sad truth [D. Howser too ill to manage the Kansas City Royals] R. Fimrite. il por *Sports Illus* 66:96 Mr 9 '87
Focusing on brain-tumor phosphates [use of nuclear magnetic resonance spectroscopy; work of Klaus Roth and others] S. Weisburd. il *Sci News* 132:375 D 12 '87
Say, brother [malignant brain tumor] D. S. Baker. por *Essence* 17:9 F '87
Genetic aspects
Identification of an amplified, highly expressed gene in a human glioma. K. W. Kinzler and others. bibl f il *Science* 236:70-3 Ap 3 '87
Diseases
See also
Alzheimer's disease
Brain damage
Cerebral palsy
Cerebrovascular disease
Parkinson's disease
AIDS: attacking the brain. E. E. Goode and J. Silberner. il *U S News World Rep* 103:48-9 S 7 '87

Brain—Diseases—*cont.*

The bad seed [connection between neurotoxins in food and brain disease; research by Peter S. Spencer and others] K. Wright. *Sci Am* 257:44 O '87

Brain damage by AIDS under active study. D. M. Barnes. bibl il *Science* 235:1574-7 Mr 27 '87

Dual infection of the central nervous system by AIDS viruses with distinct cellular tropisms. Y. Koyanagi and others. bibl f il *Science* 236:819-22 My 15 '87

Environmental hypothesis for brain diseases strengthened by new data [plant toxins] R. Lewin. il *Science* 237:483-4 Jl 31 '87

Guam amyotrophic lateral sclerosis-Parkinsonism-dementia linked to a plant excitant neurotoxin [cover story] P. S. Spencer and others. bibl f il map *Science* 237:517-22 Jl 31 '87

Plant at the root of neural disorders [research by Peter S. Spencer and others] *Sci News* 132:94 Ag 8 '87

Tumor necrosis factor (cachectin) as an essential mediator in murine cerebral malaria. G. E. Grau and others. bibl f il *Science* 237:1210-12 S 4 '87

Growth

Early hearing loss and brain development [work of Edwin W. Rubel] J. Greenberg. *Sci News* 131:149 Mr 7 '87

Growth spurts mirror mental milestones [cerebral hemisphere development; research by Robert W. Thatcher and others] R. J. Trotter. *Psychol Today* 21:13 S '87

Human cerebral hemispheres develop at different rates and ages. R. W. Thatcher and others. bibl f il *Science* 236:1110-13 My 29 '87

Hemorrhage

What happened to my daughter? [cerebral hemorrhage] M. T. Zimmermann. il por *Good Housekeep* 204:82+ Ap '87

Innervation

Asymmetry of neural feedback in the organization of behavioral states [discussion of November 7, 1986 article, The brain nucleus locus coeruleus: restricted afferent control of a broad efferent network] G. Aston-Jones and others. *Science* 237:537-8 Jl 31 '87

Blockade of "NMDA" receptors disrupts experience-dependent plasticity of kitten striate cortex. A. Kleinschmidt and others. bibl f il *Science* 238:355-8 O 16 '87

Corresponding spatial gradients of TOP molecules in the developing retina and optic tectum. D. Trisler and F. Collins. bibl f il *Science* 237:1208-9 S 4 '87

Hippocampus studied for learning mechanisms [synaptic transmission] D. M. Barnes. *Science* 236:1628-9 Je 26 '87

Neuronal coding and robotics [discussion of September 26, 1986 article, Neuronal population coding of movement direction] A. P. Georgopoulos and others. *Science* 237:300-1 Jl 17 '87

A physiological basis for a theory of synapse modification. M. F. Bear and others. bibl f il *Science* 237:42-8 Jl 3 '87

Protobrain [embryonic cat brain cells; work of Jerald J. M. Chun and others] *Sci Am* 256:68+ My '87

Retina transplant restores rat reflex [pupillary reflex; work of Henry Klassen and Raymond D. Lund] R. Weiss. il *Sci News* 132:245 O 17 '87

Thought and action [computer model of motor cortex neuron activity; work of Apostolos Georgopoulos] A. Fisher. il *Pop Sci* 230:8 F '87

Zinc: moderator in brain cell chatter? [research by D. Choi and others] *Sci News* 131:313 My 16 '87

Zinc selectively blocks the action of N-methyl-D-aspartate on cortical neurons. S. Peters and others. bibl f il *Science* 236:589-93 My 1 '87

Localization of functions

See also
 Electronic behavior control
 Laterality
 Split brain

The anatomy of memory. M. Mishkin and T. Appenzeller. bibl (p136) il *Sci Am* 256:80-9 Je '87

Auditory pathways to the frontal cortex of the mustache bat, Pteronotus parnellii. J. B. Kobler and others. bibl f il *Science* 236:824-6 My 15 '87

Cells in temporal cortex of conscious sheep can respond preferentially to the sight of faces. K. M. Kendrick and B. A. Baldwin. bibl f il *Science* 236:448-50 Ap 24 '87

Courtship in unisexual lizards: a model for brain evolution. D. Crews. bibl (p158) il *Sci Am* 257:116-21 D '87

Crazy-quilt brain. J. A. Miller. il *BioScience* 37:701-7 N '87

Creating an "electronic nose" [electronically reproduced fragment of the olfactory cortex; work of Gary Lynch and others] il *USA Today (Periodical)* 115:13 Je '87

Glut responses. R. M. Restak. *Vogue* 177:325+ Ag '87

Neuronal coding and robotics [discussion of September 26, 1986 article, Neuronal population coding of movement direction] A. P. Georgopoulos and others. *Science* 237:300-1 Jl 17 '87

Physiological evidence for serial processing in somatosensory cortex. T. P. Pons and others. bibl f il *Science* 237:417-20 Jl 24 '87

So that's why they keep giving each other those sheepish looks [sheep temporal lobe facial recognition cells; work of K. M. Kendrick and B. A. Baldwin] il *Discover* 8:6 Jl '87

Thought and action [computer model of motor cortex neuron activity; work of Apostolos Georgopoulos] A. Fisher. il *Pop Sci* 230:8 F '87

When looking sheepish counts as smarts. *Sci News* 131:313 My 16 '87

Metabolism

Brain food: eat smart to stay sharp. S. C. Finn. il *50 Plus* 27:65+ Je '87

Do 15 million cat neurons mediate the memory of a circle and a star? [discussion of September 12, 1986 article, Double-labeled metabolic maps of memory] E. R. John and others. *Science* 238:1586-8 D 11 '87

Focusing on brain-tumor phosphates [use of nuclear magnetic resonance spectroscopy; work of Klaus Roth and others] S. Weisburd. il *Sci News* 132:375 D 12 '87

Images of obsession [positron emission tomography; cover story] B. Bower. il *Sci News* 131:236-7 Ap 11 '87

Three-dimensional representation and analysis of brain energy metabolism [glucose] L. S. Hibbard and others. bibl f il *Science* 236:1641-6 Je 26 '87

Surgery

See also
 Split brain

First do no harm [education of a neurosurgeon; condensation] J. K. Rainer. il *Read Dig* 131:282-9+ N '87

The miracle of Maranda [hemispherectomy relieves Rasmussen's encephalitis] E. Sherman. il pors *Ladies Home J* 104:48+ N '87

Revolutionary brain surgery technique [stereotactic neurosurgery; work of Michael Apuzzo] il *USA Today (Periodical)* 115:7-8 F '87

Tomography

See Tomography—Medical use

Transplantation

Adrenal medulla grafts enhance recovery of striatal dopaminergic fibers. M. C. Bohn and others. bibl f il *Science* 237:913-16 Ag 21 '87

The amazing new brain surgery for Parkinson's disease. E. Kiester. il *50 Plus* 27:24-6+ O '87

Back to normal [cells from adrenal glands transplanted into brain to treat Parkinson's disease] C. Wallis. il *Time* 129:57 Ap 13 '87

Borrowed time [transplantation of suprachiasmatic nuclei restores circadian rhythm in hamsters] *Sci Am* 256:84 F '87

Brain grafts benefit Parkinson's patients [work of Ignacio Madrazo and others] R. Lewin. *Science* 236:149 Ap 10 '87

Breakthrough for Parkinson's disease? [cells from adrenal glands transplanted into brain] B. Wallace. il *Macleans* 100:46-7 My 18 '87

Cell grafts proceed, value uncertain [fetal brain cell transplants for Parkinson's disease] R. Weiss. *Sci News* 132:341 N 28 '87

Dramatic results with brain grafts [treatment of Parkinson's disease] R. Lewin. il *Science* 237:245-7 Jl 17 '87

The edge of knife [adrenal glands grafted to brain] J. Carpi. *Health* 19:25 Jl '87

Hole in the head [uncertainties surrounding adrenal cell transplants into the brain as cure for Parkinson's] R. Bazell. *New Repub* 197:13-14 Ag 10-17 '87

Human fetal-cell transplants planned [Parkinson's disease research] R. Weiss. *Sci News* 132:22 Jl 11 '87

Neocortical transplants in the mammalian brain lack a blood-brain barrier to macromolecules. J. M. Rosenstein. bibl f il *Science* 235:772-4 F 13 '87

New Parkinson's surgery [adrenal glands transplanted into brain] *Sci News* 131:244 Ap 18 '87

New tissue eases Huntington's disease [work of Paul R. Sanberg and others] J. Greenberg and B. Bower. *Sci News* 131:328 My 23 '87

Brain—Transplantation—*cont.*

Parkinson's: is this the cure? [adrenal cell transplants into the brain] K. McAuliffe. il *U S News World Rep* 102:12-13 Ap 13 '87

Progress in Parkinsonism [transferring adrenal gland cells into the brain] *Time* 129:59 Ap 20 '87

Steps toward a brave new world [treating neural disorders with brain implants of fetal nerve tissue and adrenal gland tissue] L. Jaroff. il *Time* 130:56-7 Jl 13 '87

Therapy by transplant [adrenal cells transplanted into brains of Parkinson's victims; work of Ignacio Madrazo and others] *Sci Am* 256:29-30 Je '87

Transplants in the brain [adrenal grafts for Parkinson's victims] S. Begley. il *Newsweek* 109:64 Ap 13 '87

Wounds and injuries

See Brain damage

Brain-blood barrier *See* Blood-brain barrier

Brain cells *See* Nerve cells

Brain damage

See also

Autism

Shaken child syndrome

Decreased hippocampal inhibition and a selective loss of interneurons in experimental epilepsy. R. Sloviter. bibl f il *Science* 235:73-6 Ja 2 '87

Drug may protect brains of heart attack victims [use of MK-801 to limit neuronal injury after ischemia] D. M. Barnes. il *Science* 235:632-3 F 6 '87

Epilepsy hypothesis [discussion of January 2, 1987 article, Decreased hippocampal inhibition and a selective loss of interneurons in experimental epilepsy] R. Sloviter. bibl f *Science* 238:1292-3 N 27 '87

Long-term neuropathological and neurochemical effects of nucleus basalis lesions in the rat. G. W. Arendash and others. bibl f il *Science* 238:952-6 N 13 '87

Nerve growth factor treatment after brain injury prevents neuronal death. L. F. Kromer. bibl f il *Science* 235:214-16 Ja 9 '87

Radical therapy: drugs may combat brain damage by toxic oxygen free radicals. K. Wright. *Sci Am* 257:34 S '87

Thanks for the memory [anterograde amnesia; research by Larry Squire and others] D. M. Barnes. il *Science* 238:1651-2 D 18 '87

Brain damaged children *See* Mentally handicapped children

Brain drain

May we borrow your historians? [U.S. universities' recruitment of English humanities professors] M. Kishlansky. il *Hist Today* 37:6-7 Je '87

Brain lesions *See* Brain damage

Brain stem

Asymmetry of neural feedback in the organization of behavioral states [discussion of November 7, 1986 article, The brain nucleus locus coeruleus: restricted afferent control of a broad efferent network] G. Aston-Jones and others. *Science* 237:537-8 Jl 31 '87

Brain stimulation *See* Brain—Innervation

Brain stimulation (Electronic) *See* Electronic behavior control

Brain waves

See also

Electroencephalography

Brainerd, Paul

about

How two pioneers brought publishing to the desktop. K. M. Hafner. il pors *Bus Week* p61-2 O 5 '87

BrainReserve (Firm)

Putting Faith in trends [F. Popcorn] A. Miller. il pors *Newsweek* 109:46-7 Je 15 '87

Brainstem *See* Brain stem

Brainwashing

See also

Deprogramming

An heiress vs. a pastor [E. Dovydenas vs. C. Stevens and his Bible Speaks church] G. Hackett. por *Newsweek* 109:33 Ap 20 '87

Nominating a hero for 1987 [J. Rauh's suit against CIA mind control experiments performed on Canadians] A. Fotheringham. il *Macleans* 100:64 Ja 19 '87

Psychology and religion in court—again [anticult theories of coercive persuasion] J. R. Lewis and J. G. Melton. *Christ Century* 104:914-16 O 21 '87

The women of Lexington Prison [S. L. Rosenberg and A. Torres charge they are victims of brainwashing] W. A. Reuben and C. Norman. il *Nation* 244:881-4 Je 27 '87

Braising (Cooking)

Gastronomie sans argent [braised meats] il *Gourmet* 47:60-1+ F '87

Brake lights, Automobile *See* Automobiles—Lighting

Brakes, Airplane

See also

Airplanes—Stopping

British L-1011 accident report raises questions on braking data [1985 British Airtours accident] D. A. Brown. *Aviat Week Space Technol* 127:52 O 12 '87

Brakes, Automobile

See also

Automobiles—Stopping

Anti-lock for less. D. Scott. il *Pop Sci* 231:30+ O '87

No more skids . . . [anti-lock brakes] il *U S News World Rep* 103:42 Ag 10 '87

Stopping and going [Mazda RX-7 with anti-lock brakes and Mercedes-Benz 190 2.6] il *Road Track* 38:88-9 F '87

Tough brakes. *Black Enterp* 18:80 N '87

Maintenance and repair

Car-care quiz. S. Mercaldo. il *Pop Sci* 230:100-2+ Mr '87

When your brake pedal gets the shakes. P. Weissler. il *Home Mech* 83:82+ S '87

Brakes, Motorcycle

Anti-lock brakes for motorcycles. S. F. Brown. il *Pop Sci* 230:66-7 My '87

Braking of airplanes *See* Airplanes—Stopping

Braking of automobiles *See* Automobiles—Stopping

Braman, Norman

about

Can this born salesman launch a luxury car? G. DeGeorge. il por *Bus Week* p107 My 4 '87

Norman Braman—megadealer making megabucks. J. R. Nerad. por *Mot Trend* 39:70-1 F '87

Brampton (Ont.)

Judgment of liability [reversal of personal injury damage award in M. McErlean vs. Brampton, Ont.] R. Corelli. il por *Macleans* 100:52 O 12 '87

Bramson, Robert M., and Bramson, Susan, 1940-

What kind of thinker are you? [quiz; condensed from The stressless home] il *Read Dig* 131:149-52 D '87

Bramson, Susan, 1940-

(jt. auth) See Bramson, Robert M., and Bramson, Susan, 1940-

Brancacci Chapel (Florence, Italy) *See* Santa Maria del Carmine (Church: Florence, Italy)

Branch, Ben F., d. 1987

about

Obituary

Jet por 72:55 S 14 '87

Branch, Taylor

Lessons from the fringe. *Wash Mon* 19:56-8 F '87

The Sunday school fascist. *Wash Mon* 19:46-8 Ap '87

Branch banking *See* Banks and banking—Branch banking

Branches in house decoration *See* Fruits, vegetables, etc. in decoration

Brand, Joshua

A case of bigamy. il *N Y Times Mag* p100 My 17 '87

Brand, Stewart

Mothers of invention [excerpt from The Media Lab] *Omni* 9:18+ Ag '87

Brand family

about

A family down and out. P. King. il *Newsweek* 109:44-6 Ja 12 '87

Brand names *See* Trade marks and trade names

Brandão, Carlos Rodrigues

Three continents, one people. il *Courier* 39:21-3+ D '86

Branded merchandise

See also

Private brands

The battle of the brands. J. A. Trachtenberg. il *Forbes* 139:111 F 9 '87

Creeping commercialism [Monroe Friedman's study of brand names used in novels, plays, and song lyrics] P. McCarthy. *Psychol Today* 21:16 Ag '87

The granddaddy of branded beef [Certified Angus Beef] B. Eftink. *Success Farm* 85:32 S '87

Romancing the stone [Lazare Kaplan's branded diamonds] B. Kanner. il *N Y* 20:22+ N 30 '87

Brandhuber, Barbara J., and others

Three-dimensional structure of interleukin-2. bibl f il *Science* 238:1707-9 D 18 '87

Brandies, Monica Moran, 1938-

A summer glory garden based on daylilies. il *Flower Gard* 31:24-5+ Je/Jl '87

Brandli, Hank

Earth and moon together. il *Astronomy* 15:20-2 O '87

Brandon, Charles *See* Suffolk, Charles Brandon, Duke of, d. 1545

Brandon, Dale
Chad's dad; ed. by John Grossmann. il *Health* 19:79-80 Ap '87
Brandon, Heather
The snack that crawls. il *Int Wildl* 17:16-21 Mr/Ap '87
Brandon Systems Corporation
'Tekkie' temps have this firm thriving. J. M. Laderman. *Bus Week* p98 Je 15 '87
Brandos (Musical group)
The Brandos: real contenders. D. Browne. il *Roll Stone* p20 N 19 '87
Brandt, Pam
Callan Pinckney: the thighs have it. il *Ms* 16:20+ N '87
(jt. auth) See Van Gelder, Lindsy, and Brandt, Pam
Brandt, Willy, 1913-
about
Brandt steps down. *Natl Rev* 39:20 Ap 24 '87
Too long at the table. A. Nagorski. il por *Newsweek* 109:39 Ap 6 '87
Brandt & Brandt Literary Agents Inc.
Agent Gail Hochman's role in the ascent of 'Presumed innocent'. A. O'Malley. il por *Publ Wkly* 231:35-6 Ap 3 '87
Brandy
Brandy the bountiful. M. Gersh. *Vogue* 177:496 S '87
Grand Andalusians [Spanish brandy] W. Grimes. il *Esquire* 108:44 O '87
Anecdotes, facetiae, satire, etc.
Brandy by firelight. I. Frazier. *New Yorker* 63:37 D 21 '87
Brandywine Asset Management
A cellar of stocks now ripe for buying [views of T. Hitschler] G. G. Marcial. il por *Bus Week* p114 D 7 '87
Brandywine River Museum
George A. Weymouth. M. S. Doherty. il pors *Am Artist* 51:32-7+ Ja '87
Brandywine Valley (Pa. and Del.)
Wyeth country. A. Chase. il *Vogue* 177:316+ O '87
Branham, George, III
about
Breakthrough in bowling. il pors *Ebony* 42:142+ Mr '87
Braniff, Inc.
At Braniff, no frills and few thrills. J. E. Ellis. *Bus Week* p101 My 4 '87
Exchange of stock signals Pan Am, Braniff merger. *Aviat Week Space Technol* 127:36 D 14 '87
Branigin, William
about
Beat the devil. A. Cockburn. *Nation* 244:790-1 Je 13 '87
Brann, Mark R., and Cohen, Leslie V.
Diurnal expression of transducin mRNA and translocation of transducin in rods of rat retina. bibl f il *Science* 235:585-7 Ja 30 '87
Brannigan, Augustine
Is obscenity criminogenic? bibl *Society* 24:12-19 Jl/Ag '87
Branson, Branley Allan
Burro's-tail sedum. il *Flower Gard* 31:51+ O/N '87
How to build durable, compatible garden steps. il *Flower Gard* 31:56 Je/Jl '87
Branson, Gary
Ask Handyman. See isssues of The Family Handyman beginning January 1987
Branson, Louise
'Glasnost' in print. il *World Press Rev* 34:34-5 Ag '87
Branson, Richard
about
Balloonatic Richard Branson puts his faith in hot air. R. Arias. il pors *People Wkly* 27:91-2 Je 15 '87
The big splashdown. N. Cooper. il pors *Newsweek* 110:37 Jl 13 '87
Branson Coates (Firm)
The Empire strikes back. D. Dietsch. il *Archit Rec* 175:142-51 mid-S '87
Brantes, Paul de, marquis
about
Legend of Le Fresne: Marquis and Marquise de Brantes near Tours. C. Bricker. il pors *Archit Dig* 44:176-81+ S '87
Brantes, Sue de, marquise
about
Legend of Le Fresne: Marquis and Marquise de Brantes near Tours. C. Bricker. il pors *Archit Dig* 44:176-81+ S '87

Brantley, Ben
Cinema's serene queen. por *Harpers Bazaar* 120:204-5+ F '87
Brantley, Duncan
Oh brother, here comes Carolina. il pors *Sports Illus* 66:69-70 My 4 '87
Branton, David
about
Analyzing the Mac numbers. C. O'Malley. il por *Pers Comput* 11:179+ O '87
Branton, Wiley A., 1923-
about
Marshall shows for D.C. Bar tribute to Wiley Branton. il pors *Jet* 71:6-7 Ja 12 '87
Branyon, Alaxandra
(jt. auth) See Lee, Karen, and Branyon, Alaxandra
Bras *See* Brassieres
Brasília (Brazil)
Description
Brasília: shapes of the future. G. Smith. il *Américas* 39:31-7 N/D '87
Brass beds *See* Beds
Brass work
A touch of brass [making custom hardware] W. E. Burton. il *Pop Mech* 164:82-5 Mr '87
Brasseur, Guy
The endangered ozone layer [cover story; with editorial comment by Gilbert F. White] bibl il *Environment* 29:inside cover, 6-11+ Ja/F '87
Brassica
See also
 Broccoli
 Broccoli raab
 Cabbages
 Cauliflower
 Chinese broccoli
Cabbage and its cousins: do they protect against cancer? L. Hoppe. il *Better Homes Gard* 65:82 O '87
Brassieres
See also
 Frederick's of Hollywood Bra Museum
Andre Van Pier's bras of gold and crystal inspire a boom at the top. il por *People Wkly* 28:92-3 Jl 13 '87
Big breasts, little breasts: how to make the most of yours. il *Glamour* 85:268-71 O '87
The complete guide to sports bras. C. Cummins. il *Women's Sports Fitness* 9:52-4+ S '87
Brasswork *See* Brass work
Bratcher, Twila
Thyca: underarm and underfoot. il *Sea Front* 33:286-7 Jl/Ag '87
Braud, Dominique
How to build a floating blind. il *Petersens Photogr Mag* 16:46-7 Ag '87
Braun, Frank, and Davies, Owen
The Martian Metro. il *Omni* 10:52-4+ N '87
Braun, Herbert S.
The economy according to small business. il *Nations Bus* 75:42-4+ My '87
Small-business confidence: looking good at home. il *Nations Bus* 75:32-3+ N '87
Braund, David, 1957-
The Roman revolution? il *Hist Today* 37:49-52 Ap '87
Brave Combo (Musical group)
Brave Combo. M. Point. il *Down Beat* 54:14 Je '87
Bravery *See* Courage
Bravo, Manuel Alvarez *See* Alvarez Bravo, Manuel, 1902-
Bravo, Miguel Obando y *See* Obando y Bravo, Miguel, Cardinal
Braxton, Anthony
about
Braxton [discography] T. Martin. *Down Beat* 54:43-5+ Ap '87
Braxton, Dwight *See* Qawi, Dwight Muhammad
Braxton, Edward K.
Is there an American Catholic Church? *America* 157:422-6 D 5 '87
The National Black Catholic Congress [cover story] *America* 157:29-34 Jl 18-25 '87
Bray, Rosemary L.
Facing the fear: help for women with AIDS. il por *Ms* 15:31 My '87
The miseducation of our children. il *Essence* 18:79-80+ S '87
Work in progress: the definitive Lorraine Hansberry. pors *Ms* 15:31 F '87
Bray, Rosemary L., and FitzGerald, Karen
The luxury of summer reading. il *Ms* 15:16+ Je '87

Brazeal, Aurelia
about
Aurelia Brazeal gets major U.S. embassy post in Japan. *Jet* 71:4 F 16 '87
Brazelton, T. Berry, 1918-
about
PW interviews. K. Weber. il por *Publ Wkly* 232:57-8 N 13 '87
Brazil
See also
Agriculture—Brazil
AIDS (Disease)—Brazil
Amazon River
Amazon River Valley
Americana (Brazil)
Americans—Brazil
Automobile racing—Brazil
Aviation—Brazil
Birds—Brazil
Blacks—Brazil
Brasília (Brazil)
Campos Elísios (Brazil)
Churches (Buildings)—Brazil
Crime and criminals—Brazil
Eating—Brazil
Environmental movement—Brazil
Environmental policy—Brazil
Goiania (Brazil)
Health resorts, watering places, etc.—Brazil
Industry and state—Brazil
Investments, American—Brazil
Investments, Canadian—Brazil
Investments, Foreign—Brazil
Land reform—Brazil
Loans, Bank—Brazil
Manaus (Brazil)
Motion pictures—Brazil
Natural resources—Brazil
Plantations—Brazil
Police—Brazil
Political prisoners—Brazil
Popular music—Brazil
Rain forests—Brazil
Rio de Janeiro (Brazil)
Salvador (Brazil)
Space research—Brazil
Swiss—Brazil
Theater—Brazil
Wildlife—Brazil
Wildlife conservation—Brazil

Air Force
Air Force center offers postgraduate training [Aerospace Technical Center] *Aviat Week Space Technol* 127:44 Ag 24 '87

Antiquities
Cliff notes [rock-shelter paintings] N. Guidon. il map *Nat Hist* 96:6+ Ag '87

Army
Brazil woes: Sarney plays an Army card. C. A. Robbins. il por *U S News World Rep* 103:41 Jl 13 '87
Brazilian Army to buy 260 helicopters for airmobile battalions. *Aviat Week Space Technol* 127:47 Ag 17 '87

Civilization
Brazil: 20th-century giant [special issue; with editorial comment by Edouard Glissant] il map *Courier* 39:3-46 D '86

Climate
See also
Droughts—Brazil

Commerce
United States
See United States—Commerce—Brazil
Commercial policy
Brazil's independent computer strategy [cover story] A. J. J. Botelho. il maps *Technol Rev* 90:36-45 My/Je '87
The lure of southern money. A. Shortell. il *Macleans* 100:26-7 Ja 19 '87

Cultural relations
Portugal
Return ticket [Brazilian arts in Portugal] F. A. Cristóvão. il *Courier* 39:37+ D '86

Defenses
See also
Airplanes, Military—Brazil
Aviation, Military—Brazil
Brazil—Air Force

Description and travel
See also
Automobile touring—Brazil

Brazil: moment of promise & pain. P. J. Vesilind. il maps *Natl Geogr* 171:348-85 Mr '87
Letter from Brazil. A. MacPherson. map *Focus* 37:29-31 Fall '87

Economic conditions
The wealth of a nation. il *Courier* 39:43-5 D '86

Economic policy
Brazil. M. S. Forbes, Jr. il *Forbes* 139:25 Ap 20 '87
Brazil and its creditors: who has more to lose? J. Ryser and W. Glasgall. il *Bus Week* p56-7 Mr 9 '87
Brazil says: nuts. J. S. Henry. *New Repub* 197:25+ O 12 '87
Brazil throws down the gauntlet [suspension of interest repayments] H. O'Shaughnessy. il *World Press Rev* 34:46-7 Ap '87
Brazil's Cruzado Plan. E.-S. Pang and L. Jarnagin. bibl f *Curr Hist* 86:13-16+ Ja '87
Brazil's would-be miracle worker [D. Funaro] W. Woods. il por *Fortune* 115:68 Ja 5 '87
Bungling in Brazil. N. Gall. il *Forbes* 140:39-40 Jl 27 '87
The debt crisis isn't Brazil's only liability. P. C. Roberts. il *Bus Week* p14 Ap 20 '87
Default, dear Brutus [Brazil unable to pay interest on foreign debt] *New Repub* 196:8+ Mr 16 '87
Inflation wrecks southern giant's vision of future. J. De Onis. il *U S News World Rep* 103:46-7 D 28 '87-Ja 4 '88
No more blood in the stone [Brazil suspends interest payments on foreign debt] G. Scott. il *Time* 129:46 Mr 2 '87
Settling Brazil's account. C. Wood. il *Macleans* 100:36 N 16 '87
Stonewalling the banks [Brazil suspends interest payments on debt] T. Fennell. il *Macleans* 100:34-5 Mr 9 '87
That old-time inflation hits Brazil. R. A. Manning. il por *U S News World Rep* 102:36 Mr 2 '87
"This is war" [interview with M. Colasuonno] L. Minard. il por *Forbes* 139:50 Je 29 '87

Anecdotes, facetiae, satire, etc.
Millions of Brazilians—all unreasonable. L. F. Veríssimo. *World Press Rev* 34:34 O '87

Foreign relations
Caribbean region
Caribbean cousins. C. Castilho. il *Courier* 39:16-20 D '86

Latin America
Brazil and its neighbours. E. Nepomuceno. il *Courier* 39:11-15 D '86

History
Tiradentes: a vision vindicated. por *Dep State Bull* 87:77 Mr '87
Whistling Dixie in Brazil [disillusioned southerners settle in Brazil, 1865-79] J. H. Kennedy. il *Américas* 39:26-31 Ja/F '87

Industries
See also
Aerospace industries—Brazil
Airlines—Brazil
Automobile industry—Brazil
Avibras Industria Aeroespacial SA
Banco do Brasil SA
Citrosuco Paulista (Firm)
Computer industry—Brazil
Cruzeiro do Sul SA
Distribuidora Record de Servicos de Imprensa SA
Embraer Empresa Brasileira de Aeronautica SA
Gold mines and mining—Brazil
Orbita Aerospace Systems (Firm)
Petroleo Brasileiro SA
Rubber industry—Brazil
Transbrasil SA-Linhas Aéreas
Varig SA Viação Aérea Rio-Grandense
Viacao Aerea Sao Paolo SA
Wood pulp industry—Brazil

Native peoples
See Indians of South America—Brazil

Politics and government
The beat of Brazil. C. Wood. il *World Press Rev* 34:24-6 Mr '87
Brazil woes: Sarney plays an Army card. C. A. Robbins. il por *U S News World Rep* 103:41 Jl 13 '87
Brazilian split. L. Rogers. il *World Press Rev* 34:42 S '87
Brazil's new beat [special section; with editorial comment by Kevin Doyle] il por map *Macleans* 100:2, 18-22+ Ja 19 '87
In Brazil, the president and Congress jostle for power. J. Ryser. por *Bus Week* p62 Je 8 '87

Brazil—*cont.*

Race relations

Three continents, one people [Indians, Europeans and Africans] C. R. Brandão. il *Courier* 39:21-3+ D '86

Religious institutions and affairs

See also

Church and civil rights—Brazil

Church and social problems—Brazil

Cults—Brazil

Missions—Brazil

Voodooism—Brazil

Social conditions

The beat of Brazil. C. Wood. il *World Press Rev* 34:24-6 Mr '87

Brazil's new beat [special section; with editorial comment by Kevin Doyle] il por map *Macleans* 100:2, 18-22+ Ja 19 '87

Brazilian art *See* Art, Brazilian

Brazilian arts *See* Arts, Brazilian

Brazilian cooking *See* Cooking, Brazilian

Brazilian Grand Prix *See* Automobile racing—Brazil

Brazilian helicopters *See* Helicopters

Brazilian poetry

See also

Folk poetry, Brazilian

The concrete poetry movement. S. Sarduy. il *Courier* 39:28 D '86

Breach of contract

The clearing of Vanessa Redgrave [Boston Symphony case] M. Heins. il *Nation* 245:713-15 D 12 '87

Penta files breach of contract suit against Harper & Row. *Publ Wkly* 232:25 Jl 17 '87

Bread

See also

Cornbread

Crackers

Gingerbread

Muffins

3 breads & 3 soups in 3 hours. B. Greenwood. il *Better Homes Gard* 65:128-31+ O '87

The 20 minute baker [quick breads] il *Ladies Home J* 104:98-9+ F '87

Australia's damper loaf is basically a large biscuit. il *Sunset* 179:136 Ag '87

Bake French bread like the pros. il *South Living* 22:164+ O '87

Breads fresh from your oven. C. Lyons. il *Ebony* 42:116-18+ O '87

Bread—the #1 diet food: a few grains of truth. il *Mademoiselle* 93:164 Ja '87

Fast breads and muffins. il *Better Homes Gard* 65:163-4 My '87

Fringed, fragrant, fanciful . . . Costa Ricans just call it "good bread". il *Sunset* 178:118-19 Ap '87

From Russia, Germany, and France come three hearty (and unusual) peasant breads. il *Sunset* 179:166-7 O '87

The giant pretzel that feeds six hungry sports fans [pretzel-shaped sandwich loaf] il *Sunset* 178:80-1 Mr '87

Hot biscuits: the new cool food. il *Mademoiselle* 93:270-1+ Mr '87

In New Jersey: bread that casts a spell [Italian bread from Giordano's Bakery] R. Conniff. il *Time* 129:15-16 Je 8 '87

Just how fast can you produce a loaf of yeast bread? il *Sunset* 178:214+ My '87

Popover power. S. Costner. il *Work Woman* 12:144-6 N '87

Potato yeast rolls. il *South Living* 22:206 Mr '87

Recipe of the week [cheesy grits biscuits] il *Jet* 73:30 D 28 '87-Ja 4 '88

Recipe of the week [dilly cheese bread] il *Jet* 72:33 Jl 20 '87

Sourdough. D. Holmstrom. il *Americana* 15:40-3 S/O '87

Southerners love these oldtime breads. D. G. Lowery. il *South Living* 22:82-4 F '87

A springy, light loaf that's all whole-wheat. il *Sunset* 178:166 F '87

The toast of Tuscany [Tuscan bread] E. Sahatjian. il *Esquire* 108:52 O '87

Vegetable-patch bread. il *Sunset* 179:72-3 S '87

Bread boxes

Old and new styling combined in practical breadbox. A. Gutierrez. il *Workbench* 43:120 Mr/Ap '87

Bread dough craft *See* Dough craft

Bread Loaf School of English

"Great human power or magic". M. Ludtke. il *Time* 130:76 S 14 '87

Bread Loaf Writers' Conference of Middlebury College

Writers' conferences: a short story. D. Moreau. il *Changing Times* 41:61-3 Mr '87

Breakfast foods *See* Cereal foods

Breakfasts

See also

Brunches

8 get-up-and-go breakfasts. il *Redbook* 168:144+ Mr '87

The American breakfast. B. Rupp. il *Ctry J* 14:50-5 F '87

Best breakfasts [eateries] J. Stern and M. Stern. il *Harpers Bazaar* 120:102+ O '87

Breakfast makes a comeback. il *Glamour* 85:344-7 Ap '87

Breakfast makes a comeback [work of M. Cunningham] L. Shapiro. il por *Newsweek* 110:69 S 21 '87

The breakfast special [special section] il *McCalls* 115:115-16+ O '87

Breakfasts & brunches [special section] il *South Living* 22:135+ Ap '87

The complete breakfast. J. E. Brody. il *Saturday Evening Post* 259:18+ O '87

Country inn breakfasts. H. Garrison. il *Parents* 62:143-6+ Mr '87

Delicious high-fiber breakfasts. J. B. Hurley. il *Prevention* 39:82-4+ F '87

Derby Day breakfast for 12,000! [given by Kentucky's Governor M. L. Collins] J. Siroto. il por *McCalls* 114:108-11 Ap '87

Fresh starts: five breakfast treats. C. Rossant. *McCalls* 115:107+ O '87

The hyperactive breakfast [research by C. Keith Connors and others] B. Bower. *Sci News* 132:168 S 12 '87

An innkeeper's guide to better breakfasts [Dairy Hollow House] M. Gorman. il *Rodale's Org Gard* 34:52-4 O '87

The portable breakfast. E. Hackman. il *Women's Sports Fitness* 9:56 Ap '87

Quick breakfast ideas. il *Better Homes Gard* 65:89-90 Ja '87

Rev up your day with nutritional reveille. G. Maleskey. *Prevention* 39:68+ S '87

Rise 'n' dine. il *Seventeen* 46:214-15 S '87

Sleep-late weekend breakfasts. C. Walker. il *Work Woman* 12:78-80 Jl '87

A southern breakfast in just minutes. il *South Living* 22:143 Jl '87

Surprise her with breakfast. *South Living* 22:211 My '87

A wake-up breakfast for mom . . . easy to make, clean up. il *Sunset* 178:116-17 My '87

Breakfasts, Business *See* Business entertaining

Breakfasts, Prayer *See* Prayer breakfasts

Breaking silence [television program] *See* Television program reviews—Single works

Breaking the code [drama] *See* Whitemore, Hugh

Breakpoint (Term)

Gimme a breakpoint. W. Safire. il *N Y Times Mag* p8+ Jl 5 '87

Brealey, John M.

about

Profiles. C. Tomkins. por *New Yorker* 63:44-6+ Mr 16 '87

Breast

All about breasts. K. McCoy. il *Seventeen* 46:36+ O '87

Are breast creams a bust? P. Boyer. il *Prevention* 39:76-8 My '87

Cancer

The big scare: Nancy Reagan's time comes. S. Findlay. il por *U S News World Rep* 103:16 O 26 '87

Breast cancer. M. Morra and E. Potts. *Good Housekeep* 204:153-6 My '87

It wasn't the end of the world. A. Roy. il *Work Woman* 12:126-9+ Mr '87

The new ways to detect—and treat—breast cancer. M. Castleman. il *Redbook* 169:180-1 S '87

Causes

Estrogens exonerated in breast cancer. *Sci News* 131:57 Ja 24 '87

Diagnosis

See also

Mammography

Breast cancer: earlier diagnoses and new attitudes. B. Weinhouse. *Ladies Home J* 104:112 O '87

Breast cancer: new keys to early detection. il *McCalls* 145:83+ Mr '87

Genetic aspects

Breast cancer: *neu* clue [work of Dennis J. Slamon and others] *Sci Am* 256:71+ Mr '87

Breast—Cancer—Genetic aspects—*cont.*
Genetic clue to cancer prognosis [gene amplification] J. Silberner. *Sci News* 131:46 Ja 17 '87
Human breast cancer: correlation of relapse and survival with amplification of the HER-2/*neu* oncogene. D. J. Slamon and others. bibl f il *Science* 235:177-82 Ja 9 '87
Oncogenes give breast cancer prognosis [research by Dennis J. Slamon and others] G. Kolata. *Science* 235:160-1 Ja 9 '87
Reduction to homozygosity of genes on chromosome 11 in human breast neoplasia. I. U. Ali and others. bibl f il *Science* 238:185-8 O 9 '87

Nutritional aspects
Alcohol-breast cancer link. D. D. Edwards. *Sci News* 131:292 My 9 '87
Breast cancer & alcohol. B. Weinhouse. *Ladies Home J* 104:58+ Ag '87
Breast cancer prevention: a controversial new diet program. S. Rennie. il *Ms* 15:40-51+ Ap '87
Coffee—an anticancer agent? *Prevention* 39:98+ Jl '87
Dietary fat-breast cancer link questioned [study by Walter Willett and others] G. Kolata. *Science* 235:436 Ja 23 '87
Does alcohol increase risk of breast cancer? . . . J. Kaplan. *Vogue* 177:174 N '87
Drinker's dilemma [alcohol may raise risk of breast cancer] J. D. Schwartz. il *Health* 19:24 O '87
Drinking and breast cancer. *Newsweek* 109:73 My 18 '87
Female trouble [alcohol-breast cancer link] *Sci Am* 257:24+ Jl '87
Fish oil helps prevent tumor spread [research by Debra Szeluga and others] *Prevention* 39:6+ O '87
From only one drink a week? [alcohol may trigger cancer] J. Silberner. il *U S News World Rep* 102:64-5 My 18 '87
How strong is the alcohol/breast cancer link? il *Glamour* 85:86 O '87
The new breast-cancer scare—should you say no to alcohol? E. R. Shell. il *Mademoiselle* 93:112 Ag '87
Should women drink less? [alcohol consumption linked to cancer] M. D. Lemonick. il *Time* 129:66 My 18 '87

Prevention
Thinking about breast cancer. il *U S News World Rep* 102:65 My 18 '87
Your best breast defense: how to outsmart breast cancer. E. R. Shell. il *Mademoiselle* 93:246-7+ Ap '87

Surgery
See also
Mastectomy
Psychological scars of breast surgery [lumpectomy vs. mastectomy; study by Lesley J. Fallowfield] P. McCarthy. *Psychol Today* 21:17 Ag '87

Therapy
Breast cancer: when chemotherapy works. S. Rennie. il *Ms* 16:70-4 N '87
Preventing recurrence of breast cancer [use of tamoxifen; research by Douglass Tormey] *USA Today (Periodical)* 115:7 F '87
The wisest decision I ever made [postponing chemotherapy to complete pregnancy]; ed. by Jack Hope. E. Eaton. il pors *Good Housekeep* 205:48+ Jl '87

Diseases
Breast lumps: what—and what not—to worry about. il *Glamour* 85:184-5+ Ja '87

Nutritional aspects
Painful breasts may benefit from iodine [fibrocystic breast disease; research by Bernard A. Eskin and William R. Ghent] il *Prevention* 39:12 Ap '87

Examination
The best breast exam yet [vertical-strip technique] il *Prevention* 39:14 N '87
A better breast test? [self exam] L. Piepenbrink. *Health* 19:27 O '87
Breast self-examination (BSE). il *FDA Consum* 21:7 My '87
Breast update: why women don't do self-examination. il *Glamour* 85:182-5+ Ja '87
How to examine your breasts. il *Work Woman* 12:150 Mr '87
Improving detection of breast cancer [self examination techniques; study by Kate Saunders] il *USA Today (Periodical)* 115:7 F '87
Test your breasts (a new self-exam is getting good grades). J. C. Johnson. il *Mademoiselle* 93:150 N '87

Surgery, Plastic
See Surgery, Plastic
Breast creams *See* Cosmetics
Breast feeding
See also
Milk, Human
Wet nurses
Breast-feeding and sore nipples: prevention and relief. L. MacCallum. il *Glamour* 85:252 My '87
Breast-feeding and work. K. Levine. il *Parents* 62:64+ D '87
Breast-feeding: the father factor. R. B. McCall. il *Parents* 62:182 Je '87
Breast versus bottle. V. E. Pomeranz and D. Schultz. il *Parents* 62:144 F '87
Irritable rule for breast-fed babies [research by Janet A. DiPietro and others] *Sci News* 132:94 Ag 8 '87
"Nature's contraceptive". I. Shah and J. Khanna. il *World Health* p10-12 N '87
The working nursing mother [excerpt from The complete book of breastfeeding] M. S. Eiger and S. W. Olds. *Work Woman* 12:186+ My '87

Equipment
Doctor makes mock baby breast feeder for dads [A. Goldson] il pors *Jet* 73:44 D 28 '87-Ja 4 '88
Breast implants *See* Surgery, Plastic
Breast milk *See* Milk, Human
Breast pumping
Breast milk express [bilateral pumping] D. Zevin. il *Health* 19:16 My '87
Breast reconstruction surgery *See* Surgery, Plastic
Breast X rays *See* Mammography
Breathed, Berke
Opus goes home: Bloom County's penguin returns to his roots in Antarctica. il *Life* 10:42-7+ My '87
Breathing *See* Respiration
Breathing equipment *See* Oxygen equipment; Respirators
Breathing exercises
Breathing: can you improve it? S. M. Sims. il *Vogue* 177:230+ F '87
Breazeale, Helene
Trailblazers of the US/USSR dance exchange. il *Dance Mag* 61:70-2 Ap '87
Brecht, Bertolt, 1898-1956
about
Robyn Archer sings Brecht. E. Salzman. il por *Stereo Rev* 52:116 My '87
Breckenridge, Joyce
about
"My husband wouldn't give up on me". L. Crane. il pors *Good Housekeep* 205:74+ Ag '87
Brecker, Michael
about
Michael Brecker on Impulse [interview] B. Milkowski. il pors *Down Beat* 54:16-19 Je '87
Brecker, Randy
about
Blindfold test. M. Bourne. il pors *Down Beat* 54:45 Ja '87
Bredesen, Phil
about
The battle of Nashville. T. E. Johnson. il por *Newsweek* 110:38 S 21 '87
Breeches buoys *See* Life saving equipment
Breeden, Bill
about
Street sign. *Progressive* 51:4 Ag '87
Breeder reactors *See* Nuclear reactors
Breeders' Cup (Races) *See* Horse racing
Breeding
See also
Birds—Breeding
Cattle—Breeding
Dogs—Breeding
Horses—Breeding
Hybridization
Iguanas—Breeding
Inbreeding
Plants—Breeding
Reproduction
Sheep—Breeding
Red wolf in the wilderness [captive breeding program] J. P. Cohn. il *BioScience* 37:313-16 My '87
What's new at the zoo? [breeding endangered species] D. M. Kennedy. il *Technol Rev* 90:66-73 Ap '87
Breggin, Peter R.
Mental health versus religion. *Humanist* 47:12-13 N/D '87
Breig, James
Beaver Cleaver is divorced: the growing pains of American Catholic families. il *U S Cathol* 52:48-53 Je '87

Breig, James—*cont.*
How faith helps parents raise good kids. il *U S Cathol* 52:26-31 Mr '87
How to talk to your kids about death. il *U S Cathol* 52:21-6 Ja '87
Somebody up there likes me: what U.S. Catholic readers believe about the saints [cover story] il *U S Cathol* 52:6-15 N '87

Breindel, Eric
The legal circus. *New Repub* 196:20-2 F 9 '87

Breinin, Charles M.
A complaint and a prediction. il *Phi Delta Kappan* 69:15-16 S '87

Breit, Ernst
about
Unexpected ally for the dollar? L. Minard. por *Forbes* 139:158+ Mr 23 '87

Breitman, Martin L., and others
Genetic ablation: targeted expression of a toxin gene causes microphthalmia in transgenic mice. bibl f il *Science* 238:1563-5 D 11 '87

Breitman, Patti, 1954-, and others
Condom etiquette [excerpt from How to persuade your lover to use a condom] il *Essence* 18:19+ N '87

Breitschwerdt, Werner
about
The banker behind the shakeup at Daimler-Benz. R. Ingersoll and R. Brady. il pors *Bus Week* p36-7 Jl 27 '87
The street-smart perfectionist. L. S. Richman. il por *Fortune* 116:36 Ag 3 '87
"We are still saying hello to each other". P. Berman. il *Forbes* 139:94+ My 18 '87

Breivik, Bård
about
Bård Breivik. S. H. Madoff. il por *Art News* 86:105-6 Ja '87

Breivik, Patricia Senn
Making the most of libraries [with editorial comment by Frank Newman] il *Change* 19:4-5, 44-52 Jl/Ag '87

Brekke, Michele
about
In charge at Mission Control: a conversation with Michele Brekke. M. Register. il por *Space World* X-4-280:33-6 Ap '87

Breland, Mark
about
Breland knocked out of boxing unbeaten ranks. il pors *Jet* 72:52 S 14 '87
Off the mark. il por *Sports Illus* 67:13 Ag 31 '87

Bremen (Germany)
Music
See also
Opera—Germany (West)

Bremer, L. Paul, III
Practical measures for dealing with terrorism [address, January 22, 1987] il por *Dep State Bull* 87:1-4 Mr '87
Terrorism and intelligence [address, May 26, 1987] *Vital Speeches Day* 53:578-81 Jl 15 '87
Terrorism and the media [address, June 25, 1987] *Dep State Bull* 87:72-5 S '87
Terrorism and the rule of law [address, April 23, 1987] *Dep State Bull* 87:83-6 Ag '87

Bremner, Charles
'We should have listened to Jimmy Carter'. *World Press Rev* 34:64 My '87

Bren, Donald L.
about
Owning Irvine, Calif., isn't what it used to be. J. Flynn. il por *Bus Week* p80+ Mr 9 '87
"You get to play God". L. S. Richman. il por *Fortune* 116:138-9 O 12 '87

Brenda's palace, a comedy fable [film] See Motion picture reviews—Single works

Brendel, Alfred
about
High priest of the piano. A. Rich. il por *Newsweek* 110:58 Jl 27 '87

Brennan, Christine
Manley, unchained. por *Sport Mag* 78:73-5 Ag '87

Brennan, Robert E.
about
Trying not to be a second First Jersey. C. Welles. il por *Bus Week* p44 Ja 12 '87

Brennan, William J., Jr.
about
Renaissance of an octogenarian liberal. A. Press and A. McDaniel. il por *Newsweek* 110:18 Jl 6 '87

Brenner Tank Company
Steel workers on the line [strike] M. Wettstein, Jr. and J. Gormican. *Progressive* 51:15-16 Ja '87

Brenson, Michael
Maverick sculptor makes good. il por *N Y Times Mag* p84+ N 1 '87

Brent, Frances Padorr
(tr) See Ratushinskaya, Irina. Give me a nickname, prison

Brent, Madeleine
Golden urchin [fiction] il *Good Housekeep* 204:133-6+ Ja '87

Brent, Nancy
(jt. auth) See Edwards, Linda, and Brent, Nancy

Brent, Stuart
about
Brent springs eternal. N. Barrett. il por *Publ Wkly* 232:60-2 S 11 '87

Brentham, Jerry D.
about
A coach who got back in the game. N. L. Croft. il por *Nations Bus* 75:51-2 Ag '87

Brenton, Howard, 1942-
about
Bloody poetry [drama] Reviews
N Y 20:53 Ja 19 '87. J. Simon

Brescia, Bernardo Fort- See Fort-Brescia, Bernardo

Breskin, David
Bono [cover story; interview] il pors *Roll Stone* p42-5+ O 8 '87

Bresler, Robert J.
Arms control: the Reagan legacy. il *USA Today (Periodical)* 115:6-7 Ja '87
The complexities of nuclear diplomacy. il *USA Today (Periodical)* 116:7 Jl '87
Covert action and national policy: beyond North and Poindexter. il *USA Today (Periodical)* 115:6-7 Mr '87
Politics after Reagan. il *USA Today (Periodical)* 116:7 S '87
The Reagan presidency and the deficit issue. il *USA Today (Periodical)* 115:13 My '87
A return to the center. il *USA Today (Periodical)* 116:7 N '87

Breslin, John B.
Thunder on the left. il *Publ Wkly* 232:39-41 O 9 '87

Breslow, Stephen P.
Plying the Java Sea [cover story] il map *Oceans* 20:20-7 S/O '87

Bresnick, Jan
Foods that heal. il *Prevention* 39:26-9 D '87

Bressler, Richard M.
about
All alone by the telephone. J. Cook. il por *Forbes* 140:80+ N 16 '87
Will a takeover derail Burlington Northern's makeover? J. B. Levine. il por *Bus Week* p66-7 Ag 3 '87

Bresson, Henri Cartier- See Cartier-Bresson, Henri, 1908-

Bretscher, Mark S.
How animal cells move. bibl (p158) il *Sci Am* 257:72-6+ D '87

Brett, Bob
Fitness for your strokes. il *World Tennis* 34:34-5 Ja '87

Brettell, Caroline B.
In the absence of men. il *Nat Hist* 96:52-61 F '87

The Bretts [television program] See Television program reviews—Single works

Breughel, Pieter, the Elder See Brueghel, Pieter, the Elder, 1522?-1569

Breuning, Stephen E.
about
"It was too good to be true". D. Brand. il por *Time* 129:59 Je 1 '87
NIMH finds a case of "serious misconduct". C. Holden. *Science* 235:1566-7 Mr 27 '87
Prosecution urged in fraud case. C. Norman. *Science* 236:1057 My 29 '87

Brewer, James W.
Are you a photographer or a hired gun? il *Petersens Photogr Mag* 16:64-7 O '87
Are you playing Russian roulette with your rights? il *Petersens Photogr Mag* 16:44-6 S '87

Brewer, Stephen
Tough guys grow petunias. il *50 Plus* 27:28-31 My '87
Turning your green thumb into a new career [cover story] il *50 Plus* 27:27-31 O '87

Brewery workers
See also
Trade unions—Brewery workers

Brewing
Homemade beer. C. Freeman, Jr. il *Ctry J* 14:68-73 Mr '87
"No—Bug Lite" [BioTechnica's high tech beer made with recombinant yeast] *Sci Am* 256:89 F '87

Brewing industry
 See also
 Adolph Coors Co.
 Anheuser-Busch, Inc.
 Boston Beer Company
 Catamount Brewing Company
 G. Heileman Brewing Co., Inc.
 Miller Brewing Company
A glass of handmade [beer from local breweries] W. Least Heat Moon. il *Atlantic* 260:75-9+ N '87
Roll out the barrel [small local breweries] M. Sheraton. il *Time* 130:98 N 9 '87

   Acquisitions and mergers
Heileman's Russell Cleary: brawling for breweries. M. D. Oneal. il por *Bus Week* p68+ Mr 2 '87
   International aspects
Carling goes Australian [takeover by Elders IXL Ltd.] T. Tedesco. il *Macleans* 100:36 Mr 9 '87
Is Carling Black Label worth a trip from Australia? [A. Bond's bid for G. Heileman Brewing] M. D. Oneal. il por *Bus Week* p33-4 S 21 '87
Two Australian beer barons take their brawl abroad [A. Bond and J. D. Elliott] C. Debes and P. Finch. il pors *Bus Week* p138+ O 19 '87

   Advertising
Break out the suds for Spuds: contrary to rumors, he's alive—and not only that, he's a she! il *People Wkly* 28:62-4 S 14 '87
Frothing anti-drink forces set out to nip Spuds in the Bud [objections to Spuds MacKenzie's appeal to children] il *People Wkly* 28:87 O 26 '87
Top dog [Bud Light's Spuds MacKenzie] B. Kanner. il *N Y* 20:20+ S 28 '87
Twin ads: a case of mistaken identity [Michelob and ABC Sports run commercials using song Everybody have fun tonight by Wang Chung] *Newsweek* 110:37 Ag 24 '87
Woman bites dog [J. Smith, brand director of Coors Light] E. Giltenan. il por *Forbes* 140:198 S 21 '87

   Ethical aspects
Anheuser-Busch: the scandal may be small beer after all [kickback charges] M. D. Oneal. il *Bus Week* p72-3 My 11 '87

   Export-import trade
A barroom brawl with Mexico [Canada vs. Mexico over Corona's impact] W. J. Holstein. *Bus Week* p38 Ag 10 '87
Counting the cost of protectionism [GATT ruling against Canadian beer and wine tariffs] M. Janigan. il *Macleans* 100:14 N 23 '87

   Marketing
 See also
 Askew Distributing Company
How Busch wins in a doggy market. P. Sellers. il por *Fortune* 115:99-100+ Je 22 '87
A new thirst for 'brewpubs'. G. C. Lubenow. il *Newsweek* 109:49 F 9 '87

   Australia
Two Australian beer barons take their brawl abroad [A. Bond and J. D. Elliott] C. Debes and P. Finch. il pors *Bus Week* p138+ O 19 '87

   Canada
 See also
 Carling O'Keefe Limited
 John Labatt Limited
A barroom brawl with Mexico [Canada vs. Mexico over Corona's impact] W. J. Holstein. *Bus Week* p38 Ag 10 '87
Canadian draft picks. W. Grimes. il *Esquire* 107:34 Ap '87

   Great Britain
 See also
 Allied-Lyons plc
 Guinness plc

   Philippines
 See also
 San Miguel Corp.

   United States
 See Brewing industry

Brewpubs *See* Bars and barrooms

Briand, Frédéric, and Cohen, Joel E.
Environmental correlates of food chain length. bibl f il *Science* 238:956-60 N 13 '87

Bribery
 See also
 Foreign Corrupt Practices Act of 1977

 Politics, Corruption in
Anheuser-Busch: the scandal may be small beer after all [kickback charges] M. D. Oneal. il *Bus Week* p72-3 My 11 '87
A suspicion of bribery [Canadian national soccer team members under investigation] G. Ferzoco. il *Macleans* 100:37 Ag 17 '87
The world's greatest middleman [S. Eisenberg] H. Kestin. il pors *Forbes* 140 Sp Issue:98+ O 26 '87

Brick construction
Adding on with brick: how to make a match. S. Romeo. il *Fam Handyman* 37:36+ F '87

Bricker, Charles
Antiques: art deco rugs. il *Archit Dig* 44:160-5 S '87
Legend of Le Fresne: Marquis and Marquise de Brantes near Tours. il pors *Archit Dig* 44:176-81+ S '87
Master of luxurious fakery. il por *Archit Dig* 44:238+ Ap '87

Bricker, William H.
   about
The downfall of a CEO. T. Mason. il por *Bus Week* p76-80+ F 16 '87

Brickfield, Cyril F.
   about
Brickfield to go. Who will follow his act? R. Rosenblatt. *50 Plus* 27:15+ Je '87

Brickley, Rosemarie
God isn't finished with me yet. *Commonweal* 114:410-11 Jl 17 '87

Brickmaking
The last brickmaker in America [G. Black] C. Kuralt. il *Read Dig* 130:53-6 My '87

Bricks
   Collectors and collecting
Fascinating bricks. R. P. Anjard. il *Antiques Collect Hobbies* 92:72-5 S '87

Bridal gowns *See* Wedding clothes
Bridal wreath *See* Spirea
Brides *See* Weddings

Bridge (Game)
   Tournaments
Making it in big-time bridge [R. Hamman and B. Wolff] T. Buckley. il pors *N Y Times Mag* p22-5+ Jl 26 '87

Bridge Cafe (New York, N.Y.) *See* New York (N.Y.)—Restaurants, nightclubs, bars, etc.

Bridge loans
Bridge loans: when you're between homes. T. Tilling. il *Parents* 62:54 Je '87
Bridging the house gap. L. Scheer and W. G. Flanagan. il *Forbes* 140:176 O 19 '87
Investment banking takes a new—and risky—turn. C. Farrell. il *Bus Week* p92+ Je 15 '87
Scarlett O'Hara comes to Wall Street [scramble over leveraged buyout financing] R. L. Stern and E. F. Cone. il *Forbes* 140:37-8+ S 21 '87

Bridgeport (Conn.)
   Housing
Death in the afternoon [building collapse] il *Macleans* 100:24 My 4 '87

Bridges, C. David, and Alvarez, Richard A.
The visual cycle operates via an isomerase acting on all-trans retinol in the pigment epithelium. bibl f il *Science* 236:1678-80 Je 26 '87

Bridges, Hudson
Along the avenues. See occasional issues of Gourmet

Bridges, Jeff
   about
It's a match: this time around, Basinger gets Bridges. il pors *Life* 10:61-4 Jl '87

Bridges, Linda
What hope for the courts? *Natl Rev* 39:36-7+ Ag 28 '87

Bridges, Todd
   about
Todd Bridges and mom sue managers for $2 million. *Jet* 72:15 Ap 13 '87
Todd Bridges: trying to put his troubled past behind him. il pors *Ebony* 42:27-8+ Jl '87

Bridges
 See also
 Covered bridges
 Houston (Tex.)—Bridges
 Tampa Bay (Fla.)—Bridges

   Design
Inside the Sunshine Skyway [longest concrete span in the Western Hemisphere] D. Stover. il *Pop Sci* 231:50-3 Jl '87

   Painting
Goodbye, old paint [George Washington Bridge] B. Weber. il *N Y Times Mag* p94 S 27 '87

Bridges—*cont.*

Canada

Plans for an Island link [Prince Edward Island] C. Barrett. il *Macleans* 100:18 N 30 '87

Bridges, Foot

Entry bridges: garden additions that work. il *South Living* 22:104+ Ap '87

Bridges, Wooden

See also

Covered bridges

Bridgestone Corp.

Bridgestone may try an end run around the yen [construction of U.S. plant to make car tires] Z. Schiller and J. B. Treece. il *Bus Week* p31 F 2 '87

Working for the Japanese [factory in Tenn.] il *Time* 130:60 S 14 '87

Bridgetown (Barbados)

Description

Bridgetown: sights of the Caribbean. A. R. Williams. il *Américas* 39:18-23+ N/D '87

Bridgewater State Hospital (Mass.) *See* Hospitals, Psychiatric—Massachusetts

Bridgman, Richard

The American studies of Henry Nash Smith. *Am Sch* 56:259-68 Spr '87

Briefcases

In the bag: what you carry, and how you carry it, is as important as what you wear. J. Mattera. il *Glamour* 85:102 Je '87

Anecdotes, facetiae, satire, etc.

The road warrior's survival kit. B. W. Yates. il *Car Driv* 32:25 Je '87

Briere, Alan D.

Duckweed [with photographs] il *Ctry J* 14:33-5 S '87

Brierley, Ronald

about

Market letter writer makes good. T. Jaffe. il *Forbes* 139:32-4 F 23 '87

Ron Brierley is king of the middle of the road. C. Debes. por *Bus Week* p78+ S 21 '87

Briers, David

Welsh comfort. il *House Gard* 159:112-19+ Ag '87

Briggs, Asa, 1921-

Samuel Smiles: the gospel of self-help. bibl il *Hist Today* 37:37-43 My '87

Briggs, Joe Bob

The gospel according to Joe Bob. il *Film Comment* 23:51-2+ Mr/Ap '87

Briggs, John, and Peat, F. David, 1938-

Interview [D. Bohm] por *Omni* 9:68-70+ Ja '87

Briggs, Josephine P.

(jt. auth) See Skøtt, Ole, and Briggs, Josephine P.

Briggs, Peter

about

Australian classic: the Robin and Peter Briggs house near Perth. C. Aillaud. il por *Archit Dig* 44:116-23 F '87

Briggs, Vernon M.

The growth and composition of the U.S. labor force. bibl f il *Science* 238:176-80 O 9 '87

Briggs & Stratton Corp.

Man on the bull's eye [F. Stratton] J. A. Conway. il por *Forbes* 139:8 My 4 '87

Bright, Deborah

(jt. auth) See Bright, Michael, and Bright, Deborah

Bright, John

Naming names [excerpt from Worms in a wine cup] il por *Film Comment* 23:48-51 N/D '87

Bright, Michael, and Bright, Deborah

Airbrushing your photos. il *Petersens Photogr Mag* 15:38-41 Ap '87

Bright children *See* Children, Gifted

Brightman, Adam

Fog . . . foggier . . . foggiest. il *Theatre Crafts* 21:28-9+ Mr '87

Brighton Beach memoirs [drama] See Simon, Neil

Brighton Beach memoirs [film] See Motion picture reviews—Single works

Brighton Festival *See* Music festivals—Great Britain

Brighton Grill & Oyster Bar (New York, N.Y.) *See* New York (N.Y.)—Restaurants, nightclubs, bars, etc.

Brill, Julie

South Korea. *Nation* 244:469-70 Ap 11 '87

Brill, Margaret

about

A market Prophet who ignores profits [interview] A. E. Serwer. il por *Fortune* 116:106 Ag 17 '87

Brilliance Corporation

Houghton Mifflin, Brilliance collaborate on two audio lines. *Publ Wkly* 231:42+ My 8 '87

Working a niche that works. J. Tangorra. il *Publ Wkly* 231:52+ Ja 16 '87

Brimelow, Peter, 1947-

A cautionary case of bilingualism. *Commentary* 84:63-5 N '87

Brimmer, Andrew F.

Economic perspectives. See issues of Black Enterprise

Income and wealth. il por *Ebony* 42:42+ Ag '87

Brine shrimp

Brine shrimp: curious crustaceans. R. L. Radtke. il *Sea Front* 33:128-33 Mr/Ap '87

Briner, Gordon

Stubborn stems; ed. by Doug Smith. il *Skiing* 40:218 D '87

Brining, Carmen

The lactose dilemma. il *Saturday Evening Post* 259:66-8 S '87

Brinkley, Alan

Dreams of the sixties. bibl f il *N Y Rev Books* 34:10+ O 22 '87

Brinkley, Christie

about

Fine tuning at the spa. C. Tuhy. il pors *Life* 10:68-71+ F '87

Brinley, Maryann Bucknum

10 tips on talking with your child. il *McCalls* 114:53 Ag '87

Brinsfield, James

2120 S. Michigan Ave. *Down Beat* 54:30 Mr '87

Brisbane (Australia)

Music

See also

Opera—Australia

Brisbane (Australia). Expo 88 *See* Expo 88 (Brisbane, Australia)

Brisco, Valerie

about

The gift of power [cover story] M. Kort. pors *Women's Sports Fitness* 9:40-3 N '87

Olympian Brisco-Hooks files for divorce in L.A. il por *Jet* 71:24 F 9 '87

Brister, Bob

Shooting. See issues of Field & Stream

Britain *See* Great Britain

Britains Ltd.

Peaceful toy soldiers. P. Bordan. il *Antiques Collect Hobbies* 92:40-2 Jl '87

Britannia (British national symbol)

John Bull's family arises. P. Mellini and R. T. Matthews. bibl il *Hist Today* 37:17-23 My '87

Brite, Jane

about

Jane Brite: riding the Madison Avenue express. P. Finch. il por *Bus Week* p146 D 7 '87

British

Netherlands

History

A patriot for whom? Stanley, York and Elizabeth's Catholics [1587 defection of key officers in the Netherlands] S. Adams. bibl il *Hist Today* 37:46-50 Jl '87

South Africa

The wrong tribe [English-speaking South Africans] il *Time* 129:35 My 4 '87

Spain

History

Scholar Gypsy [excerpt from The Bible in Spain] G. Borrow. il *Courier* 40:16 Ap '87

United States

May we borrow your historians? [U.S. universities' recruitment of English humanities professors] M. Kishlansky. il *Hist Today* 37:6-7 Je '87

History

Letters home: old and New England in the seventeenth century. D. Cressy. bibl il map *Hist Today* 37:37-41 O '87

"The most-hated man in America" [1842 visit of C. Dickens] E. L. Abel. bibl il pors *Am Hist Illus* 22:10-15+ D '87

West Africa

History

West Africa's Mary Kingsley. D. Birkett. bibl il pors *Hist Today* 37:10-16 My '87

British Aerospace plc

British Aerospace defines military aircraft versions. il *Aviat Week Space Technol* 126:97 Je 29 '87

British Aerospace delays missile program [air-launched antiradiation missile] *Aviat Week Space Technol* 127:23 S 21 '87

British Aerospace developing Rapier 2000 missile system. il *Aviat Week Space Technol* 126:143 F 9 '87

British Aerospace plc—*cont.*

British Aerospace, McDonnell Douglas will propose new Harrier version [AV-8B/GR. 5 Advanced Harrier] *Aviat Week Space Technol* 126:24 Je 22 '87

British Aerospace offers Terprom navigation system to U.S. military. il *Aviat Week Space Technol* 126:85 My 4 '87

British Aerospace rejects A330/A340 aid proposal. *Aviat Week Space Technol* 126:36 Mr 30 '87

British Aerospace seeks projects for EAP aircraft [Experimental Aircraft Program] *Aviat Week Space Technol* 127:69 D 7 '87

British agree on launch aid for A330/A340. *Aviat Week Space Technol* 126:33 My 18 '87

British offer Ariane deployment system for use on Titan 3 [Spelda dual satellite deployment system] il *Aviat Week Space Technol* 126:32-3 Ja 12 '87

British seek risk-sharing partners for high-agility aircraft project [Small Agile Battlefield Aircraft] D. A. Brown. il *Aviat Week Space Technol* 127:61 D 14 '87

Corporate plans [designs of business jets] J. M. McClellan. il *Flying* 114:12-13 Ap '87

T-45A trainer will be built, tested at Palmdale. *Aviat Week Space Technol* 127:136 O 12 '87

Thirteen new orders placed for British Aerospace 146s; second production line planned. *Aviat Week Space Technol* 126:267 Mr 9 '87

Wings West commuter orders 10 British Advanced Turboprops. *Aviat Week Space Technol* 127:37 S 28 '87

Wings West orders 15 Jetstream 31 commuters. *Aviat Week Space Technol* 127:36 O 19 '87

British Airways

British Airways is out to create its own united kingdom. M. Maremont. il *Bus Week* p90 D 28 '87-Ja 4 '88

British Airways places orders for 14 Boeing transports. *Aviat Week Space Technol* 127:36 Ag 24 '87

British Airways value set at $1.36 billion. *Aviat Week Space Technol* 126:36 F 2 '87

British Caledonian threatens to scuttle merger with British Airways. D. A. Brown. *Aviat Week Space Technol* 127:38 Ag 3 '87

British carriers boost service to Far Eastern destinations [transsiberian route] D. A. Brown. *Aviat Week Space Technol* 126:32-3 Je 8 '87

British government approves British Airways merger proposal [British Caledonian] *Aviat Week Space Technol* 127:36 N 16 '87

CAA chief backs move by small carriers to prevent British Airways/BCal merger; British Caledonian downplays impact of merger on competitors. D. A. Brown. *Aviat Week Space Technol* 127:56-7 Ag 3 '87

Caledonian board accepts offer to merge with British Airways. D. A. Brown. *Aviat Week Space Technol* 127:36 Jl 20 '87

Model pilots [pilot training program] R. L. Collins. *Flying* 114:90+ N '87

SAS bid for British Caledonian cleared by British government. *Aviat Week Space Technol* 127:36 D 21 '87

SAS, British Airways boost bids for stake in British Caledonian. *Aviat Week Space Technol* 127:34 D 14 '87

SAS seeks British Caledonian tie to boost international traffic. D. A. Brown. *Aviat Week Space Technol* 127:30-1 N 30 '87

U.S. denies British Airways ticket offer to continental Europe. J. Ott. *Aviat Week Space Technol* 126:34-5 Ap 6 '87

United names Wolf, shares CRS codes with British Airways. *Aviat Week Space Technol* 127:35 D 14 '87

Unloading British Airways. R. A. Melcher. *Bus Week* p48 F 9 '87

British architecture *See* Architecture, British

British art *See* Art, British

British Astronomical Association

Amateurs, professionals unite in England. N. Henbest. *Sky Telesc* 74:536-8 N '87

British authors *See* Authors, British

British Broadcasting Corporation *See* BBC

British Caledonian Airways Ltd.

British carriers boost service to Far Eastern destinations [transsiberian route] D. A. Brown. *Aviat Week Space Technol* 126:32-3 Je 8 '87

British Caledonian Group plc

British Caledonian Group cuts non-airline operations. *Aviat Week Space Technol* 126:36 Ap 6 '87

British Caledonian threatens to scuttle merger with British Airways. D. A. Brown. *Aviat Week Space Technol* 127:38 Ag 3 '87

British government approves British Airways merger proposal. *Aviat Week Space Technol* 127:36 N 16 '87

CAA chief backs move by small carriers to prevent British Airways/BCal merger; British Caledonian downplays impact of merger on competitors. D. A. Brown. *Aviat Week Space Technol* 127:56-7 Ag 3 '87

Caledonian board accepts offer to merge with British Airways. D. A. Brown. *Aviat Week Space Technol* 127:36 Jl 20 '87

SAS bid for British Caledonian cleared by British government. *Aviat Week Space Technol* 127:36 D 21 '87

SAS, British Airways boost bids for stake in British Caledonian. *Aviat Week Space Technol* 127:34 D 14 '87

SAS seeks British Caledonian tie to boost international traffic. D. A. Brown. *Aviat Week Space Technol* 127:30-1 N 30 '87

British Civil Aviation Authority *See* Great Britain. Civil Aviation Authority

British Columbia

See also

Camping—British Columbia

Columbia River

Educational laws and regulations—British Columbia

Environmental movement—British Columbia

Finance—British Columbia

Fishing—British Columbia

Gardens and gardening—British Columbia

Hotels, motels, etc.—British Columbia

Labor laws and regulations—British Columbia

Medical policy—British Columbia

Music festivals—British Columbia

Privatization—British Columbia

Queen Charlotte Islands (B.C.)

Resorts—British Columbia

Skis and skiing—British Columbia

South Moresby National Park (B.C.)

Vancouver (B.C.)

Vancouver Island (B.C.)

Victoria (B.C.)

Description and travel

See also

Cruising—British Columbia

Hot springs. E. Iglauer. *New Yorker* 63:62-9 Jl 6 '87

Fisheries

See Fisheries—Canada

Gambling

See Gambling—Canada

Industries

See also

British Columbia Hydro and Power Authority

Tourist trade—British Columbia

Politics and government

See also

Politics, Corruption in—British Columbia

Social Credit Party (B.C.)

A moderate takes over [M. Harcourt acclaimed leader of New Democratic Party] J. O'Hara. *Macleans* 100:16 Ap 27 '87

Vander Zalm's bold plans. J. O'Hara. il por *Macleans* 100:14-16 N 2 '87

Religious institutions and affairs

An unholy prayer fight [Prayer Canada's meetings in British Columbia legislature provoke protests] il *Macleans* 100:12 Ap 13 '87

Strikes

B.C.'s low-key day of protest [general strike] J. O'Hara. il *Macleans* 100:20-1 Je 15 '87

British Columbia Hydro and Power Authority

Whose power to which people? [plans for hydroelectric dam for export on the Peace River] J. Baker. il *Sierra* 72:22-4 Ja/F '87

British Columbia Social Credit Party *See* Social Credit Party (B.C.)

British Columbia Teachers' Federation

Legislation threatens B.C. Teachers' Federation. T. McConaghy. *Phi Delta Kappan* 69:310-11 D '87

British Commonwealth of Nations *See* Commonwealth of Nations

British communications satellites *See* Communications satellites, British

British correspondents in foreign countries *See* Foreign correspondents

British crown jewels *See* Crown jewels

British East India Company *See* East India Company

British Electric Traction Co. plc

See also

B E T plc

British Gas Corporation

See also

British Gas plc

British Gas plc
An oil-patch marriage [British Gas buys major stake in Bow Valley Industries] J. Howse. il *Macleans* 100:33 Ag 17 '87
British Grand Prix *See* Automobile racing—Great Britain
British helicopters *See* Helicopters
British jewelry *See* Jewelry, British
British National Space Center *See* National Space Center (Great Britain)
British Petroleum Co. plc
Adding to the wreckage [sale of shares] R. Laver. il *Macleans* 100:45 N 9 '87
Arresting new warrants. S. Miller. il *Bus Week* p126 My 25 '87
The century's best investor? [W. Churchill] P. Fuhrman. il por *Forbes* 139 Ann Directory:58 Ap 27 '87
A policeman's son enjoys tough calls [P. Walters] R. I. Kirkland, Jr. il por *Fortune* 116:30 Ag 3 '87
Why BP is going all out for all of Standard Oil. S. Miller. il *Bus Week* p50 Ap 13 '87
British Rail Pension Fund
Art for the pensioners' sake [prices of Japanese print collection] L. Scheer. il *Forbes* 140:117-18 D 28 '87
British Rail: on track [sale of old master prints from the collection of the British Rail Pension Fund] G. Barker. il *Art News* 86:25 O '87
Will British Rail sell all? [art and antiques collection amassed by British Rail Pension Fund expected to go on market] T. Trucco. il *Art News* 86:99-103 My '87
British Railways
See also
British Rail Pension Fund
British Satellite Broadcasting (Firm)
Hughes to build direct broadcast satellites. *Aviat Week Space Technol* 126:21 Je 8 '87
McDonnell Douglas receives firm commercial Delta launch orders [Hughes Aircraft to purchase for launch of British Satellite Broadcasting spacecraft] *Aviat Week Space Technol* 127:24 Jl 20 '87
British sculpture *See* Sculpture, British
British soccer fans *See* Soccer fans
British Telecom plc
First you slim your fat cats. S. Jenkins. il *U S News World Rep* 103:62 N 9 '87
British Virgin Islands
See also
Resorts—British Virgin Islands
Virgin Gorda (British Virgin Islands)
Description and travel
See also
Cruising—British Virgin Islands
Britoil plc
A squall over oil whips up the North Sea [British independents scurrying for white knights] S. Miller. il *Bus Week* p89-90 D 28 '87-Ja 4 '88
Britt, Angela M.
Showered! [poem] *Essence* 18:122 Ag '87
Britt, Bill
about
Facing eviction from his Boston hovel, hermit Bill Britt pleads there's no place like home. C. Neuhaus. il pors *People Wkly* 27:61-2 Ap 13 '87
Britt, Jim
Bathing beauties on the beach & in the studio [cover story] il *Petersens Photogr Mag* 16:16-19+ Jl '87
Brittain, Judy
Mews of the day. il *House Gard* 159:226-9 N '87
Brittany (France)
Armorica the beautiful: France's land by the sea. S. McCutcheon. il map *Travel Holiday* 168:66-71+ Jl '87
Britten, Benjamin, 1913-1976
about
Death in Venice [opera] Reviews
Dance Mag il 61:25+ Mr '87. L. M. Brooks *New Yorker* 63:61-2 Ag 3 '87. A. Porter
Ongoing Dialogues. P. G. Davis. il *N Y* 20:82+ Ap 6 '87
Britton, A. G.
Coast-to-coast pros: the best in beauty. il *Harpers Bazaar* 120:46+ S '87
Britton, Timothy
about
Philadelphia piping. M. D. Lemonick. il por *Time* 129:12+ Mr 16 '87
Brive (New York, N.Y.: Restaurant) *See* New York (N.Y.)—Restaurants, nightclubs, bars, etc.

Broad, Eli
about
Why collectors buy contemporary art [interview] M. S. Doherty. por *Am Artist* 51:10-11 Ap '87
Broad, William J.
The secrets of Soviet Star Wars. il map *N Y Times Mag* p22+ Je 28 '87
Star Wars is coming, but where is it going? il *N Y Times Mag* p80+ D 6 '87
Broad beans *See* Beans
Broadbent, Edward
about
Canada's sober socialists. H. M. Waller. il *New Leader* 70:10-11 O 5 '87
Not just another nice guy. M. Rose. il por *Macleans* 100:12-13 Ag 3 '87
Anecdotes, facetiae, satire, etc.
Alerting America to 'Red Ed'. A. Fotheringham. il *Macleans* 100:52 Ag 10 '87
Broadcast Arts (Firm)
Pee-wee's workhouse [special effects for Pee-wee's playhouse] B. Donofrio. il *N Y* 20:14 Ja 19 '87
Broadcast Music, Inc.
In the music biz, a star behind the scenes [F. W. Preston] D. L. Dennis. il por *Fortune* 115:77-8 Ja 5 '87
Broadcast news [film] *See* Motion picture reviews—Single works
Broadcast Promotion and Marketing Executives
The copycat factor [Broadcast Promotion and Marketing Executives awards] R. Buck. il *Channels* 7:17-18 Je '87
Broadcasters Promotion Association
See also
Broadcast Promotion and Marketing Executives
Broadcasting law *See* Television laws and regulations
Broadus, James M.
Seabed materials. bibl f il map *Science* 235:853-60 F 20 '87
Broadway [drama] *See* Dunning, Philip
Broadway bound [drama] *See* Simon, Neil
Broadway theater district (New York, N.Y.) *See* New York (N.Y.)—Theater
Brocard, Marie
about
Regal needles. S. De Rochambeau. il *House Gard* 159:88+ S '87
Broccoli
Beat the southern broccoli blues. B. Pleasant. il map *Rodale's Org Gard* 34:80+ N '87
Broccoli: America's rising star [cover story; special section] il *Rodale's Org Gard* 34:33-4+, 87-9 N '87
Broccoli: the anti-cancer vegetable. W. Gottlieb. il *Rodale's Org Gard* 34:66-7 Ag '87
Broccoli, Chinese *See* Chinese broccoli
Broccoli raab
See also
Cooking—Vegetables
Brassicas from abroad. J. H. Sanchez. il *Rodale's Org Gard* 34:42-5 N '87
Brochures *See* Pamphlets
Brock, Lou, Jr.
about
Young Brock ready to step from dad's shadow. il pors *Jet* 73:50 N 23 '87
Brock, William E.
Bozeman chain saw massacre. il pors *Discover* 8:78-82+ N '87
Brock, William Emerson, 1930-
Low-paying service work is a "myth" [address, March 5, 1987] *Vital Speeches Day* 53:444-6 My 1 '87
The state of the workforce [address, October 6, 1987] *Vital Speeches Day* 54:37-40 N 1 '87
about
Bill Brock's balancing act. M. E. Recio. il por *Bus Week* p146-7 F 23 '87
Fate of labor force depends on minorities' skills: Brock. *Jet* 72:38 My 4 '87
Brockhouse, Gordon
5 simple steps to highway hi-fi. il *High Fidel* 37:35-8+ My '87
Video and the digital revolution. il *High Fidel* 37:51+ N '87
Brockman, James R.
A torch held on high. *America* 156:214-16+ Mr 14 '87
Brockman, Michael
1987 Nissan Pathfinder. il *Mot Trend* 39:73-5 Mr '87
Brockmann, Stephen
In the land of the setting sun [cover story] il *America* 157:238-43 O 17 '87
Brockway, George P.
The dismal science. *See* issues of The New Leader

Brockway, Inc. (NY)
Most improved. il *Forbes* 139:202 Ja 12 '87
Brockway Air, Inc. (Vt.)
Brockway Air begins service with new SF340 transport.
il *Aviat Week Space Technol* 126:42 Je 29 '87
Broder, David S.
The story that still nags at me [excerpt from Behind
the front page] il *Wash Mon* 19:29-32+ F '87
Broder, King
about
Jury selection under way in Eddie Murphy dispute. *Jet*
71:16 Mr 23 '87
Murphy settles battle with ex-manager out of court.
il por *Jet* 72:54 Ap 6 '87
Yo, Broder! Eddie Murphy has to pay the King's ransom.
K. Gross. il pors *People Wkly* 27:103-4+ Ap 13 '87
Broder, Steve
Plowed under. il *Progressive* 51:35-40 My '87
Broderick, Damien
Thy sting [fiction] *Omni* 9:117-18 Je '87
Broderick, Matthew
about
Coping with the "cute" factor. R. Corliss. il pors *Time*
129:97 My 4 '87
Matthew Broderick ends a holiday in a tragic crash
that claims two lives. il por *People Wkly* 28:53 Ag
24 '87
Matthew Broderick leaves behind the grieving Irish town
that charges him with two lost lives. A. Richman.
il por *People Wkly* 28:92-4 S 28 '87
Broderick, Mosette Glaser
Marshall, Michigan. il *House Gard* 159:128+ Ap '87
Brodkey, Harold
Between 6:37 p.m. and 9:04 p.m. [poem] *New Yorker*
63:32 Je 15 '87
Family. *New Yorker* 63:119-33 N 23 '87
The laugh [story] *New Yorker* 62:31-8 F 2 '87
Brodoff, Ami S.
Night visitors. *Vogue* 177:446 F '87
Brodsky, Joseph, 1940-
The Belfast tune [poem] *New Yorker* 63:28 Jl 13
'87
The bust of Tiberius [poem]; tr. by Alan Myers. *N
Y Rev Books* 34:18 Je 25 '87
Eclogue V: summer [poem]; tr. by George L. Kline.
New Yorker 63:22-4 Ag 3 '87
In memoriam [poem] *New Yorker* 63:48 N 9 '87
Kelomyakki [poem]; tr. by the author. *New Yorker*
62:26-7 Ja 26 '87
October tune [poem] *New Yorker* 63:38 O 5 '87
Polonaise: a variation [poem] *New Yorker* 63:40
S 21 '87
'Slave, come to my service!' [poem] *N Y Rev Books*
34:23 N 19 '87
about
Brodsky's Nobel: what the applause was about. S. Heaney.
por *N Y Times Book Rev* 92:1+ N 8 '87
Joseph Brodsky: scrutinizing the good. D. Heim. *Christ
Century* 104:989-90 N 11 '87
Lyrics of loss, theories of gain. P. Gray; P. Elmer-DeWitt.
il pors *Time* 130:80 N 2 '87
Nobel dynamite. *Natl Rev* 39:21 N 20 '87
Poetry's laureate in exile. J. Kroll. il por *Newsweek*
110:66 N 2 '87
A talk with Joseph Brodsky [interview] A. Husarska.
New Leader 70:8-11 D 14 '87
Brody, Aileen
about
My mother's silent world. R. Brody. il *50 Plus* 27:25-7+
My '87
Brody, David
Elements of paradox in U.S. labor history. il *Mon Labor
Rev* 110:48-50 Ag '87
Brody, Jane E.
The complete breakfast. il *Saturday Evening Post* 259:18+
O '87
Eat more, weigh less, feel great [condensed from Jane
Brody's Good food book] *Read Dig* 131:159-62 N
'87
Fighting dental plaque. il *Essence* 17:17+ Ja '87
Brody, Meredith
We killed 'em in Chicago. il por *Film Comment* 23:68-70+
Ja/F '87
Brody, Robert
Taking better aim. il *Sport Mag* 78:91+ Ag '87
Brody, Steve
How I got smart. il *Read Dig* 131:176-8 N '87
Broecker, Wallace S., 1931-
The biggest chill. il maps *Nat Hist* 96:74-80+ O '87

Broeske, Pat H.
Hollywood's change of art. il *Roll Stone* p24+ F 12
'87
Broglie, Jeanne-Marie de
about
A connoisseur's esprit: Princess Jeanne-Marie de Broglie's
apartment in France. C. Aillaud. il por *Archit Dig*
44:192-5 Ap '87
Broglie, Louis de, 1892-1987
about
Obituary
Sci News 131:196 Mr 28 '87
Brokaw, Meredith
about
This Brokaw is cashing in on classy toys. M. Frons.
il por *Bus Week* p107 My 11 '87
Brokaw, Tom
about
High moments in a low key. T. Griffith. por *Time*
130:68 D 14 '87
The most trusted men in America. C. Kramer. il pors
McCalls 114:128+ Jl '87
NBC's catalytic anchor [interview] pors *Channels* 7:62-3
My '87
Anecdotes, facetiae, satire, etc.
A man and his face. D. Seligman. il *Fortune* 115:26
Ja 5 '87
Broken bones *See* Fractures
Broken homes
See also
Children of divorced parents
Children of separated parents
Broken mirrors [film] *See* Motion picture reviews—Single
works
Brokered deposits *See* Bank accounts—Brokered deposits
Brokers
See also
A.B. Tompane & Company
Aubrey G. Lanston & Company
Banks and banking—Securities handling
Bear, Stearns & Co. Inc.
Black brokers
Blinder, Robinson & Company
Charles Schwab & Co., Inc.
Commodity brokers
Dean Witter Reynolds Inc.
Drexel Burnham Lambert Incorporated
E. F. Hutton Group Inc.
Edward D. Jones & Company
First Jersey Securities, Inc.
Foreign exchange brokers
Gabelli & Company
Gruntal Financial Corporation
IDS Financial Services Inc.
Jefferies Group Inc.
Kidder, Peabody & Co., Incorporated
Matthews & Wright Inc.
Minority brokers
Money brokers
Oppenheimer & Co., Inc.
Over-the-counter securities markets
PaineWebber Group Inc.
R. D. Smith & Company
Rooney, Pace Group Inc.
Sherwood Investors Ltd.
Smith Barney, Harris Upham & Co. Incorporated
Spear Financial Services, Inc.
Specialists (Stock exchange firms)
Stuart-James Company Inc.
Thomson McKinnon Inc.
Tucker, Anthony & R. L. Day, Inc.
Women brokers
The best stockbrokers. J. Edgerton and B. Hager. il
Money Sp Issue:83-4+ Fall '87
The decline of the superstar [cover story] A. Bianco.
il *Bus Week* p90-6+ Ag 17 '87
Five experts' picks. il *U S News World Rep* 103:58-9
Ag 31 '87
The Fortune investment challenge: who can make the
most of $100,000? il *Fortune* 116 Sp Issue:175-91
Fall '87
Investment challenge: surveying the damage. J. Mendes.
il *Fortune* 116:176+ D 7 '87
It's back to the basics for your friendly broker. D.
P. Wiener. il *U S News World Rep* 103:62-3 N 16
'87
Money and freedom [retirement at age 24] M. Glickman.
il *N Y Times Mag* p62 Ap 26 '87
The stock analysts. J. Rothchild. il *Wash Mon* 19:10-14+
O '87

Brokers—*cont.*

Updating the investment challenge: five out of six players lead the S&P 500. M. McFadden. il *Fortune* 115:110-11 F 16 '87

Updating the investment challenge: for no. 1 Shearson, a big jump on the market. T. Paré. il *Fortune* 115:166-7 My 11 '87

Updating the investment challenge: who has made $100,000 grow most. T. Paré. il *Fortune* 116:104-5 Ag 17 '87

When the house always wins [performance of mutual funds operated by largest national brokerage houses] W. L. Updegrave. il *Money* 16:97-100 Jl '87

Acquisitions and mergers

Can Cohen the consolidator make Shearson-Hutton work? A. Bianco. il por *Bus Week* p96-8 D 21 '87

For sale: Wall Street giant [Shearson Lehman's bid for E.F. Hutton] J. Schwartz. il *Newsweek* 110:64 D 7 '87

For Smith Barney, the go-go years have just begun [takeover by Primerica Corp.] R. Mitchell. il por *Bus Week* p39-40 Je 8 '87

Humbled Hutton. il *Time* 130:49 D 7 '87

Trying not to be a second First Jersey [sale of retail brokerage to be named Sherwood Investors] C. Welles. il por *Bus Week* p44 Ja 12 '87

Will Sandy Weill snare Hutton? G. G. Marcial. il *Bus Week* p73 Ag 24 '87

International aspects

Jardine's giant step from Hong Kong to Wall Street [stake in Bear Stearns] D. J. Yang and others. il por *Bus Week* p39-40 O 12 '87

Small world [Sanyo Securities buys stake in Spear Financial Services] J. Heins. il *Forbes* 139:159+ My 4 '87

Advertising

And now, heeere's Johnny's brother [D. Carson appears in Dean Witter TV ad] il por *Newsweek* 109:49 F 9 '87

The honor system. B. Weberman. il *Forbes* 140:255 D 14 '87

'Spin control' on Wall Street. J. Reed. il *U S News World Rep* 102:46 Ap 20 '87

Age

Nomura: land of the rising young. B. Buell. il por *Bus Week* p51-2 N 30 '87

Anecdotes, facetiae, satire, etc.

Wall Street's new bull market: jokes. G. Parshall. *U S News World Rep* 103:16 N 9 '87

Banking services

See also

Cash management accounts

Commissions

Egad, chaps! It's a Yankee discount broker [Fidelity Management in London] L. Therrien. il *Bus Week* p97 F 16 '87

Excessive markups? [o-t-c spreads] D. Henry. il *Forbes* 139:98 Ja 26 '87

How to pick and choose among no-frills brokers. M. McFadden. il *Fortune* 115:112 Mr 16 '87

The long trail [fund companies paying brokers an annual commission] R. Simon. il *Forbes* 140:204 S 21 '87

Merrill Lynch, discount king? [Blueprint program] G. Weiss. *Bus Week* p72 Mr 30 '87

Customer relations

Battling your broker gets harder [Supreme Court upholds arbitration] D. P. Wiener. il *U S News World Rep* 102:51 Je 22 '87

Busy signals [customers' inability to get through to brokers and funds on toll free numbers during the crash] M. Schifrin. il *Forbes* 140:38+ N 16 '87

Can't sue your broker? It's no big loss [Supreme Court decision upholds arbitration] D. Zigas. il *Bus Week* p128 Je 22 '87

Choosing a good stockbroker. T. Hauser. il *McCalls* 114:179 F '87

Did you agree not to sue? [use of arbitration to settle broker-stockholder disputes] *U S News World Rep* 103:45 N 9 '87

Did your broker pick up the phone? [stock market crash] A. Miller. il *Newsweek* 110:40 N 2 '87

How to avoid a rogue broker. D. R. Katz. il *Esquire* 108:39-40 Ag '87

How to become your broker's pet. A. Lanyi. il *Nations Bus* 75:4 Ja '87

How to say no (or yes) to your broker. J. Kosnett. il *Changing Times* 41:77-81 Mr '87

How to settle a beef with your broker. *Money* 16:13 Ap '87

Keeping your broker under control. M. Hodge. il *50 Plus* 27:50-2 S '87

Managing your money pro. L. Meisler. il *Work Woman* 12:36+ F '87

Many, many are called—by pro and rookie alike. M. Schifrin. il *Forbes* 139:140-1 F 23 '87

Picking a stockbroker: 6 questions you need to ask—and answer—before you choose. B. G. Quint. il *Glamour* 85:114+ O '87

Picking the right stockbroker. il *Changing Times* 41:27 Ap '87

Small investors and the crash. C. Friday. il *Newsweek* 110:50-1 D 21 '87

Sue your stockbroker? You can't, you know [upcoming Supreme Court ruling] S. Weiss. il *Bus Week* p75-6 Mr 2 '87

Wall Street's credibility gap [cover story; special section] il *Bus Week* p92-5+ N 23 '87

We wuz robbed [arbitration in broker-customer cases] R. L. Stern. il *Forbes* 140:60-1 D 28 '87

What to do if your broker leads you astray. T. Segal. il *Bus Week* p90 F 2 '87

When you're burned by your broker. il *Changing Times* 41:77-80+ Ap '87

Why one phone is stirring up the Big Board [broker W. J. Higgins' mobile phone] J. M. Laderman. il por *Bus Week* p123 Jl 20 '87

Why stockbrokers sleep at night [Supreme Court upholds binding arbitration] M. Meyer. il *Money* 16:105-8+ Jl '87

Dismissal

The big chill on Wall Street. A. Bianco. il *Bus Week* p54-7 D 7 '87

'Down with M.B.A.'s!' [effect of stock market crash] J. Taylor. il *N Y* 20:34-7 N 2 '87

Finding work for Wall Street's exiles. *Fortune* 116:8 D 7 '87

A jolt for Wall St.'s whiz kids [wave of layoffs] B. Powell and C. Friday. il *Newsweek* 110:55-6+ O 26 '87

The Street's retreat will be felt far from the Big Apple. D. Zigas and J. Berger. il *Bus Week* p31 O 26 '87

When bad things happen to rich people [layoffs on Wall Street] D. Bleeker. *New Repub* 197:17-18 N 23 '87

Ethical aspects

See also

Drugs and brokers

Bad brokers. J. W. Merline. *Consum Res Mag* 70:38 F '87

Blind 'em and rob 'em [Blinder, Robinson & Co.] M. Schifrin. il por *Forbes* 140:8 N 2 '87

Blinder, Robinson—blind 'em and rob 'em. M. Schifrin. il *Forbes* 139:33-8 Ap 20 '87

Crime wave [securities crime; cover story] R. L. Stern and M. Schifrin. il *Forbes* 139:67-70 Je 29 '87

The day the brokers picked their own pockets [Black Monday] R. L. Stern and A. Sloan. il *Forbes* 140:32-3 N 16 '87

Dispassionate advice [conflict of interests arising from brokers sales of mutual funds] J. Heins. il *Forbes* 139:160+ Mr 9 '87

Government bond dealers: a bell is tolling. G. DeGeorge. *Bus Week* p63-4 My 25 '87

How E. F. Hutton is trying to clean its slate [industrial revenue bond imbroglio] G. Weiss. il *Bus Week* p79 Ja 26 '87

Jefferies's fall worries more than insiders. il por *Fortune* 115:8 Ap 13 '87

Meet the prince of penny stocks: Meyer Blinder. D. R. Katz. il por *Fortune* 115:108-10+ Ja 19 '87

Nabbing the stealth broker [B. Jefferies charged] B. Powell and C. Friday. il por *Newsweek* 109:48 Mr 30 '87

Poison wine in new bottles [Stuart-James Co. Inc.] D. Henry. il *Forbes* 140:32-4 O 5 '87

Requiem for a heavyweight [bank broker C. H. Howard for Thomson McKinnon] L. Jereski. il *Forbes* 140:152 N 30 '87

Serving his clients all too well [criminal charges against B. Jefferies] S. Koepp. il por *Time* 129:52 Mr 30 '87

The stranger in the corner [broker H. Kirschner launches securities scam from Greenwich office of Shearson Lehman Brothers] D. Fanning. *Forbes* 140:37-8 O 5 '87

When Boyd Jefferies talks, all of Wall Street will be listening. C. Farrell and others. il por *Bus Week* p37 Ap 6 '87

Where were the cops? [J. A. Lugo] R. L. Stern and M. Fritz. il *Forbes* 139:60-2 Ap 6 '87

Finance

The big chill on Wall Street. A. Bianco. il *Bus Week* p54-7 D 7 '87

Brokers—Finance—*cont.*

The bombs of October. J. M. Laderman and D. J. Yang. *Bus Week* p116 N 23 '87

The chaotic world of bonds. D. Pauly. il *Newsweek* 110:36 Jl 6 '87

The shrinking of Fat City [effect of stock market crash] J. Greenwald. il *Time* 130:41-2 N 2 '87

Snapped by their own suspenders [effect of stock market crash] M. Hornblower. il *Time* 130:53 N 2 '87

Upheaval ahead on Wall Street. R. E. Norton. il *Fortune* 116:68-9+ S 14 '87

Wall Street craving for capital. A. Bianco. il *Bus Week* p34-5 Ap 6 '87

Wall Street is solid—but very nervous. A. Bianco. il *Bus Week* p110 Ja 12 '87

Wall Street's new austerity [special section] il *Bus Week* p28-31 O 26 '87

Wreckage on Wall Street. D. Pauly. il *Newsweek* 110:31 N 9 '87

Management

Will the Street ever learn that good times end? C. Welles. il *Bus Week* p57 D 7 '87

Marketing

Wall Street's credibility gap [cover story; special section] il *Bus Week* p92-5+ N 23 '87

Recruiting

Bay Street bickering [Wood Gundy sues employees hired away by Walwyn Inc.] P. Best. il *Macleans* 100:30 S 28 '87

Securities

Bargains in brokerage stocks. J. J. Curran. *Fortune* 115:128 Ja 19 '87

The biggest bomb landed smack in the Street [effects of October crash] A. Bianco. il *Bus Week* p52 N 2 '87

This bull likes two brokerages [views of Mason S. Sexton] G. G. Marcial. *Bus Week* p148 Mr 23 '87

Supply and demand

Cold-call cowboys. M. Schifrin. *Forbes* 139:140-1 F 23 '87

Training

See also
Stanton C. Selbst Inc.

Canada

See also
Nesbitt Thomson Deacon Inc.
Walwyn Inc.
Wood Gundy Incorporated

Black Monday's long hangover. D. Jenish. il *Macleans* 100:32-3 D 14 '87

Countdown to an open market. T. Fennell. il *Macleans* 100:38-9 Je 1 '87

Crackdown on Bay Street [Ontario Securities Commission probes insider trading] T. Tedesco. il *Macleans* 100:22-3 Jl 13 '87

Frantic week for a broker [D. Doritty's activities during stock market crash] A. Shortell. il por *Macleans* 100:31-2 N 2 '87

The last days of the club [Bay Street] P. C. Newman. il *Macleans* 100:70 F 2 '87

Regulating deregulation. T. Fennell. il *Macleans* 100:36-7 O 12 '87

France

Now, the Bourse is in the game for real [le Big Bang] J. Rossant. il *Bus Week* p88 Jl 20 '87

Great Britain

See also
Panmure Gordon & Company
S.G. Warburg Group plc

Big bust [Big Bang aftermath] R. L. Stern and D. Henry. il *Forbes* 140:64-5 Ag 24 '87

The City of London wanted competition—but not this much. R. A. Melcher. il *Bus Week* p37 Ag 10 '87

Egad, chaps! It's a Yankee discount broker [Fidelity Management in London] L. Therrien. il *Bus Week* p97 F 16 '87

Japan

See also
Nikko Securities Co. Ltd.
Nomura Securities Co. Ltd.
Sanyo Securities Co. Ltd.

Can Japan work the Street? B. Powell. il *Newsweek* 110:60 O 19 '87

Comparative disadvantage [Japanese brokers in the United States] P. Fuhrman. il *Forbes* 139:144 My 18 '87

Deregulation: a two-way street. B. Buell. *Bus Week* p62 Je 22 '87

Japan on Wall Street [cover story] W. Glasgall. il *Bus Week* p82-6+ S 7 '87

Rising Sun on Wall Street: how Japanese money and firms are moving in. D. Burstein. il *N Y* 20:32-8 Mr 2 '87

Why banks fear Congress' help [trade bill restrictions on Japanese banks and brokers in the U.S.] M. McNamee. il *Bus Week* p35 S 14 '87

Brokers, Mortgage *See* Mortgage brokers

Brokers, Real estate *See* Real estate agencies and agents

Brolin, James

about

Altared states: Brolin & Co. B. Goodwin. pors *Harpers Bazaar* 120:136-7 Jl '87

Bromberg, Craig

Teaching tomorrow's avant-garde. il *Art News* 86:100-3 S '87

Bromeliads

See also
Puya
Spanish moss

Bromine

Therapeutic use

Drug 'nukes' ovarian cancer [estrogen linked with radioactive bromine] J. Raloff. *Sci News* 131:389 Je 20 '87

Bromke, Adam

Jaruzelski walks a fine line. *World Press Rev* 34:37 Je '87

Bromke, Adam, and Nossal, Kim Richard

A turning point in U.S.-Canadian relations. *Foreign Aff* 66:150-69 Fall '87

Bromley, Stan

about

The butler does it. P. Tyre. il por *N Y* 20:14 Ag 3 '87

Bromon Aircraft Company

Bromon plans first flight of BR2000 for late 1988. S. W. Kandebo. il *Aviat Week Space Technol* 126:329-30 Je 15 '87

Bronchial tubes

Diseases

See also
Bronchiectasis

Bronchiectasis

"Don't worry!" [daughter's bout] A. R. Roiphe. il por *McCalls* 114:58-60 Ja '87

Brondfield, Jerome

Just for kicks. il *Read Dig* 131:33-7 Ag '87

Bronfman family

about

Can the Bronfmans keep Seagram in the family? E. B. Terry. il *Bus Week* p60 Je 1 '87

A dynasty divided. P. Best. il *Macleans* 100:41 My 18 '87

Bronner, Beth

about

Building a better sundae. J. Sherman. il por *Work Woman* 12:48 Jl '87

Bronsky, Sid

about

Sections. *New Yorker* 62:24 Ja 26 '87

Bronson, Gail

Science & technology. See issues of Forbes beginning March 10, 1986

Brontosaurus *See* Dinosaurs

Bronx (New York, N.Y.)

Crime

N.Y. woman attacks ex-judge in dispute over $482 [L. Byron attempts to shoot A. Levy] il pors *Jet* 72:33 Ag 3 '87

Education

6,000 hours [Special Public School 31 in the South Bronx] *New Yorker* 62:25-7 F 16 '87

Adoption [sixth graders learn about Hudson River Striped Bass Hatchery] *New Yorker* 62:31-2 F 9 '87

The drive to excel [D. Kuo, Chinese student at Bronx High School of Science] A. Quindlen. il pors *N Y Times Mag* p32+ F 22 '87

The sound of music [St. Augustine parochial school] E. Hopkins. il *N Y* 20:54-7 N 23 '87

Motion picture theaters

Loew's Paradise. A. Corman. il *N Y* 20:76-7 D 21-28 '87

Politics and government

Charges of bribery [M. Biaggi indicted in Wedtech scandal] B. Levin. il por *Macleans* 100:30 Je 15 '87

Religious institutions and affairs

The Pope's foot soldiers [B. Frawley and R. Dlugos, parish priests; cover story] J. Buckley. il pors *U S News World Rep* 103:60-4+ S 21 '87

Bronx Zoo

It's a jungle in there [Jungleworld] il *USA Today (Periodical)* 116:96 N '87

Bronx Zoo—*cont.*
Pandas [J. A. Cohen's work in securing loan of pandas from Beijing] *New Yorker* 63:23-4 Ap 13 '87
Take a ganda at this panda, the queen of China's bear market and now the zoo's who of N.Y.C. il *People Wkly* 27:79 My 18 '87
The whole world goes pandas [Chinese pandas] G. Clarke. il *Time* 129:79 My 11 '87

Bronze Age
Mediterranean region
Oldest known shipwreck reveals splendors of the Bronze Age [cover story] G. F. Bass. il map *Natl Geogr* 172:692-733 D '87
Switzerland
Digging for Bronze Age treasures [Earthwatch's Lake Neuchâtel project] S. Ocko. il *Technol Rev* 90:70-1 F/Mr '87

Bronze figurines *See* Figurines
Bronzes
Forms of fantasy [sculpture of N. Graves] C. McGuigan. il pors *N Y Times Mag* p62-4+ D 6 '87
Keeping dance forever [sculptor E. MacQueen] G. Parks. il por *Dance Mag* 61:46-8 D '87
Conservation and restoration
Buried treasure [restoration of Roman bronzes found in Marches region of Italy] G. Armstrong. il *Art News* 86:91-2 Ap '87

Brooches
Eleanor Moty [cover story] S. Foley. il por *Am Craft* 47:34-9+ Je/Jl '87
Little big gems. il *Vogue* 177:252 My '87

Brook, Irina
about
Talent: orbiting to the top. pors *Harpers Bazaar* 120:264-73 Mr '87

Brook, Peter, 1925-
about
The Mahabharata [drama] Reviews
America 157:358+ N 14 '87. G. G. Seibert
Commonweal il 114:655-6 N 20 '87. G. Weales
N Y il 20:110-11 N 2 '87. J. Simon
N Y Times Mag il p36-8+ O 4 '87. M. Croyden
New Repub 197:26-8 N 30 '87. R. Brustein
New Yorker 63:146-8 N 2 '87. M. Kramer
Newsweek il 110:74-5 S 21 '87. J. Kroll
People Wkly il 28:134-5 N 9 '87
Theatre Crafts il 21:27-31+ N '87
Time il 130:85 O 19 '87. W. A. Henry
Vogue il por 177:444-5+ O '87. A. Harvey
Peter Brook creates a nine-hour epic. M. Croyden. il por *N Y Times Mag* p36-8+ O 4 '87

Brook trout fishing *See* Trout fishing
Brooke, James
Cuba's strange mission in Angola. il *N Y Times Mag* p24+ F 1 '87

Brooke, Peter
about
Foreign affairs of a venture capitalist. A. Ramirez. il pors *Fortune* 115:84-6+ F 2 '87

Brookehill Equities Inc.
Sweetening the pot at Holly Sugar. M. Ivey. il *Bus Week* p34 Je 29 '87

Brookes, Warren T.
Don't raise taxes. il *Read Dig* 131:163-6 O '87

Brookgreen Gardens
Green men [C. Milles' The fountain of the muses] J. Herzfeld. il *Art News* 86:13-14 N '87

Brookhaven National Laboratory
Wimps [search for axions by W. Wuensch and others] *New Yorker* 63:18-19 Jl 13 '87

Brookhiser, Richard
Born-again Bradley? il *Natl Rev* 39:44-6 S 25 '87
Call me Pete. *Natl Rev* 39:24-6 D 31 '87
Democracy in South Africa. *Natl Rev* 39:34-6 Jl 31 '87
My New York, my New York. *Natl Rev* 39:37-9 F 13 '87
Over here! Over here! *Natl Rev* 39:50+ O 9 '87
The public brawl, the secret war. il *Natl Rev* 39:34-7 Ja 30 '87
Why Dole can't do it [cover story] il por *Natl Rev* 39:30-2 D 4 '87

Brooklands (Race track) *See* Speedways—Great Britain
Brooklyn (New York, N.Y.)
See also
Coney Island (New York, N.Y.)
Arts
See also
Brooklyn Academy of Music

Child welfare
Against all odds [Jackson children living at Brooklyn Arms welfare hotel] B. Campbell. il *N Y* 20:68-74+ N 16 '87
Crime
Ex-boyfriend beheads teen girl with samurai sword in New York [E. Rodrique kills J. Mentor] por *Jet* 72:17 Je 8 '87
Husband tosses wife 18 stories in heated dispute [J. Burgos] *Jet* 73:32 O 26 '87
Machine gunman, high on crack, pumps 26 fatal bullets into boy, 3 [murder of L. Horris] il por *Jet* 73:36 D 7 '87
Festivals
Welcome Back. *New Yorker* 63:22-4 Je 22 '87
Galleries and museums
See also
Brooklyn Museum
Museum of the Borough of Brooklyn
Gardens and gardening
Operation GreenThumb. P. H. Johnson. il *Rodale's Org Gard* 34:20-2 N '87
Health facilities
An open door [Pesach Tikvah, mental health center serving the Orthodox community in Williamsburg] J. Meer. *Psychol Today* 21:17 Ap '87
Housing
Against all odds [Jackson children living at Brooklyn Arms welfare hotel] B. Campbell. il *N Y* 20:68-74+ N 16 '87
Interracial couple in N.Y. get damages from landlord. *Jet* 72:29 My 4 '87
Music
See also
Brooklyn Philharmonic Symphony Orchestra
Police
Breaking the crack murders [solving the murder of a crack dealer] R. Rosenbaum. il *N Y Times Mag* p44-6+ N 15 '87
Crack murder: a detective story [solving the murder of a crack dealer] R. Rosenbaum. il pors *N Y Times Mag* p24-30+ F 15 '87
Politics and government
U.S. Rep. Major Owens fights ex-wife on charges of race bias, back alimony. il pors *Jet* 73:16-17 N 2 '87
Restaurants, nightclubs, bars, etc.
Borscht belt [St. Petersbourg, Odessa and Kavkazian] G. Greene. il *N Y* 20:116-18 O 19 '87
Catch as chef can [chef R. Palmer of the River Cafe catches, cooks and serves tuna] M. Burros. il por *N Y Times Mag* p75-6 Je 14 '87
Spécialités de la maison:
The River Café. A. Birsh. il *Gourmet* 47:28+ Ag '87
Social history
When summers were free [Brooklyn in the 1940's] P. Hamill. il *Read Dig* 131:72-4 Jl '87
Theater
See also
Majestic Theater (Brooklyn, N.Y.)
Brooklyn Heights
See Brooklyn Heights (New York, N.Y.)
Brownsville
See Brownsville (New York, N.Y.)
Flatbush
See Flatbush (New York, N.Y.)
Brooklyn Academy of Music
See also
Next Wave Festival
BAM goes boom [cover story] A. Virshup. il *N Y* 20:38-47 O 12 '87

Brooklyn College. Museum of the Borough of Brooklyn
See Museum of the Borough of Brooklyn

Brooklyn Heights (New York, N.Y.)
Witness stand [community objection to proposed Watchtower Society residential building] P. Tyre. il *N Y* 20:14-15 Mr 16 '87

Brooklyn Museum
Brooklyn Museum [seventeenth-century iron-painted Korean dragon jar] il *Antiques Collect Hobbies* 92:58-9 My '87
Brooklyn Museum master plan design competition. il *Archit Rec* 175:45 Ja '87
Moonlight in the Brooklyn Museum [painting by R. A. Blakelock] P. Auster. il *Art News* 86:104-5 S '87

Brooklyn Philharmonia *See* Brooklyn Philharmonic Symphony Orchestra

Brooklyn Philharmonic Symphony Orchestra
Forces of nature [W. Bolcom's Songs of innocence and of experience] P. G. Davis. il *N Y* 20:71-2 Ja 26 '87
Musical events:
Songs of innocence and of experience by W. Bolcom. A. Porter. il *New Yorker* 62:70-3 F 2 '87
Reich's progress. P. G. Davis. il por *N Y* 20:110-11 N 23 '87
Tiger, tiger daring, bright [Songs of innocence and of experience by W. Bolcom] A. Rich. il por *Newsweek* 109:58 Ja 19 '87

Brookover, Wilbur B.
Distortion and overgeneralization are no substitutes for sound research. bibl f il *Phi Delta Kappan* 69:225-7 N '87

Brooks, Anne, 1938-
about
The healing of soul and body. L. Lindeman. il pors *50 Plus* 27:20-3+ D '87
Sister Anne Brooks, doctor and nun, practices without preaching to the poor. B. Shaw. il pors *People Wkly* 27:82-3+ Mr 23 '87

Brooks, Avery
about
Avery Brooks: a.k.a. Hawk. F. White, III. il pors *Ebony* 42:62+ Ap '87

Brooks, David
Good vibrations: the new peace offensive. il *Natl Rev* 39:36-9 N 6 '87
The young pol's guide to the brave new world. il *Natl Rev* 39:28-30+ Ap 10 '87

Brooks, Edward M.
The March annular-total eclipse. il *Sky Telesc* 73:12 Ja '87
The total solar eclipse of March, 1988. map *Sky Telesc* 74:21-2 Jl '87

Brooks, Gwendolyn
about
Gwendolyn Brooks—a poet for all ages. C. Whitaker. il pors *Ebony* 42:154+ Je '87

Brooks, James L., 1940-
about
Broadcast news [film] Reviews
Newsweek il 110:50 D 28 '87. C. Gould
Newsweek il por 110:44-9 D 28 '87. D. Ansen
People Wkly il 28:10 D 21 '87. P. Travers
Time il por 130:82-3 D 14 '87. R. Corliss

Brooks, James M., and others
Deep-sea hydrocarbon seep communities: evidence for energy and nutritional carbon sources. bibl f il *Science* 238:1138-42 N 20 '87

Brooks, Keith
Teaching [address, October 31, 1986] *Vital Speeches Day* 53:434-9 My 1 '87

Brooks, Linda Lockman- *See* Lockman-Brooks, Linda
Brooks, Lonnie
about
Blues breaker. S. G. Freedman. il pors *Roll Stone* p91-2+ S 24 '87

Brooks, Mel
about
The cosmos according to Mel Brooks. E. G. Carter. il por *Vogue* 177:220-1+ Je '87
May the farce be with him: Spaceballs rockets Mel Brooks back into lunatic orbit. M. Dougherty. il pors *People Wkly* 28:38-41 Jl 20 '87
The private side of Anne Bancroft. J. Goodman. il pors *Ladies Home J* 104:72+ O '87
Spaceballs [film] Reviews
Macleans il 100:46 Jl 13 '87. L. O'Toole
New Repub 197:26-7 Ag 3 '87. S. Kauffmann
Newsweek il 109:66 Je 29 '87. D. Ansen
People Wkly il 28:10 Jl 13 '87. P. Travers
Time il 130:68 Jl 13 '87. R. Schickel

Brooks, Paul
Courage of Rachel Carson [excerpt from Two Park Street] il por *Audubon* 89:12+ Ja '87

Brooks, Ron
Endless summer. il *World Tennis* 35:80 Jl '87

Brooks, Valerie F.
Art & business in the 80's: the billion-dollar merger. il *Art News* 86:19+ Ja '87

Brooks, Walter R., 1886-1958
about
Fan club organized for Walter Brooks's 'Freddy' books. J. Roginski. il *Publ Wkly* 231:105 F 27 '87

Brooks, creeks, etc.
A creek is worth the knowing. R. Schuessler. il *Conservationist* 41:54-5 Mr/Ap '87

Lessons from a little stream [Reefer Creek] J. Kulpa. il *Field Stream* 91:43+ Mr '87
Trout on edge. D. Carty. il *Outdoor Life* 179:104-5+ My '87

Brooks County (Ga.)
Police
Willie Jones becomes second black sheriff in Georgia. *Jet* 71:31 Mr 23 '87

Brookstown Mill (Winston-Salem, N.C.: Shopping center)
See Winston-Salem (N.C.)—Stores

Broome, Thomas J.
about
NBA pres. urges High Court to uphold affirm. action. por *Jet* 71:26 Ja 12 '87

Broomfield, Nicholas
about
Lily Tomlin: the film behind the show [film] Reviews *New Repub* 196:24-5 Mr 23 '87. S. Kauffmann

Broomfield, William S.
Should Congress adopt the House-passed "Gephardt Amendment"? [excerpts from debate, April 29, 1987] *Congr Dig* 66:171+ Je/Jl '87

Brooms
A clean sweep. R. Kimber. il *Ctry J* 14:13-14+ F '87

Brophy, Beth
Money issues on the job [excerpt from Everything college didn't teach you about money] il *Essence* 18:122+ S '87

Brophy, Theodore Frederick
about
Can GTE keep foiling the raiders? J. R. Norman. il por *Bus Week* p100-1 Ap 6 '87

Brosnan, Jim
The Cincinnati Kid. il pors *Life* 10:78-81 Ag '87

Brosnan, Peter L.
"Captain" Mary Patten. il por *Oceans* 20:36-9 S/O '87
Hollywood turns 100: Tinseltown glitters again. il *Travel Holiday* 168:42-7 Ag '87

Brosnan, Pierce
about
Pierce Brosnan. D. De Dubovay. il pors *McCalls* 114:148-50+ Jl '87

Bross, Tom
Great escapes: New England [special section] il *Travel Holiday* 167:67-8+ My '87
The Magnificent Mile. il *Travel Holiday* 167:10+ Je '87
Small towns, big art. il *Travel Holiday* 167:29-31 Ja '87

Brosse, Jacques
The traveller and his quest. il *Courier* 40:4-7 Ap '87

Brotak, Edward
Audio visuals about the weather. *Weatherwise* 40:159 Je '87
Audio visuals about the weather. il *Weatherwise* 40:107 Ap '87
Audio visuals about the weather. *Weatherwise* 40:218 Jl/Ag '87
Audio visuals about the weather. *Weatherwise* 40:271-2 O '87

Brotherhood of man
Eight modern myths. G. K. Shepherd. il por *Humanist* 47:15-17+ Mr/Ap '87
First word; tr. by Antonina W. Bouis. Y. A. Yevtushenko. il *Omni* 9:6 Ag '87

Brothers, Joyce
Dr. Joyce Brothers answers your questions. See issues of Good Housekeeping
How to put romance back in your marriage. il por *Good Housekeep* 204:117+ F '87
The importance of family ties. il pors *Good Housekeep* 205:96+ S '87
Why husbands walk out. il *Read Dig* 131:27-8+ Jl '87
about
Vanity is good for you. por *USA Today (Periodical)* 116:11 Ag '87

Brothers *See* Siblings
Brothers (in religious orders, congregations, etc.)
See also
Benedictines
Communauté de Taizé
Brothers and sisters *See* Siblings
Brötzmann, Peter
about
Han Bennink/Peter Brotzmann: first entrances and last exits [interview] B. Shoemaker. il pors *Down Beat* 54:24-6 Ja '87

Broun, Heywood Hale, 1918-
1944: a soldier's Christmas in Wales. il por *50 Plus* 27:35-42 D '87
Art: woodland prints. il *Archit Dig* 44:178-83 Je '87

Broun, Janice A.
Still waiting for the millennium. *Commonweal* 114:592-5 O 23 '87
Broussard, Eldridge John, Jr.
about
Going for gold or zealotry? C. O'Connor. il *Newsweek* 109:27 Je 29 '87
Brouwer, Arie R.
about
NCC officials put dispute on hold. J. C. Lyles. *Christ Century* 104:1021-2 N 18 '87
Brouwers, Elisabeth M., and others
Dinosaurs on the North Slope, Alaska: high latitude, latest Cretaceous environments. bibl f il map *Science* 237:1608-10 S 25 '87
Brow, Robert
The truth about consequences. il por *Christ Today* 31:33-4 Ap 17 '87
Brower, Brock
Spying's dirty little secret. il *Money* 16:130-4+ Jl '87
Brower, Kenneth, 1944-
Out on a limb. il *Omni* 9:56-64+ Ap '87
Brower, Michael
(jt. auth) See Clausen, Peter, and Brower, Michael
Brower, Montgomery
Vladimir Shityikov mines 'black gold' (and the good life) in some of the world's harshest weather. il pors *People Wkly* 27:61+ Ap 6 '87
Brown, Abe
Check your drug awareness: a quiz. il *Curr Health 2* 13:19-21 My '87
Emblems of medicine: serpents that bear no evil. il *Curr Health 2* 14:12-13 S '87
Hodgkin's disease: a can-win battle. il *Curr Health 2* 13:28-9 Mr '87
Summer vacation destination: health. il *Curr Health 2* 13:14-15 My '87
Brown, Ann C.
Stock trends. See issues of Forbes
Brown, Archie, 1938-
A reformer in the Kremlin. *Nation* 244:792-5 Je 13 '87
Brown, B. C.
Acne and me. il *Seventeen* 46:112+ My '87
Brown, Blair
about
Blair Brown as Molly Dodd: the bittersweet days and nights of a single woman. J. Powell. por *Glamour* 85:104 Jl '87
Molly Dodd opens new windows for Blair Brown. J. Hall. il pors *People Wkly* 28:69-71 Jl 20 '87
Brown, Bob
about
How to be safe in bear country. M. Reiss. il *Outdoor Life* 179:50-1+ Ja '87
Brown, Charles Moses, 1904-1987
about
Obituary
Am Craft il por 47:19 O/N '87. V. Schemer
Brown, Clifford, 1930-1956
about
Clifford Brown: the ultimate jazz trumpeter. S. M. Stroff. il pors *Antiques Collect Hobbies* 92:42-5 Mr '87
Brown, Cynthia G., 1943-
Pinochet's way. il por *N Y Rev Books* 34:47-9 Je 25 '87
Brown, Dave
about
The lowdown on a high-sticking. il por *Sports Illus* 67:16 N 9 '87
Brown, Donna
From hassles to hugs. il *Teen* 31:18+ D '87
Brown, Drew Bundini, d. 1987
about
Obituary
Jet il por 73:51 O 12 '87
Brown, Dwight
Morocco's mystique. il por *Essence* 18:20+ N '87
Brown, Edward A.
about
Brick breaker. D. E. Miller. il *Atlantic* 259:79-81 Ap '87
Brown, Edward Espe
(jt. auth) See Madison, Deborah, and Brown, Edward Espe
Brown, Ethan
about
Trials by Fire. M. Hunt. il pors *Dance Mag* 61:42-5 My '87

Brown, Freckles
about
Sitting atop a Tornado. W. K. Stratton. il por *Sports Illus* 66:89 My 25 '87
Brown, Gary
about
A Shakey turnaround. L. M. Keefe. il por *Forbes* 140:184 O 19 '87
Brown, George E., Jr.
Pentagon usurps civilian space program. il *Bull At Sci* 43:26-31 N '87
U.S. nuclear waste policy: flawed but feasible. il *Environment* 29:6-7+ O '87
Brown, Greg
Corrymeela: a flicker of hope in Northern Ireland. *Christ Century* 104:336-7 Ap 8 '87
Brown, Harlen
A two-time national barefoot water ski champion at 11. il *Ebony* 42:61-2+ Je '87
Brown, Harrison
Draw the line at Star Wars. *Bull At Sci* 43:3 Ja/F '87
about
Obituary
Bull At Sci il pors 43:3-8 Mr '87. J. P. Holdren
Brown, Harry C.
about
First black probate judge elected in S. Carolina. por *Jet* 71:25 F 16 '87
Brown, Hilton
Fame and fortune in the art world. bibl f il *Am Artist* 51:46-51+ Mr '87
Brown, Hunter
Counsels for the baptized. *Commonweal* 114:558-61 O 9 '87
Brown, J. Larry
Hunger in the U.S. il *Sci Am* 256:36-41 F '87
Letters [discussion of February 1987 article, Hunger in the U.S.] *Sci Am* 256:6+ Je '87
Brown, James
about
James Brown says he was mistreated by police, after alleged accident. por *Jet* 73:54 N 30 '87
James Brown undergoes dental surgery, cancels Chicago concert engagement. *Jet* 72:8 My 4 '87
Soul survivors. T. Young. por *Vogue* 177:36+ Ja '87
Brown, Jamie
about
Essence woman. L. B. Randolph. il por *Essence* 17:24 Ja '87
Brown, Jane
Transatlantic transplant. il por *House Gard* 159:90+ Je '87
Brown, Jeffrey L.
Kids and medicine: what to give them when. *Ladies Home J* 104:60+ Mr '87
Brown, Jim, 1936-
about
Bo Jackson's 'hobby' could be trouble says Jim Brown. pors *Jet* 72:46 Ag 3 '87
Brown, John F., and others
Polychlorinated biphenyl dechlorination in aquatic sediments. bibl f il *Science* 236:709-12 My 8 '87
Brown, John Y., Jr., 1933-
about
John Y. Brown Jr. is down and out in Kentucky. *Newsweek* 109:20 Je 8 '87
Brown, Joyce
about
Down and out—but determined. M. Hornblower. il *Time* 130:29 N 23 '87
Brown, Keith M.
Much ado about nothing? il *Hist Today* 37:6-8 F '87
Brown, Ken
about
Mini golf. *New Yorker* 63:31-2 O 26 '87
Brown, Kim
College knowledge. il *Seventeen* 46:118+ Ag '87
Brown, Laurence D.
Books. See issues of Phi Delta Kappan beginning September 1985
Brown, Lee Patrick
about
Houston police chief receives NOBLE award. *Jet* 72:40 Ag 3 '87
Brown, Les, 1928-
Editor's note. See issues of Channels (New York, N.Y.: 1986) beginning July/August 1986
The public eye. See issues of Channels (New York, N.Y.: 1986)

Brown, Lester Russell, 1934-, and Postel, Sandra
Thresholds of change. il pors *Futurist* 21:9-14 S/O '87
Brown, Linda *See* Smith, Linda Brown
Brown, Luther
Breaking ground. il por *Black Enterp* 18:76-8+ O '87
Charity begins with a budget. il *Black Enterp* 18:77-8+ D '87
Brown, MacAlister
Easing the burden of socialist struggle in Laos. *Curr Hist* 86:152-5+ Ap '87
Brown, Madeleine
about
LBJ's 'mistress' signs with Contemporary. il por *Publ Wkly* 232:42-3 O 16 '87
Was LBJ's final secret a son? M. Brower. il pors *People Wkly* 28:30-5 Ag 3 '87
Brown, Margaret Wise, 1910-1952
about
A moon that never sets. L. S. Marcus. *N Y Times Book Rev* 92:22 Ja 25 '87
Brown, Marie
about
Staying power in publishing. J. Simmons. il por *Essence* 18:135-6 My '87
Brown, Mary Jane
Technique: tap, tapping, and tappers. il *Dance Mag* 61:56-7 Ag '87
Brown, Mary Ward
about
With spare and powerful prose, Mary Ward Brown joins the southern literary tradition. P. Brawley. il pors *People Wkly* 28:86-7+ S 7 '87
Brown, Melanie
Is it time for you to blossom? [excerpt from Attaining personal greatness] *Redbook* 169:74-5+ Ag '87
Brown, Merrill
The business side. See issues of Channels (New York, N.Y.: 1986) beginning January-February 1986
Brown, Michael H.
Toxic wind. il map *Discover* 8:42-9 N '87
The zeal of disapproval. il por *Oceans* 20:36-41 My/Je '87
Brown, Milton H.
Camellias for colder winters. il *Rodale's Org Gard* 34:56-9 D '87
Brown, Norman
Kidney-stone surgery one day may pass. il *Nations Bus* 75:74 N '87
Stop a cold before it starts. *McCalls* 114:22 F '87
Treating ear disorders. il *Nations Bus* 75:52+ Ap '87
Brown, Olivia
about
Philip Michael Thomas and Olivia Brown sizzle in 'Miami Vice' [cover story] T. S. Moore. il pors *Jet* 73:58-9 O 12 '87
Brown, Peter H., and Pinkston, Jim
Dressing for Oscar [excerpt from Oscar dearest] il *Life* 10:89-92 Ap '87
Brown, Ralph S.
Can you be sued for letters of reference? *Educ Dig* 52:54-6 Mr '87
Brown, Raymond Edward
Scripture and dogma today. *America* 157:286-9 O 31 '87
Brown, Rexford
Who is accountable for 'thoughtfulness'? bibl f il *Phi Delta Kappan* 69:49-52 S '87
Brown, Rita Mae
You say begin, I say commence—to the victor belongs the language. il *N Y Times Book Rev* 92:13 D 20 '87
Brown, Robert A., and Giacconi, Riccardo
New directions for space astronomy. bibl f *Science* 238:617-19 O 30 '87
Brown, Robert Hamilton
(jt. auth) See Cruikshank, Dale P., and Brown, Robert Hamilton
Brown, Robert J.
about
Robert Brown oversees the enrollment of Mandela's daughter at Boston Univ. il por *Jet* 72:28 Je 8 '87
Brown, Roger, 1941-
about
Roger Brown at the Hirshhorn. K. M. Burke. il *Smithsonian* 18:148 Ag '87
Roger Brown: Phyllis Kind. J. Schwendenwein. il *Art News* 86:146 D '87
Brown, Rusty
Sister Darlene Nicgorski. il por *Ms* 15:54+ Ja '87
Verna Williamson. il por *Ms* 16:102+ Jl/Ag '87

Brown, Samuel
about
Black N.Y. police officer turns down a promotion; says he's no 'quota cop'. *Jet* 71:25 Mr 23 '87
Brown, Stuart F.
What's new in recreation. See issues of Popular Science beginning December 1985
Brown, Tim
about
Mister T [cover story] R. Reilly. il pors *Sports Illus* 67:30-2+ Ag 31 '87
Brown, Tina
English transfer. il *House Gard* 159:196-203 N '87
Brown, Tony
Economics [address, February 20, 1987] *Vital Speeches Day* 53:400-4 Ap 15 '87
Brown, Trisha
about
Dance Magazine Awards 1987. il pors *Dance Mag* 61:44-6 F '87
Dancing with Carmen. K. Kertess. il pors *Art Am* 75:180-5+ Ap '87
Newark [dance] Reviews
N Y il 20:104 O 5 '87. T. Tobias
Trisha Brown's empty flashes. L. A. Jacobs. *New Leader* 70:22 O 5 '87
Brown, Vander, Jr.
about
First black president of Greyhound's Western Division reveals plans. il pors *Jet* 72:38-9 Je 29 '87
Brown, W. L., and others
Covalent group IV atomic clusters. bibl f il *Science* 235:860-5 F 20 '87
Brown, Wesley
Anita Baker [cover story] pors *Essence* 18:48-50+ D '87
Nobel laureate Wole Soyinka [interview] por *Essence* 18:35 Ag '87
Brown, William S.
Hidden life of the timber rattler. il map *Natl Geogr* 172:128-38 Jl '87
Brown, Willie Lewis, Jr.
about
Racism charge by Brown prompts Calif. gov. to probe new history text. *Jet* 71:28 Mr 23 '87
Brown, Father (Fictional character) *See* Father Brown (Fictional character)
Brown (Trisha) Dance Company *See* Trisha Brown Dance Company
Brown dwarf stars *See* Stars, Dwarf
Brown family
about
A language spoken only by believers [Charlotte, N.C. charismatics] P. R. Range. il *U S News World Rep* 102:66 Ap 6 '87
Brown-Forman Distillers Corp.
Esteem in a $60 bottle [doing business in Japan] il *U S News World Rep* 103:41-2 Ag 24 '87
Brown rot
When brown rot attacks your summer fruit. il *Sunset* 178:224 Je '87
Brown trout fishing *See* Trout fishing
Brown University
Amy Carter gets probation for Brown apartheid protest. *Jet* 72:22 Mr 30 '87
Brown v. Board of Education decision *See* United States. Supreme Court—Decisions
Brown Zikmund, Barbara
Trinity and unity [discussion of April 15, 1987 article, The Trinity and women's experience] *Christ Century* 104:534-6 Je 3-10 '87
The Trinity and women's experience. *Christ Century* 104:354-6 Ap 15 '87
Browne, Anthony
Piggybook [story] il *Ms* 15:55-6 Mr '87
Browne, Arthur D.
Declaring academic bankruptcy: another chance at college. *Educ Dig* 53:46-9 N '87
Browne, Jackson
about
Jackson Browne [interview] A. DeCurtis. por *Roll Stone* p157-8+ N 5-D 10 '87
Video vérité: Jackson Browne makes his point about U.S. policy in Central America. A. DeCurtis. il por *Roll Stone* p12 Ja 29 '87
Browne, Malcolm W.
Can you top this? il *N Y Times Mag* p50 Je 14 '87
Browner, Julia
about
NFL Players' dinner fetes Mom of Year. il pors *Jet* 72:52-3 Ap 20 '87

Brownie, Alexander C.
(jt. auth) See Pedersen, Robert C., and Brownie, Alexander C.

Brownies (Cake)
Cookies, cupcakes & brownies. il *Ladies Home J* 104:112-13+ Mr '87

Browning, D. Dale
about
Plastic profits. A. Snitzer. il por *Forbes* 140:116 Ag 10 '87

Browning, Don S.
The Protestant church in the People's Republic of China. *Christ Century* 104:218-21 Mr 4 '87

Browning
More bad news about that tasty browning [Maillard reactions in meat produce mutagens] *Sci News* 132:25 Jl 11 '87

Brownlee, Shannon
Fostering hope for the whooper. il map *Natl Wildl* 25:38-43 Je/Jl '87

Brownlee, Walter
H.M.S. Warrior. il *Sci Am* 257:130-6 D '87

Brownstein, Larry
The 20 millimeter lens: exploring an ultrawide optic. il *Petersens Photogr Mag* 16:40-2 S '87
Deserts of the Southwest. il maps *Petersens Photogr Mag* 16:18-19+ Je '87

Brownstein, Ronald
The Hollywood primary [cover story] il *New Repub* 197:19+ N 23 '87
Raising bucks for Bush. il pors *N Y Times Mag* p42-4+ My 17 '87

Brownstone decoration See House decoration
Brownstones (Houses) See City houses
Brownsville (New York, N.Y.)
Brownsville. G. Green. il *N Y* 20:102-3 D 21-28 '87

Broxon, James William, d. 1986
about
Obituary
Phys Today 40 pt1:86 Ag '87. A. A. Bartlett

Broyard, Anatole
About books. See occasional issues of The New York Times Book Review beginning November 11, 1984

Broyles, Frank, 1924-
about
The Emperor of Arkansas. D. Whitford. il pors *Sport Mag* 78:68-73 Ja '87

Broyles, William
Conquest of Aconcagua. il pors *Read Dig* 131:144-50 N '87
Pushing the mid-life envelope. il pors *Esquire* 107:72-4+ Je '87
The wall that heals. il *Read Dig* 130:70-6 My '87

Brubach, Holly
The annals of glory. *Atlantic* 259:81-3 My '87
Fat pride. il *Atlantic* 260:111-13 N '87
Ralph Lauren's achievement. il *Atlantic* 260:70-3 Ag '87
Shakespeare's sister. il *Atlantic* 259:86-8 F '87
Twyla Tharp's return. il *Atlantic* 259:86+ Mr '87

Brubaker, Charmayne Denlinger
U.S. bases spread AIDS virus. il *Progressive* 51:14 F '87

Bruce, Earle
about
More football madness. J. Kirshenbaum. il por *Sports Illus* 67:110 N 30 '87

Bruce, James T.
(jt. auth) See Waller, Douglas C., and Bruce, James T.

Bruce, Michael G.
Europe in European curricula. *Phi Delta Kappan* 68:551-2 Mr '87
High school graduation, international style. il *Phi Delta Kappan* 69:79-81 S '87
Higher education: taking our bearings. il *Phi Delta Kappan* 69:239-40 N '87
International schools for international people. *Phi Delta Kappan* 68:707-8 My '87

Bruce Hornsby and the Range (Musical group)
Bands hitting the headlines. il por *Teen* 31:55 My '87
Rock & roll's other Bruce. S. Pond. il por *Roll Stone* p16 F 12 '87

Bruck, David
On death row in Pretoria Central. *New Repub* 197:18-21+ Jl 13-20 '87

Brucker, Roger, and Watson, Richard A.
Prehistoric adventurers explored Kentucky cave passages 3,000 years before modern cavers came along [excerpt from The longest cave] *Earth Sci* 40:23 Fall '87

Bruckheimer, Jerry
about
1+1=$935 million. M. Dougherty. il pors *Life* 10:96-8+ Ap '87
You don't know them—but they know moviegoers. R. Grover. il pors *Bus Week* p166+ My 25 '87

Bruckner, Pascal
about
Dismissing the third world. S. Englund. *Commonweal* 114:533-6 S 25 '87

Brudenell family
about
At Deene Park: the Brudenell family estate in Northamptonshire. E. Lambert. il *Archit Dig* 44:110-15+ Ja '87

Bruder, Gerry
The enduring mystery of Amelia Earhart. bibl il pors map *Am Hist Illus* 22:10-19+ My '87

Brueckmann, Dee
(jt. auth) See Brueckmann, Korte, and Brueckmann, Dee

Brueckmann, Korte, and Brueckmann, Dee
India's backwater highways. il map *Oceans* 20:24-9 Ja/F '87
Wolf Bauer's mission. il pors *Oceans* 20:48-53 Mr/Ap '87

Bruegel, Pieter See Brueghel, Pieter, the Elder, 1522?-1569

Brueggen, Frans
about
The real thing. P. G. Davis. il *N Y* 20:146+ D 7 '87

Brueghel, Pieter, the Elder, 1522?-1569
about
The serious art of Pieter the Droll. M. Feist. il *Art News* 86:163 My '87

Bruemmer, Fred
Life upon the permafrost. il *Nat Hist* 96:30-9 Ap '87

Bruffee, Kenneth A.
The art of collaborative learning. il *Change* 19:42-7 Mr/Ap '87

Bruford, Bill
about
Bill Bruford. B. Milkowski. il por *Down Beat* 54:14 Je '87

Bruggen, Coosje van
about
An outsize Oldenburg cuts a wide swath at the Guggenheim. il por *People Wkly* 27:102-3 Ja 26 '87

Brüggen, Frans See Brueggen, Frans
Bruggers, James
Forest Service steps on Blackfeet. il *Progressive* 51:14 Ap '87
The Salish-Kootenai comeback. il *Sierra* 72:22-3+ Jl/Ag '87

Bruist, Michael F., and others
Synthesis of a site-specific DNA-binding peptide. bibl f il *Science* 235:777-80 F 13 '87

Brumberg, Abraham
A new deal in Poland? bibl f il *N Y Rev Books* 33:32-6 Ja 15 '87

Brummer, Alex
The cost of Shultz. map *World Press Rev* 34:14-15 F '87
'Seven dwarfs' asleeping. il *World Press Rev* 34:64 O '87
The unbeaten Bush. il *World Press Rev* 34:64 D '87
World Bank on track. *World Press Rev* 34:48 N '87

Brunches
A beach weekend. il *Gourmet* 47:82-8 Ag '87
Best & worst brunch bets. il *Glamour* 85:316 O '87
Breakfasts & brunches [special section] il *South Living* 22:135+ Ap '87
Brunch [New York City] J. Freiman. il *N Y* 20:66-8+ Je 29-Jl 6 '87
Brunch bundle: it's gift-wrapped eggs, sausage [fila-wrapped torta] il *Sunset* 179:74-5 D '87
Date with a dish . . . continue the celebration with a New Year's brunch. C. Lyons. il *Ebony* 42:104-6+ Ja '87
Easy on the cook, an all-in-the-oven brunch. il *Sunset* 178:104-5, 195 Ap '87
A fashionable Sunday brunch. J. R. Nyenhuis. il *Saturday Evening Post* 259:20-1 O '87
Holiday brunch with your personal style. il *Glamour* 85:230-2 D '87
Join the brunch bunch. M. Greenberg and E. Greenberg. il *50 Plus* 27:74+ Ap '87
Romancing the morning. il *Mademoiselle* 93:160-2 F '87
Sunday brunch with friends. M. Schmidt. il *Work Woman* 12:82-4+ Ja '87

Brundage, Brian
about
Street crime put Brian Brundage in Sing Sing; basketball sent him to college. J. Friedman. il pors *People Wkly* 27:84+ F 2 '87
Brundtland, Gro Harlem
about
On top of the world. F. Hauptfuhrer. il pors *People Wkly* 27:34-9 Ap 20 '87
Brunei
Politics and government
His $10 million contra-bution got lost, but to the Sultan of Brunei it was (sigh) only money. M. Wilhelm. il pors *People Wkly* 27:32-3 Je 1 '87
Brunette, Frank
about
Fight judge files a suit against ex-champ Holmes. por *Jet* 72:50 Je 8 '87
Brünger, Axel T., and others
Crystallographic R factor refinement by molecular dynamics. bibl f il *Science* 235:458-60 Ja 23 '87
Solution of a protein crystal structure with a model obtained from NMR interproton distance restraints. bibl f il *Science* 235:1049-53 F 27 '87
Brunick, Tom
Comfort your sole. il *Women's Sports Fitness* 9:55-8 N '87
The latest, greatest aerobics shoes. il *Women's Sports Fitness* 9:34-6 D '87
Bruning, Nancy
When antacids won't work. *McCalls* 114:155 My '87
Brunner, Erwin
'Green death' in the Alps. *World Press Rev* 34:53 D '87
Brunner, Gerhard
about
In Vienna, Brunner has driven dance into the 1980s. il *Dance Mag* 61:99 Ap '87
Brunner, John, 1934-
The fable of the farmer and fox [fiction] *Omni* 9:110+ Je '87
Bruno, Jenny
about
Smart on-the-go getters. il pors *Harpers Bazaar* 120:290-7 Mr '87
Brunson, David
David Brunson. il por *People Wkly* 27:55 F 9 '87
Brunson, Dorothy, 1938-
about
Dorothy Brunson. K. Smikle. *Black Enterp* 17:45-6 Ap '87
Brunswick (Ga.)
Medical care
When doctors refuse to treat lawyers [obstetricians vs. women lawyers] P. Cooke. il *Read Dig* 131:100-4 O '87
Brunswick stew *See* Stew
Brush, Stephanie
Be your own woman (even if you're somebody's girl). il *Mademoiselle* 93:106-7+ Jl '87
Brush
Cutting brush [cover story] D. Thomas. il *Ctry J* 14:58-63 My '87
Brushes
See also
Fuller Brush Co.
Brushing of teeth *See* Teeth—Care and hygiene
Brussels (Belgium)
Architecture
That Palladian feeling [home in Brussels designed by C. Vandenhove] C. Jencks. il *House Gard* 159:160-5+ Je '87
Art
Art underground [mural art in the subways] B. Grauman. il *Art News* 86:69-70 My '87
Galleries and museums
See also
Musée van Buuren (Brussels, Belgium)
Historic houses, sites, etc.
Forever Ashley. H. Montgomery-Massingberd. il *House Gard* 159:158-65+ S '87
Music
See also
Opera—Belgium
Riots
Soccer: old riot, new riot [Belgian trial for British fans over 1985 riot] T. Clifton and R. Marshall. il *Newsweek* 110:8 S 21 '87
Stations
Art underground [mural art in the subways] B. Grauman. il *Art News* 86:69-70 My '87

Stores
Bountiful Belgium. D. P. Marshall. il *Travel Holiday* 167:24-5+ Je '87
Brustein, Robert, 1927-
Robert Brustein on theater. See occasional issues of The New Republic
Bryan, Alan Lyle
Points of order: excavations in Venezuela and Colombia put the Ice Age hunters of North America in a new perspective. maps *Nat Hist* 96:6+ Je '87
Bryan, C. D. B. (Courtlandt Dixon Barnes)
Artful tradition. il *Archit Dig* 44:200-5 N '87
Colonial contours: traditional lines for a Connecticut farmhouse. il *Archit Dig* 44:102-7 Jl '87
Lessons in simplicity. il por *Archit Dig* 44:92+ O '87
Peter H. Tillou's American flair. il por *Archit Dig* 44:64+ Je '87
"A society for the increase and diffusion of geographical knowledge" [excerpt from The National Geographic Society; with editorial comment by Ed Holm] il *Am Hist Illus* 22:4, 16-27 D '87
about
Abrams celebrates National Geographic 1988 centennial. il *Publ Wkly* 231:51 My 29 '87
Bryan, Courtlandt Dixon Barnes *See* Bryan, C. D. B. (Courtlandt Dixon Barnes)
Bryan, Frank L.
(jt. auth) See Michanie, Silvia, and Bryan, Frank L.
Bryan, Glenn J., and others
Heritable somatic excision of a Drosophila transposon. bibl f il *Science* 235:1636-8 Mr 27 '87
Bryan, John Henry, Jr.
about
A week in the life of a CEO. J. H. Dobrzynski. il pors *Bus Week* Sp Issue:46-50+ O 23 '87
Bryan, Richard H.
The politics and promises of nuclear waste disposal: the view from Nevada. bibl f il maps *Environment* 29:14-17+ O '87
Bryan, William Jennings, 1860-1925
about
William Jennings Bryan's last campaign. S. J. Gould. il por *Nat Hist* 96:16+ N '87
Bryant, Boudleaux, 1920-1987
about
Obituary
Roll Stone por p14 Ag 13 '87. K. Loder
Bryant, Cecelia Williams- *See* Williams-Bryant, Cecelia
Bryant, George
Oh, Canada! il *50 Plus* 27:34-8+ Ap '87
Bryant, Hugh, d. 1987
about
Obituary
Jet il por 72:56 Ag 10 '87
Bryant, John H., and Gellhorn, Alfred
A call for action. il *World Health* p12-13 Ap '87
Bryant, Steven
about
Dial om for murder. J. Hubner and L. Gruson. il pors *Roll Stone* p53-4+ Ap 9 '87
Bryce, Collin A.
Jerry Hammond: from lawbreaker to lawmaker. il *Ebony* 42:60+ My '87
Bryce Canyon National Park (Utah)
Exploring Bryce Canyon's high country on horseback. il *Sunset* 179:60 Jl '87
Bryon, Ellen
Make it merry! il *Redbook* 170:75-7+ D '87
Bryophytes
See also
Mosses
Bryozoa
Home on the grain [marine invertebrates that can colonize single grains of sand] D. D. Edwards. il *Sci News* 131:156-7 Mr 7 '87
Bryson, Bill
English village names. il *Travel Holiday* 168:94 S '87
Brzezinski, Zbigniew
The danger of disarming. il *N Y Times Mag* p51-2 Ap 5 '87
Lessons of the Iran-contra affair. por *Read Dig* 130:76-7 Je '87
The NSC's midlife crisis. *Foreign Policy* 69:80-99 Wint '87/'88
about
Off with their heads: how Zbigniew Brzezinski hawked the doctrine of nuclear decapitation. M. Kaku and D. Axelrod. il *Progressive* 51:29-31 Ja '87
The powers that shouldn't be: five Washington insiders the next Democratic president shouldn't hire [cover story] P. Glastris. pors *Wash Mon* 19:39-46+ O '87

Brzoska, Michael
Profiteering on the Iran-Iraq War. bibl f il *Bull At Sci* 43:42-5 Je '87
Bstan-'dzin-rgya-mtsho *See* Dalai Lama XIV, 1935-
Buatta, Mario, 1935-
about
A living scrapbook. C. Vogel. il *N Y Times Mag* p34-7 S 6 '87
Bubbles
See also
Foams
Soap bubbles and films
On the trail of ocean bubbles [work of S. A. Thorpe and A. J. Hall] R. Monastersky. *Sci News* 132:21 Jl 11 '87
Splish splash. S. Morris. il *Omni* 9:48-55 S '87
Sticky threadlike substances that tend to draw themselves out into bead arrays. J. Walker. il *Sci Am* 257:108-11 S '87
Bubbles, Interstellar *See* Nebulae
Bubel, Nancy
All about almanacs. il *Ctry J* 14:26-8 Ja '87
Grow your own peanuts! il *Rodale's Org Gard* 34:24-8 Je '87
Home food drying. bibl il *Ctry J* 14:50-5 Ag '87
Saving seeds. il *Mother Earth News* 107:58-63 S/O '87
The vegetable garden. See issues of Country Journal beginning October 1986
Wildflowers. il *Ctry J* 14:36-42 My '87
Buccaneers *See* Pirates
Buchan, John, 1875-1940
about
John Buchan's Richard Hannay. G. Powell. bibl il pors map *Hist Today* 37:32-9 Ag '87
Buchanan, Bob
Where's that Great Society? por *U S News World Rep* 102:6 F 23 '87
Buchanan, Edna
The hitchhiker [excerpt from The corpse had a familiar face] il por *Glamour* 85:140+ O '87
about
1987: Miami's year in the literary limelight. R. Kaye. il pors *Publ Wkly* 232:46-7 N 13 '87
Buchanan, James M., 1919-
The constitution of economic policy [adaptation of Nobel Prize address, December 8, 1986] bibl f *Science* 236:1433-6 Je 12 '87
about
Brockway's paradox. G. P. Brockway. il *New Leader* 69:10-11 D 29 '86
Buchanan, James T., and Grillner, Sten
Newly identified 'glutamate interneurons' and their role in locomotion in the lamprey spinal cord. bibl f il *Science* 236:312-14 Ap 17 '87
Buchanan, Patrick
A conservative makes a final plea. il por *Newsweek* 109:23-6 Mr 30 '87
Whom will history indict? il *Newsweek* 110:21 Jl 13 '87
about
Buchanan bows out. *Natl Rev* 39:20 F 13 '87
Fifth Amendment patriots. *New Repub* 196:4 Ja 5-12 '87
Savior on the right? M. G. Warner. il por *Newsweek* 109:18 Ja 19 '87
The spirit of Buchanan. *Natl Rev* 39:20-1 My 8 '87
White House vigilante. J. B. Judis. *New Repub* 196:17-18+ Ja 26 '87
Buchanan, Rex, 1953-
Badlands fossils. il *Earth Sci* 40:13-15 Fall '87
Buchanan, Rob
Baiting the hook. il *Roll Stone* p99-100+ Mr 26 '87
Flash and the pan. il *Roll Stone* p101-2+ N 19 '87
Buchanan, Scott Milross, 1895-1968
The power of politics and the politics of power. por *Cent Mag* 20:4-8 Jl/Ag '87
Buchanan, William J., 1926-
Attack of the midnight screamer. il *Read Dig* 130:169-70+ Ap '87
Buchen, Irving H.
Faculty for the future. il por *Futurist* 21:22-5 N/D '87
Buchheim, Lothar-Günther, 1918-
about
Buchheim vs. Duisburg: another round. J. Dornberg. il por *Art News* 86:45+ N '87
Buchman, Harit Allan
about
Piano man. I. Ross. il por *N Y* 20:24 Jl 13 '87
Buchsbaum, Alan, 1936-1987
Burma: a golden land. il *Vogue* 177:292+ F '87

about
Eye of his times. M. Filler. il *Archit Rec* 175:108-19 mid-S '87
Individualist interiors. M. Filler. il por *House Gard* 159:64+ Mr '87
Buchsbaum, Michael S.
about
Arb makes good. P. Berman and C. Brown. por *Forbes* 139:152 Je 1 '87
Sweetening the pot at Holly Sugar. M. Ivey. il *Bus Week* p34 Je 29 '87
Buck, Jerry
Jill Eikenberry and Michael Tucker: L.A. law's . . . perfect match. il pors *McCalls* 114:10-12 Ag '87
(ed) *See* Ritter, John. "I'm proud of my brother"
Buck, John E., 1946-
about
John Buck. S. Taylor. il *Art News* 86:31-2 Ap '87
Buck Baker Driving School *See* Automobile racing—Study and teaching
Buck hunting *See* Deer hunting
Buckbee Mears Co. *See* BMC Industries Inc.
Buckingham, Lindsey
about
Lindsey Buckingham leaves Fleetwood Mac. J. Ressner. *Roll Stone* p15+ S 24 '87
Buckler, James R.
A surprising new oasis blossoms at the Smithsonian. bibl (p147) il *Smithsonian* 18:120-4+ Jl '87
Buckley, C. Don
about
Jet-sitters. il pors *Life* 10:91-4 My '87
Buckley, Christopher Taylor, 1952-
Autumn on Sandbar Island: Dr. Lee Salk's retreat in Maine. il por *Archit Dig* 44:134-9 O '87
Blass country. il *House Gard* 159:132-43+ My '87
Brillig on the wave: island aerie of Nancy and Henry Luce III. il pors *Archit Dig* 44:180-3+ My '87
Casa de las Mil Flores: Harold and Matilda Stream in Guatemala. il *Archit Dig* 44:108-15 Ag '87
Folk tales: of baseballs and weathervanes in Washington, D.C. il pors *Archit Dig* 44:62-7+ Jl '87
The Highlander: aboard Malcolm Forbes' remarkable yacht. il por *Archit Dig* 44:100-9+ Ja '87
Man about town at home. il por *House Gard* 159:190-3+ O '87
Not a syllogism but a poem. il *Commonweal* 114:452-7 Ag 14 '87
Reinaldo and Carolina Herrera in Manhattan. il pors *Archit Dig* 44:128-35+ Ap '87
Buckley, Gail Lumet, 1937-
about
Keeping it all in the family. il por *Harpers Bazaar* 120:128+ Ag '87
Lena Horne and daughter receive achievement awards. *Jet* 72:57 Je 8 '87
Buckley, Priscilla L.
Father, friend. il por *Natl Rev* 39:51-4 S 11 '87
France has unveiled its spectacular science showcase. il *Smithsonian* 18:148-52+ O '87
Musée extraordinaire. il *Horizon* 30:11-13 Mr '87
Buckley, Robert Joseph
Economic Armageddon [address, January 29, 1987] *Vital Speeches Day* 53:347-9 Mr 15 '87
Buckley, Tom
Making it in big-time bridge. il pors *N Y Times Mag* p22-5+ Jl 26 '87
Buckley, William
Kidnapping
A desperate quest in Beirut [Drug Enforcement Administration used in search] G. Shamis. por *U S News World Rep* 102:22 Je 29 '87
North falls for a hostage scam [involvement of H. R. Perot in scheme to rescue W. Buckley] G. J. Church. il pors *Time* 129:25 Je 8 '87
Buckley, William F. (William Frank), 1925-
50-plussers are conservatives at heart! il pors *50 Plus* 27:56-60 Mr '87
Down to the great ship. il por *N Y Times Mag* p40-1+ O 18 '87
Notes & asides. See issues of National Review
On the right. See issues of National Review
Racing through paradise (I). *New Yorker* 62:40-4+ F 9 '87
Racing through paradise (II). *New Yorker* 62:71-88 F 16 '87
about
'Hey, bro'er!' It's William F. Buckley Jr. D. Smith. il pors *N Y* 20:36-42 Jl 27 '87
Minority report. C. Hitchens. *Nation* 244:170 F 14 '87

Buckley, William T.
(ed) See Peale, Norman Vincent. The greatest gift you can give your children for Christmas

Bucklin, Linda H.
In the light of the Bay. il por *House Gard* 159:124-33+ S '87

Buckmaster, Sheila F.
Andie MacDowell. pors *Harpers Bazaar* 120:270, 360-3 S '87
Quick makeup artistry. il *Harpers Bazaar* 120:114-15+ Ja '87

Bucknell University
Joe College: memories of a fifties education [cover story] P. Roth. il *Atlantic* 260:41-8+ D '87

Buckner, Kirk
about
Auguries of innocence. L. Zuckerman. il por *Time* 130:21 O 19 '87
A shocking arrest breaks the case of a Missouri farm family's murder—and rescues a boy's reputation. M. Green. il pors *People Wkly* 28:101-2+ O 26 '87

Bucks County (Pa.)
Description and travel
Pennsylvania's inn places: Bucks County bed & breakfast. M. M. Mason. il *Travel Holiday* 168:54-9 N '87

Buckwheat Zydeco
about
Buckwheat Zydeco makes music accordion to bayou tradition, and who can say him neigh? A. Abrahams. il pors *People Wkly* 28:151-2 D 7 '87

Budai, Livia
about
A Gypsy's way. N. Coons. il por *Opera News* 52:24-5 D 19 '87

Budd, Harold
about
Harold Budd. J. Diliberto. por *Down Beat* 54:13 Ag '87

Buddhas in art
Japan's Buddha wars [huge Buddha statues] il *Newsweek* 110:33 Ag 17 '87

Buddhism
See also
Lamas
In Vermont: a spiritual leader's farewell [cremation of C. Trungpa] G. Jaynes. il *Time* 129:10+ Je 22 '87
Canada
In search of tradition [Buddhist community in Halifax, N.S.] C. Wood. il por *Macleans* 100:15+ My 4 '87
India
How Buddhism came to Karnasuvarna [excerpt from Records of the western regions of the great T'ang dynasty] Hsüan-tsang. il *Courier* 40:24 Ap '87
Japan
Japan's Buddha wars [huge statues] il *Newsweek* 110:33 Ag 17 '87
Tibet
See also
Dalai Lama XIV, 1935-
Psychic sports [practice of toumo; excerpt from Mystiques et magiciens du Tibet] A. David-Neel. il por *Courier* 40:36-7 Ap '87
Tibetan Buddhism survives nightmare of repression. L. Wischmann. il *Christ Century* 104:529-31 Je 3-10 '87
Tibetans rally to guard a culture. J. Elbert. *Christ Century* 104:988-9 N 11 '87
Turmoil in Tibet. L. Wischmann. il map *Christ Century* 104:1118-19 D 9 '87

Buddhist art See Art, Buddhist
Budge, Don, 1915-
about
Redheads have more fun. S. Flink. il pors *World Tennis* 35:18+ S '87

Budget
See also
Astronomical research—Federal aid
Botanical research—Federal aid
Colleges and universities—Federal aid
Mathematical research—Federal aid
National Institutes of Health (U.S.)—Appropriations and expenditures
National Science Foundation (U.S.)—Appropriations and expenditures
Physics—Federal aid
Research—Federal aid
United States—Appropriations and expenditures
United States. Congress. House. Committee on the Budget
United States. Congress. Senate. Committee on the Budget

United States. Dept. of Defense—Appropriations and expenditures
United States. Dept. of Energy—Appropriations and expenditures
United States. Dept. of State—Appropriations and expenditures
United States. Federal Bureau of Investigation—Appropriations and expenditures
United States. National Aeronautics and Space Administration—Appropriations and expenditures
United States. Office of Human Development Services—Appropriations and expenditures
United States. Office of Management and Budget
Against austerity. R. Kuttner. *New Repub* 197:16-18 D 28 '87
Arms accord for domestic renewal. *America* 156:22-3 Ja 17 '87
As the world squirms, Washington acts out its budget soap opera. D. Harbrecht. il *Bus Week* p35 N 23 '87
As Washington fiddles . . . G. Borger. il *U S News World Rep* 103:20-2 N 23 '87
At long last, coming to grips with the deficit [Congress] G. Borger. il *U S News World Rep* 102:20-1 Ap 6 '87
Backing into the future [deficit] D. Gergen. il *U S News World Rep* 103:72 Ag 17 '87
Balance the budget—but not with an amendment. A. S. Blinder. il *Bus Week* p16 Jl 27 '87
The battle-ax of the republic [P. Gramm] P. Magnusson. il por *Bus Week* p78-9 Ag 31 '87
The big D: Managing the deficit. W. F. Buckley. *Natl Rev* 39:60-1 F 13 '87
Bob Dole bets it all on busting the budget deficit. R. Fly. il por *Bus Week* p45 N 23 '87
Boo to the boring budget of 1988. il *Fortune* 115:8 F 2 '87
Budget bust. *Nation* 245:667-8 D 5 '87
The budget compromise: an opportunity lost. il *Fortune* 116:8 D 21 '87
The budget compromise isn't traveling well. M. McNamee. il *Bus Week* p58 D 7 '87
Budget gridlock. B. Powell. il *Newsweek* 110:53+ N 16 '87
A clear warning to Washington. D. Francis. il *Macleans* 100:9 N 16 '87
Con game. *Natl Rev* 39:18-19 D 4 '87
Congressman Gray puts together first trillion dollar budget in history of U.S. S. Booker. il pors *Jet* 72:12-13 Jl 13 '87
Crafting a budget. il *Nations Bus* 75:14 Je '87
A cutting agreement. I. Austen. il *Macleans* 100:41+ N 30 '87
The deficit: point those fingers at the Fed. P. C. Roberts. il *Bus Week* p22 N 30 '87
Deficit summit splits over taxes, spending. *Aviat Week Space Technol* 127:24 N 9 '87
The Democrats may be losing a game of chicken on the budget. P. Magnuson and D. Harbrecht. il *Bus Week* p43 O 26 '87
Discounting the cuts [budget cuts and the stock market] J. Crudele. il *N Y* 20:16 N 30 '87
Doing the budget shuffle. D. Harbrecht and H. Gleckman. *Bus Week* p38-9 Ap 6 '87
The dollar and the deficits: what to do [cover story; special section] il *Fortune* 116:36-40+ D 7 '87
Don't let a tax increase ruin a chance to whittle debt. P. C. Roberts. il *Bus Week* p21 Mr 23 '87
Don't raise taxes [detrimental to balancing the budget] W. T. Brookes. il *Read Dig* 131:163-6 O '87
Dutch uncles [foreign reaction to budget deficit agreement] J. Crudele. il *N Y* 20:26+ D 7 '87
European economic summit meeting [address, June 15, 1987] R. Reagan. *Vital Speeches Day* 53:546-8 Jl 1 '87
Fandango over the budget [with interview with J. Miller] M. W. Karmin. il pors *U S News World Rep* 102:45-7 Ja 12 '87
The Fed sees trouble if the deficits diverge. K. Pennar. il *Bus Week* p80 Mr 30 '87
Federal and trade deficits. P. H. Abelson. *Science* 238:1211 N 27 '87
The federal deficit: how does it matter? R. Eisner. il *Science* 237:1577-82 S 25 '87
Finally, some grudging budget compromises. P. Magnusson. *Bus Week* p39 Ag 3 '87
Floundering in Washington [stock market crash] P. Magnusson and M. McNamee. il *Bus Week* p32-4 N 9 '87
Gasp! The budget crisis is easing. M. S. Forbes, Jr. il *Forbes* 139 Ann Directory:45 Ap 27 '87

Budget—*cont.*

Going once, going twice—going nowhere fast [loan sales by federal government] R. Brady. il *Bus Week* p35 Jl 13 '87

Government data are hardly an early warning system [Gramm-Rudman provision that suspends budget targets when economists agree a recession is imminent] J. Berger. *Bus Week* p32 Ja 12 '87

Gramm-Rudman isn't a 'fiscal train wreck' after all. P. Magnusson. il *Bus Week* p38 O 12 '87

Gramm-Rudman looks more than ever like a pipe dream. D. Harbrecht. il *Bus Week* p41 Jl 6 '87

Gramm-Rudman revision threatens defense cuts of $19-30 billion. P. Mann. *Aviat Week Space Technol* 127:24-5 O 5 '87

The great federal shrink begins at last. T. May, Jr. il *Fortune* 115:49+ Mr 2 '87

Higher interest rates: just what a bloated deficit doesn't need. G. Koretz. il *Bus Week* p18 Jl 6 '87

How Volcker sabotaged the president's agenda. P. C. Roberts. il *Bus Week* p18 Je 15 '87

In search of leadership. I. Austen. il *Macleans* 100:22-3 N 16 '87

In the shadow of the budget ax. M. Crawford. *Science* 238:1225 N 27 '87

In the shadows of the Twin Towers [budget and trade deficits] S. Koepp. il *Time* 130:46-8 N 2 '87

It's sleight-of-hand time—again. H. Banks. *Forbes* 139:35 Mr 9 '87

It's time to put an end to the borrowing binge. A. S. Blinder. il *Bus Week* p22 My 4 '87

The knife must fall. S. Koepp. il *Time* 130:48-50 N 23 '87

Lame duck soup [deficit reduction plan] *Commonweal* 114:691 D 4 '87

Let's not use mirrors to balance the budget. G. S. Becker. por *Bus Week* p22 D 7 '87

'Misguided' fiscal policies. P. Cook. il *World Press Rev* 34:16 D '87

A new issue for Congress to consider: "the morality of government spending". il *Nations Bus* 75:76 F '87

The next budget shell game. T. Noah. il *Newsweek* 109:22-3 Ja 12 '87

Of deficits and taxes. G. P. Brockway. *New Leader* 70:14-15 O 5 '87

One budget reform step that would pay a double dividend [two-year budget process] il *Nations Bus* 75:80 Jl '87

Partisan budget. *Natl Rev* 39:17+ Jl 17 '87

Pie in the sky [trillion dollar budget] B. Rudolph. il *Time* 129:52-3 Ja 12 '87

The politics of austerity. B. Powell. il *Newsweek* 110:18-19 N 23 '87

The politics of obscurity. R. J. Samuelson. il *Newsweek* 110:56 N 30 '87

Politics v. economics. W. F. Buckley. *Natl Rev* 39:62-3 Je 19 '87

Prescription for a slump. W. C. Peterson. *New Leader* 70:14 N 30 '87

The president's budget battler [J. A. Baker] L. Smith. il por *Fortune* 116:58 N 23 '87

Proposed budget has good and bad news. H. Fields. *Publ Wkly* 231:21 Ja 23 '87

R&D and the deficit. M. Crawford. *Science* 235:152 Ja 9 '87

Reagan cuts cause many to slip through 'net'. *Jet* 73:28 S 28 '87

The Reagan presidency and the deficit issue. R. J. Bresler. il *USA Today (Periodical)* 115:13 My '87

Reagan's 1988 wish list: already 'D.O.A.'. R. Thomas. il *Newsweek* 109:22-3 Ja 12 '87

Reagan's budget won't wash—but can Congress do better? H. Gleckman. il *Bus Week* p32 Ja 19 '87

Reagan's 'correction' [post crash assessment] *New Repub* 197:7-9 N 16 '87

Reagan's road to stabilization [deficit debate] B. D. Nossiter. il *Nation* 244:12+ Ja 10 '87

Rich people, poorer country [deficits] M. B. Zuckerman. il *U S News World Rep* 103:66 Jl 20 '87

Risks in every direction [cutting the deficit] G. J. Church. il *Time* 130:22-4+ N 9 '87

Scaling the nation's mountain of debt. J. Jaban. il *Sch Update* 119:18-19 Ja 12 '87

A search for leadership [post stock market crash] B. Levin. il *Macleans* 100:46-8 N 9 '87

A somewhat baffling budget. H. Stein. il *Fortune* 115:121-2 Ap 13 '87

Spending smarter. *New Repub* 196:5-7 F 2 '87

Stockmania revisited [Gramm-Rudman] *Natl Rev* 39:18 O 23 '87

Stumbling at the summit. S. Strasser. il *Newsweek* 110:22-3 N 30 '87

A tale of two cities [deficit] M. B. Zuckerman. il *U S News World Rep* 103:114 N 9 '87

Target practice [deficit target] F. Barnes. *New Repub* 196:10-11 Ap 13 '87

The tough choices Washington can no longer dodge. M. McNamee and P. Magnusson. il *Bus Week* p47 N 2 '87

Tradeamok [cutting federal budget deficit] *New Repub* 196:7-9 Ap 27 '87

Turkey and trimmings [spending cuts] J. V. Lamar, Jr. il *Time* 130:14-16 N 30 '87

Twin deficits and the G-7 [Paris accord] il *Natl Rev* 39:19-20 Ap 24 '87

Two messages Washington should send to the world [raising the discount rate and meaningful deficit reduction] H. Gleckman and B. Riemer. il *Bus Week* p45 My 11 '87

Uncle Sam the cosigner [off-budget financing] R. Thomas. il *Newsweek* 109:50+ Je 8 '87

Uncle Sam's loan sale: low prices, no guarantees. H. Gleckman. *Bus Week* p41-2 Ja 26 '87

Urgency on the deficit; Tax hike is not the answer. il *Nations Bus* 75:13 D '87

Vitriol in the Rose Garden [R. Reagan's opposition to revised Gramm-Rudman] T. Gup. il por *Time* 130:21 O 12 '87

"We have reached breakpoint" [budget battle between Reagan and Congress] R. Stengel. il por *Time* 129:12 Je 29 '87

When does the party end? [deficits] M. B. Zuckerman. il *U S News World Rep* 102:72 Ja 26 '87

Whose ax is gored [bipartisan move to revive the Gramm-Rudman act] R. Kuttner. *New Repub* 197:19+ O 12 '87

A 'wimp budget': Washington's best offer. G. Borger. il *U S News World Rep* 103:19-20 N 30 '87

With fiscal policy no longer stimulating growth . . . the question is: how would Greenspan fight recession? G. Koretz. il *Bus Week* p28 Je 22 '87

Yes, the federal deficit is finally narrowing. V. Brownstein. il *Fortune* 115:41+ Je 8 '87

You call this austerity? *New Repub* 197:4+ D 7 '87

Anecdotes, facetiae, satire, etc.

Trickle-up economics: JR goes to Washington. W. Gaddis. il *N Y Times Book Rev* 92:29 O 25 '87

Canada

See also
Canada—Armed Forces—Appropriations and expenditures
Canada. Office of the Auditor General

The rise of the man behind the budget [S. Hartt] B. Wallace. il por *Macleans* 100:10 Mr 2 '87

There are no sacred trusts when you're broke [address, March 26, 1987] N. J. Patterson. *Vital Speeches Day* 53:484-7 Je 1 '87

'Trying to pull it all together' [interview with M. H. Wilson] M. Drohan. il por *Macleans* 100:24 Mr 2 '87

Whittling at the deficit. T. Fennell. il *Macleans* 100:22-3 Mr 2 '87

Great Britain

See also
Great Britain—Armed Forces—Appropriations and expenditures

Sugar bowls and election fever. M. S. Serrill. il *Time* 129:43 Mr 30 '87

Israel

See also
Israel—Armed Forces—Appropriations and expenditures

Arms and the budget in Israel. E. Salpeter. il *New Leader* 70:5-6 F 9-23 '87

Japan

See also
Japan—Armed Forces—Appropriations and expenditures

United States

See Budget

Budget, Business *See* Corporations—Finance
Budget, City *See* Municipal finance
Budget, College and university *See* Colleges and universities—Finance
Budget, Household

Money. M. Daly. *See* issues of Better Homes and Gardens
Money drains: little ways big money can disappear. il *McCalls* 114:127-8 S '87

Budget, Municipal *See* Municipal finance
Budget, Personal *See* Finance, Personal
Budget Committee (House) *See* United States. Congress. House. Committee on the Budget

Budget Committee (Senate) *See* United States. Congress. Senate. Committee on the Budget
Budny, Mildred
Paperback history. *Hist Today* 37:60 O '87
Bud's (New York, N.Y.: Restaurant) *See* New York (N.Y.)—Restaurants, nightclubs, bars, etc.
Budz, Sherry
"I've kept my secret for too long"; ed. by Deidre Sullivan. il por *Redbook* 169:61-3 O '87
Buechner, David
about
Musical events. A. Porter. *New Yorker* 62:93-4 F 16 '87
Bueler, William M.
Attaining a sustainable future. il *USA Today (Periodical)* 115:34-7 My '87
Buell, Hal
about
Hal Buell leads the Associated Press into the future. H. Chapnick. il por *Pop Photogr* 94:40 Jl '87
Buenos Aires (Argentina)
Architecture
Gopher baroque [work of G. and E. Puppo] C. Bach. il por *Américas* 39:2-7+ S/O '87
Description
The new Argentina. L. Valenzuela. il *Vogue* 177:248+ Ap '87
Music
See also
Opera—Argentina
Social life and customs
The deep currents of nostalgia. M. Kogan. il *Américas* 39:26-31 Mr/Ap '87
Bueter, Robert J.
about
Of many things. G. G. Seibert. *America* 157:346 N 14 '87
Buffalo (Minn.)
Education
A creative approach to learning [high school history teacher J. Ause] C. Orange. por *Progressive* 51:12 N '87
Buffalo (N.Y.)
Education
Students speak out against textbook censorship. F. Edwords. *Humanist* 47:23-6+ Mr/Ap '87
A teacher's teacher [high school Latin teacher T. Jones; cover story] J. W. Donohue. *America* 157:495-7 D 26 '87
Buffalo Bob Smith *See* Smith, Bob, 1917-
Buffalo hunting
Burdensome bison [Yellowstone] J. Robbins. il *Audubon* 89:24+ Ja '87
Buffalo industry
Cashing in on the lean, mean buffalo. S. D. Atchison. il *Bus Week* p126-7 Je 8 '87
Buffalo meat
Cashing in on the lean, mean buffalo. S. D. Atchison. il *Bus Week* p126-7 Je 8 '87
Buffalo meat cooking *See* Cooking—Game
Buffaloes, American *See* Bison, American
Buffers (Computers)
Heathkit SK-203 printer buffer. il *Radio-Electron* 58 ComputerDigest:76 S '87
Strip-buffer vs. full-page bit-map imaging. B. Douglas. il *Byte* 12:229-30 S '87
Buffet meals
Cheese served with flair. S. Payne. il *South Living* 22:118-19 My '87
An hors d'oeuvres buffet. il *Gourmet* 48:76-8+ Je '87
No place like home. B. Kafka. il *N Y Times Mag* p25-6 D 27 '87
Salute to summer's end [Italian buffet dishes] N. H. Jenkins. il *N Y Times Mag* p43-4 Ag 23 '87
Summer weekend cookbook [buffet suppers] il *Good Housekeep* 204:118-28+ Je '87
Superstar buffet [Christmas] il *Ladies Home J* 104:152-3+ D '87
Treat your friends to a Halloween buffet. il *South Living* 22:174-5 O '87
Wonderful holiday buffet [Indian cooking] il *Glamour* 85:226-9 D '87
Buffets, sideboards, etc. (Furniture)
Elegance on the side [mahogany sideboard] R. Capotosto. il *Pop Mech* 164:116-18+ N '87
Buffett, Warren E.
Early fears about index futures. il por *Fortune* 116:191-2+ D 7 '87
What we can learn from Phil Fisher. il por *Forbes* 140:40 O 19 '87

about
The best investors of our time. il pors *Money* Sp Issue:32-6+ Fall '87
Big investors on Wall Street. pors *Fortune* 116:8 O 26 '87
Salomon and Revlon: what really happened. A. Bianco. il pors *Bus Week* p156+ O 12 '87
An unlikely savior for Gillette? G. G. Marcial. *Bus Week* p188 N 16 '87
What color is your mail? A. Sloan. il *Forbes* 140:36-7 O 19 '87
A white knight saves Salomon. B. Powell. il por *Newsweek* 110:66 O 12 '87
White-knight time on Wall Street. J. Egan. il pors *U S News World Rep* 103:60 O 12 '87
Buford, George
Keeping your mower alive. il *Rodale's Org Gard* 34:66-73 Ap '87
Buford, Sharnia Tab
about
Tab Buford resigns from Freedom National Bank. por *Jet* 71:7 F 23 '87
Bugajski, Janusz
Skeptical satellites. *New Repub* 196:15-16 My 4 '87
Bugg, Robert
about
Bugg tabbed as top ranked black city exec. in Topeka. por *Jet* 73:36 N 9 '87
Bugging *See* Electronics in criminal investigation, espionage, etc.; Lasers in criminal investigation, espionage, etc.
Bugging of telephones *See* Wiretapping
Bugner, Joe
about
G'day, Aussie Joe! W. O. Johnson. il pors *Sports Illus* 66:56+ My 25 '87
Bugs, Artificial *See* Fishing lures, flies, etc.
Bugs Burger Bug Killer Inc.
Absolutely guaranteed. J. Livingston. il por *Nations Bus* 75:51-2 N '87
Buhl, Claire
Old Tucson. il *Travel Holiday* 168:10+ Ag '87
Surrender on Lake Superior. il *Travel Holiday* 168:56-9+ Jl '87
Buhrer, Jean-Claude
The Dalai Lama speaks [interview] il por *World Press Rev* 34:21 D '87
Buick Motor Division
The Buick stops here [general manager E. Mertz] R. Ceppos. por *Car Driv* 33:46 S '87
Buie, James
The case for separate schools for pregnant teenagers. *Educ Dig* 53:50-2 D '87
Teen pregnancy: it's time for the schools to tackle the problem [cover story] il *Phi Delta Kappan* 68:737-9 Je '87
Builder (Periodical)
Building bridges: George Godwin and architectural journalism. R. Thorne. bibl il por *Hist Today* 37:11-17 Ag '87
Building
See also
Acoustics, Architectural
Arches
Brick construction
Buildings
Carpentry
Ceilings
Concrete construction
Earthquakes and building
Environmental engineering (Buildings)
Framing (Building)
Glass construction
House construction
Housing
Insulation (Heat)
Metal construction
Plywood construction
Prison construction
Roofs and roofing
Scaffolding
Stone construction
Structural engineering
Tension structures
Walls
Wood construction
Technology [address, September 9, 1987] H. L. Adams. *Vital Speeches Day* 54:83-5 N 15 '87
Costs
Construction costs. il map *Archit Rec* 175:39 O '87

Building—cont.
Finance
See also
Housing finance
Mortgages
Inspection
See Building inspection
Building, Adobe
Adobe blowup [Ron Robles remodels Santa Fe house] G. Winkel. il *House Gard* 159:122-5 Ja '87
Adobes of God [New Mexico churches] S. Zwinger. il map *Americana* 15:65-9 N/D '87
Southwest rhythms: restoring a Sante Fe adobe [home of M. Mahaffey] L. Bernikow. il por *Archit Dig* 44:130-5 F '87
Building, Ice and snow
Snow shelters. K. Bogan. il *Sierra* 72:143-5 Ja/F '87
Building codes See Building laws and regulations
Building costs See Building—Costs
Building failures
Death in the afternoon [building collapse in Bridgeport, Conn.] il *Macleans* 100:24 My 4 '87
Building fittings
New products. See issues of Architectural Record
Product reports 1988 [cover story; special issue; with editorial comment by Mildred F. Schmertz] il *Archit Rec* 175:23-7+ D '87
Building industry See Construction industry
Building inspection
Inspecting your house. J. Sherman. il *Ctry J* 14:57-61 Mr '87
It pays to let a pro check out that new house. R. W. King. il *Bus Week* p131 Ap 27 '87
Building laws and regulations
See also
Building inspection
Building code requirements. *South Living* 22:145 F '87
Compilation of sloping-glass codes shows regional differences. J. Trewhitt. il *Archit Rec* 175:37 O '87
Building materials
See also
Asbestos
Bricks
Building, Adobe
Concrete blocks
Insulation (Heat)
Lumber
Plywood
Roofs and roofing
Siding (Building)
Stucco
New products. See issues of Architectural Record
Product reports 1988 [cover story; special issue; with editorial comment by Mildred F. Schmertz] il *Archit Rec* 175:23-7+ D '87
Building materials industry
See also
Certain-Teed Corp.
Georgia-Pacific Corp.
Grossman's Inc.
Jim Walter Corp.
Owens-Corning Fiberglas Corp.
Philips Industries Inc.
Strober Organization (Firm)
Acquisitions and mergers
Are USG's walls crumbling? [Desert Partners bid] J. E. Ellis. il *Bus Week* p59 O 19 '87
Customer relations
Ear to the ground [Georgia-Pacific] D. Henry. il *Forbes* 140:71 O 19 '87
Sales reps or service reps: what do architects need from them? W. F. Koelling. il por *Archit Rec* 175:16-17 D '87
Finance
Construction. J. Willoughby. il *Forbes* 139:108+ Ja 12 '87
Marketing
See also
Home improvement centers
Building research
Federal aid
Government backing of research and development in construction urged. P. Hoffmann. il *Archit Rec* 175:37 Jl '87
Building sites
See also
Hillside architecture
Buildings
See also
Architecture
Building failures

Concert halls
Embassies (Buildings)
Office buildings
School buildings
Conservation and restoration
See Architecture—Conservation and restoration
Environmental engineering
See Environmental engineering (Buildings)
Equipment
See Building fittings
Heating and ventilation
Hvac systems: in pursuit of comfort. I. Peterson. *Archit Rec* 175:150-3 My '87
Models
See Architectural models
Security measures
Insecurities about security: face to face with the building-protection crisis. I. Wolfman. il *Archit Rec* 175:126-31 Ag '87
Buildings, Historic See Historic houses, sites, etc.
Buildings, Prefabricated
See also
Houses, Prefabricated
Prisons, Prefabricated
Buildings, Remodeled
See also
School buildings, Remodeled
Downtown Memphis: they're moving in [converted buildings] L. Joyner. il *South Living* 22:96-8 N '87
Old buildings come alive [reuse for elderly housing] L. McNickle and B. Deacon. il *Aging* no356:6-12 '87
Buildings, Restoration of See Architecture—Conservation and restoration
Buildings, Round
See also
Geodesic domes
Houses, Round
Uncommon law [U. of Iowa College of Law] G. Anderson. il *Archit Rec* 175:106-13 Ag '87
A well-rounded barn. M. Hofferber. il *Ctry J* 14:42-6 F '87
Buildings, Wrecking of See Wrecking
Buildings in art See Architecture in art
Built in furniture See Furniture, Built in
Bukhara (New York, N.Y.: Restaurant) See New York (N.Y.)—Restaurants, nightclubs, bars, etc.
Bukharin, Nikolai Ivanovich, 1888-1938
about
The ghost of an old Bolshevik. N. Cooper. pors *Newsweek* 110:76 N 16 '87
Bukovsky, Vladimir
Glasnost [address, March 11, 1987] *Vital Speeches Day* 53:596-600 Jl 15 '87
Bukowski, Charles
about
Black Sparrow: the house a poet helped to build. J. Barbato. il pors *Publ Wkly* 232:26-7 O 23 '87
Boozehound poet Charles Bukowski writes a hymn to himself in Barfly, and Hollywood starts singing too. M. Dougherty. il pors *People Wkly* 28:79-80 N 16 '87
Gin-soaked boy [cover story; interview] C. Hodenfield. il pors *Film Comment* 23:53-4+ Jl/Ag '87
Bulbs
See also
Forcing (Plants)
Hyacinths
Narcissus
Bulbs that are persistent even in shade. il *Sunset* 179:200-1 S '87
Downsizing [miniature bedding plants and bulbs] il *Sunset* 179:256-7 N '87
Flowering bulbs: pair up your plantings for twice the color. D. A. Jimerson. il *Better Homes Gard* 65:118-21 O '87
Little bulbs give lots of color. J. Glattstein. il *Flower Gard* 31:32-4+ Ag/S '87
Plant plenty of bulbs this fall. il *Flower Gard* 31:8 Ag/S '87
Putting your bulbs to bed. E. Henke. il *Saturday Evening Post* 259:34-5+ O '87
A spring bulb bed. H. P. Loewer. il *Rodale's Org Gard* 34:58-61 S '87
Sure picks. J. Glattstein. il *Home Mech* 83:32 S '87
Which bulb to buy? See what you get. il *Sunset* 179:94-6 O '87
Why didn't my bulbs bloom? R. M. Watson. *Flower Gard* 31:42-3 Ap/My '87

Bulbs, Light *See* Light bulbs
Bulbtronics (Firm)
The bulb broker. K. Harby. il por *Nations Bus* 75:58 Mr '87
Bulevardia (Helsinki, Finland: Restaurant) *See* Helsinki (Finland)—Restaurants, nightclubs, bars, etc.
Bulfinch, Charles, 1763-1844
about
The architecture of Charles Bulfinch on historical blue Staffordshire (II). H. Goldberg. bibl f il *Antiques* 131:434-43 F '87
Bulgaria
Description and travel
Laughter in the Balkans [International Biennial of Humor and Satire in the Arts in Gabrovo] B. Bernstein. *New Yorker* 63:98-101+ O 26 '87
Bulge, Battle of the, 1944-1945 *See* Ardennes, Battle of the, 1944-1945
Bulger, William M.
The new terrorism [address, September 19, 1986] *Vital Speeches Day* 53:430-4 My 1 '87
Bulgin, Russell
Unsung hero. il pors *Mot Trend* 39:115-17 F '87
Bulimarexia *See* Bulimia
Bulimia
Anorexia and bulimia: causes and cures. K. Lehrman. il *Consum Res Mag* 70:29-32 S '87
Antidepressants may curb addictions. *Prevention* 39:60 O '87
Battle of the binge [hypnosis as tool against bulimia] J. Slothower. il *Health* 19:19+ O '87
The body prison: a bulimic's compulsion to eat more, eat less, add muscle, get thinner [case of Christine Bergel] V. Kohn. il *Life* 10:44 F '87
Diabetes and eating disorders [study by Randi Birk and Martha Spencer] K. Ullman. *Psychol Today* 21:23 N '87
Dieting to bulimia. E. F. Kales. il *Psychol Today* 21:18 D '87
How effective are bulimia treatments? [study by David B. Herzog] B. Bower. *Sci News* 132:278 O 31 '87
Tips for readers of research [questionable bulimia statistics lead to warning to be wary of any research results] G. W. Bracey. il *Phi Delta Kappan* 69:236-7 N '87
Bulkheads
See also
Airplanes, Jet—Bulkheads
Bull, Evelyn L., and Henjum, Mark G.
The neighborly great gray owl [cover story] il *Nat Hist* 96:32-41 S '87
Bull, Gerald
about
The Canadian connection. A. Bilski. il map *Macleans* 100:36 O 19 '87
Bull fights *See* Bullfights
Bull riding *See* Rodeos
Bullaty, Sonja, and Lomeo, Angelo
Country flea markets [photographs] il *Ctry J* 14:54-7 Jl '87
Bulldozers (Machines)
See also
Snowcats (Machines)
Make the earth move [Caterpillar D8N] R. Ceppos. il *Car Driv* 32:67-8+ F '87
Bulletin boards
See also
Computer bulletin boards
Bulletin of the atomic scientists
Bulletin wins top award [National Magazine Award in the "single-topic issue"] *Bull At Sci* 43:2 Je '87
Bullets
See also
Ballistics
Cartridges
Shot
When the bullet gets there. J. Carmichel. il *Outdoor Life* 179:42+ Je '87
Laws and regulations
Biting the bullet. C. Simser. *Natl Rev* 39:30 Mr 13 '87
Bullfighters
See also
Martinez, Raquel
Romero, Curro
Bullfights
Mexico
Matadora in waiting [R. Martinez, first professional female bullfighter in Mexican history] P. Clark. il por *Women's Sports Fitness* 9:54 Je '87

Spain
The bullfight and Spanish national decadence. C. Graña. *Society* 24:33-7 Jl/Ag '87
Pamplona in July [excerpt from Dateline Toronto] E. Hemingway. il *50 Plus* 27:50-4 Jl '87
To fight or not to fight—bullfighter Curro Romero faces a dilemma with horns. W. Plummer. il pors *People Wkly* 28:38-9 Ag 3 '87
Bullford, Harris J.
Scaling the ivory tower. il *Change* 19:56-7 S/O '87
Scaling the ivory tower. il *Change* 19:58-60 N/D '87
Bullies *See* Bullying
Bullis, Larry
Exterior architecture: a study in natural light. il *Petersens Photogr Mag* 16:32-3 My '87
Bullpens (Baseball)
Doing time in the pen [Oakland A's relievers] A. Murphy. il *Sports Illus* 67:88-91 Jl 6 '87
Bullying
An expert finds that bullies and their victims are linked in a strange, unconscious courtship [interview with N. M Floyd] E. Levin. il por *People Wkly* 27:143-4+ Ap 13 '87
What to do if your boss is a bully. M. M. Kennedy. il *Glamour* 85:150 Mr '87
Bulter, Ron
Morelia: Mexico's candy capital. il *Américas* 39:56-7 My/Je '87
Bultman, Bethany Ewald
(jt. auth) See Church, Beverly, and Bultman, Bethany Ewald
Bumblebees *See* Bees
Bumper cars
History
Anecdotes, facetiae, satire, etc.
1947 Lusse Auto Skooter. J. Thompson. il *Road Track* 38:50-1 Ap '87
Testing
Anecdotes, facetiae, satire, etc.
Six Italian urban electrics [Soli bumper cars] il *Road Track* 38:42-9 Ap '87
Bundesbank
The Bundesbank edges closer to a rate cut. J. Templeman. il *Bus Week* p59 Je 1 '87
The Bundesbank's hardliner has a change of heart [H. Schlesinger willing to cut interest rates] B. Riemer. il por *Bus Week* p32 D 14 '87
Can Germany withstand the heat from abroad this time? J. Templeman. il *Bus Week* p50-1 O 5 '87
Bundle of Convenience (Firm)
Bundles of joy, bundles of money. il *Newsweek* 110:65 D 7 '87
Bundra, Judy Iwata
The arts in education: a search for balance. bibl f *Des Arts Educ* 89:25-30 S/O '87
Bundy, McGeorge
Arms control, not competition. il *N Y Times Mag* p46-7 Ap 5 '87
Bundy, Winifred
about
In Arizona: a rancher's bookstore. G. Jaynes. il por *Time* 129:12 My 18 '87
Bungalows, Remodeled *See* Houses, Remodeled
Bunker, Bruce C.
(jt. auth) See Michalske, Terry A., and Bunker, Bruce C.
Bunker reveries [drama] *See* Shaber, David
Bunn, Christopher C., and Mathews, Michael B.
Autoreactive epitope defined as the anticodon region of alanine transfer RNA. bibl f il *Science* 238:1116-19 N 20 '87
Bunning, Jim
about
Jim Bunning (R., Ky.). S. Wulf. il pors *Sports Illus* 66:64-8 F 23 '87
Bunting, J. Pearce
about
Wired. D. Henry. il por *Forbes* 140:454 Jl 13 '87
Bunyan, Paul (Legendary character) *See* Paul Bunyan (Legendary character)
Bunyaviruses
A G1 glycoprotein epitope of La Crosse virus: a determinant of infection of Aedes triseriatus. D. R. Sundin and others. bibl f il *Science* 235:591-3 Ja 30 '87
La buona figliuola [opera] *See* Piccinni, Niccolò, 1728-1800
Buonarroti, Michel Angelo *See* Michelangelo Buonarroti, 1475-1564
Burbank, Luther, 1849-1926
about
Burbank's legacy. J. Cox. il pors map *Rodale's Org Gard* 34:27-8+ S '87

Burch, Larry
(jt. auth) See Mueller, Peter, and Burch, Larry
Burcharth, Ewa Lajer- *See* Lajer-Burcharth, Ewa
Burcharth, Martin
Danes bristle at U.S. radar plans. il map *Bull At Sci* 43:11-13 Je '87
Burchfield, R. W. (Robert W.)
about
The building of a dictionary: how Robert Burchfield devoted 29 years to the 'OED supplement'. R. Herbert. il por *Publ Wkly* 232:38-9 O 2 '87
Burchfield, Robert W. See Burchfield, R. W. (Robert W.)
Burckhardt, Rudy
about
Rudy Burckhardt at Blue Mountain and Brooke Alexander. L. Campbell. il *Art Am* 75:186 O '87
Burden, Carter
Voluminous obsession. il *House Gard* 159:126-31+ Mr '87
Burdick, Gary S.
Finding work through an employment agency. il *Consum Res Mag* 70:27-30 F '87
Protect your home with an alarm system. il *Consum Res Mag* 70:22-5 Ag '87
Burdick, Thomas, 1950-
(jt. auth) See Mitchell, Charlene, 1950-, and Burdick, Thomas, 1950-
Burdman, Ralph
about
Tete-a-tete [drama] Reviews
Macleans il 100:50 S 21 '87. J. Bemrose
Bureaucracy
Beating back the education 'blob'. L. Solórzano. il *U S News World Rep* 102:74 Ap 27 '87
Bureaucracy as life [W. H. Whyte's Organization man] R. J. Samuelson. il *Newsweek* 109:43 Ja 12 '87
Coping with Washington. H. Sidey. il *Time* 130:22 N 23 '87
Into the vacuum stepped Ollie North [U.S. needs a bureaucracy on the European model to counteract reliance on the military] J. Keegan. por *U S News World Rep* 103:14 Ag 31 '87
The paper chase [obstacles to obtaining a proper toilet paper dispenser for the teachers' restroom] S. Ohanian. il *Phi Delta Kappan* 69:153-5 O '87
To: Corporate managers. Re: Bureaucracy. Don't send memos! T. J. Peters. il *Wash Mon* 19:12-14+ N '87
Bureaucrats See Government employees; Public officers
Burford holly See Holly
Burgdorf, Diane
about
Mark Thatcher bridles. il pors *People Wkly* 27:26-7 Mr 2 '87
Burgenland (Austria)
Description and travel
Austria's Burgenland. L. Langseth-Christensen. il map *Gourmet* 47:44-9+ Jl '87
Burger, Alvin
about
Absolutely guaranteed. J. Livingston. il por *Nations Bus* 75:51-2 N '87
Burger, George G.
Test your dental I.Q.! *McCalls* 114:111+ F '87
Burger, Janis
A mountainous appetite. il *Natl Parks* 61:28-31 Ja/F '87
Burger, Max M.
(jt. auth) See Burn, Paul, and Burger, Max M.
Burger, Warren E., 1907-
Birth of a true nation. il *Read Dig* 131:33-5 S '87
Creating a more perfect union. il *Natl Parks* 61:12-14 Mr/Ap '87
We the people. il por *Am Hist Illus* 22:10-11 Summ '87
about
The Burger Court: bad, but not that bad. D. Farber. *Wash Mon* 19:52-4 My '87
A Constitutional celebration. J. Adler. il *Newsweek* 109:21-2 Ja 19 '87
Burger Boat Company, Inc.
Full speed ahead [owner J. McMillian] B. Waitzkin. il por *Mot Boat Sail* 159:54-7+ My '87
Burger King Corporation
Burger King is hungry—for the right ad campaign. P. Engardio. il *Bus Week* p82+ Mr 16 '87
Can Burger King's man spice up Pillsbury's eateries? [J. J. Campbell] M. J. Pitzer. il por *Bus Week* p50-1 My 18 '87
N.W. Ayer bags itself a whopper. M. N. Vamos. il *Bus Week* p42 O 12 '87

Burgess, Anthony, 1917-
About oranges. il *Gourmet* 47:60+ N '87
Alex on today's youth: creeching golosses and filthy toofles! il *N Y Times Book Rev* 92:7+ My 31 '87
A clockwork orange: the missing chapter [fiction] il *Roll Stone* p74-6+ Mr 26 '87
Let's talk nonsense. il *N Y Times Book Rev* 92:1+ Ag 9 '87
Oh, James, don't stop. il *Life* 10:114-16+ Ap '87
The sainted sleuth, still on the case. bibl il *N Y Times Book Rev* 92:1+ Ja 4 '87
about
Chapter of 'A clockwork orange' restored. *Publ Wkly* 231:64 Mr 13 '87
Burgess, Don
about
Oklahoma keeps an eye on the storms. D. Young. il por *South Living* 22:134+ My '87
Burgess, Roy
about
He paints the dignity of farming [cover story] il pors *Success Farm* 85:13-15 O '87
Burghardt, Andrew F.
The outermost Hebride. il map *Focus* 37:34-5 Summ '87
Burghardt, Walter J.
Warning: God's been known to speak through a jackass [excerpt from Preaching] il *U S Cathol* 52:13-15 S '87
about
How prayer can strengthen your love for God [cover story; interview] por *U S Cathol* 52:6-13 D '87
Burghley House (Cambridgeshire, England) See Historic houses, sites, etc.—Great Britain
Burglar [film] See Motion picture reviews—Single works
Burglar alarm industry See Electronic industries
Burglar alarms See Alarms
Burglar alarms, Automobile See Automobiles—Alarms
Burglary and burglars
See also
Art thefts
Echoes of Watergate [break-ins and surveillance campaign against critics of U.S. Central American policy] B. Levin. il *Macleans* 100:22+ F 16 '87
Burglary protection
See also
Alarms
Locks and keys
Bright ideas in home security [automatic security lights] M. Morris. il *Home Mech* 83:50-1 S '87
Home, secure home. J. Hayes. il *Saturday Evening Post* 259:30+ Ap '87
Home security. J. Vara. il *Ctry J* 14:55-6 Ja '87
New security systems that break burglars' hearts. S. Woolley. il *Bus Week* p110-11 Ap 13 '87
Other measures [house protection] *Consum Res Mag* 70:24 Ag '87
Ray Johnson discovers his past crimes do pay after all. M. Neill. il pors *People Wkly* 28:155-7 S 7 '87
Securing the home front while you're away. L. Hazelton. il *Black Enterp* 17:91 Jl '87
Security door that keeps bugs out, too. M. Morris. il *Home Mech* 83:52 S '87
Smart security systems: matching wits with burglars. G. Williams. bibl il *Home Mech* 83:28-30+ N '87
Burgoo (Stew) See Stew
Burgos, Jose
about
Husband tosses wife 18 stories in heated dispute. *Jet* 73:32 O 26 '87
Burgum, Douglas
about
Plains seeking. K. Berney. il por *Nations Bus* 75:77 O '87
Burgundy (France)
History
Chasing a sphinx: Charles the Bold's Burgundy [cover story] R. Vaughan. bibl il pors map *Hist Today* 37:24-9 My '87
Burial
See also
Cryonics
Funeral rites and ceremonies
Mummies
Undertakers and undertaking
Burian, Jarka M.
Svoboda & Vychodil: Czechoslovakia's two master scenographers. il *Theatre Crafts* 21:34-7+ O '87

Buried treasure *See* Treasure trove
Burk family
about
The long agony of Shirley Fish [mother of sufferer Lauren Burk] G. Bennett. il por *McCalls* 114:148-50 Ap '87
Burkarth, Paul
about
A boy who climbed the marigold. A. Jones. il pors *Read Dig* 130:96-100 F '87
Burke, Bill
about
Seeing is deceiving. S. Piperato. il por *Pop Photogr* 94:58-9 F '87
Burke, Daniel B.
about
Not ready for prime time? G. Fabrikant. il pors *N Y Times Mag* p30+ Ap 12 '87
Burke, David A.
about
David Burke's deadly revenge. E. Magnuson. il por *Time* 130:30 D 21 '87
Gunman seen as key to crash of PSA flight that killed 43. M. A. Dornheim. il *Aviat Week Space Technol* 127:31 D 14 '87
Mass murder in the clouds. M. Satchell. il por *U S News World Rep* 103:14-15 D 21 '87
Settling a score. G. Hackett. il por *Newsweek* 110:43 D 21 '87
Burke, David T., and others
Cloning of large segments of exogenous DNA into yeast by means of artificial chromosome vectors. bibl f il *Science* 236:806-12 My 15 '87
Burke, Delta
about
Those remarkable Designing women. H. Yorkshire. il pors *McCalls* 115:78-9+ N '87
Burke, Edmund, 1729?-1797
about
Edmund Burke: history, politics and polemic. J. Black. bibl il por *Hist Today* 37:42-7 D '87
Burke, Michele
about
Stranded: Michele Burke's friendly foreigners. R. Seidenberg. il por *Theatre Crafts* 21:83-6 N '87
Burke, Richard T.
about
HMO survivor? J. Parr. il por *Forbes* 139 Ann Directory:126 Ap 27 '87
Burkett, Joe
about
Landlubber largemouths. D. Bartholomew. il por *Outdoor Life* 180:70-1+ Jl '87
Burkett, Katherine
Flying the safer skies. il *Ms* 15:33 Je '87
Burkey, Bill
about
Vintage toys and Golden Oak. A. Bahar. il por *Antiques Collect Hobbies* 92:46-9 S '87
Burkhart, Marian
Beauty in a world of schlock. il *Commonweal* 114:294-6 My 8 '87
Burkholder, Steve
Torpedoing free speech. il *Progressive* 51:15-16 My '87
Burki, Shahid Javed
Toward a world demographic balance. *World Press Rev* 34:59 Ja '87
Burkina Faso
See also
Solar energy—Burkina Faso
Politics and government
Burkina Faso [assassination of President T. Sankara] il *World Press Rev* 34:46 D '87
Upright down [assassination of President T. Sankara] por *Time* 130:52 O 26 '87
Burkitt's lymphoma *See* Lymphatic system—Cancer
Burks, Ellis
about
Ellis Burks. P. Gammons. il por *Sports Illus* 67:44 Jl 13 '87
Burks, Jean M.
English and continental brass candlesticks. bibl f il *Antiques* 132:1280-9 D '87
Burlafskii, Fedor Mikhaĭlovich
Revising Lenin's legacy. *Harpers* 275:27-8+ N '87
Burleigh, Michael, 1955-
Albert Brackmann & the Nazi adjustment of history. bibl il por *Hist Today* 37:42-6 Mr '87
Burlingame, Edward L.
about
Burlingame to have imprint at Harper; Shinker is publisher. il pors *Publ Wkly* 232:14-15 O 16 '87

Burlingame (Edward L.) Books *See* Edward L. Burlingame Books
Burlington Industries, Inc.
Burlington almost invited Edelman to attack [bid by A. B. Edelman and Dominion Textile] D. Foust. il por *Bus Week* p50+ My 11 '87
Dominion's unraveling bid. D. Foust. *Bus Week* p49-50 Je 1 '87
Burlington Northern Inc.
All alone by the telephone. J. Cook. il por *Forbes* 140:80+ N 16 '87
Will a takeover derail Burlington Northern's makeover? J. B. Levine. il por *Bus Week* p66-7 Ag 3 '87
Burma
Antiquities
See also
Pagan (Ancient city)
Description and travel
Burma: a golden land. A. Buchsbaum. il *Vogue* 177:292+ F '87
Economic conditions
A detour on Burma's road to socialism? W. A. Taylor. il map *U S News World Rep* 103:37-8 S 21 '87
Industries
See also
Ruby mines and mining—Burma
Politics and government
Burmese daze. A. Sullivan. *New Repub* 197:18-20 N 2 '87
An exchange on Burma [discussion of October 23, 1986 article, The road from Mandalay] I. Buruma. *N Y Rev Books* 34:50-2 Mr 26 '87
Burn, Paul, and Burger, Max M.
The cytoskeletal protein vinculin contains transformation-sensitive, covalently bound lipid. bibl f il *Science* 235:476-9 Ja 23 '87
Burn this [drama] *See* Wilson, Lanford, 1938-
Burnand, Eric
(jt. auth) *See* Schapiro, Mark, and Burnand, Eric
Burnens, André, and others
Epitope mapping by chemical modification of free and antibody-bound protein antigen. bibl f il *Science* 235:780-3 F 13 '87
Burnet
How to grow and use burnet. il *Sunset* 179:173 S '87
Burnett, Carol
Carol Burnett: the half sister she had to raise [excerpt from One more time] il pors *Redbook* 168:54+ Ja '87
A promise kept [condensed from One more time] il *Read Dig* 131:80-4 S '87
about
"My mom saved my life". A. W. Petrucelli. pors *Redbook* 170:108-9+ N '87
Burnett, Chrissy
about
Carol Burnett: the half sister she had to raise [excerpt from One more time] C. Burnett. il pors *Redbook* 168:54+ Ja '87
Burnett, David
Baseball's little acre [photographs] il *Sport Mag* 78:50-7 My '87
Burney, Derek
about
A man with a mandate. H. Mackenzie. il pors *Macleans* 100:10-11 My 25 '87
Burney, Mohammad Ilyas, and Lari, Faiyaz Ahmed
Motivating parents. il *World Health* p19-20 Ja/F '87
Burnham, James, 1905-1987
Liberalism v. reality: the ideology of Western suicide. *Natl Rev* 39:39-43 S 11 '87
about
Apocalypse now and then. J. B. Judis. *New Repub* 197:29-30+ Ag 31 '87
James Burnham: 1905-1987 [cover story; special section] il pors *Natl Rev* 39:31-54 S 11 '87
Burnham, James B., 1939-
Father, friend. il *Natl Rev* 39:50-1 S 11 '87
Burnham, Malin
about
Rough sailing. G. Buchalter. il por *Forbes* 140:452 Jl 13 '87
Burnham, Robert
Eye on the sky. See issues of Astronomy beginning May 1986
Burnham, Walter Dean
Elections as democratic institutions. bibl *Society* 24:38-48 My/Je '87
Burning of land
See also
Shifting cultivation

Burning of land—*cont.*
A burning question [prescribed burning of warm-season native grasses] J. Walter. il *Success Farm* 85 no6:24-5 Mr '87

Burningham, John, 1936-
about
PW interviews. M. Field. il pors *Publ Wkly* 232:168-9 Jl 24 '87

Burnout, Occupational *See* Job stress

Burns, Amy
about
The simple life [with editorial comment by Sandra Wilmot] D. Welebit. il *Americana* 15:3, 37-9 S/O '87

Burns, Arthur F. (Arthur Frank), 1904-1987
about
Obituary
Natl Rev 39:18 Jl 31 '87
Time por 130:13 Jl 6 '87

Burns, Charles R.
A priest's painful choice. por *Newsweek* 109:6 F 2 '87

Burns, Clarence H.
about
First black mayor of Baltimore begins building coalition. il por *Jet* 71:54 F 9 '87

Burns, E. Bradford
A portrait of change [excerpt from Eadweard Muybridge in Guatemala, 1875] il *Américas* 39:26-33 Jl/Ag '87

Burns, George, 1896-
about
George Burns: an American treasure. J. McCollister. il pors *Saturday Evening Post* 259:58-9 My/Je '87

Burns, James MacGregor
A call for reform. il *Life* 10:126 Fall '87

Burns, John F.
A reporter's odyssey in unseen China. il map *N Y Times Mag* p29-31+ F 8 '87

Burns, Kay
A lesson of love. il por *Ladies Home J* 104:20+ D '87

Burns, Ken
about
The simple life [with editorial comment by Sandra Wilmot] D. Welebit. il *Americana* 15:3, 37-9 S/O '87

Burns, Kenneth C., 1920-
See also
Homer and Jethro

Burns, Khephra
Ski tripping. il *Essence* 18:21+ D '87

Burns, M. Anthony
about
Tony Burns has Ryder's rivals eating dust. P. Engardio. il por *Bus Week* p104+ Ap 6 '87

Burns, Robert E., 1927-
The examined life. See issues of U.S. Catholic

Burns and scalds
12-year-old boy awarded $28 million for burns in fire that killed mother [J. Guerrier] D. M. Cheers. il pors *Jet* 73:20-1 D 28 '87-Ja 4 '88
Epithelial wound healing enhanced by transforming growth factor-α and vaccinia growth factor. G. S. Schultz and others. bibl f il *Science* 235:350-2 Ja 16 '87
Long-term skin graft survival [use of cyclosporin with cadaver skin grafts; work of Bruce Achauer] *USA Today (Periodical)* 115:13 F '87
One woman's fiery ordeal [C. G. Quintana set on fire by government troops] A. Finlayson. por *Macleans* 100:24 Mr 30 '87
Test-tube skin and other high-tech treatments for burns. D. Farley. il *FDA Consum* 21:28-31 Je '87

Burr Trail (Utah)
NPCA lawsuit helps put Burr Trail paving on hold. il *Natl Parks* 61:37 My/Je '87

Burri, René
The quirks of Korea. il *Life* 10:20-7 S '87

Burris, Keith
Religious distraction. *Commonweal* 114:310-11 My 22 '87

Burros, Marian
A chef's Easter. il *N Y Times Mag* p75-6 Ap 12 '87
Making the grade. il *N Y Times Mag* p45-6 Jl 19 '87
A road not often taken. il pors *N Y Times Mag* p67-8 Mr 8 '87

Burros, Domestic *See* Donkeys

Burroughs, Bruce
Brava Zinka! il pors *Opera News* 52:18+ D 19 '87

Burroughs, John, 1837-1921
about
In celebration of John Burroughs [special section] il pors *Conservationist* 41:2-13 Ja/F '87

Burroughs, William S., 1914-
The ghost lemurs of Madagascar [story] il *Omni* 9:48-50+ Ap '87
The Valley [story] il *Esquire* 108:215-16 S '87
about
William Burroughs [interview] R. Palmer. il por *Roll Stone* p253-4 N 5-D 10 '87

Burroughs Corporation
See also
Unisys Corp.

Burroughs Wellcome Co.
The unhealthy profits of AZT. T. Kingston. il *Nation* 245:408-9 O 17 '87
An uproar over AIDS drugs [accused of overcharging for Retrovir] J. Branegan. il *Time* 129:58 Ap 6 '87

Burrowing owls *See* Owls

Burrows, Adam
The birth of neutron stars and black holes [cover story] bibl f il *Phys Today* 40:28-37 S '87

Burrows, William E.
We have an edge in quality, but the Soviets overwhelm us in quantity. il *Discover* 8:92-3 Ap '87

Burruss, Robert Page
The long voyage from home [cover story] il por *Futurist* 21:29-33 S/O '87

Bursa Fabricii
The chicken B cell compartment. J.-C. Weill and C.-A. Reynaud. bibl f il *Science* 238:1094-8 N 20 '87

Burstall, Tim, 1929-
about
Kangaroo [film] Reviews
Commonweal 114:182-3 Mr 27 '87. T. O'Brien
Macleans 100:69 Mr 23 '87. J. Bemrose
Ms il 15:35-6 Ap '87. L. Stone
New Repub 196:24-5 Mr 30 '87. S. Kauffmann
People Wkly 27:12 Ap 13 '87. I. Hellman

Burstein, Daniel
Rising Sun on Wall Street: how Japanese money and firms are moving in. il *N Y* 20:32-8 Mr 2 '87

Burstein, Sidney
The eater-friendly grocery list that makes shopping easy. il *Work Woman* 12:168+ My '87

Burt, Elizabeth
about
The active gourmet. J. Myers. il pors *Women's Sports Fitness* 9:37-9 N '87

Burt, William G., III
Tales of two rails. il *Audubon* 89:78+ S '87

Burtchaell, James Tunstead
The Catholic legacy & abortion: a debate [transcript of debate at University of Notre Dame, February 9, 1987; with editorial comment] *Commonweal* 114:657-63+ N 20 '87
In a family way [adaptation of address] il por *Christ Today* 31:24-7 Je 12 '87
about
Abortion: the life you destroy may be your own [interview] por *U S Cathol* 52:20-7 Jl '87

Burtis, Grace
Eat to beat PMS. il *Mademoiselle* 93:180 My '87

Burtless, Gary T., 1950-
Inequality in America: where do we stand? il *Current* 297:4-10 N '87

Burton, Christine M.
Big promise from the wee hoyas. il *Flower Gard* 31:74-7 F/Mr '87

Burton, Cynthia, and Cohen-Rosenthal, Edward
Collective bargaining for the future. il pors *Futurist* 21:34-7 Mr/Ap '87

Burton, Ian
Report on reports: Our common future. bibl f *Environment* 29:25-9 Je '87

Burton, Joseph A.
about
Obituary
Phys Today por 40:108 Ap '87. W. L. Brown

Burton, LeVar
about
LeVar Burton joins cast of new 'Star trek' series. *Jet* 72:56 Je 1 '87

Burton, Linda, 1946-
"What's a smart woman like you doing at home?" [excerpt] il *Read Dig* 131:29-30+ O '87

Burton, Marda
A country called Cajun. il *Saturday Evening Post* 259:82-4 S '87

Burton, Michael
about
Up from poverty. C. Whitaker. il pors *Ebony* 42:110-11+ Ag '87
Burton, Pearlie
about
All the hours of the night: the recollections of a country midwife. M. F. Greene. il pors *Ctry J* 14:58-63 N '87
Burton, Sandra
Aquino's Philippines: the center holds. *Foreign Aff* 65 Sp Issue:524-37 ['87]
Burton, Scott, 1939-
about
Scott Burton: Max Protetch. E. Heartney. il *Art News* 86:148+ D '87
Social seating [cover story] N. Princenthal. bibl f il *Art Am* 75:130-7 Je '87
Burton, William
(jt. auth) See Barter, Christie, and Burton, William
Buruma, Ian
An exchange on Burma [discussion of October 23, 1986 article, The road from Mandalay] *N Y Rev Books* 34:50-2 Mr 26 '87
In the realm of the sensuous. il *House Gard* 159:170-3+ D '87
Korea: shame & chauvinism. bibl f il *N Y Rev Books* 34:21-6 Ja 29 '87
The last Bengali renaissance man. bibl f il *N Y Rev Books* 34:12+ N 19 '87
A new Japanese nationalism [cover story] il *N Y Times Mag* p22-7+ Ap 12 '87
Burundi
Politics and government
Catching the early plane [J.-B. Bagaza ousted in coup] por *Macleans* 100:9 S 14 '87
Bus accidents *See* Traffic accidents
Bus decoration
Panama's moving murals. M. L. Wilkinson. il *Américas* 39:44-7 Mr/Ap '87
Bus drivers
See also
Black bus drivers
Bus industry
See also
Lawson National Distributing Company
Bus lines
See also
Greyhound Corp.
Trailways Inc.
Less bus, more service. S. Shane. *Travel Holiday* 167:28 Ja '87
Acquisitions and mergers
All aboard [Greyhound to buy Trailways] il *Time* 129:46 Je 29 '87
How an ace mechanic wants to fix Greyhound Lines [takeover by F. W. Currey's investor group] J. Hurlock. *Bus Week* p45-6 Ja 12 '87
Leave the driving to Fred Currey [plan for fusing Greyhound and Trailways] J. Weber, Jr. il por *Bus Week* p62-3 Ag 24 '87
Trying to put Greyhound back on its feet. il *Newsweek* 109:40 Ja 5 '87
Unhappy Trails [Greyhound to acquire Trailways] *Newsweek* 109:49 Je 29 '87
Bus travel
The king of the road [A. Neuharth's USA today bus tour] J. Alter. il por *Newsweek* 109:66-7 My 4 '87
Buscaglia, Leo F.
A Santa suit does not a Santa Claus make [excerpt from Seven stories of Christmas love] il *Good Housekeep* 205:44+ D '87
Busch, August A., III
about
How Busch wins in a doggy market. P. Sellers. il por *Fortune* 115:99-100+ Je 22 '87
Busch, Charles
about
Psycho beach party [drama] Reviews
New Yorker 63:60 Ag 10 '87. M. Kramer
Busch, Ron
about
Obituary
Publ Wkly 232:18 Ag 28 '87
Publ Wkly por 232:32-3 O 9 '87. M. Reuter
Busch (Alice) Opera Theatre (Cooperstown, N.Y.) *See* Opera houses
Buses
See also
School buses
Trolleys

Decoration
See Bus decoration
Buses (Computers) *See* Computers—Buses
Bush, Catherine
Still life in motion. il *Theatre Crafts* 21:32-3+ F '87
Bush, Elliott J.
Conceiving Christ first within one's heart. *Christ Century* 104:1054-5 N 25 '87
Bush, George, 1924-
NATO: the best investment in peace [excerpts from address, May 23, 1987] *Dep State Bull* 87:27-8 Ag '87
Uniting against terrorism [address, January 20, 1987] *Dep State Bull* 87:3 Ap '87
about
Ambushed. F. Barnes. *New Repub* 197:14-15 O 12 '87
Baker to Bush: no. il por *Newsweek* 110:7 O 19 '87
Bush battles the 'wimp factor' [cover story] M. G. Warner. il pors *Newsweek* 110:28-30+ O 19 '87
Bush business. *Nation* 244:420-1 Ap 4 '87
The Bush connection [cover story] A. Nairn. il *Progressive* 51:19-23 My '87
The Bush defense: he saw no evil. J. Alter. por *Newsweek* 109:25 F 23 '87
Bush stumbles. il por *Time* 130:23 D 28 '87
Bush's covenants. D. Robb. *Nation* 245:616-17 N 28 '87
Bushwhacking the 'wimp factor'. K. T. Walsh. il por *U S News World Rep* 102:36-7 Mr 30 '87
Escape from Iranscam: Bush's campaign gets a boost. R. Fly. por *Bus Week* p47 Ag 17 '87
The fragile candidacy of a front-runner. K. T. Walsh. il por *U S News World Rep* 103:22 O 19 '87
George Bush on God, war and Ollie North [interview] D. Frost. il por *U S News World Rep* 103:47-8 D 14 '87
A hostage-swap headache for Bush. *U S News World Rep* 103:13 D 28 '87-Ja 4 '88
The invisible favorite. W. Lowther. il por *Macleans* 100:30-1 O 26 '87
Pay pap. D. Seligman. *Fortune* 116:165 N 9 '87
The price of loyalty. M. McDonald. il por *Macleans* 100:26 Mr 9 '87
Putting a bad business behind him? K. T. Walsh. il por *U S News World Rep* 103:27 S 21 '87
Raising bucks for Bush. R. Brownstein. il pors *N Y Times Mag* p42-4+ My 17 '87
Saying bye-bye to the wimp factor. M. Kramer. il por *U S News World Rep* 103:46 N 9 '87
Shaking off a shadow. M. McDonald. il por *Macleans* 100:28 S 7 '87
Stop beating around the Bush [cover story] R. K. Dornan. il *Natl Rev* 39:32-4 N 6 '87
Strictly Bush league. L. Fleischer. *Publ Wkly* 232:30 N 20 '87
The unbeaten Bush. A. Brummer. il *World Press Rev* 34:64 D '87
V.P. Bush tells Dillard grads racism's 'ugly head' always will be chopped off. il pors *Jet* 72:29 Je 8 '87
Vice President Sunbeam. M. Kondracke. il *New Repub* 196:20-3 Mr 30 '87
Where is the real George Bush? R. Ajemian. il pors *Time* 129:20-1 Ja 26 '87
Religion
Vice President Bush worships at black church, boosts families [Shiloh Baptist Church in Washington, D.C.] il pors *Jet* 71:24-5 Ja 19 '87
Speechwriters and speechwriting
George Bush polishes up his comedy routines [hiring of L. Parvin] *Newsweek* 109:27 Ja 5 '87
Staff
Republican dirty tricks [anti-Kemp mailing traced to G. Bush operatives] F. Barnes. *New Repub* 197:18+ Jl 27 '87
Bush, George S.
Sun Valley. il *Skiing* 39:38-44 Spr '87
Bush, George W.
about
The son also rises. R. Phalon. il por *Forbes* 139:178 Je 1 '87
Bush, Trudy Bloser
The challenge of Christian-Muslim relations. il *Christ Century* 104:694-6 Ag 12-19 '87
Bush (Vannevar) Award *See* Science—Awards
Business
See also
Advertising
Aged and business
Airplanes in business
Big business
Boats in business

Business—See also—*cont.*
Capitalism
Christmas business
Commerce
Communications satellites—Business use
Competition
Computers—Business use
Conflict of interests (Business)
Conjuring—Business use
Corporations
Desktop video—Business use
Electronic data interchange—Business use
Entrepreneurs
Goodwill in business
Humor in business
Ideas in business
Industry
Information storage and retrieval systems—Business
use
Interactive video—Business use
Inventories
Location in business and industry
Mail order business
Mentors in business
New Age movement and business
Radiotelephone in business
Real estate business
Retail trade
Rural industries
Selling
Sex in business
Sex oriented business
Small business
Stock exchanges
Tape recordings—Business use
Telecommunication in business
Telephone in business
Trade marks and trade names
Trucks in business
Videotapes—Business use
Word processors and processing—Business use
Youth and business
Business chic: the latest bulletin from the fad front.
il *Bus Week* p38 Ja 19 '87

Bibliography
1987's best business books: a rich, readable crop. M.
A. Reichek. il *Bus Week* p14+ D 14 '87
Books & business [special section] il *N Y Times Book
Rev* 92:27-30+ O 25 '87
The hottest books on business this fall. D. B. Moskowitz.
il *Bus Week* p86 Ag 31 '87
Iacocc-heads. J. Nocera. *New Repub* 196:32-6 Mr 2 '87
Samples from a vintage season [Canadian business books]
P. C. Newman. il *Macleans* 100:39 D 14 '87

Caricatures and cartoons
Nation's funny business. il *Nations Bus* 75:52-3 S '87

Conferences
Conference maneuvers. J. Malveaux. il *Essence* 18:140+
My '87

Finance
See Corporations—Finance

History
Photographs and photography
A business scrapbook. il *Nations Bus* 75:42-4+ S '87

Information services
See also
Information centers (Data processing)

International aspects
See also
Banks and banking, International
Export-import trade
America's hottest new export [special section] P. Sherrid.
il *U S News World Rep* 103:39-41 Jl 27 '87
Cultural collisions to watch out for. S. Rose. *Work
Woman* 12:21-2 Ja '87
Home-grown Americans go global. D. M. Topolnicki.
il *Money* 16:106-8+ My '87

Periodicals
See also
American City Business Journals, Inc.
Business week
Financial post (Canada)
Financial times
Forbes (Periodical)
House organs
Investment dealers' digest
Investor's daily
Nation's business (Periodical)
Venture (Periodical)
Wall Street journal

Political aspects
See also
Business Executives for National Security
Business Roundtable
Chamber of Commerce of the United States of
America
Industry and state
Lobbyists and lobbying
A backlash against business is building—and the
Democrats know it. R. Fly. il *Bus Week* p49 Ap
6 '87
Business [address, November 25, 1986] I. M. Rolland.
Vital Speeches Day 53:253-6 F 1 '87
Congressional alert. See issues of Nation's Business
How to master the politics of marketing. J. Sherman.
Work Woman 12:18+ Mr '87
In demand: Wall Street's liberals. I. Ross. il *Fortune*
115:187-8+ Ap 27 '87
Lewis F. Powell, Jr.: his warning brought a new era
of business activism. il por *Nations Bus* 75:66 Ag
'87
Playing politics on Wall Street. J. Crudele. il *N Y* 20:16+
Ag 10 '87
The political marketplace [right wing elites funded by
business] F. F. Siegel. il *Commonweal* 114:113-16 F
27 '87
Politics & policy. See issues of Fortune beginning March
5, 1984
A reasonable appeal to reason [address, October 7, 1986]
J. E. Sloan. *Vital Speeches Day* 53:168-71 Ja 1 '87
A risky tack for Democrats [antibusiness sentiment] S.
H. Wildstrom. *Bus Week* p71 Jl 20 '87
The shrug market [stock market's reaction to Iranian
arms scandal] J. K. Glassman. *New Repub* 196:15-16
Ja 5-12 '87
Washington roundup. See issues of Nation's Business
beginning September 1985
Whose business is defense? [address, January 16, 1987]
J. R. Munro. *Vital Speeches Day* 53:360-2 Ap 1 '87
Why business is bananas over Baker [H. Baker] il por
Fortune 115:8 Mr 30 '87

Psychological aspects
See Psychology, Industrial

Public relations
See also
Architectural firms—Public relations
Business and television
Business and the press
Chemical industries—Public relations
Customer relations
Motorcycle industry—Public relations
Petroleum industry—Public relations
Business week/Harris poll: is an antibusiness backlash
building? il *Bus Week* p71 Jl 20 '87
The sin of 'smelling Japanese' [trying to build a more
American image] A. Miller. il *Newsweek* 109:55 Ap
27 '87
Speakers and the bottom line [address, August 7, 1987]
R. Kelly. *Vital Speeches Day* 54:47-50 N 1 '87

Social aspects
See also
Corporations—Charitable contributions
Council on Economic Priorities
The case of the ethical ketchup [Rating America's cor-
porate conscience] D. Seligman. il *Fortune* 115:28 F
16 '87
Corporate America sucks up [Council on Economic
Priorities Corporate Conscience Awards] D. K. Mano.
Natl Rev 39:55-7 My 8 '87
Corporation as citizen [address, May 22, 1987] D. F.
Linowes. *Vital Speeches Day* 53:755-8 O 1 '87
Creeping commercialism [Monroe Friedman's study of
brand names used in novels, plays, and song lyrics]
P. McCarthy. *Psychol Today* 21:16 Ag '87
Give your dollars a political spin. A. T. Marlin and
others. il *Nation* 244:75-6+ Ja 24 '87
Giving in a material world [special section] il *Money*
Sp Issue:180-4+ Fall '87
A New York businessman settles an old score (and
his conscience) by paying a 1966 debt to 80 farmers
[W. P. Carey reimburses farmers for losses incurred
by liquidation of sugar refinery] L. Aitken. il por
People Wkly 27:74+ F 23 '87
Public service. il *Bus Week* p130 Ja 12 '87
'Radicals' on the right. il *U S News World Rep* 103:30
S 14 '87
Reaping high returns from social investments. B. Robson.
il *Black Enterp* 18:86-8+ D '87

Business airplane industry *See* Airplane industry
Business airplanes *See* Airplanes, Business
Business and alcoholism *See* Alcohol and employment
Business and art *See* Art and industry
Business and convict labor *See* Convict labor
Business and day care *See* Day care and industry
Business and education
>   *See also*
>   ConSern Program
>   Interns (Business)

Academia, Inc. [commercialization of university research] S. Shulman. il *Technol Rev* 90:11-12 N/D '87
Aid for unwed teens [job training program in Norfolk, Va. subsidized by Systems Management American Corp.] S. S. Harrison. *Black Enterp* 17:17 Mr '87
All-around achiever [IBM executive J. Donald's commitment to helping young people] J. Sands. il por *Essence* 18:102+ Je '87
Back to the basics [business and literacy] J. B. Copeland. il *Newsweek* 110:54-5 S 21 '87
Business and schools [special section] bibl f il *Phi Delta Kappan* 68:378-92 Ja '87
Business goes to college for a brain gain. J. Main. il *Fortune* 115:80-2+ Mr 16 '87
Business involvement and public school improvement (I). D. Mann. bibl f il *Phi Delta Kappan* 69:123-8 O '87
Business involvement and public school improvement (II). D. Mann. bibl f il *Phi Delta Kappan* 69:228-32 N '87
Business leaders urge more aid for poor kids. K. D. Thompson. il *Black Enterp* 18:30 D '87
Business takes an active role in education. B. E. Anderson. il *Black Enterp* 18:53 D '87
Can chicken-coop inventors help us win? [colleges assisting in start-up ventures] D. S. Greenberg. il *U S News World Rep* 103:42 Jl 27 '87
Cooperative education: learn-and-earn college programs. M. Conroy. il *Better Homes Gard* 65:66+ My '87
Corporations on campus. W. Biddle. il *Science* 237:353-5 Jl 24 '87
Franchising education. R. Hotch. il *Nations Bus* 75:30-1 Ap '87
Fun and profits at Beverly Hills High [deal with Twentieth Century-Fox Film Corp.] il *Newsweek* 110:45 Ag 31 '87
How schools sabotage a creative work force. J. A. Hershey. il *Bus Week* p16 Jl 13 '87
Keeping youth in school: a public-private collaboration [peer mentor program for high school students sponsored by Catholic University and Marriott; with reports by J. Payne and J. Smith] S. Lee and others. il *Child Today* 16:15-21 Jl/Ag '87
The Noah principle and the public sector [address, January 29, 1987] D. W. Calloway. *Vital Speeches Day* 53:357-60 Ap 1 '87
Schools and business: partners for reform. D. M. Clark. *Educ Dig* 53:23-5 D '87
Schools are my business [Rich's department store program for high school students in Atlanta] J. M. Zimmerman. por *Newsweek* 109:6-7 My 11 '87
A second-rate power? P. Choquette, Jr. por *Nations Bus* 75:4 D '87
Tainted money: the ethics and rhetoric of divestment [colleges and business] R. L. Payton. il *Change* 19:55-60 My/Je '87
The United States educational system [address, October 26, 1987] D. T. Kearns. *Vital Speeches Day* 54:150-3 D 15 '87
Upgrading the schools: business gets into the act. S. B. Garland. il *Bus Week* p51 Ag 10 '87
Will your company pay for your classes? G. Hechinger. il *Glamour* 85:278 F '87
Germany (West)
German companies serve as schools. P. Bernard. *World Press Rev* 34:47 Ap '87
Business and government *See* Industry and state
Business and politics *See* Business—Political aspects
Business and professional women *See* Businesswomen
Business and society *See* Business—Social aspects
Business and sports
Advantage, sponsors [French Open] F. J. Comes. *Bus Week* p58 Je 8 '87
An all-star entrepreneur [Drew Pearson Enterprises wins Olympic contract] L. Gite. il por *Black Enterp* 17:22 F '87
The America's Cup: just racing means winning [Australia and New Zealand interests] R. L. Miller and C. Debes. il *Bus Week* p100 Ja 19 '87
Barbara Paddock: keeping Manny Hanny ahead of the game. P. Finch. il por *Bus Week* p91 N 9 '87

Ceasing and desisting [Winter Olympics trademark protection effort in Canada] H. Quinn. il *Macleans* 100:61 D 7 '87
Cigarettes anyone? Tennis and smoking [Virginia Slims tournaments sponsored by Philip Morris] R. Doar. *Wash Mon* 19:40 Je '87
The color of money [growth of college tennis spurred by corporate sponsorship] B. Socolow. il *World Tennis* 34:47-9 Ap '87
Expanding on a fast track [K. Bernstein's drag race-related enterprises] S. Gatty. il por *Nations Bus* 75:78 O '87
Going for gold with Olympic pins [collectible lapel pins] J. Howse. il *Macleans* 100:56 N 9 '87
The gold rush [Calgary Olympics; cover story; special section; with editorial comment by Kevin Doyle] il *Macleans* 100:2, 28-39 Mr 23 '87
Hamming it up [professional baseball in Japan] H. Katayama. il *Forbes* 139:150 Ap 6 '87
A little sales pitch and a lot of slow pitches [Equitable's sponsorship of old-timers baseball games] B. Welling. il *Bus Week* p114-15 Je 22 '87
A new way to reach America's good ol' girls [corporate sponsors trying to attract women stock car fans] B. Bauer. il *U S News World Rep* 102:41 Je 29 '87
Nothing sells like sports [cover story] M. D. Oneal and P. Finch. il *Bus Week* p48-53 Ag 31 '87
OCO's symbolic victory [Olympic lapel pin distributor B. Hipson taken to court over trademark rights in Calgary] H. Quinn. il por *Macleans* 100:40 Je 8 '87
Pow! Bam! A one-two punch from Bob Arum and Budweiser [Hagler-Leonard fight] M. D. Oneal. il *Bus Week* p44 Ap 6 '87
The selling of the Olympics [official sponsor deals for Calgary Games] R. Manning. il *Newsweek* 110:40-1 D 28 '87
Business and state *See* Industry and state
Business and television
>   *See also*
>   American Business Network
Giving them the business. J. Rosen. il *Channels* 7:16 F '87
Business and the aged *See* Aged and business
Business and the arts *See* Arts and industry
Business and the church *See* Church and industry
Business and the community *See* Business—Social aspects
Business and the environment *See* Industry and the environment
Business and the New Age movement *See* New Age movement and business
Business and the press
>   *See also*
>   Cigarette industry—Press relations
>   Investment banking—Press relations
>   Petroleum industry—Press relations
Famous findings from Nexis [executives most in the news] D. Seligman. il *Fortune* 116:201+ N 23 '87
Grading the press. P. Plawin. il *Changing Times* 41:114 O '87
Not available for comment. J. Saltzman. il *USA Today (Periodical)* 116:73 S '87
Business and weather *See* Industry and weather
Business and youth *See* Youth and business
Business arbitration *See* Arbitration, Commercial
Business as usual [film] See Motion picture reviews—Single works
Business cards *See* Advertising cards
Business clothes *See* Clothing and dress—Businessmen; Clothing and dress—Businesswomen
Business communication *See* Communication in management
Business conditions
>   *See also*
>   Business cycles
>   Business depression
>   Business failures
>   Business forecasting
>   Economic conditions
>   Inflation (Finance)
>   Productivity, Industrial
Business notes. See issues of World Press Review
Economic diary. See issues of Business Week
International business. See issues of Business Week
Business consultants
>   *See also*
>   Accounting firms—Consulting services
>   Arthur D. Little, Inc.
>   Bain & Company
>   Booz, Allen & Hamilton Inc.
>   Center for Family Business
>   Executive search consultants

Business consultants—See also—*cont.*
　　Investment advisers
　　Marketing consultants
　　McKinsey & Company
　　Meret, Inc.
　　Outplacement consultant services
　　Public relations consultants
　　Real estate consultants
　　Secura Group
　　Towers, Perrin, Forster & Crosby Inc.
　　Townsend-Greenspan & Company
Before you hang out a consultant's shingle. J. A. Byrne. il *Bus Week* p138-9 N 23 '87
A cure for stress? [business stress management programs] P. Wang. il *Newsweek* 110:64-5 O 12 '87
Dad's little helper [M. Connally] M. Fritz. il por *Forbes* 140:104 Jl 27 '87
Franchising: business services. B. Gatty. il *Nations Bus* 75:38-40 Mr '87
Get paid for your advice! R. Brody. il *50 Plus* 27:67+ N '87
The green berets of corporate management [turnaround specialists] G. L. Miles and M. Rothman. il *Bus Week* p110-12+ S 21 '87
A liberal gets rich yet keeps the faith [I. Magaziner] P. Petre. il pors *Fortune* 116:69-72 Ag 31 '87

Acquisitions and mergers

Can this canary swallow a cat? [Plenum wants Arthur D. Little] K. H. Hammonds. *Bus Week* p30-1 Jl 27 '87

Taxation

Consultants will have a tougher time. P. Philipps. il *Bus Week* p91 F 2 '87
Business conventions *See* Conventions
Business cooperation
　　See also
　　Architectural firms—Cooperation
Business crimes *See* Commercial crimes
Business cycles
　　See also
　　Business depression
Endgame strategy [interview with K. R. Harrigan] J. Willoughby. il por *Forbes* 140:181-2 Jl 13 '87
Growth without end? Amen, says one theory [theory of real business cycles] K. Pennar. il *Bus Week* p100-1 Mr 2 '87
The last iceman [companies doing well in declining industries] J. Willoughby. il *Forbes* 140:183+ Jl 13 '87
Why you should hire peak-time employees. L. Washer. *Work Woman* 12:21+ F '87
Business decision making *See* Decision making
Business depression
The 1929 parallel. J. K. Galbraith. il *Atlantic* 259:62-6 Ja '87
1987 need not become 1929 [cover story; special section] il *Fortune* 116:46-8+ N 23 '87
After the fall. il *Progressive* 51:7-8 D '87
Against austerity. R. Kuttner. *New Repub* 197:16-18 D 28 '87
All eyes on the U.S. Y. Messarovitch. *World Press Rev* 34:25-6 N '87
A bad case of nerves [April's market jolts] S. Bartlett. il *Bus Week* p30-2 Ap 27 '87
Binge: end of a profligate era [cover story] I. F. Stone. *Nation* 245:469+ O 31 '87
Calm before a storm? [markets battered by weakening dollar] W. Glasgall. il *Bus Week* p30-2 D 14 '87
A case of the jitters [financial markets] L. Martz. il *Newsweek* 109:18-22+ My 4 '87
Cassandra economics. R. J. Samuelson. il *Newsweek* 109:65 My 18 '87
Coping with the markets [April jitters] B. Powell. il *Newsweek* 109:54 Ap 27 '87
The 'crash of '88' scenario. M. Meyer. il *Newsweek* 110:49-50 N 23 '87
Dear Doctor Lekachman . . . R. Lekachman. il *Nation* 244:250-2 F 28 '87
The doom merchants. J. Crudele. il *N Y* 20:19+ Ag 31 '87
Doomsday machine [trading in index futures] D. N. Dreman. il *Forbes* 139:176 Mr 23 '87
From boom to doom? [views of R. Batra] por *Time* 130:38 Ag 24 '87
The gathering gloom: is 1929 about to happen again? P. Quinn. *America* 157:105-9 Ag 29-S 5 '87
The ghost of 1929. N. Gall. il *Forbes* 140:314-16+ Jl 13 '87

Government data are hardly an early warning system [Gramm-Rudman provision that suspends budget targets when economists agree a recession is imminent] J. Berger. *Bus Week* p32 Ja 12 '87
Here's a happy thought [interview with R. Dalio] R. McGough. il por *Forbes* 139:100+ F 9 '87
Hoovernomics is no cure for Reaganomics. R. Kuttner. por *Bus Week* p22 N 23 '87
How ripe for a crash? S. Koepp. il *Time* 130:44-6 O 5 '87
If Dr. Ravi Batra's theories hold water, man the lifeboats for the great depression of 1990. E. Levin. il pors *People Wkly* 28:59-60+ O 12 '87
In Venice, an opportunity lost [fears of global recession contribute to failure of economic summit meeting] R. Fly and others. il *Bus Week* p44 Je 22 '87
Industrial structure has little impact on jobless rate of experienced workers. R. M. Devens, Jr. bibl f il *Mon Labor Rev* 110:30-2 My '87
Is the party almost over? [cover story; special section] il *Newsweek* 110:50-6+ O 26 '87
Is the sky really falling in? K. R. Sheets. il *U S News World Rep* 103:83-4 S 28 '87
Jitters! [cover story; special section] il *Bus Week* p40-5 My 11 '87
Johnny one-note sings again. A. Bladen. il *Forbes* 140:317 N 16 '87
The minority view: Bloody Monday staved off recession. G. Koretz. *Bus Week* p33 N 16 '87
The next panic: fear and trembling on Wall Street. L. J. Davis. il *Harpers* 274:35-9+ My '87
No 1929 in sight [views of J. E. Maack] R. Brady. il por *Nations Bus* 75:86 O '87
No exit [rash of closed-end investment trusts as harbinger of market crash] L. Jereski. il *Forbes* 139:170 Mr 23 '87
On the brink. F. G. Rohatyn. il *N Y Rev Books* 34:3-4+ Je 11 '87
The panic on Wall Street. T. Fennell. il *Macleans* 100:36-8 O 26 '87
Prescription for a slump. W. C. Peterson. *New Leader* 70:14 N 30 '87
The prophets of gloom '87. B. Powell. il *Newsweek* 110:56 S 14 '87
Ravi Batra's phony baloney. P. Brimelow. il por *Forbes* 140:100+ S 7 '87
Raw materials haven't been bloodied much [no sign of recession yet in commodity prices] G. Koretz. il *Bus Week* p24 N 30 '87
A recession might hit junk-bond issuers right between the eyes. G. Koretz. il *Bus Week* p24 Jl 20 '87
The rising risk of recession [situation facing new Fed chief A. Greenspan] J. Egan. il pors *U S News World Rep* 102:47+ Je 15 '87
The specter of depression. R. J. Samuelson. *Newsweek* 110:22-3 N 2 '87
The stock market is a lousy economic forecaster. J. Willoughby. il *Forbes* 140:32-4 N 30 '87
A storm in the markets. il *Macleans* 100:28-9 Ap 13 '87
Sunrise, sunset. *Nation* 244:455-6 Ap 11 '87
Talk—and fear—of a recession. M. Blondet. il *World Press Rev* 34:24-5 N '87
That rumble you hear is called 'recession'. K. Pennar. il *Bus Week* p44-6 N 2 '87
There's no depression in Ravi Batra's royalties. J. Weber, Jr. il por *Bus Week* p128 N 30 '87
To the brink of recession [Canada] D. Jenish. il *Macleans* 100:34-5 N 16 '87
Warning signs of the crash of '88. P. C. Newman. il *Macleans* 100:27 Mr 2 '87
Where to run for cover if the roof caves in. S. Bartlett. il *Bus Week* p142+ D 28 '87-Ja 4 '88
Why a depression isn't in the cards. G. S. Becker. por *Bus Week* p22 N 9 '87
Why the market crash won't cause a recession [cover story] S. Lee and C. Brown. il *Forbes* 140:120-4 N 30 '87
Why this is 1929 all over again. M. M. Thomas. *Nation* 244:641-2+ My 16 '87
With fiscal policy no longer stimulating growth . . . the question is: how would Greenspan fight recession? G. Koretz. il *Bus Week* p28 Je 22 '87
A word of caution. *America* 156:42-3 Ja 24 '87
Writing to sell in the MTV era [R. N. Batra's The great depression of 1990] A. Smith. il *Esquire* 108:87+ D '87

Business depression, 1837
1837. il *Am Herit* 38:139-40 My/Je '87

Business depression, 1893

Yesterday's lemon is today's watermelon! [Panic of 1893 and issuance of watermelon notes] E. Rochette. il *Antiques Collect Hobbies* 92:71-2 Ap '87

Business depression, 1929-1939

1929 and 1987: the differences. M. Friedman. *Natl Rev* 39:50 N 20 '87

1929? Or 1962? M. S. Forbes, Jr. il *Forbes* 140:24-5 N 16 '87

The 1929 parallel. J. K. Galbraith. il *Atlantic* 259:62-6 Ja '87

1987 is not like 1929. il *World Press Rev* 34:11-12 D '87

The big lesson from 'the other crash' [interview with C. P. Kindleberger] il *U S News World Rep* 103:32-3 N 2 '87

"Do it big, Sammy" [S. Insull] P. Fuhrman. il pors *Forbes* 140:278-80 Jl 13 '87

The ghost of 1929. N. Gall. il *Forbes* 140:314-16+ Jl 13 '87

How the book trade survived the Great Depression [reprints from March 10, 1975 issue] C. B. Grannis. il *Publ Wkly* 232:19-22 N 20 '87

Joe Folkl remembers. G. Morgenson. por *Forbes* 140:304 N 16 '87

Looking back: the crash of '29. L. Harris. il *Sch Update* 120:10-11 D 18 '87

Memories of the road [Depression era hobo life] D. Mansfield. il por *Am Hist Illus* 21:34-41 F '87

Once upon a time in October . . . [1929 stock market crash] O. Friedrich. il *Time* 130:54-5 N 2 '87

Business districts

Booming American cities [cover story; special section] il *Fortune* 116:30-7+ Ag 17 '87

The new American downtown: Tyson's Corner as a case study. R. L. Miller. il *Archit Rec* 175:79+ S '87

Spiffing up the urban heritage [downtown areas; cover story] K. Anderson. il *Time* 130:72-6+ N 23 '87

Business education

See also
Business ethics—Study and teaching
Business management—Study and teaching
Business schools and colleges
Junior Achievement

Academe and the boom in business studies. il *Change* 19:37-42 S/O '87

Blacks follow trend in pursuing business degree. *Jet* 71:39 F 23 '87

Giving kids the business. R. Thompson. il *Nations Bus* 75:43-4 Ag '87

Go back to school—this time as the teacher. J. B. Levine. il *Bus Week* p146-7 Ja 12 '87

Business enterprises

See also
Black business enterprises
Filipino American business enterprises
Minority business enterprises

History

Entrepreneurial street smarts. W. Hoffer. il *Nations Bus* 75:62-4 N '87

The tiny starts of titans [corporate founders] W. S. Wingo. il *Nations Bus* 75:38-9 Ja '87

Business entertaining

See also
Office parties

Cheers! Dressing right for holiday parties. J. Mattera. il *Glamour* 85:114 D '87

The dawn patrol [restaurants for power breakfasts] il *Harpers Bazaar* 120:26+ Ja '87

Don't know anyone in the room? How to take charge. il *Glamour* 85:108 F '87

Lunches with writers can be a succession of doors opening on new worlds; the best are as stimulating as a week's vacation. J. P. Wiley, Jr. *Smithsonian* 18:32+ Je '87

Surviving the power breakfast. L. Scheer and W. G. Flanagan. il *Forbes* 140:208+ N 2 '87

Anecdotes, facetiae, satire, etc.

Ice-cream music [pianist supplying mood music for corporate reception featuring ice cream] D. Asher. il *Harpers* 274:68-71 Je '87

Surviving the business banquet. K. Fury. il *Work Woman* 12:170 Ap '87

Taxation

Call it a seminar [writing off business entertainment as seminars in Australia] G. Buchalter. il *Forbes* 139:42 Ja 12 '87

Even the 1-martini lunch is a target [deducting business expenses] L. Wiener. *U S News World Rep* 103:64 S 7 '87

Paying the dues. L. Saunders. il *Forbes* 139:78+ Mr 9 '87

Writing it off. J. J. Buck. *Vogue* 177:206-7+ Ja '87

Business ethics

See also
Accounting ethics
Advertising ethics
Aerospace industries—Ethical aspects
Airplane industry—Ethical aspects
Appraisers—Ethical aspects
Art trade—Ethical aspects
Audio equipment stores—Ethical aspects
Automobile industry—Ethical aspects
Automobiles—Leasing and renting—Ethical aspects
Avionics industry—Ethical aspects
Banks and banking—Ethical aspects
Brewing industry—Ethical aspects
Bribery
Brokers—Ethical aspects
Business intelligence
Cable television—Ethical aspects
Cleaning services—Ethical aspects
Clothing industry—Ethical aspects
Commercial crimes
Commodity brokers—Ethical aspects
Competition
Computer industry—Ethical aspects
Construction industry—Ethical aspects
Contractors—Ethical aspects
Drug industry—Ethical aspects
Foreign exchange brokers—Ethical aspects
Fraud
Health maintenance organizations—Ethical aspects
Investment banking—Ethical aspects
Market research—Ethical aspects
Meat industry—Ethical aspects
Mortgage brokers—Ethical aspects
Nepotism
Perfume industry—Ethical aspects
Petroleum industry—Ethical aspects
Phonograph record industry—Ethical aspects
Photographic industry—Ethical aspects
Publishers and publishing—Ethical aspects
Shipbuilding—Ethical aspects
Television equipment industry—Ethical aspects
Tourist trade—Ethical aspects

The Boesky touch. T. C. Muck. il *Christ Today* 31:14-15 Mr 6 '87

Business ethics, immigrants' treatment—70 years ago and now. B. C. Forbes. il por *Forbes* 140:33-4 Jl 13 '87

Coping with ethical decisions [views of LaRue Hosmer] *USA Today (Periodical)* 116:10 Ag '87

Enterprise and double cross [excerpt from Tales of a new America] R. B. Reich. *Wash Mon* 18:13-19 Ja '87

Ethics and the free market. G. F. Cavanagh and P. J. Chmielewski. il *America* 156:79-82 Ja 31 '87

Ethics and the investment industry [Notre Dame conference] T. C. Widner. *America* 157:444-5 D 12 '87

Ethics of transnationalism. R. Vernon. *Society* 24:53-6 Mr/Ap '87

The fear of getting caught. P. Baida. il *Am Herit* 38:22+ S/O '87

Finding the ethical edge [cover story] K. Berney. il *Nations Bus* 75:18-19+ Ag '87

Have ethics disappeared from Wall Street? R. S. Bachelder. il *Christ Century* 104:628-30 Jl 15-22 '87

Integrity and trust [address, January 21, 1987] P. Dawkins. *Vital Speeches Day* 53:344-7 Mr 15 '87

The morals of the marketplace. G. P. Brockway. il *New Leader* 70:13-14 S 7 '87

Morals of the money-makers. D. Francis. por *Macleans* 100:7 My 4 '87

The need for ethical leadership [address, May 15, 1987] W. C. Butcher. *Vital Speeches Day* 53:679-81 S 1 '87

Should you ever rat on a coworker? B. L. Harragan. *Mademoiselle* 93:106 F '87

To the graduates of 1987: on losing one's self in finance [adaptation of address] J. O'Donnell. *America* 156:415-16 My 23 '87

Unfuzzing ethics for managers. W. Kiechel, III. il *Fortune* 116:229+ N 23 '87

Study and teaching

All hail the new greed. L. Wainwright. il *Life* 10:12 Je '87

Banking on ethics [J. S. R. Shad's endowment to Harvard] *Time* 129:79 Ap 13 '87

The business ethics debate. T. Noah. il *Newsweek* 109:36 My 25 '87

Business ethics—Study and teaching—_cont._

Ethics 101: can the good guys win? [J. S. R. Shad funds program at Harvard Business School] B. Brophy. il por *U S News World Rep* 102:54 Ap 13 '87

Ethics for greedheads. F. Zakaria. *New Repub* 197:18+ O 19 '87

Gatsby at the B school [use of fiction in business ethics course at Harvard] R. Coles. *N Y Times Book Rev* 92:1+ O 25 '87

Harvard's $30 million windfall for ethics 101 [J. S. R. Shad's gift] J. A. Byrne. por *Bus Week* p40 Ap 13 '87

Shad the lawgiver [J. S. R. Shad's gift to Harvard Business School] D. Seligman. il *Fortune* 115:154 My 11 '87

Business etiquette

Corporate etiquette. L. H. Lapham. *Harpers* 275:7-8 Ag '87

The new business etiquette. F. McCoy. *Black Enterp* 17:104 F '87

The new rules for on-the-job manners. M. A. Kellogg. il *Glamour* 85:120+ Ap '87

Business executives *See* Black executives; Executives; Women executives

Business Executives for National Security

Business versus Star Wars. A. M. Cunningham. il *Technol Rev* 90:17 My/Je '87

Business expansion *See* Industrial expansion

Business expenses *See* Expense accounts (Business)

Business failures

See also

Bank failures

Default (Finance)

Workout investments

40 to lose jobs when Hunters in Westwood, Beverly Hills close. L. See. *Publ Wkly* 232:23 D 25 '87

The $90 million dream: the rise and fall of Michael Hollis [failure of Air Atlanta] C. Whitaker. il pors *Ebony* 43:188-90+ N '87

Adler & Adler, lacking backlist, to fold after fall 1988 season. H. Fields. *Publ Wkly* 232:12 N 13 '87

As risky as a crapshoot [buying stock in a bankrupt firm] A. Gabor. il *U S News World Rep* 102:65 Ap 27 '87

Bankrupt ideology [L. LaRouche forced into involuntary bankruptcy] *Time* 129:80 My 4 '87

Bankruptcy court for Texaco: the lesser evil—barely. T. Thompson and others. il *Bus Week* p102-3+ Ap 27 '87

Battling a billion-dollar debt [Hunt brothers; cover story] J. A. Jenkins. il *N Y Times Mag* p24-9+ S 27 '87

Behind the scenes at Texaco's settlement [Pennzoil agreement] J. R. Norman and T. Vogel. il *Bus Week* p66-8 D 28 '87-Ja 4 '88

Bonds: the safest play on Texaco. G. G. Marcial. *Bus Week* p124 Je 8 '87

Boom in the bust market [R. D. Smith & Co.] E. Linden. il *Time* 130:52 O 12 '87

A break in the action [Texaco files for Chapter 11] J. Castro. il *Time* 129:52-3 Ap 27 '87

The bright side of economic failure. R. B. McKenzie. *Society* 24:39-42 S/O '87

Buying into Chapter 11: the method in Rorer's madness [bid for A. H. Robins] C. S. Eklund. il *Bus Week* p73-4 Jl 20 '87

Chapter 11 for Texaco. D. Pauly. il *Newsweek* 109:52 Ap 20 '87

The crash of Air Atlanta. R. Witherspoon. il por *Black Enterp* 17:59-60 Je '87

The Davis boys won't go down without one more fight [T. C. and K. Davis] T. Vogel. il pors *Bus Week* p108-9+ My 25 '87

Et tu, Pennzoil? [Texaco-Pennzoil case] *New Repub* 196:4+ My 4 '87

Francesco Galesi isn't used to losing [failure of Argo Communications Corp.] P. Finch. il por *Bus Week* p114 My 4 '87

Freundlich Books bankrupt, to be liquidated. *Publ Wkly* 232:11 O 23 '87

Frying pan to fire [Computone Systems] B. Leonard. il por *Forbes* 139:116+ Ap 6 '87

The gambler who refused $2 billion [Pennzoil's J. H. Liedtke's fight with Texaco; cover story] S. P. Sherman. il pors *Fortune* 115:50-4+ My 11 '87

Guarding the till at LTV [L. Galie, chairman of committee formed to represent unsecured creditors] M. Kuntz. il por *Forbes* 139:90 Ja 26 '87

Invisible property [bankruptcy proceedings and rights to intellectual property] D. Fanning. il *Forbes* 139:104 Mr 23 '87

It's white-knuckle time for the Hunts [bankruptcy court to decide fate of Placid Oil Gulf drilling project] T. Mason. il *Bus Week* p29 Mr 30 '87

J. R. McConnell: the ballad of a Texas tornado. T. Vogel. il por *Bus Week* p80+ N 9 '87

Jack Stanley's 30-year oil feud is sizzling [Coastal Corp's O. Wyatt stages hostile takeover of TransAmerican Natural Gas in bankruptcy court] J. R. Norman. il *Bus Week* p58-9 Ap 13 '87

Keeping your business afloat [avoiding bankruptcy] N. L. Croft. il *Nations Bus* 75:16-18+ F '87

Losing the future to the past [effects of information revolution on entrepreneurism] M. Pastin. il por *Nations Bus* 75:4 F '87

Milt Grant's fall: the moral. J. Baker. il *Channels* 7:15 F '87

Serenity on a scrap heap of dreams [failed Toronto industrialist J. Gower] J. Barber. il por *Macleans* 100:41 Ja 26 '87

A shark gets bitten [V. Posner's Sharon Steel files for bankruptcy] J. A. Conway. il *Forbes* 139:8 My 18 '87

The shootout at Texaco corral [petition for Chapter 11] J. Egan. il *U S News World Rep* 102:62+ Ap 27 '87

Silicon Valley phoenixes. C. Barron. il *Fortune* 116:128-9+ N 23 '87

Texaco starts a new life [bankruptcy] J. B. Copeland. il *Newsweek* 109:50 Ap 27 '87

Texaco's big gamble [bankruptcy gambit] T. Tedesco. il *Macleans* 100:42 Ap 27 '87

Texaco's last stand [negotiations over Pennzoil settlement] T. Tedesco. il *Macleans* 100:43 D 28 '87

Texaco's star falls. J. Castro. il *Time* 129:50-2 Ap 20 '87

Texas broke [T. C. Davis] L. M. Keefe. por *Forbes* 140 Sp Issue:8 O 26 '87

There's no word for Chapter 11 in Dutch. T. Vogel. il *Bus Week* p62+ N 30 '87

They honk when the Krohs fly by [attempt to reorganize under Chapter 11] J. Castro. il *Time* 129:56 Mr 16 '87

Too long at the party [career of Levittown developer W. Levitt] L. Gubernick. il por *Forbes* 139:40 My 4 '87

Victor Posner is on the ropes—and slipping. G. DeGeorge and P. Engardio. il por *Bus Week* p36 N 23 '87

Were STC's optical disks just a mirage? [suit brought by limited partnership investors against Storage Technology Corp.] M. Ivey. il *Bus Week* p67 Je 15 '87

When to invest in a battered stock. il *Bus Week* p162-3 Je 22 '87

A whiz kid goes wrong [B. Minkow of ZZZZ Best Co.] J. B. Copeland. il por *Newsweek* 110:40 Jl 20 '87

Why didn't they pay him to stay home? [Horn & Hardart's Bojangles' stores mismanaged by B. Florescue] B. Leonard. il por *Forbes* 139:120-1 Je 15 '87

Why Posner backed out of a bailout for Sharon Steel [bailout from Quantum Fund] P. Engardio. il por *Bus Week* p40 My 4 '87

You don't have to be broke to need Chapter 11. D. B. Moskowitz and M. Ivey. *Bus Week* p108 Ap 27 '87

ZZZZ Best may be ZZZZ worst. P. Elmer-Dewitt. por *Time* 130:56 Jl 20 '87

History

Building on failure. B. Gatty. il *Nations Bus* 75:50-1 Ap '87

Business flying *See* Airplanes in business

Business forecasting

See also

Stocks—Price forecasting

Brighter prospects for corporate profits. T. May, Jr. il *Fortune* 116:49+ S 14 '87

Business in the year 2000 [predictions by Barbara Chrispin] *USA Today (Periodical)* 115:10 My '87

Business is disillusioned. S. Lee and C. Brown. il *Forbes* 140:124 N 30 '87

Business outlook. See issues of Nation's Business

Business outlook. W. B. Franklin. See issues of Business Week through January 18, 1988

Business outlook '87 [special issue] il *Nations Bus* 75:16-17+ Ja '87

The economy according to small business. H. S. Braun. il *Nations Bus* 75:42-4+ My '87

The Fortune 500 CEO poll. B. Saporito. il *Fortune* 116:58-9 S 28 '87

Fortune forecast. See issues of Fortune

Industry outlook [special section] il *Bus Week* p65-72+ Ja 12 '87

Business forecasting—*cont.*

Numbers to help you size up the market's prospects—and yours. il *Bus Week* p186-7+ D 28 '87-Ja 4 '88

The riches in market niches [fast growing companies on fringe of Fortune 500] S. Gannes. il *Fortune* 115:227-8+ Ap 27 '87

Sluggish growth—but a recession is unlikely. J. C. Cooper and K. Madigan. il *Bus Week* p110-12 D 28 '87-Ja 4 '88

Small-business confidence: looking good at home. H. S. Braun. il *Nations Bus* 75:32-3+ N '87

Still bullish at the top. A. Ramirez. il *Fortune* 116:90-1 N 23 '87

What the forecast means for 16 industries. B. Dumaine. il *Fortune* 116:46-8 Jl 20 '87

What the forecast means for 16 industries. J. Nielsen and F. Rice. il *Fortune* 115:76+ Ja 19 '87

Business games *See* Management games

Business gifts *See* Gifts in business

Business hours
> *See also*
> Hours of labor

Business in literature

Gatsby at the B school [use of fiction in business ethics course at Harvard] R. Coles. *N Y Times Book Rev* 92:1+ O 25 '87

Business in motion pictures

The movie version [insider information as handled in movie The House of Rothschild] D. Seligman. il *Fortune* 115:27-8 F 16 '87

Business in television

The real drama's in business. H. Altman. il *Nations Bus* 75:4 Ap '87

Business intelligence

The spy who loves cars [H. G. Lehmann's photographs of prototype cars] R. Hutton. il pors *Car Driv* 32:90-1+ My '87

Business interns *See* Interns (Business)

Business Leadership Hall of Fame *See* Halls of fame

Business letters *See* Business writing

Business liability *See* Liability (Law)

Business liquidation *See* Liquidation

Business literature
> *See also*
> House organs

Business lobby *See* Lobbyists and lobbying

Business location *See* Location in business and industry

Business management
> *See also*
> Airlines—Management
> Architectural firms—Management
> Arts—Management
> Automobile industry—Management
> Automotive industries—Management
> Black executives
> Brokers—Management
> Business intelligence
> Business planning
> Cable television—Management
> Casinos—Management
> Chemical industries—Management
> Communication in management
> Computers—Business use
> Conflict of interests (Business)
> Corporations—Directors
> Crisis management in business
> Decision making
> Diversification in industry
> Electric utilities—Management
> Electronic industries—Management
> Executives
> Factory management
> Fisheries—Management
> Food industry—Management
> Genetic research industry—Management
> Hotel management
> Industrial expansion
> Information managers
> Insurance companies—Management
> Inventories
> Leveraged buyouts
> Location in business and industry
> Marketing
> Mass media industry—Management
> Mining equipment industry—Management
> Nuclear industry—Management
> Office management
> Organizational change
> Participative management
> Personnel management
> Petroleum industry—Management

> Poultry industry—Management
> Productivity, Industrial
> Restaurant management
> Retail trade—Management
> Scheduling (Management)
> Service industries—Management
> Steel industry—Management
> Task forces in industry
> Team work in industry
> Television industry—Management
> Theater management
> Women executives

39th annual report on American industry [special issue] il *Forbes* 139:61-78+ Ja 12 '87

Advice from the Dr. Spock of business [interview with P. F. Drucker] J. A. Byrne. il por *Bus Week* p61+ S 28 '87

America's leanest and meanest [cover story] G. D. Wallace. il *Bus Week* p78-82+ O 5 '87

The battle for corporate control [cover story] B. Nussbaum and J. H. Dobrzynski. il *Bus Week* p102-9 My 18 '87

Bear hug [failed mergers when big companies swallow little ones] C. Poole and J. A. Trachtenberg. il *Forbes* 140:186-7+ N 16 '87

Business leaders [address, December 8, 1986] H. R. Perot. *Vital Speeches Day* 53:337-42 Mr 15 '87

Catalysts of genius, dealers in hope [address, October 14, 1986] L. E. Reuss. *Vital Speeches Day* 53:173-6 Ja 1 '87

The challenge of global competition [address, September 17, 1987] G. H. Conrades. *Vital Speeches Day* 54:125-8 D 1 '87

Competitiveness [address, July 21, 1987] F. G. Steingraber. *Vital Speeches Day* 53:758-62 O 1 '87

The competitiveness challenge [address, August 21, 1987] J. J. Melone. *Vital Speeches Day* 54:100-4 D 1 '87

Competitiveness: getting it back. S. Nasar. il *Fortune* 115:217-18+ Ap 27 '87

The corporate elite [with CEO 1000 directory] il *Bus Week* Sp Issue:13-17+ O 23 '87

The corporation. See issues of Business Week

Endgame strategy [interview with K. R. Harrigan] J. Willoughby. il por *Forbes* 140:181-2 Jl 13 '87

The fine art of asking smart questions [excerpt from Smart questions] D. Leeds. il *Work Woman* 12:132-3+ N '87

How managers will manage [1990s] P. Nulty. il *Fortune* 115:47-8+ F 2 '87

How the best get better [R. H. Waterman's The renewal factor; cover story] J. A. Byrne. il por *Bus Week* p98-9 S 14 '87

How to cut a monster project down to size. J. Stoltenberg. il *Work Woman* 12:118-19 Mr '87

How to manage a growing company. H. Waldrop. il *Work Woman* 12:39-42 Ap '87

How to turn bright ideas into solid results [project management] T. L. Quick. il *Work Woman* 12:92-3+ Je '87

International competitiveness [address, June 8, 1987] H. Goldfeder. *Vital Speeches Day* 53:722-5 S 15 '87

Japanese challenge—American response [address, March 5, 1987] P. Cannon. *Vital Speeches Day* 53:503-9 Je 1 '87

Keeping up in the fast lane. N. L. Croft. il *Nations Bus* 75:24-6 Jl '87

The last iceman [companies doing well in declining industries] J. Willoughby. il *Forbes* 140:183+ Jl 13 '87

Learning from Reagan's debacle [applying Iran arms scandal mistakes to business management] A. R. Dowd. il por *Fortune* 115:169-72 Ap 27 '87

Lessons of leadership. See issues of Nation's Business

Making American industry competitive again [address, April 16, 1987] J. Weaver. *Vital Speeches Day* 53:560-2 Jl 1 '87

Managers' shoptalk. See issues of Working Woman beginning October 1984

The old management magic [address, October 5, 1987] T. R. Horton. *Vital Speeches Day* 54:111-13 D 1 '87

A quest for excellence [special section] B. Robson. il *Black Enterp* 17:273-4+ Je '87

The renewal factor [excerpt] R. H. Waterman, Jr. il *Bus Week* p100-1+ S 14 '87

Smart questions to ask to get ahead in your job [excerpts from Smart questions] D. Leeds. il *Glamour* 85:116+ My '87

Start-up help for your business. R. R. Roha. il *Changing Times* 41:73-4+ Je '87

Business management—cont.

Still alive at 75 [techniques for staying in business] N. L. Croft. il *Nations Bus* 75:57+ S '87

There are no excellent companies. T. J. Peters. il por *Fortune* 115:341+ Ap 27 '87

Tips for the hands-off CEO. B. Powell. il *Newsweek* 109:52 Mr 16 '87

To: Corporate managers. Re: Bureaucracy. Don't send memos! T. J. Peters. il *Wash Mon* 19:12-14+ N '87

Unbinding Gulliver [address, April 9, 1987] R. A. Voell. *Vital Speeches Day* 53:661-5 Ag 15 '87

When to lead, when to stand back. F. E. Fiedler. il *Psychol Today* 21:26-7 S '87

Winning your own game [cover story] R. Thompson. il *Nations Bus* 75:16-17+ Jl '87

Anecdotes, facetiae, satire, etc.

Corporate comeback strategies. J. Queenan. il *Commonweal* 114:340-1 Je 5 '87

Bibliography

The latest secrets of managing. D. Seligman. il *Fortune* 116:98 Jl 6 '87

Study and teaching

See also
American Management Association
Business schools and colleges
Executives—Training
General Electric Co. Management Development Institute
Junior Achievement
Women executives—Training

Behind the scenes at the Magic Kingdom [Walt Disney Co. in the management seminar business] R. Simon. il *Forbes* 140:427+ Jl 13 '87

A teacher who made a difference [G. F. Doriot] P. Fuhrman. il por *Forbes* 140:362+ Jl 13 '87

Wanted: leaders who can make a difference. J. Main. il *Fortune* 116:92-4+ S 28 '87

Aids and devices

Monday morning at the movies [videos] A. E. LaForge. il *Work Woman* 12:50+ Je '87

Think like a dolphin [role models for managers learning strategic thinking skills] *Futurist* 21:52 Mr/Ap '87

Germany (West)

Lessons from German managers. L. S. Richman. il *Fortune* 115:267+ Ap 27 '87

Italy

Italy's daredevil entrepreneurs. P. C. Newman. il *Macleans* 100:40 N 9 '87

Japan

See also
Kanrisha Yosei

Harnessing the 'yen monster'. M. R. Meyer. il *Newsweek* 110:60 S 21 '87

A puzzling toll at the top [deaths of corporate chiefs] J. M. Horowitz. il *Time* 130:46 Ag 3 '87

Where the jobs are [U.S.; special section] il *Newsweek* 109:42-8 F 2 '87

Your next boss may be Japanese. B. Powell. il *Read Dig* 130:141-4 Je '87

Korea (South)

Korea's new corporate bosses: made in America. L. Nakarmi and W. J. Holstein. il *Bus Week* p58-9 F 23 '87

Western Europe

How business is creating Europe Inc. J. Heard and J. Kapstein. il *Bus Week* p40-1 S 7 '87

Business meetings *See* Corporations—Meetings
Business names *See* Corporations—Names
Business organization *See* Business management
Business patronage of art *See* Art and industry
Business patronage of the arts *See* Arts and industry
Business planning

See also
Computers—Business use
Organizational change
Product planning
Scheduling (Management)

The corporation. See issues of Business Week

Strategic planning [address, March 18, 1987] R. D. Kennedy. *Vital Speeches Day* 53:624-7 Ag 1 '87

Strategy in a more volatile world [science of chaos and business management] R. H. Waterman, Jr. il por *Fortune* 116:181-2 D 21 '87

Where do the best goals come from? [excerpt from The human side of management] G. S. Odiorne. il *Work Woman* 12:32+ D '87

Business presentations

Act your way through a tough presentation. il *Glamour* 85:36 Jl '87

Have overhead projector, will travel [McKinsey & Co. techniques] J. Merwin. il *Forbes* 140:127 O 19 '87

Aids and devices

A better mouse trap [Freelance Plus presentation graphics program] S. R. Reed. il *Pers Comput* 11:204 My '87

Graphics come of age. K. Berney. il *Nations Bus* 75:53-5 Je '87

Lights, camera . . . briefcase: act for success [Acting for Businesspeople courses] P. Kripke. il *Work Woman* 12:122 S '87

Now playing at an office near you—desktop videos. J. Rothfeder. il *Bus Week* p85+ Je 1 '87

Business recession *See* Business depression
Business relocation *See* Location in business and industry
Business reports *See* Corporation reports
Business Roundtable

Bush business [G. Bush courting Business Roundtable] *Nation* 244:420-1 Ap 4 '87

Business schools and colleges

See also
Columbia University. Graduate School of Business
Harvard University. Graduate School of Business Administration
Sloan School of Management
Wharton School
Yale University. School of Organization and Management

Money majors. il *U S News World Rep* 103:81-3 N 2 '87

The trade crisis begins at home. T. F. Keller. por *U S News World Rep* 103:8 Ag 31 '87

Admission

See also
Graduate Management Admission Council

MBAs are hotter than ever. J. A. Byrne. il *Bus Week* p46+ Mr 9 '87

One key to B-school: your essay. J. A. Byrne. il *Bus Week* p168 Mr 23 '87

Curriculum

See also
Business ethics—Study and teaching

The business ethics debate. T. Noah. il *Newsweek* 109:36 My 25 '87

Ethics for greedheads. F. Zakaria. *New Repub* 197:18+ O 19 '87

What they don't teach you at business school. A. Gabor. il *U S News World Rep* 103:44-6 Jl 13 '87

Graduates

Group pushes MBAs for minorities with forum tour [Graduate Management Admission Council] *Jet* 72:24 Ag 31 '87

How an M.B.A. makes a difference [black women] E. C. Ray. il *Essence* 18:105-6 D '87

Leroy Nunery: working for a bigger crop of minority MBAs. M. Mallory. por *Bus Week* p76 O 26 '87

"The sex appeal is intact". D. Machan. il *Forbes* 139:156+ My 4 '87

This year's MBAs are staying off the Street. L. Helm. il *Bus Week* p40 D 14 '87

Wanted: black M.B.A.s. M. Mallory. il *Black Enterp* 18:28 O '87

You can't go home again, MBA-san [Japanese business students] il *Fortune* 116:9 Ag 3 '87

Standards

A $100,000 campus 'raid' [Columbia Business School teacher A. Edelman's finder's fee raises questions of conflict of interests] A. Gabor. por *U S News World Rep* 103:12-13 O 26 '87

A $100,000 question stirs up Columbia [A. Edelman offers his Columbia business students a finder's fee for spotting a good takeover target] B. Kantrowitz. il por *Newsweek* 110:76 O 26 '87

Don't go near the dollars [Columbia Business School vetoes professor A. Edelman's offer of finder's fee to a student who could come up with a company ripe for raiding] E. Bowen. il por *Time* 130:138-9 O 26 '87

Edelman's art of reward [offer of $100,000 finder's fee to Columbia Business School students] N. J. Perry. il por *Fortune* 116:159 N 9 '87

Great Britain

See also
Templeton College, the Oxford Centre for Management Studies

Japan

See also
Kanrisha Yosei

Business secrets *See* Trade secrets
Business Service Etc. Inc.

Close to home. J. Koblenz. il *Black Enterp* 17:22 F '87

Business training films *See* Motion pictures in industry
Business travel
> *See also*
> Automobiles in business
> Frequent flier programs
> Frequent guest programs
> Information storage and retrieval systems—Business travel use
> Midway Airlines, Inc.

American configures 747SPs to serve Tokyo first/business-class market. il *Aviat Week Space Technol* 126:54 My 11 '87

Black enterprise guide to executive travel [special section] il *Black Enterp* 17:33+ Mr '87

Business travel. D. Reed and J. E. Lasky. il *Esquire* 108:201-7 O '87

Business travel made easy. J. Malveaux. il *Essence* 17:105-6 Ap '87

The business traveler. D. Reed and J. E. Lasky. il *Esquire* 107 Summ Traveler:T49-T52+ Ap '87

Career makeover: from ticket sales to corporate travel planner [L. Lee] il por *Glamour* 85:110 F '87

Convenience outranks price. *Nations Bus* 75:36 N '87

The executive suite goes traveling. J. Castro. il *Time* 129:55 Mr 30 '87

Off on a business trip? Don't forget the diapers. S. D. Atchison. il *Bus Week* p79+ N 30 '87

Race against time [Mooney 252 vs. the airlines for business trips] G. Baxter. il *Flying* 114:78-81 Ag '87

Square meals for a Sunday night [businessmen alone in new town] B. Harte. il *Fortune* 115:311+ Ap 27 '87

Suitcase survival: how to dress smart, on the road. il *Glamour* 85:139-42+ F '87

To check or not to check [women executives] B. G. Kempton. il *Work Woman* 12:45-6 Mr '87
> **Taxation**

Paying the dues. L. Saunders. il *Forbes* 139:78+ Mr 9 '87

Business trips *See* Business travel
Business uniforms *See* Uniforms
Business week
Wake up, Business week! *Natl Rev* 39:18-19 D 18 '87
Business writing
> *See also*
> Form letters

Crying in your beer, eighties style [rejection letters] J. Sherman. *Work Woman* 12:27-8 My '87

'Nobody ever throws fruit at the speechwriter' [corporate speechwriters] J. A. Byrne. il *Bus Week* p112-13+ O 12 '87

Businessmen
> *See also*
> Clothing and dress—Businessmen
> Entrepreneurs
> Executives

Faces behind the figures. See issues of Forbes

Fortune people. N. J. Perry. See issues of Fortune beginning August 17, 1987

Making it. See issues of Nation's Business beginning September 1985

Businessmen in television
The business people and television [address, June 6, 1987] M. Eisner. *Vital Speeches Day* 53:665-7 Ag 15 '87

Businessmen's organizations
> *See also*
> Rotary International

Businesswomen
> *See also*
> Clothing and dress—Businesswomen
> Women entrepreneurs
> Women executives

2 smart women, one top job: who got the VP promotion? M. Gordon. il *Mademoiselle* 93:144-5+ Je '87

Does a working woman really need to be married? No. C. E. Rinzler. il *Work Woman* 12:60+ Ag '87

Does a working woman really need to be married? Yes. E. Lax. il *Work Woman* 12:61+ Ag '87

Making it. See issues of Nation's Business beginning September 1985

On the move. See issues of Black Enterprise

A table for one, please. H. Yorkshire. il *Work Woman* 12:132-4 S '87

Will the real president please stand up? il *Mademoiselle* 93:146-9 Je '87

Women: the second wave [cover story] S. Nelton and K. Berney. il *Nations Bus* 75:18-20+ My '87
> **Anecdotes, facetiae, satire, etc.**

Stages of a woman's career. K. Fury. il *Work Woman* 12:168 O '87

> **Photographs and photography**

How to look your best in a business photo. J. Mattera. il *Glamour* 85:172 Ap '87
> **Travel**
> *See* Business travel

Businesswomen (American) in foreign countries *See* Americans—Foreign countries
Businesswomen's organizations
> *See also*
> National Federation of Business and Professional Women's Clubs
> Professional Secretaries International

Buskin, David
> *about*

Despite their jingular success, Buskin and Batteau insist they'd rather be just folks. M. Neill. il pors *People Wkly* 28:109-10 D 21 '87

Buspirone
What, me worry? V. DeBenedette. *Health* 19:20 Mr '87

Buss, Jerry Hatten
> *about*

Who's the biggest sport in L.A.? Jerry Buss. R. Grover. il por *Bus Week* p72+ Mr 16 '87

Bustin' loose [television program] *See* Television program reviews—Single works
Butcher, Pat
The reign ended in Spain. il pors *Sports Illus* 66:34-5 Je 15 '87

Butcher, Susan
> *about*

Arctic dreams. K. McCoy. il pors *Women's Sports Fitness* 9:22-7+ F '87

Musher. *New Yorker* 63:34-5 O 5 '87

Butcher, Willard C.
The need for ethical leadership [address, May 15, 1987] *Vital Speeches Day* 53:679-81 S 1 '87

Butenko, Raissa G., and Shamina, Zlata B.
Hybrids for the year 2000. il *Courier* 40:20-1 Mr '87

Buthaud, René, b. 1886
> *about*

Deco doyen. A. Duncan. il por *House Gard* 159:36B+ Ja '87

Buthelezi, Gatsha Mangosuthu, 1928-
The future of South Africa [address, November 24, 1986] *Vital Speeches Day* 53:194-6 Ja 15 '87
> *about*

The chief. M. Massing. bibl f il por *N Y Rev Books* 34:15-22 F 12 '87

South Africa's Zulu chief. G. Behrens. il pors *World Press Rev* 34:34-5 Ja '87

Won't someone listen? *Natl Rev* 39:22 Ja 30 '87

Butler, Carmen Lopez
Georgia woman tied to Julian Bond in drug probe gets 22-year sentence. por *Jet* 72:52 S 21 '87

Butler, Henry
> *about*

Henry Butler. G. Kalbacher. il por *Down Beat* 54:45-6 O '87

Butler, Jerry
> *about*

From ballads to ballots. il pors *Ebony* 42:152+ F '87

The Iceman cometh back. B. Barol. il pors *Newsweek* 110:65 N 9 '87

Butler, John Sibley
Social research and scholarly interpretation. bibl *Society* 24:13-18 Ja/F '87

Butler, Jonathan
> *about*

South Africa's Jonathan Butler finds a new home in pop music. S. Dougherty. il pors *People Wkly* 28:97-8+ N 23 '87

Butler, Octavia E.
The evening and the morning and the night [fiction] il *Omni* 9:56-8+ My '87
> *about*

Word star. P. A. Carter. por *Essence* 18:34 S '87

Butler, Richard
> *about*

NCC officials put dispute on hold. J. C. Lyles. *Christ Century* 104:1021-2 N 18 '87

Butler, Robert N.
> *about*

"Medicare must be rewritten, now!". E. Kiester. il por *50 Plus* 27:30-2+ Ja '87

Butler, Smedley D. (Smedley Darlington), 1881-1940
> *about*

Ollie and Old Gimlet Eye. G. C. Ward. il *Am Herit* 38:14+ N '87

Butler, Steven
Vietnam has a new agenda. *World Press Rev* 34:39 Je '87

Butler, Sydney J.
about
Butler new Conservation head. por *Wilderness* 51:3 Fall '87

Butler, Victoria
Arch foe of apartheid. por *Read Dig* 130:157-62 Mr '87

Butlers
Anecdotes, facetiae, satire, etc.
Almost Jeeves [hunting for a job as butler in the Hamptons] M. Kenyon. il *Gourmet* 47:64+ Jl '87

Butler's tables *See* Tables

Butoh
See also
Dai Rakuda Kan (Dance company)
Sankai Juku (Dance company)
Butoh: dance of darkness. M. Loke. il *N Y Times Mag* p40-1+ N 1 '87

Butowsky, Harry A.
The Dryden Flight Research Facility. il *Space World* X-8-284:34-5 Ag '87
The Lyndon B. Johnson Space Center. il *Space World* X-11-287:19-20 N '87
The National Space Technology Laboratories. il *Space World* X-9-285:34-5 S '87

Butter
See also
Fruit butter
Peanut butter
Flavored butters. il *Gourmet* 47:182 F '87
Stick-to-your-mouth sun butter [sunflower seed butter] il *Sunset* 178:230 Ap '87

Butterfield, Fox
Are Asian-American kids really smarter? il *Read Dig* 130:87-90 Ja '87

Butterfield, Paul, 1942-1987
about
Obituary
Esquire il por 108:35-6 O '87. P. Moffitt
Roll Stone il pors p25 Je 18 '87

Butterflies
See also
Caterpillars
Our mysterious monarchs. il *Sunset* 178:128 Ja '87
Migration
Flight of the butterflies [monarch butterfly sanctuary in El Rosario, Mexico is open to visitors] P. Primack. il *Travel Holiday* 168:96 N '87
Guarding the monarch's kingdom [Mexico's plan to protect butterfly's wintering grounds; cover story] S. Sullivan. il map *Int Wildl* 17:4-11 N/D '87
Mass meeting on the Coast [monarch butterflies in Calif.] D. Ackerman. il *Life* 10:21+ My '87
Photographs and photography
The curious case of the flying fish [fish butterfly] il *Sea Front* 33:373 S/O '87

Butterflies, Attracting of
Butterflies: nature's music on the wing. S. Bender. il *South Living* 22:56+ Je '87
Welcome butterflies. D. A. Jimerson. il *Better Homes Gard* 65:104-7 Mr '87

Butterfly plaques *See* Plaques and plaquettes

Buttery, Thomas J.
Helping biracial children adjust. *Educ Dig* 52:38-41 My '87

Buttner, Joseph K.
Aquaculture: food for thought. *BioScience* 37:308 My '87

Buttocks exercises *See* Exercise

Buttons
Collectors and collecting
Unusual buttons of the past. B. Manas. il *Antiques Collect Hobbies* 92:60-1 O '87

Butwin, David
Baseball flannels are hot. il por *Sports Illus* 67:105 Jl 6 '87
Five new ways to sail the seven seas. il *Esquire* 107:20+ Ja '87

Butyric acid
See also
Aminobutyric acid

Buus, Soren, and others
The relation between major histocompatibility complex (MHC) restriction and the capacity of Ia to bind immunogenic peptides. bibl f il *Science* 235:1353-8 Mr 13 '87

Buxbaum, Robert E., and others
F-actin and microtubule suspensions as indeterminate fluids. bibl f il *Science* 235:1511-14 Mr 20 '87

Buxton, Jennifer
On becoming a writer. il *Seventeen* 46:89+ N '87

Buybacks (Stocks) *See* Stocks—Repurchase

Buyer protection *See* Consumer protection

BuyerGraphics research *See* Single-source research (TV audience research)

Buying *See* Compulsive shopping; Consumption (Economics); Purchasing, Household; Shopping and shoppers

Buying power *See* Income

Buyouts, Leveraged *See* Leveraged buyouts

Buzzards
See also
Turkey vultures

By-the-wind sailor (Hydrozoa)
The by-the-wind sailor: a masterpiece of natural design. S. Brownlee. il *Discover* 8:46 Ag '87

Byatt, A. S. (Antonia Susan), 1936-
Sugar [story] *New Yorker* 62:28-38+ Ja 12 '87

Byatt, Antonia Susan *See* Byatt, A. S. (Antonia Susan), 1936-

Bychkov, Semyon
about
Bychkov's stirring Shostakovich. R. Freed. por *Stereo Rev* 52:87-8 S '87

Byer, Robert L.
(jt. auth) See Faris, Gregory W., and Byer, Robert L.

Byers, John A.
Why the deer and the antelope play. il *Nat Hist* 96:54-61 My '87

Byers, Peggy
Bright, varied, berried barberries pep up your landscape. il *Flower Gard* 31:16+ F/Mr '87
Integrate ravishing irises [cover story] il *Flower Gard* 31:44-5+ Je/Jl '87
Layering: a sure way to increase your shrubs and vines. il *Flower Gard* 31:93-4 Ap/My '87

Byers, S. H. M.
How men feel in battle. il *Am Hist Illus* 22:10-17 Ap '87

Byers, T. J.
Testing semiconductors (I). il *Radio-Electron* 58:58-60+ F '87
Testing semiconductors (II). il *Radio-Electron* 58:71-2+ Mr '87
Testing semiconductors (III). il *Radio-Electron* 58:62-4+ Ap '87
Testing semiconductors (IV). il *Radio-Electron* 58:59-61 My '87
Testing semiconductors (V). il *Radio-Electron* 58:61-3+ Je '87
Testing semiconductors (VI). il *Radio-Electron* 58:61-3 S '87
Testing semiconductors (VII). il *Radio-Electron* 58:115-17+ N '87

Byline (Desktop publishing program) *See* Desktop publishing—Programming

Bylinsky, Gene
The high tech race: computers and chips. *Current* 291:17-20 Mr/Ap '87

Bypass surgery, Coronary *See* Heart—Surgery

Byrd, Charles
about
Calif.'s first black-elected sheriff: humble and proud. por *Jet* 71:30 F 23 '87

Byrd, Deborah
The sun, moon, and planets this month. See issues of Sky and Telescope beginning August 1985
about
A Texan with stars in her eyes. D. Young. il por *South Living* 22:94 D '87

Byrd, Robert C.
Should the Boren Amendment approach to curtailing PAC's be adopted? [excerpts from debate, August 11, 1986] *Congr Dig* 66:40+ F '87
Should the Byrd-Warner Amendment be adopted? [excerpts from debate, October 21, 1987] *Congr Dig* 66:304 D '87
about
Bob and Jim play a duet. G. Hackett. il pors *Newsweek* 109:29 F 9 '87
Byrd's new image. il por *Newsweek* 109:7 Ja 19 '87

Byrne, David
about
Are four Heads better than one? D. Handelman. il por *Roll Stone* p34-6+ Ja 15 '87
Start making sense. C. Coulson. *New Repub* 196:26+ Mr 23 '87

Byrne, David—about—*cont.*
True stories [film] Reviews
   Progressive il 51:36-7 Ja '87. P. Aufderheide
Byrne, Harry J.
Church, state and foster-care children. *America* 157:38-41
   Jl 18-25 '87
Byrne, Jane, 1934-
about
Chicago's two solitudes. I. Austen. il pors *Macleans*
   100:16 Mr 2 '87
A rematch in the Windy City. M. Bosc. il pors *U
   S News World Rep* 102:20 F 23 '87
Byrne, John H.
(jt. auth) See Scholz, Kenneth P., and Byrne, John H.
Byrne, Katharine
Greek: who needs it? il *America* 156:52-4 Ja 24 '87
Byron, Ellen
Priscilla Presley just gets more gorgeous [interview] il
   pors *Redbook* 168:8+ Ja '87
Byron, Louise
about
N.Y. woman attacks ex-judge in dispute over $482.
   il pors *Jet* 72:33 Ag 3 '87
Byron, William J.
Needed: a new educational partnership between govern-
   ment and families. *America* 156:460-2+ Je 6 '87
Byte (Periodical)
The "B" word [benchmarks] F. Langa. *Byte* 12:6 D
   '87
Byte gets ready for 1988. P. Lemmons. il *Byte* 12:6
   N '87
The Byte subscriber now. P. Lemmons. *Byte* 12:6 Jl
   '87

C

C (Computer language)
Advantage C + + and Guidelines C + +. M. Mallett.
   il *Byte* 12:229-30+ O '87
A C interface. D. F. Ridgway. il *Byte* 12:363-4+ N
   '87
Four C language interpreters [Run/C, Run/C Professional,
   C-terp, and Instant-C] J. Unger. il *Byte* 12:245-8+
   Je '87
The great C compiler war. J. Pournelle. *Byte* 12:264
   O '87
High C 386. M. Trask. il *Byte* 12:196+ N '87
Installing memory-resident programs with C [to extend
   DOS] B. Edginton. il *Byte* 12:129-32+ Mr '87
Macintosh C compilers revisited. J. W. West. il *Byte*
   12:219-24 Ag '87
Microsoft's two new versions of C. il *Byte* 12:45 Jl
   '87
MIX C compiler, editor, debugger. il *Radio-Electron*
   58 ComputerDigest:94 N '87
MPW compiler lets Mac II's 68020 shine. il *Byte* 12:109
   N '87
Natural-language processing in C. H. Schildt. il *Byte*
   12:269-70+ D '87
Pull-down menus in C. J. L. Pinson. il *Byte* 12:108-10+
   My '87
Reviewer's notebook [Borland's Turbo C] D. Betz. il
   Byte 12:198 Ag '87
Reviewer's notebook [MetaWare's High C compiler and
   Phar Lap Software's assembler package for 80386
   machines] R. Grehan. *Byte* 12:201 Ap '87
Reviewer's notebook [Microsoft's Quick C] D. Betz. il
   Byte 12:236 S '87
Stack machines and compiler design: the Novix CPU's
   FORTH instruction set and the design of a C compiler.
   D. L. Miller. bibl il *Byte* 12:177-8+ Ap '87
Three C language screen-utility packages for PCs [Win-
   dows for Data, C-Worthy, and Vitamin C.] J. Robie.
   il *Byte* 12:223-4+ O '87
C-5 airplanes *See* Airplanes, Military transport
C-5B airplanes *See* Airplanes, Military transport
C-17 airplanes *See* Airplanes, Military transport
C-130 airplanes *See* Airplanes, Military transport
C. F. Mueller & Co.
Adviser beware: cooked books may burn you, too [invest-
   ment bankers face fraud charges in CPC International's
   suit against McKesson and Morgan Stanley over sale
   of C. F. Mueller] L. J. Tell. il *Bus Week* p58+ O
   26 '87

C.O.M.B. Co.
One home for two home shoppers? [Home Shopping
   Network's bid for COMB and its Cable Value Network]
   G. DeGeorge. *Bus Week* p34-5 F 2 '87
**C^3I (Command, control, communications and intelligence
network)** *See* Communications, Military
Cab drivers *See* Taxicab drivers
Cabaniss, Nabers
about
The future of federal family-planning programs [interview]
   il por *Christ Today* 31:42-3 O 16 '87
Cabaret [musical] See Musicals, revues,
   etc.—Reviews—Single works
Cabbage Patch dolls *See* Dolls
Cabbages
See also
   Cooking—Vegetables
Diseases and pests
Cabbageworms. W. S. Moore. il *Flower Gard* 31:27 Ap/My
   '87
Cabernet Sauvignon (Wine) *See* Wine
Cabeza Prieta National Wildlife Refuge (Ariz.) *See* Wildlife
   sanctuaries—Arizona
Cabinet (Canada) *See* Canada. Cabinet
Cabinet (U.S.) *See* United States. Cabinet
Cabinetmakers
See also
   Chipman, John, fl. ca. 1770-1790
   Courtenay, Hercules
   Furness, Frank, 1839-1912
   Phyfe, Duncan, 1768-1854
   Seymour, John, ca. 1738-1818
Cabinets (Furniture)
See also
   Kitchen cabinets
   Vanities (Furniture)
Build-in a video corner. M. Brett. il *Pop Sci* 231:76-7
   D '87
Child's hutch. V. Stout. il *Workbench* 43:35-6 My/Je
   '87
Classic furniture series [Lincoln corner cabinet] D. A.
   Warren. il *Workbench* 43:26-34 S/O '87
Decorator wall cabinet. J. Olivari. il *Workbench* 43:26-7
   Jl/Ag '87
English country [reproduction of washstand] H. Wicks.
   il *Home Mech* 83:64-8 Mr '87
Living with TV-video. D. L. Caringer. il *Better Homes
   Gard* 65:55-61 Ja '87
Piece-keeper: an easy-to-build small-parts cabinet. R.
   Capotosto. il *Pop Mech* 164:142-4+ Jl '87
Storage dividers—two easy-to-build styles. A. W. Lees.
   il *Pop Sci* 230:95-7 F '87
Cabins
See also
   Log cabins, houses, etc.
A cottage of sticks and stones [reprint from February
   1982 issue] il *South Living* 22:124 Je '87
Cabins, Airplane *See* Airplanes, Jet—Cabins
Cabins, Spaceplane *See* Spaceplane—Cabins
Cable cars *See* Cable railroads
Cable News Network
CNN. C. Capuzzi. il *Channels* 7:44-5 O '87
Fast talk [CNN debate with Rep. J. Howard on 55-mph
   speed limit] R. Ceppos. il *Car Driv* 33:26-7 Jl '87
Fox and the hounds [reporting on Fox Broadcasting]
   L. Brown. il *Channels* 7:18 Ja '87
Cable railroads
History
The bells still toll for San Francisco's hills. B. C. Lewis.
   il *Am Hist Illus* 22:36-43 Ap '87
Cable television
See also
   Aged in cable television
   Cable Value Network
   Disney Channel
   Heritage Communications, Inc.
   Home Box Office
   Lifetime (Firm)
   Multichannel multipoint distribution service
   Network Productions Inc.
   Prime Cable Corporation
   Tele-Communications, Inc.
   Turner Broadcasting System, Inc.
   United Artists Communications, Inc.
   Viacom International Inc.
   Warner Amex Cable Communications Inc.
   Women in cable television
Cable. il *Channels* 7:42 Je '87
Cable TV [cover story; special section] il *Consum Rep*
   52:547-55 S '87
Cable-TV channels. il *Consum Rep* 52:337-41 D '87

Cable television—*cont.*

Great expectations: one more time [pay cable networks] R. Zahradnik. il *Channels* 7 Sp Issue:117-18 D '87

The importance of being patient [views of consultant P. Bortz] M. Brown. il *Channels* 7:22 O '87

A new high profile for cable's basic strengths [basic networks] L. Ballard. il *Channels* 7 Sp Issue:107-9 D '87

Opportunities abound on PBS and cable [miniseries and movies based on novels] L. See. *Publ Wkly* 231:30 Ap 3 '87

The rap on cable [special section; with editorial comment by Les Brown] il *Channels* 7:45-56 My '87

A rosy future, but proceed with caution. C. Capuzzi. il *Channels* 7 Sp Issue:100-1 D '87

SMATV keeps its niche [satellite master antenna television] M. Burgi. il *Channels* 7 Sp Issue:104 D '87

Waging the battle for ultimate consumer comfort [pay per view] A. Breznick. *Channels* 7 Sp Issue:121 D '87

Young and impulsive [pay per view] P. E. Bauer. il *Channels* 7:50-1 My '87

Acquisitions and mergers

Coveting thy neighbor's system. J. Vitale. il *Channels* 7 Sp Issue:51 D '87

Is NBC getting hooked up to cable? [deal with Disney Channel and Turner Broadcasting] D. Lieberman. il por *Bus Week* p73 D 28 '87-Ja 4 '88

The unimportance of being earners [Heritage Communications] J. Baker. il map *Channels* 7:51-6 Mr '87

What a performance [sale of United Artists Communications to Tele-Communications and spinoff of Todd-AO] A. B. Block. il *Forbes* 139:136 Ap 6 '87

Where the deals still dazzle. M. Ivey. il *Bus Week* p42-3 F 23 '87

Agricultural programs

Farm news from the sky [satellite TV] G. Vincent. il *Success Farm* 85:64 O '87

Antitrust cases

Feds pursue cable antitrust probe. S. Behrens. *Channels* 7:11 Je '87

Blues music

Black stars gather to pay dues to blues on Cinemax. *Jet* 72:64 Jl 6 '87

Children's programs

See also
Nickelodeon (Firm)

Those who want to clean up TV face a real challenge in cable's slop-happy kids' show, Double dare. il *People Wkly* 28:135 O 19 '87

Comedy programs

Ranting, raving, doing the dishes. R. Zoglin. il *Time* 129:88-9 Ap 27 '87

Copyright

See Copyright—Broadcasting rights

Do-it-yourself programs

Do-it-yourself TV. J. R. Provey. il *Home Mech* 83:1 My '87

Ethical aspects

A decade later, cable's 'rented' citizens cash in [offers of shares to prominent local citizens] J. Vitale. il *Channels* 7:9 My '87

Finance

Hooking up to a cable-TV limited partnership. M. Ivey. il *Bus Week* p152 Je 8 '87

The stuff of dreams [pay-per-view] J. A. Conway. il *Forbes* 139:8 Je 1 '87

Financial programs

The ratings game pinches the beguiling gurus of get-rich TV. il *Money* 16:13-14 Ja '87

Government use

The first decade of the TV MPs [Canada's House of Commons] G. Bain. il *Macleans* 100:56 O 19 '87

Laws and regulations

Cable's dereg dilemma. M. Brown. il *Channels* 7:22 Ja '87

The elusive compromise [must-carry rules] C. Capuzzi. il *Channels* 7:51-3 Ja '87

Fear and loathing in Palo Alto [lawsuit over franchises] L. Ballard. *Channels* 7:15 Jl/Ag '87

Is the blue sky falling? C. Capuzzi. il *Channels* 7:46-8 My '87

Must-carry's poster children [effect of regulation on independent WTZA-TV, Hudson Valley, N.Y.] C. Capuzzi. *Channels* 7:17 Ja '87

Management

Cable's ten to watch. il *Channels* 7:52-4 My '87

Marketing

Coming soon to a cable company near you [pay-per-view channels] M. Ivey and others. il *Bus Week* p55 Ag 31 '87

Starting over in Dallas. C. Capuzzi. il *Channels* 7:23-4 Jl/Ag '87

The unplugged city: the story of New York cable is a model municipal mess. P. Blauner. il map *N Y* 20:36-42 Jl 20 '87

Motion pictures

See also
American Movie Classics (Firm)

News

See also
Cable News Network
Canadian Cable News Network
News 12 Long Island (Television channel)

Activists take to the airwaves [More than the news produced in Ithaca, N.Y.] M. Schultz. il *Progressive* 51:13 S '87

News, influence and propaganda [application by the CBC for license to operate on cable an all-news-and-public-affairs channel] G. Bain. il *Macleans* 100:45 S 21 '87

Programming

Cable TV's journey from promised land to wasteland. M. Ivey. il *Bus Week* p39 S 14 '87

Cable's other calendar [fall season] C. Capuzzi. il *Channels* 7:56 S '87

Cable's strange bedfellows. M. Brown. il *Channels* 7:24 F '87

Who needs friends? [off-network series going to cable] L. Brown. il *Channels* 7:20 O '87

Rates

Cable's dereg dilemma. M. Brown. il *Channels* 7:22 Ja '87

Real estate programs

For TV gurus, the new game is self-help [retreat from real estate] C. Friday and J. B. Copeland. il *Newsweek* 109:54+ My 11 '87

Religious programs

See also
Trinity Broadcasting Network

'Farbrengen' my baby back home [cablecast of Lubavitcher gatherings] M. Pally. il por *Film Comment* 23:75-7 My/Je '87

Rock music

See also
MTV Networks Inc.

Securities

1987: for cable and radio it was a breathtaking year. M. Brown. il *Channels* 7 Sp Issue:42+ D '87

A decade later, cable's 'rented' citizens cash in [offers of shares to prominent local citizens] J. Vitale. il *Channels* 7:9 My '87

Self help programs

For TV gurus, the new game is self-help [retreat from real estate] C. Friday and J. B. Copeland. il *Newsweek* 109:54+ My 11 '87

Shopping services

See Electronic shopping

Sports

See also
Entertainment and Sports Programming Network

The cable crisis, part II [baseball broadcasts on superstations] D. Kaplan. il *Sport Mag* 78:20 Ag '87

Cable's Mr. Capable [interviewer R. Firestone] W. Taaffe. il por *Sports Illus* 66:77 F 23 '87

Unlike his hairline, Dick Vitale's persona has never sounded retreat [basketball broadcaster] R. Novak. il pors *People Wkly* 27:104-6 Mr 16 '87

Terminology

Understanding CATV lingo. il *Radio-Electron* 58:12 Mr '87

Unauthorized use

The General [General Instrument buys Video Cipher from M/A-Com] A. B. Block. il *Forbes* 139:38-9 Je 29 '87

Pay TV's descrambling wars [suit against Network Productions Inc.] C. Gerber. *Channels* 7:11 Je '87

Practical descrambling [M/A-COM scrambling system has been breached] B. Cooper, Jr. il *Radio-Electron* 58:83-4 F '87

Tri-mode cable-TV scrambling. J. Coffell. il *Radio-Electron* 58:43-7+ F '87

TV signal descrambling (VII). W. Sheets and R. F. Graf. il *Radio-Electron* 58:53-6 Ja '87

TV signal descrambling (VIII). W. Sheets and R. F. Graf. il *Radio-Electron* 58:63-5 Mr '87

TV signal descrambling (IX). W. Sheets and R. F. Graf. il *Radio-Electron* 58:58-61+ Jl '87

Cable television—Unauthorized use—*cont.*
Videocipher has been cracked. B. Cooper, Jr. il *Radio-Electron* 58:4+ Ja '87
What's next? [home-dish industry] B. Cooper, Jr. il *Radio-Electron* 58:74-5 D '87
Why Videocipher is dead. B. Cooper, Jr. il *Radio-Electron* 58:78-9 Mr '87
The ZITS fraud [VideoCipher descrambling chip] B. Cooper, Jr. il *Radio-Electron* 58:76-7+ Je '87
Zombies, ZITS, and zoweee! B. Cooper, Jr. il *Radio-Electron* 58:77-8+ My '87
Weather forecasts
See also
Weather Channel
Belize
A suburb of Chicago. S. Donziger. il *Progressive* 51:31 Mr '87
Canada
See also
Canadian Cable News Network
Rogers Communications Inc.
The contest for cable. P. Young. il *Macleans* 100:46 Ag 24 '87
The fight to rule the airwaves. M. Janigan. il *Macleans* 100:49-50 Jl 20 '87
New choices for channel-switchers. P. Young. il *Macleans* 100:58 D 14 '87
News, influence and propaganda [application by the CBC for license to operate on cable an all-news-and-public-affairs channel] G. Bain. il *Macleans* 100:45 S 21 '87
China
Guess what they watch in China on Sunday nights? [Y.-S. Kan's One world series] D. J. Yang. il *por Bus Week* p91 Ja 19 '87
Helping East meet West via TV, America's Yue-Sai Kan has become the most famous woman in China. S. K. Reed. il pors *People Wkly* 27:123-4 My 18 '87
Eastern Europe
Satellite TV transcends the Curtain. S. Masterman. il *World Press Rev* 34:54 Je '87
United States
See Cable television
Cable television, Black
See also
Barden Cablevision
Black Entertainment Television
Cable television and politics
Campaign '88 makes a cable connection. R. Fly and F. Seghers. il *Bus Week* p74 N 23 '87
Cable television in counseling
On the sunny side of 50, pop psychologist Sonya Friedman has legs as talk cable's new queen. S. Toepfer. il pors *People Wkly* 28:75-6 N 16 '87
Cable television satellites *See* Communications satellites—Television broadcasting use
Cable Value Network
One home for two home shoppers? [Home Shopping Network's bid for COMB and its Cable Value Network] G. DeGeorge. *Bus Week* p34-5 F 2 '87
Cables
See also
Electric cables
Telephone cables
Cables, Submarine
Fiber-optic feeding frenzy [telephone cables attacked by sharks] *Time* 129:77 Je 22 '87
London calling, on a beam of light [fiber optic telephone cables under the Atlantic Ocean] S. Koepp. map *Time* 129:52 Ja 19 '87
Why the shark bites [underwater telephone cables] B. D. Stutz. *Nat Hist* 96:94+ N '87
Cabo San Lucas (Mexico)
Description
"The world's greatest fish trap". M. Beauchamp and K. K. Wiegner. il *Forbes* 140:182-3+ S 21 '87
Cabot, Laurie
about
Salem's official witch, Laurie Cabot, finds grave errors in Eastwick. C. Neuhaus. il por *People Wkly* 27:52-3 Je 29 '87
Cabrera, Clotilde Helen
about
Black first runner-up in 1987 Miss USA Pageant. il pors *Jet* 71:36 Mr 9 '87
Cabrillo, Juan Rodríguez, d. 1543
about
Monument to a discoverer? B. McGinty. il *Am Hist Illus* 22:38-41 O '87

Cabrillo Slavonic Chorus
Rachmaninoff's lost chords [A. Antolini's quest for church choral piece] D. Neff. il pors *Christ Today* 31:63-4 D 11 '87
Cacaci, Joe
about
Old business [drama] Reviews
N Y 20:116-17 N 23 '87. J. Simon
Self defense [drama] Reviews
N Y 20:63 Jl 13 '87. J. Simon
New Yorker 63:68-9 Je 29 '87. M. Kramer
Caccavale, Ruth Wilford
(jt. auth) See Safford, Frances Gruber, and Caccavale, Ruth Wilford
Cache memory (Computers) *See* Computers—Memory systems
Cachectin
Tumor necrosis factor (cachectin) as an essential mediator in murine cerebral malaria. G. E. Grau and others. bibl f il *Science* 237:1210-12 S 4 '87
Cachepots
Paris cache pot decorated to fool the eye. S. Bagdade and A. Bagdade. il *Antiques Collect Hobbies* 92:39 Jl '87
Cachie, Albert E.
about
Breaking the crack murders. R. Rosenbaum. il *N Y Times Mag* p44-6+ N 15 '87
Crack murder: a detective story. R. Rosenbaum. il pors *N Y Times Mag* p24-30+ F 15 '87
Cacho, Emilie
about
In search of self. M. Rochlin. il pors *Ms* 16:58-60 N '87
Cactus
See also
Christmas cactus
Prickly pears
The saguaro cactus. F. Turner. il *Ctry J* 14:31-4+ Ag '87
Theft
Cactus rustlers. L. Frazer. il *Sierra* 72:15-16 Mr/Ap '87
The cactus snatchers. il *Time* 130:79 N 30 '87
A purloined saguaro is recovered, replanted. il *Audubon* 89:20 Jl '87
Cactus rustlers *See* Cactus—Theft
CAD (Computer-aided design) *See* Computer graphics
Cadang-cadang, Coconut *See* Palms—Diseases and pests
Cadavers *See* Dead bodies
Caddell, Patrick
about
Caddell's defeat. il por *Newsweek* 110:9 O 5 '87
Joe Biden's 'petulant genius'. H. Rainie. il por *U S News World Rep* 103:25 S 21 '87
The powers that shouldn't be: five Washington insiders the next Democratic president shouldn't hire [cover story] P. Glastris. pors *Wash Mon* 19:39-46+ O '87
Caddies (Golf)
Golf carts 'killing' caddies and blacks on PGA tour [views of C. Peete] por *Jet* 71:46 Ja 26 '87
Turning Tom around [B. Edwards, T. Watson's caddie] J. Diaz. il *Sports Illus* 66:25 Je 29 '87
Caddisflies (Fishing lures) *See* Fishing lures, flies, etc.
Cade, Henry
about
Henry Cade named new Pharmacy Board prexy. por *Jet* 72:14 Jl 13 '87
Cade, Mossy
about
Packers' Cade is found guilty of raping aunt. il por *Jet* 72:33 Ag 17 '87
Packers win one, lose one in Green Bay sex cases. il pors *Jet* 72:49 Je 15 '87
Cadenhead, Kenneth
Reading level: a metaphor that shapes practice. bibl f il *Phi Delta Kappan* 68:436-41 F '87
Cadets
See also
Black cadets
Cadigan, Pat
Patterns [fiction] il *Omni* 9:68-70+ Ag '87
Cadillac Motor Car Division
Allanté: slow off the mark. J. Flint. il *Forbes* 140:204 N 30 '87
Can Cadillac come back? M. Keller. il *Mot Trend* 39:146-7 My '87
"A delicate subject" [Cadillac Allante designed by Pininfarina rather than by GM Design Staff] R. Hutton. il *Car Driv* 32:85 Mr '87

Cadillac Motor Car Division—*cont.*
Pininfarina heads for the U.S. in a Caddy [Allante] W. C. Symonds. il por *Bus Week* p58-9 F 9 '87
Thinking big. D. Seligman. il *Fortune* 115:115+ My 25 '87

Cadillacs (Musical group)
Doo-wop. *New Yorker* 63:27-8 Mr 2 '87

Cadmium
Historical coral [El Niño-Southern Oscillation events and cadmium levels in Galapagos coral; research by Glen T. Shen] *Sci News* 132:168 S 12 '87
Regulation in vitro of metallothionein gene binding factors. C. Seguin and D. H. Hamer. bibl f il *Science* 235:1383-7 Mr 13 '87

Cadmium in the body
High-cadmium diet: recipe for stress? [increased alcohol consumption in rats; research by Jack R. Nation and others] B. Bower. *Sci News* 132:101-2 Ag 15 '87

Cadmium poisoning
Cadmium: as bad as (or worse than) lead. M. Cala. *Home Mech* 83:58 O '87

Cadwallader, Sharon
Hacienda La Trinidad: artists' retreat near Guanajuato, Mexico. il *Archit Dig* 44:126-31 Ja '87

Cady, Marlene L. S.
"My Siamese twins have brought me joy". il *Redbook* 168:32+ F '87

Cady twins *See* Siamese twins

Caedmon Audio (Firm)
Caedmon put on the market. *Publ Wkly* 231:49 Mr 20 '87
Harper & Row purchases Caedmon. il *Publ Wkly* 231:52+ Je 5 '87
TDM, Caedmon end year-old distribution deal. *Publ Wkly* 231:50 Ap 24 '87

Caelum (Constellation) *See* Constellations

Caen, Herb
Odyssey by the bay: the San Francisco peregrinations of Herb Caen. il por *Archit Dig* 44:68-71+ Jl '87

Caenorhabditis elegans embryos *See* Embryology—Nematodes

Caenorhabditis elegans mutation *See* Mutation—Nematodes

Caesar, Adolph, d. 1986
about
Adolph Caesar estate worth $295,000 goes to wife, two daughters. il pors *Jet* 71:18 F 16 '87

Caesar, Julius, 100-44 B.C.
about
Julius Caesar and the Hereford world map. P. Wiseman. bibl il maps *Hist Today* 37:53-7 N '87

Caesar, Shirley
about
Shirley Caesar belts the gospel according to God and Grammy. K. Hubbard. il pors *People Wkly* 28:85-6 N 9 '87

Caesar cometary mission *See* Space flight—Cometary missions

Caesarea (Ancient city)
Herod the Great's city on the sea. R. L. Hohlfelder. il maps *Natl Geogr* 171:260-79 F '87
Herod's great harbour. A. Raban. il *Courier* 40:30-1 N '87

Caesarean section *See* Cesarean section

CAFE (Corporate Average Fuel Economy) standard *See* Automobile engines—Energy usage

Cafe au Go Go (New York, N.Y.: Nightclub) *See* New York (N.Y.)—Restaurants, nightclubs, bars, etc.

Cafe Beaujolais (Mendocino, Calif.) *See* Mendocino (Calif.)—Restaurants, nightclubs, bars, etc.

Café Pastoral (Berkeley, Calif.) *See* Berkeley (Calif.)— Restaurants, nightclubs, bars, etc.

Cafes *See* Restaurants

Cafeterias

History
The Automat [New York City] N. Simon. il *N Y* 20:66-7 D 21-28 '87

Caffeine
Caffeine: another dietary dilemma? L. Hoppe. il *Better Homes Gard* 65:28 Ja '87
Caffeine jitters: some safety questions remain [cover story] C. Lecos. il *FDA Consum* 21:22-7 D '87/Ja '88
Caffeine jolt for ECT [work of C. Edward Coffey] J. Greenberg and B. Bower. *Sci News* 131:328 My 23 '87
Caffeine redeemed? P. Dranov. il *Health* 19:69-71 N '87
Decaf can benefit your bones [work of Linda K. Massey] il *Prevention* 39:8 My '87
Drug side effects or java jitters? [ciprofloxacin] D. D. Edwards. *Sci News* 132:255 O 17 '87

Caffrey, John M., and others
Mitogens and oncogenes can block the induction of specific voltage-gated ion channels. bibl f il *Science* 236:570-3 My 1 '87

Cagayan (Philippines: Province)
A military renaissance [Philippine Army's success against New People's Army] R. Laver. il *Macleans* 100:6+ Ja 26 '87

Cage, John
about
Jigs, japes and Joyce [Roaratorio, an Irish circus on Finnegans wake] J. Johnston. il *Art Am* 75:102-5 Ja '87

Cage, Nicolas
about
Nicolas Cage: it's no act. il pors *Teen* 31:50 Jl '87

La cage aux folles [musical] *See* Musicals, revues, etc.—Reviews—Single works

Cages
See also
Bird cages
Calf pens and sheds

Cagney, James, 1899-1986
about
Unforgettable Jimmy Cagney. R. Bellamy. il por *Read Dig* 130:107-11 My '87

Cagney & Lacey [television program] *See* Television program reviews—Single works

Cahalane, Thomas P.
about
Alienated Catholics Anonymous [interview] *America* 156:477-81 Je 13 '87

Cahan, Abraham, 1860-1951
about
Looking back to the 'Forward'. G. Tyler. il *New Leader* 70:9-10 Ap 20 '87

Cahawba site (Ala.) *See* Alabama—Antiquities

Cahill, Kevin M.
The university and revolution. *America* 157:77-8 Ag 15-22 '87

Cahill, Lisa Sowle
Divorced from experience. il *Commonweal* 114:171-6 Mr 27 '87
'A man is ethical only when life, as such, is sacred to him'. *America* 157:250+ O 17 '87
The Vatican document on bioethics: two responses. *America* 156:246-7 Mr 28 '87

Cahill, Michael O'Connell- *See* O'Connell-Cahill, Michael

Cahill, Spencer E.
The place of children in public life. il *USA Today (Periodical)* 115:87-9 Ja '87

Cahill, Tim
The Rolling stone interview: Stanley Kubrick. il *Roll Stone* p29-32+ Ag 27 '87

Cahn, Patricia, and Cahn, Robert
Coast of riches. il map *Natl Parks* 61:18-20 S/O '87

Cahn, Robert
Takeover at the Park Service. *Natl Parks* 61:53 Mr/Ap '87
Taking a count of threats. il *Natl Parks* 61:33-4 Jl/Ag '87
(jt. auth) See Cahn, Patricia, and Cahn, Robert

Cahouet, Frank V.
about
Mellon's turnaround man is racing the clock. M. Schroeder. il por *Bus Week* p146 S 14 '87

Cahuilla Indians
Eighteen holes at the oasis [proposed development of Agua Caliente land in the Indian Canyons] O. Redwine. il *Sierra* 72:83-4 N/D '87

Caillé, René, 1799-1838
Into the heart of Africa [excerpt from Journal d'un voyage à Temboctou et à Jenné] il *Courier* 40:35-6 Ap '87

Cain, Bill
Cities without crime. il *World Press Rev* 34:64 Je '87

Cain, Eugene
about
Eugene Cain: black men must help black youth. *Jet* 73:24 O 26 '87

Cain, Gordon
about
Leaning against the wind. J. Willoughby. il por *Forbes* 140:208+ Jl 13 '87

Cain, Stephen Alexis, and Adams, Gordon
Reagan's 1988 military budget. il *Bull At Sci* 43:50-2 Mr '87

Cain Chemical Inc.
Leaning against the wind. J. Willoughby. il por *Forbes* 140:208+ Jl 13 '87

Caine, Michael, 1933?-
about
The busiest actor in town [cover story] A. Richman. il pors *People Wkly* 27:104-6+ My 4 '87
Cairns, Scott
Acts [poem] *New Repub* 197:42 D 28 '87
Another song [poem] *New Repub* 197:41 O 12 '87
In praise of darkness [poem] *New Repub* 197:40 O 12 '87
Cairo (Egypt)
Historic houses, sites, etc.
Splendor in the dust [Al-Kahira district] J. Morris. il *Vogue* 177:348+ Mr '87
History
Cairo recalled [1940s] E. W. Said. il por *House Gard* 159:20+ Ap '87
Social conditions
Cairo's conflict between old and new. T. Ross. il *World Press Rev* 34:58-9 Mr '87
Cajun cooking *See* Cooking, Cajun
Cajun Craw-Tators *See* Potato chips
Cajun music
Allons danser. B. Sandmel. il *Atlantic* 260:88+ Jl '87
Cajuns *See* Acadians—Louisiana
Cake
See also
Brownies (Cake)
Cheesecake
Coffee cake
Cupcakes
Fruitcake
Gingerbread
Lloyd's Carrot Cake (Firm)
Cake mix magic: fast, fabulous goodies! A. Bailey. il *Parents* 62:185-6+ My '87
Christmas takes the cake [centerpiece cakes] S. West. il *Ladies Home J* 104:138-41+ D '87
Cooking with Jacques Pépin [orange vacherin Jeannette] J. Pépin. il *Gourmet* 48:169-71+ Je '87
Festive cakes and tortes. il *Better Homes Gard* 65:187-8 N '87
The fourth season at The Four Seasons. N. Hazelton. *Natl Rev* 39:51-2 D 31 '87
Great American cakes. B. Kafka. il *Gourmet* 47:88-9+ D '87
Have your cake—and no salt too [research by Virginia H. Holsinger] *Sci News* 131:361 Je 6 '87
Luscious valentine delight. il *McCalls* 114:170+ F '87
New variations on an old favorite [upside-down cakes] il *South Living* 22:100 Ja '87
Oregon sampler [blueberry tea cake] il *Good Housekeep* 205:196 D '87
The perfect cake. J. T. Hazard. il *Ladies Home J* 104:102-3+ My '87
Pound cake primer. F. Greenberg. il *Work Woman* 12:138 My '87
Quick and easy cakes [microwave] il *South Living* 22:200 My '87
Raspberries, mangoes, and meringue [torte] il *Sunset* 178:169 Je '87
Recipe of the week [double strawberry cake] il *Jet* 72:39 Je 15 '87
Rosemary Littman has the competition licked when it comes to making uncommon cakes. il por *People Wkly* 27:101 Mr 9 '87
Toasted almond cakes. il *Good Housekeep* 204:174 My '87
We've got to come up with a better name than bird seed cake. il *Sunset* 178:158 Mr '87
Willard Scott's favorite Christmas cake [excerpt from Willard Scott's All-American cookbook] il *Redbook* 170:18 D '87
You start by grinding the almonds [almond torte] il *Sunset* 179:174 D '87
Cake mixes
Cake mix magic: fast, fabulous goodies! A. Bailey. il *Parents* 62:185-6+ My '87
How to bake a cake in a microwave oven. il *Consum Rep* 52:330-1 Je '87
Cal-a-Vie (Vista, Calif.: Spa) *See* Health resorts, watering places, etc.—California
Calabro, Daniel
about
L.A. NAACP wants judge fired for 'nigger' slur. *Jet* 72:12 S 14 '87
Caladiums
Caladiums give landscapes a lift. C. W. Dunn. il *Flower Gard* 31:9+ Ap/My '87

Calamities *See* Disasters
Calcium
Isotopes
Calcium-41 concentration in terrestrial materials: prospects for dating of Pleistocene samples. W. Henning and others. bibl f il *Science* 236:725-7 My 8 '87
Calcium blocking agents
See also
Verapamil
Calcium in the body
See also
Hypercalcemia
The best calcium for your bones. G. Makeskey. *Prevention* 39:97-8+ F '87
The birth of the calcium business. J. Sherman. il *Work Woman* 12:46 Jl '87
Calcium/blood-pressure link confirmed. il *Prevention* 39:6+ Mr '87
Calcium. J. Kaplan. *Vogue* 177:174+ N '87
Calcium: a little dab'll do ya [EZ-Cal soft whip supplement] il *Prevention* 39:6 Ap '87
The calcium controversy: an expert warns that supplements are not the cure-all for dowager's hump [interview with B. L. Riggs] G. Breu. il pors *People Wkly* 27:69-70+ Ap 13 '87
The calcium craze. B. T. Hunter. il por *Consum Res Mag* 70:8-9 Ja '87
Calcium for steroid users. il *Prevention* 39:8+ Ja '87
Calcium ions may have their ups and downs [research by Michael Berridge] J. L. Marx. *Science* 238:616 O 30 '87
Calcium may take the pressure off pregnancy. *Prevention* 39:10 F '87
Calcium: now it's boxed, jarred, loafed and bottled. *Prevention* 39:75 Ag '87
Cellular and subcellular heterogeneity of $[Ca^{2+}]_i$ in single heart cells revealed by fura-2. W. G. Wier and others. bibl f il *Science* 235:325-8 Ja 16 '87
Decaf can benefit your bones [work of Linda K. Massey] il *Prevention* 39:8 My '87
Development of two types of calcium channels in cultured mammalian hippocampal neurons. Y. Yaari and others. bibl f il *Science* 235:680-2 F 6 '87
The dynamics of free calcium in dendritic spines in response to repetitive synaptic input. E. Gamble and C. Koch. bibl f il *Science* 236:1311-15 Je 5 '87
Effect of membrane potential changes on the calcium transient in single rat cardiac muscle cells. M. B. Cannell and others. bibl f il *Science* 238:1419-23 D 4 '87
A G protein directly regulates mammalian cardiac calcium channels. A. Yatani and others. bibl f il *Science* 238:1288-92 N 27 '87
Going crazy over calcium. A. Toufexis. il *Time* 129:88-9 F 23 '87
Good for the old bones [post-menopausal women] K. S. Zimmeth. il *Health* 19:16 F '87
High-calcium cookery. il *Health* 19:48-50+ O '87
How good are the new sources of calcium? il *Glamour* 85:91 Mr '87
Identification of an α subunit of dihydropyridine-sensitive brain calcium channels. M. Takahashi and W. A. Catterall. bibl f il *Science* 236:88-91 Ap 3 '87
No calcium fix [osteoporosis] *Sci Am* 256:72 Ap '87
Osteoporosis: most answers yet to come. J. Silberner. *Sci News* 131:116 F 21 '87
The osteoporosis protection plan from the National Institutes of Health. il *Prevention* 39:34+ Ag '87
Osteoporosis reexamined: complexity of bone biology is a challenge. B. J. Culliton. *Science* 235:833-4 F 20 '87
The personal you: calcium—how much is enough? [dancers] M. Horosko. il *Dance Mag* 61:78-9 Mr '87
Regional changes in calcium underlying contraction of single smooth muscle cells. D. A. Williams and others. bibl f il *Science* 235:1644-8 Mr 27 '87
Sodium-calcium exchange in heart: membrane currents and changes in $[Ca^{2+}]_i$. L. Barcenas-Ruiz and others. bibl f il *Science* 238:1720-2 D 18 '87
Teen-agers and the calcium crisis. P. Mann. il *Saturday Evening Post* 259:68-71 Ap '87
Three "half truths" about health. il *Glamour* 85:406 S '87
Calcium transport *See* Biological transport
Calculating machines *See* Calculators
Calculators
The latest show-offs in electronic gadgetry. S. Woolley. il *Bus Week* p204 N 2 '87
Aviation use
Battery-powered slide rules. N. Moll. il *Flying* 114:76 D '87

Calculators—*cont.*
Educational use
Let them use calculators [elementary school arithmetic] A. Ralston. il *Technol Rev* 90:30-1 Ag/S '87
Will calculators hurt math skills? F. Roberts. il *Parents* 62:50+ D '87
Investment use
Calculators that check your broker's math. D. H. Dunn. il *Bus Week* p126 S 21 '87
Calculi, Alimentary *See* Bezoars
Calculi, Biliary *See* Gallstones
Calculi, Urinary *See* Bladder stones; Kidney stones
Calculus
Study and teaching
Calculus reform: catching the wave? I. Peterson. il *Sci News* 132:317 N 14 '87
Why is calculus such a hurdle? J. Walsh. *Science* 238:749 N 6 '87
Calder, Alexander, 1898-1976
about
Some said Mary Mace had bats in her belfry, until she proved who made the toys in the basement. il por *People Wkly* 27:53 Ja 26 '87
Calderas *See* Craters
Calderón, Ricardo Arias *See* Arias Calderón, Ricardo
Calderone, Mary Steichen
about
A candid conversation with Dr. Mary Calderone. M. Fox. il por *Health* 19:75-6+ My '87
Caldwell, E. P.
about
Caldwell's curious contraptions. J. A. Wren. il *Road Track* 38:144 My '87
Caldwell, Erskine, 1903-1987
about
Obituary
  Natl Rev 39:21 My 8 '87
Caldwell, Lawrence T.
United States-Soviet relations and arms control. bibl f *Curr Hist* 86:305-8+ O '87
Caldwell, Sarah Ellison
Latin legacy in the City by the Bay. il *Américas* 39:44-9 N/D '87
Caldwell (Idaho)
Education
The prizes of first grade [incentive program at Lincoln School] P. Skreslet. por *Newsweek* 110:8 N 30 '87
Cale, David
about
The redthroats [drama] Reviews
  New Yorker 63:71 Jl 13 '87. M. Kramer
Calegari, Maria
about
Post-Balanchine breakthroughs. E. Kendall. pors *Vogue* 177:48 Je '87
Calendars
See also
Publishers and publishing—Calendars
1988 calendar update. il *Publ Wkly* 232:34 O 23 '87
1988 calendar update. il *Publ Wkly* 232:36-7 Jl 10 '87
1988 calendars. il *Publ Wkly* 231:35-6+ Ap 10 '87
Americana in calendars—1988. J. O'Dwyer. il *Americana* 15:24-5 N/D '87
Books [nature calendars] il *Conservationist* 41:53 Ja/F '87
California kids say their calendar poses no skin problem, but their school officials say it's unsuitable [student fund raising venture in Gilroy] il *People Wkly* 27:59 My 18 '87
Keeping up-to-date with the changing calendar market [photographic calendars] G. Schaub. il *Pop Photogr* 94:16 F '87
Nip-nose and freeze-toes. M. Reed. *Weatherwise* 40:344-5 D '87
Outstanding 1988 calendars. M. O'Koon. il *Good Housekeep* 205:242 N '87
Calero, Adolfo
about
The contra crack-up. M. Kondracke. *New Repub* 196:9-11 Mr 9 '87
The contras' little list. A. Nairn. il *Progressive* 51:24-6 Mr '87
The contras without Cruz? N. Cooper. il pors *Newsweek* 109:42 F 9 '87
Reinventing the contras. R. Watson. il pors *Newsweek* 109:32-4 Mr 2 '87
Calf pens and sheds
Portable calf hutch goes permanent. J. R. Borcherding and D. Wanner. il *Success Farm* 85 no3:D4-D5 F '87

Calgary (Alta.)
Climate
Confronting the warm winds of winter [chinook winds] H. Quinn. il *Macleans* 100:58 D 7 '87
Description
There's more to Calgary than the Winter Olympics. E. B. Terry. il *Bus Week* p203 N 2 '87
Festivals
See also
Olympic Arts Festival (1988: Calgary, Alta.)
Hotels, motels, etc.
No room at the inns [Winter Olympics] J. Howse. il *Macleans* 100:59 D 7 '87
Calgary Olympics, 1988 *See* Olympic Games—1988—Winter Olympics
Calgary Stampede *See* Rodeos—Canada
Calhoun, John
Where credit is due: the heads and tails of title design. il *Theatre Crafts* 21:79-82 Ag/S '87
Calibration
Misapplication: still a 'billion dollar blunder' [pesticides] *Success Farm* 85 no3:17 F '87
Calibrators
New calibrator tunes sprayer in 10 minutes. il *Success Farm* 85 no5:26F Mr '87
California
See also
Abortion clinics—California
Agriculture—California
Air pollution—California
Airports—California
Architecture—California
Architecture, Domestic—California
Art—California
Arts—California
Aviation—California
Beaches—California
Birds—California
Booksellers and bookselling—California
Camping—California
Camps—California
Central Valley (Calif.)
Coachella Valley (Calif.)
Colleges and universities—California
Contra Costa County (Calif.)
Country estates—California
Courts—California
Crime and criminals—California
Criminal justice, Administration of—California
Death Valley National Monument (Calif. and Nev.)
Earthquakes—California
Education—California
Educational laws and regulations—California
Environmental movement—California
Environmental policy—California
Express highways—California
Finance—California
Forests and forestry—California
Game laws—California
Gardens and gardening—California
Geology—California
Golden Gate National Recreation Area (Calif.)
Health resorts, watering places, etc.—California
Humboldt County (Calif.)
Hunting—California
Indian Canyons (Calif.)
Informed consent (Medical law)—California
Insurance law—California
Kings River (Calif.)
Kings River Canyon (Calif.)
Marin County (Calif.)
Mattole River (Calif.)
Medical care—California
Mendocino County (Calif.)
Merced River (Calif.)
Mono Lake (Calif.)
Monterey Bay (Calif.)
Monterey County (Calif.)
Monterey Peninsula (Calif.)
Motion picture festivals—California
Mount Shasta region (Calif.)
Music festivals—California
National parks and reserves—California
Natural areas—California
New River (Mexico and Calif.)
Orange County (Calif.)
Organic gardens and gardening—California
Point Reyes National Seashore (Calif.)
Prisons—California
Public welfare—California
Ranches—California

California—*See also*—*cont.*
Resorts—California
Roads—California
Sacramento River (Calif.)
San Francisco Bay (Calif.)
San Francisco Bay region (Calif.)
Santa Barbara County (Calif.)
Santa Clara County (Calif.)
Santa Margarita River (Calif.)
Santa Rosa Island (Calif.)
Savings and loan associations—California
Sequoia and King's Canyon National Park (Calif.)
Sierra Nevada Mountains (Calif. and Nev.)
Siskiyou County (Calif.)
Skis and skiing—California
Sonoma County (Calif.)
South Yuba River (Calif.)
Sports—California
Stanislaus River (Calif.)
Tahoe National Forest (Calif.)
Television festivals—California
Traffic regulations—California
Trails—California
Trials—California
Water pollution—California
Wetlands—California
Wilderness areas—California
Wildlife—California
Wildlife conservation—California
Wildlife sanctuaries—California
Yosemite National Park (Calif.)
Youth—California

Climate
Real-time landslide warning during heavy rainfall. D. K. Keefer and others. bibl f il map *Science* 238:921-5 N 13 '87

Description and travel
See also
Automobile touring—California
Cycling—California
Motorcycling—California
The American Riviera [southern California] R. Alleman. il *Vogue* 177:220+ My '87
California, here I come. T. Bethell. il *Natl Rev* 39:33-6 F 27 '87
Stop and smell the rosé [northern California wine tasting vacation; cover story] B. St. Pierre. il map *50 Plus* 27:31-8 Je '87

Discovery and exploration
Monument to a discoverer? [Santa Rosa Island stone linked to J. R. Cabrillo] B. McGinty. il *Am Hist Illus* 22:38-41 O '87

Fisheries
See Fisheries

Forest fires
See Forest fires

History
See also
De Anza College. California History Center

Industries
See also
Automobile industry
Gold mines and mining—California
Petroleum industry
Tourist trade—California
Wine industry

Legislature
Maxine Waters blocks controversial text in California legislature [racist charges levelled against The making of America] *Jet* 72:5 Ap 6 '87
Racism charge by Brown prompts Calif. gov. to probe new history text. *Jet* 71:28 Mr 23 '87

Missions
A question of faith in California [dispute over proposed sainthood for Father Junípero Serra] il *U S News World Rep* 102:24 My 11 '87
So you want to be a saint [Father N. F. Moholy's efforts to have J. Serra canonized] L. Gomez and W. Wynn. il pors *Life* 10:68-9+ S '87

Parks and reserves
Camping deep in the Humboldt redwoods. il map *Sunset* 179:42+ S '87
Checkbooks stop chainsaws [increasing size of Sinkyone Wilderness State Park] A. Alm. il *Sierra* 72:79-80 Mr/Ap '87
Contra Costa's cow country. il map *Sunset* 178:36+ Ja '87
A gold country Christmas [Columbia State Historic Park] N. R. Day. il map *Americana* 15:32-7 N/D '87

Jack London's "dream-ranch" . . . today a state park [Jack London State Historic Park] il map *Sunset* 178:10-11 F '87
Off the beaten path in blooming Anza-Borrego. il *Sunset* 178:60+ F '87
San Francisco's island mountain [San Bruno Mountain State and County Park] il *Sunset* 178:50+ F '87

Politics and government
See also
California—Legislature
Calif. educator makes bid for congressional seat [D. M. Ward] por *Jet* 72:9 Mr 30 '87
California, here I come. T. Bethell. il *Natl Rev* 39:33-6 F 27 '87
Can Pete Wilson keep his 'jinxed' Senate seat? R. Grover. il por *Bus Week* p70-2 D 14 '87
Glitz and gold: why candidates love California [top fund raising state] R. Grover. il *Bus Week* p147 Je 8 '87

Religious institutions and affairs
See also
Crystal Cathedral (Garden Grove, Calif.)
Matthew's Party
Clergy malpractice [suit over suicide of K. Nally] *Christ Century* 104:850 O 7 '87

Social conditions
Lotus Land isn't what it used to be [declining services] S. L. Hawkins. il *U S News World Rep* 103:23-4 O 19 '87

California. Air Resources Board
Jealousy [differences between California motorcycles and those sold in other states] P. Schilling. il *Cycle* 38:9 Jl '87

California. Dept. of Education. Reading Initiative *See* California Reading Initiative

California. Dept. of Fish and Game
Putting the sting on poachers [undercover agent K. Corey conducts sting operation on fish poachers] M. Tennesen. il *Natl Wildl* 25:26-8 O/N '87

California. Dept. of Motor Vehicles
It's a dirty job, but California's special DMV unit has to make sure that motorists clean their plates [offensive vanity plates] il *People* 28:69 Jl 13 '87

California. Division of Occupational Health and Safety
Worker safety comes under attack [plan to abolish agency] A. L. Huebner. *Progressive* 51:11-12 Jl '87

California. Task Force to Promote Self-Esteem, Personal and Social Responsibility
California esteemin'. *Harpers* 275:16 Ag '87
The esteem team. D. Seligman. *Fortune* 116:134+ S 14 '87
Okay, we make fun of California; now the state is putting money where its mouth is. Yikes! N. Faber. il por *People Wkly* 27:32+ Mr 2 '87
Pondering self-esteem. D. Gelman. il *Newsweek* 109:70 Mr 2 '87
Touchy-feely-dopey. D. Seligman. il *Fortune* 116:101 Jl 20 '87

California. University *See* University of California (System)
California, Gulf of (Mexico) *See* Gulf of California (Mexico)
California, Lower *See* Baja California (Mexico: Peninsula)
California Academy of Sciences. Natural History Museum
Gems, waterfowl in Golden Gate Park. il *Sunset* 179:15 N '87

California Child Care Initiative
California makes business a partner in day care. J. O. Hamilton. il *Bus Week* p100 Je 8 '87

California College of Arts and Crafts
Theory and practice. il *Horizon* 30:37 Ja/F '87

California Community Colleges
California college boss quits; blames red tape [chancellor J. L. Smith] *Jet* 72:38 S 14 '87

California Desert Conservation Area *See* Wilderness areas—California
California deserts *See* Deserts
California in art
Joseph Moure's California impressionist paintings [collector] I. Borger. il por *Archit Dig* 44:86+ Mr '87

California Institute of Technology
At witty Caltech, pranks aren't purely a laughing matter. J. Ellis. il *Smithsonian* 18:100-2+ S '87
What's right, what's wrong with U.S. science? [address, March 13, 1987] M. L. Goldberger. *Vital Speeches Day* 53:537-40 Je 15 '87

California Institution for Women (Chino Valley, Calif.)
See Prisons—California
California lottery winners *See* Lottery winners
California Microwave, Inc.
Companies testing Long-EZ derivative for unmanned aerial vehicle market [California Microwave CM-44 designed by Burt Rutan] W. B. Scott. il *Aviat Week Space Technol* 126:128+ Ap 27 '87

California Microwave, Inc.—*cont.*
A ride on Voyager's tail [drone aircraft designed by Burt Rutan] G. G. Marcial. *Bus Week* p117 Ja 12 '87

California Museum of Photography
Two American museums provide new homes for old cameras. E. S. Lothrop. il *Pop Photogr* 94:28 Ag '87

California Plaza (Los Angeles, Calif.) *See* Los Angeles (Calif.)—Plazas

California Reading Initiative
California plan puts quality children's books in supermarkets. M. Colin. *Publ Wkly* 232:28 O 30 '87

California tree poppies *See* Matilija poppies

California wines *See* Wine

Californians
A Californian's lament: the Raiders and Lakers are not laid-back, thank you. R. Fimrite. il por *Sports Illus* 66:108 Je 1 '87

La Calisto [opera] *See* Cavalli, Pier Francesco, 1602-1676

Call, Barbara
Six smart buys to boost productivity. il *Work Woman* 12:69 Ap '87

Calla lilies
Outdoors, indoors calla-lilies are spectacular. G. Taloumis. il *Flower Gard* 31:24+ F/Mr '87

Callahan, Daniel, 1930-
Letters [discussion of August 15-22, 1987 article, Limiting health care for the old] *Nation* 245:362+ O 10 '87
Limiting health care for the old [cover story] *Nation* 245:109+ Ag 15-22 '87
about
Examining the limits of life. B. Angelo. il por *Time* 130:76-7 N 2 '87

Callahan, Mary
Fighting for Tony [excerpt] il por *Ladies Home J* 104:66+ O '87

Callahan, Michael
about
Dispensing forgiveness and justice in equal measure, Father Mike Callahan is a man of the cloth and the law. S. K. Reed. il pors *People Wkly* 28:143-4+ D 7 '87

Callahan, Rick
"High" hurdle. il *Saturday Evening Post* 259:32-3 Jl/Ag '87

Callahan, Sidney
Lovemaking & babymaking. il *Commonweal* 114:233-9 Ap 24 '87

Callas, Maria, 1923-1977
about
A connoisseur's Callas. M. Scott. il pors *Opera News* 52:29-30+ S '87
Past masters. P. G. Davis. por *N Y* 20:64-6 Je 15 '87

Callaway Editions (Firm)
A remarkable book from the 'greatest painter of flowers' [publication of Georgia O'Keeffe: one hundred flowers] W. Goldstein. il *Publ Wkly* 232:27+ S 11 '87

Callendar, Newgate
Crime. See issues of The New York Times Book Review

Calleo, David P., 1934-
NATO's middle course. bibl f *Foreign Policy* 69:135-47 Wint '87/'88

Callister, Jerry P., and others
Profiling family preservation efforts in Utah. il *Child Today* 15:23-5+ N/D '86

Calloway, D. Wayne
The Noah principle and the public sector [address, January 29, 1987] *Vital Speeches Day* 53:357-60 Ap 1 '87
about
Wayne Calloway's nonstop cash machine. S. N. Chakravarty. il por *Forbes* 140:35-7 S 7 '87

Calls for animals *See* Animal calling

Calls for birds *See* Bird calling

Calls of birds *See* Birds—Song

Calluna *See* Heathers

Calman, Robert Frederick, 1932-
about
Men who moil for gold. H. Rudnitsky. il por *Forbes* 140:36-7 O 5 '87

Calmeadow Charitable Foundation
An investment in new hope [founder M. Connell] por *Macleans* 100:26-7 D 28 '87

Calmodulin
Fluorescence properties of calmodulin-binding peptides reflect alpha-helical periodicity. K. T. O'Neil and others. bibl f il *Science* 236:1454-6 Je 12 '87

Functional analysis of a complementary DNA for the 50-kilodalton subunit of calmodulin kinase II. R. M. Hanley and others. bibl f il *Science* 237:293-7 Jl 17 '87

Calories, Food
See also
Low calorie cooking
Can "lite" foods help you lose? D. Longobardi. il *Mademoiselle* 93:112 My '87
"Light" on the label: what does it mean? L. Hoppe. il *Better Homes Gard* 65:40 My '87

Calorimeters and calorimetry
The calorie room [USDA Energy and Protein Laboratory's Room Calorimeter] D. Starr. il *Health* 19:8 Ap '87

Calta, Marialisa
By the daunserly light. il *Read Dig* 130:167-8 F '87

Caltech *See* California Institute of Technology

Calves
Feeding
Added fat can help save calves. *Success Farm* 85:44 N '87
Put grain in stocker calves. G. Johnston. il *Success Farm* 85:7 My '87
Pens and sheds
See Calf pens and sheds

Calvet, Jacques
about
Europe: a battling bureaucrat. S. Tully. il por *Fortune* 116:86 N 9 '87
France's no-frills manager. S. Tully. il por *Fortune* 116:58 Ag 3 '87
Let them drive Peugeots. R. Morais. il por *Forbes* 139:153-4 My 18 '87

Calvi, Carlo
about
Following the money. J. Howse. il por *Macleans* 100:11 Jl 27 '87

Calvin Klein Industries
Calvin Klein: an obsession with perfection. A. Haden-Guest. il por *Harpers Bazaar* 120:178-85+ F '87

Calving
Calve heifers, then market them [single-calf heifer system] B. Eftink. il *Success Farm* 85:16-17 O '87

Calvino, Italo
about
The heirs of Calvino and the Eco effect. S. Perosa. il *N Y Times Book Rev* 92:1+ Ag 16 '87

Calypso music
Grenada
Grenada fights the calypso menace. *Newsweek* 110:38 Jl 27 '87

Calyx [dance] *See* Dance reviews—Single works

Camacho, Hector
about
You ready, Boom Boom? P. Putnam. il por *Sports Illus* 66:96 My 11 '87

Camargo Penteado, Sebastião Ferraz de
about
The man who built Brazil. J. Barham. il por *Fortune* 116:185 O 12 '87

Cambodia *See* Kampuchea

Cambodian Civil War, 1970-1975 *See* Kampuchea—History—Civil War, 1970-1975

Cambodians *See* Kampucheans

Cambrian & General Securities
Distressed merchandise. R. Phalon. por *Forbes* 139:180 Ap 6 '87

Cambrian period *See* Paleontology—Cambrian

Cambridge (Mass.)
Bookstores
See Booksellers and bookselling—Massachusetts
Galleries and museums
See also
Harvard University. Botanical Museum
Public health
Anecdotes, facetiae, satire, etc.
Smoke in Cambridge. R. Baker. il *N Y Times Mag* p26 Mr 29 '87
Stations
Interfacing cars and trains [Alewife subway station and garage] G. Anderson. il *Archit Rec* 175:72-5 Ja '87
Sculpture in the subways? Is there a better place for it? R. Wolkomir. il *Smithsonian* 18:114-18+ Ap '87
Theater
See also
Harvard University. American Repertory Theatre
Loeb Drama Center (Cambridge, Mass.)

Camcorders *See* Video cameras
Camdessus, Michel
>about
Michel Camdessus is making the IMF less of a Scrooge. M. McNamee. il *Bus Week* p36-7 O 5 '87
Camel Corps (U.S.) *See* United States. Army. Camel Corps
Camel drives
North to Cairo along the scorching Way of the Forty [camel drive from Sudan to Egypt] L. Werner. il map *Smithsonian* 17:120-4+ Mr '87
Camellias
Camellias for colder winters. M. H. Brown. il *Rodale's Org Gard* 34:56-9 D '87
The lure of the camellia. A. J. De Blasi. il *Flower Gard* 32:50-2 D '87/Ja '88
Now's the time to move a camellia. il *Sunset* 179:252 N '87
Camelopardalis (Constellation) *See* Constellations
Camels
>*See also*
>Llamas
>**Military use**
>*See also*
>United States. Army. Camel Corps
Cameo (Musical group)
Cameo! N. George. il *Essence* 18:54-5+ Jl '87
Cameo's black-rock breakthrough. M. Goldberg. il *Roll Stone* p18 Ja 15 '87
Cameos (New York, N.Y.: Restaurant) *See* New York (N.Y.)—Restaurants, nightclubs, bars, etc.
Camera bags, cases, etc.
Fitting much SLR into little space [Soligor small camera and accessory bag] H. Keppler. il *Pop Photogr* 94:74-5 S '87
A practical case [Camjacket system] K. Geller-Shinn. il *Petersens Photogr Mag* 16:12 My '87
Camera batteries *See* Electric batteries
Camera industry *See* Photographic industry
Camera lenses *See* Lenses, Photographic
Camera repairmen
Compare repair prices if they seem too high. H. Keppler. il *Pop Photogr* 94:80-1 S '87
Where to get your camera fixed. L. Nielsen and J. Wahman. il *Petersens Photogr Mag* 16:54-7 Jl '87
Camera shutters
>**Control**
A remote camera trigger for under $5! C. H. Hartley. il *Petersens Photogr Mag* 15:68-70 F '87
Camera stores
>*See also*
>Porter's Camera Store, Inc.
Camera supports
Other means of support: monopods, gunstocks, beanbags. J. Shaw. il *Pop Photogr* 94:62+ N '87
Thank you for your support: Cora's low-light photo tips. C. W. Kennedy. il *Pop Photogr* 94:24-5 My '87
Camera tripods
Bogen's amazing tripod system. K. Geller-Shinn. il *Petersens Photogr Mag* 15:10 F '87
Keppler's SLR world. H. Keppler. il *Pop Photogr* 94:76-7+ O '87
Possibilities of a "tetrapod" [tetrahedral tripod] D. Trott. il *Sky Telesc* 74:426-8 O '87
Supporting role. E. Stecker. il *Pop Photogr* 94:72-5 O '87
Three legs to stand on: tripods and field photography. J. Shaw. il *Pop Photogr* 94:32+ O '87
Cameramen, Television *See* Television cameramen
Cameras
>*See also*
>Eastman Kodak Co.
>Video cameras
Compact 35mm cameras [PMA Show] S. Pollock. il *Pop Photogr* 94:65-6 My '87
The debatable value of the disposable camera. A. Goldsmith. il *Pop Photogr* 94:22 Ag '87
Fuji and Kodak introduce disposable cameras. B. Hurter. il *Petersens Photogr Mag* 16:12 Je '87
How to build and use an all-sky camera. J. Charles and others. il *Astronomy* 15:64-70 Ap '87
Large format [PMA Show] B. Schwalberg. il *Pop Photogr* 94:71-2 My '87
Medium format [PMA Show] R. Hart. il *Pop Photogr* 94:70-1 My '87
Mobile image-makers [supercompact autofocus 35mm rangefinders] S. A. Booth. il *Pop Mech* 164:38+ Jl '87
Nikon Tele-Touch Deluxe. K. Geller-Shinn. il *Petersens Photogr Mag* 16:8 N '87
The smart new cameras [35mm] C. Begole. il *Better Homes Gard* 65:102 O '87

Snap it, scrap it [disposable cameras] il *Time* 129:50 Mr 2 '87
Snappy shooters [35mm cameras] S. A. Booth. il *Pop Mech* 164:106-8+ Ja '87
Super visions. S. A. Booth. il *Pop Mech* 164:80-2 Ja '87
Taming the Schmidt camera. R. Reeves and M. Hooley. il *Astronomy* 15:82-7 D '87
>**Care**
>*See* Cameras—Maintenance and repair
>**Collectors and collecting**
Fifty collectible cameras—an anniversary assortment. E. S. Lothrop. il *Pop Photogr* 94:30+ Ja '87
One shutterbug wears more than meets the eye [J. Naylor's collection; cover story] D. Stewart. il pors *Smithsonian* 18:108-12+ O '87
Practical classics [vintage 35mm cameras] B. Schwalberg. il *Pop Photogr* 94:22-9 Mr '87
>**Control**
>*See also*
>Camera shutters—Control
>**Design**
Are these the cameras of the future? [biodesign cameras by Luigi Colani] G. Schaub. il *Pop Photogr* 94:58-9 Ja '87
>**Equipment**
>*See* Photography—Equipment
>**Films**
>*See* Photography—Films
>**History**
50 innovations that changed the world. il *Pop Photogr* 94:52-7 Ja '87
Automatic acceptance: innovations should be embraced. N. Rothschild. il *Pop Photogr* 94:16 S '87
Fifty years of progress in camera and lens design. N. Goldberg. il *Pop Photogr* 94:16+ Ja '87
Flashback: five American-made subminiature cameras. E. S. Lothrop. il *Pop Photogr* 94:76 Ap '87
Paper, string, and leather disguised early cameras. E. S. Lothrop. il *Pop Photogr* 94:32 S '87
Some cameras take stage center, then fall on their baseplates. E. S. Lothrop. il *Pop Photogr* 94:30 Je '87
Street photography with almost-instant cameras. E. S. Lothrop. il *Pop Photogr* 94:58 D '87
>**Maintenance and repair**
>*See also*
>Camera repairmen
Clean machines. C. Gromer. il *Pop Mech* 164:111-13 Ja '87
Compare repair prices if they seem too high. H. Keppler. il *Pop Photogr* 94:80-1 S '87
How to get your camera fixed [recommendations by Marty Forscher] A. Schupack. il *Petersens Photogr Mag* 16:53 Jl '87
What to do when equipment doesn't seem to work. H. Keppler. il *Pop Photogr* 94:75 S '87
>**Mounting**
Experiments with a toothless sector. D. A. Harbour. il *Sky Telesc* 74:546-8 N '87
A portable photographic platform. W. G. Pursell. il *Astronomy* 15:91-3 Jl '87
>**Testing**
Compacts in action! Canon Sure Shot Tele. K. Geller-Shinn. il *Petersens Photogr Mag* 15:58-9 Mr '87
Compacts in action! Chinon Auto GX Tele and Splash AF. K. Geller-Shinn. il *Petersens Photogr Mag* 15:80-1 Ap '87
Compacts in action! Fuji DL-300. K. Geller-Shinn. il *Petersens Photogr Mag* 16:80-1 Je '87
Compacts in action! Minolta Freedom Dual. K. Geller-Shinn. il *Petersens Photogr Mag* 16:56+ O '87
Compacts in action! Minox 35 MB and 35 AL. K. Geller-Shinn. il *Petersens Photogr Mag* 16:60-1 S '87
Compacts in action! Nikon Fun-Touch. K. Geller-Shinn. il *Petersens Photogr Mag* 16:30-1 Ag '87
Compacts in action! Pentax IQ Zoom. K. Geller-Shinn. il *Petersens Photogr Mag* 16:80-1 My '87
Compacts in action! Ricoh TF-500. K. Geller-Shinn. il *Petersens Photogr Mag* 16:72-3 Jl '87
Compacts in action! Vivitar Trek 50. K. Geller-Shinn. il *Petersens Photogr Mag* 15:50-1 F '87
Compacts in action! Yashica L AF-D. K. Geller-Shinn. il *Petersens Photogr Mag* 15:58-9 Ja '87
Computerized cameras for the ambitious amateur. D. H. Dunn. il *Bus Week* p105 Ja 19 '87
Fuji DL-250 & DL-400: two dual focal length compacts. K. Geller-Shinn. il *Petersens Photogr Mag* 16:36+ D '87

Cameras—Testing—*cont.*

Fuji: new 6X9 wizardry [GW 690 II and GSW 690 II Professional rangefinder cameras] D. O'Neill. il *Petersens Photogr Mag* 15:48-50 Ja '87

Konica MR.70LX [compact 35mm camera] K. Geller-Shinn. il *Petersens Photogr Mag* 16:48 N '87

Medium-format rangefinders. D. Brooks. il *Petersens Photogr Mag* 16:58-61+ N '87

Medium-format view cameras. D. Brooks. il *Petersens Photogr Mag* 16:30-1+ O '87

Minolta Weathermatic Dual 35 [all-weather/waterproof dual-lens autofocus compact camera] A. Stone. il *Petersens Photogr Mag* 16:10 D '87

Sharp shooters [point and shoot 35mm compacts] T. O'Connor. il *Roll Stone* p41 Mr 12 '87

Toko cherry 4x5's [folding field camera] D. Brooks. il *Petersens Photogr Mag* 15:54-6 F '87

Wisner technical field camera [folding sheet-film camera] D. Brooks. il *Petersens Photogr Mag* 16:12 O '87

Wooden field camera review. J. A. Dickerson. il *Petersens Photogr Mag* 16:45-7+ O '87

Anecdotes, facetiae, satire, etc.

Tom Thumb. T. Steinmetz. il *Pop Photogr* 94:72-3 Ap '87

Cameras, Instant print
See also
Polaroid Corp.

The Polaroid promise [Spectra instant camera] J. A. Conway. il *Forbes* 139:8 F 9 '87

Polaroid's Spectra may be losing its flash. K. H. Hammonds. il *Bus Week* p31-2 Je 29 '87

Testing

True colors [Polaroid's Spectra system] T. O'Connor. il *Roll Stone* p50 Ja 29 '87

Cameras, Miniature

Flashback: five American-made subminiature cameras. E. S. Lothrop. il *Pop Photogr* 94:76 Ap '87

Cameras, Single-lens reflex

35mm single-lens reflex cameras [PMA Show] N. Goldberg. il *Pop Photogr* 94:64-5 My '87

Automatic rescue [overriding your autoexposure SLR] B. Hagin. il *Pop Photogr* 94:56-61 Ap '87

Canon finally challenges Minolta's mighty Maxxum [EOS autofocus SLRs] O. Port. il *Bus Week* p89-90 Mr 2 '87

EOS, Canon's autofocus SLR. D. Brooks. il *Petersens Photogr Mag* 15:10 Ap '87

"I am betting my destiny" [Canon's EOS automatic focusing camera] J. A. Trachtenberg. il *Forbes* 139:66 Mr 9 '87

Keppler's SLR world. H. Keppler. See issues of Popular Photography beginning September 1987

New AF Nikon N4004. M. Stensvold. il *Petersens Photogr Mag* 16:8 Ag '87

New Yashica AF SLR. M. Stensvold. il *Petersens Photogr Mag* 15:12 Ap '87

Pentax SF1. B. Hurter. il *Petersens Photogr Mag* 16:10 My '87

Ricoh's new XR-M SLR. K. Geller-Shinn. il *Petersens Photogr Mag* 16:16 Je '87

They're here . . . the amazing AF SLRs. J. Augustine. il *Petersens Photogr Mag* 16:6 O '87

Design

Advances in user-friendly camera features lie ahead. N. Goldberg. il *Pop Photogr* 94:26 F '87

The OM77AF: a springboard design for future AF SLRs. N. Goldberg. il *Pop Photogr* 94:34 Ap '87

Testing

Autofocus SLR update [cover story] il *Pop Photogr* 94:72-87 D '87

Canon EOS. D. Brooks. il *Petersens Photogr Mag* 16:34-8 My '87

Canon EOS 620. D. Brooks. il *Petersens Photogr Mag* 16:40-3 O '87

Canon EOS 650 [cover story] E. Stecker; N. Goldberg. il *Pop Photogr* 94:62-7 Jl '87

Contax 167 MT. D. Brooks. il *Petersens Photogr Mag* 16:32-3+ S '87

Contax 167MT [autoexposure SLR] S. Pollock; N. Goldberg. il *Pop Photogr* 94:56-60 S '87

Dawn of a new age [Canon's EOS 650 and 620 autofocus SLRs] S. A. Booth. il *Pop Mech* 164:14+ My '87

EOS: fast, quiet auto SLR. A. Fisher. il *Pop Sci* 230:114 Ap '87

Exakta 66. D. O'Neill. il *Petersens Photogr Mag* 16:60-2 My '87

Fast focus [Canon EOS 650 and 620] B. Schwalberg. il *Pop Photogr* 94:50-3 Ap '87

First look: Nikon N4004. B. Schwalberg. il *Pop Photogr* 94:52-3 Jl '87

Hasselblad 2000FCW. D. Brooks. il *Petersens Photogr Mag* 16:60-2 Je '87

Leica R5. D. Brooks. il *Petersens Photogr Mag* 15:66-9 Ap '87

Nikon N4004 [autofocus SLR] S. Pollock; N. Goldberg. il *Pop Photogr* 94:52-4 O '87

Nikon N4004 AF 35mm SLR. M. Stensvold. il *Petersens Photogr Mag* 16:34-6+ N '87

Olympus OM-77AF. D. O'Neill. il *Petersens Photogr Mag* 15:58-60 F '87

Olympus OM77AF. B. Schwalberg, N. Goldberg. il *Pop Photogr* 94:44-8 Ap '87

Painless focusing [Olympus OM-77AF] S. A. Booth. il *Pop Mech* 164:37 Mr '87

Pentax SF1 [autofocus SLR] B. Hurter. il *Petersens Photogr Mag* 16:48-52 Jl '87

Pentax SF1 [cover story] B. Schwalberg; N. Goldberg. il *Pop Photogr* 94:54-9 Ag '87

Personal programming [Leica R5] B. Schwalberg. il *Pop Photogr* 94:50-1 F '87

Ricoh XR-10. D. O'Neill. il *Petersens Photogr Mag* 15:54-6 Mr '87

Ricoh XR-M. B. Hurter and M. Stensvold. il *Petersens Photogr Mag* 16:68-70 D '87

Rollei SL66X and SE. D. Brooks. il *Petersens Photogr Mag* 16:26-8 Jl '87

Rolleiflex 3001. D. Brooks. il *Petersens Photogr Mag* 16:54-6 Ag '87

Rolleiflex 6002. G. Schaub. il *Pop Photogr* 94:40-5 F '87

Seeing-eye cameras [Pentax SF-1 and Nikon N4004 autofocus SLRs] S. A. Booth. il *Pop Mech* 164:40-1 S '87

Senior sibling [Canon EOS 620 autofocus SLR] B. Schwalberg. il *Pop Photogr* 94:57-9 O '87

Trap shooter [Yashica 230-AF] B. Schwalberg. il *Pop Photogr* 94:54-5 Ap '87

Yashica 230-AF [cover story] B. Hagin; N. Goldberg. il *Pop Photogr* 94:54-9 Je '87

Yashica 230-AF SLR. D. O'Neill. il *Petersens Photogr Mag* 16:32-4 Je '87

Cameras, Used

Practical classics [vintage 35mm cameras] B. Schwalberg. il *Pop Photogr* 94:22-9 Mr '87

Cameron, Franklin

Meet the masters. See alternate issues of Petersen's Photographic Magazine beginning March 1985

Cameron, J. M.

Is nuclear deterrence moral? bibl f il *N Y Rev Books* 34:38-43 N 5 '87

Cameron, Julia

Dennis Farina: guts & glamour. il por *Harpers Bazaar* 120:124+ Ap '87

Cameron, Ken
about
The good wife [film] Reviews
Macleans 100:46 Mr 2 '87. L. O'Toole
New Repub 196:27-8 Mr 16 '87. S. Kauffmann

Cameron, Kevin
TDC. See issues of Cycle

Cameron, Kirk
about
Kirk Cameron: growing strong. por *Teen* 31:50 F '87
Kirk's girls. il pors *Teen* 31:59 D '87

Cameron, Peter
Why I live where I live [story] il *Roll Stone* p97+ Jl 16-30 '87

Cameron family
about
Kirk's girls. il pors *Teen* 31:59 D '87

Cameroon
See also
Douala (Cameroon)
Lake Monoun (Cameroon)
Lake Nyos (Cameroon)
Lakes—Cameroon

Politics and government

The post-Ahidjo era in Cameroon. M. Azevedo. bibl f *Curr Hist* 86:217-20+ My '87

Cameroon and the United States

Tales of sister cities [Philadelphia, Pa. and Douala, Cameroon] L. Hazelton. *Black Enterp* 17:16 Mr '87

Camille (Fictional character)

Joining ranks with Garbo and Gish, Kathleen Turner proves that playing Camille is not a dying art. il por *People Wkly* 27:70-1+ Ja 5 '87

Cammile, Wayman E., Jr.
about
Deathbed confession frees Del. black after 12 years. il por *Jet* 72:16 Jl 6 '87

Camomile *See* Chamomile
Camouflage
   See also
     Mimicry (Biology)
Camouflage (Hunting)
   See also
     Blinds (Camouflage)
Blending in. N. Strung; J. Doggett. il *Field Stream* 92:64-6+ O '87
Camo: latest cover ups. S. Link. il *Outdoor Life* 179:68-9+ Ap '87
Without a trace [art of camouflage in bowhunting for deer] G. Helgeland. il *Field Stream* 91:56-7+ F '87
Camp, Joe
   about
Benji the hunted [film] Reviews
   People Wkly il 27:10 Je 29 '87. P. Travers
Camp Ahus (Sweden) *See* Church camps—Sweden
Camp cooking *See* Cooking, Outdoor
Camp Pendleton (Calif.) *See* Military training camps
Camp sites, facilities, etc.
Fort Wilderness: Disney World's "Hinterland". M. T. O'Keefe. il *Saturday Evening Post* 259:92-4+ Ja/F '87
   Directories
Campground hotline. D. Leathers. See issues of Travel Holiday
Campaign aides *See* Campaign management
Campaign consultants *See* Campaign management
Campaign ethics *See* Political ethics
Campaign for Human Development
'And the greatest of these is social justice'. C. Hays. *Natl Rev* 39:36+ D 31 '87
Campaign funds
   See also
     Political action committees
     Watergate case
But Mike's raking in money [1988 presidential candidates] L. I. Barrett. *Time* 130:34 Jl 20 '87
Free speech and free air [candidates should be given free TV time] H. Evans. il *U S News World Rep* 102:82 My 11 '87
Gary Hart's ticking debt bomb [1984 presidential campaign] K. T. Walsh. il por *U S News World Rep* 102:25 Ap 6 '87
Glitz and gold: why candidates love California [top fund raising state] R. Grover. il *Bus Week* p147 Je 8 '87
The gold mine is playing out [Republican Party direct mail fund raising] J. Novack. il *Forbes* 139:146+ Ap 6 '87
Guess who's not coming to brunch [Senator L. Bentsen accused of shaking down lobbyists for contributions] il por *Newsweek* 109:19 F 16 '87
The high cost of holding—and keeping—public office. A. Plattner. il *U S News World Rep* 102:30 Je 22 '87
The Hollywood primary [cover story] R. Brownstein. il *New Repub* 197:19+ N 23 '87
In demand: Wall Street's liberals. I. Ross. il *Fortune* 115:187-8+ Ap 27 '87
Jackson will announce bid for presidency next month; Cosby hosts big fund-raiser. il pors *Jet* 72:24-5 S 21 '87
Jesse raises $250,000 in Chicago fund-raiser. il pors *Jet* 72:4+ S 14 '87
The lady has a Midas touch [Democratic fund raising dinners hosted by P. Harriman] E. Thomas. il pors *Newsweek* 109:32-3 Je 15 '87
Letter from Washington [presidential candidates] Cato. *Natl Rev* 39:16 O 9 '87
Letter from Washington [Republican campaign coffers] Cato. *Natl Rev* 39:13 Jl 31 '87
The men who put dough behind the Democrats. R. Fly. il *Bus Week* p168+ O 12 '87
The money game [presidential candidate with most money will win] A. Kopkind. *Nation* 244:787-8 Je 13 '87
The political debt bomb. M. Greenfield. il *Newsweek* 109:76 Ap 6 '87
Raising bucks for Bush [work of fundraiser L. E. Bathgate] R. Brownstein. il pors *N Y Times Mag* p42-4+ My 17 '87
Running short on cash, Jesse Jackson works a glittering Harlem bash. il pors *People Wkly* 28:61 S 14 '87
Who's ahead in the '88 money race [presidential candidates] A. R. Dowd. il *Fortune* 115:58-9+ Je 8 '87
   Laws and regulations
   See also
     United States. Federal Election Commission
The campaign reform fraud. R. J. Samuelson. il *Newsweek* 110:43 Jl 13 '87
Evolution of federal campaign financing law. *Congr Dig* 66:34+ F '87

Indicted candidate [L. LaRouche indicted on charges of conspiring to block investigation of alleged fund raising fraud] B. Levin. *Macleans* 100:18 Jl 13 '87
Playing political hardball with soft money [views of Herbert Alexander] il *USA Today (Periodical)* 116:10 D '87
   Canada
The tastes of the Mulroney family [use of Conservative Party donations to renovate official residences] M. Janigan. il por *Macleans* 100:13 Ap 27 '87
Campaign issues
   See also
     Abortion
     Agricultural administration
     AIDS (Disease)
     Budget
     Child welfare
     Competition
     Disarmament
     Education and state
     Family
     Freedom of information
     Income
     Industry and state
     Military assistance, American
     Presidential candidates—Sexual behavior
     Space research
     Stock market crash, 1987
     United States—Commercial policy
     United States—Defenses
     United States—Economic policy
     United States—Foreign relations
     United States. Navy—Forces in the Persian Gulf region
And now, 'log cabin chic'. H. Fineman. il *Newsweek* 110:27 N 30 '87
The budget for motherhood. D. E. Koshland, Jr. *Science* 236:1501 Je 19 '87
Six candidates in search of an issue. R. Fly and D. Harbrecht. il *Bus Week* p55-6 O 19 '87
Some questions for the Democrats [presidential candidates] W. F. Buckley. *Natl Rev* 39:54 Ag 14 '87
What two of the darkest horses are running on: ideas [B. Babbitt and P. DuPont] P. Magnusson. il pors *Bus Week* p126+ D 21 '87
Where the candidates stand. L. Smith. il *Fortune* 116:129-30+ D 7 '87
Campaign management
Baker to Bush: no. il por *Newsweek* 110:7 O 19 '87
Caddell's defeat [J. Biden campaign] il por *Newsweek* 110:9 O 5 '87
Debacle for the Duke [resignation of M. Dukakis's campaign manager J. Sasso for his role in discrediting J. Biden] J. Klein. il por *N Y* 20:26+ O 12 '87
Debate distress? Call the spin doctors. E. Clift. il *Newsweek* 110:51 D 14 '87
Duke of piety [resignation of M. Dukakis's campaign manager J. Sasso] S. Lehigh and F. J. Connolly. *New Repub* 197:13-15 O 26 '87
The dwarfs in disarray [resignation of M. Dukakis's campaign manager J. Sasso] G. J. Church. il pors *Time* 130:22+ O 12 '87
Jesse Jackson names campaign leaders in quest for presidency. il por *Jet* 73:4-5 N 30 '87
Joe Biden's 'petulant genius' [P. Caddell] H. Rainie. il por *U S News World Rep* 103:25 S 21 '87
Manufacturing the next president [Harper's forum simulating process of 1988 Democratic nomination] il *Harpers* 275:43-54 D '87
Now, a Dukakis fiasco [campaign manager J. Sasso resigns] M. Kaus. il por *Newsweek* 110:40 O 12 '87
The price of deception [M. Dukakis' campaign hurt by resignations of staff members] J. Bierman. *Macleans* 100:32 O 12 '87
Campaign organizers *See* Campaign management
Campaign workers
After the fall: how Hart's workers picked up the pieces. L. Glynn and J. Mathewson. il por *Glamour* 85:362-3+ S '87
A caveat for candidates [walking away from the first campaign crisis] B. McBarton. por *Newsweek* 110:14 O 19 '87
Campaigns, Money raising *See* Fund raising
Campaigns, Political *See* Political campaigns
Campaigns, Presidential *See* Presidential campaigns
Campanelli, Luigi
   about
Luigi Campanelli: Jack Shainman. L. Malen. il *Art News* 86:159 D '87

Campanis, Al

about

40 years after Jackie Robinson, baseball still has no black managers. N. O. Unger. il pors *Jet* 72:48-51 My 4 '87

Al Campanis. F. C. Klein. il por *Sport Mag* 78:97-8 D '87

Baseball: a crisis in black and white. P. Axthelm. *Newsweek* 109:71 Ap 20 '87

Black swimmer resurfaces thanks to Campanis' slur. il por *Jet* 72:51 My 18 '87

Bowie Kuhn: Campanis did blacks a favor. por *Jet* 72:46 Jl 27 '87

Buoyancy basics. D. Seligman. *Fortune* 116:102 Jl 20 '87

The Campanis affair. P. Gammons. il por *Sports Illus* 66:31 Ap 20 '87

Edwards hires Campanis to assist baseball job. il por *Jet* 72:48 S 14 '87

The foul ball that shook baseball's front office. A. P. Sanoff. il por *U S News World Rep* 102:12-13 Ap 20 '87

In America's national pastime, says Frank Robinson, white is the color of the game off the field [interview] il pors *People Wkly* 27:46+ Ap 27 '87

Racism at bat. T. Callahan. por *Time* 129:63 Ap 20 '87

Racist remarks spark push for black execs. il por *Jet* 72:46 Ap 27 '87

Campanulas

These campanulas are blue carpet makers. il *Sunset* 178:210-11 Je '87

Campbell, Barbara

Against all odds. il *N Y* 20:68-74+ N 16 '87

Campbell, Bebe Moore

Bedroom eyes. il *Essence* 18:78-80+ My '87

Breaking the age taboo. il *Essence* 17:50-2+ F '87

Double trouble in the two-career marriage [excerpt from Successful women, angry men] *Essence* 17:51-2+ Mr '87

Is it true what they say about black men? il *Ebony* 42:116+ Jl '87

Successful women, angry men [excerpt] il por *Ebony* 42:38+ F '87

'What I wish I'd known': the surprising reality of motherhood. il *Essence* 18:116 O '87

When having fun ends with broken teeth. *Essence* 18:99 Je '87

about

Working wives, threatened husbands [interview] il por *U S News World Rep* 102:46 F 23 '87

Campbell, Blair F., and others

Linkage of functional and structural heterogeneity in proteins: dynamic hole burning in carboxymyoglobin. bibl f il *Science* 238:373-6 O 16 '87

Campbell, Craig S.

Basques in the Age of Exploration. il map *Focus* 36:24-9 Wint '86

Campbell, David

(jt. auth) See Blackwelder, Brent, and Campbell, David

Campbell, Duncan

Imperial reach. *Nation* 245:669-70 D 5 '87

Campbell, Earl

about

Campbell back in school; assists student-athletes. *Jet* 71:49 Ja 26 '87

Earl Campbell finds fame is fleeting on UT campus. por *Jet* 72:48 Ap 20 '87

Campbell, J. Jeffrey

about

Can Burger King's man spice up Pillsbury's eateries? M. J. Pitzer. il por *Bus Week* p50-1 My 18 '87

Campbell, Jane, 1951-

Growing up born again. il *Publ Wkly* 232:44-5 O 9 '87

Campbell, Jeff

Secrets of the speed cleaners [excerpts from Speed cleaning] il *Redbook* 168:114-15+ Ap '87

Campbell, Jeffrey

Don't raise the minimum wage. il por *Fortune* 116:103-4 Ag 31 '87

Campbell, John

Demythologising Nye Bevan. bibl il pors *Hist Today* 37:13-18 Ap '87

Campbell, Joseph, 1904-1987

about

Obituary

Natl Rev 39:21 D 4 '87. J. Hart

Campbell, Kurt M., 1957-

The ghost of Stalin [cover story] il *New Leader* 70:9-14 N 2 '87

Campbell, Mary Schmidt

about

Mary Campbell is cultural affairs chief of New York. il por *Jet* 72:23 Ag 17 '87

NY gets new cultural head. B. Blondin. *Black Enterp* 18:24 N '87

Campbell, Nell

about

If you want to lounge on a love seat in New York's hippest club, you'll have to get Nell Campbell's okay. M. Small. il por *People Wkly* 27:117-19 F 2 '87

Campbell, W. John, 1951-

about

When less is more. L. Fleischer. il *Publ Wkly* 231:81 Ja 9 '87

Campbell (Wallace H.) & Company *See* Wallace H. Campbell & Company

Campbell-Ewald Co.

Those heartbeat ads are a hit in the heartland [Chevrolet] C. Dugas. il *Bus Week* p107 F 23 '87

Campbell Mithun Inc.

Advertising success in Minneapolis [M. Betsch] J. Giambanco. il pors *Work Woman* 12:117-18+ O '87

Campbell Soup Company

Marketing's new look [move to regionalization] C. Dugas. il *Bus Week* p64-9 Ja 26 '87

Campeau, Robert, 1923-

about

Campeau's cash squeeze. T. Fennell. il por *Macleans* 100:26 Mr 2 '87

A Canadian with a chip on his shoulder. K. Ballen. il por *Fortune* 115:102 Ja 5 '87

Is Campeau in over his head at Allied Stores? D. Cook. il *Bus Week* p52-3 F 9 '87

Campeau Corporation

Campeau's cash squeeze [R. Campeau's takeover of Allied Stores] T. Fennell. il por *Macleans* 100:26 Mr 2 '87

A Canadian with a chip on his shoulder. K. Ballen. il por *Fortune* 115:102 Ja 5 '87

Is Campeau in over his head at Allied Stores? D. Cook. il *Bus Week* p52-3 F 9 '87

A top law firm feels the heat [Sullivan & Cromwell's G. C. Kern charged by SEC with violating disclosure rules during Campeau's bid on Allied Stores] C. Friday. *Newsweek* 110:40-1 Jl 13 '87

When companies talk turkey, investors should be told [SEC charges against G. C. Kern and Allied Stores over inadequate disclosure in Campeau hostile takeover] V. Cahan. il *Bus Week* p100 Jl 13 '87

Camper, Diane

The quest for liberty. il *Black Enterp* 17:53-6 Jl '87

Camper, Petrus, 1722-1789

about

Petrus Camper's angle. S. J. Gould. il *Nat Hist* 96:12+ Jl '87

Campers, Truck

A buyer's guide to vacation vehicles. M. Thompson and D. Prestly. il *Fam Handyman* 37:97-100+ Ap '87

Itasca's "little brother" [Phasar 220I] T. H. Cole. il *Pop Mech* 164:12 Je '87

New age RVs [cover story] B. Livingston. il *Pop Mech* 164:86-9+ Je '87

The perfect hunting and fishing rig? [pop-up camper] T. Fegely. il *Outdoor Life* 179:70 My '87

Pop-up camper for work and play. il *Home Mech* 83:20 Mr '87

Equipment

Wood-epoxy construction makes a featherweight camper cap. P. Butler and M. Butler. il *Pop Sci* 231:86-8 O '87

Leasing and renting

Get a taste of the open road by renting an RV. J. Flynn. il *Bus Week* p157 My 18 '87

Motor-home rentals. B. Humeston. il *Better Homes Gard* 65:150-1 Mr '87

Testing

Aero-motor-home [Vixen 21] J. Keebler. il *Pop Sci* 230:91 F '87

The long, long motorhome [Vogue III] P. Bingham. il *Mot Trend* 39:76-8+ S '87

The vexation of the Vixen—a short story [Vixen 21 motorhome] D. C. Ross. *Mot Trend* 39:126 S '87

Campers (Trailers) *See* Automobile trailers
Campgrounds *See* Camp sites, facilities, etc.
Camphor

See also

Menthol

Camping

See also

Backpacks and backpacking

Camping—See also—*cont.*
Camp sites, facilities, etc.
Camps
Cooking, Outdoor
1987 bonus guide to camping [special section] il *Outdoor Life* 179:39-40+ My '87
Camping. S. Netherby. See issues of Field & Stream
How camping helps children grow. J. C. Stone. *Educ Dig* 52:47-9 My '87
Memorable camps [reprint from March 1970 issue] T. Trueblood. il *Field Stream* 91:72-3+ Ap '87

Equipment
See also
Backpacks and backpacking
Survival and emergency equipment
Tents
Hints from a hikers' Heloise. E. J. Joyce. il *Sierra* 72:15-16 My/Je '87
Product update. D. Leathers. *Travel Holiday* 168:24-5 N '87
Product update. D. Leathers. il *Travel Holiday* 168:36-7 S '87
RV/camping products update. D. Leathers. *Travel Holiday* 167:30 My '87
What's new. See issues of Outdoor Life
Yurts! [ski camping shelters] E. Hermann. il *Sierra* 72:51-4 N/D '87

Outfits, supplies, etc.
See Camping—Equipment

Psychological aspects
The Indian ordeal. A. Alben. il *N Y Times Mag* p78 Mr 8 '87

British Columbia
Horseback camping. il map *Natl Geogr World* 141:7-13 My '87

California
Camping deep in the Humboldt redwoods. il map *Sunset* 179:42+ S '87

United States
See Camping

Western States
Elk camp. N. Strung. il *Field Stream* 91:62-3+ Ja '87
Camping outfits *See* Camping—Equipment
Campion, Nardi Reeder
Our Christmas Madeira. il *Gourmet* 47:100+ D '87
Campo, Richard
about
Six bites from one apple. W. P. Barrett. il por *Forbes* 140:88+ S 7 '87
Camporesi, Piero
Paradise lost. il *Courier* 40:28-31 My '87
Campos Elísios (Brazil)
Religious institutions and affairs
Letter from the Elysian Fields [work of Catholic priest D. R. Santos] J. Kramer. *New Yorker* 63:40-2+ Mr 2 '87
Camps
See also
Church camps
Baseball camps: where big league dreams come true [adult camps] L. Kaufman. il *Travel Holiday* 167:48-51 My '87
The camp spirit: bring it home. J. E. Loehr. il *World Tennis* 34:32-3 Ja '87
A guide to the summer hoop camps. M. George. il *Sport Mag* 78:93-4 Jl '87
How to get the most from summer ski camp. C. Cooper. *Skiing* 39:77-8 Spr '87
Kids' camps with a focus. M. Posner. il *Changing Times* 41:91-5 F '87
Space summer '87. G. Chitwood. il *Space World* X-4-280:38-9 Ap '87

Advertising
Her f ce is f mili r [V. White, model for B/C All-Stars Basketball camps' T shirts] R. Jackson. il por *Sports Illus* 66:24 Je 1 '87

International aspects
Directory [tennis camps] il *World Tennis* 34:38-40+ Ja '87
Summer ski camps '87. *Skiing* 39:82-7 Spr '87

Arizona
Birding's fledgling phenoms [Victor Emanuel Nature Tours birding camp in Arizona desert] F. Graham. il por *Audubon* 89:38-40+ My '87

California
Here's a camp for hulkless masses yearning to flex for a healthy fee [Pro Muscle Bodybuilding and Fitness Training Camp in Los Angeles] il *People Wkly* 28:96-7 Ag 31 '87

Hog Island (Me.)
Audubon ecology camp. P. Salmansohn. il *Ctry J* 14:60-2 Je '87

Maryland
Food for fun [Kids' Cooking Camp at L'Academie de Cuisine, Bethesda] il *Natl Geogr World* 142:10-13 Je '87

New Jersey
How I spent my summer vacation: one woman's journey to fantasy bodybuilding camp [Pro Muscle Bodybuilding and Fitness Training Camp] D. Frost. il *Women's Sports Fitness* 9:38-41 Je '87

New York (State)
Summer camp and compost [Camp Treetops and North Country School in Lake Placid] L. K. Murrow. il *Ctry J* 14:61-8 Ja '87

United States
See Camps
Camps for sick children
See also
Amanda the Panda, Inc.
Camps for the handicapped
Formation and transformation at Camp Ahus [Swedish confirmation camp] B. Webb-Mitchell. *Christ Century* 104:531-2 Je 3-10 '87
Campus ministry *See* College students—Religious life
Campus queens *See* Beauty contests
Campylobacter
A bug, not what's bugging you, may cause ulcers [development of bacteria fighting drugs] Z. Schiller and S. Siwolop. il *Bus Week* p90 Ag 3 '87
Bugged by an ulcer? You could have a bug [work of Barry Marshall] il *Discover* 8:10 My '87
Foul chickens. B. Costikyan. il *N Y* 20:44-8 Ag 10 '87
Ulcers: on the brink of a cure [work of Barry Marshall and others] D. Foley. *Prevention* 39:49-52 My '87
Can openers
Can openers. il *Consum Rep* 52:43-7 D '87
Can openers. il *Consum Rep* 52:634-8 O '87
Canada
See also
Advertising, Public service—Canada
Aged—Canada
Agricultural administration—Canada
Agriculture—Canada
AIDS (Disease)—Canada
Alberta
Aliens—Canada
Anti-Semitism—Canada
Architecture—Canada
Art—Canada
Astronomy—Canada
Aviation and state—Canada
Banks and banking—Canada
Bridges—Canada
British Columbia
Cable television—Canada
Capital punishment—Canada
Child molesting—Canada
Child welfare—Canada
Children—Canada
Children's literature—Canada
Chinese—Canada
Christmas—Canada
Christmas business—Canada
Cities and towns—Canada
Collecting of accounts—Canada
Collective bargaining—Canada
Collective bargaining—Postal service—Canada
Collective labor agreements—Airlines—Canada
Collective labor agreements—Automobile industry—Canada
Contracts, Government—Canada
Copyright—Canada
Corporations—Acquisitions and mergers—Laws and regulations—Canada
Corporations, Government—Canada
Credit cards—Canada
Crime and the press—Canada
Criminal justice, Administration of—Canada
Dairying—Canada
Dams—Canada
Dance—Canada
Day care—Canada
Discrimination in employment—Canada
Drug abuse—Canada
Drug laws and regulations—Canada
Earthquakes—Canada
Education—Canada
Energy policy—Canada

Canada—See also—*cont.*
    Engineering—Canada
    Equal pay for equal work—Canada
    Family—Canada
    Festivals—Canada
    Finance—Canada
    Financial institutions—Laws and regulations—Canada
    Fishing—Canada
    Food inspection—Canada
    Food supply—Canada
    Football, Professional—Canada
    Gambling—Canada
    Gangs—Canada
    Germans—Canada
    Government and the press—Canada
    Government liability—Canada
    Handicapped—Canada
    Homeless—Canada
    Housing—Canada
    Immigration and emigration—Canada
    Income tax—Canada
    Indians (East Indian)—Canada
    Indians of North America—Canada
    Industry and state—Canada
    Insurance, Liability—Canada
    Insurance, Unemployment—Canada
    Insurance law—Canada
    Investment banking—Canada
    Investments, American—Canada
    Investments, Australian—Canada
    Investments, British—Canada
    Investments, Canadian
    Investments, Foreign—Canada
    Investments, Hong Kong—Canada
    Investments, Japanese—Canada
    Islands—Canada
    Journalism—Canada
    Juvenile justice, Administration of—Canada
    Labor laws and regulations—Canada
    Laundromats—Canada
    Manitoba
    Maritime Provinces
    Mass media—Canada
    Medical care—Canada
    Medicare—Canada
    Missing children—Canada
    Monasteries—Canada
    Money—Canada
    Morale, National—Canada
    Motion picture laws and regulations—Canada
    Narcotics laws and regulations—Canada
    New Brunswick
    Newfoundland
    Northwest Territories
    Nova Scotia
    Nuclear power plants—Canada
    Nursing homes—Canada
    Obscenity (Law)—Canada
    Occupational health and safety—Canada
    Official residences—Canada
    Old age assistance—Canada
    Ontario
    Pollution—Canada
    Polo—Canada
    Pornography—Canada
    Postal service—Canada
    Power of attorney—Canada
    Press and politics—Canada
    Prince Edward Island
    Prisons—Canada
    Public opinion—Canada
    Québec (Province)
    Railroads—Canada
    Railroads and state—Canada
    Real estate investment—Canada
    Regionalism—Canada
    Resorts—Canada
    Rock music—Canada
    Rodeos—Canada
    Russians—Canada
    Saint Lawrence River
    Sales tax—Canada
    Saskatchewan
    Savings and loan associations—Canada
    Scots—Canada
    Securities—Canada
    Securities—Laws and regulations—Canada
    Servicewomen—Canada
    Sex crimes—Canada
    Sex education—Canada

    Shipwrecks—Laws and regulations—Canada
    Smoking—Laws and regulations—Canada
    Space research—Canada
    Stadiums—Canada
    Strikes—Airline employees—Canada
    Strikes—Department store employees—Canada
    Strikes—Postal employees—Canada
    Strikes—Publishers and publishing—Canada
    Strikes—Railroad workers—Canada
    Student aid—Canada
    Suicide—Canada
    Tamils—Canada
    Taxation—Canada
    Technology—Canada
    Technology and state—Canada
    Television broadcasting—Canada
    Television laws and regulations—Canada
    Temporary employment—Canada
    Theater—Canada
    Trade unions—Canada
    Trade unions—Fishermen—Canada
    Traffic accidents—Canada
    Traffic regulations—Canada
    Trials—Canada
    Turks—Canada
    Videotapes—Canada
    Vocational-technical education—Canada
    Water supply—Canada
    Wetlands—Canada
    Women—Canada
    Youth—Canada
    Yukon Territory
Images of '87 [special section; with editorial comment by Carl Mollins] il *Macleans* 100:34-48 D 21 '87

Anecdotes, facetiae, satire, etc.
An award-worthy guest column. S. MacLeod. por *Macleans* 100:52 Ag 17 '87
Provide the answers—but politely. A. Fotheringham. il *Macleans* 100:68 N 30 '87

Anniversaries, etc.
Canada at 120: future shocks [predictions for the year 2007] M. Nichols. il *Macleans* 100:42-4 Jl 6 '87

Antiquities
Diving for dollars [special section] il *Macleans* 100:36-42 Ag 10 '87

Appropriations and expenditures
See also
Budget—Canada
Canada. Office of the Auditor General
Fantasyland furore [annual report by the Auditor General] M. Drohan. il *Macleans* 100:14 N 9 '87

Armed Forces
See also
Royal Canadian Legion
    Appropriations and expenditures
Canada continues to scale down defense. P. Mann. *Aviat Week Space Technol* 126:20 F 23 '87
    Forces in Germany (West)
Security shock at dawn in Lahr [saboteurs attack Canadian base] M. Nichols. il *Macleans* 100:10-11 Jl 20 '87
Tracking an inside job [explosion at Canadian base] P. Lewis. *Macleans* 100:19 Ag 3 '87
    Forces in Norway
Retreating from Norway [Canada abandons NATO commitment to help defend Norway in wartime] H. Mackenzie. *Macleans* 100:14-15 F 23 '87
    Women
See Servicewomen—Canada

Capital
See also
Ottawa (Ont.)

Climate
Canadian weather briefs. See issues of Weatherwise
How we earn our place in the sun [enduring Canadian winters] C. Gordon. por *Macleans* 100:7 F 9 '87
Spring and clearer predictions ahead. J. Barber. il *Macleans* 100:44-5 Mr 16 '87

Commerce
See also
Interstate commerce—Canada
    China
A new drug deal with China. P. C. Newman. il *Macleans* 100:31 S 14 '87
    France
See France—Commerce—Canada
    Iran
See also
Iran-contra affair—Canadian participation

Canada—Commerce—*cont.*

South Africa

The Canadian connection [South Africa using Canadian-designed weaponry in Angola] A. Bilski. il map *Macleans* 100:36 O 19 '87

United States

See United States—Commerce—Canada

Commercial policy

See also

Tariff—Canada

The case for a free trade accord [U.S.-Canada talks] D. Francis. il *Macleans* 100:13 S 7 '87

Celebrations for the 'win-win' deal [final text of free trade agreement between Canada and the U.S.] M. Drohan. il *Macleans* 100:18-19 D 21 '87

Division in the house [free trade debate dominates First Ministers' meeting] M. Drohan. il *Macleans* 100:10-12 D 7 '87

Emotional divisions [Canadian debate over trade agreement with U.S.] M. Janigan. il *Macleans* 100:21 N 16 '87

The free trade countdown. M. Drohan. il *Macleans* 100:15-16 S 28 '87

Going public on trade [B. Mulroney pushes for free trade agreement with U.S.] M. Janigan. il por *Macleans* 100:16+ Mr 23 '87

In search of a trade deal [U.S. and Canada] M. Drohan. il *Macleans* 100:8-9 Jl 20 '87

Nothing to fear but the fearful [free trade accord with the U.S.] D. Francis. il *Macleans* 100:13 O 19 '87

'One hell of a fight' [Canada-U.S. free trade agreement] M. Drohan. il *Macleans* 100:26-7 O 26 '87

Personalities enter the trade talks [Canadian-U.S. negotiators] M. Janigan. il *Macleans* 100:18-19 D 14 '87

Potential victims of a trade pact [protectionist sentiment] M. Drohan. il *Macleans* 100:22-3 Ag 10 '87

Preparing for a real election [upcoming federal election in Canada seen to be focused on free trade issue] C. Gordon. il *Macleans* 100:41 N 2 '87

The pull of the American dream [free trade agreement-in-principle between Ottawa and Washington] P. C. Newman. il *Macleans* 100:42 O 19 '87

Redrawing the nation [U.S.-Canada trade accord; cover story; special section; with editorial comment by Kevin Doyle] il *Macleans* 100:2, 14-23 O 19 '87

A revolt over energy [controversy over Canada-U.S. free trade pact] M. Rose. il *Macleans* 100:15 N 23 '87

The sweep of free trade [U.S. and Canada] P. Gessell. il *Macleans* 100:24-5 Mr 16 '87

Temperatures rising [free trade debate] M. Janigan. il *Macleans* 100:10-12 N 9 '87

Tension in talking [trade talks with U.S.] D. Jenish. il *Macleans* 100:30-1 Je 29 '87

Toward the final hurdles [free trade accord discussed at First Ministers' meeting] M. Drohan. il *Macleans* 100:36-7 D 28 '87

Trade: a Canadian view. M. Drohan. *World Press Rev* 34:47 D '87

Trumpets of free trade. M. Rose. il *Macleans* 100:16 Mr 30 '87

Uneasy over free trade [Maclean's/Decima poll] M. Rose. il *Macleans* 100:38-9 Ja 5 '87

Walkout from the talks [cover story; special section; with editorial comment by Kevin Doyle] il *Macleans* 100:2, 14-20+ O 5 '87

Anecdotes, facetiae, satire, etc.

Free trade? It will not happen. A. Fotheringham. il *Macleans* 100:64 O 26 '87

Cultural policy

A question of identity [Maclean's/Decima poll] il *Macleans* 100:42 Ja 5 '87

Skepticism in the arts [reaction to U.S.-Canada free trade accord] V. Ross. il *Macleans* 100:21 O 19 '87

Cultural relations

Concerns at the summit [meeting of francophone nations in Quebec City] M. Rose. il *Macleans* 100:24 S 7 '87

Speaking with one tongue [La Francophonie conference in Quebec] M. Rose. il *Macleans* 100:8-9 S 14 '87

Troubles of a tongue *en crise* [Quebec summit] W. R. Doerner. il *Time* 130:49 S 14 '87

China

Making a legend [filming Bethune: the making of a hero in China; cover story; special section; with editorial comment by Kevin Doyle] il pors *Macleans* 100:2, 26-34 Ag 10 '87

United States

See United States—Cultural relations—Canada

Defenses

See also

Airplanes, Military—Canada

Aviation, Military—Canada

Canada. Royal Canadian Navy

Nuclear submarines, Canadian

The Canadian Arctic is a new U.S.-Soviet hot spot. W. J. Holstein. il *Bus Week* p41 Ag 10 '87

Canadian defense [special section] il *Bull At Sci* 43:9-19 O '87

Canadian defense (I) [cover story; special section] il map *Aviat Week Space Technol* 127:56-9+ S 21 '87

Canadian defense (II) [special section] il map *Aviat Week Space Technol* 127:124-9+ S 28 '87

Canadian defense (III) [special section] il map *Aviat Week Space Technol* 127:82-3+ O 5 '87

Canadian defense white paper will call for nuclear subs, more patrol aircraft. P. Mann. *Aviat Week Space Technol* 126:56-7+ My 11 '87

Canadian plan calls for sharp change in military defense strategy. J. D. Morrocco. map *Aviat Week Space Technol* 126:77-8 Je 22 '87

A defence plan for Canada. H. Mackenzie and M. Clark. il por *Macleans* 100:18+ Je 15 '87

U.S./Canadian radar research questioned. *Aviat Week Space Technol* 126:22 Ap 20 '87

Description and travel

Oh, Canada! [special section] il *50 Plus* 27:34-8+ Ap '87

Diplomatic and consular service

United States

The ambassador's tale [Canadian ambassador A. Gotlieb subpoenaed to testify in M. Deaver perjury trial] M. McDonald. il por *Macleans* 100:21 Je 8 '87

Discovery and exploration

Saved by the Indians [scurvy antidote given to French explorers; excerpt from Voyages au Canada] J. Cartier. il *Courier* 40:12 Ap '87

Economic conditions

See also

Consumption (Economics)—Canada

Steady as it goes for the new year [A. Sarlos' predictions] P. C. Newman. il por *Macleans* 100:16 Ja 5 '87

To the brink of recession. D. Jenish. il *Macleans* 100:34-5 N 16 '87

Economic policy

See also

Budget—Canada

Canada. Western Diversification Office

Building blocks for a new era. D. Cohen. por *Macleans* 100:7 F 2 '87

The decline of Lean and Mean [disenchantment with economic conservatism] C. Gordon. il *Macleans* 100:9 Ap 6 '87

The message in the NDP's book. D. Francis. il *Macleans* 100:7 Ag 24 '87

A move toward self-reliance [Maclean's/Decima poll] P. Best. il *Macleans* 100:46+ Ja 5 '87

Northern opportunity. M. S. Forbes, Jr. il *Forbes* 139:27 Je 1 '87

Economic relations

See also

Economic assistance, Canadian

United States

See United States—Economic relations—Canada

Foreign relations

See also

Economic assistance, Canadian

Africa

Mulroney, Brian—Visit to Africa, 1987

Central America

Clark's troubled tour. K. Scanlon. il por *Macleans* 100:26 D 7 '87

France

See France—Foreign relations—Canada

Poland

Searching for signs of spring [J. Clark's visit] H. Mackenzie. il *Macleans* 100:20-1 My 18 '87

South Africa

See also

South Africa—Diplomatic and consular service—Canada

Apartheid and diplomacy [J. Clark's visit] C. Wood. il por *Macleans* 100:22-3 Ag 24 '87

Clark's compromise offer [Canadian efforts to combat apartheid] H. Mackenzie. il por *Macleans* 100:24 S 21 '87

Canada—Foreign relations—South Africa—*cont.*
Oliver Tambo's war cry [visit to Canada] H. Mackenzie.
il por *Macleans* 100:25 S 7 '87
Turks and Caicos Islands
Canada's fantasy islands [with editorial comment by
Kevin Doyle] P. Gessell. il map *Macleans* 100:2, 10-12
Mr 30 '87
Clouds over paradise. il *Macleans* 100:14 My 4 '87
United States
    See United States—Foreign relations—Canada
History
    See also
World War, 1939-1945—Canada
        1914-1945
    See also
World War, 1914-1918—Canada
Industries
    See also
Advertising agencies—Canada
Air Canada
Airlines—Acquisitions and mergers—Canada
Airlines—Canada
Amoco Canada Petroleum Company Ltd.
Atomic Energy of Canada Ltd.
Audio equipment industry—Canada
Automobile factories—Canada
Barnes Investor Relations Ltd.
Barrick Resources Corp.
Bell Canada Enterprises Inc.
Bell-Northern Research Ltd.
Book industries—Canada
Bow Valley Industries Ltd.
Brewing industry—Canada
Brokers—Canada
Campeau Corporation
Canadair Ltd.
Canadian Airlines International
Canadian Tire Corp., Ltd.
Carling O'Keefe Limited
Chemical industries—Canada
Chrysler Canada Ltd.
Cigarette industry—Canada
Corporations—Acquisitions and mergers—Canada
Counsel Corporation
Crown Life Insurance Co.
CTV (Network)
Dairying—Acquisitions and mergers—Canada
DeHavilland Aircraft of Canada, Limited
Delta Hotels Ltd.
Dofasco Inc.
Dome Mines Limited
Dome Petroleum Ltd.
Dominion Textile Inc.
Echo Bay Mines Ltd.
Employment agencies—Canada
Energy industries—Canada
Film Arts Ltd.
Financial institutions—Acquisitions and mergers—
    Canada
First City Financial Corporation
Fisheries—Canada
Freight forwarders—Canada
Fur industry—Canada
Gold mines and mining—Canada
Gulf Canada Limited
Helicopter industry—Canada
Hiram Walker Resources Ltd.
Hollinger, Inc.
Hudson's Bay Co.
Husky Oil Ltd.
IKOY Partnership
Inter-City Gas Corp.
International Thomson Organisation Ltd.
Irving Oil Company
John Labatt Limited
Kimberly-Clark of Canada, Ltd.
Laurentian Group Corporation
Leopold Property Consultants Inc.
MacDonald Dettwiler and Associates
Maple sugar industry—Canada
Maritime Telegraph & Telephone Co., Ltd.
Mass media industry—Acquisitions and mergers—
    Canada
Meat industry—Canada
Medical care industry—Canada
Michelin Canada Ltd.
Mining industry—Acquisitions and mergers—Canada
Mining industry—Canada
Motion picture industry—Canada
Munitions—Canada
National Sea Products Ltd.

Newspaper publishers and publishing—Acquisitions
    and mergers—Canada
Newspaper publishers and publishing—Canada
Northern Telecom Ltd.
NovAtel Communications Ltd.
Olympia & York Developments Ltd.
Onex Capital Corporation
Palm Dairies Ltd.
Petroleum industry—Acquisitions and mergers—
    Canada
Petroleum industry—Canada
Phonograph record industry—Canada
Placer Dome Inc.
Power Corporation of Canada
Principal Group Ltd.
Publishers and publishing—Acquisitions and merg-
    ers—Canada
Quadra Logic Technologies Inc.
Quebecor Inc.
Retail trade—Acquisitions and mergers—Canada
Rogers Communications Inc.
Royal Trustco Limited
Savings and loan associations—Acquisitions and
    mergers—Canada
Seagram Company Ltd.
Sealing
Selkirk Communications Limited
Shellfish fisheries—Canada
Shipbuilding—Canada
Shipping—Canada
Small business—Canada
Sun Ice Ltd.
T. Eaton Co. Ltd.
Teck Corp.
Telecommunication—Acquisitions and mergers—
    Canada
Telefilm Canada
Telemedia Inc.
Television industry—Canada
Thompson Bousquet Gold Mines Ltd.
Tobacco industry—Canada
Tourist trade—Canada
TransCanada PipeLines Limited
Triple Five Corporation
Unicorp Canada Corporation
Venture capital companies—Canada
Versatile Corp.
Virtual Prototypes, Inc.
Walwyn Inc.
Wardair Inc.
Wine industry—Canada
Wood Gundy Incorporated
Zellers Inc.
Business watch. P. C. Newman. See issues of Maclean's
Industry's surprising revival north of the border. E.
    B. Terry and others. il *Bus Week* p38-9 Jl 27 '87
Manufacturing today [address, June 24, 1987] B. M.
    McGourty. *Vital Speeches Day* 53:752-5 O 1 '87
    Bibliography
Samples from a vintage season. P. C. Newman. il
    Macleans 100:39 D 14 '87
Intellectual life
    See also
Learned Societies Conference
Languages
A cautionary case of bilingualism [French language in
    Canada] P. Brimelow. *Commentary* 84:63-5 N '87
A tougher language bill [bilingualism requirements] P.
    Gessell. il *Macleans* 100:15 Jl 6 '87
Military policy
About-face in defence strategy. P. C. Newman. il por
    Macleans 100:28 Ja 12 '87
Canadian defense [special section] il *Bull At Sci* 43:9-19
    O '87
Canadian defense (I) [cover story; special section] il
    map *Aviat Week Space Technol* 127:56-9+ S 21 '87
Canadian defense (II) [special section] il map *Aviat Week
    Space Technol* 127:124-9+ S 28 '87
Canadian defense (III) [special section] il map *Aviat
    Week Space Technol* 127:82-3+ O 5 '87
Canadian plan calls for sharp change in military defense
    strategy. J. D. Morrocco. map *Aviat Week Space
    Technol* 126:77-8 Je 22 '87
A defence plan for Canada. H. Mackenzie and M. Clark.
    il por *Macleans* 100:18+ Je 15 '87
New views on defense [New Democratic Party] G. Dyer;
    R. J. Jackson. *World Press Rev* 34:45 N '87
Moral conditions
    See also
Prostitution—Canada

Canada—*cont.*

Nationalism
See also
Federal and provincial relations (Canada)

Politics and government
See also
Campaign funds—Canada
Canada—Prime ministers
Canada. Cabinet
Canada. Constitution
Christian Heritage Party (Canada)
Elections—Canada
Federal and provincial relations (Canada)
Political attitudes—Canada
Political campaigns—Canada
Politics, Corruption in—Canada
Reform Party of Canada
Column. A. Fotheringham. See issues of Maclean's
A hint of election fever [B. Mulroney's provincial tour]
    M. Janigan. il pors *Macleans* 100:12-13 N 30 '87
Judgment in hard-cover [books about B. Mulroney] P.
    Gessell. il *Macleans* 100:17 N 2 '87
Mulroney on his record [interview] il pors *Macleans*
    100:14-17 D 21 '87
Mulroney's red-hot summer. P. Gessell. il por *Macleans*
    100:8 Jl 13 '87
Preparing for a real election [upcoming federal election
    in Canada seen to be focused on free trade issue]
    C. Gordon. il *Macleans* 100:41 N 2 '87
The Tory revival plan [upcoming barrage of policy
    initiatives] M. Rose. il *Macleans* 100:10-11 Je 1 '87

Anecdotes, facetiae, satire, etc.
Dog days and snakes in a sponge. A. Fotheringham.
    il *Macleans* 100:60 S 14 '87
Elsewhere, confusion reigns. A. Fotheringham. il *Macleans*
    100:72 Mr 23 '87

Popular culture
The survival of Canadian culture. B. Amiel. il *Macleans*
    100:9 Ap 20 '87

Population
See also
Birth rate—Canada

Premiers
See Canada—Prime ministers

Prime ministers
Division in the house [free trade debate dominates First
    Ministers' meeting] M. Drohan. il *Macleans* 100:10-12
    D 7 '87
Toward the final hurdles [free trade accord discussed
    at First Ministers' meeting] M. Drohan. il *Macleans*
    100:36-7 D 28 '87

Provinces
See also
Federal and provincial relations (Canada)

Religious institutions and affairs
See also
Buddhism—Canada
Catholics—Canada
Church and state—Canada
Prayer Canada (Organization)
Sikhs—Canada
Divergent views on religion [Maclean's/Decima poll] R.
    Corelli. il *Macleans* 100:58+ Ja 5 '87
'Take it or leave it' religion [views of Reginald Bibby
    in The fragmented gods] D. O'Leary. *Christ Today*
    31:62-3 O 2 '87

Social conditions
See also
Sexual behavior—Canada

Statistics
See also
Canada. Statistics Canada
Canada. Air Force *See* Canada. Royal Canadian Air Force

Canada. Cabinet
Blitzing the West [Brian Mulroney and Cabinet visit
    Alberta] M. Clark. il *Macleans* 100:12 Jl 20 '87
The Minister of Everything [D. Mazankowski] P. Gessell.
    il por *Macleans* 100:12 S 14 '87
Mulroney's new team. H. Mackenzie. il *Macleans* 100:21
    Mr 23 '87
Speaking with fewer tongues. S. MacLeod. por *Macleans*
    100:52 Ag 24 '87
A timely Cabinet shuffle. *Macleans* 100:15 S 7 '87

Canada. Constitution
Breakthrough [agreement that will allow Quebec to sign
    the Constitution; cover story; special section] il
    Macleans 100:8-12+ My 11 '87
Canada's new deal [cover story; special section; with
    editorial comment by Kevin Doyle] il *Macleans* 100:2,
    8-10+ Je 15 '87

Constitutional clouds [attempt to have Quebec sign the
    Constitution] M. Rose. il *Macleans* 100:10-11 Ap 27
    '87
Constitutional discord. P. Gessell. il *Macleans* 100:13
    Ag 17 '87
Debates on the morning after [constitutional break-
    through] M. Gee. il *Macleans* 100:12-13 My 18 '87
Facing a deadline [constitutional resolution and Quebec
    endorsement] M. Janigan. il *Macleans* 100:13 Jl 6
    '87
A historic 'yes' vote [Meech Lake constitutional accord]
    P. Gessell. il *Macleans* 100:12 N 9 '87
A Liberal family feud [constitutional agreement] M. Rose.
    il *Macleans* 100:12+ My 25 '87
A strike against labor [Supreme Court of Canada's rulings
    hurt labor's right to strike and bargain collectively]
    il *Macleans* 100:15 Ap 20 '87
Tasting bitter failure [failure to find a way of entrenching
    native self-government in the Constitution] P. Gessell.
    il *Macleans* 100:21-2 Ap 6 '87
Trudeau's power punch [denunciation of constitutional
    accord] M. Janigan. il por *Macleans* 100:10-11 Je
    8 '87
Trudeau's star turn [criticism of the constitutional accord]
    M. Janigan. il por *Macleans* 100:14-16+ S 7 '87
The war among the Liberals [constitutional agreement]
    M. Rose. il *Macleans* 100:12-13 Je 22 '87

Canada. Dept. of Regional Industrial Expansion
Wrapping up an inquiry [conflict of interest charges
    against former cabinet minister S. Stevens] S. Aiken-
    head. il *Macleans* 100:13 Mr 2 '87
'Wrong by any measure' [report on S. Stevens' conflict
    of interest investigation issued] M. Rose. il por
    Macleans 100:12-14 D 14 '87

Canada. Environment Canada
Spring and clearer predictions ahead. J. Barber. il
    Macleans 100:44-5 Mr 16 '87

Canada. Health Protection Branch
Dining-room detectives. il *Macleans* 100:34+ Ap 27 '87
Canada. National Film Board *See* National Film Board
    of Canada
Canada. Navy *See* Canada. Royal Canadian Navy

Canada. Office of the Auditor General
Fantasyland furore [annual report] M. Drohan. il *Macleans*
    100:14 N 9 '87

Canada. Parliament. House of Commons
Bring on the backbenchers [TV coverage] A.
    Fotheringham. il *Macleans* 100:48 Jl 27 '87
The first decade of the TV MPs. G. Bain. il *Macleans*
    100:56 O 19 '87
Fortunately they forgot Quebec [rejection of capital
    punishment] A. Fotheringham. il *Macleans* 100:52 Jl
    13 '87
Hard choices on crime [rejection of death penalty] H.
    Mackenzie. il *Macleans* 100:6-7 Jl 13 '87
A historic 'yes' vote [Meech Lake constitutional accord]
    P. Gessell. il *Macleans* 100:12 N 9 '87
Testy tempers in Ottawa. M. Clark. il *Macleans* 100:17
    N 16 '87
A Tory who refuses to toe the line [F. Jourdenais]
    M. Clark. il por *Macleans* 100:18 N 2 '87

Canada. Parliament. Senate
Confronting the Red Chamber [with editorial comment
    by Kevin Doyle] P. Gessell. il *Macleans* 100:2, 18-19
    Ag 24 '87
Preparing for a new Senate. M. Drohan. il por *Macleans*
    100:14 My 11 '87

Anecdotes, facetiae, satire, etc.
Whimsy and the death vote. A. Fotheringham. il *Macleans*
    100:64 Ap 27 '87
**Canada. Radio-Television and Telecommunications Commis-
    sion** *See* Canadian Radio-Television and
    Telecommunications Commission

Canada. Revenue Canada
Taxing a gambler's loss [Canadian embezzler B. Molony]
    D. Jenish. il por *Macleans* 100:34+ D 14 '87

Canada. Royal Canadian Air Force
Old age of Air Force fleet complicates modernization.
    il *Aviat Week Space Technol* 127:69+ S 21 '87
Canada. Royal Canadian Mounted Police *See* Royal
    Canadian Mounted Police

Canada. Royal Canadian Navy
Blueprint for a real navy. P. C. Newman. il *Macleans*
    100:36 Je 15 '87
Canadian agency rejects nuclear subs, favors surface
    vessels and patrol aircraft. P. Mann. *Aviat Week Space
    Technol* 126:77-8 Je 1 '87

Canada. Statistics Canada
Small business on a recharge [Statistics Canada's Small
    Business Database] D. Cohen. por *Macleans* 100:9
    Ap 27 '87

Canada. Supreme Court
Judging the contenders [appointing a new judge] A. Wilson-Smith. il *Macleans* 100:10 Mr 9 '87
A new face on the bench [C. L'Heureux-Dubé] A. Wilson-Smith. il por *Macleans* 100:11 Ap 27 '87

Decisions
No to sexual harassment [rules that employers under federal jurisdiction are responsible for acts of harassment their employees commit] M. Clark. il por *Macleans* 100:44 Ag 10 '87
A strike against labor [rulings hurt labor's right to strike and bargain collectively] il *Macleans* 100:15 Ap 20 '87

Canada. Western Diversification Office
Money for the West. J. Howse. il *Macleans* 100:14-15 Ag 17 '87
New money, old refrains. S. MacLeod. por *Macleans* 100:52 Ag 31 '87

Canada and the Soviet Union
See also
Soviet Union—Foreign opinion—Canadian

Canada and the United States
Anecdotes, facetiae, satire, etc.
Uncivil liberties. C. Trillin. il *Nation* 245:116 Ag 15-22 '87

Canada Council
Attacking the left's sacred cows [refuses grant to Idler magazine] B. Amiel. il *Macleans* 100:9 D 7 '87
In the vanguard for the arts [chairman M. Forrester] il por *Macleans* 100:22-3 D 28 '87

Canada Cup (Hockey) *See* Hockey—Tournaments

Canada Development Investment Corporation
Memotec's tangled roots [takeover of Teleglobe Canada] T. Fennell. il *Macleans* 100:42+ Mr 23 '87

Canada goose shooting *See* Goose shooting

Canada-Great Britain air agreements *See* Aviation—International aspects

Canada Lands Company (Mirabel) Ltd.
A murder mystery [murder of M. Taddeo, subject of Mirabel Airport land sales investigation] L. Van Dusen. por *Macleans* 100:19-20 D 21 '87

Canada Post Corporation
Anger on the postal picket line. M. Clark. il *Macleans* 100:26+ O 19 '87
Angry words in the East [decision to appoint a francophone postmaster ignites protest in New Brunswick] M. Gee. *Macleans* 100:13 Ag 31 '87
A bitter confrontation. M. Gee. il *Macleans* 100:10-11 Je 29 '87
A bitter return to work. M. Clark. il *Macleans* 100:27 O 26 '87
CUPW at the table [talks between Canada Post and Canadian Union of Postal Workers] R. Corelli. il *Macleans* 100:35 Jl 20 '87
Drawing the battle lines [postal strike; cover story; special section; with editorial comment by Kevin Doyle] il *Macleans* 100:2, 10-14+ O 12 '87
Going down to the wire. M. Clark. il *Macleans* 100:13 Je 22 '87
Post office showdown [impending strike by Canadian Union of Postal Workers] M. Clark. il *Macleans* 100:24-5 O 5 '87
The posties' threat. M. Clark. il *Macleans* 100:16-17 Je 8 '87
Violence on the lines; The heart of the matter [strike] M. Clark. il *Macleans* 100:10-11 Jl 6 '87

Canadair Ltd.
Canadair will limit redesign, costs of Challenger upgrade [upgrade from business jet to commuter transport] il *Aviat Week Space Technol* 127:42 D 7 '87
Repairs for an image [controversy over awarding CF-18 jet fighter maintenance contract to Canadair] M. Clark. il *Macleans* 100:7 Ja 5 '87

Canadian Airlines International
Canada reallocates world service to improve efficiency, planning. *Aviat Week Space Technol* 127:36-7 O 12 '87

Canadian art *See* Art, Canadian

Canadian artificial satellites *See* Artificial satellites, Canadian

Canadian Auto Workers *See* National Automobile, Aerospace and Agricultural Implement Workers Union of Canada

Canadian Baseball Hall of Fame
Ex-pitcher Jenkins named to Canadian Hall of Fame. por *Jet* 71:46 F 23 '87

Canadian Booksellers Association
Canadians upbeat for fall: strong lists and a record convention turnout are cause for cheer. B. Slopen. il *Publ Wkly* 232:29-30+ Jl 31 '87

Canadian Broadcasting Corporation
The face of the news [retiring anchorman K. Nash] J. Bennett. il por *Macleans* 100:10+ D 21 '87
The National's new man [P. Mansbridge to anchor CBC's flagship news show] P. Young. il pors *Macleans* 100:58 N 23 '87
News, influence and propaganda [application for license to operate on cable an all-news-and-public-affairs channel] G. Bain. il *Macleans* 100:45 S 21 '87

Canadian Broadcasting Corporation. Radio Canada International
Making waves abroad. J. Careless. *Macleans* 100:61 O 19 '87

Canadian Cable News Network
A news junkie's national dream [sponsor C. Allard] P. C. Newman. il por *Macleans* 100:34 Jl 6 '87

Canadian Centre for Arms Control and Disarmament
Canadian agency rejects nuclear subs, favors surface vessels and patrol aircraft. P. Mann. *Aviat Week Space Technol* 126:77-8 Je 1 '87

Canadian cooking *See* Cooking, Canadian

Canadian fiction
Bibliography
Brevity, soul and wit. A. Manguel. il *Macleans* 100:53-4 S 21 '87

Canadian Football League
Black day for the CFL [Montreal Alouettes go out of business] H. Quinn. *Macleans* 100:21 Jl 6 '87
Staying away in flocks. R. Reilly. il *Sports Illus* 67:38-40+ N 9 '87
That empty feeling. D. Burke. il *Macleans* 100:56-7 N 16 '87

Canadian helicopters *See* Helicopters

Canadian Institute for Theoretical Astrophysics
Canadian Institute for Theoretical Astrophysics thrives in Toronto. W. Sweet. il *Phys Today* 40:100 F '87

Canadian Invasion, 1775-1776
See also
Québec (Québec)—History—Siege, 1775-1776

Canadian literature
See also
Children's literature—Canada

Canadian Medical Association
Ethical issues of AIDS. A. Steacy. *Macleans* 100:46 S 7 '87

Canadian motion picture actors and actresses *See* Motion picture actors and actresses

Canadian Museum of Civilization
Building beyond limitations [architect D. Cardinal] il por *Macleans* 100:18-19 D 28 '87

Canadian nuclear submarines *See* Nuclear submarines, Canadian

Canadian Odeon Theatres Ltd.
See also
Cineplex Odeon Corporation

Canadian Opera Company
Toronto. U. Kareda. *Opera News* 51:38 Ja 17 '87

Canadian premiers *See* Canada—Prime ministers

Canadian Radio-Television and Telecommunications Commission
The contest for cable. P. Young. il *Macleans* 100:46 Ag 24 '87
The fight to rule the airwaves. M. Janigan. il *Macleans* 100:49-50 Jl 20 '87
New choices for channel-switchers. P. Young. il *Macleans* 100:58 D 14 '87

Canadian rock groups *See* Rock groups

Canadian science fiction
Voyages of the mind. P. Giffen. il *Macleans* 100:66-7 Mr 23 '87

Canadian Security Intelligence Service
Exit of the spy master [resignation of T. D. Finn] H. Mackenzie. por *Macleans* 100:25 S 21 '87
Old worries about new spies. M. Drohan. il *Macleans* 100:10 Jl 13 '87
Reining in the spies. H. Mackenzie. il *Macleans* 100:19 D 14 '87
Spies under fire. H. Mackenzie. il *Macleans* 100:12-14 S 28 '87

Canadian Tire Corp., Ltd.
Battle to control a retail institution. T. Tedesco. il *Macleans* 100:38 Ja 19 '87
Canadian Tire showdown. T. Tedesco. il *Macleans* 100:36 Je 22 '87
The epic struggle [takeover attempt; special section] il *Macleans* 100:26-33 Ja 26 '87

Canadian Union of Postal Workers
Anger on the postal picket line. M. Clark. il *Macleans* 100:26+ O 19 '87
A bitter return to work. M. Clark. il *Macleans* 100:27 O 26 '87

Canadian Union of Postal Workers—*cont.*
CUPW at the table. R. Corelli. il *Macleans* 100:35 Jl 20 '87
Drawing the battle lines [postal strike; cover story; special section; with editorial comment by Kevin Doyle] il *Macleans* 100:2, 10-14+ O 12 '87
Post office showdown [impending strike] M. Clark. il *Macleans* 100:24-5 O 5 '87

Canadians
See also
French Canadians
The Honor Roll [cover story; special section; with editorial comment by Kevin Doyle] il *Macleans* 100:2, 11-35 D 28 '87
How we earn our place in the sun [enduring Canadian winters] C. Gordon. por *Macleans* 100:7 F 9 '87

China
History
Making a legend [filming Bethune: the making of a hero in China; cover story; special section; with editorial comment by Kevin Doyle] il pors *Macleans* 100:2, 26-34 Ag 10 '87

Great Britain
Canadian shield at the Palace [royal family media relations officer V. Chapman] il por *Macleans* 100:29 Jl 27 '87

Anecdotes, facetiae, satire, etc.
Canadians on the beat in London. A. Fotheringham. il *Macleans* 100:60 F 16 '87

Iran
A champagne homecoming [release of P. Engs] S. Aikenhead. *Macleans* 100:13 F 23 '87
The mullahs reconsider [release of P. Engs] A. Bilski. il por *Macleans* 100:19 F 16 '87

Italy
Life in a Roman limbo [Canadians M. and L. Lévesque held on charges of heroin trafficking] A. Wilson-Smith. il pors *Macleans* 100:15-16 Ja 26 '87
Triumph for two sisters [M. and L. Lévesque cleared of heroin smuggling charges in Rome] J. Barber. il pors *Macleans* 100:44 F 23 '87

United States
Canada's talent bank [Canadians in Hollywood] P. Hluchy. il *Macleans* 100:38-9 Je 8 '87

Western Europe
Europe welcomes a peaceful invasion. M. Gray. il *Macleans* 100:40 Jl 27 '87

Canal Ramírez, Gonzalo
Our aging world. *World Press Rev* 34:28 Ag '87
Canal Zone *See* Panama Canal Zone
Canals

Panama
See also
Panama Canal

Virginia
See also
Patowmack Canal (Va.)
Canapés *See* Appetizers
Canavan, Gregory H., and others
Debate on APS directed-energy weapons study. bibl f pors *Phys Today* 40:48-53 N '87
Canberra (Australia)

Description
Leisurely bike tour of Australia's Canberra. il *Sunset* 178:92 My '87
Cancellation of insurance *See* Insurance—Cancellation
Cancer
See also
Bladder—Cancer
Blood cells—Cancer
Brain—Cancer
Breast—Cancer
Cancer research
Cervix—Cancer
Colon (Anatomy)—Cancer
Colorectal cancer
Esophagus—Cancer
Eye—Cancer
Hodgkin's disease
Kidneys—Cancer
Larynx—Cancer
Leukemia
Liver—Cancer
Lungs—Cancer
Lymphatic system—Cancer
Metastasis
Nasopharynx—Cancer
Ovaries—Cancer
Pancreas—Cancer
Prostate gland—Cancer
Skin—Cancer

Testicles—Cancer
Causes
See also
Bladder—Cancer—Causes
Leukemia—Causes
Lungs—Cancer—Causes
Lymphatic system—Cancer—Causes
Nasopharynx—Cancer—Causes
Nitrosamines
Oncogenic viruses
Radiation—Physiological effects
Skin—Cancer—Causes
Stilbestrols
Urethanes
California's debate on carcinogens [Proposition 65] E. Marshall. *Science* 235:1459 Mr 20 '87
California's Proposition 65 [Safe Drinking Water and Toxic Enforcement Act] P. H. Abelson. *Science* 237:1553 S 25 '87
Cancer and the pill. S. Holck. il *World Health* p18-19 N '87
Cancer phobia. P. H. Abelson. *Science* 237:473 Jl 31 '87
Chemical carcinogenesis [discussion of July 31, 1987 article, Cancer phobia] P. H. Abelson. *Science* 238:259-60 O 16 '87
Covert chemical [methylene chloride] K. Freifeld. il *Health* 19:75 Ja '87
ELF: the current controversy. D. D. Edwards. il *Sci News* 131:107-9 F 14 '87
EPA indicts formaldehyde, 7 years later. E. Marshall. *Science* 236:381 Ap 24 '87
Gauging the value of carcinogen assays. J. Raloff. *Sci News* 131:343 My 30 '87
How safe is your food? [cancer threat from pesticides] K. McAuliffe. il *U S News World Rep* 103:70-2 N 16 '87
More bad news about that tasty browning [Maillard reactions in meat produce mutagens] *Sci News* 132:25 Jl 11 '87
Paleolithic diet, evolution, and carcinogens [discussion of April 17, 1987 article, Ranking possible carcinogenic hazards] B. N. Ames and others. *Science* 238:1633-4 D 18 '87
Power lines and cancer: the evidence grows [ELF fields] L. Slesin. il *Technol Rev* 90:52-9 O '87
Prediction of chemical carcinogenicity in rodents from in vitro genetic toxicity assays. R. W. Tennant and others. bibl f il *Science* 236:933-41 My 22 '87
Ranking possible carcinogenic hazards. B. N. Ames and others. bibl f il *Science* 236:271-80 Ap 17 '87
Regulating pesticides in food [National Academy of Sciences report] L. Tangley. il *BioScience* 37:452-6 Jl/Ag '87
Tumor promoters halt cell-cell 'talk' [research by John Holland] J. Raloff. *Sci News* 131:230-1 Ap 11 '87
Complications
New tumor factor may disrupt calcium levels [development of hypercalcemia] D. M. Barnes. bibl il *Science* 237:363-4 Jl 24 '87
A parathyroid hormone-related protein implicated in malignant hypercalcemia: cloning and expression. L. J. Suva and others. bibl f il *Science* 237:893-6 Ag 21 '87
Parathyroid hormone-related protein of malignancy: active synthetic fragments. B. E. Kemp and others. bibl f il *Science* 238:1568-70 D 11 '87
Similarity of synthetic peptide from human tumor to parathyroid hormone in vivo and in vitro. N. Horiuchi and others. bibl f il *Science* 238:1566-8 D 11 '87
Diagnosis
See also
Biopsy
Breast—Cancer—Diagnosis
Colon (Anatomy)—Cancer—Diagnosis
Colorectal cancer—Diagnosis
Lungs—Cancer—Diagnosis
Lymphatic system—Cancer—Diagnosis
Prostate gland—Cancer—Diagnosis
Skin—Cancer—Diagnosis
Genetic aspects
See also
Blood cells—Cancer—Genetic aspects
Brain—Cancer—Genetic aspects
Breast—Cancer—Genetic aspects
Colon (Anatomy)—Cancer—Genetic aspects
Colorectal cancer—Genetic aspects
Eye—Cancer—Genetic aspects
Kidneys—Cancer—Genetic aspects
Larynx—Cancer—Genetic aspects
Liver—Cancer—Genetic aspects

Cancer—Genetic aspects—See also—*cont.*
    Lungs—Cancer—Genetic aspects
    Lymphatic system—Cancer—Genetic aspects
    Pancreas—Cancer—Genetic aspects

The approaching era of the tumor suppressor genes. G. Klein. bibl f *Science* 238:1539-45 D 11 '87

Construction of a novel oncogene based on synthetic sequences encoding epidermal growth factor. D. F. Stern and others. bibl f il *Science* 235:321-4 Ja 16 '87

Elevated levels of glucose transport and transporter messenger RNA are induced by *ras* or *src* oncogenes. J. S. Flier and others. bibl f il *Science* 235:1492-5 Mr 20 '87

Epidermal growth factor-dependent transformation by a human EGF receptor proto-oncogene. T. J. Velu and others. bibl f il *Science* 238:1408-10 D 4 '87

*erb*B-2 is a potent oncogene when overexpressed in NIH/3T3 cells. P. P. Di Fiore and others. bibl f il *Science* 237:178-82 Jl 10 '87

erg, a human *ets*-related gene on chromosome 21: alternative splicing, polyadenylation, and translation. V. N. Rao and others. bibl f il *Science* 237:635-9 Ag 7 '87

Gaining on cancer. R. Corelli. il *Macleans* 100:41 Ag 24 '87

Human proto-oncogene *c-jun* encodes a DNA binding protein with structural and functional properties of transcription factor AP-1. D. Bohmann and others. bibl f il *Science* 238:1386-92 D 4 '87

Mitogens and oncogenes can block the induction of specific voltage-gated ion channels. J. M. Caffrey and others. bibl f il *Science* 236:570-3 My 1 '87

The molecular genetics of cancer. J. M. Bishop. bibl f il *Science* 235:305-11 Ja 16 '87

New family of growth factor genes identified [fibroblast growth factors] J. L. Marx. il *Science* 237:602-3 Ag 7 '87

A novel putative tyrosine kinase receptor encoded by the *eph* gene. H. Hirai and others. bibl f il *Science* 238:1717-20 D 18 '87

Oncogene linked to fruit-fly development [research by Roel Nusse and others] J. L. Marx. bibl il *Science* 238:160-1 O 9 '87

Oncogenes and transcriptional control. H. E. Varmus. bibl f *Science* 238:1337-9 D 4 '87

Oncogenes in radioresistant, noncancerous skin fibroblasts from a cancer-prone family. E. H. Chang and others. bibl f il *Science* 237:1036-9 Ag 28 '87

'Precancer' gene localized in embryo, sperm [int-1 expression] il *Sci News* 132:68 Ag 1 '87

Rapid stimulation of diacylglycerol production in Xenopus oocytes by microinjection of H-*ras* p21. J. C. Lacal and others. bibl f il *Science* 238:533-6 O 23 '87

Torn genes. T. Beardsley. *Sci Am* 257:40+ O '87

Transformation by oncogenes encoding protein kinases induces the metastatic phenotype. S. E. Egan and others. bibl f il *Science* 238:202-5 O 9 '87

Immunological aspects
Can you teach your body to fight cancer? il *Prevention* 39:6 D '87

Mortality
Cancer deaths [General Accounting Office report] J. W. Merline. il *Consum Res Mag* 70:38 N '87

Depression and cancer: a fatal link [study by Victoria W. Persky and others] B. Bower. *Sci News* 132:244 O 17 '87

Medical breakthroughs: cutting the toll of killer diseases. T. J. Gordon. il por *Futurist* 21:15-17 Ja/F '87

Recalculating the cost of Chernobyl [anticipated cancer deaths; report by the Dept. of Energy] E. Marshall. il *Science* 236:658-9 My 8 '87

Nutritional aspects
See also
    Breast—Cancer—Nutritional aspects
    Colon (Anatomy)—Cancer—Nutritional aspects
    Lungs—Cancer—Nutritional aspects

Broccoli: the anti-cancer vegetable. W. Gottlieb. il *Rodale's Org Gard* 34:66-7 Ag '87

Cabbage and its cousins: do they protect against cancer? L. Hoppe. il *Better Homes Gard* 65:82 O '87

Can your diet prevent cancer? P. Von Nostitz. il *Parents* 62:170+ Je '87

Cancer preventer? [beta-carotene] G. Bakoulis. il *Health* 19:57-9+ D '87

Coming—dietary aids to prevent cancer? [protease inhibitors; research by Ann Kennedy and others] J. Raloff. *Sci News* 131:206 Mr 28 '87

Diet and cancer. L. A. Cohen. bibl (p150) il *Sci Am* 257:42-8 N '87

Food factors that stop cancer: best news, best bets [cover story] G. Maleskey. il *Prevention* 39:88-90+ O '87

High cholesterol = high cancer risk? J. Silberner. *Sci News* 131:4 Ja 3 '87

Nature against cancer [using naturally occurring nutrients to prevent development of malignancies] N. Underwood. *Macleans* 100:60 N 2 '87

Researcher accused of plagiarism resigns [case of R. J. Shamberger] C. Holden. *Science* 237:1098 S 4 '87

Vitamin E: a new weapon against cancer. H. Rodale. *Prevention* 39:17-19 F '87

Your diet: cancer-fighting foods? J. S. Stern. *Vogue* 177:383 Ap '87

Prevention
See also
    Breast—Cancer—Prevention
    Cancer inhibiting substances
    Cervix—Cancer—Prevention
    Skin—Cancer—Prevention

9 out of 10 cases—a matter of habits. J. Carey and J. Silberner. il *U S News World Rep* 103:58+ Ag 17 '87

Cancers women get: how to reduce your risk. il *McCalls* 145:85 Mr '87

Does exercise help prevent cancer? Exercise? H. Higdon. *50 Plus* 27:16-18 Ag '87

Five-year, $4 million cancer control program set for Chicago blacks. *Jet* 71:24 F 23 '87

Psychological aspects
Blotting out cancer with a smile [research by Pirkko L. Graves] D. Zevin. il *Health* 19:14 My '87

Can you teach your body to fight cancer? il *Prevention* 39:6 D '87

Cancer & the mind: can you cure your own illness? L. Lenard. *McCalls* 114:83+ Ap '87

The character of cancer [work of Pirkko L. Graves and others] B. Bower. *Sci News* 131:120-1 F 21 '87

A degree of detachment [physician and cancer patient] B. Shragg. il *N Y Times Mag* p48 Jl 26 '87

Depression and cancer: a fatal link [study by Victoria W. Persky and others] B. Bower. *Sci News* 132:244 O 17 '87

Dr. Bernie Siegel's prescription for cancer victims (and a best-seller): 'Patient, heal thyself'. K. Gross. il pors *People Wkly* 28:61+ S 21 '87

Three medical miracles: the medicine was love; ed. by Susan Schneider. B. S. Siegel. *Redbook* 170:84-5+ D '87

Statistics
Cancer: illusory progress? [criticism of National Cancer Institute figures] *Sci Am* 256:29 Je '87

Cancer stats attacked as misleading [National Cancer Institute figures] D. D. Edwards. *Sci News* 131:260 Ap 25 '87

Cancer: what progress? [inflation of survival statistics by The National Cancer Institute] *Time* 129:64 Ap 27 '87

GAO report angers cancer officials. B. J. Culliton. il *Science* 236:380-1 Ap 24 '87

A new atlas of cancer's 'hot spots'. S. Budiansky. maps *U S News World Rep* 102:12-13 Je 22 '87

Surgery
See also
    Breast—Cancer—Surgery
    Liver—Cancer—Surgery
    Skin—Cancer—Surgery

Surgery: pain for patients and spouses [study by Merle Keitel and others] J. Meer. *Psychol Today* 21:21 Ja '87

Therapy
See also
    Breast—Cancer—Therapy
    Cancer inhibiting substances
    Hodgkin's disease—Therapy
    Leukemia—Therapy
    Lymphatic system—Cancer—Therapy
    Ovaries—Cancer—Therapy
    Prostate gland—Cancer—Therapy
    Skin—Cancer—Therapy

The anticancer company expands [Biotherapeutics] G. Bylinsky. il *Fortune* 116:121+ N 23 '87

Biologics gain influence in expanding NCI program. D. M. Barnes. il *Science* 237:848-50 Ag 21 '87

Cancer-killers from macrophages. J. Raloff. *Sci News* 131:215 Ap 4 '87

Cancer M.D.'s clash over interleukin therapy [work of Steven A. Rosenberg] M. Bloom. il por *Science* 235:154-5 Ja 9 '87

Cancer therapy risks assessed [childhood cancer; research by Margaret A. Tucker and others] R. Weiss. *Sci News* 132:165 S 12 '87

Cancer—Therapy—*cont.*

Cancer's genes and chemotherapy [research with P-glycoprotein mRNA by Ira Pastan and Michael M. Gottesman] *Sci News* 131:57 Ja 24 '87

Customized chemotherapy [Lifetrac C.S.A. (ChemoSensitive Assay)] D. Zevin. il *Health* 19:24 O '87

Drug resistance: malaria-cancer similarity? J. Silberner. *Sci News* 131:148 Mr 7 '87

The end of the beginning? [adoptive immunotherapy] D. Thompson. il *Time* 129:59 Ap 20 '87

Faulty therapy machines cause radiation overdoses [Therac-25 machines] R. C. Thompson. il *FDA Consum* 21:37-8 D '87/Ja '88

Human trials of new cancer therapy begin [stimulating cancer cells to differentiate] J. L. Marx. il *Science* 236:778-9 My 15 '87

Interleukin-2: an encouraging study. por *Newsweek* 109:74 Ap 20 '87

The lone ranger of cancer care [P. McGrady] E. Kiester. il pors *50 Plus* 27:88-94 Ap '87

Patients as research partners [privatization of research; address, August 14, 1987] R. K. Oldham. *Vital Speeches Day* 53:763-6 O 1 '87

Pay-your-own-way research [Biotherapeutics Inc.] M. Clark. il *Newsweek* 109:61 F 9 '87

Plant therapy in the fight against cancer [Chinese medicine] Xing Sishao. il *Courier* 40:20 Ag '87

Psychiatric side-effects of interleukin-2 [research by Kirk D. Denicoff and others] R. Weiss. *Sci News* 132:196 S 26 '87

Quickly. Death is going on [treating terminal cancer with heroin] W. F. Buckley. *Natl Rev* 39:63 N 6 '87

Recombinant interferon enhances monoclonal antibody-targeting of carcinoma lesions in vivo. J. W. Greiner and others. bibl f il *Science* 235:895-8 F 20 '87

Relieving cancer pain. J. Dahl and D. Joranson. il *World Health* p28-9 N '87

Resisting cancer chemotherapy. J. Silberner. il *Sci News* 131:12-13 Ja 3 '87

Scouring the globe for natural cures for cancer. *FDA Consum* 21:35 Je '87

Still looking for cancer immunotherapy. D. D. Edwards. *Sci News* 131:219 Ap 4 '87

Useless yew aids cancer fight [drug from Pacific yew bark] il *Audubon* 89:14 S '87

What are your chances of surviving cancer? M. Castleman. il *Redbook* 168:130-2+ Mr '87

Will sea animals help treat cancer? S. Eisenberg. *Sci News* 132:295 N 7 '87

Vaccines and vaccination
See also
Skin—Cancer—Vaccines and vaccination

Cancer (Constellation) *See* Constellations

Cancer cells
See also
Metastasis

Cancer's genes and chemotherapy [research with P-glycoprotein mRNA by Ira Pastan and Michael M. Gottesman] *Sci News* 131:57 Ja 24 '87

Leukemic cells rehabilitated in rats [research by Joaquin J. Jimenez and Adel A. Yunis] R. Weiss. *Sci News* 132:357 D 5 '87

Phagocytosis of Candida albicans enhances malignant behavior of murine tumor cells. I. Ginsburg and others. bibl f il *Science* 238:1573-5 D 11 '87

Resisting cancer chemotherapy. J. Silberner. il *Sci News* 131:12-13 Ja 3 '87

Tumor cell rejection through terminal cell differentiation [leukemia cells] J. J. Jimenez and A. A. Yunis. bibl f il *Science* 238:1278-80 N 27 '87

Differentiation
See Differentiation (Biology)

Cancer counseling by telephone *See* Telephone in medical care

Cancer genes *See* Cancer—Genetic aspects

Cancer in cats *See* Cats—Diseases and pests

Cancer in children
See also
Amanda the Panda, Inc.
Candlelighters Childhood Cancer Foundation
Leukemia

Anticancer genes [missing gene causes retinoblastoma] C. SerVaas. il *Saturday Evening Post* 259:98+ My/Je '87

Calls from Cosby give sick teen will to live [C. Pettaway] *Jet* 71:24 F 23 '87

Cancer therapy risks assessed [research by Margaret A. Tucker and others] R. Weiss. *Sci News* 132:165 S 12 '87

Deathwatch. P. Klass. il *Discover* 8:26+ O '87

What every teen should know about cancer. J. Moss. il *Curr Health 2* 14:27-9 O '87

Cancer in dogs *See* Dogs—Diseases and pests

Cancer inhibiting substances
See also
Cachectin
Cancer—Nutritional aspects
Mitomycin

Can garlic lick cancer? [study by Tariq Abdullah] M. S. Boyd. il *Health* 19:13 Ag '87

Combing the earth for cures to cancer, AIDS. W. Booth. il *Science* 237:969-70 Ag 28 '87

Redesigning nature's poisons to create anti-tumor reagents [immunotoxins] E. S. Vitetta and others. bibl f il *Science* 238:1098-104 N 20 '87

YIGSR, a synthetic laminin pentapeptide, inhibits experimental metastasis formation. Y. Iwamoto and others. bibl f il *Science* 238:1132-4 N 20 '87

Cancer patients

Setbacks along the way [one legged runner S. Fonyo] R. Laver. il por *Macleans* 100:42 Mr 30 '87

A survivor's bout with cancer [W. Traber] M. Maran. il por *Sch Update* 119:4-5 Ap 20 '87

A triumph of will/Barbara Shook. J. Kaplan. il por *Vogue* 177:454-5+ Mr '87

A writer at his best [R. Price] M. Ruhlman. il por *N Y Times Mag* p60-1+ S 20 '87

Civil rights
Doctor with a mission [G. Batist presses Soviet authorities to release refusenik patients with cancer] L. Van Dusen. il por *Macleans* 100:49-50 My 18 '87

Family relationships
My father's best gift [living will] N. P. Randall. il *Read Dig* 130:11-16 Ja '87

Prescription: My father spent his life healing others. Now he was the patient, and I wanted to find his cure. K. Leishman. *Glamour* 85:70+ Ja '87

Say, brother [malignant brain tumor] D. S. Baker. por *Essence* 17:9 F '87

Surgery: pain for patients and spouses [study by Merle Keitel and others] J. Meer. *Psychol Today* 21:21 Ja '87

Religious life
My cancer and the good health gospel. C. W. Colson. por *Christ Today* 31:56 Ap 3 '87

Cancer producing substances *See* Cancer—Causes

Cancer research
See also
Biotherapeutics Inc.
Memorial Sloan-Kettering Cancer Center
National Cancer Institute (U.S.)

Patients as research partners [privatization of research; address, August 14, 1987] R. K. Oldham. *Vital Speeches Day* 53:763-6 O 1 '87

Ethical aspects
Researcher accused of plagiarism resigns [case of R. J. Shamberger] C. Holden. *Science* 237:1098 S 4 '87

Cancer viruses *See* Oncogenic viruses

Candace Awards
Black women recipients of Candace Awards in N.Y. il *Jet* 72:51 Jl 6 '87

Candelaria, Michael
José Carlos Mariátegui: forgotten forerunner of liberation theology. *Christ Century* 104:885-7 O 14 '87

Candib, Claudette
about
Tranquilla: an Italianate palazzo on Biscayne Bay [cover story] J. Taylor. il pors *Archit Dig* 44:148-55 Ap '87

Candib, Murray
about
Tranquilla: an Italianate palazzo on Biscayne Bay [cover story] J. Taylor. il pors *Archit Dig* 44:148-55 Ap '87

Candid photography
History
The snapshot at 100: a tradition of spontaneous imagery. A. Goldsmith. il *Pop Photogr* 94:62+ D '87

Candida *See* Yeasts

Candidates, Political *See* Political candidates

Candidiasis
How to beat the yeast beast. B. Kevles. il *Mademoiselle* 93:58 Jl '87

Is there a "yeast connection"? Not everyone thinks so. il *Glamour* 85:246+ Je '87

Is there too much yeast in your diet? J. Storm. il *Women's Sports Fitness* 9:10-11 Jl '87

Medical disputes you should know about [views of O. Truss] G. Williams. *Ladies Home J* 104:56+ Mr '87

Yeast infections. M. Southgate. il *Essence* 18:17 O '87

Candleberry myrtle
Biological invasion by Myrica faya alters ecosystem development in Hawaii. P. M. Vitousek and others. bibl f il *Science* 238:802-4 N 6 '87
Candlelighters Childhood Cancer Foundation
Candlelighters: help for stricken families. D. Lund. il *Read Dig* 131:73-8 Ag '87
Candler, Julie
Fleet management. il *Nations Bus* 75:61-2+ My '87
Truck fever [cover story] il *Nations Bus* 75:14-16+ O '87
Candles and candleholders
English and continental brass candlesticks. J. M. Burks. bibl f il *Antiques* 132:1280-9 D '87
Candomblé (Cult) *See* Cults—Brazil
Candy
See also
Chocolate
Microwave mastery:
　Candy. il *Gourmet* 47:92-3+ D '87
Sweets for your sweet [Valentine's Day candy in the microwave] il *McCalls* 114:159-60 F '87
What's our Easter bunny's secret? Crack open an egg . . . it's chocolate inside. il *Sunset* 178:198-9 Ap '87
Candy corn plant *See* Hypocyrta
Candy industry
See also
Hershey Foods Corp.
Women in the candy industry
Mexico
Morelia: Mexico's candy capital. R. Bulter. il *Américas* 39:56-7 My/Je '87
Candy mountain [film] *See* Motion picture reviews—Single works
Candy stores
Repackaging chocolates. D. Tuller. il *Work Woman* 12:45-6 Ja '87
Candytuft
Good-looking all year . . . evergreen candytuft. il *Sunset* 179:244 N '87
Cane weaving
Hand caning chair seats. W. Shipman. il *Ctry J* 14:65-8+ F '87
Cangilla, Chris
about
Oh boy! Meet 'Teen's dream guy: Chris Cangilla. il pors *Teen* 31:64-7 Ja '87
Canin, Ethan
The year of getting to know us [story] il *Atlantic* 259:47-9+ Mr '87
about
Houghton Mifflin publishing stories by literary fellowship winner. W. Goldstein. il por *Publ Wkly* 232:19-20 D 18 '87
Caning *See* Cane weaving
Canion, Joseph R.
about
Who's afraid of IBM? [cover story] J. E. Davis. il por *Bus Week* p68-72+ Je 29 '87
Caniparoli, Val
about
SFB's Val Caniparoli: sunrise for Caniparoli. il por *Dance Mag* 61:44-5 Ag '87
Cannabis *See* Marijuana
Cannas
Cannas for summer color. L. C. Askey. il *South Living* 22:76 My '87
Cannatella, David C.
(jt. auth) *See* Poinar, George O., and Cannatella, David C.
Canned food *See* Food, Canned
Canned food cooking *See* Cooking—Canned food
Canned laughter *See* Television broadcasting—Laugh tracks
Cannell, Mark B., and others
Effect of membrane potential changes on the calcium transient in single rat cardiac muscle cells. bibl f il *Science* 238:1419-23 D 4 '87
Cannell, Stephen J.
about
Go north, young man [interview] P. E. Bauer. il pors *Channels* 7:70-1 Jl/Ag '87
Syndicating a success. G. Buchalter. il por *Forbes* 139:92 Ja 26 '87
Cannell (Stephen J.) Productions *See* Stephen J. Cannell Productions
Canneries
Shutdowns
Star-Kist's revival [reopening of St. Andrews, N.B. plant] T. Fennell. il *Macleans* 100:34 S 28 '87

Cannes Film Festival
Assault of the movie cannibals. R. Corliss. il *Time* 129:74-5 Je 1 '87
Canadian gems at a glittery festival. B. D. Johnson. il *Macleans* 100:53-4 My 25 '87
The Cannes Film Festival is a grade B movie with no good parts for Charles and Diana. il pors *People Wkly* 27:34-5 Je 1 '87
Cannes tankerous. M. Corliss; H. Jacobson. il *Film Comment* 23:60-5 Jl/Ag '87
Memo from Cannes. J. J. Buck. il *Vogue* 177:320-3+ Ag '87
Cannibalism
Are the horrors of cannibalism fact—or fiction? G. Kolata. il por *Smithsonian* 17:150-2+ Mr '87
The myths and perturbing realities of cannibalism. P. Shipman. il *Discover* 8:70-2+ Mr '87
Fish
Now here's a case of you eat what you are [work of Gary Meffe and Martha Crump with mosquitofish] il *Discover* 8:10 Je '87
Canning, Peter C.
The best Father's Day ever. il *Read Dig* 130:61-3 Je '87
Canning and preserving
See also
Canneries
Food, Canned
Pectins
Pickles and relishes
Tomatoes—Preservation
Pressure can safely [venting] S. Milius. il *Rodale's Org Gard* 34:52 Jl '87
She does all of her canning in a special harvest kitchen. il *Sunset* 179:142 Ag '87
Equipment
A canner's dream [Mason jars] E. Long. il por *Rodale's Org Gard* 34:60-1 Ag '87
Canning industry *See* Canneries
Canning jars *See* Canning and preserving—Equipment
Cannold, Mitchell
about
Fancy dancing. G. Morgenson. il por *Forbes* 140:194 S 21 '87
Cannon, Gordon C.
Sequence analysis on microcomputers. bibl f il *Science* 238:97-103 O 2 '87
Cannon, Maureen
Halfway-to-two [poem] il *Good Housekeep* 205:198 O '87
I think of flags [poem] il *Good Housekeep* 205:157 Jl '87
Sixty-third summer [poem] il *Good Housekeep* 205:193 Ag '87
Waiting for Jay [poem] il *Good Housekeep* 205:198 O '87
Winter wail [poem] *Good Housekeep* 204:153 Ja '87
Cannon, Peter
Japanese challenge—American response [address, March 5, 1987] *Vital Speeches Day* 53:503-9 Je 1 '87
Cannon Group Inc.
Is the go-go gone? [M. Golan and Y. Globus] M. Dougherty. il pors *Life* 10:102 Ap '87
Cannonball One Lap of America (Rally) *See* Automobile rallies
Canoe trips *See* Canoes and canoeing
Canoes and canoeing
See also
Kayaks and kayaking
Running rapids
Canoe-exploring the canals, rivers, and lakes of southwest Sweden. il *Sunset* 178:68 My '87
Canoeing Saskatchewan: Canada's watery highways. B. Wrenn. il *Travel Holiday* 168:22+ S '87
Float yourself a holiday. D. Moreau. il *Changing Times* 41:105-7 Mr '87
The green canoe. H. Middleton. il *South Living* 22:16+ Jl '87
The longest honeymoon [V. Fons-Kruger and V. Kruger paddling from the Arctic Ocean to Cape Horn] J. Mills. il pors map *Women's Sports Fitness* 9:80-4+ Mr '87
Roughing it in the bush [Duke and Duchess of York on a canoeing holiday in the Northwest Territories] M. McIver. il pors *Macleans* 100:46 Ag 10 '87
Canon Inc.
Canon finally challenges Minolta's mighty Maxxum [EOS autofocus SLRs] O. Port. il *Bus Week* p89-90 Mr 2 '87

Canon Inc.—*cont.*
"I am betting my destiny" [Canon's EOS automatic focusing camera] J. A. Trachtenberg. il *Forbes* 139:66 Mr 9 '87

Canonization
See also
Beatification
A new U.S. saint [R. P. Duchesne] K. L. Woodward. por *Newsweek* 109:8 Je 22 '87
A question of faith in California [dispute over proposed sainthood for Father Junípero Serra] il *U S News World Rep* 102:24 My 11 '87
So you want to be a saint [Father N. F. Moholy's efforts to have J. Serra canonized] L. Gomez and W. Wynn. il pors *Life* 10:68-9+ S '87

Canopies
Tailored for the king-size bed. il *South Living* 22:184 Ap '87
Turning the mattress into a fortress [earthquake-proof bed canopy; work of H. J. Khadivi] T. Dworetzky. il *Discover* 8:22 S '87

Canopy, Forest crown *See* Forest crown canopy

Canright, Sarah, 1941-
about
Sarah Canright. M. McCombie. il *Art News* 86:45 My '87

Cans
See also
Beverage containers
Gasoline cans
Recycling
See Recycling (Waste, etc.)

Can't buy me love [film] *See* Motion picture reviews—Single works

Cantata and cantatas
See also
Compact discs—Cantatas
Phonograph records—Cantatas
Musical events:
Boston Symphony performs D. Martino's The white island. A. Porter. *New Yorker* 63:98+ My 11 '87
Performance of J. Harbison's The flight into Egypt. A. Porter. *New Yorker* 63:86-7 Je 8 '87

Cantata Singers and Ensemble
Musical events:
Performance of J. Harbison's The flight into Egypt. A. Porter. *New Yorker* 63:86-7 Je 8 '87

Canticle for innocent comedians [dance] *See* Dance reviews—Single works

Canticum Novum Singers
Musical events:
Performance of Handel's Joshua. A. Porter. *New Yorker* 63:75-6 Je 15 '87

Canton (China) *See* Guangzhou (China)

Canton (Mass.)
Buildings
A corporate villa [Codex World Headquarters Building; cover story] il *Archit Rec* 175:120-31 N '87

Canton (Ohio)
Social conditions
The heart of Canton, Ohio [amputee C. Torrence] H. Hurt. *Read Dig* 130:49-52 Mr '87

Cantor, B. Gerald
about
Sculptural strengths: the B. Gerald Cantors in Manhattan. M. M. Thomas. il *Archit Dig* 44:118-23+ My '87

Cantor, Iris
about
Sculptural strengths: the B. Gerald Cantors in Manhattan. M. M. Thomas. il *Archit Dig* 44:118-23+ My '87

Cantrell, Ed, 1928?-
about
The last hired gun. J. Conaway. il por *Harpers* 275:58-63 Ag '87

Cantrell, Jim, 1935-
about
Jim Cantrell. B. S. Goldman. il por *Am Artist* 51:32-7 Jl '87

Cantwell, Brian J.
The Columbia River Gorge. il *Travel Holiday* 168:12-15 Jl '87

Cantwell, Mary
Joanne Woodward: a class act. il por *Vogue* 177:390-1+ N '87
The young man and the sea. il por *Vogue* 177:236-7+ Jl '87

Canvassing *See* Door-to-door selling

Canyon Colorado Equid Sanctuary (N.M.) *See* Wildlife sanctuaries—New Mexico

Canyons
See also
Barranca de Cobre (Mexico)
Colorado Plateau
Columbia River Gorge (Or. and Wash.)
Grand Canyon (Ariz.)
Hell Canyon (S.D.)
Indian Canyons (Calif.)
Kings River Canyon (Calif.)
Sycamore Canyon (Ariz.)
Amazing canyon country [Arizona and Utah] G. S. Bush. il map *Better Homes Gard* 65:128+ Je '87

Capa, Robert, 1913-1954
about
The Cultural Center. il por *Antiques Collect Hobbies* 92:54-5 S '87

Capacity, Industrial *See* Industrial capacity

Capasso, Carl
about
Bess and the mess: Myerson's slide into scandal [cover story] P. Morrisroe. il pors *N Y* 20:30-44 Mr 30 '87
Downfall of an American idol [cover story] M. Green. il pors *People Wkly* 27:44-6+ Je 29 '87

Capasso, Federico
Band-gap engineering: from physics and materials to new semiconductor devices. bibl f il *Science* 235:172-6 Ja 9 '87

CAPE *See* Cincinnati Academy of Physical Education

Cape Cod (Mass.)
See also
Beaches—Cape Cod (Mass.)
Birds—Cape Cod (Mass.)
Geology—Cape Cod (Mass.)
Description and travel
Thoreau walks the Cape. J. J. Thorndike. il *Am Herit* 38:70-5 Ap '87

Cape Hatteras Lighthouse *See* Lighthouses

Cape Hatteras National Seashore (N.C.)
Standoff at Oregon Inlet [Army Corps of Engineers proposal to build jetties] L. S. Bates. il *Oceans* 20:5-6 Mr/Ap '87

Cape Henry Lighthouse *See* Lighthouses

Cape Horn (Chile)
"Captain" Mary Patten [1854-55 voyage from New York to San Francisco via Cape Horn] P. L. Brosnan. il por *Oceans* 20:36-9 S/O '87
Passage at Cape Horn [D. and D. Hays sail 25 foot cutter around Cape Horn and back to Connecticut] A. Smith. il pors *Esquire* 107:88-90+ Mr '87

Cape Sarichef Lighthouse *See* Lighthouses—Aleutian Islands (Alaska)

Cape Vincent (N.Y.)
Historic houses, sites, etc.
Napoleonic New York. A. Keefe. *Travel Holiday* 167:32-4 Je '87

Capel, M. S., and others
A complete mapping of the proteins in the small ribosomal subunit of Escherichia coli. bibl f il *Science* 238:1403-6 D 4 '87

Capelin, Joan
Change in the blink of an eye. il *Archit Rec* 175:45+ F '87

Capen, Edgar
about
One office the Mac has conquered. il por *Fortune* 116:60 N 9 '87

Capezio, Salvatore
about
Capezio centenary: family affairs. N. V. Dalva. il pors *Dance Mag* 61:90-4 My '87

Capital
See also
Liquidity (Economics)
Capital takes advantage. E. J. McCarthy. il *Commonweal* 114:37-8 Ja 30 '87

Capital, Venture *See* Venture capital

Capital Appreciation Fund *See* T. Rowe Price Capital Appreciation Fund

Capital Cities/ABC Inc.
Cap Cities' quiet man [R. J. Doerfler] R. Buck. por *Channels* 7:55 Je '87
An exception to Murphy's Law? [Capital Cities/ABC] S. N. Chakravarty. il por *Forbes* 140:36-8 Ag 10 '87
Not ready for prime time? [Capital Cities/ABC] G. Fabrikant. il por *N Y Times Mag* p30+ Ap 12 '87
What's a flop worth? [earnings accounting] S. N. Chakravarty. *Forbes* 140:82 D 28 '87

Capital equipment industry *See* Industrial equipment industry

Capital formation *See* Capital

Capital gains tax
> *See also*
>> Real property—Taxation

Angel of death loophole [proposal to tax capital gains at death] *New Repub* 197:4 Jl 13-20 '87

Are all gains equal? Not yet. P. Philipps. il *Bus Week* p152 Mr 16 '87

Embarrassing facts. *Natl Rev* 39:17-18 S 25 '87

The environment gets a break as well [effects of closing capital gains loopholes] il *Discover* 8:13 My '87

How to pull in revenues without gutting tax reform. P. C. Roberts. il *Bus Week* p14 Ag 10 '87

The long and short of capital gains. W. G. Flanagan. il *Forbes* 139:100 Je 29 '87

Make the taxman share the losses. W. Baldwin. *Forbes* 140:48+ N 16 '87

Of capital, taxes, and death. D. R. Katz. il *Esquire* 107:55-6 Mr '87

An offer Congress shouldn't refuse—a revenue increase via a tax decrease. il *Nations Bus* 75:79 N '87

Raising venture capital now. J. C. Szabo. il *Nations Bus* 75:31-4 F '87

Take it now. J. Crudele. il *N Y* 20:16 D 14 '87

Why Congress should reconsider abolition of the capital gains differential. il *Nations Bus* 75:72 Mr '87

Capital goods investment *See* Capital investments

Capital Holding Corp.

Thank you, Tom Simons. J. Andresky. il por *Forbes* 139:99 Mr 23 '87

Capital investments
> *See also*
>> Investment tax credit

Capital spending is rising again. H. Banks. *Forbes* 140:27 Ag 10 '87

Capital spending suffers when public investment lags. G. Koretz and K. Pennar. il *Bus Week* p34 N 2 '87

Casting light on the mystery of low productivity . . . G. Koretz. il *Bus Week* p32 Je 1 '87

Don't count out a mild upsurge in capital investment. G. Koretz. il *Bus Week* p26 Ap 6 '87

The economy draws power from spending for equipment. . . but some of the benefits seem headed overseas. G. Koretz. il *Bus Week* p38 D 28 '87-Ja 4 '88

Finance: business's outlay for plants and equipment holding its own. R. Ringelstein. il *Archit Rec* 175:41+ Jl '87

How the long runup will change corporate behavior [bull market] A. L. Cowan and E. Spragins. il *Bus Week* p62-3 F 2 '87

Investment rebounds. S. Nasar. il *Fortune* 115:50 Je 22 '87

The long wait [capital spending strategy of International Paper] D. Henry. il *Forbes* 139:66-7 Je 15 '87

Still more reasons to mistrust supply siders [Stefan Welzk's study of German tax loopholes and parallel decline in capital investments] R. Kuttner. por *Bus Week* p22 O 26 '87

Why earlier outlays were starved. W. B. Franklin and J. C. Cooper. il *Bus Week* p23-4 S 28 '87

Why tax reform isn't taking a toll on investment. P. Magnusson. *Bus Week* p26 Ag 10 '87

Capital markets *See* Money markets

Capital movements

Dirty money and the debt crisis [views of T. H. Naylor] P. C. Newman. il por *Macleans* 100:39 Mr 9 '87

New capitals for raising capital? [interview with J. Hennessy] R. Morais. por *Forbes* 139:64 Mr 9 '87

Capital punishment
> *See also*
>> Executions and executioners
>> Hanging

AIDS and the death penalty as consistency tests for the prolife movement. J. R. Kelly. *America* 157:151-5 S 26 '87

The appointment of death [Supreme Court rejects view that death penalty is racially biased] M. Kempton. il *N Y Rev Books* 34:40 My 28 '87

The bench and the chair [Supreme Court's ruling that death penalty doesn't discriminate against blacks] *Natl Rev* 39:15 My 22 '87

Capital punishment: just or cruel? [interview with D. Popeo and H. Schwarzschild] A. Kenney. pors *Sch Update* 119:13 F 9 '87

Clearing a path to the chair [Supreme Court rejects argument that the death penalty discriminates against blacks] R. Lacayo. il *Time* 129:80 My 4 '87

Countdown to the electric chair [18-year-old killer P. Cooper] F. Bruning. por *Macleans* 100:13 O 26 '87

Crime and the Constitution [death penalty] D. O. Relin and C. Lawrence. il *Sch Update* 120:10-11 D 4 '87

Death row clerk [death penalty work in the Supreme Court] C. Sloan. *New Repub* 196:18+ F 16 '87

Decide on the death penalty. D. Pawelek. il *Sch Update* 119:12+ F 9 '87

Gridlock on death row [Supreme Court rejects view that death penalty is racist] A. Press. il *Newsweek* 109:60-1 My 4 '87

Group cites racism in death penalty sentence [views of Amnesty International] *Jet* 72:38 Ap 13 '87

Indiana killer, Italian martyr [Italians show support for juvenile killer P. Cooper] G. Hackett. il por *Newsweek* 110:37 S 21 '87

Minority report. C. Hitchens. *Nation* 245:150 Ag 29 '87

Open door to the execution chamber? [Supreme Court ruling that death penalty does not discriminate against blacks] T. Gest. il *U S News World Rep* 102:25 My 4 '87

Punishable by death. D. W. Van Ness. il por *Christ Today* 31:24-7 Jl 10 '87

A shared fate [Supreme Court ruling that death penalty is not racially biased] M. O. Finkelstein. *Nation* 244:599 My 9 '87

Thinking about the death penalty [Supreme Court rules death penalty not racially biased] *America* 156:393 My 16 '87

Canada

Between life and death row. A. Fotheringham. il *Macleans* 100:52 Ap 13 '87

Capital punishment: the death vote [special section; with editorial comment by Kevin Doyle] il *Macleans* 100:2, 8-12+ Mr 16 '87

The death debate begins. M. Gee. il *Macleans* 100:16-17 My 11 '87

Fortunately they forgot Quebec [rejection of capital punishment] A. Fotheringham. il *Macleans* 100:52 Jl 13 '87

Hard choices on crime [Parliament rejects death penalty] H. Mackenzie. il *Macleans* 100:6-7 Jl 13 '87

Restoring Canada's death penalty. T. Sinclair-Faulkner. *Christ Century* 104:400 Ap 29 '87

A return to the gallows? P. Gessell. il *Macleans* 100:10 F 23 '87

Saying no to the death penalty. L. K. Tarr. il *Christ Today* 31:38 Ag 7 '87

Should the state kill? [cover story; special section; with editorial comment by Kevin Doyle] il *Macleans* 100:2, 14-20+ Je 29 '87

> *Anecdotes, facetiae, satire, etc.*

Whimsy and the death vote. A. Fotheringham. il *Macleans* 100:64 Ap 27 '87

South Africa

On death row in Pretoria Central. D. Bruck. *New Repub* 197:18-21+ Jl 13-20 '87

Capital spending *See* Capital investments

Capitalism
> *See also*
>> Big business
>> Small business

Capitalism & selfishness [discussion of December 1986 article] A. Ryerson. *Commentary* 83:10-12+ Mr '87

Capitalism and its consequences [special section] *Society* 24:26-54 S/O '87

Morality and capitalism: is there virtue in profit? *Current* 292:11-17 My '87

Paying for a good squeeze. C. Gordon. por *Macleans* 100:7 Mr 9 '87

Socialism as the teflon dream. R. J. Neuhaus. *Natl Rev* 39:52 Ja 30 '87

History

Creative destruction [Forbes 70th anniversary issue; cover story; special issue] il *Forbes* 140:49-51 Jl 13 '87

How capitalism survived the twentieth century. M. Mayer. il *Am Herit* 38:46-51 N '87

Capitalists and financiers

Getting rich in America: men, money & the survival of capitalism [cover story; special issue; with editorial comment by Byron Dobell] il *Am Herit* 38:5, 34-51+ N '87

Here we go again [corporate mergers and restructurings in the last 100 years; special section] il *Forbes* 140:242-6+ Jl 13 '87

Capitalists and financiers in literature

A robber historian [M. Josephson's The robber barons] M. Klein. il *Forbes* 140 Sp Issue:46+ O 26 '87

Capitol (Washington, D.C.)
Mystery lady [J. Trumbull's wife Sarah appears in painting The resignation of General Washington in Capitol Rotunda] I. B. Jaffe. il pors *Art News* 86:34-5 Mr '87
Capitol Industries-EMI, Inc.
Capitol shake-up: EMI America merges with Manhattan. M. Goldberg. *Roll Stone* p18+ Ag 13 '87
Joe Smith named head of Capitol/EMI. A. DeCurtis. *Roll Stone* p11+ F 12 '87
Capitols
   See also
   South Carolina—Capitol
   Washington (State)—Capitol
Caplan, Frieda
   about
The Princess of Produce. P. F. Stewart. il por *Ladies Home J* 104:156 O '87
Caplan, Lincoln
The tenth justice (I). *New Yorker* 63:29-32+ Ag 10 '87
The tenth justice (II). *New Yorker* 63:30-2+ Ag 17 '87
Caplan, Richard
Crates of fresh poison. *Harpers* 275:58-9 O '87
Cap'n Sam's Riverboat Cruises
Savannah's true pilot [S. Stevens] D. Young. il pors *South Living* 22:74 Ag '87
Capolino, Peter
   about
Baseball flannels are hot. D. Butwin. il por *Sports Illus* 67:105 Jl 6 '87
Capone, Al, 1899-1947
   about
Al Capone: Chicago's "untouchable" mobster. por *Am Hist Illus* 22:50-1 O '87
Caporale, Patricia
Taking a chance on love [adoption of handicapped children] il por *Ladies Home J* 104:22+ My '87
Capos, Claudia R.
How to drive an elephant. il *Ms* 16:108 S '87
Capote, Truman, 1924-1984
Three neighbors. il pors *Esquire* 108:223-4 D '87
   about
The tiny terror: a Capote memory. L. Lerman. il pors *Vogue* 177:762-3+ S '87
Capotosto, Rosario
Workshop minicourse. See issues of Popular Mechanics beginning January 1986
Cappella Sistina (Vatican) *See* Vatican. Cappella Sistina
Cappelletti, Don
   about
Trying to unload a 90-foot-high home is one very tall order. il por *People Wkly* 28:57 N 23 '87
Capps, Kenneth
   about
Kenneth Capps at Saxon-Lee. F. Colpitt. il *Art Am* 75:189+ My '87
Caprio, Jennie
Maimed by skin cancer, this onetime sun worshipper paid a painful price for the perfect tan. il pors *People Wkly* 28:87-8+ Ag 10 '87
Capriotti, Joe
   about
Garlic you plant only once. L. Korn. il pors *Rodale's Org Gard* 34:91-2 Ap '87
Capron, André, and others
Immunity to schistosomes: progress toward vaccine. bibl f il *Science* 238:1065-72 N 20 '87
Capsicum *See* Peppers
Capsules
   See also
   Nutrient capsules
Captain EO [film] *See* Motion picture reviews—Single works
Captain Power and the soldiers of the future [television program] *See* Television program reviews—Single works
Captains of ships *See* Shipmasters
Captions (Opera) *See* Opera—Titling
Captions (Slides) *See* Slides (Photography)—Captions
Captive animals *See* Zoos
Captive breeding programs (Animals) *See* Breeding
Captive insurance companies *See* Insurance companies—Captive companies
Captive Nations Week
Captive Nations Week, 1987 [proclamation, July 17, 1987] R. Reagan. *Dep State Bull* 87:36 O '87
Captopril
A tough act to follow. K. Hannon. il por *Forbes* 139:88+ Je 15 '87
Capuchin monkeys and the handicapped *See* Handicapped and animals

Capucilli, Terese
   about
Dance. T. Tobias. il por *N Y* 20:98-9 S 21 '87
Caputo, Robert
In the pink [photograph] il *Nat Hist* 96:104-5 O '87
Car and driver (Periodical)
Guided tours, right this way [office photos] D. Sherman. il *Car Driv* 33:11 Ag '87
   Anecdotes, facetiae, satire, etc.
The deep stuff. B. W. Yates. il *Car Driv* 33:23 O '87
Car auctions *See* Auctions
Car clubs *See* Automobile clubs
Car manuals *See* Automobiles—Handbooks, manuals, etc.
Car seats (Safety seats) *See* Automobiles—Safety devices and measures
Car telephones *See* Cellular radio in automobiles
Caracas (Venezuela)
   Description
Caracas. N. N. Schofield. il *Black Enterp* 17:35-6 My '87
Caramel desserts *See* Desserts
Caras, Ingrid W., and others
Signal for attachment of a phospholipid membrane anchor in decay accelerating factor. bibl f il *Science* 238:1280-3 N 27 '87
Caras, Roger A.
Give them what they want. *Writer* 100:7-8 Je '87
Caravaggio, Michelangelo Merisi da, 1573-1610
   about
Love story. L. Tillman. il *Art Am* 75:21-3 Ja '87
Caravaggio [film] *See* Motion picture reviews—Single works
Caravans
   See also
   Wagon trains
Caravans (Gypsy wagons) *See* Gypsy wagons
Caraway thyme *See* Thyme
Carbamates
   See also
   Urethanes
Carberry, Charles M.
   about
Wall Street's top cop. il pors *Newsweek* 109:48-50 Mr 2 '87
Carbo, Bernie
   Anecdotes, facetiae, satire, etc.
Time loves a haircut. B. Cardoso. *Harpers* 274:68-9 Ap '87
Carbo, Marie
Deprogramming reading failure: giving unequal learners an equal chance. bibl f il *Phi Delta Kappan* 69:197-202 N '87
Reading styles research: 'What works' isn't always phonics. bibl f il *Phi Delta Kappan* 68:431-5 F '87
Carbohydrate metabolism
Get a daily carbo boost [glycogen burning] G. Sloan. il *Women's Sports Fitness* 9:16 Ag '87
High-carb diets questioned [theory of Gerald Reaven] G. Kolata. *Science* 235:164 Ja 9 '87
Three-dimensional representation and analysis of brain energy metabolism [glucose] L. S. Hibbard and others. bibl f il *Science* 236:1641-6 Je 26 '87
Carbohydrates
   See also
   Feeds—Carbohydrate content
Carbing up at the salad bowl. R. Schrambling. il *Work Woman* 12:140+ Je '87
Carbohydrates: today's dietary 'good buys'. L. Hoppe. il *Better Homes Gard* 65:40+ Jl '87
Carbon
   See also
   Graphite
   Plants—Carbon content
Covalent group IV atomic clusters. W. L. Brown and others. bibl f il *Science* 235:860-5 F 20 '87
Explaining carbon-cluster magic numbers [structure for 11-atom carbon molecule; research by James A. Van Vechten and Douglas A. Keszler] S. Weisburd. il *Sci News* 132:100-1 Ag 15 '87
   Isotopes
Natural abundances of carbon isotopes in acetate from a coastal marine sediment. N. E. Blair and others. bibl f il *Science* 236:66-8 Ap 3 '87
Carbon, Activated
Activated charcoal: new champion of cholesterol fighters? J. Meade. *Prevention* 39:112+ Ja '87
Carbon-14 dating *See* Radiocarbon dating
Carbon compounds
   See also
   Hydrocarbons

Carbon cycle (Biogeochemistry)
Autumn's hidden harvest [carbon in fallen leaves as energy source for stream creatures] R. H. Boyle. il *Natl Wildl* 25:4-9 O/N '87
Forests made the world frigid? [theory of James C. G. Walker and Andrew H. Knoll] S. Weisburd. *Sci News* 131:9 Ja 3 '87
Terrestrial metabolism and atmospheric CO_2 concentrations. R. A. Houghton. bibl il *BioScience* 37:672-8 O '87

Carbon dioxide
See also
Greenhouse effect
The 1986 Lake Nyos gas disaster in Cameroon, West Africa [cover story] G. W. Kling and others. bibl f il maps *Science* 236:169-75 Ap 10 '87
Cameroon clouds: soda source? R. Monastersky. il *Sci News* 131:388 Je 20 '87
Cameroon lake: new clues, new clouds? [Lake Nyos] S. Weisburd. *Sci News* 131:36-7 Ja 17 '87
A dead chief's revenge? [Lake Nyos gas burst] H. Sigurdsson. il maps *Nat Hist* 96:44-9 Ag '87
Lake Nyos reported red and rumbling. S. Weisburd. *Sci News* 131:134 F 28 '87
Lake Nyos was rigged for disaster. R. A. Kerr. il *Science* 235:528-9 Ja 30 '87
Plumbing the depths of a lethal lake [Nyos in Cameroon; work of George Kling] il map *Discover* 8:12 My '87
Prehistoric Cameroon-style lake events [ancient Arizona crater lake; research by James D. White and Richard Fisher] R. Monastersky. *Sci News* 132:335 N 21 '87
Seasonal mixing and catastrophic degassing in tropical lakes, Cameroon, West Africa. G. W. Kling. bibl f il *Science* 237:1022-4 Ag 28 '87
Silent death from Cameroon's killer lake [Lake Nyos] C. Stager. il map *Natl Geogr* 172:404-20 S '87
Terrestrial metabolism and atmospheric CO_2 concentrations. R. A. Houghton. bibl il *BioScience* 37:672-8 O '87

Carbon fibers
Medical use
Fast comeback from injury: carbon fibers can rebuild torn tendons. S. Reeder. *Women's Sports Fitness* 9:44-5 Ja '87

Carbon monoxide
Carbon monoxide: stealthy environmental pollutant. D. A. Labianca. il *USA Today (Periodical)* 116:44-6 N '87

Carbon monoxide detectors
A lifesaving key chain [Lifesign detector] *Prevention* 39:12-13 My '87

Carbon tetrachloride
Carbon tetrachloride at hepatotoxic levels blocks reversibly gap junctions between rat hepatocytes. J. C. Sáez and others. bibl f il *Science* 236:967-9 My 22 '87

Carbonated milk *See* Milk, Carbonated
Carbonates
See also
Iron carbonates
Delving deep into the Indian past [ocean hot spots] R. Monastersky. map *Sci News* 132:56 Jl 25 '87

Carboxylic acids
See also
Quinolinic acid
Carboxymyoglobin *See* Myoglobin
Carburetors
A carb named SU. P. Egan. il *Road Track* 38:20 Jl '87
Carb tune-ups: the right way [boats] T. Banse. il *Mot Boat Sail* 160:94 Ag '87

Carcasses, Cattle *See* Cattle—Carcasses
Carcasses, Swine *See* Swine—Carcasses
Carcinogens *See* Cancer—Causes
Carcinoma *See* Cancer
Card, Emily
The bottom line for women. il *Ms* 16:48+ Jl/Ag '87
The new plastic money. il *Ms* 15:80+ Ap '87
You and your 1040: how women fare under the new tax law. il *Ms* 15:68+ F '87

Cardboard boxes *See* Boxes, cases, etc.
Carden, Sarah
Live performance [story] il por *McCalls* 145:153-4 Mr '87

Carder, Frederick, 1863 or 4-1963
about
Glass. S. B. Sherrill. il *Antiques* 131:352+ F '87
The Rockwell Museum. il *Antiques Collect Hobbies* 92:53 Ag '87

Cardia, Roy A., 1940-
about
Back on track. A. A. Lappen. il por *Forbes* 140:12 Jl 13 '87

Cardiac arrhythmia defibrillators *See* Defibrillators
Cardiac catheterization
A doctor's prize catch [comparison of the retrieval of a catheter lodged in a lung with muskie fishing] P. Skalka. il *Read Dig* 130:128-32 Mr '87
The female heart [difference in numbers of men and women referred for catheterization] il *U S News World Rep* 103:6 Ag 3 '87
A tube that could be a killer [diagnostic device] *U S News World Rep* 103:65 N 23 '87

Cardiac diseases *See* Heart—Diseases
Cardiac muscle *See* Heart—Muscle
Cardiac pacemakers *See* Pacemaker, Artificial (Heart)
Cardiac patients *See* Cardiacs
Cardiacs
Psychology
See Heart—Diseases—Psychological aspects
Rehabilitation
See Heart—Diseases—Therapy
Travel
Rx for cardiac patients. E. S. Orzac. *Travel Holiday* 167:32-3+ Ap '87

Cardiff (Wales)
Race relations
Mixed marriage 67 years ago has 3 generations of mixed descendants [descendants of Joseph Dixon and Emily Ashford] J. Collins. il *Jet* 71:14-16 F 16 '87

Cardinal, Douglas
about
Building beyond limitations. il por *Macleans* 100:18-19 D 28 '87

Cardinal Industries
The lord of modular [A. Guirlinger] E. Schmuckler. il por *Forbes* 140:208+ D 14 '87

Cardinals
Political activities
Covert aid and the Church [U.S. aid to Cardinal Obando y Bravo of Nicaragua] R. Parry and T. Jacoby. il por *Newsweek* 109:27-8 Je 15 '87

Cardiopulmonary resuscitation *See* Resuscitation
Cardiovascular system
See also
Blood vessels
Heart
Do-it-yourself test for cardiovascular fitness. B. Weinhouse. il *Ladies Home J* 104:58 Je '87
How fit—heart. K. McCleary. il *Good Housekeep* 204:90 My '87

Diseases
Smoking, the pill, and coronary disease [lowered prostacyclin levels; studies by Jerry L. Nadler] il *USA Today (Periodical)* 115:4 F '87

Cardoen, Dany
about
Progress and panic at Puimichel. L. Vanhoeck. il pors *Sky Telesc* 74:543-6 N '87

Cardoso, Bill
Time loves a haircut. *Harpers* 274:68-9 Ap '87

Cards
See also
Bridge (Game)
IQ Foundation (Firm)
Poker (Game)

Cards, Advertising *See* Advertising cards
Cards, Baseball *See* Baseball cards
Cards, Greeting *See* Greeting cards
Career counseling *See* Vocational guidance
Career counseling firms *See* Employment agencies
Career criminals *See* Recidivists
Career education *See* Vocational-technical education
Career stress *See* Job stress
Career switching *See* Occupational mobility
Careers *See* Occupations
Careers for women *See* Women—Occupations
Caremark, Inc.
A booster shot for Baxter Labs [acquisition of Caremark Inc.] K. Deveny. il *Bus Week* p63 My 25 '87

Carew, Topper
about
Carew "Busts loose". S. Herbert. por *Black Enterp* 18:25 S '87

Carew-Reid, Lloyd
about
This is against my rights! Three who felt wronged—and determined to battle for redress. G. Jaynes. il pors *Time* 130:40-2 Jl 6 '87

Carey, Alan
The nature of wildlife photography. il pors *Mother Earth News* 105:60-3+ My/Je '87
Carey, Cathy, and Hommel, Carolyn L.
Cracking down on crab pickers. il *FDA Consum* 21:33-4 S '87
Carey, Ellen
about
Ellen Carey at ICP and Simon Cerigo. S. Westfall. il *Art Am* 75:181 N '87
Carey, George W., and others
U.S. youth and violent death. il maps *Focus* 37:30-2 Spr '87
Carey, Gregory D.
How to analyze waveforms. il *Radio-Electron* 58:59-60+ D '87
Carey, James W.
The press and the public discourse [cover story; with discussion] il por *Cent Mag* 20:4-32 Mr/Ap '87
Carey, John
Trouble in paradise. il map *Natl Wildl* 25:42-5 O/N '87
Carey, Richard Adams
The red fox. il *Ctry J* 14:56-61 S '87
Carey, William D.
about
William D. Carey. D. E. Koshland, Jr. *Science* 235:1553 Mr 27 '87
Carey, William Polk
about
A New York businessman settles an old score (and his conscience) by paying a 1966 debt to 80 farmers. L. Aitken. il por *People Wkly* 27:74+ F 23 '87
Carey-Thomas Awards
Carey Thomas Awards. il *Publ Wkly* 231:12 Mr 13 '87
Cargo airlines *See* Air freight service
Cargo airplanes *See* Airplanes, Freight
Cargo ships *See* Freighters
Caribbean American Chamber of Commerce and Industry
Carib trade exhibition. M. Scott. il *Black Enterp* 17:18 Jl '87
Caribbean Basin Initiative, 1983-
Caribbean Basin Initiative. E. C. Conkling. il map *Focus* 37:2-9 Summ '87
The Caribbean Basin Initiative [address, November 17, 1986] A. J. Roach. *Vital Speeches Day* 53:317-18+ Mr 1 '87
The Caribbean Basin Initiative [address, October 1, 1987] A. A. Farrelly. *Vital Speeches Day* 54:68-70 N 15 '87
Caribbean cooking *See* Cooking, Caribbean
Caribbean coral reefs *See* Coral reefs and islands
Caribbean literature (English)
See also
Caribbean writer (Periodical)
The puzzle for Caribbean writers. N. Faria. *World Press Rev* 34:62 Ja '87
Caribbean music *See* Music, Caribbean
Caribbean National Forest (Puerto Rico)
Caribbean National Forest. B. G. Norton. il map *Wilderness* 50:20-1 Spr '87
El Yunque Rain Forest, Puerto Rico. R. H. Mohlenbrock. il map *Nat Hist* 96:76-9 F '87
Elfin Forest, Puerto Rico. R. H. Mohlenbrock. il map *Nat Hist* 96:20-2 D '87
Caribbean region
See also
Arts—Caribbean region
Barbados
Children—Caribbean region
Economic assistance, American—Caribbean region
Environmental policy—Caribbean region
Hotels, motels, etc.—Caribbean region
Housing—Caribbean region
Jamaica
Medical care—Caribbean region
Medical colleges—Caribbean region
Military assistance, American—Caribbean region
Military assistance, Cuban—Caribbean region
Music—Caribbean region
Public health—Caribbean region
Real estate investment—Caribbean region
Resorts—Caribbean region
Spanish Main
Defenses
See also
Fortification—Caribbean region
Description and travel
See also
Cruising—Caribbean region

Black enterprise: guide to Caribbean travel [special section] il *Black Enterp* 17:31+ My '87
A Caribbean for all seasons [special section] K. Showker. il *Travel Holiday* 167:69+ Ap '87
The cream of the Caribbean. R. J. Christmas. il *Essence* 17:14+ Ap '87
Hidden bargains in the Caribbean. T. Grossinger. il map *Better Homes Gard* 65:198+ O '87
Island travel. L. Wolfe and J. Cecil. il *N Y* 20:64-6+ N 9 '87
Islands. M. Zellers. il *South Living* 22:129+ Mr '87
Playing house in the Caribbean. il *Esquire* 108:148-55 O '87
Summer in the Caribbean: getaway islands with come-hither-prices. il *Glamour* 85:238+ My '87
Sunspot getaways. il *Harpers Bazaar* 120:38+ F '87
Take your dream vacation now! il *Ebony* 42:128+ My '87
What's best in the Caribbean. il *Glamour* 85:264-6+ N '87

Anecdotes, facetiae, satire, etc.
Caribbean therapy. D. Mamet. il *Vogue* 177:298+ F '87
Economic conditions
See also
United Nations. Economic Commission for Latin America and the Caribbean
Foreign relations
Brazil
See Brazil—Foreign relations—Caribbean region
United States
See United States—Foreign relations—Caribbean region
Politics and government
Democracy in Latin America and the Caribbean: the promise and the challenge. il *Dep State Bull* 87:58-89 Mr '87
Latin America and the Caribbean: the paths to democracy [address, June 30, 1987] E. Abrams. *Dep State Bull* 87:81-5 S '87
Statistics
Profile of four English-speaking Caribbean nations [charts] D. Johnson. il *Black Enterp* 17:29 My '87
Caribbean writer (Periodical)
Home base for new islands literature. D. Lyon. *Américas* 39:53-4 N/D '87
Caribou
A compromise the caribou will like [oil exploration in Arctic National Wildlife Refuge] il *Fortune* 115:9 My 25 '87
Fighting a new threat to the North [proposed oil development in the Arctic National Wildlife Refuge] I. Austen. il map *Macleans* 100:12 My 4 '87
High stakes in a land of plenty [Arctic National Wildlife Refuge; cover story; with editorial comment by Jay D. Hair] T. A. Lewis. il map *Natl Wildl* 25:4-11, 28 Je/Jl '87
Caribou hunting
Four-of-a-kind caribou [Quebec and Labrador] H. L. Lawrence. il *Outdoor Life* 179:68-9+ Mr '87
Caricatures and cartoons
See also
Comic books, strips, etc.
Motion pictures—Animated films
Publishers and publishing—Cartoons
Television broadcasting—Cartoons
Videotapes—Animated films
See also subhead Caricatures and cartoons under various subjects
Collectors and collecting
Drawn to politics [political cartoons] C. Neave. il *Esquire* 107:29-30 Mr '87
Exhibitions
Barking up the family tree [The art of the New Yorker—a 60 year retrospective] T. Young. il *Vogue* 177:96 Ag '87
Photographs and photography
Blockheads: how to make dimensional photographic caricatures. J. E. Widoff. il *Petersens Photogr Mag* 16:80-1+ D '87
CARIE *See* Coalition of Advocates for the Rights of the Infirm Elderly
Caries, Dental *See* Dental caries
Carim, A. H., and others
High-resolution electron microscopy and scanning tunneling microscopy of native oxides on silicon. bibl f il *Science* 237:630-3 Ag 7 '87
Caring
See also
Helping behavior

Caring—*cont.*
"Caring from the heart" [teaching children to help the homeless] S. Lapinski. il *Ladies Home J* 104:26+ Mr '87
On not caring. M. E. Marty. *Christ Century* 104:807 S 23 '87
Caring education *See* Social education
Carino, Ralph
Restarting the wandering gooneys. il *Sea Front* 33:42-5 Ja/F '87
Carl, Beverly May
The Nicaraguan economic system. map *America* 156:155-8 F 21 '87
Carleson, Robert B.
Caging the welfare monster. il *Read Dig* 131:86-90 S '87
Carlin, David R., Jr.
Of several minds. See alternate issues of Commonweal beginning May 31, 1985
Carlin, Lottye
about
Credit where credit is due. il por *50 Plus* 27:16+ S '87
Carling O'Keefe Limited
Carling goes Australian [takeover by Elders IXL Ltd.] T. Tedesco. il *Macleans* 100:36 Mr 9 '87
Carlisle, Belinda
about
Flying solo: stars take off alone. il pors *Teen* 31:80-1 My '87
Talent: orbiting to the top. pors *Harpers Bazaar* 120:264-73 Mr '87
Carlisle, Olga Andreyev
My grandfather, Leonid Andreyev: heard again, loud and clear. il por *N Y Times Book Rev* 92:15-16 O 4 '87
Carlos, Antonio *See* Tatu
Carlos, John
about
Ex-Olympian John Carlos denies drug possession. por *Jet* 71:47 Ja 26 '87
Carlos, Walter *See* Carlos, Wendy
Carlos, Wendy
about
Wendy Carlos: A.D. (after digital). J. Diliberto. il pors *Down Beat* 54:20-2+ Mr '87
Carlsen, Henning
about
Wolf at the door [film] Reviews
America 157:162 S 26 '87. R. A. Blake
New Repub 197:26 Ag 24 '87. S. Kauffmann
Carlsen, Peter
Frames of reference: varied palette for a New York apartment. il *Archit Dig* 44:120-7 D '87
Tree house retreat: a designer's Fire Island aerie. il *Archit Dig* 44:60-5 Ag '87
Carlson, Cathy M.
(jt. auth) See Sklar, Ellen, and Carlson, Cathy M.
Carlson, Cynthia
about
Cynthia Carlson: McIntosh/Drysdale. A. Thorson. il *Art News* 86:164 D '87
Carlson, Dennis G.
about
Bootstrap time in a luckless land. J. Buckley. il pors map *U S News World Rep* 103:88-90+ D 28 '87-Ja 4 '88
Carlson, Diane
When bad dreams happen to good people. *McCalls* 114:98 My '87
Carlson, Jack
about
Under new management. C. McLaughlin. *50 Plus* 27:20-1 N '87
Carlson, John, and Trueson, John
Last word. il *Omni* 9:122 S '87
Carlson, Ken
about
Art from the heart of nature. M. Wexler. il por *Natl Wildl* 25:34-9 Ag/S '87
Carlson, Richard
What the spirit of the people provides [address, September 1987] *Vital Speeches Day* 54:104-5 D 1 '87
Carlson, Robert J.
about
Surviving the cure. J. Parr. il por *Forbes* 140:52-3 Jl 27 '87
Carlson, Robert V.
(jt. auth) See Matthes, William A., and Carlson, Robert V.

Carlson, Ron
Family ritual [story] il por *McCalls* 114:43-5 Ja '87
Carlson, Shawn
about
The scientist who makes icons weep. il por *Newsweek* 110:79 O 26 '87
Carlsson, Ingvar, 1934-
Visit of Swedish prime minister [remarks, September 9, 1987] il por *Dep State Bull* 87:40-2 N '87
Visit to the United States, 1987
Visit of Swedish prime minister [remarks, September 9, 1987] R. Reagan; I. Carlsson. il por *Dep State Bull* 87:40-2 N '87
Carlston, Doug
Crossing over the boundaries. por *Pers Comput* 11:250 O '87
Carlton, Steve
about
Lefty's last stand. P. Gammons. il por *Sports Illus* 66:48-9 Mr 30 '87
Carlton Arms Hotel (New York, N.Y.) *See* New York (N.Y.)—Hotels, motels, etc.
Carlton Hill Multiple Use Area (N.Y.)
The many uses of Carlton Hill. D. L. Kiel. il *Conservationist* 42:16-21 N/D '87
Carlucci, Frank Charles
about
Carlucci and the N.S.C. J. Bamford. il *N Y Times Mag* p16-19+ Ja 18 '87
Carlucci cleans up the act at the NSC. H. Anderson. il por *Newsweek* 109:19-20 Ja 19 '87
Carlucci is teaching the Pentagon a new word—'cutback'. D. Griffiths. *Bus Week* p49 D 21 '87
Changing of the guards. G. J. Church. il por *Time* 130:21-2 N 16 '87
A new hot seat for the cool Frank Carlucci. B. Javetski. por *Bus Week* p70 N 16 '87
'No reason ever to withdraw' [interview] por *U S News World Rep* 103:28 Ag 24 '87
Out of the basement. M. Kondracke. *New Repub* 196:10+ Ja 5-12 '87
Story of a consummate bureaucrat [cover story] J. Morley. *Nation* 245:737+ D 19 '87
Carman, James
On location. il *Natl Parks* 61:30-6 N/D '87
Carmel (Calif.)
Politics and government
Clint Eastwood: small-town mayor. W. Roessing. il pors *Saturday Evening Post* 259:42-5 S '87
Dirty Harry for president? [C. Eastwood] M. Dobbin. il por *U S News World Rep* 102:26 F 2 '87
No more baby kissing [Mayor C. Eastwood] P. A. Witteman. il por *Time* 129:34 Ap 6 '87
Carmelites
The Auschwitz Carmel [controversy over convent at Auschwitz] *America* 156:206 Mr 14 '87
Blessed Edith Stein. *America* 156:354-5 My 2 '87
Edith Stein's early years. J. W. Donohue. *America* 156:7-9+ Ja 3-10 '87
Learning from history [convent at Auschwitz] E. Fleischner. *Commonweal* 114:167-8 Mr 27 '87
A martyr of Auschwitz [E. Stein] S. M. Batzdorff. por *N Y Times Mag* p52-5+ Ap 12 '87
Saintly passions [Jews protest beatification of E. Stein, also known as Teresa Benedicta of the Cross] D. Brand. por *Time* 129:82-3 My 4 '87
Carmen [opera] See Bizet, Georges, 1838-1875
Carmichel, Jim
Shooting. See issues of Outdoor Life
Carmody, Timothy
about
A bizarre escape from Brazil. por *Newsweek* 109:35 Ja 5 '87
Carne-Ross, D. S.
The strange case of Leopardi. il *N Y Rev Books* 34:42-3 Ja 29 '87
Carnegie, Dale, 1888-1955
about
The so-so salesman who told millions how to make it big. R. Conniff. bibl (p230) il por *Smithsonian* 18:82-6+ O '87
Carnegie, Dale Breckenridge *See* Carnegie, Dale, 1888-1955
Carnegie Hall (New York, N.Y.)
Battered 'Bat' [reopening gala concert] P. G. Davis. il *N Y* 20:43-4 Ag 5 '87
Carnegie Hall: a facelift and a new sound. T. Eckert, Jr. il *High Fidel* 37:57-9 Ap '87
Carnegie's legacy restored. L. Kundell. il *Travel Holiday* 167:30-2 Mr '87

Carnegie Hall (New York, N.Y.)—*cont.*
Dich, teure halle! [reopening the Weill Recital Hall] P. G. Davis. il *N Y* 20:62-3 F 2 '87
Musical events:
Critique of acoustics in renovated Carnegie Hall. A. Porter. *New Yorker* 63:76-9 Ap 20 '87
Weill Recital Hall. A. Porter. *New Yorker* 63:101-4 F 23 '87
Sounds in the night [reopening] M. Walsh. il *Time* 129:68 F 16 '87
Viewpoint [renovation] J. W. Freeman. *Opera News* 51:4 Mr 28 '87
Carnegie Hall International American Music Competition for Vocalists *See* Singing—Competitions
Carnegie-Mellon University
Data structures in a bit-mapped text editor: how Carnegie-Mellon University displays text on the IBM RT PC. W. J. Hansen. il *Byte* 12:183-4+ Ja '87
Distributed processing: the state of the art [Carnegie-Mellon's MACH and Stanford's V] W. A. Mason. il *Byte* 12:291-7 N '87
Carnes, Bruce M.
The college cost explosion. il *Consum Res Mag* 70:16-19 S '87
Carnes, Patty
about
The million-dollar baby nobody wants. C. C. Frink. il pors *Ladies Home J* 104:48+ D '87
Carney, Cynthia J.
The emigration of innocents. *Commonweal* 114:79-82 F 13 '87
Carney, Pat
about
Ottawa's trade offensive. M. Drohan. il por *Macleans* 100:10-11 Ja 19 '87
Carney, William J.
Examine the motives of junk-bond critics. il *Bus Week* p18 Mr 30 '87
Carnie, Clive
The last working horses. il *Natl Parks* 61:30-5 Mr/Ap '87
Carnitas *See* Cooking, Mexican
Carnitine
Updating the health promise of carnitine. H. Fisher. *Prevention* 39:116+ Ap '87
Carnival (Pre-Lenten festival)
A rain of paper confetti. C. N. White. il *Commonweal* 114:134-5 Mr 13 '87
Italy
Venice: the world's greatest costume party. R. P. Crease and C. C. Mann. il *50 Plus* 27:67-71+ D '87
Trinidad and Tobago
Streets of steel. M. Rowland. il *Esquire* 108:41-2 N '87
Carnival Cruise Lines Inc.
Carnival Cruise Lines is making waves. G. DeGeorge. il *Bus Week* p34 Jl 6 '87
Carnivals
Winter carnivals. G. S. Bush. il *Better Homes Gard* 65:194+ D '87
Carolco Service, Inc.
Is there life beyond Rambo? A. B. Block. il *Forbes* 139:88+ Je 1 '87
Caroli, Betty Boyd
about
Too old, too bold, too pushy, too plastic—First Ladies hear it all, but never 'she's perfect!' [interview] M. Wilhelm. il por *People Wkly* 27:93-4+ My 18 '87
Carolina (Puerto Rico)
Sports
See also
Roberto Clemente Sports City (Carolina, Puerto Rico)
Caroline Islands
See also
Palau
Caron, Glenn
about
Dark side of the Moon. D. Handelman. il pors *Roll Stone* p52+ Mr 26 '87
Carotene
Cancer preventer? [beta-carotene] G. Bakoulis. il *Health* 19:57-9+ D '87
New evidence that carotene prevents cancer. *Prevention* 39:104 Ag '87
Carothers, Wallace Hume
about
1937. por *Am Herit* 38:108-9 F/Mr '87
Carotid arteries *See* Arteries
Carozza, Alex
about
Accordions. *New Yorker* 63:37-8+ D 14 '87

Carpal tunnel syndrome
Therapy
B₆: a solution to a painful problem. H. Fisher. il *Prevention* 39:56-8 Ja '87
Carpenter, Cris
about
The second coming of Bo Jackson. R. Wolff. il pors *Sport Mag* 78:20 Ap '87
Carpenter, Dan
Politics snarl the Pan Am Games. *Progressive* 51:12 Ag '87
Carpenter, Edmund M.
about
Ed Carpenter: ITT's field marshall and Mr. Fixit. C. Power. por *Bus Week* p68 Mr 23 '87
Carpenter, Edward, 1844-1929
about
'Commanding the heart': Edward Carpenter and friends. S. Rowbotham. bibl il pors *Hist Today* 37:41-6 S '87
Carpenter, Fay
Meat pie essentials. il *Ctry J* 14:35-7 D '87
Carpenter, Liz
Lunching over love [excerpt from Getting better all the time] il *50 Plus* 27:28-9+ N '87
A second life [excerpt from Getting better all the time] il pors *McCalls* 114:142+ Ag '87
Carpenter, Richard
about
Four years after his sister Karen's death, singer Richard Carpenter makes his debut as a solo act. J. Calio. il pors *People Wkly* 28:139-40 O 26 '87
Carpenter, Rick
about
First comes soil. M. Kane. il pors *Rodale's Org Gard* 34:60-3+ Je '87
Carpenter, Sharon
about
First comes soil. M. Kane. il pors *Rodale's Org Gard* 34:60-3+ Je '87
Carpenter, Ted Galen
Global intervention and a new imperial presidency. il *USA Today (Periodical)* 115:10-18 Mr '87
about
U.S. foreign aid: virtue or vice? [interview] P. M. Jones. pors *Sch Update* 119:26 F 23 '87
Carpenter, Will D.
Bringing new agricultural technology to the market [address, January 29, 1987] *Vital Speeches Day* 53:350-2 Mr 15 '87
Carpenters' squares
Electronic square. P. McCafferty. il *Pop Sci* 231:73 D '87
An electronic square. L. Okrend. il *Workbench* 43:60-1 N/D '87
Using a T-bevel. R. Capotosto. il *Pop Mech* 164:48 My '87
Carpentry
See also
Joints (Carpentry)
Woodworking
"Lunt" carpentry. P. Stone. il *Mother Earth News* 106:86-91 Jl/Ag '87
Carper, Jean
The clip-out catalog of super foods. il *Redbook* 168:127-30 Ap '87
Carper, Thomas
A farmstead with a hayrick and weirs beside a stream [poem] *Am Sch* 56:399 Summ '87
Rembrandt prepares for a walk along the Amstel River [poem] *Am Sch* 56:398 Summ '87
Carpets *See* Rugs and carpets
Carr, Archie Fairly, III
about
The legacy of Tortuguero. il *Nat Hist* 96:2+ Je '87
Carr, Edward G., and Durand, V. Mark
See me, help me. bibl (p65) il *Psychol Today* 21:62-4 N '87
Carr, Fred
about
Fred Carr buys some insurance. T. Carson. *Bus Week* p36 O 26 '87
Carr, Harold
Communicating during a "crisis" [address, December 2, 1986] *Vital Speeches Day* 53:248-50 F 1 '87
Carr, Joseph J.
How to design oscillator circuits (VII). il *Radio-Electron* 58:65-6+ Ja '87
Carr, Patrick
Farm Aid's founder Willie Nelson [cover story] il pors *Mother Earth News* 105:42-5 My/Je '87

Carr, Patrick, and Glass, Kathy
The long fight for Kings Canyon. il maps *Sierra* 72:38-44 Ja/F '87
Carrasco, Joe King
about
Music. G. Santoro. *Nation* 245:351-3 O 3 '87
Carrett, Laura Coti
Grand Slam menus. il *World Tennis* 35:34-5 Je '87
Carriage houses
See also
House decoration
Carriage houses, Converted *See* Houses, Remodeled
Carrier pigeons *See* Pigeons
Carrière, Jean-Claude
about
The Mahabharata [drama] Reviews
America 157:358+ N 14 '87. G. G. Seibert
Commonweal il 114:655-6 N 20 '87. G. Weales
N Y il 20:110-11 N 2 '87. J. Simon
N Y Times Mag il p36-8+ O 4 '87. M. Croyden
New Repub 197:26-8 N 30 '87. R. Brustein
New Yorker 63:146-8 N 2 '87. M. Kramer
Newsweek il 110:74-5 S 21 '87. J. Kroll
People Wkly il 28:134-5 N 9 '87
Theatre Crafts il 21:27-31+ N '87
Time il 130:85 O 19 '87. W. A. Henry
Vogue il por 177:444-5+ O '87. A. Harvey
Carriers, Aircraft *See* Aircraft carriers
Carriers, Car-top *See* Automobiles—Equipment
Carriers, Roof-top *See* Trucks—Equipment
Carriers of infection
See also
Animals as carriers of infection
Mosquitoes as carriers of infection
Carrington, Richard Christopher, 1826-1875
about
The last days of Richard Carrington. K. Weitzenhoffer. il *Astronomy* 15:24+ Ap '87
Carrington, Terri Lyne
about
Showstopper: Terri Lyne Carrington. M. Johnson. por *Essence* 18:27 My '87
Carro, Jorge L.
Education for peace [address, October 9, 1987] *Vital Speeches Day* 54:157-60 D 15 '87
Carroll, David, 1942-
(jt. auth) See Stern, Jack I., and Carroll, David, 1942-
Carroll, Devin
The humanist family and moral education. por *Humanist* 47:35-6 Mr/Ap '87
Humanists versus religiosity in the Boy Scouts. por *Humanist* 47:37 N/D '87
The well-rounded humanist. il por *Humanist* 47:35-6 Jl/Ag '87
Carroll, Diahann
about
Diahann Carroll & Suzanne Kay. pors *Teen* 31:48 D '87
Diahann Carroll and Vic Damone marry at Golden Nugget Casino. il pors *Jet* 71:12-14 Ja 19 '87
Diahann Carroll and Vic Damone: new marriage and new career on stage. il pors *Jet* 71:57-8 Ja 26 '87
Star mothers & daughters. pors *Harpers Bazaar* 120:129+ Ag '87
Carroll, Earl
about
Doo-wop. *New Yorker* 63:27-8 Mr 2 '87
Carroll, James D., and others
What do U.S. government and civics textbooks teach? [excerpt from We the people] *Educ Dig* 53:36-8 S '87
Carroll, John Bissell, 1916-
The national assessments in reading: are we misreading the findings? bibl f il *Phi Delta Kappan* 68:424-30 F '87
Carroll, John J.
The dilemma of the Philippine left: the party or the people? *America* 157:79-81 Ag 15-22 '87
Carroll, Lucille Ryman
about
MGM vet Lucille Ryman Carroll recalls the reel adventures of Liz, Rock, Marilyn and Nancy [interview] R. Natale. il por *People Wkly* 28:135-7+ N 2 '87
Carroll, Michael W.
The changing face of Mars [cover story] il *Astronomy* 15:6-22+ Mr '87
Project Galileo: the phoenix rises [cover story] il *Sky Telesc* 73:359-61 Ap '87

Carrollton (Ga.)
Crime
Georgia sisters indicted for their mother's murder [R. Golden and M. Collier] *Jet* 73:47 N 2 '87
Two Georgia sisters held for their mother's murder [M. Collier and R. Golden held in murder of Frances Golden] il pors *Jet* 72:32 Ag 17 '87
Carrots
See also
Cooking—Vegetables
The sweet taste of carrots. il *South Living* 22:64 S '87
What's up, docs? Supercarrot is on the way [Beta III carrot] il pors *People Wkly* 27:40 Mr 16 '87
Why carrots may reduce cholesterol. *Sci News* 131:409 Je 27 '87
Carry, Peter
Some guy named Erving. il *Sports Illus* 66:75-6 My 4 '87
Carry, Walter T.
Architectural education: on NCARB's horizon—a computer-adaptive exam. il *Archit Rec* 175:59 N '87
Carry-on luggage *See* Luggage
Carry-on luggage regulations *See* Airlines—Luggage handling
Cars (Automobiles) *See* Automobiles
Cars (Musical group)
Cars rev up for 'Door to door' LP. A. DeCurtis. il *Roll Stone* p15+ S 24 '87
Carson, Benjamin
about
Black surgeon works to separate Siamese twins. il por *Jet* 73:8 S 28 '87
Carson, Christopher
about
Carson's son claims AIDS to make girlfriend abort baby: judge nixes test. il por *Jet* 72:13-14 Ag 3 '87
Johnny Carson to face queries on son's support. *Jet* 72:4 Jl 6 '87
Johnny Carson's son must pay support for black child who was living on welfare. il por *Jet* 72:52-3 Ap 13 '87
Carson, Dick
about
And now, heeere's Johnny's brother. il por *Newsweek* 109:49 F 9 '87
Carson, Elizabeth
A young runner faces osteoporosis. il *Women's Sports Fitness* 9:58-9 Ja '87
Carson, Hampton L.
The process whereby species originate [cover story] bibl il por *BioScience* 37:715-20 N '87
Carson, Harry, 1953-
about
Après the Super Bowl, Giants' giant Harry Carson plans to treat his mildewed coach to le déluge. J. Friedman. il pors *People Wkly* 27:68+ Ja 26 '87
Carson, Jim
about
The King and his court. P. Fichtenbaum. il pors *Sport Mag* 78:61-2+ F '87
The Kings' crown princes. B. Anderson. il pors *Sports Illus* 66:58+ Ja 26 '87
Carson, Johnny, 1925-
about
25 years with Johnny Carson. E. Sherman. il pors *Ladies Home J* 104:44+ O '87
Johnny Carson & his ex-es [excerpt from Carson] P. Corkery. il pors *Good Housekeep* 205:120+ O '87
Johnny Carson: his private worlds [excerpt from Johnny Carson] R. L. Smith. il pors *McCalls* 114:141-4 S '87
Johnny Carson to face queries on son's support. *Jet* 72:4 Jl 6 '87
Johnny Carson's son must pay support for black child who was living on welfare. il por *Jet* 72:52-3 Ap 13 '87
Carson, Mike
Holy Name School, 1951 [poem] *Commonweal* 114:566 O 9 '87
Carson, Rachel, 1907-1964
about
Courage of Rachel Carson [excerpt from Two Park Street] P. Brooks. il por *Audubon* 89:12+ Ja '87
Carson, Russell
about
Infomaniac. L. Jereski. il por *Forbes* 140:224+ O 5 '87
Carson Productions
The business of show biz [M. A. Thomas, black woman executive] S. Herbert. il por *Essence* 18:116+ S '87
Cartagena Film Festival *See* Motion picture festivals—Colombia

Cartels

International aspects

See also
International Tin Council
Organization of Petroleum Exporting Countries

Carter, Amy

about

Amy Carter and Abbie Hoffman win acquittal, but they want to keep the C.I.A. on trial. F. A. Bernstein. il pors *People Wkly* 27:57-8+ My 4 '87

Amy Carter faces life. M. F. Hoyt. il pors *Good Housekeep* 205:143+ O '87

Amy Carter gets probation for Brown apartheid protest. *Jet* 72:22 Mr 30 '87

Amy's day. J. Nocera. *New Repub* 196:11-13 My 11 '87

No longer in the White House, a young Carter rediscovers the importance of being Amy. D. Chu. il por *People Wkly* 27:36-7 Ja 5 '87

Not guilty by necessity. por *Time* 129:71 Ap 27 '87

On trial: cheers and jeers for Amy Carter. por *Newsweek* 109:33 Ap 20 '87

Carter, Anne Babson

Scenes and stitches. il por *Americana* 15:33-6 S/O '87

Carter, Arthur L.

about

Now, the New York 'observer'. E. Diamond. il por *N Y* 20:21-3 Jl 13 '87

Carter, Benny

about

Benny Carter/American Jazz Orchestra. M. Bourne. il por *Down Beat* 54:56-7 Je '87

Carter, Calvin

about

Top two U.S. airports headed by black execs. pors *Jet* 72:8 Je 22 '87

Carter, Cris

about

Buckeyes Carter sues agents for $4 million. por *Jet* 73:50 O 5 '87

A sad goodbye to Columbus. J. Lieber. il por *Sports Illus* 67:38-9 Ag 3 '87

Carter, Dixie

about

Those remarkable Designing women. H. Yorkshire. il pors *McCalls* 115:78-9+ N '87

Carter, Don

about

Formal details. J. Gruen. il *Archit Dig* 44:186-92 D '87

Carter, E. Graydon

The cosmos according to Mel Brooks. il por *Vogue* 177:220-1+ Je '87

An eye for the best. il *House Gard* 159:218-21+ O '87

High times. por *Vogue* 177:186+ Ag '87

Carter, Gary

about

The most happy fella. D. S. Looney. il por *Sports Illus* 67:28-9 Jl 6 '87

Carter, Hurricane See Carter, Rubin

Carter, James

about

Sitting in with the big band boys, James Carter blows up an old-fashioned jazz storm. il *People Wkly* 27:117 Mr 9 '87

Carter, James Earl See Carter, Jimmy, 1924-

Carter, Jennifer

about

Formal details. J. Gruen. il *Archit Dig* 44:186-92 D '87

Carter, Jimmy, 1924-

Jimmy Carter on a nation weakened by a lack of trust. il por *Life* 10:26-7 O '87

Middle East: time for negotiations. il por *Time* 129:38-9 Ap 20 '87

about

Carter: racism could be inherent in all of us. il por *Jet* 71:15 Mr 9 '87

The Carters: building a new life. E. Sherman. pors *Ladies Home J* 104:82 Je '87

Chapter 2 for Jimmy and Rosalynn [interview] B. Brophy. il pors *U S News World Rep* 102:62 Je 1 '87

He's back! J. L. Pasley and A. P. Weisman. il *New Repub* 196:13-15 Ja 19 '87

Iran arms deal was more serious than Watergate [interview] D. Frost. por *U S News World Rep* 103:32 D 7 '87

Jimmy Carter's judges [excerpt from The judges war] G. P. Smith, II. il *Natl Rev* 39:44+ O 23 '87

Off with their heads: how Zbigniew Brzezinski hawked the doctrine of nuclear decapitation. M. Kaku and D. Axelrod. il *Progressive* 51:29-31 Ja '87

On the road with the Carters. G. D. Garcia. il pors *Time* 129:78-9 Je 15 '87

The restoration of Jimmy Carter. S. Pacher. il pors *Mother Earth News* 108:42-7 N/D '87

Homes

A presidential theme park in Plains? il *Newsweek* 110:42 O 19 '87

A visit to the Carters' home in Plains, Georgia. C. Varney. il pors *Good Housekeep* 204:110-13+ Je '87

Carter, Jimmy, 1924-, and Carter, Rosalynn

When all the glory is gone [excerpt from Everything to gain] il pors *People Wkly* 27:56-8+ My 25 '87

With our own hands [excerpt from Everything to gain] il pors *McCalls* 114:44+ Jl '87

Carter, Joe

about

Pow! Wow! R. Fimrite. il pors *Sports Illus* 66:74-6+ Ap 6 '87

Carter, Joe, d. 1987

about

Flint blacks angered by youth's 'suicide' probe. L. Ransom. il pors *Jet* 72:51-3 Ag 24 '87

Carter, John Mack

Editor's notebook. See issues of Good Housekeeping

Carter, Luther J.

Siting the nuclear waste repository: last stand at Yucca Mountain. bibl f il map *Environment* 29:8-13+ O '87

Carter, M. Joni

about

She planted Kentucky's gardens. D. Young. il por *South Living* 22:134+ S '87

Carter, Matthew

about

A personal type. A. Ward. il pors *N Y Times Mag* p146 S 20 '87

Carter, Nell

about

Nell Carter returns to nightclubs after TV show. por *Jet* 72:29 Ag 17 '87

Carter, Patrice Gaines- See Gaines-Carter, Patrice

Carter, Paul, and Wells, James A.

Engineering enzyme specificity by "substrate-assisted catalysis". bibl f il *Science* 237:394-9 Jl 24 '87

Carter, Robert A.

The war of words. il *Publ Wkly* 232:27-8+ O 2 '87

Carter, Rosalynn

(jt. auth) See Carter, Jimmy, 1924-, and Carter, Rosalynn

about

The Carters: building a new life. E. Sherman. pors *Ladies Home J* 104:82 Je '87

Chapter 2 for Jimmy and Rosalynn [interview] B. Brophy. il pors *U S News World Rep* 102:62 Je 1 '87

On the road with the Carters. G. D. Garcia. il pors *Time* 129:78-9 Je 15 '87

The restoration of Jimmy Carter. S. Pacher. il pors *Mother Earth News* 108:42-7 N/D '87

A visit to the Carters' home in Plains, Georgia. C. Varney. il pors *Good Housekeep* 204:110-13+ Je '87

Carter, Rubin

about

Court bars conviction of 'Hurricane' Carter. por *Jet* 72:50 S 14 '87

Carter, Santanya

about

From 204 pounds to 122 pounds in half a year. il pors *Ebony* 42:46+ Jl '87

Carter (Jimmy) National Historic Site See Jimmy Carter National Historic Site

Carter-Shotts, Cheryl

about

Out of Africa with Diane Sawyer. M. G. Stoddard. il pors *Saturday Evening Post* 259:52-4+ Ap '87

Carter-Wallace, Inc.

Be cautious with Carter-Wallace. G. G. Marcial. *Bus Week* p116 F 23 '87

Carthage (Ancient city)

How Carthage lost the sea [reconstruction of Punic warship] H. Frost. il maps *Nat Hist* 96:58-67 D '87

Exhibitions

Carthage [D. Soren and Carthaginian exhibit at American Museum of Natural History] *New Yorker* 63:36-7 D 14 '87

A fanciful way with ferocity [Carthage: a mosaic of ancient Tunisia] M. Stevens. il *Newsweek* 110:95-6 D 7 '87

The treasures of ancient Tunisia [Carthage: a mosaic of ancient Tunisia] R. Bacher. il *Nat Hist* 96:68+ D '87

Cartier, Jacques, 1491-1557
Saved by the Indians [excerpt from Voyages au Canada] il *Courier* 40:12 Ap '87
Cartier-Bresson, Henri, 1908-
about
Candide camera. J. Perl. il *Vogue* 177:98 N '87
Cartier-Bresson. J. Loengard. il pors *Life* 10:124-5+ D '87
Drawing on an old passion. M. Peppiatt. il *Archit Dig* 44:40+ Ja '87
Drunk on a world served straight. R. Lacayo. il *Time* 130:88 O 12 '87
Eyes behind the camera, then and now [interview] M. Horn. il *U S News World Rep* 103:88-9 N 9 '87
Henri Cartier-Bresson. A. C. Danto. *Nation* 245:346-8 O 3 '87
Henri Cartier-Bresson. R. B. Woodward. il *Art News* 86:200+ N '87
A master with a double image. D. Davis. il *Newsweek* 110:78 S 21 '87
Portraits by the artist as a young man. G. James. il *Macleans* 100:62+ N 9 '87
A question of attitude. D. Lanchner. il *Art News* 86:11 D '87
Carting (Go-carting) *See* Go-karting
Cartledge, Paul
A patriot for whom? Alcibiades of Athens. bibl il por *Hist Today* 37:15-19 O '87
Cartledge-Hayes, Mary
A Mother's Day challenge [discussion of sex with teenage daughter] il *Ms* 15:80 My '87
Cartography
See also
Computers—Cartographic use
Contours (Cartography)
Road maps, guides, etc.
Spherical projection
Cartoonists
See also
Al-Adhami, Ali Naji
Barbera, Joe, 1911-
Caricatures and cartoons
Groening, Matt
Larson, Gary
Lasswell, Fred
Steig, William, 1907-
Trudeau, G. B., 1948-
Cartoons *See* Caricatures and cartoons; Motion pictures—Animated films; Publishers and publishing—Cartoons; Television broadcasting—Cartoons; Videotapes—Animated films
Cartridge tape recorders *See* Tape recorders and recording
Cartridges
Handloads can ruin your hunt. J. Carmichel. il *Outdoor Life* 180:26+ N '87
New loads from Federal, Remington and Winchester [shotgun shells] J. Carmichel. il *Outdoor Life* 180:20+ Ag '87
Cartridges, Phonograph *See* Phonograph—Pickup
Carts
See also
Golf carts
A cart for all seasons. V. Hahn. il *Parents* 62:168-70 Mr '87
The contemporary tipcart [yard and garden cart] il *Mother Earth News* 104:67-9 Mr/Ap '87
The cook's assistant. T. H. Jones. il *Fam Handyman* 37:80-6 Mr '87
Cutting cart with refuse bin. il *Sunset* 179:143 S '87
Easy-to-assemble utility cart. M. Ferrara. il *Home Mech* 83:81 D '87
Garden tool caddy. il *Home Mech* 83:24 S '87
Grill on the go [grill cart] L. M. Dalsgaard. il *Home Mech* 83:64-6+ My '87
Just rolling along [panel caddy] il *Workbench* 43:50 S/O '87
Sturdy yard cart lightens heavy load. D. B. Stutzman. il *Workbench* 43:46-7 Mr/Ap '87
Carty, Brian T.
about
The unlikely hero of small-business finance. L. Helm. il por *Bus Week* p170 N 2 '87
Carty, Winthrop P.
Birds of a feather feed together. il *Américas* 39:28-33+ S/O '87
Carugati, Dirma Pardo de *See* Pardo de Carugati, Dirma
Caruso, Josie
about
Josie Caruso: modeling a career. B. Burns. il por *Theatre Crafts* 21:18 O '87

Carvajal SA
Today's pop-ups: more complex than ever. W. A. Rebsamen. il *Publ Wkly* 231:72+ Mr 6 '87
Carvalho, Otelo Saraiva de
about
Letter from Europe. J. Kramer. *New Yorker* 63:105-20 N 30 '87
Carver, George
Official rogues. *New Repub* 196:12-15 Ap 13 '87
Carver, Raymond
Errand [story] *New Yorker* 63:30-6 Je 1 '87
about
Love, literature and solitude link mutually admiring authors Raymond Carver and Tess Gallagher. A. Chambers. il pors *People Wkly* 28:81-2+ N 23 '87
Carver, Sally S.
The picture postcard. See issues of Hobbies through February 1985
Picture postcards. See issues of Antiques & Collecting Hobbies beginning March 1985
Carver Corp.
The rational audiophile. M. Riggs. il *High Fidel* 37:5 N '87
Carver Federal Savings Bank
Carver Federal carves out its market niche. R. Fleming. il por *Black Enterp* 17:214-16+ Je '87
Carvers and Gilders (Firm)
Goldfingers. P. Spike. il *House Gard* 159:114+ Ap '87
Carvey, Dana
about
America's second-funniest Church Lady. N. Atkins. il pors *Roll Stone* p29-30 O 22 '87
As SNL's Church Lady, comic Dana Carvey raises unholy hell. D. Hutchings. il pors *People Wkly* 27:101+ My 4 '87
Church Lady. por *People Wkly* 28:59 D 28 '87-Ja 4 '88
A nerd's sweet revenge. H. F. Waters. il por *Newsweek* 109:70 Ap 13 '87
Carving (Art industries)
See also
Soap sculpture
Wood carving
CASA *See* Construcciones Aeronauticas SA
Casa Botin (Madrid, Spain: Restaurant) *See* Madrid (Spain)—Restaurants, nightclubs, bars, etc.
Casa de las Mil Flores (Antigua, Guatemala: Historic house) *See* Antigua (Guatemala)—Historic houses, sites, etc.
Casabas *See* Melons
Casagrande, Louis B.
The five nations of Mexico. il map *Focus* 37:2-9 Spr '87
Casali, Paolo, and others
Human lymphocytes making rheumatoid factor and antibody to ssDNA belong to Leu-1+ B-cell subset. bibl f il *Science* 236:77-81 Ap 3 '87
Casanova, Montserrat
about
A new face on dance. B. Haye. il *Theatre Crafts* 21:42-3+ N '87
Casanova [television program] *See* Television program reviews—Single works
Casbah (Essaouira, Morocco) *See* Essaouira (Morocco)—Historic houses, sites, etc.
Casciero, Annick Sanjurjo de *See* Sanjurjo de Casciero, Annick
Cascio, Sam
about
Sam Cascio, nonagenarian bellhop, refuses to bag it. il por *People Wkly* 28:119 S 21 '87
Case (J. I.) Company *See* J. I. Case Company
Caselotti, Adriana
Snow White speaks. il *People Wkly* 27:102-4+ My 18 '87
about
"The fairest one of all". il por *Am Hist Illus* 22:38 D '87
Casem, Marino
about
Casem greets Southern gridders with hard work. *Jet* 72:46 Ap 13 '87
Cases *See* Boxes, cases, etc.
Casey, Kathryn
For better, for worse. il *Ladies Home J* 104:89-91+ My '87
Casey, William J.
about
Ace reporter Bob Woodward lifts the Veil on the secrets of CIA chief William Casey. M. Green. il pors *People Wkly* 28:40-1 O 12 '87

Casey, William J.—about—*cont.*
Books. L. Hirschberg. il por *N Y* 20:110-11 S 21 '87
Casey and Woodward: who used whom? M. Kempton. il *N Y Rev Books* 34:61 N 5 '87
Casey's boys. M. Kondracke. *New Repub* 197:42 Ag 24 '87
Casey's secret. *Nation* 245:363-4 O 10 '87
Casey's well-groomed successor. N. Traver. il por *Time* 129:22-3 F 16 '87
The CIA & the legacy of William Casey. J. B. Judis. il *Commonweal* 114:752-6 D 18 '87
Cleaning up the mess [cover story; special section] il pors *Newsweek* 110:24-30+ O 12 '87
Did a dead man tell no tales? R. Zoglin. il pors *Time* 130:28+ O 12 '87
Did Woodward get it right? G. Witkin. il por *U S News World Rep* 103:23 O 12 '87
Factoid time? *Natl Rev* 39:19 O 23 '87
Hard times once again in the spookhouse. W. L. Chaze. il por *U S News World Rep* 102:22-3+ Ja 26 '87
Knock on Woodward. F. Barnes. il *New Repub* 197:11-13 O 26 '87
Lifting the Veil on the CIA's secrets. M. Elfin. il pors *U S News World Rep* 103:26-7 O 5 '87
The man who wasn't there. D. M. Alpern. il por *Newsweek* 110:44-5 O 5 '87
Obituary
  Natl Rev 39:17 Je 5 '87
  Newsweek il pors 109:46 My 18 '87. T. Jacoby
  Time il por 129:37 My 18 '87. E. Magnuson
  U S News World Rep por 102:29 My 18 '87. C. Fenyvesi
Out in the cold. *Time* 130:20 S 7 '87
Reagan's secret wars and missed opportunities. J. M. Wall. *Christ Century* 104:907-8 O 21 '87
The secret wars of the CIA [excerpts from Veil] B. Woodward. il *Newsweek* 110:46-8+ O 5 '87
Silent witness: William Casey, Iranscam's mystery man, will tell no tales. E. Barnes and M. Dubrow. il pors *Life* 10:28-31 S '87
Spy master revelations. M. McDonald. il pors *Macleans* 100:30-1 O 12 '87
A spy's secret dies with him. M. Healy. por *U S News World Rep* 103:25 Jl 20 '87
William Casey. por *People Wkly* 28:84-5 D 28 '87-Ja 4 '88
With Casey out, who will fill the CIA's top job? *Newsweek* 109:21 Ja 12 '87
Woodward on Casey. T. H. Stahel. *America* 157:236-7 O 17 '87
Would you believe . . . Iranian moderates? [cover story] M. McDonald. *Wash Mon* 19:39-45+ Mr '87
Casey's General Stores Inc.
A belated crash for Casey's? G. G. Marcial. *Bus Week* p118 N 23 '87
Cash, James I.
    about
Business is his business. il pors *Ebony* 42:31-3+ O '87
Cash, Pat
    about
Australia had the Pat hand. R. Yallop. il por *Sports Illus* 66:26-7 Ja 5 '87
Cash on the line. F. Deford. il pors *Sports Illus* 67:36-9 Ag 24 '87
Cash won't stand Pat. S. Flink. il por *World Tennis* 34:18-19 Ap '87
Davis Cup '86: credit for Cash. S. Flink. il por *World Tennis* 34:54-5 Mr '87
Smash acts on centre court. C. Kirkpatrick. il pors *Sports Illus* 67:28-30+ Jl 13 '87
Cash, Rosanne, 1955-
    about
Rosanne Cash gets back to basics. A. Nash. il por *Stereo Rev* 52:147+ N '87
Cash America Investments (Firm)
The pawn king [J. R. Daugherty] M. Gill. il por *Esquire* 108:52 Jl '87
Pawnshops strike gold. D. Pedersen. il por *Newsweek* 109:53 Mr 16 '87
Cash business
    Taxation
Stash accounting. A. Snitzer. il *Forbes* 139:88+ Ap 6 '87
Cash flow
Now you see it . . . T. Pouschine. il *Forbes* 139:70 F 9 '87
The savviest investors are going with the flow. J. M. Laderman. il *Bus Week* p92-3 S 7 '87
Wagering on companies with mounds of money [views of Norman Weinger] A. E. Serwer. il *Fortune* 116:178 D 7 '87

Wall Street's new pet: the big corporate kitty. B. Nussbaum. il *Bus Week* p109+ D 7 '87
When customers don't pay. L. Kirschbaum. il *Nations Bus* 75:24+ Je '87
Cash management
Why Chrysler's cash handles like a dream [treasurer of pension fund F. W. Zuckerman] S. Weiss. il por *Bus Week* p116 Je 8 '87
Cash management accounts
Cash management accounts: getting your money's worth. G. Weiss. il *Bus Week* p104-5 Ja 19 '87
Cashen, Sara
Avalanche! il *Int Wildl* 17:36-7 My/Je '87
Cashew nuts
    Export-import trade
Meanwhile, back in Mozambique. il *Forbes* 140:110 N 16 '87
Cashin, Richard
    about
Unions fighting unions. D. Jenish. il *Macleans* 100:41-2 Ap 27 '87
Cashman, Thomas
    about
Sound picks in small stocks [interview] A. E. Serwer. il por *Fortune* 115:164 My 11 '87
Cashman Farrell & Associates
Are any stocks still worth buying? [interview with J. Farrell] A. E. Serwer. il por *Fortune* 116:100 Ag 31 '87
Casino Control Commission (N.J.) See New Jersey. Casino Control Commission
Casino gambling See Gambling
Casinos
  See also
  Del E. Webb Corp.
  Golden Nugget, Inc.
  Resorts International Inc.
  Trump's Castle Hotel and Casino
Battle royal on the old boardwalk [Atlantic City] J. Reed. il *U S News World Rep* 102:60-1 Ap 27 '87
Oaklander wins $1 mil. on Reno slot machine [P. Anderson] il por *Jet* 72:52 S 21 '87
    Acquisitions and mergers
Atlantic City roulette [competition between M. Davis and D. Trump over Resorts International] J. Crudele. il pors *N Y* 20:24 My 18 '87
The casino game: just for the highest rollers. L. Baum. il *Bus Week* p36-7 Mr 23 '87
For Bally, dumping Trump raises the ante [purchase of Golden Nugget in Atlantic City] M. D. Oneal. il *Bus Week* p45 Mr 9 '87
He who eats last . . . [D. Trump and Tweedy, Browne buy interests in Resorts International] R. Phalon. il por *Forbes* 140:130+ D 14 '87
Trump vs. Wynn: 'giant egos on the line' [Golden Nugget stock] R. Grover. il por *Bus Week* p31-2 Jl 27 '87
Zero-sum game [Bally buys Golden Nugget's Atlantic City casino] R. Phalon. il pors *Forbes* 139:110-12 Mr 23 '87
    International aspects
Asian fat cats are betting big on Vegas. R. Grover. il *Bus Week* p24 Ag 24 '87
Bucking odds in Vegas [Japanese investors] L. Brody. *Fortune* 116:84 D 7 '87
    Finance
Turmoil time in the casino business. D. Seligman. il *Fortune* 115:102-8+ Mr 2 '87
    Laws and regulations
  See also
  New Jersey. Casino Control Commission
    Management
Donald Trump gets a $200 million Christmas gift [contract to manage Resorts International Atlantic City casino approved by New Jersey Casino Control Commission] L. J. Tell and S. Benway. il por *Bus Week* p76 D 28 '87-Ja 4 '88
    Macao
Macau's casino king gets set to play with Beijing [S. Ho] M. Shao. il por *Bus Week* p98-9 Ja 19 '87
Caskey, C. Thomas
Disease diagnosis by recombinant DNA methods. bibl f il *Science* 236:1223-9 Je 5 '87
(jt. auth) See Gibbs, Richard A., and Caskey, C. Thomas
Casper, Billy
    about
Seven ahead, nine to go, and then . . . R. Reilly. il *Sports Illus* 66:62-6+ Je 15 '87
Caspi, Rachel R., and others
Organ-resident, nonlymphoid cells suppress proliferation of autoimmune T-helper lymphocytes. bibl f il *Science* 237:1029-32 Ag 28 '87

Cassell, Gail H.
(jt. auth) See Dybvig, Kevin, and Cassell, Gail H.
Cassell, Warren
What's wrong with co-op and three ways to make it better. *Publ Wkly* 232:62+ O 2 '87
Casselli, Henry, 1947-
about
Henry Casselli. J. R. Kemp. il por *Am Artist* 51:48-53+ Ag '87
Casserole cooking
See also
Skillet cooking
Terrine cooking
Casseroles! il *Good Housekeep* 204:108-18+ Ja '87
Casseroles for potluck dinners. il *South Living* 22:152-3 Jl '87
Turkey casseroles. il *Better Homes Gard* 65:149-50 D '87
Cassette books See Talking books
Cassette decks See Tape recorders and recording
Cassette recorders See Tape recorders and recording
Cassette recorders, Video See Videotape recorders and recording
Cassette recordings See Tape recordings
Cassette tape See Tape, Magnetic
Cassette tape recordings, Video See Videotapes
Cassian, Nina
Four poems [poem]; tr. by Christopher Hewitt. *New Yorker* 63:42 Ap 6 '87
September [poem]; tr. by Ruth Whitman. *New Yorker* 63:36 S 14 '87
Cassidy, Anne
Toilet training for adults: learn what you can catch in public bathrooms. il *Redbook* 169:118-19+ O '87
Cassidy, Jo
Smoking-related diseases: free with every puff. il *Curr Health 2* 14:13-15 N '87
Speaking of biopsies. il *Curr Health 2* 14:24-5 D '87
Cassidy, John
(jt. auth) See Smallwood, Christopher, and Cassidy, John
Cassidy, Joseph E.
The Nicaraguan Catholic Church vs. the Sandinista Front. il *USA Today (Periodical)* 115:31-2 Ja '87
Cassini, Oleg
Dressing for Camelot [excerpt from In my own fashion; cover story] il pors *People Wkly* 28:66-8+ Ag 24 '87
My romance with Grace Kelly [excerpt from In my own fashion] il pors *Ladies Home J* 104:32+ S '87
Cassini flights to Saturn See Space flight to Saturn
Cassiopeia (Constellation) See Constellations
Cassirer, Nadine Gordimer See Gordimer, Nadine, 1923-
Cassis (Los Angeles, Calif.: Restaurant) See Los Angeles (Calif.)—Restaurants, nightclubs, bars, etc.
Casson, Lionel, 1914-
Imagine, if you will, a time without any lawyers at all. bibl (p230) il *Smithsonian* 18:122-4+ O '87
Cassoni, Vittorio
about
AT&T may be ready to cut its losses in computers. J. J. Keller. il *Bus Week* p30 Jl 6 '87
AT&T's epic push in computers. P. Petre. il por *Fortune* 115:42-4+ My 25 '87
Cast iron
Collectors and collecting
Cast iron: heavy metal for collectors. E. Baroody. il *Antiques Collect Hobbies* 92:28-32 Jl '87
Cast iron cookware See Kitchen utensils and appliances
Cast iron outdoor furniture See Furniture, Outdoor
Cast iron plant See Aspidistra
Castaway [film] See Motion picture reviews—Single works
Le Castel (San Francisco, Calif.: Restaurant) See San Francisco (Calif.)—Restaurants, nightclubs, bars, etc.
Castelbajac, Kate de
about
American in Paris. il pors *Vogue* 177:258 Ag '87
Castellani, Loriana, and Cohen, Carolyn
Myosin rod phosphorylation and the catch state of molluscan muscles. bibl f il *Science* 235:334-7 Ja 16 '87
Castelli, Jean-Christophe
Long train coming. il *Esquire* 107:49+ Je '87
Castelli, Leo, 1907-
about
Knight unerring: Castelli becomes a chevalier. G. Henry. por *Art News* 86:18 Summ '87
Leader of the pack. K. Larson. il *N Y* 20:110+ Mr 9 '87
The past master of pop, Leo Castelli, celebrates his 30th anniversary as art's big dealer. H. Shapiro. il pors *People Wkly* 27:41-2+ F 16 '87

Castelli (Leo) Gallery See Leo Castelli Gallery
Castelli Ferrieri, Anna
about
Designing women. A. V. Anderson. il por *Ms* 16:26 D '87
Castiglione, Lawrence V.
Mythologies in arts teacher education. *Des Arts Educ* 89:14-18 S/O '87
Castile, Rand
Le style Japonesque. il por *House Gard* 159:28+ Je '87
Castile (Spain)
Social history
Hidalgo and pechero in Castile. I. A. A. Thompson. bibl f il *Hist Today* 37:23-9 Ja '87
Castilho, Carlos
Caribbean cousins. il *Courier* 39:16-20 D '86
Castillo, Jorge, 1933-
about
Jorge Castillo at Marlborough. C. Ratcliff. il *Art Am* 75:155-6 Je '87
Castillo del Lago (Hollywood, Calif.) See Hollywood (Calif.)—Historic houses, sites, etc.
Casting (Centrifugal) See Centrifugal casting
Casting (Fishing)
Bobbers on the rebound. J. Gibbs. bibl il *Outdoor Life* 180:44+ N '87
The fine art of fly fishing [women's participation in sport] R. L. Graham. il *Women's Sports Fitness* 9:52-4+ My '87
Fish dry and vote wet! C. Ford. il *50 Plus* 27:62-4 Je '87
Midstream [fly fishing for trout] T. McGuane. il *Harpers* 274:60-4 Ap '87
The problems of fly fishing deep [trout] P. Barrett. il *Field Stream* 92:70+ N '87
Schools for fly-fishers. J. I. Merritt. il *Money* 16:67-8+ Jl '87
Spinning a stream. G. Webster. il *Field Stream* 92:93+ My '87
Surfcasting with a home-run swing [technique of R. Arra] J. Skorupa. il por *Pop Mech* 164:59 N '87
Untangling the mysteries of fly-fishing. M. N. Vamos. il *Bus Week* p170-1 S 14 '87
Wet flies up, dry flies down. J. Bashline. il *Field Stream* 92:60+ My '87
Casting (Sculpture)
See also
Hoka Hey Foundry
Plaster casts (Sculpture)
The casting of Kevin Christian [drama] See Holt, Stephen
Casting of motion pictures See Motion picture production and direction
Castle, Ken
Swiss twins. il map *Travel Holiday* 168:36-43 O '87
Castle, Michael N.
The states and economic development [address, November 18, 1986] *Vital Speeches Day* 53:199-202 Ja 15 '87
Castle & Cooke, Inc.
David Murdock is picking plums. T. Carson. il por *Bus Week* p43 O 12 '87
"I just make ideas happen" [D. Murdock] J. Heins. il por *Forbes* 140 Sp Issue:32-5 O 26 '87
Castle models
Castle Lizzadro [miniature gold castle designed by W. Tolliday] A. Bahar. il por *Antiques Collect Hobbies* 92:48-52 Mr '87
Castleman, Michael
Molds, mites & pollen particles. il *Redbook* 169:24+ S '87
The new ways to detect—and treat—breast cancer. il *Redbook* 169:180-1 S '87
Silent heart disease: who's at risk? Why? il *Redbook* 169:118-19+ My '87
Sure-to-soothe cold and sore-throat remedies [excerpt from Cold cures] *Prevention* 39:99+ D '87
Surprising facts about the common cold. il *Read Dig* 130:85-8 F '87
What are your chances of surviving cancer? il *Redbook* 168:130-2+ Mr '87
Castles
See also
Sand castles
France
Arranging a stay in a French chateau. il *Sunset* 178:52-3 Mr '87
A château in bloom: Maryll and Bernard Lanvin's house in the Ile de France. A. Gordon. il *Vogue* 177:328-39 D '87

Castles—France—*cont.*
Easter in a Loire Valley château. A. Zabar. il *Gourmet* 47:72-3+ Ap '87
Legend of Le Fresne: Marquis and Marquise de Brantes near Tours. C. Bricker. il pors *Archit Dig* 44:176-81+ S '87
New life for a medieval castle: architect Roger Anger reclaims a Provençal ruin [Crestet] D. S. Aghion. il *Archit Dig* 44:184-9+ Mr '87

Mainau (Germany)
Profiles: Count and Countess Lennart Bernadotte [Schloss Mainau] D. H. Minassian. il pors *Archit Dig* 44:174-9+ D '87

Castletown (Ireland: Country estate) *See* Country estates—Ireland

Castonguay, Claude
about
Laurentian's Asian campaign. P. C. Newman. il por *Macleans* 100:24 Jl 13 '87

Castro, Fidel, 1927-
about
An American Christian's view of Castro's Cuba. R. Frame. il pors *Christ Today* 31:49+ N 6 '87
Building socialism—one more time. L. López. il por *Time* 129:67 My 4 '87
Castro takes the economy in hand. M. Perez-Stable. il *Nation* 245:298-300 S 26 '87
Fantasy island. *New Repub* 196:4 My 18 '87
Thoughts on the Church and Cuba. H. G. Cox. il *Nation* 244:595+ My 9 '87

Castro Valley (Calif.)
Stores
Denny Daughters, teenage shopkeeper, is a soft touch when it comes to helping blind customers [proprietor of Please Touch] il por *People Wkly* 28:120 O 12 '87

Castroviejo, Ramon, 1904-1987
about
Obituary
Natl Rev 39:23-4 Ja 30 '87. W. F. Buckley

Casts, Plaster (Sculpture) *See* Plaster casts (Sculpture)
Casual Quilted Giraffe (New York, N.Y.: Restaurant) *See* New York (N.Y.)—Restaurants, nightclubs, bars, etc.
Casualty insurance *See* Insurance, Property and casualty
Casualty loss deductions *See* Income tax—Deductions
Casuarinas (Nassau, Bahamas: Hotel) *See* Nassau (Bahamas)—Hotels, motels, etc.
CAT (Computerized axial tomography) *See* Tomography
Cat Cay Tuna Tournament *See* Fishing—Competitions
Cat food *See* Cats—Food and feeding
Cat litter
Kitty odor product seized [Scent-free product mislabeled as drug] D. Farley. il *FDA Consum* 21:37-8 Je '87
Learning a lot from litter: it's nothing to sniff at. P. W. Moser. il *Discover* 8:78-9 My '87

Catá, Alfonso, 1937-
about
Catá and his Ballet du Nord: France's northern lights. M. E. Willis. il *Dance Mag* 61:50-3 O '87

Cataffo, Louis
about
Graceful details: classical lines in a designer's Los Angeles villa. H. Drohojowska. il *Archit Dig* 44:66-71 Ag '87

Catalano, Susan M.
about
Susan Catalano: software keeps her on her toes. P. Finch. il por *Bus Week* p58 Ap 27 '87

Catalog houses *See* Mail order business
Catalog showrooms
See also
Best Products Co., Inc.
Service Merchandise Co., Inc.
Catalog of woes. M. Kuntz. il por *Forbes* 139:75+ My 4 '87

Catalogs, College
See also
Videotapes—College catalogs

Catalogs, Commercial
See also
Spiegel, Inc.
Don't leave home to buy it! Catalog shopping is the working woman's answer. J. Wechsler. *Work Woman* 12:91-3 Mr '87
For kids who have it all: minks and cars [F.A.O. Schwarz Christmas catalog] il *Newsweek* 110:73 N 2 '87
The good old days [prices of sporting goods in 1900 Sears catalog] E. B. Mann. il *Field Stream* 92:66-7+ Je '87
Hats, boots, chaps, neckerchiefs, dusters, and more: western wear by mail. *Sunset* 179:62-3 D '87
Shop by mail catalogs. See issues of Glamour

Anecdotes, facetiae, satire, etc.
Special attention. *New Yorker* 62:24-5 Ja 26 '87
Veblenian interlude. N. Hazelton. *Natl Rev* 39:58-60 Mr 13 '87

Catalogs, Genealogical
A bonanza of catalogs. C. E. Kraft. il *Antiques Collect Hobbies* 92:76-8 D '87

Catalogs, Library
See also
Catalogs, Union

Catalogs, Publishers'
Sprucing up the catalogue. il *Publ Wkly* 232:46-8 N 6 '87

Catalogs, Seed and plant
Five catalogs, modest to sizable, let you tap into the vegetable revolution. il *Sunset* 178:117 Ap '87
A guide to garden wish-books. il *Mother Earth News* 103:48-50 Ja/F '87
Reading the seeds. N. Bubel. il *Ctry J* 14:38-41 F '87
Seed/plant source finder 1988. *Flower Gard* 32:71-2 D '87/Ja '88

Catalogs, Trade *See* Catalogs, Commercial
Catalogs, Union
Great Britain
Acid test [Nineteenth century short title catalog on microfiche] il *Hist Today* 37:61-2 Ag '87

Catalonia (Spain)
Human high-rise [human castle builders] il map *Natl Geogr World* 147:21-3 N '87

Catalysts and catalysis
See also
Enzymes
Abzymes [catalytic antibodies] *Sci Am* 256:84-5 F '87
Cages, cavities and clefts [molecular traps; cover story] I. Peterson. il *Sci News* 132:90-3 Ag 8 '87
Catalysis: new perspectives from surface science. D. W. Goodman and J. E. Houston. bibl f il *Science* 236:403-9 Ap 24 '87
Chemical reactions on clays. P. Laszlo. bibl f il *Science* 235:1473-7 Mr 20 '87
The chemistry of self-splicing RNA and RNA enzymes. T. R. Cech. bibl f il *Science* 236:1532-9 Je 19 '87
The evolution of catalytic function. P. A. Sharp and D. Eisenberg. *Science* 238:729-30+ N 6 '87
Sound waves for activating nickel [research by Kenneth S. Suslick and Dominick J. Casadonte] I. Peterson. *Sci News* 131:388 Je 20 '87
A stereospecific cyclization catalyzed by an antibody. A. D. Napper and others. bibl f il *Science* 237:1041-3 Ag 28 '87

Catamaran racing
Iron men, plastic boats [race from Fort Lauderdale, Fla. to Virginia Beach, Va.] E. Sharp. il *Mot Boat Sail* 160:46-9+ Ag '87
Sibling rivalry [French brothers L. and B. Peyron in single-handed race from New York to England] P. Whittell. il pors *Mot Boat Sail* 159:58-61+ Je '87
Accidents and injuries
Going, going, gone . . . [Cougar Cat crashes in attempt to set world speed record] P. Whittell. il *Mot Boat Sail* 159:62-3 Je '87

Catamount Brewing Company
In Vermont: making beer the old-fashioned way. J. Skow. il *Time* 129:14+ F 23 '87

Cataracts (Eye defect)
All about cataracts. T. Shealey. *Prevention* 39:122+ N '87
Surgery
Cataract in India. G. Venkataswamy. il *World Health* p25-6 My '87

Catastrophes *See* Disasters
Catastrophic extinction of species *See* Mass extinction of species
Catastrophic health insurance *See* Insurance, Health
Catch A Rising Star Inc.
Richard Fields: catching his own rising star. il por *Bus Week* p59 Ag 17 '87

Catch basins
When a catch basin fails. H. Wicks. il *Home Mech* 83:64 Ap '87
Catching of balls *See* Ball catching
Catchings, John
about
Clairvoyant crime busters. R. Wolkomir and J. Wolkomir. il por *McCalls* 115:162-4+ O '87

Cate, William B.
Ecumenism: the future is local. *Christ Century* 104:551-2 Je 17-24 '87

Catechetics

Catholic Church

P.T. Barnum and the catechetical quest. W. J. O'Malley. il *America* 157:206-10 O 10 '87

Catecholamines

See also

Dopamine

Caterers and catering

See also

OK's Company

The dinner party as theater—feasts for the spirit and the senses [catering by N. Kalachnikoff] C. Rayner. il por *Vogue* 177:288 F '87

Joy of cooking: the life of rock caterers. L. Fissinger. il *Roll Stone* p32+ Je 4 '87

Snow peas stuffed with dollar bills: hauts hors d'oeuvres. J. Adler. il *Newsweek* 109:49 Ja 5 '87

Caterpillar Inc.

For Caterpillar, the metamorphosis isn't over. K. Deveny. il *Bus Week* p72-4 Ag 31 '87

George Schaefer. K. Deveny. il por *Bus Week* Sp Issue:258 Ap 17 '87

Most improved. il *Forbes* 139:146 Ja 12 '87

Caterpillar Tractor Co.

See also

Caterpillar Inc.

Caterpillars

See also

Gypsy moths

The snack that crawls [mopane worm caterpillars eaten as food in Africa] H. Brandon. il *Int Wildl* 17:16-21 Mr/Ap '87

Cates, Phoebe

about

New star style! il pors *Harpers Bazaar* 121:178-97 N '87

Catfish

See also

Cooking—Fish

No mud for the new catfish. L. Shapiro. il *Newsweek* 109:53 Je 29 '87

Catfish culture *See* Fish culture

Catfish fishing

The catfish connection. B. W. Dalrymple. il *Field Stream* 92:72-3+ Jl '87

Cathedral ceilings *See* Ceilings

Cathedral of St. John the Divine (New York, N.Y.)

Architecture [work of Rev. J. P. Morton] C. Wiseman. il *N Y* 20:122-3 S 21 '87

Big fish, big pond [J. Borofsky's sculpture Fish with ruby eye hanging in Cathedral] S. Staggs. il *Art News* 86:17-18 My '87

Dogs in the manger [Dean J. P. Morton's Theology of the earth] D. K. Mano. *Natl Rev* 39:65-6 Ja 30 '87

Cathedrals

California

See also

Crystal Cathedral (Garden Grove, Calif.)

New York (State)

See also

Cathedral of St. John the Divine (New York, N.Y.)

Cather, Willa, 1873-1947

about

First encounters. E. Sorel and N. C. Sorel. il *Atlantic* 260:83 Jl '87

Catherine Palace (Leningrad, Soviet Union) *See* Palaces—Soviet Union

Catheterization

See also

Cardiac catheterization

Catholic authors

See also

Greeley, Andrew M., 1928-

O'Connor, Flannery

Catholic Charities U.S.A.

Catholic Charities builds a bridge. C. J. Carney. *Commonweal* 114:80 F 13 '87

Catholic Church

See also

Beatification

Catechetics—Catholic Church

Catholicism

Catholics

Church renewal—Catholic Church

Divorce—Catholic Church

Laity—Catholic Church

Nuns

Papacy

Pentecostalism (Catholic)

Synod of Bishops (1987)

Synods of bishops

Vatican Council (2nd: 1962-1965)

Cardinal Suenens calls for a new Pentecost [interview] J. Catoir. *America* 156:457-9 Je 6 '87

Catholics plan worldwide evangelization effort [Evangelization 2000] J. Duin. *Christ Today* 31:36 F 6 '87

The good, the (sometimes) bad, and the beautiful. H. Fehren. *U S Cathol* 52:40-2 F '87

Of many things [Catholic news events of 1987] G. W. Hunt. *America* 157:490 D 26 '87

Attendance

See Church attendance

Authority

See also

Association for the Rights of Catholics in the Church

Catholic Church—Teaching office

Authority meets mystery. J. M. Wall. *America* 157:403-5 N 28 '87

Catholic authority, Catholic theology, Catholic identity [special section] *Commonweal* 114:43-51 Ja 30 '87

CUF and dissent: a case study in religious conservatism [Catholics United for the Faith] T. Iglesias. *America* 156:303-7 Ap 11 '87

Free speech in the Catholic Church [address, December 19, 1986] R. P. McBrien. *Vital Speeches Day* 53:237-40 F 1 '87

God is not elected but people are: reflections occasioned by NBC's news special "Report on America". W. H. Shannon. *America* 157:136-8 S 12-19 '87

Moral theology and public dissent: a temporary compromise. J. L. Lombardi. *America* 156:100-1+ F 7 '87

Nine Americans he won't want to meet—and why [critics of Pope John Paul II] il *People Wkly* 28:114-15 S 14 '87

Of many things. G. W. Hunt. *America* 156:inside cover F 21 '87

Our brother the Pope [discussion of November 7, 1986 article, The Pope, our brother] W. M. Shea. *Commonweal* 114:34+ Ja 30 '87

The peripatetic Pope: papal visits are a mixed blessing. P. Collins. il *Commonweal* 114:484-7 S 11 '87

Pope John Paul II and freedom. M. Negri. por *Humanist* 47:23-5+ S/O '87

Thunder on the left [new book entitled The Church in anguish: has the Vatican betrayed the Council?] J. B. Breslin. il *Publ Wkly* 232:39-41 O 9 '87

The Vatican doesn't know who its friends are. R. E. Burns. *U S Cathol* 52:2 F '87

Who's got the last word on Catholic morality? R. T. Reilly. il *U S Cathol* 52:54-8 Je '87

Whose Church is it? H. Fehren. *U S Cathol* 52:37-9 Ja '87

Blacks

See also

National Black Catholic Congress

Pope blasts U.S. racism; urges Church to continue fight for black equality. il por *Jet* 73:4 S 28 '87

Pope John-Paul's historic meeting with black bishops. il por *Jet* 73:24 N 9 '87

Charities

See also

Catholic Charities U.S.A.

Clergy

See also

Bishops

Black bishops

Cardinals

Catholic Church. National Conference of Catholic Bishops

Jesuits

Priests

Women deacons

Converts

See Converts, Catholic

Devotions

See Catholic Church—Prayer books and devotions

Discipline

See also

Celibacy

Penance

Hunthausen reinstated. *Christ Century* 104:522 Je 3-10 '87

Hunthausen restored. *Commonweal* 114:372-3 Je 19 '87

Panel probe in Seattle [R. C. Hunthausen case] *Christ Century* 104:215 Mr 4 '87

Education

See also

Catholic colleges and universities

Catholic schools

Catholic Church—Education—*cont.*
P.T. Barnum and the catechetical quest. W. J. O'Malley. il *America* 157:206-10 O 10 '87
Three views from the trenches: teaching high school religion in the city [New York City] D. H. Powell. *America* 157:212-16 O 10 '87

Finance
See also
Vatican City—Finance
Of many things. G. W. Hunt. *America* 156:inside cover Je 20-27 '87
Parish finances: are Catholics reluctant to pay their own way? [with editorial comment by Robert E. Burns] T. Unsworth. il *U S Cathol* 52:2, 32-8 S '87
A second collection on Catholic giving [discussion of September 1987 article, Parish finances] T. Unsworth. *U S Cathol* 52:46-7 D '87
Who says bingo is for losers? W. Flaherty. *U S Cathol* 52:40 Ja '87

Foreign relations
See Catholic Church—Relations (Diplomatic)

Government
John Paul: how he's changing the Church [cover story] K. L. Woodward. il pors *Newsweek* 110:22-9 S 21 '87
Of many things [Patrick Granfield's The limits of the papacy] G. W. Hunt. *America* 157:234 O 17 '87

Infallibility
See also
Catholic Church—Teaching office

Liturgy and ritual
See also
Baptism
Mass
Empirical liturgy: the search for grace. A. M. Greeley. *America* 157:379-83+ N 21 '87
Letter from Seattle. J. Whelan. *America* 156:463-5+ Je 6 '87

Marriage
See Marriage—Catholic Church

Missions
See Missions

Parishes
See Parishes

Prayer books and devotions
Don't let sleeping devotions lie. R. E. Burns. *U S Cathol* 52:2 Ja '87

Relations
Church of England
Joint Commission agrees on meaning of salvation [Anglican and Roman Catholic churches] il *Christ Today* 31:61 Mr 20 '87
Episcopal Church
Parishes for Anglican usage. J. H. Fichter. *America* 157:354-7 N 14 '87
Hinduism
Hindus vs. Catholics [Catholic priests charged with fostering anti-Hindu attitudes in India] *Christ Century* 104:353 Ap 15 '87
Judaism
The art of papal finesse [John Paul II's meeting with Jewish leaders] K. L. Woodward. il *Newsweek* 110:64 S 14 '87
The Auschwitz Carmel [controversy over convent at Auschwitz] *America* 156:206 Mr 14 '87
An historic Rome meeting. il *America* 157:124 S 12-19 '87
The invitation [Pope John Paul to meet with K. Waldheim] *Newsweek* 109:43 Je 29 '87
Jewish-Catholic dialogue: a year to remember. *America* 157:443 D 12 '87
Jews dismayed by Pope [meeting with K. Waldheim] *Christ Century* 104:586 Jl 1-8 '87
John Paul clears the air [summit with Jewish leaders] R. N. Ostling. il por *Time* 130:66 S 14 '87
Kurt Waldheim's Roman holiday [visit with Pope John Paul II] il pors *U S News World Rep* 103:14 Jl 6 '87
Learning from history [Carmelite convent at Auschwitz] E. Fleischner. *Commonweal* 114:167-8 Mr 27 '87
Long time no See [terminology in papal communiqué issued after meeting with Jewish leaders] W. Safire. il *N Y Times Mag* p34+ S 20 '87
Mr. Waldheim visits the Vatican. *America* 157:27 Jl 18-25 '87
One must bear witness [K. Waldheim's visit to John Paul II] M. B. Zuckerman. il *U S News World Rep* 103:66 Jl 13 '87
The pariah and the Pope [K. Waldheim visits the Vatican] pors *Time* 130:16 Jl 6 '87

The Pope and the Jews. I. Austen. il por *Macleans* 100:44 S 21 '87
The Pope and the pariah [visit with K. Waldheim] K. L. Woodward. pors *Newsweek* 110:45 Jl 6 '87
The Pope's letter [Holocaust letter marred by recent meeting with K. Waldheim] W. F. Buckley. *Natl Rev* 39:64-5 S 25 '87
The Pope's precedent [K. Waldheim invited to the Vatican] S. Masterman. pors *Macleans* 100:29 Je 29 '87
Ratzinger's 'land mine'. *Christ Century* 104:1138 D 16 '87
A reception and a snub [Pope John Paul meets with K. Waldheim] A. Bilski. *Macleans* 100:20 Jl 6 '87
A revolution in mutual esteem. M. H. Tanenbaum. por *U S News World Rep* 103:9 S 21 '87
Seeing Waldheim [visit to the Vatican] *Commonweal* 114:405-6 Jl 17 '87
Special delivery from the Pope [conciliatory letter from John Paul II] R. Lacayo. il *Time* 130:53 Ag 31 '87
Lutheran Church
About those Lutherans. R. J. Neuhaus. *Natl Rev* 39:43 Jl 31 '87
No joint worship [absence of Lutheran Church—Missouri Synod from Pope John Paul's ecumenical service in South Carolina] *Christ Century* 104:848 O 7 '87
Protestant churches
Catholic bishops address Protestant fundamentalism. *Christ Today* 31:54-5 D 11 '87
I wonder what the Catholics are doing tonight [interview with M. E. Marty] por *U S Cathol* 52:20-6 Je '87
Mainline Protestants help U.S. Catholic bishops spread economics message. W. Bole. il *Christ Today* 31:52+ F 20 '87
Protestant perspectives on the Catholic Church [cover story; special section; with editorial comment by George W. Hunt] il *America* 157:394, 399-408+ N 28 '87
Protestants and the Marian Year. R. M. Brown. *Christ Century* 104:520-1 Je 3-10 '87
Turning down the heat. K. S. Kantzer. il *Christ Today* 31:11 Mr 6 '87
Under the tent with John Paul [scheduled speaking appearance with B. Graham in Columbia, S.C.] *Time* 130:55 Jl 13 '87

Relations (Diplomatic)
John Paul II: the universal Pole. M. Maneli. *Humanist* 47:26-7+ S/O '87
Austria
The invitation [Pope John Paul to meet with K. Waldheim] *Newsweek* 109:43 Je 29 '87
Jews dismayed by Pope [meeting with K. Waldheim] *Christ Century* 104:586 Jl 1-8 '87
Kurt Waldheim's Roman holiday [visit with Pope John Paul II] il pors *U S News World Rep* 103:14 Jl 6 '87
Mr. Waldheim visits the Vatican. *America* 157:27 Jl 18-25 '87
One must bear witness [K. Waldheim's visit to John Paul II] M. B. Zuckerman. il *U S News World Rep* 103:66 Jl 13 '87
The pariah and the Pope [K. Waldheim visits the Vatican] pors *Time* 130:16 Jl 6 '87
The Pope and the pariah [visit with K. Waldheim] K. L. Woodward. pors *Newsweek* 110:45 Jl 6 '87
The Pope's letter [Holocaust letter marred by recent meeting with K. Waldheim] W. F. Buckley. *Natl Rev* 39:64-5 S 25 '87
The Pope's precedent [K. Waldheim invited to the Vatican] S. Masterman. pors *Macleans* 100:29 Je 29 '87
A reception and a snub [Pope John Paul meets with K. Waldheim] A. Bilski. *Macleans* 100:20 Jl 6 '87
Seeing Waldheim [visit to the Vatican] *Commonweal* 114:405-6 Jl 17 '87
Israel
The Cardinal & Israel [J. J. O'Connor] *Commonweal* 114:36-7 Ja 30 '87
The Cardinal goes calling [J. O'Connor] *New Repub* 196:9 Ja 19 '87
Diplomatic impasse [J. J. O'Connor's visit to Israel] *Christ Century* 104:48 Ja 21 '87
George Will overboard [views on Cardinal O'Connor's trip to Israel] W. F. Buckley. *Natl Rev* 39:62-3 F 27 '87
A holy row from a visit to a holy city [Cardinal J. O'Connor's controversial trip to Jerusalem] W. L. Chaze. il por *U S News World Rep* 102:14 Ja 12 '87
Jerusalem and the pluck of the Irish [Cardinal O'Connor's trip] *America* 156:41-2 Ja 24 '87

Catholic Church—Relations (Diplomatic)—Israel—*cont.*
Minority report [conflicting views of G. F. Will and W. F. Buckley regarding J. J. O'Connor's visit] C. Hitchens. *Nation* 244:170 F 14 '87
O'Connor's critics misconstrue terms [Cardinal O'Connor's comments on the Holocaust] J. M. Wall. *Christ Century* 104:75-6 Ja 28 '87
Office politics [Cardinal O'Connor's visit to Israel] *New Repub* 196:9 Ja 26 '87
On challenging a few clichés [J. J. O'Connor's visit] *America* 156:62-3 Ja 31 '87

United States
See also
Reagan, Ronald, 1911——Visit to the Vatican, 1987
Three years later: U.S. relations with the Holy See. T. J. Reese. *America* 156:29-35 Ja 17 '87

Renewal
See Church renewal—Catholic Church

Rites and ceremonies
See also
Boy bishops
Letter from Seattle. J. Whelan. *America* 156:463-5+ Je 6 '87
The R.C.I.A. misunderstood? [Rite of Christian Initiation of Adults] R. A. Duffy. il *America* 156:385+ My 9 '87

Societies
See also
Alienated Catholics Anonymous
Association for the Rights of Catholics in the Church
Opus Dei (Society)

Teaching office
One, holy, Catholic and somewhat infallible [Catholic college's allegiance to academic freedom] D. O'Brien. *America* 156:276-8 Ap 4 '87
Scripture and dogma today [Catholic doctrine] R. E. Brown. *America* 157:286-9 O 31 '87
Who speaks for the Church? T. P. Rausch. *America* 156:344-6 Ap 25 '87

Theology
See Theology

Argentina
Church and insurrection in Argentina. R. K. DeHainaut. *Christ Century* 104:582-3 Jl 1-8 '87

Bolivia
The Catholic Church in Bolivia. J. A. McCoy. *America* 157:263-5 O 24 '87

Brazil
See also
Church and social problems—Brazil

Canada
Barred from the church altar [S. Bernier prohibited from serving as altar girl in Toronto] M. McIver. por *Macleans* 100:45 Jl 6 '87
John Paul's restless Catholics [cover story; special section; with editorial comment by Kevin Doyle] il pors *Macleans* 100:2, 32-8+ S 14 '87

Chile
See also
John Paul II, Pope, 1920——Visit to Chile, 1987

Congo
A cardinal who spoke truth to power [E. Biayenda] R. Fegley. *Christ Century* 104:325-6 Ap 8 '87

Cuba
Cuba: the Church is open. T. C. Wright. *America* 157:266-9 O 24 '87
Thoughts on the Church and Cuba. H. G. Cox. il *Nation* 244:595+ My 9 '87

Czechoslovakia
Apostle of *glasnost* visits Prague. *America* 156:333 Ap 25 '87

El Salvador
See also
Church and social problems—El Salvador
A tale of two cities. J. P. Fitzpatrick. *America* 157:4-5 Jl 4-11 '87
A torch held on high [legacy of murdered priest R. Grande] J. R. Brockman. *America* 156:214-16+ Mr 14 '87

France
See also
John Paul II, Pope, 1920——Visit to France, 1986
Breaking the silence [K. Barbie and role of the Catholic Church] K. McCaffrey. il *Commonweal* 114:418-20 Jl 17 '87
The churches and the peace movement in France. M. B. Davis. il *Christ Century* 104:826-8 S 30 '87

Germany
The priests of Dachau. W. J. O'Malley. il *America* 157:351-3 N 14 '87

Guatemala
Four candles in the wind [disappearance of four Catholic activists] G. L. Bowen. il *Commonweal* 114:726-7 D 18 '87

Haiti
See also
Church and social problems—Haiti

India
See also
Church and social problems—India
Hindus vs. Catholics [Catholic priests charged with fostering anti-Hindu attitudes] *Christ Century* 104:353 Ap 15 '87

Latin America
See also
Church and social problems—Latin America
John Paul II, Pope, 1920——Visit to Latin America, 1987
Latin America and the Church [cover story; special section] *America* 157:261-73 O 24 '87

Lithuania
Lithuania, land of the unquenchable wick. J. A. Broun. *Commonweal* 114:594-5 O 23 '87
The Lithuanian cross. *America* 156:474 Je 13 '87

Nicaragua
Covert aid and the Church [U.S. aid to Cardinal Obando y Bravo] R. Parry and T. Jacoby. il por *Newsweek* 109:27-8 Je 15 '87
The Nicaraguan Catholic Church vs. the Sandinista Front. J. E. Cassidy. il *USA Today (Periodical)* 115:31-2 Ja '87
A tale of two cities. J. P. Fitzpatrick. *America* 157:4-5 Jl 4-11 '87

Nigeria
Learning from missionaries. P. Schineller. *America* 156:249-51 Mr 28 '87

Peru
See also
Church and social problems—Peru

Philippines
Church and state in the Philippines. C. Quimpo. *Christ Century* 104:647 Jl 29-Ag 5 '87
The dilemma of the Philippine left: the party or the people? J. J. Carroll. *America* 157:79-81 Ag 15-22 '87
Inextricably involved. *America* 156:414 My 23 '87
The Philippine revolution: a year later. F. F. Claver. *America* 156:232-5 Mr 21 '87

Poland
See also
John Paul II, Pope, 1920——Visit to Poland, 1987
Popieluszko, Jerzy—Murder case
A bitter anniversary [fifth anniversary of the declaration of martial law] *America* 156:1 Ja 3-10 '87

Ukraine
'Catholics of the world should know . . . '. *America* 157:419 D 5 '87
Soviet repression of the Ukrainian Catholic Church. bibl f *Dep State Bull* 87:47-52 Mr '87

United States
See also
Campaign for Human Development
Catholic Church. National Conference of Catholic Bishops
Catholics—United States
John Paul II, Pope, 1920——Visit to the United States, 1987
Parishes
United States Catholic Conference
American Catholics: what's happened to your Church in the last 25 years? [cover story; special issue; with editorial comment by Robert E. Burns] il *U S Cathol* 52:2, 6-61+ Je '87
America's most generous diocese [Springfield-Cape Girardeau, Mo.] M. F. Dorion. il *Fortune* 116:40 D 21 '87
Baltimore priest 1st black bishop for West Coast [C. A. Fisher] por *Jet* 71:36 Ja 26 '87
Being Catholic in America [cover story] J. Berger. il *N Y Times Mag* p22-7+ Ag 23 '87
Believe it or not:
Faith, institution and community. G. McCauley. *America* 156:259+ Mr 28 '87
Church/state: the first freedom [agreement between Archdiocese of San Antonio and Park Service to operate San Antonio National Historical Park] J. Freeman. il *Natl Parks* 61:18 Mr/Ap '87
God is not elected but people are: reflections occasioned by NBC's news special "Report on America". W. H. Shannon. *America* 157:136-8 S 12-19 '87

Catholic Church—United States—cont.

Is there an American Catholic Church? E. K. Braxton. *America* 157:422-6 D 5 '87

John Paul's feisty flock [cover story] R. N. Ostling. il por *Time* 130:46-51 S 7 '87

Kinds of Catholics. R. J. Neuhaus. *Natl Rev* 39:42 Jl 3 '87

Nine Americans he won't want to meet—and why [critics of Pope John Paul II] il *People Wkly* 28:114-15 S 14 '87

Our brother the Pope [discussion of November 7, 1986 article, The Pope, our brother] W. M. Shea. *Commonweal* 114:34+ Ja 30 '87

The Pope's foot soldiers [B. Frawley and R. Dlugos, parish priests; cover story] J. Buckley. il pors *U S News World Rep* 103:60-4+ S 21 '87

Profiles (I) [Cardinal J. J. O'Connor of the archdiocese of New York] N. Hentoff. por *New Yorker* 63:59-76 Mr 23 '87

Profiles (II) [Cardinal J. J. O'Connor of the archdiocese of New York] N. Hentoff. il *New Yorker* 63:37-8+ Mr 30 '87

The rise of Catholic fundamentalism. P. M. Arnold. il *America* 156:297-302 Ap 11 '87

The Vatican doesn't know who its friends are. R. E. Burns. *U S Cathol* 52:2 F '87

What's in a name? [pick-and-choose Catholicism] *Commonweal* 114:515-16 S 25 '87

History

The legacy of two leaders [G. Washington and J. Carroll] J. T. Ellis. *America* 157:149-50 S 26 '87

Yugoslavia

Medjugorje's miracles: faith and profit [appearances of the Virgin Mary] D. R. Janz. il *Christ Century* 104:724-5 Ag 26-S 2 '87

Visitations of the Virgin. K. L. Woodward. il *Newsweek* 110:54-5 Jl 20 '87

Catholic Church. Congregation for the Doctrine of the Faith

Catholic authority, Catholic theology, Catholic identity [special section] *Commonweal* 114:43-51 Ja 30 '87

Charles E. Curran: a teaching moment continues [cover story; special issue; with editorial comment by George W. Hunt] il *America* 156:inside cover, 334-46+ Ap 25 '87

A classic case of consequentialism [criticism of Cardinal Ratzinger's views on the morality of deterrence] E. W. Doherty. *Commonweal* 114:10-11 Ja 16 '87

Diagnosing the Vatican 'Instruction' [Instruction on respect for human life in its origin and on the dignity of procreation] J. C. Harvey. *Commonweal* 114:238-9 Ap 24 '87

The ethics of human manufacture [document on artificial forms of procreation; cover story] C. Krauthammer. *New Repub* 196:17-21 My 4 '87

Father Charles Curran and Canon 812. R. M. Brown. *Christ Century* 104:100 F 4-11 '87

Open letters to Archbishop John R. Quinn [discussion of February 7, 1987 article, On the pastoral care of homosexual persons] J. R. Quinn. *America* 156:238-44 Mr 21 '87

Procreation, science and sin. J. Carey. il *U S News World Rep* 102:10 Mr 23 '87

Religious leaders respond to the Vatican's ban on artificial conception [Instruction on respect for human life in its origin and on the dignity of procreation] B. Spring. il *Christ Today* 31:41-2 Ap 17 '87

Roma locuta [Vatican's statement on issues of artificial reproduction] *Natl Rev* 39:19-20 Je 19 '87

Roman Catholic sexual ethics: a dissenting view [cover story] C. E. Curran. il *Christ Century* 104:1139-42 D 16 '87

Rules for making love and babies [Vatican pronouncement] K. L. Woodward. il *Newsweek* 109:42-3 Mr 23 '87

Taking it on the chin—for life: reflections on a Vatican instruction [On respect for human life and its origin and on the dignity of procreation] D. E. Pilarczyk. *America* 156:295-6 Ap 11 '87

Technology and the womb [Catholic Church denounces advances in reproductive technology] R. N. Ostling. il *Time* 129:58-9 Mr 23 '87

Toward an understanding of the letter On the pastoral care of homosexual persons. J. R. Quinn. *America* 156:92-5+ F 7 '87

The Vatican and bioethics [interview with J. Ratzinger] H. Tincq. *World Press Rev* 34:58 Jl '87

The Vatican document on bioethics: some unsolicited suggestions. R. A. McCormick. il *America* 156:24-8+ Ja 17 '87

The Vatican document on bioethics: two responses [with editorial comment] L. S. Cahill; R. A. McCormick. *America* 156:245-8 Mr 28 '87

The Vatican weighs in. C. Holden. *Science* 235:1455 Mr 20 '87

Vatican't [document on reproduction] H. Hertzberg. *New Repub* 196:42 Ap 6 '87

What comes naturally [Vatican's Instruction on respect for human life in its origin and on the dignity of procreation] *Commonweal* 114:163-4 Mr 27 '87

What is sex for? [Vatican statement on human reproduction] S. Grenz. il por *Christ Today* 31:22-3 Je 12 '87

Catholic Church. National Conference of Catholic Bishops

Bishops: joining KKK is sinful, violates teaching. *Jet* 72:29 Ap 20 '87

The bishops' letter, world debt and the U.S. trade deficit [pastoral letter on the economy] J. A. Gylys. il *America* 157:86-7 Ag 15-22 '87

Bishops move diagonally [pastoral letter, Economic justice for all] G. P. Brockway. *New Leader* 70:10-11 Mr 23 '87

Catholic bishops address Protestant fundamentalism. *Christ Today* 31:54-5 D 11 '87

Catholic bishops meet. *Christ Century* 104:1113 D 9 '87

Don't route this pastoral to the dead-letter office [U.S. bishops' "Economic justice for all"] R. E. Burns. *U S Cathol* 52:2 Mr '87

How to implement 'Economic justice for all'. A. M. Pilla. il *America* 156:76-8+ Ja 31 '87

How to talk about economic strategy [Catholic bishops' pastoral letter and Democratic Leadership Council's conference in Williamsburg] A. Cockburn and R. Pollin. il *Nation* 244:245-7 F 28 '87

Legal attack by bishops [asking the Supreme Court to overturn an order demanding that the bishops relinquish church files to critics of their stand on abortion] *Christ Century* 104:881-2 O 14 '87

Mainline Protestants help U.S. Catholic bishops spread economics message. W. Bole. il *Christ Today* 31:52+ F 20 '87

On challenging opponents [D. E. Pilarczyk's views on the U.S. bishops' economics pastoral] *America* 156:434 My 30 '87

Our bishops and our economy [Catholic pastoral] J. Gaffney. *America* 156:44-9 Ja 24 '87

Resurrecting the common good [pastoral letter on the economy] R. N. Bellah. il *Commonweal* 114:736-41 D 18 '87

Toward a socialist strategy [discussion of February 28, 1987 article, How to talk about economic strategy] A. Cockburn and R. Pollin. *Nation* 244:748+ Je 6 '87

U.S. bishops' meeting: efficiency and openness. T. H. Stahel. *America* 157:420-1 D 5 '87

What's become of the pastoral? [letter on the economy] K. S. Smith. il *Commonweal* 114:742-7 D 18 '87

Catholic Church. National Conference of Catholic Bishops. Committee on War and Peace

Is nuclear deterrence immoral? [Catholic bishops' stand] R. E. Powaski. *America* 156:401-5 My 16 '87

Living in sin with nuclear arms [views of M. Gallagher on peace pastoral] J. M. Wall. *Christ Century* 104:155-6 F 18 '87

Sidestepping The challenge of peace [Catholic bishops' pastoral on nuclear deterrence] M. Gallagher. il *Commonweal* 114:9-13 Ja 16 '87

Catholic Church. Pontifical Commission for Social Communication

Flacking in the fields of the Lord [Archbishop J. Foley] J. Ferullo. il pors *Channels* 7:45-8 Mr '87

Catholic Church and abortion See Abortion—Moral and religious aspects

Catholic Church and AIDS (Disease) See AIDS (Disease)—Religious aspects; AIDS (Disease) and priests

Catholic Church and artificial insemination See Artificial insemination, Human—Moral and religious aspects

Catholic Church and birth control See Birth control—Moral and religious aspects

Catholic Church and civil rights See Church and civil rights

Catholic Church and disarmament See Church and disarmament

Catholic Church and economics See Christianity and economics

Catholic Church and ethics *See* Christian ethics
Catholic Church and homosexuality *See* Church work with homosexuals; Homosexuality and Christianity
Catholic Church and labor *See* Church and labor
Catholic Church and politics *See* Religion and politics
Catholic Church and race relations *See* Church and race relations
Catholic Church and reproduction *See* Reproduction—Moral and religious aspects
Catholic Church and sex *See* Sex and religion
Catholic Church and social problems *See* Church and social problems
Catholic Church and the press *See* Church and the press
Catholic Church and war *See* War and religion
Catholic Church and women *See* Women and religion
Catholic colleges and universities
> *See also*
> Association of Catholic Colleges and Universities
> Catholic University of America
> De Paul University
> Georgetown University
> University of Notre Dame

Authority and academic freedom. R. Kirtland. *America* 156:348-9 Ap 25 '87
Have Catholic colleges kept the faith? R. T. Reilly. il *U S Cathol* 52:34-40 O '87
One, holy, Catholic and somewhat infallible [Catholic college's allegiance to academic freedom] D. O'Brien. *America* 156:276-8 Ap 4 '87
The Pope and the colleges. *America* 157:180 O 3 '87
Federal aid
Religiously affiliated colleges and American freedom. K. D. Whitehead. *America* 156:96-8+ F 7 '87
Laws and regulations
Catholics and their colleges. *America* 156:225 Mr 21 '87
Father Charles Curran and Canon 812. R. M. Brown. *Christ Century* 104:100 F 4-11 '87
Lebanon
Assassination in South Lebanon [French Jesuit A. Masse] H. Madelin. *America* 157:397-8 N 28 '87
Nicaragua
> *See also*
> Universidad Centroamericana

Catholic converts *See* Converts, Catholic
Catholic education *See* Catholic colleges and universities; Catholic schools
Catholic ethics *See* Christian ethics
Catholic hymns and hymnals *See* Hymns
Catholic laity *See* Laity—Catholic Church
Catholic literature
Bibliography
Catholic books that won't go away. G. M. Costello. *U S Cathol* 52:65-7 Je '87
Catholic missions *See* Missions
Catholic parishes *See* Parishes
Catholic Pentecostals *See* Pentecostalism (Catholic)
Catholic press
> *See also*
> America (Periodical)
> Commonweal (Periodical)

Catholic Relief Services
Scandals in Catholic Relief [cover story] J. MacGuire. il *Natl Rev* 39:26-30+ Jl 3 '87
Catholic schools
> *See also*
> National Catholic Educational Association

Bashing public education [study of Catholic high school students and drug use] E. Doerr. *Humanist* 47:43 Jl/Ag '87
The case of Our Lady of Sorrows [school on the Lower East Side of New York City] D. E. DeCosse. *Commonweal* 114:210-15 Ap 10 '87
Community as social capital: James S. Coleman on Catholic schools. A. M. Greeley. *America* 157:110-12 Ag 29-S 5 '87
Minorities do better at Catholic schools: study. *Jet* 72:24 Je 22 '87
Minorities in Catholic schools: why do they read better? V. Lee. *Educ Dig* 52:20-3 F '87
No boys allowed: a smart solution? [girls attending single-sex Catholic high schools do better academically; research by Valerie E. Lee and Anthony S. Bryk] S. Vandershaf. il *Psychol Today* 21:68 F '87
Rebound for glory [St. Mary's basketball team in Trenton, N.J.] B. Doyle. il *U S Cathol* 52:26-33 O '87
Sarabeth Eason [interview with 11 year old expelled from Toledo Catholic school for supporting abortion free choice] C. Grant. il pors *Ms* 15:60-1+ Ja '87
The sound of music [St. Augustine parochial school, South Bronx] E. Hopkins. il *N Y* 20:54-7 N 23 '87

A teacher's teacher [high school Latin teacher T. Jones; cover story] J. W. Donohue. *America* 157:495-7 D 26 '87
Why Johnny drops out [interview with J. S. Coleman] B. Leonard. il por *Forbes* 140:242+ N 16 '87
Federal aid
Needed: a new educational partnership between government and families. W. J. Byron. *America* 156:460-2+ Je 6 '87
Finance
Needed: a new educational partnership between government and families. W. J. Byron. *America* 156:460-2+ Je 6 '87
Catholic theology *See* Theology
Catholic University of America
Keeping youth in school: a public-private collaboration [peer mentor program for high school students sponsored by Catholic University and Marriott; with reports by J. Payne and J. Smith] S. Lee and others. il *Child Today* 16:15-21 Jl/Ag '87
Catholicism
> *See also*
> Anti-Catholicism

Growing up Catholic & the adult search for faith [special section] *Commonweal* 114:446-57 Ag 14 '87
Protestant perspectives on the Catholic Church [cover story; special section; with editorial comment by George W. Hunt] il *America* 157:394, 399-408+ N 28 '87
What's in a name? [pick-and-choose Catholicism] *Commonweal* 114:515-16 S 25 '87
Catholicism in literature *See* Religion in literature
Catholics
Canada
John Paul's restless Catholics [cover story; special section; with editorial comment by Kevin Doyle] il pors *Macleans* 100:2, 32-8+ S 14 '87
Great Britain
History
A patriot for whom? Stanley, York and Elizabeth's Catholics [1587 defection of key officers in the Netherlands] S. Adams. bibl il *Hist Today* 37:46-50 Jl '87
Northern Ireland
Why Irish eyes frown at U.S. help [pressure to open jobs in American firms to Ulster Catholics] P. Sherrid. il *U S News World Rep* 103:32 Ag 24 '87
United States
> *See also*
> Alienated Catholics Anonymous

American Catholics: what's happened to your Church in the last 25 years? [cover story; special issue; with editorial comment by Robert E. Burns] il *U S Cathol* 52:2, 6-61+ Je '87
America's Catholics: what the Pope will encounter. W. Bole. il por *Christ Today* 31:58-9+ S 4 '87
Being Catholic in America [cover story] J. Berger. il *N Y Times Mag* p22-7+ Ag 23 '87
Chords of a dissonant choir. il *Newsweek* 110:30 S 21 '87
[Column] H. Fehren. See issues of U.S. Catholic
The examined life. R. E. Burns. See issues of U.S. Catholic
Growing up Catholic & the adult search for faith [special section] *Commonweal* 114:446-57 Ag 14 '87
If I had five minutes with the Pope [views of 10 prominent American Catholics; cover story] il *America* 157:126-32+ S 12-19 '87
John Paul's feisty flock [cover story] R. N. Ostling. il por *Time* 130:46-51 S 7 '87
Painting by number [Gallup-Castelli survey] *Commonweal* 114:101-2 F 27 '87
Phil Donahue [interview] L. Gomez. pors *Life* 10:21-2 O '87
Prime-time conversation. A. D. Achenback. *America* 156:475-6 Je 13 '87
Somebody up there likes me: what U.S. Catholic readers believe about the saints [cover story] J. Breig. il *U S Cathol* 52:6-15 N '87
Sun dances, corn pollen, & the cross [Native American Catholics] C. Vecsey. il *Commonweal* 114:345-51 Je 5 '87
'To be American and Catholic'. J. W. Malone. il por *U S News World Rep* 103:61 S 14 '87
Why Catholics stay in the Church [cover story] A. M. Greeley. il *America* 157:54-7+ Ag 1-8 '87
Anecdotes, facetiae, satire, etc.
Poll finds mix-&-match Catholics. *Commonweal* 114:516-17 S 25 '87
Catholics United for the Faith
CUF and dissent: a case study in religious conservatism. T. Iglesias. *America* 156:303-7 Ap 11 '87

CATIE *See* Centro Agronómico Tropical de Investigación y Enseñanza

Cations *See* Ions

Catlin, Paul
about
Drive & Survive. P. Bingham. il por *Mot Trend* 39:137+ Je '87

Catmint
Catmint: delicate color from a sturdy plant. il *South Living* 22:68 Je '87

Cato
Letter from Washington. See issues of National Review

Catoir, John
Cardinal Suenens calls for a new Pentecost [interview] *America* 156:457-9 Je 6 '87

Cats
Are cats smart? Yes, at being cats. P. W. Moser. il *Discover* 8:76-7+ My '87
An autumn apparition [cat perched on back of flying mallard] M. J. Walters. il *Read Dig* 131:71-4+ O '87
Get to know the animal in your pet. A. R. Marder. *Prevention* 39:73-5 Jl '87
Going to the cats. C. Murphy. il *Atlantic* 260:14+ Ag '87
The secret lives of dogs and cats [condensed from Dogwatching and Catwatching] D. Morris. il *Read Dig* 131:47-8+ D '87
What is a cat? [excerpts] B. Adler. il *Good Housekeep* 204:166 Je '87

Anecdotes, facetiae, satire, etc.
Ask the best cat in the world. K. Fury. il *50 Plus* 27:84 S '87
'The cat would never admit her mistakes' [empty nest syndrome] D. D. Jackson. il *Smithsonian* 17:140 Ja '87
Ménage à cat. T. Young. *Vogue* 177:391+ F '87

Brain
See Brain

Care
Exercising your pet. R. Kidd. il *Mother Earth News* 105:34+ My/Je '87
Grooming your cat. S. L. Gerstenfeld. il *Parents* 62:232 D '87
A safe and happy holiday for your pet. A. R. Marder. *Prevention* 39:49+ N '87
Workouts for pampered pets. A. R. Marder. *Prevention* 39:110+ O '87

Diseases and pests
Animal rightists raid USDA lab [interruption of toxoplasmosis research at Animal Parasitology Institute] C. Holden. *Science* 237:1099 S 4 '87
Dogs, cats, and cancer. H. E. Whiteley. il *Saturday Evening Post* 259:32+ Mr '87
Isolation of a T-lymphotropic virus from domestic cats with an immunodeficiency-like syndrome. N. C. Pedersen and others. bibl f il *Science* 235:790-3 F 13 '87
Letting cats out of the lab: a cautionary tale [animal activists' interruption of toxoplasmosis research at the Animal Parasitology Institute] P. Gadsby. il *Discover* 8:22 N '87
Myocardial failure in cats associated with low plasma taurine: a reversible cardiomyopathy [cover story] P. D. Pion and others. bibl f il *Science* 237:764-8 Ag 14 '87

Vaccines and vaccination
A vaccination update. A. R. Marder. *Prevention* 39:105-8 S '87

Equipment
See also
Cat litter

Eye
See Eye—Animals

Food and feeding
Morris the Cat is learning Japanese [U.S. cat food exports] B. Buell. il *Bus Week* p82 Je 15 '87
Myocardial failure in cats associated with low plasma taurine: a reversible cardiomyopathy [cover story] P. D. Pion and others. bibl f il *Science* 237:764-8 Ag 14 '87
Now thanks to Suzanna Goodin, pets can clean the bowl—and then eat the spoon that feeds them. il por *People Wkly* 27:119 Mr 9 '87

Photographs and photography
Beauty in the beasts [cover story] W. Chandoha. il *Petersens Photogr Mag* 16:18-21 D '87
Instant success . . . ! [C. Gandolfo's photograph of Cinnamon the wet cat; cover story] J. Gray. il *Petersens Photogr Mag* 15:28-9+ Mr '87

Cats, Wild
See also
Bobcats

Jaguars
Leopards
Pumas

Cats as carriers of infection *See* Animals as carriers of infection

Cats in television
Pretty cool cat [Bob the Weather Cat at KATU-TV, Portland, Or.; cover story] il *Natl Geogr World* 144:3-5 Ag '87

Catskill Mountains region (N.Y.)
See also
Architecture, Domestic—Catskill Mountains region (N.Y.)
Resorts—Catskill Mountains region (N.Y.)

Description and travel
Searching for Kaaterskill Falls. N. Bliven. il *New Yorker* 63:43-58 Ag 3 '87

Cattails
Cattails for whitetails. J. Boatner. il *Outdoor Life* 180:48-9+ D '87

Catterall, William A.
(jt. auth) *See* Takahashi, Masami, and Catterall, William A.

Cattle
See also
Beef
Calves
Calving
Cows
Beef. B. Eftink. See issues of Successful Farming through June 1987
Texas longhorns on the comeback trail. J. D. Scott. il *Read Dig* 130:56-60 Ja '87

Breeding
Derek's herd [White Galloway breeder D. Pruitt] R. Gavin. il por *Ctry J* 14:21-5 Jl '87
The latest economy model, a compact cow [work of José Manuel Berruecos with Brahman cattle] il *Discover* 8:9 Ag '87
Look! On the ground! It's a cow! [selective breeding of mini Brahman cattle] il *Newsweek* 110:37 Jl 20 '87

Carcasses
Packers don't want to pay for fat [hot fat trimming] B. Eftink. il *Success Farm* 85:60-1 Ag '87

Confinement methods
See also
Cattle feedlots

Contamination
Are you wasting 20% of your implant dollars? B. Eftink. il *Success Farm* 85:56-7 S '87
Drugged livestock [beef cattle from Gordon Riley's farm] il *FDA Consum* 21:30-1 Jl/Ag '87

Diseases and pests
Cyanamid is bullish on a cure for sick cows [acquiring stake in Applied Microbiology's protein for mastitis] G. G. Marcial. il *Bus Week* p136 My 11 '87
How to build a fly trap that really works [horn flies] il *Success Farm* 85:41B Je '87
Ohio dairy expert offers new ways to beat mastitis. il *Success Farm* 85:D1 Je '87
Predipping teats sharply cuts mastitis troubles. *Success Farm* 85:D2 Je '87

Vaccines and vaccination
War on cattle disease divides the troops [rinderpest] J. Walsh. il map *Science* 237:1289-91 S 11 '87

Feeding
See also
Calves—Feeding
Cattle feedlots
Grazing
Cheap corn makes cheap Holsteins competitive. *Success Farm* 85 no6:B17 Mr '87
Flexible forages. il *Success Farm* 85 no6:B3-B6+ Mr '87
New cattle feed additives on the way. *Success Farm* 85:B1 My '87
Silage beats hay as supplement to wheat pasture. *Success Farm* 85 no4:B13 F '87
Switching brands of ionophores won't boost gains; Reducing intake improves feed efficiency. *Success Farm* 85:B4 My '87

Marketing
See also
Better Beef Marketing
Calve heifers, then market them [single-calf heifer system] B. Eftink. il *Success Farm* 85:16-17 O '87
A cattle plan your banker will like [hedging] G. Johnston. *Success Farm* 85:7 S '87

Cattle—Marketing—cont.

Pencil shrink gives way to computer shrink [spreadsheet to figure shrinkage when marketing slaughter-weight cattle] C. Peterson, Jr. il *Success Farm* 85 no4:B21 F '87

Prices

Can livestock bubble continue to rise? G. Johnston. il *Success Farm* 85:62 Ag '87

Packers don't want to pay for fat [hot fat trimming] B. Eftink. il *Success Farm* 85:60-1 Ag '87

Weight and measurements

See also

Cattle—Carcasses

High-tech cattle call [USDA weight monitoring system] D. Eskow. il *Pop Mech* 164:12 Mr '87

Cattle egrets *See* Egrets

Cattle farm management

Electronic cowboys. il *Futurist* 21:50 My/Je '87

How Ray Muzny doubled gross sales with little extra cost. il *Success Farm* 85 no4:B20 F '87

Planning pays off for rancher [Bob Chenoweth] D. Allen and G. Johnston. il *Success Farm* 85:12 Je '87

What it costs to computerize your herd. G. Vincent. il *Success Farm* 85 no4:B4-B5 F '87

Cattle feedlots

Co-op expands choices for these farmer-feeders. D. Ohrtman. il *Success Farm* 85 no6:B10+ Mr '87

Joint feeding gives small feeders a lever. B. Eftink and R. Brunoehler. il *Success Farm* 85 no4:B6 F '87

Why big feedlots feel 'PIKed' on. B. Eftink. il *Success Farm* 85 no2:B4+ Ja '87

Location

Cattle feeding and packing too concentrated. *Success Farm* 85 no4:B24 F '87

Corn Belt states organizing to lure feedlot customers. *Success Farm* 85 no6:B20 Mr '87

Cattle futures *See* Commodity futures

Cattle industry

See also

Monfort of Colorado, Inc.

The '86 events that will affect you most in '87. *Success Farm* 85 no4:B16 F '87

Computer predicts $1/pound feeders in three years [beef industry predictions] *Success Farm* 85 no4:B12 F '87

For cattle, the svelte look is in [lower fat beef] S. D. Atchison. il *Bus Week* p154-5 N 30 '87

Good news for '87! Profits up, numbers down. *Success Farm* 85:40B Je '87

He's diversified in 6 cattle enterprises [Jeff Breker] R. Watkins. il *Success Farm* 85 no4:B14 F '87

Central America

Hamburgers are killing trees [boycott of fast-food outlets until they stop using Central American beef] il *Newsweek* 110:74 S 14 '87

One costly hamburger [importation of Central American beef contributes to tropical deforestation; views of Christopher Uhl] *Ctry J* 14:12-13 Ag '87

Cattle plague *See* Cattle—Diseases and pests

Cattle ranches *See* Ranches

Cattleya orchids *See* Orchids

Catto, Jeremy

Dissidents in an age of faith? Wyclif and the Lollards. bibl il *Hist Today* 37:46-52 N '87

Catton, William Robert, 1926-

The world's most polymorphic species. bibl f il *BioScience* 37:413-19 Je '87

CATV system *See* Cable television

Caucuses

See also

Congressional Black Caucus

Democratic Leadership Council

House Democratic Caucus (U.S.)

National Black Caucus of State Legislators

National Women's Political Caucus

Iowa

Campaign '88: why Iowa is bad for American politics. G. Borger. il *U S News World Rep* 103:22-4 Jl 6 '87

Charade on Main Street [presidential candidates] F. Barnes. *New Repub* 196:15-17 Je 15 '87

Faithful on the move [P. Robertson supporters] T. J. Curry. il *Commonweal* 114:727-9 D 18 '87

Far too much ado about little Iowa. M. Kaus. il *Newsweek* 110:20+ Jl 6 '87

Fighting for their right to the party [Democratic candidates] W. Greider. il *Roll Stone* p93-4+ N 19 '87

Harvest '87: making hay. D. Gates. il *Newsweek* 110:6 Ag 24 '87

Hog heaven: Jesse Jackson cultivates the farm vote in Iowa. J. Klein. il por *N Y* 20:42-5 S 7 '87

Jackson sets up shop. H. Sidey. il *Time* 130:20 S 7 '87

Jesse Jackson takes first step toward another run for president of United States. D. M. Cheers. il pors *Jet* 72:22-5 Ap 13 '87

Jesse Jackson urges big businesses to 'reinvest in America'. il pors *Jet* 72:4+ S 7 '87

Letter from Washington [presidential nomination] Cato. *Natl Rev* 39:18 Ja 30 '87

Making hay in Iowa. A. Plattner. il *U S News World Rep* 103:20 Ag 31 '87

Planning a secret-poll scam [tactics by R. Gephardt's organization] M. Duffy. il por *Time* 130:27 N 23 '87

A populist message hits home [J. L. Jackson and J. R. Biden; cover story] A. Kopkind. il *Nation* 245:37+ Jl 18-25 '87

Watering the Iowa economy [Iowa Caucus] il *Fortune* 116:8 Ag 3 '87

Caudill, Rowlett, Scott *See* CRS Sirrine, Inc.

Caudle, Pearl

about

Granny midwives: portrait of a timeless profession. E. I. M. Holland. il pors *Ms* 15:48-51+ Je '87

Caufield, Catherine

Fowl play. il *Omni* 9:22+ Je '87

Caulfield, Henry P., Jr.

Report on reports: Currents of change: final report, Inquiry on Federal Water Policy, Canada. *Environment* 28:25-7 D '86

Cauliflower

See also

Cooking—Vegetables

Cauliflower clinic [cover story] K. Martin. il *Rodale's Org Gard* 34:34-6+ O '87

Cauliflower mosaic virus *See* Viruses, Plant

Caulking

Bathroom caulk in a roll [3M Press-In-Place Tub & Sink Caulk] J. Wicks. il *Home Mech* 83:70 Ja '87

Confused about caulk? il *Sunset* 179:148+ N '87

Exterior caulks. il *Consum Rep* 52:393-5 Je '87

Exterior caulks. il *Consum Rep* 52:221-4 D '87

Push-method caulking. H. Wicks. il *Home Mech* 83:18 Mr '87

Recaulking your shower. il *Better Homes Gard* 65:111 Ap '87

Causation

Causality, structure, and common sense. M. M. Waldrop. il *Science* 237:1297-9 S 11 '87

Cause and effect *See* Causation

Causley, Jeremy J.

about

Can McDonnell Douglas make its computers fly? S. Toy. il por *Bus Week* p121-2 My 4 '87

Cavaco Silva, Anibal, 1939-

about

Now comes the orange crush. H. G. Chua-Eoan. il por *Time* 130:31 Ag 3 '87

Portugal turns right. il por *Fortune* 116:8 Ag 31 '87

Portugal's vote. C. D. Van De Stadt. *World Press Rev* 34:36 S '87

A small victory. E. von Kuehnelt-Leddihn. *Natl Rev* 39:46 N 6 '87

Cavalier, Alain

about

Thérèse [film] Reviews

America 156:137-8+ F 14 '87. J. W. Donohue

America 156:55-6 Ja 24 '87. R. A. Blake

Christ Century 104:260-1 Mr 18-25 '87. J. D. Lynch

Macleans il 100:54 Ap 6 '87. L. O'Toole

N Y 20:51-2 Ja 12 '87. D. Denby

New Yorker 62:73-4 Ja 26 '87. P. Kael

Newsweek il 109:61 Ja 19 '87. D. Ansen

Time il 129:75 Ja 5 '87. R. Corliss

Cavaliere, Denise

How zucchini won 5th-grade hearts [cover story] il *Child Today* 16:18-21 My/Je '87

Cavallaro, Michael

The pride that flies. il *Américas* 39:14-19 My/Je '87

Cavalli, Pier Francesco, 1602-1676

about

La Calisto [opera] Reviews

New Yorker 63:140-1 O 26 '87. A. Porter

Opera News il 52:38 Ag '87. S. Low

Giasone [opera] Reviews

New Yorker 63:63 Ag 24 '87. A. Porter

La virtù de' strali d'Amore [opera] Reviews

New Yorker 63:62-3 Ag 24 '87. A. Porter

Cavalry

See also

U.S. Horse Cavalry Association

Cavanagh, Gerald F., and Chmielewski, Philip J.
Ethics and the free market. il *America* 156:79-82 Ja 31 '87

Cavanaugh-O'Keefe, John
New questions—same old debate. *America* 156:334-5 Ap 25 '87

Cave, Hugh B.
The mission [story] il *Saturday Evening Post* 259:32+ Ap '87
The mission [story] il *Saturday Evening Post* 259:42-5+ Mr '87

Cave diving *See* Skin diving

Cave drawings and paintings
Cliff notes [rock-shelter paintings at Pedra Furada site and vicinity, Brazil] N. Guidon. il map *Nat Hist* 96:6+ Ag '87
Oasis of art in the Sahara [Tassili-n-Ajjer, Algeria] H. Lhote. il map *Natl Geogr* 172:180-91 Ag '87
Underground bestiary [Lascaux murals] J. E. Pfeiffer. il *Nat Hist* 96:84+ O '87

Cave fauna
What's in a cave? [fauna in marine caves] N. Sefton. il *Sea Front* 33:404-13 N/D '87

Cavenar, Jesse O.
about
Textbook credits bruise psychiatrists' egos. E. Marshall. por *Science* 235:835-6 F 20 '87
Textbook dispute [discussion of February 20, 1987 article, Textbook credits bruise psychiatrists' egos] E. Marshall. *Science* 236:655-7 My 8 '87

Cavendish, Grania
about
50 rooms with a view. R. Billington. il pors *Vogue* 177:314-21+ My '87

Cavendish, Hugh
about
50 rooms with a view. R. Billington. il pors *Vogue* 177:314-21+ My '87

Caves
See also
Marine caves
Underground frontiers. D. W. Bolton. il *Earth Sci* 40:16-18 Summ '87

Kentucky
Prehistoric adventurers explored Kentucky cave passages 3,000 years before modern cavers came along [excerpt from The longest cave] R. Brucker and R. A. Watson. *Earth Sci* 40:23 Fall '87

South Dakota
See also
Wind Cave National Park (S.D.)

Texas
The time of our lives: subterranean experiments on the rhythms imposed by the solar day [experiments in Midnight Cave] M. Siffre. il *Courier* 40:14-15 Je '87

Caviar
Caviar: little guide to the affordable kind. il *Good Housekeep* 204:169 Je '87
Caviar that doesn't cost a mint. T. Segal. il *Bus Week* p182 Jl 20 '87

Caviedes, Cesar, 1936-
"Running Christ against the bandits". il *Nat Hist* 96:44-53 My '87

Cavities, Dental *See* Dental caries

CAW *See* National Automobile, Aerospace and Agricultural Implement Workers Union of Canada

Cawley, Leo
The end of the rich man's boom. il *Nation* 245:675-6+ D 5 '87

Caws, Peter
The storehouse of the possible. *Wilderness* 51:64 Fall '87

Cayman Islands
Description and travel
The Caymans—from turtles to tourists. il *Saturday Evening Post* 259:68-70+ D '87
Of turtles and tax havens. W. G. Flanagan. il *Forbes* 140:432-3 Jl 13 '87

CBA *See* Christian Booksellers Association
CBC *See* Canadian Broadcasting Corporation
CBI *See* Caribbean Basin Initiative, 1983-
CBN *See* Christian Broadcasting Network, Inc.

CBS-Fox Video, Inc.
Bank shot [line of NBA basketball tapes] A. D. Frank. il *Forbes* 139:252+ Je 15 '87

CBS Inc.
Anchor away [D. Rather walks off CBS News] il *Time* 130:55 S 28 '87
The arts, Sunday morning, and Charles Kuralt. M. Rhodes. il por *Horizon* 30:6 Je '87

The bad news hits home [layoffs at CBS News] D. Fitzpatrick. por *Newsweek* 109:8 Mr 23 '87
A bear hug for CBS [L. Tisch] A. L. Taylor, III. il por *Fortune* 115:35 Ja 5 '87
CBS News with Dan Rather [distortions on Nicaragua] W. F. Buckley. *Natl Rev* 39:54-5 Je 5 '87
A close-up look at *glasnost* [special Seven days in May] J. Alter. il *Newsweek* 109:62 Je 29 '87
The cloud of seriousness [CBS evening news] T. Teachout. *Natl Rev* 39:62-4+ O 23 '87
Dan Rather draws a blank [anchor walks off telecast] H. F. Waters. il por *Newsweek* 110:47-8 S 28 '87
Dan Rather's struggle. J. Alter. il por *Newsweek* 110:51 Ag 24 '87
Did Dan Rather get this story wrong? [effect of budget cuts on news broadcasts] V. G. Sauter. il *U S News World Rep* 102:72 Mr 23 '87
An embarrassing failure [cancellation of The morning program] L. Zuckerman. il *Time* 130:91 O 12 '87
The golden parachutes open on media row [CBS deal with T. Wyman] por *Newsweek* 109:55 Ap 20 '87
Hard times at a "can-do" network [CBS News] R. Zoglin. il *Time* 129:75 Mr 23 '87
How CBS landed Grant Tinker. M. Brown. il por *Channels* 7:26 Ap '87
"If Howard had known . . . " [CBS News president H. Stringer; cover story] M. Gordon. il pors *Channels* 7:60-6 O '87
Judge blocks production of 'Amos 'n' Andy' musical [copyright owned by CBS] *Jet* 72:56 S 14 '87
The last tycoon [W. Paley] J. Cooney and G. Winslow. il pors *Channels* 7:34-5 F '87
Laurence Tisch. D. Lieberman. il por *Bus Week* Sp Issue:220 Ap 17 '87
Leahy's line: sell networks' strength. L. Brown and S. Behrens. il pors *Channels* 7:62-3 Ap '87
A legendary chairman [W. Paley] P. Baida. il *Am Herit* 38:16+ Jl/Ag '87
Lessons in job leveraging from the CBS shake-up [case of H. Stringer] J. Ciabattari. por *Work Woman* 12:67 F '87
News by the numbers [cutbacks made by H. Stringer] R. Corliss. por *Time* 129:64 Mr 16 '87
Nice cop, tough cop. E. Diamond. pors *N Y* 20:14+ F 9 '87
Nightly news update. il *Fortune* 116:16 Ag 3 '87
O.K., Larry and Bill, take your places. It's showtime [L. Tisch appointed president and CEO and W. S. Paley appointed chairman] D. Lieberman and M. N. Vamos. il por *Bus Week* p36-7 Ja 26 '87
The press on trial [R. Adler's book on Westmoreland v. CBS and Sharon v. Time] R. M. Dworkin. bibl f il *N Y Rev Books* 34:27-37 F 26 '87
Rather strange [D. Rather] E. Diamond. il por *N Y* 20:28+ S 28 '87
Rhetoric vs. real issues in the network news cutbacks. D. Lieberman. il *Bus Week* p33 Mr 30 '87
Sad news at Black Rock, good news from the field. J. Vitale. il *Channels* 7 Sp Issue:36-7 D '87
The Sawyer exception [D. Sawyer's new contract] por *Newsweek* 109:41 Ja 12 '87
Taking the heat for sagging ratings, CBS anchor Dan Rather is toughing it out in last place. J. Hall. por *People Wkly* 28:32-3 Ag 10 '87
Tampering with the nervous system [CBS News] L. Brown. il map *Channels* 7:24 My '87
Tinker's CBS deal. A. D. Frank. il por *Forbes* 140:184+ O 19 '87
A Tisch is still a Tisch. F. Dannen. il pors *Channels* 7:28-33 F '87
Tisch, Tisch, Tisch . . . [cutbacks at CBS News] E. Diamond. il por *N Y* 20:22+ Mr 30 '87
The trouble with CBS' stations. C. Capuzzi. il *Channels* 7:9 Je '87
Weighed as a future anchor, Diane Sawyer joins TV's million-dollar men's club. J. Hall. il por *People Wkly* 27:30-1 Ja 19 '87
Welcome to the Rustbelt [cutbacks by CBS News] *New Repub* 196:4+ Mr 30 '87
Westy's revenge [controversy over Gen. Westmoreland's libel suit against CBS leads to current network crisis; cover story] F. Barnes. *New Repub* 196:21+ Ap 6 '87

CBS Inc. Magazines Division
Buying out the boss at CBS Magazines [P. Diamandis' group] D. Lieberman. il por *Bus Week* p30 Jl 27 '87
Cutting the fat. R. Behar. il por *Forbes* 140:8 Ag 10 '87
Peter Diamandis is finally working for himself. P. Finch. il por *Bus Week* p48 Ag 3 '87

CBS Inc. Magazines Division—*cont.*
"We'll get back to you on that" [how Ziff-Davis magazines are faring at CBS and Murdoch group] R. Behar. il *Forbes* 139:42+ Ap 6 '87

CBS Inc. Records Division
The big money sound of music. C. P. Work. il *U S News World Rep* 103:44 O 26 '87
Born in the U.S.A., sold to Japan [Sony acquires CBS Records] S. Koepp. il *Time* 130:66 N 30 '87
CBS Records: if you can't beat 'em, sell [sold to Sony Corp.] il *Newsweek* 110:53 N 30 '87
A solid gold record deal [Sony acquires CBS Records] D. Lieberman and W. J. Holstein. il *Bus Week* p36 N 30 '87

CBS Inc. Technology Center
Interrupted melody [Copy Code system; cover story] D. Ranada. il *High Fidel* 37:44-7+ Jl '87

CCA *See* Club Corp. of America

C'Cat (Submarine) *See* Oceanographic submersibles

CCDs *See* Charge coupled devices (Electronics)

CCI/ICE (Firm)
Be true to your school. C. Meherani and R. Orr. il pors *Nations Bus* 75:46+ Je '87

CCM *See* Christian contemporary music

CCSSO *See* Council of Chief State School Officers

CCX Network Inc.
Cutting out the guesswork. M. Barrier. il *Nations Bus* 75:77-8 Jl '87

CD-ROM (Compact disc-Read only memory)
10,000 public-domain and user-supported programs on disk [PC-SIG library] il *Radio-Electron* 58 ComputerDigest:94-6 Mr '87
Dazzling data discs. G. B. Latamore. il *Pop Sci* 231:38+ D '87
Facts at your fingertips on CDs for PCs. S. Bentley. il *Black Enterp* 18:35 N '87
From Mozart to megabytes. P. Elmer-Dewitt. il *Time* 129:71 Mr 16 '87

Earth sciences use
Compact discs shrinking data storage costs. R. A. Kerr. il *Science* 237:604 Ag 7 '87

Encyclopedias
Grolier's Electronic Encyclopedia. il *Radio-Electron* 58 ComputerDigest:90-1 Ap '87
Would you believe Encyclopedia Electronica? R. R. Roha. il *Changing Times* 41:49+ Jl '87

Maps
Map storage on CD-ROM [digital street mapping] D. F. Cooke. *Byte* 12:129-30+ Jl '87

Reference books
A CD-ROM with a view [Microsoft Bookshelf] il *Pers Comput* 11:27 My '87

CD-V *See* Compact disc video

CD4 antigens *See* Antigens and antibodies

CDC *See* Centers for Disease Control (U.S.) Control Data Corp.

CDF *See* Children's Defense Fund (U.S.)

CDI (Compact disc interactive) *See* Compact disc interactive

CDs *See* Certificates of deposit

Ceaușescu, Nicolae
about
'Down with the dictator'. F. Willey. il *Newsweek* 110:27+ D 28 '87
Romania in the age of *glasnost*. W. Fisher. il *New Leader* 70:11-13 Je 29 '87

Cech, Thomas R.
The chemistry of self-splicing RNA and RNA enzymes. bibl f il *Science* 236:1532-9 Je 19 '87

Cecil, Bill
about
Selling—the computer way. J. Blackford. il por *Pers Comput* 11:167+ O '87

Cecil, Jennifer
(jt. auth) See Wolfe, Linda, and Cecil, Jennifer

Cecil, Jennifer, and Robbins, Michael W.
Weekend vacations. il *N Y* 20:58-64+ Ap 27 '87

Cecil family
about
The Oriental porcelains at Burghley House, Lincolnshire, England. G. Lang. il *Antiques* 131:236-47 Ja '87

Cecko, Ivan
about
Yugoslav youth stir it up. S. Drakulich. il *Nation* 244:601-3 My 9 '87

Cedar chests *See* Chests

Cedar closets *See* Closets

Cedar Falls (Iowa)
Stores
See also
Porter's Camera Store, Inc.

Cedar Mountain, Battle of, 1862
Red badge revivalists [reenactment] R. O'Sullivan. il *Hist Today* 37:6-8 D '87

Cedar shingles *See* Shingles and shingling

Cedar Street Tavern (New York, N.Y.) *See* New York (N.Y.)—Restaurants, nightclubs, bars, etc.

Ceiling fans *See* Fans, Electric

Ceilings
Cathedral ceilings: construction, ventilation & insulation. G. Branson and C. J. De Groote. il *Fam Handyman* 37:42-3+ F '87
Hang a hardwood ceiling. P. McCafferty. il *Pop Sci* 230:88-90 Mr '87
New ceilings: looking up. J. Hayes. il *Saturday Evening Post* 259:32 My/Je '87
The return of the tin ceiling. B. Vila. il *Pop Mech* 164:20-1+ D '87

Celadon (San Francisco, Calif.: Restaurant) *See* San Francisco (Calif.)—Restaurants, nightclubs, bars, etc.

Celebrating Gershwin [television program] See Television program reviews—Single works

Celebration [dance] See Dance reviews—Single works

Celebrities
See also
Black celebrities
Children of celebrities
Clothing and dress—Celebrities
Drugs and celebrities
Entertainers
Fans (Persons)
Walk of Fame (Hollywood, Calif.)
Walk of Fame (Philadelphia, Pa.)
8 star dishes [recipes from celebrities' restaurants] il *Redbook* 168:110-13+ Ap '87
10 'perfect 10' men. L. Hirschberg. il *Harpers Bazaar* 120:64+ My '87
10 sexy ex's. il *Harpers Bazaar* 121:148+ N '87
49 turning 50 [quiz] M. Opsata. il *50 Plus* 27:26-8 Ja '87
Altered egos [imaginary makeovers of celebrities] il *Seventeen* 46:116-21 Jl '87
America's 10 most beautiful women [cover story] il *Harpers Bazaar* 120:340-71+ S '87
America's 10 most beautiful women reveal their beauty secrets [special section] il *Harpers Bazaar* 120:30+ S '87
Are these stars sick of being stars? M. Musto. il *Mademoiselle* 93:90 Ap '87
Audio reviews: celebrity autobiographies. *Publ Wkly* 231:58-9 My 29 '87
The blond leading the blond. M. Musto. il *Mademoiselle* 93:44 Je '87
Celebrity autobiographies on audio. A. Postman. il *Publ Wkly* 231:56-7 My 29 '87
Celebs of the year. E. Sherman. il *Ladies Home J* 104:116+ D '87
A comic, a rapper, a rocker, an ex-QB and a candidate send Father's Day felicitations from the front [celebrity fathers] il *People Wkly* 27:36-8+ Je 22 '87
Could you wear this star's clothes? [celebrities' clothing lines] B. Zehme. il *Mademoiselle* 93:60 F '87
Dear Dad [letters from celebrities to their fathers; excerpts] L. N. Cox. *Ladies Home J* 104:53 Je '87
Diahann Carroll and Vanessa Williams take the bridal path, as Lee Iacocca and Leonard Nimoy trot off alone. M. Neill. il *People Wkly* 27:32-4 Ja 19 '87
Do short men make better lovers? J. V. Iovine. il *Mademoiselle* 93:92 N '87
The faces of '87. il *Seventeen* 46:84-5 Ja '87
Hairstyles of the rich & famous. il *Ladies Home J* 104:128-31+ Ap '87
Hollywood report card: grading the stars of '87. M. Musto. il *Mademoiselle* 93:58 D '87
Hollywood's top draws donate oodles of doodles for an artistic cause [auction of celebrity doodles for Los Angeles' Back Alley Theatre] il *People Wkly* 28:110-11 S 28 '87
Hot [cover story; special issue] il *Roll Stone* p29-31+ My 21 '87
Hot commodities: rich returns [celebrity comebacks] il *Harpers Bazaar* 120:128-31 Jl '87
How to catch a star [meeting and marrying a celebrity] C. Kramer. il *McCalls* 114:85-7 F '87
Inquirer. See issues of 'Teen beginning November 1983
Labors of love [celebrity couples] J. Etra. il *Harpers Bazaar* 120:186-7+ My '87
Lessons we learned from the women of '87. il *Glamour* 85:62 D '87
McCall's celebrity quiz. S. La Rosa and J. Siroto. il *McCalls* 114:19+ Ja '87

Celebrities—*cont.*

Newman and Woodward gather a 'Menagerie' of pals—like Mailer, Kennedy and Shriver—for a benefit. il *People Wkly* 28:110-11 N 9 '87

P-s-s-t. See issues of 50 Plus

People. C. Krupp. See issues of Glamour

People [media lists of who's in and who's out for 1987] G. D. Garcia. il *Time* 129:73 Ja 26 '87

Please fake me over! Beauty tricks of the stars. L. Rozen. il *Mademoiselle* 93:64 Ja '87

Post people. See issues of The Saturday Evening Post

The private lives of star moms [excerpt from Starring mothers] J. Barber. il pors *McCalls* 114:57+ My '87

Ring in the new, wring out the old. il *People Wkly* 27:26-31 Ja 5 '87

Scoop du jour [interview with N. Collins] L. Smith. il por *Vogue* 177:352-3+ Ap '87

Seventeen's greatest hits! [excerpts from interviews] il *Seventeen* 46:65-8 Jl '87

Sexy looks: celebrity secrets. il pors *Harpers Bazaar* 120:146-57 My '87

Star-studded love notes. il *Teen* 31:51 S '87

Star-track trivia. M. Ehrman. il *Teen* 31:40 Ag '87

Stars who made a difference [health-related achievements] il *Health* 19:34 D '87

Where have you gone, Woody Allen? [N.Y. celebrities have forsaken Elaine's and are now dining at Elio's, Primola, Orso, and Columbus] D. Blum. il *N Y* 20:48-53 O 12 '87

Winnie one of world's 'most important women' [W. Mandela cited by Ladies' home journal] il por *Jet* 73:38 O 26 '87

The women we love: a definitive selection [symposium] il *Esquire* 107:154-68 Je '87

The world's most controversial women [special section] il *Ladies Home J* 104:121-4+ Mr '87

The world's ten most important women. il *Ladies Home J* 104:133-5+ N '87

Agencies and agents
See Theatrical agencies and agents

Anecdotes, facetiae, satire, etc.

Here today, gone today. R. Baker. il *N Y Times Mag* p8 D 27 '87

How to be hot, part II. L. Hirschberg and L. Henricksson. il *Roll Stone* p69-70 My 21 '87

Personal glimpses. See issues of Reader's Digest

Why I never want to be a celebrity. J. Kaufman. il *Glamour* 85:68 Ap '87

Attitudes

A gaggle of New Year's guesses [forecasts] S. F. Golden and others. il *U S News World Rep* 103:116 D 28 '87-Ja 4 '88

The God letters [belief in God; excerpts] P. Rifkin. il *McCalls* 114:97-8 Ja '87

My best—and worst—date ever. L. F. McCarthy. il *Seventeen* 46:192+ Mr '87

Super Sundays of the rich and famous. il *Sport Mag* 78:51 F '87

Caricatures and cartoons

Poster artist Robbie Conal paints satiric dislikenesses of the great, the wrinkled and the powerful. il por *People Wkly* 28:138 N 23 '87

Civil rights

The clearing of Vanessa Redgrave [Boston Symphony case] M. Heins. il *Nation* 245:713-15 D 12 '87

Economic conditions

Cosby's $84 million makes him richest entertainer [Forbes' list] il por *Jet* 73:52-3 S 28 '87

The fault is not in our stars [cover story] A. D. Frank. il *Forbes* 140:120-3+ S 21 '87

Education

What's your major? K. M. Miller. il *Roll Stone* p104-6+ Mr 26 '87

Health and hygiene

All-star fitness [cover story] T. Osborne. bibl il *Curr Health 2* 14:3-8 S '87

Health styles of the rich and famous. D. Ragan. il *50 Plus* 27:92-4 Mr '87

Well-known walkers. D. Groves. il *Good Housekeep* 205:118 O '87

Words of assurance for a stricken First Lady [four celebrities tell their stories] il por *People Wkly* 28:48-50+ N 2 '87

Housing

6-page portfolio of celebrity homes. M. Fiore. il *Good Housekeep* 204:94-9 Ja '87

8-page portfolio of celebrity homes. M. Fiore. il *Good Housekeep* 205:108-15+ Ag '87

Pets

Celebrity pets. il *Teen* 31:61 O '87

Dogs' best friends. B. Astor. il *House Gard* 159:134-7 D '87

Photographs and photography

Bertmania! [celebrities posing with terrier on David Letterman show] il *People Wkly* 28:165-7 D 7 '87

Friends [K. Rogers' second book of photographs] *New Yorker* 63:43-4 N 9 '87

I do. I do. And they did. And did [celebrity weddings of 1986] il *Life* 10:72-4+ Ja '87

If your school's most (or least) likely succeeded, hang on to that mildewed yearbook—it's golden [collector W. A. Day] il *People Wkly* 27:110-11 Je 1 '87

Images 1967-1987 [reprints of original Rolling stone photographs] il *Roll Stone* p71-7+ N 5-D 10 '87

New faces of 1987. il *Roll Stone* p109-18 D 17-31 '87

Paparazzo. D. K. Mano. *Natl Rev* 39:60-1 Mr 13 '87

Reunited, the Iacoccas celebrated the ups at Churchill Downs [Kentucky Derby] il *People Wkly* 27:51-2 My 18 '87

Top Guns. il *Life* 10:30-5+ Ja '87

Uncommon images. D. Hopper. il pors *People Wkly* 27:124-7 Ap 13 '87

Political activities

The Hollywood primary [cover story] R. Brownstein. il *New Repub* 197:19+ N 23 '87

Psychology

If I were an animal, I'd be a . . . [excerpts] F. Cowles. il *Redbook* 168:78+ Mr '87

Religious life

Celebrity ads promote National Bible Week. *Jet* 73:32 N 16 '87

Sports

In Florida: sweet charity [George Plimpton Celebrity Challenge Cup Harness Race in Pompano Beach, Fla.] P. Jordan. il *Time* 129:9+ Ap 13 '87

My brilliant career [Celebrity race of New York's Liberty Cup] R. Marshall. il *Mot Boat Sail* 160:10 D '87

The new sports-lovers workouts. il *Harpers Bazaar* 120:132-7 Ja '87

Anecdotes, facetiae, satire, etc.

Me and my good friends [celebrities at the Los Angeles Lakers games] C. Kirkpatrick. il *Sports Illus* 66:24-5 Je 15 '87

Statues, portraits, etc.

Come Halloween, pumpkin carver Hugh McMahon has no trouble scaring up famous faces. V. R. Peterson. il por *People Wkly* 28:143-4 N 2 '87

Celebrities and computers *See* Computers and celebrities

Celebrities as air pilots

Who's who on the wing. G. D. Garcia. il *Time* 130:68-9 N 30 '87

Celebrities as photographers

People. G. D. Garcia. il *Time* 129:94-5 My 4 '87

Celebrity *See* Fame

Celebrity (Word processor program) *See* Word processors and processing—Programming

Celebrity product endorsements *See* Advertising—Testimonials

Celebrity roasts *See* Roasts, Celebrity

Celeriac

See also
Cooking—Vegetables

Celery

See also
Cooking—Vegetables

Celery root cooking *See* Cooking—Vegetables

Celeste, Richard F.

about

Again, sex and politics. C. O'Connor. il por *Newsweek* 109:33 Je 15 '87

Are the sex lives of all politicians now fair game? A. P. Sanoff. il por *U S News World Rep* 102:12 Je 15 '87

Celestial Arts Publishing Company

Writing for Celestial Arts. P. Reed and D. Hinds. *Writer* 100:26-7 Ja '87

Celestial mechanics *See* Mechanics, Celestial

Celgene Corporation

Cutting the golden years down to a few months [L. Fernandez] C. Power. il por *Bus Week* p114-15 Jl 20 '87

Celibacy

See also
Virginity

The church needs married priests [with readers' comments] M. O'Connell-Cahill. *U S Cathol* 52:14-19 D '87

Sweeney agonistes [case of T. Sweeney] *America* 156:413-14 My 23 '87

Celibacy—*cont.*

Sweeney responds [discussion of May 23, 1987 article, Sweeney agonistes] *America* 157:22 Jl 4-11 '87

Wanting a woman's hand to hold [priests] J. Seligmann. il *Newsweek* 109:60 F 23 '87

Céline, Louis-Ferdinand, 1894-1961

about

Writing off the deep end. A. Broyard. il *N Y Times Book Rev* 92:11 F 1 '87

Cell adhesion *See* Adhesion

Cell aggregation

See also

Blood cell aggregation

Cell communication *See* Cells—Communication

Cell death

Delayed transneuronal death of substantia nigra neurons prevented by γ-aminobutyric acid agonist. M. Saji and D. J. Reis. bibl f il *Science* 235:66-9 Ja 2 '87

Nerve growth factor treatment after brain injury prevents neuronal death. L. F. Kromer. bibl f il *Science* 235:214-16 Ja 9 '87

The science of cellular suicide. R. Weiss. *Sci News* 132:360 D 5 '87

Worm watching: the case of the suicidal sex cell [Caenorhabditis elegans and Panagrellus redivivus; research by P. Sternberg] G. Montgomery. il por *Discover* 8:44-6+ O '87

Cell degeneration *See* Cell death

Cell differentiation *See* Differentiation (Biology)

Cell division (Biology)

See also

Mitogens

A cell-cycle constraint on the regulation of gene expression by platelet-derived growth factor. B. J. Rollins and others. bibl f il *Science* 238:1269-71 N 27 '87

Growth switch [cell division gene of yeast; work of Melanie G. Lee and Paul Nurse] *Sci Am* 257:23 Jl '87

Nuclear reassembly excludes large macromolecules. J. A. Swanson and P. L. McNeil. bibl f il *Science* 238:548-50 O 23 '87

The structure of sister minichromosome DNA before anaphase in Saccharomyces cerevisiae. D. Koshland and L. H. Hartwell. bibl f il *Science* 238:1713-16 D 18 '87

Cell division (Botany)

Cell-autonomous determination of cell-type choice in Dictyostelium development by cell-cycle phase. R. H. Gomer and R. A. Firtel. bibl f il *Science* 237:758-62 Ag 14 '87

Cell fusion *See* Cell hybridization

Cell growth *See* Growth

Cell hybridization

The fragile X site in somatic cell hybrids: an approach for molecular cloning of fragile sites [cover story] S. T. Warren and others. bibl f il *Science* 237:420-3 Jl 24 '87

Identification by cell fusion of gene sequences that interact with positive trans-acting factors. T. Lufkin and C. Bancroft. bibl f il *Science* 237:283-6 Jl 17 '87

T-cell tumor elimination as a result of T-cell receptor-mediated activation. J. D. Ashwell and others. bibl f il *Science* 237:61-4 Jl 3 '87

Cell interaction *See* Cells—Communication

Cell junctions *See* Junctions (Physiology)

Cell lines *See* Cells—Culture

Cell lysis *See* Lysis

Cell membranes *See* Membranes (Biology)

Cell movement *See* Cells—Motility

Cell nuclei

Nuclear reassembly excludes large macromolecules. J. A. Swanson and P. L. McNeil. bibl f il *Science* 238:548-50 O 23 '87

Cell organelles

See also

Microtubules

Mitochondria

Ribosomes

Cell regulation *See* Cellular control mechanisms

Cell transformation *See* Gene transfer

Cellars *See* Basements

Cellars, Root *See* Root cellars

Cellars, Wine *See* Wine cellars

Cellists

See also

Haimovitz, Matt

Meneses, Antonio

Rostropovich, Mstislav, 1927-

Cello

Study and teaching

A classical education. M. Haimovitz. il por *N Y* 20:26 N 23 '87

Cello music

See also

Compact discs—Cello music

Cells

See also

Blood cells

Cancer cells

Chromatin

Chromosomes

Cytology

Differentiation (Biology)

Epithelium

Fibroblasts

Genes

Macrophages

Membranes (Biology)

Nerve cells

Phagocytes and phagocytosis

Pigments (Biology)

Plant cells and tissues

Communication

Expression of functional cell-cell channels from cloned rat liver gap junction complementary DNA. G. Dahl and others. bibl f il *Science* 236:1290-3 Je 5 '87

Restoration of LDL receptor activity in mutant cells by intercellular junctional communication. L. Hobbie and others. bibl f il *Science* 235:69-73 Ja 2 '87

Second wind for second-messenger research: how do G proteins and external signals influence intracellular activity? C. Vaughan. il *BioScience* 37:642-6 O '87

Selective disruption of gap junctional communication interferes with a patterning process in hydra. S. E. Fraser and others. bibl f il *Science* 237:49-55 Jl 3 '87

Tumor promoters halt cell-cell 'talk' [research by John Holland] J. Raloff. *Sci News* 131:230-1 Ap 11 '87

Varying influences on cell-cell interactions. D. M. Barnes. *Science* 237:1568-9 S 25 '87

Culture

Eosinophils cocultured with endothelial cells have increased survival and functional properties. M. E. Rothenberg and others. bibl f il *Science* 237:645-7 Ag 7 '87

Extended culture of mouse embryo cells without senescence: inhibition by serum. D. T. Loo and others. bibl f il *Science* 236:200-2 Ap 10 '87

OTA: property right, donor consent factors cloud "gifts" of human tissue. M. Crawford. *Science* 235:1564 Mr 27 '87

Selling a pound of flesh [biotech use of patients' cell lines] J. Schwartz. il *Newsweek* 109:55 Ap 20 '87

Who owns human tissues and cells? [report by the Office of Technology Assessment] L. Tangley. *BioScience* 37:376-8 Je '87

Fusion

See Cell hybridization

Growth

See Growth

Inclusions

A synaptic vesicle protein with a novel cytoplasmic domain and four transmembrane regions. T. C. Südhof and others. bibl f il *Science* 238:1142-4 N 20 '87

Motility

How animal cells move. M. S. Bretscher. bibl (p158) il *Sci Am* 257:72-6+ D '87

What myosin might do. F. Solomon. bibl f *Science* 236:1043-4 My 29 '87

Resistance and sensitivity

Ouabain resistance conferred by expression of the cDNA for a murine Na^+,K^+-ATPase α subunit. R. B. Kent and others. bibl f il *Science* 237:901-3 Ag 21 '87

Cellular automata

The game Life acquires some successors in three dimensions. A. K. Dewdney. il *Sci Am* 256:16-17+ F '87

Let there be life. F. Hapgood. il *Omni* 9:40-2+ Ap '87

Cellular Communications, Inc.

Beyond the beeper. M. Gill. il por *Esquire* 108:94 O '87

Cellular control mechanisms

See also

Calmodulin

Cells—Communication

The *fos* gene as "master switch". J. L. Marx. bibl il *Science* 237:854-6 Ag 21 '87

The molecular control of blood cell development. L. Sachs. bibl f il *Science* 238:1374-9 D 4 '87

Cellular differentiation *See* Differentiation (Biology)
Cellular radio
    See also
    Cellular Communications, Inc.
    McCaw Cellular Communications Inc.
    Metro Mobile CTS Inc.
Inside cellular telephone. J. Bernard. il *Radio-Electron* 58:53-5+ S '87
Space phone. *Sci Am* 256:30+ Je '87
        Finance
Hello anywhere: the cellular phone boom will change the way you live [cover story] J. J. Keller. il *Bus Week* p84-7+ S 21 '87
        Securities
Hot wires [views of M. Gabelli] T. Jaffe. *Forbes* 140 Sp Issue:402 O 26 '87
Wrong numbers? G. Morgenson. il *Forbes* 139:50-1 My 18 '87
        Security measures
Cellular security. J. W. Merline. *Consum Res Mag* 70:38 Ja '87
        Canada
    See also
    NovAtel Communications Ltd.
        Great Britain
Cellular phones in Britain are ringing off the hook. T. Peterson. il *Bus Week* p87 S 21 '87
Cellular radio, Military
Tadiran-General Dynamics team will compete as second-source for Army Sincgars radios. *Aviat Week Space Technol* 127:28 Jl 13 '87
Cellular radio crimes
Crime: dialing for dollars. T. E. Johnson. il *Newsweek* 110:42 S 14 '87
Cellular radio in automobiles
Car phone users: we've got your number [causing traffic accidents] D. C. Ross. il *Mot Trend* 39:158 Je '87
The 'celling' of America. P. Dworkin. il *U S News World Rep* 103:45-6 Ag 31 '87
A cellular phone: you can take it with you. il *Sunset* 179:122-3 O '87
High tech [VocaLink, voice-activated dialing for cellular phones] D. Sweeney. il *Car Driv* 32:38 Je '87
Phoning at 40,000 feet. G. Eichler. il *Esquire* 107:40 Ja '87
Cellular radio on ships, boats, etc.
1988 buyer's guide: radios & cellular phones [VHFs and SSBs] G. West. il *Mot Boat Sail* 160:58-60+ N '87
Marine cellular update. J. H. Rhodes. il *Mot Boat Sail* 159:76+ Mr '87
Cellular therapy
    See also
    Skin grafting
Cellulite
Cellulite: straight facts, honest answers, effective treatments. il *Glamour* 85:186-7 Ja '87
Cellulose
No-calorie substitute for flour. J. Raloff. *Sci News* 131:251 Ap 18 '87
CELSS (Controlled Ecological Life Support System) *See* Life support systems (Space environment)
Celtuce
Celtuce . . . where has it been all your life? R. M. Watson. il *Flower Gard* 31:80-1 F/Mr '87
Cement
New strong cement materials: chemically bonded ceramics. D. M. Roy. bibl f il *Science* 235:651-8 F 6 '87
Cement industry
    See also
    Giant Group Ltd.
    Lone Star Industries, Inc.
    Southdown, Inc.
Cemeteries
    See also
    Epitaphs
        Alabama
    See also
    Mobile (Ala.)—Cemeteries
Homecoming [visit to family graves in old cemetery] E. Trout. il *Ctry J* 14:26-7 Mr '87
        France
    See also
    Paris (France)—Cemeteries
        Great Britain
    See also
    Birmingham (England)—Cemeteries
    Highgate Cemetery (London, England)

        Louisiana
    See also
    New Orleans (La.)—Cemeteries
        New York (State)
Tracking New York's literary ghosts [writers' and publishers' burial places] J. Culbertson and T. Randall. il *Publ Wkly* 232:27-9 Jl 17 '87
        Virginia
    See also
    Richmond (Va.)—Cemeteries
La Cenerentola [opera] *See* Rossini, Gioacchino, 1792-1868
Censorship
    See also
    Art—Censorship
    Freedom of information
    Freedom of the press
    Government and the press
    Illustration—Censorship
    Motion pictures—Censorship
    Obscenity (Law)
    Radio broadcasting—Censorship
    Television broadcasting—Censorship
    Textbooks—Censorship
    Theater—Censorship
Book banning must be stopped. M. Cohen. por *Seventeen* 46:158 Ap '87
British official suggests ousting Viking board to stop 'Spycatcher' [effort to prevent U.S. publication of book by P. Wright] V. Menkes. *Publ Wkly* 232:311 Ag 7 '87
Censorship in children's books [symposium] il *Publ Wkly* 232:108-11 Jl 24 '87
A civics lesson at Hazelwood East [principal of Missouri high school censors student newspaper; Supreme Court case] S. Visser. il *Nation* 245:441-2 O 24 '87
Controlling ideas. H. G. Florence. *Society* 24:19-21 Jl/Ag '87
Freedom to choose. B. P. Lynch. *Society* 24:24-6 Jl/Ag '87
From Hazelwood to the High Court [principal of Missouri high school deletes articles from school newspaper] M. A. Uhlig. il *N Y Times Mag* p100-7 S 13 '87
Porn and the novelist: freedom to read [symposium] *Current* 290:27-31 F '87
The real Fahrenheit 451 [views of science fiction authors on censorship of their books] M. Long. il *Omni* 9:22 F '87
Sex, psychology and censorship: preserving the freedoms of the mind [public school curricula and libraries] P. Scales. il por *Humanist* 47:18-22+ S/O '87
Six statements/questions from the censors. K. Donelson. bibl f il *Phi Delta Kappan* 69:208-14 N '87
Students should have freedom of the press, too! D. Fuchs. por *Seventeen* 46:182 S '87
Support for the censorship fight [ABA convention meeting] J. F. Baker. il *Publ Wkly* 231:77 Je 19 '87
What's scaring Stephen King. S. King. il por *Omni* 9:16 F '87
Writers discuss their craft, and censorship, at PEN panel in Boston [children's literature] D. Hardy. *Publ Wkly* 232:43 D 25 '87
        China
China's cultural crackdown. E. A. Gargan. il *N Y Times Mag* p24-6+ Jl 12 '87
Thaw and freeze and thaw again: the cultural weather in China. S. Topping. *N Y Times Book Rev* 92:3+ D 27 '87
'Thought examination' in China. *World Press Rev* 34:59-60 Jl '87
        Hungary
The seduction of censorship [excerpt from The velvet prison] M. Haraszti. *New Repub* 197:32-4+ N 23 '87
        Nicaragua
Minority report. C. Hitchens. *Nation* 244:458 Ap 11 '87
Playing to the crowd [discussion of April 11, 1987 article, Minority report] C. Hitchens. *Nation* 244:564-5 My 2 '87
        Soviet Union
'Exodus' in samizdat: still popular and still subversive. E. McDowell. il *N Y Times Book Rev* 92:13 Ap 26 '87
Jamming flim-flam [jamming of Radio Free Europe/Radio Liberty] *Natl Rev* 39:16 Je 19 '87
Wanted: a nude *glasnost* [women's magazines in the Soviet Union] S. Drakulich. il *Nation* 244:846-8 Je 20 '87
Where *glasnost* has its limits [trying to get published in Novy mir]; tr. by John Glad and Marie Arana-Ward. V. Voinovich and S. Zalygin. por *N Y Times Mag* p30-1 Jl 19 '87

Censorship—*cont.*
United States
See Censorship
Census
See also
United States—Census
Expert group meets on 1990 World Population and Housing Census Programme. *UN Chron* 23:85 Ja '86
Cent' Anni (New York, N.Y.: Restaurant) *See* New York (N.Y.)—Restaurants, nightclubs, bars, etc.
Centaur (Launch vehicle) *See* Space vehicles—Propulsion systems
Centenarians
Florida man celebrates his 110th birthday [W. Smith] il por *Jet* 72:12 Je 22 '87
Living to 100 is within your reach. R. Rodale. il *Prevention* 39:24-7 My '87
One hundred candles [interview with T. F. Williams] E. Kiester. il *50 Plus* 27:28-30 Je '87
Centennial Exhibition (1876: Philadelphia, Pa.)
Collectibles
Women's Pavilion Centennial medallion [Philadelphia Centennial Exposition] M. Wollett and B. Wollett. il *Antiques Collect Hobbies* 91:26 Ja '87
Centeq Cos.
Six bites from one apple [R. Campo sells Houston condo investors on desyndication deal] W. P. Barrett. il por *Forbes* 140:88+ S 7 '87
Center for African, Near Eastern and Asian Cultures *See* Smithsonian Institution. Center for African, Near Eastern and Asian Cultures
Center for Contemporary Opera
The loneliness of love [performance of Tomorrow and tomorrow] il *Macleans* 100:51 Ap 13 '87
The real thing [performance of Christopher Sly] P. G. Davis. *N Y* 20:89-90 F 9 '87
Center for Democratic Renewal
National center helps victims of racist acts rampant across nation. *Jet* 71:18 F 23 '87
Center for Family Business
Passing on the dream [L. A. Danco] S. Nelton. il pors *Nations Bus* 75:56-8 D '87
Center for the Study of Democratic Institutions
See also
Robert Maynard Hutchins Center for the Study of Democratic Institutions
Centerpieces *See* Table decoration
Centers (Football players) *See* Football players
Centers for Disease Control (U.S.)
Agent Orange study hits brick wall [Vietnam veterans] W. Booth. il *Science* 237:1285-6 S 11 '87
AIDS: CDC report card . . . and lesbian transmission? *Sci News* 131:8 Ja 3 '87
Critical condition [conflicts in AIDS research lab] R. Blow. il por *Roll Stone* p67-8+ Mr 26 '87
A frustrating glimpse of the true AIDS epidemic. W. Booth. *Science* 238:747 N 6 '87
Centers for the performing arts
See also
92nd Street Y (New York, N.Y.)
Bayfront Center (Saint Petersburg, Fla.)
Brooklyn Academy of Music
Krannert Center for the Performing Arts
Orange County Performing Arts Center
Snug Harbor Cultural Center
St. Louis County Heritage and Arts Center (Duluth, Minn.)
Tampa Bay Performing Arts Center
University of Massachusetts at Amherst. Fine Arts Center
Wolf Trap Farm Park for the Performing Arts
Wortham Theater Center
Viewpoint. J. L. Poole. *Opera News* 52:7 O '87
France
See also
Centre National d'Art et de Culture Georges Pompidou
Centocor, Inc.
In treatment, Centocor is breaking new ground. C. S. Eklund. il por *Bus Week* p91 Je 1 '87
Central & South West Corp.
Mr. Malec versus the bureaucrats [SEC's involvement in Central & South West Corp's factoring operations] E. A. Finn, Jr. il por *Forbes* 140:44 D 28 '87
Central Africa
See also
Burundi
Central African Republic
Sudan
Uganda
Zaire

Central African Republic
See also
Trials—Central African Republic
Politics and government
Former emperor Bokassa is sentenced to death. *Jet* 72:9 Je 29 '87
Central America
See also
Americans—Central America
Belize
Civil rights—Central America
Costa Rica
Economic assistance, American—Central America
El Salvador
Geothermal resources—Central America
Guatemala
Honduras
Indians of Central America
Military assistance, American—Central America
Nicaragua
Panama
Public health—Central America
Rain forests—Central America
United Nations—Central America
Volcanoes—Central America
Bibliography
Book reviews. *Curr Hist* 86:429+ D '87
Economic conditions
Economic crisis: a way of life in Central America. L. Kravitz. il *Sch Update* 119:22-4 Mr 9 '87
A whiff of hope for ravaged Central America. S. Baker. il *Bus Week* p52-3 D 21 '87
Foreign relations
Canada
See Canada—Foreign relations—Central America
Nicaragua
See Nicaragua—Foreign relations—Central America
Soviet Union
See Soviet Union—Foreign relations—Central America
United States
See United States—Foreign relations—Central America
History
The war-torn roots of today's turmoil. J. Rose. il *Sch Update* 119:19-21 Mr 9 '87
Industries
See also
Cattle industry—Central America
Politics and government
See also
National Bipartisan Commission on Central America (U.S.)
And what of the contras now? [Central American peace plans] *America* 157:75-6 Ag 15-22 '87
Another useful tool [discussion of April 18, 1987 article, Democrats and the Arias plan] L. Annunziata. *Nation* 244:565 My 2 '87
Apocalypse soon [effect of Central American peace plan on contra aid] J. Smolowe. il *Time* 130:34-6 S 21 '87
The Arias plan. J. B. Hehir. il *Commonweal* 114:521-2 S 25 '87
Assembly urges support for Contadora efforts towards negotiated settlement in Central America. map *UN Chron* 24:59-61 F '87
The battle of the isthmus [Reagan administration opposition to Central American peace plan] il *Progressive* 51:8-9 O '87
Blessed are the peacemakers [O. Arias wins Nobel Peace Prize for Central American plan] *America* 157:283-4 O 31 '87
Captain Ahab vs. Moby Dick [Reagan roadblocks to Central American peace plan] G. J. Church. il *Time* 130:28 O 19 '87
Central America: why peace talks aren't just talk. B. Javetski. il *Bus Week* p41 Ag 24 '87
Central America: will it be peace now? C. A. Robbins. il *U S News World Rep* 103:39-40 O 5 '87
The Central American crisis and the Contadora process. P. M. Alvergue. *USA Today (Periodical)* 115:29-30 Ja '87
The Central American peace plan [text of agreement] *Curr Hist* 86:430+ D '87
A Central American Yalta? [peace agreement] M. Kramer. il *U S News World Rep* 103:13 Ag 24 '87
Changing Central America [cover story; special issue] bibl f map (inside back cover) *Curr Hist* 86:401-38+ D '87

Central America—Politics and government—*cont.*

The choice in Central America [peace plans] S. K. Purcell. bibl f map *Foreign Aff* 66:109-28 Fall '87

Costa Rican initiative [Arias plan; statement, March 6, 1987] E. Abrams. *Dep State Bull* 87:90-1 My '87

Cursed are the peacemakers [plans for Nicaragua] M. S. Serrill. il *Time* 130:30-1 Ag 24 '87

Deadline [peace plan] *Time* 130:68 N 2 '87

Democrats and the Arias plan [cover story] L. Annunziata. il *Nation* 244:489+ Ap 18 '87

An elusive cease-fire [peace plan] C. A. Robbins. il *U S News World Rep* 103:49-50 N 16 '87

The end of the affair? [peace plans and contra aid] J. Chace. bibl f il *N Y Rev Books* 34:24-6+ O 8 '87

Eyeing a dialogue [D. Ortega Saavedra agrees to peace talks with contras; with interview] J. Smolowe. il por *Time* 130:34-6 N 16 '87

The glimmer [Central American peace initiative] J. Klein. il *N Y* 20:16+ S 14 '87

Golden opportunity for Don Oscar [O. Arias Sanchez awarded Nobel Peace Prize] J. Smolowe. il por *Time* 130:44+ O 26 '87

Guatemalan agreement for peace in Central America. *Dep State Bull* 87:56-9 O '87

The hole in the summit agenda. M. Kramer. il *U S News World Rep* 103:40 D 21 '87

In search of change. R. Rivard. il *Newsweek* 109:40+ Ap 27 '87

The Jim Wright shuffle [Central American peace plan] J. Morley. *Nation* 245:185+ S 5 '87

A lean chain of hope [Central American peace proposal signed in Guatemala City on August 7] *Commonweal* 114:469 S 11 '87

Leaning on Arias. M. Honey and T. Avirgan. *Nation* 245:220-1 S 12 '87

Letter from Washington [effect of Central American peace initiative on contra aid] Cato. *Natl Rev* 39:15 S 11 '87

More action on Central America: follow-up to January mission. *UN Chron* 24:10 My '87

New steps to Central American peace. M. Nichols. il *Macleans* 100:18-19 Ag 17 '87

The Nobel difference [O. Arias wins Peace Prize for his Central American plan] H. Anderson. il por *Newsweek* 110:44+ O 26 '87

Nobel winner Oscar Arias makes Costa Rica the mouse that roars for peace in Central America. M. Brower. il pors *People Wkly* 28:57-8+ N 9 '87

Not just one peace plan for Nicaragua, but two: Reagan and Central Americans unveil proposals. E. Magnuson. il *Time* 130:14-15 Ag 17 '87

Odd man out [role of Honduras] J. Eldridge. *America* 157:348-9 N 14 '87

On the battle fronts [Central America and the Persian Gulf] D. Schorr. *New Leader* 70:6 O 19 '87

Oscar's Nobel [Arias peace plan] M. Kondracke. *New Repub* 197:14-16 N 9 '87

Peace, democracy, and security in Central America [statement, September 10, 1987] G. P. Shultz. *Dep State Bull* 87:13-16 N '87

Peace plan problems [Arias plan] L. S. Robinson. *Commonweal* 114:580-2 O 23 '87

Peace process at a stalemate. B. Levin. *World Press Rev* 34:23-4 Ap '87

Peace scare. *New Repub* 197:4+ S 28 '87

Peaced off [Reagan-Wright plan upstaged by Central American peace proposal] F. Barnes. *New Repub* 197:10-11 Ag 31 '87

The phony peace [Reagan peace plan for Central America] *Nation* 245:147-8 Ag 29 '87

A plea to 'give peace a chance' [aid to contras undercut by peace plan] M. McDonald. il *Macleans* 100:32 O 5 '87

Potholes on the road to peace [U.S. delays Central American summit meeting; with interview with O. Arias Sánchez] J. Smolowe. il por *Time* 129:34+ Je 29 '87

The price of peace [Central American peace plan] M. Kempton. *N Y Rev Books* 34:46 S 24 '87

'Pricing the contras' [Central American peace initiative's effect on contra aid] H. Anderson. il *Newsweek* 110:24-5 Ag 24 '87

Puzzling out a peace plan. H. Rainie. il *U S News World Rep* 103:19 S 7 '87

Reagan isn't calling the shots in Central America anymore. B. Javetski and others. il *Bus Week* p65 O 12 '87

Reagan peace plan: a win if it fails? J. Wallace. il *U S News World Rep* 103:24-5 Ag 17 '87

Revolution in Central America? C. Krauss. *Foreign Aff* 65 Sp Issue:564-81 ['87]

Rival plans, rival goals [Central American peace plans] B. Crozier. *Natl Rev* 39:30 S 25 '87

The rule of reason [Central American peace plan] *Commonweal* 114:549 O 9 '87

Sabotage and failure [Contadora process] B. Levin. il *Macleans* 100:25 F 23 '87

Secretary-General reaffirms support for Contadora efforts after four-day peace mission to region. il pors *UN Chron* 24:7-10 My '87

Should the Sandinistas be trusted? [peace plans] H. Anderson. il *Newsweek* 110:28+ Ag 31 '87

Slipping and sliding around peace [plans for Nicaragua] J. Smolowe. il *Time* 130:28+ S 7 '87

Speaking his peace [O. Arias Sanchez addresses Congress] J. Smolowe. il por *Time* 130:34-5 O 5 '87

Still gunning for peace. J. Smolowe. il *Time* 130:72 N 9 '87

Torpedoing the peace process? [Reagan's support for the contras] H. Anderson. il *Newsweek* 110:49 O 19 '87

A twisting road to peace. C. Wood. il *Macleans* 100:19 Ag 31 '87

U.S. initiative for peace in Central America. *Dep State Bull* 87:54-6 O '87

The U.S. view from Guatemala City [interview with A. M. Piedra] J. A. Briggs and J. W. Michaels. il por *Forbes* 139:174+ My 18 '87

Vacation at Club Dead. S. L. Wisenberg. il *Progressive* 51:34 Jl '87

War of words [Reagan's commitment to the contras blocks peace plan] P. R. Range. il *U S News World Rep* 103:10 O 19 '87

What's at stake in Central America: U.S. influence under fire [special issue] il map *Sch Update* 119:4-25 Mr 9 '87

A whiff of hope for ravaged Central America. S. Baker. il *Bus Week* p52-3 D 21 '87

Who wants peace? [Arias plan; cover story] M. Kondracke. *New Repub* 197:16-19 S 28 '87

Whose peace plan is it anyway? J. Smolowe. por *Time* 130:34 S 28 '87

Will Ortega play for peace—or play for time? [Central American peace agreement] J. L. Galloway. il por *U S News World Rep* 103:30-1 Ag 24 '87

Will peace break out? [initiatives by R. Reagan and Central American governments] H. Anderson. il *Newsweek* 110:16-18 Ag 17 '87

Will the Arias peace plan work? *World Press Rev* 34:22-3 O '87

Central America (Steamship)

Dredging for dollars [sonar used to find sunken sidewheel steamer] W. J. Cook. il *U S News World Rep* 103:48 Ag 3 '87

Central American refugees *See* Refugees, Central American

Central American University *See* Universidad Centroamericana

Central Arizona Project

The House abandons a desert dam [compromise on Cliff Dam on Verde River and Central Arizona Project] D. Dagget. il *Sierra* 72:84+ N/D '87

The thirsty state drinks. B. Weber. il *N Y Times Mag* p162 D 6 '87

Central Asia

See also

Afghanistan

Tibet

Description and travel

Thoughts from the roof of the world [excerpt from Silk Road] J. Myrdal. il *Courier* 40:37-8 Ap '87

Central asset accounts *See* Cash management accounts

Central Capital Corporation

High dives into a deep money pool. P. C. Newman. il por *Macleans* 100:28 F 9 '87

A victory against formidable odds. C. Wood. il *Macleans* 100:44-5 My 4 '87

Central Europe

See also

Churches (Buildings)—Central Europe

Forests and forestry—Central Europe

Nuclear energy—Central Europe

Politics and government

Borders of the mind. J. Rupnik. *New Repub* 196:17-19 Mr 9 '87

The rebirth of an idea. A. Nagorski. il *Newsweek* 109:38+ Mr 30 '87

Central Intelligence Agency (U.S.) *See* United States. Central Intelligence Agency

Central Maine Power Co.

Humble pie [nuclear problems] J. Cook. il por *Forbes* 139:50-1 Ap 20 '87

Central Maine Power Co.—*cont.*
Still in the woods. A. A. Lappen. il *Forbes* 140:8 O 5 '87

Central Michigan Hospital *See* Mount Pleasant (Mich.)—Hospitals

Central National Bank of New York
Closely watched banks: one that got away. F. A. Miller and R. A. Kessler. il por *Bus Week* p108 O 19 '87

Central nervous system *See* Nervous system

Central Park (New York, N.Y.)
The bridle path. M. Korda. il *N Y* 20:100-1 D 21-28 '87
Gondola. *New Yorker* 63:24-5 Je 1 '87
Pterodactyl eats two in park [bird watching] J. Adler. il *Newsweek* 109:86 My 18 '87

Central Park Zoo
Central Park Zoo. S. Cheever. il *N Y* 20:69 D 21-28 '87
On the wild side [renovations] B. Weber. il *N Y Times Mag* p102 N 29 '87
Zoo update. *New Yorker* 63:28-9 Ap 20 '87

Central serous chorioretinopathy *See* Eye—Diseases and defects

Central State University (Ohio)
Central State University lands Nigerian business exec. at commencement [A. Ojora] il por *Jet* 72:25 Jl 27 '87
Central State University returns sports to NAIA. *Jet* 72:48 Jl 27 '87
CSU celebrates 100th year, pays tribute to Dr. Charles H. Wesley. *Jet* 72:10 Ap 27 '87
CSU honors Stevie Wonder for role in national King holiday. il por *Jet* 71:12-13 F 9 '87
CSU kicks off season dedicated to Paul Robeson. por *Jet* 72:53 S 14 '87
CSU's Thomas visits Senegal and forms socio-economic tie. il por *Jet* 71:21 Mr 2 '87

Central Valley (Calif.)
Discovering the 'other California'. G. Hackett. il map *Newsweek* 110:68+ N 16 '87

Centre Hospitalier Universitaire au Sart Tilman (Liège, Belgium)
An unexpected surprise [C. Vandenhove's design] G. Bekaert. il *Archit Rec* 175:126-35 Jl '87

Centre National d'Art Contemporain (Grenoble, France)
Magasin: new life for an old building. T. Bell. il *Art Am* 75:53-5 S '87

Centre National d'Art et de Culture Georges Pompidou
Trading passion for boredom at the Pompidou. A. Hunt. il *Art News* 86:199 O '87

Centre National d'Études Spatiales (France)
CNES discusses Hermes-Mir compatibility with Soviets. *Aviat Week Space Technol* 126:25 My 11 '87

Centrifugal casting
The mirror maker [R. Angel] M. M. Waldrop. il pors *Discover* 8:78-84+ D '87
Spinning scopes [spin-cast telescope mirrors; work of R. Angel] A. Fisher. il pors *Pop Sci* 231:76-9+ O '87

Centrifuges
Centrifuges. *Science* 235 pt2:G37 F 27 '87

Centro Agronómico Tropical de Investigación y Enseñanza
Fighting Central America's other war. L. Tangley. il *BioScience* 37:772-7 D '87

Century 21 Real Estate Corp.
Selling the home advantage [R. and E. Trass] S. Herbert. il pors *Black Enterp* 18:90-2 O '87

Century Corporation
See also
Centeq Cos.

CEPAD *See* Evangelical Committee for Aid and Development in Nicaragua

Cephalopods
See also
Octopuses
Squid

Cepheids (Stars) *See* Stars, Variable

Cera, Russell M.
Of vanishing birds and dogs—and neckties. il *Conservationist* 42:22-5 N/D '87

Cerami, Anthony C., and others
Glucose and aging. bibl (p128) il *Sci Am* 256:90-6 My '87

Ceramic automobile engines *See* Automobile engines—Materials

Ceramic diesel engines *See* Diesel engines, Automotive—Materials

Ceramic figurines *See* Figurines

Ceramic National Exhibition *See* Pottery, American—Exhibitions

Ceramic oxides
The 1987 Nobel Prize for Physics [awarded to J. G. Bednorz and K. A. Muller] M. M. Waldrop. il pors *Science* 238:481-2 O 23 '87
Antiferromagnetism observed in La_2CuO_4 [research by David Johnston and others] A. L. Robinson. *Science* 236:780 My 15 '87
Bednorz and Müller win Nobel Prize for new superconducting materials. A. Khurana. il pors *Phys Today* 40:17-19 D '87
The chemistry of superconductivity. J. Raloff. il *Sci News* 131:247 Ag 18 '87
Current news about superconductors. D. E. Thomsen. *Sci News* 131:308 My 16 '87
The discovery of a class of high-temperature superconductors. K. A. Müller and J. G. Bednorz. bibl f il *Science* 237:1133-9 S 4 '87
Dreams into reality [superconducting material] *Time* 129:61 My 25 '87
An electrifying discovery. J. Gleick. *Read Dig* 131:131 Jl '87
Electrifying progress. il *U S News World Rep* 102:15 Mr 2 '87
Even lanthanum copper oxide is superconducting. A. Khurana. bibl f il *Phys Today* 40:17-22 S '87
Fast-food physics. il *Life* 10:38-9+ S '87
Getting warmer. T. Beardsley. il *Sci Am* 257:32+ O '87
Getting warmer . . . [superconducting material] M. Rogers. il *Newsweek* 110:42-3 Jl 6 '87
High-powered discussions on high-temperature superconductivity. K. Hartley. *Sci News* 132:359 D 5 '87
High-school students make $YBa_2Cu_3O_{7-x}$ [Gilroy, Calif. class produces superconducting material] W. Sweet. il *Phys Today* 40:111-12 O '87
High T_c may not need phonons; supercurrents increase. A. Khurana. bibl f il *Phys Today* 40:17-21 Jl '87
High-temperature superconductivity: what's here, what's near and what's unclear [cover story] K. Hartley. *Sci News* 132:106-7+ Ag 15 '87
High-temperature superconductor hints. A. L. Robinson. *Science* 236:1431 Je 12 '87
Hot questions in superconductivity [research by Paul C. W. Chu and others] S. Weisburd. *Sci News* 131:164-5 Mr 14 '87
How to make your own superconductors. B. Schechter. il *Omni* 10:72-4+ N '87
IBM superconductor leaps current hurdle. A. L. Robinson. *Science* 236:1189 Je 5 '87
In the trenches of science [new superconducting material; work of Ching-Wu (Paul) Chu] J. Gleick. il *N Y Times Mag* p28-31+ Ag 16 '87
The microstructure of high-critical current superconducting films. P. Chaudhari and others. bibl f il *Science* 238:342-4 O 16 '87
More superconductivity questions than answers [special section] A. L. Robinson. il *Science* 237:248-50 Jl 17 '87
Neutrons clarify superconductors. A. L. Robinson. il *Science* 237:1115-17 S 4 '87
A new electrical revolution [superconducting material] W. D. Marbach. il *Newsweek* 109:74 My 25 '87
New evidence at Wayne State for superconductivity at 240 K. A. L. Robinson. *Science* 236:28 Ap 3 '87
New heights in superconductivity. I. Peterson. *Sci News* 131:23 Ja 10 '87
A new route to oxide superconductors. A. L. Robinson. *Science* 236:1526 Je 19 '87
The new superconductivity. il *Sci Am* 256:32-3 Je '87
Nobel prizes: physics [use in superconductivity] J. Horgan. *Sci Am* 257:46 D '87
'Our life has changed'. il *Bus Week* p94-100 Ap 6 '87
Oxygen isotope effect in high-temperature oxide superconductors. H.-C. Zur Loye and others. bibl f il *Science* 238:1558-60 D 11 '87
An oxygen key to the new superconductors [special section] A. L. Robinson. il *Science* 236:1063-5 My 29 '87
Putting superconductors to work—superfast. E. T. Smith. il *Bus Week* p124-6 My 18 '87
Record high-temperature superconductors claimed. A. L. Robinson. il *Science* 235:531-3 Ja 30 '87
Research on high-T_c superconductivity in Japan. S. Tanaka. bibl il *Phys Today* 40:53-7 D '87
The resonating valence bond state in La_2CuO_4 and superconductivity. P. W. Anderson. bibl f il *Science* 235:1196-8 Mr 6 '87
Seeking the perfect wire [use as superconducting material] W. J. Cook. il *U S News World Rep* 102:66-71 My 11 '87

Ceramic oxides—*cont.*

Signs of a new high in ceramic superconductivity [work of Ahmet Erbil] I. Peterson. *Sci News* 132:356 D 5 '87

Superconduction possible at room temperatures? il *Radio-Electron* 58:5 Jl '87

Superconductive barriers surpassed. S. Weisburd. *Sci News* 131:116-17 F 21 '87

Superconductivity: a hard frost. D. E. Thomsen. *Sci News* 131:215 Ap 4 '87

Superconductivity: a physics rush. D. E. Thomsen. il *Sci News* 131:196-7 Mr 28 '87

Superconductivity and quantum mechanics [views of E. Teller] D. E. Thomsen. *Sci News* 131:358 Je 6 '87

Superconductivity at 40 K in the oxygen-defect perovskites $La_{2-x}Sr_xCuO_{4-y}$. J. M. Tarascon and others. bibl f il *Science* 235:1373-6 Mr 13 '87

Superconductivity at 52.5 K in the lanthanum-barium-copper-oxide system. C.-W. Chu and others. bibl f il *Science* 235:567-9 Ja 30 '87

Superconductivity glimpsed near 300 K. D. E. Thomsen. *Sci News* 132:4 Jl 4 '87

A superconductivity happening. A. L. Robinson. il *Science* 235:1571 Mr 27 '87

Superconductivity heats up. M. D. Lemonick. il *Time* 129:62 Mr 2 '87

Superconductivity: hype vs. reality. G. Maranto. il *Discover* 8:22-4+ Ag '87

Superconductivity in alkaline earth-substituted La_2CuO_{4-y}. J. G. Bednorz and others. bibl f il *Science* 236:73-5 Ap 3 '87

Superconductivity seen above the boiling point of nitrogen. A. Khurana. bibl f il *Phys Today* 40:17-23 Ap '87

Superconductor claim raised to 94 K. A. L. Robinson. *Science* 235:1137-8 Mr 6 '87

Superconductor frenzy. A. Fisher. il *Pop Sci* 231:54-8+ Jl '87

Superconductor race heats up. A. L. Robinson. *Science* 236:664 My 8 '87

Superconductors! M. D. Lemonick. il *Read Dig* 131:13-14+ N '87

Superconductors! M. D. Lemonick. il *Time* 129:64-70+ My 11 '87

Superconductors: a dimpled beauty [neutron diffraction] D. E. Thomsen. *Sci News* 131:327 My 23 '87

Superconductor's critical current at a new high. M. M. Waldrop. il *Science* 238:1655-6 D 18 '87

Superconductors: early visions. T. H. Cole. il *Pop Mech* 164:16 Ag '87

Superconductors: facing reality. T. H. Cole. il *Pop Mech* 164:32 N '87

Superconductors gain. A. Fisher. il *Pop Sci* 231:10 Ag '87

Superconductors heat up. *Sci Am* 256:64-5 Mr '87

Superconductors heat up. M. Gray. il *Macleans* 100:44 Ap 6 '87

Superconductors' promise. *World Press Rev* 34:54 S '87

Yb or not Yb? That is the question [mistake in element listing in publishing of Paul Chu's superconducting formula] G. Kolata. il *Science* 236:663-4 My 8 '87

Ceramic sculpture

Deco doyen [R. Buthaud] A. Duncan. il por *House Gard* 159:36B+ Ja '87

Howard Kottler: conceptualist and purveyor of psychosexual allusions. P. Failing. il por *Am Craft* 47:22-9 D '87/Ja '88

Exhibitions

The gifted hands of a prairie populist [work of Canadian J. Fafard] G. James. il *Macleans* 100:69-70 N 16 '87

James L. Tanner/Maurine Littleton Gallery. J. W. Larson. il *Am Craft* 47:74-5 D '87/Ja '88

Poetry in porcelain [animal sculptures of E. M. Boehm at Bellingrath Gardens] il por *South Living* 22:26 Ja '87

Ceramic tile industry *See* Tile industry
Ceramic tile laying *See* Tile laying
Ceramic tiles *See* Tiles
Ceramics

See also
Pottery

Ceramics by the solution-sol-gel route. R. Roy. bibl f il *Science* 238:1664-9 D 18 '87

Dawn of the new Stone Age [space age ceramics] L. Ponte. il *Read Dig* 131:128-33 Jl '87

Laser shaping of ultrahard materials [work of Stephen Copley and Michael Bass] *USA Today (Periodical)* 115:14-15 Je '87

New life for a cell: the ceramic solution [fuel cells] T. Dworetzky. il *Discover* 8:16 Jl '87

New strong cement materials: chemically bonded ceramics. D. M. Roy. bibl f il *Science* 235:651-8 F 6 '87

Japan

See also
Kyocera Corporation

Déjà vu—yet again [ceramic auto engines] J. Zweig. il *Forbes* 140:282+ N 16 '87

Cereal foods

See also
Cooking—Grain

The American breakfast. B. Rupp. il *Ctry J* 14:50-5 F '87

Ready-to-eat cereals. *Consum Rep* 52:381-6 D '87

Serious breakfast. P. Dranov. il *Health* 19:57-8+ Mr '87

Advertising

The great cereal wars. R. J. Samuelson. il *Newsweek* 110:49 S 7 '87

Selling high-fiber cereals. il *FDA Consum* 21:6 S '87

Packaging

Solution for soggy cereal [resealable linings] il *Time* 130:70 Jl 27 '87

Cereals *See* Grain
Cerebellum *See* Brain
Cerebral blood flow *See* Blood flow
Cerebral dominance *See* Laterality
Cerebral lesions *See* Brain damage
Cerebral palsy

"I'm proud of my brother" [T. Ritter]; ed. by Jerry Buck. J. Ritter. il pors *Redbook* 170:76+ N '87

"We have a problem". J. Marks. il *Parents* 62:58+ D '87

Cerebrovascular disease

For two New Jersey grannies misfortune sets the stage for a musical collaboration [stroke victims M. Patrick and R. Eisenberg] il pors *People Wkly* 28:121 D 14 '87

"I think your mommy's had a stroke" [excerpt from Pat Nixon: the untold story] J. N. Eisenhower. il por *Saturday Evening Post* 259:60-1+ Ap '87

Plaque hemorrhage linked to stroke [use of computer tomography to scan carotid arteries; research by Antonio Culebras and others] S. Weisburd. il *Sci News* 131:167 Mr 14 '87

Diagnosis

An early sign of stroke [transient ischemic attack] I. Pave. il *Bus Week* p91 Ag 24 '87

Mortality

Better control of hypertension has reduced stroke deaths [report by Centers for Disease Control] *FDA Consum* 21:2 Jl/Ag '87

Medical breakthroughs: cutting the toll of killer diseases [stroke] T. J. Gordon. il por *Futurist* 21:15-17 Ja/F '87

Mortality from CVD in elderly on the decline. *World Health* p30-1 Jl '87

Nutritional aspects

Block a stroke with better nutrition. M. Mihalik. il *Prevention* 39:24-8 Ag '87

Prevention

Cut your blood pressure and halve the risk [stroke] J. Carey and J. Silberner. il *U S News World Rep* 103:61 Ag 17 '87

How to avoid a stroke. S. L. Englebardt. *Read Dig* 130:93-5 Ja '87

Therapy

Drug may protect brains of heart attack victims [use of MK-801 to limit neuronal injury after ischemia] D. M. Barnes. il *Science* 235:632-3 F 6 '87

Race, sex key factors in treating strokes. *Jet* 71:53 Mr 2 '87

A stroke victim's road to recovery [J. Nekoloff] B. Perris. il por *Sch Update* 119:5 Ap 20 '87

Ceremonies *See* Rites and ceremonies
Ceres (Asteroid) *See* Asteroids
Cerezo Arévalo, Vinicio

Visit of Guatemalan president [remarks, May 13, 1987] il por *Dep State Bull* 87:87 Ag '87

about

Giving democracy a chance. J. Moody. il por *Time* 129:45 Ap 20 '87

Visit to the United States, 1987

Visit of Guatemalan president [remarks, May 13, 1987] R. Reagan; V. Cerezo Arévalo. il por *Dep State Bull* 87:87 Ag '87

Cerha, Birgit

Breaking the Persian Gulf stalemate. il *World Press Rev* 34:21-3 Mr '87

Cerkovnik, Tomaz
Real life on the pro tour. il por *Skiing* 40:152+ D '87

CERN *See* European Organization for Nuclear Research

CERN accelerators *See* Accelerators (Electrons, etc.)

Cerón family
about
What it was like to fear 'a knock on the door' [family of Mexicans living illegally in Los Angeles] W. L. Chaze. il *U S News World Rep* 102:24-6 Ja 19 '87

Cerovsek, Corey
about
Two extraordinary, ordinary children. N. Eberle. il pors *McCalls* 114:49-52 Ag '87

Cerovsek, Katja
about
Two extraordinary, ordinary children. N. Eberle. il pors *McCalls* 114:49-52 Ag '87

Cerre, Gina
about
A labor of wanderlust. L. S. Brady. il pors *Esquire* 107:48 Ja '87

Cerre, Mike
about
A labor of wanderlust. L. S. Brady. il pors *Esquire* 107:48 Ja '87

Certain-Teed Corp.
Penalizing success. T. Jaffe. il *Forbes* 139:182 My 4 '87

Certificates of deposit
Bank introduces indexed investing [Chase Manhattan's Market Investment Index] R. Brady. il *Nations Bus* 75:85-6 My '87
CDs go all out. il *Consum Rep* 52:700-2 N '87
CDs that play the market [S&P CDs] *Money* 16:13 O '87
Certificates of deposit: how to get high yields without withdrawal pains. D. W. Englander. il *Money* 16:33+ N '87
Chase chases the stock runup—and big investors [Market Index Investment] G. Weiss. il *Bus Week* p115 Je 8 '87
Do your homework before stashing that cash [money market mutual funds] F. A. Miller. il *Bus Week* p170 D 28 '87-Ja 4 '88
Gamboling with frisky new CD's. A. McGrath. il *U S News World Rep* 103:105 S 28 '87
A guide to the new CDs: from step-up to bump-up. F. A. Miller. *Bus Week* p124 O 26 '87
In the CD wars, the customers are winning. S. Weiss. il *Bus Week* p151 Je 8 '87
Saving: float like a butterfly before you sock away your cash. il *Money* 16:40 Je '87
Savings: a new insured account chases the stock market [Chase Market Index Investment] il *Money* 16:25 My '87
Savings: five ways to look for Mr. Good Bank. il *Money* 16:23 N '87
Savings: how you can catch rising rates at their peak. il *Money* 16:29 Jl '87
Savings: no-penalty CDs with penalties—and other gimmicks. il *Money* 16:29 O '87
Savings: why the days of ultrahigh rates are numbered. il *Money* 16:25 Ag '87
Why the new CollegeSure CD deserves to flunk. il *Money* 16:9 N '87

Insurance
Anything goes [CollegeSure CD marketed by College Savings Bank qualifies for FDIC insurance] L. Jereski. il *Forbes* 140:34-5 O 5 '87

Certificates of merit
Certificate Maker [computer program] *Radio-Electron* 58 ComputerDigest:103 F '87

Certification
See also
Airplane engines, Jet—Standards
Airplanes, Business—Standards
Airplanes, Freight—Standards
Airplanes, Jet—Standards
Dance teachers—Certification
Death—Proof and certification
Electronic technicians—Certification
Science teachers—Certification
Teachers—Certification
Theater teachers—Certification

Cervecería Modelo SA
A barroom brawl with Mexico. W. J. Holstein. *Bus Week* p38 Ag 10 '87

Cerveny, Randall S., and Skeeter, Brent R.
Escapers' weather. bibl il *Weatherwise* 40:248-54 O '87

Cervical caps (Contraceptives) *See* Contraceptives

Cervix

Cancer
Causes
The next sex epidemic [human papilloma virus] S. Downie. il *Mademoiselle* 93:154 N '87
A sexually transmitted cancer virus [views of D. Norman Dahm on papilloma viruses and Pap tests] C. SerVaas. il *Saturday Evening Post* 259:104-5 My/Je '87
Diagnosis
See also
Pap test
Prevention
A sound barrier [barrier birth control methods protect against cervical cancer; research by Ruth Peters] J. Carpi. *Health* 19:24 Jl '87

Cesarean section
Caesarean sections: why are they increasing? B. Weinhouse. *Ladies Home J* 104:110+ O '87
Sound advice on ultrasound: sonograms found to reduce cesarean rates. L. Piepenbrink. il *Health* 19:23 S '87
Surgery women should think about twice. A. Mereson. *McCalls* 114:139-40 Jl '87

Cesarman, Ethel, and others
Mutations in the first exon are associated with altered transcription of c-*myc* in Burkitt lymphoma. bibl f il *Science* 238:1272-5 N 27 '87

Cesium
Why is D.O.E. for food irradiation? [justifying the extraction of plutonium from commercial nuclear wastes for use in nuclear weapons] K. Terry. il *Nation* 244:142+ F 7 '87

Isotopes
Radioactive cesium from the Chernobyl accident in the Greenland ice sheet. C. I. Davidson and others. bibl f maps *Science* 237:633-4 Ag 7 '87

Cessna Aircraft Company
Cessna, Beech trim operations as jet, turboprop sales improve. il *Aviat Week Space Technol* 127:82 S 28 '87
Cessna offers modified Caravan for low-cost reconnaissance. B. D. Nordwall. il *Aviat Week Space Technol* 127:153 O 12 '87
Citation 5 debut promises altitude performance gains. il *Aviat Week Space Technol* 127:20 O 5 '87

Cetacea
See also
Dolphins
Whales
Habitats for cetaceans. *Oceans* 20:57 Jl/Ag '87

Cetera, Peter
about
Glory of love singer Peter Cetera left Chicago (the band) for Idaho (the state) and solo success. S. Dougherty. il pors *People Wkly* 27:60-2 F 2 '87
Peter Cetera fact file. por *Teen* 31:48 Ja '87
Peter Cetera hit the top when he began doing what he does best—being his own voice. E. Miller. por *Seventeen* 46:170+ Mr '87

Cetron, Marvin J.
about
Marvin Cetron says he's seen the future, and it's high-tech joy [interview] B. Cornell. il *People Wkly* 27:84-6 Ja 12 '87

Cetron, Marvin J., and Rocha, Wanda
Travel tomorrow [cover story] il pors *Futurist* 21:29-34 Jl/Ag '87

Cetus Corporation
Betting that Cetus will soar again [Interleukin-2] G. G. Marcial. il *Bus Week* p117 Ja 12 '87

Cévennes Biosphere Reserve and National Park (France)
Return of the griffon. il *Courier* 40:13-15 O '87

Ceylon *See* Sri Lanka

CF *See* Cystic fibrosis

CFCs *See* Chlorofluorocarbons

CFM International
Airbus defines new A340 to use CFM56 turbofans. J. M. Lenorovitz. *Aviat Week Space Technol* 126:36-8 Ap 13 '87
CFM plans no ultrahigh bypass competitor to IAE's SuperFan. J. M. Lenorovitz. il *Aviat Week Space Technol* 126:28-30 F 2 '87
CFM56-5C1 to receive thrust improvements for operation on the Airbus A340 transport. il *Aviat Week Space Technol* 126:44 My 4 '87
Leasing company selects CFM56-5 to power A320s [International Lease Finance Corp.] *Aviat Week Space Technol* 126:33 Ap 6 '87
Strong demand prompts increase in CF6, CFM56 engine production. J. M. Lenorovitz. *Aviat Week Space Technol* 127:35-6 N 9 '87

CFR *See* Council on Foreign Relations
CGIAR *See* Consultative Group on International Agricultural Research
Chabon, Michael
Admirals [story] *New Yorker* 63:34-8 S 14 '87
A foreign affair [story] il *Mademoiselle* 93:196+ S '87

about

Morrow pays $155,000 for first novel by 23-year-old author. W. Goldstein. por *Publ Wkly* 231:73-4 Ap 10 '87
Chabot, Joy de Rohan- *See* Rohan-Chabot, Joy de
Chace, Frederic

about

Audio alchemy. G. Buchalter. il por *Forbes* 140:188 O 5 '87
Chace, James
The end of the affair? bibl f il *N Y Rev Books* 34:24-6+ O 8 '87
Ike was right. il *Atlantic* 260:39-41 Ag '87
Chace Productions, Inc.
Audio alchemy. G. Buchalter. il por *Forbes* 140:188 O 5 '87
Chachere, Bernadette, and others
Causes for alarm. bibl *Society* 24:22-8 Ja/F '87
Chaco Culture National Historical Park (N.M.)
Ancient mansions of Chaco Canyon [work of the Hyde Exploring Expedition in excavating Anasazi artifacts] il *Nat Hist* 96:74-7 Mr '87
Chad

See also

Military assistance, American—Chad
Military assistance, French—Chad
Foreign relations
Libya
See Libya—Foreign relations—Chad
Chadbourn (N.C.)
Police
Town manager fired, mayor quits in row over new black police chief in N.C. por *Jet* 72:8 Ap 6 '87
Chadbourne, Eugene

about

Notes from underground. J. Kruth. il por *Progressive* 51:11 Ag '87
Chadds Ford (Pa.)
Galleries and museums
See also
Brandywine River Museum
Chad's Rainbow, Inc.
Chad's dad [D. Brandon uses toys to treat son's autism]; ed. by John Grossmann. D. Brandon. il *Health* 19:79-80 Ap '87
Chadwick, Douglas H.
At the crossroads of Kathmandu. il maps *Natl Geogr* 172:32-65 Jl '87
Chafee, John
Should the Levin-Nunn Amendment be approved? [excerpts from address, May 15, 1987] *Congr Dig* 66:276+ N '87
Chagall, Marc, 1887-1985

about

Broken continuities: Night and White crucifixion [cover story] K. A. Plank. il por *Christ Century* 104:963-6 N 4 '87
The return of the native. M. Satchell. il *U S News World Rep* 103:12 S 14 '87
A surprise at the Pushkin. S. Strasser. il por *Newsweek* 110:87 S 14 '87
Unforgettable Marc Chagall. E. O. Hauser. il pors *Read Dig* 130:180-7 Je '87
Whose Chagall is it, anyway? A. Decker. *Art News* 86:21 D '87
Chain saws and sawing *See* Saws and sawing
Chain stores
See also
Department stores
Discount houses (Retail trade)
Supermarkets
La Chaîne des Rôtisseurs
La Chaîne des Rôtisseurs [annual View from the Vineyards party] *New Yorker* 63:34-5 Ap 6 '87
Chains
See also
Tire chains
Chair caning *See* Cane weaving
Chairs
Bentwood chair and lamp. K. Meyers. il *Workbench* 43:54-9 S/O '87
Biedermeier chairs. A. Wilkie. il *Antiques* 132:798-807 O '87

Chairmanship [mahogany dining chair] R. Capotosto. il *Pop Mech* 164:126-30+ N '87
God's lawn chair [Adirondack chair] il *Esquire* 108:22 Ag '87
Lazy afternoon deck chair. A. Hontoir. il *Workbench* 43:50-2 Jl/Ag '87
A motorized observing chair [telescope observing] E. C. Larr. il *Sky Telesc* 74:665-7 D '87
Old-fashioned high chair. R. B. Rennaker. il *Workbench* 43:27-9 N/D '87
The perfect chair. M. D. Glass and S. Slesin. il *Ladies Home J* 104:104-9 F '87
The rocking chair. B. W. DuBois. il *McCalls* 115:70+ N '87
The shape of ourselves—Robert Venturi's chairs. V. J. Scully. il *Archit Dig* 44:62+ Ap '87
Very contemporary furniture for kids. J. Thom. il *Workbench* 43:46-50 N/D '87
Anecdotes, facetiae, satire, etc.
Raising chair awareness. A. McCarroll. il *Saturday Evening Post* 259:22 S '87
Exhibitions
Furniture in Pennsylvania [Two hundred years of chairs and chairmaking in the collection of the Chester County Historical Society] S. B. Sherrill. il *Antiques* 132:52+ Jl '87
Maintenance and repair
See also
Cane weaving
New life for an old chair. il *Glamour* 85:318 Mr '87
Rocker repair. R. Barnhart. il *Home Mech* 83:24 Mr '87
Chait, Richard P.
Third and long for enrollment managers: life inside the pressure cooker. il *Change* 19:43-5 S/O '87
Chakoumakos, Bryan C., and others
Alpha-decay-induced fracturing in zircon: the transition from the crystalline to the metamict state [cover story] bibl f il *Science* 236:1556-9 Je 19 '87
Chalets *See* Architecture, Domestic—Switzerland
Chaliapin, Feodor

about

A star in the eighties. J. Kornbluth. il por *N Y* 20:20 Ja 26 '87
Chalk, Vincent

about

AIDS tests for teachers. J. N. Baker. por *Newsweek* 110:81 O 19 '87
Chalk's International Airlines
Chalk's aweigh. E. Weiner. il *Flying* 114:58-62+ Jl '87
Chall, Jeanne Sternlicht, 1921-, and others
Adult literacy: new and enduring problems. bibl f il *Phi Delta Kappan* 69:190-6 N '87
Challenger (Space shuttle) explosion, 1986
The astronauts after Challenger. J. Reston. il *N Y Times Mag* p46-7+ Ja 25 '87
Challenger's legacy [expendable launch vehicle development program] D. E. Fink. *Aviat Week Space Technol* 126:13 Ja 26 '87
Cheryl McNair: surviving the shuttle disaster. il pors *Ebony* 42:162+ My '87
The day Challenger exploded. O. A. Fish. il *Read Dig* 130:67-9 Ja '87
The death and life of Christa McAuliffe [excerpt from I touch the future] R. T. Hohler. il pors *Good Housekeep* 204:90-3+ Ja '87
How were children affected by the space shuttle disaster? G. G. Sparks. *Educ Dig* 52:55-7 F '87
"I touch the future . . ." [teacher-astronaut C. McAuliffe; condensation] R. T. Hohler. il pors *Read Dig* 130:78-85 Je '87
Lost in space [views of M. McConnell and J. Trento] G. Easterbrook. *Wash Mon* 19:48-54 Ap '87
New factors cited in Challenger accident [undetected wind shear and a weakened attach ring that holds boosters to external tank] C. Covault. il *Aviat Week Space Technol* 126:21-2 F 23 '87
Remembering Christa [special section] il pors *Ladies Home J* 104:76+ F '87
Ronald McNair's family copes with memories of Challenger tragedy. il *Jet* 71:53 F 9 '87
A year later [effects of disaster at Kennedy Space Center] B. Dickey. il *Space World* X-1-277:14-17 Ja '87
Economic aspects
Life beyond Challenger [Morton Thiokol] C. Siler. por *Forbes* 140:44 S 21 '87
Photographs and photography
Challenger: a teacher, a mission, a nation's tragedy. il *Life* 10:56-63 Ja '87

Challenger (Space shuttle) explosion, 1986—*cont.*

Reporters and reporting

NASA, the press and Challenger. il *Space World* X-4-280:24-5 Ap '87

Suits and claims

Astronaut McNair's widow settles with rocket maker. *Jet* 72:18 My 25 '87

Can the crown do wrong? A. Press. il *Newsweek* 109:62 Ja 12 '87

Can Thiokol rise from Challenger's ashes? J. Mendes. *Fortune* 115:152+ Je 8 '87

FBI investigating fraud charges against Morton Thiokol in manufacture of shuttle solid rocket motors. *Aviat Week Space Technol* 126:41-2 Ap 27 '87

Morton Thiokol will forfeit $10 million in lieu of contract penalty. *Aviat Week Space Technol* 126:28 Mr 2 '87

Chamber music

See also

Compact discs—Chamber music

Phonograph records—Chamber music

Musical events:

Merkin Hall concerts. A. Porter. *New Yorker* 62:69-70 Ja 5 '87

Chamber of Commerce of the United States of America

Making America more competitive [annual report] il *Nations Bus* 75:71-5 My '87

Chamber of Commerce of the United States of America. American Business Network *See* American Business Network

Chamber orchestras

See also

Les Arts Florissants (Chamber orchestra)

Chambered nautilus *See* Nautilus

Chamberlain, David

Teacher of the Year. il pors *Sport Mag* 78:70-4+ D '87

Chamberlain, David M.

about

Fruit-enriched vitamins? E. Paris. il por *Forbes* 140:56 O 5 '87

Chamberlain, John, 1903-

Another Nobel for freedom. *Natl Rev* 39:36+ F 13 '87

Chamberlain, Joseph, 1836-1914

about

Joseph Chamberlain and the municipal ideal. D. Fraser. bibl il por *Hist Today* 37:33-9 Ap '87

Chamberlain, Karen

Stepping in the same river [poem] *Nation* 244:660 My 16 '87

Chamberlain, Wilt, 1936-

about

Wilt wants to throw his weight around Olympics. por *Jet* 72:50 Ag 10 '87

Chambers, Alex A.

about

Chambers inaugurated 8th prexy of Lane College. por *Jet* 71:40 Mr 9 '87

Chambers, Bette

Eyewitness to a Soviet wedding. il *Humanist* 47:13-15+ Ja/F '87

Chambers, Dennis

about

Dennis Chambers. B. Milkowski. il pors *Down Beat* 54:52-3 Jl '87

Chambers, Robert

about

Jennifer Levin and Robert Chambers: a walk with love and death. A. C. Heller. il pors *Mademoiselle* 93:145-7+ Ja '87

The people versus Robert Chambers. L. Wolfe. il pors *N Y* 20:92-9+ O 26 '87

Prosecuting Jennifer Levin's killer. M. Laurino. il pors *Ms* 16:70-2+ S '87

Chambers, Tom

about

Hey, Tom can smile! J. McCallum. il pors *Sports Illus* 67:64+ N 23 '87

Chambers Development Company

Treasure in the trash pile. J. A. Conway. il *Forbes* 139 Ann Directory:10 Ap 27 '87

Chambers of commerce

See also

Chamber of Commerce of the United States of America

Chameleons

Photographs and photography

Tongue lashing. B. Davidson. il *Nat Hist* 96:92-3 Ja '87

Chamish, Barry

Masters of the tiles. il *Atlantic* 259:54-8 Je '87

Chamomile

Chamomile. K. Kellogg. il *Rodale's Org Gard* 34:46 O '87

Chamorro, Jaime

How "La prensa" was silenced; tr. by Steven Blakemore. *Commentary* 83:39-44 Ja '87

"Our people cannot be silenced"; tr. by Steven Blakemore. *Read Dig* 130:169-70+ My '87

Chamorro, Pedro Joaquin

about

Two democrats betrayed. pors *Dep State Bull* 87:66 Mr '87

Chamot, Dennis

Unions need to confront the results of new technology. *Mon Labor Rev* 110:45 Ag '87

Champagne

Bargains in bubbly. B. Kallen. il *Forbes* 140:436+ Jl 13 '87

Brut force. B. Kanner. il *N Y* 20:9-10 Ja 19 '87

Champagne—in a class by itself. E. Fried. il *Black Enterp* 17:336 Je '87

Champagne's California twist [French wine makers in the Napa Valley] G. C. Lubenow and A. Miller. il *Newsweek* 110:40 Ag 24 '87

In a glass sparkly. M. Gersh. *Vogue* 177:272 N '87

Pardon their French, but the first of American bubbly boasts a champagne worthy of the name [product of Schramsberg Vineyards] E. Levin. il pors *People Wkly* 28:113-14 D 21 '87

Champin, Fleur

Green architecture. il *House Gard* 159:162-71+ Mr '87

Landscape of high romance. il *House Gard* 159:194-203+ O '87

CHAMPUS *See* Civilian Health and Medical Program of the Uniformed Services

Chan, Amos

about

Pro challenge. il por *Pop Photogr* 94:66 Jl '87

Pro challenge. R. Hart. il *Pop Photogr* 94:59 O '87

Chan, Chong Chi

about

Weaves of grass. B. B. Ryan. il pors *Travel Holiday* 167:34-6 Mr '87

Chan, Kwing L., and Sofia, Sabatino

Validity tests of the mixing-length theory of deep convection. bibl f il *Science* 235:465-7 Ja 23 '87

Chance, Paul

Master of mastery. bibl (p65) il pors *Psychol Today* 21:42-6 Ap '87

Chance, Paul, and Fischman, Joshua

The magic of childhood. bibl (p94) il *Psychol Today* 21:48-51+ My '87

Chance

See also

Coincidence

Probabilities

Chancellor, Alexander

The poise of Americans. il *World Press Rev* 34:33-4 Jl '87

Chancellor, John, 1927-

Pure Nantucket. il *House Gard* 159:78-85+ Ag '87

Chandigarh (India)

Architecture

Chandigarh revisited [work of Le Corbusier] R. Maass. il *Archit Rec* 175:72-5 Jl '87

Chandler, Albert B., 1898-

about

Happy days. F. Deford. il pors *Sports Illus* 67:56-60+ Jl 20 '87

Chandler, Chris

about

Time to air it out. il por *Sports Illus* 67:33 S 14 '87

Chandler, Clay

Bright lights, big MITI. *New Repub* 197:11-13 Ag 31 '87

Chandler, Colby H.

about

Why Kodak is starting to click again. L. Helm. il por *Bus Week* p134-5+ F 23 '87

Chandler, David, and Chandler, Mary

A second chance at life. il pors *People Wkly* 27:124-7+ Je 8 '87

Chandler, David Leon

about

Macmillan cancels Bingham book after challenge by family patriarch. *Publ Wkly* 232:310-11 Ag 7 '87

Chandler, Happy *See* Chandler, Albert B., 1898-

Chandler, John P. H., 1911-

about

Aide to Kemp dismissed for making racial slurs. *Jet* 73:37 S 28 '87

Chandler, Mary
(jt. auth) See Chandler, David, and Chandler, Mary
Chandler, Michael
about
Michael Chandler at Stephen Rosenberg. E. Heartney. *Art Am* 75:186-7 O '87
Chandler, Rod
about
A warden's story. F. Graham. il pors *Audubon* 89:105-21 Mr '87
Chandoha, Walter
Beauty in the beasts [cover story] il *Petersens Photogr Mag* 16:18-21 D '87
A different breed of mom. il *Good Housekeep* 204:157 My '87
Putting your beds to bed. il *Ctry J* 14:64-7 O '87
about
Gardens: autumn fields. C. Kittredge. il por *Archit Dig* 44:170-5 S '87
Chandra Maharaj, Swami
about
The swami connection. M. McDonald. il por *Macleans* 100:26+ N 9 '87
The swami of Iranamok [cover story] M. Isikoff and M. Hosenball. *New Repub* 197:21-3 N 9 '87
Chandrasekhar Rao, R. V. R.
India, Pakistan racing to be last. il *Bull At Sci* 43:32-4 N '87
Chanel (Firm)
Chanel steals the show. J. Conant. il *Newsweek* 109:50-1 Ap 6 '87
Chaneles, Sol
Growing old behind bars. bibl (p62) il *Psychol Today* 21:46-51 O '87
Chaney, John
about
Temple's Chaney wins coach of year honors. por *Jet* 72:46 Ap 6 '87
Chang, David D., and Clayton, David A.
A mammalian mitochondrial RNA processing activity contains nucleus-encoded RNA. bibl f il *Science* 235:1178-84 Mr 6 '87
Chang, Esther H., and others
Oncogenes in radioresistant, noncancerous skin fibroblasts from a cancer-prone family. bibl f il *Science* 237:1036-9 Ag 28 '87
Chang, Michael
about
No place to go but up. F. Deford. il por *Sports Illus* 67:59-60 S 14 '87
Chang, S. G., and others
Disulfate ion as an intermediate to sulfuric acid in acid rain formation. bibl f il *Science* 237:756-8 Ag 14 '87
Chang, Soo Ko
In a remote Korean village [poem] *America* 157:158 S 26 '87
Chang, Yu-che, 1902-1986
about
Obituary
Sky Telesc il por 73:481 My '87
Chang, Yung-fa
about
Taiwan's billionaire sea lord. A. Tanzer. il por *Forbes* 140:36-8 Ag 24 '87
Chang-Diaz, Franklin R., 1950-
about
Tomorrow's rockets: a conversation with Franklin Chang-Diaz. M. Freeman. il pors *Space World* X-9-285:14-16 S '87
Change
See also
Social change
Technological innovations
Change (Psychology)
Are you at a turning point? S. P. Haven. *Glamour* 85:168+ N '87
Can we change the people we love? B.-J. Raphael. il *Glamour* 85:222+ S '87
Changing to please a man: how much is too much? J. Stone. *Glamour* 85:44 O '87
"I deserve a change" [stories of A. Diehl and C. Orlaskey] S. Schneider. il pors *Redbook* 168:82-5 Ja '87
Search for a sea change. L. Wainwright. il *Life* 10:22 N '87
Taking the mystery out of change. N. K. Schlossberg. bibl (p94-5) *Psychol Today* 21:74-5 My '87
"The trouble is—you've changed". M. Klein. il *Parents* 62:71-4 Jl '87

Change in the Bible
Change—and cheer up! G. G. Seibert. *America* 157:143 S 12-19 '87
Change of life in women See Menopause
Change of sex
Differentiation and evolution of sex change in fishes. D. Y. Shapiro. bibl f il *BioScience* 37:490-7 Jl/Ag '87
"My son, my daughter". J. McDowell. il por *Ladies Home J* 104:18+ F '87
Changery, Michael J., and Quayle, Robert G.
Coastal wave energy [cover story] bibl il map *Sea Front* 33:259-62 Jl/Ag '87
Channel Four (Television station: London, England)
Channel 4. il por *Channels* 7:55 O '87
Poland's 20th-century struggles [series The struggles for Poland; cover story] N. Ascherson. il *Hist Today* 37:44-9 Je '87
Channel frequency allocation, Television See Television frequency allocation
Channel Islands
See also
Sark (Channel Islands)
Social conditions
Tight little islands [social consequences of being a tax haven] R. Phalon. il *Forbes* 140:40-1 Jl 27 '87
Channel tunnel See English Channel tunnel
Channelers
Channelers. K. Lowry. il por *Omni* 10:46-8+ O '87
Mystics on Main Street. A. Levine. il *U S News World Rep* 102:67-9 F 9 '87
Reincarnation? Channeling? Hell, no, I won't go! G. Hirshey. il *Glamour* 85:72 D '87
Theology from the Twilight Zone. B. Alexander. il por *Christ Today* 31:22-6 S 18 '87
Voices from beyond: the channelers. il *People Wkly* 27:30-3 Ja 26 '87
Channell, Carl
about
Autopen presidency. M. Hosenball. *New Repub* 196:16-18 My 11 '87
Channell's high connections. J. V. Lamar, Jr. il por *Time* 129:13 My 11 '87
One down and a few more to go. D. Baer. il por *U S News World Rep* 102:17 My 11 '87
Putting the arm on rich, right-wing widows. G. Hackett. il por *Newsweek* 109:30 Ap 20 '87
Channels (Hydraulic engineering)
The "sewer ditch" undone [dismantling the Kissimmee River channel] F. Graham. il maps *Audubon* 89:114-15 Mr '87
Channels (Periodical)
The ABC's of success. P. D. Schaeffer. *Channels* 7:4 Jl/Ag '87
New seasons. P. D. Schaeffer. il *Channels* 7:6-7 S '87
Chanteys See Sea songs
Le Chantilly (New York, N.Y.: Restaurant) See New York (N.Y.)—Restaurants, nightclubs, bars, etc.
Chants (Gregorian, plain, etc.)
See also
Compact discs—Chants (Gregorian, plain, etc.)
Chanukah See Hanukkah
Chaos (Science)
Chaos, strange attractors, and fractal basin boundaries in nonlinear dynamics. C. Grebogi and others. bibl f il *Science* 238:632-8 O 30 '87
Chaotic bursts in nonlinear dynamical systems. R. L. Devaney. bibl f il *Science* 235:342-5 Ja 16 '87
Finding order in disorder. S. Begley. il *Newsweek* 110:55-6 D 21 '87
Mr. Chaos [theories of M. Feigenbaum] A. Rosenfeld. por *N Y* 20:26 My 18 '87
New images of chaos that are stirring a science revolution. J. Gleick. bibl (p205) il *Smithsonian* 18:122-4+ D '87
Probing the strange attractions of chaos. A. K. Dewdney. il *Sci Am* 257:108-11 Jl '87
Quantum chaos? [work of Giulio Casati and others] *Sci Am* 256:62+ Mr '87
Strategy in a more volatile world [science of chaos and business management] R. H. Waterman, Jr. il por *Fortune* 116:181-2 D 21 '87
Unmashing chaos [work of Mitchell Feigenbaum and others] il *Sci Am* 256:61-2 F '87
Zeroing in on chaos [study of Newton's method; work of Scott A. Burns and others] I. Peterson. il *Sci News* 131:137-9 F 28 '87
Chaparral Steel Company
Forward's march. L. M. Keefe. il por *Forbes* 139:104-5 Ap 20 '87

Chapel, Richard J.
Bad backs: pains in the wallet. il *Nations Bus* 75:43-4
Ja '87
Chapels
See also
Wedding chapels
Great Britain
See also
Bath (England)—Chapels
Chapin, F. Stuart, 1944-, and others
Plant responses to multiple environmental factors. bibl
f il *BioScience* 37:49-57 Ja '87
Chapin, Harry, 1942-1981
about
Controversial bio of singer Harry Chapin released by
Ashley. *Publ Wkly* 232:76-7 O 2 '87
Harry Chapin is gone, but friends carry his song in
their hearts. il pors *People Wkly* 28:49-50 D 21 '87
Chapiteau (New York, N.Y.: Restaurant) *See* New York
(N.Y.)—Restaurants, nightclubs, bars, etc.
Chaplains, Military
Easter on Hill 17 [chaplain in Vietnam] G. H. Meyer.
il por *Christ Today* 31:18-22 Ap 17 '87
Worship in wartime. W. J. Leonard. *America* 157:58-60
Ag 1-8 '87
Chapline, Jake
Listener. See issues of Blair & Ketchum's Country Journal
through March 1987
Chapman, Allan
Gauging angles in the 17th century. il *Sky Telesc* 73:362-4
Ap '87
Chapman, Anthony Colin Bruce *See* Chapman, Colin,
1928-1982
Chapman, Colin, 1928-1982
about
The legacy. C. Fox. il pors *Car Driv* 32:101-5 Je '87
Chapman, Howard
about
A poignant farewell from Howard Chapman. *Natl Parks*
61:42-3 S/O '87
Chapman, Lawrence
Tomorrow's global economy: the challenge of increasing
competition. il por *Futurist* 21:26-7 Jl/Ag '87
Chapman, Mark David
about
In the shadows a killer waited. J. R. Gaines. il por
People Wkly 27:50-2+ Mr 2 '87
The killer takes his fall. J. R. Gaines. il por *People
Wkly* 27:60-2+ Mr 9 '87
The man who shot Lennon. J. R. Gaines. il pors *People
Wkly* 27:58-60+ F 23 '87
Chapman, Peter
Mexico's race is on. *World Press Rev* 34:45 Ja '87
Chapman, Rex
about
A wild new Cats' meow. C. Kirkpatrick. il pors *Sports
Illus* 66:18-19 Ja 5 '87
Chapman, Victor
about
Canadian shield at the Palace. il por *Macleans* 100:29
Jl 27 '87
Chapman, William
Big Red machine. *New Repub* 196:19-20 Ap 6 '87
Still without land: for Filipino peasants, Aquino brings
no change. il *Progressive* 51:26-8 Je '87
about
Manila fudge. J. M. Fallows. *Wash Mon* 19:53-6 S '87
Chapman School of Seamanship *See* Boats and boating—
Study and teaching
Chapnick, Howard
Markets & careers. See issues of Popular Photography
through January 1987
Profiles. See issues of Popular Photography beginning
February 1987
Chappell, George S.
about
The sky line. B. Gill. *New Yorker* 63:106-9 F 23 '87
Char fishing
The lady in pink [Arctic char in northern Canada] C.
Gammon. il *Sports Illus* 67:54-8 Ag 24 '87
Character
See also
Individuality
Personality
Responsibility
Typology (Psychology)
The character debate: how much is too much? K. A.
Lawton. il *Christ Today* 31:49-50+ D 11 '87
Character issue. W. Safire. il *N Y Times Mag* p18+
N 22 '87

The character issue: enough already [presidential can-
didates] W. Shapiro. il *Time* 130:93-4 D 7 '87
Did Gorbachev smoke pot? M. Greenfield. il *Newsweek*
110:94 N 30 '87
Character education *See* Moral education
Characterization
How well do you know your characters? R. M. Stern.
Writer 100:9-11 Je '87
People I have known. K. Paterson. *Writer* 100:22-4 Ap
'87
Roles in collision: a play begins. J. Sweet. il *Writer*
100:16-18 My '87
Writing short stories. P. Meinke. *Writer* 100:12-14 Ja
'87
Characters in literature
See also
Alex (Fictional character)
Animals in literature
Blacks in literature
Bobbsey Twins (Literary characters)
Characterization
Curious George (Fictional character)
Don Quixote (Fictional character)
Father Brown (Fictional character)
Freddy (Fictional character)
Hello Kitty (Fictional character)
Huckleberry Finn (Fictional character)
J R (Fictional character)
James Bond (Fictional character)
Richard Hannay (Fictional character)
Sherlock Holmes (Fictional character)
Winnie the Pooh (Fictional character)
Women in literature
How beautiful was Helen of Troy? What Homer never
told us [descriptions of characters' appearance] A.
Krystal. il *N Y Times Book Rev* 92:3 Jl 12 '87
Who created whom? Characters that talk back. il *N
Y Times Book Rev* 92:36-7 My 31 '87
Characters in motion pictures
See also
Daffy Duck (Fictional character)
Donald Duck (Fictional character)
Hispanic Americans in motion pictures
James Bond (Fictional character)
Jews in motion pictures
King Kong (Fictional character)
Rambo (Fictional character)
Richard Hannay (Fictional character)
Sherlock Holmes (Fictional character)
Snow White (Fictional character)
Women in motion pictures
Characters in radio
See also
Amos 'n' Andy (Fictional characters)
Characters in television
See also
ALF (Fictional character)
Amos 'n' Andy (Fictional characters)
Blacks in television
Businessmen in television
He-Man (Fictional character)
Hispanic Americans in television
Max Headroom (Fictional character)
Teachers in television
Women in television
Youth in television
Anecdotes, facetiae, satire, etc.
Jock is back. G. W. S. Trow. *New Yorker* 63:33 S
14 '87
Charade (Automobile) *See* Automobiles, Foreign
Charbeneau, Travis
Music's electronic future. il por *Futurist* 21:35-7 S/O
'87
Charcoal, Activated *See* Carbon, Activated
Chardonnay wines *See* Wine
Charen, Mona
The petty inquisitors. il *Natl Rev* 39:36+ D 18 '87
Charest, Jean-J.
about
A young and rising star. M. Rose. il por *Macleans*
100:6-7 S 21 '87
Charge coupled devices (Electronics)
See also
Metal oxide semiconductors
CCD images of supernova remnants. il *Sky Telesc* 73:27
Ja '87
Ferret: an image processor. C. Harris. il *Byte* 12:317-18+
D '87
Globular clusters in the Coma cluster of galaxies [CCD
observations by William E. Harris] il *Sky Telesc*
74:346-7 O '87

Charge coupled devices (Electronics)—*cont.*
Sky on a chip: the fabulous CCD. J. Janesick and M. Blouke. il *Sky Telesc* 74:238-42 S '87
Solid pictures, or gathering MOS. D. Ranada. il *High Fidel* 37:16 O '87
The use of a charge-coupled device for quantitative optical microscopy of biological structures. Y. Hiraoka and others. bibl f il *Science* 238:36-41 O 2 '87
Chargebacks, Credit card *See* Credit cards—Chargebacks
Charging, Battery *See* Electric batteries—Charging; Storage batteries—Charging
Charging indicator lights, Battery *See* Electric batteries—Charging
Charismatic movement *See* Pentecostalism
Charismatic movement (Catholic) *See* Pentecostalism (Catholic)
Charitable contributions as tax deductions *See* Income tax—Deductions
Charities

   See also
   Affinity cards
   Ann Arbor (Mich.)—Charities
   Combined Federal Campaign (U.S.)
   Corporations—Charitable contributions
   Foundations, Charitable and educational
   Fund raising
   Giving
   New York (N.Y.)—Charities
   Relief work
   United Way of America
America's best-run charities. G. Kinkead. il *Fortune* 116:145-6+ N 9 '87
Black philanthropy. il *Black Enterp* 18:55 D '87
Charities: a wise-giver's guide. E. McGowan. il *Good Housekeep* 205:251 O '87
Charity begins with a budget. L. Brown. il *Black Enterp* 18:77-8+ D '87
A consumer guide to charity: where to get more balm for your buck. H. Gershen. il *Esquire* 108:185-6+ D '87
Deep pockets [charitable contributions] M. S. Dolan. il *Consum Res Mag* 70:2 O '87
Faith, hope, and chicanery [mismanaged and fraudulent charities] J. Wark and G. Marx. il *Wash Mon* 18:25-31 Ja '87
Hype across America: the dangers of quick-fix giving. *Glamour* 85:52 Ja '87
Who's who in charity? C. Cox. il *Vogue* 177:396-9 N '87

         Directors
Serving on a charity: it's getting safer. D. B. Moskowitz. il *Bus Week* p120 Jl 13 '87
Charity

   See also
   Good works (Theology)
   Love (Theology)
Charlatans *See* Quacks and quackery
Charles, Duke of Burgundy, 1433-1477

         about
Chasing a sphinx: Charles the Bold's Burgundy [cover story] R. Vaughan. bibl il pors map *Hist Today* 37:24-9 My '87
Charles, Prince of Wales, 1948-

         about
Autumn of their discontent [cover story] B. Johnson. il pors *People Wkly* 28:90-2+ N 9 '87
Baba says ta ta to Wills and Harry—the question is, did Charles and Di get the nanny's goat? B. Johnson. il pors *People Wkly* 27:44+ F 2 '87
Britain's Charles shows his colors. L. S. Healy. il por *Life* 10:82-3 Ag '87
The Cannes Film Festival is a grade B movie with no good parts for Charles and Diana. il pors *People Wkly* 27:34-5 Je 1 '87
'Dallas' at the Palace. F. Willey. il por *Newsweek* 110:33 Jl 6 '87
Diana: why she and Charles can't agree [cover story] P. Leigh. il pors *Ladies Home J* 104:97-9+ Jl '87
For the Prince and Princess of Wales, a time of troubles. il pors *McCalls* 114:38 Je '87
A frame-up? Charles & Di's latest brushes with art may be unpaletteable. L. Rozen. il pors *People Wkly* 27:79-80 Je 22 '87
Happy? Or just ever after? [cover story] F. A. Bernstein. il pors *People Wkly* 27:112-14+ Je 8 '87
London marriage falling down? il pors *Newsweek* 110:85 N 9 '87
The long march of the Prince of Wales. R. Alan. il por *New Leader* 70:10-12 Ja 12-26 '87
Man in a gilded cage [cover story] A. Holden. il pors *Life* 10:32-5 S '87

The man who will be king. R. Laver. il por *Macleans* 100:30 Jl 27 '87
Much ado about Di. il pors *Newsweek* 110:65 Jl 13 '87
A no-nonsense nanny strolls into Charles and Di's nursery. il pors *People Wkly* 27:45 Mr 30 '87
No ordinary fender bender, Diana gives Prince Charles a pain in the Aston Martin. il pors *People Wkly* 28:95 Jl 6 '87
A right royal uproar. M. Janigan. il por *Macleans* 100:20 Jl 6 '87
A royal scandal [cover story; special section; with editorial comment by Kevin Doyle] il pors *Macleans* 100:2, 30-4+ N 9 '87
Royals bashing: a blood sport? M. Smilgis. il pors *Time* 130:94-5 N 9 '87

    Anecdotes, facetiae, satire, etc.
Notes and comment. *New Yorker* 63:33-4 N 23 '87

    Visit to Germany (West), 1987
Their marital woes on hold, Charles and Di wow Germany. il pors *People Wkly* 28:52-3 N 23 '87
Charles, the Bold *See* Charles, Duke of Burgundy, 1433-1477
Charles, Daniel
NATO looks for arms control loopholes. il *Bull At Sci* 43:7-12 S '87
Star Wars fell on Alabama. il *Nation* 245:748-50 D 19 '87
Charles, Jeffrey, and others
How to build and use an all-sky camera. il *Astronomy* 15:64-70 Ap '87
Charles, Pepsi
Each is one [poem] *Essence* 17:138 Ap '87
Charles, Ray

        about
Blind Ray Charles urges Congress to aid the deaf. *Jet* 72:22 My 18 '87
Calif. Links group lauds superstar Ray Charles. il pors *Jet* 71:29 Mr 2 '87
Charles J. Connick Studio (Firm)
Threatened light sources. M. E. Marty. *Christ Century* 104:295 Mr 18-25 '87
Charles K. Nishioka & Son
Slow and steady wins the race [C. K. Nishioka] R. Thompson. il pors *Nations Bus* 75:63-4 Ag '87
Charles M. Russell National Wildlife Refuge (Mont.) *See* Wildlife sanctuaries—Montana
Charles R. Drew Postgraduate Medical School
Drew U. medical study focuses on 75 twins [heart research] il *Jet* 72:36 Ap 13 '87
Leavell named prexy of Drew Med School [W. F. Leavell] *Jet* 71:24 F 9 '87
Charles Schwab & Co., Inc.
How now, Chuck Schwab? J. Heins. il por *Forbes* 139:37-8 Je 15 '87
Schwab: bear markets have been very, very good to him. J. B. Levine. il por *Bus Week* p95 N 23 '87
Schwab's stock offering looks like a winner . . . G. Weiss. il *Bus Week* p77 Ag 17 '87
Charleston (S.C.)

         Description
Southern comfort [visiting via the Intracoastal Waterway in a Grand Banks 42 motor yacht] J. Clemans. il *Mot Boat Sail* 159:42-5+ Mr '87

    Galleries and museums

   See also
   Old Slave Mart Museum

    Historic houses, sites, etc.
The Charleston inheritance. S. Abbott. il *Am Herit* 38:62-9 Ap '87

    Hotels, motels, etc.
History comes with the room in Charleston. il *South Living* 22:56+ Ap '87

    Social life and customs
A day of oyster (and ancestor) worship—in South Carolina, there's nothing finer [Tony and Julie Merck of Ashe Point farm] W. P. Rayner and C. Rayner. il *Vogue* 177:212 My '87

         Theater
A Charleston, South Carolina, playbill of 1794. J. T. Newlin. il *Antiques* 131:432-3 F '87
Charleston (W. Va.)

    Galleries and museums

   See also
   West Virginia State Museum
Charlestown (Saint Kitts-Nevis)

         Description
Charlestown, Nevis. R. Berleant-Schiller and A. Berleant. il map *Focus* 37:32-3 Fall '87

Charlesville (N.S.)

Tourist trade

Charlesville's big boom [East Indian refugee landing site generates tourist trade] B. Hatfield. il *Macleans* 100:8 O 5 '87

Charlie Watts Orchestra

The Charlie Watts interview. B. Beuttler. il pors *Down Beat* 54:16-19+ F '87

Charlie Watts's jazz dream. D. Fricke. il por *Roll Stone* p35 F 26 '87

Charlip, Remy

about

World of wonders. T. Tobias. il *N Y* 20:70 Ja 26 '87

Charlotte (N.C.)

Airports

Positive control: two TCAs, and the controllers in the ATC shuffle. P. Scott. il *Flying* 114:30-2 D '87

Buildings

Southern panache [offices of Clark Tribble Harris & Li, Architects] H. L. Smith, Jr. il *Archit Rec* 175:114-17 Je '87

Politics and government

Gantt seeks third term as Charlotte, N.C., mayor. il por *Jet* 72:32 Jl 20 '87

Charlottesville (Va.)

Architecture

Plain and fancy [Albemarle Conservatory] M. Gaskie. il *Archit Rec* 175:106-9 Ja '87

Bookstores

See Booksellers and bookselling—Virginia

Description

Garden Week in Charlottesville. T. Weeks. il *Gourmet* 47:66-71 Ap '87

Historic houses, sites, etc.

See also

Ash Lawn-Highland (Va.: Historic house)

Charlottetown (P.E.I.)

Crime

Search for a firebug. A. Steacy. *Macleans* 100:46 Ag 10 '87

Moral conditions

Charlottetown and the F-word [uproar over drama festival's censorship of play about Elvis Presley] A. Fotheringham. il *Macleans* 100:60 My 4 '87

Charlottetown Festival See Drama festivals—Prince Edward Island

Charnas, Inc.

UFO update. D. Stacey. il *Omni* 9:87 Mr '87

Charnizon, Marlene

Women at the top. il *Publ Wkly* 231:27-31 Ja 23 '87

Charno, Milt

about

Build your deck to last [interview] J. H. Ingersoll. il por *Home Mech* 83:22+ Ag '87

Charon (Satellite) See Pluto (Planet)—Satellites

Charter 77 (Organization)

Czechoslovak human rights initiative [statement, December 31, 1986] R. Reagan. *Dep State Bull* 87:45 Ap '87

Prague's kamikaze icebreakers. J. Kavan. il *Nation* 244:78-82 Ja 24 '87

Charter of the United Nations Special Committee See United Nations. Special Committee on the Charter of the United Nations and on the Strengthening of the Role of the Organization

Chartering of boats See Fishing boats—Leasing and renting; Motor boats—Leasing and renting; Yachts and yachting—Leasing and renting

Chartism

'Kindness and reason': William Lovett and education. B. H. Harrison. bibl il por *Hist Today* 37:14-22 Mr '87

Charts, Astronomical See Astronomy—Charts, diagrams, etc.

Charts, Aviation See Aviation charts

Charts, Nautical See Nautical charts

Chas. Levy Circulating Co.

Chas. Levy employees describe 'books that made a difference' [contest held as part of the Year of the Reader] il *Publ Wkly* 232:12+ O 30 '87

Chas. P. Young Co.

Pat Rooney's back—and he hasn't changed a bit. A. Bianco. il por *Bus Week* p110-11 My 4 '87

Chase, Alston

The great, green deep-ecology revolution. il *Roll Stone* p61-2+ Ap 23 '87

How to save our national parks [cover story] il *Atlantic* 260:35-44 Jl '87

Smokey would never believe this. *Wash Mon* 19:45-6+ N '87

Chase, Anthony

Wyeth country. il *Vogue* 177:316+ O '87

Chase, Chris

(ed) See Ford, Betty. The day my family saved my life

Chase, Donald

The latest Dance craze. il por *Horizon* 30:36-7 My '87

Torvill & Dean: so nice on ice. il pors *Saturday Evening Post* 259:48-9+ Ja/F '87

Chase, Sarah Leah

Easy strawberry-apricot cheesecake [excerpt from Sarah Leah Chase's Open house cookbook] il *Redbook* 169:22 S '87

Chase, William Merritt, 1849-1916

about

Dreams of summer. M. Wade. il *Horizon* 30:35 S '87

William Merritt Chase at Shinnecock Hills [cover story] N. Cikovsky. bibl f il *Antiques* 132:290-303 Ag '87

Chase Manhattan Bank, N. A.

The $2 million man [art consultant J. L. Boulton] A. Virshup. il por *Art News* 86:112-14 S '87

Bank introduces indexed investing [Market Investment Index] R. Brady. il *Nations Bus* 75:85-6 My '87

Career makeover: from ticket sales to corporate travel planner [L. Lee] il por *Glamour* 85:110 F '87

Chase chases the stock runup—and big investors [Market Index Investment] G. Weiss. il *Bus Week* p115 Je 8 '87

Putting his money where the trends are [interview with N. Miller of Intermediate Cap Growth Fund] A. E. Serwer. il por *Fortune* 115:174 Je 22 '87

Savings: a new insured account chases the stock market [Chase Market Index Investment] il *Money* 16:25 My '87

Chase-Riboud, Barbara, 1936-

Why Paris? [cover story] il *Essence* 18:65-6 O '87

Chassis, Automobile See Automobiles—Chassis

Chassler, Sey

It's your move! *Essence* 17:47+ Mr '87

Success: the Zen commandments: a doer's guide for dreamers (not schemers). il *Work Woman* 12:68-9 F '87

Chast, Roz

about

Chast-izing the world. W. Goldstein. il por *Publ Wkly* 232:82-3 Ag 14 '87

Chaste tree

Rediscover chaste tree. L. B. Trigg. il *South Living* 22:40-1 Ag '87

Chastity

See also

Celibacy

A concerned clergyman's message to teens: look, but don't leap. B. Fanning. por *People Wkly* 27:116 Ap 13 '87

How we can help teenagers wait. T. Stafford. *Christ Today* 31:24 Ja 16 '87

Religious groups denied federal funds to prevent teen pregnancy. P. P. Wong. *Christ Today* 31:41-2 Jl 10 '87

Saying no [chastity in sex education] H. Smith. il *Christ Today* 31:12-13 F 6 '87

Château Bowes (Barnard Castle, England) See Bowes Museum (Barnard Castle, England)

Château Gabriel (Deauville, France: Country estate) See Country estates—France

Château Haut-Brion (Firm)

Wine journal. G. Asher. il *Gourmet* 47:32+ F '87

Château-sur-Mer (Newport, R.I.) See Newport (R.I.)—Historic houses, sites, etc.

Chateaubriand See Cooking—Meat

Chateaux See Castles

Chatfield-Taylor, Joan

The collectors: a passion for sculpture: Patsy and Raymond D. Nasher's Dallas residence and gardens. il *Archit Dig* 44:112-21 O '87

French flavor in Napa: Provence style for a California house and winery. il *Archit Dig* 44:140-5+ Je '87

Gardens: levels of beauty. il *Archit Dig* 44:152-7 D '87

The Rene Di Rosas in Napa Valley. il por *Archit Dig* 44:258+ Je '87

Shock of the past: ancient objects accent a visionary San Francisco design. il *Archit Dig* 44:116-27 Ap '87

Sleight of hand. il por *Archit Dig* 44:146-51+ My '87

Using minerals in interior design. il *Archit Dig* 44:324+ N '87

Chatham (Mass.)

The case of Cape Cod [beach erosion] B. Sargent. *Oceans* 20:47 Mr/Ap '87

Chatham (Mass.)—*cont.*
Swept away at Chatham [breach in sand barrier at Nauset Beach] D. Thompson. il *Time* 130:43 Ag 10 '87

Chattanooga (Tenn.)
Architecture
New house over old foundation. il *South Living* 22:180-1 Ap '87
City planning
Chugging toward the future. Chattanooga contemplates a downtown revival. P. M. Sachner. il *Archit Rec* 175:53 Mr '87
Festivals
Chattanooga remembers the river [Riverbend Festival] C. Griffith. il *South Living* 22:10-11 Je '87

Chatto, Virago, Bodley Head & Jonathan Cape Ltd.
CVBC executives hail Random House takeover. V. Menkes. *Publ Wkly* 231:21 My 22 '87
Random House to acquire Chatto, Virago, Bodley and Cape group. *Publ Wkly* 231:114 My 15 '87
Virago Press completes buyout from Random House's CBC Group. il *Publ Wkly* 232:310 Ag 7 '87
Virago quits Chatto consortium as Graham Greene enters fray [management buyout of Virago Press] V. Menkes. *Publ Wkly* 231:20 Ap 17 '87

Chatwal, Sant Singh
about
Adding spice to the food chain. G. G. Marcial. *Bus Week* p113 My 4 '87
"Inner patience". P. Gupte. por *Forbes* 139:74-5 Ja 26 '87

Chatwin, Bruce
The Lizard Man. il *N Y Rev Books* 34:47-8 Ag 13 '87
A tower in Tuscany. il *House Gard* 159:78-85+ Ja '87
about
A nomadic heart. E. White. por *Vogue* 177:190+ Ag '87
PW interviews. M. Field. por *Publ Wkly* 232:430-1 Ag 7 '87

Chaudhari, P., and others
The microstructure of high-critical current superconducting films. bibl f il *Science* 238:342-4 O 16 '87

Chaume, Jacqueline Thion de la
about
Allure in the grand manner. J. Kornbluth. il por *House Gard* 159:152-9+ D '87

Chautauqua County (N.Y.)
Description and travel
New York's Chautauqua County. J. Hope. il map *Mother Earth News* 108:48-55 N/D '87

Chautauqua Opera
Chautauqua. E. T. Glasow. *Opera News* 52:55-6 N '87

Chavchavadze, Ilya, 1837-1907
about
The poetry of Ilya Chavchavadze. G. Bouatchidzé and E. Glissant. il *Courier* 40:31-2 O '87

Chaves, Judy
Using the old bean. il *Saturday Evening Post* 259:82+ Mr '87

Chávez, Julio César
about
Too good for his own good. P. Putnam. il pors *Sports Illus* 67:89-90 N 30 '87

Chavez, Linda
The next underclass? *New Repub* 197:12-13 Ag 3 '87

Chavis, Benjamin F., 1948-
Stop the torture! por *Essence* 18:146 O '87

Chavooshian, Nora
about
Matewan: Nora Chavooshian creates major miners. R. Seidenberg. il *Theatre Crafts* 21:45-8 Ap '87

Cheating in school work
The cheating industry [services selling term papers to lazy students] D. K. Mano. *Natl Rev* 39:50+ Je 5 '87
Cheating: what's the catch? il *Teen* 31:28+ Ja '87
Elementary school dilemma: cheating or helping? H. L. Miller. *Educ Dig* 52:40-1 Ap '87

Check clearing *See* Banks and banking—Float
Check-offs, Promotion (Meat industry) *See* Meat industry—Advertising
Checkerboard Press
Checkerboard Press: a backlist with a new identity. il *Publ Wkly* 231:30 Ap 24 '87

Checkers (Game)
Tournaments
Checker king 'Two-Ton' Tinsley jumps for joy—and victory [World Championship] A. Richman. il pors *People Wkly* 28:53+ S 7 '87

Checks
See also
Clearinghouse (Banking)
Telecredit, Inc.
Checks, Fraudulent
Less bounce in your checks [Federal Reserve's second chance check clearing plan] il *Consum Rep* 52:593 O '87
Checks and balances (Government) *See* Separation of powers
Checkups, Medical *See* Physical examinations
Cheek, James R.
about
A hospital 'savior' goes on the critical list. D. Foust. il por *Bus Week* p58 S 7 '87
Cheek, Leane B.
Easing the burden on Alzheimer's families. il *Aging* no355:16-19 '87
Cheerleaders *See* Cheerleading
Cheerleading
Cheer, but don't jump [restrictions at the University of Michigan] S. Stone. il *Women's Sports Fitness* 9:51 Je '87
Is cheerleading getting too dangerous? A. Frankel. il *Seventeen* 46:56+ S '87
Let's make cheerleading a sport. M. Marcaccini. il *Women's Sports Fitness* 9:78 My '87
Thirty-fourth winter. C. F. Wall. il *South Living* 22:80 Ja '87
Cheers, D. Michael
Bernard P. Randolph: the armed forces' only black four-star general. il pors *Ebony* 43:154+ N '87
TransAfrica: the black world's voice on Capitol Hill. il pors *Ebony* 42:108+ Jl '87
Cheers *See* Cheerleading
Cheese
See also
Cooking—Cheese
Cheese invites a party. S. Dosier. il *South Living* 22:124-6 Mr '87
Cheese served with flair. S. Payne. il *South Living* 22:118-19 My '87
Cheeses of America. K. Haedrich. il *Ctry J* 14:22-5 Mr '87
The cream of the crop [raw milk cheese and Devonshire, or clotted, cream] R. Sokolov. il *Nat Hist* 96:80+ D '87
Of curds and whey: do some cheeses taste better if they start out as raw milk? R. Sokolov. il *Nat Hist* 96:80+ Jl '87
Cheese bread *See* Bread
Cheese industry
Cheeses of America. K. Haedrich. il *Ctry J* 14:22-5 Mr '87
Italy
Cheesemaking in Parma. F. Ferretti. il *Gourmet* 47:74-9+ O '87
Cheese soufflés *See* Soufflés
Cheese soups *See* Soups
Cheese spreads *See* Spreads (Food)
Cheese stores *See* Food stores
Cheese tarts *See* Tarts
Cheesecake
Easy strawberry-apricot cheesecake [excerpt from Sarah Leah Chase's Open house cookbook] S. L. Chase. il *Redbook* 169:22 S '87
Teen-ager's dream cake [chocolate cooky cheesecake] il *Sunset* 178:180 My '87
Cheetahs
Bottlenecked cheetahs [research by Stephen O'Brien and others] R. Lewin. il *Science* 235:1327 Mr 13 '87
Two bottlenecks for cheetahs? *Sci News* 131:88 F 7 '87
Why isn't a leopard more like a lion? [research by Tim Caro] R. Lewin. il *Science* 236:777 My 15 '87
Photographs and photography
Cheated cheetah. J. P. Rood. il *Nat Hist* 96:42-3 D '87
Cheever, John, 1912-1982
The angel of the bridge [story] il *Read Dig* 130:99-103 Ap '87
Cheever, Susan
Central Park Zoo. il *N Y* 20:69 D 21-28 '87
Chefs *See* Cooks
Chelimsky, Eleanor
The politics of program evaluation. *Society* 25:24-32 N/D '87
Chellam, Raju
The computerization of India. il *World Press Rev* 34:52 F '87

Chelminski, Rudolph
Learning one's letters from Mme. la Comtesse. il *Smithsonian* 18:212 D '87
Chelsea, Andy
about
A girl's anger rouses her kinfolk from an alcoholic daze. M. Green. il pors *People Wkly* 27:83-4 Ja 26 '87
Chelsea, Phyllis
about
A girl's anger rouses her kinfolk from an alcoholic daze. M. Green. il pors *People Wkly* 27:83-4 Ja 26 '87
Chelsea (London, England)
Historic houses, sites, etc.
Country house in town: a designer's residence on the Thames [Lindsey House, home of J. Stefanidis] E. Lambert. il por *Archit Dig* 44:110-17+ My '87
Chelsea Flower Show *See* Flower exhibits
Chelsea pottery *See* Pottery, English
Chemical additives in food *See* Food additives
Chemical and biological weapons
See also
Convention on the Prohibition of the Development, Production and Stockpiling of Bacteriological (Biological) and Toxin Weapons and on Their Destruction (1972)
Bees did it [yellow rain story] R. Bazell. *New Repub* 196:9-10 F 2 '87
Biological research and military funding. S. Shulman. il *Technol Rev* 90:13-14 Ap '87
The birth of the U.S. biological-warfare program. B. J. Bernstein. bibl (p136) il *Sci Am* 256:116-21 Je '87
Churchill's anthrax bombs: a debate [discussion of January/February 1987 article, Churchill's secret biological weapons] B. J. Bernstein. *Bull At Sci* 43:42-5 N '87
Churchill's secret biological weapons [World War II British plans to use biological warfare] B. J. Bernstein. bibl f *Bull At Sci* 43:46-50 Ja/F '87
Funding for biological weapons research grows amidst controversy. S. Shulman. il *BioScience* 37:372-5 Je '87
Germ warfare. *Sci Am* 256:62 Ap '87
Is the Pentagon preparing for biotech warfare? R. Rhein, Jr. and M. Bluestone. il *Bus Week* p66-7 Ag 10 '87
New designs for biological weapons. S. Wright. bibl f *Bull At Sci* 43:43-6 Ja/F '87
A plague of 'hellish poison'. M. Satchell. il *U S News World Rep* 103:30+ O 26 '87
Poisons from the Pentagon [increase in funding for biological warfare research; cover story] S. Shulman. il *Progressive* 51:16-19 N '87
Security Council members condemn use of chemical weapons in Iran-Iraq conflict. *UN Chron* 24:33-4 Ag '87
The University of Wisconsin hatches toxins [biological warfare research] R. Jannaccio. il *Progressive* 51:20 N '87
Yellow rain: the story collapses. J. Robinson and others. bibl f *Foreign Policy* 68:100-17 Fall '87
Disarmament
See Disarmament
Disposal
Doing the nerve gas shuffle [Army stockpiles] S. Zakin. il *Sierra* 72:26+ Jl/Ag '87
Export-import trade
Export controls imposed on chemical weapons substances [State Dept. statement, July 31, 1987] *Dep State Bull* 87:49 O '87
Testing
Biological warfare research under fire [DOD held accountable for environmental impact] D. D. Edwards. *Sci News* 131:132 F 28 '87
DOD to reassess bioweapons' risks. M. Crawford. *Science* 235:968 F 27 '87
Fighting biological weapons research in the courts [suit to bar Defense Department from building a testing facility at Dugway Proving Grounds in Utah] *Bull At Sci* 43:45 Ja/F '87
Chemical Bank
Chemical Bank finds a home in real estate. S. Bartlett. il *Bus Week* p89 Je 15 '87
Chemical bonds
See also
Binding sites (Biochemistry)
Does ammonia hydrogen bond? D. D. Nelson, Jr. and others. bibl f il *Science* 238:1670-4 D 18 '87
Going for a molecular spin [electron stimulated desorption ion angular distribution method of probing structure and bonding at surfaces] S. Weisburd. il *Sci News* 132:199 S 26 '87

Icosahedral boron-rich solids. D. Emin. bibl f il *Phys Today* 40:55-62 Ja '87
Monitoring biosynthesis of wheat cell-wall phenylpropanoids in situ. N. G. Lewis and others. bibl f il *Science* 237:1344-6 S 11 '87
Partners for a noble element [helium; work of Gernot Frenking and others] *Sci News* 132:334 N 21 '87
The resonating valence bond state in La_2CuO_4 and superconductivity. P. W. Anderson. bibl f il *Science* 235:1196-8 Mr 6 '87
Chemical elements
See also
Beryllium
Carbon
Helium
Hydrogen
Isotopes
Nitrogen
Nucleosynthesis
Oxygen
Periodic law
Selenium
Transuranium elements
Uranium
Ytterbium
Yttrium
Chemical equipment
See also
Spectrometers
Chemical factories *See* Chemical plants
Chemical industries
See also
American Cyanamid Co.
Aristech Chemical Corporation
Chemical plants
Diamond Shamrock Corp.
Dow Chemical Co.
E. I. Du Pont de Nemours
Ethyl Corp.
Fertilizer industry
GAF Corp.
H.B. Fuller Company
Monsanto Company
Morton Thiokol, Inc.
National Distillers & Chemical Corp.
Petrochemical industry
Union Carbide Corp.
Vista Chemical Company
Acquisitions and mergers
Cornering Borg-Warner [GAF's offer] J. E. Ellis. il por *Bus Week* p39 Ap 13 '87
Will GAF cash in its Borg-Warner chips—or up the ante? [leveraged buyout led by Merrill Lynch] J. E. Ellis. *Bus Week* p34-5 Ap 27 '87
International aspects
Union Carbide sold to Rhone-Poulenc. *Success Farm* 85 no2:18T Ja '87
Finance
Chemicals. R. Simon. il *Forbes* 139:93+ Ja 12 '87
Rediscovering the formula for profits. J. H. Cutaia. il *Bus Week* p72 Ja 12 '87
Laws and regulations
See Chemicals—Laws and regulations
Management
Chemicals: an industry sheds its smokestack image. M. J. Bennett and C. H. Kline. il *Technol Rev* 90:36-45 Jl '87
Public relations
Dow and South Africa [address, April 11, 1987] R. K. Long. *Vital Speeches Day* 53:520-4 Je 15 '87
The public face of the chemical industry [Canada; address, November 11, 1986] J. M. Hay. *Vital Speeches Day* 53:178-80 Ja 1 '87
Securities
Lukewarm love. S. Lee. il *Forbes* 140:132 D 28 '87
Suits and claims
In Illinois: the longest jury trial drones on [Kemner et al. v. Monsanto] L. Griggs. il *Time* 129:1 Mr 23 '87
Never to be accused of rushing to judgment, a jury goes home after a trying 44 months [Monsanto dioxin-spill suit] M. Green. il *People Wkly* 28:48-50 N 9 '87
A piece of the action [Agent Orange litigation and lawyer compensation] D. Fanning. il *Forbes* 140:68 O 19 '87
Canada
The public face of the chemical industry [address, November 11, 1986] J. M. Hay. *Vital Speeches Day* 53:178-80 Ja 1 '87

Chemical industries—cont.
France
See also
Rhone-Poulenc SA
Germany (West)
See also
BASF AG
Bayer AG
Hoechst AG
Great Britain
See also
Imperial Chemical Industries plc
Japan
See also
Tateho Chemical Industries Co. Ltd.
Chemical lasers See Lasers
Chemical plants
Accidents and explosions
See also
Bhopal poisonous gas disaster, India, 1984
Rhine River chemical spills, 1986
Environmental aspects
See also
Love Canal case
Chemical cleanup [EPA cleanup at closed facilities of Arkansas Chemical Co. in Newark, N.J.] B. Weber. il *N Y Times Mag* p42 D 27 '87
A grassroots rebuff for Du Pont [proposed plant near Lukang, Taiwan] J. Hamilton. il *Sierra* 72:68-9 My/Je '87
Chemical pollution See Pollution
Chemical pollution of the air See Air pollution
Chemical reactions
See also
Acylation
Alkylation
Browning
Catalysts and catalysis
Hydrolysis
Methylation
Oxidation
Phosphorylation
Electron tunneling paths in proteins. A. Kuki and P. G. Wolynes. bibl f il *Science* 236:1647-52 Je 26 '87
Herschbach, Lee and Polanyi receive 1986 Chemistry Nobel. P. H. Andersen. il pors *Phys Today* 40:17-20 Mr '87
Molecular beam studies of elementary chemical processes [adaptation of Nobel Prize address, December 8, 1986] Y. T. Lee. bibl f il *Science* 236:793-8 My 15 '87
Molecular dynamics of a cytochrome c-cytochrome b$_5$ electron transfer complex. J. J. Wendoloski and others. bibl f il *Science* 238:794-7 N 6 '87
A new window onto the chemists' big bang [work of Ahmed H. Zewail and others] R. Lewin. il *Science* 238:1512-13 D 11 '87
'Snapshots' of bond breaking and making [work of Ahmed H. Zewail and others] S. Weisburd. *Sci News* 132:372 D 12 '87
Some concepts in reaction dynamics [adaptation of Nobel Prize address, December 8, 1986] J. C. Polanyi. bibl f il *Science* 236:680-90 My 8 '87
Chemical research
See also
Gordon Research Conferences
Chemical synthesis See Synthesis
Chemical warfare
See also
Chemical and biological weapons
Chemical waste disposal See Hazardous substances—Disposal; Trade waste—Disposal
Chemical wastes See Trade waste
Chemicals
See also
Agricultural chemicals
Pesticides
Laboratory chemicals. *Science* 235 pt2:G104-G106+ F 27 '87
Biodegradation
See Biodegradation
Laws and regulations
See also
Pesticides—Laws and regulations
California's debate on carcinogens [Proposition 65] E. Marshall. *Science* 235:1459 Mr 20 '87
California's Proposition 65 [Safe Drinking Water and Toxic Enforcement Act] P. H. Abelson. *Science* 237:1553 S 25 '87
New Jersey's Bhopal bill [Toxic Catastrophe Prevention Act] *Environment* 29:30 Jl/Ag '87

Physiological effects
Cancer phobia. P. H. Abelson. *Science* 237:473 Jl 31 '87
Chemical carcinogenesis [discussion of July 31, 1987 article, Cancer phobia] P. H. Abelson. *Science* 238:259-60 O 16 '87
Impact of chemicals. S. M. Sims. il *Vogue* 177:158-9+ Ja '87
Kids' leukemia from parents' exposures? J. Raloff. *Sci News* 132:38-9 Jl 18 '87
Chemistry
See also
Astrochemistry
Catalysts and catalysis
Combustion
Computers—Chemical use
Conjugation (Chemistry)
Diffusion
Electrochemistry
Immunochemistry
Lasers—Chemical use
Magnetic resonance imaging—Chemical use
Microchemistry
Nuclear chemistry
Photographic chemistry
Polymers and polymerization
Radicals (Chemistry)
Ultrasonic waves—Chemical use
Chemistry, Analytic
See also
Chromatographic analysis
Isoelectric focusing
Lasers—Chemical use
Metallurgy
Proteins—Analysis
Spectrum analysis
Water—Analysis
Chemistry, Organic
See also
Aromatic compounds
Enzymes
Synthesis
Chemistry, Physical and theoretical
See also
Colloids
Crystallization
Free energy
Periodic law
Solution (Chemistry)
Surface chemistry
Thermodynamics
Chemical physics. *Phys Today* 40:S11-S14 Ja '87
Chemists
See also
Women chemists
Chemoreceptors
See also
Drug receptors
Hormone receptors
Blockade of "NMDA" receptors disrupts experience-dependent plasticity of kitten striate cortex. A. Kleinschmidt and others. bibl f il *Science* 238:355-8 O 16 '87
Cloning, sequencing, and expression of the gene coding for the human platelet α_2-adrenergic receptor. B. K. Kobilka and others. bibl f il *Science* 238:650-6 O 30 '87
D$_1$ dopamine receptor activation required for postsynaptic expression of D$_2$ agonist effects. J. R. Walters and others. bibl f il *Science* 236:719-22 My 8 '87
Genetic reconstitution of functional acetylcholine receptor channels in mouse fibroblasts. T. Claudio and others. bibl f il *Science* 238:1688-94 D 18 '87
Histamine receptors found. *Sci News* 131:311 My 16 '87
Identification of a family of muscarinic acetylcholine receptor genes. T. I. Bonner and others. bibl f il *Science* 237:527-32 Jl 31 '87
An M2 muscarinic receptor subtype coupled to both adenylyl cyclase and phosphoinositide turnover. A. Ashkenazi and others. bibl f il *Science* 238:672-5 O 30 '87
Mapping the main immunogenic region and toxin-binding site of the nicotinic acetylcholine receptor. T. Barkas and others. bibl f il *Science* 235:77-80 Ja 2 '87
Molecular cloning of complementary DNA encoding the avian receptor for vitamin D. D. P. McDonnell and others. bibl f il *Science* 235:1214-17 Mr 6 '87
Peptide turn-on for the ACh receptor gene [research by Jean-Pierre Changeux and others] D. M. Barnes. *Science* 238:1652-3 D 18 '87

Chemoreceptors—*cont.*
Primary structure and biochemical properties of an M_2 muscarinic receptor. E. G. Peralta and others. bibl f il *Science* 236:600-5 My 1 '87
Rat brain N-methyl-D-aspartate receptors expressed in Xenopus oocytes. T. A. Verdoorn and others. bibl f il *Science* 238:1114-16 N 20 '87
Receptor families reunited [neurotransmitters] *Sci News* 132:37 Jl 18 '87
Receptors highlighted at NIH symposium [special section] J. L. Marx. il *Science* 238:615-616 O 30 '87

Chemotaxis
Cytosolic acidification as an early transductory signal of human neutrophil chemotaxis. I. Yuli and A. Oplatka. bibl f il *Science* 235:340-2 Ja 16 '87

Chemotherapy
See also
Breast—Cancer—Therapy
Cancer—Therapy
Cancer inhibiting substances
Psychopharmacology
Viruses—Inactivation

Chen, Chi-Hong B., and Sigman, David S.
Chemical conversion of a DNA-binding protein into a site-specific nuclease. bibl f il *Science* 237:1197-1201 S 4 '87

Chen, Chi-t'ung, 1851-1909
A Chinese general in Paris. il *Courier* 40:31 Ap '87

Chen, Joan
about
What you see of Joan Chen in Tai-Pan hardly tells the tale. E. Miller. por *Seventeen* 46:68 Ja '87

Chen, Kuan-I
China's food policy and population. bibl f *Curr Hist* 86:257-60+ S '87

Chen, San-Hwan, and others
Apolipoprotein B-48 is the product of a messenger RNA with an organ-specific in-frame stop codon. bibl f il *Science* 238:363-6 O 16 '87

Chen, Steve
about
Cray supercomputer axed, superstar departs. M. M. Waldrop. il por *Science* 237:1558-9 S 25 '87

Chen, T. C.
about
T.C. conquers L.A. in O.T. R. Reilly. il por *Sports Illus* 66:22-4+ Mr 2 '87

Chen Chong *See* Chen, Joan
Chen Jitong *See* Chen, Chi-t'ung, 1851-1909

Cheney, Dodo
about
Dorothy Cheney, 71. M. Kort. il por *Women's Sports Fitness* 9:20-1 O '87

Cheng, Chu-yüan
China's economy at the crossroads. bibl f *Curr Hist* 86:253-6+ S '87

Cheng, Nien, 1915-
Life and death in Shanghai [excerpts; cover story] il por *Time* 129:42-8+ Je 8 '87
about
Surviving the hurricane. J. Shapiro. il *N Y Rev Books* 34:5-6+ Jl 16 '87
The Year of the Setback? H. Smith. *Christ Today* 31:13 Ag 7 '87

Cheng, Yang-Tse, and Johnson, William L.
Disordered materials: a survey of amorphous solids. bibl f il *Science* 235:997-1002 F 27 '87

Chepesiuk, Ron
The angel of death row. por *Progressive* 51:14 My '87

Cher, 1946-
about
Cher. il por *People Wkly* 28:48-9 D 28 '87-Ja 4 '88
Cher: sensual, sensitive, seductive, sensational. B. Lovenheim. il pors *McCalls* 115:172-6 O '87
Cher's next act. B. Weber. il pors *N Y Times Mag* p42-4+ O 18 '87
The many faces of Cher. J. Wolf. pors *Ladies Home J* 104:36+ Ag '87
The many faces of Cher [cover story] C. Leerhsen. il pors *Newsweek* 110:66-9+ N 30 '87

Cherches, Peter
Reading comprehension [excerpt from Condensed book] *Harpers* 274:28+ Mr '87

Cherico, Tony
about
C'mon, Tony, lighten up. R. Telander. il pors *Sports Illus* 67:58-60+ N 2 '87

Cherimoya
See also
Cooking—Fruit

Chernobyl (Ukraine)
See also
Chernobyl nuclear disaster, 1986

Chernobyl nuclear disaster, 1986
After Chernobyl: where do we go from here? C. Reed. il *USA Today (Periodical)* 116:48-51 N '87
Bone marrow transplants: from Chernobyl to cancer therapy. M. J. Fromer. il *FDA Consum* 21:12-15 Ap '87
Can Chernobyl happen here? [comparison to Three Mile Island]; ed. by Mary Hopkins. M. Copulos. il *Consum Res Mag* 70:35-7 Ja '87
Chernobyl: a radiobiological perspective. M. Goldman. bibl f *Science* 238:622-3 O 30 '87
The Chernobyl disaster. D. R. Marples. bibl f *Curr Hist* 86:325-8+ O '87
Chernobyl public health effects [discussion of June 26, 1987 article, A visit to Chernobyl] R. Wilson. *Science* 238:10-11 O 2 '87
Chernobyl: the lessons the Soviets learned. J. Trimble. il *U S News World Rep* 103:14 Jl 20 '87
Chernobyl: what happened? D. Schoonmaker. il *Mother Earth News* 105:96-8 My/Je '87
Chernobyl—one year after. M. Edwards. il map *Natl Geogr* 171:632-53 My '87
Chernobyl's high cost [interview with R. Gale] J. Bennett. il por *Macleans* 100:6-8 Jl 6 '87
Deadly winds: one year after Chernobyl. L. Elliott. il *Read Dig* 130:129-33 My '87
An eyewitness to disaster, Soviet fireman Leonid Telyatnikov recounts the horror of Chernobyl. D. Grogan. il por *People Wkly* 28:57-8+ O 5 '87
The future of nuclear power: seeking new energy sources. C. Flavin. *Current* 298:24-9 D '87
Hard rain falls on Yugoslavia. S. Drakulich. il *Nation* 244:177-8+ F 14 '87
Ice traces of catastrophe: Chernobyl . . . and the ancient volcano Thera. *Sci News* 132:121 Ag 22 '87
In Chernobyl's grim shadow. S. Strasser. il *Newsweek* 109:38 Je 29 '87
Interview [R. Gale] M. C. Smith. il pors *Omni* 10:110-12+ O '87
Judgment at Chernobyl [trial of nuclear plant officials] J. Greenwald. il *Time* 130:44-5 Jl 20 '87
Lapp life after Chernobyl. S. Stephens. il map *Nat Hist* 96:32-41 D '87
The legacies of two disasters. il *World Press Rev* 34:55-6 Mr '87
The legacy of Chernobyl: disaster for the Lapps [reindeer meat contamination] R. Knight. il map *U S News World Rep* 102:36 Mr 23 '87
The lessons of Chernobyl. S. Begley. il map *Newsweek* 109:56-7 Ap 27 '87
Living with fallout [effect on Italy] M. J. Salter. il *Atlantic* 259:30-2+ Ja '87
A neglected lesson of the Chernobyl disaster [relationship to effects of a nuclear war] R. E. Powaski. *America* 156:167-8 F 28 '87
Nuclear power after Chernobyl [comparison to Three Mile Island] J. F. Ahearne. bibl f il *Science* 236:673-9 My 8 '87
Nuclear power's burdened future. C. Flavin. bibl f il *Bull At Sci* 43:26-31 Jl/Ag '87
Nuclear power's Faustian bargain. E. V. Kohák. *Harpers* 274:15-16+ My '87
Radioactive cesium from the Chernobyl accident in the Greenland ice sheet. C. I. Davidson and others. bibl f maps *Science* 237:633-4 Ag 7 '87
Recalculating the cost of Chernobyl [anticipated cancer deaths; report by the Dept. of Energy] E. Marshall. il *Science* 236:658-9 My 8 '87
Revising the nuclear dream. C. Flavin. il *USA Today (Periodical)* 116:60-2 Jl '87
A Soviet expert discusses Chernobyl [interview with V. Legasov] N. Vikhlyayev. il por *Bull At Sci* 43:32-4 Jl/Ag '87
Ten years in stir for Chernobyl's scapegoats. *Newsweek* 110:47 Ag 10 '87
A visit to Chernobyl. R. Wilson. bibl f *Science* 236:1636-40 Je 26 '87
World enough & time. *Commonweal* 114:227-8 Ap 24 '87

Economic aspects
West Germany pours hot milk [disposition of milk contaminated by Chernobyl] D. Egger. il *Nation* 244:392-4+ Mr 28 '87

Personal narratives
Life after Chernobyl. J. Forssell and E. Forssell. il pors *Mother Earth News* 105:94-8+ My/Je '87

Chernyshov, Mikhail
Cosmonautics: investments begin to pay off. il *Space World* X-10-286:24-7 O '87

Cherokee Group
Smoke signals? T. Jaffe. *Forbes* 139:267 My 18 '87

Cherpak, Evelyn M.
Devoted wives, determined rebels. il *Américas* 39:32-7 Mr/Ap '87

Cherry, Carol D.
about
The spy who came in from the cold cuts. P. Finch. il por *Bus Week* p101 Jl 20 '87

Cherry, Kelly
Almost the real thing [story] il *Mademoiselle* 93:127-30+ O '87
Alzheimer's [story] *Commentary* 83:50-5 Je '87
More precious than gold [story] il *Redbook* 170:49-51 D '87
The violin of his mind [story] il *Read Dig* 131:172-6 O '87

Cherry, Laurence
The contraceptive crisis. il *Glamour* 85:278-81+ My '87
My father's last year. il *Glamour* 85:300-1+ O '87

Cherry desserts *See* Desserts

Cherry Hill (N.J.)
Gardens and gardening
Gathering moss [J. Biesenkamp's garden] K. Whiteside. il *House Gard* 159:144-9+ My '87

Cherry trees
Bird cherries [excerpt from The country journal book of hardy trees and shrubs] H. L. Flint. il *Ctry J* 14:6-7 Ag '87

Chérubin [opera] *See* Massenet, Jules, 1842-1912

Chesapeake Bay (Md. and Va.)
EMP: fallout over a naval EMPRESS [Navy proposal for electromagnetic pulse simulator] J. Raloff. *Sci News* 131:182 Mr 21 '87
Hope for blighted bays: the reduction of nitrogen inflow may benefit coastal waters. T. Beardsley. *Sci Am* 257:26-7+ N '87
Nutrient enrichment of the Chesapeake Bay [cover story; with editorial comment by Alan McGowan and Abel Wolman] C. F. D'Elia. bibl f il map *Environment* 29:inside cover, 2-3, 6-11+ Mr '87
We all live downstream. F. L. Schultz. il *Ctry J* 14:10-11 Jl '87

Chesapeake Bay retrievers *See* Retrievers

Chesley, Robert, 1943-
about
Jerker [drama] Reviews
Nation 244:656+ My 16 '87. T. M. Disch

Chess
See also
Computer chess
Duel of two minds [G. Kasparov vs. A. Karpov for world title] F. Lidz. il pors *Sports Illus* 67:60-3 D 7 '87
Grand mastery [G. Kasparov defeats A. Karpov] *Newsweek* 110:29 D 28 '87
K.K. Karanja: young chess champ on a mission. U. J. Rivers. il pors *Ebony* 42:54+ F '87
Nurtured to be geniuses, Hungary's Polgar sisters put winning moves on chess masters. il *People Wkly* 27:65 My 4 '87
Paul Morphy: the pride and sorrow of chess. B. McGinty. por *Am Hist Illus* 22:50-1 Mr '87
Virtuoso performance in Seville [G. Kasparov retains title] J. D. Reed. il pors *Time* 130:70 D 28 '87
Psychological aspects
A chess player realizes the game controls his life. P. Hoffman. bibl (p147) il *Smithsonian* 18:129-30+ Jl '87
In your face, mate. J. Mostel. il *Esquire* 108:42 N '87

Chess [musical] *See* Musicals, revues, etc.—Reviews—Single works

Chester (Neb.)
Little Boy Blue of Chester, Nebraska [child found dead by roadside] H. Hurt. *Read Dig* 131:73-8 D '87

Chester County Historical Society
Furniture in Pennsylvania [Two hundred years of chairs and chairmaking in the collection of the Chester County Historical Society] S. B. Sherrill. il *Antiques* 132:52+ Jl '87

Chestnut blight
Fighting fungi with fungi. J. A. Miller. il *BioScience* 37:248-50 Ap '87

Chestnut trees
Diseases and pests
See also
Chestnut blight

Chests
See also
Toy chests
Chest full of pride [blanket chest] H. Wicks. il *Home Mech* 83:90-2+ O '87
A chest is a good first choice. il *South Living* 22:192+ Ap '87
Chippendale chest [kit] A. Rooze. il *Fam Handyman* 37:48-9 Ap '87
Country cupboard [linen chests] A. Capotosto. il *Pop Mech* 164:90-4 F '87
Fake right, go left [built-in corner dresser] il *Sunset* 178:140 My '87
How effective are cedar chests and closets? il *Workbench* 43:22 N/D '87
Pine dresser you build from plans [Shaker dresser] il *Home Mech* 83:84 F '87

Chetirkin, Peter V.
Valonia. il *Sea Front* 33:256-8 Jl/Ag '87

Chetwynd, Lionel
about
The Hanoi Hilton [film] Reviews
Macleans 100:57 My 11 '87. L. O'Toole
N Y il 20:90-1 Ap 13 '87. D. Denby
New Repub 196:26-7 Ap 27 '87. S. Kauffmann
People Wkly il 27:14 Ap 20 '87. R. Novak
Time il 129:78 Ap 13 '87. R. Schickel

Cheval mirrors *See* Mirrors

Chevannes, Paul, and Garrard, Leslie
Cross-cultural covers. il *Publ Wkly* 232:37-40 N 27 '87

Chevrolet Motor Division
GM's future may ride on two new Chevys [Beretta and Corsica] W. Zellner. il *Bus Week* p41 Ap 6 '87
Miscellaneous ramblings. J. Dinkel. il *Road Track* 38:33 My '87
The new Chevys aren't driving away with the market. W. Zellner. il *Bus Week* p34-5 Je 15 '87
Revealed! '90 Chevrolet GM 10. D. C. Ross. il *Mot Trend* 39:28-9 N '87
Those heartbeat ads are a hit in the heartland. C. Dugas. il *Bus Week* p107 F 23 '87

Chevron Chemical Company. Ortho Book Division *See* Ortho Books

Chevron Corporation
The competitiveness problem [address, September 14, 1987] G. M. Keller. *Vital Speeches Day* 54:61-4 N 1 '87
Most improved. il *Forbes* 139:199 Ja 12 '87
Still smiling over Gulf [G. M. Keller] B. O'Reilly. il por *Fortune* 116:40-1 Ag 3 '87

Chewing gum
The best bet yet for worried smokers [excerpt from The smoker's book of health] T. Ferguson. il *Prevention* 39:74-80 Je '87
Chewing away cavities [use of xylitol gum; research by Kauko Makinen] *Prevention* 39:15 S '87
Does sugarless gum really prevent cavities? il *Parents* 62:27 N '87
Pushing the panic button [nicotine chewing gum] P. SerVaas. il *Saturday Evening Post* 259:14+ Mr '87

Chewing tobacco
Now it's tobacco "gum". L. J. Brown. il *Good Housekeep* 205:251 O '87

Chez Louis (New York, N.Y.: Restaurant) *See* New York (N.Y.)—Restaurants, nightclubs, bars, etc.

Chez TJ (Mountain View, Calif.: Restaurant) *See* Mountain View (Calif.)—Restaurants, nightclubs, bars, etc.

Chiang, Antonio
about
A new voice is heard [interview] D. R. Shanor. il por *World Press Rev* 34:21 N '87

Chiang, Kai-shek, 1887-1975
about
The Xi'an Incident. J. Crossland. bibl il pors *Hist Today* 37:10-16 Jl '87

Chianti (Wine) *See* Wine

Chiat/Day Inc. Advertising
Shoot-out in Los Angeles: how Chiat/Day captured Nissan. J. Flynn and R. Grover. il *Bus Week* p70-1 Ag 17 '87

Chicago (Ill.)
Airports
General aviation fights Midway fee hike. *Aviat Week Space Technol* 127:52 O 26 '87
Lighting the way [lighting at United Airlines Terminal at O'Hare Airport] S. R. Shemitz. il *Archit Rec* 175:148-55 N '87
NTSB cites erroneous transponder code in near collision [two American Airlines Boeing 727s near O'Hare International Airport] *Aviat Week Space Technol* 126:82 Je 15 '87

Chicago (Ill.)—Airports—cont.

The temple of marketing [H. Jahn's United Airlines terminal at O'Hare Airport] H. Muschamp. il *New Repub* 197:25-8 O 26 '87

Top two U.S. airports headed by black execs [E. Hord of O'Hare] pors *Jet* 72:8 Je 22 '87

Architecture

Report from Paris: no small plans [exhibit entitled Chicago architecture, 1872-1922 at the Musée d'Orsay] K. D. Stein. il *Archit Rec* 175:69 N '87

Art

See also
　Chicago (Ill.)—Monuments, statues, etc.

Chicago's art explosion. L. Nilson. il *Art News* 86:110-19 My '87

Medium cool: new Chicago abstraction [The non-spiritual in art: abstract painting 1985-????] M. Bonesteel. il *Art Am* 75:138-47 D '87

Banks

See also
　Continental Illinois National Bank & Trust Co. of Chicago
　Exchange National Bank of Chicago
　First National Bank of Chicago

Blacks

Breaking out of the ghetto: the origins of the underclass. N. Lemann. *Current* 289:4-15 Ja '87

Brothers [cover story; special section] il *Newsweek* 109:54-66+ Mr 23 '87

Chicago: the Second City pushes to be no. 1. K. Smikle. il *Black Enterp* 17:60-2 My '87

Bookstores

See Booksellers and bookselling—Illinois

Churches (Buildings)

Blessing in disguise [Grace Place: Grace Episcopal Church and Community Center] il *Archit Rec* 175:94-9 F '87

Crime

See also
　Chicago (Ill.)—Police

Al Capone: Chicago's "untouchable" mobster. por *Am Hist Illus* 22:50-1 O '87

Chicago's modern mob: a home in the suburbs. J. McCormick. il *Newsweek* 109:35 My 11 '87

Woman shoots man during Chicago church service [R. Eaton] *Jet* 72:18 Ag 31 '87

Criminal justice, Administration of

Black Chicagoan awarded $800,000 for false arrest [G. Jones] *Jet* 72:5 Mr 30 '87

Deaf-mute must stay in mental hospital for 1971 slaying in Chicago [case of D. Lang] *Jet* 72:17 Je 8 '87

Investigating Scott Turow [possible obstruction of justice] *Time* 130:73 D 14 '87

White man gets 6 years for arson to blacks' home [K. Falk] *Jet* 72:33 Ap 27 '87

Description

The Magnificent Mile. T. Bross. il *Travel Holiday* 167:10+ Je '87

Education

Atlanta, Chicago schools among the most segregated. *Jet* 72:12 Ag 10 '87

Marva Collins may teach in Chicago and Compton. por *Jet* 72:12 Ag 17 '87

Top-grade perks for teens [program at DuSable High School] M. Oshin. il *Essence* 18:38 Je '87

Up from poverty [M. Burton, teacher and dean at The Harvard School] C. Whitaker. il pors *Ebony* 42:110-11+ Ag '87

Where high school kids learn to think [Pedro Albizu Campos High School] M. Ervin. il *Progressive* 51:11 Je '87

Which system is the worst? [views of W. Bennett] por *Time* 130:69 N 23 '87

Wynton debuts jazz in Chicago classrooms. B. Beuttler. il por *Down Beat* 54:12 Ja '87

Elections

See Chicago (Ill.)—Politics and government

Finance

Sharon Gist Gilliam: the woman in charge of Chicago's $3.8 billion budget. il pors *Ebony* 42:31-2+ Mr '87

Galleries and museums

See also
　Art Institute of Chicago
　Chicago Historical Society
　DuSable Museum of African American History, Inc.
　Hanzel Galleries
　R.H. Love Galleries, Inc.
　Struve Gallery
　Terra Museum of American Art (Chicago, Ill.)

Chicago: a guide to galleries and museums. map *Art Am* 75:68-9 My '87

Historic houses, sites, etc.

Chicago: the giants' footprints. B. Klaw. il *Am Herit* 38:28+ N '87

Hospitals

Chicago girl, 11, wins $6 mil. settlement from hospital [malpractice award to Vernette Eiland by Rush Presbyterian-St. Luke's Hospital] *Jet* 72:18 Mr 30 '87

Hotels, motels, etc.

Sam Cascio, nonagenarian bellhop, refuses to bag it [Chicago Hilton & Towers employee] il por *People Wkly* 28:119 S 21 '87

Monuments, statues, etc.

Picasso gets a hit. J. Yood. il *Art News* 86:16 N '87

Sculpture takes off from O'Hare [disappearance of B. Holden's Kill Devil Hill] S. Taylor. il *Art News* 86:13-14 S '87

Music

See also
　Chicago Opera Theater
　Chicago Symphony Orchestra
　Lyric Opera of Chicago
　Opera—Illinois

The blues: alive and well in Chicago. C. Whitaker. il *Ebony* 42:42+ My '87

Playing the blues, Chicago-style [photographs] M. PoKempner. il *N Y Times Mag* p80-1 Ja 18 '87

Music festivals

See Music festivals—Illinois

Newspapers

See also
　Chicago sun-times (Newspaper)
　Chicago tribune

Photographs and photography

Chicago ascending [then and now photographs] il *Am Herit* 38:118-19 My/Je '87

Police

Chicago mayor names city's second black police chief [L. Martin] il por *Jet* 73:5 N 16 '87

Politics and government

Big shoulders on the lakefront [H. Washington's mayoral primary victory] il por *U S News World Rep* 102:9 Mr 9 '87

Chicago: as durable as Daley? [H. Washington's mayoral victory] J. McCormick. il por *Newsweek* 109:10 Ap 20 '87

Chicago loses its mayor [death of H. Washington] J. McCormick and P. King. il *Newsweek* 110:45 D 7 '87

A Chicago-style power scramble [selection of interim mayor] il *U S News World Rep* 103:14-15 D 7 '87

Chicago: the Second City pushes to be no. 1. K. Smikle. il *Black Enterp* 17:60-2 My '87

Chicago's political circus. J. McCormick. il *Newsweek* 109:29 Ja 5 '87

Chicago's two solitudes [primary race between H. Washington and J. Byrne] I. Austen. il pors *Macleans* 100:16 Mr 2 '87

Eugene Sawyer vows to continue reforms of Mayor Washington. R. E. Johnson. il pors *Jet* 73:4-6+ D 21 '87

From ballads to ballots [J. Butler elected county commissioner] il pors *Ebony* 42:152+ F '87

Harold Washington: Chicago mayor charts new direction for next four years [cover story] R. E. Johnson. il pors *Jet* 72:4-6 My 4 '87

The Iceman cometh back [J. Butler, entertainer and Cook County Commissioner] B. Barol. il pors *Newsweek* 110:65 N 9 '87

In Chicago a machine dies [mayoral race] G. Rivlin. il *Nation* 244:424-6 Ap 4 '87

Jesse Jackson may not have the clout of a kingmaker after all [failure to dictate Harold Washington's successor] R. Fly. il por *Bus Week* p47 D 14 '87

Lakeside follies: a machine-made mayor for Chicago [E. Sawyer] M. Satchell. il por *U S News World Rep* 103:12 D 14 '87

"A loss in the family" [death of Mayor H. Washington] J. E. White. il *Time* 130:27 D 7 '87

The mayor everybody knows [H. Washington] C. Whitaker. il pors *Ebony* 43:78-80+ D '87

Mayor Washington eulogized as symbol of hope for blacks [cover story; special section] il *Jet* 73:4-6+ D 14 '87

Mayor Washington wins historic second term. il pors *Jet* 72:4+ Ap 27 '87

A rematch in the Windy City [mayoral primary] M. Bosc. il pors *U S News World Rep* 102:20 F 23 '87

Shaky start [E. Sawyer appointed interim mayor] por *Time* 130:36 D 14 '87

Chicago (Ill.)—Politics and government—*cont.*
Spoils and spoilers [H. Washington] C. Page. *New Repub* 196:13-15 Mr 2 '87
Uncle Tom Sawyer [Mayor E. Sawyer] G. Rivlin. *Nation* 245:741 D 19 '87
An unsettling victory [new mayor E. Sawyer] J. McCormick. il por *Newsweek* 110:52 D 14 '87
Anecdotes, facetiae, satire, etc.
One man, one vote [J. R. Bilski receives one vote in mayoral primary] M. E. Marty. *Christ Century* 104:319 Ap 1 '87

Poor
The urban homeless: estimating composition and size. P. H. Rossi and others. bibl f il *Science* 235:1336-41 Mr 13 '87

Public buildings
The apotheosis of the atrium [architecture of the State of Illinois Center] M. F. Schmertz. *Archit Rec* 175:9 My '87

Public health
Five-year, $4 million cancer control program set for Chicago blacks. *Jet* 71:24 F 23 '87

Race relations
Delete slave ship from Chicago seal: aldermen. il *Jet* 72:4 S 21 '87
Why be ugly when you can be beautiful [address, December 7, 1986] B. H. Alexander. *Vital Speeches Day* 53:202-4 Ja 15 '87

Religious institutions and affairs
13-year-old conducts wedding like veteran [W. Hudson] il por *Jet* 71:29 Mr 16 '87
13-year-old preacher talks about love, sex, sin and forgiveness [W. Hudson] T. S. Moore. il pors *Jet* 72:14-16 Je 29 '87
In an Eastern Orthodox Chicago church, a weeping Madonna and Child bring throngs to pray and hope for miracles [first sighted by Father P. Koufos at St. Nicholas Church] C. Tamarkin. il *People Wkly* 27:44-5 Ja 19 '87
In Chicago, God's word often comes out of the mouth of a mere babe—the Rev. William Hudson III, 13. D. Grogan. il pors *People Wkly* 28:102+ Ag 24 '87
The Insane Dragons meet the Unknown Vice Lords [Youth for Christ's work with gangs] G. Lewis. il *Christ Today* 31:10+ N 20 '87

Sanitary affairs
Of dumps, Chicago politics & herons [environmentalists fight to save wetlands threatened by landfill] J. Sullivan. il *Audubon* 89:122-6 Mr '87

Social history
The forgotten four hundred: Chicago's first millionaires. B. A. Weisberger. il *Am Herit* 38:34-45 N '87

Stores
See also
Marshall Field & Company

Street traffic
A Chicago sting: CEO scofflaws, beware [company cars ticketed] *Newsweek* 109:52 F 9 '87

Streets
See also
Michigan Avenue (Chicago, Ill.)

Theater
See also
New Regal Theater (Chicago, Ill.)

World's fair, 1893
See World's Columbian Exposition (1893: Chicago, Ill.)

Chicago (Ill.). Post Office
Chicago woman tabbed for top Post Office job [J. Norfleet] por *Jet* 72:18 Ap 6 '87
Janet Norfleet: in charge of the world's largest post office. F. White, III. il pors *Ebony* 42:80+ Jl '87

Chicago Auto Show *See* Automobiles—Exhibitions

Chicago Bar Association
Black attorney in line to head Chicago Bar Assn. [C. L. Blair] por *Jet* 72:29 Ap 13 '87

Chicago Board of Trade
Fast times in the Chicago pits. E. Williams. il *Newsweek* 110:57 S 21 '87
The Japanese are elbowing into Chicago's futures pits. J. N. Frank. il *Bus Week* p106-7 Je 1 '87
Rich list candidate: 1995 [trader T. Baldwin] S. W. Angrist. il *Forbes* 140 Sp Issue:401 O 26 '87
This veteran of the pits still has a soft spot for soybeans [K. Mahlman] M. E. Kreca. il por *Bus Week* p168 D 28 '87-Ja 4 '88

Chicago Board Options Exchange
If you think New York has it bad, take a look at Chicago. M. E. Kreca and J. M. Laderman. il *Bus Week* p132-3 N 30 '87

Tough options: an investor who hedged himself out of a bundle. J. M. Laderman. *Bus Week* p133 N 30 '87

Chicago Historical Society
Bicentennial of the Constitution—Chicago [We the people: creating a new nation, 1765-1820] S. B. Sherrill. il *Antiques* 132:420+ S '87

Chicago Lyric Opera *See* Lyric Opera of Chicago

Chicago Mercantile Exchange
Chicago's traders are trying to be their own best watchdogs. J. N. Frank. il *Bus Week* p38 Mr 2 '87
Escape from New York [trader R. Rowland] J. Clements. il por *Forbes* 140:126 S 7 '87
Fast times in the Chicago pits. E. Williams. il *Newsweek* 110:57 S 21 '87
If you think New York has it bad, take a look at Chicago. M. E. Kreca and J. M. Laderman. il *Bus Week* p132-3 N 30 '87
The Japanese are elbowing into Chicago's futures pits. J. N. Frank. il *Bus Week* p106-7 Je 1 '87
The Merc starts to clean up its pit. J. N. Frank. il *Bus Week* p114+ Mr 16 '87

Chicago Opera Theater
Chicago. J. Von Rhein. *Opera News* 52:48-50 O '87

Chicago Repertory Dance Ensemble
Reviews:
Performances at Somerset County College, N.J. B. F. Fox. *Dance Mag* 61:78-9 F '87

Chicago sun-times (Newspaper)
Dear Ann Landers: anything you can do, I can do better, write 22 dazzled but eager column hopefuls. L. Aitken. il por *People Wkly* 27:42-4+ Ap 20 '87
Defeating 12,000, odd couple Diane Crowley and Jeff Zaslow win Ann Landers' old job. M. Vespa. il pors *People Wkly* 27:49-50 Je 22 '87
Looking for Miss Lonelyhearts [Chicago sun-times holds contest to replace Ann Landers who moved to the Chicago tribune] M. Bosc. il por *U S News World Rep* 102:13 Mr 23 '87
Mr. and Ms. Lonelyhearts [J. Zaslow and D. Crowley replace A. Landers] M. Bosc. il pors *U S News World Rep* 102:12 Je 15 '87

Chicago Symphony Orchestra
The exuberant Solti at 75. A. Rich. il por *Newsweek* 110:93 O 19 '87
Morgan replaces ill Chicago Symphony conductor Solti. por *Jet* 72:38 Je 15 '87

Chicago tribune
The big leak [U.S. war plans against Germany in 1941] T. J. Fleming. il por *Am Herit* 38:64-71 D '87
Looking for Miss Lonelyhearts [Chicago sun-times holds contest to replace Ann Landers who moved to the Chicago tribune] M. Bosc. il por *U S News World Rep* 102:13 Mr 23 '87

Chicanos *See* Mexican Americans

Chichén Itzá (Mexico)
State of Yucatán: Chichén Itzá. F. W. Rosen. il *Saturday Evening Post* 259:69-70 O '87

Chick embryos *See* Embryology—Birds

Chickadees
Chickadee down. P. Schullery. il *Ctry J* 14:78-80 Mr '87
Chickadee—bird for all seasons. H. Middleton. il *South Living* 22:30+ Ja '87

Chicken contamination *See* Poultry contamination

Chicken cooking *See* Cooking—Poultry

Chicken industry *See* Poultry industry

Chicken pox

Vaccines and vaccination
Seeking antibodies against chickenpox. *USA Today (Periodical)* 115:9-10 F '87

Chicken salads *See* Salads

Chickens *See* Poultry

Chico River Dam project (Philippines) *See* Dams—Philippines

Chief executive officers (Corporations) *See* Executives

Chief information officers *See* Information managers

Chief Zabú [film] See Motion picture reviews—Single works

Chieffo, Clifford T., 1937-
Technical page. See issues of American Artist

Chien, Philip
Assembling the space station. il *Space World* X-12-288:16-17+ D '87
Nuclear power: how safe in space? il *Space World* X-9-285:11-13 S '87

Chievous, Derrick
about
Tiger of another stripe. A. Wolff. il pors *Sports Illus* 66:76-81 Ja 12 '87

Chiffon

Chiffon is back as designers unveil a look at sheer heaven. il *People Wkly* 28:180-1 D 14 '87

Child, Sir Josiah, 1630-1699

about

The East India Company and the Emperor Aurangzeb. B. Lenman. bibl il map *Hist Today* 37:23-9 F '87

Child abuse

See also

Child molesting

National Committee for Prevention of Child Abuse

Shaken child syndrome

Steinberg, Elizabeth, d. 1987—Child abuse case

Alice Miller: the cost of parental tyranny [abusive child rearing practices deny children self respect] L. Van Gelder. il por *Ms* 16:82+ O '87

Child abuse and neglect: prevention and reporting. B. J. Meddin and A. L. Rosen. *Educ Dig* 52:52-5 Ja '87

Does abuse beget abuse? [study by Joan Kaufman and Edward Zigler] A. H. Rosenfeld. *Psychol Today* 21:9 Ag '87

The face of abuse [inability of some abusive parents to correctly interpret infant facial cues; study by Joseph P. Kropp and O. Maurice Haynes] R. J. Moss. *Psychol Today* 21:20 Jl '87

How to protect abused children. B. Kantrowitz. il *Newsweek* 110:70-1 N 23 '87

If you suspect child abuse . . . M. O'Koon. il *Good Housekeep* 205:249 O '87

Interview [A. Miller] D. Connors. por *Omni* 9:72-4+ Mr '87

Middle-class child abuse worsening [study by Dean Knudsen] il *USA Today (Periodical)* 115:6-7 My '87

A personal legacy [learning problems as result of child abuse] L. Distad. bibl f il *Phi Delta Kappan* 68:744-5 Je '87

Power and the fury [childhood of tennis player P. Gonzalez]; ed. by Neil Amdur. R. A. Gonzalez. il *World Tennis* 35:25-7 S '87

Reaching out to the kids [volunteer work of Olympic athlete J. B. Brown] K. Moore. il pors *Sports Illus* 67:18-19 D 21 '87

SCAN: providing preventive services in an urban setting [Supportive Child Adult Network in Philadelphia] T. Tatara and others. il *Child Today* 15:17-22 N/D '86

Six things parents should never say to their children [verbal abuse] por *Jet* 73:14+ N 30 '87

A tale of two Minnesota mothers: one seeks the truth behind their son's death, the other stands accused [investigation into death of Dennis Jurgens] D. Chu. il pors *People Wkly* 27:28-31 Mr 2 '87

International aspects

Child-abuse charges rock UNICEF. *Newsweek* 110:33 Jl 6 '87

Statistics

The numbers game: when more is less. D. Whitman. il *U S News World Rep* 102:39-40 Ap 27 '87

Child abuse in literature

The last angry man: lawyer Andrew Vachss takes to novels to fight child abuse. E. Pooley. il por *N Y* 20:42-4+ My 25 '87

Child abuse in music

Dear Mr. Jesus [song by S. Batts] il por *Time* 130:61 D 21 '87

Child-adult relationship

See also

Generation gap

Parent-child relationship

Finding your heart . . . away from home [teenager-adult friendships] S. Nelson. il *Seventeen* 46:152-3+ My '87

Intergenerational understanding in the middle school [attitudes towards aged] J. Berkson and S. A. Griggs. *Educ Dig* 52:30-2 Ap '87

"Sold! to the young man in shorts" [bicycle bought at Kansas City, Mo. police auction] P. Harvey. il *Read Dig* 131:265-6 N '87

While demons howl, folks in a Florida nursing home scare kids every witch way but loose [Green Briar Nursing Home in Kendall] il *People Wkly* 28:98 N 2 '87

Anecdotes, facetiae, satire, etc.

Uncivil liberties. C. Trillin. il *Nation* 245:671 D 5 '87

Child Assault Prevention (Program)

Sally Cooper. C. Weaver. por *Ms* 16:112+ Jl/Ag '87

Child care *See* Children—Care and hygiene

Child care centers *See* Day care

Child custody *See* Custody of children

Child guidance *See* Child psychology

Child labor *See* Children—Employment

Child molesting

See also

Child Assault Prevention (Program)

Incest

Abuse in the name of protecting children [guarding against false accusations] R. L. Emans. *Educ Dig* 53:36-9 N '87

Abuse in the name of protecting children [guarding against false accusations] R. L. Emans. bibl f il *Phi Delta Kappan* 68:740-3 Je '87

Can the 'abused' kids be believed? [McMartin Preschool trial] T. Gest. il *U S News World Rep* 103:10 Jl 27 '87

The child abuser: how can you spot him?; ed. by Nora Harlow. G. G. Abel. il *Redbook* 169:98-100+ Ag '87

Convicted Va. minister quits council, churches [case of C. Johnson] por *Jet* 72:6 Ag 24 '87

Ex-teacher in D.C. gets 52-155 yrs. for sex abuse [J. B. Crawford] *Jet* 72:36 Jl 27 '87

A flasher from your past [non-contact sexual abuse] L. S. Dumas. il *Health* 19:22 N '87

Helping parents help their children [Girls Clubs of America's KID-ABILITY sexual abuse prevention program] *Child Today* 16:5 My/Je '87

In the journals. il *Child Today* 16:5 Jl/Ag '87

Md. day care center owner gets 10 yrs. for child abuse [S. A. Craig] *Jet* 73:37 O 19 '87

Men and child care: the plot thickens. S. Miller. il por *Ms* 16:54-6 O '87

The mind of a molester. S. A. Johnston. bibl (p64) il *Psychol Today* 21:60-3 F '87

Minister/councilman's rape conviction still stuns his church, city [Rev. C. Johnson] D. M. Cheers. il por *Jet* 72:16-17 Jl 13 '87

Minister/lawmaker may get 161 years in prison for rape, sexual battery [case of C. Johnson] il por *Jet* 72:4-6 Je 29 '87

Petersburg, Va. pastor charged with alleged sexual abuse of 6 girls [case of C. L. Johnson] *Jet* 72:10 Je 15 '87

Scarlet lettering [child molester required to post warning signs in Portland, Or.] *Time* 130:60 S 7 '87

'The Second Beast of Revelation' [M. A. Aquino of the Army Reserve accused of child molestation at the day care center at Presidio Army Base, Calif.] J. Adler. il por *Newsweek* 110:73 N 16 '87

Sex abuse in preschool: fears and facts. F. Roberts. il *Parents* 62:52 O '87

Sexual abuse or abuse of justice? [false accusations] R. Lacayo. il *Time* 129:49 My 11 '87

Shattered innocence. A. Kohn. bibl (p64) il *Psychol Today* 21:54-8 F '87

Special report on child sexual abuse. il *McCalls* 114:93-7 F '87

Touch of evil: memories of a molested child. M. E. Gordon. *Mademoiselle* 93:188+ Mr '87

Va. minister convicted of sex crimes gets 120 years [case of C. L. Johnson] por *Jet* 73:51 O 5 '87

Was I molested? The gray area of sexual abuse. C. Kirschenbaum. *Mademoiselle* 93:188+ Mr '87

"We are survivors . . .". B. Goldsmith. il *Ms* 16:88-9 Jl/Ag '87

Canada

A questionable witness to abuse [bill would eliminate need for corroboration of unsworn testimony of a child in sexual abuse cases] B. Amiel. il *Macleans* 100:9 Ja 26 '87

'We just want the truth' [child witnesses and sex abuse cases in Montreal] L. Van Dusen. il *Macleans* 100:56+ N 2 '87

Child neglect *See* Child abuse

Child oriented business *See* Youth market

Child placement *See* Adoption and adopted children; Foster home care

Child pornography *See* Pornography

Child psychology

See also

Anger in children

Children and death

Imagination in children

Infant psychology

Maternal deprivation

Moral development

Parent-child relationship

Parent education

Play

Child psychology—See also—*cont.*
Problem children
School children—Adjustment
School phobia
Sick children—Psychology
Busy, busy bees [stress on young children] L. G. Katz. il *Parents* 62:154 F '87
The child psychologist. L. Salk. See issues of McCall's beginning March 1986
Coping with trauma [preschoolers] L. G. Katz. il *Parents* 62:210 O '87
Do we push our kids too hard? [excerpt from The hurried child] D. Elkind. il *Good Housekeep* 205:117-19 S '87
Does it damage children to deceive them about Santa Claus? Ho, ho, no, says Dr. Carl Anderson [interview] L. Armstrong. il pors *People Wkly* 28:45+ D 21 '87
Elementary 'psychological accounting' [study by Helene J. Krouse] *Sci News* 131:89 F 7 '87
Helping children adjust to moving. F. A. Smardo. bibl f il *Child Today* 16:10-13 My/Je '87
Is perfectionism killing your kid? M. Conroy. il *Better Homes Gard* 65:76+ N '87
The magic of childhood. P. Chance and J. Fischman. bibl (p94) il *Psychol Today* 21:48-51+ My '87
Milestones: charting the stages in a child's emotional development. J. Taylor. il *N Y* 20:34-9 N 23 '87
One day a year we give mom flowers; the other 364 we give her grief. Why? il *Glamour* 85:106 My '87
Protecting children's innocence [with editorial comment by Elizabeth Crow] J. Gaylin. il *Parents* 62:6, 88+ O '87
Santa lives [children's beliefs; study by Cyndy Scheibe and John Condry] V. Bozzi. il *Psychol Today* 21:12 D '87
Storytelling in therapy and counseling. E. Wynne. bibl f il *Child Today* 16:11-15 Mr/Ap '87
Tender years, a terrible sadness: children of depression. C. Leerhsen. il *Newsweek* 109:50-1 My 4 '87
Understanding kids. L. Balter. See issues of Ladies' Home Journal beginning February 1984
When you're really hassled [mothers of toddlers] J. T. Gibson. il *Parents* 62:148 Jl '87
Why mothers get a hard time. J. Marzollo. il *Parents* 62:103-5+ N '87
Winning against whining. T. F. Murphy. il *Parents* 62:110-12 Ag '87
Young Type A's: the heartbreak kids [views of Carl Thoreson] J. Fischman. *Psychol Today* 21:10-11 Ja '87
Your child's temperament: easy, difficult, or slow-to-warm-up? N. Rubin. il *Parents* 62:94-6+ S '87

Child psychotherapy
See also
Toys—Therapeutic use
Children's mental health. il *Futurist* 21:50-1 Jl/Ag '87
When your child needs help. K. Levine. il *Parents* 62:126-30 Ap '87
Your child's mental health. J. Segal and Z. Segal. il *Parents* 62:156 F '87

Child raising *See* Children—Management and training
Child raising, Cost of *See* Children—Cost of raising
Child support *See* Support (Domestic relations)
Child testimony *See* Witnesses
Child welfare
See also
Adoption and adopted children
Child abuse
Child molesting
Children—Law
Children's Defense Fund (U.S.)
Custody of children
Day care
Foster home care
Group homes for children
Homeless children
National Resource Center for Children in Poverty
National Resource Center on Family Based Services
Orphans and orphanages
Parent and child (Law)
Save the Children Federation
Social work with youth
United States. Children's Bureau
Caring for children [special section] bibl f *Society* 24:5-52 Mr/Ap '87
Crusading for kids on the hustings [views of Democratic presidential candidates] A. Plattner. il *U S News World Rep* 103:29-30 S 14 '87
Family based services [special issue] il *Child Today* 15:4-32 N/D '86
FYI. See issues of Children Today

Retirees are about to see a healthier boost in benefits . . . but U.S. children are slipping past the safety net. G. Koretz. il *Bus Week* p26+ O 12 '87

Awards
Secretary Bowen's Commemorative Awards. il *Child Today* 16:8-9 S/O '87

International aspects
See also
Declaration of the Rights of the Child
UNICEF
1987 State of world's children: 'the silent emergencies' [UNICEF report] il *UN Chron* 24:64-7 My '87

Africa
From Africa, with love. L. Ullmann. il pors *Seventeen* 46:210-11+ Ap '87

California
See also
California Child Care Initiative

Canada
A young and rising star [minister of state for youth J. Charest] M. Rose. il por *Macleans* 100:6-7 S 21 '87

Developing countries
See also
UNICEF

Florida
See also
Fort Lauderdale (Fla.)—Child welfare
Intensive crisis counseling in Florida [family counseling] J. H. Paschal and L. Schwahn. il *Child Today* 15:12-16 N/D '86

Illinois
See also
Kaleidoscope, Inc.
Adoption by blacks in Illinois at record high. *Jet* 71:29 Mr 16 '87

India
See also
Bombay (India)—Child welfare

Kentucky
Moving toward family preservation services in Kentucky. B. Triplett and others. *Child Today* 15:8-11 N/D '86

Kenya
See also
Nairobi (Kenya)—Child welfare

Massachusetts
Fostering prejudice [policy prohibiting homosexuals from being foster parents] W. F. Schulz, Jr. il *Progressive* 51:15 Ja '87
In Massachusetts, an ugly battle for a little girl [child abuse charges in custody case of N. LaLonde] G. Hackett. il por *Newsweek* 110:41 O 19 '87
Massachusetts spotlights day care. il *Child Today* 16:2-3 Mr/Ap '87

Minnesota
See also
Hennepin County (Minn.)—Child welfare
Changing how society views children [Whole Child Initiative] R. Friedmann and others. il *Child Today* 16:10-14 Jl/Ag '87

Mississippi
Miss. kids finding homes thanks to preacher's wife [efforts of L. West] il por *Jet* 71:32 Ja 19 '87

Missouri
See also
Saint Louis (Mo.)—Child welfare

New York (State)
See also
Brooklyn (New York, N.Y.)—Child welfare
New York (N.Y.)—Child welfare
Church, state and foster-care children. H. J. Byrne. *America* 157:38-41 Jl 18-25 '87
The last angry man: lawyer Andrew Vachss takes to novels to fight child abuse. E. Pooley. il por *N Y* 20:42-4+ My 25 '87

Pennsylvania
See also
Philadelphia (Pa.)—Child welfare

Southern Africa
Children on the frontline. M. A. Fortune. il *Black Enterp* 17:16 My '87

Tennessee
Man sues for paternity of child that was born to his ex-girlfriend now wed [G. E. Cline] por *Jet* 71:15 Ja 26 '87

United States
See Child welfare

Utah
Profiling family preservation efforts in Utah. J. P. Callister and others. il *Child Today* 15:23-5+ N/D '86

Child welfare—*cont.*

Wisconsin

Wisconsin: getting tough on wayward fathers. D. Stoeffler. il *Sch Update* 119:23-4 Mr 23 '87

Wisconsin's child-support experiment. R. J. Margolis. il *New Leader* 70:14-16 O 19 '87

Child World, Inc.

Gift idea. T. Jaffe. il *Forbes* 139:202 Je 1 '87

Childbirth

See also
    Cesarean section
    Hospitals—Maternity care
    Midwives
    Obstetrics
    Postpartum depression
    Pregnancy
    Stillbirth
    Umbilical cord—Prolapse

As they grow/pregnancy and birth. P. A. Hillard. See issues of Parents

At last—it's a boy! [couple witnesses birth of child they hope to adopt] M. Grant. il *Life* 10:28-34 Je '87

Can natural childbirth be painless? *Psychol Today* 21:55 Ag '87

Childbirth: how it was for me [five women compare notes] G. N. Edelman. il *Good Housekeep* 205:86+ S '87

Childbirth more fatal for black women [views of Kristine A. Siefert] il *USA Today (Periodical)* 115:10 Ap '87

"Don't let my baby die!" [preeclampsia; excerpt from Intensive care] E. Heron. il por *Redbook* 168:122-4+ Ap '87

Husbands for safe blood [transfusions in the OB/GYN departments] C. SerVaas. il *Saturday Evening Post* 259:82+ N '87

Kids in the delivery room. C. Schaeffer. *Changing Times* 41:22-3 S '87

Labor-saving device [Term Guard, a device that can detect premature labor] D. Tonnessen. il *Health* 19:23 Je '87

Premature labor takes a holiday thanks to a new pregnancy monitor [Term Guard home monitoring device] *Prevention* 39:79-80 N '87

Your baby, your way [excerpt] S. Kitzinger. il *Glamour* 85:50+ Ag '87

Costs

The bundle a baby costs. R. R. Roha. il *Changing Times* 41:85+ N '87

Exhibitions

'Generations': a family album [exhibit at International Gallery] D. M. Bolz. il *Smithsonian* 18:276 N '87

Postpartum hemorrhage

See Hemorrhage

Childhood *See* Children
Childhood autism *See* Autism
Childhood memories *See* Memory
Childhood obesity *See* Obesity
Childhood poisoning *See* Poisons and poisoning
Childlessness

Motherhood's sad loss of social esteem: one couple's reaction to America's birth dearth. S. Jacob and G. Jacob. pors *U S News World Rep* 103:6 Ag 17 '87

My husband doesn't want a baby. E. Switzer. il *Ladies Home J* 104:12+ S '87

Childproof packaging (Drugs) *See* Drugs—Packaging
Children

See also
    Art and children
    Arts and children
    Birth order
    Birth rate
    Black children
    Boys
    Bullying
    Childlessness
    Christmas gifts for children
    Cooking by children
    Cosmetics for children
    Family
    Family size
    Fathers
    Gifts for children
    Girls
    Imagination in children
    Infants
    Jewish children
    Missing children
    Mothers
    Motion pictures—Children's films
    Only child

    Orphans and orphanages
    Parents
    Problem children
    Refugee children
    School children
    Siblings
    Single parent families
    Socially handicapped children
    Stepparents and stepchildren
    Telephone and children
    Television and children
    Triplets
    Twins
    Youth

All our lonely children. P. A. Hall. por *Newsweek* 110:12 O 12 '87

The baby bandwagon. S. Jacoby. il *Glamour* 85:388-9+ S '87

Childhood: then vs. now [results of survey] I. Groller. il *Parents* 62:30 Ap '87

Families and children in the year 2000. A. J. Norton. il *Child Today* 16:6-9 Jl/Ag '87

Kids did it! See issues of National Geographic World

Kids! Kids! Kids! [special section] il *McCalls* 114:43-6+ Ag '87

Mother & child. I. S. McDermott. See issues of Good Housekeeping beginning January 1986

Accidents

See Accidents

Adoption

See Adoption and adopted children

Altruism

See Altruism

Anecdotes, facetiae, satire, etc.

Can childhood be cured? A research evaluation. J. W. Smoller. *Educ Dig* 52:56-9 Ap '87

What is a perfect child? B. Adler. il *Good Housekeep* 205:104 S '87

What's the matter with kids today? [views of Jordan Smoller] G. W. Bracey. il *Phi Delta Kappan* 69:73 S '87

Anger

See Anger in children

Attitudes

Feeling good about America [survey] il *USA Today (Periodical)* 116:4-5 Ag '87

Holiday [views of second graders on Martin Luther King] *New Yorker* 62:28-9 F 2 '87

"How I'd like mom & dad to change". G. N. Edelman. il *Parents* 62:122-6 N '87

"Mommy, what's wrong with that lady?" [answering children's questions about the handicapped] C. W. Levy. il por *McCalls* 114:65-7 S '87

Today's kids with yesterday's goals. il *Parents* 62:15 Ap '87

Bibliography

Book reviews. See issues of Children Today

Care and hygiene

See also
    Baby sitters
    Child psychology
    Child welfare
    Children—Medical care
    Children—Preparation for hospital and medical care
    Parent education
    Physical education and training
    Poisons and poisoning
    Public schools—Medical care
    Shaken child syndrome
    Sick children

25 ways to help your child get fit and why that's so important. P. Krantz. il *Better Homes Gard* 65:61+ My '87

A-plus in fitness [Fitnessgram developed by the Institute for Aerobics Research] D. Zevin. il *Health* 19:18 Ap '87

Baby boomlet meets fitness boom. S. Richmond. *Changing Times* 41:46 Ag '87

Battling the bulge at an early age [physical fitness] J. Carey. il *U S News World Rep* 102:66-7 Mr 2 '87

Children of Latin America and the Caribbean. E. M. Moreno and others. il *World Health* p14-15+ O '87

C'mon now, shape it up, baby [preschool exercise programs] A. Toufexis. il *Time* 130:61 O 5 '87

Dr. Mom's page. M. R. Neifert. See issues of McCall's beginning May 1986

Fit and fun: fitness strategies for kids and their parents. C. Winters. il *Work Woman* 12:159+ S '87

Good housekeeping child care '87 [special section] il *Good Housekeep* 205:75+ S '87

Children—Care and hygiene—*cont.*
A grab bag of mothering tips from TV's favorite working mom [views of J. Lunden] il *Ladies Home J* 104:187 Ap '87
Guide to your child's health. K. Glenn. il *McCalls* 114:43-6 Ag '87
Indiana Senator Lugar hosts Fitness Festival. il por *Jet* 72:29 Jl 6 '87
Is your child fit? M. S. Williams. il *McCalls* 114:57 Ag '87
Kids aren't little grownups! J. L. Lippert. il *Health* 19:52-3+ S '87
Medical news. il *Parents* 62:26 F '87
"Mommy, I don't feel good . . ." Kids' symptoms not to ignore. G. J. Subak-Sharpe. il *Ladies Home J* 104:82+ N '87
Q&A. See issues of Parents
Shake, rattle, and roll [physical fitness programs in New York City] M. Bloom. il *N Y* 20:72-87 N 23 '87

Civil rights
See also
Children's Defense Fund (U.S.)
Declaration of the Rights of the Child
Parent and child (Law)
Decide seven Court cases that test teenagers' rights. M. Christopher. il *Sch Update* 120:16-18+ S 4 '87

Clothing and dress
See Clothing and dress—Children

Cost of raising
It's a girl . . . and a girl . . . and a girl! [financial implications of raising triplets for Bill and Eileen Lund] S. Seixas. il *Money* 16:80-3+ N '87
The spoils of success. D. Menaker. il *N Y Times Mag* p24-5+ Ag 9 '87

Anecdotes, facetiae, satire, etc.
The high cost of raising a daughter. E. Bombeck. por *Teen* 31:64 D '87

Creativity
See Creativity

Crime
See Juvenile delinquents and delinquency

Crimes against
See also
Child abuse
Child molesting
Parents of murdered children
Safety education
Little Boy Blue of Chester, Nebraska [child found dead by roadside] H. Hurt. *Read Dig* 131:73-8 D '87
"We have a problem" [mugging of a 10 yr. old] J. Marks. il *Parents* 62:61-4 S '87

Day care
See Day care

Dental care
See Pedodontics

Development
See Children—Growth and development

Diseases
See also
AIDS (Disease) and children
ALD (Disease)
Allergy
Asthma
Cancer in children
Chicken pox
Cystic fibrosis
Diarrhea
Ear—Diseases
Hib infections
Infants, Newborn—Diseases
Kawasaki syndrome
Meningitis
Reye's syndrome
Rheumatic fever
Short bowel syndrome
Xerophthalmia
Illness in day care. P. Von Nostitz. il *Parents* 62:112 Ap '87
Infectious disease in day care. *Child Today* 16:4-5 Ja/F '87
"Mommy, I feel sick". S. Evans. il *Parents* 62:120-2 O '87
Serious childhood ailments. M. Oppenheim. il *Better Homes Gard* 65:76+ F '87

Vaccines and vaccination
See also
DPT vaccine
50 per cent mark reached in world immunizations. il *World Health* p30 N '87
Boosting children's health with vaccinations. il *Consum Res Mag* 70:20-3 S '87

A chance for every child. M. Rey. il *Courier* 40:13-15 Ag '87
Declaration affirming commitment to immunization of all the world's children by 1990 signed at headquarters. il *UN Chron* 22:107 N/D '85
Immunization: a chance for every child [promoting concept with comic books and postage stamps] il *World Health* p28-9 Mr '87
Immunization: a chance for every child [special issue] il *World Health* p3-30 Ja/F '87
Immunization: the drive must continue [fear of AIDS] il *World Health* p30 Ap '87
Three new vaccines for junior [chicken pox, meningitis, and pertussis] S. Findlay. il *U S News World Rep* 103:14 N 2 '87

Economic conditions
Children and money. D. F. Bjorklund and B. Bjorklund. il *Parents* 62:202 Ap '87
Greed on Sesame Street? A. Miller. il *Newsweek* 110:38-40 Jl 20 '87
Kids and money: tots to teens, teaching the basics. J. K. Rosemond. il *Better Homes Gard* 65:52+ Jl '87

Education
See also
Education, Elementary
Education, Experimental
Education, Preschool
Moral education
Play
Readiness for school
Safety education
School age
Sex education
Social education
Teaching
Real-life learning. D. F. Bjorklund and B. Bjorklund. il *Parents* 62:194 Mr '87
School days. F. Roberts. See issues of Parents beginning January 1983

Employment
50 to 200 million children under 15 are in world's work force, ILO says [developing countries] il *UN Chron* 23:116 N '86

Food
See Children—Nutrition

Growth and development
See also
Child psychology
Infants—Growth and development
Moral development
All in the family [views of E. Maccoby] E. Hall. il pors *Psychol Today* 21:54-8+ N '87
As they grow. See issues of Parents
Bright, average, or slow? N. S. Schwartzberg. il *Parents* 62:106-8+ My '87
Growth spurts mirror mental milestones [cerebral hemisphere development; research by Robert W. Thatcher and others] R. J. Trotter. *Psychol Today* 21:13 S '87
How camping helps children grow. J. C. Stone. *Educ Dig* 52:47-9 My '87
How many friends are enough? [children's social development] C. Berman. il *Parents* 62:64-6+ Ja '87
An image in time [concept of time; research by William Friedman] S. Vandershaf. il *Psychol Today* 21:20 Jl '87
Keeping up with the Joneses. J. W. Hilton. il *Parents* 62:86-8+ Je '87
Kids suddenly gain in grasp of symbols [research by Judy S. DeLoache] B. Bower. *Sci News* 132:389 D 19-26 '87
Learning from the children [Listen to the children by Jean Reiss Berlfein] il *Child Today* 16:3 Mr/Ap '87
Logical leaps [children's understanding of inference; study by Beate Sodian and Heinz Wimmer] J. Rubin. *Psychol Today* 21:13 Ag '87
The magic of childhood. P. Chance and J. Fischman. bibl (p94) il *Psychol Today* 21:48-51+ My '87
Making kids smarter. L. J. Greene. il *Parents* 62:94-8+ D '87
Margins of sexuality [developmental difficulties associated with abnormal sex chromosomes] D. B. Berch and B. G. Bender. bibl (p63) il *Psychol Today* 21:54-7 D '87
Milestones: charting the stages in a child's emotional development. J. Taylor. il *N Y* 20:34-9 N 23 '87
Our images of children: where will they take us? D. Elkind. *Educ Dig* 53:2-4 N '87

Children—Growth and development—*cont.*
Rapid change in the symbolic functioning of very young children. J. S. DeLoache. bibl f il *Science* 238:1556-7 D 11 '87
What's it like to be one year old? P. La Farge. il *Parents* 62:124-6+ S '87
Zinc: a key element for growth. *Prevention* 39:17 D '87

Health
See Children—Care and hygiene

Height
See Stature

Hospital care
See also
Children—Preparation for hospital and medical care
Infants, Newborn—Hospital care
Baby came in sick, baby getting better, baby go home soon. P. Klass. il *Discover* 8:18+ My '87
If your child goes to the hospital. H. Roiphe. *McCalls* 114:60 Ja '87
The million-dollar baby nobody wants [P. Carnes, suffering from diffuse myelitis, lives in Texas hospital] C. C. Frink. il pors *Ladies Home J* 104:48+ D '87
When your child needs a hospital. H. R. Kennedy. *U S News World Rep* 103:91 D 7 '87
Your child is in the hospital, and you're blanketed by guilt. P. Klass. il *Discover* 8:20+ Ja '87

Hospitals
See also
Children's Hospital (San Diego, Calif.)
Anita Baker benefit raises $135,032.50 for Chicago's LaRabida Children's Hospital. il por *Jet* 72:58 My 4 '87

Humor
See Humor

Imprisonment
See Refugee children—Imprisonment

Institutional care
See also
Orphans and orphanages

Intelligence
See Intelligence

Language
Associations or rules in learning language? G. Kolata. il *Science* 237:133-4 Jl 10 '87
By the daunserly light. M. Calta. il *Read Dig* 130:167-8 F '87
No language but a cry [infants] M. Roberts. il *Psychol Today* 21:57-8 Je '87
Prattling with purpose [infant speech development; research by D. Kimbrough Oller] D. Zevin. *Health* 19:18 F '87
See and say, say, say! [one year olds] J. T. Gibson. il *Parents* 62:200 S '87
What is my baby saying? N. S. Schwartzberg. il *Parents* 62:78-82 Jl '87

Anecdotes, facetiae, satire, etc.
One nation and a vegetable. R. Keyes. il *Good Housekeep* 204:76+ Je '87

Law
See also
Children—Civil rights
Children—Employment
Children's Defense Fund (U.S.)
Curfew
Guardian and ward
Juvenile delinquents and delinquency
Parent and child (Law)
Author and publisher groups make filings in two Supreme Court cases [challenge to a Virginia law on how certain books may be displayed] H. Fields. *Publ Wkly* 232:12 S 4 '87
High Court to review Va. minors access law. M. Yen. *Publ Wkly* 231:30 Mr 6 '87
Supreme Court justices quiz both sides in Virginia minors access law. H. Fields. *Publ Wkly* 232:16 N 20 '87

Management and training
See also
Child abuse
Child psychology
Children's chores
Corporal punishment
Moral education
Parent-child relationship
Parent education
Problem children
6 easy ways to get kids to behave [excerpt from How to discipline effectively] F. Dodson. il *Redbook* 169:76-7+ Jl '87
Are you raising a yuppie-puppy? B. M. Katz. il *Parents* 62:74-6 Ja '87

Avoiding sex-role stereotypes. J. Segal and Z. Segal. il *Parents* 62:200 D '87
Becoming independent [two year olds] B. Weissbourd. il *Parents* 62:192 Ag '87
Big and little bigots. E. Crow. il *Parents* 62:6 Jl '87
Boys will be boys . . . [problems in raising non-sexist children] G. Witkin-Lanoil. il *Health* 19:6 Ag '87
"Buy me, buy me": how to cope when kids get greedy. L. Werner. il *Ladies Home J* 104:76-8 D '87
Changing childrearing practices in Sudan: an early stimulation demonstration program. E. H. Grotberg and others. bibl f il *Child Today* 16:26-9 Ja/F '87
The children of Narcissus. C. Lasch. *Des Arts Educ* 88:45-8 My/Je '87
Control [teaching children how to take control in their lives] D. F. Bjorklund and B. Bjorklund. il *Parents* 62:156 Jl '87
A diary's the best medicine. S. Kayne. il *Parents* 62:85-6+ N '87
Disorderly conduct [results of survey] I. Groller. il *Parents* 62:33 Ag '87
Does it have to hurt to punish your kids? R. Greene. il *U S Cathol* 52:24-31 N '87
Driven crazy by advice? L. Felder. il *Parents* 62:94-6+ My '87
Expert identifies best way to raise your child [views of Cynthia Baum] *Jet* 72:36 My 25 '87
The good enough parent's parent [views of B. Bettelheim] M. J. Bandler. il pors *Parents* 62:189-90+ N '87
The greatest gift you can give your children for Christmas [positive thinking]; ed. by William T. Buckley. N. V. Peale. il *Good Housekeep* 205:116+ D '87
How to stop fighting with your kids [excerpt from Loving your child is not enough]; ed. by Martha Moraghan Jablow. N. Samalin. il *Good Housekeep* 205:98+ S '87
How to stop spanking: try a lot of tenderness. S. S. Oliver. il *Essence* 17:98+ Ap '87
How useful are telephone consultation services for parents? [NYU Warmline] J. Samuels and L. Balter. bibl f il *Child Today* 16:27-30 My/Je '87
"If I knew then, what I know now" [views of experienced mothers] E. Davidowitz. il *Redbook* 170:100-3+ N '87
In praise of praise. P. Theroux. il *Parents* 62:60+ Ag '87
Is your child too dependent on you? B. Spock. il *Redbook* 169:28 Jl '87
Mother to mother. See issues of McCall's beginning March 1986
News for parents. M. Mohler. See occasional issues of Ladies' Home Journal beginning September 1984 through August 1987
The parent as an effective and loving manager [excerpt from When your child needs you] E. Weisberger. *Work Woman* 12:176+ N '87
Parenting. J. K. Rosemond. See issues of Better Homes and Gardens beginning June 1985
Parents' discipline style affects timing of teen sex. *Jet* 71:31 F 23 '87
Parents' journal. M. Mohler. See issues of Ladies' Home Journal beginning September 1987
Parents, use your heads [views of B. Bettelheim] B. Kantrowitz. il por *Newsweek* 109:78-9 Je 22 '87
The place of children in public life. S. E. Cahill. il *USA Today (Periodical)* 115:87-9 Ja '87
Punishment & preschoolers. L. G. Katz. il *Parents* 62:205 My '87
Q&A. See issues of Parents
Questions on child raising you'd be too embarrassed to ask. H. Roiphe and A. R. Roiphe. *McCalls* 114:77-9 S '87
A 'R'-rated book on Raising 'PG' kids [work of T. Gore] B. Summer. *Publ Wkly* 231:44 Ap 24 '87
Raising a responsible child. C. Berman. il *Parents* 62:110-12+ O '87
A report card for parents. S. F. Enos. il *Ladies Home J* 104:87-9+ Je '87
Spare the rod—and the child? [results of survey; with editorial comment by Elizabeth Crow] I. Groller. il *Parents* 62:6, 27 S '87
Superkids and super problems [parents are pushing their children too fast] D. Elkind. il *Psychol Today* 21:60-1 My '87
Superkids and superparents. H. Smith. il *Christ Today* 31:14-15 S 18 '87
Teaching children to give. B. Spock. il por *Redbook* 170:34+ D '87
The terrible twos. J. K. Rosemond. il *Better Homes Gard* 65:81 Ap '87

Children—Management and training—*cont.*

There goes my song again. L. Wainwright. il *Life* 10:18 Mr '87

The trouble with Emily [spoiled child] J. Gaylin. il *Parents* 62:54+ Mr '87

Trying to raise children in the city [New York City] M. Stone. il *N Y* 20:26-33 F 2 '87

We reap what we sow [child rearing practices and adult ego development; study by Eric F. Dubow] S. Chollar. *Psychol Today* 21:12 D '87

What are you teaching your child about love & marriage? B. Spock. por *Redbook* 169:40 S '87

You can be a more sensitive parent. F. Rogers. il por *Redbook* 168:88-9+ Ap '87

Your child: is she hiding something? L. Salk. il *McCalls* 115:67 N '87

Your wild child. B. Weissbourd. il *Parents* 62:114 Ja '87

Caricatures and cartoons

"They'll outgrow it" and other myths about children [excerpt] L. Yarrow. il *Parents* 62:78-80+ Ja '87

Medical care

See also

Pediatricians

3 children who needed a medical miracle [special section] il *Redbook* 168:110-12+ F '87

Emergency advice for your babysitter. *Parents* 62:40+ Jl '87

Kids and medicine: what to give them when. J. L. Brown. *Ladies Home J* 104:60+ Mr '87

Medical identification

See Medical identification

Mortality

New benefits seen in vitamin A therapy. J. Raloff. *Sci News* 131:325 My 23 '87

Nutrition

See also

Malnutrition

Obesity

School lunches

Breakfasts for little champions. M. S. Williams. il *McCalls* 115:124+ O '87

Food for all—the 'Paris appeal' [universal free access to basic foodstuffs] Y. Coutsocheras. il *Courier* 40:34 O '87

Good nutrition for your growing child. E. Hale. il *FDA Consum* 21:20-7 Ap '87

Goody-goodies! [snacks] il *Redbook* 169:200+ S '87

Kids, food and fitness [special section] il *Work Woman* 12:149-51+ S '87

Let them eat cake—with tomato sauce [controversial eating guide, "Are you hungry?"] *Newsweek* 110:48 Jl 27 '87

The littlest dieters. J. Seligmann. il *Newsweek* 110:48 Jl 27 '87

Nutrition, diet, fitness. il *Good Housekeep* 205:110 S '87

Picky-eater defeaters. J. A. Reimer. il *Parents* 62:80-1+ S '87

Should children diet? B. T. Hunter. il *Consum Res Mag* 70:8-9 S '87

Anecdotes, facetiae, satire, etc.

Salad days. P. Theroux. il *N Y Times Mag* p22 N 22 '87

Obesity

See Obesity

Only child

See Only child

Preparation for hospital and medical care

Helping children cope [anatomically correct Zaadi dolls] il *Ms* 16:28 D '87

Playing doctor with Gail Zayka's lifelike dolls helps kids facing surgery get over their fears [Zaadi dolls] B. Taubman. il pors *People Wkly* 28:57-8 S 14 '87

Psychology

See Child psychology

Recreation

See also

Games

Play

Play groups

Playgrounds

Toys

At the beach [toddlers] J. T. Gibson. il *Parents* 62:156 Je '87

Eight days a week [special events and activities in New York City] L. Schnurnberger. il *N Y* 20:88-99 N 23 '87

Getting out and about [outings] B. Weissbourd. il *Parents* 62:150 Jl '87

A host of holiday projects for children. il *McCalls* 115:47 D '87

Keeping kids amused while you entertain. il *McCalls* 115:50 D '87

Kids and summer: when plans create a problem. L. Salk. il *McCalls* 114:54 Je '87

Kids' time. D. Pines. il *McCalls* 114:73 Ap '87

Kids: what to do with them, where to do it [summer in New York City] L. Schnurnberger. il *N Y* 20:114+ Je 29-Jl 6 '87

Mother's children. See issues of The Mother Earth News

Superfun special [special section] il *Natl Geogr World* 140:17-24 Ap '87

Superfun special [special section] il *Natl Geogr World* 147:17-20 N '87

Superfun special [special section] il *Natl Geogr World* 145:17-20 S '87

Religious life

See also

Church work with children

Sunday schools

Talking about God [young children] J. Segal and Z. Segal. il *Parents* 62:208 S '87

Where does God live? T. McCarroll. il *Parents* 62:102-4+ D '87

Anecdotes, facetiae, satire, etc.

Growing up born again. J. Campbell. il *Publ Wkly* 232:44-5 O 9 '87

Self confidence

See Self confidence

Self reliance

See Self reliance

Self respect

See Self respect

Sexual behavior

See also

Sex education

Sleep

See Sleep

Social development

See Children—Growth and development

Speech

See Children—Language

Sports

See also

Baseball, Children's

Basketball, Children's

Ice skating

Karate

School athletics

Skis and skiing, Children's

Tennis

Breaks of the game [injuries] S. Findlay. il *U S News World Rep* 103:75-7 O 5 '87

Don't feel sorry for my kids. M. Weiss. il *Women's Sports Fitness* 9:78 F '87

Giving kids the edge in sports. L. Salk. il *McCalls* 114:80 Ag '87

High-flying household [sports-oriented Mills clan of Northfield, Ill.] H. Hersch. il *Sports Illus* 66:44-6+ Je 22 '87

Suicide

See Suicide

Surgery

See also

Children—Preparation for hospital and medical care

Mind games taken to heart [post-operative cardiac patients at Children's Hospital in San Diego] N. Benford and D. Gage. il *Health* 19:25 N '87

Taxation

See also

Gifts to minors

It's more taxing to be a kid. L. Wiener. il *U S News World Rep* 102:51-2 Je 1 '87

Put the kids on the payroll and give yourself a break. P. Philipps. il *Bus Week* p154 Je 8 '87

Training

See Children—Management and training

Travel

See also

Travel with children

The youngest jet-setters. B. Kantrowitz. il *Newsweek* 109:52-3 Je 29 '87

Volunteer service

See Volunteer service

Writing

The write stuff. B. G. Polikoff. il *Parents* 62:140-4 O '87

Children—*cont.*

Canada

Growing pains [cover story; special section; with editorial comment by Kevin Doyle] il *Macleans* 100:2, 36-9+ S 7 '87

Caribbean region

Children of Latin America and the Caribbean. E. M. Moreno and others. il *World Health* p14-15+ O '87

China

Bringing up baby, one by one [single child policy] H. G. Chua-Eoan. il *Time* 130:38 D 7 '87

China's only child. E. Hall. bibl (p68) il *Psychol Today* 21:44-7 Jl '87

Developing countries

50 to 200 million children under 15 are in world's work force, ILO says. il *UN Chron* 23:116 N '86

Child survival: an achievable goal in hunger relief [cover story] T. Peterson. il *Christ Century* 104:594-5 Jl 1-8 '87

Preventing child mortality [Child survival: risks and the road to health report] il *Futurist* 21:41 N/D '87

Latin America

Children of Latin America and the Caribbean. E. M. Moreno and others. il *World Health* p14-15+ O '87

Photographs and photography

Photo '87 winners [Americas Photo Contest] C. Healy. il *Américas* 39:20-7 My/Je '87

Mexico

Children-power in Mexico [immunization program] L. Taylor. il *World Health* p24-5 Ja/F '87

New York (State)

See also

New York (N.Y.)—Children

South Africa

Apartheid's troubled children. A. Getz. *World Press Rev* 34:34-5 D '87

Children on the front line. S. Reiss. il *Newsweek* 110:39 Jl 27 '87

Why deny the children? [effects of American publishers' boycott] G. Miklowitz. por *Publ Wkly* 232:66 O 9 '87

Sudan

Changing childrearing practices in Sudan: an early stimulation demonstration program. E. H. Grotberg and others. bibl f il *Child Today* 16:26-9 Ja/F '87

United States

See Children

Vietnam

See also

Vietnamese War, 1957-1975—Children

Children, Exceptional

See also

Children, Gifted

Children, Handicapped

Learning disabilities

Problem children

Slow learning children

Education

See Special education

Children, Gifted

See also

Children as musicians

The fine art of child appreciation. M. Mantle. *U S Cathol* 52:30-1 S '87

The hamlet handicap [effect of village life on talented youth] K. Seelinger. por *Newsweek* 109:10-11 My 18 '87

Education

See also

High school students, Gifted

Classes for the gifted: a bright idea? F. Roberts. *Parents* 62:58 Ag '87

Curriculum-based programs for the gifted. B. L. Barrington. *Educ Dig* 52:48-51 Ja '87

Education of the gifted and talented in the world community. B. M. Mitchell and W. G. Williams. *Phi Delta Kappan* 68:531-4 Mr '87

Genius in the slow track [programs for gifted students; views of Julian Stanley] P. Chance. il *Psychol Today* 21:14 Mr '87

Gifted education boondoggles: a few bad apples or a rotten bushel? L. A. Sosniak. bibl f il *Phi Delta Kappan* 68:535-8 Mr '87

Oh, to be young and gifted. B. Kantrowitz. il *Newsweek* 109:62-3 F 23 '87

Television literacy programs for gifted children. R. Abelman. *Educ Dig* 52:30-2 My '87

Why smart kids get bad grades and what parents can do about it. P. Krantz. il *Better Homes Gard* 65:62+ F '87

Children, Handicapped

See also

Cerebral palsy

Hyperactivity

Mentally handicapped children

Parents of the handicapped

Socially handicapped children

For kids who can use an assist, Judi Emens designs clothing that doesn't add to their handicaps. L. Rozen. il pors *People Wkly* 28:59+ S 28 '87

The littlest Marine [honorary Marine J. Zimmerman] J. Stuller. il pors *Read Dig* 131:123-7 Jl '87

Yetta Galiber: Christmas every day of the year [special store for disabled children in Washington, D.C.] il pors *Ebony* 43:27-30 D '87

Adoption

See Adoption and adopted children

Education

Early help for handicapped preschoolers. F. Roberts. *Parents* 62:58+ Ap '87

The Full Employment for Attorneys Act [Handicapped Children's Protection Act] P. A. Zirkel. bibl f il *Phi Delta Kappan* 69:165-6 O '87

Handicapped views [study by Heidi M. Inderbitzen and Deborah L. Best] S. Walton. *Psychol Today* 21:15 O '87

Making a difference [work of J. Pyfer with children with motor problems] D. Young. il pors *South Living* 22:98+ Je '87

Federal aid

A windfall for disabled kids. J. N. Baker. il *Newsweek* 110:72 N 9 '87

Family relationships

"We have a problem". J. Marks. il *Parents* 62:58+ D '87

Children, Handicapped, and animals *See* Handicapped and animals

Children, Hyperactive *See* Hyperactivity

Children, Mentally superior *See* Children, Gifted

Children, Wild *See* Wild children

Children and adults *See* Child-adult relationship

Children and alcohol *See* Alcohol and youth

Children and animals

Animal magnetism. S. Isaacs and C. Soares. il *Parents* 62:92-6+ Mr '87

Children and pets: forging the right relationship. L. Salk. il *McCalls* 114:75 Ap '87

Lessons that pets can teach your children and how pets help kids grow. P. Hodgins. il *Better Homes Gard* 65:181+ My '87

Pets give youngsters a real head start [views of Michael M. Levine] *Prevention* 39:63 Ag '87

Pets plus [study by Michael Levine] J. R. Goldberg. il *Health* 19:14 Ap '87

Picking the purr-fect pet. il *Teen* 31:112 O '87

Pig at the Pacific! [Kevin Feaster and his pet pig Wilbur] il *Natl Geogr World* 143:15-17 Jl '87

The question of pets [infants] K. Karlsrud and D. Schultz. il *Parents* 62:192 D '87

Children and art *See* Art and children; Children in art; Children's art

Children and automobiles

See also

Travel with children

Children and business *See* Youth and business

Children and Christmas

See also

Santa Claus

The greatest gift you can give your children for Christmas [positive thinking]; ed. by William T. Buckley. N. V. Peale. il *Good Housekeep* 205:116+ D '87

Children and computers *See* Computers and youth

Children and death

Helping a child understand death. H. R. Kennedy. *U S News World Rep* 103:87 O 12 '87

How to handle death in the school. R. G. Stevenson and H. L. Powers. *Educ Dig* 52:42-3 My '87

How to talk to your kids about death. J. Breig. il *U S Cathol* 52:21-6 Ja '87

How were children affected by the space shuttle disaster? G. G. Sparks. *Educ Dig* 52:55-7 F '87

Learning to cope with death. J. P. Comer. il *Parents* 62:210 My '87

Roses for Yolande [condensed from Enchanted summer] G. Roy. il *Read Dig* 130:137-40 Ap '87

"We have a problem" [child's acceptance of brother's death] J. Marks. il *Parents* 62:70+ Je '87

"We have a problem" [child's guilt caused by wishing for the death of stepfather's family] J. Marks. il *Parents* 62:62+ F '87

Children and death—cont.

When a child dies, a therapist warns, the grief of brothers and sisters may leave lasting scars [interview with J. Rothman] C. Tamarkin. il por *People Wkly* 27:77-8+ Mr 23 '87

When a young mother dies. J. Gaylin. *Ladies Home J* 104:78+ F '87

Children and drugs *See* Drugs and youth

Children and grandparents *See* Grandparents

Children and mass media *See* Mass media and youth

Children and music *See* Music and children

Children and nuclear warfare

How do you see nuclear war? il *Sch Update* 120:10+ N 20 '87

Learning to live with the bomb [with editorial comment by Elizabeth Crow] P. La Farge. il *Parents* 62:6, 121-2+ Mr '87

Politics and "peace education". A. Ryerson. *Read Dig* 130:133-8 Je '87

Children and parents *See* Parent-child relationship

Children and pets *See* Children and animals

Children and sickness

See also
Sick children

Children and television *See* Television and children

Children and the arts *See* Arts and children

Children and the environment

News from It's Your World clubs. il *Natl Geogr World* 148:26-7 D '87

Children and the telephone *See* Telephone and children

Children and war

See also
Vietnamese War, 1957-1975—Children
World War, 1939-1945—Children

Living in fear. B. Golomb. il *Sch Update* 119:5-6 My 4 '87

Children as acrobats

It's time to jump! [Skip Its, acrobatic rope skipping troupe] il *Natl Geogr World* 139:4-9 Mr '87

Children as actors and actresses

Baby on set [infant star of motion picture Baby boom]; ed. by Roberta Grant. K. Kennedy. il pors *Ladies Home J* 104:61-2+ Je '87

A childhood of sorrows [excerpt from Call me Anna] P. Duke and K. Turan. il pors *People Wkly* 28:70-2+ Jl 13 '87

A troubled coming of age [excerpt from Call me Anna] P. Duke and K. Turan. il pors *People Wkly* 28:54-6+ Jl 20 '87

Children as astronomers

The children of Stellafane. S. J. O'Meara. il *Sky Telesc* 74:417-19 O '87

A child's perspective of Halley's comet. B. Johnston. il *Astronomy* 15:24+ F '87

Hot tub astronomy: a star for everybody. B. Mosier. *Astronomy* 15:32+ D '87

Children as baseball fans *See* Baseball fans

Children as consumers *See* Youth market

Children as dancers

A kid lands every child's dream job: fighting mice in The Nutcracker [M. Parvin dancing with New York City Ballet] il pors *People Wkly* 28:119-21 D 21 '87

Children as guests *See* Guests

Children as inventors

Little wizards. A. A. Lappen. il *Forbes* 139:156-7 Ap 6 '87

Maurice Scales—brother of invention [7 year old inventor of Baby-No-Mash] il pors *Ebony* 42:51-2+ O '87

Now thanks to Suzanna Goodin, pets can clean the bowl—and then eat the spoon that feeds them. il por *People Wkly* 27:119 Mr 9 '87

Children as journalists

Heather Cook's pint-size publication runs all the Family news that's fit to print. K. Hubbard. il por *People Wkly* 27:101-2 Je 1 '87

Children as ministers

13-year-old conducts wedding like veteran [W. Hudson of Chicago] il por *Jet* 71:29 Mr 16 '87

13-year-old preacher talks about love, sex, sin and forgiveness [W. Hudson] T. S. Moore. il pors *Jet* 72:14-16 Je 29 '87

In Chicago, God's word often comes out of the mouth of a mere babe—the Rev. William Hudson III, 13. D. Grogan. il pors *People Wkly* 28:102+ Ag 24 '87

Children as musicians

Blind boy, 3, learns to play 50 songs on piano [J. Gardner] D. M. Cheers. il pors *Jet* 72:22-3 My 25 '87

Blind piano player, 3, visits Stevie Wonder [J. Gardner] il pors *Jet* 72:18 Je 22 '87

Blind piano prodigy, age 4, gets free facial surgery [J. Gardner] il por *Jet* 72:24 S 14 '87

Blind since birth and barely 4, Jermaine Gardner happily hits all the right keys—and heartstrings. K. Hubbard. il pors *People Wkly* 27:53+ Je 22 '87

Dear Mr. Jesus [song by S. Batts] il por *Time* 130:61 D 21 '87

The genius of teaching geniuses [interview with D. DeLay] M. Horn. il por *U S News World Rep* 103:59 Jl 27 '87

Stefan Milenkovic, who plays like a kid when he isn't playing a violin. M. Runnion. il pors *People Wkly* 28:93-4 S 7 '87

Two extraordinary, ordinary children [K. and C. Cerovsek] N. Eberle. il pors *McCalls* 114:49-52 Ag '87

Children as poets

Russian poetry finds a prodigy in 12-year-old Nika Turbina. M. Brower. il por *People Wkly* 27:67 Ap 6 '87

Children as prisoners *See* Refugee children—Imprisonment

Children as witnesses *See* Witnesses

Children in art

A naïf vision of paradise [paintings of M. Lepe] M. Kroll. il por *Américas* 39:20-4 S/O '87

Children of a lesser god [film] *See* Motion picture reviews—Single works

Children of alcoholics

Carol Burnett: the half sister she had to raise [excerpt from One more time] C. Burnett. il pors *Redbook* 168:54+ Ja '87

Daughter's blues: coping with being the adult child of an alcoholic. L. E. Cary. bibl *Essence* 18:76+ My '87

Dependent on disorder. M. Malone. il *Ms* 15:50+ F '87

Forgotten victims: children of alcoholics. E. Stark. bibl (p63) il *Psychol Today* 21:58-62 Ja '87

This mother's daughter. R. Weems. il *Essence* 18:75-6+ My '87

Too late to say, 'I'm sorry'. J. M. Queenan. il *Newsweek* 110:7 Ag 31 '87

Children of artists

The special problems faced by children of famous artists. D. Grant. *Am Artist* 51:76+ O '87

Children of celebrities

Bette Davis talks back! [excerpt from This 'n that]; ed. by Michael Herskowitz. B. Davis. il pors *Redbook* 168:34+ Ap '87

Does a famous name help or hurt? [children of black celebrities] il *Ebony* 43:60+ N '87

Father's Day: celebrity dads talk about their children. il *Jet* 72:14-16 Je 22 '87

How children of celebrities cope with privilege and prejudice [black celebrities] il *Jet* 72:58-9+ Jl 27 '87

How stars make time for their children. il *Jet* 73:58-60 O 26 '87

You're handsomer than Jimmy Stewart, and you will always live in Beverly Hills. N. Wynn. il pors *Roll Stone* p79+ O 8 '87

Children of divorced parents

The best Father's Day ever. P. C. Canning. il *Read Dig* 130:61-3 Je '87

Child of divorce. S. Grobman. il *USA Today (Periodical)* 116:40-2 Jl '87

A curfew for Karin. D. Spencer. il *N Y Times Mag* p26 Jl 5 '87

Divorce: do it for the kids? [study by Nicholas Long and Rex Forehand] J. Meer. *Psychol Today* 21:21 Jl '87

"It was their divorce. Now it's my problem!". A. Wood. *Seventeen* 46:42+ F '87

Missing fathers. E. Teyber and C. D. Hoffman. bibl (p65) il *Psychol Today* 21:36-9 Ap '87

Never a right age [divorce of parents is hardest on adolescents] E. Collins. *Sci Am* 257:32 S '87

Reconciliation, remarriage: the trauma continues [study by D. M. Fergusson] P. Nicholas. *Psychol Today* 21:11 Ja '87

You'd better sit down, kids. J. Conant. il *Newsweek* 110:58 Ag 24 '87

Young children of divorce: depressed, wary, subdued [views of Neil Kalter] *USA Today (Periodical)* 116:10 S '87

Children of drug addicts

Fla. man who used child for drug deal collateral jailed [case of F. W. Cook] il *Jet* 71:32 F 23 '87

Man turns in mother, but won't testify against her [19 year old P. DeRosa] *Jet* 71:29 F 16 '87

Children of executives

"Dad, I know I can handle it". E. F. Cone. il *Forbes* 140 Sp Issue:370+ O 26 '87

Children of executives—*cont.*

Educate, preach and pray. D. Machan. il *Forbes* 139:146+ Mr 9 '87

Executive guilt: who's taking care of the children? F. S. Chapman. il *Fortune* 115:30-7 F 16 '87

Keeping it in the family: should kids inherit fortunes? R. I. Kirkland, Jr. *Current* 289:16-20 Ja '87

Like father, like daughter [father-daughter corporations] R. Rooney. il *Good Housekeep* 204:108-9+ Je '87

Off on a business trip? Don't forget the diapers. S. D. Atchison. il *Bus Week* p79+ N 30 '87

Succeeding in family businesses [women] S. Nelton and K. Berney. il *Nations Bus* 75:26 My '87

Children of hippies

Son of sixties parents. R. Metzner. il *Seventeen* 46:14+ F '87

Children of Holocaust survivors

"We have a problem" [overprotective mother] J. Marks. il *Parents* 62:76+ Ag '87

Children of homosexuals

Gay gothic [two homosexual couples jointly raise a child] L. Van Gelder. il *Ms* 16:146-7+ Jl/Ag '87

Children of interracial parents

Carson's son claims AIDS to make girlfriend abort baby: judge nixes test [child support suit against C. Carson] il por *Jet* 72:13-14 Ag 3 '87

Helping biracial children adjust. T. J. Buttery. *Educ Dig* 52:38-41 My '87

'It's not easy being green' [difficulties of being biracial] L. Mahdesian. por *U S News World Rep* 103:8 N 23 '87

Johnny Carson to face queries on son's support. *Jet* 72:4 Jl 6 '87

Johnny Carson's son must pay support for black child who was living on welfare. il por *Jet* 72:52-3 Ap 13 '87

Mixed but equal [study by Ronald C. Johnson and Craig T. Nagoshi] M. Roberts. *Psychol Today* 21:18 Ap '87

Children of migrant laborers

Education

A teacher pushes migrants' kids into college—and gets fired by his California school board [case of G. Shirley at Alisal High in East Salinas] M. Green. il pors *People Wkly* 27:50+ F 2 '87

Children of prisoners

Prison parenting: a challenge for children's advocates [male prisoners in New York State] V. Bauhofer. il *Child Today* 16:15-16 Ja/F '87

When mothers serve time. M. Christopher. il *Sch Update* 119:8 F 9 '87

Women behind bars [separation from children] N. Rubin. il *McCalls* 114:36+ Ag '87

Children of prostitutes

Bombay's 'red-light' children. B. Sadasivam. *World Press Rev* 34:54 Jl '87

Children of rock musicians

Love the outfit, Mrs. Harleman, but your kids want to just die. D. Grogan. il pors *People Wkly* 28:141-3 O 12 '87

Photographs and photography

The kids are alright. D. Handelman. il *Roll Stone* p167-71 N 5-D 10 '87

Children of separated parents

Parental separation and school problems. F. Roberts. *Parents* 62:53 D '87

"We have a problem". J. Marks. il *Parents* 62:64+ Jl '87

Children of servicemen

"I am Bryan, your brother" [Australian son fathered by an American serviceman is united with his sisters in the U.S.] J. L. Block. il por *Good Housekeep* 204:82+ Mr '87

Children of the deaf

The empty crib [deaf parents struggle to retain custody of child; case of S. Timmons in Florida] L. A. Walker. il por *Ladies Home J* 104:76+ Mr '87

I was my parents' radio. L. Konner. il *Glamour* 85:228+ My '87

My mother's silent world. R. Brody. il *50 Plus* 27:25-7+ My '87

Children of the mentally ill

A wrenching separation ends an Iowa couple's hope of adopting the five Cooper kids [P. and L. Mick fight to keep children of mentally ill mother] G. Pick. il *People Wkly* 27:40-3 F 2 '87

Children of the rich

"My son, I brought him up like an immigrant". R. McGough. il *Forbes* 140 Sp Issue:70+ O 26 '87

Rich kids: cashing in on happiness? J. Romberger. il *Teen* 31:32+ Ag '87

Children of working mothers *See* Children of working parents

Children of working parents

See also

Day care

Are working moms good mothers? Ask their kids [results of study] D. Hales. *Redbook* 168:95+ Mr '87

Helping your kids understand your work. M. Cantarella. *McCalls* 114:135 Ag '87

How do kids really feel about being home alone? [latchkey children] E. Gray and P. Coolen. bibl f il *Child Today* 16:30-2 Jl/Ag '87

Kids and two-career parents. J. P. Comer. il *Parents* 62:125 Ja '87

Latchkey kids: who are they? [study by Sandra Hofferth and Virginia Cain] S. Chollar. *Psychol Today* 21:12 D '87

Quality time—what's that? K. Levine. il *Parents* 62:76+ N '87

Safety for latchkey children. C. Loomis. il *Parents* 62:13 D '87

Sick at school. B. D. Colen. il *Health* 19:8 Ja '87

Statistics

Census Bureau estimate of number of latchkey children disputed. *Phi Delta Kappan* 68:638 Ap '87

Children's art

Art mailbag [drawings] il *Natl Geogr World* 141:30-1 My '87

Unicorn mailbag [children's drawings of unicorns] il *Natl Geogr World* 147:24-5 N '87

Competitions

Detroit girl stays in school; wins trip to Japan [C. McKinnon wins art contest] *Jet* 72:12 S 7 '87

Here they are! The top winning cards in the 1987 Mother's Day contest! il *Good Housekeep* 204:36+ My '87

Children's Book Press

Broadening niches: multilingual children's books and movie technology guides. L. See. *Publ Wkly* 231:144 F 27 '87

Children's books *See* Children's literature

Children's bookstores *See* Booksellers and bookselling—Children's literature

Children's Bureau (U.S.) *See* United States. Children's Bureau

Children's camps *See* Camps

Children's chores

Child labor. E. McCoy. il *Parents* 62:94-9 Ag '87

Chores & children. L. G. Katz. il *Parents* 62:152 Jl '87

Every child should have a chore. B. Spock. por *Redbook* 169:30+ O '87

Children's clothes *See* Clothing and dress—Children

Children's clothing stores *See* Clothing stores

Children's costumes *See* Costume

Children's cribs *See* Cribs (Beds)

Children's Defense Fund (U.S.)

Marian Wright Edelman. K. Bouton. por *Ms* 16:98-100+ Jl/Ag '87

"They cannot fend for themselves" [lobbyist M. Edelman] N. Traver. il por *Time* 129:27 Mr 23 '87

Children's electronics

Babes in techland. P. Hoban. il *N Y* 20:20+ Mr 23 '87

Children's emotions *See* Emotions

Children's fantasies

The dream that grew in our garden [daughter "grows" a Cabbage Patch doll] S. Alexander. il *Good Housekeep* 204:58 Mr '87

The great pretender. B. Weissbourd. il *Parents* 62:158 Je '87

Let's pretend. P. Theroux. il *Parents* 62:66+ My '87

Children's fears *See* Fear

Children's festivals *See* Festivals

Children's friends *See* Friendship

Children's furniture *See* Furniture, Children's

Children's games *See* Games

Children's gardens and gardening

See also

School gardens and gardening

Children's homes *See* Orphans and orphanages

Children's Hospital (San Diego, Calif.)

Mind games taken to heart [post-operative cardiac patients] N. Benford and D. Gage. il *Health* 19:25 N '87

Children's hospitals *See* Children—Hospitals

Children's humor *See* Humor

Children's hunting *See* Hunting

Children's lies *See* Lying

Children's literature

See also

Booksellers and bookselling—Children's literature

Children's literature—See also—*cont.*
Children's periodicals
Children's poetry
Children's reading
Children's stories
Fairy tales
Picture books for children
Publishers and publishing—Children's literature
Scientific literature for children
Story telling
Young adults' literature

Advertising
See Books—Advertising

Authorship
See also
Society of Children's Book Writers
Flying starts: new faces of 1987. D. E. Roback; K. O. Fakih. il *Publ Wkly* 232:36-8+ D 25 '87
The growing market for juvenile books. *Writer* 100:28-30 O '87
A moon that never sets [work of M. W. Brown] L. S. Marcus. *N Y Times Book Rev* 92:22 Ja 25 '87
PW interviews [J. Burningham and H. Oxenbury] M. Field. il pors *Publ Wkly* 232:168-9 Jl 24 '87
PW interviews [J. Stevenson] K. O. Fakih. por *Publ Wkly* 231:148-9 F 27 '87
A sense of audience. J. Paton Walsh. *Writer* 100:19-21 F '87
Steig: nobody is grown-up. S. Kroll. *N Y Times Book Rev* 92:26 Je 28 '87
Thacher Hurd: a talent in his own right. D. E. Roback. il por *Publ Wkly* 231:33+ Ja 23 '87
Where the Wild Things began [childhood fears] M. Sendak. il *N Y Times Book Rev* 92:1+ My 17 '87
William Steig at 80. D. Allender. il por *Publ Wkly* 232:116-18 Jl 24 '87
Words & pictures: the right order [adaptation of address] R. Wells. por *Publ Wkly* 231:146 F 27 '87

Awards
See also
Picture books for children—Awards

Bibliography
. . . and to all a good book [children's books for Christmas] C. Loomis. il *Parents* 62:92+ N '87
Books your children will enjoy and learn from [depictions of the handicapped] C. W. Levy. *McCalls* 114:68 S '87
Children's books. See issues of The New York Times Book Review
Children's books [religious books] *Publ Wkly* 231:56-7 Mr 6 '87
Children's books: fall 1987. il *Publ Wkly* 232:123-53+ Jl 24 '87
Children's books for Christmas. F. McNulty. *New Yorker* 63:132+ N 30 '87
Children's books: spring 1987. il *Publ Wkly* 231:107-37 F 27 '87
Enchantments for children [best of 1986] S. Kanfer. il *Time* 129:80-1 Ja 5 '87
For giving: a 'read to me' wrap-up. L. Shapiro. il *Newsweek* 110:51-2 D 28 '87
Forecasts. See issues of Publishers Weekly
Great new books for kids [excerpt from The RIF guide to encouraging young readers] R. Graves. il *Good Housekeep* 205:105 S '87
Liberating youthful spirits [Christmas gifts] S. Kanfer. il *Time* 130:78-9 D 14 '87
Lives of the rich and famous [biographies for children] C. C. Epstein. il *Parents* 62:71-3+ Ap '87
Timeless stories with timely morals. il *Esquire* 108:146-7 D '87

Book reviews
See Book reviews and reviewing

Censorship
See Censorship

Illustration
See Illustration

Marketing
See Books—Marketing

Technique
How to make believe. A. Lindbergh. *Writer* 100:17-19 D '87
Remembering how it was [using childhood memories in writing for children] L. Lowry. il *Writer* 100:16-19 Jl '87
Writing biographies for children. G. Kamen. *Writer* 100:19-21 Mr '87

Themes
A boy's own author [J. R. Tunis] J. Epstein. *Commentary* 84:50-6 D '87

The challenge of children's history: making it vivid, getting it right. P. Maier. il *N Y Times Book Rev* 92:42-3 My 17 '87
The truth about Black Beauty [unrealistic portrayal of animals in children's literature; views of H. N. Christensen] D. Sobel. *Omni* 9:27 Mr '87
Yooks, zooks and the bomb. R. Sutton. *N Y Times Book Rev* 92:22 F 22 '87

Canada
Bibliography
Child's garden of print. P. Young. il *Macleans* 100:50-1 Jl 13 '87
Joys for young readers. P. Young. il *Macleans* 100:54+ D 7 '87

Japan
A Washington, D.C. conference: Japanese children's books. D. E. Roback. il *Publ Wkly* 232:42 D 25 '87

Children's magic window (Periodical)
New ventures in the Snow State. K. O. Fakih. *Publ Wkly* 231:102-3 F 27 '87

Children's Museum of Indianapolis
Minds-on museum. M. Wade. il *Horizon* 30:24 Je '87
New Children's Museum gallery celebrates global themes [Passport to the World gallery] P. Rowe. il *Child Today* 16:14-17 My/Je '87

Children's museums
See also
Children's Museum of Indianapolis
Exploratorium
Please touch the exhibits. B. Kantrowitz. il *Newsweek* 110:98 O 19 '87

Children's music *See* Music and children
Children's music phonograph records *See* Phonograph records—Children's music
Children's opinions *See* Children—Attitudes
Children's parties
See also
Birthday parties

Children's periodicals
See also
Children's magic window (Periodical)
Juvenile articles that sell. M. Johnston. *Writer* 100:28-9 S '87

Children's poetry
Read-aloud rhymes for the very young [excerpt] J. Prelutsky. il *Parents* 62:141-2+ S '87

Children's pottery *See* Pottery
Children's programs (Television) *See* Cable television—Children's programs; Television broadcasting—Children's programs

Children's questions and answers
Why in the world? See occasional issues of National Geographic World

Children's reading
See also
Children's literature
Reading aloud
7 ways to turn a TV-kid on to reading. D. Stillman. il *McCalls* 115:61 O '87
Huckleberry Finn: or, Something exotic in Czechoslovakia. J. Škvorecký. *N Y Times Book Rev* 92:47-8 N 8 '87

Anecdotes, facetiae, satire, etc.
Growing up born again. J. Campbell. il *Publ Wkly* 232:44-5 O 9 '87

Projects
See also
California Reading Initiative
1987 Reading rainbow selections. *Publ Wkly* 231:106 F 27 '87
A reading program that works as a community effort [Reading Incentive Program at Samuel Bowles School in Springfield, Mass.] M. R. McGrath. il *Phi Delta Kappan* 68:475-6 F '87

Children's rights *See* Children—Civil rights
Children's rooms
Beat the messy room rap [teen bedrooms] S. Harris. il *Teen* 31:26+ N '87
Kids' rooms: not for sleeping only. V. Hahn. il *Parents* 62:162-4 S '87
Kidstyle decorating. D. L. Caringer and R. E. Dittmer. il *Better Homes Gard* 65:132-7 My '87
Learning to live with a sloppy kid. C. Berman. il *Parents* 62:128-30+ N '87
Pretty rooms [girls' rooms] V. Hahn. il *Parents* 62:163+ My '87
Room to grow [girl's bedroom] L. E. Oberwager. il *Home Mech* 83:48-50+ O '87
Stairwell gives them play area and storage. il *Sunset* 179:152-3 O '87

Children's rooms—*cont.*
Understanding kids [different aged children sharing a bedroom] L. Balter. il *Ladies Home J* 104:110 N '87

Children's safety seats *See* Automobiles—Safety devices and measures

Children's songs
Take a gander at Mother Goose's newest champions, Pam Beall and Susan Nipp of Wee Sing. A. Chambers. il pors *People Wkly* 28:66+ S 14 '87

Children's stories
See also
Story telling

Single works
See name of author for full entry
The Clown-Arounds go on vacation. Cole, Joanna
The day dad made toast. Durkee, Sarah
Five minutes' peace. Murphy, Jill, 1949-
Get well, Clown-Arounds. Cole, Joanna
Ima on the bima. Portnoy, Mindy Avra
Marcella and the moon. Coats, Laura Jane
My brother, Will. Robins, Joan
The oak tree. Coats, Laura Jane
Piggybook. Browne, Anthony

Children's stories (by children)
Smart, magical, funny 3-year-olds [work of V. G. Paley at the University of Chicago Laboratory Nursery School] P. La Farge. il pors *Parents* 62:160-4+ N '87

Children's tape recordings *See* Tape recordings—Children's use

Children's Television Workshop
Big Bird's mother hen [cover story; interview with J. Cooney] R. Robinson. il pors *50 Plus* 27:24-7 D '87
Street smart. P. Hellman. il por *N Y* 20:48-53 N 23 '87

Children's theater *See* Theater, Children's
Children's thinking *See* Thought and thinking
Children's videotapes *See* Videotapes—Children's use
Childress, Alice, 1920-
about
Moms [drama] Reviews
N Y 20:128 F 23 '87. J. Simon
New Yorker 63:105 F 23 '87. E. Oliver
Childress, James J., and others
Symbiosis in the deep sea. il *Sci Am* 256:114-20 My '87
Childs, David M.
about
David Childs: the classicist. B. Dumaine. il por *Fortune* 115:153-5 Je 22 '87
Childs, Lucinda
about
Acting aside, Childs readies troupe for NYC season. por *Dance Mag* 61:6 My '87
Portraits in reflection [dance] Reviews
Theatre Crafts il 21:32-3+ F '87. C. Bush
Childs, Richard L. MacKenzie *See* MacKenzie-Childs, Richard L.
Childs (Lucinda) Dance Company *See* Lucinda Childs Dance Company
A child's Christmas in Wales [television program] *See* Television program reviews—Single works
Chile
See also
Airplanes, Training—Chile
Andes
Astronomical observatories—Chile
Birds—Chile
Cape Horn (Chile)
Civil rights—Chile
College education and state—Chile
Earthquakes—Chile
Easter—Chile
Easter Island
Festivals—Chile
Patagonia (Argentina and Chile)
Rain forests—Chile
Space research—Chile
Student protests, demonstrations, etc.—Chile
Antiquities
By the banks of the Chinchihuapi. T. D. Dillehay. il map *Nat Hist* 96:8+ Ap '87
Commerce
United States
See United States—Commerce—Chile
Defenses
See also
Airplanes, Military—Chile

Economic policy
"Relax, Mr. President". E. A. Finn, Jr. il *Forbes* 140:100+ N 30 '87
The tricoteuse of counterrevolution [S. Christian's reporting] A. Cockburn. *Nation* 245:44-5 Jl 18-25 '87
Foreign relations
United States
See United States—Foreign relations—Chile
Industries
See also
Empresa Nacional de Aeronautica
Ladeco (Firm)
Native peoples
See Indians of South America—Chile
Politics and government
See also
Press and politics—Chile
Chile's impending choice. V. Horne. *Natl Rev* 39:40 Ag 28 '87
Chile's student leaders under fire. T. Rosenberg. il *Roll Stone* p97+ S 24 '87
Life goes on under Pinochet's yoke. S. J. Ungar. il *U S News World Rep* 103:40 N 30 '87
Pinochet's grip on Chile. P. Constable. bibl f *Curr Hist* 86:17-20+ Ja '87
Pinochet's way. C. G. Brown. il por *N Y Rev Books* 34:47-9 Je 25 '87
Situation in Chile [statement, July 21, 1987] E. Abrams. *Dep State Bull* 87:63-6 O '87
A tight grip on the reins. C. Lane. il por *Newsweek* 110:29 Jl 6 '87
Under the dictator [regime of A. Pinochet]; tr. by Robert Cox. J. Timerman. *New Yorker* 63:47-50+ N 2 '87
Bibliography
Going to extremes [cover story] M. Falcoff. il *New Repub* 197:26-33 S 7 '87
Religious institutions and affairs
See also
Church and civil rights—Chile
John Paul II, Pope, 1920-—Visit to Chile, 1987
Chiles, James R.
Breaking codes was this couple's lifetime career. bibl (p154) il pors *Smithsonian* 18:128-30+ Je '87
NASA's giant research balloons are out of sight. bibl (p132) il *Smithsonian* 17:82-8+ Ja '87
Titanium: for when you care enough to use the very best. bibl (p184) il *Smithsonian* 18:86-90+ My '87
Chiles, Lawton
about
Will a new chairman polarize the Senate Budget Committee? D. Harbrecht. *Bus Week* p49 D 21 '87
Chili
A chili winter. J. Pruess. il *N Y Times Mag* p57-8 Ja 18 '87
Choose-the-color chili. il *Sunset* 178:86-7 Mr '87
What makes chili chili? J. Taylor and T. P. Wolf. il *Better Homes Gard* 65:72-3+ Ja '87
Chili peppers *See* Peppers
Chillida, Eduardo, 1924-
about
Eduardo Chillida. L. Goldman. il *Art News* 86:27 F '87
Chilstrom, Herbert W., 1931-
about
Chilstrom installed. *Christ Century* 104:936 O 28 '87
Chilton, W. E., III
about
Obituary
Nation 244:205 F 21 '87
Chimeras (Biology) *See* Mosaics (Biology)
Chimney cleaning
New techniques in chimney cleaning [interview with R. Edwards] S. Maviglio. il por *Home Mech* 83:30+ O '87
Sweeping out the soot. R. Kimber. il *Ctry J* 14:13-15 O '87
Chimney sweeps *See* Chimney cleaning
Chimneys
Romance in the rooftops [condominiums] P. Langdon. il *Atlantic* 260:85-7 Jl '87
Where there's fire there is smoke—and usually a 'chimney'. R. Wernick. bibl (p187) il *Smithsonian* 18:140-4+ S '87
Maintenance and repair
Dealing with old chimneys. B. Vila. il *Pop Mech* 164:37-8 O '87
When your chimney needs relining. S. Maviglio. il *Home Mech* 83:67-8+ O '87

Chimpanzee to human transplants *See* Xenografts

Chimpanzees

Calculating apes [cover story] B. Bower. il *Sci News* 131:334-5 My 23 '87

The challenge of testing chimps [AIDS vaccine research] S. Weisburd. *Sci News* 131:331 My 23 '87

Outward bound for chimps [reintroduction to the wild at Abuko Nature Reserve, Gambia] B. McBride. il map *Int Wildl* 17:18-21 S/O '87

Simian star of a new toy line, Michael Jackson's pet, Bubbles, plays second banana to no one. il *People Wkly* 28:189 N 16 '87

War among the chimps [cover story] M. P. Ghiglieri. il *Discover* 8:66-70+ N '87

Treatment

A plea for the chimps. J. Goodall. il *N Y Times Mag* p108-10+ My 17 '87

Chimpanzees as actors

A chimp for all seasons [Zippy the Chimp] il *N Y* 20:28 Ap 13 '87

Chimpanzees as artists

The artist in us all [chimp drawings; research by Sarah T. Boysen] A. H. Rosenfeld. il *Psychol Today* 21:20 S '87

China

See also

Abortion—Laws and regulations—China
Aged—China
Agricultural administration—China
Agriculture—China
AIDS (Disease)—China
Air pollution—China
Air traffic control—China
Americans—China
Automation—China
Aviation and state—China
Beijing (China)
Benxi (China)
Birth control—China
Cable television—China
Canadians—China
Censorship—China
Children—China
Chinese
Copyright—China
Divorce—China
Education—China
Education and state—China
Environmental policy—China
Express highways—China
Food supply—China
Foreign correspondents—China
Forests and forestry—China
Government and the press—China
Government entertaining—China
Guangdong Province (China)
Guangzhou (China)
Investments, American—China
Investments, Foreign—China
Investments, Hong Kong—China
Law—China
Literacy education—China
Literature and state—China
Medical care—China
Mount Everest (China and Nepal)
Nepotism—China
Nutrition—China
Paleontology—China
Political prisoners—China
Psychiatry—China
Public opinion—China
Restaurants—China
Science—China
Shanghai (China)
Shenyang (China)
Shenzhen (China)
Space centers—China
Space research—China
Street trades—China
Student movement—China
Student protests, demonstrations, etc.—China
Taiwan
Technology—China
Television advertising—China
Theater—China
Trade routes—China
Wildlife conservation—China
Wildlife sanctuaries—China
Women—China
Youth—China

Air Force

Chinese Air Force developing few new aircraft designs. R. G. O'Lone. il *Aviat Week Space Technol* 127:55+ D 7 '87

Antiquities

See also

Tombs—China

Acoustics of ancient Chinese bells. S. Shen. il map *Sci Am* 256:104-10 Ap '87

Armed Forces

See also

China. People's Liberation Army

Bibliography

Book reviews. *Curr Hist* 86:270 S '87

Civilization

Vive la différence! [comparison of Chinese and Western civilizations in the 1880s; excerpt from Nouvelles lettres édifiantes et curieuses d'Extrême-Occident par des voyageurs lettrés chinois à la Belle Epoque] T.-C. Yuan. il *Courier* 40:28-9 Ap '87

Commerce

Canada

See Canada—Commerce—China

Iran

What's the Chinese word for chutzpah? [sale of missiles to Iran] *Newsweek* 110:59 N 9 '87

Soviet Union

See Soviet Union—Commerce—China

Taiwan

Taiwan is in the throes of 'mainland-mania'. D. J. Yang. il *Bus Week* p46-7 O 26 '87

United States

See United States—Commerce—China

Commercial policy

The China bubble bursts. L. Kraar. il *Fortune* 116:86-9 Jl 6 '87

Cultural policy

China's cultural crackdown. E. A. Gargan. il *N Y Times Mag* p24-6+ Jl 12 '87

Let a hundred flowers wilt. R. Dorfman. il *Progressive* 51:19-23 Mr '87

Some flowers bloom. *World Press Rev* 34:27 S '87

Thaw and freeze and thaw again: the cultural weather in China. S. Topping. *N Y Times Book Rev* 92:3+ D 27 '87

Cultural relations

Canada

See Canada—Cultural relations—China

United States

See United States—Cultural relations—China

Defenses

See also

Airplanes, Military—China
China—Air Force
Guided missiles, Chinese

Defending China in 1987. H. W. Jencks. bibl f *Curr Hist* 86:266-9+ S '87

Description and travel

On the road in China. P. Plawin. il *Changing Times* 41:89-92+ D '87

A reporter's odyssey in unseen China. J. F. Burns. il map *N Y Times Mag* p29-31+ F 8 '87

Riding the Silk Road in China [cover story] G. Woodcock. il *New Leader* 70:10-15 S 21 '87

Economic conditions

China's standing in the developing world. V. Smil. bibl f il *Curr Hist* 86:245-8+ S '87

Economic policy

Cabbages and capitalists [storeowner Guan Guangmei] D. Elliott. il por *Newsweek* 110:37 Jl 20 '87

China's economy at the crossroads. C.-Y. Cheng. bibl f *Curr Hist* 86:253-6+ S '87

Deng's policy: to get rich is glorious. J. Martin. il *Sch Update* 120:19+ S 18 '87

Deng's reforms will prevail—but at a price. D. J. Yang and M. Shao. il por *Bus Week* p70-1+ O 19 '87

Deng's second revolution: prosperity vs. ideology. M. Lord. il por *U S News World Rep* 103:41-3 O 12 '87

Development of a more market-oriented economy in China. G. C. Chow. bibl f *Science* 235:295-9 Ja 16 '87

Economic reforms may have begun a long march backward. D. J. Yang and R. T. Grieves. il *Bus Week* p54-5 Mr 16 '87

From long march to great leap. S. Sen. *Commonweal* 114:648-9 N 20 '87

In China, the buck starts here. N. D. Kristof. il map *N Y Times Mag* p40-2+ D 20 '87

Is Beijing about to take two steps back? J. Becker and D. J. Yang. il *Bus Week* p69 Je 22 '87

China—Economic policy—*cont.*

A touch of capitalism. S. Simmie. il *Macleans* 100:24 N 9 '87

Zhao gives China a swift kick toward a free market. M. Shao. il por *Bus Week* p89 N 16 '87

Foreign relations

China's confident nationalism. M. Oksenberg. bibl f *Foreign Aff* 65 Sp Issue:501-23 ['87]

East Asia

Next door to the People's Republic of China [special section] il map *Sch Update* 120:27-9+ S 18 '87

Great Britain

See Great Britain—Foreign relations—China

India

Chinese deploy J-7 fighters in Tibet to counter Indian threat. C. Covault. il *Aviat Week Space Technol* 127:103-4 O 19 '87

To the west: fearful neighbors. *Sch Update* 120:32 S 18 '87

Japan

To the east: worried smiles. il *Sch Update* 120:32 S 18 '87

Portugal

Macao returns to 'the motherland'. *Newsweek* 109:39 Ap 6 '87

Macau's casino king gets set to play with Beijing [S. Ho] M. Shao. il por *Bus Week* p98-9 Ja 19 '87

Soviet Union

See Soviet Union—Foreign relations—China

Taiwan

Taiwan begins to bend to the new reality. D. Doder. il *U S News World Rep* 103:51-2 N 9 '87

Taiwan: the other China. il *Sch Update* 120:27-8 S 18 '87

Tibet

China still battles for Tibet. S. Simons. il *World Press Rev* 34:29-31 My '87

Fire at the top of the world. F. Willey. il map *Newsweek* 110:50+ O 19 '87

Fire in a snowy land [pro-independence rioting in Tibet] W. E. Smith. il map *Time* 130:26-7 O 19 '87

The monks' rebellion. M. Nichols. il *Macleans* 100:33 O 19 '87

Spirit in exile: the Dalai Lama pleads for the Tibetan people. R. Gere and R. A. F. Thurman. il por *Roll Stone* p68-9 D 3 '87

Tibet [special section] il *World Press Rev* 34:19-22 D '87

Tibetan air operations [special section] il *Aviat Week Space Technol* 127:103-4+ O 19 '87

Tibetan Buddhism survives nightmare of repression. L. Wischmann. il *Christ Century* 104:529-31 Je 3-10 '87

Tibetans rally to guard a culture. J. Elbert. *Christ Century* 104:988-9 N 11 '87

A tinderbox in Tibet inflames U.S.-China relations. J. Becker and B. Javetski. il *Bus Week* p53 O 26 '87

To the west: fearful neighbors. *Sch Update* 120:32 S 18 '87

Turmoil in Tibet. L. Wischmann. il map *Christ Century* 104:1118-19 D 9 '87

Unrest rocks the calm of 'Shangri-La' [anti-Chinese demonstrations] il *U S News World Rep* 103:10 O 19 '87

Tibet—Anecdotes, facetiae, satire, etc.

Uncivil liberties. C. Trillin. il *Nation* 245:778 D 26 '87-Ja 2 '88

United States

See United States—Foreign relations—China

Vietnam

To the south: a friend turned foe. il *Sch Update* 120:29 S 18 '87

History

China's long struggle to rid itself of foreign domination. I. Peck. il *Sch Update* 120:24-6 S 18 '87

Ch'in dynasty, 221-207 B.C.

Treasures from an ancient Chinese tomb [Duke of Qin Tomb No. 1] Wen Ruitang. il *Courier* 40:32-3 Ja '87

Ming dynasty, 1368-1644

China studies [The Chinese scholar's studio: artistic life in the late Ming period at the Asia Society] K. Larson. il *N Y* 20:108-9 N 2 '87

Xi'an Incident, 1936

The Xi'an Incident. J. Crossland. bibl il pors *Hist Today* 37:10-16 Jl '87

Cultural Revolution, 1966-1969

Life and death in Shanghai [excerpts; cover story] N. Cheng. il por *Time* 129:42-8+ Je 8 '87

The loving penance of Hu Bo [caring for former teacher after Cultural Revolution; condensed from After the nightmare] H. Liang and J. Shapiro. il *Read Dig* 130:104-9 Ap '87

Mao's student revolution. P. M. Jones. il *Sch Update* 120:11-12+ S 18 '87

Running dogs and credit cards: class struggle and a Chinese dictionary. O. Schell. il *N Y Times Book Rev* 92:3+ Je 7 '87

Surviving the hurricane [Nien Cheng] J. Shapiro. il *N Y Rev Books* 34:5-6+ Jl 16 '87

Industries

See also
Aerospace industries—China
Airlines—China
Airplane industry—China
Computer industry—China
Electronic industries—China
Munitions—China
Shanghai Metallurgical & Mining Machinery Mfg.
Silk industry—China
Tourist trade—China
Xian Aircraft Corp.

Don't discount China's potential to succeed as industrial power. L. Bertain. por *Aviat Week Space Technol* 127:61-2 D 7 '87

Intellectual life

China: intellectuals at bay. M. Goldman and R. Wagner. il *N Y Rev Books* 34:17-20 Mr 26 '87

China's cultural crackdown. E. A. Gargan. il *N Y Times Mag* p24-6+ Jl 12 '87

Some flowers bloom. *World Press Rev* 34:27 S '87

Thaw and freeze and thaw again: the cultural weather in China. S. Topping. *N Y Times Book Rev* 92:3+ D 27 '87

Military policy

See also
China—Defenses

Nationalism

China's confident nationalism. M. Oksenberg. bibl f *Foreign Aff* 65 Sp Issue:501-23 ['87]

Photographs and photography

Images of contemporary China. I. M. Elliott. il por *Archit Dig* 44:166+ Ja '87

Politics and government

See also
Communism—China
Communist Party (China)
Politics, Corruption in—China

Balancing act [13th Communist Party Congress] S. Tifft. il *Time* 130:64-5 N 9 '87

Battle of the octogenarians [weakening power of Deng Xiaoping] M. S. Serrill. il *Time* 129:50 Mr 9 '87

Broken China. J. Mirsky. *Foreign Policy* 66:57-76 Spr '87

Can Deng protect his reforms from the 'angry old men'? M. Shao and others. por *Bus Week* p53 F 2 '87

China [cover story; special section] il *World Press Rev* 34:11-16 Mr '87

China drops the copilot [firing Hu Yaobang] R. Watson. il por *Newsweek* 109:30-1 Ja 26 '87

China hits the clutch [forced resignation of Hu Yaobang] M. Hopkins. por *New Leader* 70:3-4 Ja 12-26 '87

China passes the torch. M. Hopkins. por *New Leader* 70:5-6 N 30 '87

China puts off the millennium. E. MacFarquhar. il *U S News World Rep* 103:50-1 N 9 '87

The China syndrome [student demonstrations] B. I. Schwartz. *New Repub* 196:15-16 F 9 '87

China takes the reformist road. A. Joyce. il *Nation* 245:752-4 D 19 '87

China's changing of the guard [elevation of Zhao Ziyang] F. Willey. il por *Newsweek* 110:78 N 16 '87

China's ghastly tragedy. *Natl Rev* 39:16-17 F 13 '87

China's heir apparent [Zhao Ziyang] D. Elliott. il por *Newsweek* 110:69 N 2 '87

China's last emperor [Deng Xiaoping] M. Hopkins. il *New Leader* 70:7-10 O 19 '87

China's new math. S. Leys. *New Repub* 196:13 Mr 2 '87

China's new Year of the Mule [Peng Zhen's rivalry with Deng Xiaoping] F. Willey. il por *Newsweek* 109:43 F 9 '87

China's reform consumes one of its creators [forced resignation of Hu Yaobang] M. Lord. il por *U S News World Rep* 102:34 Ja 26 '87

China's student protests. il *World Press Rev* 34:19 F '87

China's student rebels are playing into Deng's hands. M. Shao. il por *Bus Week* p48-9 Ja 19 '87

China—Politics and government—cont.

A crackdown campaign goes on. T. A. Sancton. il Time 129:45-6 F 2 '87

Deng cracks down [Hu Yaobang forced to resign] J. Smolowe. il por Time 129:24-5 Ja 26 '87

Deng's balancing act. F. Willey. il por Newsweek 110:33 Ag 17 '87

Deng's reforms will prevail—but at a price. D. J. Yang and M. Shao. il por Bus Week p70-1+ O 19 '87

Deng's second revolution: prosperity vs. ideology. M. Lord. il por U S News World Rep 103:41-3 O 12 '87

The end of a beginning [departure of Hu Yaobang] M. Janigan. il por Macleans 100:24 Ja 26 '87

Free speech Chinese style [special section] il por Newsweek 109:30-1+ Ja 5 '87

Hu's not on first [ouster of Hu Yaobang] F. Schurmann. Nation 244:100-1 Ja 31 '87

Let a hundred flowers wilt. R. Dorfman. il Progressive 51:19-23 Mr '87

Liberalization digs in. A. Giarelli. World Press Rev 34:38 Je '87

The long shadow of Mao. F. Willey. il por Newsweek 109:40 Mr 16 '87

More wintry days of discontent [student protests] W. R. Doerner. il Time 129:38 Ja 12 '87

The Moscow/Peking dilemma. B. Crozier. Natl Rev 39:26 D 18 '87

The new thunder out of China—what it means [student protests] R. A. Manning. il U S News World Rep 102:12 Ja 12 '87

The old man and the mountains [comeback for Deng Xiaoping's reform campaign] H. G. Chua-Eoan. il Time 130:41 Jl 13 '87

Opening the windows [student protests] A. Bilski. il Macleans 100:19 Ja 12 '87

The People's Republic of China, 1987 [special issue] bibl f il map (inside back cover) Curr Hist 86:241-81+ S '87

Political reform in China. M. Gottschalk. il Nation 244:677-80 My 23 '87

Reading the fortune cookies. H. Trewhitt. il por U S News World Rep 102:37-8 Mr 16 '87

The reformists strike back. R. Delfs. il World Press Rev 34:25-6 S '87

Rumblings. New Repub 196:7-9 Ja 19 '87

Running dogs and credit cards: class struggle and a Chinese dictionary. O. Schell. il N Y Times Book Rev 92:3+ Je 7 '87

Settling for a stalemate [National People's Congress] J. Greenwald. il Time 129:38-9 Ap 6 '87

There's a dragon out there [government reaction to student dissent] M. S. Serrill. il Time 129:45 Ja 19 '87

Three for tomorrow [Zhao Ziyang] R. Thomson. il por World Press Rev 34:23 D '87

Today's changing China: can the new freedom last? [cover story; special issue] il maps Sch Update 120:6-12+ S 18 '87

Two crossroads of reform. J. Kohan. il Time 130:66-8+ N 9 '87

"We will march!" [student protests] M. S. Serrill. il Time 129:50-2 Ja 5 '87

'You cannot arrest us' [defiant students] D. Elliott. il Newsweek 109:28-30 Ja 12 '87

Popular culture

Food and TV for 1 billion. E. Dzik. il Sch Update 120:41 S 18 '87

Population

China's food policy and population. K.-I. Chen. bibl f Curr Hist 86:257-60+ S '87

Religious institutions and affairs

  See also

  Christians—China

  Evangelistic work—China

  Protestant churches—China

Social conditions

  See also

  Women—China

Today's changing China: can the new freedom last? [cover story; special issue] il maps Sch Update 120:6-12+ S 18 '87

China. Army See China. People's Liberation Army

China. People's Liberation Army

Too important for the politicians. F. Willey. il Newsweek 109:30-1 Ja 26 '87

China (Porcelain) See Pottery

China and the United States

Pandas [J. A. Cohen's work in securing loan of pandas from Beijing for the Bronx Zoo] New Yorker 63:23-4 Ap 13 '87

China Grill (New York, N.Y.) See New York (N.Y.)—Restaurants, nightclubs, bars, etc.

China in motion pictures

Glimpse of the Forbidden City [The last emperor] D. Leigh-Kile. il Life 10:36-40 Ap '87

Model citizen: Bernardo Bertolucci on location in China [making of The last emperor; cover story] T. Rayns. il por Film Comment 23:31-2+ N/D '87

China International Trust and Investment Corporation

China's Mister Right [Rong Yiren] L. Kraar. il por Fortune 115:109 Ja 5 '87

China Moon Cafe (San Francisco, Calif.) See San Francisco (Calif.)—Restaurants, nightclubs, bars, etc.

China National Opera and Dance Drama Theater

Reviews:

Performance of A dancer on the bronze phoenix terrace in Beijing. J.-P. Ou. il Dance Mag 61:18-19 D '87

China trade porcelain

Chine de commande. R. Fischell. il House Gard 159:70+ D '87

Chinese export porcelain [State Dept. Building] E. Gordon. il Antiques 132:182-7 Jl '87

The shipwrecked remainders of Europe's china boom. C. R. Boxer. il Hist Today 37:45-8 Ap '87

China-United States air agreements See Aviation—International aspects

Chincoteague National Wildlife Refuge (Va.) See Wildlife sanctuaries—Virginia

Chinese

Canada

Rich and powerful [cover story; special section; with editorial comment by Kevin Doyle] il Macleans 100:2, 24-31 Ag 17 '87

Young and merciless [Chinese gangs in Vancouver] J. O'Hara. il Macleans 100:59 O 26 '87

Religious life

Ethnic Chinese churches prepare for influx of Hong Kong immigrants. L. Mackey. il Christ Today 31:54-5 Mr 20 '87

France

  History

A Chinese general in Paris [late 19th century] C.-T. Chen. il Courier 40:31 Ap '87

India

  History

How Buddhism came to Karnasuvarna [excerpt from Records of the western regions of the great T'ang dynasty] Hsüan-tsang. il Courier 40:24 Ap '87

United States

  See also

  Chinese Americans

Activist abroad: an agenda for reform in China [Ni Yuxian] W. J. Holstein. Bus Week p49 Ja 19 '87

A feather on the wind [watercolorist Lei Yu] D. Frankel. il por N Y 20:21 F 9 '87

  History

Let's eat Chinese tonight. B. R. Johnson. il Am Herit 38:98-103+ D '87

Chinese Americans

Being Chinese in America. T. Fung. il por Sch Update 120:37 S 18 '87

Education

The drive to excel [D. Kuo, student at Bronx High School of Science] A. Quindlen. il pors N Y Times Mag p32+ F 22 '87

Chinese art See Art, Chinese

Chinese artificial satellites See Artificial satellites, Chinese

Chinese astronomy See Astronomy, Chinese

Chinese broccoli

  See also

  Cooking—Vegetables

Brassicas from abroad. J. H. Sanchez. il Rodale's Org Gard 34:42-5 N '87

Chinese cooking See Cooking, Chinese

Chinese dictionaries See Chinese language—Dictionaries

Chinese frozen food See Food, Frozen

Chinese hibiscus

Chinese hibiscus. B. Gould. il Flower Gard 31:48+ O/N '87

Chinese house decoration See House decoration, Chinese

Chinese kale See Chinese broccoli

Chinese language

Understanding the Chinese language. E. Dzik. il Sch Update 120:42 S 18 '87

Dictionaries

Running dogs and credit cards: class struggle and a Chinese dictionary. O. Schell. il N Y Times Book Rev 92:3+ Je 7 '87

Chinese medicine *See* Medicine, Chinese
Chinese People's Liberation Army *See* China. People's Liberation Army
Chinese pottery *See* Pottery, Chinese
Chinese space vehicles *See* Space vehicles, Chinese
Chinese students in the United States *See* Foreign students—United States
Chinn, W. Franklyn
> *about*
> The Meese mess gets muddier. P. Dwyer. por *Bus Week* p68 D 28 '87-Ja 4 '88
> Meese's troubles go way beyond Wedtech. P. Dwyer and H. Collingwood. il por *Bus Week* p26-7 Jl 27 '87

Chinnici, Madeline
> A frog's day in court. il *Discover* 8:42-3 D '87
Chino, Tetsuo
> *about*
> Culture shock. A. Tanzer. il por *Forbes* 140:196+ S 21 '87

Chino Valley (Ariz.)
> Chino Valley changes. G. Beverly. il por *Mother Earth News* 103:64-5 Ja/F '87
Chinsman, B.
> Food irradiation. il *World Health* p10-11 Mr '87
Chintz
> The ubiquitous chintz. J. Simpson. il *Archit Dig* 44:226+ Mr '87

Chiodo, Beverly
> Choose wisely [address, August 14, 1987] *Vital Speeches Day* 54:40-2 N 1 '87
Chiodo, John J.
> The effects of exam anxiety on grandma's health. *Educ Dig* 52:45-7 Ja '87

Chip cards *See* Memory cards
Chip circuit copyright *See* Copyright—Integrated circuits
Chip circuits *See* Integrated circuits
Chip components (Electronics) *See* Surface mounting (Electronics)
Chipman, John, fl. ca. 1770-1790
> *about*
> John Chipman, cabinetmaker of Salem, Massachusetts. P. A. Louis and D. R. Sack. il *Antiques* 132:1318-25 D '87

Chippendale tables *See* Tables
Chippendales (Striptease revue) *See* Male striptease
Chippewa Indians
> Las Vegas North: buying chips from the Chippewa [Vegas Kewadin casino in Mich.] J. A. Seamonds. il *U S News World Rep* 102:31 F 9 '87
Chippindale, Christopher
> Tempting providence with the Turin Shroud? il *Hist Today* 37:5-6 S '87
Chirac, Jacques, 1932-
> Visit of French prime minister [remarks, March 31, 1987] il por *Dep State Bull* 87:56-7 Jl '87
> *about*
> Can France's great sell-off sell Chirac as president? J. Rossant. il *Bus Week* p76 My 25 '87
> Chirac's chance to remake France may be slipping away. F. J. Comes and J. Rossant. por *Bus Week* p44-5 Mr 30 '87
> 'Chirac's Yalta': the selling of French TV. J. Rossant. il *Bus Week* p48 F 16 '87
> A choice menu from Jacques Chirac. M. McFadden. il *Fortune* 115:18-19 Ja 5 '87
> Dark time in the City of Light. M. Whitaker. il por *Newsweek* 109:27 Ja 19 '87
> The future of cohabitation in France. J. Valls-Russell. il *New Leader* 70:3-4 Mr 9 '87
> Giving French lessons in *le scandale*. R. Z. Chesnoff. il pors *U S News World Rep* 103:56 N 16 '87
> Liberté, egalité, chaos. J. Bonfante. il por *Time* 129:36-7 Ja 19 '87
> The perils of power sharing [with interview] W. R. Doerner. il pors *Time* 129:43-4 Ap 6 '87
> The rail strike may break—or make—Chirac. J. Rossant. il *Bus Week* p50 Ja 19 '87
> A talk with Chirac: privatization was 'a psychological revolution'. S. B. Shepard and others. *Bus Week* p45 Mr 30 '87
> > **Visit to the Soviet Union, 1987**
> > Zeroing in on Moscow. J. Smolowe. il por *Time* 129:50-1 My 25 '87
> > **Visit to the United States, 1987**
> > Visit of French prime minister [remarks, March 31, 1987] R. Reagan; J. Chirac. il por *Dep State Bull* 87:56-7 Jl '87
Chirambo, Moses C.
> Ophthalmic medical assistants [Malawi] il *World Health* p9-11 My '87

Chiron
> Your horoscope. See issues of McCall's beginning August 1986
Chiropody *See* Podiatry
Chiropractic
> Chiropractic for animals? R. H. Pitcairn. il *Prevention* 39:81-4 Ja '87
> Should you trust the touch of a chiropractor? L. Morice. il *Mademoiselle* 93:82 Je '87
Chisels
> Chisels. J. Truini. il *Pop Mech* 164:104+ N '87
Chitawan National Park (Nepal) *See* National parks and reserves—Nepal
Chitin
> How an old crab could keep you in stitches [use of chitin from discarded crabshells for surgical sutures; work of Paul Austin] T. Dworetzky. il *Discover* 8:16 F '87
> New life for crab shells [use of chitin for sutures; work of Paul Austin] *Oceans* 20:3-4 Mr/Ap '87
> Stop—don't throw those crab shells away. M. Bluestone. il *Bus Week* p112+ Mr 23 '87
Chiu Chow cooking *See* Cooking, Chinese
Chivalry
> *See also*
> Knights and knighthood
> > **Exhibitions**
> An Age of Chivalry [Age of Chivalry: art in Plantagenet England 1200-1400 at the Royal Academy; cover story; special issue] il *Hist Today* 37:2-57 N '87
> Blazing exceptions to nature [Age of Chivalry exhibit] R. Hughes. il *Time* 130:94+ N 30 '87
Chives
> Savor the beauty of chives. L. B. Trigg. il *South Living* 22:74-5 Mr '87
Chlordane
> Chlordane sales halted [EPA ruling] *Sci News* 132:102 Ag 15 '87
> Chlordane's health threat. D. Baxter. *Rodale's Org Gard* 34:83+ D '87
Chlorides
> *See also*
> Carbon tetrachloride
Chlorine
> Reviving an old route to chlorine [work of Sidney W. Benson and Mohammed Hisham] *Sci News* 132:121 Ag 22 '87
Chlorine in sea water *See* Sea water
Chlorine monoxide
> Antarctic ozone: the plot thickens. R. Monastersky. *Sci News* 131:326 My 23 '87
> Halocarbons linked to ozone hole [research by Philip Solomon and others] R. A. Kerr. il *Science* 236:1182-3 Je 5 '87
Chlorofluorocarbons
> *See also*
> Vienna Convention for the Protection of the Ozone Layer (1985)
> Antarctic ozone reaches lowest levels. R. Monastersky. *Sci News* 132:230 O 10 '87
> Assessing the threat to the ozone [cover story] S. F. Singer and C. Crandall. il *Consum Res Mag* 70:11-14 Jl '87
> Can we close the ozone hole? F. S. Rowland. il *Technol Rev* 90:50-8 Ag/S '87
> Chlorofluorocarbons and the incredible shrinking ozone. J. P. Cohn. il *FDA Consum* 21:32-5 D '87/Ja '88
> Chlorofluorocarbons and the ozone layer. J. P. Cohn. *BioScience* 37:647-50 O '87
> Culprits of the stratosphere [study by Crofton Farmer on the Antarctic ozone hole] M. D. Lemonick. il *Time* 130:57 S 21 '87
> EPA to cut U.S. CFC production to protect ozone in stratosphere. M. Crawford. il *Science* 238:1505 D 11 '87
> Flying into an ozone hole [Airborne Antarctic Ozone Experiment] *Sci News* 132:95 Ag 8 '87
> Forecast for disaster. R. H. Boyle. il *Sports Illus* 67:78-84+ N 16 '87
> The heat is on [cover story] M. D. Lemonick. il *Time* 130:58-63+ O 19 '87
> How to protect the ozone layer. D. Starr. il *Natl Wildl* 26:26-8 D '87/Ja '88
> A lethal filibuster. H. Evans. il *U S News World Rep* 102:72 Je 22 '87
> Made in the shade? No way [Antarctic ozone hole] G. Taubes. il *Discover* 8:62-7] Ag '87
> The Missouri standard [U.S. failure to curb acid rain and chlorofluorocarbons] H. Evans. il *U S News World Rep* 103:90 O 12 '87

Chlorofluorocarbons—*cont.*
More clues to the mysterious ozone hole. R. Monastersky. *Sci News* 132:182 S 19 '87
New threats to the sky [depletion in Antarctic ozone layer] A. Steacy. il *Macleans* 100:44-5 S 14 '87
The ozone hole [Antarctic] *Sci Am* 257:19-20 Ag '87
Ozone hole updates. *Sci News* 132:302 N 7 '87
Ozone watch [Antarctic ozone hole] T. Beardsley. *Sci Am* 257:18 N '87
Watch this space [Antarctic ozone hole] E. R. Shell. il *Omni* 9:36-8+ Ag '87
Weather versus chemicals [controversy over Antarctic ozone hole] E. R. Shell. il *Atlantic* 259:27-31 My '87
Winds, pollutants drive ozone hole. R. A. Kerr. il map *Science* 238:156-8 O 9 '87

Chloroform
Shower shudders [breathing toxins; research by Julian Andelman] G. Woolley. il *Sierra* 72:13-14 Jl/Ag '87

Chlorophyll
See also
Chloroplasts
Climate and chlorophyll a: long-term trends in the central North Pacific Ocean. E. L. Venrick and others. bibl f il maps *Science* 238:70-2 O 2 '87
How purple was my valley [bacteriorhodopsin; work of Andrew Goldsworthy] il *Discover* 8:14+ N '87

Chloroplasts
Stop-transfer regions do not halt translocation of proteins into chloroplasts. T. H. Lubben and others. bibl f il *Science* 238:1112-14 N 20 '87

Chloroquine
An antidrug malaria pump? [resistance to chloroquine] *Sci News* 132:359 D 5 '87
Efflux of chloroquine from Plasmodium falciparum: mechanism of chloroquine resistance. D. J. Krogstad and others. bibl f il *Science* 238:1283-5 N 27 '87
Parkinson's protection? [chloroquine offers partial protection from MPTP-induced symptoms; research by Robert J. D'Amato and others] B. Bower. *Sci News* 131:359 Je 6 '87
Reversal of chloroquine resistance in Plasmodium falciparum by verapamil. S. K. Martin and others. bibl f il *Science* 235:899-901 F 20 '87

Chmielewski, Philip J.
(jt. auth) See Cavanagh, Gerald F., and Chmielewski, Philip J.

Chmielinski, Piotr
Kayaking the Amazon. il pors map *Natl Geogr* 171:460-73 Ap '87

Chocolate
See also
Cooking—Chocolate
Hershey Foods Corp.
Chocolate bars. *Consum Rep* 52:352-6 D '87
Present dessert in a shell of chocolate. S. Payne. il *South Living* 22:134-6 Jl '87
What's our Easter bunny's secret? Crack open an egg . . . it's chocolate inside. il *Sunset* 178:198-9 Ap '87

Contamination
Sweet spirits [alcohol] il *FDA Consum* 21:43-4 F '87
Chocolate desserts See Desserts
Chocolate stores See Candy stores
Chodosh, Lewis A., and others
The adenovirus major late transcription factor activates the rat γ-fibrinogen promoter. bibl f il *Science* 238:684-8 O 30 '87

Chogyam Trungpa See Trungpa, Chogyam, 1939-1987
Choi, Un Hui

Kidnapping
Kidnapped by Beloved Leader Comrade. D. Reed. il *Read Dig* 130:105-12 Mr '87

Choice, Janie
The mystique of jade. il *Antiques Collect Hobbies* 91:12-15+ Ja '87

CHOICE See Concerned Helpers of Inner Community Endeavors

Choice (Psychology)
See also
Decision making
Risk taking (Psychology)

Choice of college See College, Choice of
Choice of school See School, Choice of

Choirs
See also
Canticum Novum Singers
Dessoff Choirs

Choking
See also
Heimlich maneuver

Cholakian, Ed
about
Rancho Cadillac. T. Assenza. il pors *Car Driv* 32:101+ Mr '87

Cholecystokinin
Eat to remember [role of the vagus nerve; research by James F. Flood and others] S. Weisburd. *Sci News* 131:327 My 23 '87
Modulation of memory processing by cholecystokinin: dependence on the vagus nerve. J. F. Flood and others. bibl f il *Science* 236:832-4 My 15 '87

Cholesterol
See also
Hypercholesteremia
Activated charcoal: new champion of cholesterol fighters? J. Meade. *Prevention* 39:112+ Ja '87
Another up/down side of trimming the fat. D. D. Edwards. *Sci News* 131:261-2 Ap 25 '87
The battle of the lipoproteins [Helsinki study shows gemfibrozil lowers LDL levels while raising HDL levels] C. Gorman. il *Time* 130:68 N 23 '87
Beyond a safe diet [Mevacor, cholesterol reducing drug] N. Underwood. il *Macleans* 100:61 Mr 23 '87
Bypass breakthrough [University of Southern California study on lowering cholesterol through diet and drugs] il *Time* 129:52 Je 29 '87
Cholesterol. il *World Tennis* 35:28-30 Ag '87
Cholesterol control. B. T. Hunter. il *Consum Res Mag* 70:8-9 Mr '87
Cholesterol drug approved [lovastatin] *Sci News* 132:166 S 12 '87
Cholesterol guidelines released. *Sci News* 132:254 O 17 '87
Cholesterol: the heart of the matter. M. Callahan. il *Parents* 62:221-6 O '87
Cholesterol vs. saturated fats [discussion of March 1987 article, Planning a diet for a healthy heart] C. Lecos. il *FDA Consum* 21:5 Jl/Ag '87
Controlling cholesterol [new guidelines issued by expert panel] M. Clark. il *Newsweek* 110:94-5+ O 19 '87
Curbing killer cholesterol. S. Siwolop. il *Bus Week* p122-3 O 26 '87
Cutting cholesterol? Look to the label. C. Lecos. il *FDA Consum* 21:8-13 F '87
Cyclosporine, low cholesterol: bad mix? [neurological side effects] D. D. Edwards. *Sci News* 132:212 O 3 '87
The devil we know [Mevacor vs. niacin for reducing cholesterol] S. N. Chakravarty. il *Forbes* 140:203-4 N 2 '87
Diet, drugs slow heart-felt 'insults' [lowering cholesterol; University of Southern California study] D. D. Edwards. il *Sci News* 131:407 Je 27 '87
The diet that can clear your arteries [low-fat diet] L. Vaughn. *Prevention* 39:44+ O '87
Eggs O.K. on low-fat diet. il *Prevention* 39:6 Jl '87
Fat and the cholesterol connection. il *Glamour* 85:310-13 O '87
Fish oil and cholesterol: a megadose of hype? [diet supplements] T. Monmaney. il *Newsweek* 109:67-8 Ap 13 '87
Fish oil slows plaque deposits. *Prevention* 39:100-1 Ap '87
Grapefruit pectin reduces cholesterol [research by James Cerda] *Sci News* 132:63 Jl 25 '87
High cholesterol = high cancer risk? J. Silberner. *Sci News* 131:4 Ja 3 '87
Hope for clogged arteries [lovastatin] S. Begley. il *Newsweek* 110:74 S 14 '87
How to check out your cholesterol. S. Zarrow. *Prevention* 39:78-82 S '87
A how-to guide on cholesterol [new guidelines issued by blue ribbon panel] D. Thompson. il *Time* 130:45 O 19 '87
Is now the time for cholesterol screening? D. D. Edwards. *Sci News* 131:343 My 30 '87
Killer cholesterol: the news is good [study by University of Southern California] il *U S News World Rep* 102:11 Je 29 '87
A laser to lighten the heart [vaporizing cholesterol] M. Nichols. il *Macleans* 100:45 Ag 31 '87
Life in the slow lane [research by Walker Buckalew] il *Prevention* 39:8 O '87
Measuring cholesterol is as tricky as lowering it [guidelines issued by federal panel] L. Roberts. il *Science* 238:482-3 O 23 '87
Metamucil may move cholesterol out. *Prevention* 39:67-8 N '87
More good news about 'good cholesterol' [gemfibrozil increases HDL levels] *U S News World Rep* 103:14 N 23 '87

Cholesterol—*cont.*

New ally against heart disease [lovastatin] C. Gorman. il *Time* 130:69 S 14 '87

New blast at cholesterol [new guidelines issued by blue ribbon panel] J. Silberner. il *U S News World Rep* 103:76-7 O 19 '87

A new drug that fights cholesterol [lovastatin] I. Ross. il *Read Dig* 131:91-4 D '87

A new weapon in the battle against heart disease [lovastatin] D. Farley. il *FDA Consum* 21:26-8 N '87

News for women only: the cholesterol connection. J. C. Johnson. *Mademoiselle* 93:146 Ap '87

NIH moves to debar cholesterol researcher [case of C. J. Glueck] C. Holden. por *Science* 237:718-19 Ag 14 '87

Odorless garlic lowers blood fats [research by Benjamin Lau and others] *Prevention* 39:8+ S '87

One for the heart [University of Southern California study on lowering cholesterol through diet and drugs] T. Monmaney. il *Newsweek* 109:56-7 Je 29 '87

Pectin promises [lowers cholesterol] D. Welch. il *Health* 19:13 D '87

Pectin—the super fiber. G. Maleskey. il *Prevention* 39:60-4 Mr '87

A pill to cut cholesterol: hope for hearts [lovastatin] il *Newsweek* 109:66 Mr 2 '87

A powerful tonic for Warner-Lambert [anticholesterol drug Lopid] L. Baum. il por *Bus Week* p144+ N 30 '87

A sizzling food fight [high cholesterol products push nutrition in ads] A. Miller. il *Newsweek* 109:56 Ap 20 '87

Steroidogenesis-activator polypeptide isolated from a rat Leydig cell tumor. R. C. Pedersen and A. C. Brownie. bibl f il *Science* 236:188-90 Ap 10 '87

Study bolsters case against cholesterol [University of Southern California research] L. Roberts. il *Science* 237:28-9 Jl 3 '87

Therapy by mimicry [thyromimetic SK&F L-94901 reduces blood cholesterol without increasing heart rate] *Sci Am* 256:88 F '87

U.S. cholesterol guidelines are off-target. E. M. Whelan and R. E. Olsen. il *Consum Res Mag* 70:36-7 D '87

Vitamin C KO's cholesterol. *Prevention* 39:67 N '87

Walking up your HDL [study of mailmen by Timothy Cook] il *Prevention* 39:6 My '87

Watching cholesterol [blood tests] J. W. Merline. il *Consum Res Mag* 70:38 Ap '87

Which fat is worst? *Prevention* 39:18 D '87

Why carrots may reduce cholesterol. *Sci News* 131:409 Je 27 '87

Your cholesterol, more or less [blood tests] *U S News World Rep* 103:64 N 23 '87

Cholula (Mexico)

Description

Puebla and Cholula. C. Hunt. il *Travel Holiday* 167:23-4+ Ap '87

Chomsky, Noam

about

Noam Chomsky: an American dissident [interview; excerpt from The Chomsky reader] J. Peck. il *Progressive* 51:22-5 Jl '87

Chong, Ping

about

Angels of Swedenborg [dance] Reviews
  Dance Mag il 61:93-5 Ap '87. S. Sommer
Kindness [dance] Reviews
  Dance Mag 61:93-5 Ap '87. S. Sommer

Choppin, Purnell W.

about

Choppin takes reins at Howard Hughes. B. J. Culliton. il por *Science* 237:1406-7 S 18 '87

Chopra, Deepak

Are your thoughts killing you? il *Nations Bus* 75:87 O '87

Choquet, Daniel, and others

Cyclic AMP-modulated potassium channels in murine B cells and their precursors. bibl f il *Science* 235:1211-14 Mr 6 '87

Choquette, Paul, Jr.

A second-rate power? por *Nations Bus* 75:4 D '87

Choral groups and societies

See also
  Amor Artis Chorale and Orchestra
  Cabrillo Slavonic Chorus
  Cantata Singers and Ensemble
  Mannes Camerata
  University Glee Club of New York City

Choral music

See also
  Compact discs—Choral music

Choral singing *See* Singing

Chordal schemes *See* Harmony

Chordeleg (Ecuador)

Galleries and museums

Saving cultural assets [OAS-backed Community Museum project] G. Urriolagoitia V. il *Américas* 39:56 Ja/F '87

Chords *See* Harmony

Choreographers

See also
  Abdul, Paula
  Armitage, Karole
  Balanchine, George, 1904-1983
  Bennett, Michael
  Childs, Lucinda
  Clarke, Martha, 1944?-
  Cunningham, Merce
  Dean, Laura
  Dorfman, David
  Dunham, Katherine
  Field, Ron
  Forsythe, William
  Graham, Martha
  Hawkins, Erick
  Holby, Grethe Barrett
  House, Christopher
  Hughes, Jim
  Keersmaeker, Anne Teresa de
  Komatsubara, Yoko
  Kovich, Robert
  Kresnik, Johann
  Kylián, Jiři
  Lara, Reyes de
  Laurin, Ginette
  Marin, Maguy
  Martin, Barry
  Martins, Peter
  Newman, Rosalind
  Pennison, Marleen
  Petronio, Stephen
  Prokovsky, André
  Robbins, Jerome
  Scholz, Uwe
  Self, Jim
  Streb, Elizabeth
  Taylor, Paul, 1930-
  Tetley, Glen
  Tharp, Twyla
  Tomasson, Helgi
  Tudor, Antony, 1909-1987

Modern dance: a growing presence [family tree] K. Matheson. il *Dance Mag* 61:151-3 Je '87

Choreographers, Handicapped

Take it again from the fall [B. Martin] A. Fadiman. il pors *Life* 10:13-14+ My '87

Choreography

See also
  Copyright—Choreography

Aboard the Starlight Express: choreographing human trains [work of A. Phillips] K. Grubb. il *Dance Mag* 61:86-7 Ap '87

Dancing with Carmen [L. Wertmuller's and T. Brown's collaboration on experimental production of Carmen in Naples] K. Kertess. il pors *Art Am* 75:180-5+ Ap '87

Twenty years later . . . Ron Field revisits Cabaret. K. Grubb. il *Dance Mag* 61:66-7 O '87

Chores

See also
  Children's chores

Chou, Hubert S., and others

Germline organization of the murine T cell receptor β-chain genes. bibl f il *Science* 238:545-8 O 23 '87

Chow, Gregory C., 1929-

Development of a more market-oriented economy in China. bibl f *Science* 235:295-9 Ja 16 '87

Chow, Ida

(jt. auth) See Young, Steven H., and Chow, Ida

Chow, Tina

about

Clearly different. il *Vogue* 177:334-7 Ag '87

Chowder

In the soup. S. Bashline. il *Field Stream* 91:78 Mr '87

Choyce, Alice Swafford- *See* Swafford-Choyce, Alice
Chris-Craft Industries, Inc.
The feud at Warner just keeps getting hotter [H. J. Siegel vs S. J. Ross] S. Benway. il pors *Bus Week* p76-8+ Je 29 '87
The Warner war: why Steve Ross and Herb Siegel can't get along [cover story] J. Taylor. il pors *N Y* 20:34-42 Jl 13 '87
What might have been. H. Rudnitsky. il *Forbes* 140:138 N 2 '87
Chrisley, John
about
John Chrisley is a sweet kid of 17 who plays a big, mean harmonica. il por *People Wkly* 27:97 Ja 12 '87
Christ *See* Jesus Christ
Christ the King, Feast of *See* Jesus Christ the King, Feast of
Christening *See* Baptism
Christensen, Dale
about
On the road again [interview] K. Houk. il por *Space World* X-12-288:29 D '87
Christensen, Halvor N.
about
The truth about Black Beauty. D. Sobel. *Omni* 9:27 Mr '87
Christensen, Lillian Langseth- *See* Langseth-Christensen, Lillian
Christensen, Norman L.
(jt. auth) See Peet, R. K., and Christensen, Norman L.
Christensen, Todd
about
'I can catch the rock'. P. Zimmerman. il pors *Sports Illus* 67:74-8+ Ag 10 '87
Christenson, Reo M.
Shame, shame on the entertainment industry. il *USA Today (Periodical)* 115:92-5 My '87
Christian, Rebecca
Belter style. il pors *Americana* 15:46-50 S/O '87
Festive, ethnic, historic. il *Americana* 15:56-9 N/D '87
Christian, Shirley, 1938-
about
The tricoteuse of counterrevolution. A. Cockburn. *Nation* 245:44-5 Jl 18-25 '87
Christian art and symbolism
See also
Altarpieces
Church decoration and ornament
Icons
Illumination of books and manuscripts
Jesus Christ—Art
Jesus Christ—Crucifixion—Art
Last Supper in art
Santos (Art)
Stations of the Cross in art
Crucifying machine [sculptor T. Prescott] D. Neff. il *Christ Today* 31:58 N 6 '87
Gruesome images, signs of hope [work of E. Knippers] D. Neff. il por *Christ Today* 31:63-4 Mr 6 '87
Tombs and inner temples [paintings of S. Keefe] D. Neff. il por *Christ Today* 31:72 O 2 '87
A visit with Vincent van Gogh [Van Gogh in Saint Rémy and Auvers exhibit] J. F. Cotter. *America* 156:50-1+ Ja 24 '87
William Schickel's 'Salvation suite'. J. W. Goetz. il *America* 157:304-5 O 31 '87
Christian book publishing *See* Publishers and publishing—Religious literature
Christian Booksellers Association
Christian Booksellers in Anaheim. W. Griffin. il *Publ Wkly* 232:21-5 Ag 21 '87
Disneyland of the spirit: Christian Booksellers are on their way to Anaheim. W. Griffin. *Publ Wkly* 231:28+ Je 26 '87
Christian Broadcasting Network, Inc.
Con man of the cloth [P. Robertson and the Fairness Doctrine] W. A. Henry. il *Channels* 7:16 Ja '87
Will Pat run? [P. Robertson's Christian television network faces fallout from his possible presidential bid] B. Spring. il pors *Christ Today* 31:34-6 Ag 7 '87
Christian camps *See* Church camps
Christian century (Periodical)
'30'. M. E. Marty. *Christ Century* 104:95 Ja 28 '87
Christian Church (Disciples of Christ)
Disciples meet. *Christ Century* 104:1023-4 N 18 '87
Reagan and the Disciples: a widening chasm. M. S. Lord. *Christ Century* 104:1055-6 N 25 '87

Christian colleges *See* Church colleges and universities
Christian contemporary music
Christian music enters the New Age. S. Rabey. il *Christ Today* 31:52-3 F 6 '87
Happy hour at Mr. C's [Episcopal pastor S. Boehmig brings his band into Pittsburgh clubs] R. Frame. il por *Christ Today* 31:12-13 O 16 '87
Hard times rock the Christian music industry. S. Rabey. il *Christ Today* 31:56+ O 2 '87
If he had a rocket launcher . . . [B. Cockburn] S. Rabey. il por *Christ Today* 31:57-8 N 6 '87
Stryper: a holy hit. S. Pond. il *Roll Stone* p32 F 26 '87
South Africa
Can music be the instrument of racial reconciliation? J. Long. il *Christ Today* 31:47+ My 15 '87
Christian Dior (Firm)
Bohan: the power behind Dior. P. McColl. il pors *Harpers Bazaar* 120:162+ S '87
Dior: 40 years of triumph. A. Kurzweil. il pors *Harpers Bazaar* 120:152+ S '87
Dior's new look . . . then and now. J. J. Buck. il por *Vogue* 177:478-9+ Mr '87
Christian ethics
See also
Christianity and economics
Church and social problems
Clergy—Ethics
Love (Theology)
Sin
Sociology, Christian
Stewardship, Christian
War and religion
Alternative universes: literature, ethics and the American dream. C. A. Rubino. *America* 157:332+ N 7 '87
Caulking while Rome burns. P. Yancey. il *Christ Today* 31:64 F 20 '87
Decadence à la mode. J. I. Packer. il *Christ Today* 31:13 O 2 '87
A farewell to harms. K. S. Kantzer. il *Christ Today* 31:14-15 D 11 '87
Josef Pieper and the pursuit of virtue. D. Heim. *Christ Century* 104:1076-7 D 2 '87
Moral theologian under attack: Saint Alphonsus Liguori. B. Häring. *America* 156:362-6 My 2 '87
Moral theology and public dissent: a temporary compromise [Catholic Church] J. L. Lombardi. *America* 156:100-1+ F 7 '87
On honesty and self-deception: 'you are the man'. L. Steffen. *Christ Century* 104:403-5 Ap 29 '87
A passion for morality. G. G. Seibert. *America* 157:175 S 26 '87
Sliding into paganism. T. C. Muck. il *Christ Today* 31:14-15 N 6 '87
Today's issues in ethics [special section] il *America* 156:64-82 Ja 31 '87
Who's got the last word on Catholic morality? R. T. Reilly. il *U S Cathol* 52:54-8 Je '87
Christian giving
Biblical guidelines for asking and giving. E. B. Habecker. il por *Christ Today* 31:32-4 My 15 '87
Christian Heritage Party (Canada)
Christian political activist launches a new party [E. Vanwoudenberg] L. Mackey. il *Christ Today* 31:36-7 Ap 3 '87
Christian leadership
Calling the next generation of Christian leaders [Singapore 87 conference] J. D. Douglas. *Christ Today* 31:39 Ag 7 '87
Fallen leaders are not "damaged goods". R. W. Dingman. il por *Christ Today* 31:12 D 11 '87
Remembering other Christian leaders [obituaries] il *Christ Today* 31:40+ D 11 '87
The road to restoration: how should the church treat its fallen leaders? [cover story] K. S. Kantzer. il *Christ Today* 31:19-22 N 20 '87
So where's the crisis? T. C. Muck. *Christ Today* 31:17 N 20 '87
Vacation by objectives. K. S. Kantzer. il *Christ Today* 31:15 S 4 '87
Christian life
See also
Christian ethics
Faith
Good works (Theology)
Prayer
Self denial
Spiritual life
Stewardship, Christian
The examined life. R. E. Burns. See issues of U.S. Catholic

Christian life—cont.

The fragrant season. P. Yancey. il *Christ Today* 31:64 Ap 17 '87

The never-ending story [soap operas vs. a Christian view of life] Q. J. Schultze. il por *Christ Today* 31:26-9 Ap 17 '87

The new Dark Ages. R. Clapp. *Christ Today* 31:15 S 18 '87

A theology to die by. V. G. Beers. *Christ Today* 31:11 F 6 '87

Who pays for the roof? [costs of God's work] G. K. Brushaber. il *Christ Today* 31:15 Ja 16 '87

The Word. M. K. Hellwig. See issues of America beginning June 23-30, 1984 through June 20-27, 1987

The Word. P. J. Ryan. See issues of America beginning November 21, 1987

The Word. G. G. Seibert. See issues of America beginning July 4-11, 1987 through November 14, 1987

Anecdotes, facetiae, satire, etc.

Growing up born again. J. Campbell. il *Publ Wkly* 232:44-5 O 9 '87

Christian literature

See also

Publishers and publishing—Religious literature

Publish bad tidings. T. Stafford. il *Christ Today* 31:30 F 20 '87

Authorship

An accidental author. J. I. Packer. il *Christ Today* 31:11 My 15 '87

PW interviews [W. Wangerin] W. Griffin. por *Publ Wkly* 231:95-6 Mr 6 '87

Bibliography

Current religious bestsellers. *Publ Wkly* 231:28 Je 26 '87

Current religious bestsellers. *Publ Wkly* 231:24 Ap 17 '87

Favorite books and how they influence [cover story] il *Christ Century* 104:490-5 My 20-27 '87

Gold, frankincense, and books. L. Sibley. il *Christ Today* 31:58-60 D 11 '87

Religious bestsellers. il *Publ Wkly* 232:41 O 9 '87

Religious bestsellers. *Publ Wkly* 231:43 Mr 6 '87

Christian love *See* Love (Theology)

Christian missions *See* Missions

Christian Reconstruction movement

Democracy as heresy. R. Clapp. il *Christ Today* 31:17-23 F 20 '87

Getting out God's vote: Pat Robertson and the evangelicals [cover story] F. Edwords and S. McCabe. il *Humanist* 47:5-10+ My/Je '87

Christian renewal *See* Church renewal

Christian schools *See* Accelerated Christian Education; Church schools

Christian Science Church *See* Church of Christ, Scientist

Christian Science monitor

The many lives of Kay Fanning. I. Nelson. il por *50 Plus* 27:78+ Ja '87

Christian sociology *See* Sociology, Christian

Christian stewardship *See* Stewardship, Christian

Christian union *See* Church union

Christianity

See also

Bible

Catholicism

Christian ethics

Christian Reconstruction movement

Church history

Ecumenical movement

Fundamentalism

God

Grace (Theology)

Homosexuality and Christianity

Kingdom of God

Sociology, Christian

Theology

Philosophy

Suddenly, respect. K. Christlieb. il por *Christ Today* 31:30-2 Ap 17 '87

The tyranny of subjectivism [address, September 18, 1987] G. Leonard. *Vital Speeches Day* 54:50-7 N 1 '87

Christianity and AIDS (Disease) *See* AIDS (Disease)—Religious aspects

Christianity and communism *See* Communism and religion

Christianity and culture

Culture shock on the prairie. M. S. Van Leeuwen. il *Christ Today* 31:9 N 20 '87

The ease of distraction [decline of a common cultural memory and rise of secularism, convenience, and distraction] J. Garvey. il *Commonweal* 114:520-1 S 25 '87

Garrison Keillor and culture Protestantism. D. Heim. *Christ Century* 104:517-19 Je 3-10 '87

Jim Bakker made me do it. P. Yancey. il *Christ Today* 31:64 O 16 '87

Christianity and economics

See also

Church and industry

The bishops' letter, world debt and the U.S. trade deficit [pastoral letter on the economy] J. A. Gylys. il *America* 157:86-7 Ag 15-22 '87

Bishops move diagonally [pastoral letter, Economic justice for all] G. P. Brockway. *New Leader* 70:10-11 Mr 23 '87

The Boesky touch. T. C. Muck. il *Christ Today* 31:14-15 Mr 6 '87

A call to transform the marketplace [Inter-Varsity Christian Fellowship conference called Marketplace '86] L. Lau. *Christ Today* 31:41+ F 6 '87

Challenging the private sector. M. E. Marty. *Christ Century* 104:871 O 7 '87

Christianity today talks to Michael Novak. D. Neff. por *Christ Today* 31:54-5 Jl 10 '87

Don't route this pastoral to the dead-letter office [U.S. bishops', "Economic justice for all"] R. E. Burns. *U S Cathol* 52:2 Mr '87

Have ethics disappeared from Wall Street? R. S. Bachelder. il *Christ Century* 104:628-30 Jl 15-22 '87

How to implement 'Economic justice for all' [Catholic bishops' pastoral] A. M. Pilla. il *America* 156:76-8+ Ja 31 '87

How to talk about economic strategy [Catholic bishops' pastoral letter and Democratic Leadership Council's conference in Williamsburg] A. Cockburn and R. Pollin. il *Nation* 244:245-7 F 28 '87

Mainline Protestants help U.S. Catholic bishops spread economics message. W. Bole. il *Christ Today* 31:52+ F 20 '87

Mortgaging a house of cards [ethics of international debt] K. P. Jameson. il *Commonweal* 114:105-7 F 27 '87

On challenging opponents [D. E. Pilarczyk's views on the U.S. bishops' economics pastoral] *America* 156:434 My 30 '87

Our bishops and our economy [Catholic pastoral] J. Gaffney. *America* 156:44-9 Ja 24 '87

Resurrecting the common good [Catholic bishops' pastoral letter] R. N. Bellah. il *Commonweal* 114:736-41 D 18 '87

The skewing of America: disparities in wealth and income. R. D. Pasquariello. il *Christ Century* 104:164-6 F 18 '87

Toward a socialist strategy [discussion of February 28, 1987 article, How to talk about economic strategy] A. Cockburn and R. Pollin. *Nation* 244:748+ Je 6 '87

What's become of the pastoral? [Catholic bishops' letter] K. S. Smith. il *Commonweal* 114:742-7 D 18 '87

Christianity and education *See* Church and education

Christianity and humanism

Alabama board to appeal ban on 'humanist' texts. M. Yen. *Publ Wkly* 231:14 Mr 27 '87

Alabamboozle [secular humanist textbook ruling] E. Doerr. *Humanist* 47:39-40 My/Je '87

Books and schools [fundamentalists' attacks on public school books] *Nation* 244:705-6 My 30 '87

Christianity & mental health [cover story; with reply by P. R. Breggin] W. W. Watters. il *Humanist* 47:5-13+ N/D '87

God's right Hand [W. Brevard Hand's decision that secular humanism is a religion in Alabama textbook case] D. R. Carlin, Jr. il *Commonweal* 114:263-4 My 8 '87

The humanist. E. Doerr. *Humanist* 47:2 N/D '87

Humanists and talk of God. D. E. Marietta. il por *Humanist* 47:8-10+ S/O '87

Is 'humanism' a religion? [Judge W. Brevard Hand bans certain textbooks in Alabama] T. Gest. il *U S News World Rep* 102:10-11 Mr 16 '87

Nondenominational humanism? [Alabama secular humanist textbook case] *Natl Rev* 39:19 Ap 10 '87

Other sides to the textbook controversy [discussion of May 6, 1987 articles, Voltaire arraigned in Alabama: the textbook humanism case and Curriculum in the public schools: can compromise be reached?] D. Underhill; C. L. Glenn. il *Christ Century* 104:631-2 Jl 15-22 '87

Religion: an obstacle to a better world? G. K. Griswold. il por *Humanist* 47:18-19+ Mr/Ap '87

Religious bias [Judge W. Brevard Hand bans "secular humanist" textbooks from Alabama schools] il *Time* 129:66 Mr 16 '87

Christianity and humanism—*cont.*

Shuttered windows. C. Heath. *Humanist* 47:27-8 N/D '87

Striking down the textbook rulings. K. A. Lawton. il *Christ Today* 31:50-1 O 2 '87

Students speak out against textbook censorship [Buffalo, N.Y.] F. Edwords. *Humanist* 47:23-6+ Mr/Ap '87

Survival in the apocalyptic era. G. A. Larue. il *Humanist* 47:11-17 S/O '87

Textbook cases. T. C. Muck. *Christ Today* 31:17 Ap 17 '87

Textbook ruling sparks concern [secular humanism ruling in Alabama] C. Holden. *Science* 235:1459 Mr 20 '87

Textbooks on trial [Alabama decision banning textbooks from public schools because they promote secular humanism] *America* 156:265 Ap 4 '87

Tillich in an Alice-in-Wonderland world [court decisions pertaining to school textbooks and secular humanism] J. McBride. *Christ Century* 104:519-20 Je 3-10 '87

Voltaire arraigned in Alabama: the textbook humanism case. D. Underhill. *Christ Century* 104:438-40 My 6 '87

Christianity and industry *See* Church and industry
Christianity and justice *See* Religion and justice
Christianity and marriage *See* Marriage
Christianity and occult sciences

Pruning time for Shirley MacLaine? C. V. Anderson. *Christ Century* 104:182-3 F 25 '87

Theology from the Twilight Zone [New Age spiritism] B. Alexander. il por *Christ Today* 31:22-6 S 18 '87

Under fire [cover story] il *Christ Today* 31:17-21 S 18 '87

Christianity and other religions

See also

Catholic Church—Relations—Hinduism
Catholic Church—Relations—Judaism
Christianity and humanism

Broken continuities: Night and White crucifixion [M. Chagall and E. Wiesel; cover story] K. A. Plank. il por *Christ Century* 104:963-6 N 4 '87

The challenge of Christian-Muslim relations. T. B. Bush. il *Christ Century* 104:694-6 Ag 12-19 '87

Coming to terms with Judaism [Presbyterian Church U.S.A.] R. N. Ostling. il *Time* 129:57 Je 29 '87

Constantine's pagan triumph [R. Lane Fox's Pagans and Christians] P. Pettingell. *New Leader* 70:15-16 Ap 6 '87

Differences that bind. J. Garvey. il *Commonweal* 114:103-4 F 27 '87

How could the Iran-Iraq War affect Christianity? [interview with C. G. Fry] S. Mumper. il por *Christ Today* 31:46-7 N 6 '87

Interfaith dialogue [discussion of May 1987 article, The rise & fall of interfaith dialogue] H. Singer. *Commentary* 84:4-6+ S '87

Out of India: karma & Christ. M. Moynihan. il *Commonweal* 114:446-52 Ag 14 '87

Pagans, Christians, Jews. C. Raphael. *Commentary* 84:39-44 O '87

Presbyterians: politics and responsibility [statement on Jewish-Christian relations] G. Telford. *Christ Century* 104:614-16 Jl 15-22 '87

Reflections on solitude [encounters with Muslims in 15th century India] A. Nikitin. il *Courier* 40:15 Ap '87

Religions of the one God [interview with H. Küng] D. Toolan. *Commonweal* 114:143+ Mr 13 '87

Reviving Judaica—without Jews—in Poland. J. B. Miller. il *Christ Century* 104:916-17 O 21 '87

The rise & fall of interfaith dialogue [Jews and Christians] H. Singer. *Commentary* 83:50-5 My '87

Seeing Israel in full perspective. J. M. Wall. *Christ Century* 104:515-17 Je 3-10 '87

Shoah: enough already? [Christian resistance to dishonestly polemical uses of the Holocaust] R. J. Neuhaus. *Natl Rev* 39:38 Je 5 '87

We can love Israel too much. B. Spradlin. il por *Christ Today* 31:14 Jl 10 '87

White Protestants polled on Jews. *Society* 24:2 Mr/Ap '87

Christianity and politics *See* Religion and politics
Christianity and psychology *See* Psychology, Religious
Christianity and science *See* Religion and science
Christianity and sex *See* Sex and religion
Christianity and social problems *See* Church and social problems
Christianity and socialism *See* Socialism and religion
Christianity and the arts *See* Arts and religion
Christianity and the environment *See* Religion and the environment

Christianity and the world *See* Church and the world
Christianity and war *See* War and religion
Christianity today (Periodical)

Focus on the family. T. C. Muck. il *Christ Today* 31:11 S 18 '87

What makes CT laugh? T. C. Muck. il *Christ Today* 31:11 D 11 '87

Christians

China

The church the Gang of Four built [cover story] S. Mumper. il *Christ Today* 31:17-21 My 15 '87

The Protestant church in the People's Republic of China. D. S. Browning. *Christ Century* 104:218-21 Mr 4 '87

Israel

Seeing Israel in full perspective. J. M. Wall. *Christ Century* 104:515-17 Je 3-10 '87

We can love Israel too much. B. Spradlin. il por *Christ Today* 31:14 Jl 10 '87

Korea (North)

To the North: signs of hope. H. Smith. il *Christ Today* 31:38 N 20 '87

Korea (South)

Korean Christians hold out hope for democracy. S. Rabey and L. Cryderman. il *Christ Today* 31:48 Ag 7 '87

Will success spoil the South Korean church? il *Christ Today* 31:29-44 N 20 '87

Soviet Union

Believers test the limits of Gorbachev's *glasnost*. B. Spring. il *Christ Today* 31:40 S 18 '87

An Orthodox monk and a Lutheran pastor witness the survival of faith in an atheistic state [Methody and V. Raudsepp] M. Brower. il pors *People Wkly* 27:110-13 Ap 6 '87

The religious climate under *glasnost* [cover story] L. Howe. il *Christ Century* 104:883-5 O 14 '87

Soviet believers: still paying a high cost for commitment. K. A. Lawton. il *Christ Today* 31:40-2 Je 12 '87

Sri Lanka

How can Christians bring reconciliation to Sri Lanka? [interview with R. Ebenezer] S. Mumper. il por *Christ Today* 31:46 Ag 7 '87

Christians, Hindu *See* Converts from Hinduism
Christians, Jewish *See* Converts from Judaism
Christians and Jews *See* Christianity and other religions
Christians and Muslims *See* Christianity and other religions
Christiansen, Drew

Ethical guidelines for assisting the elderly. il *America* 156:72-5 Ja 31 '87

Christianson, Gale E.

Newton's Principia: a retrospective. il por *Sky Telesc* 74:18-20 Jl '87

Christie, William

about

The real thing. P. G. Davis. il *N Y* 20:146+ D 7 '87

Christie's (London, England)

Christie's and Cristallina settle [fraud and negligent misrepresentation suit against Christie's] R. W. Walker. il *Art News* 86:21-2 Ap '87

Christison, Kathleen

Myths about Palestinians. bibl f *Foreign Policy* 66:109-27 Spr '87

Christlieb, Kristine

Suddenly, respect. il por *Christ Today* 31:30-2 Ap 17 '87

Christmas, Rachel J.

Collage of cultures. il *Travel Holiday* 168:22-4 D '87
The cream of the Caribbean. il *Essence* 17:14+ Ap '87
Travels with my father: what we learned from working together. il por *Ms* 15:66+ Mr '87

Christmas

See also

Advent
Children and Christmas
Jesus Christ—Nativity
Santa Claus

The busy woman's guide to the holidays. il *Ladies Home J* 104:144-7+ D '87

Busy woman's holiday survival guide [special section] il *Essence* 18:81-4+ D '87

Captain Midlife faces Christmas. R. Rosenblatt. il *Time* 130:96 D 14 '87

Celebrating Christmas in public schools. W. Bole. *Christ Today* 31:35-6 D 11 '87

Celebrities express their thoughts at Christmastime. il *Jet* 73:56 D 28 '87-Ja 4 '88

"Christmas at my house". K. Rogers. il pors *Redbook* 170:94-5 D '87

Christmas in Bethlehem [Pa.] S. Ferrell. il *Saturday Evening Post* 259:66-70 D '87

"Christmas in November is okay with me". E. Berg. il *Parents* 62:136-7 N '87

Christmas—*cont.*

Christmas shame [cover story] E. H. Peterson. il por *Christ Today* 31:17-19 D 11 '87

Christmas thoughts. L. Radziwill. por *McCalls* 115:164 D '87

Christmas yesterday, today and tomorrow. G. W. Hunt. *America* 157:467-8 D 19 '87

Christmases past. E. Hoagland. *Nation* 245:776-7 D 26 '87-Ja 2 '88

Clement C. Moore: "A visit from St. Nicholas". B. McGinty. por *Am Hist Illus* 22:28-9 D '87

The December dilemma [gentile-Jewish marriages face Christmas and Hanukkah] B. Kantrowitz. il *Newsweek* 110:56 D 28 '87

Do holidays spell trouble? [effects on unhappy marriages; views of Robert L. Barker] *USA Today (Periodical)* 116:4-5 D '87

Dolly Parton: "We had nothing but love" [cover story] A. W. Petrucelli. por *Redbook* 170:64 D '87

Family ties [special section] *Harpers Bazaar* 121:126-7+ D '87

Festive, ethnic, historic. R. Christian. il *Americana* 15:56-9 N/D '87

The gift of a Yellowstone Christmas. R. S. Fuller. il *Natl Wildl* 26:4-11 D '87/Ja '88

A glow on Main Street. il *South Living* 22:70-5 D '87

A gold country Christmas [Columbia State Historic Park, Calif.] N. R. Day. il map *Americana* 15:32-7 N/D '87

Gourmet holidays: Christmas in Nantucket. T. Weeks. il map *Gourmet* 47:66-71+ D '87

Have an old-fashioned Huntsville Christmas. J. T. Black. il *South Living* 22:10-11+ D '87

Holiday almanac. K. Stechert. il *Better Homes Gard* 65:22+ D '87

Holiday helper [special section] S. La Rosa and J. Siroto. il *McCalls* 115:47-8+ D '87

The holiday spirit. S. L. Taylor. il *Essence* 18:47 D '87

A holiday survival-manual [special section] L. Werner. il *Ladies Home J* 104:70+ D '87

Holiday time in New York. il *Glamour* 85:174-6+ D '87

Holidays and single moms. V. Gallman. il *Essence* 18:102 D '87

How to avoid Christmas stress [views of Wallace Denton] *USA Today (Periodical)* 116:4 D '87

I can't take one more Christmas with this man! S. F. Enos. il *Ladies Home J* 104:10+ D '87

Isn't this what Christmas is all about? [helping others] R. Rooney. il *Good Housekeep* 205:120+ D '87

It's coming on Christmas. P. Quinn. *Commonweal* 114:731-2 D 18 '87

"Joy comes from sharing". C. L. Player. il *McCalls* 115:133-5 D '87

Letting Christmas grow. K. Fury. il *50 Plus* 27:76 D '87

The magic of babylove. il *Harpers Bazaar* 121:118-25 D '87

Make it merry! E. Bryon. il *Redbook* 170:75-7+ D '87

Making it through the holidays. J. Marzollo. il *Parents* 62:110-14 N '87

Merry Christmas. *Natl Rev* 39:16-17 D 31 '87

'My best Christmas ever' [black celebrities] il *Ebony* 43:34+ D '87

Now [reminiscences of seven American writers] il *Seventeen* 46:97-101+ D '87

Of many things. G. W. Hunt. *America* 157:466 D 19 '87

Our Christmas Madeira. N. R. Campion. il *Gourmet* 47:100+ D '87

Pennsylvania's own Star of Bethlehem. C. La VO. *Travel Holiday* 168:14-15 D '87

Put more spirit in the season. M. Golin. *Prevention* 39:52-4 D '87

The stars who make Christmas special. L. Feldman. il pors *McCalls* 115:90+ D '87

'Tis the season [events in national parks] L. Tuttle. il *Natl Parks* 61:38-9 N/D '87

The unholy ghost of Christmas yet to come. R. E. Burns. *U S Cathol* 52:2 D '87

Why I am crazy about Christmas (even though it's crazy to be crazy about Christmas). E. Crow. il *Parents* 62:6 N '87

Yuletide strife [family conflict; views of Sidney Russak] il *USA Today (Periodical)* 116:16 D '87

Anecdotes, facetiae, satire, etc.

Christmas at my house [excerpt from Family] E. Bombeck. il por *Ladies Home J* 104:160-1+ D '87

Getting ready for the holidays [excerpt from Christmastime] S. Boynton. il *Ladies Home J* 104:126+ D '87

A hipster's holidaze. B. Houston-Montgomery. il *Harpers Bazaar* 121:64+ D '87

Collectibles

See also
Santa Claus—Collectibles

Collecting Christmas paper memorabilia [cover story] S. B. Nicholson. il *Antiques Collect Hobbies* 92:52-3+ D '87

Economic aspects

See also
Christmas business
Christmas shopping
Christmas stores

Photographs and photography

Christmas in America. il *Good Housekeep* 205:129-39 D '87

Holiday pictures that celebrate a family's life together. C. Begole. il *Glamour* 85:78 D '87

Terminology

Anecdotes, facetiae, satire, etc.

The season to talk jolly. R. Baker. il *N Y Times Mag* p24 D 20 '87

Bolivia

Slouching toward Bethlehem. J. Warner. il *America* 157:472-4 D 19 '87

Canada

A Canadian Christmas feast: bringing out the British [hotels in British Columbia offering special medieval Christmas feasts] A. Satterfield. il *Travel Holiday* 168:66-9 N '87

France

Christmas chic: Gallic galas. J. B. Rafferty. il *Harpers Bazaar* 121:80+ D '87

Great Britain

Boy into bishop: a festive role-reversal. N. Mackenzie. bibl il *Hist Today* 37:10-16 D '87

Photographs and photography

A Dickens Christmas. D. Montgomery. il *Good Housekeep* 205:160-5 D '87

Honduras

Slouching toward Bethlehem. J. Warner. il *America* 157:472-4 D 19 '87

Mali

African Noel [excerpt from An African journey] M. Patinkin. il *Omni* 10:26+ D '87

United States

See Christmas

Wales

1944: a soldier's Christmas in Wales. H. H. Broun. il por *50 Plus* 27:35-42 D '87

Christmas and children *See* Children and Christmas

Christmas business

See also
Christmas stores

Christmas 1986: customers bought across the board [booksellers' reports] S. Bolle. *Publ Wkly* 231:364-5 Ja 30 '87

Good news for the holidays [bookstore sales of audiotapes] il *Publ Wkly* 232:29-30 D 18 '87

Have yourself a wary Christmas. N. L. Croft. il *Nations Bus* 75:40 D '87

A mildly merry Christmas. il *Fortune* 115:6 Ja 5 '87

Movies for Christmas [videotapes] il *Publ Wkly* 232:37-8 Ag 21 '87

Power retailers [cover story] A. Dunkin and M. D. Oneal. il *Bus Week* p86-9+ D 21 '87

PW business survey: plunging stocks boost books. S. Bolle and others. il *Publ Wkly* 232:24+ D 18 '87

Retailers got most of their Christmas wishes. M. N. Vamos. il *Bus Week* p47 Ja 12 '87

'Tis the season to be shopping. J. Schwartz. il *Newsweek* 110:52 D 21 '87

Too many goodies under Hollywood's tree. R. Grover. il *Bus Week* p39 D 21 '87

Toymakers could wake up to coal-filled stockings. K. H. Hammonds. il *Bus Week* p131 O 12 '87

Video games make a Christmas comeback. il *Fortune* 116:8 D 7 '87

Will the crash steal Christmas? What two retailers expect [K Mart and Bloomingdale's] il *Bus Week* p60-2 D 7 '87

The year the feds stole Christmas [unavailability of dual deck videocassette recorders and digital audio tape technology] Z. Lazarevič. il *Forbes* 140:286 N 16 '87

Canada

Black Monday's long hangover. D. Jenish. il *Macleans* 100:32-3 D 14 '87

Christmas cactus

Christmas cactus is for keeping. M. C. Pindar. il *South Living* 22:48-9 D '87

Make Christmas cactus rebloom. R. Keller. il *Rodale's Org Gard* 34:20-1 D '87

Christmas cake See Cake

Christmas cards

"Etching" for fourth-graders [drypoint etching in plaster] il *Sunset* 179:106-7 N '87

Mola cards: you layer paper. il *Sunset* 179:112-13 D '87

Wishing it was just the thought. T. Friend. il *Harpers* 275:68-9 D '87

Exhibitions

Doing it their way [Photographers' Christmas Show at the California Museum of Photography] J. O'Dwyer. il *Americana* 15:54-5 N/D '87

Christmas cookies See Cookies

Christmas cooking

   See also

     Christmas dinners

     Christmas entertaining

     Cooking, Ornamental

     Food as gifts

Christmas cookbook. il *McCalls* 115:105-17 D '87

Christmas treats from early cookbooks. H. Garrison. il *Parents* 62:154-6+ D '87

Fabulous holiday food for busy, busy families. B. Greenwood. il *Better Homes Gard* 65:114-21+ D '87

Festive first courses [microwaving] il *Good Housekeep* 205:243-4 D '87

Food. B. Livermore. il *Health* 19:46-8 D '87

Holiday baking in minutes [microwaved] il *South Living* 22:216 N '87

Holiday baking spices the air [cover story] S. Payne. il *South Living* 22:118-19+ D '87

Holiday brunch with your personal style. il *Glamour* 85:230-2 D '87

Masterpiece cookbook. il *Good Housekeep* 205:166-76+ D '87

The new Noel [special section] il *Harpers Bazaar* 121:132-9+ D '87

Recipes for a tree-hunt tradition. il *South Living* 22:126+ D '87

Season's eatings. il *Redbook* 170:86-91+ D '87

Strong breads, dark sweets [Italian and Spanish cooking] L. Forbes. il *House Gard* 159:88+ D '87

Trimming your holiday recipes [cutting fat] L. Phelps. il *Better Homes Gard* 65:95 D '87

Christmas cribs

An ornamental holiday scene [cover story] R. N. Hoffman. il *Workbench* 43:34-7 N/D '87

Christmas decorations

   See also

     Christmas wreaths

24 quick tips for holiday parties. J. Williams and others. il *Better Homes Gard* 65:74-9 D '87

Acetate meets copy machine for cards, decorations. il *Sunset* 179:110-11 D '87

Apples at Christmas. L. C. Askey. il *South Living* 22:80-1 D '87

Beribbon a tree. R. J. Katz. il *Redbook* 170:79-81 D '87

Bring home the joy! Celebrate and decorate with country-Christmas spirit. il *Redbook* 170:67-73 D '87

Christmas all through the house. il *McCalls* 115:69-71+ D '87

Christmas, country style. J. Williams and J. Severson. il *Better Homes Gard* 65:99-107 D '87

Christmas, Victorian style. il *Better Homes Gard* 65:108-13+ D '87

Country touches for Christmas [hand crafted tree trims] J. Williams and J. Severson. il *Better Homes Gard* 65:122-3 O '87

A Dickens of a Christmas [Victorian interiors] M. D. Glass. il *Ladies Home J* 104:154-9 D '87

Electronic Xmas tree. T. L. Jozwiak. il *Radio-Electron* 58:47-8+ D '87

Festive reindeer. A. Cook. il *Workbench* 43:32 N/D '87

Gearing up for the holidays [Lord & Taylor Christmas windows] B. Weber. il *N Y Times Mag* p110 N 15 '87

Heirloom ornaments. il *Good Housekeep* 205:140-1 D '87

Holiday accents by the bowlful. J. Williams and J. Severson. il *Better Homes Gard* 65:144-5 N '87

A home for the holidays [Lookout Mountain, Tenn.] L. Hallam. il *South Living* 22:98-100 D '87

In the dough. R. Hinderstein. il *Mother Earth News* 108:30 N/D '87

Kids' style: fun-to-make holiday trees and wreaths. V. Hahn. il *Parents* 62:151-2 D '87

Ornaments with the scent of applesauce and cinnamon. il *Sunset* 179:92 D '87

Our merry little Christmas house. il *Good Housekeep* 205:142-7 D '87

Paper and plants, simple and cheerful. il *Sunset* 179:64-7 D '87

Puffy ornaments from cloth or new cellophane. il *Sunset* 179:106 D '87

Scents of the season [Victorian crafts] il *Redbook* 170:14 N '87

Slot-togethers. il *Sunset* 179:82-3 D '87

A Swiss Christmas tree shop [Johann Wanner] L. Langseth-Christensen. il *Gourmet* 47:78-81+ D '87

Wood appliqué art [ornaments created by Lillian Renko Bledow] J. Williams. il *Better Homes Gard* 65:58-60+ O '87

A wooden reindeer [from logs] G. Rubin. il *Ctry J* 14:40 D '87

Christmas decorations, Outdoor

Big-scale and bright, architectural lighting makes a Bay Area comeback. il *Sunset* 179:14-15 D '87

Christmas dinners

A Canadian Christmas feast: bringing out the British [hotels in British Columbia offering special medieval Christmas feasts] A. Satterfield. il *Travel Holiday* 168:66-9 N '87

Christmas at Colette's [Christmas Eve feast] C. Rossant. il *McCalls* 115:101+ D '87

Christmas dinner. il *Gourmet* 47:138-46+ D '87

A Christmas dinner "for sale" [served at R. J. White home] J. Siroto. il por *McCalls* 114:63-5 Ja '87

A Christmas feast [reinterpreting standard English dishes] N. H. Jenkins. il *N Y Times Mag* p95-6 D 13 '87

Christmas feast with an Oriental flavor [Chinese duckling] A. Simon. il *Saturday Evening Post* 259:18-20 D '87

A country Christmas [roast goose] E. Frell. il *Mother Earth News* 108:84-6 N/D '87

Entrées with flair. P. Y. Cordell. il *South Living* 22:76-7 D '87

The Esquire Christmas dinner. il *Esquire* 108:217-20 D '87

Holiday dinners [special section] il *South Living* 22:101+ N '87

Holiday shortcuts [microwaving] J. B. Hurley. *Prevention* 39:64+ D '87

Savory merriment [Christmas at London's Connaught Hotel] S. M. Dinhofer. il *Harpers Bazaar* 121:82+ D '87

Superstar buffet. il *Ladies Home J* 104:152-3+ D '87

Wonderful holiday buffet [Indian cooking] il *Glamour* 85:226-9 D '87

Christmas entertaining

   See also

     Christmas dinners

A caroling party. il *Gourmet* 47:102-4+ D '87

Come by for dessert. J. Nash. il *Essence* 18:82-3+ D '87

Creating a lavish holiday party. E. Fried. il *Black Enterp* 18:106-8+ D '87

Delicious tradition: a holiday party with a history [dessert party of R. Lazarus] F. Greenberg. il pors *Work Woman* 12:94-8+ D '87

McCall's holiday party cookbook. M. Langan. il *McCalls* 114:67-72+ Ja '87

An old-fashioned tree-hunt party. D. G. Lowery. il *South Living* 22:88-9 D '87

One hell of a party: how to throw a holiday open house for forty. il *Esquire* 108:148-51 D '87

Pouring the wassail with care. D. B. Moskowitz. il *Bus Week* p154 D 7 '87

'Twas the bite before Christmas . . . W. P. Rayner and C. Rayner. il *Vogue* 177:214 D '87

Anecdotes, facetiae, satire, etc.

Fête accompli. P. Mehlman. il *Harpers Bazaar* 121:68+ D '87

Christmas fire prevention measures See Fire prevention

Christmas gift wrapping See Wrapping of packages

Christmas gifts

   See also

     Books as gifts

     Christmas projects

     Christmas shopping

     Food as gifts

     Gifts in business

     Phonograph records as gifts

     Plants as gifts

     Videotapes as gifts

     Wrapping of packages

Christmas gifts—*cont.*
$5 to $70: how to sort through all those blinking, beeping choices. C. Begole. il *Glamour* 85:48 D '87
45 gifts under $35. J. Ristsoo. il *Good Housekeep* 205:32+ D '87
Best buy gifts. il *Consum Rep* 52:678-82 N '87
Christmas gift guide [photographic equipment] il *Pop Photogr* 94:22+ D '87
Christmas gift shop [for boat owners] B. Gladstone and others. il *Mot Boat Sail* 160:59-66 D '87
Christmas giftbook. il *Good Housekeep* 205:70+ N '87
Christmas gifts [cover story] C. Pollan. il *N Y* 20:57-77+ D 7 '87
Christmas gifts under $50. il *Gourmet* 47:90-1 D '87
Christmas kicks [boating gifts; cover story] D. Hoover. il *Mot Boat Sail* 160:50-3 D '87
Fail-safe gifts. L. Werner. il *Ladies Home J* 104:78+ D '87
For the fan who has everything [sports-oriented gifts] il *Sport Mag* 78:79-80+ Ja '87
The gifted skier. D. White. il *Skiing* 40:138-41 D '87
Gifts that make your Christmas dance. M. Horosko. il *Dance Mag* 61:58-9 N '87
Gifts they won't expect. D. Moreau. il *Changing Times* 41:74-7 N '87
Gourmet's Christmas gifts. il *Gourmet* 47:98-106 N '87
Great gear. il *Women's Sports Fitness* 9:76-7 D '87
Hi-fi holiday gifts [with editorial comment by Louise Boundas] il *Stereo Rev* 52:8, 79-83 D '87
Holiday shopping guide [gifts for artists] il *Am Artist* 51:46-7 N '87
Innovations. il *Essence* 18:92-3 D '87
Innovations. il *Essence* 18:98-100 N '87
Loot for friends & lovers. il *Ms* 16:56-7 D '87
The pleasures of giving. il *N Y Times Mag* p106-11 N 8 '87
The Post goes shopping. M. G. Stoddard. il *Saturday Evening Post* 259:48-51 D '87
Practical little photo gifts. K. Geller-Shinn. il *Petersens Photogr Mag* 16:16 D '87
Practical or just pretty, these gift ideas help give a garden its character. il *Sunset* 179:183-4 D '87
Present & accounted for. P. Nelson. *Harpers Bazaar* 121:127+ D '87
Seeds 'n' greetings [gardening gifts] J. Burnett. il *Rodale's Org Gard* 34:77-81 D '87
Twice as nice gifts to give. M. O'Koon. *Good Housekeep* 205:243 N '87
Watts for Christmas. P. Hoban. il *N Y* 20:30+ D 14 '87

Anecdotes, facetiae, satire, etc.
Yoo hoo, Santa! J. Miller. il *Ms* 16:28 D '87

Shipping
See Parcel post

Christmas gifts for children
See also
Books as gifts
Toys
The 10 best gift ideas under $10. M. Mohler and M. D. Rosen. il *Ladies Home J* 104:66 D '87
"Buy me, buy me": how to cope when kids get greedy. L. Werner. il *Ladies Home J* 104:76-8 D '87
The children's closet. *New Yorker* 63:132-4+ N 16 '87
Loot for fun & games. il *Ms* 16:58-9 D '87
On and off the avenue. *New Yorker* 63:118+ D 7 '87
Presents perfect (for giving!) [teens] il *Teen* 31:58 D '87

Christmas gifts for men
On and off the avenue. *New Yorker* 63:106-18 D 14 '87

Christmas gifts for pets
Playing Santa to your pet. H. E. Whiteley. il *Saturday Evening Post* 259:22+ D '87

Christmas gifts for the home
8 gifts to give your favorite do-it-yourselfer. il *Workbench* 43:24-5 N/D '87
Food in Vogue. B. Kafka. il *Vogue* 177:216+ D '87
High-tech toys for homebodies. T. Segal. il *Bus Week* p150-1 D 7 '87
Microwave gifts & gadgets. il *Redbook* 170:140+ D '87
On and off the avenue. *New Yorker* 63:105-18 N 23 '87
Sharing your favorite recipes: three ways to go. il *Sunset* 179:116-17 D '87

Christmas gifts for women
29 gifts for her. il *Good Housekeep* 205:58+ D '87
50 perfect big-impact extras. il *Harpers Bazaar* 121:238-41 N '87
The best of everything. il *Seventeen* 46:118-19 D '87
On and off the avenue. *New Yorker* 63:114-32 N 16 '87

Anecdotes, facetiae, satire, etc.
Home-shopping Santa. M. G. Stoddard. il *Saturday Evening Post* 259:46-7 D '87

Christmas greens
See also
Christmas trees
Christmas wreaths
Mistletoe
Bowls of vigorous greens. W. Shipman. il *Ctry J* 14:38-9 D '87

Christmas in literature
See also
Christmas poems
Christmas stories

Christmas Island (Indian Ocean)
See also
Phosphate industry—Christmas Island (Indian Ocean)
Wildlife—Christmas Island (Indian Ocean)

Christmas Island (Indian Ocean) postage stamps *See* Postage stamps

Christmas lighting *See* Christmas decorations
Christmas mail order business *See* Mail order business
Christmas music
See also
Compact discs—Christmas music
Phonograph records—Christmas music

Christmas pageants
The perfect Christmas pageant. M. L. Lindvall. il *Good Housekeep* 205:56-7 D '87

Christmas parties *See* Christmas entertaining
Christmas plants *See* House plants
Christmas poems

Single works
See name of author for full entry
Advent awakening. Shepherd, J. Barrie
And a light shines in darkness. Brady, Charles
La bella notizia. Porter, Anne
Christmas. Gronseth, Charlotte M.
December. Updike, John
Gifts. Mott, Michael
Greetings, friends! Angell, Roger
Mary at the manger. Shepherd, J. Barrie
A mother's Christams Eve wish. Bariteau, Corinne Adria
No sign of Santa. Wise, William
The oxen. Hardy, Thomas, 1840-1928
Persistent suitor. Hillila, Bernhard
Storm window. Smith, Antony
Wishes. De Vito, E. B.

Christmas presents *See* Christmas gifts
Christmas projects
See also
Christmas decorations
Charming Christmas gifts to make now. il *Good Housekeep* 205:124-5+ Ag '87
Christmas crafts to make, bake & sew. il *McCalls* 115:79-82+ D '87
Christmas, Southwest style. J. Williams and J. Severson. il *Better Homes Gard* 65:37-48+ D '87
Fun for all! il *Redbook* 170:14 D '87
Gifts to make [special section] il *Workbench* 43:27-9+ N/D '87
A host of holiday projects for children. il *McCalls* 115:47 D '87
One-of-a-kind glass gifts . . . with easy chemical etching. il *Sunset* 179:95-6 D '87

Christmas safety devices and measures *See* Accidents—Prevention
Christmas seals

Collectors and collecting
Four score (and more) Christmas seals. S. A. Sprecher. il *Antiques Collect Hobbies* 92:26-30 D '87

Christmas shopping
See also
Christmas business
Christmas shopping [with toddlers] J. T. Gibson. il *Parents* 62:194 D '87
Christmas shopping on the Drive [Rodeo Drive] D. P. Marshall. il *Travel Holiday* 168:20-1+ D '87
Emeryville's Stroll, a chance to buy unusual gifts. il *Sunset* 179:60 D '87
How to avoid the shopping daze. B. Bauer. il *U S News World Rep* 103:64-6 N 30 '87
Shopping tips from the pros. il *Glamour* 85:173 D '87

Anecdotes, facetiae, satire, etc.
Joy to the mall! C. Dolson. *Christ Today* 31:25 D 11 '87

Photographs and photography
Christmas shopping around the world. J. Fierman. il *Fortune* 116:92-100 D 21 '87

Christmas Star *See* Star of Bethlehem
Christmas stores
    See also
      Johann Wanner (Firm)
  Yetta Galiber: Christmas every day of the year [special store for disabled children in Washington, D.C.] il pors *Ebony* 43:27-30 D '87
Christmas stories
    Single works
    See name of author for full entry
  Bless the child. Stewart, Isobel
  The cabbie wore red. Serotta, Edward
  A Carol Christmas. Allen, Richard
  Caroling on command. Toner, Gerald R.
  Chester's Christmas surprise. Stanton, Will
  Christmas 1940. Roosevelt, Eleanor, 1884-1962
  Christmas in Lake Wobegon. Keillor, Garrison
  A drummer's gift. Sechler, Teena
  Family ritual. Carlson, Ron
  The girl with the gift. Ford, John
  Home for Christmas. Stewart, Isobel
  Horatio's trick. Beattie, Ann
  A love song for Christmas. Doig, D. T.
  More precious than gold. Cherry, Kelly
  Mr. Pat's magical ride. Johnson, Timothy J.
  Santa knows. Woodruff, Elvira
Christmas table setting *See* Table setting
Christmas toys *See* Toys
Christmas tree ornaments *See* Christmas decorations
Christmas trees
  Christmas shame [cover story] E. H. Peterson. il por *Christ Today* 31:17-19 D 11 '87
  A Christmas tradition that grows and grows. S. Miller. il *Good Housekeep* 205:206 D '87
  Christmas trees: a field guide. T. Krautwurst. il map *Mother Earth News* 108:87-9 N/D '87
  Pick the best Christmas tree on the lot. il *South Living* 22:66 D '87
  A tree for the birds. il *South Living* 22:54 D '87
  What to do with your old Christmas tree. il *Glamour* 85:51 Ja '87
  When you team up two scrawny Douglas firs . . . il *Sunset* 179:187 D '87
    Decoration
    See Christmas decorations
    Export-import trade
  Anger over a tree tax [protesting Ottawa's decision to impose a tariff on Christmas trees imported from United States] M. Clark. il *Macleans* 100:11 F 9 '87
Christmas vacations *See* Vacations
Christmas wreaths
  Deck the halls . . . il *Redbook* 170:82-3 D '87
  From the jungle to your front door: "air plants" in wreaths. il *Sunset* 179:190-1 D '87
  Kids' style: fun-to-make holiday trees and wreaths. V. Hahn. il *Parents* 62:151-2 D '87
  A treasury of holiday wreaths. il *McCalls* 114:38-40 Ja '87
  Wreaths made from nature's gifts. K. King. il *South Living* 22:66+ N '87
Christophe, Henri, King of Haiti, 1767-1820
    about
  'We will confound the calumniators of our race . . .'. F. Maclean. il por map *Smithsonian* 18:160-6+ O '87
Christopher, Dean
  Last word. por *Omni* 10:178 D '87
Christopher, H. W.
  Kind words for the mother-in-law's tongue. il *Flower Gard* 31:47 O/N '87
Christopher, Nicholas
  Blizzard [poem] *Nation* 244:22 Ja 10 '87
  Circe revisited [poem] *New Repub* 197:48 D 14 '87
  Desperate character [poem] *New Yorker* 63:30 Ag 31 '87
  Krazy Kat's confession [poem] *Nation* 245:280 S 19 '87
  Miranda in Reno [poem] *New Repub* 196:40 Ja 26 '87
Christopher Sly [opera] *See* Argento, Dominick
Christy, Shawna Lyn
    about
  All-American Girl talk. por *Teen* 31:72 Ag '87
Chromatid exchange, Sister *See* Crossing over (Genetics)
Chromatin
  Sequence-specific packaging of DNA in human sperm chromatin. J. M. Gatewood and others. bibl f il *Science* 236:962-4 My 22 '87
Chromatographic analysis
  Chromatography. *Science* 235 pt2:G43-G46+ F 27 '87

Chromatography with supercritical fluids. M. L. Lee and K. E. Markides. bibl f il *Science* 235:1342-7 Mr 13 '87
High-performance liquid chromatography, gas chromatography, and supercritical fluid chromatography. H. M. McNair. *Science* 235 pt2:G43 F 27 '87
Polychlorinated biphenyl dechlorination in aquatic sediments [river sediments] J. F. Brown and others. bibl f il *Science* 236:709-12 My 8 '87
The role of protein structure in chromatographic behavior. F. E. Regnier. bibl f *Science* 238:319-23 O 16 '87
Chromium in the body
  Refined sugars can polish off chromium. *Prevention* 39:113 S '87
Chromodynamics, Quantum *See* Quantum chromodynamics
Chromosome abnormalities
    See also
      Down syndrome
      Fragile X syndrome
  Absence of duplication of chromosome 21 genes in familial and sporadic Alzheimer's disease. P. H. St George-Hyslop and others. bibl f il *Science* 238:664-6 O 30 '87
  Amyloid β protein gene: cDNA, mRNA distribution, and genetic linkage near the Alzheimer locus. R. E. Tanzi and others. bibl f il *Science* 235:880-4 F 20 '87
  Anticancer genes [missing gene causes retinoblastoma] C. SerVaas. il *Saturday Evening Post* 259:98+ My/Je '87
  Avian v-*myc* replaces chromosomal translocation in murine plasmacytomagenesis. M. Potter and others. bibl f il *Science* 235:787-9 F 13 '87
  Characterization and chromosomal localization of a cDNA encoding brain amyloid of Alzheimer's disease. D. Goldgaber and others. bibl f il *Science* 235:877-80 F 20 '87
  Defect in Alzheimer's is on chromosome 21. D. M. Barnes. *Science* 235:846-7 F 20 '87
  Detection of minimal residual cells carrying the t(14;18) by DNA sequence amplification. M.-S. Lee and others. bibl f il *Science* 237:175-8 Jl 10 '87
  Fragile sites at 16q22 are not at the breakpoint of the chromosomal rearrangement in AMMoL. R. N. Simmers and others. bibl f il *Science* 236:92-4 Ap 3 '87
  Gene for manic depression? [study of Amish families by Janice Egeland and others] B. Bower. *Sci News* 131:132 F 28 '87
  Gene of the week [studies of five families in Jerusalem] *Time* 129:62 Mr 30 '87
  The genetic defect causing familial Alzheimer's disease maps on chromosome 21. P. H. St George-Hyslop and others. bibl f il *Science* 235:885-90 F 20 '87
  Hunting 'the black dog' [study of manic depression among the Amish] il *U S News World Rep* 102:8 Mr 9 '87
  Introduction of a normal human chromosome 11 into a Wilms' tumor cell line controls its tumorigenic expression. B. E. Weissman and others. bibl f il *Science* 236:175-80 Ap 10 '87
  Is mental illness inherited? [study of Amish families; research by Janice Egeland and others] C. Wallis. il *Time* 129:67 Mr 9 '87
  Key to Alzheimer's? [defect tracked to chromosome 21] *Sci Am* 256:68 Ap '87
  Manic depression: a new gene defect [X chromosome; research by Miron Baron and others] B. Bower. *Sci News* 131:199 Mr 28 '87
  Manic-depression gene tied to chromosome 11. G. Kolata. *Science* 235:1139-40 Mr 6 '87
  Margins of sexuality [developmental difficulties associated with abnormal sex chromosomes] D. B. Berch and B. G. Bender. bibl (p63) il *Psychol Today* 21:54-7 D '87
  Molecular analysis of a constitutional X-autosome translocation in a female with muscular dystrophy. S. E. Bodrug and others. bibl f il *Science* 237:1620-4 S 25 '87
  Mutations in the first exon are associated with altered transcription of c-*myc* in Burkitt lymphoma [chromosomal translocations] E. Cesarman and others. bibl f il *Science* 238:1272-5 N 27 '87
  Reduction to homozygosity of genes on chromosome 11 in human breast neoplasia. I. U. Ali and others. bibl f il *Science* 238:185-8 O 9 '87
  Relationship between the c-*myb* locus and the 6q-chromosomal aberration in leukemias and lymphomas. C. Barletta and others. bibl f il *Science* 235:1064-7 F 27 '87

Chromosome abnormalities—*cont.*

Unique forms of the *abl* tyrosine kinase distinguish Ph[1]-positive CML Ph[1]-positive ALL. S. S. Clark and others. bibl f il *Science* 235:85-8 Ja 2 '87

When manic depression is part of the family legacy [Amish research by Janice Egeland and others] T. Monmaney. il *Newsweek* 109:53 My 4 '87

X marks the spot [manic depression; research on five families in Jerusalem] *Sci News* 131:376 Je 13 '87

Chromosome mapping

See also

Linkage (Genetics)

Locus (Genes)

The causes of Down syndrome. D. Patterson. il *Sci Am* 257:52-7+ Ag '87

Construction of a general human chromosome jumping library, with application to cystic fibrosis. F. S. Collins and others. bibl f il *Science* 235:1046-9 F 27 '87

Genetic promise [restriction fragment length polymorphism mapping] *Sci Am* 257:30-1 Ag '87

Homozygosity mapping: a way to map human recessive traits with the DNA of inbred children. E. S. Lander and D. Botstein. bibl f il *Science* 236:1567-70 Je 19 '87

Megabase-scale mapping of the HLA gene complex by pulsed field gel electrophoresis [major histocompatibility complex] S. K. Lawrance and others. bibl f il *Science* 235:1387-90 Mr 13 '87

A physical map of the Escherichia coli K12 genome. C. L. Smith and others. bibl f il *Science* 236:1448-53 Je 12 '87

Variable number of tandem repeat (VNTR) markers for human gene mapping. Y. Nakamura and others. bibl f il *Science* 235:1616-22 Mr 27 '87

Chromosome translocations *See* Chromosome abnormalities

Chromosomes

See also

Chromatin

Crossing over (Genetics)

Genes

Genomes

Linkage (Genetics)

Transposons

A chicken transferrin gene in transgenic mice escapes X-chromosome inactivation. M. A. Goldman and others. bibl f il *Science* 236:593-5 My 1 '87

Genetic recombination. F. W. Stahl. il *Sci Am* 256:90-101 F '87

High-speed chromosome sorting. J. W. Gray and others. bibl f il *Science* 238:323-9 O 16 '87

Is she or isn't she? [growing movement to end gender testing in the Olympics] L. Fink. il *Women's Sports Fitness* 9:71 D '87

Mammals need moms and dads. J. A. Miller. il *BioScience* 37:379-82 Je '87

A new oyster for all seasons [triploids edible year-round; research by Standish Allen and Sandra Downing] R. M. Strickland and L. Bevan. il *Oceans* 20:7-8 S/O '87

Chromosomes, Artificial

Artificial chromosomes. A. W. Murray and J. W. Szostak. bibl (p150) il *Sci Am* 257:62-6+ N '87

Cloning of large segments of exogenous DNA into yeast by means of artificial chromosome vectors. D. T. Burke and others. bibl f il *Science* 236:806-12 My 15 '87

Chromosomes (Botany)

Electrophoretic evidence for genetic diploidy in the bracken fern (Pteridium aquilinum). P. G. Wolf and others. bibl f il *Science* 236:947-9 My 22 '87

Chronic fatigue syndrome

Stealthy epidemic of exhaustion. D. Thompson. il *Time* 129:52 Je 29 '87

Chronic illness *See* Sickness

Chronicle Books

Chronicle Books hires New York editor to start children's list [V. Rock] *Publ Wkly* 232:26+ O 30 '87

Chronicle Publications Inc.

ABA to be exclusive distributor of 'Chronicle of 20th century' [distribution handled through BOS] *Publ Wkly* 231:14 Ap 3 '87

Chronobiology *See* Biological rhythms

Chronograph

Time the speeding bullet. J. Carmichel. il *Outdoor Life* 179:38+ Ja '87

Chronology

See also

Geological time

Chronology, Historical

Computer dating [astronomical dating] F. R. Stephenson. il *Nat Hist* 96:24+ Ja '87

Chrysanthemum balsamita *See* Costmary

Chrysanthemums

The biggest of the big: exhibition chrysanthemums. il *Sunset* 178:118-19 Ja '87

Five basics for glorious chrysanthemums. V. C. Fisher. il *Flower Gard* 31:72-3 Ap/My '87

Chrysler Canada Ltd.

A pension breakthrough [agrees to index pensions against inflation] D. Jenish. il *Macleans* 100:32-3 S 28 '87

Chrysler Corp.

Any more rabbits in the hat, Lee? J. Flint. il *Forbes* 140:108-9 N 30 '87

Can Chrysler make a comeback in Europe, too? J. B. Treece. il *Bus Week* p168-9 N 16 '87

Chrysler courts AMC. P. Lienert. il *Road Track* 38:110+ Mr '87

Chrysler to go Grand Prix racing! N. Wollheim and others. *Mot Trend* 39:18 Ag '87

Chrysler's aerospace involvement grows with takeover of Texas firm [Electrospace Systems, Inc.] C. A. Shifrin. *Aviat Week Space Technol* 127:66-7 Jl 20 '87

Chrysler's conundrum [no factory available to produce Omni/Horizon] S. Flack. il por *Forbes* 139:104 Ap 20 '87

Chrysler's crystal ball. P. Lienert. *Road Track* 38:98 My '87

A daredevil wheel deal [Chrysler buys AMC] G. Russell. il *Time* 129:40-1 Mr 23 '87

The first Chrysler bail-out: the M-1 tank. R. A. Mendel. il *Wash Mon* 19:17-23 F '87

A free ride at Chrysler [odometer scandal] G. Carroll and J. B. Copeland. il *Newsweek* 110:37 Jl 6 '87

Iacocca: 'Did we screw up? You bet' [odometer scandal] *Newsweek* 110:42 Jl 13 '87

Jeep/Eagle: preview of an evolution [Chrysler's acquisition of AMC] M. Keller. il *Mot Trend* 39:150 N '87

Lee Iacocca's production whiz [R. E. Dauch] A. L. Taylor, III. il pors *Fortune* 115:36-8+ Je 22 '87

Living as a legend [L. A. Iacocca] A. L. Taylor, III. il por *Fortune* 116:43 Ag 3 '87

The nonsense of a "post-industrial society" [address, January 15, 1987] R. A. Lutz. *Vital Speeches Day* 53:330-3 Mr 15 '87

Now, for Chrysler's next trick . . . [acquisition of American Motors Corp.] W. J. Hampton. il *Bus Week* p32-3 Mr 23 '87

The payoff to customers from Chrysler-AMC merger. J. A. Seamonds. il *U S News World Rep* 102:58-9 Mr 23 '87

Survival of the fleetest [acquisition of AMC and Lamborghini] J. Lamm. il *Road Track* 39:118+ O '87

Tooling into the luxury market in a Lamborghini. W. C. Symonds. il *Bus Week* p45+ My 4 '87

A U-turn for Chrysler's fund [pension fund sells bonds to buy stocks] S. Weiss. *Bus Week* p146 Mr 23 '87

Why Chrysler can't afford to go off its diet. W. J. Hampton. il *Bus Week* p84 O 5 '87

Why Chrysler's cash handles like a dream [treasurer of pension fund F. W. Zuckerman] S. Weiss. il por *Bus Week* p116 Je 8 '87

Would you buy a used Chrysler from this man? [disconnected odometers] C. P. Work. *U S News World Rep* 103:44 Jl 6 '87

'Zip, overnight': a Chrysler Jeep [Chrysler's bid for AMC] B. Powell. il *Newsweek* 109:38-9 Mr 23 '87

Chrysler Museum

Order out of hodgepodge. J. Meyer. il *Art News* 86:28+ D '87

Chrystal, John

about

Gorbachev's prairie pals. T. Jacoby. il por *Newsweek* 109:31 Ap 6 '87

Chu, Ching-Wu

about

In the trenches of science. J. Gleick. il *N Y Times Mag* p28-31+ Ag 16 '87

Chu, Ching-Wu, and others

Superconductivity at 52.5 K in the lanthanum-barium-copper-oxide system. bibl f il *Science* 235:567-9 Ja 30 '87

Chu, Ellen W.

(jt. auth) See Coder, David M., and Chu, Ellen W.

Chu, Paul *See* Chu, Ching-Wu

Chua, Jonalo Ace

America: the 'great fish trap'. por *U S News World Rep* 103:16 O 5 '87

Chua, Victor

about

Victor Chua: studying hard for Singapore. J. O'Connor. por *Sch Update* 119:4-5 Ap 6 '87

Chubb, John E.
States rights and the national interests [address, July 22, 1987] *Vital Speeches Day* 53:702-4 S 1 '87
Chubin, Daryl E.
Replies to progress [discussion of April 1986 article, Scientific progress: an interim report] *BioScience* 37:108-9 F '87
A soap opera for science. bibl f *BioScience* 37:259-61 Ap '87
Chuck Barris Productions Inc.
What's his line? [B. Sugarman of Giant Group buys Chuck Barris Productions] A. B. Block. il por *Forbes* 139:70-1 Ja 26 '87
Chuck Berry Hail! Hail! Rock 'n' roll [film] See Motion picture reviews—Single works
Chucks (Machine work)
Chuck key eliminator [Chucklok] J. R. Provey. il *Home Mech* 83:100 My '87
Multipurpose chucks for woodturning lathes [excerpt from Handbook of woodturning] L. H. Hodges. il *Workbench* 43:96-9 Mr/Ap '87
Chun, Doo Hwan
about
Brinkmanship in South Korea. R. Watson. il por *Newsweek* 110:26-7 Jl 6 '87
A cautious victory. B. Levin. il por *Macleans* 100:16 Jl 13 '87
Chun switches signals. F. Willey. il por *Newsweek* 109:39 Ap 27 '87
Chun's hard line can only deepen Korea's unrest. L. Nakarmi and B. Javetski. il *Bus Week* p49 Jl 6 '87
Chun's option: to crush or concede. M. Lord. il map *U S News World Rep* 102:26-8 Je 29 '87
How South Korea's Chun is trying to bypass the opposition. R. J. Dowling. il *Bus Week* p49 My 4 '87
Old friends. M. S. Serrill. il pors *Time* 129:40 Je 15 '87
Olympian hurdle in Korea. D. Kirk. il *New Leader* 70:3-5 Je 29 '87
Onslaughts of force and fury. J. Greenwald. il *Time* 129:50-1 Mr 16 '87
Reforms on hold. H. G. Chua-Eoan. por *Time* 129:38-9 Ap 27 '87
A successor in his own image. B. Levin. il por *Macleans* 100:18 Jl 6 '87
Talk and fight. W. R. Doerner. il por *Time* 130:14-15 Jl 6 '87
Tradition and change at war. W. L. Chaze. il por *U S News World Rep* 103:31-2 Jl 6 '87
A volcano of unrest. W. R. Doerner. il *Time* 129:46-7 My 25 '87
Chung, Ju Yung
about
A patriarch relaxes his control. il por *Newsweek* 110:26-7 Ag 31 '87
Chunnel See English Channel tunnel
Church, Beverly, and Bultman, Bethany Ewald
Party disasters: what to do, say, serve when things go wrong [excerpt from The joys of entertaining] il *Glamour* 85:58 D '87
Church, F. Forrester
A just-war theory for abortion. *Christ Century* 104:733-4 Ag 26-S 2 '87
Church
See also
Catholic Church
Christianity
House churches
Laity
Parishes
Church advertising See Religious advertising
Church and AIDS (Disease) See AIDS (Disease)—Religious aspects
Church and aliens See Church and social problems
Church and civil rights
Public exorcism in Forsyth County ["Brotherhood" March to protest racism] K. Sehested. *Christ Century* 104:238-9 Mr 11 '87
International aspects
Religion and the future of human rights. R. F. Drinan. il *Christ Century* 104:683-7 Ag 12-19 '87
UN official seeks data on repression of believers [A. Ribeiro of the Commission on Human Rights] B. Spring. *Christ Today* 31:34-5 F 6 '87
Brazil
A miracle, a universe (I) [involvement of Presbyterian minister J. Wright and Cardinal Arns in project to document torture by Brazilian military governments, 1964-1979] L. Weschler. *New Yorker* 63:69-84+ My 25 '87

A miracle, a universe (II) [involvement of Presbyterian minister J. Wright and Cardinal Arns in project to document torture by Brazilian military governments, 1964-1979] L. Weschler. *New Yorker* 63:72-80+ Je 1 '87
Chile
Business as usual: life after the Pope's visit. V. M. Bouvier. il *Commonweal* 114:373-5 Je 19 '87
A fraternal broadside [visit by Pope John Paul II] il por *Macleans* 100:22 Ap 13 '87
Human rights and the Pope's visit to Chile. R. F. Drinan. *America* 156:227-8 Mr 21 '87
'Only fifty yards away' [Pope's Chilean tour] *America* 156:313 Ap 18 '87
The Pope's battalions. F. Willey. il por *Newsweek* 109:37 Ap 13 '87
The Pope's new weapon. P. Yancey. il *Christ Today* 31:56 Ag 7 '87
Paraguay
The 'red' bishop of Benjamín Aceval [M. Medina] T. H. Stahel. *America* 156:453-4 Je 6 '87
United States
See Church and civil rights
Church and disarmament
Catholic thought on war & peace [discussion of September 11 and September 25, 1987 articles, The heritage abandoned?] P. Steinfels. *Commonweal* 114:690+ D 4 '87
The churches and the peace movement in France. M. B. Davis. il *Christ Century* 104:826-8 S 30 '87
A classic case of consequentialism [criticism of Cardinal Ratzinger's views on the morality of deterrence] E. W. Doherty. *Commonweal* 114:10-11 Ja 16 '87
An editorial dissent [discussion of May 8, 1987 article, Is deterrence moral?] P. Jordan. *Commonweal* 114:309-10 My 22 '87
The heritage abandoned? (I) [G. Weigel's critique of the Catholic position on war and peace, Tranquillitas ordinis] P. Steinfels. *Commonweal* 114:487-92 S 11 '87
The heritage abandoned? (II) [G. Weigel's critique of the Catholic position on war and peace, Tranquillitas ordinis] P. Steinfels. il *Commonweal* 114:530-3 S 25 '87
Is deterrence moral? [Catholic view] *Commonweal* 114:259-61 My 8 '87
Is nuclear deterrence immoral? [Catholic bishops' stand] R. E. Powaski. *America* 156:401-5 My 16 '87
Is nuclear deterrence moral? [Catholic views] J. M. Cameron. bibl f il *N Y Rev Books* 34:38-43 N 5 '87
Living in sin with nuclear arms [views of M. Gallagher on Catholic bishops' peace pastoral] J. M. Wall. *Christ Century* 104:155-6 F 18 '87
Ministering to the collective soul amid the arms race. J. Smith. il *Christ Century* 104:17-20 Ja 7-14 '87
A nuclear free Pacific: enlisting U.S. support [South Pacific Nuclear Free Zone Treaty] R. A. Evans. *Christ Century* 104:373-4 Ap 22 '87
Sidestepping The challenge of peace [Catholic bishops' pastoral on nuclear deterrence] M. Gallagher. il *Commonweal* 114:9-13 Ja 16 '87
'The things that make for peace' [United Methodist pastoral In defense of creation] W. H. Willimon. *Christ Century* 104:453-4 My 6 '87
Willimon hollering at bishops? [discussion of May 6, 1987 article, The things that make for peace] W. H. Willimon. *Christ Century* 104:632-4 Jl 15-22 '87
Church and economic problems See Christianity and economics
Church and education
See also
Accelerated Christian Education
Church colleges and universities
Church schools
Public schools and religion
Is education going to the technicians? S. Ulstein. il por *Christ Today* 31:28 S 4 '87
Church and homosexuality See Church work with homosexuals; Homosexuality and Christianity
Church and hunger See Church and social problems
Church and industry
Profiting with help from above. E. C. Baig. il *Fortune* 115:36-8+ Ap 27 '87
Church and labor
See also
United Methodist Church—Employees
Civilizing work [Catholic view] J. C. Haughey. *America* 156:382-4 My 9 '87
Labor & the limits of the market place. *Commonweal* 114:3-4 Ja 16 '87

Church and labor—*cont.*

Labor-saving devices [cover story] D. Kusnet. il *Commonweal* 114:526-9 S 25 '87

Making the case for full employment. M. Hope and J. Young. *Christ Century* 104:715-18 Ag 26-S 2 '87

Rethinking hunger in America: adapting the Sullivan principles. N. Amidei. il *Christ Century* 104:51-4 Ja 21 '87

Toward a civilization of work [Catholic view] R. Barta. *America* 156:187-8 Mr 7 '87

Church and law *See* Religion and law

Church and marriage *See* Marriage

Church and peace *See* Religion and peace

Church and politics *See* Religion and politics

Church and race relations

    See also

    Church colleges and universities—Race relations

Bishops: joining KKK is sinful, violates teaching [Catholic bishops] *Jet* 72:29 Ap 20 '87

Black Methodist minister heads white Texas church [J. D. Phillips of St. Andrew's United Methodist Church in Killeen] por *Jet* 72:22 Jl 13 '87

A cause for alarm. *Commonweal* 114:5-6 Ja 16 '87

Lingering racism. L. Cryderman. *Christ Today* 31:15 Mr 6 '87

Martin Luther King's inner spiritual church. M. E. Marty. por *Christ Century* 104:44 Ja 21 '87

Pope blasts U.S. racism; urges Church to continue fight for black equality. il por *Jet* 73:4 S 28 '87

Pope John-Paul's historic meeting with black bishops. il por *Jet* 73:24 N 9 '87

The signal from Howard Beach. *America* 156:61 Ja 31 '87

Untold story of black founder of Pentecostal church body rocked by sex scandal of whites [W. J. Seymour of the Assemblies of God and reaction to J. Bakker scandal] S. Booker. il pors *Jet* 72:12-14+ My 18 '87

International aspects

WCC antiracism grants. *Christ Century* 104:1137 D 16 '87

Australia

Australian bicentenary: 1988. A. Lyons. il *America* 157:451-4 D 12 '87

Fiji

Methodists involved in Fiji coup. D. C. White. *Christ Century* 104:548-9 Je 17-24 '87

South Africa

Afrikaner church needs 'critical solidarity' [Dutch Reformed Church] H. W. Turner. *Christ Century* 104:645-6 Jl 29-Ag 5 '87

Apartheid persecution [clergy opposed to the government's policies] *Christ Century* 104:49-50 Ja 21 '87

Bishop Tutu calls for dismantling of apartheid system, beginning of dialogue with blacks. por *UN Chron* 22:17 N/D '85

Can music be the instrument of racial reconciliation? J. Long. il *Christ Today* 31:47+ My 15 '87

A congregation divided [Dutch Reformed Church] C. Erasmus. *Macleans* 100:24 Jl 20 '87

Methodists will cut some stocks linked to S. Africa. *Jet* 72:14 S 14 '87

Peter Storey: hope for South Africa. W. H. Willimon. *Christ Century* 104:1109-11 D 9 '87

Sanctions in context [Catholic bishops reaffirm support] R. E. Lambert. *Commonweal* 114:166-7 Mr 27 '87

Shell game [Shell Oil accused of using former church leader James Armstrong to neutralize religious opposition to Shell's South African activities] *Christ Century* 104:937 O 28 '87

South African retaliation: a blessing in disguise? R. A. Evans and A. F. Evans. *Christ Century* 104:79-80 Ja 28 '87

U.S. Advisory Committee cites church's role in South African reconciliation. il *Christ Today* 31:63-4 Mr 20 '87

United States

    See Church and race relations

Church and refugee problems *See* Church and social problems

Church and reproduction *See* Reproduction—Moral and religious aspects

Church and social problems

    See also

    Abortion—Moral and religious aspects

    Birth control—Moral and religious aspects

    Campaign for Human Development

    Church and civil rights

    Church and industry

    Church and labor

    Church and race relations

    Church work with families

    Church work with homosexuals

    Church work with the handicapped

    Evangelicals for Social Action

    Feed the Children (Organization)

    Liberation theology

    People in Faith United Housing Corporation

    Sanctuary movement (Refugee aid)

    Socialism and religion

    Sociology, Christian

    Television broadcasting—Moral and religious aspects

    World Conference on Church, Community, and State (1937)

    World Vision (Organization)

Admiring what works [10th anniversary of Catholic Church's A call to action] A. McCarthy. *Commonweal* 114:73-4 F 13 '87

Brief encounter [discussing the plight of Harlem with white man on Manhattan's East Side] J. M. McConnell. il *America* 157:101 Ag 29-S 5 '87

Casa Romero closes: where do they go from here? [INS closes Catholic Church-run shelter for Central American refugees in Brownsville, Tex.] C. McElroy. il map *Focus* 37:28-9 Spr '87

The celebrity illusion. C. W. Colson. il *Christ Today* 31:72 D 11 '87

Church businesses spread the gospel of self help [community development and black churches] il *Ebony* 42:61-2+ F '87

Churches band together to help register undocumented aliens. R. Frame. il *Christ Today* 31:34-5 Jl 10 '87

A fellowship of suffering [refugees] B. R. Thompson. il por maps *Christ Today* 31:24-9 F 20 '87

How Catholics have grown up on the works of mercy. G. M. Costello. il *U S Cathol* 52:27-33 Je '87

On challenging opponents [D. E. Pilarczyk's views on the U.S. bishops' economics pastoral] *America* 156:434 My 30 '87

Papa do preach [state of Hispanic Catholicism] A. Sullivan. *New Repub* 197:13-14+ O 5 '87

Rethinking hunger in America: adapting the Sullivan principles. N. Amidei. il *Christ Century* 104:51-4 Ja 21 '87

Seminary, ministry and social responsibility. J. F. Fishburn. *Christ Century* 104:100-2 F 4-11 '87

Should the poor earn their keep? [Christian values and welfare policy] S. V. Monsma. il por *Christ Today* 31:28-31 Je 12 '87

Strong medicine. *America* 156:166-7 F 28 '87

Two kinds of thanks [evening at a shelter for homeless women] E. Bence. il por *Christ Today* 31:34 Ja 16 '87

The unholy ghost of Christmas yet to come. R. E. Burns. *U S Cathol* 52:2 D '87

What does the rabbi see? H. Fehren. *U S Cathol* 52:38-40 Ag '87

When I was homeless, you sat in your La-Z-Boy. R. E. Burns. *U S Cathol* 52:2 Ap '87

Brazil

The great Brazilian land grab. A. Powers. *Commonweal* 114:288-90 My 8 '87

Land and violence in Brazil. A. Powers. *America* 156:324-6 Ap 18 '87

Letter from the Elysian Fields [work of Catholic priest D. R. Santos in poor town of Campos Elísios] J. Kramer. *New Yorker* 63:40-2+ Mr 2 '87

Ecuador

Sowing justice in Ecuador [liberation theology practitioners L. Proaño and J. Gómez Izquierdo] P. R. Greene. *Christ Century* 104:910-12 O 21 '87

El Salvador

Accompaniment: an invitation. R. A. Howard. *America* 157:455-7 D 12 '87

El Salvador: the new face of war. P. Shiras. il *Commonweal* 114:275-8 My 8 '87

The long trip home [A. Nenzel's work with refugees] G. Palumbo. *Commonweal* 114:377 Je 19 '87

Ruben Zamora: politics & belief [interview] G. Palumbo. il *Commonweal* 114:733-5 D 18 '87

Haiti

The priest who fights the regime [J.-B. Aristide; cover story] A. Wilentz. *Nation* 245:217+ S 12 '87

Uprooting Duvalierism [Catholic Church] J. P. Hogan. *Commonweal* 114:518-19 S 25 '87

India

Mother Teresa's work of grace. C. Tower. il pors *Read Dig* 131:163-75+ D '87

The poor break through. J. McGowan. il *Commonweal* 114:383-6 Je 19 '87

Church and social problems—*cont.*

Latin America

Looking north at a world of self [watching W. Allen's movies in Latin America] M. Gallagher. *America* 157:82-3 Ag 15-22 '87

Quelling the fire of 'liberation theology'. R. A. Manning. il *U S News World Rep* 102:48-9 Mr 30 '87

Bibliography

Books on the Americas. B. Ramsey. *America* 157:168+ S 26 '87

Nicaragua

Death and resurrection in Matiguás [death of Franciscan brother T. Zavaleta] E. Rivera. *America* 157:261-2 O 24 '87

Ministry amid adversity. R. Lee. il *Christ Today* 31:32-4 F 6 '87

Pakistan

Sister Gertrude and the children of Karachi. L. Weber. il *Christ Century* 104:887-9 O 14 '87

Peru

Indigenous moral problems in Peru. C. Gudorf. *America* 157:270-3 O 24 '87

José Carlos Mariátegui: forgotten forerunner of liberation theology. M. Candelaria. *Christ Century* 104:885-7 O 14 '87

José María Arguedas: godfather of liberationism. S. B. Wall-Smith. *Christ Century* 104:1034-9 N 18 '87

Philippines

The slum behind the Sheraton. J. DeParle. il *Wash Mon* 19:32-44 D '87

Sri Lanka

The roots of conflict in Sri Lanka. V. Rebeck. *Christ Century* 104:792-4 S 23 '87

United States

See Church and social problems

Western Europe

See also

Sanctuary movement (Refugee aid)—Western Europe

Zambia

The Zambian debt dilemma: a just repayment plan. J. B. Straus, Jr. *Christ Century* 104:855-6 O 7 '87

Zimbabwe

Zimbabwe's 'situation' and prayers for unity. E. Jorstad. *Christ Century* 104:710-11 Ag 26-S 2 '87

Church and state

See also

Public schools and religion

Religion and law

Religion and politics

Religious liberty

Taxation, Exemption from

World Conference on Church, Community, and State (1937)

The bicentennial and church-related schools. T. A. Rayer. *America* 157:427-9+ D 5 '87

Can Christians hand out gospel tracts in airports? [Supreme Court case involving Jews for Jesus at Los Angeles International Airport] B. Spring. il *Christ Today* 31:43-4 Ap 3 '87

Charges of break-ins and infiltration [FBI investigation of the sanctuary movement] J.-M. Andriote. il *Christ Today* 31:44-5 Ap 17 '87

Church and state. E. Doerr. See issues of The Humanist

Church and state: the ramparts besieged. R. L. Maddox. il *Christ Century* 104:191-2 F 25 '87

Church, state and foster-care children [New York State] H. J. Byrne. *America* 157:38-41 Jl 18-25 '87

Churches band together to help register undocumented aliens. R. Frame. il *Christ Today* 31:34-5 Jl 10 '87

Clergy malpractice [suit over suicide of K. Nally] *Christ Century* 104:850 O 7 '87

The Constitution and the congregation: time to celebrate. M. E. Marty. il *Christ Century* 104:523-5 Je 3-10 '87

The Constitution at 200 [cover story; special section] il *Christ Today* 31:18-30 Jl 10 '87

God vs. Caesar? G. G. Seibert. *America* 157:231 O 10 '87

A Guatemalan family's flight to sanctuary in the U.S. P. M. Jones. il *Sch Update* 119:18 Mr 9 '87

Imposing standards [recent cases questioning right of religious institutions to require doctrinal orthodoxy of employees] D. Neff. *Christ Today* 31:17 Jl 10 '87

Jews for Jesus ministers settle out of court [suit against UCLA for prohibiting distribution of religious literature on campus] B. Bird. il *Christ Today* 31:46 Mr 6 '87

Kinds of Catholics. R. J. Neuhaus. *Natl Rev* 39:42 Jl 3 '87

The legacy of two leaders [G. Washington and J. Carroll] J. T. Ellis. *America* 157:149-50 S 26 '87

A look at Robert Bork and rulings affecting the church. K. A. Lawton. il por *Christ Today* 31:42-3 Ag 7 '87

Religion cases declined [Supreme Court cases] *Christ Century* 104:961 N 4 '87

Religious groups denied federal funds to prevent teen pregnancy. P. P. Wong. *Christ Today* 31:41-2 Jl 10 '87

Sanctuary: should parishes break the law for a stranger? R. McClory. il *U S Cathol* 52:32-8 My '87

Secular and religious America. E. C. Ladd. *Society* 24:63-8 Mr/Ap '87

Should a Mormon-owned corporation be able to fire a Mormon who does not tithe? [Supreme Court considers discrimination case of F. Mayson] R. F. Drinan. il *America* 156:375-6 My 9 '87

Should a priest serve on a jury? V. A. Lapomarda. il *America* 156:495-6 Je 20-27 '87

Sister Darlene Nicgorski [sanctuary movement worker] R. Brown. il por *Ms* 15:54+ Ja '87

Suit challenges Christian employment service practices [discrimination suit against Intercristo] R. Frame. *Christ Today* 31:48 Ap 3 '87

Supreme Court hears challenge to church hiring policies [discrimination case filed by F. Mayson against the Mormon church] E. J. Larson. *Christ Today* 31:49-50 My 15 '87

Threatening the wall: church-state separation has powerful new critics. R. N. Ostling. il *Time* 130:70-1 Jl 6 '87

U.S. judge rules prayer before a game is illegal [high school football] *Jet* 71:6 Mr 2 '87

Vanity of vanities [allowing GOD on license plates in Maryland] H. H. Morris. *Christ Century* 104:932 O 28 '87

The wall that never was [First Amendment] T. C. Muck. il *Christ Today* 31:16-17 Jl 10 '87

Bolivia

See also

Catholic Church—Bolivia

Canada

See also

Christian Heritage Party (Canada)

An unholy prayer fight [Prayer Canada's meetings in British Columbia legislature provoke protests] il *Macleans* 100:12 Ap 13 '87

China

See also

Christians—China

Cuba

See also

Catholic Church—Cuba

An American Christian's view of Castro's Cuba [J. Ballard] R. Frame. il pors *Christ Today* 31:49+ N 6 '87

Thoughts on the Church and Cuba. H. G. Cox. il *Nation* 244:595+ My 9 '87

Czechoslovakia

See also

Catholic Church—Czechoslovakia

Guatemala

See also

Catholic Church—Guatemala

Haiti

What's ahead for the church in Haiti? [interview with C. Noel] il por *Christ Today* 31:60-1 N 20 '87

Korea (South)

Korean Christians hold out hope for democracy. S. Rabey and L. Cryderman. il *Christ Today* 31:48 Ag 7 '87

Politics test Korean church. H. Smith. *Christ Today* 31:15 My 15 '87

Lithuania

See also

Catholic Church—Lithuania

Nicaragua

See also

Catholic Church—Nicaragua

Evangelical leader named to national peace commission [G. Parajon] S. Wykstra. il por *Christ Today* 31:52 O 2 '87

Religion and the Nicaraguan constitution. J. E. Mulligan. il *Christ Century* 104:398-9 Ap 29 '87

Philippines

See also

Catholic Church—Philippines

Are church groups backing opponents of Corazon Aquino? K. A. Lawton. *Christ Today* 31:46-7 Ja 16 '87

Poland

See also

Catholic Church—Poland

Church and state—*cont.*

Romania

Romania could lose its trade status because of rights abuses. *Christ Today* 31:37 Jl 10 '87

Soviet Union

See also

Christians—Soviet Union

Orthodox Eastern Church, Russian

Still waiting for the millennium. J. A. Broun. *Commonweal* 114:592-5 O 23 '87

United States

See Church and state

Western Europe

Europe's sanctuary movement: grappling with governments. M. McConnell. il *Christ Century* 104:1001-3 N 11 '87

Yugoslavia

See also

Catholic Church—Yugoslavia

Church and the poor *See* Church and social problems

Church and the press

See also

Catholic Church. Pontifical Commission for Social Communication

Minority report [conflicting views of G. F. Will and W. F. Buckley regarding J. J. O'Connor's visit to Israel] C. Hitchens. *Nation* 244:170 F 14 '87

Pearlygate satires are weak on substance [press coverage of J. Bakker scandal] L. I. Sweet. *Christ Century* 104:644-5 Jl 29-Ag 5 '87

Preacher-bashing and the public life [J. Bakker scandal and media overkill] J. M. Wall. *Christ Century* 104:347-8 Ap 15 '87

Secular journalism: a ripe opportunity for Christians [interview with D. Aikman] il por *Christ Today* 31:58 Mr 6 '87

The value of preacher-bashing [discussion of April 15, 1987 article, Preacher-bashing and the public life] J. M. Wall. *Christ Century* 104:532-4 Je 3-10 '87

Church and the world

See also

Stewardship, Christian

World Council of Churches

Church/world watch. J. B. Hehir. See occasional issues of *Commonweal*

Counsels for the baptized. H. Brown. *Commonweal* 114:558-61 O 9 '87

The new Dark Ages. R. Clapp. *Christ Today* 31:15 S 18 '87

Church architecture *See* Churches (Buildings)

Church art *See* Christian art and symbolism

Church attendance

Blacks more frequent churchgoers than whites. *Jet* 71:36 Ja 26 '87

Bull market for religion. R. Clapp. *Christ Today* 31:15 Ap 3 '87

Let's take the must out of Sunday Mass [with readers' comments] T. Unsworth. *U S Cathol* 52:14-20 Ja '87

The secular society: a myth? [study by Michael Hout and Andrew M. Greeley] V. Bozzi. *Psychol Today* 21:20 D '87

Church bonds *See* Church securities

Church camps

Sweden

Formation and transformation at Camp Ahus [confirmation camp] B. Webb-Mitchell. *Christ Century* 104:531-2 Je 3-10 '87

Church colleges and universities

See also

Catholic colleges and universities

Mercer University

Pillsbury Baptist Bible College

Southern Methodist University

The class of 2000. il *Christ Today* 31:64+ N 6 '87

Race relations

Minn. Bible College jock says he was expelled for dating white girl there [case of C. Addison of Pillsbury Baptist Bible College] il por *Jet* 72:14 My 11 '87

Probe interracial dating policy at Bible College [Pillsbury Baptist Bible College] *Jet* 71:21 F 23 '87

Church conferences *See* Religious conferences

Church decoration and ornament

See also

Altarpieces

Glass painting and staining

The art of persuasion [Central European baroque] Ç. Norberg-Schulz. il *Courier* 40:42-5 S '87

Big fish, big pond [J. Borofsky's sculpture Fish with ruby eye hanging in Cathedral of St. John the Divine] S. Staggs. il *Art News* 86:17-18 My '87

Splendid sanctuary [baroque decoration in Atotonilco, Mexico church built by L. F. N. de Alfaro] J. Richardson. il *House Gard* 159:104-7+ D '87

The triumph of O Aleijadinho [Brazilian baroque] A. C. D. S. Telles. il *Courier* 40:39-41 S '87

Church discipline

See also

Catholic Church—Discipline

Church employees

See also

Mormons and Mormonism—Employees

United Methodist Church—Employees

Dear Betty Harragan [sexual harassment by religious employers] B. L. Harragan. il *Work Woman* 12:30+ Jl '87

Imposing standards [recent cases questioning right of religious institutions to require doctrinal orthodoxy of employees] D. Neff. *Christ Today* 31:17 Jl 10 '87

Suit challenges Christian employment service practices [discrimination suit against Intercristo] R. Frame. *Christ Today* 31:48 Ap 3 '87

Church finance

See also

Catholic Church—Finance

Evangel Temple (Washington, D.C.)—Finance

Evangelical Council for Financial Accountability

Evangelistic work—Finance

National Religious Broadcasters. Ethics and Financial Integrity Commission

Taxation, Exemption from

Black Monday aftershocks [effect of crash on church investments] *Christ Century* 104:992 N 11 '87

Church government

See also

Catholic Church—Government

Congregationalism

Elders (Church officers)

Church growth

America's Pentecostals: see how they grow. C. P. Wagner. il *Christ Today* 31:28-9 O 16 '87

Church history

See also

Bible

Heresy

Middle Ages

See also

Crusades

Reformation

Primitive and early church

Constantine's pagan triumph [R. Lane Fox's Pagans and Christians] P. Pettingell. *New Leader* 70:15-16 Ap 6 '87

Pagans, Christians, Jews. C. Raphael. *Commentary* 84:39-44 O '87

Church leadership *See* Christian leadership

Church membership

See also

Alienated Catholics Anonymous

Church membership. *Christ Century* 104:713 Ag 26-S 2 '87

Religion's social ladders [decline of liberal Protestant churches] R. J. Neuhaus. *Natl Rev* 39:52 O 23 '87

Why Catholics stay in the Church [cover story] A. M. Greeley. il *America* 157:54-7+ Ag 1-8 '87

Church music *See* Religious music

Church of Christ, Scientist

The graying of a church. K. L. Woodward. il *Newsweek* 110:60 Ag 3 '87

"We thought our faith could save our son" [death of M. Swan from meningitis after Christian Scientist parents withhold medical treatment] K. Delaney. il pors *Redbook* 168:104-6 Ja '87

Church of England

See also

Catholic Church—Relations—Church of England

Anglicans compromise on gay clergy. T. Beeson. *Christ Century* 104:1080-1 D 2 '87

Anglicans in turmoil [G. V. Bennett's suicide after attacks on R. Runcie] K. L. Woodward. il pors *Newsweek* 110:57 D 21 '87

Anglicans move toward women's ordination. K. Slack. il *Christ Century* 104:374-5 Ap 22 '87

Choosing new Anglican bishops [Birmingham, England] K. Slack. *Christ Century* 104:460-1 My 13 '87

Death and the archbishop [G. Bennett commits suicide following publication of his critical essay on R. Runcie] R. N. Ostling. il pors *Time* 130:60 D 21 '87

Hour of decision for women priests. M. P. Harris. il *Time* 129:43 Mr 2 '87

Church of England—*cont.*
Keeping the Church for 'Young Fogies' [reprint from November 5, 1986 issue] K. Slack. *Christ Century* 104:933-4 O 28 '87
Oxford election draws clergy interest [chancellorship] K. Slack. *Christ Century* 104:303 Ap 1 '87
Sailing to the edge of the world [role of women] S. Fletcher. il *Hist Today* 37:10-11 S '87

Church of Jesus Christ of Latter-Day Saints *See* Mormons and Mormonism

Church of Scientology *See* Scientology

Church of South India
Tensions beset Church of South India. M. L. Stackhouse. *Christ Century* 104:743-4 S 9-16 '87

Church parishes *See* Parishes

Church related colleges *See* Church colleges and universities

Church related schools *See* Church schools

Church renewal

Catholic Church
Does the RENEW program renew? J. R. Kelly. *America* 156:197-9 Mr 7 '87

Church schools
See also
Accelerated Christian Education
Catholic schools
Sunday schools
The fourth "R" [Christian schools; cover story] P. F. Parsons. il por *Christ Today* 31:21-7 S 4 '87

Federal aid
The bicentennial and church-related schools. T. A. Rayer. *America* 157:427-9+ D 5 '87
Parochiaid challenged again. E. Doerr. *Humanist* 47:43-4 Jl/Ag '87
Should government help kids attend private schools? J. H. DeDakis. il *Christ Today* 31:52-3 My 15 '87

Church securities
Fear and salvation [church bond underwriter W. May] R. Koselka. por *Forbes* 139:38-9 Je 1 '87

Church services
See also
Worship

Church union
See also
Ecumenical movement
World Council of Churches
Evangelical denomination gains official acceptance into the Orthodox Church [Evangelical Orthodox Church will join the Antiochian Orthodox Church] B. Nassif. il *Christ Today* 31:40 F 6 '87
Merging Lutherans: a dying and a birth [Evangelical Lutheran Church in America] J. C. Lyles. *Christ Century* 104:461-3 My 13 '87
A mightier fortress [formation of Evangelical Lutheran Church in America] il *Time* 129:60 My 11 '87
The new Lutheran Church: the gift of Augustana [Evangelical Lutheran Church in America; cover story] R. E. Koenig. il *Christ Century* 104:555-8 Je 17-24 '87
Pentecostals and NCC begin dialogue. K. Houghland. *Christ Century* 104:87-9 Ja 28 '87
Three Lutheran denominations become one [Evangelical Lutheran Church in America] il *Christ Today* 31:55-6 Je 12 '87

United States
See Church union

Church Universal and Triumphant
Cult builds complex at Yellowstone borders. *Natl Parks* 61:36-7 My/Je '87

Church work
See also
Christian leadership
Church and social problems
Evangelistic work
Missions
Pastoral counseling
Melting accomplishments. G. K. Brushaber. il *Christ Today* 31:13 Mr 20 '87

Church work with AIDS patients
High-risk ministry. A. Tapia. il por *Christ Today* 31:15-19 Ag 7 '87
Houston facility wages a war against AIDS [work of D. G. Moreschi at the Institute for Immunological Disorders] E. Fudge. *Christ Today* 31:52+ Mr 6 '87
Pastoral care for persons with AIDS and for their families. R. L. Schaper. il *Christ Century* 104:691-4 Ag 12-19 '87
A priest's painful choice. C. R. Burns. por *Newsweek* 109:6 F 2 '87
Why some God-fearing folks are so frightening [Catholic judgmental behavior] R. E. Burns. *U S Cathol* 52:2 Jl '87

Church work with children
See also
Church camps
Church, state and foster-care children [New York State] H. J. Byrne. *America* 157:38-41 Jl 18-25 '87

Church work with divorcees
Does the Church have good news for divorced Catholics? [cover story; interview with J. V. Flosi] il por *U S Cathol* 52:6-13 My '87

Church work with families
Beaver Cleaver is divorced: the growing pains of American Catholic families. J. Breig. il *U S Cathol* 52:48-53 Je '87
Home-grown kids need a full-time mom. W. Metts, Jr. il por *Christ Today* 31:12 Mr 6 '87
Reinforcing the fragile family. P. Uhlenberg. il por *Christ Today* 31:31-3 Ja 16 '87

Church work with farmers
What role does the church play in agriculture? P. Smith. il *Success Farm* 85:19 Ap '87

Church work with homosexuals
See also
Dignity (Organization)
Homosexuals Anonymous Fellowship Services
Open letters to Archbishop John R. Quinn [discussion of February 7, 1987 article, On the pastoral care of homosexual persons] J. R. Quinn. *America* 156:238-44 Mr 21 '87
Toward an understanding of the letter On the pastoral care of homosexual persons [Catholic Church] J. R. Quinn. *America* 156:92-5+ F 7 '87
Why some God-fearing folks are so frightening [Catholic judgmental behavior] R. E. Burns. *U S Cathol* 52:2 Jl '87

Church work with leprosy patients
A mission of service to leprosy sufferers [R. Lamburn's work in Tanzania] F. Nowikowski. *Christ Century* 104:782-3 S 23 '87

Church work with prisoners
And you visited me. H. Fehren. *U S Cathol* 52:41-3 O '87
The angel of death row [work of Rev. M. Davis in Jackson, Ga.] R. Chepesiuk. por *Progressive* 51:14 My '87
The celebrity illusion. C. W. Colson. il *Christ Today* 31:72 D 11 '87

Church work with single mothers
Upstairs, downstairs in a house of peace [Resurrection Life, home for unwed mothers in Aurora, Ill.] R. Clapp. il *Christ Today* 31:16-17 Ja 16 '87

Church work with single people
See also
Church work with divorcees
Appropriate vulnerability: a sexual ethic for singles. K. Lebacqz. il *Christ Century* 104:435-8 My 6 '87
Onward Christian singles [questionnaire distributed by the Christian Dating Club] *Harpers* 274:22 Mr '87
Sexuality and vulnerability [discussion of May 6, 1987 article, Appropriate vulnerability: a sexual ethic for singles] K. Lebacqz. *Christ Century* 104:596-8 Jl 1-8 '87

Church work with the aged
The graying of the church [cover story] T. Stafford. il *Christ Today* 31:17-22 N 6 '87

Church work with the bereaved
Can faith survive a suicide in the family? J. Davidson. il *U S Cathol* 52:16-21 N '87
A pastoral and theological response to losses in pregnancy. J. S. Peterman. *Christ Century* 104:750-3 S 9-16 '87

Church work with the handicapped
Formation and transformation at Camp Ahus [Swedish confirmation camp] B. Webb-Mitchell. *Christ Century* 104:531-2 Je 3-10 '87
Respite care: help goes both ways [church programs] J. B. Gehret. *Christ Century* 104:76-7 Ja 28 '87

Church work with the mentally handicapped
See also
Rainbow Acres (Organization)

Church work with youth
See also
National Teen Challenge (Organization)
Project 714 (Organization)
Youth for Christ (Organization)

Church World Service *See* National Council of Churches. Church World Service

Churches (Buildings)
See also
Monasteries

Conservation and restoration
Adobes of God [New Mexico] S. Zwinger. il map *Americana* 15:65-9 N/D '87

Churches (Buildings) — Conservation and restoration — cont.

Requiem and jubilate [restoration of St. Luke in the Fields, New York City] D. Brenner. il *Archit Rec* 175:130-7 Je '87

Saviors of an island church [St. Mary's Roman Catholic Church in Indian River, P.E.I.] B. MacAndrew. il *Macleans* 100:43 N 2 '87

Maintenance and repair

On the stewardship of property. S. A. Portaro. *Christ Century* 104:846-7 O 7 '87

Photographs and photography

Heavenly photos. M. Grimm and T. Grimm. il *Travel Holiday* 168:19-20 N '87

Brazil

The triumph of O Aleijadinho [Brazilian baroque] A. C. D. S. Telles. il *Courier* 40:39-41 S '87

Central Europe

The art of persuasion [Central European baroque] C. Norberg-Schulz. il *Courier* 40:42-5 S '87

Three great domes. G. C. Argan. il *Courier* 40:10 S '87

Florida

See also

Saint Augustine (Fla.)—Churches (Buildings)

Great Britain

See also

Etchingham (England)—Churches (Buildings)

Illinois

See also

Chicago (Ill.)—Churches (Buildings)

Mexico

See also

Atotonilco (Mexico)—Churches (Buildings)

Netherlands

See also

Amsterdam (Netherlands)—Churches (Buildings)

New Mexico

Adobes of God [churches] S. Zwinger. il map *Americana* 15:65-9 N/D '87

Ohio

See also

Cleveland (Ohio)—Churches (Buildings)

Prince Edward Island

See also

Indian River (P.E.I.)—Churches (Buildings)

Washington (D.C.)

See Washington (D.C.)—Churches (Buildings)

Churches (Buildings) in art

The pleasure of the image [Dutch paintings of church interiors] S. Sontag. il *Art Am* 75:122-31 N '87

Churchill, Caryl

about

Serious money [drama] Reviews

New Yorker 63:119-20 D 14 '87. M. Kramer

Vogue 177:134 N '87. R. Koenig

Churchill, Joan

about

Lily Tomlin: the film behind the show [film] Reviews *New Repub* 196:24-5 Mr 23 '87. S. Kauffmann

Churchill, Naomi

about

Black appointed to USDA office; fourth director. *Jet* 72:22 Je 15 '87

Churchill, Robert, and Jones, Kimberly

Kennecott's boom and bust. il *Focus* 37:1-5 Fall '87

Churchill, Sir Winston, 1874-1965

about

The century's best investor? P. Fuhrman. il por *Forbes* 139 Ann Directory:58 Ap 27 '87

Churchill at war. E. A. Cohen. *Commentary* 83:40-9 My '87

Churchill envy. A. Sullivan. il *New Repub* 197:14-16 D 7 '87

Churchill's anthrax bombs: a debate [discussion of January/February 1987 article, Churchill's secret biological weapons] B. J. Bernstein. *Bull At Sci* 43:42-5 N '87

Churchill's secret biological weapons. B. J. Bernstein. bibl f *Bull At Sci* 43:46-50 Ja/F '87

A day in the life of Winston Churchill [condensed from The last lion] W. Manchester. il pors *Read Dig* 131:156-62 O '87

In the Churchill museum. T. Garton Ash. bibl f il *N Y Rev Books* 34:22-7 My 7 '87

The lion caged [with editorial comment by Byron Dobell] W. Manchester. il pors *Am Herit* 38:6-7, 65-88 F/Mr '87

Churchill (Man.)

Camping out in polar bear country. D. Matthews. il map *50 Plus* 27:44-8+ F '87

Church's Fried Chicken, Inc.

Blacks buy Ohio chain. P. A. Jones. il *Black Enterp* 17:20 F '87

Flying high with Church's Chicken [black franchisers E. Horton and A. Whitmore] il pors *Ebony* 42:72+ Jl '87

Chute, David

A zoo for films. il *Film Comment* 23:71-3 N/D '87

Chutneys *See* Pickles and relishes

CIA *See* United States. Central Intelligence Agency

Ciani, Judithe

about

Elegant strides in the paper chase. F. Greenberg. il por *Work Woman* 12:60-1 F '87

Ciarcia, Steve

Ask Byte. See issues of Byte

Ciarcia's circuit cellar. See issues of Byte

Ciardi, John, 1916-1986

about

Of many things. G. W. Hunt. *America* 156:inside cover Ap 4 '87

Ciba-Geigy AG

A promise comes of age [Ciba-Geigy takes over Spectra-Physics] R. Addis. il *Forbes* 140:8 Ag 24 '87

Cicadas

The cicadas are coming [17-year locusts] P. H. Johnson. *Rodale's Org Gard* 34:9 Je '87

The cicadas are coming, the cicadas are coming [seventeen-year cicada] map *Nat Hist* 96:4 My '87

Jiminy Cricket sings again [terminology] W. Safire. il *N Y Times Mag* p10+ My 31 '87

Tick, buzz, it's that time again [17-year cicada] D. Brand. il *Time* 129:61 My 25 '87

Cicciolina

about

The body politic. M. Lilla. *New Repub* 197:14-16 S 28 '87

In a naked play for power, porn queen Cicciolina wins a seat in Italy's Parliament. W. Plummer. il pors *People Wkly* 28:34-5 Jl 6 '87

Letter from Rome. A. Lee. *New Yorker* 63:133-6+ N 9 '87

Ciccolini, Aldo

about

Ciccolini's basic Satie on compact disc. R. Freed. por *Stereo Rev* 52:101-2 Je '87

Cicely, Sweet *See* Sweet cicely

Cicerone, Ralph J.

Changes in stratospheric ozone. bibl f il *Science* 237:35-42 Jl 3 '87

Cichan, Cecilia

about

Miracle girl. il por *Time* 130:15 Ag 31 '87

Cid, ca. 1043-1099

about

The Cid of history and the history of The Cid. P. Linehan. bibl il *Hist Today* 37:26-32 S '87

Cid Campeador *See* Cid, ca. 1043-1099

Cider

See also

Cooking—Cider

Cigar industry

See also

Culbro Corp.

Cigar store Indians

Collectors and collecting

The cigar-store Indian. M. T. Baker. il *Antiques Collect Hobbies* 92:52-4+ Je '87

Cigarette industry

See also

American Brands, Inc.

Liggett & Myers Tobacco Company

Philip Morris, Inc.

R. J. Reynolds Tobacco Co.

Beverages and tobacco. H. Seneker. il *Forbes* 139:78+ Ja 12 '87

Don't bet against cigarette makers. D. Seligman. il *Fortune* 116:70-2+ Ag 17 '87

Puffing up a second wind. D. P. Wiener. il *U S News World Rep* 103:80-1 S 28 '87

Advertising

Advertising pleads the First. M. L. Wulf. *Commonweal* 114:75-9 F 13 '87

Ban cigarette advertising? il *Consum Rep* 52:565-9 S '87

Cigarette ads and the press [symposium] il *Nation* 244:283-8 Mr 7 '87

Cigarettes anyone? Tennis and smoking [Virginia Slims tournaments sponsored by Philip Morris] R. Doar. *Wash Mon* 19:40 Je '87

Cigarette industry—Advertising—*cont.*
Exchange [discussion of March 7, 1987 article, Cigarette ads and the press] *Nation* 244:526+ Ap 25 '87
Hazards of tobacco advertising [report by William L. Weis and Chauncey Burke] *Society* 24:2 S/O '87
Here's one tough cowboy [Marlboro Man] J. A. Trachtenberg. il *Forbes* 139:108-10 F 9 '87
Taking the tobacco war too far [Canadian plan to ban cigarette advertising] D. Francis. il *Macleans* 100:11 N 30 '87

Anecdotes, facetiae, satire, etc.
Exit laughing [making cigarette TV commercials at a salmon fishing camp] E. Zern. il *Field Stream* 92:142 Jl '87

Employees
See Tobacco workers
Export-import trade
Tainted tobacco could poison a hot market [RJR Nabisco exports cigarettes tainted by weed killer to Japan] N. Gross and S. Ticer. il *Bus Week* p45+ Je 15 '87
Where cigarettes and spirits are still booming [Japan] L. Armstrong. il *Bus Week* p94 S 14 '87
Press relations
Cigarette ads and the press [symposium] il *Nation* 244:283-8 Mr 7 '87
Exchange [discussion of March 7, 1987 article, Cigarette ads and the press] *Nation* 244:526+ Ap 25 '87
Canada
A long, hard fight back. B. Wallace. il *Macleans* 100:28-9 Je 22 '87
Cigarette smoking *See* Smoking
Cigarettes
See also
Smokeless cigarettes
Advertising
See Cigarette industry—Advertising
Contamination
Tainted tobacco could poison a hot market [RJR Nabisco exports cigarettes tainted by weed killer to Japan] N. Gross and S. Ticer. il *Bus Week* p45+ Je 15 '87
Labeling
Caveat fumator [rulings in favor of Liggett & Myers and American Brands in product liability cases] J. Castro. il *Time* 130:43 S 7 '87
A judicial smoke alert [pro-industry rulings in Liggett & Myers Tobacco Co. cases] il *U S News World Rep* 103:12 S 7 '87
Tobacco wins one in court [ruling that warning labels on cigarettes shielded Liggett & Myers from liability claim] D. Pauly. il *Newsweek* 110:44 S 7 '87
Taxation
Bob Dole and the tobacco connection. D. Corn. il *Nation* 244:381+ Mr 28 '87
Ciguatoxin *See* Toxins and antitoxins
Cikovsky, Nicolai
William Merritt Chase at Shinnecock Hills [cover story] bibl f il *Antiques* 132:290-303 Ag '87
Cimbala, Stephen J.
Doctrine and deterrence. *Society* 24:61-6 Jl/Ag '87
Cimino, Michael
about
The Sicilian [film] Reviews
People Wkly 28:14 N 16 '87. R. Novak
Cincinnati (Ohio)
Anniversaries, etc.
Commemorating an anniversary that never was [1936 Stephen Foster Cincinnati commemorative half-dollar] E. Rochette. il *Antiques Collect Hobbies* 92:74-5 Mr '87
Education
See also
Cincinnati Academy of Physical Education
The last day of school is usually a zoo, but for 11 Ohio kids it was meant to be [Cincinnati's Zoo School] il *People Wkly* 27:60 Je 15 '87
Hospitals
Lethal doses [orderly D. Harvey accused of 34 murders] por *Time* 130:17 Ag 24 '87
Cincinnati Academy of Physical Education
The CAPE of good hopes. C. Neff. il *Sports Illus* 67:84+ O 26 '87
Cincinnati Zoological Garden
The last day of school is usually a zoo, but for 11 Ohio kids it was meant to be [Cincinnati's Zoo School] il *People Wkly* 27:60 Je 15 '87
Move over, Felix and Oscar, move way over—these two are a really heavy-duty odd couple [elephant and hippo living together] il *People Wkly* 28:116 D 21 '87

Cinco de Mayo (New York, N.Y.: Restaurant) *See* New York (N.Y.)—Restaurants, nightclubs, bars, etc.
Cinderella
Anecdotes, facetiae, satire, etc.
I am Cinderella's stepmother and I know my rights. J. Rossner. il *N Y Times Book Rev* 92:3 Ap 19 '87
Cinderella [ballet] *See* Ballet reviews—Single works
Cinderella [film] *See* Motion picture reviews—Single works
Cinecom Entertainment Group
The Amir Malin story. D. Machan. il pors *Forbes* 140:178+ O 19 '87
Cinema *See* Motion pictures
Cinema 'N' Drafthouse International Inc.
Hold the popcorn; pass the chablis. D. Marth. il pors *Nations Bus* 75:60 Jl '87
Cinematographers
See also
Hall, Conrad, 1927-
Cinematography *See* Motion picture photography
Cineplex Corp.
See also
Cineplex Odeon Corporation
Cineplex Odeon Corporation
King of the silver screen [G. Drabinsky; cover story; special section; with editorial comment by Kevin Doyle] il pors *Macleans* 100:2, 38-42+ S 28 '87
CIO *See* AFL-CIO
Cipher, Babe
Square root, root, root for the home team. il *Discover* 8:87-8+ O '87
Ciphers *See* Cryptography
Cipriani, Harry
about
In a gastronomic grudge match, a seasoned contender from Italy taunts the Times's top taster. A. Richman. il por *People Wkly* 28:67-8 D 7 '87
The trouble with Harry's: behind the coup at Cipriani. J. Taylor. il por *N Y* 20:62-7 O 19 '87
Cipriani (Venice, Italy: Hotel) *See* Venice (Italy)—Hotels, motels, etc.
Ciprofloxacin
Drug side effects or java jitters? D. D. Edwards. *Sci News* 132:255 O 17 '87
Circadian rhythms *See* Biological rhythms
Circassians
Israel
A scandal in the ranks [I. Napsu's claims against Shin Bet arouses Circassian community] E. Silver. *Macleans* 100:28+ My 4 '87
Circle Theatre (Indianapolis, Ind.)
A full Circle. B. Golightly. il *Horizon* 30:23 Je '87
Circuit breakers, Electric *See* Electric circuit breakers
Circuits, Integrated *See* Integrated circuits
Circular saws *See* Saws and sawing
Circulation, Ocean *See* Ocean circulation
Circulatory system *See* Cardiovascular system
Circumcision
Calculating the odds [uncircumcised men more likely to be infected after exposure to AIDS] *Time* 130:40 O 19 '87
Circumcision: the medical perspective. K. Donnan. *McCalls* 114:149-50 S '87
Circumcision: why no pain relief? *Redbook* 169:185 O '87
Doubts about circumcision. T. Monmaney. il *Newsweek* 109:74+ Mr 30 '87
Like father, like son. B. Livermore. il *Health* 19:15 D '87
Circumnavigation *See* Voyages around the world
Circus
See also
Ringling Bros.-Barnum & Bailey Combined Shows, Inc.
Circus, Miniature
Little big top [work of A. Kveck] J. Colihan. il *Am Herit* 38:42-7 D '87
Circus models *See* Circus, Miniature
Circus performers
See also
Acrobats and acrobatism
Clowns
Cirker, Hayward
about
How to succeed in publishing with nary a best-seller. D. Cohen. il pors *Smithsonian* 18:83-6+ Jl '87
Le Cirque (New York, N.Y.: Restaurant) *See* New York (N.Y.)—Restaurants, nightclubs, bars, etc.
Cisneros, Henry
San Antonio: laying the foundation for the future. il *USA Today (Periodical)* 116:24-33 Jl '87

Cisneros, Henry—*cont.*
about
San Antonio: putting family first. D. Pedersen. il por *Newsweek* 110:8 S 14 '87
Cisó, Lake (Spain) *See* Lake Cisó (Spain)
CISPES *See* U.S. Committee in Solidarity with the People of El Salvador
Citadel (Military academy)
S.C. panel tells Citadel to stop playing 'Dixie!'. *Jet* 71:33 Mr 23 '87
Citadelle (Haiti) *See* Fortification—Haiti
Citation airplanes *See* Airplanes, Business
La Cité des Sciences et de l'Industrie (Paris, France)
France has unveiled its spectacular science showcase. P. L. Buckley. il *Smithsonian* 18:148-52+ O '87
Citibank N.A.
Citibank wows the consumer. R. E. Norton. il *Fortune* 115:48-50+ Je 8 '87
CITIC *See* China International Trust and Investment Corporation
Citicorp
Bank stockholders should applaud [write-off of third world debt] M. S. Forbes, Jr. il *Forbes* 139:25 Je 15 '87
Bank to the future [former chairman G. S. Moore] E. A. Finn, Jr. il por *Forbes* 140:450+ Jl 13 '87
The Citi squeezes its lemons [move to clean up third world debt with debt for equity swaps] S. Bartlett. il *Bus Week* p31 Je 15 '87
Citibank wows the consumer. R. E. Norton. il *Fortune* 115:48-50+ Je 8 '87
Citicorp breaks ranks [write-off of third world loans] S. Koepp. il *Time* 129:48-50 Je 1 '87
Citicorp faces reality—and finds it doesn't hurt [third world debt] D. Pauly. il *Newsweek* 109:42+ Je 1 '87
Citicorp pulls out [South Africa] A. Edmond, Jr. *Black Enterp* 18:22 S '87
Good-bye Peru, hello Peoria [Citicorp buys sick S&Ls] J. Heins. il *Forbes* 140:34-5 D 28 '87
How to take a $1 billion loss and look good [write-off of third world loans] P. M. Scherschel. il *U S News World Rep* 102:46-7 Je 1 '87
John Reed's bold stroke [third world debt loan loss reserves; cover story] J. Fierman. il por *Fortune* 115:26-30+ Je 22 '87
The never-sleeping precedent setter [stock issue] il *Fortune* 116:7 S 14 '87
Soon, Citicorp 'branches' could be all over Japan [sharing automated teller machines with Dai-Ichi Kangyo] J. B. Treece. *Bus Week* p82 Ja 19 '87
A stunner from the Citi [reserve to cushion third world loans] S. Bartlett. il por *Bus Week* p42-3 Je 1 '87
Teaching old banks new tricks. E. A. Finn, Jr. and J. Willoughby. il por *Forbes* 139:34-6 Je 15 '87
Three cheers for Citicorp's initiative [write-off of third world debt] J. S. Henry. il *U S News World Rep* 102:48 Je 1 '87
Citicorp Investment Bank Ltd.
How Citicorp landed in an Irish stew [trading gaffe in Dublin] R. A. Melcher. *Bus Week* p40-1 D 21 '87
Look who's charging into the merger business. S. Bartlett. il *Bus Week* p44 Mr 9 '87
Citicorp Mortgage, Inc.
Casting a spell over employees. S. Nelton. il *Nations Bus* 75:52 D '87
Cities and towns
See also
Business districts
Education, Urban
Housing
Location in business and industry
Metropolitan areas
Neighborhoods
Sister Cities International
Slums
Squatter settlements
United States—Urban policy
United States. Dept. of Housing and Urban Development
Villages
Winter cities
5 top metros for black professionals [cover story; with editorial comment by Earl G. Graves] il *Black Enterp* 17:7, 55-8+ My '87
Are American cities becoming obsolete? [views of Jon Teaford] il *USA Today (Periodical)* 116:7 Ag '87
The best places to live in America. R. Eisenberg and D. W. Englander. il map *Money* 16:34-42+ Ag '87
City lights U S A. il *Glamour* 85:262-4+ Ap '87

Destination U.S.A.: America's surprising cities. il *Better Homes Gard* 65:186+ My '87
Great places to live: the ten best cities for active women. C. Abbott and J. Starker. il map *Women's Sports Fitness* 9:42-6 My '87
Utopia by computer [attributes of U.S. cities and towns] il *Harpers* 275:28 S '87
The well-married manager [effect of cities on marriage] S. Blotnick. il *Forbes* 139:176-7 My 4 '87
Defenses
See also
Civil defense
Finance
See Municipal finance
Fortification
See Fortification
Growth
See also
Metropolitan areas
Suburbs
Booming American cities [cover story; special section] il *Fortune* 116:30-7+ Ag 17 '87
Cities. R. M. Salas. il map *Courier* 40:10-17 Ja '87
City flight and suburb blight [views of Jon Teaford] il *Futurist* 21:49 Jl/Ag '87
Urban population growth: blessing or burden? R. M. Salas. il *USA Today (Periodical)* 116:74-7 Jl '87
International aspects
World urban areas: the anatomy of cities. il *Current* 293:28-35 Je '87
The world's most underrated cities. P. Dragadze. il *Harpers Bazaar* 120:84+ Ap '87
Names
See Names, Geographical
Planning
See City planning
Transit systems
See Local transit
Arab countries
The city-builders of Islam. M. A. Sinaceur. bibl f il *Courier* 40:20-4 Jl '87
Canada
Anecdotes, facetiae, satire, etc.
Whistler, Baie Comeau or Hearne [choosing a location for the 1988 economic summit] A. Fotheringham. il *Macleans* 100:52 Je 15 '87
Developing countries
Cities. R. M. Salas. il map *Courier* 40:10-17 Ja '87
Urban population growth: blessing or burden? R. M. Salas. il *USA Today (Periodical)* 116:74-7 Jl '87
Persian Gulf region
Cities without crime. B. Cain. il *World Press Rev* 34:64 Je '87
United States
See Cities and towns
Cities and towns, Miniature *See* Models of cities, towns, etc.
Cities and towns, Ruined, extinct, etc.
Burma
See also
Pagan (Ancient city)
Guatemala
See also
El Mirador site (Guatemala)
Honduras
See also
Copán (Ancient city)
Iraq
See also
Babylon (Ancient city)
Israel
See also
Caesarea (Ancient city)
Italy
See also
Pompeii (Ancient city)
Libya
See also
Apollonia (Libya: Ancient city)
Mexico
See also
Chichén Itzá (Mexico)
Life among Mexico's ruins: ancient cities, modern inns. D. A. Thomas. il map *Travel Holiday* 167:51-5+ F '87
Pakistan
See also
Mohenjo-Daro site (Pakistan)
Peru
See also
Ciudad Perdida (Colombia)

Cities and towns, Ruined, extinct, etc.—Peru—See also
—*cont.*
Machu Picchu (Peru)
Syria
See also
Ugarit (Ancient city)
Tunisia
See also
Carthage (Ancient city)
Citizens' Action for Safe Energy
The woman who tackled Black Fox [C. Dickerson's fight against Black Fox plant in Oklahoma] N. H. Perreault. il por *Progressive* 51:12 D '87
Citizens' associations
See also
ACORN (Organization)
Crime prevention—Citizen participation
Special interest groups
Citizen's Clearinghouse for Hazardous Wastes, Inc.
Citizen's Clearinghouse for Hazardous Wastes. W. Collette. il *Environment* 29:44-5 N '87
Citizens for Sensible Control of Acid Rain
How a disinformation campaign quashed an acid rain bill. J. R. Luoma. *Audubon* 89:48 Mr '87
Citizens Savings & Loan Assn.
See also
Independent American Savings & Loan Association
Citizens Utility Board (Ill.)
Consumers out in the cold [rate hikes approved for Commonwealth Edison] M. Ervin. il *Progressive* 51:17 Mr '87
Citizenship
See also
Aliens
Patriotism
The changing shape of U.S. citizenship. R. J. Shapiro. il *U S News World Rep* 102:28-31 Ap 27 '87
Fraternalist manifesto [excerpt from address, November 1986] C. Lasch. *Harpers* 274:17-20 Ap '87
A letter to Lendl [advising tennis star not to play Davis Cup for the U.S.] S. Flink. il *World Tennis* 35:10-11 D '87
Public affairs journalism. A. Ross. *Cent Mag* 20:33-5 Mr/Ap '87
Resurrecting common sense [address, December 17, 1986] J. A. Howard. *Vital Speeches Day* 53:240-2 F 1 '87
United States
See Citizenship
Citizenship education
Education for democracy: the changes we need to make. *Educ Dig* 53:10-13 O '87
Nothing less will do. G. L. Bauer. por *Saturday Evening Post* 259:14+ N '87
Operation scare-the-pants-off-'em [Tennessee National Guard stages mock invasions of high schools to promote patriotism] *Harpers* 274:22-3 Ap '87
The public conversation [universities] E. H. O'Neil. *Cent Mag* 20:60-1 Jl/Ag '87
A true test or a trivia game? [Maryland's citizenship test] M. Henry. por *Newsweek* 109:10-11 Je 22 '87
What do U.S. government and civics textbooks teach? [excerpt from We the people] J. D. Carroll and others. *Educ Dig* 53:36-8 S '87
What we must teach our children about freedom. G. L. Bauer. il *Read Dig* 130:102-4 My '87
Citroën (Automobile) *See* Automobiles, Foreign
Citron
Sweetening the season to be jolly [Puerto Rico] K. Robinson. il *Américas* 39:2-7 N/D '87
Citrosuco Paulista (Firm)
Profiting in the third world [founder K. Fischer] il por *U S News World Rep* 102:61-2 My 11 '87
Citrus (Los Angeles, Calif.: Restaurant) *See* Los Angeles (Calif.)—Restaurants, nightclubs, bars, etc.
Citrus ants *See* Ants
Citrus desserts *See* Desserts
Citrus fruit industry
See also
Dole Citrus
Sunkist Growers, Inc.
The changing Florida orange industry. M. D. Winsberg. map *Focus* 36:30-1 Wint '86
Brazil
See also
Citrosuco Paulista (Firm)
Puerto Rico
Sweetening the season to be jolly [citron industry] K. Robinson. il *Américas* 39:2-7 N/D '87
Citrus fruit trees
Talk about good timing . . . citrus that grow their own ornaments. il *Sunset* 179:68-9 D '87

Citrus fruits
See also
Citron
Cooking—Fruit
Grapefruits
Diseases and pests
Suckers, mites, snails: summer troubles for citrus. il *Sunset* 179:146-7 Ag '87
City and country
See also
Country life
Suburban life
Village life
City vs. rural environment: which is healthier? L. L. Guidry. il *Curr Health 2* 14:24-5 S '87
City and town life
See also
Suburban life
Village life
The idiocy of urban life. H. Fairlie. *New Repub* 196:21-3 Ja 5-12 '87
City bicycles *See* Bicycles
City budget *See* Municipal finance
City cycling *See* Cycling
City ecology *See* Urban ecology
City flora *See* Urban flora
City gardens and gardening
See also
Brooklyn (New York, N.Y.)—Gardens and gardening
San Francisco (Calif.)—Gardens and gardening
A city sanctuary [J. O'Brien's garden in Long Beach, Calif.] K. Wilson. il por *Rodale's Org Gard* 34:18+ My '87
Easing the city squeeze [S. Obern's and S. Stotts' garden in Madison, Wis.] K. Martin. il pors *Rodale's Org Gard* 34:78+ Ap '87
Food for thought. il *Courier* 40:12 O '87
City gates
Restoring Hull's medieval past [Beverley Gate] S. Barclay. il *Hist Today* 37:4-5 Jl '87
City halls
See also
Atlanta (Ga.)—City hall
Hague (Netherlands)—City hall
City houses
See also
House decoration
Row houses
Chronicles of a [New York] brownstone (I). G. Talese. il por *Archit Dig* 44:44+ N '87
Chronicles of a New York brownstone (II). G. Talese. il por *Archit Dig* 44:28+ D '87
City Lights Books (San Francisco, Calif.: Bookstore) *See* Booksellers and bookselling—California
City Lights Books Inc.
City Lights: still doing things its own way. L. See. *Publ Wkly* 231:34 Je 26 '87
City National Bank (Beverly Hills, Calif.)
Bank to the stars. L. Gubernick. il por *Forbes* 140:65-6 D 28 '87
City of Faith Medical and Research Center (Tulsa, Okla.)
A price tag on salvation [O. Roberts' plea for funds] L. Black. *Macleans* 100:43 Mr 2 '87
City planning
See also
Business districts
Gentrification
Regional planning
Victory City
Waterfronts
Winter cities
Designing to deter crime. E. Krupat and P. E. Kubzansky. bibl (p62) il *Psychol Today* 21:58-61 O '87
Group consciousness [with introd. by Paul M. Sachner] il *Archit Rec* 175:107-19 N '87
In the public interest: design guidelines. J. Barnett. il *Archit Rec* 175:114-25 Jl '87
Urban planning: what went wrong? M. Kimmelman. il *U S News World Rep* 102:76-7 Mr 30 '87
History
Planning, American style. G. Sternlieb. *Society* 25:21-3 N/D '87
Alabama
See also
Tannin (Ala.)—City planning
California
See also
San Francisco (Calif.)—City planning
San Jose (Calif.)—City planning

City planning—*cont.*

Florida

See also
Heathrow (Fla.)

France

See also
Paris (France)—City planning

Georgia

See also
Madison (Ga.)—City planning

Italy

See also
Venice (Italy)—City planning

Japan

See also
Osaka (Japan)—City planning

Massachusetts

See also
Boston (Mass.)—City planning
Lowell (Mass.)—City planning

Minnesota

See also
Duluth (Minn.)—City planning

New York (State)

See also
New York (N.Y.)—City planning

North Carolina

See also
Raleigh (N.C.)—City planning

Scotland

See also
Glasgow (Scotland)—City planning

Southeast Asia

Review of 'geological risks' in ESCAP urban areas planned. *UN Chron* 23:22 Ja '86

Tennessee

See also
Chattanooga (Tenn.)—City planning

Texas

See also
Austin (Tex.)—City planning
Las Colinas (Tex.)
San Antonio (Tex.)—City planning

Virginia

See also
Tysons Corner (Va.)—City planning

Washington (D.C.)

See Washington (D.C.)—City planning

Washington (State)

See also
Seattle (Wash.)—City planning

City services *See* Municipal services
City Slickers (Lake Geneva, Wis.: Nightclub) *See* Lake Geneva (Wis.)—Restaurants, nightclubs, bars, etc.
City taxation *See* Local taxation
City traffic

See also
Chicago (Ill.)—Street traffic
Las Colinas (Tex.)—Street traffic
Lodi (Ohio)—Street traffic
Los Angeles (Calif.)—Street traffic
New York (N.Y.)—Street traffic
Rome (Italy)—Street traffic
Tysons Corner (Va.)—Street traffic
Vancouver (B.C.)—Street traffic
Auto use and cities [research by Jodi L. Jacobson] il *Futurist* 21:46 N/D '87

City transit *See* Local transit
City University of New York
Life in remedial English: learning about teaching and learning. L. Forstall. *Phi Delta Kappan* 68:796-7 Je '87

City University of New York. Manhattan Community College *See* Manhattan Community College
CityFed Financial Corp.
Mystery profits [accrual accounting] L. Jereski. il *Forbes* 139:54 Ap 20 '87

Citytrust
A new bond for small business [Citytrust Capital Market industrial development bonds] R. W. King. *Bus Week* p109 Je 1 '87

Ciudad Perdida (Colombia)
An ancient emerald city. R. MacGregor. il *Américas* 39:40-5 S/O '87

Ciulla, Joanne B.
The legacy of Baby Doe. il *Psychol Today* 21:70-1+ Ja '87

Civics *See* Citizenship education
Civil defense

See also
Atomic bomb shelters

Evacuation of civilians
United States. Federal Emergency Management Agency
Star Wars revives civil defense. J. Leaning. il *Bull At Sci* 43:42-6 My '87

Oregon

County blocks bomb exercise [Clatsop County, self-declared nuclear free zone, subjected to mock nuclear attack by Federal Emergency Management Agency] D. Friedrich. *Progressive* 51:16 My '87
Civil disobedience *See* Government, Resistance to
Civil engineering

See also
Public works
Civil liberty *See* Liberty
Civil-military relations *See* Civil supremacy over the military
Civil Reserve Air Fleet (U.S.) *See* United States. Civil Reserve Air Fleet
Civil rights

See also
Australian aborigines—Civil rights
Baseball fans—Civil rights
Blacks—Civil rights
Cancer patients—Civil rights
Celebrities—Civil rights
Children—Civil rights
Church and civil rights
Citizenship
Deaf—Civil rights
Deaf-mutes—Civil rights
Due process of law
Equality before the law
Freedom of information
Freedom of speech
Freedom of the press
Handicapped—Civil rights
Indians of North America—Civil rights
Law students—Civil rights
Liberty
Mentally ill—Civil rights
Minorities—Civil rights
Privacy, Right of
Searches and seizures
Students—Civil rights
Torture Victims Protection Act (Proposed)
United States. Dept. of Justice. Civil Rights Division
United States Commission on Civil Rights
Women—Equal rights
Echoes of Watergate [break-ins and surveillance campaign against critics of U.S. Central American policy] B. Levin. il *Macleans* 100:22+ F 16 '87
Epidemics and civil rights [AIDS] D. E. Koshland, Jr. *Science* 235:729 F 13 '87
The Meese factor: packing the lower courts. I. Silver. *Commonweal* 114:102 F 27 '87
An old anti-bias law's widened bite [Supreme Court rulings on 1866 statute] T. Gest. il *U S News World Rep* 102:10-11 Je 1 '87
Some truths are not self-evident. H. Zinn. *Nation* 245:87-8 Ag 1-8 '87
This is against my rights! Three who felt wronged—and determined to battle for redress. G. Jaynes. il pors *Time* 130:40-2 Jl 6 '87
What the spirit of the people provides [address, September 1987] R. Carlson. *Vital Speeches Day* 54:104-5 D 1 '87

International aspects

See also
Captive Nations Week
Convention against Torture and Other Cruel, Inhuman, or Degrading Treatment or Punishment (1984)
United Nations. Commission on Human Rights
United Nations. Human Rights Committee
United Nations. Social, Humanitarian and Cultural Committee
1986 human rights report released [statement, February 19, 1987] R. Schifter. *Dep State Bull* 87:37-8 Ap '87
Assembly adopts Declaration on Right to Development, acts on wide range of issues related to human rights. il *UN Chron* 24:119-25 F '87
Human rights and U.S. foreign policy [address, May 18, 1987] R. Schifter. *Dep State Bull* 87:75-7 Ag '87
Human rights progress in 1986 [address, December 10, 1986] R. Schifter. *Dep State Bull* 87:67-9 F '87
Human rights: the ageless issue [special section] il *Seventeen* 46:122-3 My '87
U.S. human rights policy: origins and implementation [address, May 26, 1987] G. Lister. *Dep State Bull* 87:73-5 Ag '87

Civil rights—International aspects—*cont.*
Understanding human rights [address, October 10, 1987] M. Decter. *Vital Speeches Day* 54:139-42 D 15 '87
The world got a bit freer in '86. il *U S News World Rep* 102:13 Ja 12 '87

Africa
The human rights dimension in Africa [address, November 6, 1986] C. W. Freeman. *Dep State Bull* 87:42-5 F '87

Argentina
Closing the book. *Nation* 244:239-40 F 28 '87
The dirty war's dirty laundry [human rights trials] F. Willey. il por *Newsweek* 109:40 F 23 '87
Fitting justice to reality [prosecution of human rights violators] J. De Onis. il *U S News World Rep* 102:38 Ja 26 '87
Identifying Argentina's 'disappeared'. S. G. Michaud. il *N Y Times Mag* p18-21+ D 27 '87
Kissinger and the 'dirty war' [human rights violations during the 1970s] M. Andersen. il *Nation* 245:477-80 O 31 '87
Time out or time's up [R. Alfonsin's request for legislation that would free most of the military officers currently up on charges of human rights abuse] P. Lacefield. *Commonweal* 114:375-7 Je 19 '87
Torturers saved by the bell, almost [R. Alfonsin signs bill stopping the initiation of human rights abuse cases] D. L. Boroughs. il *Progressive* 51:13 Ap '87
Undue obedience [military officers convicted of human rights abuses granted amnesty] W. E. Smith. il *Time* 130:17 Jl 6 '87

Bibliography
Further reading [disappeareds] J. Polk. *Nation* 244:90 Ja 24 '87

Central America
Elliott Abrams: the teflon Assistant Secretary. E. Alterman. por *Wash Mon* 19:19-22+ My '87

Chile
Bearer of unwelcome tidings. W. Svoboda. il por *Time* 129:47 Ap 13 '87
Getting away with murder. H. Evans. il *U S News World Rep* 102:80 Mr 23 '87
In Chile, all sides angle for a nod from the Pope. M. Santini. il por *U S News World Rep* 102:38 Ap 6 '87
One woman's fiery ordeal [C. G. Quintana set on fire by government troops] A. Finlayson. por *Macleans* 100:24 Mr 30 '87
Pinochet's way. C. G. Brown. il por *N Y Rev Books* 34:47-9 Je 25 '87
The Pontiff's even hand: blessing for all in Chile. C. A. Robbins. il pors *U S News World Rep* 102:33 Ap 13 '87
Under the dictator [regime of A. Pinochet]; tr. by Robert Cox. J. Timerman. *New Yorker* 63:47-50+ N 2 '87

Colombia
A society torn apart by violence. P. Lernoux. il *Nation* 245:512-14+ N 7 '87

Cuba
See also
Political prisoners—Cuba
Human rights in Castro's Cuba. il *Dep State Bull* 87:62-7 F '87
Human rights in Cuba [statement, March 5, 1987] V. A. Walters. *Dep State Bull* 87:71-4 My '87
A spotlight on Cuba [address, October 22, 1986] K. N. Skoug, Jr. *Dep State Bull* 86:81-4 D '86

Czechoslovakia
Reform and dissidence in Czechoslovakia. V. V. Kusin. *Curr Hist* 86:361-4+ N '87
The regime within [interview with V. Havel]; tr. by A. G. Brain. E. Blair. *Harpers* 274:24+ Je '87

Eastern Europe
See also
Helsinki Human Rights Day

El Salvador
Anaya's murder. A. Cockburn. *Nation* 245:546-7 N 14 '87
Beat the devil. A. Cockburn. *Nation* 244:206-7 F 21 '87
Minority report. C. Hitchens. *Nation* 245:674 D 5 '87
'The same old assassins' [slaying of human-rights activist H. Anaya] *Commonweal* 114:646 N 20 '87

Ethiopia
Gray pushes for sanctions against Ethiopia atrocity. *Jet* 73:4 O 12 '87

Guatemala
See also
Political prisoners—Guatemala

Iran
See also
Political prisoners—Iran
A chronicle of abuse. J. Bierman. *Macleans* 100:20 My 25 '87

Kenya
Moi? Yes, Moi. *World Press Rev* 34:41 My '87

Korea (South)
The human rights issue in Korea [statement, May 6, 1987] R. Schifter. *Dep State Bull* 87:77-8 Ag '87

Nicaragua
Beat the devil [pro contra reporting by W. Branigin of the Washington post] A. Cockburn. *Nation* 244:790-1 Je 13 '87
The contra contradiction. A. Neier. il *N Y Rev Books* 34:5-6 Ap 9 '87
The right books [Nicaragua in focus] C. Williamson. *Natl Rev* 39:50 My 22 '87

Philippines
Forensic experts aid Philippine search for disappeared. K. Hannibal. il *Science* 235:535-6 Ja 30 '87
Human rights problems persist in the Philippines. D. Friesen. *Christ Century* 104:348 Ap 15 '87
Leandro Alejandro: victim of militarism. D. Friesen. *Christ Century* 104:877-8 O 14 '87

Romania
Romania could lose its trade status because of rights abuses. *Christ Today* 31:37 Jl 10 '87

Saudi Arabia
Anguish and languishing in Saudi Arabia [case of American businessman S. Bamieh] por *Newsweek* 109:32 Ja 12 '87

South Africa
See also
Apartheid

Soviet Union
See also
Political prisoners—Soviet Union
Countering Gorbachev [glasnost campaign] M. Whitaker. il por *Newsweek* 109:32-3 F 23 '87
Emigrés express caution on Soviet human rights. C. Holden. il *Science* 235:738-40 F 13 '87
The evolving Soviet approach to human rights [addresses, January 27 and February 20, 1987] W. Zimmermann. *Dep State Bull* 87:67-9 Je '87
The 'glasnost' test. R. Pipes. *New Repub* 196:16-17 F 2 '87
Gorbachev has planted the seeds, but will they grow? P. Galuszka and others. il por *Bus Week* p44-5 F 2 '87
Gorbachev's dilemma. E. H. Methvin. *Natl Rev* 39:42+ D 4 '87
Gorbachev's gamble [cover story; special section] por *World Press Rev* 34:9-12+ Ap '87
A hard bargain [special section] il pors *Newsweek* 109:12-23 Ja 5 '87
Human rights and Soviet-American relations [address, October 31, 1986] G. P. Shultz. *Dep State Bull* 86:26-9 D '86
Human rights, the Soviet Union, and the Helsinki process [address, January 28, 1987] R. Schifter. *Dep State Bull* 87:42-8 Ap '87
The issue that will not fade. N. Traver. il *Time* 130:33 D 14 '87
A meeting with Sakharov [interview] H. Feshbach. il pors *Phys Today* 40:7+ Ap '87
More glazed than *glasnost*. I. F. Stone. *Nation* 244:240-1 F 28 '87
The Moscow Book Fair: *glasnost* has its limits. J. Laber. il *N Y Times Book Rev* 92:13-14 O 11 '87
Moscow's mixed signals. B. Levin. il *Macleans* 100:29 F 23 '87
A new Russian revolution? *America* 157:371 N 21 '87
Orlov provides perspectives on Gorbachev's reforms [interview] W. Sweet. por *Phys Today* 40:79-82 My '87
Picking up where he left off [A. Sakharov freed] J. Smolowe. il pors *Time* 129:53-4 Ja 5 '87
Planning the 'second revolution'. *World Press Rev* 34:31 Mr '87
Raising the stakes in Soviet reform [with interview with A. Sakharov] S. Powell. il por *U S News World Rep* 102:30-1 Ja 12 '87
The reality about human rights in the U.S.S.R. [address, February 16, 1987] R. Schifter. *Dep State Bull* 87:38-41 Ap '87
Rumblings. *New Repub* 196:7-9 Ja 19 '87
Sounds of freedom. W. E. Smith. il *Time* 129:52-3 F 23 '87
Soviet reforms. il *World Press Rev* 34:18 F '87

Civil rights—Soviet Union—*cont.*
The systematic repression of Soviet Jews [address, September 28, 1986] R. Pilon. *Dep State Bull* 86:67-70 D '86

Testing *glasnost*: an exile visits his homeland [cover story] A. Goldfarb. il pors *N Y Times Mag* p46-9+ D 6 '87

Through the *glasnost*, darkly. V. P. Aksenov. *Harpers* 274:65-7 Ap '87

Wedded by hate. I. F. Stone. *Nation* 244:492-3 Ap 18 '87

Yevtushenko feels a fresh wind blowing [cover story; interview] K. Vanden Heuvel. il pors *Progressive* 51:24-31 Ap '87

Anecdotes, facetiae, satire, etc.
Glasnost and the condom. W. Goodman. il *New Leader* 70:11-12 Mr 9 '87

United States
See Civil rights

Zimbabwe
Zimbabwe's tortured path. B. Berkeley. *New Repub* 196:21-3 F 16 '87

Civil Rights Commission (U.S.) *See* United States Commission on Civil Rights

Civil rights demonstrations
Amy Carter gets probation for Brown apartheid protest. *Jet* 72:22 Mr 30 '87

Beyond Forsyth [new civil rights activism in the South] M. Eaton. *Black Enterp* 17:62 Je '87

Blacks protest at Univ. of Virginia on race bias. *Jet* 73:6 N 9 '87

C.T. Vivian faces threat of losing right to vote [participation in civil rights demonstration in Ga.] *Jet* 72:23 Je 22 '87

On the march again: protesters hit the South with '60s-style rights rally [Cumming, Ga.] il *Ebony* 42:156+ My '87

Public exorcism in Forsyth County ["Brotherhood" March to protest racism] K. Sehested. *Christ Century* 104:238-9 Mr 11 '87

Racial intolerance in Cumming, Ga., protested. il *Jet* 71:56 F 9 '87

Racism on the rise [civil rights march in Cumming, Ga.] O. Friedrich. il *Time* 129:18-21 F 2 '87

Yale anti-apartheid protest. il *Jet* 72:15 Je 15 '87

History
Rustin, organizer of 1963 march on Washington, dies [B. Rustin] il *Jet* 72:54 S 7 '87

A visit from Rosa Parks: power of the ordinary [Montgomery bus boycott catalyst] D. C. Skinner. *Christ Century* 104:300-1 Ap 1 '87

Civil Rights Division (Dept. of Justice) *See* United States. Dept. of Justice. Civil Rights Division

Civil rights organizations
See also
American-Arab Anti-Discrimination Committee
American Civil Liberties Union
Amnesty International
Center for Democratic Renewal
Congress of Racial Equality
National Association for the Advancement of Colored People
People for the American Way
People United to Serve Humanity (Organization)

Argentina
See also
Conciencia (Organization)
Grandmothers of the Plaza de Mayo (Organization)

Czechoslovakia
See also
Charter 77 (Organization)

Civil Rights Restoration Act
Good intentions aren't enough. G. Roche. por *U S News World Rep* 102:6 My 4 '87

Prolifers say civil rights measure could expand the practice of abortion. *Christ Today* 31:46 Ap 17 '87

Trouble in Grove City [Civil Rights Restoration Act and abortion concerns] M. Gallagher. *Natl Rev* 39:40 Jl 17 '87

Civil service
See also
Bureaucracy
Government employees

United States
See Civil service

Western Europe
Into the vacuum stepped Ollie North [U.S. needs a bureaucracy on the European model to counteract reliance on the military] J. Keegan. por *U S News World Rep* 103:14 Ag 31 '87

Civil service pensions
Dotson transferred to save pension in alleged mishap [case of B. L. Dotson] *Jet* 72:18 Ap 20 '87

Laws and regulations
Out of South Africa: divestment hits a snag [Baltimore ordinance requiring public pension funds to sell stocks challenged] E. Weiner and L. J. Tell. il *Bus Week* p53 Jl 6 '87

Civil supremacy over the military
The colonels' coup [involvement of military officers in Iran arms scandal] F. Zakaria. *New Repub* 197:15 Jl 13-20 '87

To provide for the common defense. Publius. *New Leader* 70:12-14 N 16 '87

Civil war
See also
El Salvador—Civil War, 1980-
Great Britain—History—Civil War, 1642-1649
Greece—History—Civil War, 1944-1949
Spain—History—Civil War, 1936-1939
United States—History—Civil War, 1861-1865

The CIVIL warS [drama] *See* Wilson, Robert, 1941-

Civilian defense *See* Civil defense

Civilian Health and Medical Program of the Uniformed Services
The $600 bedpan? J. Novack. il *Forbes* 139:128-9 Je 15 '87

Civilization
See also
Animals and civilization
Anthropology
Archeology
Brazil—Civilization
China—Civilization
History
Humanism
Iceland—Civilization
Intellectuals and intellectual life
Latin America—Civilization
Madagascar—Civilization
Ocean and civilization
Philosophical anthropology
Plants and civilization
Popular culture
Progress
Science and civilization
Slovenia (Yugoslavia)—Civilization
Social change
United States—Civilization
Western Europe—Civilization
Edith Piaf among the pygmies [importance of translation in the passage of ideas from one civilization to another]; tr. by Helen R. Lane. O. Paz. il *N Y Times Book Rev* 92:1+ S 6 '87

Eight modern myths. G. K. Shepherd. il por *Humanist* 47:15-17+ Mr/Ap '87

The philosopher and the everyday. T. Todorov. *New Repub* 197:34-7+ S 14-21 '87

The third parent [excerpt from address, March 25, 1987] G. W. S. Trow. *Harpers* 275:34-5 Jl '87

The tyranny of subjectivism [address, September 18, 1987] G. Leonard. *Vital Speeches Day* 54:50-7 N 1 '87

Civilization, Ancient
See also
Institute for the History of Ancient Civilizations (China)
Man, Prehistoric
Mayas
The search for a common heritage through the study of ancient civilizations has become a truly international effort. R. M. Adams. il *Smithsonian* 18:10 D '87

Civilization, Arab
The silence in Arab culture. F. Ajami. *New Repub* 196:27-33 Ap 6 '87

Civilization, Baroque
The baroque [cover story; special issue] bibl il *Courier* 40:3-46+ S '87

Civilization, Christian
See also
Christianity and culture

Civilization, Hispanic
See also
Latin America—Civilization

Civilization, Islamic
The city-builders of Islam. M. A. Sinaceur. bibl f il *Courier* 40:20-4 Jl '87

Civilization, Medieval
Pugin & the medieval dream. N. Yates. bibl il *Hist Today* 37:33-40 S '87

Civilization, Slavic
Baroque in the Slav countries. G. D. Gatchev. il *Courier* 40:46 S '87
Civilization and computers *See* Computers and civilization
CJI Industries Inc.
Who's getting the deal in the Triangle shuffle? [N. Peltz and P. W. May construct deal to sell Triangle to its affiliate] C. Power. il por *Bus Week* p78 N 23 '87
CKVU (Vancouver, B.C.: Television station) *See* Television stations
Claar, Nancy
about
A child for Christmas. W. Barnhill. il pors *Good Housekeep* 205:66+ D '87
Claas, Fern
about
Keeping the Cardinals in stitches. J. E. Vader. il pors *Sports Illus* 67:44 O 26 '87
Clad, James
Putting Corypower to the test. il *World Press Rev* 34:24-6 Ja '87
Cladistic analysis
Asymmetry of lineages and the direction of evolutionary time. S. J. Gould and others. il *Science* 236:1437-41 Je 12 '87
Claflin, Edward Beecher
How menacing is the Red menace? il *Publ Wkly* 232:23-4 N 20 '87
When is a true story true? il por *Publ Wkly* 232:23-6 Ag 14 '87
Clague, Ewan, 1896-1987
about
Obituary
Mon Labor Rev 110:2 My '87. R. Fisher
Claiborne, Craig, and Franey, Pierre
Food. See issues of The New York Times Magazine
Claiborne, Liz
about
The rag trade's reluctant revolutionary. P. Sellers. por *Fortune* 115:36-8 Ja 5 '87
Claiborne (Liz), Inc. *See* Liz Claiborne, Inc.
Claire, José Hernandez- *See* Hernandez-Claire, José
Claire (New York, N.Y.: Restaurant) *See* New York (N.Y.)— Restaurants, nightclubs, bars, etc.
Clairvoyance
See also
Extrasensory perception
Clam fisheries *See* Shellfish fisheries
Clampitt, Amy
Man feeding pigeons [poem] *New Yorker* 62:30 Ja 26 '87
Meadowlark country [poem] *New Yorker* 63:32 Jl 13 '87
Clamps
A basic clamp collection. H. Wicks. il *Home Mech* 83:18+ Ag '87
Making your own mat-cutting clamp and guide. G. R. Cohen. il *Am Artist* 51:84+ N '87
Clams
See also
Cooking—Shellfish
Chemical energy fuels ecosystems [gutless clam able to oxidize and get energy directly from sulfides] il *Sea Front* 33:62-4 Ja/F '87
The domestication of reef-dwelling clams [giant clams; cover story] G. A. Heslinga and W. K. Fitt. il *BioScience* 37:332-9 My '87
Contamination
Nobody here but us tamales [smuggling unsafe clams across Baja border] il *FDA Consum* 21:40-1 Mr '87
Clanagan, Russell
about
Black wins case against Pennsylvania state police; will receive $485,000. *Jet* 72:38 My 11 '87
Clancy, Tom, 1947-
about
How to stop a Russian 'surge' [interview] W. J. Cook and R. Kaylor. il por *U S News World Rep* 102:43 Je 15 '87
Tom Clancy: "By God, I'm going to do it.". W. Hoffer. il por *Nations Bus* 75:46-7 D '87
Clapper, Gregory S.
Finding a place for emotions in Christian theology. il *Christ Century* 104:409-11 Ap 29 '87
Clapping *See* Applause
Clapton, Eric
about
Eric Clapton. M. Coleman. il por *Roll Stone* p16 Ja 15 '87
Eric Clapton. M. Peel. por *Stereo Rev* 52:77 Mr '87

Music. G. Santoro. *Nation* 244:776-8 Je 6 '87
Claptrap [drama] *See* Friedman, Ken
Claremont Economics Institute
The saving of America [views of J. Rutledge] P. Brimelow. il por *Forbes* 139:71 Ap 20 '87
Claremore (Okla.)
Galleries and museums
See also
Will Rogers Memorial
Clarendon, Edward Hyde, 1st Earl of, 1609-1674
about
Clarendon and the Great Rebellion. R. Ollard. bibl il por *Hist Today* 37:47-52 S '87
Clarendon Park (Wiltshire, England)
Historic houses, sites, etc.
In the shadow of Clarendon House [living in converted stables] B. Neil. il por *House Gard* 159:230-8 N '87
Clarens, Carlos, 1930-1987
about
Obituary
Film Comment il por 23:75 Mr/Ap '87. M. Corliss *New Yorker* 63:22-3 Mr 30 '87
Clarinet music
See also
Phonograph records—Clarinet music
Mr. Personality [P. Schimmel, clarinet player in New York City subways] *New Yorker* 63:25-7 Ap 13 '87
Clarinetists
See also
Daniels, Eddie
Clarion Music Society
Musical events:
A. Steffani's Le rivali concordi. A. Porter. *New Yorker* 63:91-2 My 25 '87
Clarity, James F.
Softball immortality. il *N Y Times Mag* p52 Mr 22 '87
Clark, Bob
about
From the hip [film] Reviews
Macleans 100:52 F 23 '87. L. O'Toole
N Y 20:72+ F 16 '87. D. Denby
People Wkly il 27:12 Mr 9 '87. S. Haller
Clark, Carol, 1947-
Charles Deas. il por *Am Hist Illus* 22:18-33 Ap '87
Clark, Charles Joseph *See* Clark, Joe, 1939-
Clark, David L. (David Louis), 1929-
High school seniors react to their teachers and their schools. il *Phi Delta Kappan* 68:503-9 Mr '87
(jt. auth) See Gallup, Alec, and Clark, David L. (David Louis), 1929-
Clark, Diane
about
Diane Clark: the mayor of Peace City. P. Skalka. il pors *McCalls* 114:134 Ap '87
Clark, Dick, 1929-
about
American Bandstand's Dick Clark . . . not the boy next door. D. Heyn. il pors *McCalls* 114:115-17 Ja '87
American handstand. M. Barrier. il pors *Nations Bus* 75:89-91 O '87
Dick Clark grows up [cover story] A. Snyder. il pors *Channels* 7:28-31+ My '87
Clark, Donald M.
Schools and business: partners for reform. *Educ Dig* 53:23-5 D '87
Clark, Earl
Emulating the great age of organ building. il *Am Craft* 47:56-63 O/N '87
Oregon's covered bridges. il map *Travel Holiday* 167:71-2 Ja '87
Clark, Earnest Hubert, Jr.
about
Why the Baker-Hughes merger almost didn't happen. C. S. Eklund and T. Vogel. il pors *Bus Week* p110-11 My 11 '87
Clark, Georgie
Tales from a river woman; ed. by Deborah Whitford. il pors *Women's Sports Fitness* 9:38-41+ Ap '87
Clark, Gloria
Two eyes named Aston. il *McCalls* 114:64-5 S '87
Clark, Gwen
about
A walker in the city. B. Kevles. il por *N Y* 20:32 S 28 '87
Clark, Jack, 1955-
about
Jack the Ripper. R. Wiley. il pors *Sports Illus* 67:38-41 Jl 20 '87

Clark, Joe, 1939-
Secretary visits Canada [text of joint press conference, November 21, 1986] *Dep State Bull* 87:45-8 F '87
about
Apartheid and diplomacy. C. Wood. il por *Macleans* 100:22-3 Ag 24 '87
Clark's compromise offer. H. Mackenzie. il por *Macleans* 100:24 S 21 '87
Clark's troubled tour. K. Scanlon. il por *Macleans* 100:26 D 7 '87
Searching for signs of spring. H. Mackenzie. il *Macleans* 100:20-1 My 18 '87

Clark, Jonathan
about
Tot gets liver thanks to help from Cosby, Jackson. por *Jet* 72:9 My 18 '87

Clark, Kate Freeman
about
Rediscovering a forgotten painter. il por *South Living* 22:38 Mr '87

Clark, Kim
about
Career makeover: from aerobics instructor to high-tech medical equipment sales. il por *Glamour* 85:68 Jl '87

Clark, Mary Higgins
Always a storyteller. *Writer* 100:9-11 Ag '87
Weep no more my lady [story] il *Redbook* 169:38-40+ Je '87
Weep no more, my lady [story] il *Redbook* 169:70-2+ My '87

Clark, Michael
about
No fire escape in hell [dance] Reviews
Dance Mag 61:81-2 Mr '87. O. Stuart

Clark, Michelle
about
A teenager's tragedy: birth and death in a Florida town. C. Mitchell and T. Burdick. il por *Ms* 16:60-3 D '87

Clark, Nancy, 1951-
A week of healthy eating. il *Women's Sports Fitness* 9:41-4 S '87

Clark, Roy Peter
about
Kids can learn to write—and enjoy it [interview] il *U S News World Rep* 102:68 Ap 6 '87

Clark, Russell G.
about
Can a judge raise taxes? J. Seligmann. il por *Newsweek* 110:98 O 12 '87

Clark, Steven C., and Kamen, Robert
The human hematopoietic colony-stimulating factors. bibl f il *Science* 236:1229-37 Je 5 '87

Clark, Steven S., and others
Unique forms of the *abl* tyrosine kinase distinguish Ph[1]-positive CML Ph[1]-positive ALL. bibl f il *Science* 235:85-8 Ja 2 '87

Clark, William, Jr.
Korea: moving quickly toward democracy [statement, September 17, 1987] *Dep State Bull* 87:29-31 N '87
Clark (Dick) Productions Inc. *See* Dick Clark Productions Inc.
Clark (Kate Freeman) Art Gallery *See* Kate Freeman Clark Art Gallery
Clark (Michael) and Company *See* Michael Clark and Company
Clark (Sterling and Francine) Art Institute *See* Sterling and Francine Clark Art Institute
Clark Air Base (Philippines) *See* Air bases
Clark County Detention Center (Las Vegas, Nev.) *See* Las Vegas (Nev.)—Prisons and reformatories
Clark Tribble Harris & Li, Architects
Southern panache [Charlotte, N.C. offices] H. L. Smith, Jr. il *Archit Rec* 175:114-17 Je '87

Clarke, Alan
about
Rita, Sue and Bob too [film] Reviews
New Repub 197:24-5 Ag 10-17 '87. S. Kauffmann
Newsweek 110:67 Ag 3 '87. D. Ansen

Clarke, Arthur C., 1917-
Looking into the future. il *Radio-Electron* 58:81-3 My '87
On golden seas [fiction] il *Omni* 9:88-90 My '87
The sentinel [fiction] il *Read Dig* 131:153-7 D '87

Clarke, Duncan L.
Why State can't lead. bibl f *Foreign Policy* 66:128-42 Spr '87

Clarke, Jay
Hooked on cruising. il *50 Plus* 27:44-5+ My '87

Clarke, John H.
Building a lecture that really works. *Educ Dig* 53:52-5 O '87

Clarke, Mae, 1910-
Mae Clarke. il pors *People Wkly* 27:79 F 9 '87

Clarke, Martha, 1944?-
about
Clarke flies again. S. Reiter. il por *N Y* 20:25 Je 1 '87
Clarke work. M. Gussow. il pors *N Y Times Mag* p30-4+ Ja 18 '87
The garden of earthly delights [drama] Reviews
New Yorker 63:68 Je 29 '87. E. Oliver
The hunger artist [drama] Reviews
Dance Mag il 61:174-5+ Je '87. S. Sommer
N Y il 20:97-8 Mr 9 '87. J. Simon
Nation 244:446-8 Ap 4 '87. M. Hodgson
New Repub 196:26-7 Mr 9 '87. R. Brustein
New Yorker 63:74 Mr 9 '87. E. Oliver
Time il 129:88 Mr 9 '87. W. A. Henry
Vogue il 177:96 Ap '87. J. Hobhouse

Clarke, Mary
Princess Di's nanny remembers . . . the custody battle for Diana. il pors *Redbook* 169:88-9+ Ag '87

Clarke, Stephen H.
Young wildlife: look—don't touch! il *Conservationist* 41:26-8 My/Je '87

Clarkson, Elizabeth
about
Wing Haven. K. Whiteside. il *House Gard* 159:166-73+ Je '87

Clary, Michael
Down on the levy. il *Channels* 7:53-5 N '87
The human dimension in hurricane forecasting. il *Weatherwise* 40:197-9 Jl/Ag '87
Local TV fights back in Palm Beach. il map *Channels* 7:21-2 Ap '87

Class distinction *See* Social classes
Class reunions *See* College reunions; High school reunions
Class size
Small is beautiful—and effective [research by Sid Bourke] G. W. Bracey. il *Phi Delta Kappan* 68:703 My '87
Classes, Social *See* Social classes
Classic Aircraft Corporation
Reborn Roundy [Waco Classic YMF-5] R. L. Collins. il *Flying* 114:28-35 Ja '87
Classic automobiles *See* Automobiles—History
Classical compact discs *See* Compact discs
Classical education
See also
Humanities
Liberal education
Classical languages
See also
Greek language
Latin language
Classical music *See* Music
Classical music broadcasting *See* Radio broadcasting—Music
Classical phonograph record industry *See* Phonograph record industry
Classical phonograph records *See* Phonograph records
Classical sculpture *See* Sculpture, Classical
Classical tape recordings *See* Tape recordings
Classicism
See also
Neoclassicism
Classicism in architecture
See also
Neoclassicism (Architecture)
Villa civility [J. Crepain creates modern classical house for De Wachter family in Belgium] C. Amery. il *House Gard* 159:184-9+ S '87
Classicism in art
Exhibitions
American decorative arts [exhibition entitled Motif and meaning: classicism in America] S. B. Sherrill. il *Antiques* 132:1194+ D '87
Classics (Books) *See* Books and reading—Best books
Classification
See also
Biology—Classification
Botany—Classification
Climate—Classification
Fish—Classification
Classified advertising *See* Advertising, Classified
Classified information
See also
Official secrets
Pentagon Papers

Classified information—*cont.*

The anti-space act of 1986 [restricting access to NASA tech briefs] J. Rhea. il *Space World* X-7-283:3 Jl '87

Black holes in the budget [line item requests for Air Force research and development programs that are classified] D. C. Morrison. il *Harpers* 274:50-1 Ja '87

Coming: the big chill? J. Raloff. il *Sci News* 131:314-17 My 16 '87

Congressman urges public disclosure of spy satellite data [views of George Brown] il *Aviat Week Space Technol* 126:30-1 Ap 6 '87

Death of a data directive [automated databases] R. Chalk. il *Technol Rev* 90:13-14 Jl '87

Export controls and research results. *Sci News* 132:73 Ag 1 '87

Forbidden facts. P. Bagne. il *Omni* 9:18+ F '87

Furor over embassy security points to tighter screening of architects. P. Hoffmann. il *Archit Rec* 175:39 Je '87

In rough waters, White House cancels controls on databases. I. Goodwin. *Phys Today* 40:66 My '87

Investing in the dark [investors in black programs] M. Beauchamp. il *Forbes* 140:131+ S 21 '87

Making waves: Poindexter sails into scientific databases. I. Goodwin. por *Phys Today* 40:51-2 Ja '87

NASA panel would withhold accident witness accounts [Space Flight Safety Panel] il *Aviat Week Space Technol* 127:128-9 S 7 '87

Secrets storm [R. W. Pelton sentenced to life imprisonment] *Nation* 244:4-5 Ja 10 '87

Security risk. J. B. Montague, Jr. il *Progressive* 51:34 S '87

Sworn to silence [restrictions on government employees] D. A. Demac. il *Progressive* 51:29-32 My '87

Tapping new secrets [government initiatives to control database information] M. McIver. il *Macleans* 100:60-1 S 28 '87

Vindication for a blacklist victim [case of P. Kimball] D. Gates. il por *Newsweek* 110:8 S 28 '87

What is federal policy on scientific communication? D. R. Corson. *Phys Today* 40:144 Ja '87

Classroom furniture, equipment, etc. *See* School furniture, equipment, etc.

Classroom management

    See also

    Class size

Is high school the place to teach thinking? F. Schrag. *Educ Dig* 53:16-19 D '87

Teaching ethics [confronting a defiant student] S. M. Masiclat. il *Phi Delta Kappan* 69:275-6 D '87

Using positive reinforcement. T. R. McDaniel. *Educ Dig* 53:36-9 O '87

    Anecdotes, facetiae, satire, etc.

Scaling the ivory tower. H. J. Bullford. il *Change* 19:58-60 N/D '87

Classroom observation *See* School supervision and supervisors

Classrooms

Keeping classroom walls from distracting learners. W. N. Creekmore. *Educ Dig* 53:44-6 O '87

Clathrin

Assembly of clathrin-coated pits onto purified plasma membranes. M. S. Moore and others. bibl f il *Science* 236:558-63 My 1 '87

Clathrin light chains LCA and LCB are similar, polymorphic, and share repeated heptad motifs. T. Kirchhausen and others. bibl f il *Science* 236:320-4 Ap 17 '87

Clathrin requirement for normal growth of yeast. S. K. Lemmon and E. W. Jones. bibl f il *Science* 238:504-9 O 23 '87

Clatsop County (Or.)

County blocks bomb exercise. D. Friedrich. *Progressive* 51:16 My '87

Claudio, Toni, and others

Genetic reconstitution of functional acetylcholine receptor channels in mouse fibroblasts. bibl f il *Science* 238:1688-94 D 18 '87

Claus, Jim

    about

The case of the poisoned wildlife refuge. R. Fitzgerald. il por *Read Dig* 131:133-7 O '87

Claus, Karen E.

Kesterson: an unsolvable problem? bibl f *Environment* 29:4-5 Jl/Ag '87

Clausen, A. W. (Alden Winship)

    about

Deja vu at BankAmerica. J. B. Levine. il por *Bus Week* p59 My 25 '87

Tom Clausen. J. B. Levine. il por *Bus Week* Sp Issue:216 Ap 17 '87

Clausen, Alden Winship *See* Clausen, A. W. (Alden Winship)

Clausen, John

(jt. auth) See McGlashan, Sandy, and Clausen, John

Clausen, Peter, and Brower, Michael

The confused course of SDI. il *Technol Rev* 90:60-5+ O '87

Clauser, Francis H.

    about

A better 12-meter. P. A. Janssen. il por *Mot Boat Sail* 159:64-5 F '87

Claver, Francisco F.

The Philippine revolution: a year later. *America* 156:232-5 Mr 21 '87

Claverie, Laura

Blue moods. il *Health* 19:47-51 S '87

Clavière d'Hust, Bernard, de, Count

    about

The art of Count Bernard de Clavière d'Hust. C. Styles-McLeod. il *Archit Dig* 44:208-15+ My '87

Clawson, John

Miniature wideband amplifier. il *Radio-Electron* 58:45-6+ My '87

Clay, Carolyn

Unfinished symphonies. il pors *Esquire* 107:106-9 My '87

Clay, Cassius *See* Ali, Muhammad, 1942-

Clay

    See also

    Ceramics

Chemical reactions on clays. P. Laszlo. bibl f il *Science* 235:1473-7 Mr 20 '87

Clay animation

Filmmaker Will Vinton and his feats of clay are giving animation a new raisin d'être. D. Van Biema. il pors *People Wkly* 27:76+ Mr 9 '87

What's to become of me? Claymation! [cover story] il *Natl Geogr World* 148:3-7 D '87

Clay sculpture *See* Ceramic sculpture

Clay tennis courts *See* Tennis courts

Clayman, Barbara

Penetrating the mystery of migraine. il *Nations Bus* 75:71-2 Jl '87

Claypool, Norma

    about

"If we don't take them, who will?". A. Steinbach. il por *McCalls* 115:135-7 D '87

Clayton, David A.

(jt. auth) See Chang, David D., and Clayton, David A.

Clayton, Ellen Wright

Surrogate motherhood: a legal labyrinth. il *USA Today (Periodical)* 116:68-9 N '87

Clayton, Jack

    about

The lonely passion of Judith Hearne [film] Reviews *New Yorker* 63:92-3 D 28 '87. P. Kael

Clayton, Sara

How do you do? May I marry you? [story] il *Redbook* 168:32+ Ja '87

Clayton, Xernona

    about

Broadcasting exec gets apology from organization following racial insult. il por *Jet* 72:32 My 18 '87

Southern exposure. M. Scott. il pors *Essence* 17:97-8+ Mr '87

Clean Air Act

Clean Air advocates: still (wheezing, gasping, crying) trying after all these years. A. Stine. il *Sierra* 72:13-14 S/O '87

Clean Air: Congress must get tough. G. J. Mitchell. il por *Natl Parks* 61:12-13 Jl/Ag '87

Clean Air should start in the parks. P. C. Pritchard. *Natl Parks* 61:5 Jl/Ag '87

Clean Air: the promise is unfulfilled. J. D. Hair. il *Natl Wildl* 25:30 F/Mr '87

Deadlines for Clean Air. il *Sunset* 179:207 D '87

The EPA may just be blowing smoke on Clean Air. T. Smart. *Bus Week* p49 Je 8 '87

High noon for smog control. D. S. Strait and R. E. Ayres. bibl f *Environment* 29:43-5 S '87

L.A. to E.P.A.: don't hold your breath. M. Cone. il *Sierra* 72:27+ N/D '87

Missing the deadline on ozone. M. D. Uehling. il *Natl Wildl* 25:34-7 O/N '87

The new soldier in the clean-air war: you. S. N. Wellborn. il *U S News World Rep* 103:50-1 Ag 10 '87

Once more, with compliance. C. Pope. il *Sierra* 72:34+ S/O '87

Clean Air Act—*cont.*
Searching for a breath of Clean Air. I. Peterson. map *Sci News* 132:340 N 28 '87
Smog-ozone policy shift. J. Raloff. *Sci News* 131:244 Ap 18 '87
A smogbound quest for Clean Air [EPA delays penalties for noncompliance] il *U S News World Rep* 103:10 N 30 '87
When will we stop breathing polluted air? [extending deadline for compliance] M. Engel. il *Glamour* 85:136 D '87

Clean Air Associates
A crusader who helps offices go smoke-free [R. Addison] P. Finch. il por *Bus Week* p105 Mr 23 '87

Clean rooms
Dustbusting: how they build the cleanest rooms on earth. E. M. Gabler. il *Archit Rec* 175:128-33 Ap '87

Clean Water Act
Citizen enforcement of environmental laws. N. S. Marks. bibl f *Environment* 29:5+ Je '87
Clean Water bill sent back to Reagan. J. Raloff. *Sci News* 131:71 Ja 31 '87
Clean Water, the next act. A. Stine. il *Sierra* 72:14 My/Je '87
Reauthorize the Clean Water Act. il *Oceans* 20:65 Ja/F '87

Cleaning
See also
Automobile engines—Cleaning
Automobiles—Cleaning
Boats and boating—Cleaning
House cleaning
Motorcycles—Cleaning
Photographs—Cleaning

Cleaning compositions
See also
Bleaching materials
Paint and varnish removers
Soap
Bathroom cleaners. il *Consum Rep* 52:262-4 D '87
Cleaning an oven. G. Branson. il *Fam Handyman* 37:85 My/Je '87
Glass cleaners. il *Consum Rep* 52:264-6 D '87
Oven cleaners. il *Consum Rep* 52:140-1 Mr '87
Oven cleaners. il *Consum Rep* 52:35-7 D '87
S100 cleaner [for motorcycles] il *Cycle* 38:71 Ja '87

Cleaning machinery and appliances
See also
Brooms
Pressure washers
Vacuum cleaners

Cleaning of fish See Fish, Dressing of

Cleaning of lakes, rivers, etc.
Cleaner waters pay off in better fishing [New York] L. Smith and E. Stegemann. il *Conservationist* 41:6-15 Mr/Ap '87

Cleaning services
See also
Hawley Group, Inc.
ServiceMaster Industries Inc.
ZZZZ Best Company

Ethical aspects
Wall-to-wall trouble for the carpet-cleaning king [B. Minkow of ZZZZ Best] K. Kelly. il por *Bus Week* p83 Jl 13 '87
A whiz kid goes wrong [B. Minkow of ZZZZ Best Co.] J. B. Copeland. il por *Newsweek* 110:40 Jl 20 '87
ZZZZ Best may be ZZZZ worst. P. Elmer-Dewitt. por *Time* 130:56 Jl 20 '87

Clearcutting
End of the old-growth canopy [destruction of Pacific Northwest forests endangers spotted owls] L. Tuttle. il *Natl Parks* 61:16-21 My/Je '87
The Forest Service's road to nowhere [timber contracts and roadbuilding projects threaten Tongass National Forest] K. E. Franklin. il *Progressive* 51:12 Je '87
Paradise in peril [clearcutting of Tongass National Forest] R. Robotham. il map *Life* 10:92-6 N '87
Public dismay over private cuts [clearcutting by Plum Creek Timber Company on private land in the Pacific Northwest] J. Sher. il *Sierra* 72:83-4 Mr/Ap '87
Razing the giant redwoods [Pacific Lumber Co.] P. Abramson. il por *Newsweek* 110:38 Jl 6 '87
The shrinking province of the primeval [Pacific Northwest; cover story] K. Ervin. il map *Sierra* 72:38-45 Jl/Ag '87
The South Moresby war [Haida Indians protest logging on Queen Charlotte Islands] M. Gee. il *Macleans* 100:12 Jl 6 '87

Threat to the spotted owl [destruction of Pacific Northwest forests] L. Burnham. il *Sci Am* 257:34+ O '87
Trashing the Tongass. G. Laycock. il maps *Audubon* 89:110-12+ N '87

Clearing house (Banking) See Clearinghouse (Banking)

Clearing of land
See also
Shifting cultivation

Clearinghouse (Banking)
Risky moments in the money markets. M. W. Karmin. il *U S News World Rep* 102:44-5 Mr 2 '87

Cleary, Russell George
about
Heileman's Russell Cleary: brawling for breweries. M. D. Oneal. il por *Bus Week* p68+ Mr 2 '87

Cleaver, Carole
Haiti robbed of hope [cover story] il *New Leader* 70:8-10 D 28 '87
In the eye of Haiti's hurricane. il *New Leader* 70:5-7 S 21 '87

Cleaver, Chester
about
English transfer. T. Brown. il *House Gard* 159:196-203 N '87

Cleaver, Eldridge, 1935-
about
Cleaver is arrested in L.A. on cocaine charges. por *Jet* 73:38 O 26 '87
Eldridge Cleaver fights charge; holds fund-raiser. por *Jet* 73:26 N 16 '87

Cleese, John
about
The Bingo Long traveling all-star industrialists. D. M. Kimmel. il por *Film Comment* 23:41-3 Ja/F '87

Cleland, Max, 1942-
The South will rise again. por *U S News World Rep* 102:5 Ja 19 '87
about
Words that give us strength. C. T. Rowan. il pors *Read Dig* 130:49-50+ Ap '87

Clematis
Know your clematis. il *South Living* 22:54 Je '87

Clemens, Roger
about
Off to a troubled start. P. Axthelm. il pors *Newsweek* 109:66-7 Ap 13 '87

Clemens, Samuel Langhorne See Twain, Mark, 1835-1910

Clemente, Francesco
about
Realm of the senses. R. Storr. bibl f il *Art Am* 75:132-45+ N '87

Clemente, Lilia C.
about
Family portfolio. R. Phalon. il por *Forbes* 140:148+ S 7 '87

Clemente, Roberto, 1934-1972
about
It's a dream come true. J. Kaplan. il por *Sports Illus* 67:95 O 5 '87

Clemente (Roberto) Sports City (Carolina, Puerto Rico) See Roberto Clemente Sports City (Carolina, Puerto Rico)

Clemente Capital Inc.
Family portfolio. R. Phalon. il por *Forbes* 140:148+ S 7 '87

Clements, George
about
'The Father Clements story' dramatizes fight of Chicago priest to adopt a son. C. Waldron. il por *Jet* 73:30-2 D 14 '87

Clements, Kevin P.
New Zealand paying for nuclear ban. bibl f il *Bull At Sci* 43:41-4 Jl/Ag '87
New Zealand's antinuclear stand. il *Bull At Sci* 43:32-4 Mr '87

Clements, Robert
Say, brother. por *Essence* 18:6 O '87

Clements, William P., 1917-
about
A bad case of foot-in-mouth disease is alarming the Texas GOP. T. Mason. por *Bus Week* p39 Ag 31 '87
Payoff, hike! E. Magnuson. il *Time* 129:34 Mr 16 '87
Playing for pay in Texas. T. E. Johnson. por *Newsweek* 109:32 Mr 16 '87

La clemenza di Tito [opera] See Mozart, Wolfgang Amadeus, 1756-1791

Clemon, U. W.
about
Black judge disqualified in Ala. segregation case. por *Jet* 73:4 O 26 '87

Clerc, Jean-Pierre
The Vatican's money troubles. *World Press Rev* 34:46 S '87
Clergy
See also
Bishops
Black clergy
Chaplains, Military
Children as ministers
Elders (Church officers)
Missionaries
Preaching
Priests
Seminarians
Women clergy

Anecdotes, facetiae, satire, etc.
Why are these pastors smiling? M. E. Marty. *Christ Century* 104:367 Ap 15 '87

Appointment, call and election
Hick rejected [bid to be accepted as a Presbyterian minister] *Christ Century* 104:304-5 Ap 1 '87

Crime
A cloud falls on a Dallas preacher [attack on wife of W. Railey] D. Pedersen. il por *Newsweek* 109:23 My 25 '87
The condom preacher—and his pantless past [Rev. C. F. Thitchener] il por *Newsweek* 109:69 Mr 2 '87
A late indictment may close the case behind TV's Murder ordained. J. Calio. il pors *People Wkly* 27:107-8+ Je 8 '87
Strangled in Dallas: an ungodly mystery [Rev. W. Railey held in attack on his wife] *Newsweek* 109:30 My 11 '87
A troubled minister's tale [strangulation of W. Railey's wife] S. Peterson. il por *U S News World Rep* 102:28 My 25 '87

Dismissal
The restoration of Maurice McCrackin [Presbyterian activist minister] D. Peerman. il *Christ Century* 104:998-1000 N 11 '87

Education
See also
Theological seminaries

Ethics
Fallen leaders are not "damaged goods". R. W. Dingman. il por *Christ Today* 31:12 D 11 '87
The private lives of public leaders. D. Augsburger. il por *Christ Today* 31:23-4 N 20 '87
The road to restoration: how should the church treat its fallen leaders? [cover story] K. S. Kantzer. il *Christ Today* 31:19-22 N 20 '87

Political activities
See also
Black clergy—Political activities
Cardinals—Political activities
Con man of the cloth [P. Robertson and the Fairness Doctrine] W. A. Henry. il *Channels* 7:16 Ja '87
Getting out God's vote: Pat Robertson and the evangelicals [cover story] F. Edwords and S. McCabe. il *Humanist* 47:5-10+ My/Je '87
God's on his side [P. Robertson] A. Kopkind. *Nation* 245:400-1 O 17 '87
His eyes have seen the glory [P. Robertson] L. I. Barrett. il pors *Time* 130:22-3 S 28 '87
Pat Robertson: why he can't win. il por *U S News World Rep* 103:16 S 28 '87
Pat Robertson's bid: good for democracy. T. B. Lynch. *Christ Century* 104:908-9 O 21 '87
Will Pat run? [P. Robertson's Christian television network faces fallout from his possible presidential bid] B. Spring. il pors *Christ Today* 31:34-6 Ag 7 '87

Anecdotes, facetiae, satire, etc.
Beseeching the Great Decider [candidacies of J. Jackson and P. Robertson] A. Fotheringham. il *Macleans* 100:72 D 7 '87

Retirement
Mandatory retirement: its time has passed. R. L. Minker. *Christ Century* 104:463-4 My 13 '87

Salaries, pensions, etc.
Anecdotes, facetiae, satire, etc.
The latest academic fad. F. Sprock. por *Newsweek* 109:8 Je 1 '87

Sexual behavior
See also
Ordination of homosexuals
Ankerberg discusses the part he played [uncovering the J. Bakker sex scandal] il por *Christ Today* 31:52 Je 12 '87
Bakker quits [J. Bakker] *Christ Century* 104:328 Ap 8 '87

The Bakker tragedy [danger of mixing television and ministry] T. C. Muck. il por *Christ Today* 31:14-15 My 15 '87
Baring body and soul [J. Hahn, J. Bakker and PTL scandal; cover story] il pors *People Wkly* 28:32-7 O 5 '87
Beyond Bakker. W. F. Buckley. *Natl Rev* 39:59 Jl 3 '87
Breaking faith, two TV idols fall [J. and T. Bakker] J. Wadler. il pors *People Wkly* 27:80-2+ My 18 '87
Clergy troubles. *Christ Century* 104:961-2 N 4 '87
A crackdown at PTL. il por *Christ Today* 31:51+ Je 12 '87
Fresh out of miracles [J. Bakker loses TV ministry] R. Watson. il por *Newsweek* 109:70-2 My 11 '87
Gays in the clergy. K. L. Woodward. il *Newsweek* 109:58-60 F 23 '87
God and money [PTL scandal; cover story; special section] il pors *Time* 130:48-55 Ag 3 '87
God and money [TV evangelists; cover story; special section] il pors *Newsweek* 109:16-23 Ap 6 '87
Gordon MacDonald leaves the helm of InterVarsity. il por *Christ Today* 31:38-9 Jl 10 '87
Hahn bares her soul, etc. G. Hackett. il pors *Newsweek* 110:43 O 12 '87
Heaven can wait [J. and T. Bakker; cover story; special section] il pors *Newsweek* 109:58-62+ Je 8 '87
Heaven in 15 minutes or less [J. Bakker sex scandal] A. Fotheringham. il *Macleans* 100:56 Ap 20 '87
Hellfire, brimstone—and a TV scandal [J. Bakker sex scandal] B. Levin. il pors *Macleans* 100:42-3 Ap 6 '87
The Jim Bakker affair. il pors *Christ Today* 31:36-7 Ap 17 '87
Jim Bakker's lost America. A. Kopkind. il pors *Esquire* 108:174-8+ D '87
New Bakker charge [sexual misconduct charges by J. Hahn] K. L. Woodward. il por *Newsweek* 109:6 Ap 13 '87
On having fun with fundamentalists [J. Bakker sex scandal] W. F. Buckley. *Natl Rev* 39:60 My 8 '87
Ousting two from the clergy [J. Bakker and R. Dortch fired from the Assemblies of God] R. N. Ostling. il por *Time* 129:65 My 18 '87
An "outrageous" ministry [J. Bakker scandal] D. Brand. il por *Time* 129:82 My 4 '87
Paying the wages of sin [PTL's J. Bakker] G. Hackett. il por *Newsweek* 109:28 Mr 30 '87
Preaching & practice [case of J. Bakker] D. R. Carlin, Jr. *Commonweal* 114:342-3 Je 5 '87
A really bad day at Fort Mill [J. Bakker forced to resign from PTL in wake of sex scandal] R. N. Ostling. il por *Time* 129:70 Mr 30 '87
Religious distraction [PTL affair] K. Burris. *Commonweal* 114:310-11 My 22 '87
Spring cleaning at Jim Bakker's PTL. J. L. Sheler and J. Thornton. il *U S News World Rep* 102:8-9 My 11 '87
Taking command at Fort Mill [J. Bakker loses TV ministry] R. N. Ostling. il pors *Time* 129:60 My 11 '87
Thou shalt not smirk [J. Bakker sex scandal] *Natl Rev* 39:17 Ap 24 '87
Tragic confusion [homosexual clergy] *Natl Rev* 39:21 Mr 13 '87
TV's raging holy wars [J. Bakker scandal] L. Black. il por *Macleans* 100:54 My 11 '87
TV's unholy row [sex scandal involving J. Bakker; cover story] R. N. Ostling. il pors *Time* 129:60-4+ Ap 6 '87
Untold story of black founder of Pentecostal church body rocked by sex scandal of whites [W. J. Seymour of the Assemblies of God and reaction to J. Bakker scandal] S. Booker. il pors *Jet* 72:12-14+ My 18 '87
Clergy conferences
See also
Catholic Church. National Conference of Catholic Bishops
Synods of bishops
Clergy malpractice trials *See* Trials (Malpractice)
Clerks (Retail trade)
See also
United Food and Commercial Workers International Union
Cleveland, Harlan, 1918-
The abolition of retirement. il *Change* 19:8-10 N/D '87
Western Europe's dilemma: is a strong defense possible without nuclear arms? il *USA Today (Periodical)* 116:52-4 S '87

Cleveland, Paul M.
New Zealand and an interdependent world [address, March 13, 1987] map *Dep State Bull* 87:80-3 Je '87
Cleveland (Ohio)

Banks
See also
Bank One, Cleveland, NA

Churches (Buildings)
Climbing Jacob's ladder [St. Andrew Abbey Church] M. Gaskie. il *Archit Rec* 175:132-7 N '87

Education
Black elected president of Cleveland school board [S. E. Tolliver] *Jet* 71:5 F 2 '87
Cleveland pays for its A's [Scholarship-in-Escrow Program] il *Newsweek* 110:66 Ag 31 '87

Galleries and museums
See also
Cleveland Museum of Art

Geology
The geology of art: Cleveland Museum of Art has walls and sculptures made of rock, and sidewalks made of skeletons [cover story] J. T. Hannibal and M. T. Schmidt. il *Earth Sci* 40:12-15 Summ '87

Newspapers
See also
Cleveland plain dealer (Newspaper)

Police
Shot by a cop [J. Yates] D. O. Relin. il por *Sch Update* 120:7 D 4 '87

Politics and government
Carl Stokes considering comeback in Cleveland. por *Jet* 72:24 Jl 6 '87

Stores
Cleveland's splendor under glass [shopping arcade] il *Am Herit* 38:90-1 Jl/Ag '87
A novel union role: picketing for the boss [supermarkets enlist workers in push against nonunion rivals] S. Phillips. il *Bus Week* p80 D 28 '87-Ja 4 '88
Cleveland Ballet
Reviews:
Performances of Swan Lake. W. Salisbury. il *Dance Mag* 61:19+ S '87
Cleveland-Cliffs, Inc.
Dilution control [stockholders vs. management over share value] P. Fuhrman. il *Forbes* 140:174 O 5 '87
Cleveland Museum of Art
The geology of art: Cleveland Museum of Art has walls and sculptures made of rock, and sidewalks made of skeletons [cover story] J. T. Hannibal and M. T. Schmidt. il *Earth Sci* 40:12-15 Summ '87
Warrant for Lee's arrest dropped [dispute between French government and former Cleveland Museum of Art director S. E. Lee over the export of a N. Poussin painting] R. W. Walker. *Art News* 86:30 Summ '87
Cleveland plain dealer (Newspaper)
Cleveland rock critic Jane Scott may be pushing 70, but she's still got the beat. K. Myers. il pors *People Wkly* 27:91-2 Je 8 '87
Cliburn, Van, 1934-
about
Van Cliburn's disturbing legacy. P. Moor. il por *High Fidel* 37:82-3 N '87
Clichés
Platitudes and natural selection. G. F. Kreyche. il *USA Today (Periodical)* 115:98 My '87
Click and Clack, the Tappet Brothers [radio program] See Radio program reviews—Single works
Cliff, Stafford, and Tresidder, Jane
Dazzling sunrooms [excerpt from Living under glass] il *Redbook* 169:114-19 Je '87
Clifford, Geoffrey C.
At home in Vietnam. il *Life* 10:58-61+ D '87
Clifford, Martin, 1910-
The early days of radio (III). il *Radio-Electron* 58:59-61+ Ap '87
The early days of radio (IV). il *Radio-Electron* 58:52+ Jl '87
The early days of radio (V). il *Radio-Electron* 58:64-6+ D '87
Clifford, Thomas Hugh, 1948-
about
A tale of two Cliffords. R. Hutton. il por *Hist Today* 37:8-9 Jl '87
Clifford of Chudleigh, Thomas Clifford, Baron, 1630-1673
about
A tale of two Cliffords. R. Hutton. il por *Hist Today* 37:8-9 Jl '87
Cliff's Notes Inc.
Fast food for thought [founder C. Hillegass] N. Atkins. il por *Roll Stone* p110-12+ Mr 26 '87

Clift Hotel (San Francisco, Calif.) *See* San Francisco (Calif.)—Hotels, motels, etc.
Clifton, Nat
about
Sweetwater [excerpt from From set shot to slam dunk] C. Salzberg. il por *Sport Mag* 78:63 Jl '87
Clifton, Sweetwater *See* Clifton, Nat
Climate
See also
Climatic changes
Droughts
Paleoclimatology
Plants, Effect of climate on
Trees, Effect of climate on
Weather
See also subhead Climate under names of continents, countries, states, cities, etc.

Classification
The Koeppen climate classification system [computer program] A. Viterito. il *Weatherwise* 40:160-1 Je '87
Climate and health *See* Weather—Mental and physiological effects
Climate models *See* Meteorological models
Climate-ocean interaction *See* Ocean-atmosphere interaction
Climate-solar relationships *See* Sun and meteorology
Climatic changes
See also
El Niño (Ocean current)
Greenhouse effect
International Geosphere-Biosphere Program
Nuclear winter
Earthly belches perturb the weather [effect of volcanoes] I. Teinowitz. il map *U S News World Rep* 103:65+ D 7 '87
Impact of deforestation on local weather. *Sea Front* 33:64 Ja/F '87
Milankovitch climate cycles through the ages. R. A. Kerr. il *Science* 235:973-4 F 27 '87
Probing the permafrost [work of Arthur H. Lachenbruch and B. Vaughn Marshall] il *Sci Am* 256:62 F '87
Volcanic history in the Aleutian arc [research by Thomas P. Miller and Robert L. Smith] R. Monastersky. il *Sci News* 131:357 Je 6 '87
Weird weather patterns aren't forever [views of Robert Stinson] il *USA Today (Periodical)* 115:13 Ap '87
Climatology *See* Climate
Climbing
See also
Mountaineering
Snow and ice climbing
Climbing by animals *See* Animal locomotion
Climbing plants
See also
Clematis
Fatshedera
Hardenbergia
Passionflowers
Wax plants
Vines and arbors: a superb combination. T. A. Steadman. il *South Living* 22:38-9 Jl '87
Vines for every purpose. T. Martin. il *Ctry J* 14:54-9 Je '87

Training
See Plants—Training
Cline, George Edward
about
Man sues for paternity of child that was born to his ex-girlfriend now wed. por *Jet* 71:15 Ja 26 '87
Clinical Homecare Corporation
From nurse to medical-supply executive [K. Parker] J. Giambanco. il pors *Work Woman* 12:77-8+ Ag '87
Clinical laboratories *See* Medical laboratories
Clinical thermometers *See* Thermometers, Clinical
Clinics *See* Health facilities
Clinics, Legal *See* Law firms
Clinton, Bill, 1946-
about
Whistling Dixie. pors *Time* 129:32 Ap 6 '87
Clinton, Gary
about
Itty Bitty monster hits. J. Culpepper and S. Dark. il pors *Nations Bus* 75:58 Jl '87
Clinton, Jean
about
Itty Bitty monster hits. J. Culpepper and S. Dark. il pors *Nations Bus* 75:58 Jl '87
Clinton (Md.)
Crime
D.C. mayor's mother-in-law pleads guilty to arson [P. L. Harris] *Jet* 72:8 Jl 13 '87

Clip-on watches See Watches
Clipper ships
See also
Neptune's Car (Clipper ship)
Cliques See Groups (Sociology)
Clive Museum (Wales)
A passage from India. K. Nurse. il *Hist Today* 37:2-3 S '87
Clock industry
See also
E. Howard & Company
Howard Clock Products, Inc.
Clocks
See also
Astronomical clocks
Beeping the faith [Prayer Times Clock and international lunar date line calculations for Moslem travelers] map *Sci Am* 256:74 Mr '87
Build a clock and create an heirloom [kit clocks] B. Gould. il *Workbench* 43:42+ Ja/F '87
Clock kits for every taste and budget . . . il *Workbench* 43:48-9 Ja/F '87
Kuempel wall clock [kit] P. Barry. il *Fam Handyman* 37:50-1 Ap '87
Quartz mantel clock. M. Selwood. il *Workbench* 43:22 My/Je '87

Collectors and collecting
Collecting French clocks. M. Forrest. il *Antiques Collect Hobbies* 91:24-8 F '87
Clocks, Electronic
Build a clock board for your PC. V. D. Martin. il *Radio-Electron* 58 ComputerDigest:97-100 Mr '87
TSM 201 clock module. il *Radio-Electron* 58:122-3 N '87
Clodagh, Ross & Williams Inc.
Partners in the next wave. il *Vogue* 177:206 My '87
Clofazimine
New drug against leprosy. *FDA Consum* 21:2 Mr '87
Clog plant See Hypocyrta
Clogston, A. M.
Applied research: key to innovation. bibl f *Science* 235:12-13 Ja 2 '87
Clones (Biology)
See also
Monoclonal antibodies
Clonal analysis of human colorectal tumors [use of restriction fragment length polymorphisms] E. R. Fearon and others. bibl f il *Science* 238:193-7 O 9 '87
Clonal gene therapy: transplanted mouse fibroblast clones express human α1-antitrypsin gene in vivo. R. I. Garver, Jr. and others. bibl f il *Science* 237:762-4 Ag 14 '87
Clonal restriction boundaries in Xenopus embryos shown with two intracellular lineage tracers. P. Sheard and M. Jacobson. bibl f il *Science* 236:851-4 My 15 '87
Cloned gene of rickettsia rickettsii surface antigen: candidate vaccine for Rocky Mountain spotted fever. G. A. McDonald and others. bibl f il *Science* 235:83-5 Ja 2 '87
Cloning and detection of DNA from a nonculturable plant pathogenic mycoplasma-like organism. B. C. Kirkpatrick and others. bibl f il *Science* 238:197-200 O 9 '87
Cloning of complementary DNA for GAP-43, a neuronal growth-related protein. L. R. Karns and others. bibl f il *Science* 236:597-600 My 1 '87
Cloning of genomic and complementary DNA from Shaker, a putative potassium channel gene from Drosophila. D. M. Papazian and others. bibl f il *Science* 237:749-53 Ag 14 '87
Cloning of human mineralocorticoid receptor complementary DNA: structural and functional kinship with the glucocorticoid receptor. J. L. Arriza and others. bibl f il *Science* 237:268-75 Jl 17 '87
Cloning of large segments of exogenous DNA into yeast by means of artificial chromosome vectors. D. T. Burke and others. bibl f il *Science* 236:806-12 My 15 '87
Cloning, sequencing, and expression of the gene coding for the human platelet α2-adrenergic receptor. B. K. Kobilka and others. bibl f il *Science* 238:650-6 O 30 '87
Derivation of clones close to *met* by preparative field inversion gel electrophoresis. F. Michiels and others. bibl f il *Science* 236:1305-8 Je 5 '87
The fragile X site in somatic cell hybrids: an approach for molecular cloning of fragile sites [cover story] S. T. Warren and others. bibl f il *Science* 237:420-3 Jl 24 '87

Human CSF-1: molecular cloning and expression of 4-kb cDNA encoding the human urinary protein. G. G. Wong and others. bibl f il *Science* 235:1504-8 Mr 20 '87
Identification of putative human T cell receptor δ complementary DNA clones. S. Hata and others. bibl f il *Science* 238:678-82 O 30 '87
Immunochemical proof that a novel rearranging gene encodes the T cell receptor δ subunit. H. Band and others. bibl f il *Science* 238:682-4 O 30 '87
Isolation of an olfactory cDNA: similarity to retinol-binding protein suggests a role in olfaction. K.-H. Lee and others. bibl f il *Science* 235:1053-6 F 27 '87
Molecular cloning and expression of a human B-cell growth factor gene in Escherichia coli. S. Sharma and others. bibl f il *Science* 235:1489-92 Mr 20 '87
Molecular cloning of complementary DNA encoding the avian receptor for vitamin D. D. P. McDonnell and others. bibl f il *Science* 235:1214-17 Mr 6 '87
Clones (Botany)
Artificial seed breakthrough [work of Dennis Gray] *USA Today (Periodical)* 115:7 Je '87
Clonidine
Hot flash! [use of clonidine transdermal patches to counter menopausal flashes] P. McCarthy. *Health* 19:29 N '87
Cloninger, C. Robert
Neurogenetic adaptive mechanisms in alcoholism. bibl f il *Science* 236:410-16 Ap 24 '87
Cloonan, James B.
about
The "nonprofit" with the fat profit margin. R. Simon. il por *Forbes* 140:37-8 N 2 '87
Clos Pegase Winery
The Graves of wrath [M. Graves' design] D. Ketcham. il *Vogue* 177:110 Ap '87
A shrine to wine [Napa Valley winery designed by M. Graves] M. Filler. il *House Gard* 159:154-7+ S '87
Close, Glenn
about
Crazy Alex, foxy Glenn. C. McGuigan. il pors *Newsweek* 110:76-7 O 12 '87
Getting Close to stardom. D. Goodgame. il por *Time* 130:81 N 16 '87
Glenn Close. por *People Wkly* 28:80-1 D 28 '87-Ja 4 '88
Close air support
AFTI F-16 testbed to evaluate sensors for close air support. il *Aviat Week Space Technol* 127:76 N 2 '87
Army's analysis of LHX helicopters will omit close air support issue. *Aviat Week Space Technol* 126:18 F 16 '87
Battle brews over follow-on close air support aircraft [successor to A-10 Thunderbolt] *Aviat Week Space Technol* 126:19 F 2 '87
The case against the Air Force [developing planes designed to deliver smart bombs behind enemy lines at the expense of providing close air support] R. Coram. il *Wash Mon* 19:17-24 Jl/Ag '87
Defense Dept. asks USAF to broaden design options for new CAS aircraft. il *Aviat Week Space Technol* 127:28-9 N 23 '87
Let the Army fly its own close air support. B. M. Greeley, Jr. *Aviat Week Space Technol* 126:11 F 9 '87
Speed, stealth, maneuverability sought for survivable close air support. B. M. Greeley, Jr. *Aviat Week Space Technol* 126:143+ Ap 27 '87
Study supports call for design of new close air support aircraft [Institute for Defense Analysis] J. D. Morrocco. il *Aviat Week Space Technol* 127:29-30 S 28 '87
USAF, Army grapple with key issues of close air support mission. B. M. Greeley, Jr. *Aviat Week Space Technol* 126:50-1+ Mr 23 '87
USAF, Defense Dept. reach compromise on new CAS aircraft. *Aviat Week Space Technol* 127:33 D 7 '87
USAF panel urges separate CAS, interdiction aircraft. *Aviat Week Space Technol* 127:22-3 Jl 27 '87
USAF seeks designs for close air support successor to A-10. *Aviat Week Space Technol* 126:37 Je 22 '87
Close corporations See Closely held corporations
Close-Out Merchandise Buyers Co. See C.O.M.B. Co.
Close-up lenses See Lenses, Photographic
Close-up photography See Photography, Close-up
Closed Circuit Aquatic Television (Submarine) See Oceanographic submersibles
Closed ecological systems
See also
Biosphere II

Closed-end funds *See* Investment trusts

Closely held corporations

The 400 largest private companies in the U.S. il *Forbes* 140:150-2+ D 14 '87

The freest enterprise. P. Glastris. *Wash Mon* 19:51-4 F '87

Taxation

Congress, spare us this reform. G. W. Padwe. il *Nations Bus* 75:58 Ag '87

Closets

The closet case—set your clothes straight. W. Smolen. il *Mademoiselle* 93:174+ Ap '87

Do it yourself super organized closet. il *Seventeen* 46:202-3 Ap '87

How effective are cedar chests and closets? il *Workbench* 43:22 N/D '87

Put every inch of closet space to work. S. Ross. il *Fam Handyman* 37:43-6 D '87

Shape up your closet. il *Redbook* 168:116-19 Ap '87

Clotfelter, Charles T.

Life after tax reform [cover story] il *Change* 19:12-18 Jl/Ag '87

Cloth *See* Textile fabrics

Clothes cupboards *See* Armoires

Clothes dryers

Clothes dryers. il *Consum Rep* 52:75-9 D '87

Clothes washing machines *See* Washing machines

Clothestime Inc.

Buy cheap. C. Siler. il por *Forbes* 140:109 Jl 27 '87

Clothier, Peter, 1936-

Douglas Cramer: passionate perfectionist. il por *Art News* 86:146-50 Summ '87

New-Age visions: Zangezi goes west. il *Art Am* 75:25+ My '87

Clothing, Cold weather

See also

Coats

Handwarmers (Clothing)

4 surprising facts about what works to keep you warm. il *Glamour* 85:51 Ja '87

Bates Thermal Vest [for motorcyclists] il *Cycle* 38:74 Ja '87

How to stay warm on the slopes, rink, track and trail. J. Mattera. il *Glamour* 85:106 D '87

Inside the ice cube [testing winter motorcycle riding suits] P. Gordon. il *Cycle* 38:31-7 Ja '87

New wrinkles in old clothing. M. Scherer. il *Sierra* 72:120-4 Ja/F '87

Clothing, Protective

See also

Arms and armor

Clothing, Cold weather

Clothing, Waterproof

Gloves

Helmets

Knee pads

Dressed for excess. il *Esquire* 107:78-81 Ja '87

Personal protection from pesticides. C. Tevis. il *Success Farm* 85 no1:26D-26E Ja '87

Clothing, Waterproof

Coat views [women's raincoats] il *Vogue* 177:274 Ap '87

Hondaline one-piece rainsuit [for motorcyclists] il *Cycle* 38:23 My '87

How to stay dry and look great when it rains. il *Glamour* 85:197-200 Mr '87

New life for waterproof/breathables. E. Perlman. *Skiing* 39:101 Spr '87

Splashy rain gear. il *Harpers Bazaar* 120:46-9 F '87

Waiting for rain [men's raincoats] R. La Ferla. il *N Y Times Mag* p60 Mr 1 '87

Walking in the rain. il *Prevention* 39:72-3+ Ap '87

Clothing and dress

See also

Bathing suits

Bathrobes

Clothing industry

Coats

Collars

Costume

Costume designers

Cuffs (Clothing)

Dress accessories

Fashion

Fashion designers

Fashion shows

Folding of clothes

Footwear

Fur coats, wraps, etc.

Gloves

Hats

Hosiery

Indians of South America—Costume and adornment

Jackets

Leather garments

Models (Persons)

Pants

Personal shoppers

Scarves

Sewing

Shawls

Shirts

Shorts (Clothing)

Shoulder pads

Skirts (Clothing)

Sleepwear

Sweaters

Tailoring

Underwear

Uniforms

Vests

Wedding clothes

Western wear

A cool hand [white suits] K. Madden. il *Vogue* 177:366+ Mr '87

Dish-towel chic [towels made into clothing] il *Good Housekeep* 205:126-7 Jl '87

Dos & don'ts. See issues of Glamour

The dress solution. il *Vogue* 177:330-5 My '87

Dress to dazzle during the holidays: best advice from some top professionals. il *Glamour* 85:55 D '87

Fashion failures: don't fall for them. il *Teen* 31:102 Ap '87

Fashion questions. See issues of Glamour

Mergers & acquisitions: manstyle for women. il *Harpers Bazaar* 120:154-63 F '87

Metamorphosis [style according to your yin and yang; excerpt] D. Kibbe. il *Ladies Home J* 104:126-33 O '87

Multiple-choice dressing. il *Teen* 31:88-9 Ag '87

Only on Sunday [black women dressing to worship] il *Essence* 18:56-63 My '87

Party patter [evening dress] il *Teen* 31:74 N '87

The perfect vacation: a first-class beauty and fashion guide. L. J. Johnson. il *Ladies Home J* 104:110-17 Jl '87

Putting pizzazz into holiday dressing. il *Glamour* 85:45 Ja '87

Quality: how to spot it, why to buy it. il *Glamour* 85:202 S '87

Smart moves—nonstop style. il *Vogue* 177:322-33 Ap '87

Smart new fashion buys: clothes to wear in any season. il *Glamour* 85:74 Ag '87

The suit story. il *N Y Times Mag* p52-5 Ag 30 '87

What went wrong here? How to make it right. See issues of Mademoiselle

Businessmen

Business suits. il *Consum Rep* 52:172-7 D '87

The fabric of success [views of M. Levitt] W. Hoffer. il pors *Nations Bus* 75:53+ Jl '87

How to dress with style: a guide for the fifty plus man [interview with L. Fenton] il *50 Plus* 27:48-51 Mr '87

The proper business look. W. S. Wingo. il *Nations Bus* 75:42-3 Mr '87

Tweed business. R. La Ferla. il *N Y Times Mag* p82 S 27 '87

What is professional style? S. L. Hilliard. il *Black Enterp* 18:66-8+ Ag '87

Anecdotes, facetiae, satire, etc.

Suit-burning [rejection of corporate culture] *New Yorker* 63:24 Ag 31 '87

Businesswomen

42 ways to look better, feel more comfortable at work. il *Glamour* 85:199-202 O '87

Advertising success in Minneapolis [M. Betsch at Campbell-Mithun] J. Giambanco. il pors *Work Woman* 12:117-18+ O '87

The best of the new career clothes. il *Work Woman* 12:57+ Mr '87

Business suits. il *Consum Rep* 52:172-7 D '87

Career builders: the pay-as-you-go wardrobe. il *Mademoiselle* 93:38+ Ja '87

Checklist for working women. *Redbook* 169:83 Ag '87

Clothes strategies. J. Mattera. See issues of Glamour beginning October 1986

Confident looks from head to toe [cover story; special section] il *Work Woman* 12:57+ S '87

Connecticut's on-air authority [TV anchorwoman J. Peckinpaugh] J. Giambanco. il pors *Work Woman* 12:91-2+ Ja '87

Clothing and dress—Businesswomen—_cont._

A crash course in suit selection. P. Kripke. _Work Woman_ 12:118 N '87

Crossing the magic threshold [creating a look of affluence and self-assurance] J. Ciabattari. il _Work Woman_ 12:94-7+ Je '87

The death of dress for success. T. Minsky. il _Mademoiselle_ 93:308-9+ S '87

Dressed for excess [job interviews; study by Robert A. Baron] S. Walton. _Psychol Today_ 21:8 Ag '87

Dresses for success. il _Work Woman_ 12:117-20 Ap '87

Dressing in the rich tradition [banker E. Patterson] W. Konrad. il pors _Work Woman_ 12:83-4+ Jl '87

Executive quality [A. Magnin's job dressing strategy] il por _Harpers Bazaar_ 120:54+ Mr '87

Exercising options in Florida [Y. Rubio, public relations director of Safety Harbor Spa] J. Giambanco. il pors _Work Woman_ 12:105-6+ Je '87

From nurse to medical-supply executive [K. Parker] J. Giambanco. il pors _Work Woman_ 12:77-8+ Ag '87

How to get more mileage out of your interview suit. J. Mattera. il _Glamour_ 85:146 My '87

Investing in a confident style [broker K. Reiman] J. Giambanco. il pors _Work Woman_ 12:103-4+ D '87

Jewelers woo the working woman. S. Caminiti. il _Fortune_ 115:71-2 Je 8 '87

L.A.'s eclectic entertainment executive [B. Mutchnick] J. Giambanco. il pors _Work Woman_ 12:128+ Ap '87

The look that got the job. M. L. O'Hana. il _Ladies Home J_ 104:138-41 N '87

The new success looks: young & easy [L. Coffey's look] il por _Harpers Bazaar_ 120:76 O '87

A new work style. il _Essence_ 17:58-63 Mr '87

A new working advantage . . . il _Vogue_ 177:276-85 Ag '87

Perfect suits: the million-dollar checks. il _Work Woman_ 12:98-101 O '87

Personal elegance with the look of power. il _Work Woman_ 12:106-7 O '87

Post-grad job-smart dressing. il _Harpers Bazaar_ 120:100-3 Je '87

Professional power [P. Crespi's dressing ideas] il pors _Harpers Bazaar_ 120:68+ Mr '87

Suitcase survival: how to dress smart, on the road. il _Glamour_ 85:139-42+ F '87

What is professional style? S. L. Hilliard. il _Black Enterp_ 18:66-8+ Ag '87

When toys mean business [marketing manager C. Irving of Mattel] J. Giambanco. il pors _Work Woman_ 12:133-4+ My '87

Which look got the job? il _Glamour_ 85:304-5 Ap '87

Care

Fabric care that works [excerpt from The clothing care handbook] K. Robinson. _Work Woman_ 12:112 S '87

How to care for spring clothes. il _Ladies Home J_ 104:80+ Ap '87

Treat your clothes right. K. Beckett. il _Redbook_ 169:172-3 S '87

An unwrinkle in time . . . A. Oshins. il _Work Woman_ 12:94+ Mr '87

Celebrities

Dressing for Oscar [excerpt from Oscar dearest] P. H. Brown and J. Pinkston. il _Life_ 10:89-92 Ap '87

Style '87—dash and trash [cover story] il _People Wkly_ 28:48-58+ N 16 '87

Worn in the USA: where big looks are born. G. Sikes. il _Mademoiselle_ 93:148-51+ D '87

Children

See also
Oshkosh B'Gosh, Inc.
Special Clothes (Firm)

Autumn is in the air. A. Skinner. il _N Y Times Mag_ p34-9+ Ag 16 '87

Baby Steps are the socks of choice for toddlers who don't want to hit the skids early [marketed by V. Reisman and R. Lerner] il _People Wkly_ 28:183 N 16 '87

The children's closet [Christmas gifts] _New Yorker_ 63:132-4+ N 16 '87

Dress without stress. C. Loomis. il _Parents_ 62:15 F '87

Fireproof kids' clothes. C. Loomis. il _Parents_ 62:13 Jl '87

Nice and easy. A. Skinner. il _N Y Times Mag_ p56-61+ Mr 8 '87

Shopping without tears (or tantrums) [shopping with and for children] L. Schnurnberger. il _Parents_ 62:88-92 My '87

Some do's and don't's for dressing kids [ski clothes] K. Brizzolara. _Skiing_ 39:136 Ja '87

Homemakers

Good housedressing. H. Brubach. il _Vogue_ 177:337+ Ap '87

Infants

See also
Diapers

Lawyers

A case for the unconventional [S. Handler] J. Giambanco. il pors _Work Woman_ 12:80+ F '87

Leasing and renting

See also
One Night Stand (Firm)

Lifeguards

I dreamed I saved a swimmer in my Maidenform pantyhose [protection from jellyfish] S. Brownlee. il _Discover_ 8:52 Ag '87

Men

See also
Ascots
Bathing suits
Clothing and dress—Businessmen
Clothing stores
Hats
Neckties
Shirts
Suspenders
Sweaters
Vests

'Air' Jordan rates high marks in men's fashion. por _Jet_ 71:29 F 23 '87

Altering tradition [suits for spring] R. La Ferla. il _N Y Times Mag_ p54 Ja 18 '87

Boy toys! il _Mademoiselle_ 93:218-21 Ag '87

The Esquire Collection [special section] il _Esquire_ 107:F1+ Mr '87

The Italians. R. La Ferla. il _N Y Times Mag_ p35 Ag 2 '87

Little shopping horrors: getting your guy to buy. P. Mehlman. il _Mademoiselle_ 93:170+ Ap '87

A man's stylebook. K. J. Gross and J. Mather. il _Esquire_ 108:133-51 S '87

Role models. R. La Ferla. il _N Y Times Mag_ p128 D 6 '87

The shape of suits to come. G. B. Boyer. il _Esquire_ 108:130-5 O '87

Summer essentials. R. La Ferla. il _N Y Times Mag_ p36 My 24 '87

Three-button revival [suits] R. La Ferla. il _N Y Times Mag_ p58 Ap 12 '87

To sew a fine seam [hand tailoring of men's suits] R. La Ferla. il _N Y Times Mag_ p50+ Je 7 '87

Anecdotes, facetiae, satire, etc.

Why can't men dress themselves? M. Policastro. il _50 Plus_ 27:56+ S '87

Presidential candidates

Winning looks for November. il _Esquire_ 108:107-13 N '87

Psychological aspects

See also
Sex and fashion

Rock musicians

Caught in the act: the secret lives of rock 'n' roll style stealers. il _Seventeen_ 46:124-9 Jl '87

Clothes make the musician. J. Pareles. il _Mademoiselle_ 93:124+ Ap '87

Rock style: 1967-1987 [cover story; special issue] il _Roll Stone_ p74-7+ Ap 23 '87

Size

Body-smart summer fashion. il _Ladies Home J_ 104:104-7 Je '87

Clothes that fight figure flaws. il _Mademoiselle_ 93:40+ F '87

Executive dressing in size 16 and up. G. Bakoulis. _Work Woman_ 12:117 S '87

Fat pride. H. Brubach. il _Atlantic_ 260:111-13 N '87

Fit to be tried; In the height of fashion. il _Teen_ 31:56-9 Ja '87

How to dress 10 lbs. thinner. il _Glamour_ 85:150-7 Jl '87

In fashion, bigger is now beautiful [stores catering to larger size women] J. Castro. il _Time_ 129:76-7 My 4 '87

Petite power for night. il _Harpers Bazaar_ 120:118-25 Ja '87

Petites: short & sexy. pors _Harpers Bazaar_ 120:400-3 S '87

Shape your shape. il _Redbook_ 168:76-9 Ja '87

Think you're too fat? [with introd. by Melody Trask] N. Roberts. pors _McCalls_ 114:34, 38-9 S '87

Clothing and dress—Size—cont.

Anecdotes, facetiae, satire, etc.

Why I'm not wearing miniskirts, I think. K. Fury. il *Work Woman* 12:184 N '87

Social aspects

See also

Sex and fashion

Sports clothes

See also

Custom Jockeys' Apparel (Firm)

The 1987 guide to huntingwear [special section] il *Field Stream* 92:75+ S '87

Aerostich Wind Scarf and Wind Triangle [for motorcyclists] il *Cycle* 38:87 Mr '87

The athlete's new clothes. M. L. K. Doyle and K. J. Gross. il *Esquire* 107:155-7 My '87

Bates Thermal Vest [for motorcyclists] il *Cycle* 38:74 Ja '87

Bicycle high-gear. il *Harpers Bazaar* 120:28-31 Ap '87

Blending in [hunting or fishing] N. Strung; J. Doggett. il *Field Stream* 92:64-6+ O '87

Camo: latest cover ups [hunters] S. Link. il *Outdoor Life* 179:68-9+ Ap '87

Colors rally on the court [tennis fashions] il *Women's Sports Fitness* 9:60 Ap '87

Dainese Lucky and Monza leathers [for motorcyclists] il *Cycle* 38:52-3+ S '87

Fitness now [exercise gear] il *Vogue* 177:76 Jl '87

A guide to smart shopping [skiwear] H. Brooks. il *Skiing* 40:165+ S '87

High-tech workout wear: how to choose the right clothes at the right price. il *Glamour* 85:298 F '87

Hondaline one-piece rainsuit [for motorcyclists] il *Cycle* 38:23 My '87

How to stay warm on the slopes, rink, track and trail. J. Mattera. il *Glamour* 85:106 D '87

Inside the ice cube [testing winter motorcycle riding suits] P. Gordon. il *Cycle* 38:31-7 Ja '87

Knit one, hunt too [sweaters for the outdoorsman] K. Etling. bibl il *Outdoor Life* 180:96-7+ N '87

New life for waterproof/breathables [ski clothes] E. Perlman. il *Skiing* 39:101 Spr '87

New wrinkles in old clothing. M. Scherer. il *Sierra* 72:120-4 Ja/F '87

Orange helps bring 'em back alive [hunting clothes] R. Deigh. il *U S News World Rep* 103:70 D 14 '87

Outdoor style. il *Health* 19:33-7 Ag '87

Pedaling a new look [cycling wear] G. Carroll. il *Newsweek* 110:47 Jl 27 '87

Quiet clothes make the man [quiet hunting clothes] T. Huggler. il *Outdoor Life* 180:84-6+ Jl '87

The right tack [men's yachting and sailing clothes] R. La Ferla. il *N Y Times Mag* p44 F 1 '87

Risky business. il *Harpers Bazaar* 120:86-91+ Jl '87

A short guide to long johns [ski underwear] E. Perlman. il *Skiing* 39:87-9 F '87

The shorts story. C. Cummins. il *Women's Sports Fitness* 9:34-7+ Ap '87

Snow job [skiwear] il *Women's Sports Fitness* 9:24 S '87

Some do's and don't's for dressing kids [ski clothes] K. Brizzolara. il *Skiing* 39:136 Ja '87

What the terms mean [fabrics for skiwear] H. Brooks. il *Skiing* 40:178+ S '87

White-water wear. W. Withers. il *Women's Sports Fitness* 9:56 Ap '87

Students

Campus fashions: what today's college students are wearing. M. M. Horowitz. il *USA Today (Periodical)* 115:64-8 Mr '87

Dress code unrest: a peek at the past. il *Teen* 31:100 O '87

Clothing industry

See also

Albert Nipon, Inc.

Calvin Klein Industries

Cherokee Group

CP Shades (Firm)

Custom Shop Shirtmakers Inc.

Dan River Inc.

Esprit de Corp. (Firm)

Garment workers

Gitano (Firm)

Guess?, Inc.

H₂O Swimwear Ltd.

Halston Enterprises

Hartmarx Corporation

Jordache Enterprises Inc.

Kellwood Co.

Levi Strauss & Co.

Liz Claiborne, Inc.

Neuma Inc.

Oshkosh B'Gosh, Inc.

Polo/Ralph Lauren, Inc.

Special Clothes (Firm)

Tailors

VF Corp.

Warnaco Inc.

Ruth Kavenoff liked what she saw in her microscope, so she's putting genes and germs on her T-shirts. il por *People Wkly* 28:133 N 9 '87

Who's who in American style: the people, the success, the impact. G. Y. Dryansky. il *Vogue* 177:171-4+ O '87

Acquisitions and mergers

A big deal for little Beeba's [J. C. Penney's investment] G. G. Marcial. *Bus Week* p61 Jl 27 '87

Advertising

BlueJean-Luc Godard. H. A. Rodchenko. il *Film Comment* 23:2+ N/D '87

Ethical aspects

Does Guess have a friend in the IRS? [Guess vs. Jordache] R. Behar. il map *Forbes* 140:146-50+ N 16 '87

The IRS mess [corruption charges surrounding Guess, Inc. feud with Jordache] R. Behar. il *Forbes* 140:8 N 30 '87

Export-import trade

See also

Beeba's Creations Inc.

Consumer protection? [Textile Apparel Trade Act] J. W. Merline. il *Consum Res Mag* 70:38 O '87

The locomotive needs help [Jamaica and the U.S.] A. D. Frank. por *Forbes* 139:100 Ja 26 '87

Finance

Apparel, shoes and textiles. E. Pomice. il *Forbes* 139:68-70 Ja 12 '87

History

The Garment Center [New York City] J. Weidman. il *N Y* 20:90 D 21-28 '87

Licensing agreements

'Eefningwear' for America [Soviet designer V. Zaitsev's fashions to be licensed in the U.S.] A. Miller. il por *Newsweek* 110:64 O 19 '87

Marketing

See also

Clothing industry—Licensing agreements

Can you find a swimsuit to buy in July? il *Glamour* 85:40 Jl '87

Could you wear this star's clothes? [celebrities' clothing lines] B. Zehme. il *Mademoiselle* 93:60 F '87

What's in a name? Store brands offer the best value for your money. il *Glamour* 85:84 Je '87

Canada

See also

Sun Ice Ltd.

France

See also

Chanel (Firm)

Christian Dior (Firm)

Groupe Financière Agache

Pierre Balmain (Firm)

High fashion, high finance—high drama. F. J. Comes. il *Bus Week* p132-3 Jl 20 '87

Italy

See also

Benetton SpA

Krizia SpA

Salvatore Ferragamo SpA

Jamaica

The locomotive needs help. A. D. Frank. por *Forbes* 139:100 Ja 26 '87

Japan

See also

Kashiyama & Co., Ltd.

Latin America

Fashion with a flair [Latin American couturiers] C. Healy. il *Américas* 39:2-7 My/Je '87

Soviet Union

'Eefningwear' for America [Soviet designer V. Zaitsev's fashions to be licensed in the U.S.] A. Miller. il por *Newsweek* 110:64 O 19 '87

Red Square chic. G. Perrelli and E. Regazzoni. il *World Press Rev* 34:19-20 Ap '87

United States

See Clothing industry

Western Europe

High fashion, high finance—high drama. F. J. Comes. il *Bus Week* p132-3 Jl 20 '87

Clothing stores

See also

Aca Joe (Firm)

Clothing stores—See also—*cont.*
   Clothestime Inc.
   Gap, Inc.
   Hemisphere (Firm)
   Marui Co. Ltd.
   One Night Stand (Firm)
   One Price Clothing Stores
   Petrie Stores Corp.
   Polo/Ralph Lauren, Inc.
   Workers for Freedom (Firm)
The age of McFashion [specialty stores] J. Conant. il *Newsweek* 110:66-8 S 28 '87
Franchising: T-shirt on your back. M. Whittemore. il *Nations Bus* 75:58-9 My '87
In fashion, bigger is now beautiful [stores catering to larger size women] J. Castro. il *Time* 129:76-7 My 4 '87
Passing through customs [made-to-order clothes] G. B. Boyer. il *Esquire* 108:218-20+ S '87
Setting the proper scene [interiors of men's stores] R. La Ferla. il *N Y Times Mag* p60-1+ Jl 19 '87
Some stores have all the fun [men's stores] il *Esquire* 107:F56-F60 Mr '87
Toddlers in $90 suits? You gotta be kidding. J. B. Levine and A. Dunkin. il *Bus Week* p52+ S 21 '87
Clothing workers *See* Garment workers
Clotting of blood *See* Blood—Coagulation
Cloudgate Taipei Contemporary Dance Theatre
Reviews:
   Performances at the Lyric Theatre in Hong Kong. D. Ries. *Dance Mag* 61:99 Ja '87
Clouds
   See also
   Noctilucent clouds
Billow clouds, wind pressure. T. Schlatter. il *Weatherwise* 40:156-8 Je '87
Cloud conundrums [possible methane plumes in Soviet Arctic; cover story] S. Weisburd. il map *Sci News* 131:204-6 Mr 28 '87
Effect of ship-stack effluents on cloud reflectivity. J. A. Coakley, Jr. and others. bibl f il *Science* 237:1020-2 Ag 28 '87
Hoodwinked over Oklahoma [flying in the clouds] M. Coan. il *Flying* 114:104-5 Ap '87
Out of control. J. M. McClellan. il *Flying* 114:48-50+ Jl '87
U.S. weather waxing cloudy. *Sci News* 131:200 Mr 28 '87
UFO update [August 12, 1986 cloud formed by liquid fuel released from Japanese rocket] J. E. Oberg. il *Omni* 9:83 Ja '87
What your windshield shows about the clouds [origin of clouds and dew] R. Williams. il *Weatherwise* 40:260-1 O '87
Clouds, Intergalactic *See* Matter, Interstellar
Clouds, Magellanic *See* Magellanic clouds
Clough, Charles
   about
A fan of smokestack America [interview] A. E. Serwer. il por *Fortune* 116:192 O 26 '87
Clouse, John
   about
Jet-sitters. il pors *Life* 10:91-4 My '87
Kings of the road. B. Rice. il pors *50 Plus* 27:22-5+ Mr '87
The race to visit every country on earth. B. Rice. il *50 Plus* 27:17 Ap '87
Cloutier, Chantal
   about
Total communication. F. Greenberg. il por *Work Woman* 12:102-3 My '87
Cloutier (Firm)
Total communication [C. Cloutier's styling agency office] F. Greenberg. il por *Work Woman* 12:102-3 My '87
Clownfish
The anemone is not its enemy. D. G. Fautin. il *Natl Wildl* 25:22-5 O/N '87
      Larvae
   See Larvae
Clowns
   See also
   Irwin, Bill
Chester the clown: a brief autobiography. K. Cummins. il *Child Today* 16:14 Ja/F '87
Clowns [ballet] See Ballet reviews—Single works
Clozapine
Sanity saver [study by Herbert Y. Meltzer] M. Mintzer. il *Health* 19:17 S '87
Schizophrenia: new hope from an old drug. B. Bower. *Sci News* 131:324 My 23 '87

Club Corp. of America
Cheap capital. P. Newcomb. il por *Forbes* 140:154 D 14 '87
Club Méditerranée SA
Now Club Med wants an antidote for competition. A. Dunkin. il *Bus Week* p120-1 N 2 '87
Club Nouveau (Musical group)
Club Nouveau Svengali Jay King boasts a platinum hit and a double-platinum ego. S. Dougherty. il pors *People Wkly* 27:109-10 Ap 27 '87
Club Nouveau's King-size hit. R. Hoerburger. il *Roll Stone* p15 My 7 '87
Let's dance! Top tunemakers. il por *Teen* 31:55 Jl '87
Clubs
   See also
   Astronomical societies
   Automobile clubs
   Club Corp. of America
   Collectors and collecting—Clubs and societies
   Computer clubs
   Discotheques
   Fan clubs
   Health clubs
   Investment clubs
   Literary clubs and societies
   Political clubs and associations
   Radio clubs
   Rotary International
   Sports clubs
   Warehouse clubs
   Wine societies
   Yacht clubs
Boys continue to be boys. B. Kallen. il *Forbes* 139 Ann Directory:93-4+ Ap 27 '87
Getting clubbed [men's clubs and sex discrimination] *New Repub* 196:4+ Mr 16 '87
A sense of belonging. W. McGowan. il *N Y Times Mag* p46-8 Ag 23 '87
A small moral quandary [dining at men's club that bars women] O. Friedrich. il *Time* 129:94 Mr 16 '87
Tap, tap, tap on the clubhouse door [men-only clubs] L. Rosellini. il *U S News World Rep* 102:72+ My 11 '87
Cluchey, Rick
   about
Columnist Barbara Bladen sees her love story with a convict flower onscreen in Weeds. J. Stark. il pors *People Wkly* 28:83-4+ D 7 '87
Clumsiness *See* Awkwardness
Cluster housing
Clustered for leisure: the changing home [cover story] C. Vogel. il *N Y Times Mag* p12-17+ Je 28 '87
Cluster theory (Nuclear physics)
The coupled-cluster method. R. F. Bishop and H. Kümmel. bibl f il *Phys Today* 40:52-60 Mr '87
Covalent group IV atomic clusters. W. L. Brown and others. bibl f il *Science* 235:860-5 F 20 '87
Explaining carbon-cluster magic numbers [structure for 11-atom carbon molecule; research by James A. Van Vechten and Douglas A. Keszler] S. Weisburd. il *Sci News* 132:100-1 Ag 15 '87
Clusters, Galactic *See* Galaxies
Clutches (Machinery)
   See also
   Automobiles—Clutches
CML Group, Inc.
This 'boutique' looks like a buy. G. G. Marcial. *Bus Week* p80 Mr 2 '87
CMOs (Collateralized mortgage obligations) *See* Mortgage bonds and notes
CMOS integrated circuits *See* Integrated circuits
CMV *See* Cytomegalovirus
CNES *See* Centre National d'Études Spatiales (France)
CNN *See* Cable News Network
Co-op colleges *See* Business and education
Coach House (New York, N.Y.: Restaurant) *See* New York (N.Y.)—Restaurants, nightclubs, bars, etc.
Coachella Valley (Calif.)
Lizard and the links [Coachella Valley fringe-toed lizard] D. Holing. il map *Audubon* 89:38-42+ N '87
Coaches (Academic) *See* Tutors and tutoring
Coaches (Athletics)
   See also
   Baseball coaches
   Basketball coaches
   Football coaches
   Tennis coaches
And where are the black head coaches? N. Cohen. *Sport Mag* 78:6 Ag '87

Coaches (Athletics)—*cont.*
Black coaches remain scarce in college ranks. D. J. Dent. il *Black Enterp* 18:34 D '87
Strike one and you're out [racism in sports] L. Rosellini. il *U S News World Rep* 103:52-7 Jl 27 '87
Women who coach. G. Hechinger. il *Glamour* 85:238-9 D '87
Coagulation of blood *See* Blood—Coagulation
Coakley, James A., Jr., and others
Effect of ship-stack effluents on cloud reflectivity. bibl f il *Science* 237:1020-2 Ag 28 '87
Coal
Lung cancer and indoor air pollution in Xuan Wei, China [burning of smoky coal] J. L. Mumford and others. bibl f il map *Science* 235:217-20 Ja 9 '87
Prices
Who will decide the future of coal? [address, April 16, 1987] A. W. Dahlberg. *Vital Speeches Day* 53:562-4 Jl 1 '87
Coal-fired electric power plants *See* Electric plants
Coal fly ash *See* Ashes
Coal gasification
A mild alternative? T. Beardsley. *Sci Am* 257:37+ D '87
Off-design performance of power plants: an integrated gasification combined-cycle example. M. R. Erbes and others. bibl f il *Science* 237:379-83 Jl 24 '87
Coal industry
See also
Coal mines and mining
Collective bargaining—Coal industry
Nacco Industries
Peter Kiewit Sons, Inc.
Environmental aspects
Dubious mining operations continue at New River. *Natl Parks* 61:40 S/O '87
Rethinking energy security: the case for coal in the United States. H. H. Landsberg. il *Environment* 29:18-20+ Jl/Ag '87
Finance
Coal. K. Hannon. il *Forbes* 139:97-8 Ja 12 '87
Who will decide the future of coal? [address, April 16, 1987] A. W. Dahlberg. *Vital Speeches Day* 53:562-4 Jl 1 '87
Laws and regulations
See Strip mining—Laws and regulations
United States
See Coal industry
Coal laws and regulations
See also
Strip mining—Laws and regulations
Coal miners
See also
Collective bargaining—Coal industry
United Mine Workers of America
Coal mines and mining
See also
Coal industry
Coal supply
Strip mining
Environmental aspects
See Coal industry—Environmental aspects
Laws and regulations
See Strip mining—Laws and regulations
Siberia (Soviet Union)
Vladimir Shityikov mines 'black gold' (and the good life) in some of the world's harshest weather. M. Brower. il pors *People Wkly* 27:61+ Ap 6 '87
West Virginia
Dubious mining operations continue at New River. *Natl Parks* 61:40 S/O '87
Coal stoves *See* Stoves
Coal supply
Rethinking energy security: the case for coal in the United States. H. H. Landsberg. il *Environment* 29:18-20+ Jl/Ag '87
Coale, John P.
about
In the wake of a tragic hotel fire, disaster attorneys seek compensation for the victims—and for themselves. J. S. Kunen. il pors *People Wkly* 27:36-8 Ja 26 '87
Coalition of Advocates for the Rights of the Infirm Elderly
A voice for the frail elderly. J. Alwang. il *Aging* no355:10-13 '87
Coalition to Preserve the American Copyright Tradition
Coalition is formed to fight U.S. joining Berne convention. H. Fields. *Publ Wkly* 232:13 S 11 '87
Coan, Marc
Hoodwinked over Oklahoma. il *Flying* 114:104-5 Ap '87

Coan, Peter M.
about
Controversial bio of singer Harry Chapin released by Ashley. *Publ Wkly* 232:76-7 O 2 '87
Coard, Bernard
about
Some fell slow and some fell fast. G. Wagner. *Natl Rev* 39:32-3 Je 5 '87
Coast changes
Beaches and barrier islands. R. Dolan and H. F. Lins. il map *Sci Am* 257:68-73+ Jl '87
The case of the vanishing beaches. R. A. Taylor. il *U S News World Rep* 102:33 Je 22 '87
"It can't happen to me". G. Reiger. il *Field Stream* 92:34+ Jl '87
Louisiana's bayou blues. F. Gibney. il map *Newsweek* 109:54-5 Je 22 '87
On the beach [erosion in Westhampton, Long Island] S. Weinstein. il *N Y* 20:21 Jl 20 '87
Our troubled coasts [cover story; special issue; with editorial comment by Michael W. Robbins] il *Oceans* 20:2, 8-53+ Mr/Ap '87
Shrinking shores [cover story] M. D. Lemonick. il maps *Time* 130:38-42+ Ag 10 '87
Coast Guard (U.S.) *See* United States. Coast Guard
Coastal (New York, N.Y.: Restaurant) *See* New York (N.Y.)—Restaurants, nightclubs, bars, etc.
Coastal Corporation
Jack Stanley's 30-year oil feud is sizzling [Coastal Corp's O. Wyatt stages hostile takeover of TransAmerican Natural Gas in bankruptcy court] J. R. Norman. il *Bus Week* p58-9 Ap 13 '87
Coastal disturbances [drama] See Howe, Tina
Coastal photography *See* Marine photography
Coastal protection *See* Shore protection
Coastal Zone Management Act *See* Shore protection—Laws and regulations
Coasts
See also
Atlantic coast
Fjords
Shore protection
Coated Sales Inc.
"This was a business of old men". B. Leonard. il por *Forbes* 139:120+ Mr 9 '87
Coates, Ruth Allison
Hurry up and love me [story] il *Teen* 31:42+ F '87
Coats, Dan
Should Congress approve the Fairness Doctrine? [excerpts from debate, June 3, 1987] *Congr Dig* 66:243+ O '87
Coats, Laura Jane
Marcella and the moon [story] il *Parents* 62:135-40 My '87
The oak tree [story] il *Parents* 62:125-6+ Ag '87
Coats
See also
Fur coats, wraps, etc.
Jackets
The pea coat. J. Berendt. il *Esquire* 108:32 N '87
Trenchcoats. il *Consum Rep* 52:538-45 S '87
Trenchcoats. il *Consum Rep* 52:168-72 D '87
Care
How to care for your coat. il *Good Housekeep* 205:238 S '87
Coats, Rain *See* Clothing, Waterproof
Cobb, Ann Porter, d. 1987
about
Obituary
Jet il por 72:52 Jl 20 '87
Cobb, Charles E.
Awash in change. il maps *Natl Geogr* 172:484-513 O '87
The Great Lakes' troubled waters. il supp (folded map) maps *Natl Geogr* 172:2-31 Jl '87
Haiti: against all odds. il supp (folded map) maps *Natl Geogr* 172:644-71 N '87
Cobb, Randall
about
Pug philosopher Tex Cobb turns Hollywood heavyweight. J. Kelley. il pors *People Wkly* 28:87-8+ Ag 3 '87
Cobb, Tex *See* Cobb, Randall
Cobb, Vicki
A,B,C, or F: test your child's school. il *Parents* 62:138-42+ N '87
A little science, a little magic. il *Parents* 62:97-100+ F '87
Cobb, William
Looking for Mr. Faulkner. il *South Living* 22:128 Mr '87

Cobblers (Pie) *See* Pie
Cobe, Patricia
Nutrition all-stars. il *Ladies Home J* 104:142-5+ O '87
COBE (Cosmic Background Explorer) *See* Artificial satellites—Astronomical use
Cober, Alan E., 1935-
On tour with the Pope. il *Roll Stone* p85-9 N 19 '87
Cobham, Billy
about
Billy Cobham: on the attack [interview] B. Beuttler. il pors *Down Beat* 54:19-21 Ap '87
Coble, Howard
Should Congress approve the Fairness Doctrine? [excerpts from remarks, June 3, 1987] *Congr Dig* 66:245+ O '87
Cobos, Daniel
about
SAC sergeant says no to spy flights. B. E. Johansen. il por *Progressive* 51:12 O '87
Coburn, Alvin Langdon, 1882-1966
about
Alvin Langdon Coburn. J. Sturman. il *Art News* 86:154+ My '87
Coburn, Christopher M.
National economic competitiveness [address, February 6, 1987] *Vital Speeches Day* 53:478-80 My 15 '87
Coburn, John W.
about
Coburn elected 1988 president in Vacuum Society balloting. por *Phys Today* 40:72 Ap '87
Coburn, Marcia Froelke, 1950-
Rough sex gets real. il *Mademoiselle* 93:238-9+ My '87
You get ahead, he gets mad . . . will success spoil your romance? *Mademoiselle* 93:186-7+ O '87
Coca
See also
Cocaine
Coca-Cola Bottling Co. Consolidated
Are we there yet? E. F. Cone. il por *Forbes* 139:110+ Mr 9 '87
Promises, promises [M. W. Griffin leaves] J. A. Conway. il por *Forbes* 139 Ann Directory:10+ Ap 27 '87
Coca-Cola Bottling Company of Philadelphia
A trailblazer's trip to the top [J. B. Llewellyn] F. McCoy. il por *Bus Week* p129+ N 16 '87
Coca-Cola Company
At Columbia, things might go better with Tri-Star [Coca-Cola merging two studios] R. Grover. il por *Bus Week* p74-5 N 30 '87
Coca-Cola: a flexible highflier. S. Ticer. il *Bus Week* p82 O 5 '87
Coca-Cola USA awards seven scholarships in Black History sweepstakes [Black History Month "Share the Dream" sweepstakes] il *Jet* 72:26-7 Jl 6 '87
Coke may be going where the beef is [merger with Wendy's] G. G. Marcial. *Bus Week* p74 Mr 30 '87
Coke's latest movie deal could be boffo [backing J. Weintraub] R. Grover. il por *Bus Week* p44 F 23 '87
Cuba libre, sans Coke. G. García Márquez. *World Press Rev* 34:34 N '87
Foot and Falconetti are TV's most popular penguin pitchmen, and it serves them right. il por *People Wkly* 28:50 Ag 24 '87
He put the kick back into Coke [R. C. Goizueta] T. Moore. il por *Fortune* 116:46-8+ O 26 '87
If Coke has its way, blacks will soon own 'the real thing' [bid to sell off stake in South African bottler] S. Mufson. il *Bus Week* p56 Mr 23 '87
In Belize, Coke goes better [Coca-Cola vs. rain forest] D. Voelker. il map *Sierra* 72:12 S/O '87
Max Headroom speaks the dreaded 'P-word' [new ads] S. Ticer. il *Bus Week* p40-1 Mr 16 '87
These guys don't blink [C. Ware and C. Morrison] A. Edmond, Jr. il pors *Black Enterp* 17:310-12+ Je '87
Coca-Cola Television (Firm)
Planting for Coke's harvest [views of F. Biondi] M. Brown and C. Capuzzi. il pors *Channels* 7:78-9 Je '87
Cocaine
See also
Crack (Cocaine)
Alice Bond, Carmen Butler meet before magistrate to argue battery charge [Mrs. J. Bond's accusations of cocaine abuse directed against husband Julian] il por *Jet* 72:6 My 11 '87
Andrew Young's ill-timed call [A. Bond's accusations of cocaine use] il por *Time* 129:34 My 25 '87
Atlanta grand jury not questioning Julian Bond in city's drug scandal. *Jet* 72:4 Je 15 '87

Atlanta mayor testifies in drug probe; says his family shaken by slurs [A. Young] il pors *Jet* 72:4 Je 1 '87
Atlanta mayor Young to testify before grand jury in city's drug scandal. por *Jet* 72:4 My 25 '87
Atlanta's coke controversy [charges against J. Bond] il por *Newsweek* 109:36 Ap 27 '87
Breakthrough against cocaine [antidepressants] P. Mann. *Read Dig* 130:185-6+ Ap '87
Can cocaine conquer America? [symposium] il *Read Dig* 130:30-8 Ja '87
Charge two in drug probe of U-Texas cager's death [case of H. Jackson] *Jet* 72:52 Je 1 '87
Cocaine cardiology: problems, mysteries [research by Jeffrey M. Isner and others] J. Silberner. *Sci News* 131:69 Ja 31 '87
Coke and a pitching ace [D. Gooden case] il por *Macleans* 100:26 Ap 13 '87
A crash landing for an ace [D. Gooden enters clinic for cocaine abuse treatment] S. Wulf. il pors *Sports Illus* 66:32-4 Ap 13 '87
D.C. mayor Marion Barry denies cocaine usage. il por *Jet* 72:4 Jl 6 '87
The downfall of a champion [cocaine use during basketball career at Villanova and afterwards]; ed. by Jeffrey Marx. G. McLain. il pors *Sports Illus* 66:42-6+ Mr 16 '87
Dr. K strikes out [D. Gooden enters drug rehabilitation] por *Time* 129:67 Ap 13 '87
Driesell denies saying cocaine helps athletes. *Jet* 72:50 Jl 6 '87
Ex-Olympian John Carlos denies drug possession. por *Jet* 71:47 Ja 26 '87
Getting fooled by drugs: the perils of taking NBA cocaine users at their word. J. McCallum. il por *Sports Illus* 66:70 Ja 26 '87
Going to bat against the fear of failure [D. Gooden cocaine case] J. M. Wall. *Christ Century* 104:371-2 Ap 22 '87
Gooden sheds light on his problem with cocaine. *Jet* 72:52 Jl 13 '87
Gooden to start working back into Mets rotation. il por *Jet* 72:48 My 18 '87
Ike Turner arrested again for cocaine possession. por *Jet* 72:65 S 7 '87
Indiana coach Knight has no sympathy for Bias; 'He was so cool'. *Jet* 72:46 Ag 3 '87
Julian Bond denies using cocaine and lashes media; Mayor Young implicated. pors *Jet* 72:8 My 4 '87
Julian Bond's wife accuses him of using drugs daily; she later recants story. il por *Jet* 72:54 Ap 27 '87
Loving a coke addict. C. Jacobs. il *Glamour* 85:298-9+ My '87
LT: living on the edge [football player's cocaine use; excerpt; cover story] L. Taylor and D. Falkner. il pors *Sport Mag* 78:68-72+ S '87
Mets moral support may speed up Gooden's return after drug rehabilitation. il pors *Jet* 72:50 Ap 20 '87
Off to a troubled start [D. Gooden case] P. Axthelm. il pors *Newsweek* 109:66-7 Ap 13 '87
Rockets' pair bombed out of NBA for cocaine use [M. Wiggins and L. Lloyd] pors *Jet* 71:50 F 2 '87
Say it ain't snow, Doc! Baseball hero Dwight Gooden is knocked out of the box by cocaine. J. S. Kunen. il por *People Wkly* 27:123-4 Ap 20 '87
A scandal scars Atlanta [cocaine charges against A. Young and J. Bond] T. E. Johnson. il pors *Newsweek* 109:28 Je 1 '87
Tony Elliott: just back from the dead, a too well-traveled NFL star bears witness to a chilling drug odyssey. W. Plummer. il pors *People Wkly* 27:81-4+ Ja 5 '87
Turner pleads innocent to cocaine charges [I. Turner] por *Jet* 71:61 Ja 26 '87
Urban murders: on the rise [cocaine-related killings] T. E. Johnson. il *Newsweek* 109:30 F 9 '87
We can conquer cocaine. T. Armbrister. il *Read Dig* 130:63-8 F '87
Young clear in drug probe, fellow Democrats cheer; ponders bid for governor. il pors *Jet* 72:24 Jl 6 '87
Laws and regulations
See Narcotics laws and regulations
Cocaine receptors *See* Drug receptors
Cocaine trade *See* Narcotics trade
Cochineal
How a bug made the world see red. N. Vietmeyer. il *Int Wildl* 17:42-7 Mr/Ap '87

Cochlea *See* Labyrinth (Ear)
Cochlear implants *See* Ear, Artificial
Cochran, David
about
'Life is like basketball'. R. L. Mahon. por *Newsweek* 109:10 F 23 '87
Cochran, Leonard
Acts [poem] *Christ Century* 104:877 O 14 '87
Cochrane, Elizabeth, 1867-1922
about
Columbian Exposition satchel. M. Wollett and B. Wollett. il *Antiques Collect Hobbies* 92:39 Ag '87
Nellie Bly. C. Bergman and M. Nussbaum. il pors *Am Hist Illus* 22:22-6+ Mr '87
Cochrane, Harwood
about
From two used trucks to a $1.2-billion deal. A. B. Rea. il por *Fortune* 115:67 Ja 5 '87
Cock fighting *See* Cockfighting
Cockburn, Alexander
Artful presents. il *House Gard* 159:22+ D '87
Beat the devil. See issues of The Nation
California Xanadu. il pors *House Gard* 159:222-30+ O '87
The surreal life of Edward James. il por *House Gard* 159:198-206+ Je '87
A taste of the New World. il *House Gard* 159:38+ Ap '87
Cockburn, Alexander, and Pollin, Robert
How to talk about economic strategy. il *Nation* 244:245-7 F 28 '87
Toward a socialist strategy [discussion of February 28, 1987 article, How to talk about economic strategy] *Nation* 244:748+ Je 6 '87
Cockburn, Andrew
Ascot of the air. il *House Gard* 159:34+ My '87
Cockburn, Bruce, 1945-
about
If he had a rocket launcher . . . S. Rabey. il por *Christ Today* 31:57-8 N 6 '87
Cocke, W. John
(jt. auth) *See* Tifft, William G., and Cocke, W. John
Cocker spaniels
See also
English cocker spaniels
Cockfighting
The gamecockers' call to arms. B. Haws. *Harpers* 275:34 O '87
Cocking, Edward C., and Davey, Michael R.
Gene transfer in cereals. bibl f *Science* 236:1259-62 Je 5 '87
Cockpit simulators *See* Flight simulators
Cockpit voice recorders *See* Flight recorders
Cockpits, Airplane *See* Airplanes, Jet—Cockpits; Airplanes, Military—Cockpits
Cockpits, Helicopter *See* Helicopters—Cockpits
Cockpits, Spaceplane *See* Spaceplane—Cockpits
Cockroaches
The Asian roach invasion. P. G. Koehler and R. S. Patterson. il *Nat Hist* 96:28+ N '87
Unwelcome immigrant: the Asian cockroach. il *Discover* 8:10 Mr '87
Will the real Asian roach please stand up? K. Hartley. il *Sci News* 132:23 Jl 11 '87
Control
Adiós, la cucaracha. G. Slutsker. il *Forbes* 140:174-5 S 21 '87
Cocktails
Chill out! Serve 'em luscious slushes with a kick of liquor. il *Mademoiselle* 93:136-7+ Jl '87
Cool drinks for hot days. J. Friedrich. il *Mademoiselle* 93:182 Je '87
Favorite drinks of James Bond. J. F. Mariani. il *Mot Boat Sail* 160:30 Ag '87
Frozen spirits. il *Gourmet* 47:62-3+ Ag '87
Getting juiced [fruit-based cocktails] J. F. Mariani. il *Harpers Bazaar* 120:98+ Ag '87
Gin without the tonic. W. Grimes. il *Esquire* 108:24 Ag '87
Louisiana lightnin': the martini for many a Cajun. il *Esquire* 107:106-7 Ap '87
Martini redux. L. Gruson. il *N Y Times Mag* p56 Ag 30 '87
New-Age cocktails. L. Bailey. il *Vogue* 177:212 D '87
Oddballs. il *Esquire* 108:194-5 O '87
A peach of a drink [Bellini] il *Time* 130:63 Ag 24 '87
Tropical icebreakers [summer cocktails] J. Etra. il *Harpers Bazaar* 120:48+ Jl '87

Cocoa futures *See* Commodity futures
Cocoa mixes *See* Beverage mixes
Cocom *See* Coordinating Committee on Multilateral Export Controls
Coconut cadang-cadang *See* Palms—Diseases and pests
Coconut palms *See* Palms
Cocteau, Jean, 1889-1963
Witness at the free-for-all [excerpts from Past tense, vol. 1]; tr. by Richard Howard. il pors *N Y Times Book Rev* 92:1+ Ja 25 '87
Cod fisheries (Commercial) *See* Fisheries
Cod fishing
In a tizzy over tommy cod [ice fishing for spawning tommycod in Quebec's Ste.-Anne River] S. Homer. il *Int Wildl* 17:18-24 Ja/F '87
CoDanceCo
Reviews:
Performances at the Bessie Schönberg Theater, New York City. L. Garafola. *Dance Mag* 61:41-2 Ap '87
Coder, David M., and Chu, Ellen W.
Extending portable computing. il *BioScience* 37:420-4 Je '87
Codes
See also
Cryptography
Codes, Building *See* Building laws and regulations
Codes, Secret *See* Cryptography
Codetermination in industry *See* Participative management
Codevilla, Angelo M., 1943-
How eminent physicists have lent their names to a politicized report on strategic defense. *Commentary* 84:21-6 S '87
Codex Corp.
A corporate villa [World Headquarters Buildings, Canton, Mass; cover story] il *Archit Rec* 175:120-31 N '87
Codina, Juan, and others
The α subunit of the GTP binding protein G_k opens atrial potassium channels. bibl f il *Science* 236:442-5 Ap 24 '87
Coding, Bar *See* Bar coding
Coding theory
See also
Data compression (Computer science)
Codons *See* Genetic code
Cody, Robin
Shooting star. il pors *Women's Sports Fitness* 9:42-4+ Ap '87
Coe, Andrew
Slugfests del sur. il *Film Comment* 23:27-8+ Jl/Ag '87
Coe, Christopher
about
Christopher Coe: "I find people without any affectation terrifying, and certainly irritating". A. Hempel. il por *Vogue* 177:455-7 S '87
Coe, Sue, 1951-
about
Sue Coe's inferno [cover story] S. Gill. il pors *Art News* 86:110-15 O '87
Coe, Susan
about
Career makeover: from secretary to assistant vice president. il por *Glamour* 85:84+ Ja '87
Coed sports
Climb every mountain: how to neutralize your male opponent. C. Evert. il *World Tennis* 34:22-4 F '87
The great sports debate. L. Villarosa. il *Health* 19:27-30+ Jl '87
Sexism in "men-only" sports: why I'm not a victim. N. Lieberman. il por *Glamour* 85:64 Ag '87
With a name like Wynne . . . [W. Haemisegger, female lacrosse player on men's team at Southwestern University] S. Shuger. il *Women's Sports Fitness* 9:21 Ap '87
Coeducation
At an all-girls school you're taught to believe in yourself. K. Odean. il *Glamour* 85:112 Ag '87
The one and only [J. Monheit, first male student at Goucher College] por *Time* 129:68 My 18 '87
A sisterhood under siege [Wheaton to go coed] E. Salholz. il *Newsweek* 109:77 Mr 30 '87
Coelacanths
A distant cousin's secret shuffle. il *U S News World Rep* 103:14 O 5 '87
'Living fossils' display unusual behavior. R. Monastersky. il *Sci News* 132:213 O 3 '87
Coelenterates
See also
Corals
Hydra (Zoology)
Jellyfish

Coelenterates—See also—*cont.*
Sponges
Coelho, Duarte Pinto *See* Pinto Coelho, Duarte
Coen, Ethan
about
The brothers from another planet. D. Handelman. pors *Roll Stone* p59+ My 21 '87
Praising 'Arizona'. J. Barth. il por *Film Comment* 23:18-20+ Mr/Ap '87
Warped in America: the dark vision of moviemakers Joel and Ethan Coen. E. Pooley. il pors *N Y* 20:44-8 Mr 23 '87
Coen, Joel
about
The brothers from another planet. D. Handelman. pors *Roll Stone* p59+ My 21 '87
Praising 'Arizona'. J. Barth. il por *Film Comment* 23:18-20+ Mr/Ap '87
Raising Arizona [film] Reviews
Christ Century 104:598 Jl 1-8 '87. J. H. Mahan
Commonweal 114:242-3 Ap 24 '87. T. O'Brien
Glamour il 85:243 Ap '87. J. G. Boyum
Macleans il 100:69 Mr 23 '87. L. O'Toole
N Y il 20:60+ Mr 16 '87. D. Denby
Natl Rev 39:52-4 My 8 '87. J. Simon
New Leader 70:22-3 Ap 6 '87. J. Gardner
New Repub 196:24 Ap 13 '87. S. Kauffmann
New Yorker 63:81-2 Ap 20 '87. P. Kael
People Wkly il 27:8 Mr 23 '87. P. Travers
Time il 129:86 Mr 23 '87. R. Corliss
USA Today (Periodical) 116:43 Jl '87. K. R. Hey
Vogue il 177:62 Ap '87. M. Haskell
Warped in America: the dark vision of moviemakers Joel and Ethan Coen. E. Pooley. il pors *N Y* 20:44-8 Mr 23 '87
Coenzyme Q
Miracle nutrient? G. L. Hunt. il *Omni* 9:24 F '87
Coffee
See also
Caffeine
Bitter jitters [panic attack patients exhibit sensitivity to coffee's bitter taste] M. O'Brian. il *Health* 19:22 N '87
Coffee with a kick. C. Lamalle. il *Mademoiselle* 93:284 N '87
Decaf can benefit your bones [work of Linda K. Massey] il *Prevention* 39:8 My '87
Ground coffee. il *Consum Rep* 52:527-33 S '87
Ground coffee. il *Consum Rep* 52:359-63 D '87
Winter day antidote: a perfect cup of coffee or tea. il *Glamour* 85:58 F '87
Prices
See also
International Coffee Agreement
Coffee growers are in for lots of sleepless nights. G. Weiss. il *Bus Week* p67 F 2 '87
Coffee cake
Choose-your-fruit coffee cake. il *Better Homes Gard* 65:180 N '87
Coffee cake for Christmas. il *South Living* 22:144 D '87
A dessert to wait all year for: this kuchen's made with early summer's fresh apricots. il *Sunset* 178:196 Je '87
Fresh-baked sugar cake. il *South Living* 22:169 O '87
Sweet almond twist. il *Good Housekeep* 204:38 Ja '87
Coffee industry
See also
General Foods Corp. Maxwell House Division
Export-import trade
Coffee growers are in for lots of sleepless nights. G. Weiss. il *Bus Week* p67 F 2 '87
Marketing
Maxwell House serves up a yuppie brew [Private Collection gourmet line] A. Dunkin. il *Bus Week* p62 Mr 2 '87
Coffee pots, percolators, etc.
Coffee makers. il *Consum Rep* 52:534-7 S '87
Coffee makers. il *Consum Rep* 52:54-8 D '87
Coffee tables *See* Tables
Coffee trees
Anecdotes, facetiae, satire, etc.
Dangerous to the last drop. R. Baker. il *N Y Times Mag* p28 D 13 '87
Coffeeville (Miss.)
Education
Blacks boycott schools in Coffeeville, Miss. [protest over transfer of black teacher, Gwendolyn English] *Jet* 72:12 S 7 '87

Coffell, Jimmy
Tri-mode cable-TV scrambling. il *Radio-Electron* 58:43-7+ F '87
Coffer, Helene Lewis
Play it again, Sam [poem] il *Good Housekeep* 205:157 Jl '87
Coffey, Linda
about
The new success looks: young & easy. il por *Harpers Bazaar* 120:76 O '87
Coffey, Paul
about
Edgy from lack of Coffey. A. Murphy. il *Sports Illus* 67:26-7 N 16 '87
The Penguins are percolating. E. M. Swift. il por *Sports Illus* 67:20-1 D 14 '87
Coffey, Susanna
about
Susanna Coffey. S. Taylor. il *Art News* 86:58+ Ja '87
Coffey, Wayne
Cram at your own risk. il *Seventeen* 46:48+ My '87
Coffin, John M.
(jt. auth) See Herman, Steven A., and Coffin, John M.
Cofide *See* Compagnia Finanziaria De Benedetti
Cogan, Marshall Stuart
about
The sour smell of success. G. Slutsker. il pors *Forbes* 139:54-5 Ja 26 '87
Coghlan, Eamonn
about
Pluck of the Irish. C. Neff. il pors *Sports Illus* 66:158+ F 9 '87
Cognac *See* Brandy
Cognac (France)
A delightful tour of Bordeaux and Cognac. F. E. Ruffin. il *Black Enterp* 18:109-10 O '87
Cognition
See also
Perception
The cognitive unconscious. J. F. Kihlstrom. bibl f *Science* 237:1445-52 S 18 '87
Cognitive maps *See* Geographical perception
Cognitive science *See* Cognition
Cognitive therapy
Six mind traps to avoid. J. Borysenko. il *Health* 19:74-8 Jl '87
Cohabitation *See* Unmarried couples
Coheleach, Guy
about
Guy Coheleach—artist and hunter [cover story] A. Fornora. il *Conservationist* 42:26-33 N/D '87
Cohen, Avner, 1951-, and Frankel, Ben
Israel's nuclear ambiguity. bibl f il *Bull At Sci* 43:15-19 Mr '87
Israel's nuclear ambiguity. *Current* 294:34-8 Jl/Ag '87
Cohen, Barney
"You were great, Dad". il *Read Dig* 131:124-6 D '87
Cohen, Benjamin V., 1894-1983
about
Ben Cohen: one who took a different path. J. Eisendrath. *Wash Mon* 19:44-5 F '87
Cohen, Bennett
about
Cold comfort. D. C. Craig. il pors *Life* 10:58-9 S '87
Cohen, Carolyn
(jt. auth) See Castellani, Loriana, and Cohen, Carolyn
Cohen, Daniel, 1936-
Charles Tiffany's 'fancy goods' shop and how it grew. bibl (p204) il por *Smithsonian* 18:52-6+ D '87
How to succeed in publishing with nary a best-seller. il pors *Smithsonian* 18:83-6+ Jl '87
Cohen, Dian
Budgeting for Canadian babies. por *Macleans* 100:9 Mr 30 '87
Building blocks for a new era. por *Macleans* 100:7 F 2 '87
The growing claims of the aged. por *Macleans* 100:7 Mr 2 '87
Small business on a recharge. por *Macleans* 100:9 Ap 27 '87
Cohen, E. Richard, and Taylor, Barry N.
The fundamental physical constants. bibl il *Phys Today* 40 pt2:BG11-BG15 Ag '87
Cohen, Eliot A.
Churchill at war. *Commentary* 83:40-9 My '87
Computer combat [cover story] *New Repub* 196:15-17 Ap 20 '87
Cohen, Gregory R.
Making your own mat-cutting clamp and guide. il *Am Artist* 51:84+ N '87

Cohen, Jacqueline
Games runners play. il *Women's Sports Fitness* 9:70-1 My '87
Cohen, Jacqueline
(jt. auth) See Blumstein, Alfred, and Cohen, Jacqueline
Cohen, Jeffrey
Converting home movies to video. il *Consum Res Mag* 70:32-4 Jl '87
Electronic review. il *Consum Res Mag* 70:19-22 F '87
The new unified remote controls. il *Consum Res Mag* 70:29-30 D '87
A review of coming electronics. il *Consum Res Mag* 70:24-6 O '87
Cohen, Jeffrey Todd
Joe Henderson's solo on Song for my father—a tenor saxophone transcription. il *Down Beat* 54:58-9 S '87
Steve Winwood's solo on Empty pages—an electric piano transcription. il *Down Beat* 54:60-1 Ag '87
Cohen, Jerome Alan
about
Law and China. *New Yorker* 62:25-6 Ja 19 '87
Pandas. *New Yorker* 63:23-4 Ap 13 '87
Cohen, Jerry S., and Cuneo, Jonathan W.
Pulling the plug on antitrust law. il *Nation* 245:296-7 S 26 '87
Cohen, Joel E.
(jt. auth) See Briand, Frédéric, and Cohen, Joel E.
Cohen, Jon
'Gone up north, gone out west, gone!'. il *Smithsonian* 18:72-6+ My '87
Cohen, Joyce
For weary women only—how to get energy to go. il *Mademoiselle* 93:128 Mr '87
Cohen, Leonard, 1934-
about
Jennifer Warnes sings songs of Leonard Cohen. A. Nash. il pors *Stereo Rev* 52:78+ My '87
Jenny sings Lenny. S. Pond. pors *Roll Stone* p16 Mr 12 '87
Cohen, Leonard A.
Diet and cancer. bibl (p150) il *Sci Am* 257:42-8 N '87
Cohen, Leslie V.
(jt. auth) See Brann, Mark R., and Cohen, Leslie V.
Cohen, Marcia
Book banning must be stopped. por *Seventeen* 46:158 Ap '87
Cohen, Martin
about
It's 1987. Do you know where your love life is? D. Kent. *Mademoiselle* 93:138-9+ F '87
Cohen, Martin
about
A fund manager who separates REITs from wrongs. G. Anrig, Jr. il por *Money* 16:232 Ap '87
Cohen, Martin
about
Tough options: an investor who hedged himself out of a bundle. J. M. Laderman. *Bus Week* p133 N 30 '87
Cohen, Michael
State boards in an era of reform. il *Phi Delta Kappan* 69:60-4 S '87
Cohen, Neil
about
Cut-rate moguls. D. C. Craig. il pors *Life* 10:44-5+ Ap '87
Cohen, Paul
To skip or hop? il *World Tennis* 35:82-3 S '87
Cohen, Paul W.
Can the Mennonites survive success? il *N Y Times Mag* p114-16+ N 8 '87
Cohen, Peter
about
Can Cohen the consolidator make Shearson-Hutton work? A. Bianco. il por *Bus Week* p96-8 D 21 '87
Cohen, Randy
Diary of a flying man. *New Yorker* 63:34-5 S 21 '87
The New First Lady. *New Yorker* 63:36-7 My 18 '87
Cohen, Raquel E., 1922-
The psychological aftermath of disasters. il *USA Today (Periodical)* 116:70-2 S '87
Cohen, Richard Martin
Rites of passage. il *Read Dig* 131:145-6 S '87
Suddenly I'm the adult? *Psychol Today* 21:70-1 My '87
Cohen, Sherry Suib
The cheater's diet. il *Ladies Home J* 104:58+ D '87
How to find your body map to sexual pleasure. il *Glamour* 85:298-9+ Ap '87
Test your sex I.Q. il *Ladies Home J* 104:58+ Ja '87

Understanding the reasons behind men's new sexual fears. il *Glamour* 85:206-7+ Je '87
Cohen, Stephen F.
Sovieticus. See issues of The Nation
Cohen, Stephen R.
about
A shareholder revolt at Telecom. B. Dumaine. il por *Fortune* 115:58-60 Mr 2 '87
Cohen, Stephen S., and Zysman, John
The myth of a post-industrial economy. il *Technol Rev* 90:54-60+ F/Mr '87
Cohen, Steve, 1950-, and Colina, Paulo
How to decide which job to take [excerpt from Getting to the right job] il *Glamour* 85:132 Ag '87
Cohen, Susan Phillips
about
Therapy. *New Yorker* 63:30-1 O 26 '87
Cohen, Wilbur Joseph, 1913-1987
Needed: a new political agenda for the 1990s. por *U S News World Rep* 102:7 Mr 16 '87
Cohen, William S.
Should the Levin-Nunn Amendment be approved? [excerpts from address, September 17, 1987] *Congr Dig* 66:278+ N '87
Cohen, Yehuda
(jt. auth) See Alldredge, Alice L., and Cohen, Yehuda
Cohen Brothers Realty Corporation
Outflanked, outmaneuvered [Integrated Resources vs. Cohen Brothers Realty over 666 5th Ave., New York City] H. Rudnitsky. il *Forbes* 140:343-4 Jl 13 '87
Cohen-Rosenthal, Edward
(jt. auth) See Burton, Cynthia, and Cohen-Rosenthal, Edward
Cohen-Solal, Annie
about
Jean-Paul Sartre: an 'ethical compass' [interview] R. Z. Chesnoff. il pors *U S News World Rep* 103:67 N 2 '87
Cohn, Carol
Nuclear language and how we learned to pat the bomb [cover story] bibl f il *Bull At Sci* 43:17-24 Je '87
Sex, power, and nuclear language [discussion of June 1987 article, Nuclear language and how we learned to pat the bomb] *Bull At Sci* 43:58-61 S '87
Cohn, Jeffrey P.
Applauding the beleaguered bat. il *Américas* 39:14-17+ N/D '87
The beginnings: laboratory and animal studies. il *FDA Consum* 21:6-9 N '87
Chlorofluorocarbons and the incredible shrinking ozone. il *FDA Consum* 21:32-5 D '87/Ja '88
Chlorofluorocarbons and the ozone layer. *BioScience* 37:647-50 O '87
Doctors' do-it-yourself lab tests: how reliable? il *FDA Consum* 21:36-9 F '87
Encouraging conservation. *Américas* 39:58-9 My/Je '87
The molecular biology of aging. il *BioScience* 37:99-102 F '87
Nights—and days—of the iguana. il por *Américas* 39:34-9 Jl/Ag '87
Cohn, Jordan E.
The art (and science) of concentration. il *Seventeen* 46:50 Ap '87
Coiffure *See* Hairstyling
Coils
See also
Induction coils
Coin banks *See* Banks, Coin
Coin collecting *See* Numismatics
Coin operated machines
See also
Gambling machines
Coinage *See* Coins
Coincidence
Our wild, weird world of coincidence. R. Blodgett. il *Read Dig* 131:125-8 S '87
Coins
See also
Tokens
Abolishing the penny makes good sense. A. S. Blinder. il *Bus Week* p29 Ja 12 '87
America's thank you for the Statue of Liberty [Lafayette dollar] E. Rochette. il *Antiques Collect Hobbies* 92:81-2 My '87
Cents are nonsense [abolishing the penny] A. S. Blinder. il *Read Dig* 131:79-80 Ag '87
Commemorating an anniversary that never was [1936 Stephen Foster Cincinnati commemorative half-dollar] E. Rochette. il *Antiques Collect Hobbies* 92:74-5 Mr '87

Coins—*cont.*

Finding wealth on the wings of Mercury [F. E. Townsend's 1933 request for dime contributions to pension plan] E. Rochette. il *Antiques Collect Hobbies* 91:81-2 F '87

New silver dollars: a case of deja vu! E. Rochette. il *Antiques Collect Hobbies* 91:83-4 Ja '87

Penny puzzlers. il *Natl Geogr World* 142:14-15 Je '87

The toy money that was not! [plastic trial cents of 1942] E. Rochette. il *Antiques Collect Hobbies* 92:27+ N '87

Collectors and collecting
See Numismatics

Coins as an investment

Coins that glitter for collectors—and investors. T. Segal. il *Bus Week* p166 Mr 23 '87

Getting your gold fix from coins. A. McGrath. il *U S News World Rep* 102:53-4 Je 15 '87

No higher yields exist [Salomon Brothers' survey on coins and stamps] *Changing Times* 41:126 N '87

Coit, David M.

about

Maine: the financier's new frontier. A. Beam. il por *Bus Week* p81 Ja 19 '87

Coker, Homer

(jt. auth) *See* Medley, Donald M. (Donald Matthias), and Coker, Homer

Cokliss, Harley

about

Malone [film] Reviews
   People Wkly il 27:10 My 18 '87. R. Novak

COLA's *See* Cost of living adjustments

Colasuonno, Miguel

about

"This is war" [interview] L. Minard. il por *Forbes* 139:50 Je 29 '87

Colbert, Claudette

about

One classy lady. A. Richman. il pors *People Wkly* 27:67-8+ F 16 '87

A weekend with Claudette. W. Walton. il *House Gard* 159:156-9+ Je '87

Colbert, Evelyn

United States policy in Southeast Asia. bibl f *Curr Hist* 86:145-7+ Ap '87

Colbert, Richard

about

The art of decay. M. Wade. il *Horizon* 30:39-40 D '87

Colburn, Forrest D.

Cuba chases the dollar. il *New Leader* 70:13-14 Mr 9 '87

Embattled Nicaragua. bibl f *Curr Hist* 86:405-8+ D '87

The Colbys [television program] *See* Television program reviews—Single works

Colchicine

Back from the past [used to alleviate disk disease] J.-B. Shoemaker. il *Health* 19:21 F '87

Cold

See also
   Low temperatures

Physiological effects
See also
Birds, Effect of temperature on
Fish, Effect of temperature on
Hibernation
Hypothermia
Insects, Effect of temperature on
Marine fauna, Effect of temperature on
Plants, Effect of temperature on

Baby, it's cold outside. K. Karlsrud and D. Schultz. il *Parents* 62:256 N '87

Out in the cold [emergency camping gear] S. Netherby. il *Field Stream* 92:75-6 Ag '87

Protection against winter woes. D. Farley. il *FDA Consum* 21:28-35 F '87

Warm up to cold-weather workouts. S. Garland. il *Prevention* 39:68+ D '87

Therapeutic use
See also
Cryosurgery

Cold (Disease)

See also
Common Cold Unit (Great Britain)

The bugs that bug us: what you should know about colds. L. Ponte. il *Read Dig* 131:85-9 O '87

Cold cure, prevention: nothing to sneeze at. D. D. Edwards. *Sci News* 132:261 O 24 '87

The complete book of colds and flu. M. Mercer. il *Good Housekeep* 205:62+ N '87

Flying with a cold: save your ears. G. Weiss. il *Bus Week* p148 Ja 12 '87

Stop a cold before it starts. N. Brown. *McCalls* 114:22 F '87

Surprising facts about the common cold. M. Castleman. il *Read Dig* 130:85-8 F '87

The truth about the common cold (and similar ills). S. Montgomery. il *Work Woman* 12:142+ Ap '87

Will you get a cold this month? P. C. Bartel. il *Mademoiselle* 93:152 N '87

Cold (Disease) remedies

Hot new cold treatment [Viralizer nasal spray] D. Pine. il *Health* 19:21 Ap '87

Quick tips for cold comfort [excerpt from Listen to your body] E. Michaud and L. Anastas. *Prevention* 39:66 N '87

Sure-to-soothe cold and sore-throat remedies [excerpt from Cold cures] M. Castleman. *Prevention* 39:99+ D '87

When you absolutely, positively have to be there: how to take your cold to the office. A. Oshins. *Work Woman* 12:60 F '87

Cold frames

A better cold frame for gardeners. J. Cook. il *Ctry J* 14:63-5 Ap '87

Real gardeners have coldframes. J. Glattstein. il *Flower Gard* 31:44-5 O/N '87

Test garden update. D. A. Jimerson and J. A. McKeon. il *Better Homes Gard* 65:34 Ja '87

Cold fronts (Meteorology) *See* Fronts (Meteorology)

Cold Lake Air Base (Canada) *See* Air bases

Cold war (U.S. and Soviet Union) *See* United States— Foreign relations—Soviet Union

Cold water swimming *See* Swimming

Cold weather

See also
   Winter cities

Cold weather clothing *See* Clothing, Cold weather

Cold weather cruising *See* Cruising—Cold weather conditions

Cold weather photography *See* Photography—Cold weather conditions

Cold weather swimming *See* Swimming

Cold weather videotaping *See* Videotape recorders and recording—Cold weather conditions

Coldframes *See* Cold frames

Colds *See* Cold (Disease)

Cole, Charlie

Our spy on high. il *N Y Times Mag* p30-4 My 10 '87

Cole, Diane

A feminist reader's guide. *Ms* 16:73 O '87

It might have been: mourning the unborn. *Psychol Today* 21:64-5 Jl '87

Cole, Duane

about

Flip side. J. M. McClellan. il por *Flying* 114:56-9 My '87

Cole, Jacqueline

about

The miraculous story of a coma survivor. J. R. Heilman. il por *Redbook* 169:90-1+ Jl '87

Cole, Joanna

The Clown-Arounds go on vacation [story] il *Parents* 62:103-4+ Jl '87

Get well, Clown-Arounds [story] il *Parents* 62:129-33 Mr '87

Cole, Johnnetta B.

about

Johnnetta B. Cole: Spelman's "sister" president [interview] P. Giddings. il por *Essence* 18:34+ N '87

Johnnetta Cole: serving by example [interview] A. Bernstein. il pors *Change* 19:46-55 S/O '87

Spelman College gets its first "sister president". S. McHenry. il por *Ms* 16:58-61+ O '87

Spelman College names 1st black woman president. *Jet* 72:7 My 11 '87

Cole, Jonathan R., and Zuckerman, Harriet

Letters [discussion of February 1987 article, Marriage, motherhood and research performance in science] *Sci Am* 257:4+ Ag '87

Marriage, motherhood and research performance in science. il *Sci Am* 256:119-25 F '87

Cole, K. C.

A theory of everything [cover story] il pors *N Y Times Mag* p20-6+ O 18 '87

Who needs women? *Omni* 9:35 My '87

Cole, Natalie

about

Natalie Cole says success for her is better second time around [cover story] il pors *Jet* 72:58-60 Ag 10 '87

Cole, Robert W., Jr.
The editor's page. See issues of Phi Delta Kappan through January 1988

Cole, Stephen
Superpower pact links initial Mars missions. il *Astronomy* 15:26-8 N '87

Cole, Thomas, 1801-1848
about
Editorial. W. Garrett. il *Antiques* 132:1082-3 N '87

Cole, Timothy H.
Outdoors. See issues of Popular Mechanics beginning August 1985 through June 1987
Science. See issues of Popular Mechanics beginning July 1987

Cole, Tommy
about
Supreme Life sales mgr. wins prestigious honor. il pors *Jet* 72:36 Ap 6 '87

Coleco Industries, Inc.
Coleco: out of the Cabbage Patch and into the fire. S. Benway. il por *Bus Week* p54 Mr 30 '87

Coleman, Alton
about
Alton Coleman was his own lawyer, had fool for client. por *Jet* 72:16 Je 8 '87

Coleman, Anne
about
A very special home for the elderly. L. Stone and L. Snyder-Stone. il *McCalls* 114:68-9 Jl '87

Coleman, Beatrice, 1916-
about
The mother figure of Maidenform. M. Morris. il pors *Work Woman* 12:82-3+ Ap '87

Coleman, Bob, 1949-
Science writing: too good to be true? il *N Y Times Book Rev* 92:1+ S 27 '87

Coleman, Dabney
about
Dabney Coleman, TV's coolest jerk. B. Zehme. il por *Roll Stone* p39-40+ N 19 '87
Slap crackles and pops. J. McCallum. il por *Sports Illus* 67:66 N 16 '87

Coleman, David
about
North star: a shining presence in woodland Vermont. L. Atwill. il *Archit Dig* 44:154-7 Mr '87

Coleman, Debi
about
Apple Computer's Debi Coleman. M. Dowie. il por *Ms* 15:60-2+ My '87
Good, better, best. F. M. Henley. il pors *Work Woman* 12:86-9 D '87

Coleman, E. Thomas
about
A champion for developing rural areas. *Success Farm* 85:49 Ag '87

Coleman, Ellen
Anemia—are you at risk? il *Women's Sports Fitness* 9:12 Mr '87

Coleman, Gary
about
Gary Coleman, 19, and on his own. A. Collier. il pors *Jet* 72:36-8 Mr 30 '87

Coleman, James Samuel, 1926-
about
Community as social capital: James S. Coleman on Catholic schools. A. M. Greeley. *America* 157:110-12 Ag 29-S 5 '87
Why Johnny drops out [interview] B. Leonard. il por *Forbes* 140:242+ N 16 '87

Coleman, Janet
Leaving the corporate nest. il *Work Woman* 12:42 O '87

Coleman, Kate
Taking the plunge: how a fitness dabbler learned to love the open water. il por *Women's Sports Fitness* 9:23-6 Je '87

Coleman, Mike
about
A very special home for the elderly. L. Stone and L. Snyder-Stone. il *McCalls* 114:68-9 Jl '87

Coleman, Mitch, and Jaffe, Dave
Last word. il *Omni* 9:138 My '87

Coleman, Ornette
about
Ornette Coleman: the color of music [cover story; interview] H. Mandel. il pors *Down Beat* 54:16-19 Ag '87
Unfinished symphonies. C. Clay. il pors *Esquire* 107:106-9 My '87

Coleman, Roger W., 1929-
about
What's the hurry? E. Paris. il por *Forbes* 140:112+ N 2 '87

Coleman, Sue
about
Sue Coleman starts up interior design showroom. il pors *Jet* 72:23 Ap 20 '87

Coleman-Karger Showroom
Sue Coleman starts up interior design showroom. il pors *Jet* 72:23 Ap 20 '87

Colen, B. D.
Hot seat. See occasional issues of Health (New York, N.Y.) beginning July 1986

Colen, Bruce David
Architectural digest visits: Dinah Shore. il por *Archit Dig* 44:158-63+ D '87
Cabin in the sky: a designer's retreat in the Montana Rockies. il por *Archit Dig* 44:132-9+ Je '87
An eye for detail: the Paris apartment of Michel and Noémi Ermelin. il *Archit Dig* 44:132-42 Ja '87
Stonepine: sophisticated equestrian retreat in California's Carmel Valley. il *Archit Dig* 44 Archit Dig Travels:32-7+ O '87
View from Malibu: Michael and Kim McCarty in California. il pors *Archit Dig* 44:96-101+ Jl '87

Coles, Katharine
Letter from a friend on her anniversary [poem] *New Repub* 197:39 Jl 27 '87

Coles, Robert
Gatsby at the B school. *N Y Times Book Rev* 92:1+ O 25 '87
My parents, my children. il *50 Plus* 27:100 F '87
The power of prayer. il *50 Plus* 27:44-6 D '87
about
The crayon man. P. Yancey. il pors *Christ Today* 31:14-20 F 6 '87
Does Dr. Ruth talk to your kids more than you do? [interview] por *U S Cathol* 52:22-9 Ag '87

Coles, Roberts, III
about
Jefferson's descendant becomes a living memorial. J. Sanderson. il por *People Wkly* 27:80-1 Ja 26 '87

Coleslaw *See* Salads

Colgate-Palmolive Co. (Delaware)
The man brushing up Colgate's image [R. Mark] H. J. Steinbreder. il pors *Fortune* 115:106-7+ My 11 '87
Most improved. il *Forbes* 139:115 Ja 12 '87

Colglazier, Bruce
Planning a ceramic tile project. il pors *Home Mech* 83:12+ F '87

Colic
A case of colic. J. C. Berman. il *N Y Times Mag* p64 N 29 '87
Colic: "cause" and "cure". K. Karlsrud and D. Schultz. il *Parents* 62:198 S '87

Colin, Molly
California plan puts quality children's books in supermarkets. *Publ Wkly* 232:28 O 30 '87
Giving no ground, Avon and NCBA settle suit. *Publ Wkly* 232:9 N 13 '87
Judge limits trade books in Marin college stores. *Publ Wkly* 232:10 O 30 '87
The 'San Francisco chronicle' focuses on children's books. il *Publ Wkly* 231:39-40 My 29 '87

Colina, Paulo
(jt. auth) See Cohen, Steve, 1950-, and Colina, Paulo

Colino, Richard R.
about
The mysterious fall of a star. J. S. DeMott. il por *Time* 130:51 O 5 '87

Colitis
Inflammatory bowel disease: recognizing the symptoms. P. A. Banks. por *McCalls* 114:108 Ja '87
Less colitis among smokers. *Sci News* 131:213 Ap 4 '87

Collaboration, Artistic *See* Art—Collaboration
Collaboration, Literary *See* Authorship—Collaboration
Collaborative learning *See* Group work in education
Collaborative Research, Inc.
Flap arises over genetic map. L. Roberts. il *Science* 238:750-2 N 6 '87

Collage
See also
Photomontage

Collagen
Diabetics need vitamin C for healthy skin. *Prevention* 39:124 Ja '87
Youth in a bottle [Avon's Collagen Booster Line Controlling Lotion] M. Fox. il *Health* 19:18 My '87

Collective labor agreements—Airlines—*cont.*
TWA pilots extend current contract. *Mon Labor Rev* 110:42 Mr '87

Canada
Air Canada resumes flights after reaching pact with union. *Aviat Week Space Technol* 127:38 D 21 '87
Returning to the air [Air Canada strike ends] L. Van Dusen. il *Macleans* 100:49 D 28 '87

Automobile industry
Can GM afford this deal? *Newsweek* 110:63 O 19 '87
A different sort of victory for the UAW [agreement with Ford] *Newsweek* 110:65 S 28 '87
Ford-UAW contract bolsters job security. il *Mon Labor Rev* 110:31-3 N '87
A Ford vehicle doomed to stall at General Motors [UAW contract] J. A. Seamonds. il *U S News World Rep* 103:16 S 28 '87
General Motors' new uphill course. J. A. Seamonds. il *U S News World Rep* 103:9 O 19 '87
How GM and the UAW kept from butting heads. W. Zellner. il *Bus Week* p32 O 26 '87
One down, tougher one to go [UAW settles with Ford] J. Castro. il *Time* 130:52 S 28 '87
Smiling fender to fender [Ford's UAW contract] W. Zellner and A. Bernstein. il *Bus Week* p39 O 5 '87

Canada
A pension breakthrough [Chrysler Canada agrees to index pensions against inflation] D. Jenish. il *Macleans* 100:32-3 S 28 '87

Food industry
Victory on Cannery Row [settlement of strike at Watsonville Canning] R. Erlich. il *Progressive* 51:26-7 Jl '87

Hospitals
Kaiser Foundation in California settles. *Mon Labor Rev* 110:56-7 Je '87

Postal service
Postal Service contract. il *Mon Labor Rev* 110:47 O '87

Shipbuilding
Shipyard contracts feature labor cost relief. *Mon Labor Rev* 110:57 Ag '87

Shipping
Maritime settlements. *Mon Labor Rev* 110:72 S '87

Steel industry
USX contract ends 6-month strike. *Mon Labor Rev* 110:55-6 Ap '87

Supermarkets
Grocery store settlements. il *Mon Labor Rev* 110:56-7 Ag '87
Kroger workers forgo bonus plan to save jobs. *Mon Labor Rev* 110:42-3 Mr '87
A novel union role: picketing for the boss [Ohio supermarkets enlist workers in push against nonunion rivals] S. Phillips. il *Bus Week* p80 D 28 '87-Ja 4 '88

Teachers
Teachers' negotiations generally peaceful. *Mon Labor Rev* 110:33 N '87

Truck industry
Mack Trucks, Auto Workers settle. *Mon Labor Rev* 110:44 Jl '87

Collective settlements
See also
Shakers

Israel
See also
Kibbutzim

Northern Ireland
See also
Corrymeela Community (Northern Ireland)

Tennessee
See also
The Farm (Tenn.)

Collectors and collecting
See also
Americana
Black collectibles
Display of antiques, art objects, etc.
See also subheads Collectibles; Collectors and collecting under various subjects
Avon calling! [100 years of collectibles] il *Antiques Collect Hobbies* 92:77-9 Jl '87
Common sense investing [collectibles] M. Thorne. *Antiques Collect Hobbies* 92:51-2 S '87
Finger-lap firkin in original paint. W. Shipman. il *Ctry J* 14:52-9 D '87
In a mess. J. Fowles. il por *Archit Dig* 44:24+ Je '87
In the marketplace. F. Donegan. See issues of Americana
Information desk. E. Edwards. See issues of Antiques & Collecting Hobbies beginning January 1987
"It's just not fair" [investing in collectibles] S. Blotnick. il *Forbes* 139:302-3 Ja 12 '87

Solid investments you can get your hands around [tangible assets] B. Bauer. il *U S News World Rep* 103:106 D 28 '87-Ja 4 '88
Some men collect . . . others just won't let go. il *Esquire* 107:194-9 Je '87
Tomorrow's antiques [views of Charles J. Jordan] il *Futurist* 21:57 Jl/Ag '87
Trivial pursuits: investing for fun in the toys and kitsch of the fabulous '50s. H. Wheelwright. il *Money* 16:65-6+ D '87
What's hot, what's not. M. C. Paulson. il *Changing Times* 41:123-4+ N '87
Where a grand buys a great time. B. Hager. il *Money* 16:64 Jl '87

Bibliography
Book reviews. See issues of Hobbies through February 1985

Clubs and societies
Collector club corner. *Antiques Collect Hobbies* 92:47 Ap '87

College, Choice of
Campus visits: how helpful are they? G. Hechinger. il *Glamour* 85:314+ Ag '87
College bound, without a map [inability of overworked guidance counselors to offer good advice] J. E. Gallagher. il *Time* 129:74 F 23 '87
College-hunting? Ask someone who majors in it. P. Cole. il *Bus Week* p157 N 30 '87
How to get the most from a college trip. J. Dyer. *Seventeen* 46:72+ Ap '87
Let the student decide. F. H. T. Rhodes. il *U S News World Rep* 103:72-4 O 26 '87
Smoothing the transition from high school to college. E. L. Boyer. *Educ Dig* 52:2-5 My '87

College administrators *See* College officials
College admission *See* Colleges and universities—Admission
College alumni *See* College graduates
College and high school cooperation *See* Educational cooperation
College and public school cooperation *See* Educational cooperation
College and school drama
Teen sues for being denied love role opposite white [J. L. Mosley's suit over role in school musical in Oxford, Miss.] *Jet* 72:22 Mr 30 '87

College and school journalism
See also
Columbia Missourian
Federalist paper
Yale daily news
A civics lesson at Hazelwood East [principal of Missouri high school censors student newspaper; Supreme Court case] S. Visser. il *Nation* 245:441-2 O 24 '87
From Hazelwood to the High Court [principal of Missouri high school deletes articles from school newspaper] M. A. Uhlig. il *N Y Times Mag* p100-7 S 13 '87
Students should have freedom of the press, too! D. Fuchs. por *Seventeen* 46:182 S '87

College and the community *See* Colleges and universities—Public relations
College architecture
See also
Dormitories
Aldo Rossi makes his American debut [design of new architecture school for the University of Miami] K. D. Stein. il por *Archit Rec* 175:67 My '87
Finding the "Ole" in Ole Miss [early campus buildings] il *South Living* 22:20 Mr '87
Gwathmey Siegel & Associates: coming soon to a school near you. il *Archit Rec* 175:53 Je '87
In the Northeast [George M. Low Center for Industrial Innovation, Rensselaer Polytechnic Institute] G. Anderson. il *Archit Rec* 175:90-5 Jl '87
Independent studies [with introd. by Margaret Gaskie] il *Archit Rec* 175:95-111 Mr '87
The nationality rooms [Cathedral of Learning on the campus of the University of Pittsburgh] M. A. Zimmermann. il *Focus* 36:34-5 Wint '86
Over-achiever [Wallace Building, University of Manitoba] P. M. Sachner. il *Archit Rec* 175:130-3 My '87
They stood guard in Tuscaloosa [Jasons' Shrine at the University of Alabama] il *South Living* 22:53 S '87
Uncommon law [circular building houses the U. of Iowa College of Law] G. Anderson. il *Archit Rec* 175:106-13 Ag '87

College art galleries and museums
See also
Hood Museum of Art
Jane Baerwald Aron Art Center
Mount Holyoke College. Art Museum
Smith College. Museum of Art

College art galleries and museums—See also—*cont.*
Tweed Museum of Art (Duluth, Minn.)
University of Massachusetts at Amherst. Fine Arts Center
Williams College. Museum of Art
College athletes *See* Athletes
College athletes, Women *See* Women athletes
College athletics
See also
Baseball, College
Basketball, College
Football, College
Gymnastics
Hockey, College
Lacrosse, College
National Association of Intercollegiate Athletics
National Collegiate Athletic Association
Rowing
Soccer, College
Swimming
Tennis
Volleyball, College
Wrestling, College
What's in a nickname? [college and professional sports teams] J. Leo. il *Time* 129:82 Ja 19 '87
Cheerleading
See Cheerleading
Directors
Dismissal
White charges Lincoln U. violated his civil rights [former athletic director D. A. Bennice] *Jet* 72:23 Ag 31 '87
Economic aspects
NCAA union: no pay, no play? [compensating major college athletes; views of Dick DeVenzio] D. Whitford. il *Sport Mag* 78:14 Ja '87
Ethical aspects
Another NCAA fumble [judge rules against drug testing policy] B. Newman. il por *Sports Illus* 67:100 D 7 '87
Big-time college athletics: academic eligibility rules are elitist. G. R. Roberts. il *USA Today (Periodical)* 116:68-70 Jl '87
Big-time college athletics: commercialization and corruption. T. A. Luken. il *USA Today (Periodical)* 116:64-7 Jl '87
College athletics reform: losing through intimidation [survey of college presidents] J. W. Gilley. *Educ Dig* 52:57-9 Mr '87
A failed game plan [college sports and black youth] M. Naison. il *Commonweal* 114:199-200 Ap 10 '87
Jan Kemp [professor's stand against college athletes' low academic standards at the Univ. of Georgia] C. Reece. il por *Ms* 15:44+ Ja '87
Mr. Clean comes to the NCAA [R. D. Schultz] M. Ivey. il por *Bus Week* p51+ S 7 '87
Trapped in an 'athletics arms race'. I. M. Heyman. por *U S News World Rep* 103:7 Jl 20 '87
College bands *See* Bands (Music)
College bookstores
See also
National Association of College Stores (U.S.)
Laws and regulations
Judge limits trade books in Marin college stores [Marin County Community College] M. Colin. *Publ Wkly* 232:10 O 30 '87
College buildings *See* College architecture
College chapels
See also
Duke University—Chapel
College clubs and societies
See also
College fraternities
College sororities
Hasty Pudding Club
College coaches *See* Coaches (Athletics)
College commencements *See* Commencements
College dormitories *See* Dormitories
College drama *See* College and school drama
College dropouts *See* Dropouts
College education
See also
Adult education
Aged—Education
Coeducation
College teaching
Colleges and universities
Community and junior colleges
Computers—Educational use
Liberal education
Police—Education
Women—Education

The adventures of education in Wonderland: implementing education reform [cover story] K. P. Cross. bibl f il *Phi Delta Kappan* 68:496-502 Mr '87
Death of the university. H. I. London. il por *Futurist* 21:17-22 My/Je '87
Death of the university [cover story] H. I. London. il *USA Today (Periodical)* 116:32-6 S '87
Higher education circa 2005. F. D. Fisher. il *Change* 19:40-5 Ja/F '87
The ivory foxhole. J. Hart. See occasional issues of National Review beginning September 26, 1986
Aims and objectives
Competition or cooperation? [address, March 1987] A. W. Astin. il *Change* 19:12-19 S/O '87
Education and values [address, October 12, 1987] T. Ehrlich. *Vital Speeches Day* 54:106-9 D 1 '87
Higher education [address, September 8, 1987] J. A. Howard. *Vital Speeches Day* 54:13-17 O 15 '87
The quality of the university today: an exchange at Harvard [address, October 1986] W. J. Bennett; D. C. Bok. *Current* 291:4-11 Mr/Ap '87
The skillful baccalaureate. G. A. Woditsch and others. il *Change* 19:48-57 N/D '87
Teaching and research as student responsibilities: integrating community and academic work. J. Wagner. il *Change* 19:26-31+ S/O '87
Troubles in the groves of academe [views of college presidents; panel discussion] il *U S News World Rep* 102:67-8 Ap 20 '87
Bibliography
Books. See issues of Change beginning November/December 1984
Saving the soul of higher education. M. A. Marty. *Christ Century* 104:659-62 Jl 29-Ag 5 '87
Costs
See also
ConSern Program
Michigan Education Trust
Scholarships and fellowships
Student aid
The college cost explosion. B. M. Carnes. il *Consum Res Mag* 70:16-19 S '87
College tuition: paying in advance. T. Tilling. il *Parents* 62:52 Ap '87
College without Clifford. M. Fritz. il *Forbes* 139:135-6 F 23 '87
Coping with costs the Wyoming way. il *U S News World Rep* 103:83-4+ O 26 '87
Does college cost too much? L. Solórzano. il *U S News World Rep* 102:54-5 Mr 9 '87
Facing up to sticker shock. J. E. Gallagher. il *Time* 129:70 Ap 20 '87
Fuming over college costs. H. Anderson. il *Newsweek* 109:66-8+ My 18 '87
The high finance of higher education. T. Segal. il *Bus Week* p80-1 Jl 27 '87
How to cut the cost of tomorrow's tuition. T. Segal. il *Bus Week* p181 O 12 '87
How to pay a $94,000 tuition bill. S. E. Polson. il *Changing Times* 41:133-6 Ja '87
Insure the parent, not the child, even when the policy is a college fund. R. A. Lynch. il *Money* 16:51 Ja '87
Kids and college: how to build a nest egg. B. G. Quint. il *Glamour* 85:180 Ap '87
A new look at college costs [case studies of six institutions; cover story; with editorial comment by Theodore J. Marchese] M. O'Keefe. il *Change* 19:4, 11-27+ N/D '87
Save more, borrow less. T. J. Marchese. *Change* 19:4 Mr/Ap '87
Saving for college: one scheme has survived [minor's Section 2503(c) trust] P. Philipps. il *Bus Week* p147 Ja 12 '87
Taking on Secretary Bennett [issue of college costs and student aid] M. P. McPherson and P. Korshin. pors *U S News World Rep* 102:6 Je 29 '87
A tax-exempt muni that's good college material. B. Hitchings. *Bus Week* p106 Ja 26 '87
Ten great tuition deals for your dollars. J. Stickney. il *Money* 16:100-2+ S '87
Tuition aid 1980s style. J. B. Quinn. il *Newsweek* 110:74 O 12 '87
Tuition prepurchase plans. R. E. Anderson. il *Change* 19:36-41 Mr/Ap '87
The untouchables. P. Brimelow. il *Forbes* 140:140-2+ N 30 '87
With large tuition bills ahead, a widow plans a flexible portfolio of income investments [Joanne Venutolo] B. Hager. il *Money* 16:61 Je '87

College education—Costs—*cont.*

Worries about pay-now, study-later plans. J. Bodnar. *Changing Times* 41:9 Jl '87

Your child's college education: how to afford the cost. T. Fischer. il *McCalls* 114:21+ Ap '87

Evaluation

See Colleges and universities—Evaluation

Federal aid

See Colleges and universities—Federal aid; Student aid

Philosophy

Are student heads full of emptiness? [books by A. Bloom and E. D. Hirsch] E. Bowen. il *Time* 130:56-7 Ag 17 '87

A best-seller's puzzling sizzle [A. Bloom's The closing of the American mind] F. Bruning. por *Macleans* 100:7 Ag 31 '87

Bloom and doom [views of A. Bloom] W. Greider. il *Roll Stone* p39-40 O 8 '87

Campus 1987 [A. Bloom's views on college education; cover story; special section; with editorial comment by Richard Vigilante] *Natl Rev* 39:34-8+ O 9 '87

Chicago philosophy professor Allan Bloom warns that America's universities are crumbling [interview] S. K. Reed. il por *People Wkly* 28:141-2+ S 14 '87

Clark Kerr: the masterbuilder at 75 [cover story] A. Levine. il pors *Change* 19:12-27+ Mr/Ap '87

The closing of the American mind [views of A. D. Bloom] R. K. Bennett. *Read Dig* 131:81-4 O '87

Community, conflict, and ways of knowing [address, March 1987] P. J. Palmer. il *Change* 19:20-5 S/O '87

A dunce cap for America [views of E. D. Hirsch and A. D. Bloom] D. Gates. il pors *Newsweek* 109:72-4 Ap 20 '87

Nietzsche by another name [views of A. Bloom] E. Bowen. por *Time* 129:79 Ap 13 '87

Rethinking the university: design for a new academy. F. Turner. *Current* 290:22-6 F '87

Sex and drugs and Heidegger [views of A. D. Bloom] J. Weisberg. *Wash Mon* 19:49-53 S '87

Today's university: where democracy is anarchy. A. D. Bloom. *Current* 297:22-7 N '87

Undemocratic vistas [views of A. Bloom] M. C. Nussbaum. bibl f il *N Y Rev Books* 34:20-6 N 5 '87

Writing to sell in the MTV era [A. D. Bloom's The closing of the American mind] A. Smith. il *Esquire* 108:87+ D '87

College education, Experimental

Antidote to obscurity: innovation [lesser-known schools with innovative programs] il *U S News World Rep* 103:68-9 O 26 '87

College education, Value of

The untouchables. P. Brimelow. il *Forbes* 140:140-2+ N 30 '87

College education and state

See also
Michigan Education Trust

Assessment: where are we? The implications of new state mandates. P. Ewell. il *Change* 19:23-8 Ja/F '87

The courts and the colleges [address, December 8, 1986] S. R. Spencer. *Vital Speeches Day* 53:310-14 Mr 1 '87

The public and the university [address, February 17, 1987] D. Kennedy. *Vital Speeches Day* 53:412-14 Ap 15 '87

Chile

Uncertainties over University of Chile. J. Walsh. *Science* 238:1037 N 20 '87

France

France. D. Ireland. *Nation* 244:464-6 Ap 11 '87

Student protests block university changes. D. Dickson. il *Science* 235:24-5 Ja 2 '87

Great Britain

Universities and the government: a lesson from Britain. D. Bouchier. *Educ Dig* 52:50-2 My '87

India

Politics and the university [examination fixing scandal at the University of Bombay] P. G. Altbach. il *Change* 19:56-9 Jl/Ag '87

Nicaragua

The university and revolution [University of Central America] K. M. Cahill. *America* 157:77-8 Ag 15-22 '87

United States

See College education and state

College ethics *See* Business schools and colleges—Standards; Colleges and universities—Standards

College extension *See* University extension

College facilities

See also
College sports facilities

College fraternities

Alphas move to erect King memorial in D.C. [Alpha Phi Alpha] *Jet* 71:28 F 9 '87

The Greek rites of exclusion. M. G. Lord. il *Nation* 245:10-13 Jl 4-11 '87

Phi Beta Sigma 1st blacks on U. of Miss. frat row. *Jet* 72:24 Ag 31 '87

Vanderbilt orders frats to integrate or close. *Jet* 71:21 F 23 '87

College graduates

See also
Baccalaureate addresses
Black college graduates
Business schools and colleges—Graduates
College education, Value of
Colleges and universities—Graduate work
Minority college graduates
Women college graduates

The graduates [four collegiate student-athletes] il *Sports Illus* 66:60-4 Je 8 '87

Attitudes

Alone together: the unromantic generation [cover story] B. Weber. il *N Y Times Mag* p22-6+ Ap 5 '87

Employment

Baiting the hook [businesses recruiting on campus] R. Buchanan. il *Roll Stone* p99-100+ Mr 26 '87

The C.I.A. goes back to college. J. Wiener. il *Nation* 245:719-20 D 12 '87

Jobs for new college grads. P. Plawin. il *Changing Times* 41:43-6+ F '87

Looking for that first job. P. Plawin. *Changing Times* 41:78+ Ag '87

What every June graduate should be doing right now. il *Glamour* 85:168 Ap '87

Ethics

Choose wisely [address, August 14, 1987] B. Chiodo. *Vital Speeches Day* 54:40-2 N 1 '87

College libraries

See also
Annenberg Library and Communications Center (Mass.)
Research libraries
Rush Rhees Library

Making the most of libraries [with editorial comment by Frank Newman] P. S. Breivik. il *Change* 19:4-5, 44-52 Jl/Ag '87

College mascots *See* Mascots

College museums

See also
Harvard University. Botanical Museum
University of Arkansas, Fayetteville. University Museum

College of Environmental Science and Forestry. New York State Ranger School (Wanakena, N.Y.) *See* New York State Ranger School (Wanakena, N.Y.)

College officials

See also
College presidents

Third and long for enrollment managers: life inside the pressure cooker. R. P. Chait. il *Change* 19:43-5 S/O '87

College presidents

See also
Freedman, James O.
Godsey, R. Kirby
Kerr, Clark, 1911-
McLaughlin, David

The university presidency today. S. Muller. *Science* 237:705 Ag 14 '87

Attitudes

America's best colleges [cover story; special section] il *U S News World Rep* 103:48-51+ O 26 '87

College athletics reform: losing through intimidation. J. W. Gilley. *Educ Dig* 52:57-9 Mr '87

Top training for top jobs [evaluation of graduate schools; special section] il *U S News World Rep* 103:70-3+ N 2 '87

Troubles in the groves of academe [panel discussion] il *U S News World Rep* 102:67-8 Ap 20 '87

College professors and instructors *See* College teachers

College radio stations *See* Radio stations

College Retirement Equities Fund

Clifton R. Wharton Jr.: the nation's highest-paid black executive. il pors *Ebony* 42:29-30+ S '87

Wharton to head fund. P. A. Jones. por *Black Enterp* 17:16 Ja '87

College reunions

The real 'Big chill' in Michigan [reunion of 1960s Ann Arbor activists] E. Frank. il *Nation* 245:480-2 O 31 '87

College Savings Bank

Anything goes [CollegeSure CD qualifies for FDIC insurance] L. Jereski. il *Forbes* 140:34-5 O 5 '87

Why the new CollegeSure CD deserves to flunk. il *Money* 16:9 N '87

College scholarships *See* Scholarships and fellowships

College sororities

The Greek rites of exclusion. M. G. Lord. il *Nation* 245:10-13 Jl 4-11 '87

College sports *See* College athletics

College sports facilities

A picture of health [Wellesley College Sports Center] D. Dietsch. il *Archit Rec* 175:90-5 Ag '87

College students

See also

Black students
Coeducation
College graduates
Foreign students
Law students

College knowledge [coping with freshman year] K. Brown. il *Seventeen* 46:118+ Ag '87

On campus 1987 [special section] il *Roll Stone* p92-4+ Mr 26 '87

On campus 1987 [special section] il *Roll Stone* p86-9+ S 24 '87

Sending a daughter to college. J. Fonda. il pors *Ladies Home J* 104:22+ Ja '87

The Seventeen honor roll: most likely to succeed. C. Hanauer. il *Seventeen* 46:210-13 S '87

Admission

See Colleges and universities—Admission

Aid

See Student aid

Attitudes

College daze [career and family expectations; research by Hedwin Naimark and others] E. Stark. il *Psychol Today* 21:14 N '87

How college women and men feel today about sex, AIDS, condoms, marriage, kids. il *Glamour* 85:261-3 Ag '87

Kudos for Emma, thumbs down on Becky [responses to 19th century English literature] B. F. Williamson. por *Publ Wkly* 232:159 Jl 24 '87

The one who has the most toys when he dies, wins [life goals of college freshmen] P. Chance. il *Psychol Today* 21:54 My '87

Place maps [regional distortions in map drawing by college freshman; study by Thomas F. Saarinen] C. Simon. maps *Psychol Today* 21:15 N '87

Science and religion: divided we stand? [surveys by Robert W. Suchner] R. Camer. *Psychol Today* 21:61 Je '87

Awards

See also

Robinson Student Humanitarian Achievement Award

Cheating

See Cheating in school work

Clothing and dress

See Clothing and dress—Students

Counseling

See Educational counseling

Employment

See Youth—Employment

Federal aid

See Student aid

Housing

See also

Dormitories

Geek House [Georgetown University's Right House, a conservatives-only group house] C. Lane. *New Repub* 196:16-17 Ja 5-12 '87

Political activities

See also

Student protests, demonstrations, etc.
Students for a Democratic Society

Geek House [Georgetown University's Right House, a conservatives-only group house] C. Lane. *New Repub* 196:16-17 Ja 5-12 '87

Student Pugwash awarded major grants. R. Hart. *Phys Today* 40:110-11 O '87

Protests, demonstrations, etc.

See Student protests, demonstrations, etc.

Psychology

The Jung and the restless [college students' nightmares about exams] H. Ward. il *N Y* 20:23 Je 8 '87

Recreation

At witty Caltech, pranks aren't purely a laughing matter. J. Ellis. il *Smithsonian* 18:100-2+ S '87

Caution: geniuses at work and play [MIT students] A. Theroux. il *Read Dig* 131:215-18+ O '87

Hanging out 101 [off-campus haunts] E. Wing. il *Roll Stone* p123-4+ Mr 26 '87

Spring break at South Padre Island. R. Woodbury. il *Time* 129:87 Ap 6 '87

Recruiting

See Black colleges and universities—Student recruiting; Colleges and universities—Student recruiting

Religious life

See also

Inter-Varsity Christian Fellowship

Going first class on the Titanic. S. Garber. il por *Christ Today* 31:25-7 N 20 '87

Remedial teaching

See Remedial teaching

Sexual behavior

Extremism on campus: symbols of hate, symbols of hope [collegiate gay baiting] E. D. Howard. il *Christ Century* 104:625-7 Jl 15-22 '87

Have gays taken over Yale? J. Adler. il *Newsweek* 110:96 O 12 '87

Is Yale now colored mauve? [gay and lesbian presence] J. Hart. *Natl Rev* 39:30 O 9 '87

Liberty, equality, sexuality. A. D. Bloom. *Commentary* 83:24-30 Ap '87

Poison-pen mail [anti-gay form letters] *Harpers* 275:16+ S '87

'Safe sex' and the presence of the absence [Dartmouth College's safe sex kit] J. Hart. *Natl Rev* 39:43+ My 8 '87

Show opening in New Haven [homosexuality at Yale] J. Hart. *Natl Rev* 39:26 N 20 '87

University 'madam' gets $1000 fine, probation [J. Owens' business at De Paul] il por *Jet* 73:22 N 16 '87

Statistics

Foreign students: a valuable link. il *Change* 19:39-43 Jl/Ag '87

Volunteer service

See Volunteer service

College students, Black *See* Black students

College students, Women *See* Women college students

College students and alcohol *See* Alcohol and youth

College students and teachers *See* College teachers and students

College teachers

See also

Black college teachers
College teaching
Executives as college teachers

The 21st-century professor. J. R. Hoyle and G. R. Johnson. il pors *Futurist* 21:26-7 N/D '87

Bridging the gap between a public school system and a university [Texas Tech faculty members adopt school classes in Lubbock] R. E. Ishler and E. C. Leslie. *Phi Delta Kappan* 68:615-16 Ap '87

Faculty for the future. I. H. Buchen. il por *Futurist* 21:22-5 N/D '87

The two-person career on college campuses. E. Zencey. *Educ Dig* 53:56-8 O '87

Where are all the young brains? [views of R. Jacoby] E. Bowen. il por *Time* 130:70 N 30 '87

Anecdotes, facetiae, satire, etc.

Fallowships: fertilizing the groves of academe. A. A. Blum. il *Phi Delta Kappan* 69:71-2 S '87

Dismissal

Contract not renewed [faculty member E. Bettenhausen charges sexism in dispute with Boston University School of Theology] *Christ Century* 104:936 O 28 '87

Financial exigency is alive and well in Idaho [justification for Boise State University's dismissal of tenured faculty members] T. J. Flygare. *Phi Delta Kappan* 68:550-1 Mr '87

Jan Kemp [professor's stand against college athletes' low academic standards at the Univ. of Georgia] C. Reece. il por *Ms* 15:44+ Ja '87

Teachers can be ousted for swearing at students [case of Midland College professor J. D. Martin] *Jet* 71:23 F 23 '87

White professor wins reverse bias law suit against black college [D. Voiku wins case against Albany State College] *Jet* 72:32 Ap 20 '87

Education in service

Life in remedial English: learning about teaching and learning [writing course at the City University of New York] L. Forstall. *Phi Delta Kappan* 68:796-7 Je '87

College teachers—*cont.*

Political activities

Academic post-communism. J. Hart. *Natl Rev* 39:40 Jl 31 '87

The academy [discussion of October 1986 article, The tenured left] S. H. Balch and H. I. London. *Commentary* 83:11-12 Ja '87

Blood lust in academia [S. P. Huntington denied membership in National Academy of Sciences] F. Zakaria. *New Repub* 197:16-18 Jl 27 '87

The class struggle [Communist professors; views of E. Schrecker] T. Draper. *New Repub* 196:29-36 Ja 26 '87

Letters [discussion of September 19, 1987 article, Radicals in academia] R. Jacoby. *Nation* 245:434 O 24 '87

The odyssey of Daniel Boorstin [legacy of HUAC testimony; cover story] J. Wiener. il *Nation* 245:289+ S 26 '87

Oh, if I could only be a Communist [E. Schrecker's No ivory tower] J. Hart. *Natl Rev* 39:44 Je 19 '87

Radicals in academia [excerpt from The last intellectuals] R. Jacoby. il *Nation* 245:263-4+ S 19 '87

When historians judge their own [historian N. Davies sues Stanford University over denial of professorship because of his views on Jews] J. Wiener. il *Nation* 245:584-6+ N 21 '87

Professional ethics

A matter of mission: the dilemma of teaching in expensive places. B. DeMott. *Change* 19:62 My/Je '87

Publications

The case for book burning [publishing mania] *New Repub* 197:7-8+ S 14-21 '87

Anecdotes, facetiae, satire, etc.

Scaling the ivory tower [publishing mediocre articles] H. J. Bullford. il *Change* 19:56-7 S/O '87

Recruiting

Raiders in the groves of academe. E. Bowen. il *Time* 130:69 N 23 '87

Retirement

The abolition of retirement. H. Cleveland. il *Change* 19:8-10 N/D '87

Salaries, pensions, etc.

See also
Teachers Insurance and Annuity Association

Supply and demand

May we borrow your historians? [U.S. universities' recruitment of English humanities professors] M. Kishlansky. il *Hist Today* 37:6-7 Je '87

Tenure

Black Harvard professor protests tenure policy [views of D. Bell] *Jet* 72:28 Je 29 '87

Professor sues MIT over tenure [D. Noble] D. L. Goodman. *Progressive* 51:13 Je '87

Tenure or The great chain of being. A. Ross. il *Change* 19:54-5 Jl/Ag '87

College teachers, Part time

Academia's new "gypsies". E. Bowen. il *Time* 129:65 Ja 12 '87

Tales of a freeway flyer or Why I left college teaching after 10 years. C. Maitland. *Change* 19:8-9+ Ja/F '87

College teachers and students

I thought I was a terrific teacher until one day . . . [dealing with older women returning to college] M. Yudkin. il *Ms* 16:66-7 O '87

Martha meets her mentor: the power of teaching relationships. L. A. Daloz. il *Change* 19:35-7 Jl/Ag '87

Student evaluation. J. Epstein. *Am Sch* 56:177-84 Spr '87

What Charles knew: homage to an English teacher [Howard University teacher C. Watkins; excerpt from An apple for my teacher] H. A. Baker. pors *N Y Times Book Rev* 92:3+ Mr 22 '87

College teaching

See also
College teachers

Building a lecture that really works. J. H. Clarke. *Educ Dig* 53:52-5 O '87

Commonplaces about teaching: second thoughts. B. Fong. il *Change* 19:28-34 Jl/Ag '87

Teaching [address, October 31, 1986] K. Brooks. *Vital Speeches Day* 53:434-9 My 1 '87

What one teacher learned becoming an undergraduate. R. Starling. *Educ Dig* 53:30-3 S '87

Anecdotes, facetiae, satire, etc.

Scaling the ivory tower. H. J. Bullford. il *Change* 19:58-60 N/D '87

College theatricals *See* College and school drama

College tuition *See* College education—Costs

College yearbooks

See also
Video yearbooks

Colleges and business *See* Business and education

Colleges and universities

See also
Black colleges and universities
Business schools and colleges
Catholic colleges and universities
Church colleges and universities
Colleges for women
Community and junior colleges
Engineering colleges
Foreign students
International Space University
Law schools
Medical colleges
Summer schools
Theological seminaries

Death of the university. H. I. London. il por *Futurist* 21:17-22 My/Je '87

Death of the university [cover story] H. I. London. il *USA Today (Periodical)* 116:32-6 S '87

Goodbye to some of that. G. McCauley. il *America* 157:328-30 N 7 '87

Reaching for community [cover story; special section; with editorial comment by Russell Edgerton] il *Change* 19:6, 12-31+ S/O '87

Where not to find new ideas. K. Sale. *Nation* 244:320-3 Mr 14 '87

Administration

See also
College officials
College presidents

Admission

At the gates of California [blind student applies for college admission in 1952] V. Mehta. *New Yorker* 63:82-97 My 11 '87

The big rush on campus. L. Solórzano. il *U S News World Rep* 103:14 Jl 6 '87

Black admissions director hired at Oberlin College [J. L. Washington] *Jet* 73:22 S 28 '87

Declaring academic bankruptcy: another chance at college. A. D. Browne. *Educ Dig* 53:46-9 N '87

Do colleges set Asian quotas? E. Salholz. il *Newsweek* 109:60 F 9 '87

Help! I've been wait-listed. H. Rubin. *Seventeen* 46:152+ Ap '87

How to survive the admissions maze. il *U S News World Rep* 103:77-80 O 26 '87

SAT's, school by school. il *U S News World Rep* 103:90 O 26 '87

What it'll take [getting into a prestige graduate school] il *U S News World Rep* 103:85 N 2 '87

Why preferential admission? G. C. Loury. *Current* 296:27-9 O '87

Why preferential admission is not enough for blacks. G. C. Loury. *Educ Dig* 53:42-5 S '87

Anecdotes, facetiae, satire, etc.

Campus comedy. See occasional issues of Reader's Digest

Terms of complaint. D. McAdam. *Change* 19:7 Mr/Ap '87

Budget

See Colleges and universities—Finance

Buildings

See College architecture

Business activities

See Business and education

Choice

See College, Choice of

Commencements

See Commencements

Computer installations

See Computers—Educational use

Cooperation

See also
Southeastern Universities Research Association

Curriculum

See also
Art—Study and teaching
Arts—Study and teaching
Biology—Study and teaching
Citizenship education
Comedy—Study and teaching
Creative writing—Study and teaching
English language—Study and teaching
English literature—Study and teaching
Humanities—Study and teaching
International education
Liberal education
Moral education
Nuclear weapons—Study and teaching
Science—Study and teaching
Science and the humanities—Study and teaching

Colleges and universities—Curriculum—See also—*cont.*
Soviet studies
Theological seminaries—Curriculum
Thought and thinking—Study and teaching
Cool schools. J. B. Meigs. il *Roll Stone* p92-4+ Mr 26 '87
How to pick a major. G. Hechinger. *Glamour* 85:420-1 S '87
The quality of the university today: an exchange at Harvard [address, October 1986] W. J. Bennett; D. C. Bok. *Current* 291:4-11 Mr/Ap '87
Rocks and rockets [colleges with highly regarded specific programs] il *U S News World Rep* 103:67 O 26 '87
What's your major? [celebrities] K. M. Miller. il *Roll Stone* p104-6+ Mr 26 '87

Departments of economics
And you thought Harvard was only keen on Keynes [economist R. Barro appointed to faculty] N. Jonas. il por *Bus Week* p78+ S 7 '87

Desegregation
Black judge disqualified in Ala. segregation case [U. W. Clemon] por *Jet* 73:4 O 26 '87
Phi Beta Sigma 1st blacks on U. of Miss. frat row. *Jet* 72:24 Ag 31 '87
Vanderbilt orders frats to integrate or close. *Jet* 71:21 F 23 '87

Enrollment
The alarming decline in the number of black college students. M. Marshall. il *Ebony* 42:44+ S '87
Black enrollments: the case of the missing students. S. Arbeiter. il *Change* 19:14-19 My/Je '87
Blacks push Md. colleges' enrollment to record high. *Jet* 73:22 N 9 '87
Minority access: a question of equity. il *Change* 19:35-9 My/Je '87
Third and long for enrollment managers: life inside the pressure cooker. R. P. Chait. il *Change* 19:43-5 S/O '87

Entrance examinations
See also
Colleges and universities—Admission
Scholastic Aptitude Test
Entrance requirements
See Colleges and universities—Admission
Ethical aspects
See Colleges and universities—Standards
Evaluation
The adventures of education in Wonderland: implementing education reform [cover story] K. P. Cross. bibl f il *Phi Delta Kappan* 68:496-502 Mr '87
America's best colleges [survey of college presidents; cover story; special section] il *U S News World Rep* 103:48-51+ O 26 '87
Assessment: fact or fad? T. J. Marchese. *Change* 19:4 Ja/F '87
Assessment: where are we? The implications of new state mandates. P. Ewell. il *Change* 19:23-8 Ja/F '87
Highest education [world's best universities are in the U.S.] H. Rosovsky. *New Repub* 197:13-14 Jl 13-20 '87
How goes it with the colleges? [Carnegie report, College: the undergraduate experience in America] J. W. Donohue. *America* 156:269-73+ Ap 4 '87
How to grade a college [excerpt from College: the undergraduate experience in America] E. L. Boyer. *Money* 16:112-13 S '87
Insomnia and the Pious Parchment Pile [Carnegie report, College: the undergraduate experience in America] D. E. Koshland, Jr. *Science* 235:1125 Mr 6 '87
Judging a good college: the importance of the 'voice' of the institution. B. DeMott. *Change* 19:5 Ja/F '87
The push to assess. S. D. Spangehl. il *Change* 19:35-9 Ja/F '87
Storm warnings [report of the National Commission on the Role and Future of State Colleges and Universities] *Cent Mag* 20:58 Ja/F '87
Supermarket U. [Carnegie report, College: the undergraduate experience in America] A. Hacker. il *Fortune* 115:327+ Ap 27 '87
Ten great tuition deals for your dollars. J. Stickney. il *Money* 16:100-2+ S '87
Time to deliver [assessment] T. H. Kean. il *Change* 19:10-11 S/O '87
Top training for top jobs [college presidents' evaluation of graduate schools; special section] il *U S News World Rep* 103:70-3+ N 2 '87

Extension
See University extension
Faculty
See College teachers
Federal aid
See also
Colleges and universities—Research—Federal aid
A 'pay up or else' ultimatum from William Bennett [threatening to withhold federal aid from colleges with 20% student loan default rate] R. A. Taylor. il *U S News World Rep* 103:16 N 16 '87
Staying on top. D. Gergen. il *U S News World Rep* 103:92 O 26 '87
What's in the future for women's sports? [demise of gymnastics at Southwest Texas State University as an example of effects of weakened Title IX regulations] C. L. Hogan. il *Women's Sports Fitness* 9:42-7 Je '87

Finance
See also
CCI/ICE (Firm)
College education—Costs
Colleges and universities—Gifts, legacies, etc.
Colleges and universities—Investments
Financial exigency is alive and well in Idaho [justification for Boise State University's dismissal of tenured faculty members] T. J. Flygare. *Phi Delta Kappan* 68:550-1 Mr '87
Life after tax reform [cover story] C. T. Clotfelter. il *Change* 19:12-18 Jl/Ag '87
A new look at college costs [case studies of six institutions; cover story; with editorial comment by Theodore J. Marchese] M. O'Keefe. il *Change* 19:4, 11-27+ N/D '87
The untouchables. P. Brimelow. il *Forbes* 140:140-2+ N 30 '87
Gifts, legacies, etc.
B is for billion [Stanford fund raising drive] *Time* 129:61 F 16 '87
Banking on ethics [J. S. R. Shad's endowment to Harvard for business ethics studies] *Time* 129:79 Ap 13 '87
Big man on campus [A. Khashoggi's pledge to contribute $5 million to American University] C. McCarthy. *Nation* 244:252-4 F 28 '87
Ethics 101: can the good guys win? [J. S. R. Shad funds business ethics program at Harvard Business School] B. Brophy. il por *U S News World Rep* 102:54 Ap 13 '87
Harvard's $30 million windfall for ethics 101 [J. S. R. Shad's gift] J. A. Byrne. por *Bus Week* p40 Ap 13 '87
Longhorns 8, Crimson 4 [endowments at Univ. of Texas and Harvard] W. P. Barrett. il *Forbes* 140:116+ O 19 '87
Minorities get $25 million boost from Columbia gift [gift by J. W. Kluge] *Jet* 72:32 My 18 '87
Real estate deals that help ol' alma mater—and you. D. B. Moskowitz. il *Bus Week* p126 O 26 '87
Shad the lawgiver [J. S. R. Shad's gift to Harvard Business School] D. Seligman. il *Fortune* 115:154 My 11 '87
Graduate work
Top training for top jobs [college presidents' evaluation of graduate schools; special section] il *U S News World Rep* 103:70-3+ N 2 '87
Investments
Harvard to the rescue [divestiture of portfolio in South Africa; candidates for overseer] W. F. Buckley. *Natl Rev* 39:58 Jl 3 '87
How an educated guess is paying off for George Keane [Common Fund's manager calls the crash] G. G. Marcial. il por *Bus Week* p106 D 21 '87
How the richest colleges handle their billions. C. Knowlton. il *Fortune* 116:106-8+ O 26 '87
Longhorns 8, Crimson 4 [endowments at Univ. of Texas and Harvard] W. P. Barrett. il *Forbes* 140:116+ O 19 '87
Shotgun approach [Common Fund's asset pool] R. Phalon. il por *Forbes* 139:132+ Je 15 '87
Tainted money: the ethics and rhetoric of divestment [colleges and business] R. L. Payton. il *Change* 19:55-60 My/Je '87
Laws and regulations
The courts and the colleges [address, December 8, 1986] S. R. Spencer. *Vital Speeches Day* 53:310-14 Mr 1 '87
Public relations
The public and the university [address, February 17, 1987] D. Kennedy. *Vital Speeches Day* 53:412-14 Ap 15 '87

Colleges and universities—Public relations—*cont.*
Teaching and research as student responsibilities: integrating community and academic work. J. Wagner. il *Change* 19:26-31+ S/O '87
University-based public service [adaptation of address, November 10, 1987] R. G. Mawby. *Science* 238:1491 D 11 '87

Publications
See also
University presses

Race relations
Back to the future: Columbia replays the battles of '68. P. Blauner. il *N Y* 20:30-3 My 18 '87
Black colleges vs. white colleges: the fork in the road for black students. W. R. Allen. il *Change* 19:28-31+ My/Je '87
Blacks protest at Univ. of Virginia on race bias. *Jet* 73:6 N 9 '87
Blacks protest campus racism. B. Kantrowitz. il *Newsweek* 109:30 Ap 6 '87
Campus controversy [racial tension at Columbia University] S. McConnell. *New Repub* 196:13-14 My 25 '87
An ebony view of the ivory power: memories of a black faculty member. W. B. Harvey. *Change* 19:46-9 My/Je '87
The Greek rites of exclusion [fraternities and sororities] M. G. Lord. il *Nation* 245:10-13 Jl 4-11 '87
The new racists. C. C. R. White. il *Ms* 16:68 O '87
Racial jokes bring end of campus radio station [University of Michigan] *Jet* 71:33 Mr 23 '87
Racism on campus. A. Edwards. il *Seventeen* 46:166-7+ N '87
Racism on campus. E. T. Louis. *Essence* 18:53+ Ag '87
University of Michigan agrees to blacks' demands; Jesse Jackson assists. *Jet* 72:5 Ap 13 '87
Why fewer blacks are graduating [college students] R. A. Taylor. il *U S News World Rep* 102:75-6 Je 8 '87
Wrong message from academe [racist incidents] E. Bowen. il *Time* 129:57-8 Ap 6 '87

Rating
See Colleges and universities—Evaluation

Real estate operations
Real estate deals that help ol' alma mater—and you. D. B. Moskowitz. il *Bus Week* p126 O 26 '87

Recruiting
See Colleges and universities—Student recruiting

Relations with business
See Business and education

Religious life
See also
Inter-Varsity Christian Fellowship

Research
Academia, Inc. [commercialization of university research] S. Shulman. il *Technol Rev* 90:11-12 N/D '87
Berkeley changes tack on reactor [decision to shut down reactor used for military-related research] J. Walsh. *Science* 235:273 Ja 16 '87
Business goes to college for a brain gain. J. Main. il *Fortune* 115:80-2+ Mr 16 '87
Corporations on campus. W. Biddle. il *Science* 237:353-5 Jl 24 '87
Export controls and research results. *Sci News* 132:73 Ag 1 '87
Inquiry in the undergraduate science classroom. C. D'Avanzo. *BioScience* 37:540 S '87
Research reactor closed at Berkeley for mixed reasons. W. Sweet. *Phys Today* 40:56 Je '87
Use of Berkeley reactor questioned on military-related research [views of Charles Schwartz] J. Walsh. *Science* 235:23 Ja 2 '87
What's right, what's wrong with U.S. science? [address, March 13, 1987] M. L. Goldberger. *Vital Speeches Day* 53:537-40 Je 15 '87

Federal aid
See also
Research grants
Adapting to pork-barrel science. J. Walsh. il *Science* 238:1639-40 D 18 '87
The CIA-Harvard controversy over secrecy. T. A. Idinopulos. il *USA Today (Periodical)* 115:38-40 My '87
Congress considers upgrading labs. J. Walsh. il *Science* 237:351-2 Jl 24 '87
Funding facilities: who's getting what [research universities and the pork barrel issue] I. Peterson. *Sci News* 131:246 Ap 18 '87
Geographical limit on research funds in bill seen as swipe at peer review [University Research Initiative program] J. Walsh. *Science* 238:1506 D 11 '87

A halt to earmarking [vote of the Association of American Universities] *Sci News* 131:341 My 30 '87
Military funding: does it add up? [support for math research] I. Peterson. *Sci News* 131:71 Ja 31 '87
NASA selects seven new Centers for Commercial Development of Space. *Aviat Week Space Technol* 127:31 Ag 3 '87
NSF centers: yes, but . . . C. Norman. *Science* 237:21 Jl 3 '87
NSF puts big stake on research centers. J. Walsh. il *Science* 236:18-19 Ap 3 '87
NSF supercomputer centers plan for next leap into research. I. Goodwin. il map *Phys Today* 40:61-4 O '87
Plant science grant program nears approval. M. Crawford. *Science* 236:1620 Je 26 '87
Pork barrel science: no end in sight. C. Norman. *Science* 236:16-17 Ap 3 '87
The University of Wisconsin hatches toxins [biological warfare research] R. Jannaccio. il *Progressive* 51:20 N '87
The ups and downs of federal funding for R&D. il *Change* 19:35-9 N/D '87

Segregation
Study: 10 states continue college racial segregation. *Jet* 73:24 O 26 '87

Standards
AASCU's clarion call to state colleges and universities. S. Kaplan. il *Change* 19:48-51+ Mr/Ap '87
Ethnophobia, heterophobia, & liberal fascism [campus values] J. Hart. *Natl Rev* 39:46 F 13 '87
Harvard title for sale? [John F. Kennedy School of Government's offer to donor C. C. Dickson] por *Newsweek* 110:24 N 23 '87
Software piracy [responsibilities of colleges] K. C. Green and S. W. Gilbert. il *Change* 19:46-9 Ja/F '87

Statistics
See also
Colleges and universities—Enrollment

Student recruiting
Essay [National College Fair] *New Yorker* 63:32-3 O 19 '87
Smoothing the transition from high school to college. E. L. Boyer. *Educ Dig* 52:2-5 My '87
Take a leaf from Joe Paterno . . . [recruiting of blacks; interview with W. A. Blakey] R. Edgerton. il pors *Change* 19:40-3 My/Je '87

Alabama
See also
Talladega College
Tuskegee University
University of Alabama
Black judge disqualified in Ala. segregation case [U. W. Clemon] por *Jet* 73:4 O 26 '87

Arizona
See also
University of Arizona

Arkansas
See also
Arkansas State University

Atlantic States
Eastern liberal arts colleges. il *U S News World Rep* 103:66 O 26 '87
Engineering awareness [comprehensive institutions] il *U S News World Rep* 103:60-1 O 26 '87

California
See also
California College of Arts and Crafts
California Community Colleges
California Institute of Technology
Compton Community College
De Anza College
Mills College
Pomona College
Stanford University
University of California, Berkeley
University of California, Los Angeles
University of California, Santa Cruz
University of California (System)
California urged to update master plan. J. Walsh. *Science* 237:720 Ag 14 '87

Chile
See also
Universidad de Chile

Colorado
See also
University of Colorado at Boulder

Connecticut
See also
Wesleyan University (Middletown, Conn.)
Yale University

Colleges and universities—*cont.*

Florida

See also
Florida A & M University
University of Miami

Georgia

See also
Albany State College (Ga.)
Atlanta University
Mercer University
Morehouse College
Morehouse School of Medicine
Morris Brown College
Savannah State College
Spelman College
University of Georgia

Great Britain

See also
University of Oxford
Not waving, but drowning [teaching of history] *Hist
   Today* 37:2-3 Jl '87
U.K. science: survival of the fittest—or fattest? D.
   Dickson. il *Science* 236:512-13 My 1 '87

Idaho

See also
Boise State University

Illinois

See also
De Paul University
Harold Washington College
Southern Illinois University at Carbondale

India

See also
University of Bombay

Indiana

See also
DePauw University
University of Notre Dame

Iowa

See also
Maharishi International University

Italy

See also
American Academy in Rome

Japan

See also
United Nations University

Kansas

See also
University of Kansas

Lebanon

See also
American University of Beirut

Louisiana

See also
Dillard University
Grambling State University

Manitoba

See also
University of Manitoba

Maryland

See also
Goucher College
Johns Hopkins University
University of Maryland at Baltimore
Blacks push Md. colleges' enrollment to record high.
   Jet 73:22 N 9 '87
Md. Caucus to submit plan to aid black collegians.
   Jet 73:22 S 28 '87

Massachusetts

See also
Boston University
Harvard University
Massachusetts Institute of Technology
Tufts University
Wellesley College
Wheaton College (Norton, Mass.)

Mexico

See also
Universidad Autónoma de Guadalajara

Michigan

See also
Michigan Education Trust
University of Michigan

Middle East

See also
Birzeit University

Minnesota

See also
Pillsbury Baptist Bible College
University of Minnesota, Duluth

Mississippi

See also
Jackson State University
Tougaloo College
University of Mississippi

Missouri

See also
Concordia Seminary (Saint Louis, Mo.)

Montana

See also
Montana State University (Bozeman)

New Hampshire

See also
Dartmouth College

New Jersey

See also
Princeton University
Rider College
Stevens Institute of Technology
N.J. officials pushing for more minority college grads.
   Jet 72:25 Ag 31 '87

New York (State)

See also
City University of New York
Columbia University
Community College of the Finger Lakes
Cornell University
Manhattan Community College
Manhattan School of Music
New York University

North Carolina

See also
Black Mountain College (N.C.)
Duke University
Southeastern Baptist Theological Seminary
St. Augustine's College

Ohio

See also
Central State University (Ohio)
Columbus State Community College
Oberlin College
Ohio State University

Pennsylvania

See also
Bucknell University
Carnegie-Mellon University
Indiana University of Pennsylvania
Lincoln University (Pa.)
Swarthmore College
University of Pennsylvania
University of Pittsburgh

Rhode Island

See also
Brown University

Senegal

See also
University of Dakar

South Africa

See also
University of Stellenbosch
Universities and apartheid. A. Pifer. *Cent Mag* 20:61-2
   Mr/Ap '87

South Carolina

See also
Allen University
Citadel (Military academy)
South Carolina State College

Southern States

See also
Southeastern Universities Research Association
Booked up for learning [comprehensive institutions] il
   U S News World Rep 103:59 O 26 '87
The gamble paid off [liberal arts colleges] il *U S News
   World Rep* 103:63 O 26 '87
Study: 10 states continue college racial segregation. *Jet*
   73:24 O 26 '87
Treasures on campus [cultural keepsakes] il *South Living*
   22:66-71 O '87

Soviet Union

See also
Moscow M. V. Lomonosov State University

Sudan

See also
University of Khartoum

Switzerland

See also
Art Center College of Design (Pasadena, Calif.).
   European campus

Tennessee

See also
Fisk University

Colleges and universities—Tennessee—See also—*cont.*
    Lane College
    Meharry Medical College
    University of Tennessee, Knoxville
    Vanderbilt University
              Texas
    See also
    Bishop College
    Midland College (Tex.)
    Southern Methodist University
    Texas A & I University
    Texas Southern University
    Texas Tech University
    University of Texas (System)
    University of Texas at Austin
              United States
    See Colleges and universities
              Vermont
    See also
    Saint Michael's College
              Virginia
    See also
    Hampton University
    Saint Paul's College
    University of Virginia
          Washington (D.C.)
    See also
    American University (Washington, D.C.)
    Catholic University of America
    Georgetown University
    Howard University
    University of the District of Columbia
    Wesley Theological Seminary
             West Virginia
    See also
    West Virginia University
Off again, on again [early closings cancelled] *Time* 129:70 Ap 20 '87
           Western Europe
Higher education: taking our bearings [comparative study of U.S. and European systems] M. G. Bruce. il *Phi Delta Kappan* 69:239-40 N '87
           Western States
Testing for eight skills [liberal arts colleges] il *U S News World Rep* 103:62 O 26 '87
Up and atom in the labs [comprehensive institutions] il *U S News World Rep* 103:60-1 O 26 '87
Colleges and universities, Choice of *See* College, Choice of
Colleges and universities, Cooperative *See* Business and education
Colleges and universities, Experimental *See* College education, Experimental
Colleges for women
    See also
    Spelman College
    Wellesley College
    Wheaton College (Norton, Mass.)
A sisterhood under siege. E. Salholz. il *Newsweek* 109:77 Mr 30 '87
Why can't a woman be more? E. Bowen. il *Time* 130:75-6 O 5 '87
Collegiate Tennis Hall of Fame
Georgia nets hall of fame. il *South Living* 22:73 My '87
Collembola *See* Springtails
Collett, Merrill
The cross and the flag: right-wing evangelicals invade Latin America. il *Progressive* 51:18-20 D '87
Collett, Peter
(jt. auth) See Marsh, Peter E., and Collett, Peter
Collett, Rosemary K.
A favor returned. il *Flower Gard* 32:56-7 D '87/Ja '88
Collette, Will
Citizen's Clearinghouse for Hazardous Wastes. il *Environment* 29:44-5 N '87
Colletti, Roseanne, and others
Underpaid? Check our salary list. il *Good Housekeep* 204:80+ Je '87
Collier, Aldore
Doctor of sports and sociology. il pors *Ebony* 42:101-2+ O '87
If your problem is earthshaking, call Waverly Person. il pors *Ebony* 42:134+ S '87
Jackée Harry: how her TV role is ruining her love life. il pors *Ebony* 42:128+ Je '87
Collier, June M. *See* Mason, June-Collier
Collier, Melinda
        about
Georgia sisters indicted for their mother's murder. *Jet* 73:47 N 2 '87

Two Georgia sisters held for their mother's murder. il pors *Jet* 72:32 Ag 17 '87
Collier, Michael
Feedback [poem] *New Yorker* 62:34 F 2 '87
Collier, Peter
(jt. auth) See Horowitz, David, 1939-, and Collier, Peter
Collier, Peter, and Horowitz, David, 1939-
Another "low dishonest decade" on the left. *Commentary* 83:17-24 Ja '87
Cristina [excerpt from The Fords] il pors *Good Housekeep* 205:58+ O '87
Collier, Reggie
        about
Cowboys cleaning house, toss Collier on waivers. por *Jet* 72:50 Jl 6 '87
Collier's (Periodical)
Lunar fantasies [work of C. Bonestell and F. Freeman] R. Miller and F. C. Durant. il *Omni* 9:50-5 F '87
Starman [1950's sketches by W. von Braun] G. Williams. il *Omni* 9:86-93 Jl '87
Collins, Billy
The Brooklyn Museum of Art [poem] *New Yorker* 63:109 My 18 '87
Collins, Cardiss
        about
Collins: United Airlines must hire more blacks. *Jet* 71:8 Mr 23 '87
Collins, Dean
Collins on basics. See occasional issues of Petersen's Photographic Magazine beginning July 1983 through April 1987
Collins, Francis S., and others
Construction of a general human chromosome jumping library, with application to cystic fibrosis. bibl f il *Science* 235:1046-9 F 27 '87
Collins, Frank
(jt. auth) See Trisler, David, and Collins, Frank
Collins, Jackie
Why do we love the queens of evil? il por *Redbook* 168:62+ F '87
        about
Jackie Collins husbands her energies to turn out steamy Hollywood sagas. A. Chambers. il pors *People Wkly* 27:80-2 Ja 12 '87
Collins, Jess *See* Jess
Collins, Joan
        about
Daytime's steamy new soap. G. Clarke. il pors *Time* 130:68 Ag 3 '87
Divorcing for dollars [cover story] E. Hoover and D. Lindeman. il pors *People Wkly* 28:40-2+ Ag 10 '87
The gorge also rises. L. Fleischer. *Publ Wkly* 232:153 S 18 '87
I married Alexis. P. Holm. il *Harpers* 275:17-20 Ag '87
    Anecdotes, facetiae, satire, etc.
Imaginary interview: Peter Holm. G. W. S. Trow. *New Yorker* 63:25 Ag 24 '87
    Photographs and photography
Beauty lighting. G. Bernstein. il *Petersens Photogr Mag* 16:30-1 Je '87
Collins, Joseph, 1945-
Cory's broken promise. il *Nation* 245:549-50+ N 14 '87
Collins, Judy, 1939-
        about
Collins autobio inspires sound track. S. Bolle. *Publ Wkly* 232:50 O 16 '87
Switching from singer to scribe with amazing grace, Judy Collins writes a searing self-portrait. M. Small. il pors *People Wkly* 28:109-10+ D 7 '87
Collins, Martha Layne, 1936-
        about
Derby Day breakfast for 12,000! J. Siroto. il por *McCalls* 114:108-11 Ap '87
Collins, Marva
        about
Kevin Ross' explosion ends in Chicago with new beginning in Calif. il pors *Jet* 72:14+ Ag 10 '87
Marva Collins may teach in Chicago and Compton. por *Jet* 72:12 Ag 17 '87
Collins, Michael, 1930-
        about
Destination Mars: a conversation with Michael Collins. T. Reichhardt and I. Gilman. il pors *Space World* X-7-283:16-20 Jl '87
Collins, Nancy
Gotcha! [cover story; interview with R. Giuliani] il pors *N Y* 20:28-40 My 25 '87
Mikhail Baryshnikov [interview] pors *Roll Stone* p56-60+ O 8 '87

Collins, Nancy—*cont.*
about
Scoop du jour [interview] L. Smith. il por *Vogue* 177:352-3+ Ap '87
Collins, Paul
The peripatetic Pope: papal visits are a mixed blessing. il *Commonweal* 114:484-7 S 11 '87
Collins, Philip
about
Radio daze. R. Rapoport. il por *Americana* 15:49-52 N/D '87
Collins, Philip Arthur William
Dickens and his readers. bibl il pors *Hist Today* 37:32-40 Jl '87
Collins, Richard L., 1933-
On top. See issues of Flying
Collins, Thomas M.
about
Kareem fights English's suit with one of his own. *Jet* 72:48 Ap 6 '87
A lot of hurt: inaction got Kareem creamed. J. Papanek. il pors *Sports Illus* 67:89-92+ O 19 '87
Collins (William) plc *See* William Collins plc
Collins Avionics Group *See* Rockwell International Corp. Avionics Group
Collins family
about
Faces of middle class America: the Collins family believes in togetherness in New Orleans. il *Ebony* 42:150+ Ag '87
Collins Publishers Inc.
U.S.S.R. opens up to Day in the life crew. S. Bolle. il *Publ Wkly* 232:35-7 Ag 28 '87
Collinsworth, Millicent
about
A bus melee provides grim insight into the life of the blind. D. Chu. il pors *People Wkly* 27:105-6 Je 29 '87
Collischon, David
about
The little black book becomes a mania. M. Maremont. il por *Bus Week* p82 Ap 20 '87
Collision avoidance systems *See* Airplanes—Collision avoidance systems
Collision insurance *See* Insurance, Automobile
Collisions (Nuclear physics)
See also
Scattering (Physics)
Collisions between spinning protons. A. D. Krisch. bibl (p116) il *Sci Am* 257:42-50 Ag '87
Colloids
See also
Foams
Ceramics by the solution-sol-gel route. R. Roy. bibl f il *Science* 238:1664-9 D 18 '87
Colman, Cathy
about
A meeting of the twain. J. Biggar. bibl (p65) il *Psychol Today* 21:46-50+ N '87
Cologne *See* Perfumes
Cologne (Germany)
Music
See also
Opera—Germany (West)
Cologne for men *See* Perfumes for men
La Colombe d'Or (Saint-Paul-de-Vence, France: Hotel) *See* Saint-Paul-de-Vence (France)—Hotels, motels, etc.
Colombia
See also
Amazon River
Bogotá (Colombia)
Civil rights—Colombia
Medical care—Colombia
Motion picture festivals—Colombia
Narcotics laws and regulations—Colombia
Narcotics trade—Colombia
Paleontology—Colombia
Relief work—Colombia
United Nations—Colombia
Antiquities
See also
Ciudad Perdida (Colombia)
Points of order: excavations in Venezuela and Colombia put the Ice Age hunters of North America in a new perspective. A. L. Bryan. maps *Nat Hist* 96:6+ Je '87
Economic policy
Colombian politics: crisis or continuity? B. M. Bagley. bibl f *Curr Hist* 86:21-4+ Ja '87

Industries
See also
Carvajal SA
Emerald mines and mining—Colombia
Politics and government
Colombian politics: crisis or continuity? B. M. Bagley. bibl f *Curr Hist* 86:21-4+ Ja '87
A society torn apart by violence. P. Lernoux. il *Nation* 245:512-14+ N 7 '87
Colombo, C.
Space exploration: 1957-1987. il *Space World* X-4-280:3 Ap '87
Colombo, Cristoforo *See* Columbus, Christopher
Colon, Janette
about
Street inspirations. D. Prince. il pors *N Y* 20:32-7 Ag 17 '87
Colon, Vanessa
about
Street inspirations. D. Prince. il pors *N Y* 20:32-7 Ag 17 '87
Colon (Anatomy)
Cancer
See also
Colorectal cancer
Identification of nuclear receptors for VIP on a human colonic adenocarcinoma cell line. M. B. Omary and M. F. Kagnoff. bibl f il *Science* 238:1578-81 D 11 '87
Diagnosis
Colon cancer curb [test measures complex sugar changes in bowel mucus] M. Mintzer. *Health* 19:26 O '87
Genetic aspects
Colon cancer's culprit gene. J. Silberner. *U S News World Rep* 103:11 Ag 24 '87
Gene defects may predict colon cancer. *Newsweek* 110:46 Ag 24 '87
The gene for familial polyposis coli maps to the long arm of chromosome 5. M. Leppert and others. bibl f il *Science* 238:1411-13 D 4 '87
New clues to detecting a killer. C. Gorman. il *Time* 130:47 Ag 24 '87
ras oncogene activated in human colon cancers. J. L. Marx. *Science* 237:603 Ag 7 '87
Nutritional aspects
Sleuthing to prevent cancer [skin tags help identify persons at risk for colon polyps] C. SerVaas. il *Saturday Evening Post* 259:98+ Jl/Ag '87
Diseases
See also
Diverticular disease
Colon bacteria
See also
Yersinia
Colonial gardens *See* Gardens and gardening, Colonial
Colonial history (U.S.) *See* United States—History—Colonial period, ca. 1600-1775
Colonial manuscripts *See* Manuscripts, American
Colonial Williamsburg *See* Williamsburg (Va.)
Colonies
See also
Space colonies
United Nations. Decolonization Committee
United Nations. Special Committee on the Situation with Regard to the Implementation of the Declaration on the Granting of Independence to Colonial Countries and Peoples
United Nations. Trusteeship Council
Colonization
See also
Space colonies
Colony-stimulating factors
See also
G-CSF
GM-CSF
The human hematopoietic colony-stimulating factors. S. C. Clark and R. Kamen. bibl f il *Science* 236:1229-37 Je 5 '87
Color
See also
Dyes and dyeing
White
Yellow
Psychology
A change of hue. il *Curr Health 2* 13:24-5 Mr '87
Color: analyze yourself. il *Teen* 31:52 My '87
Extra! Extra! Red all about it! [influence of color use in newspapers; study by Robert Bohle and Mario R. Garcia] J. Goetz. il *Psychol Today* 21:24 Jl '87

Color—Psychology—*cont.*

Pink and blue: the power of suggestion [influence of color on strength; research by Jeffrey M. Smith] P. McCarthy. *Psychol Today* 21:24-5 Jl '87

The sound of purple [colors associated with music; study by Robert A. Cutietta and Kelly J. Haggerty] A. H. Rosenfeld. *Psychol Today* 21:18-19 D '87

Color bar generators *See* Signal generators

Color blindness

The case of the colorblind painter. O. W. Sacks and R. Wasserman. bibl f il *N Y Rev Books* 34:25-34 N 19 '87

Color computer graphics *See* Computer graphics

Color computers *See* Computers

Color films *See* Photography—Films

Color in fashion

Christmas glow in gold. il *Harpers Bazaar* 121:140-3 D '87

The new color shock! Black & white. il *Harpers Bazaar* 120:94-8 Ja '87

Anecdotes, facetiae, satire, etc.

Paint it black. B. Staples. il *N Y Times Mag* p22 N 15 '87

Color in house decoration

Be bold with color. il *South Living* 22:130 Jl '87

Decorating with color. D. L. Caringer and others. il *Better Homes Gard* 65:83-91 F '87

Flying colors [Rosemary Gilman decorates Hamptons home for Marifé Hernández] A. Gordon. il *House Gard* 159:180-3 S '87

Let the sun shine in [yellow] M. D. Glass. il *Ladies Home J* 104:96-101 Je '87

Mistaken identity [converted carriage house of W. Hodgins in Manchester, Mass.] C. Vogel. il *N Y Times Mag* p36-40 Ag 23 '87

Old World white [W. Hodgin's house in Manchester-by-the-Sea, Mass.] E. Greene. il *House Gard* 159:94-9 Ja '87

Paris: painting the town [J. de Rohan-Chabot] S. Drucker. il por *Vogue* 177:228-33+ Je '87

The versatility of white. il *Glamour* 85:182-4 Jl '87

Color in house painting *See* House painting

Color of animals

See also

Mimicry (Biology)

Color of birds

Looking for Mr. Goodbird [relationship between garish plumage and parasite resistance; research by Andrew Read] il *Discover* 8:8 O '87

Color of crustaceans

Crustacean blue genes [work of Anthony D'Agostino] il *Oceans* 20:4-5 Ja/F '87

Color of fish

Fugitive color [photographs] D. Hall. il *Oceans* 20:30-5 My/Je '87

Color of insects

Color-conscious mosquitoes [homochromy; work of Mark Q. Benedict and Jack A. Seawright] il *Sci Am* 257:24+ Ag '87

Color of leaves

Autumn leaves. J. H. Moerschel. il *Conservationist* 42:32-5 S/O '87

Autumn leaves. F. Roth. il *Sierra* 72:96-9 S/O '87

Leaf magic [fall color changes] A. Raver. il *Read Dig* 131:9-10+ S '87

Riding the leaves [fall foliage cycling trips] F. Lunzer. il *Forbes* 140:101+ Ag 24 '87

Color of man

Painting skin the color of life. F. Alexander. il *Am Artist* 51:66-70 Mr '87

An universal freckle [views of S. S. Smith] S. J. Gould. il por *Nat Hist* 96:14+ Ag '87

The color of money [film] *See* Motion picture reviews—Single works

Color of plants

How purple was my valley [bacteriorhodopsin; work of Andrew Goldsworthy] il *Discover* 8:14+ N '87

Color perception *See* Color vision

Color photography *See* Photography

Color printing

See also

Newspapers—Color printing

Color processing (Photography) *See* Photography—Processing

The color purple [film] *See* Motion picture reviews—Single works

Color television receivers *See* Television receivers

Color temperature

Determining the color of light. il *Pop Photogr* 94:33 Mr '87

Color vision

See also

Color blindness

Color vision and the retinex theory [discussion of February 8, 1985 article, The goldfish as a retinex animal] D. J. Ingle. il *Science* 238:1731-2 D 18 '87

Colorado

See also

Agriculture—Colorado

Architecture, Domestic—Colorado

Baca Grande (Colo.)

Booksellers and bookselling—Colorado

Colorado Plateau

Daylight saving—Colorado

Dolores River (Colo. and Utah)

Education—Colorado

Environmental policy—Colorado

Grand Mesa (Colo.)

Irrigation—Colorado

Mesa Verde National Park (Colo.)

Motion picture festivals—Colorado

Music festivals—Colorado

North Saint Vrain Creek (Colo.)

Paleontology—Colorado

Prisons—Colorado

Public health—Colorado

Radon pollution—Colorado

Ranches—Colorado

Resorts—Colorado

Vegetable gardens and gardening—Colorado

Water pollution—Colorado

Wilderness areas—Colorado

Industries

See also

Aerospace industries

Uranium mines and mining—Colorado

Rocky Mountain high-tech. E. Truitt. il *Space World* X-1-277:22-4 Ja '87

Moral conditions

Colorado booksellers challenge obscenity law. *Publ Wkly* 231:87 F 27 '87

Parks and reserves

The red rocks of Roxborough . . . new state park 25 miles southwest of Denver. il *Sunset* 179:48-9 S '87

Colorado National Bank

Plastic profits [D. D. Browning] A. Snitzer. il por *Forbes* 140:116 Ag 10 '87

Colorado Plateau

Bibliography

Six recent books on the "spiritual heart of the West". il *Sunset* 178:42+ Mr '87

Colorado River (Colo.-Mexico)

See also

Central Arizona Project

Grand Canyon (Ariz.)

Tales from a river woman [raft trip guide]; ed. by Deborah Whitford. G. Clark. il pors *Women's Sports Fitness* 9:38-41+ Ap '87

History

A river changes. V. Ryan. il map *Earth Sci* 39:15-17 Wint '86

Colorado River (Colo.-Mexico) dams *See* Dams

Colorado State Penitentiary (Cañon City, Colo.) *See* Prisons—Colorado

Colorado tick fever *See* Rocky Mountain spotted fever

Colorectal cancer

Diagnosis

The talking tumor's guide to surgery? D. D. Edwards. *Sci News* 131:232 Ap 11 '87

Genetic aspects

Clonal analysis of human colorectal tumors [use of restriction fragment length polymorphisms] E. R. Fearon and others. bibl f il *Science* 238:193-7 O 9 '87

Colon-cancer defect found [research by Walter F. Bodmer and others] *Sci News* 132:102 Ag 15 '87

Colorectal oncogenes found. *Sci News* 131:343 My 30 '87

Torn genes. T. Beardsley. *Sci Am* 257:40+ O '87

Therapy

Cancer study patients being sought. D. D. Edwards. *Sci News* 131:232 Ap 11 '87

The colored museum [drama] *See* Wolfe, George C.

Colored pencil drawing *See* Pencil drawing

Coloring matter in cosmetics, food, etc.

Amaranth: the color of soy sauce. *Prevention* 39:53-4 O '87

Coloring of motion pictures See Motion pictures—Coloring
Colors See Color
Colson, Bill
  Olympic tennis: a bad idea. por *Sports Illus* 66:96 Je 29 '87
Colson, Charles W.
  The celebrity illusion. il *Christ Today* 31:72 D 11 '87
  Criminals are made, not born. il *Christ Today* 31:72 Ja 16 '87
  The fear of doing nothing. il *Christ Today* 31:72 My 15 '87
  Must governments deal in deceit? il *Christ Today* 31:66 F 6 '87
  My cancer and the good health gospel. por *Christ Today* 31:56 Ap 3 '87
  The myth of the money tree. il *Christ Today* 31:64 Jl 10 '87
                    about
  A convert's convictions. il por *Newsweek* 110:10 O 19 '87
Colt Industries Inc.
  One year later, Colt is at a steady gallop. C. Power. il por *Bus Week* p134+ O 19 '87
Colter, Warren Z.
                    about
  Philadelphia In the black. W. J. Dawkins. il pors *Black Enterp* 17:66 Je '87
Coltrane, Alice
  John Coltrane. il pors *Essence* 18:73 N '87
Coltrane, John, 1926-1967
                    about
  John Coltrane. A. Coltrane. il pors *Essence* 18:73 N '87
  Tribute to John Coltrane. R. Woessner. *Down Beat* 54:47 My '87
  What Coltrane wanted. E. Strickland. il por *Atlantic* 260:100-2 D '87
Columba (Constellation) See Constellations
Columbia (S.C.)
                    Blacks
                    History
  Richard Samuel Roberts [exhibit of photographs at Columbia Museum] J. Meyer. il *Art News* 86:35+ Mr '87
            Historic houses, sites, etc.
  A long time building [South Carolina State House] G. D. Ford. il *South Living* 22:86-7 N '87
          Religious institutions and affairs
  The Pope came to South Carolina: unfortunately, so did the Yankee press. D. Moniz. il por *Wash Mon* 19:28-9 D '87
                    Stores
  Things are looking up for the Vista [Congaree Vista] G. D. Ford. il *South Living* 22:24+ O '87
Columbia Bar & Grill (Hollywood, Calif.) See Hollywood (Calif.)—Restaurants, nightclubs, bars, etc.
Columbia Broadcasting System, Inc. See CBS Inc.
Columbia Glacier (Alaska) See Glaciers
Columbia Law School See Columbia University. School of Law
Columbia Missourian
  'Missourian' daily gets 1st black managing editor [B. Johnson] *Jet* 72:40 S 7 '87
Columbia Pictures Entertainment Inc.
  At Columbia, things might go better with Tri-Star [Coca-Cola merging two studios] R. Grover. il por *Bus Week* p74-5 N 30 '87
Columbia Pictures Industries, Inc.
  Amelia Batchler: for 51 years she's carried the torch for Columbia [model for motion picture logo] A. Batchler. il por *People Wkly* 27:48-9 F 9 '87
  Felled in Hollywood's 'killing fields' [D. Puttnam resigns] J. Egan. por *U S News World Rep* 103:82 S 28 '87
  He rode into Hollywood on a Chariot of fire, but David Puttnam's job at Columbia went up in smoke. M. Dougherty. il pors *People Wkly* 28:125-6+ N 16 '87
  A Hollywood outsider's exit [D. Puttnam quits] M. Reese and J. Foote. il por *Newsweek* 110:65 S 28 '87
Columbia Presbyterian Medical Center (New York, N.Y.)
  Heart to heart: can a chimp transplant save human life? N. Taylor. il *N Y* 20:44-8 Jl 13 '87
Columbia Records (Firm) See CBS Inc. Records Division
Columbia River
  Big river walleyes. J. Gibbs. il *Outdoor Life* 179:100-1+ My '87
Columbia River Gorge (Or. and Wash.)
  The Columbia River Gorge. B. J. Cantwell. il *Travel Holiday* 168:12-15 Jl '87
  The gorge. il map *Sunset* 178:72+ My '87

Columbia Savings & Loan Assoc.
  The thrift that junk bonds built. T. Carson. il por *Bus Week* p86 Je 29 '87
Columbia Star (Ship)
  Sailors of the Fourth Coast try to look ahead. M. Agar. il *Smithsonian* 18:116-20+ S '87
Columbia State Historic Park (Calif.) See California—Parks and reserves
Columbia University
  1787. K. Ide. il *Am Herit* 38:108-9 Ap '87
  Back to the future: Columbia replays the battles of '68 [eviction battles and racial tensions] P. Blauner. il *N Y* 20:30-3 My 18 '87
  Campus controversy [racial tension] S. McConnell. *New Repub* 196:13-14 My 25 '87
  The Federalist paper [conservative student journal] D. K. Mano. *Natl Rev* 39:58-9 F 13 '87
  Friends in high places [M. Frankel, L. Grossman, R. Wald and R. Arledge of Columbia's Class of 1952] B. Yagoda. il pors *Channels* 7:54-61 Ja '87
  Hail, Columbia, where losing isn't everything, it's the only thing—just ask the fans. J. Friedman. il *People Wkly* 28:110-11 O 19 '87
  Minorities get $25 million boost from Columbia gift [gift by J. W. Kluge] *Jet* 72:32 My 18 '87
Columbia University. Graduate School of Business
  A $100,000 campus 'raid' [teacher A. Edelman's finder's fee raises questions of conflict of interests] A. Gabor. por *U S News World Rep* 103:12-13 O 26 '87
  A $100,000 question stirs up Columbia [A. Edelman offers his Columbia business students a finder's fee for spotting a good takeover target] B. Kantrowitz. il por *Newsweek* 110:76 O 26 '87
  Don't go near the dollars [vetoes professor A. Edelman's offer of finder's fee to a student who could come up with a company ripe for raiding] E. Bowen. il por *Time* 130:138-9 O 26 '87
  Edelman's art of reward [offer of $100,000 finder's fee to students] N. J. Perry. il por *Fortune* 116:159 N 9 '87
Columbia University. School of Law
  Columbia Law School gets its first housewife-scholar-dean [B. A. Black] C. M. Eckhardt. il por *Ms* 16:62-5+ O '87
Columbian Exposition (1893: Chicago, Ill.) See World's Columbian Exposition (1893: Chicago, Ill.)
Columbiana (Ala.)
                Galleries and museums
                    See also
  Smith-Harrison Museum
Columbus, Chris
                    about
  Adventures in babysitting [film] Reviews
    Newsweek 110:60 Jl 13 '87. D. Ansen
    People Wkly 28:10 Jl 20 '87. S. Haller
Columbus, Christopher
  The earthly paradise [excerpt from The four voyages of Christopher Columbus] il *Courier* 40:8-9 Ap '87
                    about
  Columbus's biggest discovery. R. Sokolov. il *Nat Hist* 96:66-7 Ag '87
  Retracing the path of Christopher Columbus. il *Sea Front* 33:307 Jl/Ag '87
  Searching for Columbus's lost colony [La Navidad in Haiti] K. A. Deagan. il *Natl Geogr* 172:672-5 N '87
Columbus (New York, N.Y.: Restaurant) See New York (N.Y.)—Restaurants, nightclubs, bars, etc.
Columbus (Ohio)
              Politics and government
  Jerry Hammond: from lawbreaker to lawmaker [City Council president] C. A. Bryce. il *Ebony* 42:60+ My '87
Columbus (Space station) See Space stations, European
Columbus-America Discovery Group
  Dredging for dollars [sonar used to find sunken sidewheel steamer Central America] W. J. Cook. il *U S News World Rep* 103:48 Ag 3 '87
Columbus Center (New York, N.Y.)
  The shadow [cover story] J. Taylor. il maps *N Y* 20:40-8 O 5 '87
  The sky line [redevelopment plans] B. Gill. *New Yorker* 63:113-18+ N 9 '87
Columbus Circle (New York, N.Y.)
                    See also
  Columbus Center (New York, N.Y.)
Columbus State Community College
  Ohio converts college to aid black education. *Jet* 72:28 Je 29 '87
Columbus Technical Institute See Columbus State Community College

Columns
See also
Porticoes
Columns, Advice (Newspapers) *See* Newspapers—Advice
columns
Columns (Newspapers) *See* Newspapers—Sections, columns,
etc.
Colussy, Dan
about
A successful decontamination. K. Hannon. il por *Forbes*
140:68 Ag 24 '87
Colvin, Gordon C.
Managing New York's marine fishery. il *Conservationist*
42:10-17 S/O '87
Colwin, Laurie
Flank steak: the neglected cut. il *Gourmet* 47:52+ My
'87
How to make gingerbread. il *Gourmet* 47:98+ D '87
Potato salad. il *Gourmet* 47:222+ O '87
Stuffing: a confession. il *Gourmet* 47:120+ N '87
Colyton, Henry John
The countess and the devil [story] il *Saturday Evening
Post* 259:68-71+ Ja/F '87
The countess and the devil [story] il *Saturday Evening
Post* 259:36+ Mr '87
Coma
Coming back to life [K. Ryan survives coma after almost
drowning] F. M. Henley. il pors *Ladies Home J* 104:34+
Jl '87
Common scents [multi-sensory stimulation for comatose
patients with head injuries] J. D. Schwartz. il *Health*
19:21 S '87
Is it wrong to cut off feeding? R. N. Ostling. il *Time*
129:71 F 23 '87
The miraculous story of a coma survivor [J. Cole] J.
R. Heilman. il por *Redbook* 169:90-1+ Jl '87
"My son was hit by lightning"; ed. by Lorene Hanley
Duquin. S. Schunk. il por *Redbook* 169:17+ Ag '87
A tornado took away his world [adoptee A. Sferrino
gets kidney from natural mother] J. Grazier. il pors
McCalls 114:130-2 Je '87
We got our son back for Christmas [automobile accident
victim E. Erwig] J. L. Block. il por *Good Housekeep*
205:111-13 D '87
Comacho Solis, Manuel
Mexico-United States relations [address, November 12,
1986] *Vital Speeches Day* 53:222-4 Ja 15 '87
Comair, Inc.
Two regional commuters expand market base beyond
traditional areas. *Aviat Week Space Technol* 127:52
S 28 '87
Comas, Beatrice H.
Supermarket and then some [poem] *McCalls* 114:140
S '87
Combe Inc.
Feet first [H. Lapidus] G. Morgenson. il por *Forbes*
140:113+ Ag 10 '87
Combinatorial analysis
See also
Permutations
Tessellations (Mathematics)
Combined Federal Campaign (U.S.)
UNCF seeks support of federal employees. il *Jet* 72:38
S 14 '87
Combines *See* Harvesting machinery
Combs, Nina
Is your love life going down "the tube"? il *Read Dig*
131:146-8 O '87
Combustion
See also
Detonation
Flames
Spontaneous human combustion
Dropping smoothly to a fiery end [fuel combustion
research by Thomas Avedisian and Jiann Yang] I.
Peterson. il *Sci News* 132:71 Ag 1 '87
Researchers climb inside of the fire to tweak the flame.
B. Fellman. bibl (p229) il *Smithsonian* 18:70-2+ O
'87
Combustion Engineering Inc.
From dirt to glamour and mixed reviews. R. McGough.
il por *Forbes* 139:112+ Mr 23 '87
Combustion engines *See* Automobile engines; Gas and oil
engines; Motorcycle engines
Comdex (Trade show)
The curse of Chaos Manor. J. Pournelle. *Byte* 12:251-2+
Mr '87
Report from Atlanta. il *Radio-Electron* 58
ComputerDigest:73-4 S '87
Come and see [film] *See* Motion picture reviews—Single
works

Comedians
See also
Anderson, Louie
Black comedians
Brooks, Mel
Carvey, Dana
Economists as comedians
Fields, W. C., 1879-1946
Gayle, Jackie
Gleason, Jackie
Goldthwait, Bob
Gottfried, Gilbert
Homer and Jethro
Jones, Spike, 1911-1965
Kolson, Rob
Leno, Jay
Mason, Jackie
Sahl, Mort
Saint Silicon
Short, Martin
Sinbad
Is comedy making a comeback or what? [cover story]
T. Shales. il *Esquire* 108:118-22+ O '87
Magnum farce. C. Rubin. il *Harpers Bazaar* 120:222+
Ap '87
My funny valentine: is living with a comedian a laugh
a minute? J. Powell. il *Glamour* 85:182+ F '87
Ranting, raving, doing the dishes. R. Zoglin. il *Time*
129:88-9 Ap 27 '87
Stand-up comedy on a roll. R. Zoglin. il *Time* 130:56-7
Ag 24 '87
Your favorite funnymen. il *Teen* 31:54 Jl '87
Comedy
See also
Cable television—Comedy programs
Duck's Breath Mystery Theatre
Humor
Motion pictures—Comedy films
Phonograph records—Comedy records
Radio broadcasting—Comedy programs
Tape recordings—Comedy
Television broadcasting—Comedy programs
Videotapes—Comedy
Is comedy making a comeback or what? [cover story]
T. Shales. il *Esquire* 108:118-22+ O '87
Benefit performances
See also
Comic Relief (Project)
Study and teaching
This course is a joke [M. Helitzer's comedy course
at Ohio University] N. Karlen. il por *Roll Stone* p106+
S 24 '87
Comedy nightclubs
See also
Catch A Rising Star Inc.
Comedy clubs. A. Mermelstein. il *Travel Holiday* 167:56-8
Mr '87
Magnum farce. C. Rubin. il *Harpers Bazaar* 120:222+
Ap '87
Stand-up comedy on a roll. R. Zoglin. il *Time* 130:56-7
Ag 24 '87
Comedy of errors [drama] *See* Shakespeare, William,
1564-1616
Comer, Gary C.
about
Steering his own course to success. S. Caminiti. il por
Fortune 115:95 Ja 5 '87
Comer, James P.
As they grow/11 through 13. See issues of Parents
Education is the way out and up. il pors *Ebony* 42:61-2+
Ag '87
about
A call for Comer. S. S. Harrison. por *Black Enterp*
17:20 Ap '87
Comet dust *See* Matter, Interstellar
Comets
See also
Halley's comet
Space flight—Cometary missions
Alien comets: no threat to earth [work of Alan Stern]
il *Sky Telesc* 73:154 F '87
Anatomy of a comet [cover story; special issue] il *Sky
Telesc* 73:236+ Mr '87
The comet-asteroid connection [research by William K.
Hartmann and others] *Sky Telesc* 74:343 O '87
Comet Bradfield: a northern sky showpiece. il *Astronomy*
15:90 N '87
Comet digest. J. E. Bortle. See issues of Sky and Telescope
Comets: life in an imperfect icebox. J. Eberhart. *Sci
News* 131:219 Ap 4 '87

Comets—*cont.*

The discovery of Comet Levy, 1987a. D. H. Levy. il *Sky Telesc* 73:546-7 My '87

The godfather of disaster [cometary theory of W. Whiston] S. J. Gould. il *Nat Hist* 96:20+ S '87

How to discover a comet. D. H. Levy. il *Astronomy* 15:74-7 D '87

More clues to asteroid-dead comet connections. R. A. Kerr. *Science* 235:29-30 Ja 2 '87

A new light in the sky [Comet Wilson] J. Horowitz. il *N Y Times Mag* p52+ Mr 29 '87

Observing the elusive Comet Wilson. A. Hale. il *Astronomy* 15:79-81 Ja '87

Oort cloud comets: blasted, bumped, and baked? [work of Alan Stern] *Sky Telesc* 74:459 N '87

Signs of Nemesis: meteors, magnetism. D. E. Thomsen. *Sci News* 131:100 F 14 '87

Tracking comets with a stepping motor. E. Everhart. il por *Sky Telesc* 73:208-12 F '87

Tracking down a comet [computer program] E. Everhart. il *Sky Telesc* 73:196-7 F '87

What to do if you discover a comet. D. W. E. Green. il *Sky Telesc* 74:420-1 O '87

Orbits

Realm of the comets [Oort cloud] P. R. Weissman. il *Sky Telesc* 73:238-41 Mr '87

Photographs and photography

A camera that tracks comets. R. Arbour. il *Sky Telesc* 74:428-30 O '87

Spectra and spectroscopy

Evidence for chain molecules enriched in carbon, hydrogen, and oxygen in Comet Halley [Giotto data] D. L. Mitchell and others. bibl f il *Science* 237:626-8 Ag 7 '87

First polymer in space identified in Comet Halley [Giotto data] W. F. Huebner. bibl f il *Science* 237:628-30 Ag 7 '87

ComFed Savings Bank

After the feast. J. Willoughby. por *Forbes* 140:38+ O 5 '87

Comfort

The quality of comfort [views of N. Pierrepont] S. M. Alsop. il por *Archit Dig* 44:250+ Je '87

Comfort stations *See* Public comfort stations

Comic books, strips, etc.

See also
Doonesbury (Comic strip)
Graphic novels
Opus (Fictional character)
Spider Man (Fictional character)
Superman (Fictional character)

Comic books are winning new respect. A. Levine. il *U S News World Rep* 103:69 S 21 '87

Creatures from the black cartoon [G. Larson's The far side] P. Richmond. il por *Roll Stone* p79-80+ S 24 '87

A doodle god makes good [Life in hell creator M. Groening] J. Foote. il por *Newsweek* 110:70+ S 28 '87

Kartes licenses Peanuts from sister company [arrangement with United Media for home video rights] il *Publ Wkly* 231:50+ Ap 24 '87

Snuffy Smith's pappy [F. Lasswell] D. Young. il por *South Living* 22:106 Jl '87

Bibliography

Batman at midlife: or, The funnies grow up. M. Richler. il *N Y Times Book Rev* 92:35 My 3 '87

Economics use

Cartoons? Strip joints? Economics 101 was never like this [Comic: an introduction to the Japanese economy] il *Newsweek* 110:44 Jl 27 '87

Exhibitions

The Far side of NMNH. C. Bond. il *Smithsonian* 18:168 Ap '87

History

World of funnies is 'warped with fancy, woofed with dreams'. B. Daviss. bibl (p271) il *Smithsonian* 18:180-3+ N '87

Political aspects

Comics and catastrophe [A. Spiegelman's Maus] A. Gopnik. il *New Repub* 196:29-34 Je 22 '87

Mauschwitz [excerpt from Maus, part II] A. Spiegelman. il *Esquire* 107:67-9+ My '87

Canada

The comic book's quest for maturity. P. Young. il *Macleans* 100:66-7 S 28 '87

Japan

Cartoons? Strip joints? Economics 101 was never like this [Comic: an introduction to the Japanese economy] il *Newsweek* 110:44 Jl 27 '87

Comic books, strips, etc. and fashion

Funnies business. il *Vogue* 177:256 My '87

Comic Relief (Project)

Comics spell relief for the homeless with laughter. il *People Wkly* 28:66-7 N 30 '87

Comic strips *See* Comic books, strips, etc.

Comins, Neil, and Marschall, Laurence A.

How do spiral galaxies spiral? [cover story] il *Astronomy* 15:6-23 D '87

Comissiona, Sergiu, 1928-

Vitamins of happiness. il *Opera News* 52:26-7 Jl '87

Commager, Henry Steele, 1902-

Firm yet flexible. il *Life* 10:118 Fall '87

Command, control, communications and intelligence network

See Communications, Military

Commandos, Russian

Soviet break-ins? [Spetsnaz unit suspected in U.S. naval base espionage] L. Howard. il *Newsweek* 110:6 N 9 '87

Soviet saboteurs: on-site training [Spetsnaz unit] D. Stanglin. il *U S News World Rep* 102:46 Mr 30 '87

Commemorative coins *See* Coins

Commencement addresses *See* Baccalaureate addresses

Commencements

Those growls at Brooke's commencement weren't coming from the Princeton Tiger. il pors *People Wkly* 27:34-5 Je 22 '87

Commerce

See also
Asia-Pacific International Trade Fair
Balance of trade
Barter
Business
Competition
Embargo
Export-import trade
Interstate commerce
Mercantile system
Merchant marine
Ports
Shipping
Smuggling
Tariff
Trade marks and trade names
Trade routes
Trading companies
World Trade Week
See also subhead Commerce under names of countries

International spotlight. H. Eason. See issues of Nation's Business

Commerce Clearing House, Inc.

Commerce Clearing: cashing in on tax confusion. *Money* 16:8 Ja '87

Commerce Dept. (U.S.) *See* United States. Dept. of Commerce

Commerce, Science, and Transportation Committee *See* United States. Congress. Senate. Committee on Commerce, Science, and Transportation

Commercial blacklisting *See* Blacklisting

Commercial canning *See* Canneries

Commercial catalogs *See* Catalogs, Commercial

Commercial conferences *See* Economic conferences

Commercial correspondence *See* Business writing

Commercial Credit Company

Sandy Weill is doing just fine on Main Street, thank you. S. Bartlett. il *Bus Week* p96-7+ S 21 '87

Sanford Weill. C. S. Eklund. il por *Bus Week* Sp Issue:230 Ap 17 '87

Will Sandy Weill snare Hutton? G. G. Marcial. il *Bus Week* p73 Ag 24 '87

Commercial crimes

See also
Bribery
Computer crimes
Embezzlement
Employee theft
Insider trading
Tax evasion

Having it all, then throwing it all away. S. Koepp. il *Time* 129:22-3 My 25 '87

Making punishment fit white-collar crime. L. J. Tell. il *Bus Week* p84-5 Je 15 '87

Stiffer penalties needed [corporate fraud; views of W. Holder and Theodore Mock] *USA Today (Periodical)* 116:6 D '87

White-collar crime: stopping a sneaky business. L. Eskin. il *Sch Update* 120:9 D 4 '87

Women: the new white-collar criminals. C. Kirschenbaum. *Glamour* 85:306-7+ Mr '87

Commercial fisheries *See* Fisheries
Commercial law
> *See also*
> Antitrust law
> Arbitration, Commercial
> Contracts
> Corporation law
> Landlord and tenant
> Maritime law
> Trade marks and trade names
> United Nations. Commission on International Trade Law

Business can't bank on Judge Kennedy's vote. P. Dwyer. il por *Bus Week* p33 N 30 '87
Deadlock at the Court [business cases before the Supreme Court] P. Dwyer. il *Bus Week* p36-7 O 12 '87
The great debate inside Robert Bork [business rulings and writings] P. Dwyer. il por *Bus Week* p34-5 S 14 '87
On the docket. See issues of Forbes
What Congress is pushing now. A. C. Isgrò. il *Fortune* 115:99+ My 11 '87
Commercial mortgage securities *See* Mortgage bonds and notes
Commercial photography *See* Photography, Commercial
Commercial policy
> *See also*
> Brazil—Commercial policy
> Canada—Commercial policy
> China—Commercial policy
> Commodity control
> Competition
> Dumping (Commercial policy)
> Free trade and protection
> Japan—Commercial policy
> Korea (South)—Commercial policy
> Mercantile system
> Québec (Province)—Commercial policy
> Soviet Union—Commercial policy
> Taiwan—Commercial policy
> United States—Commercial policy

International spotlight. H. Eason. See issues of Nation's Business
Commercial products
> *See also*
> Animal products
> Private brands
> Products, New
> Quality of products

Fiesta Ware and Tide, b'gosh [how yesterday's products get a second wind] J. Sherman. *Work Woman* 12:41 Ag '87
Reeboks, Swatches, Calvins and 36 other things you'd never heard of in 1972. il *Money* Sp Issue:58-63 Fall '87
> **Endorsements**
> *See* Advertising—Testimonials
> **Recall**

Product recalls. See issues of Consumer Reports
Recalls: an up-to-date list. J. Gillis. See issues of Good Housekeeping beginning May 1987
> **Safety devices and measures**
> *See also*
> U.S. Consumer Product Safety Commission
> **Testing**
> *See also*
> Consumers Union of United States
Commercial treaties and agreements
> *See also*
> General Agreement on Tariffs and Trade
> International Coffee Agreement
> United States—Commercial treaties and agreements
Commercials *See* Radio advertising; Television advertising
Commission des Valeurs Mobilières du Québec *See* Quebec Securities Commission
Commission on Central America (U.S.) *See* National Bipartisan Commission on Central America (U.S.)
Commission on Defense Management (U.S.) *See* United States. President's Commission on Defense Management
Commissioner of baseball *See* Baseball, Professional—Organization and administration
Commissions, Independent regulatory *See* Regulatory agencies
Commissions (Compensation)
> *See also*
> Brokers—Commissions
> Real estate agencies and agents—Commissions
> Sales personnel—Salaries, commissions, pensions, etc.
> Travel agencies and agents—Commissions

Commitment (Psychology)
She says monogamy, he says monotony: closing the guy/girl gap. W. D. Leight. *Mademoiselle* 93:220-1+ Ap '87
Today's troubled men. H. J. Freudenberger. bibl (p63) il *Psychol Today* 21:46-7 D '87
Committee on the Constitutional System (U.S.)
Prescription for democratic change. W. Lowther. il *Macleans* 100:21 F 9 '87
You can't take politics out of politics. M. S. Forbes, Jr. *Forbes* 139:25 F 23 '87
Commodity brokers
> *See also*
> Geldermann Inc.
> Philipp Brothers, Inc.
> Refco Group Ltd.
> Yancy Minerals Inc.

Epitaph for a trader [suicide of broker J. Markle] W. P. Barrett. il por *Forbes* 140:121 D 14 '87
Escape from New York [trader R. Rowland] J. Clements. il por *Forbes* 140:126 S 7 '87
Rich list candidate: 1995 [trader T. Baldwin] S. W. Angrist. il *Forbes* 140 Sp Issue:401 O 26 '87
> **Ethical aspects**

A giant trader under fire [Philipp Brothers] D. Pauly and B. Powell. il *Newsweek* 109:36-40 Ja 19 '87
A trader runs amok [oil trader L. Borget] T. Mack. por *Forbes* 140:8 N 16 '87
> **Great Britain**
> *See also*
> Mocatta Group
> **Japan**

The Japanese are elbowing into Chicago's futures pits. J. N. Frank. il *Bus Week* p106-7 Je 1 '87
Commodity control
UNCTAD committee assesses impact of commodity crisis on developing countries [Committee on Commodities] *UN Chron* 24:79 My '87
Commodity exchanges
> *See also*
> Chicago Board of Trade
> Chicago Board Options Exchange
> Chicago Mercantile Exchange
> Commodity brokers
> New York Mercantile Exchange
> United States. Commodity Futures Trading Commission
> **Acquisitions and mergers**

A hot commodity [W. Bradt of the New York Merc pushes for mergers] S. W. Angrist. il por *Forbes* 139:256 Je 15 '87
> **Membership**

Exchange seats are hot commodities. S. Weiss. il *Bus Week* p107 Je 1 '87
> **Australia**
> *See also*
> Sydney Futures Exchange
Commodity funds
> *See also*
> Tudor Investment Corporation

A beef about commodities. J. B. Quinn. il *Newsweek* 110:45 Jl 20 '87
Every dog has his day. S. W. Angrist. il *Forbes* 140:138 D 28 '87
Silk purses or sows' ears? J. Kosnett. il *Changing Times* 41:59-63 Jl '87
Commodity futures
> *See also*
> Chicago Board of Trade
> Commodity brokers
> Commodity funds
> Commodity Research Bureau, Inc.
> Hedging (Finance)
> Interest rate futures
> Price index futures
> Stock index futures
> United States. Commodity Futures Trading Commission

Commodities. S. W. Angrist. See issues of Forbes
Farmers shouldn't count their chickens quite yet. J. N. Frank. il *Bus Week* p61 My 25 '87
Hopes high for new feeder cattle options; Futures survive censure for now. *Success Farm* 85 no6:B13 Mr '87
The wave of the futures may be good ol' commodities. M. E. Kreca. il *Bus Week* p164+ D 28 '87-Ja 4 '88
What's causing commodity fever. J. N. Frank. il *Bus Week* p111 My 4 '87
The world of cocoa: life in the trading pits. P. Wang. il *Newsweek* 109:38-9 Ja 19 '87

Commodity futures—*cont.*
Bibliography
More reading for fun and profit. S. W. Angrist. il *Forbes* 140:240 N 2 '87
Commodity Futures Trading Commission *See* United States. Commodity Futures Trading Commission
Commodity options
See also
  Chicago Board Options Exchange
  Stock index options
A computer in your futures [Personal Options Advisor] S. W. Angrist. il *Forbes* 140:130 Ag 10 '87
Hopes high for new feeder cattle options; Futures survive censure for now. *Success Farm* 85 no6:B13 Mr '87
The hot new low-stakes play in oil [crude options] T. Thompson. il *Bus Week* p80 Ja 26 '87
Not so crude options [oil options] S. W. Angrist. il *Forbes* 139:176 Mr 9 '87
Trading tips from a poker player turned options pro [J. Keller] il por *Money* 16:242 N '87
Commodity prices *See* Prices
Commodity Research Bureau, Inc.
A glimpse today of tomorrow [futures price index] S. W. Angrist. il *Forbes* 139:109 Ja 26 '87
Commodore (Ship)
Commodore wreck: prototype "Open boat". B. Belleville. *Oceans* 20:58-9 My/Je '87
Found: Crane's 'Open boat'. S. Begley. il *Newsweek* 109:52 Ja 5 '87
Commodore International Ltd.
Commodore is anything but dead [Amiga 500] G. Lewis. il por *Bus Week* p96-7 Mr 9 '87
Curtain up on enhanced Amiga [A2000] il *Pers Comput* 11:27 Ap '87
Why did heads roll at Commodore? G. Lewis. il por *Bus Week* p114 My 11 '87
Commodore Savings Association
Cutting Commodore with a Bowie knife [L. Connell] J. Weber, Jr. il por *Bus Week* p74 N 9 '87
Commodores (Musical group)
Commodores' King arrested in L.A. investment scheme. por *Jet* 72:12 Ap 13 '87
Common Cold Unit (Great Britain)
A feverish vacation spot. D. Foote. il *Newsweek* 110:64 Ag 31 '87
The subjects came in for a cold [effects of common cold on coordination and memory; study by Andrew P. Smith] V. Bozzi and G. Lowe. il *Psychol Today* 21:14 D '87
Common Fund
How an educated guess is paying off for George Keane. G. G. Marcial. il por *Bus Week* p106 D 21 '87
Shotgun approach. R. Phalon. il por *Forbes* 139:132+ Je 15 '87
Common Market *See* European Economic Community
The common pursuit [drama] *See* Gray, Simon James Holliday, 1936-
Common sense
Causality, structure, and common sense. M. M. Waldrop. il *Science* 237:1297-9 S 11 '87
Common stocks *See* Stocks
Commoner, Barry
The environment. *New Yorker* 63:46-7+ Je 15 '87
Commonweal (Periodical)
A change of editors [P. Steinfels replaced by M. Steinfels] *Commonweal* 114:693 D 4 '87
The new look. il *Commonweal* 114:4-5 Ja 16 '87
Commonwealth Edison Co.
Consumers out in the cold [rate hikes approved] M. Ervin. il *Progressive* 51:17 Mr '87
Commonwealth of Nations
Conferences
Britain's assault on the Commonwealth [Britain refuses to agree to wider sanctions against South Africa] H. Mackenzie. il *Macleans* 100:24-5 O 26 '87
Charting a new course [meeting in Vancouver, B.C.] H. Mackenzie. il *Macleans* 100:28 O 19 '87
Communauté de Taizé
In the one Spirit [video of John Paul II's visit to Taizé] *America* 156:453 Je 6 '87
Communicable diseases
See also
  Animals as carriers of infection
  Centers for Disease Control (U.S.)
  Cold (Disease)
  Epidemiology
  Gonorrhea
  Malaria
  Measles
  Rift Valley fever
  Rocky Mountain spotted fever

Smallpox
Typhoid fever
Vaccines and vaccination
Venereal diseases
Waterborne infection
Infectious diseases; ed. by Maxine Abrams. D. Kaye. *Good Housekeep* 204:69-72 F '87
Communication
See also
  Automobiles—Communication systems
  Aviation—Communication systems
  Communications satellites
  Conversation
  Cybernetics
  Infrared communications
  Interstellar communication
  Language and languages
  Lasers—Communication use
  Mass media
  Neurolinguistics
  Persuasion (Psychology)
  Public relations
  Radio
  Speech
  Spread spectrum communications
  Telecommunication
  United Nations. Committee on Information
Psychological aspects
See me, help me [children's bizarre behavior as communication] E. G. Carr and V. M. Durand. bibl (p65) il *Psychol Today* 21:62-4 N '87
Social aspects
10 tips on talking with your child. M. B. Brinley. il *McCalls* 114:53 Ag '87
Can you small talk? (Women who can have better marriages). D. Hales. *Redbook* 169:166-7+ S '87
Depressed moms: mixed messages for kids [research by Zvia Breznitz and Tracy Sherman] E. Grant. *Psychol Today* 21:14 O '87
Fatherese & motherese. P. Perry. il *Parents* 62:100-4 Mr '87
Fragile communication between the sexes [views of Margaret L. McLaughlin] il *USA Today (Periodical)* 115:11 My '87
Games babies play [research by Hildy S. Ross and Susan P. Lollis] J. Fischman. il *Psychol Today* 21:14 O '87
The go-between [mothers] P. Theroux. il *Parents* 62:80+ N '87
How to be your husband's best friend. C. Jabs. *McCalls* 114:40+ Ap '87
How to talk to your parents. J. A. Baggett. il *Sch Update* 119:21 Mr 23 '87
I've spent years listening to men talk about their interests. When will they ask me about mine? S. M. Volchok. il *Glamour* 85:19 Ja '87
Lying in bed: can you believe his pillow talk? B. Weber. *Mademoiselle* 93:72 Jl '87
Man talk. B. Lustig. il *Glamour* 85:252 F '87
Personal politics: a lesson in straight talk [mentioning one's lesbianism in conversation] L. Van Gelder. il *Ms* 16:95 N '87
Public pillow talk [secret codes used by lovers; study by Robert A. Bell] C. Simon. il *Psychol Today* 21:18 O '87
Say, brother [lack of communication between black men] C. Marberry. por *Essence* 18:9 My '87
Talk is not cheap [communication among blacks] C. James. por *Essence* 18:130 Ag '87
Talking more easily with older people. il *Glamour* 85:100 N '87
What couples should talk about before marriage. il *Jet* 72:14+ S 7 '87
What's a nice couple like you doing in a fight like this? Why guys and girls can't talk. C. Jakobson. il *Mademoiselle* 93:190+ N '87
Why you can't talk to your parents anymore. W. Lamb. il *Seventeen* 46:114-15 F '87
Study and teaching
Aids and devices
An enthusiasm to learn through video [Santo Domingo Indian children] B. Atencio. *Phi Delta Kappan* 68:632-3 Ap '87
Communication, Animal *See* Animal communication
Communication, Chemical *See* Pheromones
Communication, Fiber optic *See* Fiber optics
Communication, Nonverbal
See also
  Facial expression
  Smiles
  Touch

Communication, Nonverbal—*cont.*

Body language [1 yr. olds] J. T. Gibson. il *Parents* 62:192 Ap '87

Body language: silent signals you send. il *Teen* 31:18+ F '87

Body language: your body's silent movie. S. R. Arbetter. il *Curr Health 2* 13:11-13 F '87

Image makers—or breakers [businesswomen] S. Young. il *Glamour* 85:32 O '87

The ring of untruth. J. Rosenthal. il *N Y Times Mag* p12+ Ag 2 '87

Communication (Theology)

See also

Radio broadcasting—Religious programs

Television broadcasting—Religious programs

A matter of being, and a matter of being right. W. Wangerin. il *Christ Century* 104:591-3 Jl 1-8 '87

Communication in education

Fighting teacher isolation. J. B. Davis. *Educ Dig* 52:27-9 My '87

Student exams: accentuating the positive [communication between teachers and students] M. McMullen-Pastrick and M. G. Weimer. *Educ Dig* 52:14-17 My '87

Communication in government

See also

Government publicity

Communication in management

See also

Business presentations

Business writing

Telecommunication in business

Communicating during a "crisis" [address, December 2, 1986] H. Carr. *Vital Speeches Day* 53:248-50 F 1 '87

Communications [address, April 23, 1987] R. T. Cottier. *Vital Speeches Day* 53:556-9 Jl 1 '87

Corporate and private sector communications responsibility [address, October 10, 1986] J. E. Lukaszewski. *Vital Speeches Day* 53:305-10 Mr 1 '87

Defensive employees? Here's what you can do. L. Grensing. *Work Woman* 12:20 S '87

Discussing the undiscussable [views of Kathleen Wiseman] S. Nelton. il *Nations Bus* 75:56 Mr '87

Giving—and getting—feedback [excerpt from The art of managing people] P. L. Hunsaker and A. J. Alessandra. il *Work Woman* 12:30+ Ap '87

How to say no—and live. S. Bing. il *Esquire* 107:66 Ap '87

Image makers—or breakers [businesswomen] S. Young. il *Glamour* 85:32 O '87

Learn how to listen. W. Kiechel, III. il *Fortune* 116:107-8 Ag 17 '87

Listen up: be a better manager. T. Callahan. il *Work Woman* 12:54 Jl '87

Lost com [airlines] L. Morgan. il *Flying* 114:12-13 Jl '87

There's a reason big shots are lonely at the top. L. Washer. *Work Woman* 12:21 Ja '87

Communication in politics

See also

Television and politics

Communication in science

See also

Exchanges, Literary and scientific

Science news

Information please. *Courier* 40:24 O '87

Communication of technical information

See also

Aviation—Communication systems

Science news

Communication satellites *See* Communications satellites

Communication theory *See* Information theory

Communication with the dead *See* Spiritualism

Communications, Military

See also

Cellular radio, Military

Communications satellites—Military use

Radio, Military

Submarines—Communication systems

Television in military art and science

World War, 1914-1918—Communications

AI 'fair' demonstrates application of expert systems to C³I operations. K. J. Stein. *Aviat Week Space Technol* 126:104-5+ Je 1 '87

Battle management definition advances at Ford Aerospace. *Aviat Week Space Technol* 127:19 N 30 '87

Distributed battle management favored for space-based defense system. il *Aviat Week Space Technol* 127:63+ N 23 '87

Forecast 2 programs may revolutionize USAF command, control technology. K. J. Stein. il *Aviat Week Space Technol* 126:68-9+ Mr 23 '87

Four teams will study system to track USAF airlift missions. D. Hughes. *Aviat Week Space Technol* 127:85+ D 7 '87

GTE adapts off-the-shelf hardware to improve command and control [WWMCCS Information System] W. H. Gregory. il *Aviat Week Space Technol* 126:73+ F 23 '87

How many fingers on the button? [views of D. Aaron in novel State scarlet] B. Van Voorst. il por *Time* 129:32 Ap 20 '87

Reagan's funding of C³ program yields hardware, systems. P. J. Klass. *Aviat Week Space Technol* 126:231+ Mr 9 '87

Communications, Privileged *See* Confidential communications

Communications Satellite Corp.

Comsat is forced to narrow its orbit [restructuring] S. Payne. por *Bus Week* p74 Jl 20 '87

Comsat is left in the lurch [Contel backs out of proposed merger] S. Payne. *Bus Week* p38-9 Ap 27 '87

Communications satellites

See also

Communications Satellite Corp.

Hughes Aircraft Co.

International Telecommunications Satellite Organization

Aviation use

Aerospatiale's Toulouse data center helps speed A320 certification program [use of French Telecom 1 communications satellite] map *Aviat Week Space Technol* 126:44-5 My 18 '87

Airlines criticize call to share exclusive aviation radio bands. P. J. Klass. *Aviat Week Space Technol* 126:28-9 Je 1 '87

Arinc files request to deploy AvSat communications system. P. J. Klass. map *Aviat Week Space Technol* 126:50+ Ap 27 '87

Arinc to initiate space service with leased satellites. *Aviat Week Space Technol* 127:47 D 7 '87

FAA plans Inmarsat satellite surveillance of oceanic routes. P. J. Klass. *Aviat Week Space Technol* 127:47+ D 7 '87

FCC proposes plan to offer competitive air-to-ground links. *Aviat Week Space Technol* 126:36 My 4 '87

FCC rejects Arinc proposal to form global aviation satellite system. P. J. Klass. *Aviat Week Space Technol* 127:27 S 21 '87

Business use

Corporate use of transponders could turn glut to shortage. J. C. Lowndes. il *Aviat Week Space Technol* 126:122-3+ Mr 9 '87

Data transmission use

Globesat designing satellite for Unisys. *Aviat Week Space Technol* 127:29 O 19 '87

The satellite the White House hates [Advanced Communications Technology Satellite; cover story] J. Rhea. il *Space World* X-8-284:21-3 Ag '87

Design

Hughes develops HS 601 communications satellite. *Aviat Week Space Technol* 127:29 O 19 '87

Direction finding use

Inventor proposes locator system using one geosynchronous satellite [R. Halavais's Starfind] il *Aviat Week Space Technol* 126:89+ Je 22 '87

Economic aspects

Aussat orbital delivery plan confirms satellite user trend. M. A. Dornheim. il *Aviat Week Space Technol* 127:59+ S 7 '87

Aussat tender requires orbital delivery. *Aviat Week Space Technol* 127:19 S 21 '87

Hughes focuses on new market ventures with its HS 601 communications satellite. B. A. Smith. il *Aviat Week Space Technol* 127:67+ O 26 '87

Mobile satellite networks attracting investors. *Aviat Week Space Technol* 126:65 Mr 23 '87

Partnerships reflect growing role of European firms in spacecraft bids. *Aviat Week Space Technol* 127:48 N 16 '87

The satellite the White House hates [Advanced Communications Technology Satellite; cover story] J. Rhea. il *Space World* X-8-284:21-3 Ag '87

Satellites seen as strong optical fiber competitors. *Aviat Week Space Technol* 126:127 Mr 9 '87

Severe drop in satellite orders follows 1986 launch failures. T. M. Foley. *Aviat Week Space Technol* 126:19-21 Je 8 '87

Communications satellites—cont.

Educational use
An old satellite finds a new calling [ATS-1 becomes PEACESAT] G. Jordahl. *Space World* X-8-284:22 Ag '87

Satellites for the classroom [joint U.S.-U.S.S.R. course on the nuclear arms race] S. Begley. il *Newsweek* 110:103 N 16 '87

Ground stations
Corporate use of transponders could turn glut to shortage. J. C. Lowndes. il *Aviat Week Space Technol* 126:122-3+ Mr 9 '87

The dish crowd fights for a pipeline in the sky. C. Gerber. il *Channels* 7 Sp Issue:99 D '87

Farm news from the sky [satellite TV] G. Vincent. il *Success Farm* 85:64 O '87

Space phone. *Sci Am* 256:30+ Je '87

TVRO antenna pointer program. E. T. Tyson. il *Radio-Electron* 58 ComputerDigest:6-8 Ja '87

What's next? [home-dish industry] B. Cooper, Jr. il *Radio-Electron* 58:74-5 D '87

Insurance
See Insurance, Space flight

Journalistic use
Eosat to mount challenge to Landsat restrictions [use by news media] *Aviat Week Space Technol* 127:26-7 N 2 '87

Government reins on private satellites [coping with press use of photos from space] J. Eberhart. *Sci News* 132:87 Ag 8 '87

Media satellite could complicate military, foreign policy activities [news gathering] *Aviat Week Space Technol* 126:22-3 Je 8 '87

The media's new spies in the sky. C. R. Mohan. il *World Press Rev* 34:55-6 Je '87

Newswatch from space [cover story] J. Eberhart. *Sci News* 132:28-9 Jl 11 '87

Space censors? [satellite photos] A. A. Lappen. il *Forbes* 140:12 S 7 '87

A spy satellite for the press? E. Marshall. il *Science* 238:1346-8 D 4 '87

Launching
Ariane success boosts Europe's hopes. D. Dickson. *Science* 237:1561 S 25 '87

Ariane V19 launches dual satellite payload [with editorial comment by Donald E. Fink] J. M. Lenorovitz. il *Aviat Week Space Technol* 127:11, 18-20 S 21 '87

Europeans prepare TVSat 1 for launch on Ariane V20 [direct broadcast satellite] K. F. Mordoff. il *Aviat Week Space Technol* 127:65+ N 2 '87

Eutelsat weighs candidates for alternate launcher. *Aviat Week Space Technol* 126:101 Ja 12 '87

GM wants to use Soviet launchers. E. Marshall. *Science* 238:23 O 2 '87

Martin pursuing 15 additional Titan launch contracts. T. M. Foley. *Aviat Week Space Technol* 126:66+ Ap 20 '87

Martin signs contract to launch Intelsat 6 satellites on Titan 3s. *Aviat Week Space Technol* 127:22 Ag 17 '87

McDonnell Douglas Astronautics receives nine $50,000 deposits for commercial satellite launches [Delta 2s] *Aviat Week Space Technol* 126:29 Ap 13 '87

McDonnell Douglas studies larger payload assist modules. *Aviat Week Space Technol* 127:136 Ag 10 '87

Satellite builders want change in U.S. anti-Proton policy. T. M. Foley. *Aviat Week Space Technol* 127:138-9 S 28 '87

Severe drop in satellite orders follows 1986 launch failures. T. M. Foley. *Aviat Week Space Technol* 126:19-21 Je 8 '87

State Dept. denies license to export U.S. satellites to the Soviet Union [use of Proton] *Aviat Week Space Technol* 127:59 Jl 27 '87

Laws and regulations
FCC permits broadcast satellite operators to broaden services. *Aviat Week Space Technol* 126:149 F 9 '87

Seven companies seek FCC approval for new communications satellites. *Aviat Week Space Technol* 127:48 O 5 '87

Maritime use
See also
International Maritime Satellite Organization

Military use
FltSatCom lost when Atlas Centaur launch fails [Fleet Satellite Communications spacecraft] *Aviat Week Space Technol* 126:20 Mr 30 '87

NATO orders two military satellites from British firms [versions of the Skynet 4 series] *Aviat Week Space Technol* 126:27 Ja 26 '87

Tight government budgets threaten Lightsat program. M. A. Dornheim. *Aviat Week Space Technol* 127:28 O 19 '87

Radiotelephone use
Airlines criticize call to share exclusive aviation radio bands. P. J. Klass. *Aviat Week Space Technol* 126:28-9 Je 1 '87

Groups seek FCC approval for mobile satellite systems. *Aviat Week Space Technol* 127:136 Ag 10 '87

Mobile satellite networks attracting investors. *Aviat Week Space Technol* 126:65 Mr 23 '87

Two mobile satellite groups compete for FCC monopoly. il *Aviat Week Space Technol* 127:47 O 5 '87

Solar energy use
Europeans to use apogee motor in attempt to free TVSat solar array. K. F. Mordoff. *Aviat Week Space Technol* 127:27-8 D 14 '87

German TVSat experiences solar array problem following launch by Ariane V20. J. M. Lenorovitz and K. F. Mordoff. il *Aviat Week Space Technol* 127:24-5 N 30 '87

Television broadcasting use
See also
American Business Network
Cable News Network
Direct broadcast satellite services
Satellite Broadcasting and Communications Association

The dish crowd fights for a pipeline in the sky. C. Gerber. il *Channels* 7 Sp Issue:99 D '87

Satellite TV. B. Cooper, Jr. See issues of Radio-Electronics beginning November 1984

Satellite TV transcends the Curtain [Eastern and Central Europe] S. Masterman. il *World Press Rev* 34:54 Je '87

SMATV keeps its niche [satellite master antenna television] M. Burgi. il *Channels* 7 Sp Issue:104 D '87

Stop press! Launch satellite! J. Heckman. il *Space World* X-8-284:24-6 Ag '87

Too many transponders or not nearly enough? R. M. Feazel. il *Channels* 7 Sp Issue:96-7 D '87

Unauthorized use
The international connection (I). B. Cooper, Jr. il *Radio-Electron* 58:87-8 S '87

The international connection (II). B. Cooper, Jr. il *Radio-Electron* 58:80+ O '87

Communications satellites, Australian

Aussat considering proposals for next-generation satellite. *Aviat Week Space Technol* 127:22 D 21 '87

Aussat orbital delivery plan confirms satellite user trend. M. A. Dornheim. il *Aviat Week Space Technol* 127:59+ S 7 '87

Aussat tender requires orbital delivery. *Aviat Week Space Technol* 127:19 S 21 '87

Australia will use satellite purchase to foster domestic space industry. T. M. Foley. *Aviat Week Space Technol* 126:78-9 Ap 6 '87

Communications satellites, British

Hughes to build direct broadcast satellites. *Aviat Week Space Technol* 126:21 Je 8 '87

McDonnell Douglas receives firm commercial Delta launch orders [Hughes Aircraft to purchase for launch of British Satellite Broadcasting spacecraft] *Aviat Week Space Technol* 127:24 Jl 20 '87

NATO orders two military satellites from British firms [versions of the Skynet 4 series] *Aviat Week Space Technol* 126:27 Ja 26 '87

Communications satellites, European

See also
European Telecommunications Satellite Organization

Europeans prepare TVSat 1 for launch on Ariane V20 [direct broadcast satellite] K. F. Mordoff. il *Aviat Week Space Technol* 127:65+ N 2 '87

Communications satellites, French

Aerospatiale's Toulouse data center helps speed A320 certification program [use of French Telecom 1 communications satellite] map *Aviat Week Space Technol* 126:44-5 My 18 '87

Matra wins Telecom 2 contest, resolves constraints on TRW for Intelsat bid. *Aviat Week Space Technol* 127:24-5 N 30 '87

Communications satellites, German

Europeans to use apogee motor in attempt to free TVSat solar array. K. F. Mordoff. *Aviat Week Space Technol* 127:27-8 D 14 '87

German TVSat experiences solar array problem following launch by Ariane V20. J. M. Lenorovitz and K. F. Mordoff. il *Aviat Week Space Technol* 127:24-5 N 30 '87

Communications satellites, Luxembourg

Eutelsat to decide whether to drop opposition to SES. *Aviat Week Space Technol* 127:20 S 21 '87

Intelsat, Eutelsat favor not opposing Astra's marketing of TV broadcast service [Astra satellite program] *Aviat Week Space Technol* 127:26-7 N 2 '87

Communications satellites, Pacific region

An old satellite finds a new calling [ATS-1 becomes PEACESAT] G. Jordahl. *Space World* X-8-284:22 Ag '87

Communications software

Clearing on-line hurdles. R. Lockwood. il *Pers Comput* 11:69-70+ Ag '87

Communicating . . . in the background [RAM-resident software] P. Honan. il *Pers Comput* 11:100-3+ Jl '87

The shareware connection [ProComm and Red Ryder] M. Bryan. il *Pers Comput* 11:83-4+ N '87

Solving the riddle of on-line searches. T. Badgett. il *Pers Comput* 11:157-9+ D '87

What's new in communications software. C. Keaveney. il *Pers Comput* 11:159-61+ N '87

Testing

BackComm and SideTalk: two multitasking communications programs for IBM PC compatibles. R. Fixmer. *Byte* 12:229-32 Ag '87

The Brooklyn Bridge and Direc-Link. il *Radio-Electron* 58 ComputerDigest:74+ S '87

Carbon Copy Plus. R. DeMaria. il *Byte* 12:180+ D '87

Communications. B. N. Meeks. il *Byte* 12 Sp Issue:91-9 Summ '87

Micro-to-mainframe communications [Relay Gold] J. Bell. il *Pers Comput* 11:145 Ja '87

Mycroft Labs' Mite. R. Grossblatt. il *Radio-Electron* 58 ComputerDigest:88-9 O '87

The right connection [HyperAccess communications and terminal-emulator package] J. Bell. il *Pers Comput* 11:154 F '87

Smarter communications [Smartcom III] R. Lockwood. il *Pers Comput* 11:250+ N '87

Useful stuff: a speller for Works and a duo of telecommunications packages for MCI Mail. E. Shapiro. *Byte* 12:283-4+ Jl '87

When the post office won't do [Desktop Express electronic mail program] J. Bell. il *Pers Comput* 11:280+ D '87

Working together via modem. R. Lockwood. *Pers Comput* 11:42 D '87

Communications Workers of America

Cooperative training in telecommunications: case studies [Communications Workers of America and American Telephone and Telegraph] M. Hilton and R. Straw. bibl f *Mon Labor Rev* 110:32-6 My '87

Communism

See also
Anti-Communist movements
Motion picture industry—Communist activities
Trade unions and communism

Communism without Marx. F. Lewis. il *N Y Times Mag* p44+ Je 7 '87

China

The Leninist quandary. B. Crozier. *Natl Rev* 39:26+ Mr 13 '87

Reluctant reform in the Communist world. J. H. Wolfe. *USA Today (Periodical)* 115:29 My '87

Cuba

Marx's carbuncles. J. Beatty. il *Atlantic* 259:20+ Ja '87

Czechoslovakia

See also
Communist Party (Czechoslovakia)

Ethiopia

Out of Africa. R. D. Kaplan. *New Repub* 197:12-13 Jl 6 '87

Hungary

See also
Communist Party (Hungary)

Soviet Union

The Bolshevik Revolution turns 70. W. Leonhard. *Foreign Aff* 66:388-409 Wint '87/'88

From Stalin's grim legacy, new weapons for reform. D. Stanglin. il por *U S News World Rep* 103:36 Ag 10 '87

The horrors of war behind her, Galina Fedyanina emerges as a triumph of socialist labor. J. W. Seymore. il pors *People Wkly* 27:88+ Ap 6 '87

The Leninist quandary. B. Crozier. *Natl Rev* 39:26+ Mr 13 '87

Marx had it wrong. Does Gorbachev? S. Bialer. il *U S News World Rep* 103:41-2 O 19 '87

Reluctant reform in the Communist world. J. H. Wolfe. *USA Today (Periodical)* 115:29 My '87

Revising Lenin's legacy [imaginary debate between two brothers] F. M. Burlatskii. *Harpers* 275:27-8+ N '87

The Soviet system today. P. M. Kennedy. il *Current* 296:16-26 O '87

The Soviet Union at seventy. R. V. Daniels. il *New Leader* 70:11-13 O 19 '87

Sovieticus. S. F. Cohen. *Nation* 244:315 Mr 14 '87

Sovieticus [resurgent anti-Stalinism] S. F. Cohen. *Nation* 244:104 Ja 31 '87

The threat from a failed system [address, June 8, 1987] M. Tugwell. *Vital Speeches Day* 53:645-7 Ag 15 '87

What Gorbachev is up against. P. M. Kennedy. il *Atlantic* 259:29-38+ Je '87

United States

Congress's Red Army [pro-Communist Democrats; cover story] J. M. Waller and J. Sobran. il *Natl Rev* 39:25-8 Jl 31 '87

Crockett and the patriots [pro-Communist views of Congressman G. Crockett] *Natl Rev* 39:18-19 Ag 14 '87

Communism and blacks

Black Americans need their own agenda [with discussion] S. Fisher. il por *Cent Mag* 20:25-36 My/Je '87

Red in the rainbow [J. Jackson's participation in Peace and Justice in Central America and South Africa march] *Natl Rev* 39:17-18 My 22 '87

Communism and democracy

The democracy syndrome, cont'd. B. Crozier. *Natl Rev* 39:26 Je 19 '87

The importance of Sidney Hook. H. Kramer. *Commentary* 84:17-24 Ag '87

Philosophy & faith [discussion of August 1987 article, The importance of Sidney Hook] H. Kramer. *Commentary* 84:2+ N '87

The threat from a failed system [address, June 8, 1987] M. Tugwell. *Vital Speeches Day* 53:645-7 Ag 15 '87

Communism and education

Academic post-communism. J. Hart. *Natl Rev* 39:40 Jl 31 '87

The class struggle [Communist professors; views of E. Schrecker] T. Draper. *New Repub* 196:29-36 Ja 26 '87

The odyssey of Daniel Boorstin [legacy of HUAC testimony; cover story] J. Wiener. il *Nation* 245:289+ S 26 '87

Oh, if I could only be a Communist [E. Schrecker's No ivory tower] J. Hart. *Natl Rev* 39:44 Je 19 '87

Communism and religion

See also
Albania—Religious institutions and affairs
Catholic Church—Cuba
Catholic Church—Czechoslovakia
Catholic Church—Lithuania
Catholic Church—Poland
Catholic Church—Yugoslavia
Christians—China
Christians—Soviet Union
Church and state—Cuba
Church and state—Soviet Union
Soviet Union—Religious institutions and affairs

Pannenberg on Marxism: insights and generalizations. S. Grenz. *Christ Century* 104:824-6 S 30 '87

Communism and trade unions See Trade unions and communism

Communist countries

See also
Albania
China
Czechoslovakia
Eastern Europe
Germany (East)
Kampuchea
Poland
Romania
Soviet Union
Vietnam
Yugoslavia

Foreign relations
United States

See United States—Foreign relations—Communist countries

Communist Party (China)

Balancing act [13th Congress] S. Tifft. il *Time* 130:64-5 N 9 '87

China puts off the millennium [Party Congress] E. MacFarquhar. il *U S News World Rep* 103:50-1 N 9 '87

Is Beijing about to take two steps back? J. Becker and D. J. Yang. il *Bus Week* p69 Je 22 '87

A touch of capitalism. S. Simmie. il *Macleans* 100:24 N 9 '87

Communist Party (China)—*cont.*
Waiting for October in China [13th Party Congress] M. Hopkins. il *New Leader* 70:3-4 Ap 6 '87
Who's who after Hu. il *World Press Rev* 34:15 Mr '87
Zhao gives China a swift kick toward a free market. M. Shao. il por *Bus Week* p89 N 16 '87
Communist Party (Czechoslovakia)
The sons of communism [Hungarian L. Rajk and Czechoslovak R. Slansky] M. T. Kaufman. il pors *N Y Times Mag* p50+ Mr 8 '87
Communist Party (Hungary)
The sons of communism [Hungarian L. Rajk and Czechoslovak R. Slansky] M. T. Kaufman. il pors *N Y Times Mag* p50+ Mr 8 '87
Communist Party (Italy)
Back in the game. G. Conti. *Nation* 244:706-7 My 30 '87
Decline of the Italian left. L. Rosenthal. il *Nation* 244:878-81 Je 27 '87
Communist Party (Philippines)
See also
New People's Army (Philippines)
Are church groups backing opponents of Corazon Aquino? K. A. Lawton. *Christ Today* 31:46-7 Ja 16 '87
Big Red machine. W. Chapman. *New Repub* 196:19-20 Ap 6 '87
The careful Communists. W. Steif. il *Progressive* 51:24-7 F '87
The dilemma of the Philippine left: the party or the people? J. J. Carroll. *America* 157:79-81 Ag 15-22 '87
Communist Party (South Africa)
The Red and the black [role of Communist Party member J. Slovo in the African National Congress] W. R. Doerner. il por *Time* 129:36 Mr 2 '87
Uncle Joe [J. Slovo] S. Mufson. *New Repub* 197:20-3 S 28 '87
Communist Party (Soviet Union)
Gorbachev takes a bearlike grip on the Politburo. J. Trimble. il por *U S News World Rep* 103:12-13 Jl 6 '87
Key men in the Kremlin. P. Taubman. il *N Y Times Mag* p98 D 6 '87
Planning the 'second revolution'. *World Press Rev* 34:31 Mr '87
States of two unions [M. Gorbachev's speech at Party plenum contrasted with Reagan's State of the Union] *Nation* 244:129 F 7 '87
Was there scuffling in the Kremlin? [Central Committee meeting] il *Newsweek* 110:53 N 9 '87
Communist Party (U.S.)
The importance of Sidney Hook. H. Kramer. *Commentary* 84:17-24 Ag '87
Philosophy & faith [discussion of August 1987 article, The importance of Sidney Hook] H. Kramer. *Commentary* 84:2+ N '87
Communist Party (Vietnam)
A new gerontocracy. M. Hiebert. *World Press Rev* 34:30 F '87
Vietnam moves toward pragmatism. W. J. Duiker. bibl f *Curr Hist* 86:148-51+ Ap '87
Communities (Ecology) *See* Ecology
Community
The demands of the community [with discussion] P. Selznick. por *Cent Mag* 20:33-54 Ja/F '87
Ferdinand Toennies: dark times for a liberal intellectual. J. Samples. bibl *Society* 24:65-8 S/O '87
Fraternalist manifesto [excerpt from address, November 1986] C. Lasch. *Harpers* 274:17-20 Ap '87
Community and business *See* Business—Social aspects
Community and junior colleges
See also
California Community Colleges
Columbus State Community College
Community College of the Finger Lakes
Compton Community College
Who says you have to be rich to go to college? L. Egle. por *Seventeen* 46:106 Mr '87
Community and the college *See* Colleges and universities—Public relations
Community and the school *See* School and the community
Community centers
See also
Senior centers
Community College of the Finger Lakes
Our classroom is the whole outdoors [environmental conservation program] C. White. il *Conservationist* 41:42-7 My/Je '87

Community development
See also
Community Reinvestment Act of 1977
Community development loan funds
Realizing happy returns, even if they're small. J. Rachlin. il *U S News World Rep* 103:68 N 30 '87
Community education
Reaching for community [cover story; special section; with editorial comment by Russell Edgerton] il *Change* 19:6, 12-31+ S/O '87
The second coming of community education. T. J. Kowalski. *Educ Dig* 52:52-4 F '87
Community gardens and gardening
See also
Operation GreenThumb (New York, N.Y.)
Community life
See also
Community organization
Neighborhoods
Community of Peace People of Northern Ireland
Of many things [Nobel Peace Prize winner M. Corrigan] G. W. Hunt. *America* 157:370 N 21 '87
Community of Taizé *See* Communauté de Taizé
Community organization
See also
ACORN (Organization)
Crime prevention—Citizen participation
Local Initiatives Support Corporation
Changing how society views children [Whole Child Initiative in Minnesota] R. Friedmann and others. il *Child Today* 16:10-14 Jl/Ag '87
How healthy is your town? (I) [community regeneration] R. Rodale. il *Rodale's Org Gard* 34:19-20 O '87; Same. *Prevention* 39:18-20+ O '87
How healthy is your town? (II) [community regeneration] R. Rodale. il *Rodale's Org Gard* 34:18-19 N '87
Resurrecting common sense [address, December 17, 1986] J. A. Howard. *Vital Speeches Day* 53:240-2 F 1 '87
Community power
See also
Community organization
Community Reinvestment Act of 1977
Take it from the bank. M. Ruoff. il *Progressive* 51:13 D '87
Community service *See* Community organization; Volunteer service
Community-Supported Agriculture (Organization)
Vegetables for all. J. Vandertuin. il *Rodale's Org Gard* 34:72+ S '87
Community theater *See* Theater, Amateur
Commuter Air Transports (Firm)
Beech King Air turboprops modified to regional airline configuration. P. Proctor. il *Aviat Week Space Technol* 126:71 Ap 20 '87
Commuter airlines *See* Airlines—Local service
Commuter airplanes *See* Airplanes, Jet
Commuters
Floating the Hudson: Big Apple commuters get mellow [ferries] G. Langer. il *Sierra* 72:12 N/D '87
Getting there [boat owners who commute via boat] C. Davis. il *Mot Boat Sail* 159:56-9+ Ap '87
Me and my cocoon. M. E. Marty. *Christ Century* 104:1071 N 25 '87
Riding the waves to work [ferries] P. Nulty. il *Fortune* 116:100-4 O 26 '87
Trapped behind the wheel. M. Smilgis. il *Time* 130:64-5 Jl 20 '87
The unknown commuter [Metro-North commute between Connecticut and Grand Central Terminal] *New Yorker* 63:29 Mr 9 '87
Como, William, 1925-
American Ballet Theatre's early years: the way it was. il *Dance Mag* 61:100-21 Je '87
Béjart mounts Malraux and The Kabuki. il *Dance Mag* 61:84-9 My '87
The Bolshoi in America: here's . . . Andris! il pors *Dance Mag* 61:42-5 D '87
Celebration! See issues of Dance Magazine beginning June 1987
Editors log. See issues of Dance Magazine
Looking back: divertimento 1986. il *Dance Mag* 61:56-63+ Ja '87
Como (Italy)
Hotels, motels, etc.
Landscape of high romance [history of Villa d'Este] F. Champin. il *House Gard* 159:194-203+ O '87
Comoros
See also
United Nations—Comoros

Comoros—*cont.*

Foreign relations

France

See France—Foreign relations—Comoros

Comp-U-Card International

How Comp-U-Card hooks home shoppers. R. Mitchell. il por *Bus Week* p73-4 My 18 '87

Compa, Lance

A 'yes' for democracy: constitutional plebiscite. il *Commonweal* 114:262-3 My 8 '87

Compact cameras *See* Cameras

Compact disc industry

CD boom! C. Greenleaf. il map *Stereo Rev* 52:89-92 Je '87

CD gripes. D. Pope. *High Fidel* 37:58 O '87

The LP's wobbly future. P. Wang. il *Newsweek* 109:52 F 9 '87

Things are looking up [classical music outlook] T. W. Libbey, Jr. il *High Fidel* 37:63 D '87

Compact disc interactive

The future of the compact disc—interactive. S. Assael. *Roll Stone* p77 S 10 '87

How CD-I will change our use of computers. W. M. Hawkins. por *Pers Comput* 11:246 O '87

Compact disc players

See also

Compact disc video

Car CD players: big sound, big price, big problem. N. Henderson. il *Changing Times* 41:93-6 Ap '87

CD players. il *Stereo Rev* 52:152-3+ F '87

CD players. E. B. Meyer. il *High Fidel* 37:45-6 S '87

CDs on the road [car stereo] J. C. Taylor. il *High Fidel* 37:22 Jl '87

The compleat CD player [new features] D. Ranada. il *High Fidel* 37:20 Mr '87

Discs, DATs and all that jazz. N. Henderson. il *Changing Times* 41:103-6 Ja '87

How to shop for a compact disc player. C. Begole. il *Glamour* 85:72 My '87

My first CD. A. Lange. *Down Beat* 54:6 Mr '87

Pop goes the disc. H. Fantel. il *Roll Stone* p46+ Ja 15 '87

The sounds of silence. F. Vizard. il *Pop Mech* 164:96-8 D '87

Upgrading to hear the sonic boom. L. Wiener. il *U S News World Rep* 103:96+ N 9 '87

Yamaha's hi-bit CD players. C. J. Esse. il *High Fidel* 37:13 Je '87

Changers

Don't stop the music! Compact disc changers. W. Burton. il *Stereo Rev* 52:63-5 O '87

JVC XL-M700 automatic CD changer. J. D. Hirsch. il *Stereo Rev* 52:27-8 F '87

Pioneer PD-M90X compact disc changer. J. D. Hirsch. il *Stereo Rev* 52:35+ N '87

Sony CDP-C10 compact disc changer. il *High Fidel* 37:46+ Ja '87

Equipment

Compact disc for your car [CD adapters] M. Thompson. il *Fam Handyman* 37:92-3 S '87

Optical equipment

Light-headed: optical links. D. Ranada. il *High Fidel* 37:13 N '87

Light music [fiber optic beam connects Kenwood CD player to amplifiers] W. J. Hawkins. il *Pop Sci* 230:14 My '87

Testing

ADC Model 16/2R compact disc player. J. D. Hirsch. il *Stereo Rev* 52:71-2 N '87

Alpine 7902 car tuner/CD player. il *High Fidel* 37:37-8+ Jl '87

The best sound on wheels [car CD players] A. Eisenberg. il *Stereo Rev* 52:59-63 My '87

CD players. il *Consum Rep* 52:341-6 D '87

Clearing the cobwebs. J. D. Hirsch. il *Stereo Rev* 52:24+ S '87

Compact-disc players [cover story] il *Consum Rep* 52:283-8 My '87

DBX DX5 CD player. J. D. Hirsch. il *Stereo Rev* 52:49-51 S '87

Denon DCD-3300 CD player. J. D. Hirsch. il *Stereo Rev* 52:26-7+ My '87

Direct-cueing CD players [Technics SL-P720 and SL-P520] C. J. Esse. il *High Fidel* 37:14 F '87

Getting smaller, digitally. C. J. Esse. il *High Fidel* 37:12+ Ja '87

Hitachi DA-005 compact disc player. il *High Fidel* 37:32+ Ja '87

Magnavox CDB-650 compact disc player. il *High Fidel* 37:27-8+ Ap '87

Marantz CD50 compact disc player. J. D. Hirsch. il *Stereo Rev* 52:47-8 Ap '87

Mission PCM-4000 compact disc player. il *High Fidel* 37:20-1 My '87

Nakamichi OMS-2A compact disc player. J. D. Hirsch. il *Stereo Rev* 52:41+ Ag '87

NEC CD-500E CD player. J. D. Hirsch. il *Stereo Rev* 52:38+ Ja '87

Onkyo DX-530 compact disc player. J. D. Hirsch. il *Stereo Rev* 52:31-2 S '87

Sharp DX-620 compact disc player. J. D. Hirsch. il *Stereo Rev* 52:59-60 Ja '87

Shure D-6000 compact disc player. il *High Fidel* 37:26-7 Jl '87

Sony CDP-505ESD compact disc player. il *High Fidel* 37:23+ D '87

Sony CDP-605ESD compact disc player. J. D. Hirsch. il *Stereo Rev* 52:26+ O '87

Sony Discman D-10. M. Smolen. il *Stereo Rev* 52:212-13 F '87

Testing CD players. J. D. Hirsch. il *Stereo Rev* 52:25-6 Ag '87

Vector Research VCD-770 compact disc player. J. D. Hirsch. il *Stereo Rev* 52:40+ Mr '87

Yamaha CD-2000 compact disc player. il *High Fidel* 37:27-8 Mr '87

Yamaha CDX-1100 compact disc player. J. D. Hirsch. il *Stereo Rev* 52:25-6+ Jl '87

Yamaha CDX-1100U compact disc player. il *High Fidel* 37:24+ O '87

Compact disc video

The CD goes single. H. Fantel. il *Roll Stone* p77-8 Je 18 '87

CD video. L. Feldman. il *Pop Sci* 231:50-2 N '87

CD video arrives. M. Smolen. il *Stereo Rev* 52:51 My '87

Compact disks for the eye and ear. D. Zigas. il *Bus Week* p100 Jl 6 '87

Disc-o-mania. P. Hoban. il *N Y* 20:16+ My 25 '87

The future of CD-V. M. Riggs. il *High Fidel* 37:5 O '87

Hey, this CD plays videos. W. J. Cook. il *U S News World Rep* 102:54 Je 15 '87

New video. E. B. Meyer. il *High Fidel* 37:53-4 S '87

The union of audio and video. W. Wolfe. il *Stereo Rev* 52:22-3 Ja '87

Vain attempts? [Sony's ED Beta system and Philips CD-V format] D. Ranada. il *High Fidel* 37:19 Je '87

Testing

Pioneer CLD-1010 combination CD-V player. il *High Fidel* 37:25-7 S '87

Pioneer CLD-909 CD/laserdisc player. il *High Fidel* 37:62+ Ja '87

Compact discs

See also

CD-ROM (Compact disc-Read only memory)

Compact disc interactive

Compact disc video

CD gripes. D. Pope. *High Fidel* 37:58 O '87

The CD spread. See issues of High Fidelity (New York, N.Y.) beginning February 1986

CDs, take 2. A. Lange. *Down Beat* 54:6 Jl '87

Coping with CD. H. Foster. il *High Fidel* 37:56 Ap '87

The digital revolution. I. Masters. il *Stereo Rev* 52:58-62+ O '87

Gold-plated CDs [Ultradisc from Mobile Fidelity] D. Ranada. il *High Fidel* 37:13 My '87

The good old days are back [classical reissues] T. W. Libbey, Jr. il *High Fidel* 37:64-5+ D '87

A little less noise, please. T. W. Libbey, Jr. il *High Fidel* 37:57-9 Mr '87

Longer audiotape [taping compact discs] F. Vizard. il *Pop Mech* 164:42+ N '87

Mozart: the basic repertoire on compact disc. R. Freed. il *Stereo Rev* 52:78-9 Jl '87

Muddy waters in laser land: new formats take the plunge. R. L. Miller. il *Channels* 7 Sp Issue:129 D '87

Past masters. P. G. Davis. por *N Y* 20:64-6 Je 15 '87

The shadow glows [Nonesuch re-issues] P. G. Davis. *N Y* 20:104+ S 14 '87

The shape of things to come [preview 1988] il *High Fidel* 37:61-71 S '87

Sound on disc. R. De Toledano. See occasional issues of National Review

The stunning success of CD's. J. Egan. il *U S News World Rep* 102:41-2 F 23 '87

Compact discs—*cont.*

American music

An American original [works by J. K. Paine] R. Freed. il *Stereo Rev* 52:109 Je '87

Arias

Edita Gruberova: Famous opera arias. P. Moor. il *High Fidel* 37:70 Jl '87

Strauss, Richard: Dance of the seven veils and final scene from "Salome"; Monologue, Recognition scene and final scene from "Elektra". R. E. Benson. il *High Fidel* 37:69 Mr '87

Ballet music

Stravinsky's ballet music. R. Freed. il por *Stereo Rev* 52:150 D '87

"The three-cornered hat". R. Freed. il *Stereo Rev* 52:194 N '87

Black music

Michael Jackson: Bad. R. Wynn. *High Fidel* 37:89+ D '87

Motown twofers. R. Wynn. *High Fidel* 37:78-9 Ap '87

Stax collections. H. Bordowitz. il *High Fidel* 37:79+ O '87

Blues music

Easy listening blues. J. McDonough. *Down Beat* 54:48-9 D '87

Cantatas

Handel, George Frideric: Apollo e Dafne; Concerto for oboe and orchestra. P. Moor. il *High Fidel* 37:62 Ap '87

Martinů, Bohuslav: Field mass; Janáček, Leoš: Amarus [Czech Philharmonic] R. R. Reilly. il *High Fidel* 37:64 Je '87

Cello music

Dvořák's cello concerto [recording by Angelica May] D. Hall. il *Stereo Rev* 52:183 N '87

Chamber music

An American original [works by J. K. Paine] R. Freed. il *Stereo Rev* 52:109 Je '87

Beyond bombast: the intimate Shostakovich. R. R. Reilly. il *High Fidel* 37:61-2 Jl '87

Chants (Gregorian, plain, etc.)

Hildegard of Bingen: Symphonia armonie celestium revelationum (selections). P. Moor. *High Fidel* 37:68 Ap '87

Choral music

Choirs of exultation [Mahler: Symphony no.8; Sir Michael Tippett: The mask of time] J. Pearce. *Macleans* 100:60 S 7 '87

Duruflé, Maurice: Choral music; Bruckner, Anton: Choral music; Britten, Benjamin: Choral music. T. Teachout. *High Fidel* 37:86 N '87

Sibelius, Jean: Choral and symphonic works. B. Zakariasen. il *High Fidel* 37:64-5 Mr '87

Christmas music

Hark! The herald angels sing—on compact disks. R. Hoffman and T. Segal. il *Bus Week* p134 D 21 '87

Concertos

See also

Compact discs—Cello music

Compact discs—Piano music

Defects

Digital slop. D. Ranada. il *High Fidel* 37:26 Ja '87

Domesticating digital. D. Hurwitz. il *High Fidel* 37:62-4+ O '87

Error-correction myths exploded. D. Ranada. il *High Fidel* 37:45+ O '87

Electronic music

Carlos, Wendy: Beauty in the beast. J. Wierzbicki. il *High Fidel* 37:63 Jl '87

Subotnick, Morton: Key to songs; Return—a triumph of reason. J. Wierzbicki. *High Fidel* 37:69-70 Ag '87

English music

English strings [recordings by the English String Orchestra] D. Hall. il *Stereo Rev* 52:180 F '87

Experimental music

Frank Zappa. R. C. Walls. *High Fidel* 37:74-5 Ap '87

Reich, Steve: Sextet; Six marimbas. K. R. Schwartz. *High Fidel* 37:65-6 Je '87

Strange bedfellows. F. Bouchard. il *Down Beat* 54:41-2 Mr '87

Zorn, John: Big gundown. K. R. Schwarz. *High Fidel* 37:68-9 Ap '87

Folk music

Rounder artists. L. Berman. il *High Fidel* 37:88 O '87

Jazz music

Blue Note artists. R. C. Walls. il *High Fidel* 37:82-3 O '87

Bluebird jazz reissues. J. Blum. il *High Fidel* 37:76+ O '87

CD-enriched jazz. H. Mandel. il *Down Beat* 54:42-4 Ja '87

Classics. A. Lange. il *Down Beat* 54:47-50 Jl '87

Columbia jazz reissues. M. Ullman. *High Fidel* 37:76 O '87

Creed Taylor's jazz [CTI/Kudu catalog] C. Albertson. il *Stereo Rev* 52:82 Ag '87

Digitized bop. T. Martin. *Down Beat* 54:42-3 Ag '87

Gordon, Dexter: Our man in Paris. S. Futterman. *High Fidel* 37:94-5 D '87

Jazz: from LP to CD. R. De Toledano. *Natl Rev* 39:61-2 S 25 '87

Keynotes & OJC's. A. Lange. *Down Beat* 54:39+ O '87

MCA/Impulse! Jazz. S. Futterman. il *High Fidel* 37:73-4 Ap '87

Old wine in new bottles: vintage music on compact discs. S. M. Stroff. il *Antiques Collect Hobbies* 92:48-51 My '87

Parker's mood [classics remastered by R. Parker] J. Sohmer. *Down Beat* 54:47-8+ D '87

Strange bedfellows. F. Bouchard. il *Down Beat* 54:41-2 Mr '87

Sweet & sour CDs. F. Bouchard. il *Down Beat* 11:44+ N '87

Upscale CDs. H. Nolan. il *Down Beat* 54:42 F '87

Marketing

Compact-disc single to hit market this year. R. Love. *Roll Stone* p21 Jl 16-30 '87

Mass (Music)

Mackerras's blazing Janáček Mass [recording of the Glagolitic Mass by the Prague Philharmonic Chorus and Czech Philharmonic Orchestra] D. Hall. il *Stereo Rev* 52:85-6 Ap '87

Motets

Bach, Johann Sebastian: Motets. K. R. Schwarz. *High Fidel* 37:62-3 Jl '87

Motion picture music

Horner, James: Gorky Park (soundtrack); Aliens (soundtrack). N. A. Trudeau. *High Fidel* 37:67 My '87

Movie music [discography] S. Simels. il *Stereo Rev* 52:59-61+ Ap '87

Musicals, revues, etc.

Rodgers and Hammerstein: South Pacific. P. Moor. *High Fidel* 37:69 Ap '87

Oboe music

Handel, George Frideric: Apollo e Dafne; Concerto for oboe and orchestra. P. Moor. il *High Fidel* 37:62 Ap '87

Opera

See also

Compact discs—Arias

Abbado's Verdi: newly minted on CD. T. Eckert, Jr. il por *High Fidel* 37:63-5 Ap '87

Bellini, Vincenzo: I Capuleti e i Montecchi. T. Eckert, Jr. il *High Fidel* 37:62+ My '87

Chausson, Ernest: Le roi Arthus. B. Zakariasen. il *High Fidel* 37:85-6 N '87

Handel, George Frideric: Imeneo. S. Lincoln. *Stereo Rev* 52:146 D '87

Monteverdi's modernity [recordings of L'Orfeo] W. H. Youngren. il *Atlantic* 259:82-5 Ap '87

Opera on CD: a basic library (I). R. Ackart. il *Stereo Rev* 52:72-4+ S '87

Opera on CD: a basic library (II). R. Ackart. il *Stereo Rev* 52:106-8+ D '87

Past masters [works by M. Callas] P. G. Davis. por *N Y* 20:64-6 Je 15 '87

Smetana, Bedřich: Bartered bride. R. Ackart. il *Stereo Rev* 52:175 F '87

Tchaikovsky, Peter Ilich: Iolanta. B. Zakariasen. il *High Fidel* 37:95 Ja '87

Verdi, Giuseppe: Un ballo in maschera. T. Eckert, Jr. il *High Fidel* 37:66-7 Je '87

Verdi, Giuseppe: Otello. T. Eckert, Jr. *High Fidel* 37:92-3 N '87

Wagner's "Ring" cycle on CD. W. Livingstone. il *Stereo Rev* 52:156-7 D '87

Operetta

Kálmán, Emmerich: Die Csárdásfürstin. B. Zakariasen. *High Fidel* 37:65 Mr '87

Orchestral music

Bernstein, Leon: Orchestral music [recording by Leonard Slatkin] T. Teachout. il *High Fidel* 37:84-5 N '87

Misunderstanding Toscanini [RCA series] T. Hathaway. il pors *High Fidel* 37:63-5 Ag '87

Vaughan Williams, Ralph: A London symphony; The lark ascending [André Previn and the Royal Philharmonic] D. Hurwitz. *High Fidel* 37:68+ Jl '87

Organ music

Virgil Fox: Digital Fox—volumes I and II. D. Hall. *Stereo Rev* 52:120 S '87

Compact discs—*cont.*

Piano music

Brahms first from Serkin and Shaw [Piano concerto no. 1, in D minor] D. Hall. por *Stereo Rev* 52:104 Je '87

Carter, Elliott: Piano concerto; variations for orchestra. J. Wierzbicki. *High Fidel* 37:64-5 My '87

Cherkassky, Shura: In concert 1984, v1 and 2. T. Hathaway. *High Fidel* 37:83 D '87

Ciccolini's basic Satie on compact disc. R. Freed. por *Stereo Rev* 52:101-2 Je '87

Crumb, George: A little suite for Christmas; Wernick, Richard: Sonata for piano [recordings by Lambert Orkis] J. Wierzbicki. il *High Fidel* 37:63-4 Jl '87

Hummel, Johann Nepomuk: Sonatas for piano. R. R. Reilly. il *High Fidel* 37:65+ Ag '87

Schubert, Franz: Sonata in B flat, op. posth. R. R. Reilly. *High Fidel* 37:78 D '87

Serkin, Peter: Peter Serkin. K. R. Schwarz. *High Fidel* 37:70 Jl '87

Van Cliburn's disturbing legacy. P. Moor. il por *High Fidel* 37:82-3 N '87

Popular music

East St. Louis Toodle-oo [pop reissues on compact disc] J. Miller. il *Newsweek* 109:57-8 Ja 19 '87

Easy listening on compact disc. W. Livingstone. il *Stereo Rev* 52:72-4 My '87

Editor on the loose! K. Richardson. il *High Fidel* 37:75+ S '87

In short order. See issues of High Fidelity (New York, N.Y.)

Mini-a-tour. il *High Fidel* 37:70-2+ My '87

Old wine in new bottles no. 2: vintage music on compact discs. S. M. Stroff. il *Antiques Collect Hobbies* 92:66-7+ N '87

The software parade [special section] il *High Fidel* 37:70+ Ap '87

You got the silver [special section] il *High Fidel* 37:75-6+ O '87

Prices

Midprice CDs are here. D. Hurwitz. il *High Fidel* 37:73-4 D '87

Quintets, Instrumental

Compelling Shostakovich [Borodin Quartet's recording of Piano quintet in G minor; String quartets nos. 7 and 8] R. Freed. il *Stereo Rev* 52:93 Ap '87

Requiems

Mozart, Wolfgang Amadeus: Requiem, K. 626; Church sonatas. K. R. Schwarz. *High Fidel* 37:90+ N '87

Rock music

Beatles CDs generate strong sales. D. Wild. il *Roll Stone* p13+ Ap 9 '87

The Beatles on compact disc. S. Simels. il *Stereo Rev* 52:122 Je '87

Beatles: Sgt. Pepper's Lonely Hearts Club Band. S. Simels. il *Stereo Rev* 52:81 Ag '87

Capitol to release Beatles CD's. D. Fricke. *Roll Stone* p25+ F 26 '87

Compact discontent. D. Handelman. *Roll Stone* p88 D 17-31 '87

Controversy surrounds Beatles CDs. M. Walker and D. Handelman. *Roll Stone* p25+ Ap 23 '87

The digital Fab Four [Beatles CD's] S. Pond. il *Roll Stone* p129+ Jl 16-30 '87

The digital revolution: why is rock falling behind? M. Walker. *Roll Stone* p15+ My 21 '87

Frank Zappa. R. C. Walls. *High Fidel* 37:74-5 Ap '87

Glimpse the truth [Help!; Rubber soul; Revolver; Sgt. Pepper's Lonely Hearts Club Band] il *High Fidel* 37:94-9+ N '87

Here come the CD Beatles. il *U S News World Rep* 102:42 F 23 '87

Hiatt, John: Bring the family. J. Nesin. il *High Fidel* 37:89 D '87

Jackson, Michael: Bad. R. Wynn. *High Fidel* 37:89+ D '87

Jefferson Airplane: 2400 Fulton Street. S. Futterman. il *High Fidel* 37:74 Ag '87

King Crimson. K. Richardson. il *High Fidel* 37:83-4+ O '87

Mop-top pop [Beatles and Rolling Stones] G. Santoro. *Down Beat* 54:44-5 S '87

Motown twofers. R. Wynn. *High Fidel* 37:78-9 Ap '87

One, two, three, four! [Beatles on CD and video] il *High Fidel* 37:70-2+ Je '87

Rock music on compact disc. S. Simels. il *Stereo Rev* 52:134 Ja '87

The Rolling Stones. M. Moses. il *High Fidel* 37:70+ Ap '87

Stax collections. H. Bordowitz. il *High Fidel* 37:79+ O '87

The Stones on CD. S. Simels. il *Stereo Rev* 52:88-9 Mr '87

When stereo isn't stereo [releasing early non-stereo Beatles albums on stereo compact discs] M. Riggs. il *High Fidel* 37:5 D '87

Sonatas

See also

Compact discs—Piano music

Haydn, Beethoven & old instruments [sonatas for piano and violin by Eugene Istomin and Isaac Stern] R. De Toledano. *Natl Rev* 39:53-4 Ap 10 '87

Songs

Lieder evenings worth remembering . . . [Salzburg Festival live recordings by D. Fischer-Dieskau] P. Moor. il por *High Fidel* 37:61-2 Je '87

Margaret Price sings Liszt gems. R. Freed. il por *Stereo Rev* 52:82 Jl '87

Robyn Archer sings Brecht. E. Salzman. il por *Stereo Rev* 52:116 My '87

Spanish music

"The three-cornered hat". R. Freed. il *Stereo Rev* 52:194 N '87

String ensemble music

English strings [recordings by the English String Orchestra] D. Hall. il *Stereo Rev* 52:180 F '87

String quartet music

Compelling Shostakovich [Borodin Quartet's recording of Piano quintet in G minor; String quartets nos. 7 and 8] R. Freed. il *Stereo Rev* 52:93 Ap '87

Haydn, Joseph: String quartets. K. R. Schwarz. *High Fidel* 37:65+ Ap '87

Persuasive Brahms from the Tokyo Quartet [no. 1 in C minor and no. 3 in B-flat major] R. Freed. il *Stereo Rev* 52:80 My '87

Suites (Music)

Holst, Gustav: "The planets". D. Hurwitz. il *High Fidel* 37:77 D '87

Schwarz: masterly Prokofiev [recording of Romeo and Juliet, Suites nos. 1 and 2; Pushkin Waltz no. 2] D. Hall. por *Stereo Rev* 52:74 Ag '87

Symphonic poems

Sibelius, Jean: Kullervo. B. Zakariasen. il *High Fidel* 37:64-5 Mr '87

Symphonies

Beethoven, Ludwig van: Symphonies no. 8 and 9 [recordings by A. Toscanini and M. T. Thomas] T. Hathaway. il por *High Fidel* 37:84 N '87

Choirs of exultation [Mahler: Symphony no.8; Sir Michael Tippett: The mask of time] J. Pearce. *Macleans* 100:60 S 7 '87

Coming to terms with an Estonian symphonist [E. Tubin] R. R. Reilly. il por *High Fidel* 37:78-9 Ja '87

Danacord's first CD [Furtwängler's Beethoven Symphony no. 5; Brahms Alto rhapsody; Von ewiger liebe; Wir wandelten] B. Wechsler. *High Fidel* 37:63 F '87

Mahler, Gustav: Symphony no. 3, in D minor. D. Hall. *Stereo Rev* 52:113-14 S '87

Mahler, Gustav: Symphony no. 8. D. Hurwitz. il *High Fidel* 37:68 Ag '87

Martinů, Bohuslav: Symphonies: no. 3; no. 6. D. Hurwitz. il *High Fidel* 37:68-9 Ag '87

Messiaen, Olivier: Turangalîla symphony [Philharmonia Orchestra] K. R. Schwarz. *High Fidel* 37:64 Je '87

Nielsen, Carl: Symphony no. 4 [Swedish Radio Symphony Orchestra] K. R. Schwarz. *High Fidel* 37:85 Ja '87

Schuman, William: Symphony no. 7; Balada, Leonardo: Steel symphony. D. Hurwitz. il *High Fidel* 37:69 Ag '87

Shostakovich, Dimitri Dmitrievich: Symphony no. 5 [Berlin Philharmonic] D. Hurwitz. *High Fidel* 37:65 Jl '87

Sibelius, Jean: Symphony no. 1, in E minor. J. Wierzbicki. *High Fidel* 37:66-7 My '87

The symphonic Furtwängler. W. H. Youngren. il *Atlantic* 259:77-80 Ja '87

Tchaikovsky, Peter Ilich: Symphony no. 6, in B minor. D. Hurwitz. il *High Fidel* 37:78+ D '87

Tubin, Eduard: Symphonies no. 4; no. 9. R. R. Reilly. *High Fidel* 37:70 Ag '87

Test discs

Philips compact disc test set. il *Radio-Electron* 58:27-8+ F '87

Unauthorized recording

The sound of money [battle over digital audio tape] J. B. Copeland. il *Newsweek* 110:72-3 O 5 '87

The spoilers. L. G. Boundas. il *Stereo Rev* 52:6 Je '87

Violin music

Mozart, Wolfgang Amadeus: Concertos for violin and orchestra: nos. 1, 2, and 4. K. R. Schwartz. *High Fidel* 37:64-5 Je '87

Compact discs—Violin music—*cont.*
Tchaikovsky, Peter Ilich: Concerto for violin and orchestra; Bartók, Bela: Sonata for solo violin; Ellington, Duke: Mainly black [recordings by Nigel Kennedy] K. R. Schwarz. il *High Fidel* 37:68 Jl '87

Vocal music
See also
Compact discs—Arias
Danacord's first CD [Furtwängler's Beethoven Symphony no. 5; Brahms Alto rhapsody; Von ewiger liebe; Wir wandelten] B. Wechsler. *High Fidel* 37:63 F '87

Waltzes
Schwarz: masterly Prokofiev [recording of Romeo and Juliet, Suites nos. 1 and 2; Pushkin Waltz no. 2] D. Hall. por *Stereo Rev* 52:74 Ag '87

Compagnia Finanziaria De Benedetti
Conglomeration Italian style. S. Solomon. il por *Forbes* 139:36-8 Mr 23 '87
Dealmaker De Benedetti [cover story] W. C. Symonds. il pors *Bus Week* p42-7 Ag 24 '87
Olivetti's global deal maker [C. De Benedetti] P. C. Newman. il por *Macleans* 100:51 N 30 '87

Compagnie Européenne de Publication
Quiet group. H. R. Lottman. *Publ Wkly* 231:28 My 22 '87

Compagnie Francaise des Petroles
See also
TOTAL-Compagnie Française des Pétroles

Compagnie Générale de Constructions Téléphoniques
The Swedes give AT&T, and the U.S., painful black eyes [L. M. Ericsson captures piece of Compagnie Générale de Constructions Téléphoniques] T. Peterson and F. J. Comes. il *Bus Week* p44-5 My 4 '87

Compagnie Générale d'Électricité
Now that CGE is a heavyweight, it will have to fight like one. T. Peterson and F. J. Comes. il por *Bus Week* p98+ My 18 '87
Sir Jimmy pulls the plug on his French connection [J. Goldsmith sells out stake in Générale Occidentale to Compagnie Générale d'Electricité] J. Rossant. il por *Bus Week* p24 Ag 10 '87

Compagnie Maguy Marin
Comfort me with apples [performance of M. Marin's Eden at Next Wave Festival] T. Tobias. il *N Y* 20:129-30 N 9 '87
A new face on dance [designer M. Casanova's collaboration with M. Marin] B. Haye. il *Theatre Crafts* 21:42-3+ N '87

La Compañia de Teatro de Albuquerque
A universal voice. J. P. Forsthoffer. il *Horizon* 30:31 O '87

Compania Telefonica Nacional de España SA
This Spanish stock is ringing bells. G. G. Marcial. *Bus Week* p101 Jl 13 '87

Companies *See* Corporations

Companion crops
Beans in wheat . . . and weeds in both [relay intercropping] D. Ohrtman. il *Success Farm* 85 no4:18AH F '87
Companion planting. P. G. McWilliams. il *Ctry J* 14:42-5 Je '87

Company [musical] *See* Musicals, revues, etc.—Reviews—Single works
Company names *See* Corporations—Names
Company publications *See* House organs
Company towns
See also
Kennecott (Alaska)
Company uniforms *See* Uniforms
Compaq Computer Corporation
Who's afraid of IBM? [cover story] J. E. Davis. il por *Bus Week* p68-72+ Je 29 '87
Compaq Telecommunications Corporation
A machine that only its makers could love [Telecompaq PC/telephone] J. E. Davis. il *Bus Week* p71 Je 29 '87
Comparable worth wage concept *See* Equal pay for equal work
Comparative anatomy *See* Anatomy, Comparative
Comparative education *See* Education, Comparative
Comparative genetics *See* Genetics, Comparative
Comparative psychology *See* Psychology, Comparative
Compassion *See* Sympathy
Compatibility (Audio systems) *See* Audio systems—Compatibility
Compatibility (Computers) *See* Computers—Compatibility
Compensation (Law)
See also
Damages
Insurance, Workers' compensation

No taking without paying [Supreme Court decision on compensation for confiscated land] A. L. Sanders. il *Time* 129:64-5 Je 22 '87
Compensatory education
Chapter 1 students score higher than other disadvantaged students. *Phi Delta Kappan* 68:638+ Ap '87
Combining categorical program services can make a major difference [discussion of April 1987 article, Why Chapter 1 hasn't made much difference] D. G. Savage. *Phi Delta Kappan* 68:787-8 Je '87
Making Chapter 1 make a difference. R. E. Slavin. bibl f il *Phi Delta Kappan* 69:110-19 O '87
Reauthorizing or restructuring Chapter 1? [parent involvement] A. C. Lewis. il *Phi Delta Kappan* 69:4-5 S '87
Why Chapter 1 hasn't made much difference. D. G. Savage. il *Phi Delta Kappan* 68:581-4 Ap '87
Competency tests *See* Educational tests and measurements
Competency tests for teachers *See* Teachers—Examinations
Competition
See also
Business intelligence
Dumping (Commercial policy)
Mercantile system
Trade marks and trade names
An advocate for competitiveness. A. Holzinger. il *Nations Bus* 75:12 Mr '87
American competitiveness is healthier than it looks. P. C. Roberts. il *Bus Week* p18 Jl 13 '87
America's leanest and meanest [cover story] G. D. Wallace. il *Bus Week* p78-82+ O 5 '87
America's love-hate view of competition. J. Rose. il *Sch Update* 119:18-20 Ja 26 '87
Blueprint for competitiveness [Making America work again: jobs, small business and the international challenge] il *Nations Bus* 75:12 My '87
The boom in service industries will not solve U.S. trade problems [report from the Office of Technology Assessment] E. Marshall. *Science* 237:243 Jl 17 '87
Can America compete? [growth crisis; cover story; special section] il *Bus Week* p44-9+ Ap 20 '87
Can American industry make it? G. de Jonquieres and A. Kaletsky. il *World Press Rev* 34:22-6 Jl '87
Can anyone compete? [Business week's cover story] *Natl Rev* 39:18-19 My 8 '87
Can we make U.S. industry competitive again? H. A. Poling. il *USA Today (Periodical)* 116:22-4 N '87
The challenge of global competition [address, September 17, 1987] G. H. Conrades. *Vital Speeches Day* 54:125-8 D 1 '87
The challenge to U.S. competitiveness. R. M. White. *Science* 236:1041 My 29 '87
Competing for political gain on competitiveness. K. R. Sheets. il *U S News World Rep* 102:42 Mr 2 '87
Competitive confusion. R. J. Samuelson. il *Newsweek* 109:39 Ja 26 '87
Competitiveness [address, July 21, 1987] F. G. Steingraber. *Vital Speeches Day* 53:758-62 O 1 '87
"Competitiveness" bill goes to Congress [Trade, Employment, and Productivity Act of 1987] M. Crawford. *Science* 235:967 F 27 '87
The competitiveness challenge [address, August 21, 1987] J. J. Melone. *Vital Speeches Day* 54:100-4 D 1 '87
The competitiveness craze [cover story] R. Kuttner. *New Repub* 197:22+ N 2 '87
The 'competitiveness' craze: a new name, an old idea. C. Welles. il *Bus Week* p31 Ja 19 '87
"Competitiveness" fever [engineering] J. I. Mattill. il *Technol Rev* 90:13-14 Ag/S '87
Competitiveness: getting it back. S. Nasar. il *Fortune* 115:217-18+ Ap 27 '87
Competitiveness in America: is protectionism the answer? [address, May 27, 1987] D. W. McMinn. *Dep State Bull* 87:56-9 Ag '87
The competitiveness problem [address, September 14, 1987] G. M. Keller. *Vital Speeches Day* 54:61-4 N 1 '87
Don't let the Grinch steal Christmas. G. F. Gilder. il *Natl Rev* 39:40-4 Ap 24 '87
The economic black hole [U.S. trade deficit and foreign debt] L. C. Thurow and L. D. Tyson. bibl f *Foreign Policy* 67:3-21 Summ '87
Engineers hear a competitive parable. W. Booth. *Science* 238:474 O 23 '87
Helping small firms compete [Small Business Trade Competitiveness and Innovation Act] *Nations Bus* 75:12 Je '87
How the best get better [R. H. Waterman's The renewal factor; cover story] J. A. Byrne. il por *Bus Week* p98-9 S 14 '87

Competition—*cont.*

In order to [address, August 10, 1987] L. A. Iacocca. *Vital Speeches Day* 53:745-8 O 1 '87

International competitiveness [address, June 8, 1987] H. Goldfeder. *Vital Speeches Day* 53:722-5 S 15 '87

Japanese challenge—American response [address, March 5, 1987] P. Cannon. *Vital Speeches Day* 53:503-9 Je 1 '87

Making America more competitive [annual report of the U.S. Chamber of Commerce] il *Nations Bus* 75:71-5 My '87

Making American industry competitive again [address, April 16, 1987] J. Weaver. *Vital Speeches Day* 53:560-2 Jl 1 '87

Making human resources more competitive. M. Simms. il *Black Enterp* 17:37 Jl '87

National economic competitiveness [Ohio's Thomas Edison Program; address, February 6, 1987] C. M. Coburn. *Vital Speeches Day* 53:478-80 My 15 '87

NSF's budget and economic competitiveness. E. Bloch. *Science* 235:621 F 6 '87

The pedagogy of competition. M. L. Weidenbaum. *Society* 25:46-54 N/D '87

Physics, Japan and US competitiveness. G. E. Pake. por *Phys Today* 40:9+ D '87

The quest for the '88 issue [competitiveness] L. Martz. il *Newsweek* 109:14-16 Ja 19 '87

The renewal factor [excerpt] R. H. Waterman, Jr. il *Bus Week* p100-1+ S 14 '87

Shaping America's future competitiveness [address, September 30, 1986] J. F. Beré. *Vital Speeches Day* 53:208-10 Ja 15 '87

The Sputnik of the eighties [economic competitiveness and federal role in education; cover story] J. F. Jennings. bibl f il *Phi Delta Kappan* 69:104-9 O '87

A surge in inequality [international competition and the feminization of poverty are distorting the distribution of income] L. C. Thurow. bibl (p128) il *Sci Am* 256:30-7 My '87

Taking on the world [special section] il *Time* 130:46-50+ O 19 '87

Technology and global industry. P. H. Abelson. *Science* 236:1609 Je 26 '87

Tomorrow's global economy: the challenge of increasing competition. L. Chapman. il por *Futurist* 21:26-7 Jl/Ag '87

The trade crisis begins at home [putting the blame on business schools] T. F. Keller. por *U S News World Rep* 103:8 Ag 31 '87

Unbinding Gulliver [address, April 9, 1987] R. A. Voell. *Vital Speeches Day* 53:661-5 Ag 15 '87

The United States-Japan economic Olympics [address, December 11-12, 1986] R. A. Morse. *Vital Speeches Day* 53:409-11 Ap 15 '87

The view from Main Street: America is slipping. M. Doan. il *U S News World Rep* 102:20-1 F 2 '87

What can America sell? *New Repub* 196:5-7 My 25 '87

Why business is at a loss in a free market. R. Kuttner. *Bus Week* p18 S 28 '87

Will the U.S. stay number one? [with interview with P. Drucker] M. W. Karmin. il *U S News World Rep* 102:18-23 F 2 '87

Winning your own game [cover story] R. Thompson. il *Nations Bus* 75:16-17+ Jl '87

The year of living competitively. D. Grossman. il *Technol Rev* 90:16 N/D '87

Competition (Biology)

Complex dynamics link islands' predators [research by Thomas Schoener and David Spiller] R. Lewin. *Science* 236:917 My 22 '87

Effect of lizards on spider populations: manipulative reconstruction of a natural experiment. T. W. Schoener and D. A. Spiller. bibl f il *Science* 236:949-53 My 22 '87

The human psyche was forged by competition [theory of Richard Alexander] R. Lewin. *Science* 236:668-9 My 8 '87

A sharp competitive edge [research by Ezra Zubrow] R. Lewin. *Science* 237:1293 S 11 '87

Competition (Plants) *See* Plant competition

Competition (Psychology)

See also

Sports—Psychological aspects

Commonsense competition. C. Schaeffer. *Changing Times* 41:97-8 F '87

Cooperation over competition: how to succeed. A. Kohn. *Current* 289:21-4 Ja '87

It isn't greed alone. S. Blotnick. il *Forbes* 139:178 Mr 23 '87

When lovers compete: sometimes romance takes a beating in the push to achieve. C. L. Mithers. *Glamour* 85:304 My '87

Why I like being competitive and why I'd like to stop. J. Kaufman. il *Glamour* 85:124+ N '87

Competitions

See also

All-American Girl Contest

Beauty contests

Odyssey of the Mind

Pole sitting

Prize contests

Tractor pulling

See also subhead Competitions under various subjects

Sur-prize, sur-prize! [contests designed for high school students] K. B. Fader. *Seventeen* 46:144-5 N '87

When chickens and chips fly [offbeat competitions] C. Julian. *Travel Holiday* 167:102 F '87

Competitiveness *See* Competition

Compilers (Computers)

See also

Silicon compilers (Computers)

Ada moves to micros. N. C. Shammas. il *Byte* 12:239-43 Jl '87

ALS Prolog. A. Lane. il *Byte* 12:269-72 S '87

Basic compilers for the Macintosh. S. L. Norman. il *Byte* 12:241-4+ My '87

Benchmarking dBASE III Plus compilers [Quicksilver, Clipper, and FoxBase] M. Rubel. il *Byte* 12:277-81 S '87

The CADcompiler. A. W. Crooke. il *Byte* 12:187-8+ Je '87

Comparing dBase compilers. M. Liskin. il *Pers Comput* 11:75-6+ Je '87

Faster, bigger, better [Turbo Basic and QuickBasic] J. Pournelle. il *Byte* 12:243-4+ Ag '87

The great C compiler war. J. Pournelle. *Byte* 12:264 O '87

High C 386. M. Trask. il *Byte* 12:196+ N '87

Lahey Personal Fortran 77. N. Baran. *Byte* 12:97-8 D '87

Logic grammars [Prolog] S. Szpakowicz. bibl il *Byte* 12:185-6+ Ag '87

Macintosh C compilers revisited. J. W. West. il *Byte* 12:219-24 Ag '87

MacScheme + Toolsmith [interactive development environment for the Macintosh] E. White. *Byte* 12:102+ D '87

Marshal Pascal and Pascal-2. M. Bridger. il *Byte* 12:185-6+ D '87

MIX C compiler, editor, debugger. il *Radio-Electron* 58 ComputerDigest:94 N '87

MPW compiler lets Mac II's 68020 shine. il *Byte* 12:109 N '87

MTBASIC. F. D. Davis. il *Byte* 12:336-9 Ja '87

Optimizing compilers. M. Roberts. bibl *Byte* 12:165-6+ O '87

Processor wars [Mac II and Professional Pascal] B. F. Webster. il *Byte* 12:297-8+ Je '87

QuickBasic 4.0. G. M. Vose. il *Byte* 12:111-12+ N '87

Reviewer's notebook [Borland's Turbo C] D. Betz. il *Byte* 12:198 Ag '87

Reviewer's notebook [MetaWare's High C compiler and Phar Lap Software's assembler package for 80386 machines] R. Grehan. *Byte* 12:201 Ap '87

Reviewer's notebook [Turbo Basic vs. QuickBasic] C. Baskin and G. A. Stewart. il *Byte* 12:227 Je '87

Stack machines and compiler design: the Novix CPU's FORTH instruction set and the design of a C compiler. D. L. Miller. bibl il *Byte* 12:177-8+ Ap '87

Three Fortran 77 compilers. D. W. Burleigh. il *Byte* 12:187-8+ N '87

Three Modula-2 programming systems. P. A. Sand. il *Byte* 12:333-6 Ja '87

Turbo Basic. G. A. Stewart. il *Byte* 12:101-6+ Mr '87

Turbo Pascal 4.0. G. A. Stewart. *Byte* 12:97 N '87

Complaints

Air travelers' gripes climb into the clouds. C. P. Work. il *U S News World Rep* 103:8 Jl 27 '87

Airline hassles: how to hassle back. M. Schiffres. il *Changing Times* 41:64-6 Jl '87

Bending an ear [consumer complaints] M. S. Dolan. *Consum Res Mag* 70:2 O '87

Flying complaints. J. W. Merline. il *Consum Res Mag* 70:38 Ja '87

Getting your gripe heard [dealing with travel operators] B. Bauer. il *U S News World Rep* 103:105 N 9 '87

How to complain and make it count. N. Barrett. il *Ladies Home J* 104:38+ O '87

Complaints—*cont.*

Northwest, TWA and Continental targets of most service complaints. *Aviat Week Space Technol* 127:41 S 14 '87

Travel complaints: how to get what you want. *Glamour* 85:101 N '87

Ways to get your money back [consumers] D. Sova. il *Read Dig* 130:25-6 Ja '87

What you can and can't do about airline snafus. il *Glamour* 85:91 O '87

Complements (Immunity)

A parasite with the guts of a burglar [Leishmania; research by David M. Mosser and Paul J. Edelson] K. Hartley. *Sci News* 131:359 Je 6 '87

Complex numbers *See* Numbers, Complex

Complexes (Chemistry)

See also

Host-guest complexes (Chemistry)

Complexion *See* Skin

Compliments *See* Praise

Composers

Stereo review's calender of classical composers. W. Livingstone. il *Stereo Rev* 52:105-9 N '87

Composers, American

See also

Adams, John

American Society of Composers, Authors and Publishers

Bernstein, Leonard, 1918-

Bolcom, William

Dean, Laura

Ellington, Duke, 1899-1974

Foster, Stephen Collins, 1826-1864

Fry, William Henry, 1813-1864

Gershwin, George, 1898-1937

Harbison, John

Loh, Sandra Tsing

Perle, George, 1915-

Powell, Mel, 1923-

Rouse, Mikel

Sondheim, Stephen

Walden, Narada Michael

Young, La Monte, 1935-

Composers, Austrian

See also

Mozart, Wolfgang Amadeus, 1756-1791

Schoenberg, Arnold, 1874-1951

Schubert, Franz, 1797-1828

Composers, Belgian

See also

Laporte, André, 1931-

Composers, Brazilian

See also

Villa-Lobos, Heitor

Composers, Czech

See also

Dvořák, Antonín, 1841-1904

Smetana, Bedřich, 1824-1884

Composers, English

See also

Benjamin, George

Birtwistle, Harrison

Britten, Benjamin, 1913-1976

Harvey, Jonathan, 1939-

Lloyd, George

Lloyd Webber, Andrew, 1948-

Composers, Finnish

See also

Salonen, Esa-Pekka

Composers, French

See also

Boulez, Pierre, 1925-

Massenet, Jules, 1842-1912

Rameau, Jean Philippe

Composers, German

See also

Beethoven, Ludwig van, 1770-1827

Gurlitt, Manfred, 1890-1973

Henze, Hans Werner, 1926-

Stockhausen, Karlheinz, 1928-

Strauss, Richard, 1864-1949

Wagner, Richard, 1813-1883

Weill, Kurt, 1900-1950

Zimmermann, Bernd Alois, 1918-1970

Composers, Hungarian

See also

Kurtág, György, 1926-

Ligeti, György

Liszt, Franz, 1811-1886

Composers, Italian

See also

Alfano, Franco, 1876-1954

De Banfield, Raffaello, 1922-

Geminiani, Francesco, 1687-1762

Morricone, Ennio

Puccini, Giacomo, 1858-1924

Composers, Polish

See also

Lutoslawski, Witold, 1913-

Penderecki, Krzysztof

Composers, Russian

See also

Stravinsky, Igor, 1882-1971

Composite materials

See also

Automobiles, Experimental—Materials

Carbon fibers

Helicopters—Materials

Composite photographs *See* Photomontage

Composition, English *See* English language—Composition

Composition (Music)

See also

Computers—Musical use

Harmony

Jazz music—Writing

Melody

Musicals, revues, etc.—Writing

Rock music—Writing

Has somebody stolen their song? M. Walsh. il *Time* 130:86 O 19 '87

Composition (Photography)

Contemporary design. A. Stone. il *Petersens Photogr Mag* 16:38-40 Jl '87

Double takes [paired images; work of G. Thorp] J. Hughes. il *Pop Photogr* 94:62-7 Ap '87

The effective use of primary and secondary shapes. F. Patterson. il *Petersens Photogr Mag* 16:46-7 My '87

Framework [views of J. Loengard] S. Piperato. il por *Pop Photogr* 94:60-1 Ag '87

Lines and edges as dynamics of composition. F. Patterson. il *Petersens Photogr Mag* 16:58-9 Jl '87

Compost

See also

Humus

Breaking down. P. L. Spencer. *Consum Res Mag* 70:2 Ap '87

Composting for spring. J. Burnett. il *Rodale's Org Gard* 34:30-2 Ag '87

Cultivating virtue. M. Pollan. il *Harpers* 274:66-9 My '87

Cultivating virtue. M. Pollan. por *Rodale's Org Gard* 34:95-6 O '87

How to make a simple compost pile. il *Sunset* 178:234 Ap '87

The instant garden. J. Cox. il *Rodale's Org Gard* 34:90-1 D '87

A one-man recycling program [O. Smith] P. H. Johnson. por *Rodale's Org Gard* 34:94-5 S '87

What you can and shouldn't compost. il *Sunset* 179:242-3 N '87

Marketing

Thoroughbred compost you can bet on [Nutra-Gro compost from Louisiana Downs spent stable bedding] F. Westergaard. il por *Rodale's Org Gard* 34:77-80 F '87

Compotes *See* Cooking—Fruit

Comprehension

See also

Memory

Reading comprehension

Comprehensive test ban *See* Nuclear weapons—Testing—Suspension

Compression of data (Computer science) *See* Data compression (Computer science)

Compton (Calif.)

Education

Marva Collins may teach in Chicago and Compton. por *Jet* 72:12 Ag 17 '87

Compton Community College

Twins joined at head enter Calif. college at age 38 [Yvonne and Yvette McCarther] il *Jet* 72:6 My 18 '87

Comptrollers *See* Controllers

Compulsive-obsessive behavior *See* Obsessive-compulsive behavior

Compulsive shopping

Are you a shopaholic? D. Tkac. il *Prevention* 39:62-5 Ap '87

The big, bad buy—shopping addiction: the nice girl's vice. D. Heyn. il *Mademoiselle* 93:198-9+ Ag '87

Compulsive shopping—*cont.*
Lifestyles of the rich and tyrannical. J. L. Goldstein. *Am Sch* 56:235-47 Spr '87
Compulsory military service *See* Military service, Compulsory
Compulsory retirement *See* Retirement
Computer-aided design *See* Computer graphics
Computer animation
Computer graphics are animating another market [industrial design] K. M. Hafner. il *Bus Week* p88+ Mr 16 '87

Programming
CAD-3D [three-dimensional modeling program for the Atari ST.] R. DeMaria. *Byte* 12:238+ Mr '87
Computer-assisted instruction *See* Computers—Educational use
Computer Associates International Inc.
Computer Associates buys its way to the top [acquisition of Uccel] A. Field. il *Bus Week* p68 Je 15 '87
Computer bulletin boards
CompuServe information service; Computer bulletin-board systems (BBS's) [astronomy] il *Sky Telesc* 74 Sky Telesc Handb:18-21 S '87
Custom-built bulletin boards. C. Keaveney. il *Pers Comput* 11:91-3+ Ag '87
Hi-tech racism. S. Miller. *Black Enterp* 18:22 O '87
TAXACOM, an online service for systematic botany. R. H. Zander. il *BioScience* 37:616-18 S '87
Using the RE-BBS. *Radio-Electron* 58:122 My '87
Computer chess
The space of one breath [fifth world championship] B. Leithauser. *New Yorker* 63:41-2+ Mr 9 '87
Speeding to a chess championship. *Sci News* 132:335 N 21 '87

Programming
Heeeere's Les Crane—and he's talking software. P. Finch. il por *Bus Week* p101 Jl 20 '87
Computer circuits *See* Integrated circuits
Computer clubs
See also
Boston Computer Society
Events and clubs. See issues of Byte beginning September 1986 through October 1987
Computer consultants
See also
Corporate Information Group
Custom Software (Firm)
Cashing in on computer confusion. C. L. Harris. il *Bus Week* p85-6 Ap 20 '87
Programmed for success [R. Y. Thomas] M. Whigham. il por *Essence* 17:103+ F '87
Computer control *See* Automation
Computer crimes
See also
Computer programming—Unauthorized use
Computer viruses
Cash-machine magician [R. Post's use of magnetic encoding machine to rob automated bank teller machines] *Time* 129:61 Je 1 '87
Computer fraud at VW [foreign exchange fraud] P. Lewis. il *Macleans* 100:32 Mr 30 '87
Hacking through NASA [penetration of Space Physics Analysis Network] W. D. Marbach. il *Newsweek* 110:38 S 28 '87
Computer dating (Social customs) *See* Computers—Social use
Computer equipment industry *See* Computer industry
Computer furniture
Contemporary computer desk. J. Olivari. il *Workbench* 43:54-5 My/Je '87
Old office, new office [special section] il *Work Woman* 12:49+ Ap '87
Computer games *See* Video games
Computer graphics
See also
Computer animation
Desktop video
Digitizers (Computers)
Manhattan Graphics Corporation
Pixar (Firm)
Publishing Technology Inc.
Affordable digital color page assembly—it's closer than you think. il *Publ Wkly* 232:405-8 Ag 7 '87
AT&T's TrueVision image processing system. R. Tinney. *Byte* 12:215-17 Mr '87
The changing face of news graphics [computer graphics for television news] C. C. Cortes. il *Technol Rev* 90:10+ F/Mr '87
Color separations: a new level of quality. J. P. Frank. il *Publ Wkly* 232:145-50 S 18 '87

Computers: practical tips for CAD selection and management. H.-C. Lischewski. il *Archit Rec* 175:51+ Ag '87
Designer bones—computers prescribe the prosthesis. S. F. Brown. *Pop Sci* 230:89 Je '87
Digital disinformation. S. Ditlea. il *Omni* 9:26 F '87
Distinctive coloring. D. Pountain. *Byte* 12:311-14 Ap '87
EGA times 12 [enhanced graphics adapter boards] C. H. Pappas and W. H. Murray. il *Byte* 12:313-14+ Ja '87
The electronic pencil; one small-firm approach [computer-aided design] I. McDougall. il *Archit Rec* 175:45+ Je '87
Faces, couches, cats . . . [efforts to mimic reality] J. Horgan. il *Sci Am* 257:34-5+ N '87
Fractal fairy tales. B. Schechter. il *Omni* 10:86-91 O '87
Graphics co-processors. J. Bernard. il *Radio-Electron* 58 ComputerDigest:82-5 S '87
Hercules discovers color graphics [InColor Card] A. C. Hixson. il *Pers Comput* 11:162 Jl '87
Hercules Graphics Card Plus. il *Radio-Electron* 58 ComputerDigest:85+ Ap '87
In news graphics, Macintosh makes the front page. F. Seghers. il *Bus Week* p87 Ja 19 '87
Inside the 82786 graphics chip. B. Nicholls. il *Byte* 12:135-41 Ag '87
A Mac on every drafting table [K. Shafton's use of computers] P. Honan. il por *Pers Comput* 11:185+ O '87
The Micro Clipper Graphics subsystem. C. D. Weston. il *Byte* 12:257-8+ S '87
A multi-display board from NEC [GB-1 graphics board] P. Honan. il *Pers Comput* 11:208 My '87
Picture this [work of C. A. Pickover; cover story] I. Peterson. il *Sci News* 131:392-5 Je 20 '87
Pictures worth a million bytes [scientists' use] M. D. Lemonick. il *Time* 129:64-5 My 18 '87
Polaroid Palette Computer Image Recorder. S. Drafahl. il *Petersens Photogr Mag* 16:48-51 My '87
Portraits of equations [cover story] I. Peterson. il *Sci News* 132:184-6 S 19 '87
Tseng Labs' EVA/480 [enhanced graphics adapter card] il *Radio-Electron* 58 ComputerDigest:135-6 My '87
Twists of space [visualization of the Romboy homotopy; cover story] I. Peterson. il *Sci News* 132:264-6 O 24 '87
VGA arrives for PCs [VGA Extra board] P. Honan. il *Pers Comput* 11:260 D '87
Zeroing in on chaos [study of Newton's method; work of Scott A. Burns and others] I. Peterson. il *Sci News* 131:137-9 F 28 '87

Exhibitions
Type-X: drawing a bead on book publishers. J. P. Frank. il *Publ Wkly* 231:30+ My 1 '87

Programming
3-D graphs for impact [Perspective] C. Spencer. il *Pers Comput* 11:150 Ja '87
Around and around [cycloids] R. T. Kurosaka. il *Byte* 12:307-8+ My '87
The art of computer graphics [work of Donald Greenberg and others] I. Peterson. il *Sci News* 132:87 Ag 8 '87
A better mouse trap [Freelance Plus presentation graphics program] S. R. Reed. il *Pers Comput* 11:204 My '87
Build the GT180 color graphics board (III). S. Ciarcia. il *Byte* 12:85-92 Ja '87
CAD-3D [three-dimensional modeling program for the Atari ST.] R. DeMaria. *Byte* 12:238+ Mr '87
A CAD for all incomes. P. R. Robinson. *Byte* 12:232+ Ag '87
Certificate Maker. *Radio-Electron* 58 ComputerDigest:103 F '87
Charts for the budget-minded [Stella Business Graphics] C. Spencer. il *Pers Comput* 11:188 Ap '87
Colorizer 1.0. T. Thompson. il *Byte* 12:104 N '87
CompDes—computer-aided circuit design. il *Radio-Electron* 58 ComputerDigest:136-7 My '87
Computer-aided design [special section] il *Byte* 12:173-5+ Je '87
Creating fractals. W. A. McWorter and J. M. Tazelaar. bibl il *Byte* 12:123-8+ Ag '87
Data structures in a bit-mapped text editor: how Carnegie-Mellon University displays text on the IBM RT PC. W. J. Hansen. il *Byte* 12:183-4+ Ja '87
Designing PC boards on your computer (I). R. Grossblatt. il *Radio-Electron* 58 ComputerDigest:97-9 Je '87
Designing PC boards on your computer (II). R. Grossblatt. il *Radio-Electron* 58 ComputerDigest:69-71+ Ag '87
Drawing, drafting, and design [Macintosh CAD programs] P. R. Robinson. *Byte* 12:251-2+ Jl '87

Computer graphics—Programming—*cont.*

Electronic drawing [GEM Draw Plus] S. Quigley. il *Pers Comput* 11:150 F '87

FastCAD 1.10. P. R. Robinson. il *Byte* 12:178-80 D '87

Graphics come of age [presentations] K. Berney. il *Nations Bus* 75:53-5 Je '87

Graphics software. S. Quigley. il *Pers Comput* 11:203+ Je '87

Holiday cheer [MacCalligraphy, Spellin!, spelling checker, and FastTRAP trackball device] E. Shapiro. il *Byte* 12:215-16+ D '87

Mimicking mountains. T. Jeffery. il *Byte* 12:337-8+ D '87

Mostly Mac [Illustrator] E. Shapiro. *Byte* 12:293 My '87

PS/2 video programming. R. Wilton. il *Byte* 12 no12 Sp Issue:67-70+ '87

RegionMaker [Macintosh program] H. Katz. il *Byte* 12:145-6+ Ja '87

Simple special effects illustrate the art of converting algorithms into programs. A. K. Dewdney. il *Sci Am* 257:142-6 D '87

Software reviews for architects [A/E Marketing Manager, version 2 and HICAD GM-1000, version 6.0] S. S. Ross. il *Archit Rec* 175:163+ N '87

Spraying and smudging [color mixing algorithms] D. Pountain. il *Byte* 12:317-18+ N '87

A stellar graphics tool for the Mac [Adobe Illustrator] A. C. Hixson. il *Pers Comput* 11:180 Jl '87

Text and graphics: together at last [Inset 2 RAM-resident utility program] P. Honan. il *Pers Comput* 11:164 Mr '87

Three-dimensional perspective plotting. T. Daulton. il *Byte* 12:307-8+ D '87

Vector-to-raster algorithms. D. Pountain. *Byte* 12:177-8+ S '87

Visual decision making [business chart producing software] C. Spencer. il *Pers Comput* 11:93-7 Ja '87

What does the graphics interface mean to you? R. Lockwood. il *Pers Comput* 11:138-41+ O '87

Standards

IGES [Initial Graphics Exchange Specification] R. J. Mayer. il *Byte* 12:209-14 Je '87

The many splendors of VGA [IBM's video graphics array] J. Blackford. il *Pers Comput* 11:279-80 S '87

PHIGS: Programmer's Hierarchical Interactive Graphics Standard. M. Plaehn. il *Byte* 12:275-6+ N '87

A 'super' EGA standard [Vega Deluxe "Super" EGA high-resolution graphics board] il *Pers Comput* 11:29-30 Je '87

Today's high resolution standards: EGA & VGA. P. Honan. il *Pers Comput* 11:119+ D '87

Computer industry

See also

3Com Corp.

Adaptec Inc.

Amdahl Corporation

American Telephone & Telegraph Co.

Apple Computer Inc.

Blue Chip Electronics (Firm)

Commodore International Ltd.

Compaq Computer Corporation

Computer service industries

Conner Peripherals Inc.

Control Data Corp.

Cray Research, Inc.

Data General Corp.

Dell Computer Corporation

Digital Equipment Corp.

Gtech Corporation

Hewlett-Packard Co.

Honeywell Bull Inc.

Honeywell Inc.

Intel Corp.

International Business Machines Corp.

LaPine Technology Corporation

Lin Data Corporation

Masstor Systems Corporation

National Semiconductor Corp.

Next Inc.

Novell Inc.

Paradyne Corp.

Pixar (Firm)

Seagate Technology

Sequent Computer Systems Inc.

Storage Technology Corp.

Stratus Computer, Inc.

Sun Microsystems Inc.

Systems Management American Corporation

Tandem Computers Inc.

Tandy Corp.

Telex Corporation

Texas Instruments Incorporated

Unisys Corp.

Women in the computer industry

Wyse Technology

Zenith Electronics Corp.

Computing in America: products and applications in an era of change [cover story; special issue; with editorial comment by Fred Abatemarco] il *Pers Comput* 11:13, 25-7+ O '87

Industry watch. R. A. Shaffer. See issues of Personal Computing beginning January 1985

Is the computer business dying? E. Dyson. *Omni* 9:31 Ap '87

Microbytes. See issues of Byte

Random access. E. Dyson. See issues of Forbes beginning May 18, 1987

View from the Valley. S. R. Reed. See issues of Personal Computing beginning June 1987

Acquisitions and mergers

Why Nashua looks even richer now [acquisition of Lin Data] G. G. Marcial. *Bus Week* p126 Jl 20 '87

International aspects

AT&T may be ready to cut its losses in computers [Olivetti to join in a spinoff] J. J. Keller. il *Bus Week* p30 Jl 6 '87

Can a turnaround wizard make Honeywell Bull work? [J. Stern] T. Peterson. il por *Bus Week* p84-5 Ap 20 '87

Advertising

Apples, frogs, and animal rights [Apple Computer television commercial] C. Holden. *Science* 238:1345 D 4 '87

New sales tool: computer lingo [Wang Labs] il *Newsweek* 109:47 Ap 6 '87

Cooperation

See also

Microelectronics and Computer Technology Corporation

Customer relations

The hunt for tech support [cover story; with editorial comment by Fred Abatemarco] R. Lockwood. il *Pers Comput* 11:5, 104-9+ Ag '87

The IBM-DEC wars: it's 'the year of the customer'. A. Beam and G. Lewis. il *Bus Week* p86-8 Mr 30 '87

Employees

See Computer personnel

Ethical aspects

Were STC's optical disks just a mirage? [suit brought by limited partnership investors against Storage Technology Corp.] M. Ivey. il *Bus Week* p67 Je 15 '87

Export-import trade

Brazil's independent computer strategy [cover story] A. J. J. Botelho. il maps *Technol Rev* 90:36-45 My/Je '87

A cautionary tale [LaPine Technology's joint venture with Kyocera] K. K. Wiegner. il por *Forbes* 140:52-3 Ag 10 '87

Don't let the Grinch steal Christmas. G. F. Gilder. il *Natl Rev* 39:40-4 Ap 24 '87

High-tech tariffs boomerang on the U.S. G. Lewis. il *Bus Week* p26-7 S 7 '87

Hyundai computers are stuck in the slow lane. G. Lewis. il *Bus Week* p50 Je 15 '87

Japan is building a cozy lead in laptops. L. Armstrong. il *Bus Week* p128+ F 23 '87

The Japanese strategy for computer supremacy [interview with C. H. Ferguson] N. Gall. il por *Forbes* 139:76+ F 9 '87

Taking the cuffs off exports to the East bloc [rules on high tech] S. J. Dryden. il *Bus Week* p48-9 Je 1 '87

Tracking a technobandit [C. J. McVey captured for illegal sales of computer equipment to the Soviet Union] D. Pauly. il por *Newsweek* 110:66 D 7 '87

Finance

Computers and electronics. M. Beauchamp. il *Forbes* 139:101+ Ja 12 '87

Desktop makers have it made [personal computers] G. Lewis. il *Bus Week* p65 N 16 '87

'The first sign of spring' for IBM and its rivals. G. Lewis. il *Bus Week* p35-6 Ap 27 '87

Going from gloom to boom [personal computer sales] G. M. Bock. il *Time* 129:52 My 11 '87

It all adds up to another so-so year. G. M. Bock. il *Bus Week* p88-9 Ja 12 '87

No more downtime [personal computer market] G. Bock. il *Time* 130:48-9 Ag 17 '87

Computer industry—Finance—*cont.*

Technology: back from the bottom. K. Berney. il *Nations Bus* 75:29 Ja '87

Why the hardware giants are hustling into software. A. Field. il *Bus Week* p53-4 Jl 27 '87

History

The greatest capitalist in history [cover story] T. J. Watson, Jr. il pors *Fortune* 116:24-32+ Ag 31 '87

International aspects

Applying tomorrow's technology today [address, September 9, 1986] G. G. Probst. *Vital Speeches Day* 53:166-8 Ja 1 '87

The high tech race: computers and chips. G. Bylinsky. *Current* 291:17-20 Mr/Ap '87

Laws and regulations

See Computers—Laws and regulations

Management

DEC's democracy [Digital Equipment] D. Machan. il *Forbes* 139:154+ Mr 23 '87

A quartet of high-tech pioneers. B. O'Reilly. il pors *Fortune* 116:148-9 O 12 '87

View from the top. il *Pers Comput* 11:285+ O '87

Marketing

See also

Computer stores

Apple cracks the business market. il *Fortune* 116:10 Ag 17 '87

Apple finally invades the office. B. O'Reilly. il *Fortune* 116:52-3+ N 9 '87

Apple goes for a bigger bite of corporate America. K. M. Hafner. il *Bus Week* p74-5 Ag 24 '87

Apple's big Mac attack [Macintosh SE and Macintosh II] J. Schwartz. il *Newsweek* 109:48 Mr 9 '87

Apple's comeback [concentrating on Macintosh sales to business] K. M. Hafner. il por *Bus Week* p84-9 Ja 19 '87

AT&T's epic push in computers. P. Petre. il por *Fortune* 115:42-4+ My 25 '87

Career makeover: high school teacher to high-tech sales [F. Monteleon, computer components distributer] il por *Glamour* 85:156 Mr '87

Commodore is anything but dead [Amiga 500] G. Lewis. il por *Bus Week* p96-7 Mr 9 '87

Computer warfare on campus [marketing computers to colleges] D. P. Wiener. il *U S News World Rep* 103:53-4 S 14 '87

Computers: the new look [change from mainframes to PCs in the office; cover story] J. W. Verity and G. Lewis. il *Bus Week* p112-15+ N 30 '87

'Day of the living clones,' starring IBM [unveiling of new line called Personal System/2] C. P. Work. il *U S News World Rep* 102:41 Ap 13 '87

Hewlett-Packard may have come up with a winner [RISC technology] R. Brandt. il *Bus Week* p48 Je 1 '87

How do you chase a $17 billion market? With everything you've got [computer makers campaigning to win government megacontracts] F. Seghers. il *Bus Week* p120+ N 23 '87

How IBM hopes to skin the copycats [new lineup of PCs] G. Lewis. il *Bus Week* p40 Ap 6 '87

The hungry pack nipping at Cray's heels. J. W. Verity and O. Port. il *Bus Week* p110+ O 26 '87

IBM and Tandy turn up the heat [personal computers] il *Fortune* 116:12 Ag 31 '87

IBM, clonebuster. P. Nulty. il *Fortune* 115:225 Ap 27 '87

IBM squares off against DEC [midrange office computers] il *Fortune* 116:8 Jl 20 '87

IBM tries another remedy [launching new mainframes and an improved laptop] G. M. Bock. *Bus Week* p32-3 F 9 '87

IBM unveils the sons of PC. W. D. Marbach. il *Newsweek* 109:61 Ap 13 '87

IBM's new family of personal computers taps greater power and compatibility [Personal System/2] S. Miller. il *Black Enterp* 17:90 Je '87

IBM's new PCs: homegrown and harder to clone. G. Lewis. il *Bus Week* p71 Ap 13 '87

Into the wild blue yonder [IBM's Personal System/2] P. Elmer-Dewitt. il *Time* 129:68 Ap 13 '87

Intriguing tales from the early days of the PS/2. P. Lemmons. il *Byte* 12:6 Ag '87

The new crop of muscle PC's. M. Schiffres. il *U S News World Rep* 102:56 Mr 16 '87

Playing second banana to desktops [sales of terminals] J. W. Verity. il *Bus Week* p85-6+ D 14 '87

Resurgence at Tandy. R. A. Shaffer. il *Pers Comput* 11:35 Ap '87

Riding a product to the top. R. A. Shaffer. il *Pers Comput* 11:39 Ja '87

Secrets to mail order success. C. O'Malley. il *Pers Comput* 11:109-13+ Jl '87

Some modest proposals [survival in the computer business] K. K. Wiegner. il *Forbes* 139:38+ Ap 20 '87

Stalking the corporate buyer [IBM's new series of personal computers] R. A. Shaffer. il *Pers Comput* 11:45 Ag '87

Suddenly the heavyweights smell money in computer networks [special section] J. W. Wilson. il *Bus Week* p110-12+ Ap 27 '87

A survival manual for the new PC's. W. J. Cook. il *U S News World Rep* 102:50 Ap 20 '87

Tandy finds a cold, hard world outside the Radio Shack [struggling to land business clients] T. Mason. il *Bus Week* p68+ Ag 31 '87

Tandy wants to be your computer company—can they be? [cover story; special section] il *Pers Comput* 11:102-9+ S '87

'Two-computer yuppies' fuel a new boom. G. Lewis. il *Bus Week* p130+ N 9 '87

The verdict on IBM's System/2: clonemakers are still in the game. G. Lewis. il *Bus Week* p118+ My 4 '87

Wait no more for the floppy disk [makers of hard disk drives] A. Snitzer. il *Forbes* 139:132 F 23 '87

What the major companies do best [personal computers] *Pers Comput* 11:108-9 S '87

Who's afraid of IBM? [Compaq Computer; cover story] J. E. Davis. il por *Bus Week* p68-72+ Je 29 '87

Who's who in desktop publishing [with editorial comment by F. Abatemarco] D. Needle. il *Pers Comput* 11:5, 110-15+ Ja '87

Securities

A high-tech play—but only for the fearless [companies that make hard storage disks] G. Lewis. *Bus Week* p118 Je 1 '87

Super stocks for tomorrow: computers. M. C. Paulson. il *Changing Times* 41:40-4+ Jl '87

Watching for $100 million flameouts. K. K. Wiegner. il *Forbes* 140:162+ N 16 '87

What's bringing down the high-tech highfliers. G. Weiss. *Bus Week* p72-3 Jl 20 '87

Brazil

Brazil's independent computer strategy [cover story] A. J. J. Botelho. il maps *Technol Rev* 90:36-45 My/Je '87

China

The state of Chinese computing. J. H. Maier. *Byte* 12:301-2 D '87

Great Britain

Byte U.K. D. Pountain. See issues of Byte through April 1987

India

The computerization of India. R. Chellam. il *World Press Rev* 34:52 F '87

Italy

See also

Ing. C. Olivetti & Co., SpA

Japan

See also

Fujitsu Ltd.

Hattori Seiko Co. Ltd.

Hitachi, Ltd.

Sony Corp.

Japan is building a cozy lead in laptops. L. Armstrong. il *Bus Week* p128+ F 23 '87

The Japanese strategy for computer supremacy [interview with C. H. Ferguson] N. Gall. il por *Forbes* 139:76+ F 9 '87

Just when IBM was roaring back in Japan . . . A. Borrus. il por *Bus Week* p70-1 F 2 '87

The power of information [address, June 15, 1987] R. W. Galvin. *Vital Speeches Day* 53:647-9 Ag 15 '87

Korea (South)

See also

Hyundai Electronics Industry Co., Ltd.

Taiwan

See also

Multitech Industrial Corp.

United States

See Computer industry

Computer integrated manufacturing *See* Automation

Computer languages

See also

Actor (Computer language)

Ada (Computer language)

AdvSys (Computer language)

Assembler language (Computer language)

Basic (Computer language)

BERTL (Computer language)

Computer languages—See also—cont.
    C (Computer language)
    Compilers (Computers)
    Forth (Computer language)
    Fortran (Computer language)
    Illinois Functional Programming (Computer language)
    Interpreters (Computer programs)
    Lisp (Computer language)
    Logo (Computer language)
    Modula-2 (Computer language)
    Natural language processing
    Pascal (Computer language)
    PostScript (Computer language)
    Prolog (Computer language)
    Simscript (Computer language)
    Smalltalk (Computer language)
    Structured Query Language (Computer language)
    Translators (Computer programs)
Computer literacy *See* Computers—Study and teaching
Computer literature
    See also
    Computers—Bibliography
Computer logic circuits *See* Logic circuits
Computer manuals *See* Computers—Handbooks, manuals, etc.
Computer maps
    Driving by the glow of a screen [Etak Navigator and DriverGuide] P. Elmer-Dewitt. il *Time* 129:63 Ap 20 '87
    Harris Corp. offering digital map generator for airborne operations. E. H. Kolcum. il *Aviat Week Space Technol* 126:84-5+ Mr 16 '87
    'A map is worth 10,000 words'. C. Gatti. *World Press Rev* 34:54 Ag '87
    These maps can almost read people's minds. M. Bluestone and E. Clark. il *Bus Week* p138-9 My 11 '87
Computer matchmaking *See* Computers—Social use
Computer music *See* Computers—Musical use
Computer network architecture
    IBM's software 'road map': a magic carpet to the future? [Systems Application Architecture] G. Lewis. il *Bus Week* p159 My 11 '87
    The meaning of SAA [IBM's Systems Application Architecture] G. M. Vose. *Byte* 12 no12 Sp Issue:6 '87
Computer networks
    See also
    American Telephone & Telegraph Co.
    Communications software
    Computer bulletin boards
    Distributed data processing
    Information storage and retrieval systems
    Local area networks
    MountainNET (Firm)
    Packet switching (Data transmission)
    Best of BIX. See issues of Byte beginning February 1986 through October 1987
    BIX's new Pyramid 9820. P. Lemmons. *Byte* 12:6 O '87
    Computer networking as a global-scale tool. P. Rossman. *Futurist* 21:10-11 Mr/Ap '87
    Computers with connections [tables] il *Pers Comput* 11:253 Jl '87
    'Diskless' computing. M. Liskin. il *Pers Comput* 11:59-60+ Jl '87
    The electronic Peace Corps. D. H. Rothman. *Natl Rev* 39:43-4 Mr 27 '87
    The IBM RT gets connected. J. Levitt. il *Byte* 12 no12 Sp Issue:133-6+ '87
    Interactive journalism and computer networking: exploring a new medium. M. Greenly. il pors *Futurist* 21:12-16 Mr/Ap '87
    Modem madness: telecommunications at a crossroads. S. Shulman. il *Technol Rev* 90:8 Jl '87
    A network for all computers [Sun Microsystems] S. R. Reed. il *Pers Comput* 11:217 Ag '87
    Networking by computer. C. Bullock. il *Black Enterp* 18:30 O '87
    Networking the colleges. *U S News World Rep* 103:54 S 14 '87
    Networks for advanced computing. R. E. Kahn. bibl (p184) il *Sci Am* 257:136-43 O '87
    The new networkers. F. Schwartz. il *Futurist* 21:8-11 Mr/Ap '87
    The next frontier of computer users. L. W. Krause. por *Pers Comput* 11:240 O '87
    On-line contacts. H. Fersko-Weiss. il *Pers Comput* 11:83-5+ Ja '87
    Online junkies. G. Fjermedal. il *Omni* 9:22+ Jl '87
    Pen pals: from quills to keyboards [Keylink computer network] *Newsweek* 110:60 D 21 '87

ScholarNet: the beginning of a world academic community. R. W. Slatta. il por *Futurist* 21:17-19 Mr/Ap '87
Strategic connections [personal computers and mainframe data] J. Blackford. il *Pers Comput* 11:131-3+ My '87
Suddenly the heavyweights smell money in computer networks [special section] J. W. Wilson. il *Bus Week* p110-12+ Ap 27 '87
Computer novels
    Adventures in computerland. W. R. Schroeder. il *Consum Res Mag* 70:24-7 Ap '87
    Interactive fiction as literature. M. A. Buckles. bibl f *Byte* 12:135-8+ My '87
    The next chapter in interactive novels. D. Caruso. il *Pers Comput* 11:130-1 Jl '87
    The sleuth in the machine [Deja vu and T. M. Disch's Amnesia] J. Ledbetter. *Nation* 244:613-14 My 9 '87
    You are what you read [T. Disch's Amnesia and R. Pinsky's Mindwheel] D. Lehman. il pors *Newsweek* 109:67 Ja 12 '87
Computer personnel
    Dorothy Terrell [black woman manager at Digital Equipment] L. Gite. il por *Black Enterp* 17:46+ Ap '87
    Who manages the network? [local area networks in business] H. Fersko-Weiss. il *Pers Comput* 11:107-9+ Mr '87

Supply and demand

    See also
    Systemp (Firm)
Computer printers *See* Computers—Print-out equipment
Computer programming
    See also
    Communications software
    Compilers (Computers)
    Computer animation—Programming
    Computer chess—Programming
    Computer graphics—Programming
    Computer service industries
    Computer viruses
    Computers—Accounting use—Programming
    Computers—Agricultural use—Programming
    Computers—Architectural use—Programming
    Computers—Art use—Programming
    Computers—Astronomical use—Programming
    Computers—Aviation use—Programming
    Computers—Banking use—Programming
    Computers—Biological use—Programming
    Computers—Business use—Programming
    Computers—Cartographic use—Programming
    Computers—Cooking use—Programming
    Computers—Earth sciences use—Programming
    Computers—Educational use—Programming
    Computers—Financial services use—Programming
    Computers—Indexing use—Programming
    Computers—Industrial use—Programming
    Computers—Investment use—Programming
    Computers—Literary use—Programming
    Computers—Mathematical use—Programming
    Computers—Medical use—Programming
    Computers—Meteorological use—Programming
    Computers—Military use—Programming
    Computers—Motion picture use—Programming
    Computers—Musical use—Programming
    Computers—Navigational use—Programming
    Computers—Oceanographic use—Programming
    Computers—Operating systems
    Computers—Photographic use—Programming
    Computers—Physics use—Programming
    Computers—Police use—Programming
    Computers—Political use—Programming
    Computers—Psychological use—Programming
    Computers—Real estate use—Programming
    Computers—Scientific use—Programming
    Computers—Social use—Programming
    Computers—Space flight use—Programming
    Computers—Sports use—Programming
    Computers—Statistical use—Programming
    Computers—Tax return use—Programming
    Computers—Theatrical use—Programming
    Copyright—Computer programming
    Data structures (Computer science)
    Desktop publishing—Programming
    Emulators (Computer programs)
    File organization (Computers)
    Floating-point arithmetic
    Hashing (Computer science)
    Heuristic programming
    HyperCard (Computer program)
    Hypertext
    Interpreters (Computer programs)
    Linear programming

Computer programming—See also—*cont.*

Logic programming
Machine translating
Macroprocessors
Menus (Computer programming)
MIDI (Musical instrument digital interface)—Programming
Multiprogramming (Computers)
Natural language processing
Programmable array logic
Sorting (Computers)
Spreadsheets (Computer programs)
Transformation (Computers)
Translators (Computer programs)
Windows (Computer programs)
Word processors and processing—Programming

286/386 protected-mode programming [IBM PC] J. Barnum. il *Byte* 12 no12 Sp Issue:125-9 '87
Answers. See issues of Personal Computing
Applications software today [with editorial comment by G. Michael Vose] il *Byte* 12 Sp Issue:6, 10-12+ Summ '87
Artificial intelligence moves into mainstream. M. M. Waldrop. il *Science* 237:484-5 Jl 31 '87
Ask Byte. S. Ciarcia. See issues of Byte
Buying software [with editorial comment by Fred Abatemarco] D. Caruso. il *Pers Comput* 11:5, 104-7+ F '87
Computing in America: products and applications in an era of change [cover story; special issue; with editorial comment by Fred Abatemarco] il *Pers Comput* 11:13, 25-7+ O '87
The limits of software reliability. R. L. Enfield. il *Technol Rev* 90:36-40+ Ap '87
On your computer. See alternate issues of Changing Times beginning September 1984
A programmer's introduction to OS/2. R. Duncan. *Byte* 12:101-2+ S '87
Programming for advanced computing. D. Gelernter. bibl (p183) il *Sci Am* 257:90-6+ O '87
Putting the byte on computer software. C. Begole. il *Seventeen* 46:124+ S '87
Teaching old screens new tricks: create fancy screen displays for your homegrown programs. M. J. Sorens. il *Byte* 12:129-33 S '87
Tips. M. Liskin. See issues of Personal Computing beginning January 1986 through May 1987
TSRs past and future: MS-DOS and OS/2. R. Duncan. il *Byte* 12 no12 Sp Issue:49-52+ '87
What's new? See issues of Byte

Bibliography

Book reviews. See issues of Byte

Debugging

See Debugging in computer science

Development

Software catches the team spirit [groupware] L. S. Richman. il *Fortune* 115:125+ Je 8 '87

Manuals

See Computers—Handbooks, manuals, etc.

Prices

For buyers of business programs, money is no object. R. Brandt. il *Bus Week* p70 Ag 10 '87

Standards

The application program interface: the SideKick Plus kernel, a proposed TSR standard. S. R. Boye and P. Kahn. il *Byte* 12 Sp Issue:19-23 Summ '87
Seybold on standards [desktop publishing; interview with J. Seybold] D. Needle. por *Pers Comput* 11:114 Ja '87
A standard for all? [coding TSR programs to interact with MS-DOS] R. Nelson. il *Pers Comput* 11:85 Mr '87
Taming the circus of TSR software. E. Tolson. por *Pers Comput* 11:228 O '87
TSR: an acronym worthy of amnesia. P. Kahn. por *Pers Comput* 11:238 O '87

Study and teaching

High road, low road, end of the road for CAI and programming? G. W. Bracey. il *Phi Delta Kappan* 68:547-8 Mr '87
A potpourri of computers [influence on children's thinking skills] G. W. Bracey. il *Phi Delta Kappan* 69:235-6 N '87

Aids and devices

Software Masters' Visible Computer: 8088. il *Radio-Electron* 58 ComputerDigest:95-6 Je '87

Testing

See also
Debugging in computer science

10,000 public-domain and user-supported programs on disk [PC-SIG library] il *Radio-Electron* 58 ComputerDigest:94-6 Mr '87
According to Webster. B. F. Webster. See issues of Byte beginning July 1985 through June 1987
ACT! Gets you organized [integrated program for MS-DOS personal computers] S. R. Reed. il *Pers Comput* 11:254 N '87
Applications only. E. Shapiro. See issues of Byte beginning March 1986
Close-up: solving remote problems. S. R. Reed. *Pers Comput* 11:148 Ja '87
Computing at Chaos Manor. J. Pournelle. See issues of Byte beginning June 1984
Dark horse applications. E. Shapiro. il *Byte* 12 Sp Issue:33-5 Summ '87
DOS utilities. S. Quigley. il *Pers Comput* 11:173-7+ S '87
Equation solvers [Eureka and TK Solver Plus] G. A. Stewart. il *Byte* 12:237-8+ O '87
Finding it fast: new software features that search your system [utilities] C. Bermant. il *Pers Comput* 11:125-7+ N '87
Flash-up [user interface utility program] R. Malloy. *Byte* 12:101 D '87
Gofer finds what you've lost [RAM-resident utility] C. Bermant. il *Pers Comput* 11:294 D '87
High-performance software analysis on the IBM PC [high-resolution timer] B. Sheppard. il *Byte* 12:157-8+ Ja '87
Hot products: software. M. Bryan. il *Pers Comput* 11:38+ O '87
Lotus Metro does it all [RAM-resident set of utilities] S. R. Reed. il *Pers Comput* 11:182 Ap '87
MacScheme + Toolsmith [interactive development environment for the Macintosh] E. White. *Byte* 12:102+ D '87
PFS: First Choice. L. D. Allen. *Byte* 12:235-7 Mr '87
Public domain software for the Amiga. W. Block. *Byte* 12:256-8 F '87
A RAM-hungry Partner [RAM-resident set of utilities] R. Lockwood. *Pers Comput* 11:176 Jl '87
RAM-resident utilities. J. Edwards. il *Byte* 12 Sp Issue:103-8+ Summ '87
Readers pick best of bunch [Personal computing survey] P. Honan. il *Pers Comput* 11:41-2 F '87
Reviewer's notebook. C. Baskin. See issues of Byte beginning March 1987 through October 1987
Reviewer's notebook. J. Edwards. See issues of Byte beginning May 1986 through February 1987
Running the Works [Microsoft Works] J. Bell. il *Pers Comput* 11:146+ Ja '87
Simulation modeling on the Macintosh using Stella. R. Costanza. il *BioScience* 37:129-32 F '87
The software robot [Automator mi] D. Pountain. *Byte* 12:383-4+ Ja '87
Taming the cursor [Cruise Control] J. Bell. il *Pers Comput* 11:160 Ja '87
Three C language screen-utility packages for PCs [Windows for Data, C-Worthy, and Vitamin C.] J. Robie. il *Byte* 12:223-4+ O '87

Unauthorized use

Can we end software piracy? [special section] il *Pers Comput* 11:142-5+ My '87
Central Point Software: the Option Board [COPY II PC tape backup] il *Radio-Electron* 58 ComputerDigest:87-8 O '87
The InJustice of it all [Dept. of Justice found guilty of stealing computer program from Inslaw] il *Time* 130:52 O 12 '87
The KEPROM: sinking the software pirates. J. Holtzman. il *Radio-Electron* 58 ComputerDigest:100-4 Je '87
Software piracy [responsibilities of colleges] K. C. Green and S. W. Gilbert. il *Change* 19:46-9 Ja/F '87
Sue 'em? Or love 'em? E. Dyson. il *Forbes* 140:307 S 7 '87

Computer science *See* Computers
Computer Sciences Corp.
Most improved. il *Forbes* 139:150 Ja 12 '87
Computer security *See* Computers—Security measures
Computer service industries

See also
Action Technologies (Firm)
AdaSoft Inc.
Adobe Systems Inc.
Aldus Corporation
Anacomp, Inc.
Ashton-Tate, Inc.
Asymetrix Corporation
Autodesk Inc.
AutoInfo Inc.

Computer service industries—See also—*cont.*
    Borland International
    Computer Associates International Inc.
    Computer Sciences Corp.
    Computone Systems, Inc.
    Control Data Corp.
    Cullinet Software, Inc.
    Custom Software (Firm)
    Electronic Data Systems Corp.
    Electronic Data Technologies
    General Sciences Corp.
    George Banta Company, Inc.
    Great Plains Software, Inc.
    Hewlett-Packard Co.
    Inslaw (Firm)
    Intel Corp.
    Interleaf Inc.
    International Business Machines Corp.
    Javelin Software Corporation
    Lotus Development Corporation
    Maxima Corporation
    MicroPro International Corporation
    Microsoft Corporation
    Penta Systems International, Inc.
    Phoenix Technologies Ltd.
    Pick Systems Inc.
    Policy Management Systems Corp.
    Software Resource (Firm)
    Software Toolworks Inc.
    Sterling Software, Inc.
    System Industries, Inc.
    Technical Support Services Inc.
    Theos Software Corporation
    Uccel Corporation
    Women in the computer service industries
Closing down the garage of the little guy [shakeout among personal computer software makers] D. P. Wiener. il *U S News World Rep* 103:45 Ag 17 '87
Home software kaboings again. il *Fortune* 115:10 F 16 '87
The Mac means opportunity [personal software industry] R. A. Shaffer. il *Pers Comput* 11:39 F '87
Now, computer paramedics. W. D. Marbach. il *Newsweek* 110:38 D 28 '87
Software plays hardball [Apple's proposed programming company and IBM's deal with Lotus] *Time* 129:52 My 11 '87
Why the hardware giants are hustling into software. A. Field. il *Bus Week* p53-4 Jl 27 '87

Accounting
Soft numbers. L. Jereski. il *Forbes* 140:89 Ag 10 '87

Acquisitions and mergers
Computer Associates buys its way to the top [acquisition of Uccel] A. Field. il *Bus Week* p68 Je 15 '87
How G.M. bought itself a lemon [tracing the Electronic Data Systems acquisition] M. M. Thomas. il *Nation* 244:108-9 Ja 31 '87
Infomaniac [R. Carson manages leveraged buyouts of information companies] L. Jereski. il por *Forbes* 140:224+ O 5 '87
Sam Wyly: will the hunter become the hunted? [Sterling Software] T. Mason. il pors *Bus Week* p110 Jl 13 '87

Customer relations
The hunt for tech support [cover story; with editorial comment by Fred Abatemarco] R. Lockwood. il *Pers Comput* 11:5, 104-9+ Ag '87
One size of software doesn't fit all. F. Gibbons. por *Pers Comput* 11:232 O '87
Revolutions don't happen overnight. J. P. Manzi. por *Pers Comput* 11:223 O '87
Who worries about 'the rest of us'? J. Rotenberg. por *Pers Comput* 11:252 O '87

Export-import trade
Will Lotus overrun Microsoft's Japanese garden? B. Buell. il por *Bus Week* p76 Ap 13 '87

Marketing
The billion-dollar whiz kid [W. Gates gets IBM to endorse Microsoft operating system; cover story] R. Brandt. il pors *Bus Week* p68-72+ Ap 13 '87
The changing corporate market. A. Osborne. por *Pers Comput* 11:256 O '87
Crossing over the boundaries. D. Carlston. por *Pers Comput* 11:250 O '87
The free-for-all has begun. A. Field. il *Bus Week* p148-51+ My 11 '87
Lotus' dream-come-true: a sweet deal with IBM [1-2-3/M spreadsheet] A. Field and A. Beam. il *Bus Week* p116 My 25 '87
PC software that helps you think. A. Field. il *Bus Week* p142 N 2 '87

Return of the home market [consumer software] R. A. Shaffer. il *Pers Comput* 11:47 S '87
The software imitators. R. A. Shaffer. il *Pers Comput* 11:41 Mr '87
Where to buy software. D. Needle. il *Pers Comput* 11:114-15 F '87

Securities
Both sides may win this war [spreadsheet market war between Lotus and Microsoft] A. Field. il *Bus Week* p104-5 O 19 '87
Early drum beats [personal computer software companies] S. Lee. il *Forbes* 139:298 Ja 12 '87

Suits and claims
Software liability. F. Lowenstein. il *Technol Rev* 90:9-10 Ja '87

United States
    See Computer service industries
Computer simulation
    See also
    Flight simulators
    Virtual computer systems
Business simulations. S. Morgenstern. il *Work Woman* 12:54+ My '87
Curbing abuses in computer modeling. B. R. Herrick. il *Technol Rev* 90:24-5 O '87
Future histories: a new approach to scenarios [SIGMA computer simulation] W. L. Renfro. il por *Futurist* 21:38-41 Mr/Ap '87
A look at Apple's Cray simulation engine. *Byte* 12:37-8 S '87
Now, 'artificial reality'. M. Rogers. il *Newsweek* 109:56-7 F 9 '87
PC Simscript II. 5. Z. A. Karian. *Byte* 12:244-6 Jl '87
Simulating a microprocessor [Prolog program] A. Lane. il *Byte* 12:161+ Ag '87
Simulation modeling on the Macintosh using Stella. R. Costanza. il *BioScience* 37:129-32 F '87
Computer software *See* Computer programming
Computer software industry *See* Computer service industries
Computer storage devices *See* Computers—Memory systems
Computer stores
    See also
    ComputerLand Corporation
    Computone Systems, Inc.
    Egghead Inc.
    PC Network (Firm)
    Tandy Corp.
Computer retailers: things have gone from worse to bad. K. M. Hafner. il *Bus Week* p104+ Je 8 '87
The retail route [post-sales support] R. Lockwood. il *Pers Comput* 11:111 Ag '87
Where to buy software. D. Needle. il *Pers Comput* 11:114-15 F '87
Computer terminal industry *See* Computer industry
Computer terminals
    See also
    Information display systems
    Keyboards
    Video monitors
Playing second banana to desktops [sales of terminals] J. W. Verity. il *Bus Week* p85-6+ D 14 '87
The right connection [HyperAccess communications and terminal-emulator package] J. Bell. il *Pers Comput* 11:154 F '87
Computer text processing *See* Text processing (Computer science)
Computer viruses
A program called MICE nibbles its way to victory at the first Core War tournament. A. K. Dewdney. il *Sci Am* 256:14-16+ Ja '87
Computer vision *See* Vision systems (Machines)
Computer workstations *See* Workstations
Computer worms *See* Computer viruses
Computerized axial tomography *See* Tomography
Computerized cameras *See* Cameras
Computerized mail systems *See* Electronic mail systems
Computerized speech *See* Speech processing systems
Computerized tomography *See* Tomography
ComputerLand Corporation
A billionaire no longer [W. Millard's sellout] K. K. Wiegner and J. Littman. il por *Forbes* 140:37-8 O 19 '87
ComputerLand celebrates a sea change [founder W. Millard sells out] K. M. Hafner. *Bus Week* p70 Je 15 '87
Computerphones
Are you ready for Pacific Bell's 'wonder phone'? [Project Victoria] il *U S News World Rep* 102:61 Mr 30 '87
Beating phone frenzy. A. Oshins. il *Work Woman* 12:86 N '87

Computerphones—*cont.*

A machine that only its makers could love [Telecompaq PC/telephone] J. E. Davis. il *Bus Week* p71 Je 29 '87

New use for your phone [Telegence Corp.] A. A. Lappen. *Forbes* 139:132 F 23 '87

Computers

See also

Artificial intelligence
Automation
Calculators
Hackers (Computer enthusiasts)
Information storage and retrieval systems
Instruction sets (Computers)
Interactive computer systems
Multiprocessors
Neural network computers
Reduced instruction set computers
Supercomputers
Turing machines

68000 update. il *Radio-Electron* 58 ComputerDigest:63 Ag '87

Answers. See issues of Personal Computing

Ask Byte. S. Ciarcia. See issues of Byte

Best of BIX. See issues of Byte beginning February 1986 through October 1987

BIX's new Pyramid 9820. P. Lemmons. *Byte* 12:6 O '87

Build the Circuit Cellar AT computer (I). S. Ciarcia. il *Byte* 12:115-20 S '87

Build the Circuit Cellar AT computer (II). S. Ciarcia. il *Byte* 12:135-43 O '87

Build the MC 68000. T. Schrader and others. il *Radio-Electron* 58 ComputerDigest:101-4 Mr '87

Build the PT-68K (I). P. Stark. il *Radio-Electron* 58 ComputerDigest:90-5 O '87

Build the PT-68K (II). P. Stark. il *Radio-Electron* 58 ComputerDigest:101-5 N '87

Build the PT-68K (III). P. Stark. il *Radio-Electron* 58 ComputerDigest:95-8+ D '87

Commodore is anything but dead [Amiga 500] G. Lewis. il por *Bus Week* p96-7 Mr 9 '87

Compute anywhere with PCs to go [LCD portables] W. J. Hawkins. il *Pop Sci* 230:88-90 F '87

Computer recreations. A. K. Dewdney. See issues of Scientific American

Computers: the new look [change from mainframes to PCs; cover story] J. W. Verity and G. Lewis. il *Bus Week* p112-15+ N 30 '87

Computers to go: you can take it with you [portable computers] D. M. Coder and E. W. Chu. il *BioScience* 37:350-5 My '87

Computing in America: products and applications in an era of change [cover story; special issue; with editorial comment by Fred Abatemarco] il *Pers Comput* 11:13, 25-7+ O '87

Data bank. See issues of Personal Computing beginning July 1987

Distinctive coloring. D. Pountain. *Byte* 12:311-14 Ap '87

Editorial [results of Microcomputer Opinion Poll] P. Lemmons. *Byte* 12:6 S '87

Fixes. See issues of Byte

IBM tries another remedy [launching new mainframes and an improved laptop] G. M. Bock. *Bus Week* p32-3 F 9 '87

IBM's new family of personal computers taps greater power and compatibility [Personal System/2] S. Miller. il *Black Enterp* 17:90 Je '87

Information processing. See issues of Business Week

Inside IBM's PS/2 line. J. Blackford. il *Pers Comput* 11:245-6+ Jl '87

Inside the IBM PCs [cover story; with editorial comment by G. Michael Vose] bibl il *Byte* 12 no12 Sp Issue:6+ '87

The MC 68000. T. Schrader and others. il *Radio-Electron* 58 ComputerDigest:138-40 My '87

The new crop of muscle PC's. M. Schiffres. il *U S News World Rep* 102:56 Mr 16 '87

The next computer revolution [cover story; special issue] bibl (p183-4) il *Sci Am* 257:56-64+ O '87

On your computer. See alternate issues of Changing Times beginning September 1984

PCs & DOS 3.x: still living after all these years. C. O'Malley. il *Pers Comput* 11:158-60+ S '87

The power of pizzazz [Macintosh II] R. A. Shaffer. il *Pers Comput* 11:61 Je '87

Random access. E. Dyson. See issues of Forbes beginning May 18, 1987

Shopping wisely for your first PC. S. Bentley. il *Black Enterp* 17:41 F '87

Star tech. P. Hoban. See issues of New York beginning September 24, 1984

Super PC [IBM Personal System/2] W. J. Hawkins. il *Pop Sci* 230:34-6 Je '87

A survival manual for the new PC's. W. J. Cook. il *U S News World Rep* 102:50 Ap 20 '87

The Tandy anniversary product explosion [cover story] R. Malloy and others. il *Byte* 12:100-6 O '87

Technology. J. Blackford. See issues of Personal Computing beginning July 1987

Tips. M. Liskin. See issues of Personal Computing beginning January 1986 through May 1987

Update. See issues of Personal Computing beginning January 1986

What's new? See issues of Byte

With a laptop computer, you can take it with you. S. Miller. il *Black Enterp* 18:35 Ag '87

Access control

See Computers—Security measures

Accounting use

386 buying spree [Coopers & Lybrand's purchase of Compaq Deskpro 386s] S. R. Reed. il *Pers Comput* 11:65 Mr '87

Programming

Accounting with a twist [NewViews] A. C. Hixson. il *Pers Comput* 11:226+ Je '87

DAC's easier accounting [DAC-Easy Accounting] T. Badgett. il *Pers Comput* 11:290+ D '87

Designing modern accounting software. G. W. Hedge. il *Byte* 12 Sp Issue:47-9+ Summ '87

An eye on the bottom line [Arthur Young/Audit Smarter, Quicker package] D. Garfinkel. il *Pers Comput* 11:69-70 Je '87

Light but full-bodied [Dac-Easy Light] C. O'Malley. il *Pers Comput* 11:89-90+ D '87

What's new in accounting software. A. C. Hixson. il *Pers Comput* 11:121-5+ My '87

Advertising

See Computer industry—Advertising

Agricultural use

Ag computerization steams on. G. Vincent. il *Success Farm* 85 no6:18AR-18AS Mr '87

Computer predicts $1/pound feeders in three years [beef industry predictions] *Success Farm* 85 no4:B12 F '87

Computer spies on college cows [Westfalia system at University of Delaware] D. Wanner. il *Success Farm* 85:50D Ag '87

A dandy farm computer for under $3,000. G. Vincent. il *Success Farm* 85 no3:18P F '87

Electronic cowboys. il *Futurist* 21:50 My/Je '87

New computers, new programs. G. Vincent. il *Success Farm* 85 no4:18AR F '87

'Ole eyeball' gets infrared view of weed problems [Soilection Systems of Soil Teq, Inc.] il *Success Farm* 85 no2:18P Ja '87

Rancher believes KIS theory of computer use [keep it simple] *Success Farm* 85:62P O '87

So you have a computer! Now what do you need? J. Anderson and others. il *Success Farm* 85 no5:26X-26Y Mr '87

What it costs to computerize your herd. G. Vincent. il *Success Farm* 85 no4:B4-B5 F '87

Programming

Buy it or build it? [cow-calf software] C. Henry. il *Success Farm* 85:B2 My '87

Computers can simplify chemical buying choices. *Success Farm* 85 no5:26F Mr '87

'Expert systems' are newest breed of computer help. *Success Farm* 85 no5:26AF Mr '87

'Flight simulator' helps you learn to pilot combine [Deere's HarvesTrainer] D. Mowitz. il *Success Farm* 85:18 Ag '87

He sorts cows; computer sorts rations. D. Ohrtman. il *Success Farm* 85:72 Ag '87

Pencil shrink gives way to computer shrink [spreadsheet to figure shrinkage when marketing slaughter-weight cattle] C. Peterson, Jr. il *Success Farm* 85 no4:B21 F '87

Prefab clues for soybean disease sleuths. il *Success Farm* 85 no1:26V Ja '87

Program guides you through marketing blizzard [Grain Marketing Advisor expert system] *Success Farm* 85 no6:18AX Mr '87

Spreadsheets: the computer's crystal ball. G. Vincent. il *Success Farm* 85:F1 My '87

Computers—*cont.*

Air traffic control use

See Computers—Aviation use

Airline use

See Airlines—Automation

Anecdotes, facetiae, satire, etc.

10 questions (and answers) to test your personal computing savvy and etiquette (with apologies to Cosmopolitan magazine). il *Pers Comput* 11:206 O '87

Build this IBM incompatible. J. Holtzman. il *Radio-Electron* 58 ComputerDigest:98-101 Ap '87

Chip thrills: the joke of Silicon Valley [Saint Silicon] J. Stone. il *Discover* 8:54-6+ D '87

Last word. C. Graybill. il *Omni* 9:114 Ja '87

Architectural use

Architectural education: on NCARB's horizon—a computer-adaptive exam. W. T. Carry. il *Archit Rec* 175:59 N '87

Computer show once again outdoes previous performances [A/E/C Systems '87] C. K. Hoyt. il *Archit Rec* 175:43 S '87

Computers: changing the legal rules. P. M. Lurie and B. D. Weiss. *Archit Rec* 175:35+ Ap '87

Computers: practical tips for CAD selection and management. H.-C. Lischewski. il *Archit Rec* 175:51+ Ag '87

The electronic pencil; one small-firm approach [computer-aided design] I. McDougall. il *Archit Rec* 175:45+ Je '87

In facility management, there are opportunities and pitfalls for architects. E. Teicholz and M. Sena. il *Archit Rec* 175:23+ Ja '87

Using your micro to specify [with editorial comment by Mildred F. Schmertz] S. S. Ross. il *Archit Rec* 175:9, 134-7 S '87

Programming

See also

Autodesk Inc.

Designing where less is best [software developed by Neeley/Lofrano Inc.] E. King. il por *Pers Comput* 11:161+ O '87

Software reviews for architects. S. S. Ross. il *Archit Rec* 175:154-6+ O '87

Software reviews for architects [A/E Marketing Manager, version 2 and HICAD GM-1000, version 6.0] S. S. Ross. il *Archit Rec* 175:163+ N '87

Art use

He didn't paint by the numbers, but he's getting digitized now [restoration of Michelangelo's Sistine Chapel frescoes] il *Discover* 8:8 My '87

Painting by numbers. J. Kluger. il *Discover* 8:56-8+ O '87

Programming

The art of computer graphics [work of Donald Greenberg and others] I. Peterson. il *Sci News* 132:87 Ag 8 '87

Colorizer 1.0. T. Thompson. il *Byte* 12:104 N '87

Electronic drawing [GEM Draw Plus] S. Quigley. il *Pers Comput* 11:150 F '87

Holiday cheer [MacCalligraphy, Spellin!, spelling checker, and FastTRAP trackball device] E. Shapiro. il *Byte* 12:215-16+ D '87

Mostly Mac [Illustrator] E. Shapiro. *Byte* 12:293 My '87

Spraying and smudging [color mixing algorithms] D. Pountain. il *Byte* 12:317-18+ N '87

A stellar graphics tool for the Mac [Adobe Illustrator] A. C. Hixson. il *Pers Comput* 11:180 Jl '87

Astronomical use

Advanced computing for science [simulating collisions between galaxies] P. Hut and G. J. Sussman. bibl (p184) il *Sci Am* 257:144-8+ O '87

The ATI "CAT": the wave of the future? [Computer Aided Telescope] D. J. Eicher. il *Astronomy* 15:66-71 D '87

Birth of a quasar [supercomputer model developed by Stuart Shapiro and Saul Teukolsky] A. Fisher. il *Pop Sci* 231:10 S '87

Birth of the moon [giant impact theory] A. Fisher. il *Pop Sci* 230:60-4+ Ja '87

Observing with the CAT [Computer Aided Telescope] G. H. East. il *Sky Telesc* 74:484-6 N '87

Programming

Astronomical computing. R. W. Sinnott. See issues of Sky and Telescope beginning April 1984

Computer dating [astronomical dating] F. R. Stephenson. il *Nat Hist* 96:24+ Ja '87

Finding the planets. A. Blackadar. il *Weatherwise* 40:45-9 F '87

Floppy Almanac. J. E. Mosley. *Sky Telesc* 73:85 Ja '87

Floppy Almanac is a real deal. B. L. Gotwols. *Astronomy* 15:47-8+ D '87

Simulating clusters on your computer. T. B. Woods. il *Astronomy* 15:63-7 S '87

Study dinosaurs, galaxies, and more with earth-science software. *Earth Sci* 40:10 Fall '87

What time is it? [sidereal time program] R. C. Walter, Jr. il *Astronomy* 15:38-40 F '87

Authors' use

Anecdotes, facetiae, satire, etc.

Computer fallout. R. Baker. il *N Y Times Mag* p30 O 11 '87

Automobile factory use

See Automobile factories—Automation

Automotive use

See also

Automobiles—Electronic equipment

Automobiles, Foreign—Electronic equipment

The happiest man at Ford. G. Baxter. il *Car Driv* 32:23 Mr '87

How IBM wooed Ford into a more meaningful relationship. W. J. Hampton. il *Bus Week* p87 Mr 30 '87

Microchip mechanic [Buick's Computerized Automotive Maintenance System] T. Swan. il *Pop Sci* 231:73-4+ Jl '87

Aviation use

See also

Airlines—Automation

Inertial guidance systems

A320 fly-by-wire controls pass basic flight testing. J. M. Lenorovitz. il *Aviat Week Space Technol* 126:41+ My 18 '87

Advanced computing for manufacturing. A. M. Erisman and K. W. Neves. bibl (p184) il *Sci Am* 257:162-9 O '87

Advanced raster monitors provide quick, accurate color ATC displays. D. Hughes. il *Aviat Week Space Technol* 127:109-10 N 9 '87

AI 'fair' demonstrates application of expert systems to C³I operations. K. J. Stein. *Aviat Week Space Technol* 126:104-5+ Je 1 '87

ARTI researchers assess feasibility of varied single-pilot operations [helicopters] il *Aviat Week Space Technol* 126:61+ Ja 19 '87

Automated flight engineer functions ease crew workload in MD-11 cockpit. M. A. Dornheim. il *Aviat Week Space Technol* 126:147+ My 11 '87

Boeing evaluating new control laws in 7J7 advanced-technology simulator [fly-by-wire control system] B. D. Nordwall. il *Aviat Week Space Technol* 126:54-6+ Je 29 '87

British Aerospace offers Terprom navigation system to U.S. military. il *Aviat Week Space Technol* 126:85 My 4 '87

Computer and software advances will boost controller productivity. W. B. Scott. il *Aviat Week Space Technol* 127:95+ N 9 '87

Crouzet, Bendix will develop voice command system [military aircraft] *Aviat Week Space Technol* 127:77 Jl 20 '87

Digital protests terms of Air Force call for computer bids. *Aviat Week Space Technol* 127:157 O 12 '87

FAA plans Inmarsat satellite surveillance of oceanic routes. P. J. Klass. *Aviat Week Space Technol* 127:47+ D 7 '87

Fly-by-wire, digital avionics ease A320 transition training [evaluation flight] D. M. North. il *Aviat Week Space Technol* 127:40-1+ N 30 '87

Forum stresses Air Force's dependence on computers [conference with vendors] D. Hughes. *Aviat Week Space Technol* 127:85+ N 2 '87

Four teams will study system to track USAF airlift missions. D. Hughes. *Aviat Week Space Technol* 127:85+ D 7 '87

Future airports. *World Press Rev* 34:58 O '87

Hidec tests show potential for thrust, fuel improvements through propulsion, flight control link [highly integrated digital engine control] W. B. Scott. *Aviat Week Space Technol* 126:62+ Ap 6 '87

IBM Host computer system operational at Boston center [FAA air traffic control system] *Aviat Week Space Technol* 127:56 O 26 '87

Lack of hardware delays use of traffic forecast system. *Aviat Week Space Technol* 127:34 O 5 '87

Lockheed developing electronic copilot in support of ATF program effort. K. J. Stein. il *Aviat Week Space Technol* 127:73+ Ag 17 '87

NASA uses supercomputer for aerodynamic simulation [Numerical Aerodynamic Simulator] il *Aviat Week Space Technol* 126:264-5 Mr 9 '87

Computers—Aviation use—*cont.*

New automated testing system aids SAC FB-111 maintenance. K. J. Stein. il *Aviat Week Space Technol* 126:91+ Mr 2 '87

New Boeing facility will play key role in ATF competition [advanced tactical fighter] *Aviat Week Space Technol* 126:89+ Ja 26 '87

New-generation Airbus A320 transport demonstrates fly-by-wire technology. il *Aviat Week Space Technol* 126:284-5 Je 15 '87

New modular system monitors engine, airframe parameters automatically [digital flight data acquisition unit] K. J. Stein. il *Aviat Week Space Technol* 126:99+ Mr 30 '87

Page Avjet, Kollsman completing design for Boeing 727 flight deck conversion. E. H. Kolcum. *Aviat Week Space Technol* 127:52+ S 28 '87

Production of ATC modernization equipment moves into high gear [National Airspace System Plan] J. Ott. *Aviat Week Space Technol* 126:31-2 Mr 23 '87

Red for La Guardia, brown for J.F.K. [FAA's new air traffic control system] P. Elmer-Dewitt. il *Time* 129:60-1 Je 1 '87

Researchers urge further tests to improve rotorcraft models. W. B. Scott. il *Aviat Week Space Technol* 126:50-3+ Ap 20 '87

Screen test. R. L. Collins. il *Flying* 114:74 D '87

Silicosms [Numerical Aerodynamic Simulator] R. Schultz. il *Omni* 9:52-7 Ag '87

South Korea activates automated civil air traffic control system. il *Aviat Week Space Technol* 126:157 My 11 '87

Speed briefs [automated flight service station at Millville, N.J.] P. Scott. il por *Flying* 114:70-2+ O '87

A super-supercomputer [Numerical Aerodynamic Simulator] *Sci News* 131:166 Mr 14 '87

USAF demonstrates electro-optical reconnaissance system on RF-4C. J. D. Morrocco. *Aviat Week Space Technol* 126:123+ My 18 '87

Wisdom of the gauges [future of avionics] J. M. McClellan. il *Flying* 114:146-7 S '87

Programming

CF-18 revolutionizes Cold Lake test data, software operations [Canada] il *Aviat Week Space Technol* 127:128-9+ S 28 '87

Datalog flight planner. J. M. McClellan. *Flying* 114:94 Mr '87

Swedish Gripen's first flight delayed by software problems [fly-by-wire flight control system] D. A. Brown. *Aviat Week Space Technol* 127:25 O 5 '87

Banking use

See also

Automated teller machines
Clearinghouse (Banking)
Debit cards
Plus System, Inc.

Managing the needs of others [R. Schnitzer controls direction of computer users in the corporate finance department at Bankers Trust] P. Honan. il por *Pers Comput* 11:164-5 O '87

Visa's back-office strategy in the credit-card wars [cutting the cost of electronic transactions] J. B. Levine. il *Bus Week* p75 Ap 20 '87

Programming

Desktop banking. C. García-Barrio. il *Essence* 18:138 My '87

Bibliography

Back-to-school booklist. il *Radio-Electron* 58 ComputerDigest:93 N '87

Book reviews. See issues of Byte

Biological use

Automated DNA sequence analysis. L. M. Smith. bibl f *Science* 235 pt2:G89 F 27 '87

The biologist's toolbox. See issues of BioScience beginning February 1985

Computer simulations of the diffusion of a substrate to an active site of an enzyme. K. Sharp and others. bibl f il *Science* 236:1460-3 Je 12 '87

Corn borers, beware the chips [computer model] D. D. Edwards. il *Sci News* 131:20 Ja 10 '87

Interview [L. E. Hood, developer of automated DNA sequencer] J. Davis. il por *Omni* 10:116-18+ N '87

Laboratory experimentation with a personal computer. J. I. Peterson. *Science* 235 pt2:G162 F 27 '87

Neural nets catch the ABCs of DNA [research by Alan Lapedes and others] S. Weisburd. *Sci News* 132:76 Ag 1 '87

Opening new frontiers in molecular biology [automated DNA sequencer] T. Dworetzky. il *Discover* 8:14-15 Mr '87

Thought and action [computer model of motor cortex neuron activity; work of Apostolos Georgopoulos] A. Fisher. il *Pop Sci* 230:8 F '87

Programming

Creating an "electronic nose" [electronically reproduced fragment of the olfactory cortex; work of Gary Lynch and others] il *USA Today (Periodical)* 115:13 Je '87

Sequence analysis on microcomputers. G. C. Cannon. bibl f il *Science* 238:97-103 O 2 '87

Book industries use

See also

Bookland EAN system

The electronics front. J. P. Frank. See issues of Publishers Weekly beginning May 15, 1987

Botanical use

Dynamic ecosystem consequences of tree birth and death patterns [computer models] H. H. Shugart. bibl il *BioScience* 37:596-602 S '87

Buses

The 32-bit Micro Channel. J. Shiell. il *Byte* 12 no12 Sp Issue:59-60+ '87

Comparing IBM's Micro Channel and Apple's NuBus. C. Cornejo and R. Lee. il *Byte* 12 no12 Sp Issue:83-6+ '87

IBM's Micro Channel: the next step. J. Blackford. *Pers Comput* 11:167 S '87

PC-601 bus extender, Chenesko Products. il *Radio-Electron* 58 ComputerDigest:94 N '87

The significance of the Micro Channel. M. Swavely. por *Pers Comput* 11:258 O '87

Three bus interface designs for the PC. J. R. Drummond. il *Byte* 12 no12 Sp Issue:225-30+ '87

Under the covers: the new IBM Micro Channel as seen from inside the PS/2 Model 50. S. Ciarcia. il *Byte* 12:101-6+ Ag '87

Business use

See also

Electronic data processing departments
Information centers (Data processing)
Offices—Automation
Telecommuting

Apple cracks the business market. il *Fortune* 116:10 Ag 17 '87

Apple finally invades the office. B. O'Reilly. il *Fortune* 116:52-3+ N 9 '87

Apple goes for a bigger bite of corporate America. K. M. Hafner. il *Bus Week* p74-5 Ag 24 '87

Apple's comeback [concentrating on Macintosh sales to business] K. M. Hafner. il por *Bus Week* p84-9 Ja 19 '87

'Big Brother' in the office. *Newsweek* 110:78 O 5 '87

Big Brother is counting your keystrokes [report by the Office of Technology Assessment] W. Booth. *Science* 238:17 O 2 '87

Business computing in flux [tables] P. Honan. il *Pers Comput* 11:369 D '87

The changing workplace [special section] il *Pers Comput* 11:151-3+ O '87

Choosing sides in the PC wars. H. McCandless. *Work Woman* 12:36+ N '87

Computer headaches. J. Schwartz. il *Newsweek* 110:34-5 Jl 6 '87

Computerizing with confidence (III). K. Berney. il *Nations Bus* 75:33-5 Ja '87

Computerizing with confidence (IV). K. Berney. il *Nations Bus* 75:55-7 F '87

Computerizing with confidence (V). K. Berney. il *Nations Bus* 75:23-4 Mr '87

Computerizing with confidence (VI). K. Berney. il *Nations Bus* 75:22-4 Ap '87

Computerizing your business [special section] il *Work Woman* 12:33+ S '87

Computers in corporations [tables] P. Honan. il *Pers Comput* 11:215 Ag '87

Computers in small business [tables] P. Honan. il *Pers Comput* 11:277 S '87

Computers: the new look [change from mainframes to PCs in the office; cover story] J. W. Verity and G. Lewis. il *Bus Week* p112-15+ N 30 '87

Computers with connections [tables] il *Pers Comput* 11:253 Jl '87

Creative solutions with everyday systems. A. C. Hixson. il *Pers Comput* 11:138-41+ S '87

Electronic taskmasters [monitoring of employees] T. Beardsley. *Sci Am* 257:32+ D '87

I couldn't learn to use a computer at work. il *Good Housekeep* 204:28+ Je '87

In business. See occasional issues of Personal Computing beginning June 1987

Information management. See issues of Business Week

Computers—Business use—*cont.*

It knows if you've been bad or good [monitoring of employees] il *Discover* 8:16 D '87

The Mac is back [cover story; special section; with editorial comment by Fred Abatemarco] A. C. Hixson. il *Pers Comput* 11:5, 102-7+ Ap '87

Managing people and their computers. A. S. Grove. por *Pers Comput* 11:228 O '87

The nerve-racking job of setting up a network. J. W. Wilson. il *Bus Week* p112+ Ap 27 '87

Now, live experts on a floppy disk. A. Kupfer. il *Fortune* 116:69-70+ O 12 '87

Office automation: making it pay off [special section] C. L. Harris. il *Bus Week* p134-8+ O 12 '87

Old office, new office [special section] il *Work Woman* 12:49+ Ap '87

Old office, new office: reaching decisions that get results [special section] il *Work Woman* 12:47+ O '87

Professionals and their computers [Apple's Macintosh] J. Sculley. por *Pers Comput* 11:236 O '87

Putting PCs to work. il *Nations Bus* 75:38 N '87

Tandy finds a cold, hard world outside the Radio Shack [struggling to land business clients] T. Mason. il *Bus Week* p68+ Ag 31 '87

Technology in action [special section] il *Work Woman* 12:67+ N '87

View from the top. il *Pers Comput* 11:285+ O '87

Who manages the network? [local area networks in business] H. Fersko-Weiss. il *Pers Comput* 11:107-9+ Mr '87

Costs

Stalking the corporate buyer [IBM's new series of personal computers] R. A. Shaffer. il *Pers Comput* 11:45 Ag '87

Programming

3-D graphs for impact [Perspective] C. Spencer. il *Pers Comput* 11:150 Ja '87

ACT! Gets you organized [integrated program for MS-DOS personal computers] S. R. Reed. il *Pers Comput* 11:254 N '87

Applications in transition [special section] il *Pers Comput* 11:87-91+ O '87

A better mouse trap [Freelance Plus presentation graphics program] S. R. Reed. il *Pers Comput* 11:204 My '87

Central intelligence: tapping the power of project management software. E. King. il *Pers Comput* 11:134-7+ N '87

The changing corporate market. A. Osborne. por *Pers Comput* 11:256 O '87

Charts for the budget-minded [Stella Business Graphics] C. Spencer. il *Pers Comput* 11:188 Ap '87

Decision Pad weighs choices. S. R. Reed. *Pers Comput* 11:262-3 D '87

Financial modeling: going beyond spreadsheets. C. Spencer. il *Pers Comput* 11:68-71+ Ap '87

For buyers of business programs, money is no object. R. Brandt. il *Bus Week* p70 Ag 10 '87

Games that grownups play. P. Elmer-Dewitt. il map *Time* 130:68 Jl 27 '87

Graphics come of age [presentations] K. Berney. il *Nations Bus* 75:53-5 Je '87

Help for project management [InstaPlan] P. Honan. *Pers Comput* 11:170 Jl '87

How to tell good software by its cover. C. J. Mullins. *Work Woman* 12:44+ D '87

Management by the book [Putting The One Minute Manager to Work] C. O'Malley. *Pers Comput* 11:206 S '87

The next generation of business software. G. Kawasaki. por *Pers Comput* 11:244 O '87

Professionals and their setups. C. Spezzano. il *Pers Comput* 11:127-9+ S '87

Should we move to Milpitas? [Decision Pad software] E. Dyson. il *Forbes* 140:102 Ag 10 '87

Software catches the team spirit [groupware] L. S. Richman. il *Fortune* 115:125+ Je 8 '87

Strategic connections [personal computers and mainframe data] J. Blackford. il *Pers Comput* 11:131-3+ My '87

Visual decision making [business chart producing software] C. Spencer. il *Pers Comput* 11:93-7 Ja '87

Cartographic use

'A map is worth 10,000 words'. C. Gatti. *World Press Rev* 34:54 Ag '87

These maps can almost read people's minds. M. Bluestone and E. Clark. il *Bus Week* p138-9 My 11 '87

Programming

Contour mapping and SURFACE II. J. C. Davis. bibl f il *Science* 237:669-72 Ag 7 '87

A contouring subroutine [Basic program] P. D. Bourke. il *Byte* 12:143-6+ Je '87

Mapping the world in Pascal. R. Miller and F. Reddy. il maps *Byte* 12:329-32+ D '87

Methods of map encoding. il *Byte* 12:134-5 Jl '87

Chemical use

Computer-aided molecular design. J. A. McCammon. bibl f il *Science* 238:486-91 O 23 '87

Free energy calculations by computer simulation. P. A. Bash and others. bibl f il *Science* 236:564-8 My 1 '87

Circuits

See Integrated circuits

Compatibility

The Apple Macintosh II [cover story; with editorial comment by Phil Lemmons] G. Williams and T. Thompson. il *Byte* 12:6, 85-8+ Ap '87

Benchmarks of compatibility. T. Badgett. il *Pers Comput* 11:99-101+ F '87

Build an IBM-compatible clone computer. J. Flack. il *Radio-Electron* 58 ComputerDigest:104-9 F '87

The complete guide to IBM compatibles. S. Makrias and P. Honan. il *Pers Comput* 11:141-3+ Ap '87

Connections. C. Lu. *BioScience* 37:422 Je '87

A head full of cotton [Magic Sac to run Macintosh software on the Atari] B. F. Webster. il *Byte* 12:289-90+ Ap '87

IBM PC AT compatibles. J. C. Dermody and J. Punater. il *Byte* 12:328-9 Ja '87

Intriguing tales from the early days of the PS/2. P. Lemmons. il *Byte* 12:6 Ag '87

The knockoffs head for a knockdown fight with IBM. K. M. Hafner. il *Bus Week* p112-13 D 21 '87

A link between operating systems [MacLinkPlus] A. C. Hixson. il *Pers Comput* 11:152 Ag '87

Microsolutions' Matchpoint-PC. il *Radio-Electron* 58 ComputerDigest:94-5 Je '87

Reconcilable differences: data transfer between mismatched disk formats. R. Cook. il *Pers Comput* 11:143+ D '87

A timing-independent BIOS. H. N. Cohen and J. Hanel. il *Byte* 12 no12 Sp Issue:219-20+ '87

A trio of 8-MHz PC AT compatibles [NCR PC8 Victor V286 and QIC AT-Plus 1800] S. Miastkowski. il *Byte* 12:209-12 Mr '87

Two high-performance PC AT compatibles [ITT XTRA/ 286 ATW and AST Premium/286] J. Unger. il *Byte* 12:207-11 Ag '87

The wall comes tumbling down [IBM and Apple personal computers] P. Elmer-Dewitt. il *Time* 129:68 F 2 '87

What's compatible with PS/2? *Pers Comput* 11:106 Je '87

Working with clone software. M. Liskin. il *Pers Comput* 11:39-40+ My '87

Conferences

Amiga Developers Conference. B. F. Webster. *Byte* 12:291-2+ Mr '87

Journeys [Apple IIGS Developers Conference] B. F. Webster. *Byte* 12:303+ F '87

Control use

Computer-controlled robot [Armatron] J. Barbarello. il *Radio-Electron* 58 ComputerDigest:144-7 My '87

Taking control. D. Pountain. *Byte* 12:279-80+ Mr '87

Cooking use

Programming

Chinese food by computer [CHEF program expands AI; work of Kristan Hammond] il *USA Today (Periodical)* 115:12-13 Je '87

Credit rating use

See Credit—Rating—Automation

Dance use

Computerography [use of personal computers by Limon Company] B. Hamblett. *Dance Mag* 61:86-7 Ja '87

Design

See also

Massachusetts Institute of Technology. Media Laboratory

How IBM hopes to skin the copycats [new lineup of PCs] G. Lewis. il *Bus Week* p40 Ap 6 '87

IBM, clonebuster. P. Nulty. il *Fortune* 115:225 Ap 27 '87

IBM's new PCs: homegrown and harder to clone. G. Lewis. il *Bus Week* p71 Ap 13 '87

The next computers [personal computers] M. Rogers. il *Newsweek* 109:60+ Ap 6 '87

Pied Piper of the computer [A. Kay] F. Rose. il por *N Y Times Mag* p56+ N 8 '87

The technical implications of the PS/2. G. M. Vose. il *Byte* 12 no12 Sp Issue:33-4+ '87

Earth sciences use

Programming

Study dinosaurs, galaxies, and more with earth-science software. *Earth Sci* 40:10 Fall '87

Computers—*cont.*

Economics use
Nuclear crash [computer simulation of the post-attack economy] C. Norman. *Science* 236:1517 Je 19 '87

Educational use
See also
National Geographic Kids Network

Computer warfare on campus [marketing computers to colleges] D. P. Wiener. il *U S News World Rep* 103:53-4 S 14 '87

Computing gets an overhaul at Stanford University. J. N. Shurkin. il *Pers Comput* 11:179-81+ D '87

Do freshmen really need computers? C. Tuzzolino. il *Bus Week* p83 Ag 10 '87

Educational computing [special section] il *Byte* 12:146-7+ F '87

From campus to business [D. Patnaude's use of computers while a student at Stevens Institute of Technology] J. Schwartz. il por *Pers Comput* 11:189+ O '87

Hidden effects of computers on teachers and students. M. W. Apple. *Educ Dig* 53:2-6 O '87

High road, low road, end of the road for CAI and programming? G. W. Bracey. il *Phi Delta Kappan* 68:547-8 Mr '87

Microcomputers and the pro-innovation bias. P. Jorde. *Educ Dig* 52:36-9 F '87

Overselling technology on campus. L. H. Fleit. *Educ Dig* 53:19-21 N '87

Pen pals: from quills to keyboards [Keylink computer network] *Newsweek* 110:60 D 21 '87

A potpourri of computers [influence on children's thinking skills] G. W. Bracey. il *Phi Delta Kappan* 69:235-6 N '87

Programming
Acid-base balance: an educational computer game. J. Boyle and G. Robinson. il *BioScience* 37:511-13 Jl/Ag '87

Computers in the classroom [Project Headlight at Hennigan Elementary School, Roxbury, Mass.] A. Bass. il por *Technol Rev* 90:52-62+ Ap '87

A hard look at educational software. A. Naiman. *Byte* 12:193-4+ F '87

Magical tools for the 1980s [math and science software created by E. Goldstein] H.-J. Taferner. il por *Pers Comput* 11:173+ O '87

Software for learning. H. Brady. il *Parents* 62:296+ N '87

Typing tutors. N. Henderson and M. Schiffres. il *Changing Times* 41:76 Ag '87

Energy usage
5-volt only: introducing the new MAX 232. R. A. Kreuter. il *Radio-Electron* 58 ComputerDigest:10-11 Ja '87

Engineering use
Programming
See also
Silicon compilers (Computers)

Environmental use
Artificial intelligence and natural resource management. R. N. Coulson and others. bibl f il *Science* 237:262-7 Jl 17 '87

Equipment
80286 accelerators. R. G. A. Cote. il *Byte* 12:161-6 N '87

80386 accelerator boards [American Computer and Peripheral's 386 Turbo and Intel's Inboard 386] D. E. Crabb. il *Byte* 12:213-16 Ag '87

Accelerator boards [BIX product focus] C. Franklin, Jr. *Byte* 12:169-70+ N '87

Accelerator boards for the Macintosh SE [Prodigy SE and HyperCharger 020] L. H. Loeb. il *Byte* 12:177-80 N '87

The All Card AT1/M. J. Angel. il *Byte* 12:324-6 Ja '87

Awesome I/O card. R. Grehan. il *Byte* 12:101-2 D '87

Build a clock board for your PC. V. D. Martin. il *Radio-Electron* 58 ComputerDigest:97-100 Mr '87

Build the GT180 color graphics board (III). S. Ciarcia. il *Byte* 12:85-92 Ja '87

The Cheetah Adapter/386 [translator card] J. Shiell. il *Byte* 12:135-7 Ap '87

Commodore pulse generator. J. Barbarello. il *Radio-Electron* 58 ComputerDigest:96-100 O '87

Computer maladies [remedies for external annoyances] S. A. Booth. il *Pop Mech* 164:34+ Ap '87

Curtain up on enhanced Amiga [A2000] il *Pers Comput* 11:27 Ap '87

EGA times 12 [enhanced graphics adapter boards] C. H. Pappas and W. H. Murray. il *Byte* 12:313-14+ Ja '87

Expanding past on-board slots. *Pers Comput* 11:197 F '87

Extending portable computing. D. M. Coder and E. W. Chu. il *BioScience* 37:420-4 Je '87

Fax boards: is your office complete without one? E. King. il *Pers Comput* 11:121+ O '87

First PS/2 expansion board [RamQuest 50/60] R. Lockwood. il *Pers Comput* 11:276 N '87

A flood of fax boards. J. Blackford. il *Pers Comput* 11:33 S '87

Hauppauge 386 Motherboard. R. Malloy. *Byte* 12:102 N '87

Hercules discovers color graphics [InColor Card] A. C. Hixson. il *Pers Comput* 11:162 Jl '87

Hercules Graphics Card Plus. il *Radio-Electron* 58 ComputerDigest:85+ Ap '87

High-speed memory boards for ATs. B. Nance. il *Byte* 12:124-8+ D '87

Hot products: hardware. M. Bryan. il *Pers Comput* 11:25-7+ O '87

Memory-expansion boards for the IBM PC AT [BIX product focus] C. Franklin, Jr. il *Byte* 12:133-6 D '87

The Micro Clipper Graphics subsystem. C. D. Weston. il *Byte* 12:257-8+ S '87

A multi-display board from NEC [GB-1 graphics board] P. Honan. il *Pers Comput* 11:208 My '87

New life for Lucy [upgrading IBM PC] J. Pournelle. *Byte* 12:251-2+ O '87

Nine PC AT multifunction cards. W. Rash, Jr. il *Byte* 12:318-20+ Ja '87

The open MACs and family. il *Pers Comput* 11:110-12 Ap '87

Orchid PC turbo 286e IBM-PC accelerator card. il *Radio-Electron* 58:24+ F '87

A PAL programmer [board for IBM PC] R. A. Freedman. il *Byte* 12:263-6+ Ja '87

PC-Elevator 386 [80386 add-in board] F. Langa. il *Byte* 12:98 D '87

Readers pick best of bunch [Personal computing survey] P. Honan. il *Pers Comput* 11:41-2 F '87

Six smart buys to boost productivity. B. Call. il *Work Woman* 12:69 Ap '87

So you have a computer! Now what do you need? J. Anderson and others. il *Success Farm* 85 no5:26X-26Y Mr '87

A 'super' EGA standard [Vega Deluxe "Super" EGA high-resolution graphics board] il *Pers Comput* 11:29-30 Je '87

Three accelerator boards for the Macintosh Plus. C. Crawford. il *Byte* 12:161-2+ D '87

Tseng Labs' EVA/480 [enhanced graphics adapter card] il *Radio-Electron* 58 ComputerDigest:135-6 My '87

Turbo-Amiga: a peripheral for the Amiga 1000 that's actually another computer. W. Block. il *Byte* 12:235-8 Je '87

Turbocharge your PC. J. Holtzman. il *Radio-Electron* 58 ComputerDigest:95-100+ N '87

VGA arrives for PCs [VGA Extra board] P. Honan. il *Pers Comput* 11:260 D '87

What's new in computer accessories. S. Quigley. il *Pers Comput* 11:215-25 D '87

Errors
See also
Spreadsheets (Computer programs)—Errors

The limits of software reliability. R. L. Enfield. il *Technol Rev* 90:36-40+ Ap '87

Software liability. F. Lowenstein. il *Technol Rev* 90:9-10 Ja '87

Exhibitions
See also
Comdex (Trade show)
Infomart (Dallas, Tex.: Trade mart)

The big do [Digital Equipment Corp.'s trade show] il *Time* 130:53 S 21 '87

Computer show once again outdoes previous performances [A/E/C Systems '87] C. K. Hoyt. il *Archit Rec* 175:43 S '87

Events and clubs. See issues of Byte beginning September 1986 through October 1987

"Ouch! Oooh! Cut it out!" [Robots and beyond at the Boston Museum of Science] J. M. Nash. il *Time* 129:78 F 9 '87

Publish and/or perish: serious business at the MacWorld Exposition, and a look at desktop publishing. B. F. Webster. *Byte* 12:279-82+ My '87

Techniques for getting the tools you need. H. McCandless. il *Work Woman* 12:64+ O '87

Facility management use
See Facility management—Automation

Failure
Now, computer paramedics. W. D. Marbach. il *Newsweek* 110:38 D 28 '87

Computers—*cont.*

Financial services use
See also
Computers—Tax return use
Canned plans get panned [computerized financial plans] E. Schurenberg. il *Money* 16:117-18+ S '87
Planning your future, byte by byte. P. M. Scherschel. il *U S News World Rep* 102:54 Ja 19 '87
Programming
Software programs to simplify your money matters. S. Miller. il *Black Enterp* 17:87-8 Je '87

Forestry use
Curbing abuses in computer modeling [Forest Service's FORPLAN] B. R. Herrick. il *Technol Rev* 90:24-5 O '87

Gambling use
See also
Electronic Data Technologies
Lotteries—Automation
Anecdotes, facetiae, satire, etc.
The spreadsheet follies. D. Seligman. il *Fortune* 115:100 Mr 30 '87

Geological use
Saga of a speed upgrade [work of J. Johnston] C. Spencer. il *Pers Comput* 11:79 Ja '87

Government use
See also
Computers—Military use
Iran-contra affair—Computer tapes
United States. Federal Bureau of Investigation. National Stolen Art File
330 megabytes gobble it down [processing evidence to be used in Iran-contra hearings] *U S News World Rep* 102:24 My 4 '87
Haste makes waste [SEC's Edgar computer system] G. Slutsker and J. Novack. il *Forbes* 140:94+ Ag 24 '87
How do you chase a $17 billion market? With everything you've got [computer makers campaigning to win government megacontracts] F. Seghers. il *Bus Week* p120+ N 23 '87
The taxman goes on-line [electronic filing] H. Fersko-Weiss. il *Pers Comput* 11:82-3 Ap '87

Grocery trade use
Brave new shopping. il *Newsweek* 109:67 Je 15 '87
High-tech grocery shopping. il *Futurist* 21:54 Jl/Ag '87
Russian-dressing roulette [Telepanel electronic price tag system] W. J. Hawkins. il *Pop Sci* 231:14 D '87
Smart shopping. il *Fortune* 115:9 My 11 '87

Handbooks, manuals, etc.
Career makeover: from newspaper sportswriter to computer publications manager [A. Seelig] il por *Glamour* 85:106 Je '87
How to tell good software by its cover. C. J. Mullins. *Work Woman* 12:44+ D '87
Mac insights and the power user's manual. B. L. Walker. *Byte* 12:72+ My '87
Turning computer babble into plain English [S. Smith and L. Ruffolo of Software Resource] T. Engstrom. il pors *Work Woman* 12:61+ My '87

History
The 'first computer' controversy [discussion of March 1987 article, The first electronic computer] A. R. Mackintosh. *Phys Today* 40:13+ D '87
The first electronic computer [work of J. V. Atanasoff] A. R. Mackintosh. bibl f il pors *Phys Today* 40:25-32 Mr '87

Home use
The automated house. P. Langdon. il *Atlantic* 260:93-6 O '87
Butler in a box [Butler-In-A-Box voice-recognition system] J. Schefter. il *Pop Sci* 230:62 Mr '87
Computers come home to work [tables] P. Honan. il *Pers Comput* 11:393 N '87
The home of the future. J. Seisler. il *Consum Res Mag* 70:34-7 F '87
The home of the future [Smart House] D. J. MacFadyen. il *Radio-Electron* 58:115-17 My '87
Home office. C. O'Malley. See issues of Personal Computing beginning July 1987
Houses with high IQs. P. E. Godwin. il *Changing Times* 41:103-4 S '87
On the home front. P. Honan. il *Pers Comput* 11:28 Ag '87
Return of the home market [consumer software] R. A. Shaffer. il *Pers Comput* 11:47 S '87
A skylight for all seasons [Roto-Lids] D. Stover. il *Pop Sci* 231:70-2 Jl '87
The smart house. il *Futurist* 21:52-3 S/O '87
'Two-computer yuppies' fuel a new boom. G. Lewis. il *Bus Week* p130+ N 9 '87

Data banks
See Information storage and retrieval systems
Image processing use
See Image processing
Indexing use
Programming
Search and destroy [book index program] D. Pountain. il *Byte* 12:257-60 Ag '87
Sorting out the sorts [book index program] D. Pountain. il *Byte* 12:275-6+ Jl '87
WordCruncher [text indexing and retrieval program] R. Rabinovitz. *Byte* 12:216+ N '87

Industrial use
See also
Automation
Flexible manufacturing systems
Programming
This video 'game' is saving manufacturers millions [computer simulation] W. G. Wild, Jr. and O. Port. il *Bus Week* p82+ Ag 17 '87

Input-output equipment
See also
Buffers (Computers)
Computer terminals
Computers—Buses
Computers—Print-out equipment
Digitizers (Computers)
Information display systems
Interactive computer systems
Keyboards
MIDI (Musical instrument digital interface)
Modems
Speech processing systems
Video monitors
5-volt only: introducing the new MAX 232. R. A. Kreuter. il *Radio-Electron* 58 ComputerDigest:10-11 Ja '87
All about interfacing (II). J. Holtzman. il *Radio-Electron* 58 ComputerDigest:13-16 Ja '87
Application input drivers [device-independent interface] J. Sagan. il *Byte* 12 no12 Sp Issue:143-4+ '87
Atari 520ST projects: an interface board for the Atari ST cartridge port. T. G. Hunkler. il *Byte* 12:161-2+ Je '87
Clumsy mouse ascends. M. Antonoff. il *Pers Comput* 11:375-6 D '87
The Complete Answering Machine. N. Baran. il *Byte* 12:100-1 D '87
Controller chips add more zip to SCSI [small computer system interface] *Byte* 12:14 N '87
Flash-up [user interface utility program] R. Malloy. *Byte* 12:101 D '87
Hall-Comsec's Wiretap, Hayes' Transet 1000, Disc Instruments' µLynx Trackball, and Finot Group's Keep Track. il *Radio-Electron* 58 ComputerDigest:92 Ap '87
Holiday cheer [MacCalligraphy, Spellin!, spelling checker, and FastTRAP trackball device] E. Shapiro. il *Byte* 12:215-16+ D '87
IBM PC family BIOS comparison. J. Shiell. il *Byte* 12 no12 Sp Issue:173-4+ '87
Interfaces for advanced computing [cover story] J. D. Foley. bibl (p183-4) il *Sci Am* 257:126-30+ O '87
Pencept Penpad 320. il *Radio-Electron* 58:22-5+ Ja '87
Pick of the litter [mice] W. H. Murray and C. H. Pappas. il *Byte* 12:238+ Je '87
Taming the cursor [Cruise Control] J. Bell. il *Pers Comput* 11:160 Ja '87
Three bus interface designs for the PC. J. R. Drummond. il *Byte* 12 no12 Sp Issue:225-30+ '87
Using the Macintosh on a Unix network. H. T. Smith and others. il *Byte* 12:159-60+ Jl '87
What does the graphics interface mean to you? R. Lockwood. il *Pers Comput* 11:138-41+ O '87
The writer's support group. C. O'Malley. il *Pers Comput* 11:51-2+ My '87

Investment use
See also
Program trading (Securities)
Bear Stearns: hitting its stride while others trip [computerized mortgage securities trading] D. Zigas. il por *Bus Week* p59-60 Ag 31 '87
Computers amplify Black Monday [role in stock market crash] M. M. Waldrop. il *Science* 238:602-4 O 30 '87
Instant relic: the new exchange floor [computers on the London Exchange] R. A. Melcher. il *Bus Week* p60 Ja 12 '87
Machine over money: a new twist on investing. J. Maranoff. il *Work Woman* 12:34+ Jl '87
Street smarts: the supercomputer becomes a stock strategist. J. W. Verity. il *Bus Week* p84-5 Je 1 '87

Computers—Investment use—*cont.*

Strictly by the numbers [Disciplined Investment Advisors Inc.] C. Siler. il por *Forbes* 140:184+ N 2 '87

Too much number-crunching. E. Dyson. il *Forbes* 140:216 N 30 '87

A war of the generations [crash ignites feud between Wall Street old-timers and quants] B. Powell. il *Newsweek* 110:48-9 N 30 '87

Wired [Toronto Stock Exchange president J. P. Bunting] D. Henry. il por *Forbes* 140:454 Jl 13 '87

The wizardry of the 'rocket scientists' [investment house researchers] P. M. Scherschel. il *U S News World Rep* 102:48-9 My 25 '87

Programming

The computer as an investment tool. A. Glossbrenner. il *Work Woman* 12:47-8 F '87

A computer in your futures [Personal Options Advisor] S. W. Angrist. il *Forbes* 140:130 Ag 10 '87

Desk-top investing aids. M. O'Brien. il *Nations Bus* 75:45-6 Mr '87

Dress rehearsal for your next career step. S. Morgenstern. *Work Woman* 12:56 My '87

Fire that computer. P. Newcomb and M. Ozanian. il *Forbes* 140:122-3 Ag 10 '87

How's the Dow? Check it on your PC [stock quote services and software] B. Hitchings. il *Bus Week* p105 Ja 26 '87

Money machines [commodities trading] S. W. Angrist. il *Forbes* 140:240 O 5 '87

Of bulls, bears and programs in the pit. A. K. Dewdney. il *Sci Am* 256:16+ My '87

Speculating systematically? [commodities trading] S. W. Angrist. il *Forbes* 139:120 Je 29 '87

Thrive without a broker. R. Cullen. il *Pers Comput* 11:91-5+ Ap '87

What's new in software for investors. A. Kupfer. il *Fortune* 116 Sp Issue:233+ Fall '87

Journalistic use

Interactive journalism and computer networking: exploring a new medium. M. Greenly. il pors *Futurist* 21:12-16 Mr/Ap '87

Laws and regulations

Computers: changing the legal rules [architects' use] P. M. Lurie and B. D. Weiss. *Archit Rec* 175:35+ Ap '87

Legal use

Laying down the PC law [A. Pucillo] C. O'Malley. il por *Pers Comput* 11:170-1 O '87

Literary use
Programming

Recursion + data structures = anagrams. M. Morton. bibl il *Byte* 12:325-8+ N '87

Logic circuits
See Logic circuits

Maintenance and repair
See also
Technical Support Services Inc.

What, me worry? N. Henderson. il *Changing Times* 41:110 O '87

Map making use
See Computers—Cartographic use

Marketing use
See Electronic marketing

Mathematical use
See also
Computers—Statistical use

Chaotic bursts in nonlinear dynamical systems. R. L. Devaney. bibl f il *Science* 235:342-5 Ja 16 '87

Fast math [Motorola's 68882 math coprocessor] T. Thompson. il *Byte* 12:120-1 D '87

Pi wars: dueling supercomputers [work of Peter and Jonathan Borwein] I. Peterson. *Sci News* 131:118 F 21 '87

Pieces of a polyomino puzzle [work of K. A. Dahlke] I. Peterson. il por *Sci News* 132:310 N 14 '87

Portraits of equations [cover story] I. Peterson. il *Sci News* 132:184-6 S 19 '87

Solving linear equations [discussion of June 14, 1985 article, Solving linear systems faster] G. Kolata. *Science* 236:461-3 Ap 24 '87

Twists of space [visualization of the Romboy homotopy; cover story] I. Peterson. il *Sci News* 132:264-6 O 24 '87

Zeroing in on chaos [study of Newton's method; work of Scott A. Burns and others] I. Peterson. il *Sci News* 131:137-9 F 28 '87

Programming

ANSYS-PC/Linear and MSC/pal 2. N. Baran. il *Byte* 12:205-6+ N '87

Around and around [cycloids] R. T. Kurosaka. il *Byte* 12:307-8+ My '87

Calculating the area of an irregular shape. R. Stolk and G. Ettershank. il *Byte* 12:135-6 F '87

Complex math in Pascal. D. Gedeon. il *Byte* 12:121-2+ Jl '87

Craps, the Monkey Test, and other ways of proving that a series of numbers isn't random [work of George Marsaglia] il *Discover* 8:78-9 Ja '87

Creating fractals. W. A. McWorter and J. M. Tazelaar. bibl il *Byte* 12:123-8+ Ag '87

Daily Wheel, Scientific Wheel, and Professional Wheel. G. A. Stewart. *Byte* 12:98+ N '87

Equation solvers [Eureka and TK Solver Plus] G. A. Stewart. il *Byte* 12:237-8+ O '87

Mathematical reasoning: a Prolog program uses heuristic methods to solve equations. L. Sterling. il *Byte* 12:177-80 O '87

Once more through the Sieve [Sieve of Eratosthenes prime number generator] S. Ciarcia. il *Byte* 12:36+ D '87

Polynomial curve fitter [Basic program] W. G. Hood. il *Byte* 12:155-6+ Je '87

A ternary state of affairs. R. T. Kurosaka. il *Byte* 12:319-20+ F '87

Medical use
See also
Thermography—Medical use
Tomography—Medical use

Advanced computing for medicine. G. D. Rennels and E. H. Shortliffe. bibl (p184) il *Sci Am* 257:154-61 O '87

Computer heartthrobs [CPR training system developed by Actronics, Inc.] M. D. Brown. *Health* 19:22 F '87

Computers for nurses. J. I. Mattill. il *Technol Rev* 90:8+ Ap '87

Designer bones—computers prescribe the prosthesis. S. F. Brown. *Pop Sci* 230:89 Je '87

Programming

Does your computer know how sick you are? [diagnostic system DXplain] *Newsweek* 110:47 Jl 13 '87

Saying SCRAM to the sun [Skin Cancer Risk Assessment on Microcomputer] M. Fox. *Health* 19:14 Ag '87

Memory systems
See also
Data tapes
LaPine Technology Corporation
Masstor Systems Corporation
Nashua Corporation
Optical storage devices
Random access memory
Read only memory
Storage Technology Corp.

80286 accelerators. R. G. A. Cote. il *Byte* 12:161-6 N '87

Accelerator boards [BIX product focus] C. Franklin, Jr. *Byte* 12:169-70+ N '87

Add a disk drive. H. Friedman. il *Radio-Electron* 58 ComputerDigest:96-7 Ap '87

All or nothing in local mass storage. P. Lemmons. il *Byte* 12:6 My '87

An AT clone with hard disks to go [Tandon Pac 286] C. O'Malley. il *Pers Comput* 11:144+ Ag '87

The Atari SH204 and SupraDrive hard disk drives. il *Byte* 12:234 F '87

Bernoulli update for the road [Bernoulli Box II external disk drive system] P. Honan. il *Pers Comput* 11:287+ D '87

Central Point Software: the Option Board [COPY II PC tape backup] il *Radio-Electron* 58 ComputerDigest:87-8 O '87

Comparing disk-allocation methods [PC-DOS] G. Weissman. il *Byte* 12 no12 Sp Issue:185-8+ '87

Constructing an associative memory. B. Kosko. bibl il *Byte* 12:137-8+ S '87

Data-storage technologies for advanced computing [magnetic devices] M. H. Kryder. il *Sci Am* 257:116-25 O '87

Dynamic memory allocation. A. Fernandes. il *Byte* 12:169-73 Ja '87

A faster, bigger hard disk card [Rodime R-card 45] P. Honan. il *Pers Comput* 11:280 N '87

Floppy-disk data storage (I). R. Grossblatt. il *Radio-Electron* 58 ComputerDigest:91-4+ D '87

A hard disk menu shell [PreCursor] R. Lockwood. il *Pers Comput* 11:242 Je '87

Hard disks: when bigger is better. D. Caruso. il *Pers Comput* 11:118-21+ Jl '87

High-capacity hard disk card [Hardcard 40] P. Honan. il *Pers Comput* 11:154 Ag '87

Computers—Memory systems—*cont.*

A high-tech play—but only for the fearless [companies that make hard storage disks] G. Lewis. *Bus Week* p118 Je 1 '87

Internal hard disks. H.-J. Taferner. il *Pers Comput* 11:135-7+ F '87

The Konan KXP-230Z drive maximizer [hard disk controller] R. Cook and P. Schauble. il *Byte* 12:233-6 Jl '87

Lightning and Flash [disk cache programs] W. F. Bolton. il *Byte* 12:260+ Ap '87

Mac mass storage [AST-2000, hard disk with tape backup] J. Bell. il *Pers Comput* 11:190 Ap '87

Micro-floppy retrofit. H. Friedman. il *Radio-Electron* 58 ComputerDigest:67-8+ Ag '87

Much more than War and Peace [experimental high density magnetic disk] *Sci News* 132:377 D 12 '87

New life for Lucy [upgrading IBM PC] J. Pournelle. *Byte* 12:251-2+ O '87

Perpendicular disk allows very-high density recording [Maxell] il *Radio-Electron* 58:14 Ja '87

Reconcilable differences: data transfer between mismatched disk formats. R. Cook. il *Pers Comput* 11:143+ D '87

Reviewer's notebook [ShareData hard disk drive] R. Grehan. *Byte* 12:204 Jl '87

Rock solid 20mb hard disk drive [Core HC82] J. Blackford. *Pers Comput* 11:186 Jl '87

Safeguarding a hard disk [use of batch files] R. Wallace. *Pers Comput* 11:197+ Mr '87

SCSI hard disk drives for the Macintosh. C. Crawford and E. White. il *Byte* 12:237-40 My '87

Speed to burn [DataFrame XP hard disk drive] J. Bell. il *Pers Comput* 11:152 F '87

Straight talk about hard disks. J. Blackford. il *Pers Comput* 11:371-2 D '87

Sysgen's hard disk to go [DuraPak] J. Blackford. il *Pers Comput* 11:152 Ja '87

Timely hard disk backup on floppies [Intelligent Backup] H.-J. Taferner. il *Pers Comput* 11:162 Ja '87

Wait no more for the floppy disk [makers of hard disk drives] A. Snitzer. il *Forbes* 139:132 F 23 '87

The Zenith Z-183. J. Unger. il *Byte* 12:145-8 D '87

Care

Memory Minder, disk-drive analyzer from J&M Systems. il *Radio-Electron* 58 ComputerDigest:66+ Ag '87

Meteorological use

Another El Niño surprise in the Pacific, but was it predicted? R. A. Kerr. il *Science* 235:744-5 F 13 '87

Climate modeling [cover story] S. H. Schneider. il *Sci Am* 256:72-8+ My '87

Cloudy crystal balls. D. Bjerklie. il *Time* 130:64 O 19 '87

Federal Express starts 24-hr. weather forecasting system [Man-Computer Integrative Data Access System] J. Ott. il *Aviat Week Space Technol* 126:38 F 2 '87

Improved weather alerts offset by poor delivery to cockpit. J. Ott. *Aviat Week Space Technol* 127:33-4 O 5 '87

Man and machine forecast big snow [Washington, D.C.] R. A. Kerr. il *Science* 235:1460-1 Mr 20 '87

Stormbusters [Sperry's LSZ-850 lightning sensor and Primus 870 turbulence-detecting radar] J. M. McClellan. il *Flying* 114:64-6+ Mr '87

Tomorrow's weather: looking further ahead. J. Heckman. il por *Futurist* 21:27-9 Mr/Ap '87

Programming

Using your computer. A. Blackadar. See issues of Weatherwise beginning June 1984

Military use

See also

Autonomous land vehicles

The chip behind TI's smart weapons [Lisp chip] T. Mason. il *Bus Week* p104-6 Mr 9 '87

Facing reality: computer scientists aid war efforts. J. Weizenbaum. il *Technol Rev* 90:22-3 Ja '87

GTE adapts off-the-shelf hardware to improve command and control [WWMCCS Information System] W. H. Gregory. il *Aviat Week Space Technol* 126:73+ F 23 '87

National Test Bed facility demonstrates initial capability. T. M. Foley. *Aviat Week Space Technol* 127:22-3 O 5 '87

Some researchers concerned with Defense funding of AI projects [Strategic Computing Initiative] *Byte* 12:40 O '87

Programming

Black runs company that develops computer ware for Defense Department [W. A. Rolling of AdaSoft] *Jet* 72:23 My 4 '87

Joint STARS intensifies reliance on software in development phase. E. H. Kolcum. il *Aviat Week Space Technol* 126:81-2+ F 23 '87

Name, rank and computer log-on [Ada computer language foul-ups] K. Healy. il *Forbes* 139:87+ Ap 20 '87

Science Board urges major changes in Pentagon software purchasing. B. D. Nordwall. *Aviat Week Space Technol* 127:72-3 D 21 '87

Moral and religious aspects

Community & computers: Babel, bytes & bits. W. H. Willimon. *Christ Century* 104:740-1 S 9-16 '87

Coping with computers [discussion of September 9-16, 1987 article, Community & computers: Babel, byte & bits] W. H. Willimon. il *Christ Century* 104:1064-6 N 25 '87

Teaching computer ethics in the schools. W. Weintraub. *Educ Dig* 52:34-5 F '87

Motion picture use

Programming

Simple special effects illustrate the art of converting algorithms into programs. A. K. Dewdney. il *Sci Am* 257:142-6 D '87

Multiuser systems

A multiuser MS-DOS clone [PC-MOS multiuser operating system] J. Devlin. *Pers Comput* 11:282 N '87

Multiuser programming. F. D. Davis. *Byte* 12:177-80+ Jl '87

Split your computer in two [PC Share] P. Honan. il *Pers Comput* 11:158 F '87

Two-read record locking in multiuser systems. *Byte* 12 Sp Issue:50-1 Summ '87

Music industry use

Computing is just a song [Steppenwolf's J. Kay's use of computers] C. Bermant. il por *Pers Comput* 11:182-3 O '87

Musical use

See also

MIDI (Musical instrument digital interface)

The computer as a musical instrument. M. V. Mathews and J. R. Pierce. il *Sci Am* 256:126-33 F '87

Music's electronic future. T. Charbeneau. il por *Futurist* 21:35-7 S/O '87

Programming

Deluxe Music Construction Set 1.1. G. Williams. *Byte* 12:249-50 Jl '87

Enjoying the brave new world of computer music. L. Van Gelder. il *Ms* 16:42+ O '87

The sound of computing is music to the ears of some. A. K. Dewdney. il *Sci Am* 256:14+ Ap '87

Navigational use

See also

Boats and boating—Electronic equipment

Programming

Great circle navigation [Basic program] A. Blackadar. il *Weatherwise* 40:273-4 O '87

Newspaper publishing use

In news graphics, Macintosh makes the front page. F. Seghers. il *Bus Week* p87 Ja 19 '87

Nuclear industry use

Foreseeing failure [computers that predict problems may make nuclear plants safer] *Futurist* 21:42 Ja/F '87

Oceanographic use

Computer modeling in physical oceanography from the global circulation to turbulence. W. R. Holland and J. C. McWilliams. bibl f il *Phys Today* 40:51-7 O '87

Modeling tidal power [tidal power dam in the Bay of Fundy would raise tide levels in the Gulf of Maine] D. A. Greenberg. il maps *Sci Am* 257:128-128C+ N '87

Programming

The tide at Tarawa. D. W. Olson. il map *Sky Telesc* 74:526-8 N '87

Operating systems

See also

Pick Systems Inc.

286/386 protected-mode programming [IBM PC] J. Barnum. il *Byte* 12 no12 Sp Issue:125-9 '87

The 386 and DOS 5.0: hard questions and not-so-easy answers [Compaq Deskpro 386; cover story] S. R. Reed and P. Honan. il *Pers Comput* 11:62-5+ Mr '87

The application program interface: the SideKick Plus kernel, a proposed TSR standard. S. R. Boye and P. Kahn. il *Byte* 12 Sp Issue:19-23 Summ '87

Balancing chips and operating systems [OS/2] W. H. Gates. por *Pers Comput* 11:242 O '87

The billion-dollar whiz kid [W. Gates gets IBM to endorse Microsoft operating system; cover story] R. Brandt. il pors *Bus Week* p68-72+ Ap 13 '87

Computers—Operating systems—*cont.*

Comparing disk-allocation methods [PC-DOS] G. Weissman. il *Byte* 12 no12 Sp Issue:185-8+ '87

Concurrent PC DOS. W. Rash, Jr. *Byte* 12:226-8 Mr '87

Curtain up on enhanced Amiga [A2000] il *Pers Comput* 11:27 Ap '87

Deciphering old files with a new PC. S. Gelfond. il *Bus Week* p130 O 5 '87

Design goals [Microsoft OS/2] G. Letwin. *Byte* 12:119 Je '87

DOS in English [Turbo Prolog program] A. Lane. *Byte* 12:261-2+ D '87

DOS utilities. S. Quigley. il *Pers Comput* 11:173-7+ S '87

Dueling lasers (I) [Mac vs. MS-DOS desktop publishing system] M. Antonoff and J. Bell. il *Pers Comput* 11:85-7+ My '87

Dueling lasers (II) [Cordata Intellipress System and AST Premium Publisher; MS-DOS systems] A. C. Hixson and C. Spencer. il *Pers Comput* 11:121-3+ Je '87

Exploring the 386 offerings. M. Liskin. il *Pers Comput* 11:45-6+ F '87

IBM's new operating system(s): the M & M's. il *Radio-Electron* 58 ComputerDigest:93-4 Je '87

Installing memory-resident programs with C [to extend DOS] B. Edginton. il *Byte* 12:129-32+ Mr '87

A link between operating systems [MacLinkPlus] A. C. Hixson. il *Pers Comput* 11:152 Ag '87

Microsoft's new DOS. E. White and R. Grehan. il *Byte* 12:116-18+ Je '87

Microsoft's OS/2: chipping away at change. S. R. Reed. il *Pers Comput* 11:104-5 Je '87

MultiFinder for the Macintosh [multitasking operating system] G. Williams. il *Byte* 12:123-6+ N '87

A multiuser MS-DOS clone [PC-MOS multiuser operating system] J. Devlin. *Pers Comput* 11:282 N '87

Not everyone needs everything in OS/2. A. Ashton. por *Pers Comput* 11:230 O '87

The old shell game [DOS shells] J. Pournelle. *Byte* 12:199-200 D '87

The OS/2 applications family. R. Duncan. *Byte* 12:109-10+ O '87

PageMaker goes MS-DOS. M. Antonoff. *Pers Comput* 11:155-6 Jl '87

PC-MOS/386. R. Grehan. il *Byte* 12:263-6 S '87

PCs & DOS 3.x: still living after all these years. C. O'Malley. il *Pers Comput* 11:158-60+ S '87

Pipes and filters: creating filters to work with MS-DOS's pipe and redirection functions. P. Baker. il *Byte* 12 no12 Sp Issue:215-17 '87

A programmer's introduction to OS/2. R. Duncan. *Byte* 12:101-2+ S '87

SCO Xenix 386. E. J. Lau. il *Byte* 12:190-2+ D '87

The software robot [Automator mi] D. Pountain. *Byte* 12:383-4+ Ja '87

Some like it Hot; some may not [DOS application management utilities] S. Makrias. il *Pers Comput* 11:164 Ja '87

Some modest proposals [survival in the computer business] K. K. Wiegner. il *Forbes* 139:38+ Ap 20 '87

A standard for all? [coding TSR programs to interact with MS-DOS] R. Nelson. il *Pers Comput* 11:85 Mr '87

Taming the circus of TSR software. E. Tolson. por *Pers Comput* 11:228 O '87

TSR: an acronym worthy of amnesia. P. Kahn. por *Pers Comput* 11:238 O '87

TSRs past and future: MS-DOS and OS/2. R. Duncan. il *Byte* 12 no12 Sp Issue:49-52+ '87

Two programs bundled with 1-megabyte Macs [MultiFinder and HyperCard] G. Williams and T. Thompson. il *Byte* 12:45 S '87

Using the Macintosh on a Unix network. H. T. Smith and others. il *Byte* 12:159-60+ Jl '87

Welcome to the new age of DOS [cover story; with editorial comment by Fred Abatemarco] S. R. Reed. il *Pers Comput* 11:5, 72-5+ My '87

Wendin's Operating System Toolbox. J. Levitt. il *Byte* 12:228-30+ Mr '87

Optical equipment

See also

Optical scanners

Optical storage devices

Paleontological use

Periodic mass extinctions at random [computer model developed by Michael L. McKinney] R. Monastersky. *Sci News* 132:319 N 14 '87

Performing arts use

The performing arts. A. C. Hixson. il *Pers Comput* 11:144-5 S '87

Periodical publishing use

See Computers—Publishing use

Periodicals

See also

Byte (Periodical)

Interactive computer periodicals

Personal computing (Periodical)

Petroleum engineering use

One office the Mac has conquered [Atlantic Richfield uses Apple Macintosh in exploration strategy] il por *Fortune* 116:60 N 9 '87

Photographic use

A gray area for page printers—photography. il *Byte* 12:192-3 S '87

Picture-perfect photos. M. Rogers. il *Newsweek* 110:64 D 28 '87

Polaroid Palette Computer Image Recorder. S. Drafahl. il *Petersens Photogr Mag* 16:48-51 My '87

Slideless slide show for groups [Datashow System electronic transparency system for displaying computer images through an overhead projector] S. Makrias. il *Pers Comput* 11:162 Mr '87

Programming

Computer programs for photographers. J. Spragens, Jr. il *Petersens Photogr Mag* 15:32-4 F '87

Physics use

See also

Computers in physics (Periodical)

Computational physics [cover story; special section] bibl f il *Phys Today* 40:25-37+ O '87

Editor of new AIP magazine-journal discusses computers in physics [interview with R. R. Borchers] por *Phys Today* 40:109 O '87

Programming

An introduction to relaxation methods [problem solving] G. William. il *Byte* 12:111-14+ Ja '87

Police use

Programming

Taking a byte out of crime [Scorecard program used to track federal fugitives] E. Shannon. il *Time* 129:63 My 25 '87

Political use

See also

Computers—Government use

Programming

Computer congressmen [National Association of Manufacturers video game, Congressional Insight] T. Noah. *New Repub* 196:10-12 Ap 6 '87

Prices

Affordable personal computers. J. Worley. il *Essence* 18:114+ My '87

Blue Chip chips away [PC clone] W. J. Hawkins. il *Pop Sci* 230:28+ F '87

Finding a bargain in IBM clones. S. Miller. il *Black Enterp* 17:29 Mr '87

Hooray! Your computer's down [PCs] il *Money* 16:13+ Ag '87

More bang for your buck. il *Pers Comput* 11:76 O '87

PC clones: $500 to $800. N. Henderson. il *Changing Times* 41:154 Ja '87

Secrets to mail order success. C. O'Malley. il *Pers Comput* 11:109-13+ Jl '87

Print-out equipment

See also

Buffers (Computers)

24-pin sophistication [NEC Pinwriter P9XL dot matrix printer] S. Quigley. il *Pers Comput* 11:202 S '87

Better printing for charts [ImagEnhancer board] P. Honan. il *Pers Comput* 11:160 F '87

A better way to control that laser [JLaser Plus AT board] M. Antonoff. il *Pers Comput* 11:147 Mr '87

Brother's letter quality printer [HR-20 daisywheel] S. Makrias. il *Pers Comput* 11:212 My '87

C. Itoh's 24-pin color printer [ProWriter C-715 Reliant] H.-J. Taferner. il *Pers Comput* 11:148 Mr '87

Chaos Manor [MT-910 laser printer] A. Pournelle and D. Moore. il *Byte* 12:202+ D '87

Computer printers [dot-matrix models] il *Consum Rep* 52:309-13 My '87

Computer printers [dot-matrix models] il *Consum Rep* 52:308-12 D '87

Daisywheel printers. S. Makrias. il *Pers Comput* 11:137-9+ Ja '87

Departmental laser [Texas Instruments Omnilaser 2015] J. Blackford. il *Pers Comput* 11:58 Mr '87

Epson's laser contender. C. O'Malley. il *Pers Comput* 11:276 D '87

Computers—Print-out equipment—*cont.*

Four ink-jet printers. R. D. Swearengin. il *Byte* 12:239-40+ F '87

Four laser printers [Canon LBP-8, BDS Model 630/8-E, QMS Kiss and Quadram QuadLaser] A. Little. il *Byte* 12:217-20 Mr '87

Genicom's 5010: the laser's edge. H.-J. Taferner. il *Pers Comput* 11:150 Ag '87

High-impact color in a small box [HP PaintJet] S. Quigley. il *Pers Comput* 11:284 D '87

High-speed color printing [Brother M-4018 dot matrix printer] S. Makrias. il *Pers Comput* 11:268 N '87

Kyocera F-2010: 7 printers in 1 [laser printer] S. R. Reed. il *Pers Comput* 11:168 Jl '87

Laser lets you have it your way [Mannessman Tally MT910 laser printer] H.-J. Taferner. il *Pers Comput* 11:266 N '87

Laser printer times four. W. Rash, Jr. il *Byte* 12:214-16+ O '87

Laser printers. H.-J. Taferner. il *Pers Comput* 11:121-5+ Ag '87

Mastering printer drivers. M. Liskin. il *Pers Comput* 11:43-4 Mr '87

Near-letter quality with fonts [Star Micronics NB24-15 dot matrix] H.-J. Taferner. il *Pers Comput* 11:202 My '87

The new LaserJet. M. Antonoff. il *Pers Comput* 11:58 Ap '87

Okidata does a budget laser [Laserline 6] S. Makrias. il *Pers Comput* 11:156 Ag '87

Print it or copy it on this double-duty printer [Xerox 4045 CP laser printer/photocopier] D. B. Trivette. il *Pop Sci* 230:42 Ja '87

Printer has power and speed [Nissho NP-2410 letter quality dot matrix printer] S. R. Reed. il *Pers Comput* 11:152 Mr '87

Printer technologies [cover story; special section] il *Byte* 12:161-4+ S '87

Printers for professionals. C. Spezzano. il *Pers Comput* 11:133 S '87

Printing what you see [screen printouts] M. Liskin. il *Pers Comput* 11:41-2+ Ja '87

State of the art in dot-matrix impact printers. G. A. Stewart and J. M. Tazelaar. il *Byte* 12:203-13 Ap '87; Correction. 12:254 My '87

Toshiba PageLaser12. S. J. Wszola. il *Byte* 12:97 D '87

Toshiba's versatile 3-in-one printer [dot matrix printer] A. C. Hixson. il *Pers Comput* 11:188 S '87

Xerox's laser with copier option. P. Honan. il *Pers Comput* 11:154 Ja '87

Printing use

From desktop to typesetter. C. Strehlo. il *Pers Comput* 11:188-93+ D '87

Printer technologies [cover story; special section] il *Byte* 12:161-4+ S '87

Prison use

PCs convert convicts [computer education program at Washington State Reformatory] il por *Pers Comput* 11:397 N '87

Programs

See Computer programming

Psychological aspects

Computer headaches [business environment] J. Schwartz. il *Newsweek* 110:34-5 Jl 6 '87

I couldn't learn to use a computer at work. il *Good Housekeep* 204:28+ Je '87

Psychological use

Programming

The dream machine [DreamWorks] S. Ditlea. il *Omni* 10:34 O '87

Head Coach [personal advocate program created by T. Leary] S. Ditlea. por *Omni* 9:23 Ap '87

Psychotherapeutic use

Computer "analysis". *Vogue* 177:480 O '87

Technotherapy. P. Garrison. il *Omni* 10:162 D '87

Uncovering amnesiacs' hidden memories [work of Daniel L. Schacter] J. Greenberg. *Sci News* 131:118 F 21 '87

Publishing use

See also
Computers—Newspaper publishing use
Computers—Printing use
Desktop publishing

Affordable digital color page assembly—it's closer than you think. il *Publ Wkly* 232:405-8 Ag 7 '87

Bits and bytes [new computer subscription fulfillment system for Sky and telescope] il *Sky Telesc* 73:427 Ap '87

High tech in the country? [use of personal computers] B. Woods. *Mother Earth News* 105:10 My/Je '87

Penta files breach of contract suit against Harper & Row. *Publ Wkly* 232:25 Jl 17 '87

Type-X: drawing a bead on book publishers. J. P. Frank. il *Publ Wkly* 231:30+ My 1 '87

Programming

See also
Interleaf Inc.

Purchasing use

See Electronic shopping

Real estate use

Programming

Real-estate management made easy [D. C. Gardner's Custom Software] J. Wechsler. il por *Work Woman* 12:70+ My '87

Scientific use

See also
Computers—Biological use
Computers—Chemical use
Sun Microsystems Inc.

Advancements in the application of computers to scientific research. F. R. Hume. *Science* 235 pt2:G54+ F 27 '87

Computers and data handling. *Science* 235 pt2:G54-G60 F 27 '87

Pictures worth a million bytes [computer graphics] M. D. Lemonick. il *Time* 129:64-5 My 18 '87

Programming

The Asyst software for scientific computing. D. Hary and others. bibl f il *Science* 236:1128-32 My 29 '87

Security measures

See also
Iverson Technology Corporation

American begins operations at secure computer center [underground center in Tulsa, Okla.] *Aviat Week Space Technol* 126:43+ Ap 20 '87

Can a system keep a secret? [privacy issue raised by Iran arms-contra aid case] P. Elmer-Dewitt. il *Time* 129:68-9 Ap 6 '87

Data security. P. Honan. il *Pers Comput* 11:101-3+ Ja '87

Making sure your equipment and information are safe. A. Oshins. *Work Woman* 12:28+ My '87

Zero-knowledge proofs [data encryption] P. Wayner. il *Byte* 12:149-52 O '87

Social aspects

See Computers and civilization

Social use

Moonlight, violins, briefs, and bytes [dating contracts and computer dating] E. S. Cornish. il *Futurist* 21:2+ Ja/F '87

The sexy computer [Minitel system in France] J. De Lacy. il *Atlantic* 260:18+ Jl '87

Programming

Diverse personalities search for social equilibrium at a computer party. A. K. Dewdney. il *Sci Am* 257:112-15 S '87

Programming—Anecdotes, facetiae, satire, etc.

The latest version [Compusit dinner party seating program] D. Seligman. il *Fortune* 115:141+ Je 8 '87

Legal seating [Compusit, a dinner party seating program] D. Seligman. il *Fortune* 115:108 Mr 16 '87

Space flight use

Computer simulates multi-spacecraft deployment from Ariane 4 launcher. il *Aviat Week Space Technol* 126:70-1 F 2 '87

Nanotechnology [Space Development Conference] J. Rhea. il *Space World* X-6-282:8-9 Je '87

Programming

Industrial space: the modeler [work of A. Cutler] W. H. Ganoe. il *Space World* X-7-283:35 Jl '87

Logica will manage software definition for Columbus module. *Aviat Week Space Technol* 126:24 Mr 23 '87

The next small step [T. L. Keller's Space M*A*X space station construction simulation program] S. Ditlea. il *Omni* 10:22 D '87

Profits into orbit [Space M*A*X and EOS: earth orbit station system] J. L. Wilson. *Space World* X-6-282:21 Je '87

Speed

80286 accelerators. R. G. A. Cote. il *Byte* 12:161-6 N '87

Accelerator boards [BIX product focus] C. Franklin, Jr. *Byte* 12:169-70+ N '87

Accelerator boards for the Macintosh SE [Prodigy SE and HyperCharger 020] L. H. Loeb. il *Byte* 12:177-80 N '87

Beyond turbo: PC's Limited's 286[12] and Wells American's A*Star II, two 12-MHz machines. W. Rash, Jr. il *Byte* 12:229-33 Je '87

Computers—Speed—*cont.*

A closer look [relative speeds of 80386- and 68020-based machines] R. Grehan. il *Byte* 12:110-11 S '87

Speed! Speed! Speed! C. Spencer. il *Pers Comput* 11:73-5+ Ja '87

Three accelerator boards for the Macintosh Plus. C. Crawford. il *Byte* 12:161-2+ D '87

A timing-independent BIOS. H. N. Cohen and J. Hanel. il *Byte* 12 no12 Sp Issue:219-20+ '87

Turbocharge your PC. J. Holtzman. il *Radio-Electron* 58 ComputerDigest:95-100+ N '87

Sports use

The America's Cup: may the best technology win. O. Port. il *Bus Week* p74-5 F 2 '87

Hearing where the bullet will hit [Penn State research device lets you listen to your shooting faults] H. Berger. il *Outdoor Life* 180:126+ N '87

Panting by the numbers [computerized scoring allows members of FitLab health club to compete against each other] M. Maran. *Women's Sports Fitness* 9:54 Jl '87

Sails & science [America's Cup] T. H. Cole. il *Pop Mech* 164:67-70 F '87

Square root, root, root for the home team. B. Cipher. il *Discover* 8:87-8+ O '87

Stars & Stripes [yacht design; cover story] J. S. Letcher, Jr. and others. il *Sci Am* 257:34-40+ Ag '87

Techno-yachts [America's Cup] H. Aldersey-Williams. il *Pop Sci* 230:84-7+ F '87

When athletes and machines meet. T. Osborne. il *Curr Health 2* 13:16-17 F '87

Working out in the Twilight Zone [Powercise, exercise machines designed by Richard Keelor and Rick Dyer] L. Kleinmann. il *Health* 19:16 Ap '87

Working out with R2-D2 [Powercise, exercise machines designed by Richard Keelor and Rick Dyer] M. Kaufman. il *Women's Sports Fitness* 9:100 S '87

Programming

Strange news from the diamond market [computer program comparing baseball player salaries to performance] D. Seligman. il *Fortune* 115:118 My 25 '87

Workout wizardry: how to turn your personal computer into a personal coach. S. Reeder. il *Women's Sports Fitness* 9:52-5 F '87

Standards

Can IBM continue to call the tune? G. Lewis. il *Bus Week* p74 Je 29 '87

The next frontier of computer users. L. W. Krause. por *Pers Comput* 11:240 O '87

This is the year of non-confusion. E. N. Torresi. por *Pers Comput* 11:254 O '87

Statistical use
Programming

BiTurbo STATA. G. A. Stewart. *Byte* 12:98+ D '87

Forecast Master. L. Rosen. *Byte* 12:255-6 F '87

Statistics on the Macintosh. R. S. Lehman. il *Byte* 12:207-14 Jl '87

Stock exchange use
See Computers—Investment use

Study and teaching

Computer courses: changing for the better. G. Hechinger. *Glamour* 85:238-9 D '87

Computer school while you cruise. il *Sunset* 179:59+ N '87

Computerizing with confidence (IV). K. Berney. il *Nations Bus* 75:55-7 F '87

Making your investment pay off. R. Zemke. il *Work Woman* 12:49+ S '87

PCs convert convicts [program at Washington State Reformatory] il por *Pers Comput* 11:397 N '87

Teaching computer ethics in the schools. W. Weintraub. *Educ Dig* 52:34-5 F '87

Aids and devices

Software Masters' Visible Computer: 8088. il *Radio-Electron* 58 ComputerDigest:95-6 Je '87

Videos that teach computer basics. J. Koblenz. *Black Enterp* 17:24 Ja '87

Tax return use
Programming

Income tax window [discussion of December 1986 article, Tax strategies for the age of reform] P. Davidson. *Pers Comput* 11:13-14 Mr '87

A program that speeds your 1040 [HowardSoft's Tax Preparer] B. Boynton. il *Bus Week* p122 Mr 9 '87

Taxes as easy as 1-2-3 [templates for spreadsheets] T. Badgett. il *Pers Comput* 11:71-4 D '87

Taxware for the computer-driven. G. Hedberg. *Money* 16:161 F '87

Tips on tax software. N. Henderson. *Changing Times* 41:154-5 Ja '87

What's new in tax software. H. Fersko-Weiss. il *Pers Comput* 11:79-81+ Ap '87

Telephone management systems
See Computerphones

Television broadcasting use

The books go electronic. S. Behrens. il *Channels* 7:15 O '87

The changing face of news graphics [computer graphics for television news] C. C. Cortes. il *Technol Rev* 90:10+ F/Mr '87

Programming

TVRO antenna pointer program. E. T. Tyson. il *Radio-Electron* 58 ComputerDigest:6-8 Ja '87

Terminology

Beware the hypervapor! E. Dyson. il *Forbes* 140:478 Jl 13 '87

A user-friendly glossary of terms for the computer novice. M. Walker and P. Davis. *Black Enterp* 18:37 O '87

Testing

386 computers head to head: IBM Model 80 vs. Compaq 386 [cover story; with editorial comment by Fred Abatemarco] R. Lockwood and P. Honan. il *Pers Comput* 11:5, 106-111+ N '87; Correction. 12:13 Ja '88

According to Webster. B. F. Webster. See issues of Byte beginning July 1985 through June 1987

Acer 1100 and Micro 1 386+. E. McNierney. il *Byte* 12:153-6+ N '87

The Acer 1100: clone power [80386-based MS-DOS computer] J. Devlin. il *Pers Comput* 11:274 N '87

An affordable portable [Spark] S. Makrias. il *Pers Comput* 11:192 N '87

The ALR Access 386 and the Compaq Deskpro 386. S. J. Wszola and C. Franklin, Jr. il *Byte* 12:215-19 F '87

An analysis of Tandy's new products. J. Blackford. il *Pers Comput* 11:114-17+ S '87

And more clones [Amstrad PC1512 and Apricot Xen-i] D. Pountain. *Byte* 12:287-9+ F '87

The Apple IIGS. P. Chien. il *Byte* 12:223-4+ Ap '87

The Apple Macintosh II [cover story; with editorial comment by Phil Lemmons] G. Williams and T. Thompson. il *Byte* 12:6, 85-8+ Ap '87

Apple's new Mac. R. Scibilia. il *Pop Mech* 164:30+ Je '87

An AT clone with hard disks to go [Tandon Pac 286] C. O'Malley. il *Pers Comput* 11:144+ Ag '87

The Atari 1040ST. D. Menconi. il *Byte* 12:231-3+ F '87

Atari's Mega 4. J. Kent. il *Byte* 12:153-6 D '87

The "B" word [benchmarks] F. Langa. *Byte* 12:6 D '87

Beyond turbo: PC's Limited's 286¹² and Wells American's A*Star II, two 12-MHz machines. W. Rash, Jr. il *Byte* 12:229-33 Je '87

A chance to design your own business partner [Panasonic Business Partner 286] P. Honan. il *Pers Comput* 11:156 Ja '87

A closer look [relative speeds of 80386- and 68020-based machines] R. Grehan. il *Byte* 12:110-11 S '87

Colorful new Apple [Apple IIGS] S. A. Booth. il *Pop Mech* 164:16 Ja '87

The Commodore 64C. A. J. W. Mayer. il *Byte* 12:229-32 My '87

The Commodore A2000 [Amiga] G. Williams and others. il *Byte* 12:84-90+ Mr '87

The Compaq Portable 386 [cover story] T. Thompson. il *Byte* 12:134-8 N '87

Compaq's new carryon [Compaq Portable III Model 20] J. Unger. il *Byte* 12:221-5 My '87

The complete guide to IBM compatibles. S. Makrias and P. Honan. il *Pers Comput* 11:141-3+ Ap '87

Computing at Chaos Manor. J. Pournelle. See issues of Byte beginning June 1984

The Data General/One Model 2 [laptop computer] W. Rash, Jr. il *Byte* 12:303-4 Ja '87

Epson remakes the Equity One. S. R. Reed. il *Pers Comput* 11:196 My '87

Epson's 286-based Equity III Plus. S. Makrias. il *Pers Comput* 11:230 Je '87

An evolutionary quartet of AT clones [IBM PC AT, NEC APC IV, Tandy 3000 HD, HP Vectra] W. Rash, Jr. il *Byte* 12:217-21 Ap '87

A fast computer in a small package [NEC MultiSpeed laptop] S. Makrias. il *Pers Comput* 11:191 My '87

First impressions: the IBM PS/2 computers [cover story; special section] il *Byte* 12:100-4+ Je '87

Four portable computers: IBM PC-compatible offerings from Toshiba, Zenith, Bondwell and IBM. J. Unger. il *Byte* 12:221-4+ F '87

The GRiDLite laptop. J. Unger. il *Byte* 12:202+ O '87

Computers—*Testing*—*cont.*

Head to head: the IBM PS/2 Model 80 and the Apple Macintosh II. G. M. Vose and others. il *Byte* 12:113-14 Ag '87

Hot products: hardware. M. Bryan. il *Pers Comput* 11:25-7+ O '87

IBM PC AT compatibles. J. C. Dermody and J. Punater. il *Byte* 12:328-9 Ja '87

The IBM PS/2 Model 30. C. Franklin, Jr. il *Byte* 12:225-9 Jl '87

The IBM PS/2 Model 50. R. Grehan. il *Byte* 12:217-24 Jl '87

The IBM PS/2 Model 80. C. Franklin, Jr. and R. Grehan. il *Byte* 12:143-6+ N '87

IBM's new Model 30 and Model 50 PC's. il *Radio-Electron* 58 ComputerDigest:63-6 Ag '87

IBM's new systems: what do you do now? [cover story; special section; with editorial comment by Fred Abatemarco] il *Pers Comput* 11:5, 94-7+ Je '87

IBM's Personal System/2. il *Radio-Electron* 58 ComputerDigest:66-7 Jl '87

IBM's PS/2 Model in the middle. R. Lockwood. il *Pers Comput* 11:139-40 Ag '87

JC Lips Model IV's different processor. S. R. Reed. *Pers Comput* 11:166 Jl '87

The Kaypro 386 [PC AT compatible] R. Duncan. il *Byte* 12:239-42 S '87

Life in the fastlane [80386-based computers] il *Pers Comput* 11:118-21 N '87

The Mac is back [cover story; special section; with editorial comment by Fred Abatemarco] A. C. Hixson. il *Pers Comput* 11:5, 102-7+ Ap '87

The Mac takes to the open road [Macintosh II] J. Bell. il *Pers Comput* 11:247-8 N '87

The Macintosh II. B. F. Webster. il *Byte* 12:197-201 O '87

The Macintosh SE. L. H. Loeb. il *Byte* 12:201-5 Ag '87

Mail-order performance [Proteus-286GT and PC Designs GV-286] F. D. Davis. il *Byte* 12:245-50 S '87

Me and my Z [Zenith Z-181 laptop] V. Klinkenborg. il *Esquire* 107:41-2 Je '87

Mega Mac [Apple Mac II] J. Schefter. il *Pop Sci* 230:30+ My '87

Multitech Accel 900 goes mainstream. S. R. Reed. il *Pers Comput* 11:50+ Ja '87

The NEC MultiSpeed [portable computer] D. Satz. il *Byte* 12:253-6 S '87

Of price and performance [PC's Limited 386] C. O'Malley. il *Pers Comput* 11:174-5 N '87

On the road with the Z-181. P. Honan. il *Pers Comput* 11:55 Ap '87

The PC's Limited 386[16]. M. L. Van Name. il *Byte* 12:141-4 D '87

Portable computers. J. Holtzman. il *Radio-Electron* 58 ComputerDigest:77-81 S '87

Portable computers [with editorial comment by Fred Abatemarco] S. Makrias. il *Pers Comput* 11:5, 137-9+ Jl '87

Processor wars [Mac II and Professional Pascal] B. F. Webster. il *Byte* 12:297-8+ Je '87

Rating the IBM compatibles. R. G. Brookshire. bibl il *Byte* 12 no12 Sp Issue:193-6+ '87

Reviewer's notebook [ALR 386/2] C. Franklin, Jr. il *Byte* 12:194 O '87

Reviewer's notebook. C. Baskin. See issues of Byte beginning March 1987 through October 1987

Reviewer's notebook. J. Edwards. See issues of Byte beginning May 1986 through February 1987

The SE: Mac Plus plus power. A. C. Hixson. il *Pers Comput* 11:223-4 Je '87

A slimmer Mac [Dynamac portable Macintosh] J. Bell. il *Pers Comput* 11:194 S '87

Small and easy—but limited [Zenith Eazy PC] C. O'Malley. il *Pers Comput* 11:204 S '87

Speedy portable from Compaq. J. Bell. il *Pers Comput* 11:63-4 My '87

The Stride 440. P. A. Sand. il *Byte* 12:295-8+ Ja '87

The Tandon PAC 286. J. Erickson and others. il *Byte* 12:85-90+ My '87

Tandy enters the 80386 fray [Tandy 4000 desktop computer] R. Lockwood. il *Pers Comput* 11:264+ D '87

Tandy's low-priced MS-DOS computer [1000 EX] S. Makrias. il *Pers Comput* 11:148 F '87

A trio of 8-MHz PC AT compatibles [NCR PC8 Victor V286 and QIC AT-Plus 1800] S. Miastkowski. il *Byte* 12:209-12 Mr '87

Two high-performance PC AT compatibles [ITT XTRA/286 ATW and AST Premium/286] J. Unger. il *Byte* 12:207-11 Ag '87

Upward mobility [NEC MultiSpeed laptop PC] S. A. Booth. il *Pop Mech* 164:52+ Mr '87

Value in price and performance [GV-386 80386-based personal computer] P. Honan. il *Pers Comput* 11:259-60 D '87

Value in price and performance [Kaypro 386] P. Honan. il *Pers Comput* 11:158 Jl '87

The Video Technology Laser 128 [Apple II-compatible system] V. E. White. il *Byte* 12:307-10 Ja '87

VIPC 386: top-flight price and performance. A. C. Hixson. il *Pers Comput* 11:187-8 S '87

The Wang LapTop. A. Lane. il *Byte* 12:203+ O '87

Who needs the new IBMs? [Personal System/2] N. Henderson and M. Schiffres. *Changing Times* 41:76-7 Ag '87

Workstations: a hands-on evaluation of three IBM PC-compatible models offers a tantalizing glimpse of where personal computers are going. C. D. Weston and G. A. Stewart. il *Byte* 12:85-6+ F '87

The Wyse choice [Wyse PC 286] C. Spencer. il *Pers Comput* 11:53 F '87

The Zenith Z-183. J. Unger. il *Byte* 12:145-8 D '87

Theatrical use

Computer-assisted lighting controllers. D. F. Sisk. il *Theatre Crafts* 21:36-41 F '87

Programming

Computers in theatre. D. F. Sisk. *Theatre Crafts* 21:38+ Ag/S '87

Load your own: software to turn your PC into a lighting controller. *Theatre Crafts* 21:38+ Ag/S '87

Time sharing systems

See also

Multiprogramming (Computers)

Translating use

See Machine translating

Typesetting use

See Computers—Printing use

Workstations

See Workstations

Computers and air travel

Airlines zigzag on in-seat computing. M. Antonoff. *Pers Comput* 11:141 Jl '87

On the road to Karlsruhe. J. Pournelle. *Byte* 12:225-6+ N '87

Computers and celebrities

Soap star computes [M. Swan] il por *Pers Comput* 11:282 S '87

Computers and civilization

Applying tomorrow's technology today [address, September 9, 1986] G. G. Probst. *Vital Speeches Day* 53:166-8 Ja 1 '87

'Big Brother Inc.' may be closer than you thought. A. Field. il *Bus Week* p84-6 F 9 '87

Computers everywhere. J. W. Merline. il *Consum Res Mag* 70:38 Mr '87

Don't tread on my data: protecting individual privacy in the information age. P. Elmer-Dewitt. il *Time* 130:84 Jl 6 '87

Luddites and computers. G. F. Kreyche. il *USA Today (Periodical)* 115:98 Ja '87

The new networkers. F. Schwartz. il *Futurist* 21:8-11 Mr/Ap '87

The power of information [address, June 15, 1987] R. W. Galvin. *Vital Speeches Day* 53:647-9 Ag 15 '87

Telecommunications and computers: whither privacy policy? J. E. Katz. *Society* 25:81-6 N/D '87

When robots rule the world [views of Carl Hewitt and George Williams] G. Fjermedal. il *Omni* 10:24 N '87

Computers and crime *See* Computer crimes

Computers and society *See* Computers and civilization

Computers and the aged

See also

Information storage and retrieval systems—Aged

Computers and the blind

Release [blind author R. Russell and his talking word processor] *New Yorker* 63:28-32 S 28 '87

Computers and the handicapped

In the blink of an eye. G. Bronson. il *Forbes* 139:140+ Mr 23 '87

Making computers accessible to disabled people. F. Bowe. il *Technol Rev* 90:52-9+ Ja '87

With Thomas Hutchinson's marvelous ERICA, a flick of an eye brings help to the helpless. L. Albrecht. il por *People Wkly* 28:85-6 Jl 20 '87

Computers and youth

See also

Hackers (Computer enthusiasts)

Computers and your child. J. Segal and Z. Segal. il *Parents* 62:212 O '87

Computers and youth—*cont.*
Pied Piper of the computer [A. Kay] F. Rose. il por *N Y Times Mag* p56+ N 8 '87

Computers in art
Exhibitions
Computer-part art [exhibition at the Computer Museum, Boston] il *Natl Geogr World* 145:3-5 S '87

Computers in physics (Periodical)
AIP will start a new magazine, Computers in physics, in 1988. il *Phys Today* 40:71-2 Ap '87
Editor of new AIP magazine-journal discusses computers in physics [interview with R. R. Borchers] por *Phys Today* 40:109 O '87

Computone Systems, Inc.
Frying pan to fire. B. Leonard. il por *Forbes* 139:116+ Ap 6 '87

Comsat *See* Communications Satellite Corp.

Comstock Editions Inc.
Regional reissues are new directions in San Francisco and Honolulu. L. See. *Publ Wkly* 231:34 Ap 24 '87

Comstock Partners
Fancying the Rust Belt and the oil patch [interview with S. Salvigsen] A. E. Serwer. il por *Fortune* 116:112 Jl 20 '87

Conable, Barber B., Jr.
about
Conable's year of living dangerously at the World Bank. B. Javetski. il por *Bus Week* p118-19 Jl 20 '87

ConAgra, Inc.
How ConAgra grew big—and now, beefy [acquisition of Monfort] M. Ivey. il por *Bus Week* p87-8 My 18 '87
Were investors wrong to fly this coop? J. Mendes. *Fortune* 115:122+ My 25 '87

Conal, Robbie
about
Poster artist Robbie Conal paints satiric dislikenesses of the great, the wrinkled and the powerful. il por *People Wkly* 28:138 N 23 '87

Conant, Jennet
Ceramics in Wonderland. il *Newsweek* 110:78 O 12 '87

Conatec, Inc.
Microrockets for microgravity. W. H. Ganoe. il *Space World* X-11-287:39 N '87

Conaway, James, 1941-
The last hired gun. il por *Harpers* 275:58-63 Ag '87

Concanavalins
Concanavalin A alters synaptic specificity between cultured Aplysia neurons. S. S. Lin and I. B. Levitan. bibl f il *Science* 237:648-50 Ag 7 '87

Concentration *See* Attention

Concentration camps
Germany
The priests of Dachau. W. J. O'Malley. il *America* 157:351-3 N 14 '87
Poland
The Auschwitz Carmel [controversy over convent at Auschwitz] *America* 156:206 Mr 14 '87
Beyond judgment; tr. by Raymond Rosenthal. P. Levi. il *N Y Rev Books* 34:10+ D 17 '87
Learning from history [Carmelite convent at Auschwitz] E. Fleischner. *Commonweal* 114:167-8 Mr 27 '87
Soviet Union
A day in the depths of the gulag [I. Begun describes prison regimen] J. O. Jackson. il por *Time* 129:52 Mr 9 '87
Gateway to the gulag [Magadan] J. O. Jackson. il *Time* 129:46 Ap 20 '87
Houses of the dead [relevance of F. Dostoyevsky's Notes from the House of the Dead to G. Herling's A world apart] F. Eberstadt. *Commentary* 83:43-7 F '87
Photographs and photography
Gulag eyewitness: daring photographs by a Soviet prisoner. il pors *Life* 10:73-5 S '87

Concepcion, Dave
about
The half-million-dollar pay cut. M. Chass. il por *Sport Mag* 78:38 Je '87

Conception
See also
North Carolina Memorial Hospital. Preconception Clinic
Planning parenthood: can you time the birth of your child? S. Montgomery. il *Work Woman* 12:139-40+ O '87

Conceptual art
Talk about lines! A guy paid $26,400 for this drawing—and then they demolished it [auction of conceptual art by S. LeWitt] M. Small. il por *People Wkly* 27:43-4 My 25 '87

Wall painting [American politics as conceptual art] L. H. Lapham. *Harpers* 275:12+ O '87

Concerned Helpers of Inner Community Endeavors
Marla Gibbs hosts gala Los Angeles fund-raiser. il pors *Jet* 71:58-60 Mr 2 '87

Concerned Women for America
Powerhouse of the religious right? K. A. Lawton. il por *Christ Today* 31:34-6 N 6 '87
Watch on the right [work of B. LaHaye] C. Paige. por *Ms* 15:24-8 F '87

Concert Dance Company
Boston's Concert Dance enters 21st season. I. M. Fanger. il *Dance Mag* 61:5 N '87

Concert halls
See also
Mechanics Hall (Worcester, Mass.)
Acoustics
See Acoustics, Architectural
Conservation and restoration
Carnegie Hall: a facelift and a new sound. T. Eckert, Jr. il *High Fidel* 37:57-9 Ap '87
Carnegie's legacy restored. L. Kundell. il *Travel Holiday* 167:30-2 Mr '87
Musical events:
Critique of acoustics in renovated Carnegie Hall. A. Porter. *New Yorker* 63:76-9 Ap 20 '87
Viewpoint [renovation of Carnegie Hall] J. W. Freeman. *Opera News* 51:4 Mr 28 '87
New York (State)
See also
Alice Tully Hall (New York, N.Y.)
Carnegie Hall (New York, N.Y.)

Concert Opera of Manhattan
Musical events:
Rossini's Il viaggio a Reims. A. Porter. *New Yorker* 63:149-50 N 9 '87

Concert Royal
Bringing back baroque [performance of Les fêtes d'Hébé] P. J. Rosenwald. il *Horizon* 30:42 Mr '87
Reviews:
Performances of Les fêtes d'Hébé and Ariodante at Hunter College, New York City. L. Garafola. il *Dance Mag* 61:20+ F '87

Concerto and concertos
See also
Tape recordings—Concertos

Concerts
See also
Benefit performances
Blues concerts
Dance concerts
Jazz concerts
Rock concerts
Canta e pasta [annual concert sponsored by the Frisari family at the Veronica Ristorante Italiano in Manhattan] *New Yorker* 63:27-9 Mr 23 '87

Concessions (Food, etc.)
See also
Airports—Concessions (Food, etc.)
Stadiums—Concessions (Food, etc.)

Conchology *See* Shells (Conchology)

Conciencia (Organization)
Conciencia and the future of democracy. il *Dep State Bull* 87:64 Mr '87

Concierges
Those magicians at the desk. M. Smilgis. il *Time* 130:68 D 28 '87

Concord (Calif.)
Health facilities
When picketing pays [Adopt-a-Picket program run by NOW to raise money for abortions] D. G. Albrecht. il *Ms* 16:91 N '87

Concord (N.H.)
The town that remembers Christa. D. Waldman. il *Ladies Home J* 104:76+ F '87
Climate
The "fist" of a tornado? [letter] M. D. Hill. il *Weatherwise* 40:69-70 Ap '87

Concord Capital Management
Money men, California style. il por *Fortune* 116:34 Jl 20 '87

Concorde airplanes *See* Airplanes, Supersonic

Concordia Seminary (Saint Louis, Mo.)
Finding the lost. M. E. Marty. *Christ Century* 104:543 Je 3-10 '87

Concrete, Reinforced
Protecting skyscrapers against earthquakes [use of fiber reinforced concrete called SIFCON; work of Antoine E. Naaman] *USA Today (Periodical)* 115:3 Je '87

Concrete blocks
Changing the shape of things to come [ideas from National Concrete Masonry Association] D. Rastorfer. il *Archit Rec* 175:20-1 D '87
Fast foundations [concrete block foundation] R. Day. il *Pop Sci* 230:72-3 My '87
How to stucco over concrete block. G. Branson. il *Fam Handyman* 37:49-52 S '87

Concrete Blonde (Musical group)
Concrete Blonde has more fun. A. DeCurtis. il *Roll Stone* p27-8 Je 4 '87

Concrete bridges *See* Bridges

Concrete construction
See also
National Concrete Masonry Association
Portland Cement Association 1986 Concrete Building Awards. il *Archit Rec* 175:44 Ja '87
Prestressed Concrete Institute 1986 design awards. il *Archit Rec* 175:66-7 F '87

Concrete walls *See* Walls, Concrete

Concrete work
See also
Concrete blocks
10 most-asked questions about concrete. G. Branson. il *Fam Handyman* 37:82+ Ap '87
Coloring concrete. R. Day. il *Pop Sci* 231:108-9 N '87

Concurrency (Computers) *See* Parallel processing (Computers)

Condee, Nancy P., and Padunov, Vladimir
Reforming Soviet culture/Retrieving Soviet history. il *Nation* 244:815-20 Je 13 '87

Condensation (Meteorology)
Dew drops on a bathroom mirror. C. F. Bohren. il *Weatherwise* 40:102-6 Ap '87
Skylight condensation problem licked. il *Workbench* 43:12 S/O '87
What your windshield shows about the clouds [origin of clouds and dew] R. Williams. il *Weatherwise* 40:260-1 O '87
Window watching [dew on windows] C. F. Bohren. il *Weatherwise* 40:150-3 Je '87

Condensed matter *See* Matter

Condiments
See also
Mustard, Prepared
Pickles and relishes

Condit, William H.
The watercolor page. por *Am Artist* 51:50-3+ S '87

Conditioned responses
See also
Biofeedback training
Reinforcement (Psychology)
Can you teach your body to fight cancer? il *Prevention* 39:6 D '87
Long-term sensitization in Aplysia: biophysical correlates in tail sensory neurons. K. P. Scholz and J. H. Byrne. bibl f il *Science* 235:685-7 F 6 '87
Neural models yield data on learning [special section] D. M. Barnes. *Science* 236:1628-9 Je 26 '87

Conditioners (Hair) *See* Hair care products

Conditioners (Soil) *See* Soil conditioners

Condominiums
Bargain condos: going once, going twice . . . A. Fins. il *Bus Week* p163 Je 22 '87
Fortress Fisher [Fisher Island, Fla.] W. G. Flanagan. il map *Forbes* 140:232+ D 14 '87
Home sweet condo. R. Louv. il *Read Dig* 130:27-8+ Ap '87
Mondo condo [ski area condominiums] A. H. Greenberg. *Skiing* 40:30 O '87
The right mix [R. Millican's mixed-use building provides housing for the elderly in New York City] G. Wen. il por *N Y* 20:42 S 21 '87
Romance in the rooftops. P. Langdon. il *Atlantic* 260:85-7 Jl '87
Six bites from one apple [R. Campo sells Houston condo investors on desyndication deal] W. P. Barrett. il por *Forbes* 140:88+ S 7 '87

Timesharing ownership
See Timesharing (Real estate)

Condominiums (Boat docking)
A boat slip can be your castle, too. R. W. King. il *Bus Week* p114 Je 15 '87
Dockbroker Ed [E. J. Doherty] R. Behar. il por *Forbes* 140:166+ S 21 '87

Condoms
AIDS education: the moral substance [statement issued by United States Catholic Conference] D. Hollenbach. *America* 157:493-4 D 26 '87
America's bishops rule on condoms. *Newsweek* 110:57 D 21 '87

The bishops' split on AIDS [controversy over condoms divides the Catholic hierarchy] R. N. Ostling. il *Time* 130:64 D 28 '87
The bishops' statement on AIDS. *America* 157:491-2 D 26 '87
Catholics, AIDS and condoms [statement by bishops] *Time* 130:60 D 21 '87
Common sense about condoms. il *Glamour* 85:38 Jl '87
The condom conundrum: a sermon on AIDS to raise the conscience of our times. C. Thitchener. il pors *Humanist* 47:11-14+ Jl/Ag '87
Condom etiquette [excerpt from How to persuade your lover to use a condom] P. Breitman and others. il *Essence* 18:19+ N '87
The condom preacher—and his pantless past [Rev. C. F. Thitchener] il por *Newsweek* 109:69 Mr 2 '87
Condom sense. K. Freifeld. il *Health* 19:92 Je '87
Condoms: a straight girl's best friend. P. Hendricks. il *Ms* 16:98+ S '87
Condoms may not stop AIDS. J. Carey. il *U S News World Rep* 103:83 O 19 '87
Don't spend a night without armor: the condom. L. Bernikow. il *Mademoiselle* 93:116-18+ Ja '87
Get smart: a buyer's guide to condoms. il *Glamour* 85:94 Ap '87
How men really feel about condoms. P. Richmond. il *Glamour* 85:304-5+ N '87
Is preventing AIDS the responsibility of women? The media seem to think so [excerpt from Advice for life] C. Norwood. il *Glamour* 85:18 Jl '87
Married N.Y. inmates get condoms to battle AIDS. *Jet* 71:38 Ja 26 '87
Minister gives condoms to stop AIDS, starts a controversy on subject [C. Thitchener] il por *Jet* 71:10 F 23 '87
Playing safe: the new sexual landscape. il *Vogue* 177:226-7+ Je '87
Walden, WPS just say 'no' to condoms [refusal to carry cassette packaged with condoms] il *Publ Wkly* 232:48 O 30 '87
Young Reagan makes a pitch for condoms [TV documentary] il por *Newsweek* 109:24 Je 22 '87

Advertising
Ads that shatter an old taboo; Campaigns round the world [TV commercials aimed at preventing AIDS] A. Toufexis. il *Time* 129:63 F 2 '87
America gets 'condomized'. G. F. Will. il *Newsweek* 109:82 F 16 '87
The days of the condom. B. Kanner. il *N Y* 20:10-12 Ja 5 '87
A different way of saying it [Telecaster Committee of Canada's rejection of AIDS-prevention ads] S. MacLeod. por *Macleans* 100:64 Mr 30 '87
Just say no to condom ads. J. Piper. il por *Christ Today* 31:16 S 4 '87
A necessary offense [various New York groups objecting to advertising aimed at preventing AIDS] H. Evans. il *U S News World Rep* 102:80 My 25 '87
Responding to the AIDS crisis [advertising on television and broadening sex education efforts] K. A. Lawton. il *Christ Today* 31:34-6 Ap 3 '87
This is what you thought: 90% want condom ads on TV [results of survey] *Glamour* 85:57 Jl '87
An unflinching AIDS campaign [ads in New York City] T. E. Johnson. il *Newsweek* 109:24 My 25 '87

Anecdotes, facetiae, satire, etc.
Glasnost and the condom. W. Goodman. il *New Leader* 70:11-12 Mr 9 '87

History
Condoms to the rescue: New Zealand's Ettie Rout "made vice safe" in World War I. J. Tolerton. il pors *Ms* 15:28-30 My '87
Fit for a king [evidence that Louis XV used British contraceptives] J. Black. por *Hist Today* 37:3 Ap '87
The venerable condoms of Dudley Castle. il *Discover* 8:7 Mr '87

Marketing
Age of precautions. A. Finlayson. il *Macleans* 100:36 Ja 12 '87
Protection money. J. A. Conway. il *Forbes* 139:8 F 23 '87

Songs and music
The Fat Boys say: 'Protect yourself' [rap song] *Harpers* 274:18 Je '87

Condon, Eddie, 1904-1973
about
Eddie Condon's. V. Ziegel. il por *N Y* 20:70-1 D 21-28 '87

Condon, Elizabeth A.
Will *glasnost* reunite Soviet-American couples? por *U S News World Rep* 102:10 Mr 2 '87

Condor, Bob
A book store for the betting man. il *Sport Mag* 78:94 Mr '87
How the polls really work. il *Sport Mag* 78:41-3+ Ja '87
The market report. il *Esquire* 107:F8+ Mr '87

Condors
Age and diet of fossil California condors in Grand Canyon, Arizona. S. D. Emslie. bibl f il *Science* 237:768-70 Ag 14 '87
Ancient death and modern survival [California condor; work of Steven D. Emslie] *Sci News* 132:136 Ag 29 '87
Caged: the last wild condor [California condor] J. S. Lang. il *U S News World Rep* 102:62-3 My 4 '87
Caring for the condor [California condor keeper D. J. Sterner of San Diego Wild Animal Park] B. Weber. il por *N Y Times Mag* p106 O 4 '87
El condor pasa [Andean condor release program to help save California condors; work of Michael Wallace] C. Senders. il *Omni* 9:98 Ag '87
Fossils extend condor's range, pose questions [discovery in upstate New York of three fossil California condor bones] il *Audubon* 89:14 Jl '87
Fresh start for condor recovery [California condor] *Audubon* 89:144 Mr '87
Last chance for the condor [California condor] J. Nielsen. il *Sports Illus* 66:62+ Mr 23 '87
Last wild condor caught [California condor] *Sci News* 131:263 Ap 25 '87
Saga of AC-9, the last free condor [California condors] R. L. Di Silvestro. il *Audubon* 89:12+ Jl '87
Searching for the condors' next home [California condors] *Sci News* 132:319 N 14 '87

Conduct of life
See also
Advice
Altruism
Ambition
Anger
Apologies
Avarice
Caring
Character
Christian ethics
Christian life
Comfort
Conscience
Counterculture
Courtesy
Ethics
Etiquette
Faith
Forgiveness
Friendship
Habits
Hedonism
Honesty
Human relations
Humanity
Individuality
Leisure
Life skills
Love
Loyalty
Obedience
Organization
Patriotism
Pleasure
Principles
Procrastination
Responsibility
Spiritual life
Time management
Values
Virtue
Work
Zeal
Choose wisely [address, August 14, 1987] B. Chiodo. *Vital Speeches Day* 54:40-2 N 1 '87
Let yourself go! [adaptation of address, December 19, 1986] B. Hatcher. *Read Dig* 131:169-70 N '87
Living with abandon! [address, December 19, 1986] B. Hatcher. *Vital Speeches Day* 53:296-7 Mr 1 '87
Make the most of your day! A. Stoddard. *McCalls* 114:76 Jl '87
My father's song [condensed from God's best for you] M. M. Helleberg. il *Read Dig* 131:53-6 S '87
Pursue not just the material [address, May 7, 1987] A. M. Schindler. *Vital Speeches Day* 53:659-60 Ag 15 '87

Three lessons for living [adaptation of address, May 24, 1986] J. C. Gardner. il *Read Dig* 130:185-7 Mr '87
We learned it all in kindergarten. R. Fulghum. il *Read Dig* 131:115 O '87

Conducting (Music)
See also
Conductors (Music)
Double play [J. Mauceri and P. Gemignani, conductors of both opera and musical theater; cover story] S. Flatow. il pors *Opera News* 51:10-13+ Je '87
Fournet—à la française [opera conductor to bow at the Met] A. Ulrich. il por *Opera News* 51:38-9+ Ap 11 '87
Rien de trop [opera conductor M. Rosenthal] D. Harris. por *Opera News* 51:10-11+ My '87
Seeking the light [Z. Mehta to conduct at the Metropolitan Opera; cover story] M. Mayer. il pors *Opera News* 52:12-15 D 5 '87

Conductors, Electric *See* Electric conductors and conductivity

Conductors, Super *See* Superconductors and superconductivity

Conductors (Music)
See also
Abbado, Claudio
Bernstein, Leonard, 1918-
Boulez, Pierre, 1925-
Brueggen, Frans
Bychkov, Semyon
Christie, William
Crosby, John O'Hea, 1926-
DeMain, John
Domingo, Placido
Dunner, Leslie B.
Fournet, Jean, 1913-
Gemignani, Paul
Giulini, Carlo Maria
Hogwood, Christopher
Marriner, Neville, 1924-
Mauceri, John, 1945-
McArthur, Edwin, 1907-1987
Mehta, Zubin
Morgan, Michael
Muti, Riccardo
Ozawa, Seiji
Previn, André, 1929-
Rattle, Simon
Rosenthal, Manuel, 1904-
Rostropovich, Mstislav, 1927-
Rozhdestvenski, Gennadi
Sinopoli, Giuseppe
Solti, Sir Georg, 1912-
Tennstedt, Klaus, 1926-
Thomas, Michael Tilson, 1944-
Toscanini, Arturo, 1867-1957
Wolff, Hugh
Baton twirlers [opera releases by various conductors] P. G. Davis. il *N Y* 20:127-8 S 28 '87
Musical chairs [star conductors] T. W. Libbey, Jr. il *High Fidel* 37:55-7 Jl '87

Cone, Marla
L.A. to E.P.A.: don't hold your breath. il *Sierra* 72:27+ N/D '87

Cone, Richard
The gospel according to Ermel. il *Antiques Collect Hobbies* 92:35-6 My '87

Cone, Roger D., and others
Tissue-specific expression of functionally rearranged λ1 Ig gene through a retrovirus vector. bibl f il *Science* 236:954-7 My 22 '87

Cone cells *See* Rods and cones

Cones, Ice cream *See* Ice cream cones

Coney Island (New York, N.Y.)
Walking the Cyclone [W. Williams, head repairman at the Coney Island Cyclone] *New Yorker* 63:28-9 S 14 '87

Photographs and photography
Return to Coney Island: back to realistic photography. N. Rothschild. il *Pop Photogr* 94:12 My '87

Confectionery
See also
Candy
Candy industry
Marzipan
Pralines
Invite friends for dainties [almond cream confections] il *South Living* 22:183 S '87

Confederate money
The dog notes of Virginia. E. Rochette. il *Antiques Collect Hobbies* 92:80-1 Ag '87

Confederate money—*cont.*
Exhibitions
He saved the South's money [Thian Collection at Duke University] il *South Living* 22:24 Jl '87
Confederate States of America
See also
United States—History—Civil War, 1861-1865
Whistling Dixie in Brazil [disillusioned southerners settle in Brazil, 1865-79] J. H. Kennedy. il *Américas* 39:26-31 Ja/F '87
Confederate States of America in art
Exhibitions
Lost cause art [prints the North published for the South; Confederate image exhibit] M. E. Neely, Jr. and others. il *Americana* 15:59-62 Jl/Ag '87
Confédération des Syndicats Nationaux
Showdown in Quebec [police raids] M. Rose. il *Macleans* 100:12 Je 29 '87
Confederation of African Medical Associations and Societies
CAMAS: born amid turmoil. O. Adekunle. il *World Health* p24-6 Je '87
Confederation of National Trade Unions *See* Confédération des Syndicats Nationaux
Conference on Confidence and Security-Building Measures and Disarmament in Europe
The other negotiations. C. Hardenbergh. il *Bull At Sci* 43:48-9 Mr '87
Conference on Security and Cooperation in Europe
CSCE semiannual report. *Dep State Bull* 87:92 Mr '87
The evolving Soviet approach to human rights [addresses, January 27 and February 20, 1987] W. Zimmermann. *Dep State Bull* 87:67-9 Je '87
Human rights, the Soviet Union, and the Helsinki process [address, January 28, 1987] R. Schifter. *Dep State Bull* 87:42-8 Ap '87
Pursuing the promise of Helsinki [address, November 5, 1986] G. P. Shultz. *Dep State Bull* 87:47-50 Ja '87
Vienna CSCE followup meeting. *Dep State Bull* 87:50-1 Ja '87
Vienna CSCE followup meeting resumes [statement, January 26, 1987] R. Reagan. *Dep State Bull* 87:34 Ap '87
Conferences
See also
Authors' conferences
Conventions
Economic conferences
International conferences
Religious conferences
Seminars
Teleconferencing
Conferencing, Computer *See* Computer networks
Confession
The no-fault confession. M. Greenfield. il *Newsweek* 109:80 Je 15 '87
Prayers of confession: let's get unspecific. B. Barr. *Christ Century* 104:844 O 7 '87
Confession (Catholic Church) *See* Penance
Confession (Law)
The case of common sense vs. Miranda. E. H. Methvin. il *Read Dig* 131:96-100 Ag '87
Crime and the Constitution [Miranda Rule] D. O. Relin and C. Lawrence. il *Sch Update* 120:10-11 D 4 '87
The Meese lie [effort to overturn Miranda decision] S. Gillers. *Nation* 244:205 F 21 '87
Viva Miranda [Justice Dept. offensive against Miranda decision] J. Toobin. *New Repub* 196:11-12 F 16 '87
Confidence, Self *See* Self confidence
Confidences, Professional *See* Confidential communications
Confidential communications
See also
Official secrets
Privacy, Right of
Banking
Luxembourg: color it green [cover story] E. A. Finn, Jr. il *Forbes* 139:42-5 Ap 20 '87
Opening a Swiss account is no big secret. S. Woolley. il *Bus Week* p95 Ag 3 '87
Swiss secrecy: don't bank on it. G. Bock. il *Time* 130:49 D 7 '87
Press
Breaking a confidence [O. North revealed as source of government leaks to news organizations] L. Zuckerman. il *Time* 130:61 Ag 3 '87
Inside dopes [press treatment of O. L. North] J. L. Pasley. *New Repub* 196:14-16 F 23 '87
Means and ends. R. K. Manoff. *Progressive* 51:39 Mr '87

Of loose lips and stock tips [Supreme Court upholds conviction of R. F. Winans for insider trading] J. Castro. il por *Time* 130:63 N 30 '87
When sources get immunity [press treatment of O. North] J. Alter. il *Newsweek* 109:54 Ja 19 '87
Confinement feeding of swine *See* Swine—Confinement methods
Confino-Addor, Catherine
about
Building on the past. C. de Liagre. il *House Gard* 159:124-31+ Ag '87
Confiscations
Filling Uncle Sam's auction house. R. N. Ostling. il *Time* 130:73 D 14 '87
No taking without paying [Supreme Court decision on compensation for confiscated land] A. L. Sanders. il *Time* 129:64-5 Je 22 '87
Conflict (Psychology)
See also
Competition (Psychology)
"There's got to be a better way" [conflict resolution] J. Marks. il *Parents* 62:106-8+ S '87
Conflict (Psychology) in drama
Conflict: the heartbeat of a play. D. R. Andersen. *Writer* 100:14-17+ S '87
Conflict of generations *See* Generation gap
Conflict of interests (Business)
The day the brokers picked their own pockets [Black Monday] R. L. Stern and A. Sloan. il *Forbes* 140:32-3 N 16 '87
Dispassionate advice [conflict of interests arising from brokers sales of mutual funds] J. Heins. il *Forbes* 139:160+ Mr 9 '87
Egad, a conflict! D. Fanning. il *Forbes* 140:99 S 21 '87
Conflict of interests (Lawyers)
The Bakkers vs. the hired gun [charges brought against lawyer N. R. Grutman] G. Carroll. il por *Newsweek* 110:61-2 S 7 '87
Fee-busting [lawyers serving as executors and estate attorneys] D. Fanning. il *Forbes* 140:64 S 7 '87
Rambo & Rambo, attorneys-at-law [lawyers acting as prosecutors in trademark counterfeit cases] D. Fanning. *Forbes* 139:76 Ja 26 '87
Conflict of interests (Public office)
See also
Deaver, Michael K.—Conflict of interests case
The aides virus [ex-congressional aides working as lobbyists] J. L. Pasley. *New Repub* 197:22+ O 19 '87
All the president's men. il *U S News World Rep* 103:16-17 Jl 27 '87
Banning the free lunch [executive branch officials prohibited from accepting free lunches] E. Clift. il *Newsweek* 110:19 D 28 '87
A Bronx scandal tars Meese [Wedtech] C. O'Connor. il por *Newsweek* 109:20 My 25 '87
Conflicts and credibility gaps [Canadian media coverage of case against S. Stevens] G. Bain. il *Macleans* 100:52 D 21 '87
Document links NSF official to biotech firm [case of D. T. Kingsbury] M. Crawford. *Science* 238:742 N 6 '87
Edwin Meese and the Wedtech web. D. Baer. il por *U S News World Rep* 102:14 My 18 '87
Edwin Meese's quiet year turns unquiet [Wedtech case] D. Baer and P. Cary. il por *U S News World Rep* 102:14-15 My 25 '87
Fall of the Californians [Reagan's once proud team] C. O'Connor. il *Newsweek* 110:19 Jl 27 '87
Fever in a climate of scandal [reporting on the Oerlikon affair in Canada] G. Bain. il *Macleans* 100:49 F 23 '87
Harsh lessons from an inquiry [S. Stevens affair and the Canadian press] G. Bain. il *Macleans* 100:44 Ag 24 '87
Jim Wright makes it the old-fashioned way [influence peddling charges; cover story] R. C. Kirkwood. il por *Natl Rev* 39:36-7+ O 23 '87
Jim Wright: pork-barrel politician as statesman. M. Miller and R. Thomas. il pors *Newsweek* 110:26-7 N 30 '87
The Meese mess gets muddier. P. Dwyer. por *Bus Week* p68 D 28 '87-Ja 4 '88
Meese's legal troubles have him hog-tied at Justice. P. Dwyer. por *Bus Week* p39 Je 29 '87
Meese's troubles go way beyond Wedtech. P. Dwyer and H. Collingwood. il por *Bus Week* p26-7 Jl 27 '87
The new questions about Ed Meese's finances [Wedtech scandal] P. Dwyer. il por *Bus Week* p46-7 My 11 '87

Conflict of interests (Public office)—*cont.*

A new senator's troubled debut [J. Bazin's involvement in Oerlikon land speculation controversy in Canada] M. Gee. il por *Macleans* 100:14 F 16 '87

NSF official's finances probed by Justice [case of D. T. Kingsbury] M. Crawford. por *Science* 238:478 O 23 '87

The police and the MP [A. Bissonnette charged in Oerlikon land sale scandal in Canada] M. Rose. *Macleans* 100:9 Ag 31 '87

A political minefield [resignation of Canadian transport minister A. Bissonnette over land sale to Oerlikon Aerospace; special section; with editorial comment by Kevin Doyle] il pors *Macleans* 100:2, 8-9+ F 2 '87

Resign, Ed Meese. il *New Repub* 197:7-9 N 9 '87

The resilient loyalist [problems of E. Meese] E. Shannon. il por *Time* 130:15 Ag 3 '87

The Tories strike back [resignation of A. Bissonnette over land sale to Oerlikon Aerospace] M. Gee. il por *Macleans* 100:10-11 F 9 '87

The trial and errors of Edwin Meese. D. Baer. il pors *U S News World Rep* 103:16-18 Ag 3 '87

An untimely departure [conflict of interest charges force resignation of Highways Minister C. Michael in British Columbia] J. O'Hara. *Macleans* 100:20 N 30 '87

Washington's shameful revolving door [lobbying by former government officials] R. Evans and R. D. Novak. *Read Dig* 130:118-22 My '87

Wrapping up an inquiry [conflict of interest charges against former cabinet minister S. Stevens in Canada] S. Aikenhead. il *Macleans* 100:13 Mr 2 '87

'Wrong by any measure' [report on S. Stevens' conflict of interest investigation issued in Canada] M. Rose. il por *Macleans* 100:12-14 D 14 '87

Conformational analysis

Left-handed DNA in vivo. A. Jaworski and others. bibl f il *Science* 238:773-7 N 6 '87

New assay identifies southpaw DNA [work of Robert D. Wells and others] R. Weiss. *Sci News* 132:308 N 14 '87

Conformity

See also

Eccentrics and eccentricities

Confucius

about

Confucius. il *Sch Update* 120:26 S 18 '87

Congenital malformations *See* Birth defects

Conger, Clement E.

Introduction. il *Antiques* 132:120-1 Jl '87

Conglomerate corporations

Conglomerates. L. Jereski. il *Forbes* 139:106-7 Ja 12 '87

Royal Little: the conglomerator. D. A. Saunders. il pors *Forbes* 140:264+ Jl 13 '87

Conglomerate stocks *See* Stocks

Congo

Religious institutions and affairs

See also

Catholic Church—Congo

Congo River

Where jungle meets river [Zaire] D. Jacobs. il *World Press Rev* 34:62 O '87

Congregate housing

Congregate housing development guide for small communities. *Aging* no356:31 '87

Congregation for the Doctrine of the Faith *See* Catholic Church. Congregation for the Doctrine of the Faith

Congregationalism

Is elder rule a threat? [Consultation on Congregationalism] S. Grenz. *Christ Today* 31:48+ Jl 10 '87

Congress (U.S.) *See* United States. Congress

Congress of Racial Equality

CORE's Farmer gives his personal papers to Univ. of Texas [J. Farmer] *Jet* 72:22 S 21 '87

Congress of South African Trade Unions

Labor: now it's showdown time. S. Mufson. il *Bus Week* p48 My 4 '87

Why black workers may say 'thanks, but no thanks' to Ford [partial worker ownership of Samcor] S. Mufson. il *Bus Week* p47 Jl 6 '87

Congressional aides *See* Congressmen—Staff

Congressional Black Caucus

Blacks' education, political welfare major subjects of the Caucus weekend in D.C. il *Jet* 73:6+ O 19 '87

CBC pushes for new African agenda. G. McKinney. il *Black Enterp* 17:19 My '87

Mervyn Dymally takes the helm of the Black Caucus. il por *Jet* 71:5 Ja 12 '87

NBL, Black Caucus at odds over status of the MBDA. *Jet* 72:30 My 4 '87

Savage heads up Black Caucus business trust. por *Jet* 72:40 Je 29 '87

Congressional Science Fellows *See* Scientists in government

Congressmen

See also

AIDS (Disease) and congressmen

Alcohol and congressmen

Black congressmen

Conflict of interests (Public office)

Senators

See also names of congressmen

The best of Capitol Hill. il *U S News World Rep* 103:47-9 D 21 '87

Congress's Red Army [pro-Communist Democrats; cover story] J. M. Waller and J. Sobran. il *Natl Rev* 39:25-8 Jl 31 '87

For U.S. lawmakers, life in the fast lane. M. Christopher. il *Sch Update* 119:16-17 Ja 12 '87

The lawmakers [100th Congress] R. Seligman. il *Sch Update* 119:5-6 Ja 12 '87

The NIH legislators. W. Booth. il *Science* 237:844-5 Ag 21 '87

The view from the 100th Congress [congressional history; special section] il *People Wkly* 27:26-33 Mr 23 '87

Ethics

See Political ethics

Financial disclosure

Capitol gains: where lawmakers invest. D. Harbrecht. il *Bus Week* p60 Je 29 '87

Free George Hansen? [jailed for incomplete financial disclosure] D. Klinghoffer. *Natl Rev* 39:41 Ag 14 '87

Public relations

Aids and devices

Letter from Washington [Congressman C. Hecht's video newsletter] Cato. *Natl Rev* 39:15 O 23 '87

Retirement

In Tip-top shape [T. O'Neill] il por *Time* 129:18 Ja 26 '87

Salaries, allowances, etc.

The lost amendment [congressional pay amendment] R. Zagarri. *New Repub* 196:13 F 2 '87

Take the money and run [pay increases] H. G. Chua-Eoan. *Time* 129:18 Ja 26 '87

Washington may get a raise—but not without a fight. D. Harbrecht. il *Bus Week* p36 F 2 '87

Staff

The aides virus [ex-congressional aides working as lobbyists] J. L. Pasley. *New Repub* 197:22+ O 19 '87

Congressmen's wives

Fed up with the demands of her husband's career, a congressman's wife drops out of the race; ed by Annette Kornblum. P. Kostmayer. il pors *People Wkly* 28:71-2+ O 12 '87

Coniston Partners

Allegis flies into debt [fending off Coniston Partners] il *Fortune* 115:8 Je 22 '87

Bust-up artists on Wall Street. D. P. Wiener. il *U S News World Rep* 102:45 Je 22 '87

Coniston stalks Allegis. J. E. Ellis. il *Bus Week* p37 Je 8 '87

Even if Allegis wins, the victory could be pyrrhic. J. E. Ellis. por *Bus Week* p37 Je 15 '87

The trio that humbled Allegis. S. P. Sherman. il pors *Fortune* 116:52-4+ Jl 20 '87

Conjugation (Biology)

New questions in Strobel case [field test of Dutch elm disease] L. Roberts. *Science* 237:1097-8 S 4 '87

Conjugation (Chemistry)

A small gold-conjugated antibody label: improved resolution for electron microscopy [cover story] J. F. Hainfeld. bibl f il *Science* 236:450-3 Ap 24 '87

Conjunctions (Astronomy)

The Greeks had a word for it [syzygy] T. D. Nicholson. *Nat Hist* 96:70 My '87

Lunar and solar alignments caused high tides on earth [syzygy] *Earth Sci* 40:8-9 Summ '87

Conjunctions (Grammar) *See* English language—Conjunctions

Conjuring

See also

Jugglers and juggling

Grand illusions. R. Jay. il *Omni* 9:44-6+ Mr '87

Business use

Casting a spell over employees [Citicorp Mortgage, Inc.] S. Nelton. il *Nations Bus* 75:52 D '87

Conkling, Edgar C.

Caribbean Basin Initiative. il map *Focus* 37:2-9 Summ '87

Made in U.S.A./Mexico: a new industrial partnership. map *Focus* 36:32-3 Wint '86

Conlan, Garth
about
Fighting to stave off foreclosure, farmer Garth Conlan ends up taking his bank to the cleaners. D. Grogan. il por *People Wkly* 28:50-2 Ag 10 '87
Conley, David T.
Critical attributes of teacher evaluation systems. *Educ Dig* 53:32-5 O '87
Conley, Mike
about
Soaring to unseen heights. P. Putnam. il por *Sports Illus* 66:24-5 Mr 9 '87
Connally, John B., Jr.
about
Dad's little helper. M. Fritz. il por *Forbes* 140:104 Jl 27 '87
John Connally goes belly up after betting big on a Texas oil economy that ran out of gas. W. Plummer. il pors *People Wkly* 28:36-7 Ag 17 '87
Connally, Mark
about
Dad's little helper. M. Fritz. il por *Forbes* 140:104 Jl 27 '87
Connaught Hotel (London, England) *See* London (England)—Hotels, motels, etc.
Connecticut
See also
  Architecture—Connecticut
  Architecture, Domestic—Connecticut
  Birds—Connecticut
  Country estates—Connecticut
  Gardens and gardening—Connecticut
  Historic houses, sites, etc.—Connecticut
  Housatonic River (Conn. and Mass.)
  Litchfield County (Conn.)
  Medical policy—Connecticut
  Music festivals—Connecticut
  Opera—Connecticut
  Shore protection—Connecticut
  Vegetable gardens and gardening—Connecticut
  Wetlands—Connecticut
Connection Machine *See* Parallel processing (Computers)
Connective tissues
See also
  Collagen
Diseases
See also
  Lupus erythematosus
Smooth muscle-mediated connective tissue remodeling in pulmonary hypertension. R. P. Mecham and others. bibl f il *Science* 237:423-6 Jl 24 '87
Connell, Anthea M. S.
Eye services in the Caribbean. il *World Health* p27-8 My '87
Connell, Elizabeth B.
The crisis in contraception. il *Technol Rev* 90:46-55 My/Je '87
Connell, Lawrence
about
Cutting Commodore with a Bowie knife. J. Weber, Jr. il por *Bus Week* p74 N 9 '87
Connell, Martin
about
An investment in new hope. por *Macleans* 100:26-7 D 28 '87
Connelly, John F., 1905-
about
These penny-pinchers deliver a big bang for their bucks. C. S. Eklund and J. Flynn. pors *Bus Week* p52 My 4 '87
Conner, Bruce, 1933-
about
San Francisco exhibits exceed photography's boundaries. L. Lufkin. il *Pop Photogr* 94:26+ Ja '87
Conner, Dennis
Mission accomplished. il por *Sports Illus* 66:18-19 F 16 '87
about
The America's Cup goes home again. R. L. Miller. il por *Macleans* 100:50 F 16 '87
Boat warrior. B. Lewis. il pors *Sport Mag* 78:43-4+ D '87
The Cup comes back. T. Gibbs. il *New Yorker* 63:86-90+ Mr 2 '87
Dennis Conner clobbers the Kiwis. D. Wallace. il por *Mot Boat Sail* 159:36-41+ Mr '87
Dennis Conner's crusade. P. A. Janssen. il *Mot Boat Sail* 159:9+ Mr '87
Dragster in the danger zone. J. D. Reed. il por *Time* 129:75 Ja 26 '87

Fremantle says good on yer, mates. T. Callahan. il por *Time* 129:66 F 16 '87
Going for the Cup. T. Callahan. il pors *Time* 129:42-5 F 9 '87
Master on a mission. S. Ballard. il por *Sports Illus* 66:66-71 F 9 '87
Of brains, brawn and boats. W. D. Marbach. il por *Newsweek* 109:79 F 2 '87
Return of the wave warrior. il por *People Wkly* 27:88-9+ F 9 '87
A sea dog primes his guns. C. Neff. il pors *Sports Illus* 66:56-62 Ja 5 '87
Smooth sailing up Madison Ave. A. Miller. il por *Newsweek* 109:53 Mr 30 '87
Stars & Stripes . . . forever? C. Leerhsen. il por *Newsweek* 109:23 F 16 '87
Victory at sea. S. Ballard. il por *Sports Illus* 66:10-17 F 16 '87
Conner, Finis F., 1943-
about
The disk-drive maker that's driving to a record. R. Brandt. il por *Bus Week* p134+ S 14 '87
Conner Peripherals Inc.
The disk-drive maker that's driving to a record. R. Brandt. il por *Bus Week* p134+ S 14 '87
Connery, Sean
about
So . . . we meet at last, Mr. Bond. B. Greene. il por *Esquire* 107:45-6 Ap '87
Connick (Charles J.) Studio (Firm) *See* Charles J. Connick Studio (Firm)
Connie, Blitt, and Bernstein, Dennis
Mercenary with a cause. *Progressive* 51:13 Ag '87
Conniff, Richard
How the world puts gourds to work. il *Int Wildl* 17:18-24 My/Je '87
An intimate grandeur. il *Archit Dig* 44:80-5 Ag '87
The little suckers have made a comeback. il *Discover* 8:84-6+ Ag '87
Profiles: Denton A. Cooley, M.D. il pors *Archit Dig* 44:194-201+ My '87
Rejuvenating a Connecticut parsonage: a designer's Litchfield County colonial. il *Archit Dig* 44:108-17+ Je '87
The so-so salesman who told millions how to make it big. bibl (p230) il por *Smithsonian* 18:82-6+ O '87
The stage manager: Off-Broadway or on, the buck stops here. il pors *Smithsonian* 17:92-4+ F '87
When the music in our parlors brought death to darkest Africa. il *Audubon* 89:76-93 Jl '87
Connolly, Francis J.
(jt. auth) *See* Lehigh, Scot, and Connolly, Francis J.
Connolly, James E. (James Edward), 1949-
Walk on the dry side. il *Conservationist* 42:26-7 Jl/Ag '87
Connolly, Jane
Why not try union democracy? il *Nation* 245:192-4+ S 5 '87
Connolly, John W. D.
about
SURA gets new president from DOE: NSF loses two computer chiefs. I. Goodwin. *Phys Today* 40:60-1 D '87
Connors, Diane
Interview [A. Miller] por *Omni* 9:72-4+ Mr '87
Connors, Jimmy, 1952-
about
Rock of ages [cover story] N. Amdur. il por *World Tennis* 35:36-8 S '87
Conover, Adele
Expedition to a 'lost' world. il map *Int Wildl* 17:38-42 My/Je '87
Conrad, Barnaby, III
From Paris, with love, a new palace for art now shines on the Seine. il *Smithsonian* 17:82-8+ Mr '87
Ich bin ein ballooner. il map *Forbes* 140:116-20+ Ag 24 '87
Los Angeles: the new Mecca. il *Horizon* 30:17-30 Ja/F '87
Conrad, Barnaby, 1922-
A woeful gallery of the world's lost masterpieces. bibl (p271) il *Smithsonian* 18:239-40+ N '87
Conrades, George H.
The challenge of global competition [address, September 17, 1987] *Vital Speeches Day* 54:125-8 D 1 '87
Conradt, Jody
about
She's stealing the heart of Texas. S. Hollandsworth. il pors *Women's Sports Fitness* 9:49-51+ F '87

Conrail *See* Consolidated Rail Corporation
Conran family
about
The Conrans: a genuine dynasty. L. Nickson. il *Time* 130:67-8 Jl 20 '87
Conroy, Frank, 1936-
How sex feels: a reverie. il *Esquire* 107:205-6+ Je '87
Lester Lanin. il pors *People Wkly* 28:79-80+ D 21 '87
Conroy, Pat
Death of a marriage. il *Read Dig* 131:107-10 O '87
The prince of tides [fiction] il *Ladies Home J* 104:109-13 Ja '87
Consanguinity
See also
Incest
Conscience
See also
Guilt
Justice without conscience is dead. J. T. Burtchaell. *Christ Today* 31:26 Je 12 '87
Conscientious objectors
See also
Vietnamese War, 1957-1975—Conscientious objectors
World War, 1914-1918—Conscientious objectors
No benefit of appeal: registration & basic rights. P. J. Riga. *Commonweal* 114:582-4 O 23 '87
SAC sergeant says no to spy flights [D. Cobos objects to espionage missions over Nicaragua] B. E. Johansen. il por *Progressive* 51:12 O '87
Consciousness
See also
Self
Subconsciousness
Make believers [therapeutic use of enhanced states; work of M. M. Watkins] R. Katz. il *Omni* 10:126-8+ N '87
Conscription, Military *See* Military service, Compulsory
Consent (Law)
See also
Informed consent (Medical law)
ConSern Program
Banks, colleges design new student loan program. *Jet* 72:22 My 4 '87
Conservation and Research Center *See* Smithsonian Institution. Conservation and Research Center
Conservation areas *See* Wilderness areas
Conservation associations *See* Environmental associations
Conservation awards *See* Conservation of resources—Awards
Conservation biology (Periodical)
For those biologists who want to save life as well as study it, a sense of hope is the most important equipment. J. P. Wiley, Jr. *Smithsonian* 18:30+ Ag '87
Conservation easements *See* Easements
Conservation law *See* Conservation of resources—Laws and regulations
Conservation movement *See* Environmental movement
Conservation of books *See* Books—Conservation and restoration
Conservation of historic sites *See* Historic houses, sites, etc.
Conservation of resources
See also
Energy conservation
Environmental movement
Environmental policy
Estuarine area conservation
Forest conservation
Nature conservation
Reclamation of land
Shore protection
Soil conservation
United Nations. Committee on Natural Resources
United States. Dept. of the Interior
Water conservation
Watersheds
Wilderness areas
Wildlife conservation
Artificial intelligence and natural resource management. R. N. Coulson and others. bibl f il *Science* 237:262-7 Jl 17 '87
Conservation. G. Reiger. See issues of Field & Stream
The great outdoors. J. Walter. See issues of Successful Farming beginning February 1987
Taking a count of threats [natural resource inventories and monitoring in the national parks] R. Cahn. il *Natl Parks* 61:33-4 Jl/Ag '87
Awards
NPCA names Sen. Graham Conservationist of Year. il por *Natl Parks* 61:36 Ja/F '87

NWF "Connie" Awards presented to the nation's top conservationists. il *Natl Wildl* 25:27 Je/Jl '87
Wayne Trimm receives Ernest F. Trad Award. il por *Conservationist* 41:56 Mr/Ap '87
Economic aspects
The Midas touch. G. Reiger and M. Nichols. *Field Stream* 91:14+ Ja '87
International aspects
See also
International Union for Conservation of Nature and Natural Resources
Laws and regulations
See also
Endangered Species Act (1973)
Wildlife conservation—Laws and regulations
The unrealized potential of SARA: mobilizing new protection for natural resources [superfund; with editorial comment by Alan McGowan] T. Atkeson and R. C. Dower. bibl f *Environment* 29:2, 6-8+ My '87
Periodicals
See also
Audubon (Periodical)
The longer view. P. Steinhart. il *Audubon* 89:10+ Mr '87
Central America
See also
Centro Agronómico Tropical de Investigación y Enseñanza
New Mexico
In New Mexico: desert healer [work of A. Savory] G. Ehrlich. il por *Time* 130:10-11 D 7 '87
United States
See Conservation of resources
Conservation of works of art *See* Art—Conservation and restoration
Conservation Reserve Program (U.S.) *See* United States. Dept. of Agriculture. Conservation Reserve Program
Conservation tillage *See* Tillage
Conservationists *See* Ecologists
Conservatism
See also
Concerned Women for America
Democratic Leadership Council
Heritage Foundation (Washington, D.C.)
Liberty Federation
Moral Majority
Philadelphia Society
50-plussers are conservatives at heart! [mellowness of maturity] W. F. Buckley. il pors *50 Plus* 27:56-60 Mr '87
AIDS becomes a political issue. A. Stanley. il *Time* 129:24 Mr 23 '87
Ambitions and strategies of the religious right [contenders for the 1988 Republican presidential nomination] M. Negri. *Humanist* 47:29-32 My/Je '87
Apocalypse now and then [views of J. Burnham] J. B. Judis. *New Repub* 197:29-30+ Ag 31 '87
As the new right stumbles, its PACs pick up speed. R. Fly. il *Bus Week* p72-3 Mr 2 '87
As the right searches for a champion— [presidential candidates] G. Borger. il *U S News World Rep* 102:25-6 F 2 '87
Backing away from Armageddon [right wing criticism of Reagan as peacemaker] D. Schorr. *New Leader* 70:3-4 D 28 '87
The Columbus argument. D. C. Stove. *Commentary* 84:57-8 D '87
Conservatism [discussion of October 1986 article, Our conservatism and theirs] B. Berger and P. L. Berger. *Commentary* 83:6-8+ F '87
A conservative makes a final plea [Reagan agenda and legacy] P. Buchanan. il por *Newsweek* 109:23-6 Mr 30 '87
A convert's convictions [views of C. W. Colson] il por *Newsweek* 110:10 O 19 '87
Dateline Washington: the conservative crackup. S. Blumenthal. *Foreign Policy* 69:166-88 Wint '87/'88
Death of a conservative [T. Dolan] J. Alter. il *Newsweek* 109:23 Ja 12 '87
Disowning the Surgeon General [C. E. Koop excoriated] P. Schlafly and P. Weyrich. *Harpers* 275:16-17 Ag '87
Do conservatives discriminate against blacks? *Society* 25:4+ N/D '87
Don't count out conservatism. I. Kristol. il *N Y Times Mag* p30+ Je 14 '87
A fall from grace on the right [views of Surgeon-General C. E. Koop] D. deF. Whitman. il por *U S News World Rep* 102:27-8 My 25 '87
For want of a nail [losing the Bork fight] M. Gallagher. il *Natl Rev* 39:32+ N 20 '87

Conservatism—*cont.*

Fulfilling the promise of American life [address, February 19, 1987] J. A. Courter. *Vital Speeches Day* 53:398-400 Ap 15 '87

Geek House [Georgetown University's Right House, a conservatives-only group house] C. Lane. *New Repub* 196:16-17 Ja 5-12 '87

George Will among the polysyllables. W. A. Henry. il por *Esquire* 107:87-92 Ja '87

The Ginsburg generation. *Nation* 245:577 N 21 '87

How the new right is undermining Howard Baker [aides G. L. Bauer and T. K. Cribb] R. Fly. il por *Bus Week* p43 S 21 '87

INF deal faces conservative opposition. L. V. Sigal. il *Bull At Sci* 43:14-16 My '87

Is Reagan conservative? C. Krauthammer. *New Repub* 197:12-14 Jl 27 '87

It dare not speak its name: fear and self-loathing on the gay right. C. Hitchens. *Harpers* 275:70-2 Ag '87

Kemp and the cons. F. Barnes. *New Repub* 197:10+ D 28 '87

The kosher majority [Orthodoxy and political conservatism] D. Feder. *Natl Rev* 39:40+ Ap 10 '87

Letter from Washington [conservatives and the INF Treaty] Cato. *Natl Rev* 39:11 D 31 '87

Letter from Washington [young conservatives] Cato. *Natl Rev* 39:15 My 8 '87

Life after the Red menace [conservatives' split] G. Borger. il *U S News World Rep* 103:41-2 D 21 '87

Lost momentum [the religious right; interview with C. F. H. Henry] B. Spring. il por *Christ Today* 31:30-2 S 4 '87

The mouse that roars [G. L. Bauer] J. B. Judis. *New Repub* 197:23-5 Ag 3 '87

Nice guys do finish first—just ask Al Simpson. D. Harbrecht. por *Bus Week* p94 N 9 '87

No right-on for Reagan. G. J. Church. il *Time* 130:25 S 14 '87

On the problem of America's policy myopia [address, October 22, 1986] E. H. Crane. *Vital Speeches Day* 53:184-8 Ja 1 '87

The political marketplace [right wing elites funded by business] F. F. Siegel. il *Commonweal* 114:113-16 F 27 '87

Putting the arm on rich, right-wing widows [C. Channell's fund raising activities for the contras] G. Hackett. il por *Newsweek* 109:30 Ap 20 '87

Reagan: eyes right [conservatives worried over Reagan legacy] T. Morganthau. il por *Newsweek* 109:20-1+ Mr 30 '87

Reagan's court revolution comes up short. D. Whitman. il *U S News World Rep* 102:27-8 F 2 '87

Red-baiting Ron [conservative criticism of INF Treaty] *Nation* 245:739-40 D 19 '87

Right rock [rock icons from the '60s turn to the right] J. L. Pasley. *New Repub* 196:22 Mr 23 '87

The right wing opens fire [sniping at INF and the summit] R. Watson. il *Newsweek* 110:36-7 N 30 '87

Selective conservatism. *Commonweal* 114:371-2 Je 19 '87

The spirit of Buchanan. *Natl Rev* 39:20-1 My 8 '87

Stop beating around the Bush [cover story] R. K. Dornan. il *Natl Rev* 39:32-4 N 6 '87

When right isn't right. M. Greenfield. il *Newsweek* 109:88 My 4 '87

Whom are the conservatives backing? [1988 presidential race] W. F. Buckley. *Natl Rev* 39:56-7 My 22 '87

Why the Reagan era won't end in 1989. R. Fly and others. il por *Bus Week* p33 Jl 13 '87

Will the Senate kill the treaty? [INF Treaty] T. Morganthau. il *Newsweek* 110:29 D 21 '87

The young pol's guide to the brave new world [grueling confirmation hearings] D. Brooks. il *Natl Rev* 39:28-30+ Ap 10 '87

Anecdotes, facetiae, satire, etc.

Literacy on the right. D. Seligman. il *Fortune* 116:133 S 14 '87

Nuts to nomenclature. R. Baker. il *N Y Times Mag* p20 Ag 16 '87

Conferences

The backstabbers [Conservative Political Action Conference] D. Corn. *Nation* 244:276-7 Mr 7 '87

Minority report [Second Thoughts Conference] C. Hitchens. *Nation* 245:511+ N 7 '87

The second thinkers [Second Thoughts Conference] A. Cockburn. *Nation* 245:475 O 31 '87

Tacking further to the right [J. Kemp's appearance at Conservative Political Action Conference] L. I. Barrett. il por *Time* 129:19 Mr 2 '87

Washington diarist [Second Thoughts Conference] M. Peretz. *New Repub* 197:42 N 9 '87

Federal aid

A taste for pork. C. Coulson. *New Repub* 196:18-20 Mr 2 '87

Periodicals

See also
Federalist paper

France

Fanning French fears [presidential candidate J.-M. Le Pen] R. Bernstein. il por *N Y Times Mag* p50+ O 4 '87

New fire on the far right [J.-M. Le Pen emerges as a serious force in presidential politics] W. R. Doerner. il por *Time* 129:40 Je 8 '87

The summer of French discontent. J. Valls-Russell. il *New Leader* 70:8-9 S 21 '87

Great Britain

The Heritage Foundation goes abroad [cover story] il *Nation* 244:747+ Je 6 '87

United States

See Conservatism

Western Europe

"Full steam ahead for conservatism". il *Fortune* 116:8 Jl 6 '87

Conservative Judaism *See* Judaism

Conservative Party (Canada)

A dissident is shut out [Alberta Tory MP D. Kilgour disciplined for comments about lack of party commitment to the West] por *Macleans* 100:13 Ap 20 '87

Fortunately they forgot Quebec [rejection of capital punishment] A. Fotheringham. il *Macleans* 100:52 Jl 13 '87

Government under siege [accusations of Tory corruption] M. Janigan and A. Wilson-Smith. il *Macleans* 100:10-12 F 16 '87

A hint of election fever [B. Mulroney's provincial tour] M. Janigan. il pors *Macleans* 100:12-13 N 30 '87

How the free-trade talks are clobbering Canada's Tories. E. B. Terry. il *Bus Week* p61 Mr 9 '87

It is déjà vu all over again [Tories out of favor] S. MacLeod. por *Macleans* 100:84 F 2 '87

Mulroney's new offensive [government scandals] M. Janigan. il por *Macleans* 100:6-8 F 23 '87

A new senator's troubled debut [J. Bazin's involvement in Oerlikon land speculation controversy] M. Gee. il por *Macleans* 100:14 F 16 '87

A political minefield [resignation of Canadian transport minister A. Bissonnette over land sale to Oerlikon Aerospace; special section; with editorial comment by Kevin Doyle] il pors *Macleans* 100:2, 8-9+ F 2 '87

The tastes of the Mulroney family [use of Conservative Party donations to renovate official residences] M. Janigan. il por *Macleans* 100:13 Ap 27 '87

Temperatures rising [free trade debate] M. Janigan. il *Macleans* 100:10-12 N 9 '87

The Tories strike back [resignation of A. Bissonnette over land sale to Oerlikon Aerospace in Quebec] M. Gee. il por *Macleans* 100:10-11 F 9 '87

The Tory revival plan [upcoming barrage of policy initiatives] M. Rose. il *Macleans* 100:10-11 Je 1 '87

A Tory who refuses to toe the line [F. Jourdenais] M. Clark. il por *Macleans* 100:18 N 2 '87

Turning up the heat [L. Grossman's Ontario campaign] S. Aikenhead. il por *Macleans* 100:8-9 Ag 31 '87

'Yukon Erik' steps down [Tory MP E. Nielsen] C. Barrett. il por *Macleans* 100:26 F 2 '87

Conservative Party (Great Britain)

Thatcher is looking more like a three-time winner. R. A. Melcher. il *Bus Week* p53 Ap 13 '87

Thatcher on dangerous ground [poll tax scheme] N. Gelb. il *New Leader* 70:5-6 N 2 '87

Conservative political action committees *See* Political action committees

The conservatives [television program] *See* Television program reviews—Single works

Conservatories *See* Greenhouses

Considine, Tim

Hi, spy! il *N Y Times Mag* p8 Jl 26 '87

Consolidated Foods Corp.

See also
Sara Lee Corp.

Consolidated Gold Fields plc

Munk's glittering gamble [purchase of Consolidated Gold Fields stock by Barrick Resources] D. Jenish. il por *Macleans* 100:22-3 Ja 12 '87

Consolidated Hydro Inc.

A power company that could heat up. J. M. Laderman. *Bus Week* p82 Ja 26 '87

The value of a dam. J. Merwin. il por *Forbes* 139:160 Mr 23 '87

Consolidated Rail Corporation
Arriving soon: the biggest-ever IPO [initial public offering] il *Fortune* 115:9 Mr 30 '87
Conrail sale aids bankers. M. A. Fortune. *Black Enterp* 17:22 Ap '87
The Conrail sale: how much is it worth? C. Hawkins and C. S. Eklund. il *Bus Week* p78+ Mr 23 '87
Is this any way to sell a railroad? [public offering] L. Smith. il *Fortune* 115:91-2+ My 25 '87

Consolidated Stores Corp.
Can the closeout king unload its woes? S. Phillips. il por *Bus Week* p94 D 7 '87

Consortium for Superconducting Materials and Instrumentation
Superconductivity consortium pursues aerospace applications. il *Aviat Week Space Technol* 127:59+ N 16 '87

Consortiums, Social agency *See* Social agencies—Cooperation

Conspiracy
Conspiracy theories [basis of criminal prosecutions in Iran arms-contra aid case] il *Time* 129:33 My 25 '87

Conspiracy: the trial of the Chicago 8 [television program] *See* Television program reviews—Single works

Constable, Pamela
Pinochet's grip on Chile. bibl f *Curr Hist* 86:17-20+ Ja '87

Constants, Physical *See* Physical constants

Constellation Growth Fund
A patient card player's picks [interview with H. Hutzler] J. P. Newport, Jr. il por *Fortune* 116:176 N 9 '87

Constellations
See also
Pleiades
The backyard astronomer:
Aries. il *Astronomy* 15:110-13 O '87
Bootes. il *Astronomy* 15:102-5 My '87
Caelum, Columba, Pictor. il *Astronomy* 15:110-13 D '87
Camelopardalis. il *Astronomy* 15:102-5 Ja '87
Cancer, Hydra. il *Astronomy* 15:106-9 Mr '87
Cassiopeia. il *Astronomy* 15:86-9 Ag '87
Delphinus, Sagitta. il *Astronomy* 15:102-4 S '87
Draco. il *Astronomy* 15:106-9 Ap '87
Fornax. il *Astronomy* 15:106-9 N '87
Lupus, Norma. il *Astronomy* 15:102-5 Je '87
Pavo. il *Astronomy* 15:94-7 Jl '87
Vela, Pyxis. il *Astronomy* 15:94-7 F '87
Eye on the sky. R. Burnham. *See* issues of Astronomy beginning May 1986
Finding variable stars by fishhooks, lampshades, and candlesticks. G. Dyck. il *Sky Telesc* 73:658-9 Je '87
The Perseus flasher: mystery solved! [momentary reflections of sunlight by rotating artificial satellites] *Sky Telesc* 73:604 Je '87
Perseus flasher: satellite glints [momentary reflections of sunlight by rotating artificial satellites] *Sci News* 131:397 Je 20 '87
Rambling through the skies. G. Lovi. *See* issues of Sky and Telescope
Summer reverie with Cygnus overhead. J. J. Falout. il *Astronomy* 15:24+ Je '87
What's in the Bootes void? [work of Robert P. Kirshner and others] il *Sky Telesc* 74:232-3 S '87

Constipation
Digestive distress! Signals of a system in trouble. J. I. Stern and D. Carroll. il *Redbook* 169:90-1+ Ag '87

Constitution (Frigate)
"Her thunders shook the mighty deep". H. Holzer. il *Am Hist Illus* 22:24-31 N '87
"The most remarkable series of naval tactics and maneuvers ever known". E. S. Maclay. il *Am Hist Illus* 22:16-17 N '87
"Not a look of fear was seen" [USS Constitution vs. HMS Guerrière; cover story] J. Seiken. il *Am Hist Illus* 22:12-15+ N '87

Constitutional amendments *See* United States. Constitution—Amendments

Constitutional conventions
See also
United States. Constitutional Convention (1787)
How hard it is to change. M. F. Berry. il *N Y Times Mag* p93-4+ S 13 '87
If a convention were held today. L. Kravitz. il *Sch Update* 120:14 S 4 '87
Is it broke? Should we fix it? Changing the Constitution is not easy, but plenty of people keep trying. R. Lacayo. il map *Time* 130:54-5 Jl 6 '87

Letting 'We the people' speak [fear of a runaway constitutional convention; cover story] R. S. Kay. il *New Leader* 70:8-10 Jl 13-27 '87

Constitutional law
See also
Civil rights
Civil supremacy over the military
Due process of law
Equality before the law
Judicial review
Rule of law
Separation of powers
Veto

Constitutions
See also
Canada. Constitution
Great Britain. Constitution
Haiti. Constitution
Korea (South). Constitution
Nicaragua. Constitution
Philippines. Constitution
Soviet Union. Constitution
Space constitution
United States. Constitution
Custom framer [A. P. Blaustein] il por *Life* 10:92 Fall '87
A gift to all nations: America's example has inspired documents of every imaginable hue. J. Greenwald. il *Time* 130:92-3+ Jl 6 '87

Constraint logic programming *See* Logic programming

Construcciones Aeronauticas SA
Spanish/Indonesian CN-235 transport nears initial commercial operations [pilot report; cover story] R. R. Ropelewski. il *Aviat Week Space Technol* 126:102-3+ Ap 27 '87

Construction equipment
See also
Conveying equipment
Tower cranes

Construction equipment industry
See also
Caterpillar Inc.
Petroleum equipment industry

Construction industry
See also
American Continental Corp.
Black contractors
Building materials industry
Cardinal Industries
Contractors
Directions Metropolitan (Firm)
Fusco Corporation
H. J. Russell Construction Co., Inc.
Highway engineering
International American Homes Inc.
Peter Kiewit Sons, Inc.
Ryan Homes, Inc.
Ryland Group Inc.
Sabine Consolidated Inc.
Schiavone Construction Company
Space Master Enterprises Inc.
U.S. Home Corp.
Building toward 'shakeout city'. E. Spragins. il *Bus Week* p112 Ja 12 '87
Construction. J. Willoughby. il *Forbes* 139:108+ Ja 12 '87
Construction economy outlook: down we go but, with luck, not too far. G. A. Christie. il *Archit Rec* 175:38+ N '87
Construction economy outlook: winding down the up cycle. G. A. Christie. il *Archit Rec* 175:39+ My '87
Construction-economy update: rising interest rates won't help the short-term outlook. G. A. Christie. il *Archit Rec* 175:37+ S '87
Construction heads into the doldrums. W. B. Franklin and J. C. Cooper. *Bus Week* p30 S 14 '87
Finance: improvement in trade renews our real growth. P. E. Kidd. il *Archit Rec* 175:44 Ag '87
Healthy housing. T. May, Jr. il *Fortune* 115:54 Ap 27 '87
Homebuilders won't come to the rescue. W. B. Franklin and J. C. Cooper. il *Bus Week* p21-2 Ag 3 '87
Interest rates may nail housing. W. B. Franklin and J. C. Cooper. il *Bus Week* p27-8 My 4 '87
Rising interest rates dim economic prospects. P. E. Kidd. il *Archit Rec* 175:43 Je '87
The roof won't fall in on the housing market. S. Toy. il *Bus Week* p27 Je 29 '87
Slump in dollar's value clouds interest-rate outlook. P. E. Kidd. il *Archit Rec* 175:41 Mr '87

Construction industry—*cont.*
Whither housing in the next decade? J. M. Abraham. il *Archit Rec* 175:33 Ap '87

Acquisitions and mergers

Pyrrhic possibilities [NV Homes' acquisition of Ryan Homes] K. Hannon. il por *Forbes* 139:94 Je 15 '87

Ethical aspects

Crafty builders palm dollars earmarked for escrow. H. Porter. il *Fam Handyman* 37:14 Jl/Ag '87

Federal aid

Government backing of research and development in construction urged. P. Hoffmann. il *Archit Rec* 175:37 Jl '87

Securities

No bust in sight for these builders. J. Mendes. il *Fortune* 115:302 Ap 27 '87

Taxation

Adjusting to tax reform will slow real growth in the first half of the year. P. E. Kidd. il *Archit Rec* 175:31 Ja '87

Taking it on the chin: what tax reform means to the construction industry and you. J. M. Abraham. il *Archit Rec* 175:39+ F '87

Hawaii

Peacocks, geysers, marble stallions—Mr. Mega-Resort strikes again [C. Hemmeter] J. B. Levine. il por *Bus Week* p64-5 Mr 30 '87

Construction materials *See* Building materials

Constructivism

Gabo's progeny [influence of N. Gabo's work on contemporary American sculptors] C. Nadelman. il por *Art News* 86:123-7 D '87

Consultants

See also
  Business consultants
  Computer consultants
  Executive search consultants
  Image consultants
  Marketing consultants
  Personal shoppers
  Political consultants
  Public relations consultants
  Real estate consultants
  Tax consultants
  Wine consultants

Consultative Group on International Agricultural Research

Report on reports: Partners against hunger. D. Pimentel. bibl f *Environment* 29:25-7 S '87

Consumer complaints *See* Complaints

Consumer education *See* Consumer protection

Consumer Electronics Show

CES picks and pans [Super VHS] M. Riggs. il *High Fidel* 37:3 S '87

CES report: video moves further into mainstream markets. *Publ Wkly* 231:358+ Ja 30 '87

CES show stoppers. W. Burton. il *Stereo Rev* 52:66-70 Ap '87

CES show stoppers. W. Burton. il *Stereo Rev* 52:12-16 S '87

Consumer Electronics update. W. J. Hawkins. il *Pop Sci* 230:22+ Ap '87

Drumming up interest at the electronic show of shows. M. Schiffres. il *U S News World Rep* 102:54-5 Ja 26 '87

Electronics roundup [camcorders] P. Sealfon. il *Petersens Photogr Mag* 16:12+ S '87

For the fan of tomorrow [high tech sports equipment] R. Cahan. il *Sport Mag* 78:83-4 S '87

Games bounce back. J. B. Meigs. il *Pop Mech* 164:28+ O '87

Look, listen, and smile. W. J. Hawkins. il *Pop Sci* 231:22+ S '87

Pieces of '88. R. Long and E. B. Meyer. il *High Fidel* 37:40-1+ S '87

Products at an exhibition [cover story] R. Long and E. B. Meyer. il *High Fidel* 37:44-55 Ap '87

Road warriors 1987 [auto sound systems] J. C. Taylor. il *High Fidel* 37:46-8+ My '87

Sight and sound: DAT's what it's all about. H. Fantel. il *Opera News* 52:48+ N '87

Sight and sound: odds-on favorites. H. Fantel. il *Opera News* 51:52-3 Mr 14 '87

Summer CES: an abbreviated look. J. Augustine. il *Petersens Photogr Mag* 16:6 Ag '87

Taking the fifth [camcorders at the Winter Show] G. Schaub and E. Stecker. il *Pop Photogr* 94:74-5 Ap '87

Video sales market continues to expand. il *Publ Wkly* 231:39-40 Je 26 '87

Consumer fraud *See* Fraud

Consumer goods *See* Commercial products

Consumer loans *See* Loans, Personal

Consumer Price Index *See* Price indexes

Consumer Price Index futures *See* Price index futures

Consumer Product Safety Commission (U.S.) *See* U.S. Consumer Product Safety Commission

Consumer protection

See also
  Citizens Utility Board (Ill.)
  Consumer reports (Periodical)
  Consumers' research magazine
  Consumers Union of United States
  Quality of products
  Warranty

Are you buying used goods? H. R. Kennedy. *U S News World Rep* 103:75 D 14 '87

Consumer tips. See issues of Consumers' Research Magazine

Consuming interest. K. Freifeld. See issues of Health (New York, N.Y.) beginning July 1984

It's still full speed ahead for Ralph Nader. I. Wolfman. il por *50 Plus* 27:24-7 N '87

Speaker for the house. J. Keely. See issues of Good Housekeeping

History

The Constitution and the consumer: discovering the connections. W. F. Janssen. il *FDA Consum* 21:8-11 S '87

Ralph Nader [interview] W. Greider. il por *Roll Stone* p115-16+ N 5-D 10 '87

Laws and regulations

See also
  U.S. Consumer Product Safety Commission
  United States. Federal Trade Commission
  United States. Food and Drug Administration

Dateline Washington. See issues of Consumers' Research Magazine

Product liability legislation. *Congr Dig* 66:3-32 Ja '87

Consumer relations *See* Customer relations

Consumer reports (Periodical)

Memo to members. R. H. Karpatkin. See issues of Consumer Reports

When Consumer reports talks, buyers listen—and so do companies. M. Bluestone. il *Bus Week* p135 Je 8 '87

Consumers

See also
  Aged market
  Asian American market
  Black consumers
  Blind market
  Compulsive shopping
  Consumer protection
  Consumption (Economics)
  Electronic shopping
  Hispanic American market
  Homosexual market
  Middle age market
  Shopping and shoppers
  Singles market
  Women consumers
  Youth market

Consumers Power Co.

Most improved. il *Forbes* 139:120 Ja 12 '87

Consumers' research magazine

Consumers' history. J. W. Merline. *Consum Res Mag* 70:38 Je '87

Consumers Union of United States

CU wins a round in fight to stay out of advertising [use of ratings in Regina vacuum cleaner commercials] *Consum Rep* 52:526 S '87

Consumption (Economics)

See also
  Christmas business
  Cost and standard of living
  Supply and demand

1987 taxes—worse than you think. H. Banks. *Forbes* 139:27 Mr 23 '87

Can the shifting economy keep on an even keel? K. Pennar. il *Bus Week* p27-8 Jl 27 '87

Confidence is up, misery is down—that spells spending. G. Koretz. il *Bus Week* p22 Ag 31 '87

The Consumer Expenditure Survey: quality control by comparative analysis. R. Gieseman. bibl f il *Mon Labor Rev* 110:8-14 Mr '87

Employment and wage changes of families from CE Survey data [Consumer Expenditure Survey] M. F. Kokoski. bibl f il *Mon Labor Rev* 110:31-3 F '87

Fighting the urge to splurge. S. Koepp. il *Time* 130:58-61 D 14 '87

Consumption (Economics)—*cont.*

Gazing into Bergdorf's window. P. Freundlich. *Harpers* 275:73-6 D '87

How the bull market has enriched the economy. J. Berger and N. Jonas. il *Bus Week* p54-5 Ag 10 '87

Job growth explains why consumers keep on spending . . . and interest income may give them more to burn. K. Pennar. il *Bus Week* p24 O 26 '87

Measuring consumer confidence. J. C. Szabo. il *Nations Bus* 75:10 D '87

The question of confidence. R. H. Bork, Jr. il *U S News World Rep* 103:30 N 9 '87

The sacrifice buy. C. Lorenz. *World Press Rev* 34:50 N '87

The shopping malls haven't emptied out—so far [stock market crash] J. Berger. il *Bus Week* p35-6 N 9 '87

Slow wage growth means more sag in sales. W. B. Franklin and J. C. Cooper. il *Bus Week* p23-4 F 9 '87

Some signs that the consumer is alive and kicking . . . and is spending in ways that may help the economy. G. Koretz. il *Bus Week* p24 My 25 '87

What the sober spenders will buy [1990s] A. L. Taylor, III. il *Fortune* 115:35-7 F 2 '87

Why Americans aren't likely to start buying American. L. Therrien. il *Bus Week* p34 N 23 '87

Why higher rates won't clobber consumer spending. G. Koretz. il *Bus Week* p17 S 7 '87

Canada

The confident consumer [results of Maclean's/Decima poll] D. Jenish. il *Macleans* 100:44 N 9 '87

Japan

Is Japan as rich as you think? B. Powell. il *Newsweek* 109:48-50 Je 8 '87

Japan's economic masochism. R. C. Wood. il *Forbes* 140:138+ S 21 '87

A shopping spree starts turning Japan around. L. Armstrong. il *Bus Week* p50-1 Ag 17 '87

Contact dermatitis *See* Skin—Diseases

Contact lens industry *See* Optical industry

Contact lens solutions

Care required to clean contacts. il *FDA Consum* 21:2 D '87/Ja '88

Contact lenses

See also

CooperVision, Inc.

Am I blue! [lenses that change eyecolor] G. Blair. il *Mademoiselle* 93:270-1+ S '87

Are your contact lenses as safe as you think? M. Tolbert and R. E. Lippman. il *FDA Consum* 21:16-19 Ap '87

Blur-less [Hydrocurve Elite soft contact lenses] A. P. Farah. il *Health* 19:12 Ja '87

Bright sights: contact closeup. il *Harpers Bazaar* 120:38 Ap '87

A contact-lens bulletin. *U S News World Rep* 103:63 Ag 10 '87

Eye-opening news for contact lens wearers. il *Glamour* 85:240-3+ F '87

Eyes prefer plasma-coated contacts [work of Hirotsugu Yasuda] J. Raloff. *Sci News* 131:251 Ap 18 '87

More than meets the eye. F. Lunzer. il *Forbes* 140:186+ S 21 '87

A promising look at contact lenses [rigid gas-permeable lenses] C. Schaeffer. *Changing Times* 41:16+ Jl '87

Safer contacts may ease the strain on lensmakers. S. Siwolop. il *Bus Week* p121 Ja 12 '87

Seeing red: lenses for the vision unimpaired [tinted contact lenses] il *Esquire* 108:233 S '87

Soft lens users: clean 'em or weep [risk of acanthamoeba keratitis] R. Weiss. *Sci News* 132:6 Jl 4 '87

Throw-aways. A. Pratt. *Health* 19:20 D '87

What's new in contact lenses. L. J. Brown. il *Good Housekeep* 204:201 Mr '87

Contacts (Employment) *See* Networking

Contadora group proposals *See* Central America—Politics and government

Contagious diseases *See* Communicable diseases

Container gardens and gardening

See also

Bonsai

Flower boxes, planters, etc.

Hanging plants

House plants

Eight ways to save work and water when you garden in containers. il *Sunset* 179:154-5 Jl '87

Four-season showoffs. il *Sunset* 179:108-11 N '87

Managing the unmanageable berries . . . in pots. il *Sunset* 178:52-3 Ja '87

My patio eggplant plantation. N. Bubel. il *Ctry J* 14:61-3 Ag '87

Container industry

See also

Anchor Glass Container Corp.

Ball Corporation

Brockway, Inc. (NY)

Crown Cork & Seal Company, Inc.

Diamond-Bathurst Inc.

Packaging Corp. of America

Shorewood Packaging Corporation

Stone Container Corp.

Tupperware International

West Co., Inc.

Acquisitions and mergers

What keeps Anchor Glass steady: buying shaky rivals [acquisition of Diamond-Bathurst] G. DeGeorge. il por *Bus Week* p72-3 Jl 27 '87

Finance

Packaging. S. Flack. il *Forbes* 139:202-3 Ja 12 '87

Container ships

Malcom McLean's pirate ships. A. D. Frank. il por *Forbes* 139:32-3 Mr 23 '87

Containerization (Freight)

See also

McLean Industries Inc.

Sea-Land Corp.

Containers

See also

Bags

Beverage containers

Bottles

Boxes, cases, etc.

Sacks

Tin containers

Vases

Containment policy *See* United States—Foreign relations—Soviet Union

Contamination

See also

Airplane engines—Fuel—Contamination

Alcoholic beverages—Contamination

Apples—Contamination

Cattle—Contamination

Chocolate—Contamination

Cigarettes—Contamination

Clams—Contamination

Cosmetics—Contamination

Crabs—Contamination

Feeds—Contamination

Fish contamination

Food contamination

Mangoes—Contamination

Mars (Planet)—Contamination

Meat contamination

Milk contamination

Paper products—Contamination

Pasta—Contamination

Potatoes—Contamination

Poultry contamination

Rapeseed oil—Contamination

Shellfish contamination

Trace elements—Contamination

Contamination (Technology)

See also

Clean rooms

Contee, Christine E.

(jt. auth) *See* Sewell, John W., and Contee, Christine E.

Contel Corp.

Comsat is left in the lurch [Contel backs out of proposed merger] S. Payne. *Bus Week* p38-9 Ap 27 '87

The Contel express switches tracks. J. J. Keller. *Bus Week* p39-40 O 5 '87

Contel's revolving door may soon spin again [president J. N. Lemasters leaving] S. Ticer and S. Payne. *Bus Week* p47 My 11 '87

Contemplation *See* Meditation

Contemporary Books, Inc.

Contemporary Books challenges New York and frontlist publishing. M. Reuter. il *Publ Wkly* 231:118+ My 15 '87

LBJ's 'mistress' signs with Contemporary [M. Brown] il por *Publ Wkly* 232:42-3 O 16 '87

Contemporary Crafts Association (Portland, Or.)

Golden service: Portland's Contemporary Crafts Gallery marks its 50th year. J. Van Cleve. il *Am Craft* 47:38-41 O/N '87

Contemporary furniture *See* Furniture
Contests *See* Competitions; Prize contests
Conti, Anthony
            about
Updating a classic. B. Kanner. il pors *N Y* 20:19-20
Jl 13 '87
Conti, Gregory
Back in the game. *Nation* 244:706-7 My 30 '87
Continental Air Lines, Inc.
Airlines follow Continental's lead in setting fares, ticket
restrictions. C. A. Shifrin. *Aviat Week Space Technol*
127:32-3 Ag 17 '87
Can this airline be saved? C. P. Work. il por *U S
News World Rep* 103:37-8 Ag 3 '87
Continental: full planes may not mean full coffers. J.
E. Davis. il *Bus Week* p37 Mr 16 '87
Continental upgrades commuter fleet with purchase of
ATR42 aircraft. D. M. North. il *Aviat Week Space
Technol* 127:40-1 N 16 '87
Continental's Maxsaver becomes a minisaver. C. Hawkins
and J. E. Davis. il *Bus Week* p37 My 4 '87
Eastern will transfer six A300s to Continental. *Aviat
Week Space Technol* 126:34 F 16 '87
Has Lorenzo fired the first salvo in a fare war? C.
Hawkins and J. E. Ellis. *Bus Week* p37-8 S 14 '87
Kind words for Continental [FAA accused of suppressing
critical report] J. S. DeMott. il *Time* 129:30 Ja 12
'87
Lorenzo again faces problems at helm of Continental
Airlines. C. A. Shifrin. il *Aviat Week Space Technol*
127:48-9+ Ag 3 '87
Lorenzo sees Continental's problems easing. *Aviat Week
Space Technol* 127:41 S 28 '87
Operational problems at Newark hub reducing Continental
traffic. M. Feazel. il *Aviat Week Space Technol* 126:44-5
Mr 30 '87
People Express, New York Air merging under Continental
umbrella. C. Preble. *Aviat Week Space Technol* 126:32-3
Ja 19 '87
Plaskett replaced as Continental chief; Lorenzo takes
over. *Aviat Week Space Technol* 127:32 Jl 27 '87
Regional airlines play key role in Continental's pilot
development. *Aviat Week Space Technol* 127:40-1 N
16 '87
Shareholders fail to block Texas Air's Continental buy.
Aviat Week Space Technol 126:32 F 16 '87
Taking over the controls [F. Lorenzo ousts president
T. Plaskett] pors *Time* 130:43 Ag 3 '87
Texas Air, Continental agree on stock price. *Aviat Week
Space Technol* 126:40 F 2 '87
U.S., Australian officials deadlock over Continental Air-
lines schedule. *Aviat Week Space Technol* 126:41 Je
1 '87
What it's like to work for Frank Lorenzo. J. E. Davis.
il por *Bus Week* p76+ My 18 '87
What's keeping new airports from getting off the ground
[Stapleton Airport] M. Ivey. il *Bus Week* p32 Jl 27
'87
            Anecdotes, facetiae, satire, etc.
Milking a deadbeat. R. Baker. il *N Y Times Mag* p18
O 18 '87
Continental crust *See* Earth—Crust
Continental drift
            See also
      Polar wander
Making the world's roof. R. A. Kerr. *Science* 236:911
My 22 '87
The rifting of continents. E. Bonatti. bibl (p128) il maps
Sci Am 256:96-103 Mr '87
Travels of an ancient reef. G. D. Stanley, Jr. il maps
Nat Hist 96:36-43 N '87
Unlocking the amazing mystery of our continent. R.
Schiller. il map *Read Dig* 131:152-6+ S '87
Continental Illinois National Bank & Trust Co. of Chicago
Still drifting after all these years. J. N. Frank. il *Bus
Week* p130+ My 11 '87
Ten on the Richter scale [move into investment banking]
C. Siler. il por *Forbes* 140:96-7 N 30 '87
Tom Theobald has second thoughts. N. J. Perry. il
por *Fortune* 116:92 Ag 31 '87
Tom Theobald's big question. J. N. Frank. por *Bus
Week* p28 Ag 10 '87
Continental Marketing and Research Ltd.
Kamasura contretemps [mail order motorcycles turn out
to be mopeds] T. Carrithers. il *Cycle* 38:93-6 Ag '87
Continental Telecom, Inc.
            See also
      Contel Corp.
Continents
            See also
      Continental drift

Contingent workers
Hi ho, Silver. S. Lee and S. Flack. il *Forbes* 139:90+
Mr 9 '87
The 'just in time' worker. B. Brophy. il *U S News
World Rep* 103:45-6 N 23 '87
Continuing education *See* Adult education; University exten-
sion
Continuously variable transmission *See* Automobiles—
Transmission; Automobiles, Foreign—Transmission
Contou-Carrère, Enrique Jorge
Pulitzer [story] il *Américas* 39:25-7 S/O '87
Contour farming
Native grass buffer strips [modified contour strip-
cropping] J. Walter. il *Success Farm* 85 no5:26AJ
Mr '87
Contours (Cartography)
Contour mapping and SURFACE II. J. C. Davis. bibl
f il *Science* 237:669-72 Ag 7 '87
A contouring subroutine [Basic program] P. D. Bourke.
il *Byte* 12:143-6+ Je '87
Geoquiz. J. V. O'Connor. il *Earth Sci* 40:24 Spr '87
Contra aid *See* Military assistance, American—Nicaragua
Contra aid-Iran arms case *See* Iran-contra affair
Contra Costa County (Calif.)
            Description and travel
Contra Costa's cow country. il map *Sunset* 178:36+ Ja
'87
Contra-Sandinista conflict *See* Nicaragua—Politics and gov-
ernment
Contraband trade *See* Smuggling
Contraception *See* Birth control
Contraceptives
            See also
      Condoms
      Spermicides
Blocks and barriers [tubal infertility risk reduced by
use of barrier contraceptives] *Time* 129:66 My 18
'87
Caveat-laden, the copper IUD returns. *Sci News* 132:318
N 14 '87
Contraception fights STD's [sexually transmitted diseases]
M. Adero and M. Whigham. il *Essence* 17:13+ F
'87
The contraceptive crisis. L. Cherry. il *Glamour* 85:278-81+
My '87
The crisis in contraception. E. B. Connell. il *Technol
Rev* 90:46-55 My/Je '87
Does Miami Vice's Sonny Crockett carry condoms? Is
Dynasty's Alexis on the pill? Did Dallas's Jenna Wade
wear a diaphragm? C. Krupp. il *Glamour* 85:232+
Mr '87
Gerald Zatuchni plays midwife to innovations in birth
control [interview] G. Breu. il pors *People Wkly*
27:101-2+ F 9 '87
Here's a shocker: a contraceptive with electric potential
[electric field device invented by Steven Kaali] T.
Dworetzky. il *Discover* 8:16 Ja '87
Immune to pregnancy. *Sci Am* 256:70 Ap '87
Kids and contraceptives. B. Kantrowitz. il *Newsweek*
109:54-8+ F 16 '87
The most intimate crisis. L. Kleinmann. il *Health* 19:25-8
F '87
New device's advantages over the pill [vaginal ring]
USA Today (Periodical) 115:10-11 F '87
New-tech contraception. M. Fox. il *Health* 19:30-3 F
'87
The newest contraceptive [cervical cap] *Redbook* 168:9
Ap '87
Pill/cancer: another look [protection from ovarian cancer]
Sci News 131:180 Mr 21 '87
'The pill' may not mix well with other drugs. J. Willis.
il *FDA Consum* 21:26-8 Mr '87
The real contraceptive shock [electric field device invented
by Steven Kaali] il *Glamour* 85:92 O '87
The sad legacy of the Dalkon Shield. G. Kolata. *N
Y Times Mag* p120 D 6 '87
Sex, love and the family [cover story; special issue]
il *World Health* p2-27 N '87
Smoking, the pill, and coronary disease [lowered prostacy-
clin levels; studies by Jerry L. Nadler] il *USA Today
(Periodical)* 115:4 F '87
A sound barrier [barrier birth control methods protect
against cervical cancer; research by Ruth Peters] J.
Carpi. *Health* 19:24 Jl '87
'Two birds, one stone' birth control? *Sci News* 131:296
My 9 '87
Update on contraceptives. P. Kripke. *Work Woman*
12:156 O '87
Update: the pill's risks—and benefits. B. D. Shephard.
il *McCalls* 114:85-6 S '87

Contraceptives—*cont.*

Where have all the contraceptives gone? E. Frank. il *Mademoiselle* 93:70+ Je '87

Women's contraceptives: technologies of the future. A. E. Wilbur. il *McCalls* 114:88 Ag '87

Advertising

Networks nix contraceptives ad. C. Holden. *Science* 238:887 N 13 '87

Contract labor

See also

Indentured servants

Contraction, Muscular *See* Muscle contraction

Contractors

See also

Black contractors

Fischbach Corporation

Above all . . . a good roof. S. Carmichael. il *Home Mech* 83:48-9 Ap '87

Hiring a landscape contractor. C. Crandall. il *Home Mech* 83:42 My '87

How to work with a contractor. L. Green. *Good Housekeep* 204:210+ Ap '87

Working with contractors. B. Vila. il *Pop Mech* 164:22+ Ja '87

Ethical aspects

Poor construction: will it pay to sue? T. Tilling. il *Parents* 62:47 My '87

Remodeling woes? Don't get mad, get arbitration. D. Stover. *Pop Sci* 230:83 Ap '87

Contracts

See also

Breach of contract

Collective labor agreements

Commodity options

Labor contracts

Partnership

Put and call transactions

Repurchase agreements

Service contracts

Negotiating a remodeling contract [interview with R. Enfield] J. H. Ingersoll. il por *Home Mech* 83:18-19 Jl '87

Opening the doors to corporate contracts. B. Robson. il *Black Enterp* 17:282 Je '87

What you don't sign can still hurt you [excerpt from What every executive better know about the law] M. G. Trachtman. *Work Woman* 12:26+ Je '87

Contracts, Agricultural

'Contracting is here to stay' [swine] B. Freese. il *Success Farm* 85:50A Ag '87

Contracts, Authors' *See* Authors and publishers

Contracts, Government

See also

Military-industrial complex

Munitions

Privatization

United States. Air Force—Procurement

United States. Army—Procurement

United States. Dept. of Defense—Procurement

United States. Federal Aviation Administration—Appropriations and expenditures

United States. General Services Administration

United States. Marine Corps—Procurement

United States. National Aeronautics and Space Administration—Procurement

United States. Navy—Procurement

$4 billion worth of temptation [corruption of set-aside programs for minority firms as evidenced in Wedtech scandal] W. Shapiro. il *Time* 129:20 Je 15 '87

The 8(a) follies [minority set-asides] il *Fortune* 115:17-18 F 2 '87

Black businessman charges conspiracy behind losses [J. N. Grayson of Univox California, Inc.] il por *Jet* 71:15 Mr 23 '87

Desperately seeking defense contracts [black businesses] D. C. Ruffin. il *Black Enterp* 18:43 D '87

"Give me back my reputation!" [ex-Labor Secretary R. Donovan] G. J. Church. il por *Time* 129:31 Je 8 '87

A good deed that pays. *Consum Rep* 52:329 Je '87

Hello? This is Uncle Sam. Where's my phone system? F. Seghers. il *Bus Week* p102 S 7 '87

How do you chase a $17 billion market? With everything you've got [computer makers campaigning to win government megacontracts] F. Seghers. il *Bus Week* p120+ N 23 '87

'A political snake pit' comes under the spotlight [Wedtech scandal] P. Cary. il *U S News World Rep* 102:22-4 Je 15 '87

The return of the blacklist [Justice Department's use of suspension orders against government contractors] D. Fanning. il *Forbes* 139:84 Ap 6 '87

International aspects

The world's greatest middleman [S. Eisenberg] H. Kestin. il pors *Forbes* 140 Sp Issue:98+ O 26 '87

Canada

The battle of the subs [nuclear subs contract] M. Clark. il *Macleans* 100:16 D 7 '87

Repairs for an image [controversy over awarding CF-18 jet fighter maintenance contract to Canadair] M. Clark. il *Macleans* 100:7 Ja 5 '87

Seeking new salvation [Versatile Corp. seeks contract to build Polar 8 icebreaker] J. O'Hara. il *Macleans* 100:36 Mr 16 '87

Contracts, Marriage *See* Marriage contracts

Contrarian speculation *See* Speculation

Contrast in photography *See* Photography—Light and lighting

Contrast media

Making X-ray procedures safer [Omnipaque contrast agent] il *USA Today (Periodical)* 115:14-15 F '87

Contraves AG

Contraves seeks production contract for Hermes spaceplane bay doors. il *Aviat Week Space Technol* 126:58-9 F 23 '87

Control (Psychology)

Anecdotes, facetiae, satire, etc.

Creativity or control? [what desk tops communicate] M. E. Marty. *Christ Century* 104:983 N 4 '87

Control Communications Standard Committee *See* United States Institute for Theatre Technology. Control Communications Standard Committee

Control Data Corp.

A computer firm rebounds. S. Koepp. il *Time* 129:48 F 16 '87

The corporate perspective [acting as test site for Zenith Data Systems Z-386] S. R. Reed. il *Pers Comput* 11:69 Mr '87

How Bob Price is reprogramming Control Data. P. Houston. il pors *Bus Week* p102+ F 16 '87

Control mechanisms, Cellular *See* Cellular control mechanisms

Control panels (Airplanes) *See* Airplanes—Instrument panels

Control systems, Biological *See* Biological control systems

Control theory of learning *See* Learning, Psychology of

Controlled forest fires *See* Forest fires—Controlled fires

Controllers

New niche for accountants [part-time controller service] il *Nations Bus* 75:12 Ja '87

Controls, Wage-price *See* Wage-price policy

Controls (Accounting) *See* Auditing—Internal control

Convection of heat *See* Heat—Convection

Convenience foods

See also

Cooking—Convenience foods

Food, Frozen

Spam

The fast-food diet. C. A. Pearce. il *Harpers Bazaar* 120:84+ Mr '87

How the food industry is catering to consumers who want it now. M. N. Vamos. il *Bus Week* p88-9 Ap 27 '87

It's 10 p.m.: where can you get some food? il *Glamour* 85:242 Je '87

Meals in store for the future [trade show at Chicago's McCormick Place] L. Shapiro. il *Newsweek* 109:66-7 Je 15 '87

What "lite" and "lean" don't always mean. il *USA Today (Periodical)* 115:3 F '87

Convenience industries *See* Service industries

Convenience stores

See also

Getty Petroleum Corp.

Southland Corp.

Anecdotes, facetiae, satire, etc.

My store of grievances. J. Welter. il *Atlantic* 260:26 Ag '87

Convention against Torture and Other Cruel, Inhuman, or Degrading Treatment or Punishment (1984)

Human Rights Committee reviews reports of four states, considers individual complaints. *UN Chron* 24:45 Ag '87

Torture prevention: dragging our heels. M. D. Wilde. *Christ Century* 104:616-17 Jl 15-22 '87

Convention facilities

See also

Atlanta (Ga.)—Auditoriums, convention facilities, etc.

Denver (Colo.)—Auditoriums, convention facilities, etc.

Convention facilities—See also—*cont.*
   Indianapolis (Ind.)—Auditoriums, convention facilities, etc.

Convention on the Law of the Sea (1982)
Assembly lauds agreement on pioneer investment formula. *UN Chron* 24:82 F '87
United Nations at seabed. M. Schwabe. *World Press Rev* 34:44 O '87

Convention on the Prohibition of the Development, Production and Stockpiling of Bacteriological (Biological) and Toxin Weapons and on Their Destruction (1972)
Second treaty review conference calls for measures to strengthen biological weapons ban. *UN Chron* 23:72-3 N '86
Updating the biological weapons ban. B. H. Rosenberg. *Bull At Sci* 43:40-3 Ja/F '87
Review conference held on Biological and Toxin Weapons Convention [statements, reports, and text of final declaration, September 9-26, 1986] D. S. Lowitz. *Dep State Bull* 86:40-7 D '86

Conventional war *See* War
Conventions
   See also
   National conventions (Political)
Networking update [Black Enterprise Professional Exchange] C. Bullock. il *Black Enterp* 18:26 S '87
Planning exciting meetings and conventions. L. Hazelton. il *Black Enterp* 17:40-1 Mr '87

Convents

Estonia
Photographs and photography
Sisters of the mists. M. Yurchenko. il *Life* 10:134-5+ N '87

Poland
The Auschwitz Carmel [controversy over convent at Auschwitz] *America* 156:206 Mr 14 '87
Learning from history [Carmelite convent at Auschwitz] E. Fleischner. *Commonweal* 114:167-8 Mr 27 '87

Conversation
Converging character [interactions between introverts and extraverts; study by Avril Thorne] P. Chance. il *Psychol Today* 21:22-3 D '87
How to succeed at small talk. il *Glamour* 85:71 Ag '87
How to talk to a boy. D. Seeley. il *Seventeen* 46:306-7+ Ag '87
Interruptions: an equal-opportunity disturber [study by Kathryn Dindia] V. Bozzi. *Psychol Today* 21:15 S '87
Just talkin'. J. Barsness. il *Field Stream* 92:23-5 Ag '87
Never be nervous again [condensation]; ed. by Gaylen Moore. D. Sarnoff. *Read Dig* 131:27-8+ D '87
Seeing connections. K. Kolenda. il *Humanist* 47:43 My/Je '87

Anecdotes, facetiae, satire, etc.
In judgment [1987 Delectations contest] N. Hazelton. *Natl Rev* 39:62-4 O 9 '87

Conversation programs *See* Radio broadcasting—Conversation programs; Television broadcasting—Conversation programs
Conversion, Economic *See* Economic conversion
Conversion franchising *See* Franchise system
Converters, Analog to digital *See* Digital electronics
Converters, Frequency *See* Frequency changers
Converters, Radio frequency *See* Frequency changers
Convertible bonds
15% with little risk. K. L. Fisher. il *Forbes* 139:256 My 18 '87
Falling off a limb at Harcourt [Salomon and Mutual Shares lost on convertible bond gamble] D. Zigas. por *Bus Week* p32 Jl 6 '87
Fence-sitter bonds. B. Weberman. il *Forbes* 139:143 F 9 '87
Judge backs Harcourt in ruling on debentures. *Publ Wkly* 232:12 Jl 3 '87
Rewarding ragtops. J. Edgerton and J. E. Goodman. *Money* 16:8 Ap '87
What you need to know about convertible bonds. T. Tilling. *Parents* 62:54+ F '87
Convertible mortgages *See* Mortgages
Convertible securities
Four ways to tame this bear market. J. Edgerton. il *Money* 16:145-6 D '87
Mr. Convertibles [A. S. Lyons of Value Line convertibles] P. Brimelow. por *Forbes* 139:109 My 18 '87
A note of caution on the rush to convertibles. B. Hitchings. *Bus Week* p158 My 18 '87
Time for a shiny new convertible? R. Brady. il *Nations Bus* 75:57-8 Ag '87

Convertibles (Automobiles)
Allanté: slow off the mark. J. Flint. il *Forbes* 140:204 N 30 '87
On the downside of drop tops. B. Nagy. il *Mot Trend* 39:50 My '87
Rebirth of top-down driving. J. A. Seamonds. il *U S News World Rep* 103:52-3 Jl 13 '87
Two for the road [two-seaters] P. Bedard. il *Esquire* 107:31-2 Ap '87

Design
The breeze is back [open top sports cars from Chrysler] D. McCosh. il *Pop Sci* 230:10+ Mr '87
"A delicate subject" [Cadillac Allante designed by Pininfarina rather than by GM Design Staff] R. Hutton. il *Car Driv* 32:85 Mr '87
Hope springs eternal [Riviera convertible] W. Hoyt. il *Pop Mech* 164:23 Ag '87
Pininfarina heads for the U.S. in a Caddy [Allante] W. C. Symonds. il por *Bus Week* p58-9 F 9 '87
Zero hour in Munich [BMW Z1] P. Frère. il *Road Track* 39:92-3 D '87

History
1948 Type 135 M Delahaye. T. C. Browne. il *Mot Trend* 39:125-8+ D '87
1954 Kaiser Darrin. H. Rasmussen. il *Mot Trend* 39:115-18+ Mr '87
Buick [1954 Roadmaster] T. West. il *Road Track* 39:22 O '87
Saab Sonett I: so neat it is. M. Knepper. il *Mot Trend* 39:110+ N '87

Materials
Plastic BMW [Z1 roadster] D. McCosh. il *Pop Sci* 231:18 D '87

Remodeled automobiles
See Automobiles, Remodeled

Testing
1949 Talbot-Lago T 26 Grand Sport. J. Ethridge. il *Mot Trend* 39:117-19+ Ap '87
1987 Chevrolet Cavalier Z24. D. C. Ross. il *Mot Trend* 39:74-7 F '87
Beauty & the beast: Vette vs. Cobra: 25 years of performance history; cover story. R. Titus. il *Mot Trend* 39:46-9+ Jl '87
BMW 325i Cabrio. P. L. Albrecht. il *Road Track* 39:86+ O '87
BMW 325i Convertible. P. Lyons. il *Car Driv* 33:115-16 O '87
Cadillac Allanté. R. Ceppos. il *Car Driv* 32:81-3+ Mr '87
Chrysler LeBaron Convertible. J. R. Nerad. il *Mot Trend* 39:133-6 N '87
Corvette Convertible. il *Road Track* 38:190-4 Je '87
Gambling with a convertible, gambolling with a convertible [Saab 9000 Turbo] R. Homan. il *Road Track* 38:80+ Ag '87
The heartland highway [traveling U.S. 50 from Ocean City, Md. to Sacramento, Calif. in Porsche 911 Cabriolet] L. Griffin. il map *Car Driv* 32:84-7+ Ap '87
Maserati Biturbo i Spyder. R. Grable. il *Mot Trend* 39:49-50 O '87
Maserati Biturbo i Spyder. L. Griffin. il *Car Driv* 33:51-3+ S '87
More power to the Japanese [Mazda RX-7 Cabriolet and Nissan Skyline GTS-R] J. K. Yamaguchi. il *Road Track* 39:112+ D '87
Performance ragtops [Chevrolet Camaro Z28, Ford Mustang GT, Toyota Celica GT] J. Keebler. il *Pop Sci* 231:26-7+ Ag '87
PM long-term car tests: Dodge Shadow Turbo, Tempo 4WD, Corvette Convertible. M. Allen and J. Oldham. il *Pop Mech* 164:120-1+ D '87
PM's long-term test reports [Corvette Roadster, Dodge Shadow Turbo, Ford Tempo 4WD] il *Pop Mech* 164:53-5+ Ag '87
Porsche 911 Carrera Cabrio. il *Road Track* 38:112-13 Ap '87
Porsche 911 Turbo Cabriolet. B. W. Yates. il *Car Driv* 33:32-7+ S '87
Ragtop fever. il *Pop Mech* 164:71-5+ Je '87
Reliant Scimitar 1800Ti. R. Hutton. il *Car Driv* 33:25 S '87
Road test: the Cadillac Allanté. L. J. Nonkin. *Vogue* 177:152+ D '87
Saab 900 Turbo Convertible. J. R. Nerad. il *Mot Trend* 39:67+ Ja '87
Stop the presses! Chrysler's newest is here! [LeBaron] J. R. Nerad. il *Mot Trend* 39:49 My '87

Convertibles (Automobiles)—Testing—*cont.*
Topless models [Alfa Romeo Spider, Chevrolet Cavalier RS, Ford Mustang, Pontiac Sunbird, Renault GTA, Toyota Celica and VW Cabriolet; cover story] J. R. Nerad. il *Mot Trend* 39:36-41+ My '87
Toyota Celica GT Convertible. T. Assenza. il *Car Driv* 33:113-14+ Ag '87

Converts, Catholic
Of many things [C. B. Luce] J. W. Donohue. *America* 157:282 O 31 '87
Parishes for Anglican usage. J. H. Fichter. *America* 157:354-7 N 14 '87
The R.C.I.A. misunderstood? [Catholic Church's Rite of Christian Initiation of Adults] R. A. Duffy. il *America* 156:385+ My 9 '87

Converts, Jewish
Israel's new conversion crisis [case of S. Miller] R. N. Ostling. il por *Time* 129:75 Ja 19 '87
On becoming a Jew. R. Owen. *Commentary* 84:55-62 N '87

Converts from Hinduism
Hindus vs. Catholics [Catholic priests charged with fostering anti-Hindu attitudes in India] *Christ Century* 104:353 Ap 15 '87

Converts from Judaism
Blessed Edith Stein. *America* 156:354-5 My 2 '87
Edith Stein's early years. J. W. Donohue. *America* 156:7-9+ Ja 3-10 '87
A martyr of Auschwitz [E. Stein] S. M. Batzdorff. por *N Y Times Mag* p52-5+ Ap 12 '87
My mother's conversion. D. V. Segre. *Commentary* 83:27-37 F '87
Saintly passions [Jews protest beatification of E. Stein, also known as Teresa Benedicta of the Cross] D. Brand. por *Time* 129:82-3 My 4 '87

Conveying equipment
Product reports 1988. il *Archit Rec* 175:188+ D '87

Convict labor
Turning penance to profit [P. Eaton instructs other Delaware Correctional Center inmates in prison construction] R. Arias. il por *People Wkly* 27:30-3 Mr 30 '87

Convicts *See* Ex-convicts; Prisoners

Convulsions
See also
Anticonvulsants
Epilepsy
Mapping patterns of c-*fos* expression in the central nervous system after seizure. J. I. Morgan and others. bibl f il *Science* 237:192-7 Jl 10 '87
The miracle of Maranda [hemispherectomy relieves Rasmussen's encephalitis] E. Sherman. il pors *Ladies Home J* 104:48+ N '87

Conway, Gordon R.
Report on reports: Sustainable development of the biosphere. *Environment* 29:25-7 N '87

Conway, John A.
Trends. See issues of Forbes

Conwell, Tommy
about
Local heroes. D. Handelman. il pors *Roll Stone* p68-70+ O 22 '87

Conwy, Peter A. Rowley- *See* Rowley-Conwy, Peter A.

Conyers, John, 1929-
about
Conyers hits plan to open the FBI's arrest records. *Jet* 73:12 N 9 '87
John Conyers asks that Edwin Meese resign. *Jet* 72:29 Ag 31 '87

Coogan, Keith
about
"Adventures in babysitting": the mad movie about the pitfalls of making pocket money. E. Miller. il pors *Seventeen* 46:71-2+ Jl '87

Cook, Barbara, 1927-
about
Barbara Cook: a concert for the theatre [musical] Reviews
N Y 20:139-40 Ap 27 '87. J. Simon
New Yorker 63:127 My 4 '87. E. Oliver

Cook, Colin
about
Leading ex-gay figure resigns counseling post. R. Frame. il *Christ Today* 31:57 Mr 6 '87

Cook, Dan
Taft Broadcasting may become a Carl Lindner production. il por *Bus Week* p37-8 Ap 27 '87

Cook, David
Vintage New York PolaGraphs. il *Petersens Photogr Mag* 16:28-30 S '87

Cook, Floyd W.
about
Fla. man who used child for drug deal collateral jailed. *Jet* 71:32 F 23 '87

Cook, Gerald
(ed) See Taylor, Frank C. Blues singer Alberta Hunter: the forgotten years

Cook, Heather
about
Heather Cook's pint-size publication runs all the Family news that's fit to print. K. Hubbard. il por *People Wkly* 27:101-2 Je 1 '87

Cook, J. Edward
about
The art of mingei at Kuromatsu. H. Junker. il por *Archit Dig* 44:98+ My '87

Cook, Jack
A better cold frame for gardeners. il *Ctry J* 14:63-5 Ap '87
Elm Street revisited. il *Ctry J* 14:52-6+ O '87
General Kline's secret army. il pors *Ctry J* 14:36-41 Jl '87
Headstart garden. il *Ctry J* 14:34-5 My '87

Cook, James, 1728-1779
Festivities in the Friendly Islands [excerpt from Captain Cook's voyages of discovery] il *Courier* 40:12-13 Ap '87

Cook, Janet Saad- *See* Saad-Cook, Janet

Cook, John Michael
about
John 3:16 Cook has saving words for Vegas losers. K. Hubbard. il pors *People Wkly* 27:115-16+ My 11 '87

Cook, Karen
Marketing the 'lowdown on high tech'. il por *Work Woman* 12:74+ My '87

Cook, Kathleen Sue, and others
Adipsin: a circulating serine protease homolog secreted by adipose tissue and sciatic nerve. bibl f il *Science* 237:402-5 Jl 24 '87

Cook, L. Katherine
From songs of protest to hymns of praise. por *Christ Century* 104:279-80+ Mr 18-25 '87

Cook, Lodwrick M.
about
Dancing into the limelight. B. O'Reilly. por *Fortune* 116:62 Ag 3 '87
How Arco is priming the pump. R. Grover. il por *Bus Week* p80+ Je 1 '87

Cook, Marshall
How to write good article leads. *Writer* 100:16-18 Je '87

Cook, Mattie, 1921-1987
about
Obituary
Change por 19:38 Jl/Ag '87. A. Bernstein

Cook, Paul Maxwell, 1924-
about
Raychem: "faster, better, quicker". A. A. Lappen. il por *Forbes* 140:200+ N 2 '87

Cook, Peter
'Misguided' fiscal policies. il *World Press Rev* 34:16 D '87

Cook, Sam
The importance of "tweety birds". il *Natl Wildl* 25:46-7 O/N '87

Cook, Will Mercer, d. 1987
about
Obituary
Jet por 73:25 O 26 '87

Cook, William E.
Adventures of a birder. il *Conservationist* 41:36-41 My/Je '87

Cook, Wilson W., III
Of space walks and wolves: the incredible flight of Voskhod 2. il *Space World* X-1-277:11-13 Ja '87

Cookbooks
See also
Booksellers and bookselling—Cookbooks
My mother's cookbook [discovery of cookbook prompts memories of recently deceased mother] S. Flynn. il por *McCalls* 114:47+ My '87
Authorship
Always a new word on southern cooking [work of J. Egerton and A. B. Egerton] B. Summer. *Publ Wkly* 232:15 Jl 17 '87
La professoressa della cucina [M. Hazan] C. Hemphill. il por *House Gard* 159:24+ My '87
Bibliography
All-American kitchens. L. Shapiro. il *Newsweek* 110:90+ D 7 '87

Cookbooks—Bibliography—cont.

The cookbook shelf. L. Lerman. il *Gourmet* 47:68+ N '87

The cookbook shelf. L. Lerman. il *Gourmet* 47:74+ Mr '87

Cookbooks. F. Fabricant. il *N Y Times Book Rev* 92:38+ D 6 '87

Cookbooks. F. Fabricant. *N Y Times Book Rev* 92:50 My 31 '87

Down-home around the world. M. Sheraton. il *Time* 130:102-3 N 30 '87

Eating right. *Vogue* 177:244 Ja '87

Eating their words. N. Hazelton. *Natl Rev* 39:54+ Ap 10 '87

Food in Vogue. B. Kafka. il *Vogue* 177:488+ S '87

Food in Vogue. B. Kafka. il *Vogue* 177:302+ O '87

Food in Vogue [seafood cookbooks] B. Kafka. il *Vogue* 177:280+ N '87

Food in Vogue. B. Kafka. il *Vogue* 177:128+ Jl '87

Six good cookbooks. K. Haedrich. il *Ctry J* 14:18-23 My '87

Super books for healthy cooks. M. Wagner. il *Women's Sports Fitness* 9:62-3 Je '87

A taste of the New World. A. Cockburn. il *House Gard* 159:38+ Ap '87

Cooke, Bernard

What God has jointed together . . . il *Commonweal* 114:178-82 Mr 27 '87

Cooke, Hope, 1940-

about

Palimpsests. *New Yorker* 63:24-5 Ap 13 '87

Cooke, Jack Kent, 1912-

about

Words that give us strength. C. T. Rowan. il pors *Read Dig* 130:49-50+ Ap '87

Cooke, James *See* Cook, James, 1728-1779

Cooke, Patrick

When doctors refuse to treat lawyers. il *Read Dig* 131:100-4 O '87

Cookery *See* Cooking

Cookie houses, ornaments, etc. *See* Cooking, Ornamental

Cookie industry *See* Bakers and bakeries

Cookie tins *See* Tin containers

Cookies

48 quick holiday cookies [special section] il *Redbook* 170:113-16+ D '87

Bar cookies. il *Gourmet* 47:274 D '87

Biscotti. N. V. Barr. il *Gourmet* 47:108-9+ N '87

Brandy snaps. il *Good Housekeep* 205:32 S '87

Busy woman's cookie collection [Christmas cookies] il *McCalls* 115:118-20+ D '87

Christmas-toy cookies. il *Good Housekeep* 205:96+ D '87

Cookies and wine [Biscotti di Prato and Vin Santo] C. Kummer. il *Atlantic* 259:71-3 Je '87

Cookies, cupcakes & brownies. il *Ladies Home J* 104:112-13+ Mr '87

Cookies for a Hanukkah party [rugelach] il *Redbook* 170:121 D '87

Good little ghosts. il *Redbook* 169:28 O '87

Heartthrob cookies [valentine treats] T. P. Wolf. il *Better Homes Gard* 65:132 F '87

Heavenly angel cookies [Christmas cookies] il *Redbook* 170:23 D '87

Holiday cookies. il *Better Homes Gard* 65:149-50 D '87

Holiday kitchen fun: cookies kids can bake. A. Bailey. il *Parents* 62:175+ D '87

LHJ's cookie collection [Christmas cookies] J. T. Hazard. il *Ladies Home J* 104:162-3+ D '87

Mother's Christmas cookie contest: the top ten. C. Taylor. il *Mother Earth News* 108:90-2+ N/D '87

Recipe of the week [candied window cookies] il *Jet* 73:30 N 23 '87

Spooky cookies [Halloween] B. Greenwood. il *Better Homes Gard* 65:138 O '87

Sweet & speedy: old-fashioned bar cookies. A. Bailey. il *Parents* 62:184+ S '87

When the call's for Christmas cookies. il *Sunset* 179:162+ D '87

You don't have to be southern to appreciate a Moon Pie's gooey sweetness—but it helps. J. Hevrdejs. il *People Wkly* 28:111+ N 23 '87

Cooking

See also

Appetizers

Baking

Barbecue cooking

Braising (Cooking)

Breakfasts

Brunches

Buffet meals

Candy

Canning and preserving

Casserole cooking

Caterers and catering

Chowder

Christmas cooking

Computers—Cooking use

Confectionery

Cookbooks

Curry

Custards

Desserts

Diet

Dinners and dining

Easter cooking

Entertaining

Fondues

Food as gifts

Food mixes

Frying

Gastronomy

Halloween cooking

Ice cream, ices, etc.

Jelly, jam, etc.

Kabobs

Kitchen utensils and appliances

Low calorie cooking

Low sodium cooking

Luncheons

Lunches

Marinades

Mayonnaise

Meals

Menus

Meringue

Microwave cooking

Oils and fats, Edible

Outdoor meals

Pancakes, waffles, etc.

Papillote cooking

Pickles and relishes

Puddings

Quantity cooking

Roulades

Roux (Cooking)

Salads

Sandwiches

Sauces

Skillet cooking

Snacks

Soufflés

Soups

Spreads (Food)

Stew

Stocks (Cooking)

Stuffing (Food)

Suppers

Tarts

Television broadcasting—Cooking programs

Terrine cooking

Thanksgiving dinners

Wedding meals

Wood stove cooking

8 star dishes [recipes from celebrities' restaurants] il *Redbook* 168:110-13+ Ap '87

Cooking from the cupboard [three chefs create meals from foods on hand] il *Ladies Home J* 104:110-14+ My '87

Cook's tour. K. Haedrich. See issues of Country Journal beginning January 1987

Date with a dish. C. Lyons. See issues of Ebony

Easy eating: a month of summertime menus. J. T. Hazard. il *Ladies Home J* 104:118-24+ Jl '87

Fix food fast. J. Nash. See issues of Essence

Food. C. Claiborne and P. Franey. See issues of The New York Times Magazine

Food. M. Greenberg and E. Greenberg. See issues of 50 Plus beginning May 1983

Food editor's tips. M. Ying. See issues of Good Housekeeping

Food first-aid [excerpt from How to repair food] M. Bear and J. Bear. il *Ladies Home J* 104:82+ Jl '87

Food in Vogue. B. Kafka. See issues of Vogue beginning September 1983

Food tips to clip. M. Langan. See issues of McCall's beginning May 1986

From mom's kitchen. il *Teen* 31:67 D '87

From our kitchen to yours. See issues of Southern Living

Gourmet's menus. See issues of Gourmet

Gourmet's pantry. See issues of Gourmet

Cooking—*cont.*

Great chefs, great kitchens [workspaces and favorite recipes of Debbi Fields, Pierre Franey, and Martha Stewart] M. D. Glass. il *Ladies Home J* 104:124-9+ S '87

Great dinners for small families [entrees] il *Redbook* 169:76-9 Ag '87

High-calcium cookery. il *Health* 19:48-50+ O '87

How America eats. J. T. Hazard. il *Ladies Home J* 104:98-106+ Ja '87

In short order. See issues of Gourmet beginning June 1984

Kitchen express. See issues of Parents beginning July 1986

Kitchen management [special section] il *Work Woman* 12:145+ My '87

Kitchen to kitchen. See issues of Rodale's Organic Gardening beginning September 1985 through February 1987

Main dish cookbook. il *Good Housekeep* 204:200-10+ My '87

A matter of taste. R. Sokolov. See issues of Natural History

McCall's cooking school. See issues of McCall's

[Month] menus. See issues of Sunset (Central edition)

The most requested recipes [from newspaper food sections] il *Ladies Home J* 104:114-17+ Ap '87

Now you're cooking. See issues of Seventeen through June 1987

Nutrition all-stars. P. Cobe. il *Ladies Home J* 104:142-5+ O '87

Recipes. J. Nash. See issues of Essence

Simple, but savory, entrées. il *South Living* 22:154+ F '87

Soup or sauce? It surrounds salmon, peas, or chicken. il *Sunset* 178:206+ My '87

Specialties of the house [most often ordered dishes from well-known restaurants] il *Ladies Home J* 104:104-5+ Mr '87

Stocking up [preparing food in advance] K. Lee and A. Branyon. il *N Y Times Mag* p51-2 O 18 '87

Summer cooking. J. Taylor. il *Better Homes Gard* 65:22-5+ Jl '87

Summer's finest: bite into the best. il *Glamour* 85:234-7+ Je '87

Sunset's kitchen cabinet. See issues of Sunset (Central edition)

Where to call to ask questions about food [food manufacturers' toll-free hot lines] *Sunset* 179:158 D '87

You asked for it. See issues of Gourmet

Your kitchen's emergency relief kit. il *Glamour* 85:194 Jl '87

Beer

Recipe of the week [beer barbecue sauce] il *Jet* 72:37 Jl 6 '87

Bibliography

See Cookbooks—Bibliography

Canned food

Canned food entrées. il *Better Homes Gard* 65:125-6 F '87

Cereals

See Cooking—Grain

Cheese

See also
Cheesecake

Churns for the better [American cheeses] L. Land. il *N Y Times Mag* p53-4 F 8 '87

Quick teamwork: cheese and salad. il *Sunset* 179:186+ O '87

Recipe of the week [grits 'n' cheese bake] il *Jet* 73:32 O 5 '87

Recipe of the week [savory cheese ball] il *Jet* 72:37 Jl 27 '87

Stir in flavor with cottage cheese. il *South Living* 22:170 S '87

They look like madeleines, but they're laced with cheese, zucchini. il *Sunset* 179:128 Jl '87

Chocolate

Charming Easter creations. M. Langan. il *McCalls* 114:52-4+ Ap '87

Easy, irresistible chocolate treats. il *Redbook* 168:154 Ap '87

Paris' haute chocolaterie. N. Barry. il *Gourmet* 47:58-63+ Mr '87

Sample a chip off the old chocolate block. il *South Living* 22:194+ O '87

Sensational, sensuous chocolate! J. Nash. il *Essence* 17:94 F '87

Cider

Ways with cider. K. Haedrich. il *Ctry J* 14:26-30 O '87

Competitions

50 winners from 50 years. T. P. Wolf. il *Better Homes Gard* 65:110-18+ S '87

Canadian content in the kitchen [World Culinary Arts Festival in Vancouver, B.C.] M. Gray. il *Macleans* 100:40-1 Jl 20 '87

Making the grade [winners of competition sponsored by Citymeals-on-Wheels] M. Burros. il *N Y Times Mag* p45-6 Jl 19 '87

Mother's Christmas cookie contest: the top ten. C. Taylor. il *Mother Earth News* 108:90-2+ N/D '87

What's cooking? [Seventeen's Now You're Cooking National Competition] C. Gigi. il *Seventeen* 46:91-2+ Mr '87

Winning cooking contests. il *Essence* 18:97-100+ S '87

Convenience foods

See also
Cooking—Canned food

Cornbread mix offers possibilities. il *South Living* 22:119 Ag '87

Have a box of corn bread mix? il *Glamour* 85:324 My '87

No time to cook. See issues of McCall's

Nothing to eat? il *Glamour* 85:330 Mr '87

Peek into my pantry. C. Rossant. il *McCalls* 114:95 Je '87

Pick up a dinner party on your way home. il *Glamour* 85:408 S '87

Quick cooking for career women. J. Nash. il *Essence* 17:78+ Mr '87

Start with a can of pie filling. il *South Living* 22:140 D '87

Anecdotes, facetiae, satire, etc.

Three great meals. W. White. *New Yorker* 63:28-9 Je 1 '87

Corn meal

T.G.I. Domenica. C. Walker. il *Work Woman* 12:144 Mr '87

Dried food

Dried tomatoes add intensity, color, chewiness . . . to an appetizer or butter, with artichokes or pasta. il *Sunset* 178:182+ My '87

Eggs

See also
Omelets
Soufflés

Bunny bonus! 10 terrific ways to use hard-cooked eggs. A. Bailey. il *Parents* 62:170+ Ap '87

Eggs Benedict with a twist. il *South Living* 22:178 S '87

Gastronomie sans argent. il *Gourmet* 47:76-7+ Ap '87

Recipe of the week [ham 'n' swiss scramble] il *Jet* 73:28 N 9 '87

Recipes for eggs-tras. il *Natl Geogr World* 140:23 Ap '87

Fish

See also
Chowder
Cooking—Shellfish
Stew

A 30-minute spicy-salmon dinner. il *Glamour* 85:314 O '87

A 30-minute summer supper [catfish] il *Glamour* 85:190 Jl '87

Bass recipes for large and small mouths. S. Bashline. il *Field Stream* 91:64 Ap '87

A Cajun fish story [blackened fish] K. Haedrich. il *Ctry J* 14:65-7 Mr '87

Catch as chef can [chef R. Palmer of the River Cafe catches, cooks and serves tuna] M. Burros. il por *N Y Times Mag* p75-6 Je 14 '87

The charm of trash fish. J. F. Mariani. il *Mot Boat Sail* 159:32 Mr '87

Fast fish [microwaving] C. Kummer. il *Atlantic* 260:96-9 D '87

Fish: food for a healthy heart. H. Garrison. il *Parents* 62:92-4+ Ja '87

Fish in a flash [microwave] il *South Living* 22:206 Ap '87

Fish is fine on your low-sodium diet. B. E. Templeton. il *South Living* 22:96+ Ja '87

Fish out of water [Gordon Naccarato's Chippewa salmon sandwich] B. Costikyan. il *N Y* 20:62 Je 8 '87

Fish with flair. P. Perry. il *Saturday Evening Post* 259:18-20 Mr '87

Fixing fish. C. Taylor. il *Mother Earth News* 105:76-9 My/Je '87

Fresh fish! [microwaving] il *Good Housekeep* 205:169-70 Jl '87

Giving albacore the Swedish treatment [gravad albacore] il *Sunset* 178:164+ Je '87

Cooking—Fish—cont.

The low-cholesterol meal [sauces to complement fish] S. Bashline. il *Field Stream* 92:31 Ag '87

Micro-way cooking. il *McCalls* 114:113-14+ Je '87

Microwave your fish and game. P. J. Del Giudice. il *Outdoor Life* 179:72-4+ Je '87

The miracle cure for holiday indulgence . . . the new Q.V., a worthy splurge. B. Kafka. il *Vogue* 177:112+ Ja '87

A new angle on trout. A. J. McClane. il *Esquire* 107:36 My '87

New-wave fish. R. Schrambling. il *Work Woman* 12:112-14 O '87

The nine lives of the catfish. A. J. McClane. il *Esquire* 107:25-6 F '87

Northern delights [pike] S. Bashline. il *Field Stream* 92:56 Je '87

Out of the stream, into the frying pan . . . fresh trout. il *Sunset* 179:116-17 Ag '87

Puget Sound gefillte fish [salmon] il *Sunset* 179:192-3 S '87

Quick or Southwest? [broiled swordfish] il *Sunset* 179:206+ N '87

The recipe that launched a thousand boats [blackened redfish] P. Prudhomme. il por *Oceans* 20:12 My/Je '87

Salmon-devilishly good. R. Sax. il *Work Woman* 12:159 Mr '87

Salmon en croûte. il *Good Housekeep* 205:104 Ag '87

Seafood en papillote [salmon and halibut steak] il *Good Housekeep* 204:42 Mr '87

Singing the blues [bluefish] S. Bashline. il *Field Stream* 92:59 Jl '87

Some fry it hot [Bajan fried fish] R. Schrambling. il *Esquire* 108:48 D '87

Steak dinners from the sea. T. Ney. il *Prevention* 39:62+ S '87

Flowers

Cooked or raw, squash blossoms taste and look good. il *Sunset* 179:132+ Jl '87

Frankfurters

New ways with franks. il *Good Housekeep* 204:263 My '87

You dog, you! il *Seventeen* 46:133-4 Jl '87

Fruit

See also
Applesauce

American apple specialties. il *Americana* 15:59 S/O '87

Autumn's apples: 10 quick dishes. A. Bailey. il *Parents* 62:186+ O '87

Avocado gazpacho . . . and more adventure with the July abundance. il *Sunset* 179:136 Jl '87

A citrus sampler. E. Schneider. il *Gourmet* 47:60-3+ Ja '87

Crab apple recipes to smile about. B. Greenwood. il *Better Homes Gard* 65:118 Ag '87

Cranberries! B. Greenwood. il *Better Homes Gard* 65:146-7 N '87

Cranberries—sweet and savory. il *Gourmet* 47:312 N '87

Dried apricots. *Gourmet* 47:206 Mr '87

Dried fruit is always in season. il *South Living* 22:176 O '87

Grape expectations. il *Better Homes Gard* 65:40 N '87

Melon. *Gourmet* 47:168 Jl '87

A most finicky fruit [cherimoya] R. Sokolov. il *Nat Hist* 96:88-91 Ja '87

Mystery citrus . . . kumquats. il *Sunset* 178:76-7, 162-4 F '87

Not your everyday melon. S. Payne. il *South Living* 22:64-5 Ag '87

Orange-wine-herb sauce with berries [compote] il *Sunset* 178:226 My '87

Perfect partners [meat and fruit combinations] il *Redbook* 169:83-7+ Je '87

Persimmons . . . the soft and the hard and the confusing. il *Sunset* 179:102-4+ O '87

Poaching in red wine transforms humble dried prunes. il *Sunset* 178:228 Ap '87

Preserving persimmons. il *Sunset* 179:168+ O '87

Ripe, juicy berries. H. Garrison. il *Parents* 62:119-22+ Jl '87

September's fresh figs meet some new friends. il *Sunset* 179:167 S '87

Spirited fruit [Christmas gifts] il *Sunset* 179:130 D '87

Strawberries. *Gourmet* 47:238 My '87

Tutti fruity. il *Seventeen* 46:346-7 Ag '87

When you find kiwis at a good price . . . cake, tart, seviche. il *Sunset* 179:196+ N '87

The winning kiwi (fruit). J. F. Mariani. il *Mot Boat Sail* 159:63 F '87

Game

Best recipes for game. il *Good Housekeep* 205:182+ O '87

Convenient pheasants. S. Bashline. il *Field Stream* 92:70 O '87

Deer camp recipes (I). J. Zumbo and L. Zumbo. il *Outdoor Life* 179:44 Ja '87

Deer camp recipes (II). J. Zumbo and L. Zumbo. *Outdoor Life* 179:89 F '87

The great indoor venison barbecue. A. D. Livingston. il *Outdoor Life* 179:76-7+ Mr '87

Ground buffalo. il *Sunset* 178:220+ My '87

If there's a successful hunter around your house [venison] il *Sunset* 179:160+ O '87

If you've been intimidated by pheasant . . . il *Sunset* 179:160 D '87

McCall's Thanksgiving game & bird cookbook. il *McCalls* 115:115-20+ N '87

Microwave your fish and game. P. J. Del Giudice. il *Outdoor Life* 179:72-4+ Je '87

Random recipes. S. Bashline. il *Field Stream* 91:78+ Ja '87

The rise of rabbit: hare apparent. J. Etra. il *Harpers Bazaar* 121:116+ N '87

Ruff recipes [grouse] S. Bashline. il *Field Stream* 92:36 N '87

Salam-ease [venison salami] R. P. Stuart. il *Outdoor Life* 179:58-9+ Ja '87

Semiwild game. J. B. Hurley. il *Prevention* 39:90-2+ N '87

Versatile venison. S. Bashline. il *Field Stream* 92:27 D '87

Garnishes

Pretty to look at, good to eat [marinated vegetable garnishes] S. Payne. il *South Living* 22:80-1 Je '87

Grain

See also
Muesli

Know your oats! S. C. Finn. il *50 Plus* 27:62-6 D '87

Oats. il *Sunset* 178:134-6 F '87

Oats: good food for a healthy heart. L. Hoppe. il *Better Homes Gard* 65:64 Ag '87

Recipe of the week [grits 'n' cheese bake] il *Jet* 73:32 O 5 '87

Whole grain side dishes. il *Better Homes Gard* 65:145-6 Mr '87

Herbs and spices

From our kitchen to yours. K. Adams. *South Living* 22:125 D '87

Get a crush on mint. il *South Living* 22:188 My '87

Japanese herbs do great things for simple Western-style dishes. il *Sunset* 179:112+ Ag '87

Put some spice in your cooking. T. P. Wolf. il *Better Homes Gard* 65:74-8+ Ja '87

Seasoning with saffron [seafood stir-fry with saffron] il *Better Homes Gard* 65:105 Ap '87

Sensational summer herbs. B. Livermore. il *Health* 19:38-41+ Ag '87

A side order of sea slugs [Chinese herbal cookery at Emperor Herbal Restaurant, San Francisco] L. Shapiro. il *Newsweek* 110:77 S 14 '87

Spice up dishes with Italian seasonings. il *South Living* 22:168 F '87

Spicing it up. P. G. McWilliams. il *Ctry J* 14:49 Ag '87

Surprising spices. M. Fox. il *Health* 19:46-7+ My '87

When you roast garlic, you turn it soft, sweet, and unassertive. il *Sunset* 179:194 O '87

Leftovers

The day after the feast before [turkey leftovers] C. Claiborne and P. Franey. il *N Y Times Mag* p63-4 N 22 '87

Great ways with meat leftovers. il *Good Housekeep* 204:155 Mr '87

Leftover turkey for company [turkey-cheese puffs] il *South Living* 22:145 D '87

Real meals from doggie-bag leftovers. il *Glamour* 85:300 Ag '87

Turn Thanksgiving leftovers into something special. il *Glamour* 85:336 N '87

Use up that leftover ham. il *South Living* 22:204-5 Ap '87

What do I do with all this turkey? il *Redbook* 170:134 D '87

Liquors

Spirited fruit [Christmas gifts] il *Sunset* 179:130 D '87

Marshmallows

Marshmallow magic. il *Good Housekeep* 205:192 D '87

Cooking—*cont.*

Meat
See also
Barbecue cooking

A 30-minute bistro dinner for two [filet mignon with wild mushrooms] il *Glamour* 85:204 Ja '87

A 30-minute spring preview [pork chops with ginger sauce] il *Glamour* 85:348 Ap '87

The all new ground meat & potato cookbook. J. T. Hazard. il *Ladies Home J* 104:120-3+ S '87

And just a little thinly sliced prosciutto. il *Sunset* 178:204 My '87

Australia's answer to the hamburger? It's meat pie, big or small. il *Sunset* 178:162-3 Je '87

Beef entrées [microwaving] il *McCalls* 115:131-2 N '87

Beef, lamb, pork . . . here are holiday roast showpieces. il *Sunset* 179:133-5 D '87

Bliss is a 30-minute meatball dish. il *Redbook* 169:162-5+ S '87

Crown roast of pork. il *Good Housekeep* 205:72 D '87

A dozen delicious dinner pies. il *Redbook* 168:135-8+ Mr '87

Easy dinner party entrées? Four caterers tell their favorites. il *Sunset* 178:178+ Je '87

The feasts of spring—baby lamb. B. Kafka. il *Vogue* 177:226 Ap '87

Flank steak: the neglected cut. L. Colwin. il *Gourmet* 47:52+ My '87

Florentine beef roulades. il *Redbook* 168:14 Ja '87

Four fabulous meat loaves [microwaving] il *McCalls* 114:115-16 S '87

Gastronomie sans argent [beef chuck] il *Gourmet* 47:94-5+ D '87

Gastronomie sans argent [braised meats] il *Gourmet* 47:60-1+ F '87

The great American meat loaf. F. Ferretti. il *50 Plus* 27:46-9 Jl '87

Great ways with meat leftovers. il *Good Housekeep* 204:155 Mr '87

Ground beef wrapped up in lettuce, rolled up in fila. il *Sunset* 178:160-1 Mr '87

Have you cooked corned beef lately? il *South Living* 22:202-3 Mr '87

Holy cow! Steaks are high [steak houses] J. Stern and M. Stern. il *Harpers Bazaar* 120:72+ My '87

How Italians say shanks [osso buco] J. F. Mariani. il *Esquire* 108:56 S '87

Instant luxury, no waiting [veal chop with wild-mushroom sauce] R. Sax. *Work Woman* 12:157 N '87

Lean meat. il *Sunset* 179:86-97 N '87

Lean meat and little oil . . . for soup, curry, ragout, or chili. il *Sunset* 179:176 N '87

Let them eat meat. J. T. Hazard. il *Ladies Home J* 104:96-7+ Mr '87

Meat loaf, an old favorite. il *South Living* 22:202 O '87

Meat pie essentials. F. Carpenter. il *Ctry J* 14:35-7 D '87

More bad news about that tasty browning [Maillard reactions in meat produce mutagens] *Sci News* 132:25 Jl 11 '87

The new home cooking! [beef and pork recipes] B. Greenwood. il *Better Homes Gard* 65:140-4+ My '87

A new light touch for beef & veal. H. Garrison. il *Parents* 62:170-6+ My '87

Nine quick burgers from one recipe. J. Nash. il *Essence* 18:104 Jl '87

Oranges join with mint to glaze lamb. il *Sunset* 178:231-2 My '87

Pepper chateaubriand. il *Good Housekeep* 205:186 S '87

The perfect hamburger. C. Claiborne and P. Franey. il *N Y Times Mag* p65-6 Je 21 '87

Perfect partners [meat and fruit combinations] il *Redbook* 169:83-7+ Je '87

Perk up your burgers. il *South Living* 22:168 S '87

Quick & easy meat cookbook. il *Good Housekeep* 205:162-72+ O '87

Roast beef with herbs [microwave] il *Good Housekeep* 204:231 My '87

Savor veal. il *South Living* 22:200 O '87

Savory pot roasts. il *South Living* 22:180 O '87

Sensational stuffed entrées. B. E. Templeton. il *South Living* 22:218+ N '87

Summery veal cutlets. il *Good Housekeep* 205:30 Jl '87

Use up that leftover ham. il *South Living* 22:204-5 Ap '87

Veal medallions with mushroom sauce. il *Good Housekeep* 204:110 Mr '87

Mushrooms
The master of mushroom cookery [J. Czarnecki] il por *Mother Earth News* 104:84-6 Mr/Ap '87

Morel conquests. J. H. Lang. il *N Y Times Mag* p47-8 My 24 '87

The shaggy mane. S. Bashline. il *Field Stream* 92:38+ S '87

Nuts
Macadamia nuts. F. Levy. il *Gourmet* 47:82-3+ My '87

Pecans and peanuts, plain and fancy. P. Y. Cordell. il *South Living* 22:156-8 S '87

Pistachio nuts. *Gourmet* 47:154 Ja '87

Organic food
See also
Muesli

Gardeners' kitchen. See issues of Rodale's Organic Gardening through February 1987

Pasta
See also
Ravioli

Fast family favorites: pasta! B. Greenwood. il *Better Homes Gard* 65:122-4 Mr '87

From our kitchen to yours. K. Adams. il *South Living* 22:108-9 Ag '87

Gastronomie sans argent [pasta entrées] il *Gourmet* 47:78-9+ S '87

Italian stir-fry? [tortellini with broccoli and gorgonzola] il *Sunset* 179:190+ O '87

Lee Bailey's fabulous fettuccine [excerpt from Lee Bailey's Good parties] il *Redbook* 168:22 F '87

Macaroni: winning combinations for summer meals. H. Garrison. il *Parents* 62:127-30+ Je '87

One recipe—four international flavor choices [stuffed manicotti] il *Better Homes Gard* 65:78+ Ja '87

Pasta. M. Ying. il *Good Housekeep* 204:140-50+ F '87

Pasta appeal? C. Lyons. il *Ebony* 42:108-10+ Mr '87

Pasta: new sauces, new shapes. M. Scicolone. il *Ladies Home J* 104:122-3+ Ap '87

Pasta perfect. il *Seventeen* 46:159 O '87

Pasta: using the old noodle. il *Saturday Evening Post* 259:78-9+ O '87

Posh pasta. il *Better Homes Gard* 65:111-12 Je '87

Quick and easy pasta special! il *Redbook* 169:145-8+ O '87

Peanut butter
Peanut butter treats. il *Better Homes Gard* 65:171-2 Ap '87

Potatoes
The all new ground meat & potato cookbook. J. T. Hazard. il *Ladies Home J* 104:120-3+ S '87

Potato eaters [glycoalkaloid dangers] E. Collins. *Sci Am* 257:31 S '87

The sweetest . . . potatoes of all. M. Gorman. il *Rodale's Org Gard* 34:58-61 N '87

Try these sweet potato favorites. il *South Living* 22:232 N '87

Warning: peel potatoes before cooking [glycoalkaloid dangers] *Sci News* 132:8 Jl 4 '87

Poultry
See also
Thanksgiving dinners

5 meals from one chicken! il *Glamour* 85:355 Ap '87

A 30-minute spring dinner [chicken with mustard sauce] il *Glamour* 85:318 My '87

Christmas feast with an Oriental flavor [Chinese duckling] A. Simon. il *Saturday Evening Post* 259:18-20 D '87

Cooking with Jacques Pépin [braised duck] J. Pépin. il *Gourmet* 47:211-15 My '87

A country Christmas [roast goose] E. Frell. il *Mother Earth News* 108:84-6 N/D '87

The day after the feast before [turkey leftovers] C. Claiborne and P. Franey. il *N Y Times Mag* p63-4 N 22 '87

Easy dinner party entrées? Four caterers tell their favorites. il *Sunset* 178:178+ Je '87

Everyday turkey dishes. il *Redbook* 168:152 Ap '87

Fast-fixin' chicken. il *Better Homes Gard* 65:49-50 Jl '87

Handle with care: this bird can make you sick [turkey cooking] *Consum Rep* 52:602 O '87

How to roast a turkey. il *Parents* 62:228 N '87

Keep chicken on the menu. il *South Living* 22:208 O '87

Leftover turkey for company [turkey-cheese puffs] il *South Living* 22:145 D '87

Mad about duck. L. Van Gelder. il *Ms* 16:44+ S '87

Marmalade chicken with orange rice. il *Redbook* 170:20 N '87

McCall's chicken cookbook. il *McCalls* 114:89-94+ Ap '87

Cooking—Poultry—cont.

McCall's Thanksgiving game & bird cookbook. il *McCalls* 115:115-20+ N '87

Poultry: go from good to great. J. B. Hurley. il *Prevention* 39:66-8+ My '87

Recipe of the week [sesame chicken nuggets] il *Jet* 73:38 D 14 '87

Sensational stuffed entrées. B. E. Templeton. il *South Living* 22:218+ N '87

Southern fried chicken. K. Haedrich. il *Ctry J* 14:14-17 S '87

Spring chicken! [microwaving] il *Good Housekeep* 204:183-4 Ap '87

"Steamroller" chicken. il *Sunset* 178:72-3 F '87

Stuffed turkey breast. il *Good Housekeep* 205:30 N '87

Summer chicken cookbook. il *Good Housekeep* 205:128-38+ Ag '87

Terrific turkey. L. Hoppe. il *Better Homes Gard* 65:148-9+ N '87

Thanksgiving turkey. il *Good Housekeep* 205:175 N '87

Trimming with turkey. P. Perry. il *Saturday Evening Post* 259:26+ My/Je '87

Turkey casseroles. il *Better Homes Gard* 65:149-50 D '87

Turkey roasting guide. il *Better Homes Gard* 65:179 N '87

Turkey roasting kit. il *McCalls* 115:153+ O '87

Turkey with a twist. R. Kowalski. il *50 Plus* 27:74-6+ N '87

What do I do with all this turkey? il *Redbook* 170:134 D '87

Rhubarb

Rhubarb. il *Better Homes Gard* 65:104 Ap '87

Rice

Going with the grain [risotto alla parmigiana] E. Sahatjian. il *Esquire* 107:26 Ja '87

Not the same old rice [American adaptations of long-grain basmati rice] J. Pruess. il *N Y Times Mag* p49-50 S 6 '87

Pilafs. il *Gourmet* 47:266 O '87

Rice: a versatile southern tradition. il *South Living* 22:182-3 Mr '87

Risotto . . . Italy's creamy rice. il *Sunset* 178:200 Ap '87

Shrimp risotto—the real thing. il *Good Housekeep* 204:212+ My '87

A stirring dish [risotto] C. Kummer. il *Atlantic* 260:90-2 S '87

Worldwide companions: beans and rice. il *Sunset* 178:204 Ap '87

Sausage

Gastronomie sans argent. il *Gourmet* 47:86-7+ O '87

Links with Dixie [Cajun sausage] R. Lundy. il *Esquire* 107:38+ Mr '87

Sausage: a Texas tradition. D. G. Lowery. il *South Living* 22:212-14 N '87

Tamale sausages. il *Sunset* 178:186-7 My '87

Seafood

See also
 Chowder
 Cooking—Fish
 Cooking—Shellfish

Fish and seafood entrées. il *Better Homes Gard* 65:145-6 Mr '87

Food in Vogue [cookbooks] B. Kafka. il *Vogue* 177:280+ N '87

Fresh from the sea [recipes by J.-L. Palladin] J. Nathan. il *N Y Times Mag* p67-8 Mr 22 '87

Microwave mastery:
 Seafood. il *Gourmet* 47:62-3+ Jl '87

Seafood of the desert [Southwest food] S. H. Loomis. il *N Y Times Mag* p47-8 Ag 30 '87

This is a fish fry? il *Sunset* 179:78-9, 164 S '87

Try a seafood entrée for two. il *South Living* 22:186 My '87

Shellfish

See also
 Chowder

A 30-minute seafarer's dinner [sautéed shrimp and vegetables] il *Glamour* 85:402 S '87

Claws for celebration [lobster fricasee] A. J. McClane. il *Esquire* 108:21-2 Ag '87

Deep-sea treasures [mollusks] J. Torrey. il *Health* 19:40-2+ F '87

Dim sum quick and easy [based on puréed shrimp] il *Sunset* 178:148+ F '87

Incredible crab [microwaving] J. B. Hurley. il *Prevention* 39:74 My '87

Luxurious lobster. S. Purdy. il *Saturday Evening Post* 259:92-4 Jl/Ag '87

Oysters are versatile. il *South Living* 22:164-5 F '87

Seafood brochette with a tomato-champagne sauce. il *Sunset* 179:200 O '87

Seasoning with saffron [seafood stir-fry with saffron] il *Better Homes Gard* 65:105 Ap '87

Shrimp & crab puffs. il *Good Housekeep* 205:134 N '87

Shrimp risotto—the real thing. il *Good Housekeep* 204:212+ My '87

Shrimp, wonderful shrimp! il *South Living* 22:116 Ag '87

Start with three dozen steamers. il *Sunset* 178:228-9 My '87

Anecdotes, facetiae, satire, etc.

More than a meal [memories of disastrous Italian octopus dinner] N. Hazelton. *Natl Rev* 39:54-5 My 8 '87

Snails

The trail of the snail. E. Fried. il *Harpers Bazaar* 120:166+ Mr '87

Sour cream

Enjoy the taste of sour cream. il *South Living* 22:158 F '87

Soybean products

Gastronomie sans argent [tofu] il *Gourmet* 47:64-5+ Ja '87

Spices

See Cooking—Herbs and spices

Study and teaching

See also
 Badia a Coltibuono (Cooking school)
 Culinary Institute of America
 École de Cuisine Française S. de Mirbeck

Cooking up a new career. G. Hechinger. il *Glamour* 85:216 Ja '87

A cook's fantasy comes true. A. L. Ball. il *Work Woman* 12:164 N '87

Food for fun [Kids' Cooking Camp at L'Academie de Cuisine, Bethesda, Md.] il *Natl Geogr World* 142:10-13 Je '87

Vegetables go to school [healthful cooking classes] A. Hirsch. il *Rodale's Org Gard* 34:99-103 F '87

What's cooking in Europe: schools with flavor. M. Polvay. il *Travel Holiday* 167:56-60 F '87

Vegetables

See also
 Vegetarianism

25 summer side dishes. J. T. Hazard. il *Ladies Home J* 104:90-1+ Ag '87

Add eggplant to the menu. il *South Living* 22:106 Ag '87

Asparagus . . . with a light touch. J. B. Hurley. il *Rodale's Org Gard* 34:86-9 Ap '87

At last, tomato time. J. Pruess. il *N Y Times Mag* p37-8 Ag 9 '87

Bring on black-eyed peas. D. G. Lowery. il *South Living* 22:72-3 Ja '87

Cauliflower at its best. S. Milius. il *Rodale's Org Gard* 34:40-3 O '87

Cauliflower is best now. il *South Living* 22:172 O '87

Cooking with pumpkin! A classy entrée, a classic pie. il *Better Homes Gard* 65:141 O '87

Corn in the husk [microwaved] J. B. Hurley. il *Prevention* 39:66 S '87

Dieter's delight [low calorie vegetables] P. Vargas. il *Flower Gard* 31:8+ Je/Jl '87

Dried tomatoes add intensity, color, chewiness . . . to an appetizer or butter, with artichokes or pasta. il *Sunset* 178:182+ My '87

Dutiful, wholesome, satisfying . . . celery root is the winter cook's friend. il *Sunset* 178:150+ Mr '87

The fine art of cooking and eating asparagus. P. G. McWilliams. il *Ctry J* 14:51 My '87

Food in Vogue [tomatoes] B. Kafka. il *Vogue* 177:128+ Jl '87

Fresh spring vegetables. il *Good Housekeep* 204:126 Ap '87

Garden cookbook. M. Langan. il *McCalls* 114:113-18+ Ag '87

Gastronomie sans argent [celery] il *Gourmet* 47:112-13+ N '87

Gastronomie sans argent [green beans] il *Gourmet* 47:84-5+ My '87

Gastronomie sans argent [lentils] il *Gourmet* 47:72-3+ Mr '87

Gastronomie sans argent [summer garden harvest] il *Gourmet* 47:64-5+ Ag '87

Get ready for fresh vegetables [cover story] S. Dosier. il *South Living* 22:182-4 My '87

Good-for-you greens. J. T. Hazard. il *Ladies Home J* 104:132-4+ Ap '87

The great pumpkin. il *Good Housekeep* 205:192+ O '87

Cooking—Vegetables—_cont._

The Greens cookbook. D. Madison and E. E. Brown. il *Gourmet* 47:74-5+ Ap '87

The inside scoop on pumpkins. A. J. Sheinman. il *50 Plus* 27:58-60 O '87

It's a wonderful loaf [Andy D'Amico's eggplant terrine] B. Costikyan. il *N Y* 20:50 Jl 13 '87

Little vegetables, big show. il *Sunset* 178:92-3, 182 Je '87

Low-calorie okra! M. Gorman. il *Rodale's Org Gard* 34:42-4+ Jl '87

Mexican vegetables and salads. E. L. Ortiz. il *Gourmet* 47:80-1+ My '87

Micro-way cooking. il *McCalls* 114:131-2 My '87

Microwave mastery:
Winter vegetables. il *Gourmet* 47:64+ F '87

A new leaf [leafy green vegetables] il *Mademoiselle* 93:224-5+ My '87

No-fuss asparagus [microwaving] J. B. Hurley. il *Prevention* 39:48 Ap '87

Paste tomatoes. J. B. Hurley. il *Rodale's Org Gard* 34:38+ Ag '87

Pepper pleasures. J. B. Hurley. il *Rodale's Org Gard* 34:40-2+ Je '87

Pointers for red heads [red cabbage] M. Gorman. il *Rodale's Org Gard* 34:94-6+ F '87

Prime time for pumpkin. J. R. Nyenhuis. il *Saturday Evening Post* 259:90-3 N '87

Pumpkin dishes. L. Furgatch. il *Ctry J* 14:48-51 O '87

Quick-cooking garden fare [microwaving] il *South Living* 22:141-2 Jl '87

Roman meal [artichokes] B. Costikyan. il *N Y* 20:79 Ap 6 '87

Savor sprouting broccoli [Chinese broccoli and broccoli raab] J. H. Sanchez. il *Rodale's Org Gard* 34:46+ N '87

Season's best: crisp garden vegetables. H. Garrison. il *Parents* 62:153-6+ Ap '87

Serve carrots anytime. il *South Living* 22:162 F '87

The Spanish know how to wake up winter vegetables. il *Sunset* 178:160 F '87

Stuffed artichokes Amalfi. il *Good Housekeep* 204:52 Ap '87

Stuffed with style. B. Livermore. il *Health* 19:58-60+ S '87

Sweet taste of summer [corn] O. Woodier. il *Americana* 15:46-50 Jl/Ag '87

Taste tempters from the garden. J. R. Nyenhuis. il *Saturday Evening Post* 259:18+ S '87

They look like madeleines, but they're laced with cheese, zucchini. il *Sunset* 179:128 Jl '87

The tomato and I. D. Massey. il *Gourmet* 47:76-7+ S '87

Turn squash . . . into low-cal pasta [zucchini] J. B. Hurley. il *Rodale's Org Gard* 34:66-7 S '87

Twist on sprouts [Anne Rosenzweig's carrot custard] B. Costikyan. il *N Y* 20:71 N 30 '87

The uncommon artichoke. H. Salloum. il *Saturday Evening Post* 259:20+ Ap '87

Using the old bean. J. Chaves. il *Saturday Evening Post* 259:82+ Mr '87

Vegetable adventure. C. Lyons. il *Ebony* 42:100-2+ Jl '87

The vegetable cookbook [microwaving] il *Good Housekeep* 205:118+ N '87

Vegetables galore! B. Fritz. il *Prevention* 39:74+ O '87

Vegetables go to school. A. Hirsch. il *Rodale's Org Gard* 34:99-103 F '87

Vegetables you can rely on. il *South Living* 22:182 S '87

What makes an onion work? il *Sunset* 178:122-6, 210+ My '87

Winter vegetables. J. Pruess. il *N Y Times Mag* p73-4 N 29 '87

Worldwide companions: beans and rice. il *Sunset* 178:204 Ap '87

Zucchini ideas. il *Better Homes Gard* 65:111-12 Ag '87

Wine

New uses, old wines. C. Claiborne and P. Franey. il *N Y Times Mag* p91-2 S 20 '87

Poaching in red wine transforms humble dried prunes. il *Sunset* 178:228 Ap '87

Cooking, American
See also
Barbecue cooking
Cooking, Black
Cooking, Tex-Mex

All-American favorites. B. Livermore. il *Health* 19:42-7 Jl '87

All-American kitchens [cookbooks] L. Shapiro. il *Newsweek* 110:90+ D 7 '87

American classics [recipes inspired by meals in American literature] il *Ladies Home J* 104:106-9+ Jl '87

The American scene [Ozark forager B. J. Tatum] E. Jones. il *Gourmet* 47:62+ F '87

The best of Southwest cuisine. il *Ladies Home J* 104:160-2+ N '87

Columbus's biggest discovery. R. Sokolov. il *Nat Hist* 96:66-7 Ag '87

Country cooking. il *Good Housekeep* 205:210-20+ S '87

Country style. il *Redbook* 169:111-14+ Jl '87

An elegant sufficiency [J. Egerton's book Southern food] il *Time* 130:76 S 28 '87

Expect the unexpected in new southwestern cuisine. D. Lowery. il *South Living* 22:86-9, 146+ Je '87

Favorite recipes from Kutztown's Country Kitchen. il *Americana* 15:37 Jl/Ag '87

Garden Week in Charlottesville [with regional recipes from Virginia] T. Weeks. il *Gourmet* 47:66-71 Ap '87

Gourmet holidays: Christmas in Nantucket. T. Weeks. il map *Gourmet* 47:66-71+ D '87

Home cooking. D. C. Craig. il *Life* 10:67+ Jl '87

The homecoming [dishes by John E. Sola and Leonard Schwartz] C. Claiborne and P. Franey. il *N Y Times Mag* p33-5 Ja 4 '87

Low Country cuisine [southern cooking] il *Ladies Home J* 104:92-3+ My '87

Making the grade [winners of competition sponsored by Citymeals-on-Wheels] M. Burros. il *N Y Times Mag* p45-6 Jl 19 '87

Manna from Amana. D. Swift. il *Mother Earth News* 107:54-7 S/O '87

McCall's Americana cookbook. il *McCalls* 114:99-104+ S '87

McCall's country favorites cookbook. il *McCalls* 115:135-40+ O '87

Native and natural. B. Livermore. il *Health* 19:62-6+ N '87

New southern cooking [excerpts] N. Dupree. il *Redbook* 168:115-18+ F '87

A road not often taken [work of J. and M. Stern] M. Burros. il pors *N Y Times Mag* p67-8 Mr 8 '87

Roadfood [work of J. and M. Stern] K. Haedrich. il pors *Ctry J* 14:14-18 Jl '87

Seafood of the desert [Southwest food] S. H. Loomis. il *N Y Times Mag* p47-8 Ag 30 '87

A southwestern Thanksgiving. il *Gourmet* 47:114-16+ N '87

Taste of Texas [food show in Manhattan] *New Yorker* 63:32 S 28 '87

Tombstone in the kitchen. K. T. Windham. il *Mother Earth News* 107:72-5 S/O '87

Traditional southern foods go light. B. E. Templeton. il *South Living* 22:102-4 Ag '87

Western classics. il *Sunset* 178:59-67 Ja '87

Cooking, Argentine
Of maize and meat: culinary traditions and cultural identity in Mexico and Argentina. P. Petrich. il *Courier* 40:10-13 My '87

Cooking, Asian
30 minutes to a taste of Asia. il *Glamour* 85:330 N '87

Cooking, Australian
Australia's answer to the hamburger? It's meat pie, big or small. il *Sunset* 178:162-3 Je '87

Australia's damper loaf is basically a large biscuit. il *Sunset* 179:136 Ag '87

Down Under cooking. G. Newman. il *Outdoor Life* 180:56-7+ D '87

From Melbourne meat pies . . . to Brisbane mud crabs. F. Ferretti. il *Gourmet* 47:42+ S '87

Cooking, Austrian
Austria's Burgenland. L. Langseth-Christensen. il map *Gourmet* 47:44-9+ Jl '87

Cooking, Barbadian
Some fry it hot [Bajan fried fish] R. Schrambling. il *Esquire* 108:48 D '87

Cooking, Black
Black heritage cooking. C. Lyons. il *Ebony* 42:120-2+ F '87

Specialties of the house [black women restaurant owners] J. Nash. il *Essence* 18:97-100+ My '87

Cooking, Brazilian
Feijoada . . . it's Brazil's party dish. il *Sunset* 179:92-3 O '87

Hot stuff! J. B. Harris. il *Black Enterp* 18:84 Ag '87

The meal is the message: the language of Brazilian cuisine. R. DaMatta. il *Courier* 40:22-3 My '87

Cooking, Cajun

Cajun and Creole dishes. il *Better Homes Gard* 65:187-8 N '87

A Cajun fish story [blackened fish] K. Haedrich. il *Ctry J* 14:65-7 Mr '87

Cooked up in the bayous. P. Y. Cordell. il *South Living* 22:72-3 O '87

Links with Dixie [Cajun sausage] R. Lundy. il *Esquire* 107:38+ Mr '87

The recipe that launched a thousand boats [blackened redfish] P. Prudhomme. il por *Oceans* 20:12 My/Je '87

Welcome to Mardi Gras. il *Seventeen* 46:275-6 Mr '87

Cooking, Canadian

Canadian content in the kitchen [World Culinary Arts Festival in Vancouver, B.C.] M. Gray. il *Macleans* 100:40-1 Jl 20 '87

Cooking, Caribbean

Caribbean catch. J. L. Lippert. il *Health* 19:42-7 Ap '87

Caribbean forecast: cool times, hot tastes. B. Karoff. il *Work Woman* 12:130-2+ Mr '87

Gourmet holidays [Anguilla and Saint Martin] D. Beal. il map *Gourmet* 47:42-7+ Ja '87

Gourmet holidays [Saint Barthelemy and Saint Eustatius] D. Beal. il maps *Gourmet* 47:46-51+ Mr '87

It's a tropical heat wave [Caribbean-style restaurants] M. Sheraton. il *Time* 130:64 Ag 31 '87

A taste of the Caribbean. C. Lyons. il *Ebony* 42:108-10+ Ap '87

A taste of the islands: spicy, sweet and savory. J. B. Harris. il *Black Enterp* 17:47-8 My '87

Twin islands cuisine [Trinidad and Tobago] J. Nash and C. Cherry. il *Essence* 17:82-4+ Ap '87

Cooking, Chinese

See also
Dim sum
Egg rolls
Soy sauce
Wok cooking

Canton. F. Ferretti. il *Gourmet* 47:56-63+ My '87

Chicken cloud and egg crêpe: they're light and mild Chinese soups. il *Sunset* 179:145 D '87

China's health food tradition. L. Ruifen. il *Courier* 40:24-7 My '87

Chinese food: sensational with less salt! J. Nash. il *Essence* 18:75-8+ Ag '87

Christmas feast with an Oriental flavor [Chinese duckling] A. Simon. il *Saturday Evening Post* 259:18-20 D '87

A different barbecue [Chinese influences] K. Lee and A. Branyon. il *N Y Times Mag* p59-60 Jl 12 '87

An exotic pilgrimage [Chinese-Moslem food] C. Rossant. il *N Y Times Mag* p72-4 Ap 26 '87

The flavors of China [microwave cooking] J. R. Nyenhuis. il *Saturday Evening Post* 259:16+ Mr '87

From Peking to Canton. M. Sheraton. il *Time* 129:82-3+ Ap 13 '87

Let's eat Chinese tonight. B. R. Johnson. il *Am Herit* 38:98-103+ D '87

A new taste from China [Chiu Chow cuisine] G. Lang and J. H. Lang. il *N Y Times Mag* p49-50 Ja 25 '87

Shanghai secrets. F. Lin. il *N Y Times Mag* p63-4 S 27 '87

A side order of sea slugs [herbal cookery at Emperor Herbal Restaurant, San Francisco] L. Shapiro. il *Newsweek* 110:77 S 14 '87

Cooking, Costa Rican

Fringed, fragrant, fanciful . . . Costa Ricans just call it "good bread". il *Sunset* 178:118-19 Ap '87

Cooking, Creole

Cajun and Creole dishes. il *Better Homes Gard* 65:187-8 N '87

Cooked up in the bayous. P. Y. Cordell. il *South Living* 22:72-3 O '87

Gumbo: soul in a bowl. il *Mademoiselle* 93:316-17+ S '87

Cooking, English

A Christmas feast [reinterpreting standard English dishes] N. H. Jenkins. il *N Y Times Mag* p95-6 D 13 '87

The Cotswolds. C. P. Reynolds. il map *Gourmet* 47:54-9+ S '87

A menagerie of delights [recipes of A. Worrall-Thompson] C. Claiborne and P. Franey. il *N Y Times Mag* p41-2 Ja 11 '87

The new English cooking. F. Bissell. il *Harpers Bazaar* 120:104+ Ap '87

The renaissance of English cookery. L. Forbes. il *House Gard* 159:124+ N '87

The Royal Windsor Horse Show. S. Wilding. il *Gourmet* 47:60-5+ Ap '87

Cooking, European

European dining. W. Schemmel. *Travel Holiday* 167:73-6 Mr '87

What's cooking in Europe: schools with flavor. M. Polvay. il *Travel Holiday* 167:56-60 F '87

Cooking, Foreign *See* Cooking, International

Cooking, French

See also
Crêpes
École de Cuisine Française S. de Mirbeck

After quiche [open-faced tarts] P. Wells. il *N Y Times Mag* p61-2 O 4 '87

Best of bistro. S. Costner. il *Work Woman* 12:122-4+ Ap '87

Bistro maestros. P. Wells. il *N Y Times Mag* p99-100 N 8 '87

Bistro's new simplicity [Chez Louis in New York City] C. Claiborne and P. Franey. il *N Y Times Mag* p51-2 My 10 '87

Bourride: bouillabaisse's country cousin [Provençal fish stew] il *Sunset* 179:188-9 N '87

Cooking with Jacques Pépin. J. Pépin. See issues of Gourmet beginning January 1985

Deconstructing dinner [nouvelle cuisine] R. Sokolov. il *Nat Hist* 96:74-7 My '87

The French evolution [Le Cirque, Le Régence, Le Chantilly and Le Festival in New York City] G. Greene. il *N Y* 20:50-5 Mr 23 '87

From platter to plate [nouvelle cuisine] R. Sokolov. il *Nat Hist* 96:62-3 Je '87

The gastronomic world of Balzac. N. Barry. il *Gourmet* 47:48-53+ S '87

Gourmet holidays: France's Atlantic islands. D. Beal. il map *Gourmet* 47:50-5+ Ag '87

Gourmet holidays: the coast of Languedoc. P. T. Mitchell. il map *Gourmet* 47:60-5+ O '87

Of truffles and lavender [harvesting and Provençal recipes] L. Forbes. il *House Gard* 159:42+ S '87

Parisian fare extraordinaire! J. Nash. il *Essence* 18:100-1 O '87

Potage provençal [Antoine Bouterin's cream-of-garlic soup] B. Costikyan. il *N Y* 20:57 Ja 26 '87

Reaping the harvest [grape-picking season] P. Wells. il *N Y Times Mag* p55-6 O 25 '87

The rules of the game [entertaining in France] J. Kramer. il *House Gard* 159:86+ O '87

Simply delicious la belle cuisine [women chefs in France] A. Stone-Sweet. il por *Harpers Bazaar* 120:292+ S '87

Vinegar and ham . . . another French secret. il *Sunset* 179:190+ N '87

When things go right [preparing a birthday luncheon in Provence] P. Wells. il *N Y Times Mag* p123-4+ S 13 '87

Cooking, German

Gourmet holidays: cross-country skiing from Baden-Baden. P. J. Wade. il map *Gourmet* 47:48-53+ F '87

Heidelberg. S. Wilding. il *Gourmet* 47:48-53+ Ja '87

A meister chef's legacy [A. Walterspiel] L. Langseth-Christensen. il por *Gourmet* 47:80-1+ O '87

Cooking, Hawaiian

Barbecue island style. il *Ladies Home J* 104:96-7+ Ag '87

Limu: a Hawaiian delicacy. C. Bates. il *Gourmet* 47:72-3+ S '87

Cooking, Indian (East Indian)

Delhi's cuisine and craftsmen. L. Nicholson. il *Gourmet* 47:66-71+ S '87

Entertaining [hostess S. Pitember in Bombay] W. P. Rayner and C. Rayner. il por *Vogue* 177:128 Je '87

Indian summer, East Indian style. il *Glamour* 85:400-1 S '87

Playing with fire [Mangalore cuisine] J. Sahni. il *N Y Times Mag* p93-4 O 11 '87

Wonderful holiday buffet. il *Glamour* 85:226-9 D '87

Cooking, Indonesian

An exotic buffet [rijsttafel] C. Claiborne and P. Franey. il *N Y Times Mag* p47-8 Mr 15 '87

Cooking, International

Family dinners with foreign flair [microwaving] il *Good Housekeep* 204:177-8 F '87

Knowing no boundary [chef J. Robert] B. Cost. il *N Y Times Mag* p69-70 Ap 19 '87

McCall's international cookbook. M. Langan. il *McCalls* 114:131-8+ F '87

Cooking, Islamic

An exotic pilgrimage [Chinese-Moslem food] C. Rossant. il *N Y Times Mag* p72-4 Ap 26 '87

Cooking, Italian

See also
Badia a Coltibuono (Cooking school)

Cooking, Italian—See also—*cont.*
  Cooking—Pasta
  Ravioli
Cheesemaking in Parma. F. Ferretti. il *Gourmet* 47:74-9+ O '87
An excursion from Milan: Bergamo. D. L. Parker. il *Gourmet* 47:60-5+ S '87
Going with the grain [risotto alla parmigiana] E. Sahatjian. il *Esquire* 107:26 Ja '87
Have an Italian-style picnic. J. B. Hurley. il *Prevention* 39:60+ Jl '87
How Italians say shanks [osso buco] J. F. Mariani. il *Esquire* 108:56 S '87
Salute to summer's end [buffet dishes] N. H. Jenkins. il *N Y Times Mag* p43-4 Ag 23 '87
A stirring dish [risotto] C. Kummer. il *Atlantic* 260:90-2 S '87
Strong breads, dark sweets [Christmas cooking] L. Forbes. il *House Gard* 159:88+ D '87
T.G.I. Domenica. C. Walker. il *Work Woman* 12:144 Mr '87
Waiter, what's that ribollita doing in my soup? E. Sahatjian. il *Esquire* 108:38 N '87
  Anecdotes, facetiae, satire, etc.
More than a meal [memories of disastrous Italian octopus dinner] N. Hazelton. *Natl Rev* 39:54-5 My 8 '87
Cooking, Japanese
  See also
  Surimi
  Sushi
Paris, Tokyo, New York: Hanae Mori's style goes everywhere—and so does her chef. W. P. Rayner and C. Rayner. il por *Vogue* 177:300 O '87
  Photographs and photography
Good enough to eat [work of R. Wolf] R. Sokolov. il *Nat Hist* 96:58-64 S '87
Cooking, Jewish
Cookies for a Hanukkah party [rugelach] il *Redbook* 170:121 D '87
Festive Passover feast. D. Meadow. il *McCalls* 114:116-18 Ap '87
Happy Hanukkah from the Boresow family. J. Taylor. il *Better Homes Gard* 65:87-92 D '87
A Passover seder [created by B. Wine] J. Nathan. il *N Y Times Mag* p63-4 Ap 5 '87
Puget Sound gefillte fish [salmon] il *Sunset* 179:192-3 S '87
Cooking, Marine
Sumptuous sea fare [J. Ruette's use of vacuum-sealed precooked food] S. Ballard. il por *Sports Illus* 66:81 Je 15 '87
Cooking, Mexican
  See also
  Chili
  Cooking, Tex-Mex
Dessert tostadas . . . you use crisp tortillas as bowls and spoons. il *Sunset* 178:224 My '87
For gringos only [tortillas] L. Sombke. il *Esquire* 107:38 Ap '87
Just tell your guests: build your own carnitas. il *Sunset* 178:102-3+ Je '87
Mexican fiesta! B. Greenwood. il *Better Homes Gard* 65:136 O '87
Mexican vegetables and salads. E. L. Ortiz. il *Gourmet* 47:80-1+ My '87
Of maize and meat: culinary traditions and cultural identity in Mexico and Argentina. P. Petrich. il *Courier* 40:10-13 My '87
A place for fresh tortillas [La Villita Tortillas in San Antonio, Tex.] il *South Living* 22:32 Je '87
Quick & easy Mexican meals. P. Perry. il *Saturday Evening Post* 259:92+ S '87
Real Mexican, at last. C. Andrews. il *Harpers Bazaar* 120:108+ F '87
Sweetness and heat together . . . a Mexican secret [chilies rellenos and pico de gallo salad] il *Sunset* 179:125-6 Jl '87
Tamale sausages. il *Sunset* 178:186-7 My '87
A taste of Mexico. P. Quintana. il *Americana* 15:56-9 My/Je '87
Cooking, Moroccan
A 30-minute Moroccan dinner. il *Glamour* 85:266 F '87
Moroccan feast. il *Sunset* 179:174+ S '87
Oasis food. B. Fritz. il *Prevention* 39:74-6+ Mr '87
Cooking, North African
Marvelous no-meat stew [vegetarian couscous] il *McCalls* 145:123-4 Mr '87
Cooking, Norwegian
Food fit for a Viking. M. Polvay. il *Travel Holiday* 167:67 Je '87

Cooking, Ornamental
  See also
  Cooking—Garnishes
24 quick tips for holiday parties. J. Williams and others. il *Better Homes Gard* 65:74-9 D '87
Charming Easter creations. M. Langan. il *McCalls* 114:52-4+ Ap '87
Christmas takes the cake [centerpiece cakes] S. West. il *Ladies Home J* 104:138-41+ D '87
Create a Christmas cookie cottage. il *Redbook* 170:74+ D '87
Create a Christmas fantasy [S. Demers' gingerbread village] I. Jones. il por *Ctry J* 14:41-2 D '87
A fruit wreath to eat [della robbia fruit wreath] il *South Living* 22:133 D '87
Gingerbread gallery. il *Good Housekeep* 205:150-5+ D '87
How to make our little country church [gingerbread; cover story] il *Good Housekeep* 205:1G+ D '87
Little chickadees [Easter cookies] il *Redbook* 168:12 Ap '87
Santa's here! Sensational cookie creations. il *McCalls* 115:32-6+ D '87
With sturdy gingerbread, you can build almost anything [cover story] il *Sunset* 179:84-7 D '87
Cooking, Outdoor
  See also
  Barbecue cooking
  Outdoor meals
Field tests. S. Bashline. il *Field Stream* 92:76 My '87
Food care in camp. T. Thomas. *Field Stream* 92:54-5 Jl '87
Cooking, Peruvian
Peru's sophistication. B. H. Fussell. il *N Y Times Mag* p49-50 F 1 '87
Cooking, Puerto Rican
The spirits of Puerto Rico [rum] R. L. Balzer. il *Travel Holiday* 168:10-11+ S '87
Cooking, Russian
Borscht belt [St. Petersbourg, Odessa and Kavkazian; restaurants in New York City] G. Greene. il *N Y* 20:116-18 O 19 '87
A gourmet at large [Moscow's food] F. Ferretti. il *Gourmet* 47:48+ Ag '87
Cooking, Scandinavian
  See also
  Smorgasbord
Cooking, Shaker
A simple Shaker meal. K. Haedrich. il *Ctry J* 14:60-2+ Ap '87
Cooking, Southeast Asian
This is a fish fry? il *Sunset* 179:78-9, 164 S '87
Cooking, Spanish
  See also
  Tapas
Columbus's biggest discovery. R. Sokolov. il *Nat Hist* 96:66-7 Ag '87
Foods and finos of Spain [Jerez] T. Lydecker. il *Travel Holiday* 167:16+ F '87
Gourmet holidays: La Rioja. P. T. Mitchell. il map *Gourmet* 47:74-9+ N '87
The original tortilla [in Spain it's an egg-potato omelet] il *Sunset* 178:196-7 Ap '87
The Spanish know how to wake up winter vegetables. il *Sunset* 178:160 F '87
Spanish salads. il *Sunset* 179:182-3 S '87
Spanish soup: fresh clams and dry fava beans. il *Sunset* 178:170 Mr '87
Strong breads, dark sweets [Christmas cooking] L. Forbes. il *House Gard* 159:88+ D '87
Cooking, Swedish
Giving albacore the Swedish treatment [gravad albacore] il *Sunset* 178:164+ Je '87
Cooking, Swiss
  See also
  Muesli
Cooking, Syrian
Are you ready for sumac? [zahtar] il *Sunset* 179:185 N '87
Cooking, Tex-Mex
Fry this appetizer [Tex-Mex wontons] il *South Living* 22:166 S '87
The nacho experience. K. Haedrich. il *Ctry J* 14:22-5 F '87
Picante sauce burns with flavor. D. G. Lowery. il *South Living* 22:72-3 S '87
Speedy Tex-Mex fajitas. il *Redbook* 169:20 Je '87
Tech Mex. il *Seventeen* 46:185-6 N '87
Tex-Mex: hot and getting hotter. T. Segal. il *Bus Week* p99 Jl 6 '87
Zest of the West. il *Seventeen* 46:174-5 My '87

Cooking, Thai
High Thai [Bangkok House and Thai Taste in New York City] J. Freiman. il *N Y* 20:76 Mr 16 '87
Nothing like a Thai grill. E. Sahatjian. il *Esquire* 107:52+ Je '87

Cooking, Turkish
Homage to Anatolia. R. Sokolov. il *Nat Hist* 96:94+ F '87
Talking Turkey [International Food Congress] R. Sokolov. il *Nat Hist* 96:92-5 Mr '87

Cooking, Vietnamese
Serve your guests a "two-jewel" dinner . . . Asian fondue and soup. il *Sunset* 178:214+ Ap '87

Cooking, West Indian
Winds of the Antilles [French West Indies] B. Kafka. il *N Y Times Mag* p61-2 F 15 '87

Cooking by children
Food for fun [Kids' Cooking Camp at L'Academie de Cuisine, Bethesda, Md.] il *Natl Geogr World* 142:10-13 Je '87
Holiday kitchen fun: cookies kids can bake. A. Bailey. il *Parents* 62:175+ D '87
Junior chefs on their own with a microwave. il *Sunset* 179:116-17 Jl '87
Microwave cooking for kids. D. W. Hansen. il *Ladies Home J* 104:66+ S '87
Recipes for eggs-tras. il *Natl Geogr World* 140:23 Ap '87
Recipes for little chefs. il *Good Housekeep* 205:124 S '87
Teaching kids to cook [microwaving] il *Good Housekeep* 205:116 N '87
Thought for food. A. Jungreis. il *Sch Update* 120:24-5 N 20 '87
The working kids' cookbook [microwave cooking] R. Coyle. il *Work Woman* 12:168+ S '87

Cooking by firefighters
Out of the fire and into the frying pan [J. Sineno's The firefighters cookbook] il *Newsweek* 109:58 Mr 9 '87

Cooking by men
Chefs of the West. See issues of Sunset (Central edition)
Entrées men like to cook. il *South Living* 22:212+ My '87
Essence woman [L. Turner's Men Who Cook benefit in New York City] M. Southgate. il por *Essence* 17:28 Ap '87
Men do cook. J. Nash. il *Essence* 18:89-92+ N '87

Anecdotes, facetiae, satire, etc.
Confessions of a non-cook. P. J. O'Rourke. il *Read Dig* 130:67-9 Mr '87
Singing the cordon bleus. R. H. Bell. *Commonweal* 114:70-1 F 13 '87

Cooking contests *See* Cooking—Competitions
Cooking oils *See* Oils and fats, Edible
Cooking on boats *See* Cooking, Marine
Cooking programs *See* Television broadcasting—Cooking programs
Cooking utensils and appliances *See* Kitchen utensils and appliances
Cooks, R. G.
(jt. auth) See Delgass, W. Nicholas, and Cooks, R. G.
Cooks

See also
Boulud, Daniel
Bourdin, Michel
Delaveyne, Jean
Dunton, Graham
Hill, Jon
Le Coze, Gilbert
Little, Alastair
Palladin, Jean-Louis
Palmer, Charles
Smith, Jeff
Tower, Jeremiah
Walterspiel, Alfred
Women cooks
Flash and the pan [celebrity chefs] R. Buchanan. il *Roll Stone* p101-2+ N 19 '87
Great chefs, great kitchens [workspaces and favorite recipes of Debbi Fields, Pierre Franey, and Martha Stewart] M. D. Glass. il *Ladies Home J* 104:124-9+ S '87

Anecdotes, facetiae, satire, etc.
Not quite Escoffier [summer job as a cook for a family in the Hamptons] M. Kenyon. il *Gourmet* 47:68+ Ag '87

Cookson, Catherine
Love's own dream [fiction] il por *Good Housekeep* 204:247-50+ My '87

Cookstoves *See* Stoves
Cookware *See* Kitchen utensils and appliances
Cool, Lisa Collier, 1952-
Fatigue: are you fighting your internal clock? il *McCalls* 115:144+ D '87
Coolant hoses, Automobile *See* Automobile engines—Hoses
Coolen, Peter
(jt. auth) See Gray, Ellen, and Coolen, Peter
Coolers, Wine *See* Wine coolers
Cooley, Archie
about
Mississippi Valley coach leads FB exodus to Ark. por *Jet* 71:50 Ja 12 '87
Cooley, Denton A., 1920-
about
Profiles: Denton A. Cooley, M.D. R. Conniff. il pors *Archit Dig* 44:194-201+ My '87
Cooley, Denton A., 1920-, and Moore, Carolyn E.
Eat healthy—and love it! il *Redbook* 169:101-5 O '87
Cooling

See also
Air conditioning
Airplane engines—Cooling
Automobile engines—Cooling
Diesel engines, Marine—Cooling
Food—Cooling
Quenching
Techniques for keeping cool. J. Seisler. il *Consum Res Mag* 70:23-5 Jl '87
Cooner, James Robert
Introduction to Buddhist collectibles. il *Antiques Collect Hobbies* 92:28-32 Mr '87
Cooney, Gerry
about
A bout against doubt. G. Smith. il pors *Sports Illus* 66:76-80+ Je 8 '87
Say good night, Gerry. W. Nack. il pors *Sports Illus* 66:22-3 Je 22 '87
Spinks cleared to fight, but Cooney camp is quiet. por *Jet* 72:47 Ap 13 '87
Spinks-Cooney 'title' fight boasts equal opportunity. *Jet* 72:46 Je 1 '87
Spinks loses round one in bid to fight Cooney. por *Jet* 71:48 Ja 19 '87
Spinks says victory tells little guys to stand tall. il por *Jet* 72:48 Jl 6 '87
Why Cooney can't win . . . J. Ryan. il pors *Sport Mag* 78:13 Jl '87
Cooney, Joan Ganz
about
Big Bird's mother hen [cover story; interview] R. Robinson. il pors *50 Plus* 27:24-7 D '87
Street smart. P. Hellman. il por *N Y* 20:48-53 N 23 '87
Cooney, John, and Winslow, George
The last tycoon. il pors *Channels* 7:34-5 F '87
Coons, Nancy
A Gypsy's way. il por *Opera News* 52:24-5 D 19 '87
Coons, Richard
about
High tech: big returns from small stocks [interview] J. Mendes. il por *Fortune* 116:128 S 28 '87
Coons *See* Raccoons
Coonts, Stephen, 1946-
about
Once a Navy bomber pilot, Stephen Coonts soars again with a supersonic first novel. R. Arias. il pors *People Wkly* 27:51-2 Ja 19 '87
Cooper, Allene Bary- *See* Bary-Cooper, Allene
Cooper, Bob, Jr.
Satellite TV. See issues of Radio-Electronics beginning November 1984
Cooper, Bruce S.
Retooling teachers: the New York experience. il *Phi Delta Kappan* 68:606-9 Ap '87
Cooper, Christin
How to get the most from summer ski camp. *Skiing* 39:77-8 Spr '87
Inside racing. See issues of Skiing beginning September 1985
Cooper, Dennis
Art on the Amstel. il *Art Am* 75:32-5+ O '87
Cooper, Ellen
about
Fast-tracking the first AIDS drug [interview] B. Stone. pors *FDA Consum* 21:13-15 O '87
Cooper, Henry S. F.
Letter from the Space Center. *New Yorker* 63:71-81 Je 8 '87
Cooper, Kevin
Aero age. il *Cycle* 38:38-41+ Ap '87

Cooper, Matthew
Beware of Republicans bearing voting rights suits. *Wash Mon* 19:11-15 F '87
Hot chain nixes wingo, buscapades—nabs Pulitzers, big bucks. *Wash Mon* 19:17-22 S '87

Cooper, Michael
about
And . . . it's super sub! R. Wiley. il pors *Sports Illus* 66:50-2+ My 11 '87

Cooper, Paula
about
Contemporary energies at the Paula Cooper Gallery. A. Haden-Guest. il por *Archit Dig* 44:78+ Ap '87

Cooper, Paula R.
about
Indiana killer, Italian martyr. G. Hackett. il por *Newsweek* 110:37 S 21 '87

Cooper, Ralph
Headlining the Apollo; ed. by Steven Dougherty. il pors *People Wkly* 28:71+ O 19 '87

Cooper, Richard A.
A heroic theater for the rational mind. *Humanist* 47:33-4 Jl/Ag '87

Cooper, Sally
about
Sally Cooper. C. Weaver. por *Ms* 16:112+ Jl/Ag '87

Cooper, Theodore M.
How high a priority will society accord to health care? [address, December 5, 1986] *Vital Speeches Day* 53:242-5 F 1 '87

Cooper, Wendy A.
The installation of American furniture from the Kaufman Collection at the National Gallery of Art. bibl f il *Antiques* 131:1096-1105 My '87

Cooper (Paula) Gallery *See* Paula Cooper Gallery

Cooper Companies
A fire sale at Cooper? [P. G. Montgomery's leveraged buyout scheme] J. O. Hamilton. il por *Bus Week* p37 N 23 '87

Cooper Development Co.
Inside Parker Montgomery's tangle of troubled companies. J. O. Hamilton and J. H. Dobrzynski. il por *Bus Week* p110-11 F 23 '87

Cooper family
about
A wrenching separation ends an Iowa couple's hope of adopting the five Cooper kids. G. Pick. il *People Wkly* 27:40-3 F 2 '87

Cooper-Hewitt Museum
Cooper-Hewitt Museum [exhibition entitled Recollections: a decade of collection] il *Antiques Collect Hobbies* 91:57-8 Ja '87

Cooper Lasersonics Inc.
Inside Parker Montgomery's tangle of troubled companies. J. O. Hamilton and J. H. Dobrzynski. il por *Bus Week* p110-11 F 23 '87

Cooper Tire & Rubber Company
Good merchandise and a square deal. J. Parr. *Forbes* 140:416+ Jl 13 '87

Cooperation
See also
Educational cooperation
International cooperation
Competition or cooperation? [address, March 1987] A. W. Astin. il *Change* 19:12-19 S/O '87
Cooperation over competition: how to succeed. A. Kohn. *Current* 289:21-4 Ja '87
Managing sideways. R. E. Lefton. il *Work Woman* 12:34+ O '87

Cooperative advertising, Television *See* Television advertising—Cooperative advertising

Cooperative agriculture *See* Agriculture, Cooperative

Cooperative associations
See also
Artistic License (Organization)
Operation Get Down Food Co-op

Cooperative associations, Agricultural *See* Agriculture, Cooperative

Cooperative education *See* Business and education

Cooperative Extension Service *See* United States. Extension Service

Cooperative learning *See* Group work in education

Cooperative Marketing Company
An upstart is upsetting Actmedia's shopping carts. R. Mitchell. il *Bus Week* p28-9 S 7 '87

Cooperman, Jeff
Learning to love Sauternes. il *Esquire* 108:34+ N '87

Cooperman, Robert
The empress of the laundromat [poem] *Commonweal* 114:357 Je 5 '87

Coopers & Lybrand
386 buying spree [purchase of Compaq Deskpro 386s] S. R. Reed. il *Pers Comput* 11:65 Mr '87

Cooperstown (N.Y.)
Music
See also
Glimmerglass Opera Theater

CooperVision, Inc.
Inside Parker Montgomery's tangle of troubled companies. J. O. Hamilton and J. H. Dobrzynski. il por *Bus Week* p110-11 F 23 '87
Who's making eyes at CooperVision? G. G. Marcial. *Bus Week* p98 S 28 '87

Coordinating Committee on Multilateral Export Controls
CoCom tightening high technology export controls. *Aviat Week Space Technol* 127:33 Ag 3 '87
Strategic technology export controls [White House statement, September 18, 1987] *Dep State Bull* 87:33 N '87
Taking the cuffs off exports to the East bloc [rules on high tech] S. J. Dryden. il *Bus Week* p48-9 Je 1 '87
The technobandits [U.S. export controls] N. R. Gibbs. il *Time* 130:42-4 N 30 '87

Coordination, Muscular *See* Motor ability

Coors (Adolph) Co. *See* Adolph Coors Co.

Cop 1 (Drug)
Drug shows potential as MS treatment. *Sci News* 132:120 Ag 22 '87
New hope for MS victims. L. Drew. il *Newsweek* 110:46 Ag 24 '87

Cop television shows *See* Television broadcasting—Crime programs

Copán (Ancient city)
Cache withdrawal at classic Maya site. B. Bower. il *Sci News* 131:212 Ap 4 '87

Cope, Julian
about
Julian Cope: from obscurity to sainthood. M. Kaplan. por *Roll Stone* p21 My 21 '87

Copeland, Alvin
about
Popeye's punch. C. Davis. il *Mot Boat Sail* 159:46-9+ Ja '87

Copeland, Irene
Cosmopolitan. il *Writer* 100:27 F '87

Copeland, Miles
Activist, strategist. *Natl Rev* 39:37-8 S 11 '87

Copier art *See* Photocopying—Art use

Coping behavior *See* Adjustment (Psychology)

Coping behavior in school children *See* School children—Adjustment

Copland, Aaron, 1900-
about
The tender land [opera] Reviews
N Y il 20:96 My 18 '87. P. G. Davis

Copley, Teri
about
Micki Free says he likes his wife's sexy image. pors *Jet* 72:59 Ag 24 '87

Coplon, Jeff
Barnstorming, NBA style. il map *Sport Mag* 78:65-6+ Ap '87
By the numbers. por *New Yorker* 63:56+ D 21 '87
Globetrotter stooge for a day. il *Sport Mag* 78:84 Je '87
The secret of my new success. il pors *Sport Mag* 78:50-1+ N '87

Coppélia [ballet] *See* Ballet reviews—Single works

Copper Canyon (Mexico) *See* Barranca de Cobre (Mexico)

Copper cookware *See* Kitchen utensils and appliances

Copper in the body
Copper: what a difference sex makes [research by Meira Fields and others] J. Raloff. *Sci News* 131:70 Ja 31 '87

Copper industry
See also
ASARCO Inc.
Phelps Dodge Corporation

Copper mines and mining
Alaska
Kennecott's boom and bust. R. Churchill and K. Jones. il *Focus* 37:1-5 Fall '87
Tennessee
The death of Ducktown [desert created in Tennessee 100 years ago when copper smelter fumes killed vegetation] W. Barnhardt. il map *Discover* 8:34-6+ O '87

Copper Mountain (Colo.: Resort) *See* Resorts—Colorado
Copper smelters *See* Smelters
Copper sulfate
Stealing from thieves [use of copper sulfate in Bordeaux vineyards] F. J. Prial. il *N Y Times Mag* p74 Mr 15 '87

Coppola, Francis, 1939-
about
Captain EO [film] Reviews
USA Today (Periodical) 115:33 Ja '87. J. Saltzman
Gardens of stone [film] Reviews
America 156:506+ Je 20-27 '87. R. A. Blake
Commonweal 114:320 My 22 '87. T. O'Brien
Macleans il 100:57 My 11 '87. L. O'Toole
N Y 20:93 My 18 '87. D. Denby
New Repub 196:24-5 My 25 '87. S. Kauffmann
New Yorker 63:84-6 My 18 '87. P. Kael
Newsweek il 109:79 My 11 '87. D. Ansen
People Wkly il 27:10 My 11 '87. P. Travers
Time 129:74 Je 15 '87
Vogue il 177:90 Mr '87. T. Young
Peggy Sue got married [film] Reviews
Christ Century 104:61 Ja 21 '87. J. M. Wall
Humanist il 47:44-5 Ja/F '87. H. M. Geduld
Progressive 51:36 Ja '87. P. Aufderheide
USA Today (Periodical) il 115:97 Ja '87. K. R. Hey

Coppola, Mary Anne
The "perfect" student: being alert to autism. *Educ Dig* 52:33-5 My '87
Coprocessors *See* Multiprocessors
Coproduction of airplanes *See* Airplane industry—International aspects
Copulos, Milton
Can Chernobyl happen here?; ed. by Mary Hopkins. il *Consum Res Mag* 70:35-7 Ja '87
Copy photography *See* Photography—Copying
Copy stands (Photography) *See* Photography—Equipment
Copying equipment
See also
Photocopying
Photocopying equipment
Photography—Copying
Signature writing machines
Slides (Photography)—Copying
Copyright
See also
Coalition to Preserve the American Copyright Tradition
National Committee for the Berne Convention
New York Rights & Permissions Group
Royalties
AAP meeting to hear Bale and Kastenmeier. H. Fields. *Publ Wkly* 231:16 Ja 16 '87
A busy summer for copyright law. C. E. Rinzler. il *Publ Wkly* 232:25-6 S 11 '87
Demise of the Manufacturing Clause elicits mostly publishers' yawns. J. P. Frank. *Publ Wkly* 232:42-3 Jl 3 '87
For five-year report, publishers and librarians split on copying [impact of photocopying law] H. Fields. *Publ Wkly* 231:12 Ap 24 '87
'Moral rights' provision is now moot for joining Berne Convention, officials say. H. Fields. *Publ Wkly* 232:309 Ag 7 '87
A new lease on life for old books [permitting authors and heirs to terminate contracts before the end of their book's copyright term] C. E. Rinzler. il *Publ Wkly* 232:27-9 Jl 10 '87
Oman endorses inclusion of 'moral rights' proviso [proposed revision of the 1976 Copyright Act] H. Fields. *Publ Wkly* 232:13 Jl 3 '87
Rights. P. S. Nathan. See issues of Publishers Weekly
Sen. Cochran again introduces writers' work-for-hire bill. H. Fields. *Publ Wkly* 231:16 Je 19 '87
The year in rights. P. S. Nathan. *Publ Wkly* 231:42 Ja 9 '87
Art
Artists sue over posters: San Francisco battle focuses on rights to psychedelic artwork from the sixties. M. Goldberg. *Roll Stone* p29 Ap 23 '87
Broadcasting rights
The Betamax case (I). J. Lardner. *New Yorker* 63:45-8+ Ap 6 '87
The Betamax case (II). J. Lardner. *New Yorker* 63:60-81 Ap 13 '87
Judge blocks production of 'Amos 'n' Andy' musical [copyright owned by CBS] *Jet* 72:56 S 14 '87
Superstation super mess. P. Hersch. il *Channels* 7:45-6 Ja '87

Choreography
Choreography and copyright. K. Rowe. il *Dance Mag* 61:42-3 Mr '87
Computer programming
See also
Computer programming—Unauthorized use
The decline of copy protection. M. Antonoff. il *Pers Comput* 11:155-7 My '87
Lotus takes the offensive: targets 1-2-3 clones; add-in market. il *Pers Comput* 11:29-30 Mr '87
The market for mainframes will never be the same [IBM-Fujitsu software copyright fight] J. W. Verity. il *Bus Week* p62 O 5 '87
New product or knockoff? E. Dyson. il *Forbes* 139:272 Je 15 '87
Software copyrights: keep out the pirates—but let innovators in. L. J. Tell. *Bus Week* p31 Ag 31 '87
Conferences
See also
World Congress on Copyright Teaching and Information
Integrated circuits
The knockoffs head for a knockdown fight with IBM. K. M. Hafner. il *Bus Week* p112-13 D 21 '87
International aspects
See also
Berne Convention for the Protection of Literary and Artistic Works
The changing foreign rights market [children's books] L. E. Owen. il *Publ Wkly* 231:28-30+ Mr 20 '87
Copyright official challenges linking of copyright to trade negotiators. H. Fields. *Publ Wkly* 231:16 Ap 3 '87
Danish agent fights to disburse copying fees to foreign authors [payment for school photocopying] H. R. Lottman. *Publ Wkly* 232:14 Ag 14 '87
Frankfurt '87: fair guide for rights buyers & sellers. il *Publ Wkly* 232:77-121 S 18 '87
Legally bound [publishers in France dismayed by red tape involved in selling rights to Americans] H. R. Lottman. *Publ Wkly* 231:34 Je 12 '87
Orchestrating Gorbachev [foreign rights to M. Gorbachev's book *Perestroika*] P. S. Nathan. *Publ Wkly* 232:21 N 6 '87
Toward a worldwide copyright era. P. G. Altbach. il *Publ Wkly* 232:44 D 11 '87
Motion pictures
The battle for Platoon [video rights] J. Vitale. il *Channels* 7:59 O '87
A jungle war over the 'Platoon' video. il *Newsweek* 110:56 N 23 '87
Legal shadings [colorization of motion pictures] W. S. Strong. *Society* 24:19-21 My/Je '87
Lights, camera, lawyers! [battle over video rights to Platoon] W. Harris. il *Forbes* 140:33 Ag 10 '87
Music
See also
American Society of Composers, Authors and Publishers
A cruel cut for Sergeant Pepper [losing copyright in Japan] N. Gross. il *Bus Week* p62 Je 22 '87
The fight over golden oldies [rock music] N. Jennings. il *Macleans* 100:36-7 Mr 2 '87
Has somebody stolen their song? M. Walsh. il *Time* 130:86 O 19 '87
Imports under fire. M. Goldberg. *Roll Stone* p14+ Jl 2 '87
Little Richard sues over ownership of new hit song. por *Jet* 71:59 Mr 9 '87
More than Feelings [L. Gasté sues M. Albert for copyright infringement] il por *Time* 130:37 Ag 10 '87
Musician Willie Dixon satisfied out of court. *Jet* 72:58 Mr 30 '87
Prince's sis says he stole lyrics from her. *Jet* 72:62 S 7 '87
The push to end blanket licensing hits a sour note with songwriters [music on television] P. E. Bauer. *Channels* 7:17 Ap '87
Photographs and photography
Are you a photographer or a hired gun? J. W. Brewer. il *Petersens Photogr Mag* 16:64-7 O '87
Are you playing Russian roulette with your rights? J. W. Brewer. il *Petersens Photogr Mag* 16:44-6 S '87
Television rights
See Copyright—Broadcasting rights
Unauthorized reprints
See Copyright infringement
Canada
A defeat for Scientology [Canadian publication of Russell Miller's biography of L. R. Hubbard allowed] D. Todd. *Macleans* 100:54 D 14 '87

Copyright—*cont.*

China
Oman is optimistic on copyright protection in China and Russia. C. Reid. *Publ Wkly* 232:14 D 4 '87

Japan
A cruel cut for Sergeant Pepper [losing copyright] N. Gross. il *Bus Week* p62 Je 22 '87

Scandinavia
Danish agent fights to disburse copying fees to foreign authors [payment for school photocopying] H. R. Lottman. *Publ Wkly* 232:14 Ag 14 '87

Soviet Union
See also
Soviet Union. Copyright Agency
Oman is optimistic on copyright protection in China and Russia. C. Reid. *Publ Wkly* 232:14 D 4 '87

United States
See Copyright

Copyright Agency of the USSR *See* Soviet Union. Copyright Agency

Copyright infringement
AAP and seven authors ask to join Random House in Salinger appeal [blocked publication of I. Hamilton's biography of J. D. Salinger] H. Fields. *Publ Wkly* 232:11 S 25 '87

AAP files amicus brief for Random House in appeal of Salinger decision [appeals court decision to bar publication of I. Hamilton's biography of J. D. Salinger] M. Yen. *Publ Wkly* 231:90 F 27 '87

Citing copyright infringement, judge halts Stravinsky biography [suit brought by R. Craft against J. Kobler] J. Mutter. *Publ Wkly* 232:14 Ag 21 '87

Groups deny states' immunity from copyright infringement. H. Fields. *Publ Wkly* 232:17 Jl 31 '87

Holden Caulfield goes to law school [court blocks publication of I. Hamilton's biography of J. D. Salinger] A. Delbanco. *New Repub* 196:27-8+ Mr 9 '87

Morrow to sue 'Washington times' over excerpts from Deaver book. H. Fields. *Publ Wkly* 232:19 D 25 '87

Random House seeks review of Salinger decision [decision to bar publication of I. Hamilton's biography of J. D. Salinger] M. Yen. *Publ Wkly* 231:24 F 13 '87

Return to sender [I. Hamilton's unauthorized biography of J. D. Salinger blocked in court] por *Time* 129:62 F 9 '87

Salinger and 'The bell jar': what do they mean to publishers? C. E. Rinzler. il *Publ Wkly* 231:20-2 Ap 24 '87

The Salinger file [J. D. Salinger's attempt to block unauthorized biography by I. Hamilton] P. Hoban. il pors *N Y* 20:36-42 Je 15 '87

When the going gets tough, the tough go to court [chipmakers wage intellectual property battles] K. K. Wiegner. il *Forbes* 140:36-7 D 28 '87

Whose mail is it, anyway? [J. D. Salinger blocks use of his correspondence by biographer I. Hamilton] A. Press. il pors *Newsweek* 109:58 F 9 '87

Whose words are they, anyway? [J. D. Salinger's suit against I. Hamilton and Random House] D. Margolick. il *N Y Times Book Rev* 92:1+ N 1 '87

International aspects
Sen. Pete Wilson introduces measure to fight piracy. H. Fields. *Publ Wkly* 231:90 F 27 '87

East Asia
Farewell to pirate printing in Asia? S. A. Taylor. il *Publ Wkly* 231:23-4 Ap 24 '87

Korea (South)
Korea says piracy accord can't be enforced. H. Fields. il *Publ Wkly* 232:11 N 20 '87

Korea sells 2 million unauthorized U.S. books. H. Fields. *Publ Wkly* 232:13 O 2 '87

Coqui frogs *See* Frogs

Coral Gables (Fla.)

Bookstores
See Booksellers and bookselling—Florida

Coral reef algae *See* Algae

Coral reef fauna
See also
Sponges
Deep questions about shallow seas [diversity of species in the waters around the Hawaiian Islands] K. E. F. Watt. il *Nat Hist* 96:60-5 Jl '87

Diadema antillarum was not a keystone predator in cryptic reef environments. J. B. C. Jackson and K. W. Kaufmann. bibl f il *Science* 235:687-9 F 6 '87

Differentiation and evolution of sex change in fishes. D. Y. Shapiro. bibl f il *BioScience* 37:490-7 Jl/Ag '87

The spangled reef. il *Sea Front* 33:183-5 My/Je '87

Coral reefs and islands
See also
Coral reef fauna
Florida Keys (Fla.)
Great Barrier Reef (Australia)
Lighthouse Reef (Belize)
Palau
Coral bleaching threatens Atlantic reefs [Caribbean coral reefs] L. Roberts. il map *Science* 238:1228-9 N 27 '87

Food production in low-nutrient seas. W. H. Adey. bibl f il *BioScience* 37:340-8 My '87

Photographs and photography
Coral gardens: a textured treasure [Palau] D. Faulkner. il *Int Wildl* 17:46-51 N/D '87

Corals
Historical coral [El Niño-Southern Oscillation events and cadmium levels in Galapagos coral; research by Glen T. Shen] *Sci News* 132:168 S 12 '87

Corals, Fossil
Precise timing of the last interglacial period from mass spectrometric determination of thorium-230 in corals. R. L. Edwards and others. bibl f il *Science* 236:1547-53 Je 19 '87

Travels of an ancient reef. G. D. Stanley, Jr. il maps *Nat Hist* 96:36-43 N '87

Coram, Robert
The case against the Air Force. il *Wash Mon* 19:17-24 Jl/Ag '87

Corbett, Jim, 1875-1955
about
Jim Corbett: the reluctant executioner. G. C. Ward. il por maps *Audubon* 89:44-9+ Jl '87

Corbett National Park (India) *See* National parks and reserves—India

Corchard, Judith H.
about
This stock picker just follows a few homespun rules. G. G. Marcial. por *Bus Week* p113 My 4 '87

Corchia Woliner Associates
The art of the cold call. D. Shilling. il pors *Work Woman* 12:50-3 D '87

Corcoran, Thomas
about
Tommy the Cork: the secret world of Washington's first modern lobbyist. A. J. Lichtman. il por *Wash Mon* 19:41-9 F '87

Corcoran, Thomas B., and Wilson, Bruce L.
Successful secondary schools [excerpt from The search for successful secondary schools] *Educ Dig* 53:22-4 S '87

Corcoran Gallery of Art. Biennial Exhibition of Contemporary American Painting
Washington, D.C.: an inevitable gathering. S. H. Madoff. il *Art News* 86:153 S '87

Cordele (Ga.)
Restaurants, nightclubs, bars, etc.
A Georgia truck stop asks the question: haute enough for you? [Mon Petit] il *People Wkly* 28:65 Ag 17 '87

Cordero, Angel
about
Uncrowned prince of the Triple Crown. J. Rolfe and P. Demartini. il pors *Sport Mag* 78:63+ Je '87

Cordero, León Febres *See* Febres Cordero, León, 1931-

Cordials *See* Liqueurs

Cordis Corporation
Why Cordis' heart wasn't in pacemakers. P. Engardio. il *Bus Week* p80 Mr 16 '87

Cordless power tools *See* Tools

Cordless telephone *See* Radiotelephone

Cordless vacuum cleaners *See* Vacuum cleaners

CORE *See* Congress of Racial Equality

Core curriculum *See* Courses of study

Corey, D. R., and Schultz, Peter G.
Generation of a hybrid sequence-specific single-stranded deoxyribonuclease. bibl f il *Science* 238:1401-3 D 4 '87

Corey, Elias J., and others
Antiarthritic gold compounds effectively quench electronically excited singlet oxygen. bibl f il *Science* 236:68-9 Ap 3 '87

Corey, Kristyn
about
Putting the sting on poachers. M. Tennesen. il *Natl Wildl* 25:26-8 O/N '87

Corfield, Penelope
From rank to class: innovation in Georgian England. bibl il *Hist Today* 37:36-42 F '87

Cork, Richard
Site reading: British art in public spaces. il *Art Am* 75:144-51 S '87

Corkery, Paul
Johnny Carson & his ex-es [excerpt from Carson] il pors *Good Housekeep* 205:120+ O '87

Corliss, Mary
Cannes tankerous. il *Film Comment* 23:60+ Jl/Ag '87

Corliss, Richard
70-millimeter nerves [interview with R. Roud] por *Film Comment* 23:36+ S/O '87

Cormack, William S., and Sydenham, Michael
Counter-revolution? Toulon, 1793. bibl il *Hist Today* 37:49-55 O '87

Corman, Avery
Loew's Paradise. il *N Y* 20:76-7 D 21-28 '87

Cormick, Gerald W., and Knaster, Alana
Oil and fishing industries negotiate: mediation and scientific issues. bibl il *Environment* 28:6-15+ D '86

Cormie, Donald Mercer
about
Giving business a bad name. P. C. Newman. il por *Macleans* 100:35 Ag 17 '87

Corn, David
The big ones that got away. il *Nation* 245:152-4 Ag 29 '87
Bob Dole and the tobacco connection. il *Nation* 244:381+ Mr 28 '87
Futures shock. *Nation* 245:509-10 N 7 '87
Inside Gephardt's PACscam [cover story] il *Nation* 244:559+ My 2 '87
Mellowing of a muckraker [cover story] il *Nation* 245:541+ N 14 '87

Corn, David, and Morley, Jefferson
Beltway bandits. See issues of The Nation beginning July 18-25, 1987
A guide to Iran/contra theories [cover story] *Nation* 245:73+ Ag 1-8 '87
Lost in Afghanistan. *Nation* 245:43 Jl 18-25 '87

Corn, Robert
The F.C.C. cleans up the airways. il *Nation* 245:679-81 D 5 '87

Corn
See also
Cooking—Vegetables
Feeds—Corn
Discovery of transposable element activity among progeny of tissue culture-derived maize plants. V. M. Peschke and others. bibl f il *Science* 238:804-7 N 6 '87
The maize transposable element Ds is spliced from RNA. S. R. Wessler and others. bibl f il *Science* 237:916-18 Ag 21 '87
Meet the supersweets [cover story; with editorial comment by S. Daniels] K. Martin. il *Rodale's Org Gard* 34:4, 32-7 My '87
Ode to corn [excerpt from A rocking horse on Mars] P. West. il *Harpers* 275:30-1 S '87
Of maize and meat: culinary traditions and cultural identity in Mexico and Argentina. P. Petrich. il *Courier* 40:10-13 My '87
Revolutionary corn [supersweet corn] W. Shipman. il *Ctry J* 14:51-3 Je '87
Stalking the perfect ear [supersweet corn; cover story] B. Pleasant. il *Rodale's Org Gard* 34:28-30 My '87
Transposon tagging and molecular analysis of the maize regulatory locus opaque-2. R. J. Schmidt and others. bibl f il *Science* 238:960-3 N 13 '87
Cultivation
About corn. S. Pacher. il *Mother Earth News* 106:20-2+ Jl/Ag '87
Bend, but don't break, starter placement [fertilizer placement for corn] R. Fee. il *Success Farm* 85 no4:18E F '87
The Corn Belt: waning in importance? M. D. Winsberg. il *Focus* 37:32 Summ '87
The land that corn farmers forgot [Nebraska] J. Walter. il *Success Farm* 85 no3:18K F '87
No-hands handling of corn insecticides [hopper system] J. Walter. il *Success Farm* 85 no1:26H Ja '87
Scepter carryover stunts cotton and corn. *Success Farm* 85:62 S '87
Spike starter with extra nitrogen. R. Fee. il *Success Farm* 85:18Y Ap '87
Super sweet corns. il *Flower Gard* 31:18 Ap/My '87
They read the leaves to target fertilizer [DRIS analysis] M. Holmberg. il *Success Farm* 85 no3:18AH F '87
Diseases and pests
See also
Bollworms
Borers (Insects)
Corn rootworms

Gene transfer in corn. D. D. Edwards. *Sci News* 131:37 Ja 17 '87
New corn blight has little effect on seed marketing. *Success Farm* 85:10 My '87
New southern corn leaf blight threatens U.S. *Success Farm* 85:18 Ap '87
No-bug bins. il *Success Farm* 85:34 S '87
Seed companies abandon C cytoplasm [threat from southern corn leaf blight] *Success Farm* 85:62I O '87
Field experiments
Bottom-line tillage trials [Minnesota demonstration plots] R. Fee. il *Success Farm* 85 no4:18P F '87
Harvesting
A yield against the odds: harvest time on a Missouri farm. R. Rhodes. il *Harpers* 274:53-7 Ap '87
Marketing
The synthetic hedge: reducing market risk. G. Vincent. il *Success Farm* 85 no6:5 Mr '87
Prices
This market pays $2.40 for corn! [food grade corn] *Success Farm* 85:62G O '87
Seed
Production
See Seed industry
Storage
Storage sprouts in cornfield. il *Success Farm* 85:70K Ag '87

Corn (Term)
Corn, glorious corn. R. Lynes. il *Archit Dig* 44:42+ Mr '87

Corn bisque *See* Bisques (Cooking)
Corn borers *See* Borers (Insects)
Corn bread *See* Cornbread
Corn earworms *See* Bollworms
Corn meal
See also
Cooking—Corn meal
From our kitchen to yours. K. Adams. *South Living* 22:161 F '87

Corn price supports *See* Agricultural administration
Corn rootworms
Control
Wind hurts pattern, but not control [insecticide application] R. Fee. il *Success Farm* 85 no1:20-1 Ja '87

Corn seed industry *See* Seed industry
Cornbread
Cornbread mix offers possibilities. il *South Living* 22:119 Ag '87
From our kitchen to yours. K. Adams. *South Living* 22:161 F '87

Cornea
Surgery
A living contact lens [epikeratophakia] P. Spencer. *50 Plus* 27:82-3 Je '87
Radial keratotomy: a cure for myopia? J. Pace. il *Consum Res Mag* 70:27-31 O '87
Transplantation
The gift of sight [case of J. McGuire; with editorial comment by Bard Lindeman] P. Spencer. il pors *50 Plus* 27:4, 24-7+ Je '87

Corned beef cooking *See* Cooking—Meat
Cornejo, Dennis
For the desert toad, rain starts a race to metamorphosis. il *Smithsonian* 17:98-105 Mr '87

Cornelissen, Michael
about
Royal Trust challenges the banks. P. C. Newman. il por *Macleans* 100:25 Jl 27 '87

Cornell, Joseph, 1903-1972
about
Joseph Cornell. N. Grimes. il *Art News* 86:143 Mr '87

Cornell, Katharine, 1893-1974
about
In the dunes. C. Vogel. il *N Y Times Mag* p70-4 My 31 '87

Cornell University
Cornell's supercomputer building at the brink. I. Goodwin. il *Phys Today* 40:63 O '87

Cornell University. Cooperative Extension
General Kline's secret army [agent R. A. Kline] J. Cook. il pors *Ctry J* 14:36-41 Jl '87

Cornell University. Medical Center *See* New York Hospital-Cornell Medical Center
Cornell University. Medical College
NIH finally resolves 7-year dispute [case of J. S. Borer] C. Holden. *Science* 238:151 O 9 '87

Corner cupboards See Cupboards
Corner shelves See Shelves and racks
Cornerstone Theater Company
Prairie town companions. J. Conant. il *Newsweek* 110:68-9
S 21 '87
Cornfeld, Betty
The "interactive" generation. il *Ms* 16:79-81 D '87
Cornfield, Jim
Meet the masters. il *Petersens Photogr Mag* 16:22-4+
S '87
Corning Glass Works
See also
Steuben Glass
Cornish, Samuel E.
about
Founders of the black press. L. Bennett. il pors *Ebony*
42:96+ F '87
Cornish pumps See Mine pumps
Cornman, Reba
(jt. auth) See Poppleton, Lou Anne, and Cornman, Reba
Cornrow hairstyles See Hairstyling
Cornwell, David
about
NFL appoints black to monitor minority hiring. *Jet*
73:46 O 12 '87
Cornwell, Rupert
Campaigning in Moscow. *World Press Rev* 34:11-12 My
'87
Gorbachev tackles the Academy. *World Press Rev* 34:53
Ag '87
Corona, Solar See Sun—Corona
Corona beer See Beer
Coronado National Forest (Ariz. and N.M.)
Mount Graham, Arizona. R. H. Mohlenbrock. il map
Nat Hist 96:88-90 Mr '87
Coronary artery catheterization See Cardiac catheterization
Coronary artery disease See Arteriosclerosis
Coronary artery surgery See Blood vessels—Surgery
Coronary bypass surgery See Heart—Surgery
Coronary diseases See Heart—Diseases
Coronel, Leandro V.
A new road in the Philippines spurs development. il
UN Chron 24:66-7 Ag '87
Corporal punishment
Blacks more likely to be suspended, punished in nation's
public schools. *Jet* 72:32 Ap 20 '87
Dads who hit. R. B. McCall. il *Parents* 62:242 O '87
Paddling: still a sore point [school discipline] J. N.
Baker. il *Newsweek* 109:61 Je 22 '87
Punitiveness and public policy: child abuse in American
schools. I. A. Hyman. il *USA Today (Periodical)*
116:44-7 S '87
Spare the rod—and the child? [results of survey; with
editorial comment by Elizabeth Crow] I. Groller. il
Parents 62:6, 27 S '87
White woman jailed for hitting black principal who
paddled her son [incident in Moody, Ala.] il por *Jet*
73:6-7 N 30 '87

Religious aspects
Anecdotes, facetiae, satire, etc.
Manufacturer not responsible [marketing "Rod of Correction"] M. E. Marty. *Christ Century* 104:1159 D 16
'87

Corporate airplanes See Airplanes, Business
Corporate art collections See Art and industry
Corporate Average Fuel Economy standard See Automobile
engines—Energy usage
Corporate bonds See Bonds
Corporate campaigns See Trade unions—Corporate cam-
paigns
Corporate classrooms See Employees—Training
Corporate couples See Married couples—Employment
Corporate crimes See Commercial crimes
Corporate culture See Organizational behavior
Corporate debt See Corporations—Finance
Corporate ethics See Business ethics
Corporate flying See Airplanes in business
Corporate founders See Entrepreneurs
Corporate giving See Corporations—Charitable contribu-
tions
Corporate headhunters See Executive search consultants
Corporate income tax See Corporations—Taxation
Corporate Information Group
Marketing the 'lowdown on high tech'. K. Cook. il
por *Work Woman* 12:74+ My '87

Corporate law See Corporation law
Corporate liquidation See Liquidation
Corporate lobby See Lobbyists and lobbying
Corporate management See Business management
Corporate names See Corporations—Names
Corporate nepotism See Nepotism
Corporate patronage of art See Art and industry
Corporate patronage of the arts See Arts and industry
Corporate planning See Business planning
Corporate power See Big business
Corporate profit See Corporations—Finance
Corporate profit forecasting See Business forecasting
Corporate recruiting See Employees—Recruiting
Corporate reorganization See Corporations—Reorganization
Corporate responsibility See Business—Social aspects
Corporate secrets See Trade secrets
Corporate sponsorship of sports events See Business and
sports
Corporate training films See Motion pictures in industry
Corporation for Public Broadcasting
'You can't yank the rug out' [interview with W. Hanley]
pors *Channels* 7:62-3 Mr '87
Corporation law
See also
Antitrust law
Corporations—Acquisitions and mergers—Laws and
regulations
Liability (Law)
Small business—Laws and regulations
United States. Securities and Exchange Commission
The battle for corporate control [cover story] B. Nussbaum
and J. H. Dobrzynski. il *Bus Week* p102-9 My 18
'87
David Boies: the ace litigator playing Texaco's hand.
L. J. Tell. il por *Bus Week* p79 Ap 20 '87
Judicial imperialism [cover story; special section] il *Forbes*
139:109-12+ Je 1 '87
Meet Larry Tribe, Pennzoil's hole card [bested Texaco
in Supreme Court] L. Helm and P. Dwyer. il por
Bus Week p78-9 Ap 20 '87
On the docket. See issues of Forbes
Corporation lawyers See Lawyers
Corporation reports
See also
Financial statements
Annual report illustration. M. Olson. il *Petersens Photogr
Mag* 16:70-1 S '87
Beware of what you don't see [annual reports] L. Jereski.
il *Forbes* 139:102 Mr 23 '87
The corporate report striptease. R. Brady. il *Nations
Bus* 75:45 Je '87
Haste makes waste [SEC's Edgar computer system] G.
Slutsker and J. Novack. il *Forbes* 140:94+ Ag 24 '87
Reading between the lines of an annual report. G. Weiss.
il *Bus Week* p164-5 Mr 23 '87
This year's annual reports: show business as usual. J.
A. Byrne. il *Bus Week* p42 Ap 13 '87
Corporations
See also
Big business
Black business enterprises
Black executives
Closely held corporations
Executives
Family corporations
Minority business enterprises
Proxies
Small business
Stockholders
Stocks
Women executives
America's most admired corporations [Fortune survey]
E. C. Baig. il *Fortune* 115:18-31+ Ja 19 '87
The corporation. See issues of Business Week
Corporation as citizen [address, May 22, 1987] D. F.
Linowes. *Vital Speeches Day* 53:755-8 O 1 '87
Goodbye, corporate staff. T. Moore. il *Fortune* 116:65+
D 21 '87

Accounting
See also
Automobile industry—Accounting
Corporation reports
Insurance companies—Accounting
Pensions—Accounting
Real estate agencies and agents—Accounting
Small business—Accounting
Telephone companies—Accounting
Television industry—Accounting
Numbers game. See issues of Forbes
Victory at last? [inflation accounting] J. Andresky. il
Forbes 139:65-6 Je 1 '87

Corporations—*cont.*
Acquisitions and mergers
See also
Advertising agencies—Acquisitions and mergers
Aerospace industries—Acquisitions and mergers
Airlines—Acquisitions and mergers
Airplane industry—Acquisitions and mergers
Automobile industry—Acquisitions and mergers
Avionics industry—Acquisitions and mergers
Bank holding companies—Acquisitions and mergers
Banks and banking—Acquisitions and mergers
Boatbuilding—Acquisitions and mergers
Book industries—Acquisitions and mergers
Bottled water industry—Acquisitions and mergers
Brewing industry—Acquisitions and mergers
Brokers—Acquisitions and mergers
Building materials industry—Acquisitions and mergers
Bus lines—Acquisitions and mergers
Cable television—Acquisitions and mergers
Casinos—Acquisitions and mergers
Chemical industries—Acquisitions and mergers
Clothing industry—Acquisitions and mergers
Computer industry—Acquisitions and mergers
Computer service industries—Acquisitions and mergers
Construction industry—Acquisitions and mergers
Container industry—Acquisitions and mergers
Cosmetics industry—Acquisitions and mergers
Dairying—Acquisitions and mergers
Department stores—Acquisitions and mergers
Drug industry—Acquisitions and mergers
Electric industries—Acquisitions and mergers
Electric utilities—Acquisitions and mergers
Electronic industries—Acquisitions and mergers
Electronic shopping—Acquisitions and mergers
Employment agencies—Acquisitions and mergers
Entertainment industry—Acquisitions and mergers
Fast food restaurants—Acquisitions and mergers
Finance companies—Acquisitions and mergers
Financial institutions—Acquisitions and mergers
Firearms industry—Acquisitions and mergers
Food industry—Acquisitions and mergers
Gas industry—Acquisitions and mergers
Genetic research industry—Acquisitions and mergers
Greenmail
Hair care products industry—Acquisitions and mergers
Household appliances industry—Acquisitions and mergers
Household furnishings industry—Acquisitions and mergers
Insurance companies—Acquisitions and mergers
Investment advisers—Acquisitions and mergers
Investment banking—Acquisitions and mergers
Investment trusts—Acquisitions and mergers
Leveraged buyouts
Liquor industry—Acquisitions and mergers
Lumber industry—Acquisitions and mergers
Market research—Acquisitions and mergers
Mass media industry—Acquisitions and mergers
Mattress industry—Acquisitions and mergers
Meat industry—Acquisitions and mergers
Medical care industry—Acquisitions and mergers
Mining industry—Acquisitions and mergers
Mortgage banks—Acquisitions and mergers
Motion picture industry—Acquisitions and mergers
Newspaper publishers and publishing—Acquisitions and mergers
Paper industry—Acquisitions and mergers
Personal care products industry—Acquisitions and mergers
Petrochemical industry—Acquisitions and mergers
Petroleum equipment industry—Acquisitions and mergers
Petroleum industry—Acquisitions and mergers
Phonograph record industry—Acquisitions and mergers
Printing industry—Acquisitions and mergers
Publishers and publishing—Acquisitions and mergers
Radio industry—Acquisitions and mergers
Railroads—Acquisitions and mergers
Real estate business—Acquisitions and mergers
Retail trade—Acquisitions and mergers
Steel industry—Acquisitions and mergers
Sugar industry—Acquisitions and mergers
Supermarkets—Acquisitions and mergers
Telecommunication—Acquisitions and mergers
Telephone companies—Acquisitions and mergers
Telephone equipment industry—Acquisitions and mergers

Television industry—Acquisitions and mergers
Textile industry—Acquisitions and mergers
Tire industry—Acquisitions and mergers
Toy and game industry—Acquisitions and mergers
Transportation—Acquisitions and mergers
Wine industry—Acquisitions and mergers
A $100,000 campus 'raid' [Columbia Business School teacher A. Edelman's finder's fee raises questions of conflict of interests] A. Gabor. por *U S News World Rep* 103:12-13 O 26 '87
A $100,000 question stirs up Columbia [A. Edelman offers his Columbia business students a finder's fee for spotting a good takeover target] B. Kantrowitz. il por *Newsweek* 110:76 O 26 '87
The battle for USX: Icahn retreats for now. *Newsweek* 109:42 Ja 19 '87
Bear hug [failed mergers when big companies swallow little ones] C. Poole and J. A. Trachtenberg. il *Forbes* 140:186-7+ N 16 '87
Bullish on takeovers [Merrill Lynch] J. Crudele. il *N Y* 20:14 My 25 '87
Buy-outs on Wall Street [merger activity rises in spite of insider trading scandal] L. Black. il *Macleans* 100:29 Mr 30 '87
Buying companies the old-fashioned way [R. S. Jepson] C. Siler. il por *Forbes* 140 Sp Issue:357+ O 26 '87
Can UAL and its Hilton wing fly in formation? J. E. Ellis. il *Bus Week* p45 Ja 12 '87
Corporate clients feel seduced and abandoned [faith in investment firms] J. A. Byrne. il *Bus Week* p34 Mr 2 '87
Creative destruction [Forbes 70th anniversary issue; cover story; special issue] il *Forbes* 140:49-51 Jl 13 '87
The credibility gap widens [raiders] T. Jaffe. *Forbes* 139:110 Ja 26 '87
Deal mania: tax reform is no tranquilizer after all. S. Weiss. il *Bus Week* p66-7 Mr 30 '87
Deals of the year. D. P. Wiener. il *Fortune* 115:68-72+ F 2 '87
Dear Betty Harragan [anti-nepotism policy instituted after corporate merger] B. L. Harragan. il *Work Woman* 12:38+ D '87
Don't go near the dollars [Columbia Business School vetoes professor A. Edelman's offer of finder's fee to a student who could come up with a company ripe for raiding] E. Bowen. il por *Time* 130:138-9 O 26 '87
Edelman's art of reward [offer of $100,000 finder's fee to Columbia Business School students] N. J. Perry. il por *Fortune* 116:159 N 9 '87
Everybody's doing it, doing it [hostile takeover game] A. Sloan. il *Forbes* 139:32 Ap 20 '87
For better or for worse? [1983-86] J. H. Dobrzynski. il *Bus Week* p38-40 Ja 12 '87
Ford's Bruce Blythe has a big blank check—and a mission. J. B. Treece. il por *Bus Week* p79+ D 21 '87
From street kid to superstar? [bid for Cyclops by S. Rose] D. Cook. il por *Bus Week* p33 F 16 '87
General Eclectic [General Electric] E. A. Finn, Jr. il *Forbes* 139:74-8+ Mr 23 '87
General Electric is stalking big game again. J. R. Norman. il por *Bus Week* p112-13 Mr 16 '87
Going hunting for sitting ducks [takeover targets] J. Edgerton and J. E. Goodman. il *Money* 16:7 Je '87
Harold Simmons is set to roll another seven [proposal to merge NL Industries into Valhi] G. G. Marcial. il por *Bus Week* p106 O 5 '87
Home-equity loans, Wall Street style [recapitalization as takeover defense] J. Egan. il *U S News World Rep* 102:50-1 Je 22 '87
How the 12 top raiders rate. T. Moore. il *Fortune* 116:44-5+ S 28 '87
How to be a raider. J. Crudele. il *N Y* 20:14+ Jl 13 '87
Irv Jacobs is calling 'time out'. P. Houston. il *Bus Week* p46 Je 1 '87
Is the merger mania good for the nation? [address, February 19, 1987] D. F. Linowes. *Vital Speeches Day* 53:423-6 My 1 '87
Just merged [cover story] K. Berney. il *Nations Bus* 75:30-2+ D '87
Look who's charging into the merger business [big banks] S. Bartlett. il *Bus Week* p44 Mr 9 '87
Mega mergers [address, September 7, 1987] R. H. Guest. *Vital Speeches Day* 54:20-2 O 15 '87
Merger mania: a high-stakes game. M. Christopher. il *Sch Update* 119:10-11 Ja 26 '87
Merger phobia has unions wheeling and dealing. Z. Schiller. il *Bus Week* p118+ Mr 23 '87
Money managing in a bell jar. M. M. Thomas. il *Nation* 244:318-20 Mr 14 '87

Corporations—Acquisitions and mergers—*cont.*

Natalie Koether: the lady is a raider. P. Finch. il por *Bus Week* p118-19 F 23 '87

Need a quick billion or two? Just ask your banker [lending for mergers and LBOs] S. Bartlett. il *Bus Week* p98-9 O 26 '87

The next takeover artist you meet could be Jeff Steiner [Banner Industries takeover of Rexnord Inc.] Z. Schiller. il por *Bus Week* p33+ F 9 '87

Now introducing son of greenmail [recapitalization as a takeover defense] *Time* 129:62 Je 8 '87

Paul Bilzerian still don't get no respect. P. Engardio. il por *Bus Week* p62+ N 23 '87

The raiders may be sniffing 'round USX again. G. G. Marcial. il *Bus Week* p74 Mr 30 '87

Raiders retreat—for now [effect of stock market crash] G. Bock. il *Time* 130:39 N 9 '87

Rating the raiders. J. Crudele. *N Y* 20:22 Ag 31 '87

Responding to corporate takeovers. M. L. Weidenbaum. *Society* 24:26-9 S/O '87

The takeover controversy [address, March 17, 1987] M. C. Jensen. *Vital Speeches Day* 53:426-9 My 1 '87

The takeover game: many were forced to punt [effects of October crash] C. Hawkins and others. il por *Bus Week* p53 N 2 '87

Terrorists in three-piece suits [address, March 3, 1987] R. E. Mercer. *Vital Speeches Day* 53:421-3 My 1 '87

To sell or not to sell . . . [black business enterprises] M. King. il *Black Enterp* 17:287-8+ Je '87

The top 200 deals. G. Weiss. il *Bus Week* Sp Issue:273-4+ Ap 17 '87

Wall Street ponders the continuing dearth of dividends . . . and wonders how long the merger boom can carry the ball. G. Koretz. il *Bus Week* p16+ Ag 3 '87

Waterloo at USX [chairman D. Roderick fends off takeover attempt by C. Icahn] J. Castro. il por *Time* 129:51 Ja 19 '87

What the Boesky scandal means to you and your money [takeover stocks] J. Edgerton. il *Money* 16:64-7 Ja '87

When going gets rough, corporate raiders get scarce. il *U S News World Rep* 102:36 F 23 '87

When Jack Welch takes over: a guide for the newly acquired [GE takeovers] R. Mitchell. il *Bus Week* p95 D 14 '87

Where pros are fishing in the wake of the crash [takeover stocks] G. G. Marcial. il *Bus Week* p136 N 30 '87

Who said takeovers were dead? B. Rudolph. il *Time* 129:42 Mr 23 '87

Who's afraid of the big bad bear? Not the dealmakers. J. H. Dobrzynski. il *Bus Week* p62-3 N 16 '87

Who's getting the deal in the Triangle shuffle? [N. Peltz and P. W. May construct deal to sell Triangle to its affiliate CJI Industries Inc.] C. Power. il por *Bus Week* p78 N 23 '87

Why nothing seems to make a dent in dealmaking. J. H. Dobrzynski. il *Bus Week* p75 Jl 20 '87

Why so many mergers fail [clash of corporate cultures] M. Lefkoe. il por *Fortune* 116:113-14 Jl 20 '87

With Lindner in charge, Penn Central is on the prowl. R. Mitchell. il *Bus Week* p80-1 Ap 20 '87

International aspects

The 100 largest foreign investments in the U.S. il *Forbes* 140:146-50 Jl 27 '87

Belzbergs on the prowl. T. Fennell. il *Macleans* 100:32 Je 29 '87

The British raider who sneaked up on ADT [M. Ashcroft] M. Maremont. il por *Bus Week* p33+ Ag 31 '87

Hanson and Kidde: a marriage made in low tech; A portrait of the raider as respected industrialist. L. Baum and R. A. Melcher. il *Bus Week* p36-7 Ag 17 '87

The lucky gambler [J. Goldsmith] O. Friedrich. il por *Time* 130:60-2 N 23 '87

A promise comes of age [Ciba-Geigy takes over Spectra-Physics] R. Addis. il *Forbes* 140:8 Ag 24 '87

Raiders of the cheap buck [foreign raiders after the crash] D. Pauly. il *Newsweek* 110:51 N 30 '87

Laws and regulations

See also

Antitrust law

An acid test for antitakeover laws [Minnesota law could help Alberto-Culver land Lamaur] M. J. Pitzer. il *Bus Week* p31 S 28 '87

. . . and Proxmire takes aim at takeover abuses. V. Cahan. *Bus Week* p35 Ap 20 '87

Are we hissing the wrong guys? G. J. Stigler. il *Forbes* 140:52-3+ Jl 13 '87

Beware of state takeover laws. J. W. Bartlett. il *Fortune* 116:179+ N 9 '87

The blight on Wall Street. F. G. Rohatyn. il *N Y Rev Books* 34:21-3 Mr 12 '87

Corporate socialism [anti-takeover bill in Delaware] R. J. Samuelson. il *Newsweek* 110:42 D 28 '87

Examine the motives of junk-bond critics. W. J. Carney. il *Bus Week* p18 Mr 30 '87

Free gifts [Minnesota passes anti-takeover measure influenced by Dayton Hudson's charity] J. K. Glassman. *New Repub* 197:10+ Jl 27 '87

A lawyer justified [J. Tobin] A. A. Lappen. il por *Forbes* 139:8 Je 29 '87

Merge while the merging's good [views of National Association of Attorneys General] il *Fortune* 116:12 N 23 '87

No news is bad news [quicker corporate disclosure to discourage insider trading] J. Crudele. il *N Y* 20:20-1 Je 8 '87

"Play me—or trade me" [NFL draft compared to impending merger rules] S. Blotnick. il *Forbes* 140:176 Jl 27 '87

Raiders could get some very short leashes. V. Cahan. il *Bus Week* p34 Ap 27 '87

Regulating "hostile" takeovers [views of Michael Bradley] il *USA Today (Periodical)* 115:6 Ap '87

States vs. raiders: will Washington step in? V. Cahan. il *Bus Week* p56-7 Ag 31 '87

The Supreme Court [barriers to hostile takeover bids upheld] M. S. Forbes, Jr. il *Forbes* 139:33 My 18 '87

Takeover artists take a direct hit [Supreme Court upholds states' power to restrict hostile bids] P. Dwyer. il *Bus Week* p35 My 4 '87

Takeover hurdle [Supreme Court decision allows state regulation of corporate takeovers] *Time* 129:74 My 4 '87

Takeover—a positive force. M. S. Forbes, Jr. il *Forbes* 140:25 O 19 '87

A top law firm feels the heat [Sullivan & Cromwell's G. C. Kern charged by SEC with violating disclosure rules during Campeau's bid on Allied Stores] C. Friday. *Newsweek* 110:40-1 Jl 13 '87

Two lawyers turning Cravath into a force in takeovers [A. Finkelson and R. S. Rolfe] M. Frons. pors *Bus Week* p103 Ja 26 '87

The war on takeovers [closing tax loopholes] L. Saunders. il *Forbes* 140:116-17 N 30 '87

When companies talk turkey, investors should be told [SEC charges against G. C. Kern and Allied Stores over inadequate disclosure in Campeau hostile takeover] V. Cahan. il *Bus Week* p100 Jl 13 '87

Zuckerman bound [J. Zuckerman of the Federal Trade Commission] G. Slutsker. il por *Forbes* 139:123 F 9 '87

Laws and regulations—Canada

Battle to control a retail institution [Canadian Tire Corp. Ltd.] T. Tedesco. il *Macleans* 100:38 Ja 19 '87

Canadian Tire showdown. T. Tedesco. il *Macleans* 100:36 Je 22 '87

The epic struggle [Canadian Tire takeover attempt; special section] il *Macleans* 100:26-33 Ja 26 '87

Unicorp fuels a fight [sale of Palm Dairies blocked by Competition Act tribunal] T. Fennell. il *Macleans* 100:14-15 Ja 5 '87

Australia

The raiders Down Under may be down and out [stock market crash] C. Debes. il por *Bus Week* p55 N 9 '87

Canada

Building a first for Canada [Onex Capital Corp.] D. Jenish. il por *Macleans* 100:22+ Jl 27 '87

Hidden costs of takeovers. A. Shortell. il *Macleans* 100:30-1 D 7 '87

The new debate about takeovers. D. Jenish. il *Macleans* 100:38-9 My 4 '87

France

Moet and Vuitton: the dernier cri in chic. F. J. Comes. *Bus Week* p49 Je 15 '87

Les raiders are on the rampage in Europe. J. Kapstein and F. J. Comes. il *Bus Week* p44-5 S 28 '87

Sir Jimmy pulls the plug on his French connection [J. Goldsmith sells out stake in Générale Occidentale to Compagnie Générale d'Electricité] J. Rossant. il por *Bus Week* p24 Ag 10 '87

Takeover fever spreads to France. S. Marti. il *World Press Rev* 34:48 Mr '87

Great Britain

Table for two [Waterford-Wedgwood merger] A. A. Lappen. il *Forbes* 140:8 D 28 '87

Corporations—Acquisitions and mergers—*cont.*

Japan

Japanese takeover artists are learning fast. B. Buell. il *Bus Week* p40-1 Ag 3 '87

Sweden

A financial gambler tries to trump the Wallenbergs again [E. Penser's moves on Swedish Match] J. Kapstein. *Bus Week* p50+ Ja 19 '87

Western Europe

Conglomeration Italian style [C. De Benedetti's empire] S. Solomon. il por *Forbes* 139:36-8 Mr 23 '87

Europe's takeover kings. S. Tully. il *Fortune* 116:95-6+ Jl 20 '87

Hands across Europe: deals that could redraw the map. J. Templeman. il *Bus Week* p64-5 My 18 '87

How business is creating Europe Inc. J. Heard and J. Kapstein. il *Bus Week* p40-1 S 7 '87

Les raiders are on the rampage in Europe. J. Kapstein and F. J. Comes. il *Bus Week* p44-5 S 28 '87

Advertising

See Advertising

Charitable contributions

Free gifts [Minnesota passes anti-takeover measure influenced by Dayton Hudson's charity] J. K. Glassman. *New Repub* 197:10+ Jl 27 '87

Reaping high returns from social investments. B. Robson. il *Black Enterp* 18:86-8+ D '87

Survivor's debt. D. A. Tate. il *N Y Times Mag* p38 Ag 30 '87

Crime

See Commercial crimes

Directories

America's leading exporters [with introd. by Alan Farnham] il *Fortune* 116:72-3 Jl 20 '87

The corporate elite [with CEO 1000 directory] il *Bus Week* Sp Issue:13-17+ O 23 '87

The Forbes 500s [cover story] il *Forbes* 139 Ann Directory:128-30+ Ap 27 '87

The Forbes foreign rankings [special section] il *Forbes* 140:111-14+ Jl 27 '87

The Fortune 500: the largest U.S. industrial corporations [cover story; special section; with introd. by Stephen J. Madden and Julianne Slovak] il *Fortune* 115:359-61+ Ap 27 '87

The international 500 [with introd. by Terence P. Paré and Wilton Woods] il *Fortune* 116:214-15+ Ag 3 '87

No one is safe [Forbes top 100 companies over the last 70 years] P. Newcomb. il *Forbes* 140:121-3+ Jl 13 '87

The service 500 [cover story; special section] il *Fortune* 115:191-4+ Je 8 '87

The U.S. news 100: market bonanzas [cover story; special section] il *U S News World Rep* 103:48-57+ Jl 6 '87

The world's 50 biggest industrial CEOs [with introd. by Terence Paré and Wilton Woods; cover story] il *Fortune* 116:23-31+ Ag 3 '87

Directors

Blue collars in the boardroom: putting business first. J. Hoerr. il *Bus Week* p126+ D 14 '87

Directors aren't doing their jobs. D. J. Dunn. il por *Fortune* 115:117-19 Mr 16 '87

How to fire the CEO. R. B. Stolley. il *Fortune* 116:38-41+ Ag 31 '87

How to get on a board [strategy for getting more women aboard] il por *Nations Bus* 75:57 N '87

Is it safe to go back in the boardroom? [exempting directors from liability] B. Powell. il *Newsweek* 109:45-6 My 4 '87

New look for corporate directors. P. Plawin. *Changing Times* 41:116-17 O '87

Responding to corporate takeovers. M. L. Weidenbaum. *Society* 24:26-9 S/O '87

Ten reasons for an outside board [family businesses] S. Nelton. il *Nations Bus* 75:48+ O '87

Top black directors on major corporate boards. D. C. Lyons. il *Ebony* 42:77-80+ O '87

Vernon Jordan named to board of Revlon. por *Jet* 73:39 O 26 '87

Divestiture

AT&T may be ready to cut its losses in computers [Olivetti to join in a spinoff] J. J. Keller. il *Bus Week* p30 Jl 6 '87

Beyond book [breakup value] M. Ozanian. il *Forbes* 139:166 Mr 23 '87

Can Santa Fe outrun the raiders? K. Deveny. il *Bus Week* p60-1 N 2 '87

The decline of Lorimar's instant empire. R. Grover. il por *Bus Week* p29 Jl 6 '87

Eaton sees its future—and it's on the ground. S. Phillips. il por *Bus Week* p113+ N 16 '87

Eaton to sell AIL, all other defense electronics units. *Aviat Week Space Technol* 127:29 N 2 '87

Getting antsy [boom in sales of businesses] J. Crudele. il *N Y* 20:35 O 19 '87

Give it to the stockholders? [Mobil may spinoff Montgomery Ward] C. Siler. il *Forbes* 140:55-6 S 7 '87

Kinder-Care may stick to its sitting. D. Foust. il por *Bus Week* p36 Jl 13 '87

Kraft, minus some extra baggage, is picking up speed. K. Dreyfack. il por *Bus Week* p74-5 Mr 9 '87

A random walk through Euclid [spinoff subsidiaries in the new issues market] R. Phalon. il *Forbes* 140:170+ S 21 '87

RJR Nabisco may cut down on tobacco. G. G. Marcial. il *Bus Week* p116 F 23 '87

Santa Fe's pursuers may have to settle for pieces. S. Toy. il *Bus Week* p74 D 28 '87-Ja 4 '88

This Penn Central spinoff may soar [Sprague Technologies] G. G. Marcial. *Bus Week* p61 Ag 31 '87

U.S. Shoe isn't dragging its feet. G. G. Marcial. *Bus Week* p101 Jl 13 '87

Why IC is uncoupling itself from the past. K. Deveny. il por *Bus Week* p120+ O 12 '87

Will a spinoff rev up GM? [General Motors Acceptance Corp.] G. G. Marcial. *Bus Week* p100 F 16 '87

Employees

See Employees

Finance

See also

Bonds

Capital

Corporations—Accounting

Corporations—Valuation

Corporations, International—Finance

Cost control

Dividends

Employees as stockholders

Securities

Small business—Finance

Stocks—Marketing

Swap financing

Caution in the boardroom [effect of stock market crash] J. Castro. il *Time* 130:34+ N 9 '87

A cloud over stock prices [corporate profits] D. Pauly. il *Newsweek* 109:50 Mr 16 '87

Companies are staying cool—but moving fast [stock market crash] C. Farrell. il *Bus Week* p37 N 9 '87

Corporate finance. See issues of Business Week

Corporate profits: reading between the bottom lines [operating earnings] K. Pennar. il *Bus Week* p102+ Je 15 '87

Financial modeling: going beyond spreadsheets. C. Spencer. il *Pers Comput* 11:68-71+ Ap '87

How corporate America is coping with the aftershocks [stock market crash] C. Power. il *Bus Week* p105+ N 16 '87

How the long runup will change corporate behavior [bull market] A. L. Cowan and E. Spragins. il *Bus Week* p62-3 F 2 '87

Industry outlook [special section] il *Bus Week* p65-72+ Ja 12 '87

Making more debt do double duty [securitization] C. Farrell. il *Bus Week* p67-8 Mr 30 '87

The market crash batters corporate balance sheets [corporate debt] G. Koretz. il *Bus Week* p24 D 7 '87

The meanest and leanest sit down to just deserts. B. Nussbaum. il *Bus Week* p30-1 F 9 '87

Over the ears in debt [views of Time's Board of Economists] G. Russell. il *Time* 129:58-60 Mr 9 '87

Over their heads? [mounting corporate debt] J. Crudele. il *N Y* 20:19-20 Je 22 '87

Pleasing profit prospects. S. Nasar. il *Fortune* 115:65 Mr 30 '87

Profits are up—but caveat investor. C. Power. il *Bus Week* p36-7 My 4 '87

Strategic budgeting in good times and bad. K. Stechert. il *Work Woman* 12:88-90+ Je '87

Statistics

See also

Corporations, International—Finance—Statistics

39th annual report on American industry [special issue] il *Forbes* 139:61-78+ Ja 12 '87

The 400 largest private companies in the U.S. il *Forbes* 140:150-2+ D 14 '87

Corporate scoreboard. il *Bus Week* p101-6+ Ag 17 '87

Corporate scoreboard. il *Bus Week* p131-6+ My 18 '87

Corporate scoreboard. L. Baum. il *Bus Week* p196-9+ N 16 '87

The Forbes 500s [cover story] il *Forbes* 139 Ann Directory:128-30+ Ap 27 '87

Corporations—Finance—Statistics—*cont.*

The Fortune 500: the largest U.S. industrial corporations [cover story; special section; with introd. by Stephen J. Madden and Julianne Slovak] il *Fortune* 115:359-61+ Ap 27 '87

No one is safe [Forbes top 100 companies over the last 70 years] P. Newcomb. il *Forbes* 140:121-3+ Jl 13 '87

Numbers to help you size up the market's prospects—and yours. il *Bus Week* p186-7+ D 28 '87-Ja 4 '88

Paltry gains almost everywhere. il *Bus Week* p125-9+ Mr 16 '87

A preview of second-quarter profits. il *Bus Week* p28 Jl 27 '87

A preview of third-quarter profits. il *Bus Week* p61 N 2 '87

The top 1000. il *Bus Week* Sp Issue:30-3+ Ap 17 '87

The U.S. news 100: market bonanzas [cover story; special section] il *U S News World Rep* 103:48-57+ Jl 6 '87

Foreign subsidiaries
See Corporations, International
Founders
See Entrepreneurs
Laws and regulations
See Corporation law
Lawyers
See Lawyers
Liquidation
See Liquidation
Location
See Location in business and industry
Management
See Business management
Meetings

Do you spend too much time in meetings? [excerpt from Effective listening] K. J. Murphy. *Work Woman* 12:30 D '87

The fine art of leading a meeting. J. Bailey. il *Work Woman* 12:68-70+ Ag '87

How to run a really good meeting [interview with W. Green] por *U S News World Rep* 103:80 O 12 '87

Howdy Letzring can make your company meetings immortal [videotapes] M. Frons. il por *Bus Week* p103 Ja 26 '87

Making the most out of meetings. J. A. Byrne. il *Bus Week* p120 Jl 13 '87

Planning exciting meetings and conventions. L. Hazelton. il *Black Enterp* 17:40-1 Mr '87

Names

The new name game. B. Kanner. il *N Y* 20:16+ Mr 16 '87

What really is in a name? J. Schwartz. il *Newsweek* 110:55 N 30 '87

Price policies
See Price policies
Public relations
See Business—Public relations
Regulation
See Industry and state
Reorganization
See also
Recapitalization
Workout investments

Allegis will live on—in the nightmares of CEOs. J. H. Dobrzynski. il *Bus Week* p29 Je 29 '87

The basics come back. il *Fortune* 116:8 Ag 31 '87

Creative destruction [Forbes 70th anniversary issue; cover story; special issue] il *Forbes* 140:49-51 Jl 13 '87

Drexel's heavy hand [bid to restructure Western Union] C. Friday. il *Newsweek* 110:53+ N 23 '87

How Dick Ferris blew it [Allegis Corp.] K. Labich. il por *Fortune* 116:42-4+ Jl 6 '87

Investors' breakup of Allegis prompts Ferris resignation. *Aviat Week Space Technol* 126:82 Je 15 '87

Make-over fever. J. Crudele. il *N Y* 20:14+ Ag 17 '87

The new corporate environment [cover story; special section; with editorial comment by Earl G. Graves] il *Black Enterp* 18:9, 40-2+ Ag '87

Old-line industry shapes up [restructuring] T. Moore. il *Fortune* 115:22-6+ Ap 27 '87

One man's dream comes down to earth [R. Ferris' failed strategy for Allegis] C. P. Work and H. Wells. il por *U S News World Rep* 102:44-5 Je 22 '87

Our changing capital markets [address, April 30, 1987] D. B. Marron. *Vital Speeches Day* 53:586-8 Jl 15 '87

Restructuring really works. M. Magnet. il *Fortune* 115:38-44+ Mr 2 '87

The restructuring regimen. il *Fortune* 115:6-7 Ja 5 '87

The sad saga of Western Union's decline. A. Bianco. il pors *Bus Week* p108-10+ D 14 '87

Special report on corporate restructuring: rebuilding to survive. il *Time* 129:44-8 F 16 '87

Stopping a Ferris wheel. D. Pauly. il por *Newsweek* 109:42-3 Je 22 '87

The takeover controversy [address, March 17, 1987] M. C. Jensen. *Vital Speeches Day* 53:426-9 My 1 '87

There are no excellent companies. T. J. Peters. il por *Fortune* 115:341+ Ap 27 '87

There's no word for Chapter 11 in Dutch. T. Vogel. il *Bus Week* p62+ N 30 '87

Trying to make Lockheed over—before a raider does. S. Toy. il *Bus Week* p38 Jl 13 '87

United once more [Allegis drops new name and failed strategy] J. Castro. il *Time* 129:46-7 Je 22 '87

The unraveling of an idea [R. J. Ferris ousted at Allegis] J. E. Ellis and C. Hawkins. il por *Bus Week* p42-3 Je 22 '87

What the rally really means [massive revaluation of corporate assets; special section] il *Bus Week* p58-63 F 2 '87

Who's afraid of the new Kurt Wulff? J. R. Norman. il por *Bus Week* p74 Je 15 '87

Why nothing seems to make a dent in dealmaking. J. H. Dobrzynski. il *Bus Week* p75 Jl 20 '87

Will black managers survive corporate downsizing? [special section; with editorial comment by Earl G. Graves] il *Black Enterp* 17:7, 49-52+ Mr '87

Social aspects
See Business—Social aspects
Spinoffs
See Corporations—Divestiture
Statistics
See also
Corporations—Finance—Statistics
Subsidiaries

Invisible debt [accounting treatment of unconsolidated subsidiaries] L. Jereski. il *Forbes* 139:68 F 9 '87

A random walk through Euclid [spinoff subsidiaries in the new issues market] R. Phalon. il *Forbes* 140:170+ S 21 '87

Taxation
See also
Closely held corporations—Taxation
Construction industry—Taxation
Corporations, International—Taxation
Eskimos—Industries—Taxation
Insurance companies—Taxation
Inventories—Taxation
Investment trusts—Taxation
Petroleum industry—Taxation
Real estate business—Taxation
S corporations
Service industries—Taxation
Small business—Taxation

13 ways tax reform will change your company. M. Rowland. *Work Woman* 12:114-15 Ap '87

Beyond tax populism. R. Darman. *Society* 24:35-8 S/O '87

Corporate taxpayers are about to say 'ouch' again. D. Harbrecht and P. Magnusson. il *Bus Week* p34 D 14 '87

Deal mania: tax reform is no tranquilizer after all. S. Weiss. il *Bus Week* p66-7 Mr 30 '87

How golden are your parachutes? G. W. Padwe. il *Nations Bus* 75:62 Mr '87

Populism and tax reform. R. Darman. il *USA Today (Periodical)* 116:29-31 S '87

Still more reasons to mistrust supply siders [Stefan Welzk's study of German tax loopholes and parallel decline in capital investments] R. Kuttner. por *Bus Week* p22 O 26 '87

Taxing matters. See issues of Forbes

Tough times living with tax reform. K. Labich. il *Fortune* 116:113-14+ N 9 '87

The war on takeovers [closing tax loopholes] L. Saunders. il *Forbes* 140:116-17 N 30 '87

Who'll win with the tax law. T. Minsky. il *Esquire* 107:44 F '87

Why tax reform isn't taking a toll on investment. P. Magnusson. *Bus Week* p26 Ag 10 '87

Widening the net [Canada] P. Best. il *Macleans* 100:41 Je 29 '87

Winners and losers. L. Saunders. il *Forbes* 139:286 Ja 12 '87

World War III accounting [deferred taxes] L. Saunders. il *Forbes* 139:74+ N 9 '87

Valuation

Are stocks too high? [cover story] J. J. Curran. il pors *Fortune* 116:28-30+ S 28 '87

Corporations—Valuation—*cont.*

As risky as a crapshoot [buying stock in a bankrupt firm] A. Gabor. il *U S News World Rep* 102:65 Ap 27 '87

Beyond book [breakup value] M. Ozanian. il *Forbes* 139:166 Mr 23 '87

Big, medium or small cap? D. N. Dreman. il *Forbes* 140:215 O 19 '87

Bird-in-hand theory [dividend discount valuation] M. Ozanian. il *Forbes* 139:104+ F 23 '87

Bottom fishing for value when all else fails. A. E. Serwer. il *Fortune* 116:103 Jl 6 '87

Business appraising: beware of amateur hour. S. Weiss. il *Bus Week* p74 F 9 '87

Cheapskates in a pricey stock market [value investing] B. D. Fromson. il *Fortune* 116 Sp Issue:41-2+ Fall '87

Fishing season? T. Jaffe. il *Forbes* 140:322 N 16 '87

Giving stocks a 'rational value' [views of Charles C. Hickox and Parry v. S. Jones of Ashland Management] G. G. Marcial. *Bus Week* p136 My 11 '87

A Grahamite finds value in the rubble [interview with M. Gabelli] J. P. Newport, Jr. il por *Fortune* 116:212 N 23 '87

Hidden gems in a high market [interview with P. Hoffmann] A. E. Serwer. il por *Fortune* 115:126 My 25 '87

If a correction comes, it may be short and sweet. J. M. Laderman. il *Bus Week* p71 Ap 6 '87

Judging whether stocks are overvalued. J. Rachlin. il *U S News World Rep* 102:60-1 Mr 23 '87

Losers you can love. J. Kosnett. il *Changing Times* 41:35-8+ N '87

Medium is beautiful [stocks with medium market capitalizations] K. L. Fisher. il *Forbes* 140:134 Ag 24 '87

A message from Ben Graham. M. Schifrin. *Forbes* 140:258 N 30 '87

The savviest investors are going with the flow [cash flow] J. M. Laderman. il *Bus Week* p92-3 S 7 '87

Shearson's summer stocks ['uncommon values' list] G. Weiss. *Bus Week* p124 Jl 20 '87

Some contrarian picks [value stocks] D. N. Dreman. il *Forbes* 140:174 Jl 27 '87

Strategic planning [address, March 18, 1987] R. D. Kennedy. *Vital Speeches Day* 53:624-7 Ag 1 '87

The top 1000. il *Bus Week* Sp Issue:30-3+ Ap 17 '87

An unending quest for value [interview with A. Snyder] A. E. Serwer. il por *Fortune* 115:114 Mr 16 '87

A value seeker says there's plenty left [interview with K. Simons] A. E. Serwer. il por *Fortune* 116:200 Ag 3 '87

Wagering on companies with mounds of money [views of Norman Weinger] A. E. Serwer. il *Fortune* 116:178 D 7 '87

Wall Street's new pet: the big corporate kitty. B. Nussbaum. il *Bus Week* p109+ D 7 '87

What the rally really means [massive revaluation of corporate assets; special section] il *Bus Week* p58-63 F 2 '87

When to invest in a battered stock. il *Bus Week* p162-3 Je 22 '87

Where pros are fishing in the wake of the crash [takeover stocks] G. G. Marcial. il *Bus Week* p136 N 30 '87

Corporations, Government
See also
Privatization

Canada
See also
Air Canada
Canada Development Investment Corporation
Manitoba Consumers Gas Corporation
Potash Corporation of Saskatchewan

A case against the Crown [excerpts from Uneasy lies the head] W. Stewart. il *Macleans* 100:44-6+ My 11 '87

France
See also
Elf Aquitaine

Great Britain
See also
British Airways

Japan
See also
Nippon Telegraph & Telephone Corporation

Corporations, International
See also
Banks and banking, International
Business—International aspects
United Nations. Commission on Transnational Corporations

Ethics of transnationalism. R. Vernon. *Society* 24:53-6 Mr/Ap '87

The Forbes foreign rankings [special section] il *Forbes* 140:111-14+ Jl 27 '87

The lessons of Bhopal. F. M. Bordewich. il *Atlantic* 259:30-3 Mr '87

Most U.S. companies are innocents abroad. il *Bus Week* p168-9 N 16 '87

We've met the enemy, and they are us? [effect of proposed tariffs on multinationals] E. A. Finn, Jr. and K. Healy. il *Forbes* 139:78+ F 9 '87

Why U.S. companies don't always win friends abroad. P. M. Jones. il *Sch Update* 120:31-2 O 2 '87

You don't have to be a giant to score big overseas. il *Bus Week* p62-3 Ap 13 '87

Finance
High time [stock performance of multinationals] M. Ozanian. il *Forbes* 139:178 Ap 6 '87

Statistics
The 100 largest U.S. multinationals. il *Forbes* 140:152+ Jl 27 '87

500 largest foreign companies. il *Forbes* 140:116-19+ Jl 27 '87

America's leading exporters [with introd. by Alan Farnham] il *Fortune* 116:72-3 Jl 20 '87

The international 500 [with introd. by Terence P. Paré and Wilton Woods] il *Fortune* 116:214-15+ Ag 3 '87

International corporate scoreboard. il *Bus Week* p136-43+ Jl 20 '87

The world's 50 biggest industrial CEOs [with introd. by Terence Paré and Wilton Woods; cover story] il *Fortune* 116:23-31+ Ag 3 '87

Regulation
See Industry and state

Taxation
A Eurobond bombshell [U.S. ends tax treaty with Netherlands Antilles] R. Brady and V. English. *Bus Week* p100 Jl 13 '87

Innocent victims [multinational corporations getting caught in trap set for tax haven abusers] L. Saunders. il *Forbes* 140:64+ O 5 '87

The sun isn't setting on this tax haven [Netherlands Antilles] G. DeGeorge. il *Bus Week* p57-8 Ag 31 '87

A tempest hits the Treasury [cancels Antilles tax treaty] D. Zigas and V. English. il *Bus Week* p124 Jl 20 '87

Corporations and art *See* Art and industry
Corporations and day care *See* Day care and industry
Corporations and education *See* Business and education
Corporations and government *See* Industry and state
Corporations and state *See* Industry and state
Corporations and the arts *See* Arts and industry
Corps of Engineers *See* United States. Army. Corps of Engineers
Corpulence *See* Obesity
Corpus Christi (Tex.)

Education
An alternative to alternative education [dropout prevention program] D. Banks. *Educ Dig* 53:33-5 D '87

History
Photographs and photography
The unknown photographer [1934] B. Klaw. il *Am Herit* 38:42-7 Jl/Ag '87

Corpus Christi festival
Manna in the wilderness. M. K. Hellwig. il *America* 156:inside back cover Je 13 '87

Correctional institutions *See* Prisons
Correlation (Education)
The arts in education: a search for balance. J. I. Bundra. bibl f *Des Arts Educ* 89:25-30 S/O '87

Goodbye to some of that. G. McCauley. il *America* 157:328-30 N 7 '87

Hidden agendas in writing across the curriculum. S. N. Tchudi. *Educ Dig* 52:33-5 Ap '87

STS science teaching emphasizes problem solving [science/technology/society focus] R. E. Yager. *Educ Dig* 53:39-41 S '87

Correspondence *See* Business writing; Letters
Correspondence schools and courses
See also
Aviation Training Center

Do you really want to be rich? [mail order finance courses] M. Schiffres. il *Changing Times* 41:73-4+ O '87

Is woodland management for you? [home study course] D. J. Decker. il *Conservationist* 41:38-41 Ja/F '87

Correspondents, Foreign *See* Foreign correspondents
Corridors *See* Halls
Corridos! [television program] *See* Television program reviews—Single works

Corrigan, E. Gerald

about

Gerry Corrigan's solutions to a banking 'hodgepodge'. S. Bartlett. il por *Bus Week* p78 Ap 6 '87

Corrigan, Mairead, 1944-

about

Of many things. G. W. Hunt. *America* 157:370 N 21 '87

Corrigan, Wilfred J.

about

"I know I sound protectionistic". K. K. Wiegner. il por *Forbes* 139:54+ Je 29 '87

Corrosion and anticorrosives

Bacterial methanogenesis and growth from CO_2 with elemental iron as the sole source of electrons. L. Daniels and others. bibl f il *Science* 237:509-11 Jl 31 '87

Making a meal of iron [role of methanogens in biocorrosion; work of Lacy Daniels and others] *Sci News* 132:104 Ag 15 '87

Corrsin, Stanley, 1930-1986

about

Obituary

Phys Today 40:126 F '87. J. Lumley

Corrugated cardboard boxes *See* Boxes, cases, etc.

Corruption in politics *See* Politics, Corruption in

Corrymeela Community (Northern Ireland)

Corrymeela: a flicker of hope in Northern Ireland. G. Brown. *Christ Century* 104:336-7 Ap 8 '87

Corson, Dale R.

What is federal policy on scientific communication? *Phys Today* 40:144 Ja '87

Cortada, Rafael L.

about

Cortada faces myriad of problems as new UDC chief. *Jet* 72:16 Ag 24 '87

Cortés, Carlos E., and Fleming, Dan B.

Social studies texts need a global perspective. *Educ Dig* 52:42-5 Mr '87

Cortex (Brain) *See* Brain

Corticosteroids

See also

Prednisone

Corticosterone

Virus-induced increases in plasma corticosterone [with reply by J. Edwin Blalock] il *Science* 238:1423-5 D 4 '87

Corticotropin *See* ACTH

Corticotropin releasing factor *See* Pituitary hormone releasing factors

Cortina D'Ampezzo Olympics, 1956 *See* Olympic Games—1956—Winter Olympics

Cortisol *See* Hydrocortisone

Cortisone

See also

Hydrocortisone

Cortissoz, Royal, 1869-1948

about

An epitaph for Mr. Lincoln. H. W. Morgan. il por *Am Herit* 38:58-63 F/Mr '87

The idea of tradition in American art criticism. H. Kramer. *Am Sch* 56:319-27 Summ '87

Cortright, David

The arms race—intervention link. *Cent Mag* 20:58-9 My/Je '87

Corvette (Automobile) *See* Sports cars

Corwell, Marion

Best of the '88 auto buys! il *Essence* 18:103-4 N '87

Do-it-yourself car repair. il *Essence* 17:91-2 Mr '87

Corya, George

about

The heretics of the heartland. J. McCormick. il por *Newsweek* 109:46-7 Mr 30 '87

Corylus *See* Filbert trees

COs *See* Conscientious objectors

COSATU *See* Congress of South African Trade Unions

Cosby, Anna Pearl

about

Bill Cosby tells how wife saved his mother's life. R. E. Johnson. il pors *Jet* 73:14+ O 19 '87

Cosby, Bill, 1937-

Cosby comes of age [condensed from Time flies] il *Read Dig* 131:111-14 N '87

Dr. Spock never promised us a rose garden [excerpt from Fatherhood] il pors *Saturday Evening Post* 259:60-2 Mr '87

Time flies [excerpt] il por *Good Housekeep* 205:60+ S '87

about

Behind the scenes with Bill Cosby. R. E. Johnson. il pors *Ebony* 42:160+ F '87

Bill and Camille Cosby make $1.3 million gift to aid Fisk University. *Jet* 71:52 Ja 12 '87

Bill Cosby: 'I did not read the script . . . Lisa made the decision'. pors *Jet* 71:62 Mr 23 '87

Bill Cosby: "My wife helped me become a better person" [interview] M. Berle. il pors *Redbook* 169:72+ Je '87

Bill Cosby tells how wife saved his mother's life. R. E. Johnson. il pors *Jet* 73:14+ O 19 '87

Bill Cosby wins three People's Choice Awards. il por *Jet* 72:55 Mr 30 '87

Bill Cosby's 'Leonard part 6' film funny and outrageous [cover story] il pors *Jet* 73:54-7 D 21 '87

Calls from Cosby give sick teen will to live. *Jet* 71:24 F 23 '87

Cosby heads 'Unlock Apartheid Jails' drive; hits reporter's insult. il por *Jet* 73:56 O 19 '87

Cosby helps save black-owned airline; brokers a $3.5 million loan from E. F. Hutton Group Inc. il *Jet* 71:28 Mr 9 '87

Cosby, Inc. [cover story] R. Zoglin. il pors *Time* 130:56-60 S 28 '87

Cosby named top hero in World almanac poll. *Jet* 71:52 Ja 12 '87

Cosby ranks highest in TV ad 'believability,' too. *Jet* 71:28 Mr 9 '87

Cosby raps network execs for not hiring more blacks. *Jet* 72:59 Je 22 '87

'The Cosby show' starts 4th season with surprises and changes [cover story] il pors *Jet* 72:58-60 S 21 '87

Cosby to speak at Wesleyan for daughter's graduation. *Jet* 72:58 My 18 '87

Cosby's $84 million makes him richest entertainer. il por *Jet* 73:52-3 S 28 '87

The fault is not in our stars [cover story] A. D. Frank. il *Forbes* 140:120-3+ S 21 '87

Fisk president tells meaning of the Cosbys' gift of $1.3 million. il por *Jet* 71:16 Ja 19 '87

"I do believe in control". D. Goodgame. il pors *Time* 130:62-4 S 28 '87

Jackson will announce bid for presidency next month; Cosby hosts big fund-raiser. il pors *Jet* 72:24-5 S 21 '87

Kodak hopes Cosby video will boost market share. il por *Jet* 72:16 S 14 '87

The most popular man in America. R. Schoenstein. il pors *50 Plus* 27:24-6 Ja '87

Reception at JPC honors author of Bill Cosby book. il pors *Jet* 72:59-60 My 18 '87

Son of 'Fatherhood'. H. F. Waters. il pors *Newsweek* 110:78-9 S 14 '87

Untold story—real reason the Cosbys gave Fisk $1.3 million. il por *Jet* 71:14-15 F 9 '87

Cosby, Camille

about

Bill Cosby tells how wife saved his mother's life. R. E. Johnson. il pors *Jet* 73:14+ O 19 '87

Camille Cosby delivers Howard graduation address; receives honorary degree. il por *Jet* 72:24 Je 1 '87

The Cosby show [television program] *See* Television program reviews—Single works

Cosmetic dentistry *See* Dentistry

Cosmetic surgery *See* Surgery, Plastic

Cosmeticians *See* Makeup artists

Cosmetics

See also

Department stores—Cosmetics departments

Lipstick

Makeup

Powder (Face, toilet, etc.)

Suntan products

The anti-age war. S. Lord. il *Vogue* 177:400-1+ O '87

Are breast creams a bust? P. Boyer. il *Prevention* 39:76-8 My '87

Beauty exotica. il *Health* 19:47-8+ Ag '87

Beauty in the making [homemade cosmetics] il *Seventeen* 46:56 O '87

Beauty: serious business. il *Essence* 17:64-7+ Mr '87

Enhancing black skin. L. Wells. il *N Y Times Mag* p53 Ja 18 '87

Erasing wrinkles: easier said than done [cover story] D. Stehlin. il *FDA Consum* 21:20-2 Jl/Ag '87

A firm foundation. L. Wells. il *N Y Times Mag* p66 My 3 '87

First, base: beauty foundation that's better than bare. il *Mademoiselle* 93:304-7 S '87

Foundation—how to choose it, how to use it. il *Mademoiselle* 93:26 Ja '87

Fountains of youth [anti-aging products] J. B. Copeland. il *Newsweek* 109:48-9 Mr 16 '87

Holding action [moisturizers] L. Wells. il *N Y Times Mag* p56 S 6 '87

Cosmetics—*cont.*

Mascara application: worth a closer look. D. Groves. il *McCalls* 114:144 Jl '87

The new anti-aging products. il *Glamour* 85:34 Mr '87

Now, the eyes have it [creams designed for skin around eyes] L. Wells. il *N Y Times Mag* p70 F 22 '87

Skin moisturizers. il *Consum Rep* 52:192-6 D '87

Skin progress [special section] il *Vogue* 177:456-61+ Mr '87

Stressed-skin savers [facial masks] il *Harpers Bazaar* 120:48 Mr '87

True colors. L. Wells. il *N Y Times Mag* p78 D 13 '87

Was Alfin's beauty only skin-deep? [Glycel skin care line] C. Power. il *Bus Week* p62-3 Ja 19 '87

Youth in a bottle [Avon's Collagen Booster Line Controlling Lotion] M. Fox. il *Health* 19:18 My '87

Contamination

Contaminated cosmetics [manufactured by Tori Laboratories Inc.] il *FDA Consum* 21:3 My '87

Labeling

The science of beauty. J. Torrey. il *Health* 19:34-6+ F '87

Packaging

Touch-up touch. il *Harpers Bazaar* 121:46 D '87

Traveling with the pack [travel-sized containers] L. Wells. il *N Y Times Mag* p72 Ap 19 '87

Terminology

Beauty glossary. il *Ladies Home J* 104:24 F '87

Cosmetics for children

The bloom of youth. L. Wells. il *N Y Times Mag* p86 Ap 5 '87

Cosmetics for men

See also

Perfumes for men

Good grooming. D. Welch. il *Health* 19:40-1 N '87

The masculine presence. S. Lord. *Vogue* 177:187-8+ Je '87

Peak performance: skincare. il *Harpers Bazaar* 120:30 My '87

Cosmetics industry

See also

Alfin Fragrances, Inc.

American Health and Beauty Aids Institute

Avon Products, Inc.

Bonne Bell Inc.

Dudley Products, Inc.

Elizabeth Arden, Inc.

Estée Lauder, Inc.

Faberge Inc.

Hair care products industry

Johnson Products Company, Inc.

Luster Products Inc.

Merle Norman Cosmetics, Inc.

Noxell Corporation

Perfume industry

Revlon Inc.

Shulton Group

Soft Sheen Products

Worlds of Curls (Firm)

Acquisitions and mergers

Faberge lands Arden: 'Now we've got mass—and class'. S. Benway. il por *Bus Week* p38-9 Ag 17 '87

Advertising

Avon picks UniWorld. K. Smikle. il *Black Enterp* 17:24 F '87

Make-over at Revlon. B. Kanner. il *N Y* 20:12-13 Ja 12 '87

Marketing

Fountains of youth [anti-aging products] J. B. Copeland. il *Newsweek* 109:48-9 Mr 16 '87

Making millions on women over 30 [Noxell] F. Rice. il *Fortune* 115:75+ My 25 '87

Securities

Was Alfin's beauty only skin-deep? [Glycel skin care line] C. Power. il *Bus Week* p62-3 Ja 19 '87

Japan

See also

Shiseido Company Ltd.

Cosmic Background Explorer *See* Artificial satellites—Astronomical use

Cosmic background radiation

Light from the depths of time. R. Kippenhahn. il *Sky Telesc* 73:140-2 F '87

True ZITs: can such things be? [anisotropies] D. E. Thomsen. *Sci News* 131:4-5 Ja 3 '87

Cosmic Contact Psychic Services

For those who see the past and the future, but can't find their way to the bank, Michael Goodrich offers—himself. D. Van Biema. il pors *People Wkly* 27:113-14+ My 18 '87

Cosmic dust *See* Matter, Interstellar

Cosmic jets *See* Plasma (Ionized gases)

Cosmic rays

Balloon flights view sun and gather cosmic rays. *Sky Telesc* 73:481-2 My '87

Hunting for the heliosphere [research by William R. Webber] il *Sky Telesc* 74:578-9 D '87

Marvelous mystery cosmic radiation [muons; work of Marvin Marshak] D. E. Thomsen. *Sci News* 131:228-9 Ap 11 '87

Cosmic strings

Cosmic strings. A. Vilenkin. bibl (p158) il *Sci Am* 257:94-8+ D '87

Gathering cosmic string [gravitational lens; work of Lennox L. Cowie and Esther M. Hu] *Sci Am* 257:19 Ag '87

Getting vibes from cosmic strings [research by Arif Babul and others] *Sci News* 131:345 My 30 '87

Keeping current with cosmic strings [research by Edward Witten and others] M. M. Waldrop. il *Science* 235:283-4 Ja 16 '87

Strings that blow bubbles in the cosmos. D. E. Thomsen. *Sci News* 131:22 Ja 10 '87

Cosmic superstring theories *See* Superstring theories (Physics)

Cosmochemistry *See* Astrochemistry

Cosmology *See* Universe

Cosmopolitan (Periodical)

Cosmopolitan [manuscript submission policy] I. Copeland. il *Writer* 100:27 F '87

Cosmos missions *See* Artificial satellites—Cosmos missions

Cost, Bruce, 1945-

Knowing no boundary. il *N Y Times Mag* p69-70 Ap 19 '87

Cost

See also

Labor costs

Cost (Law)

See also

Lawyers—Salaries, fees, etc.

Cost accounting

Accounting bores you? Wake up. F. S. Worthy. il *Fortune* 116:43-4+ O 12 '87

Cost and standard of living

See also

Budget, Household

Children—Cost of raising

Finance, Personal

Home economics

Income

Inflation (Finance)

Price indexes

Prices

Saving and savings

Do we live as well as we used to? [cover story] S. Nasar. il *Fortune* 116:32-4+ S 14 '87

The Forbes four hundred cost of living index. C. Brown. il *Forbes* 140 Sp Issue:54+ O 26 '87

Inflating our cost of living. il *Money* Sp Issue:18+ Fall '87

Life at the edge (I). il *Consum Rep* 52:375-8 Je '87

Life at the edge (II). il *Consum Rep* 52:436-9 Jl '87

Life at the edge (III). il *Consum Rep* 52:504-7 Ag '87

Living well on less. P. E. Godwin. il *Changing Times* 41:26-30+ Mr '87

The silver lining in Houston [low cost of living] W. P. Barrett. il *Forbes* 140:174+ O 19 '87

Too much ain't enough. J. Flint. il *Forbes* 140:92-4+ Jl 13 '87

Warning: the standard of living is slipping. A. Bernstein. il *Bus Week* p48-9+ Ap 20 '87

What things cost [New York City; cover story] il *N Y* 20:32-40 S 7 '87

International aspects

The good life costs princely sums abroad. S. Tully. il *Fortune* 115:29 Ap 13 '87

The wealth of nations: the world is getting richer. L. Smith. il *Fortune* 116:35 S 14 '87

Germany (West)

See the world—and pinch pfennigs [effect of weak dollar on American G.I.s] J. D. Reed. il *Time* 130:24 D 28 '87

Japan

The Oriental dilemma. M. Clugston. il *Macleans* 100:26-8+ N 30 '87

United States

See Cost and standard of living

Cost benefit analysis *See* Cost effectiveness

Cost control

Cutting costs without cutting people [cover story] B. Saporito. il *Fortune* 115:26-32 My 25 '87

Cost control—*cont.*
The pedagogy of competition. M. L. Weidenbaum. *Society* 25:46-54 N/D '87
Cost effectiveness
Anecdotes, facetiae, satire, etc.
Analyzing the cost. B. Stein. il *N Y Times Mag* p22 O 25 '87
Cost of living adjustments
See also
Social security—Cost of living adjustments
Diet COLA: miracle cure for the budget? T. Jacoby. il *Newsweek* 110:56 N 16 '87
Costa, Rita
about
Jailed Mafia men face the wrath of Sicilian widows. il pors *People Wkly* 27:40-2+ My 18 '87
La Costa (Calif.: Resort) *See* Health resorts, watering places, etc.—California
Costa Brava (Spain)
See also
Architecture, Domestic—Costa Brava (Spain)
Costa Mesa (Calif.)
Theater
See also
South Coast Repertory
Costa-Pierce, Barry A.
Aquaculture in ancient Hawaii. bibl f il maps *BioScience* 37:320-31 My '87
Costa Rica
See also
Forests and forestry—Costa Rica
Military assistance, American—Costa Rica
National parks and reserves—Costa Rica
Rain forests—Costa Rica
Wildlife conservation—Costa Rica
Antiquities
Archaeology from above. N. McAleer. il map *Space World* X-2-278:21-5 F '87
Economic policy
Costa Rica's Arias at midterm. L. Gudmundson. bibl f *Curr Hist* 86:417-20+ D '87
More than a peacemaker [views of O. Arias] J. S. Fuerst. il *Commonweal* 114:701-3 D 4 '87
Foreign relations
Nicaragua
The C.I.A.'s war in Costa Rica. T. Avirgan and M. Honey. *Nation* 244:105-7 Ja 31 '87
Nicaragua asks for World Court to consider cases against Costa Rica and Honduras. *UN Chron* 23:88 N '86
United States
See United States—Foreign relations—Costa Rica
Politics and government
Costa Rica. E. Bibb. il *Sch Update* 119:13-14 Mr 9 '87
Costa Rica's Arias at midterm. L. Gudmundson. bibl f *Curr Hist* 86:417-20+ D '87
Nobel winner Oscar Arias makes Costa Rica the mouse that roars for peace in Central America. M. Brower. il pors *People Wkly* 28:57-8+ N 9 '87
Costa Rican cooking *See* Cooking, Costa Rican
Costanza, Robert
Simulation modeling on the Macintosh using Stella. il *BioScience* 37:129-32 F '87
Social traps and environmental policy. bibl f il *BioScience* 37:407-12 Je '87
Costanzo, Janice A.
(jt. auth) See Lichter, Daniel T., and Costanzo, Janice A.
Costas, Bob
about
The rules of the game [interview] J. Vitale. il pors *Channels* 7:61-2 N '87
Costello, Cynthia B.
Technological change and unionization in the service sector. bibl f *Mon Labor Rev* 110:45-6 Ag '87
Costello, Elvis
about
Elvis Costello. B. Milkowski. il por *Down Beat* 54:52 F '87
Costello, Gerald M.
[Column] See issues of U.S. Catholic beginning January 1985
How Catholics have grown up on the works of mercy. il *U S Cathol* 52:27-33 Je '87
Costello, Robert B.
about
Acquisition chief's successor named. *Aviat Week Space Technol* 127:30-1 S 28 '87
Costikyan, Barbara
Foreign intrigue. il *N Y* 20:46-52 My 4 '87
Foul chickens. il *N Y* 20:44-8 Ag 10 '87

Great new places to have a party (I). il *N Y* 20:52-66+ F 16 '87
Great new places to have a party (II). il *N Y* 20:40-57 F 23 '87
Jaunts: follow the Hudson back to a better age. il *N Y* 20:48-52+ Je 29-Jl 6 '87
Costin, Lela B.
Is the family neglectful or neglected? bibl f *Society* 24:27-32 Mr/Ap '87
Costmary
Costmary. B. Reppert. il *Rodale's Org Gard* 34:55 D '87
Costner, Kevin
about
Hollywood rediscovers romance. D. Worrell. por *Time* 130:74 S 7 '87
Kevin Costner: an irresistible rascal, but an untouchable family man. C. Krupp. por *Glamour* 85:156 Je '87
Costner, Susan
Best of bistro. il *Work Woman* 12:122-4+ Ap '87
Popover power. il *Work Woman* 12:144-6 N '87
Costume
See also
Fashion
Hats
Wearable art
Dressed to thrill [no-sew Halloween costumes] R. J. Katz. il *Redbook* 169:16+ O '87
Halloween redux. J. Miller. il *Ms* 16:24 O '87
Exhibitions
See also
Metropolitan Museum of Art (New York, N.Y.). Costume Institute
The annals of glory [The best of the best-dressed lists: 1934-1984 at the Museum of the City of New York] H. Brubach. *Atlantic* 259:81-3 My '87
Designing women [Three women at the Fashion Institute of Technology] D. Drier. il pors *Art Am* 75:21-3 My '87
Designing women [Three women: Vionnet, McCardell, Kawakubo] K. Beckett. il *Vogue* 177:222+ Mr '87
A glimpse of beauty past and present [Eye of the beholder exhibition at the Royal Ontario Museum] il *Macleans* 100:50-1 Ap 13 '87
In fashion [Fashion Institute of Technology's exhibition Three women: Madeleine Vionnet, Claire McCardell, Rei Kawakubo] *New Yorker* 63:29-30 Mr 16 '87
Latin America
Keeping guayabera cool [lightweight shirts] T. A. Remas. il *Américas* 39:32-7 Ja/F '87
Soviet Union
A fashion designer recommends . . . V. Zaitsev. il por *World Press Rev* 34:58 My '87
Anecdotes, facetiae, satire, etc.
Garbed in *glasnost*. R. Baker. *N Y Times Mag* p14 Ap 12 '87
Costume, Indian (American) *See* Indians of South America—Costume and adornment
Costume, Theatrical
See also
Baum's, Inc.
Costume designers
Television advertising—Costume
Wigs
Create armour from junkyard scrap. P. McCrory. il *Theatre Crafts* 21:66 F '87
Flexibility & fine fabrics: Jess Goldstein's costume designs. M. L. Gavenas. il por *Theatre Crafts* 21:18-21+ F '87
The gift of garb [P. Zipprodt's costumes for New York City Ballet's Sleeping beauty] B. Weber. il por *N Y Times Mag* p94 N 1 '87
Greek-born designer decorates Paris stage [Y. Kokkos] E. Lampert. il *Theatre Crafts* 21:18 N '87
If looks could kill, some film careers would be finished. M. Musto. il *Mademoiselle* 93:90 Mr '87
Jean-Louis [motion picture costume design] Jean-Louis. il por *People Wkly* 27:76 F 9 '87
Jens-Jacob Worsaae sets a sparkling stage: designing the light fantastic. M. Hunt. il por *Dance Mag* 61:48-52 Ap '87
Make custom dress forms. K. Kearney. il *Theatre Crafts* 21:96-8 N '87
A new face on dance [designer M. Casanova's collaboration with M. Marin] B. Haye. il *Theatre Crafts* 21:42-3+ N '87
Period perfect: Van Broughton Ramsey costumes Horton Foote's Texas. R. Seidenberg. il *Theatre Crafts* 21:99-102 My '87
Rosi Zingales, costume draper. T. Hardin. il por *Seventeen* 46:233 Ag '87

Costume, Theatrical—*cont.*
Sarah Lemire: creating the "Cosby" look [television costume designer] A. Radakovich. il pors *Seventeen* 46:87-8+ Jl '87
Wardrobe [touring theater] C. Houlihan. il *Theatre Crafts* 21:22+ Ag/S '87
Collectors and collecting
Dressing dreams: costumier Umberto Tirelli's residences in Rome and Capri. C. Aillaud. il por *Archit Dig* 44:140-5 O '87
Costume accessories *See* Dress accessories
Costume designers
> *See also*
> Casanova, Montserrat
> Fashion designers
> Goldstein, Jess
> Higby, Sha Sha
> Kokkos, Yannis
> Lemire, Sarah
> Ramsey, Van Broughton
> Tirelli, Umberto
> Zaccaro, Dolores
> Zipprodt, Patricia

Designers at work [cover story; special section] il *Theatre Crafts* 21:23-42+ My '87
Costume Institute (New York, N.Y.) *See* Metropolitan Museum of Art (New York, N.Y.). Costume Institute
Costume jewelry *See* Jewelry
Cosumnes River Preserve (Calif.) *See* Natural areas—California
Cosworth engines *See* Automobiles, Racing—Engines
Cotinine
How much do you smoke? Spit it out [testing saliva levels of cotinine; research by David B. Abrams] *Sci News* 132:25 Jl 11 '87
Cotoneasters
Cotoneaster [excerpt from Flowers for all seasons] J. Cox and M. Cox. il *Rodale's Org Gard* 34:57 N '87
Cotswolds (England)
Description and travel
The Cotswolds. C. P. Reynolds. il map *Gourmet* 47:54-9+ S '87
Cott, Johnathan *See* Cott, Jonathan
Cott, Jonathan
Fasting for life. il por *Roll Stone* p33+ My 7 '87
Is there life after life? A scholar goes out on a limb. il *Vogue* 177:312+ My '87
A matter of life and death. il por *Roll Stone* p48-9+ F 26 '87
The strange visions of J.G. Ballard [interview] il por *Roll Stone* p76+ N 19 '87
Walk like an Egyptian [excerpt from The search for Omm Sety] il *Omni* 9:66-8+ Jl '87
Cottage cheese
> *See also*
> Cooking—Cheese
Cottage industries
Dear Betty Harragan [client relations] B. L. Harragan. il *Work Woman* 12:40+ Je '87
Home-based business—a moving experience [W. Lazar revives Glendale Industries] L. L. Small. il pors *Ms* 16:76+ S '87
Homing in on home-based businesses. il *Success Farm* 85 no4:18D F '87
Your home business: starting it right. P. Plawin. il *Changing Times* 41:71-5 Ag '87
Cottage seminars
Prospecting in the home. B. J. Bigham. il *Nations Bus* 75:55-6 N '87
Cottages
> *See also*
> House decoration
Carolina cottage. il *South Living* 22:142 F '87
The comforts of a colonial. il *South Living* 22:182 Ap '87
Garden view cottage. il *South Living* 22:88 Ja '87
In the Chalk Hills: Sir Nicholas and Lady Henderson's West Country cottages. M. Henderson, Lady. il pors *Archit Dig* 44:184-7+ Je '87
A shingle-style cottage. il *South Living* 22:96 Ag '87
Leasing and renting
The Bermuda Collection [cottage colonies] A. S. Blask. *Travel Holiday* 168:30-3 N '87
Cottages, Remodeled *See* Houses, Remodeled
Cottages, Restored
Cottage charm awakens a tired old house. R. E. Jaffin and B. A. Lewis. il *Better Homes Gard* 65:97-103 Mr '87
Filled with art and style [renovated New Orleans cottage] L. Hallam. il *South Living* 22:84-5 Je '87

Cottages, Seashore *See* Beach architecture
Cotten, Elizabeth, 1893-1987
> *about*

Obituary
Jet il por 72:18 Ag 17 '87
Cotter, Holland
Advertisements for a mean utopia. il *Art Am* 75:82-9 Ja '87
Art from the Exiled City. il *Art Am* 75:43-5+ O '87
Eight artists interviewed. il *Art Am* 75:162-79+ My '87
Fontana's post-Dada operatics. il *Art Am* 75:80-5 Mr '87
Portraits of the artists. il *Art Am* 75:154-7 N '87
Cotter, James Finn
A visit with Vincent van Gogh. *America* 156:50-1+ Ja 24 '87
Cottier, Roy T.
Communications [address, April 23, 1987] *Vital Speeches Day* 53:556-9 Jl 1 '87
Cotting, James Charles, 1933-
> *about*
Can the man who saved Navistar run it, too? K. Deveny. il por *Bus Week* p88 Mr 9 '87
Cotton
Cultivation
Scepter carryover stunts cotton and corn. *Success Farm* 85:62 S '87
Disease and pest resistance
Induced resistance and interspecific competition between spider mites and a vascular wilt fungus [verticillium wilt] R. Karban and others. bibl f il *Science* 235:678-80 F 6 '87
Mite and fungus: foe and friend? [spider mites and verticillium wilt; research by Richard Karban and others] D. D. Edwards. *Sci News* 131:101 F 14 '87
Cotton fabrics
> *See also*
> Denim
Cotton workers *See* Textile workers
Cottontails *See* Rabbits
Cotugno, Gianluca
> *about*
Incident at Exit 20. M. Stone. il pors *N Y* 20:50-4+ O 5 '87
Coturnix *See* Quails
Couch, Frank, and Stephens, Ken
The Good Book can be good for you. il *Publ Wkly* 232:67-8 O 9 '87
Couch potatoes
Cocooner, this spud's for you. J. Schwartz. il *Newsweek* 110:73 O 26 '87
Couch potatoes and lounge lizards. W. Safire. il *N Y Times Mag* p10+ Mr 8 '87
Couch potatoes need exercise [research by Larry Tucker] P. McCarthy. *Psychol Today* 21:13 Ag '87
Couch potatoes: the new nightlife [stay-at-home New Yorkers] D. Blum. il *N Y* 20:24-30 Jl 20 '87
Couches *See* Sofas
Coudert, Jo
Donald Thornton's magnificent dream. il por *Read Dig* 130:121-5 F '87
Endometriosis: one woman's struggle. *McCalls* 114:86-8 S '87
Coues deer hunting *See* Deer hunting
Coufal, James E.
(jt. auth) *See* Smith, Kathy, and Coufal, James E.
Cougar, John *See* Mellencamp, John Cougar
Cougars *See* Pumas
Cough medicines
Final rule issued on OTC cough medicines. *FDA Consum* 21:3 N '87
Strong medicine [FDA investigates high concentrations of menthol in cough syrup] *FDA Consum* 21:38-9 Je '87
Coughlin, Mary Jane
Supermodel Monika Schnarre. il pors *Seventeen* 46:192-5 Ap '87
Coulette, Henri
Late love, a comic opera [poem] *New Yorker* 62:68 F 16 '87
Coulson, Crocker
Pulling punches. *New Repub* 196:10-12 My 25 '87
Start making sense. *New Repub* 196:26+ Mr 23 '87
Too much too soon? il *Art News* 86:115-19 S '87
Coulson, Robert N. (Robert Norris), 1943-, and others
Artificial intelligence and natural resource management. bibl f il *Science* 237:262-7 Jl 17 '87
Coulters (Cultivators) *See* Cultivators—Equipment
Coulthard, Leslie Jean
Growth [poem] *Commonweal* 114:618 N 6 '87

Council Bluffs (Iowa)
Description
Next stop: Council Bluffs. R. C. Gildart. *Travel Holiday* 168:106+ O '87
Council for International Organizations of Medical Sciences
Health, ethics and human values [conference in Athens, Greece] Z. Bankowski and F. Gutteridge. il *World Health* p9-11 Je '87
Council of Chief State School Officers
New president of school chiefs outlines plan to focus on at-risk youth [views of D. Hornbeck] *Phi Delta Kappan* 68:407 Ja '87
Council of Economic Advisers (U.S.)
Why Reagan still needs an economic guru in the White House. P. Magnusson. il *Bus Week* p47 O 5 '87
Anecdotes, facetiae, satire, etc.
Dear Doctor Lekachman . . . R. Lekachman. il *Nation* 244:390-2 Mr 28 '87
Council on Economic Priorities
Corporate America sucks up [Corporate Conscience Awards] D. K. Mano. *Natl Rev* 39:55-7 My 8 '87
Council on Foreign Relations
Travelers to a changing land. J. Greenwald. il *Time* 129:34-5 F 16 '87
Councils and synods
See also
Synod of Bishops (1987)
Synods of bishops
Vatican Council (2nd: 1962-1965)
Counsel Corporation
Banking in the big leagues. P. C. Newman. il por *Macleans* 100:25 Ag 10 '87
Counseling
See also
Cable television in counseling
Credit counseling
Crisis management (Psychology)
Educational counseling
Employee counseling
Marriage counseling
Pastoral counseling
Peer counseling
Telephone in counseling
Television in counseling
Vocational guidance
Intensive crisis counseling in Florida [family counseling] J. H. Paschal and L. Schwahn. il *Child Today* 15:12-16 N/D '86
Prepping to be a stepparent [stepparent counseling] I. Pave. il *Bus Week* p149 Mr 16 '87
Counseling, Financial *See* Investment advisers
Counselors
See also
Educational counselors
Count Basie Orchestra
The common law of Count Basie. J. McDonough. il por *Down Beat* 54:61 My '87
Counter, S. Allen
The Eskimo offspring of Matthew Henson. il pors *Ebony* 42:50+ Ja '87
about
No slouches at breaking the ice, polar explorers Peary and Henson each left behind a son in the Arctic. C. Neuhaus. il pors *People Wkly* 27:41-2 Je 1 '87
Counter culture *See* Counterculture
Counter Intelligence Corps (U.S. Army) *See* United States. Army. Counter Intelligence Corps
Counterculture
Corporate countercultures. *Society* 24:2-3 My/Je '87
Counterfeiting *See* Counterfeits and counterfeiting
Counterfeits and counterfeiting
See also
Credit card crimes
The almost-perfect crime [counterfeit shilling stamps of 1872] H. Herst, Jr. il *Antiques Collect Hobbies* 92:73 Ag '87
The hidden threat to air safety [bogus parts] A. C. Isgrò. il *Fortune* 115:81-2+ Ap 13 '87
Is it real? Counterfeit goods are a big business—how to avoid getting ripped off. il *Glamour* 85:210 My '87
The Monet of money paints himself into a corner [J. S. G. Boggs to be prosecuted in England for his reproductions of legal tender] il por *People Wkly* 27:77 Mr 2 '87
'Obsession' by any other name sells sweetly [perfumes] A. Dunkin. il *Bus Week* p97 Je 1 '87
Rambo & Rambo, attorneys-at-law [lawyers acting as prosecutors in trademark counterfeit cases] D. Fanning. *Forbes* 139:76 Ja 26 '87

Repair parts: the name-brand game [counterfeit boat parts] T. Banse. il *Mot Boat Sail* 159:104 F '87
Counters, Kitchen *See* Kitchen furniture
Counties (U.S.)
The boom towns [megacounties] G. J. Church. il maps *Time* 129:14-17 Je 15 '87
Counting
Calculating apes [cover story] B. Bower. il *Sci News* 131:334-5 My 23 '87
Countries *See* Nations
Country and city *See* City and country
Country and western music *See* Country music
Country clubs
See also
Club Corp. of America
Country estates
California
Places in the heart [A. Getty's Sacramento Valley estate] L. Blandford. il pors *Vogue* 177:326-33+ Ag '87
Connecticut
Traditional comforts on the Sound: a welcoming Connecticut residence [decorated by Arthur E. Smith] L. Bernikow. il *Archit Dig* 44:70-5 F '87
Finland
A dacha in Finland [Honkala, summer home of the Gullichsen family; excerpt from Scandinavia] E. Gaynor. il *House Gard* 159:86-93+ Ag '87
France
Architectural digest visits: Baron and Baroness Guy de Rothschild: the evolution of the chalet at Ferrières [decorated by François Catroux] C. Aillaud. il pors *Archit Dig* 44:208-18+ Ap '87
Architectural digest visits: Maud Frizon [Les Hautes Belles in the Loire Valley] C. Aillaud. il pors *Archit Dig* 44:118-25+ Je '87
Gardens: Château Gabriel: Yves Saint Laurent and Pierre Bergé at Deauville [cover story] C. Aillaud. il *Archit Dig* 44:172-9+ My '87
Moulin refuge [B. Fouret's remodeled mill outside Paris] C. de Liagre. il por *House Gard* 159:138-47+ Ap '87
Great Britain
December at Great Dixter [excerpt from The year at Great Dixter] C. Lloyd. il *Archit Dig* 44:84+ D '87
Editorial. W. Garrett. il *Antiques* 131:1262-3 Je '87
In the Chalk Hills: Sir Nicholas and Lady Henderson's West Country cottages. M. Henderson, Lady. il pors *Archit Dig* 44:184-7+ Je '87
Power and the early-Tudor courtier's house [excerpt from The early Tudor country house] M. Howard. bibl il por *Hist Today* 37:44-50 My '87
Ireland
Castletown, County Kildare. D. J. V. Fitz-Gerald. il *House Gard* 159:184-96+ Mr '87
Memories of an eccentric world. M. Girouard. il *Archit Dig* 44:54+ Je '87
Italy
Gardens: plotting an alpine cliffhanger: the Bagatti Valsecchi villa above Lake Como. M. Spark. il por *Archit Dig* 44:124-9+ F '87
Gardens: Villa Melzi: Count Gallarati Scotti's flowering hills on Lake Como. N. Shrady. il *Archit Dig* 44:126-31 Ag '87
Landscape of high romance [history of Villa d'Este] F. Champin. il *House Gard* 159:194-203+ O '87
Neoclassic beauty [Villa Melzi] A. Lambton. il *House Gard* 159:190-9+ S '87
A royal family heritage [cover story; Villa Polissena] A. González-Palacios. il *House Gard* 159:162-72+ Jl '87
Villa Rocca nel Circeo: Nathalie Volpi's creation on the Tyrrhenian Sea. C. Aillaud. il *Archit Dig* 44:116-25 Ja '87
Villar Perosa. M. Agnelli. il *House Gard* 159:144-53+ S '87
Long Island (N.Y.)
Reminiscing in Great Gatsbyland. J. Kern. il *Travel Holiday* 168:28+ O '87
Sound choice: a Georgian revival estate on Long Island's North Shore [decorated by Georgina Fairholme] J. Kornbluth. il *Archit Dig* 44:190-5 Mr '87
Mexico
Hacienda La Trinidad: artists' retreat near Guanajuato, Mexico [home and studio of C. and J. W. Summers] S. Cadwallader. il *Archit Dig* 44:126-31 Ja '87
Mustique (Saint Vincent and the Grenadines)
Caribbean folly: Lord Glenconner's villa on Mustique. Suzy. il *Archit Dig* 44:132-9 S '87
New York (State)
A garden heritage [estate called the Meadows] U. G. Dietz. il *House Gard* 159:176-9+ S '87

Country estates—*cont.*
Portugal
The classical villa restated [D. Hicks's design for Vila Verde] M. Hampton. il *House Gard* 159:114-23 Je '87
Courting pleasure in Portugal [C. Pereira, owner of Azinhal estate] il *Vogue* 177:488-95 Mr '87
Quinta da Bacalhoa [restoration by O. Scoville] J. Taboroff. il por *House Gard* 159:180-5+ D '87
Switzerland
Music, art and country pleasures [Château de Lully, home of H. Cuénod] N. Barry. il *House Gard* 159:140-7+ Mr '87
Tennessee
Alex Haley's hideaway. H. J. Massaquoi. il pors *Ebony* 42:52-4+ S '87
Country furniture, American *See* Furniture, American
Country ham *See* Ham
Country houses
See also
Farmhouses
House decoration
Buy the beloved country: finding an affordable retreat [within striking distance of New York City] M. W. Robbins. il *N Y* 20:48-56+ My 25 '87
Classic modern [Westchester County home designed by R. Meier] C. Vogel. il *N Y Times Mag* p60-4 F 1 '87
Country houses [cover story; special issue] il *Archit Dig* 44:108-208+ Je '87
Magnificent obsession: a house in the country [cover story] E. Abeel. il *N Y Times Mag* p20-6+ Ap 19 '87
Together in the country [Foster family compound in the Texas Hill Country] E. Wood. il *South Living* 22:80-2 Ag '87
Country inns *See* Hotels, motels, etc.
Country life
See also
City and country
Farm life
Village life
Country lore. See issues of The Mother Earth News
Listener. J. Chapline. See issues of Blair & Ketchum's Country Journal through March 1987
Listener. W. Shipman. See issues of Country Journal beginning April 1987
Rural persuasion. See issues of Country Journal beginning June 1987
Rural sprawl: of junked cars and spent refrigerators. P. G. Quinnett. il *Ctry J* 14:68-71 N '87
A working vacation [instructional workshops that teach rural skills] il *Ctry J* 14:57-60 Ja '87
Photographs and photography
This country life. See issues of Country Journal beginning October 1986
Great Britain
Bibliography
Paperback history. J. Patrick. *Hist Today* 37:59 N '87
Country music
See also
Gospel music
Phonograph records—Country music
America's new honky-tonk heroes. D. Shewey. il *Harpers Bazaar* 120:238-9+ O '87
The backbone of country. L. Berman. il *High Fidel* 37:71-2+ Mr '87
Riding high on a down-home revival. N. Jennings. il *Macleans* 100:50-1 Ag 3 '87
Rural-free country. J. Blum. il *High Fidel* 37:56 S '87
County contracts
See also
Fulton County (Ga.)—County contracts
Prince Georges County (Md.)—County contracts
County employees
See also
Santa Clara County (Calif.)—Employees
County officers
See also
Sheriffs
Couples, Unmarried *See* Unmarried couples
Coupons
Book coupon launch elicits low consumer response. A. Symons. *Publ Wkly* 231:68+ F 6 '87
Upscale dogs: clipping coupons for chow. il *Newsweek* 109:62 My 18 '87
Courage
See also
Heroes and heroines
Are you a courageous manager? J. Sherman. *Work Woman* 12:24 My '87

On political courage [excerpt from address] M. Kunin. por *Ms* 16:84 N '87
Summoning managerial courage. W. Kiechel, III. il *Fortune* 115:149-50+ Ja 19 '87
Courant, Ernest D.
about
DOE bestows Fermi awards on Courant and Livingston. por *Phys Today* 40:83 Je '87
Courbier, Jim
about
Say goodby to the office. S. Stapleton. il por *Mot Boat Sail* 159:44-7+ My '87
Courchevel (France: Resort) *See* Resorts—France
Courier-Journal & Louisville Times Co.
After a woman is scorned, a publishing family cashes out [S. Bingham] J. Nielsen. il por *Fortune* 115:93 Ja 5 '87
Courses of study
See also
Colleges and universities—Curriculum
Correlation (Education)
Correspondence schools and courses
Curriculum planning
Jewish studies
Peace studies
Vocational-technical education
See also subhead Study and teaching under various subjects
Franchising education. R. Hotch. il *Nations Bus* 75:30-1 Ap '87
A new look at core curriculum. J. I. Goodlad. *Educ Dig* 52:6-9 My '87
Texts, tests don't match—but does it matter? [research by William Mehrens and S. E. Phillips] G. W. Bracey. il *Phi Delta Kappan* 68:397 Ja '87
Anecdotes, facetiae, satire, etc.
Setting things right in school. G. V. Griffith. por *Newsweek* 110:16-17 S 21 '87
Coursing hounds *See* Gazehounds
Court, Edward R.
Liability roulette. por *Nations Bus* 75:4 N '87
Court, Robert Holmes à *See* Holmes à Court, Robert
Court martial *See* Courts martial and courts of inquiry
Court reporting (By newspapers) *See* Newspaper court reporting
Courtaulds plc
Turning around an old industry [chairman C. Hogg] il por *U S News World Rep* 102:62-3 My 11 '87
Courtenay, Hercules
about
Philadelphia carving shops: Hercules Courtenay and his school. L. Beckerdite. bibl f il *Antiques* 131:1044-63 My '87
Courter, James A.
Fulfilling the promise of American life [address, February 19, 1987] *Vital Speeches Day* 53:398-400 Ap 15 '87
Step by step [address, May 2, 1987] *Vital Speeches Day* 53:581-5 Jl 15 '87
Time to end corporate welfare. *Read Dig* 130:35-40 Je '87
Courtesy
See also
Etiquette
The down side of civility [evangelical courtesy; study by James Davison Hunter] D. Neff. *Christ Today* 31:13 F 6 '87
Public conduct [adolescents] J. P. Comer. il *Parents* 62:216 O '87
The six rudest restaurants in America. M. Willens. il *Money* 16:115-16+ O '87
What ever happened to common courtesy? *Read Dig* 131:168-70 Jl '87
Anecdotes, facetiae, satire, etc.
Bug slaying and other minor chivalries for the man of the eighties. V. Klinkenborg. il *Glamour* 85:390 S '87
Hey you! Make way for my technology! [rudeness and consumer technology] D. Lyon. il *Technol Rev* 90:28-9 Ag/S '87
Courthouses
See also
Courtrooms
Old Court House Museum-Eva Whitaker Davis Memorial
A classic courthouse [Tarrant County Courthouse, Fort Worth, Tex.] il *South Living* 22:59 N '87
A glimpse of the past [Fayette County Courthouse] il *South Living* 22:16 Ja '87
Courtillot, Vincent, and Besse, Jean
Magnetic field reversals, polar wander, and core-mantle coupling. bibl f il maps *Science* 237:1140-7 S 4 '87

Courtois, Gilles, and others
Interaction of a liver-specific nuclear factor with the fibrinogen and α_1-antitrypsin promoters. bibl f il *Science* 238:688-92 O 30 '87

Courtot, Philippe
about
Philippe Courtot: champion of mammography. il por *Saturday Evening Post* 259:16 My/Je '87

Courtrooms
Astrodome, anyone? [mega courtrooms to accommodate supersize lawsuits] D. Fanning. il *Forbes* 139:222 Je 15 '87

Courts
See also
Courtrooms
Courts martial and courts of inquiry
Family courts
Grand jury
Judges
Judicial power
Judicial review
Jury
Legal procedure
Small claims courts
Television broadcasting—Trials
Trials
United States. Supreme Court
The politicalization of America's courts [address, October 16, 1987] R. Neely. *Vital Speeches Day* 54:147-50 D 15 '87

California
See also
Glendale (Calif.)—Courts
Los Angeles (Calif.)—Courts
Bork and Bird [pro-Bork campaign contrasted with pro-Bird campaign] H. Meyerson. *New Repub* 197:21+ S 14-21 '87
The 'Onion Field' parole: Rose Bird's parting shot. por *Newsweek* 109:26 Ja 12 '87

Canada
See also
Canada. Supreme Court

Florida
A brief for impeachment [case of Judge A. Hastings] il por *U S News World Rep* 102:9 Mr 30 '87
Hastings: critics are motivated by racism [ethics charges against judge] por *Jet* 71:29 F 16 '87
Judge fights impeachment [A. L. Hastings] L. Brown. il por *Black Enterp* 18:18 Ag '87
Judge Hastings faces congressional hearing on charges of bribery. por *Jet* 73:6+ N 2 '87

Michigan
Federal judge Damon Keith honored by Mich. governor for 20 years on bench. il pors *Jet* 73:14 D 21 '87

Oklahoma
See also
Tulsa (Okla.)—Courts

Pennsylvania
See also
Philadelphia (Pa.)—Courts

South Carolina
First black probate judge elected in S. Carolina [H. C. Brown] por *Jet* 71:25 F 16 '87

Texas
The best justice money can buy. W. P. Barrett. il *Forbes* 139:122+ Je 1 '87
More of the same. W. P. Barrett. il *Forbes* 140:8 S 7 '87

Vermont
And in Vermont . . . [5 high court judges accused of misconduct] *Time* 129:72 F 23 '87

Virginia
Fairfax County, Va. gets its first black judge [M. D. Williams] *Jet* 72:36 Ag 17 '87

Washington (D.C.)
See Washington (D.C.)—Courts

Courts (for games)
See also
Tennis courts

Courts martial and courts of inquiry
The example of Private Slovik [WWII soldier executed for desertion] B. B. Kimmelman. il pors *Am Herit* 38:97-104 S/O '87
Military justice comes to attention [Marine guard spy case] R. Lacayo. il por *Time* 129:62 My 18 '87

Courtship
See also
Dating (Social customs)
Since he got Connie Powers' number, long-distance operator Scott Luczak is hearing a steady aisle tone. il pors *People Wkly* 27:57 Mr 30 '87

Courtyards
See also
Atriums
Flag-flying trellis and fence create a private entry court. il *Sunset* 178:177 My '87
Former driveway is now a private entry court. il *Sunset* 179:86-7 Ag '87
Splashing oasis just inside this Fresno front entry. il *Sunset* 179:158 Jl '87

Coury, John
Medicine today and tomorrow [address, April 13, 1987] *Vital Speeches Day* 53:621-4 Ag 1 '87

Couscous *See* Cooking, North African

Cousins
How cousins enrich our lives. J. Garfield. il *Read Dig* 130:80-2 Ap '87

Cousteau, Jacques Yves
Cousteau's plea for the Mediterranean. por *World Press Rev* 34:53 Je '87

Cousy, Bob, 1928-
about
Hey, shorty, wanna play ball? A. Beam. il por *Bus Week* p82 Mr 2 '87

Coutsocheras, Yannis
Food for all—the 'Paris appeal'. il *Courier* 40:34 O '87

Couturier collections *See* Fashion shows

Couvelier, Mel
about
A bid for major-league banking. P. C. Newman. il por *Macleans* 100:33 F 16 '87
Touching the right-wing bases. P. C. Newman. il por *Macleans* 100:48 Mr 23 '87

Couvreux family
about
In Florida: everyman's dream. G. Jaynes. il *Time* 129:16-17 Mr 9 '87

Covenant House (New York, N.Y.)
Helping dropouts drop in [Covenant House-St. Michael's College program] J. N. Baker. il *Newsweek* 110:63 Ag 3 '87

Covenants (Theology)
Promises, promises [international treaties and Christian morality] T. C. Muck. il *Christ Today* 31:18-19 Ja 16 '87

Covent Garden Opera House *See* Royal Opera House (London, England)

Cover crops
Cover crop update [work at the Rodale Research Center] P. H. Johnson. il *Rodale's Org Gard* 34:32-3 O '87
Cover design *See* Book covers; Periodical covers

Coverdale, David
about
Critics hiss and fans cheer as David Coverdale's Whitesnake slithers up the charts. S. Dougherty. il pors *People Wkly* 28:85-6 O 5 '87

Covered bridges
Oregon's covered bridges. E. Clark. il map *Travel Holiday* 167:71-2 Ja '87
Covered calls *See* Put and call transactions
Covered wagon trains *See* Wagon trains
Covers, Book *See* Book covers
Covers, Periodical *See* Periodical covers
Covers, Phonograph record *See* Phonograph record covers
Covers (Philately)
Maximum philately [first day covers] H. Herst, Jr. *Antiques Collect Hobbies* 91:82 Ja '87
Covert American military assistance *See* Military assistance, American
Covetousness *See* Avarice
Cow manure *See* Feces—Animals
Cowan, Connell, and Kinder, Melvyn
Are you too hard to please? [excerpt from Women men love/women men leave] *Redbook* 169:96-7+ Jl '87
Fear of intimacy: not for men only [excerpt from Women men love/women men leave] il *Glamour* 85:96+ O '87
Wise women/wonderful marriages [excerpt from Women men love/women men leave] *Redbook* 169:106-7+ O '87

Cowan, Ruth Schwartz, 1941-
"Labor saving" means more work. il *Read Dig* 131:181-4 D '87
Less work for mother? il *Am Herit* 38:68-70+ S/O '87
Cowan, Wade
about
Building a foundry for fine art. L. Thomas. il por *South Living* 22:162 Ap '87

Coward, Noel
about
Blithe spirit [drama] Reviews
    N Y il 20:103-4 Ap 13 '87. J. Simon
    New Leader 70:21 Ap 6 '87. L. Sauvage
    New Yorker 63:86+ Ap 13 '87. E. Oliver
    Newsweek il 109:79 Ap 13 '87. J. Kroll
    Time il 129:74 Ap 13 '87. W. A. Henry
Cowart, Virginia S.
Athletes and steroids: the bad bargain. il *Saturday Evening Post* 259:56-9 Ap '87
Cowboy and Indian Alliance
Trouble in Hell Canyon [Indians oppose Honeywell's proposed munitions testing site in South Dakota] T. E. Johnson. il *Newsweek* 110:30 S 28 '87
Cowboy art *See* Western States in art
Cowboy hats *See* Hats
Cowboy poetry
Sentiment straight from the saddle [Cowboy Poetry Gathering in Elko, Nev.] R. B. Stolley. il *Life* 10:19-21 Jl '87
Cowboys
    See also
    Prisoners as cowboys
    Rodeos
Cowboy. J. P. Sisk. *Am Sch* 56:400-6 Summ '87
    Photographs and photography
Focusing on one telling detail evokes the full story. J. Loengard. il *Pop Photogr* 94:34 S '87
Cowboys in motion pictures *See* Motion pictures—Westerns
Cowell, Alan
A farewell to South Africa. il *N Y Times Mag* p36-9+ Ja 25 '87
Cowen, Robert C.
[Column] See issues of Technology Review
Cowles, Fleur
If I were an animal, I'd be a . . . [excerpts] il *Redbook* 168:78+ Mr '87
Cowley, John Maxwell
    about
Cowley and Moodie honored for work in crystallography. por *Phys Today* 40:105 D '87
Cowpeas
    See also
    Cooking—Vegetables
Cowper, William, 1731-1800
    about
The meticulous melancholia of a poet. por *Discover* 8:12-13 My '87
Cowpox virus *See* Pox viruses
Cows
    See also
    Adopt-A-Cow (Firm)
    Calving
    Dairying
Dairy. J. R. Borcherding. See occasional issues of Successful Farming through June 1987
    Breeding
    See Cattle—Breeding
    Care
Predipping teats sharply cuts mastitis troubles. *Success Farm* 85:D2 Je '87
    Diseases and pests
    See Cattle—Diseases and pests
    Feeding
Bean "soup" for bossy [soybeans] J. R. Borcherding. il *Success Farm* 85:38-9 N '87
The best forage grower in Indiana [David Forgey] J. R. Borcherding. il *Success Farm* 85:56-7 Ag '87
He sorts cows; computer sorts rations. D. Ohrtman. il *Success Farm* 85:72 Ag '87
Manage NPN to boost or hold dairy profits [nonprotein nitrogen] *Success Farm* 85:D8 My '87
Nutrient balance revs up dairy cows [soluble carbohydrate] J. R. Borcherding. il *Success Farm* 85:36 S '87
Product report: Megalac [protected fat for cows] J. R. Borcherding and D. Wanner. il *Success Farm* 85:54 N '87
Should you add selenium to your dairy rations? *Success Farm* 85:D6 My '87
Thrifty cow feeding, New England style [Knoxland Farm, Weare, N.H.] il *Success Farm* 85 no5:D2-D3 Mr '87
    Identification
Smart ID tags coming for U.S. cows and sows. il *Success Farm* 85:70 Ag '87

Milk production
    See Milk—Production
Cowslips (Dodecatheon) *See* Shooting stars (Flowers)
Cox, Alex
    about
Contra-courant. G. Fuller. il *Film Comment* 23:50-1 Jl/Ag '87
Nicaragua: radical flick. R. Nordland. il por *Newsweek* 109:44 Ap 20 '87
Rebel rouser. F. Schruers. il por *Roll Stone* p29+ S 10 '87
Walker [film] Reviews
    Macleans il 100:67 D 14 '87. L. O'Toole
    New Repub 197:26-7 D 28 '87. S. Kauffmann
    Newsweek il 110:88+ D 7 '87. D. Ansen
    Time il 130:79 D 7 '87. R. Schickel
Cox, Archibald, 1912-
Iranian arms and contra aid [address, March 6, 1987] *Vital Speeches Day* 53:531-3 Je 15 '87
    about
This smoking gun won't shoot. M. Kramer. il por *U S News World Rep* 103:16 S 21 '87
Cox, Christopher
Dressed to kill. il por *Vogue* 177:196 My '87
Who's who in charity? il *Vogue* 177:396-9 N '87
Cox, Claude C.
Radio marketing [address, September 16, 1987] *Vital Speeches Day* 54:88-92 N 15 '87
Cox, Courtney
    about
After her attention-getting spin with the Boss, Courtney Cox revs up a film career with the Masters of the universe. il por *People Wkly* 27:109 Mr 16 '87
Michael J. Fox and his Family ties flame Courtney Cox have a big announcement to make—they're not dating. M. Alexander. il pors *People Wkly* 28:72-4 D 7 '87
Cox, Dan
New York's own ballet competition: fighting for glitter and gold in NYC. il *Dance Mag* 61:62-3 O '87
Cox, Edwin L., Jr.
    about
A meat-packing magnate gets boxed in. J. Weber, Jr. il por *Bus Week* p50+ Je 22 '87
Cox, Harvey Gallagher
Thoughts on the Church and Cuba. il *Nation* 244:595+ My 9 '87
Cox, James A.
How good food and Harvey 'skirts' won the West. il *Smithsonian* 18:130-4+ S '87
Sneaker chic. il *Read Dig* 130:17-18 Je '87
Cox, Jeff, and Cox, Marilyn, 1951-
Bellflowers, cranesbills and lilies [excerpt from The perennial garden] il *Rodale's Org Gard* 34:46-8+ F '87
Cotoneaster [excerpt from Flowers for all seasons] il *Rodale's Org Gard* 34:57 N '87
Hardy ageratums, chrysanthemums and petunias [excerpt from The perennial garden] il *Rodale's Org Gard* 34:48 S '87
Cox, L. Norma, 1939-
Dear Dad [excerpts] *Ladies Home J* 104:53 Je '87
Cox, Lynne
    about
A cold swim to promote warm U.S.-U.S.S.R. ties. il pors *Discover* 8:8+ Jl '87
Lynne Cox comes in from the cold. R. L. Graham. il *Women's Sports Fitness* 9:12-13 N '87
Lynne Cox's brave swim across the frigid Bering Strait breaks the ice with the Russians. K. Hubbard. il pors *People Wkly* 28:32-4 Ag 24 '87
Swimmer Lynne Cox braces for an ice water ordeal, a dire crossing in the Bering Strait. J. Friedman. il por *People Wkly* 27:46-7 My 4 '87
Cox, Marilyn, 1951-
(jt. auth) See Cox, Jeff, and Cox, Marilyn, 1951-
Cox, Richard Hubert Francis, 1931-
Writing thrillers. *Writer* 100:10-12+ Mr '87
Cox, Robert
(tr) See Timerman, Jacobo, 1923-. Under the dictator
Cox, Roger W.
The Adriatic connection. il map *Travel Holiday* 167:46-51+ Je '87
A Hilton Head footnote. il *Travel Holiday* 168:24-6 Ag '87
Sentosa Island [cover story] il *Travel Holiday* 168:12+ O '87
Trekking in Nepal. il map *Travel Holiday* 167:42-7+ My '87
Cox Enterprises Inc.
Big decisions [J. C. Kennedy] L. Gubernick. il por *Forbes* 140:222 N 2 '87

Coyle, Rena
The working kids' cookbook. il *Work Woman* 12:168+ S '87

Coyne, Judith
A cathode ray tube is. il *Glamour* 85:118+ Ag '87

The coyote cycle [drama] See Mednick, Murray

Coyote hunting
A coyote coat for Lue. E. Park. il *Outdoor Life* 179:58-9+ F '87

Coyotes
Don Coyote [condensation] D. O. Hyde. il *Read Dig* 130:70-8+ Mr '87
The old couple [coyotes and badgers hunting together] P. Schullery. il *Ctry J* 14:86-8 O '87
        Control
The last predator. J. Walter. il *Success Farm* 85:18 S '87

CP Shades (Firm)
CP Shades's David Weinstein is cashing in on color and comfort—no haute couture need apply. B. Johnson. il por *People Wkly* 28:106-7 O 19 '87

CPC International Inc.
Adviser beware: cooked books may burn you, too [investment bankers face fraud charges in CPC International's suit against McKesson and Morgan Stanley over sale of C. F. Mueller] L. J. Tell. il *Bus Week* p58+ O 26 '87
Back to business [effects of R. Perelman's raid] J. Cook. il por *Forbes* 140:40-1 O 5 '87

CPI (Consumer Price Index) See Price indexes

CPR (Cardiopulmonary resuscitation) See Resuscitation

Crab apples
        See also
        Cooking—Fruit

Crab industry See Shellfish industry

Crabb, Michael
Kain is able. il pors *Dance Mag* 61:68-9 Mr '87
The widow's a peak [cover story] il *Dance Mag* 61:62-7 Mr '87

Crabeater seals See Seals (Animals)

Crabs
        See also
        Cooking—Shellfish
Down under a sand dollar: world of the tiniest crab [Dissodactylus mellitae] J. L. Bell. il *Sea Front* 33:210-15 My/Je '87
Identification of a juvenile hormone-like compound in a crustacean. H. Laufer and others. bibl f il *Science* 235:202-5 Ja 9 '87
Red crabs on the march on Christmas Island. J. W. Hicks. il map *Natl Geogr* 172:822-31 D '87
        Contamination
Cracking down on crab pickers [processors in Alabama] C. Carey and C. L. Hommel. il *FDA Consum* 21:33-4 S '87

Crabs, Horseshoe See Horseshoe crabs

Crack (Cocaine)
Breaking the crack murders [solving the murder of a crack dealer in Brooklyn] R. Rosenbaum. il *N Y Times Mag* p44-6+ N 15 '87
Crack: cheap, quick, deadly. M. S. Kreiter. il *Curr Health 2* 14:9-11 S '87
Crack murder: a detective story [solving the murder of a crack dealer in Brooklyn] R. Rosenbaum. il pors *N Y Times Mag* p24-30+ F 15 '87
Cracking up. J. Nelson. il *Essence* 17:65-6+ Ja '87
Drug use: down, but not in the ghetto. M. Miller. il *Newsweek* 110:33 N 23 '87
'Fat Cat' and the crack wars: brash young dealers muscle the drug establishment [Queens, N.Y.] P. Blauner. il por *N Y* 20:46-54 S 7 '87
L.A. law: gangs and crack. G. Hackett and M. A. Lerner. il *Newsweek* 109:35-6 Ap 27 '87
Machine gunman, high on crack, pumps 26 fatal bullets into boy, 3 [murder of L. Horris in Brooklyn] il por *Jet* 73:36 D 7 '87

Crackers
Cheddar crisps. il *Good Housekeep* 205:196+ O '87
It's a snap to make these crackers. S. Payne. il *South Living* 22:68-9 Ja '87

Cracow (Poland) See Kraków (Poland)

Cracraft, James
The Gorbachev regime after two years. bibl f *Bull At Sci* 43:31-3 My '87

Cradles
Heirloom cradle. D. Watson. il *Fam Handyman* 37:88-91 Ap '87

Cradles, Doll See Doll furniture

Craft, Robert
Amorous in Amherst. bibl f pors *N Y Rev Books* 34:18-21 Ap 23 '87

        about
Citing copyright infringement, judge halts Stravinsky biography. J. Mutter. *Publ Wkly* 232:14 Ag 21 '87

Craft fairs See Arts and crafts—Exhibitions

Crafts, Lisa
        about
Mini golf. *New Yorker* 63:31-2 O 26 '87

Crafts See Arts and crafts

Craftsmanship
        See also
        Arts and crafts

Craftsmen See Artisans

Cragg, Tony
        about
Tony Cragg, L. Goldman. *Art News* 86:62 Ja '87

Craig, Gordon Alexander, 1913-
After the Reich. il *N Y Rev Books* 34:38-41 O 8 '87
Waldheim's Austria [discussion of October 9, 1986 article, The Waldheim file] *N Y Rev Books* 34:44 F 26 '87
The war of the German historians. il *N Y Rev Books* 33:16-19 Ja 15 '87

Craig, H., and Hayward, T.
Oxygen supersaturation in the ocean: biological versus physical contributions. bibl f il *Science* 235:199-202 Ja 9 '87

Craig, Pamela Tudor- See Tudor-Craig, Pamela

Craig, Peter
Waterfalls in black and white. il *Petersens Photogr Mag* 15:16-18 Mr '87

Craig, Sandra A.
        about
Md. day care center owner gets 10 yrs. for child abuse. *Jet* 73:37 O 19 '87

Craik, Charles S., and others
The catalytic role of the active site aspartic acid in serine proteases. bibl f il *Science* 237:909-13 Ag 21 '87

Crain, Gertrude
        about
The keeper (and stoker) of the company flame. S. Wilkinson. il pors *Work Woman* 12:70-1+ O '87

Crain, Joyce
        about
Engineering light and movement. P. Scheinman. bibl f il *Am Craft* 47:22-9+ F/Mr '87

Crain Communications Inc.
The keeper (and stoker) of the company flame [G. Crain] S. Wilkinson. il pors *Work Woman* 12:70-1+ O '87

Cram, Donald J., 1919-
        about
Chemistry in the image of biology. R. Lewin. il pors *Science* 238:611-12 O 30 '87
Nobel prizes: chemistry. J. Horgan. *Sci Am* 257:46 D '87
What's in a middle name? Ask Donald Cram, carpet cleaner, and Donald Cram, Nobel laureate. il pors *People Wkly* 28:61 N 2 '87

Cram, Donald O.
        about
What's in a middle name? Ask Donald Cram, carpet cleaner, and Donald Cram, Nobel laureate. il pors *People Wkly* 28:61 N 2 '87

Cram courses See Tutors and tutoring

Cramer, Douglas S.
        about
Douglas Cramer: passionate perfectionist. P. Clothier. il por *Art News* 86:146-50 Summ '87
La Quinta Norte: Douglas S. Cramer's ranch in the Santa Ynez Valley. L. Bernikow. il por *Archit Dig* 44:136-47 Ap '87

Cramer, James J.
Casino Royale. *New Repub* 196:10-11 F 16 '87

Cramer, Richard Ben
Citizen Ueberroth [interview] il pors *Esquire* 107:69-72+ F '87
Fore play: a celebration of golf the glorious. il *Esquire* 107:99-101 Je '87

Cramps, Menstrual See Menstruation—Disorders

Crampton, Bruce
        about
Uh-oh! He's at it again. D. S. Looney. il pors *Sports Illus* 66:77-8+ My 11 '87

Crampton, Michael
        about
Bringing the office home. R. Lockwood. il por *Pers Comput* 11:176-7 O '87

Cranberries
        See also
        Cooking—Fruit

Cranbrook (England)
Description
Cranbrook. B. Wallach. il *Focus* 37:16-19 Spr '87
Crandall, Candace
(jt. auth) See Singer, S. Fred, and Crandall, Candace
Crandall, Robert L.
Solving the crisis in the skies. il por *Fortune* 116:203-4 S 28 '87
The volatile airline industry [address, February 23, 1987] *Vital Speeches Day* 53:468-72 My 15 '87
about
American vs. its unions: double trouble. T. Mason. il por *Bus Week* p45 F 23 '87
Crandall proposes commission empowered to limit flights. J. Ott. *Aviat Week Space Technol* 126:32-3 Je 29 '87
Crandall proposes filing of on-time reports. *Aviat Week Space Technol* 126:39 Mr 30 '87
Crandall seeks Congress' support for restrictions on general aviation. *Aviat Week Space Technol* 127:41 S 14 '87
Who will be Sky King? A. Miller. il pors *Newsweek* 109:54 Mr 2 '87
Crandall-Millar, Debbie
about
Woman awarded $6 million after doctor/husband sewed her vagina shut. *Jet* 73:12 N 23 '87
Crandell, Hugh
Shenandoah [excerpt] il *Natl Parks* 61:54-5 Mr/Ap '87
Crane, Edward H., 1944-
On the problem of America's policy myopia [address, October 22, 1986] *Vital Speeches Day* 53:184-8 Ja 1 '87
Crane, Janet
Viewpoint. See issues of Focus (New York, N.Y.: 1950)
Crane, Jill
Reservations. il *Atlantic* 260:32 Jl '87
Today's radio selections. il *Atlantic* 260:39 D '87
Crane, Les
about
Heeeere's Les Crane—and he's talking software. P. Finch. il por *Bus Week* p101 Jl 20 '87
Crane, Lucy
"My husband wouldn't give up on me". il pors *Good Housekeep* 205:74+ Ag '87
Crane, Philip M., 1930-
Should the financing of U.S. catastrophic health care emphasize private insurance methods? [excerpts from remarks, February 5, 1987] *Congr Dig* 66:104+ Ap '87
Crane, Stephen, 1871-1900
about
Commodore wreck: prototype "Open boat". B. Belleville. *Oceans* 20:58-9 My/Je '87
Found: Crane's 'Open boat'. S. Begley. il *Newsweek* 109:52 Ja 5 '87
Crane, Tricia
Age anxiety: dealing with a new decade. *Harpers Bazaar* 120:164 O '87
Desperate & demanding. il *Harpers Bazaar* 120:300+ S '87
Crane Duplicating Service Inc.
Crane Duplicating: still king of the bound galleys. il *Publ Wkly* 232:22-4 Jl 17 '87
Cranes, derricks, etc.
See also
Tower cranes
Cranes (Birds)
Fostering hope for the whooper. S. Brownlee. il map *Natl Wildl* 25:38-43 Je/Jl '87
Migration
Making whoopers. map *Nat Hist* 96:4 Ag '87
Cranfield, Michael
about
His life is a zoo. D. Young. il por *South Living* 22:145 Mr '87
Craniometry
Petrus Camper's angle. S. J. Gould. il *Nat Hist* 96:12+ Jl '87
Crankbaits (Fishing lures) See Fishing lures, flies, etc.
Cranston, Alan
about
Banking on deregulation. J. McLaughlin. *Natl Rev* 39:24 O 23 '87
Crappie fishing
Fail-safe crappies. M. Bleech. il *Outdoor Life* 179:96-7+ My '87
Crash barriers See Roads—Guard fences
Crash testing of automobiles See Automobiles—Testing; Automobiles, Foreign—Testing

Craters
Big splash from an ancient fall [Montagnais crater off Nova Scotia coast] R. Monastersky. *Sci News* 131:404 Je 27 '87
Correlation of volcanic activity with sulfur oxyanion speciation in a crater lake [cover story] B. Takano. bibl f il map *Science* 235:1633-5 Mr 27 '87
Fission-track dating of Haughton Astrobleme and included biota, Devon Island, Canada. G. Omar and others. bibl f il map *Science* 237:1603-5 S 25 '87
Impact cratering looks clustered, not periodic. R. A. Kerr. *Science* 236:1426-7 Je 12 '87
Outward-dipping ring-fault structure at Rabaul caldera as shown by earthquake locations. J. Mori and C. McKee. bibl f il map *Science* 235:193-5 Ja 9 '87
Point of impact: Manson, Iowa? R. Monastersky. *Sci News* 132:396 D 19-26 '87
Searching land and sea for the dinosaur killer. R. A. Kerr. il *Science* 237:856-7 Ag 21 '87
There's a hole in the bottom of the sea [impact crater off Nova Scotia coast; research by Lubomir Jansa and Georgia Pe-Piper] map *Discover* 8:20 S '87
Crates
See also
Milk crates
Cravath, Swaine & Moore
Two lawyers turning Cravath into a force in takeovers [A. Finkelson and R. S. Rolfe] M. Frons. pors *Bus Week* p103 Ja 26 '87
Cravens, Gwyneth
Wedding [story] *New Yorker* 62:32-40 F 16 '87
Cravings, Food See Eating—Psychological aspects
Crawford, Alan
Why we mustn't create an "industrial policy" in space. il *USA Today (Periodical)* 115:21-5 Ja '87
Crawford, Betty
about
Getting ahead in government. L. Gite. il por *Black Enterp* 17:93-4+ F '87
Crawford, Chris, 1950-
about
Hardguy software. J. Ledbetter. *Nation* 244:150-3 F 7 '87
Crawford, Hank
about
Hank Crawford/Jimmy McGriff. M. Bourne. il pors *Down Beat* 54:14 S '87
Crawford, James B.
about
Ex-teacher in D.C. gets 52-155 yrs. for sex abuse. *Jet* 72:36 Jl 27 '87
Crawford, Kay
about
For his opening act in L.A. the Pope can thank Kay Crawford, mother of the modern drill team. J. Calio. il pors *People Wkly* 28:105-6 S 21 '87
Crawford, Lynn
'I think it's broken'. il *Work Woman* 12:150+ Ap '87
Crawley, Nicholas
about
London's Dolphin Brasserie. J. Robinson. il *Gourmet* 47:60-1+ Ag '87
Crawmer, Robert
Flexibility for interiors. *Nations Bus* 75:44 Mr '87
Craxi, Bettino
about
Craxi leaves behind 'a new Italy'. J. Wyles. *World Press Rev* 34:37 Ap '87
Cray, Robert
about
Blues with a bullet . . . and Robert Cray holds the smoking gun [cover story] M. Gilmore. il pors *Roll Stone* p40-2+ Je 18 '87
Robert Cray: the blues . . . and a little bit more. J. Roberts. il pors *Down Beat* 54:23-5 Mr '87
Robert Cray's new blues power. J. Pareles. il por *Roll Stone* p45-6 Ja 29 '87
Showstopper: Robert Cray. M. Johnson. il por *Essence* 18:35 Je '87
Strong persuader Robert Cray sings to prove there's pop life left in the blues. S. Dougherty. il pors *People Wkly* 27:133-4 Ap 13 '87
Cray Research, Inc.
Cray supercomputer axed, superstar departs. M. M. Waldrop. il por *Science* 237:1558-9 S 25 '87
The hungry pack nipping at Cray's heels. J. W. Verity and O. Port. il *Bus Week* p110+ O 26 '87
Now, Cray is only way ahead. M. J. Pitzer. il *Bus Week* p109 Jl 13 '87

Crayfish

The greatest smallmouth catcher of all [crayfish as bass bait] J. Bashline. il *Field Stream* 92:52+ Ag '87

Tails for steelies [crayfish as bait for steelhead trout] J. Gibbs. il *Outdoor Life* 180:42+ Jl '87

Crazy Eddie Inc.

The net drops on Crazy Eddie [E. Zinn's proxy] T. Vogel. il *Bus Week* p62 N 2 '87

Creach, Terry

about

Hold me tight. T. Tobias. il *N Y* 20:81-2 N 30 '87

Cream

The cream of the crop [raw milk cheese and Devonshire, or clotted, cream] R. Sokolov. il *Nat Hist* 96:80+ D '87

Cream (Musical group)

Cream: the Royal Albert Hall, London, November 26th, 1968. D. Fricke. il *Roll Stone* p49-50 Je 4 '87

Cream puffs See Pastry

Creamer, Robert W.

Once upon a time in Cleveland . . . il *Sports Illus* 66:78 Ap 6 '87

One fan's tribute to baseball greats—and almost-greats [cover story] il por *Smithsonian* 18:102-6+ Ap '87

Creams, Breast See Cosmetics

Creams, Facial See Cosmetics

Crease, Robert P.

None but the bald. il *50 Plus* 27:74+ F '87

Crease, Robert P., and Mann, Charles C.

UNK: the accelerator that couldn't shoot straight. il *Omni* 9:63-6+ Je '87

Venice: the world's greatest costume party. il *50 Plus* 27:67-71+ D '87

Creation

Cosmic groanings. R. Goetz. il *Christ Century* 104:1083-7 D 2 '87

Creationists: of two minds about science. il *Discover* 8:6 Mr '87

From the beginning. M. K. Hellwig. *America* 156:inside back cover F 7 '87

The godfather of disaster [cometary theory of W. Whiston] S. J. Gould. il *Nat Hist* 96:20+ S '87

The return of the God-hypothesis. B. Durbin, Jr. il por *Christ Today* 31:22-3 Ap 3 '87

Science & the ways to God [views of S. L. Jaki] H. Rolston. *Commonweal* 114:313-16 My 22 '87

What did Noah do with the manure? and other burning questions of creation science. J. Hitt. il *Wash Mon* 19:25-8 F '87

Where does space end? H. Fehren. *U S Cathol* 52:39-41 S '87

Will creationism rise again? S. Boxer. il *Discover* 8:80-5 O '87

Study and teaching

Back talk [discussion of February 1987 article, Censoring science] K. Stein. il *Omni* 9:12+ S '87

Censoring science [fundamentalists] K. Stein. il *Omni* 9:42-4+ F '87

Creation/evolution update. F. Edwords. See issues of The Humanist

The creation-science case: is it science or religion? [Louisiana case to be heard by Supreme Court] E. J. Larson. *Christ Today* 31:50-1 Ja 16 '87

Creationism case argued before Supreme Court [Louisiana case] R. Lewin. *Science* 235:22-3 Ja 2 '87

Creationism in Ontario [threat to astronomy curriculum] D. E. Thomsen. *Sci News* 132:24 Jl 11 '87

Evolution and creation: one missed opportunity [booklet published by the American Scientific Affiliation] F. J. Ayala. *BioScience* 37:450 Jl/Ag '87

First word [attempts to impose creation science on public schools] M. Gell-Mann. il *Omni* 9:8 F '87

High Court rejects creationism law [Louisiana case] J. Raloff. *Sci News* 131:404 Je 27 '87

High Court: the day God and Darwin collided [teaching of creationism in Louisiana ruled unconstitutional] T. Gest and L. Solórzano. il *U S News World Rep* 102:12 Je 29 '87

Justice Scalia's misunderstanding [dissenting opinion on Louisiana creationism case] S. J. Gould. il *Nat Hist* 96:14+ O '87

Keep guard up after evolution victory. M. Zimmerman. *BioScience* 37:636 O '87

Keeping God out of the classroom [Supreme Court ruling on Louisiana creation science law] L. Martz. il *Newsweek* 109:23-4 Je 29 '87

Memories of the monkey trial [Supreme Court rules against creationism law in Louisiana] A. L. Sanders. il *Time* 129:54 Je 29 '87

One case: a step-by-step account of its progress through the Supreme Court [Louisiana creationism case] il *Life* 10:114-15 Fall '87

Schools can not require religious and scientific evolution teachings: Court. *Jet* 72:17 Jl 6 '87

Science, 7; creationism, 2 [Supreme Court ruling on Louisiana statute] *Sci Am* 257:14 Ag '87

Should public schools teach creation science? W. S. Morrow; J. Wiester. il *Christ Today* 31:50 S 18 '87

Supreme Court abolishes Louisiana creationism law. H. Fields. *Publ Wkly* 232:13 Jl 3 '87

Supreme Court bars creationism in schools [Louisiana law] I. Goodwin. *Phys Today* 40:56-7 S '87

Supreme Court hears arguments on teaching 'creation science' [Louisiana case] I. Goodwin. il *Phys Today* 40:64-6 F '87

Supreme Court on 'flat souls' [ruling on Louisiana law ordering equal treatment of creationism with evolution] J. M. Wall. *Christ Century* 104:579 Jl 1-8 '87

Supreme Court strikes down "creation science" law as promotion of religion [Louisiana case] C. Norman. *Science* 236:1620 Je 26 '87

Supreme Court strikes down Louisiana creationism act. T. J. Flygare. il *Phi Delta Kappan* 69:77-9 S '87

The verdict on creationism [Supreme Court ruling on Louisiana law] S. J. Gould. il *N Y Times Mag* p32+ Jl 19 '87

Creation (Literary, artistic, etc.) See Creativity

Creative ability See Creativity

Creative education

See also

Dramatization in education

Creative imagination See Imagination

Creative Label Inc.

Creative Label takes its decorative finishing closer to eastern printers [building of new plant in Martin, Tenn.] J. P. Frank. il *Publ Wkly* 231:260 My 15 '87

Creative Resources Management Inc.

Jones opens new agency. por *Black Enterp* 17:24 F '87

Creative thinking See Creativity

Creative writing

See also

English language—Composition

Study and teaching

Let's not talk down to ourselves [college courses] M. Robinson. *N Y Times Book Rev* 92:11 Ap 5 '87

On becoming a writer [teenager attends workshop with adults] J. Buxton. il *Seventeen* 46:89+ N '87

Staying alive by learning to write [college courses] A. Muschg. il *N Y Times Book Rev* 92:1+ F 1 '87

What I teach in creative writing classes. M. Wojciechowska. *Writer* 100:5-6 Jl '87

The write stuff. B. G. Polikoff. il *Parents* 62:140-4 O '87

Creativity

See also

Odyssey of the Mind

Acid test [LSD and creativity; study by Oscar Janigar] R. B. Tucker. *Omni* 10:16 N '87

Art for art's sake [work of T. Amabile] A. Kohn. il pors *Psychol Today* 21:52-7 S '87

The creative process and libel. I. R. Kaufman. il *N Y Times Mag* p28-30+ Ap 5 '87

Creative solutions with everyday systems [creative computing] A. C. Hixson. il *Pers Comput* 11:138-41+ S '87

Creativity and enterprise [address, June 1, 1987] A. W. Elliott. *Vital Speeches Day* 53:637-40 Ag 1 '87

Creativity and the troubled mind [association with manic depression] C. Holden. il *Psychol Today* 21:9-10 Ap '87

Exercise your creativity [research by Joan C. Gondola] *Prevention* 39:12 Jl '87

How schools sabotage a creative work force. J. A. Hershey. il *Bus Week* p16 Jl 13 '87

How to think like an innovator. D. Waitley and R. B. Tucker. il *Futurist* 21:9-15 My/Je '87

Laughter: a creative muse? [mood and creativity; research by Alice M. Isen] C. Russo. *Psychol Today* 21:21 S '87

Mood swings and creativity: new clues [research by Nancy C. Andreasen] B. Bower. *Sci News* 132:262 O 24 '87

Origins of creativity. J. Croghan. il *Am Artist* 51:14+ Ag '87

Perfectionism: a serious impediment to creativity. J. Croghan. *Am Artist* 51:14+ Je '87

Releasing blocked creativity. J. Croghan. *Am Artist* 51:16+ D '87

Creativity—cont.

Second wind: capitalizing on your full creative potential [address, December 7, 1986] R. L. Weaver. *Vital Speeches Day* 53:235-7 F 1 '87

The spark: personal testimonies of creativity [cover story] S. Weisburd. il *Sci News* 132:298-300 N 7 '87

The spirit of creativity [two-year olds] B. Weissbourd. il *Parents* 62:186 Mr '87

Tapping your creativity [advice for business people from Michael Ray and Rochelle Myers] H. Bacas. il *Nations Bus* 75:48 Mr '87

Trying to transcend copycat science [Japan] G. Bylinsky. il *Fortune* 115:42-4+ Mr 30 '87

What becomes an artist most. G. Danto. il *Art News* 86:149-53 N '87

Wisdom from the well. R. T. Harwood. il *Mother Earth News* 108:8+ N/D '87

Anecdotes, facetiae, satire, etc.

Creativity or control? [what desk tops communicate] M. E. Marty. *Christ Century* 104:983 N 4 '87

Crèches *See* Christmas cribs

Credit

See also
Agricultural credit
Collecting of accounts
Debit cards
Debt
Finance companies
Government lending
Interest (Economics)
Loans, Bank
Loans, Personal

How to find the best loans now. K. McCormally. il *Changing Times* 41:22-7+ F '87

It's time to rethink debt [special section] il *Money* 16:90-1+ Ap '87

Information services

See Credit bureaus

Rating

See also
Credit bureaus

Credit where credit is due [L. Carlin sues Southeast Banking Corp. over credit rating dispute] il por *50 Plus* 27:16+ S '87

Credit where it's due. B. Kallen. il *Forbes* 140:100-1 Ag 24 '87

Dun & Bradstreet's overheard Dialog [access to Dun's Financial Records] *Newsweek* 110:39 D 28 '87

How lenders size you up. W. L. Updegrave. il *Money* 16:145-7+ Ap '87

How to improve your credit rating. G. L. Beiswinger. *McCalls* 145:32 Mr '87

Maintaining a good credit record. D. Lamaute. il *Black Enterp* 17:25-6 Ja '87

Money for nothing [TRW Credentials' marketing of credit information] A. Snitzer. il *Forbes* 139:212+ My 18 '87

Take control of your credit [TRW Credentials program] il *Consum Rep* 52:412 Jl '87

Your credit-profile rights. M. Jasper. il *Essence* 18:120 O '87

Automation

Your humble servant [American Express' Authorizer's Assistant AI-based system] E. Dyson. il *Forbes* 140:204 N 2 '87

Credit bureaus

See also
Telecredit, Inc.

Fixing your credit file. A. McGrath. il *U S News World Rep* 102:49 Je 29 '87

Credit card crimes

See also
Credit cards—Security measures

Bankrupt ideology [L. LaRouche forced into involuntary bankruptcy] *Time* 129:80 My 4 '87

Caution prevents credit-card fraud. J. Malveaux. il *Essence* 18:102 Ag '87

Indicted candidate [L. LaRouche indicted on charges of conspiring to block investigation of alleged fund raising fraud] B. Levin. *Macleans* 100:18 Jl 13 '87

Credit card equipment

See also
Bartizan Corporation

Credit cards

See also
Affinity cards
American Express Co.
Credit counseling
Mastercard International
Memory cards
Visa International Inc.

Charge-a-lawyer is here. R. R. Roha. il *Changing Times* 41:112+ Mr '87

Credit cards: getting the best deal [bank cards] M. Daly. il *Better Homes Gard* 65:24+ Ap '87

Credit cards offer new incentives for travelers. il *Black Enterp* 17:30 Ap '87

Don't go abroad without your trusty cash card. D. Zigas. il *Bus Week* p179 Jl 20 '87

Getting on top of your debt. E. Schurenberg. il *Money* 16:95-6+ Ap '87

House of credit cards. M. Sivy. il *Money* 16:57-8 F '87

Me-generation credit cards. il *Money* 16:13 O '87

Playing your cards right. E. Schmuckler. il *Forbes* 140:116 D 28 '87

Playing your credit cards for all they're worth. B. Hitchings. il *Bus Week* p102-3 Mr 2 '87

Should you switch credit cards? H. Manley. il *Good Housekeep* 204:204 Mr '87

Take a card—but not just any card [premium cards] P. M. Scherschel. il *U S News World Rep* 102:64-5 Mr 23 '87

Tax reform and your credit: a consumer update. B. G. Quint. il *Glamour* 85:76+ F '87

When you're too far in debt. il *Read Dig* 131:49-52 S '87

Your most fantastic plastic. P. Tai. il *Money* 16:162 Ap '87

Advertising

You must know me [AmEx ads] A. Miller. il *Newsweek* 110:64 Ag 17 '87

Chargebacks

Don't get mad, get credited. A. McGrath. il *U S News World Rep* 102:61 My 4 '87

The hidden power of plastic. *Consum Rep* 52:119-22 F '87

Fees

Borrowing: a dire fate awaits those who pay late. il *Money* 16:28 S '87

Interest (Economics)

Borrowing: a political Robin Hood takes from a rich bank. il *Money* 16:36 Mr '87

Borrowing: credit-card junkies overdose as rates stay high. il *Money* 16:40 Ja '87

Borrowing: credit-card lenders show grace under pressure. il *Money* 16:26 Ag '87

Borrowing: credit-card rates refuse to return to earth. il *Money* 16:44 F '87

Card rates. J. W. Merline. il *Consum Res Mag* 70:38 Jl '87

Cardholders get cranky. il *Fortune* 116:10 S 14 '87

Cheaper plastic cash [Canadian rates] D. Jenish. il *Macleans* 100:32+ Ap 6 '87

Check out "too easy" credit. D. Lamaute. *Black Enterp* 17:94 Je '87

Counting the true cost of credit cards. D. Lamaute. il *Black Enterp* 18:47-8 D '87

Credit card caps curtail consumer choices. M. Becker. il *Consum Res Mag* 70:24-7 S '87

Credit card wars—how you can win. M. Asnes. *Vogue* 177:271 S '87

Credit cards: hey, big spender, the Optima is for you [variable-rate card] il *Money* 16:26 My '87

Does lower interest mean lower cost? *Consum Rep* 52:121 F '87

High-stakes cards. *Fortune* 115:6-7 Ap 27 '87

More is less [squeeze on bank credit card profits] B. Weberman. il *Forbes* 139:60-1 Je 29 '87

Marketing

Charge of the plastic brigade [Optima card issued by American Express] J. Castro. il *Time* 129:52 Mr 23 '87

Credit cards: more combat, more casualties [bank cards] F. A. Miller. il *Bus Week* p104+ D 21 '87

Credit cards that say: 'fly me'. T. Segal. il *Bus Week* p139 N 23 '87

From American Express—revolving credit [Optima card] J. B. Levine and C. Farrell. *Bus Week* p146 Mr 23 '87

The rise of Discover. S. B. Weiner. il *Forbes* 139:46-7 My 4 '87

Security measures

See also
SafeCard Services Inc.

Credit card registries: a help or a headache? il *Bus Week* p142 N 9 '87

Protecting your credit cards. G. L. Beiswinger. il *McCalls* 114:127 S '87

Canada

Cheaper plastic cash. D. Jenish. il *Macleans* 100:32+ Ap 6 '87

Credit cards—*cont.*

Japan

The U.S. is getting Japan hooked on plastic. A. Borrus. il *Bus Week* p100+ My 25 '87

Western Europe

Europe's credit-card market is ripe for invasion, too. F. A. Miller. il *Bus Week* p104 My 25 '87

Credit counseling

Keeping big spenders on a leash. B. Bauer. il *U S News World Rep* 102:47-8 F 23 '87

Credit rating *See* Credit—Rating

Credit reporting agencies *See* Credit bureaus

Credit Suisse First Boston Ltd.

Trying to patch up a family quarrel in banking. R. A. Melcher. il por *Bus Week* p66 F 2 '87

Credits, Motion picture *See* Motion picture credits

Cree Indians

Culture and conflict [Calgary's Olympic Arts Festival] P. Young. il *Macleans* 100:52+ N 9 '87

A people's last stand [Lubicon Albertan band] J. Howse. il *Macleans* 100:20 N 16 '87

Seeking a new direction [violence and drug abuse plague Cree Indian reserve of Shamattawa, Man.] C. Barrett. il *Macleans* 100:24 F 2 '87

Creech, John L.

Japanese solomon's-seal. il *Flower Gard* 31:46+ Ap/My '87

Creech, Wendy Goodall

The myth [story] il *Teen* 31:40+ Je '87

Creedence Clearwater Revival (Musical group)

John Fogerty [interview] J. Henke. por *Roll Stone* p146-8+ N 5-D 10 '87

Creekmore, W. N.

Keeping classroom walls from distracting learners. *Educ Dig* 53:44-6 O '87

Creeks *See* Brooks, creeks, etc.

Creeping red (Plant) *See* Penstemons

Creepshow 2 [film] *See* Motion picture reviews—Single works

CREF *See* College Retirement Equities Fund

Creiger, Joyce

about

A brand-new way to organize fine art. A. Oshins. il por *Work Woman* 12:66+ My '87

Creighton, John

The autonomous kingdoms of Opus Dei. il por *Humanist* 47:9-13+ Mr/Ap '87

Crémant (Wine) *See* Wine

Crème brûlée *See* Custards

Cremonini, Leonardo, 1925-

about

Leonardo Cremonini. L. Malen. il *Art News* 86:178 O '87

Creole cooking *See* Cooking, Creole

Creole dialects

See also

Gullah dialect

Crépain, Jo

about

Villa civility. C. Amery. il *House Gard* 159:184-9+ S '87

Crêpes

End the meal with crêpes [raspberry crêpes] il *South Living* 22:143 Je '87

Crespi, Pilar

about

Professional power. il pors *Harpers Bazaar* 120:68+ Mr '87

Cressy, David

Letters home: old and New England in the seventeenth century. bibl il map *Hist Today* 37:37-41 O '87

Crestet (Provençe, France: Castle) *See* Castles—France

Cretaceous period *See* Geology, Stratigraphic—Cretaceous; Paleoclimatology—Cretaceous; Paleontology—Cretaceous

Creviston, John

about

The tale of a remarkably loyal husband. *Newsweek* 110:45 D 21 '87

Creviston, Shirley

about

The tale of a remarkably loyal husband. *Newsweek* 110:45 D 21 '87

Crew, Spencer R.

The Great Migration of Afro-Americans, 1915-40 [cover story] il *Mon Labor Rev* 110:34-6 Mr '87

Crew racing *See* Rowing

Crews, David

Courtship in unisexual lizards: a model for brain evolution. bibl (p158) il *Sci Am* 257:116-21 D '87

Crews, Frederick C.

Pressure under grace. bibl f il por *N Y Rev Books* 34:30-7 Ag 13 '87

'Pressure under grace': an exchange [discussion of August 13, 1987 article] il *N Y Rev Books* 34:59-60 O 22 '87

Crews, Harry, 1935-

about

Life-scarred and wary of battle, a literary guerrilla calls truce. M. Green. il pors *People Wkly* 27:75-6+ Je 8 '87

Crews, Airplane *See* Airplane crews

Crews, Boat *See* Seamen

Crews, Guided missile base *See* Guided missile bases—Crews

Crib deaths *See* Sudden infant death syndrome

Cribb, T. Kenneth, Jr.

about

How the new right is undermining Howard Baker. R. Fly. il por *Bus Week* p43 S 21 '87

Cribs (Beds)

Room with view: no adults [baby tender designed by Stephen Ledoux and Carl Cheney] P. Chance. il *Psychol Today* 21:14 Ap '87

Crichton, Jean

Warehouse clubs: an expanding market. il *Publ Wkly* 231:56-8+ F 13 '87

Crichton, Jennifer

Branded! The red-hot tales of a chronic blusher. il *Seventeen* 46:54 My '87

Cricket (Sport)

Great Britain

Black Botham. M. Weiss. il pors *Esquire* 107:82-6 Ja '87

Going to bat for Britain. T. Stoppard. il por *House Gard* 159:22+ N '87

Crime and age

Felonies decline as population ages [views of Darrell J. Steffensmeier and Miles D. Harer] *USA Today (Periodical)* 116:4 Ag '87

Crime and criminals

See also

Airplane hijacking
Arson
Asian Americans—Crimes against
Assassination
Assault and battery
Athletes—Crime
Black clergy—Crime
Black markets
Black women—Crimes against
Blacks—Crime
Blacks—Crimes against
Body snatching
Bribery
Burglary and burglars
Capital punishment
Cellular radio crimes
Children—Crimes against
Clergy—Crime
Commercial crimes
Computer crimes
Convict labor
Counterfeits and counterfeiting
Credit card crimes
Crime and age
Crime and the press
Crime prevention
Criminal investigation
Criminal psychology
Drugs and crime
Education and crime
Embezzlement
Escapes
Extortion
Fraud
Fugitives from justice
Gangs
Government employees—Crime
Insurance crimes
Juvenile delinquents and delinquency
Mafia
Murder
Narcotics trade
Nurses and nursing—Crime
Organized crime
Parole
Pillage
Pirates
Poaching
Prisoners

Crime and criminals—See also—*cont.*
    Prisons
    Puerto Ricans—United States—Crime
    Punishment
    Rape
    Recidivists
    Robberies and assaults
    Salvadorans—United States—Crimes against
    Self defense for women
    Sex crimes
    Shoplifting
    Smuggling
    Stealing
    Suburban crimes
    Tax evasion
    Teachers—Crime
    Telephone crimes
    Television broadcasting—Crime programs
    Terrorism
    Trials
    United States. Army Reserve—Crimes and misdemeanors
    Victims of crime
    Women—Crime
    Women—Crimes against
Crime and punishment: forces shaping the future. G. Stephens. il por *Futurist* 21:18-26 Ja/F '87
Crime: fighting public enemy No. 1 [cover story; special issue] il *Sch Update* 120:2-20 D 4 '87
Crime in America: the shocking truth [results of survey] R. Hillhouse. *McCalls* 145:144 Mr '87
Criminals are made, not born. C. W. Colson. il *Christ Today* 31:72 Ja 16 '87
It was the perfect crime . . . M. Long. il *Omni* 9:78 My '87
When diplomatic immunity is a crime [condensed from Diplomatic crime] C. R. Ashman and P. Trescott. *Read Dig* 131:129-32 D '87

Biography
    See also
    Son of Sam laws

Economic aspects
    See also
    Laundering of money

History
200 years of crime, coppers, and criminals. I. Peck. il *Sch Update* 120:14-17 D 4 '87

    Photographs and photography
Rogues' gallery [exhibit at Pace/MacGill Gallery] il *N Y Times Mag* p20-3 F 1 '87

Identification
    See also
    Computers—Police use

International aspects
Fighting world crime. P. M. Jones. il *Sch Update* 120:22-3 D 4 '87

Rehabilitation
    See also
    Prisoners—Rehabilitation

Terminology
Deliver a verdict on terms of crime and punishment. T. Rothenberg. *Sch Update* 119:15 F 9 '87
Wordpower. C. K. Lawrence. *Sch Update* 120:23 D 4 '87

Alberta
    See also
    Edmonton (Alta.)—Crime

Arkansas
    See also
    West Memphis (Ark.)—Crime

Brazil
Scenes from Brazilian Vice. C. Wood. il *Macleans* 100:24-5 Ja 19 '87

British Columbia
    See also
    Vancouver (B.C.)—Crime

California
    See also
    Humboldt County (Calif.)—Crime
    Los Angeles (Calif.)—Crime
    Manhattan Beach (Calif.)—Crime
    Milpitas (Calif.)—Crime
    Orange County (Calif.)—Crime
    Sacramento (Calif.)—Crime
    San Diego (Calif.)—Crime
If you're missing milk crates, Mike Massey will crack the case. il por *People Wkly* 28:114 S 21 '87
In Manson's eyes [interview with C. Manson] R. Healy. il pors *Life* 10:54-6 Mr '87

Canada
    See also
    Mafia

Florida
    See also
    Arcadia (Fla.)—Crime
    Daytona Beach (Fla.)—Crime
    Golden Gate (Fla.)—Crime
    Malabar (Fla.)—Crime
    Miami (Fla.)—Crime
    Palm Bay (Fla.)—Crime
    Palm Beach Gardens (Fla.)—Crime
Family business: murder would settle it, and Debra Banister knew who to ask [hit man J. W. Hearn] J. Wadler. il pors *People Wkly* 28:57-8+ Jl 6 '87

Georgia
    See also
    Atlanta (Ga.)—Crime
    Blakely (Ga.)—Crime
    Carrollton (Ga.)—Crime

Great Britain
    See also
    Great Britain. Army—Crimes and misdemeanors
    Hungerford (Berkshire, England)—Crime

Idaho
Claude Dallas update. R. P. Stuart. por *Outdoor Life* 179:49 Mr '87
In Idaho: a killer becomes a mythic hero [C. Dallas] M. Riley. il por *Time* 129:10-11 Ja 26 '87

Illinois
    See also
    Chicago (Ill.)—Crime
    Small, Stephen, d. 1987—Kidnapping

Iowa
    See also
    Mount Pleasant (Iowa)—Crime

Italy
    See also
    Association of Sicilian Women Against the Mafia
    Mafia
    Milan (Italy)—Crime

Jamaica
More intrigue involved in Peter Tosh's murder. por *Jet* 73:32 O 26 '87
Reggae great Peter Tosh murdered. M. Goldberg. por *Roll Stone* p24+ O 22 '87
Reggae star Peter Tosh fatally shot in Jamaica. por *Jet* 73:62 S 28 '87

Kansas
    See also
    Emporia (Kan.)—Crime
The gang that couldn't rob straight [bank robberies] il *Newsweek* 110:30 S 28 '87

Maryland
    See also
    Clinton (Md.)—Crime
    Suitland (Md.)—Crime

Massachusetts
    See also
    Boston (Mass.)—Crime
    Haverhill (Mass.)—Crime

Missouri
    See also
    Elkland (Mo.)—Crime

Montana
A made-for-television movie brings biathlete Kari Swenson face-to-face with her past. M. Neill. il pors *People Wkly* 27:76-8+ Mr 16 '87

New Jersey
    See also
    Highland Park (N.J.)—Crime
    Manalapan (N.J.: Township)—Crime

New York (State)
    See also
    Bronx (New York, N.Y.)—Crime
    New York (N.Y.)—Crime
    Westchester County (N.Y.)—Crime
    Woodmere (N.Y.)—Crime

Ontario
    See also
    Toronto (Ont.)—Crime
Search for a serial killer. R. Corelli. il *Macleans* 100:54 O 5 '87

Oregon
    See also
    Springfield (Or.)—Crime

Pennsylvania
    See also
    Homestead (Pa.)—Crime
    Honesdale (Pa.)—Crime
    Philadelphia (Pa.)—Crime

Crime and criminals—Pennsylvania—See also—*cont.*
Pittsburgh (Pa.)—Crime

Persian Gulf region
Cities without crime. B. Cain. il *World Press Rev* 34:64 Je '87

Prince Edward Island
See also
Charlottetown (P.E.I.)—Crime

Québec (Province)
See also
Montreal (Québec)—Crime
A murder mystery [murder of M. Taddeo, subject of Mirabel Airport land sales investigation] L. Van Dusen. por *Macleans* 100:19-20 D 21 '87

Rhode Island
Stalking the nighttime sniper. S. Doherty. il *Newsweek* 109:29 Ja 26 '87

Rwanda
I didn't kill Dian. She was my friend [murder of gorilla protector D. Fossey]; ed. by Beverly Trainer and Gina Maranto. W. McGuire. il pors maps *Discover* 8:28-32+ F '87

Southwestern States
The Southwest drug connection. S. Strasser. il map *Newsweek* 110:29-30+ N 23 '87

Tennessee
See also
Nashville (Tenn.)—Crime

Texas
See also
Dallas (Tex.)—Crime
Houston (Tex.)—Crime
Midlothian (Tex.)—Crime

Utah
A hand from the grave [E. LeBaron and the polygamy murders case] P. Abramson. il pors *Newsweek* 110:45 D 21 '87

Virginia
See also
Petersburg (Va.)—Crime

Washington (State)
See also
Seattle (Wash.)—Crime
Casting a net at Green River [serial murderer manhunt] C. Garcia. il *Time* 130:61 Jl 27 '87
Epidemic of murder [Vancouver, B.C. murders thought to be linked to Washington State serial murderer] J. O'Hara. *Macleans* 100:12 Jl 20 '87
A killer still on the loose [Green River serial murderer] M. Ryan. il *People Wkly* 28:24-9 Ag 24 '87

Wisconsin
See also
Norwalk (Wis.)—Crime
Why are there Angels in the Dells? [Guardian Angels in Wisconsin] il *Newsweek* 110:21 Ag 24 '87

Wyoming
The last hired gun [range detective E. Cantrell] J. Conaway. il por *Harpers* 275:58-63 Ag '87
Crime and drugs *See* Drugs and crime
Crime and education *See* Education and crime
Crime and punishment [drama] *See* Lyubimov, Yuri
Crime and the press
See also
Newspaper court reporting
N.Y. sax player labeled criminal in Daily news in case of mistaken identity [case of D. Foster] il por *Jet* 72:38 My 11 '87
The Police Shack [old hangout for police reporters in New York City] N. Pileggi. il por *N Y* 20:95 D 21-28 '87
Puzzling evidence [pretrial publicity and juries; study by Roger W. Davis] S. Walton. il *Psychol Today* 21:10 Ag '87

Canada
Only news that's nice to print [suppression of racial identification in criminal cases] G. Bain. il *Macleans* 100:47 Ja 26 '87
Crime and weather
Predicting crime from the weather. S. P. Lab and J. D. Hirschel. il pors *Futurist* 21:30-2 Mr/Ap '87
Crime detection *See* Criminal investigation
Crime films *See* Motion pictures—Crime films
Crime novels *See* Detective and mystery stories
Crime prevention
See also
Electronics in criminal investigation, espionage, etc.
Police
Sheriffs
Designing to deter crime. E. Krupat and P. E. Kubzansky. bibl (p62) il *Psychol Today* 21:58-61 O '87

The public fights back. T. Gest. il *U S News World Rep* 102:16-17 Je 29 '87
Citizen participation
Citizen crime-fighters: do they help or hurt police efforts? il *Sch Update* 120:12-13 D 4 '87
Demand for crime fighter Isiah is Piston's problem [I. Thomas] por *Jet* 71:51 Ja 12 '87
Screams from somewhere else. R. Rosenblatt. il *Time* 130:98 N 16 '87
Crime programs *See* Television broadcasting—Crime programs
Crime story [television program] See Television program reviews—Single works
Crimean Tatars *See* Tatars
Crimes of the heart [film] See Motion picture reviews—Single works
Criminal investigation
See also
Computers—Police use
Electronics in criminal investigation, espionage, etc.
Fingerprints
Forensic anthropology
Forensic illustration
Fugitives from justice
Informers
Lie detectors and detection
Medical jurisprudence
Missing persons
Parapsychology and criminal investigation
Police questioning
Public prosecutors
United States. Federal Bureau of Investigation
Getting away with murder [forensics] E. Larson. il *Omni* 9:72-4+ My '87
Lab evidence = tougher sentences [views of Joseph Peterson] il *USA Today (Periodical)* 115:15 Ap '87
Criminal jury *See* Jury
Criminal justice, Administration of
See also
Courts martial and courts of inquiry
Criminal investigation
Jury
Justice, Miscarriage of
Juvenile justice, Administration of
Legal procedure
Pardon
Parole
Pleas (Legal procedure)
Political prisoners
Preventive detention
Probation
Public prosecutors
Punishment
Searches and seizures
United States. Dept. of Justice
Considering the alternatives [punishment other than prison] R. Lacayo. il *Time* 129:60-1 F 2 '87
Crime and punishment: forces shaping the future. G. Stephens. il por *Futurist* 21:18-26 Ja/F '87
Crime and punishment (U.S.A.). il *Read Dig* 131:54-8 Jl '87
Crime: fighting public enemy No. 1 [cover story; special issue] il *Sch Update* 120:2-20 D 4 '87
Doing hard time, fairly [sentencing guidelines] A. Press. il *Newsweek* 109:79 F 16 '87
How many times does a victim have to pay? A. Smith. il *Esquire* 108:83-4 N '87
Lab evidence = tougher sentences [views of Joseph Peterson] il *USA Today (Periodical)* 115:15 Ap '87
The released killers who walk among us [sentencing reform drive] T. Gest. il *U S News World Rep* 102:18 Ap 27 '87
Restorative justice: does it work? [conference in Guelph, Ont.] R. Rempel. *Christ Century* 104:156-7 F 18 '87
Sentences by the book [guidelines established by the U.S. Sentencing Commission] R. Lacayo. il *Time* 129:71 Ap 27 '87
Will counterrevolution continue? [criminal procedure and the Rehnquist Court; views of Charles Whitebread] il *USA Today (Periodical)* 116:11 Ag '87
Alabama
Avenging a murder [D. Thompson seeks justice for murdered son] D. O. Relin. il por *Sch Update* 120:7 D 4 '87
Deaf mute cleared of murdering Ala. woman [case of J. Green] *Jet* 73:36 O 19 '87
California
See also
San Diego (Calif.)—Criminal justice, Administration of

Criminal justice, Administration of—California—*cont.*
Not in my town [problems of paroled rapist L. Singleton] il por *Time* 129:31 Je 1 '87
The 'Onion Field' parole: Rose Bird's parting shot [case of G. Powell] por *Newsweek* 109:26 Ja 12 '87
Prison versus probation [report of Joan Petersilia and Susan Turner] *Society* 24:3 My/Je '87

Canada
Redress for victims of crime. M. Rose. *Macleans* 100:21 N 16 '87

Delaware
Deathbed confession frees Del. black after 12 years [case of W. Cammile] il por *Jet* 72:16 Jl 6 '87

Florida
See also
Miami (Fla.)—Criminal justice, Administration of
The agony did not end for Roswell Gilbert, who killed his wife to give her peace. L. Marx. il pors *People Wkly* 27:30-2+ Ja 12 '87

Georgia
See also
Fort Valley (Ga.)—Criminal justice, Administration of
Georgia murder conviction overturned: black jurors struck for racial reasons [case of W. Gamble] *Jet* 72:40 Ag 3 '87
A shared fate [Supreme Court ruling that death penalty is not racially biased] M. O. Finkelstein. *Nation* 244:599 My 9 '87
Thinking about the death penalty [Supreme Court rules death penalty not racially biased] *America* 156:393 My 16 '87

Illinois
See also
Chicago (Ill.)—Criminal justice, Administration of
Oak Park (Ill.)—Criminal justice, Administration of

Louisiana
"Everyone's a victim in this" [execution of murderer S. Rault] R. Woodbury. il por *Time* 130:22 S 7 '87

Maryland
Md. day care center owner gets 10 yrs. for child abuse [S. A. Craig] *Jet* 73:37 O 19 '87

Michigan
See also
Wayne County (Mich.)—Criminal justice, Administration of
Michigan woman jailed; can't serve time at home [case of C. Doa] *Jet* 72:25 My 18 '87

Minnesota
Black man's teeth a deadly weapon, jury rules [case of J. V. Moore] il por *Jet* 72:24 Jl 13 '87

Mississippi
Minority report [capital punishment] C. Hitchens. *Nation* 245:150 Ag 29 '87

Missouri
Witnessing for peace [update on Silo Pruning Hooks case] R. Pollak. *Nation* 244:567-8 My 2 '87

New Jersey
See also
Englewood (N.J.)—Criminal justice, Administration of
Innocent man's eight-year prison ordeal [case of N. Walker] W. Leavy. il pors *Ebony* 42:86+ Mr '87

New York (State)
See also
Queens (New York, N.Y.)—Criminal justice, Administration of
Convictions and conflict: a top cop's tale [U.S. Attorney R. Giuliani] D. Baer. il pors *U S News World Rep* 102:23-4+ Mr 23 '87
Gotcha! [cover story; interview with R. Giuliani] N. Collins. il pors *N Y* 20:28-40 My 25 '87
Keep your eye on Giuliani. G. F. Will. il *Newsweek* 109:84 Mr 2 '87
The lady killer: should Jean Harris go free? B. G. Harrison. *Mademoiselle* 93:164 Ag '87
New York's 'Eliot Ness' [R. Giuliani] L. Black. il por *Macleans* 100:6-7 Ap 6 '87
Wall Street's top cop [U.S. Attorney C. M. Carberry] il pors *Newsweek* 109:48-50 Mr 2 '87

Nova Scotia
See also
Sydney (N.S.)—Criminal justice, Administration of

Ontario
Crackdown on defaulters [support payment defaulters] J. Bennett. *Macleans* 100:48 Jl 6 '87

Oregon
See also
Portland (Or.)—Criminal justice, Administration of

Québec (Province)
See also
Montreal (Québec)—Criminal justice, Administration of

Soviet Union
Linnas and the long war [deportation to the Soviet Union] *Natl Rev* 39:19-20 My 22 '87
The Linnas case: was justice done? [deportation to Soviet Union of Estonian war criminal] N. Cooper. il por *Newsweek* 109:33-4 My 4 '87
Nazis and Communists [case of K. Linnas] *New Repub* 196:4+ My 11 '87
Problems of crime and punishment [ethics of U.S. use of Soviet evidence against Nazi war criminal K. Linnas] R. Lacayo. il *Time* 129:60 Ap 20 '87

Texas
An everyday death [E. Moreno] I. Austen. il por *Macleans* 100:16+ Mr 16 '87

United States
See Criminal justice, Administration of

Utah
See also
Salt Lake City (Utah)—Criminal justice, Administration of

Virginia
Guilty of theft, Bethea awaits sentencing in Va. [L. Bethea] *Jet* 71:49 Ja 19 '87

Washington (D.C.)
See Washington (D.C.)—Criminal justice, Administration of

Wisconsin
See also
Milwaukee (Wis.)—Criminal justice, Administration of

Criminal law
See also
Capital punishment
Conspiracy
Criminal justice, Administration of
Legal procedure
Liability (Law)
Libel and slander
Obscenity (Law)
Pardon
Racketeer Influenced and Corrupt Organizations Act of 1970
Rape
Son of Sam laws
Tax evasion

Criminal procedure *See* Legal procedure

Criminal psychology
See also
Forensic psychiatry
Prison psychology
Violence
Advances reported in predicting violence [study by Antonio Convit and others] J. Greenberg. *Sci News* 131:324-5 My 23 '87
Hidden histories on death row [neurological disorders and homicidal behavior; study of death row juveniles by Dorothy Otnow Lewis] *Sci News* 132:287 O 31 '87
Murder in mind [neurological disorders and homicidal behavior; study of death row juveniles by Dorothy Otnow Lewis] J. Meer. *Psychol Today* 21:62 Mr '87
Psychologist with a badge [T. H. Blau of Manatee County, Fla.] R. J. Trotter. il pors *Psychol Today* 21:26+ N '87
Sin, psychopathology and Father Brown [comparison with M. Mann's Manhunter] M. Horst. *Christ Century* 104:46-7 Ja 21 '87

Criminal records
Cocaine arrests prompt efforts to investigate airline employee records [smuggling rings uncovered at Kennedy Airport] *Aviat Week Space Technol* 126:36 Mr 16 '87
Conyers hits plan to open the FBI's arrest records [impact on black employment] *Jet* 73:12 N 9 '87

Criminal violence *See* Violence
Criminals *See* Crime and criminals
Criminology *See* Crime and criminals

Crisis management (Psychology)
Teaching young people to help others in crises. W. W. Crowder. *Educ Dig* 53:46-9 S '87

Crisis management in business
Communicating during a "crisis" [address, December 2, 1986] H. Carr. *Vital Speeches Day* 53:248-50 F 1 '87
Corporate and private sector communications responsibility [address, October 10, 1986] J. E. Lukaszewski. *Vital Speeches Day* 53:305-10 Mr 1 '87

Crisis management in business—*cont.*
Crash course in crisis management. M. R. Feinberg. il *Work Woman* 12:24+ Ja '87
Crisis management in education
Help for principals in managing school crises. W. D. St. John. *Educ Dig* 52:36-9 Ap '87
Crisis management in government
Black Monday's reign of terror. M. Greenfield. il *Newsweek* 110:86 N 2 '87
Crise du jour. *Natl Rev* 39:19-20 My 8 '87
The Cuban Missile Crisis revisited. J. G. Blight and others. bibl f *Foreign Aff* 66:170-88 Fall '87
Time to recall this model? [Cuban Missile Crisis model] M. Greenfield. il *Newsweek* 110:84 S 21 '87
Anecdotes, facetiae, satire, etc.
Crisis, crisis, who's got the crisis? G. F. Kreyche. il *USA Today (Periodical)* 116:98 Jl '87
Crisis pregnancy centers *See* Alternative pregnancy centers
Crist, Kathy
For the rivers, come hell or high water. il pors *Sierra* 72:61-5 My/Je '87
Crista Ministries
Christian nursing center adopts life-support policy. E. J. Larson. *Christ Today* 31:59 O 16 '87
Cristallina SA
Christie's and Cristallina settle [fraud and negligent misrepresentation suit against Christie's] R. W. Walker. il *Art News* 86:21-2 Ap '87
Cristóvão, Fernando Alves
Return ticket. il *Courier* 39:37+ D '86
Criterion Group Inc.
Paying the piper. W. P. Barrett. il *Forbes* 140:124 Ag 10 '87
Critical condition [film] *See* Motion picture reviews—Single works
Critical thinking *See* Thought and thinking
Criticism *See* Critics and criticism
Criticism, Personal
The art of constructive criticism. E. Davidowitz. il *Work Woman* 12:101 My '87
How to handle a picky boyfriend. S. Squire. il *Seventeen* 46:206-7+ S '87
How to stop being so tough on yourself. B. Hilbert. il *Ladies Home J* 104:70+ My '87
"Was it something I said?" How not to take things personally. J. Stone. *Glamour* 85:82 Je '87
Why everyone hates "friendly advice". S. Isaacs. il *Parents* 62:89-93 D '87
The world's worst critics [authors' self criticism] J. C. Oates. il *N Y Times Book Rev* 92:1+ Ja 18 '87
Critics and criticism
See also
Art critics and criticism
Book reviews and reviewing
Drama critics and criticism
Education critics and criticism
Food critics and criticism
Hermeneutics
Literary critics and criticism
Music critics and criticism
A little matter of sense. J. Barzun. il *N Y Times Book Rev* 92:1+ Je 21 '87
Critser, Greg
The feud that toppled a TV empire. il pors *Channels* 7:24-31 Ja '87
Tough New World. il *Channels* 7:20-6 Mr '87
Cro-Magnon man *See* Man, Prehistoric
Croce, Arlene
Dancing. See occasional issues of The New Yorker
Crocheting
Pick-up-and-go crafts [tablecloth] J. Williams and J. Severson. il *Better Homes Gard* 65:126-7+ Ag '87
Crocker, Chester A.
South Africa: toward peace and stability [address, December 1, 1986] *Dep State Bull* 87:40-2 F '87
U.S. policy toward Mozambique [statement, June 24, 1987] *Dep State Bull* 87:19-22 S '87
U.S. policy toward Southern Africa [address, December 1, 1986] *Vital Speeches Day* 53:197-9 Ja 15 '87
Crockett, George W., Jr.
about
Crockett and the patriots. *Natl Rev* 39:18-19 Ag 14 '87
Crockett heads committee exposing racism within the U.S. Foreign Service. il por *Jet* 72:5 Ag 17 '87
Crockett heads drive for a day honoring Mandela. pors *Jet* 73:4 N 9 '87
Rep. Crockett appointed to United Nations post. por *Jet* 72:8 S 7 '87

Crockett, Rita
about
Black star leads women's volleyball team to title. *Jet* 72:48 Je 15 '87
Crofters
Scotland
'Having and holding': the Highland land war of the 1880s. I. C. Bradley. bibl il *Hist Today* 37:23-8 D '87
Croghan, Jerry
The psychology of art. See issues of American Artist beginning November 1986
Crohn's disease *See* Regional ileitis
Cronin, John
about
The riverkeeper. A. Wilkinson. il *New Yorker* 63:49-50+ My 11 '87
Cronkite, Walter
about
Walter Cronkite [interview] J. Alter. il por *Roll Stone* p87+ N 5-D 10 '87
Crook, Martha, and Crook, Warren
Clean up your photos. bibl il *Petersens Photogr Mag* 15:47-8 Mr '87
Crook, Warren
(jt. auth) See Crook, Martha, and Crook, Warren
Crooker, Barbara
Ripening [poem] *McCalls* 114:20 My '87
Crop genetics *See* Plant genetics
Crop Over (Festival) *See* Festivals—Barbados
Crop protection *See* Plants—Protection
Crop research *See* Agricultural research
Crop rotation *See* Rotation of crops
Crop yields
See also
Grain—Yield
Soybeans—Yield
Unlocking plants' secret potential [use of triethylamine DCPTA] J. Raloff. *Sci News* 131:265 Ap 25 '87
Cropland utilization *See* Land utilization
Cropping of photographs *See* Photographs—Trimming, mounting, etc.
Cropping of slides *See* Slides (Photography)—Trimming, mounting, etc.
Crops
See also
Companion crops
Forage plants
Grain
Rotation of crops
Soybeans
Crop costs edge up next year. D. Allen. *Success Farm* 85:8 N '87
Marketing
See Farm produce—Marketing; Produce trade
Crops, Effect of air pollution on *See* Plants, Effect of air pollution on
Cropsey, Jasper Francis, 1823-1900
about
American painting. S. B. Sherrill. il *Antiques* 132:894+ N '87
Cropsey, Seth
Moscow in the Pacific. *Natl Rev* 39:28-30 Je 5 '87
Croquet
Big-league croquet in the Bay Area. il *Sunset* 179:50+ Jl '87
A comeback for croquet. K. Springen. il *Newsweek* 110:49 Jl 27 '87
Crosby, David
The happy Lazarus of rock 'n' roll [cover story] il pors *People Wkly* 27:52-4+ Ap 27 '87
Crosby, John O'Hea, 1926-
about
Opera in the desert. J. P. Forsthoffer. il por *Horizon* 30:57-9 O '87
Crosby, Stills, Nash and Young (Musical group)
Young rejoins CSN. M. Goldberg. *Roll Stone* p29+ Mr 26 '87
Crosetti, Ronald
about
A versatile retreat: designer's Lake Tahoe apartment. H. Junker. il *Archit Dig* 44:132-7 Mr '87
Cross, K. Patricia
The adventures of education in Wonderland: implementing education reform [cover story] bibl f il *Phi Delta Kappan* 68:496-502 Mr '87
Cross, Michael C., and Osheroff, Douglas D.
Novel magnetic properties of solid helium-3. bibl f il *Phys Today* 40:34-41 F '87

Cross, Peter S., and others
Ultrahigh-power semiconductor diode laser arrays. bibl f il *Science* 237:1305-9 S 11 '87

Cross, Roger L.
Eastern north Pacific tropical cyclones. il map *Weatherwise* 40:25-6 F '87

Cross, Theodore L., 1924-
about
Harper & Row gets $190 million offer from private investor. M. Reuter. il por *Publ Wkly* 231:10 Mr 20 '87
Lawyer, writer, activist, millionaire. A. Kupfer. il por *Fortune* 115:62 Ja 5 '87

Cross (A. T.) Co. *See* A. T. Cross Co.

The cross and the crescent [radio program] *See* Radio program reviews—Single works

Cross country running
Rolling a six the hard way [P. Porter wins TAC title] C. Neff. il por *Sports Illus* 67:42-3 D 7 '87
Running for redemption [J. Falcon] A. Murphy. il pors *Sports Illus* 67:103-4 O 26 '87

Cross country ski camping *See* Camping

Cross country ski exercisers *See* Exercising equipment

Cross country ski racing *See* Ski racing

Cross country skiing *See* Skis and skiing

Cross Creek (Ohio)
Cross Creek. K. McCafferty. il *Field Stream* 91:60-1+ Mr '87

Cross cultural studies *See* Intercultural research

Cross my heart [film] *See* Motion picture reviews—Single works

Crossair AG
Switzerland's Crossair considers purchase of stretched Saab SF340. J. M. Lenorovitz. il *Aviat Week Space Technol* 126:42-3 Je 8 '87

Crossbow
The hybrid compound crossbow. il *Mother Earth News* 104:74-5 Mr/Ap '87

Crossbreeding *See* Hybridization

Crossen, Craig
Observing spring galaxies with binoculars. il *Astronomy* 15:62-7 My '87

Crossick, Geoffrey
Classes and the masses in Victorian England. bibl il *Hist Today* 37:29-35 Mr '87

Crossing over (Genetics)
Meiotic recombination in yeast: alteration by multiple heterozygosities. R. H. Borts and J. E. Haber. bibl f il *Science* 237:1459-65 S 18 '87
The structure of sister minichromosome DNA before anaphase in Saccharomyces cerevisiae. D. Koshland and L. H. Hartwell. bibl f il *Science* 238:1713-16 D 18 '87

Crossland, John
The Xi'an Incident. bibl il pors *Hist Today* 37:10-16 Jl '87

Crossland, Steve
about
Be true to your school. C. Meherani and R. Orr. il pors *Nations Bus* 75:46+ Je '87

Crosson, James D., d. 1987
about
Obituary
Jet por 71:52 F 2 '87

Crossover, Electronic (Loudspeakers) *See* Loudspeakers

Crossword puzzles
38 down: oops! [errors in puzzles] E. T. Maleska. il *N Y Times Mag* p50+ Ap 26 '87
Note from the editor [crossword puzzler W. Lutwiniak] S. Wilmot. il por *Americana* 15:3 My/Je '87
Tournaments
Coble and tenk [Stamford Marriott Crossword Puzzle Tournament] E. J. Kahn. *New Yorker* 63:103-4+ My 11 '87

Croswell, Ken
Looking for a few good stars [cover story] il *Space World* X-7-283:12-15 Jl '87
A mission to Pluto. il *Space World* X-9-285:22-4 S '87
Visit the nearest stars. il *Astronomy* 15:16-22 Ja '87

Crouch, Edmund A. C.
(jt. auth) See Wilson, Richard, 1926-, and Crouch, Edmund A. C.

Crouch, Jan
about
They're not the Bakkers. K. L. Woodward. il pors *Newsweek* 110:61 Ag 31 '87

Crouch, Paul
Is TV appropriate for mass evangelism? por *Christ Today* 31:50 O 16 '87

about
They're not the Bakkers. K. L. Woodward. il pors *Newsweek* 110:61 Ag 31 '87

Crouch, Stanley
Wynton Marsalis: 1987 [cover story; interview] il por *Down Beat* 11:16-19+ N '87

Crouse, Lindsay
about
Life visits David Mamet & Lindsay Crouse. D. E. Haupt. il pors *Life* 10:64-5+ O '87
Psycho therapy. M. Haskell. il por *Vogue* 177:140+ S '87

Crouzet (Firm)
Crouzet, Bendix will develop voice command system [military aircraft] *Aviat Week Space Technol* 127:77 Jl 20 '87

Crovitz, L. Gordon
Crime, the Constitution, and the Iran-contra affair. *Commentary* 84:23-30 O '87

Crow, C. P.
Profiles [R. J. Kusse] *New Yorker* 63:34-8+ Je 22 '87

Crow, Elizabeth
Inside Parents. See issues of Parents

Crow, Thomas E., 1948-
Saturday disasters: trace and reference in early Warhol [cover story] bibl f il por *Art Am* 75:128-36 My '87

Crow, Trammell
about
The U.S. Business Hall of Fame. A. M. Louis. il por *Fortune* 115:104 Ap 13 '87

Crowd control
See also
National parks and reserves—Crowd control

Crowded House (Musical group)
Crowded House. il *Teen* 31:80 Ag '87
Crowded House [performance at The Bottom Line] D. Handelman. il *Roll Stone* p12 My 7 '87
Crowded House: a pop showplace. D. Wild. il *Roll Stone* p22 F 12 '87
Take heart from Neil Finn's Crowded House. E. Miller. il por *Seventeen* 46:80-1 Jl '87

Crowder, William W.
Teaching young people to help others in crises. *Educ Dig* 53:46-9 S '87

Crowding stress
Facing the crowd. il *Curr Health 2* 13:16-17 Ja '87

Crowds
See also
Riots
Lost in the crowd [group size and composition can affect behavior; research by Brian Mullen] J. Goetz. il *Psychol Today* 21:60 Je '87

Crowe, William J., 1925-
about
Joint Chiefs chairman counsels long-term strategic view of Soviets. il *Aviat Week Space Technol* 126:117+ Je 15 '87

Crowell, Nancy K.
Summer adventures—under $500! il *Women's Sports Fitness* 9:49-51 My '87

Crowfoot, John
(tr) See Yemelyanov, Vasily S. The making of the Soviet bomb

Crowley, Bob
about
Les liaisons dangereuses [cover story] M. Sommers. il por *Theatre Crafts* 21:26-31+ Ag/S '87

Crowley, Diane
about
Defeating 12,000, odd couple Diane Crowley and Jeff Zaslow win Ann Landers' old job. M. Vespa. il pors *People Wkly* 27:49-50 Je 22 '87
Mr. and Ms. Lonelyhearts. M. Bosc. il pors *U S News World Rep* 102:12 Je 15 '87

Crowley's Ridge (Ark. and Mo.)
Crowley's Ridge, Arkansas. R. H. Mohlenbrock. il map *Nat Hist* 96:84-6 N '87

Crown Books Corporation
Crown to countersue NCBA and individual booksellers [antitrust suit] M. Reuter. *Publ Wkly* 231:19 F 13 '87
Crown to launch books based on songs of popular singer [Raffi] il por *Publ Wkly* 231:42 My 29 '87
A new agent and a new publisher for June Flaum Singer. *Publ Wkly* 232:24 Jl 31 '87

Crown Cork & Seal Company, Inc.
These penny-pinchers deliver a big bang for their bucks [J. F. Connelly] C. S. Eklund and J. Flynn. pors *Bus Week* p52 My 4 '87

Crown corporations *See* Corporations, Government—Canada

Crown jewels

The family jewels [L. Field's book about Queen Elizabeth's jewels] R. Koenig. por *N Y* 20:40 O 19 '87

The Queen's jewels [Queen Elizabeth II] il pors *Life* 10:44-6+ O '87

Crown Life Insurance Co.

The tangle of disability claims [D. McTaggart suing Crown Life for disability benefits] D. Francis. il *Macleans* 100:11 D 14 '87

Crown Publishers Inc.

Crown and Walden to launch mass market category line. il *Publ Wkly* 232:16 Jl 31 '87

Multipurpose new video promo for Crown Publishers by American Made. A. Symons. *Publ Wkly* 232:48 O 16 '87

Crown Video (Firm)

Crown moves up Sistine Chapel video [documentary on restoration of Michelangelo's frescoes] il *Publ Wkly* 231:32 Mr 27 '87

Crowns (Dentistry) See Dentures

Crowther, Prudence

Knowing S. J. Perelman. il *N Y Rev Books* 34:14-19 Jl 16 '87

Croyden, Margaret

Peter Brook creates a nine-hour epic. il por *N Y Times Mag* p36-8+ O 4 '87

Croyle, John

about

John Croyle's speck of heaven. R. Exum. il *Read Dig* 130:85-9 My '87

Crozier, Brian

Activist, strategist. il *Natl Rev* 39:36-7 S 11 '87

The protracted conflict. See issues of National Review

CRS Sirrine, Inc.

Sirrine serene [stock price] T. Jaffe. *Forbes* 140:246 O 5 '87

Crucifixion

See also

Jesus Christ—Crucifixion

Greg Withrow's neo-Nazi past returns to inflict the ultimate scourge: crucifixion. M. Green. il pors *People Wkly* 28:41-2+ S 21 '87

Crude oil See Petroleum

Crude oil options See Commodity options

Crudele, John

The bottom line. See issues of New York beginning April 20, 1987

Ten lessons. il *N Y* 20:38-9 N 2 '87

Cruelty

See also

Aged—Mistreatment

Animals—Treatment

Child abuse

Police cruelty

Sadomasochism

Cruglas (Wales: Historic house) See Historic houses, sites, etc.—Wales

Cruickshank, Alexander M.

Gordon Research Conferences. *Science* 235:1233-60 Mr 6 '87

Gordon Research Conferences. *Science* 238:212-17 O 9 '87

Cruikshank, Dale P.

Cometary studies come of age. il *Sky Telesc* 73:236 Mr '87

Cruikshank, Dale P., and Brown, Robert Hamilton

Organic matter on asteroid 130 Elektra. bibl f il *Science* 238:183-4 O 9 '87

Cruise, Tom

about

Now married to Mimi Rogers, Tom's Cruising days are over. pors *People Wkly* 27:83 My 25 '87

Paul Newman and Tom Cruise spend a so-so day at the races, but fans lap it up anyway. il pors *People Wkly* 28:36-7 Jl 13 '87

The straight men: Michael J. Fox, Huey Lewis, Tom Cruise. C. Krupp. il pors *Glamour* 85:250 Ap '87

Tom Cruise: Hollywood's new Top Gun. E. Sherman. por *Ladies Home J* 104:113+ Ap '87

Tom Cruise: nothing but the facts. il pors *Teen* 31:28 Ap '87

Cruise control (Automobiles) See Automobiles—Speed control

Cruise lines See Steamship lines

Cruise missiles See Guided missiles

Cruise ships See Ocean liners

Cruisers (Pleasure boats)

Pocket cruisers. S. Stapleton. il *Mot Boat Sail* 160:28 O '87

Testing

Creatures of comfort [Cape Dory 300, Nauticat 33, Gulfstar 54, Cheoy Lee 53 and Shannon 38] R. Marshall. il *Mot Boat Sail* 159:52-5+ Ap '87

European elegance [Euromarine 43] R. Marshall. il *Mot Boat Sail* 160:62-3+ Jl '87

Express cruisers [Wellcraft 34 Grand Sport, Chris Craft 332 Amerosport, Sea Ray 34 and Trojan 10-Meter Express] il *Mot Boat Sail* 159:70-7 F '87

Grand cruise: Mackinac Island's Grand Hotel provides an elegant setting for a weekend on the new extended bridge Cruisers 42. D. Fales. il *Mot Boat Sail* 160:46-9+ D '87

Pearson powers up [Pearson 38] D. Fales. il *Mot Boat Sail* 159:58-61 My '87

Cruises See Cruising

Cruising

See also

River trips

Voyages

Voyages around the world

Computer school while you cruise. il *Sunset* 179:59+ N '87

Cruises: the young, fun, affordable vacation. il *Glamour* 85:248-54 O '87

Cruising '88. K. Showker. il *Travel Holiday* 168:65-6+ O '87

Going it alone [singlehanded cruising] S. Stapleton. il *Mot Boat Sail* 160:28 N '87

Hooked on cruising. J. Clarke. il *50 Plus* 27:44-5+ My '87

New-wave fitness. D. Tkac. il *Prevention* 39:100-3 Ja '87

Sun and fun—just a cruise away. il *Ebony* 42:118+ Ja '87

Theme cruises. il *Harpers Bazaar* 120:10+ Ja '87

The top ten cruising grounds. S. Stapleton. il *Mot Boat Sail* 160:24 D '87

Cold weather conditions

Cold-weather cruising. S. Stapleton. il *Mot Boat Sail* 160:22 S '87

Photographs and photography

Cruising photography. S. Stapleton. il *Mot Boat Sail* 159:28 F '87

Atlantic coast

The longest ride [trip from Miami to Maine in 38-foot Tempest speedboat] P. A. Janssen. il *Mot Boat Sail* 160:38-41 S '87

Baja California (Mexico: Peninsula)

Blazing the charter trail in Baja. B. Duke and S. Duke. il *Mot Boat Sail* 160:56-9+ Ag '87

British Columbia

Rocky Mountain high [Williston Lake] D. Fales. il *Mot Boat Sail* 160:38-41+ N '87

British Virgin Islands

Blissed out in the B.V.I. P. A. Janssen. il *Mot Boat Sail* 160:52-5+ Ag '87

Caribbean charters: luxury yachting in the British Virgin Islands. G. Watts. il *Archit Dig* 44 Archit Dig Travels:4+ O '87

Caribbean region

Yachting for the not-so-rich [Caribbean charters] B. Bauer. il *U S News World Rep* 103:87 N 16 '87

Fiji

Amnesia in Polynesia. D. A. Rose. il *Esquire* 108:47+ O '87

Indian Ocean

Hal Roth: on to Bali [tenth leg of circumnavigation] H. Roth. *Mot Boat Sail* 159:170+ Ja '87

Hal Roth: sailing to the Seychelles [eleventh leg of circumnavigation] H. Roth. *Mot Boat Sail* 159:158+ F '87

Java Sea

Plying the Java Sea [traditional wooden prahu; cover story] S. P. Breslow. il map *Oceans* 20:20-7 S/O '87

Pacific coast

You can sail on a tall ship. il *Sunset* 178:48+ My '87

Utah

Lake Powell by boat . . . day or less trips. il map *Sunset* 178:58+ Ap '87

Yugoslavia

Slavic splendor. C. Davis. il *Mot Boat Sail* 160:60-3+ Ag '87

Crum, Bartley C.

about

Memories of HUAC. P. Bosworth. *Nation* 245:436-7 O 24 '87

Crum and Forster

World's largest up & comer [Xerox's acquisition] H. Rudnitsky. il *Forbes* 139:78+ My 18 '87

Crumpler, L. S.
(jt. auth) See Head, James, and Crumpler, L. S.

Crusaders (Musical group)
The Crusaders. G. Kalbacher. *Down Beat* 54:53 F '87

Crusades
Mediawatch [BBC's The cross and the crescent series on the Crusades] H. David. il *Hist Today* 37:4-5 Ap '87
Saladin's triumph over the crusader states: the Battle of Hattin, 1187 [cover story] N. Housley. bibl il map *Hist Today* 37:17-23 Jl '87

Cruse, William
about
Carnage at a shopping mall. *Macleans* 100:24 My 4 '87

Crushes (Emotions)
Crushes: why you fall so hard. A. Bell. il *Teen* 31:36+ Ag '87

Anecdotes, facetiae, satire, etc.
How I got smart [reading encyclopedias to impress an intelligent classmate] S. Brody. il *Read Dig* 131:176-8 N '87
The rush of the crush. D. Seeley. il *Seventeen* 46:174-5+ N '87

Crust (Earth) *See* Earth—Crust
Crust (Pie) *See* Pie
Crustaceans
See also
 Color of crustaceans
 Crabs
 Crayfish
 Krill
 Mysids
 Nervous system—Crustaceans
 Ostracods
 Pillbugs
 Sexual behavior—Crustaceans
 Sowbugs

Crutchfield, Edward Elliott, 1941-
about
How 'Fast Eddie' is pulling First Union out ahead. S. Ticer. il por *Bus Week* p142+ Mr 23 '87
This gorilla can putt. J. Willoughby. *Forbes* 140:154 O 19 '87

Crutchfield, Will
An open ear. il *Opera News* 52:18-20+ Ag '87
Twin glories (I). il pors *Opera News* 52:10-13 D 19 '87

Crutchley, John Brennan
about
Count Malabar. S. Baker. il por *Omni* 9:84 Ja '87

Cruvinet dispensers *See* Wine—Equipment

Cruz, Arturo
about
The contra crack-up. M. Kondracke. *New Repub* 196:9-11 Mr 9 '87
A contra defection. M. Satchell. il por *U S News World Rep* 102:18-19 Mr 23 '87
The contras without Cruz? N. Cooper. il pors *Newsweek* 109:42 F 9 '87
The contretemps of the contras. M. Satchell. il por *U S News World Rep* 102:10 F 9 '87
Pack it in. C. Lane. il *New Repub* 196:17-19 Ap 6 '87
Reinventing the contras. R. Watson. il pors *Newsweek* 109:32-4 Mr 2 '87

Cruz, Arturo, Jr.
One hundred years of turpitude [cover story] il *New Repub* 197:26-8+ N 16 '87
about
The ballad of Fawn and Arturo [cover story] J. Morley. il *Nation* 245:397+ O 17 '87

Cruz, Stevie
about
A real nobody did it better. R. Wiley. il pors *Sports Illus* 66:32-4+ Ja 12 '87

Cruz-Stark Associates PA
Faces of middle class America: architect Craig Stark puts his hope in the future of Miami. il pors *Ebony* 42:144-5 Ag '87

Cruzeiro do Sul SA
Varig, Cruzeiro share directors, facilities. *Aviat Week Space Technol* 127:44 Ag 31 '87

Cry freedom [film] See Motion picture reviews—Single works

Cryer, Jon
about
Jon Cryer. E. Miller. il pors *Seventeen* 46:75-6+ D '87

Crying
See also
 Infants—Crying

Big boys don't cry—but why not? J. Dyer. *Seventeen* 46:56-7+ Mr '87
Crying it out. J. R. Goldberg. il *Health* 19:64-6 F '87
Twenty good reasons to cry [men] S. Bing. il *Esquire* 107:225 Je '87
Why do we cry? S. A. Schreiner. il *Read Dig* 130:141-4 F '87

Cryobiology
See also
 Cryonics
Beyond the cutting edge of cold [vitrification of organs; cover story] S. Weisburd. il *Sci News* 132:138-41 Ag 29 '87
The miracle baby [frozen embryo in vitro fertilization] B. Weinhouse and F. Feldinger. il *Ladies Home J* 104:104+ Ap '87
Musseling in on novel cryoprotectants [research by Stephen Loomis and others] S. Weisburd. *Sci News* 132:9 Jl 4 '87
Sealed in time: ice entombs an Eskimo family for five centuries. A. A. Dekin, Jr. il map *Natl Geogr* 171:824-36 Je '87
Sweet success in freezing islets. S. Weisburd. *Sci News* 132:47 Jl 18 '87

Cryogenic interment *See* Cryonics
Cryogenics *See* Low temperatures
Cryonics
A clinically doggone beagle, medical miracle Miles is a former chilly dog back from the beyond [work of P. Segall] il *People Wkly* 27:85 Ap 20 '87
On ice. C. Kahn. il *Health* 19:70-2+ Mr '87
Today a frozen dog, tomorrow the iceman [beagle named Miles brought back from the dead; work of Hal Sternberg] il *Discover* 8:9 Je '87

Cryosurgery
In cold blood [bloodless surgery] C. Kahn. *Health* 19:76 Ja '87
Putting the freeze on liver tumors. S. Weisburd. *Sci News* 132:20-1 Jl 11 '87

Cryptography
Breaking codes was this couple's lifetime career [W. and E. Friedman] J. R. Chiles. bibl (p154) il pors *Smithsonian* 18:128-30+ Je '87
Ciphernauts [search for treasure buried by T. J. Beale in the 1820's in Virginia] P. Hoffman. il *Omni* 9:26+ My '87
How randomness protects you and your banker during an automated transaction. il *Discover* 8:76-7 Ja '87
Zero-knowledge proofs [data encryption] P. Wayner. il *Byte* 12:149-52 O '87

Cryptology *See* Cryptography
Crypton, Dr.
Extraterrestrial congress: the case of the bed-hopping aliens. il *Discover* 8:104 O '87

Cryptozoology
See also
 Loch Ness monster
 Sasquatch
 Sea monsters

Crystal Beach (Tex.)
Politics and government
The city that isn't [vote to dissolve government] il *Time* 129:33 Ap 27 '87

Crystal Cathedral (Garden Grove, Calif.)
Dr. Robert Schuller: TV's minister of hope. D. De Dubovay. il pors *McCalls* 114:44+ Ap '87
Problems for Schuller. *Christ Century* 104:818 S 30 '87

Crystal oscillators *See* Oscillators, Crystal
Crystalline lens
See also
 Cataracts (Eye defect)
Double-duty proteins [research by Graeme Wistow and Joram Piatigorsky] *Sci News* 131:409 Je 27 '87
In situ detection of β-galactosidase in lenses of transgenic mice with a γ-crystallin/lacZ gene. D. R. Goring and others. bibl f il *Science* 235:456-8 Ja 23 '87
Oncogenesis of the lens in transgenic mice. K. A. Mahon and others. bibl f il *Science* 235:1622-8 Mr 27 '87
Recruitment of enzymes as lens structural proteins. G. Wistow and J. Piatigorsky. bibl f il *Science* 236:1554-6 Je 19 '87

Crystallins
Lens crystallins may be moonlighting [determination of nucleotide sequence for mole rat crystallin gene; work of Wiljan Hendriks and others] *Sci News* 132:104 Ag 15 '87

Crystallization
Artificially structured thin-film materials and interfaces. V. Narayanamurti. bibl f il *Science* 235:1023-8 F 27 '87

Crystallography

See also
American Crystallographic Association
Ewald Prize

An amylose antiparallel double helix at atomic resolution. W. Hinrichs and others. bibl f il *Science* 238:205-8 O 9 '87

The atomic structure of Mengo virus at 3.0 Å resolution. M. Luo and others. bibl f il *Science* 235:182-91 Ja 9 '87

Atomic structure of thymidylate synthase: target for rational drug design. L. W. Hardy and others. bibl f il *Science* 235:448-55 Ja 23 '87

Bacterial resistance to β-lactam antibiotics: crystal structure of β-lactamase from Staphylococcus aureus PC1 at 2.5 Å resolution. O. Herzberg and J. Moult. bibl f il *Science* 236:694-701 My 8 '87

Crystallographic R factor refinement by molecular dynamics. A. T. Brünger and others. bibl f il *Science* 235:458-60 Ja 23 '87

Crystallography. *Phys Today* 40:S20-S23 Ja '87

Designer therapeutics [structure of thymidylate synthase; work of Larry W. Hardy and others] il *Sci Am* 256:69-70 Ap '87

A flash in the crystalline pan [triboluminescence; research by Linda M. Sweeting and Arnold L. Rheingold] *Sci News* 131:360 Je 6 '87

Helix geometry, hydration, and G·A mismatch in a B-DNA decamer. G. G. Privé and others. bibl f il *Science* 238:498-504 O 23 '87

Immune molecule's 3-D structure revealed [X ray crystallography of human leukocyte antigen; work of Donald C. Wiley and others] R. Weiss. il *Sci News* 132:228 O 10 '87

Magnetic properties of hydrothermally recrystallized magnetite crystals. F. Heider and others. bibl f il *Science* 236:1287-90 Je 5 '87

More superconductivity questions than answers [special section] A. L. Robinson. il *Science* 237:248-50 Jl 17 '87

A new method for analyzing powder diffraction patterns: confirmation of a predicted phase of SF_6 [neutron diffraction experiments] L. S. Bartell and others. bibl f il *Science* 236:1463-5 Je 12 '87

New opportunities in synchrotron X-ray crystallography. C. T. Prewitt and others. bibl f il *Science* 238:312-19 O 16 '87

Solution of a protein crystal structure with a model obtained from NMR interproton distance restraints. A. T. Brünger and others. bibl f il *Science* 235:1049-53 F 27 '87

Structure of MHC protein solved [work of Jack Strominger and others] J. L. Marx. il *Science* 238:613-14 O 30 '87

The structure of poliovirus. J. M. Hogle and others. bibl (p128) il *Sci Am* 256:42-9 Mr '87

Structures of two thermolysin-inhibitor complexes that differ by a single hydrogen bond. D. E. Tronrud and others. bibl f il *Science* 235:571-4 Ja 30 '87

Superconductors: a dimpled beauty [neutron diffraction of ceramic oxides] D. E. Thomsen. *Sci News* 131:327 My 23 '87

The surface of crystalline helium-4. H. J. Maris and A. F. Andreev. bibl f il *Phys Today* 40:25-30 F '87

A tunnel in the large ribosomal subunit revealed by three-dimensional image reconstruction. A. Yonath and others. bibl f il *Science* 236:813-16 My 15 '87

X-ray snapshots of proteins in motion. I. Peterson. *Sci News* 132:182 S 19 '87

Crystals

See also
Electrides
Oscillators, Crystal
Quasicrystals

A metal's many faces [research by John W. Cahn and Jean E. Taylor] I. Peterson. il *Sci News* 131:76-7 Ja 31 '87

Defects

Butterfly catcher [gettering process for crystalline silicon] G. Greenwell. il *Sci Am* 257:28-9 S '87

Direct observation of dissociated dislocations in garnet. F. M. Allen and others. bibl f il *Science* 238:1695-7 D 18 '87

Disorder in Al-Li-Cu and Al-Mn-Si icosahedral alloys. P. A. Heiney and others. bibl f il *Science* 238:660-3 O 30 '87

Magic butterfly cleans up chips [gettering process for crystalline silicon] J. Raloff. il *Sci News* 132:55 Jl 25 '87

Growth

See Crystallization

Therapeutic use

Crystal cruise [plan to scatter magic crystals in the waters around Manhattan] il *New Yorker* 63:18-20 Ag 10 '87

Pet rocks. *Harpers* 274:20 Ja '87

Rock power for health and wealth. M. Smilgis. il *Time* 129:66 Ja 19 '87

The rocks with good vibrations. il *Newsweek* 110:78 O 12 '87

Supreme quartz. J. Page. il *Omni* 10:94-6+ O '87

You don't need a crystal ball to see that New Age rocks are clearly on a roll. L. Aitken. il *People Wkly* 27:67+ Je 15 '87

Crystals in house decoration

Using minerals in interior design. J. Chatfield-Taylor. il *Archit Dig* 44:324+ N '87

Csaky, Adrian

about

Rare and early. E. Greene. il *House Gard* 159:162-7+ N '87

CSCE See Conference on Security and Cooperation in Europe

CSFs See Colony-stimulating factors

Csikszentmihalyi, Mihaly

about

The ups and downs of teenage life. J. Fischman. il *Psychol Today* 21:56-7 My '87

CSIS See Canadian Security Intelligence Service

CSX Corporation

CSX may have charted a treacherous course [purchase of Sea-Land] T. Ichniowski. il *Bus Week* p36+ F 16 '87

If it isn't profitable, don't do it. J. Cook. il por *Forbes* 140:54+ N 30 '87

CT (Computerized tomography) See Tomography

CTS Corp.

And then? And then? T. Jaffe. *Forbes* 139:126-7 Ap 20 '87

CTV (Network)

Bringing the Games to the world [Winter Olympics] J. Howse. il *Macleans* 100:60-1 D 7 '87

CTV's bitter family feud. R. Corelli. il *Macleans* 100:57+ Mr 23 '87

CTW See Children's Television Workshop

Cuadra, Pablo Antonio, 1912-

about

Poetry and power in Nicaragua. F. Goldman. il por *N Y Times Mag* p44-6+ Mr 29 '87

Cuadrado, John A.

Antiques: samplers. il *Archit Dig* 44:152-7 Je '87

Antiques: steel furniture. il *Archit Dig* 44:178-83 N '87

Collectors' finds in Paris: discoveries in painting, wallpaper and posters. il *Archit Dig* 44:210+ D '87

French virtuosity at Galerie Schmit. il por *Archit Dig* 44:86+ Je '87

Cuau, Yves

'Reasonable goals'. il *World Press Rev* 34:13+ Ja '87

Cuba

See also
Agricultural administration—Cuba
Birds—Cuba
Civil rights—Cuba
Cubans
Dance festivals—Cuba
Intelligence service—Cuba
Money—Cuba
Political prisoners—Cuba
Science and state—Cuba

Economic policy

Building socialism—one more time. L. López. il por *Time* 129:67 My 4 '87

Castro takes the economy in hand. M. Perez-Stable. il *Nation* 245:298-300 S 26 '87

Cuba chases the dollar [austerity measures] F. D. Colburn. il *New Leader* 70:13-14 Mr 9 '87

'Cuba is living on borrowed time'. P. Engardio. il *Bus Week* p52+ D 14 '87

Foreign relations

Latin America

Cuba's declining fortunes. J. M. Del Aguila. bibl f *Curr Hist* 86:425-8+ D '87

United States

See United States—Foreign relations—Cuba

History

Two democrats betrayed [J. Marti and P. J. Chamorro] pors *Dep State Bull* 87:66+ Mr '87

1959-

Cuba libre, sans Coke. G. García Márquez. *World Press Rev* 34:34 N '87

Cuba—History—*cont.*

Invasion, 1961

Miami: 'la lucha'. J. Didion. il *N Y Rev Books* 34:15-18 Je 11 '87

New look at an old failure [views of ex-CIA historian J. Pfeiffer on the Bay of Pigs] J. Peterzell. il por *Time* 129:29 Je 1 '87

Missile Crisis, 1962

See Cuban Missile Crisis, 1962

Industries

See also

Soft drink industry—Cuba

Politics and government

See also

Communism—Cuba

Cuba's declining fortunes. J. M. Del Aguila. bibl f *Curr Hist* 86:425-8+ D '87

Cuba's growing crisis [address, May 27, 1987] K. N. Skoug, Jr. *Dep State Bull* 87:85-90 S '87

A spotlight on Cuba [address, October 22, 1986] K. N. Skoug, Jr. *Dep State Bull* 86:81-4 D '86

Whispers behind the slogans. P. Iyer. il *Time* 130:46-7 S 21 '87

Religious institutions and affairs

See also

Catholic Church—Cuba

Church and state—Cuba

Social conditions

Whispers behind the slogans. P. Iyer. il *Time* 130:46-7 S 21 '87

Cuban, Larry

Teacher-centered instruction versus education reform. *Educ Dig* 52:2-5 F '87

Cuban Americans

Can Miami save itself? [cover story] R. Sherrill. il *N Y Times Mag* p18-24+ Jl 19 '87

Miami. J. Didion. il *N Y Rev Books* 34:43-8 My 28 '87

Miami: exiles. J. Didion. il *N Y Rev Books* 34:35-9 Je 25 '87

Miami: 'la lucha'. J. Didion. il *N Y Rev Books* 34:15-18 Je 11 '87

The second Havana [Miami] D. Rieff. il *New Yorker* 63:65-9+ My 18 '87

Political activities

Revenge in a hot place [views of J. Didion] J. Rothchild. *Wash Mon* 19:45-6+ D '87

Washington in Miami. J. Didion. il *N Y Rev Books* 34:22+ Jl 16 '87

Cuban defectors *See* Defectors, Political

Cuban military assistance *See* Military assistance, Cuban

Cuban Missile Crisis, 1962

Class reunion: Kennedy's men relive the Cuban Missile Crisis [cover story] J. A. Lukas. il *N Y Times Mag* p22-7+ Ag 30 '87

Cuba: even dicier than we knew. R. L. Garthoff. il *Newsweek* 110:34 O 26 '87

The Cuban Missile Crisis revisited. J. G. Blight and others. bibl f *Foreign Aff* 66:170-88 Fall '87

October tremors. *Nation* 245:507-8 N 7 '87

Time to recall this model? M. Greenfield. il *Newsweek* 110:84 S 21 '87

When the other guy blinked. D. McComas. il *Sch Update* 120:27-9 N 20 '87

Cubans

United States

See also

Cuban Americans

Come home to roost [prison riots] *Nation* 245:701 D 12 '87

A Cuban explosion [Marielitos seize two U.S. prisons] A. Press. il *Newsweek* 110:38-40 D 7 '87

Excludable from justice [Cuban detainees at U.S. penitentiary in Atlanta] G. Galbaugh. *America* 156:315-16 Ap 18 '87

The flames of fear [Marielitos riot in two U.S. prisons] B. Duffy. il *U S News World Rep* 103:20-2 D 7 '87

A flight to freedom [Cuban Air Force general R. del Pino Diaz defects to the U.S.] *Macleans* 100:24 Je 8 '87

Hero to go [Air Force General R. del Pino Diaz defects to the U.S.] *Time* 129:26 Je 8 '87

Imprisoned in limbo [Cubans in U.S. jails] K. S. Smith. *Commonweal* 114:552-3 O 9 '87

Just how big a fish is the man from Havana? [defection of General R. del Pino Diaz] C. A. Robbins. por *U S News World Rep* 102:12 Je 8 '87

Lessons of the Cuban prison crisis: what the Marielitos won. G. Hackett. il *Newsweek* 110:53 D 14 '87

The men behind the prison walls: profiling the Marielitos. T. Jacoby. il *Newsweek* 110:43 D 7 '87

Miami's bishop Agustin Roman defuses a human time bomb to end the Cuban prison riots peacefully [Marielito uprising] R. Arias. il pors *People Wkly* 28:104-6 D 21 '87

Once a Cuban hero, Roberto Urrutia aims to give the U.S. a boost—and Castro a lesson—in the Pan American Games. P. Jordan. il pors *People Wkly* 28:105-6+ Ag 10 '87

Promises, promises [Marielitos and prison riots] E. Magnuson. il *Time* 130:36 D 14 '87

Revolt of the Cubans [Marielitos riot in two U.S. prisions] A. Bilski. il *Macleans* 100:24 D 7 '87

Spilled beans [defection of Cuban intelligence chief F. Aspillaga Lombard] K. M. Pierce. il *Time* 130:17 Ag 24 '87

Their man from Havana: true confessions? [defector R. del Pino Diaz] *Newsweek* 109:42 Je 8 '87

'This is a moment of peace' [Miami bishop A. Román helps end Cuban prisoner takeovers] *America* 157:468-9 D 19 '87

"We are the abandoned ones" [Marielitos riot in two U.S. prisons] J. V. Lamar, Jr. il *Time* 130:23-4 D 7 '87

Cubic Corp.

How Walter Zable missed his wake-up call. M. Beauchamp. il por *Forbes* 140:72-3 D 28 '87

Cubism

Exhibitions

Echoes of a creative earthquake [1912: break up of tradition] G. James. il *Macleans* 100:61 S 7 '87

Cucurbits

See also

Melons

Cuellar, Javier Pérez de *See* Pérez de Cuellar, Javier

Cuénod, Hugues, 1902-

about

Hugues Cuénod. *New Yorker* 63:28-9 Mr 16 '87

Music, art and country pleasures. N. Barry. il *House Gard* 159:140-7+ Mr '87

Vintage debut. N. Kenyon. il pors *Opera News* 51:24+ Mr 28 '87

Cuffs (Clothing)

The cuff [men's shirts] P. Deitz. il *Esquire* 107:F63 Mr '87

Culbertson, Judi, and Randall, Tom, 1945-

Tracking New York's literary ghosts. il *Publ Wkly* 232:27-9 Jl 17 '87

Culbro Corp.

A tobacco dynasty that's cutting down on cigars. C. Power. il pors *Bus Week* p62 F 9 '87

Culhane, Brien, and Tuttle, Liza

Landscape of the mind. il map *Natl Parks* 61:24-5 S/O '87

Culhane, John

Angela Lansbury takes the lead. il pors *Read Dig* 130:20-2+ Je '87

The front porch connection. il *Read Dig* 130:106-9 Je '87

The greatest two minutes in sports. il *Read Dig* 130:236-8+ My '87

The hobby that lifts your heart. il *Read Dig* 130:56-60 F '87

John Huston: Hollywood's giant. il pors *Read Dig* 131:136-43 N '87

Keep a happiness calendar. il *Read Dig* 130:63-6 Ja '87

Oscar: little statue of dreams. il *Read Dig* 130:53-8 Mr '87

Unforgettable Snow White. il *Read Dig* 131:114-19 D '87

Culinary Institute of America

Fine dining on the Hudson: the Culinary Institute of America. L. Kundell. *Travel Holiday* 168:25+ O '87

Cullen (Lillie and Hugh Roy) Sculpture Garden *See* Museum of Fine Arts (Houston, Tex.). Lillie and Hugh Roy Cullen Sculpture Garden

Cullinet Software, Inc.

Cullinet's comeback trail is full of thorns. K. H. Hammonds. il *Bus Week* p132 S 14 '87

Cullman, Edgar M., Jr.

about

A tobacco dynasty that's cutting down on cigars. C. Power. il pors *Bus Week* p62 F 9 '87

Cullman, Edgar M., 1918-

about

A tobacco dynasty that's cutting down on cigars. C. Power. il pors *Bus Week* p62 F 9 '87

Cult films *See* Motion pictures—Cult films
Cultivation *See* Tillage
Cultivators
How the Ro-Till system handles northern soils. M. Holmberg. il *Success Farm* 85 no3:18AF F '87
Multi-task tiller/tractor. E. F. Lindsley. il *Pop Sci* 230:80 My '87
Rotary tiller update. il *Ctry J* 14:3 S '87
Rotary tillers. D. Thomas. il *Ctry J* 14:21-7 Ap '87
    Equipment
A double-barreled shot [use of coulters] C. Finck. il *Success Farm* 85 no6:18Z Mr '87
New guidance systems offer row-crop precision. C. Finck. il *Success Farm* 85:18K My '87
   Maintenance and repair
Winterize your tiller. J. Burnett. il *Rodale's Org Gard* 34:67-8 N '87
Cults
  See also
  Church Universal and Triumphant
  Santería (Cult)
  Temple of Set
The new victims of cults [middle aged and aged women] D. Salvatore. *Ladies Home J* 104:46+ Ag '87
Psychology and religion in court—again [anticult theories of coercive persuasion] J. R. Lewis and J. G. Melton. *Christ Century* 104:914-16 O 21 '87
    Brazil
Bahia's Candomblé. J. B. Harris. *Black Enterp* 18:82+ Ag '87
Brazil's black magic [Macumba] H. J. Maier, Jr. il *Travel Holiday* 167:100 Mr '87
Cultural Affairs Dept. (New York, N.Y.) *See* New York (N.Y.). Dept. of Cultural Affairs
Cultural centers *See* Centers for the performing arts
Cultural differences *See* Ethnopsychology
Cultural education *See* Intercultural education
Cultural literacy
Are student heads full of emptiness? [books by A. Bloom and E. D. Hirsch] E. Bowen. il *Time* 130:56-7 Ag 17 '87
Bring class back to the classroom. N. King. *Des Arts Educ* 89:8-11 N/D '87
A cathode ray tube is [views of E. D. Hirsch] J. Coyne. il *Glamour* 85:118+ Ag '87
Cultural literacy: what every American needs to know [condensation] E. D. Hirsch. *Read Dig* 131:79-83 D '87
The Department of Factual Verification [E. D. Hirsch's Cultural literacy] H. Kenner. *Natl Rev* 39:37-8+ O 9 '87
If you can read this, says E.D. Hirsch, you may still be illiterate [interview] J. Cramer. il por *People Wkly* 28:69-71+ Ag 10 '87
Literacy at the barricades [E. D. Hirsch's Cultural literacy and H. J. Graff's The legacies of literacy] J. W. Tuttleton. *Commentary* 84:45-8 Jl '87
A meditation on education. K. Kolenda. il *Humanist* 47:39 S/O '87
What Americans should know [cover story] A. P. Sanoff. bibl il *U S News World Rep* 103:86-8+ S 28 '87
Cultural policy
  See also
  China—Cultural policy
  Soviet Union—Cultural policy
Cultural property
    Protection
  See also
  Architecture—Conservation and restoration
  Art—Conservation and restoration
  United States. Federal Bureau of Investigation. National Stolen Art File
Preserving the past. il *Futurist* 21:40-1 Ja/F '87
    Conferences
  See also
  World Heritage Convention
   International aspects
Assembly calls for steps to combat illicit traffic in cultural property. il *UN Chron* 23:19-20 Ja '86
   Laws and regulations
Olmsted Heritage Landscapes Act. J. H. Kay. *Nation* 244:552-4 Ap 25 '87
Violating history [American archeological sites] J. Robbins. il *Natl Parks* 61:26-31 Jl/Ag '87
    Egypt
An answer to the sphinx's problem [salt damage] R. Monastersky. *Sci News* 132:301 N 7 '87
   Great Britain
Roads to ruins [destruction of archeological sites by road crews] K. Nurse. il *Hist Today* 37:2 Mr '87

    Italy
Going undercover for art's sake [special police unit] R. Suro. il *N Y Times Mag* p42-3+ D 13 '87
    Mexico
Restoring Mexican murals. *Américas* 39:56 Mr/Ap '87
Cultural relations
  See also
  Brazil—Cultural relations
  Canada—Cultural relations
  Declaration of the Principles of International Cultural Co-operation
  Soviet Union—Cultural relations
  United States—Cultural relations
    Conferences
Miss Muse [World Congress of Cultures] *New Yorker* 63:29-31 S 14 '87
Cultural Revolution (China) *See* China—History—Cultural Revolution, 1966-1969
Culturally deprived children *See* Socially handicapped children
Culture
  See also
  Civilization
  Intercultural research
  Language and culture
  Popular culture
Culture, American *See* United States—Civilization; United States—Popular culture
Culture, Corporate *See* Organizational behavior
Culture and Christianity *See* Christianity and culture
Culture conflict
An Amazon love story [marriage of anthropologist K. Good to Yanomamo Indian Yarima] R. Arias. il pors *People Wkly* 27:24-9 Ja 19 '87
When good intentions aren't enough [culture conflict between student and teacher] S. S. Wineburg. il *Phi Delta Kappan* 68:544-5 Mr '87
Culture of cells *See* Cells—Culture
Culture of nerve cells *See* Nerve cells—Culture
Culture of tissues *See* Tissues—Culture
Cumberland County (Tenn.)
   Description and travel
Tennessee's Cumberland County. S. Pacher. il map *Mother Earth News* 104:92-6+ Mr/Ap '87
Cumberland Farms, Inc.
A new life for Come By Chance [reopening of oil refinery in Newfoundland] D. Jenish. il *Macleans* 100:32-3 S 7 '87
Cummer Gallery of Art
Jacksonville, Florida's three museums offer a variety of culture, education, and fun. M. Wade. il *Horizon* 30:49-51 D '87
Cumming (Ga.)
    Race relations
Beyond Forsyth. M. Eaton. *Black Enterp* 17:62 Je '87
C.T. Vivian faces threat of losing right to vote [participation in civil rights demonstration] *Jet* 72:23 Je 22 '87
On the march again: protesters hit the South with '60s-style rights rally. il *Ebony* 42:156+ My '87
Public exorcism in Forsyth County ["Brotherhood" March to protest racism] K. Sehested. *Christ Century* 104:238-9 Mr 11 '87
Racial intolerance in Cumming, Ga., protested. il *Jet* 71:56 F 9 '87
Racism on the rise [civil rights march] O. Friedrich. il *Time* 129:18-21 F 2 '87
Cummings, Gordon
    about
Newfound riches for National Sea. P. C. Newman. il por *Macleans* 100:39 Ja 19 '87
Cummings, Sally
Fear-free! il *Health* 19:44-6+ N '87
Cummins, Cynthia
The complete guide to sports bras. il *Women's Sports Fitness* 9:52-4+ S '87
The shorts story. il *Women's Sports Fitness* 9:34-7+ Ap '87
Cummins, James
The little professor [poem] *New Repub* 196:36 Mr 23 '87
Cummins, Jim, 1949-
Bilingual education and politics. *Educ Dig* 53:30-3 N '87
Cummins, Kent
Chester the clown: a brief autobiography. il *Child Today* 16:14 Ja/F '87
ChildFest. il *Child Today* 16:12-13 Ja/F '87

Cuna Indians
Kuna Indians: building a bright future [preservation of virgin rain forest] N. Myers. il map *Int Wildl* 17:18-24 Jl/Ag '87

Cuneo, Ernest L., 1905-1988
Present at the creation: professional football in the twenties. *Am Sch* 56:487-501 Aut '87

Cuneo, Jonathan W.
(jt. auth) See Cohen, Jerry S., and Cuneo, Jonathan W.

Cunkelman, Jack
Transistor amplifier design. il *Radio-Electron* 58:55-6+ Ag '87

Cunningham, Bruce A., and others
Neural cell adhesion molecule: structure, immunoglobulin-like domains, cell surface modulation, and alternative RNA splicing. bibl f il *Science* 236:799-806 My 15 '87

Cunningham, Doug
(jt. auth) See Williams, B. David, and Cunningham, Doug

Cunningham, Lawrence S.
Letters from 'The Kingdom of Night'. il *Commonweal* 114:316-18 My 22 '87
Urgency and security in the coming Marian Year. il *Christ Century* 104:334-6 Ap 8 '87
We dare to say 'Our Father'. il *Commonweal* 114:291-2 My 8 '87

Cunningham, Marion
Muffins. il *Gourmet* 47:74-5+ S '87
about
Breakfast makes a comeback. L. Shapiro. il por *Newsweek* 110:69 S 21 '87

Cunningham, Mary Elizabeth
about
Why Martin Marietta loves Mary Cunningham. T. Moore. il *Fortune* 115:66-8+ Mr 16 '87

Cunningham, Merce
about
Fabrications [dance] Reviews
N Y il 20:73 Mr 23 '87. T. Tobias
Roaratorio, an Irish circus on Finnegans wake [dance] Reviews
Art Am il por 75:102-5 Ja '87. J. Johnston
Dance Mag 61:80-1 F '87. E. Zimmer
Visible spirit: the Cunningham continuum. N. V. Dalva. il por *Dance Mag* 61:46-8 Ag '87

Cunningham, Randall
about
Black QBs' face-off: first in NFL in 5 years. por *Jet* 73:46 O 5 '87

Cunningham, Terri Lynn
about
W. Va. Univ. elects first black homecoming queen. *Jet* 71:27 Ja 19 '87

CUNY *See* City University of New York

Cuomo, Mario
A brief on the freedom of the press [address, November 25, 1986] *Vital Speeches Day* 53:265-9 F 15 '87
The Constitution, the courts, and judicial competence. por *USA Today (Periodical)* 116:34-6 Jl '87
about
The best possible way for Cuomo and Bradley to run. M. S. Forbes. *Forbes* 140:17 D 14 '87
Cuomo and Bradley: second thoughts? J. Alter. il pors *Newsweek* 110:28 N 9 '87
Cuomo and those rumors: getting to the bottom of all the 'Mob' talk [cover story] N. Pileggi. il pors *N Y* 20:44-8+ N 2 '87
Cuomo pulls out and scrambles the 1988 race. T. Noah. il pors *Newsweek* 109:28-9 Mr 2 '87
Cuomo: the most visible noncandidate. M. Kramer. il por *U S News World Rep* 103:29 O 12 '87
Cuomo's decision. F. F. Siegel. *Commonweal* 114:133-6 Mr 13 '87
Cuomo's out and the money game is in. G. Borger. il por *U S News World Rep* 102:20-1 Mr 2 '87
The Democrats to Mario: put up or shut up. D. Harbrecht and R. Fly. il por *Bus Week* p47 N 30 '87
Down and out in L.A. A. Kopkind. il *Nation* 244:309+ Mr 14 '87
Exit Cuomo. *Natl Rev* 39:17 Mr 27 '87
In place of giants and ogres. por *Time* 130:24 N 30 '87
Just teasing. por *Time* 129:30 Je 1 '87
The kibitzer. J. Klein. il por *N Y* 20:9+ Ag 10 '87
Letting the cup pass. R. Stengel. il por *Time* 129:18 Mr 2 '87
A little spice for the tapioca. G. Witkin. il pors *U S News World Rep* 103:14 S 21 '87

Make strides to help minority youths: N.Y. gov. *Jet* 72:30 My 25 '87
The man Gorbachev didn't circle. M. Kramer. por *U S News World Rep* 103:20 D 14 '87
Mario Cuomo's coy politics. *Newsweek* 109:28 Je 1 '87
Mario's moves. por *Time* 129:26 F 23 '87
Moscow bound. *Natl Rev* 39:17 S 25 '87
The New York idea. A. Logan. *New Yorker* 63:84-6+ Mr 23 '87
Notes and comment. *New Yorker* 63:36 O 12 '87
Shrinking violets. *New Repub* 196:4+ Je 22 '87
Taking shots at the 'Sphinx of Albany'. H. Fineman. il por *Newsweek* 109:25-6 Ja 26 '87
The "turn-to" scenarios. L. I. Barrett. il pors *Time* 129:26 Ap 13 '87
A visitation of phantoms. M. Kaus. il pors *Newsweek* 110:32-3 S 21 '87
We hardly knew ye. *Nation* 244:275-6 Mr 7 '87
While others are running, Mario Cuomo's stature is growing. M. S. Forbes. *Forbes* 140:17-18 O 5 '87

Cupboards
See also
Armoires
Kitchen cabinets
Corner cupboard. B. Jones. il *Fam Handyman* 37:50-2 Ja '87
Corner cupboard blends with decor. il *South Living* 22:151 S '87
Country in a corner. il *Home Mech* 83:32 Ag '87
A cupboard for the corner. il *South Living* 22:187 Ap '87
Holds-anything storage unit: low-cost, easy-to-build, versatile. C. M. Stowers. il *Better Homes Gard* 65:166+ Mr '87

Cupcakes
Cookies, cupcakes & brownies. il *Ladies Home J* 104:112-13+ Mr '87
Stars & spice cupcakes! il *Redbook* 169:12 Jl '87

Curators *See* Museum directors

Curbstone Press
Left, but not left out. J. Mutter. il *Publ Wkly* 232:18-19 Jl 17 '87

Curcio, Christine A., and others
Distribution of cones in human and monkey retina: individual variability and radial asymmetry [cover story] bibl f il *Science* 236:579-82 My 1 '87

Cure (Musical group)
Cure, Arab group reach accord on song. A. DeCurtis. *Roll Stone* p30 F 26 '87
Cure releases double album. M. Coleman. il *Roll Stone* p15+ Je 4 '87
The Cure's cruel passions. M. Peel. il *Stereo Rev* 52:97 O '87
The Cure's Robert Smith likes his music to shake you up. E. Miller. il por *Seventeen* 46:88+ Ap '87

Curfew
City curfews. il *Teen* 31:45 N '87
A curfew for Karin. D. Spencer. il *N Y Times Mag* p26 Jl 5 '87
The late show: curfew crisis [teenagers] A. Bell. il *Teen* 31:20+ N '87

Curing (Preservation process)
See also
Bacon—Curing
Tobacco—Curing

Curiosities and wonders
Look! Up in the sky! It's a bird! It's a fish! It's grist for oddity archivist Robert Rickard. R. Wolmuth. il pors *People Wkly* 27:55-6 My 18 '87
With tales of Learned pigs & fireproof women, Ricky Jay conjures up a memorable book. J. Jerome. il por *People Wkly* 27:67+ My 11 '87
The wizard of odd [R. Jay] R. Tannenbaum. il por *Roll Stone* p69-70+ Ap 23 '87

Curiosity Killed the Cat (Musical group)
England's latest Curiosity. R. Tannenbaum. il *Roll Stone* p30-1 S 24 '87

Curious George (Fictional character)
Curious George and his literary mama, Margret Rey, celebrate a half-century of monkeyshines. il por *People Wkly* 27:98 Je 1 '87

Curley, John J.
about
The growing gets tougher. S. N. Chakravarty. il pors *Forbes* 139:68+ Je 15 '87
Invasion of the Gannettoids. P. Weiss. il *New Repub* 196:18-20+ F 2 '87

Curling (Sport)
Sweeping success? [demonstration sport at the Winter Olympics] M. Goldberg. il *Women's Sports Fitness* 9:67 N '87

Curly filbert trees *See* Filbert trees
Curly top disease of tomatoes *See* Tomatoes—Diseases and pests
Curran, Charles E.
Roman Catholic sexual ethics: a dissenting view [cover story] il *Christ Century* 104:1139-42 D 16 '87
A teaching moment continues. il *America* 156:336-40 Ap 25 '87

about

Catholic authority, Catholic theology, Catholic identity [special section] *Commonweal* 114:43-51 Ja 30 '87
Charles E. Curran: a teaching moment continues [cover story; special issue; with editorial comment by George W. Hunt] il *America* 156:inside cover, 334-46+ Ap 25 '87
Father Charles Curran and Canon 812. R. M. Brown. *Christ Century* 104:100 F 4-11 '87
Curran, Dolores
Envy: how green are my values? il *U S Cathol* 52:6-7 Ag '87
Family fights don't have to be fatal. il *U S Cathol* 52:22-9 S '87
Five ways to fight family stress [condensed from Stress and the healthy family] il *Read Dig* 130:169-70+ F '87
Stress survival manual: how faith can help your family cope [cover story] il *U S Cathol* 52:6-13 Ap '87
What's so bad about being a yuppie? *U S Cathol* 52:31-3 F '87
Curran, James

about

Critical condition. R. Blow. il por *Roll Stone* p67-8+ Mr 26 '87
Curran, James F., and Yarus, Michael
Reading frame selection and transfer RNA anticodon loop stacking. bibl f il *Science* 238:1545-50 D 11 '87
Curren, Maureen
You and sports: finding the right fit. il *McCalls* 114:39+ My '87
Curren, Tommy

about

Chairman of the board: Tom Curren. K. Nunn. il pors *Roll Stone* p81-4 Jl 16-30 '87
Currency *See* Money
Currency exchange warrants
The $4.50 window [Bear, Stearns introduces currency exchange warrants] E. A. Finn, Jr. il *Forbes* 140:345-6 Jl 13 '87
Current events
Events and people. See issues of The Christian Century
Images of '87 [special section; with editorial comment by Carl Mollins] il *Macleans* 100:34-48 D 21 '87
Intelligencer. J. Kasindorf. See issues of New York beginning August 19, 1985
The month in review. See issues of Current History
Nadirism [ten most depressing events of 1986] D. Seligman. il *Fortune* 115:119-20 Ja 19 '87
The national interest: winners and sinners [1987] J. Klein. il *N Y* 20:20+ D 21-28 '87
Notebook. See issues of The New Republic
Oliver North and the music of the night: reflections on a year out of tune [1987] L. Eisenberg. il *Esquire* 108:141+ D '87
Points of reference [how impersonal numbers take on a life of their own in crises] E. Levin. il *People Wkly* 28:40-1 N 2 '87
Three balls, two strikes [1986] G. F. Will. il *Newsweek* 109:64 Ja 5 '87
The top 10 news stories of 1986. B. Shelby. il *World Press Rev* 34:8+ F '87
World beat. J. R. Moskin. See issues of World Press Review through April 1987
The zeitgeist checklist. C. P. Freund. See issues of The New Republic beginning September 8, 1986
Anecdotes, facetiae, satire, etc.
Small favors. M. Ivins. See issues of The Progressive beginning March 1986
The year that fell to earth [1987] P. J. O'Rourke. il *Roll Stone* p123-32+ D 17-31 '87
The year that was [1986] M. Ivins. il *Progressive* 51:18 F '87
Caricatures and cartoons
The world in cartoons. See issues of World Press Review
Photographs and photography
And let us not forget [with introd. by Nadine Gordimer] il *Esquire* 108:229-35 D '87
Images 1987. il *Time* 130:36-44+ D 28 '87
October news in pictures. il *UN Chron* 22:110 N/D '85
Snapshots. See issues of Life beginning July 1987

The year in pictures '86 [special issue; with editorial comment by Judith Daniels] il *Life* 10:5, 8-19+ Ja '87
Current events in advertising
Current events. E. F. Cone. il *Forbes* 139:90-1 Je 29 '87
Currents, Ocean *See* Ocean currents
Currey, Frederick W.

about

How an ace mechanic wants to fix Greyhound Lines. J. Hurlock. *Bus Week* p45-6 Ja 12 '87
Leave the driving to Fred Currey. J. Weber, Jr. il por *Bus Week* p62-3 Ag 24 '87
Curriculum *See* Colleges and universities—Curriculum; Courses of study
Curriculum development *See* Curriculum planning
Curriculum planning
Curriculum-based programs for the gifted. B. L. Barrington. *Educ Dig* 52:48-51 Ja '87
Currie, John

about

A future in smart boxes. il por *Macleans* 100:40 Ap 20 '87
Currie, Kathleen
(jt. auth) See Levine, Art, and Currie, Kathleen
Currie, Leonard J.

about

Pro bono architecture in Appalachia and elsewhere. M. F. Schmertz. *Archit Rec* 175:9 Mr '87
Curry, Bill

about

Bad Tidings from 'Bama. R. Reilly. por *Sports Illus* 66:78 Ja 19 '87
A stranger in the family. D. Whitford. il pors *Sport Mag* 78:45+ S '87
Curry, Donald

about

Loud left from a quiet champ. P. Putnam. il pors *Sports Illus* 67:34-5 Jl 27 '87
Curry, Rick
May we come in? il *America* 156:442-4 My 30 '87
Curry, Thomas J.
Faithful on the move. il *Commonweal* 114:727-9 D 18 '87
Curry
The curry connection. J. F. Mariani. il *Mot Boat Sail* 160:30 N '87
Curry in a Hurry (New York, N.Y.: Restaurant) *See* New York (N.Y.)—Restaurants, nightclubs, bars, etc.
Cursing *See* Swearing
Curtain Bluff Resort Hotel (Antigua, Antigua and Barbuda) *See* Resorts—Antigua (Antigua and Barbuda)
Curtains and draperies
See also
Shower curtains
Don't hide the woodwork. il *South Living* 22:211 N '87
How to make swags and cascades. il *Fam Handyman* 37:46+ My/Je '87
Simple, fresh look for windows [balloon-style curtains] il *South Living* 22:91 Ag '87
Top windows with swags. il *South Living* 22:123 Je '87
Curtis, Charles
Strategies for equipment shopping. il *Stereo Rev* 52:68-71 My '87
Curtis, James M., 1940-
Solzhenitsyn's October 1916: a preview. il por *USA Today (Periodical)* 115:90-2 Ja '87
Curtis, Jeannette
The corners of my mind remember [poem] *Essence* 18:137 O '87
Curtis, Lawrence A.
Vertical distribution of an estuarine snail altered by a parasite. bibl f il *Science* 235:1509-11 Mr 20 '87
Curtis, Patricia
Contact with dolphins. il *Oceans* 20:18-23 Ja/F '87
Curtis, Richard
Merger, he wrote. il *Publ Wkly* 231:46 Ja 9 '87
A taxing issue. por *Publ Wkly* 231:52 Mr 20 '87
Curtis, Robert

about

Ordeal on Bay Ledge Buoy. D. J. Snyder. il por *Read Dig* 130:112-17 My '87
Curtis, Wayne
Here comes the repo man. *Nation* 244:570+ My 2 '87
Curtis, William J. R.
The Aga Khan Award for Architecture 1986: "third-world myths and first-world fashions": a critical view. il *Archit Rec* 175:104-5 Ja '87

Curtis Benjamin Award *See* Publishers and publishing—
Awards
Curves
See also
Cycloids
Fractals
Cusack, Isabel Langis
Love song [story] il *Good Housekeep* 204:138-9
F '87
Cushions
See also
Pillows
Custard, John Goss- *See* Goss-Custard, John
Custards
Custard. il *Gourmet* 47:70-1+ Mr '87
It's a fruit and custard classic . . . but prettier and
easier to make [crackle brûlée] il *Sunset* 179:60-1 Ag
'87
It's just plain custard up to some new tricks. il *Sunset*
179:210 N '87
Microwave custard in just 5 minutes. il *Sunset* 178:172-3
Mr '87
Peaches, berries, and zabaglione . . . light, quick, grand.
il *Sunset* 179:178 S '87
Custody of children
See also
Baby M case
Guardian and ward
Bitter battles over kids in the middle. A. Fine and
others. il *People Wkly* 27:52+ Mr 23 '87
Child-custody issues and the schools. A. H. Hempe and
W. Decker. *Educ Dig* 53:50-1 O '87
The child custody murder [battle for P. A. Taylor] P.
Maas. il pors *Good Housekeep* 205:154-5+ O '87
His fundamentalist mother and his father's gay lover
square off over custody of young Brian Batey. M.
Brower. il pors *People Wkly* 28:112-14 N 9 '87
In Massachusetts, an ugly battle for a little girl [child
abuse charges in custody case of N. LaLonde] G.
Hackett. il por *Newsweek* 110:41 O 19 '87
Legacy of a mother's murder [custody battle for P.
A. Taylor] P. Maas. il pors *N Y Times Mag* p40-4+
Ap 12 '87
When fathers have custody. R. B. McCall. il *Parents*
62:211 Ag '87
When mommy moves out: women who choose to give
up custody of their children. L. Rogak. il *N Y* 20:36-41
Ja 5 '87
Winning back a child [custody battle for P. A. Taylor
concludes] P. Maas. il por *N Y Times Mag* p42+
Je 7 '87
A wrenching separation ends an Iowa couple's hope
of adopting the five Cooper kids [P. and L. Mick
fight to keep children of mentally ill mother] G. Pick.
il *People Wkly* 27:40-3 F 2 '87
Custom Energy Services Inc.
See also
Customedix Corporation
Custom 'could be a sizzler'. G. G. Marcial. *Bus Week*
p83 Ja 19 '87
Custom Jockeys' Apparel (Firm)
Win, place and sew. D. Marth. il por *Nations Bus*
75:65 F '87
Custom Shop Shirtmakers Inc.
The fabric of success. W. Hoffer. il pors *Nations Bus*
75:53+ Jl '87
Custom Software (Firm)
Real-estate management made easy. J. Wechsler. il por
Work Woman 12:70+ My '87
Customedix Corporation
Putting teeth into Customedix. G. G. Marcial. *Bus Week*
p148 S 14 '87
Customer relations
See also
Airplane industry—Customer relations
Automobile industry—Customer relations
Banks and banking—Customer relations
Brokers—Customer relations
Building materials industry—Customer relations
Computer industry—Customer relations
Computer service industries—Customer relations
Customer service
Department stores—Customer relations
Electric utilities—Customer relations
Investment trusts—Customer relations
1-800 . . . [use of toll-free telephone numbers by
consumers of packaged goods] B. Wallraff. il *Atlantic*
260:18+ O '87
Eight small ways to build big sales. M. Stevens. *Work
Woman* 12:54 F '87

Making changes: how to budge the office mule. M.
J. Parson. il *Work Woman* 12:139-41 S '87
Training customers [views of David Bowen] *USA Today
(Periodical)* 116:5-6 D '87
Anecdotes, facetiae, satire, etc.
My store of grievances. J. Welter. il *Atlantic* 260:26
Ag '87
Customer service
See also
Return of goods
Companies that serve you best. B. Uttal. il *Fortune*
116:98-101+ D 7 '87
In the service sector, nothing is 'free' anymore. J. Berger.
il *Bus Week* p144 Je 8 '87
Little things mean a lot. S. Nelton. il *Nations Bus* 75:4
O '87
Make it right for the customer. H. Bacas. il *Nations
Bus* 75:49-51 N '87
Productivity in a customer vein [address, February 23,
1987] R. A. Ferchat. *Vital Speeches Day* 53:602-5
Jl 15 '87
Pul-eeze! Will somebody help me? [special section] il
Time 129:48-57 F 2 '87
Customs Service (U.S.) *See* U.S. Customs Service
CUT *See* Church Universal and Triumphant
Cut glass *See* Glassware
Cutaneous T-cell lymphoma *See* Lymphatic system—Cancer
Cuthbert, Saint, 653?-687
about
Conservationist before Assisi: the foolishness of St. Cuth-
bert. E. P. Echlin. il *America* 157:478-9 D 19 '87
Cuticle
Insects
Aromatic cross-links in insect cuticle: detection by solid-
state ^{13}C and ^{15}N NMR. J. Schaefer and others. bibl
f il *Science* 235:1200-4 Mr 6 '87
Cutler, Andrew
about
Industrial space: the modeler. W. H. Ganoe. il *Space
World* X-7-283:35 Jl '87
Cutler, Jonathan C.
Youth participation [address, July 20, 1987] *Vital Speeches
Day* 54:11-13 O 15 '87
Cutler, M. Rupert
Human population [address, June 22, 1987] *Vital Speeches
Day* 53:691-6 S 1 '87
Cutler, Roger Randall- *See* Randall-Cutler, Roger
Cutter, Susan L.
Airborne toxic releases: are communities prepared? bibl
f il map *Environment* 29:12-17+ Jl/Ag '87
Cutthroat trout fishing *See* Trout fishing
Cutting Crew (Musical group)
Cutting Crew. E. Miller. il *Seventeen* 46:79-80+ O '87
Cutting tools
See also
Knives
Pastry cutters
Saws and sawing
Taps and dies
Cuttler, Simon H.
A patriot for whom? The treason of Saint-Pol, 1474-75.
bibl f il *Hist Today* 37:43-8 Ja '87
Cutworms
Control
Put the crunch on cutworms. S. Sides. il *Mother Earth
News* 104:62-3 Mr/Ap '87
Cuyler, Susanna
Daydream believers. il *Omni* 9:16+ Je '87
Cuzzi, Jeffrey N., and Esposito, Larry W.
The rings of Uranus. bibl (p116) il *Sci Am* 257:52-4+
Jl '87
CVR (Contraceptive vaginal ring) *See* Contraceptives
Cyanide poisoning
See also
Tylenol poisoning case, 1982
Cyanuric acid
An acid cure for acid rain [injection into diesel vehicle's
exhaust system] il *U S News World Rep* 102:72 F
16 '87
Cybernetics
See also
Computers
Braitenberg memoirs: vehicles for probing behavior roam
a dark plain marked by lights. A. K. Dewdney. il
Sci Am 256:16-18+ Mr '87
Cycle (Periodical)
Editorial. P. Schilling. See issues of Cycle
Famous last words [concluding paragraphs of motorcycle
road tests] C. Hodenfield. il *Cycle* 38:41-3 S '87

Cycles

See also
Biogeochemical cycles
Biological rhythms
Business cycles
Solar cycle

Cyclic adenosine monophosphate See Adenosine monophosphate

Cyclic compounds

See also
Propellanes

Cyclic GMP See Guanosine monophosphate

Cycling

See also
Bicycle racing
Motorcycling
Rail cycling

Autumn adventures. S. Festa. il *Women's Sports Fitness* 9:92-3 S '87

Bicycle tours built for comfort. S. Woolley. il *Bus Week* p164 My 11 '87

For your thighs only: the big wheel workout. il *Mademoiselle* 93:108-11 Jl '87

Riding the leaves [fall foliage cycling trips] F. Lunzer. il *Forbes* 140:101+ Ag 24 '87

Tour de fun. il *Seventeen* 46:202 Ag '87

Training in the commuter lane. N. Bloom. il *Women's Sports Fitness* 9:66-7 Ap '87

Two-wheeling in the urban jungle [use of mountain bikes] R. McManus. il *Sierra* 72:107-8 N/D '87

Accidents and injuries

Get rid of that pain in your neck. C. R. Wolpert. il *Women's Sports Fitness* 9:56 Ja '87

How to avoid cyclist's knee. L. Rogak. il *Women's Sports Fitness* 9:11-12 Je '87

Clothing and dress

See Clothing and dress—Sports clothes

History

When the wheels began to turn [women and cycling] B. J. Mitchell. il *Women's Sports Fitness* 9:14 Mr '87

International aspects

Getting back in the saddle [tours] J. Orsini. *Travel Holiday* 167:66 My '87

Laws and regulations

"Scaring the public to death" [reckless bicyclists] F. Trippett. il *Time* 130:29 O 5 '87

Physiological effects

Pedaling down the pressure. il *Prevention* 39:6 O '87

Turbocharge on wheels [fitness benefits of mountain biking] J. Poppy. il *Esquire* 107:57-8 Ap '87

Australia

Leisurely bike tour of Australia's Canberra. il *Sunset* 178:92 My '87

California

Biking and birding around southern San Francisco Bay. il *Sunset* 178:10-11 Ja '87

Biking the quieter wine valleys . . . Alexander and Dry Creek. il map *Sunset* 178:12-14 Ap '87

Loop trips for mountain bikes [Bay Area] il map *Sunset* 179:12-13 N '87

Great Britain

Cycling in Suffolk. P. J. Wade. il maps *Gourmet* 48:54-9+ Je '87

Vermont

Pedaling Vermont. M. Pennacchia. il map *Travel Holiday* 167:62-6+ My '87

Western States

Back-country biking . . . on a guided tour. il *Sunset* 178:66+ Mr '87

Cycling trips See Cycling

Cycloids

Around and around. R. T. Kurosaka. il *Byte* 12:307-8+ My '87

Cyclones

Eastern north Pacific tropical cyclones [1986] R. L. Cross. il map *Weatherwise* 40:25-6 F '87

Cyclops Corp.

From street kid to superstar? [bid for Cyclops by S. Rose] D. Cook. il por *Bus Week* p33 F 16 '87

Cyclosporin

Cyclosporine, low cholesterol: bad mix? [neurological side effects] D. D. Edwards. *Sci News* 132:212 O 3 '87

Diabetes autoimmunity seen, stopped. D. D. Edwards. *Sci News* 132:292 N 7 '87

Long-term skin graft survival [use of cyclosporin with cadaver skin grafts; work of Bruce Achauer] *USA Today (Periodical)* 115:13 F '87

Cyclothymia See Depression, Mental

Le Cygne (New York, N.Y.: Restaurant) See New York (N.Y.)—Restaurants, nightclubs, bars, etc.

Cygnus (Constellation) See Constellations

Cygnus X-3 (Star) See Stars, Double

Cylinders (Engines, etc.)

See also
Automobile engines—Cylinders

Cypripedium See Lady's slipper

Cyprus

See also
United Nations—Cyprus

29th report on Cyprus [message to the Congress, November 14, 1986] R. Reagan. *Dep State Bull* 87:58 F '87

30th report on Cyprus [message to Congress, January 29, 1987] R. Reagan. *Dep State Bull* 87:34 Ap '87

31st report on Cyprus [message to Congress, April 21, 1987] R. Reagan. *Dep State Bull* 87:57 Jl '87

32d report on Cyprus [message to Congress, July 17, 1987] R. Reagan. *Dep State Bull* 87:42 S '87

Intrigue is big business on Cyprus. S. Powell. il map *U S News World Rep* 102:33 F 23 '87

Security Council extends mandate of Cyprus force until 15 December 1987. il *UN Chron* 24:28-32 Ag '87

Security Council extends mandate of Cyprus Force until 15 June 1987. il map *UN Chron* 24:75-8 F '87

Defenses

See also
United Nations—Armed Forces—Forces in Cyprus

Cyrille, Andrew

about

Andrew Cyrille. J. Macnie. il por *Down Beat* 54:53 Ag '87

Cysteine

The role of individual cysteine residues in the structure and function of the v-*sis* gene product. N. A. Giese and others. bibl f il *Science* 236:1315-18 Je 5 '87

Cystic fibrosis

Construction of a general human chromosome jumping library, with application to cystic fibrosis. F. S. Collins and others. bibl f il *Science* 235:1046-9 F 27 '87

Derivation of clones close to *met* by preparative field inversion gel electrophoresis. F. Michiels and others. bibl f il *Science* 236:1305-8 Je 5 '87

Diagnosis

By a nose [testing newborns; procedure developed by C. W. Gowen and others] R. Mason. *Health* 19:23+ Ja '87

Therapy

The hearts of the matter [domino donors at Johns Hopkins Hospital] C. Wallis. il *Time* 129:60 My 25 '87

Cystitis

Cystitis crisis: when a little lovesickness spells big trouble. H. Marsh. *Mademoiselle* 93:84 F '87

In pain, sleepless—and ignored [interstitial cystitis] K. McAuliffe. il *U S News World Rep* 103:79 S 21 '87

The infection that strikes 38 million women. S. Berkman. il *Good Housekeep* 204:250-1 Ap '87

Cysts

The inside story on your ovarian-cyst risk. E. Kunes. il *Mademoiselle* 93:112 O '87

Cysts (Zoology)

Encystation and expression of cyst antigens by Giardia lamblia in vitro. F. D. Gillin and others. bibl f il *Science* 235:1040-3 F 27 '87

Cytochromes

Cytochrome P-450-catalyzed formation of Δ^4-VPA, a toxic metabolite of valproic acid. A. E. Rettie and others. bibl f il *Science* 235:890-3 F 20 '87

Molecular dynamics of a cytochrome c-cytochrome b_5 electron transfer complex. J. J. Wendoloski and others. bibl f il *Science* 238:794-7 N 6 '87

Neurosteroids: cytochrome $P-450_{scc}$ in rat brain. C. Le Goascogne and others. bibl f il *Science* 237:1212-15 S 4 '87

Cytogenetics See Chromosomes

Cytokines

Cytokine-induced expression of HIV-1 in a chronically infected promonocyte cell line. T. Folks and others. bibl f il *Science* 238:800-2 N 6 '87

Cytokines alter AIDS virus production [research by Anthony Fauci and Thomas Folks] D. M. Barnes. il *Science* 236:1627 Je 26 '87

Cytology

See also
Cells

Methodology

Cell culture, fusion, manipulation, and tissue culture. *Science* 235 pt2:G35-G36 F 27 '87

Cytomegalovirus
Vaccines and vaccination
Heaven sent? [priests test vaccine for pregnant women]
D. Tonnessen. il *Health* 19:18 D '87
Cytoplasm
See also
Cytosol
Liposomes
Mitochondria
Cytosol
Cytosolic acidification as an early transductory signal
of human neutrophil chemotaxis. I. Yuli and A. Oplat-
ka. bibl f il *Science* 235:340-2 Ja 16 '87
Czar Saltan [opera] *See* Rimsky-Korsakov, Nikolay,
1844-1908
Czarnecki, Jack
about
The master of mushroom cookery. il por *Mother Earth
News* 104:84-6 Mr/Ap '87
Czechoslovakia
See also
Arts and state—Czechoslovakia
Charter 77 (Organization)
Civil rights—Czechoslovakia
Foreign correspondents—Czechoslovakia
Government and the press—Czechoslovakia
Literature and state—Czechoslovakia
Palaces—Czechoslovakia
Political prisoners—Czechoslovakia
Slovakia (Czechoslovakia)
Theater—Czechoslovakia
United States—Diplomatic and consular service—
Czechoslovakia
Foreign relations
See also
Espionage, Czech
Soviet Union
See Soviet Union—Foreign relations—Czechoslo-
vakia
Politics and government
See also
Communist Party (Czechoslovakia)
A new face, an old policy in Prague [M. Jakes succeeds
G. Husak] il por *Newsweek* 110:27 D 28 '87
Reform and dissidence in Czechoslovakia. V. V. Kusin.
Curr Hist 86:361-4+ N '87
A reluctant reformer bows out [G. Husak steps down
as leader of the Communist Party] W. R. Doerner.
il por *Time* 130:34 D 28 '87
Religious institutions and affairs
See also
Catholic Church—Czechoslovakia
Cziffra, György
about
Cziffra's incomparable Liszt. R. Freed. il por *Stereo
Rev* 52:105 Ja '87
Czyz, Bobby
about
Tough in so many ways. F. Lidz. il pors *Sports Illus*
66:66-9 F 16 '87

D

D-Day Invasion, 1944
The first wave [disastrous 741st amphibious tank battalion
assault] A. D. Wiener. il *Am Herit* 38:136-8 My/Je
'87
D-form substances
The significances of form. B. T. Hunter. il *Consum
Res Mag* 70:8-9 Je '87
D. H. Blair & Co., Inc.
Blair's Morty Davis: the prince of going public. P. Finch.
il por *Bus Week* p176+ N 2 '87
D W G Corporation
Three sparkling turnarounds: can this really be Victor
Posner? P. Engardio. il por *Bus Week* p56-7 Jl 27
'87
Da Silva, Adroaldo Moura *See* Silva, Adroaldo Moura
da
Da Vinci, Leonardo *See* Leonardo, da Vinci, 1452-1519
Daalder, Ivo H.
A tactical defense initiative for Western Europe? bibl
f il *Bull At Sci* 43:34-9 My '87
D'Abo, Maryam
about
Maryam D'Abo: Bond bombshell. il por *Vogue* 177:322-3
Ag '87

Maryam D'Abo hopes to bring the James Bond girl
out of the dark ages in The living daylights. M.
Alexander. il pors *People Wkly* 28:48-9 Ag 24 '87
Dachau (Germany: Concentration camp) *See* Concentration
camps—Germany
Dackman, Linda
Sex & the single-breasted woman. *Vogue* 177:420+ S
'87
Dadaism
Exhibitions
Modern Arp: the Boston Museum shows a playful Dada.
J. Perl. il *Vogue* 177:52 Jl '87
Daddona, Joe
This mayor elected to have a fitter future; ed. by Maria
Mihalik. il pors *Prevention* 39:81-2+ O '87
D'Adesky, Anne-Christine
Breaking the F.D.A. drugjam. il *Nation* 245:405-6+ O
17 '87
Daedalus Project
Preparing to pedal into history. il *Sci News* 132:302
N 7 '87
Daeshik, Seo
about
Mac gets a new Mr. Fix-it. R. Sullivan. il pors *Sports
Illus* 67:26-7 Ag 17 '87
Daewoo Corporation
Korea's export king [Kim Woo-Choong] L. Kraar. il
por *Fortune* 115:74 Ja 5 '87
The master of joint ventures [chairman Kim Woo-
Choong] il por *U S News World Rep* 102:61 My
11 '87
Daffodils *See* Narcissus
Daffy Duck (Fictional character)
A duck amuck, one more time [new theatrical short
The duxorcist] B. Barol. il *Newsweek* 110:83 N 30
'87
Dafoe, Willem
about
Oliver's army. F. Schruers. il por *Roll Stone* p24 Ja
29 '87
Platoon's real trouper. F. Schruers. por *Roll Stone* p49+
My 21 '87
Radical cheek to cheek. L. Liebmann. pors *Vogue* 177:90
Ap '87
Willem Dafoe: saintly Sergeant Elias. J. M. Saul. il
por *People Wkly* 27:53 Mr 9 '87
Daggett, Stephen
(jt. auth) *See* English, Robert, and Daggett, Stephen
Dagon Burmese Restaurant (New York, N.Y.) *See* New
York (N.Y.)—Restaurants, nightclubs, bars, etc.
D'Agresta, David
about
Choke-hold death of black sparks violence in Tampa.
Jet 71:15 Mr 9 '87
White cop cleared in choke hold death of black man.
Jet 72:33 Ap 27 '87
Daguerreotypes
The moon on a silver plate [experimenting with daguer-
reotype process] J. K. Herman and M. S. Barger.
il *Astronomy* 15:98-103 O '87
Dahl, G., and others
Expression of functional cell-cell channels from cloned
rat liver gap junction complementary DNA. bibl f
il *Science* 236:1290-3 Je 5 '87
Dahl, June, and Joranson, David
Relieving cancer pain. il *World Health* p28-9 N '87
Dahlberg, A. W.
Who will decide the future of coal? [address, April 16,
1987] *Vital Speeches Day* 53:562-4 Jl 1 '87
Dahlem Konferenzen
Anatomy of a conference. il *BioScience* 37:707-8 N '87
Dahlias
Dahlias for the 21st century. il *Sunset* 178:184-7, 190
Mr '87
Dahlin, Bob
about
Monster in the closet [film] Reviews
People Wkly il 27:8 Je 1 '87. R. Novak
Dahlin, Donald
about
Arizona high. S. N. Chakravarty. il por *Forbes* 140:178+
N 2 '87
Dahlke, Dieter
The 'Kids for Peace' reach out. il *World Press Rev*
34:45 Ap '87
Dahlke, Karl A.
about
Pieces of a polyomino puzzle. I. Peterson. il por *Sci
News* 132:310 N 14 '87

Dahlsten, Donald L.
(jt. auth) See Dreistadt, Steve H., and Dahlsten, Donald L.

Dahm, Arnold J., and Vinen, W. F.
Electrons and ions at the helium surface. bibl f il *Phys Today* 40:43-50 F '87

Dai-Ichi Kangyo Bank, Ltd.
Don't blame the bureaucrats. M. Beauchamp. il *Forbes* 139 Ann Directory:124 Ap 27 '87
Soon, Citicorp 'branches' could be all over Japan [sharing automated teller machines] J. B. Treece. *Bus Week* p82 Ja 19 '87

Dai Rakuda Kan (Dance company)
Faux pas [performance of The five rings at City Center, New York City] T. Tobias. il *N Y* 20:137-8 Ap 27 '87

Daihatsu (Automobile) See Automobiles, Foreign
Daihatsu Motor Co. Ltd.
Just what the U.S. needs: an even smaller car from Japan [Daihatsu's Charade] S. Toy. il *Bus Week* p26 Ap 20 '87

Dailey, Dan

about
At the Renwick: Dan Dailey. K. M. Burke. il *Smithsonian* 18:158+ Je '87

Daily news (New York, N.Y.)
Blacks file bias suit against N.Y. Daily news. *Jet* 71:15 Mr 2 '87
Blacks win lawsuit filed against N.Y. Daily news. *Jet* 72:24 My 4 '87
Daily news makes $3.1 mil. settlement in job bias case. *Jet* 72:22 Jl 6 '87
Guilty of race bias. *Newsweek* 109:63 Ap 27 '87
Journalists win bias suit [black journalists vs. Daily news] Y. Rice. il *Black Enterp* 17:15-16 Jl '87
N.Y. sax player labeled criminal in Daily news in case of mistaken identity [case of D. Foster] il por *Jet* 72:38 My 11 '87
The 'News' news. E. Diamond. il por *N Y* 20:19+ F 16 '87
Tabloid pays a big tab [settlement in discrimination case] *Time* 129:65 Je 22 '87

Daily racing form
Get warm to the Form [learning to handicap] J. Rolfe. il *Sport Mag* 78:91+ Jl '87

Daimler-Benz AG
The banker behind the shakeup at Daimler-Benz [A. Herrhausen] R. Ingersoll and R. Brady. il pors *Bus Week* p36-7 Jl 27 '87
Putsch and shove at Daimler-Benz [new chairman E. Reuter] N. J. Perry. il por *Fortune* 116:92 Ag 17 '87
The street-smart perfectionist [W. Breitschwerdt] L. S. Richman. il por *Fortune* 116:36 Ag 3 '87
"We are still saying hello to each other" [squabbling among the directors] P. Berman. il *Forbes* 139:94+ My 18 '87

Dairy cows See Cows
Dairy equipment
Coming: new dairy ideas from Europe and Israel. S. Spahr. il *Success Farm* 85:50 O '87
Dairy farming See Dairying
Dairy farms

Equipment
See Dairy equipment
Dairy Hollow House (Eureka Springs, Ark.: Inn) See Eureka Springs (Ark.)—Hotels, motels, etc.
Dairy industry See Dairying
Dairy price supports See Agricultural administration
Dairy products
See also
Butter
Cheese
Cream
Ice cream, ices, etc.
Milk
Yogurt
Dairying
See also
Cheese industry
Cows
Farmland Dairies
National Dairy Board
Computer spies on college cows [Westfalia system at University of Delaware] D. Wanner. il *Success Farm* 85:50D Ag '87
Dairy. J. R. Borcherding. See occasional issues of Successful Farming through June 1987
Dairy buyout ends. J. R. Borcherding. il *Success Farm* 85:44+ O '87

Green forage to white milk to green $$$ [Koepke dairy] D. Allen and G. Johnston. il *Success Farm* 85:13 Je '87

Acquisitions and mergers
Canada
Unicorp fuels a fight [sale of Palm Dairies blocked by Competition Act tribunal] T. Fennell. il *Macleans* 100:14-15 Ja 5 '87

Canada
See also
Palm Dairies Ltd.
It all began with Daisy [condensation] S. Jones. il *Read Dig* 131:82-90+ Ag '87
Daisies
Daisies speak of summer. il *South Living* 22:45 Ag '87
Which daisy? Here's a guide to today's nursery choices. il *Sunset* 178:240+ My '87
Daisywheel printers (Computers) See Computers—Print-out equipment
Daix, Pierre
Picasso's time of decisive encounters; tr. by Tom Repensek. il *Art News* 86:136-41 Ap '87
Dakota Grill & Bar (Berkeley, Calif.) See Berkeley (Calif.)—Restaurants, nightclubs, bars, etc.
Dakota Indians
See also
Cowboy and Indian Alliance
Give it back to the Indians? [P. Stevens leads Sioux claim to the Black Hills] T. Jacoby. il pors *Newsweek* 110:47 D 7 '87
The heart of everything that is [Sioux Indians battle for return of the Black Hills] W. Greider. il *Roll Stone* p37-8+ My 7 '87
The Sioux reject nuclear waste [Cheyenne River Sioux reservation] J. W. Wilson. *Progressive* 51:11-12 S '87
Photographs and photography
The Americanization of Indian girls [exhibit at the Voorhees Zimmerli Art Museum at Rutgers University] M. N. Powers. il *Society* 24:83-6 Ja/F '87
Dalai Lama XIV, 1935-
about
The Dalai Lama speaks [interview] J.-C. Buhrer. il por *World Press Rev* 34:21 D '87
Spirit in exile: the Dalai Lama pleads for the Tibetan people. R. Gere and R. A. F. Thurman. il por *Roll Stone* p68-9 D 3 '87
Anecdotes, facetiae, satire, etc.
Uncivil liberties. C. Trillin. il *Nation* 245:778 D 26 '87-Ja 2 '88
Dalbey, Ross E., and Wickner, William T.
Leader peptidase of Escherichia coli: critical role of a small domain in membrane assembly. bibl f il *Science* 235:783-7 F 13 '87
Dale, Don
Drip irrigation. il *Ctry J* 14:42-7 Jl '87
D'Aleo, Angela
The watercolor page. il por *Am Artist* 51:48-51+ Jl '87
D'Alessandro, Bill
Dark days for solar. il *Sierra* 72:34-7 Jl/Ag '87
Daley, George Q., and others
The CML-specific P210 *bcr/abl* protein, unlike v-*abl*, does not transform NIH/3T3 fibroblasts. bibl f il *Science* 237:532-5 Jl 31 '87
Daley, Tammy K.
When a good word takes on a negative meaning. por *U S News World Rep* 102:9 Ja 12 '87
Dalfo, Michael J., d. 1982
about
The case against Brian Spencer. P. Dexter. il *Sports Illus* 66:98-102+ My 11 '87
A hockey player's victory in court. M. Gray. il pors *Macleans* 100:46-7 O 26 '87
Dalio, Ray
about
Here's a happy thought [interview] R. McGough. il por *Forbes* 139:100+ F 9 '87
Dalkon Shield (Contraceptive) See Contraceptives
Dall'Acqua, Joyce
Making of a desert. il map *Earth Sci* 40:19-21 Spr '87
Dallas, Claude, Jr.
about
Claude Dallas update. R. P. Stuart. por *Outdoor Life* 179:49 Mr '87
In Idaho: a killer becomes a mythic hero. M. Riley. il por *Time* 129:10-11 Ja 26 '87
Dallas, Gregor
New York 1865. bibl il *Hist Today* 37:17-22 D '87

Dallas (Tex.)
Starting over in Dallas [cable TV] C. Capuzzi. il *Channels* 7:23-4 Jl/Ag '87

Airports
Atlantic Southeast expects to double service at Dallas/Ft. Worth hub. C. Preble. il *Aviat Week Space Technol* 126:41+ My 4 '87

Buildings
See also
Infomart (Dallas, Tex.: Trade mart)
Lone star [showroom of Herman Miller, Inc.] C. K. Gandee. il *Archit Rec* 175:110-15 My '87

Crime
A cloud falls on a Dallas preacher [attack on wife of W. Railey] D. Pedersen. il por *Newsweek* 109:23 My 25 '87
Daughter alleges father sired his own grandkids [case of Rev. L. Elliott] il por *Jet* 72:16+ Ag 31 '87
Strangled in Dallas: an ungodly mystery [Rev. W. Railey held in attack on his wife] *Newsweek* 109:30 My 11 '87
Texas preacher guilty of siring 12 of his grandkids [L. Elliott] il por *Jet* 73:16 D 7 '87
A troubled minister's tale [strangulation of W. Railey's wife] S. Peterson. il por *U S News World Rep* 102:28 My 25 '87

Galleries and museums
See also
Dallas Museum of Art
Southwest Museum of Science and Technology, The Science Place

Health facilities
'This is a good place' [West Dallas Youth Clinic] B. Turque. il *Newsweek* 109:61 F 16 '87

Housing
Demolition dilemma [West Dallas housing projects] L. Gite. il *Black Enterp* 18:26 O '87
Major breakup of Dallas housing project planned. *Jet* 72:22 Je 1 '87

Music
See also
Dallas Opera

Newspapers
See also
Dallas morning news

Politics and government
Breakthrough in Dallas [black city manager R. Knight] il pors *Ebony* 42:120+ Ap '87
First black city manager appointed in Dallas, Tex. [R. Knight] *Jet* 71:13 Ja 12 '87
A new man heads Dallas [R. Knight] R. Witherspoon. il por *Black Enterp* 17:15 Mr '87

Stores
See also
Neiman Marcus

Dallas Ballet
Reviews:
Performance of Phaedra in Dallas. J. Neal. *Dance Mag* 61:25 O '87
Performances of Swan Lake in Dallas. J. Neal. *Dance Mag* 61:29+ Mr '87

Dallas-Fort Worth Regional Airport *See* Dallas (Tex.)—Airports

Dallas morning news
Jury selection series cited by Marshall wins an award [series on jury discrimination] *Jet* 72:23 Jl 20 '87

Dallas Museum of Art
Art has a place in the South. il *South Living* 22:62-7 F '87

Dallas Museum of Art. Decorative Arts Wing
An art-filled villa finds a special setting in Texas [donation by W. R. Reves of Villa La Pausa Collection] H. Dudar. il pors *Smithsonian* 17:50-9 Ja '87

Dallas Opera
Dallas. W. Albright. il *Opera News* 51:34 F 28 '87

Dallmann, Daniel
about
Daniel Dallmann. T. Bolt. il *Am Artist* 51:56-61 Mr '87

Dallmeyer, Dorinda G.
National security and the semiconductor industry. il *Technol Rev* 90:46-52+ N/D '87

Daloz, Laurent A.
Martha meets her mentor: the power of teaching relationships. il *Change* 19:35-7 Jl/Ag '87

Dalton, Hugh Dalton, Baron, 1887-1962
about
Writing our own history. T. Benn. il pors *Hist Today* 37:9-12 Ap '87

Dalton, Stephen
Jumping blues. il *Nat Hist* 96:96-7 Mr '87

Split seconds [excerpt from Split second] il *Read Dig* 131:155-61 Ag '87

Dalton, Timothy
about
Bond at 25: back to basics. C. McGuigan. il pors *Newsweek* 110:56-7 Jl 27 '87
Meet the new Bond. G. Hirshey. il por *Roll Stone* p37-9 Jl 16-30 '87
Timothy Dalton: a bold new Bond. E. Sherman. il por *Ladies Home J* 104:74 Ag '87

Dalton (B.) Booksellers *See* B. Dalton Booksellers

Dalva, Nancy Vreeland
Capezio centenary: family affairs. il pors *Dance Mag* 61:90-4 My '87
Visible spirit: the Cunningham continuum. il por *Dance Mag* 61:46-8 Ag '87

Daly, Bridget, and Skeels, Janet
Boy talk [excerpt from The 100th boyfriend] *Harpers* 275:31-2 S '87

Daly, Macdonald
'All heaven in a rage'. il *Hist Today* 37:7-9 My '87

Daly, Margaret
Money. See issues of Better Homes and Gardens

Daly, Michael
The Fat Man: the life and high times of Irwin Schiff [cover story] il pors *N Y* 20:46-61 O 19 '87
I spy: how a Queens College student helped catch a KGB agent and set off a superpower showdown [cover story] il pors *N Y* 20:34-47 Ap 6 '87

Daly, Timothy
about
Winning raves is no stretch for Tyne Daly's baby brother Timothy. D. Hutchings. il pors *People Wkly* 27:141-2 Je 8 '87

Daly, Tyne
about
Sharon Gless & Tyne Daly. M. Gordon. il pors *Ms* 15:40-1+ Ja '87

Damadian, Raymond, 1936-
about
The inventor. K. McAuliffe. il por *U S News World Rep* 102:66 Ja 26 '87

Damages
See also
Liability (Law)
Libel and slander
12-year-old boy awarded $28 million for burns in fire that killed mother [J. Guerrier] D. M. Cheers. il pors *Jet* 73:20-1 D 28 '87-Ja 4 '88
Accident victim's son, 2, awarded nearly $1.7 million [son of traffic accident victim H. Fisher] pors *Jet* 72:36 Ag 17 '87
Chicago boy gets $2.5 mil. in injury case: his arm destroyed by electricity [L. Mance] por *Jet* 72:36 Jl 27 '87
Damage control [Supreme Court to decide on damages awarded in suit against Bankers Life] D. Fanning. il *Forbes* 139:84 Je 29 '87
The lawyer who wins $100 million damage suits [personal injury specialist W. Gary] C. Whitaker. il pors *Ebony* 42:127-30+ O '87
Wrangling over the booty from insider trading. C. Yang. il *Bus Week* p158+ O 12 '87

Damask, A. C.
Forensic physics of vehicle accidents [cover story] bibl f il *Phys Today* 40:36-44 Mr '87

DaMatta, Roberto
The meal is the message: the language of Brazilian cuisine. il *Courier* 40:22-3 My '87

D'Ambrosio, Nancy
Visions of magic. il *Horizon* 30:46-52 O '87

Damin Aviation Corp. Manhattan Helicopter Tours *See* Manhattan Helicopter Tours

Daminozide
An apple a day is O.K.—for now [food processing industry rejects apples treated with growth regulator Alar] il *Consum Rep* 52:594 O '87

Damone, Vic
about
Diahann Carroll and Vic Damone marry at Golden Nugget Casino. il pors *Jet* 71:12-14 Ja 19 '87
Diahann Carroll and Vic Damone: new marriage and new career on stage. il pors *Jet* 71:57-8 Ja 26 '87
Diahann's hubby rebounds after kidney stone scare. *Jet* 71:23 F 9 '87

Damper bread *See* Bread

Dampness in buildings
See also
Waterproofing

Damrosch, Barbara
Keeping the pool cool. il *Esquire* 108:24 Jl '87

Dams
See also
Hetch Hetchy Water Supply Project
BuRec gives up plan to mine in Grand Teton [reconstruction of the Jackson Lake Dam] il *Natl Parks* 61:35 Jl/Ag '87
A city says no to canyon dams [North St. Vrain Creek] T. Turner. il *Sierra* 72:133-5 Ja/F '87
The Corps (Marine) and the only natural river [Camp Pendleton and proposed Santa Margarita dams in Calif.] J. Sunila. il map *Audubon* 89:114-16+ S '87
Dryland farmers say no to water [Colorado farmers sue Bureau of Reclamation over Dolores River Project] J. Price. il *Progressive* 51:11 Jl '87
An end to ecstasy. D. E. Worster. il *Wilderness* 51:18-21+ Fall '87
The House abandons a desert dam [compromise on Cliff Dam on Verde River and Central Arizona Project] D. Dagget. il *Sierra* 72:84+ N/D '87
The last big dam? [proposed Two Forks Project on the South Platte River] S. Stuller. *Wilderness* 51:34-6 Fall '87
The long fight for Kings Canyon [proposed Rodgers Crossing dam site] P. Carr and K. Glass. il maps *Sierra* 72:38-44 Ja/F '87
A nonrenewable river [proposed hydroelectric dams on the South Yuba] D. Carter. il *Sierra* 72:66-7 My/Je '87
A river changes [dams on the Colorado] V. Ryan. il map *Earth Sci* 39:15-17 Wint '86

Bangladesh
They stopped the sea. H. van Duivendijk. il *Natl Geogr* 172:92-101 Jl '87

Canada
See also
Bassano Dam (Alta.)
Modeling tidal power [tidal power dam in the Bay of Fundy would raise tide levels in the Gulf of Maine] D. A. Greenberg. il maps *Sci Am* 257:128-128C+ N '87
A reservoir of concerns [controversy over proposed Old-man River dam] M. Nemeth. il *Macleans* 100:8 D 21 '87
Voices against the tide [Annapolis Tidal Power Plant on Bay of Fundy is accused of harming clam fishery] D. Holt. il *Macleans* 100:11-12 N 2 '87
Whose power to which people? [B. C. Hydro's plans for hydroelectric dam for export on the Peace River] J. Baker. il *Sierra* 72:22-4 Ja/F '87

Philippines
One for the spirits [defeat of Chico River Dam project by tribal peoples] C. Fay. il *Sierra* 72:22-4 Mr/Ap '87

Sri Lanka
Still waters run deep [remains of earth embankment dam found] A. Bingham. il *Hist Today* 37:5-6 O '87

United States
See Dams

Dan, Freda
about
Freda Dan: an open style in Hong Kong. J. O'Connor. por *Sch Update* 119:5 Ap 6 '87

Dan River Inc.
How Dan River's ESOP missed the boat. D. Foust. il *Bus Week* p34-5 O 26 '87

Dana, Leo I.
Life in the Kamerlingh Onnes lab. *Phys Today* 40:42 Ap '87
about
Leo Dana: cryogenic science and technology. R. J. Donnelly. il por *Phys Today* 40:38-41+ Ap '87

Danazol
The frightening side effects of a "miracle drug" for infertility. S. Edmiston. il *Glamour* 85:220-1+ D '87

Danbrot, Margaret
(ed) See Wurtman, Judith J. Mood foods to raise your energy or lower your stress

Dance, Charles
about
The latest Dance craze. D. Chase. il por *Horizon* 30:36-7 My '87

Dance
See also
Alvin Ailey American Dance Theater
Armitage Ballet
Ballet
Ballroom dancing
Belly dancing
Bill T. Jones/Arnie Zane & Company
Chicago Repertory Dance Ensemble
CoDanceCo

Computers—Dance use
Concert Dance Company
Dance Alloy (Dance company)
Dance Kaleidoscope
David Dorfman Dance
David Gordon/Pick Up Company
David Parsons Company
Dennis Wayne's Dancers
Discotheques
Drill teams
Elisa Monte Dance Company
Erick Hawkins Dance Company
Fiji Theater Company
Garth Fagan's Bucket Dance Theatre
HARRY (Dance company)
Hula (Dance)
Information storage and retrieval systems—Dance use
Jonathon Apples Plus Company
Lar Lubovitch Dance Company
Laura Dean Dancers and Musicians
Limón Dance Company
Lucinda Childs Dance Company
Mark Morris Dance Group
Martha Graham Dance Company
Merce Cunningham Dance Company
Minnesota Dance Theatre
Momix (Dance company)
Motion pictures—Dance films
Murray Louis Dance Company
National Dance Week
Nevada Dance Theatre
New York Baroque Dance Company
Nina Wiener and Dancers
North Carolina Dance Theater
Paul Taylor Dance Company
Peridance
Pilobolus Dance Theatre
Ririe-Woodbury Dance Company
Rosalind Newman and Dancers
Tap dance
Trisha Brown Dance Company
Twyla Tharp Dance Company
Videotapes—Dance
Wil Swanson and Dancers
Changes in ballet and modern dance techniques: crossovers/fallouts. M. Horosko. il *Dance Mag* 61:168-71 Je '87
Dance. T. Tobias. See issues of New York
Dance magazine summer dance calendar '87 [special section] il *Dance Mag* 61:SC1-SC8+ My '87
Dancing:
Twyla Tharp Dance Company's appearance at the Brooklyn Academy occasions thoughts on relationship of modern dance and ballet. A. Croce. *New Yorker* 63:118-20 F 23 '87
Editors log. W. Como. See issues of Dance Magazine
I won't dance—don't ask me! B. Stepko. il *Seventeen* 46:126 Ap '87
Looking back: divertimento 1986. W. Como. il *Dance Mag* 61:56-63+ Ja '87
Modern dance: a growing presence [family tree] K. Matheson. il *Dance Mag* 61:151-3 Je '87
Performance calendar. See issues of Dance Magazine
Presstime news. See issues of Dance Magazine

Awards
See also
Dance Magazine Awards
Isadora Duncan Dance Awards

Benefit performances
New frontiers [AIDS benefit program Dancing for life] T. Tobias. il *N Y* 20:119-20 O 26 '87
To fight AIDS, American troupes will dance for life. il *Dance Mag* 61:6 S '87

Bibliography
Dancebooks. See issues of Dance Magazine

Choreography
See Choreography

Conferences
Conference explores Judaism and dance [92nd Street Y, New York City] L. Garafola. il *Dance Mag* 61:14 Ja '87
Critics to investigate Rite of spring this fall. L. Garafola. il *Dance Mag* 61:6 O '87
In its first meeting, New England's dance world finds it has a lot to discuss. E. Zimmer. il *Dance Mag* 61:6 Jl '87

Copyright
See Copyright—Choreography

Directories
Dance directory. See issues of Dance Magazine

Dance—*cont.*

Federal aid

Dancing:

Grant for preservation of Martha Graham Dance Company works. A. Croce. *New Yorker* 63:147-8 N 23 '87

History

See also

New English Song and Daunce Companie

Society of Dance History Scholars

Exploding a favored myth: ballet and its booms. C. Barnes. il *Dance Mag* 61:88-95 Je '87

A wishbook of danceworks we'd like to see again: revivals. R. Philp. il *Dance Mag* 61:136-49 Je '87

Photographs and photography

Celebration! W. Como. See issues of Dance Magazine beginning June 1987

International aspects

Stepping out. O. Stuart. il *Harpers Bazaar* 120:152+ O '87

Management

See also

Pentacle (DanceWorks, Inc.)

Photographs and photography

The photogenic art of dance in the studio and on the stage. A. B. Smith. il *Petersens Photogr Mag* 16:32-3+ Ag '87

Production and direction

See Dance production

Stage setting and scenery

Roz Newman forms a multi-national alliance [Canadian artist P. Hebert's designs for new dance] E. Zimmer. il por *Dance Mag* 61:4 F '87

Still life in motion [L. Childs' Portraits in reflection] C. Bush. il *Theatre Crafts* 21:32-3+ F '87

Study and teaching

See also

Dance schools

Education. M. Horosko. See issues of Dance Magazine

Is creative dance responsive to research? A. Riley. bibl f il *Des Arts Educ* 88:36-40 My/Je '87

Aids and devices

Instructional video directory. D. Towers. il *Dance Mag* 61:44-50 Mr '87

Themes

See also

Sex in dance

Belgium

See also

Rosas (Dance company)

Canada

See also

Les Ballets Jazz de Montréal

National Tap Dance Company of Canada

Celebrating body and soul. P. Hluchy. il *Macleans* 100:50-2+ Mr 9 '87

Reviews:

Multimedia presentation There's always been dance during Expo 86. L. Windreich. *Dance Mag* 61:28-9+ F '87

China

See also

China National Opera and Dance Drama Theater

France

See also

Compagnie Maguy Marin

Reviews:

Groupe de recherche choréographique de l'Opera de Paris at the Holland Festival in Amsterdam. H. Klooss. *Dance Mag* 61:98-9 Ja '87

Germany (West)

See also

Berlin (Germany: West)—Dance

Heidelberg (Germany)—Dance

Great Britain

See also

Ballet Rambert

Michael Clark and Company

Hong Kong

See also

Hong Kong Dance Company

Japan

See also

Ballet Español de Yoko Komatsubara

Dai Rakuda Kan (Dance company)

Sankai Juku (Dance company)

Netherlands

See also

Netherlands Dance Theater

New England

In its first meeting, New England's dance world finds it has a lot to discuss. E. Zimmer. il *Dance Mag* 61:6 Jl '87

New York (State)

See also

New York (N.Y.)—Dance

Rochester (N.Y.)—Dance

Quebec (Province)

See also

Montréal Danse

Soviet Union

Trailblazers of the US/USSR dance exchange. H. Breazeale. il *Dance Mag* 61:70-2 Ap '87

Spain

See also

Madrid (Spain)—Dance

Spain's dance scene is burgeoning. L. Kumin. il *Dance Mag* 61:104 F '87

Taiwan

See also

Cloudgate Taipei Contemporary Dance Theatre

Texas

See also

International Theatrical Arts Society

United States

See Dance

Dance, Aerobic *See* Aerobics

Dance, Black

Katherine Dunham: a living legend. B. Allen. il por *Essence* 18:54-5+ D '87

Dance, Chinese

See also

China National Opera and Dance Drama Theater

Dance, Haitian

Driven to dance. M. Fox. il *Health* 19:48-51 Jl '87

Dance, Indian (East Indian)

Celebration of dance [S. Mansingh] K. C. Reinhart. il *Horizon* 30:30 Mr '87

Dance, Japanese

See also

Butoh

Dance, Jewish

Conference explores Judaism and dance [92nd Street Y, New York City] L. Garafola. il *Dance Mag* 61:14 Ja '87

Reviews:

Women of Yemen: interpretations in theatrical dance presented as part of Jews and Judaism in dance at the Joyce Theater, New York City. L. Garafola. *Dance Mag* 61:83+ Mr '87

Dance, Latin American

Reviews:

Dance events at the Public Theater's Festival Latino, New York City. J. R. Acocella. *Dance Mag* 61:28+ Ja '87

Dance, Spanish

See also

Ballet Español de Yoko Komatsubara

Flamenco

Dance Alloy (Dance company)

Reviews:

Performances at Chatham College, Pittsburgh. K. Dacko. *Dance Mag* 61:79-80 F '87

Dance and fashion

"Dance" at Met Museum is lavish but laconic. B. Laine. il *Dance Mag* 61:14-15 Ap '87

Dance and industry

See also

National Corporate Fund for Dance

Dance and literature

See also

Ballet adaptations

Dance and state

See also

Dance—Federal aid

State arts councils: what educational role? A personal review. S. Hodes. *Des Arts Educ* 88:11-14 N/D '86

Dance and the aged

Comfort me with apples [L. Lerman's dances for senior performers at Dance Theater Workshop] T. Tobias. il *N Y* 20:129-30 N 9 '87

The official wiggle jiggle bump & grind program [belly dancing by Farouché] E. Kiester. il pors *50 Plus* 27:46-9 O '87

Dance and the handicapped

See also

Choreographers, Handicapped

Dance therapy

Dance associations
See also
Regional Dance America (Organization)
Dance clubs See Discotheques
Dance companies See Dance
Dance concerts
Close encounters [concerts staged by A. Gamson at St. Mark's Church, New York City] T. Tobias. il *N Y* 20:84-5 F 16 '87
Reviews:
"Dive in", Danspace Project at St. Mark's Church, New York City. S. Sommer. *Dance Mag* 61:43-4 Ap '87
P. Hunter at Merce Cunningham Studio, New York City. M. Aloff. *Dance Mag* 61:38-9 Ja '87
S. Forti and D. Zambrano at the Ethnic Folk Arts Center, New York City. C. Hardy. *Dance Mag* 61:40-1 Ap '87
S. Paxton and L. Nelson at The Kitchen, New York City. S. Sommer. pors *Dance Mag* 61:22 S '87
Taking stock [D. Parsons at the Joyce Theater, New York City] T. Tobias. il *N Y* 20:58-9 F 2 '87
World of wonders [R. Charlip at the Joyce Theater, New York City] T. Tobias. il *N Y* 20:70 Ja 26 '87
Netherlands
Reviews:
No fixed abode, solo performance by P. Daniels in Utrecht. H. Klooss. *Dance Mag* 61:21 O '87
Dance costume See Costume, Theatrical
Dance critics and criticism
See also
Dance reviews
Denby, Edwin, 1903-1983
Dance festivals
Australia
Australia's bicentennial will feature festivals of dance. P. Laughlin. il *Dance Mag* 61:12 S '87
Cuba
Cuban festival shows worldwide diversity [Havana International Ballet Festival] M. Hunt. il *Dance Mag* 61:12+ Mr '87
Denmark
More than make-believe [Royal Danish Ballet Festival] M. Hunt. il *Dance Mag* 61:58-60 O '87
France
Reviews:
Performance at the American Festival, Roubaix, France [Ballet du Nord] S. Ueno. il *Dance Mag* 61:20+ Mr '87
Hong Kong
London troupe highlights Hong Kong's fifteenth arts festival. D. Ries. il *Dance Mag* 61:32 Je '87
Massachusetts
See also
Jacob's Pillow Dance Festival
Reviews:
1987 Discovery Festival in Boston. I. M. Fanger. *Dance Mag* 61:73-4 S '87
Mexico
Oaxaca's gift of music and dance [Guelaguetza Festival] L. DeLaRosa. il *Américas* 39:58-60 Ja/F '87
Netherlands
Reviews:
Groupe de recherche choréographique de l'Opera de Paris at the Holland Festival in Amsterdam. H. Klooss. *Dance Mag* 61:98-9 Ja '87
New York (State)
Reviews:
Dance events at the Public Theater's Festival Latino, New York City. J. R. Acocella. *Dance Mag* 61:28+ Ja '87
Festival of Dance Stars 1987 at Brooklyn College. M. Hunt. *Dance Mag* 61:191+ Je '87
Liberty Dances festival, part of the French/American Dance Exchange. L. A. Small. *Dance Mag* 61:22+ Ja '87
Women of Yemen: interpretations in theatrical dance presented as part of Jews and Judaism in dance at the Joyce Theater, New York City. L. Garafola. *Dance Mag* 61:83+ Mr '87
Ontario
Portrait of a country in motion [Canada Dance Festival] L. Howe-Beck. il *Macleans* 100:44 Jl 20 '87
Retail complex hosts premier dance fair [Harbourfront in Toronto] P. Citron. il *Dance Mag* 61:5 Mr '87
Québec (Province)
Nouvelle cuisine of dance cooking up in Montreal [International Festival of New Dance] L. Howe-Beck. *Dance Mag* 61:7 S '87

Reviews:
Moment'homme festival at Tangente: Danse Actuelle in Montreal. L. Howe-Beck. *Dance Mag* 61:102+ Ja '87
Sicily
Editor's log [Basel Ballet at the Taormina Music and Ballet Festival] W. Como. il *Dance Mag* 61:30 N '87
Spain
Reviews:
Cumbre Flamenca in Madrid. L. Kumin. *Dance Mag* 61:34-5 Ja '87
Various companies at the Muestra de Danza en Madrid. L. Kumin. *Dance Mag* 61:26-7 F '87
Texas
See also
San Antonio Festival
Dance films See Motion pictures—Dance films
Dance Films Association
Dance Films Association guards the past, promotes the future. *Dance Mag* 61:14-15 My '87
Dance halls
France
See also
Paris (France)—Dance halls
New York (State)
See also
New York (N.Y.)—Dance halls
Dance in America [television program] See Television program reviews—Single works
Dance in art
Keeping dance forever [sculptor E. MacQueen] G. Parks. il por *Dance Mag* 61:46-8 D '87
Dance in motion pictures
'Giselle' goes to Hollywood [making of Dancers] M. Pally. il por *Film Comment* 23:80+ S/O '87
Dance institutes and workshops
See also
Dance Theater Workshop
Jacob's Pillow Dance Festival
School of American Ballet
Dance Kaleidoscope
Diver Greg Louganis returns to dancing, his first love, before the eyes of his pal Ryan White. W. Plummer. il pors *People Wkly* 28:44-5 N 9 '87
Reviews:
Performances at Ford Theatre, Los Angeles. D. Perlmutter. *Dance Mag* 61:24-5 Ja '87
Dance libraries
See also
New York Public Library. Dance Collection
Dance magazine
Dance magazine 1927-1987 [special issue] il *Dance Mag* 61:17+ Je '87
Dance magazine's 60th birthday party was a glittering affair. il *Dance Mag* 61:10 S '87
Dance Magazine Awards
Dance Magazine Awards 1954-1987. il *Dance Mag* 61:124-6 Je '87
Dance Magazine Awards 1987. il pors *Dance Mag* 61:44-6 F '87
Dance museums
See also
National Museum of Dance (U.S.)
Dance production
The Met's Jane Hermann: offstage assoluta. J. Gruen. il por *Dance Mag* 61:48-51 Jl '87
Taylor-made design. S. Flatow. il *Theatre Crafts* 21:24-5+ Ja '87
Dance reviews
Dance. M. Aloff. See occasional issues of The Nation
Dancing. A. Croce. See occasional issues of The New Yorker
On dance. L. A. Jacobs. See occasional issues of The New Leader
Reviews. See issues of Dance Magazine
Single works
Angels of Swedenborg
Dance Mag il 61:93-5 Ap '87. S. Sommer
The animal trilogy
Dance Mag 61:23-4 Jl '87. C. Hardy
N Y il 20:47 Ja 5 '87. T. Tobias
Ballare
N Y il 20:110 Mr 2 '87. T. Tobias
Black and white
N Y il 20:80 Ap 6 '87. T. Tobias
Calyx
N Y 20:64+ Je 1 '87. T. Tobias
Canticle for innocent comedians
N Y il 20:102 N 2 '87. T. Tobias

Dance reviews—Single works—*cont.*
  Celebration
    N Y il 20:102-3 N 2 '87. T. Tobias
  A dancer on the bronze phoenix terrace
    Dance Mag il 61:18-19 D '87. J.-P. Ou
  Eden
    N Y 20:129 N 9 '87. T. Tobias
    New Leader 70:23 N 2 '87. L. A. Jacobs
  Elena's aria
    N Y il 20:108 N 23 '87. T. Tobias
    New Leader 70:23 N 30 '87. L. A. Jacobs
  L'enfant et les sortilèges
    Dance Mag 61:66-7 S '87. J. Gruen
  Fabrications
    N Y il 20:73 Mr 23 '87. T. Tobias
  Fierce attachments
    N Y il 20:81 N 30 '87. T. Tobias
  The five rings
    N Y 20:137-8 Ap 27 '87. T. Tobias
  Goya: luz y sombra
    Dance Mag 61:75+ Ap '87. L. Kumin
  In the upper room
    N Y il 20:123 F 23 '87. T. Tobias
  Kindness
    Dance Mag 61:93-5 Ap '87. S. Sommer
  Kith and kin
    N Y il 20:100 My 18 '87. T. Tobias
  Land's edge
    N Y il 20:84 F 16 '87. T. Tobias
  Magnetic
    N Y il 20:137 Ap 27 '87. T. Tobias
  Multiple/choice crimes
    N Y 20:80 Ap 6 '87. T. Tobias
  Mythologies
    New Yorker 63:83-4 Je 8 '87. A. Croce
  New moon stories
    Dance Mag 61:26-8 Ap '87. C. Hardy
    New Leader 69:19 D 29 '86. L. A. Jacobs
  Newark
    N Y il 20:104 O 5 '87. T. Tobias
  No fire escape in hell
    Dance Mag 61:81-2 Mr '87. O. Stuart
  Portraits in reflection
    Theatre Crafts il 21:32-3+ F '87. C. Bush
  Presley pieces
    N Y il 20:155 D 7 '87. T. Tobias
  Roaratorio, an Irish circus on Finnegans wake
    Art Am il por 75:102-5 Ja '87. J. Johnston
    Dance Mag 61:80-1 F '87. E. Zimmer
  Rosas danst Rosas
    Dance Mag 61:36-7 Ap '87. N. V. Dalva
  Six dances
    New Leader 70:22 Jl 13-27 '87. L. A. Jacobs
  Stabat mater
    Dance Mag 61:35-6 Ap '87. J. R. Acocella
  Sunset
    New Yorker 63:75 Jl 6 '87. A. Croce
  Syzygy
    N Y 20:77 My 11 '87. T. Tobias
  Tamago netsu
    Dance Mag il 61:20+ Mr '87. S. Ueno
Dance schools
    See also
    School of American Ballet
China
    See also
    Beijing Dance Conservatory
Soviet Union
  Reviews:
    Washington, D.C. performance by Soviet students
    from the Perm State Ballet School. G. Jackson.
    Dance Mag 61:74+ S '87
Dance studios
  Tampa tower gives dance a boost [Tampa Ballet's dance
  studio in Ashley Tower] H. Ostlere. il *Dance Mag*
  61:14-15 F '87
Dance teachers
    See also
    Williams, Stanley
Certification
  Dance education certification: current status and
  significance. S. H. Gingrasso. bibl f *Des Arts Educ*
  89:31-5 S/O '87
Dance Theater Workshop
  David Parsons takes off. L. Friedman. il por *Vogue*
  177:46 Je '87
  Hold me tight [performances by T. Creach and S. Koester]
  T. Tobias. il *N Y* 20:81-2 N 30 '87
  Sixties in the eighties: programming the revolution [artistic
  director D. White] J. R. Acocella. il pors *Dance Mag*
  61:70-3 F '87

Stepping out [solo concert by S. Krieckhaus] T. Tobias.
  il *N Y* 20:110 Mr 2 '87
Dance Theatre of Harlem
  D.T.H. *New Yorker* 63:35-6 D 28 '87
  Reviews:
    Performances at Davis Hall, New York City. J.
    R. Acocella. *Dance Mag* 61:90-4 O '87
  Shall we dance? [performance of Fancy free] T. Tobias.
  il *N Y* 20:92-3 Mr 30 '87
Dance therapy
  Health: American Dance Therapy Association, a
  kinesthetic approach. A. Stark. il *Dance Mag* 61:56-7
  N '87
  Shall we dance? *Vogue* 177:260 Jl '87
A dancer on the bronze phoenix terrace [dance] *See* Dance
  reviews—Single works
Dancers
    See also
    Children as dancers
      See also names of dancers
  Dancescape. See issues of Dance Magazine
  Editors log. W. Como. See issues of Dance Magazine
  Presstime news. See issues of Dance Magazine
Attitudes
  The personal you: what you told us about yourself.
  M. Horosko. *Dance Mag* 61:70 S '87
Health and hygiene
  The personal you. M. Horosko. See issues of Dance
  Magazine
Nutrition
  The personal you: calcium—how much is enough? M.
  Horosko. il *Dance Mag* 61:78-9 Mr '87
Psychology
  The personal you: finding a balance [views of J. Kupers-
  smith] M. Horosko. il *Dance Mag* 61:52-5 Ag '87
Taxation
  Education [effect of new tax laws] M. Horosko. bibl
  il *Dance Mag* 61:107-9 Ja '87
Dancers, Handicapped
  A dancer's nightmare [S. Lavery] L. Leivick. il pors
  N Y Times Mag p66+ N 8 '87
Dancers [film] *See* Motion picture reviews—Single works
Dances (Balls) *See* Balls (Parties)
Danco, Léon A., 1923-
    about
  Passing on the dream. S. Nelton. il pors *Nations Bus*
  75:56-8 D '87
Dandois, Ariane
    about
  Global treasure trove. C. Vogel. il por *N Y Times Mag*
  p62-6 Mr 1 '87
Dandridge, Ray
    about
  Negro League star gets Hall of Fame surprise. il por
  Jet 71:46 Mr 23 '87
Dandridge, Ruby, d. 1987
    about
  Obituary
    Jet por 73:16 N 16 '87
Dandruff
  Dealing with dandruff. A. Kozlov. il *McCalls* 115:99
  N '87
Danforth, Douglas D.
    about
  Danforth picks his heirs. G. L. Miles and M. Rothman.
  Bus Week p26-7 Ag 10 '87
Danforth, John C.
  Should Congress approve the Fairness Doctrine? [excerpts
  from debate, April 21, 1987] *Congr Dig* 66:242+ O
  '87
  Should the proposed Product Liability Reform Act be
  approved? [excerpts from debate, September 17, 1986]
  Congr Dig 66:10+ Ja '87
    about
  The Danforth bill [with editorial comment by Phil
  Schilling] P. Gordon. il *Cycle* 38:7, 66-9+ N '87
Danger: memory! [drama] *See* Miller, Arthur, 1915-
Dangerous goods *See* Hazardous substances
Daniel, Ana
    about
  Hamptons homestead: the D. Ronald Daniels' converted
  barn. D. Harris. il *Archit Dig* 44:158-63 Je '87
Daniel, Charles W.
  (jt. auth) *See* Silberstein, Gary B., and Daniel, Charles
  W.
Daniel, D. Ronald
    about
  Guiding the flock. J. Merwin. il por *Forbes* 140:128
  O 19 '87
  Hamptons homestead: the D. Ronald Daniels' converted
  barn. D. Harris. il *Archit Dig* 44:158-63 Je '87

Daniel', Ĩŭlii, 1925-
about
What Yevgeny knew. D. Jameson. *New Repub* 196:39-41 Je 22 '87
Daniele, Graciela
about
Presley pieces [dance] Reviews
N Y il 20:155 D 7 '87. T. Tobias
Daniell, Robert F.
about
"Achieve or leave". H. Banks. por *Forbes* 140:344-5 Jl 13 '87
Finally, some new blood at the top. C. Leinster. il por *Fortune* 116:56 Ag 3 '87
UTC's diet hasn't been much help—yet. R. Mitchell. il por *Bus Week* p53 My 18 '87
Daniels, Barbara
about
No nonsense. T. Eckert, Jr. il pors *Opera News* 51:16-19 Ja 3 '87
Daniels, Billy
about
Billy Daniels doing well after heart bypass surgery. por *Jet* 73:60 O 12 '87
'Mr. Black Magic' singer Billy Daniels serenades Orange Bowl. il pors *Jet* 71:55-6 Ja 19 '87
Daniels, Eddie
about
Clarinetist for all seasons: Eddie Daniels. Z. Stewart. il pors *Down Beat* 54:23-4+ Je '87
Daniels, Elizabeth
Riddle of Gettysburg's vultures. il *Audubon* 89:82-4+ Ja '87
Daniels, Lacy, and others
Bacterial methanogenesis and growth from CO_2 with elemental iron as the sole source of electrons. bibl f il *Science* 237:509-11 Jl 31 '87
Daniëls, Pauline
about
Reviews:
No fixed abode, solo performance by P. Daniels in Utrecht. H. Klooss. *Dance Mag* 61:21 O '87
Daniels, Robert Vincent
Moscow's rubber Marx. il *New Leader* 70:5-7 D 28 '87
The Soviet Union at seventy. il *New Leader* 70:11-13 O 19 '87
Daniels, Stevie O.
Garden gate. See issues of Rodale's Organic Gardening beginning February 1987
Inside. See issues of Rodale's Organic Gardening beginning August 1985 through January 1987
Danielson, Romina
about
The enigmatic Passion Flower opens up. il pors *People Wkly* 28:47 Ag 10 '87
Daniloff, Nicholas
See also
Daniloff-Zakharov espionage case, 1986
Daniloff-Zakharov espionage case, 1986
I spy: how a Queens College student helped catch a KGB agent and set off a superpower showdown [L. Bhoge; cover story] M. Daly. il pors *N Y* 20:34-47 Ap 6 '87
The USSR and the press. P. Taubman. *Current* 291:28-33 Mr/Ap '87
Dann, Jack, and Dann, Jeanne Van Buren
The apotheosis of Isaac Rosen [fiction] *Omni* 9:113+ Je '87
Dannen, Fredric
MTV's great leap backward. il *Channels* 7:45-7 Jl/Ag '87
A Tisch is still a Tisch. il pors *Channels* 7:28-33 F '87
Danner, Braden
about
Sitting pretty in two hits on Broadway, Braden Danner looks like a waif of the future. V. Burns. il por *People Wkly* 27:87 Je 1 '87
Danner, Mark D.
The struggle for a democratic Haiti. il *N Y Times Mag* p38-42+ Je 21 '87
Dannie Heineman Prize *See* Physics—Awards
Danocrine *See* Danazol
Dansby, Mozella, d. 1987
about
Denied promotion, woman shoots supervisors and kills self in Atlanta. *Jet* 72:25 My 18 '87
Whispering hope. R. Weems. il *Ms* 16:40-1 D '87

Danson, Ted
about
Meet the new "Mr. Moms" [interview] K. Henderson. il pors *Redbook* 170:44+ N '87
Ted Danson leers again on Cheers [cover story] L. Rozen. il pors *People Wkly* 27:108-9+ My 11 '87
Who is the father of this baby? [interview] il pors *Good Housekeep* 205:106+ N '87
Dansource *See* Information storage and retrieval systems—Dance use
Dante, Joe
about
Innerspace [film] Reviews
Macleans 100:46 Jl 13 '87. L. O'Toole
N Y 20:51 Jl 20 '87. D. Denby
New Yorker 63:65 Jl 27 '87. P. Kael
Newsweek il 110:60 Jl 13 '87. D. Ansen
People Wkly il 28:10 Jl 20 '87. S. Haller
Time il 130:68-9 Jl 13 '87. R. Corliss
Dantley, Adrian
about
NBA star Dantley aids Hershey track program. *Jet* 72:48 Ag 3 '87
Danto, Arthur Coleman, 1924-
Addressing Gettysburg. il *Harpers* 275:36+ Jl '87
Art. See issues of The Nation beginning October 20, 1984
Art's grime and place [excerpt from address, May 1987] *Harpers* 275:13-14 S '87
On public art and the public interest. *Art News* 86:208 O '87
about
Post-history on parade. R. Krauss. *New Repub* 196:27-30 My 25 '87
Danto, Ginger
What becomes an artist most. il *Art News* 86:149-53 N '87
Danza, Tony
about
Tony Danza shows Who's the boss. E. Sherman. il pors *Ladies Home J* 104:52+ F '87
Danzberger, Jacqueline P., and others
School boards: the forgotten players on the education team. il *Phi Delta Kappan* 69:53-9 S '87
Dapping (Fishing)
The dap does it [dapping for trout] A. Jennings. il *Field Stream* 91:70-1+ Ap '87
D'Arby, Terence Trent
about
Terence Trent D'Arby makes American debut. M. Gilmore. il pors *Roll Stone* p17+ N 19 '87
Dare (Term)
Love that dare. W. Safire. il *N Y Times Mag* p10+ My 17 '87
Daresh, John C.
Support for beginning principals. *Educ Dig* 52:10-13 Ja '87
Darío, Rubén, 1867-1916
about
Stranded by politics and war: Nicaragua's loved, neglected poet. S. Kinzer. por *N Y Times Book Rev* 92:3 Ja 18 '87
Dark eyes [film] *See* Motion picture reviews—Single works
Dark glasses *See* Sunglasses
Dark matter (Astronomy)
The 'dark matter' problems. P. H. Andersen. *Phys Today* 40:34 Ap '87
Density determines destiny of the universe [work of Edwin Loh and Earl Spillar] *Astronomy* 15:78 F '87
Large-scale structure, streaming and galaxy formation. P. H. Andersen. bibl il *Phys Today* 40:19-21 O '87
Missing mass: what it's not. *Sky Telesc* 73:150 F '87
Probing cosmic geometry suggests the universe is flat [work of Edwin Loh and Earl Spillar] B. M. Schwarzschild. il *Phys Today* 40:17-20 My '87
Darkness
See also
Night
Darkroom equipment *See* Photography—Processing—Equipment
Darkroom technique in photography *See* Photography—Processing
Darkroom timers *See* Photography—Processing—Equipment
Darling, David J.
Star trek (I). il *Astronomy* 15:94-9 Mr '87
Star trek (II). il *Astronomy* 15:94-9 Ap '87
Darling, Grace
about
Grace Darling—the lighthouse heroine. J. Mitford. il por *Archit Dig* 44:30+ S '87

Darling, Ron
about
More than a media Darling. P. Gammons. il pors *Sports Illus* 66:56-8+ Ap 6 '87
Darling-Hammond, Linda, 1951-
Teacher "professionalization" versus democratic control. *Educ Dig* 53:15-17 S '87
Darman, Richard
And now for Ronald Reagan's finale. il *U S News World Rep* 103:31 D 28 '87-Ja 4 '88
Beyond tax populism. *Society* 24:35-8 S/O '87
Populism and tax reform. il *USA Today (Periodical)* 116:29-31 S '87
What's wrong with Japan bashing. il *U S News World Rep* 103:53-4 O 5 '87
about
Dick Darman calls it quits. E. Thomas. il por *Newsweek* 109:27 Ap 13 '87
Richard Darman: why he's joining the 'corpocracy' [interview] L. Walczak. il por *Bus Week* p36-7 Ap 13 '87
Darmstadt (Germany)
Historic houses, sites, etc.
Historic architecture: Joseph Maria Olbrich: a jugendstil design at the Mathildenhöhe artists' colony. J. Rykwert. il por *Archit Dig* 44:180-5+ Ap '87
Darmstadter, Joel, 1928-
Report on reports: Energy security: a report to the president of the United States. bibl f il *Environment* 29:25-7 Jl/Ag '87
Darr, Jack
Service clinic. See issues of Radio-Electronics through September 1987
Darrach, Brad
Meryl [cover story] il pors *Life* 10:72-4+ D '87
Darsee, John
about
Integrity of research papers questioned. B. J. Culliton. *Science* 235:422-3 Ja 23 '87
A long-disputed paper goes to press. M. Murray. il *Sci News* 131:52-3 Ja 24 '87
A soap opera for science. D. E. Chubin. bibl f *BioScience* 37:259-61 Ap '87
Dart, Richard Pousette- *See* Pousette-Dart, Richard, 1916-
Dart Drug Corp.
High yield, high risk [aftermath of 1984 Dart Drug leveraged buyout] P. Berman. il *Forbes* 140:38 Ag 24 '87
Dart Group Corporation
The Hafts may mean it [bid for Dayton Hudson] M. J. Pitzer. il *Bus Week* p37 O 5 '87
The most feared family in retailing [Haft family] B. Saporito. il *Fortune* 115:65-6+ Je 22 '87
Will Dart bag a grocer this time? [Supermarkets General] T. Ichniowski. *Bus Week* p35-6 Mr 23 '87
Dartmouth College
"Civility" for Dartmouth [new president J. Freedman] por *Time* 129:85 Ap 27 '87
'Safe sex' and the presence of the absence [safe sex kit] J. Hart. *Natl Rev* 39:43+ My 8 '87
Dartmouth College. Hood Museum of Art *See* Hood Museum of Art
Darts (Game)
Tournaments
Darts [champion S. Reitan] *New Yorker* 63:33-5 D 21 '87
Darwin, Charles, 1809-1882
about
The process whereby species originate [cover story] H. L. Carson. bibl il por *BioScience* 37:715-20 N '87
Darwin, Charles Robert *See* Darwin, Charles, 1809-1882
Darwinism *See* Evolution; Natural selection
Darwinism, Social *See* Social Darwinism
Darwisch, Tiffany *See* Tiffany
Das Furlines (Musical group)
When punk begins sounding passé, Das Furlines and other rockers prove they're not too proud to polka. M. Small. il *People Wkly* 28:71-2+ N 9 '87
Das Gupta, Chidananda, and Hoberman, J.
Pols of India. il pors *Film Comment* 23:20-4 My/Je '87
Dash, Robert, 1934-
A painter's garden. il *House Gard* 159:100-11 Ag '87
Dashboards, Automobile *See* Automobiles—Dashboards
DaSilva, Edgar J., and others
Rhizobium, the farmer's Mr. Fixit. il *Courier* 40:27-8 Mr '87
Dass, Ram *See* Ram Dass
Dassault Breguet Aviation (Avions Marcel)
Dassault-Breguet plans to cut 1,261 workers. *Aviat Week Space Technol* 127:25 O 26 '87

Dassault foresees problems in sales of new aircraft. il *Aviat Week Space Technol* 127:73+ S 28 '87
Dassault proposes Rafale program with 1996 service introduction. *Aviat Week Space Technol* 126:25 Ap 20 '87
French accelerate Falcon production. *Aviat Week Space Technol* 126:26-7 F 16 '87
Weak aircraft sales dictate new layoffs at Dassault-Breguet. *Aviat Week Space Technol* 127:127 O 12 '87
Data (Statistics) *See* Statistics
Data banks *See* Information storage and retrieval systems
Data base management *See* Information storage and retrieval systems—Management
Data base systems *See* Information storage and retrieval systems
Data buses *See* Computers—Buses
Data compression (Computer science)
Another approach to data compression [Basic programs explore the Nyquist sampling theorem] R. J. Sciamanda. il *Byte* 12:137-8+ F '87
Packing it in. I. Peterson. il *Sci News* 131:283-5 My 2 '87
Run-length encoding. D. Pountain. il *Byte* 12:317-20+ Je '87
Data General Corp.
Data General gets the call [deal with Japan's NTT] L. Helm and N. Gross. il *Bus Week* p96 O 19 '87
The new Data General is leaner—but is it meaner? L. Helm. il *Bus Week* p86+ Ag 17 '87
Data processing departments *See* Electronic data processing departments
Data processing personnel *See* Computer personnel
Data structures (Computer science)
See also
Hashing (Computer science)
Data structures in a bit-mapped text editor: how Carnegie-Mellon University displays text on the IBM RT PC. W. J. Hansen. il *Byte* 12:183-4+ Ja '87
Data structures in CAD software. L. Pfortmiller. il *Byte* 12:177-80+ Je '87
Dynamic memory allocation. A. Fernandes. il *Byte* 12:169-73 Ja '87
Recursion + data structures = anagrams. M. Morton. bibl il *Byte* 12:325-8+ N '87
RegionMaker [Macintosh program] H. Katz. il *Byte* 12:145-6+ Ja '87
Data tapes
See also
Masstor Systems Corporation
Central Point Software: the Option Board [COPY II PC tape backup] il *Radio-Electron* 58 ComputerDigest:87-8 O '87
Timely hard disk backup on floppies [Intelligent Backup] H.-J. Taferner. il *Pers Comput* 11:162 Ja '87
Data transmission systems
See also
American Telephone & Telegraph Co.
Communications satellites—Data transmission use
Communications software
Computer networks
Computerphones
Computers—Buses
Electronic data interchange
Electronic mail systems
Facsimile transmission
Integrated services digital network
Local area networks
MCI Communications Corp.
Offices—Automation
Packet switching (Data transmission)
Superconductors and superconductivity—Data transmission use
Teleconferencing
By land? By air? By sea? W. A. Kleinschrod. il *Work Woman* 12:82+ N '87
Date line, International *See* International date line
Date rape
Date rape: familiar strangers [study by Charlene L. Muehlenhard and Melaney A. Linton] J. Meer. *Psychol Today* 21:10 Jl '87
Too close to home. G. Witkin-Lanoil. il *Health* 19:6+ Ja '87
When the date turns into rape. J. Leo. il *Time* 129:77 Mr 23 '87
Date with an angel [film] See Motion picture reviews—Single works

Dates (History) *See* Chronology, Historical
Dating (Archeology) *See* Archeology—Methodology
Dating (Geology) *See* Geological time
Dating (Radioactive) *See* Radioactive dating
Dating (Social customs)
    See also
        Date rape
        Interracial dating
1 doll + 3 guys = dating complications. C. Rickey. *Mademoiselle* 93:70 Jl '87
Ask him out—stop the waiting game. il *Teen* 31:78 Ja '87
Ask me out—but ask me nice. B. Weber. *Mademoiselle* 93:159 Ag '87
Best & worst "first-date" restaurants. il *Glamour* 85:294 Ag '87
The business of dating: it's in the cards [use of business cards] S. Mernit. il *Work Woman* 12:91 Ap '87
Dating disasters: how to handle them. il *Teen* 31:52+ Ap '87
Dating games you can't win. D. Raffel. il *Seventeen* 46:72+ Ja '87
Group dating: safety—and fun—in numbers. S. Goodman. il *Curr Health 2* 14:12-13 D '87
A healthy interest. D. Elkind. il *Parents* 62:218 O '87
How to break a date. G. Waggoner. *Esquire* 107:24 Ja '87
It happened one date. D. Heyn. il *Mademoiselle* 93:158-67 D '87
Looking for Ms. Right: the black male side of the dating game. C. Whitaker. il *Ebony* 42:128+ S '87
Moonlight, violins, briefs, and bytes [dating contracts and computer dating] E. S. Cornish. il *Futurist* 21:2+ Ja/F '87
My best—and worst—date ever. L. F. McCarthy. il *Seventeen* 46:192+ Mr '87
The new rectangle [dating divorced fathers] L. Schnurnberger. il *Glamour* 85:240+ N '87
Onward Christian singles [questionnaire distributed by the Christian Dating Club] *Harpers* 274:22 Mr '87
Surviving the first date. il *Teen* 31:72 S '87
Understanding kids. L. Balter. il *Ladies Home J* 104:62 S '87
What couples should talk about before marriage. il *Jet* 72:14+ S 7 '87
        Anecdotes, facetiae, satire, etc.
The art of lite dating. S. Bird. il *Mademoiselle* 93:340+ S '87
How do you rate as a first date? R. Schulman. il *Mademoiselle* 93:118+ S '87
Dating (Social customs) by computer *See* Computers—Social use
Dating (Social customs) by videotape *See* Videotapes—Social aspects
Dating (Social customs) services
    See also
        Escorts (Dating service)
        Matchmaking
        Peace of Mind (Organization)
Paying for peace of mind [dating services offer screening tests for AIDS] J. Castro. il *Time* 129:26 My 11 '87
Profile of a New-Age date [dating services requiring screening tests for AIDS] G. Sikes. *Mademoiselle* 93:187+ Ag '87
DATs (Digital audio tape recorders and recording) *See* Digital audio tape recorders and recording
Datsun *See* Nissan Motor Co. Ltd.
Dau, Mary
Nudging the East into high technology. *World Press Rev* 34:51 Je '87
D'Aubuisson, Roberto
        about
Grave encounters. H. G. Chua-Eoan. il pors *Time* 130:32-4 D 7 '87
Dauch, Richard Eugene
        about
Lee Iacocca's production whiz. A. L. Taylor, III. il pors *Fortune* 115:36-8+ Je 22 '87
Daudet, Janyck
        about
Club Med's recipe for success: the chef de village. A. Dunkin. il por *Bus Week* p121 N 2 '87
Daugherty, Jack R.
        about
The pawn king. M. Gill. il por *Esquire* 108:52 Jl '87
Pawnshops strike gold. D. Pedersen. il por *Newsweek* 109:53 Mr 16 '87

Daugherty, Joe
        about
Tell the tooth! Dr. Joe Daugherty's rock repast may look filling, but it's a real jawbreaker. il por *People Wkly* 27:123 My 25 '87
Daugherty, Tracy
Low rider [story] *New Yorker* 63:40-8 N 23 '87
Daughters, Denny
        about
Denny Daughters, teenage shopkeeper, is a soft touch when it comes to helping blind customers. il por *People Wkly* 28:120 O 12 '87
Daughters and parents *See* Parent-child relationship
Daughtry, Sylvester
        about
First black police chief in Greensboro, N.C. is used to being a first. por *Jet* 72:12 Ap 13 '87
D'Aulaire, Emily
Our best friend. il por *Good Housekeep* 204:36+ F '87
(jt. auth) See D'Aulaire, Per Ola, and D'Aulaire, Emily
D'Aulaire, Per Ola, and D'Aulaire, Emily
60 billion burgers—and counting. il *Read Dig* 131:39-40+ D '87
Chain of circumstance. il *Read Dig* 131:143-8 D '87
Rescue in midair! il *Read Dig* 131:100-5 N '87
The Starduster's last flight. il *Read Dig* 131:75-80 Jl '87
D'Avanzo, Charlene
Inquiry in the undergraduate science classroom. *BioScience* 37:540 S '87
Davao City (Philippines)
They saw the future and it didn't work. R. Vokey. *Newsweek* 109:38-9 F 16 '87
Vigilantes resurgent [right wing Alsa Masa movement] D. Friesen. il *Progressive* 51:21-3 N '87
Davenport, John A., 1904-1987
        about
Obituary
    Natl Rev 39:21 Jl 3 '87. W. F. Buckley
Davenport, Lawrence F.
        about
Massie, Davenport get high level Energy Dept. posts. *Jet* 72:22 Je 15 '87
Davey, Jocelyn *See* Raphael, Chaim
Davey, Michael R.
(jt. auth) See Cocking, Edward C., and Davey, Michael R.
David, King of Israel
        about
David and the sin cycle. P. Yancey. *Christ Today* 31:32 Mr 6 '87
David, Hugh
Mediawatch. il *Hist Today* 37:4-5 Ap '87
Mediawatch. il *Hist Today* 37:4-5 Ja '87
Mediawatch. il *Hist Today* 37:6-8 Jl '87
Mediawatch. *Hist Today* 37:8-9 O '87
David, Irene
(jt. auth) See David, Lester, and David, Irene
David, Jay *See* Adler, Bill, 1929-
David, Leonard
America in space: where next? [cover story] il *Sky Telesc* 74:23-9 Jl '87
David, Lester
Caroline Kennedy at 30. il pors *McCalls* 114:14-15+ S '87
David, Lester, and David, Irene
How we can save our babies. il *Health* 19:29-31+ Ag '87
David, Walter W.
Investing for a brighter future [excerpt from 50 plus guide to retirement investing] il *50 Plus* 27:68+ Mr '87
Keep your estate safe for your family [excerpt from 50 plus guide to retirement investing] il *50 Plus* 27:68-73 Ap '87
David Dorfman Dance
Reviews:
    Performance at the Bessie Schönberg Theater, New York City. O. Stuart. *Dance Mag* 61:106-7 My '87
David Gordon/Pick Up Company
Reviews:
    Performances at Brooklyn Academy of Music. B. Newman. *Dance Mag* 61:29+ Ap '87
David K's (New York, N.Y.: Restaurant) *See* New York (N.Y.)—Restaurants, nightclubs, bars, etc.
David-Neel, Alexandra, 1868-1969
Psychic sports [excerpt from Mystiques et magiciens du Tibet] il por *Courier* 40:36-7 Ap '87

David Parsons Company
Reviews:
Performances at Bessie Schönberg Theater, New York City. S. Sommer. *Dance Mag* 61:77-8 D '87
David Sarnoff Research Center
GE gift-wraps a landmark lab [donating the Center to SRI International] O. Port. il *Bus Week* p35 F 16 '87
Davidovich, Bella
about
For pianist Bella Davidovich, Dmitry Sitkovetsky is more than just 'my son, the violinist'. D. Chu. il pors *People Wkly* 27:107-9 F 2 '87
Davidowitz, Esther
The history of makeup. il *Seventeen* 46:123-4+ Mr '87
"If I knew then, what I know now". il *Redbook* 170:100-3+ N '87
Davidson, Abraham A.
The wretched life and death of an 'American van Gogh'. il por *Smithsonian* 18:80-6+ D '87
Davidson, Bill, 1918-
All about nightmares. il *Seventeen* 46:40 Ja '87
Her life since Elvis: Priscilla Presley. il pors *McCalls* 145:12-14+ Mr '87
Our largest minority: Americans with handicaps [special section] il *McCalls* 114:61-8 S '87
Shedding light on lasers. il *McCalls* 115:90+ O '87
Davidson, Bruce, 1933-
Tongue lashing [photograph] il *Nat Hist* 96:92-3 Ja '87
Davidson, Carla
Steamboat on the upper Mississippi. il *Am Herit* 38:24+ Ap '87
Davidson, Cliff I., and others
Radioactive cesium from the Chernobyl accident in the Greenland ice sheet. bibl f maps *Science* 237:633-4 Ag 7 '87
Davidson, Donald
The Indy book of weird records. il *Mot Trend* 39:118-23+ Je '87
Davidson, Frank Paul, 1918-
about
Interview. D. Lessem. por *Omni* 9:80-2+ My '87
Davidson, Jean
Can faith survive a suicide in the family? il *U S Cathol* 52:16-21 N '87
Davidson, Margaret G.
High-flying Oshkosh. *Travel Holiday* 167:34+ Je '87
Davidson, Mark
Hope amid hopelessness: a conversation about arms control with Arvid Pardo. il por *USA Today (Periodical)* 115:26-8 Ja '87
"You've got a long way to go, baby": a conversation about the women's movement with Ruth Hubbard. por *USA Today (Periodical)* 116:92-5 S '87
Davidson, Mark
Anniversary [poem] il *Good Housekeep* 204:272 Ap '87
Davidson, Osha
Farms without farmers. il *Progressive* 51:25-7 Ag '87
Pentagon gives lifts to bosses. *Progressive* 51:14 Jl '87
Recruiters for peace. *Nation* 244:175-7 F 14 '87
Davidson, Paul
Whose debt crisis is it anyway? il *New Leader* 70:14-15 Ag 10-24 '87
Davidson, Sara
On tour with Rock Hudson. il *N Y Times Mag* p54+ My 3 '87
Davidson, Willard
about
Casting for a better bait. D. Young. il por *South Living* 22:138 My '87
Davie, Donald
North & south [poem] *Am Sch* 56:574-5 Aut '87
Davies, Jack L.
about
Pardon their French, but the first of American bubbly boasts a champagne worthy of the name. E. Levin. il pors *People Wkly* 28:113-14 D 21 '87
Davies, John K.
The extreme ultraviolet: a promising new window on the universe. il *Astronomy* 15:82-7 Jl '87
Davies, Laura
about
Muscling her way to the fore. D. Scheiber. il por *Sports Illus* 67:82 D 14 '87
A new force in the game. J. Diaz. il pors *Sports Illus* 67:66+ Ag 10 '87
Davies, M. Wyn
Like a John Wayne movie. *World Press Rev* 34:16 S '87

Davies, Norman
about
When historians judge their own. J. Wiener. il *Nation* 245:584-6+ N 21 '87
Davies, Owen
Addicted! *Health* 19:71-3+ Jl '87
Cyberwars. il *Omni* 9:76-8 Ja '87
Repair shop. il *Omni* 10:140 N '87
(jt. auth) See Braun, Frank, and Davies, Owen
Davies, P. C. W., 1946-
Particle physics for everybody [cover story] il *Sky Telesc* 74:582-7+ D '87
Davies, P. J., and others
Horizontal plate motion: a key allocyclic factor in the evolution of the Great Barrier Reef. bibl f il map *Science* 238:1697-700 D 18 '87
Davies, Paul See Davies, P. C. W., 1946-
Davies, Ray
about
Ray Davies. M. Small. il pors *People Wkly* 28:86-8+ Jl 6 '87
Ray Davies on film. L. Meredith. por *Stereo Rev* 52:94 Ag '87
Davies, Robert F.
Be a healthy traveller. il *World Health* p8-9 Mr '87
Davies, Robertson, 1913-
about
A master's sharp eye [interview] E. Seidner. il pors *Macleans* 100:8-9+ O 19 '87
Davies, William Robertson See Davies, Robertson, 1913-
Davis, Al
about
Al Davis: on the move again? il por *Bus Week* p34 Ag 10 '87
Al the bad. M. Lupica. il por *Esquire* 108:75-6+ O '87
Davis, Anthony
about
X [opera] Reviews
Down Beat 54:50 Ja '87. H. Mandel
Davis, Bernard David
Bacterial domestication: underlying assumptions. bibl f *Science* 235:1329+ Mr 13 '87
Davis, Bette, 1908-
Bette Davis talks back! [excerpt from This 'n that]; ed. by Michael Herskowitz. il pors *Redbook* 168:34+ Ap '87
about
Bette Davis is back, thank you, and will not be going gentle into anybody's damned good night. S. Haller. il pors *People Wkly* 28:62-4 N 2 '87
Grand old Lillian Gish makes a big splash in The whales of August. B. Darrach. il pors *People Wkly* 28:70-2+ D 14 '87
Davis, Carl
about
The sound of silents. D. Shaw. il por *N Y* 20:22 Mr 2 '87
Davis, Cheryl A.
A day on wheels. *Progressive* 51:34 N '87
Davis, Clifton
about
'Amen' star Clifton Davis denies TV guide story. por *Jet* 71:30 F 23 '87
A star is reborn. F. White, III. il pors *Ebony* 42:104+ F '87
Davis, Sir Colin
about
Enthusiastic response. P. G. Davis. il por *N Y* 20:114-15 O 5 '87
Davis, Cullen
about
The Davis boys won't go down without one more fight. T. Vogel. il pors *Bus Week* p108-9+ My 25 '87
Texas broke. L. M. Keefe. por *Forbes* 140 Sp Issue:8 O 26 '87
Davis, D. Jack
From research to practice. bibl f *Des Arts Educ* 88:15-20 My/Je '87
Davis, Damon
I've learned from my female boss; ed. by Julie Chenault. il por *Essence* 18:111 N '87
Davis, Dan M.
(jt. auth) See Sykes, Lynn R., and Davis, Dan M.
Davis, Debby
about
Debby Davis at Piezo Electric. H. Cotter. *Art Am* 75:151 Je '87

Davis, Don
about
Mr. Davis builds his dream house. P. Skalka. il por *Read Dig* 131:100-4 S '87
Davis, Douglas, 1933-
Late postmodern: the end of style. bibl f il *Art Am* 75:14-19+ Je '87
Davis, Eric
about
The Cincinnati Kid. J. Brosnan. il pors *Life* 10:78-81 Ag '87
Hailing the first Eric Davis. T. Callahan. il pors *Time* 129:73 My 18 '87
The Reds' menace. S. McManis. il por *Sport Mag* 78:22-4 Mr '87
Say hey! Is Eric Davis the next . . . C. Siebert. il pors *N Y Times Mag* p42+ My 3 '87
These are Red letter days [cover story] R. Wiley. il pors *Sports Illus* 66:36-8+ My 25 '87
Warm-up for a hot career. P. Axthelm. il pors *Newsweek* 109:88 My 18 '87
Davis, Flora
News. See issues of Mademoiselle
Davis, Francis
Creator by proxy. il *Atlantic* 259:83-5 F '87
Large-scale jazz. il *Atlantic* 260:76-7 Ag '87
West Coast ghost. il *Atlantic* 260:97-9 O '87
Davis, George E., and others
Human amnion membrane serves as a substratum for growing axons in vitro and in vivo. bibl f il *Science* 236:1106-9 My 29 '87
Davis, Gwen
The private pain of infertility. il por *N Y Times Mag* p106+ D 6 '87
Davis, Hardge, Jr.
about
First black named deputy surrogate in New Jersey. *Jet* 72:8 Ag 31 '87
Davis, Henry Fuller
about
Twelve-foot Davis's revenge. P. C. Newman. *Macleans* 100:44-5 O 12 '87
Davis, Howard
about
You ready, Boom Boom? P. Putnam. il por *Sports Illus* 66:96 My 11 '87
Davis, J. Morton
about
Blair's Morty Davis: the prince of going public. P. Finch. il por *Bus Week* p176+ N 2 '87
Davis, J. P.
Confessions of a leg man. il *Glamour* 85:142-3 Jl '87
The erotic art of undressing. il *Glamour* 85:206-7+ D '87
What men really want from women in bed. il *Glamour* 85:178-9+ Ja '87
Davis, James Kotsilibas- See Kotsilibas-Davis, James
Davis, Jerry B.
Fighting teacher isolation. *Educ Dig* 52:27-9 My '87
Davis, Jimmie
about
Morehouse quarterback, 19, has straight A's; majors in math, engineering, physics. D. M. Cheers. il pors *Jet* 73:52-4 D 7 '87
Davis, Joann, and Goldstein, William
Trade news. See issues of Publishers Weekly
Davis, Joe, 1957?-
about
Extraterrestrials in Alphabetland. G. Henry. il por *Art News* 86:17 My '87
Davis, Joel
Interview [L. E. Hood, developer of automated DNA sequencer] il por *Omni* 10:116-18+ N '87
Davis, John C.
Contour mapping and SURFACE II. bibl f il *Science* 237:669-72 Ag 7 '87
Davis, Kenneth, Jr.
about
The Davis boys won't go down without one more fight. T. Vogel. il pors *Bus Week* p108-9+ My 25 '87
Davis, L. J. (Lawrence J.)
The next panic: fear and trembling on Wall Street. il *Harpers* 274:35-9+ My '87
William Simon's Pacific overtures. il pors *N Y Times Mag* p14-17+ D 27 '87
Davis, Lawrence J. See Davis, L. J. (Lawrence J.)
Davis, Lorraine
Between us. See issues of Vogue

Davis, Louzon
about
Boy, 9, clad in underwear, rescues 6 sisters, brothers from fire on 22-degree night. il por *Jet* 71:40 F 16 '87
Davis, Martin S.
about
Can a tough boss mellow? M. J. Williams. il pors *Fortune* 116:105+ D 21 '87
Gulf & Western: from grab bag to lean, mean, marketing machine. D. Lieberman. il *Bus Week* p152-3+ S 14 '87
Davis, Marvin
about
Atlantic City roulette. J. Crudele. il pors *N Y* 20:24 My 18 '87
Marvin Davis wants back into Tinseltown. R. Grover. por *Bus Week* p64 D 7 '87
Davis, Mary B.
The churches and the peace movement in France. il *Christ Century* 104:826-8 S 30 '87
Davis, Michael, 1956-
about
Michael Davis at Art Galaxy. S. Tillim. il *Art Am* 75:126 Jl '87
Davis, Miles
about
Marcus Miller: Miles' man in the studio. B. Milkowski. il pors *Down Beat* 54:20-2 F '87
Miles Davis' solo on Tutu—a trumpet transcription. B. Bergstein. il *Down Beat* 54:51 My '87
Davis, Millard C.
Summer at Windmill Point. il *Conservationist* 42:2-5 Jl/Ag '87
Davis, Murphy
about
The angel of death row. R. Chepesiuk. por *Progressive* 51:14 My '87
Davis, Nancy
about
Not necessarily the First Lady. J. Wiener. *Nation* 245:337 O 3 '87
Davis, Natalie Zemon, 1928-
about
The hot History Department. M. Silk. il pors *N Y Times Mag* p42-3+ Ap 19 '87
Davis, Paul, 1938-
about
The first sign of a Wimsey. B. Weber. il por *N Y Times Mag* p62 Ag 30 '87
Paul Davis. S. DiLauro. il *Am Artist* 51:48-53 Ja '87
Davis, Peter, 1937-
Exploring the kingdom of AIDS. il *N Y Times Mag* p32-6+ My 31 '87
Managua is waiting [excerpt from Where is Nicaragua?] il *Esquire* 107:171-4+ Mr '87
about
If it's Tuesday, this must be Managua. C. Lane. *Wash Mon* 19:48-51 Je '87
Davis, Peter G.
Jimmy's Met. il por *N Y* 20:52-4+ Ap 20 '87
The man Turandot finished. il por *Opera News* 51:14-17 Mr 28 '87
Music. See issues of New York
Saying it all. *Opera News* 51:12 F 14 '87
Davis, Reyn
Little by little . . . il *Sports Illus* 66:54-5 Mr 2 '87
Davis, Robert
Retrofitting the sixties: taking the temperature of your theatre. il *Theatre Crafts* 21:36-9 Ja '87
Davis, Robert C.
Let's be careful out there. *Psychol Today* 21:10 Ag '87
Davis, Rodney M., d. 1967
about
Navy commissions 1st war war ship named for a black medal of honor winner. il por *Jet* 72:38 Je 1 '87
Davis, Sammi
about
Luck, love and lots of nerve make Hope and glory's Sammi Davis the cat's meow of British bombshells. M. Dougherty. il pors *People Wkly* 28:142-4 N 30 '87
Davis, Sammy, Jr.
about
Dr. A.E. Smith installed as S.C. State president; Sammy Davis gives speech. il pors *Jet* 72:29 Mr 30 '87
Sammy and Frank treat L.A. to rare duo performances. il pors *Jet* 72:55 S 21 '87
Sammy brings Broadway to Newark for fundraiser. il pors *Jet* 72:53 Je 8 '87

Davis, Sammy, Jr.—about—*cont.*

Sammy Davis among five Kennedy Center honorees. *Jet* 73:60 O 12 '87

Sammy Davis and Jerry Lewis star on telethon to fight muscular dystrophy [cover story] il pors *Jet* 72:60-1 S 7 '87

Sammy Davis, Frank Sinatra, Dean Martin together again for historic concert tour. il pors *Jet* 73:36 D 21 '87

Sammy Davis gets Kennedy Center Honor for Christmas. il por *Jet* 73:55 D 28 '87-Ja 4 '88

Sammy Davis Jr. saluted at Black Filmmakers' weekend. il pors *Jet* 71:12-13 Mr 16 '87

Sammy Davis refuses to cross line of pickets. *Jet* 72:10 Ag 31 '87

Teaming up in the new Vegas. C. Leerhsen. pors *Newsweek* 109:83 Ap 13 '87

Davis, Scott
about
Scott Davis at Laurie Rubin. E. Saxon. il *Art Am* 75:180-1 O '87

Davis, T. Cullen *See* Davis, Cullen

Davis, Tami R., and Lynn-Jones, Sean M.
"Citty upon a hill". bibl f *Foreign Policy* 66:20-38 Spr '87

Davis, Walter
about
Suns' Walter Davis seeks to build drug clinic. *Jet* 73:50 O 12 '87

Davis, William, d. 1987
about
Obituary
    Jet 71:18 Ja 26 '87

Davis, William C.
The detonation of explosives. bibl (p128) *Sci Am* 256:106-12 My '87

Davis (Rodney M.) (Warship) *See* Rodney M. Davis (Warship)

Davis (Russel) Planetarium *See* Russel Davis Planetarium

Davis (Sammy Jr.) National Liver Institute *See* Sammy Davis Jr. National Liver Institute

Davis Mountains (Tex.)
An Old West autumn. D. Young. il *South Living* 22:38+ O '87

Davison, James E.
Organ donation: giving the gift of life. il *Christ Century* 104:1146-8 D 16 '87

Daviss, Bennett
World of funnies is 'warped with fancy, woofed with dreams'. bibl (p271) il *Smithsonian* 18:180-3+ N '87

Davitz, Lois Leiderman
Why men divorce. *McCalls* 145:26+ Mr '87

Davitz, Michael A., and others
A glycan-phosphatidylinositol-specific phospholipase D in human serum. bibl f il *Science* 238:81-4 O 2 '87

Davos (Switzerland)
The magic mountains of Davos. N. Howe. il *Skiing* 39:66-72 Ja '87

Daw, Leila
about
Leila Daw. M. King. il *Art News* 86:31 Ap '87
Leila Daw at Atrium. J. Frueh. il *Art Am* 75:133 Jl '87

Dawat (New York, N.Y.: Restaurant) *See* New York (N.Y.)—Restaurants, nightclubs, bars, etc.

Dawber, Pam
about
Dawber hits the Mark! F. A. Bernstein. il pors *People Wkly* 27:44-6+ Mr 2 '87
Pam Dawber: "I'm traditional about marriage" [interview] S. Russell. il pors *Redbook* 168:20+ Ap '87
Pam Dawber: what, a producer too? H. Yorkshire. il pors *McCalls* 114:83-4+ Je '87

Dawdling *See* Procrastination

Dawidowicz, Lucy S.
The curious case of Marek Edelman. *Commentary* 83:66-9 Mr '87
Poles and Jews [discussion of March 1987 article, The curious case of Marek Edelman] *Commentary* 84:2-4+ Ag '87

Dawkins, Darryl
about
Darryl Dawkins tells his story in new book. por *Jet* 72:50 Ap 13 '87
Police probe mystery death of Dawkins' wife. pors *Jet* 73:8 N 16 '87

Dawkins, Kelly Barnes, d. 1987
about
Police probe mystery death of Dawkins' wife. pors *Jet* 73:8 N 16 '87

Dawkins, Pete
Integrity and trust [address, January 21, 1987] *Vital Speeches Day* 53:344-7 Mr 15 '87

Dawson, Andre
about
A bargain at any price. B. Anderson. il por *Sports Illus* 66:36-7 Je 15 '87
Bell, Dawson, capture baseball's MVP Awards. pors *Jet* 73:17 D 7 '87
Cubs' dismal finish may dim Dawson's MVP hopes. il por *Jet* 73:50 O 19 '87
The last laugh. D. Whitford. il pors *Sport Mag* 78:16-18+ D '87
An MVP (boo) and lights (sigh) for the Cubs. P. Gammons. il por *Sports Illus* 67:18 N 30 '87
My quarrel with Andre: a hit with bosses? J. McCormick. il *Newsweek* 110:76 O 5 '87
No Series for the Cubbies, but at least they have Andre the Awesome. J. Friedman. il pors *People Wkly* 28:121-2 O 5 '87

Dawson, Bertrand Edward *See* Dawson of Penn, Bertrand Edward Dawson, 1st Viscount, 1864-1945

Dawson, Carol G.
Buying safe for your baby. il *Consum Res Mag* 70:33-4 S '87

Dawson, Doug
about
Man down on the field. J. D. Miller. il *Sport Mag* 78:102 Ag '87

Dawson International Ltd.
Branding a success [Dawson International's P. Kemp now running J.E. Morgan] L. Gubernick. por *Forbes* 139:91 Ja 26 '87

Dawson of Penn, Bertrand Edward Dawson, 1st Viscount, 1864-1945
about
Was the king murdered? K. Slack. *Christ Century* 104:6-7 Ja 7-14 '87

Daxor Corporation
Seeing red. S. N. Chakravarty. il por *Forbes* 139:76+ Je 1 '87

Day, Ken
Canadian conundrum. por *Space World* X-8-284:40 Ag '87

Day, Nancy R.
A clearing-house for Victorian crafts [cover story] il *Americana* 15:36-41 Mr/Ap '87
A gold country Christmas. il map *Americana* 15:32-7 N/D '87

Day, Samuel H., Jr.
Be your own peacemaker. il *Progressive* 51:17-18 Ap '87
Before we cheer. *Progressive* 51:14-15 N '87

Day, Walter A.
about
If your school's most (or least) likely succeeded, hang on to that mildewed yearbook—it's golden. il *People Wkly* 27:110-11 Je 1 '87

Day care
See also
California Child Care Initiative
Play groups
Can the 'abused' kids be believed? [McMartin Preschool trial] T. Gest. il *U S News World Rep* 103:10 Jl 27 '87
Caring about child care [cover story; with list of resources] K. Rubin. bibl il *Ms* 15:31-6+, 60+ Mr '87
The child-care dilemma [cover story; special section] il *Time* 129:54-60+ Je 22 '87
Child care issues [report of Population Reference Bureau, Inc.] *Child Today* 16:3-4 My/Je '87
Child care: the bottom line [report by AT&T] *Child Today* 16:3 Jl/Ag '87
Child-care workers speak up. J. Marzollo. il *Parents* 62:114-16+ Ap '87
Crisis in child care. J. Shannon. il *Health* 19:29-31+ O '87
Day-care considerations. K. Karlsrud and D. Schultz. il *Parents* 62:198 My '87
The day care dilemma: from infants to pre-teens. M. Frank and M. E. Lang. il *USA Today (Periodical)* 115:59-62 My '87
Day care's unfair burden [report of Center for Public Advocacy Research, Inc.] *Child Today* 16:4 My/Je '87
Daycare for sick children. D. M. Topolnicki. il *Good Housekeep* 205:245 N '87
Executive guilt: who's taking care of the children? F. S. Chapman. il *Fortune* 115:30-7 F 16 '87
Family day care dos and don'ts. C. Loomis. il *Parents* 62:17 Ja '87

Day care—*cont.*
  Finding quality child care. C. Loomis. il *Parents* 62:15
    Ag '87
  For-profit vs. not-for-profit. G. G. Morgan. il *Parents*
    62:108-9 Ap '87
  For working parents with a sick child, hospital day
    care centers may spell instant relief [Sick Bay in Oak
    Park, Ill.] D. Grogan. il *People Wkly* 28:63+ Jl 13
    '87
  Good grades for day-care [IQ tests and infant-mother
    bond; studies by Margaret Burchinal] R. J. Moss.
    il *Psychol Today* 21:20 F '87
  Helping your child learn [excerpt from The parents'
    guide to daycare] J. A. Miller and S. Weissman. *Work
    Woman* 12:146+ Mr '87
  House rules for care-givers. B. Holcomb. il *Parents* 62:56+
    My '87
  How to keep your kids safe [protection against sexual
    abuse] M. Jacobbi and R. Wright. *McCalls* 114:95-6
    F '87
  Improving your child's day care. E. Klavan. il *Parents*
    62:68+ N '87
  Infectious disease in day care. *Child Today* 16:4-5 Ja/F
    '87
  Massachusetts spotlights day care. il *Child Today* 16:2-3
    Mr/Ap '87
  Md. day care center owner gets 10 yrs. for child abuse
    [S. A. Craig] *Jet* 73:37 O 19 '87
  Men and child care: the plot thickens [child molesting
    accusations] S. Miller. il por *Ms* 16:54-6 O '87
  Preschool children in the public schools: good investment?
    Or bad? D. B. Strother. bibl f il *Phi Delta Kappan*
    69:304-8 D '87
  Quality day-care and social growth [study by Deborah
    Phillips and others] B. Bower. *Sci News* 132:54-5 Jl
    25 '87
  Second thoughts about infant day care. A. Levine. il
    U S News World Rep 102:73-4 My 4 '87
  Sex abuse in preschool: fears and facts. F. Roberts.
    il *Parents* 62:52 O '87
  Substitute parents can be beneficial [views of Rebecca
    New and Jaipaul Roopnarine] *USA Today (Periodical)*
    115:10-11 Ap '87
  Three generations of love [Foster Grandparents work
    in child care center for teenage parents in Detroit,
    Mich.] N. Walls. il *Aging* no355:2-5 '87
  "What's a smart woman like you doing at home?" [search
    for child care; excerpt] L. Burton. il *Read Dig*
    131:29-30+ O '87
  Where's mommy? The great debate over the effects
    of day care. B. Holcomb. il *N Y* 20:72-8+ Ap 13
    '87
  Who's minding the kids? [results of survey] il *Parents*
    62:106-10+ Ap '87
      Anecdotes, facetiae, satire, etc.
  Minutes of the parents' meeting. R. H. Bell. *Commonweal*
    114:582-3 O 23 '87
      Chain and franchise operations
    See also
    Kinder-Care Learning Centers Inc.
    Kinderberry Hill (Firm)
    Sleepy Hollow Educational Centers
      Federal aid
  Project Day-care [views of E. F. Zigler] R. J. Trotter.
    bibl (p63) il pors *Psychol Today* 21:32-8 D '87
  Who will mind the children? A. C. Lewis. *Phi Delta
    Kappan* 69:252-3 D '87
      International aspects
  Children of the world. il *Time* 129:60 Je 22 '87
      Laws and regulations
  Child care: a national crisis. D. C. Ruffin. il *Black
    Enterp* 18:33 O '87
  Day care regulation: serving children or bureaucrats?
    K. Lehrman and J. Pace. *USA Today (Periodical)*
    115:63-6 My '87
      Canada
  Budgeting for Canadian babies. D. Cohen. por *Macleans*
    100:9 Mr 30 '87
  The long wait for day care. M. McIver. il *Macleans*
    100:50 N 16 '87
  The new day care policy. M. Clark. il por *Macleans*
    100:14+ D 14 '87
  Taking care of the kids. il *Macleans* 100:8-9 Ap 13
    '87
Day care and industry
    See also
    California Child Care Initiative
  Child care: get the ball rolling at work. il *Glamour*
    85:95 Ap '87

Corporate child care: playpens in the boardroom or
  productivity investment? [Hoffmann-La Roche Inc.]
  L. Silverman. il *USA Today (Periodical)* 115:67-9 My
  '87
Family ties: the day-care center a TV show built [G.
  D. Goldberg and Paramount studio's day care center]
  N. Gittelson. il *McCalls* 114:61-4 Ag '87
Who's minding the children? J. L. Greene. il *Black
  Enterp* 17:106+ F '87
Day care and the military
  'The Second Beast of Revelation' [M. A. Aquino of
    the Army Reserve accused of child molestation at
    the day care center at Presidio Army Base, Calif.]
    J. Adler. il por *Newsweek* 110:73 N 16 '87
Day care for the aged
  Day care for the elderly. H. Manley. *Good Housekeep*
    204:214 Je '87
  Finding day care for your aging parent. C. Siler. il
    Money 16:199-200+ D '87
Day lilies *See* Daylilies
Day of Judgment *See* Judgment Day
Day of Solidarity with South African Political Prisoners
  Day of Solidarity with South African Political Prisoners
    observed; immediate release of all such detainees asked.
    il *UN Chron* 22:14-15 N/D '85
Dayco Corp.
  "The most corrupt person" [fabricating fraudulent Soviet
    orders for goods made by Dayco; case of E. Reich]
    N. J. Perry. por *Fortune* 116:93 Ag 17 '87
Daydreams *See* Children's fantasies; Fantasy
Daylight
  Formed to light: thirteen projects by Gunnar Birkerts
    [daylighting design] D. Rastorfer. il *Archit Rec* 175:141-9
    Mr '87
Daylight saving
      Colorado
  Time out for clear air [using daylight-saving time year
    round to improve Denver's air] B. Most. *Pop Sci*
    231:115 N '87
Daylilies
  A summer glory garden based on daylilies. M. M.
    Brandies. il *Flower Gard* 31:24-5+ Je/Jl '87
Days
    See also
    Birthdays
    Monday
The days and nights of Molly Dodd [television program]
  See Television program reviews—Single works
Days Inns Corp.
  Days Inns could turn out to be a sleeper. C. Farrell.
    il *Bus Week* p69 F 2 '87
Dayton (Ohio)
      Bookstores
    See Booksellers and bookselling—Ohio
      Newspapers
    See also
    Dayton Newspapers, Inc.
      Politics and government
  Richard Dixon second black mayor in Dayton, Ohio.
    il por *Jet* 71:14 Mr 23 '87
Dayton Ballet Company
  Dayton Ballet to shine for golden anniversary. W. Salis-
    bury. il *Dance Mag* 61:7 S '87
Dayton-Hudson Corp.
  Dayton Hudson: a 16-year winning streak is over. M.
    J. Pitzer. il *Bus Week* p38-9 Mr 16 '87
  Free gifts [Minnesota passes anti-takeover measure] J.
    K. Glassman. *New Repub* 197:10+ Jl 27 '87
  The Hafts may mean it [bid for Dayton Hudson] M.
    J. Pitzer. il *Bus Week* p30 O 5 '87
  Hey Wall Street, wanna buy the Brooklyn Bridge?
    [takeover hoax surrounding Dayton Hudson shows
    market's vulnerability to rumor] G. Weiss. il por *Bus
    Week* p31 Jl 6 '87
Dayton Newspapers, Inc.
  Dayton Newspapers Inc. names asst. business mgr. [K.
    G. Milton] por *Jet* 73:25 O 5 '87
Daytona 500 *See* Automobile racing
Daytona Beach (Fla.)
      Crime
  Fla. man who used child for drug deal collateral jailed
    [case of F. W. Cook] *Jet* 71:32 F 23 '87
      Galleries and museums
    See also
    Museum of Arts and Sciences (Daytona Beach, Fla.)
      Sports
  The dawn of speed [origins of auto racing] B. R. Kimes.
    il *Am Herit* 38:92-4+ N '87
Daytona Speed Week *See* Motorcycle racing
dBase (Data base management systems) *See* Information
  storage and retrieval systems—Management

dB's (Musical group)
The dB's try again. M. McCormick. il *Roll Stone* p23 D 3 '87
DCPTA (Dichlorophenoxy-triethylamine) *See* Ethylamines
De Acuña, Cristóbal *See* Acuña, Cristóbal de, 1597-1676?
De Alfaro, Luis Felipe Neri *See* Alfaro, Luis Felipe Neri de
De Angelis, Barbara
Are you losing each other? [excerpt from How to make love all the time] *McCalls* 114:88 F '87
Seven truths about sex [condensed from How to make love all the time] *Read Dig* 131:127-30 Ag '87
De Angelo, Michael P.
about
Buy cheap. C. Siler. il por *Forbes* 140:109 Jl 27 '87
De Anza College. California History Center
Political quilts. il *Sunset* 178:40-1 Mr '87
De Balzac, Honoré *See* Balzac, Honoré de, 1799-1850
De Banfield, Raffaello, 1922-
about
Decoration for a dynasty. W. Weaver. il *House Gard* 159:100-11+ F '87
De Barbin, Lucy
about
Daughters of the King? D. Chu. il pors *People Wkly* 27:28-31 Je 22 '87
A hot property. L. Fleischer. *Publ Wkly* 231:69 Mr 13 '87
De Barbin, Lucy, and Matera, Dary
Are you lonesome tonight? [excerpt] il pors *Redbook* 169:106-8+ Jl '87
De Bartolo, Edward J., Jr.
about
At Zayre, the skies were just starting to clear. C. Brown. *Bus Week* p59-60 O 19 '87
De Beaumarchais, Pierre Augustin Caron *See* Beaumarchais, Pierre Augustin Caron de, 1732-1799
De Benedetti, Carlo
about
Conglomeration Italian style. S. Solomon. il por *Forbes* 139:36-8 Mr 23 '87
Dealmaker De Benedetti [cover story] W. C. Symonds. il pors *Bus Week* p42-7 Ag 24 '87
More rabbits, please, Signor De Benedetti. S. Solomon. por *Forbes* 139:114+ Mr 9 '87
Olivetti's global deal maker. P. C. Newman. il por *Macleans* 100:51 N 30 '87
De Blasi, Anthony J.
The lure of the camellia. il *Flower Gard* 32:50-2 D '87/Ja '88
Tree peonies. il *Flower Gard* 31:70-1+ Ap/My '87
De Blij, Harm J.
African wine frontiers. il *Focus* 37:37 Fall '87
Vintage years and wine futures. *Focus* 37:36 Summ '87
Wines of the Southeast. *Focus* 37:36 Spr '87
De Borchgrave, Arnaud
about
Underdog to an 800-pound gorilla. L. Zuckerman. il por *Time* 129:64-5 Je 15 '87
De Borondy, Laszlo
about
For sale: the Gloved One's cast-off main squeeze. il por *People Wkly* 27:88 My 25 '87
De Botton, Gilbert
about
A confident British 'fundamentalist'. R. A. Melcher. il por *Bus Week* p154-5 D 28 '87-Ja 4 '88
De Brantes, Paul *See* Brantes, Paul de, marquis
De Brantes, Sue *See* Brantes, Sue de, marquise
De Broglie, Jeanne-Marie *See* Broglie, Jeanne-Marie de
De Broglie, Louis *See* Broglie, Louis de, 1892-1987
De Camargo Penteado, Sebastião Ferraz *See* Camargo Penteado, Sebastião Ferraz de
De Caro, Chuck
The zap gap. il *Atlantic* 259:24+ Mr '87
De Carvalho, Otelo Saraiva *See* Carvalho, Otelo Saraiva de
De Castelbajac, Kate *See* Castelbajac, Kate de
De Clavière d'Hust, Bernard *See* Clavière d'Hust, Bernard de, Count
De Dubovay, Diane
Dr. Robert Schuller: TV's minister of hope. il pors *McCalls* 114:44+ Ap '87
Pierce Brosnan. il pors *McCalls* 114:148-50+ Jl '87
Robert Wagner: Hollywood's incurable romantic. il pors *McCalls* 145:158+ Mr '87
De Geer, Annette
about
She sells springboks by the seashore. T. Ryan. il por *Sierra* 72:17 Ja/F '87

De Gennes, Pierre-Gilles
Bubbles. il *Phys Today* 40:7+ Jl '87
De Gregorio, Domenico
The new world of artificial intelligence. il *Courier* 40:14-15 Jl '87
De Havilland Aircraft of Canada, Limited *See* DeHavilland Aircraft of Canada, Limited
De Hemptinne, Marc *See* Hemptinne, Marc de, 1902-1986
De Jonge, Peter
The golfing machine. por *N Y Times Mag* p88+ Ap 5 '87
De Jonquieres, Guy *See* Jonquieres, Guy de
De Keersmaeker, Anne Teresa *See* Keersmaeker, Anne Teresa de
De Koenigsberg, Paula
about
Rate it X [film] Reviews
Christ Today il pors 31:64 Mr 6 '87. S. Ulstein
De Kwiatkowski, Henry K.
about
Back country Greenwich. S. M. L. Aronson. il *House Gard* 159:132-9+ Ag '87
De la Chaume, Jacqueline Thion *See* Chaume, Jacqueline Thion de la
De la Madrid Hurtado, Miguel *See* Madrid Hurtado, Miguel de la
De Lacy, Justine
The sexy computer. il *Atlantic* 260:18+ Jl '87
De Lafayette, Gilbert *See* Lafayette, Gilbert de
De Lara, Reyes *See* Lara, Reyes de
De Laurentiis, Dino
about
Dino De Laurentiis needs a hit—and fast. R. Grover. il por *Bus Week* p130-1 N 2 '87
Tar Heel Tinseltown: De Laurentiis does it in North Carolina. D. Myers and D. Ewing. il *Theatre Crafts* 21:53-4 Ap '87
De Laurentiis Entertainment Group
Dino De Laurentiis needs a hit—and fast. R. Grover. il por *Bus Week* p130-1 N 2 '87
De Lena Fialco, Diane *See* Fialco, Diane De Lena
De Liagre, Christina *See* Liagre, Christina de
De' Liguori, Alfonso Maria *See* Liguori, Alfonso Maria de', Saint, 1696-1787
De Lozanne, Arturo, and Spudich, James A.
Disruption of the Dictyostelium myosin heavy chain gene by homologous recombination. bibl f il *Science* 236:1086-91 My 29 '87
De Lucia, Fernando, 1860-1925
about
Twin glories (I). W. Crutchfield. il pors *Opera News* 52:10-13 D 19 '87
De Malleray, Pierre *See* Malleray, Pierre de
De Mayo, Cathy
Orange County: a place in the sun. il *Horizon* 30:56-62+ Ja/F '87
De' Medici, Lorenza *See* Medici, Lorenz de'
De Mejo, Oscar, 1911-
"I'll call this land Virginia". il *Am Herit* 38:49-57 F/Mr '87
De Mello, Anthony, 1931-1987
The temple bells [excerpt from The song of the bird] *America* 157:449 D 12 '87
about
"Tell us," they asked, "what is God like?" An appreciation of Tony de Mello, S.J. [cover story] T. H. Stahel. *America* 157:446-50 D 12 '87
De Melo Neto, João Cabral *See* Melo Neto, João Cabral de, 1920-
De Menil, Dominique
about
A gift of vision. R. Bernier. il por *House Gard* 159:120-9+ Jl '87
De Menil Collection (Houston, Tex.)
Chez Dominique. K. Larson. il *N Y* 20:52-3 Jl 13 '87
Dream museum. B. Rose. il *Vogue* 177:222-5+ Je '87
How to start a museum. R. Hughes. il *Time* 130:48-50 Ag 10 '87
In the neighborhood of art. R. Banham. il *Art Am* 75:124-9 Je '87
Menil Collection: the power of modesty. K. Gregor. il *Art News* 86:31-2 S '87
A quiet place for art. M. Filler. il *House Gard* 159:74+ Jl '87
De Mille, Agnes
De Mille on Tudor [address, December 6, 1986] *Dance Mag* 61:42 My '87

De Mille, Cecil B., 1881-1959
about
Historic houses: Cecil B. De Mille: family scenario for a Hollywood legend. M. Webb. il por *Archit Dig* 44:144-53+ Mr '87
De Mola, Yolanda T.
Let's get rid of 'minority'. *America* 157:284-5 O 31 '87
De Mornay, Rebecca
about
Spring—hot for dots. il pors *Harpers Bazaar* 120:200-3 F '87
De Mota, Atico Vilas-Boas *See* Mota, Atico Vilas-Boas da
De Niro, Robert, 1945?-
about
De Niro as Capone: the magnificent obsessive. J. Kroll. il por *Newsweek* 109:64-5 Je 22 '87
De Nora, Vittoria
about
Did Bricker give a little too much help to a friend? T. Mason. *Bus Week* p79 F 16 '87
De Oliveira, Paulo *See* Colina, Paulo
De Palma, Brian
Brian De Palma's guilty pleasures. il por *Film Comment* 23:52-3 My/Je '87
about
Brian De Palma. J. Jerome. il pors *People Wkly* 27:72-6+ Je 29 '87
Brian De Palma [interview] K. Loder. il por *Roll Stone* p157+ D 17-31 '87
The Untouchables [film] Reviews
America 157:66 Ag 1-8 '87. R. A. Blake
Christ Century 104:598 Jl 1-8 '87. J. M. Wall
Commonweal 114:354-6 Je 5 '87. T. O'Brien
Humanist il 47:43 S/O '87. H. M. Geduld
Macleans il 100:51 Je 15 '87. L. O'Toole
N Y il 20:68-9 Je 8 '87. D. Denby
Nation 244:900-2 Je 27 '87. T. Rafferty
New Repub 196:26-7 Je 22 '87. S. Kauffmann
New Yorker 63:70-2 Je 29 '87. P. Kael
Newsweek il 109:78 Je 8 '87. D. Ansen
Newsweek il 109:62-6+ Je 22 '87. T. Mathews
People Wkly il 27:12 Je 15 '87. R. Novak
Roll Stone il p47-8+ Mr 26 '87. F. Schruers
Time il 129:83 Je 8 '87. R. Schickel
Time il 129:78-9 Je 22 '87. R. Corliss
Vogue il 177:58+ Je '87. J. Salamon
De Passe, Suzanne
about
Motown's other mogul. J. Hopewell. il por *Channels* 7:38-9 S '87
De Paul University
University 'madam' gets $1000 fine, probation [J. Owens' business] il por *Jet* 73:22 N 16 '87
De Plessix Gray, Francine *See* Gray, Francine du Plessix
De Prato, Bruno
about
The road not taken. M. Lindemann. il *Cycle* 38:86-7 S '87
De Rochambeau, Sheila
Regal needles. il *House Gard* 159:88+ S '87
De Rohan-Chabot, Joy *See* Rohan-Chabot, Joy de
De Rojas, Fernando *See* Rojas, Fernando de, d. 1541
De Rosnay, Jenna
about
Surfer, sailor, model, mom. L. Kleinmann. il pors *Health* 19:36 My '87
De Rothschild, David *See* Rothschild, David de
De Rothschild, Guy *See* Rothschild, Guy de
De Rothschild, Marie-Hélène *See* Rothschild, Marie-Hélène de
De Rothschild, Philippine *See* Rothschild, Philippine de
De Roy, Tui
In the society of lions. il *Int Wildl* 17:30-5 N/D '87
When aliens take over. il *Int Wildl* 17:34-7 Ja/F '87
De Saint-Aubin, Horace *See* Balzac, Honoré de, 1799-1850
De Saint-Phalle, Niki *See* Saint-Phalle, Niki de
De San Martín, José *See* San Martín, José de, 1778?-1850
De Soto, Hernando *See* Soto, Hernando de
De Soto (Mo.)
Photographs and photography
The invisible reach: how the Constitution touches Main Street U.S.A. R. Robotham. il *Life* 10:128-35 Fall '87
De St. Jorre, John
South Africa embattled. bibl f *Foreign Aff* 65 Sp Issue:538-63 ['87]
De Stefano, George
Family lies. il *Film Comment* 23:22-4+ Jl/Ag '87

De Toledano, Ralph
Sound on disc. See occasional issues of National Review
De Vaucouleurs, Antoinette *See* Vaucouleurs, Antoinette de
De Vaucouleurs, Gerard Henri *See* Vaucouleurs, Gerard Henri de
De Vere, Edward *See* Oxford, Edward De Vere, Earl of, 1550-1604
De Vito, Danny
about
An all-round, lovable louse. M. Reese. il pors *Newsweek* 109:72-3 Ap 27 '87
Danny De Vito & Rhea Perlman. W. Urbanska. il pors *McCalls* 145:36+ Mr '87
Throw momma from the train [film] Reviews
Macleans il 100:61 D 21 '87. L. O'Toole
Newsweek il 110:69 D 21 '87. D. Ansen
De Vito, E. B.
Wishes [poem] *America* 157:481 D 19 '87
De Vries, Paul
The deadly sin. il por *Christ Today* 31:22-4 My 15 '87
De Wire, Elinor
Fog songs [cover story] il *Sea Front* 33:164-73 My/Je '87
Women of the lights. il *Am Hist Illus* 21:42-9 F '87
De Zurbarán, Francisco *See* Zurbarán, Francisco de, 1598-1664
Deacidification of books *See* Books—Conservation and restoration
Deacon, Beverly
(jt. auth) See McNickle, Larry, and Deacon, Beverly
Deacons
See also
Women deacons
Dead
See also
Epitaphs
Undertakers and undertaking
The dead [film] See Motion picture reviews—Single works
Dead bodies
Body donation: an enigmatic subject. K. M. Wilson. *Humanist* 47:30+ Mr/Ap '87
A British lord wants to go to the dogs . . . literally! [Lord Avebury's intention to donate his body for dog food] il por *People Wkly* 27:94 F 23 '87
'This incredible machine' [cadaver studied in New York Academy of Art anatomy class] R. Bass. il *Art News* 86:182 Mr '87
Dead Kennedys (Musical group)
Dead Kennedys break up; Jello Biafra's legal problems persist. D. Fricke. *Roll Stone* p14 Ja 29 '87
Rockin' with the First Amendment [J. Biafra acquitted on charges of distributing harmful matter to minors] S. Wishnia. il *Nation* 245:444-6 O 24 '87
Dead of winter [film] See Motion picture reviews—Single works
Dead Sea scrolls
The Dead Sea scrolls and the Bible: after forty years. J. A. Fitzmyer. il *America* 157:300-3 O 31 '87
Deadline [film] See Motion picture reviews—Single works
Deadly sins *See* Sin
Deaf
See also
Children of the deaf
Civil rights
Can justice be deaf, too? [deaf jurors] G. Carroll. il *Newsweek* 109:69 Mr 2 '87
The empty crib [deaf parents struggle to retain custody of child; case of S. Timmons in Florida] L. A. Walker. il por *Ladies Home J* 104:76+ Mr '87
Employment
Against all odds [A. Sadovsky, hearing impaired motivational speaker] P. F. Stewart. il por *Ladies Home J* 104:148 O '87
Equipment
See also
Ear, Artificial
Hearing aids
Vocoders
Sports
A true Jet fighter [hockey player J. Kyte] B. Newman. il pors *Sports Illus* 67:108-12 O 12 '87
Deaf-mutes
Civil rights
Deaf mute cleared of murdering Ala. woman [case of J. Green] *Jet* 73:36 O 19 '87
Deaf-mute must stay in mental hospital for 1971 slaying in Chicago [case of D. Lang] *Jet* 72:17 Je 8 '87

Deafness
See also
Deaf
Noise—Physiological effects
Early hearing loss and brain development [work of Edwin
W. Rubel] J. Greenberg. *Sci News* 131:149 Mr 7 '87
Loud noise from little headphones [effect on hearing
of Walkman-type radios and tape players] M. Dobbin.
il *U S News World Rep* 103:77-8 O 12 '87
Federal aid
Blind Ray Charles urges Congress to aid the deaf. *Jet*
72:22 My 18 '87
Deagan, Kathleen A.
Searching for Columbus's lost colony. il *Natl Geogr*
172:672-5 N '87
Deak, Istvan
The convert. il *N Y Rev Books* 34:39-44 Mr 12 '87
Dealers, Agricultural equipment *See* Agricultural equipment
dealers
Dealers, Automobile *See* Automobile dealers; Black
automobile dealers
Dean, Andrea Oppenheimer
He was an acrobat on the leading edge of Jazz Age
art. bibl (p229) il por *Smithsonian* 18:58-64+ O '87
Dean, Christopher
about
Fighting drugs on ice. P. SerVaas. il pors *Saturday Evening
Post* 259:50 Ja/F '87
Torvill & Dean: so nice on ice. D. Chase. il pors *Saturday
Evening Post* 259:48-9+ Ja/F '87
Dean, John W. (John Wesley), 1938-
John Dean on Ollie: the ugly road ahead. il por *Newsweek*
110:28-9 Jl 20 '87
Dean, Jonathan
Gorbachev's arms control moves. il *Bull At Sci* 43:34-40
Je '87
Military security in Europe. *Foreign Aff* 66:22-40 Fall
'87
Dean, Laura
about
Deanmusicdance. G. Parks. il por *Dance Mag* 61:54-5
Ap '87
Magnetic [dance] Reviews
N Y il 20:137 Ap 27 '87. T. Tobias
Dean, Maureen
about
Maureen Dean makes a steamy literary debut with a
tale of passion on the Potomac. A. Chambers. il por
People Wkly 28:46-7 N 9 '87
Dean, William
about
The Dean of pro bono law. A. Prud'homme. il por
N Y 20:36 N 9 '87
Dean (Laura) Dancers and Musicians *See* Laura Dean
Dancers and Musicians
Dean Witter Reynolds Inc.
And now, heeere's Johnny's brother [D. Carson appears
in TV ad] il por *Newsweek* 109:49 F 9 '87
Deane, Andrea
Ice cream for adults. il *Work Woman* 12:72-4 Ag '87
Dear, William
about
Harry and the Hendersons [film] Reviews
Glamour 85:101+ Jl '87. J. G. Boyum
Macleans 100:51 Je 15 '87. L. O'Toole
Mademoiselle il 93:146+ S '87. R. Rosenbaum
Newsweek il 109:78 Je 8 '87. D. Ansen
People Wkly il 28:10 Jl 6 '87. T. Cunneff
Time 129:74 Je 15 '87
Deas, Charles, 1818-1867
about
Charles Deas. C. Clark. il por *Am Hist Illus* 22:18-33
Ap '87
Death
See also
Annihilationism (Theology)
Euthanasia
Funeral rites and ceremonies
Future life
Immortality
Longevity
Near-death experiences
Resurrection
Right to die
Suicide
Dying in character: the myth of the impish chuckle.
P. Klass. il *Discover* 8:20+ F '87
Reminders of man's mortality. A. Fotheringham. il
Macleans 100:64 S 7 '87

Causes
See also
Asphyxia
Mortality
Proof and certification
AIDS: how wide the cover-up? il *U S News World
Rep* 102:8 F 23 '87
Counting the AIDS victims. T. Monmaney. il *Newsweek*
109:65 F 23 '87
Psychology
See also
Children and death
Grief
Youth and death
A case of colic. J. C. Berman. il *N Y Times Mag*
p64 N 29 '87
Death in the mountains [terminal home care for old
man] J. Smoot. il *South Living* 22:100 N '87
The last stop [letter] M. M. Rice. *Harpers* 274:4-7 My
'87
The room where Scott died [F. S. Fitzgerald] S. Graham.
il por *N Y Times Mag* p20-1 Jl 26 '87
Religious aspects
See also
Church work with the bereaved
Because I could not stop for death, he kindly stopped
for me. K. S. Devassy. il *U S Cathol* 52:33-7 Ap
'87
Embarrassed physicians. R. Clapp. il *Christ Today*
31:16-17 N 20 '87
Gentle into that good night [son learns to accept father's
impending death] W. Wangerin. il por *Christ Today*
31:23-5 N 6 '87
How to talk to your kids about death. J. Breig. il
U S Cathol 52:21-6 Ja '87
The inevitability of death. R. R. MacGregor. il por
Christ Today 31:24-6 Mr 6 '87
A meditation on death and life. W. A. Barry. *America*
157:409-10 N 28 '87
More tears of God. M. E. Marty. *Christ Century* 104:639
Jl 15-22 '87
Politics won't cure death. J. Garvey. il *Commonweal*
114:584-5 O 23 '87
A rain of paper confetti. C. N. White. il *Commonweal*
114:134-5 Mr 13 '87
The tears of God [N. Wolterstorff's Lament for a son]
M. E. Marty. *Christ Century* 104:607 Jl 1-8 '87
A theology to die by. V. G. Beers. *Christ Today* 31:11
F 6 '87
What's in a name? [death of a son] W. T. Hanlon.
America 157:317-18 N 7 '87
Study and teaching
The long-term effects of death education and counseling.
E. Morgan. *Humanist* 47:27-8+ Mr/Ap '87
Death (Biology)
See also
Cell death
Last rights [redefining death; cover story] K. Stein. il
Omni 9:58-60+ S '87
Life and death [discussion of September 1987 article,
Last rights] K. Stein. *Omni* 10:18 D '87
Death and children *See* Children and death
Death and the king's horseman [drama] See Soyinka, Wole
Death and youth *See* Youth and death
Death Angel (Musical group)
Death Angel's noisy cherubs thrash toward rock's top.
il *People Wkly* 28:106 S 7 '87
Death before dishonor [film] *See* Motion picture
reviews—Single works
Death certificates *See* Death—Proof and certification
Death education *See* Death—Study and teaching
Death in music
Penderecki and Shostakovich: death affirms life. L. Men-
des. *Christ Century* 104:287-8 Mr 18-25 '87
Death in Venice [opera] *See* Britten, Benjamin, 1913-1976
Death notices *See* Obituaries
Death of the heart [television program] *See* Television
program reviews—Single works
Death penalty *See* Capital punishment
Death rate *See* Mortality
Death Valley National Monument (Calif. and Nev.)
Scotty's Castle [excerpt] S. W. Paher. il *Natl Parks* 61:46-7
S/O '87
Deauville (France)
Gardens and gardening
Gardens: Château Gabriel: Yves Saint Laurent and Pierre
Bergé at Deauville [cover story] C. Aillaud. il *Archit
Dig* 44:172-9+ My '87
Deaver, Michael K.
Peephole on the presidency [excerpt from Behind the
scenes] il pors *Life* 10:49-50+ D '87

Deaver, Michael K.—*cont.*

about

Morrow to sue 'Washington times' over excerpts from Deaver book. H. Fields. *Publ Wkly* 232:19 D 25 '87

Conflict of interests case

The ambassador's tale [Canadian ambassador A. Gotlieb subpoenaed to testify in perjury trial] M. McDonald. il por *Macleans* 100:21 Je 8 '87

The bill comes due for Deaver. J. S. DeMott. il por *Time* 129:23 Mr 30 '87

The confused Reagan twilight. D. Schorr. il *New Leader* 70:4 N 16 '87

The Deaver defense: the drink made me do it. D. Baer. il por *U S News World Rep* 103:60 N 2 '87

Deaver's wrong turn in a limousine [convicted under government ethics law] il por *U S News World Rep* 103:12-13 D 28 '87-Ja 4 '88

Downfall of 'The Acid Rainmaker'. M. McDonald. il por *Macleans* 100:22-3 Mr 30 '87

Guilty in court and shunned by the Reagans. il por *Newsweek* 110:19 D 28 '87

Have influence, will travel. por *Time* 130:25 N 16 '87

The high price of friendship [convicted of lying about his lobbying activities] D. Beckwith. il por *Time* 130:23 D 28 '87

Mike Deaver's rise and fall. E. Thomas and T. M. DeFrank. il pors *Newsweek* 109:22-3 Mr 23 '87

On the outside, cashing in. E. Alterman. *Harpers* 275:48-9 Jl '87

Pondering a high-proof defense [alcoholism used as legal defense] A. Wilentz. il por *Time* 130:60 N 2 '87

Washington's power game. T. Noah. il pors *Newsweek* 110:44 D 7 '87

DeBakey, Lois

Our national priority [address, February 27, 1987] *Vital Speeches Day* 53:496 Je 1 '87

DeBakey, Michael E. (Michael Ellis), 1908-

When your doctor needs to know—fast. il *Read Dig* 131:110-13 Jl '87

DeBarge, El

about

El DeBarge fails to show for concert; warrant issued. por *Jet* 72:24 Ag 24 '87

El DeBarge's sentence: benefit concert for kids. por *Jet* 71:36 F 2 '87

Showstopper El DeBarge. G. Summers. por *Essence* 17:21 Ja '87

Debategate case

Minority report. C. Hitchens. *Nation* 244:842 Je 20 '87

Minority report. C. Hitchens. *Nation* 245:7 Jl 4-11 '87

Debates, Presidential *See* Presidential debates

DeBerg, Steve

about

Battlin' Buccaneer. J. Lieber. il pors *Sports Illus* 67:50+ D 7 '87

DeBevoise, Charles R.

Quiz show kids: cashing in on their smarts. il *Teen* 31:70+ N '87

Debit cards

Debit cards: who needs them? R. R. Roha. il *Changing Times* 41:51-2 S '87

The new plastic money. E. Card. il *Ms* 15:80+ Ap '87

Visa's back-office strategy in the credit-card wars [cutting the cost of electronic transactions] J. B. Levine. il *Bus Week* p75 Ap 20 '87

DeBrask, Bob A.

Graphic self-promotion. il *Petersens Photogr Mag* 15:42-3 F '87

Debt

See also
Bankruptcy
Credit counseling

Calm down about debt [consumer debt] S. Nasar. il *Fortune* 115:52 Mr 2 '87

Debt trap. W. Greider. il *Roll Stone* p46+ S 24 '87

House of credit cards. M. Sivy. il *Money* 16:57-8 F '87

How to know if you owe too much. G. Williams. *Vogue* 177:142 F '87

It's time to rethink debt [special section] il *Money* 16:90-1+ Ap '87

New directions in the relation between public and private debt. B. M. Friedman. bibl f il *Science* 236:397-403 Ap 24 '87

Over the ears in debt [views of Time's Board of Economists] G. Russell. il *Time* 129:58-60 Mr 9 '87

Too much debt? How to tell if you're heading for the danger zone. B. G. Quint. il *Glamour* 85:216+ S '87

When you're too far in debt. il *Read Dig* 131:49-52 S '87

Debt-to-equity swaps *See* Swap financing

Debtor and creditor

See also
Collecting of accounts

Debts, Corporate *See* Corporations—Finance

Debts, External

Accounts receivable [third world debt] P. T. Bauer. *New Repub* 196:10-12 Je 15 '87

American bank loans line the pockets of the third world's elite [views of R. T. Naylor] S. C. Gwynne. *Wash Mon* 19:51-2 O '87

And now the bill comes due [U.S. foreign debt] B. Nussbaum. il *Bus Week* p160-1+ N 16 '87

Are big-bank shares a bargain? [market reaction to Brazil's suspension of interest payments] J. Egan. *U S News World Rep* 102:68 Mr 30 '87

Assembly reaches consensus on approach to external debt of developing countries. *UN Chron* 24:109 F '87

Bank stockholders should applaud [Citicorp's write-off of third world debt] M. S. Forbes, Jr. il *Forbes* 139:25 Je 15 '87

Bank stocks and the Brazil factor. M. McFadden. il *Fortune* 115:103-5 Mr 30 '87

BankAmerica's new tight spot [reserve set aside against third world debt] J. B. Levine and S. Bartlett. il *Bus Week* p50 Je 22 '87

The banks get tough [third world debt] D. Jenish. il *Macleans* 100:28 Je 8 '87

Beggaring our Latin neighbors. P. Lernoux. il *Nation* 245:709-10+ D 12 '87

Best buys among banks [value adjusted for Latin debt] J. Edgerton and others. il *Money* 16:7 Jl '87

The bishops' letter, world debt and the U.S. trade deficit [pastoral letter on the economy] J. A. Gylys. il *America* 157:86-7 Ag 15-22 '87

Biting half a bullet [further write-offs of foreign loan losses by big banks] A. Sloan. il *Forbes* 140:38-9 Jl 27 '87

Blues south of the border [Latin America] H. Eason. il *Nations Bus* 75:35-6 Jl '87

Bolivia swaps debt for conservation. J. Walsh. map *Science* 237:596-7 Ag 7 '87

Brazil and its creditors: who has more to lose? J. Ryser and W. Glasgall. il *Bus Week* p56-7 Mr 9 '87

Brazil says: nuts. J. S. Henry. *New Repub* 197:25+ O 12 '87

Brazil throws down the gauntlet [suspension of interest repayments] H. O'Shaughnessy. il *World Press Rev* 34:46-7 Ap '87

Buying debt, saving nature [offers to suspend debt payments for tropical countries which protect forests] J. B. Copeland. il *Newsweek* 110:46 Ag 31 '87

A case of bottom-line blues [banks raise the prime rate and reclassify loans to Brazil as nonperforming] B. Rudolph. il *Time* 129:63 Ap 13 '87

Cashing in on debt [Latin debt-to-equity swaps] T. Tedesco. il *Macleans* 100:34-5 O 5 '87

The Citi squeezes its lemons [move to clean up third world debt with debt for equity swaps] S. Bartlett. il *Bus Week* p31 Je 15 '87

Citicorp breaks ranks [write-off of third world loans] S. Koepp. il *Time* 129:48-50 Je 1 '87

Citicorp faces reality—and finds it doesn't hurt [third world debt] D. Pauly. il *Newsweek* 109:42+ Je 1 '87

Cutting the debt, saving the forest. D. Page. *Environment* 29:4-5+ S '87

Dance of debt isn't over yet [third world loans] J. S. Henry. il *U S News World Rep* 103:39-41 Ag 31 '87

Dealing with debt. J. Amuzegar. *Foreign Policy* 68:140-58 Fall '87

Debt and the dollar: the markets are making all the rules [meetings of the World Bank and International Monetary Fund] W. Glasgall and M. McNamee. il *Bus Week* p57 O 12 '87

Debt crisis. il *Black Enterp* 18:47 S '87

The debt crisis isn't Brazil's only liability. P. C. Roberts. il *Bus Week* p14 Ap 20 '87

Debt to democracy [Philippines] S. C. Monsod. *New Repub* 197:16-18 D 7 '87

The debtors' revolt is spreading in Latin America. J. Ryser and others. il *Bus Week* p88-9 D 28 '87-Ja 4 '88

Deep red: the international debt crisis and its historical precedents. H. James. *Am Schol* 56:331-41 Summ '87

Default, dear Brutus [Brazil unable to pay interest on foreign debt] *New Repub* 196:8+ Mr 16 '87

Debts, External—_cont._

Dirty money and the debt crisis [views of T. H. Naylor] P. C. Newman. il por *Macleans* 100:39 Mr 9 '87

Dominoes in a grim game of debt [Canadian banks' reaction to Brazil's decision to suspend interest payments] P. C. Newman. il *Macleans* 100:40 Mr 16 '87

The economic black hole [U.S. trade deficit and foreign debt] L. C. Thurow and L. D. Tyson. bibl f *Foreign Policy* 67:3-21 Summ '87

Exchanging debt for conservation [debt for nature scheme] A. L. Spitler. il *BioScience* 37:781 D '87

Fast bucks in Latin loan swaps [debt-equity swaps] J. Fierman. il *Fortune* 116:91-2+ Ag 3 '87

A golden deal: debt for nature. J. D. Hair. il *Int Wildl* 17:30 S/O '87

Hard times in store for international debtors. R. D. Hylton. il *Black Enterp* 18:19-20 S '87

Here comes the repo man [debt-equity swaps in Latin America] W. Curtis. *Nation* 244:570+ My 2 '87

How 'experts' caused the third world debt crisis. P. C. Roberts. il *Bus Week* p28 N 2 '87

How to take a $1 billion loss and look good [Citicorp write-off of third world loans] P. M. Scherschel. il *U S News World Rep* 102:46-7 Je 1 '87

In debt? Ring up the Louvre [work of Paris Club in rescheduling third world debt] F. Ungeheuer. il *Time* 130:50 Jl 13 '87

It's time to put an end to the borrowing binge. A. S. Blinder. il *Bus Week* p22 My 4 '87

John Reed's bold stroke [Citicorp's third world debt loan loss reserves; cover story] J. Fierman. il por *Fortune* 115:26-30+ Je 22 '87

A 'junk' king takes on the third world [M. R. Milken's debt crisis offensive] B. Powell and C. Friday. il por *Newsweek* 110:56 S 21 '87

Latin America's new dance of debt. R. H. Bork, Jr. il *U S News World Rep* 102:55 Mr 16 '87

Learning to love stocks and bonds [U.S. as a debtor nation] G. Bock. il *Time* 130:56 S 14 '87

Mexico's development crisis. J. H. Street. bibl f *Curr Hist* 86:101-4+ Mr '87

Michel Camdessus is making the IMF less of a Scrooge. M. McNamee. il *Bus Week* p36-7 O 5 '87

Mortgaging a house of cards [ethics of international debt] K. P. Jameson. il *Commonweal* 114:105-7 F 27 '87

No more blood in the stone [Brazil suspends interest payments on foreign debt] G. Scott. il *Time* 129:46 Mr 2 '87

The outlook for Latin America debt. P.-P. Kuczynski. il *Foreign Aff* 66:129-49 Fall '87

Preparing for the worst [Canadian banks and third world loans] T. Tedesco. il *Macleans* 100:32-3 Ag 3 '87

Pulling the plug [North Korean default on foreign debt] G. Bock. il *Time* 130:43 S 7 '87

A secret bank deal with South Africa. L. Howard. il *Newsweek* 109:7 Mr 16 '87

Settling Brazil's account. C. Wood. il *Macleans* 100:36 N 16 '87

Stonewalling the banks [Brazil suspends interest payments on debt] T. Fennell. il *Macleans* 100:34-5 Mr 9 '87

A stunner from the Citi [reserve to cushion third world loans] S. Bartlett. il por *Bus Week* p42-3 Je 1 '87

A talk with Alfonsin: 'the debt cannot be paid'. J. Ryser and R. A. Kessler. por *Bus Week* p66 Je 22 '87

There goes the neighborhood [M. Schubert's mastery of Latin loan swaps] E. A. Finn, Jr. il por *Forbes* 139:35-7 Je 29 '87

The third world debt crisis [address, October 29, 1986] J. J. LaFalce. *Vital Speeches Day* 53:162-6 Ja 1 '87

"This is war" [Brazilian debt; interview with M. Colasuonno] L. Minard. il por *Forbes* 139:50 Je 29 '87

Three cheers for Citicorp's initiative [write-off of third world debt] J. S. Henry. il *U S News World Rep* 102:48 Je 1 '87

The U.S. gets foreign aid [Treasury bond sale] J. B. Copeland. il *Newsweek* 109:58 My 18 '87

View from the middle [interview with A. M. da Silva] E. A. Finn, Jr. il por *Forbes* 140:60+ N 16 '87

Welcome to the Nassau branch! [condensed from Selling money] S. C. Gwynne. il *Read Dig* 130:127-30 Ap '87

Who's afraid of Solita Monsod? U.S. bankers, that's who [Economic Planning Minister of the Philippines] D. J. Yang. il por *Bus Week* p54 Ja 26 '87

Whose debt crisis is it anyway? [U.S. as debtor compared to Latin America] P. Davidson. il *New Leader* 70:14-15 Ag 10-24 '87

Why the dollar could head south again . . . and send the economy into recession next year [U.S. as debtor nation] G. Koretz. il *Bus Week* p20 Jl 13 '87

Will U.S. banks do more for the LDCs? H. Banks. *Forbes* 140:27 N 2 '87

The World Bank's turn [debt quagmire] J. Egan. il *U S News World Rep* 103:54 O 12 '87

The Zambian debt dilemma: a just repayment plan. J. B. Straus, Jr. *Christ Century* 104:855-6 O 7 '87

Debts, Public
See also
Debts, External
Treasury bills and notes

Accounting and accountability [address, May 6, 1987] D. R. Kullberg. *Vital Speeches Day* 53:606-8 Jl 15 '87

Beyond our means [views of A. Malabre] A. Bladen. il *Forbes* 140:178 Jl 27 '87

Debt trap. W. Greider. il *Roll Stone* p46+ S 24 '87

The federal deficit: how does it matter? R. Eisner. il *Science* 237:1577-82 S 25 '87

Going down with the ship. A. Bladen. il *Forbes* 140:252 N 30 '87

How much does Uncle Sam owe? J. C. Szabo. il *Nations Bus* 75:42 Ag '87

How the government cooks the books. P. Longman. *Wash Mon* 19:47-52 Jl/Ag '87

Liberty to all [address, June 22, 1987] W. E. Simon. *Vital Speeches Day* 54:7-11 O 15 '87

Living beyond our means [condensed from Beyond our means] A. L. Malabre. *Read Dig* 131:123-6 N '87

New directions in the relation between public and private debt. B. M. Friedman. bibl f il *Science* 236:397-403 Ap 24 '87

Of many things [views of A. L. Malabre in Beyond our means] G. W. Hunt. *America* 156:inside cover Ap 18 '87

Over the ears in debt [views of Time's Board of Economists] G. Russell. il *Time* 129:58-60 Mr 9 '87

Scaling the nation's mountain of debt. J. Jaban. il *Sch Update* 119:18-19 Ja 12 '87

Third world debt: a flawed solution [debt-equity swaps] R. Kuttner. il *Bus Week* p18 Ja 19 '87

Uncle Sam the cosigner [off-budget financing] R. Thomas. il *Newsweek* 109:50+ Je 8 '87

Anecdotes, facetiae, satire, etc.
Easy ways to retire the debt. E. G. Flagell. por *Newsweek* 109:8 Ja 26 '87

International aspects
Sound financial reporting by nation states [address, September 29, 1986] M. Egol. *Vital Speeches Day* 53:176-8 Ja 1 '87

United States
See Debts, Public

Debugging in computer science
A fast CRC [XMODEM cyclic redundancy check algorithm] J. LeVan. bibl il *Byte* 12:339-41 N '87

Periscope. il *Radio-Electron* 58 ComputerDigest:87-8 D '87

Shareware assembler/debugger, Eric Isaacson; MIX C compiler, editor debugger. il *Radio-Electron* 58 ComputerDigest:94 N '87

Spreadsheets can be hazardous to your health. S. Ditlea. il *Pers Comput* 11:60-1+ Ja '87

Spying on Windows. M. Geary. il *Byte* 12 no12 Sp Issue:97-8+ '87

Turbo Pascal debuggers. il *Radio-Electron* 58 ComputerDigest:88-90 D '87

DEC *See* Digital Equipment Corp.; New York (State). Dept. of Environmental Conservation

Decade of Disabled Persons *See* United Nations Decade of Disabled Persons, 1983-1992

Decay (Biology) *See* Biodegradation

Decay (Dental) *See* Dental caries

Decay of wood *See* Wood—Deterioration

Decedents' estates *See* Estates, Decedents'

Deceit *See* Fraud

December
The December almanac. il *Atlantic* 260:16 D '87

December at Great Dixter [excerpt from The year at Great Dixter] C. Lloyd. il *Archit Dig* 44:84+ D '87

Deception *See* Fraud; Lying

Deceptive behavior in animals *See* Animals—Habits and behavior

Decibels
Clearing the cobwebs. J. D. Hirsch. il *Stereo Rev* 52:24+ S '87

Decibels. I. Masters. il *Stereo Rev* 52:22 Je '87

DeCindis, John
Rodeo! il *Petersens Photogr Mag* 16:26-8 My '87

Decision/Capital Fund Inc.
A closed-end fund with its eyes open. G. G. Marcial. *Bus Week* p113 My 4 '87
Decision making
See also
Risk taking (Psychology)
University of Chicago. Center for Decision Research
Decision-making in the presence of risk. M. J. Machina. bibl f il *Science* 236:537-43 My 1 '87
Decision Pad weighs choices [computer program] S. R. Reed. *Pers Comput* 11:262-3 D '87
Hard choices: the tough decisions women must make today [roundtable discussion] S. S. Stautberg. il *Ladies Home J* 104:96-7+ Ja '87
Health and safety risk analyses: information for better decisions. L. B. Lave. bibl f *Science* 236:291-5 Ap 17 '87
How to make a no-lose decision. S. Jeffers. *McCalls* 114:53-4 Ja '87
The human dimension of data-based decision making [interview with Newman Walker] D. B. Strother. il por *Phi Delta Kappan* 68:470-3 F '87
Making snap decisions that don't snap back [business] S. Dark. *Work Woman* 12:25 O '87
Should we move to Milpitas? [Decision Pad software] E. Dyson. il *Forbes* 140:102 Ag 10 '87
Tennis at Harvard [experimental findings on rationality and economic theory] D. Seligman. il *Fortune* 116:204 N 23 '87
Visual decision making [business chart producing software] C. Spencer. il *Pers Comput* 11:93-7 Ja '87
What's the best way to deal with an indecisive boss? *Glamour* 85:164 O '87
When no decision is the best decision [excerpt from Managing people at work desk guide] T. L. Quick. *Work Woman* 12:18 Mr '87
Study and teaching
The fourth R? [social decision making; study by John Clabby and Maurice Elias] J. Meer. *Psychol Today* 21:68-9 F '87
Teaching middle-schoolers decision-making skills. S. Bergmann. *Educ Dig* 52:48-50 Mr '87
The wisdom of Solomon. J. McCormick. il *Newsweek* 110:62-3 Ag 17 '87
Deck, Allan Figueroa
Ministry and vocations: going back to the drawing board. *America* 156:212-13+ Mr 14 '87
Deck boats *See* Motor boats
Deck chairs *See* Chairs
Decker, Andrew
The battle over Georgia O'Keeffe's multimillion-dollar legacy. il pors *Art News* 86:120-7 Ap '87
Real and fake in the 'Zagreb Louvre'. il pors *Art News* 86:151-8 Summ '87
Decker, Daniel J.
Is woodland management for you? il *Conservationist* 41:38-41 Ja/F '87
Decker, Mary *See* Slaney, Mary Decker
Decker, William
(jt. auth) *See* Hempe, A. Henry, and Decker, William
Decks, patios, terraces, etc.
See also
Pergolas
Porches
10 ways to build a sturdier, safer deck. R. Barnhart. il *Home Mech* 83:36-40+ Ag '87
Best outdoor projects. il *Fam Handyman* 37:30-2+ My/Je '87
A big 1980s deck for a 1920s house. il *Sunset* 178:134 Je '87
Build your deck to last [interview with M. Charno] J. H. Ingersoll. il por *Home Mech* 83:22+ Ag '87
Creative patio crafting. N. P. Pierce. il *Flower Gard* 31:16+ Ag/S '87
Deck design saves vintage orange tree. il *South Living* 22:150 S '87
A deck in one weekend. R. Scharff. il *Fam Handyman* 37:71-4 Mr '87
Decks—right wood is worthwhile investment. *South Living* 22:126-7 Je '87
Double decker. A. Capotosto and S. Capotosto. il *Pop Mech* 164:92-6+ My '87
Drawn to the deck [multilevel deck] T. A. Steadman. il *South Living* 22:92-3 N '87
Elegant decks—low or high. A. W. Lees. il *Pop Sci* 230:60-4 Ap '87
Hot tub and decks for a steep slope. il *Sunset* 179:97 Ag '87
No room for a deck? Have you looked at your garage roof? il *Sunset* 178:120-3 Ap '87

Outdoor living. G. D. Cook and others. il *Better Homes Gard* 65:33-43+ Je '87
The outdoor room idea. il *Sunset* 179:68-71 S '87
Step-up deck for sloping yards. A. W. Lees. il *Pop Sci* 231:64-7 Ag '87
Their deck has bloom built in. il *Sunset* 178:78-9 Mr '87
They made the most of only 22 feet. il *Sunset* 178:76 Ja '87
They wanted the look of the beach, and wind protection. il *Sunset* 179:110 Jl '87
Tips on deck building. il *South Living* 22:98+ Mr '87
Two decks and a sunroom make the difference. il *Sunset* 179:90-1 Ag '87
Declaration of Independence *See* United States. Declaration of Independence
Declaration of the Principles of International Cultural Co-operation
Twenty years of cultural co-operation. E. Pouchepadass. il *Courier* 40:9 Ja '87
Declaration of the Rights of the Child
The true sprit of Christmas. A. B. Heath. il *Natl Rev* 39:27-9 D 31 '87
The decline of the American empire [film] *See* Motion picture reviews—Single works
Deco art *See* Art deco
Decoders, Sound effects *See* Sound equipment
Decoding (Telecommunication) *See* Scrambling systems (Telecommunication)
Decoding of ciphers *See* Cryptography
Decolonization Committee (United Nations) *See* United Nations. Decolonization Committee
Decommissioning of nuclear facilities *See* Nuclear facilities—Decommissioning
Decommissioning of nuclear power plants *See* Nuclear power plants—Decommissioning
Decomposition (Biology) *See* Biodegradation
Decompression (Physiology)
Avascular necrosis: occurrence in diving Cretaceous mosasaurs. B. Rothschild and L. D. Martin. bibl f il *Science* 236:75-7 Ap 3 '87
Decompression sickness *See* Decompression (Physiology)
DeConcini, Dennis
Protecting against patent piracy. il *USA Today (Periodical)* 116:25-6 N '87
Deconstruction
Descartes, Nietzsche and the search for the unsayable. M. C. Taylor. il *N Y Times Book Rev* 92:3+ F 1 '87
Bibliography
Truth and consequences [J. Derrida] A. Nehamas. *New Repub* 197:31-6 O 5 '87
Decontrol of natural gas prices *See* Natural gas—Prices
Decorated eggs *See* Eggs, Decorated
Decoration and ornament
See also
Antiques
Art deco
Arts and crafts
Baskets
Buttons
Candles and candleholders
Christmas decorations
Church decoration and ornament
Cooking, Ornamental
Decoupage
Design
Eggs, Decorated
Firearms—Decoration
Flower arrangement
Flowers, Artificial
Frescoes
Fruits, vegetables, etc. in decoration
Glassware
Hardware
House decoration
Monograms
Mosaics
Mounts (Decorative arts)
Needlework
Ormolu
Paneling
Paper work (Art)
Pottery—Decoration
Shellwork
Silk screen printing
Stencil work
Table decoration
Terracotta
Tiles

Decoration and ornament—*cont.*
Create the look of malachite. il *South Living* 22:158 Mr '87
Napoleon's grand designs [influence on French decorative arts] O. Bernier. il *House Gard* 159:146-51+ D '87
Painting a world [decorative artist S. Gemberling] E. Greene. il por *House Gard* 159:40+ D '87

Exhibitions
See also
Dallas Museum of Art. Decorative Arts Wing
Metropolitan Museum of Art (New York, N.Y.). American Wing
Musée des Arts Décoratifs (Paris, France)
American decorative arts [exhibition entitled Motif and meaning: classicism in America] S. B. Sherrill. il *Antiques* 132:1194+ D '87
American decorative arts [Federal Philadelphia, 1785-1825] S. B. Sherrill. il *Antiques* 132:42+ Jl '87
Athens on these shores [Federal Philadelphia, 1785-1825] S. Weaver. il *Americana* 15:22-5 Jl/Ag '87
Cooper-Hewitt Museum [exhibition entitled Recollections: a decade of collection] il *Antiques Collect Hobbies* 91:57-8 Ja '87
Decorative arts in New England [The decorative arts and crafts of Nantucket] S. B. Sherrill. il *Antiques* 132:64+ Jl '87

Decoration and ornament, Architectural
See also
Floor painting and decoration
G. Jackson & Sons
Latticework
Moldings (Architecture)
Mural painting and decoration
Terracotta
Special effects: how to use paint to create eye-catching, inexpensive home furnishings. S. Wood. il *Home Mech* 83:44-50 Ja '87
Urban animals [building ornaments] K. C. Bloomer. il *Audubon* 89:68-75 Ja '87
Decoration of food *See* Cooking—Garnishes
Decorations of honor
See also
Legion of Honor
Decorative arts *See* Decoration and ornament
DeCosse, David E.
The case of Our Lady of Sorrows. *Commonweal* 114:210-15 Ap 10 '87
Decoupage
Decorate a screen with decoupage! S. Wood. il *McCalls* 145:162+ Mr '87
DeCourcy, Michael Hinds *See* Hinds, Michael deCourcy
Decoys (Hunting)
Editorial [live decoys] D. Barnes. *Field Stream* 91:7 F '87
Flagging for geese [Canada geese] B. Sayler. il *Outdoor Life* 180:58-60+ D '87
My hunting comrade, Pete [live turkey as decoy; reprint from January 1900 issue] J. Gordon. il *Field Stream* 91:60-1 F '87

Collectors and collecting
Brackets show off decoy collection. il *South Living* 22:198 N '87
Decter, Midge
Understanding human rights [address, October 10, 1987] *Vital Speeches Day* 54:139-42 D 15 '87
DeCurtis, Anthony
George Harrison gets back [cover story] pors *Roll Stone* p36-8+ O 22 '87
Dedications (in books)
To squalor, with love. A. Broyard. il *N Y Times Book Rev* 92:11 Ag 30 '87
Dedman, Robert H.
about
Cheap capital. P. Newcomb. il por *Forbes* 140:154 D 14 '87
Deductions, Income tax *See* Income tax—Deductions
Deeds
Sure, it's your property, but . . . D. Moreau. il *Changing Times* 41:57-9 Ag '87
Deedy, John
Does evil have a life of its own? il *U S Cathol* 52:20-5 D '87
Last will and testament: how to do God's will with your own. il *U S Cathol* 52:32-7 Mr '87
The new baptism: you can't get the water and run [cover story] il *U S Cathol* 52:6-13 F '87
Will you be in the hot seat on Judgment Day? il *U S Cathol* 52:6-12 Jl '87
Deen, Rosemary
Eyes that do not sleep at dawn. *Commonweal* 114:322-3 My 22 '87

Deene Park (Northamptonshire, England: Historic house)
See Historic houses, sites, etc.—Great Britain
Deep ecology
The great, green deep-ecology revolution. A. Chase. il *Roll Stone* p61-2+ Ap 23 '87
Deep Rover (Oceanographic submersible) *See* Oceanographic submersibles
Deep sea deposits *See* Marine sediments
Deep sea diving *See* Diving, Submarine
Deep sea fishing *See* Salt water fishing
Deep sea mining *See* Ocean mining
Deer
See also
Antlers
Caribou
Elk
Dogs and deer [dogs as deer killers] B. Shipman. il *Ctry J* 14:17-20 Ap '87
Much ado about pudu [work of M. MacNamara] J. P. Cohn. il *Int Wildl* 17:38 Ja/F '87
Peregrinations and permutations of a contrary eight-toed beast [whitetailed deer; photographs by Carl R. Sams; cover story; with editorial comment by Les Line] il *Audubon* 89:4, 52-81 My '87
Trouble in paradise [Key deer] J. Carey. il map *Natl Wildl* 25:42-5 O/N '87

Photographs and photography
Deer wars [test of wills by whitetail deer] D. E. Petzal. il *Field Stream* 92:62-3 Je '87
The deerstalker [C. R. Sams] L. Line. il por *Audubon* 89:4 My '87
Non-typical, near mythical. M. Biggs. il *Field Stream* 92:50-1 Ag '87
This country life. G. Stockey. il *Ctry J* 14:80 Jl '87
Deer, Dressing of *See* Game, Dressing of
Deer baits and repellents
A deer-proof garden. P. Holm. il *Rodale's Org Gard* 34:31-3 D '87
The deer still visit, but they ignore most of the plants [deer-resistant plants] il *Sunset* 179:224-5 O '87
Essence of deer. B. W. Dalrymple and C. W. Virnig. il *Field Stream* 92:60-1 S '87
Some scentsible advice. J. Weiss. il *Field Stream* 92:48-9+ D '87
Deer calling *See* Animal calling
Deer drives
The art of driving deer. J. Bashline. il *Field Stream* 92:62-3+ O '87
Deer farming
Deer ranching: do fallow deer offer hope for struggling farms? H. Smith. il *Ctry J* 14:48-53 N '87
Deer hunting
100 deer with a bow [C. Yates] J. E. Phillips. il *Outdoor Life* 179:52-3+ F '87
1986 Big Buck Club winners. il *Conservationist* 42:46-7 S/O '87
After opening day [hunting whitetailed deer] G. Clancy. il *Outdoor Life* 180:75-7+ N '87
All about rattling [antlers used as deer calls] K. Etling. il *Outdoor Life* 179:58-9+ Ap '87
The art of driving deer. J. Bashline. il *Field Stream* 92:62-3+ O '87
Be ready when the deer is. B. W. Dalrymple. il *Field Stream* 92:86-7+ My '87
The big little deer [Coues deer] S. Fadala. bibl il *Outdoor Life* 180:82-3+ N '87
Boat seats for bucks. C. Slovensky. il *Outdoor Life* 180:136-7 O '87
Breaking the rules for deer [New York hunter P. Fiduccia] K. Etling. il *Outdoor Life* 180:68-9+ O '87
Bucks around the clock. K. L. Peterson. il *Outdoor Life* 180:64-5+ Ag '87
Bucks at the edge [mule deer] W. L. Prothero. il *Field Stream* 92:46+ N '87
Cattails for whitetails. J. Boatner. il *Outdoor Life* 180:48-9+ D '87
Deer calling secrets [whitetails] B. McGuire. il *Outdoor Life* 179:48-9+ F '87
Deer forecast '87 [cover story] M. C. Toth. il *Outdoor Life* 180:87-9+ S '87
Deer hunting's big stink [controlling body odor to get closer] J. Weiss. il *Outdoor Life* 180:56-7+ Ag '87
A deer to believe in [Vermont hunt] H. F. Blaisdell. il *Read Dig* 131:25-6+ N '87
Editorial [whitetail trophy deer] D. Barnes. *Field Stream* 92:7 Ag '87
Empty days: a journal of two weeks afield. C. Fergus. il *Ctry J* 14:64-9 D '87
Essence of deer. B. W. Dalrymple and C. W. Virnig. il *Field Stream* 92:60-1 S '87

Deer hunting—*cont.*

Farther back. J. Barsness. il *Field Stream* 91:55+ Ja '87

Getting there. J. Byers. il *Outdoor Life* 180:106-8+ S '87

The grand deer slammer [bowhunter B. Long] T. Stienstra. il por *Outdoor Life* 179:54-5+ Ja '87

Hard time mule deer. S. Curtis. il *Outdoor Life* 180:78-9+ N '87

Home on the range [habits of whitetail deer] H. Buck. il *Field Stream* 92:58-9+ N '87

Hunt structure for deer. J. Byers. il *Outdoor Life* 180:61-3+ O '87

Hunt with a grunt [calls for whitetailed deer; cover story] K. Etling. il *Outdoor Life* 180:65-7+ Jl '87

Jack O'Connor on mule deer hunting [reprint from January 1960 issue] J. O'Connor. il *Outdoor Life* 180:54-5+ D '87

The least factor. T. Jones. il *Outdoor Life* 179:47-9+ Ja '87

The masters of scarce [whitetails] J. Weiss. il *Field Stream* 92:67+ S '87

Mule deer metamorphoses. G. Webster. il *Field Stream* 92:53+ N '87

Muleys where you want them. S. Curtis. il *Outdoor Life* 180:98-9+ S '87

Public vs. private hunting [stag stalking in Scotland] G. Reiger. *Field Stream* 91:38+ Mr '87

The quality of mercy. K. McCafferty. il *Field Stream* 92:40+ O '87

Shooting a buck. R. K. Nelson. *Harpers* 274:29-30 Ja '87

Sitting out the season. S. Curtis. il *Field Stream* 92:26+ N '87

Some scentsible advice. J. Weiss. il *Field Stream* 92:48-9+ D '87

The sportiest way for whitetails. B. W. Dalrymple. il *Field Stream* 91:78-9+ Ap '87

The stuff that counts. B. Brister. il *Field Stream* 92:75-8 N '87

Take an intelligent stand for whitetails. J. H. Williams. il *Field Stream* 92:44-5+ Ag '87

A tale of two bucks [C. Van Lith and B. Kontras take trophy whitetail deer with bow and arrow] J. Murray and M. Pearce. il pors *Outdoor Life* 180:68-9+ Jl '87

A thin disguise [life of a farmer imitated by author] R. Rhodes. il *N Y Times Mag* p62 Jl 19 '87

Things look up when you look down [mule deer] W. Van Zwoll. il *Field Stream* 92:69+ S '87

Watch a trail to take a trophy. W. L. Prothero. il *Outdoor Life* 180:72-3+ Jl '87

What deer? G. Clancy. il *Outdoor Life* 179:59+ Mr '87

Where whitetails travel. J. Barsness. il *Field Stream* 92:71-2 S '87

Whitetails: east and west. J. Zumbo. il *Outdoor Life* 180:72-3+ O '87

Without a trace [art of camouflage in bowhunting for deer] G. Helgeland. il *Field Stream* 91:56-7+ F '87

Your farmland buck. J. O. Cartier. il *Outdoor Life* 180:94-5+ S '87

Anecdotes, facetiae, satire, etc.

Taking care of your dear. K. Cowgill. il *Field Stream* 92:45-7 O '87

The wackiest ways to whitetails. J. Weiss. il *Outdoor Life* 179:70-1+ Je '87

Deer hunting trophies *See* Hunting trophies

Deer meat cooking *See* Cooking—Game

Deere & Company

Deere contract protects employees against layoffs. *Mon Labor Rev* 110:56-7 Ap '87

Deerfield (Mass.)

See also

Historic Deerfield, Inc.

Deering, James

about

The residence of James Deering's winters. il *South Living* 22:38 N '87

Dees, Benny

about

They're jumping for joy. C. Kirkpatrick. il pors *Sports Illus* 67 Sp Issue:20-3+ N 18 '87

Def Leppard (Musical group)

Def Leppard unleashes 'Hysteria'. R. Tannenbaum. il *Roll Stone* p16 S 10 '87

Deffer than ever. K. Loder. il *Roll Stone* p127-8 S 24 '87

Defamation *See* Libel and slander

Default (Finance)

See also

Bonds—Default

Bonds, Industrial development—Default

Municipal bonds—Default

Accounting in the West [outraged investors demand inquiry into Principal Group Ltd.'s default] D. Jenish. il *Macleans* 100:20-1 Jl 27 '87

Giving business a bad name [Principal Group's D. Cormie] P. C. Newman. il por *Macleans* 100:35 Ag 17 '87

Government bond dealers: a bell is tolling. G. DeGeorge. *Bus Week* p63-4 My 25 '87

A meat-packing magnate gets boxed in [Swift's E. L. Cox] J. Weber, Jr. il por *Bus Week* p50+ Je 22 '87

Picking up the pieces [Metropolitan Life's purchase offer for Principal Group's assets] J. Howse. il *Macleans* 100:26-7 Ag 31 '87

Principal's stunning loss. D. Jenish. il *Macleans* 100:30-1 Ag 24 '87

Threats of another failure [Principal Group Ltd.] D. Jenish. il *Macleans* 100:23 Jl 13 '87

Defeat (Psychology) *See* Failure (Psychology)

Defectors, Political

See also

Asylum, Right of

Black man returns home after 47 years in Russia [R. Robinson] S. Booker. il pors *Ebony* 42:67+ Je '87

Confession of a 'good soldier' [A. Fernandez Larios' account of Letelier assassination] M. R. Meyer. il por *Newsweek* 109:43 F 16 '87

A dance for détente [M. Baryshnikov invited to dance in Moscow] P. Young. il por *Macleans* 100:74 F 2 '87

A defector's damaging tale [Nicaraguan defector R. Miranda's revelations] N. Cooper. il por *Newsweek* 110:49 D 21 '87

Derailing Pinochet [A. Pinochet implicated in A. Fernandez's account of Letelier assassination] J. Dinges and S. Landau. il *Nation* 244:280-2 Mr 7 '87

Fallout from a defector [revelations from Nicaraguan defector R. Miranda] H. Anderson. il por *Newsweek* 110:26 D 28 '87

A flight to freedom [Cuban Air Force general R. del Pino Diaz defects to the U.S.] *Macleans* 100:24 Je 8 '87

Hero to go [Cuban Air Force General R. del Pino Diaz defects to the U.S.] *Time* 129:26 Je 8 '87

Just how big a fish is the man from Havana? [defection of General R. del Pino Diaz] C. A. Robbins. por *U S News World Rep* 102:12 Je 8 '87

'Little worm' or big fish? [Sandinista R. Miranda defects to the U.S.] N. Cooper. por *Newsweek* 110:80 N 16 '87

Miranda's tempest [Nicaraguan defector R. Miranda used to manipulate U.S. press] A. Cockburn. *Nation* 245:780-1 D 26 '87-Ja 2 '88

A Moscow mystery [Lockshin family from Houston defects to Moscow] J. Fayard. il *Life* 10:42-3+ Mr '87

Mother Russia's new Red carpet [M. Baryshnikov and others invited to perform in their homeland] por *U S News World Rep* 102:10 F 2 '87

Once a Cuban hero, Roberto Urrutia aims to give the U.S. a boost—and Castro a lesson—in the Pan American Games. P. Jordan. il pors *People Wkly* 28:105-6+ Ag 10 '87

Siren songs from Moscow [M. Baryshnikov and other Soviet defectors invited to perform] M. S. Serrill. il por *Time* 129:46 F 2 '87

Spilled beans [defection of Cuban intelligence chief F. Aspillaga Lombard] K. M. Pierce. il *Time* 130:17 Ag 24 '87

Tales of a Sandinista defector [Sandinista defector R. Miranda] J. Smolowe. il por *Time* 130:47 D 21 '87

Their man from Havana: true confessions? [Cuban defector R. del Pino Diaz] *Newsweek* 109:42 Je 8 '87

Defects, Crystal *See* Crystals—Defects

Defense, Civil *See* Civil defense

Defense (Legal procedure) *See* Legal procedure

Defense Advanced Research Projects Agency (U.S.) *See* United States. Defense Advanced Research Projects Agency

Defense appropriations *See* United States. Dept. of Defense—Appropriations and expenditures

Defense contracts *See* Contracts, Government

Defense Dept. (U.S.) *See* United States. Dept. of Defense

Defense industries *See* Military-industrial complex; Munitions

Defense information, Classified *See* Classified information

Defense Intelligence Agency (U.S.) *See* United States. Defense Intelligence Agency

Defense lawyers *See* Lawyers
Defense mechanisms (Biology)
See also
   Mimicry (Biology)
Bat predation and its influence on calling behavior in neotropical katydids. J. J. Belwood and G. Morris. bibl f il *Science* 238:64-7 O 2 '87
Driven batty, katydids change tune [influence of predator bats; research by J. J. Belwood and G. Morris] R. Weiss. *Sci News* 132:231 O 10 '87
The smell of fear [rats; research by Michael Fanselow] P. Chance. *Psychol Today* 21:16 Jl '87
Defense mechanisms (Botany)
See also
   Mimicry (Botany)
Allocating resources to reproduction and defense. F. A. Bazzaz and others. bibl f il *BioScience* 37:58-67 Ja '87
Punching holes in a sticky defense [insect vein-cutting behavior counters plant latex defenses; research by David E. Dussourd and Thomas Eisner] D. D. Edwards. il *Sci News* 132:134 Ag 29 '87
Vein-cutting behavior: insect counterploy to the latex defense of plants. D. E. Dussourd and T. Eisner. bibl f il *Science* 237:898-901 Ag 21 '87
War & passion [passionflowers] P. Fogden. il *Int Wildl* 17:12-17 Ja/F '87
Defense mechanisms (Psychology)
See also
   Denial (Psychology)
   Repression (Psychology)
Defensive employees? Here's what you can do. L. Grensing. *Work Woman* 12:20 S '87
Defense of the realm [film] *See* Motion picture reviews—Single works
Defense Science Board (U.S.) *See* United States. Defense Science Board
Defense spending, International *See* Armed Forces—Appropriations and expenditures
Defense stocks *See* Munitions—Securities
Deferred compensation
See also
   401(k) plan
Deferred taxation
Accounting
World War III accounting. L. Saunders. il *Forbes* 139:74+ Mr 9 '87
Defibrillators
Rural elderly need new heart attack rescue rules. *Success Farm* 85:54 O '87
Deficiency diseases
See also
   Malnutrition
   Scurvy
   Xerophthalmia
Spot your nutritional deficiencies. M. Mihalik. *Prevention* 39:26-8 Je '87
Deficits, Budget *See* Budget
Deficits, Trade *See* Balance of trade
Deflation (Finance)
The problem is not inflation at home but deflation abroad. P. C. Roberts. il *Bus Week* p31 My 18 '87
DeFoe, Mark
Pale ambience: browsing a bookstore in Appalachia [poem] *America* 157:34 Jl 18-25 '87
Defoliants *See* Herbicides
Deford, Frank
America the beautiful's team. il *Sports Illus* 67:66-72+ Ag 3 '87
Bigger but not better. por *Sports Illus* 66:86 Mr 30 '87
Cash on the line. il pors *Sports Illus* 67:36-9 Ag 24 '87
Eleven is a big fat crowd. il *Sports Illus* 67 Sp Issue:42-5 S 9 '87
The guard who would be quarterback. il pors *Sports Illus* 67:64-9+ S 14 '87
Happy days. il pors *Sports Illus* 67:56-60+ Jl 20 '87
Let's count boxing out. il por *Sports Illus* 66:222 F 9 '87
Look who's on top again. il por *Sports Illus* 67:40-3 S 21 '87
Look who's on top still. il por *Sports Illus* 67:44+ S 21 '87
No losers in St. Loo. il por *Sports Illus* 67:116 O 19 '87
No place to go but up. il por *Sports Illus* 67:59-60 S 14 '87
Oh, the woes of the O's. por *Sports Illus* 67:102 S 21 '87

Rabbit ball: whodunit? por *Sports Illus* 67:94 Jl 27 '87
Score one more for Steffi. il pors *Sports Illus* 66:38-42 Je 15 '87
A star's legacy. il *Sports Illus* 66:83-4 My 4 '87
This Bud's not for you. il pors *Sports Illus* 67:67-8+ N 2 '87
Troubled times in Titletown. il *Sports Illus* 66:70-4+ My 25 '87
DeForest, Joe
about
What goes up comes down. W. Nack. il pors *Sports Illus* 67:68+ D 14 '87
Deforestation
Acid rain in Europe [cover story; special section; with editorial comment by Leen Hordijk] bibl f il maps *Environment* 29:inside cover, 4-15+ N '87
Battles and treaties for tropical forests. *Environment* 29:21 Jl/Ag '87
Bolivia swaps debt for conservation. J. Walsh. map *Science* 237:596-7 Ag 7 '87
Buying debt, saving nature [offers to suspend debt payments for tropical countries which protect forests] J. B. Copeland. il *Newsweek* 110:46 Ag 31 '87
Crisis in the rain forest. D. Schoonmaker. il map *Mother Earth News* 106:94-6+ Jl/Ag '87
Cutting the debt, saving the forest. D. Page. *Environment* 29:4-5+ S '87
Exchanging debt for conservation [debt for nature scheme] A. L. Spitler. il *BioScience* 37:781 D '87
Forests are dying but is acid rain really to blame? J. R. Luoma. il map *Audubon* 89:36-8+ Mr '87
A golden deal: debt for nature. J. D. Hair. il *Int Wildl* 17:30 S/O '87
Green devolution [West Germany] il map *Natl Parks* 61:17 S/O '87
Hamburgers are killing trees [boycott of fast-food outlets until they stop using Central American beef] il *Newsweek* 110:54 S 14 '87
A hope for the Himalayas and its people. il *Environment* 29:10-11 Ap '87
Idaho batholith. B. G. Norton. il map *Wilderness* 50:30-1 Spr '87
Impact of deforestation on local weather. *Sea Front* 33:64 Ja/F '87
In the tropics, still rolling back the rain forest primeval [Costa Rica] J. Omang. bibl (p182) il *Smithsonian* 17:56-60+ Mr '87
Is Nepal going bald? T. Kerasote. il map *Audubon* 89:28-30+ S '87
The last frontier [Brazil's Amazon policy] B. Levin. il *Macleans* 100:28 Ja 19 '87
Life, the great chemistry experiment [State of the earth 1987] S. Postel. il *Nat Hist* 96:41-8 Ap '87
MacArthur Foundation grants to combat deforestation. il *BioScience* 37:236 Mr '87
Mike Benge and his marvelous tree [leucaena used to halt deforestation] J. G. Hubbell. il por *Read Dig* 131:103-7 Ag '87
'Mount Everest is a junk pile' [Himalayan pollution] S. Begley. il *Newsweek* 110:104-5 N 16 '87
One costly hamburger [importation of Central American beef contributes to tropical deforestation; views of Christopher Uhl] *Ctry J* 14:12-13 Ag '87
Peter Raven [tropical deforestation expert] B. Lawren. *Omni* 9:38+ S '87
Preserving old-growth forests. D. B. Edelson. bibl f il *Environment* 29:3-5 O '87
Public dismay over private cuts [clearcutting by Plum Creek Timber Company on private land in the Pacific Northwest] J. Sher. il *Sierra* 72:83-4 Mr/Ap '87
Root rot turns back the clock on the Yosemite Valley [trees destroyed by fungus Fomes annosus] il *Discover* 8:10+ Ja '87
Rubber and Amazon alliances. S. Schwartzman. il map *Technol Rev* 90:15-16 Ap '87
The shrinking province of the primeval [Pacific Northwest; cover story] K. Ervin. il map *Sierra* 72:38-45 Jl/Ag '87
Tree death: cause and consequence [cover story; special issue] il *BioScience* 37:542-6+ S '87
Trouble ahead for the Canal? [deforestation may cause water shortage in Panama Canal] J. Borrell. il *Time* 129:63 Mr 2 '87
We're killing our world [address, February 14, 1987] P. H. Raven. *Vital Speeches Day* 53:472-8 My 15 '87
Deformation, Tectonic *See* Geology
Deformation (Mechanics)
See also
   Crystals—Defects

Deformation (Mechanics)—See also—*cont.*
Rheology
DeFrain, John
(jt. auth) See Stinnett, Nick, and DeFrain, John
DeFrantz, Anita
about
1987 Essence Awards. A. Edwards. pors *Essence* 18:121+ My '87
Black woman named prexy of Olympic surplus fund. por *Jet* 72:48 Jl 27 '87
Olympic veteran becomes 1st black woman on IOC. por *Jet* 71:51 F 9 '87
Defrosters, Windshield *See* Automobiles—Windshield defrosters
DEG Film Studio
Tar Heel Tinseltown: De Laurentiis does it in North Carolina. D. Myers and D. Ewing. il *Theatre Crafts* 21:53-4 Ap '87
Degnan, Daniel A.
Bound by the Constitution. *Commonweal* 114:481-3 S 11 '87
Degradable plastics *See* Plastics—Deterioration
Degradation (Biology) *See* Biodegradation
DeGraff, Lee, and Dell, Joseph
Restoring New York's wildlife. il *Conservationist* 42:2-11+ N/D '87
Degrassi Junior High [television program] *See* Television program reviews—Single works
Degré, Alain
Together we stand . . . [photographs; cover story] il *Nat Hist* 96:34-9 Je '87
Degree days
Degree days: heating and cooling by the numbers. J. M. Mitchell. il *Weatherwise* 40:334-6 D '87
Degrees, Academic
See also
International baccalaureate
Academe and the boom in business studies. il *Change* 19:37-42 S/O '87
Advice on applying for a postdoc. P. W. Anderson. por *Phys Today* 40:7+ S '87
High school-community college cooperation creates a degree [2 + 2 tech-prep/associate degree] D. Parnell. *Educ Dig* 52:40-1 Mr '87
Survey of physics bachelors finds that more plan to teach. *Phys Today* 40:76 S '87
Degrees, Honorary
Camille Cosby delivers Howard graduation address; receives honorary degree. il por *Jet* 72:24 Je 1 '87
Central State University lands Nigerian business exec. at commencement [A. Ojora] il por *Jet* 72:25 Jl 27 '87
CSU honors Stevie Wonder for role in national King holiday [Central State University] il por *Jet* 71:12-13 F 9 '87
Dr. Gloster weeps as he awards Wonder last degree as president of Morehouse. il pors *Jet* 72:24 Je 8 '87
Nobel winner will accept a Morehouse degree only [African writer W. Soyinka] il por *Jet* 72:28 Ap 27 '87
DeHainaut, Raymond K.
Church and insurrection in Argentina. *Christ Century* 104:582-3 Jl 1-8 '87
DeHavilland Aircraft of Canada, Limited
Americanization of a high-flyer [since the Boeing takeover] P. C. Newman. il *Macleans* 100:42 F 23 '87
De Havilland rolls out stretched Dash 8-300. P. Proctor. il *Aviat Week Space Technol* 126:32-3 Mr 30 '87
Workers strike at Bell Helicopter, De Havilland plants. *Aviat Week Space Technol* 126:27 Je 29 '87
Dehmlow, Louis
A one-size-fits-all leave policy? por *U S News World Rep* 103:11 D 7 '87
Dehumidifiers
Dehumidifier buying guide. il *Consum Res Mag* 70:21-3 Je '87
Humidity capacities. P. L. Spencer. il *Consum Res Mag* 70:2 Jl '87
Deibel, Terry L.
Hidden commitments. *Foreign Policy* 67:46-63 Summ '87
Deieso, Donald A.
(jt. auth) See Nicholls, Gerald P., and Deieso, Donald A.
Deigh, Robb
Celebrating the Constitution. il *Saturday Evening Post* 259:54-6+ My/Je '87
Deinstitutionalization of the mentally ill *See* Mentally ill—Care and treatment

Deitz, Paula
The cuff. il *Esquire* 107:F63 Mr '87
DeJohnette, Jack
about
The Jack DeJohnette interview [cover story] B. Beuttler. il pors *Down Beat* 54:16-19 S '87
Dekin, Albert A., Jr.
Sealed in time: ice entombs an Eskimo family for five centuries. il map *Natl Geogr* 171:824-36 Je '87
Dekker, Fred
about
The Monster Squad [film] Reviews
People Wkly 28:14 S 7 '87. T. Cunneff
DeKoevend, Derk
about
Mothers, don't raise your sons to drive snow-cats. A. Pospisil. il *Skiing* 40:220 O '87
Del Aguila, Juan M.
Cuba's declining fortunes. bibl f *Curr Hist* 86:425-8+ D '87
Del E. Webb Corp.
Del Webb's turnaround turns out to be a mirage. T. Carson. il *Bus Week* p132+ D 7 '87
Don't read too much into Del Webb's downturn [stock price] G. G. Marcial. il *Bus Week* p61 Ag 31 '87
Fast-track stumble. J. A. Conway. il *Forbes* 139:8 Ap 6 '87
Del Guidice, Robert
about
Singing the company blues. M. Antonoff. il por *Pers Comput* 11:155+ O '87
Del Mar (Calif.)
Architecture
A coastal contradiction in terms [beach house designed for Bill and Lila Jaeger by R. W. Quigley] P. M. Sachner. il *Archit Rec* 175:146-9 Je '87
Del Tredici, Robert
about
The bomb we never see. J. Schell. il *Progressive* 51:25-8 D '87
Dela Peña, Andrew
about
Racing for life. J. Korman. il pors *N Y Times Mag* p62-4+ S 20 '87
Delabar, Jean-Maurice, and others
β amyloid gene duplication in Alzheimer's disease and karyotypically normal Down syndrome. bibl f il *Science* 235:1390-2 Mr 13 '87
Delaney, Kevin
"We thought our faith could save our son". il pors *Redbook* 168:104-6 Ja '87
Delaney, Robert V.
Saving on trucking costs. il *Consum Res Mag* 70:31-3 My '87
Tilting at the windmills of transportation policy [address, May 27, 1987] *Vital Speeches Day* 53:627-30 Ag 1 '87
Delaney Clause *See* Food laws and regulations
Delano, William Adams, 1874-1960
about
William Adams Delano and the Muttontown enclave. M. A. Hewitt. bibl f il *Antiques* 132:316-27 Ag '87
DeLaRosa, Lupe
Oaxaca's gift of music and dance. il *Américas* 39:58-60 Ja/F '87
Delatiner, Barbara
When it's time to quit your job. il *McCalls* 114:21+ Ap '87
Delaveyne, Jean
about
Chefs of influence. N. Barry. il pors *Gourmet* 47:82-3+ D '87
Delaware
See also
Brandywine Valley (Pa. and Del.)
Criminal justice, Administration of—Delaware
Education—Delaware
Kent County (Del.)
Legislation—Delaware
Prisons—Delaware
Delaware Bay (Del. and N.J.)
Birds of a feather feed together [feeding on horseshoe crab eggs by migrating shore birds] W. P. Carty. il *Américas* 39:28-33+ S/O '87
Delaware Correctional Center (Smyrna, Del.) *See* Prisons—Delaware
Delaware furniture *See* Furniture, American
DeLay, Dorothy, 1917-
about
The genius of teaching geniuses [interview] M. Horn. il por *U S News World Rep* 103:59 Jl 27 '87

Delay devices
Sound Concepts SSD550 time-delay system. J. D. Hirsch. il *Stereo Rev* 52:39-40 O '87
Very simple delay circuits. R. Grossblatt. il *Radio-Electron* 58:34-5 S '87

Delbanco, Andrew, 1952-
Holden Caulfield goes to law school. *New Repub* 196:27-8+ Mr 9 '87

Delchamps, Oliver H., Jr.
about
Looking ahead. D. Marth. il pors *Nations Bus* 75:69-70 Je '87

Delchamps, Inc.
Looking ahead [O. H. Delchamps] D. Marth. il pors *Nations Bus* 75:69-70 Je '87

Delegation of authority in business *See* Personnel management

Delehanty, Hugh
(jt. auth) See Mills, Judy, and Delehanty, Hugh

Delfi American Corporation
No free samples. J. Willoughby. il por *Forbes* 140:165 S 7 '87

Delfs, Robert
The reformists strike back. il *World Press Rev* 34:25-6 S '87

Delgass, W. Nicholas, and Cooks, R. G.
Focal points in mass spectrometry. bibl f il *Science* 235:545-53 Ja 30 '87

Delhagen, Kate
2001 a sports odyssey. il *Women's Sports Fitness* 9:32-3 Ag '87
Be your own bike mechanic. bibl il *Women's Sports Fitness* 9:68-9 My '87
The many shapes of sport. il *Women's Sports Fitness* 9:28-31 F '87
Test yourself. il *Women's Sports Fitness* 9:32-6+ Ja '87
Turn your living room into a velodrome. il *Women's Sports Fitness* 9:10-11 N '87
Weatherproof workout. il *Women's Sports Fitness* 9:50+ O '87

Delhi (India) *See* New Delhi (India)

D'Elia, Christopher F.
Nutrient enrichment of the Chesapeake Bay [cover story; with editorial comment by Alan McGowan and Abel Wolman] bibl f il map *Environment* 29:inside cover, 2-3, 6-11+ Mr '87

Delinquents *See* Juvenile delinquents and delinquency

Delivery of goods
See also
United Parcel Service of America, Inc.

Dell, Joseph
(jt. auth) See DeGraff, Lee, and Dell, Joseph

Dell, Michael
about
Computer technology to go. D. Garfinkel. il pors *Pers Comput* 11:168-71+ N '87
The hottest little computer maker in Texas. G. Lewis. il por *Bus Week* p71-2 F 2 '87

Dell Computer Corporation
Computer technology to go. D. Garfinkel. il pors *Pers Comput* 11:168-71+ N '87
The hottest little computer maker in Texas. G. Lewis. il por *Bus Week* p71-2 F 2 '87

Dell Publishing Co., Inc.
Random House, Dell launch series for younger readers. il *Publ Wkly* 232:24 S 25 '87

Della Femina, Jerry, 1936-
Miss Rheingold. il *N Y* 20:74-5 D 21-28 '87
about
An aging boy wonder shakes up the ad business. P. Nulty. il pors *Fortune* 115:86-8 Ap 13 '87

Della Femina, Travisano & Partners
An aging boy wonder shakes up the ad business [J. Della Femina] P. Nulty. il pors *Fortune* 115:86-8 Ap 13 '87

Della Illien, Phyllis
about
Big wig. J. Roberts. il por *N Y* 20:16 Ja 12 '87

Delle Chiaie, Stefano
about
Delle Chiaie: from Bologna to Bolivia [cover story] G. Black. il *Nation* 244:525+ Ap 25 '87

Delloff, Linda-Marie
Distorted images: the elderly and the media. il *Christ Century* 104:12-16 Ja 7-14 '87

Dellums, Ronald V., 1935-
about
The Dellums record [discussion of January 1987 article, Another "low dishonest decade" on the left] D. Horowitz and P. Collier. *Commentary* 84:2-3+ Jl '87

DeLoache, Judy S.
Rapid change in the symbolic functioning of very young children. bibl f il *Science* 238:1556-7 D 11 '87

DeLong, Kari
about
Jefferson graduate aims for the top. M. U. West. por *Dance Mag* 61:100-1 S '87

Delphi Management Inc.
Stocks even a skeptic can love [views of S. M. Black] C. Farrell. *Bus Week* p69 F 2 '87

Delphinus (Constellation) *See* Constellations

Delta (Launch vehicle) *See* Space vehicles—Propulsion systems

Delta Air Lines, Inc.
A case of Delta blues. il *Time* 130:53 Jl 27 '87
Dark clouds over Delta [four near misses] il *Newsweek* 110:41 Jl 20 '87
Delta Air Lines officials baffled by series of unrelated mishaps. C. Preble. il *Aviat Week Space Technol* 127:31-2 Jl 20 '87
FAA investigation focuses on Delta operations, training. C. Preble. il *Aviat Week Space Technol* 127:31 Jl 27 '87
FAA urges use of standard procedures, more discipline in Delta cockpits. E. H. Phillips. *Aviat Week Space Technol* 127:44 S 28 '87
Supreme Court overturns injunction blocking Delta-Western merger. C. Preble. map *Aviat Week Space Technol* 126:32-3 Ap 6 '87
There's more choppiness ahead for Delta. S. Ticer. il *Bus Week* p30-1 Ag 3 '87
What's wrong with Delta? T. E. Johnson. il *Newsweek* 110:25 Jl 27 '87

Delta Hotels Ltd.
Delta's spreading welcome mat. P. C. Newman. il por *Macleans* 100:35 Ag 3 '87

Delta Waterfowl and Wetlands Research Station (Man.)
Working their magic on ducks. G. Turbak. il *Int Wildl* 17:24-8 Mr/Ap '87

Deltas
See also
Yazoo River (Miss.)—Delta

DeLuca, Liza N.
Open your eyes to vision training. il *World Tennis* 35:16-17 Ag '87

DeLuise, Peter
about
Class acts: guys who make the grade. M. L. Baer. il pors *Teen* 31:59-60 N '87

DeLynn, Jane
Booked up! Undercover attractions. il *Harpers Bazaar* 120:30+ Jl '87
John Sayles mines new film territory. por *Harpers Bazaar* 120:382+ S '87

Demac, Donna A.
Sworn to silence. il *Progressive* 51:29-32 My '87

DeMaeyer, Edouard M.
A three-pronged programme. il *World Health* p22 My '87

DeMain, John
about
Music director John DeMain: the real thing. G. Heymont. il por *Opera News* 52:22 O '87

Demak, Richard
Fighting the enemy within. il pors *Sports Illus* 66:40-3 Je 22 '87
The pain that won't go away. il *Sports Illus* 66:60-2+ Ap 27 '87

Demand and supply *See* Supply and demand

DeMarco, Mario A.
Western movie stars: yesterday's heroes. il *Antiques Collect Hobbies* 92:50-4 O '87

DeMarinis, Rick, 1934-
Before the beginning. *Writer* 100:12-14 Ag '87
Mole [story] il *Harpers* 274:63-5 Mr '87

Demartini, Pablo
(jt. auth) See Rolfe, John, and Demartini, Pablo

Dembner Books
Dembner Books [manuscript submission policy] T. Eiben. *Writer* 100:31 O '87

Dembo, Fennis
about
They're jumping for joy. C. Kirkpatrick. il pors *Sports Illus* 67 Sp Issue:20-3+ N 18 '87

DeMello, Dennis
about
Pro challenge. il por *Pop Photogr* 94:58 Je '87

Dementia
See also
AIDS (Disease)
Alzheimer's disease

Dementia—See also—*cont.*
  Senility
Demers, Jacques, 1944-
about
New model in Motown. A. Murphy. il pors *Sports Illus* 66:30-2 Mr 16 '87
Demers, Rock
about
Movie magic for the child in everyone. B. D. Johnson. il por *Macleans* 100:57 Mr 16 '87
Demers, Shirley
about
Create a Christmas fantasy. I. Jones. il por *Ctry J* 14:41-2 D '87
Deming, W. Edwards
about
The American who saved Japan. P. M. Jones. por *Sch Update* 119:8 Ap 6 '87
Demjanjuk, John
about
Demjanjuk in Jerusalem. L. Wieseltier. *New Repub* 196:15-16 Mr 30 '87
Eerie echoes of the Nazi death camps. M. McIver. por *Macleans* 100:42 Ag 17 '87
The hell of Treblinka. K. Scanlon. il por *Macleans* 100:23 Mr 23 '87
"I can't even kill a chicken". M. S. Serrill. il por *Time* 130:23 Ag 10 '87
Ivan the Terrible? *Natl Rev* 39:18-19 Mr 27 '87
'Like long-gone history'. N. Cooper. il por *Newsweek* 109:36 Mr 2 '87
'A trial against forgetting'. R. Rosenberg. il por *U S News World Rep* 102:36 Mr 9 '87
Trial by bitter recollection. W. E. Smith. il por *Time* 129:31 Mr 2 '87
Trials of an expert witness. E. F. Loftus. por *Newsweek* 109:10-11 Je 29 '87
Demme, Jonathan
about
Jonathan Demme. J. Hammer. il pors *People Wkly* 27:91-2+ My 25 '87
Something wild [film] Reviews
  Glamour 85:131 Ja '87. J. G. Boyum
Swimming to Cambodia [film] Reviews
  Glamour 85:218 My '87. J. G. Boyum
  Macleans 100:62 Ap 27 '87. L. O'Toole
  Mademoiselle il 93:46-7+ Jl '87. R. Rosenbaum
  N Y il 20:82+ Mr 23 '87. D. Denby
  N Y Times Mag il p40+ Mr 8 '87. M. Simpson
  Nation 244:518-20 Ap 18 '87. T. Rafferty
  New Repub 196:24 Mr 23 '87. S. Kauffmann
  New Yorker 63:84-5 Ap 6 '87. P. Kael
  Time 129:79 Ap 27 '87. R. Schickel
Democracy
See also
  Black suffrage
  Communism and democracy
  Education and democracy
  Liberty
  National Endowment for Democracy
Above the battle, democracy gains. H. Trewhitt. il *U S News World Rep* 103:26-7 Jl 27 '87
The age of media democracy [interview with P. Johnson] A. P. Sanoff. por *U S News World Rep* 102:68 Je 22 '87
Democracy and Colonel North. L. Wieseltier. *New Repub* 196:22-5 Ja 26 '87
Democracy and its heroes. J. R. Silber. *Current* 294:16-19 Jl/Ag '87
Democracy expanding worldwide [views of Seymour Martin Lipset] il *USA Today (Periodical)* 116:13-14 D '87
Democracy in Latin America and the Caribbean: the promise and the challenge. il *Dep State Bull* 87:58-89 Mr '87
Democracy is not easy. A. Vasinsky. *World Press Rev* 34:18-19 Ap '87
Diplomacy for democracy [Reagan administration policy] W. Lowther. il *Macleans* 100:18 Jl 27 '87
The expansion of democracy [address, July 24, 1987] S. M. Lipset. *Vital Speeches Day* 53:748-51 O 1 '87
The fragile polity. B. Crozier. *Natl Rev* 39:30 Ja 30 '87
Guerrillas who came in from the cold [restoration of democracy in Uruguay, Argentina, and Brazil] C. A. Robbins. il *U S News World Rep* 102:33-4 My 11 '87
The price of power [relationship of democracy to foreign policy] C. Krauthammer. *New Repub* 196:23-5 F 9 '87

The surge to democracy [with discussion] R. A. Falk. il por *Cent Mag* 20:44-50 My/Je '87
Democratic Caucus (U.S.) See House Democratic Caucus (U.S.)
Democratic congressmen See Congressmen
Democratic conventions See National conventions, Democratic
Democratic Leadership Council
The DLC: seeking a party shift to the right. D. C. Ruffin. il *Black Enterp* 17:19 Mr '87
How to talk about economic strategy [Catholic bishops' pastoral letter and Democratic Leadership Council's conference in Williamsburg] A. Cockburn and R. Pollin. il *Nation* 244:245-7 F 28 '87
Toward a socialist strategy [discussion of February 28, 1987 article, How to talk about economic strategy] A. Cockburn and R. Pollin. *Nation* 244:748+ Je 6 '87
Democratic National Committee
Kirk's cant [P. Kirk's proposal to arrest the decline of voter participation in elections] T. Ferguson. *Nation* 244:385 Mr 28 '87
Democratic Party (U.S.)
See also
  Democratic Leadership Council
  National conventions, Democratic
The 100th Congress: the Democrats take charge [special issue] il maps *Sch Update* 119:2-24 Ja 12 '87
Another useful tool [discussion of April 18, 1987 article, Democrats and the Arias plan] L. Annunziata. *Nation* 244:565 My 2 '87
Aspin's scalp [House Armed Services Committee chairman L. Aspin deposed] *New Repub* 196:7 F 2 '87
Baby-boomerang: why the Democrats can't count on generational politics. F. F. Siegel. *Commonweal* 114:442-5 Ag 14 '87
The closing of the Democratic mind. *New Repub* 197:7-10 O 19 '87
Congress's Red Army [pro-Communist Democrats; cover story] J. M. Waller and J. Sobran. il *Natl Rev* 39:25-8 Jl 31 '87
A Democrat looks at foreign policy. A. M. Schlesinger. *Foreign Aff* 66:263-83 Wint '87/'88
Democratic jubilation has given way to sober reality. il *Nations Bus* 75:87 D '87
Democrats and the Arias plan [cover story] L. Annunziata. il *Nation* 244:489+ Ap 18 '87
Democrats award King Scholarships to 5 youths. *Jet* 72:8 Mr 30 '87
The Democrats' glass chin [opposition to R. Bork nomination to Supreme Court] G. F. Will. il *Newsweek* 110:66 Jl 20 '87
The Democrats go home licking their wounds. D. Harbrecht. il por *Bus Week* p72 D 28 '87-Ja 4 '88
The Democrats may be losing a game of chicken on the budget. P. Magnuson and D. Harbrecht. il *Bus Week* p43 O 26 '87
The Democrats: no more cover. G. Borger. il *U S News World Rep* 102:18-19 Mr 23 '87
The Democrats' zero options [foreign policy leadership] P. Osterlund. *Natl Rev* 39:36+ Je 19 '87
Dixie fix: can the Democrats win the South? F. Barnes. *New Repub* 197:10+ N 2 '87
Edward Kennedy [interview] W. Greider. il por *Roll Stone* p99-100 N 5-D 10 '87
The fall and rise of Les Aspin. J. D. Isaacs. il por *Bull At Sci* 43:4-5 Ap '87
Farewell to reform—almost. A. Ranney. bibl *Society* 24:29-38 My/Je '87
Happy days are here again. *Natl Rev* 39:17 F 27 '87
How to win in '88: meld the unmeldable. N. J. Ornstein. il *U S News World Rep* 103:31-2+ O 12 '87
In the House, an abrasive defender of defense [L. Aspin] D. Griffiths. por *Bus Week* p53 Ag 24 '87
Job training: the Democrats are stealing the show. M. E. Recio. il *Bus Week* p53 Mr 9 '87
Labels can be misleading [study by Warren E. Miller and M. Kent Jennings] il *USA Today (Periodical)* 116:12 D '87
The lady has a Midas touch [Democratic fund raising dinners hosted by P. Harriman] E. Thomas. il pors *Newsweek* 109:32-3 Je 15 '87
Letter from Washington. Cato. *Natl Rev* 39:15 Mr 13 '87
A lot of Nunnsense [agenda for 1988] W. Greider. il *Roll Stone* p57+ Mr 26 '87
The men who put dough behind the Democrats. R. Fly. il *Bus Week* p168+ O 12 '87
The new Senate Democrats: no bunch of rookies. D. Harbrecht. il *Bus Week* p74-5 Ja 26 '87

Democratic Party (U.S.)—*cont.*

The Old Breed strikes back [backlash against L. Aspin] C. J. Matthews. il *New Repub* 196:21-3 Mr 2 '87

A party of outsiders. D. R. Carlin, Jr. *Commonweal* 114:553-4 O 9 '87

Pas de scandale à gauche [congressional Democrats' relations with the Sandinistas] *Natl Rev* 39:17 Je 19 '87

Rebuilding the parties [address, April 7, 1987] R. J. Dole. *Vital Speeches Day* 53:482-4 Je 1 '87

Sam Nunn is sticking to his guns. D. Griffiths. il por *Bus Week* p52-3 Ag 24 '87

Selling higher taxes. R. Kuttner. *New Repub* 197:23-5 Ag 24 '87

Targeting youth. J. McLaughlin. *Natl Rev* 39:24 Je 19 '87

Trade: the Democrats come out swinging—at one another. D. Harbrecht and B. Javetski. il *Bus Week* p41 Mr 30 '87

Whose ax is gored [bipartisan move to revive the Gramm-Rudman act] R. Kuttner. *New Repub* 197:19+ O 12 '87

Why the Democrats lose elections [cover story] G. F. Will. il *Natl Rev* 39:28-9+ D 18 '87

Year of the donkey. J. McLaughlin. *Natl Rev* 39:28 Ja 30 '87

Democratic presidential candidates *See* Presidential candidates

Demography

See also

Population forecasting

Demolition derbies, Automobile *See* Automobile demolition derbies

Demolition of buildings *See* Wrecking

Demonology

See also

Temple of Set

Suicide and satanism [case of 16 yr. old D. Shaw in Canada] C. Wood. il *Macleans* 100:54 Mr 30 '87

Demonstrations *See* Protests, demonstrations, etc.

DeMott, Benjamin

Changing teaching practices: what school-college collaboration is all about. *Change* 19:36 S/O '87

Judging a good college: the importance of the 'voice' of the institution. *Change* 19:5 Ja/F '87

A matter of mission: the dilemma of teaching in expensive places. *Change* 19:62 My/Je '87

Dempsey, Patrick

about

The spotlight's on . . . Patrick Dempsey. il pors *Teen* 31:62 N '87

Dempsey, Paul Stephen

Fear of flying frequently. por *Newsweek* 110:12 O 5 '87

Demuth, Charles, 1883-1935

about

Charles Demuth amid the silos. R. Hughes. il *Time* 130:91 D 7 '87

He was an acrobat on the leading edge of Jazz Age art. A. O. Dean. bibl (p229) il por *Smithsonian* 18:58-64+ O '87

History painting. K. Larson. il *N Y* 20:121-2 N 9 '87

Technical page. J. R. Doyle. il *Am Artist* 51:32+ S '87

Demyelination

Genetic aspects

Shiverless deportment [gene surgery for mice lacking myelin basic protein; work of Leroy E. Hood] il *Sci Am* 256:64 My '87

Denali National Park and Preserve (Alaska)

Caribou, tundra, whitewater, Mount McKinley . . . Alaska adventures. il map *Sunset* 178:72-4+ Je '87

Giants of the wilderness: Alaskan moose. V. Van Ballenberghe. il map *Natl Geogr* 172:260-80 Ag '87

Denby, David

Movies. See issues of New York

Ollie North, the movie. il *New Repub* 197:7-9 Ag 3 '87

(jt. auth) See Schine, Cathleen, and Denby, David

Denby, Edwin, 1903-1983

about

Denby on dance. D. Kaufman. il pors *Horizon* 30:38-40 Jl/Ag '87

Dendrites *See* Nerve cells

Deneuve, Catherine

about

Cinema's serene queen. B. Brantley. por *Harpers Bazaar* 120:204-5+ F '87

Deng Xiaoping, 1904-

about

Battle of the octogenarians. M. S. Serrill. il *Time* 129:50 Mr 9 '87

Broken China. J. Mirsky. *Foreign Policy* 66:57-76 Spr '87

Can Deng protect his reforms from the 'angry old men'? M. Shao and others. por *Bus Week* p53 F 2 '87

China [cover story; special section] il *World Press Rev* 34:11-16 Mr '87

China drops the copilot. R. Watson. il por *Newsweek* 109:30-1 Ja 26 '87

China hits the clutch. M. Hopkins. por *New Leader* 70:3-4 Ja 12-26 '87

China takes the reformist road. A. Joyce. il *Nation* 245:752-4 D 19 '87

China's last emperor. M. Hopkins. il *New Leader* 70:7-10 O 19 '87

China's new Year of the Mule. F. Willey. il por *Newsweek* 109:43 F 9 '87

China's student rebels are playing into Deng's hands. M. Shao. il por *Bus Week* p48-9 Ja 19 '87

Deng cracks down. J. Smolowe. il por *Time* 129:24-5 Ja 26 '87

Deng's balancing act. F. Willey. il por *Newsweek* 110:33 Ag 17 '87

Deng's reforms will prevail—but at a price. D. J. Yang and M. Shao. il por *Bus Week* p70-1+ O 19 '87

Deng's second revolution: prosperity vs. ideology. M. Lord. il por *U S News World Rep* 103:41-3 O 12 '87

Free speech Chinese style [special section] il por *Newsweek* 109:30-1+ Ja 5 '87

The long shadow of Mao. F. Willey. il por *Newsweek* 109:40 Mr 16 '87

The old man and the mountains. H. G. Chua-Eoan. il *Time* 130:41 Jl 13 '87

Political reform in China. M. Gottschalk. il *Nation* 244:677-80 My 23 '87

Reading the fortune cookies. H. Trewhitt. il por *U S News World Rep* 102:37-8 Mr 16 '87

Deng Yuzhen

Reaching the grass-roots. il *World Health* p20-1 Je '87

Denial (Psychology)

Healthy denial [helping bypass patients to improve health; research by David G. Folks and Arthur M. Freeman] L. Crawford. il *Psychol Today* 21:24 O '87

If I've got it, it can't be that bad [downplaying the seriousness of an illness; study by John Jemmott] V. Bozzi. *Psychol Today* 21:18 Ja '87

Reality? Just say no [R. Reagan's denial syndrome] G. Sheehy. *New Repub* 196:16-18 Mr 30 '87

Denim

Denim: its popularity never fades. il *Teen* 31:70-3 F '87

Denison, Ray

Protecting workers in the marketplace: new union benefit privileges. *Mon Labor Rev* 110:39-40 Ag '87

Denman, Rose Mary

about

A Methodist on trial. M. Starr. il por *Newsweek* 110:62 S 7 '87

Denmark

See also

Allerød (Denmark)

Dance festivals—Denmark

Pollution—Denmark

Pornography—Denmark

Sex crimes—Denmark

Stone Age—Denmark

Defenses

Danes bristle at U.S. radar plans [phased-array radar planned for Thule, Greenland complicates ABM Treaty] M. Burcharth. il map *Bull At Sci* 43:11-13 Je '87

Foreign relations

United States

See United States—Foreign relations—Denmark

Military policy

Denmark OK's radar [upgrading of the U.S. early warning system at Thule in Greenland] D. Dickson. *Science* 235:1456 Mr 20 '87

Denneny, Michael

The universal voice of gay writers. por *Publ Wkly* 232:48 Jl 3 '87

Denning, Robert

about

Entertaining. W. P. Rayner and C. Rayner. il *Vogue* 177:222 Ap '87

Dennis, Clue Tyler

October farewell. il *Conservationist* 42:56 S/O '87

Dennis, Ed
Diesels. See issues of Motor Boating & Sailing

Dennis, James W., and others
β1-6 branching of Asn-linked oligosaccharides is directly associated with metastasis. bibl f il *Science* 236:582-5 My 1 '87

Dennis, Landt
Contemporary caravansary: the Hotel Tichka in Marrakesh. il *Archit Dig* 44:52-9+ Ja '87
Habitation Pécoul: Vicomte and Vicomtesse d'Origny on Martinique. il *Archit Dig* 44:192-7+ O '87

Dennis, Paul, Jr.
Deep mulch. bibl il *Mother Earth News* 105:89-90+ My/Je '87

Dennis, Shirley M.
about
Shirley Dennis hailed as new Women's Bureau boss. il por *Jet* 71:4 Mr 23 '87

Dennis Wayne's Dancers
Reviews:
Performances at the Triplex, Manhattan Community College. E. Zimmer. *Dance Mag* 61:26+ Ag '87

Dennison, Joe
Steve Morse's The whistle—a guitar transcription. il *Down Beat* 54:59 Ap '87
Terje Rypdal's The curse—a guitar transcription. il *Down Beat* 54:56 O '87

Dennon, A. R.
Are the elderly overinsured? il *Consum Res Mag* 70:16-19 Mr '87

Denny's Inc.
The first name in coffee shops [Marriott's bid for Denny's] T. Ichniowski. il *Bus Week* p35-6 Je 15 '87
TW's numbers man throws caution to the winds [F. L. Salizzoni buys Denny's] L. Baum. il por *Bus Week* p67-9 Ag 3 '87

Dens (Rooms)
Redwood renovation. J. Truini. il *Pop Mech* 164:112-14+ Ap '87

Dental caries
Chewing away cavities [use of xylitol gum; research by Kauko Makinen] *Prevention* 39:15 S '87
Does sugarless gum really prevent cavities? il *Parents* 62:27 N '87
Prevention
See Teeth—Care and hygiene
Vaccines and vaccination
Vaccination against tooth decay. H. Donoghue. il *World Press Rev* 34:52 My '87

Dental equipment
See also
Dental materials
Toothbrushes
Toothpastes, powders, etc.

Dental hygiene See Teeth—Care and hygiene
Dental materials
How safe are your dental fillings? [mercury amalgam fillings] il *Glamour* 85:330+ My '87
Titanium tooth crowns. *Pop Sci* 231:34 Jl '87

Dental plaque
Fighting dental plaque. J. E. Brody. il *Essence* 17:17+ Ja '87
Glorious gargle [chlorhexidine gluconate] D. Groves. *Health* 19:22-3 F '87

Dentifrices See Toothpastes, powders, etc.
Dentistry
See also
AIDS patients—Dental care
Dentures
Indians of North America—Dental care
Orthodontics
Pedodontics
Teeth
Dental advances: what's here now, what's ahead? il *Glamour* 85:236+ D '87
Dentistry: forecasting the future. D. Born. il *Saturday Evening Post* 259:30-1+ S '87
Dentists polish up their image. D. Boetig. il *Saturday Evening Post* 259:28-9+ N '87
A different kind of oral sensation [electronic dental anesthesia] *Sci News* 132:268 O 24 '87
Flash a fabulous smile with new dental methods. il *Ladies Home J* 104:20 Ja '87
Giving teeth a face-lift [bonding] L. S. Senz. il *Saturday Evening Post* 259:30-1 O '87
Great teeth [cosmetic dentistry] J. Mandelbaum-Schmid. *Vogue* 177:212+ Mr '87
No-fear dentistry: 4 breakthroughs. M. Mihalik. il *Prevention* 39:81+ N '87
Pain-free dentistry? [electronic anesthesia] L. S. Senz. *Health* 19:20 D '87

Smile, America: a special dental health-care section. il *McCalls* 114:107-8+ F '87
Smile makeovers [bonding] il *McCalls* 114:41 F '87
Terrific teeth. R. Lewis. il *Health* 19:74-9 Je '87
Your brightest, whitest smile: the newest ways to get it. il *Glamour* 85:302-5 Mr '87
Psychological aspects
Dental esthetics: a bridge too far? [study by Naham C. Cons and others] E. Bird. il *Psychol Today* 21:16 S '87
Fighting your fear of the dentist. P. C. Bartel. il *Seventeen* 46:235 Ag '87

Dentists
See also
AIDS (Disease) and dentists
National Dental Association
Dentists polish up their image. D. Boetig. il *Saturday Evening Post* 259:28-9+ N '87
Health and hygiene
How safe is your dentist? D. Born. il *Saturday Evening Post* 259:28-9+ Jl/Ag '87

Dentists and patients
Do dentists know when it hurts? [facial expressions of juvenile patients; study by Ann Rowland] G. Lowe. *Psychol Today* 21:12 Ag '87
Patients. M. L. Magie. *Commentary* 83:48-52 F '87
Anecdotes, facetiae, satire, etc.
The crime of the tooth. P. Freundlich. *Harpers* 275:65-8 S '87

Denton, James S., and Schweizer, Peter, 1964-
Murdering SDI. *Natl Rev* 39:37-9 Jl 31 '87

Denton, John R.
Lower back pain: coping with a common problem. por *McCalls* 114:84 Ag '87

Dentsu Inc.
Japan is getting too small for Dentsu. T. Holden and A. Dunkin. il *Bus Week* p62+ O 26 '87

Dentures
Titanium tooth crowns. *Pop Sci* 231:34 Jl '87

Denver, John
about
The John Denver '87 farm program. *Success Farm* 85:62K O '87
The stars who make Christmas special. L. Feldman. il pors *McCalls* 115:90+ D '87

Denver (Colo.)
Air pollution
Time out for clear air [using daylight-saving time year round to improve Denver's air] B. Most. *Pop Sci* 231:115 N '87
Airports
FAA assessing impact of regulation setting airline noise budget at Denver's Stapleton Airport. *Aviat Week Space Technol* 126:33 Mr 30 '87
Pilots glean shear information from operational LLWAS tests [low-level wind shear alert system at Stapleton International Airport] *Aviat Week Space Technol* 127:25 Ag 24 '87
What's keeping new airports from getting off the ground [Stapleton Airport] M. Ivey. il *Bus Week* p32 Jl 27 '87
Auditoriums, convention facilities, etc.
Denver's quiet billionaire comes out fighting [P. Anschutz] M. Ivey. il por *Bus Week* p70-1 Jl 27 '87
A dogfight in Denver [fight between Mayor F. Peña and billionaire P. F. Anschutz] M. Ivey. il por *Bus Week* p38 Ap 27 '87
Banks
See also
Colorado National Bank
Bookstores
See Booksellers and bookselling—Colorado
Music
See also
Opera Colorado
Parks and playgrounds
Biking, walking, fishing Denver's Platte River Greenway. il map *Sunset* 178:52-4 Je '87
Politics and government
Webb wins, becomes 1st black auditor of Denver. por *Jet* 72:38 Ag 10 '87
Sanitary affairs
Recycled waste water: Denver's scheme [Potable Water Reuse Demonstration Plant] R. A. Marcus. il *Pop Sci* 231:44 S '87
Sports
How about it, Mr. Pete? Ten good reasons Denver deserves a major league team. R. Reilly. por *Sports Illus* 67:90 Ag 24 '87

Denver (Colo.)—*cont.*

Transit systems

He's been working on the railroad in Denver [G. M. Wallace's mass transit link] S. D. Atchison. il por *Bus Week* p42 Je 8 '87

Water supply

The last big dam? [proposed Two Forks Project on the South Platte River] S. Stuller. *Wilderness* 51:34-6 Fall '87

Denzau, Arthur T.

Made in America: the Japanese auto cartel. *Society* 24:30-5 S/O '87

Denzin, Norman K.

Postmodern children. *Society* 24:32-5 Mr/Ap '87

Deom, Carl M., and others

The 30-kilodalton gene product of tobacco mosaic virus potentiates virus movement. bibl f il *Science* 237:389-94 Jl 24 '87

Deoxyribonuclease

Generation of a hybrid sequence-specific single-stranded deoxyribonuclease. D. R. Corey and P. G. Schultz. bibl f il *Science* 238:1401-3 D 4 '87

Deoxyribonucleic acid *See* DNA

DePalma, Anthony

Ruben Blades: up from salsa. il pors *N Y Times Mag* p24+ Je 21 '87

Depardieu, Gérard

about

France's leading man. J. Dupont. il pors *N Y Times Mag* p38-41+ Je 14 '87

DeParle, Jason

The slum behind the Sheraton. il *Wash Mon* 19:32-44 D '87

Department stores

See also

Abraham & Straus
Allied Stores Corp.
Ames Department Stores, Inc.
Associated Dry Goods Corp.
B. Altman & Co.
Bloomingdale's
Dayton-Hudson Corp.
F. W. Woolworth Co.
Federated Department Stores, Inc.
Henri Bendel Inc.
J. C. Penney Company, Inc.
Lord & Taylor
Marshall Field & Company
May Department Stores Co.
Montgomery Ward & Co., Inc.
Neiman Marcus
Nordstrom, Inc.
R. H. Macy & Co., Inc.
Rich's (Firm)
Sears, Roebuck and Co.
Shopping centers

Can you find a swimsuit to buy in July? il *Glamour* 85:40 Jl '87

Acquisitions and mergers

The battle of Bendel's [takeover by L. Wexner] J. Kornbluth. il pors *N Y* 20:26-33 F 23 '87

David Farrell [acquisition of Associated Dry Goods by May Department Stores] M. D. Oneal. il por *Bus Week* Sp Issue:236 Ap 17 '87

Hey Wall Street, wanna buy the Brooklyn Bridge? [takeover hoax surrounding Dayton Hudson shows market's vulnerability to rumor] G. Weiss. il por *Bus Week* p31 Jl 6 '87

The new show at Neiman-Marcus [General Cinema takeover] J. P. Newport, Jr. il por *Fortune* 115:103-4+ Ap 27 '87

Powerhouse potential [May Department Stores buys Associated Dry Goods] T. Jaffe. il *Forbes* 139:110 Ja 26 '87

International aspects

Sir Jimmy goes shopping again [Federated Department Stores] G. G. Marcial. *Bus Week* p188 N 16 '87

Cosmetics departments

Big names are opening doors for Avon. A. Dunkin. il *Bus Week* p96-7 Je 1 '87

Customer relations

Sexist sales [men receive more prompt service; study by Bette Ann Stead and George M. Zinkhan] V. Bozzi. *Psychol Today* 21:11 Jl '87

Why rivals are quaking as Nordstrom heads east. J. O. Hamilton. il *Bus Week* p99-100 Je 15 '87

Employees

See also

Strikes—Department store employees

Training

Schools are my business [Rich's department store program for high school students in Atlanta] J. M. Zimmerman. por *Newsweek* 109:6-7 My 11 '87

Canada

See also

T. Eaton Co. Ltd.

Great Britain

See also

Marks & Spencer plc

DePauw University

Olympian Wilma Rudolph gets DePauw college post. por *Jet* 71:52 F 2 '87

Dependency (Psychology)

See also

Addictive behavior

Do you feel like his mother or his wife? C. K. Ostrom. il *Ladies Home J* 104:100+ N '87

Have you declared your independence? [quiz] J. Adams. *Essence* 18:95+ S '87

Interdependence: rely on others but maintain your sense of control. B. L. Stern. *Vogue* 177:266 Je '87

Is your child too dependent on you? B. Spock. il *Redbook* 169:28 Jl '87

Some day my prince will come and other lies Snow White told us. il *Glamour* 85:78 Ag '87

Submitting to freedom. P. Yancey. il *Christ Today* 31:64 Je 12 '87

Dependency deductions *See* Income tax—Deductions

Depilation *See* Hair—Removal

Depletion allowances

The petroleum industry at its crossroads [address, February 19, 1987] M. T. Halbouty. *Vital Speeches Day* 53:381-4 Ap 1 '87

Deportation

See also

Asylum, Right of

Linnas and the long war [deportation to the Soviet Union] *Natl Rev* 39:19-20 My 22 '87

The Linnas case: was justice done? [deportation to Soviet Union of Estonian war criminal] N. Cooper. il por *Newsweek* 109:33-4 My 4 '87

Nazis and Communists [case of K. Linnas] *New Repub* 196:4+ My 11 '87

No place to hide [K. Linnas deported to the Soviet Union] il por *Time* 129:70 My 4 '87

Problems of crime and punishment [ethics of U.S. use of Soviet evidence against Nazi war criminal K. Linnas] R. Lacayo. il *Time* 129:60 Ap 20 '87

Soviet firing squad awaits [U.S. deportation of suspected Estonian war criminal K. Linnas] por *U S News World Rep* 102:14 Ap 13 '87

Deposit brokers *See* Money brokers

Deposits, Bank *See* Bank accounts

Depp, Johnny

about

Class acts: guys who make the grade. M. L. Baer. il pors *Teen* 31:59-60 N '87

Depression, Business *See* Business depression

Depression, Mental

See also

Postpartum depression
Seasonal affective disorder

The aging of immunity [research by Steven J. Schleifer and others] J. Greenberg and B. Bower. *Sci News* 131:328 My 23 '87

Brokenhearted me. E. Pell. il *Ms* 15:80 Je '87

Bummer blues. A. Bell. il *Teen* 31:100-1 Ap '87

Clinical depression: when the blues won't go away. R. M. A. Hirschfeld. por *McCalls* 145:88 Mr '87

Coping with a partner's depression. A. H. Rosenfeld. il *Psychol Today* 21:24 N '87

Creativity and the troubled mind [association with manic depression] C. Holden. il *Psychol Today* 21:9-10 Ap '87

Cyclothymia: when mood swings are serious. Z. Hedden-Sellman. il *McCalls* 114:87 Ag '87

Depressed about life, or just depressed? [research by Clive J. Robins] C. Wood. *Psychol Today* 21:22 F '87

Depressed moms: mixed messages for kids [research by Zvia Breznitz and Tracy Sherman] E. Grant. *Psychol Today* 21:14 O '87

Depression [cover story; special section] il *Newsweek* 109:48-54+ My 4 '87

Depression [teenagers] D. Elkind. il *Parents* 62:206 D '87

Depression and cancer: a fatal link [study by Victoria W. Persky and others] B. Bower. *Sci News* 132:244 O 17 '87

Depression, Mental—*cont.*

Getting over the breakup blues. K. McCoy. *Seventeen* 46:34+ Mr '87

'I was full of terror and fright' [actor R. Young] L. Marx. il pors *People Wkly* 27:35-6 Ja 12 '87

The meticulous melancholia of a poet [W. Cowper] por *Discover* 8:12-13 My '87

Mood swings and creativity: new clues [research by Nancy C. Andreasen] B. Bower. *Sci News* 132:262 O 24 '87

My son tried to kill himself [17 year old] il *Good Housekeep* 204:30+ My '87

Second-hand woes. When you wallow in his worries, are you hiding from your own? J. Stone. *Glamour* 85:259 Mr '87

Stop blaming yourself [linking explanatory style with learned helplessness, depression, and illness; research by M. E. P. Seligman] R. J. Trotter. bibl (p64) il pors *Psychol Today* 21:30-2+ F '87

Stressed out: learned helplessness in rats sheds light on human depression. E. Collins. *Sci Am* 257:30 N '87

Why depression is different for high-achieving women. H. B. Braiker. il *Work Woman* 12:79-83 D '87

Genetic aspects

Gene for manic depression? [study of Amish families by Janice Egeland and others] B. Bower. *Sci News* 131:132 F 28 '87

Gene of the week [studies of five families in Jerusalem] *Time* 129:62 Mr 30 '87

Hunting 'the black dog' [study of manic depression among the Amish] il *U S News World Rep* 102:8 Mr 9 '87

Is mental illness inherited? [study of Amish families; research by Janice Egeland and others] C. Wallis. il *Time* 129:67 Mr 9 '87

Manic depression: a new gene defect [X chromosome; research by Miron Baron and others] B. Bower. *Sci News* 131:199 Mr 28 '87

Manic-depression gene tied to chromosome 11. G. Kolata. *Science* 235:1139-40 Mr 6 '87

When manic depression is part of the family legacy [Amish research by Janice Egeland and others] T. Monmaney. il *Newsweek* 109:53 My 4 '87

X marks the spot [manic depression; research on five families in Jerusalem] *Sci News* 131:376 Je 13 '87

Therapy

See also
Antidepressants
Cognitive therapy

Caffeine jolt for ECT [work of C. Edward Coffey] J. Greenberg and B. Bower. *Sci News* 131:328 My 23 '87

Can exercise beat the blues? [research by Joel Thirer] E. Grant. il *Psychol Today* 21:22 S '87

Depression: is there a quick fix for this dangerous disease? C. D. Gurin. il *Ms* 16:48-9+ D '87

Heartbreak hotel [Debora Phillips' learning vacations to deal with problems of love] D. Zevin. il *Health* 19:18 Ja '87

Shock therapy's return to respectability. S. Squire. il *N Y Times Mag* p78-9+ N 22 '87

What's in the cards for manic depression? [cover story] B. Bower. *Sci News* 131:410 Je 27 '87

Why (perhaps) lithium is doubly effective [manic depression] il *Discover* 8:12 F '87

Deprivation, Maternal *See* Maternal deprivation
Deprivation, Paternal *See* Paternal deprivation
Deprogramming

Psychology and religion in court—again [anticult theories of coercive persuasion] J. R. Lewis and J. G. Melton. *Christ Century* 104:914-16 O 21 '87

Dept. of State Building (Washington, D.C.) *See* State Dept. Building (Washington, D.C.)
Depth indicators

Probing new depths [1988 depthsounders and fishfinders] G. West and D. Fales. il *Mot Boat Sail* 160:58-62+ O '87

Transducer installations—the right way [small boats] B. Stearns. il *Field Stream* 91:83+ Ja '87

Depth sounders *See* Depth indicators
Der Hovanessian, Diana

Fisherman's wife [poem] *McCalls* 115:147 O '87
Derbyshire (England)

Historic houses, sites, etc.

Doing up Derbyshire. A. Hills. il *Hist Today* 37:3-4 Je '87
Dere, Kenneth P., and others

Ultraviolet observations of solar fine structure. bibl f il *Science* 238:1267-9 N 27 '87

Deregulation of airlines *See* Aviation—Laws and regulations
Deregulation of banking *See* Banks and banking—Laws and regulations
Deregulation of industry *See* Industry and state
Deregulation of transportation *See* Transportation—Laws and regulations
Deressa, Yonas

Rebel aid. *Natl Rev* 39:36-9 Ap 24 '87
Derham, Anthony

Ixing. il *House Gard* 159:36-41+ F '87
Derivation of words *See* English language—Etymology
Dermatology *See* Skin
Dern, Laura

about

A coupla nice kids. D. Mason. il pors *Vogue* 177:92 Mr '87

Laura Dern & Diane Ladd. pors *Teen* 31:48 D '87
DeRosa, Paul

about

Man turns in mother, but won't testify against her. *Jet* 71:29 F 16 '87
Derrick, Christopher, 1921-

Our great blind spot. *America* 156:437-9+ My 30 '87
Derrida, Jacques

about

Descartes, Nietzsche and the search for the unsayable. M. C. Taylor. il *N Y Times Book Rev* 92:3+ F 1 '87

Bibliography

Truth and consequences. A. Nehamas. *New Repub* 197:31-6 O 5 '87
Dershowitz, Alan M.

Collectible adolescence. il *N Y Times Mag* p46 My 31 '87

First word. il *Omni* 9:6 S '87
Dervan, Peter B.

(jt. auth) *See* Moser, Heinz E., and Dervan, Peter B.
Derwinski, Edward J.

Budgetary resources and foreign policy [statement, March 19, 1987] *Dep State Bull* 87:84-7 Je '87
Dery, Mark

An interview with Bob Ludwig. il por *Stereo Rev* 52:113-15 N '87
DES (Diethylstilbestrol) *See* Stilbestrols
Des Moines (Iowa)

Stores

See also
Beeler's Meat Market and Bakery
Des Plaines (Ill.)

Police

An Illinois policeman puts his job on the line by rushing to the aid of his family [C. Launius] il por *People Wkly* 28:59 O 19 '87
DeSantis, Stanley

about

Stanley DeSantis: turning 'my neuroses' into fashion. K. Kelly. il por *Bus Week* p146 D 7 '87
Descent *See* Genealogy
Desegregation *See* Blacks—Segregation
Desegregation in education *See* Colleges and universities—Desegregation; Public schools—Desegregation
Desert architecture

Architecture: Antoine Predock [home of Nat and Connie Troy] R. Morris. il por *Archit Dig* 44:90-7+ Ag '87
Desert ecology

See also
Desertification

Herbivory in rocks and the weathering of a desert [impact of lichen feeding by snails] M. Shachak and others. bibl f il *Science* 236:1098-9 My 29 '87

Snails dine at desert dust depot [research by Clive G. Jones and others] K. Hartley. il *Sci News* 131:373 Je 13 '87
Desert flora

See also
Cactus

When spring paints the desert [condensed from Beyond the wall] E. Abbey. il *Read Dig* 130:164-7 Ap '87
Desert National Wildlife Range (Nev.) *See* Wildlife sanctuaries—Nevada
Desert Partners

Are USG's walls crumbling? J. E. Ellis. il *Bus Week* p59 O 19 '87
The desert song [operetta] *See* Romberg, Sigmund, 1887-1951
Desert survival

The desert as a way of life. H. A. Sidikou. il *Courier* 40:16-19 Je '87
Desertification

Africa's Sahel: the stricken land [cover story] W. S. Ellis. il map *Natl Geogr* 172:140-79 Ag '87

Desertification—*cont.*

Expanding deserts, shrinking resources. C. Norman. il *Science* 235:963 F 27 '87

In New Mexico: desert healer [work of A. Savory] G. Ehrlich. il por *Time* 130:10-11 D 7 '87

Making of a desert [Landsat images help study effects of 20-year drought on the Inland Niger Delta in Mali; work of Patricia Jacobberger] J. Dall'Acqua. il map *Earth Sci* 40:19-21 Spr '87

Desertion, Military

See also

Afghanistan—Russian invasion, 1979- —Desertions

World War, 1939-1945—Desertions

Deserts

See also

Sonoran Desert

The death of Ducktown [desert created in Tennessee 100 years ago when copper smelter fumes killed vegetation] W. Barnhardt. il map *Discover* 8:34-6+ O '87

Desert sojourn [Southwestern States] C. Haas. il *Esquire* 108:136-43 O '87

A worldly wilderness: California Desert. B. H. Lopez. il map *Natl Geogr* 171:42-77 Ja '87

Photographs and photography

Cameras on caravan. M. Grimm and T. Grimm. *Travel Holiday* 167:6+ Mr '87

Deserts of the Southwest. L. Brownstein. il maps *Petersens Photogr Mag* 16:18-19+ Je '87

The first three steps to seeing photographically. F. Patterson. il *Petersens Photogr Mag* 15:26-7 Mr '87

Africa

Africa's Sahel: the stricken land [cover story] W. S. Ellis. il map *Natl Geogr* 172:140-79 Ag '87

Egypt

See also

Western Desert (Egypt)

Israel

See also

Negev (Israel)

Niger

The desert as a way of life. H. A. Sidikou. il *Courier* 40:16-19 Je '87

North Africa

See also

Sahara

Design

See also

Architectural design

Book design

Environmental design

Exploring the new materialism [best of 1986] K. Andersen. il *Time* 129:76-7 Ja 5 '87

Innovations. See issues of Essence beginning August 1987

Living. B. Plumb. See issues of Vogue

Exhibitions

See also

Cooper-Hewitt Museum

Modern remastered [design section of the Metropolitan Museum's Lila Acheson Wallace Wing] M. Filler. il *House Gard* 159:136-43+ Ja '87

Morris to Memphis: modern design at the Metropolitan Museum of Art. R. C. Miller. il *Antiques* 131:278-81 Ja '87

Study and teaching

See also

Art Center College of Design (Pasadena, Calif.). European campus

Japan

Japan is on the go. K. Andersen. il *Time* 130:68-70+ S 21 '87

Design, Decorative

See also

Book covers

Decoupage

Monograms

Pottery—Decoration

Stencil work

Design, Industrial

See also

Computers—Design

Electronic equipment—Design

Engineering design

Computer graphics are animating another market. K. M. Hafner. il *Bus Week* p88+ Mr 16 '87

Exhibitions

The embodiment of ingenuity [Craft today; In pursuit of beauty: Americans and the aesthetic movement; The Machine Age in America: 1918-1941] M. Kangas. bibl f il *Am Craft* 47:46-53 Ag/S '87

The Machine Age in America, 1918-1941. C. Willis. il *Archit Rec* 175:77+ F '87

The Machine Age on display [The Machine Age in America: 1918-1941] P. Bob. il *Esquire* 107:132 F '87

Mario Bellini: designer on view at the Museum of Modern Art. il por *Archit Rec* 175:59 Ag '87

Ode to a locomotive [The Machine Age in America, 1918-1941] G. Slutsker. il *Forbes* 139:105-6+ Ap 6 '87

History

Dresser's success. M. Filler. il *House Gard* 159:32+ N '87

Design firms

See also

Frogdesign Inc.

G N Associates

J. Robert Scott (Firm)

M & Company

Meret, Inc.

Nissan Design International

Italy

See also

Industrie Pininfarina SpA

Zagato (Firm)

Designer Referral Service, Inc.

How two owners handled the tax changes. D. Shilling. il pors *Work Woman* 12:40-1 Mr '87

Designers

See also

Conran family

Costume designers

Deskey, Donald

Fashion designers

Gray, Eileen, 1879-1976

Lighting designers

Manwaring, Michael

Set designers

Vanderbyl, Michael

Designing women [television program] See Television program reviews—Single works

Desire

The joy—no kidding—of sex. L. Bernikow. il *Mademoiselle* 93:248-9+ N '87

Lust in your heart: at what point does a fantasy about someone become infidelity? C. L. Mithers. *Glamour* 85:304 O '87

Lust: it can be wrong when it feels so right. J. Bacik. il *U S Cathol* 52:10-11 Ag '87

Not tonight, dear [lack of sexual desire] D. Gelman. il *Newsweek* 110:64-6 O 26 '87

Sexual chemistry. J. Wilson. il *Ladies Home J* 104:40+ Ag '87

"Why don't I enjoy sex more?". N. Friedman. *Read Dig* 130:141-4 Ap '87

Why you want sex—and why you don't. E. Rapp. *Mademoiselle* 93:176 S '87

Anecdotes, facetiae, satire, etc.

The shame of wanting. B. McCormick. il *Atlantic* 259:36-7 F '87

Desk furnishings

See also

Inkwells and inkstands

Letter holders

Decorative headquarters. il *Harpers Bazaar* 120:136 Mr '87

End desk-top clutter [desk organizer] R. J. DeCristoforo. il *Workbench* 43:46 My/Je '87

Objets d'office: executive security blankets. B. Andrews. il *Work Woman* 12:121 S '87

Ultimate desk set. L. M. Dalsgaard. il *Home Mech* 83:64-8 D '87

Desk organizers See Desk furnishings

Deskey, Donald

about

Donald Deskey's decorative designs. D. A. Hanks and J. Toher. bibl f il *Antiques* 131:838-45 Ap '87

The screens and screen designs of Donald Deskey. M. Komanecky. bibl f il *Antiques* 131:1064-77 My '87

Desks

See also

Computer furniture

Contemporary rolltop desk. K. Collier. il *Fam Handyman* 37:84-91 S '87

Fancy veneer gives new life to cast-off relic [writing desk] B. Gould. il *Workbench* 43:10+ Ja/F '87

Lap desk or bed tray . . . sturdy but lightweight. il *Sunset* 179:114-17 O '87

A roll-top desk you can build. il *Home Mech* 83:38-9 O '87

Desks—*cont.*

Rolltop desk [kit] M. Thompson. il *Fam Handyman* 37:48-50 Ap '87

Secret secretary. R. Wilkes. il *Pop Mech* 164:76-80 Ag '87

Storage and work space built of interlocking custom-milled maple. il *Sunset* 179:107 Ag '87

Anecdotes, facetiae, satire, etc.

Creativity or control? [what desk tops communicate] M. E. Marty. *Christ Century* 104:983 N 4 '87

Desktop computers *See* Computers

Desktop publishing

See also

Aldus Corporation

Interleaf Inc.

10 top desktop publishing projects. H.-J. Taferner. il *Pers Comput* 11:201-5+ N '87

Desktop publishing. W. C. Banks. il *Money* 16:119-20+ Jl '87

Desktop publishing [cover story; special section] il *Byte* 12:147-50+ My '87

Desktop publishing. P. Saffo. See issues of Personal Computing beginning May 1987

Desktop publishing: one solution to your printing needs. S. Miller. il *Black Enterp* 18:51 D '87

Dueling lasers (I) [Mac vs. MS-DOS desktop publishing system] M. Antonoff and J. Bell. il *Pers Comput* 11:85-7+ My '87

Dueling lasers (II) [Cordata Intellipress System and AST Premium Publisher; MS-DOS systems] A. C. Hixson and C. Spencer. il *Pers Comput* 11:121-3+ Je '87

From desktop to typesetter. C. Strehlo. il *Pers Comput* 11:188-93+ D '87

Publish and/or perish: serious business at the MacWorld Exposition, and a look at desktop publishing. B. F. Webster. *Byte* 12:279-82+ My '87

PW special report. il *Publ Wkly* 232:26+ N 13 '87

Setting up for desktop publishing [cover story] M. Antonoff. il *Pers Comput* 11:74-7+ Jl '87

Who's who in desktop publishing [with editorial comment by F. Abatemarco] D. Needle. il *Pers Comput* 11:5, 110-15+ Ja '87

Handbooks, manuals, etc.

Aldus guide to basic design. J. Bell. il *Pers Comput* 11:28 Jl '87

Programming

See also

PostScript (Computer language)

Custom publishing [Harvard Professional Publisher] S. Quigley. *Pers Comput* 11:164+ Jl '87

Desktop publishing software. M. Antonoff. il *Pers Comput* 11:223+ N '87

Entry publishing [Clickart Personal Publisher] S. Quigley. il *Pers Comput* 11:158 Ja '87

How two pioneers brought publishing to the desktop [J. E. Warnock and P. Brainerd] K. M. Hafner. il pors *Bus Week* p61-2 O 5 '87

Leap-frogging the competition [Quark's XPress] J. Bell. il *Pers Comput* 11:182+ Jl '87

Make my page! T. Holmes. il *Byte* 12:159-66 My '87

A new Interleaf. *Byte* 12:45 O '87

Page design made easy [NewsMaster] P. Honan. il *Pers Comput* 11:244 Je '87

PageMaker goes MS-DOS. M. Antonoff. *Pers Comput* 11:155-6 Jl '87

PreScript. K. Sheldon. il *Byte* 12:197-8 Mr '87

Putting it all together with Ventura Publisher. M. Antonoff. il *Pers Comput* 11:55-6 Mr '87

Quick publishing for the non-expert [Byline] C. O'Malley. il *Pers Comput* 11:272+ D '87

Real competition for PageMaker [Ready Set Go 3.0] J. Bell. il *Pers Comput* 11:64+ My '87

Rosenberg and Abbott: giant steps in desktop publishing [M. Rosenberg and K. Abbott of Manhattan Graphics Corp.] P. Finch. il pors *Bus Week* p81 F 9 '87

Seybold on standards [interview with J. Seybold] D. Needle. por *Pers Comput* 11:114 Ja '87

Streamlining author interaction in typesetting [TeXtures 1.0 typesetting software package for the Apple Macintosh] *Publ Wkly* 232:25 Jl 17 '87

Taking the pain out of document design. M. Antonoff. il *Pers Comput* 11:128-31+ O '87

Three PC-based desktop-publishing programs [PageMaker, Ventura Publisher and GEM Desktop Publisher] J. Cavuoto. il *Byte* 12:169-72+ D '87

Desktop video

Pictures for everywoman. A. Oshins. il *Work Woman* 12:72 N '87

Business use

Now playing at an office near you—desktop videos. J. Rothfeder. il *Bus Week* p85+ Je 1 '87

Home use

Giving home movies a Hollywood flair. M. Rogers. il *Newsweek* 110:60-1 Ag 10 '87

Desmarais, Paul Guy

about

Power's new Siberian connection. P. C. Newman. il por *Macleans* 100:44 Je 1 '87

Desormeaux, Kent

about

Make way for superbug. D. Stathoplos. il por *Sports Illus* 67:91 Jl 13 '87

Desorption

Going for a molecular spin [electron stimulated desorption ion angular distribution method of probing structure and bonding at surfaces] S. Weisburd. il *Sci News* 132:199 S 26 '87

Despard, Lucy Edwards

Recent books on international relations. See issues of Foreign Affairs

Desrosiers, Robert

about

Blue snake [ballet] Reviews

Dance Mag 61:74 Ja '87. J. Gruen

Desserts

See also

Cake

Cookies

Custards

Ice cream, ices, etc.

Meringue

Pastry

Pie

Puddings

Soufflés

Tarts

150 desserts averaging less than 200 calories a serving. il *Sunset* 179:142+ Jl '87

All-new, all-chocolate cookbook. il *Good Housekeep* 204:138-48+ Mr '87

Apple desserts. il *Better Homes Gard* 65:175-6 O '87

Autumn treats [microwaving] il *Good Housekeep* 205:237-8 O '87

Berries: the just dessert. J. R. Nyenhuis. il *Saturday Evening Post* 259:22+ My/Je '87

Burnt sugar [caramel] S. Tager. il *Gourmet* 47:110-11+ N '87

Caramel makes it rich. il *South Living* 22:160 F '87

Chocolate and . . . J. T. Hazard. il *Ladies Home J* 104:120-2+ F '87

Chocolate basket with berry cream. il *Good Housekeep* 205:30 D '87

A chocolate-lover's dream. il *Redbook* 168:78-81+ F '87

Come by for dessert. J. Nash. il *Essence* 18:82-3+ D '87

Cooking with Jacques Pépin [summer cornet susy and double-decker ambrosia] J. Pépin. il *Gourmet* 47:147-50 Jl '87

Dazzling desserts: half the time, just as good. il *Ladies Home J* 104:110-11+ S '87

Decadent desserts. J. Pruess. il *N Y Times Mag* p63-4 My 3 '87

Delicious tradition: a holiday party with a history [dessert party of R. Lazarus] F. Greenberg. il pors *Work Woman* 12:94-8+ D '87

Dessert cookbook. M. Langan. il *McCalls* 114:105-10+ Jl '87

Dessert for the sentimental [Valentine's Day] S. Payne. il *South Living* 22:152-3 F '87

Desserts: step-saving, streamlined cooking [microwaving] il *Better Homes Gard* 65:144-5+ Ap '87

Favorite recipes from Kutztown's Country Kitchen. il *Americana* 15:37 Jl/Ag '87

Fresh fruit desserts. J. Taylor. il *Better Homes Gard* 65:32-3+ Jl '87

Fruitful endings. J. Borkoski. il *Ladies Home J* 104:104-5+ Ag '87

Hazelnut cookie curls. il *McCalls* 115:135-6 N '87

Home sweet home. il *Redbook* 169:112-14+ Ag '87

Just a bowl of cherries. M. D. Higgins. il *Ladies Home J* 104:94-5+ Je '87

Just desserts (and champagne): a party for 12. il *Mademoiselle* 93:196-8 D '87

Low-calorie desserts with high appeal. il *South Living* 22:208+ Ap '87

McCall's chocolate-dessert cookbook. M. Langan. il *McCalls* 145:95-100+ Mr '87

Microwave cookbook. il *Good Housekeep* 204:185-6 Je '87

Microwave desserts. il *Better Homes Gard* 65:111-12 Je '87

Desserts—*cont.*

New England apple-peach betty. il *Redbook* 169:26 My '87

Peaches, berries, and zabaglione . . . light, quick, grand. il *Sunset* 179:178 S '87

Present dessert in a shell of chocolate. S. Payne. il *South Living* 22:134-6 Jl '87

Puzzled about white chocolate? S. Payne. il *South Living* 22:118-19 Mr '87

Quick desserts making use of winter citrus. il *Sunset* 178:144 Mr '87

Rhubarb and strawberries in a rosy sauce [Valentine's Day dessert] il *Sunset* 178:128+ F '87

A spirit-raising sweet [tirami su] il *McCalls* 114:163-4 F '87

Start with a can of pie filling. il *South Living* 22:140 D '87

Strawberry sensations. il *Better Homes Gard* 65:163-4 My '87

A sweetheart dessert [microwave poached pears] J. B. Hurley. il *Prevention* 39:58 F '87

Valentine Day dessert [cherries en gelée] il *Good Housekeep* 204:114 F '87

Valentine desserts. il *Better Homes Gard* 65:125-6 F '87

Dessoff Choirs

Musical events:

Performance of Handel's Saul. A. Porter. *New Yorker* 63:75-6 Je 15 '87

Destouches, Henri-Louis *See* Céline, Louis-Ferdinand, 1894-1961

Destruction of buildings *See* Wrecking

Desuetude (Term)

The penumbra of desuetude. W. Safire. il *N Y Times Mag* p16+ O 4 '87

DESY accelerators *See* Accelerators (Electrons, etc.)

Detailing (Automobile cleaning) *See* Automobiles—Cleaning

Detaining Mr. Trotsky [drama] *See* Fothergill, Robert

Detection of crime *See* Criminal investigation

Detective and mystery plays

Mystery plays in Madison [festival in Georgia] C. Griffith. il *South Living* 22:8-10 Ag '87

Mystery weekend vacations. il *Glamour* 85:86 O '87

Detective and mystery stories

See also

Motion pictures—Crime films

Crime in every hamlet. M. Stasio. il *N Y Times Book Rev* 92:1+ Ag 2 '87

Authorship

See also

International Association of Crime Writers

A gift of reasonable terror [R. Rendell] D. Lehman. il por *Newsweek* 110:77 S 21 '87

How do you learn to write? R. Rendell. il *Writer* 100:7-10 N '87

Murder never dies. M. Spillane. il *Harpers Bazaar* 120:152-3+ Ja '87

Mysteries from a novelist nun [C. A. O'Marie] J. Horowitz. il por *N Y Times Mag* p34-5 Ag 30 '87

PW interviews. S. S. Steinberg. por *Publ Wkly* 231:78-9 F 6 '87

The sainted sleuth, still on the case [centenary of first appearance of A. C. Doyle's Sherlock Holmes] A. Burgess. bibl il *N Y Times Book Rev* 92:1+ Ja 4 '87

A taste for life's seamy side [interview with E. Leonard] A. P. Sanoff. il por *U S News World Rep* 102:64 Mr 9 '87

The terribly English mysteries of Martha Grimes are a welcome addition to the pub-lic domain. A. Chambers. il pors *People Wkly* 27:64+ F 2 '87

Wide world of intrigue [R. Thomas] D. Lehman. il por *Newsweek* 110:89 O 19 '87

Bibliography

The case of the missing woman [women mystery writers] C. G. Heilbrun. il *Ms* 16:76+ O '87

Crime. N. Callendar. See issues of The New York Times Book Review

The hard-boiled go to brunch. C. Nicol. il *Harpers* 275:61-5 O '87

To be or not to be continued [sequels] W. A. Henry. il *Time* 130:63-4 Ag 17 '87

Single works

See name of author for full entry

Brothers in honor. LeClaire, Anne D.

Hiram's ghost. Wilds, Mary Catherine

Sylvia Smith-Smith and . . . the cigar-smoking ghost. Nelson, Peter

Weep no more, my lady. Clark, Mary Higgins

Technique

Creating suspense in the young mystery. J. L. Nixon. *Writer* 100:19-21+ O '87

Plotting the realistic detective novel. M. Muller. *Writer* 100:12-15+ Je '87

The reader as partner. T. Hillerman. *Writer* 100:14-16 O '87

Seeing around curves. M. Grimes. *Writer* 100:11-13+ S '87

Writing thrillers. R. H. F. Cox. *Writer* 100:10-12+ Mr '87

Detectives

See also

Women detectives

Daylighting: going undercover with Gillian Farrell and the new private eyes. N. Pileggi. il pors *N Y* 20:44-8 Ap 20 '87

Training

See also

G. Gordon Liddy Academy of Corporate Security and Private Investigation

Detectors

See also

Biosensors

Bomb detectors

Carbon monoxide detectors

Fire detectors

Gas detectors

Moisture meters

Oxygen detectors

Radar detectors

Radon detectors

Wind shear detectors

Dashboards for humans [lifesign detectors; work of Charles Lessard] D. Lampe. *Pop Sci* 231:33 S '87

Detectors, Gravity *See* Gravity and gravitation—Measurement

Detectors, Infrared

AFTI F-16 testbed to evaluate sensors for close air support. il *Aviat Week Space Technol* 127:76 N 2 '87

Airborne Optical Adjunct [infrared system mounted in aircraft for missile tracking as part of SDI] il *Aviat Week Space Technol* 127:69+ N 23 '87

Boost-phase requirements lead sensor development program. il *Aviat Week Space Technol* 127:54-5 N 23 '87

Emphasis on stealth will spur improvements in Flir sensors. il *Aviat Week Space Technol* 127:101+ S 7 '87

GE/Martin selected to provide ATF electro-optic sensor [YF-22A advanced tactical fighter] *Aviat Week Space Technol* 126:73 Je 15 '87

Getting the picture in the infrared. D. E. Thomsen. il *Sci News* 131:295 My 9 '87

Imagery comes to infrared astronomy [infrared array detector] M. M. Waldrop. il *Science* 236:1525-6 Je 19 '87

Infrared imaging system will record flow fields during shuttle reentry. il *Aviat Week Space Technol* 127:65+ D 7 '87

An invisible eye to stand a watch [infrared sensors instead of radar on military planes] S. Budiansky. il *U S News World Rep* 103:61-2 Jl 20 '87

Martin develops simplified Flir for night-vision attack capability. *Aviat Week Space Technol* 127:101 S 21 '87

New infrared line scanner to enter Air Force service [Honeywell AN/AAD-5B] il *Aviat Week Space Technol* 127:108 S 7 '87

Northrop developing tactical infrared focal plane array. il *Aviat Week Space Technol* 127:82-3 N 2 '87

USAF demonstrates electro-optical reconnaissance system on RF-4C. J. D. Morrocco. *Aviat Week Space Technol* 126:123+ My 18 '87

VHSIC demonstrates significant benefits in performing signal processing functions [use in Flir imagery] *Aviat Week Space Technol* 127:98-9 S 7 '87

Détente policy *See* United States—Foreign relations—Soviet Union

Detergent industry *See* Soap industry

Detergents

The great soap opera [cover story] il *Consum Rep* 52:413-22 Jl '87

Laundry detergents. il *Consum Rep* 52:72-5 D '87

Labeling

Label claims: the science behind the sell. il *Consum Rep* 52:415-18 Jl '87

Deterioration of plastics *See* Plastics—Deterioration

Deterioration of wood *See* Wood—Deterioration

Determined Productions (Firm)

Determined Productions: bringing children's books to life [book-and-doll packages] K. O. Fakih. il *Publ Wkly* 232:27-8 Ag 28 '87

Detert, Yvonne Lembi- *See* Lembi-Detert, Yvonne

Detmers, Maruschka

about

Maruschka Detmers makes sex erotic, dangerous—even funny. D. Denby. por *Vogue* 177:78 Ag '87

Detonation

The detonation of explosives. W. C. Davis. bibl (p128) *Sci Am* 256:106-12 My '87

Detonography *See* Explosives in art

Detroit (Mich.)

Economic conditions

The Monaco of the Midwest [Grand Prix racing] K. Springen. il *Newsweek* 110:42 Jl 13 '87

Education

Detroit girl stays in school; wins trip to Japan [C. McKinnon wins art contest] *Jet* 72:12 S 7 '87

In Detroit, kids kill kids [searching students for weapons used in school-related attacks] E. Salholz. il *Newsweek* 109:74 My 11 '87

Not gunmen, but smarties [principal J. Greene at Redford High School] B. Dolan. il por *Time* 129:85 Ap 27 '87

Employees

Cicero case prompts bias charges against Detroit suburbs: Justice Dept. *Jet* 71:7 Ja 19 '87

Galleries and museums

See also

Detroit Gallery of Contemporary Crafts

Hospitals

Detroit couple awarded $5 mil. in hospital suit [suit by George Hollis and wife against North Detroit General Hospital] *Jet* 72:30 Ap 6 '87

Housing

See also

People in Faith United Housing Corporation

Music

See also

Michigan Opera Theatre

Newspapers

See also

Detroit news

Photographs and photography

Time and Detroit . . . and New York . . . and Santa Barbara. il *Am Herit* 38:100-5 Ap '87

Police

Detroit man gets $1 million in police brutality case [R. Steward] *Jet* 72:29 My 4 '87

Jury awards $900,000 to black female officer in Detroit police case [case of C. Preston] *Jet* 72:33 Ap 27 '87

Prisons and reformatories

Ali makes new friends during Detroit jail visit. *Jet* 72:28 Je 22 '87

Public welfare

See also

Operation Get Down Food Co-op

Religious institutions and affairs

See also

People in Faith United Housing Corporation

Detroit Gallery of Contemporary Crafts

Detroit Gallery celebrates 10th year. il *Am Craft* 47:96 F/Mr '87

Detroit Grand Prix *See* Automobile racing

Detroit news

Bill Johnson hired as Detroit news editorialist. *Jet* 72:32 Jl 6 '87

Detroit Symphony Orchestra

Detroit Symphony hires black assistant conductor [L. B. Dunner] *Jet* 72:30 Jl 20 '87

Deutch, Howard

about

Some kind of wonderful [film] Reviews

People Wkly il 27:12 Mr 9 '87. P. Travers

Time il 129:86 Mr 9 '87. R. Schickel

Deuterium

Deuterium, dust, and infant stars [study of Kleinmann-Low nebula; work of Malcolm Walmsley and others] *Sky Telesc* 74:236 S '87

Was Venus wet? Deuterium reconsidered. D. H. Grinspoon. bibl f il *Science* 238:1702-4 D 18 '87

Deuterium oxide

Heavy water cheaters. G. Milhollin. bibl f *Foreign Policy* 69:100-19 Wint '87/'88

Deutsch, Cynthia

Love and marriage. See issues of Parents

Deutsch, David, 1943-

about

David Deutsch. M. E. Haus. il *Art News* 86:128 S '87

Deutsch, Steven

Successful worker training programs help ease impact of technology. bibl f *Mon Labor Rev* 110:14-20 N '87

Deutsche Airbus

German government commits funds to Airbus A330/A340 development. *Aviat Week Space Technol* 126:35 Je 8 '87

Deutsche Bank AG

The banker behind the shakeup at Daimler-Benz [A. Herrhausen] R. Ingersoll and R. Brady. il pors *Bus Week* p36-7 Jl 27 '87

Deutsche Luftverkehrsgesellschaft mbH *See* DLT German Domestic Airlines

Deutsches Hygiene-Museum (Dresden, Germany)

The German Hygiene Museum. B. Golde and I. Köper. il *World Health* p16-17 Je '87

Devaluation of money *See* Money

Devaney, Robert L.

Chaotic bursts in nonlinear dynamical systems. bibl f il *Science* 235:342-5 Ja 16 '87

Devassy, Karen Stevens

Because I could not stop for death, he kindly stopped for me. il *U S Cathol* 52:33-7 Ap '87

Developing (Photography) *See* Photography—Developing and developers

Developing countries

See also

Agriculture—Developing countries

Birth control—Developing countries

Children—Developing countries

Cities and towns—Developing countries

Economic assistance, American—Developing countries

Economic assistance, Russian—Developing countries

Economic assistance, Swedish—Developing countries

Electric power—Developing countries

Environment—Developing countries

Environmental policy—Developing countries

Foreign correspondents—Developing countries

Genetic research—Developing countries

Government and the press—Developing countries

Industry and the environment—Developing countries

Information storage and retrieval systems—Developing countries

Investments, Foreign—Developing countries

Journalism—Developing countries

Loans, Bank—Developing countries

Loans, Foreign—Developing countries

Medical care—Developing countries

Military assistance, American—Developing countries

Missions—Developing countries

Munitions—Developing countries

Power resources—Developing countries

Public health—Developing countries

Relief work—Developing countries

Sports—Developing countries

Technical assistance, American—Developing countries

Technology—Developing countries

United Nations—Developing countries

Water supply—Developing countries

Women—Developing countries

All in the name of aid. P. Adams. il *Sierra* 72:45-50 Ja/F '87

Dismissing the third world [P. Bruckner's The tears of the white man] S. Englund. *Commonweal* 114:533-6 S 25 '87

Hard times for foreign aid. J. Greenwald. il *Time* 129:38-9 F 9 '87

"What a legacy for our children!" [interview with S. Aga Khan] P. Gupte. il por *Forbes* 139:100+ Je 15 '87

Commerce

See also

United Nations Conference on Trade and Development

Low costs, high growth. G. Garelik. il *Time* 130:52 O 19 '87

Soviet Union

See Soviet Union—Commerce—Developing countries

United States

See United States—Commerce—Developing countries

Communication

See also

United Nations. Committee on Information

Developing countries—*cont.*
Economic conditions
Does wealth equal health? D.-C. Lambert. il *Courier* 40:8-12 Ag '87
Poverty and progress [special section] bibl f il *Courier* 40:20-7 Ja '87
Third world income just can't catch up [report by Organization for Economic Cooperation & Development] G. Koretz. il *Bus Week* p21 F 9 '87
Economic policy
Development under siege. S. Sen. *Commonweal* 114:647-52 N 20 '87
How 'experts' caused the third world debt crisis. P. C. Roberts. il *Bus Week* p28 N 2 '87
Economic relations
See also
United Nations. Committee for Development Planning
United Nations. Industrial Development Organization
United Nations Conference on Trade and Development
United Nations Pledging Conference for Development Activities
Domination and deprivation. V. K. Nguyên. il *Courier* 40:24-6 Ja '87
The plant germplasm controversy [cover story; with reply by H. G. Wilkes] J. Kloppenburg, Jr. and D. L. Kleinman. bibl f il maps *BioScience* 37:190-8, 215-18 Mr '87
Seeds of struggle: the geopolitics of genetic resources. J. Kloppenburg, Jr. and D. L. Kleinman. il map *Technol Rev* 90:46-53 F/Mr '87
United States
See United States—Economic relations—Developing countries
Foreign opinion
American
Southern attitudes and world affairs [Main Street America and the third world] J. H. Wolfe. *USA Today (Periodical)* 115:9 Ja '87
Foreign relations
The arms race is a universal issue. P. Ochieng. il *World Press Rev* 34:36-7 Ja '87
Soviet Union
See Soviet Union—Foreign relations—Developing countries
United States
See United States—Foreign relations—Developing countries
Industries
See also
United Nations. Industrial Development Organization
Low costs, high growth. G. Garelik. il *Time* 130:52 O 19 '87
Literature
A map upside down: third world artists explore their territory [conference at Duke University's Center for International Studies] P. Aufderheide. il *Progressive* 51:36-8 Mr '87
Population
Cigarettes smoked outstrip population growth. il *World Health* p30 Mr '87
Population scares. P. T. Bauer. *Commentary* 84:39-42 N '87
Development, Biological *See* Developmental biology; Morphogenesis
Development, Economic *See* Economic development
Development, Neurological *See* Developmental neurology
Development, Organizational *See* Organizational change
Development, Real estate *See* Real estate business
Development banks
See also
African Development Bank
World Bank
Bank balance: economy and ecology. *Sci News* 132:238 O 10 '87
Banks should be part of the solution [multilateral development banks and the environment] J. D. Hair. il *Int Wildl* 17:30 Mr/Ap '87
Eco-bucks: going for the purse strings. *Sci News* 132:137 Ag 29 '87
Development of children *See* Children—Growth and development
Development of infants *See* Infants—Growth and development
Development Programme (United Nations) *See* United Nations Development Programme
Developmental biology
See also
Insects—Development

Homeo boxes in the study of development. W. J. Gehring. bibl f il *Science* 236:1245-52 Je 5 '87
Making contacts in the developing embryo [research by Masatoshi Takeichi and others] J. L. Marx. il *Science* 236:30-1 Ap 3 '87
Molecular events guide embryonic development. D. M. Barnes. il *Science* 238:893-4 N 13 '87
Worm watching: the case of the suicidal sex cell [Caenorhabditis elegans and Panagrellus redivivus; research by P. Sternberg] G. Montgomery. il por *Discover* 8:44-6+ O '87
Developmental neurology
See also
Brain—Growth
Blockade of "NMDA" receptors disrupts experience-dependent plasticity of kitten striate cortex. A. Kleinschmidt and others. bibl f il *Science* 238:355-8 O 16 '87
Formation of retinal ganglion cell topography during prenatal development [cats] B. Lia and others. bibl f il *Science* 236:848-51 My 15 '87
A nervous disposition [embryo skin cells; research by Colin R. Sharpe and John B. Gurdon] J. Horgan. il *Sci Am* 257:40+ D '87
Neural Darwinism: an exchange [discussion of October 9, 1986 article, Neural Darwinism: a new approach to memory and perception] I. Rosenfield. *N Y Rev Books* 34:44-5 Mr 12 '87
Transient morphological features of identified ganglion cells in living fetal and neonatal retina. A. S. Ramoa and others. bibl f il *Science* 237:522-5 Jl 31 '87
Developmental Sciences (Firm)
Developmental Sciences tests parafoil recovery on Skyeye RPV. il *Aviat Week Space Technol* 126:92 Je 1 '87
Deverell, Rex
about
Quartet for three actors [drama] Reviews
Macleans 100:55 Ja 26 '87. M. Scholar
Deviation, Sexual *See* Sexual deviation
Devil
See also
Demonology
The devil is ambidextrous. G. K. Brushaber. il *Christ Today* 31:11 O 16 '87
Devil in literature
Speak of the devil [J. B. Russell's books about the devil] J. J. Pelikan. *Commentary* 83:63-6 Ap '87
Devil in the flesh [film] *See* Motion picture reviews—Single works
Devil worship *See* Demonology
Devine, Grant
Canadian-United States trade [address, September 14, 1987] *Vital Speeches Day* 54:76-9 N 15 '87
about
Devine's tough talk. T. Tedesco. *Macleans* 100:47 Mr 23 '87
DeVito, Paul L.
The pain-pleasure connection. il *USA Today (Periodical)* 115:47-9 Ja '87
Devlin, Tom
about
Lender of last resort. D. Henry. por *Forbes* 139:73+ My 18 '87
Devonian period *See* Paleontology—Devonian
Devonshire cream *See* Cream
DeVore, James
Painting atmospheric effects in watercolor. il *Am Artist* 51:58-61 Ap '87
Devotions, Catholic *See* Catholic Church—Prayer books and devotions
DeVries, Eileen
about
Big fish, nice pond. F. Greenberg. il por *Work Woman* 12:54-5 Jl '87
Dew, Fred
about
Cmdr. Dew is first black to head Seabee battalion. por *Jet* 72:6 Ag 17 '87
Dew, Robb Forman
The unmaking of a southern belle. il pors *Ms* 16:92+ O '87
Dew
See also
Acid dew
Build a heated dew cap for less than $10 [telescopes] H. Hammond. il *Astronomy* 15:72-4 N '87
Much ado about dewing. G. A. Lucas. *Astronomy* 15:72-3 N '87
What your windshield shows about the clouds [origin of clouds and dew] R. Williams. il *Weatherwise* 40:260-1 O '87

Dew—*cont.*
Window watching [dew on windows] C. F. Bohren. il *Weatherwise* 40:150-3 Je '87
Dewdney, A. K.
Computer recreations. See issues of Scientific American
Dewey, Thomas E. (Thomas Edmund), 1902-1971
about
In Dewey's steps. por *U S News World Rep* 102:24 Mr 23 '87
Dewhurst, Colleen
about
Colleen Dewhurst. D. K. Mano. il pors *People Wkly* 27:80-2+ Mr 9 '87
Cultural exchange within the global village. M. Rhodes. por *Horizon* 30:9 D '87
DeWitt, Bryce S. (Bryce Seligman), 1923-
about
Bruno Zumino and Bryce Dewitt receive Dirac medals. pors *Phys Today* 40:111 N '87
Dexter, King
Laser light on film. il *Petersens Photogr Mag* 15:12-15+ Ja '87
about
His classic eye catches light from the laser. il por *Smithsonian* 17:118-21 F '87
Dexter, Pete, 1943-
Battling for her place. il pors *Sports Illus* 66:48-52 F 23 '87
The case against Brian Spencer. il *Sports Illus* 66:98-102+ My 11 '87
about
From the publisher. D. J. Barr. il por *Sports Illus* 66:4 F 23 '87
Dextrans
Nuclear reassembly excludes large macromolecules. J. A. Swanson and P. L. McNeil. bibl f il *Science* 238:548-50 O 23 '87
Dey, Susan
about
Once a simple, singing Partridge, a grown-up Susan Dey tries her wings as TV's sultry legal eagle. J. Yarbrough. il pors *People Wkly* 27:82-3 F 2 '87
Susan Dey: "Hollywood almost killed me" [cover story] A. W. Petrucelli. il pors *Redbook* 169:58+ Ag '87
DFS Dorland Worldwide
How they do it [TV time analysts B. Frank and D. Myers] J. Traub. pors *Channels* 7:39 My '87
DHL Worldwide Courier Express
Downdraft [chairman C. Lynch] L. Scheer. il por *Forbes* 140:196 S 21 '87
Di Cicco, Dennis
Observer's page. See issues of Sky and Telescope
Di Fiore, Pier Paolo, and others
erbB-2 is a potent oncogene when overexpressed in NIH/3T3 cells. bibl f il *Science* 237:178-82 Jl 10 '87
Di Gennaro, Giuseppe
How should we attack the drug problem? il *Courier* 40:10-13 Jl '87
Di Montezemolo, Catherine
about
Stylish ease. W. P. Rayner. il *House Gard* 159:80-9 Jl '87
Di Piero, W. S.
Gulls on dumps [poem] *New Yorker* 63:38 Mr 9 '87
Di Rosa, Rene
about
The Rene Di Rosas in Napa Valley. J. Chatfield-Taylor. il por *Archit Dig* 44:258+ Je '87
Di Salvatore, Bryan
Vehement fire (I). *New Yorker* 63:42-4+ Ap 27 '87
Vehement fire (II). *New Yorker* 63:38-42+ My 4 '87
Di Silvestro, Roger L.
Nature stories. See issues of Audubon beginning July 1987
Dia Art Foundation
Bound for glory. K. Larson. il *N Y* 20:112-13 O 19 '87
Diabetes
Diabetics and the elderly—special care for vulnerable feet. il *Prevention* 39:125-6+ Mr '87
Living with diabetes. W. D. Roberts. il *Parents* 62:306+ N '87
Protein defect in diabetes? D. D. Edwards. *Sci News* 131:327 My 23 '87
Diagnosis
Life-saving screening prescribed [skin symptoms of adult-onset diabetes; views of Carl S. Korn] *USA Today (Periodical)* 115:12-13 F '87

Genetic aspects
HLA is factor in diabetes [human leukocyte antigen; research by John A. Todd and others] *Sci News* 132:247 O 17 '87
Three recessive loci required for insulin-dependent diabetes in nonobese diabetic mice. M. Prochazka and others. bibl f il *Science* 237:286-9 Jl 17 '87
Nutritional aspects
Diabetes and eating disorders [study by Randi Birk and Martha Spencer] K. Ullman. *Psychol Today* 21:23 N '87
Diabetic? Diet means more than ever. I. Pare. il *Bus Week* p132 D 14 '87
Diabetics need vitamin C for healthy skin. *Prevention* 39:124 Ja '87
Diabetics should lose weight, avoid diet fads. G. Kolata. *Science* 235:163-4 Ja 9 '87
Fish oil prevents insulin resistance induced by high-fat feeding in rats. L. H. Storlien and others. bibl f il *Science* 237:885-8 Ag 21 '87
Niacin: sweet hope for slowing diabetes [niacinamide] *Prevention* 39:52-3 O '87
Psychological aspects
Diabetes and stress: a Type A connection? [research by Brian Stabler and Richard S. Surwit] M. Roberts. *Psychol Today* 21:22 Jl '87
Therapy
See also
Insulin
Diabetes autoimmunity seen, stopped [cyclosporine therapy] D. D. Edwards. *Sci News* 132:292 N 7 '87
Islet allograft survival after a single course of treatment of recipient with antibody to L3T4. J. A. Shizuru and others. bibl il *Science* 237:278-80 Jl 17 '87
Diacylglycerol *See* Glycerol
Diagnosis
See also
Abbott Laboratories/Diagnostics Division
Biopsy
Computers—Medical use
Gene probes
Genetic screening
Hair analysis
Hospitals—Diagnostic services
Image processing—Medical use
Instant Medical Tests (Firm)
Radiography, Medical
Thermography—Medical use
Tomography—Medical use
Ultrasonic waves—Medical use
Urine—Analysis
See also subhead Diagnosis under names of diseases
Are we hooked on tests? [cover story] S. Findlay. il *U S News World Rep* 103:60-5+ N 23 '87
Can fingerprints be clues to disease? P. Gadsby. il *Good Housekeep* 204:275 My '87
Can you really trust a lab test? The scary truth. M. Lawrence. il *Glamour* 85:74+ N '87
Disease diagnosis by recombinant DNA methods. C. T. Caskey. bibl f il *Science* 236:1223-9 Je 5 '87
How to help your doctor diagnose your pain. P. Gadsby. il *Good Housekeep* 205:182-3 Ag '87
Knowing when to call the doctor [sizing up symptoms; study by George D. Bishop] A. H. Rosenfeld. il *Psychol Today* 21:12 O '87
"Mommy, I don't feel good . . ." Kids' symptoms not to ignore. G. J. Subak-Sharpe. il *Ladies Home J* 104:82+ N '87
Office tests for doctors. R. Simon. il *Forbes* 139 Ann Directory:90+ Ap 27 '87
Serious childhood ailments. M. Oppenheim. il *Better Homes Gard* 65:76+ F '87
Those lips, those eyes . . . what your looks reveal about your health. K. P. Behan. il *Mademoiselle* 93:76+ Ja '87
Tune in to your feet and head off serious problems. il *Prevention* 39:131-2 Mr '87
What to do when your doctor says there's nothing wrong with you and you still feel awful. S. Berger. *Good Housekeep* 204:129+ Ap '87
Women's medical tests: what your doctor may not tell you. P. Gadsby. il *Good Housekeep* 205:239-40 N '87
Women's symptoms not to ignore. G. J. Subak-Sharpe. *Ladies Home J* 104:31-2 Ap '87
Wrong tests. J. W. Merline. *Consum Res Mag* 70:38 My '87

Diagnostic equipment *See* Medical equipment
Dial, Aleize Rena
about
Ralph Sampson, bride miss wedding—already married. il pors *Jet* 72:57 Ag 3 '87
Ralph Sampson, wife may be headed for divorce. il pors *Jet* 72:12 S 14 '87
Sampson, wife reconcile, divorce suit shelved. *Jet* 73:51 N 16 '87
Dial (Periodical)
Rediscovering an early modern vision. J. Richardson. il por *House Gard* 159:158-63+ F '87
Dial-a-porn *See* Telephone pornography
Dial Collection *See* Art—Collectors and collecting
Dialing systems, Telephone *See* Telephone dialing systems
Dialogue
Ghosts to believe in: recalling Bateson and Mead [learning to bridge the gap between speech and writing] M. C. Bateson. *N Y Times Book Rev* 92:49 N 15 '87
Dialogues of the Carmelites [opera] See Poulenc, Francis, 1899-1963
Diamandis, Peter G.
about
Buying out the boss at CBS Magazines. D. Lieberman. il por *Bus Week* p30 Jl 27 '87
Cutting the fat. R. Behar. il por *Forbes* 140:8 Ag 10 '87
Peter Diamandis is finally working for himself. P. Finch. il por *Bus Week* p48 Ag 3 '87
Diamandis, Peter H., and Sunshine, Kenneth H.
Your career in space. il *Space World* X-4-280:8-13 Ap '87
Diamant, Anita
Big time, small time: the widening gap. *Writer* 100:13-15+ Jl '87
Diamond, Edwin
Attack of the people meters. il *N Y* 20:38-41 Ag 24 '87
Gotcha! The media's frenzied patrol of the candidates. il *N Y* 20:50-3 O 26 '87
Media. See issues of New York beginning January 28, 1985
Stay tuned for the evening news: the networks downsize. il *N Y* 20:30-3 Mr 16 '87
The Times of Frankel [cover story] il pors *N Y* 20:26-34 Ag 10 '87
Diamond, Harvey, 1945-, and Diamond, Marilyn
Detox your body [excerpt from Living health] pors *Redbook* 169:84-5+ Jl '87
Diamond, I. A. L., 1920-1988
I. A. L. Diamond. il por *People Wkly* 27:66+ F 9 '87
Diamond, Jared M.
The worst mistake in the history of the human race. il *Discover* 8:64-6 My '87
about
All by their lonesome. S. Budiansky. il *U S News World Rep* 102:71 My 4 '87
Diamond, Larry
Nigeria between dictatorship and democracy. bibl f *Curr Hist* 86:201-4+ My '87
Diamond, Marilyn
(jt. auth) See Diamond, Harvey, 1945-, and Diamond, Marilyn
Diamond-Bathurst Inc.
What keeps Anchor Glass steady: buying shaky rivals. G. DeGeorge. il por *Bus Week* p72-3 Jl 27 '87
Diamond industry
See also
Lazare Kaplan International Inc.
Export-import trade
The big money in cheap rock [India's Jains dominate U.S. market for low-priced diamonds] P. Gupte. il *Forbes* 140:64+ Ag 10 '87
Marketing
Romancing the stone [Lazare Kaplan's branded diamonds] B. Kanner. il *N Y* 20:22+ N 30 '87
India
The big money in cheap rock [India's Jains dominate U.S. market for low-priced diamonds] P. Gupte. il *Forbes* 140:64+ Ag 10 '87
Diamond Shamrock Corp.
The downfall of a CEO [W. H. Bricker] T. Mason. il por *Bus Week* p76-80+ F 16 '87
Diamonds
Diamonds from outer space [research by Roy Lewis] il *USA Today (Periodical)* 115:4-5 Je '87
Getting clear on diamonds. L. Kanakis. il *Consum Res Mag* 70:20-2 Jl '87
Star dust in the sky with diamonds [research by Edward Anders and others] I. Peterson. *Sci News* 131:166 Mr 14 '87

Stardust on earth [interstellar diamonds] J. K. Beatty. il *Sky Telesc* 73:610 Je '87
Starlight reflected in a diamond. D. Lago. il *Astronomy* 15:28+ My '87
Diana, Princess of Wales, 1961-
about
Autumn of their discontent [cover story] B. Johnson. il pors *People Wkly* 28:90-2+ N 9 '87
Baba says ta ta to Wills and Harry—the question is, did Charles and Di get the nanny's goat? B. Johnson. il pors *People Wkly* 27:44+ F 2 '87
The Cannes Film Festival is a grade B movie with no good parts for Charles and Diana. il pors *People Wkly* 27:34-5 Je 1 '87
'Dallas' at the Palace. F. Willey. il por *Newsweek* 110:33 Jl 6 '87
Diana, no dipso, knocks those risible bubbly rumors flat. il por *People Wkly* 28:34 Ag 10 '87
Diana: why she and Charles can't agree [cover story] P. Leigh. il pors *Ladies Home J* 104:97-9+ Jl '87
Fashion mavens snub a "sandwich-board" princess. il pors *People Wkly* 27:138 Ap 13 '87
For the Prince and Princess of Wales, a time of troubles. il pors *McCalls* 114:38 Je '87
A frame-up? Charles & Di's latest brushes with art may be unpaletteable. L. Rozen. il pors *People Wkly* 27:79-80 Je 22 '87
Happy? Or just ever after? [cover story] F. A. Bernstein. il pors *People Wkly* 27:112-14+ Je 8 '87
How far will these girls go? P. Junor. il pors *McCalls* 115:14-16+ N '87
London marriage falling down? il pors *Newsweek* 110:85 N 9 '87
Look inside Diana's closet. il *Good Housekeep* 204:99-101+ Je '87
Much ado about Di. il pors *Newsweek* 110:65 Jl 13 '87
A no-nonsense nanny strolls into Charles and Di's nursery. il pors *People Wkly* 27:45 Mr 30 '87
No ordinary fender bender, Diana gives Prince Charles a pain in the Aston Martin. il pors *People Wkly* 28:95 Jl 6 '87
No titters, you two, this is serious! B. Johnson and L. Rozen. il pors *People Wkly* 28:24-8+ Jl 20 '87
The Princess and the Duchess. N. Underwood. il pors *Macleans* 100:32-3 Jl 27 '87
Princess Di's nanny remembers . . . the custody battle for Diana. M. Clarke. il pors *Redbook* 169:88-9+ Ag '87
A right royal uproar. M. Janigan. il por *Macleans* 100:20 Jl 6 '87
A royal scandal [cover story; special section; with editorial comment by Kevin Doyle] il pors *Macleans* 100:2, 30-4+ N 9 '87
Royals bashing: a blood sport? M. Smilgis. il pors *Time* 130:94-5 N 9 '87
Their marital woes on hold, Charles and Di wow Germany. il pors *People Wkly* 28:52-3 N 23 '87
When in doubt, run the Royals. L. Zuckerman. il pors *Time* 130:52 Jl 13 '87
Anecdotes, facetiae, satire, etc.
Notes and comment. *New Yorker* 63:33-4 N 23 '87
Princess Diana. il pors *People Wkly* 28:40-2 D 28 '87-Ja 4 '88
Dianetics
See also
Scientology
Dianthus *See* Pinks (Plants)
Diaper service
See also
Bundle of Convenience (Firm)
Diapers
The bottom line [superabsorbent diapers] K. Freifeld. il *Health* 19:82 Ap '87
Disposable diapers. il *Consum Rep* 52:181-3 D '87
Disposable diapers. il *Consum Rep* 52:510-12 Ag '87
Diaries
Design your own diary [tennis match diary] I. Lendl. il *World Tennis* 34:20-1 F '87
A diary's the best medicine. S. Kayne. il *Parents* 62:85-6+ N '87
A Fathers' Day gift for the whole family [Grandfather remembers, a journal for personal memories] C. Loomis. il *Parents* 62:15 Je '87
Keep a happiness calendar. J. Culhane. il *Read Dig* 130:63-6 Ja '87
Secrets of success [I. Lendl's tennis match diary] K. Cunningham. il *World Tennis* 34:18-21 F '87
Should you keep a diary? [writers] M. Raphael. *Writer* 100:30 Ja '87

Diaries—*cont.*

Small moments [mother captures fleeting magic of childhood] E. Berg. il *Parents* 62:108-10+ D '87

Writing our own history [contribution of H. Dalton's political diary and others to British post-war history] T. Benn. il pors *Hist Today* 37:9-12 Ap '87

Your diary: a very special friend. il *Teen* 31:38+ F '87

El diario-La prensa (New York, N.Y.)

Notes and comment. *New Yorker* 63:27-8 O 26 '87

Diarrhea

Coping with turista. F. Lunzer. il *Forbes* 139:136 F 23 '87

Digestive distress! Signals of a system in trouble. J. I. Stern and D. Carroll. il *Redbook* 169:90-1+ Ag '87

Food-borne diarrhea. B. T. Hunter. il *Consum Res Mag* 70:8-9 Jl '87

Infant diarrhea in research spotlight [rotavirus-associated diarrhea] D. D. Edwards. *Sci News* 132:255 O 17 '87

The October-to-April trek of the 'stomach bug' [childhood diarrhea] J. Silberner. il *U S News World Rep* 103:90 N 9 '87

Spin-off from space travel [hazard analysis critical control point in preventing food associated diarrheal diseases] S. Michanie and F. L. Bryan. il *World Health* p26-7 Ag/S '87

Therapy

A major child-killer. *UN Chron* 24:66 My '87

Diaz, Franklin R. Chang- *See* Chang-Diaz, Franklin R., 1950-

Diaz, Jaime

And the surfer ate the shark. il por *Sports Illus* 66:73 My 18 '87

Another era, same Player. il por *Sports Illus* 67:18-19 Jl 20 '87

At last Tom has a fling. il por *Sports Illus* 67:44-5 N 9 '87

Big Cat on the prowl. il por *Sports Illus* 66:91-2 Ap 20 '87

Bringing lives up to par. il pors *Sports Illus* 67:28-9 D 21 '87

Chi Chi has a last laugh. il pors *Sports Illus* 67:38-40+ N 23 '87

Cool customer in a hot PGA. il pors *Sports Illus* 67:28-30+ Ag 17 '87

A cup for the old world. il *Sports Illus* 67:58-61 O 5 '87

Getting fed to the Dawgs. il *Sports Illus* 66:68+ Je 1 '87

Grooving on a Sunday afternoon. il pors *Sports Illus* 66:73-4 Je 8 '87

Has golf gotten too groovy? il *Sports Illus* 67:52-9 Ag 3 '87

Kicking with both his heels. il por *Sports Illus* 67:80 N 23 '87

Mac is back and right on track. il por *Sports Illus* 66:50-1 Ja 19 '87

Mayfairest of them all. il por *Sports Illus* 67:75 S 7 '87

A new force in the game. il pors *Sports Illus* 67:66+ Ag 10 '87

On and up with Steffi. il por *Sports Illus* 67:92 N 30 '87

The power of Love. il pors *Sports Illus* 66:44-6+ Mr 23 '87

The shirtless wonder. il pors *Sports Illus* 66:66+ Mr 9 '87

Shootout down at the Shore. il *Sports Illus* 66:57-8 Ap 13 '87

A Tennessee waltz. il *Sports Illus* 66:124+ Ap 6 '87

Time for the Pat and Nancy show. il pors *Sports Illus* 66:84+ F 9 '87

The trials of a phenom. il por *Sports Illus* 66:50-1 Mr 2 '87

A victory for the System. il *Sports Illus* 67:70-1 Ag 24 '87

Diaz, Leonel Hildago- *See* Hildago-Diaz, Leonel

Díaz, Rafael del Piño *See* Piño Díaz, Rafael del

Díaz de Vivar, Rodrigo *See* Cid, ca. 1043-1099

Diaz Herrera, Roberto

about

Defying the strong man. B. Levin. il por *Macleans* 100:18 Ag 10 '87

Dibbets, Jan, 1941-

about

Spotlight; tr. by Beth O'Brien. R. Fuchs. il por *Art News* 86:67-8 S '87

Dibenzodioxin *See* Dioxin

DIC Enterprises

Babe in Toyland. P. E. Bauer. il pors *Channels* 7:48-51 Jl/Ag '87

Dichter, Marc A., and Ayala, G. F.

Cellular mechanisms of epilepsy: a status report. bibl f il *Science* 237:157-64 Jl 10 '87

Dick, Miri, and others

Parallel and serial processes in motion detection. bibl f il *Science* 237:400-2 Jl 24 '87

Dick Clark Productions Inc.

American handstand. M. Barrier. il pors *Nations Bus* 75:89-91 O '87

Dick Clark grows up [cover story] A. Snyder. il pors *Channels* 7:28-31+ My '87

Dickens, Charles, 1812-1870

about

A Christmas carol. B. Burns. il *Theatre Crafts* 21:38-41+ O '87

Dickens and his readers. P. A. W. Collins. bibl il pors *Hist Today* 37:32-40 Jl '87

"The most-hated man in America". E. L. Abel. bibl il pors *Am Hist Illus* 22:10-15+ D '87

Dickens, Hazel

about

A movie about mining unearths a gem by bringing mountain singer Hazel Dickens into the spotlight. R. Wolmuth. il pors *People Wkly* 28:134-6 N 16 '87

Dickens, Monica, 1915-

When I lost my husband. *Read Dig* 130:114-17 Mr '87

Dickerson, Carrie

about

The woman who tackled Black Fox. N. H. Perreault. il por *Progressive* 51:12 D '87

Dickerson, Eric

about

Break up the Colts! [cover story] A. Murphy. il *Sports Illus* 67:18-23 N 9 '87

Courted by college cash, Dickerson knew his worth. por *Jet* 72:33 Je 1 '87

Dickerson files $12 million suit vs. Norton's agency. il por *Jet* 72:48 Je 8 '87

Dickerson trade shifts NFL balance of power. il *Jet* 73:50 N 30 '87

Eric Dickerson must pay pregnant ex-girlfriend. pors *Jet* 72:25 S 7 '87

NFL bachelors consider fine points of marriage. pors *Jet* 71:50 F 16 '87

White ex-girlfriend hits Dickerson with paternity and palimony lawsuits. pors *Jet* 72:52 Ag 3 '87

Dickerson, Karle

BMX racer: beating the boys at their own game. il *Teen* 31:67 S '87

The messenger [story] il *Teen* 31:46-8+ Ap '87

Dickerson, R. R., and others

Thunderstorms: an important mechanism in the transport of air pollutants. bibl f il *Science* 235:460-5 Ja 23 '87

Dickey, Christopher

Assad and his allies: irreconcilable differences? bibl f *Foreign Aff* 66:58-76 Fall '87

Dickey, James

The captains [fiction] il *Esquire* 107:176-8+ Ap '87

Spring-shock [poem] *Harpers* 274:27 F '87

about

PW interviews. S. Staggs. por *Publ Wkly* 231:62-3 My 29 '87

Dickinson, Angie

about

Angie Dickinson is riding high [interview] F. Robbins. por *50 Plus* 27:32-3+ Ap '87

Dickinson, Austin, d. 1895

about

Amorous in Amherst. R. Craft. bibl f pors *N Y Rev Books* 34:18-21 Ap 23 '87

Dickinson, Charles, 1951-

Abundance [story] *New Yorker* 63:46-53 N 9 '87

Dickinson, Charles C., III

about

Harvard title for sale? por *Newsweek* 110:24 N 23 '87

Dickinson, Emily, 1830-1886

about

Amorous in Amherst. R. Craft. bibl f pors *N Y Rev Books* 34:18-21 Ap 23 '87

The Jeffery Amherst Bookshop: cultivating a narrow specialty. K. McCune. il pors *Publ Wkly* 232:29-31 Jl 3 '87

Dickinson, Emily, 1830-1886—*cont.*
Anecdotes, facetiae, satire, etc.
Emily Dickinson: the movie. J. Karasik. il *N Y Times Book Rev* 92:25 F 1 '87

Dickinson, John, 1732-1808
about
Editorial. W. Garrett. *Antiques* 132:775 O '87
John Dickinson's Poplar Hall, Kent County, Delaware. J. A. H. Sweeney. il *Antiques* 132:820-7 O '87

Dickinson, Warren W.
Stable isotopes. il *Earth Sci* 40:19-20 Summ '87

Dickinson Press Inc.
Dickinson Press, in new plant, moves into tradebook sizes. il *Publ Wkly* 231:52 Ap 3 '87

Dickman, Gregory
Backyard superbees. il *Rodale's Org Gard* 34:69-71 N '87

Dickson, Jim
about
On eye opening. W. F. Buckley. *Natl Rev* 39:73 S 11 '87

Dickson, John
The steeple [poem] *Am Sch* 56:391-2 Summ '87

Dickson, L. C.
(jt. auth) See Karasek, Francis W., 1919-, and Dickson, L. C.

Dickson, Paul
Don't knock knock-knocks! *Read Dig* 130:21-2 Ja '87
An ode to newspaper fillers, those rich tidbits of the mind. il *Smithsonian* 18:280 N '87

Dickstein, Morris
Call it an awakening. il pors *N Y Times Book Rev* 92:1+ N 29 '87

Dictators' wives
Lifestyles of the rich and tyrannical. J. L. Goldstein. *Am Sch* 56:235-47 Spr '87

Dictionaries
  See also
  Chinese language—Dictionaries
  Economics—Dictionaries
  English language—Dictionaries
  Music, American—Dictionaries
  Publishers and publishing—Dictionaries

Dictionary stands *See* Stands (Furniture)

Diddley, Bo
about
Bo Diddley [interview] K. Loder. il pors *Roll Stone* p76-8+ F 12 '87

Didion, Joan
Miami. il *N Y Rev Books* 34:43-8 My 28 '87
Miami: exiles. il *N Y Rev Books* 34:35-9 Je 25 '87
Miami: 'la lucha'. il *N Y Rev Books* 34:15-18 Je 11 '87
Washington in Miami. il *N Y Rev Books* 34:22+ Jl 16 '87
about
1987: Miami's year in the literary limelight. R. Kaye. il pors *Publ Wkly* 232:46-7 N 13 '87
Didion & Dunne: the rewards of a literary marriage. L. Garis. il pors *N Y Times Mag* p18-24+ F 8 '87
Revenge in a hot place. J. Rothchild. *Wash Mon* 19:45-6+ D '87

Didrikson, Babe *See* Zaharias, Babe Didrikson, 1911-1956

Diebenkorn, Richard, 1922-
about
Profiles. D. Hofstadter. il *New Yorker* 63:54-5+ S 7 '87

Dieckmann, Katherine
Good films in small packages. il *Roll Stone* p153+ D 17-31 '87
Young rascal. pors *Roll Stone* p37-8+ S 24 '87

Diehl, Ann
about
"I deserve a change". S. Schneider. il pors *Redbook* 168:82-5 Ja '87

Diehl, Dorothy
The space educator. See issues of Space World beginning June 1987

Dieppe Raid, 1942
Honoring the Dieppe dead [Canadian participation] D. Eisler. il *Macleans* 100:11-12 Ag 31 '87

Dierdorf, Dan
about
Monday man. W. Taaffe. il pors *Sports Illus* 67 Sp Issue:124-7+ S 9 '87

Diery, Ian
about
Mr. Outside. G. Slutsker. il por *Forbes* 140:194+ S 21 '87

Dies and taps *See* Taps and dies

Diesel engines, Automotive
Energy usage
Diesels—do they get better mileage? R. Grable. il *Mot Trend* 39:156-7 Je '87
Fuel consumption
See Diesel engines, Automotive—Energy usage
Materials
The slow road to ceramic engines. I. Peterson. *Sci News* 132:214 O 3 '87
Pollution control devices
An acid cure for acid rain [injection of cyanuric acid into exhaust system] il *U S News World Rep* 102:72 F 16 '87
Superchargers
Aero-motor-home [Vixen 21] J. Keebler. il *Pop Sci* 230:91 F '87
Mercedes-Benz 300TD. il *Road Track* 38:56-8 Ja '87

Diesel engines, Marine
Diesels. E. Dennis. See issues of Motor Boating & Sailing
Cooling
Scoops, seacocks, strainers. E. Dennis. il *Mot Boat Sail* 160:71 Jl '87
Maintenance and repair
10 diesel lay-up tips. E. Dennis. il *Mot Boat Sail* 160:87-8 O '87
Emergency repairs at sea. E. Dennis. *Mot Boat Sail* 159:70 My '87
Superchargers
Lydia engine room report [pair of 1500-hp Detroit Diesel 16V92 turbo-charged and intercooled diesels] E. Dennis. *Mot Boat Sail* 160:95 Jl '87
Testing
Bertram 50 engine room report. E. Dennis. *Mot Boat Sail* 160:106 S '87
Diagnostic tools for diesels. E. Dennis. il *Mot Boat Sail* 159:70 Mr '87

Dieskau, Dietrich Fischer- *See* Fischer-Dieskau, Dietrich, 1925-

Diet
  See also
  Aged—Nutrition
  Aging—Nutritional aspects
  Aluminum in the body
  Athletes—Nutrition
  Baseball players—Nutrition
  Calcium in the body
  Carbohydrates
  Children—Nutrition
  Chromium in the body
  Copper in the body
  Dancers—Nutrition
  Deficiency diseases
  Diet Center, Inc.
  Digestion
  Fasting
  Fiber in diet
  Firefighters—Nutrition
  Hypnotism—Diet use
  Infants—Nutrition
  Iodine in the body
  Iron in the body
  Low calorie cooking
  Low sodium cooking
  Magnesium in the body
  Minerals in the body
  Nutrition
  Nutrition education
  Pregnancy—Nutritional aspects
  Pritikin Longevity Centers
  Proteins
  Shapedown (Program)
  Skiers—Nutrition
  Tennis players—Nutrition
  Trace elements
  Vegetarianism
  Vitamins
  Women—Nutrition
  Women athletes—Nutrition
  Youth—Nutrition
  Zinc in the body
7 strategies: how to eat, drink and be merry—without blowing your diet! S. S. Lang. il *McCalls* 114:99 Ja '87
The 8 biggest diet don'ts and how to deep-six them. E. Royte. il *Mademoiselle* 93:80+ F '87
The 10 commonest dieting downfalls. K. Koontz. *McCalls* 114:37 My '87
29 little ways to lose a lot of weight. M. Mihalik. *Prevention* 39:28-30+ My '87

Diet—*cont.*

126 pounds lighter through diet, prayer and hard work [S. A. Flake] il pors *Ebony* 42:70+ S '87

232 pounds lost: half the size and twice as happy [G. Langford] il pors *Ebony* 42:60+ Ja '87

After 27 years in his bedroom, 1,200-lb. Walter Hudson decides to take a load off [D. Gregory to help] W. Plummer. il pors *People Wkly* 28:60-1 O 26 '87

After the baby: shedding 25 inches and 25 pounds [M. Spletzer-Newman] See issues of Glamour beginning June 1987 through December 1987

All new rotation diet dishes. M. Katahn and T. Katahn. il *Redbook* 169:108-13+ My '87

The anti-cellulite diet [low fat diet] il *Mademoiselle* 93:254+ Ag '87

Being thin isn't always being happy [interview with H. Schwartz] il por *U S News World Rep* 102:74 F 9 '87

Bob Jordan: tops in news and health. il pors *Ebony* 42:145-6+ F '87

Body-beautiful diet guide. J. Romberger. il *Teen* 31:16+ Je '87

Body management: weight loss/energy gain [special section] il *Work Woman* 12:85-6+ F '87

Can your marriage survive your diet? J. G. Fitzpatrick. il *Parents* 62:58-62 Ja '87

The cheater's diet. S. S. Cohen. il *Ladies Home J* 104:58+ D '87

Chew the drumstick slowly. L. C. Garrett. il *World Tennis* 35:44-6 D '87

Count your calories now, feast later. I. Pave. il *Bus Week* p154 D 7 '87

Cut it out! J.-A. Heslin and A. B. Natow. il *Redbook* 169:65-9 Jl '87

Dangerous diet drugs from south of the border [Mexican diet] R. C. Thompson. il *FDA Consum* 21:29-30 My '87

Detox! The big beauty cleanup. il *Mademoiselle* 93:250-5 Mr '87

Diet boosts to keep you on the right track in 1987. L. Gordon. il *Glamour* 85:136 F '87

Diet news. See issues of Mademoiselle

Diet Q & A. See issues of Mademoiselle

Diet spoilers: how to keep people from driving you crazy while you're losing weight. L. Gordon. il *Glamour* 85:242 Mr '87

The diet that can clear your arteries [low-fat diet] L. Vaughn. *Prevention* 39:44+ O '87

The diet that nurtures your nature. S. Waldman. il *Mademoiselle* 93:167-9+ F '87

Diet warm-up: how to get ready to lose [quiz] J. H. Tanne. il *Mademoiselle* 93:194-5+ My '87

Dieters, don't bypass breakfast! D. Webb. *McCalls* 115:128 O '87

Dieting figures. J. W. Merline. il *Consum Res Mag* 70:38 O '87

Dieting with Debbie [D. Fraser] P. A. Taylor. por *Essence* 17:109 Ap '87

Dining out with a healthy appetite. il *FDA Consum* 21:18-23 Mr '87

A doctor's new popcorn diet makes excess pounds go poof. P. Brawley. il por *People Wkly* 27:137-8 Je 8 '87

Eat out and lose weight! E. Padus. il *Prevention* 39:68-74 Ag '87

Eggs O.K. on low-fat diet. il *Prevention* 39:6 Jl '87

Famous diets that don't work. D. Fortino. *Harpers Bazaar* 120:94+ O '87

The fast-food diet. C. A. Pearce. il *Harpers Bazaar* 120:84+ Mr '87

Fat & muscle. R. B. Pearce. il *Women's Sports Fitness* 9:36-9 Jl '87

Fat or fantasy? P. Von Nostitz. il *Parents* 62:200+ Mr '87

The fat to muscle diet [excerpt] V. Zak and others. il *Ladies Home J* 104:70+ Je '87

The feel like a million diet. S. C. Finn. il *50 Plus* 27:32-6+ My '87

Flab fighters. il *Teen* 31:80-3 Je '87

The flavor factor [research by Susan Schiffman] D. Tonnessen. il *Health* 19:8 Ag '87

For babies, fat's not so bad [dangers of putting infants on a diet] J. Silberner. il *U S News World Rep* 103:75 S 14 '87

From 204 pounds to 122 pounds in half a year [S. Carter] il pors *Ebony* 42:46+ Jl '87

Get in swimsuit shape by summer. il *Teen* 31:86-7 Ap '87

Get started. J. Rogers. *Good Housekeep* 204:88 My '87

Get your mate to help you lose weight [cover story] H. Rodale. il *Prevention* 39:26-9 Mr '87

The great food face-off. il *Seventeen* 46:174 Ag '87

Gregory comes to rescue of 1,000-pound Walter Hudson. il pors *Jet* 73:17-18 N 9 '87

A guide to successful weight loss from the Health, Weight and Stress Clinic of Johns Hopkins Medical Institutions. il *Prevention* 39:34-6+ Ja '87

The healthy-hair diet. il *Mademoiselle* 93:38 Ag '87

Help him lose extra pounds . . . while you get in shape, too. il *Glamour* 85:206+ Ja '87

Her 'extraordinary dream' came true [weight loss on Weight Watchers program]; ed. by Eileen Nechas. F. Mark. il pors *Prevention* 39:54+ Mr '87

Her goal: to help others trim down as she did. D. Pyles. il pors *Prevention* 39:100+ My '87

Holiday temptations: how to keep your shape and your sanity through all the eating. L. Gordon. il *Glamour* 85:44+ D '87

How the top models stay on course. il *Essence* 17:48-50+ Ja '87

How to get off the diet roller coaster. S. C. Finn. il *50 Plus* 27:63-4 Jl '87

How to stay thin after 25. J. Wilson. il *Read Dig* 130:41-2+ My '87

I lost 117 lbs. and won back my husband; ed. by Barbara Raymond. S. Keeton. il pors *Good Housekeep* 204:96+ Ap '87

I was a junk food addict [dieting with the aid of a dietician] B. Prescott. il *Health* 19:12+ S '87

Indiana's health chief got sick of life in the fat lane, and he's never svelte better [W. A. Myers] M. Neill. il pors *People Wkly* 28:185-6 N 16 '87

Inside the super spas [with Golden Door diet plan] L. J. Johnson. il *Ladies Home J* 104:96-101+ My '87

Life is sunnier for this now-fit Florida man; ed. by Maria Mihalik. M. Prelee. il *Prevention* 39:98-100+ S '87

The littlest dieters. J. Seligmann. il *Newsweek* 110:48 Jl 27 '87

Lose 10 stubborn pounds forever! [cover story] E. Padus. il *Prevention* 39:104-6+ N '87

Make your kitchen a dieter's dream. D. Tkac. il *Prevention* 39:30-2+ D '87

The Mexican way: easy but dangerous [Mexican diet] F. Gibney. *Newsweek* 109:76-7 F 2 '87

Never say diet. N. Malkin. il *Mademoiselle* 93:52 Ja '87

The new and improved Martha Hamilton. il pors *Ebony* 43:84-6+ N '87

New diet/exercise basics. *Vogue* 177:367 Ap '87

The no-diet diet. W. Korn. il *Ladies Home J* 104:94+ N '87

The pizza diet. L. Bellini-Gergley. il *Harpers Bazaar* 120:107+ Je '87

Popular diets don't work [views of Adam Drewnowski] il *USA Today (Periodical)* 115:3 F '87

Pritikin gets respect. M. S. Balter. il *Health* 19:67-8+ Je '87

Run, or diet? C. Schaeffer. *Changing Times* 41:18 Ag '87

The save-his-life weight loss diet [excerpt from The underburner's diet] B. Edelstein. il *Ladies Home J* 104:62+ F '87

Shaping up for summer. M. Marshall. il *Ebony* 42:84-6+ Je '87

She lost weight following her father's footsteps; ed. by Denise Foley. C. Dunn. il pors *Prevention* 39:81-2+ Ag '87

Should children diet? B. T. Hunter. il *Consum Res Mag* 70:8-9 S '87

Slim & trim: the pineapple diet. L. Bellini-Gergley. il *Harpers Bazaar* 120:172-3+ My '87

Slim and fit. L. Bellini-Gergley. il *Harpers Bazaar* 120:128+ Ag '87

Slim pickings [quick fix diets] J. Poppy. il *Esquire* 108:59-60 N '87

Slimming secrets from the body-makeover specialists. M. Mihalik. il *Prevention* 39:90-1+ D '87

Summer power: diet and exercise for hot times. J. M. Toal. il *Mademoiselle* 93:54+ Jl '87

Sweet tooth diet: the latest scoop. C. A. Pearce. il *Harpers Bazaar* 120:62+ Jl '87

Take the plunge: slim for summer 1987 [cover story; special section] il *Health* 19:25-8+ My '87

Thin thighs in 3 weeks. C. A. Pearce. il *Harpers Bazaar* 120:116-17+ Ja '87

This diet could be your last: but not for the reasons you think [harmful diets] D. Kagan. *Mademoiselle* 93:262-3+ Mr '87

The UCLA diet. il *Redbook* 168:100-3+ Ap '87

Diet—*cont.*
The underburner's diet [excerpt] B. Edelstein. il *Ladies Home J* 104:81-3+ Ja '87
Victoria's diet Principals [excerpt from The diet Principal] V. Principal. il pors *Redbook* 168:8+ F '87
Wanted: someone to watch my weight while I get on with the rest of my life. T. Mendoza. il *Curr Health 2* 13:25-7 F '87
"We lost 239 lbs.". il *Seventeen* 46:166-71 My '87
We lost—and how! [UCLA diet] il *Redbook* 168:96-9 Ap '87
Why smart women don't diet anymore. il *Glamour* 85:306-11 N '87
Your diet. J. S. Stern. See issues of Vogue beginning October 1984
Your diet: clear-skin nutrition. J. S. Stern. *Vogue* 177:362 My '87
Your diet: selling weight loss. J. S. Stern. *Vogue* 177:814 S '87
Your diet: smart vacation eating. J. S. Stern. *Vogue* 177:448 N '87
     Anecdotes, facetiae, satire, etc.
The Bing diet for big guys. S. Bing. il *Esquire* 107:40 Ap '87
     Bibliography
Diet books with no sugarcoating. T. Monmaney. il *Newsweek* 109:76-8 F 2 '87
To have and have not: the avoirdupois collection. H. Dudar. il *N Y Times Book Rev* 92:30-1 Ap 5 '87
Diet, Prehistoric *See* Man, Prehistoric—Food
Diet Center, Inc.
Pounds to dollars [founder S. Ferguson] P. F. Stewart. il por *Ladies Home J* 104:150 O '87
Trimming down to size. A. Kinamore. il *Essence* 18:142+ My '87
Diet cooking *See* Low calorie cooking
Diet in disease
     See also
     ALD (Disease)—Nutritional aspects
     Alzheimer's disease—Nutritional aspects
     Anorexia nervosa
     Arteriosclerosis—Nutritional aspects
     Arthritis—Nutritional aspects
     Breast—Cancer—Nutritional aspects
     Breast—Diseases—Nutritional aspects
     Bulimia
     Cancer—Nutritional aspects
     Cerebrovascular disease—Nutritional aspects
     Colon (Anatomy)—Cancer—Nutritional aspects
     Diabetes—Nutritional aspects
     Dietitians
     Diverticular disease—Nutritional aspects
     Gallstones—Nutritional aspects
     Gingivitis—Nutritional aspects
     Headache—Nutritional aspects
     Heart—Diseases—Nutritional aspects
     Hyperactivity—Nutritional aspects
     Hypertension—Nutritional aspects
     Lungs—Cancer—Nutritional aspects
     Premenstrual syndrome—Nutritional aspects
     Regional ileitis—Nutritional aspects
     Stress—Nutritional aspects
     Xerophthalmia—Nutritional aspects
Foods that heal. J. Bresnick. il *Prevention* 39:26-9 D '87
Putting dizziness on a diet. *Prevention* 39:132 S '87
Why vitamin A may fight infections [research by Susan Smith and Colleen Hayes] *Sci News* 132:46 Jl 18 '87
Diet pills *See* Weight reducing preparations
Dietary supplements
     See also
     Fish oil supplements
     Weider Health & Fitness Corporation
Extras, extras! Which food supplements do you need? G. Goldenberg. il *Mademoiselle* 93:144 Ap '87
A Meals on Wheels program adds liquid nutrient supplements. *Aging* no355:31-2 '87
Dietary supplements industry
     See also
     Shaklee Corp.
     United Sciences of America Inc.
Diethylstilbestrol *See* Stilbestrols
Dietitians
I was a junk food addict [dieting with the aid of a dietician] B. Prescott. il *Health* 19:12+ S '87
The "weight shrinks" dig in [nutrition counseling] P. Blake. il *Time* 129:64 Ja 12 '87
Diets *See* Diet
Dietz, James J.
Grass roots of the maned wolf. il *Nat Hist* 96:52-9 Mr '87

Dietz, Sharon
     about
How two owners handled the tax changes. D. Shilling. il pors *Work Woman* 12:40-1 Mr '87
Dietz, Susan
     about
Opening-night cast party. C. Rossant. il por *McCalls* 114:107-8+ My '87
Dietz, Ulysses G. (Ulysses Grant), 1955-
A garden heritage. il *House Gard* 159:176-9+ S '87
Dietz, Ulysses Grant *See* Dietz, Ulysses G. (Ulysses Grant), 1955-
Differences, Individual *See* Individual differences
Differences, Race *See* Race differences
A different world [television program] *See* Television program reviews—Single works
Differential gear *See* Gearing
Differentials, Wage *See* Wage differentials
Differentiation (Biology)
     See also
     Morphogenesis
Cell-autonomous determination of cell-type choice in Dictyostelium development by cell-cycle phase. R. H. Gomer and R. A. Firtel. bibl f il *Science* 237:758-62 Ag 14 '87
Human trials of new cancer therapy begin [stimulating cancer cells to differentiate] J. L. Marx. il *Science* 236:778-9 My 15 '87
Leukemic cells rehabilitated in rats [research by Joaquin J. Jimenez and Adel A. Yunis] R. Weiss. *Sci News* 132:357 D 5 '87
"Switching" in yeast and slime molds [research by David Soll and others] il *Science* 236:30 Ap 3 '87
Tumor cell rejection through terminal cell differentiation [leukemia cells] J. J. Jimenez and A. A. Yunis. bibl f il *Science* 238:1278-80 N 27 '87
Difficult children *See* Problem children
Diffraction
     See also
     X rays—Diffraction
Keeping it together [avoiding diffractive spreading of a laser beam; work of James Durnin and others] *Sci Am* 257:28-9 Jl '87
Stars and spikes [finding stellar diffraction patterns for different telescope types; computer program] R. W. Sinnott. il *Sky Telesc* 74:294-6 S '87
Diffraction gratings
Picosecond holographic-grating spectroscopy. D. A. Wiersma and K. Duppen. bibl f il *Science* 237:1147-54 S 4 '87
Diffuse myelitis *See* Myelitis
Diffusion
     See also
     Biological transport
Fluid interfaces, including fractal flows, can be studied in a Hele-Shaw cell. J. Walker. il *Sci Am* 257:134-6+ N '87
Diffusion filters *See* Light filters
Diffusion technique (Photography) *See* Photography—Focusing
Digestion
     See also
     Dyspepsia
Nutrient interactions: the inner-digestive struggle. il *Curr Health 2* 13:11-13 My '87
Digestive system
     See also
     Colon (Anatomy)
     Intestines
     Pancreas
     Stomach
          Diseases
     See also
     Dyspepsia
     Flatulence
     Regional ileitis
Gut reactions! M. Mylander. il *Ladies Home J* 104:80+ Ag '87
Digges, Deborah
Circadian rhythms [poem] *New Yorker* 63:36 Mr 23 '87
Sycamores [poem] *New Yorker* 63:44 N 16 '87
Diggs, Charles
     about
Charles Diggs defeated in race for Wayne County board of commissioners. *Jet* 73:25 O 12 '87
Charles Diggs wins back his mortuary license. por *Jet* 73:39 O 26 '87
Ex-rep. Diggs enters Wayne County commission race. *Jet* 72:29 Ag 3 '87

Dight, Janet
How to handle a parent's visit [excerpt from Do your parents drive you crazy?] il *Glamour* 85:153-4 N '87
Your parents' house—or his? [excerpt from Do your parents drive you crazy?] il *Ladies Home J* 104:70+ D '87
DiGiacomo, James
All you need is love. il *America* 156:126-9 F 14 '87
Digital amplifiers *See* Amplifiers
Digital audio tape recorders and recording
DAT finally released [Aiwa's XD-001 DAT deck] B. Harrell. il *Stereo Rev* 52:18+ Ap '87
DAT flash. D. Ranada. il *High Fidel* 37:13 My '87
DAT: going mobile. F. Vizard. il *Pop Mech* 164:36 Jl '87
DAT spat. il *Time* 129:67 F 23 '87
DAT update. S. A. Booth. *Pop Mech* 164:14+ S '87
Digital audio tape. S. Birchall. il *Stereo Rev* 52:56-9 Mr '87
Digital audio tape. B. C. Fenton. il *Radio-Electron* 58:45-7+ O '87
Digital audio tape. J. D. Hirsch. il *Stereo Rev* 52:24 O '87
Digital audiotape recorders cause new stir. M. Goldberg. *Roll Stone* p11 Ja 29 '87
Discs, DATs and all that jazz. N. Henderson. il *Changing Times* 41:103-6 Ja '87
Japanese audio [cover story] B. Harrell. il *Stereo Rev* 52:48-57 Jl '87
The new sound of music. M. Schiffres. il *U S News World Rep* 102:54-5 Ja 26 '87
A new tape to record your favorite numbers. T. Dworetzky. il *Discover* 8:14-15 My '87
Origins of a species. D. Ranada. il *High Fidel* 37:52-3+ Ag '87
Ready or not, here come DATs. L. Feldman. il *Pop Sci* 231:44+ N '87
Sight and sound: DAT's what it's all about. H. Fantel. il *Opera News* 52:48+ N '87
Stacking the decks [latest technology] P. Hoban. il *N Y* 20:14 F 16 '87
What's DAT? J. Augustine. il *Petersens Photogr Mag* 16:4 Jl '87

Testing
DAT certain feeling. D. Ranada. il *High Fidel* 37:20 Jl '87
Digital audio cassettes: small tape, big sound. S. A. Booth and F. Vizard. il *Pop Mech* 164:106-9+ Jl '87
Onkyo DT-2001. C. Stark. il *Stereo Rev* 52:66-9 O '87
Sony DTC-1000 digital audio tape recorder. il *High Fidel* 37:19-21 O '87
Two DAT decks [Sony DTC-1000ES and Victor XD-Z1100] J. D. Hirsch. il *Stereo Rev* 52:60-4 Jl '87

Unauthorized recording
Another attack on home taping. *Radio-Electron* 58:4 O '87
Copy-coding misconceptions. M. Riggs. il *High Fidel* 37:4 Je '87
The Copycode controversy. il *Pop Sci* 231:48 N '87
DAT at the crossroads. M. Riggs. *High Fidel* 37:5 Ap '87
The DAT debate. L. G. Boundas. il *Stereo Rev* 52:8 Ag '87
Enemies of promise. S. A. Booth. il *Pop Mech* 164:46+ Jl '87
Interrupted melody [CBS Copy Code system; cover story] D. Ranada. il *High Fidel* 37:44-7+ Jl '87
It can't happen here. C. J. Esse. il *High Fidel* 37:11+ Ap '87
Looking for the Jolly Roger [record industry vs. digital audio tape recorders] M. Riggs. *High Fidel* 37:4 My '87
Record executives are on pins and needles. B. Buell and others. il *Bus Week* p112 F 16 '87
Record industry battles digital tape. A. DeCurtis. *Roll Stone* p13+ Ap 9 '87
The sound of money. J. B. Copeland. il *Newsweek* 110:72-3 O 5 '87
The spoilers. L. G. Boundas. il *Stereo Rev* 52:6 Je '87
Viewpoint. J. W. Freeman. *Opera News* 52:4 N '87
What is DAT, and why are the record companies trying to keep it away from you? P. Wilkinson. il *Roll Stone* p69-70+ S 10 '87
What's all this about DAT? J. W. Merline. il *Consum Res Mag* 70:35-7 Je '87
Who DAT? M. Costello. *Omni* 10:43 D '87
Why digital audio tape isn't here. B. C. Fenton. il *Radio-Electron* 58:4 Je '87

The year the feds stole Christmas [unavailability of dual deck videocassette recorders and digital audio tape technology] Z. Lazarević. il *Forbes* 140:286 N 16 '87
Digital clocks *See* Clocks, Electronic
Digital compact disc players *See* Compact disc players
Digital compact discs *See* Compact discs
Digital computers *See* Computers
Digital electronics
See also
    Integrated circuits
All about A-to-D converters. H. L. Trietley. il *Radio-Electron* 58:71-7 F '87
Digital Equipment Corp.
The big do [trade show] il *Time* 130:53 S 21 '87
Clean-room controversy [study on toxic hazards that affect a worker's ability to have children] R. Wilson. il *Technol Rev* 90:10+ Ag/S '87
DEC's democracy. D. Machan. il *Forbes* 139:154+ Mr 23 '87
Digital protests terms of Air Force call for computer bids. *Aviat Week Space Technol* 127:157 O 12 '87
Dorothy Terrell. L. Gite. il por *Black Enterp* 17:46+ Ap '87
The IBM-DEC wars: it's 'the year of the customer'. A. Beam and G. Lewis. il *Bus Week* p86-8 Mr 30 '87
IBM squares off against DEC [midrange office computers] il *Fortune* 116:8 Jl 20 '87
Just how high can Digital Equipment climb? L. Helm. il *Bus Week* p110+ Jl 20 '87
Digital radiotelephone *See* Radiotelephone
Digital sound recording and reproducing *See* Sound—Recording and reproducing
Digital television receivers *See* Television receivers
Digital timers *See* Timing devices
Digital videodiscs *See* Videodiscs
Digital videotape recorders and recording *See* Videotape recorders and recording
Digitalis (Plant) *See* Foxgloves
Digitizers (Computers)
AT&T's TrueVision image processing system. R. Tinney. *Byte* 12:215-17 Mr '87
Build a gray-scale video digitizer (I). S. Ciarcia. il *Byte* 12:95-106 My '87
Build a gray-scale video digitizer (II). S. Ciarcia. il *Byte* 12:129-38 Je '87
Reading pictures into your computer [Princeton Graphic Systems LS-300] R. Lockwood. il *Pers Comput* 11:240 Je '87
Scanning images into your computer [Microtek MS-300A] J. Bell. il *Pers Comput* 11:158 Mr '87
Using the ImageWise video digitizer (I). S. Ciarcia. il *Byte* 12:113-19 Jl '87
Using the ImageWise video digitizer (II). S. Ciarcia. il *Byte* 12:117-21 Ag '87
A video data base [PicturePower] R. Lockwood. il *Pers Comput* 11:178 Jl '87
Dignity (Organization)
Dignity groups barred [conflict between Roman Catholic homosexuals and the Archdiocese of New York] *Christ Century* 104:376-7 Ap 22 '87
DiIanni, Albert
Vocations and the laicization of religious life. *America* 156:207-11 Mr 14 '87
Dika, Vera
A feminist fairy tale. il *Art Am* 75:31-3 Ap '87
Dikov, Nikolai N.
Beringia. il map *Courier* 40:32-4 N '87
DiLauro, Stephen
Paul Davis. il *Am Artist* 51:48-53 Ja '87
Diliberto, Gioia, 1950-
about
Brenda Frazier biographer turns to Hadley Hemingway. W. Goldstein. *Publ Wkly* 232:79-80 Ag 14 '87
Diliberto, John
Wendy Carlos: A.D. (after digital). il pors *Down Beat* 54:20-2+ Mr '87
Dilip Hiro *See* Hiro, Dilip
Dilks, Carol
Life in the slow lane. il *Nations Bus* 75:61-2 Mr '87
The massage break is catching on. il *Nations Bus* 75:56-7 Ag '87
Dill, Howard
about
The Babe Ruth of pumpkin growers. il por *50 Plus* 27:61 O '87
Dillard, Annie
The French and Indian War in Pittsburgh: a memoir. il por *Am Herit* 38:49-53 Jl/Ag '87
Mother told jokes [condensed from An American childhood] il *Read Dig* 131:122-5 O '87

Dillard, Annie—*cont.*
about
Annie Dillard: her pilgrimage this time is into her past. A. Chambers. il pors *People Wkly* 28:99-100+ O 19 '87
Remembrances of things past [interview] A. P. Sanoff. por *U S News World Rep* 103:78 N 16 '87

Dillard, Peggy
about
Peggy's still Turning Heads. R. Houston. il *Essence* 18:50+ N '87

Dillard University
V.P. Bush tells Dillard grads racism's 'ugly head' always will be chopped off. il pors *Jet* 72:29 Je 8 '87

Dillehay, Tom D.
By the banks of the Chinchihuapi. il map *Nat Hist* 96:8+ Ap '87

Dillenberger, John
Controversy over the Sistine ceiling. *Christ Century* 104:708-9 Ag 26-S 2 '87

Diller, Barry
about
Storming television's toll bridge [interview] P. E. Bauer. il *Channels* 7:70-1 S '87

Diller, Calvin
Using the new generation oscilloscopes. il *Radio-Electron* 58:55-7 F '87

Dillon, Clarence
about
Clarence Dillon: using other people's money. L. Jereski. il por *Forbes* 140:270+ Jl 13 '87

Dillon, Kevin
about
Kevin Dillon. E. Miller. il pors *Seventeen* 46:153-4+ Ag '87

Dillon, Ned
When my wife's mother died, the loss tore us apart. *Glamour* 85:234+ Mr '87

Dillon, Richard
Spanning the Golden Gate. il *Am Hist Illus* 22:34-45 My '87

Dillon Read & Co. Inc.
Clarence Dillon: using other people's money. L. Jereski. il por *Forbes* 140:270+ Jl 13 '87
The wonder woman of muni bonds [C. A. Fitts] A. Bianco. il por *Bus Week* p112-13 F 23 '87

Dillons Bookstore (London, England) *See* Booksellers and bookselling—Great Britain

DiLorenzo, Thomas J.
The rhetoric of antitrust. bibl *Society* 24:43-6 S/O '87

Dilsizian, Rick
Gaining confidence with piggyback astrophotography. il *Astronomy* 15:39-46 Ap '87
Photographing our nearest star. il *Astronomy* 15:38-43 My '87

Dim sum
Dim sum quick and easy [based on puréed shrimp] il *Sunset* 178:148+ F '87

Dime novels
Dime novels. E. T. Leblanc. il *Antiques Collect Hobbies* 92:84-6+ D '87

Dimensional Fund Advisors
Sounds good . . . R. Simon. il *Forbes* 140:168 Jl 27 '87

Dimensions (Firm)
Essence woman [D. May-Pressley, founder] J. C. McAdams. il por *Essence* 18:38 Je '87

Dimes *See* Coins
Dimethyl sulfide *See* Methyl sulfide
Dimethyl sulfoxide *See* DMSO
Dimitrios I
about
Mission to Moscow. il por *Time* 130:66 S 14 '87
A new vision for Eastern Orthodoxy? [cover story] Y. Eldar and T. A. Idinopulos. il *Christ Century* 104:995-8 N 11 '87

Dimmer switches *See* Electric switches
Dinelli, Carol, and Dinelli, Jerry
Early German tin toy autos 1900-1925. il *Antiques Collect Hobbies* 92:55-8+ O '87

Dinelli, Jerry
(jt. auth) *See* Dinelli, Carol, and Dinelli, Jerry

Diners (Restaurants)
Nostalgia food: the diner updated and fond memories of forties and fifties fare. A. Batterberry. il por *House Gard* 159:54+ Mr '87

Dinerstein, Eric
(jt. auth) *See* Mishra, Hemanta Raj, and Dinerstein, Eric

Ding Ling
The silent speech of love [story]; tr. by Mary Ann Hurst. il *Ms* 16:64-5+ D '87

Dingell, John D.
Should Congress adopt the House-passed "Gephardt Amendment"? [excerpts from debate, April 29, 1987] *Congr Dig* 66:170+ Je/Jl '87
about
Corporate watchdog. T. Noah. il por *Newsweek* 109:50-1 Ap 20 '87
Detroit powerhouse. J. McLaughlin. *Natl Rev* 39:24 F 27 '87

Dinges, John, and Landau, Saul
Derailing Pinochet. il *Nation* 244:280-2 Mr 7 '87

Dinghies *See* Boats and boating

Dingman, Michael D.
about
'Betting on the genius' of Henley's chairman. G. G. Marcial. il por *Bus Week* p118 N 23 '87
Mike Dingman tunes 'em up, turns 'em around, spins 'em off. S. Toy. il por *Bus Week* p90-2+ O 5 '87
Trying to turn Henley into more than 'assets and a dream'. L. Baum. il por *Bus Week* p80 F 2 '87
The turnaround king investors love. B. Dumaine. il por *Fortune* 115:66 Ja 5 '87

Dingman, Robert W.
Fallen leaders are not "damaged goods". il por *Christ Today* 31:12 D 11 '87

Dings, Fred
Late marsh [poem] *New Yorker* 62:38 F 9 '87

Dinham, Sarah M.
The possibilities for research on architecture teaching. bibl f por *Archit Rec* 175:41+ Ap '87

Dinhofer, Shelly Mehlman
The new Provence allure. il *Harpers Bazaar* 120:86+ My '87
Savory merriment. il *Harpers Bazaar* 121:82+ D '87

Dining *See* Dinners and dining

Dining alcoves, etc.
Antiques with a built-in look [morning room] il *South Living* 22:128-9 Ap '87

Dining establishments *See* Restaurants
Dining room chairs *See* Chairs
Dining rooms
Ceiling raised for spacious dining area. il *South Living* 22:178 My '87
Dining room is small, yet elegant. il *South Living* 22:192-3 N '87
Elegant addition for dining. il *South Living* 22:86-7 Ja '87
Frothy and fun for dining. il *South Living* 22:170 My '87
No kidding, a Gothic cathedral inspired this L.A. dining room. il *Sunset* 178:87 Ja '87
Paintings of the table [art considered suitable for the dining room] L. Blanch. il *Archit Dig* 44:24+ Mr '87
Small space, big ideas. il *Better Homes Gard* 65:160 Mr '87

Dining tables *See* Tables
Dinitrophenol
Diet drug danger déjà vu. A. Hecht and W. F. Janssen. il *FDA Consum* 21:22-7 F '87

Dinkel, John
Miscellaneous ramblings. See issues of Road & Track

Dinks
Dinks: a practical partnership. A. Oston. *Harpers Bazaar* 120:139+ Jl '87
Here come the dinks [double income, no kids couples] M. Smilgis. il *Time* 129:75 Ap 20 '87
The new American family. L. C. Thurow. il *Technol Rev* 90:26-7 Ag/S '87

Dinner parties *See* Dinners and dining
Dinners and dining
See also
  Buffet meals
  Christmas dinners
  Easter dinners
  Gastronomy
  Government entertaining
  Outdoor meals
  Roasts, Celebrity
  Table setting
  Thanksgiving dinners
4 at eight. il *Mademoiselle* 93:218-19+ Ap '87
30 fast spring dinners. il *Good Housekeep* 204:152-64+ Ap '87
April, come she will: celebrate spring with the first fresh foods of the season. P. G. McWilliams. il *Ctry J* 14:75-8 Ap '87
A beach weekend. il *Gourmet* 47:82-8 Ag '87

Dinners and dining—*cont.*

Catered by Cupid [Valentine's Day dinner] M. Greenberg and E. Greenberg. il *50 Plus* 27:36-8 F '87

Come for dinner! P. Y. Cordell. il *South Living* 22:132-4+ Je '87

Come to dinner! Elegant meals in sixty minutes or less. J. T. Hazard. il *Ladies Home J* 104:152-3+ N '87

The dinner party as theater—feasts for the spirit and the senses [catering by N. Kalachnikoff] C. Rayner. il por *Vogue* 177:288 F '87

Dinner-party fights: how to keep the mayhem minimal. B.-J. Raphael. *Glamour* 85:59 Ja '87

Dinner's ready in less than an hour. S. Dosier. il *South Living* 22:112+ Ag '87

Elegant but easy. il *Gourmet* 47:80-2+ S '87

Elegant party dinners [microwaved entrees] il *Good Housekeep* 205:113-14 N '87

Enjoy a candlelight dinner for two [low calorie menu] B. Fannin. il *South Living* 22:134+ D '87

An evening with Carolina and Reinaldo Herrera: strong opinions, European style. W. P. Rayner and C. Rayner. il pors *Vogue* 177:342 Mr '87

A family reunion. il *Gourmet* 47:84-90 Jl '87

A February dinner for four. il *Gourmet* 47:92-8+ F '87

Five times great: what working girls work up for dinner in under 30 minutes. il *Mademoiselle* 93:220-1+ O '87

Gazebo dinners. il *Gourmet* 48:100-6+ Je '87

A late spring dinner. il *Gourmet* 47:124-32 My '87

Midnight meals. J. Nash. il *Essence* 17:92-3+ F '87

New Year's Eve dinner for two. il *Gourmet* 47:66-8+ Ja '87

One from the heart [Valentine's Day dinner] il *Seventeen* 46:135-6 F '87

Opening-night cast party [dinner given by S. Dietz] C. Rossant. il por *McCalls* 114:107-8+ My '87

Paris, Tokyo, New York: Hanae Mori's style goes everywhere—and so does her chef. W. P. Rayner and C. Rayner. il por *Vogue* 177:300 O '87

A pretheater dinner. il *Gourmet* 47:108-15 Mr '87

A spring dinner. il *Gourmet* 47:82-4+ Ap '87

Stew pour vous [bistro beef stew and accompaniments] il *Seventeen* 46:125-6 D '87

Wendy Goldberg: "the most gracious hostess in town". N. Gittelson. il pors *McCalls* 114:124-6+ F '87

Anecdotes, facetiae, satire, etc.

And after all, isn't that what eggs are for? S. Dooley. il *Smithsonian* 17:152 F '87

Are you dinner-party paranoid? W. D. Leight. *Mademoiselle* 93:166+ Mr '87

The latest version [Compusit dinner party seating program] D. Seligman. il *Fortune* 115:141+ Je 8 '87

Legal seating [Compusit, a dinner party seating program] D. Seligman. il *Fortune* 115:108 Mr 16 '87

Where the bodies are buried [dinner parties] I. Frazier. il *Atlantic* 259:26 Je '87

Exhibitions

The arts of dining [exhibition entitled Savory suppers and fashionable feasts: dining in Victorian America] S. B. Sherrill. il *Antiques* 131:356+ F '87

Dinners and dining in the Bible

Come to the feast. G. G. Seibert. il *America* 157:199 O 3 '87

Dinnerware *See* Tableware

Dinning Sisters (Musical group)

Dreamgirls [F. Lenger, ardent fan] B. Greene. il por *Esquire* 107:39-40 My '87

Dinoflagellates

See also
Red tide

Deadly blooms and curious clocks [Gonyaulax; research by Donald M. Anderson and Bruce A. Keafer] *Sci News* 131:122 F 21 '87

The domestication of reef-dwelling clams [giant clams; cover story] G. A. Heslinga and W. K. Fitt. il *BioScience* 37:332-9 My '87

Propagation in cell culture of the dinoflagellate Amyloodinium, an ectoparasite of marine fishes. E. J. Noga. bibl f il *Science* 236:1302-4 Je 5 '87

Dinosaur models *See* Paleontological models and exhibits

Dinosaurs

Announcing the birth of a heresy [cover story] V. Morell. il *Discover* 8:26-8+ Mr '87

Artist rearranges plates along dinosaur's back [Stegosaurus; work of Stephen Czerkas] il *Earth Sci* 40:10-11 Spr '87

Bringing up baby [live birth for Brontosaurs; work of Robert T. Bakker] *Sci Am* 256:68+ Mr '87

A daring gamble in the Gobi Desert took the jackpot [R. C. Andrews' search for dinosaur fossils] D. J. Preston. il pors *Smithsonian* 18:94-8+ D '87

Digging for dinosaurs [Dinosaur Project findings in China and Alberta] J. Howse. il *Macleans* 100:62 N 30 '87

Dinosaur country. il maps *Sunset* 178:82-91 Je '87

Dinosaurs: decline or fall? *Sci Am* 256:62-3 Ja '87

Dinosaurs on the North Slope, Alaska: high latitude, latest Cretaceous environments. E. M. Brouwers and others. bibl f il map *Science* 237:1608-10 S 25 '87

Drop that bone! [deposits of dinosaur bones in Alberta] P. Johnston. il *Hist Today* 37:4-6 D '87

Finding a family for an Ultrasaurus. *Sci News* 132:136 Ag 29 '87

How dumb was the dinosaur, anyway? [theories of R. T. Bakker] S. Budiansky. il por *U S News World Rep* 103:66-7 Jl 6 '87

The lesson of the dinosaurs: evolution didn't inevitably lead to us. S. J. Gould. il *Discover* 8:51 Mr '87

Make no bones about it, dinosaur theory challenged [Alaskan Hadrosaur remains found by Elisabeth Brouwers and William Clemens] il *Earth Sci* 40:6 Wint '87

New fossil finds give clues about dinosaurs. il *Earth Sci* 40:10-11 Summ '87

They dig dinos [Colorado dig] il map *Natl Geogr World* 146:6-9 O '87

What killed the dinosaurs? [asteroid impact theory; work of Eric Essene and Daniel Fisher] il *USA Today (Periodical)* 115:9 Je '87

Who killed the dinosaurs? [impact-generated extinction theory] *Space World* X-8-284:9 Ag '87

Collectibles

The incredible mystery of dinomania! R. Micheli. il *Money* 16:150-2 D '87

Nests

Dinosaur eggs unscrambled [discovered in Wells Gulch, Colo.] il *Time* 130:56 Ag 3 '87

Dinosaurs in art

Exhibitions

Dinosaur art exhibits tour North America [Dinosaurs past and present; cover story] il *Earth Sci* 40:9-10 Fall '87

Dinosaurs shake the ground in paint and sculpture. J. P. Wiley, Jr. bibl (p153-4) il *Smithsonian* 18:84-9 Je '87

Evolving views of dinosaurs [Dinosaurs past and present exhibit; cover story] il *Nat Hist* 96:46-55 D '87

Traveling dinosaurs [Dinosaurs past and present] A. Fisher. il *Pop Sci* 231:10 D '87

Dinucleotides *See* Nucleotides

Diodes

High-temperature cubic boron nitride P-N junction diode made at high pressure. O. Mishima and others. bibl f il *Science* 238:181-3 O 9 '87

Lasers light the way for computer links. S. Weisburd. *Sci News* 131:408 Je 27 '87

Light-bulb savers: not a bright idea [work of Alexander Emanuel] D. Stover. *Pop Sci* 230:34 My '87

Putting the heat on new semiconductors [cubic boron nitride diode; work of Osamu Mishima and others] I. Peterson. *Sci News* 132:247 O 17 '87

Silicon devices: LED there be light. S. Weisburd. il *Sci News* 131:294-5 My 9 '87

SMT project: LED flasher [surface-mountable components] F. M. Mims. il *Radio-Electron* 58:73-4+ S '87

Ultrahigh-power semiconductor diode laser arrays. P. S. Cross and others. bibl f il *Science* 237:1305-9 S 11 '87

Testing

Testing semiconductors (I). T. J. Byers. il *Radio-Electron* 58:58-60+ F '87

Testing semiconductors (III). T. J. Byers. il *Radio-Electron* 58:62-4+ Ap '87

Diodoros I

about

A new vision for Eastern Orthodoxy? [cover story] Y. Eldar and T. A. Idinopulos. il *Christ Century* 104:995-8 N 11 '87

Diodorov, Boris

about

Illustrator Boris Diodorov gives a winning Russian accent to a bear called 'Vinni-Pukh'. J. W. Seymore. il por *People Wkly* 37:52-4 Ap 6 '87

Dionne, E. J., Jr.

Gary Hart: the elusive front-runner [cover story] il pors *N Y Times Mag* p28-34+ My 3 '87

Dionne, Marcel
    about
The King and his court. P. Fichtenbaum. il pors *Sport Mag* 78:61-2+ F '87
Diop, Amadou Moustapha
Women on the sidelines. bibl f il *Courier* 40:20-2 Ja '87
Dior, Christian, 1905-1957
    about
Dior: 40 years of triumph. A. Kurzweil. il pors *Harpers Bazaar* 120:152+ S '87
Dior's new look . . . then and now. J. J. Buck. il por *Vogue* 177:478-9+ Mr '87
Dior (Christian) (Firm) *See* Christian Dior (Firm)
Dioramas
Toybot. K. McKinney. il *Omni* 9:52-7 Ja '87
Diouf, Abdou
        Visit to the United States, 1987
Top African leaders Diouf, Odhiambo hailed for fight against hunger. il pors *Jet* 73:6 O 5 '87
Dioxin
    See also
    Agent Orange
Alarm over paper goods [dioxin contamination] M. Gray. *Macleans* 100:57-8 O 26 '87
Garbage: to burn or not to burn? T. Davis. il *Technol Rev* 90:19 F/Mr '87
In Illinois: the longest jury trial drones on [Kemner et al. v. Monsanto] L. Griggs. il *Time* 129:1 Mr 23 '87
Is mother's milk safe? Dioxin climbs to the top of the food chain. K. Hart. il *Progressive* 51:32-4 Mr '87
Keeping dioxins down in the dumps. I. Peterson. *Sci News* 132:118-19 Ag 22 '87
Model studies of polychlorinated dibenzo-*p*-dioxin formation during municipal refuse incineration [fly ash] F. W. Karasek and L. C. Dickson. bibl f il *Science* 237:754-6 Ag 14 '87
Never to be accused of rushing to judgment, a jury goes home after a trying 44 months [Monsanto dioxin-spill suit] M. Green. il *People Wkly* 28:48-50 N 9 '87
Diphtheria
        Vaccines and vaccination
    See also
    DPT vaccine
Diphtheria toxin *See* Toxins and antitoxins
Diploidy (Botany) *See* Chromosomes (Botany)
Diplomacy
Public diplomacy in the information age [address, September 15, 1987] G. P. Shultz. *Dep State Bull* 87:16-18 N '87
Diplomat Samurai Band
Diplomats. *New Yorker* 63:29-30 Ap 20 '87
Diplomatic and consular service
    See also
    Ambassadors
    Canada—Diplomatic and consular service
    Foreign propagandists
    Iran—Diplomatic and consular service
    Japan—Diplomatic and consular service
    South Africa—Diplomatic and consular service
    Soviet Union—Diplomatic and consular service
    United States—Diplomatic and consular service
Diplomatic documents, Classified *See* Classified information
Diplomatic privileges and immunities
The ambassador's tale [Canadian ambassador A. Gotlieb subpoenaed to testify in M. Deaver perjury trial] M. McDonald. il por *Macleans* 100:21 Je 8 '87
Diplomatic immunity and U.S. interests [statement, August 5, 1987] S. Roosevelt. *Dep State Bull* 87:29-32 O '87
When diplomatic immunity is a crime [condensed from Diplomatic crime] C. R. Ashman and P. Trescott. *Read Dig* 131:129-32 D '87
Diplomats
    See also
    Ambassadors
Dips *See* Appetizers
Dirac Medal *See* Physics—Awards
Direct Broadcast Satellite Association
    See also
    Satellite Broadcasting and Communications Association
Direct broadcast satellite services
    See also
    Satellite Broadcasting and Communications Association
The dish crowd fights for a pipeline in the sky. C. Gerber. il *Channels* 7 Sp Issue:99 D '87

FCC permits broadcast satellite operators to broaden services. *Aviat Week Space Technol* 126:149 F 9 '87
Satellite TV. B. Cooper, Jr. See issues of Radio-Electronics beginning November 1984
        Agricultural programs
Farm news from the sky [satellite TV] G. Vincent. il *Success Farm* 85:64 O '87
        Germany (West)
Europeans to use apogee motor in attempt to free TVSat solar array. K. F. Mordoff. *Aviat Week Space Technol* 127:27-8 D 14 '87
German TVSat experiences solar array problem following launch by Ariane V20. J. M. Lenorovitz and K. F. Mordoff. il *Aviat Week Space Technol* 127:24-5 N 30 '87
        Great Britain
    See also
    British Satellite Broadcasting (Firm)
        Western Europe
Europeans prepare TVSat 1 for launch on Ariane V20. K. F. Mordoff. il *Aviat Week Space Technol* 127:65+ N 2 '87
Eutelsat to decide whether to drop opposition to SES. *Aviat Week Space Technol* 127:20 S 21 '87
Intelsat, Eutelsat favor not opposing Astra's marketing of TV broadcast service [Luxembourg's Astra satellite program] *Aviat Week Space Technol* 127:26-7 N 2 '87
Direct energy conversion
    See also
    Biomass energy
    Fuel cells
    Heat engines
    Ocean thermal power plants
    Solar cells
Direct mail advertising *See* Advertising, Direct mail
Direct mail advertising, Political *See* Advertising, Political
Direct marketing *See* Direct selling
Direct Pharmaceutical Corp.
Drug money. J. Wynn. il por *Forbes* 139:254 Je 15 '87
Direct selling
    See also
    Advertising, Direct mail
    CCX Network Inc.
    Door-to-door selling
    Mail order business
    Telephone selling
    Tupperware International
Direct marketing success stories [publishers] L. Shanley. il *Publ Wkly* 232:48-50 N 13 '87
Farmers overlook million-dollar direct markets. *Success Farm* 85 no4:5 F '87
Direction, Sense of *See* Orientation
Direction, Theatrical *See* Musicals, revues, etc.—Production and direction; Theater—Production and direction
Direction finding equipment
    See also
    Communications satellites—Direction finding use
    Radio direction finders
Directions Metropolitan (Firm)
Building an empire [black woman contractor J. Bradley] P. F. Stewart. il por *Ladies Home J* 104:158 O '87
Directories
    See also
    Telephone directories
Directors, College athletics *See* College athletics—Directors
Directors, Corporation *See* Corporations—Directors
Directors, Motion picture *See* Motion picture directors
Directors, Television *See* Television directors
Directors, Theatrical *See* Theatrical directors
Directors Guild of America
Hollywood directors: lights, camera, walkout? R. Grover. il *Bus Week* p66 My 25 '87
Make money, not war. A. Gibney and A. Thompson. il *Film Comment* 23:17-18+ N/D '87
Dirr, Michael
    about
A passion for plants. S. Bender. il por *South Living* 22:102 Je '87
Dirt
    See also
    Soils
The joy of dirt. T. Kornheiser. il *Esquire* 107:145-6 Je '87
Dirty dancing [film] *See* Motion picture reviews—Single works

Dirty tricks (Political ethics) See Political ethics
Dirty words See Words, Obscene
Disability insurance See Insurance, Disability
Disabled See Handicapped
Disadvantaged children See Socially handicapped children
Disarmament

> See also
>
> Anti-nuclear movement
> Canadian Centre for Arms Control and Disarmament
> Church and disarmament
> Convention on the Prohibition of the Development, Production and Stockpiling of Bacteriological (Biological) and Toxin Weapons and on Their Destruction (1972)
> European Nuclear Disarmament (Organization)
> Guided missiles—Testing—Suspension
> Nuclear-free zones
> Nuclear weapons—Testing—Suspension
> Parapsychology and disarmament
> Press and disarmament
> Pugwash movement
> SANE/FREEZE (Organization)
> United Nations. Disarmament Commission
> United States. Arms Control and Disarmament Agency

ABM must go. W. F. Buckley. *Natl Rev* 39:62 Ap 24 '87
ABM, SDI, SOS. *Natl Rev* 39:16-17 Ap 10 '87
The ABM Treaty and the Soviets. *Bull At Sci* 43:2 Ap '87
The ABM Treaty controversy. *Congr Dig* 66:257-88 N '87
About arms control [discussion of June 6, 1986 article, Rethinking arms control and June 20, 1986 article, SALT free] *Commonweal* 114:2+ Ja 16 '87
About-face on arms [Soviet strategy] *World Press Rev* 34:10-12 Ap '87
Administration wrong on ABM Treaty [criticism of A. D. Sofaer's interpretation] C. Levin. il *Bull At Sci* 43:30-3 Ap '87
Advancing U.S.-Soviet relations: the challenge of arms control [address, September 9, 1987] E. L. Rowny. *Dep State Bull* 87:24-5 N '87
After arms control: what does NATO do now? D. Griffiths. il *Bus Week* p124-5 O 19 '87
Again, Mikhail the acrobat displays his tricks [global double zero proposal] P. R. Range. il *U S News World Rep* 103:6 Ag 3 '87
Allies weigh new deployments to offset proposed INF cuts. J. D. Morrocco. *Aviat Week Space Technol* 126:18-19 My 18 '87
'Ample opportunities' for arms pact [interview with E. Honecker] R. Knight. il por *U S News World Rep* 102:34-5 Ja 12 '87
April's spy scare [Soviet espionage and the INF proposals] D. Schorr. il *New Leader* 70:3-4 Ap 20 '87
Arms and the ban. *Nation* 245:616 N 28 '87
Arms and the men. D. E. Koshland, Jr. *Science* 238:9 O 2 '87
Arms control. J. B. Hehir. *Commonweal* 114:38-9 Ja 30 '87
Arms control [address, December 10, 1986] K. L. Adelman. *Vital Speeches Day* 53:226-9 F 1 '87
Arms Control Agency challenges Nunn's contention on legality of testing kinetic systems [ABM Treaty restrictions] *Aviat Week Space Technol* 126:29 Mr 23 '87
Arms control and SDI. *Natl Rev* 39:20-1 F 27 '87
Arms control: decision time [INF Treaty] H. Trewhitt. il *U S News World Rep* 103:32-3 S 21 '87
Arms-control frenzy [INF breakthrough] T. Bethell. il *Natl Rev* 39:26-8+ O 23 '87
Arms control in the new Congress. J. D. Isaacs. il *Bull At Sci* 43:4-5 Ja/F '87
Arms control protests force delay in next stage of SDI research [risking abrogation of the Antiballistic Missile Treaty] P. Mann. *Aviat Week Space Technol* 126:16-17 F 16 '87
Arms control: the Reagan legacy. R. J. Bresler. il *USA Today (Periodical)* 115:6-7 Ja '87
An arms offer is accepted [eliminating medium-range missiles in Europe; with interview with M. Kampelman] M. Satchell. il *U S News World Rep* 102:26-7 Mr 16 '87
The arms race—intervention link. D. Cortright. *Cent Mag* 20:58-9 My/Je '87
Aspin believes INF unworkable without SALT 2 compliance. M. Mecham. *Aviat Week Space Technol* 127:135 O 12 '87
Backing away from Armageddon [right wing criticism of Reagan as peacemaker] D. Schorr. *New Leader* 70:3-4 D 28 '87

Ballistic missiles and SDI [address, November 13, 1986] K. L. Adelman. *Vital Speeches Day* 53:181-4 Ja 1 '87
Battle of the bean counters [effect of zero option proposal on NATO and Warsaw Pact forces] C. Redman. il map *Time* 129:33-4 Je 15 '87
Before we cheer [comparison between impending INF Treaty and the nuclear test ban treaty of 1963] S. H. Day, Jr. *Progressive* 51:14-15 N '87
Blundering into disaster [address, February 17, 1987] R. S. McNamara. *Vital Speeches Day* 53:390-4 Ap 15 '87
Bombs away [INF deal] *New Repub* 197:7-8 O 12 '87
'Breakthrough' on arms control [intermediate range nuclear forces in Europe] R. Watson. il *Newsweek* 109:36-7 Mr 16 '87
Breakthrough unlikely in nuclear diplomacy. A. Geyer. *Christ Century* 104:211-12 Mr 4 '87
Can NATO survive an arms deal? [views of B. W. Rogers] J. Keegan. il *U S News World Rep* 103:30 Jl 27 '87
Can SDI survive house arrest? *Sci Am* 256:59 Ja '87
Captain Zero Option [Gorbachev's latest proposal concerning European INF forces] C. Krauthammer. *New Repub* 196:12-14 Mr 30 '87
Closer to an arms deal [M. Gorbachev's INF concession on Asian missiles] I. Austen. *Macleans* 100:28 Ag 3 '87
Closing the gap [INF agreement] J. Greenwald. il *Time* 130:12-13 S 7 '87
Collision in space [SDI deployment and compliance with ABM Treaty] R. English and S. Daggett. *New Repub* 196:11-13 Je 29 '87
The complexities of nuclear diplomacy [INF proposals] R. J. Bresler. il *USA Today (Periodical)* 116:7 Jl '87
Congress and arms control. D. B. Fascell. bibl f *Foreign Aff* 65:730-49 Spr '87
Congress questions wisdom, savings of expanded antimissile tests [broad interpretation of the ABM Treaty] P. Mann. *Aviat Week Space Technol* 126:18-19 Mr 2 '87
Congress tries again on arms control. J. D. Isaacs. il *Bull At Sci* 43:3-4 Je '87
Congressional defense leaders, White House agree on SDI tests [compromise on ABM Treaty compliance] *Aviat Week Space Technol* 127:24-5 N 16 '87
Congressional leaders outline terms of arms control agreement [dropping references to ABM and SALT 2 treaties] *Aviat Week Space Technol* 127:24-5 N 23 '87
Controlling deadly weapons [special section] *Society* 24:38-79 Jl/Ag '87
Conventional forces in Europe [special section] bibl f il *Bull At Sci* 43:9-20 D '87
Cruisin' for a bruisin' [INF reductions expose the Germans] J. Joffe. *New Repub* 197:17-18 O 5 '87
Danes bristle at U.S. radar plans [phased-array radar planned for Thule, Greenland complicates ABM Treaty] M. Burcharth. il map *Bull At Sci* 43:11-13 Je '87
Dateline Washington: INF: a hollow victory? M. R. Gordon. *Foreign Policy* 68:159-79 Fall '87
The Democrats' zero options. P. Osterlund. *Natl Rev* 39:36+ Je 19 '87
Disarmament is no bargain. M. S. Forbes, Jr. il *Forbes* 139:33 My 18 '87
Disarmament issues, especially nuclear matters, acted on by General Assembly. il *UN Chron* 24:87-92 F '87
A disarming surprise [Soviet concession on medium-range nuclear missiles in Asia] I. Austen. *Macleans* 100:20 Ag 10 '87
A dispute over Soviet ABM plans. C. Norman. *Science* 235:524-6 Ja 30 '87
Draw the line at Star Wars. H. Brown. *Bull At Sci* 43:3 Ja/F '87
East-West missile deal: Helmut Kohl feels the heat. D. Stanglin. il por *U S News World Rep* 102:13 Je 1 '87
Effective arms control demands a broad approach [address, April 27, 1987] E. L. Rowny. *Dep State Bull* 87:22-4 Jl '87
Equitable arms control [secure deterrence; address, February 19, 1987] A. M. Haig. *Vital Speeches Day* 53:387-90 Ap 15 '87
Euromissile pact may affect NATO's conventional/high-technology balance. J. D. Morrocco. il map *Aviat Week Space Technol* 126:122+ Je 15 '87
A European deterrent? B. Crozier. *Natl Rev* 39:24 Jl 31 '87

Disarmament—*cont.*

Europe's decoupling anxiety [disarmament proposals frighten Western European leaders] N. Gelb. il *New Leader* 70:7-8 Ap 20 '87

Europe's security dilemmas. C. Bertram. *Foreign Aff* 65:942-57 Summ '87

Farewell, Dark Prince [resignation of R. Perle from Defense Dept.] il por *Time* 129:14 Mr 23 '87

Fasting for life [C. Hyder's hunger strike for disarmament] J. Cott. il por *Roll Stone* p33+ My 7 '87

Final reductions [Soviet Euromissile proposal] M. Kondracke. *New Repub* 196:15-16 My 11 '87

Finlandizing Europe. J. McLaughlin. *Natl Rev* 39:20 D 31 '87

First Committee's disarmament debate: towards fewer weapons, more hope. il *UN Chron* 23:43-50 Ja '86

For INF, with regrets. *New Repub* 197:9-10 D 28 '87

From Star Wars to smart rocks [ABM Treaty threatened by SDI] B. Van Voorst. il *Time* 129:27 F 23 '87

Future missile cuts would force NATO to improve conventional arms planning. *Aviat Week Space Technol* 126:212-14 Je 15 '87

The game of perceptions in arms racing [with discussion] S. Kull. por *Cent Mag* 20:43-57 S/O '87

Generals can be right [B. Rogers on proposed INF Treaty] W. F. Buckley. *Natl Rev* 39:56 Jl 31 '87

Germany's decision on proposed INF reductions [statement, June 4, 1987] R. Reagan. *Dep State Bull* 87:50 Ag '87

Getting over the summit. L. V. Sigal. il *Bull At Sci* 43:12-13 Ja/F '87

Gorbachev's long reach [proposal to eliminate intermediate range nuclear missiles in Europe] K. Scanlon. il por map *Macleans* 100:31-2 Mr 16 '87

Gorbachev's next move. M. A. Evangelista. il *Harpers* 274:24+ Ja '87

The harm is done [treaty arranged by Reagan-Shultz to remove intermediate nuclear weapons from Europe] W. F. Buckley. *Natl Rev* 39:66 N 20 '87

Heading toward a 4% solution [need for strategic arms reductions beyond those gained through INF negotiations] S. Talbott. il *Time* 130:28-9 S 21 '87

The hearings ahead [INF Treaty] W. F. Buckley. *Natl Rev* 39:54 D 31 '87

Hope amid hopelessness: a conversation about arms control with Arvid Pardo. M. Davidson. il por *USA Today (Periodical)* 115:26-8 Ja '87

How the cold war might end. J. L. Gaddis. il *Atlantic* 260:88-92+ N '87

If Labour wins. W. B. Messmer. *Foreign Policy* 67:137-53 Summ '87

In defense of ABM—and Star Wars. S. D. Drell. *Harpers* 274:21-3 Je '87

In defense of the zero option [eliminating medium-range missiles] R. N. Perle. il *U S News World Rep* 102:36-7 My 25 '87

Independent initiatives: an alternative peace process. M. Sommer and G. Feller. *Current* 292:36-9 My '87

INF deal faces conservative opposition. L. V. Sigal. il *Bull At Sci* 43:14-16 My '87

The INF trap [Gorbachev's gambit] E. V. Rostow. *New Repub* 197:16-17 Ag 24 '87

International views of the superpowers [cover story; special section; with editorial comment by Len Ackland] il *Bull At Sci* 43:2, 28-47 Mr '87

Interpreting the ABM Treaty [address, April 1, 1987] P. H. Nitze. *Dep State Bull* 87:31-3 Je '87

The Iran/arms control connection [R. Perle's efforts to damage existing arms control agreements] M. Krepon. il *Bull At Sci* 43:9-10 Mr '87

Kissinger: a new era for NATO. H. Kissinger. il *Newsweek* 110:57-8+ O 12 '87

Kissinger and INF. il *Natl Rev* 39:17 N 6 '87

Kohl is nudged, but will he budge? [INF disarmament proposal] *Newsweek* 109:39 Je 1 '87

Kohl vows to scrap Pershing 1As if U.S., Soviets agree on treaty [INF] *Aviat Week Space Technol* 127:18 Ag 31 '87

The Kremlin's new cards [Soviets tie INF agreement to SDI] J. V. Lamar, Jr. il *Time* 130:30 Jl 20 '87

Labor's defense [interview with N. Kinnock] J. Lloyd and P. Kellner. *World Press Rev* 34:15-16 My '87

A Labour Britain, NATO and the bomb. D. Healey. *Foreign Aff* 65:716-29 Spr '87

The last hurrahs [Reagan administration moves on contra aid, arms control and R. Bork nomination] *Nation* 245:291-2 S 26 '87

Latest ABM ploy—old is new [dispute over legality of kinetic weapons] T. K. Longstreth. il *Bull At Sci* 43:3-4 D '87

Let's make a deal [removal of medium-range missiles from Europe] J. Smolowe. il map *Time* 129:38-9 Mr 16 '87

Letter from Washington [conservatives and the INF Treaty] Cato. *Natl Rev* 39:11 D 31 '87

Looking this gift horse in the mouth [Soviet INF proposal] W. F. Buckley. *Natl Rev* 39:60 Ap 10 '87

Lost horizons. *Nation* 244:35-6 Ja 17 '87

Major SDI tests—compliance with alternative treaty regimes [ABM Treaty] il *Aviat Week Space Technol* 127:31 S 14 '87

A matter of life and death [fast for disarmament; interview with C. Hyder] J. Cott. il por *Roll Stone* p48-9+ F 26 '87

Medium gains [medium-range missile treaty] *Nation* 245:327-8 O 3 '87

Medium-range missile cuts pose unclear impact on ABM research [Soviet proposal] P. Mann. *Aviat Week Space Technol* 126:262 Mr 9 '87

A mellower Moscow. R. Watson. il *Newsweek* 110:42-4 S 21 '87

Memo to the Senate [views of B. Rogers on INF deal] *Natl Rev* 39:15 Jl 17 '87

Military security in Europe. J. Dean. *Foreign Aff* 66:22-40 Fall '87

The missile treaty: down the stretch. H. Trewhitt. il *U S News World Rep* 103:32 O 26 '87

The missile treaty is only a 3% solution. B. Javetski and D. Griffiths. il *Bus Week* p24 S 7 '87

Moscow's arms-control offer has Kohl in a corner. J. E. Pluenneke and F. Thelen. il *Bus Week* p69 My 18 '87

Moscow's chemical candor. N. Cooper. il *Newsweek* 110:56 O 19 '87

Much ado about zero [INF forces] *Bull At Sci* 43:2 S '87

NATO defense ministers back INF agreement. B. A. Smith. *Aviat Week Space Technol* 127:26-7 N 9 '87

NATO looks for arms control loopholes [prospect of an INF accord] D. Charles. il *Bull At Sci* 43:7-12 S '87

NATO planning group to discuss post-INF tactical nuclear strategy. J. D. Morrocco. *Aviat Week Space Technol* 127:125+ O 12 '87

The need for nuclear arms [interview with B. W. Rogers] R. Knight. por *U S News World Rep* 102:22-3 Je 22 '87

New rules for war [H. Kohl drops objection to Soviet offer on Euromissiles] P. Lewis. il por *Macleans* 100:20-1 Je 8 '87

'New thinking' in foreign policy [Soviet initiatives] M. A. Evangelista. *Nation* 244:795-9 Je 13 '87

Nine SDI tests planned in 1988-89 amid ABM debate over 'exotic' weapons. P. Mann. *Aviat Week Space Technol* 126:28 Ap 6 '87

Nonproliferation and the peaceful uses of nuclear energy [address, May 20, 1987] J. Negroponte. *Dep State Bull* 87:67-70 Jl '87

North Atlantic Council meets in Brussels [texts of final communique, declaration on conventional arms control, and press conference, December 12, 1986] *Dep State Bull* 87:42-6 Mr '87

North Atlantic Council meets in Iceland [texts of final communique and news conference, June 12, 1987] G. P. Shultz. *Dep State Bull* 87:59-63 Ag '87

Notes and comment [bargaining on Star Wars] *New Yorker* 63:35 D 7 '87

Now to the summit: high risks for high stakes [special section; with editorial comment by David Gergen] il *U S News World Rep* 103:38-40+, 94 D 7 '87

Nuclear cooperation with EURATOM [letter to Congress, February 28, 1986] R. Reagan. *Dep State Bull* 87:77 Je '87

Nuclear disarmament [address, February 28, 1987] M. Gorbachev. *Vital Speeches Day* 53:386-7 Ap 15 '87

The nuclear opening. Sir S. Zuckerman. bibl f il *N Y Rev Books* 34:42-6 My 7 '87

Nuclear proliferation: who's next? L. S. Spector. bibl f il *Bull At Sci* 43:17-20 My '87

Nuclear shysters [early deployment of SDI and the ABM Treaty] *New Repub* 196:7-8 Mr 9 '87

Nuclear weapons, arms control, and the future of deterrence [address, November 17, 1986] G. P. Shultz. *Dep State Bull* 87:31-5 Ja '87

Nunn affirms 1972 ABM pact, finding kinetic tests illegal. P. Mann. *Aviat Week Space Technol* 126:21-3 Mr 16 '87

Nunn calls for conventional upgrades to balance possible nuclear cuts. K. F. Mordoff. *Aviat Week Space Technol* 126:30-1 Ap 20 '87

Disarmament—*cont.*

Nunn threatens INF pact with link to ABM Treaty. P. Mann. *Aviat Week Space Technol* 126:30 My 11 '87

Of arms and reforms [adaptations of three addresses] A. D. Sakharov. il por *Time* 129:40-3 Mr 16 '87

An offer that Reagan can't refuse? [M. Gorbachev's INF concession on Asian SS-20s] J. Young. il por *Newsweek* 110:27 Ag 3 '87

An offer they can refuse [Republican presidential candidates' reaction to the INF Treaty] J. V. Lamar, Jr. il *Time* 130:32 D 14 '87

The Ogarkov factor [Soviet arms control proposals linked to views of N. Ogarkov] B. Crozier. *Natl Rev* 39:22 Je 5 '87

On accepting a prize. A. D. Sakharov. il *N Y Rev Books* 34:49 Ag 13 '87

One small step for mankind [INF agreement] *America* 157:235 O 17 '87

One way to arms-control unity: twist allied arms. P. Hassner. il *U S News World Rep* 102:24-5 Je 22 '87

The opiate of arms control. G. F. Will. il *Newsweek* 109:86 Ap 27 '87

Opponents focus on kinetic-kill research, ABM Treaty violations [SDI] *Aviat Week Space Technol* 127:84+ N 23 '87

The Pakistan syndrome [halting nuclear proliferation] *New Repub* 197:7-8+ S 28 '87

Peacedrunk [INF Treaty] W. F. Buckley. *Natl Rev* 39:71 O 23 '87

Permitted and prohibited activities under the ABM Treaty [address, October 31, 1986] P. H. Nitze. *Dep State Bull* 87:39-40 Ja '87

Physicist Hyder fasts for peace. W. Sweet. il por *Phys Today* 40:68 Ap '87

Pledges to World Disarmament Campaign total $360,000. *UN Chron* 22:83 N/D '85

The political trials of SDI. R. N. Perle. il *U S News World Rep* 103:45-6 S 14 '87

Presidential memo. W. F. Buckley. *Natl Rev* 39:62-3 D 4 '87

The 'Prince of Darkness' calls it quits [R. Perle leaves Defense Dept.] T. Jacoby. il por *Newsweek* 109:27 Mr 23 '87

Problems of assurance of nuclear supplies [address, May 27, 1987] F. McGoldrick. *Dep State Bull* 87:48-52 S '87

Progress on a chemical arms treaty. E. Marshall. il *Science* 238:471-2 O 23 '87

The promise—and problems—of Gorbachev's offer. B. Javetski and D. Griffiths. il por *Bus Week* p36 Mr 16 '87

A promising Soviet ploy [M. Gorbachev's proposal to eliminate intermediate and shorter range missiles from Europe and Asia] B. Van Voorst. por *Time* 130:18 Ag 3 '87

The proposed Euromissile agreement: an important step toward nuclear sanity [INF agreement] R. E. Powaski. *America* 157:183-4+ O 3 '87

The proposed treaty [Soviet INF proposal] *Natl Rev* 39:13-15 My 22 '87

A ray of light in arms control [R. Reagan attempts to boost weakened status] H. Trewhitt. il por *U S News World Rep* 103:28-9 Ag 10 '87

Reagan & Gorbachev: arms-control breakthrough? [cover story; special issue] il map *Sch Update* 120:4-10+ N 20 '87

Reagan breaks his fall [new arms proposal and H. Baker made chief of staff] R. Fly and others. il pors *Bus Week* p34-5 Mr 16 '87

Reagan, Congress on collision course over treaty limits [SALT 2 and ABM restrictions] *Aviat Week Space Technol* 127:32 O 12 '87

Reagan still has a shot at arms control—but it's a long one. B. Javetski. il *Bus Week* p63 F 23 '87

Reagan's de facto détente. D. Schorr. il *New Leader* 70:3-4 S 21 '87

Red-baiting Ron [conservative criticism of INF Treaty] *Nation* 245:739-40 D 19 '87

Red star blazes on [M. Gorbachev's tactics] B. Crozier. *Natl Rev* 39:26 Ag 14 '87

Rejecting the suicide pact [opposition to proposed INF agreement] *Natl Rev* 39:12-13 Je 5 '87

Removing Gorbachev's edge. M. Svec. il *Foreign Policy* 69:148-65 Wint '87/'88

'Renegotiate the ABM Treaty' [interview with S. Nunn] por *U S News World Rep* 103:30-1 D 14 '87

Richard Perle did his best [leaving the Defense Dept.] *Natl Rev* 39:21 Ap 10 '87

The right wing opens fire [conservatives snipe at INF and the summit] R. Watson. il *Newsweek* 110:36-7 N 30 '87

Rocky road to INF accord. M. Krepon. il *Bull At Sci* 43:3-4 S '87

Roiling the arms control waters [impact of Canada's defense white paper on disarmament policy] J. M. Lamb. il *Bull At Sci* 43:17-19 O '87

A rush to the summit [INF agreement] R. Watson. il *Newsweek* 110:14-16 S 7 '87

The saver? [latest Soviet zero option proposal] M. Kramer. il *N Y* 20:14-15 Mr 30 '87

SDI: incentive for arms control [with discussion] F. J. Gaffney, Jr. *Cent Mag* 20:33-8 S/O '87

Secretary's interview on "This week with David Brinkley" [interview with G. P. Shultz; transcript of program, February 8, 1987] *Dep State Bull* 87:8-11 Ap '87

Secretary's interview on "This week with David Brinkley" [interview with G. P. Shultz; transcript of program, September 21, 1987] *Dep State Bull* 87:21-3 N '87

Senate Committee boosts conventional forces, limits ABM reinterpretation [Armed Services] M. Mecham. *Aviat Week Space Technol* 126:28-9 My 11 '87

Senate infighting on treaty [INF] J. D. Isaacs. il *Bull At Sci* 43:3-4 N '87

Senate minority could imperil treaty. J. D. Isaacs. il *Bull At Sci* 43:5-6 S '87

Seven nations curb nuclear weapon launch system exports [Missile Technology Control Regime] D. M. North. *Aviat Week Space Technol* 126:28-9 Ap 20 '87

A shield against arms control [C. Weinberger calls for early deployment] S. Talbott. il por *Time* 129:25 F 2 '87

Showdown nears on ABM Treaty. C. Norman. il *Science* 238:147-9 O 9 '87

The singular threat to the Atlantic Alliance [excerpts from address, May 28, 1987] H. Kissinger. *Natl Rev* 39:18-19 Jl 3 '87

A Soviet leap in arms control—in theory. J. Trimble. il *U S News World Rep* 102:42-3 My 18 '87

Soviet Union accused of treaty violations [Antiballistic Missile Treaty] C. Norman. *Science* 235:1456-7 Mr 20 '87

Soviets indicate acceptance of INF proposal [White House statement, July 22, 1987] *Dep State Bull* 87:17 O '87

Star Wars block. I. F. Stone. *Nation* 245:508-9 N 7 '87

Star Wars: Shultz's goal [bargaining chip in arms talks] il *Newsweek* 109:4 F 2 '87

Stemming the spread of nuclear weapons. M. M. Miller. il *Technol Rev* 90:68-75 Ag/S '87

The Strategic Defense Initiative and arms control [cover story; special section] il *Cent Mag* 20:4-24 My/Je '87

The superpower dispute over radars [large phased-array radars and the ABM Treaty] J. P. Rubin. bibl f *Bull At Sci* 43:34-7 Ap '87

The superpower tango [INF agreement] J. L. Galloway. il *U S News World Rep* 103:30-1 S 7 '87

Thunder over Britain. W. F. Buckley. *Natl Rev* 39:62-3 Ap 24 '87

A thunderclap [proposal that all nuclear missiles be removed from European soil] E. von Kuehnelt-Leddihn. *Natl Rev* 39:44 Jl 17 '87

To get an impactful feel for how upsetting . . . [views of F. J. Strauss on upcoming arms agreement between U.S. and Soviet Union] M. S. Forbes, Jr. il por *Forbes* 140:25 Ag 24 '87

To ratify or not to ratify? [outlook for Senate ratification of proposed arms control deal with the Soviets] J. McLaughlin. *Natl Rev* 39:28 S 25 '87

To win the peace [Russian offer on Euromissiles sets stage for peace movement] *Nation* 244:561-2 My 2 '87

Two ways to zero. *Natl Rev* 39:15-16 Jl 3 '87

U.S. ABM Treaty withdrawal possible but not imminent. P. Mann. il *Aviat Week Space Technol* 127:85+ S 14 '87

U.S. proposes INF reductions [statement, September 14, 1987] R. Reagan. *Dep State Bull* 87:25 N '87

U.S., West German concessions improve prospects for INF Treaty with Soviets. *Aviat Week Space Technol* 127:19 Ag 31 '87

The uneasy nuclear balance [Soviet offers to reduce the number of nuclear missiles deployed in Europe] D. E. Fink. *Aviat Week Space Technol* 126:25 Ap 27 '87

United States-Soviet relations and arms control. L. T. Caldwell. bibl f *Curr Hist* 86:305-8+ O '87

Disarmament—*cont.*

Voodoo treaty-reading [ABM Treaty and the Strategic Defense Initiative] *Commonweal* 114:131-2 Mr 13 '87

A way out of Reykjavik. B. Scowcroft and others. il *N Y Times Mag* p40+ Ja 25 '87

We'd be nuts to agree to a nuclear wipeout. M. S. Forbes. *Forbes* 139:17 Ap 6 '87

Wedded by hate [U.S. and Soviet Union] I. F. Stone. *Nation* 244:492-3 Ap 18 '87

West Germany to dismantle Pershing IA missiles [White House statement, August 26, 1987] *Dep State Bull* 87:49 O '87

Western Europe's dilemma: is a strong defense possible without nuclear arms? H. Cleveland. il *USA Today (Periodical)* 116:52-4 S '87

What the ABM Treaty means. S. Talbott. il *Time* 129:15 Mr 23 '87

Why an INF agreement makes sense [address, May 1, 1987] K. L. Adelman. *Vital Speeches Day* 53:514-18 Je 15 '87

Why Gorbachev's arms offer gives NATO the jitters. D. Griffiths. il *Bus Week* p49 Mr 30 '87

Why Reagan and Gorbachev need an arms agreement. M. I. Goldman. il por *Technol Rev* 90:18+ Jl '87

Why the Soviets want an arms-control agreement, and why they want it now. E. V. Rostow. *Commentary* 83:19-26 F '87

Why the Soviets want arms control. M. K. MccGwire. il *Technol Rev* 90:36-45 F/Mr '87

A world without nuclear weapons [address, November 13, 1986] K. L. Adelman. *Dep State Bull* 87:35-8 Ja '87

A world without nuclear weapons? [special section] il *N Y Times Mag* p45-9+ Ap 5 '87

Yalta II [implications of Soviet Union's zero option INF proposal] J. Morley. *New Repub* 196:14-15 Mr 30 '87

Zero option II [latest Soviet proposal] *Natl Rev* 39:16-17 Mr 27 '87

The 'zero option'—a Western idea. H. Schmidt. il *World Press Rev* 34:28-30 Jl '87

Zero plus zero [options for nuclear-arms cuts in Europe] *Natl Rev* 39:15 Je 19 '87

See also **Conferences**

Conference on Confidence and Security-Building Measures and Disarmament in Europe
International Forum for a Nuclear-Free World
Reagan-Gorbachev summit conference, 1986
Reagan-Gorbachev summit conference, 1987
Strategic Arms Limitation Talks
Strategic Arms Reduction Talks
United Nations. Conference on Disarmament
United Nations. General Assembly (Special Session on Disarmament: 1988)
United Nations. Preparatory Committee for the International Conference on the Relationship between Disarmament and Development

Arms and the man [adviser P. Nitze] S. Talbott. por *Time* 130:76-8 D 21 '87

Arms control and openness [address, February 5, 1987] K. L. Adelman. *Dep State Bull* 87:19-22 My '87

Arms control: the East Asian and Pacific focus [address, December 30, 1986] E. L. Rowny. *Dep State Bull* 87:37-9 Mr '87

Arms control: 'the fix is in' [missiles in Europe] R. Watson. il *Newsweek* 109:28-30 My 4 '87

Arms talks [cover story; special section] il *World Press Rev* 34:9-15 Je '87

An arms tango in Moscow [G. P. Shultz meets with M. Gorbachev] A. Finlayson. il pors *Macleans* 100:18-19 Ap 27 '87

Asymmetry [meeting of the International Physicians for the Prevention of Nuclear War in Moscow] J. Hersey. *New Yorker* 63:36-40+ S 7 '87

At long last, an arms deal [negotiators in Washington reach agreement to scrap INF forces] R. Watson. il *Newsweek* 110:18-21 S 28 '87

Bargaining chips [upcoming meeting between George Shultz and Eduard Shevardnadze] il *Newsweek* 109:7 Ap 6 '87

The beginning of the big thaw? [Washington, D.C. agreement on INF forces] B. Javetski and D. Griffiths. il *Bus Week* p32-3 O 5 '87

Beginning of the end game? [INF talks in Geneva] J. Barry. il *Newsweek* 110:28 Jl 13 '87

Benefits of an INF agreement [response to R. M. Nixon and H. Kissinger] G. P. Shultz. *Dep State Bull* 87:17-18 Jl '87

Comrades in arms control [signing INF Treaty; special section] il *Bus Week* p34-7 D 21 '87

Confusion abounding [G. Shultz' visit to Moscow] *Natl Rev* 39:18-19 N 20 '87

Dealing at last [M. Gorbachev's offer to cut back Euromissiles; cover story; special section] il pors map *Newsweek* 109:20-8+ Ap 27 '87

Developments in NST issues after Reykjavik [nuclear and space talks; statement, December 4, 1987] P. H. Nitze. *Dep State Bull* 87:33-6 Mr '87

Disarming [INF agreement; cover story; special section] il *World Press Rev* 34:11-18 N '87

Failure in Moscow [G. Shultz' visit] B. Levin. il por *Macleans* 100:20-1 N 2 '87

A Gorbachev arms offer even Europe may not refuse. B. Javetski and P. Galuszka. il por *Bus Week* p53 Ap 27 '87

Gorbachev's arms control moves. J. Dean. il *Bull At Sci* 43:34-40 Je '87

The Hamburg disarmament proposals [excerpts from statement at the International Scientists' Peace Congress in Hamburg, West Germany, November 14-16, 1986] *Bull At Sci* 43:52 Ja/F '87

History on the wing [Reagan-Gorbachev summit] *Nation* 245:737 D 19 '87

If Gorbachev loses . . . [intermediate range missiles] il *Progressive* 51:9-10 My '87

INF agreement in principle. M. Krepon. il *Bull At Sci* 43:5-6 N '87

INF extended session ends [statements, March 26 and 27, 1987] M. W. Glitman; R. Reagan. *Dep State Bull* 87:18-19 My '87

INF talks resume [statement, April 23, 1987] R. Reagan. *Dep State Bull* 87:35 Je '87

An interview with Richard Nixon [views on zero option proposal] J. F. Stacks and S. Talbott. il por *Time* 129:23 My 4 '87

Last call to arms talks? [Geneva talks] il *Newsweek* 109:24-5 Ja 26 '87

'The last chance we have' [Reagan-Gorbachev summit; cover story; special section] il *Newsweek* 110:14-20+ D 21 '87

Last tango in Geneva [INF talks] B. Levin. *Macleans* 100:29-30 S 7 '87

Looking at a summit [agreement on INF Treaty] G. J. Church. il *Time* 130:14-16 S 28 '87

A major sticking point [disagreement over West German Pershing IAs stalls INF pact] il *Time* 130:14 Ag 10 '87

Making a safer world [Washington accord on INF forces] B. Levin. il *Macleans* 100:20-2 S 28 '87

MBFR talks resume [State Dept. statement, May 14, 1987] *Dep State Bull* 87:19 Jl '87

Meeting of NATO's Special Consultative Group [statement, December 10, 1986] A. Holmes. *Dep State Bull* 87:46 Mr '87

Missile pact edges closer. C. Norman. il *Science* 236:378-9 Ap 24 '87

The Moscow agenda [visit to Russia by G. Shultz] T. Jacoby. il *Newsweek* 109:24 Ap 20 '87

Moscow and Washington agree to deal. J. L. Galloway. il *U S News World Rep* 103:14-15 S 28 '87

Nearing a deal on Euromissiles. H. Trewhitt. il por *U S News World Rep* 102:48-9 Ap 27 '87

Negotiations on Intermediate-range Nuclear Forces. il *Dep State Bull* 87:24-7 S '87

Nervous about nuclear security [NATO allies object to possible removal of INF missiles] C. Redman. il *Time* 129:37 My 11 '87

New prospects for agreement in INF and START [address, March 20, 1987] E. L. Rowny. *Dep State Bull* 87:33-6 Je '87

Nitty-gritty time for arms control [Euromissile talks] P. R. Range. il map *U S News World Rep* 102:44-5 Mr 30 '87

A no-frills summit. E. Magnuson. il *Time* 130:50-1 N 9 '87

Nonproliferation agreement with allies [White House statement, April 16, 1987] *Dep State Bull* 87:68 Jl '87

Now, super-zero? [M. Gorbachev's proposal to NATO] G. J. Church. il pors *Time* 129:20-3 Ap 27 '87

Nuclear and space arms talks close round seven [statement, March 6, 1987] M. M. Kampelman. *Dep State Bull* 87:18 My '87

Nuclear and space arms talks close round six [statements, November 12, 1986] R. Reagan; M. M. Kampelman. *Dep State Bull* 87:41-2 Ja '87

Nuclear and space arms talks open round eight [statements, May 4, 1987] R. Reagan; M. M. Kampelman. *Dep State Bull* 87:24-6 Jl '87

Disarmament—Conferences—*cont.*

Nuclear and space arms talks open round six [statement, September 17, 1986] R. Reagan. *Dep State Bull* 86:39 D '86

Nuclear and space arms talks resume round seven [statement, January 12, 1987] R. Reagan. *Dep State Bull* 87:36-7 Mr '87

The nuclear and space negotiations: translating promise to progress [address, January 14, 1987] P. H. Nitze. *Dep State Bull* 87:29-33 Mr '87

On to the summit, as Star Wars waits. S. Budiansky and H. Trewhitt. il *U S News World Rep* 103:13-14 N 9 '87

The other negotiations. C. Hardenbergh. *Bull At Sci* 43:52-3 S '87

The other negotiations [Vienna negotiations on Mutual and Balanced Force Reductions] C. Hardenbergh. il *Bull At Sci* 43:48-9 Mr '87

Post-Moscow blues [Soviet INF proposal] W. F. Buckley. *Natl Rev* 39:57 My 22 '87

President meets with arms negotiators [statement, March 6, 1987] R. Reagan. il por *Dep State Bull* 87:17 My '87

The problem: the other guy says 'yes' [INF talks; with editorial comment by Mortimer B. Zuckerman] H. Trewhitt. il *U S News World Rep* 102:41, 78 My 4 '87

Reagan/Gorbachev summit [special section; with editorial comment by Donald E. Fink] il *Aviat Week Space Technol* 127:11, 18-24 D 14 '87

The Reagan method. M. Kondracke. *New Repub* 197:12-14 N 30 '87

Reagan's disarmament [summit with Gorbachev] G. F. Will. il *Newsweek* 110:78 D 21 '87

Reagan's no suicide [defense of Reagan's Euromissile disarmament stance] W. A. Rusher. *Natl Rev* 39:36 Je 5 '87

Reagan's suicide pact [Soviet INF proposals; cover story; special section] il *Natl Rev* 39:27-30+ My 22 '87

The red queen. L. H. Lapham. *Harpers* 275:10-12 Jl '87

A reply to Nixon and Kissinger [defense of zero option proposal] G. P. Shultz. il por *Time* 129:40 My 18 '87

Scientists urge new stance on SDI testing in U.S.-Soviet arms talks. T. M. Foley. *Aviat Week Space Technol* 127:30 S 14 '87

Secretary's interview on "Face the nation" [interview with G. P. Shultz; transcript of program, September 13, 1987] *Dep State Bull* 87:19-21 N '87

Secretary's interview on "Meet the press" [interview with G. P. Shultz; transcript of program, October 19, 1986] *Dep State Bull* 86:29-32 D '86

Secretary's trip to Helsinki, Moscow, and Brussels. G. P. Shultz. il por *Dep State Bull* 87:12-24 Je '87

Senate leadership warns president against 'rushing' into Euromissile pact. P. Mann. *Aviat Week Space Technol* 126:40-1 Ap 27 '87

Shevardnadze schmooze [U.S.-Soviet agreement in principle on INF forces] F. Barnes. *New Repub* 197:10+ O 19 '87

Snuffing a summit [Soviets demand concession on SDI] J. Kohan. il por *Time* 130:56-7 N 2 '87

The spirit of Washington [Reagan-Gorbachev summit; special section] il *Time* 130:16-23+ D 21 '87

Striking a missile deal [Shultz-Shevardnadze talks in Geneva] I. Austen. il *Macleans* 100:22 D 7 '87

Summit breakthrough. I. Austen. il *Macleans* 100:18-19 N 9 '87

Summit gazing. *Commonweal* 114:723-4 D 18 '87

The summit: on again. R. Watson. il *Newsweek* 110:52-4 N 9 '87

A summit with style [cover story; special section; with editorial comment by Kevin Doyle] il *Macleans* 100:2, 24-9 D 21 '87

A superpowers' October surprise [SDI blocks summit and arms treaty] H. Trewhitt. il *U S News World Rep* 103:36-7 N 2 '87

A Twilight Zone defense? [U. Geller's influence on U.S.-Soviet negotiations] D. Gates. il por *Newsweek* 109:5 My 11 '87

U.S. arms control initiatives. *Dep State Bull* 87:16-18 Ap '87

U.S. arms control initiatives: an update. *Dep State Bull* 87:27-9 Jl '87

U.S.-Soviet nuclear and space arms negotiations [statement, May 8, 1987] R. Reagan. *Dep State Bull* 87:25 Jl '87

U.S. tables draft INF Treaty [remarks, March 3, 1987] R. Reagan. *Dep State Bull* 87:16-17 My '87

Waiting for the postman [Soviets use Star Wars as bargaining ploy in meetings with G. Shultz] R. Watson. il por *Newsweek* 110:60-1+ N 2 '87

The wary warlords [views of Joint Chiefs on Euromissile treaty] D. Gates. il *Newsweek* 109:5 My 11 '87

'A way out of the nuclear dilemma' [INF talks] *America* 156:393-4 My 16 '87

West urges acceptance of verification at MBFR Talks [U.S. statement, October 23, 1986] *Dep State Bull* 86:37-9 D '86

Why arms talks unnerve NATO. J. Keegan. il *U S News World Rep* 102:28-30 Ap 20 '87

Economic aspects

See also

International Conference on the Relationship between Disarmament and Development

Arms accord for domestic renewal. *America* 156:22-3 Ja 17 '87

It's time for economic conversion. J. Ritter-Murray. *Humanist* 47:30+ S/O '87

Less bang may mean more bucks for growth. K. Pennar. il *Bus Week* p128 O 19 '87

History

Arms control: is it good for us? H. Trewhitt. il map *U S News World Rep* 103:24-7+ D 14 '87

Evolution of nuclear arms control policy. *Congr Dig* 66:258+ N '87

Leo Szilard: giving peace a chance in the nuclear age. B. J. Bernstein. il pors *Phys Today* 40:40-7 S '87

The long struggle to strike a major new arms deal. R. Schaeffer. il *Sch Update* 120:6-9 N 20 '87

The road to zero. S. Talbott. il *Time* 130:18-21+ D 14 '87

Slouching toward an arms agreement [zero option] S. Talbott. il *Time* 129:24+ Ap 27 '87

Wars aren't 'accidental'. G. F. Will. il *Newsweek* 110:104 O 26 '87

Inspection

Administration disputes findings of U.S. visit to Soviet radar [Krasnoyarsk] P. Mann. il map *Aviat Week Space Technol* 127:26-8 S 14 '87

. . . and I'll show you mine [U.S. congressmen tour Krasnoyarsk radar facility in Siberia] il *Time* 130:28 S 21 '87

Arms control pacts can be verified. K. Tsipis. il maps *Discover* 8:79-93 Ap '87

An arms deal may be Reagan's last chance to triumph . . . B. Javetski and D. Griffiths. *Bus Week* p83 Jl 20 '87

Chemical weapons pact edging closer. D. Dickson. *Science* 235:1452-3 Mr 20 '87

A close-up look at a secret Soviet radar [Krasnoyarsk] C. Norman. il map *Science* 237:1408-9 S 18 '87

Explaining Soviet compliance. G. Duffy. *Society* 24:66-72 Jl/Ag '87

Gorbachev calls the 'verification' bluff. *Newsweek* 110:49 S 14 '87

Hercules prepares for INF verification inspections. il *Aviat Week Space Technol* 127:23-4 D 14 '87

High stakes in INF verification. M. Krepon. *Bull At Sci* 43:14-16 Je '87

How to negotiate a treaty [compliance] P. J. Farley. il *Bull At Sci* 43:33-6 O '87

How to put more backbone into the bioweapons treaty. M. Bluestone. il *Bus Week* p67 Ag 10 '87

INF Treaty could mean intrusive inspections of defense plants. M. Mecham. *Aviat Week Space Technol* 127:29-30 D 7 '87

The limitations of on-site inspection [cover story] S. N. Graybeal and M. Krepon. il *Bull At Sci* 43:22-6 D '87

Long on data, short on intelligence [spy satellites] W. M. Arkin. il *Bull At Sci* 43:5-6 Je '87

Long-range signals [Americans inspect Soviet radar complex in Krasnoyarsk] *Commonweal* 114:516-17 S 25 '87

Memorandum details methods of verifying treaty compliance [INF Treaty] il *Aviat Week Space Technol* 127:21-2 D 14 '87

Mobile missile verification slows START negotiators. P. J. Klass. *Aviat Week Space Technol* 127:24-5 D 21 '87

Pact would allow Soviet officials to inspect U.S. missile plants. M. Mecham. il *Aviat Week Space Technol* 127:16-19 N 30 '87

Parsing the INF Treaty [on-site inspection] map *U S News World Rep* 103:28 D 21 '87

Report from Krasnoyarsk [U.S. congressmen visit radar facility in Siberia] T. J. Downey and others. il *Bull At Sci* 43:11-14 N '87

Disarmament—Inspection—cont.

Rocky road to the summit. J. Bierman. il *Macleans* 100:19 N 23 '87

The Russians are coming [verification agreement] il *Time* 130:16 D 7 '87

SDI watch [Krasnoyarsk radar inspection by group of Democratic congressmen and staffers] *Natl Rev* 39:18-19 O 9 '87

Soviet INF plant visits concern Pentagon. *Aviat Week Space Technol* 127:25 N 9 '87

Soviet noncompliance with arms control agreements [report to Congress, March 10, 1987] R. Reagan. *Dep State Bull* 87:37-42 Je '87

A Soviet official on verification. R. Timerbaev. *Bull At Sci* 43:8-10 Ja/F '87

Soviets in San Diego? [U.S. proposal for on-site inspection plan to guarantee compliance with INF Treaty] E. Magnuson. il *Time* 129:14 Mr 23 '87

Study finds treaty compliance. G. Duffy. *Bull At Sci* 43:30-2 O '87

Swords into plowshares [dismantling Titan II missiles] W. S. Malone and others. il *Life* 10:26-30+ N '87

Tagging nuclear weapons. *Sci Am* 256:88 F '87

Treaty compliance rated good. C. Norman. *Science* 235:839 F 20 '87

U.S. compliance with arms control agreements [report to Congress, February 17, 1987] R. Reagan. *Dep State Bull* 87:42-7 Je '87

U.S. presents views on INF verification [State Dept. statement, August 25, 1987] *Dep State Bull* 87:18-19 O '87

Unlocking the riddle of Krasnoyarsk [Americans visit Soviet radar complex] W. D. Marbach. map *Newsweek* 110:43 S 21 '87

Verification and arms control [with editorial comment by Daniel E. Koshland, Jr.] S. D. Drell; M. Eimer. bibl f *Science* 235:406-14 Ja 23 '87

Verification bind. il *Newsweek* 109:6 Je 29 '87

Verification in an age of mobile missiles [address, June 26, 1987] K. L. Adelman. *Dep State Bull* 87:27-31 S '87

Verification: the devil is in the details. T. Jacoby. il *Newsweek* 110:20 S 28 '87

Verification: will it work? [cover story] D. Aaron. il *N Y Times Mag* p36-40+ O 11 '87

Washington notebook. D. Schorr. il *New Leader* 70:3-4 Mr 23 '87

What are 'they' up to? [Krasnoyarsk radar station inspected in the Soviet Union] W. F. Buckley. *Natl Rev* 39:62 N 6 '87

Disarmament and parapsychology *See* Parapsychology and disarmament

Disarmament and the press *See* Press and disarmament

Disarmament Commission (United Nations) *See* United Nations. Disarmament Commission

Disarmament Week

Disarmament Week observed around the world by United Nations. *UN Chron* 24:92 F '87

Political and Security Committee holds special meeting to observe Disarmament Week to highlight need for arms control. il *UN Chron* 22:82-3 N/D '85

Disaster relief *See* Relief work

Disaster Relief Co-ordinator Office (United Nations) *See* Office of the United Nations Disaster Relief Co-ordinator

Disasters

See also
Avalanches
Building failures
Earthquakes
Floods
Forest fires
Hurricanes
Nuclear power plants—Accidents and explosions
Tornadoes

Airborne toxic releases: are communities prepared? S. L. Cutter. bibl f il map *Environment* 29:12-17+ Jl/Ag '87

The godfather of disaster [cometary theory of W. Whiston] S. J. Gould. il *Nat Hist* 96:20+ S '87

It can happen to you! [advance preparation] N. S. Walker. il *Mother Earth News* 103:88+ Ja/F '87

"What a legacy for our children!" [interview with S. Aga Khan] P. Gupte. il por *Forbes* 139:100+ Je 15 '87

The year the warning lights flashed on [technological disasters] T. Ferris. il *Life* 10:67-8+ Ja '87

Photographs and photography

Tape at 11:00 [when you encounter a news event, keep the camcorder running] E. Stecker. il *Pop Photogr* 94:98-9 D '87

Psychological aspects

The psychological aftermath of disasters. R. E. Cohen. il *USA Today (Periodical)* 116:70-2 S '87

Statistics

See also
Sage Analytics International Inc.

Disc jockeys

See also
Purtan, Dick

Disc mowing machines *See* Mowing machines

Disch, Thomas M.

Brigazoon. il *Omni* 9:74-7 S '87

Dreams: a Darwinian view [poem] *New Repub* 196:36 Je 1 '87

Nightmare on Elm Street [poem] *New Repub* 196:36 My 11 '87

Palindrome [fiction] il *Omni* 9:42-4+ S '87

Rude awakening [fiction] il *Omni* 9:64-9 My '87

The village alien. il *Nation* 244:328-34+ Mr 14 '87

about

The sleuth in the machine. J. Ledbetter. *Nation* 244:613-14 My 9 '87

You are what you read. D. Lehman. il pors *Newsweek* 109:67 Ja 12 '87

Discharge of employees *See* Employees—Dismissal

Discharges, Electric *See* Electric discharges

Disciples of Christ *See* Christian Church (Disciples of Christ)

Discipline

See also
Children—Management and training
Corporal punishment
Labor discipline
Presidents—Discipline
School discipline

Disciplined Investment Advisors Inc.

Strictly by the numbers. C. Siler. il por *Forbes* 140:184+ N 2 '87

Disclosure Information Group

Losing ground. L. Scheer. il *Forbes* 140:8 O 5 '87

Disclosure of personal finances *See* Congressmen—Financial disclosure; Public officers—Financial disclosure

Discos *See* Discotheques

Discotheques

See also
Art in discotheques
New York (N.Y.)—Restaurants, nightclubs, bars, etc.

Lighting

Stars come in at night [light projection system at Saint nightclub in New York City] il *Pop Mech* 164:125 Mr '87

Discount airline fares *See* Airlines—Fares

Discount brokers *See* Brokers—Commissions

Discount coupons *See* Coupons

Discount houses (Retail trade)

See also
Consolidated Stores Corp.
Crazy Eddie Inc.
Family Dollar Stores, Inc.
K Mart Corp.
One Price Clothing Stores
Wal-Mart Stores, Inc.
Warehouse clubs
Zayre Corp.

Discounters in the dumps [electronics retailers] B. Saporito. il *Fortune* 116:103+ Ag 3 '87

Reading redux [Pa.] J. Merwin. il *Forbes* 139:48-9+ Mr 9 '87

Discourtesy *See* Courtesy

Discover (Credit card) *See* Credit cards

Discover (Periodical)

Discover is headed for a new family [Family Media] D. Lieberman. il *Bus Week* p40 Je 8 '87

From the editor. P. Hoffman. See issues of Discover beginning September 1987

From the editor. G. L. Rogin. See issues of Discover through August 1987

Discovery (Space shuttle vehicle) *See* Space vehicles

Discovery Hall Marine Biology Institute

Share the secrets of Discovery Hall. il *South Living* 22:25 Jl '87

Discrimination

See also
Ageism
Anti-Semitism
Race discrimination
Sex discrimination
Toleration

Affirmative action: cure or contradiction? [discussion] il *Cent Mag* 20:20-8 N/D '87

Discrimination—*cont.*

The new McCarthyism. G. F. Kreyche. il *USA Today (Periodical)* 116:98 S '87

Resolute ignorance: social science and affirmative action. W. R. Beer. *Society* 24:63-9 My/Je '87

Discrimination in education

See also

Asian Americans—Education
Blacks—Education
Colleges and universities—Desegregation
Colleges and universities—Segregation
Public schools—Desegregation
Public schools—Segregation

Running the rights scam at DOE. L. A. Uzzell. *Natl Rev* 39:39-40+ Mr 13 '87

Discrimination in employment

See also

Aged—Employment
Asian Americans—Employment
Black women—Employment
Blacks—Employment
Equal pay for equal work
Handicapped—Employment
United States. Equal Employment Opportunity Commission
Women—Employment

Affirmative action: after the debate, opportunity [Supreme Court decision in Santa Clara case] P. Dwyer. il *Bus Week* p37 Ap 13 '87

Affirmative reaction. R. A. Epstein. *New Repub* 197:17-19 O 12 '87

Age bias is his business [V. P. Donnelly] D. Katz. il por *50 Plus* 27:18-20 Mr '87

Age bias: the uphill battle. J. Mitchell. *50 Plus* 27:32+ Mr '87

Age bias: the uphill battle [interview with C. G. Mackaronis] F. Greve. il por *50 Plus* 27:33-6 Mr '87

Balancing act [Supreme Court expands affirmative action in Santa Clara County, Calif. case] R. Stengel. il *Time* 129:18-20 Ap 6 '87

Bound by freedom [discussion of September 23, 1987 article, Victimized by justice] G. Hewitt. *Christ Century* 104:1022-3 N 18 '87

Brennanism [Supreme Court decision in Santa Clara, Calif. affirmative action case] D. Seligman. *Fortune* 115:283+ Ap 27 '87

A case goes unheard at the EEOC [Navy waitress M. Farrell] F. Greve. il por *50 Plus* 27:16+ N '87

Court ruling affirmative [Supreme Court decides Santa Clara affirmative action case] J. C. Baker. *Black Enterp* 17:20 Jl '87

Don't be age biased against the young or old. S. Rose. *Work Woman* 12:27+ O '87

Employer beware [age discrimination suits] D. Fanning. il *Forbes* 139:82+ My 18 '87

Gender-based hiring and promotions approved [Supreme Court decision in Santa Clara County, Calif. affirmative action case] *Mon Labor Rev* 110:41-2 My '87

Imposing standards [recent cases questioning right of religious institutions to require doctrinal orthodoxy of employees] D. Neff. *Christ Today* 31:17 Jl 10 '87

Ladies' day [Supreme Court ruling in Santa Clara affirmative action case] *New Repub* 196:4+ Ap 20 '87

Normal nonsense [reverse discrimination seen in U.S. Employment Service rankings of General Aptitude Test Battery scores] D. Seligman. il *Fortune* 116:165-6 N 9 '87

Resolute ignorance: social science and affirmative action. W. R. Beer. *Society* 24:63-9 My/Je '87

Saying "yes" to affirmative action [Supreme Court ruling in Santa Clara case] M. Takas. *Vogue* 177:58 N '87

Should a Mormon-owned corporation be able to fire a Mormon who does not tithe? [Supreme Court considers discrimination case of F. Mayson] R. F. Drinan. il *America* 156:375-6 My 9 '87

Suit challenges Christian employment service practices [discrimination suit against Intercristo] R. Frame. *Christ Today* 31:48 Ap 3 '87

Supreme Court extends affirmative action goals for women, minorities. *Jet* 72:5 Ap 13 '87

Supreme Court hears challenge to church hiring policies [discrimination case filed by F. Mayson against the Mormon church] E. J. Larson. *Christ Today* 31:49-50 My 15 '87

The Supreme Court puts the mike in Diane Joyce's hands, giving feminists a major victory [Santa Clara County, Calif. affirmative action case] W. Plummer. il pors *People Wkly* 27:49-50+ Ap 13 '87

Tribal justice [Supreme Court majority opinion upholding the legality of Santa Clara, Calif. affirmative action plan] *Natl Rev* 39:17-18 Ap 24 '87

The tyranny of beauty [Adam Cohen's article on facial discrimination in Harvard law review] *New Repub* 197:4 O 12 '87

Victimized by justice [affirmative-action policies] G. Hewitt. *Christ Century* 104:780-1 S 23 '87

The wages of discrimination: comparing salaries. W. R. Beer. *Current* 297:33-6 N '87

White charges Lincoln U. violated his civil rights [former athletic director D. A. Bennice] *Jet* 72:23 Ag 31 '87

White professor wins reverse bias law suit against black college [D. Voiku wins case against Albany State College] *Jet* 72:32 Ap 20 '87

A woman's day in court [Supreme Court decision in Santa Clara County, Calif. affirmative action case] A. Press. il *Newsweek* 109:58-9 Ap 6 '87

The women win—again [Supreme Court decision in Santa Clara County, Calif. affirmative action case] T. Gest. il *U S News World Rep* 102:18-19 Ap 6 '87

Anecdotes, facetiae, satire, etc.

Fat rights. D. Seligman. il *Fortune* 115:25-6 Ja 5 '87

Ugly rights. D. Seligman. *Fortune* 116:95-6 Ag 31 '87

Canada

When women do men's work [guarding both male and female prisoners] B. Amiel. il *Macleans* 100:9 O 12 '87

Northern Ireland

Why Irish eyes frown at U.S. help [pressure to open jobs in American firms to Ulster Catholics] P. Sherrid. il *U S News World Rep* 103:32 Ag 24 '87

United States

See Discrimination in employment

Discrimination in housing

See also

Black women—Housing
Blacks—Housing

Bush's covenants [G. Bush's stand on civil rights and restrictive housing covenants] D. Robb. *Nation* 245:616-17 N 28 '87

Discrimination in mortgages

Leaning on banks to lend to the poor [activists citing redlining are holding up mergers] D. Foust. *Bus Week* p76 Mr 2 '87

Discrimination in sports

See also

Baseball Network
National Organization on the Status of Minorities in Sports
Sex discrimination in sports

40 years after Jackie Robinson, baseball still has no black managers. N. O. Unger. il pors *Jet* 72:48-51 My 4 '87

40th anniversary: biggest breakthrough in sports [J. Robinson; excerpt from Negro firsts in sports] A. S. Young. il pors *Ebony* 42:66-8+ My '87

'Actions' aren't racist Yankee boss tells NAACP [G. Steinbrenner's comments] *Jet* 73:48 O 12 '87

Al Campanis [loss of job with Dodgers after remarks about lack of black baseball managers] F. C. Klein. il por *Sport Mag* 78:97-8 D '87

And where are the black head coaches? N. Cohen. *Sport Mag* 78:6 Ag '87

Another blow to Jim Crow [Mississippi State's first game against integrated team in 1963 NCAA basketball tournament] R. Jackson. il *Sports Illus* 67 Sp Issue:113 N 18 '87

Atlanta NAACP targets Turner's Hawks, Braves. *Jet* 73:48 D 14 '87

Baseball: a crisis in black and white [furor over remarks of A. Campanis regarding black managers] P. Axthelm. *Newsweek* 109:71 Ap 20 '87

Baseball exec defended after 'blackface' remark. *Jet* 72:13 Jl 6 '87

Baseball manager candidates seeking a try with control [blacks] il *Jet* 72:46 Je 8 '87

Baseball missing black fans for many reasons. *Jet* 72:48 Jl 6 '87

Baseball takes steps [attempting to end racial discrimination] il *Sports Illus* 66:11 Je 22 '87

Billy Williams' speech fans Hall of Fame fires. il por *Jet* 72:51+ Ag 10 '87

Black coaches remain scarce in college ranks. D. J. Dent. il *Black Enterp* 18:34 D '87

Black managers far off, say Williams, Roseboro. il por *Jet* 73:46 O 19 '87

Black NFL executives plan job finders dept. *Jet* 72:50 Ag 24 '87

Discrimination in sports—*cont.*

Black NY group seeks Harry Edwards' ouster [Black United Fund of New York] il por *Jet* 72:46 S 14 '87

Black swimmer resurfaces thanks to Campanis' slur [C. Silva] il por *Jet* 72:51 My 18 '87

Black tennis stars winning big bucks but snubbed for commercials. pors *Jet* 72:48 Jl 20 '87

Bob Gibson fears baseball will fail to promote blacks. por *Jet* 72:50 Jl 27 '87

Bowie Kuhn: Campanis did blacks a favor. por *Jet* 72:46 Jl 27 '87

Buoyancy basics [A. Campanis' remarks] D. Seligman. *Fortune* 116:102 Jl 20 '87

The Campanis affair [Los Angeles Dodgers VP's remarks on dearth of black managers in baseball] P. Gammons. il por *Sports Illus* 66:31 Ap 20 '87

The complexities of complexions. T. Callahan. il *Time* 129:80 Je 22 '87

Detroit's Thomas sees Bird in black & white [I. Thomas' comments on L. Bird] pors *Jet* 72:50 Je 22 '87

Doby honored by Indians as 1st black AL player. por *Jet* 72:50 S 21 '87

Doctor of sports and sociology [H. Edwards] A. Collier. il pors *Ebony* 42:101-2+ O '87

Edwards and Ueberroth, classmates now teammates [racism in baseball] pors *Jet* 72:51 Je 29 '87

Edwards hires Campanis to assist baseball job. il por *Jet* 72:48 S 14 '87

Essence woman [golfer M. Hathaway's fight against segregation] F. Newby and R. D. Manuel. por *Essence* 17:26 F '87

Ex-Army boss to examine baseball's plan for action [C. Alexander to review affirmative action plans] por *Jet* 72:46 Je 29 '87

Ex-Dodger Joe Black hurls pitch to owners on how to strike out baseball bias. il pors *Jet* 72:50 My 18 '87

Ex-manager Martin tells Jesse: stick to politics [views of B. Martin] por *Jet* 72:46 Jl 13 '87

Ex-pros plan conference, as bias talks continue. *Jet* 72:28 My 25 '87

Former Army Secretary and woman scientist try to change baseball image [C. Alexander and J. Hill] il pors *Jet* 73:50-1 N 9 '87

The foul ball that shook baseball's front office [Dodgers VP, A. Campanis, reveals bias against blacks as managers] A. P. Sanoff. il por *U S News World Rep* 102:12-13 Ap 20 '87

The fuse that lit the fire [J. Robinson] G. F. Will. il *Newsweek* 109:88 Ap 13 '87

Harry Edwards hints at college sports boycott. *Jet* 73:51 O 26 '87

Howard U. battles NCAA over grid playoff snub. *Jet* 73:50 D 14 '87

In America's national pastime, says Frank Robinson, white is the color of the game off the field [interview] il pors *People Wkly* 27:46+ Ap 27 '87

Isiah & Bernhard. J. Morley. *Nation* 245:4-5 Jl 4-11 '87

Jesse vs. the big leagues. A. Edmond, Jr. il por *Black Enterp* 17:16 Jl '87

Mandatory drug testing may spark racism: Page [views of A. Page] por *Jet* 72:46 Ag 31 '87

Minorities in his office a priority, Ueberroth says. *Jet* 72:50 S 7 '87

Minority hiring issue faces increased focus. il *Jet* 73:47 D 21 '87

NBA leading pro sports in hiring of minorities. *Jet* 73:46 N 9 '87

NCAA panel to address minorities in management. *Jet* 73:50 O 12 '87

NFL appoints black to monitor minority hiring [D. Cornwell] *Jet* 73:46 O 12 '87

Phils boss ignored blacks when hiring new manager. il *Jet* 72:47 Jl 6 '87

Racism at bat [A. Campanis forced to resign from Dodger organization after remarks on lack of black baseball managers] T. Callahan. por *Time* 129:63 Ap 20 '87

Racist remarks spark push for black execs [remarks concerning black baseball managers by A. Campanis] il por *Jet* 72:46 Ap 27 '87

Racist, sexist comment by CBS sports anchors riles nation's women's groups [comments by B. Packer about J. Gillom during Pan Am Games] il por *Jet* 72:54 S 14 '87

Reggie picks Winfield to go to bat for blacks. pors *Jet* 72:50 Je 15 '87

Remembering . . . Jackie Robinson. S. A. Robinson. il pors *Essence* 17:49 Ap '87

Rowers snub South Boston club race that bans blacks. *Jet* 72:16 Je 8 '87

Rozelle says black coach is an NFL owners' problem. *Jet* 72:46 Jl 20 '87

Shamefully lily-white: NFL head-coach opening? Blacks need not apply. R. Telander. il por *Sports Illus* 66:80 F 23 '87

South Boston club ends it's ban against blacks [rowing club] *Jet* 72:4 Je 15 '87

Strike one and you're out. L. Rosellini. il *U S News World Rep* 103:52-7 Jl 27 '87

The stuff dreams are made of [L. Bird and M. Johnson clash in NBA finals] D. Halberstam. il pors *Sports Illus* 66:38-40+ Je 29 '87

Teacher of the Year [H. Edwards] D. Chamberlain. il pors *Sport Mag* 78:70-4+ D '87

Ueberroth vows baseball will lead in hiring. *Jet* 72:47 Ag 17 '87

Upshaw claims racism influences NFL strike. por *Jet* 73:49 O 19 '87

"We have a serious problem that isn't going away" [discrimination against blacks in baseball; cover story]; ed. by Peter Gammons. R. Jackson. il pors *Sports Illus* 66:40-2+ My 11 '87

Where are the black fans? [baseball; cover story] B. Staples. il *N Y Times Mag* p26-32+ My 17 '87

Who will be the first black head coach in NFL? W. Leavy. il *Ebony* 42:36+ Ja '87

Winning is only half the battle [problems of black women tennis players Z. Garrison and L. McNeil] M. Witherell. il pors *World Tennis* 34:38-41+ My '87

Yankees owner points to 'black boy' in office as affirmative action [remarks by G. Steinbrenner] *Jet* 72:52 Jl 20 '87

Discs, Compact *See* Compact discs
Discs, Video *See* Videodiscs
Discussion
> *See also*
> Argument
> Negotiation

Disease Control Centers *See* Centers for Disease Control (U.S.)
Disease models, Animal *See* Diseases—Animal models
Disease prevention *See* Medicine, Preventive
Disease resistance *See* Immunity
Disease resistance of plants *See* Plants—Disease and pest resistance
Diseases
> *See also*
> Animals as carriers of infection
> Arteries—Diseases
> Blood vessels—Diseases
> Bone—Diseases
> Brain—Diseases
> Breast—Diseases
> Cardiovascular system—Diseases
> Cerebrovascular disease
> Children—Diseases
> Connective tissues—Diseases
> Deficiency diseases
> Diagnosis
> Digestive system—Diseases
> Ear—Diseases
> Epidemics
> Eye—Diseases and defects
> Fetus—Diseases
> Foot—Diseases
> Gums—Diseases
> Heart—Diseases
> Heredity of disease
> Iatrogenic diseases
> Immunologic diseases
> Infants, Newborn—Diseases
> Infection
> Liver—Diseases
> Lungs—Diseases
> Nervous system—Diseases
> Neural tube—Diseases
> Prostate gland—Diseases
> Reproductive organs—Diseases
> Skin—Diseases
> Throat—Diseases
> Women—Diseases
> > *See also* names of diseases; *also* subhead Diseases and pests under names of plants and animals

Common winter ailments and their cures. G. J. Subak-Sharpe. il *Ladies Home J* 104:102+ D '87

Generic disposition for disease? *Sci News* 132:46 Jl 18 '87

Just ask us . . . [questions and answers] See issues of Current Health 2

Diseases—*cont.*

Animal models

Better animal models for genetic defects [technique developed by Mario R. Capecchi and Kirk R. Thomas] S. Eisenberg. *Sci News* 132:327 N 21 '87

Paleolithic diet, evolution, and carcinogens [discussion of April 17, 1987 article, Ranking possible carcinogenic hazards] B. N. Ames and others. *Science* 238:1633-4 D 18 '87

Ranking possible carcinogenic hazards. B. N. Ames and others. bibl f il *Science* 236:271-80 Ap 17 '87

Causes

See also
Medicine, Psychosomatic
Stress

Bad habits that can ruin your health. W. Korn. il *Ladies Home J* 104:36+ S '87

Oxygen free radicals linked to many diseases. J. L. Marx. *Science* 235:529-31 Ja 30 '87

Toilet training for adults: learn what you can catch in public bathrooms. A. Cassidy. il *Redbook* 169:118-19+ O '87

Nutritional aspects

See Diet in disease

Transmission by water

See Waterborne infection

Diseases, Industrial *See* Occupational health and safety
Diseases, Mental *See* Mental illness
Diseases, Prehistoric *See* Paleopathology
Dish gardens *See* Miniature gardens and gardening
Dish towels *See* Towels

Dishwashers

Change color, quickly. il *South Living* 22:186 Ap '87
Dishwashers. il *Consum Rep* 52:384-91 Je '87
Dishwashers. il *Consum Rep* 52:30-4 D '87
New dishwashers [choosing options] *Better Homes Gard* 65:72 O '87

Disinfection and disinfectants

How safe is your dentist? D. Born. il *Saturday Evening Post* 259:28-9+ Jl/Ag '87

Disinflation (Finance) *See* Deflation (Finance)
Disinformation *See* Propaganda
Disk drive memory systems (Computers) *See* Computers—Memory systems
Disk surgery *See* Spine—Surgery
Disks, Slipped *See* Spine—Abnormalities
Dismissal of clergymen *See* Clergy—Dismissal
Dismissal of employees *See* Employees—Dismissal
Dismissal of public officers *See* Public officers—Dismissal
Dismissal of school principals *See* School superintendents and principals—Dismissal
Dismissal of teachers *See* Teachers—Dismissal

Dismore, Margaret

A lost people. map *Opera News* 51:32-3+ Ap 11 '87

Disney, Walt, 1901-1966

about

Disney's enduring masterpiece. E. Oxford. il por *Am Hist Illus* 22:30-9 D '87

The lost Snow White: working sketches reveal how Disney's fairy tale came true. M. Dougherty. il *Life* 10:52-4+ Ap '87

Ordeal by Disney. J. Scott. il pors *Film Comment* 23:52-4+ N/D '87

Unforgettable Snow White. J. Culhane. il *Read Dig* 131:114-19 D '87

Disney (Walt) Company *See* Walt Disney Company

Disney Channel

The Disney Channel. P. Ellis-Simons. il *Channels* 7:43-4 O '87

Is NBC getting hooked up to cable? [deal with Disney Channel and Turner Broadcasting] D. Lieberman. il por *Bus Week* p73 D 28 '87-Ja 4 '88

Disneyland (Anaheim, Calif.)

Disney: coast to coast [historical reconstruction] R. F. Snow. il *Am Herit* 38:22+ F/Mr '87

State-of-the-art pap [Captain EO] J. Saltzman. *USA Today (Periodical)* 115:33 Ja '87

Technologies merge in fantasy simulators [Star Tours at Disneyland and Toronto's Tour of the Universe] il *Pop Mech* 164:65 Je '87

Disneyland (France) *See* Euro Disneyland

Disneyland (Tokyo, Japan)

Disneyland abroad: today Tokyo, tomorrow the world. L. Armstrong. il *Bus Week* p68-9 Mr 9 '87

Disneyworld (Fla.) *See* Walt Disney World (Fla.)
Disorderliness *See* Messiness

Dispensers

See also
Wine—Equipment

Dispensing physicians *See* Physicians—Pharmaceutical services

Dispersal (Ecology)

Getting the drift [behavioral drift of aquatic insects] P. Schullery. il *Ctry J* 14:66-9 Ag '87

Displaced Homemakers Network

Network reaches out to aid displaced minority homemakers seeking jobs. il *Jet* 71:26 Ja 12 '87

Display of antiques, art objects, etc.

Brackets show off decoy collection. il *South Living* 22:198 N '87

Decorating by the book [antique books being bought for display purposes] E. Felber. il por *Publ Wkly* 232:76 Ag 14 '87

An eye for detail: the Paris apartment of Michel and Noémi Ermelin. B. D. Colen. il *Archit Dig* 44:132-42 Ja '87

French door display case. T. H. Jones. il *Fam Handyman* 37:54-6+ D '87

Protect your collectibles [acrylic display case] E. Waltner and W. Waltner. il *Workbench* 43:78-80 S/O '87

Display of merchandise

See also
Show windows

Photographs and photography

Rep photographer makes camera his marketing tool [Doubleday sales rep R. Williams takes photographs of bookstore displays] B. List. il *Publ Wkly* 231:53-4 My 29 '87

Display systems, Airplane *See* Airplanes—Electronic equipment; Airplanes, Jet—Electronic equipment
Display systems, Information *See* Information display systems
Display systems, Space vehicle *See* Space vehicles—Electronic equipment
DisplayWrite (Word processor program) *See* Word processors and processing—Programming
Disposable cameras *See* Cameras
Disposable diapers *See* Diapers
Disposable workers *See* Contingent workers
Disposal of medical waste *See* Medical waste disposal
Disposal of radioactive waste *See* Radioactive waste disposal
Disposal of refuse *See* Refuse and refuse disposal

Dissection

Apples, frogs, and animal rights [Apple Computer television commercial] C. Holden. *Science* 238:1345 D 4 '87

A teen fights for frog rights, and bio may never be the same [J. Graham refuses to dissect frog in biology class in Victorville, Calif.] il por *People Wkly* 27:109 My 25 '87

Dissent (Periodical)

Delirious New York [publication of special issue] J. Leonard. *Nation* 245:636-40+ N 28 '87

Dissenters

See also
Political prisoners
Protests, demonstrations, etc.

The dialectics of dissent [excerpt from The velvet prison] M. Haraszti. *Harpers* 275:28+ D '87

'Informing on ourselves'. G. Konrád. *Nation* 244:237+ F 28 '87

The sons of communism [Hungarian L. Rajk and Czechoslovak R. Slansky] M. T. Kaufman. il pors *N Y Times Mag* p50+ Mr 8 '87

Dissentshik, Ido

about

'The PLO cannot be a partner' [interview] J. R. Moskin. por *World Press Rev* 34:18-19 Jl '87

Distad, Lois

A personal legacy. bibl f il *Phi Delta Kappan* 68:744-5 Je '87

Starting the day with a good book. *Phi Delta Kappan* 68:476-7 F '87

Distances, Astronomical *See* Astronomical distances

Distelheim, Rochelle

A day in the life of an abortion clinic. il *Glamour* 85:238-9+ F '87

Two mothers for Laura. il pors *McCalls* 114:135-7 S '87

Distillation equipment

Super still [vapor compression water processor invented by Stephan Sears] M. Bowker. il *Pop Sci* 230:56-8 Ap '87

Distilling industries *See* Liquor industry
Distortion, Audio *See* Audio systems—Noise

Distribuidora Record de Servicos de Imprensa SA

Banta to print 85 titles for Brazil's Distribuidora. J. P. Frank. *Publ Wkly* 231:24 Ja 23 '87

Distributed data processing

Distributed processing: the state of the art [Carnegie-Mellon's MACH and Stanford's V] W. A. Mason. il *Byte* 12:291-7 N '87

Distributed data processing—*cont.*
Distributing the workload. M. Liskin. il *Pers Comput* 11:79-80+ D '87
The IBM RT gets connected. J. Levitt. il *Byte* 12 no12 Sp Issue:133-6+ '87
Linking all the company data: we're not there yet. R. Brandt. il *Bus Week* p151 My 11 '87
Toward a shared data base. T. Badgett. il *Pers Comput* 11:111+ O '87
Distribution of food *See* Food industry—Marketing
Distribution of goods
See also
Marketing channels
Distribution of income *See* Income
Distribution of wealth *See* Wealth
Distributors, Book *See* Book wholesalers and distributors
District of Columbia *See* Washington (D.C.)
Disulfides *See* Sulfides
Ditka, Diana
about
Diana Ditka: a lonely vigil in the Bear's den. J. Friedman. il por *People Wkly* 27:69 Ja 5 '87
Ditka, Mike, 1939-
about
Ditka praises Payton as best running back. il pors *Jet* 73:48 D 28 '87-Ja 4 '88
Staring down his rowdy ruffians, Chicago coach Mike Ditka prods the Bears to the Super Bowl. J. Friedman. il pors *People Wkly* 27:66-7+ Ja 5 '87
Ditlea, Steve
The big link. il *Omni* 9:16+ S '87
Digital disinformation. il *Omni* 9:26 F '87
The dream machine. il *Omni* 10:34 O '87
Head Coach. por *Omni* 9:23 Ap '87
The next small step. il *Omni* 10:22 D '87
Dittmer, Thomas H.
about
Trading machine. S. B. Weiner. il por *Forbes* 140:168+ N 30 '87
Diuretics and diuresis
See also
Furosemide
Diurnal rhythms *See* Biological rhythms
Divad gun system *See* Guns, Anti-aircraft
Divarkar, Parmananda R.
A letter from Rome: on the Synod of Bishops. *America* 157:349-50 N 14 '87
Divers *See* Diving; Diving, Submarine
Diversification in agriculture
He's diversified in 6 cattle enterprises [Jeff Breker] R. Watkins. il *Success Farm* 85 no4:B14 F '87
Diversification in industry
American Brands is breaking its cigarette habit. R. W. King. il *Bus Week* p86+ S 14 '87
The corporation. See issues of Business Week
Diversity is the secret weapon [Martin Marietta] T. Smart. il *Bus Week* p36 D 14 '87
Lessening the risks through diversification. B. Robson. il *Black Enterp* 17:280 Je '87
Diversity (Biology) *See* Variation (Biology)
Diversity reception, Radio *See* Radio reception
Diverticular disease
Nutritional aspects
New hope for those with diverticular disease. E. Weck. il *FDA Consum* 21:23-5 Jl/Ag '87
Diverticulosis *See* Diverticular disease
Divestiture by corporations *See* Corporations—Divestiture
Dividend reinvestment
Drip, drip, drip. J. A. Conway. il *Forbes* 139:8 Ap 6 '87
Stocks that reinvest your dividends. J. H. Green. il *Money* 16:147-50 S '87
Turning dividends into a quick capital gain. G. Weiss. *Bus Week* p204 N 2 '87
Dividends
53 stocks that always pay. J. Kosnett. il *Changing Times* 41:47-50+ Je '87
Bird-in-hand theory [dividend discount valuation] M. Ozanian. il *Forbes* 139:104+ F 23 '87
Farewell buybacks, hello dividends. J. J. Curran. il *Fortune* 115:129-31 Mr 2 '87
How to get on Wall Street's map: trade 19 million shares a day [Japanese investors taking advantage of high dividends on utility stocks] J. M. Laderman. il *Bus Week* p85 S 7 '87
The low-risk path to a high-income portfolio. G. G. Marcial. il *Bus Week* p120+ D 28 '87-Ja 4 '88
The lowdown on high-dividend stocks. G. Weiss. il *Bus Week* p100-1 F 9 '87
Shining your light on a bushel of dividends. il *Fortune* 115:106+ F 2 '87

Wall Street ponders the continuing dearth of dividends . . . and wonders how long the merger boom can carry the ball. G. Koretz. il *Bus Week* p16+ Ag 3 '87
Dividers, Room *See* Room dividers
Divination
See also
Astrology
Divine healing *See* Faith cure
Divine love *See* Love (Theology)
Divine providence *See* God—Providence
Diving
Competitions
Diver just says no [Stanford's S. LeVant refuses to submit to drug tests] A. Ferber. il por *Women's Sports Fitness* 9:25 My '87
Gaining at last on the top guy [G. Louganis's losses in the U.S. indoor championships] P. Putnam. il por *Sports Illus* 66:40-1 Ap 27 '87
Diving, Submarine
See also
Decompression (Physiology)
Skin diving
An ugly feeling [macho feelings while salvage diving] S. Toperoff. il *N Y Times Mag* p64 O 25 '87
Diving, Umbilical *See* Diving, Submarine
Diving by animals *See* Animal locomotion
Divinity of Christ *See* Jesus Christ—Divinity
Divinity schools *See* Theological seminaries
Division of powers *See* Separation of powers
Division Street [drama] *See* Tesich, Steve, 1942-
Divorce
See also
Alimony
Children of divorced parents
Custody of children
Palimony
Remarriage
Separation (Law)
Support (Domestic relations)
Blood and money: the unsolved murder of a Long Island woman leads to a novel suit against her husband [case of M. S. Schwartz] M. Ryan. il pors *N Y* 20:38-44 Je 8 '87
Daytime's steamy new soap [J. Collins wins case against P. Holm] G. Clarke. il pors *Time* 130:68 Ag 3 '87
Death of a marriage. P. Conroy. il *Read Dig* 131:107-10 O '87
The demise of a marriage. J. Nelson. *Essence* 18:63+ N '87
Diahann Carroll and Vanessa Williams take the bridal path, as Lee Iacocca and Leonard Nimoy trot off alone. M. Neill. il *People Wkly* 27:32-4 Ja 19 '87
Diary of a divorce. I. Miller. il por *Ladies Home J* 104:67-70+ Ja '87
Dick and Joni [bitter divorce battle between J. Evans and R. Snyder] J. Kasindorf. il pors *N Y* 20:60-4+ D 14 '87
Divorce in America [results of survey] O. S. Nordberg. il *Parents* 62:32 Ja '87
Divorcing for dollars [J. Collins and P. Holm; cover story] E. Hoover and D. Lindeman. il pors *People Wkly* 28:40-2+ Ag 10 '87
The dollar side of divorce. R. R. Roha. il *Changing Times* 41:94-6+ My '87
Dumped: how I survived the first six months. C. Hope. il por *Glamour* 85:236+ Ap '87
Everyone said it wouldn't last . . . [Madonna and S. Penn; cover story] J. Kaufman. il pors *People Wkly* 28:138-9+ D 14 '87
A fair share [N.Y. divorce ruling holds M. O'Brien's medical license to be form of property]; ed. by Micki Siegel. R. Maloney. il por *Good Housekeep* 205:54+ N '87
Fifth wife pregnant again, Pryor re-files for divorce [R. Pryor] *Jet* 72:56 Ap 6 '87
I married Alexis [P. Holm's request for spousal support from J. Collins] P. Holm. il *Harpers* 275:17-20 Ag '87
Jermaine Jackson's wife files for divorce in L.A. il pors *Jet* 73:54 N 2 '87
A lawyer tells women what they should know about divorce. F. Garber. *Good Housekeep* 205:64+ Jl '87
New policies on divorce and speaking in tongues [Southern Baptists] *Christ Today* 31:51+ S 18 '87
Olympian Brisco-Hooks files for divorce in L.A. il por *Jet* 71:24 F 9 '87
Portrait of divorce in America. B. Kantrowitz. il *Newsweek* 109:78 F 2 '87
Postnuclear family. M. K. Blakely. il por *Ms* 16:134+ Jl/Ag '87

Divorce—cont.

Pre-divorce survival [special section] il *Harpers Bazaar* 120:140-1+ Ag '87

Richard Pryor talks about what caused his fifth marriage to fall. il por *Jet* 72:16-17 Ap 20 '87

Richard Pryor's estranged wife tells why their marriage failed. A. Collier. il pors *Jet* 72:54-6 My 4 '87

Sly says bye, bye, Brigitte, and so a rocky marriage ends with a split decision. A. Richman. il pors *People Wkly* 28:38-9 Jl 27 '87

The Stallones: sex on the Sly? [cover story] J. Ash and others. pors *People Wkly* 28:48-9 Ag 10 '87

What the new divorce laws are doing to women. M. M. Hunt. il *Good Housekeep* 205:64+ Jl '87

When divorce is not the answer. D. Heyn. *McCalls* 114:28+ Ag '87

Why men divorce. L. L. Davitz. *McCalls* 145:26+ Mr '87

Anecdotes, facetiae, satire, etc.

Imaginary interview: Peter Holm. G. W. S. Trow. *New Yorker* 63:25 Ag 24 '87

Remember the alimony. M. G. Stoddard. il *Saturday Evening Post* 259:62-3 Jl/Ag '87

Catholic Church

Does the Church have good news for divorced Catholics? [cover story; interview with J. V. Flosi] il por *U S Cathol* 52:6-13 My '87

International aspects

Just married—but will it last? [anthropologist Helen Fisher's cross cultural study] K. McAuliffe. il *U S News World Rep* 102:68-9 Je 8 '87

Mary Ann Glendon: "We have let our love of individual liberty trump everything else, such as our sense of community" [interview] M. Asnes. il por *Vogue* 177:238+ N '87

Statistics

The divorce game: slippery numbers [Louis Harris' projections] *Newsweek* 110:55 Jl 13 '87

The four-year itch: do divorce patterns reflect our evolutionary heritage? H. E. Fisher. il *Nat Hist* 96:22+ O '87

Now for the good news. E. E. Goode. il *U S News World Rep* 102:68-9 Je 8 '87

One in two? Not true [study by Louis Harris] *Time* 130:21 Jl 13 '87

"Statistical nonsense" [Harris poll] L. Cryderman. *Christ Today* 31:19 S 4 '87

China

Divorce, Chinese style. T. K. Hareven. il *Atlantic* 259:70-6 Ap '87

Dominican Republic

Divorce, Dominican style [I. Felt's divorce case] L. Saunders. il por *Forbes* 140:79 D 28 '87

India

Where divorce is a fate better than death. M. Jain. il *World Press Rev* 34:57 Mr '87

United States

See Divorce

Divorce lawyers *See* Lawyers

Divorced fathers

See also

Support (Domestic relations)

The best Father's Day ever. P. C. Canning. il *Read Dig* 130:61-3 Je '87

A curfew for Karin. D. Spencer. il *N Y Times Mag* p26 Jl 5 '87

Missing fathers. E. Teyber and C. D. Hoffman. bibl (p65) il *Psychol Today* 21:36-9 Ap '87

The new rectangle [dating divorced fathers] L. Schnurnberger. il *Glamour* 85:240+ N '87

Divorced mothers

When mommy moves out: women who choose to give up custody of their children. L. Rogak. il *N Y* 20:36-41 Ja 5 '87

Divorcees

10 sexy ex's. il *Harpers Bazaar* 121:148+ N '87

Baby divorcée. D. Kent. il *Mademoiselle* 93:206-7+ Ap '87

The divorced personality [study by Edward W. McCranie and Joel Kahan] J. Folkenberg. il *Psychol Today* 21:66 Ja '87

How I survived divorce [experience of black divorcees] il *Ebony* 42:148+ O '87

Pre-divorce survival [special section] il *Harpers Bazaar* 120:140-1+ Ag '87

Suddenly single (and looking). J. Viorst. il *Redbook* 169:54+ O '87

Women should blame men for breakup of marriage. *Jet* 71:22 Mr 23 '87

Economic conditions

Divorce settlements: lump sum versus alimony. T. Hauser. il *McCalls* 114:75 Jl '87

The dollar side of divorce. R. R. Roha. il *Changing Times* 41:94-6+ My '87

A newly divorced woman's sudden fall from middle-class comfort into despair and struggle [Pam Jantzen] J. Nathan. il *Sch Update* 119:9 Mr 23 '87

What the new divorce laws are doing to women. M. M. Hunt. il *Good Housekeep* 205:64+ Jl '87

Religious life

See also

Church work with divorcees

Taxation

Divorce tricks. L. Saunders. il *Forbes* 140:74+ D 28 '87

Taking a less taxing road to divorce. D. Lamaute. il *Black Enterp* 17:29-30 Jl '87

Dixie National Rodeo and Livestock Show (Jackson, Miss.)

See Rodeos

Dixon, Bernard

The gene revolution. il *Courier* 40:13-16 Mr '87

Dixon, David A.

(jt. auth) *See* Miller, Joel S., and Dixon, David A.

Dixon, Ian

Seizing the moment for teaching pastoral care. *Christ Century* 104:103-4 F 4-11 '87

Dixon, Leslie

about

Some down and dirty zingers. D. Ansen. il *Newsweek* 109:76 Ja 26 '87

Dixon, Peter Eichner- *See* Eichner-Dixon, Peter

Dixon, Richard Clay

about

Richard Dixon second black mayor in Dayton, Ohio. il por *Jet* 71:14 Mr 23 '87

Dixon, Robert S., 1939-

about

Bob Dixon: still waiting for a long distance call. M. J. Mackowski. il por *Space World* X-8-284:17-20 Ag '87

Dixon, Ronald

about

D.C. judge assailed for remark to black prosecutor. *Jet* 72:17 Jl 20 '87

Dixon, Willie

about

Musician Willie Dixon satisfied out of court. *Jet* 72:58 Mr 30 '87

Dizziness

Putting dizziness on a diet. *Prevention* 39:132 S '87

DL-form substances

The significances of form. B. T. Hunter. il *Consum Res Mag* 70:8-9 Je '87

Dlamini, Zenani Mandela, Princess

about

Robert Brown oversees the enrollment of Mandela's daughter at Boston Univ. il por *Jet* 72:28 Je 8 '87

DLT German Domestic Airlines

German airline begins service with Fokker 50 transport. il *Aviat Week Space Technol* 127:36-7 S 7 '87

Dlugos, Ray

about

The Pope's foot soldiers. J. Buckley. il pors *U S News World Rep* 103:60-4+ S 21 '87

Dlugozima, Hope

A short (guy) love story. il *Seventeen* 46:134 My '87

DM news

Anecdotes, facetiae, satire, etc.

Uncivil liberties. C. Trillin. *Nation* 245:42 Jl 18-25 '87

DMM (Digital multimeters) *See* Multimeters

D'Monte, Darryl

Gandhi under the gun. il *New Leader* 70:8-10 Je 29 '87

DMSO

The truth about DMSO. S. Festa. il *Women's Sports Fitness* 9:62 My '87

DNA

See also

Genetic code

Genetic research

Nitrogenous bases

Plasmids

Transposons

Bushes all the way down: we are all products of a recent African twig [mitochondrial DNA] S. J. Gould. *Nat Hist* 96:12+ Je '87

Cloning and detection of DNA from a nonculturable plant pathogenic mycoplasma-like organism. B. C. Kirkpatrick and others. bibl f il *Science* 238:197-200 O 9 '87

DNA—*cont.*

Detection of minimal residual cells carrying the t(14;18) by DNA sequence amplification. M.-S. Lee and others. bibl f il *Science* 237:175-8 Jl 10 '87

Direct evidence for DNA bending at the lambda replication origin. K. Zahn and F. R. Blattner. bibl f il *Science* 236:416-22 Ap 24 '87

Disease diagnosis by recombinant DNA methods. C. T. Caskey. bibl f il *Science* 236:1223-9 Je 5 '87

Everyone's genealogical mother [study of mtDNA indicates "Eve" lived in sub-Saharan Africa; research by Allan Wilson and others] M. D. Lemonick. il *Time* 129:66 Ja 26 '87

Functional analysis of a complementary DNA for the 50-kilodalton subunit of calmodulin kinase II. R. M. Hanley and others. bibl f il *Science* 237:293-7 Jl 17 '87

Genetic recombination. F. W. Stahl. il *Sci Am* 256:90-101 F '87

Helix geometry, hydration, and G·A mismatch in a B-DNA decamer. G. G. Privé and others. bibl f il *Science* 238:498-504 O 23 '87

Identification of putative human T cell receptor δ complementary DNA clones. S. Hata and others. bibl f il *Science* 238:678-82 O 30 '87

Immunochemical proof that a novel rearranging gene encodes the T cell receptor δ subunit. H. Band and others. bibl f il *Science* 238:682-4 O 30 '87

Isolation and structure of a covalent cross-link adduct between mitomycin C and DNA. M. Tomasz and others. bibl f il *Science* 235:1204-8 Mr 6 '87

Isolation of an olfactory cDNA: similarity to retinol-binding protein suggests a role in olfaction. K.-H. Lee and others. bibl f il *Science* 235:1053-6 F 27 '87

Left-handed DNA in vivo. A. Jaworski and others. bibl f il *Science* 238:773-7 N 6 '87

Metalloregulator DNA-binding protein encoded by the *mer*R gene: isolation and characterization. T. O'Halloran and C. Walsh. bibl f il *Science* 235:211-14 Ja 9 '87

The mitochondrial genotype can influence nuclear gene expression in yeast. V. S. Parikh and others. bibl f il *Science* 235:576-80 Ja 30 '87

Molecular cloning of complementary DNA encoding the avian receptor for vitamin D. D. P. McDonnell and others. bibl f il *Science* 235:1214-17 Mr 6 '87

Neural nets catch the ABCs of DNA [research by Alan Lapedes and others] S. Weisburd. *Sci News* 132:76 Ag 1 '87

New assay identifies southpaw DNA [work of Robert D. Wells and others] R. Weiss. *Sci News* 132:308 N 14 '87

A promoter with an internal regulatory domain is part of the origin of replication in BPV-1 [bovine papilloma virus] A. Stenlund and others. bibl f il *Science* 236:1666-71 Je 26 '87

A sequence in M13 phage detects hypervariable minisatellites in human and animal DNA. G. Vassart and others. bibl f il *Science* 235:683-4 F 6 '87

Sequence-specific cleavage of double helical DNA by triple helix formation. H. E. Moser and P. B. Dervan. bibl f il *Science* 238:645-50 O 30 '87

Sequence-specific packaging of DNA in human sperm chromatin. J. M. Gatewood and others. bibl f il *Science* 236:962-4 My 22 '87

Site-specific nick in the T-DNA border sequence as a result of Agrobacterium vir gene expression. K. Wang and others. bibl f il *Science* 235:587-91 Ja 30 '87

A small viral RNA is required for in vitro packaging of bacteriophage φ29 DNA. P. Guo and others. bibl f il *Science* 236:690-4 My 8 '87

Structure of a psoralen cross-linked DNA in solution by nuclear magnetic resonance. M. T. Tomic and others. bibl f il *Science* 238:1722-5 D 18 '87

Synthesis of a sequence-specific DNA-cleaving peptide. J. P. Sluka and others. bibl f il *Science* 238:1129-32 N 20 '87

Synthesis of a site-specific DNA-binding peptide. M. F. Bruist and others. bibl f il *Science* 235:777-80 F 13 '87

The unmasking of mitochondrial Eve. R. Lewin. il *Science* 238:24-6 O 2 '87

Unwinding of duplex DNA from the SV40 origin of replication by T antigen. M. Dodson and others. bibl f il *Science* 238:964-7 N 13 '87

DNA fingerprints

DNA fingerprinting of birds. *Sci News* 131:344 My 30 '87

DNA prints [analysis of nuclear DNA patterns in criminal investigations] *Time* 129:66 Ja 26 '87

Leaving Holmes in the dust. S. Begley. il *Newsweek* 110:81 O 26 '87

DNA gene probes *See* Gene probes

DNA ligase *See* Synthetases

DNA methylation *See* Methylation

DNC *See* Democratic National Committee

Do-it-yourself diagnosis *See* Diagnosis

Do-it-yourself house building *See* House construction

Do-it-yourself medical kits *See* Medical equipment

Do-it-yourself work

100 ideas under $100. S. Coulter. il *Better Homes Gard* 65:63-90+ Jl '87

Beat the clock in your home and shop. G. Williams. il *Home Mech* 83:48-50+ F '87

D-I-Y Analyzer: what it means to you. J. R. Provey. il *Home Mech* 83:6 Ap '87

Doing it yourself. S. Willson. il *Pop Mech* 164:110-11 Ap '87

Bibliography

Books. See issues of Workbench

Literature for the workshop library. See issues of Workbench

Competitions

Home Mechanix D-I-Y Contest winners. il *Home Mech* 83:54-6+ D '87

Study and teaching

Aids and devices

See also

Cable television—Do-it-yourself programs

Videotapes—Do-it-yourself work

Great Britain

Watch out, Yanks! We're right behind you! A. Taylor. il *Workbench* 43:66-8 Mr/Ap '87

Doa, Connie

about

Michigan woman jailed; can't serve time at home. *Jet* 72:25 My 18 '87

Doar, Robert

Cigarettes anyone? Tennis and smoking. *Wash Mon* 19:40 Je '87

Dobbelmann, Pierre F.

The perils of protectionism [address, May 19, 1987] *Vital Speeches Day* 53:590-4 Jl 15 '87

Dobell, Byron

Letter from the editor. See issues of American Heritage

Dobie, Kathy, and Goodman, Amy

Playing with poison. il *Progressive* 51:19-23 F '87

Dobija, Jane

Coming up from underground. *Progressive* 51:13 N '87

Doble, John

Interpreting public opinion: five common fallacies. *Current* 294:20-5 Jl/Ag '87

Doboujinsky, Rostislav

about

Master of luxurious fakery. C. Bricker. il por *Archit Dig* 44:238+ Ap '87

Dobson, Jerome E., and others

Lake acidification [with reply by A. H. Johnson, D. F. Charles, and S. B. Andersen] bibl f il *Environment* 29:2-5 Je '87

Dobsonian telescopes *See* Telescopes

Doby, Larry

about

Doby honored by Indians as 1st black AL player. por *Jet* 72:50 S 21 '87

Senator tabs Larry Doby for congressional medal. por *Jet* 72:46 Ag 10 '87

Docekal, Eileen

Tale of the tallgrass. il map *Sierra* 72:76-9 My/Je '87

Dock workers *See* Longshoremen

Docking in space *See* Orbital rendezvous (Space flight)

Docking of boats *See* Boats and boating—Handling

Dockominiums *See* Condominiums (Boat docking)

Docks, wharves, etc.

See also

Condominiums (Boat docking)

New York (N.Y.)—Docks, wharves, etc.

Ports

Great Britain

See also

London (England)—Docks, wharves, etc.

Dockser, Amy

Nice PAC you've got here . . . a pity if anything should happen to it: how politicians shake down the special interests. *Wash Mon* 18:21-2+ Ja '87

Dockstader, Frederick J.

Tradition updated. il *Am Craft* 47:39-45 Ag/S '87

Doctorates *See* Degrees, Academic
Doctorow, E. L., 1931-
America's sacred text. *Current* 294:8-15 Jl/Ag '87
A citizen reads the Constitution [adaptation of address, September 1986] il *Nation* 244:208-9+ F 21 '87
Doctors *See* Physicians
Doctors, Women *See* Women physicians
Doctors for Artists (Organization)
The healing art. S. Staggs. *Art News* 86:21+ My '87
Doctors' offices *See* Physicians' offices
Doctrine, Religious *See* Theology
Docudramas (Television) *See* Television broadcasting—Docudramas
Documenta
Documenta 8: the social dimension? N. Marmer. il *Art Am* 75:128-39+ S '87
Documenta: making the pointed pointless. S. H. Madoff. il *Art News* 86:160-1 S '87
Flying blind into the future of art. G. James. il *Macleans* 100:53-5 Je 29 '87
Documentary photography *See* Photography, Documentary
Documentary television programs *See* Television broadcasting—Documentary programs
Documents
See also
Government publications
Documents, Household *See* Household records
DOD *See* United States. Dept. of Defense
Dodd, Christopher J.
about
Should the contras get more U.S. aid? [interview] S. Manning. pors *Sch Update* 119:10 Mr 9 '87
Dodds, Johnny, 1892-1940
about
35th annual International Critics Poll [with editorial comment by Art Lange] J. McDonough. il pors *Down Beat* 54:5, 20-4 Ag '87
Dodecahedrane
Crafting a miniature pagoda [synthesis of pagodane by Wolf-Dieter Fessner and others] il *Sci News* 132:104 Ag 15 '87
Dodecatheon *See* Shooting stars (Flowers)
Dodeles, Giselle
(jt. auth) See Teich, Mark, and Dodeles, Giselle
Dodgson, Judith
Do women in education need mentors? *Educ Dig* 52:26-8 Ja '87
Dodson, Fitzhugh, 1923-
6 easy ways to get kids to behave [excerpt from How to discipline effectively] il *Redbook* 169:76-7+ Jl '87
Dodson, Mark, and others
Unwinding of duplex DNA from the SV40 origin of replication by T antigen. bibl f il *Science* 238:964-7 N 13 '87
DOE *See* United States. Dept. of Energy
Doe hunting *See* Deer hunting
Doerfler, Ronald John
about
Cap Cities' quiet man. R. Buck. por *Channels* 7:55 Je '87
Doerr, Edd
Church and state. See issues of The Humanist
Does religion belong in our public schools? *USA Today (Periodical)* 116:48-50 S '87
Doesken, Nolan J., and Eckrich, William P.
How often does it rain where you live? il maps *Weatherwise* 40:200-3 Jl/Ag '87
Dofasco Inc.
Union-free workplace. A. Steacy. il *Macleans* 100:35 Jl 13 '87
Dog bites
Your dog bit someone: what now? il *Glamour* 85:50 Ja '87
Dog fighting *See* Dogfighting
Dog food *See* Dogs—Food and feeding
Dog racing
Arctic dreams [S. Butcher and L. Riddles, Iditarod Trail Sled Dog Race champions] K. McCoy. il pors *Women's Sports Fitness* 9:22-7+ F '87
Musher [S. Butcher, two-time winner of the Iditarod Trail Sled Dog Race] *New Yorker* 63:34-5 O 5 '87
Dog shows
The canine crowd puts on the dog [Westminster Kennel Club show] il *Sports Illus* 66:10 F 23 '87
Social aspects
The status game is afoot. G. Buchalter. il *Forbes* 140:160+ N 2 '87
Dog sleds and sledding
Ann Bancroft [first woman to reach North Pole by dogsled] S. Margolis. il pors *Ms* 15:71-2+ Ja '87

The Arctic adventures of Ann Bancroft. M. Specktor. il pors *McCalls* 114:101 Ja '87
Dog-sledder goes it alone [P. Flowers attempts solo trek from Ellsmere Island, Canada to North Pole] N. Klouda. il por *Women's Sports Fitness* 9:20 Mr '87
Everything is North/Ann Bancroft [first woman to reach North Pole by dogsled] J. Kaplan. il por *Vogue* 177:452-3+ Mr '87
Running on sled dog power. il *Natl Geogr World* 148:28-31 D '87
Racing
See Dog racing
Dog walking *See* Dogs—Care
Dogfighting
A boy and his dog in hell [illegal dog fighting with pit bull terriers in Philadelphia] M. Sager. il *Roll Stone* p36-7+ Jl 2 '87
Dogg, John
about
John Dogg at 303 and American Fine Arts. J. Rian. il *Art Am* 75:180-1 S '87
Doggy Court
Bones of contention get buried in Doggy Court, where justice is tempered with mercy. il por *People Wkly* 27:135 My 11 '87
Dogma, Catholic *See* Theology
Dogs
See also
Beagles (Dogs)
Dog racing
Doggy Court
English cocker spaniels
English setters
Gordon setters
Guide dogs
Hounds
Hunting dogs
Mountain curs
Pit bull terriers
Retrievers
Sheep dogs
Can Fido save this marriage? il *Prevention* 39:6 F '87
The dog with nine lives. F. H. Hurt. il *Read Dig* 130:115-18 Ja '87
Dogs' best friends [celebrities' pets] B. Astor. il *House Gard* 159:134-7 D '87
Get to know the animal in your pet. A. R. Marder. *Prevention* 39:73-5 Jl '87
Our best friend [Bintang, family dog] E. D'Aulaire. il por *Good Housekeep* 204:36+ F '87
The perfect country dog. D. Russell. il *Ctry J* 14:28-34 D '87
The secret lives of dogs and cats [condensed from Dogwatching and Catwatching] D. Morris. il *Read Dig* 131:47-8+ D '87
The stately dogs of England. S. Gray. il *House Gard* 159:142+ N '87
What to do when man's best friend is your garden's worst enemy? il *Sunset* 178:106-9 Ap '87
Anecdotes, facetiae, satire, etc.
Exclusive! Martina's dog tells all. H. Delehanty. il por *Women's Sports Fitness* 9:62 Ja '87
Hounded by woes, Miamians beg for more of Ryan the Advice Dog. il por *People Wkly* 28:113 O 19 '87
Our dog won't retire. M. G. Stoddard. il *Saturday Evening Post* 259:48-9 Mr '87
This is one candidate who's not afraid to admit he's a dog [Punch Burger is registered with the Federal Election Commission] il *People Wkly* 28:45 Jl 13 '87
Breeding
Do you know your dogs? H. E. Whiteley. il *Saturday Evening Post* 259:28+ Ap '87
Puppy love. M. S. Dolan. il *Consum Res Mag* 70:2 D '87
Care
At last there's something more for the pooch who has everything (including odor)—doggie perfume [work of L. Gilford] il por *People Wkly* 28:117 S 21 '87
Exercising your pet. R. Kidd. il *Mother Earth News* 105:34+ My/Je '87
A safe and happy holiday for your pet. A. R. Marder. *Prevention* 39:49+ N '87
Taking care of the older dog. S. L. Gerstenfeld. il *Parents* 62:244 S '87
Walk your dog to trimness. D. Foley. il *Prevention* 39:72+ Ja '87
Workouts for pampered pets. A. R. Marder. *Prevention* 39:110+ O '87

Dogs—*cont.*

Diseases and pests

See also

Fleas

Dogs, cats, and cancer. H. E. Whiteley. il *Saturday Evening Post* 259:32+ Mr '87

Vaccines and vaccination

A vaccination update. A. R. Marder. *Prevention* 39:105-8 S '87

Equipment

See also

Haut Dog (Firm)

Great ideas for dog men. L. Mueller. il *Outdoor Life* 180:34+ O '87

Food and feeding

See also

Lick Your Chops (Firm)

A British lord wants to go to the dogs . . . literally! [Lord Avebury's intention to donate his body for dog food] il por *People Wkly* 27:94 F 23 '87

Upscale dogs: clipping coupons for chow. il *Newsweek* 109:62 My 18 '87

Grooming

See Dogs—Care

Laws and regulations

Dogs and deer [dogs as deer killers] B. Shipman. il *Ctry J* 14:17-20 Ap '87

Parks that say yes (and no) to dogs [Bay Area] il *Sunset* 179:47-8 N '87

Photographs and photography

Beauty in the beasts [cover story] W. Chandoha. il *Petersens Photogr Mag* 16:18-21 D '87

Bertmania! [celebrities posing with terrier on David Letterman show] il *People Wkly* 28:165-7 D 7 '87

William Wegman: the artist and his dog. A. Hempel. il pors *N Y Times Mag* p40-2+ N 29 '87

Training

Playing the egg game [training a dog to gather eggs] M. Smith. il *Mother Earth News* 108:22 N/D '87

'Why is my dog so hyper?'. R. H. Pitcairn. *Prevention* 39:80 F '87

Treatment

From smoking gun to smoking dog: a 'Beat the devil' investigation [killing of dogs at Topeka's Forbes Field Airport before arrival of R. Reagan] A. Cockburn. map *Nation* 245:332-3 O 3 '87

Dogs, Effect of temperature on

Handling heat [conditioning hunting dogs for hot weather] B. Tarrant. il *Field Stream* 92:130+ Jl '87

A warm welcome for newborn pups. L. Mueller. il *Outdoor Life* 179:41+ Ap '87

Dogs as actors

Box office bite. J. Zweig and A. D. Frank. il *Forbes* 140:123 S 21 '87

Take a bowwow, Bowser! G. Clarke. il *Time* 130:75 D 7 '87

Dogs in advertising

See also

Spuds MacKenzie (Advertising character)

Dogs in motion pictures

Unleashed by Hollywood, the star of Benji the hunted has tongues wagging all over America. J. Jarvis. il por *People Wkly* 28:78-80 Jl 20 '87

Dogs in television

Maybe John Ritter is bitter about his canine co-star, but Hooperman won't be dropping Britches. il por *People Wkly* 28:82+ D 14 '87

Doherty, Craig A.

Gardening the Zuni way. il *Rodale's Org Gard* 34:62-4 Ag '87

Doherty, Edward J.

about

Dockbroker Ed. R. Behar. il por *Forbes* 140:166+ S 21 '87

Doherty, Edward W.

A classic case of consequentialism. *Commonweal* 114:10-11 Ja 16 '87

Doherty, Jim

The hobby that challenges you to think like a bee. bibl (p146-7) il *Smithsonian* 18:62-70+ Jl '87

Doherty, M. Stephen

Eight artists open their studios. il *Am Artist* 51:48-57 F '87

Eleven artists paint the same location. il *Am Artist* 51:30-41 F '87

Expanding your market with multiples. il *Am Artist* 51:52-9 My '87

George A. Weymouth. il pors *Am Artist* 51:32-7+ Ja '87

Pen & ink: John Anderson. il *Am Artist* 51:64-7 Ag '87

Wendell Minor. il por *Am Artist* 51:42-7 Ja '87

Doi, Norihisa, and others

The search for a thinking computer. il *Courier* 40:16-19 Jl '87

Doig, D. T.

A love song for Christmas [story] il *Good Housekeep* 205:248+ D '87

The man who married Mom [story] il *Good Housekeep* 204:182-3+ My '87

Doig, Ivan

about

PW interviews. W. Smith. por *Publ Wkly* 232:156-7 S 18 '87

Dolan, Robert, and Lins, Harry F.

Beaches and barrier islands. il map *Sci Am* 257:68-73+ Jl '87

Dolan, Terry

about

From Dolan to da Vinci. A. Cockburn. *Nation* 244:135 F 7 '87

Obituary

Natl Rev 39:24 Ja 30 '87

Newsweek por 109:23 Ja 12 '87. J. Alter

Dolby, Thomas

about

Thomas Dolby settles suit over name. M. Coleman. *Roll Stone* p10 My 7 '87

Dolby Laboratories Inc.

Dolby. R. Hodges. il *Stereo Rev* 52:168 Ja '87

Thomas Dolby settles suit over name. M. Coleman. *Roll Stone* p10 My 7 '87

Dolby noise reduction system *See* Audio systems—Noise

Dolce, Joe

Beyond the first novel. il *Harpers Bazaar* 120:108+ Ag '87

Designer cheek. il *Harpers Bazaar* 120:210+ Mr '87

Dole, Elizabeth Hanford, 1936-

about

Charming her way to the White House [cover story] P. Weiss. *Wash Mon* 19:29+ S '87

A Dole 'fast-track'. D. Gates. il pors *Newsweek* 109:7 Je 15 '87

Dole proposes upgrade of nine radar service areas to TCA status. *Aviat Week Space Technol* 127:33 Ag 31 '87

Dole resigns, raising concerns about Department's leadership. *Aviat Week Space Technol* 127:34 S 21 '87

Secretary Dole, meet Mrs. Dole. A. Stanley. il por *Time* 130:30 S 21 '87

The time is not yet. A. McCarthy. il *Commonweal* 114:554-5 O 9 '87

Dole, Robert J., 1923-

Rebuilding the parties [address, April 7, 1987] *Vital Speeches Day* 53:482-4 Je 1 '87

Should the Byrd-Warner Amendment be adopted? [excerpts from debates, October 9 and 12, 1987] *Congr Dig* 66:305 D '87

about

Bob Dole and the tobacco connection. D. Corn. il *Nation* 244:381+ Mr 28 '87

Bob Dole bets it all on busting the budget deficit. R. Fly. il por *Bus Week* p45 N 23 '87

Bob Dole: ready to lead, but where? G. Borger. il pors *U S News World Rep* 103:27-8 N 16 '87

Bush stumbles. il por *Time* 130:23 D 28 '87

The contradictions of Bob Dole. M. Tolchin and J. Gerth. il pors *N Y Times Mag* p62-5+ N 8 '87

The contradictory character of Bob Dole. H. Fineman. il pors *Newsweek* 110:65+ N 16 '87

Dole buries his hatchet. A. Stanley. il por *Time* 130:25 N 16 '87

A Dole 'fast-track'. D. Gates. il pors *Newsweek* 109:7 Je 15 '87

The Dole moment. F. Barnes. il *New Repub* 196:14-15 Ja 26 '87

Dole's dilemma. il por *Newsweek* 110:5 N 23 '87

For whom the Doles toil. J. Klein. il por *N Y* 20:24+ S 28 '87

Leonard is lionized on Capitol Hill as guest of Kan. Sen. Robert Dole. il pors *Jet* 72:12 My 11 '87

A loner's quest. G. F. Gilder. il pors *Life* 10:62-4+ S '87

The market for Dole. F. Barnes. *New Repub* 197:9-11 N 16 '87

Secretary Dole, meet Mrs. Dole. A. Stanley. il por *Time* 130:30 S 21 '87

The Senate's former majority leader urges compromise in the 100th Congress [interview] M. Christopher. il *Sch Update* 119:10 Ja 12 '87

Suddenly a hot property. H. Fineman. il por *Newsweek* 109:27 Ja 5 '87

Dole, Robert J., 1923-—about—*cont.*
Survivor on the track. J. E. White. il por *Time* 129:23-4
Mr 23 '87
The time is not yet. A. McCarthy. il *Commonweal*
114:554-5 O 9 '87
A veteran's campaign. M. McDonald. il por *Macleans*
100:16-17 N 23 '87
Why Dole can't do it [cover story] R. Brookhiser. il
por *Natl Rev* 39:30-2 D 4 '87

Dole Citrus
David Murdock is picking plums. T. Carson. il por
Bus Week p43 O 12 '87

Doleman, Edgar C.
How I built a real live telescope. il *Astronomy* 15:63-6
Ja '87

Doll furniture
Rustic doll crate-l. T. Havenga. il *Workbench* 43:51
N/D '87

Doll house furniture *See* Furniture, Miniature

Doll houses
High-rise dollhouse . . . or whatever children make
of it. il *Sunset* 178:96+ Mr '87

Dollar *See* Money

Dollar coins *See* Coins

Dollar cost averaging *See* Investment trusts—Dollar cost
averaging; Stocks—Dollar cost averaging

Dollar devaluation *See* Money

Dollar sign
Notes on the sign of the dollar. E. Rochette. il *Antiques
Collect Hobbies* 92:72-3 Je '87

Dollhouses *See* Doll houses

Dolls

See also
Alexander Doll Company
Paper dolls
Tia's Doll Emporium

Bagged in Boston [Sher-Stuff's Bag Lady dolls] *Time*
129:78 Ap 27 '87
The dolls' Christmas. il *Good Housekeep* 205:148-9 D
'87
The dream that grew in our garden [daughter "grows"
a Cabbage Patch doll] S. Alexander. il *Good Housekeep*
204:58 Mr '87

Collectors and collecting
America's "primitive" dolls. M. Jailer. il *Antiques Collect
Hobbies* 92:33-5 Ag '87
Autoperipatetikos: the self-walking doll. M. Jailer. il
Antiques Collect Hobbies 91:32-4+ F '87
Charming all-bisque dolls. M. Jailer. il *Antiques Collect
Hobbies* 92:38-40+ S '87
The compelling German "characters". M. Jailer. il
Antiques Collect Hobbies 92:34-6 Jl '87
Dolls of fashion. M. Jailer. il *Antiques Collect Hobbies*
92:40-2 Je '87
How dolls began to talk. M. Jailer. il *Antiques Collect
Hobbies* 92:34-6 Mr '87
Käthe Kruse: creator of the beloved classic. M. Jailer.
il *Antiques Collect Hobbies* 92:36-8 Ap '87
Lenci dolls. M. Jailer. il *Antiques Collect Hobbies* 92:44-6
O '87
A look at china-head dolls. M. Jailer. il *Antiques Collect
Hobbies* 92:59-60 N '87
Nineteenth-century dollmakers as viewed by the profes-
sionals. M. Jailer. il *Antiques Collect Hobbies* 92:38-40
My '87

Exhibitions
Dolls and toys at home for Christmas. M. Jailer. il
Antiques Collect Hobbies 92:34-8 D '87

Repairing
The care and repair of precious bisque. M. Jailer. il
Antiques Collect Hobbies 91:30-2 Ja '87

Therapeutic use
Helping children cope [anatomically correct Zaadi dolls]
il *Ms* 16:28 D '87
Playing doctor with Gail Zayka's lifelike dolls helps
kids facing surgery get over their fears [Zaadi dolls]
B. Taubman. il pors *People Wkly* 28:57-8 S 14 '87

Dolly [television program] *See* Television program
reviews—Single works

Dolman, Nancy
about
Couples. M. Orth. il pors *Vogue* 177:393 F '87

Dolnick, Edward
Closer encounters. *New Repub* 197:15-16 Ag 10-17 '87
He's the wisest of wise guys. il por *Discover* 8:82-4+
Ja '87
Inventing the future. il por *N Y Times Mag* p30-3+
Ag 23 '87
Is a yawn really contagious? il *Read Dig* 131:99-102
Jl '87

Dolores River (Colo. and Utah)
Dryland farmers say no to water [Colorado farmers
sue Bureau of Reclamation over Dolores River Project]
J. Price. il *Progressive* 51:11 Jl '87

Dolphin Brasserie (London, England) *See* London
(England)—Restaurants, nightclubs, bars, etc.

Dolphins
See also
Killer whales
Dolphin talk [interview with D. Reiss] G. Hartwell.
Oceans 20:62-3 Mr/Ap '87
Joe and Rosie go for it [captive dolphins retrained and
released] E. Linden. il *Time* 130:72 Ag 17 '87
Strange pool-fellows [dolphin swim seminar at Sealand
Aquarium, West Brewster, Mass.] L. W. Kloss. il *Travel
Holiday* 167:8+ Ap '87
Think like a dolphin [role models for managers learning
strategic thinking skills] *Futurist* 21:52 Mr/Ap '87
Who in Solihull cares about dolphins? [Catholic theology]
E. P Echlin. *America* 157:15-17 Jl 4-11 '87

Food and feeding
Sonic punch: dolphins and whales generate "bangs" that
may stun prey [research by Kenneth Marten and
Kenneth S. Norris] T. Beardsley. *Sci Am* 257:36 O
'87

Mortality
The dolphin die-off [along the East Coast] il *U S News
World Rep* 103:12 Ag 24 '87
Mysterious deaths at sea [dead dolphins washing ashore
from New Jersey to Virginia] M. Gray. il *Macleans*
100:42 Ag 24 '87
What is killing the Atlantic's dolphins? il *Newsweek*
110:51 Ag 24 '87

Dolphins Plus (Key Largo, Fla.)
Contact with dolphins. P. Curtis. il *Oceans* 20:18-23
Ja/F '87

Dolson, Chris
Joy to the mall! *Christ Today* 31:25 D 11 '87

Dombek, George
(jt. auth) See Porter, Tom, and Dombek, George

Dombois, Dieter Mueller- *See* Mueller-Dombois, Dieter,
1925-

Dome Mines Limited
Defence of a gold mine. D. Jenish. il *Macleans* 100:32-3
Ag 17 '87

Dome Petroleum Ltd.
Amoco becomes bolder [bid for Dome] C. Siler. il *Forbes*
140:88 N 2 '87
A bidding war shapes up for debt-ridden Dome [bid
by TransCanada PipeLines] E. B. Terry. il *Bus Week*
p50 Ap 27 '87
Desperate times for Dome. il *Macleans* 100:28-9 Ap
20 '87
Dome's day of reckoning [creditors disappointed with
Amoco Canada bid] T. Tedesco. il *Macleans* 100:29
My 25 '87
Dome's deepening saga [proposed sale of Dome to Amoco
Canada Petroleum Co. Ltd.] D. Jenish. il *Macleans*
100:26 Jl 6 '87
Dome's last deal [bid by Amoco Canada; cover story;
special section; with editorial comment by Kevin Doyle]
il *Macleans* 100:2, 34-42 My 4 '87
Dome's light at the end of the tunnel [Amoco raises
its takeover offer] D. Jenish. il *Macleans* 100:50 N
30 '87
Dome's lingering drama [agreement with Amoco Canada
Petroleum] T. Tedesco. il *Macleans* 100:40 My 18
'87
Dome's trans-Canadian vision [bid by TransCanada
PipeLines] T. Fennell. il *Macleans* 100:45 Ap 27 '87
A special interest in Dome [J. P. Gallagher wants Dome
to stay in Canadian hands] P. C. Newman. il por
Macleans 100:48 Ap 27 '87
A threat to the public interest [loss to Canada of Dome
to Amoco] P. C. Newman. il *Macleans* 100:31 Jl
6 '87

Dome stadiums *See* Stadiums

Domes
See also
Geodesic domes
Three great domes [church domes] G. C. Argan. il *Courier*
40:10 S '87

Domes (Geology)
See also
Salt domes

Domesday book
High-tech printing techniques create an 'elaborately forged'
Domesday book. S. D. Bell. il *Publ Wkly* 231:50-2
Ap 17 '87

Domesday book—*cont.*
William the Conqueror ordered England's first land and resource survey. The record is the Domesday book. il *Earth Sci* 40:29 Spr '87

Domestic animals
See also
Cats
Dogs
Horses
Pets

Laws and regulations
Little horse, big deal—protestors cry 'There goes the neighborhood' [P. Fairchild fights to keep her miniature horse in Thousand Oaks, Calif.] il pors *People Wkly* 27:96-7 Je 1 '87

Domestic appliances *See* Household appliances
Domestic architecture *See* Architecture, Domestic
Domestic economy *See* Home economics
Domestic employees *See* Household employees
Domestic finance *See* Finance, Personal
Domestic quarrels *See* Quarrels
Domestic relations
See also
Divorce
Family
Marriage
Marriage counseling
Married couples
Support (Domestic relations)
Unmarried couples
Wife abuse

Domestic violence *See* Family violence
Dominance, Lateral *See* Laterality
Domingo, Placido
about
Domingo: giving his best [cover story] J. Scovell. il pors *Opera News* 52:14-17 S '87

Dominica
Description and travel
Trekking in nature's terrarium. R. Okey. il map *Américas* 39:8-13 S/O '87

Dominican refugees *See* Refugees, Dominican
Dominican Republic
See also
Americans—Dominican Republic
Architecture, Domestic—Dominican Republic
Baseball—Dominican Republic
Divorce—Dominican Republic
Paleontology—Dominican Republic
San Pedro de Macoris (Dominican Republic)

Dominick, Anne Westbrook
The first "fruit" of spring: rhubarb. il *Flower Gard* 31:30 F/Mr '87

Dominion Federal Savings & Loan Assn.
The better idea. M. Schifrin. il *Forbes* 140:57-8 O 5 '87

Dominion Textile Inc.
Burlington almost invited Edelman to attack [bid by A. B. Edelman and Dominion Textile] D. Foust. il por *Bus Week* p50+ My 11 '87
Dominion's unraveling bid [bid for Burlington Industries] D. Foust. *Bus Week* p49-50 Je 1 '87

Dominoes
Calculating the real domino effect [work of Bill Stronge] il *Discover* 8:5 Ap '87

Domm, Bill
about
An ardent advocate [interview] H. Mackenzie. il por *Macleans* 100:11 Mr 16 '87

Domning, Daryl P.
Sea cow family reunion. il *Nat Hist* 96:64+ Ap '87

Don Giovanni [opera] *See* Mozart, Wolfgang Amadeus, 1756-1791

Don Quixote (Fictional character)
A Don Quixote discovery [ninth plate in Don Quixote series of transfer-printed earthenware attributed to Staffordshire potters James and Ralph Clews] E. H. Gustafson. il *Antiques* 132:740+ O '87
Don Quixote's Spain. M. Picchi. il *World Press Rev* 34:61 N '87

Donahue, Christine
Linda Wachner. il por *Ms* 15:78+ Ja '87

Donahue, Elinor
about
Elinor Donahue of Father knows best is a mother to six, plus Beans Baxter. L. Armstrong. il pors *People Wkly* 28:97-8+ S 28 '87

Donahue, Phil
about
Phil Donahue [interview] L. Gomez. pors *Life* 10:21-2 O '87

Stirring up the comrades. R. Zoglin. il por *Time* 129:79 F 16 '87

Donahue, William H., d. 1987
about
Murder hits home. S. G. Freedman. il *N Y Times Mag* p20+ My 31 '87

Donahue [television program] *See* Television program reviews—Single works

Donald, Beulah Mae
about
Seeking justice for her lynched son, an Alabama mother ruins the Klan that killed him. J. S. Kunen. il pors *People Wkly* 27:55-6+ Je 8 '87
The woman who beat the Klan. J. Kornbluth. il pors *N Y Times Mag* p26-32+ N 1 '87

Donald, David Herbert, 1920-
Wolfe in love. il por *N Y Times Book Rev* 92:1+ Ja 11 '87
about
PW interviews. S. Staggs. por *Publ Wkly* 231:366-7 Ja 30 '87

Donald, Jacquelyn
about
All-around achiever. J. Sands. il por *Essence* 18:102+ Je '87

Donald, Michael
about
Black lawyer forces KKK to pay $7 million for lynching black, 19. T. S. Moore. il pors *Jet* 71:6-8 Mr 9 '87
Going after the Klan. A. Press. il *Newsweek* 109:29 F 23 '87
Mother of slain black son takes possession of KKK building won in lawsuit. il por *Jet* 72:8 Je 8 '87
Seeking justice for her lynched son, an Alabama mother ruins the Klan that killed him. J. S. Kunen. il pors *People Wkly* 27:55-6+ Je 8 '87
The woman who beat the Klan. J. Kornbluth. il pors *N Y Times Mag* p26-32+ N 1 '87

Donald Duck (Fictional character)
If it quacks like this odd duck, it must be Tony Anselmo. il por *People Wkly* 27:127 My 18 '87

Donaldson, Barry
Stone: new technology and design. il *Archit Rec* 175:136-45 Jl '87

Donaldson, Jeffery
Mandelstam [poem] *New Repub* 196:30 Mr 16 '87

Donaldson, Roger
about
No way out [film] Reviews
Glamour il 85:297 S '87. J. G. Boyum
Macleans il 100:46 Ag 31 '87. B. D. Johnson
N Y il 20:62-3 Ag 17 '87. D. Denby
Natl Rev 39:59-61 S 25 '87. J. Simon
New Yorker 63:98-100 S 7 '87. P. Kael
People Wkly il 28:6 Ag 24 '87. S. Haller
Time il 130:62 Ag 17 '87. R. Schickel

Donaldson, Sam
about
Newsman as predator. J. Alter. il pors *Newsweek* 109:58-9 Mr 2 '87
Of many things. G. W. Hunt. *America* 156:inside cover My 9 '87
Pushiness we can respect. J. Powell. *Wash Mon* 19:55-6 F '87

Donation of organs, tissues, etc.
Body donation: an enigmatic subject. K. M. Wilson. *Humanist* 47:30+ Mr/Ap '87
A British lord wants to go to the dogs . . . literally! [Lord Avebury's intention to donate his body for dog food] il por *People Wkly* 27:94 F 23 '87
A father's special gift of love [J. Garn donates kidney to diabetic daughter] M. F. Hoyt. il por *Good Housekeep* 204:74+ F '87
Last rights [redefining death; cover story] K. Stein. il *Omni* 9:58-60+ S '87
Life and death [discussion of September 1987 article, Last rights] K. Stein. *Omni* 10:18 D '87
Organ donation: giving the gift of life. J. E. Davison. il *Christ Century* 104:1146-8 D 16 '87
Transplants come of age. G. Bronson. il *Forbes* 139 Ann Directory:86+ Ap 27 '87
Vital organs of black doctor killed in holdup given to Pasadena hospital [S. Y. Morgan] *Jet* 73:28 D 14 '87
Why blacks are reluctant to donate organs for transplants. il *Jet* 73:52-3 N 2 '87
Laws and regulations
First word [rejection of anencephalic newborn as organ donor] G. Marell. il *Omni* 9:8 My '87

Donation of organs, tissues, etc.—Laws and regulations —cont.

OTA: property right, donor consent factors cloud "gifts" of human tissue. M. Crawford. *Science* 235:1564 Mr 27 '87

Selling a pound of flesh [biotech use of patients' cell lines] J. Schwartz. il *Newsweek* 109:55 Ap 20 '87

Who owns human tissues and cells? [report by the Office of Technology Assessment] L. Tangley. *BioScience* 37:376-8 Je '87

Donegan, Frank
In the marketplace. See issues of Americana

Donelson, Ken
Six statements/questions from the censors. bibl f il *Phi Delta Kappan* 69:208-14 N '87

Dönhoff, Marion, Gräfin, 1909-
Subtle changes in South Africa? il *World Press Rev* 34:26-8 My '87

Doniger, Joanna
about
Serving Cinderellas on both sides of the ocean. Joanna Doniger rents out gowns fit for a princess. L. Lague. il pors *People Wkly* 28:51-2 D 21 '87

Donkey Sanctuary (Devonshire, England)
In a seaside hee-haw haven, 1,700 donkeys bray each day for Elisabeth Svendsen. M. Neill. il pors *People Wkly* 27:84-7 My 25 '87

Donkeys
Treatment
See also
Donkey Sanctuary (Devonshire, England)
Donkey business and asinine journalism [British mass circulation dailies' coverage of false Spanish donkey abuse story fed them by an animal rights group] J. Valls-Russell. il *New Leader* 70:5-7 Ap 6 '87

La donna del lago [opera] *See* Rossini, Gioacchino, 1792-1868

Donnelley (R. R.) & Sons Co. *See* R. R. Donnelley & Sons Co.

Donnelly, Russell J.
Leo Dana: cryogenic science and technology. il por *Phys Today* 40:38-41+ Ap '87

Donnelly, V. Paul
about
Age bias is his business. D. Katz. il por *50 Plus* 27:18-20 Mr '87

Donner, Richard
about
Lethal weapon [film] Reviews
New Repub 196:24 Ap 13 '87. S. Kauffmann
Newsweek il 109:72 Mr 16 '87. D. Ansen
People Wkly il 27:8 Mr 23 '87. T. Cunneff
Time il 129:86 Mr 23 '87. R. Schickel

Donoghue, Denis
Feelings of and and if, of and but. il *N Y Times Book Rev* 92:10 Ja 25 '87
Relax, it's only a theory. il *N Y Times Book Rev* 92:14 Mr 1 '87
What makes life worth writing? il *N Y Times Book Rev* 92:11-12 Mr 29 '87

Donoghue, Helen
Vaccination against tooth decay. il *World Press Rev* 34:52 My '87

Donoghue, Sue
Fitness tips from the stars' trainers. il *McCalls* 114:35 My '87

Donohue, John W.
Better than rubies. il *America* 157:319-26 N 7 '87
Edith Stein's early years. *America* 156:7-9+ Ja 3-10 '87
How goes it with the colleges? *America* 156:269-73+ Ap 4 '87
Recovering black history. *America* 157:35-7 Jl 18-25 '87
A teacher's teacher [cover story] *America* 157:495-7 D 26 '87

Donors, Organ *See* Donation of organs, tissues, etc.
Donors, Sperm *See* Artificial insemination, Human

Donoso, José
about
Stormy adventures of the spirit. M. Kogan. il pors *Américas* 39:8-13 N/D '87

Donovan, Arthur J.
Football's fat man [ed. by Jerome Cramer] il pors *People Wkly* 28:79-80+ N 9 '87
The greatest game never played [excerpt from Fatso] il *Sport Mag* 78:53-5 Jl '87

Donovan, Carrie
Fashion. See occasional issues of The New York Times Magazine
The swagger of Christian Lacroix. il pors *N Y Times Mag* p22-5+ S 6 '87

Donovan, Raymond James, 1930-
about
Black lawyer keys Donovan's trial win. il pors *Jet* 72:6 Je 22 '87
"Give me back my reputation!". G. J. Church. il por *Time* 129:31 Je 8 '87

Don't get God started [musical] *See* Musicals, revues, etc.—Reviews—Single works

Donziger, Steven
Peace Corps follies. il *Progressive* 51:28-31 Mr '87

Doo Dah Parade (Pasadena, Calif.) *See* Pasadena (Calif.)— Parades

Doo-wop concerts *See* Rock concerts

Doodles
Hollywood's top draws donate oodles of doodles for an artistic cause [auction of celebrity doodles for Los Angeles' Back Alley Theatre] il *People Wkly* 28:110-11 S 28 '87

Doohan, Peter
about
Boris's blunder. C. Kirkpatrick. il pors *Sports Illus* 67:21 Jl 6 '87

Dooley, Susan
And after all, isn't that what eggs are for? il *Smithsonian* 17:152 F '87
Bitches in business. il *Harpers Bazaar* 120:308+ S '87

Doomsday *See* End of the world; Judgment Day

Doonesbury (Comic strip)
'Doonesbury' in Arizona [depiction of Governor E. Mecham] il *Newsweek* 110:41 S 14 '87

Door locks *See* Locks and keys

Door mats, etc.
Color your floors bright [stenciled doormat and painted floor cloth] V. Hahn. il *Parents* 62:147-8+ Ag '87
Mud stompers. il *Sunset* 178:110+ F '87

Door pulls *See* Doorknobs, pulls, etc.

Door-to-door selling
See also
Fuller Brush Co.
Anecdotes, facetiae, satire, etc.
The door-to-door salesman: an endangered species. M. G. Stoddard. il *Saturday Evening Post* 259:46-7+ Ja/F '87

Doorknobs, pulls, etc.
Plumbing plastic as door handles. il *Sunset* 178:117 F '87

Doorpersons
Buster of Bendel's. G. Stutz. il *N Y* 20:68 D 21-28 '87

Doors
See also
Garage doors
Spaceplane—Doors
Door remodeling. J. Gaynor. il *Home Mech* 83:96 My '87
Glass doors for light and for temperature control. il *Sunset* 178:114 Mr '87
How to install a space-saving pocket door. G. Branson. il *Fam Handyman* 37:36 Ja '87
How to replace a sliding glass door. M. Thompson. il *Fam Handyman* 37:94-5 O '87
Product reports 1988. il *Archit Rec* 175:79-83+ D '87
Security door that keeps bugs out, too. M. Morris. il *Home Mech* 83:52 S '87
Turn a window into a door. il *Mother Earth News* 105:46-9 My/Je '87
Unmask hidden style at your front door [cover story] S. Ross. il *Fam Handyman* 37:27-9+ Ap '87
Maintenance and repair
Fix your sticky doors. T. R. Kovach. il *Workbench* 43:65 Ja/F '87

Doors, Mechanically operated
See also
Garage doors—Control

Doors, Screen *See* Screens (Doors, windows, etc.)

Doorways
Replacing your threshold. A. Rooze. il *Fam Handyman* 37:59 Mr '87

Doozie (Term)
'When I make a mistake . . .'. W. Safire. il *N Y Times Mag* p10 F 22 '87

Dopamine
Cocaine receptors on dopamine transporters are related to self-administration of cocaine. M. C. Ritz and others. bibl f il *Science* 237:1219-23 S 4 '87
The shyness chemical [low dopamine levels] *Time* 129:78 Mr 16 '87

Dopamine receptors *See* Chemoreceptors
Dope trade *See* Narcotics trade
Doppler radar in meteorology *See* Radar meteorology
Dorcas Place Parent Literacy Center
The ABC's of literacy [Providence, R.I. program serves women] J. F. Rodriquez. il *Ms* 16:74 D '87
Doré, Jean
about
Montreal's controversial reformers. A. Wilson-Smith. il por *Macleans* 100:36 F 9 '87
Dorfman, David
about
Reviews:
Performance at the Bessie Schönberg Theater, New York City. O. Stuart. *Dance Mag* 61:106-7 My '87
Dorfman, Ron
Let a hundred flowers wilt. il *Progressive* 51:19-23 Mr '87
Dorfman (David) Dance *See* David Dorfman Dance
Doria, John J.
(jt. auth) *See* Doria, Suzanne S., and Doria, John J.
Doria, Suzanne S., and Doria, John J.
Out of the past. *Earth Sci* 39:29 Wint '86
D'Origny, Henri *See* Origny, Henri d', vicomte
D'Origny, Sybil *See* Origny, Sybil d', vicomtesse
Doriot, Georges Frederic, 1899-1987
about
A teacher who made a difference. P. Fuhrman. il por *Forbes* 140:362+ Jl 13 '87
Doritty, David
about
Frantic week for a broker. A. Shortell. il por *Macleans* 100:31-2 N 2 '87
Dorler, Bernd
The fantasy world of Gunpoint U. il *World Press Rev* 34:60 Mr '87
Dormen, Lesley
Rewriting your romantic résumé. il *Glamour* 85:316-17+ N '87
Water, water everywhere . . . but not for me, thanks! il *Health* 19:43 My '87
When everyone has more money than you. il *Seventeen* 46:29-30+ D '87
When you like your stepparent too much. il *Seventeen* 46:152-3+ O '87
Dormen, Lesley, and Zussman, Mark
How to meet a man/how to meet a woman. il *Glamour* 85:288-9+ My '87
Is he marriage material? 74 sneaky ways to separate the possibilities from the deadbeats. il *Glamour* 85:226-7+ F '87
The secret life of boys. il *Seventeen* 46:222-4 Ap '87
Dormer rooms *See* Rooms
Dormitories
Quadrangle keep [Feinberg Hall, Princeton University] il *Archit Rec* 175:100-5 Mr '87
Dornan, Robert K., 1933-
Stop beating around the Bush [cover story] il *Natl Rev* 39:32-4 N 6 '87
Dornberg, John
Art vandals: why do they do it? il por *Art News* 86:102-9 Mr '87
Dornbusch, Rudiger
European unemployment: the challenge of the '80s. il *Current* 289:25-31 Ja '87
Dörner, Günter
about
Sexual destinies. L. Murray. il *Omni* 9:100-2+ Ap '87
Dornier GmbH
Dornier begins full-scale development of 30-passenger DO. 328 commuter. K. F. Mordoff. il *Aviat Week Space Technol* 126:36 My 25 '87
Dornier designs DO. 328 cabin for comfort, reduced sound levels. il *Aviat Week Space Technol* 126:43 Je 22 '87
Dornier readies Seastar CD2 for Paris flight demonstrations. K. F. Mordoff. il *Aviat Week Space Technol* 126:125 My 11 '87
Martin Marietta selects Dornier to build Titan component. *Aviat Week Space Technol* 127:27 O 19 '87
Dornoch (Scotland: Golf course) *See* Golf courses—Scotland
Doron, Daniel
about
The enemy within [interview] P. Brimelow. il por *Forbes* 140:54+ D 28 '87
Doronila, Amando
'After Aquino'. *World Press Rev* 34:41 D '87
Dorr, Les, Jr.
The cosmokremlinologists. il *Space World* X-10-286:28-30+ O '87

Russki business. il *Space World* X-7-283:31-4 Jl '87
When the doctor is 200 miles away [cover story] il *Space World* X-3-279:33-6 Mr '87
Dorrance, Anson
about
Kicking with both his heels. J. Diaz. il por *Sports Illus* 67:80 N 23 '87
Dorrance, John T., Jr.
about
If life hands you a silver spoon—gild it. B. Dumaine. il por *Fortune* 116:160-1 O 12 '87
Dorrance family
about
How long will Campbell retain its family flavor? A. Bianco. il *Bus Week* p68-9 Ja 26 '87
Dorrie, Doris
about
Men . . . [film] Reviews
New Leader 70:21-2 Ja 12-26 '87. J. Gardner
Dorris, Michael
The best of pen pals. il *Seventeen* 46:272 Ag '87
Hard luck [fiction] il *Seventeen* 46:262-3+ Mr '87
The queen of Christmas. *Seventeen* 46:128-9 D '87
Dorsett, Beryl
about
Beryl Dorsett lauded in new education post with a $5.4 billion budget. il pors *Jet* 73:22+ N 23 '87
Dorsey, Lee, 1927-1986
about
Obituary
Roll Stone p22 Ja 15 '87
Dortch, Richard
about
Ousting two from the clergy. R. N. Ostling. il por *Time* 129:65 My 18 '87
Dory building *See* Boatbuilding
DOS operating systems *See* Computers—Operating systems
Dosage forms of drugs *See* Drugs—Dosage forms
Dosage of drugs *See* Drugs—Dosage
Dosimeters, Radiation *See* Radiation dosimeters and dosimetry
Dossena, Alceo, 1878-1937
about
The eye of the beholder. R. Lynes. il por *Archit Dig* 44:26+ Ap '87
Dostal, John
Over the river and through the woods. bibl il *Women's Sports Fitness* 9:40-4 D '87
Dostoevskii, Fedor Mikhaĭlovich *See* Dostoyevsky, Fyodor, 1821-1881
Dostoyevsky, Fyodor, 1821-1881
Dostoyevsky: prisoner, gambler, prophet. il *N Y Times Book Rev* 92:1+ Je 14 '87
about
Houses of the dead. F. Eberstadt. *Commentary* 83:43-7 F '87
DOT *See* United States. Dept. of Transportation
Dot matrix printers (Computers) *See* Computers—Print-out equipment
Dotson, Betty Lou
about
Dotson transferred to save pension in alleged mishap. *Jet* 72:18 Ap 20 '87
Dotson, Donald
about
Dotson's exit: a lot more than politics. A. Bernstein and S. B. Garland. por *Bus Week* p114 N 9 '87
Doty, Paul
A nuclear test ban. bibl f *Foreign Aff* 65:750-69 Spr '87
Doty, Roy, 1922-
Wordless workshop. See issues of Popular Science
Douala (Cameroon)
Tales of sister cities [Philadelphia, Pa. and Douala, Cameroon] L. Hazelton. *Black Enterp* 17:16 Mr '87
Doubilet, David
Scorpionfish: danger in disguise. il *Natl Geogr* 172:634-43 N '87
Double barreled shotguns *See* Shotguns
Double bass players
See also
Berlin, Jeff
East, Nathan
Edwards, Bernard
Haden, Charlie
Meyer, Edgar
Double Cola Co.-USA
The mouse that roared at Pepsi. S. Tefft. il *Bus Week* p42 S 7 '87
Double dare [television program] See Television program reviews—Single works

Double income, no kids couples *See* Dinks
Double stars *See* Stars, Double
Double taxation *See* Taxation, Double
Doubleday, Nelson
about
A big winner, in two leagues. N. J. Perry. il por *Fortune* 115:32-5 Ja 5 '87
Doubleday & Company, Inc.
Bantam's Vitale to head Doubleday-Dell trade group [changes in wake of Bertelsmann takeover] *Publ Wkly* 231:24 Ja 9 '87
A big winner, in two leagues [N. Doubleday] N. J. Perry. il por *Fortune* 115:32-5 Ja 5 '87
Boorstin joins Doubleday as editor-at-large. por *Publ Wkly* 232:33 O 9 '87
D'day Manufacturing reorganized with Bertelsmann. J. P. Frank. *Publ Wkly* 232:71 O 2 '87
Doubleday Book & Music Clubs
New options (positive) for the troubled Doubleday clubs [interview with P. von Puttkamer] R. A. Roel. il pors *Publ Wkly* 232:21-3 O 23 '87
Doublespeak *See* Jargon
Doucet, Jean Alfred
about
At the eye of a blistering storm. M. Rose. il pors *Macleans* 100:9 F 23 '87
Doudna, Christine
Vicki Frankovich. por *Ms* 15:74-6+ Ja '87
Dougan, Cindy
3 children who needed a medical miracle; ed. by Joan Rodman Goulianos. il *Redbook* 168:112+ F '87
Dough, Frozen *See* Food, Frozen
Dough craft
In the dough [ornaments] R. Hinderstein. il *Mother Earth News* 108:30 N/D '87
Dougherty, Steven
(ed) *See* Cooper, Ralph. Headlining the Apollo
Doughnuts
See also
Dunkin' Donuts Incorporated
Douglas, Barry
about
Music for three pianos. R. Freed. pors *Stereo Rev* 52:132 O '87
Douglas, Bobby
about
ASU grappling mentor named to Wrestling Hall. por *Jet* 73:46 O 26 '87
Douglas, Charlotte, 1936-
Report from Leningrad. il *Art Am* 75:25+ Ap '87
Douglas, J. D. (James Dixon)
Calling the next generation of Christian leaders. *Christ Today* 31:39 Ag 7 '87
Douglas, James Dixon *See* Douglas, J. D. (James Dixon)
Douglas, Kirk, 1916-
about
Sophia Loren and Kirk Douglas waltz through their latest roles as Hollywood honorees. il pors *People Wkly* 27:72-3 Ja 26 '87
Douglas, Michael
about
A bull market in sin. C. McGuigan. il por *Newsweek* 110:78-9 D 14 '87
Michael Douglas. por *People Wkly* 28:60-1 D 28 '87-Ja 4 '88
Michael Douglas [interview] R. Wallace. por *Roll Stone* p247-50 N 5-D 10 '87
Douglass, Carroll
about
Lost together in paradise. J. Kelly. il pors *Time* 129:73 F 23 '87
Douglis, Carole A.
The beat goes on. il *Psychol Today* 21:36-9+ N '87
Worldly healers. il *Omni* 9:18+ Mr '87
Doutrelant, Pierre-Marie, d. 1987
about
A reporter's reporter. F. J. Prial. il por *N Y Times Mag* p96 N 8 '87
Dove, Rita
about
Blacks win Pulitzer prizes in drama, poetry categories. pors *Jet* 72:9 My 4 '87
Introducing: Pulitzer Prize-winning poet Rita Dove. R. E. McKinney. il pors *Ebony* 42:44+ O '87
Word star. P. Giddings. por *Essence* 18:26 Ag '87
Dove shooting *See* Mourning dove shooting
Dover (N.H.)
Religious institutions and affairs
A Methodist on trial [trial of lesbian clergywoman R. Denman] M. Starr. il por *Newsweek* 110:62 S 7 '87

Dover Publications, Inc.
How to succeed in publishing with nary a best-seller. D. Cohen. il pors *Smithsonian* 18:83-6+ Jl '87
Dovichi, Norman J.
about
Very, very, very small scale [cover story] J. Raloff. il *Sci News* 132:74-5 Ag 1 '87
Dovlatov, Sergei
Father [story]; tr. by Anne Frydman. *New Yorker* 63:34-6 N 30 '87
Uncle Leopold [story]; tr. by Anne Frydman. *New Yorker* 63:25-30 Jl 13 '87
Dovring, Folke
New directions in Soviet agriculture. bibl f il *Curr Hist* 86:329-32+ O '87
Dovydenas, Elizabeth Dayton
about
An heiress vs. a pastor. G. Hackett. por *Newsweek* 109:33 Ap 20 '87
Dow, Jim
A flash in the dark. il *Pop Photogr* 94:50-5 Mr '87
A flash of color. il *Pop Photogr* 94:94-7 D '87
Dow Chemical Co.
Dow and South Africa [address, April 11, 1987] R. K. Long. *Vital Speeches Day* 53:520-4 Je 15 '87
Meanwhile in Midland. S. Flack. il *Forbes* 139:132 My 18 '87
Dow Jones averages *See* Stocks—Price indexes and averages
Dowd, Jamie
about
Career makeover: from typist to training specialist without a college degree. il *Glamour* 85:144+ My '87
Dowd, Maureen
Hot shots: why nice girls take off their clothes. il *Mademoiselle* 93:205-6+ S '87
Is Jack Kemp Mr. Right? il pors *N Y Times Mag* p18-21+ Je 28 '87
The new flirt. il *N Y Times Mag* p18 Mr 1 '87
Women with Capital clout. *Harpers Bazaar* 121:46+ N '87
Dowel joints *See* Joints (Carpentry)
Dowell, Coleman, 1925-1985
City Sundays [story] *Harpers* 274:34-5 Ap '87
Dowels
Dialing for dowel joints [doweling jig] R. Capotosto. il *Pop Mech* 164:45 O '87
Dower, John W.
The end of innocence. il *Nation* 245:224-6+ S 12 '87
Dower, Roger C.
(jt. auth) *See* Atkeson, Timothy, and Dower, Roger C.
Dower houses *See* Widows—Housing
Dowie, Mark
Apple Computer's Debi Coleman. il por *Ms* 15:60-2+ My '87
A hotel of one's own. il por *Ms* 16:38-9 D '87
Nancy Ascher, M.D.: on the frontiers of medicine. il por *Ms* 16:86+ N '87
Down beat (Periodical)
The 52nd annual Down Beat Readers Poll [with editorial comment by Art Lange] il *Down Beat* 54:6, 20-2 D '87
On the beat. See issues of Down Beat
Down Beat Student Music Awards
The 10th annual Down Beat Student Music Awards. B. Beuttler. il *Down Beat* 54:26-8 Je '87
Down syndrome
Alzheimer/Down syndrome bond tightens. *Sci News* 131:188 Mr 21 '87
β amyloid gene duplication in Alzheimer's disease and karyotypically normal Down syndrome. J.-M. Delabar and others. bibl f il *Science* 235:1390-2 Mr 13 '87
A boy who climbed the marigold [P. Burkarth's participation in horseback riding program for the handicapped] A. Jones. il pors *Read Dig* 130:96-100 F '87
Building a better mouse. J. A. Miller. il *BioScience* 37:103-6 F '87
The causes of Down syndrome. D. Patterson. il *Sci Am* 257:52-7+ Ag '87
Evidence for reduced recombination on the nondisjoined chromosomes 21 in Down syndrome. A. C. Warren and others. bibl f il *Science* 237:652-4 Ag 7 '87
My friend Emily. P. Theroux. il *Parents* 62:56+ S '87
Special talents. C. Turkington. il *Psychol Today* 21:42-6 S '87
To confound the wise and the strong. P. H. Samway. *America* 157:372 N 21 '87
Downey, Thomas J., and others
Report from Krasnoyarsk. il *Bull At Sci* 43:11-14 N '87
Downie, Sue
The next sex epidemic. il *Mademoiselle* 93:154 N '87

Downing, A. J. (Andrew Jackson), 1815-1852
about
Philosopher of the country house. R. Lynes. il por *Archit Dig* 44:35+ Je '87
Downing, Andrew Jackson *See* Downing, A. J. (Andrew Jackson), 1815-1852
Downing, Beulah
about
Bootstrap time in a luckless land. J. Buckley. il pors map *U S News World Rep* 103:88-90+ D 28 '87-Ja 4 '88
Downriggers (Fishing) *See* Trawls and trawling—Equipment
Downs, Diane
about
Unmasking a murderous mother, crime writer Ann Rule closes the book on another psychopath. M. Brower. il pors *People Wkly* 28:125 S 14 '87
Downs, Diane
Natural flea control. il *Mother Earth News* 106:29+ Jl/Ag '87
Downs, Hugh
First word. il *Omni* 9:6 Mr '87
Downs, Peter
Your money or your life. il *Progressive* 51:24-8 Ja '87
Down's syndrome *See* Down syndrome
Downspouts *See* House drainage
Downtown areas *See* Business districts
Dox family
about
"I am Bryan, your brother". J. L. Block. il por *Good Housekeep* 204:82+ Mr '87
Doyle, Sir Arthur Conan, 1859-1930
about
The enduring cult of Sherlock Holmes. D. Todd. il por *Macleans* 100:60-1 N 16 '87
The game is still afoot. S. Kanfer. il *Time* 130:76 Ag 17 '87
The game's still afoot. C. Murphy. il *Atlantic* 259:58-62+ Mr '87
The sainted sleuth, still on the case. A. Burgess. bibl il *N Y Times Book Rev* 92:1+ Ja 4 '87
Doyle, Brian
If I can make it there, I'll make it anywhere. il *U S Cathol* 52:26-33 D '87
Rebound for glory. il *U S Cathol* 52:26-33 O '87
Doyle, Conan *See* Doyle, Sir Arthur Conan, 1859-1930
Doyle, Frank P.
Labor and management [address, September 18, 1986] *Vital Speeches Day* 53:293-5 Mr 1 '87
Doyle, J. Ray
Technical page. il *Am Artist* 51:32+ S '87
Doyle, John
The economic superstate. il *Commonweal* 114:549-51 O 9 '87
Doyle, Kevin
From the editor's desk. See issues of Maclean's beginning March 14, 1983
Doyle Graf Mabley (Firm)
Nothing but the best. B. Kanner. il *N Y* 20:20-1 Jl 27 '87
DP departments *See* Electronic data processing departments
DPT vaccine
The DPT dilemma. C. Levine. il *Parents* 62:228+ Ap '87
DTP shots: benefit outweighs risk. *FDA Consum* 21:4 S '87
Dr. J *See* Erving, Julius
Dr. Lacey Kirk Williams Educational Trust
Religious leaders guide trust for black schools. *Jet* 72:13 S 14 '87
Drabble, Margaret, 1939-
The dying year [story] il *Harpers* 275:59-69 Jl '87
about
Margaret Drabble: the magic of the ordinary. M. Atwood. il *Ms* 16:62+ N '87
Two Margarets on Maggie [interview] M. Atwood. por *Ms* 16:65-6 N '87
Drabelle, Dennis
The lifeblood of wilderness. il *Wilderness* 51:36-8 Fall '87
Drabinsky, Garth, 1948-
about
King of the silver screen [cover story; special section; with editorial comment by Kevin Doyle] il pors *Macleans* 100:2, 38-42+ S 28 '87

Draco (Constellation) *See* Constellations
Draconakis, Anthimos *See* Anthimos, Bishop of Denver
Draft, Military *See* Military service, Compulsory
Draft horses *See* Horses, Draft
Draft resisters *See* Military service, Compulsory—Draft resisters
Drafting of basketball players *See* Basketball, Professional—Draft
Drafting of football players *See* Football, Professional—Draft
Drag racing
More pro, less stock [motorcycle drag racing] N. Mayersohn. il *Pop Mech* 164:48-9 Ap '87
The Teacher and the Crows [street racing in L.A.] D. Barry. il *Car Driv* 32:109+ My '87
Economic aspects
Expanding on a fast track [K. Bernstein's drag race-related enterprises] S. Gatty. il por *Nations Bus* 75:78 O '87
Drag racing cars *See* Automobiles, Racing
Dragadze, Peter
The house of Orange-Nassau's modest queen. il pors *Forbes* 140 Sp Issue:66-7 O 26 '87
The world's most underrated cities. il *Harpers Bazaar* 120:84+ Ap '87
Dragnet [film] *See* Motion picture reviews—Single works
Dragon Airlines Ltd.
A free market? J. Willoughby. il por *Forbes* 139:158 Mr 23 '87
Dragonflies
Photographs and photography
Children of the sun [excerpts from Grassroot jungles; with photographs by Frank Cocco] E. W. Teale. il *Audubon* 89:63-71 Jl '87
Dragonflies, Artificial *See* Fishing lures, flies, etc.
Dragsters *See* Automobiles, Racing
Drain, Sharon Cramer
A mechanic gave the world a lift. il *Am Hist Illus* 22:42-6+ N '87
Drain cleaning *See* Plumbing—Maintenance and repair
Drainage
See also
Catch basins
House drainage
Runoff
Drake, Charles
about
It may be a case of the 'word-blind' leading the 'word-blind,' but Charles Drake unscrambles dyslexia. K. Gross. il pors *People Wkly* 27:105-7 Mr 30 '87
Drake, J. A.
(jt. auth) *See* Mooney, Harold A., and Drake, J. A.
Drake, Jim
about
Police Academy 4 [film] Reviews
People Wkly il 27:14 Ap 20 '87. R. Novak
Drake, Teddy Millington- *See* Millington-Drake, Teddy
Drakulich, Slavenka
Hard rain falls on Yugoslavia. il *Nation* 244:177-8+ F 14 '87
Wanted: a nude *glasnost*. il *Nation* 244:846-8 Je 20 '87
Yugoslav youth stir it up. il *Nation* 244:601-3 My 9 '87
DRAM (Dynamic random access memory) *See* Random access memory
Drama
See also
Black drama
College and school drama
Detective and mystery plays
Indian drama (East Indian)
Opera
Television broadcasting—Drama
Theater
Study and teaching
See also
College and school drama
Shakespeare, William, 1564-1616—Study and teaching
Yale University. School of Drama
Technique
Conflict: the heartbeat of a play. D. R. Andersen. *Writer* 100:14-17+ S '87
Roles in collision: a play begins. J. Sweet. il *Writer* 100:16-18 My '87
Themes
See also
AIDS (Disease) in drama
Anti-Semitism in drama
Black family in drama

Drama—Themes—See also—*cont.*
    Conflict (Psychology) in drama
    Holocaust, Jewish (1939-1945), in drama
    Zionism in drama
Drama, Filmed *See* Motion picture adaptations
Drama critics and criticism
    See also
    Theater reviews
    Tynan, Kenneth, 1927-1980
Snarls from the bedclothes. R. Brustein. *New Repub*
196:27-9 F 2 '87
Drama festivals

Alabama
    See also
    Alabama Shakespeare Festival

Georgia
Mystery plays in Madison. C. Griffith. il *South Living*
22:8-10 Ag '87

New York (State)
Not acting their age [Young Playwrights Festival] J.
Simon. il *N Y* 20:110 O 5 '87
Theater [Ensemble Studio Theater's Marathon '87] T.
M. Disch. *Nation* 245:30-2 Jl 4-11 '87
The theatre [Young Playwrights Festival] E. Oliver. *New
Yorker* 63:109 O 5 '87

Nova Scotia
The agitprop players [Standin' the Gaff, international
festival of leftist political theater in Sydney] C. Wood.
il *Macleans* 100:55 Je 8 '87

Ontario
    See also
    Stratford Festival (Ont.)
Breezy summer concoctions at Shaw. J. Bemrose. il
Macleans 100:49 Je 15 '87
Domestic drama that hits home [Blyth Festival] J. Bem-
rose. il *Macleans* 100:49 Ag 17 '87

Prince Edward Island
Charlottetown and the F-word [uproar over drama
festival's censorship of play about Elvis Presley] A.
Fotheringham. il *Macleans* 100:60 My 4 '87
F-words at Green Gables [Charlottetown Festival] A.
Thurlow. il *Macleans* 100:49 Jl 13 '87
Drama in education *See* Dramatization in education
Drama production and direction *See* Theater—Production
and direction
Drama reviews *See* Theater reviews
Dramatic censorship *See* Theater—Censorship
Dramatic criticism *See* Drama critics and criticism
Dramatic production *See* Theater—Production and direction
Dramatists, American
    See also
    Mamet, David
    Norman, Marsha
    Wilson, August
Anticipated communications. M. Stitt. il *Horizon* 30:10
O '87
Are directors necessary? M. Stitt. il *Horizon* 30:12 My
'87
Opportunities for today's playwrights [list of 33 theaters]
Writer 100:24-7 D '87
Dramatists, Canadian
    See also
    Dubois, René-Daniel
    Tremblay, Michel, 1942-
Dramatists, Czech
    See also
    Havel, Václav
Dramatists, English
    See also
    Orton, Joe
    Shakespeare, William, 1564-1616
Dramatists, Irish
    See also
    Beckett, Samuel, 1906-
    Wilde, Oscar, 1854-1900
Dramatists, Mexican American
    See also
    Valdez, Luis
Dramatization in education
Campus report: is there a drinker in the house? [Welles-
ley's Alcohol Informational Theater] K. FitzGerald.
il *Ms* 15:30 F '87
Smart, magical, funny 3-year-olds [work of V. G. Paley
at the University of Chicago Laboratory Nursery
School] P. La Farge. il pors *Parents* 62:160-4+ N
'87
Dranov, Paula
Caffeine redeemed? il *Health* 19:69-71 N '87
Change of life. il *N Y* 20:70-6 O 19 '87
Serious breakfast. il *Health* 19:57-8+ Mr '87

Draper, Carolyn
    about
One business owner tells her story. H. Waldrop. il por
Work Woman 12:40-1 Ap '87
Draper, Patricia
(jt. auth) See Belsky, Jay, 1952-, and Draper, Patricia
Draper, Theodore, 1912-
American hubris: from Truman to the Persian Gulf.
bibl f il *N Y Rev Books* 34:40-8 Jl 16 '87
An autopsy. bibl f il *N Y Rev Books* 34:67-77 D 17
'87
The class struggle. *New Repub* 196:29-36 Ja 26 '87
The fall of an American junta. bibl f il *N Y Rev Books*
34:45-57 O 22 '87
Reagan's junta. bibl f il *N Y Rev Books* 34:5+ Ja 29
'87
Reagan's junta [discussion of January 29, 1987 article]
N Y Rev Books 34:47-8 Ap 23 '87
The rise of the American junta. bibl f il *N Y Rev
Books* 34:47-58 O 8 '87
Draperies *See* Curtains and draperies
Dravo Corp.
Anyone got a raft? K. Hannon. il *Forbes* 140:91-2 S
7 '87
A case of rank vs. privilege [Senator A. Specter's attempt
to get Navy to reimburse Dravo Corp. for plant
construction cost overruns] T. Gup. il *Time* 130:29
S 14 '87
Drawers
Cedar lining a drawer. G. Branson. il *Fam Handyman*
37:82 My/Je '87
Sticking drawers. G. Branson. il *Fam Handyman* 37:56
F '87
Drawing
    See also
    Architectural drawing
    Doodles
    Illustration
    Landscape drawing
    Pastel drawing
    Pen drawing
    Pencil drawing
    Portrait drawing
    Scratchboard drawing
    Still life drawing
Art: details of old-master drawings. C. Eisler. il *Archit
Dig* 44:146-51+ O '87
Drawing on an old passion [work of H. Cartier-Bresson]
M. Peppiatt. il *Archit Dig* 44:40+ Ja '87
To take paper, to draw. J. Berger. il *Harpers* 275:57-60
S '87

Collectors and collecting
Da Vinci drawing tops 'triumphant' Gaines sale [J. R.
Gaines Collection] R. W. Walker. *Art News* 86:16
Ja '87
Drawn to the masters—David Tunick. J. Kornbluth.
il por *Archit Dig* 44:74+ My '87
The old master [collector I. Woodner] P. Gardner. il
por *Art News* 86:120-3 S '87

Exhibitions
The art behind the dots [work of R. Lichtenstein] D.
Solomon. il por *N Y Times Mag* p42-6+ Mr 8 '87
Drawings in the Golden Anniversary National Art Exhibi-
tion. il *Am Artist* 51:52-5 Je '87
The interpretive link. H. Drohojowska. il *Art News* 86:29+
F '87
The luck of the draw [The drawings of Roy Lichtenstein
at the Museum of Modern Art] K. Larson. il *N Y*
20:98-9 My 18 '87
Mike Parr at Ruth Siegel. E. Heartney. il *Art Am* 75:132-3
Ja '87
Polished work, divine doodles [Raphael and his circle
at the Morgan Library] il *Newsweek* 110:77 N 30
'87
A question of attitude [work of H. Cartier-Bresson] D.
Lanchner. il *Art News* 86:11 D '87
Raphael and his circle: Pierpont Morgan Library. M.
E. Haus. il *Art News* 86:144 D '87
Raphael's drawings. A. C. Danto. *Nation* 245:765-7 D
19 '87
Roy Lichtenstein: master of the Benday dot [The drawings
of Roy Lichtenstein at the Museum of Modern Art]
E. Heartney. il *Art News* 86:210 Summ '87
Susanna Coffey. S. Taylor. il *Art News* 86:58+ Ja '87
Toddling toward modernism [Interpretive link exhibit]
J. Perl. il *Vogue* 177:106 Mr '87
View points [P. Ireland's paper and rope drawings] C.
Ratcliff. il *Art Am* 75:96-103 Mr '87

Drawing—*cont.*

Study and teaching

Watching the artist watch nature [J. Arnosky's Drawing from nature TV series] K. O. Fakih. il por *Publ Wkly* 231:43-4 My 29 '87

Technique

Techniques of drawing: Richard C. Hoff [graphite drawing] R. C. Hoff. il por *Am Artist* 51:64-7 S '87

Drawing, Children's *See* Children's art

Drawing from nature [television program] *See* Television program reviews—Single works

Drawing rooms

Museum accessions [restoration of R. Adam's drawing room from the Lansdowne House at the Philadelphia Museum of Art] E. H. Gustafson. il *Antiques* 131:1228-9 Je '87

Drawings *See* Drawing

Drayton, Leslie

about

Leslie Drayton. E. Tiegel. il por *Down Beat* 54:47-8 Ja '87

DrDesign (Firm)

1990 Cessna? [Cessna 210 update by DrDesign] il *Flying* 114:66-70 F '87

Dreamgirls [musical] *See* Musicals, revues, etc.—Reviews—Single works

Dreams

See also

Nightmares

Daydream believers [aborigines] S. Cuyler. il *Omni* 9:16+ Je '87

The dream machine [DreamWorks computer program] S. Ditlea. il *Omni* 10:34 O '87

Dreams: a journey into the mind. S. Perry. il *Curr Health 2* 13:11-13 Ja '87

Family dreams [work of Edward Taub-Bynum] S. Baker. il *Omni* 9:112 Ap '87

Heavy traffic on the royal road [dreamwork movement] A. Toufexis. il *Time* 130:76 O 12 '87

Power trips: controlling your dreams [cover story] S. LaBerge and J. Gackenbach. il *Omni* 9 Omni Exper:1-3 Ap '87

Recurrent dreams [study by psychologists Ronald Brown and Donald Donderi] L. Wallach. il *Omni* 9:35 F '87

REM sleep: pilot light of the mind? L. Miller. il *Psychol Today* 21:8+ S '87

Sleep on it. M. Nelson. il *Nations Bus* 75:72+ D '87

A vision of murder [S. Linscott tried for murder on basis of dream] M. Green. il pors *People Wkly* 27:30-2 My 25 '87

What pregnant dreams mean. M. Vogel. il *Parents* 62:120-2+ My '87

Your dreams: what you can learn from them! J. Morris. il *Good Housekeep* 204:12+ Ap '87

Dred Scott case

In pursuit of civil rights. M. Corbett. il *Natl Parks* 61:20-1 Mr/Ap '87

Dreifus, Claudia

If anything good comes from the farm crisis, it will be a new respect for the skills of rural women. il *Glamour* 85:190-1+ Ja '87

Margarita Papandreou [interview] il *Progressive* 51:21-4 D '87

No refugees need apply. il *Atlantic* 259:32-5 F '87

Sergio Ramirez: the view from Managua [interview] il por *Progressive* 51:19-20 S '87

Dreistadt, Steve H., and Dahlsten, Donald L.

Report on reports: Pesticide resistance: strategies and tactics for management [report of National Research Council conference, 1984] bibl f *Environment* 29:25-7 Ap '87

Drell, Sidney D. (Sidney David), 1926-

In defense of ABM—and Star Wars. *Harpers* 274:21-3 Je '87

Stop early SDI deployment. *Bull At Sci* 43:3 Ap '87

Thoughts of a retiring APS president. il *Phys Today* 40 pt1:56-62 Ag '87

Verification and arms control [with editorial comment by Daniel E. Koshland, Jr.] bibl f *Science* 235:406-14 Ja 23 '87

Dreman, David N.

The contrarian. See alternate issues of Forbes

Dresden (Germany)

Galleries and museums

See also

Deutsches Hygiene-Museum (Dresden, Germany)

Dresden Festival *See* Music festivals—Germany (East)

Dress *See* Clothing and dress

Dress accessories

Accessories: the decorative edge! il *Vogue* 177:466-77 Mr '87

Accessory update: what to revive, pack away and splurge on this summer. il *Glamour* 85:57 Je '87

Details! Details! M. C. Stevens. *Redbook* 169:82-3 Ag '87

Extra accessory status. il *Harpers Bazaar* 120:112+ S '87

Great finds. il *Harpers Bazaar* 120:54+ Ap '87

New breed accessories . . . il *Vogue* 177:234-9 Je '87

Special effects: do-it-yourself chic. il *Mademoiselle* 93:44 Ja '87

Dress codes (Students) *See* Clothing and dress—Students

Dress designers *See* Fashion designers

Dress forms

Make custom dress forms. K. Kearney. il *Theatre Crafts* 21:96-8 N '87

Dresser, Christopher, 1834-1904

about

Dresser's success. M. Filler. il *House Gard* 159:32+ N '87

Dressers (Furniture) *See* Chests

Dresses *See* Clothing and dress

Dressing (Stuffing) *See* Stuffing (Food)

Dressing booths

Portable dressing booth [for portrait, fashion or figure photography] T. F. Fuller. il *Petersens Photogr Mag* 16:74-5 Jl '87

Dressing of fish *See* Fish, Dressing of

Dressing of game *See* Game, Dressing of

Dressler, Alan

The large-scale streaming of galaxies. bibl (p120) il *Sci Am* 257:46-54 S '87

Drew, Elizabeth

Letter from Washington. *New Yorker* 63:140-6+ My 4 '87

Letter from Washington. *New Yorker* 62:95-102+ F 16 '87

Letter from Washington. *New Yorker* 63:112+ D 21 '87

Letter from Washington. *New Yorker* 63:124-32+ D 14 '87

Letter from Washington. *New Yorker* 63:150-4+ N 2 '87

Letter from Washington. *New Yorker* 63:71-89 Ag 31 '87

Letter from Washington. *New Yorker* 63:75-6+ Je 22 '87

Letter from Washington. *New Yorker* 63:111-19 Mr 30 '87

Drew, John, 1954-

about

Ex-Hawks star John Drew sentenced in drug case. *Jet* 71:49 F 2 '87

Drew, Nicholas *See* Harling, Robert, 1910-

Drew (Charles R.) Postgraduate Medical School *See* Charles R. Drew Postgraduate Medical School

Drew Pearson Enterprises

An all-star entrepreneur. L. Gite. il por *Black Enterp* 17:22 F '87

Drexel Burnham Lambert Incorporated

Buying 30-year Treasuries is 'the last thing I would do right now' [views of M. F. Ramirez] D. Zigas. il por *Bus Week* p163 D 28 '87-Ja 4 '88

The case against Drexel: will the government come up short? C. Welles. il por *Bus Week* p56-60 Ag 10 '87

A chat with Michael Milken. A. Sloan. il por *Forbes* 140:248+ Jl 13 '87

Did Drexel bully takeover candidates? [suit brought by Staley Continental] C. Welles. *Bus Week* p43-4 Mr 9 '87

Does Drexel have a game plan for Mattel? G. G. Marcial. il *Bus Week* p76 F 9 '87

The Drexel connection [potential partners in Western Union takeover offer scared off by Pacific Asset's dealings with Drexel] J. Crudele. *N Y* 20:24 Ap 20 '87

Drexel in the cross hairs [SEC investigation] B. Powell and C. Friday. il *Newsweek* 109:48 F 16 '87

Drexel sweats the SEC probe. S. P. Sherman. il *Fortune* 115:38-42 Mr 16 '87

Drexel's clients are rallying 'round Milken. C. Welles. il *Bus Week* p74 Ap 20 '87

Drexel's heavy hand [bid to restructure Western Union] C. Friday. il *Newsweek* 110:53+ N 23 '87

An extra slice of the pie [special investment in I. Boesky's arbitrage fund] A. Sloan. il *Forbes* 139:32-3 F 9 '87

Drexel Burnham Lambert Incorporated—*cont.*
Frederick Joseph. A. Bianco. por *Bus Week* Sp Issue:212 Ap 17 '87
A 'junk' king takes on the third world [M. R. Milken's debt crisis offensive] B. Powell and C. Friday. il por *Newsweek* 110:56 S 21 '87
Let's-make-a-deal time on the Street. A. Gabor. il *U S News World Rep* 102:48 F 2 '87
Mattel has to play harder than ever [main shareholders, Warburg and Drexel, want a turnaround] J. Flynn. il *Bus Week* p60-1 My 25 '87
Me too, me too [Drexel Burnham Lambert's killing in the leveraged buyout and breakup of the old Beatrice Cos.] L. Jereski. *Forbes* 140:38 S 21 '87
Mystery man of mergers [M. Milken] A. E. Serwer. il por *Fortune* 115:50 Ja 5 '87
Now Drexel Burnham is fighting on two fronts [SEC allegations] C. Welles. il por *Bus Week* p90-3+ F 16 '87
'An outrageous violation' of fairness [interview with F. Joseph] il por *U S News World Rep* 102:39 F 23 '87
A record turnout for Drexel's junk-bond bash [conference in Beverly Hills] A. Bianco. il por *Bus Week* p80 Ap 13 '87
Rivals refuse to be out on a limb with Drexel Burnham. C. P. Work. il *U S News World Rep* 102:41 Ap 6 '87
'Spin control' on Wall Street. J. Reed. il *U S News World Rep* 102:46 Ap 20 '87
Were Drexel and Boesky in cahoots? J. Egan and D. Baer. il por *U S News World Rep* 102:45 F 16 '87
Why Mike Milken is suddenly taking himself public. C. Welles. il pors *Bus Week* p27-8 S 7 '87

Drexler, Jerome, 1927-
about
Hurry up and wait for optical-memory cards. J. W. Wilson. il por *Bus Week* p89+ F 9 '87

Drexler, Millard S.
about
Put the zipper on the back. H. Rudnitsky. il por *Forbes* 139:89-90 Je 29 '87

Drexler Technology Corp.
Hurry up and wait for optical-memory cards. J. W. Wilson. il por *Bus Week* p89+ F 9 '87

Dreyfus, Alfred, 1859-1935
about
The Dreyfus affair: Jewish Museum. M. Moorman. il *Art News* 86:152+ D '87
The other fin de siècle. K. Silver. bibl f il *Art Am* 75:104-11+ D '87

Dreyfus, René
about
Rising to greatness. T. West. il pors *Road Track* 38:56-60 Mr '87

Dreyfus Capital Value Fund
Knowing when to say 'when' made his fund no. 1 [S. Salvigsen] G. Weiss. il por *Bus Week* p160 D 28 '87-Ja 4 '88

Dreyfus Corp.
Has the lion been tamed? R. L. Stern. il por *Forbes* 140:76+ S 21 '87
Liquid lion. T. Jaffe. il *Forbes* 139:122 Je 29 '87

Dreyfuss, Richard, 1947-
about
The Dreyfuss affair [cover story] J. Kaplan. il pors *Esquire* 108:144-8+ N '87
A wise guy's resurrection. D. Ansen. il pors *Newsweek* 110:56-7 Ag 10 '87

Drier, Deborah
The defiant ones. il pors *Art Am* 75:47-9+ S '87
Designing women. il pors *Art Am* 75:21-3 My '87

Driesell, Lefty
about
Driesell denies saying cocaine helps athletes. *Jet* 72:50 Jl 6 '87

Driessen, Paul K.
Oil rigs and sea life: a shotgun marriage that works. il *Sea Front* 33:362-72 S/O '87

Drift (Dispersal) *See* Dispersal (Ecology)
Drift bottles
Drift bottle update [1981-82 Pacific Ocean launch] il map *Natl Geogr World* 146:20 O '87
Drifting of continents *See* Continental drift
Drill press *See* Drilling and boring machinery
Drill teams
For his opening act in L.A. the Pope can thank Kay Crawford, mother of the modern drill team. J. Calio. il pors *People Wkly* 28:105-6 S 21 '87

Drilling and boring (Earth and rocks)
Borehole measurement of the Newtonian gravitational constant. A. T. Hsui. bibl f il map *Science* 237:881-3 Ag 21 '87
Drilling into a deep controversy [deep-earth-gas theory of Thomas Gold] R. Monastersky. *Sci News* 131:380-1 Je 13 '87
Getting to the bottom of the San Andreas [Cajon Pass hole] S. Weisburd. *Sci News* 131:70 Ja 31 '87
Is the San Andreas weak at heart? R. A. Kerr. il *Science* 236:388-9 Ap 24 '87
Sounding the inner earth for gas and oil [deep-earth-gas theory of Thomas Gold] *Environment* 29:22-3 Jl/Ag '87

Drilling and boring machinery
See also
Jigs (Tools)
Build a drillpress. G. D. Lydecker. il *Theatre Crafts* 21:75 F '87
Cordless drill with punch [Ryobi Driver-Drill] H. Wicks. il *Home Mech* 83:75 Je '87
Quick-draw drill [Black & Decker cordless drill/screwdriver] R. Capotosto. il *Pop Mech* 164:48 Je '87
Triple-duty drill [Skil Xtra] R. Capotosto. il *Pop Mech* 164:19 Ag '87

Equipment
See also
Bits (Drilling and boring)
Portable drill accessories. H. Wicks. il *Home Mech* 83:28 Je '87

Drilling funds (Oil wells) *See* Petroleum investment trusts
Drilling rig workers *See* Petroleum workers
Drilling rigs, Oil well *See* Oil well drilling rigs
Drills, Fire *See* Fire drills
Drills (Machinery) *See* Drilling and boring machinery
Drinan, Robert F.
Human rights and the Pope's visit to Chile. *America* 156:227-8 Mr 21 '87
Religion and the future of human rights. il *Christ Century* 104:683-7 Ag 12-19 '87
Should a Mormon-owned corporation be able to fire a Mormon who does not tithe? il *America* 156:375-6 My 9 '87
A thousand days' detention. il *America* 157:247-9 O 17 '87

Drinking and driving *See* Alcohol and automobile drivers
Drinking and employment *See* Alcohol and employment
Drinking and the aged *See* Alcohol and the aged
Drinking customs
The unsocial drinker: another round? [study by R. Lorraine Collins] C. Greene. il *Psychol Today* 21:66 Mr '87

History
The geography of drinking. C. J. Smith. il map *Focus* 36:16-23 Wint '86

Drinking problem *See* Alcoholics and alcoholism
Drinking vessels
See also
Mugs

Collectors and collecting
GAR tumbler: Gen. George H. Thomas [Grand Army of the Republic] M. Wollett and B. Wollett. il *Antiques Collect Hobbies* 92:53 Mr '87
Garfield memorial tumbler. M. Wollett and B. Wollett. il *Antiques Collect Hobbies* 92:53 S '87

Drinking water
See also
Bottled water
International Drinking Water Supply and Sanitation Decade, 1981-1990
Water coolers
How safe is the water your family drinks? M. Cala. bibl il *Home Mech* 83:60-2+ F '87
How trustworthy is your tap water? il *Consum Rep* 52:48 Ja '87
Is our drinking water safe? J. Schmid. il *Vogue* 177:406-7+ O '87

Analysis
See Water—Analysis

Laws and regulations
See also
Safe Drinking Water Act

Drinking water—*cont.*
Pollution
See Water pollution
Purification
See Water purification
Drinks *See* Alcoholic beverages; Beverages
Drip irrigation *See* Watering of gardens, lawns, etc.
Drip irrigation equipment *See* Irrigation equipment
Driscoll, Dennis M.
Windchill. bibl il *Weatherwise* 40:321-6 D '87
Driscoll, Ellen
about
Ellen Driscoll. J. Sturman. il por *Art News* 86:83-4 My
'87
Drive-in restaurants
The bargainburger makes a new stand. J. B. Copeland.
il *Newsweek* 109:45 Je 1 '87
Driver, Senta
about
Reviews:
Performances at the Joyce Theater, New York City.
S. Sommer. *Dance Mag* 61:38-9 Ap '87
Driver education *See* Automobile driving—Study and
teaching
Driveways
Hidden driveway ahead . . . what should you do? D.
Chaikin. il *Home Mech* 83:22 Jl '87
Maintenance and repair
Seal a blacktop drive. G. Branson. il *Fam Handyman*
37:74 O '87
Driving, Automobile *See* Automobile driving
Driving, Motor vehicle *See* Motor vehicle driving
Driving gloves *See* Gloves
Driving Miss Daisy [drama] See Uhry, Alfred
Driving tests, Automobile *See* Automobile drivers—Testing
Drohan, Madelaine
Trade: a Canadian view. *World Press Rev* 34:47 D '87
Drohojowska, Hunter
Beyond flower power. il por *Harpers Bazaar* 121:224-5+
N '87
Graceful details: classical lines in a designer's Los Angeles
villa. il *Archit Dig* 44:66-71 Ag '87
New directions in style. il por *Archit Dig* 44:252+ My
'87
Drone aircraft *See* Remotely piloted vehicles
Dropouts
An alternative to alternative education [dropout preven-
tion program in Corpus Christi, Tex.] D. Banks. *Educ
Dig* 53:33-5 D '87
Budget constraints hinder school dropout programs. *Phi
Delta Kappan* 68:716-17 My '87
Business offers a hand to education. M. J. Justiz and
M. C. Kameen. bibl f il *Phi Delta Kappan* 68:379-83
Ja '87
A "culture of concern" for at-risk students. R. Valdivieso.
Educ Dig 52:29-31 Ag '87
Declaring academic bankruptcy: another chance at college.
A. D. Browne. *Educ Dig* 53:46-9 N '87
Graduation-contingent student aid: fighting the high costs
of dropping out. F. J. Fischer. il *Change* 19:40-7
N/D '87
Helping dropouts drop in [Covenant House-St. Michael's
College program] J. N. Baker. il *Newsweek* 110:63
Ag 3 '87
Looking at America's dropouts: who are they? L. W.
Barber and M. C. McClellan. il *Phi Delta Kappan*
69:264-7 D '87
One community's response to the dropout problem [Er-
win, N.C.] G. H. Arnold and V. Biggers. *Phi Delta
Kappan* 68:708-9 My '87
Reaching out to America's dropouts: what to do? [cover
story] A. Hahn. il *Phi Delta Kappan* 69:256-63 D
'87
Top-grade perks for teens [program at DuSable High
School, Chicago] M. Oshin. il *Essence* 18:38 Je '87
Drops
Dew drops on a bathroom mirror. C. F. Bohren. il
Weatherwise 40:102-6 Ap '87
Dropping smoothly to a fiery end [fuel combustion
research by Thomas Avedisian and Jiann Yang] I.
Peterson. il *Sci News* 132:71 Ag 1 '87
Soap bubble meteorology. M. J. Iacono and D. C.
Blanchard. il *Weatherwise* 40:141-2 Je '87
Drosophila
Cloning of genomic and complementary DNA from
Shaker, a putative potassium channel gene from
Drosophila. D. M. Papazian and others. bibl f il *Science*
237:749-53 Ag 14 '87

Genomic organization and deduced amino acid sequence
of a putative sodium channel gene in Drosophila.
L. Salkoff and others. bibl f il *Science* 237:744-9 Ag
14 '87
Heritable somatic excision of a Drosophila transposon.
G. J. Bryan and others. bibl f il *Science* 235:1636-8
Mr 27 '87
Homeo boxes in the study of development. W. J. Gehring.
bibl f il *Science* 236:1245-52 Je 5 '87
Hybrid dysgenesis in D. melanogaster is not a general
release mechanism for DNA transpositions. R. C.
Woodruff and others. bibl f il *Science* 237:1206-8
S 4 '87
The lords of the flies. S. Brownlee. il *Discover* 8:26-9+
Ap '87
On the rescue gene and the origin of species [work
of Michael Ashburner and Pierre Hutter] *Discover*
8:6-7 Ag '87
Purification and properties of Drosophila heat shock
activator protein. C. Wu and others. bibl f il *Science*
238:1247-53 N 27 '87
Sequence of a probable potassium channel component
encoded at Shaker locus of Drosophila. B. L. Tempel
and others. bibl f il *Science* 237:770-5 Ag 14 '87
Single-channel and genetic analyses reveal two distinct
A-type potassium channels in Drosophila. C. K. Solc
and others. bibl f il *Science* 236:1094-8 My 29 '87
Development
See Insects—Development
Embryology
See Embryology—Insects
Droste, Bernd von
Sustainable development. il *Courier* 40:4-7 O '87
Droughts
In the United States—flash floods and drought [1986]
D. Le Comte. il *Weatherwise* 40:12-16 F '87
The role of drought in outbreaks of plant-eating insects.
W. J. Mattson and R. A. Haack. bibl f il *BioScience*
37:110-18 F '87
Africa
African drought subject of regional seminar. *UN Chron*
23:60 Ja '86
Drought in Africa. M. H. Glantz. il maps *Sci Am*
256:34-40 Je '87
Brazil
A land of contrasts [waters of the Amazon contrasted
with drought-stricken Northeast] T. de Mello. il map
Courier 39:4-10 D '86
Mali
Making of a desert [Landsat images help study effects
of 20-year drought on the Inland Niger Delta in Mali;
work of Patricia Jacobberger] J. Dall'Acqua. il map
Earth Sci 40:19-21 Spr '87
United States
See Droughts
Zimbabwe
Where elephants die [Hwange National Park] G. Haynes.
il *Nat Hist* 96:28-33 Je '87
Drowning
Coming back to life [K. Ryan survives coma after almost
drowning] F. M. Henley. il pors *Ladies Home J* 104:34+
Jl '87
Prevention
Teach your child swimming safety. il *Glamour* 85:38
Jl '87
What to do if your car hits deep water. D. McCluggage.
Glamour 85:144+ Je '87
Drowning rescues *See* Rescue work
Drownproofing *See* Drowning—Prevention
Drozak, Frank
The Soviet maritime threat [address, March 17, 1987]
Vital Speeches Day 53:534-7 Je 15 '87
Drucker, David J.
Money management: 5 mistakes you don't have to make.
il por *Changing Times* 41:27-8+ Ag '87
Drucker, Peter Ferdinand, 1909-
Japan's choices. bibl f *Foreign Aff* 65:923-41 Summ
'87
Japan's economic choices. *Current* 296:33-40 O '87
about
Advice from the Dr. Spock of business [interview] J.
A. Byrne. il por *Bus Week* p61+ S 28 '87
Where Japan will turn next [interview] il por *U S News
World Rep* 103:45 Ag 24 '87
'The worst thing is to modernize' [interview] por *U
S News World Rep* 102:23 F 2 '87
Drucker, Stephen
The look of glitz. il *Vogue* 177:320-1 D '87
Psyching it out. *Vogue* 177:208-9+ Ja '87

Drug abuse
See also
Alcoholics and alcoholism
Children of drug addicts
Cocaine
Crack (Cocaine)
Drug education
Drugs and air pilots
Drugs and airplane accidents
Drugs and artists
Drugs and brokers
Drugs and celebrities
Drugs and crime
Drugs and employment
Drugs and judges
Drugs and mass media
Drugs and musicians
Drugs and physicians
Drugs and politicians
Drugs and public officers
Drugs and sports
Drugs and the aged
Drugs and the mentally ill
Drugs and the press
Drugs and women
Drugs and youth
Heroin
Marijuana
United States. Congress. House. Select Committee
on Narcotics Abuse and Control
9 days in June. il *Life* 10:83-5 Ja '87
Addicted! O. Davies. *Health* 19:71-3+ Jl '87
Black mayors rap funding for U.S. war on drugs. *Jet* 73:6 N 16 '87
Citizen Ueberroth [interview] R. B. Cramer. il pors *Esquire* 107:69-72+ F '87
The debate over drug use. B. Brophy. il *U S News World Rep* 103:26 N 16 '87
Drug addicts with dirty needles [AIDS connection] W. A. Schwartz. il *Nation* 244:843-6 Je 20 '87
Fighting drugs. M. S. Kreiter. il *Curr Health 2* 13:12-15 Ap '87
Grave new world. M. Jacobson. il *Esquire* 108:65+ S '87
Reefer madness [Reagan antidrug campaign] A. Hoffman. *Nation* 245:580-1 N 21 '87
This is what you thought: 56% say kids should report drug-using parents [results of survey] *Glamour* 85:125 Mr '87
The toll: bad news for women and I.V. users [AIDS deaths] *Newsweek* 110:85 N 2 '87
What's behind 'Jar Wars'. H. Levine and C. Reinarman. il *Nation* 244:388-90 Mr 28 '87
Who's cool today—and who isn't. J. Kelly. por *U S News World Rep* 102:9 Ap 20 '87

Conferences
See also
International Conference on Drug Abuse and Illicit Trafficking
Meeting on NGO involvement in combating drug use held in Sweden. *UN Chron* 23:108 N '86

International aspects
Enforcement alone is not enough to fight drug abuse. il *World Health* p30-1 O '87
'A perverse logic'. J. Baudrillard. il *Courier* 40:7-9 Jl '87

Rehabilitation
See also
Health Concepts IV Inc.
KIDS of Bergen County (Program)
Naltrexone
National Teen Challenge (Organization)
An ex-con's journey to the right side of the law [D. Streater] L. B. Randolph. il pors *Ebony* 42:38-40+ O '87
A letter from one who knows [Smithers Center program] *Sports Illus* 66:33 Ap 13 '87
The long road back. S. Begley. il *Newsweek* 109:66 My 11 '87
Sobering facts on rehab. R. Phalon. il *Forbes* 139:140+ Mr 9 '87
Suns' Walter Davis seeks to build drug clinic. *Jet* 73:50 O 12 '87

Testing
See also
Sports Medicine Drug Identification Laboratory
Air traffic controllers sue to block FAA drug testing. C. Preble. *Aviat Week Space Technol* 126:32-3 Mr 2 '87
Another NCAA fumble [judge rules against testing policy] B. Newman. il por *Sports Illus* 67:100 D 7 '87

Big John [guidelines for administering drug tests to federal workers] il *Time* 129:19 Mr 2 '87
Black federal workers oppose drug testing. *Jet* 72:23 Je 22 '87
"But I've never used drugs". F. Lunzer. il *Forbes* 140:442 Jl 13 '87
The case against drug testing. A. M. O'Keefe. *Psychol Today* 21:34-5+ Je '87
Did she or didn't she? [pentathlete L. Norwood banned after positive drug test] S. Francis. il *Women's Sports Fitness* 9:22 Ap '87
Diver just says no [Stanford's S. LeVant refuses to submit to drug tests] A. Ferber. il por *Women's Sports Fitness* 9:25 My '87
Doctors square off on employee drug testing. C. Holden. il *Science* 238:744-5 N 6 '87
Drug charges lose steam as Suns' trio pass tests [Phoenix Suns basketball team] il *Jet* 72:47 My 11 '87
Drug testing OK with most black pilots, execs say. *Jet* 71:32 F 23 '87
Drug tests in the workplace: are they reliable? D. Groves. *McCalls* 114:155 My '87
Drug tests may explain why Vida Blue retired. por *Jet* 71:50 Mr 23 '87
Drugs, AIDS and the threat to privacy. Y. Kamisar. il *N Y Times Mag* p108-10+ S 13 '87
Free enterprise rushes to fill a delicate need [mail order urine samples circumvent drug testing regulations] D. Collins. il *U S News World Rep* 102:10 F 23 '87
Getting tough on drugs [Calgary Olympics] H. Quinn. il *Macleans* 100:46-7 O 5 '87
Just say no [testing pilots] E. Weiner. *Flying* 114:24+ Ap '87
Just say no . . . to mandatory drug testing [athletes] N. Cohen. *Sport Mag* 78:6 My '87
Mandatory drug testing may spark racism: Page [sports testing; views of A. Page] por *Jet* 72:46 Ag 31 '87
Maury Wills favors drug testing for all players. il por *Jet* 71:46 Mr 2 '87
On-the-job drug tests: what to know. C. Kitch. il *Good Housekeep* 204:145 Ja '87
Pissing contests [guidelines for drug testing of federal employees] *Harpers* 274:19-20 My '87
Reagan administration drug testing program [federal employees] *Congr Dig* 66:131-60 My '87
Urine tests can be misleading [views of Roger P. Maickel] *USA Today (Periodical)* 115:13 F '87
What managers must know about drug testing. S. Rose. *Work Woman* 12:20 Ap '87

Canada
New campaigns in the war on drugs. M. McIver. il *Macleans* 100:44 Je 8 '87

Eastern Europe
Shooting up under a Red star. J. Hull. il *Time* 129:46 Ja 19 '87

Great Britain
See also
Institute for the Study of Drug Dependence

Kenya
The street boys of Nairobi. I. Ndirangu. *World Press Rev* 34:57 S '87

Mexico
Puppets versus drugs [Youth Integration Centres] E. Massün. il *World Health* p2-5 Je '87

Soviet Union
Shooting up under a Red star. J. Hull. il *Time* 129:46 Ja 19 '87

United States
See Drug abuse
Drug addicts See Drug abuse
Drug and food interactions in the body See Drugs—Physiological effects
Drug control See Narcotics laws and regulations
Drug delivery systems in the body See Drugs—Dosage forms
Drug education
Drug programs show mixed results [views of Robert Bangert-Drowns] *USA Today (Periodical)* 116:7+ Ag '87
Howard, Grambling get fed. funds for anti drug plans. *Jet* 73:32 N 2 '87
One mother's crusade against drug abuse [interview with L. Bias] pors *Christ Today* 31:50+ My 15 '87
School-based drug education: what is wrong? M. S. Goodstadt. *Educ Dig* 52:44-7 F '87
"We're teaching our kids to use drugs". P. Mann. il *Read Dig* 131:106-10 N '87

International aspects
How should we attack the drug problem? G. Di Gennaro. il *Courier* 40:10-13 Jl '87
Learning to live. N. Friderich. il *Courier* 40:5-6 Jl '87

Drug education—International aspects—*cont.*
　Unesco and drugs. il *Courier* 40:6-7 Jl '87
Drug Enforcement Administration (U.S.) *See* United States.
　Drug Enforcement Administration
Drug industry
　　See also
　　A. H. Robins Company, Inc.
　　Baxter Travenol Laboratories Inc.
　　Bolar Pharmaceutical Co.
　　Burroughs Wellcome Co.
　　Carter-Wallace, Inc.
　　Direct Pharmaceutical Corp.
　　Eli Lilly and Company
　　Enzon, Inc.
　　Generix Drug Corporation
　　Hoffmann-La Roche Inc.
　　ICN Pharmaceuticals, Inc.
　　Lee Pharmaceuticals
　　McKesson Corp.
　　Medi-Rx America, Inc.
　　Merck & Co., Inc.
　　Merrell Dow Pharmaceutical Inc.
　　Miles Laboratories, Inc.
　　Monsanto Company
　　Mylan Laboratories Inc.
　　Nova Pharmaceutical Corp.
　　Ortho Pharmaceutical Corporation
　　Pfizer Inc.
　　Procter & Gamble Co.
　　Rorer Group Inc.
　　Schering-Plough Corp.
　　SmithKline Beckman Corp.
　　Squibb Corp.
　　Sterling Drug Inc.
　　Syntex Corp.
　　VLI Corporation
　　Warner-Lambert Company
　　Zenith Laboratories, Inc.
The generic drug industry: an overview [address, October 8, 1987] M. Zeiger. *Vital Speeches Day* 54:142-7 D 15 '87

Acquisitions and mergers
Buying into Chapter 11: the method in Rorer's madness [bid for A. H. Robins] C. S. Eklund. il *Bus Week* p73-4 Jl 20 '87
Has Perelman taken a shine to Sterling Drug? [R. O. Perelman] G. G. Marcial. il por *Bus Week* p101 Jl 13 '87

Advertising
Block, Block, fizz, fizz [Alka-Seltzer and H&R Block join advertising forces] S. D. Atchison. il *Bus Week* p36 Mr 30 '87
Six months and half a million dollars, all for 15 seconds [Young & Rubicam does a television commercial for Warner-Lambert's Rolaids] J. E. Pfeiffer. il *Smithsonian* 18:134-8+ O '87

Ethical aspects
Playing hide and seek with FDA [Generix Corp.'s fraudulent activities] R. C. Thompson. il *FDA Consum* 21:36-7 Ap '87
Scandal in Sweden: how the Fermenta dream turned sour. J. Kapstein. il por *Bus Week* p68-9 Je 8 '87
What's not in the prospectus [Medi-Rx management linked to drug diversion business] G. Morgenson. il *Forbes* 140:61-2 Jl 27 '87

Export-import trade
Japan's push in pharmaceuticals. J. Dreyfuss. il *Fortune* 116:85-6 Jl 20 '87
A new drug deal with China [Canada and China] P. C. Newman. il *Macleans* 100:31 S 14 '87

Finance
The cost of new drugs raises the roof. S. Budiansky. il *U S News World Rep* 102:47 Ap 6 '87
For drugmakers, these will be the good old days. J. H. Cutaia. il *Bus Week* p94 Ja 12 '87
Health. M. Fritz. il *Forbes* 139:140+ Ja 12 '87
Who has the next wonder drug? il *Fortune* 116:8 S 28 '87

International aspects
Overdose. G. Peters. il *Courier* 40:21-4 Ag '87

Laws and regulations
See Drug laws and regulations

Marketing
　See also
　Orphan drugs
The big lie about generic drugs. il *Consum Rep* 52:480-5 Ag '87
The birth of the calcium business. J. Sherman. il *Work Woman* 12:46 Jl '87

Securities
AIDS stocks worth the gamble. M. McFadden. il *Fortune* 115:113-14 Ap 13 '87
Counting on a cure [AIDS-related stocks] D. R. Katz. il *Esquire* 108:71-2 N '87
Prescription for profits [views of D. Paisley] G. Bronson. il por *Forbes* 140:65-6 O 19 '87
The quest for an AIDS cure is igniting stocks. K. Deveny. il *Bus Week* p82-3 Je 29 '87
Still prescribing drug stocks [interview with W. J. Hayes] A. E. Serwer. il por *Fortune* 115:112 F 16 '87
These stocks are not drugs on the market. K. R. Sheets. il *U S News World Rep* 102:53 Mr 30 '87

Suits and claims
Deformed D.C. boy gets $95 million award in product liability suit [award to S. Ealy in Bendectin case] por *Jet* 72:26 Ag 3 '87
The sad legacy of the Dalkon Shield. G. Kolata. *N Y Times Mag* p120 D 6 '87

Canada
　See also
　Quadra Logic Technologies Inc.

Great Britain
　See also
　Glaxo Holdings plc
　Wellcome Foundation Ltd.

Japan
Japan's push in pharmaceuticals. J. Dreyfuss. il *Fortune* 116:85-6 Jl 20 '87

Sweden
　See also
　Fermenta AB

Switzerland
　See also
　Ciba-Geigy AG

United States
　See Drug industry
Drug insurance *See* Insurance, Pharmaceutical services
Drug interactions in the body *See* Drugs—Physiological effects
Drug laws and regulations
　See also
　Drugs—Labeling
　Narcotics laws and regulations
　United States. Food and Drug Administration
Benefit vs. risk: how FDA approves new drugs. D. Farley. il *FDA Consum* 21:6-18 D '87/Ja '88
Breaking the F.D.A. drugjam [AIDS drugs] A.-C. D'Adesky. il *Nation* 245:405-6+ O 17 '87
Compassion vs. control: FDA investigational drug regulation. D. H. Gieringer. il *USA Today (Periodical)* 115:69-73 Mr '87
Dying for drugs. R. Bazell. *New Repub* 197:17-19 N 9 '87
Experimental drugs for the desperately ill. F. E. Young. il *FDA Consum* 21:2-3 Je '87
Experimental drugs for the desperately ill. F. E. Young. il *Consum Res Mag* 70:34-5 Ag '87
For athletes and dealers, black market steroids are risky business. D. Stehlin. il *FDA Consum* 21:24-5 S '87
From test tube to patient: new drug development in the United States [cover story; special section] il *FDA Consum* 21:4-15 N '87
Genentech's custody case over an orphan drug [gene-spliced human growth hormone] J. O. Hamilton. il *Bus Week* p39 Mr 23 '87
The generic drug industry: an overview [address, October 8, 1987] M. Zeiger. *Vital Speeches Day* 54:142-7 D 15 '87
Jailed [J. Bradshaw convicted of illegally distributing steroids] il *FDA Consum* 21:31 My '87
Myths and facts of generic drugs. il *FDA Consum* 21:12-14 S '87
"Operation Rx" sting [D. Hall helps break pharmacists' prescription drug scam in Los Angeles] J. Fincher. il *Read Dig* 131:36-41 S '87
A prescription for cutting the red tape. J. Seligmann. il *Newsweek* 109:52-3 Je 1 '87
Rushing drugs to market. T. Kiely. il *Technol Rev* 90:12-13 Ag/S '87

Canada
Ending a bitter stalemate [patent protection bill passed] P. Gessell. il *Macleans* 100:19 N 30 '87
Drug plants *See* Botany, Medical
Drug receptors
Cocaine receptors on dopamine transporters are related to self-administration of cocaine. M. C. Ritz and others. bibl f il *Science* 237:1219-23 S 4 '87

Drug research *See* Pharmaceutical research

Drug resistance

Cancer's genes and chemotherapy [research with P-glycoprotein mRNA by Ira Pastan and Michael M. Gottesman] *Sci News* 131:57 Ja 24 '87

Drug resistance: malaria-cancer similarity? J. Silberner. *Sci News* 131:148 Mr 7 '87

Expression of the multidrug-resistant gene in hepatocarcinogenesis and regenerating rat liver. S. S. Thorgeirsson and others. bibl f il *Science* 236:1120-2 My 29 '87

Resisting cancer chemotherapy. J. Silberner. il *Sci News* 131:12-13 Ja 3 '87

Drug testing *See* Drug abuse—Testing; Pharmaceutical research

Drug tolerance *See* Drugs—Physiological effects

Drug trade *See* Drug industry

Drug traffic *See* Narcotics trade

Druggists *See* Pharmacists

Drugs

See also
Adrenergic blocking agents
Alcohol antagonists
Amphetamines
Antacids
Antibiotics
Antidepressants
Antihistamines
Biotherapeutics
Botany, Medical
Cancer inhibiting substances
Hospitals—Pharmaceutical services
Medicines, Nonprescription
Orphan drugs
Physicians—Pharmaceutical services
Tranquilizing drugs
Veterinary drugs
See also names of drugs

Check your drug awareness: a quiz. A. Brown. il *Curr Health 2* 13:19-21 My '87

Myths and facts of generic drugs. il *FDA Consum* 21:12-14 S '87

Overdose. G. Peters. il *Courier* 40:21-4 Ag '87

Questions about your medicine? Go ahead—ask. F. E. Young. il *FDA Consum* 21:2-3 O '87

Vitamin or drug? A clarification. H. Fisher. *Prevention* 39:121-4+ My '87

Advertising

See Drug industry—Advertising

Dosage

Just another swallow away [doses for tension headache] F. Lunzer. il *Forbes* 139:224 My 18 '87

Know the right way to take your medicines. A. Hecht. il *FDA Consum* 21:22-4 My '87

Dosage forms

See also
Eye drops, washes, etc.
Nasal sprays
Pills
Transdermal patches

Camouflaged drugs make Enzon stand out [coating enzymes with polyethylene glycol] M. Bluestone. il *Bus Week* p115-16 Ap 27 '87

Cancer-killers from macrophages. J. Raloff. *Sci News* 131:215 Ap 4 '87

Feeling no pain. F. Lunzer. il *Forbes* 140:210+ N 2 '87

Firing squad [antibiotic pump implant developed by Clayton R. Perry] W. Barnhill. *Health* 19:24 Jl '87

Liposomes [use in drug delivery] M. J. Ostro. il *Sci Am* 256:102-4+ Ja '87

Making drugs stick to your stomach [work of David Harris] J. Raloff. *Sci News* 131:251 Ap 18 '87

Self-administered pain-killer. B. Bialick. il *McCalls* 114:144 Jl '87

Stuck like glue [adhesive Carbopol in time release drugs] L. Lang. *Health* 19:21 D '87

These tiny bubbles could make a big splash [liposomes] S. Siwolop and C. S. Eklund. il *Bus Week* p87-8 Jl 6 '87

Labeling

Bug spray-drug spray mix-up [pesticide mislabeled as an aerosol drug] *FDA Consum* 21:40 Mr '87

Laws and regulations

See Drug laws and regulations

Packaging

See also
West Co., Inc.

Protecting tots from drug poisonings. B. Rados. il *FDA Consum* 21:24-5 Mr '87

Patents

Ending a bitter stalemate [patent protection bill passed in Canada] P. Gessell. il *Macleans* 100:19 N 30 '87

Physiological effects

Drugs that can cause serious side effects [excerpt from The essential guide to prescription drugs] J. W. Long. il *Good Housekeep* 204:202-3 F '87

Dysaphrodisiacs [sexual dysfunction caused by prescribed drugs] E. Collins. *Sci Am* 257:42+ O '87

Food and drugs: what mixes, what doesn't. P. Gadsby. il *Good Housekeep* 205:247-8 O '87

Kids and medicine: what to give them when. J. L. Brown. *Ladies Home J* 104:60+ Mr '87

Know the right way to take your medicines. A. Hecht. il *FDA Consum* 21:22-4 My '87

Monitoring drugs for the aged. W. I. Bennett. il *N Y Times Mag* p73-4 D 13 '87

Ordinary medicines can have extraordinary side effects. C. Hallowell. il *Redbook* 169:132-4+ My '87

'The pill' may not mix well with other drugs [birth control pills] J. Willis. il *FDA Consum* 21:26-8 Mr '87

Some foods and drugs don't mix. J. Schein. il *Consum Res Mag* 70:33-7 Mr '87

Wonder drugs with hidden dangers. K. McAuliffe. il *U S News World Rep* 103:63 S 14 '87

Prices

The big lie about generic drugs. il *Consum Rep* 52:480-5 Ag '87

Prescription drugs: how your doctor can cut your medicine bill in half [generic drugs] J. Reid. il *Money* 16:63 F '87

Psychological effects

See Psychopharmacology

Research

See Pharmaceutical research

Side effects

See Drugs—Physiological effects

Testing

See Drug abuse—Testing; Pharmaceutical research

Drugs and air pilots

Drug testing OK with most black pilots, execs say. *Jet* 71:32 F 23 '87

Just say no [testing pilots] E. Weiner. *Flying* 114:24+ Ap '87

Drugs and airplane accidents

Air traffic controllers sue to block FAA drug testing. C. Preble. *Aviat Week Space Technol* 126:32-3 Mr 2 '87

Drugs and artists

Acid test [LSD and creativity; study by Oscar Janigar] R. B. Tucker. *Omni* 10:16 N '87

Drugs and brokers

From hot tips to hard drugs—another Wall Street bust [brokers as cocaine dealers] K. R. Sheets. il *U S News World Rep* 102:55 Ap 27 '87

Self-loathing on the Street [cocaine on Wall Street] il *Newsweek* 109:53 Ap 27 '87

Sniffing out a line of coke brokers [drug dealing on Wall Street] S. Koepp. il *Time* 129:54 Ap 27 '87

Drugs and celebrities

Mackenzie Phillips comes clean. D. Maychick. il por *Mademoiselle* 93:54 Ja '87

"My mom saved my life" [daughter of comedienne C. Burnett] A. W. Petrucelli. pors *Redbook* 170:108-9+ N '87

A TV child grows up [D. Arnaz Jr.] M. Cooper. il por *Macleans* 100:8 Ja 19 '87

Drugs and children *See* Drugs and youth

Drugs and crime

Urban murders: on the rise [cocaine-related killings] T. E. Johnson. il *Newsweek* 109:30 F 9 '87

Drugs and employment

Big John [guidelines for administering drug tests to federal workers] il *Time* 129:19 Mr 2 '87

Black federal workers oppose drug testing. *Jet* 72:23 Je 22 '87

"But I've never used drugs". F. Lunzer. il *Forbes* 140:442 Jl 13 '87

The case against drug testing. A. M. O'Keefe. *Psychol Today* 21:34-5+ Je '87

Doctors square off on employee drug testing. C. Holden. il *Science* 238:744-5 N 6 '87

Drug tests in the workplace: are they reliable? D. Groves. *McCalls* 114:155 My '87

High on the job: a growing problem? [survey by James W. Schreier] J. Goetz. il *Psychol Today* 21:16 My '87

On-the-job drug tests: what to know. C. Kitch. il *Good Housekeep* 204:145 Ja '87

Drugs and employment—*cont.*
Pissing contests [guidelines for drug testing of federal employees] *Harpers* 274:19-20 My '87
Reagan administration drug testing program [federal employees] *Congr Dig* 66:131-60 My '87
What managers must know about drug testing. S. Rose. *Work Woman* 12:20 Ap '87

Drugs and judges
Betrayal. H. S. Scott. *New Repub* 197:12-13 D 14 '87
Exit the smoking judge [D. Ginsburg] I. Austen. il por *Macleans* 100:32 N 16 '87
The Ginsburg test: bad logic. C. Krauthammer. il *Time* 130:102 N 23 '87
Pot & politics [D. H. Ginsburg's Supreme Court nomination; cover story] A. Press. il pors *Newsweek* 110:46-52 N 16 '87
Sins of the past [drug use by D. Ginsburg derails Supreme Court nomination] M. Hornblower. por *Time* 130:18-20 N 16 '87
Up in smoke: the undoing of a High Court nominee [D. Ginsburg] B. Duffy and D. Baer. il por *U S News World Rep* 103:24-6 N 16 '87

Drugs and mass media
Public service and the bottom line [National Association of Broadcasters antidrug public service announcements] J. L. Swerdlow. il *Channels* 7:66 Ja '87

Drugs and musicians
Boy George comes clean—and tries to come back—after heroin addiction and his pals' drug deaths. L. S. Healy. il pors *People Wkly* 28:92-3+ Ag 24 '87
The happy Lazarus of rock 'n' roll [cover story] D. Crosby. il pors *People Wkly* 27:52-4+ Ap 27 '87
Ike Turner arrested again for cocaine possession. por *Jet* 72:65 S 7 '87
More problems for Boy George. M. Goldberg. *Roll Stone* p13 Ja 15 '87
Mr. Clean: Boy George straightens up his act. M. Goldberg. il pors *Roll Stone* p87-8+ O 8 '87
Rocker Sly Stone jailed for parole violation. *Jet* 72:17 Je 22 '87
Turner pleads innocent to cocaine charges [I. Turner] por *Jet* 71:61 Ja 26 '87

Drugs and physicians
Doctors who use drugs. J. Pekkanen. il *Good Housekeep* 205:198-9+ S '87
My 17 years as a drug addict [woman psychiatrist]; ed. by Dick Harris. M. Morrison. il por *Read Dig* 130:123-6 My '87

Drugs and politicians
After the Ginsburg debacle, a chronicler of the sixties ponders the new politics of pot [interview with T. Gitlin] M. Wilhelm. il por *People Wkly* 28:124+ N 23 '87
Alice Bond, Carmen Butler meet before magistrate to argue battery charge [Mrs. J. Bond's accusations of cocaine abuse directed against husband Julian] il por *Jet* 72:6 My 11 '87
Andrew Young's ill-timed call [A. Bond's accusations of cocaine use] il por *Time* 129:34 My 25 '87
Atlanta grand jury not questioning Julian Bond in city's drug scandal. *Jet* 72:4 Je 15 '87
Atlanta mayor testifies in drug probe; says his family shaken by slurs [A. Young] il pors *Jet* 72:4 Je 1 '87
Atlanta mayor Young to testify before grand jury in city's drug scandal. por *Jet* 72:4 My 25 '87
Atlanta's coke controversy [charges against J. Bond] il por *Newsweek* 109:36 Ap 27 '87
Georgia woman tied to Julian Bond in drug probe gets 22-year sentence [C. Butler] por *Jet* 72:52 S 21 '87
Julian Bond denies using cocaine and lashes media; Mayor Young implicated. pors *Jet* 72:8 My 4 '87
Julian Bond's wife accuses him of using drugs daily; she later recants story. il por *Jet* 72:54 Ap 27 '87
A scandal scars Atlanta [cocaine charges against A. Young and J. Bond] T. E. Johnson. il pors *Newsweek* 109:28 Je 1 '87
Test cases for a new political generation. J. Alter. il *Newsweek* 110:48-9 N 16 '87
Young clear in drug probe, fellow Democrats cheer; ponders bid for governor. il pors *Jet* 72:24 Jl 6 '87

Drugs and public officers
D.C. mayor Marion Barry denies cocaine usage. il por *Jet* 72:4 Jl 6 '87

Drugs and sports
See also
Sports Medicine Drug Identification Laboratory
Another NCAA fumble [judge rules against testing policy] B. Newman. il por *Sports Illus* 67:100 D 7 '87
Athletes and steroids: playing a deadly game. R. W. Miller. il *FDA Consum* 21:16-21 N '87

Athletes and steroids: the bad bargain. V. S. Cowart. il *Saturday Evening Post* 259:56-9 Ap '87
Banned NBAer files suit over his '86 drug relapse [M. R. Richardson] *Jet* 72:50 My 25 '87
Bias' friend Tribble glad 'system did not fail me'. pors *Jet* 72:48 Je 22 '87
Bosworth faces the music [casualty of the NCAA's steroid crackdown] C. Neff. il pors *Sports Illus* 66:20-2+ Ja 5 '87
Boxing slips the drug punch. J. Ryan. il *Sport Mag* 78:19 Ag '87
The case for the defence [lawyer's account of baseball player F. Jenkins' narcotics case; excerpt from Greenspan] E. L. Greenspan and G. Jonas. il pors *Macleans* 100:48-50+ O 19 '87
Charge two in drug probe of U-Texas cager's death [case of H. Jackson] *Jet* 72:52 Je 1 '87
Coke and a pitching ace [D. Gooden case] il por *Macleans* 100:26 Ap 13 '87
A crash landing for an ace [D. Gooden enters clinic for cocaine abuse treatment] S. Wulf. il pors *Sports Illus* 66:32-4 Ap 13 '87
Dark clouds over Sun country [drug bust implicating present and former members of the Phoenix Suns basketball team] A. Keteyian. il *Sports Illus* 66:24-5 Ap 27 '87
Did she or didn't she? [pentathlete L. Norwood banned after positive drug test] S. Francis. il *Women's Sports Fitness* 9:22 Ap '87
Diver just says no [Stanford's S. LeVant refuses to submit to drug tests] A. Ferber. il por *Women's Sports Fitness* 9:25 My '87
The downfall of a champion [cocaine use during basketball career at Villanova and afterwards]; ed. by Jeffrey Marx. G. McLain. il pors *Sports Illus* 66:42-6+ Mr 16 '87
Dr. K strikes out [D. Gooden enters drug rehabilitation] por *Time* 129:67 Ap 13 '87
Driesell denies saying cocaine helps athletes. *Jet* 72:50 Jl 6 '87
Drug charges lose steam as Suns' trio pass tests [Phoenix Suns basketball team] il *Jet* 72:47 My 11 '87
Drug free Bronco feels good, chats with Hollywood [C. Kay] *Jet* 71:46 F 16 '87
Drug scandal witness dies, Phoenix case loses steam. por *Jet* 72:47 Jl 6 '87
Drug tests may explain why Vida Blue retired. por *Jet* 71:50 Mr 23 '87
Expos' Youmans enters drug treatment clinic. *Jet* 73:50 N 2 '87
For athletes and dealers, black market steroids are risky business. D. Stehlin. il *FDA Consum* 21:24-5 S '87
Getting fooled by drugs: the perils of taking NBA cocaine users at their word. J. McCallum. il por *Sports Illus* 66:70 Ja 26 '87
Getting tough on drugs [Calgary Olympics] H. Quinn. il *Macleans* 100:46-7 O 5 '87
Going to bat against the fear of failure [D. Gooden cocaine case] J. M. Wall. *Christ Century* 104:371-2 Ap 22 '87
Gooden sheds light on his problem with cocaine. *Jet* 72:52 Jl 13 '87
Gooden to start working back into Mets rotation. il por *Jet* 72:48 My 18 '87
Head winds and scandals. H. Quinn. *Macleans* 100:39 Ag 31 '87
How many athletes are high? [female drug use] il *Women's Sports Fitness* 9:26 Ap '87
Indiana coach Knight has no sympathy for Bias; 'He was so cool'. *Jet* 72:46 Ag 3 '87
Just say no . . . to mandatory drug testing. N. Cohen. *Sport Mag* 78:6 My '87
LT: living on the edge [football player's cocaine use; excerpt; cover story] L. Taylor and D. Falkner. il pors *Sport Mag* 78:68-72+ S '87
Mandatory drug testing may spark racism: Page [views of A. Page] por *Jet* 72:46 Ag 31 '87
Maury Wills favors drug testing for all players. il por *Jet* 71:46 Mr 2 '87
Mets moral support may speed up Gooden's return after drug rehabilitation. il pors *Jet* 72:50 Ap 20 '87
Mets provide protection while 'Dr. K' heals himself [D. Gooden] por *Jet* 72:46 My 25 '87
Milner quietly beat drugs, but he's talking about it [E. Milner] *Jet* 72:46 S 7 '87
New NBA trio implicated in Phoenix drug probe. il *Jet* 72:49 Je 1 '87
New Triple Crown threat [medication given to race horses] J. Rolfe. il *Sport Mag* 78:16 Je '87
NFL MVP Taylor reveals trap of drugs caught him. por *Jet* 72:51 Ap 6 '87

Drugs and sports—*cont.*

Off to a troubled start [D. Gooden case] P. Axthelm. il pors *Newsweek* 109:66-7 Ap 13 '87

Offshore racing's image problems. D. Wallace and C. Davis. il *Mot Boat Sail* 160:42-5+ D '87

Quiz sports stars after probe produces pictures [connections to heroin kingpin J. Jackson] il *Jet* 72:46 Je 1 '87

Raiders' star Robinson facing Calif. drug charge [J. Robinson] por *Jet* 72:50 Ag 10 '87

Rockets' pair bombed out of NBA for cocaine use [M. Wiggins and L. Lloyd] pors *Jet* 71:50 F 2 '87

Say it ain't snow, Doc! Baseball hero Dwight Gooden is knocked out of the box by cocaine. J. S. Kunen. il por *People Wkly* 27:123-4 Ap 20 '87

A showdown at the shore: Bet Twice beat Alysheba in the Haskell at Monmouth, but Lasix lurked in the shadows. C. Gammon. il *Sports Illus* 67:36-8+ Ag 10 '87

A star flunks his test [B. Bosworth found using steroids] P. Axthelm. il por *Newsweek* 109:48-9 Ja 5 '87

Steroids: the stuff of synthetic supermen? [anabolic steroids] M. S. Kreiter. il *Curr Health 2* 14:14-16 D '87

Three strikes and he's . . . back [cocaine abuser J. Lucas playing basketball for the Milwaukee Bucks] B. Newman. il pors *Sports Illus* 66:18-19 Mr 2 '87

Time to rise and shine [drug charges against Phoenix Suns players] C. Neff. il *Sports Illus* 67:30-2+ N 23 '87

Tony Elliott: just back from the dead, a too well-traveled NFL star bears witness to a chilling drug odyssey. W. Plummer. il pors *People Wkly* 27:81-4+ Ja 5 '87

Drugs and the aged

Monitoring drugs for the aged. W. I. Bennett. il *N Y Times Mag* p73-4 D 13 '87

New trends in over-the-counter care. B. S. Rabin. il *50 Plus* 27:20+ Ja '87

Treating the mind, risking the body [drugs linked to hip fractures; study by Wayne A. Ray and others] *Sci News* 131:122 F 21 '87

Drugs and the mentally ill

Bad trips for the doubly troubled [problems of street drugs and alcohol] C. Gorman. il *Time* 130:58 Ag 3 '87

Drugs and the press

Bond criticizes media on personal life prying [J. Bond] por *Jet* 72:22 Jl 6 '87

Drugs and women

"Boy, could I use a . . ." (a) drink, (b) pill, (c) joint. If you filled in the blank you could be a preaddict. W. Gallagher. *Mademoiselle* 93:210-11+ O '87

The day my family saved my life [excerpt from Betty]; ed. by Chris Chase. B. Ford. il pors *Good Housekeep* 204:132-3+ F '87

Don't mess with magic pills, darling: they're bad medicine [tranquilizers] M. Sandmaier. il *Mademoiselle* 93:128-9+ Jl '87

Drugs. L. Van Gelder. il *Ms* 15:42 F '87

How many athletes are high? [female drug use] il *Women's Sports Fitness* 9:26 Ap '87

A mild dose of candor [K. Dukakis reveals former amphetamine dependency] W. Shapiro. il pors *Time* 130:34 Jl 20 '87

Swearing off social drugging. J. Levine. *Mademoiselle* 93:276-8+ S '87

The ten drugs most often prescribed for women. *McCalls* 145:81-3 Mr '87

Drugs and youth

See also

Drug education

Just Say No (Organization)

KIDS of Bergen County (Program)

National Teen Challenge (Organization)

Project 714 (Organization)

Bashing public education [study of Catholic high school students and drug use] E. Doerr. *Humanist* 47:43 Jl/Ag '87

Drinking, drugs and kids: what to say. L. Salk. il *McCalls* 115:65 O '87

Drug abuse and teenagers. D. Elkind. il *Parents* 62:164 F '87

Drug abuse: who says it can't happen to your kid? M. O'Connell-Cahill. il *U S Cathol* 52:20-5 O '87

The drug trip: a rough detour. I. S. Abrams. il *Curr Health 2* 14:11-13 O '87

Drug use: down, but not in the ghetto. M. Miller. il *Newsweek* 110:33 N 23 '87

Fighting drugs on ice [Torvill and Dean benefit for N. Reagan's anti-drug crusade] P. SerVaas. il pors *Saturday Evening Post* 259:50 Ja/F '87

How to stop teen drug use. il *Consum Res Mag* 70:27-31 Ja '87

I said no to drugs [high school student] J. Lifton. il *Seventeen* 46:120-1 O '87

Kids and drugs [roundtable discussion] S. S. Stautberg. il *Ladies Home J* 104:74+ My '87

Kids can be drink and drug free. il *Parents* 62:22 O '87

The law and youth substance abuse [American Bar Association report] il *Child Today* 16:4 Ja/F '87

Looking for peace in the war on drugs. R. Sagor. *Educ Dig* 52:50-2 Ap '87

The new kid [undercover narcotics cop G. Raffield murdered at Midlothian High School in Texas] por *Time* 130:61 N 9 '87

Parents vs. drugs. I. Groller. il *Parents* 62:126-8+ My '87

Puppets versus drugs [Mexico's Youth Integration Centres] E. Massún. il *World Health* p2-5 Je '87

Schoolchildren and drugs: the fancy that has not passed. R. A. Hawley. il *Phi Delta Kappan* 68:K1-K8 My '87

The street boys of Nairobi. I. Ndirangu. *World Press Rev* 34:57 S '87

Students and drugs [University of Michigan survey] il *Child Today* 15:2-3 N/D '86

Teen to teen: drugs aren't cool. il *Curr Health 2* 14:19-21 N '87

Young people and drugs. il *UN Chron* 23:40-1 Ja '86

Drugs from the sea *See* Marine pharmacology

Drugstores

See also

Dart Drug Corp.

Pay N Save Inc.

Revco D.S., Inc.

Rite Aid Corp.

Drum

Wanted: snare drums [overuse of drum machines] K. Richardson. il *High Fidel* 37:54 Je '87

Drummers

See also

Bennink, Han

Bruford, Bill

Chambers, Dennis

Cobham, Billy

Cyrille, Andrew

DeJohnette, Jack

Gottlieb, Danny

Hart, Mickey

Hooper, Stix

Horton, Yogi, d. 1987

Kodo (Musical group)

Kreutzmann, Bill

Previte, Bobby

Roach, Max

Watts, Charlie

Watts, Jeff

Weckl, Dave

Drummond, Hugh

Condoms: the offer you can't refuse. il *Vogue* 177:226+ Je '87

Drummond, Sarah

Antiques: seals: assuring identity and privacy with style. il *Archit Dig* 44:182-7 O '87

Art: gardens by design. il *Archit Dig* 44:164-9+ Ap '87

Drums *See* Drum

Drunk driving *See* Alcohol and automobile drivers

Drunkenness *See* Alcoholics and alcoholism

Drury, David

about

Defense of the realm [film] Reviews

New Yorker 63:99-100 Mr 9 '87. P. Kael

Newsweek il 109:61 Ja 19 '87. D. Ansen

Drury, John

Sonnet to Orpheus [poem] *New Repub* 197:30 N 23 '87

Drury, Michael

The legacy [poem] *Good Housekeep* 205:157 Jl '87

Dry cell electric batteries *See* Electric batteries

Dry flies *See* Fishing lures, flies, etc.

Dry tropical forests *See* Forests and forestry

Dryansky, G. Y.

Architectural digest visits: King Hussein and Queen Noor of Jordan. il pors *Archit Dig* 44:68-77+ Ja '87

A charmed life. il *Vogue* 177:446-53+ O '87

Orientalist opulence in Belgravia: the London residence of Princess Firyal of Jordan. il *Archit Dig* 44:216-20 My '87

Traces of the future's past: Nicola Trussardi's palazzo in Bergamo. il por *Archit Dig* 44:152-9 My '87

Dryansky, G. Y.—*cont.*
Who's who in American style: the people, the success, the impact. il *Vogue* 177:171-4+ O '87
Dryden (Hugh L.) Flight Research Center *See* Hugh L. Dryden Flight Research Center
Dryers, Clothes *See* Clothes dryers
Drying
> *See also*
> Food—Drying
> Fruit—Drying
> Tomatoes—Drying
> Vegetables—Drying
> Wood—Dryers and drying

Drying (Crops)
> *See also*
> Grain—Drying

Drying equipment
> *See also*
> Clothes dryers
> Grain dryers
> Kilns
> Wood—Dryers and drying

Drypoint
"Etching" for fourth-graders. il *Sunset* 179:106-7 N '87
Drywall materials *See* Wallboard
D'Souza, Dinesh, 1961-
What the Soviets think about American liberals. *Natl Rev* 39:39-41+ Ja 30 '87
DTMF *See* Dual-tone multifrequency signalling
Du Bois, W. E. B. (William Edward Burghardt), 1868-1963
> *about*
> The black and the red. C. V. Woodward. por *New Repub* 196:32-6 Mr 16 '87
> **Bibliography**
> A man for all seasons. T. Bolden Davis. por *Black Enterp* 17:50+ Je '87
Du Bois, William Edward Burghardt *See* Du Bois, W. E. B. (William Edward Burghardt), 1868-1963
Du Page County (Ill.)
Du Page County, Illinois. il map *Time* 129:17 Je 15 '87
Du Pont, Pierre S., IV
> *about*
> A blueblood with bold ideas. A. Stanley. il pors *Time* 130:16+ S 7 '87
> Call me Pete. R. Brookhiser. *Natl Rev* 39:24-6 D 31 '87
> How dark a horse? J. Hart. *Natl Rev* 39:16 Ag 28 '87
> Letter from Washington. Cato. *Natl Rev* 39:14 Jl 3 '87
> Patrician populist. F. Barnes. il *New Repub* 196:12-13+ Mr 9 '87
> The right's free lunch. M. Kaus. *New Repub* 196:14 Mr 9 '87
> Throwing the 'long bomb'. M. Kaus. pors *Newsweek* 109:20 Je 8 '87
> What two of the darkest horses are running on: ideas. P. Magnusson. il pors *Bus Week* p126+ D 21 '87
Du Pont de Nemours (E. I.) *See* E. I. Du Pont de Nemours
Dual photon absorptiometry *See* Absorptiometry
Dual purpose investment trusts *See* Investment trusts
Dual-tone multifrequency signalling
A DTMF receiver [dual tone multi-frequency receiver] R. Grossblatt. il *Radio-Electron* 58:82-3 Mr '87
An output decoder. R. Grossblatt. il *Radio-Electron* 58:76-8 Ap '87
Phonlink interactive remote control (I). G. Roseth. il *Radio-Electron* 58:39-41 My '87
Phonlink interactive remote control (II). G. Roseth. il *Radio-Electron* 58:53-7 Je '87
Remote-control transmitter. R. Grossblatt. il *Radio-Electron* 58:82-4 Ja '87
Dualism
> *See also*
> Mind and body
Duarte, José Napoleón
> *about*
> All states asked to provide emergency assistance to El Salvador after devastating earthquake; President Duarte addresses United Nations on earthquake assistance. il por *UN Chron* 24:65 F '87
> Duarte's last stand. T. Golden. *New Repub* 196:12-14 Je 22 '87
> Duarte's secret friends. F. Smyth. il *Nation* 244:316-18 Mr 14 '87
> Duarte's unkept promises. J. Contreras. il por *Newsweek* 109:35 Mr 2 '87
> Grave encounters. H. G. Chua-Eoan. il pors *Time* 130:32-4 D 7 '87

Hard times for Duarte. B. Levin. il por *Macleans* 100:29 Je 15 '87
Meanwhile, in El Salvador . . . J. Smolowe. il por *Time* 130:30-1 Ag 24 '87
Mess in El Salvador: Duarte takes the heat. J. C. Erlick. il por *U S News World Rep* 102:33 My 25 '87
Minority report. C. Hitchens. *Nation* 245:674 D 5 '87
Will Duarte see peace in his time? C. A. Robbins. il por *U S News World Rep* 103:29 Ag 31 '87
Duato, Nacho
> *about*
> Spanish dancer finally achieves success in his native country. L. Kumin. por *Dance Mag* 61:104 S '87
Dubai (United Arab Emirates: Emirate)
> *See also*
> Airports—Dubai (United Arab Emirates: Emirate)
Dubbing of motion pictures *See* Motion pictures—Sound editing
Dubé, Claire L'Heureux- *See* L'Heureux-Dubé, Claire
Dubik, James M.
An officer and a feminist. por *Newsweek* 109:8-9 Ap 27 '87
Dublin (Ireland)
> **Description**
> Dublin for the stout of heart. B. Barich. il *Esquire* 107 Summ Traveler:T12-T16+ Ap '87
Dubofsky, Melvyn, 1934-
The extension of solidarity conflicts with the spirit of individualism. *Mon Labor Rev* 110:36-7 Ag '87
DuBois, Bessie Wilson
The rocking chair. il *McCalls* 115:70+ N '87
Dubois, Mark
> *about*
> For the rivers, come hell or high water. K. Crist. il pors *Sierra* 72:61-5 My/Je '87
Dubois, René-Daniel
> *about*
> At centre stage with a message. il por *Macleans* 100:28-9 D 28 '87
> Drama's daring new voice. J. Goddard. il por *Macleans* 100:61 Ap 27 '87
> Pericles Prince of Tyre by William Shakespeare [drama] Reviews
> *Macleans* il por 100:61 Ap 27 '87. J. Bemrose
Dubus, Elizabeth Nell
Always room for one more [story] il *Redbook* 170:48+ N '87
Duchamp, Marcel, 1887-1968
> *about*
> Marcel Duchamp. E. Heartney. il *Art News* 86:160+ Ap '87
> Notorious. J. Perl. il por *Vogue* 177:160+ S '87
Duchenne dystrophy *See* Muscular dystrophy
Duchesne, Rose Philippine, d. 1842
> *about*
> A new U.S. saint. K. L. Woodward. por *Newsweek* 109:8 Je 22 '87
Duchin, Dian
New grafting technique. il *Rodale's Org Gard* 34:62-6 Ja '87
Duck, Robert W.
> *about*
> The improbable Mr. Duck proves that it takes one to race one. J. Kaufman. il pors *People Wkly* 28:141+ N 23 '87
Duck blinds *See* Blinds (Camouflage)
Duck cooking *See* Cooking—Poultry
Duck racing
The improbable Mr. Duck proves that it takes one to race one [R. W. Duck] J. Kaufman. il pors *People Wkly* 28:141+ N 23 '87
Duck shooting
> *See also*
> Blinds (Camouflage)
> Ducks and disaster. G. Reiger. il *Field Stream* 92:14+ O '87
> Ducks with a difference. G. Clancy. il *Outdoor Life* 180:66-7+ O '87
> Grandpa and the kid [jumpshooting end of season ducks on the Umpqua River with a Chesapeake Bay retriever] D. Sisson. il *Field Stream* 91:49+ F '87
> A morning under the Missions [duck shooting with stepson in Montana] J. Barsness. il *Field Stream* 92:44+ Je '87
> Sea ducks. G. Reiger. il *Field Stream* 91:56-7+ Ja '87
> The small-water factor. B. W. Dalrymple. il *Field Stream* 92:60-1+ O '87

Ducklow, Hugh W., and others
Bacteria: link or sink? [discussion of May 16, 1986 article, Bacterioplankton: a sink for carbon in a coastal marine plankton community] *Science* 235:88-9 Ja 2 '87

Ducks

Training
Lucky ducks! [trained ducks at Peabody Hotel, Memphis, Tenn.] il *Natl Geogr World* 140:3-5 Ap '87

Ducks, Wild
An autumn apparition [cat perched on back of flying mallard] M. J. Walters. il *Read Dig* 131:71-4+ O '87
Black duck decline: an acid rain link. J. R. Luoma. il map *Audubon* 89:18-20+ My '87
A deadly rain [effect of acid rain on wild ducks] L. Williamson. il *Outdoor Life* 179:46+ Je '87
Too many mallards [Storrs, Conn.] R. Holland. il *Audubon* 89:64-7 Ja '87
The wings of spring [return of migrating ducks; cover story] G. Lemmo. il *Conservationist* 41:26-31 Mr/Ap '87

Control
Ducks and disaster. G. Reiger. il *Field Stream* 92:14+ O '87
Working their magic on ducks [Delta Waterfowl and Wetlands Research Station in the Canadian prairies] G. Turbak. il *Int Wildl* 17:24-8 Mr/Ap '87

Shooting
See Duck shooting

Duck's Breath Mystery Theatre
The comedy conglomerate. C. McGuigan. il *Newsweek* 110:87 O 12 '87

Ducks in art
DEC's 1987 migratory waterfowl print and stamp. il *Conservationist* 42:54 Jl/Ag '87

Ducks on revenue stamps *See* Revenue stamps

Duckweeds

Photographs and photography
Duckweed. A. D. Briere. il *Ctry J* 14:33-5 S '87

Duclos, Clovis
about
*How to become Arnold Palmer. D. Goodgame. il por *Time* 130:51 Ag 17 '87

Dudar, Helen
An art-filled villa finds a special setting in Texas. il pors *Smithsonian* 17:50-9 Ja '87
New treasures on the Mall. il *Smithsonian* 18:44-63 S '87
New York's Metropolitan enters the 20th century with a bang. bibl (p183) il *Smithsonian* 18:46-54+ My '87
To have and have not: the avoirdupois collection. il *N Y Times Book Rev* 92:30-1 Ap 5 '87

Dude ranches *See* Ranches

Dudek, Joe
about
Joe Dudek shows how to be a (union) football hero. il por *People Wkly* 28:52 O 12 '87

Dudley, Trevania
A chutney sampler. il *Ctry J* 14:58-60 Jl '87
Hanging gardens. il *Ctry J* 14:60-3 D '87
In a pickle. il *Ctry J* 14:36-9 S '87

Dudley Products, Inc.
Dudley Products draws 2,000 to beauty seminar. il *Jet* 72:6 Je 1 '87

I due litiganti [opera] *See* Sarti, Giuseppe, 1729-1802

Due process of law
See also
Jury
The blessings of liberty [judicial authority and due process] A. Press. il *Newsweek* 109:66-7 My 25 '87

Duet for one [film] *See* Motion picture reviews—Single works

Duff, Susan, 1945-
Fresh start: a great body. *Harpers Bazaar* 120:210+ O '87
Old: fall's beauty focus. il *Harpers Bazaar* 120:390-3+ S '87

Duffield, Ian
Billy Blue: a legend of early Sydney. bibl il *Hist Today* 37:43-8 F '87

Duffy, Gloria
Explaining Soviet compliance. *Society* 24:66-72 Jl/Ag '87
Study finds treaty compliance. *Bull At Sci* 43:30-2 O '87

Duffy, Jim
about
Hold the popcorn; pass the chablis. D. Marth. il pors *Nations Bus* 75:60 Jl '87

Duffy, John
about
Hold the popcorn; pass the chablis. D. Marth. il pors *Nations Bus* 75:60 Jl '87

Duffy, Julia
about
Newhart's brat, Julia Duffy, says she's not like that at all. M. Dougherty. il pors *People Wkly* 28:111-12 O 5 '87

Duffy, Regis A.
The R.C.I.A. misunderstood? il *America* 156:385+ My 9 '87

Duffy, Robert
about
A conversation with Robert Duffy. C. Movalli. il *Am Artist* 51:54-9+ N '87

Dugas, Gaetan
about
The appalling saga of Patient Zero. W. A. Henry. il pors *Time* 130:40+ O 19 '87
The Columbus of AIDS. *Natl Rev* 39:19 N 6 '87
Patient Zero. por *People Wkly* 28:47 D 28 '87-Ja 4 '88
'Patient Zero' and the AIDS virus. A. Steacy. il por *Macleans* 100:53 O 19 '87

Dugger, Edward Anthony
Aunt Sadie's visit [poem] *Essence* 18:149 S '87

Duhé, Camille
Hair frenzy fix-up. il *Harpers Bazaar* 120:110-13+ Ja '87
Perfect skin: the clean sweep. il *Harpers Bazaar* 120:214-19+ O '87

Duignan, Peter
The U.S. and apartheid. *Current* 297:11-17 N '87

Duiker, William J.
Vietnam moves toward pragmatism. bibl f *Curr Hist* 86:148-51+ Ap '87

Duinker, Peter
(jt. auth) *See* Nilsson, Sten, and Duinker, Peter

Duisburg (Germany)

Galleries and museums
See also
Wilhelm-Lehmbruck-Museum der Stadt Duisburg

Music
See also
Opera—Germany (West)

Duivendijk, Hans van
They stopped the sea. il *Natl Geogr* 172:92-101 Jl '87

Dukakis, Kitty
about
A mild dose of candor. W. Shapiro. il pors *Time* 130:34 Jl 20 '87

Dukakis, Michael
about
The Bay State puts up its Duke. D. Chu. il por *People Wkly* 27:38-9 Ap 13 '87
A break for Cuomo's look-alike. il por *Newsweek* 109:29 Mr 2 '87
Cool Hand Duke [cover story] M. Kondracke. *New Repub* 197:17-18+ Ag 31 '87
Debacle for the Duke. J. Klein. il por *N Y* 20:26+ O 12 '87
Dollars for the Duke. K. T. Walsh. il por *U S News World Rep* 103:24 Jl 6 '87
The Dukakis design. J. Siegal. il *New Leader* 70:10-13 Ag 10-24 '87
The Duke of economic uplift. W. Shapiro. il pors *Time* 130:22-3 Jl 27 '87
Duke of piety. S. Lehigh and F. J. Connolly. *New Repub* 197:13-15 O 26 '87
The dwarfs in disarray. G. J. Church. il pors *Time* 130:22+ O 12 '87
Have we seen the future? [cover story] A. Kopkind. il *Nation* 244:631+ My 16 '87
Letters [discussion of May 16, 1987 article, Have we seen the future?] A. Kopkind. *Nation* 244:872+ Je 27 '87
A long shot takes aim. D. Collins. il por *U S News World Rep* 102:37 Mr 30 '87
Marathon man. W. Shapiro. il por *Time* 129:26 Mr 30 '87
Mike Dukakis has ideas—but will they travel? L. Helm. il por *Bus Week* p61 Mr 23 '87
A mild dose of candor. W. Shapiro. il pors *Time* 130:34 Jl 20 '87
A miracle—and the man who would take credit for it. H. Rainie. il por *U S News World Rep* 103:18-19 Ag 10 '87
Now, a Dukakis fiasco. M. Kaus. il por *Newsweek* 110:40 O 12 '87

Dukakis, Michael—about—*cont.*
The price of deception. J. Bierman. *Macleans* 100:32 O 12 '87
Ready for the Duke? [cover story] J. Klein. il pors *N Y* 20:24-31 Ag 17 '87
A second look at an economic 'miracle'. il por *Newsweek* 110:31 N 30 '87
A sort of memoir. P. Green. *Nation* 245:158-60+ Ag 29 '87
Yes, we have a front runner. M. Kaus. il por *Newsweek* 110:31 Jl 20 '87

Duke, Daniel L.
Understanding what it means to be a teacher. *Educ Dig* 52:20-3 Mr '87

Duke, Daryl
about
Delightful, lovable chaos. A. Fotheringham. il *Macleans* 100:52 Jl 20 '87

Duke, James
about
Homespun doc James 'Red' Duke preaches what he practices—and inspires a new TV show. A. Maier. il pors *People Wkly* 27:65+ Je 29 '87

Duke, James A., 1929-
Help rediscover an American vegetable: apios. il *Rodale's Org Gard* 34:98-101 Ja '87

Duke, Patty, and Turan, Kenneth
A childhood of sorrows [excerpt from Call me Anna] il pors *People Wkly* 28:70-2+ Jl 13 '87
Patty Duke's personal miracle [excerpt from Call me Anna] il pors *Ladies Home J* 104:42+ S '87
A troubled coming of age [excerpt from Call me Anna] il pors *People Wkly* 28:54-6+ Jl 20 '87

Duke University
Duke's heart center in bureaucratic jam. M. Basgall. *Science* 238:882-3 N 13 '87
Chapel
Duke's Gothic chapel. il *South Living* 22:47 D '87

Dukes, Paul, 1934-
'Glasnost' and the Russian Revolution [cover story] il *Hist Today* 37:11-14 O '87
Klyuchevsky and the course of Russian history. il por *Hist Today* 37:51-4 Jl '87

Dukes, Rufus L., d. 1987
about
Obituary
Jet por 73:51 O 12 '87

Dula, Arthur
about
A Texas lawyer markets Soviet rockets. D. Pedersen. il por *Newsweek* 110:58 Ag 17 '87

Dulles, Avery Robert, 1918-
about
Principles & politics. J. B. Hehir. il *Commonweal* 114:169-70 Mr 27 '87

Dulles International Airport See Washington (D.C.)—Airports

Duluth (Minn.)
Arts
See also
St. Louis County Heritage and Arts Center (Duluth, Minn.)
Duluth [special section] E. Beck. il *Horizon* 30:13-26+ Ap '87
City planning
Making a comeback. B. Beck. il *Horizon* 30:16-18 Ap '87
Description
Duluth [special section] E. Beck. il *Horizon* 30:13-26+ Ap '87

Dulwich Picture Gallery (London, England)
A stubborn Englishness. T. Trucco. il *Art News* 86:103+ N '87

Dumaine, Frederic C., 1866-1951
about
Frederic Dumaine: upstreaming the profits. D. A. Saunders. il por *Forbes* 140:258-9+ Jl 13 '87

Dumas, Lynne S.
When opposites attract. il *Health* 19:35-9+ S '87

Dumas, Rena
about
French ensemble: the Paris apartment of Rena Dumas and Jean-Louis Dumas-Hermès. C. Aillaud. il por *Archit Dig* 44:132-6 Jl '87

Dumas-Hermès, Jean-Louis
about
French ensemble: the Paris apartment of Rena Dumas and Jean-Louis Dumas-Hermès. C. Aillaud. il por *Archit Dig* 44:132-6 Jl '87

Dumbarton Oaks
Washington after the cherry blossoms fall. C. H. Crowley. il *Saturday Evening Post* 259:84-6+ Ap '87

Dumbwaiters
A dumbwaiter for the home. L. D. Armstrong. il *Workbench* 43:22-5+ Ja/F '87
Dumbwaiter to the laundry room. il *Sunset* 179:85 Ag '87

Dumont, James P. C., and Robertson, R. Meldrum
Neuronal circuits and evolution [discussion of August 22, 1986 article, Neuronal circuits: an evolutionary perspective] *Science* 236:1681-2 Je 26 '87

Dumping (Commercial policy)
Dumping: it's a jungle out there [microchips] il *Time* 129:32 Ap 13 '87
Dumping? Or just defending markets? [prices of imported goods] G. Slutsker. il *Forbes* 139:166+ My 18 '87
The Europeans start to play a little rough [antidumping proposals against Japan] T. Peterson. il *Bus Week* p47 F 9 '87
"I know I sound protectionistic" [LSI Logic's W. Corrigan] K. K. Wiegner. il por *Forbes* 139:54+ Je 29 '87
Shell game at the docks [U.S. Customs not enforcing antidumping restrictions] G. Slutsker. il *Forbes* 139:34-5 Je 29 '87

Dun & Bradstreet Corp.
Dun & Bradstreet's overheard Dialog [access to Dun's Financial Records] *Newsweek* 110:39 D 28 '87
Nielsen boosts its ratings [acquisition of Information Resources Inc.] A. Dunkin. il *Bus Week* p40 S 14 '87

Dunbar, Maxwell J.
Arctic seas that never freeze. il map *Nat Hist* 96:50-3 Ap '87

Dunbar, R. I. M. (Robin Ian MacDonald), 1947-
Changing of the guard. il *Int Wildl* 17:30-3 Ja/F '87
Getting the author's goat [discussion of November 1986 article, Rhum deal for goats] il *Nat Hist* 96:2+ Mr '87

Dunbar, Robin Ian MacDonald See Dunbar, R. I. M. (Robin Ian MacDonald), 1947-

Duncan, Alastair, 1942-
A deco discovery. il *House Gard* 159:156-9+ My '87
Deco doyen. il por *House Gard* 159:36B+ Ja '87

Duncan, David
about
Old-timey medicine. il por *South Living* 22:146 Mr '87

Duncan, Dayton
about
Of prairie dogs, VCR's and Indian scouts [interview] A. P. Sanoff. il por map *U S News World Rep* 103:72 Jl 6 '87

Duncan, Evan
Chronology of relations between the United States and Nepal, 1947-87. il *Dep State Bull* 87:63-7 S '87

Duncan, Isadora, 1878-1927
about
Dance historians honor Duncan. S. J. Cohen. por *Dance Mag* 61:6-7 Jl '87

Duncan, James S.
(jt. auth) See Hennayake, Shantha K., and Duncan, James S.

Duncan, John Alastair See Duncan, Alastair, 1942-

Duncan, Lois, 1934-
"Memories are wrecking our marriage". il *Ladies Home J* 104:10+ Ja '87
My husband is never there for me. il *Ladies Home J* 104:14+ Ag '87

Duncan, Robert
about
Riding DEC's coattails. I. Chithelen. il por *Forbes* 140:225 N 2 '87

Duncan, William H.
about
Picking small high-tech winners. G. G. Marcial. *Bus Week* p72 Ap 6 '87

Duncan (Isadora) Dance Awards See Isadora Duncan Dance Awards

Dundee, Angelo
about
The corner man. G. Smith. il pors *Sports Illus* 67:92-6+ N 2 '87

Dung beetles
Will livestock drug cause dung crisis? [ivermectin; research by Richard Wall and Les Strong] J. Raloff. *Sci News* 131:358 Je 6 '87

Dunham, Katherine
about
Ailey launches a Katherine Dunham renaissance: Miss D's day. R. Philp. il pors *Dance Mag* 61:50-5 D '87

Dunham, Katherine—about—*cont.*
Dance break. L. Friedman. il pors *Vogue* 177:98 D '87
Dancing:
Program of K. Dunham dances. A. Croce. *New Yorker* 63:102 D 21 '87
Katherine Dunham: a living legend. B. Allen. il por *Essence* 18:54-5+ D '87

Dunkeld Ranching Ltd.
Following the money [Banco Ambrosiano scandal aftermath] J. Howse. il por *Macleans* 100:11 Jl 27 '87

Dunkin' Donuts Incorporated
Two doughnuts and a martini, please. K. Hannon. il por *Forbes* 139:128+ Mr 9 '87

Dunkle, Joseph
about
Even entrepreneurs can make it. il por *Fortune* 116:82 Ag 31 '87

Dunkley, Christopher
TV's distorted window on the world. *World Press Rev* 34:64 Ap '87

Dunlap, Paul D., 1930-
about
Back from the brink. C. Siler. il por *Forbes* 140:8 Ag 24 '87

Dunlap, Riley E.
Polls, pollution, and politics revisited: public opinion on the environment in the Reagan era [cover story; with editorial comment by Gilbert F. White] bibl f il *Environment* 29:6-11+ Jl/Ag '87
Public opinion on the environment [discussion of July/August 1987 article, Polls, pollution and politics revisited] il *Environment* 29:2-3 N '87

Dunlap, Tony
about
Walkabout. *New Yorker* 63:23-4 Jl 27 '87

Dunlop, Lane
(tr) See Abé, Kobo. The red cocoon

Dunlop, Richard
RV safety on the road. *Travel Holiday* 167:30-1 Je '87

Dunmire, Delbert
about
Ex-bank thief Delbert Dunmire busts loose with a classy high school reunion in the Bahamas. R. Arias. il pors *People Wkly* 28:30-1 Ag 31 '87

Dunn, Charles W.
Caladiums give landscapes a lift. il *Flower Gard* 31:9+ Ap/My '87

Dunn, Cynthia
She lost weight following her father's footsteps; ed. by Denise Foley. il pors *Prevention* 39:81-2+ Ag '87

Dunn, David J.
Directors aren't doing their jobs. il por *Fortune* 115:117-19 Mr 16 '87

Dunn, Donald H.
Personal business. See issues of Business Week

Dunn, Joni
about
The iron courage of Joni Dunn. J. G. Hubbell. il pors *Read Dig* 130:39-44 Ja '87

Dunn, Nora
about
Hip comedienne Nora Dunn brings gab and gams to Saturday night. T. Cunneff. il pors *People Wkly* 28:95-6+ N 30 '87

Dunn, Stephen, 1939-
Collecting future lives [poem] *Nation* 245:102 Ag 1-8 '87
Companionship [poem] *Nation* 244:122 Ja 31 '87

Dunn, Susan
about
Make me a star [cover story] M. Mayer. il pors *Opera News* 52:10-12+ Jl '87

Dunne, Dominick
An author's maison de plume: Dominick Dunne in his New York penthouse. il por *Archit Dig* 44:146-9+ S '87

Dunne, Jim, 1931-
Inside Detroit. See issues of Popular Mechanics beginning January 1986
about
Goin' fishin' with Jim. R. Ceppos. il por *Car Driv* 32:96-7 My '87

Dunne, John Gregory, 1932-
On writing. See issues of Esquire beginning October 1986 through May 1987
This year in Jerusalem. il *Esquire* 108:237-40+ D '87
about
Didion & Dunne: the rewards of a literary marriage. L. Garis. il pors *N Y Times Mag* p18-24+ F 8 '87

Dunner, Leslie B.
about
Detroit Symphony hires black assistant conductor. *Jet* 72:30 Jl 20 '87

Dunning, Brian
America in London. il *Am Herit* 38:76-9+ Ap '87

Dunning, Philip
about
Broadway [drama] Reviews
N Y 20:63 Jl 13 '87. J. Simon
New Yorker 63:57-8 Jl 6 '87. M. Kramer

Dunphy, Paul H.
Peas and potatoes. il *Ctry J* 14:53-9 Ap '87

Dunson, Sonja
about
Actress suing Farrah Fawcett is attacked in Los Angeles. pors *Jet* 72:26 Je 22 '87

Dunton, Graham
about
Chefs of influence. N. Barry. il pors *Gourmet* 47:82-3+ D '87

Duodenal ulcers *See* Peptic ulcers
Duplex apartments *See* Apartments
Duplex houses *See* Two family houses
Duplicating processes *See* Photocopying

Dupont, Joan
France's leading man. il pors *N Y Times Mag* p38-41+ Je 14 '87

Dupont Plaza (San Juan, Puerto Rico: Hotel) *See* San Juan (Puerto Rico)—Hotels, motels, etc.

Duppen, K.
(jt. auth) See Wiersma, D. A., and Duppen, K.

Dupre, D.
Macrovision stabilizer [cover story] il *Radio-Electron* 58:49-54 D '87

Dupree, Louis
The Soviet Union and Afghanistan in 1987. bibl f *Curr Hist* 86:333-5 O '87

Dupree, Nathalie
New southern cooking [excerpts] il *Redbook* 168:115-18+ F '87

Dupuy, René Jean
Is the international community a myth? il *Courier* 40:4-8 Ja '87

Duquin, Lorene Hanley
(ed) See Schunk, Sharon. "My son was hit by lightning"

Durakon Industries
No longer just hitching a ride on pickups. J. B. Treece. il por *Bus Week* p85-6 My 25 '87

Dural, Stanley *See* Buckwheat Zydeco

Durand, Enrique
Bogotá: echoes of the past. il *Américas* 39:24-30 N/D '87

Durand, V. Mark
(jt. auth) See Carr, Edward G., and Durand, V. Mark

Durang, Christopher, 1949-
about
Laughing wild [drama] Reviews
New Yorker 63:153 N 23 '87. E. Oliver

Durant, Frederick C., 1916-
(jt. auth) See Miller, Ron, 1947-, and Durant, Frederick C., 1916-

Durant, W. Clark, III
Maximizing access to justice [address, February 12, 1987] *Vital Speeches Day* 53:540-4 Je 15 '87

Duration of bonds *See* Bonds—Duration
Duration of life *See* Longevity

Durbin, Bill, Jr.
The return of the God-hypothesis. il por *Christ Today* 31:22-3 Ap 3 '87

Durenberger, David
Investing in parks. il *Natl Parks* 61:10-11 Ja/F '87
Should the Boren Amendment approach to curtailing PAC's be adopted? [excerpts from debate, August 11, 1986] *Congr Dig* 66:49+ F '87
Should the Byrd-Warner Amendment be adopted? [excerpts from debate, October 21, 1987] *Congr Dig* 66:308+ D '87

Durham, Michael
Keeper of the Attic. il pors *Americana* 15:43-8 N/D '87

Durham (England)
Galleries and museums
See also
Bowes Museum (Barnard Castle, England)
Museum of Archaeology (Durham, England)

Durham (N.C.)
Banks
See also
Mechanics & Farmers Bank

Durham (N.C.)—*cont.*
Chapels
See also
Duke University—Chapel
Duriron Co.
Rust Belt belle [stock price] T. Jaffe. *Forbes* 140:219 O 19 '87
Durkee, Sarah
The day dad made toast [story] il *Ms* 16:70-2 D '87
Durner, Pat
How safe are the pesticides on food? il *Rodale's Org Gard* 34:69-76 Je '87
Durnin, John
The ones that get away. il *Courier* 40:17 My '87
Durocher, Leo, 1905-
about
An error for baseball: why aren't Leo Durocher and Roger Maris in the Hall? S. Wulf. il por *Sports Illus* 67:92 Ag 10 '87
D'Urso, Joe, 1943-
about
The poetics of space. P. Goldberger. il por *Archit Dig* 44:266+ N '87
D'Urso, Mary Ann
Massage for the masses. il *Health* 19:63-4+ Ap '87
Durston, Chris
Signs & wonders & the English Civil War. bibl il *Hist Today* 37:22-8 O '87
DuSable Museum of African American History, Inc.
Blind tour guide describes exhibits at famous museum [J. Luckett] il pors *Jet* 72:24-5+ Ag 17 '87
Mrs. Eunice W. Johnson, Warren Bacon reign at regal Carnaval [charity ball] il pors *Jet* 72:33 S 7 '87
Düsseldorf (Germany)
Music
See also
Opera—Germany (West)
Dussourd, David E., and Eisner, Thomas
Vein-cutting behavior: insect counterploy to the latex defense of plants. bibl f il *Science* 237:898-901 Ag 21 '87
Dust, Interstellar *See* Matter, Interstellar
Dust, Volcanic *See* Volcanic ash, tuff, etc.
Dust collectors
Shopsmith Dust Collector. K. Collier. il *Fam Handyman* 37:48-9 D '87
Dust jackets *See* Book covers
Dust masks
Don't pollute yourself: wear the right protective mask. A. Rooze. il *Fam Handyman* 37:8+ Mr '87
Duster, Troy
Purpose and bias. bibl *Society* 24:8-12 Ja/F '87
Dusty millers (Plant)
How do you grow your dusty millers? As annuals, or perennials? S. B. Bonino. il *Flower Gard* 31:81-2 F/Mr '87
Dutch, Pennsylvania *See* Pennsylvania Germans
Dutch elm disease *See* Elm—Diseases and pests
Dutch National Ballet
Reviews:
Performances in Amsterdam. H. Klooss. *Dance Mag* 61:25-6 F '87
Performances in Amsterdam at the Muziektheater. H. Klooss. *Dance Mag* 61:19+ D '87
Dutch painting *See* Painting, Dutch
Dutch Reformed Church (South Africa) *See* Reformed churches—South Africa
Dutchess County (N.Y.)
Climate
Notes and comment [unseasonal snowstorm] *New Yorker* 63:31 O 19 '87
Duties (Tariff) *See* Tariff
Dutoit, Charles
about
Charles Dutoit: a surpassing "Firebird". R. Freed. il por *Stereo Rev* 52:72+ Mr '87
Duty free importation
Airport shopping. D. P. Marshall. *Travel Holiday* 167:28-31 F '87
Those airport deals aren't always a steal. B. Bauer. il *U S News World Rep* 102:48-9 Ap 20 '87
Duvalier, Jean-Claude
about
Judge: $115,000 Duvalier aide's condo in Miami belongs to Haiti Republic. *Jet* 71:6 Mr 2 '87
What's up, Baby Doc? il por *Time* 129:42 F 16 '87
Duvalier, Michèle
about
Lifestyles of the rich and tyrannical. J. L. Goldstein. *Am Sch* 56:235-47 Spr '87

Duvall, Camille
about
No one beats slalom champ Camille Duvall at making waves where the buoys are. M. Neill. il pors *People Wkly* 28:58-60 Jl 13 '87
Duvall, Shelley
about
Shelley Duvall comes home to the movie roost in Roxanne. M. A. Fischer. il pors *People Wkly* 28:85-6 Jl 27 '87
Duveil, Jenny
Oh, brother! A sort of love story. il *Mademoiselle* 93:182-3+ D '87
Duxbury (Mass.)
Historic houses, sites, etc.
History in towns: Duxbury, Massachusetts. A. B. Earle. bibl f il *Antiques* 131:614-27 Mr '87
The duxorcist [film] *See* Motion picture reviews—Single works
Dvořák, Antonín, 1841-1904
about
New world symphonietta. E. Rothstein. *New Repub* 196:27-30 Je 1 '87
Rusalka [opera] Reviews
N Y il 20:114 My 25 '87. P. G. Davis
Opera News il 51:32-3 F 28 '87. Y. S. Graff
Dwarf bamboo *See* Bamboo
Dwarf fruit trees *See* Fruit trees, Dwarf
Dwarf stars *See* Stars, Dwarf
Dwarf trees *See* Trees, Dwarf
Dwarfs and dwarfism
Rising above a prehistoric handicap [adolescent male dwarf skeleton from southern Italy; research by David W. Frayer and others] *Sci News* 132:334 N 21 '87
Dwellings *See* Architecture, Domestic
Dwight, Edward J., Jr.
about
He used to soar with eagles, but now sculptor Ed Dwight has landed on his feet. M. Neill. il pors *People Wkly* 27:115-16 My 25 '87
Dwork, Melvin
about
Tree house retreat: a designer's Fire Island aerie. P. Carlsen. il *Archit Dig* 44:60-5 Ag '87
Dworkin, Andrea
. . . and Dworkin's treatise on intercourse [excerpt from Intercourse] por *Ms* 15:28 Ap '87
Dworkin, Ronald Myles, 1931-
The Bork nomination. bibl f il *N Y Rev Books* 34:3+ Ag 13 '87
'The Bork nomination': an exchange [discussion of August 13, 1987 article] il *N Y Rev Books* 34:59-61 O 8 '87
From Bork to Kennedy. bibl f il *N Y Rev Books* 34:36+ D 17 '87
The press on trial. bibl f il *N Y Rev Books* 34:27-37 F 26 '87
Dworkin, Sidney
about
Why going private didn't bring Sidney Dworkin happiness. Z. Schiller. *Bus Week* p43+ O 12 '87
Dworkin, Susan
Roseanne Barr. il pors *Ms* 16:106-8+ Jl/Ag '87
Dwyer, Andrew Thompson, 1948-
about
If at first you don't succeed. J. Cook. il por *Forbes* 139:61-2 Je 29 '87
Dwyer, Augusta
Closing the door. *Nation* 244:384-5 Mr 28 '87
Dybvig, Kevin, and Cassell, Gail H.
Transposition of gram-positive transposon Tn916 in Acholeplasma laidlawii and Mycoplasma pulmonis. bibl f il *Science* 235:1392-4 Mr 13 '87
Dye, Dale
about
How the war was won. D. Goodgame. il por *Time* 129:58 Ja 26 '87
Dye, James L.
Electrides [cover story] il *Sci Am* 257:66-75 S '87
Dye, Kenneth M.
about
Fantasyland furore. M. Drohan. il *Macleans* 100:14 N 9 '87
Dye, Norman E.
Understanding data sheets of RF power transistors. il *Radio-Electron* 58:109-12+ N '87
Dyer, Alan
The refractor advantage: quality over size. il *Astronomy* 15:66-71 O '87
Dyer, Gwynne
Buying revolutions. *World Press Rev* 34:15 F '87

Dyer, Gwynne—*cont.*
New views on defense. *World Press Rev* 34:45 N '87
Dyer, Ira, and others
Ocean dynamics and acoustic fluctuations in the Fram Strait marginal ice zone. bibl f il *Science* 236:435-6 Ap 24 '87
Dyer, Joyce
Big boys don't cry—but why not? *Seventeen* 46:56-7+ Mr '87
How to get the most from a college trip. *Seventeen* 46:72+ Ap '87
Dyer, Susan
Look at Violet now! [story] il *Redbook* 168:16+ Ja '87
Two's a crowd [story] il por *McCalls* 114:99-100 Ag '87
Dyes and dyeing
See also
Cochineal
Coloring matter in cosmetics, food, etc.
Hair—Dyeing and bleaching
Indigo
Textile painting
Hippies meet yuppies as a new generation is fit to be tie-dyed. il *People Wkly* 28:65 Ag 24 '87
Dyett, Linda
Adult education: classes of '87. il *N Y* 20:38-42+ Ag 17 '87
Adults: what to do, where—and when—to do it. il *N Y* 20:90+ Je 29-Jl 6 '87
Dying *See* Death
Dylan, Bob, 1941-
about
Blowin' in the ear. R. O'Connor. por *Vogue* 177:54 Jl '87
Bob Dylan [interview] K. Loder. por *Roll Stone* p301-3 N 5-D 10 '87
Bob Dylan and The Band: U.S. tour, January-February 1974. D. Fricke. il pors *Roll Stone* p85-7+ Je 4 '87
Bob Dylan and the Grateful Dead. D. Browne. il por *Roll Stone* p22-3 S 10 '87
The Dead and Dylan. *New Yorker* 63:24-5 Jl 27 '87
Dylan stirs controversy in Israel. K. Loder. *Roll Stone* p15 O 22 '87
Dymally, Mervyn M.
about
Congressman Merv Dymally leads trade mission to Japan and Seoul, Korea. il por *Jet* 72:37 My 18 '87
Dymally pushing for fair black count in 1990 census. por *Jet* 73:34 N 30 '87
Mervyn Dymally takes the helm of the Black Caucus. il por *Jet* 71:5 Ja 12 '87
Dynamic random access memory *See* Random access memory
Dynamics
See also
Fluid dynamics
Molecular dynamics
Thermodynamics
Chaos, strange attractors, and fractal basin boundaries in nonlinear dynamics. C. Grebogi and others. bibl f il *Science* 238:632-8 O 30 '87
Dynamite
Vehement fire (I). B. Di Salvatore. *New Yorker* 63:42-4+ Ap 27 '87
Vehement fire (II). B. Di Salvatore. *New Yorker* 63:38-42+ My 4 '87
Dynamometers
Ducatis on the dyno [desmo twin engines] K. Vreeke. il *Cycle* 38:31-2 My '87
Engine performance: beyond the dyno [motorcycle engines] K. Cameron. il *Cycle* 38:63-7 S '87
Engine performance: the dyno room [motorcycle engines] K. Cameron. il *Cycle* 38:72-5+ Ag '87
Dyomin, Victor
about
Mad Russian [interview] A. Batchan. il por *Film Comment* 23:48-51 My/Je '87
Dysgenesis
Hybrid dysgenesis in D. melanogaster is not a general release mechanism for DNA transpositions. R. C. Woodruff and others. bibl f il *Science* 237:1206-8 S 4 '87
Dyslexia
Dyslexia [cover story] F. R. Vellutino. bibl (p128) il *Sci Am* 256:34-41 Mr '87
Dyslexia: reading both ends against the middle [study by Gad Geiger and Jerome Lettvin] C. Greene. *Psychol Today* 21:18 N '87

Dyslexia: recognizing shapes, not sounds [research by Karen Gross-Glenn] S. Vandershaf. il *Psychol Today* 21:12 Mr '87
Here's not looking at U [skewed peripheral masking in dyslexics; work of Gad Geiger and Jerome Lettvin] *Discover* 8:10-11 O '87
I was a teacher, but my son couldn't learn. G. Greenwood. il *Work Woman* 12:180+ N '87
It may be a case of the 'word-blind' leading the 'word-blind,' but Charles Drake unscrambles dyslexia. K. Gross. il pors *People Wkly* 27:105-7 Mr 30 '87
Letters [discussion of March 1987 article, Dyslexia] F. R. Vellutino. *Sci Am* 257:8+ S '87
Unravelling the mystery of dyslexia [work of Franklin R. Manis] il *USA Today (Periodical)* 116:10-11 D '87
Dysmenorrhea *See* Menstruation—Disorders
Dyson, Esther
Random access. See issues of Forbes beginning May 18, 1987
Dyson, Freeman J., 1923-
Demystifying the bomb. il *N Y Times Mag* p52+ Ap 5 '87
Dyson, John, 1943-
The great Cup race. il *Read Dig* 130:90-5 F '87
Dyson, Marianne J.
What color is your spacecraft? [cover story] il *Space World* X-12-288:9-11 D '87
Dyspepsia
When antacids won't work. N. Bruning. *McCalls* 114:155 My '87
Dystrophy, Muscular *See* Muscular dystrophy
Dziedzic, J. M.
(jt. auth) See Ashkin, A., and Dziedzic, J. M.
Dziewonski, Adam M., and Woodhouse, John H.
Global images of the earth's interior. bibl f il maps *Science* 236:37-48 Ap 3 '87

E

E., Sheila
about
Prince's intriguing women [cover story] L. Norment. il pors *Ebony* 43:162-3+ N '87
E. & J. Gallo Winery
Some vintage advertising [use of Bartles and Jaymes takeoffs to promote Iowa State football program] il *Sports Illus* 67:18 O 12 '87
E-2C airplanes *See* Airplanes, Military
E. coli *See* Escherichia coli
E. F. Hutton Group Inc.
Can Cohen the consolidator make Shearson-Hutton work? A. Bianco. il por *Bus Week* p96-8 D 21 '87
Cosby helps save black-owned airline; brokers a $3.5 million loan from E. F. Hutton Group Inc. il *Jet* 71:28 Mr 9 '87
The fall of the House of Hutton. S. Bartlett. il pors *Bus Week* p98-9+ D 21 '87
For sale: Wall Street giant [Shearson Lehman's bid] J. Schwartz. il *Newsweek* 110:64 D 7 '87
How E. F. Hutton is trying to clean its slate [industrial revenue bond imbroglio] G. Weiss. il *Bus Week* p79 Ja 26 '87
Humbled Hutton. il *Time* 130:49 D 7 '87
Welsh: making his firm a better listener [J. C. Welsh] M. N. Vamos. il por *Bus Week* p94 N 23 '87
Will Sandy Weill snare Hutton? G. G. Marcial. il *Bus Week* p73 Ag 24 '87
E. G. Smith Color Socks (Firm)
E.G. Smith, sockmeister. L. Grunwald. il pors *Esquire* 107:F41+ Mr '87
E. Howard & Company
Made in the U.S.A. R. Koselka. il pors *Forbes* 139:80-1+ Je 15 '87
E. I. Du Pont de Nemours
A boss like Reagan [R. E. Heckert] P. Sellers. il por *Fortune* 116:36-7 Ag 3 '87
Buried treasure [Du Pont discard, Vista Chemical] J. Willoughby. il *Forbes* 139:201 My 18 '87
A grassroots rebuff for Du Pont [proposed plant near Lukang, Taiwan] J. Hamilton. il *Sierra* 72:68-9 My/Je '87
The pros like what they see in Du Pont. G. G. Marcial. *Bus Week* p78 Ag 3 '87
Rape prevention: Du Pont's model program. A. Hornaday. il *Ms* 15:31 Je '87

E. I. Du Pont de Nemours—*cont.*
Selling—the computer way [B. Cecil] J. Blackford. il por *Pers Comput* 11:167+ O '87
E.M. Warburg, Pincus & Co., Inc.
Mattel has to play harder than ever [main shareholders, Warburg and Drexel, want a turnaround] J. Flynn. il *Bus Week* p60-1 My 25 '87
E-Prime Aerospace Corporation
Priming the ELV business. W. H. Ganoe. il *Space World* X-12-288:38 D '87
E Street Band
Bruce Springsteen and The E Street Band: The Bottom Line, New York City, August 13th-17th, 1975. D. Fricke. il pors *Roll Stone* p89-90 Je 4 '87
E-Systems, Inc.
E-Systems growth plan includes acquisitions, more joint ventures. C. A. Shifrin. il *Aviat Week Space Technol* 126:69 My 4 '87
Eady, Dorothy *See* Omm Sety, 1904-1981
Eagan, Andrea Boroff, 1943-
The girl in 1-A: sexual harassment hits home. il *Mademoiselle* 93:252-3+ Ap '87
The new doctors. il *Health* 19:25-9+ Ap '87
Eagar, Thomas W.
The real challenge in materials engineering. il *Technol Rev* 90:24-35 F/Mr '87
Eagle League *See* Lacrosse, Professional
Eagles (Musical group)
Don Henley [interview] M. Gilmore. por *Roll Stone* p287-91 N 5-D 10 '87
Ealing (London, England)
Historic houses, sites, etc.
Soane country [Pitshanger Manor] M. Filler. il por *House Gard* 159:172-9+ N '87
Soane's Ealing home [Pitshanger Manor] C. Robinson. il *Hist Today* 37:6-7 O '87
Ealy, Sekou
about
Deformed D.C. boy gets $95 million award in product liability suit. por *Jet* 72:26 Ag 3 '87
EAPs (Employee assistance programs) *See* Employee counseling
Ear
See also
Deafness
Labyrinth (Ear)
Birds
Developmental stability of the tonotopic organization of the chick's basilar papilla. G. A. Manley and others. bibl f il *Science* 237:655-6 Ag 7 '87
Care and hygiene
Sound savers [sinusitis and air travel] E. S. Orzac. il *Travel Holiday* 168:30 Ag '87
Diseases
See also
Tinnitus
Children's all-too-common ear infections. M. Patlak. il *FDA Consum* 21:28-31 D '87/Ja '88
Flying with a cold: save your ears. G. Weiss. il *Bus Week* p148 Ja 12 '87
Getting an earful [swimmer's ear and surfer's ear] S. Berne. il *Women's Sports Fitness* 9:20 Je '87
Nothing to fear but ear itself [malfunctions of ear as cause of phobic behavior] L. S. Dumas. il *Health* 19:19 Je '87
Treating ear disorders. N. Brown. il *Nations Bus* 75:52+ Ap '87
Protection
Shooting for safety [Gentex 1030 Active Hearing Protector] D. Geary. il *Pop Mech* 164:150 F '87
Ear, Artificial
3 children who needed a medical miracle [T. Simpson receives cochlear implant]; ed. by Linda Lee. M. Simpson. il por *Redbook* 168:110+ F '87
The sound of a miracle [cochlear implants for K. McCoy and B. Jones] T. Rademacher. il pors *Seventeen* 46:96-8 My '87
Sweet music for the deaf [cochlear implant] M. Clark. il *Newsweek* 110:73 N 9 '87
Earhart, Amelia, 1898-1937
about
1937. K. Ide. por *Am Herit* 38:108-9 Jl/Ag '87
The enduring mystery of Amelia Earhart. G. Bruder. bibl il pors map *Am Hist Illus* 22:10-19+ My '87
Earl, John
Stage or stepping stone? il *Hist Today* 37:5-7 Ag '87
Earle, Alexandra B.
History in towns: Duxbury, Massachusetts. bibl f il *Antiques* 131:614-27 Mr '87

Earle, Steve
about
Country's Steve Earle has it all: a hit album and 'the fastest Chevelle in Tennessee'. S. Dougherty. il pors *People Wkly* 28:103-5 Ag 10 '87
Earle, Sylvia A., 1935-
about
The siren of scuba: a top diver bubbles about life at the bottom. D. E. Haupt. il pors *Life* 10:46-51 Je '87
Earle, Victor M., III
The fantasy of life without risk. il por *Fortune* 115:113-14+ F 16 '87
Earle, W. H.
The phantom amendment & the Duchess of Baltimore. il pors *Am Hist Illus* 22:32-9 N '87
Earles, Beverley
Dora who? [adaptation of address, June 1987] il pors *Humanist* 47:17-19+ N/D '87
Early, Steve, and Wilson, Rand
High-tech workers: do unions have a future? *Current* 292:24-31 My '87
Early childhood education *See* Education, Preschool
Early retirement *See* Retirement
Early stars
See also
A stars
B stars
O stars
Early warning airplanes *See* Airplanes, Military
Earnhardt, Dale
about
Dale turns 'em pale. S. Moses. il pors *Sports Illus* 67:32-5 S 7 '87
Earnings, Corporate *See* Corporations—Finance
Earth
See also
Atmosphere
Biosphere
Creation
Geophysics
Magnetism, Terrestrial
The round walls of home. D. Ackerman. *Omni* 9:27 Ja '87
Core
See Earth—Internal structure
Crust
See also
Faults (Geology)
Folds (Geology)
Ocean bottom
Getting a full view of the earth's innards [seismic surveys] R. A. Kerr. *Science* 235:433-4 Ja 23 '87
Lateral isotopic discontinuity in the lower crust: an example from Antarctica. R. I. Kalamarides and others. bibl f il maps *Science* 237:1192-5 S 4 '87
Precision of Global Positioning increases [monitoring changes in the earth's crust] R. A. Kerr. *Science* 236:1625 Je 26 '87
Seeing bright spots in the middle crust. R. A. Kerr. *Science* 238:891 N 13 '87
Internal structure
All is flux [hot spots; research by Peter Molnar and Joann Stock] R. Kunzig. *Sci Am* 257:24+ S '87
Central heating [estimating temperature of the earth's core from the melting point of iron at immense pressure] *Sci Am* 256:25-6 Je '87
Core columns [research by David Gubbins and Jeremy Bloxham] *Sci Am* 256:67-8 Ap '87
Core questions [use of seismic tomography to probe earth's core] *Sci Am* 256:60-1 F '87
Earth's most abundant mineral [perovskite; research by Elise Knittle and Raymond Jeanloz] S. Weisburd. *Sci News* 131:103 F 14 '87
Global images of the earth's interior. A. M. Dziewonski and J. H. Woodhouse. bibl f il maps *Science* 236:37-48 Ap 3 '87
Helium loss, tectonics, and the terrestrial heat budget. E. R. Oxburgh and R. K. O'Nions. bibl f il map *Science* 237:1583-8 S 25 '87
How hot is the heart of the earth? [research by Quentin Williams and others] S. Weisburd. *Sci News* 131:245 Ap 18 '87
The inner earth is coming out. S. Weisburd. map *Sci News* 131:222-3 Ap 4 '87
Is the core pure iron no more? [research by Andrew Jephcoat and Peter Olson] *Sci News* 131:106 F 14 '87
Journey to the center of the earth [seismic tomography studies] T. A. Heppenheimer. il map *Discover* 8:86-90+ N '87

Earth—Internal structure—*cont.*

Magnetic field reversals, polar wander, and core-mantle coupling. V. Courtillot and J. Besse. bibl f il maps *Science* 237:1140-7 S 4 '87

The melting curve of iron to 250 gigapascals: a constraint on the temperature at earth's center. Q. Williams and others. bibl f il *Science* 236:181-2 Ap 10 '87

Mountains and valleys are at earth's core mantle boundary [seismic tomography studies] *Earth Sci* 40:9 Summ '87

Opening doors to the core, and more. S. Weisburd. *Sci News* 131:9 Ja 3 '87

Pioneering middle earth. B. Lawren. il *Omni* 9:44-6+ Jl '87

Set adrift by wandering hotspots [cover story] R. Monastersky. il map *Sci News* 132:250-2 O 17 '87

Synthesis and equation of state of (Mg,Fe)SiO₃ perovskite to over 100 gigapascals. E. Knittle and R. Jeanloz. bibl f il *Science* 235:668-70 F 6 '87

Mantle

See Earth—Internal structure

Observations from space

See also

Artificial satellites—Earth sciences use

Earth—Photographs and photography

Space stations—Earth sciences use

A mission to planet earth [interview with S. K. Ride] L. Sherr. il *Ms* 16:180-1 Jl/Ag '87

Orbit

Milankovitch climate cycles through the ages. R. A. Kerr. il *Science* 235:973-4 F 27 '87

Photographs and photography

Astronauts discover new planet! P. Jones. il *Space World* X-3-279:18-20 Mr '87

Business as usual . . . but not with the Soviets? [GeoSpectra hesitant to handle Soviet satellite photographs] *Space World* X-12-288:7-8 D '87

Crescent earth. il *Natl Geogr World* 145:33 S '87

Earth and moon together. H. Brandli. il *Astronomy* 15:20-2 O '87

Geology from 37,000 feet. H. M. Mogil. il *Earth Sci* 40:20-2 Wint '87

Rotation

See also

Planetesimal hypothesis

Polar wander

A matter of time [leap second] E. Marshall. il *Science* 238:1641-3 D 18 '87

Surface

See Earth—Crust

Temperature

See Earth temperature

Earth, Effect of man on *See* Man—Influence on nature

Earth First! (Organization)

Monkey-wrenching around. J. Malanowski. il *Nation* 244:568-70 My 2 '87

Mother Nature's army. J. Kane. il *Esquire* 107:98-102+ F '87

Earth movements *See* Geology

Earth Radiation Budget Satellite *See* Artificial satellites—Meteorological use

Earth sciences

See also

Artificial satellites—Earth sciences use

CD-ROM (Compact disc-Read only memory)—Earth sciences use

Climate

Computers—Earth sciences use

Geology

Geophysics

Image processing—Earth sciences use

Lasers—Earth sciences use

Meteorology

Videotapes—Earth sciences use

Talking about earth. See issues of Earth Science

Bibliography

Books & maps. See issues of Earth Science

Measurement

Geoquiz [scales] J. V. O'Connor. il *Earth Sci* 39:24 Wint '86

Earth scientists

See also

Geographers

Earth sheltered houses *See* Houses, Earth sheltered

Earth stations (Communications satellites) *See* Communications satellites—Ground stations

Earth temperature

Central heating [estimating temperature of the earth's core from the melting point of iron at immense pressure] *Sci Am* 256:25-6 Je '87

How hot is the heart of the earth? [research by Quentin Williams and others] S. Weisburd. *Sci News* 131:245 Ap 18 '87

The melting curve of iron to 250 gigapascals: a constraint on the temperature at earth's center. Q. Williams and others. bibl f il *Science* 236:181-2 Ap 10 '87

Earth tremors *See* Earthquakes

Earthquake prediction

See also

National Earthquake Information Center

All shook up: Los Angeles earthquake reveals new signposts of seismic danger [research by Thomas L. Davis] J. Horgan. il *Sci Am* 257:18+ D '87

All's not quiet on the northwestern front [work of Thomas H. Heaton and Stephen H. Hartzell] map *Discover* 8:9-10 Je '87

Awaiting the next Mexico City earthquake. R. A. Kerr. *Science* 237:1118 S 4 '87

Earthquake hazards on the Cascadia subduction zone. T. H. Heaton and S. H. Hartzell. bibl f il maps *Science* 236:162-8 Ap 10 '87

Earthquakes are giving little warning [crustal deformation] *Science* 235:165-6 Ja 9 '87

Getting to the bottom of the San Andreas [Cajon Pass hole] S. Weisburd. *Sci News* 131:70 Ja 31 '87

It's amazing when a foreseer hits the mark [California earthquake] M. S. Forbes. *Forbes* 140:18 N 30 '87

The Juan de Fuca plate: a sticky situation [Cascadia subduction zone] R. Monastersky. il map *Sci News* 132:42-3 Jl 18 '87

Predicting Parkfield . . . and other California quakes [cover story] J. Silberner. il map *Sci News* 131:268-9 Ap 25 '87

Quake prediction: magnetic signals? [research by Malcolm Johnston and Robert Mueller] R. Monastersky. il *Sci News* 132:167 S 12 '87

Seismomagnetic observation during the 8 July 1986 magnitude 5.9 North Palm Springs earthquake. M. J. S. Johnston and R. J. Mueller. bibl f il maps *Science* 237:1201-3 S 4 '87

Statistical short-term earthquake prediction. Y. Y. Kagan and L. Knopoff. bibl f il *Science* 236:1563-7 Je 19 '87

Successfully predicted earthquake [1986 quake near Monterey, Calif. predicted by Max Wyss and Robert O. Burford] *Sci News* 132:238 O 10 '87

Taking the pulse of Parkfield. R. A. Kerr. il *Science* 236:145 Ap 10 '87

Earthquake protection

Make the right moves before that quake hits. S. Woolley. il *Bus Week* p118 Jl 13 '87

Turning the mattress into a fortress [earthquake-proof bed canopy; work of H. J. Khadivi] T. Dworetzky. il *Discover* 8:22 S '87

Earthquakes

See also

Seismic waves

Delving into faults and earthquake behavior [special section] il *Science* 235:165-6 Ja 9 '87

Geologic events. See issues of Earth Science

Link between earthquakes and El Niños? [research by Daniel A. Walker] R. Monastersky. *Sci News* 132:373-4 D 12 '87

Number of U.S. earthquakes increased in 1986. *Earth Sci* 40:9-10 Summ '87

UFO update [Michael A. Persinger's theory of relationship between earthquakes and UFOs] P. McCarthy. il *Omni* 10:131 D '87

Measurement

See Seismometers and seismometry

Prediction

See Earthquake prediction

Protection

See Earthquake protection

California

All shook up: Los Angeles earthquake reveals new signposts of seismic danger [research by Thomas L. Davis] J. Horgan. il *Sci Am* 257:18+ D '87

A better fit for the plate tectonic puzzle [San Andreas fault discrepancy] R. A. Kerr. il *Science* 238:30 O 2 '87

Blacks seek aid for big losses in Calif. quake. il *Jet* 73:14 N 16 '87

A chilling dress rehearsal for calamity [Los Angeles area quake] S. Budiansky. il map *U S News World Rep* 103:14-15 O 12 '87

Earthquake aftershocks [Los Angeles area] il *Newsweek* 110:39 O 26 '87

Earthquakes are giving little warning [crustal deformation] *Science* 235:165-6 Ja 9 '87

Earthquakes—California—_cont._

It's amazing when a foreseer hits the mark. M. S. Forbes. _Forbes_ 140:18 N 30 '87

Jarring notice of California quake dangers [Los Angeles area quake] S. Weisburd. _Sci News_ 132:228 O 10 '87

Living with the threat of a quake. M. McIver. il _Macleans_ 100:49 O 12 '87

Notes and comment. _New Yorker_ 63:31-2 O 19 '87

Predicting Parkfield . . . and other California quakes [cover story] J. Silberner. il map _Sci News_ 131:268-9 Ap 25 '87

Quake prediction: magnetic signals? [research by Malcolm Johnston and Robert Mueller] R. Monastersky. il _Sci News_ 132:167 S 12 '87

Seismomagnetic observation during the 8 July 1986 magnitude 5.9 North Palm Springs earthquake. M. J. S. Johnston and R. J. Mueller. bibl f il maps _Science_ 237:1201-3 S 4 '87

Successfully predicted earthquake [1986 quake near Monterey predicted by Max Wyss and Robert O. Burford] _Sci News_ 132:238 O 10 '87

Taking the pulse of Parkfield. R. A. Kerr. il _Science_ 236:145 Ap 10 '87

A ten-second wake-up call [centered between Whittier and Pasadena] E. Magnuson. il _Time_ 130:32 O 12 '87

Tense moments between two quakes [Imperial Valley] R. Monastersky. _Sci News_ 132:358 D 5 '87

Waiting for 'the big one' [Los Angeles area quake] T. E. Johnson. il _Newsweek_ 110:42 O 12 '87

What is worse than "the big one"? [quake within the Los Angeles basin] R. A. Kerr. il map _Science_ 238:269-70 O 16 '87

History

San Francisco (Calif.)—Earthquake and fire, 1906

Dating earthquakes [work of Gordon Jacoby and others] J. Silberner. _Sci News_ 131:255 Ap 18 '87

Canada

In Canada: strong acceleration . . . and mysterious objects. J. Silberner. _Sci News_ 131:233 Ap 11 '87

Chile

Trees of the trembling earth [southern beech forest] T. T. Veblen. il _Nat Hist_ 96:42-7 S '87

Ecuador

Slow killers. M. S. Serrill. il _Time_ 129:35 Mr 23 '87

El Salvador

All states asked to provide emergency assistance to El Salvador after devastating earthquake; President Duarte addresses United Nations on earthquake assistance. il por _UN Chron_ 24:65 F '87

San Salvador: small quake, big problems [volcanic ash amplifies earthquake] J. Silberner. _Sci News_ 131:212 Ap 4 '87

Hawaii
History

Disruption of the Mauna Loa magma system by the 1868 Hawaiian earthquake: geochemical evidence. R. I. Tilling and others. bibl f il map _Science_ 235:196-9 Ja 9 '87

Mexico

Awaiting the next Mexico City earthquake. R. A. Kerr. _Science_ 237:1118 S 4 '87

Follow-up meeting on Mexican relief held 30 October. _UN Chron_ 22:104 N/D '85

Middle Western States
History

Midwest earthquakes. A. G. Unklesbay. il map _Earth Sci_ 40:11-13 Wint '87

Mississippi River Valley

Earthquake threat to the Mississippi Valley. J. Miller and M. Miller. il _USA Today (Periodical)_ 116:66-9 S '87

Montana
History

Scars and legends of Montana's 1959 earthquake. il _Sunset_ 179:44-5 Ag '87

Pacific Northwest

All's not quiet on the northwestern front [work of Thomas H. Heaton and Stephen H. Hartzell] map _Discover_ 8:9-10 Je '87

Earthquake hazards on the Cascadia subduction zone. T. H. Heaton and S. H. Hartzell. bibl f il maps _Science_ 236:162-8 Ap 10 '87

The Juan de Fuca plate: a sticky situation [Cascadia subduction zone] R. Monastersky. il map _Sci News_ 132:42-3 Jl 18 '87

Papua New Guinea

Outward-dipping ring-fault structure at Rabaul caldera as shown by earthquake locations. J. Mori and C. McKee. bibl f il map _Science_ 235:193-5 Ja 9 '87

Washington (State)

Coastal ups and downs point to a big quake. R. A. Kerr. _Science_ 235:166 Ja 9 '87

History

Evidence for great Holocene earthquakes along the outer coast of Washington State. B. F. Atwater. bibl f il maps _Science_ 236:942-4 My 22 '87

Earthquakes and building

Protecting skyscrapers against earthquakes [use of fiber reinforced concrete called SIFCON; work of Antoine E. Naaman] _USA Today (Periodical)_ 115:3 Je '87

Waiting for the next big earthquake [views of Robert V. Whitman] _Technol Rev_ 90:80 Ja '87

What is worse than "the big one"? [quake within the Los Angeles basin] R. A. Kerr. il map _Science_ 238:269-70 O 16 '87

Earthwatch (Organization)

The business of selling adventure. S. Ocko. il _Technol Rev_ 90:64-9+ F/Mr '87

Earthwork
See also
Dams
Filling (Earthwork)

Earthworms

Wormin' [taking trout on worms] W. G. Tapply. il _Field Stream_ 91:26+ F '87

Earwigs
Control

Are earwigs eating seedlings? _Sunset_ 178:202 Mr '87

Earwig solutions. P. H. Johnson. il _Rodale's Org Gard_ 34:64 Jl '87

Earworms, Corn _See_ Bollworms

Easements

The farm opportunity [conservation easements] P. A. A. Berle. _Audubon_ 89:4 Ja '87

The Trust for Public Land [donating conservation easements to land trusts] il _Mother Earth News_ 104:64-6 Mr/Ap '87

Eason, Henry

International spotlight. See issues of Nation's Business

Eason, Sarabeth
about

Sarabeth Eason [interview] C. Grant. il pors _Ms_ 15:60-1+ Ja '87

East, Nathan
about

Nathan East. R. Tolleson. il pors _Down Beat_ 54:47-8 F '87

East, Sarita Kenedy, d. 1961
about

Three-decades-long Texas estate feud being chronicled in Norton book. M. J. O'Brien. _Publ Wkly_ 232:29 O 23 '87

East Africa
See also
Ethiopia
Kenya
Mozambique
Trade routes—East Africa
Wildlife—East Africa
Description and travel

Africa. L. Morrow. il _Time_ 129:44-8+ F 23 '87
Native peoples
See also
Masai (African people)
Swahili (African people)

East and West

America's chance. C. W. Maynes. _Foreign Policy_ 68:88-99 Fall '87

The arms race is a universal issue. P. Ochieng. il _World Press Rev_ 34:36-7 Ja '87

German 'togetherness' could cause trouble for East and West. F. A. Miller. il _Bus Week_ p41 Ap 20 '87

East Asia
See also
Copyright infringement—East Asia
Economic assistance, American—East Asia
Education—East Asia
Investment banking—East Asia
Investments, Canadian—East Asia
Labor—East Asia
Motion pictures—East Asia
Pacific region
Women—East Asia

East Asia—*cont.*

Commerce

United States

See United States—Commerce—East Asia

Defenses

See also

Soviet Union—Armed Forces—Forces in East Asia

Description and travel

New adventure & romance in East Asia [special section] J. Powell. il map *Travel Holiday* 167:61-2+ F '87

Economic conditions

Are Asians really that much smarter? A. Smith. il *Esquire* 108:99-100 S '87

Foreign relations

China

See China—Foreign relations—East Asia

Soviet Union

See Soviet Union—Foreign relations—East Asia

United States

See United States—Foreign relations—East Asia

Industries

See also

Paper industry—East Asia

Printing industry—East Asia

East Berlin *See* Berlin (Germany: East)

East End (London, England)

History

East Enders recalled [Celebration of the Jewish East End] il *Hist Today* 37:61-2 My '87

East Germany *See* Germany (East)

East Hampton (N.Y.)

Architecture

Out of sight [home of architect R. Fisher] C. Vogel. il *N Y Times Mag* p58-62 Je 14 '87

Out of the woods [house built and decorated by Noel Jeffrey] S. Slesin. il *N Y Times Mag* p58-9 Jl 19 '87

The sticks [Pardo weekend house] D. Brenner. il *Archit Rec* 175:134-9 mid-Ap '87

East Hampton Historical Society

The William Efner Wheelock Collection at the East Hampton Historical Society [American furniture] J. A. Graybeal and P. M. Kenny. bibl f il *Antiques* 132:328-39 Ag '87

East India Company

The East India Company and the Emperor Aurangzeb. B. Lenman. bibl il map *Hist Today* 37:23-9 F '87

East Pacific Rise *See* Ocean bottom

East Saint Louis (Ill.)

Politics and government

E. St. Louis mayor wins 3rd term, but spectre of dead man may mar victory [reelected Mayor C. Officer] il por *Jet* 72:38 Ag 24 '87

East St. Louis mayor in dispute over election [C. Jordan vs. C. Officer] *Jet* 72:29 Ap 13 '87

East Salinas (Calif.)

Education

A teacher pushes migrants' kids into college—and gets fired by his California school board [case of G. Shirley at Alisal High] M. Green. il pors *People Wkly* 27:50+ F 2 '87

East Side House Settlement Winter Antiques Show *See* Antiques—Exhibitions

East Stoke (England)

Historic houses, sites, etc.

Stoke Field's last stand [500th anniversary of the Battle of Stoke Field] N. Bainbridge. il map *Hist Today* 37:2-3 Je '87

East Texas Television Network

Texas TV pioneer: Clara McLaughlin is first black woman to own stations. M. Marshall. il pors *Ebony* 42:78+ Mr '87

East Village (New York, N.Y.) *See* Greenwich Village (New York, N.Y.)

East-West trade

See also

Coordinating Committee on Multilateral Export Controls

ECE seminar in Greece considers East-West trade prospects. *UN Chron* 23:113 N '86

Eastcott, John

(jt. auth) See Momatiuk, Yva, and Eastcott, John

Eastdil Realty Inc.

More than a yen [Nomura Securities buys interest in Eastdil Realty] J. Willoughby. il por *Forbes* 139:122 F 9 '87

Easter, Dwayne

about

19 hours in "Devil's Icebox". S. Kelly. il *Read Dig* 131:60-6 Ag '87

Easter

See also

Jesus Christ—Resurrection and Ascension

Easter meditation:

Believing Thomas. B. L. Rohrig. il *Christ Century* 104:350-1 Ap 15 '87

Easter on Hill 17 [chaplain in Vietnam] G. H. Meyer. il por *Christ Today* 31:18-22 Ap 17 '87

The fragrant season. P. Yancey. il *Christ Today* 31:64 Ap 17 '87

Letters to Reinhold: Easter memories. U. M. Niebuhr. il *Christ Century* 104:357-8 Ap 15 '87

A meditation after Easter. D. K. Mano. *Natl Rev* 39:60 Ap 24 '87

Chile

"Running Christ against the bandits" [horsemen carry on Easter tradition] C. Caviedes. il *Nat Hist* 96:44-53 My '87

France

Easter in a Loire Valley château. A. Zabar. il *Gourmet* 47:72-3+ Ap '87

Easter candy *See* Candy

Easter cooking

See also

Cooking, Ornamental

An Easter luncheon. il *Gourmet* 47:108-14+ Ap '87

Easter dinners

A chef's Easter [A. Soltner] M. Burros. il *N Y Times Mag* p75-6 Ap 12 '87

Easter eggs *See* Eggs, Decorated

Easter Island

See also

Airports—Easter Island

Antiquities

Sleuthing around on Easter Island. L. Sitler. il *Travel Holiday* 167:62-3 Ja '87

Toppled statues and upended theories [views of Jo Anne Van Tilburg] il map *Discover* 8:9 My '87

Description and travel

Sleuthing around on Easter Island. L. Sitler. il *Travel Holiday* 167:62-3 Ja '87

Easterbrook, Gregg

Larceny at the launch pad. il *Read Dig* 131:209-16 D '87

Lost in space. *Wash Mon* 19:48-54 Ap '87

The revolution in medicine. il *Newsweek* 109:40-4+ Ja 26 '87

Sack Weinberger, bankrupt General Dynamics, and other procurement reforms. il *Wash Mon* 18:33-8+ Ja '87

The sky isn't falling [cover story] *New Repub* 197:18+ N 30 '87

Eastern Air Lines, Inc.

Can this airline be saved? C. P. Work. il por *U S News World Rep* 103:37-8 Ag 3 '87

Did the mechanics say too much? [Eastern disciplines mechanics who talked to press] il *U S News World Rep* 103:8 Ag 10 '87

Eastern Airlines agrees to pay fine of $9.5 million for safety violations. *Aviat Week Space Technol* 126:34 F 16 '87

Eastern begins replacing hundreds of pilots who quit in midst of dispute. C. Preble. *Aviat Week Space Technol* 127:36 Ag 10 '87

Eastern refuses to deal with ALPA until pilots end safety campaign. E. H. Kolcum. *Aviat Week Space Technol* 127:37+ N 9 '87

Eastern seeks early meeting with unions. E. H. Kolcum. *Aviat Week Space Technol* 126:34 F 2 '87

Eastern to enroll 4,000 a year in college-based pilot training. *Aviat Week Space Technol* 127:94 O 5 '87

Eastern-union stalemate expected to spur more layoffs. *Aviat Week Space Technol* 127:34 N 30 '87

Eastern will slash labor costs by $490 million this year. E. H. Kolcum. *Aviat Week Space Technol* 126:35+ Ja 26 '87

Eastern will transfer six A300s to Continental. *Aviat Week Space Technol* 126:34 F 16 '87

FAA faults Eastern's maintenance procedures; airline disputes findings. P. Proctor. *Aviat Week Space Technol* 127:34 D 7 '87

Has Lorenzo fired the first salvo in a fare war? C. Hawkins and J. E. Ellis. *Bus Week* p37-8 S 14 '87

It's that time at Eastern. P. Engardio. il *Bus Week* p33 F 2 '87

Judge blocks transfer of Eastern workers. *Aviat Week Space Technol* 127:31 Jl 13 '87

Lorenzo starts his attack [cost cutting] D. Pauly. il por *Newsweek* 109:49 F 2 '87

Questions about Eastern [maintenance procedures] J. Castro. il *Time* 130:41 Ag 24 '87

Eastern Air Lines, Inc.—*cont.*
Texas Air will maintain Eastern's identity. *Aviat Week Space Technol* 126:32 Ja 19 '87
Why Eastern is backing off from a union showdown. P. Engardio. il *Bus Week* p108-9 O 12 '87

Eastern Europe
See also
Cable television—Eastern Europe
Drug abuse—Eastern Europe
Food supply—Eastern Europe
Poland
Romania
Technology—Eastern Europe
Videotapes—Eastern Europe
Yugoslavia

Bibliography
Book reviews. *Curr Hist* 86:382+ N '87

Commerce
See also
Coordinating Committee on Multilateral Export Controls
East-West trade

Defenses
See also
Warsaw Treaty Organization

Economic policy
Bracing for trouble. A. Nagorski. il *Newsweek* 110:38 N 30 '87
Confronting the perils of *perestroika*. S. Sullivan. il *Newsweek* 110:39 N 30 '87

Foreign relations
Soviet Union
See Soviet Union—Foreign relations—Eastern Europe
United States
See United States—Foreign relations—Eastern Europe

Photographs and photography
Photographic pleasures outweigh pitfalls in Eastern Europe. C. Purcell and A. Purcell. il *Pop Photogr* 94:17 My '87

Politics and government
East Europe [special issue] bibl f il map (inside back cover) *Curr Hist* 86:353-94+ N '87
Gorbachev and Eastern Europe. C. Gati. *Foreign Aff* 65:958-75 Summ '87
New kid on the bloc: Gorbachev's reforms spill into Eastern Europe. S. H. Loory. il *Progressive* 51:21-3 Je '87
Reform? Few fans in East bloc. D. Stanglin. il *U S News World Rep* 102:26 F 23 '87
Skeptical satellites. J. Bugajski. *New Repub* 196:15-16 My 4 '87
Top down or bottom up? D. Singer. il *Nation* 244:756-8 Je 6 '87
Worried and nervous neighbors. S. Allis. il *Time* 129:51 Mr 9 '87

Eastern New Mexico University, Portales. Museum of Natural History *See* Museum of Natural History (Portales, N.M.)

Eastern Orthodox Church *See* Orthodox Eastern Church

Eastern River Expeditions (Firm)
Big drops and standing waves [whitewater rafting] R. Kimber. il *Ctry J* 14:36-41 Je '87

Eastern Test Range (Air Force) *See* United States. Air Force. Eastern Test Range

Eastland, Terry
The use and abuse of liberty. il por *Christ Today* 31:28-30 Jl 10 '87

Eastman, Lester F.
(jt. auth) See Heiblum, Mordehai, and Eastman, Lester F.

Eastman Kodak Co.
Back in focus. A. A. Lappen. il *Forbes* 140:8 Ag 24 '87
Focus on a new image [doing business in Japan] il *U S News World Rep* 103:40 Ag 24 '87
Kodak electronic photos [still video systems] S. A. Booth. il *Pop Mech* 164:40 O '87
Kodak hopes Cosby video will boost market share. il por *Jet* 72:16 S 14 '87
Straw in the wind? [A. Sieg, president of Kodak Japan] A. Tanzer. il por *Forbes* 139:122-3 F 9 '87
Why Kodak is starting to click again. L. Helm. il por *Bus Week* p134-5+ F 23 '87

Eastman Opera Theatre
Rochester. S. Low. il *Opera News* 52:38 Ag '87

Eastman Philharmonia
A tough course in orchestral realities. A. Rich. il *Newsweek* 109:55 Ja 5 '87

Easton, Robert
about
Uzing fo-netix, Robert Easton tranes moovey grates inn most evry axsent there iz. K. Hubbard. il pors *People Wkly* 28:69-70+ S 21 '87

Easton, Sheena
about
Prince's intriguing women [cover story] L. Norment. il pors *Ebony* 43:162-3+ N '87
A wedding belle gives Miami spice [cover story] R. Sanders. il pors *People Wkly* 28:132-7 N 23 '87

Easton (Md.)
Festivals
Follow the call of the wild goose [Waterfowl Festival] K. Lingo. il *South Living* 22:10-11+ N '87

Eastwood, Clint
about
Charismatic Clint. R. Gentry. il pors *McCalls* 114:136+ Je '87
Clint Eastwood: small-town mayor. W. Roessing. il pors *Saturday Evening Post* 259:42-5 S '87
Dirty Harry for president? M. Dobbin. il por *U S News World Rep* 102:26 F 2 '87
Eastwood asked Van Peebles to play role in new flick. por *Jet* 71:57 Ja 19 '87
Heartbreak Ridge [film] Reviews
N Y il 20:45 Ja 5 '87. D. Denby
New Repub 196:24-5 Ja 5-12 '87. S. Kauffmann
People Wkly il por 27:10 Ja 5 '87. R. Novak
No more baby kissing. P. A. Witteman. il por *Time* 129:34 Ap 6 '87

Eat the peach [film] See Motion picture reviews—Single works

Eating
See also
Appetite
Diet
Gastronomy
Gluttony
Nutrition

Anecdotes, facetiae, satire, etc.
The domestic silly food person speaks out. M. Frances. il *Teen* 31:20 S '87

Competitions
Miss Pancake [contest held on Shrove Tuesday at Peggy's Restaurant in Manhattan] *New Yorker* 63:30-1 Mr 16 '87

International aspects
The spice of life: food and culture [cover story; special issue; with editorial comment by Edouard Glissant] il *Courier* 40:3-34 My '87

Psychological aspects
Being thin isn't always being happy [interview with H. Schwartz] il por *U S News World Rep* 102:74 F 9 '87
Comfort food says "I love you". H. Garrison. il *Parents* 62:111-16+ F '87
Danger! Marriage can make you fat [excerpt from Weight, sex and marriage] R. B. Stuart and B. Jacobson. il *Redbook* 169:92-3+ Ag '87
Eat to remember [role of the vagus nerve; research by James F. Flood and others] S. Weisburd. *Sci News* 131:327 My 23 '87
Eating healthfully: for appearance' sake [study by Diane Hayes and Catherine E. Ross] S. Walton. *Psychol Today* 21:18 D '87
Food for thought [drop in concentration after meals; research by Andrew Smith and Christopher Miles] G. Lowe. *Psychol Today* 21:14 F '87
Foods that please the spirit [fruits and vegetables] R. Rodale. il *Prevention* 39:17-20 Je '87
How to conquer food cravings. H. C. Spencer. il *Ladies Home J* 104:69-70+ Ap '87
Let them eat cake—with tomato sauce [controversial eating guide, "Are you hungry?"] *Newsweek* 110:48 Jl 27 '87
Modulation of memory processing by cholecystokinin: dependence on the vagus nerve. J. F. Flood and others. bibl f il *Science* 236:832-4 My 15 '87
Never say diet. N. Malkin. il *Mademoiselle* 93:52 Ja '87
No butts [food cravings of ex-smokers; research by Neil E. Grunberg] D. Tonnessen. il *Health* 19:10 Je '87
Why you crave what you crave. E. Rapp. il *Mademoiselle* 93:142 Ap '87
Your diet: food cravings. J. S. Stern. *Vogue* 177:522 Mr '87

Africa
A grain revolution: the impact of imported rice on millet-based African civilizations. T. Ndoye and M. M'Baye. il *Courier* 40:8-9 My '87

Eating—*cont.*

Argentina

Of maize and meat: culinary traditions and cultural identity in Mexico and Argentina. P. Petrich. il *Courier* 40:10-13 My '87

Brazil

The meal is the message: the language of Brazilian cuisine. R. DaMatta. il *Courier* 40:22-3 My '87

Mediterranean region

Beneficial beans? [fava bean consumption in the Mediterranean region] *Courier* 40:13 My '87

Mexico

Of maize and meat: culinary traditions and cultural identity in Mexico and Argentina. P. Petrich. il *Courier* 40:10-13 My '87

Netherlands

Holland's feast of life [eating habits in the 17th and 18th centuries; excerpt from The embarrassment of riches] S. Schama. il *House Gard* 159:68+ Je '87

Papua New Guinea

The ones that get away [low protein diet] J. Durnin. il *Courier* 40:17 My '87

Philippines

Reflections on the potato. N. M. Joaquin. il *Courier* 40:14-15 My '87

Eating areas *See* Dining alcoves, etc.

Eating disorders

See also

Anorexia nervosa
Bulimia
Pica (Pathology)

Body image and self-esteem. *Society* 25:7 N/D '87

Food. L. Van Gelder. il *Ms* 15:39 F '87

Paradise lost. P. Camporesi. il *Courier* 40:28-31 My '87

Eaton, Eileen

The wisest decision I ever made; ed. by Jack Hope. il pors *Good Housekeep* 205:48+ Jl '87

Eaton, Mark

about

Clash of the titans. R. Goldberg. il *Sport Mag* 78:56-8+ Ja '87

Eaton, Phil

about

Turning penance to profit. R. Arias. il por *People Wkly* 27:30-3 Mr 30 '87

Eaton, Quaintance

Beau idéal. il pors *Opera News* 51:10-14 Ap 11 '87

Eaton, Rosie

about

Woman shoots man during Chicago church service. *Jet* 72:18 Ag 31 '87

Eaton (T.) Co. Ltd. *See* T. Eaton Co. Ltd.

Eaton Corporation

Eaton sees its future—and it's on the ground. S. Phillips. il por *Bus Week* p113+ N 16 '87

Eaton to sell AIL, all other defense electronics units. *Aviat Week Space Technol* 127:29 N 2 '87

USAF suspends AIL from new contracts pending billing inquiry. *Aviat Week Space Technol* 127:30 N 16 '87

Eaves, A. Reginald

about

Two Georgia commissioners indicted for extortion. *Jet* 73:12 N 2 '87

Eavesdropping, Electronic *See* Electronics in criminal investigation, espionage, etc.

Eavesdropping, Laser *See* Lasers in criminal investigation, espionage, etc.

Ebalo, Dan

The star story [poem] *New Yorker* 63:34 Jl 20 '87

Ebenezer, Reggie

about

How can Christians bring reconciliation to Sri Lanka? [interview] S. Mumper. il por *Christ Today* 31:46 Ag 7 '87

Eber, Shirley

(tr) See Hanniya, Akram. A death in Palestine

Eberhard, William G.

Runaway sexual selection. *Nat Hist* 96:4+ D '87

Eberhardt, Susan

about

Reader of the Year. il pors *McCalls* 115:41-6+ O '87

Eberhart, Richard, 1904-

How I became a Royal White Elephant, Third Class. il por *Am Herit* 38:44-7 F/Mr '87

about

The poet at age 82. N. R. Campion. *Am Herit* 38:46-7 F/Mr '87

Eberle, Nancy

Teaching parents to be better parents. il *McCalls* 114:49+ Je '87

Two extraordinary, ordinary children. il pors *McCalls* 114:49-52 Ag '87

Eberstadt, Fernanda, 1960-

Houses of the dead. *Commentary* 83:43-7 F '87

Moses [discussion of June 1987 article, The uses of Exodus] *Commentary* 84:8+ O '87

The uses of Exodus. *Commentary* 83:25-33 Je '87

Eberstadt, Frederick

The adobe island. il *Vogue* 177:324+ O '87

Don't call me Fred. il *Vogue* 177:267 Ap '87

Last man at a spa. *Vogue* 177:186+ Mr '87

Power tipping. il *Vogue* 177:148+ D '87

Eberstadt, Nick, 1955-

The latest myths about the Soviet Union. *Commentary* 83:17-27 My '87

Ebert, George

about

Saying 'no' to psychiatry. M. Schultz. il por *Progressive* 51:17 F '87

Ebert, Roger

about

"It stinks!" "You're crazy!". R. Zoglin. il pors *Time* 129:64 My 25 '87

Siskel on Ebert—Ebert on Siskel [interview] *Omni* 9:52+ Je '87

Eble, Diane

Too young to die [cover story] il por *Christ Today* 31:19-24 Mr 20 '87

Ebner, Tim

about

Tim Ebner at Wolff. K. Sofer. il *Art Am* 75:135-6 Ja '87

Ebony (Periodical)

Ebony examines new black middle class. il *Jet* 72:40 Ag 17 '87

Lerone Bennett Jr. named executive editor of Ebony; two others also promoted. il por *Jet* 73:19 D 28 '87-Ja 4 '88

The ebony tower [television program] *See* Television program reviews—Single works

Ebsary, Roy Newman

about

Strange and contradictory testimony. M. Gee. il pors *Macleans* 100:23 S 21 '87

EBV *See* Epstein-Barr virus

ECA *See* United Nations. Economic Commission for Africa

Ecaré, Désiré

about

Faces of women [film] Reviews

New Repub 196:24-5 F 16 '87. S. Kauffmann

Eccentrics and eccentricities

See also

Hermits

Indulge your quirks! H. H. Broun. il *50 Plus* 27:88 O '87

Anecdotes, facetiae, satire, etc.

What's your EQ? [Bing Eccentricity Quotient] S. Bing. il *Esquire* 108:70 D '87

Eccles, Margaret

The AgeLine database. *Aging* no355:23-5 '87

Ecclesia Athletic Association

Going for gold or zealotry? C. O'Connor. il *Newsweek* 109:27 Je 29 '87

Ecclesiastical architecture *See* Churches (Buildings)

Ecclesiastical art *See* Christian art and symbolism

Ecco Press

Ecco—selling beyond the 'core' audience [publisher D. Halpern] J. Barbato. *Publ Wkly* 232:39 D 18 '87

Ecenbarger, William

The astonishing flight of pigeon 309. il *Read Dig* 130:94-8 Mr '87

Bingo! il *Read Dig* 131:155-6+ Jl '87

ECG *See* Electrocardiography

Echinoderms

See also

Embryology—Echinoderms
Sea urchins
Sexual behavior—Echinoderms
Starfish

Rings on coral fingers [Astroporpa annulata] N. Sefton. il *Sea Front* 33:134-5 Mr/Ap '87

Echinoderms, Fossil

Spiny sea dwellers. D. B. Blake. il *Earth Sci* 40:17-19 Wint '87

Echlin, Edward P.

Conservationist before Assisi: the foolishness of St. Cuthbert. il *America* 157:478-9 D 19 '87

Echlin, Edward P.—*cont.*
Who in Solihull cares about dolphins? *America* 157:15-17 Jl 4-11 '87

Echlin Inc.
Service is our most important product. L. R. Walbert. il por *Forbes* 139:48+ Ap 6 '87

ECHO *See* Educational Concerns for Hunger Organization

Echo and the Bunnymen (Musical group)
Echo and the Bunnymen's slow hop to the top. M. Goldberg. il *Roll Stone* p20 D 3 '87

Echo Bay Mines Ltd.
Men who moil for gold. H. Rudnitsky. il por *Forbes* 140:36-7 O 5 '87

Echo sounders *See* Depth indicators

Echolocation (Physiology)
Auditory pathways to the frontal cortex of the mustache bat, Pteronotus parnellii. J. B. Kobler and others. bibl f il *Science* 236:824-6 My 15 '87
Sonic punch: dolphins and whales generate "bangs" that may stun prey [research by Kenneth Marten and Kenneth S. Norris] T. Beardsley. *Sci Am* 257:36 O '87

Eckardt, Allison M.
Books about antiques. See issues of Antiques
A collection of American neoclassical furnishings on the East Coast. il *Antiques* 131:858-63 Ap '87

Eckardt, Roy A.
Beyond zero-sum thinking in the Arab-Israeli struggle. il *Christ Century* 104:1143-5 D 16 '87

Eckart, Christian
about
Christian Eckart at Massimo Audiello. S. Westfall. *Art Am* 75:147 F '87

Eckert, Thor, Jr.
No nonsense. il pors *Opera News* 51:16-19 Ja 3 '87
Singer for life. il por *Opera News* 51:26 F 28 '87
Videocassettes. See occasional issues of Opera News beginning January 17, 1987

Eckhardt, Celia Morris, 1935-
Columbia Law School gets its first housewife-scholar-dean. il por *Ms* 16:62-5+ O '87

Eckhardt, Linda West
Mail-order morsels: good tastes to go. *Harpers Bazaar* 121:137-8+ D '87

Eckman, Fern Marja
Battered women. *McCalls* 115:157+ N '87
Teen suicide. *McCalls* 115:71-4 O '87

Eckrich, William P.
(jt. auth) See Doesken, Nolan J., and Eckrich, William P.

ECLAC *See* United Nations. Economic Commission for Latin America and the Caribbean

Eclipses
See also
Occultations
Computer dating [astronomical dating] F. R. Stephenson. il *Nat Hist* 96:24+ Ja '87
Mysterious Pluto may shrink no longer [Pluto-Charon mutual events; research by David Tholen and others] R. A. Kerr. il *Science* 235:30 Ja 2 '87
Timing eclipses of Jupiter's moons. J. E. Westfall. il *Sky Telesc* 74:634-6 D '87

Eclipses, Lunar
A deep penumbral eclipse of the moon. il *Sky Telesc* 74:399 O '87
Lunar coverups. T. D. Nicholson. il *Nat Hist* 96:92 O '87
A shallow eclipse [April 13, 1987 penumbral eclipse] il *Sky Telesc* 73:414 Ap '87
Photographs and photography
October's total lunar eclipse. il *Sky Telesc* 73:224-5 F '87

Eclipses, Solar
A Far-Eastern annular eclipse. il *Sky Telesc* 74:172 Ag '87
The March annular-total eclipse. E. M. Brooks. il *Sky Telesc* 73:12 Ja '87
October's remarkable "totality". G. Schneider. il *Sky Telesc* 73:222 F '87
A one-second total eclipse. P. Maley. il *Sky Telesc* 74:102-3 Jl '87
The Philippines: a land in shadow [visit in preparation for 1988 solar eclipse expedition] S. J. O'Meara. il *Sky Telesc* 73:432-3 Ap '87
Prospects for the March 1988 total solar eclipse [cover story] J. Anderson. il maps *Astronomy* 15:38-42 Ag '87
Shadow bands explained. *Sky Telesc* 73:27-8 Ja '87
The total solar eclipse of March, 1988. E. M. Brooks. map *Sky Telesc* 74:21-2 Jl '87

Photographs and photography
October's solar eclipse. il *Sky Telesc* 73:113 Ja '87

Eclipsing binaries *See* Stars, Eclipsing binary

ECM (Electronic countermeasures) on military airplanes
See Airplanes, Military—Electronic equipment

Ecofeminism
Ecofeminism—a new perspective. K. Sale. il *Nation* 245:302-5 S 26 '87
What is ecofeminism? [discussion of September 26, 1987 article, Ecofeminism—a new perspective] K. Sale. *Nation* 245:702+ D 12 '87

École de Cuisine Française S. de Mirbeck
French with an English accent. J. Pruess. il *N Y Times Mag* p50-2 F 22 '87

Ecole de Rouen
Collectors' finds in Paris: discoveries in painting, wallpaper and posters. J. A. Cuadrado. il *Archit Dig* 44:210+ D '87

Ecological art *See* Environment (Art)

Ecological models
Dynamic ecosystem consequences of tree birth and death patterns [computer models] H. H. Shugart. bibl il *BioScience* 37:596-602 S '87
Modeling the climate dynamics of tree death. P. J. Michaels and B. P. Hayden. bibl il maps *BioScience* 37:603-10 S '87

Ecological movement *See* Environmental movement

Ecologists
Now (I think) I understand the ecologists better. J. Simon. il por *Futurist* 21:18-19 S/O '87

Ecology
See also
Adaptation (Biology)
Agricultural ecology
Animal ecology
Birds—Ecology
Botany—Ecology
Competition (Biology)
Deep ecology
Desert ecology
Dispersal (Ecology)
Environment
Estuarine ecology
Food chains (Ecology)
Forest ecology
Fresh water ecology
Geographical distribution of animals and plants
Human ecology
Indians of North America—Influence on nature
Information storage and retrieval systems—Ecological use
Island ecology
Landscape ecology
Man and the Biosphere Programme
Marine ecology
Marsh ecology
Mountain ecology
Paleoecology
Pond ecology
Population biology
Prairie ecology
Predation (Biology)
Productivity, Biological
Religion and the environment
Reptiles—Ecology
Soil ecology
Urban ecology
Community diversity: relative roles of local and regional processes. R. E. Ricklefs. bibl f il *Science* 235:167-71 Ja 9 '87
Earth diary. T. Turner. See issues of The Mother Earth News beginning January/February 1987
Models
See Ecological models
Study and teaching
See Environmental education
Ethiopia
Ethiopian landscapes. D. Stevens. il *Commonweal* 114:652-4 N 20 '87
Hawaii
Biological invasion by Myrica faya alters ecosystem development in Hawaii. P. M. Vitousek and others. bibl f il *Science* 238:802-4 N 6 '87
Ecological invasions offer opportunities. R. Lewin. il *Science* 238:752-3 N 6 '87
Kenya
Beating the odds in arid Africa [Turkana] J. T. McCabe and J. E. Ellis. il map *Nat Hist* 96:32-41 Ja '87
Salina (Italy)
Pirates, parasites and population. il *Courier* 40:23 O '87

Ecology camps *See* Camps

Econometrics

Economic power [use of Compaq Deskpro 386 by H. Bowen] S. R. Reed. *Pers Comput* 11:71 Mr '87

Economic and Financial Committee (United Nations) *See* United Nations. Economic and Financial Committee

Economic and Social Commission for Asia and the Pacific *See* United Nations. Economic and Social Commission for Asia and the Pacific

Economic and Social Council (United Nations) *See* United Nations. Economic and Social Council

Economic assistance

See also

Relief work

World Bank

Developing countries

See Developing countries

Economic assistance, American

See also

National Endowment for Democracy

United States. Agency for International Development

Critics fault U.S. aid programs. P. M. Jones. il *Sch Update* 119:23-4 F 23 '87

The foreign aid cancer [address, May 28, 1987] R. T. Montoya. *Vital Speeches Day* 53:616-18 Ag 1 '87

FY 1988 request for foreign assistance programs [statement, March 17, 1987] M. P. McPherson. *Dep State Bull* 87:61-6 Je '87

Matching foreign policy resources with goals [statement, August 7, 1987] G. P. Shultz. *Dep State Bull* 87:6-11 O '87

U.S. foreign aid: virtue or vice? [interview with H. J. Hyde and T. Carpenter] P. M. Jones. pors *Sch Update* 119:26 F 23 '87

U.S. national interest and the budget crisis [address, May 7, 1987] M. H. Armacost. *Dep State Bull* 87:43-5 S '87

Africa

African development: an administration perspective [address, May 7, 1987] J. C. Whitehead. *Dep State Bull* 87:15-17 Jl '87

FY 1988 assistance requests for Sub-Saharan Africa [statement, March 12, 1987] R. A. Stacy. *Dep State Bull* 87:11-16 My '87

New and needed help for Africa [Africa Famine Recovery and Development Act] J. D. Hair. il *Int Wildl* 17:26 My/Je '87

Report on reports: Continuing the commitment: agricultural development in the Sahel [Office of Technology Assessment report] L. Olsson. il *Environment* 29:25-7 Mr '87

Science gets short end in foreign aid funding. J. Walsh. *Science* 235:742-3 F 13 '87

Secretary visits Bermuda and Africa [address, January 8, 1987] G. P. Shultz. maps *Dep State Bull* 87:23-8 Mr '87

U.S. development strategy for Sub-Saharan Africa [statement, February 26, 1987] M. P. McPherson. *Dep State Bull* 87:56-8 My '87

Caribbean region

See also

Caribbean Basin Initiative, 1983-

FY 1988 assistance requests for Latin America and the Caribbean [statement, March 25, 1987] E. Abrams. il *Dep State Bull* 87:84-90 My '87

Central America

Economic assistance for Central America [message to Congress, March 3, 1987] R. Reagan. *Dep State Bull* 87:82-3 My '87

A plan for fully funding NBCCA recommendations. il *Dep State Bull* 87:59-86 Ap '87

Developing countries

See also

Overseas Development Network

Aid, arms, and friends. B. Crozier. *Natl Rev* 39:32 O 9 '87

Ethnocentrism and third world development. H. J. Wiarda. bibl *Society* 24:55-64 S/O '87

Foreign aid and Gramm-Rudman. J. W. Sewell and C. E. Contee. bibl f *Foreign Aff* 65:1015-36 Summ '87

The moral implications of our population policy. W. Fornos. il por *Humanist* 47:30-2 Ja/F '87

The short end of the stick [advocating a program to send used sports equipment to the third world] D. O'Connell. il *World Tennis* 35:80+ O '87

Why foreign aid? il *Dep State Bull* 87:1-22 Ja '87

East Asia

FY 1988 assistance requests for East Asia and the Pacific [statement, February 25, 1987] G. J. Sigur. *Dep State Bull* 87:30-6 My '87

El Salvador

Minority report. C. Hitchens. *Nation* 245:742 D 19 '87

Europe

FY 1988 assistance requests for Europe [statements, February 3 and March 3, 1987] R. L. Ridgway. *Dep State Bull* 87:48-54 My '87

Latin America

See also

ACCION International

Alliance for Progress

FY 1988 assistance requests for Latin America and the Caribbean [statement, March 25, 1987] E. Abrams. il *Dep State Bull* 87:84-90 My '87

Liberia

Liberia's new moneymen. *Newsweek* 110:81 N 16 '87

Middle East

FY 1988 assistance requests for the Middle East and South Asia [statement, March 23, 1987] R. W. Murphy. *Dep State Bull* 87:59-64 My '87

Nicaragua

Covert aid and the Church [aid to Cardinal Obando y Bravo] R. Parry and T. Jacoby. il por *Newsweek* 109:27-8 Je 15 '87

Fighting the Sandinistas with dollars. M. D. Wilde. *Christ Century* 104:957-8 N 4 '87

Pacific region

FY 1988 assistance requests for East Asia and the Pacific [statement, February 25, 1987] G. J. Sigur. *Dep State Bull* 87:30-6 My '87

Philippines

Cory hallelujah. *New Repub* 196:7-9 Mr 2 '87

Last call for Cory? *Commonweal* 114:643-4 N 20 '87

Save Cory. *New Repub* 197:7-9 N 2 '87

South Asia

FY 1988 assistance requests for the Middle East and South Asia [statement, March 23, 1987] R. W. Murphy. *Dep State Bull* 87:59-64 My '87

Southern Africa

Congress seeks $800 mil. for new front-line states shipping ports, routes. *Jet* 72:4 Mr 30 '87

A truly constructive step: helping South Africa's neighbors. E. Weiner and S. Mufson. map *Bus Week* p48 Mr 2 '87

U.S. initiative for Southern Africa [address, February 5, 1987] M. P. McPherson. *Dep State Bull* 87:54-5 My '87

Sudan

The humanitarian side of the Reagan administration: the rescue of Ethiopian Jews. M. Bard and H. M. Lenhoff. *Humanist* 47:25-6+ N/D '87

Economic assistance, Canadian

Developing countries

See also

Calmeadow Charitable Foundation

Nicaragua

Canada's helping hand. H. Mackenzie. il *Macleans* 100:26-7 F 23 '87

Economic assistance, Domestic

See also

Government lending

Grants-in-aid

Old age assistance

Public welfare

Rent subsidies

Arms accord for domestic renewal. *America* 156:22-3 Ja 17 '87

Diet COLA: miracle cure for the budget? T. Jacoby. il *Newsweek* 110:56 N 16 '87

We need to rethink the "unthinkable". R. D. Lamm. il *USA Today (Periodical)* 116:20-1 S '87

United States

See Economic assistance, Domestic

Economic assistance, European

Nicaragua

Selling the rope. R. C. Kirkwood. *Natl Rev* 39:29 Mr 13 '87

Economic assistance, Japanese

Panama

"Everyone wants us". A. D. Frank. il *Forbes* 139:37-8 F 23 '87

Economic assistance, Russian

Developing countries

Aid, arms, and friends. B. Crozier. *Natl Rev* 39:32 O 9 '87

Economic assistance, Swedish

Developing countries

The poorest had most to gain [participation in smallpox eradication program] J. Tranaeus. il *World Health* p14-15 Ag/S '87

Economic Commission for Africa *See* United Nations. Economic Commission for Africa

Economic Commission for Europe *See* United Nations. Economic Commission for Europe
Economic conditions
See also
Business conditions
Business cycles
Business depression
Cost and standard of living
Inflation (Finance)
See also subhead Economic conditions under names of continents, countries, states, cities, etc.
International business. See issues of Business Week
The outlook is earthbound [world economy in charts] C. Gottlieb. il *Fortune* 116:70-5 Ag 3 '87
The world economy. See issues of World Press Review
Economic conferences
See also
United Nations. Preparatory Committee for the International Conference on the Relationship between Disarmament and Development
Another Nobel for freedom [Mont Pelerin Society's 1986 meeting] J. Chamberlain. *Natl Rev* 39:36+ F 13 '87
Another summit? *Natl Rev* 39:20 Jl 3 '87
Back to the Wall [Venice summit] G. J. Church. il pors *Time* 129:18-20 Je 22 '87
European economic summit meeting [Venice; address, June 15, 1987] R. Reagan. *Vital Speeches Day* 53:546-8 Jl 1 '87
For Reagan, missed opportunities at a soufflé summit [Venice] W. L. Chaze. il por *U S News World Rep* 102:20-1 Je 22 '87
In Venice, an opportunity lost [fears of global recession contribute to failure of economic summit meeting] R. Fly and others. il *Bus Week* p44 Je 22 '87
Is the dollar doomed? [economic conference in Venice] A. Smith. il *Esquire* 107:51-2 Ja '87
Limping into Venice. R. Fly. il *Bus Week* p34-5 Je 8 '87
Navigating with care [Venice summit] S. Koepp. il *Time* 129:58-9+ Je 8 '87
News briefing of May 8, 1987 [upcoming Venice summit] G. P. Shultz. *Dep State Bull* 87:13-14 Jl '87
Playing the summit game [Venice] K. T. Walsh. il *U S News World Rep* 102:28-9 Je 8 '87
The prospect for the summit: political gridlock [Venice summit] R. Kuttner. il *Bus Week* p22 Je 8 '87
Showdown in Venice. T. Fennell. il *Macleans* 100:29 Je 8 '87
Vagueness in Venice. D. Jenish. il *Macleans* 100:34-5 Je 22 '87
Venice economic summit [cover story] il pors *Dep State Bull* 87:1-21 Ag '87
Waiting for Gorbachev [results of Venice economic summit] R. Watson. il pors *Newsweek* 109:18-19 Je 22 '87
What the seven want—and may get [Venice summit] il *U S News World Rep* 102:30+ Je 8 '87
Anecdotes, facetiae, satire, etc.
Whistler, Baie Comeau or Hearne [choosing a location for the 1988 economic summit] A. Fotheringham. il *Macleans* 100:52 Je 15 '87
Economic conversion
It's time for economic conversion. J. Ritter-Murray. *Humanist* 47:30+ S/O '87
Soviets interested in study on economic conversion. M. Crawford. *Science* 235:1133 Mr 6 '87
Economic cycles *See* Business cycles
Economic development
See also
Developing countries
Development banks
International Conference on the Relationship between Disarmament and Development
Organisation for Economic Co-operation and Development
United Nations. Committee for Development Planning
United Nations. Industrial Development Organization
United Nations. Intergovernmental Committee on Science and Technology for Development
United Nations Conference on Trade and Development
United Nations Pledging Conference for Development Activities
United States. Agency for International Development
World Bank
World Commission on Environment and Development
See also subhead Economic conditions under names of countries

Attaining a sustainable future. W. M. Bueler. il *USA Today (Periodical)* 115:34-7 My '87
A declining dollar is just one piece in the puzzle. A. M. Solomon. il *Bus Week* p20 Ap 13 '87
Development under siege. S. Sen. *Commonweal* 114:647-52 N 20 '87
Five billion and counting. P. A. A. Berle. *Audubon* 89:6 Jl '87
Lyrics of loss, theories of gain [Nobel Prize awarded to R. Solow for economics] P. Gray; P. Elmer-DeWitt. il pors *Time* 130:80 N 2 '87
Nobel Prize for theory of economic growth [theories of R. M. Solow] E. Marshall. il por *Science* 238:754-5 N 6 '87
The results are in: overregulation kills growth. G. S. Becker. il *Bus Week* p24 Je 22 '87
World development report—1987. *UN Chron* 24:38-9 N '87
Economic education *See* Economics—Study and teaching
Economic forecasting
See also
Business forecasting
Econometrics
Economic indicators
Stocks—Price forecasting
Townsend-Greenspan & Company
The 21st century economy. W. V. D. Wishard. il por *Futurist* 21:23-8 My/Je '87
1986 World economic survey forecasts slow growth and falling commodity prices. *UN Chron* 23:103 N '86
1987 & beyond [special issue] il *Changing Times* 41:27-47+ Ja '87
The 1990s [special section] il *Fortune* 115:22-4+ F 2 '87
After a stumble, faster growth. T. May, Jr. il *Fortune* 116:38-42+ Jl 20 '87
American enterprise: then, now and tomorrow: 75th anniversary issue [cover story; special issue] il *Nations Bus* 75:10-12+ S '87
Backing into the future. D. Gergen. il *U S News World Rep* 103:72 Ag 17 '87
Business outlook. See issues of Nation's Business
Confusion—but hope [results of Time's poll of economists] N. R. Gibbs. il *Time* 130:52-4 D 21 '87
Economic Armageddon [address, January 29, 1987] R. J. Buckley. *Vital Speeches Day* 53:347-9 Mr 15 '87
Economic forecasting [address, May 29, 1987] J. Maxwell. *Vital Speeches Day* 53:685-6 S 1 '87
The economic outlook for 1987 and beyond [address, January 5, 1987] R. P. Forrestal. *Vital Speeches Day* 53:273-7 F 15 '87
The economy: down, not out. V. Brownstein. il *Fortune* 116:61+ N 23 '87
The economy of 1987—and beyond [address, January 26, 1987] M. Loeb. *Vital Speeches Day* 53:371-5 Ap 1 '87
Europe's recovery keeps rolling [views of Time's European Board of Economists] C. Redman. il *Time* 129:50-1 F 9 '87
Fifteen trends that will shape your financial future. M. Sivy. *Money* Sp Issue:26-30 Fall '87
Finding a prescription for black wealth [Black enterprise Board of Economists] D. T. Dingle. il *Black Enterp* 17:38-40+ Ja '87
Forecasting's dim prognosis. S. Dentzer and R. Thomas. il por *Newsweek* 110:42 Jl 27 '87
Fortune forecast. See issues of Fortune
The good times roll on for investors [midyear investment outlook; cover story; special section] il *Bus Week* p56-62+ Jl 6 '87
A hard rain is going to fall. M. W. Karmin. il *U S News World Rep* 103:76-7+ D 28 '87-Ja 4 '88
Has Europe's growth peaked? [views of Time's European Board of Economists] C. Redman. il *Time* 130:34 Ag 10 '87
Healthy signs for the economy. R. Thompson. il *Nations Bus* 75:8-9 Ap '87
The hidden issues facing America [address, January 6, 1987] W. E. Hoadley. *Vital Speeches Day* 53:270-3 F 15 '87
The international economic outlook for 1987. R. Bendiner. il *World Press Rev* 34:20-1 Ja '87
Keep your hopes up and your parachute handy [Money Roundtable] il *Money* 16:68-70+ Ja '87
The morning after [cover story] P. G. Peterson. il *Atlantic* 260:43-50+ O '87
The new economy: say hello to the lean years. K. Pennar. il *Bus Week* p164-6 N 16 '87
Observations. A. Bladen. See occasional issues of Forbes

Economic forecasting—*cont.*

An optimist with a different twist [interview with D. A. Levine] G. Slutsker. il por *Forbes* 139:54+ My 18 '87

Over the ears in debt [views of Time's Board of Economists] G. Russell. il *Time* 129:58-60 Mr 9 '87

Overall, a decent year ahead. M. S. Forbes, Jr. il *Forbes* 139:29 Ja 12 '87

Pick a forecast, any forecast. K. Pennar. il *Bus Week* p30-2 N 30 '87

Pollyanna and Cassandra. *New Repub* 197:4+ N 2 '87

Projections 2000 [special section] bibl f il *Mon Labor Rev* 110:3-63 S '87

Rising interest rates dim economic prospects. P. E. Kidd. il *Archit Rec* 175:43 Je '87

A rough road ahead. B. Rudolph. il *Time* 129:54-5 My 25 '87

Steady as it goes for the new year [A. Sarlos' predictions for Canada] P. C. Newman. il por *Macleans* 100:16 Ja 5 '87

Surprise: faster growth lies ahead. T. May, Jr. il *Fortune* 115:68-70+ Ja 19 '87

Tomorrow's global economy: the challenge of increasing competition. L. Chapman. il por *Futurist* 21:26-7 Jl/Ag '87

What lies ahead? [views of Paul W. McCracken] il *USA Today (Periodical)* 115:3 Ap '87

What's ahead for business. H. Banks. See issues of Forbes beginning January 16, 1984

Where to invest in 1988 [cover story; special section] il *Bus Week* p95-9+ D 28 '87-Ja 4 '88

Why Greenspan is bullish [cover story] S. Nasar. il pors *Fortune* 116:28-32+ O 26 '87

The world after Volcker. C. Smallwood and J. Cassidy. il *World Press Rev* 34:44-5 Ag '87

Economic growth *See* Economic development

Economic history

See also
Business depression, 1837
Business depression, 1893
Business depression, 1929-1939
Great Britain—Economic history
Japan—Economic history
Philadelphia (Pa.)—Economic history
United States—Economic history

Bibliography

Fun reading for bankers. C. P. Kindleberger. il *Forbes* 140:292+ Jl 13 '87

Economic indicators

See also
Price indexes

Government data are hardly an early warning system [Gramm-Rudman provision that suspends budget targets when economists agree a recession is imminent] J. Berger. *Bus Week* p32 Ja 12 '87

Economic models *See* Econometrics

Economic news

See also
Stock market crash, 1987—Reporters and reporting

The best and the worst of 1987. P. C. Newman. il *Macleans* 100:32 D 21 '87

Can anyone compete? [Business week's cover story] *Natl Rev* 39:18-19 My 8 '87

Current accounts. See issues of Money through December 1987

"I didn't see my name, either . . . " [press reports on Forbes four hundred] il *Forbes* 140 Sp Issue:390-1+ O 26 '87

News/Trends. See issues of Fortune beginning March 5, 1984

$$$$-saver: money-gram. See issues of Good Housekeeping

Winners and sinners: the bottom line [1987] J. Crudele. il *N Y* 20:26+ D 21-28 '87

Economic planning *See* Economic policy

Economic policy

See also
Commercial policy
Deflation (Finance)
Economic development
Full employment
Inflation (Finance)
Mercantile system
Sanctions (International law)
United Nations. Economic and Financial Committee
United Nations. Economic and Social Council
United Nations. Special Commission of the Economic and Social Council on the In-depth Study of the United Nations Intergovernmental Structure and Functions in the Economic and Social Fields

See also subhead Economic policy under names of countries and states

The constitution of economic policy [adaptation of Nobel Prize address, December 8, 1986] J. M. Buchanan. bibl f *Science* 236:1433-6 Je 12 '87

Economic imbalances and world politics. C. F. Bergsten. bibl f *Foreign Aff* 65:770-94 Spr '87

Global economic powers with global responsibilities [address, August 3, 1987] D. W. McMinn. *Dep State Bull* 87:24-6 O '87

A global new deal. G. Soros. il *N Y Rev Books* 34:52-3 Ag 13 '87

Managing the global economy [address, September 29, 1987] R. Reagan. *Dep State Bull* 87:5-8 N '87

The president of France speaks out [interview with F. Mitterrand] M. S. Forbes. il pors *Forbes* 140:22-3+ D 28 '87

Thresholds of change. L. R. Brown and S. Postel. il pors *Futurist* 21:9-14 S/O '87

Economic relations

See also
Balance of payments
European Economic Community
General Agreement on Tariffs and Trade
Organisation for Economic Co-operation and Development

Economic research

See also
Claremont Economics Institute
Econometrics

Economic statistics

See also
Economic indicators
Employment—Statistics
Gross national product
Unemployment—Statistics

The Forbes index. See issues of Forbes

Quality [excerpts from address, March 30, 1987] J. L. Norwood. *Mon Labor Rev* 110:2 Ap '87

Economic status of women *See* Women—Economic conditions

Economic theory *See* Economics

Economic value of man *See* Man—Economic value

Economics

See also
American Economic Association
Business
Business cycles
Capital
Capitalism
Claremont Economics Institute
Comic books, strips, etc.—Economics use
Competition
Computers—Economics use
Consumption (Economics)
Cost and standard of living
Debt
Deflation (Finance)
Employment
Finance
Income
Inflation (Finance)
Labor
Law and economics
Liquidity (Economics)
Money
Prices
Saving and savings
Socialism
Stock exchanges
Supply and demand
Urban economics
Wealth

The dismal science. G. P. Brockway. See issues of The New Leader

Is the dismal science really a science? H. Stein. il *Discover* 8:96-9 N '87

Lights! Camera! Economists! G. Hedberg. il *Money* 16:148-50+ O '87

The newest name in economics: John Maynard Keynes. N. Jonas and J. Berger. *Bus Week* p42 Ja 12 '87

Tennis at Harvard [experimental findings on rationality and economic theory] D. Seligman. il *Fortune* 116:204 N 23 '87

Bibliography

Book reviews. See issues of Monthly Labor Review

Dictionaries

$550 'Dictionary of economics' announced by Stockton Press [The new Palgrave] *Publ Wkly* 232:63 O 9 '87

Economics—Dictionaries—*cont.*
Explaining economics from A to Z [The new Palgrave] S. Dentzer. il *U S News World Rep* 103:64 D 21 '87

History
See Economic history
Mathematical models
See Econometrics
Study and teaching
See also
Colleges and universities—Departments of economics
The economists take their lumps [free market economy theory] R. H. Bork, Jr. *U S News World Rep* 103:46 Jl 13 '87
Readin', ritin' and real estate [opposition to courses for children] G. Merkin. por *U S News World Rep* 103:9 N 2 '87
Terminology
A profitable supply of hard working words. J. Ferber. *Sch Update* 119:22 Ja 26 '87
Economics and Christianity *See* Christianity and economics
Economics and education
See also
School children—Social and economic status
Higher learning means higher earnings, study. *Jet* 73:12 N 16 '87
The impact of money. D. O. Relin. il *Sch Update* 120:13 N 6 '87
The Sputnik of the eighties [economic competitiveness and federal role in education; cover story] J. F. Jennings. bibl f il *Phi Delta Kappan* 69:104-9 O '87
The states and economic development [address, November 18, 1986] M. N. Castle. *Vital Speeches Day* 53:199-202 Ja 15 '87
Would it pay you to go back to school? D. S. Johnson. il *Better Homes Gard* 65:34+ Ap '87
Economics and law *See* Law and economics
Economics and politics
Brockway's paradox [theories of J. M. Buchanan] G. P. Brockway. il *New Leader* 69:10-11 D 29 '86
The constitution of economic policy [adaptation of Nobel Prize address, December 8, 1986] J. M. Buchanan. bibl f *Science* 236:1433-6 Je 12 '87
Politics v. economics. W. F. Buckley. *Natl Rev* 39:62-3 Je 19 '87
Economist (Periodical)
Glass houses [criticism of U.S. economic policy] *Natl Rev* 39:20-1 O 9 '87
Economists
See also
Abalkin, Leonid
American Economic Association
Barro, Robert J.
Buchanan, James M., 1919-
Burns, Arthur F. (Arthur Frank), 1904-1987
Greenspan, Alan
Heller, Walter W.
Keynes, John Maynard, 1883-1946
Kolson, Rob
Monnet, Jean, 1888-1979
Sen, Amartya Kumar
Thurow, Lester C.
Lights! Camera! Economists! G. Hedberg. il *Money* 16:148-50+ O '87
Why we can't live without economists. G. S. Becker. il *Bus Week* p20 F 2 '87
Economists as comedians
The case of the popular economist [R. Kolson] D. Seligman. il *Fortune* 116:166 N 9 '87
Economy *See* Thrift
Economy cars *See* Automobiles; Automobiles, Foreign
ECOSOC *See* United Nations. Economic and Social Council
Ecstatic orange [ballet] *See* Ballet reviews—Single works
ECT (Electroconvulsive therapy) *See* Shock therapy
Ectopic pregnancy *See* Pregnancy—Complications
Ecuador
See also
Arts and crafts—Ecuador
Chordeleg (Ecuador)
Earthquakes—Ecuador
Galapagos Islands
Indians of South America—Ecuador
Quito (Ecuador)
Rain forests—Ecuador
Politics and government
Kidnapping a president [L. Febres Cordero] K. Scanlon. *Macleans* 100:24 Ja 26 '87
Religious institutions and affairs
See also
Church and social problems—Ecuador

Ecumenical Council (2nd: 1962-1965) *See* Vatican Council (2nd: 1962-1965)
Ecumenical movement
See also
Catholic Church—Relations—Church of England
Catholic Church—Relations—Episcopal Church
Catholic Church—Relations—Protestant churches
Church union
Communauté de Taizé
International Seminar on the Future of Mankind and Cooperation Among Religions
World Council of Churches
Denominational moves raise questions [relocating church offices out of New York City has implications for ecumenism] C. Iosso. *Christ Century* 104:484-6 My 20-27 '87
Differences that bind. J. Garvey. il *Commonweal* 114:103-4 F 27 '87
Ecumenism enroute. *America* 156:42 Ja 24 '87
Ecumenism: the future is local. W. B. Cate. *Christ Century* 104:551-2 Je 17-24 '87
State ecumenism explored [Catholic, Protestant and Orthodox leaders meet in Indianapolis] *Christ Century* 104:848 O 7 '87
Ed Debevic's Diner (Beverly Hills, Calif.) *See* Beverly Hills (Calif.)—Restaurants, nightclubs, bars, etc.
EDB (Ethylene dibromide) pesticides *See* Pesticides
Edberg, Stefan
about
Heads up! [cover story] K. Cunningham. pors *World Tennis* 35:22-6 Ag '87
Edberg, Stephen J.
about
Inside the IHW: the amateurs [interview] A. MacRobert. il por *Sky Telesc* 73:264-5 Mr '87
Eddie Condon's (New York, N.Y.: Jazz club) *See* New York (N.Y.)—Restaurants, nightclubs, bars, etc.
Eddies
See also
Vortex motion
Ice-edge eddies in the Fram Strait marginal ice zone. O. M. Johannessen and others. bibl f il maps *Science* 236:427-9 Ap 24 '87
Eddison, Sydney
Garden generosity. il *House Gard* 159:142-7+ Je '87
Eddy, Don, 1944-
about
Don Eddy at Nancy Hoffman. G. Henry. il *Art Am* 75:148 F '87
Eddy, William
Rhythms of survival. il map *Natl Parks* 61:21-3 S/O '87
Edelman, Asher B.
about
A $100,000 campus 'raid'. A. Gabor. por *U S News World Rep* 103:12-13 O 26 '87
A $100,000 question stirs up Columbia. B. Kantrowitz. il por *Newsweek* 110:76 O 26 '87
Asher the arb. R. L. Stern. por *Forbes* 139:35 F 23 '87
Burlington almost invited Edelman to attack. D. Foust. il por *Bus Week* p50+ My 11 '87
Don't go near the dollars. E. Bowen. il por *Time* 130:138-9 O 26 '87
Edelman: a new Lucky strike? K. M. Hafner. il por *Bus Week* p49 F 23 '87
Edelman's art of reward. N. J. Perry. il por *Fortune* 116:159 N 9 '87
Inside Wall Street: these pros have already started betting on a rebound. G. G. Marcial. il por *Bus Week* p44 N 9 '87
Edelman, Gay Norton
Childbirth: how it was for me. il *Good Housekeep* 205:86+ S '87
"How I'd like mom & dad to change". il *Parents* 62:122-6 N '87
Edelman, Gerald M., 1929-
about
Neural Darwinism: an exchange [discussion of October 9, 1986 article, Neural Darwinism: a new approach to memory and perception] I. Rosenfield. *N Y Rev Books* 34:44-5 Mr 12 '87
Edelman, Hendrik, 1937-, and Muller, Karen, 1948-
A new look at the library market. il *Publ Wkly* 231:30-5 My 29 '87
Edelman, Marek, 1921-
about
The curious case of Marek Edelman. L. S. Dawidowicz. *Commentary* 83:66-9 Mr '87
Poland's 'Jewish problem' [interview] *Harpers* 275:21-2 Ag '87

Edelman, Marek, 1921——about—*cont.*
Poles and Jews [discussion of March 1987 article, The curious case of Marek Edelman] L. S. Dawidowicz. *Commentary* 84:2-4+ Ag '87

Edelman, Marian Wright
How to prevent teenage pregnancy [excerpt from Families in peril] il pors *Ebony* 42:60+ Jl '87
about
Edelman raps U.S. high black infant death rate. por *Jet* 71:9 F 23 '87
Marian Wright Edelman. K. Bouton. por *Ms* 16:98-100+ Jl/Ag '87
"They cannot fend for themselves". N. Traver. il por *Time* 129:27 Mr 23 '87

Edelmann, Sergei
about
Edelmann: Irresistible Chopin. R. Freed. por *Stereo Rev* 52:76 Ag '87

Edelson, Burt
about
Outlook for space science: conversations with Burt Edelson and Lennard Fisk. M. Freeman; T. Reichhardt. pors *Space World* X-11-287:26-31 N '87

Edelson, David B.
Preserving old-growth forests. bibl f il *Environment* 29:3-5 O '87

Edelson, Richard I.
about
New clues to the immune system. S. Squire. il por *N Y Times Mag* p32-3+ F 1 '87

Edelstein, Barbara, 1931-
The save-his-life weight loss diet [excerpt from The underburner's diet] il *Ladies Home J* 104:62+ F '87
The underburner's diet [excerpt] il *Ladies Home J* 104:81-3+ Ja '87

Edema
See also
Reye's syndrome
Heart peptide goes to the head [research by James A. Nathanson and Luca Steardo] D. D. Edwards. *Sci News* 131:68 Ja 31 '87

Eden, Anthony, Earl of Avon, 1897-1977
about
Anthony Eden & the decline of Britain. O. Harries. *Commentary* 83:34-43 Je '87

Eden
The earthly paradise [Orinoco River as Eden; excerpt from The four voyages of Christopher Columbus] C. Columbus. il *Courier* 40:8-9 Ap '87
Has the Garden of Eden been located at last? [views of J. Zarins] D. J. Hamblin. bibl (p184) il map *Smithsonian* 18:127-35 My '87

Eden [dance] See Dance reviews—Single works

Edgar, Joanne
Iceland's feminists: power at the top of the world. il *Ms* 16:30+ D '87

Edgartown (Mass.)
Historic houses, sites, etc.
History in towns: Edgartown, Martha's Vineyard. W. N. Banks. il *Antiques* 132:1302-17 D '87

Edgell, Robert Louis, 1922-
about
HBJ shows the leveraged deal is alive and well. G. DeGeorge. *Bus Week* p36-7 N 30 '87

Edgell Communications Inc.
HBJ sells units to Edgell group for $334.1 million. C. Reid. *Publ Wkly* 232:11 N 27 '87
HBJ shows the leveraged deal is alive and well [R. L. Edgell acquires magazine unit] G. DeGeorge. *Bus Week* p36-7 N 30 '87

Edgerton, Harold Eugene, 1903-
about
"Doc" Edgerton: the man who made time stand still. E. Zwingle. il pors *Natl Geogr* 172:464-83 O '87

EDI See Electronic data interchange
Edible greens See Greens, Edible
Edible plants See Plants, Edible
Edinburgh, Philip, Duke of See Philip, Prince, consort of Elizabeth II, Queen of Great Britain, 1921-
Edinburgh Film Festival See Motion picture festivals—Scotland

Edinger, Claudio
about
Claudio Edinger: portraiture is a way to understand mankind. S. Piperato. il por *Pop Photogr* 94:40 D '87

Edison Brothers Stores, Inc.
Where's that wake-up call? J. Parr. *Forbes* 140:168 S 21 '87

Edison Institute See Henry Ford Museum and Greenfield Village

Edison National Historic Site
Where Edison brought good things to life. S. Alcorn. il *Travel Holiday* 168:32-4 Ag '87

Edison Winter Home and Museum (Fort Myers, Fla.)
Fort Myers houses the Edison legacy. il *South Living* 22:28+ Mr '87

Editing of motion pictures See Motion pictures—Editing
Editing of slides See Slides (Photography)—Editing
Editing of tape recordings See Tape recordings—Editing
Editing of television programs See Television editing
Editing of videotapes See Videotapes—Editing
Editors, Videotape See Videotape recorders and recording—Equipment

Editors and editing
See also
Authors and editors
Jenks, Tom
McDonald, Erroll
Mehta, A. S. (Ajai Singh)
Motion pictures—Editing
Proofreading
Television editing
Whitehead, William Grant, d. 1987
Women editors
Fanfare for the common editor. E. Hitchner. por *Publ Wkly* 232:40 S 4 '87
On the road to mediocrity [decline of copy editing] T. Rogers. il *Publ Wkly* 232:42 D 4 '87
Textbook credits bruise psychiatrists' egos [R. Michels vs. J. O. Cavenar] E. Marshall. por *Science* 235:835-6 F 20 '87
Textbook dispute [discussion of February 20, 1987 article, Textbook credits bruise psychiatrists' egos] E. Marshall. *Science* 236:655-7 My 8 '87
Awards
Bantam's Deborah Futter wins Tony Godwin Award. por *Publ Wkly* 231:26 F 13 '87
Political activities
286 editors sign letter against Bork nomination. *Publ Wkly* 232:13 O 16 '87
Salaries, pensions, etc.
The importance of copy editing [boosting pay and prestige] L. Stearns. il *Publ Wkly* 232:48 Jl 10 '87

Edmiston, Susan
The frightening side effects of a "miracle drug" for infertility. il *Glamour* 85:220-1+ D '87

Edmond, Alfred, Jr.
Can this man keep Team Xerox no. 1? il *Black Enterp* 18:58-60+ Ag '87
These guys don't blink. il pors *Black Enterp* 17:310-12+ Je '87

Edmonds, Frank N., 1919-1986
about
Obituary
Phys Today 40:108+ Ap '87. G. H. de Vaucouleurs

Edmondson, Daisy
Open wide! il *Parents* 62:112-16+ Mr '87
The surprising truth about children's height. il *Parents* 62:133-6+ S '87

Edmondson, Jolee
Hazards of the game. il *Audubon* 89:24-8+ N '87

Edmondson, Simon, 1955?-
about
Simon Edmondson: between two worlds. J. Higgins. il por *Art News* 86:89-90 Mr '87

Edmonton (Alta.)
Buildings
A cluster of one-room schoolhouses [Julia Kiniski School] H. L. Smith, Jr. il *Archit Rec* 175:98-101 S '87
Climate
A disaster in Edmonton [tornado] J. Howse. il *Macleans* 100:8-9 Ag 10 '87
Edmonton after the storm [July tornado] J. Howse. *Macleans* 100:12 O 26 '87
Pain and hope after the killer winds [aftermath of tornado] M. Gray. il *Macleans* 100:39-40 Ag 17 '87
Crime
Fears of a serial killer. *Macleans* 100:14 Ap 13 '87

Edmunds, Lavinia
Barbara Mikulski. por *Ms* 15:63+ Ja '87
Women who won. il *Ms* 15:29+ Ja '87

Edo (Japan) in art
Views of Edo: high and low [Hiroshige] K. Varnedoe. il *Art Am* 75:98-105 Jl '87

Edsall, Thomas Byrne
The political impasse. il *N Y Rev Books* 34:8-10+ Mr 26 '87

EDTA See Ethylenediamine tetraacetic acid
Educating Rita [drama] See Russell, Willy

Education

See also

Ability grouping in education
Accountability (Education)
Adult education
Aged—Education
Agricultural education
Art teachers—Education
Arts teachers—Education
Asian Americans—Education
Athletes—Education
Bilingual education
Black athletes—Education
Blacks—Education
Blind—Education
Business and education
Calculators—Educational use
Catholic schools
Celebrities—Education
Children—Education
Children, Gifted—Education
Children of migrant laborers—Education
Chinese Americans—Education
Citizenship education
Coeducation
College education
Colleges and universities
Communication in education
Communications satellites—Educational use
Community and junior colleges
Community education
Compensatory education
Computers—Educational use
Correlation (Education)
Dramatization in education
Drug education
Economics and education
Educators
Environmental education
Ex-convicts—Education
Farmers—Education
Foreign students
Forestry education
Grade repetition (Education)
Grading and marking (Students)
Group work in education
Handicapped—Education
Health education
Hispanic Americans—Education
Home education
Incentives in education
Indians of North America—Education
Information storage and retrieval systems—Educational use
Interactive video—Educational use
Intercultural education
International education
Journalism, Educational
Labor—Education
Learning, Psychology of
Liberal education
Literacy education
Measurement-driven instruction
Medical education
Mentally handicapped children—Education
Mexican Americans—Education
Minorities—Education
Montessori method of education
Moral education
Motion pictures in education
Motivation (Education)
Motorcycles in education
Music teachers—Education
Nature study
Nutrition education
Palestinian Arabs—Education
Parent education
Photocopying—Educational use
Physical education and training
Police—Education
Private schools
Problem children—Education
Public schools
Rich—Education
Safety education
Self improvement
Sex discrimination in education
Sick children—Education
Single mothers—Education
Slow learning children—Education
Social education

Socially handicapped children—Education
Special education
Study
Summer schools
Teachers
Teaching
Television in education
Textbooks
Videodiscs—Educational use
Videotapes—Educational use
Visually handicapped—Education
Vocational-technical education
Volunteer workers in education
Women—Education

A complaint and a prediction [teachers as focus of school reform efforts] C. M. Breinin. il *Phi Delta Kappan* 69:15-16 S '87
Education. See occasional issues of Better Homes and Gardens
Education reforms. R. W. Tyler. il *Phi Delta Kappan* 69:277-80 D '87
Mr. Bennett warns lotus eaters [speech on educational reform to National Seminar of the Education Writers' Association] J. W. Donohue. *America* 156:373-4 My 9 '87
New thinking in America's schools: does your school district offer these programs? M. Conroy. il *Better Homes Gard* 65:52+ O '87
Teachers are writing the ABCs of school reform. J. Tasini. il *Bus Week* p74-5 S 7 '87
Unlocking school reform: uncertainty as a condition of professionalism. C. D. Glickman. bibl f il *Phi Delta Kappan* 69:120-2 O '87

Aims and objectives

See also

College education—Aims and objectives
Educational sociology

A call for radical changes in educational delivery. C. E. Finn. *Educ Dig* 52:2-5 Ja '87
Discover yourself [address, May 10, 1987] E. L. Boyer. *Vital Speeches Day* 53:686-8 S 1 '87
In defense of our common culture. W. J. Bennett. il por *USA Today (Periodical)* 115:45-7 Mr '87
Teaching ethics [confronting a defiant student] S. M. Masiclat. il *Phi Delta Kappan* 69:275-6 D '87
What education reform? [local reforms preferred over state mandates] P. Welsh. *Educ Dig* 52:6-9 F '87

Awards

See also

High schools—Awards
Teachers—Awards

Bibliography

Books. L. D. Brown. See issues of Phi Delta Kappan beginning September 1985
New materials. See issues of The Education Digest beginning September 1986

Conferences

Calendar. See issues of The Education Digest beginning September 1986

Curricula

See Courses of study

Evaluation

See also

Accountability (Education)
National Assessment of Educational Progress

A,B,C, or F: test your child's school. V. Cobb. il *Parents* 62:138-42+ N '87
American schools rate a "B" [survey of children] *USA Today (Periodical)* 116:5 Ag '87
Does your child's school make the grade? il *Parents* 62:24 Je '87
Does your child's school make the grade? M. Mohler. il *Ladies Home J* 104:58 S '87
Good and/or effective schools: what do we want? C. D. Glickman. bibl f il *Phi Delta Kappan* 68:622-4 Ap '87
How schools sabotage a creative work force. J. A. Hershey. il *Bus Week* p16 Jl 13 '87
It's time we changed the effective schools formula [with reply by W. B. Brookover] L. C. Stedman. bibl f il *Phi Delta Kappan* 69:215-27 N '87
National Governors' Association report on education reform. L. Alexander. *Educ Dig* 52:2-5 Ap '87
Neocentralists vs. neopluralists: the battle over educational reform. L. A. Uzzell. il *USA Today (Periodical)* 115:70-3 Ja '87
The schools we deserve. R. J. Samuelson. il *Newsweek* 110:79 O 5 '87
The United States educational system [address, October 26, 1987] D. T. Kearns. *Vital Speeches Day* 54:150-3 D 15 '87

Education—Evaluation—*cont.*

What do you need to know? A close look at U.S. education [cover story; special issue] il *Sch Update* 120:1-8+ N 6 '87

Whither education reform? S. W. White. *Humanist* 47:24-6+ My/Je '87

Experimental methods
See Education, Experimental

Federal aid
See also

Black medical colleges—Federal aid
Catholic colleges and universities—Federal aid
Catholic schools—Federal aid
Colleges and universities—Federal aid
Literacy education—Federal aid
Private schools—Federal aid
Science—Study and teaching—Federal aid
Student aid
Voucher plan in education

AAP endorses Senate bill to change educational block grants. H. Fields. *Publ Wkly* 232:20 Ag 14 '87

Combining categorical program services can make a major difference [discussion of April 1987 article, Why Chapter 1 hasn't made much difference] D. G. Savage. *Phi Delta Kappan* 68:787-8 Je '87

Evolution of public education legislation. *Congr Dig* 66:69-71 Mr '87

A feast for federal policy makers. A. C. Lewis. il *Phi Delta Kappan* 68:420-1 F '87

Get involved—write a letter! [restoration of Title IX to original strength to aid women's sports] *Women's Sports Fitness* 9:64 Je '87

The learning curve. *New Repub* 196:7-8 F 23 '87

Making Chapter 1 make a difference. R. E. Slavin. bibl f il *Phi Delta Kappan* 69:110-19 O '87

Reauthorizing or restructuring Chapter 1? [parent involvement] A. C. Lewis. il *Phi Delta Kappan* 69:4-5 S '87

The Sputnik of the eighties [economic competitiveness and federal role in education; cover story] J. F. Jennings. bibl f il *Phi Delta Kappan* 69:104-9 O '87

Why Chapter 1 hasn't made much difference. D. G. Savage. il *Phi Delta Kappan* 68:581-4 Ap '87

Finance
See also

Catholic schools—Finance
Colleges and universities—Finance
Education—State aid
Foundations, Charitable and educational
Voucher plan in education

Budget constraints hinder school dropout programs. *Phi Delta Kappan* 68:716-17 My '87

Can a judge raise taxes? [R. G. Clark's attempt to end school segregation by ordering tax increases in Kansas City] J. Seligmann. il por *Newsweek* 110:98 O 12 '87

Kansas judge raises taxes to desegregate schools [Russell Clark] *Jet* 73:22 O 19 '87

The lottery luster [educational funds raised in state lotteries] C. Pipho. *Phi Delta Kappan* 69:254-5 D '87

Outlook brightens for nation's schools [views of Allan Odden] il *USA Today (Periodical)* 116:11-12 D '87

Spelling for dollars [school Spell-a-Thon] M. J. Valentine. *Phi Delta Kappan* 69:312-13 D '87

History
Five who pushed for change in schools. P. M. Conniffe. il *Sch Update* 120:14-15 N 6 '87

International aspects
See also

Student exchange programs

Education abroad [special section] bibl f il *Phi Delta Kappan* 68:352-78 Ja '87

Education of the gifted and talented in the world community. B. M. Mitchell and W. G. Williams. *Phi Delta Kappan* 68:531-4 Mr '87

Laws and regulations
See Educational laws and regulations

Philosophy
See also

College education—Philosophy

Bring class back to the classroom. N. King. *Des Arts Educ* 89:8-11 N/D '87

Cultural literacy: what every American needs to know [condensation] E. D. Hirsch. *Read Dig* 131:79-83 D '87

Is education going to the technicians? S. Ulstein. il por *Christ Today* 31:28 S 4 '87

Learning from the giants. G. F. Will. il *Newsweek* 110:96 S 14 '87

A meditation on education. K. Kolenda. il *Humanist* 47:39 S/O '87

The well-rounded humanist. D. Carroll. il por *Humanist* 47:35-6 Jl/Ag '87

What Americans should know [cover story] A. P. Sanoff. bibl il *U S News World Rep* 103:86-8+ S 28 '87

What is an American education? R. Rodriguez. *Des Arts Educ* 89:44-6 N/D '87

Research
See Educational research

Social aspects
See Educational sociology

Standards
See also

Colleges and universities—Standards

State aid
Making hard choices. C. Pipho. il *Phi Delta Kappan* 69:182-3 N '87

Statistics
See also

School attendance

Annual wall chart shows test scores steady, dropout rate up. *Phi Delta Kappan* 68:640-1 Ap '87

Study and teaching
See Teachers—Education

Taxation for
See Education—Finance

Terminology
A quick guide to educational lingo. J. Ferber. *Sch Update* 120:18 N 6 '87

Alabama
See also

Colleges and universities—Alabama
Educational laws and regulations—Alabama

Alberta
Internships in Alberta. T. McConaghy. *Phi Delta Kappan* 68:794-5 Je '87

Arizona
See also

Glendale (Ariz.)—Education
Globe (Ariz.)—Education

How zucchini won 5th-grade hearts [gardening program; cover story] D. Cavaliere. il *Child Today* 16:18-21 My/Je '87

Arkansas
See also

Little Rock (Ark.)—Education

Scholarships given in honor of Daisy Bates and her late husband. *Jet* 72:23 Ag 3 '87

Atlantic States
See also

Colleges and universities—Atlantic States

Australia
How the Japanese beat us in school [comparison with Australia] G. Sheridan. il *World Press Rev* 34:32-3 My '87

British Columbia
See also

Educational laws and regulations—British Columbia

California
See also

Beverly Hills (Calif.)—Education
Colleges and universities—California
Compton (Calif.)—Education
East Salinas (Calif.)—Education
Gilroy (Calif.)—Education
Glendale (Calif.)—Education
Hope University
Los Angeles (Calif.)—Education
Milpitas (Calif.)—Education
Policy Analysis for California Education
Victorville (Calif.)—Education

'My favorite subject is gardening!'. G. Hanauer. il *Rodale's Org Gard* 34:42+ Ap '87

Pen pals: from quills to keyboards [Keylink computer network] *Newsweek* 110:60 D 21 '87

The value of 'values education'. P. Dworkin. il *U S News World Rep* 102:61 F 23 '87

Canada
See also

Vocational-technical education—Canada

Learning a living. M. Gray. il *Macleans* 100:42-3 S 7 '87

Teachers as researchers: learning through teaching. T. McConaghy. il *Phi Delta Kappan* 68:630-1 Ap '87

Chile
See also

College education and state—Chile

Education—*cont.*

China

See also
Education and state—China
Literacy education—China
Children of China. M. H. Lystad. bibl f il *Child Today* 16:20-2 Mr/Ap '87

Colorado

Learning to homestead [Malachite Small Farm School] S. Voynick. il *Ctry J* 14:60 Ja '87

Delaware

The states and economic development [address, November 18, 1986] M. N. Castle. *Vital Speeches Day* 53:199-202 Ja 15 '87

East Asia

Are Asians really that much smarter? A. Smith. il *Esquire* 108:99-100 S '87

France

See also
College education and state—France
Private schools—France

Georgia

See also
Atlanta (Ga.)—Education
Educational laws and regulations—Georgia
Royston (Ga.)—Education
Savannah (Ga.)—Education

Germany (West)

See also
Business and education—Germany (West)

Great Britain

See also
College education and state—Great Britain
Colleges and universities—Great Britain
History and controversy in the classroom. J. Slater. il *Hist Today* 37:6-7 Ja '87
What works in education. N. Macrae. il *Current* 290:14-21 F '87

History
'Kindness and reason': William Lovett and education [Victorian England] B. H. Harrison. bibl il por *Hist Today* 37:14-22 Mr '87

Idaho

See also
Caldwell (Idaho)—Education

Illinois

See also
Chicago (Ill.)—Education
Illinois leads U.S. with most school segregation. *Jet* 72:8 Mr 30 '87
Teaching history—alive and well [Lincoln Log Cabin project] H. Malehorn. il *Phi Delta Kappan* 69:166-8 O '87

India

See also
College education and state—India
The power of schooling [Motilal Nehru School of Sports] B. R. Joyce and B. Showers. bibl f il *Phi Delta Kappan* 68:352-5 Ja '87

Indiana

See also
Indianapolis (Ind.)—Education
Kokomo (Ind.)—Education

Iowa

See also
Ames (Iowa)—Education
Hampton (Iowa)—Education
Rural education [cooperation among school districts] C. Pipho. il *Phi Delta Kappan* 69:6-7 S '87

Israel

Middle East oasis of hope [Jewish and Arab families run the School for Peace in Neve Shalom] L. Press. *Macleans* 100:8 F 16 '87
Water from the rock [Jewish-Arab cooperation at the School for Peace in Neve Shalom, Israel] *Commonweal* 114:198 Ap 10 '87

Italy

See also
Venice (Italy)—Education

Japan

See also
Gakkyusha (Firm)
Are Japanese preschools really better? F. Roberts. *Parents* 62:54+ N '87
Can Americans learn from foreign schools? P. M. Jones. il *Sch Update* 120:16-17 N 6 '87
Confucius say, learn from international neighbors. A. C. Lewis. *Phi Delta Kappan* 68:492-3 Mr '87
Gradgrind's heirs. J. M. Fallows. il *Atlantic* 259:16+ Mr '87

How the Japanese beat us in school [comparison with Australia] G. Sheridan. il *World Press Rev* 34:32-3 My '87
Ikuko's bout with 'exam hell'. M. Lord. il *U S News World Rep* 102:63 Ja 19 '87
Japanese education in America? S. Ohanian. *Educ Dig* 53:10-14 S '87
Japanese versus U.S. texts: Dept. of Ed. assessment. H. Fields. *Publ Wkly* 231:21 F 6 '87
Kyoiku mama: secret of Japan's schools. C. Simons. il *Read Dig* 131:117-20 Jl '87
Memorizing vs. thinking [Americans study the Japanese and vice versa] J. Seligmann. il *Newsweek* 109:60-1 Ja 12 '87
Notes on Japan from an American schoolteacher. S. Ohanian. il *Phi Delta Kappan* 68:360-7 Ja '87
Pacific overtures [reform] N. Paleologos. il *Phi Delta Kappan* 68:368 Ja '87
A society where students are no. 1 [interview with M. White] il por *U S News World Rep* 102:65 Ja 19 '87
They get by with a lot of help from their kyoiku mamas [cover story] C. Simons. bibl (p182) il *Smithsonian* 17:44-53 Mr '87
U.S.-Japan study aim is education reform. J. Walsh. *Science* 235:274-5 Ja 16 '87
Zen and the art of cultural misappropriation [work of M. White] J. Rowe. *Wash Mon* 19:49-52 My '87

Kansas

See also
Manhattan (Kan.)—Education
Topeka (Kan.)—Education

Kentucky

See also
Jefferson County (Ky.)—Education
Lincoln County (Ky.)—Education

Kenya

Struggling against the odds: Harambee secondary schools in Kenya. D. A. Shiman and K. Mwiria. bibl f *Phi Delta Kappan* 68:369-72 Ja '87

Lebanon

See also
Catholic colleges and universities—Lebanon

Louisiana

See also
Educational laws and regulations—Louisiana

Maine

Superintendent found guilty of slander for teacher recommendation [M. True v. R. Ladner] T. J. Flygare. il *Phi Delta Kappan* 68:629-30 Ap '87

Maryland

See also
Baltimore (Md.)—Education
Colleges and universities—Maryland
Educational laws and regulations—Maryland

Massachusetts

See also
Boston (Mass.)—Education
Sandwich (Mass.)—Education
Springfield (Mass.)—Education
Taunton (Mass.)—Education
The new common school. C. L. Glenn. il *Phi Delta Kappan* 69:290-4 D '87

Mexico

See also
Education and state—Mexico

Michigan

See also
Detroit (Mich.)—Education
Monroe (Mich.)—Education
Ypsilanti (Mich.)—Education

Minnesota

See also
Buffalo (Minn.)—Education
The Minnesota dialogue on education. R. E. Randall. il *Phi Delta Kappan* 68:539-43 Mr '87

Mississippi

See also
Coffeeville (Miss.)—Education
Oxford (Miss.)—Education
Senatobia (Miss.)—Education

Missouri

See also
Hazelwood (Mo.)—Education
Kansas City (Mo.)—Education

Nepal

Educating the 'most beautiful children in the world'. T. Sagnier. il *UN Chron* 24:74-5 N '87

New Brunswick

See also
Moncton (N.B.)—Education

Education—*cont.*

New Hampshire

See also
Winchester (N.H.)—Education

New Jersey

See also
Colleges and universities—New Jersey
Educational laws and regulations—New Jersey
Moorestown (N.J.)—Education

New Mexico

See also
Santo Domingo Pueblo (N.M.)—Education
Involving children and youth in community projects.
N. Kalishman and others. bibl f il *Child Today* 16:23-6
Mr/Ap '87

New York (State)

See also
Buffalo (N.Y.)—Education
Lake Placid (N.Y.)—Education
New York (N.Y.)—Education

Nicaragua

See also
College education and state—Nicaragua

North Carolina

See also
Erwin (N.C.)—Education

Ohio

See also
Cincinnati (Ohio)—Education
Cleveland (Ohio)—Education
Toledo (Ohio)—Education

Ontario

See also
Educational laws and regulations—Ontario
Toronto (Ont.)—Education
Learning to compete [address, April 23, 1987] D. R.
Peterson. *Vital Speeches Day* 53:528-31 Je 15 '87

Pennsylvania

See also
Pottsville (Pa.)—Education

Portugal

Breaking down the barriers for visually handicapped
children. M. A. M. de M. Alves. il *Courier* 40:30-2
Jl '87

South Africa

See also
Colleges and universities—South Africa
Educational laws and regulations—South Africa

South Dakota

Giving kids the business. R. Thompson. il *Nations Bus*
75:43-4 Ag '87

Southern States

See also
Colleges and universities—Southern States
Historic architecture teaches preservation. il *South Living*
22:92 O '87

Soviet Union

See also
Leningrad (Soviet Union)—Education
Exhuming the corpse [American studies] S. Strasser. il
Newsweek 110:44 D 14 '87

Sudan

Building the Sudan. B. Wallach. il map *Focus* 37:12-15
Fall '87

Switzerland

See also
Private schools—Switzerland

Tennessee

See also
Educational laws and regulations—Tennessee
Memphis (Tenn.)—Education
Operation scare-the-pants-off-'em [Tennessee National
Guard stages mock invasions of high schools to promote
patriotism] *Harpers* 274:22-3 Ap '87

Texas

See also
Corpus Christi (Tex.)—Education
Fort Worth (Tex.)—Education
Lubbock (Tex.)—Education

United States

See Education

Virginia

See also
Alexandria (Va.)—Education
Educational laws and regulations—Virginia
Norfolk (Va.)—Education

Washington (D.C.)

See Washington (D.C.)—Education

Washington (State)

See also
Pasco (Wash.)—Education

Vancouver (Wash.)—Education

West Virginia

See also
Colleges and universities—West Virginia

Western Europe

See also
Colleges and universities—Western Europe
Europe in European curricula. M. G. Bruce. *Phi Delta
Kappan* 68:551-2 Mr '87
The unraveling of European education. E. von Kuehnelt-
Leddihn. *Natl Rev* 39:46 Ap 24 '87

Western States

See also
Colleges and universities—Western States
Education, Bilingual *See* Bilingual education
Education, Boards of *See* School boards

Education, Comparative

Are Asians really that much smarter? A. Smith. il *Esquire*
108:99-100 S '87
Are Japanese preschools really better? F. Roberts. *Parents*
62:54+ N '87
Bad news about math [American students compared
with others] E. Bowen. il *Time* 129:65 Ja 26 '87
The brain battle. L. J. Lord. il *U S News World Rep*
102:58-64 Ja 19 '87
Can Americans learn from foreign schools? P. M. Jones.
il *Sch Update* 120:16-17 N 6 '87
Confucius say, learn from international neighbors. A.
C. Lewis. *Phi Delta Kappan* 68:492-3 Mr '87
Education abroad [special section] bibl f il *Phi Delta
Kappan* 68:352-78 Ja '87
Education: math and aftermath. I. Peterson. *Sci News*
131:72 Ja 31 '87
Higher education: taking our bearings [study of U.S.
and European systems] M. G. Bruce. il *Phi Delta
Kappan* 69:239-40 N '87
How the Japanese beat us in school [comparison with
Australia] G. Sheridan. il *World Press Rev* 34:32-3
My '87
Memorizing vs. thinking [Americans study the Japanese
and vice versa] J. Seligmann. il *Newsweek* 109:60-1
Ja 12 '87
U.S.-Japan study aim is education reform. J. Walsh.
Science 235:274-5 Ja 16 '87

Education, Compulsory

See also
School age
Education, Cooperative *See* Business and education

Education, Elementary

See also
Economics—Study and teaching
History—Study and teaching
Mathematics—Study and teaching
Montessori method of education
Reading—Study and teaching
Social sciences—Study and teaching
Classroom capers [First lessons: a report on elementary
education in America] H. R. Kohl. *Nation* 244:368-71
Mr 21 '87

Education, Experimental

See also
Montessori method of education
Central Park East: an alternative story. D. Meier. il
Phi Delta Kappan 68:753-7 Je '87
Inside a school of choice [Alternative Learning Center
in Vancouver, Wash.] R. L. Fizzell. il *Phi Delta Kappan*
68:758-60 Je '87
Something is missing from the education reform move-
ment [lesson of open education] M. Henley. il *Phi
Delta Kappan* 69:284-5 D '87
Education, Humanistic *See* Liberal education

Education, Preschool

See also
Kindergarten
Montessori method of education
Nursery schools
Project Head Start (U.S.)
Are Japanese preschools really better? F. Roberts. *Parents*
62:54+ N '87
Choosing a preschool. M. Mohler. il *Ladies Home J*
104:86 My '87
Differential treatment in preschool [research by Lorene
Quay and Olga Jarrett] G. W. Bracey. il *Phi Delta
Kappan* 68:703-4 My '87
Helping your child learn [excerpt from The parents'
guide to daycare] J. A. Miller and S. Weissman. *Work
Woman* 12:146+ Mr '87
How a male teacher sees early childhood education.
W. Ayers. *Educ Dig* 52:27-9 Ap '87
'Kids need time to be kids'. E. Salholz. il *Newsweek*
109:56-8 F 2 '87

Education, Preschool—*cont.*
Miseducation. D. Elkind. il *Parents* 62:124-8+ O '87
Our images of children: where will they take us? D. Elkind. *Educ Dig* 53:2-4 N '87
Policy options for preschool programs. L. J. Schweinhart and others. bibl f il *Phi Delta Kappan* 68:524-9 Mr '87
Preparing for preschool. L. G. Katz. il *Parents* 62:194 Ag '87
Preschool children in the public schools: good investment? Or bad? D. B. Strother. bibl f il *Phi Delta Kappan* 69:304-8 D '87
Preventive preschool programming that works [Ypsilanti, Mich.] J. A. Harper. il *Phi Delta Kappan* 69:81-2 S '87
Project Transition [from preschool to elementary school] il *Child Today* 16:2 Ja/F '87
School's out for 4-year-olds [views of Edward Zigler] R. J. Trotter. il *Psychol Today* 21:35 D '87
Should prekindergarten be public? F. Roberts. il *Parents* 62:58 F '87
The states and economic development [address, November 18, 1986] M. N. Castle. *Vital Speeches Day* 53:199-202 Ja 15 '87
Summer with a preschooler. F. Roberts. *Parents* 62:59-60 Je '87
What should preschoolers be taught? L. G. Katz. il *Parents* 62:207 S '87
Education, Primary *See* Education, Elementary
Education, Rural
Rural education [cooperation among Iowa school districts] C. Pipho. il *Phi Delta Kappan* 69:6-7 S '87
Summer camp and compost [Camp Treetops and North Country School in Lake Placid, N.Y.] L. K. Murrow. il *Ctry J* 14:61-8 Ja '87
Why do teachers choose rural schools? [results of survey] W. A. Matthes and R. V. Carlson. *Educ Dig* 52:27-9 F '87
A working vacation [instructional workshops that teach rural skills] il *Ctry J* 14:57-60 Ja '87
Education, Secondary
See also
    High schools
Struggling against the odds: Harambee secondary schools in Kenya. D. A. Shiman and K. Mwiria. bibl f *Phi Delta Kappan* 68:369-72 Ja '87
Education, Urban
Alternative certification and urban schools. M. Haberman. *Educ Dig* 52:22-5 Ja '87
Bureaucracy and the neutering of teachers [study of urban teachers; cover story] J. R. Frymier. il *Phi Delta Kappan* 69:8-14 S '87
High schools that work. R. E. McKinney. il *Ebony* 43:34+ N '87
Improving urban schools. E. L. Boyer. *Educ Dig* 53:6-9 S '87
Education, Value of
See also
    College education, Value of
Education and business *See* Business and education
Education and Christianity *See* Church and education
Education and church *See* Church and education
Education and communism *See* Communism and education
Education and crime
Educators and police working together. P. Blauvelt. *Educ Dig* 53:26-9 N '87
Education and democracy
Using a hidden curriculum for moral education [democratic processes can teach values] C. Power and L. Kohlberg. *Educ Dig* 52:10-13 My '87
Education and economic problems *See* School and social and economic problems
Education and economics *See* Economics and education
Education and manpower *See* Labor—Education
Education and mass media *See* Mass media and education
Education and politics *See* Politics and education
Education and social problems *See* School and social and economic problems
Education and socialism *See* Socialism and education
Education and society *See* Educational sociology
Education and sociology *See* Educational sociology
Education and state
See also
    Black medical colleges—Federal aid
    Catholic colleges and universities—Federal aid
    College education and state
    Colleges and universities—Federal aid
    Colleges and universities—Laws and regulations
    Colleges and universities—Research—Federal aid
    Education—Federal aid
    Education—State aid

    Educational laws and regulations
    United States. Dept. of Education
    Voucher plan in education
Bureaucracy and the neutering of teachers [study of urban teachers; cover story] J. R. Frymier. il *Phi Delta Kappan* 69:8-14 S '87
Media and arts education policy. S. Hope. *Des Arts Educ* 88:20-8 Jl/Ag '87
The Minnesota dialogue on education. R. E. Randall. il *Phi Delta Kappan* 68:539-43 Mr '87
National Governors' Association report on education reform. L. Alexander. *Educ Dig* 52:2-5 Ap '87
National literacy campaigns: historical and comparative lessons. R. F. Arnove and H. J. Graff. bibl f il *Phi Delta Kappan* 69:202-6 N '87
Neocentralists vs. neopluralists: the battle over educational reform. L. A. Uzzell. il *USA Today (Periodical)* 115:70-3 Ja '87
Policy options for preschool programs. L. J. Schweinhart and others. bibl f il *Phi Delta Kappan* 68:524-9 Mr '87
Quo vadis arts education: a national agenda. J. Remer. *Des Arts Educ* 89:38-40 N/D '87
Results and future prospects of state efforts to increase choice among schools. J. Nathan. bibl f il *Phi Delta Kappan* 68:746-52 Je '87
State/local boards [special section] il *Phi Delta Kappan* 69:53-68 S '87
Stateline. C. Pipho. See issues of Phi Delta Kappan
Teacher-centered instruction versus education reform. L. Cuban. *Educ Dig* 52:2-5 F '87
Teacher "professionalization" versus democratic control. L. Darling-Hammond. *Educ Dig* 53:15-17 S '87
Testing ideas on education [presidential candidates] G. J. Church. il *Time* 130:32 S 21 '87
Toward an integrated study of cultural and educational policy. D. B. Pankratz. bibl f *Des Arts Educ* 89:12-21 N/D '87
Washington news. A. C. Lewis. See issues of The Education Digest beginning September 1986
Washington report. A. C. Lewis. See issues of Phi Delta Kappan

China
Education reform in China. A. D. Swanson and Zhang Zhian. bibl f il *Phi Delta Kappan* 68:373-8 Ja '87
Mexico
The quest for change in Mexican education. K. Kovacs. bibl f *Curr Hist* 86:117-20+ Mr '87
United States
See Education and state
Education and technology *See* Educational technology
Education and the press *See* Educational news
Education critics and criticism
Kid bashing is in. A. C. Lewis. il *Phi Delta Kappan* 69:180-1 N '87
Education Dept. (U.S.) *See* United States. Dept. of Education
Educational achievements *See* Student achievements
Educational administration *See* School management and organization
Educational associations
See also
    National Education Association of the United States
    Parents' and teachers' associations
Educational censorship *See* Censorship
Educational Concerns for Hunger Organization
A seed of prayer [work of M. Price] M. Kane. il pors *Rodale's Org Gard* 34:80-2+ Mr '87
Educational conferences *See* Education—Conferences
Educational consultants
See also
    MBA/Strategies (Firm)
Educational cooperation
Board/staff partnership: the key to the effectiveness of state and local boards. G. McGonagill. bibl f *Phi Delta Kappan* 69:65-8 S '87
Bridging the gap between a public school system and a university [Texas Tech faculty members adopt school classes in Lubbock] R. E. Ishler and E. C. Leslie. *Phi Delta Kappan* 68:615-16 Ap '87
Changing teaching practices: what school-college collaboration is all about. B. DeMott. *Change* 19:36 S/O '87
High school-community college cooperation creates a degree [2 + 2 tech-prep/associate degree] D. Parnell. *Educ Dig* 52:40-1 Mr '87
The policy and public relations role of higher education with respect to K-12 arts education. R. Gilmore. *Des Arts Educ* 88:28-9 Ja/F '87
Project Transition [from preschool to elementary school] il *Child Today* 16:2 Ja/F '87

Educational cooperation—*cont.*
Rural education [Iowa school districts] C. Pipho. il *Phi Delta Kappan* 69:6-7 S '87
Teacher collaboration: new partnerships to attack old problems [classroom teachers and university professors in Institute for Research on Teaching program] A. C. Porter. bibl f il *Phi Delta Kappan* 69:147-52 O '87

Educational counseling
See also
Peer counseling
After-school discussion helps problem students [program at Central High School in Indianapolis] W. Bourke and R. D. Furniss. il *Phi Delta Kappan* 69:241-2 N '87
Do women in education need mentors? J. Dodgson. *Educ Dig* 52:26-8 Ja '87
Guiding minority students into adulthood [Yukon-Koyukuk School District Postsecondary Counselor Program] J. Kleinfeld. il *Phi Delta Kappan* 68:553-4 Mr '87
Martha meets her mentor: the power of teaching relationships. L. A. Daloz. il *Change* 19:35-7 Jl/Ag '87
Needs of gay students for acceptance and support [high schoolers] G. J. Krysiak. *Educ Dig* 53:44-7 D '87

Educational counselors
College bound, without a map [inability of overworked guidance counselors to offer good advice] J. E. Gallagher. il *Time* 129:74 F 23 '87
College-hunting? Ask someone who majors in it. P. Cole. il *Bus Week* p157 N 30 '87

Educational criticism *See* Education critics and criticism
Educational discrimination *See* Discrimination in education
Educational equalization
The unraveling of European education. E. von Kuehnelt-Leddihn. *Natl Rev* 39:46 Ap 24 '87
Educational evaluation *See* Education—Evaluation
Educational exchanges
See also
Foreign students
Student exchange programs
CSU's Thomas visits Senegal and forms socio-economic tie. il *por Jet* 71:21 Mr 2 '87
Universities and apartheid. A. Pifer. *Cent Mag* 20:61-2 Mr/Ap '87
Educational extension *See* University extension
Educational films *See* Motion pictures in education
Educational forecasting
The 21st-century professor. J. R. Hoyle and G. R. Johnson. il *pors Futurist* 21:26-7 N/D '87
Death of the university. H. I. London. il *por Futurist* 21:17-22 My/Je '87
Death of the university [cover story] H. I. London. il *USA Today (Periodical)* 116:32-6 S '87
Faculty for the future. I. H. Buchen. il *por Futurist* 21:22-5 N/D '87
The future of U.S. education [views of John D. Haas] *Futurist* 21:49-50 Jl/Ag '87
Higher education circa 2005. F. D. Fisher. il *Change* 19:40-5 Ja/F '87
Learning needs in a changing world. M. Elmandjra. *Futurist* 21:60 Mr/Ap '87
Teaching the great issues of the future [textbooks] D. B. Fleming. il *por Futurist* 21:27-8 Ja/F '87
Educational foundations *See* Foundations, Charitable and educational
Educational games
See also
Simulation games in education
Fractions as fun [board games] il *Sunset* 179:125-6 O '87
Educational innovations
See also
Educational technology
Educational journalism *See* Journalism, Educational
Educational laws and regulations
See also
Colleges and universities—Laws and regulations
Education—Federal aid
United States. Dept. of Education
De jure. T. J. Flygare. See issues of Phi Delta Kappan
How government helps shape what you learn in school. R. Morell. il *Sch Update* 120:6-7 N 6 '87
No-pass/no-play hurts minorities more than whites [high school students] il *Phi Delta Kappan* 68:561 Mr '87
Stateline. C. Pipho. See issues of Phi Delta Kappan
Washington news. A. C. Lewis. See issues of The Education Digest beginning September 1986
Washington report. A. C. Lewis. See issues of Phi Delta Kappan

Watching a changing Court: will the center hold? [Supreme Court and education cases] D. G. Savage. *Phi Delta Kappan* 69:135-7 O '87

Alabama
Alabama board to appeal ban on 'humanist' texts. M. Yen. *Publ Wkly* 231:14 Mr 27 '87
Alabamboozle [secular humanist textbook ruling] E. Doerr. *Humanist* 47:39-40 My/Je '87
Fundamentalists lose two textbook cases in federal appeals courts. *Publ Wkly* 232:11 S 11 '87
God's right Hand [W. Brevard Hand's decision that secular humanism is a religion in Alabama textbook case] D. R. Carlin, Jr. il *Commonweal* 114:263-4 My 8 '87
Going back to the books [fundamentalists lose court case] R. Lacayo. il *Time* 130:60 S 7 '87
Is 'humanism' a religion? [Judge W. Brevard Hand bans certain textbooks] T. Gest. il *U S News World Rep* 102:10-11 Mr 16 '87
Mark of Darrow [fundamentalists lose textbook court battle] il *U S News World Rep* 103:10 S 7 '87
Nondenominational humanism? [secular humanist textbook case] *Natl Rev* 39:19 Ap 10 '87
Other sides to the textbook controversy [discussion of May 6, 1987 articles, Voltaire arraigned in Alabama: the textbook humanism case and Curriculum in the public schools: can compromise be reached?] D. Underhill; C. L. Glenn. il *Christ Century* 104:631-2 Jl 15-22 '87
Religious bias [Judge W. Brevard Hand bans "secular humanist" textbooks] il *Time* 129:66 Mr 16 '87
The textbook cases: secularism on appeal. P. A. Zirkel. bibl f *Phi Delta Kappan* 69:308-10 D '87
Textbook ruling sparks concern [secular humanism ruling] C. Holden. *Science* 235:1459 Mr 20 '87
Textbooks on trial [decision banning textbooks from public schools because they promote secular humanism] *America* 156:265 Ap 4 '87
Voltaire arraigned in Alabama: the textbook humanism case. D. Underhill. *Christ Century* 104:438-40 My 6 '87

British Columbia
Legislation threatens B.C. Teachers' Federation. T. McConaghy. *Phi Delta Kappan* 69:310-11 D '87

California
Battling the IQ-test ban [M. Amaya contests ruling that bars black students from taking IQ tests] J. N. Baker. il *por Newsweek* 110:53 Mr 16 '87
Teach the children well [Catholic response to pending legislation requiring AIDS prevention education] W. J. Wood. il *America* 156:397-400 My 16 '87

Georgia
Teachers fail Georgia test [competency testing] A. Press. il *Newsweek* 110:65 S 7 '87

Louisiana
The creation-science case: is it science or religion? [case to be heard by Supreme Court] E. J. Larson. *Christ Today* 31:50-1 Ja 16 '87
Creationism case argued before Supreme Court. R. Lewin. *Science* 235:22-3 Ja 2 '87
High Court rejects creationism law. J. Raloff. *Sci News* 131:404 Je 27 '87
High Court: the day God and Darwin collided [teaching of creationism ruled unconstitutional] T. Gest and L. Solórzano. il *U S News World Rep* 102:12 Je 29 '87
Justice Scalia's misunderstanding [dissenting opinion on creationism case] S. J. Gould. il *Nat Hist* 96:14+ O '87
Keeping God out of the classroom [Supreme Court ruling on creation science law] L. Martz. il *Newsweek* 109:23-4 Je 29 '87
Memories of the monkey trial [Supreme Court rules against creationism law] A. L. Sanders. il *Time* 129:54 Je 29 '87
One case: a step-by-step account of its progress through the Supreme Court [creationism case] il *Life* 10:114-15 Fall '87
Schools can not require religious and scientific evolution teachings: Court. *Jet* 72:17 Jl 6 '87
Science, 7; creationism, 2 [Supreme Court ruling] *Sci Am* 257:14 Ag '87
Supreme Court abolishes Louisiana creationism law. H. Fields. *Publ Wkly* 232:13 Jl 3 '87
Supreme Court bars creationism in schools. I. Goodwin. *Phys Today* 40:56-7 S '87
Supreme Court hears arguments on teaching 'creation science'. I. Goodwin. il *Phys Today* 40:64-6 F '87
Supreme Court on 'flat souls' [ruling on Louisiana law ordering equal treatment of creationism with evolution] J. M. Wall. *Christ Century* 104:579 Jl 1-8 '87

Educational laws and regulations—Louisiana—cont.
Supreme Court strikes down "creation science" law as promotion of religion. C. Norman. *Science* 236:1620 Je 26 '87
Supreme Court strikes down Louisiana creationism act. T. J. Flygare. il *Phi Delta Kappan* 69:77-9 S '87
The verdict on creationism [Supreme Court ruling] S. J. Gould. il *N Y Times Mag* p32+ Jl 19 '87
Maryland
A true test or a trivia game? [citizenship test] M. Henry. por *Newsweek* 109:10-11 Je 22 '87
New Jersey
Can a state require public schools to allow a moment of silence? H. Hagerman; R. L. Maddox. il *Christ Today* 31:52 N 20 '87
Supreme Court considers a second moment-of-silence law. *Christ Today* 31:56 N 6 '87
Supreme Court will rule on moment-of-silence law. B. Spring. il *Christ Today* 31:56+ Mr 20 '87
Ontario
Creationism in Ontario [threat to astronomy curriculum] D. E. Thomsen. *Sci News* 132:24 Jl 11 '87
South Africa
Is protest losing steam? [new curriculum for black students] il *U S News World Rep* 102:32-3 Ja 19 '87
New rules for black schools. W. R. Doerner. *Time* 129:48 Ja 12 '87
Tennessee
See also
Tennessee evolution controversy
AAP joins in appeal of Tennessee textbook ruling. H. Fields. *Publ Wkly* 231:30 Mr 6 '87
Book ban overturned [textbook case] *Christ Century* 104:745 S 9-16 '87
Fundamentalists lose two textbook cases in federal appeals courts. *Publ Wkly* 232:11 S 11 '87
Going back to the books [fundamentalists lose court case] R. Lacayo. il *Time* 130:60 S 7 '87
Mark of Darrow [fundamentalists lose textbook court battle] il *U S News World Rep* 103:10 S 7 '87
The significance of the decision in 'Scopes II' [fundamentalists vs. school system in textbook case] E. B. Jenkinson. bibl f *Phi Delta Kappan* 68:445-50 F '87
Some thoughts on the Tennessee textbook case. T. J. Flygare. bibl f il *Phi Delta Kappan* 68:474-5 F '87
The textbook cases: secularism on appeal. P. A. Zirkel. bibl f *Phi Delta Kappan* 69:308-10 D '87
Textbook controversies: a 'disaster for public schools'? [fundamentalists vs. school system in textbook case] C. L. Glenn. bibl f *Phi Delta Kappan* 68:451-5 F '87
Wins and losses [referenda on church-state issues and Tennessee textbook case] E. Doerr. *Humanist* 47:40+ Ja/F '87
United States
See Educational laws and regulations
Virginia
ACLU sues to end school bd. appointments in Va. [black discrimination cited] *Jet* 73:37 N 2 '87
Educational literature
See also
Self help literature
Authorship
Anecdotes, facetiae, satire, etc.
Scaling the ivory tower [publishing mediocre articles] H. J. Bullford. il *Change* 19:56-7 S/O '87
Educational measurements *See* Educational tests and measurements
Educational news
Education briefs. See issues of The Education Digest
Improving relations between schools and the press. S. B. Zakariya. *Educ Dig* 53:8-11 N '87
Newsnotes. See issues of Phi Delta Kappan
Educational organization *See* School management and organization
Educational philosophy *See* Education—Philosophy
Educational planning
See also
Curriculum planning
Educational policy *See* College education and state; Education and state
Educational records *See* School reports and records
Educational reform *See* Education
Educational research
See also
Michigan State University. Institute for Research on Teaching
Policy Analysis for California Education

Does "What works" work in the classroom? [criticism of Dept. of Education publication] A. Franza. *Educ Dig* 52:10-13 F '87
It's time we changed the effective schools formula [with reply by W. B. Brookover] L. C. Stedman. bibl f il *Phi Delta Kappan* 69:215-27 N '87
The possibilities for research on architecture teaching. S. M. Dinham. bibl f por *Archit Rec* 175:41+ Ap '87
Research. G. W. Bracey. See alternate issues of Phi Delta Kappan beginning March 1984
Research: who cares? [arts education; special issue] bibl f il *Des Arts Educ* 88:2-44 My/Je '87
Restructuring teaching: a call for research. M. H. Futrell. *Educ Dig* 53:2-5 S '87
The role of music research in teacher training programs [music education research] J. N. Anderson. bibl f *Des Arts Educ* 88:42-4 My/Je '87
Taking the terror out of research. R. Gable and V. Rogers. il *Phi Delta Kappan* 68:690-5 My '87
Teachers as researchers: learning through teaching. T. McConaghy. il *Phi Delta Kappan* 68:630-1 Ap '87
Toward an integrated study of cultural and educational policy. D. B. Pankratz. bibl f *Des Arts Educ* 89:12-21 N/D '87
When research does not help teachers. M. Myers. *Educ Dig* 52:14-17 Ja '87
Educational sociology
See also
School and social and economic problems
Social education
Socially handicapped children—Education
A child resource policy beyond school and family. S. B. Heath and M. W. McLaughlin. *Educ Dig* 53:19-21 O '87
A child resource policy: moving beyond dependence on school and family [cover story] S. B. Heath and M. W. McLaughlin. bibl f il *Phi Delta Kappan* 68:576-80 Ap '87
Let's not throw out the baby with the bath water [discussion of April 1987 article, A child resource policy: moving beyond dependence on school and family] S. B. Heath and M. W. McLaughlin. bibl f *Phi Delta Kappan* 68:784-6 Je '87
Educational software *See* Computers—Educational use—Programming
Educational statistics *See* Education—Statistics
Educational supplies *See* School furniture, equipment, etc.
Educational technology
See also
Communications satellites—Educational use
Computers—Educational use
Information storage and retrieval systems—Educational use
Higher education circa 2005. F. D. Fisher. il *Change* 19:40-5 Ja/F '87
Educational television *See* Television in education
Educational tests and measurements
See also
Aptitude tests
Intelligence tests
Reading—Testing
Scholastic Aptitude Test
Courses and test scores yield mixed results. G. W. Bracey. il *Phi Delta Kappan* 68:397-8 Ja '87
Good news, bad news: black performance on standardized tests. J. Baratz-Snowden. il *Change* 19:50-4 My/Je '87
The high-schooler's informational IQ test [proposal for test as requirement for teenage driver's license] W. F. Buckley. *Natl Rev* 39:57 Jl 17 '87
The merits of measurement-driven instruction [with reply by G. W. Bracey] W. J. Popham. bibl f il *Phi Delta Kappan* 68:679-89 My '87
Teaching teachers about testing: another mismatch? G. W. Bracey. il *Phi Delta Kappan* 68:546-7 Mr '87
Test scores—are they a distorted proxy for achievement? [report from the Congressional Budget Office] J. Walsh. *Science* 237:1100 S 4 '87
Testing students may raise legal issues for reformers [St. Louis lawsuit over evaluating teachers partly on the basis of how their students perform on competency tests] *Phi Delta Kappan* 68:481-3 F '87
Texts, tests don't match—but does it matter? [research by William Mehrens and S. E. Phillips] G. W. Bracey. il *Phi Delta Kappan* 68:397 Ja '87
Time enough to learn [measurement of summer learning gains; work of Maxine Wintre] P. Chance. *Psychol Today* 21:14 Ap '87

Educational tests and measurements—*cont.*
Tips for readers of research [distinction between ability and achievement] G. W. Bracey. *Phi Delta Kappan* 69:76-7 S '87

Educational theory *See* Education—Philosophy

Educational toys *See* Toys

Educational workshops
See also
Bread Loaf School of English

Educators
See also
College presidents
College teachers
Teachers

Attitudes
Differences between educators and the public on questions of education policy. S. M. Elam. il *Phi Delta Kappan* 69:294-6 D '87

Edward VIII, King of Great Britain *See* Windsor, Edward, Duke of, 1894-1972

Edward, Duke of Windsor *See* Windsor, Edward, Duke of, 1894-1972

Edward, Prince of Great Britain, 1964-
about
Edward goes his own way. L. Aitken. il pors *People Wkly* 27:44-6+ Ja 26 '87

Edward Albert, Prince of Wales *See* Windsor, Edward, Duke of, 1894-1972

Edward D. Jones & Company
Biggest little brokerage. W. Cole. il *Time* 130:52 Jl 27 '87

Edward L. Burlingame Books
Burlingame to have imprint at Harper; Shinker is publisher. il pors *Publ Wkly* 232:14-15 O 16 '87

Edwards, Audrey, 1947-
Black working women: a report from the front. il *Glamour* 85:162-3+ Jl '87
Racism on campus. il *Seventeen* 46:166-7+ N '87

Edwards, Bernard
about
Bernard Edwards: hit man on the production line. G. Santoro. il pors *Down Beat* 54:20-2 Je '87

Edwards, Blake, 1922-
about
Blind date [film] Reviews
Macleans il 100:54 Ap 6 '87. L. O'Toole
New Leader 70:23 Ap 6 '87. J. Gardner
New Repub 196:27 Ap 27 '87. S. Kauffmann
Newsweek il 109:77-8 Ap 13 '87. J. Kroll
People Wkly il 27:12 Ap 13 '87. P. Travers
Time il 129:76 Ap 20 '87. R. Schickel

Edwards, Edwin W.
about
The GOP smells more than gumbo in Louisiana. R. Fly. il por *Bus Week* p56 O 26 '87
Is it Edwin's last stand? D. Pedersen. il por *Newsweek* 110:39 O 26 '87
The trials and jubilations of Governor Edwin Edwards. N. Lemann. il por *Esquire* 107:79-82+ My '87

Edwards, Ernest
Information desk. See issues of Antiques & Collecting Hobbies beginning January 1987

Edwards, Harry
about
Black NY group seeks Harry Edwards' ouster. il por *Jet* 72:46 S 14 '87
Doctor of sports and sociology. A. Collier. il pors *Ebony* 42:101-2+ O '87
Edwards and Ueberroth, classmates now teammates. pors *Jet* 72:51 Je 29 '87
Edwards hires Campanis to assist baseball job. il por *Jet* 72:48 S 14 '87
Group to monitor black progress in white colleges. *Jet* 72:27 Je 1 '87
Harry Edwards hints at college sports boycott. *Jet* 73:51 O 26 '87
Owens fouls with Edwards; now pitches to Ueberroth. por *Jet* 73:49 N 2 '87
Teacher of the Year. D. Chamberlain. il pors *Sport Mag* 78:70-4+ D '87

Edwards, Jon
Reviewer's notebook. See issues of Byte beginning May 1986 through February 1987

Edwards, Linda, and Brent, Nancy
Issues for school clinics. *Educ Dig* 53:52-5 N '87

Edwards, Mike
Chernobyl—one year after. il map *Natl Geogr* 171:632-53 My '87
Ukraine. il maps *Natl Geogr* 171:594-631 My '87

Edwards, R. Lawrence, and others
Precise timing of the last interglacial period from mass spectrometric determination of thorium-230 in corals. bibl f il *Science* 236:1547-53 Je 19 '87

Edwards, Royal
about
New techniques in chimney cleaning [interview] S. Maviglio. il por *Home Mech* 83:30+ O '87

Edwige
about
Edwige. *New Yorker* 63:38-9 N 16 '87

Edwords, Frederick
Creation/evolution update. See issues of The Humanist
The religious character of American patriotism. il por *Humanist* 47:20-4+ N/D '87
Students speak out against textbook censorship. *Humanist* 47:23-6+ Mr/Ap '87

Edwords, Frederick, and McCabe, Stephen
Getting out God's vote: Pat Robertson and the evangelicals [cover story] il *Humanist* 47:5-10+ My/Je '87

EEC *See* European Economic Community

EEG *See* Electroencephalography

Eek, Nat
Media as a transmitter not a barrier. *Des Arts Educ* 88:33-5 Jl/Ag '87

EEOC *See* United States. Equal Employment Opportunity Commission

Effective (Term)
Effective immediately. W. Safire. il *N Y Times Mag* p6+ Je 28 '87

Effective Government Committee
Inside Gephardt's PACscam [cover story] D. Corn. il *Nation* 244:559+ My 2 '87

Effeminacy
Homosexuality: an effeminate beginning? [study by Richard Green] J. Meer. il *Psychol Today* 21:66 Ap '87

Efficiency, Household *See* Home economics

Efficiency, Industrial
See also
Factory management
Office management
Productivity, Industrial
Team work in industry

EFIS (Electronic flight instrument system) display *See* Airplanes—Electronic equipment; Airplanes, Jet—Electronic equipment

Eftink, Bill
Beef. See issues of Successful Farming through June 1987

Egan, Deborah
Coupling [photographs] il *Society* 24:78-81 My/Je '87

Egan, James E., and others
Efficacy of murine malaria sporozoite vaccines: implications for human vaccine development. bibl f il *Science* 236:453-6 Ap 24 '87

Egan, Peter
Side glances. See issues of Road & Track beginning November 1983

Egan, Sean E., and others
Transformation by oncogenes encoding protein kinases induces the metastatic phenotype. bibl f il *Science* 238:202-5 O 9 '87

Egerton, Ann Bleidt
about
Always a new word on southern cooking. B. Summer. *Publ Wkly* 232:15 Jl 17 '87

Egerton, John
about
Always a new word on southern cooking. B. Summer. *Publ Wkly* 232:15 Jl 17 '87
An elegant sufficiency. il *Time* 130:76 S 28 '87

Egg decoration *See* Eggs, Decorated

Egg rolls
With repossession you get egg rolls [Whittaker brothers' factory 4W in Oklahoma] P. M. Fielding. il pors *Nations Bus* 75:60 Mr '87

Egg salads *See* Salads

Egg tempera painting *See* Tempera painting

Egger, Daniel
West Germany pours hot milk. il *Nation* 244:392-4+ Mr 28 '87

Egghead Inc.
about
Egghead Software. D. Caruso. il *Pers Comput* 11:116-19 F '87

Egginton, Joyce
Blue flame, black gunk. il map *Audubon* 89:106-12 S '87

Eggleston, Niles
Strawberry strategies [cover story] il *Rodale's Org Gard* 34:74-6 Ap '87

Eggplant
See also
Cooking—Vegetables
My patio eggplant plantation. N. Bubel. il *Ctry J* 14:61-3 Ag '87

Eggs
See also
Cooking—Eggs
Insects—Eggs
Reptiles—Eggs
An ancient shell game: balancing eggs to celebrate the spring. S. Morris. il *Omni* 9:114-15 Mr '87
Eggs O.K. on low-fat diet. il *Prevention* 39:6 Jl '87
Playing the egg game [training a dog to gather eggs] M. Smith. il *Mother Earth News* 108:22 N/D '87

Eggs, Decorated
Easter egg tips. il *Good Housekeep* 204:255 Ap '87

Eggs, Fossil
A daring gamble in the Gobi Desert took the jackpot [R. C. Andrews' search for dinosaur fossils] D. J. Preston. il pors *Smithsonian* 18:94-8+ D '87
Dinosaur eggs unscrambled [discovered in Wells Gulch, Colo.] il *Time* 130:56 Ag 3 '87

Eggs (Ova) *See* Ova

Egle, Lisa
Who says you have to be rich to go to college? por *Seventeen* 46:106 Mr '87

Eglin Air Force Base (Fla.) *See* Air bases

Ego *See* Self

Egoism
See also
Narcissism

Egol, Morton
Sound financial reporting by nation states [address, September 29, 1986] *Vital Speeches Day* 53:176-8 Ja 1 '87

Egoyan, Atom
about
Family viewing [film] Reviews
Macleans il 100:64 D 7 '87. B. D. Johnson

EGR (Exhaust gas recirculation) system *See* Automobiles—Pollution control devices

Egremont, Sir George O'Brien Wyndham, 3rd Earl of, 1751-1837
about
Painting Petworth. M. Egremont. il *House Gard* 159:116+ N '87

Egremont, Max
Painting Petworth. il *House Gard* 159:116+ N '87

Egrets
Migration
An African bird makes its move around the world [cattle egret] J. H. Heminway. bibl (p183) il map *Smithsonian* 18:60-6+ My '87

Egypt
See also
Bedouins—Egypt
Cairo (Egypt)
Cultural property—Protection—Egypt
Investments, American—Egypt
Iran-contra affair—Egyptian participation
Opera—Egypt
Red Sea
Sexual behavior—Egypt
Western Desert (Egypt)
Women—Egypt
Antiquities
See also
Mummies
Pyramids—Egypt
Ships, Ancient—Egypt
Sphinxes
Walk like an Egyptian [excerpt from The search for Omm Sety] J. Cott. il *Omni* 9:66-8+ Jl '87
Defenses
See also
Remotely piloted vehicles—Egypt
Foreign relations
Israel
See also
Israel-Arab Wars, 1967-
United States
See United States—Foreign relations—Egypt
Industries
See also
General Motors Egypt S.A.E.
Nasr Automotive Manufacturing Company

Politics and government
See also
Political campaigns—Egypt
An Arab embrace revives prodigal's wounded pride. L. Lief. il map *U S News World Rep* 103:50 D 28 '87-Ja 4 '88
Egypt: repression and liberalization. H. Ansari. *Curr Hist* 86:77-80+ F '87
Egypt: the Islamic issue. M. Sid-Ahmed. *Foreign Policy* 69:22-39 Wint '87/'88
A flood of radicalism in the land of the Nile [Shiite fundamentalists] J. L. Galloway. il *U S News World Rep* 103:35-6 Jl 6 '87

Religious institutions and affairs
See also
Muslims—Egypt

Egyptian art *See* Art, Egyptian

Ehlenbeck, Steve
In hiding [story] il *Seventeen* 46:196-7+ S '87

Ehmann, James
The elephant as artist. il *Natl Wildl* 25:26-8 F/Mr '87
An elephant who draws pictures. il por *Read Dig* 131:96-9 O '87

Ehrenfeld, David
Beyond the farming crisis. il *Technol Rev* 90:46-56 Jl '87

Ehrenkrantz, Louis
Geriatric autos. por *Forbes* 140:136 Ag 24 '87

Ehrenreich, Barbara
In praise of 'best friends'. por *Ms* 15:35-6 Ja '87
The next wave. il *Ms* 16:166-8+ Jl/Ag '87
A step back to the workhouse? il por *Ms* 16:40-2 N '87

Ehrenreich, Barbara, and O'Reilly, Jane
Femme is fatal. *New Repub* 196:15-16 Je 1 '87

Ehrenreich, Henry
Electronic theory for materials science. bibl f *Science* 235:1029-35 F 27 '87

Ehrlich, Anne H., and Ehrlich, Paul R.
Back from the abyss [excerpt from Earth] il *Sierra* 72:54-60 Mr/Ap '87

Ehrlich, Gretel
Surrender to the landscape. il *Harpers* 275:24+ S '87

Ehrlich, Paul R.
Habitats in crisis. il *Wilderness* 50:12-15 Spr '87
Population biology, conservation biology, and the future of humanity [address, August 10, 1987] *BioScience* 37:757-63 N '87
(jt. auth) See Ehrlich, Anne H., and Ehrlich, Paul R.

Ehrlich, Thomas
Education and values [address, October 12, 1987] *Vital Speeches Day* 54:106-9 D 1 '87

Ehrman, Mark
Star-track trivia. il *Teen* 31:40 Ag '87

Eiben, Therese
Dembner Books. *Writer* 100:31 O '87

Eichenwald, Kurt
Braving epilepsy's storm. il *N Y Times Mag* p30-3+ Ja 11 '87

Eicher, David J.
(jt. auth) See Higgins, David, and Eicher, David J.

Eichinger, Bernd, 1953-
about
Germany's 'international' producer. A. Fisher. *World Press Rev* 34:58 Ap '87

Eichler, Glenn
An affinity for flying. il *Esquire* 108:82 O '87
Airline seats, and why they're like that. il *Esquire* 108:46 Jl '87
Getting into first class. il *Esquire* 107:56 Mr '87
Getting less for less. il *Esquire* 107:62 Ap '87
In search of the perfect (okay, decent) airline meal. il *Esquire* 108:68 D '87
Phoning at 40,000 feet. il *Esquire* 107:40 Ja '87
Picking up a suite deal. il *Esquire* 107:34 F '87
Renting a dream machine. il *Esquire* 107:62 My '87
Vis-à-visas: how to cut the red tape. il *Esquire* 108:72 N '87
A wait that's worth the wait. il *Esquire* 108:80 S '87
Welcome to the U.S.: let's have your wallet. il *Esquire* 108:40 Ag '87

Eichner-Dixon, Peter
Daniel Sprick. il por *Am Artist* 51:32-7 Ag '87

Eickhoff, Janie
about
Woman to watch: Janie Eickhoff. H. R. Madison. por *Women's Sports Fitness* 9:25 Ap '87

Eidetics International (Firm)
Eidetics proposes upgrades to improve F-16 performance. M. A. Dornheim. il *Aviat Week Space Technol* 127:59+ S 28 '87

Eidetics International (Firm)—*cont.*
USAF, Eidetics plan vortex flow, high-angle-of-attack studies. *Aviat Week Space Technol* 126:31 Ja 19 '87

Eidsvik, Harold
International defense. il *Natl Parks* 61:12-13 S/O '87

Eidus, Janice
Where art and commerce coexist. por *Publ Wkly* 232:43 D 18 '87

Eiffel Tower (Paris, France)
For the City of Light, a Ring of Light that's out of this world [space structure to mark the 100th anniversary] il *Discover* 8:6 F '87
France's Ring of Light [space structure to mark 100th anniversary] P. Lewis. il *Macleans* 100:22 Ja 5 '87
Twinkle, twinkle, great big bauble [proposed Ring of Light to mark 100th anniversary] G. Taubes. il *Discover* 8:60-2+ N '87
A "yes" for the French space ring. C. Raymo. *Sky Telesc* 74:5 Jl '87

Eiger, Marvin S., and Olds, Sally Wendkos
The working nursing mother [excerpt from The complete book of breastfeeding] *Work Woman* 12:186+ My '87

Eight is enough [television program] See Television program reviews—Single works

Eikenberry, Jill
about
Jill Eikenberry and Michael Tucker: L.A. law's . . . perfect match. J. Buck. il pors *McCalls* 114:10-12 Ag '87
L.A. law's closest couple. K. Koontz. il pors *Health* 19:34 Je '87

Eiko
about
New moon stories [dance] Reviews
Dance Mag 61:26-8 Ap '87. C. Hardy
New Leader 69:19 D 29 '86. L. A. Jacobs

Eilber, Charles R.
The North Carolina School of Science and Mathematics. *Phi Delta Kappan* 68:773-7 Je '87

Eimer, Manfred
Verification and arms control [with editorial comment by Daniel E. Koshland, Jr.] bibl f *Science* 235:406-14 Ja 23 '87

Eimers, Nancy
Magnolia season [poem] *Nation* 244:544 Ap 25 '87

Einarsson, Lars
Jewels from the Crown. il *Courier* 40:26-9 N '87

Einhorn, Steven G.
about
Stocks for a difficult market [interview] A. E. Serwer. il por *Fortune* 116:176 D 21 '87

Einstein, Albert, 1879-1955
about
Einstein and ether drift experiments. J. Stachel. bibl f *Phys Today* 40:45-7 My '87
Einstein and Germany [discussion of February 1986 article] F. R. Stern. *Phys Today* 40:15+ Jl '87
Einstein and Michelson-Morley [discussion of August 1982 article, How I created the theory of relativity] A. I. Miller. bibl f *Phys Today* 40:9+ My '87

Eis, Joel
A practicing artist-in-residence looks at the view from back stage. *Des Arts Educ* 88:34-9 N/D '86

Eiseley, Loren C., 1907-1977
Our path leads upward [adaptation of address] il *Read Dig* 131:35-6+ N '87
Reading nature [excerpt from The lost notebooks of Loren Eiseley] *Harpers* 275:27 S '87
Silent bones and fallen kingdoms [excerpts from The lost notebooks of Loren Eiseley] *Nat Hist* 96:20+ Je '87

Eisenberg, Amee
The best sound on wheels. il *Stereo Rev* 52:59-63 My '87

Eisenberg, David
(jt. auth) See Sharp, Phillip A., and Eisenberg, David

Eisenberg, Deborah
A cautionary tale [story] *New Yorker* 63:32-42+ Mr 23 '87
Presents [story] *New Yorker* 63:25-36+ Jl 20 '87

Eisenberg, Howard
So many books so little space: what makes a book review editor pick up a book? il *Publ Wkly* 231:25-30 Ap 10 '87

Eisenberg, Lawrence
17 hours with Mariette Hartley. il pors *Good Housekeep* 204:180-1+ My '87
365 tips for a year of health. il *Good Housekeep* 204:77-80+ Ja '87
Loni Anderson: "Why are people so cruel to us?". il pors *Redbook* 168:82+ Mr '87

Eisenberg, Lee, 1946-
Oliver North and the music of the night: reflections on a year out of tune. il *Esquire* 108:141+ D '87
Welcome to the magazine of the 1990s. il *Esquire* 107:1 Ap '87

Eisenberg, Ronni
What-to-do checklist before the baby arrives [excerpt from Organize yourself!]; ed. by Kate Kelly. il *Glamour* 85:160+ F '87
Where to find more time for yourself [excerpt from Organize yourself!]; ed. by Kate Kelly. il *Redbook* 168:74-5+ Ja '87

Eisenberg, Ruth
about
For two New Jersey grannies misfortune sets the stage for a musical collaboration. il pors *People Wkly* 28:121 D 14 '87

Eisenberg, Shoul
about
The world's greatest middleman. H. Kestin. il pors *Forbes* 140 Sp Issue:98+ O 26 '87

Eisendrath, John
Ben Cohen: one who took a different path. *Wash Mon* 19:44-5 F '87
You think the NSC is screwed up? Take a look at Washington's worst run program. il *Wash Mon* 19:13-16 Ap '87

Eisenhower, David, 1948-
Howard Baker: fighting the president's final battles [cover story] il pors *N Y Times Mag* p18-21+ S 6 '87
about
At home with Julie and David (I). B. Yagoda. il pors *Saturday Evening Post* 259:64-7+ Ja/F '87
At home with Julie and David (II). B. Yagoda. il pors *Saturday Evening Post* 259:68-70+ Mr '87

Eisenhower, Dwight D. (Dwight David), 1890-1969
about
Can he be more like Ike? R. Watson. il pors *Newsweek* 109:27 Mr 2 '87
Eight (years) is enough. G. F. Will. il *Newsweek* 110:92 N 23 '87

Eisenhower, Julie Nixon, 1947-
"I think your mommy's had a stroke" [excerpt from Pat Nixon: the untold story] il por *Saturday Evening Post* 259:60-1+ Ap '87
about
At home with Julie and David (I). B. Yagoda. il pors *Saturday Evening Post* 259:64-7+ Ja/F '87
At home with Julie and David (II). B. Yagoda. il pors *Saturday Evening Post* 259:68-70+ Mr '87

Eisenhower, William D.
Sleepers in the hands of an angry God. il por *Christ Today* 31:26-8 Mr 20 '87

Eisenreich, Jim
about
Fighting the enemy within. R. Demak. il pors *Sports Illus* 66:40-3 Je 22 '87
When anxiety comes to bat. J. Shear. il pors *N Y Times Mag* p72+ Mr 8 '87

Eisenstadt, Jill
The girl from Rockaway [fiction] il *Mademoiselle* 93:106+ D '87
about
Girl From Rockaway. B. Treitler. il por *N Y* 20:28 Ag 31 '87
Jill Eisenstadt, a young novelist from farthest Queens, exploring a literary shore close to home. M. Dougherty. il pors *People Wkly* 28:133-4 O 26 '87
The selling of the young. J. Giles. *Natl Rev* 39:64-5 N 20 '87

Eisler, Colin
Art: details of old-master drawings. il *Archit Dig* 44:146-51+ O '87

Eisler, Riane Tennenhaus
The ERA renewal drive. *Humanist* 47:35-6 Ja/F '87
about
The chalice and the blade: an interview with Riane Eisler. F. P. Hosken. *Humanist* 47:26-30+ Jl/Ag '87

Eisner, Elliot W.
Why arts are basic. *Educ Dig* 53:20-2 D '87

Eisner, Michael
The business people and television [address, June 6, 1987] *Vital Speeches Day* 53:665-7 Ag 15 '87
about
Disney's magic. R. Grover. il por *Bus Week* p62-5+ Mr 9 '87
Putting magic back in the Magic Kingdom. M. Magnet. il por *Fortune* 115:65 Ja 5 '87

Eisner, Robert, 1922-
The federal deficit: how does it matter? il *Science* 237:1577-82 S 25 '87

Eisner, Thomas
(jt. auth) See Dussourd, David E., and Eisner, Thomas
Eiszner, James R., 1927-
about
Back to business. J. Cook. il por *Forbes* 140:40-1 O 5 '87
Ejection devices (Airplanes) *See* Airplanes, Military—Escape devices
El Al Israel Airlines Ltd.
El Al proposes two-tier pay scale for pilots. D. A. Brown. *Aviat Week Space Technol* 127:36-7 S 14 '87
Israeli airline seeks partners to survive deregulated era. *Aviat Week Space Technol* 127:37 S 14 '87
"We were overweight". M. Fritz. il por *Forbes* 140:226 O 5 '87
El Chichón (Mexico)
Going star-crazy [aerosols resulting from sulfurous materials ejected by El Chichon believed to cause cloudy airliner windows] R. Gannon. il *Earth Sci* 40:16-17 Fall '87
El Greco, 1541-1614
about
Picasso's apocalyptic whorehouse. J. Richardson. bibl f il *N Y Rev Books* 34:40-7 Ap 23 '87
El Malpais National Monument (N.M.)
Lavaland. P. Guthrie. il map *Natl Parks* 61:22-7 My/Je '87
Senators propose El Malpais as park area. il *Natl Parks* 61:40 Mr/Ap '87
El Mirador site (Guatemala)
El Mirador: an early Maya metropolis uncovered. R. T. Matheny. il map *Natl Geogr* 172:316-39 S '87
El Morocco (New York, N.Y.: Nightclub) *See* New York (N.Y.)—Restaurants, nightclubs, bars, etc.
El Niño (Ocean current)
Another El Niño surprise in the Pacific, but was it predicted? R. A. Kerr. il *Science* 235:744-5 F 13 '87
Capturing El Niño in models. R. A. Kerr. *Science* 238:1507-8 D 11 '87
Historical coral [El Niño-Southern Oscillation events and cadmium levels in Galapagos coral; research by Glen T. Shen] *Sci News* 132:168 S 12 '87
Link between earthquakes and El Niños? [research by Daniel A. Walker] R. Monastersky. *Sci News* 132:373-4 D 12 '87
Natural selection: bird seeds of change [research by Peter R. Grant and H. Lisle Gibbs] R. Monastersky. il *Sci News* 131:373-4 Je 13 '87
Warming up to an El Niño. S. Weisburd. *Sci News* 131:55 Ja 24 '87
El Paso (Tex.)
Water supply
On the outskirts of El Paso, 20,000 survive without water. L. Gomez. il *Life* 10:152-4+ N '87
El Rukn (Gang)
Gaddafi's goons [Chicago gang members convicted of terrorism] il *Time* 130:27 D 7 '87
El Salvador
See also
Civil rights—El Salvador
Earthquakes—El Salvador
Economic assistance, American—El Salvador
Espionage, American—El Salvador
Espionage, Salvadoran
Military assistance, American—El Salvador
Relief work—El Salvador
Repatriation—El Salvador
Salvadorans
Trade unions—El Salvador
United Nations—El Salvador
Civil War, 1980-
Anaya's murder. A. Cockburn. *Nation* 245:546-7 N 14 '87
Bloody setback at El Paraíso [U.S. military adviser killed during rebel attack] J. Borrell. il *Time* 129:49 Ap 13 '87
Death squads—primed to pounce? il *U S News World Rep* 103:14 D 7 '87
Duarte's last stand. T. Golden. *New Repub* 196:12-14 Je 22 '87
El Salvador. L. Hopping. il *Sch Update* 119:13 Mr 9 '87
El Salvador: heading home [guerrilla R. Zamora returns] C. Lane. il por *Newsweek* 110:50 S 21 '87
El Salvador: riddled with fear. J. Moody. il *Time* 130:44 N 16 '87
El Salvador's forgotten war. F. Smyth. il *Progressive* 51:22-4 Ag '87
Hard times for Duarte. B. Levin. il por *Macleans* 100:29 Je 15 '87

Meanwhile, in El Salvador . . . [effect of proposed peace plan] J. Smolowe. il por *Time* 130:30-1 Ag 24 '87
The night fighters of El Salvador [U.S. military adviser dies during FMLN attack] J. L. Sheler. il *U S News World Rep* 102:12-13 Ap 13 '87
Notes and comment. *New Yorker* 63:23 Ap 13 '87
Remember El Salvador? R. Backmann. *World Press Rev* 34:24-5 Ag '87
Salvador's rebels: alive and deadly [attack by Farabundo Marti National Liberation Front kills U.S. adviser] N. Cooper. il *Newsweek* 109:32 Ap 13 '87
'The same old assassins' [slaying of human-rights activist H. Anaya] *Commonweal* 114:646 N 20 '87
The seven plagues of El Salvador. E. A. Baloyra. *Curr Hist* 86:413-16+ D '87
'We came to fight'. N. Cooper. il *Newsweek* 110:51-2 D 7 '87
Moral and religious aspects
Accompaniment: an invitation. R. A. Howard. *America* 157:455-7 D 12 '87
El Salvador: the new face of war. P. Shiras. il *Commonweal* 114:275-8 My 8 '87
Grave encounters [J. N. Duarte links R. D'Aubuisson to murder of O. A. Romero] H. G. Chua-Eoan. il pors *Time* 130:32-4 D 7 '87
The long trip home [A. Nenzel's work with refugees] G. Palumbo. *Commonweal* 114:377 Je 19 '87
Stop all military aid now! [views of I. Martín-Baro] L. Hufford. *America* 156:146-7 F 21 '87
A tale of two cities. J. P. Fitzpatrick. *America* 157:4-5 Jl 4-11 '87
Peace and mediation
Will Duarte see peace in his time? C. A. Robbins. il por *U S News World Rep* 103:29 Ag 31 '87
Description and travel
Holiday in hell. P. J. O'Rourke. il *Roll Stone* p45-6+ F 26 '87
Foreign relations
United States
See United States—Foreign relations—El Salvador
Politics and government
See also
El Salvador—Civil War, 1980-
Duarte's last stand. T. Golden. *New Repub* 196:12-14 Je 22 '87
Duarte's unkept promises. J. Contreras. il por *Newsweek* 109:35 Mr 2 '87
Hard times for Duarte. B. Levin. il por *Macleans* 100:29 Je 15 '87
Holiday in hell. P. J. O'Rourke. il *Roll Stone* p45-6+ F 26 '87
Mess in El Salvador: Duarte takes the heat. J. C. Erlick. il por *U S News World Rep* 102:33 My 25 '87
Minority report. C. Hitchens. *Nation* 245:674 D 5 '87
Ruben Zamora: politics & belief [interview] G. Palumbo. il *Commonweal* 114:733-5 D 18 '87
The seven plagues of El Salvador. E. A. Baloyra. *Curr Hist* 86:413-16+ D '87
A visit to Salvador. M. Kondracke. *New Repub* 197:10-12 Ag 10-17 '87
Religious institutions and affairs
See also
Church and social problems—El Salvador
Evangelistic work—El Salvador
El Salvador [drama] See Lima, Rafael
El Sayed, Refaat
about
A golden boy who lost his luster. P. Sherrid. il por *U S News World Rep* 103:41 Jl 27 '87
Scandal in Sweden: how the Fermenta dream turned sour. J. Kapstein. il por *Bus Week* p68-9 Je 8 '87
Elaine's (New York, N.Y.: Restaurant) *See* New York (N.Y.)—Restaurants, nightclubs, bars, etc.
Elam, Stanley M.
Differences between educators and the public on questions of education policy. il *Phi Delta Kappan* 69:294-6 D '87
Elastase
Heparin promotes the inactivation of antithrombin by neutrophil elastase. R. E. Jordan and others. bibl f il *Science* 237:777-9 Ag 14 '87
Elastin
Smooth muscle-mediated connective tissue remodeling in pulmonary hypertension. R. P. Mecham and others. bibl f il *Science* 237:423-6 Jl 24 '87
Elba (Italy)
Description and travel
Taking refuge on Elba. M. H. Sedge. il *Travel Holiday* 167:36-8 F '87

Elber, R., and Karplus, Martin
Multiple conformational states of proteins: a molecular dynamics analysis of myoglobin. bibl f il *Science* 235:318-21 Ja 16 '87

Elbert, Joan
Tibetans rally to guard a culture. *Christ Century* 104:988-9 N 11 '87

Eldar, Yishai, and Idinopulos, Thomas A.
A new vision for Eastern Orthodoxy? [cover story] il *Christ Century* 104:995-8 N 11 '87

Elder, Jean K.
The role of intergenerational programs in: the "Youth 2000" campaign. il *Aging* no356:17-19 '87
Youth 2000. por *Child Today* 16:32-3 Mr/Ap '87

Elder, Lee
about
Lee Elder recovering from mild heart attack. por *Jet* 73:46 D 21 '87

Elder, Mimi
Ohio. il map *Gourmet* 47:80-5+ N '87

Elderhostel
These 'student' hostels aren't for youngsters. I. Pave. il *Bus Week* p117 Jl 13 '87

Elderly *See* Aged

Elderly services programs *See* Industry—Elderly services programs

Elders (Church officers)
Is elder rule a threat? [Consultation on Congregationalism] S. Grenz. *Christ Today* 31:48+ Jl 10 '87

Elders IXL Limited
Australia's apostle of beer and business [J. D. Elliott] L. Kraar. il por *Fortune* 115:88 Ja 5 '87
Carling goes Australian [takeover by Elders IXL Ltd.] T. Tedesco. il *Macleans* 100:36 Mr 9 '87
Two Australian beer barons take their brawl abroad [A. Bond and J. D. Elliott] C. Debes and P. Finch. il pors *Bus Week* p138+ O 19 '87

Eldon (Iowa)
Historic houses, sites, etc.
An Iowa town debates the fate of Grant Wood's gothic backdrop. il *People Wkly* 28:111 S 7 '87

Eldridge, Joseph
Odd man out. *America* 157:348-9 N 14 '87

Election (Theology)
The chosen. M. K. Hellwig. *America* 156:inside back cover Mr 21 '87
God is not elected but people are: reflections occasioned by NBC's news special "Report on America". W. H. Shannon. *America* 157:136-8 S 12-19 '87

Election bets *See* Gambling

Election districts
See also
  Apportionment (Election law)
  Gerrymander

Election expenses *See* Campaign funds

Election laws
See also
  Black suffrage
  Campaign funds—Laws and regulations
  Proportional representation
  United States. Federal Election Commission
  Voter registration
Pittsburgh voters approve new system; ups chances for black candidates. *Jet* 72:12 Je 8 '87
The right not to know [universal poll-closing time bill] D. Olin. *New Repub* 197:18-19 Ag 10-17 '87
What went wrong with the Voting Rights Act [views of A. M. Thernstrom] P. H. Schuck. *Wash Mon* 19:51-5 N '87

United States
See Election laws

Elections
See also
  Black suffrage
  Election laws
  National conventions (Political)
  Political campaigns
  Political candidates
  Presidential candidates
  Presidential primaries
  Presidents—Election
  Proportional representation
  Referendum
  Television broadcasting—Election results
  Trade unions—Elections
  United States. Federal Election Commission
  Voting
    See also subhead Politics and government under names of states and cities
An on-year for the Democrats. J. P. Shapiro. il *U S News World Rep* 103:20 N 16 '87

Argentina
Argentina casts a 'punishment vote' [Peronist resurgence] il *Newsweek* 110:50 S 21 '87

Australia
Hawke's sweeping victory. P. Kopvillem. il por *Macleans* 100:25 Jl 20 '87

Bahamas
Pindling reelected as Bahamian prime minister. il por *Jet* 72:8 Jl 6 '87

Canada
See also subhead Politics and government under names of provinces and cities
On the march [New Democratic Party; cover story; special section; with editorial comment by Kevin Doyle] il *Macleans* 100:2, 8-16 Ag 3 '87

Germany (West)
East-West missile deal: Helmut Kohl feels the heat. D. Stanglin. il por *U S News World Rep* 102:13 Je 1 '87
Kohl is nudged, but will he budge? [INF disarmament proposal] *Newsweek* 109:39 Je 1 '87
Kohl on a roll [British prospects in light of German election] W. Laqueur. *New Repub* 196:17-18 Mr 2 '87
Kohl's second term: Washington may feel a chilly breeze. F. A. Miller and J. E. Pluenneke. il por *Bus Week* p48 F 9 '87

Great Britain
Aiming for three straight [results of local elections and possibility of general election in June] C. Ogden. il por *Time* 129:44 My 18 '87
All revved up [with interview with M. Thatcher] D. Brand. il pors *Time* 129:34-8 Je 22 '87
Beat the devil [Thatcher victory] A. Cockburn. *Nation* 244:876-7 Je 27 '87
Blacks in Parliament. D. J. Dent. il *Black Enterp* 18:22 S '87
First 3 blacks elected to British Parliament. il *Jet* 72:36 Jl 6 '87
"Full steam ahead for conservatism". il *Fortune* 116:8 Jl 6 '87
The long reign of Britain's 'Maggie III'. R. Knight. il por *U S News World Rep* 102:14 Je 22 '87
No slacking [M. Thatcher's victory] A. Lejeune. *Natl Rev* 39:38 Jl 17 '87
Now the other Britain needs Thatcher's attention. R. A. Melcher. il por *Bus Week* p43 Je 29 '87
One determined lady [M. Thatcher] R. Laver. il por *Macleans* 100:20 Je 22 '87
Power in the name of ideas [reelection of M. Thatcher] G. F. Will. il *Newsweek* 109:84 Je 22 '87
Thatcher wins again. K. Slack. *Christ Century* 104:581-2 Jl 1-8 '87
Thatcher's two Britains. M. Whitaker. il por *Newsweek* 109:28-30 Je 22 '87
The two Britains. *Nation* 244:873-4 Je 27 '87
Anecdotes, facetiae, satire, etc.
Against all odds [betting on the election] D. Seligman. il *Fortune* 116:101-2 Jl 20 '87

Haiti
Blood at the ballot boxes. B. Levin. il *Macleans* 100:25+ D 14 '87
Blood in the ballot box. J. Smolowe. il *Time* 130:38-40 D 14 '87
Bloodshed blocks a ballot. J. Greenwald. il *Time* 130:34 D 7 '87
Cry Haiti. M. S. Hooper. *Nation* 245:740-1 D 19 '87
Democracy in Haiti. W. F. Buckley. *Natl Rev* 39:54-5 D 31 '87
Haiti: democracy derailed. D. Peerman. *Christ Century* 104:1135-6 D 16 '87
Haiti robbed of hope [cover story] C. Cleaver. il *New Leader* 70:8-10 D 28 '87
How the U.S. miscalculated in Haiti. C. A. Robbins. il *U S News World Rep* 103:36-7 D 14 '87
Living with a nightmare [H. Namphy's junta] J. Smolowe. il *Time* 130:48+ D 21 '87
Terror keeps Haiti in line. N. Cooper. il *Newsweek* 110:54-5 D 14 '87
Violence stops the vote. N. Cooper. il *Newsweek* 110:57 D 7 '87
Voodoo foreign policy. *New Repub* 197:7-8 D 21 '87
What not to do in Haiti. *Commonweal* 114:724 D 18 '87

India
End of an enchanted honeymoon [Congress (I) Party loses in state elections] E. W. Desmond. il por *Time* 129:40 Ap 6 '87
For Gandhi, everything turns sour. M. Satchell. il por *U S News World Rep* 102:34-5 Ap 6 '87

Elections—*cont.*

Ireland

After the Irish elections. T. P. O'Mahony. *America* 156:267-8 Ap 4 '87

Economic agendas. P. Kirby. *Commonweal* 114:136-7 Mr 13 '87

Hollow victory [minority government led by C. Haughey] por *Time* 129:31 Mr 2 '87

The Irish Houdini [C. Haughey wins general election] R. Laver. il por *Macleans* 100:17 Mr 2 '87

Italy

The body politic [Cicciolina] M. Lilla. *New Repub* 197:14-16 S 28 '87

Changing Italy. E. von Kuehnelt-Leddihn. *Natl Rev* 39:42 Ag 14 '87

In a naked play for power, porn queen Cicciolina wins a seat in Italy's Parliament. W. Plummer. il pors *People Wkly* 28:34-5 Jl 6 '87

Korea (South)

How to have it all: mix old stability with new freedom. M. Tharp. il por map *U S News World Rep* 103:42-4 D 28 '87-Ja 4 '88

Korea votes for economic stability [election of Roh Tae Woo] L. Nakarmi. il por *Bus Week* p69 D 28 '87-Ja 4 '88

Roh wins—but can he rule? [with interview] N. Cooper. il por *Newsweek* 110:22-4 D 28 '87

Roh's bloody victory. M. Nichols. il por *Macleans* 100:40-1 D 28 '87

A vote for stability [Roh Tae Woo wins presidential election] J. Greenwald. il pors *Time* 130:28-31 D 28 '87

Philippines

Cory Aquino and the psychology of bubbles [legislative election of May 11, 1987] M. Singer. il *Natl Rev* 39:34-8 Ag 14 '87

Giant step for democracy [C. Aquino's candidates victorious in congressional elections] T. A. Sancton. il por *Time* 129:48 My 25 '87

Inextricably involved. *America* 156:414 My 23 '87

Philippines. L. Reaves. *Bus Week* p81 My 25 '87

Unclean elections. M. Singer. *New Repub* 197:9-10 Ag 3 '87

Portugal

Now comes the orange crush [A. Cavaco Silva and the Social Democratic Party win majority] H. G. Chua-Eoan. il por *Time* 130:31 Ag 3 '87

Portugal turns right. il por *Fortune* 116:8 Ag 31 '87

Portugal's vote. C. D. Van De Stadt. *World Press Rev* 34:36 S '87

A small victory [A. Cavaco Silva's election] E. von Kuehnelt-Leddihn. *Natl Rev* 39:46 N 6 '87

South Africa

Botha's triumph: South Africa's tragedy? J. Jones. il *U S News World Rep* 102:12-13 My 18 '87

In South Africa, white makes right. K. Owen. il *World Press Rev* 34:43 Jl '87

A lurch to the right. W. E. Smith. il *Time* 129:42-3 My 18 '87

A stunning roar for apartheid. S. Reiss. il *Newsweek* 109:52 My 18 '87

A sweeping shift to the right. A. Bilski. il *Macleans* 100:22 My 18 '87

Taiwan

Taiwan's generation-long political evolution [address, June 1, 1987] J. A. Robinson. *Vital Speeches Day* 53:633-7 Ag 1 '87

United States

See Elections

Western Europe

Vote for the quasi-status quo. C. D. Van de Stadt. *World Press Rev* 34:32-3 Ag '87

Elections in art

British election ceramics. J. Priestley. bibl f il *Antiques* 131:1304-13 Je '87

Electric automobiles *See* Automobiles, Electric

Electric batteries

See also
Fuel cells
Storage batteries

Batteries, from alkaline to lithium. S. Woolley. *Bus Week* p132 D 14 '87

Dry-cell batteries. il *Consum Rep* 52:703-6 N '87

Flexible battery. D. Scott. il *Pop Sci* 231:48 D '87

High-energy battery [zinc-bromine battery] D. Scott. il *Pop Sci* 230:60 Mr '87

Lithium batteries: are they really better? [camera batteries] H. Keppler. il *Pop Photogr* 94:113+ N '87

The portable power roundup [camera batteries] K. Geller-Shinn. il *Petersens Photogr Mag* 15:20+ F '87

Quantum Turbo battery [power pack for electronic flash] G. Lewis. il *Petersens Photogr Mag* 16:32+ D '87

Using the Polapulse battery. F. Blechman. il *Radio-Electron* 58:61-3+ F '87

Charging

Over-voltage indicator. R. Grossblatt. il *Radio-Electron* 58:101-2 O '87

An under-voltage monitor. R. Grossblatt. il *Radio-Electron* 58:41-2 N '87

Electric battery industry

See also
Rayovac Corporation

Advertising

The big charge. B. Kanner. il *N Y* 20:29+ N 16 '87

Marketing

Electrifying [Rayovac Corp.] S. B. Weiner. il *Forbes* 140:196+ N 30 '87

Electric bills *See* Electric utilities—Rates

Electric Boat Division *See* General Dynamics Corp. Electric Boat Division

Electric cables

See also
Electric lines

Fault location

Finding cable faults [use of time-domain reflectometry] V. D. Martin. il *Radio-Electron* 58:66-70+ Mr '87

Electric circuit breakers

Installing shock protection. il *Home Mech* 83:76 N '87

Electric coils

See also
Induction coils

Electric conductors and conductivity

See also
Semiconductors
Superconductors and superconductivity

Conductive inks and adhesives. F. M. Mims. il *Radio-Electron* 58:81-4 N '87

Currents in plastics [doping polyacetylene; work of Herbert Naarmann and N. Theophilou] J. Horgan. *Sci Am* 257:26-7 S '87

New uses for plastics. G. Bronson. il *Forbes* 139:216-17 My 18 '87

Electric control

See also
Electric switches

Electric control, Remote *See* Remote control

Electric current converters

See also
Electric current inverters
Frequency changers

Electric current inverters

5-volt only: introducing the new MAX 232. R. A. Kreuter. il *Radio-Electron* 58 ComputerDigest:10-11 Ja '87

Electric current rectifiers

See also
Thyristors

Electric currents

See also
Transients (Electricity)

Electric discharges

See also
Electric sparks

How to capture on film the faint glow emitted when sticky tape is peeled off a surface. J. Walker. il *Sci Am* 257:138-41 D '87

Electric dishwashers *See* Dishwashers

Electric drills *See* Drilling and boring machinery

Electric engineering

See also
Frequency response (Electric engineering)

Electric equipment

See also
Automobiles—Electric equipment
Boats and boating—Electric equipment
Electric generators
Remote control
Transducers

Electric equipment industry *See* Electric industries

Electric fans *See* Fans, Electric

Electric fault location

See also
Electric cables—Fault location

Electric fences *See* Fences, Electric

Electric fields

Physiological effects

See Electricity—Physiological effects

Electric filters

See also
Radio filters

Electric fish *See* Electric organs in fish
Electric furnaces *See* Furnaces
Electric generators
Emergency generator. J. Gaynor. il *Home Mech* 83:102 F '87
A man who defies the laws [J. W. Newman's electric motor] D. Noland. por *Discover* 8:46-8+ My '87
Wave-driven air turbine [Norwegian plant] D. Scott. il *Pop Sci* 231:96-7 N '87
Electric heaters *See* Heaters
Electric household appliances *See* Household appliances
Electric industries
  See also
  Bulbtronics (Firm)
  Collective bargaining—Electric industries
  Electric utilities
  Electronic industries
  General Electric Co.
  Graybar Electric Co., Inc.
  GTE Corp.
  Molex Incorporated
  Reliance Electric Co.
  Westinghouse Electric Corp.
    Acquisitions and mergers
      Western Europe
Power surge in Scandinavia [ASEA merger with BBC Brown Boveri Ltd.] B. Childs and T. Peterson. il *Bus Week* p36 Ag 24 '87
    Advertising
Battle of the bulbs. B. Kanner. il *N Y* 20:22+ Ap 13 '87
    Finance
Electrical equipment. E. Giltenan. il *Forbes* 139:116 Ja 12 '87
    Great Britain
  See also
  General Electric Company plc
    Japan
  See also
  Hitachi, Ltd.
  Matsushita Electric Industrial Co. Ltd.
  Toshiba Corporation
    Netherlands
  See also
  Philips Industries, NV
    United States
  See Electric industries
Electric lamps
  See also
  Lighting fixtures
Bentwood chair and lamp. K. Meyers. il *Workbench* 43:54-9 S/O '87
Lamps that are special. il *South Living* 22:116 Je '87
    Repairing
How to repair an incandescent lamp. M. Henkenius. il *Pop Mech* 164:129-30 D '87
Lamp repair. H. Wicks. il *Home Mech* 83:22-3 N '87
Electric lamps, Flashing
Sequential flasher. M. Ciric. il *Radio-Electron* 58:36-7 F '87
SMT project: LED flasher [surface-mountable components] F. M. Mims. il *Radio-Electron* 58:73-4+ N '87
Electric lamps, Halogen
Halogen lights: what you should know. il *Glamour* 85:86 Mr '87
Electric light bulbs *See* Light bulbs
Electric light fixtures *See* Lighting fixtures
Electric lighting *See* Lighting
Electric lines
    Environmental aspects
Cutting through a sacred forest [Ojo power line and sacred sites in the Jemez Mountains, N.M.] D. Gibson. il *Sierra* 72:135-6 Ja/F '87
    Photographs and photography
Those dreaded utility lines. A. Baget. il *Petersens Photogr Mag* 16:34-5 Ag '87
Electric measurements
  See also
  Electric meters
  Strain gages
Electric meters
  See also
  Ammeters
  Multimeters
  Spectrum analyzers
  Voltohmmeters
Sencore LC75 "Z Meter II". il *Radio-Electron* 58:24-7 Ap '87

Electric motors
  See also
  Electric generators
  Stepping motors
More on motors [reversing electric motors] il *Radio-Electron* 58:10+ O '87
    Control
  See also
  Frequency changers
Electric organs in fish
Watts new, pussycat? [work of Carl D. Hopkins] *Oceans* 20:4 Mr/Ap '87
Electric outlets *See* Electric wire and wiring
Electric plants
  See also
  Electric utilities
  Hydroelectric plants
  Nuclear power plants
  Ocean thermal power plants
New technologies in the generation of electricity. P. H. Abelson. *Science* 236:373 Ap 24 '87
Off-design performance of power plants: an integrated gasification combined-cycle example. M. R. Erbes and others. bibl f il *Science* 237:379-83 Jl 24 '87
    Energy usage
Coal-fired power plants for the future. R. E. Balzhiser and K. E. Yeager. il *Sci Am* 257:100-7 S '87
Utilities kick the crude habit. M. Brody. il *Fortune* 115:56-7 Mr 16 '87
Who will decide the future of coal? [address, April 16, 1987] A. W. Dahlberg. *Vital Speeches Day* 53:562-4 Jl 1 '87
    Environmental aspects
A $2.5-billion acid rain plan [coal-burning power plants] M. Crawford. *Science* 235:1567 Mr 27 '87
Cleaning up with a smokestack's siren song [use of acoustic agglomeration to control particle emissions from coal-fired power plants] I. Peterson. *Sci News* 131:342 My 30 '87
Fighting acid rain with gold [use as catalyst to reduce nitrogen oxide after coal is burned for fuel; work of Arun Someshwar] *USA Today (Periodical)* 115:5-6 Je '87
People, power plants, and manatees [Florida] J. E. Reynolds, III and J. R. Wilcox. il map *Sea Front* 33:263-9 Jl/Ag '87
Profit without pollution [Northern States Power] S. B. Weiner. il *Forbes* 139:46 My 18 '87
Spending more for cleaner coal. I. Peterson. *Sci News* 131:199 Mr 28 '87
Electric power
  See also
  Electric plants
  Electric utilities
  Hydroelectric power
    Rates
  See Electric utilities—Rates
    British Columbia
  See also
  British Columbia Hydro and Power Authority
    Developing countries
Electricity in the developing world [cover story] C. Flavin. bibl f il *Environment* 29:12-15+ Ap '87
    New York (State)
  See also
  Power Authority of the State of New York
Electric power, Solar *See* Solar energy
Electric power distribution
Freewheeling. B. Weberman and A. Snitzer. il map *Forbes* 140:35-6 Ag 10 '87
Electric power failures
Blackout! What happens in a power failure. M. Parfit. il *Read Dig* 130:197-8+ Je '87
Coping with blackout: what happens when the lights go out? M. Parfit. bibl (p143) il *Smithsonian* 17:38-49 F '87
Electric power lines *See* Electric lines
Electric power plants *See* Electric plants
Electric power production
  See also
  Electric plants
  Hydroelectric plants
  Nuclear power plants
  Ocean thermal power plants
Energy technology in the 21st century. S. B. Kuznetsov. il *Radio-Electron* 58:107-11 My '87
Electric power production from chemical action
  See also
  Fuel cells

Electric rates *See* Electric utilities—Rates
Electric receptacles *See* Electric wire and wiring
Electric resistors
　　See also
　　Potentiometers
Electric saws *See* Saws and sawing
Electric shock
　Burning alive! [C. Marsh saves S. Moses from farm accident electrocution] S. Kelly. il *Read Dig* 131:95-9 S '87
　Chicago boy gets $2.5 mil. in injury case: his arm destroyed by electricity [L. Mance] por *Jet* 72:36 Jl 27 '87
Electric shock treatment *See* Shock therapy
Electric signs
　　See also
　　Neon signs
Electric sparks
　Plastic shocks and visible sparks. I. Peterson. il *Sci News* 132:152 S 5 '87
Electric stoves *See* Stoves
Electric switches
　　See also
　　Packet switching (Data transmission)
　　Telephone switching systems, Electronic
　　Thyristors
　Digital arming switch [remote alarm system switch] D. Petraglia. il *Pop Sci* 230:127 F '87
　Simple switches. il *Home Mech* 83:75 N '87
　Sunrise to sunset simulator [automatic lamp dimmer] il *Radio-Electron* 58:8+ Ag '87
　USITT dimmer standards. D. F. Sisk. *Theatre Crafts* 21:16+ F '87
　Wiring multi-switches. R. Day. il *Pop Sci* 230:85+ Ja '87
Electric tools *See* Tools
Electric trains *See* Railroad models
Electric transmission
　　See also
　　Electric lines
　　Electric power
Electric utilities
　　See also
　　Central & South West Corp.
　　Central Maine Power Co.
　　Commonwealth Edison Co.
　　Consumers Power Co.
　　Georgia Power Co.
　　Middle South Utilities, Inc.
　　Northern States Power Co. (Minn.)
　　Northwest Power Company
　　Nuclear industry
　　Pinnacle West Capital Corporation
　　Portland General Electric Co.
　　Power Authority of the State of New York
　　Public Service Co. of N. H.
　　Public Service Co. of New Mexico
　　Puget Sound Power & Light Co.
　　Washington Public Power Supply System
Acquisitions and mergers
　Who says utilities can't be raider bait? [M. J. Whitman's play for Public Service of N.H. includes debt by Seabrook nuclear plant] C. Brown. il por *Bus Week* p112 N 23 '87
Customer relations
　Buy your next appliance from your utility and you may just get a rebate! H. Porter. *Fam Handyman* 37:8 N '87
Energy usage
　See Electric plants—Energy usage
Environmental aspects
　See Electric plants—Environmental aspects
Finance
　Electric utilities. B. Stavro. il *Forbes* 139:120+ Ja 12 '87
Government ownership
　Power to the people. J. Cook. il por *Forbes* 140:110+ O 19 '87
Laws and regulations
　　See also
　　Citizens Utility Board (Ill.)
　Freewheeling. B. Weberman and A. Snitzer. il map *Forbes* 140:35-6 Ag 10 '87
　How to cut the cost of electricity. il *Consum Res Mag* 70:24-6 F '87
　Mr. Malec versus the bureaucrats [SEC's involvement in Central & South West Corp's factoring operations] E. A. Finn, Jr. il por *Forbes* 140:44 D 28 '87
Management
　The utility industry [address, March 9-11, 1987] R. M. Flynn. *Vital Speeches Day* 53:463-5 My 15 '87

Rates
　Consumers out in the cold [rate hikes approved for Commonwealth Edison] M. Ervin. il *Progressive* 51:17 Mr '87
　Fall of the light brigade. L. Wiener. il *U S News World Rep* 102:55 Ja 26 '87
　Freewheeling. B. Weberman and A. Snitzer. il map *Forbes* 140:35-6 Ag 10 '87
　How to cut the cost of electricity. il *Consum Res Mag* 70:24-6 F '87
　Still surviving—maybe [Middle South Utilities] M. Fritz. il *Forbes* 139:8 Je 29 '87
Regulation
　See Electric utilities—Laws and regulations
Securities
　Are diversified utilities better stock picks? G. Weiss. il *Bus Week* p132 Ap 27 '87
　Beam me up, Scotty. S. Lee. il *Forbes* 140:214 O 19 '87
　Dirty tricks [bonds and call protection] B. Weberman. il *Forbes* 139:173 My 4 '87
　How to get on Wall Street's map: trade 19 million shares a day [Japanese investors taking advantage of high dividends on utility stocks] J. M. Laderman. il *Bus Week* p85 S 7 '87
　Putting the juice back into utilities. J. P. Newport, Jr. il *Fortune* 116:125-6 S 28 '87
　Should you pull the plug on utility stocks? Y. Potts. il *50 Plus* 27:76-9+ S '87
Canada
　　See also
　　British Columbia Hydro and Power Authority
Electric vehicles
　　See also
　　Automobiles, Electric
　　Bumper cars
Electric waves
　　See also
　　Electromagnetic waves
Electric wire and wiring
　　See also
　　Automobiles—Electric wiring
　　Electric circuit breakers
　　Electric switches
　Adding an electrical receptacle box. M. Morris. il *Home Mech* 83:82 Jl '87
　How to defuse the hazards of aluminum house wiring. M. Henkenius. il *Pop Mech* 164:107-8 Ag '87
　Install a grounding receptacle. G. Branson. il *Fam Handyman* 37:49 F '87
　Upgrading home electricals. B. McPartland. il *Home Mech* 83:74-7 N '87
　Upgrading home electricals. M. Morris. il *Home Mech* 83:44-6 Jl '87
　When to upgrade your electrical service [interview with B. McPartland] il *Home Mech* 83:18-19+ S '87
　Wiring multi-switches. R. Day. il *Pop Sci* 230:85+ Ja '87
　Wiring tips from the pros. R. Day. il *Pop Sci* 230:71 Ap '87
Electricity
　　See also
　　Fuel cells
　　Lightning
　　Transients (Electricity)
Conservation
　See Energy conservation
Distribution
　See Electric power distribution
Physiological effects
　　See also
　　Electric shock
　　Electrotherapy
　Behavioral recovery induced by applied electric fields after spinal cord hemisection in guinea pig. R. B. Borgens and others. bibl f il *Science* 238:366-9 O 16 '87
　Frequency dependence of electric field modulation of fibroblast protein synthesis. K. J. McLeod and others. bibl f il *Science* 236:1465-9 Je 12 '87
Electricity generation *See* Electric power production
Electricity in medicine *See* Electrotherapy
Electricity in the home
　　See also
　　Electric wire and wiring
Conservation
　See Energy conservation
Electricity supply
　　See also
　　Computers—Energy usage
　　Electronic equipment—Energy usage

Electricity supply—See also—*cont.*
Integrated circuits—Energy usage
Refrigerators—Energy usage

Electrides
Electrides [cover story] J. L. Dye. il *Sci Am* 257:66-75 S '87

Electro-optics Industries, Ltd.
Bendix, Israeli firm demonstrate high-accuracy helmet sight. il *Aviat Week Space Technol* 127:148 Ag 10 '87

Electrobiology *See* Electrophysiology

Electrocardiography
Take heart—the doctor's on call [heart monitored via telephone] il *Prevention* 39:10 N '87
Watch Q-Med as it stalks a silent killer [portable EKG machine to detect silent ischemia] G. G. Marcial. il *Bus Week* p88 Ap 13 '87

Electrochemistry
See also
Fuel cells
Electrochemistry. *Science* 235 pt2:G61-G63 F 27 '87

Electrochromic windows *See* Windows

Electroconvulsive therapy *See* Shock therapy

Electrodes, Biomedical *See* Biosensors

Electroencephalograms *See* Electroencephalography

Electroencephalography
Growth spurts mirror mental milestones [cerebral hemisphere development; research by Robert W. Thatcher and others] R. J. Trotter. *Psychol Today* 21:13 S '87
Human cerebral hemispheres develop at different rates and ages. R. W. Thatcher and others. bibl f il *Science* 236:1110-13 My 29 '87

Electromagnetic propulsion
See also
Railguns

Electromagnetic pulse simulators
Environmental aspects
EMP: fallout over a naval EMPRESS [Navy proposal for simulator in Chesapeake Bay] J. Raloff. *Sci News* 131:182 Mr 21 '87

Electromagnetic theory
See also
Field theory (Physics)

Electromagnetic therapy
Non-invasive treatment for hypothermia. *Sea Front* 33:307-8 Jl/Ag '87

Electromagnetic waves
Airlines zigzag on in-seat computing. M. Antonoff. *Pers Comput* 11:141 Jl '87
Army modifies UH-60s to cut electromagnetic interference in controls. *Aviat Week Space Technol* 127:27-8 N 16 '87
Army will shield UH-60 hydraulics against EMI. *Aviat Week Space Technol* 127:29 N 23 '87
Physiological effects
See also
Electromagnetic therapy
An electrifying new hazard. S. N. Wellborn. il *U S News World Rep* 102:72-4 Mr 30 '87
ELF: the current controversy. D. D. Edwards. il *Sci News* 131:107-9 F 14 '87
ELF under suspicion in new report. D. D. Edwards. *Sci News* 132:39 Jl 18 '87
Magnetic fields and leukemia [power line radiation] *Newsweek* 110:56 Jl 20 '87
Power lines and cancer: the evidence grows [ELF fields] L. Slesin. il *Technol Rev* 90:52-9 O '87
Zapped? [women at Greenham Common peace camp fear they are victims of non-ionizing electromagnetic radiation] L. Slesin. *Nation* 244:313 Mr 14 '87

Electromagnetic weapons
The zap gap [Soviet edge in development of radio frequency weapons] C. De Caro. il *Atlantic* 259:24+ Mr '87

Electromagnetism
See also
Magnetic materials
Magnetohydrodynamics
Electromagnetic stabilization of weakly conducting fluids. C. F. Ivory and others. bibl f il *Science* 238:58-61 O 2 '87

Electromagnetism in medicine *See* Electromagnetic therapy

Electron beam lithography
Dancing on the head of a pin. G. Bronson. il *Forbes* 139:152-3 Ap 6 '87

Electron beams
Going for a molecular spin [electron stimulated desorption ion angular distribution method of probing structure and bonding at surfaces] S. Weisburd. il *Sci News* 132:199 S 26 '87

Electron microscopes and microscopy
Altering atomic structures [use of scanning tunneling microscope] T. H. Cole. il *Pop Mech* 164:10 S '87
High-resolution electron microscopy and scanning tunneling microscopy of native oxides on silicon. A. H. Carim and others. bibl f il *Science* 237:630-3 Ag 7 '87
Not-so-naked ancestors [electron microscope study of naked algae] G. McFadden. il *Sea Front* 33:46-51 Ja/F '87
Physics Nobel Prize. P. F. Schewe. bibl f *Phys Today* 40:S70 Ja '87
Physics Nobel Prize awarded for microscopies old and new. B. M. Schwarzschild. il pors *Phys Today* 40:17-21 Ja '87
Playing with atoms, one at a time [use of the scanning tunneling microscope] S. Budiansky. il *U S News World Rep* 102:72 F 16 '87
A small gold-conjugated antibody label: improved resolution for electron microscopy [cover story] J. F. Hainfeld. bibl f il *Science* 236:450-3 Ap 24 '87

Electron transfer reactions *See* Chemical reactions

Electron transport
Ballistic electrons in semiconductors. M. Heiblum and L. F. Eastman. il *Sci Am* 256:102-11 F '87
Gallium arsenide transistors. W. R. Frensley. bibl (p116) il *Sci Am* 257:80-7 Ag '87

Electronic alarm system industry *See* Electronic industries

Electronic anesthesia *See* Anesthesia and anesthetics

Electronic Arts Inc.
Trip Hawkins wants to be the Walt Disney of software. R. Brandt. il por *Bus Week* p134 N 9 '87

Electronic astronomy
Electric eyes. T. Beardsley. il *Sci Am* 257:35-7 S '87

Electronic banking *See* Computers—Banking use

Electronic behavior control
Probing the mind's eye [visual sensation induced by electronic stimulation of the brain] *Sci Am* 256:85 F '87

Electronic bulletin boards *See* Computer bulletin boards

Electronic church *See* Television broadcasting—Religious programs

Electronic circuits
See also
Integrated circuits
Printed circuits
Transistors
Design
CompDes—computer-aided circuit design. il *Radio-Electron* 58 ComputerDigest:136-7 My '87
Designer's notebook. R. Grossblatt. See issues of *Radio-Electronics* beginning March 1984
The drawing board. R. Grossblatt. See issues of *Radio-Electronics*

Electronic clocks *See* Clocks, Electronic

Electronic communication *See* Telecommunication

Electronic components *See* Electronic equipment

Electronic control
See also
Airplane engines, Jet—Control
Camera shutters—Control
Household appliances—Control
Radio receivers—Control
Remote control
Robots—Control
Television receivers—Control
A bang-bang IC [CMOS controller] R. F. Scott. il *Radio-Electron* 58:124-5 N '87

Electronic cooking *See* Microwave cooking

Electronic countermeasures on military airplanes *See* Airplanes, Military—Electronic equipment

Electronic crossover (Loudspeakers) *See* Loudspeakers

Electronic data interchange
Business use
An electronic pipeline that's changing the way America does business. C. L. Harris and D. Foust. il *Bus Week* p80+ Ag 3 '87

Electronic data processing
See also
Computers
Data transmission systems
Distributed data processing
Electronic data interchange
File organization (Computers)
Information storage and retrieval systems
On line searching
Optical data processing
Parallel processing (Computers)
Real-time data processing
Sorting (Computers)

Electronic data processing departments
See also
    Information centers (Data processing)
Strategic connections [personal computers and mainframe data] J. Blackford. il *Pers Comput* 11:131-3+ My '87
Electronic data processing personnel *See* Computer personnel
Electronic Data Systems Corp.
The $750 million muzzle [R. Smith forces H. R. Perot out at GM] D. Sherman. il *Car Driv* 32:7 Mr '87
A billionaire for the common man [H. R. Perot] B. O'Reilly. il por *Fortune* 115:47 Ja 5 '87
Business leaders [address, December 8, 1986] H. R. Perot. *Vital Speeches Day* 53:337-42 Mr 15 '87
Career makeover: from newspaper sportswriter to computer publications manager [A. Seelig] il por *Glamour* 85:106 Je '87
Detroit [H. R. Perot ousted at General Motors] P. Lienert. il pors *Road Track* 38:110 Mr '87
How G.M. bought itself a lemon [tracing the Electronic Data Systems acquisition] M. M. Thomas. il *Nation* 244:108-9 Ja 31 '87
Sprint's chance to gallop [contract to supply network services to GM] J. J. Keller. il *Bus Week* p33 Je 15 '87
True-life adventures of H. Ross Perot. D. Remnick. por *Read Dig* 131:165-6+ S '87
You don't lose 'em all [GM's buyout of H. R. Perot] C. Siler. il por *Forbes* 140:34 Ag 10 '87
Electronic Data Technologies
Winning at one-arm bandits. G. G. Marcial. *Bus Week* p114 D 7 '87
Electronic display systems *See* Information display systems
Electronic document interchange *See* Electronic data interchange
Electronic equipment
See also
    Airplanes—Electronic equipment
    Automobiles—Electronic equipment
    Automobiles, Foreign—Electronic equipment
    Boats and boating—Electronic equipment
    Children's electronics
    Computers
    Home electronics
    Intercom systems
    Surface mounting (Electronics)
    Television equipment
    Transducers
New-Age consumer products for high-tech homes and offices. C. McClean. il *Black Enterp* 17:88 Je '87
New products. See issues of Radio-Electronics
Product reports 1988. il *Archit Rec* 175:201-4+ D '87
What's new in electronics. W. J. Hawkins. See issues of Popular Science

Design
Silicon Valley's newest wizards. M. Rogers. il *Newsweek* 109:36-7 Ja 5 '87

Energy usage
Computer-assisted regulator design. J. Cunkelman. il *Radio-Electron* 58 ComputerDigest:110-11 F '87

Prices
Discounters in the dumps. B. Saporito. il *Fortune* 116:103+ Ag 3 '87
Electronics 'superstores' may have blown a fuse [price wars] M. J. Pitzer. il *Bus Week* p90+ Je 8 '87
FX vs. high-tech. M. Riggs. il *High Fidel* 37:2 Jl '87

Testing
Electronic review. J. Cohen. il *Consum Res Mag* 70:19-22 F '87
Equipment reports. See issues of Radio-Electronics
Electronic equipment industry *See* Electronic industries
Electronic flight instrument system display *See* Airplanes—Electronic equipment; Airplanes, Jet—Electronic equipment
Electronic funds transfer systems *See* Computers—Banking use
Electronic games
See also
    International Game Technology
    Video games
Electronic industries
See also
    A.T. & E. Corp.
    Acuson Corporation
    Advanced Micro Devices, Inc.
    Ampex Corporation
    Audio equipment industry
    Avionics industry
    Bally Manufacturing Corp.
    Bendix Corp.
    Commodore International Ltd.

    Computer industry
    Cubic Corp.
    Drexler Technology Corp.
    E-Systems, Inc.
    Eaton Corporation
    Emerson Radio Corp.
    Energy Conversion Devices, Inc.
    Fairchild Semiconductor Corporation
    General Electric Co.
    General Instrument Corp.
    Gould Inc.
    GTE Corp.
    Harris Corp.
    Haynes Environmental Systems, Inc.
    Hewlett-Packard Co.
    Honeywell Inc.
    Hughes Aircraft Co.
    Hypres Inc.
    Intel Corp.
    Kaiser Aerospace & Electronics Corp.
    Loral Corp.
    LSI Logic Corporation
    M/A-COM Inc.
    Marantz Co., Inc.
    Micron Technology, Inc.
    Mosaic Systems, Inc.
    MultiVision Products, Inc.
    National Semiconductor Corp.
    North American Philips Corp.
    Paradyne Corp.
    RCA Corp.
    Regency Electronics, Inc.
    Rockwell International Corp.
    Sanders Associates, Inc.
    Silicon Compiler Systems Corporation
    Silicon Compilers, Inc.
    Sprague Technologies Inc.
    Symbol Technologies Inc.
    Tandy Corp.
    Tech-Sym Corp.
    Teledyne, Inc.
    Television equipment industry
    Texas Instruments Incorporated
    UTL Corp.
    Western Digital Corp.
    Westinghouse Electric Corp.
    Zenith Electronics Corp.
Hope or hyperbole? High tech and economic development. E. J. Malecki. il *Technol Rev* 90:44-51 O '87
View from the Valley. S. R. Reed. See issues of Personal Computing beginning June 1987

Acquisitions and mergers
The deals ahead in defense. G. G. Marcial. *Bus Week* p122 Mr 16 '87
Little Orphan Ampex looks for Daddy Warbucks. J. B. Levine. *Bus Week* p39-40 Ap 13 '87
Why National came to the Fairchild fire sale [National Semiconductor] J. B. Levine and O. Port. il *Bus Week* p38-9 S 14 '87

International aspects
And then there was one [GE sells consumer electronics division to Thomson SA] J. B. Copeland. il *Newsweek* 110:36 Ag 3 '87
Chipping away at Silicon Valley [Japanese interests in American companies] R. H. Bork, Jr. il *U S News World Rep* 102:58 Mr 30 '87
Cold feet [Fujitsu drops bid for Fairchild] *Time* 129:52 Mr 30 '87
Ferranti plans to merge with U.S. defense company. *Aviat Week Space Technol* 127:28 S 28 '87
Fighting the chip wars: Fujitsu loses Fairchild. J. B. Copeland. il *Newsweek* 109:50 Mr 30 '87
Jumping Jack strikes again [J. Welch sells GE's consumer electronics division] P. Elmer-Dewitt. il *Time* 130:44 Ag 3 '87
Overnight, Thomson has the stuff to take on the titans [purchase of GE's consumer electronics business] T. Peterson. il *Bus Week* p36-7 Ag 10 '87
A sweet swap for GE and Thomson. *Fortune* 116:8 Ag 17 '87
What the Fairchild fiasco signals for trade policy [Fujitsu deal collapses] J. W. Wilson and S. J. Dryden. il *Bus Week* p28 Mr 30 '87

Western Europe
An Italian chipmaker shows the way [SGS's merger with Thomson] W. C. Symonds. il por *Bus Week* p134+ My 25 '87

Automation
Do-it-yourself chips get easier [circuit design machines] O. Port. *Bus Week* p92 Mr 30 '87

Electronic industries—Automation—*cont.*

ITT uses process control methods to increase plant productivity [use of Taguchi method in electronic warfare manufacturing] B. D. Nordwall. il *Aviat Week Space Technol* 126:69+ My 11 '87

Cooperation

See also
Sematech

Environmental aspects

Childbearing: the dangers of high tech [AT&T policy regarding pregnant semiconductor workers] il *U S News World Rep* 102:12 Ja 26 '87

Clean-room controversy [study by Digital Equipment Corp. on toxic hazards that affect a worker's ability to have children] R. Wilson. il *Technol Rev* 90:10+ Ag/S '87

Danger in the clean room [semiconductor workers have increased risk of miscarriage at AT&T] il *Time* 129:48 Ja 26 '87

Moms-to-be banned from 'chip room' [AT&T policy] *Sci News* 131:73 Ja 31 '87

Export-import trade

China markets EW systems for export [electronic warfare] il *Aviat Week Space Technol* 126:95 F 16 '87

Chip wars [U.S. tariffs on Japanese semiconductors] *Natl Rev* 39:20-1 Ap 24 '87

Explaining the war of the chips [U.S. tariff imposed on Japanese products] il *World Press Rev* 34:48 Je '87

Fighting off the suitcase brigade [Japanese violations of semiconductor trade pact] P. Elmer-Dewitt. il *Time* 129:49 Mr 2 '87

Fighting the trade tilt [tariffs on Japanese electronics products] S. Koepp. il *Time* 129:50-1 Ap 6 '87

Fixing a tariff blooper [U.S. tariff on Japanese electronic products] G. Lewis. *Bus Week* p35 D 14 '87

"I know I sound protectionistic" [LSI Logic's W. Corrigan] K. K. Wiegner. il por *Forbes* 139:54+ Je 29 '87

Japan can't make a quick yen in the U.S. any more [consumer electronics] K. Dreyfack. il *Bus Week* p120-1 F 23 '87

Japan may be listening, but it's not about to change [U.S. imposes tariffs on electronic products] A. Borrus. il *Bus Week* p35-6 Ap 13 '87

The Japanese strategy for computer supremacy [interview with C. H. Ferguson] N. Gall. il por *Forbes* 139:76+ F 9 '87

Let's not bash the Japanese [U.S. tariff action] L. Smith. il *Fortune* 115:175-6 Ap 27 '87

National security and the semiconductor industry. D. G. Dallmeyer. il *Technol Rev* 90:46-52+ N/D '87

No more Mr. Nice Guy [U.S. tariffs on Japanese imports] D. Pauly. il *Newsweek* 109:42 Ap 6 '87

Punishing Japan: Reagan walks a fine line [imposition of tariffs for failure to uphold semiconductor pact] B. Javetski and others. il *Bus Week* p34-5 Ap 13 '87

Semi-tough [federal action to help American semiconductor companies] M. Gladwell. *New Repub* 196:9-11 My 18 '87

Silicon Valley's vale of tears [Advanced Micro Devices' battle with Japanese semiconductor makers] P. Dworkin. il por *U S News World Rep* 102:47 Mr 2 '87

Toward a trade war [semiconductor wars between U.S. and Japan] W. Hutton. *World Press Rev* 34:19 Ag '87

Trade face-off [U.S.-Japan confrontation over semiconductor trade; cover story; special section] il *Time* 129:28-32+ Ap 13 '87

Trade with Japan [tariff on semiconductors] R. Reagan. *Dep State Bull* 87:35-7 Jl '87

The truce in the chip war may be temporary [U.S.-Japan] J. W. Wilson. *Bus Week* p46-7 F 23 '87

U.S.-Japan semiconductor trade [statement, June 8, 1987] R. Reagan. *Dep State Bull* 87:55 Ag '87

Federal aid

See also
Sematech

Finance

Computers and electronics. M. Beauchamp. il *Forbes* 139:101+ Ja 12 '87

U.S. chipmakers are learning to cope. J. W. Wilson. il *Bus Week* p92 Ja 12 '87

International aspects

The high tech race: computers and chips. G. Bylinsky. *Current* 291:17-20 Mr/Ap '87

Making deals that won't give technology away. R. Neff. il *Bus Week* p62-3 Ap 20 '87

Management

A high-tech repairman who 'can fix anything' [Q. T. Wiles] il por *Bus Week* p111 S 21 '87

How chipmakers can survive. B. Uttal. il *Fortune* 115:89+ Ap 13 '87

Silicon Valley phoenixes. C. Barron. il *Fortune* 116:128-9+ N 23 '87

Marketing

Chipmakers are taking a gamble on RISC [reduced instruction-set computing] R. Brandt. il *Bus Week* p104-5 Jl 20 '87

Intel and Sequent kiss and make up [80386 microprocessors] J. W. Wilson. il *Bus Week* p120 My 25 '87

Silicon Valley's newest wizards [product designers] M. Rogers. il *Newsweek* 109:36-7 Ja 5 '87

To catch a thief [alarm industry] E. Paris. il *Forbes* 140:92-3 Ag 24 '87

Quality control

ITT uses process control methods to increase plant productivity [use of Taguchi method in electronic warfare manufacturing] B. D. Nordwall. il *Aviat Week Space Technol* 126:69+ My 11 '87

Securities

A new crop of high-tech stocks. A. E. Serwer. il *Fortune* 115:156 Je 8 '87

Why the high-tech bubble could pop. S. Weiss. il *Bus Week* p118 Mr 16 '87

Suits and claims

When the going gets tough, the tough go to court [chipmakers wage intellectual property battles] K. K. Wiegner. il *Forbes* 140:36-7 D 28 '87

Barbados

The case of a Chicago electronics company [relocation of assembly operations] *Focus* 37:4 Summ '87

Canada

See also
Internav Ltd.
Micronav Ltd.

China

China markets EW systems for export [electronic warfare] il *Aviat Week Space Technol* 126:95 F 16 '87

The next 'Asian miracle' may be under way—in China. D. J. Yang. il *Bus Week* p144-5 N 2 '87

France

See also
Compagnie Générale d'Électricité
Thomson-C S F

Germany (West)

See also
Siemens AG

Great Britain

See also
Ferranti plc
Marconi Co. Ltd.
Plessey Co. plc

Israel

See also
Tadiran Israel Electronics Industries Ltd.

Italy

See also
SGS Ates Componeti Elettronici SpA

Japan

See also
Hitachi, Ltd.
Kyocera Corporation
Matsushita Electric Industrial Co. Ltd.
NEC Corp.
Sony Corp.

Japan can't make a quick yen in the U.S. any more [consumer electronics] K. Dreyfack. il *Bus Week* p120-1 F 23 '87

Silicon Valley's vale of tears [Advanced Micro Devices' battle with Japanese semiconductor makers] P. Dworkin. il por *U S News World Rep* 102:47 Mr 2 '87

The submicron era may belong to the Japanese [dynamic random access memory chips] O. Port. il *Bus Week* p98 Mr 16 '87

Korea (South)

See also
Samsung Group

Netherlands

See also
Philips Industries, NV

United States

See Electronic industries

Electronic locks *See* Locks and keys

Electronic mail systems

See also
Computer bulletin boards
Electronic data interchange
Voice mail systems

In dubious battle [TCOM Systems] J. Novack. il *Forbes* 139:72 My 18 '87

Electronic mail systems—*cont.*

No LAN is an island, E-mail panel says. *Byte* 12:40 O '87

Reach out and touch—with electronic mail. S. Miller. il *Black Enterp* 17:27 My '87

Useful stuff: a speller for Works and a duo of telecommunications packages for MCI Mail. E. Shapiro. *Byte* 12:283-4+ Jl '87

When the post office won't do [Desktop Express electronic mail program] J. Bell. il *Pers Comput* 11:280+ D '87

Security measures

E-mail and the law. P. Honan. *Pers Comput* 11:105 Ja '87

Malaysia

Modern times [use of pay phones in Kuala Lumpur to connect with MCI Mail via Singapore] J. M. Fallows. il *Atlantic* 259:24+ F '87

Electronic marketing

If only Willy Loman had used a laptop. J. B. Levine. il *Bus Week* p137 O 12 '87

Let the computer do it [market research] T. Mack. il *Forbes* 140:94 Ag 10 '87

Selling—the computer way [B. Cecil at E.I. Du Pont] J. Blackford. il por *Pers Comput* 11:167+ O '87

Seven strategies for gaining the competitive edge. J. M. Thompson. il *Work Woman* 12:56+ O '87

Tools of the sales trade. H. Fersko-Weiss. il *Pers Comput* 11:78-81+ Ag '87

Electronic measurements

See also
Biotelemetry

Electronic music *See* Music, Electronic

Electronic musical instruments *See* Musical instruments, Electronic

Electronic newspapers *See* Information storage and retrieval systems

Electronic noise

See also
Audio systems—Noise
Tape recorders and recording—Noise
Videotape recorders and recording—Noise

Electronic novels *See* Computer novels

Electronic ovens *See* Microwave ovens

Electronic parts *See* Electronic equipment

Electronic publishing *See* Computers—Publishing use; Information storage and retrieval systems

Electronic shopping

See also
Cable Value Network
Comp-U-Card International
Home Shopping Network Inc.

Automating the personal shopper. H. McCandless. il *Work Woman* 12:78-9 N '87

Home shopping is forever. L. Brown. il *Channels* 7:24 Ap '87

New-Age shopping: the video kiosk. il *Consum Rep* 52:593 O '87

Operators are standing by . . . D. Moreau. il *Changing Times* 41:79-81 Jl '87

Tele-shopping: warnings for smart shoppers. il *Glamour* 85:77 Ag '87

Television shopping: how it works. il *McCalls* 114:25 Ap '87

A year after the frenzy, order starts to set in. C. Capuzzi. il *Channels* 7 Sp Issue:111+ D '87

Acquisitions and mergers

One home for two home shoppers? [Home Shopping Network's bid for COMB and its Cable Value Network] G. DeGeorge. *Bus Week* p34-5 F 2 '87

Electronic surveillance *See* Electronics in criminal investigation, espionage, etc.

Electronic technicians

Certification

Certification for electronics technicians. W. C. Small. il *Radio-Electron* 58:52-4 Ag '87

Electronic toys *See* Toys

Electronic typewriters *See* Typewriters, Electronic

Electronic warfare *See* Electronics—Military use; Superconductors and superconductivity—Military use

Electronic warfare industry *See* Electronic industries

Electronic watches *See* Watches, Electronic

Electronics

See also
Children's electronics
Cybernetics
Delay devices
Digital electronics
Home electronics
Microelectronics
Optoelectronics

Oscillators, Crystal
Photoelectronics
Pulse techniques (Electronics)
Semiconductors
Surface mounting (Electronics)
Transistors

2001: electronics in the next century [cover story; special section; with editorial comment by Brian C. Fenton] il *Radio-Electron* 58:4, 79-119 My '87

Electronics. See issues of Popular Mechanics beginning June 1984

Electronics newsfront. W. J. Hawkins. See issues of Popular Science beginning February 1986

History

Making news—39 years ago. il *Radio-Electron* 58:63 Ja '87

Military use

See also
Air Force Avionics Laboratory (U.S.)
Airplanes, Military—Electronic equipment
Communications satellites—Military use
Computers—Military use
E-Systems, Inc.
Ferranti plc
Loral Corp.
Sanders Associates, Inc.
Tech-Sym Corp.

Bringing SDI down to earth [development of smart conventional weapons] D. Charles. il *Science* 237:713-15 Ag 14 '87

Electronics will gain larger share of budget. B. D. Nordwall. il *Aviat Week Space Technol* 126:227+ Mr 9 '87

ITT uses process control methods to increase plant productivity [use of Taguchi method in electronic warfare manufacturing] B. D. Nordwall. il *Aviat Week Space Technol* 126:69+ My 11 '87

One shot, one kill: a new era of 'smart' weapons [offsetting Soviet Union's edge in conventional firepower; special section] il *U S News World Rep* 102:28-35 Mr 16 '87

Special report: electronic warfare—the operational challenge. il *Aviat Week Space Technol* 126:49-51+ F 9 '87

Special report: electronic warfare—the technological response. il *Aviat Week Space Technol* 126:48-9+ F 16 '87

Electronics, Automotive *See* Automobiles—Electronic equipment

Electronics in agriculture

Electronic cowboys. il *Futurist* 21:50 My/Je '87

Smart ID tags coming for U.S. cows and sows. il *Success Farm* 85:70 Ag '87

Electronics in criminal investigation, espionage, etc.

See also
Lasers in criminal investigation, espionage, etc.
Wiretapping

The art of high-tech snooping [bugs planted by Soviets in U.S. embassy] G. J. Church. il *Time* 129:22-4 Ap 20 '87

Bugging [cover story] J. Free and others. il *Pop Sci* 231:44-9+ Ag '87

Cheaper electronics makes it a snap to snoop. S. Budiansky. il *U S News World Rep* 102:54-6 My 18 '87

The high cost of the FBI's high-tech crime wars. P. Cary. il *U S News World Rep* 103:22-3 N 30 '87

High-tech conversation stoppers. S. Begley. il *Newsweek* 109:20-1 Ap 20 '87

A tough new breed of bugs. S. Budiansky. il *U S News World Rep* 102:20 Ap 20 '87

Electronics in fishing

See also
Depth indicators

Anecdotes, facetiae, satire, etc.

Exit laughing [superconductors used in fishing tackle] E. Zern. il *Field Stream* 92:138 Je '87

Electronics in medicine *See* Medical electronics

Electronics in sports

See also
Electronics in fishing

For the fan of tomorrow [high tech sports equipment at the Consumer Electronics Show] R. Cahan. il *Sport Mag* 78:83-4 S '87

Electronics industry *See* Electronic industries

Electronics research

See also
Microelectronics and Computer Technology Corporation
Sematech

Electronics research—*cont.*
Western Europe
Europe still fails the challenge. G. de Jonquieres. por *World Press Rev* 34:46-7 My '87
Electronics stores
See also
Audio/Video Affiliates, Inc.
Crazy Eddie Inc.
Discounters in the dumps. B. Saporito. il *Fortune* 116:103+ Ag 3 '87
Electronics 'superstores' may have blown a fuse [price wars] M. J. Pitzer. il *Bus Week* p90+ Je 8 '87
Electronics workers
See also
Trade unions—Electronics workers
Women electronics workers
Electrons
See also
Electrides
Electron transport
Exciton theory
Energetic electrons: an ozone killer? *Sci News* 131:377 Je 13 '87
Beams
See Electron beams
Energy levels
See Energy levels (Quantum mechanics)
Electrophoresis
See also
Isoelectric focusing
Derivation of clones close to *met* by preparative field inversion gel electrophoresis. F. Michiels and others. bibl f il *Science* 236:1305-8 Je 5 '87
Electrophoresis. *Science* 235 pt2:G65-G68 F 27 '87
Electrophoresis and large-scale databases. N. G. Anderson. bibl f *Science* 235 pt2:G65 F 27 '87
Electrophoretic evidence for genetic diploidy in the bracken fern (Pteridium aquilinum). P. G. Wolf and others. bibl f il *Science* 236:947-9 My 22 '87
Megabase-scale mapping of the HLA gene complex by pulsed field gel electrophoresis [major histocompatibility complex] S. K. Lawrance and others. bibl f il *Science* 235:1387-90 Mr 13 '87
Electrophysiology
See also
Electric organs in fish
Electricity—Physiological effects
Electrocardiography
Electroencephalography
Cyclic AMP-modulated potassium channels in murine B cells and their precursors. D. Choquet and others. bibl f il *Science* 235:1211-14 Mr 6 '87
Depolarization without calcium can release γ-aminobutyric acid from a retinal neuron. E. A. Schwartz. bibl f il *Science* 238:350-5 O 16 '87
Direct activation of mammalian atrial muscarinic potassium channels by GTP regulatory protein G_k. A. Yatani and others. bibl f il *Science* 235:207-11 Ja 9 '87
Divalent cations directly affect the conductance of excised patches of rod photoreceptor membrane. J. H. Stern and others. bibl f il *Science* 236:1674-8 Je 26 '87
Effect of membrane potential changes on the calcium transient in single rat cardiac muscle cells. M. B. Cannell and others. bibl f il *Science* 238:1419-23 D 4 '87
Electrical responses of eggs to acrosomal protein similar to those induced by sperm. M. Gould and J. L. Stephano. bibl f il *Science* 235:1654-6 Mr 27 '87
External calcium ions are required for potassium channel gating in squid neurons. C. M. Armstrong and J. Lopez-Barneo. bibl f il *Science* 236:712-14 My 8 '87
Forskolin and phorbol esters reduce the same potassium conductance of mouse neurons in culture. D. S. Grega and others. bibl f il *Science* 235:345-8 Ja 16 '87
Full-wave rectification from a mixed electrical-chemical synapse [lobsters] K. Graubard and D. K. Hartline. bibl f il *Science* 237:535-7 Jl 31 '87
Hippocampus studied for learning mechanisms [synaptic transmission] D. M. Barnes. *Science* 236:1628-9 Je 26 '87
Human neuroelectric patterns predict performance accuracy. A. S. Gevins and others. bibl f il *Science* 235:580-5 Ja 30 '87
Long-term sensitization in Aplysia: biophysical correlates in tail sensory neurons. K. P. Scholz and J. H. Byrne. bibl f il *Science* 235:685-7 F 6 '87
Neuronal circuits and evolution [discussion of August 22, 1986 article, Neuronal circuits: an evolutionary perspective] J. P. C. Dumont and R. M. Robertson. *Science* 236:1681-2 Je 26 '87

Neuronal coding and robotics [discussion of September 26, 1986 article, Neuronal population coding of movement direction] A. P. Georgopoulos and others. *Science* 237:300-1 Jl 17 '87
Single-channel and genetic analyses reveal two distinct A-type potassium channels in Drosophila. C. K. Solc and others. bibl f il *Science* 236:1094-8 My 29 '87
Sodium-calcium exchange in heart: membrane currents and changes in $[Ca^{2+}]_i$. L. Barcenas-Ruiz and others. bibl f il *Science* 238:1720-2 D 18 '87
Thought and action [computer model of motor cortex neuron activity; work of Apostolos Georgopoulos] A. Fisher. il *Pop Sci* 230:8 F '87
Windows on the mind [work of A. S. Gevins] E. Smith. il *Omni* 9:92-6 My '87
Xenopus oocytes injected with rat uterine RNA express very slowly activating potassium currents. M. B. Boyle and others. bibl f il *Science* 235:1221-4 Mr 6 '87
Electrophysiology of plants
The electric life of plants gives fungal spores a charge [research by Charles M. Leach] S. Weisburd. il *Sci News* 132:53 Jl 25 '87
Electrospace Systems, Inc.
Chrysler's aerospace involvement grows with takeover of Texas firm. C. A. Shifrin. *Aviat Week Space Technol* 127:66-7 Jl 20 '87
Electrostatics
See also
Electric discharges
Electric sparks
The electric life of plants gives fungal spores a charge [research by Charles M. Leach] S. Weisburd. il *Sci News* 132:53 Jl 25 '87
Electrotherapy
See also
Shock therapy
Electricity may have the potential to heal injured back muscles. *Prevention* 39:63 O '87
Equipment
Going through the motions [continuous passive motion devices aid in fracture healing; work of Robert Salter] R. Boling. *Health* 19:21 D '87
Collectors and collecting
Collecting early electro-medical apparatuses. F. Polansky. il *Antiques Collect Hobbies* 92:61-2+ D '87
Elementary education *See* Education, Elementary
Elementary particles *See* Particles (Nuclear physics)
Elementary school teachers *See* Teachers
Elena's aria [dance] *See* Dance reviews—Single works
Elephant garlic *See* Garlic
Elephant Man *See* Merrick, Joseph Carey, 1862 or 3-1890
Elephant poaching *See* Poaching
Elephants
Elephants in musth, lust [Kenya's Amboseli National Park] J. H. Poole. il *Nat Hist* 96:46-55 N '87
How to drive an elephant [Royal Chitawan National Park] C. R. Capos. il *Ms* 16:108 S '87
Move over, Felix and Oscar, move way over—these two are a really heavy-duty odd couple [elephant and hippo living together at Cincinnati Zoo] il *People Wkly* 28:116 D 21 '87
When the music in our parlors brought death to darkest Africa [19th century use of ivory for piano keys] R. Conniff. il *Audubon* 89:76-93 Jl '87
Where elephants die [Hwange National Park, Zimbabwe] G. Haynes. il *Nat Hist* 96:28-33 Je '87
With three extra inches on top of young Smokey, he often gets caught in a sticky situation [Oakland Zoo] il *People Wkly* 27:87 Je 29 '87
Care
San Francisco's Tinkerbell stands corrected: the truncated account of a major feat [surgery to remove papilloma] il *People Wkly* 27:37 Ja 19 '87
Photographs and photography
Pssst . . . [baby African elephants playing] il *Natl Geogr World* 144:30-1 Ag '87
Sexual behavior
See Sexual behavior—Animals
Elephants, Fossil
See also
Mammoths
Elephants as artists
The elephant as artist [work of D. Gucwa with Siri] J. Ehmann. il *Natl Wildl* 25:26-8 F/Mr '87
An elephant who draws pictures [work of D. Gucwa with Siri] J. Ehmann. il por *Read Dig* 131:96-9 O '87
Elettronica SpA
Italians develop RF memory for deception jammer system. il *Aviat Week Space Technol* 126:73 F 16 '87

Eleuthera Island (Bahamas)
>*See also*
>Architecture, Domestic—Eleuthera Island (Bahamas)

Elevators
>*See also*
>Fujitec Company
>Otis Elevator Co., Ltd.

ELF (Extremely low frequency) military radio communications system *See* Radio, Military

ELF (Extremely low frequency) waves *See* Electromagnetic waves

Elf Aquitaine
Turning Elf into a giant [M. Pecqueur] S. Tully. il por *Fortune* 116:52 Ag 3 '87

Elflein, Cynthia
Are his friends crowding you out? il *Seventeen* 46:240-1+ Mr '87

Elfman, Danny
>*about*
Oingo Boingo's Danny Elfman. il pors *Seventeen* 46:158+ Ag '87

Elfring, Chris
Americans and the great outdoors. il *BioScience* 37:778-80 D '87

Eli Lilly and Company
All that strong medicine is doing Lilly good [stock price] G. G. Marcial. il *Bus Week* p148 S 14 '87

Elias, Eliane
>*about*
Blindfold test. M. Bourne. il pors *Down Beat* 54:45 Ja '87

Elio's (New York, N.Y.: Restaurant) *See* New York (N.Y.)—Restaurants, nightclubs, bars, etc.

Eliot, John L.
Glaciers on the move. il map *Natl Geogr* 171:104-19 Ja '87

Eliot Feld Ballet *See* Feld Ballet

Elisa Monte Dance Company
>Reviews:
>Performance in Philadelphia. B. Dixon-Stowell. *Dance Mag* 61:104-5 My '87

Elish, Herbert, 1933-
>*about*
Class consciousness raising. S. W. Angrist. il *Forbes* 140:77-8 N 30 '87

Elite (Social sciences)
The benefits of elitism [views of E. D. Baltzell] E. F. Cone. il por *Forbes* 140 Sp Issue:380 O 26 '87
Corporate etiquette. L. H. Lapham. *Harpers* 275:7-8 Ag '87

Elizabeth II, Queen of Great Britain, 1926-
>*about*
The family jewels. R. Koenig. por *N Y* 20:40 O 19 '87
'A lily cast in steel'. M. McIver. il por *Macleans* 100:33 N 9 '87
The Queen and Prince Philip toast a 40-year Windsor knot. il pors *People Wkly* 28:54 N 23 '87
The Queen's jewels. il pors *Life* 10:44-6+ O '87
Shrewd managers of regal riches. T. Paré. il pors *Fortune* 116:134-5 O 12 '87
>**Visit to Canada, 1987**
Quebec's quiet welcome. B. Wallace. il por *Macleans* 100:16 N 2 '87

Elizabeth Arden, Inc.
Faberge lands Arden: 'Now we've got mass—and class'. S. Benway. il por *Bus Week* p38-9 Ag 17 '87
'My deah, have you heard the news on Fifth Avenue?'. A. Garbor. il *U S News World Rep* 103:44 Ag 3 '87

Elizabethan period *See* Great Britain—History—Elizabethan period, 1558-1603

Elk
>*See also*
>Antlers
>**Photographs and photography**
Stalking the shot that doesn't want to happen. G. A. Rowell. il *Petersens Photogr Mag* 16:38-9 Je '87

Elk calling *See* Animal calling

Elk hunting
Are you tough enough to hunt elk? J. Zumbo. il *Outdoor Life* 180:94-5+ N '87
The basin. B. Brister. il *Field Stream* 92:54-5+ N '87
Bulls on a budget. N. Rodgers. il *Outdoor Life* 180:90-1+ S '87
Don't bugle up a grizzly bear [bowhunting bugling bull elk] B. McRae. il *Outdoor Life* 179:54-5+ Ap '87
Easy way elk. R. Mumford. il *Outdoor Life* 180:60-1+ Ag '87
Elk camp. N. Strung. il *Field Stream* 91:62-3+ Ja '87

Elk on your own. R. Spomer. il *Outdoor Life* 179:102-3+ My '87
My last hunter [Rocky Mountain elk hunt] M. Lapinski. il *Outdoor Life* 179:60-1+ F '87
The other kind of elk [Roosevelt elk] N. Nelson. il *Field Stream* 92:54-5+ S '87
Pattern for elk. D. Dobie. il *Outdoor Life* 180:64-5+ O '87
A week with the wapiti. J. Barsness. il *Field Stream* 92:64-5+ N '87
Where the elk are. S. Curtis. il *Field Stream* 92:56-7+ O '87

Elk Lake Lodge (North Hudson, N.Y.) *See* Resorts—New York (State)

Elkind, David, 1931-
As they grow/14 through 18. See issues of Parents beginning January 1987
Do we push our kids too hard? [excerpt from The hurried child] il *Good Housekeep* 205:117-19 S '87
Miseducation. il *Parents* 62:124-8+ O '87
Our images of children: where will they take us? *Educ Dig* 53:2-4 N '87
Superkids and super problems. il *Psychol Today* 21:60-1 My '87
Teachers can help parents with educational choices. *Educ Dig* 52:24-6 Ap '87

Elkins, Ann
What's new! See issues of Good Housekeeping

Elkland (Mo.)
>**Crime**
Auguries of innocence [K. Buckner posthumously cleared of murdering his family] L. Zuckerman. il por *Time* 130:21 O 19 '87
A shocking arrest breaks the case of a Missouri farm family's murder—and rescues a boy's reputation [J. Schnick charged; K. Buckner cleared] M. Green. il pors *People Wkly* 28:101-2+ O 26 '87

Elko County (Nev.)
>**Description and travel**
Sentiment straight from the saddle [Cowboy Poetry Gathering] R. B. Stolley. il *Life* 10:19-21 Jl '87

Ellenby, Kiki
>*about*
New Rx: try an atemoya a day. L. Shapiro. il pors *Newsweek* 110:77-77A+ N 23 '87

Ellenby, Marc
>*about*
New Rx: try an atemoya a day. L. Shapiro. il pors *Newsweek* 110:77-77A+ N 23 '87

Eller, Claudia
Lighting to sculpt shadows. il *Theatre Crafts* 21:26-7+ Mr '87
Non-linear nuances: Ediflex is cutting up Hollywood. il *Theatre Crafts* 21:89-90+ O '87
USA all the way. *Theatre Crafts* 21:14-15+ Mr '87

Ellerbee, Linda, and Veselka, Vanessa
Mother/daughter. pors *Ms* 16:126-8+ Jl/Ag '87

Ellesmere Island (N.W.T.)
>*See also*
>Wildlife—Ellesmere Island (N.W.T.)

Ellesmere Island National Park (N.W.T.)
A n-n-new p-p-park for C-C-Canada. J. F. King. il *Sierra* 72:13 Ja/F '87

Ellington, Duke, 1899-1974
>*about*
Charm of the Duke led Gordon to be musician. *Jet* 72:62 Ag 31 '87
D.C. festival in April to salute Duke Ellington. por *Jet* 71:16 Mr 23 '87
Duke & Co. [discography] J. McDonough. *Down Beat* 54:41+ Ap '87
Large-scale jazz. F. Davis. il *Atlantic* 260:76-7 Ag '87
Slyest of the foxes. E. J. Hobsbawm. bibl f il *N Y Rev Books* 34:3-4+ N 19 '87
>**Archives**
Congress buys Ellington collection for Smithsonian. il por *Jet* 71:27 Mr 9 '87

Elliott, A. Wright
Creativity and enterprise [address, June 1, 1987] *Vital Speeches Day* 53:637-40 Ag 1 '87

Elliott, Bill
>*about*
Good to the last drop. S. Moses. il *Sports Illus* 66:32-3 F 23 '87

Elliott, C. Phillip
>*about*
A nest-egg deal that turned rotten. P. Engardio. il por *Bus Week* p98 Ap 27 '87

Elliott, David K., 1947-
A reassessment of Astraspis desiderata, the oldest North American vertebrate. bibl f il *Science* 237:190-2 Jl 10 '87
Elliott, Inger McCabe
Images of contemporary China. il por *Archit Dig* 44:166+ Ja '87
Elliott, John D.
about
Australia's apostle of beer and business. L. Kraar. il por *Fortune* 115:88 Ja 5 '87
The raiders Down Under may be down and out. C. Debes. il por *Bus Week* p55 N 9 '87
Two Australian beer barons take their brawl abroad. C. Debes and P. Finch. il pors *Bus Week* p138+ O 19 '87
Elliott, Lawrence
Deadly winds: one year after Chernobyl. il *Read Dig* 130:129-33 My '87
Elliott, Lewis
about
Daughter alleges father sired his own grandkids. il por *Jet* 72:16+ Ag 31 '87
Texas preacher guilty of siring 12 of his grandkids. il por *Jet* 73:16 D 7 '87
Elliott, Michael
Naipaulia. *New Repub* 197:12+ N 16 '87
Elliott, Miriam Adderholdt- *See* Adderholdt-Elliott, Miriam, 1957-
Elliott, Tony
about
Tony Elliott: just back from the dead, a too well-traveled NFL star bears witness to a chilling drug odyssey. W. Plummer. il pors *People Wkly* 27:81-4+ Ja 5 '87
Elliott Enterprises Inc.
A nest-egg deal that turned rotten [investment fraud charges] P. Engardio. il por *Bus Week* p98 Ap 27 '87
Elliott Wave theorist (Newsletter) *See* Investment newsletters
Ellipses
Draw an ellipse without math, strings or tacks. W. J. Larsen. il *Workbench* 43:104 S/O '87
Ellis, Albert, 1913-
about
Their own worst enemy. C. Wood. il *Psychol Today* 21:18 F '87
Ellis, Bret Easton
about
Two divine decadents. D. Lehman. il pors *Newsweek* 110:72 S 7 '87
Ellis, Dale
about
The joy of getting even. J. McCallum. il por *Sports Illus* 66:28-30 My 4 '87
Ellis, George
(jt. auth) See Rothman, Tony, and Ellis, George
Ellis, J. E.
(jt. auth) See McCabe, J. Terrence, and Ellis, J. E.
Ellis, John Tracy, 1905-
The legacy of two leaders. *America* 157:149-50 S 26 '87
Ellis, John W., 1928-
about
The waiting game. J. Cook. il por *Forbes* 140:130+ N 30 '87
Ellis, Junius
At witty Caltech, pranks aren't purely a laughing matter. il *Smithsonian* 18:100-2+ S '87
Ellis, Richard, 1938-
Australia's southern seas. il map *Natl Geogr* 171:286-319 Mr '87
Stranded whales [discussion of June 1987 article, Why do whales strand?] *Oceans* 20:3+ Jl/Ag '87
Why do whales strand? il *Oceans* 20:24-9+ My/Je '87
Ellis, Stephen
Expanded pictograms. bibl f il *Art Am* 75:204-9 Ap '87
Ellis, Todd
about
A pair extraordinaire. D. S. Looney. il *Sports Illus* 67:100+ N 9 '87
Ellis, Walter, Jr.
Should the "Minimum Wage Restoration Act of 1987" be approved? [excerpts from testimony, July 23, 1987] *Congr Dig* 66:201+ Ag/S '87
Ellis, William S.
Africa's Sahel: the stricken land [cover story] il map *Natl Geogr* 172:140-79 Ag '87
Ellis-Simons, Pamela
The Disney Channel. il *Channels* 7:43-4 O '87

Ellman, Lee J.
Finding your own secret fishing hole. il *Conservationist* 41:16-19 Mr/Ap '87
Ellmann, Richard, 1918-1987
Oscar meets Walt. bibl f il *N Y Rev Books* 34:43-4 D 3 '87
Wilde in New York: beauty packed them in. il por *N Y Times Book Rev* 92:15-16 N 1 '87
Ellroy, James
about
The nightmare of his mother's murder is echoed in James Ellroy's grisly new novel, The black dahlia. S. Dougherty. il pors *People Wkly* 28:122-4 D 14 '87
Ellsberg, Daniel, 1931-
about
Daniel Ellsberg [interview] D. Sheff. il por *Roll Stone* p221-2+ N 5-D 10 '87
Elm
Diseases and pests
Bozeman chain saw massacre [G. A. Strobel's Dutch elm disease experiment] W. E. Brock. il pors *Discover* 8:78-82+ N '87
Elm Street revisited [Dutch elm disease] J. Cook. il *Ctry J* 14:52-6+ O '87
Montana State's troublesome elms [G. Strobel illegally injects diseased trees with genetically altered bacteria] M. D. Lemonick. il por *Time* 130:67 S 14 '87
MSU faults Strobel for Dutch elm test. L. Roberts. *Science* 237:1286 S 11 '87
New questions in Strobel case [field test of Dutch elm disease] L. Roberts. *Science* 237:1097-8 S 4 '87
Researcher flouts gene-splicing rules [G. Strobel's Dutch elm disease experiment] M. Crawford. *Science* 237:838-9 Ag 21 '87
Elman, Philip
about
A judge's breach of confidence. R. Lacayo. il pors *Time* 129:71 Ap 6 '87
Elman, Richard M.
Cool lightning over Tucson [poem] *New Yorker* 63:87 My 25 '87
Elmandjra, Mahdi
Learning needs in a changing world. *Futurist* 21:60 Mr/Ap '87
Elmblad, Mary
A sense of place. *Writer* 100:22-4 O '87
Elmi, Ross
about
Color forms. B. Hagin. il *Pop Photogr* 94:46-9 F '87
Elmore, David, and Phillips, Fred M., 1954-
Accelerator mass spectrometry for measurement of long-lived radioisotopes. bibl f il *Science* 236:543-50 My 1 '87
Elocution
See also
Public speaking
Elon, Amos
Letter from Israel. *New Yorker* 63:33-8+ Jl 27 '87
Elorriaga, John A., 1923-
about
Buy or be bought. J. Heins. il por *Forbes* 139:48 My 18 '87
Elred, Stephen
Eros between men [discussion of December 26, 1986 article, Gay rights/gay plight] *Commonweal* 114:300-3 My 8 '87
Elsberry, Richard B.
A farewell to arms. il *N Y Times Mag* p54 S 27 '87
Set free. il *N Y Times Mag* p37 Ja 4 '87
Elsen, Albert Edward, 1927-
What isn't modern sculpture? il *Art News* 86:144-7 Ja '87
Elsevier (Firm)
Elsevier hunts for 'high margin' acquisitions in United States. H. R. Lottman. *Publ Wkly* 231:22 My 29 '87
Kluwer battles Elsevier's hostile takeover attempt. H. R. Lottman. *Publ Wkly* 232:15 Jl 10 '87
Elshtain, Jean Bethke, 1941-
Fingerprints on file: the search for missing children. il *Commonweal* 114:229-30 Ap 24 '87
Elson, Andrea
about
Face to face with Andrea Elson. il pors *Teen* 31:122-3 S '87
Elswick, Brent
Pick of the crop [cover story] il *Mother Earth News* 104:26-33 Mr/Ap '87

ELTs (Emergency locator transmitters) *See* Radio beacons
Eltzroth, Thomas E.
Put color where you want it with wall planters. il *Flower Gard* 31:28+ Ap/My '87
Elvin-Lewis, Memory
about
A boy who died in 1969 may have been America's first AIDS victim. D. Chu. il pors *People Wkly* 28:179-80 N 16 '87
Elvis [television program] *See* Television program reviews—Single works
Elway, John
about
Tough guy in the clutch. R. Telander. il pors *Sports Illus* 66:30-3 Ja 26 '87
Elwes, Cary
about
A rake's progress. por *Vogue* 177:188-9 Je '87
Emancipation of slaves *See* Slavery—Emancipation
Emancipation Proclamation (1863)
1862. K. Ide. *Am Herit* 38:110 S/O '87
Emans, Robert L.
Abuse in the name of protecting children. *Educ Dig* 53:36-9 N '87
Abuse in the name of protecting children. bibl f il *Phi Delta Kappan* 68:740-3 Je '87
Emanuel, Victor
about
Birding's fledgling phenoms. F. Graham. il por *Audubon* 89:38-40+ My '87
Embalming
See also
Mummies
Embargo
Message to Iran [U.S. bans imports] il *Time* 130:42 O 12 '87
Strict implementation of 1977 arms embargo against South Africa asked by Council. *UN Chron* 24:46 F '87
Your Constitution: can the president ban private arms sales? D. Pawelek. *Sch Update* 119:20 Mr 9 '87
Embarrassment
'My most embarrassing moment' [black celebrities] il *Ebony* 42:110+ S '87
Our favorite readers are fools! J. Viorst. il *Redbook* 168:14+ Ap '87
The stupid things we do. J. Bernard. il *Seventeen* 46:60 Mr '87
Embassies (Buildings)
See also
Iranian seizure of United States embassy, 1979-1981
Getting "snookered" [comparison of locations of Soviet embassy in Washington and U.S. embassy in Moscow] il *Time* 129:18 Ap 20 '87
Legation in Tangier. il *Dep State Bull* 87:13 S '87
Open house in Prague [Petschek Palace functions as U.S. embassy] W. W. Luers. il pors *House Gard* 159:150-5+ My '87
A Vienna success [R. S. and J. C. Lauder decorate ambassador's residence] T. Lessing. il por *House Gard* 159:100-5+ Jl '87
Employees
"Do you want any more secret documents put in the safe, Mr. Ambassador?" "No, Ivan, that's all for tonight" [hiring foreign service nationals for American embassies] P. Witt. *Wash Mon* 19:17-18+ Ap '87
Why our embassies are nests for spies [hiring foreign service nationals for American embassies] P. Witt. il *Read Dig* 131:111-14 O '87
Security measures
The art of high-tech snooping [bugs planted by Soviets in U.S. embassy] G. J. Church. il *Time* 129:22-4 Ap 20 '87
The battle of the bugs [Soviet and American embassies; special section] il map *Newsweek* 109:18-22 Ap 20 '87
Bugproofing the embassy [plan to salvage part of U.S. embassy in Moscow] il por *Time* 130:14 Jl 13 '87
Challenges facing the Foreign Service [address, May 1, 1987] R. I. Spiers. *Dep State Bull* 87:30-4 Jl '87
Countering today's security challenges [statement, April 23, 1987] R. I. Spiers. *Dep State Bull* 87:52-4 Je '87
Deep in the Bear's den [R. Helms leads investigation into security breaches at U.S. embassy in Moscow] H. Sidey. il por *Time* 129:14 Je 29 '87
An expert says tear down our bugged embassy in Moscow [interview with J. Bamford] M. Ryan. il por *People Wkly* 27:91+ Ap 27 '87

Furor over embassy security points to tighter screening of architects. P. Hoffmann. il *Archit Rec* 175:39 Je '87
How much security is enough? [address, January 22, 1987] R. E. Lamb. *Dep State Bull* 87:27-9 My '87
How to protect U.S. embassies. W. L. Chaze. il *U S News World Rep* 102:18-20 Ap 20 '87
The mission in Moscow. G. F. Kennan. por *Newsweek* 110:7 Jl 13 '87
News conference of April 8, 1987. G. P. Shultz. *Dep State Bull* 87:24-7 Je '87
Notes and comment [security breaches in the U.S. embassy in Moscow] *New Yorker* 63:25-6 My 4 '87
Our new Moscow embassy—bungled and bugged [failure of Foreign Buildings Office to get properly built embassies] J. Barron. *Read Dig* 130:100-4 Je '87
President meets with Foreign Intelligence Advisory Board [White House statement, July 14, 1987] *Dep State Bull* 87:31 S '87
Security at the U.S. embassy in Moscow [remarks and question-and-answer session, April 7, 1987] R. Reagan. *Dep State Bull* 87:60-1 Je '87
Trying to undo the damage [State Dept. admits role in embassy security lapses] M. Santini. il *U S News World Rep* 102:23 My 25 '87
Washington diarist [vilification of A. Hartman over neglect of security of American embassy in Moscow] L. Wieseltier. *New Repub* 196:42 My 11 '87
Where Moscow embassy went awry. C. M. Perkins. por *U S News World Rep* 102:8 My 18 '87
Anecdotes, facetiae, satire, etc.
Uncivil liberties [bugging of U.S. embassy in Moscow] C. Trillin. *Nation* 244:674 My 23 '87
Embassy Suites Hotels
Service starts with the man at the top. B. Saporito and M. J. Williams. il pors *Fortune* 116:108 D 7 '87
Embellishment (Music)
In defense of embellishment [ornamenting Mozart's vocal music] K. Stern. il *Opera News* 51:18-21 F 14 '87
Embezzlement
A wave of embezzlement hits banking. G. DeGeorge. il *Bus Week* p49 My 18 '87
Emblems
"More than a map . . ." [United Nations emblem] il *UN Chron* 24:78 N '87
Showing the colors: classy patches from National Audubon Society chapters [portfolio] il *Audubon* 89:68-73 Mr '87
Embraced waltzes [ballet] *See* Ballet reviews—Single works
Embracing
Hugging your way to health. F. S. Goulart. il *Saturday Evening Post* 259:26+ Mr '87
A touching story [children's need for physical reassurance from teachers] P. Chance. il *Psychol Today* 21:14 My '87
Embraer Empresa Brasileira de Aeronautica SA
Embraer moves to solidify role as leading aircraft manufacturer. il *Aviat Week Space Technol* 127:40-3+ Ag 17 '87
Sales results cause Embraer to hike Brasilia delivery rates [30-40-passenger aircraft class] *Aviat Week Space Technol* 127:78 N 9 '87
Embroidery
See also
Samplers
Creative machine stitchery. J. Williams and J. Severson. il *Better Homes Gard* 65:46-9+ Ja '87
Scenes and stitches [work of S. Young] A. B. Carter. il por *Americana* 15:33-6 S/O '87
Embryo transplantation *See* Ova—Transplantation
Embryology
See also
Developmental biology
Developmental neurology
Fetus
Morphogenesis
Neural tube
Ova
Ovaries
Placenta
Umbilical cord
'Precancer' gene localized in embryo, sperm [int-1 expression] il *Sci News* 132:68 Ag 1 '87
Amphibia
Clonal restriction boundaries in Xenopus embryos shown with two intracellular lineage tracers. P. Sheard and M. Jacobson. bibl f il *Science* 236:851-4 My 15 '87
Birds
The chicken B cell compartment. J.-C. Weill and C.-A. Reynaud. bibl f il *Science* 238:1094-8 N 20 '87

Embryology—Birds—*cont.*

Corresponding spatial gradients of TOP molecules in the developing retina and optic tectum. D. Trisler and F. Collins. bibl f il *Science* 237:1208-9 S 4 '87

Form-fitting genes [identification of morphogen; research by Christina Thaller and Gregor Eichele] *Discover* 8:8+ S '87

Shape-inducing chemical identified [retinoic acid; research by Christina Thaller and Gregor Eichele] R. Weiss. il *Sci News* 131:406 Je 27 '87

Tolerance induced by thymic epithelial grafts in birds. H. Ohki and others. bibl f il *Science* 237:1032-5 Ag 28 '87

Echinoderms

A sea urchin gene encodes a polypeptide homologous to epidermal growth factor. D. A. Hursh and others. bibl f il *Science* 237:1487-90 S 18 '87

Insects

Determination of anteroposterior polarity in Drosophila. C. Nüsslein-Volhard and others. bibl f il *Science* 238:1675-81 D 18 '87

Dorsal, an embryonic polarity gene in Drosophila, is homologous to the vertebrate proto-oncogene, c-rel. R. Steward. bibl f il *Science* 238:692-4 O 30 '87

Nematodes

Worm watching: the case of the suicidal sex cell [Caenorhabditis elegans and Panagrellus redivivus; research by P. Sternberg] G. Montgomery. il por *Discover* 8:44-6+ O '87

Rodents

Diversity of alpha-fetoprotein gene expression in mice is generated by a combination of separate enhancer elements. R. E. Hammer and others. bibl f il *Science* 235:53-8 Ja 2 '87

Extended culture of mouse embryo cells without senescence: inhibition by serum. D. T. Loo and others. bibl f il *Science* 236:200-2 Ap 10 '87

Genetic ablation: targeted expression of a toxin gene causes microphthalmia in transgenic mice. M. L. Breitman and others. bibl f il *Science* 238:1563-5 D 11 '87

Region-specific expression of two mouse homeo box genes. M. F. Utset and others. bibl f il *Science* 235:1379-82 Mr 13 '87

Embryology, Experimental

See also
Clones (Biology)
Fertilization in vitro
Ova—Transplantation

Ethics in embryo [Harper's forum; cover story] *Harpers* 275:37-47 S '87

Mammals need moms and dads. J. A. Miller. il *BioScience* 37:379-82 Je '87

When life begins: embryo research. *Current* 292:9-10 My '87

Emens, Jan

about
Jan Emens' "penny jug". S. Bagdade and A. Bagdade. il *Antiques Collect Hobbies* 92:43 Ag '87

Emens, Judi

about
For kids who can use an assist, Judi Emens designs clothing that doesn't add to their handicaps. L. Rozen. il pors *People Wkly* 28:59+ S 28 '87

Emerald mines and mining

Colombia
There's green in them thar hills. L. López. il *Time* 130:40 Ag 31 '87

Emergencies *See* Accidents

Emergencies, Assistance in *See* Assistance in emergencies

Emergency ambulance service *See* Ambulance service

Emergency first aid *See* First aid in illness and injury

Emergency locator transmitters *See* Radio beacons

Emergency Position Indicating Radio Beacon *See* Radio beacons

Emergency powers *See* War and emergency powers

Emergency services, Hospital *See* Hospitals—Emergency services

Emerging growth stocks *See* Stocks

Emerson, Ralph Waldo, 1803-1882

about
1837. K. Ide. il por *Am Herit* 38:107-8 Jl/Ag '87

Human, all too inhuman. R. Poirier. *New Repub* 196:29-32+ F 2 '87

Over here! Over here! R. Brookhiser. *Natl Rev* 39:50+ O 9 '87

Where is Emerson now that we need him? or, Why literature can't save us [excerpt from The renewal of literature] R. Poirier. il *N Y Times Book Rev* 92:3+ F 8 '87

Where would Emerson find his scholar now? [adaptation of address, June 1987] A. Kazin. il *Am Herit* 38:93-6 D '87

Emerson Radio Corp.

Copycat. L. R. Walbert. il *Forbes* 139:92-3 My 18 '87

Emeryville (Calif.)

Stores
Emeryville's Stroll, a chance to buy unusual gifts. il *Sunset* 179:60 D '87

Emfinger, Max

about
Mad Max, video recruiter. D. Whitford. il por *Sport Mag* 78:19 Ag '87

Emigration *See* Immigration and emigration

Emilia-Romagna (Italy)

Emilia-Romagna: Italy's best-kept vacation secret. J. L. Greene. il *Black Enterp* 18:90-1 S '87

Emin, David

Icosahedral boron-rich solids. bibl f il *Phys Today* 40:55-62 Ja '87

Emirates (Firm)

Emirates plans Airbus A310-300 service to Europe this summer. il *Aviat Week Space Technol* 126:44 Je 1 '87

Emission control devices (Automobiles) *See* Automobiles—Pollution control devices

Emission control devices (Diesel engines) *See* Diesel engines, Automotive—Pollution control devices

Emission control devices (Motorcycles) *See* Motorcycles—Pollution control devices

Emission reduction credits

How to cut pollution and the deficit at the same time. A. S. Blinder. il *Bus Week* p10 Ag 24 '87

Emlen, Robert P.

Shaker village views. il *Nat Hist* 96:48-57 S '87

Emmerson, Donald K.

Invisible Indonesia. bibl f map *Foreign Aff* 66:368-87 Wint '87/'88

Emmet, Alan

Our Regency rental. il *House Gard* 159:52+ Jl '87

Emmons, Deborah

about
Design for a small business. C. O'Malley. il por *Pers Comput* 11:158-9 O '87

Emmons Advertising (Firm)

Design for a small business [use of computers] C. O'Malley. il por *Pers Comput* 11:158-9 O '87

Emmy Awards

'Cosby,' Woodard shine in Emmy nominations. il *Jet* 72:60 Ag 17 '87

Oprah Winfrey sweeps daytime Emmy Awards. il por *Jet* 72:22 Jl 20 '87

Emonds, Tom

From dragon slayers. il *Mother Earth News* 107:80-3+ S/O '87

Emotional distress (Law)

'Emotional distress' briefs to High Court [Hustler vs. J. Falwell] il *Publ Wkly* 232:13 Jl 17 '87

High Court queries leave outcome of 'Hustler'-Falwell case uncertain. H. Fields. *Publ Wkly* 232:15 D 18 '87

Jerry Falwell vs. Larry Flynt [emotional distress suit goes to Supreme Court] A. Press. il pors *Newsweek* 110:76 D 14 '87

Emotional illness *See* Mental illness

Emotionally disturbed children *See* Problem children

Emotions

See also
Anger
Anxiety
Avoidance (Psychology)
Bashfulness
Crying
Desire
Embarrassment
Empathy
Envy
Facial expression
Fear
Grief
Guilt
Hostility (Psychology)
Innocence (Psychology)
Jealousy
Love
Mind and body
Moods
Peeves
Security and insecurity (Psychology)
Sensitivity
Shame

Emotions—See also—*cont.*
  Smiles
  Temper
  Temperament
  Worry
The elusive language of pleasure and pain. R. Selzer. il *N Y Times Book Rev* 92:38-9 Ap 5 '87
An emotional back burner. J. Stone. *Glamour* 85:52 Jl '87
Emotional escalator. M. O'Brian. il *Health* 19:18 Jl '87
Faces of emotion: social or innate? [research by Ross Buck and Wan-Cheng Teng] B. Bower. *Sci News* 132:150 S 5 '87
Finding a place for emotions in Christian theology. G. S. Clapper. il *Christ Century* 104:409-11 Ap 29 '87
How to help when your child feels bad. N. Samalin and M. M. Jablow. il *Parents* 62:73-8 F '87
Reading between the lines [role of age in interpreting emotional expression; study by Carol Zander Malatesta] A. H. Rosenfeld. *Psychol Today* 21:16 O '87
Wedded faces [facial mimicry in married couples; study by Robert B. Zajonc] H. Hall. *Psychol Today* 21:10 D '87
The word's out: put your feelings on paper. il *Teen* 31:88 My '87
Your not-so-nice-side: when to let it show. il *Teen* 31:58+ Ag '87

Empathy
Striking a balance between others' feelings and your own self-interests. B. L. Stern. *Vogue* 177:364 My '87

Emperor Herbal Restaurant (San Francisco, Calif.) See San Francisco (Calif.)—Restaurants, nightclubs, bars, etc.
Emperor penguin sexual behavior See Sexual behavior—Birds

Emphysema
I can breathe again! P. Ruff. il pors *Saturday Evening Post* 259:100-2+ D '87

Therapy
Mending a torn screen in the lung [antitrypsin therapy] D. D. Edwards. il *Sci News* 131:277 My 2 '87
Empire of the sun [film] See Motion picture reviews—Single works
Employee absenteeism See Absenteeism
Employee assistance programs See Employee counseling
Employee benefits See Fringe benefits
Employee counseling
Help on the job [employee assistance programs] *Psychol Today* 21:48 Ag '87
Employee-employer relations See Industrial relations; Personnel management; Psychology, Industrial
Employee incentives See Incentives in industry
Employee leasing
How to delegate when there's no one to delegate to [small businesses using outside service contractors] E. Alvarez. il *Work Woman* 12:51-2 F '87
Employee morale
  See also
  Incentives in industry
  Job satisfaction
The best way to boost employee morale. B. Serlen. *Work Woman* 12:24+ My '87
From Platoon to Pan Am [views on morale by J. W. Gibson] R. McGough. il por *Forbes* 139:105 Ap 20 '87
Employee motivation See Motivation (Psychology)
Employee ownership
  See also
  Leveraged buyouts
Air pockets around United [pilots propose employee buyout] G. M. Bock. il *Time* 129:52-3 Ap 20 '87
Class consciousness raising [Weirton Steel] S. W. Angrist. il *Forbes* 140:77-8 N 30 '87
Enterprise and double cross [excerpt from Tales of a new America] R. B. Reich. *Wash Mon* 18:13-19 Ja '87
Friendly guy, unfriendly skies [United's pilots choose W. R. Howard as the executive to help them buy the company] N. J. Perry. il por *Fortune* 116:122 S 14 '87
How workers saved their steel mill [Weirton Steel] P. Gaynor. il *Sch Update* 119:9 Ja 26 '87
Move over Boone, Carl, and IRV—here comes labor. A. Bernstein. il *Bus Week* p124-5 D 14 '87
Pan Am union coalition attempts buyout. *Aviat Week Space Technol* 127:32 Jl 27 '87
Pilot ownership concept takes several forms at world carriers. *Aviat Week Space Technol* 126:49+ My 11 '87

Pilots' offer to buy United meets company, union opposition. J. Ott. *Aviat Week Space Technol* 126:32-3 Ap 20 '87
Sans Simon, Wesray cleans up on Avis. il *Fortune* 116:8-9 O 26 '87
UAL's pilots may put the airline into play. J. E. Ellis. il *Bus Week* p25 Ap 20 '87
United's pilots are inching closer to a coup. J. E. Ellis. il por *Bus Week* p32-3 Ag 31 '87
United's pilots get a captain and cash [mounting a buyout] *Newsweek* 110:32 Ag 24 '87
'We're not going to sit around and allow management to louse things up'. J. Hoerr. il *Bus Week* p107 My 18 '87
What it takes to succeed [Seymour Specialty Wire Company] M. Daniel. il *U S News World Rep* 102:48 Je 8 '87
When workers get in the takeover game. C. P. Work. il *U S News World Rep* 102:47-8 Je 8 '87
When you own the company, you try harder [employee buyout at Avis] E. Spragins. *Bus Week* p32-3 S 28 '87
Worker ownership: a commitment that's more often a con. R. Kuttner. il *Bus Week* p16 Jl 6 '87

South Africa
Why black workers may say 'thanks, but no thanks' to Ford [partial worker ownership of Samcor] S. Mufson. il *Bus Week* p47 Jl 6 '87
Employee physical fitness programs See Industry—Physical fitness programs
Employee stock ownership See Employees as stockholders
Employee tardiness See Tardiness
Employee theft
To stop a thief [cover story] H. Bacas. il *Nations Bus* 75:16-17+ Je '87
Employee uniforms See Uniforms
Employees
  See also
  Executives
  Government employees
  Household employees
  Job satisfaction
  Labor turnover
  Personnel management
  Supervisors

Attitudes
How you can find out what employees are thinking [attitude survey] G. Bakoulis. *Work Woman* 12:20+ S '87

Discipline
  See Labor discipline
Dismissal
  See also
  Layoffs
  Outplacement consultant services
  Severance pay
Friendly firing: do you warn a pal about a pink slip? C. Rickey. *Mademoiselle* 93:106 Je '87
Goodbye, corporate staff. T. Moore. il *Fortune* 116:65+ D 21 '87
The revenge of the fired. J. B. Copeland. il *Newsweek* 109:46-7 F 16 '87
Trouble on the firing line. S. A. Ploscowe and M. M. Goldstein. il *Nations Bus* 75:36-7 Mr '87

Education
  See Labor—Education
Health and hygiene
  See Occupational health and safety
Monitoring
'Big Brother' in the office. *Newsweek* 110:78 O 5 '87
Big Brother is counting your keystrokes [report by the Office of Technology Assessment] W. Booth. *Science* 238:17 O 2 '87
Electronic taskmasters [computer monitoring of employees] T. Beardsley. *Sci Am* 257:32+ D '87
It knows if you've been bad or good [computer monitoring of employees] il *Discover* 8:16 D '87

Personnel records
  See Personnel records
Promotion
  See Promotions
Psychology
  See Psychology, Industrial
Rating
  See also
  Employment tests
How am I doing? [excerpt from The human side of management] G. S. Odiorne. il *Work Woman* 12:32+ Je '87
How to appraise performance. W. Kiechel, III. il *Fortune* 116:239-40 O 12 '87

Employees—*cont.*

Recruiting

See also

Employment agencies
Employment interviewing

Baiting the hook [businesses recruiting on campus] R. Buchanan. il *Roll Stone* p99-100+ Mr 26 '87

How to sell the job you have to the person you want. M. McFadden. il *Work Woman* 12:86-7+ Je '87

The new art of hiring smart. B. Dumaine. il *Fortune* 116:78-81 Ag 17 '87

Nine rules for hiring [excerpt from The human side of management] G. S. Odiorne. *Work Woman* 12:40+ N '87

Understanding women [excerpt from Ortho Pharmaceuticals recruiting memo] *Harpers* 274:23-4 Ap '87

Relocation

See Labor mobility

Resignation

Bye bye, so long. S. Bign. il *Esquire* 108:78 N '87

Moving on. P. Plawin. *Changing Times* 41:100 F '87

When it's time to quit your job. B. Delatiner. il *McCalls* 114:21+ Ap '87

Tenure

See Labor turnover

Testing

See Employment tests

Training

See also

Motion pictures in industry
Retraining, Occupational

Computerizing with confidence (IV). K. Berney. il *Nations Bus* 75:55-7 F '87

Corporate mind control [New Age gurus] A. Miller. il *Newsweek* 109:38-9 My 4 '87

Don't promote "one of the boys". M. E. Moore. por *Nations Bus* 75:4 Mr '87

Help wanted [cover story] A. Bernstein. il *Bus Week* p48-53 Ag 10 '87

Helping workers to work smarter. M. Brody. il *Fortune* 115:86-8 Je 8 '87

Jobs without people and people without jobs: the coming mismatch in the information society. W. H. Kolberg. il *USA Today (Periodical)* 116:18-20 Jl '87

Lessons for teacher education from corporate practice. W. R. Houston. bibl f il *Phi Delta Kappan* 68:388-92 Ja '87

Making your investment pay off [computers] R. Zemke. il *Work Woman* 12:49+ S '87

Merchants of inspiration [motivational speakers] J. Main. il *Fortune* 116:69-71+ Jl 6 '87

The Russian who makes pros out of amateurs [L. Landa] J. Main. il por *Fortune* 116:79 O 12 '87

Successful worker training programs help ease impact of technology. S. Deutsch. bibl f *Mon Labor Rev* 110:14-20 N '87

The U.S. can't compete without a top-notch work force. R. Kuttner. il *Bus Week* p20 F 16 '87

Videos are starring in more and more training programs. R. Neff. il *Bus Week* p108-10 S 7 '87

Writing the book on staff training [method used at Books & Co. bookstore, Dayton, Ohio] S. Bolle. il *Publ Wkly* 232:140-2 S 18 '87

Employees as stockholders

Behind the ESOP surge. L. Jereski. il *Forbes* 140:212+ D 14 '87

The foibles of ESOP's. S. Dentzer. il *Newsweek* 110:58-9 O 19 '87

HCA may breathe new life into ESOPs [Hospital Corp. of America] G. Weiss. il *Bus Week* p94 Je 15 '87

How Dan River's ESOP missed the boat. D. Foust. il *Bus Week* p34-5 O 26 '87

How employee stock ownership plans work. T. Tilling. *Parents* 62:50 N '87

Physician, heal thy chain [plan to sell Hospital Corp. of America hospitals to employee-owned company] S. Ticer. *Bus Week* p52 Je 1 '87

Taxation

For the quick, a $20 billion estate tax loophole. P. Philipps. il *Bus Week* p152 F 23 '87

Employees' associations

See also

Ex-employees' associations

Employees' disability insurance *See* Insurance, Disability

Employees' health insurance *See* Insurance, Health

Employees' mental health insurance *See* Insurance, Mental health

Employees' representation in management *See* Participative management

Employees' whistle blowing *See* Whistle blowing (Public interest)

Employer-employee relations *See* Industrial relations; Personnel management; Psychology, Industrial

Employment

See also

Absenteeism
Aged—Employment
AIDS (Disease) and employment
Americans—Foreign countries—Employment
Asian Americans—Employment
Blacks—Employment
Contingent workers
Discrimination in employment
Drugs and employment
Full employment
Handicapped—Employment
Hours of labor
Husbands—Employment
Information storage and retrieval systems—Employment use
Married couples—Employment
Mothers—Employment
Networking
Part time employment
Retirement
Self employed
Single mothers—Employment
Smoking and employment
Supplementary employment
Temporary employment
Unemployment
Veterans—Employment
Videotapes—Employment use
Widows—Employment
Women—Employment
Youth—Employment

The American job machine. R. J. Samuelson. il *Newsweek* 109:57 F 23 '87

The crash jolts a shifting job market. G. Koretz. il *Bus Week* p33 N 16 '87

The debate over new jobs is turning into mudslinging. R. Kuttner. il *Bus Week* p22 Ap 13 '87

Employment: something to cheer about. W. B. Franklin and J. C. Cooper. il *Bus Week* p53-4 My 25 '87

The future of employment [address, October 18, 1986] J. L. Norwood. *Current* 292:18-23 My '87

How imports and exports color the U.S. job picture. G. Koretz. *Bus Week* p24 O 5 '87

The job engine is going great guns . . . but it's one reason the productivity motor is backfiring. G. Koretz. il *Bus Week* p20 Mr 30 '87

Job growth explains why consumers keep on spending . . . and interest income may give them more to burn. K. Pennar. il *Bus Week* p24 O 26 '87

Jobilism, or, Is the world really flat? R. B. McKenzie. il *Forbes* 140:68-70 Jl 13 '87

The labor force grows, but so do jobs. W. B. Franklin and J. C. Cooper. il *Bus Week* p39-40 Je 22 '87

Labor news is mostly good. H. Banks. il *Forbes* 140:29 D 14 '87

A monster jump in employment. W. B. Franklin and J. C. Cooper. il *Bus Week* p27-8 N 23 '87

The myth of 'McJobs'. *Natl Rev* 39:19-20 Ap 10 '87

New technologies good for employment [report by the National Academy of Sciences] C. Holden. *Science* 236:1622 Je 26 '87

Protectionism can't protect jobs. M. McFadden. il *Fortune* 115:121+ My 11 '87

Sorting out job trends. R. Thompson. il *Nations Bus* 75:8 Mr '87

A surge from the job machine. K. Pennar. il *Bus Week* p56-7 My 25 '87

Technological change. *Mon Labor Rev* 110:2 Jl '87

U.S. affairs annual: jobs and the economy [special issue] il *Sch Update* 119:2-12+ Ja 26 '87

Statistics

See also

Wage differentials

The defense buildup, 1977-85: effects on production and employment. D. K. Henry and R. P. Oliver. bibl f il *Mon Labor Rev* 110:3-11 Ag '87

Employment and wage changes of families from CE Survey data [Consumer Expenditure Survey] M. F. Kokoski. bibl f il *Mon Labor Rev* 110:31-3 F '87

Employment data from the household survey. See issues of Monthly Labor Review

Employment, hours, and earnings data from establishment surveys. See issues of Monthly Labor Review

Employment—Statistics—*cont.*

The employment situation during 1986: job gains continue, unemployment dips. S. E. Shank and S. E. Haugen. bibl f il *Mon Labor Rev* 110:3-10 F '87

An evaluation of state projections of industry, occupational employment. H. A. Goldstein and A. M. Cruze. bibl f il *Mon Labor Rev* 110:29-38 O '87

Industry output and employment through the end of the century. V. A. Personick. bibl f il *Mon Labor Rev* 110:30-45 S '87

A look at occupational employment trends to the year 2000. G. T. Silvestri and J. M. Lukasiewicz. il *Mon Labor Rev* 110:46-63 S '87

March was a chilly month for employment. W. B. Franklin and J. C. Cooper. il *Bus Week* p19-20 Ap 20 '87

New data on workers belonging to unions, 1986. *Mon Labor Rev* 110:36 My '87

On their own: the self-employed and others in private business. S. E. Haber and others. bibl f il *Mon Labor Rev* 110:17-23 My '87

Strong employment growth highlights first half of 1987. W. J. Howe. il *Mon Labor Rev* 110:64-9 S '87

Technological change and employment: some results from BLS research. J. A. Mark. il *Mon Labor Rev* 110:26-9 Ap '87

The turbulent job market. J. Clements. il *Forbes* 140:114-17+ Jl 13 '87

Work experience of the labor force during 1985. S. J. Smith. il *Mon Labor Rev* 110:40-4 Ap '87

Japan

Insecurely secure. D. Watts; J. Tokuyama. *World Press Rev* 34:17-18 Ag '87

Western Europe

Cathedrals in the desert. H. Banks. il *Forbes* 140:225-6+ Jl 13 '87

Employment ads *See* Advertising, Classified

Employment agencies
> *See also*
> Executive search consultants
> Insight Personnel Agency of New York Inc.
> Intercristo (Organization)
> Manpower, Inc.
> Royalpar Industries, Inc.
> Systemp (Firm)
> Theatrical agencies and agents
> Uniforce Temporary Personnel, Inc.
> United States Employment Service

Finding work through an employment agency. G. S. Burdick. il *Consum Res Mag* 70:27-30 F '87

Acquisitions and mergers
International aspects

A whiz kid bids for Manpower [A. Berry's Blue Arrow plc] M. D. Oneal and R. A. Melcher. il por *Bus Week* p37-8 Ag 17 '87

Canada

A temporary workforce. R. K. Heft. il *Macleans* 100:48-9 N 30 '87

Great Britain
> *See also*
> Blue Arrow plc

Employment and AIDS (Disease) *See* AIDS (Disease) and employment

Employment and alcoholism *See* Alcohol and employment

Employment and drugs *See* Drugs and employment

Employment and smoking *See* Smoking and employment

Employment contracts *See* Labor contracts

Employment counseling *See* Vocational guidance

Employment discrimination *See* Discrimination in employment

Employment interviewing

Dressed for excess [study by Robert A. Baron] S. Walton. *Psychol Today* 21:8 Ag '87

Hire me, I'm yours. S. Bing. il *Esquire* 108:86 S '87

Hiring the best. H. Bacas. il *Nations Bus* 75:68+ O '87

How to get more mileage out of your interview suit. J. Mattera. il *Glamour* 85:146 My '87

The interview as mating ritual. D. Friedman. il *Work Woman* 12:106-8 Ap '87

Interviews: the best face is your own. J. A. Byrne. il *Bus Week* p122 F 16 '87

Little things that mean a lot [dressing for interviews] J. Mattera. il *Glamour* 85:106 F '87

The look that got the job. M. L. O'Hana. il *Ladies Home J* 104:138-41 N '87

Six steps to a winning job interview. B. Nivens. il *Essence* 18:122 O '87

What do interviewers want to hear? *Glamour* 85:148 N '87

What to ask a prospective boss at a job interview. M. M. Kennedy. il *Glamour* 85:166 Ap '87

Which look got the job? il *Glamour* 85:304-5 Ap '87

You blew the job interview—now what? *Glamour* 85:112 D '87

Employment references

Checking references? Here are ten tough questions to ask. R. Half. *Work Woman* 12:21 F '87

How to help a friend get hired by your company. *Glamour* 85:49 Ja '87

Job references: handle with care. I. Pave. il *Bus Week* p124 Mr 9 '87

Superintendent found guilty of slander for teacher recommendation [M. True v. R. Ladner] T. J. Flygare. il *Phi Delta Kappan* 68:629-30 Ap '87

Employment security *See* Job security

Employment tests

Brainstorms [IQ tests as job performance predictor; findings reported in the Journal of vocational behavior] D. Seligman. *Fortune* 116:206+ Ag 3 '87

How often do you think about sex? [various forms of job testing] E. Hopkins. *Mademoiselle* 93:124-5+ Ja '87

Lying in Congress [bill to bar lie detector testing] D. Seligman. il *Fortune* 116:186+ D 7 '87

The new art of hiring smart. B. Dumaine. il *Fortune* 116:78-81 Ag 17 '87

Normal nonsense [reverse discrimination seen in U.S. Employment Service rankings of General Aptitude Test Battery scores] D. Seligman. il *Fortune* 116:165-6 N 9 '87

Personality tests are back [Myers-Briggs Type Indicator] T. Moore. il *Fortune* 115:74-6+ Mr 30 '87

Emporia (Kan.)
Crime

A late indictment may close the case behind TV's Murder ordained. J. Calio. il pors *People Wkly* 27:107-8+ Je 8 '87

Empresa Nacional de Aeronautica

Chile's Enaer seeks larger aerospace role. il *Aviat Week Space Technol* 127:62-3 Ag 17 '87

Empty nest syndrome *See* Parents

Emshwiller, Carol

The circular library of stones [story] il *Omni* 9:74-6+ F '87

Emslie, A. Gordon

Explosions in the solar atmosphere. il *Astronomy* 15:18-23 N '87

Emslie, Steven D.

Age and diet of fossil California condors in Grand Canyon, Arizona. bibl f il *Science* 237:768-70 Ag 14 '87

Emulators (Computer programs)

The right connection [HyperAccess communications and terminal-emulator package] J. Bell. il *Pers Comput* 11:154 F '87

Enaer *See* Empresa Nacional de Aeronautica

Encephalitis
> *See also*
> Rasmussen's encephalitis

Encephalography
> *See also*
> Electroencephalography
> Magnetoencephalography

Encyclopedias
> *See also*
> CD-ROM (Compact disc-Read only memory)—Encyclopedias
> Information storage and retrieval systems—Encyclopedias
> Publishers and publishing—Encyclopedias

Looking for knowledge, in volumes. S. N. Wellborn. il *U S News World Rep* 103:48-9 Jl 27 '87

Anecdotes, facetiae, satire, etc.

How I got smart [reading encyclopedias to impress an intelligent classmate] S. Brody. il *Read Dig* 131:176-8 N '87

END *See* European Nuclear Disarmament (Organization)

End of the world
> *See also*
> Judgment Day

End of the world: you won't feel a thing. D. E. Thomsen. *Sci News* 131:391 Je 20 '87

'The things that make for peace' [United Methodist pastoral In defense of creation] W. H. Willimon. *Christ Century* 104:453-4 My 6 '87

This is the way the world ends [cover story] T. Rothman. il *Discover* 8:82-4+ Jl '87

When the sun swallows the earth [research by Jeff Goldstein] il *Sky Telesc* 74:575 D '87

End of the world—*cont.*

Willimon hollering at bishops? [discussion of May 6, 1987 article, The things that make for peace] W. H. Willimon. *Christ Century* 104:632-4 Jl 15-22 '87

Endangered species *See* Rare animals

Endangered Species Act (1973)

Congress considers species legislation. A. L. Spitler. *BioScience* 37:383 Je '87

Endangered Species Act: uncertain prospects in 100th Congress. L. Hannah. *BioScience* 37:16 Ja '87

Political animals. il *Sci Am* 256:65+ Mr '87

Endocrine glands

See also

Adrenal glands

Pancreas

Growing up with the endocrine system. il *Curr Health 2* 13:3-10 F '87

Endocrinology

See also

Hormone receptors

Hormones

Endometriosis

Endometriosis: one woman's struggle [case of M. L. Ballweg] J. Coudert. *McCalls* 114:86-8 S '87

Endometriosis: the new young women's infertility disease. L. Morice. il *Mademoiselle* 93:94 D '87

New bone-loss risk factors in young women [research by Pamela Jensen] S. Weisburd. *Sci News* 132:347 N 28 '87

Surgery

Treating endometriosis [use of lasers] P. Gadsby and L. J. Brown. il *Good Housekeep* 204:213 Je '87

Therapy

Endometriosis: new ways to ease the pain. il *Glamour* 85:310+ Ag '87

"Reversible menopause" may help some women who have endometriosis or fibroid tumors [use of gonadotropin releasing hormone] *Prevention* 39:62-3 O '87

Endorphins

Opioids moonlighting in cell growth? D. D. Edwards. *Sci News* 131:230 Ap 11 '87

The pain-pleasure connection. P. L. DeVito. il *USA Today (Periodical)* 115:47-9 Ja '87

Endorsements in advertising *See* Advertising—Testimonials

Endoscopes and endoscopy

See also

Arthroscopes and arthroscopy

Endothelium *See* Epithelium

Endowments

See also

Black colleges and universities—Gifts, legacies, etc.

Colleges and universities—Gifts, legacies, etc.

Endurance

Can you go the distance? [endurance sports] G. Bakoulis. il *Health* 19:34-6+ O '87

Stamina! How to get it, how to keep it. L. Schnurnberger. il *Ladies Home J* 104:56+ O '87

The stamina to succeed. B. W. Bloch. il *Work Woman* 12:130+ O '87

Enduro motorcycles *See* Motorcycles

Energetics, Biological *See* Bioenergetics

Energy, Vital *See* Vitality

Energy and Commerce Committee *See* United States. Congress. House. Committee on Energy and Commerce

Energy asset insurance *See* Insurance, Energy asset

Energy conservation

See also

Agriculture—Energy usage

Air conditioning equipment—Energy usage

Alliance to Save Energy

Automobile engines—Energy usage

Boilers—Energy usage

Electric plants—Energy usage

Energy policy

Environmental engineering (Buildings)

Grain dryers—Energy usage

Hood River Conservation Project

Household appliances—Energy usage

Industry—Energy usage

Insulation (Heat)

Motorcycle engines—Energy usage

Refrigerators—Energy usage

Weatherproofing

Windbreaks

Alternate-energy answers. J. F. Kreider. See alternate issues of Popular Science through January 1987

Conservation up front. G. Nelson. *Wilderness* 51:2 Wint '87

Energy [Environmental Quality Index] il *Natl Wildl* 25:37 F/Mr '87

Energy answers. See issues of Workbench beginning May/June 1986

Energy Q & A. J. F. Kreider. See issues of Popular Science beginning March 1987

Government still backs energy-saving improvements [Energy Efficient Mortgage] H. Porter. *Fam Handyman* 37:22 F '87

What's in an energy efficient home. B. Howard. il *Consum Res Mag* 70:11-15 Mr '87

Energy Conversion Devices, Inc.

An investment that turned into a nightmare [S. R. Ovshinsky sues W. Manning] E. T. Smith. il por *Bus Week* p102+ N 30 '87

The promised land may be near for 'Ovonics'. E. T. Smith. il por *Bus Week* p58 Je 15 '87

Energy costs *See* Power resources—Economic aspects

Energy crisis *See* Petroleum supply; Power resources

Energy Dept. (U.S.) *See* United States. Dept. of Energy

Energy efficiency standard of appliances *See* Household appliances—Energy usage

Energy industries

See also

Archer-Daniels-Midland Co.

Coal industry

Coastal Corporation

Combustion Engineering Inc.

Exxon Corporation

Gas industry

Mapco Inc.

Oil shale industry

Pennzoil Company

Petroleum industry

Phillips Petroleum Company

Solar energy industry

Canada

See also

Barrick Resources Corp.

New life stirs for natural resource companies. E. B. Terry. il *Bus Week* p47 Mr 2 '87

Energy levels (Quantum mechanics)

Electronic theory for materials science. H. Ehrenreich. bibl f *Science* 235:1029-35 F 27 '87

The impossible dream [excited rubidium atom in resonant cavity; work of Gerhard Rempe and others] *Sci Am* 256:25 Je '87

Quantum chaos? [work of Giulio Casati and others] *Sci Am* 256:62+ Mr '87

Some concepts in reaction dynamics [adaptation of Nobel Prize address, December 8, 1986] J. C. Polanyi. bibl f il *Science* 236:680-90 My 8 '87

Some halfway steps give scientists a look at a quantum leap. il *Discover* 8:9 Ja '87

Energy policy

See also

United States. Congress. House. Committee on Energy and Commerce

United States. Dept. of Energy

United States. Federal Energy Regulatory Commission

Amory and Hunter Lovins. B. Lawren. *Omni* 9:97 S '87

Another oil crisis? *Futurist* 21:57 S/O '87

The avoidable oil crisis. A. B. Lovins and L. H. Lovins. il *Atlantic* 260:22+ D '87

Back to the energy crisis. M. Crawford. bibl il *Science* 235:626-7 F 6 '87

Bailing out oil. *Progressive* 51:11-12 My '87

Conservation up front. G. Nelson. *Wilderness* 51:2 Wint '87

Energy security [message to Congress, May 6, 1987] R. Reagan. *Dep State Bull* 87:51-2 Jl '87

Foreign oil: the scourge of the '70s may be a blessing now. B. Starr and T. Smart. il *Bus Week* p40 Mr 23 '87

Get ready for the coming oil crisis. J. P. Newport, Jr. il *Fortune* 115:46-52+ Mr 16 '87

Give the people light [address, June 9, 1987] M. T. Halbouty. *Vital Speeches Day* 53:653-5 Ag 15 '87

The great oil giveaway [address, September 4, 1987] R. G. Wallace. *Vital Speeches Day* 54:17-20 O 15 '87

New directions for oil policy. R. W. Fri. bibl f il *Environment* 29:16-20+ Je '87

The new energy challenge [address, February 3, 1987] G. M. Keller. *Vital Speeches Day* 53:314-17 Mr 1 '87

The next oil crisis. *Commonweal* 114:132-3 Mr 13 '87

The next oil crisis [cover story] M. Lynch. il *Technol Rev* 90:38-45+ N/D '87

Oil together now. F. Barnes. *New Repub* 196:12-13 F 9 '87

Energy policy—*cont.*

Report on reports: Energy security: a report to the president of the United States. J. Darmstadter. bibl f il *Environment* 29:25-7 Jl/Ag '87

Rethinking energy security: the case for coal in the United States. H. H. Landsberg. il *Environment* 29:18-20+ Jl/Ag '87

States rights and the national interests [address, July 22, 1987] J. E. Chubb. *Vital Speeches Day* 53:702-4 S 1 '87

The third oil crisis. J. Cook. il map *Forbes* 140:37+ D 14 '87

International aspects

See also

International Energy Agency

Canada

'One hell of a fight' [Canada-U.S. free trade agreement] M. Drohan. il *Macleans* 100:26-7 O 26 '87

Ottawa aids the oilmen [western Canada] T. Tedesco. *Macleans* 100:31 Ap 6 '87

A revolt over energy [controversy over Canada-U.S. free trade pact] M. Rose. il *Macleans* 100:15 N 23 '87

New York (State)

See also

Power Authority of the State of New York

Oregon

See also

Hood River Conservation Project

United States

See Energy policy

Energy resources *See* Power resources

Energy Simulation Specialists

Full speed ahead [use of Compaq Deskpro 386] S. R. Reed. il *Pers Comput* 11:67 Mr '87

Energy storage

See also

Heat storage

Energy supply *See* Power resources

L'enfant et les sortilèges [dance] *See* Dance reviews—Single works

L'enfant et les sortilèges [television program] *See* Television program reviews—Single works

Enfield, Roger

about

Negotiating a remodeling contract [interview] J. H. Ingersoll. il por *Home Mech* 83:18-19 Jl '87

Enfield, Ronald L.

The limits of software reliability. il *Technol Rev* 90:36-40+ Ap '87

Engel, Bob

about

Bob's job is his calling. B. Newman. il pors *Sports Illus* 67:86-7 Jl 6 '87

Engel, Bruce

about

Paul Bunyan in pinstripes. J. Willoughby. il por *Forbes* 139:118+ Ap 6 '87

Engel, J. Ronald

Teaching the eco-justice ethic: the parable of the Billerica Dam. il *Christ Century* 104:466-9 My 13 '87

Engel, Margaret

Newslines from Washington. See issues of Glamour

Engelhard, Jane

about

A passion for history. J. Fleming. il *House Gard* 159:122-5+ Mr '87

Engelhart, Kelly

about

'This is a miracle!' came the cry of disbelief—'My God, we're alive!'. il por *People Wkly* 28:103 D 21 '87

Engels, Vincent

In the hush of the night. il *Conservationist* 41:14-17 My/Je '87

Engen, Donald D.

Administrator's admission. il *Flying* 114:176 S '87

about

Engen warns against local challenges to national airspace system. *Aviat Week Space Technol* 126:50 Ap 13 '87

Engine knock *See* Automobile engines—Detonation

Engine ping *See* Automobile engines—Detonation

Engineering

See also

Audio engineering
Automobile engineering
Building materials
Highway engineering
Motorcycle engineering
Petroleum engineering
Structural engineering

The challenge to U.S. competitiveness. R. M. White. *Science* 236:1041 My 29 '87

Interview [macroengineering; F. Davidson] D. Lessem. por *Omni* 9:80-2+ My '87

Awards

See also

Presidential Young Investigators Awards

Engineering Academy honors two, elects new members. il *Phys Today* 40:109-11 My '87

International aspects

Strengthening U.S. engineering [need for international cooperation; report by the National Academy of Engineering] P. H. Abelson. *Science* 237:961 Ag 28 '87

Social aspects

Engineering: an ideal profession for idealists. S. C. Florman. il *Technol Rev* 90:18 O '87

Study and teaching

"Competitiveness" fever. J. I. Mattill. il *Technol Rev* 90:13-14 Ag/S '87

The impact of foreign graduate students on engineering education in the United States. E. G. Barber and R. P. Morgan. bibl f il *Science* 236:33-7 Ap 3 '87

Lifelong learning. P. H. Abelson. *Science* 235:521 Ja 30 '87

Making a robot out of rubbish [CHICO project for Hispanic students sponsored by University of Maryland] il *Natl Geogr World* 141:25-9 My '87

Schools for whistle blowers [ethical engineers] C. Mitcham. bibl il *Commonweal* 114:201-5 Ap 10 '87

Canada

Manufacturing today [address, June 24, 1987] B. M. McGourty. *Vital Speeches Day* 53:752-5 O 1 '87

Engineering colleges

Nuts and bolts. il *U S News World Rep* 103:75-6 N 2 '87

Engineering construction companies

See also

CRS Sirrine, Inc.
Dravo Corp.
Fluor Corp.
Ove Arup Partnership
Vollmer Associates

Japan

See also

Kumagai Gumi Co. Ltd.

Engineering design

Study and teaching

Why we need hands-on engineering education. A. D. Kerr and R. B. Pipes. il *Technol Rev* 90:36-42 O '87

Engineering ethics *See* Engineers—Professional ethics

Engineering research

See also

Aviation research
George M. Low Center for Industrial Innovation

Magnetic engineering. R. M. White. *Phys Today* 40:89 N '87

Engineering research, Genetic *See* Genetic research

Engineering societies

See also

Institute of Electrical and Electronics Engineers
National Academy of Engineering

Engineers

See also

United States. Army. Corps of Engineers
Women engineers

Making the architect-engineer relationship work. S. M. Sessler. *Archit Rec* 175:43 F '87

Professional ethics

Schools for whistle blowers. C. Mitcham. bibl il *Commonweal* 114:201-5 Ap 10 '87

Religious life

Called to broaden my horizon. J. Scheible. *Commonweal* 114:523-5 S 25 '87

Supply and demand

Engineers and immigration [illegal employment] S. Shulman. il *Technol Rev* 90:15 Ja '87

Engineers Corps *See* United States. Army. Corps of Engineers

Engines

See also

Airplane engines
Automobile engines
Automobiles, Racing—Engines
Gas and oil engines
Heat engines
Marine engines
Motor boat engines
Motorcycle engines
Rotary engines

England, Robert
Aging in America: wealth and the elderly. *Current* 294:26-9 Jl/Ag '87
England
See also
Bath (England)
Birmingham (England)
Chelsea (London, England)
Clarendon Park (Wiltshire, England)
Cotswolds (England)
Cranbrook (England)
Derbyshire (England)
East Stoke (England)
Etchingham (England)
Great Britain
Headington (England)
Hull (England)
Hungerford (Berkshire, England)
Lake District (England)
Leeds (England)
Lincolnshire (England)
London (England)
Manchester (England)
Newcastle Upon Tyne (England)
Saltaire (England)
Slapton Sands (England)
Suffolk (England)
Twickenham (London, England)
Walthamstow (England)
Wye River (Wales and England)
Englander, David
Troops & trade unions, 1919. il *Hist Today* 37:8-13 Mr '87
Englebardt, Stanley L.
Be safe in the sun. il *Read Dig* 130:173-4+ Je '87
Drive defensively—and live. il *Read Dig* 131:81-2+ N '87
How to avoid a stroke. *Read Dig* 130:93-5 Ja '87
How to escape a fire. *Read Dig* 131:163-4+ Ag '87
Hypothermia, the chilling killer. *Read Dig* 131:160-2 D '87
It can be prevented. *Read Dig* 131:97-8 Jl '87
Engles, Eric C.
Jacksonville/Charleston [poem] *Essence* 18:122 D '87
Englewood (N.J.)
Criminal justice, Administration of
Singer Wilson Pickett convicted of gun charge. il por *Jet* 72:56 Jl 20 '87
English, Alex
about
Kareem fights English's suit with one of his own. *Jet* 72:48 Ap 6 '87
English, Robert, and Daggett, Stephen
Collision in space. *New Repub* 196:11-13 Je 29 '87
English art *See* Art, English
English Channel
See also
Channel Islands
English Channel ferries *See* Ferries
English Channel tunnel
The big dig. B. Weber. il *N Y Times Mag* p142 N 8 '87
The Chunnel's chances. il *Fortune* 116:9 D 21 '87
Troubled crossing. P. Roberge. *Macleans* 100:55 Mr 16 '87
English cocker spaniels
The English cocker. B. Tarrant. il *Field Stream* 92:96-8 D '87
English composition *See* English language—Composition
English cooking *See* Cooking, English
English dictionaries *See* English language—Dictionaries
English East India Company *See* East India Company
English fiction
Assaults on the British novel. G. Smith. *New Leader* 70:17-18 D 14 '87
English furniture *See* Furniture, English
English gardens and gardening *See* Gardens and gardening, English
English historians *See* Historians, English
English history *See* Great Britain—History
English house decoration *See* House decoration, English
English language
See also
Sex discrimination in language
Vocabulary
The battle over preserving the English language [English Language Amendment] G. Imhoff and G. Bikales. il *USA Today (Periodical)* 115:63-5 Ja '87

The sun never sets on the English novel [authors of many nations writing in English] M. Gorra. il *N Y Times Book Rev* 92:1+ Jl 19 '87
U.S. language debate rages. E. Branch. *Black Enterp* 17:20+ Jl '87
Why English should be our official language. S. I. Hayakawa. *Educ Dig* 52:36-7 My '87
Bibliography
Talk talk. L. Menand. *New Repub* 196:28-33 F 16 '87
Composition
See also
Creative writing
Ghosts to believe in: recalling Bateson and Mead [learning to bridge the gap between speech and writing] M. C. Bateson. *N Y Times Book Rev* 92:49 N 15 '87
Good writing [address, April 6, 1987] D. M. Stewart. *Vital Speeches Day* 53:630-3 Ag 1 '87
"Great human power or magic" [Bread Loaf program] M. Ludtke. il *Time* 130:76 S 14 '87
Hidden agendas in writing across the curriculum. S. N. Tchudi. *Educ Dig* 52:33-5 Ap '87
Johnny can't write, either [report of the National Assessment of Educational Progress] il *Consum Res Mag* 70:18-21+ Ag '87
Kids can learn to write—and enjoy it [interview with R. P. Clark] il *U S News World Rep* 102:68 Ap 6 '87
Let's not teach bad writing: five commonly taught fallacies. P. Osborn. *Educ Dig* 52:42 Ap '87
Life in remedial English: learning about teaching and learning [writing course at the City University of New York] L. Forstall. *Phi Delta Kappan* 68:796-7 Je '87
National writing assessments: trends across 10 years [excerpt from Writing] A. N. Applebee and others. *Educ Dig* 52:24-6 F '87
Presidential perspectives on university writing requirements [address, March 7, 1987] S. Altman. *Vital Speeches Day* 53:494-6 Je 1 '87
Students lack skills in writing and critical thinking: NAEP. *Phi Delta Kappan* 68:484-5 F '87
What do I do while they're writing? M. K. Simpson. *Educ Dig* 52:44-6 My '87
Conjunctions
Feelings of and and if, of and but. D. Donoghue. il *N Y Times Book Rev* 92:10 Ja 25 '87
Dictionaries
See also
Publishers and publishing—Dictionaries
All the words that are fit to print—and some that aren't—fill the hefty new Random House dictionary [editor S. B. Flexner] E. Levin. il por *People Wkly* 28:167-9 N 23 '87
The building of a dictionary: how Robert Burchfield devoted 29 years to the 'OED supplement'. R. Herbert. il por *Publ Wkly* 232:38-9 O 2 '87
'Chocoholic'? Look it up [second edition of Random House dictionary of the English language] C. Leerhsen. il *Newsweek* 110:69 S 14 '87
Lifted lexicons [dictionaries at San Francisco's Stanford Court hotel] *Time* 129:87 Ap 6 '87
Of many things [J. Ciardi's A second browser's dictionary and native's guide to the unknown American language] G. W. Hunt. *America* 156:inside cover Ap 4 '87
Quoth the maven 'evermore' [Supplement to the Oxford English dictionary] J. Simon. *New Leader* 69:5-7 D 1-15 '86
Surveying the state of the lingo [second edition of the Random House dictionary of the English language] C. Porterfield. il *Time* 130:85-6 N 2 '87
Bibliography
Know ye by these presents. W. Safire. il *N Y Times Mag* p14+ D 13 '87
Errors
See Errors, Speech
Etymology
Of many things [J. Ciardi's A second browser's dictionary and native's guide to the unknown American language] G. W. Hunt. *America* 156:inside cover Ap 4 '87
Gender
See also
Sex discrimination in language
Grammar
See also
English language—Usage
History
You say begin, I say commence—to the victor belongs the language. R. M. Brown. il *N Y Times Book Rev* 92:13 D 20 '87

English language—*cont.*

Jargon

See Jargon

Prepositions

Feelings of and and if, of and but. D. Donoghue. il *N Y Times Book Rev* 92:10 Ja 25 '87

Pronunciation

Fawn Hall's shredding, ek-setera. W. Safire. il *N Y Times Mag* p8+ Je 21 '87

The world's hardest pronunciation test. S. Morris. il *Omni* 9:124-5 Jl '87

Spelling

See Spelling

Study and teaching

See also
Bread Loaf School of English
English language—Composition
English literature—Study and teaching

Leprous past belief. J. Hart. *Natl Rev* 39:33 D 31 '87

The realities of teaching remedial English in college. R. C. Reynolds. *Educ Dig* 52:58-60 F '87

Japan

See English language in Japan

Terms and phrases

See also
Allusions
Clichés
Jargon
Slogans

Notes & asides [use of unusual words] W. F. Buckley. *Natl Rev* 39:22+ F 13 '87

On language. W. Safire. See issues of The New York Times Magazine

Word watch. A. H. Soukhanov. See issues of The Atlantic beginning January 1987

Wordwise. See issues of National Geographic World beginning August 1987

Usage

Old and novel. G. Jennings. il *N Y Times Mag* p16+ N 29 '87

On language. W. Safire. See issues of The New York Times Magazine

Pigskin English [language of pro football broadcasters] R. MacNeil. il por *Sport Mag* 78:46-7 F '87

English language in Great Britain

History

Classes and the masses in Victorian England. G. Crossick. bibl il *Hist Today* 37:29-35 Mr '87

Estates, degrees and sorts in Tudor and Stuart England. K. Wrightson. bibl f il *Hist Today* 37:17-22 Ja '87

From rank to class: innovation in Georgian England. P. Corfield. bibl il *Hist Today* 37:36-42 F '87

English language in India

Doing the needful. S. R. Weisman. il *N Y Times Mag* p6+ Jl 12 '87

English language in Japan

Struggling with English. *World Press Rev* 34:60 O '87

English language in the United States *See* English language

English literature

Study and teaching

See also
Shakespeare, William, 1564-1616—Study and teaching

Kudos for Emma, thumbs down on Becky [responses of college students to 19th century literature] B. F. Williamson. por *Publ Wkly* 232:159 Jl 24 '87

Leprous past belief. J. Hart. *Natl Rev* 39:33 D 31 '87

English manuscripts *See* Manuscripts, English

English National Opera

London/Glasgow. N. Goodwin. *Opera News* 51:39-40 F 14 '87

London. N. Goodwin. il *Opera News* 51:42-3 Ap 11 '87

English novelists *See* Novelists, English

English painting *See* Painting, English

English people *See* British

English portraits *See* Portraits, English

English pottery *See* Pottery, English

English prints *See* Prints

English Reformation *See* Reformation

English setters

The beauty contest [views of E. Laverack] B. Tarrant. il *Field Stream* 92:102+ Ag '87

English Shakespeare Company

Turned-on Shakespeare. J. Bemrose. il *Macleans* 100:54 Je 1 '87

English sparrows *See* Sparrows

Englund, Robert

about

Hold the cutting words, please, for Robert Englund, the friendly cuss who plays Elm Street's nightmare stalker. J. Yarbrough. il pors *People Wkly* 27:42+ Mr 23 '87

Englund, Steven

Dismissing the third world. *Commonweal* 114:533-6 S 25 '87

Engman, Ronda

The finer points of tool buying. il *Flower Gard* 31:10-12 O/N '87

Engraving

See also
Drypoint
Portrait prints
Wood engraving

Engraving on firearms *See* Firearms—Decoration

Engs, Philip

about

A champagne homecoming. S. Aikenhead. *Macleans* 100:13 F 23 '87

The mullahs reconsider. A. Bilski. il por *Macleans* 100:19 F 16 '87

Engstrom, Theresa

Seven business reasons to turn to telecommunications. il *Work Woman* 12:44+ Ag '87

Turning computer babble into plain English. il pors *Work Woman* 12:61+ My '87

Enhanced states of consciousness *See* Consciousness

ENI *See* Ente Nazionale Idrocarburi

Enid A. Haupt Garden (Washington, D.C.)

A surprising new oasis blossoms at the Smithsonian. J. R. Buckler. bibl (p147) il *Smithsonian* 18:120-4+ Jl '87

Enlargers (Photography) *See* Photography—Enlargers and enlarging

Enlarging lenses *See* Lenses, Photographic

Ennis, Michael

Mexican open house. il *House Gard* 159:130-5+ F '87

Texas formality. il *Archit Dig* 44:170-5 Ap '87

Virtues of nuance. il *Archit Dig* 44:62-9 F '87

Enos, Clive, and Enos, Sondra Forsyth

The private life of the American woman. il *Ladies Home J* 104:98+ Ap '87

Enos, Sondra Forsyth

I can't take one more Christmas with this man! il *Ladies Home J* 104:10+ D '87

A report card for parents. il *Ladies Home J* 104:87-9+ Je '87

(jt. auth) See Enos, Clive, and Enos, Sondra Forsyth

Enough said [ballet] See Ballet reviews—Single works

Enquirer *See* National enquirer

Enrico Fermi Award

DOE bestows Fermi awards on Courant and Livingston. por *Phys Today* 40:83 Je '87

Enright, Joseph F., and Ryan, James W.

The sinking of a supercarrier. il *Wash Mon* 19:13-18 My '87

Enrile, Juan Ponce

about

Putting Corypower to the test. J. Clad. il *World Press Rev* 34:24-6 Ja '87

Enrollment, College *See* Colleges and universities—Enrollment

Enrollment, Medical college *See* Medical colleges—Enrollment

Enrollment, School *See* School enrollment

Enrollment, Theological seminary *See* Theological seminaries—Enrollment

Enron Corp.

Orderly mind in a disorderly market. T. Mack. il por map *Forbes* 140:62+ S 21 '87

A trader runs amok [oil trader L. Borget] T. Mack. por *Forbes* 140:8 N 16 '87

Ensor, R. C. K., 1877-1958

about

Robert Ensor, Edwardian rationalist. P. J. Waller. bibl f il por *Hist Today* 37:49-54 Ja '87

Ente Nazionale Idrocarburi

Business recovery by the book [F. Reviglio] R. I. Kirkland, Jr. il por *Fortune* 116:42 Ag 3 '87

Entertainers

See also
Actors and actresses
Black entertainers
Clowns
Comedians
Vaudeville

Entertainers—*cont.*

Quirky perks of the stars. C. Krupp. il *Glamour* 85:108 Jl '87

Taxation

After tax reform, what? B. Hanlon. il *Theatre Crafts* 21:12 Ja '87

The code is dead! Long live the code! B. Hanlon. il *Theatre Crafts* 21:12+ Mr '87

Entertaining

See also

Balls (Parties)
Birthday parties
Buffet meals
Business entertaining
Caterers and catering
Christmas entertaining
Dinners and dining
Etiquette
Government entertaining
Guests
Hospitality
Luncheons
Table decoration
Table setting
Teas

America entertains. C. Rossant. See issues of McCall's beginning February 1987

Black & white night [teen party] il *Seventeen* 46:158-63+ N '87

Breezing along [easy summer weekend suggestions by D. Boulud] C. Claiborne and P. Franey. il *N Y Times Mag* p43-5 Jl 26 '87

Celebrate with a party. il *South Living* 22:194+ My '87

Celebration cookbook. M. Langan. il *McCalls* 114:115-20+ My '87

Easy and elegant entertaining [summer] J. T. Hazard. il *Ladies Home J* 104:108-12+ Je '87

Entertaining. See issues of Vogue

Five styles of summer. C. Rayner and W. P. Rayner. il *Vogue* 177:226-33 Jl '87

Focus: party! [teenage parties] il *Seventeen* 46:100-1 Je '87

Great new places to have a party (I) [New York City] B. Costikyan. il *N Y* 20:52-66+ F 16 '87

Great new places to have a party (II) [New York City] B. Costikyan. il *N Y* 20:40-57 F 23 '87

Holiday entertaining [cover story] J. Freiman. il *N Y* 20:55-70+ O 26 '87

Instant parties: the take-out advantage. F. Greenberg. il *Work Woman* 12:161-2+ My '87

Make-ahead party menu. il *Better Homes Gard* 65:182-3 N '87

Malcolm Forbes's ultra-bash boasted French fizz and prom queen named Liz. T. Cunneff. il por *People Wkly* 27:97-9 Je 15 '87

Mini golf [theme party given by K. Brown and L. Crafts] *New Yorker* 63:31-2 O 26 '87

New Year's Eve roundup [public celebrations suitable for teenagers] C. Hanauer. il *Seventeen* 46:64-5 D '87

Party disasters: what to do, say, serve when things go wrong [excerpt from The joys of entertaining] B. Church and B. E. Bultman. il *Glamour* 85:58 D '87

Party girls [slumber party] il *Teen* 31:120-1 S '87

Ring in the new: set a festive table [New Year's Eve party] S. Wood. il *McCalls* 114:29+ Ja '87

The rules of the game [entertaining in France] J. Kramer. il *House Gard* 159:86+ O '87

Social grazes [light party treats] M. Fox. il *Health* 19:42-4+ Je '87

Summer entertaining [cover story] J. Freiman. il *N Y* 20:34-52+ My 18 '87

A swellegant party [M. Forbes' bash] K. Ames. il por *Newsweek* 109:57 Je 8 '87

You call this a party? [L. Baldrige's Complete guide to a great social life] J. Adler. il por *Newsweek* 110:90 O 5 '87

Anecdotes, facetiae, satire, etc.

Fear of entertaining. B.-J. Raphael. il *Glamour* 85:124+ D '87

Entertainment and Sports Programming Network

ESPN is finding the sailing smoother [America's Cup coverage] R. W. King. il *Bus Week* p96 F 9 '87

Entertainment industry

See also

MCA Inc.
National Amusements, Inc.
SBK Entertainment World Inc.
Walt Disney Company

Leisure and recreation. A. D. Frank. il *Forbes* 139:158-9 Ja 12 '87

Most of '86. il *Time* 129:74 Ja 5 '87

Shame, shame on the entertainment industry. R. M. Christenson. il *USA Today (Periodical)* 115:92-5 My '87

Acquisitions and mergers

Now Redstone is a media giant [S. Redstone wins Viacom] D. Lieberman and L. Therrien. il por *Bus Week* p42 Mr 16 '87

Collectibles

Joe Franklin's show biz memorabilia. S. Andacht. il por *Antiques Collect Hobbies* 91:78-81 Ja '87

Taxation

The code is dead! Long live the code! B. Hanlon. il *Theatre Crafts* 21:12+ Mr '87

Entertainment Marketing, Inc.

The net drops on Crazy Eddie [E. Zinn's proxy] T. Vogel. il *Bus Week* p62 N 2 '87

Die Entführung aus dem Serail [opera] See Mozart, Wolfgang Amadeus, 1756-1791

Entitlement programs (U.S.) See Economic assistance, Domestic

Entrance halls See Halls

Entrance requirements, College See Colleges and universities—Admission

Entrance walks See Walks (Paths)

Entrances (Doorways) See Doorways

Entranceway landscape architecture See Landscape architecture

Entranceway landscape gardening See Landscape gardening

Entrepreneurs

See also

Aged and business
Black entrepreneurs
Business enterprises
Incubators (Entrepreneurship)
Women entrepreneurs
Youth and business

America's hottest new export [special section] P. Sherrid. il *U S News World Rep* 103:39-41 Jl 27 '87

The best of their class [billionaires] J. Fierman. il por *Fortune* 116:144-5 O 12 '87

Breaking out of the company. J. Main. il *Fortune* 115:82-6+ My 25 '87

Desktop publishing. W. C. Banks. il *Money* 16:119-20+ Jl '87

Enterprise. G. D. Wallace. See issues of Business Week beginning July 27, 1987

The entrepreneurial family and its future [address, December 9, 1986] G. L. Bernstein. *Vital Speeches Day* 53:205-7 Ja 15 '87

Entrepreneurial street smarts. W. Hoffer. il *Nations Bus* 75:62-4 N '87

Entrepreneurs. il *Bus Week* p128-9 Ja 12 '87

Entrepreneurs: a tide is changing. S. Nelton. il *Nations Bus* 75:28 Ja '87

Entrepreneurs are cashing in while the price is right. K. R. Sheets. *U S News World Rep* 102:42 Je 22 '87

Europe's new entrepreneurs. R. I. Kirkland, Jr. il *Fortune* 115:253+ Ap 27 '87

How to start your own business (I) [New York City; cover story] S. M. Pollan and M. Levine. il *N Y* 20:28-37 Je 8 '87

How to start your own business (II) [New York City] S. M. Pollan and M. Levine. il *N Y* 20:44-8+ Je 15 '87

Italy's daredevil entrepreneurs. P. C. Newman. il *Macleans* 100:40 N 9 '87

Keeping up in the fast lane. N. L. Croft. il *Nations Bus* 75:24-6 Jl '87

Leaving the corporate nest. H. Bacas. il *Nations Bus* 75:14-16+ Mr '87

Losing the future to the past [effects of information revolution on entrepreneurism] M. Pastin. il por *Nations Bus* 75:4 F '87

Making it. See issues of Nation's Business beginning September 1985

My partner, my spouse. D. Machan. il *Forbes* 140:240+ D 14 '87

A 'New Age' look at business [interview with P. Hawken] P. Dworkin. por *U S News World Rep* 103:51 N 30 '87

On their own: the self-employed and others in private business. S. E. Haber and others. bibl f il *Mon Labor Rev* 110:17-23 My '87

Silicon Valley phoenixes. C. Barron. il *Fortune* 116:128-9+ N 23 '87

Some guys have all the luck: how to do for a living what you do for love. il *Esquire* 107:104-7 Je '87

Entrepreneurs—*cont.*

Start-up help for your business. R. R. Roha. il *Changing Times* 41:73-4+ Je '87

Starting up a business in 1988: a postcrash course. J. Rachlin. il *U S News World Rep* 103:70-2 D 21 '87

The tiny starts of titans [corporate founders] W. S. Wingo. il *Nations Bus* 75:38-9 Ja '87

Unleashed [immigrants] S. Blotnick. il *Forbes* 139:108 Ja 26 '87

The up & comers. See issues of Forbes

Winning your own game [cover story] R. Thompson. il *Nations Bus* 75:16-17+ Jl '87

The year of living dangerously [first year for start-ups] D. Harris. il *Money* 16:162-6 F '87

You don't have to be a young upstart to run a startup. il *Bus Week* p114-15 · Jl 20 '87

Entropy

Alas, entropy too is in the eye of the beholder. T. Rothman. il *Discover* 8:76-7 F '87

Demons, engines and the second law. C. H. Bennett. bibl (p150-1) il *Sci Am* 257:108-16 N '87

Entryway bridges *See* Bridges, Foot

Entryway walks *See* Walks (Paths)

Envelopes (Philately) *See* Covers (Philately)

Envirodyne Industries, Inc.

Envirodyne ain't glamorous—but oh, how it grows. J. M. Laderman. *Bus Week* p100 Ap 27 '87

Environment

  See also

  Adaptation (Biology)
  Air bases—Environmental aspects
  All terrain vehicles—Environmental aspects
  Automobiles—Environmental aspects
  Blacks and the environment
  Children and the environment
  Computers—Environmental use
  Ecology
  Electric lines—Environmental aspects
  Electromagnetic pulse simulators—Environmental aspects
  Express highways—Environmental aspects
  Filling (Earthwork)—Environmental aspects
  Gas pipelines—Environmental aspects
  Genetic research—Environmental aspects
  Golf courses—Environmental aspects
  Greenbelts
  Heredity and environment
  Human ecology
  Industry and the environment
  Man—Influence of environment
  Man—Influence on nature
  Military and the environment
  Minorities and the environment
  Nuclear energy—Environmental aspects
  Nuclear warfare—Environmental aspects
  Pest control services—Environmental aspects
  Pesticides—Environmental aspects
  Radio towers—Environmental aspects
  Religion and the environment
  Stadiums—Environmental aspects
  Television and the environment
  Tourist trade—Environmental aspects
  World Commission on Environment and Development

The environment. B. Commoner. *New Yorker* 63:46-7+ Je 15 '87

A portrait of our environmental quality. il *Curr Health 2* 13:16-18 My '87

Worldly healers. C. A. Douglis. il *Omni* 9:18+ Mr '87

  Bibliography

Books of note. See issues of Environment

  Conferences

  See also

  United Nations Conference on the Human Environment

Another country, another world [journalists discuss tourism, ecology, and development in Yugoslavia] P. C. Pritchard. *Natl Parks* 61:5 S/O '87

  Economic aspects

Attaining a sustainable future. W. M. Bueler. il *USA Today (Periodical)* 115:34-7 My '87

Chlorofluorocarbons and the ozone layer. J. P. Cohn. *BioScience* 37:647-50 O '87

Now (I think) I understand the ecologists better. J. Simon. il por *Futurist* 21:18-19 S/O '87

Paying the piper. G. Reiger. *Field Stream* 92:15-16+ My '87

Report on reports: Sustainable development of the biosphere. G. R. Conway. *Environment* 29:25-7 N '87

Scholarship for sustainable development. W. C. Clark. *Environment* 29:inside cover Ap '87

  Laws and regulations

  See Environmental policy

  Periodicals

  See also

  High country news
  Sierra (Periodical)

  Research

  See Environmental research

  Statistics

19th Environmental Quality Index: a nation troubled by toxics. il *Natl Wildl* 25:33-40 F/Mr '87

  Study and teaching

  See Environmental education

  Developing countries

Trouble in the third world's environment. M. Westlake. *World Press Rev* 34:53 Jl '87

  Madagascar

Madagascar: a world apart. A. Jolly. il maps *Natl Geogr* 171:148-83 F '87

  Nepal

A question of balance [life in Phalabang] D. Zurick. il *Sierra* 72:46-50 Jl/Ag '87

  Washington (State)

New life under the volcano [Mount St. Helens] P. A. Witteman. il *Time* 129:63 Je 15 '87

Replanting Mt. St. Helens. S. Kaveski. il *Technol Rev* 90:14-15 Ag/S '87

Environment (Art)

Beyond the image [Boyle Family exhibit in London] W. Feaver. il *Art News* 86:99+ Ja '87

Dream space [J. Turrell's new site installation at P.S. 1 and observatory at Roden Crater] S. Gablik. il *Art Am* 75:132-3+ Mr '87

A forest grows in Manhattan [A. Sonfist's Time Landscape] P. Hagan. il *Sierra* 72:16+ Mr/Ap '87

A man and his bridge [K. Farris' McKee Street Bridge Park, Houston] K. Gregor. il por *Art News* 86:11 Ap '87

Roden's eye [J. Turrell's Roden Crater] F. Hapgood. il por *Atlantic* 260:46-52 Ag '87

Walking into art [work of R. Long] J. Johnston. il map *Art Am* 75:160-9 Ap '87

Environment (Human) *See* Human ecology

Environment and state *See* Environmental policy

Environment Canada *See* Canada. Environment Canada

Environment in literature

Siberian writer Valentin Rasputin fears for the planet's fate. S. K. Reed. il pors *People Wkly* 27:127-8 Ap 6 '87

Environment software *See* Computer programming

Environmental allergy *See* Allergy

Environmental associations

  See also

  Anti-nuclear movement
  Audubon societies
  Bat Conservation International
  Citizen's Clearinghouse for Hazardous Wastes, Inc.
  Earth First! (Organization)
  Environmental Task Force
  Friends of the River (Organization)
  Greenpeace Foundation
  Indonesian Environmental Forum
  International Union for Conservation of Nature and Natural Resources
  International Wildlife Coalition
  National Audubon Society
  National Coalition Against the Misuse of Pesticides
  National Parks and Conservation Association
  National Wildlife Federation
  Natural Resources Defense Council
  Nature Conservancy (U.S.)
  North American Blue-Bird Society
  Oceanic Society
  Sierra Club
  Trust for Public Land (U.S.)
  Wilderness Society
  World Wildlife Fund

The growth in environmental organization memberships. il *Environment* 29:35 Jl/Ag '87

Environmental auditing

New test for clean practice. J. I. Mattill. il *Technol Rev* 90:12-13 F/Mr '87

Environmental camps *See* Camps

Environmental Conservation Dept. (N.Y.) *See* New York (State). Dept. of Environmental Conservation

Environmental design

  See also

  City planning
  Space (Architecture)

Environmental design—*cont.*
Designing to deter crime. E. Krupat and P. E. Kubzansky. bibl (p62) il *Psychol Today* 21:58-61 O '87
Environmental education
See also
Forestry education
Garden as teacher [regeneration lessons] R. Rodale. il *Rodale's Org Gard* 34:23-4 D '87
Our classroom is the whole outdoors [conservation program at Community College of the Finger Lakes] C. White. il *Conservationist* 41:42-7 My/Je '87
Population biology, conservation biology, and the future of humanity [address, August 10, 1987] P. R. Ehrlich. *BioScience* 37:757-63 N '87
Environmental engineering
See also
Environmental auditing
Environmental impact statements
Terraforming
Environmental engineering (Buildings)
See also
Solar houses
Climate as context [Bay Island Hotel, Port Blair, India] M. F. Schmertz. il *Archit Rec* 175:114-19 Ag '87
An envelope of air around this house keeps it cool in summer, warm in winter. il *Sunset* 178:94-6 F '87
House with vision [the Avalon House designed by Kevin Jeffrey] R. Barnhart. il *Home Mech* 83:74-5 Ag '87
The new regional classics: updated for energy efficiency [houses] D. Freedman and B. A. Lewis. il *Better Homes Gard* 65:33-41 S '87
Saving energy. R. D. Roslansky. il *Nations Bus* 75:40 Ja '87
Environmental health
See also
Allergy
Occupational health and safety
United States. Occupational Safety and Health Administration
City vs. rural environment: which is healthier? L. L. Guidry. il *Curr Health 2* 14:24-5 S '87
Environmental hazards [pregnancy] P. A. Hillard. il *Parents* 62:140+ F '87
Find your hot spots of health. R. Rodale. il *Prevention* 39:20-1 N '87
Health hoax and a health scare [address, September 22, 1987] E. M. Whelan. il *Vital Speeches Day* 54:57-61 N 1 '87
Our bodies, our world: how the environment affects health [special section] il *Vogue* 177:402-7+ O '87
Transboundary pollution and environmental health [Canadian perspective; cover story] E. Somers. il *Environment* 29:6-9+ Je '87
Environmental impact statements
See also
Environmental auditing
Painting the future [visual impact analysis used to chart changes in Sweden's landscape] il *Courier* 40:18-19 O '87
Environmental impairment liability insurance *See* Insurance, Pollution liability
Environmental indexes *See* Environment—Statistics
Environmental law *See* Environmental policy
Environmental lobby *See* Environmental movement
Environmental mediation
Oil and fishing industries negotiate: mediation and scientific issues [conflicts arising off California coast] G. W. Cormick and A. Knaster. bibl il *Environment* 28:6-15+ D '86
Environmental mitigation
Mitigation isn't. P. Steinhart. il *Audubon* 89:8+ My '87
Environmental movement
See also
Anti-nuclear movement
Bioregionalism
Blacks and the environment
Cleaning of lakes, rivers, etc.
Ecofeminism
Environmental associations
Industry and the environment
Minorities and the environment
Religion and the environment
19th Environmental Quality Index: a nation troubled by toxics. il *Natl Wildl* 25:33-40 F/Mr '87
Ecotimidity. T. Turner. il *Mother Earth News* 105:20 My/Je '87
The freedom to be free. J. D. Hair. il *Natl Wildl* 26:30 D '87/Ja '88
The new environmentalists. J. Kaplan. *Vogue* 177:403-4+ O '87

People who make a difference. il *Natl Wildl* 25:4-13 Ap/My '87
A portrait of our environmental quality. il *Curr Health 2* 13:16-18 My '87
History
Courage of Rachel Carson [excerpt from Two Park Street] P. Brooks. il por *Audubon* 89:12+ Ja '87
How Leopold learned to think like a mountain. C. Meine. *Wilderness* 51:57-8+ Wint '87
A man called Bird [G. B. Grinnell] J. G. Mitchell. il pors map *Audubon* 89:81-104 Mr '87
The natural magic of Olaus Murie. J. Glover and R. Glover. il pors *Sierra* 72:69-73 S/O '87
Sand County's conservation prophet [A. Leopold] D. R. Wallace. il pors *Sierra* 72:62-7 N/D '87
Typewritten on both sides: the conservation career of Wallace Stegner. T. H. Watkins. il por *Audubon* 89:88-90+ S '87
International aspects
See also
World Environment Day
Alberta
A reservoir of concerns [controversy over proposed Old-man River dam] M. Nemeth. il *Macleans* 100:8 D 21 '87
Brazil
Saving the whales—and the turtles. il *World Press Rev* 34:54-5 Ap '87
British Columbia
The South Moresby war [Haida Indians protest logging on Queen Charlotte Islands] M. Gee. il *Macleans* 100:12 Jl 6 '87
California
Along the Mattole, helping hands heal the watershed. il *Sierra* 72:62-3 Mr/Ap '87
Respecting the law [environmental protest against Louisiana-Pacific in California] P. Steinhart. il *Audubon* 89:10+ N '87
Illinois
Of dumps, Chicago politics & herons [environmentalists fight to save wetlands threatened by landfill] J. Sullivan. il *Audubon* 89:122-6 Mr '87
India
A hope for the Himalayas and its people. il *Environment* 29:10-11 Ap '87
Indonesia
See also
Indonesian Environmental Forum
Minnesota
Old adversaries guard the woods [protest against proposed Minnesota National Guard training facility] M. Helmberger. il *Sierra* 72:81-2 Mr/Ap '87
Strategic Air Command bombs out [residents block low-altitude bomber training flights] M. Helmberger. il *Progressive* 51:11-12 Ag '87
Mississippi
The Army's giant swampbuster [proposed draining of Yazoo Backwater Swamp] J. McCafferty. il *Sierra* 72:84-5 Jl/Ag '87
North Dakota
Citizens douse a hazardous burn [plan to incinerate PCBs at University of North Dakota's Energy Research Center] J. Hamilton. il *Sierra* 72:88-9 N/D '87
Philippines
One for the spirits [defeat of Chico River Dam project by tribal peoples] C. Fay. il *Sierra* 72:22-4 Mr/Ap '87
South Dakota
See also
Cowboy and Indian Alliance
Taiwan
A grassroots rebuff for Du Pont [proposed plant near Lukang] J. Hamilton. il *Sierra* 72:68-9 My/Je '87
United States
See Environmental movement
Environmental news
Afield. See issues of Sierra beginning March/April 1986
Another country, another world [journalists discuss tourism, ecology, and development in Yugoslavia] P. C. Pritchard. *Natl Parks* 61:5 S/O '87
Gallery. See issues of National Parks beginning March/April 1987
The latest word. See issues of National Parks
The longer view. P. Steinhart. il *Audubon* 89:10+ Mr '87
Lowering the gloom. S. F. Singer. por *Newsweek* 110:12 S 14 '87
News update. See issues of National Parks beginning March/April 1984

Environmental news—*cont.*

Reporting on radon: the role of local newspapers [Pennsylvania] S. M. Friedman and others. *Environment* 29:4-5+ Mr '87

Spectrum. See issues of Environment beginning January/February 1987

Wildlife digest. See issues of International Wildlife

Environmental policy

See also

Acid rain—Laws and regulations
Air pollution—Laws and regulations
Conservation of resources—Laws and regulations
Environmental auditing
Environmental impact statements
Environmental mediation
Environmental mitigation
Genetic research—Environmental aspects
Industry and the environment
Land utilization—Laws and regulations
Man—Influence on nature
Marine resources—Laws and regulations
Military and the environment
Minorities and the environment
Pollution
Proving grounds—Environmental aspects
Radioactive waste disposal—Laws and regulations
Shore protection—Laws and regulations
Soil pollution—Laws and regulations
Strip mining—Laws and regulations
Trade waste—Disposal—Laws and regulations
United States. Dept. of the Interior
United States. Environmental Protection Agency
Water pollution—Laws and regulations
Wilderness areas

The 99th Congress: action on the environment. R. Livernash. *Environment* 28:5+ D '86

America's issue [Reagan record] *New Repub* 196:7-9 Ja 26 '87

Biological diversity and public policy [Office of Technology Assessment report] S. Shen. il *BioScience* 37:709-12 N '87

Earth diary: Justice Rehnquist and the land. T. Turner. il *Mother Earth News* 103:112+ Ja/F '87

The environment gets a break as well [effects of closing capital gains loopholes] il *Discover* 8:13 My '87

The environment wins in most state polls. *Environment* 28:22-4 D '86

Environmental protection for the 1990s and beyond. M. Russell. bibl f *Environment* 29:12-15+ S '87

The great outdoors. J. Walter. See issues of Successful Farming beginning February 1987

Law. See occasional issues of Environment

Policies on global warming and ozone depletion. B. Green. *Environment* 29:5+ Ap '87

Polls, pollution, and politics revisited: public opinion on the environment in the Reagan era [cover story; with editorial comment by Gilbert F. White] R. E. Dunlap. bibl f il *Environment* 29:6-11+ Jl/Ag '87

Public opinion on the environment [discussion of July/August 1987 article, Polls, pollution and politics revisited] R. E. Dunlap. il *Environment* 29:2-3 N '87

Report urges funds for conservation biology [report by the Office of Technology Assessment] R. Lewin. il *Science* 236:257-9 Ap 17 '87

Respecting the law. P. Steinhart. il *Audubon* 89:10+ N '87

Scorecard [99th Congress record on environmental issues] *Sierra* 72:16-17 Ja/F '87

Social traps and environmental policy. R. Costanza. bibl f il *BioScience* 37:407-12 Je '87

Tax reform as environmental policy. B. Blackwelder and D. Campbell. *Sierra* 72:33-6 Mr/Ap '87

Voting on the environment. D. D. Schmidt. il *Technol Rev* 90:15-16 Ag/S '87

"We the people . . . " [proposed Environmental Quality Amendment; excerpts from address, March 1987] J. D. Hair. il *Natl Wildl* 25:25-6 Je/Jl '87

Citizen participation

Citizen enforcement of environmental laws. N. S. Marks. bibl f *Environment* 29:5+ Je '87

International aspects

See also

Man and the Biosphere Programme
United Nations Environment Programme

The 1987 State of the world describes a planet crossing thresholds. A global science effort will look for some answers. J. P. Wiley, Jr. il *Smithsonian* 18:28+ Ap '87

The environmental agenda and foreign policy [addresses, April 16, 1987] J. Negroponte; R. E. Benedick. *Dep State Bull* 87:52-5 Jl '87

Inexorable laws and the ecosystem. D. E. Koshland, Jr. *Science* 237:9 Jl 3 '87

Life, the great chemistry experiment [State of the earth 1987] S. Postel. il *Nat Hist* 96:41-8 Ap '87

Report on reports: Our common future. I. Burton. bibl f *Environment* 29:25-9 Je '87

Report on reports: Sustainable development of the biosphere. G. R. Conway. *Environment* 29:25-7 N '87

Scholarship for sustainable development. W. C. Clark. *Environment* 29:inside cover Ap '87

Thresholds of change. L. R. Brown and S. Postel. il pors *Futurist* 21:9-14 S/O '87

U.S.-Mexico Binational Commission meets [remarks, January 29, 1987] G. P. Shultz; B. Sepulveda Amor. il *Dep State Bull* 87:54-6 Ap '87

What a few can do for the environment [State of the world 1987] *Sci News* 131:153 Mr 7 '87

Brazil

Tightening up on third world loans [tying loans to environmental policy] J. De Onis. il *U S News World Rep* 103:41 O 5 '87

California

California's debate on carcinogens [Proposition 65] E. Marshall. *Science* 235:1459 Mr 20 '87

California's Proposition 65 [Safe Drinking Water and Toxic Enforcement Act] P. H. Abelson. *Science* 237:1553 S 25 '87

The long fight for Kings Canyon [proposed Rodgers Crossing dam site] P. Carr and K. Glass. il maps *Sierra* 72:38-44 Ja/F '87

Waste dump wanted [desirability of low level dumps] il *Time* 130:70 Jl 20 '87

Canada

See also

Canada. Environment Canada

Caribbean region

Developing islands. il *Futurist* 21:51-2 Jl/Ag '87

China

Environmental policy in post-Mao China [cover story] L. Ross. bibl f il map *Environment* 29:12-17+ My '87

How China views its resources. J. D. Hair. il *Int Wildl* 17:26 N/D '87

Colorado

A city says no to canyon dams [North St. Vrain Creek] T. Turner. il *Sierra* 72:133-5 Ja/F '87

Developing countries

All in the name of aid. P. Adams. il *Sierra* 72:45-50 Ja/F '87

Bank balance: economy and ecology. *Sci News* 132:238 O 10 '87

Banks should be part of the solution [multilateral development banks and the environment] J. D. Hair. il *Int Wildl* 17:30 Mr/Ap '87

Changes underway at the World Bank. L. Hannah. *BioScience* 37:186 Mr '87

Eco-bucks: going for the purse strings. *Sci News* 132:137 Ag 29 '87

A new international lending environment [adoption of guidelines by the World Bank] il *Discover* 8:10+ F '87

A turning point for environmentally sound development [World Bank initiatives] L. Hannah. *BioScience* 37:464 Jl/Ag '87

The World Bank and the environment. D. A. Wirth. bibl *Environment* 28:33-4 D '86

World Bank launches new environment policy. C. Holden. il *Science* 236:769 My 15 '87

Europe

In harmony with nature [Alps] L. Lienert. il map *Courier* 40:4-8 F '87

When men and mountains meet [Alps] J. Schaller. il map *Courier* 40:9-10 F '87

Florida

Consensus on the 'Glades. *Wilderness* 50:3 Spr '87

The "sewer ditch" undone [dismantling the Kissimmee River channel] F. Graham. il maps *Audubon* 89:114-15 Mr '87

Germany (West)

'Green death' in the Alps. E. Brunner. *World Press Rev* 34:53 D '87

India

Assessing development costs in India [cover story] R. Sharma. bibl f il *Environment* 29:6-11+ Ap '87

Lake Tahoe region (Calif. and Nev.)

Battle-weary Lake Tahoe combatants try compromise. J. Stuller. il *Audubon* 89:44-6+ My '87

Environmental policy—*cont.*
Louisiana
Atchafalaya [Army Corps of Engineers' Old River Control operation] J. A. McPhee. *New Yorker* 63:39-44+ F 23 '87
New Jersey
New Jersey's Bhopal bill [Toxic Catastrophe Prevention Act] *Environment* 29:30 Jl/Ag '87
New York (State)
See also
New York (State). Dept. of Environmental Conservation
Pacific Islands (Trust territory)
Developing islands. il *Futurist* 21:51-2 Jl/Ag '87
Soviet Union
The bear's view: Soviet environmentalism. C. E. Ziegler. il *Technol Rev* 90:44-51 Ap '87
Glasnost and the Soviet environment. D. Dickson. *Science* 236:1180 Je 5 '87
Sweden
Painting the future [visual impact analysis used to chart changes in Sweden's landscape] il *Courier* 40:18-19 O '87
United States
See Environmental policy
Environmental pollution *See* Pollution
Environmental portrait photography *See* Photography—Portraits
Environmental Protection Agency (U.S.) *See* United States. Environmental Protection Agency
Environmental psychology
See also
Color—Psychology
Weather—Mental and physiological effects
Environmental regulations *See* Environmental policy
Environmental research
Expanding adaptive management principles [discussion of November 1986 article, The place of science in environmental problem solving] G. H. Orians. *Environment* 29:3-4 Ja/F '87
R&D eroding at EPA. M. Crawford. il *Science* 236:904-5 My 22 '87
International aspects
National security and the environment. W. C. Clark. bibl *Environment* 29:inside cover+ Je '87
Environmental Task Force
Environmental Task Force. J. Pierce. *Environment* 28:3-4 D '86
Environmentalists *See* Ecologists
Envy
See also
Jealousy
Envy: how green are my values? D. Curran. il *U S Cathol* 52:6-7 Ag '87
Envy: the enemy you should befriend. W. White. il *Teen* 31:62+ My '87
How to understand and handle jealousy and envy. il *Glamour* 85:99 My '87
The root of all envy is a painful comparison, but it can be useful. B. L. Stern. *Vogue* 177:450 N '87
Anecdotes, facetiae, satire, etc.
Envy (Freud had it all wrong). K. Fury. il *Work Woman* 12:160 Mr '87
Enzon, Inc.
Camouflaged drugs make Enzon stand out. M. Bluestone. il *Bus Week* p115-16 Ap 27 '87
Enzyme inhibitors *See* Enzymes—Inactivation
Enzymes
See also
Adenosine triphosphatase
Elastase
Esterases
Galactosidases
Hydrolases
Invertase
Isomerases
Kinases
Lactamases
Lipases
Luciferase
Neuraminidase
Nucleases
Oxidases
Papain
Peptidases
Phosphatases
Phosphorylases
Plasminogen
Proteases
Ribonucleases
Superoxide dismutase

Synthases
Synthetases
Transcriptases
Transferases
Trypsin
CDC25: a component of the RAS-adenylate cyclase pathway in Saccharomyces cerevisiae. L. C. Robinson and others. bibl f il *Science* 235:1218-21 Mr 6 '87
Coexistence of guanylate cyclase and atrial natriuretic factor receptor in a 180-kD protein. A. K. Paul and others. bibl f il *Science* 235:1224-6 Mr 6 '87
Double-duty proteins [research by Graeme Wistow and Joram Piatigorsky] *Sci News* 131:409 Je 27 '87
Engineering enzyme specificity by "substrate-assisted catalysis". P. Carter and J. A. Wells. bibl f il *Science* 237:394-9 Ja 24 '87
An M2 muscarinic receptor subtype coupled to both adenylyl cyclase and phosphoinositide turnover. A. Ashkenazi and others. bibl f il *Science* 238:672-5 O 30 '87
New drugs with that enzymatic touch. D. D. Edwards. *Sci News* 131:407-8 Je 27 '87
Recruitment of enzymes as lens structural proteins. G. Wistow and J. Piatigorsky. bibl f il *Science* 236:1554-6 Je 19 '87
Tinkering with enzymes: what are we learning? J. R. Knowles. bibl f il *Science* 236:1252-8 Je 5 '87
Inactivation
Enzyme blockers slay AIDS 'giants' [castanospermine and dNM] D. D. Edwards. *Sci News* 132:294 N 7 '87
Similarity of cruzin, an inhibitor of Trypanosoma cruzi neuraminidase, to high-density lipoprotein. R. P. Prioli and others. bibl f il *Science* 238:1417-19 D 4 '87
Therapeutic use
See also
Streptokinase
Camouflaged drugs make Enzon stand out [coating enzymes with polyethylene glycol] M. Bluestone. il *Bus Week* p115-16 Ap 27 '87
Enzymes, Fungal
Many random sequences functionally replace the secretion signal sequence of yeast invertase. C. A. Kaiser and others. bibl f il *Science* 235:312-17 Ja 16 '87
Yeast KEX2 protease has the properties of a human proalbumin converting enzyme. I. C. Bathurst and others. bibl f il *Science* 235:348-50 Ja 16 '87
Eocene period *See* Paleontology—Eocene
Eosat (Firm)
Congress to provide $62.5 million for Landsat follow-on program, pending compromise with administration. T. M. Foley. *Aviat Week Space Technol* 127:29-30 Jl 6 '87
Eosat to mount challenge to Landsat restrictions [use by news media] *Aviat Week Space Technol* 127:26-7 N 2 '87
Eosat will market Landsat data from Chinese ground stations. il *Aviat Week Space Technol* 127:52-3 Jl 20 '87
Landsat commercialization stumbles again. M. M. Waldrop. *Science* 235:155 Ja 9 '87
New Landsat plans could terminate Eosat contract. *Aviat Week Space Technol* 127:139-40 S 28 '87
Eosinophils *See* Leukocytes
EPA *See* United States. Environmental Protection Agency
EPCOT (Fla.)
Ride through the human body [new Body Wars attraction] il *Pop Mech* 164:53 D '87
Ephron, Amy
about
Nora Ephron's kid sister Amy proves to be a scribbler too. il pors *People Wkly* 27:83 My 4 '87
Ephron, Nora
Etheleen Grossberg takes stock [story] il *Esquire* 108:215-16 N '87
Insider trading [story] il *Esquire* 108:94-5 Jl '87
Landscaping [story] il *Esquire* 107:102-4 Ap '87
Ms. Grossberg's legs [story] il *Esquire* 108:225-6+ S '87
Parallel play [story] il *Esquire* 107:110-11 My '87
Revision and life: take it from the top—again. *Writer* 100:7-8 Ap '87
Taking the road not taken [story] il *Esquire* 108:197-9 O '87
Epic poetry, Greek
The heroic women of Greek epic. M. R. Lefkowitz. *Am Sch* 56:503-18 Aut '87
Epicondylitis
Tennis elbow rounds the bend [devices that attempt to alleviate pain] N. Amdur. il *World Tennis* 35:18-19 Ag '87

Epidemics
    See also
    AIDS (Disease)
    Influenza
    Syphilis
         History
Killer illnesses of history. S. Wells. il *U S News World Rep* 102:69 Ja 12 '87
Unlike AIDS, says a historian, ancient plagues swept the world scythelike and suddenly [interview with W. McNeill] G. Breu. il por *People Wkly* 28:123-4+ O 12 '87
Will AIDS make the Black Death look pale? il *Discover* 8:4 Ap '87
Epidemiology
    See also
    Centers for Disease Control (U.S.)
The risks of risk studies. E. R. Shell. il *Atlantic* 260:114-15 N '87
Epidermal growth factor
Beyond the Band-Aid. G. Bronson. il *Forbes* 139:160-1 Je 1 '87
Construction of a novel oncogene based on synthetic sequences encoding epidermal growth factor. D. F. Stern and others. bibl f il *Science* 235:321-4 Ja 16 '87
The heart & mind of a genius [R. Levi-Montalcini] F. Randall. il por *Vogue* 177:480-1+ Mr '87
A sea urchin gene encodes a polypeptide homologous to epidermal growth factor. D. A. Hursh and others. bibl f il *Science* 237:1487-90 S 18 '87
Trophic stimulation of cultured neurons from neonatal rat brain by epidermal growth factor. R. S. Morrison and others. bibl f il *Science* 238:72-5 O 2 '87
Epidermal growth factor receptors *See* Hormone receptors
Epidermis *See* Skin
Epikeratophakia *See* Cornea—Surgery
Epilepsy
Braving epilepsy's storm. K. Eichenwald. il *N Y Times Mag* p30-3+ Ja 11 '87
Cellular mechanisms of epilepsy: a status report. M. A. Dichter and G. F. Ayala. bibl f il *Science* 237:157-64 Jl 10 '87
Decreased hippocampal inhibition and a selective loss of interneurons in experimental epilepsy. R. Sloviter. bibl f il *Science* 235:73-6 Ja 2 '87
Epilepsy hypothesis [discussion of January 2, 1987 article, Decreased hippocampal inhibition and a selective loss of interneurons in experimental epilepsy] R. Sloviter. bibl f *Science* 238:1292-3 N 27 '87
Magnetoencephalography and epilepsy research. D. F. Rose and others. bibl f il *Science* 238:329-35 O 16 '87
         Therapy
Cytochrome P-450-catalyzed formation of Δ^4-VPA, a toxic metabolite of valproic acid. A. E. Rettie and others. bibl f il *Science* 235:890-3 F 20 '87
New drug controls seizures [McN-4853] *USA Today (Periodical)* 115:8-9 F '87
Epiphany
Universal manifestation. P. J. Ryan. *America* 157:511 D 26 '87
Epiphytes *See* Air plants
EPIRB (Emergency Position Indicating Radio Beacon) *See* Radio beacons
Episcopal Church
    See also
    Catholic Church—Relations—Episcopal Church
         United States
Admen for heaven [Episcopal Ad Project] D. Neff. il pors *Christ Today* 31:12-13 S 18 '87
A battle over sexual morals. J. Duin. il *Christ Today* 31:46-7 Ap 3 '87
Dogs in the manger [Dean J. P. Morton's Theology of the earth at Saint John the Divine, New York City] D. K. Mano. *Natl Rev* 39:65-6 Ja 30 '87
Episcopal 'gentlemen's club' now open? [women bishops] J. C. Lyles. *Christ Century* 104:909-10 O 21 '87
Happy hour at Mr. C's [Episcopal pastor S. Boehmig brings his band into Pittsburgh clubs] R. Frame. il por *Christ Today* 31:12-13 O 16 '87
Renewal leaders issue a call to biblical morality. A. Hibbard. il *Christ Today* 31:42+ Je 12 '87
Epistles of Paul *See* Bible. N.T. Epistles of Paul
Epitaphs
An epitaph for Mr. Lincoln [inscription on the Lincoln Memorial by R. Cortissoz] H. W. Morgan. il por *Am Herit* 38:58-63 F/Mr '87

Epithelium
Absence of significant cellular dilution during ADH-stimulated water reabsorption. K. Strange and K. R. Spring. bibl f il *Science* 235:1068-70 F 27 '87
Eosinophils cocultured with endothelial cells have increased survival and functional properties. M. E. Rothenberg and others. bibl f il *Science* 237:645-7 Ag 7 '87
The regulation of natural anticoagulant pathways [protein C] C. T. Esmon. bibl f il *Science* 235:1348-52 Mr 13 '87
EPLF *See* Eritrean People's Liberation Front
EPO *See* Erythropoietin
Epoxy compounds
    See also
    Wood epoxy compounds
Epp, Jake
         about
The new day care policy. M. Clark. il por *Macleans* 100:14+ D 14 '87
Eppenbach, Sarah
Alaska in the rough: the frontier spirit of Wrangell. il maps *Travel Holiday* 167:40-5+ Je '87
Artists prefer Haines. il map *Travel Holiday* 168:48-53 D '87
Eppinger, Josh
Pitcher perfect. il por *50 Plus* 27:56-7+ Ag '87
Epps, Garrett
The discreet charms of a demogogue. bibl f il *N Y Rev Books* 34:31-5 My 7 '87
Epstein, Connie C.
Lives of the rich and famous. il *Parents* 62:71-3+ Ap '87
Looking harder at the backlist. il *Publ Wkly* 232:119-21 Jl 24 '87
Epstein, Daniel Mark
The banner yet waves [condensed from Star of wonder] il *Read Dig* 131:114-16 Jl '87
Epstein, Joseph
A boy's own author. *Commentary* 84:50-6 D '87
The gentle art of the resounding put-down. *Am Sch* 56:311-18 Summ '87
Señor Borges's portico. *Commentary* 83:55-62 Ap '87
Sid, you made the prose too thin. *Commentary* 84:53-60 S '87
Student evaluation. *Am Sch* 56:177-84 Spr '87
You probably don't know me. *Am Sch* 56:463-70 Aut '87
Epstein, Richard Allen, 1943-
Affirmative reaction. *New Repub* 197:17-19 O 12 '87
Epstein, William, 1912-
New stance tarnishes Canada's reputation. il *Bull At Sci* 43:11-12 O '87
Nuclear testing: illusion and reality. *Bull At Sci* 43:8 Ap '87
Epstein-Barr virus
Chinese folk remedy may promote cancer [plants containing phorbal esters linked to nasopharyngeal cancer; research by L. David Tomei and others] R. Weiss. *Sci News* 132:148 S 5 '87
The Epstein-Barr virus: beyond mono. I. A. Oppenheim. il *Curr Health 2* 13:18-19 Ja '87
Journey into fear: the growing nightmare of Epstein-Barr virus (I). H. Johnson. il *Roll Stone* p56-8+ Jl 16-30 '87
Journey into fear: the growing nightmare of Epstein-Barr virus (II). H. Johnson. il *Roll Stone* p42-4+ Ag 13 '87
Medicine: the new enigma. E. Switzer. il *Vogue* 177:220+ N '87
Stealthy epidemic of exhaustion [fatigue syndrome sufferers] D. Thompson. il *Time* 129:52 Je 29 '87
The yuppie disease: Epstein-Barr. il *Glamour* 85:414 S '87
Yuppie plague. R. Bazell. *New Repub* 196:13-14 Ap 27 '87
Equal Access to Justice Act *See* Small business—Laws and regulations
Equal Employment Opportunity Commission (U.S.) *See* United States. Equal Employment Opportunity Commission
Equal pay for equal work
Pay discrimination against women settled [San Francisco, Tennessee Valley Authority and Sumitomo Corp. of America cases] *Mon Labor Rev* 110:56 Je '87
Pay pap [views of G. Bush] D. Seligman. *Fortune* 116:165 N 9 '87
Pulling for pay equity. L. Bethel. *Black Enterp* 17:100+ F '87
Your Constitution: equal pay for similar work? D. Pawelek. *Sch Update* 119:11 My 18 '87

Equal pay for equal work—*cont.*
Canada
Legislating fair wages [Ontario's controversial new pay equity legislation] A. Walmsley. il *Macleans* 100:31-2 Jl 20 '87
Equal protection of the law *See* Equality before the law
Equal Rights Amendment (Proposed) *See* United States. Constitution. Equal Rights Amendment (Proposed)
Equal rights for women *See* Women—Equal rights
Equal Time Doctrine *See* Fairness Doctrine (Broadcasting)
Equality
> *See also*
> Democracy
> Educational equalization
Equality before the law
The Constitution and the 14th Amendment [with discussion] W. F. Murphy. il por *Cent Mag* 20:9-30 Jl/Ag '87
Equality before the law: the Civil War amendments [cover story; with discussion] H. Belz. il por *Cent Mag* 20:4-19 N/D '87
Maximizing access to justice [address, February 12, 1987] W. C. Durant, III. *Vital Speeches Day* 53:540-4 Je 15 '87
Equalization, Educational *See* Educational equalization
Equalizers, Audio *See* Audio systems—Equipment
Equations
> *See also*
> Simultaneous equations
Mathematical reasoning: a Prolog program uses heuristic methods to solve equations. L. Sterling. il *Byte* 12:177-80 O '87
Zeroing in on chaos [study of Newton's method; work of Scott A. Burns and others] I. Peterson. il *Sci News* 131:137-9 F 28 '87
Equatorial mounts for telescopes *See* Telescopes—Mounting
Equestrianism *See* Horsemanship
Equiano, Olaudah, b. 1745
How I became Gustavus Vasa [excerpt from Equiano's travels] por *Courier* 40:17 Ap '87
Equids
El Jefe is building a desert 'ark' to keep zebras and other equids afloat [Canyon Colorado Equid Sanctuary] J. Fincher. bibl (p184) il pors *Smithsonian* 18:138-42+ My '87
Equilibrium (Physiology)
> *See also*
> Labyrinth (Ear)
Equilibrium (Thermal) *See* Thermodynamics
Equimark Corp.
'Nice guys don't get paid' [A. Fellheimer] il por *Bus Week* p110 S 21 '87
Equinoxes
> *See also*
> Vernal equinox
Equinox may be a misnomer. T. D. Nicholson. *Nat Hist* 96:78 S '87
Equipment industry, Industrial *See* Industrial equipment industry
Equitable Life Assurance Society of the United States
Growth stocks prosper in the new year [interview with portfolio manager L. Wang] A. E. Serwer. il por *Fortune* 115:114 F 2 '87
A little sales pitch and a lot of slow pitches [sponsorship of old-timers baseball games] B. Welling. il *Bus Week* p114-15 Je 22 '87
Equity conversion, Home *See* Home equity conversion
ERA *See* United States. Constitution. Equal Rights Amendment (Proposed)
Erasable optical storage devices *See* Optical storage devices
Erbe, Margaret A.
> *about*
Moscow "radicals" stop a nuclear plant. J. Lawless. il por *Sierra* 72:125-30 Ja/F '87
Erbes, M. R., and others
Off-design performance of power plants: an integrated gasification combined-cycle example. bibl f il *Science* 237:379-83 Jl 24 '87
ERCs *See* Emission reduction credits
Erdman, Paul Emil, 1932-
> *about*
Facts stranger than fiction [interview] il por *U S News World Rep* 102:52 F 9 '87
Erdős, Paul, 1913-
> *about*
The man who loves only numbers. P. Hoffman. il por *Atlantic* 260:60-8+ N '87
Erdrich, Louise
Christmas lights. *Seventeen* 46:128 D '87
Snares [story] il *Harpers* 274:60-4 My '87

about
Offbeat auction. P. S. Nathan. *Publ Wkly* 232:40 N 13 '87
Erick Hawkins Dance Company
Reviews:
Performances at the Joyce Theater, New York City. C. Hardy. *Dance Mag* 61:40-2 F '87
Erickson, Bonnie
> *about*
Bonnie Erickson: graduating from Sesame Street. P. Finch. il por *Bus Week* p81 F 9 '87
Erickson, John R., 1943-
> *about*
Maverick. L. Fleischer. *Publ Wkly* 231:52 Je 26 '87
Erickson, Paul A.
Fans of the worms. il *Oceans* 20:62-3 S/O '87
Ericsson (L.M.) Telephone Co. *See* L.M. Ericsson Telephone Co.
Ericsson Radio Systems AB
Radar designed for intense EW environment [Swedish airborne phased-array early warning radar] *Aviat Week Space Technol* 127:130 O 19 '87
Erigena, John Scotus, ca. 810-ca. 877
> *about*
John Scotus Erigena. C. E. White. il *Christ Today* 31:39 Mr 20 '87
Erikson, Raymond J.
Settle cislunar space before heading to Mars. por *Aviat Week Space Technol* 126:87 Je 22 '87
Erisman, Albert M., and Neves, Kenneth W.
Advanced computing for manufacturing. bibl (p184) il *Sci Am* 257:162-9 O '87
Eritrea (Ethiopia)
Politics and government
> *See also*
> Eritrean People's Liberation Front
In Eritrea. T. Keneally. il map *N Y Times Mag* p42-4+ S 27 '87
Eritrean People's Liberation Front
Attacking the victims [cuts UN food supply lines] S. Seibert. il *Newsweek* 110:56 N 9 '87
In Eritrea. T. Keneally. il map *N Y Times Mag* p42-4+ S 27 '87
Eriugena, John Scotus *See* Erigena, John Scotus, ca. 810-ca. 877
Erlich, Reese
Victory on Cannery Row. il *Progressive* 51:26-7 Jl '87
Ermelin, Michel
> *about*
An eye for detail: the Paris apartment of Michel and Noémi Ermelin. B. D. Colen. il *Archit Dig* 44:132-42 Ja '87
Ermenonville (France)
Historic houses, sites, etc.
Folies de grandeur. R. M. Adams. il map *House Gard* 159:48+ Ja '87
Ermey, Lee
> *about*
Hup, two, three, four, who do movie critics adore? Full metal jacket's blistering sergeant, Lee Ermey. F. A. Bernstein. il pors *People Wkly* 28:43-4 Ag 17 '87
Ermione [opera] *See* Rossini, Gioacchino, 1792-1868
Ermshar, Rick
Viewfinder. See issues of Petersen's Photographic Magazine beginning June 1986 through March 1987
Ernest Orlando Lawrence Memorial Awards
DOE honors six physicist with 1987 Lawrence Awards. il *Phys Today* 40:111-12 N '87
Ernst, Max, 1891-1976
> *about*
The importance of being Ernst. M. Feist. il *Art News* 86:170 Ja '87
Romance to the Max. L. Liebmann. il por *Vogue* 177:200 My '87
Ernst, Mensen
> *about*
Marathon man. B. Berntsen. il por *Courier* 40:33-4 Je '87
Erosion
> *See also*
> Coast changes
> Contour farming
> Sedimentation and deposition
> Terraces (Agriculture)
> Weathering
Keeping topsoil down on the farm [Washington study of effect of farming techniques on soil; work of John P. Reganold] I. Peterson. *Sci News* 132:357-8 D 5 '87
Soil study shows abundance will outrun erosion. *Success Farm* 85:66B S '87

Erosion—*cont.*
World agriculture and soil erosion. D. Pimentel and others. bibl f il *BioScience* 37:277-83 Ap '87

Erotic art
Howard Kottler: conceptualist and purveyor of psychosexual allusions. P. Failing. il por *Am Craft* 47:22-9 D '87/Ja '88

Erotic photography
See also
Photography of the nude
Hot shots: why nice girls take off their clothes [boudoir photography] M. Dowd. il *Mademoiselle* 93:205-6+ S '87

Erotic poetry
Amorous fantasies [Uruguayan poetess D. Agustini] L. Fox-Lockert. por *Américas* 39:38-41 Ja/F '87

Errazuriz, Eugenia, d. 1954
about
Eugenia Errazuriz. J. Richardson. il por *House Gard* 159:76+ Ap '87

Errors
See also
Accuracy
Asleep at the switch: the human machine. il *Newsweek* 109:62 Ap 27 '87
How to learn from your mistakes [excerpt from Managing people at work desk guide] T. L. Quick. *Work Woman* 12:27 My '87

Errors, Computer *See* Computers—Errors

Errors, Literary
All the corrections that are fit to print [New York times] J. Alter. *Newsweek* 110:52-3 Jl 27 '87

Errors, Scientific
Integrity of research papers questioned [study by Walter W. Stewart and Ned Feder] B. J. Culliton. *Science* 235:422-3 Ja 23 '87
Isaac Newton goofed, and it took student Robert Garisto to get to the core of the matter. R. Wolmuth. il por *People Wkly* 27:43 Je 29 '87
A long-disputed paper goes to press [Walter W. Stewart's and Ned Feder's critical study of publications by J. Darsee and coauthors] M. Murray. il *Sci News* 131:52-3 Ja 24 '87
New superhero at Sigma Xi [R. Garisto finds error in I. Newton's Principal] il por *Time* 129:77 Je 22 '87
Physics, Hollywood style [J. Weyland, physicist who critiques science fiction films] B. Lawren. *Omni* 9:35 Je '87
A soap opera for science [study by Walter Stewart and Ned Feder] D. E. Chubin. bibl f *BioScience* 37:259-61 Ap '87
Yb or not Yb? That is the question [mistake in element listing in publishing of Paul Chu's ceramic oxide superconducting formula] G. Kolata. il *Science* 236:663-4 My 8 '87

Errors, Speech
Mr. Bonaprop [malapropisms] W. Safire. il *N Y Times Mag* p8+ F 15 '87
What I meant to say. M. T. Motley. bibl (p64) il *Psychol Today* 21:24-8 F '87

Errors, Typographical
Bulletins. M. E. Marty. *Christ Century* 104:903 O 14 '87
Drawer-cleaning. M. E. Marty. *Christ Century* 104:927 O 21 '87
For our collectors. M. E. Marty. *Christ Century* 104:231 Mr 4 '87
Liturgical trends. M. E. Marty. *Christ Century* 104:575 Je 17-24 '87
Spring cleaning. M. E. Marty. *Christ Century* 104:455 My 6 '87
Spring cleaning, two. M. E. Marty. *Christ Century* 104:479 My 13 '87

Ershad, Hussain Mohammad
about
A revolt against poverty. C. Wood. il *Macleans* 100:28-9 D 14 '87

Ertegun, Ahmet M.
about
In the listening room of Ahmet Ertegun. il por *Esquire* 108:156-7 S '87

Ertegun, Mica
about
Classical cool. S. M. L. Aronson. il por *House Gard* 159:100-11+ Mr '87

Ertegun, Nesuhi
about
Atlantic at 40. G. Santoro. por *Down Beat* 54:63 Ag '87

Erucic acid
They won't let their son die [Odone family battles ALD] J. Adler. il *Newsweek* 110:98-100 N 16 '87

Ervin, Keith
The shrinking province of the primeval [cover story] il map *Sierra* 72:38-45 Jl/Ag '87

Ervin, Michael
Consumers out in the cold. il *Progressive* 51:17 Mr '87
Where high school kids learn to think. il *Progressive* 51:11 Je '87

Erving, Julius
about
All-star weekend salutes the greatness of Dr. J. il por *Jet* 71:53 F 23 '87
Dr. J goes out on top, but raps parade violence. il por *Jet* 72:48 My 11 '87
'Dr. J,' 'Magic' honored at NBA players dinner. il por *Jet* 73:48 O 5 '87
Dr. J will be busy during off-season counting gifts. por *Jet* 72:39 My 25 '87
Exit dunking. T. Kornheiser. il pors *Sport Mag* 78:56-61 Je '87
Last rounds for the Doctor [cover story; special section] il pors *Sports Illus* 66:72-6+ My 4 '87
Totaling Dr. J'$ farewell tour. C. Weinschenk. il por *Sport Mag* 78:15 S '87

Erwig, Eric
about
We got our son back for Christmas. J. L. Block. il por *Good Housekeep* 205:111-13 D '87

Erwin, Morris Homer
Strange encounter on Coho Creek. il *Read Dig* 130:11-16 My '87

Erwin (N.C.)
Education
One community's response to the dropout problem. G. H. Arnold and V. Biggers. *Phi Delta Kappan* 68:708-9 My '87

Erythrocytes
See also
Blood boosting
Erythropoietin
Glycophorin
Hemoglobin

Erythropoietin
Clinical promise with new hormones [hematologic growth factors] G. Kolata. il *Science* 236:517-19 My 1 '87
The hormone that's making Amgen grow. J. Flynn. il *Bus Week* p96+ Mr 16 '87

ESA *See* European Space Agency

Esalen Institute
In California: being 25 and following your bliss. P. Iyer. il *Time* 130:10+ S 14 '87

Esber, Ed, Jr.
Why most of us need to learn to speak SQL. por *Pers Comput* 11:224 O '87

ESCAP *See* United Nations. Economic and Social Commission for Asia and the Pacific

Escape devices (Airplanes) *See* Airplanes, Military—Escape devices

Escape devices (Space stations) *See* Space stations—Escape devices

Escape devices (Space vehicles) *See* Space vehicles—Escape devices

Escape from Sobibor [television program] See Television program reviews—Single works

Escapes
A bizarre escape from Brazil [American mercenary T. Carmody] por *Newsweek* 109:35 Ja 5 '87
Escape from a Dutch jail [Peruvian E. Barreto-Morales wanted by Canada for cocaine trafficking] D. Burke. por *Macleans* 100:44 Je 15 '87
Escapers' weather [World War II] R. S. Cerveny and B. R. Skeeter. bibl il *Weatherwise* 40:248-54 O '87
Not without my daughter [escape of American woman trapped by husband in Iran; excerpt]; ed. by William Hoffer. B. Mahmoody. il por *Ladies Home J* 104:20+ Ag '87
Please don't hurt me! [woman taken hostage after Texas prison break] R. Williams. il por *Ladies Home J* 104:18+ S '87

Escargot cooking *See* Cooking—Snails

Eschatology
See also
Apocalyptic literature
End of the world
Millennium
Second Advent
Our future hope: eschatology and its role in the church [special section] il *Christ Today* 31:1I-14I F 6 '87

Eschatology—cont.

Survival in the apocalyptic era. G. A. Larue. il *Humanist* 47:11-17 S/O '87

Escherichia coli

A complete mapping of the proteins in the small ribosomal subunit of Escherichia coli [neutron scattering data] M. S. Capel and others. bibl f il *Science* 238:1403-6 D 4 '87

Expression and processing of the AIDS virus reverse transcriptase in Escherichia coli. W. G. Farmerie and others. bibl f il *Science* 236:305-8 Ap 17 '87

Leader peptidase of Escherichia coli: critical role of a small domain in membrane assembly. R. E. Dalbey and W. T. Wickner. bibl f il *Science* 235:783-7 F 13 '87

Molecular cloning and expression of a human B-cell growth factor gene in Escherichia coli. S. Sharma and others. bibl f il *Science* 235:1489-92 Mr 20 '87

A physical map of the Escherichia coli K12 genome. C. L. Smith and others. bibl f il *Science* 236:1448-53 Je 12 '87

Escorial (San Lorenzo, Spain)

Philip II's grand design for the glory of God and empire. R. Wernick. bibl (p205) il pors *Smithsonian* 18:152-6+ D '87

Escorts (Dating service)

Going out solo [finding platonic escorts] C. Rickey. *Mademoiselle* 93:180 Ap '87

Escrow accounts

Crafty builders palm dollars earmarked for escrow. H. Porter. il *Fam Handyman* 37:14 Jl/Ag '87

Esiason, Boomer

about

Beers with [interview] J. Price. il pors *Sport Mag* 78:23-5 O '87

Eskenazi, Giuseppe

about

Eskenazi's early Chinese art. E. Lambert. il por *Archit Dig* 44:156+ Ja '87

Eskilson, Melissa Dodd

Minimize your mite problem. il *Rodale's Org Gard* 34:77-80+ Je '87

Eskimos

Alaskan adventure [Christmas vacation with the Eskimos] E. Murphy. map *Seventeen* 46:90+ D '87

The Eskimo offspring of Matthew Henson. S. A. Counter. il pors *Ebony* 42:50+ Ja '87

Eskimo son of explorer Matthew Henson dies in Greenland of cancer. pors *Jet* 72:12 Jl 27 '87

Explorers' Eskimo offspring visit America [children of M. Henson and R. Peary] il *Ebony* 42:84+ S '87

Matthew Henson's Eskimo son comes to U.S. for a reunion with relatives. il pors *Jet* 72:6 Je 15 '87

No slouches at breaking the ice, polar explorers Peary and Henson each left behind a son in the Arctic. C. Neuhaus. il pors *People Wkly* 27:41-2 Je 1 '87

A Russian on the coast of Alaska [excerpt from Peregrinations of the Russian merchant Grigori Shelikhov from Okhotsk to the coasts of America by the Eastern Ocean] G. I. Shelekhov. il *Courier* 40:13-14 Ap '87

Antiquities

Sealed in time: ice entombs an Eskimo family for five centuries. A. A. Dekin, Jr. il map *Natl Geogr* 171:824-36 Je '87

Fishing

The lady in pink [Arctic char in northern Canada] C. Gammon. il *Sports Illus* 67:54-8 Ag 24 '87

Government relations

Willie Kasayulie: guardian of the promised land [leader of Yup'ik native sovereignty movement in Alaska] A. Fadiman. il pors *Life* 10:17-18 F '87

Health and hygiene

Alaska native youth: a new approach to serving emotionally disturbed children and youth. J. VanDenBerg and B. A. Minton. il *Child Today* 16:15-18 S/O '87

Helping our children [mentally disturbed Alaskan Eskimo youth] S. Polk. il *Child Today* 16:19-20 S/O '87

Hunting

Is saving the seals killing the Eskimos? E. Wiedemann. il *World Press Rev* 34:35-7 Jl '87

Industries

Taxation

Saving Eskimo capitalism [tax reform bill allows sales of tax losses] D. Pauly. il *Newsweek* 109:42 Ja 12 '87

Migration

An epic Arctic journey [expedition retracing Inuit migration and demonstrating Canadian Arctic sovereignty; special section; with editorial comment by Kevin Doyle] il map *Macleans* 100:2, 20-8+ My 11 '87

Eskimos in art

Alaskan marine life and the Eskimo—through art [work of Huong] B. Rush and H. Lebelson. il por *Sea Front* 33:84-9 Mr/Ap '87

Eskow, Dennis

Aviation. See issues of Popular Mechanics beginning January 1986 through January 1987

Science. See issues of Popular Mechanics through June 1987

Esmon, Charles T.

The regulation of natural anticoagulant pathways. bibl f il *Science* 235:1348-52 Mr 13 '87

Esophagus

Cancer

Baltimore's favorite anchorman returns despite serious malady [J. Turner of WJZ] S. Salmans. il por *Channels* 7:8 Je '87

ESP *See* Extrasensory perception

Espaillat, Rhina P.

Counterclockwise [poem] *America* 157:505 D 26 '87

In this photograph [poem] *America* 157:405 N 28 '87

Espaliers

Espalier: sculpted fruit trees for tight spaces (I). J. Ruttle. il *Rodale's Org Gard* 34:82-5+ F '87

Espalier: sculpted fruit trees for tight spaces (II). J. Ruttle. il *Rodale's Org Gard* 34:30+ Mr '87

Esperanto

Doing away with all babble from the Tower of Babel. I. Shenker. bibl (p132) il *Smithsonian* 17:112-23+ Ja '87

The hope of Esperanto. J. D. Reed. il *Time* 130:72 Ag 3 '87

In search of a common language. J. Lee. il *U S News World Rep* 102:72 Mr 2 '87

Espionage

See also

Electronics in criminal investigation, espionage, etc.

Intelligence service

Iranian-Iraqi War, 1980- —Secret service

Lasers in criminal investigation, espionage, etc.

Trials (Espionage)

World War, 1939-1945—Secret service

That other old profession. R. Alan. *New Leader* 70:15-16 My 4-18 '87

Economic aspects

Spying's dirty little secret [financial motives] B. Brower. il *Money* 16:130-4+ Jl '87

Terminology

Hi, spy! T. Considine. il *N Y Times Mag* p8 Jl 26 '87

United States

Foggy Bottom's feeble fight [security lapses at the State Dept.] C. Fenyvesi and G. Borger. il *U S News World Rep* 102:16 My 11 '87

Spying's dirty little secret [financial motives] B. Brower. il *Money* 16:130-4+ Jl '87

Espionage, American

See also

United States. Army. Counter Intelligence Corps

Covert action and open society. G. F. Treverton. bibl f *Foreign Aff* 65:995-1014 Summ '87

How a Macy's engineer and his pals became rogue American agents [K. Kattke] N. M. Renfrew and P. Blauner. il pors *N Y* 20:102-4+ D 7 '87

The secret Army. G. J. Church. il *Time* 130:12-14 Ag 31 '87

History

FDR's own network: gentlemen spies [views of Phillip Knightley] il por *U S News World Rep* 102:22 Ja 12 '87

El Salvador

Varelli: in from the cold [involvement in FBI spying] D. R. Gordon. *Nation* 244:273+ Mr 7 '87

Israel

I spy, you spy [J. Pollard case and alleged U.S. spying on Israel] W. Blitzer. *New Repub* 196:15-16 Ap 13 '87

Kuwait

An American spy in Kuwait [case of M. Powe] S. Emerson. *U S News World Rep* 102:18-19 Ap 13 '87

Nicaragua

'Little worm' or big fish? [Sandinista R. Miranda defects to the U.S.] N. Cooper. por *Newsweek* 110:80 N 16 '87

SAC sergeant says no to spy flights [D. Cobos objects to espionage missions over Nicaragua] B. E. Johansen. il por *Progressive* 51:12 O '87

Espionage, American—*cont.*

Soviet Union
See also
Daniloff-Zakharov espionage case, 1986
Casey vs. Moscow: win and lose. il *Newsweek* 110:52-3 O 5 '87
Long on data, short on intelligence [spy satellites] W. M. Arkin. il *Bull At Sci* 43:5-6 Je '87

Espionage, British

Southern Africa
History
John Buchan's Richard Hannay [character modeled after E. Ironside, amateur spy among Germans and Boers] G. Powell. bibl il pors map *Hist Today* 37:32-9 Ag '87

Espionage, Czech

Great Britain
Falling for a Warsaw Pact dame [British journalist's experiences] J. Simpson. il *Harpers* 274:58-62 Je '87

Espionage, Industrial *See* Business intelligence

Espionage, Israeli

United States
Brothers with blood in their eyes [views of U.S. Jewish leaders on J. Pollard case] W. E. Smith. il *Time* 129:40 Mr 30 '87
I spy, you spy [J. Pollard case and alleged U.S. spying on Israel] W. Blitzer. *New Repub* 196:15-16 Ap 13 '87
Israel and Pollard [spy case] *World Press Rev* 34:36-7 My '87
Israelamok [Iranamok and the Pollard affair] *New Repub* 196:9 Mr 30 '87
Jay Pollard's peculiar tale. M. Satchell. il pors *U S News World Rep* 102:23-5 Je 1 '87
Life for an Israeli spy [J. Pollard case] H. Anderson. il por *Newsweek* 109:26+ Mr 16 '87
Official rogues [Israeli government coverup of J. Pollard espionage case] G. Carver. *New Repub* 196:12-15 Ap 13 '87
One step ahead, two backward [J. Pollard case] J. Branegan. il por *Time* 129:53 Ap 13 '87
A pileup of scandals in Israel [government reports on the Pollard case and role of Shin Bet in I. Napsu's imprisonment] N. Cooper. il por *Newsweek* 109:42 Je 8 '87
The Pollard case. *Nation* 244:457 Ap 11 '87
Security on trial [J. Pollard and I. Napsu cases] B. Levin. il por *Macleans* 100:22 Je 8 '87
The spy who came between friends [J. Pollard case] M. Satchell. il por *U S News World Rep* 102:32-3 Mr 30 '87
Spying between friends [J. Pollard sentenced to life imprisonment] W. E. Smith. il por *Time* 129:44+ Mr 16 '87
Spying between friends: Pollard case simmers on. S. Powell. il por *U S News World Rep* 102:12 Mr 16 '87
Strains in the family [Pollard case sets off spat between U.S. Jews and Israel] M. Whitaker. il por *Newsweek* 109:32-4 Mr 30 '87
Thrice rebuked [cases of J. Pollard and I. Napsu] il por *Time* 129:40 Je 8 '87
Triple trouble in Israel [with editorial comment] E. Salpeter. il *New Leader* 70:2, 5-7 Mr 23 '87
Uproar over a spy [J. Pollard case] W. E. Smith. il *Time* 129:30-2 Mr 23 '87

Espionage, Russian
Soviet industrial espionage. P. Hanson. bibl f il *Bull At Sci* 43:25-9 Ap '87
Spy time. *Natl Rev* 39:17-19 Ap 10 '87

France
All for love [French expel Soviet diplomats in spy scandal] il *Time* 129:53 Ap 13 '87
France expels Soviets for spying on Ariane. D. Dickson. *Science* 236:142 Ap 10 '87

Great Britain
The conscientious spy [K. Fuchs] S. E. Toulmin. bibl f il *N Y Rev Books* 34:54-60 N 19 '87
Minority report [P. Wright's Spycatcher] C. Hitchens. *Nation* 245:223 S 12 '87
Spooked [controversy surrounding publication of Spycatcher by P. Wright] M. Hosenball. *New Repub* 197:13-14 Ag 31 '87
The 'Spycatcher' secrets [excerpt] P. Wright. il por *Macleans* 100:38-40 Ag 3 '87
Tales of a spy writer [excerpts from P. Wright's controversial book Spycatcher printed in British press despite government ban] M. McIver. il por *Macleans* 100:52 My 11 '87

United States
See also
Daniloff-Zakharov espionage case, 1986
Walker family espionage case
April's spy scare [Soviet espionage and the INF proposals] D. Schorr. il *New Leader* 70:3-4 Ap 20 '87
The battle of the bugs [Soviet and American embassies; special section] il map *Newsweek* 109:18-22 Ap 20 '87
Black Marine's parents cry their son is a 'scapegoat' in sex for secrets case [A. Bracy's family] il por *Jet* 72:5 Ap 20 '87
Booze, brawls and skirt chasing [U.S. Marine guard spy scandal at Moscow embassy] E. Magnuson. il *Time* 129:20+ Ap 13 '87
Bugproofing the embassy [plan to salvage part of U.S. embassy in Moscow] il por *Time* 130:14 Jl 13 '87
Can an open society protect its secrets? D. Baer. il *U S News World Rep* 102:26-8 Je 1 '87
The case of espionage in the embassy [Marine guards in the Soviet Union] B. Duffy. il *U S News World Rep* 102:18-20 Ap 13 '87
Charges of espionage and seduction [Marine guards in the Soviet Union] il *Macleans* 100:20 Ap 20 '87
The conscientious spy [K. Fuchs] S. E. Toulmin. bibl f il *N Y Rev Books* 34:54-60 N 19 '87
Countering today's security challenges [statement, April 23, 1987] R. I. Spiers. *Dep State Bull* 87:52-4 Je '87
Crawling with bugs [Moscow embassy spy scandal; cover story; special section] il *Time* 129:14-18+ Ap 20 '87
The declining wages of espionage [fees for selling secrets to the Russians] il *Fortune* 115:12 My 11 '87
Deep in the Bear's den [R. Helms leads investigation into security breaches at U.S. embassy in Moscow] H. Sidey. il por *Time* 129:14 Je 29 '87
Expelled! How we ousted 80 Soviet spies. R. K. Bennett. il *Read Dig* 130:47-52 Ja '87
An expert says tear down our bugged embassy in Moscow [interview with J. Bamford] M. Ryan. il por *People Wkly* 27:91+ Ap 27 '87
Fallout from the scandal [Marine guard spy case] il *Time* 129:22-3 Ap 27 '87
The fiasco in Moscow [security breach at U.S. embassy] L. Martz. il *Newsweek* 109:20-2 Ap 13 '87
From Russia with love and espionage [charges against C. Lonetree and A. Bracy, Marine guards at U.S. embassy in Moscow] il pors *Macleans* 100:18-19 Ap 13 '87
High-tech treachery [arrest of Ivan Batinic and others for attempting to sell supercomputer technology to the Soviets] *Newsweek* 110:56 N 2 '87
Holes in a spy scandal [Moscow embassy case] S. W. Cloud. il por *Time* 130:31 Jl 20 '87
The honey-trap spy case widens [charges against C. Lonetree and A. Bracy, Marine guards at the U.S. Embassy in Moscow] il pors *U S News World Rep* 102:12 Ap 6 '87
How the Soviets are bugging America. D. P. Moynihan. il map *Pop Mech* 164:102-5 Ap '87
How to protect U.S. embassies. W. L. Chaze. il *U S News World Rep* 102:18-20 Ap 20 '87
Innocent man [charges against A. Bracy dropped] por *Time* 129:23 Je 22 '87
The intelligence community [address, December 8, 1986] W. H. Webster. *Vital Speeches Day* 53:324-7 Mr 15 '87
Is the Marine spy case unraveling? G. Witkin. il *U S News World Rep* 102:14 My 4 '87
A Marine and his "swallow" [security guard at U.S. Embassy in Moscow accused of spying] B. Duffy. il por *U S News World Rep* 102:25 Ja 26 '87
The Marine case falls apart [charges dropped against A. Bracy] M. Kaus. il por *Newsweek* 109:23 Je 22 '87
The Marine spy scandal: "It's a biggie" [Moscow embassy guards C. Lonetree and A. Bracy] A. Wilentz. il pors *Time* 129:21-2 Ap 6 '87
The Marine traitors [U.S. embassy in Moscow] *Natl Rev* 39:18 Ap 24 '87
Military justice comes to attention [Marine guard spy case] R. Lacayo. il por *Time* 129:62 My 18 '87
The mission in Moscow. G. F. Kennan. por *Newsweek* 110:7 Jl 13 '87
Moonlighting in Moscow? [Marine guards C. Lonetree and A. Bracy charged with espionage] R. Watson. il pors *Newsweek* 109:32-3 Ap 6 '87
News conference of April 8, 1987. G. P. Shultz. *Dep State Bull* 87:24-7 Je '87
No entry [C. Lonetree denies allowing Soviets into Moscow embassy] il por *Time* 130:22 N 23 '87

Espionage, Russian—United States—*cont.*

Notes and comment [security breaches in the U.S. embassy in Moscow] *New Yorker* 63:25-6 My 4 '87

President meets with Foreign Intelligence Advisory Board [White House statement, July 14, 1987] *Dep State Bull* 87:31 S '87

Secrets storm [R. W. Pelton sentenced to life imprisonment] *Nation* 244:4-5 Ja 10 '87

Security at the U.S. embassy in Moscow [remarks and question-and-answer session, April 7, 1987] R. Reagan. *Dep State Bull* 87:60-1 Je '87

Semper fie [Marine security guard C. Lonetree arrested for spying] por *Time* 129:19 Ja 26 '87

Soviet break-ins? [Spetsnaz unit suspected in U.S. naval base espionage] L. Howard. il *Newsweek* 110:6 N 9 '87

Spy charges against black Marine dropped [case of A. Bracy] por *Jet* 72:9 Je 29 '87

Spy woes [testimony retracted in Marine guard spy case] *Time* 129:22 My 11 '87

Trying to undo the damage [State Dept. admits role in embassy security lapses] M. Santini. il *U S News World Rep* 102:23 My 25 '87

Washington diarist [vilification of A. Hartman over neglect of security of American embassy in Moscow] L. Wieseltier. *New Repub* 196:42 My 11 '87

Why Moscow is winning [with interview with A. Hartman] W. L. Chaze. il *U S News World Rep* 102:36-8 Ap 27 '87

Why the secrets slip out [cover story] M. Satchell. il *U S News World Rep* 102:20-2 Je 1 '87

Anecdotes, facetiae, satire, etc.

Uncivil liberties [bugging of U.S. embassy in Moscow] C. Trillin. *Nation* 244:674 My 23 '87

Espionage, Salvadoran

United States

The death squads hit home: which side is the FBI on? [attacks against Salvadoran exiles in the U.S.] V. Bielski and others. il *Progressive* 51:15-19 O '87

Death squads invade California [threats to Salvadorans living in Los Angeles] C. Garcia. il *Time* 130:20-1 Ag 3 '87

Espionage in literature *See* Spy stories

Espionage in motion pictures *See* Motion pictures—Spy films

ESPN *See* Entertainment and Sports Programming Network

Esposito, Larry W.

The changing shape of planetary rings [cover story; with editorial comment by Richard Berry] il *Astronomy* 15:6-17, 45 S '87

(jt. auth) See Cuzzi, Jeffrey N., and Esposito, Larry W.

Esposito, Phil, 1942-

about

Beers with [interview] P. Fichtenbaum. il por *Sport Mag* 78:19-21 N '87

Esprit de Corp. (Firm)

Clothes make the man [interior design and Esprit] C. K. Gandee. il por *Archit Rec* 175:120-3 mid-S '87

The spirit of Esprit! M. Altman. il *Seventeen* 46:83-4+ Je '87

Susie Tompkins: the spirit in Esprit [interview] E. Klensch. il por *Vogue* 177:344-7+ Ag '87

Espy, Michael

about

A man of the people. W. Rabb. il por *Black Enterp* 17:19 F '87

Esquire (Periodical)

Dubious achievements of 1986! il *Esquire* 107:55-8+ Ja '87

Esquire magazine [manuscript submission policy] P. Moffitt. *Writer* 100:28 F '87

The selling of Esquire [Hearst acquisition] J. Alter. il *Newsweek* 109:80 F 16 '87

Welcome to the magazine of the 1990s. L. Eisenberg. il *Esquire* 107:1 Ap '87

Ess, Barbara

about

Barbara Ess: the mind's eye. M. E. Haus. il *Art News* 86:119-20+ N '87

Essaouira (Morocco)

Historic houses, sites, etc.

In the Casbah: transforming a labyrinthine Moroccan residence. S. Anderson. il *Archit Dig* 44:198-204 O '87

Essays

One key to B-school: your essay. J. A. Byrne. il *Bus Week* p168 Mr 23 '87

Competitions

Arabs anonymous [National Association of Arab Americans sponsorship of essay contest on America's Middle East policy] J. L. Pasley. *New Repub* 197:17-18 Ag 10-17 '87

Audubon essay winners. A. Hogge and G. Musick. il *Audubon* 89:104-5 S '87

Sixth annual North American Essay Contest [special section] il *Humanist* 47:14-22+ Mr/Ap '87

Esseff, John

Lebanon: a pawn in the Middle East. il *USA Today (Periodical)* 115:74-7 My '87

Essen (Germany)

Monuments, statues, etc.

Essen: Scenes; Münster: Sculptural projects. M. Hübl. il *Art News* 86:200 O '87

Essence (Periodical)

1987 Essence Awards. A. Edwards. pors *Essence* 18:121+ My '87

Essence [manuscript submission policy] S. L. Taylor. *Writer* 100:22 My '87

Essence brides: one staff, six styles. I. Wilkerson. il *Essence* 17:82-4+ F '87

Essence: the television program [television program] See Television program reviews—Single works

Esslinger, Hartmut

about

Hartmut Esslinger: high tech's one-man Bauhaus. K. M. Hafner. il por *Bus Week* p59 Ag 17 '87

Esswood, Paul

about

No mere curiosity. A. Kozinn. il por *Opera News* 52:26+ Ag '87

Estate jewelry *See* Jewelry

Estate planning

See also

Executors and administrators

Inheritance tax

Joint ownership

Living trusts

Trusts and trustees

Videotapes—Estate planning use

Wills

It's never too early to plan your estate. D. Lamaute. il *Black Enterp* 17:25-6 Mr '87

Keep your estate safe for your family [excerpt from 50 plus guide to retirement investing] W. W. David. il *50 Plus* 27:68-73 Ap '87

Keeping it in the family. C. Hutton. il *Fortune* 116 Sp Issue:111-12+ Fall '87

Keeping it in the family: should kids inherit fortunes? R. I. Kirkland, Jr. *Current* 289:16-20 Ja '87

A short course in estate planning. E. Schurenberg. il *Money* 16:74-6+ O '87

Terminology

All that legalese. J. Reid. *Money* 16:96+ O '87

Estate tax *See* Inheritance tax

Estates, Country *See* Country estates

Estates, Decedents'

$¼ million estate of Bayard Rustin, 77, left to son, 38, adopted in 1982. por *Jet* 73:4 O 12 '87

Adolph Caesar estate worth $295,000 goes to wife, two daughters. il pors *Jet* 71:18 F 16 '87

The outsider [children of C. Payson take V. Payson to court] L. Gubernick. il pors *Forbes* 140 Sp Issue:38+ O 26 '87

The ultimate family feud [Horvitz family] L. Gubernick and R. King, Jr. il *Forbes* 139:80-1 Je 29 '87

Taxation

See Inheritance tax

Estates, Unclaimed

See also

Locater of Missing Heirs Inc.

Finders, keepers. B. Weberman. il *Forbes* 139:90 Mr 23 '87

Estée Lauder, Inc.

The make-over at Estee Lauder. L. Belkin. il pors *N Y Times Mag* p32-3+ N 29 '87

Esterases

Selective inactivation of influenza C esterase: a probe for detecting 9-O-acetylated sialic acids. E. A. Muchmore and A. P. Varki. bibl f il *Science* 236:1293-5 Je 5 '87

Esterly, David

Homage to Grinling Gibbons. il por *House Gard* 159:18+ Ja '87

Esterow, Milton

Changing the look of art education. il *Art News* 86:112-13 Ap '87

The Soviet Culture Fund: "setting this up is an amazing thing". il *Art News* 86:108-9 O '87

Esters
　See also
　Benzoates
　Phorbol esters
Why nature chose phosphates. F. H. Westheimer. bibl f il *Science* 235:1173-8 Mr 6 '87
Estes, Merion
　　about
Merion Estes at Jan Baum. C. Mallinson. il *Art Am* 75:187+ N '87
Estevez, Emilio, 1963-
　　about
Wisdom [film] Reviews
　People Wkly il 27:14 Ja 26 '87. T. Cunneff
Esther [oratorio] See Handel, George Frideric, 1685-1759
Esthetics See Aesthetics
Estill Springs (Tenn.)
　　Religious institutions and affairs
Maybe it's not the freezer of Turin, but Arlene Gardner says she sees Jesus on her G.E. il por *People Wkly* 27:80 Je 29 '87
A modern miracle [claims that the face of Jesus appears on A. Garner's freezer] il *Esquire* 108:159-61 D '87
Estimated tax
Estimated tax trauma. G. W. Padwe. *Nations Bus* 75:44 Je '87
Figuring your estimated taxes. L. Wiener. il *U S News World Rep* 102:60 F 9 '87
Estimates, Building See Building—Costs
Estonia
　See also
　Sex education—Estonia
The Tyniste twins of Estonia jibe as sailing's double threat. S. K. Reed. il pors *People Wkly* 27:108-9 Ap 6 '87
　　Religious institutions and affairs
　See also
　Convents—Estonia
Estonian war criminals See World War, 1939-1945—War criminals
Estoppel
Enough is enough [collateral estoppel in product liability cases] D. Fanning. il *Forbes* 139:56 Ap 20 '87
Estrada, Alfredo J.
Quietly keeping them out: the dark side of immigration reform. il *Harpers* 275:42-3 Ag '87
Estremadura (Spain)
　　Description and travel
Birthplace of the conquerors. L. Bindernagel. il *World Press Rev* 34:63 Mr '87
Estrogen receptors See Hormone receptors
Estrogens
Drug 'nukes' ovarian cancer [estrogen linked with radioactive bromine] J. Raloff. *Sci News* 131:389 Je 20 '87
Estrogens exonerated in breast cancer. *Sci News* 131:57 Ja 24 '87
Female trouble [menopause-heart disease link] *Sci Am* 257:24+ Jl '87
A little estrogen, fewer broken hips [osteoporosis] il *Newsweek* 110:99 N 16 '87
More about estrogen skin patches. C. SerVaas. il *Saturday Evening Post* 259:52-4+ Ja/F '87
No calcium fix [osteoporosis] *Sci Am* 256:72 Ap '87
Osteoporosis: most answers yet to come. J. Silberner. *Sci News* 131:116 F 21 '87
Osteoporosis reexamined: complexity of bone biology is a challenge. B. J. Culliton. *Science* 235:833-4 F 20 '87
Xenopus oocytes injected with rat uterine RNA express very slowly activating potassium currents. M. B. Boyle and others. bibl f il *Science* 235:1221-4 Mr 6 '87
Estuaries
　See also
　Estuarine area conservation
　Estuarine ecology
Estuarine area conservation
Preserving estuaries. *Oceans* 20:69 My/Je '87
Estuarine ecology
Fecund mysteries [Padilla Bay, Wash.] P. Johnson. il *Wilderness* 50:37-44+ Summ '87
Hope for blighted bays: the reduction of nitrogen inflow may benefit coastal waters. T. Beardsley. *Sci Am* 257:26-7+ N '87
Nutrient enrichment of the Chesapeake Bay [cover story; with editorial comment by Alan McGowan and Abel Wolman] C. F. D'Elia. bibl f il map *Environment* 29:inside cover, 2-3, 6-11+ Mr '87
Vertical distribution of an estuarine snail altered by a parasite. L. A. Curtis. bibl f il *Science* 235:1509-11 Mr 20 '87

We all live downstream [Chesapeake Bay] F. L. Schultz. il *Ctry J* 14:10-11 Jl '87
Esty (William) Company See William Esty Company
ETA (Organization)
Offering retirement to the ETA. J. Valls-Russell. il *New Leader* 70:9-10 N 30 '87
Eta Carinae (Star) See Stars, Variable
Etageres See Shelves and racks
Etch A Sketch See Toys
Etching
　See also
　Drypoint
　Glass etching
　Portrait prints
Etchingham (England)
　　Churches (Buildings)
Etchingham Church, East Sussex. N. Saul. il *Hist Today* 37:62-3 Je '87
Ethanol as fuel See Alcohol as fuel
Ethel Percy Andrus Gerontology Center
Aging has its place: the Andrus Center. J. Meer. il *Psychol Today* 21:88 My '87
Ethical education See Moral education
Ethics
　See also
　Accounting ethics
　Advertising ethics
　Altruism
　Anthropology—Ethical aspects
　Apologies
　Art and morals
　Automobile mechanics (Persons)—Professional ethics
　Automobile sales personnel—Professional ethics
　Bioethics
　Business ethics
　Character
　Christian ethics
　College graduates—Ethics
　College teachers—Professional ethics
　Conscience
　Courage
　Crime and criminals
　Fishing—Ethical aspects
　Hedonism
　Honesty
　Hunting—Ethical aspects
　Hypocrisy
　Integrity
　Journalistic ethics
　Judicial ethics
　Justice
　Law and ethics
　Legal ethics
　Loyalty
　Lying
　Medical ethics
　Military ethics
　Modesty
　Moral education
　Obedience
　Police ethics
　Political ethics
　Principles
　Professional ethics
　Puritans and puritanism
　Research—Ethical aspects
　Responsibility
　Secularism
　Sexual ethics
　Sin
　Sports agencies and agents—Ethical aspects
　Teachers—Professional ethics
　Technology and ethics
　Values
　Virtue
Compromising positions: can you get out of moral dilemmas gracefully? J. Stone. *Glamour* 85:133+ F '87
The demands of the community [with discussion] P. Selznick. *Cent Mag* 20:33-54 Ja/F '87
If moral decay is the question, is a feminist ethic the answer? G. Steinem. il *Ms* 16:57-9+ S '87
John XXIII and the hand grenade [views of H. Arkes] R. J. Neuhaus. *Natl Rev* 39:51 S 25 '87
Ms. Right and Mr. Wrong [women athletes score higher than male athletes in tests of moral reasoning] L. Howard. il *Women's Sports Fitness* 9:45 O '87
Prophets with tenure [views of M. Walzer] R. J. Neuhaus. *Commentary* 84:49-52 Jl '87
What's wrong [hypocrisy, betrayal and greed; cover story; special section] il *Time* 129:14-23+ My 25 '87

Ethics—*cont.*

Anecdotes, facetiae, satire, etc.

Mother was right about my permanent record. R. H. Bell. *Commonweal* 114:730 D 18 '87

Ethics and technology *See* Technology and ethics

Ethiopia

See also
Agriculture—Ethiopia
Americans—Ethiopia
Civil rights—Ethiopia
Ecology—Ethiopia
Eritrea (Ethiopia)
Famines—Ethiopia
Jews—Ethiopia
Land settlement—Ethiopia
Military assistance, American—Ethiopia
Missions, Medical—Ethiopia
Relief work—Ethiopia
United Nations—Ethiopia
Watersheds—Ethiopia
Wildlife—Ethiopia

Foreign relations
United States

See United States—Foreign relations—Ethiopia

Politics and government

See also
Communism—Ethiopia

Does helping really help? [political situation interfering with famine relief work] O. Friedrich. il *Time* 130:44-5 D 21 '87

Famine [cover story] M. S. Serrill. il map *Time* 130:34-8+ D 21 '87

Rebel aid. Y. Deressa. *Natl Rev* 39:36-9 Ap 24 '87

A state of permanent revolution. M. Thomas. il *Harpers* 274:53-6+ Ja '87

While famine looms, Ethiopia's leaders fiddle. J. L. Galloway. il *U S News World Rep* 103:12 O 5 '87

Popular culture

And in Ethiopia, the cult of the Gloved One [M. Jackson craze] por *Newsweek* 109:31 My 25 '87

Ethnic conflict *See* Culture conflict

Ethnic food stores *See* Food stores

Ethnic jokes *See* Humor

Ethnic minorities *See* Minorities

Ethnic studies *See* Intercultural education

Ethnicity

Your child's cultural identity. J. Segal and Z. Segal. il *Parents* 62:154 Jl '87

Ethnobotany

Dr. Plotkin's jungle pharmacy: an ethnobotanist goes native for science [work among the Tirió tribe in Suriname] A. Fadiman. il pors *Life* 10:15-17 Je '87

Ethnocentrism

Ethnocentrism and third world development. H. J. Wiarda. bibl *Society* 24:55-64 S/O '87

Place maps [regional distortions in map drawing by college freshman; study by Thomas F. Saarinen] C. Simon. maps *Psychol Today* 21:15 N '87

Ethnology

See also
Anthropology
Cannibalism
Ethnicity
Ethnobotany

A nasty, empty, dangerous word [homogeneity] M. Robinson. il *N Y Times Book Rev* 92:10-11 Mr 15 '87

An universal freckle [views of S. S. Smith] S. J. Gould. il por *Nat Hist* 96:14+ Ag '87

Samoan Islands

Letters [discussion of November 1986 article, Untrashing Margaret Mead] *Sci Am* 256:6 F '87

Ethnopsychology

See also
Blacks—Psychology
Blacks—Race identity

Making the world safe for difference. R. J. Neuhaus. *Natl Rev* 39:24 N 20 '87

A meeting of the twain [American psychologists C. Colman and D. McGill practice family therapy in Japan] J. Biggar. bibl (p65) il *Psychol Today* 21:46-50+ N '87

Therapists: a cultural bias? [study by Steven Lopez and Priscilla Hernandez] P. Chance. *Psychol Today* 21:16-17 S '87

Ethology *See* Animals—Habits and behavior

Ethyl alcohol as fuel *See* Alcohol as fuel

Ethyl carbamate *See* Urethanes

Ethyl Corp.

Life after lead. K. Hannon. il *Forbes* 139:65 My 18 '87

Ethylamines

Unlocking plants' secret potential [use of triethylamine DCPTA] J. Raloff. *Sci News* 131:265 Ap 25 '87

Ethylene

See also
Plants, Effect of ethylene on

Ethylene dibromide pesticides *See* Pesticides

Ethylenediamine tetraacetic acid

Synthesis of a sequence-specific DNA-cleaving peptide. J. P. Sluka and others. bibl f il *Science* 238:1129-32 N 20 '87

Etienne, Jean-Louis

about

Solo to the Pole [interview] il pors *Courier* 40:30-2 Je '87

Etiquette

See also
Business etiquette
Courtesy

Don't call me Fred. F. Eberstadt. il *Vogue* 177:267 Ap '87

Etiquette: doing it right. C. Ford. See issues of McCall's beginning January 1987

Etiquette for every day. E. L. Post. See issues of Good Housekeeping

The etiquette of eating out. L. Lufkin. il *Seventeen* 46:26+ My '87

How to butter an ear of corn and other dining dilemmas. il *Glamour* 85:290-1 Ag '87

Manners for the eighties: how to master the daily dance of life in New York [cover story] G. Mahon. il *N Y* 20:46-54 D 14 '87

(Table) manners makyth man. N. Ishige. il *Courier* 40:18-21 My '87

Anecdotes, facetiae, satire, etc.

How to be a totally awesome beach babe. B. Stepko. il *Seventeen* 46:59 Jl '87

Miss Manners' convention etiquette [guidelines for American Booksellers convention in Washington, D.C.] J. Martin. il por *Publ Wkly* 231:143 My 15 '87

Mister Marty's manners. M. E. Marty. *Christ Century* 104:1103 D 2 '87

Etna, Mount (Sicily) *See* Mount Etna (Sicily)

Etra, Jon

The art of getting what you want. *Harpers Bazaar* 120:298+ Mr '87

Candice Bergen. pors *Harpers Bazaar* 120:204, 354-7 S '87

High hats & coronets: nothing succeeds like excess. il *Harpers Bazaar* 121:70+ D '87

Labors of love. il *Harpers Bazaar* 120:186-7+ My '87

The rise of rabbit: hare apparent. il *Harpers Bazaar* 121:116+ N '87

Tropical icebreakers. il *Harpers Bazaar* 120:48+ Jl '87

Ettlinger, Catherine

Skiing with the guys. il *Work Woman* 12:76-9 F '87

Etymology *See* English language—Etymology

Eubanks, Eugene E., and Parish, Ralph

An inside view of change in schools. il *Phi Delta Kappan* 68:610-15 Ap '87

Eubanks, Kevin

about

Kevin Eubanks: a new breed of guitarist. M. Bourne. il pors *Down Beat* 54:20-2 Jl '87

Eucalyptus

Diseases and pests

The bird that farms the dell [relationship between bell miners, psyllids, and eucalyptus dieback] R. H. Loyn. il *Nat Hist* 96:54-60 Je '87

Euphorbias *See* Spurges

Eurailpass *See* Railroads—Western Europe

Euratom

Nuclear cooperation with EURATOM [letter to Congress, February 28, 1986] R. Reagan. *Dep State Bull* 87:77 Je '87

US and EC conclude fusion agreement [magnetic fusion] W. Sweet. *Phys Today* 40:56-7 Je '87

Eureka (Program)

The club that breeds success. D. S. Greenberg. il *U S News World Rep* 102:44-5 Ap 20 '87

Europeans approve more Eureka projects. *Aviat Week Space Technol* 127:29 O 5 '87

Eureka Springs (Ark.)

Hotels, motels, etc.

An innkeeper's guide to better breakfasts [Dairy Hollow House] M. Gorman. il *Rodale's Org Gard* 34:52-4 O '87

Euripides, ca. 485-ca. 406 B.C.

about

The Bacchae [drama] Reviews
Nation 245:246 S 12 '87. T. M. Disch

Eurman, Nina
Fake fat. il *Health* 19:8 O '87
Euro Disneyland
Hi-ho! Hi-ho! Culture high and low [mastermind R. J. Fitzpatrick] il por *Harpers Bazaar* 120:210 S '87
It's King Kong vs. the 'ravenous rat' [MCA and Disney compete for theme park market] K. Kelly. il *Bus Week* p54 O 5 '87
Eurobond market
The Assad connection [Eurobond frauds masterminded by H. Zubaidi] R. Morais. il *Forbes* 139:32-3 Je 15 '87
A Eurobond bombshell [U.S. ends tax treaty with Netherlands Antilles] R. Brady and V. English. *Bus Week* p100 Jl 13 '87
A tempest hits the Treasury [cancels Antilles tax treaty] D. Zigas and V. English. il *Bus Week* p124 Jl 20 '87
Eurocontrol *See* Air traffic control—Western Europe
Eurojet (Firm)
Eurojet stresses thrust, maintainability in design of EJ200 engine for EFA [European fighter aircraft] il *Aviat Week Space Technol* 126:94 Je 29 '87
Euromarket *See* Eurobond market
Europa (Satellite), Life on *See* Life on Europa (Satellite)
Europe
> *See also*
> Air pollution—Europe
> Alps
> Anti-nuclear movement—Europe
> Central Europe
> Economic assistance, American—Europe
> Environmental policy—Europe
> Europeans
> Forests and forestry—Europe
> Jews—Europe
> Lakes—Europe
> Music festivals—Europe
> Prostitution—Europe
> Research—Europe
> Resorts—Europe
> Restaurants—Europe
> Roads—Europe
> Witchcraft—Europe
Regional report: Europe. D. R. Shanor. See issues of World Press Review beginning October 1986
Climate
Waiting out the big chill. T. A. Sancton. il *Time* 129:34-5 Ja 26 '87
Winter's bitter changes. A. Steacy. il *Macleans* 100:42-3 Ja 26 '87
Defenses
> *See also*
> Conference on Confidence and Security-Building Measures and Disarmament in Europe
> Conference on Security and Cooperation in Europe
> Guided missiles, European
Description and travel
Europe '87: continental savings. H. Koenig. il *Travel Holiday* 167:59-60+ Mr '87
Flora Lewis: "I don't have the same power a political figure might, but I like the freedom to write what I think". J. A. Simon. por *Vogue* 177:237-8 N '87
Economic conditions
> *See also*
> United Nations. Economic Commission for Europe
Foreign relations
> *United States*
> *See* United States—Foreign relations—Europe
History
1517-1648
> *See also*
> Thirty Years' War, 1618-1648
1871-1918
> *See also*
> World War, 1914-1918
1918-1945
> *See also*
> World War, 1939-1945—Campaigns and battles—Western
Europe faces its Nazi past. S. Sullivan. il pors *Newsweek* 109:34-6 Ap 20 '87
Population
Europe faces population decline [views of Dirk J. van de Kaa] *Futurist* 21:53 Jl/Ag '87
Religious institutions and affairs
> *See also*
> Reformation

Study and teaching
> *See* European studies
Europe, Central *See* Central Europe
Europe, Eastern *See* Eastern Europe
Europe, Western *See* Western Europe
Europe (Musical group)
Europe: conquering America. M. L. Baer. il *Teen* 31:57 O '87
Europe and the United States
> *See also*
> United States—Foreign opinion—European
Love and hate across the Atlantic. N. Gelb. il *New Leader* 70:3-4 N 30 '87
European art *See* Art, European
European astronauts *See* Astronauts
European Atomic Energy Community *See* Euratom
European Civil Aviation Conference
ECAC approves liberalizing fare, capacity regulations. *Aviat Week Space Technol* 126:36 Ja 12 '87
ECAC, U.S. renew North Atlantic pact. *Aviat Week Space Technol* 126:32 F 23 '87
European communications satellites *See* Communications satellites, European
European cooking *See* Cooking, European
European Economic Community
Common Market threats force carriers toward liberalization. *Aviat Week Space Technol* 127:146+ N 9 '87
The economic superstate. J. Doyle. il *Commonweal* 114:549-51 O 9 '87
EEC research program in jeopardy [Framework Program] D. Dickson. *Science* 235:158 Ja 9 '87
EEC: uniting to meet high-tech's challenge. D. Dickson. il *Science* 237:1103-4 S 4 '87
Europe at 30. R. J. Gwyn. il *World Press Rev* 34:21-3 My '87
Europe without borders. A. Vernholes. *World Press Rev* 34:56 O '87
European skies are freer but no friendlier. J. Heard. il *Bus Week* p54 D 21 '87
The Europeans start to play a little rough [antidumping proposals against Japan] T. Peterson. il *Bus Week* p47 F 9 '87
"Eye for eye, tooth for tooth" [U.S. trade dispute] G. Russell. il *Time* 129:54 Ja 12 '87
Imports from the EEC [proclamation, January 21, 1987] R. Reagan. *Dep State Bull* 87:30 Ap '87
Trade wars: Reagan plays with fire [U.S. duties imposed on European agricultural products] *Natl Rev* 39:21-2 Ja 30 '87
Transatlantic showdown [U.S.-European Community agricultural trade war] P. Lewis. il *Macleans* 100:30 Ja 19 '87
U.K. lifts veto on plans for EEC [Framework Program] D. Dickson. *Science* 237:126 Jl 10 '87
U.S.-EC relations and the international trading system [address, October 8, 1986] W. A. Wallis. *Dep State Bull* 87:43-7 Ja '87
Wanted: leaders with vision [J. Monnet] J. M. Wall. *Christ Century* 104:779 S 23 '87
With IT in the scientific jet set [Framework Program to promote scientific collaboration] F. Pearce. *World Press Rev* 34:55 Ja '87
European Helicopter Industries
Anglo-Italian EH101 prototype expanding envelope in early flights. D. A. Brown. il *Aviat Week Space Technol* 127:111 N 23 '87
EH 101 helicopter favored in Canadian bid. il *Aviat Week Space Technol* 127:28-9 Ag 10 '87
EH101 helicopter rolled out; British to order utility version. D. A. Brown. il *Aviat Week Space Technol* 126:30 Ap 13 '87
Joint development complications delay first flight of EH-101. *Aviat Week Space Technol* 127:25 S 14 '87
Two firms vie for new Canadian helicopter program [E. H. Industries' EH101 and Aerospatiale's AS332 Mk. 2 Super Puma] il *Aviat Week Space Technol* 126:28-9 Je 22 '87
European Molecular Biology Laboratory
EMBL: "small science" on a European scale. D. Dickson. il *Science* 237:1108-9 S 4 '87
European Nuclear Disarmament (Organization)
The peace movement's next task [cover story] E. P. Thompson. *Nation* 245:701+ D 12 '87
European Organization for Nuclear Research
Abragam and Rubbia reports chart future for CERN. W. Sweet. il *Phys Today* 40:71-5 S '87
CERN: adapting to middle age. D. Dickson. il *Science* 237:1104-5 S 4 '87
CERN urged to cut 400 posts. D. Dickson. *Science* 237:20 Jl 3 '87

European Organization for Nuclear Research—*cont.*
Rubbia in line to head CERN. D. Dickson. por *Science* 238:1223 N 27 '87
European painting *See* Painting, European
European pottery *See* Pottery, European
European Research Coordination Agency *See* Eureka (Program)
European Security Conference *See* Conference on Security and Cooperation in Europe
European Space Agency
British refusal to boost space funding threatens European Space Agency unity. *Aviat Week Space Technol* 127:26-7 O 19 '87
Europe in space: the program is in French. D. Dickson. il *Science* 238:1645-6 D 18 '87
Europe maintains cautious attitude on U.S. station cooperation. J. M. Lenorovitz. il *Aviat Week Space Technol* 126:23-4 Ap 20 '87
Europe votes to expand space program. E. Marshall. *Science* 238:1034 N 20 '87
Europeans approve development of Ariane 5, Hermes, Columbus. J. M. Lenorovitz. *Aviat Week Space Technol* 127:22-4 N 16 '87
Europeans confront problems in forming long-term space plan. il *Aviat Week Space Technol* 126:127-9 Mr 9 '87
Europeans disagree on future station negotiation plans. J. M. Lenorovitz. *Aviat Week Space Technol* 126:43-5 Ap 27 '87
Europe's aerospace companies are in seventh heaven. T. Peterson. il *Bus Week* p54 N 23 '87
Europe's space planning goals [special section] J. M. Lenorovitz. il *Aviat Week Space Technol* 127:22-5 S 28 '87
Governments must strive to make private enterprise work in space. R. Gibson. por *Aviat Week Space Technol* 127:91-2 N 2 '87
The model of a modern director general: a conversation with Roy Gibson. T. Furniss. il por *Space World* X-5-281:26-7 My '87
Panel calls for interim manned capsule [Assn. for European Astronauts comment on Hermes program] *Aviat Week Space Technol* 127:48-9 Jl 27 '87
Proposed Caesar comet encounter vies for ESA authorization. il *Aviat Week Space Technol* 126:128 F 9 '87
Space: it is expensive in the major leagues. D. Dickson. il *Science* 237:1110-11 S 4 '87
Space station partners resolve key issue on polar platform. *Aviat Week Space Technol* 127:28 D 14 '87
U.K. space chief resigns over funding; ESA reevaluates impact on polar platform. J. M. Lenorovitz. il *Aviat Week Space Technol* 127:26-7 Ag 10 '87
U.S., Europe seek to conclude station talks at final bilateral meeting. *Aviat Week Space Technol* 127:28 S 7 '87
European space stations *See* Space stations, European
European studies
Europe in European curricula. M. G. Bruce. *Phi Delta Kappan* 68:551-2 Mr '87
European Telecommunications Satellite Organization
Eutelsat to decide whether to drop opposition to SES. *Aviat Week Space Technol* 127:20 S 21 '87
Eutelsat weighs candidates for alternate launcher. *Aviat Week Space Technol* 126:101 Ja 12 '87
Intelsat, Eutelsat favor not opposing Astra's marketing of TV broadcast service [Luxembourg's Astra satellite program] *Aviat Week Space Technol* 127:26-7 N 2 '87
European War, 1914-1918 *See* World War, 1914-1918
Europeans
United States
The jittery 'other illegals'. T. Morganthau. il *Newsweek* 110:35-6 O 5 '87
Europium compounds
A flash in the crystalline pan [triboluminescence; research by Linda M. Sweeting and Arnold L. Rheingold] *Sci News* 131:360 Je 6 '87
Eurotunnel (Firm)
The Chunnel's chances. il *Fortune* 116:9 D 21 '87
Eutelsat *See* European Telecommunications Satellite Organization
Euthanasia
See also
Right to die
The agony did not end for Roswell Gilbert, who killed his wife to give her peace. L. Marx. il pors *People Wkly* 27:30-2+ Ja 12 '87
Death by choice. G. Ferrieri. *World Press Rev* 34:51 D '87
Forces line up to do battle over euthanasia. il *Christ Today* 31:57-8 N 20 '87

Was the king murdered? [George V] K. Slack. *Christ Century* 104:6-7 Ja 7-14 '87
Eutrophication
See also
Water bloom
Euzkadi Ta Askatasuna *See* ETA (Organization)
EVA (Extravehicular activity) *See* Space flight—Extravehicular activity
Evacuation of airplanes *See* Airplane evacuation
Evacuation of civilians
Controversy over nuclear evacuation planning. J. Raloff. *Sci News* 131:100 F 14 '87
Legality of new NRC rule is challenged [licensing of nuclear power plants] R. Weiss. *Sci News* 132:309 N 14 '87
NRC to vote on new evacuation rule. R. Weiss. *Sci News* 132:279 O 31 '87
Evaluation (Education) *See* Colleges and universities—Evaluation; Education—Evaluation
Evaluation research
Evaluating social programs: what have we learned? C. H. Weiss. *Society* 25:40-5 N/D '87
The politics of program evaluation. E. Chelimsky. *Society* 25:24-32 N/D '87
Evangel Temple (Washington, D.C.)
Finance
Black members who gave white minister money to build church change minds and sue. D. M. Cheers. il pors *Jet* 72:24-7 Ag 10 '87
Evangelical churches
See also
Assemblies of God
Evangelical Orthodox Church
National Association of Evangelicals
Conferences
See Religious conferences
Argentina
War, political change fuel church growth in Argentina. D. Smith. il *Christ Today* 31:40 Jl 10 '87
Latin America
War of the evangelists: unfunny reflections [J. Bakker and J. Swaggart] T. H. Stahel. *America* 156:293 Ap 11 '87
Philippines
Christian outreach: one year after the revolution. S. Mumper. il *Christ Today* 31:45-6 F 20 '87
Evangelical Committee for Aid and Development in Nicaragua
Evangelical leader named to national peace commission [G. Parajon] S. Wykstra. il por *Christ Today* 31:52 O 2 '87
Evangelical conferences *See* Religious conferences
Evangelical Council for Financial Accountability
ECFA standards for fund raising. *Christ Today* 31:38 My 15 '87
Trying to tighten the belt of financial accountability. R. Frame. il *Christ Today* 31:50-1+ N 20 '87
Evangelical Lutheran Church in America *See* Lutheran Church—United States
Evangelical Orthodox Church
Evangelical denomination gains official acceptance into the Orthodox Church [Evangelical Orthodox Church will join the Antiochian Orthodox Church] B. Nassif. il *Christ Today* 31:40 F 6 '87
Evangelical Presbyterian Church *See* Presbyterian Church—United States
Evangelical television programs *See* Television broadcasting—Religious programs
Evangelical Theological Society
The battle of the lexicons [meeting titled Male and female in biblical and theological perspective] D. Neff. il *Christ Today* 31:44+ Ja 16 '87
Evangelical Women's Caucus
Christian feminists form new organization. *Christ Today* 31:44 O 16 '87
Women explore formation of alternative feminist group [Christian feminists] D. Neff. il *Christ Today* 31:45-6 Ap 17 '87
Evangelicalism
See also
Fundamentalism
Liberty Federation
Moral Majority
Christianity today talks to James Davison Hunter. D. Neff and B. Spring. por *Christ Today* 31:64-5 N 20 '87
The down side of civility [evangelical courtesy; study by James Davison Hunter] D. Neff. *Christ Today* 31:13 F 6 '87
Faith in a true believer [O. North's evangelical Christianity] A. Stanley. por *Time* 129:23 F 16 '87

Evangelicalism—*cont.*
A farewell to harms. K. S. Kantzer. il *Christ Today* 31:14-15 D 11 '87
What can liberals and evangelicals teach each other? D. W. Shriver. il *Christ Century* 104:687-90 Ag 12-19 '87
Who are the evangelicals? R. Webber. il *USA Today (Periodical)* 115:88-9 My '87

Bibliography
Giving God a hand. M. Gardner. il *N Y Rev Books* 34:17-18+ Ag 13 '87

History
Calling evangelicals to repentance [D. Frank's Less than conquerers] M. E. Marty. *Christ Century* 104:830-1 S 30 '87

Evangelicalism and politics *See* Religion and politics

Evangelicals for Social Action
With the religious right in disarray, two groups consider new opportunities [with interview with R. J. Sider] B. Spring. il por *Christ Today* 31:46, 48 Jl 10 '87

Evangelista, Matthew A.
Exploiting the Soviet "threat" to Europe. bibl f *Bull At Sci* 43:14-16+ Ja/F '87
Gorbachev's next move. il *Harpers* 274:24+ Ja '87
'New thinking' in foreign policy. *Nation* 244:795-9 Je 13 '87
Sakharov and Gorky. *Bull At Sci* 43:21 Ap '87

Evangelistic conferences *See* Religious conferences

Evangelistic work
See also
Church growth
Inter-Varsity Christian Fellowship
Jews for Jesus movement
Missions
National Association of Evangelicals
"We may never go home" [Billy Graham crusade organizers J. and J. Bigham] B. Spring. il pors *Christ Today* 31:14-15 Mr 20 '87

Finance
See also
Evangelical Council for Financial Accountability
National Religious Broadcasters. Ethics and Financial Integrity Commission
Auctioning an empire [PTL Network] M. Green. il pors *People Wkly* 27:40-3 Je 8 '87
Christianity today surveys the top TV preachers. il *Christ Today* 31:46, 48-9 O 16 '87
A crackdown at PTL. il por *Christ Today* 31:51+ Je 12 '87
Evangelists in Babylon [televangelists] H. Fairlie. *New Repub* 196:22-4 Ap 27 '87
The fall of the House of Bakker [TV evangelists] J. M. Wall. *Christ Century* 104:323-4 Ap 8 '87
False profits [televangelists] T. McNichol. *New Repub* 196:11-12 Ap 13 '87
Falwell and the PTL: 'send money'. D. Gates. il por *Newsweek* 109:6 My 25 '87
Falwell says media ministers need more accountability. por *Christ Today* 31:42 Jl 10 '87
Falwell throws in the towel [resignation from PTL] R. N. Ostling. il por *Time* 130:74 O 19 '87
Financing the Great Commission [special section] il *Christ Today* 31:25-40 My 15 '87
God and money [PTL scandal; cover story; special section] il pors *Time* 130:48-55 Ag 3 '87
God and money [TV evangelists; cover story; special section] il pors *Newsweek* 109:16-23 Ap 6 '87
God's green acres: at home with the televangelists. R. Healy and D. E. Haupt. il *Life* 10:54-8+ Je '87
The gospel according to the free market [shakeout among TV evangelists] T. Mason and S. Ticer. il por *Bus Week* p43-4 Ap 6 '87
Gospelgate II: target Falwell. L. Martz. il pors *Newsweek* 109:56-7+ Je 1 '87
Heaven can wait [J. and T. Bakker; cover story; special section] il pors *Newsweek* 109:58-62+ Je 8 '87
Holy hoaxers? [overzealous preachers giving Christian fund raisers a bad name] il *U S News World Rep* 102:10 Mr 23 '87
How much money did Jim and Tammy need? il por *Newsweek* 110:60-1 Ag 3 '87
Of God and greed [J. Bakker-J. Falwell feud] R. N. Ostling. il pors *Time* 129:70-2+ Je 8 '87
Pearlygate satires are weak on substance [press coverage of J. Bakker scandal] L. I. Sweet. *Christ Century* 104:644-5 Jl 29-Ag 5 '87
PTL: a battle of words in the holy war [J. Bakker hires lawyer M. Belli] il pors *Newsweek* 110:25 Jl 6 '87
Questioning tactics [results of Gallup poll on fund raising by evangelical groups] *Time* 129:70 Mr 30 '87

The state of Christian broadcasting. R. Frame. il *Christ Today* 31:48-50 Mr 20 '87
Stones fly in the TV temple [J. Bakker-J. Falwell feud] G. Witkin. il pors *U S News World Rep* 102:10-11 Je 8 '87
Taking yet another look at television evangelism [congressional hearings] il por *Christ Today* 31:48-9+ S 18 '87
The televangelist fiasco: top '87 religion story. *Christ Century* 104:1163-5 D 23-30 '87
Televangelist takeover. *Nation* 244:419-20 Ap 4 '87
This is what you thought: 97% say TV preachers are too concerned with raising money [results of survey] *Glamour* 85:135 S '87
A trio of fraud cases. *Christ Century* 104:488-9 My 20-27 '87
A troubled homecoming [PTL files for bankruptcy] L. Martz. il pors *Newsweek* 109:21+ Je 22 '87
TV ministries and taxation. B. Spring. il *Christ Today* 31:36+ N 6 '87
TV preachers to testify. *Newsweek* 110:64 Ag 31 '87
TV's endless holy wars [Bakkers' attempt to regain ministry] M. Gray. *Macleans* 100:45 Jl 6 '87
An unholy war in the TV pulpits [cover story; special section; with editorial comment by David R. Gergen] il *U S News World Rep* 102:58-66, 72 Ap 6 '87
What profits a preacher? [televangelists] K. L. Woodward. il *Newsweek* 109:68 My 4 '87
Why do Americans distrust Christian fund raisers? L. Cryderman. il *Christ Today* 31:38 Ap 17 '87
Will those cards and letters keep coming? [televangelists] A. Press. il *Newsweek* 109:72 My 11 '87
Anecdotes, facetiae, satire, etc.
Hostile takeovers. M. E. Marty. *Christ Century* 104:343 Ap 8 '87

International aspects
See also
Lausanne Committee for World Evangelization
Black Christians find unity in missions and evangelism. J. W. Reapsome. il *Christ Today* 31:54+ My 15 '87
The call of Destiny [black Christians to play major role in world evangelization] R. Frame. il *Christ Today* 31:64 S 4 '87
Cardinal Suenens calls for a new Pentecost [interview] J. Catoir. *America* 156:457-9 Je 6 '87
Catholics plan worldwide evangelization effort [Evangelization 2000] J. Duin. *Christ Today* 31:36 F 6 '87

China
Billy Graham postpones China trip. il por *Christ Today* 31:54 O 2 '87

El Salvador
Swaggart swings through El Salvador. P. Lacefield. il por *Commonweal* 114:279-80+ My 8 '87

Israel
We can love Israel too much. B. Spradlin. il por *Christ Today* 31:14 Jl 10 '87

Latin America
The cross and the flag: right-wing evangelicals invade Latin America. M. Collett. il *Progressive* 51:18-20 D '87
Offering the hope of heaven [work of J. Swaggart] R. N. Ostling. il por *Time* 129:69 Mr 16 '87

Nicaragua
See also
Evangelical Committee for Aid and Development in Nicaragua

Evangelists
See also
Bakker, Jim
Crouch, Paul
Falwell, Jerry
Graham, Billy, 1918-
Roberts, Oral
Robertson, Pat
Sims, Jack
Swaggart, Jimmy Lee
I saw it in the funnies, and then I didn't. M. E. Marty. *Christ Century* 104:207 F 25 '87

Evangelization *See* Evangelistic work

Evans, Alice Frazer
(jt. auth) *See* Evans, Robert A., 1937-, and Evans, Alice Frazer

Evans, Craig, 1949-
Bringing walkways to your doorstep. il *Prevention* 39:90+ S '87

Evans, David
about
David Evans: the longest-running legs on Broadway. K. Grubb. il pors *Dance Mag* 61:70-1 D '87

Evans, David L.
Self-help at its best. por *Newsweek* 109:8 Mr 16 '87
Evans, Dennis
about
Single and free—of AIDS. T. Gallant-Stokes. por *Black Enterp* 18:24 Ag '87
Evans, Diane
about
The unsung heroines of Vietnam. J. McRobbie. il pors *McCalls* 114:159 My '87
Evans, Dilys
The YA cover story. il *Publ Wkly* 232:112-15 Jl 24 '87
Evans, Gil
about
Creator by proxy. F. Davis. il *Atlantic* 259:83-5 F '87
Evans, Glenn
about
Primed to kill, an angry young man shoots his dead sister's boyfriend, leaving two families in ruins. J. Hammer. il *People Wkly* 28:159-60+ N 16 '87
Evans, James
Tone Vigeland. il por *Am Craft* 47:24-31 Ap/My '87
Evans, Janet
about
America's new golden girl. B. Anderson. il pors *Sports Illus* 67:28-30+ Ag 10 '87
Evans, Jewell
about
Flour power: mixing pleasure with business. H. G. Miller. il por *Saturday Evening Post* 259:48-9+ Ap '87
Evans, Jo Ann Hall- *See* Hall-Evans, Jo Ann
Evans, Joni
about
After the un-Random showdown. M. Reuter. il pors *Publ Wkly* 232:11 O 30 '87
Dick and Joni. J. Kasindorf. il pors *N Y* 20:60-4+ D 14 '87
Joni Evans leaves Simon & Schuster; to head imprint at Random House. J. Mutter. por *Publ Wkly* 232:10 S 4 '87
Joni Evans replaces Kaminsky at Random. *Publ Wkly* 232:11 O 23 '87
Once half of publishing's dynamic duo, Joni Evans is now throwing the book at her husband, Dick Snyder. M. Vespa. il pors *People Wkly* 28:149-50+ N 16 '87
The rumble at Random House. J. Alter. il pors *Newsweek* 110:62 O 26 '87
Evans, Karen
Meet designer Jessica McClintock. il pors *Seventeen* 46:206-9+ Ap '87
Evans, Karen
Balancing act at Point Reyes [cover story] il *Natl Parks* 61:16-21 Jl/Ag '87
Evans, Larry
Making a career of it. il *Progressive* 51:34 D '87
Evans, Lee
about
Giants on the earth. K. Moore. il pors *Sports Illus* 66:48-50+ Je 29 '87
Evans, Mary Ellen
British television's Catholic pioneer. il *America* 157:501-3 D 26 '87
Evans, Paul
about
Can't anybody coach these guys? T. Kertes. il pors *Sport Mag* 78:53-4+ F '87
Maybe Pitt is it. C. Kirkpatrick. il por *Sports Illus* 66:20-2+ F 16 '87
Evans, Phillip W.
about
Phillip Evans named Interpreter of Year. il por *Natl Parks* 61:41 Ja/F '87
Evans, Robert A., 1937-
A nuclear free Pacific: enlisting U.S. support. *Christ Century* 104:373-4 Ap 22 '87
Evans, Robert A., 1937-, and Evans, Alice Frazer
South African retaliation: a blessing in disguise? *Christ Century* 104:79-80 Ja 28 '87
Evans, Robert O.
about
A super stargazer. il por *Time* 129:66 Mr 23 '87
Evans, Rowland, and Novak, Robert D.
Gorbachev: the man with a nice smile and iron teeth. por *Read Dig* 131:90-5 O '87
High drama in the Persian Gulf. il map *Read Dig* 131:133-6 D '87
Washington's shameful revolving door. *Read Dig* 130:118-22 My '87

Evans, Samuel
about
The Katzenjammer Falcon: an elaborate government sting gets fouled up in Reagan's Iranscam. J. Traub. il por *N Y* 20:36-42 F 9 '87
Evans, Sara
"Mommy, I feel sick". il *Parents* 62:120-2 O '87
A note for the teacher. il *Parents* 62:90-2 S '87
Evans, Vince
about
Ex-Bears' QB Evans sues USFL for $1.3 million pay. por *Jet* 71:49 F 2 '87
QB Vince Evans benefits from breaking NFL strike. por *Jet* 73:46 N 9 '87
USFL Blitz ordered to pay QB Evans $1.6 million. por *Jet* 72:50 Ap 27 '87
Evans (Gil) Orchestra *See* Gil Evans Orchestra
Evans (Jewel) Family Foods *See* Jewel Evans Family Foods
Evans-Pritchard, Ambrose
Poor in Washington. il *World Press Rev* 34:64 N '87
Evaporation
See also
Evapotranspiration
Evapotranspiration
Can only evapotranspiration make a tree? [variation in biodiversity by locale; research by David J. Currie and Viviane Paquin] map *Sci News* 132:215 O 3 '87
Evarts, Prescott
Rt. 91, Vermont [poem] *Ctry J* 14:73 D '87
Eveland, Ruth A.
Troy, N.Y.: where 1225 volunteers sat in a window and read. il *Publ Wkly* 232:15 Jl 3 '87
Evening and continuation schools
See also
Adult education
University extension
Evening clothes *See* Clothing and dress
Evening primrose oil
Luring consumers down the primrose path. C. Ballentine and S. Maifarth. il *FDA Consum* 21:34-5 N '87
Everest, Mount (China and Nepal) *See* Mount Everest (China and Nepal)
Everest (New York, N.Y.: Restaurant) *See* New York (N.Y.)—Restaurants, nightclubs, bars, etc.
Everest & Jennings International
The perils of being too successful. E. Paris. il *Forbes* 139:88+ F 9 '87
Everett, Rupert
about
The emancipation of Rupert Everett. R. Nadelson. il por *Vogue* 177:80 My '87
Everglades (Fla.)
Consensus on the 'Glades. *Wilderness* 50:3 Spr '87
The promised land [largemouth bass fishing in the Everglades] P. Kaminsky. il *Field Stream* 92:62-3+ N '87
Recovery plan focuses on panther survival [Florida panther] il *Natl Parks* 61:45 Mr/Ap '87
Evergreen Group
Taiwan's billionaire sea lord [Chang Yung-fa] A. Tanzer. il por *Forbes* 140:36-8 Ag 24 '87
Evergreens
See also
Christmas trees
Holly
Yews
Everling, Anna
Waterspouts. il *Weatherwise* 40:206-8 Jl/Ag '87
Everly, Don
about
Everly Brothers. *New Yorker* 63:24-5 Ag 31 '87
Everly, Phil
about
Everly Brothers. *New Yorker* 63:24-5 Ag 31 '87
Evernden, Jack F., and Marsh, Gerald E.
Yields of US and Soviet nuclear tests [cover story] bibl il *Phys Today* 40 pt1:36-44 Ag '87
Evers, Lisa *See* Sliwa, Lisa
Evers, Marie A.
about
A welfare mother's battle to clean up the Medicaid mess. S. B. Garland. il *Bus Week* p42 D 21 '87
Evers, Myrlie
about
Myrlie Evers asks for protection during threat. *Jet* 72:16 Ap 6 '87
Everson, Mark W.
about
How will the new law affect you? [interview] R. Thompson. il por *Nations Bus* 75:34 Ap '87

Evert, Chris
Climb every mountain: how to neutralize your male opponent. il *World Tennis* 34:22-4 F '87
Don't be a clay pigeon! il por *World Tennis* 34:48-50 My '87
How I developed my volley. il por *World Tennis* 35:30-1 N '87
Passing shots. il *World Tennis* 34:28 Ap '87
Planned playerhood. il *World Tennis* 34:22-3 Ja '87
Travelers advisory. il *World Tennis* 35:96-7+ S '87
                    about
Turning pain into gain. D. Scheiber. il pors *Sports Illus* 66:93-4 My 11 '87
            Anecdotes, facetiae, satire, etc.
Golden girls. M. Lupica. il *World Tennis* 35:40-2+ S '87
Eviction
Back to the future: Columbia replays the battles of '68. P. Blauner. il *N Y* 20:30-3 My 18 '87
Musical 'Mama' eviction cleared by N.Y. judge. *Jet* 72:53 Jl 13 '87
Evidence, Expert
            See also
    Forensic psychiatry
    Medical jurisprudence
Accuracy v. advocacy. M. J. Saks. il *Technol Rev* 90:42-9 Ag/S '87
Experts up to here. D. Fanning. il *Forbes* 140:378 Jl 13 '87
From the people who brought you the Twinkie defense: the ride of the expert witness industry. B. Fleetwood. il *Wash Mon* 19:33-7 Je '87
Evidence (Law)
            See also
    Confession (Law)
    Estoppel
    Evidence, Expert
    Police questioning
    Searches and seizures
    Wiretapping
    Witnesses
Lab evidence = tougher sentences [views of Joseph Peterson] il *USA Today (Periodical)* 115:15 Ap '87
Problems of crime and punishment [ethics of U.S. use of Soviet evidence against Nazi war criminal K. Linnas] R. Lacayo. il *Time* 129:60 Ap 20 '87
Evil *See* Good and evil
Evins, Melissa
                    about
Sole mates. J. Roberts. il pors *N Y* 20:28 Mr 9 '87
Evins, Reed
                    about
Sole mates. J. Roberts. il pors *N Y* 20:28 Mr 9 '87
Evolution
            See also
    Adaptation (Biology)
    Biology
    Creation
    Galaxies—Evolution
    Homology (Biology)
    Life (Biology)—Origin
    Man, Prehistoric
    Moon—Evolution
    Natural selection
    Phylogeny
    Plants—Evolution
    Species
    Stars—Evolution
    Tennessee evolution controversy
    Variation (Biology)
Bacterial bedfellows [symbiotic theory of evolution] D. Sagan and L. Margulis. il *Nat Hist* 96:26+ Mr '87
Creationists: of two minds about science. il *Discover* 8:6 Mr '87
Darwinism defined: the difference between fact and theory. S. J. Gould. il *Discover* 8:64-5+ Ja '87
Ecology of modern humans [views of Robert Foley] R. Lewin. *Science* 237:1295 S 11 '87
Ervin Laszlo. B. Lawren. *Omni* 9:96 S '87
Everyone's genealogical mother [study of mtDNA indicates "Eve" lived in sub-Saharan Africa; research by Allan Wilson and others] M. D. Lemonick. il *Time* 129:66 Ja 26 '87
The evolution of catalytic function. P. A. Sharp and D. Eisenberg. *Science* 238:729-30+ N 6 '87
Evolution, sex, and sex allocation [special issue] *BioScience* 37:466-96+ Jl/Ag '87
Four legs bad, two legs good [bipedal locomotion] R. Lewin. bibl *Science* 235:969-71 F 27 '87

The four-year itch: do divorce patterns reflect our evolutionary heritage? H. E. Fisher. il *Nat Hist* 96:22+ O '87
Gene flow and the geographic structure of natural populations. M. Slatkin. bibl f il *Science* 236:787-92 My 15 '87
The lesson of the dinosaurs: evolution didn't inevitably lead to us. S. J. Gould. il *Discover* 8:51 Mr '87
Multidimensional analysis of an evolving lineage. D. B. Wake and A. Larson. bibl f il *Science* 238:42-8 O 2 '87
Neuronal circuits and evolution [discussion of August 22, 1986 article, Neuronal circuits: an evolutionary perspective] J. P. C. Dumont and R. M. Robertson. *Science* 236:1681-2 Je 26 '87
Red pond [Lake Cisó evidence for L. Margulis' theory of evolution by symbiosis] B. Lawren. il *Omni* 9:20 Ja '87
Stephen Jay Gould [interview] J. Tierney. il por *Roll Stone* p38-9+ Ja 15 '87
This view of life. S. J. Gould. See issues of Natural History
Tics in the tocks of molecular clocks. I. Amato. il *Sci News* 131:74-5 Ja 31 '87
What did Noah do with the manure? and other burning questions of creation science. J. Hitt. il *Wash Mon* 19:25-8 F '87
Will creationism rise again? S. Boxer. il *Discover* 8:80-5 O '87
            Bibliography
The metaphor and the rock [works by S. J. Gould] F. J. Sulloway. il *N Y Rev Books* 34:37-40 My 28 '87
            Mathematical models
Asymmetry of lineages and the direction of evolutionary time. S. J. Gould and others. il *Science* 236:1437-41 Je 12 '87
            Study and teaching
Creation/evolution update. F. Edwords. See issues of The Humanist
The creation-science case: is it science or religion? [Louisiana case to be heard by Supreme Court] E. J. Larson. *Christ Today* 31:50-1 Ja 16 '87
Creationism case argued before Supreme Court [Louisiana case] R. Lewin. *Science* 235:22-3 Ja 2 '87
Evolution and creation: one missed opportunity [booklet published by the American Scientific Affiliation] F. J. Ayala. *BioScience* 37:450 Jl/Ag '87
First word [attempts to impose creation science on public schools] M. Gell-Mann. il *Omni* 9:8 F '87
High Court rejects creationism law [Louisiana case] J. Raloff. *Sci News* 131:404 Je 27 '87
High Court: the day God and Darwin collided [teaching of creationism in Louisiana ruled unconstitutional] T. Gest and L. Solórzano. il *U S News World Rep* 102:12 Je 29 '87
Justice Scalia's misunderstanding [dissenting opinion on Louisiana creationism case] S. J. Gould. il *Nat Hist* 96:14+ O '87
Keep guard up after evolution victory. M. Zimmerman. *BioScience* 37:636 O '87
Keeping God out of the classroom [Supreme Court ruling on Louisiana creation science law] L. Martz. il *Newsweek* 109:23-4 Je 29 '87
Memories of the monkey trial [Supreme Court rules against creationism law in Louisiana] A. L. Sanders. il *Time* 129:54 Je 29 '87
One case: a step-by-step account of its progress through the Supreme Court [Louisiana creationism case] il *Life* 10:114-15 Fall '87
Schools can not require religious and scientific evolution teachings: Court. *Jet* 72:17 Jl 6 '87
Science, 7; creationism, 2 [Supreme Court ruling on Louisiana statute] *Sci Am* 257:14 Ag '87
Should public schools teach creation science? W. S. Morrow; J. Wiester. il *Christ Today* 31:50 S 18 '87
Supreme Court abolishes Louisiana creationism law. H. Fields. *Publ Wkly* 232:13 Jl 3 '87
Supreme Court bars creationism in schools [Louisiana law] I. Goodwin. *Phys Today* 40:56-7 S '87
Supreme Court hears arguments on teaching 'creation science' [Louisiana case] I. Goodwin. il *Phys Today* 40:64-6 F '87
Supreme Court on 'flat souls' [ruling on Louisiana law ordering equal treatment of creationism with evolution] J. M. Wall. *Christ Century* 104:579 Jl 1-8 '87
Supreme Court strikes down "creation science" law as promotion of religion [Louisiana case] C. Norman. *Science* 236:1620 Je 26 '87
Supreme Court strikes down Louisiana creationism act. T. J. Flygare. il *Phi Delta Kappan* 69:77-9 S '87

Evolution—Study and teaching—*cont.*
The verdict on creationism [Supreme Court ruling on Louisiana law] S. J. Gould. il *N Y Times Mag* p32+ Jl 19 '87
Evolution, Social *See* Social change
Evolution USA (Firm)
The perfect ski. C. Leocha. il *Esquire* 108:35-6 D '87
Ewald Prize
Cowley and Moodie honored for work in crystallography. por *Phys Today* 40:105 D '87
Ewell, Peter
Assessment: where are we? The implications of new state mandates. il *Change* 19:23-8 Ja/F '87
Ewing, Darrell
(jt. auth) See Myers, Dennis, and Ewing, Darrell
Ewing, Joseph H.
The new Sherman letters [cover story] il pors *Am Herit* 38:24-7+ Jl/Ag '87
Ewing, Lauren, 1947?-
about
Lauren Ewing at Diane Brown. E. Heartney. *Art Am* 75:181-2 O '87
Ex-convicts
Ex-bank thief Delbert Dunmire busts loose with a classy high school reunion in the Bahamas. R. Arias. il pors *People Wkly* 28:30-1 Ag 31 '87
Murph the Surf rides again [J. Murphy] J. Lombardi. il por *Esquire* 108:114-16+ N '87
The released killers who walk among us. T. Gest. il *U S News World Rep* 102:18 Ap 27 '87
Education
An ex-con's journey to the right side of the law [D. Streater] L. B. Randolph. il pors *Ebony* 42:38-40+ O '87
Sports
Street crime put Brian Brundage in Sing Sing; basketball sent him to college. J. Friedman. il pors *People Wkly* 27:84+ F 2 '87
Ex-employees' associations
Office pals: it pays to stay in touch. J. A. Byrne. il *Bus Week* p126 Ap 6 '87
Ex-Im Bank *See* Export-Import Bank of the United States
Ex-offenders *See* Ex-convicts
Ex-prisoners *See* Ex-convicts
Examination tutors *See* Tutors and tutoring
Examinations
See also
Educational tests and measurements
Physical examinations
Teachers—Examinations
Cram at your own risk. W. Coffey. il *Seventeen* 46:48+ My '87
The effects of exam anxiety on grandma's health. J. J. Chiodo. *Educ Dig* 52:45-7 Ja '87
The Jung and the restless [college students' nightmares about exams] H. Ward. il *N Y* 20:23 Je 8 '87
Student exams: accentuating the positive [communication between teachers and students] M. McMullen-Pastrick and M. G. Weimer. *Educ Dig* 52:14-17 My '87
Excel (Computer program) *See* Spreadsheets (Computer programs)
Excel Beef Corporation
Buyers say Excel is OK [vacuum-packed beef] il *Success Farm* 85:48 O '87
Exchange, Foreign *See* Foreign exchange
Exchange (Barter) *See* Barter
Exchange National Bank of Chicago
Photographic masterpieces from a midwestern bank. H. Kahn. il *USA Today (Periodical)* 115:42-53 My '87
Exchange rates *See* Foreign exchange
Exchanges, Commodity *See* Commodity exchanges
Exchanges, Educational *See* Educational exchanges
Exchanges, Literary and scientific
At the summit meeting [Soviet-American climb of Mount Elbrus] G. Warner. il map *Sierra* 72:57-60 Jl/Ag '87
Black scientist is named Soviet exchange scholar [S. K. Mtingwa] por *Jet* 73:36 O 12 '87
Council adopts statement on US-Soviet scientific cooperation [American Physical Society] *Phys Today* 40:121 F '87
National security and the environment. W. C. Clark. bibl *Environment* 29:inside cover+ Je '87
A new candor at Issyk-Kul [U.S.-Soviet cultural exchange] A. Miller. por *Newsweek* 109:8 Ja 19 '87
Report on scientific and technological activities [message to Congress, June 17, 1987] R. Reagan. *Dep State Bull* 87:61-2 S '87
Science and technology exchanges with the Soviet Union [statement, June 25, 1987] J. Negroponte. *Dep State Bull* 87:58-61 S '87

Soviet science and technology at the Boston meeting. A. W. Trivelpiece. *Science* 238:1631 D 18 '87
Strains in U.S.-Japan exchanges. M. Sun. il *Science* 237:476-8 Jl 31 '87
Time for Sakharov's global dialogue. R. E. Marshak. il pors *Bull At Sci* 43:7-8 O '87
U.S. policy on exchanges with the Soviets called a "shambles" [hearing by House Subcommittee on International Scientific Cooperation] C. Norman. *Science* 237:18 Jl 3 '87
U.S., Soviets renew an exchange [nuclear safety] E. Marshall. *Science* 235:1568 Mr 27 '87
Unsung force in science exchanges [work of NATO] C. Norman. *Science* 237:1113 S 4 '87
Update on AAAS cooperative efforts with Soviet scientific and engineering community. S. M. Burns. *Science* 237:85 Jl 3 '87
Excise tax
Congress is lusting after higher excise taxes. D. Harbrecht. il *Bus Week* p26 Je 29 '87
Loopholes at large. R. S. McIntyre. *New Repub* 196:12+ Je 15 '87
Restoring New York's wildlife [Pittman-Robertson program] L. DeGraff and J. Dell. il *Conservationist* 42:2-11+ N/D '87
Excited states *See* Energy levels (Quantum mechanics)
Exciton theory
Light switch [work of André Mysyrowicz and others] *Sci Am* 256:74-5 Mr '87
Exclusive Economic Zone
East Coast EEZ mapping. *Oceans* 20:4-5 My/Je '87
Mapping the nation's underseas wealth. R. C. Cowen. il *Technol Rev* 90:23 N/D '87
Nothing fishy about new tuna treaty [U.S. and the Pacific region] D. G. Knibb. il *Oceans* 20:6-7 Jl/Ag '87
Pulling the plug on ocean minerals. R. Monastersky. *Sci News* 132:86 Ag 8 '87
Sea-bottom road maps. il *Sea Front* 33:381-3 S/O '87
Excretion
See also
Feces
Urine
Excuses
The devil made me do it. H. Fehren. *U S Cathol* 52:38-40 Jl '87
Managing the excusaholic employee [excerpt from Managing people at work desk guide] T. L. Quick. *Work Woman* 12:15 Ag '87
Execucoach (Firm)
Unique concept [limousine service using elegant vans] *New Yorker* 63:19-21 Jl 13 '87
Executions and executioners
See also
Capital punishment
Hanging
An everyday death [E. Moreno in Texas] I. Austen. il por *Macleans* 100:16+ Mr 16 '87
"Everyone's a victim in this" [execution of murderer S. Rault] R. Woodbury. il por *Time* 130:22 S 7 '87
An execution in Tehran [execution of M. Hashemi] K. Scanlon and C. Jerome. il por *Macleans* 100:32 O 12 '87
Executive Air Fleet
At your service. N. Moll. il *Flying* 114:38-41 Mr '87
Executive assistants *See* Administrative assistants
Executive departments (U.S.) *See* United States—Executive departments
Executive Jet Aviation, Inc.
EJA gears for major increase in executive charter business. il *Aviat Week Space Technol* 127:95-6 S 28 '87
Ohio group offers shared ownership of business jets. *Aviat Week Space Technol* 127:102+ S 28 '87
Executive power
See also
Civil supremacy over the military
Executive privilege (Government information)
Judicial review
Pardon
Presidents—Powers and duties
Veto
War and emergency powers
Executive privilege (Government information)
History deleted [Justice Dept.'s attempt to win R. M. Nixon the right to keep secret thousands of historically significant documents] *Nation* 244:669-70 My 23 '87
Executive search consultants
See also
Heidrick & Struggles, Inc.
Korn/Ferry International
The executive woman's guide to headhunters. B. G. Kempton. il *Work Woman* 12:110-12+ Ap '87

Executive search consultants—*cont.*
Going head-to-head with a headhunter. J. A. Byrne.
il *Bus Week* p180-1 O 12 '87
How to attract the attention of headhunters. *Glamour*
85:64 Jl '87
Job strategy: how to be "discovered" by an executive
recruiter. il *Glamour* 85:90-1 Mr '87
Pounding the pavement by computer. D. H. Dunn. il
Bus Week p166 My 11 '87
Executive secretaries *See* Administrative assistants
Executive stock options *See* Stock purchase options
Executives

> *See also*
> Black executives
> Clothing and dress—Businessmen
> Corporations—Directors
> Entrepreneurs
> Information managers
> Women executives

25 executives to watch. il *Bus Week* Sp Issue:208-9+
Ap 17 '87
Bosses small but powerful. il *Forbes* 140:220+ N 16
'87
Catalysts of genius, dealers in hope [address, October
14, 1986] L. E. Reuss. *Vital Speeches Day* 53:173-6
Ja 1 '87
The corporate elite [with CEO 1000 directory] il *Bus
Week* Sp Issue:13-17+ O 23 '87
Faces behind the figures. See issues of Forbes
Famous findings from Nexis [executives most in the
news] D. Seligman. il *Fortune* 116:201+ N 23 '87
Fortune people. N. J. Perry. See issues of Fortune
beginning August 17, 1987
Global movers and shakers [special section] il *U S News
World Rep* 102:61-4 My 11 '87
How managers will manage [1990s] P. Nulty. il *Fortune*
115:47-8+ F 2 '87
How to work without a secretary. E. W. Allison and
M. A. Allison. *Work Woman* 12:22 Ag '87
Korea's new corporate bosses: made in America. L.
Nakarmi and W. J. Holstein. il *Bus Week* p58-9 F
23 '87
Lessons of leadership. See issues of Nation's Business
News/Trends. See issues of Fortune beginning March
5, 1984
Top guns who will come out firing. J. Egan. il *U S
News World Rep* 103:84-5 D 28 '87-Ja 4 '88
The U.S. Business Hall of Fame. A. M. Louis. il *Fortune*
115:102-7 Ap 13 '87
The world's 50 biggest industrial CEOs [with introd.
by Terence Paré and Wilton Woods; cover story] il
Fortune 116:23-31+ Ag 3 '87
The year's 50 most fascinating business people [special
issue] il *Fortune* 115:30-42+ Ja 5 '87
You survived a cutback—now, make the most of it.
J. A. Byrne. il *Bus Week* p131 D 14 '87

Age
The ages of a manager. W. Kiechel, III. il *Fortune*
115:170-1+ My 11 '87
Lessons from late bloomers. F. Rice. il *Fortune* 116:87-91
Ag 31 '87
Pushed out at 45—now what? P. Nulty. il *Fortune*
115:26-30 Mr 2 '87

Anecdotes, facetiae, satire, etc.
At play in the corporate tree. S. Bing. il *Esquire* 108:44
Ag '87
Corporate comeback strategies. J. Queenan. il
Commonweal 114:340-1 Je 5 '87

Applications for positions
> *See* Job applications

Attitudes
America's most admired corporations [Fortune survey]
E. C. Baig. il *Fortune* 115:18-31+ Ja 19 '87
Business week/Harris poll. See issues of Business Week
The economy according to small business. H. S. Braun.
il *Nations Bus* 75:42-4+ My '87
The Fortune 500 CEO poll. B. Saporito. il *Fortune*
116:58-9 S 28 '87
Small-business confidence: looking good at home. H.
S. Braun. il *Nations Bus* 75:32-3+ N '87
Still bullish at the top. A. Ramirez. il *Fortune* 116:90-1
N 23 '87

Biography
Book mania hits the corner office. D. Demong. il *Bus
Week* Sp Issue:61-2+ O 23 '87

Compensation
> *See* Executives—Salaries, pensions, etc.

Dismissal
> *See also*
> Outplacement consultant services

How to fire the CEO. R. B. Stolley. il *Fortune* 116:38-41+
Ag 31 '87
Pushed out at 45—now what? P. Nulty. il *Fortune*
115:26-30 Mr 2 '87
The tales of four hunters. R. B. Stolley. il *Fortune*
115:31-4 Mr 2 '87
You're fired! [cover story; special section] il *U S News
World Rep* 102:50-7 Mr 23 '87

Health and hygiene
Death wishes [executive health and stock market analysis]
J. Crudele. il *N Y* 20:14 Jl 27 '87
Extra pounds can weigh down your career. L. Baum.
il *Bus Week* p96 Ag 3 '87
Parting MCI's veil of secrecy [secrecy surrounding presi-
dent W. G. McGowan's heart transplant surgery] J.
J. Keller. *Bus Week* p54 My 18 '87
To your health. See issues of Nation's Business beginning
May 1983

Mortality
A puzzling toll at the top [deaths of corporate chiefs
in Japan] J. M. Horowitz. il *Time* 130:46 Ag 3 '87

Promotion
And some fall by the wayside. D. Machan. il *Forbes*
139:162+ Ap 6 '87
Why not second best? W. Kiechel, III. il *Fortune*
115:129-30+ Mr 16 '87

Psychology
Are you a courageous manager? J. Sherman. *Work
Woman* 12:24 My '87
Attack of the obsessive managers. W. Kiechel, III. il
Fortune 115:127-8 F 16 '87
Personality tests are back [Myers-Briggs Type Indicator]
T. Moore. il *Fortune* 115:74-6+ Mr 30 '87
The role of the manager: the use of power. F. Bartolomé
and A. Laurent. *Current* 291:12-16 Mr/Ap '87
Self-help for executives. *U S News World Rep* 102:68
F 9 '87
Something in the way he works . . . why we have
an eye for the driven guy. B. G. Harrison. il
Mademoiselle 93:262-3+ S '87
Successful supervisory secrets. M. B. Silber. il *USA Today
(Periodical)* 116:92-4 Jl '87
Summoning managerial courage. W. Kiechel, III. il
Fortune 115:149-50+ Ja 19 '87
Unlocking the managerial memory. W. Kiechel, III. il
Fortune 116:183-4 D 21 '87
What makes top managers different? R. Jelinek. *Work
Woman* 12:109 My '87
What's black and blue and floats in the Monongahela
River? [executives' humor] D. Machan. il *Forbes*
140:216+ N 2 '87
When to lead, when to stand back. F. E. Fiedler. il
Psychol Today 21:26-7 S '87
Why not second best? W. Kiechel, III. il *Fortune*
115:129-30+ Mr 16 '87
"You bet I'm scared" [anxiety] S. Blotnick. il *Forbes*
139:124 Ap 20 '87
You're probably working too hard. F. S. Worthy. il
Fortune 115:133+ Ap 27 '87

Reading
Advice without platitudes. S. Blotnick. il *Forbes* 139:119
Je 29 '87
Books bosses read. M. Wellemeyer. il *Fortune* 115:145-6+
Ap 27 '87
Classic tales of captains and castles . . . and corporations.
B. G. Kempton. il *Work Woman* 12:102-5+ O '87
Classics revisited. P. S. Green. il *Forbes* 140:171+ O
19 '87

Recreation
The art of vacationing. S. A. Franzmeier. il *Nations
Bus* 75:83+ My '87
In pursuit of outside pursuits. il *Nations Bus* 75:46
My '87
On your own time. M. Wellemeyer. See alternate issues
of Fortune

Recruiting
> *See also*
> Executive search consultants

Religious life
Profiting with help from above. E. C. Baig. il *Fortune*
115:36-8+ Ap 27 '87

Relocation
Does it pay to move the corporate headquarters? L.
Baum. il *Bus Week* p68-9 S 7 '87
A job for the 'trailing spouse,' too. J. A. Byrne. il
Bus Week p239 N 16 '87
Moving in without moving down [trailing spouse mort-
gages] P. E. Godwin. il *Changing Times* 41:20 Jl
'87
Relocating? Get the best deal you can. R. Neff. il *Bus
Week* p102 F 9 '87

Executives—Relocation—_cont._

The well-married manager [effect of cities on marriage] S. Blotnick. il *Forbes* 139:176-7 My 4 '87

When the boss wants you to move. W. Kiechel, III. *Fortune* 115:125+ Ap 13 '87

Why they hate New York. W. G. Flanagan. il *Forbes* 140:189 S 21 '87

Resignation

Breaking out of the company. J. Main. il *Fortune* 115:82-6+ My 25 '87

Leaving the corporate nest. H. Bacas. il *Nations Bus* 75:14-16+ Mr '87

Life in the outside lane [A. M. Shaver] D. Machan. il pors *Forbes* 140:220+ O 5 '87

Retirement

You don't have to be a young upstart to run a startup. il *Bus Week* p114-15 Jl 20 '87

Salaries, pensions, etc.

See also
Executives—Taxation
Expense accounts (Business)

The boss [cover story; special section] il *Forbes* 139:145-7+ Je 15 '87

Executive pay: a slower rise. E. T. Redling and K. Gorman. il *Nations Bus* 75:41-2 F '87

Executive pay: who got what in '86 [cover story] J. A. Byrne. il *Bus Week* p50-4+ My 4 '87

The golden parachutes open on media row [CBS deal with T. Wyman] por *Newsweek* 109:55 Ap 20 '87

How golden are your parachutes? G. W. Padwe. il *Nations Bus* 75:62 Mr '87

Job-hopping your way to more money. J. A. Byrne. il *Bus Week* p108 Ja 19 '87

Options, bonuses, and plain old cash. il *Fortune* 116:12 D 7 '87

Ross gets a few dollars more [S. Ross of Warner Communications] B. Dumaine. il pors *Fortune* 115:57-8+ Ap 13 '87

This year's corner-office motto: in cash we trust. B. Nussbaum. *Bus Week* p134 D 21 '87

Who gets the parachutes? J. Flint. il *Forbes* 139:38-40 Ja 12 '87

Sexual behavior

Researcher says pay hike boosts sex drive in men [research by Srully Blotnick] *Jet* 71:15 Mr 23 '87

Sports

CEOs on the slow track [long slow distance running] N. J. Perry. il *Fortune* 116:167 D 7 '87

Skiing out of a suitcase. D. P. Wiener. il *Fortune* 115:135-6+ Ja 19 '87

Taxation

How golden are your parachutes? G. W. Padwe. il *Nations Bus* 75:62 Mr '87

Training

See also
General Electric Co. Management Development Institute
Kanrisha Yosei

Behind the scenes at the Magic Kingdom [Walt Disney Co. in the management seminar business] R. Simon. il *Forbes* 140:427+ Jl 13 '87

Business simulations. S. Morgenstern. il *Work Woman* 12:54+ My '87

Danger in the wilderness. il *Fortune* 116:6 S 14 '87

Does survival training make better managers? P. Plawin. il *Changing Times* 41:78 Ag '87

Tapping your creativity [advice for business people from Michael Ray and Rochelle Myers] H. Bacas. il *Nations Bus* 75:48 Mr '87

Trying to bend managers' minds [human potential gurus] J. Main. il *Fortune* 116:95-6+ N 23 '87

Wanted: leaders who can make a difference. J. Main. il *Fortune* 116:92-4+ S 28 '87

Transfer

Job-hopping your way to more money. J. A. Byrne. il *Bus Week* p108 Ja 19 '87

Lessons from late bloomers. F. Rice. il *Fortune* 116:87-91 Ag 31 '87

Travel

See Business travel

Executives as authors

Book mania hits the corner office. D. Demong. il *Bus Week* Sp Issue:61-2+ O 23 '87

Executives as college teachers

Go back to school—this time as the teacher. J. B. Levine. il *Bus Week* p146-7 Ja 12 '87

Executives' families

See also
Children of executives

Executives in advertising

C.E.O., TV [F. Perdue's television commercials] T. Whiteside. *New Yorker* 63:39-40+ Jl 6 '87

Can a CEO buy celebrity? [W. Farley stars in his own commercials] P. King and A. Miller. il por *Newsweek* 109:44 Je 22 '87

Executone/Long Island, Inc.

A personal best [president H. Whittelsey] W. Hoffer. il pors *Nations Bus* 75:93-4 My '87

Executors and administrators

See also
Probate law and practice
Trusts and trustees

Fee-busting [lawyers serving as executors and estate attorneys] D. Fanning. il *Forbes* 140:64 S 7 '87

Exemption from taxation *See* Taxation, Exemption from

Exer-Dance Fitness Center (Butte, Mont.)

"I had to shape up my life"; ed. by Teresa Jordan. R. Hall. il pors *Redbook* 169:54+ S '87

Exercise

See also
Aerobics
Aerobikata
Body building
Body by Jake (Firm)
Breathing exercises
Exer-Dance Fitness Center (Butte, Mont.)
Exercising equipment
Eye exercises
Gymnasiums
Gymnastics
Health clubs
Muscle strength
Plyometrics
Pregnancy exercises
Rope jumping
Running
Sports
Stretching exercises
Videotapes—Exercise use
Walking
Water exercises
Weight lifting
Winter sports
Yoga

7 step swimsuit shape-up. M. Clarke. il *McCalls* 114:28-9+ My '87

The abdominal showmen [athletic training] J. Hanc. il *Sport Mag* 78:81+ O '87

The American way of fitness [special issue; with editorial comment by Judith Daniels] il *Life* 10:4, 22-31+ F '87

At-home toning with Wendy Workout. il *Seventeen* 46:200-1 Ap '87

Back aid. G. Riedel. il *World Tennis* 34:25-7 F '87

Basic muscle moves. J. Mandelbaum-Schmid. il *Vogue* 177:370-1+ Ap '87

Be fit and well—even with arthritis. il *Prevention* 39:34-6+ Je '87

Beauty workshop. See issues of Mademoiselle

The body elastic: snap into shape—the rubber-band workout. il *Mademoiselle* 93:208-11 Ap '87

Body make-over [Dan Isaacson's three week workout] L. J. Johnson. il *Ladies Home J* 104:106-11 Mr '87

Body management: leveling off at terrific [special section] il *Work Woman* 12:117-18+ Je '87

Body management: weight loss/energy gain [special section] il *Work Woman* 12:85-6+ F '87

The body vulnerable: how to strengthen your soft spots. E. Kunes. il *Mademoiselle* 93:108 My '87

Bouncing back from surgery. E. Alvarez and S. Fuchs. il *Health* 19:49-50+ Mr '87

Brooke Shields: getting back on the fitness track [cover story] A. K. Leopold. il pors *Vogue* 177:340-7+ D '87

Callan Pinckney: the thighs have it. P. Brandt. il *Ms* 16:20+ N '87

Can you outrun the flu? C. Potera. il *Women's Sports Fitness* 9:43 Ja '87

C'mon now, shape it up, baby [preschool exercise programs] A. Toufexis. il *Time* 130:61 O 5 '87

Competing couples [working out with your partner] S. Friedlander. il *Health* 19:38-40 N '87

A Cup in the balance [Karen Smith's exercises used by Star & Stripes' America's Cup crew] L. Kleinmann. il *Health* 19:51-2 F '87

Curves make a comeback. il *Mademoiselle* 93:170-3 F '87

Drop one size by Saturday: the wonder workout for thunder thighs. il *Mademoiselle* 93:152-5 D '87

Eat and run. il *Good Housekeep* 204:116+ My '87

Exercise—*cont.*

Exercise built for two. C. Schaeffer. il *Changing Times* 41:22 N '87

Exercise for life: new expert thinking [interview with W. McCarty] il *Vogue* 177:346-7+ D '87

Exercise solutions: firm up thighs & buttocks fast! il *Glamour* 85:188-9 Ja '87

Exercise: what now? *Vogue* 177:367+ Ap '87

Exercise—or how the other half lives. P. A. Feuerstein. il *Curr Health 2* 13:10-11 Mr '87

Exercises for low back pain. il *Consum Rep* 52:380-1 Je '87

The fall fitness gap [adapting outdoor workouts to indoors] S. Duff. il *Mademoiselle* 93:104+ S '87

Fashionably fit! N. Folkes. il *Essence* 18:22 S '87

First-rate shape-up! Fanny firmers [exercises by Radu] il *Harpers Bazaar* 120:80 O '87

Fit at forty: the new "middle age". A. Gottlieb. *Vogue* 177:270 O '87

Fitness at zero-G [program for astronauts] E. Smith. il *Women's Sports Fitness* 9:86 Mr '87

Fitness facts and fables. S. B. Hanson. *McCalls* 114:76 F '87

Fitness for your strokes. B. Brett. il *World Tennis* 34:34-5 Ja '87

Fitness matters. G. Legwold. il *Better Homes Gard* 65:90 O '87

Fitness matters. G. Legwold. il *Better Homes Gard* 65:82 N '87

Fitness now. L. F. McCarthy. il *Vogue* 177:162+ Ag '87

Fitness times two. H. Platt. *Harpers Bazaar* 120:132+ Ja '87

Flab fighters. il *Teen* 31:80-3 Je '87

For your thighs only: the big wheel workout. il *Mademoiselle* 93:108-11 Jl '87

Get hard, girls! Your tummy—flat out. il *Mademoiselle* 93:234-7 My '87

Get in swimsuit shape by summer. il *Teen* 31:86-7 Ap '87

Get turned on [winter workouts] T. Monahan. *Women's Sports Fitness* 9:28-9 O '87

Getting high on exercise. il *Harpers Bazaar* 120:20 F '87

Good for the old bones [post-menopausal women] K. S. Zimmeth. il *Health* 19:16 F '87

Great legs! il *McCalls* 114:23-7 Ag '87

Gut strength [abdominal exercises] J. Poppy. il *Esquire* 108:71+ S '87

Her goal: to help others trim down as she did. D. Pyles. il pors *Prevention* 39:100+ My '87

How food/fitness breakthroughs can take you from mush to muscle. il *Glamour* 85:312-15 My '87

How the top models stay on course. il *Essence* 17:48-50+ Ja '87

How to exercise without really exercising (almost). N. Stedman. il *Redbook* 168:70-3 Ja '87

How to get a superstar stomach. il *Women's Sports Fitness* 9:41 Je '87

Jane Fonda: from Barbarella . . . to barbells. S. Levin. il pors *Women's Sports Fitness* 9:24-8 D '87

Jane Fonda's 3 best potbelly exercises. il *Redbook* 169:100-3 My '87

Keep it simple [cover story; excerpt from Always beautiful] K. Pickford. il por *50 Plus* 27:26-30 Ag '87

Lean and leggy [thigh exercises; cover story] L. Kleinmann. il pors *Health* 19:50-3 Ag '87

Learning to (sort of) love exercise. A. K. Leopold. *Vogue* 177:161-2 Ap '87

Leg shape-up. C. Straley. il *Parents* 62:30 N '87

Legs, legs, legs! The short-skirt workout. il *Mademoiselle* 93:258-61 N '87

Legs! The sexy, sensory, sublime joys of legs. il *Glamour* 85:140-5 Jl '87

Life is sunnier for this now-fit Florida man; ed. by Maria Mihalik. M. Prelee. il *Prevention* 39:98-100+ S '87

Little moves matter. T. Bennett-Goleman; P. Perry. il *Good Housekeep* 205:106 O '87

The long, strong body. il *Mademoiselle* 93:212-15 O '87

'Middle aged' spread tied to lack of exercise. *Jet* 73:28 S 28 '87

More from your workouts: 16 no-strain strategies. il *Glamour* 85:228-31 F '87

Mother & daughter workout [excerpt from How to keep your child fit from birth to six] B. Prudden. il pors *Good Housekeep* 205:138 S '87

The moves you hate most and how to (finally) make them work for you. M. Fox and L. Kleinmann. il *Health* 19:54-6 S '87

Muscle movers & shapers: new body-sculpting workouts. il *Glamour* 85:276-9 Ag '87

New diet/exercise basics. *Vogue* 177:367 Ap '87

One-minute exercises [excerpts from Denise Austin's 1-minute exercises] D. Austin. il pors *Good Housekeep* 204:82+ F '87

One-minute exercises for busy bodies. D. Austin. il *Redbook* 169:97-100 O '87

Paddle-perfect upper-body builders. il *Health* 19:32-4 Ja '87

The personal you: the inner circle [Pilates exercises for the inner thighs] M. Horosko. il *Dance Mag* 61:74-5 O '87

Pilates power—all over warm-up exercises (III). M. Horosko. il *Dance Mag* 61:84-5 Ja '87

Pilates power—all over warm-up exercises (IV). M. Horosko. il *Dance Mag* 61:82-3+ F '87

Pressure points . . . active answers [special section] il *Vogue* 177:352-9+ Ag '87

The price you'll pay to sweat [special section] il *Changing Times* 41:38-44+ Ag '87

Pro advice: learning to like exercise . . . il *Vogue* 177:136 F '87

Pumping rubber [use of giant rubber bands] il *Health* 19:26-7 Ja '87

Rate your shape. J. Jones. il *Redbook* 168:88-93 F '87

Regular, easy exercise keeps pounds off best. *Prevention* 39:14 D '87

Relax your back. P. Rudolf. il *Redbook* 168:92-3 Mr '87

The shape of you to come: how fast can you get fit? P. Stein-Novack. il *Mademoiselle* 93:144+ N '87

Shape-up for stronger arms. C. Straley. il *Parents* 62:28 Ap '87

Shape-up: legs. S. M. Sims. il *Vogue* 177:338+ S '87

Shape-up now. B. Pearlman. il *Vogue* 177:72 Jl '87

Shaping up for summer. M. Marshall. il *Ebony* 42:84-6+ Je '87

The six best ways to flatten your belly. D. Foley. il *Prevention* 39:65-8 F '87

Slim and fit. L. Bellini-Gergley. il *Harpers Bazaar* 120:128+ Ag '87

Slimming secrets from the body-makeover specialists. M. Mihalik. il *Prevention* 39:90-1+ D '87

Spinal tip: building a sport-safe back. S. Beitler. il *Sport Mag* 78:79-80 F '87

Spring workout: 15 minutes a day to a better body. L. Gordon. il *Glamour* 85:187-8 Ap '87

State-of-the-art exercise. J. Kaplan. il *Vogue* 177:416+ N '87

Staying firm: a model's workout [Callanetics] M. Scott. il *Essence* 17:54-5 Ja '87

Summer power: diet and exercise for hot times. J. M. Toal. il *Mademoiselle* 93:54+ Jl '87

Sunrise beauty. il *Glamour* 85:264-7 Ag '87

Super body: tan and fit. C. Schrader. il *Harpers Bazaar* 120:54+ Je '87

Super stress-relieving routine. il *McCalls* 114:85 Ap '87

Take the plunge: slim for summer 1987 [cover story; special section] il *Health* 19:25-8+ My '87

Taking shape [legs] L. Wells. il *N Y Times Mag* p64 F 8 '87

Taking the routine out of fitness. C. Schaeffer. *Changing Times* 41:16-17 Mr '87

The taming of stress. T. Osborne. il *Curr Health 2* 14:22-3 O '87

A tough assignment—working out inside [J. Prinzmetal runs exercise program at California Institution for Women] M. Kort. il por *Ms* 16:32 O '87

Tough enough. il *Mademoiselle* 93:318-21 S '87

Travelers advisory [staying in shape on the road] C. Evert. il *World Tennis* 35:96-7+ S '87

Trim tummy toners for two [waist and stomach] il *Harpers Bazaar* 120:38 My '87

Trim your middle! C. Straley. il *Parents* 62:28 My '87

Trim your trouble spots [abdominals, buttocks, hips] C. Straley. il *Parents* 62:28 Je '87

Watch out, don't droop! il *Mademoiselle* 93:126-9 Ja '87

The whole-body workout. S. Levin. il *Mademoiselle* 93:130 Mr '87

Women and exercise. J. H. Wilmore. *Vogue* 177:90 Ja '87

Accidents and injuries

Avoiding injury. il *Vogue* 177:134 Ag '87

Exercise ailments: when your used parts break down. T. Naughton. il *Curr Health 2* 14:26-7 S '87

Exercise—*cont.*

Bibliography

Making love is not aerobic—so what? R. Blount. il *N Y Times Book Rev* 92:27-8 Ap 5 '87

Moral and religious aspects

See also

Believercise (Firm)

Physiological effects

9 mean little diet lies (and the truth about getting lean). K. Keller. il *Mademoiselle* 93:328 S '87

Can exercise cure PMS? D. Fortino. il *Women's Sports Fitness* 9:44-7 N '87

Counting calories: your metabolism may be slower than you think. B. Kevles. *Women's Sports Fitness* 9:16 Je '87

Does exercise help prevent cancer? Exercise? H. Higdon. *50 Plus* 27:16-18 Ag '87

Exercise and fluid replacement: your body's balancing act. T. Osborne. il *Curr Health 2* 14:16-17 N '87

Exercise: does doctor know best? *Vogue* 177:187 My '87

Exercise may worsen NO_2 toxicity. J. Raloff. *Sci News* 131:169 Mr 14 '87

Exercise O.K. for many with angina [research by Mayer M. Bassan] il *Prevention* 39:15 Je '87

Hamster jet lag: running it off [research by Nicholas Mrosovsky and Peggy A. Salmon] B. Bower. *Sci News* 132:358 D 5 '87

How exercise can K-O your period. S. Festa. il *Mademoiselle* 93:120 Ag '87

Keep your sunny side up [benefits of exercising in the sun] P. Cowan. il *Women's Sports Fitness* 9:13 Ag '87

Lactic acid [substance responsible for burning sensations during exercise] J. Widman. il *Women's Sports Fitness* 9:19 N '87

Life in the slow lane [research by Walker Buckalew] il *Prevention* 39:8 O '87

Metabolic catch-22 of exercise regimens. G. Kolata. il *Science* 236:146-7 Ap 10 '87

New sickle cell trait raises risk for blacks [risk of sudden death during strenuous exercise] *Jet* 73:14 N 2 '87

Postexercise headaches. P. Ennis. il *Women's Sports Fitness* 9:14 Ag '87

Quit telling women to slow down. E. Pell. il *Women's Sports Fitness* 9:68 Je '87

Sickle-cell alert [risk of sudden death during strenuous exercise] *Time* 130:61 O 5 '87

Sudden death tied to sickle-cell trait [risks of strenuous exercise] D. D. Edwards. *Sci News* 132:197 S 26 '87

Sun smarts [dangers of exercising with a sunburn] A. Ranard. *Vogue* 177:372 Ag '87

That time of month: when menstrual cramps hit, will exercise help? S. Festa. il *Women's Sports Fitness* 9:29-31 Ag '87

Walking away from fatigue [views of Harold Kohl] il *Prevention* 39:8 N '87

Warm up to cold-weather workouts. S. Garland. il *Prevention* 39:68+ D '87

Well-rounded exercise may build more bone [work of Jon E. Block] il *Prevention* 39:12 Ag '87

Why your body doesn't want to work out. A. Kaplan. il *Mademoiselle* 93:76 Je '87

Psychological aspects

The anti-exerciser. B. D. Colen. il *Health* 19:8 Je '87

Bored with exercise? How to get motivated! C. Straley. il *Parents* 62:25 S '87

Can exercise beat the blues? [research by Joel Thirer] E. Grant. il *Psychol Today* 21:22 S '87

Exercise your creativity [research by Joan C. Gondola] *Prevention* 39:12 Jl '87

The fizzle phenomenon. J. L. Lippert. il *Health* 19:55-7+ F '87

Get smart! Foods and workouts that sharpen your outlook. L. Manske. il *Mademoiselle* 93:182 S '87

Get started. J. Rogers. *Good Housekeep* 204:88 My '87

How to get—and keep—it. K. Donnan. *McCalls* 114:41 My '87

Life in the slow lane. S. A. Toth. *Vogue* 177:246 N '87

Making time to work out. L. L. Griffith and D. Pine. *Women's Sports Fitness* 9:28-33 S '87

Mental games: ten strategies for staying motivated [excerpt from The total runner] J. Lynch. il *Women's Sports Fitness* 9:26-8 Mr '87

You can make exercise fun. J. L. Lippert. il *Read Dig* 131:108-10 Ag '87

Exercise clothes *See* Clothing and dress—Sports clothes

Exercise clubs *See* Health clubs

Exercise for cats *See* Cats—Care

Exercise for dogs *See* Dogs—Care

Exercise teachers

Fitness tips from the stars' trainers. S. Donoghue. il *McCalls* 114:35 My '87

One-on-one: the future of exercise? [personal trainers] J. Kaplan. *Vogue* 177:349+ D '87

Personal fitness trainers: customized workouts. C. Schaeffer. *Changing Times* 41:20+ S '87

Exercise testing *See* Physical fitness—Testing

Exercise videotapes *See* Videotapes—Exercise use

Exercises, Military *See* Military maneuvers

Exercising equipment

Aching back? Arthur Jones says he has the answer. M. Frons. il por *Bus Week* p59+ D 14 '87

Big-league machines for the home. D. Groves. il *Sport Mag* 78:80 Je '87

Cross-country ski exercisers. il *Consum Rep* 52:187-9 D '87

Exercise bikes. il *Consum Rep* 52:189-92 D '87

The exercise extra [hand and ankle weights] il *Mademoiselle* 93:88 F '87

Exercise for homebodies. J. Hayes. il *Saturday Evening Post* 259:26 Jl/Ag '87

For chinning, the bar adjusts. il *Sunset* 178:116 Mr '87

Foul-weather friends. P. Perry. il *Good Housekeep* 205:90 O '87

High-tech body shapers. il *Harpers Bazaar* 120:40 My '87

Outfitting for fitness. *50 Plus* 27:31 Ag '87

Revving up [high tech equipment] L. Wells. *N Y Times Mag* p58 F 15 '87

Stair climbing: aerobic benefits, safety tips. il *Glamour* 85:103 N '87

Toning tables [passive exercise] M. Fiere. il *Women's Sports Fitness* 9:12 O '87

Turn your living room into a velodrome [exercise bicycles] K. Delhagen. il *Women's Sports Fitness* 9:10-11 N '87

Weatherproof workout [treadmills] K. Delhagen. il *Women's Sports Fitness* 9:50+ O '87

What should you look for in an exerciser? il *Sunset* 178:74-5 F '87

Working out in the Twilight Zone [Powercise, exercise machines designed by Richard Keelor and Rick Dyer] L. Kleinmann. il *Health* 19:16 Ap '87

Working out with R2-D2 [Powercise, exercise machines designed by Richard Keelor and Rick Dyer] M. Kaufman. il *Women's Sports Fitness* 9:100 S '87

Exercising equipment industry

See also

Hydra-Fitness Industries, Inc.

LivingWell Inc.

Weider Health & Fitness Corporation

Exhaust control devices (Automobiles) *See* Automobiles—Pollution control devices

Exhaust control devices (Diesel engines) *See* Diesel engines, Automotive—Pollution control devices

Exhaust systems

See also

Automobile engines—Exhaust

Marine engines—Exhaust

Motorcycle engines—Exhaust

Exhaustion *See* Fatigue

Exhibition buildings

See also

Infomart (Dallas, Tex.: Trade mart)

Exhibitions

See also

Asia-Pacific International Trade Fair

Book exhibits

EPCOT (Fla.)

World's fairs

Exhibitions, Traveling

See also

Art—Exhibitions

Kaleidoscope (Program)

Exiles

Director without a country [Soviet exile Y. Lyubimov of Moscow's Taganka Theater] R. B. Cullen. il por *Newsweek* 109:60 Ja 19 '87

The émigrés speak out [views of Soviet émigrés on changes in the Soviet Union] *Nation* 244:812-14 Je 13 '87

From Russia—with real love [exiled writer V. Aksenov living in the U.S.] J. Podhoretz. il por *U S News World Rep* 103:49-50 Ag 17 '87

Exiles—*cont.*

The man without a country [Soviet émigré writer E. Sevela] M. L. Grisanti. il pors *N Y* 20:38-43 Ja 12 '87

A Soviet emigre takes the 'A' Train [roots of Soviet feelings about America] V. P. Aksenov. il *N Y Times Mag* p60+ My 3 '87

Spirit in exile: the Dalai Lama pleads for the Tibetan people. R. Gere and R. A. F. Thurman. il por *Roll Stone* p68-9 D 3 '87

Testing *glasnost*: an exile visits his homeland [cover story] A. Goldfarb. il pors *N Y Times Mag* p46-9+ D 6 '87

What's up, Baby Doc? il por *Time* 129:42 F 16 '87

Exley, Frederick

A fan's further notes. il pors *Esquire* 107:150-2 Je '87

Exodus, Book of *See* Bible. O.T. Exodus

Expanding universe *See* Universe

Expansion, House *See* Houses, Remodeled

Expansion, Industrial *See* Industrial expansion

Expatriation

Rootless. D. Backer. *Am Sch* 56:269-74 Spr '87

Expectation of life *See* Longevity

Expeditions, Scientific *See* Scientific expeditions

Expenditures, Government *See* United States—Appropriations and expenditures

Expenditures, Municipal *See* Municipal finance

Expense accounts (Business)

Job strategy: what does your expense account say about you? il *Glamour* 85:100-1 My '87

Money issues on the job [excerpt from Everything college didn't teach you about money] B. Brophy. il *Essence* 18:122+ S '87

Experimental Aircraft Association

Aviation's twin meccas [Sun 'n' Fun and Oshkosh] F. Mackerodt. *Pop Mech* 164:40 Je '87

EAA thrill theater [wide-screen film Sport aviation] J. M. McClellan. *Flying* 114:88 Ja '87

Hardcore Oshkosh. P. Scott. il *Flying* 114:42-7+ D '87

High-flying Oshkosh. M. G. Davidson. *Travel Holiday* 167:34+ Je '87

Prairie homebuilt companions [Chapter 622 of Danville, Ill.] G. Baxter. il *Flying* 114:104 My '87

Experimental automobiles *See* Automobiles, Experimental

Experimental colleges *See* College education, Experimental

Experimental drug regulations *See* Drug laws and regulations

Experimental education *See* Education, Experimental

Experimental education, College *See* College education, Experimental

Experimental films *See* Motion pictures—Experimental films

Experimental motorcycles *See* Motorcycles, Experimental

Experimental music *See* Music, Experimental

Experimental Prototype Community of Tomorrow *See* EPCOT (Fla.)

Experimentation on animals *See* Animal experimentation

Experimentation on man *See* Medical research—Experimentation on man; Pharmaceutical research—Experimentation on man; Psychiatric research—Experimentation on man; Psychological research—Experimentation on man

Experiments *See* Science—Experiments

Experiments, Field *See* Field experiments (Agriculture)

Expert evidence *See* Evidence, Expert

Expert systems (Computers)

Acquaint: a frame-based knowledge-development system for the IBM PC. E. R. Tello. *Byte* 12:265-6+ Je '87

AI, AI, oh! [VP-Expert] E. Shapiro. il *Byte* 12:321-4 Je '87

AI 'fair' demonstrates application of expert systems to C³I operations. K. J. Stein. *Aviat Week Space Technol* 126:104-5+ Je 1 '87

Computerizing with confidence (VI). K. Berney. il *Nations Bus* 75:22-4 Ap '87

'Expert systems' are newest breed of computer help. *Success Farm* 85 no5:26AF Mr '87

Expert systems in the office. S. E. Bleecker. *Futurist* 21:17 Jl/Ag '87

The future of artificial intelligence. G. Heilmeier. il *Radio-Electron* 58:85-90 My '87

Lockheed developing electronic copilot in support of ATF program effort. K. J. Stein. il *Aviat Week Space Technol* 127:73+ Ag 17 '87

The morning after. R. Simon. il *Forbes* 140:164+ O 19 '87

Now, live experts on a floppy disk. A. Kupfer. il *Fortune* 116:69-70+ O 12 '87

Personal Consultant Plus. E. R. Tello. *Byte* 12:242-4 O '87

Program guides you through marketing blizzard [Grain Marketing Advisor expert system] *Success Farm* 85 no6:18AX Mr '87

RuleMaster: an expert-system software package for MS-DOS machines. M. Van Horn. il *Byte* 12:341-2 Ja '87

Expertising of American manuscripts *See* Manuscripts, American—Expertising

Expertising of art *See* Art—Expertising

Explanation (Psychology)

Stop blaming yourself [linking explanatory style with learned helplessness, depression, and illness; research by M. E. P. Seligman] R. J. Trotter. bibl (p64) il pors *Psychol Today* 21:30-2+ F '87

Exploration

See also
Aleutian Islands (Alaska)—Exploring expeditions
Amazon River Valley—Discovery and exploration
America—Discovery and exploration
Antarctic exploration
Arctic exploration
California—Discovery and exploration
Canada—Discovery and exploration
Mississippi River Valley—Exploring expeditions
Tonga—Discovery and exploration
United States—Exploring expeditions
West Africa—Exploring expeditions

Exploratorium

Exploratorium influences science museums new and old. W. Sweet. il *Phys Today* 40:65-8 Mr '87

Explorers

See also
Women explorers

Travellers' tales [cover story; special issue; with editorial comment by Edouard Glissant] bibl il *Courier* 40:3-38 Ap '87

Explorers, American

See also
Henson, Matthew Alexander, 1866-1955
Peary, Robert Edwin, 1856-1920

Explorers, Canadian

See also
Larsen, Henry A.

Explorers, French

See also
Etienne, Jean-Louis

Explosions

See also
Detonation

Plastic shocks and visible sparks. I. Peterson. il *Sci News* 132:152 S 5 '87

Explosions, Atomic weapon *See* Nuclear weapons—Testing

Explosives

See also
Detonation
Dynamite

The electronic look of explosives [work of J. William Rogers and others] *Sci News* 132:121 Ag 22 '87

Explosives in art

She's an artist whose explosives make a lasting impression [E. Rosenberg] R. Wolkomir. il pors *Smithsonian* 18:166-8+ D '87

Expo 86 (Vancouver, B.C.)

Reviews:
Multimedia presentation There's always been dance during Expo 86. L. Windreich. *Dance Mag* 61:28-9+ F '87

Expo 88 (Brisbane, Australia)

Here comes Australia's Expo 88. il *Sunset* 179:52-3 S '87

Export controls, American *See* United States—Commercial policy

Export-Import Bank of the United States

Congress approves air show deductions, cuts Exim funding. *Aviat Week Space Technol* 127:23 Jl 13 '87

Exim Bank backs 767 sale to All Nippon to foil Airbus bid. *Aviat Week Space Technol* 126:31 Je 29 '87

Expanded Exim credit could aid Douglas aircraft negotiations. *Aviat Week Space Technol* 126:31 My 11 '87

Export-import trade

See also
Aerospace industries—Export-import trade
Agricultural industries—Export-import trade
Airplane industry—Export-import trade
Audio equipment industry—Export-import trade
Automobiles—Export-import trade
Avionics industry—Export-import trade
Balance of trade
Books—Export-import trade
Brewing industry—Export-import trade

Export-import trade—See also—*cont.*

Chemical and biological weapons—Export-import trade
Christmas trees—Export-import trade
Cigarette industry—Export-import trade
Clothing industry—Export-import trade
Coffee industry—Export-import trade
Computer industry—Export-import trade
Computer service industries—Export-import trade
Diamond industry—Export-import trade
Drug industry—Export-import trade
Dumping (Commercial policy)
Electronic industries—Export-import trade
Fish industry—Export-import trade
Food industry—Export-import trade
Free trade and protection
Gas industry—Export-import trade
Grain trade
Gray market (Export-import trade)
Guided missile industries—Export-import trade
Hazardous substances—Export-import trade
Helicopter industry—Export-import trade
Hides and skins—Export-import trade
Hydroelectric power—Export-import trade
Liquor industry—Export-import trade
Lumber industry—Export-import trade
Meat industry—Export-import trade
Motorcycles—Export-import trade
Munitions—Export-import trade
Nuclear industry—Export-import trade
Paper industry—Export-import trade
Pesticides—Export-import trade
Pet industries—Export-import trade
Petroleum equipment industry—Export-import trade
Petroleum industry—Export-import trade
Potash industry—Export-import trade
Produce trade
Rice—Export-import trade
Service industries—Export-import trade
Shoe industry—Export-import trade
Small business—Export-import trade
Soybean industry—Export-import trade
Steel industry—Export-import trade
Sugar industry—Export-import trade
Tea industry—Export-import trade
Telecommunication—Export-import trade
Television industry—Export-import trade
Textile industry—Export-import trade
Tile industry—Export-import trade
Trading companies
United States—Commercial policy
Wheat trade
Wine industry—Export-import trade
See also subhead Commerce under names of countries

America's leading exporters [with introd. by Alan Farnham] il *Fortune* 116:72-3 Jl 20 '87
Are exporters settling for a fast buck? W. B. Franklin and J. C. Cooper. il *Bus Week* p30 Ag 17 '87
Dumping? Or just defending markets? [prices of imported goods] G. Slutsker. il *Forbes* 139:166+ My 18 '87
East Coast redux [ports] E. A. Finn, Jr. il *Forbes* 139:162 My 18 '87
Guess who's stuck with the check [U.S. trade deficit results in higher prices for imported goods] B. Bauer. il *U S News World Rep* 102:52-3 F 2 '87
Home-grown Americans go global. D. M. Topolnicki. il *Money* 16:106-8+ My '87
Import price declines in 1986 reflected reduced oil prices. E. Gibbons and G. F. Halpin. bibl f il *Mon Labor Rev* 110:3-17 Ap '87
Imports cost more—and they'll keep going up. W. B. Franklin and J. C. Cooper. il *Bus Week* p43-4 My 18 '87
International spotlight. H. Eason. See issues of Nation's Business
Most U.S. companies are innocents abroad. il *Bus Week* p168-9 N 16 '87
U.S. exporters need first-rate global banking networks. H. R. Heller. il *Bus Week* p20 Je 8 '87
Why Americans aren't likely to start buying American. L. Therrien. il *Bus Week* p34 N 23 '87

Anecdotes, facetiae, satire, etc.
Made elsewhere. R. Baker. il *N Y Times Mag* p18 Ap 26 '87

Exposure (Photography) See Photography—Exposure
Express highway construction See Highway engineering
Express highways
Cruising into the 21st century [manufacturing along Interstate 75] E. A. Finn, Jr. il map *Forbes* 140:80+ Ag 24 '87

Environmental aspects
Manhattan highway plan resurfaces [West Side Highway] W. F. Hewitt. il *Sierra* 72:23-4+ My/Je '87
Pompeii: a new eruption. B. Hewitt. il *Newsweek* 109:46 F 23 '87
Small eruption at Pompeii [plan to build a highway near archeological site] *World Press Rev* 34:59 Mr '87

Federal aid
Congress smells blood after Reagan's highway-bill defeat . . . R. Fly and D. Harbrecht. *Bus Week* p35 Ap 20 '87
Despite a college try, the Gipper loses one [congressional override of highway bill veto] il *Newsweek* 109:23 Ap 13 '87
The Gipper goes down [Congress overrides R. Reagan's highway legislation veto] A. Plattner. il *U S News World Rep* 102:22 Ap 13 '87
Minority claims in state contracts being probed [road construction in Illinois] *Jet* 73:32 N 2 '87
Road warriors [Congress overrides R. Reagan's veto of highway bill] W. Shapiro. il por map *Time* 129:16-19 Ap 13 '87
Whose credibility? [congressional override of R. Reagan's veto of highway bill] W. F. Buckley. *Natl Rev* 39:61 My 8 '87

Finance
Freeway privatization [address, April 10, 1987] R. W. Poole. *Vital Speeches Day* 53:553-6 Jl 1 '87

Arkansas
See also
Arkansas. State Highway Commission

Atlantic States
A separate reality on I-95. J. O'Reilly. il *Time* 130:10 N 30 '87

California
Gunfire in traffic [shooting on Los Angeles freeways] A. Steacy. il *Macleans* 100:41 Ag 17 '87
Gunplay on the freeway [shootings in Los Angeles] M. Kaus. il *Newsweek* 110:18 Ag 10 '87
Highway to homicide [freeway shootings in Los Angeles area] F. Trippett. il *Time* 130:18 Ag 17 '87
Mayhem on the freeways [drivers' responses to congestion] A. Lobue. por *U S News World Rep* 103:9 S 28 '87
Rambo's brothers cruise clogged expressways [Los Angeles freeway shootings] T. Gest. il *U S News World Rep* 103:6 Ag 10 '87

China
The man who envisions a New Jersey Turnpike in China [G. Wu] L. Kraar. il por *Fortune* 116:89 Jl 6 '87

Illinois
Minority claims in state contracts being probed. *Jet* 73:32 N 2 '87

Italy
Pompeii: a new eruption. B. Hewitt. il *Newsweek* 109:46 F 23 '87
Small eruption at Pompeii [plan to build a highway near archeological site] *World Press Rev* 34:59 Mr '87

New York (State)
Incident at Exit 20 [A. Salomon shoots G. Cotugno on the Hutchinson River Parkway] M. Stone. il pors *N Y* 20:50-4+ O 5 '87
Manhattan highway plan resurfaces [West Side Highway] W. F. Hewitt. il *Sierra* 72:23-4+ My/Je '87

Pennsylvania
On the road [A. Paulson's Highway to heaven sculpture on Route 15, Pa.] S. Staggs. il por *Art News* 86:15-16 O '87

Express mail service See Air freight service
Expression
See also
Communication, Nonverbal
Rhetoric
Expression, Facial See Facial expression
Expression, Genetic See Genetic regulation
Expressionism (Art)
See also
Abstract expressionism
Blaue Reiter (Group)
Neo-expressionism (Art)
Expulsion and suspension, Student See Student suspension and expulsion
Extemporization (Music) See Improvisation (Music)
Extended warranty See Warranty
Extension education
See also
University extension

Extension Service *See* United States. Extension Service
Extermination of termites *See* Termites—Control
Exterminators *See* Pest control services
External combustion engines *See* Heat engines
External Tanks Corporation
Company seeks funds for orbiting laboratory [proposing to take over shuttle external tanks in orbit and convert them] il *Aviat Week Space Technol* 126:102-3 Ja 12 '87
Tank land: a conversation with Thomas F. Rogers. T. Reichhardt. il por *Space World* X-8-284:27-30 Ag '87
Extinct animals *See* Animals, Extinct
Extinct fish *See* Fish, Extinct
Extinction of species, Mass *See* Mass extinction of species
Extortion
Two Georgia commissioners indicted for extortion [A. R. Eaves and C. Williams] *Jet* 73:12 N 2 '87
Extra! Extra! (New York, N.Y.: Restaurant) *See* New York (N.Y.)—Restaurants, nightclubs, bars, etc.
Extracorporeal photopheresis *See* Photopheresis
Extracurricular activities *See* Student activities
Extramarital relationships *See* Adultery
Extrasensory perception
Test your psychic abilities [remote viewing] P. Weintraub. il *Omni* 10:19-20+ O '87
Extraterrestrial life *See* Life on other planets
Extraterrestrial material *See* Matter, Interstellar
Extraterrestrial sightings *See* UFOs
Extravehicular activity *See* Space flight—Extravehicular activity
Extreme prejudice [film] *See* Motion picture reviews—Single works
Extremely low frequency waves *See* Electromagnetic waves
Extroversion *See* Introversion and extroversion
Extrude Hone Corp.
The inside mirror. P. Schilling. il *Cycle* 38:109-12 My '87
Exum, Roy
John Croyle's speck of heaven. il *Read Dig* 130:85-9 My '87
Exxon Corporation
Despite cuts, basic research survives and revives at Exxon. W. Sweet. il *Phys Today* 40:59-60 Jl '87
Exxon becomes 87th U.S. firm to quit S. Africa. *Jet* 71:4 Ja 19 '87
Exxon pulls the plug [sale of South African holdings] T. Fennell. il *Macleans* 100:27 Ja 12 '87
"I love to step on toes" [L. Rawl] C. Leinster. il por *Fortune* 116:27-8 Ag 3 '87
The little motor that couldn't [Exxon sells Reliance Electric in a leveraged buyout] J. A. Conway. il *Forbes* 139:8 F 9 '87
Tainted money: the ethics and rhetoric of divestment [colleges and business] R. L. Payton. il *Change* 19:55-60 My/Je '87
Eyck, Hubert van, ca. 1366-1426
about
A canary in an aquarium. B. Grauman. il *Art News* 86:101-2 Ja '87
Eyck, Jan van, ca. 1390-1441
about
A canary in an aquarium. B. Grauman. il *Art News* 86:101-2 Ja '87
Eye
See also
Cornea
Crystalline lens
Photoreceptors
Retina
Rods and cones
Vision
Visual purple
Amphibia
Intracellular topography of rhodopsin bleaching [toads] C. L. Makino and others. bibl f il *Science* 238:1716-17 D 18 '87
Animals
See also
Vision—Animals
Distribution of cones in human and monkey retina: individual variability and radial asymmetry [cover story] C. A. Curcio and others. bibl f il *Science* 236:579-82 My 1 '87
Formation of retinal ganglion cell topography during prenatal development [cats] B. Lia and others. bibl f il *Science* 236:848-51 My 15 '87
Cancer
Genetic aspects
Anticancer genes [missing gene causes retinoblastoma] C. SerVaas. il *Saturday Evening Post* 259:98+ My/Je '87

Human cancer gene sequenced [retinoblastoma; work of Wen-Hwa Lee and others] G. Kolata. *Science* 235:1323 Mr 13 '87
Human retinoblastoma susceptibility gene: cloning, identification, and sequence. W.-H. Lee and others. bibl f il *Science* 235:1394-9 Mr 13 '87
Light cast on a darkling gene [retinoblastoma] N. Angier. il *Discover* 8:84-96 Mr '87
Oncogenesis of the lens in transgenic mice. K. A. Mahon and others. bibl f il *Science* 235:1622-8 Mr 27 '87
Structural evidence for the authenticity of the human retinoblastoma gene. Y.-K. T. Fung and others. bibl f il *Science* 236:1657-61 Je 26 '87
Care and hygiene
See also
Eye exercises
Ophthalmic assistants
Bloodshot eyes, red rims, puffiness and dark circles: how to keep your eyes looking their best. L. Rosch. il *Glamour* 85:16 D '87
For your eyes only: how to protect those baby blues, browns, grays . . . [quiz] K. P. Behan. *Mademoiselle* 93:114 My '87
For your eyes only: solutions to seven common eye problems. il *Glamour* 85:22 Ag '87
Save sight [cover story; special issue] il *World Health* p3-15+ My '87
Sightsaving tips [travel tips] E. S. Orzac. *Travel Holiday* 168:16-17 O '87
Stay-young care for beautiful eyes. C. Straley. il *Parents* 62:24 Jl '87
Diseases and defects
See also
Blindness
Cataracts (Eye defect)
Color blindness
Myopia
Onchocerciasis
Xerophthalmia
Are your contact lenses as safe as you think? M. Tolbert and R. E. Lippman. il *FDA Consum* 21:16-19 Ap '87
Genetic ablation: targeted expression of a toxin gene causes microphthalmia in transgenic mice. M. L. Breitman and others. bibl f il *Science* 238:1563-5 D 11 '87
Insights on eyesight. C. Schrader. il *Harpers Bazaar* 120:40+ Ap '87
Mascara application: worth a closer look. D. Groves. il *McCalls* 114:144 Jl '87
Organ-resident, nonlymphoid cells suppress proliferation of autoimmune T-helper lymphocytes. R. R. Caspi and others. bibl f il *Science* 237:1029-32 Ag 28 '87
Soft lens users: clean 'em or weep [risk of acanthamoeba keratitis] R. Weiss. *Sci News* 132:6 Jl 4 '87
Summer eye infections. P. Von Nostitz. il *Parents* 62:37+ Je '87
VDT comfort. M. S. Dolan. *Consum Res Mag* 70:2 Ag '87
Diagnosis
Red flag for lazy eye [rapid screening device] C. Bushnell. il *Health* 19:15 Ja '87
Psychological aspects
Blinding stress [central serous chorioretinopathy; research by Gary S. Gelber and Howard Schatz] P. Chance. *Psychol Today* 21:22-3 Jl '87
Eye of the (emotional) storm [central serous chorioretinopathy; research by Gary S. Gelber and Howard Schatz] *Sci News* 131:40 Ja 17 '87
Examination
Do you need dime-store glasses? T. Shealey. il *Prevention* 39:118+ Ag '87
The eyes have it [National Eye Care Project] *50 Plus* 27:18 Ag '87
Taking a look at eye exams. E. Weck. il *FDA Consum* 21:14-17 My '87
Fish
Photographs and photography
Optical marvels, fish eyes are visual feasts themselves. J. Rotman. bibl (p271) il *Smithsonian* 18:172-7 N '87
Innervation
An in vitro neurite-promoting antigen functions in axonal regeneration in vivo. A. W. Sandrock, Jr. and W. D. Matthew. bibl f il *Science* 237:1605-8 S 25 '87
Insects
Developmental control gene sequenced [fruit flies; work of Gerald Rubin and others] J. L. Marx. *Science* 236:26-7 Ap 3 '87

Eye—Insects—_cont._

Sevenless, a cell-specific homeotic gene of Drosophila, encodes a putative transmembrane receptor with a tyrosine kinase domain. E. Hafen and others. bibl f il *Science* 236:55-63 Ap 3 '87

Movements

With Thomas Hutchinson's marvelous ERICA, a flick of an eye brings help to the helpless. L. Albrecht. il por *People Wkly* 28:85-6 Jl 20 '87

Protection

See also
Goggles

Rodents

In situ detection of β-galactosidase in lenses of transgenic mice with a γ-crystallin/*lacZ* gene. D. R. Goring and others. bibl f il *Science* 235:456-8 Ja 23 '87

Surgery

See also
Cataracts (Eye defect)—Surgery
Cornea—Surgery

Automation and microsurgery [Moscow Scientific Research Institute of Eye Microsurgery] S. Fedorov. il *Courier* 40:33-4 Ag '87

Surgery, Plastic

See Surgery, Plastic

Wounds and injuries

See also
Snowblindness

A beaut of a shiner [black eye assumed to be result of wife beating] J. Slaughter. il *Progressive* 51:50 My '87

What's your eye-Q? il *Curr Health 2* 13:22-3 Ja '87

Eye drops, washes, etc.

Eye care for the summer. M. Hopkins. il *Consum Res Mag* 70:11-14 Je '87

Eye exercises

Focus! [development of eye-tracking skills in athletes] S. Schneider. il *Women's Sports Fitness* 9:18 Je '87

Focusing on 'vision therapy'. S. Findlay. *U S News World Rep* 103:78 O 12 '87

Open your eyes to vision training [improving athletes' vision; views of Harvey Ratner] L. N. DeLuca. il *World Tennis* 35:16-17 Ag '87

Eye makeup *See* Makeup

Eye movements *See* Eye—Movements

Eyebrow makeup *See* Makeup

Eyebrows

At last! Shape your brows like a pro with our expert tips. il *Ladies Home J* 104:28 F '87

Eyeglasses

See also
Contact lenses
Goggles
Sunglasses

Athletic specs: the eyes have it. S. Krasnow. il *Sport Mag* 78:97+ Ag '87

Do you need dime-store glasses? T. Shealey. il *Prevention* 39:118+ Ag '87

Keeping an eye out. A. P. Farah. il *Health* 19:14 Ag '87

Low-cost spectacles. R. Homeier. il *World Health* p18-19 My '87

Make a spectacle of yourself: a guide to eyeglass shopping. M. Hickey. il *Mademoiselle* 93:162+ Ap '87

Seeing double [bi-level telemicroscopic vision system] P. Everett. il *Pop Sci* 231:34 S '87

Specs shield eyes from UV. il *Prevention* 39:14 Ap '87

What the best-dressed eyes have on. S. Woolley. il *Bus Week* p150 Mr 16 '87

Anecdotes, facetiae, satire, etc.

Framed! J. Schneller. il *Seventeen* 46:122-3+ O '87

Prices

Buying eyeglasses: a Money survey finds disturbing defects at any price. M. Willens. il *Money* 16:157 Jl '87

Eyelash makeup *See* Makeup

Eyes *See* Eye

Eyes on the prize [television program] See Television program reviews—Single works

Eyesight *See* Vision

Eyewear stores

See also
Sunglass Hut of America Inc.

Eyewitnesses *See* Witnesses

F

F-4 airplanes *See* Airplanes, Military
F-5 airplanes *See* Airplanes, Military
F-14 airplanes *See* Airplanes, Military
F-15 airplanes *See* Airplanes, Military
F-16 airplanes *See* Airplanes, Military
F-18 airplanes *See* Airplanes, Military

F. A. O. Schwarz

For kids who have it all: minks and cars [F.A.O. Schwarz Christmas catalog] il *Newsweek* 110:73 N 2 '87

Toying around [buyers at the American International Toy Fair in New York] B. Kanner. il *N Y* 20:22+ Mr 9 '87

F. H. Tomkins plc

A raider's new world [G. Hutchings' bid for Smith & Wesson] M. Maremont. il por *Bus Week* p49-50 Je 15 '87

F stars

The temperate F stars. J. B. Kaler. il *Sky Telesc* 73:131-4 F '87

F. W. Woolworth Co.

A once dowdy retailer fashions a chic new look. il *Money* 16:8 Jl '87

FAA *See* United States. Federal Aviation Administration

FAAD (Forward area air defense) *See* Air defenses

Faber, Adele, and Mazlish, Elaine

Equal is less [with editorial comment by Elizabeth Crow] il *Parents* 62:10, 96-100 Ap '87

The perils of comparisons. il *Parents* 62:82-6 My '87

Faberge Inc.

Faberge lands Arden: 'Now we've got mass—and class'. S. Benway. il por *Bus Week* p38-9 Ag 17 '87

Fabric crafts *See* Textile crafts

Fabric roofs *See* Roofs and roofing

Fabric softeners

Fabric softeners. il *Consum Rep* 52:79-81 D '87

The true performance of fabric softeners. il *Consum Rep* 52:420-2 Jl '87

Fabrica Argentina de Material Aerospacial

Argentina takes steps to boost growth in aerospace industry. *Aviat Week Space Technol* 127:57+ Ag 17 '87

Fabrica Militar de Aviones

See also
Fabrica Argentina de Material Aerospacial

Fabricant, Florence

Christmas de-lights. *Harpers Bazaar* 121:133-4+ D '87

Cookbooks. *N Y Times Book Rev* 92:50 My 31 '87

Cookbooks. il *N Y Times Book Rev* 92:38+ D 6 '87

Fabricated foods *See* Food substitutes

Fabrications [dance] See Dance reviews—Single works

Fabrics *See* Textile fabrics

Fabrikant, Geraldine

Not ready for prime time? il pors *N Y Times Mag* p30+ Ap 12 '87

Façades

Facade guidelines. J. Barnett. il *Archit Rec* 175:120-1 Jl '87

Stone: new technology and design. B. Donaldson. il *Archit Rec* 175:136-45 Jl '87

Turn-of-the-century false front for a Denver cottage. il *Sunset* 178:98 F '87

Face

See also
Facial expression

Baby face-off: the roots of attraction [study by Judith H. Langlois and others] B. Bower. *Sci News* 131:310 My 16 '87

Beauty is in the eye of the baby [infants prefer attractive faces; research by Judith H. Langlois] H. Hall. il *Psychol Today* 21:12 Ag '87

Care and hygiene

See Skin—Care and hygiene

Surgery, Plastic

See Surgery, Plastic

Face lifting *See* Surgery, Plastic

Face masks *See* Masks

Face recognition *See* Recognition (Psychology)

Faces of women [film] See Motion picture reviews—Single works

Fachler, Nimrod

about

A world investor's favorite markets [interview] J. Mendes. il por *Fortune* 116:130 S 14 '87

Facial creams *See* Cosmetics
Facial expression
See also
　Smiles
Bringing up baby: emotion's early role [research by Jeannette M. Haviland and Mary Lelwica] B. Bower. *Sci News* 131:104 F 14 '87
Do dentists know when it hurts? [facial expressions of juvenile patients; study by Ann Rowland] G. Lowe. *Psychol Today* 21:12 Ag '87
The face of abuse [inability of some abusive parents to correctly interpret infant facial cues; study by Joseph P. Kropp and O. Maurice Haynes] R. J. Moss. *Psychol Today* 21:20 Jl '87
Faces of emotion: social or innate? [research by Ross Buck and Wan-Cheng Teng] B. Bower. *Sci News* 132:150 S 5 '87
Facial gestures: do you get the message? W. J. Rohr. il *Teen* 31:20+ Ap '87
Facing up to booze [drinking impairs ability to interpret facial expressions; research by J. Borrill] G. Lowe. *Psychol Today* 21:23 S '87
Honesty: look them in the eye and smile [research by George Rotter and Naomi Rotter] P. Chance. *Psychol Today* 21:23 S '87
Reading between the lines [role of age in interpreting emotional expression; study by Carol Zander Malatesta] A. H. Rosenfeld. *Psychol Today* 21:16 O '87
Wedded faces [facial mimicry in married couples; study by Robert B. Zajonc] H. Hall. *Psychol Today* 21:10 D '87
Facial masks *See* Cosmetics
Facial tumors (Benign) *See* Tumors (Benign)
Facility management
The architect as facility manager—fiction and fact. M. C. P. McElroy. il *Archit Rec* 175:42-3 O '87
Automation
In facility management, there are opportunities and pitfalls for architects. E. Teicholz and M. Sena. il *Archit Rec* 175:23+ Ja '87
Fackre, Gabriel
Sober hope: some themes in Protestant theology today. *Christ Century* 104:790-2 S 23 '87
Facsimile transmission
Fax boards: is your office complete without one? E. King. il *Pers Comput* 11:121+ O '87
A flood of fax boards. J. Blackford. il *Pers Comput* 11:33 S '87
Just the fax, ma'am. T. McCarroll. il *Time* 130:38 Ag 31 '87
Will there be a fax in every foyer? S. Gelfond. il *Bus Week* p82 Ap 3 '87
Facsimiles of manuscripts *See* Manuscripts—Facsimiles
Factions (Special interest groups) *See* Special interest groups
Factories
See also
　Airplane factories
　Automobile factories
　Chemical plants
　Factory management
　Tire factories
　Tractor factories
Automation
See Automation
Clean rooms
See Clean rooms
Location
See Location in business and industry
Quiet rooms
See Quiet rooms
Shutdowns
BLS surveys mass layoffs and plant closings in 1986. L. B. Siegel. il *Mon Labor Rev* 110:39-40 O '87
Main Street feels the pinch. J. Castro. il *Time* 129:47 F 16 '87
Worker dislocation report. *Mon Labor Rev* 110:2 F '87
Laws and regulations
Advance notice of plant closings [Office of Technology Assessment report] *Futurist* 21:49-50 Mr/Ap '87
The battle over a plant-closing bill. M. I. Finney. il *Nations Bus* 75:84 O '87
Congress is closing in on a plant-closing law. S. B. Garland. il *Bus Week* p35 Jl 27 '87
How often do workers receive advance notice of layoffs? S. P. Brown. il *Mon Labor Rev* 110:13-17 Je '87
Job training: the Democrats are stealing the show. M. E. Recio. il *Bus Week* p53 Mr 9 '87
New York State acts to reduce plant closings. *Mon Labor Rev* 110:39 F '87
A warning for workers. T. Noah. il *Newsweek* 110:37 Ag 24 '87

Factories in space *See* Space processing
Factoring (Finance)
Mr. Malec versus the bureaucrats [SEC's involvement in Central & South West Corp's factoring operations] E. A. Finn, Jr. il por *Forbes* 140:44 D 28 '87
Sell abroad; you can collect. S. Golob. il *Nations Bus* 75:44+ N '87
Factory and trade waste *See* Trade waste
Factory management
See also
　Industrial revolution
　Quality control
　Team work in industry
Getting man and machine to live happily ever after. J. Hoerr. il *Bus Week* p61-2 Ap 20 '87
Making brawn work with brains. O. Port. il *Bus Week* p56-8+ Ap 20 '87
Wait 'til next year [interview with H. Shaiken] J. Flint. *Forbes* 139:112 Je 15 '87
Japan
Working for the Japanese [Bridgestone Tire Co.'s factory in Tenn.] il *Time* 130:60 S 14 '87
Korea (South)
Korea's newest export: management style [U.S. operations] L. Baum. il *Bus Week* p66 Ja 19 '87
Factory outlets *See* Discount houses (Retail trade)
Factrel
Clarifying cause of multiple pregnancy [work of Oscar A. Kletzky] il *USA Today (Periodical)* 115:10 F '87
Facts
The case of the falling nightwatchmen: in behavorial biology, not all facts are created equal. R. M. Sapolsky. il *Discover* 8:42-5 Jl '87
Far-out facts. See issues of National Geographic World
Of many things [David Feldman's Why do clocks run clockwise? and other imponderables] G. W. Hunt. *America* 157:418 D 5 '87
Facts on File, Inc.
Facts on File [submission policy] G. Helferich. *Writer* 100:44 D '87
Facts on File offers database that contains author contracts. *Publ Wkly* 232:12 S 11 '87
Faculty, College *See* College teachers
Fader, Kim Brown
Sur-prize, sur-prize! *Seventeen* 46:144-5 N '87
Fadiman, Anne
American dreamer. See issues of Life beginning February 1986 through October 1987
Fads
Are you hip to what's cool? M. Musto. il *Mademoiselle* 93:74 O '87
Business chic: the latest bulletin from the fad front. il *Bus Week* p38 Ja 19 '87
The importance of being hippest: a 60-second history of trends. M. Musto. *Mademoiselle* 93:147+ D '87
Anecdotes, facetiae, satire, etc.
It's hip to be: (a) square, (b) cool, (c) hot. E. Weiner. *Mademoiselle* 93:146-7+ D '87
Last word. T. Runté. il *Omni* 9:126 Jl '87
Exhibitions
Fully employed [Fad Fair III] *New Yorker* 63:32-3 N 30 '87
Photographs and photography
Showing our true colors: trends covered the spectrum— and then some. D. C. Craig. il *Life* 10:104-5+ Ja '87
Fafard, Joe
about
The gifted hands of a prairie populist. G. James. il *Macleans* 100:69-70 N 16 '87
Fagan, Brian M.
Life with Ayla and her friends: Jean Auel and the new phenomenon of Ice Age fiction. *Sci Am* 256:132-5 Je '87
Fagan, Garth
about
Dancing:
　Performances at the Joyce Theater. A. Croce. *New Yorker* 63:102-3 D 21 '87
Fagan's (Garth) Bucket Dance Theatre *See* Garth Fagan's Bucket Dance Theatre
Fager, Chuck
Friends United Meeting: a new beginning. *Christ Century* 104:742-3 S 9-16 '87
Fahlen, Charles
about
Chuck Fahlen at Lawrence Oliver. D. S. Rubin. *Art Am* 75:164 D '87
Failing, Patricia
Howard Kottler: conceptualist and purveyor of psychosexual allusions. il por *Am Craft* 47:22-9 D '87/Ja '88

Failure (Psychology)
See also
Fear of success
Cultural failure: the American preoccupation. W. F. Gavin. *Current* 293:16-19 Je '87
Facing a flop [failed motion picture] J. Boorstin. il *N Y Times Mag* p102 O 11 '87
Going to bat against the fear of failure [D. Gooden cocaine case] J. M. Wall. *Christ Century* 104:371-2 Ap 22 '87
In life, what's important is that you lose [imaginative failure] D. Radavich. por *U S News World Rep* 103:5 Ag 24 '87
Lets hear it for losers! M. J. O'Neill. por *Newsweek* 110:9 N 2 '87
My father, Mr. Lincoln and me. E. Ziegler. il *Read Dig* 130:35-40 F '87
Self-imposed limits. G. Witkin-Lanoil. il *Health* 19:10+ N '87
These beliefs are for the birds [views of Gary Emery] il *USA Today (Periodical)* 116:16 Ag '87
Why smart people fail [interview with C. Hyatt] il por *U S News World Rep* 102:55 Ap 6 '87
Your first flop: not fun, but very, very useful. J. Stone. *Glamour* 85:172 Ag '87
Failures, Business See Business failures
Fair Housing Act See Discrimination in housing
Fairbrother, Trevor J.
Edmund C. Tarbell's paintings of interiors. bibl f il *Antiques* 131:224-35 Ja '87
Fairchild, John
about
Of power, glory and the rich and famous. A. Gabor. il por *U S News World Rep* 103:55 Ag 24 '87
Fairchild, Patty
about
Little horse, big deal—protestors cry 'There goes the neighborhood'. il por *People Wkly* 27:96-7 Je 1 '87
Fairchild Aircraft Corporation
Sale will enable Fairchild Aircraft to end uncertainty, pursue growth. C. A. Shifrin. il *Aviat Week Space Technol* 127:105+ D 14 '87
Fairchild Industries Inc.
Fairchild delivers Metro 3 AEW testbed to Sweden [airborne early warning] C. A. Shifrin. il *Aviat Week Space Technol* 127:127+ O 19 '87
Fairchild seeks launch orders for new Metro 3 versions [Metro 5 and 6] *Aviat Week Space Technol* 126:46 Ap 13 '87
Sale will enable Fairchild Aircraft to end uncertainty, pursue growth. C. A. Shifrin. il *Aviat Week Space Technol* 127:105+ D 14 '87
T-46 termination will force closure of Fairchild facility on Long Island. *Aviat Week Space Technol* 126:27 Mr 23 '87
Fairchild Semiconductor Corporation
Cold feet [Fujitsu drops bid for Fairchild] *Time* 129:52 Mr 30 '87
Fighting the chip wars: Fujitsu loses Fairchild. J. B. Copeland. il *Newsweek* 109:50 Mr 30 '87
What the Fairchild fiasco signals for trade policy [Fujitsu deal collapses] J. W. Wilson and S. J. Dryden. il *Bus Week* p28 Mr 30 '87
Why National came to the Fairchild fire sale [National Semiconductor] J. B. Levine and O. Port. il *Bus Week* p38-9 S 14 '87
Fairfax County (Va.)
Fairfax County, Virginia. il map *Time* 129:16 Je 15 '87
Arts
Fairfax County [special section] il *Horizon* 30:17-30+ Jl/Ag '87
Description and travel
Fairfax County [special section] il *Horizon* 30:17-30+ Jl/Ag '87
Historic houses, sites, etc.
Several sites in Fairfax County relive early American history. K. Milam. il *Horizon* 30:17-18 Jl/Ag '87
Fairfax Symphony Orchestra
Sounds of success. M. Wade. il *Horizon* 30:21-2 Jl/Ag '87
Fairfield (Iowa)
Economic conditions
The karma of capitalism [impact of Maharishi International University] P. King and P. Wang. il *Newsweek* 110:44 Ag 3 '87
Fairhall, James
The case for the $435 hammer. *Wash Mon* 18:47-8+ Ja '87

Fairings (Motorcycle) See Motorcycles—Fairings
Fairlie, Henry
Curtain call. *New Repub* 197:16-19 S 7 '87
Evangelists in Babylon. *New Repub* 196:22-4 Ap 27 '87
The idiocy of urban life. *New Repub* 196:21-3 Ja 5-12 '87
Fairmont Fund
A hard charger for harder times. il *Money* 16:35 S '87
Fairness See Justice
Fairness Doctrine (Broadcasting)
Advertising pleads the First. M. L. Wulf. *Commonweal* 114:75-9 F 13 '87
The broadcasting Fairness Doctrine. *Congr Dig* 66:227-56 O '87
A compromise that could clear the static over the airwaves. F. Seghers. il *Bus Week* p28 Jl 6 '87
Con man of the cloth [P. Robertson and the Fairness Doctrine] W. A. Henry. il *Channels* 7:16 Ja '87
Crying foul over fairness: should the government require that broadcasting be balanced? R. Zoglin. il *Time* 130:80-1 Jl 6 '87
Edging the government out of TV. O. Friedrich. il *Time* 130:58 Ag 17 '87
FCC doublespeak. L. P. Sheinfeld. il *Film Comment* 23:87-90 S/O '87
A fight for time on the air. D. Bollier. il *Sierra* 72:18-20 S/O '87
Final say on Fairness yet to come. M. Friedman. *Channels* 7:17 S '87
In Fairness . . . and out of it. L. Brown. il *Channels* 7:24 S '87
Unfair air? R. Coorsh. il *Consum Res Mag* 70:4 S '87
Fairs
See also
Book fairs
World's fairs
Fairstein, Linda
about
Prosecuting Jennifer Levin's killer. M. Laurino. il pors *Ms* 16:70-2+ S '87
Fairway Fruits & Vegetables (New York, N.Y.)
On display [S. Jenkins, maker of signs used at food market in Manhattan] *New Yorker* 63:37-8 D 7 '87
Fairy tales
Anecdotes, facetiae, satire, etc.
How to grow beans [Jack and the Beanstalk] E. Zern. il *Field Stream* 91:138 Ja '87
Bibliography
Kissing off Snow White. J. D. Zipes. *N Y Times Book Rev* 92:32 Mr 22 '87
Faith
See also
Hope
Truth
Believe it or not:
Faith in Jesus. G. McCauley. *America* 156:282 Ap 4 '87
Faith, institution and community. G. McCauley. *America* 156:259+ Mr 28 '87
New Testament perspectives on faith (I). G. McCauley. il *America* 156:200 Mr 7 '87
New Testament perspectives on faith (II). G. McCauley. *America* 156:217 Mr 14 '87
New Testament perspectives on faith (III). G. McCauley. *America* 156:236 Mr 21 '87
Old Testament forms of faith. G. McCauley. *America* 156:177 F 28 '87
An eye on the cradle. C. F. H. Henry. il por *Christ Today* 31:26-7 N 6 '87
Fear's antidote: faith; Growing pains. G. G. Seibert. *America* 157:71 Ag 1-8 '87
God isn't finished with me yet. R. Brickley. *Commonweal* 114:410-11 Jl 17 '87
The God letters [celebrities' belief in God; excerpts] P. Rifkin. il *McCalls* 114:97-8 Ja '87
Growing up Catholic & the adult search for faith [special section] *Commonweal* 114:446-57 Ag 14 '87
Lenten meditation:
A question of faith. J. F. Scholer. *Christ Century* 104:237-8 Mr 11 '87
What's God got to do with it? R. E. Burns. *U S Cathol* 52:2 My '87
You've got to believe in something. H. S. Kushner. *Redbook* 170:92-3+ D '87
Faith cure
See also
Miracles

Faith cure—*cont.*
"A faith healer gave us our child" [work of F. Hunter] J. Grazier. il pors *McCalls* 115:164-6 O '87
Faith healers: moving toward the mainstream? B. Barron. il *Christ Today* 31:50+ Jl 10 '87
Fleecing the flock [faith healer P. Popoff debunked by J. Randi; with editorial comment by Paul Hoffman] J. Tierney. il pors *Discover* 8:50-4+ N '87
Fuller Seminary releases study on the miraculous. il *Christ Today* 31:44-5 F 6 '87
Metaphysical healing [interview with P. A. Valentine] K. J. Halliburton. il por *Essence* 18:20 S '87
"We thought our faith could save our son" [death of M. Swan from meningitis after Christian Scientist parents withhold medical treatment] K. Delaney. il pors *Redbook* 168:104-6 Ja '87

Faith healing *See* Faith cure

Faithfull, Marianne
about
Holding tight, letting go. J. Cocks. il pors *Time* 130:84 D 7 '87
Marianne Faithfull. B. Milkowski. por *Down Beat* 11:15 N '87
Tears gone by. R. O'Connor. il por *Vogue* 177:114 N '87

Fakers *See* Quacks and quackery

Fakih, Kimberly Olson
A blizzard of children's book activity in Minnesota. il *Publ Wkly* 231:101-3 F 27 '87

Falashas *See* Jews—Ethiopia

Falcão, Roberto
Discovering Bolivia's spirit. il *World Press Rev* 34:61 D '87

Falcoff, Mark, 1941-
Going to extremes [cover story] il *New Repub* 197:26-33 S 7 '87
Why Europeans support the Sandinistas. *Commentary* 84:61-5 Ag '87

Falcon, Joe
about
Running for redemption. A. Murphy. il pors *Sports Illus* 67:103-4 O 26 '87

Falcon airplanes *See* Airplanes, Business

Faldo, Nick
about
Very British Open. R. Reilly. il pors *Sports Illus* 67:18-23 Jl 27 '87

Fales, Martha Gandy
Federal Bostonians and their London jeweler, Stephen Twycross. bibl f il *Antiques* 131:642-9 Mr '87

Falick, James
Joint ventures or associations; do they work? il *Archit Rec* 175:29 Ja '87

Falk, Keith
about
White man gets 6 years for arson to blacks' home. *Jet* 72:33 Ap 27 '87

Falk, Lillian
Should Congress enact the Quayle amendments to the Bilingual Education Act? [excerpts from testimony, June 5, 1986] *Congr Dig* 66:90+ Mr '87

Falk, Pamela S.
Cuba in Africa. map *Foreign Aff* 65:1077-96 Summ '87

Falk, Richard A.
An opportunity to end the arms race. il *Bull At Sci* 43:28-32 Mr '87
South Africa's war on children. il *Nation* 245:516-17 N 7 '87
The surge to democracy [with discussion] il por *Cent Mag* 20:44-50 My/Je '87

Falke, Joseph J., and Koshland, Daniel E., Jr.
Global flexibility in a sensory receptor: a site-directed cross-linking approach. bibl f il *Science* 237:1596-600 S 25 '87

Falkenheim, Victor C.
The limits of political reform. bibl f *Curr Hist* 86:261-5+ S '87

Falkenstein, Claire, 1908-
about
Claire Falkenstein at Jack Rutberg. R. L. Pincus. il *Art Am* 75:145+ Mr '87

Falkland Islands
See also
United Nations—Falkland Islands
Politics and government
Assembly asks Argentina and United Kingdom to initiate negotiations on Falklands (Malvinas). *UN Chron* 24:81 F '87

Call for negotiations for peaceful, definitive resolution of Falklands (Malvinas) issue. map *UN Chron* 23:8-10 Ja '86

Falkner, David
(jt. auth) See Taylor, Lawrence, and Falkner, David

Fall *See* Autumn

Fall armyworms *See* Armyworms

Fall vacations *See* Vacations

Falla, Jack
Just what the doctor ordered. il pors *Sports Illus* 67:91-2 O 26 '87

Falla, Manuel de, 1876-1946
about
"The three-cornered hat". R. Freed. il *Stereo Rev* 52:194 N '87

Falla y Matheu, Manuel de *See* Falla, Manuel de, 1876-1946

Falling bodies
The bigger they are, the faster they fall [research by Barry Holstein and John Donoghue] il *Discover* 8:15-16 S '87

Fallot, Evelyne
AIDS and democracy. map *World Press Rev* 34:51-2 S '87

Fallout, Radioactive *See* Radioactive pollution

Fallout shelters *See* Atomic bomb shelters

Fallows, James M.
Asia: nobody wants a melting pot. il *U S News World Rep* 102:39 Je 22 '87
The burden of omnipotence. il *Atlantic* 260:20-1+ O '87
A damaged culture. il *Atlantic* 260:49-54+ N '87
Gradgrind's heirs. il *Atlantic* 259:16+ Mr '87
Japanese yearnings. il *Atlantic* 259:16-18 Je '87
Manila fudge. *Wash Mon* 19:53-6 S '87
Modern times. il *Atlantic* 259:24+ F '87
Playing by different rules. il *Atlantic* 260:22+ S '87
Putting the brakes on the Orient Express. *Wash Mon* 19:39-45 Ap '87
The rice plot. il *Atlantic* 259:22-6 Ja '87
What Washington should worry about. il *U S News World Rep* 102:37 Ja 12 '87
The white peril. il *Atlantic* 259:18+ My '87

Falls Church (Va.)
Housing
Jury awards $5 to black in housing bias case [Cynthia S. Bryant] *Jet* 72:22 Je 1 '87

False arrest *See* Justice, Miscarriage of

Falsehood *See* Lying

Falsey, John
about
A case of bigamy. J. Brand. il *N Y Times Mag* p100 My 17 '87

Faludi, Susan
The marriage trap. il *Ms* 16:62+ Jl/Ag '87

Falwell, Carey
about
My father's house [excerpt from Strength for the journey] J. Falwell. il pors *Good Housekeep* 205:137+ N '87

Falwell, Jerry
My father's house [excerpt from Strength for the journey] il pors *Good Housekeep* 205:137+ N '87
about
At the helm of PTL. C. Neuhaus. il pors *People Wkly* 27:30-3 Je 15 '87
Author and publisher groups make filings in two Supreme Court cases. H. Fields. *Publ Wkly* 232:12 S 4 '87
Can Jim and Tammy make a comeback? G. Witkin. il por *U S News World Rep* 103:21 O 19 '87
Dropping the reins at PTL. il por *Christ Today* 31:40 N 6 '87
'Emotional distress' briefs to High Court. il *Publ Wkly* 232:13 Jl 17 '87
Falwell and the PTL: 'send money'. D. Gates. il por *Newsweek* 109:6 My 25 '87
Falwell: fighting fundamentalist. por *Time* 129:62 Ap 6 '87
Falwell puts politics behind him—for the most part. *Christ Today* 31:53-4 D 11 '87
Falwell says media ministers need more accountability. por *Christ Today* 31:42 Jl 10 '87
Falwell throws in the towel. R. N. Ostling. il por *Time* 130:74 O 19 '87
For Falwell: new job, new questions. S. Emerson and G. Witkin. il por *U S News World Rep* 102:60-1 Ap 6 '87
Goodbye to all that. M. Miller. por *Newsweek* 110:10 N 16 '87
Gospelgate II: target Falwell. L. Martz. il pors *Newsweek* 109:56-7+ Je 1 '87
Heaven can wait [cover story; special section] il pors *Newsweek* 109:58-62+ Je 8 '87

Falwell, Jerry—about—*cont.*

High Court queries leave outcome of 'Hustler'-Falwell case uncertain. H. Fields. *Publ Wkly* 232:15 D 18 '87

A Jerry-built coalition regroups. R. N. Ostling. il por *Time* 130:68-9 N 16 '87

Jerry Falwell vs. Larry Flynt. A. Press. il pors *Newsweek* 110:76 D 14 '87

Jerry Falwell's anti-AIDS dollar drive. M. Doan. il por *U S News World Rep* 102:12-13 My 4 '87

Jim and Tammy rise again. J. Adler. il por *Newsweek* 110:77 O 19 '87

The Jim Bakker affair. il pors *Christ Today* 31:36-7 Ap 17 '87

Of God and greed. R. N. Ostling. il pors *Time* 129:70-2+ Je 8 '87

Silence does not a statesman make. J. K. Hadden. por *U S News World Rep* 102:8 Ap 13 '87

Stones fly in the TV temple. G. Witkin. il pors *U S News World Rep* 102:10-11 Je 8 '87

Taking command at Fort Mill. R. N. Ostling. il pors *Time* 129:60 My 11 '87

Toll-free woes. *Time* 129:63 Ja 26 '87

FAMA *See* Fabrica Argentina de Material Aerospacial

Fame

See also

Black celebrities
Celebrities
Halls of fame

Americans seek life, liberty and the pursuit of fame [views of Leo Braudy] il *USA Today (Periodical)* 115:10 My '87

The haul of fame. S. Gray. il por *Roll Stone* p30-1+ My 21 '87

How fleet it is! [people famous for a very brief time in 1987] il *People Wkly* 28:88-91 D 28 '87-Ja 4 '88

The new seductress [D. Rice, F. Hall, and J. Hahn] N. Scovell. il pors *Mademoiselle* 93:244-7 N '87

Ollie North and the trajectory of fame. C. Krauthammer. il *Time* 130:76 Jl 27 '87

On the springboard of notoriety [J. Hahn, D. Rice and F. Hall] F. Trippett. il pors *Time* 130:64-5 O 12 '87

Stars until the tape runs out [sports fans and other spectators viewing themselves on videotape] C. Gordon. il *Macleans* 100:37 My 18 '87

A visit from Rosa Parks: power of the ordinary. D. C. Skinner. *Christ Century* 104:300-1 Ap 1 '87

You probably don't know me. J. Epstein. *Am Sch* 56:463-70 Aut '87

Anecdotes, facetiae, satire, etc.

Hooked on fame. G. Radner. il por *Ms* 15:56-7+ F '87

Sweet fifteen. J. Martel. *Roll Stone* p91 My 21 '87

Uncivil liberties. C. Trillin. il *Nation* 244:352 Mr 21 '87

Familial hypercholesteremia *See* Hypercholesteremia

Family

See also

Aged—Family relationships
AIDS patients—Family relationships
Alcoholics' families
Alzheimer's disease patients—Family relationships
Artists' families
Aunts
Birth order
Black family
Cancer patients—Family relationships
Childlessness
Children
Children, Handicapped—Family relationships
Church work with families
Cousins
Divorce
Fathers
Foster home care
Grandparents
Home
Home education
Husbands
Marriage
Marriage counseling
Married couples
Mentally handicapped—Family relationships
Mothers
Mothers-in-law
Only child
Parent-child relationship
Parents
Patriarchy
Presidential candidates—Families

Servicemen's families
Siblings
Sick—Family relationships
Single parent families
Sons
Sons-in-law
Stepparents and stepchildren
Trade unions and the family

39 ways to destress your home life. il *Prevention* 39:34-6+ S '87

Addressing family issues [1988 presidential election] il *Christ Today* 31:53+ N 20 '87

The American dream: the family's tie. K. Zinsmeister. *Current* 290:9-13 F '87

Are home based services effective? A public child welfare agency's experiment [Hennepin County, Minn.] P. AuClaire and I. M. Schwartz. il *Child Today* 16:6-9 My/Je '87

Are you a family, or just living together? M. Golin. il *Prevention* 39:58-61 My '87

Calling all cousins—who connects the family [role of women] C. Tavris. *Vogue* 177:122 My '87

The children of Narcissus. C. Lasch. *Des Arts Educ* 88:45-8 My/Je '87

Families and children in the year 2000. A. J. Norton. il *Child Today* 16:6-9 Jl/Ag '87

Family. H. Brodkey. *New Yorker* 63:119-33 N 23 '87

Family based services [special issue] il *Child Today* 15:4-32 N/D '86

Family dreams [work of Edward Taub-Bynum] S. Baker. il *Omni* 9:112 Ap '87

Family network. See issues of Better Homes and Gardens beginning May 1986

Family ties [liking relatives; results of survey] I. Groller. il *Parents* 62:27 D '87

Family ties [special section] *Harpers Bazaar* 121:126-7+ D '87

Federal report backs policies that support the family [White House Working Group on the Family] *Christ Today* 31:47 Ja 16 '87

Five ways to fight family stress [condensed from Stress and the healthy family] D. Curran. il *Read Dig* 130:169-70+ F '87

Gays: a family phenomenon? [study by Richard Pillard and James Weinrich] J. Meer. *Psychol Today* 21:66-7 Ap '87

Golden scrapbooks of the mind [family memories] B. Bartocci. il *Read Dig* 131:137-40 D '87

How to avoid Christmas stress [views of Wallace Denton] *USA Today (Periodical)* 116:4 D '87

The hurricane hour [end-of-day family stress] K. W. Wiley. il *Health* 19:54-8 Ag '87

The impact of the women's movement(s) on the family: a father's perspective. E. Marciniak. *America* 156:194-6 Mr 7 '87

The importance of family ties. J. Brothers. il pors *Good Housekeep* 205:96+ S '87

Men in the eighties: multiplying roles: the next stage. D. Hellerstein. il *Ms* 16:48-50 O '87

Monitoring government's impact on the family. *Christ Today* 31:52+ O 16 '87

The new American family. L. C. Thurow. il *Technol Rev* 90:26-7 Ag/S '87

The new rules and new roles at family holiday get-togethers. il *Glamour* 85:99 N '87

On behalf of families. K. Greer. il *Better Homes Gard* 65:19 F '87

Preserving values in a changing world [views of B. Friedan] il por *USA Today (Periodical)* 116:2-3 Ag '87

Six secrets of strong families [condensed from Secrets of strong families] N. Stinnett and J. DeFrain. il *Read Dig* 131:132-5 N '87

What's new for American families in '87 [special section] K. Stechert. il *Better Homes Gard* 65:15+ Ja '87

Work and family [Conference Board report entitled Corporations and families] il *Child Today* 16:3-4 Ja/F '87

Yuletide strife [family conflict; views of Sidney Russak] il *USA Today (Periodical)* 116:16 D '87

Anecdotes, facetiae, satire, etc.

Family: the ties that bind . . . and gag! [excerpt] E. Bombeck. il *Redbook* 169:186-8+ S '87

Caricatures and cartoons

It's all in the family. S. Berenstain and J. Berenstain. See occasional issues of Good Housekeeping

History

A gift to the future [family oral histories] R. Long. il *High Fidel* 37:21 D '87

(Table) manners makyth man. N. Ishige. il *Courier* 40:18-21 My '87

Family—History—*cont.*

Exhibitions
Accepted notions of the family and its function have changed profoundly; how do we exhibit this in a museum? R. M. Adams. il *Smithsonian* 18:10 Je '87

Photographs and photography
Beyond the family photo album. A. McGrath. *U S News World Rep* 103:73 N 30 '87

A father's pictures [family history through photographs] D. Pitchford. il *N Y Times Mag* p44 Jl 12 '87

A few snapshots, a few regrets [memories evoked by photographs] S. Freeman. il *Parents* 62:100-1 Jl '87

Holiday pictures that celebrate a family's life together. C. Begole. il *Glamour* 85:78 D '87

Religious life
Beaver Cleaver is divorced: the growing pains of American Catholic families. J. Breig. il *U S Cathol* 52:48-53 Je '87

Career change [choosing motherhood] E. W. Fielding. il por *Christ Today* 31:26-8 D 11 '87

Family fights don't have to be fatal. D. Curran. il *U S Cathol* 52:22-9 S '87

My children's father: a self-portrait for Father's Day. M. Finley. *America* 156:499-500 Je 20-27 '87

Past imperfect: is it time to let your parents off the hook? [cover story] M. O'Connell. il *U S Cathol* 52:6-13 Ja '87

Stress survival manual: how faith can help your family cope [cover story] D. Curran. il *U S Cathol* 52:6-13 Ap '87

William Bloomer's footprints. V. G. Beers. il *Christ Today* 31:11 Je 12 '87

Yours, mine, and ours: can stepfamilies ever blend? R. Greene. il *U S Cathol* 52:31-7 Jl '87

Canada
A new emphasis on the family [Maclean's/Decima poll] A. Finlayson. il *Macleans* 100:71-2 Ja 5 '87

Japan
Absentee fathers. P. Hartcher. il *World Press Rev* 34:59 O '87

A meeting of the twain [American psychologists C. Colman and D. McGill practice family therapy] J. Biggar. bibl (p65) il *Psychol Today* 21:46-50+ N '87

Family budget *See* Budget, Household
Family business *See* Family corporations

Family corporations
See also
Center for Family Business

"Dad, I know I can handle it". E. F. Cone. il *Forbes* 140 Sp Issue:370+ O 26 '87

The entrepreneurial family and its future [address, December 9, 1986] G. L. Bernstein. *Vital Speeches Day* 53:205-7 Ja 15 '87

The family business [special section] il *Nations Bus* 75:45+ O '87

A hotel of one's own [Y. Lembi-Detert partnered with father in the Hotel Group of America] M. Dowie. il por *Ms* 16:38-9 D '87

How to bequeath the family business. il *Fortune* 116 Sp Issue:120 Fall '87

Like father, like daughter [father-daughter corporations] R. Rooney. il *Good Housekeep* 204:108-9+ Je '87

Succeeding in family businesses [women] S. Nelton and K. Berney. il *Nations Bus* 75:26 My '87

Taking over: how to decide, what to do [woman who inherits a family-owned company when her husband dies] L. Sorenson. *Work Woman* 12:40 Jl '87

Thicker than water. P. Plawin. *Changing Times* 41:102 Ap '87

Family counseling *See* Counseling

Family courts
Nova Scotia
Unorthodox behavior [Judge R. J. White] G. Emerson. il *Macleans* 100:17 Je 8 '87

Family doctors *See* Physicians

Family Dollar Stores, Inc.
The family feud at Family Dollar Stores. D. Foust. il *Bus Week* p32-3 S 21 '87

Guess who lost. L. M. Keefe. il por *Forbes* 140:60+ S 7 '87

Family education
See also
Parent education

Family finance *See* Finance, Personal

Family handyman (Periodical)
Editor's letter [use of new typeface] G. Havens. *Fam Handyman* 37:2 Ap '87

From the editor [new logo] G. Havens. *Fam Handyman* 37:6 Ja '87

Family Home Entertainment (Firm)
Scholastic leaves Lorimar, sets up label at IVE. *Publ Wkly* 232:137-8 S 18 '87

Family in literature
See also
Parent-child relationship in literature

Family in motion pictures
Homebody heat: the family triumphs over the libido. M. Haskell. *Vogue* 177:74 D '87

Family in television
TV families. M. Norman. il *Ms* 16:38+ Jl/Ag '87

Family income *See* Income

Family Media, Inc.
Discover is headed for a new family. D. Lieberman. il *Bus Week* p40 Je 8 '87

Family planning *See* Birth control

Family Planning International Assistance
Abortion more precious than $20 mil. grant: Wattleton [grant from U.S. Agency for International Development] *Jet* 72:36 My 11 '87

In the shadow of Uncle Sam [effect on Bangladesh of USAID cutoff of funds] A. Boggan. il *Ms* 16:69 N '87

Wattleton raps Reagan's cut of overseas abortion funds. por *Jet* 72:9 Ag 17 '87

Family psychotherapy
See also
Ackerman Institute for Family Therapy

A meeting of the twain [American psychologists C. Colman and D. McGill practice family therapy in Japan] J. Biggar. bibl (p65) il *Psychol Today* 21:46-50+ N '87

"We have a problem". J. Marks. See issues of Parents beginning February 1987

Family quarrels *See* Quarrels
Family resorts *See* Resorts

Family reunions
12 terrific ideas to make your next family reunion better than ever! M. Ingebretsen. il *Better Homes Gard* 65:18+ Ag '87

Cooking for a family reunion. P. A. Toussaint. il *Essence* 18:92-4+ Jl '87

Family reunions helping blacks face unsure future. il *Jet* 73:20+ O 5 '87

"I am Bryan, your brother" [Australian son fathered by an American serviceman is united with his sisters in the U.S.] J. L. Block. il por *Good Housekeep* 204:82+ Mr '87

Jackee visits N.C. roots for grandmother's 103rd birthday, clan reunion. il pors *Jet* 73:46-7 D 28 '87-Ja 4 '88

Organize a family reunion. M. C. Polk. il *Americana* 15:14-16 Jl/Ag '87

Reunion. *New Yorker* 63:21-3 Jl 20 '87

A show of strength: celebrating the black family with 'reunions'. B. Kantrowitz. il *Newsweek* 110:73 Ag 17 '87

"Where are my children?" [Walters family of Marshall County, Ky. reunited after fifty years] S. Kelly. il *Read Dig* 130:151-2+ Je '87

Family rooms
Build-in a video corner. M. Brett. il *Pop Sci* 231:76-7 D '87

Down with three walls, up with a glass roof. il *Sunset* 178:146 Ap '87

Everything's built in! il *South Living* 22:188 N '87

Filled with family memories. il *South Living* 22:66-7 Ag '87

For more light and drama, they "bashed" through the ceiling. il *Sunset* 179:88-9 Jl '87

Light and open for family entertaining. il *South Living* 22:168 My '87

More than just a room. il *South Living* 22:201 N '87

A room for the whole family. il *South Living* 22:210 N '87

Family safety education *See* Safety education

Family Savings & Loan Association (Los Angeles, Calif.)
Chairman acquires control of Family Savings & Loan has assets of $144 mil. [O. A. Trigg] *Jet* 72:6 Ag 24 '87

S&L eyes black support. M. Bernstein. por *Black Enterp* 18:22 N '87

Family size
See also
Childlessness
Only child

One big happy family [Mikowski family] M. Miller. il *People Wkly* 27:22-9 Ja 12 '87

Secrets of enormous families. K. Schlaerth. il *Parents* 62:114-19+ D '87

Family social work
Developing partnerships between families and service providers in rural Vermont [work of the Milton Family Community Center] L. Horel. il *Child Today* 16:17-19 Ja/F '87

Family souvenirs *See* Souvenirs (Keepsakes)
Family therapy *See* Family psychotherapy
Family ties [television program] *See* Television program reviews—Single works
Family vacations *See* Vacations
Family viewing [film] *See* Motion picture reviews—Single works
Family violence
See also
Wife abuse
Aftermath of a romance [K. Inwood of Toronto charged with assaulting his Russian wife and child] R. Corelli. il pors *Macleans* 100:58 S 28 '87
Life with father was nasty, brutish and scary, so Johnny Junatanov tried to have him murdered—repeatedly. A. Richman. il pors *People Wkly* 27:83+ Ja 19 '87
Sexual and family violence: a growing issue for the churches [cover story] L. G. Livezey. il *Christ Century* 104:938-42 O 28 '87

Famine relief *See* Relief work
Famines
Does more food mean less famine? A. Smith. il *Esquire* 108:55-6 Jl '87
Famine: causes, prevention, and relief. J. W. Mellor and S. Gavian. bibl f il *Science* 235:539-45 Ja 30 '87

Africa
See also
Live Aid concert, 1985
United Nations. Office of Emergency Operations in Africa
USA for Africa

Ethiopia
Famine [cover story] M. S. Serrill. il map *Time* 130:34-8+ D 21 '87
Of many things [Paulist Productions' TV movie We are the children] J. W. Donohue. *America* 156:inside cover Mr 14 '87
Saving Ethiopia from itself. D. MacKenzie. il *World Press Rev* 34:52 D '87
Secret exodus: the story of Operation Moses [excerpt] C. Safran. il *Read Dig* 130:96-104+ Ja '87
The spectre of famine. A. Bilski. il map *Macleans* 100:18-19 D 7 '87
Tourists in hell [excerpt from Breakfast in hell] M. Harris. *Harpers* 274:28-31 F '87
While famine looms, Ethiopia's leaders fiddle. J. L. Galloway. il *U S News World Rep* 103:12 O 5 '87

Lebanon
On the brink of cannibalism [food shortage at Beirut refugee camps] il *Time* 129:55 F 23 '87
Famous men and women *See* Celebrities
Famularo, Joseph J.
Young chefs' full-baked ideas. il *N Y Times Mag* p71-2 Mr 29 '87
Fan, Kenneth
about
Miss Muse. *New Yorker* 63:29-31 S 14 '87
Fan belts (Automobile) *See* Automobile engines—Fan belts
Fan clubs
See also
Sons of the Desert (Organization)
A Celebration: U2 fans join the club. S. Hochman. il *Roll Stone* p16-17 Jl 2 '87
Fan club organized for Walter Brooks's 'Freddy' books. J. Roginski. il *Publ Wkly* 231:105 F 27 '87
Fan mail
Soap star computes [M. Swan] il por *Pers Comput* 11:282 S '87
Fan worms *See* Annelids
Fancy Food and Confection Show *See* Food—Exhibitions
Fancy free [ballet] *See* Ballet reviews—Single works
Fandel, John
Memorial days [poem] *Commonweal* 114:321 My 22 '87
Miss Dickinson, no Emily, still makes me nervous. *Commonweal* 114:538-9 S 25 '87
Fanfares
Musical events:
Houston Symphony's series of fanfares. A. Porter. *New Yorker* 63:71-3 Jl 20 '87
Fangmeier, Robert A.
Ideological contradictions in U.S. policy toward Angola. il *Christ Century* 104:1061-3 N 25 '87

Fannie Mae *See* Federal National Mortgage Association
Fanning, Buckner
A concerned clergyman's message to teens: look, but don't leap. por *People Wkly* 27:116 Ap 13 '87
Fanning, John
about
Will success be merely temporary? F. McCoy. il por *Bus Week* p86 My 25 '87
Fanning, Katherine
about
The many lives of Kay Fanning. I. Nelson. il por *50 Plus* 27:78+ Ja '87
Fans, Automobile racing *See* Automobile racing fans
Fans, Baseball *See* Baseball fans
Fans, Basketball *See* Basketball fans
Fans, Electric
See also
Ventilators
Blowing away the ceiling fan myths. J. Hayes. il *Saturday Evening Post* 259:28-9 S '87
Easy summer breezes [ceiling fan installation] C. Johnson and N. Johnson. il *Workbench* 43:58-9 My/Je '87
Even with air conditioning you need a whole-house fan. P. McCafferty. il *Pop Sci* 230:76+ Ap '87
Install a fan control [ceiling fan] G. Branson. il *Fam Handyman* 37:53 F '87
Fans, Football *See* Football fans
Fans, Tennis *See* Tennis fans
Fans, Ventilating *See* Ventilators
Fans (Persons)
See also
Sports fans
Caught in the act: the secret lives of rock 'n' roll style stealers. il *Seventeen* 46:124-9 Jl '87
Dreamgirls [F. Lenger, ardent fan of the Dinning Sisters] B. Greene. il por *Esquire* 107:39-40 My '87
Letter from Europe [lives of singer L. Mariano and a Portuguese fan] J. Kramer. il *New Yorker* 63:66-70+ Ag 24 '87
Starstruck. D. Geigis. il *Glamour* 85:100+ Mr '87
Fantasies, Literary
How to make believe. A. Lindbergh. *Writer* 100:17-19 D '87
Fantastic art *See* Art, Fantastic
The fantasticks [musical] *See* Musicals, revues, etc.—Reviews—Single works
Fantasy
See also
Children's fantasies
Fairy tales
Fantasies of the stars [women athletes] il *Women's Sports Fitness* 9:18-19 Mr '87
If I were an animal, I'd be a . . . [excerpts] F. Cowles. il *Redbook* 168:78+ Mr '87
Lust in your heart: at what point does a fantasy about someone become infidelity? C. L. Mithers. *Glamour* 85:304 O '87
Make believers [therapeutic use of enhanced states; work of M. M. Watkins] R. Katz. il *Omni* 10:126-8+ N '87
The power of daydreams. E. Klinger. bibl (p62) il *Psychol Today* 21:36-9+ O '87
What about sexual daydreams? il *Psychol Today* 21:39 O '87
Fante, John, 1909-1983
about
Forgotten son of the lost generation. B. Shacochis. il pors *Vogue* 177:190+ D '87
Fantel, Hans
Sight and sound: buyer beware! *Opera News* 51:44 Je '87
Sight and sound: DAT's what it's all about. il *Opera News* 52:48+ N '87
Sight and sound: mighty bantams: small speakers now deliver big. il *Opera News* 52:32-3 Ag '87
Sight and sound: odds-on favorites. il *Opera News* 51:52-3 Mr 14 '87
Sight and sound: the big picture. il *Opera News* 51:30-1 Ja 3 '87
Fanthorpe, Ursula
Questions and answers on writing poetry. *Writer* 100:22-3 Ag '87
Fanuc Ltd.
Japan's robot king wins again [GE joint venture] G. Bylinsky. il pors *Fortune* 115:53-4+ My 25 '87
FAO *See* Food and Agriculture Organization of the United Nations

Far East *See* East Asia
Far Hills (N.J.)
Social life and customs
Blueblood boating [Far Hills Yacht Club regatta for yacht models] D. Wallace. il *Mot Boat Sail* 160:42-5+ Ag '87
Far side (Comic strip) *See* Comic books, strips, etc.
Farabundo Martí National Liberation Front
Bloody setback at El Paraíso. J. Borrell. il *Time* 129:49 Ap 13 '87
The night fighters of El Salvador [U.S. military adviser dies during attack] J. L. Sheler. il *U S News World Rep* 102:12-13 Ap 13 '87
Salvador's rebels: alive and deadly [attack kills U.S. adviser] N. Cooper. il *Newsweek* 109:32 Ap 13 '87
Faraggi, Henriette Mathieu- *See* Mathieu-Faraggi, Henriette, 1915-1985
Faragher, Ray
about
The World. *New Yorker* 63:24-5 Je 22 '87
Farah, Charles
America's Pentecostals: what they believe. il por *Christ Today* 31:22-6 O 16 '87
Farber, Dan
The Burger Court: bad, but not that bad. *Wash Mon* 19:52-4 My '87
Farber, Henry S.
The recent decline of unionization in the United States. bibl f il *Science* 238:915-20 N 13 '87
Farber, Jim
Blood, sweat, & fears: why are horror movies such a slashing success? il *Seventeen* 46:108-9+ Jl '87
New sirens of song: note worthy. il *Harpers Bazaar* 120:234+ S '87
Farber, M. A.
The con man. il por *N Y Times Mag* p34+ Je 21 '87
Farentinos, Robert C., 1941-
Power training for explosive turns. il *Skiing* 40:253-5 O '87
Fares, Airline *See* Airlines—Fares
Farese, Robert V., and others
Insulin rapidly increases diacylglycerol by activating de novo phosphatidic acid synthesis. bibl f il *Science* 236:586-9 My 1 '87
Farhad, Shukri
Shooting a self-promotional poster. il *Petersens Photogr Mag* 16:38-9 N '87
Faria, Norman
The puzzle for Caribbean writers. *World Press Rev* 34:62 Ja '87
Farina, Dennis
about
Dennis Farina: guts & glamour. J. Cameron. il por *Harpers Bazaar* 120:124+ Ap '87
Faris, Gregory W., and Byer, Robert L.
Quantitative three-dimensional optical tomographic imaging of supersonic flows. bibl f il *Science* 238:1700-2 D 18 '87
Faris, Sadeg
about
He's walking tall where IBM wouldn't tread. O. Port. il por *Bus Week* p124 My 4 '87
Farley, Cathy
Techniques of scratchboard drawing. il *Am Artist* 51:62-5 Mr '87
Farley, Dixie
Benefit vs. risk: how FDA approves new drugs. il *FDA Consum* 21:6-18 D '87/Ja '88
The eyes of Texas (and FDA) were upon them. il *FDA Consum* 21:29-31 O '87
From tainted feed to mothers' milk. il *FDA Consum* 21:38-40 Mr '87
Incontinence comes out of the closet. il *FDA Consum* 21:4-9 Mr '87
Kitty odor product seized. il *FDA Consum* 21:37-8 Je '87
Laser treatment to go: outpatient uses of healing light abound [cover story] il *FDA Consum* 21:22-7 O '87
A new weapon in the battle against heart disease. il *FDA Consum* 21:26-8 N '87
Protection against winter woes. il *FDA Consum* 21:28-35 F '87
Test-tube skin and other high-tech treatments for burns. il *FDA Consum* 21:28-31 Je '87
Farley, Frank H.
about
The big thrill. C. Zweig. il *Omni* 9:26+ Ap '87

Farley, Lee, 1955-
about
Techniques of scratchboard drawing. C. Farley. il *Am Artist* 51:62-5 Mr '87
Farley, Philip J., 1916-
How to negotiate a treaty. il *Bull At Sci* 43:33-6 O '87
Farley, William F.
about
The buyout man. C. Skrzycki. il por *U S News World Rep* 102:63 Ja 26 '87
Can a CEO buy celebrity? P. King and A. Miller. il por *Newsweek* 109:44 Je 22 '87
Look who wants to be president. B. Saporito. il pors *Fortune* 116:141+ N 23 '87
Some things are easier said than done. S. B. Weiner. il por *Forbes* 139 Ann Directory:56-7 Ap 27 '87
Farley Industries Inc.
The buyout man [W. F. Farley] C. Skrzycki. il por *U S News World Rep* 102:63 Ja 26 '87
Can a CEO buy celebrity? [W. Farley stars in his own commercials] P. King and A. Miller. il por *Newsweek* 109:44 Je 22 '87
Look who wants to be president [executive W. Farley] B. Saporito. il pors *Fortune* 116:141+ N 23 '87
Farley/Northwest Industries, Inc.
Some things are easier said than done [W. Farley] S. B. Weiner. il por *Forbes* 139 Ann Directory:56-7 Ap 27 '87
The Farm (Tenn.)
Revisiting 'The Farm': from commune to suburb. J. T. Baker. il *Christ Century* 104:918-20 O 21 '87
Farm accidents *See* Agriculture—Accidents
Farm accounting *See* Agriculture—Accounting
Farm Aid (Organization)
Farm Aid's founder Willie Nelson [cover story] P. Carr. il pors *Mother Earth News* 105:42-5 My/Je '87
Willie Nelson's harvest of hope. E. Hawkes. il pors *Ladies Home J* 104:88+ S '87
Farm animals *See* Livestock
Farm animals, Treatment of *See* Animals—Treatment
Farm buildings
See also
Barns and stables
Calf pens and sheds
Swine houses
Farm cooperatives *See* Agriculture, Cooperative
Farm credit *See* Agricultural credit
Farm Credit System (U.S.)
Bailout coming for Farm Credit System. P. Smith. il *Success Farm* 85:18W My '87
Barnyard quandary: how to get farm banks back in clover? K. R. Sheets. *U S News World Rep* 102:40 Ap 20 '87
A bushel of farm debt lands on Congress. T. Smart. il *Bus Week* p44 Mr 16 '87
The Farm Credit System slouches toward recovery. P. Houston. il por *Bus Week* p114 N 23 '87
FCS rates lag market rate drop by two years. C. Tevis. il *Success Farm* 85 no4:9 F '87
Fear for FCS stock spurs loan payments. D. Allen. *Success Farm* 85:18K Ap '87
Hot air—and hope—for Iowa. H. Sidey. il *Time* 130:14 Ag 10 '87
Move over Ginnie Mae, here comes Farmer Mac. T. Smart. *Bus Week* p72 Ag 24 '87
Mysteries of the Farm Credit System. P. Smith. il *Success Farm* 85:52 S '87
Farm education *See* Agricultural education
Farm equipment *See* Agricultural equipment
Farm equipment industry *See* Agricultural equipment industry
Farm finance *See* Agriculture—Economic aspects
Farm foreclosure *See* Foreclosure
Farm houses *See* Farmhouses
Farm labor
See also
Migrant labor
Strikes—Farm labor
United Farm Workers of America
Health and hygiene
Farmworkers out on the line again [proposed UFW grape boycott] A. Stine. il *Sierra* 72:14+ Jl/Ag '87
Farm legislation *See* Agricultural administration
Farm life
Country medicine. H. H. Price. il *Gourmet* 47:58+ O '87
In Nebraska, persistence pays off [E. Krajicek and family] C. Kenney. il por *50 Plus* 27:14+ D '87

Farm machinery *See* Agricultural equipment
Farm management
> *See also*
> Cattle farm management
> Computers—Agricultural use
> Farm records
> Farms—Size
> Swine farm management

'The best free advice I ever got'. G. Johnston. il *Success Farm* 85:62L O '87
Beyond the farming crisis. D. Ehrenfeld. il *Technol Rev* 90:46-56 Jl '87
How to diversify your farm this year. B. Freese. il *Success Farm* 85 no4:11-17 F '87
The joys of paperwork. D. Allen. il *Success Farm* 85:26-8 S '87
Opportunities abound [cover story; special section] D. Allen and others. il *Success Farm* 85:9-15 N '87
Profit. See occasional issues of Successful Farming
We're businessmen first. D. Allen and G. Johnston. il *Success Farm* 85:11-13+ Je '87
Farm mechanization
> *See also*
> Harvesting machinery

Farm policy *See* Agricultural administration
Farm price supports *See* Agricultural administration
Farm produce
> *See also*
> Surplus products, Agricultural

Marketing
> *See also*
> Farmers' markets
> Produce trade
> Supermarkets—Produce departments

Farmers overlook million-dollar direct markets. *Success Farm* 85 no4:5 F '87
It's not easy to find a market, but it sure pays off [alternative crops] il *Success Farm* 85 no4:19 F '87
Marketing. See issues of Successful Farming
Marketing miniatures [baby vegetables for upscale restaurants raised at Overbrook Herb Farm] K. Pechter. il por *Rodale's Org Gard* 34:72-6 D '87
Specialty farm crops offer marketing control. il *Success Farm* 85 no4:18A F '87

Prices
> *See also*
> Agricultural administration

Farm records
> *See also*
> Computers—Agricultural use

The joys of paperwork. D. Allen. il *Success Farm* 85:26-8 S '87
On-farm records beginning to tell what works, and doesn't [hog records] G. Johnston. il *Success Farm* 85:H2 My '87
We're businessmen first. D. Allen and G. Johnston. il *Success Farm* 85:11-13+ Je '87
A year on records yields paper plug for profit leaks [swine] B. Freese. il *Success Farm* 85:H4 Ap '87
Farm rents
Land rental market 'amazingly stable'. J. Walter. il *Success Farm* 85:18J My '87
Farm shops *See* Workshops
Farm size *See* Farms—Size
Farm taxation *See* Farmers—Taxation
Farm teams (Baseball) *See* Baseball, Professional
Farm tenancy
> *See also*
> Crofters
> Farm rents

Fertilizer strategies for short-term leases. M. Holmberg. il *Success Farm* 85 no3:18Q F '87
Farm toys *See* Toys
Farm women
Bullish on calves and sheep [J. Snyder, broker and farmer] H. Zelinsky. il por *Ms* 15:23 Ap '87
If anything good comes from the farm crisis, it will be a new respect for the skills of rural women. C. Dreifus. il *Glamour* 85:190-1+ Ja '87
Joint venture. C. Tevis. See issues of Successful Farming beginning September 1984

Economic conditions
Farm women sue USDA [farm program payment discrimination] C. Tevis. il *Success Farm* 85:24 S '87
Learning to survive on the land. M. Bosc. il *U S News World Rep* 102:30 F 2 '87
This land is their land. M. Vold. il *Ms* 16:76+ N '87

Farm woodlands *See* Woodlots
Farm workers *See* Farm labor
Farmer, James
> *about*

CORE founder Farmer mends after heart attack. il por *Jet* 71:13 F 9 '87

Archives
CORE's Farmer gives his personal papers to Univ. of Texas. *Jet* 72:22 S 21 '87
Farmer, Linda Neuviller
> *about*

"An accident destroyed my face". A. Fischer. il pors *Redbook* 169:36+ O '87
Farmer-hunter relations
Passwords to posted signs [getting hunting permission on posted lands] J. Weiss. il *Outdoor Life* 180:74-5+ Jl '87
Farmerie, William G., and others
Expression and processing of the AIDS virus reverse transcriptase in Escherichia coli. bibl f il *Science* 236:305-8 Ap 17 '87
Farmers
> *See also*
> Agriculture
> Black farmers
> Farmer-hunter relations

A thin disguise [life of a farmer imitated by author] R. Rhodes. il *N Y Times Mag* p62 Jl 19 '87

Economic conditions
See Agriculture—Economic aspects

Education
When mom and dad go off to college. C. Tevis. il *Success Farm* 85 no3:22-3 F '87

Health and hygiene
One washing won't remove pesticides from clothing. *Success Farm* 85:D My '87
Pesticide health risks. B. Freese and D. Mowitz. il *Success Farm* 85 no3:18AB F '87

Political activities
Farmers plow up Pentagon's budget [movement to transfer funding from the military budget to Iowa's FmHA program] M. Helmberger. *Progressive* 51:15-16 Mr '87
The heretics of the heartland [farmers that want off the public dole] J. McCormick. il por *Newsweek* 109:46-7 Mr 30 '87

Religious life
> *See also*
> Church work with farmers

Suits and claims
Court: accused farmers deserve due process, too [farm program payments] *Success Farm* 85:46 S '87
'I wish I would have known more about the legal system'. C. Tevis. il *Success Farm* 85 no6:18AV Mr '87

Taxation
Family farm group says tax law needs further reform. *Success Farm* 85:6 Ap '87
IRAs still lovely. M. Zall. il *Success Farm* 85:F4 My '87
Lease loophole preserves investment tax credit. C. Finck. il *Success Farm* 85:18T My '87
Tax reform and the part-time farmer. J. Alper. il *Ctry J* 14:73-9 F '87
Tax reform changes investment strategies. M. Zall. *Success Farm* 85 no6:19 Mr '87
Farmers, Handicapped
New program gives more hope to the disabled. *Success Farm* 85:41 Ag '87
Farmers . . . entrepreneurs [television program] *See* Television program reviews—Single works
Farmers Group Inc.
An insurer gets eyed from abroad. G. G. Marcial. *Bus Week* p112 O 19 '87
Farmers Home Administration (U.S.) *See* United States. Farmers Home Administration
Farmers' markets
Farm fresh [Bay Area] il *Sunset* 179:10-11+ S '87
Market watch [Greenmarket system in New York City] L. Sombke. il *N Y* 20:23 Jl 27 '87
Farmers' wives *See* Farm women
Farmhouses
> *See also*
> House decoration

Colonial contours: traditional lines for a Connecticut farmhouse [decorated by Thomas Britt] C. D. B. Bryan. il *Archit Dig* 44:102-7 Jl '87
The country life [three historic farmhouses] il *Redbook* 169:191-6 S '87
Farmhouse for the 80s: open but energy-efficient. il *Sunset* 178:164-5 Ap '87

Farmhouses—*cont.*

Image makers [Garmelow Manor, home of A. and P. Machin] E. Greene. il pors *House Gard* 159:180-7 N '87

A Texas-style farmhouse. il *South Living* 22:157 O '87

Farmhouses, Remodeled *See* Houses, Remodeled

Farming *See* Agriculture

Farming, Organic *See* Organic farming

Farming, Truck *See* Truck farming

Farming cooperatives *See* Agriculture, Cooperative

Farmland Dairies

Taste of victory. M. Fritz. il por *Forbes* 139:234 My 18 '87

Farmland investment *See* Real estate investment

Farmland utilization *See* Land utilization

Farmland values *See* Land values

Farms

> See also
> Agriculture
> Plantations

Size

> See also
> Farms, Small

The 400 largest farms in the U.S. P. Smith. il map *Success Farm* 85 no2:7-14 Ja '87

Proposed changes threaten big farms [$50,000 payment rules] D. Allen and P. Smith. il *Success Farm* 85:42-4 Ag '87

Farms, Historic *See* Agricultural museums

Farms, Model

> See also
> Agricultural museums

Farms, Small

Sugar City goes sour [Colorado] A. A. Rooney. il *Saturday Evening Post* 259:26 Ja/F '87

UC told to review impact of research [ruling primarily benefits small farmers] M. Sun. *Science* 238:1221 N 27 '87

Farnborough Air Show *See* Aviation—Exhibitions

Farnsworth, Cherrill

> about

From medical breakthrough to health-care tool. D. Holder. il por *Work Woman* 12:69-70 My '87

Faroe Islands

Industries

> See also
> Whaling—Faroe Islands

Farouché

> about

The official wiggle jiggle bump & grind program. E. Kiester. il pors *50 Plus* 27:46-9 O '87

Farrakhan, Louis

> about

Islam's new entrepreneur. S. Monroe and J. Schwartz. il por *Newsweek* 110:38-9 Jl 13 '87

Farrar, Eleanor, and Hampel, Robert L.

Social services in American high schools. il *Phi Delta Kappan* 69:297-303 D '87

Farrar Straus & Giroux, Inc.

FS & G garners three fiction nominees for National Book Award. *Publ Wkly* 232:14 O 30 '87

FSG to distribute R & S Books of Stockholm. il *Publ Wkly* 232:30 Ag 28 '87

Nobel House: publisher Roger Straus just keeps on winning. J. Reginato. il pors *N Y* 20:56-60+ N 9 '87

Farrell, David C., 1933-

> about

David Farrell. M. D. Oneal. il por *Bus Week* Sp Issue:236 Ap 17 '87

Farrell, Gillian

> about

Daylighting: going undercover with Gillian Farrell and the new private eyes. N. Pileggi. il pors *N Y* 20:44-8 Ap 20 '87

Farrell, James

> about

Are any stocks still worth buying? [interview] A. E. Serwer. il por *Fortune* 116:100 Ag 31 '87

Farrell, Mary

> about

A case goes unheard at the EEOC. F. Greve. il por *50 Plus* 27:16+ N '87

Farrell, Mary H. J.

Savvy. il *Writer* 100:25 N '87

Farrell, Suzanne, 1945-

> about

Editor's log. W. Como. il por *Dance Mag* 61:32 F '87

Farrell, Warren

> about

When women fight for equality, says Warren Farrell, fairness to men may be one of the casualties. L. Powell. il pors *People Wkly* 27:49-50+ Je 15 '87

Farrelly, Alexander A.

The Caribbean Basin Initiative [address, October 1, 1987] *Vital Speeches Day* 54:68-70 N 15 '87

Farris, Kirk

> about

A man and his bridge. K. Gregor. il por *Art News* 86:11 Ap '87

Farrow, Mia

> about

Mama Mia! "My daughter has a gift with children" [interview with M. O'Sullivan] K. Henderson. il pors *Redbook* 169:50+ S '87

FASB *See* Financial Accounting Standards Board

Fascell, Dante B.

Congress and arms control. bibl f *Foreign Aff* 65:730-49 Spr '87

Fascism

> See also
> National socialism

Anti-'fascism'. E. von Kuehnelt-Leddihn. *Natl Rev* 39:50 Ja 30 '87

Fasel, Ida

Chapel [poem] *Christ Century* 104:623 Jl 15-22 '87

Cologne [poem] *Christ Century* 104:379 Ap 22 '87

Fashion

> See also
> Clothing and dress
> Color in fashion
> Comic books, strips, etc. and fashion
> Costume
> Dance and fashion
> Dress accessories
> Hairstyling
> Sex and fashion
> Tailoring

Aesthetics in fashion [Paris] C. Worthington. il *Harpers Bazaar* 120:88+ Ag '87

Are your looks up-to-date? [quiz] *Teen* 31:28 Ag '87

Back to the 'fifties. K. Beckett. *Vogue* 177:168+ F '87

Chiffon is back as designers unveil a look at sheer heaven. il *People Wkly* 28:180-1 D 14 '87

Couture goes daring and wacky. M. Smilgis. il *Time* 130:74-5 Ag 17 '87

Discreet maneuvers. C. Donovan. il *N Y Times Mag* p56-7 Jl 19 '87

Fab '50s [special section] il *Harpers Bazaar* 120:254-63 Mr '87

Fab '50s: the now look. R. Horn. il *Harpers Bazaar* 120:274-7+ Mr '87

Fall '87: other voices. il *Vogue* 177:296-9 My '87

Fall advance: definitive directions. il *Harpers Bazaar* 120:18-21+ Je '87

Fall signals: the clothes, the hair, the look. il *Vogue* 177:168-83+ Jl '87

Fashion. C. Donovan. See occasional issues of The New York Times Magazine

Fashion and the stars [views of Adolfo] M. Luther. il *Good Housekeep* 204:210 F '87

Fashion and the stars [views of Carolyne Roehm] M. Luther. il *Good Housekeep* 204:21 My '87

Fashion and the stars [views of Givenchy] M. Luther. il *Good Housekeep* 204:48 Mr '87

Fashion and the stars [views of Louis Dell'Olio] M. Luther. il *Good Housekeep* 205:80 Ag '87

Fashion and the stars [views of Nolan Miller] M. Luther. il *Good Housekeep* 204:36 Ja '87

Fashion and the stars [views of Norma Kamali] M. Luther. il *Good Housekeep* 205:19 Jl '87

Fashion and the stars [views of Sonia Rykiel] M. Luther. il *Good Housekeep* 204:21 Je '87

Fashion and the stars [views of William Travilla] M. Luther. il *Good Housekeep* 204:54 Ap '87

Fashion workshop. See issues of Glamour

The fashion world heeds the call of the wild: animal prints. il *People Wkly* 28:128-9 O 5 '87

Femininity: do you buy it? K. Madden. il *Vogue* 177:444-6 Mr '87

The frill of it all [petticoated look vs. classic simplicity] K. Beckett. *Vogue* 177:178 Ap '87

La gamine: fun and flirty. il *Harpers Bazaar* 120:86+ Ap '87

Imitation of life [animal prints] L. Wells. il *N Y Times Mag* p62-5 N 1 '87

In style. il *Ladies Home J* 104:55-6+ My '87

Fashion—*cont.*

Look back with glamour [1950s] il *Vogue* 177:388+ Mr '87

The new créateurs [Paris] C. Worthington. il *Harpers Bazaar* 120:246+ S '87

Off-the-street chic. T. Janowitz. *Vogue* 177:620 S '87

A passion for fashion [Paris] L. Chaplin. il *Harpers Bazaar* 120:158+ Mr '87

Ready to wear. C. Rickey. See issues of Mademoiselle beginning March 1985

Secrets of great style [Paris] L. J. Johnson. il *Ladies Home J* 104:116-19 F '87

Spring '87 international report. il *Vogue* 177:162-91 Ja '87

Style '87. il *People Wkly* 27:63 Ja 5 '87

Vogue's view. See issues of Vogue

Periodicals
See also
   W (Periodical)
   Women's wear daily

Magazines for the hip. J. Schwartz. il *Newsweek* 109:46-7 Ap 6 '87

Making the scene [advertising in avant garde magazines to reach yuppie market] B. Kallen. il *Forbes* 140:230 D 14 '87

Fashion and art
See also
   Wearable art

Aesthetics in fashion [Paris] C. Worthington. il *Harpers Bazaar* 120:88+ Ag '87

Art: a sense of fashion: paintings that capture the elements of style. L. Nochlin. il *Archit Dig* 44:110-15+ F '87

Clothed in magic [fashion, art, and surrealism] B. Adams. il *Harpers Bazaar* 120:240-1 O '87

Exhibitions
A hat is a rose is a chicken [Fashion and surrealism at Fashion Institute of Technology] J. Conant. il *Newsweek* 110:85+ N 30 '87

Fashion and dance *See* Dance and fashion

Fashion and music

Caught in the act: the secret lives of rock 'n' roll style stealers. il *Seventeen* 46:124-9 Jl '87

Rock style: 1967-1987 [cover story; special issue] il *Roll Stone* p74-7+ Ap 23 '87

Fashion and sex *See* Sex and fashion

Fashion catalogs *See* Catalogs, Commercial

Fashion designers
See also
   Alaïa, Azzedine
   August, Bonnie
   Beene, Geoffrey
   Biagiotti, Laura
   Blair, Alistair
   Blass, Bill
   Bohan, Marc
   Claiborne, Liz
   Dior, Christian, 1905-1957
   Gaultier, Jean-Paul
   Givenchy, Hubert de
   Halston
   Hamnett, Katharine
   Hawes, Elizabeth, 1903-1971
   Herrera, Carolina
   Julian, Alexander
   Karan, Donna
   Kawakubo, Rei
   Kelly, Patrick
   King, Charmaine
   Lacroix, Christian
   Mandelli, Mariuccia
   McClintock, Jessica
   Monacella, Suzana
   Mtume, A. Kamili
   Nichols, Lisa
   Nipon, Albert
   Oldfield, Bruce
   Oppenheimer, Helga
   Pennathur, Sudha Messerly
   Restivo, Mary Ann
   Saint Laurent, Yves
   Smith, Paul
   Smith, Willi
   Sprouse, Stephen
   Sy, Mommadou
   Tompkins, Susie
   Trussardi, Nicola
   Valentino
   Van Pier, Andre
   Vionnet, Madeleine, 1876-1975
   Walls, Michael
   Westwood, Vivienne

   Yamamoto, Yohji
   Zaitsev, Vyacheslav

The Americans who lead. C. Donovan. il *N Y Times Mag* p48-53 Je 28 '87

Designer, client: the modern equation. P. Sinclaire and L. J. Nonkin. il *Vogue* 177:338+ N '87

The designers who lead. C. Donovan. il *N Y Times Mag* p50-6 Je 21 '87

Fashion with a flair [Latin American couturiers] C. Healy. il *Américas* 39:2-7 My/Je '87

A man's stylebook. K. J. Gross and J. Mather. il *Esquire* 108:133-51 S '87

Of power, glory and the rich and famous. A. Gabor. il por *U S News World Rep* 103:55 Ag 24 '87

When designers dress . . . [women] il *Vogue* 177:316 F '87

Who's who in American style: the people, the success, the impact. G. Y. Dryansky. il *Vogue* 177:171-4+ O '87

Awards
And the winner is . . . [Council of Fashion Designer Awards] il *Vogue* 177:132 Ja '87

Fashion dolls *See* Dolls

Fashion industry *See* Clothing industry

Fashion photography *See* Photography, Fashion

Fashion shows

Autumn in Paris. P. McColl. il *N Y Times Mag* p54-60 Mr 15 '87

Chanel steals the show. J. Conant. il *Newsweek* 109:50-1 Ap 6 '87

Couture Paris/Rome: the week that was. il *Vogue* 177:562+ S '87

Everything's coming up roses [Paris spring couture] il *Vogue* 177:240 My '87

Fall advance: definitive directions. il *Harpers Bazaar* 120:18-21+ Je '87

Fashion front [spring collections] il *Vogue* 177:314 F '87

Feminine flourishes [spring 1988 collections] C. Donovan. il *N Y Times Mag* p70-6 O 25 '87

Great expectations [Paris couture collections for fall] P. McColl. il *N Y Times Mag* p30-4 Jl 26 '87

Hot stuff from Paris. C. Donovan. il *N Y Times Mag* p84-7 S 27 '87

The House of Zaitsev [New York show] *New Yorker* 63:36-7 N 16 '87

It couldn't be worse for wear [New York spring collections] J. Conant. il *Newsweek* 110:74 N 23 '87

London: shorter and sweeter. il *Vogue* 177:248 D '87

Milan: easy does it. il *Vogue* 177:244 D '87

Milan: sexy & flirty sweeps in. il *Harpers Bazaar* 120:100-9 Ja '87

Milan's gentle air. R. La Ferla. il *N Y Times Mag* p78-9+ Ap 12 '87

Milan's modern waifs. C. Sabino. il *Harpers Bazaar* 120:182+ S '87

Milan's mood. P. McColl. il *N Y Times Mag* p78-84 O 4 '87

A new mix [London fall collections] J.-A. Jenkins. il *N Y Times Mag* p88-91 Mr 8 '87

The New York collections. il *Vogue* 177:342-83+ F '87

New York collections [cover story] il *Vogue* 177:682-753+ S '87

New York collections: spring's fling. il *Harpers Bazaar* 120:154-63 Ja '87

New York fall: the headlines. il *Vogue* 177:146+ Jl '87

New York revs up for fall. C. Donovan. il *N Y Times Mag* p88-95 Mr 29 '87

News: Paris/Milan. il *Vogue* 177:144+ Je '87

Oh la la, Lacroix [New York show] J. Conant. il por *Newsweek* 110:60-1 N 9 '87

Paris: luxe, leggy . . . a new allure. il *Vogue* 177:290-305 Ap '87

Paris: shades of difference. il *Vogue* 177:212-19 Je '87

Paris shapes [spring collections] C. Donovan. il *N Y Times Mag* p56-9 Ja 25 '87

Paris when it sizzles. C. Donovan. il *N Y Times Mag* p64-7 F 22 '87

Paris: younger than springtime. il *Harpers Bazaar* 120:138-51 Ja '87

Parisian palette [ready-to-wear spring] P. McColl. il *N Y Times Mag* p72-8+ O 11 '87

The rag collectors [Paris fashions] J. Fayard. il *Life* 10:72-3+ O '87

Report from Milan. R. La Ferla. il *N Y Times Mag* p84-5 N 15 '87

The season's riches [fall shows] L. J. Nonkin and P. Sinclaire. il *Vogue* 177:226+ Ag '87

Those mournful Milanese. J. Conant. il *Newsweek* 109:60-1 Mr 30 '87

Fashion shows—*cont.*
Up, down and around [Milan] P. McColl. il *N Y Times Mag* p80-6 Mr 8 '87
Why short is chic. C. Donovan. il *N Y Times Mag* p70-1 Ap 26 '87
Will sexy sell? [1988 spring fashions] C. Donovan. il *N Y Times Mag* p126-7 D 6 '87

Fass, Virginia
Explore the forts of a fabled land. il *Horizon* 30:26-7 Mr '87
Princely palaces. il *Horizon* 30:24-5 Mr '87

Fassbinder, Rainer Werner, 1946-1982
about
Trash, the city and death [drama] Reviews
  Nation 244:478-9 Ap 11 '87. T. M. Disch

Fast, Larry
about
Larry Fast. J. Diliberto. il por *Down Beat* 54:50+ S '87

Fast food restaurant management
See also
Women in fast food restaurant management
Blacks buy Ohio chain [Church's Fried Chicken] P. A. Jones. il *Black Enterp* 17:20 F '87
Flying high with Church's Chicken [black franchisers E. Horton and A. Whitmore] il pors *Ebony* 42:72+ Jl '87
A McDonald's coins big McMoney [A. Lencioni's restaurants in Chicago] J. Alexander. il *Money* 16:37+ D '87

Fast food restaurants
See also
Arby's Inc.
Bojangles' of America Inc.
Burger King Corporation
Church's Fried Chicken, Inc.
Drive-in restaurants
Foodmaker, Inc.
Hardee's Food Systems, Inc.
McDonald's Corp.
Pepsico, Inc.
Sbarro, Inc.
Wendy's International Inc.
Dog days [hot dog stands and restaurants around the U.S.] J. Martel. il *Roll Stone* p117+ Jl 16-30 '87
Fast food and fast lodging. R. Simon. il *Forbes* 139:78-9 Ja 26 '87
The fast food industry is slowing down. il *Bus Week* p50-1 My 18 '87
Fit, fast food. il *Good Housekeep* 204:120+ My '87
Hamburgers are killing trees [boycott of fast-food outlets until they stop using Central American beef] il *Newsweek* 110:74 S 14 '87

Acquisitions and mergers
Coke may be going where the beef is [merger with Wendy's] G. G. Marcial. *Bus Week* p74 Mr 30 '87
The first name in coffee shops [Marriott's bid for Denny's] T. Ichniowski. il *Bus Week* p35-6 Je 15 '87
TW's numbers man throws caution to the winds [F. L. Salizzoni buys Denny's] L. Baum. il por *Bus Week* p67-9 Ag 3 '87

Advertising
Burger King is hungry—for the right ad campaign. P. Engardio. il *Bus Week* p82+ Mr 16 '87
N.W. Ayer bags itself a whopper [Burger King account] M. N. Vamos. il *Bus Week* p42 O 12 '87
Pizza wars. B. Kanner. il *N Y* 20:20+ S 21 '87
Wendy's tries warming up the basic burger. D. Cook. il *Bus Week* p51 My 18 '87

Fast foods *See* Convenience foods

Fasteners
See also
Bolts and nuts
Nails
Rivets and riveting
Screws
Staples and stapling machines
Zippers
Clever carpentry connectors. P. McCafferty. il *Pop Sci* 230:63-5 My '87
Dealing with stuck fasteners. M. Thompson. il *Fam Handyman* 37:70 Jl/Ag '87
Wall grabbers. G. Branson. il *Fam Handyman* 37:64 O '87
Woodworking fasteners: a boat builder's view. L. Montgomery. il *Workbench* 43:72-5 Jl/Ag '87

Anecdotes, facetiae, satire, etc.
Open sesame, my foot! M. G. Stoddard. il *Saturday Evening Post* 259:44-5 My/Je '87

Fasting
See also
Hunger strikes
Half the man he used to be: Rev. Charles Williams loses 188 pounds. il pors *Ebony* 42:86+ O '87
Is fasting safe for quick weight loss? il *Glamour* 85:326 Mr '87

Fasts and feasts
See also
Advent
All Saints' Day
Ash Wednesday
Carnival (Pre-Lenten festival)
Christmas
Easter
Epiphany
Lent

Catholic Church
See also
Corpus Christi festival
Jesus Christ the King, Feast of

Judaism
See also
Hanukkah
Passover
Sukkoth

Fat
See also
Cellulite
Lipids
Obesity
Fat & muscle. R. B. Pearce. il *Women's Sports Fitness* 9:36-9 Jl '87
How food/fitness breakthroughs can take you from mush to muscle. il *Glamour* 85:312-15 My '87
Off the scales and into the tub [measuring body fat percentage] A. Toufexis. il *Time* 130:94 N 16 '87

Fat Boys (Musical group)
The Fat Boys say: 'Protect yourself' [rap song about condoms] *Harpers* 274:18 Je '87

Fat content of feeds *See* Feeds—Fat content
Fat content of foods *See* Food—Fat content
Fat farms *See* Health resorts, watering places, etc.
Fat shan *See* Chinese broccoli

Fat substitutes
See also
Sucrose polyesters

Fat tissues *See* Adipose tissues
Fat-to-muscle diet *See* Diet
Fat vacuuming (Cosmetic surgery) *See* Surgery, Plastic
Fatal attraction [film] *See* Motion picture reviews—Single works
Fatal beauty [film] *See* Motion picture reviews—Single works

Fathalla, Mahmoud F.
The challenge still stands. il *World Health* p6-7 N '87

Father Brown (Fictional character)
Sin, psychopathology and Father Brown [comparison with M. Mann's Manhunter] M. Horst. *Christ Century* 104:46-7 Ja 21 '87

The Father Clements story [television program] *See* Television program reviews—Single works
Father-daughter corporations *See* Family corporations

Fathers
See also
Divorced fathers
Parent education
Paternal deprivation
Paternity
Paternity leaves
Patriarchy
Single fathers
Stepparents and stepchildren
Support (Domestic relations)
About fathers. R. B. McCall. See issues of Parents beginning July 1985
A comic, a rapper, a rocker, an ex-QB and a candidate send Father's Day felicitations from the front [celebrity fathers] il *People Wkly* 27:36-8+ Je 22 '87
The expectant father. J. L. Shapiro. bibl (p63) il *Psychol Today* 21:36-9+ Ja '87
A fatherless father. H. Mungin. por *Essence* 18:10 N '87
Father's Day: celebrity dads talk about their children. il *Jet* 72:14-16 Je 22 '87
A fulfillment [late fatherhood] R. Taylor. il *N Y Times Mag* p62 Mr 29 '87
I'm a new father who takes his role seriously: why doesn't anyone else? R. Greene. il *Glamour* 85:94 Je '87

Fathers—cont.

My children's father: a self-portrait for Father's Day. M. Finley. *America* 156:499-500 Je 20-27 '87

My father is my patient. Z. Rosen. il *Newsweek* 109:10-11 Mr 30 '87

My father's last year [death from Lou Gehrig's disease] L. Cherry. il *Glamour* 85:300-1+ O '87

The new fatherhood. J. A. Levine. il *McCalls* 114:121-2+ Je '87

Say, brother. G. Powell. por *Essence* 17:10 Mr '87

Say, brother [considering fatherhood] G. W. Amos. por *Essence* 17:9 Ap '87

Truths my father never told me. P. Wilkes. *America* 156:497-8 Je 20-27 '87

What fathers really think [excerpt from Fathers] il *Parents* 62:82-5 Je '87

"Will the real 'new father' please stand up?". M. E. Lamb. il *Parents* 62:77-80 Je '87

Anecdotes, facetiae, satire, etc.

Dr. Spock never promised us a rose garden [excerpt from Fatherhood] B. Cosby. il pors *Saturday Evening Post* 259:60-2 Mr '87

Seeing him through a dad-o-scope: how well would he cope with a kid? B.-J. Raphael. *Glamour* 85:42 S '87

Photographs and photography

Like father, like son [look alikes] il *Good Housekeep* 205:70 Ag '87

Like father, like son [look alikes] il *Good Housekeep* 205:84-5 S '87

Fathers, Unmarried *See* Single fathers
Fathers and children *See* Parent-child relationship
Father's Day gifts *See* Gifts
Fathers in poetry

The poet's quest for the father. S. Kunitz. il *N Y Times Book Rev* 92:1+ F 22 '87

Fatigue

See also
Boredom
Chronic fatigue syndrome
Relaxation

Fatigue: are you fighting your internal clock? L. C. Cool. il *McCalls* 115:144+ D '87

Ready to drop [pilot fatigue] P. Bradley. il *Flying* 114:54-7 Ja '87

Tired of fatigue? J. Lewis. il *Curr Health 2* 13:28-9 Ja '87

Walking away from fatigue [views of Harold Kohl] il *Prevention* 39:8 N '87

Fatisha

Karma causes condensation [poem] *Essence* 18:140 S '87

Fatjo, Tom

about

So long, bench press. Thanks for the pep talk. J. E. Davis. il por *Bus Week* p72+ Ja 26 '87

Fats *See* Oils and fats, Edible
Fatshedera

Tree ivy. T. E. Smith. il *Flower Gard* 32:45 D '87/Ja '88

Fattal, Vahé

about

Vahé Fattal at Davies Long. M. Laurence. il *Art Am* 75:227-8 Ap '87

Fauber, Bernard

about

Nickels and dimes no more. J. A. Seamonds. il por *U S News World Rep* 102:42 Je 29 '87

Faujas, Alain

All's fair in the airliner war. *World Press Rev* 34:49-50 Je '87

Botswana: beauty and the beasts. il *World Press Rev* 34:62 Ap '87

Wardair flies high. *World Press Rev* 34:48 D '87

Faulkner, Douglas

Coral gardens: a textured treasure [with photographs] il *Int Wildl* 17:46-51 N/D '87

Faulkner, Frank

about

Frank Faulkner: Davis/McClain. M. McCombie. il *Art News* 86:169-70 D '87

Faulkner, William, 1897-1962

about

A Faulkner flirtation. L. A. Westoff. il por *N Y Times Mag* p69+ My 10 '87

Looking for Mr. Faulkner. W. Cobb. il *South Living* 22:128 Mr '87

Rowan Oak—Faulkner's Mississippi refuge. il *South Living* 22:19 Ag '87

Fault finding

See also
Self blame

The dynamics of blame. A. Gross. *Vogue* 177:783+ S '87

Why mothers get a hard time. J. Marzollo. il *Parents* 62:103-5+ N '87

Faults (Geology)

A better fit for the plate tectonic puzzle [San Andreas fault discrepancy] R. A. Kerr. il *Science* 238:30 O 2 '87

Delving into faults and earthquake behavior [special section] il *Science* 235:165-6 Ja 9 '87

Earthquake threat to the Mississippi Valley. J. Miller and M. Miller. il *USA Today (Periodical)* 116:66-9 S '87

Getting to the bottom of the San Andreas [Cajon Pass hole] S. Weisburd. *Sci News* 131:70 Ja 31 '87

Is the San Andreas weak at heart? R. A. Kerr. il *Science* 236:388-9 Ap 24 '87

New evidence on the state of stress of the San Andreas fault system. M. D. Zoback and others. bibl f il maps *Science* 238:1105-11 N 20 '87

Outward-dipping ring-fault structure at Rabaul caldera as shown by earthquake locations. J. Mori and C. McKee. bibl f il map *Science* 235:193-5 Ja 9 '87

Pollen and spores date origin of rift basins from Texas to Nova Scotia as early late Triassic. A. Traverse. bibl f il map *Science* 236:1469-72 Je 12 '87

The rifting of continents. E. Bonatti. bibl (p128) il maps *Sci Am* 256:96-103 Mr '87

Slowly sinking in the West [subsidence in Arizona and New Mexico] F. Turner. il *Wilderness* 51:47-50 Fall '87

Taking the pulse of Parkfield. R. A. Kerr. il *Science* 236:145 Ap 10 '87

What is worse than "the big one"? [quake within the Los Angeles basin] R. A. Kerr. il map *Science* 238:269-70 O 16 '87

Fauntroy, Walter E.

about

Fauntroy renews bid to gain statehood for D.C. *Jet* 71:5 Mr 23 '87

Walter Fauntroy closer to gaining statehood for D.C. *Jet* 72:4 Je 22 '87

Fauss, Geral

about

The foam finger. A. D. Frank. il por *Forbes* 139:136+ My 4 '87

Faust, Gerry

about

Starting out from Zip. P. Putnam. il por *Sports Illus* 67:33 N 9 '87

Fautin, Daphne Gail

The anemone is not its enemy. il *Natl Wildl* 25:22-5 O/N '87

Fauvism

Picasso's time of decisive encounters; tr. by Tom Repensek. P. Daix. il *Art News* 86:136-41 Ap '87

Fava beans *See* Beans

Favier, Philippe

about

Philippe Favier. J. Sturman. il *Art News* 86:179 Ap '87

Favorite child problem *See* Parent-child relationship
Favors

Asking a fellow for a favor. G. Blair. *Mademoiselle* 93:144 O '87

Fawcett, Farrah

about

Actress suing Farrah Fawcett is attacked in Los Angeles. pors *Jet* 72:26 Je 22 '87

Farrah: 40 & loving it [cover story] il pors *Harpers Bazaar* 120:124-7+ Ag '87

The Farrah Fawcett/Barbara Hutton connection [interview] M. J. Bandler. il pors *McCalls* 115:186-8 N '87

Farrah Fawcett [interview] J. Grant. il pors *Life* 10:15+ N '87

Farrah Fawcett: happy as can be [interview] M. J. Bandler. il por *McCalls* 115:12-16+ O '87

Fax *See* Facsimile transmission

Fay, Chip

One for the spirits. il *Sierra* 72:22-4 Mr/Ap '87

Fay, Martha

Why your family doctor is a group. il *N Y Times Mag* p16-20+ Je 7 '87

Fay, Michael

about

Does K stand for killjoy? E. Bowen. il *Time* 130:84 D 14 '87

Fay, Monique
   Photometrics. bibl il *Petersens Photogr Mag* 16:26+ Je '87
Fayard (Arthème Librairie) *See* Librairie Arthème Fayard
Fayer, Eric
   about
   A fashionable Canadian connection. B. Janssen. il por *Macleans* 100:37 N 16 '87
Fayetteville (Ark.)
      Galleries and museums
      See also
      University of Arkansas, Fayetteville. University Museum
FBD (Fibrocystic breast disease) *See* Breast—Diseases
FBI *See* United States. Federal Bureau of Investigation
FBI informers *See* Informers
FCC *See* United States. Federal Communications Commission
FDA *See* United States. Food and Drug Administration
FDIC *See* Federal Deposit Insurance Corporation
Feakes, Carolyn R.
   (jt. auth) *See* Retallack, Gregory J., and Feakes, Carolyn R.
Fear
      See also
      Anxiety
      Bashfulness
      Nervousness
      NIMBY syndrome
      Phobias
      Stage fright
   Five ways to overcome fear. M. Dalloway. il *Women's Sports Fitness* 9:15 Je '87
   Prowlers, prayers and a dream. M. A. King. *Christ Century* 104:959-60 N 4 '87
   Where the Wild Things began [childhood fears] M. Sendak. il *N Y Times Book Rev* 92:1+ My 17 '87
   Your child's fears. J. Segal and Z. Segal. il *Parents* 62:207 My '87
      Anecdotes, facetiae, satire, etc.
   The hugs of A. M. Rosenthal and the fear of cod. J. Gorman. il *Discover* 8:22+ My '87
Fear of flying
   The 11 worst flying fears—and how they can't, won't or hardly ever come true [excerpt from White knuckles] L. Ridley. il *Glamour* 85:112+ Je '87
   Readers' survey: overcoming fear of flying. il *Prevention* 39:24-6 Jl '87
   Taking control of your fear of flying. I. Pave. il *Bus Week* p90-1 Ag 24 '87
   Watch your language. G. Baxter. il *Flying* 114:95+ N '87
Fear of snakes
   Snakes alive! When Fergie met this party animal in Greenwich, her skin just started to crawl. il pors *People Wkly* 28:100-1 O 5 '87
Fear of success
   The great impostor: do you feel less qualified than others think you are? B. L. Stern. *Vogue* 177:374 Ag '87
Fear of water *See* Aquaphobia
Fearnside, Philip M. (Philip Martin)
   Rethinking continuous cultivation in Amazonia. bibl f il *BioScience* 37:209-14 Mr '87
   Yurimaguas technology [discussion of March 1987 article, Rethinking continuous cultivation in Amazonia] *BioScience* 37:638-40 O '87
Fearon, Eric R., and others
   Clonal analysis of human colorectal tumors. bibl f il *Science* 238:193-7 O 9 '87
Fearon, Francesca
   The slow march of Asian women. *World Press Rev* 34:56 Ag '87
A feast in the plague-time [drama] *See* Lyubimov, Yuri
Feathers
   Feathers. L. Minden. il *Sierra* 72:90-1 Mr/Ap '87
   Roxie Laybourne: feather detective. R. Wolkomir. il pors *Natl Wildl* 26:20-5 D '87/Ja '88
   A salmon delights in gaudy colors [cover story; with editorial comment by Les Line] T. Rosenbauer. il *Audubon* 89:4, 64-73 S '87
Featherstone, Mickey
   about
   The lords of Hell's Kitchen. J. Traub. il pors *N Y Times Mag* p38+ Ap 5 '87
Feaver, William
   The British accent in 20th-century art. il *Art News* 86:114-19 Ap '87
   A reasonable definition of love. il *Archit Dig* 44:34+ Jl '87

Feazel, Charles T.
   The rise and fall of Neptune's kingdom. il *Sea Front* 33:4-11 Ja/F '87
Febres Cordero, León, 1931-
      Kidnapping
   Kidnapping a president. K. Scanlon. *Macleans* 100:24 Ja 26 '87
February
   12 easy mood and image boosters to make February fly by. il *Glamour* 85:57 F '87
   The February almanac. il *Atlantic* 259:20 F '87
Feces
   Will livestock drug cause dung crisis? [ivermectin; research by Richard Wall and Les Strong] J. Raloff. *Sci News* 131:358 Je 6 '87
      Animals
   As drama it was a waste, but financially, Michigan's first cow-drop raffle was no flop. il *People Wkly* 28:85 Jl 6 '87
      Bees
   Bees did it [yellow rain story] R. Bazell. *New Repub* 196:9-10 F 2 '87
   Yellow rain: the story collapses. J. Robinson and others. bibl f *Foreign Policy* 68:100-17 Fall '87
      Marine fauna
   Can microscale chemical patches persist in the sea? Microelectrode study of marine snow, fecal pellets. A. L. Alldredge and Y. Cohen. bibl f il *Science* 235:689-91 F 6 '87
Fechin, Nicolai, 1881-1955
   about
   Russian folk in Taos. M. Morse. il *House Gard* 159:198-203 Ap '87
Fedders, Charlotte O'Donnell
   Survivor of a violent marriage, a former Washington official's wife recalls years of abuse; ed. by Jane Sims Podesta. il pors *People Wkly* 28:113-14+ D 14 '87
   about
   Can you beat this? L. Fleischer. *Publ Wkly* 232:56 N 13 '87
Fedders, John
   about
   Can you beat this? L. Fleischer. *Publ Wkly* 232:56 N 13 '87
   Survivor of a violent marriage, a former Washington official's wife recalls years of abuse; ed. by Jane Sims Podesta. C. O. Fedders. il pors *People Wkly* 28:113-14+ D 14 '87
Feder, Don
   The kosher majority. *Natl Rev* 39:40+ Ap 10 '87
Federal agencies *See* United States—Executive departments
Federal aid
      See also
      Economic assistance, Domestic
      Government lending
      Grants-in-aid
Federal and provincial relations (Canada)
      See also
      Canada. Constitution
      Canada. Western Diversification Office
      Québec (Province)—Nationalism
   Blitzing the West [Brian Mulroney and Cabinet visit Alberta] M. Clark. il *Macleans* 100:12 Jl 20 '87
   Breakthrough [agreement that will allow Quebec to sign the Constitution; cover story; special section] il *Macleans* 100:8-12+ My 11 '87
   Canada's new deal [cover story; special section; with editorial comment by Kevin Doyle] il *Macleans* 100:2, 8-10+ Je 15 '87
   Constitutional clouds [attempt to have Quebec sign the Constitution] M. Rose. il *Macleans* 100:10-11 Ap 27 '87
   Constitutional discord. P. Gessell. il *Macleans* 100:13 Ag 17 '87
   Debates on the morning after [constitutional breakthrough] M. Gee. il *Macleans* 100:12-13 My 18 '87
   Disillusionment in the region. M. Janigan. il *Macleans* 100:17-18 F 2 '87
   A dissident is shut out [Alberta Tory MP D. Kilgour disciplined for comments about lack of party commitment to the West] por *Macleans* 100:13 Ap 20 '87
   Division in the house [free trade debate dominates First Ministers' meeting] M. Drohan. il *Macleans* 100:10-12 D 7 '87
   Facing a deadline [constitutional resolution and Quebec endorsement] M. Janigan. il *Macleans* 100:13 Jl 6 '87
   Filling a western vacuum [Reform Association of Canada] J. Howse. il *Macleans* 100:12 Je 1 '87
   A historic 'yes' vote [Meech Lake constitutional accord] P. Gessell. il *Macleans* 100:12 N 9 '87

Federal and provincial relations (Canada)—*cont.*
In search of a trade deal [U.S. and Canada] M. Drohan. il *Macleans* 100:8-9 Jl 20 '87
A Liberal family feud [constitutional agreement] M. Rose. il *Macleans* 100:12+ My 25 '87
The new embassy wars [Quebec and Ottawa jockey for position in relations with France] A. Wilson-Smith. *Macleans* 100:14 Ap 27 '87
Ottawa aids the oilmen [western Canada] T. Tedesco. *Macleans* 100:31 Ap 6 '87
Rebellion in the West. M. Janigan. il *Macleans* 100:12+ Mr 30 '87
Regional racism from sea to sea. A. Fotheringham. il *Macleans* 100:72 N 9 '87
Toward the final hurdles [free trade accord discussed at First Ministers' meeting] M. Drohan. il *Macleans* 100:36-7 D 28 '87
Trudeau's power punch [denunciation of constitutional accord] M. Janigan. il por *Macleans* 100:10-11 Je 8 '87
Trudeau's star turn [criticism of the constitutional accord] M. Janigan. il por *Macleans* 100:14-16+ S 7 '87
Federal and state relations
See also
  Intergovernmental tax relations
Ebb tide for states' rights. il *Life* 10:117 Fall '87
Groups deny states' immunity from copyright infringement. H. Fields. *Publ Wkly* 232:17 Jl 31 '87
Power to the people [9th and 10th Amendments] W. B. Reynolds. il *N Y Times Mag* p116-18+ S 13 '87
Resolve two federal-state conflicts. D. Pawelek. il *Sch Update* 119:21 Ja 26 '87
States rights and the national interests [address, July 22, 1987] J. E. Chubb. *Vital Speeches Day* 53:702-4 S 1 '87
Federal Asset Disposition Association
Feuding among the ruins of failed thrifts. J. B. Levine. il *Bus Week* p116 My 18 '87
Federal Aviation Administration (U.S.) *See* United States. Federal Aviation Administration
Federal Bureau of Investigation (U.S.) *See* United States. Federal Bureau of Investigation
Federal Communications Commission (U.S.) *See* United States. Federal Communications Commission
Federal debt *See* Debts, Public
Federal Deposit Insurance Corporation
Anything goes [CollegeSure CD marketed by College Savings Bank qualifies for FDIC insurance] L. Jereski. il *Forbes* 140:34-5 O 5 '87
A billion-dollar bailout, Texas style [A. R. Abboud takeover of First City Bancorporation] K. R. Sheets. il por *U S News World Rep* 103:54 S 21 '87
Bob Abboud is back in banking—but what a bank [taking over First City Bancorp of Texas] T. Vogel. il por *Bus Week* p30 S 21 '87
Here comes the cavalry [A. R. Abboud takeover of First City Bancorporation of Texas] G. Bock. il por *Time* 130:52 S 21 '87
"Nobody thought it would be us" [FDIC liquidates Unitedbank-Houston] R. Woodbury. il *Time* 129:53 My 11 '87
Nothing like money in the bank. il *Fortune* 116:8 O 12 '87
Sweet charity [Bowery Savings Bank] A. A. Lappen. il *Forbes* 140:8 N 2 '87
Why the Bowery deal wasn't a ripoff. S. Bartlett. il *Bus Week* p105 O 19 '87
Federal Election Commission (U.S.) *See* United States. Federal Election Commission
Federal Emergency Management Agency (U.S.) *See* United States. Federal Emergency Management Agency
Federal employees *See* Government employees
Federal Energy Regulatory Commission (U.S.) *See* United States. Federal Energy Regulatory Commission
Federal Express Corp.
Federal Express delivers a price shock. D. Foust. il *Bus Week* p31-2 Mr 30 '87
Federal Express plans new hub, buys McDonnell Douglas freighters. J. Ott. il *Aviat Week Space Technol* 126:45+ Ja 26 '87
Federal Express starts 24-hr. weather forecasting system [Man-Computer Integrative Data Access System] J. Ott. il *Aviat Week Space Technol* 126:38 F 2 '87
The man in the pilot's seat [F. W. Smith] il por *Fortune* 116:35 Ag 17 '87
Small package carrier expands aerial feeder system to meet U.S. demands for next-day service. il *Aviat Week Space Technol* 126:39-40 F 2 '87
Stretch runner [Cessna Caravans] R. L. Collins. il *Flying* 114:32-7 Jl '87

Why Federal Express has overnight anxiety. D. Foust. il *Bus Week* p62+ N 9 '87
Federal grants *See* Grants-in-aid
Federal Home Loan Bank Board *See* United States. Federal Home Loan Bank Board
Federal Housing Administration (U.S.) *See* United States. Federal Housing Administration
Federal lands *See* Public lands
Federal National Mortgage Association
Most improved. il *Forbes* 139:128 Ja 12 '87
Federal prisons *See* Prisons
Federal Railroad Administration *See* United States. Federal Railroad Administration
Federal regulatory agencies *See* Regulatory agencies
Federal Reserve banks
Gerry Corrigan's solutions to a banking 'hodgepodge' [president of New York Fed] S. Bartlett. il por *Bus Week* p78 Ap 6 '87
Federal Reserve System (U.S.)
Act I at Alan Greenspan's Fed [increase in discount rate] por *Newsweek* 110:56 S 14 '87
Alan Greenspan is headed for a quiet honeymoon. M. McNamee. il por *Bus Week* p27 Ag 3 '87
Are we ready for life after Volcker? B. Riemer. il *Bus Week* p41 Ja 26 '87
The deficit: point those fingers at the Fed. P. C. Roberts. il *Bus Week* p22 N 30 '87
A delicate balance [new chairman A. Greenspan] S. Koepp. il *Time* 130:32-3 Ag 10 '87
Exit Volcker, enter Greenspan. *Natl Rev* 39:17+ Jl 3 '87
Expecting the Fed to ease? Don't hold your breath. B. Reimer. il *Bus Week* p30 F 16 '87
The Fed's bloodhounds are panting for clues. M. McNamee. il *Bus Week* p32 N 30 '87
Greenspan isn't a Volcker clone. L. Smith. il pors *Fortune* 116:34-6 Jl 6 '87
Greenspan's big test [dealing with stock market crash] il por *Time* 130:29 N 2 '87
Greenspan's debut draws raves. J. C. Szabo. il por *Nations Bus* 75:9-10 O '87
How does the Street spell relief? G-r-e-e-n-s-p-a-n. S. Weiss. il por *Bus Week* p122-3 Je 22 '87
How the bond market is forcing the Fed's hand. S. Bartlett. il *Bus Week* p42 My 11 '87
How the Fed can sway the fortunes of presidents. R. Kuttner. por *Bus Week* p26 D 21 '87
How Volcker sabotaged the president's agenda. P. C. Roberts. il *Bus Week* p18 Je 15 '87
An inflation fighter steps down [A. Greenspan replaces P. Volcker] I. Austen. il pors *Macleans* 100:34-5 Je 15 '87
Is Alan Greenspan really such a hero? S. Zucker. por *Bus Week* p35 D 14 '87
Is the Fed behind the stock boom? D. Pauly. il *Newsweek* 109:36-7 Ja 26 '87
Is the Fed playing it too close to the vest? G. Koretz. il *Bus Week* p24 D 14 '87
The last line of defense. M. W. Karmin. il *U S News World Rep* 103:26-7 N 9 '87
Less bounce in your checks [Federal Reserve's second chance check clearing plan] il *Consum Rep* 52:593 O '87
Money gods [views of W. Greider] R. Hornik. il por *Time* 130:50-1 D 7 '87
Mr. Volcker: higher interest is the last thing we need. A. S. Blinder. il *Bus Week* p30 Je 1 '87
The new Mr. Dollar [resignation of P. Volcker and nomination of A. Greenspan; cover story; special section] il pors *Time* 129:46-53 Je 15 '87
Owning a bank isn't for just anybody [letting nonfinancial companies own commercial banks] S. Bartlett. *Bus Week* p123 Je 22 '87
Paul Volcker was the Babe Ruth of central banking. A. S. Blinder. il *Bus Week* p12 Je 29 '87
The price of money (I). W. Greider. *New Yorker* 63:54-6+ N 9 '87
The price of money (II). W. Greider. *New Yorker* 63:68-72+ N 16 '87
The price of money (III). W. Greider. *New Yorker* 63:49-50+ N 23 '87
The rate shift that's handcuffing the Fed [views of Mickey D. Levy] G. Koretz. il *Bus Week* p16 Ap 20 '87
The Reagan Fed can put a Democrat in the White House. P. C. Roberts. il *Bus Week* p21 O 5 '87
Reagan's man at the Fed [resignation of P. Volcker and nomination of A. Greenspan; special section] il pors *Newsweek* 109:16-20+ Je 15 '87
The rising risk of recession [situation facing new Fed chief A. Greenspan] J. Egan. il pors *U S News World Rep* 102:47+ Je 15 '87

Federal Reserve System (U.S.)—*cont.*

Stop procrastinating on interest rates. H. Banks. *Forbes* 139:27 F 9 '87

The task ahead for Alan Greenspan. T. May, Jr. il *Fortune* 116:49+ Ag 17 '87

Testing time for Greenspan. J. Egan. il por *U S News World Rep* 103:49-50 S 21 '87

Tight money and loose fiscal policy. A. S. Blinder. bibl *Society* 24:80-3 Jl/Ag '87

Time for the Fed to tighten. H. E. Heinemann. il *Fortune* 115:129-30+ My 25 '87

Time to tighten. *Natl Rev* 39:15-16 Je 5 '87

Two guardians of the nation's economy. il *Sch Update* 120:13 D 18 '87

Vale, Volcker [cover story] G. P. Brockway. il *New Leader* 70:9-11 Jl 1-15 '87

Volcker isn't all the Fed has lost lately [ability to shape the course of economic events] K. Pennar. il *Bus Week* p47 Je 22 '87

Volcker on the crash. L. S. Silk. il por *N Y Times Mag* p40+ N 8 '87

Volcker: the absent 'icon'. R. Thomas. por *Newsweek* 110:39 N 9 '87

Volcker tries wrestling a bear called bank reform. B. Riemer and V. Cahan. por *Bus Week* p51 Mr 16 '87

Volcker: will he stay? [cover story] B. Riemer. il pors *Bus Week* p76-80+ Mr 30 '87

Weak dollar begets weak stocks and bonds [stemming the dollar's fall] M. S. Forbes, Jr. il *Forbes* 140:25 S 21 '87

Weaving a dollar crisis out of whole cloth [weak dollar] P. C. Roberts. il *Bus Week* p31 F 23 '87

What investors should ask of Alan Greenspan [letting gold be his guide] M. S. Forbes, Jr. il por *Forbes* 139:25 Je 29 '87

What's in store at the Fed [resignation of P. Volcker and nomination of A. Greenspan; cover story; special section] il pors *Bus Week* p26-30 Je 15 '87

Why Greenspan is bullish [cover story] S. Nasar. il pors *Fortune* 116:28-32+ O 26 '87

Why the Fed may zero in on the money targets. J. Berger. il *Bus Week* p73+ Jl 13 '87

Will tighter money really help? Nudging up rates may not be enough to stem inflation fears. M. McNamee. il *Bus Week* p28-9 S 21 '87

With fiscal policy no longer stimulating growth . . . the question is: how would Greenspan fight recession? G. Koretz. il *Bus Week* p28 Je 22 '87

The world after Volcker. C. Smallwood and J. Cassidy. il *World Press Rev* 34:44-5 Ag '87

Anecdotes, facetiae, satire, etc.

And now, the Fed letters. pors *U S News World Rep* 103:43 Jl 27 '87

Federal Savings and Loan Insurance Corporation

And you get to pick up the bill. J. Novack. il *Forbes* 139:32-3 My 4 '87

Après moi . . . [recapitalization plan] A. Sloan. il *Forbes* 140:35-6 O 5 '87

Banking reform has two chances: slim and none. V. Cahan. *Bus Week* p45 Ap 13 '87

Bonds away at the Bank Board [new issues from The Financing Corp.] V. Cahan. *Bus Week* p102 O 5 '87

Deep in the hole in Texas. R. E. Norton. il *Fortune* 115:61-2+ My 11 '87

Feuding among the ruins of failed thrifts. J. B. Levine. il *Bus Week* p116 My 18 '87

How safe is your money? J. B. Quinn. il *Newsweek* 109:55 Ap 13 '87

Playing politics [FSLIC bailout bonds] B. Weberman. il *Forbes* 140:209 S 21 '87

Troubled temples of thrift. G. Russell. il *Time* 129:56 My 18 '87

The Wright man to see [J. Wright's efforts on behalf of Texas thrifts] R. Thomas and D. Pauly. il por *Newsweek* 109:44-5 Je 29 '87

Federal spending policy *See* United States—Appropriations and expenditures

Federal-state tax relations *See* Intergovernmental tax relations

Federal Trade Commission (U.S.) *See* United States. Federal Trade Commission

Federalism *See* Federal and state relations

Federalist (Ship)

A new "Federalist" [replica of 1788 ship] il *Am Hist Illus* 22:38 S '87

Pint-sized ship of state [The Federalist, highlight of Maryland's 1788 Constitution ratification celebration] B. B. Ryan. il por *Am Hist Illus* 22:36-7+ S '87

Federalist paper

The Federalist paper. D. K. Mano. *Natl Rev* 39:58-9 F 13 '87

Federalist Society

Federalists all. *Natl Rev* 39:23 Ja 30 '87

Federated Department Stores, Inc.

Sir Jimmy goes shopping again. G. G. Marcial. *Bus Week* p188 N 16 '87

Federated States of Micronesia *See* Micronesia (Federated States)

Federated Stock Trust

Sticking with big-company stocks [interview with P. Anderson] A. E. Serwer. por *Fortune* 116:200 O 12 '87

Federation of American Scientists

Scientists urge new stance on SDI testing in U.S.-Soviet arms talks. T. M. Foley. *Aviat Week Space Technol* 127:30 S 14 '87

Fedorov, Svyatoslav

Automation and microsurgery. il *Courier* 40:33-4 Ag '87

Fedyanina, Galina

about

The horrors of war behind her, Galina Fedyanina emerges as a triumph of socialist labor. J. W. Seymore. il pors *People Wkly* 27:88+ Ap 6 '87

Feed supplements, Antibiotic *See* Antibiotic feed supplements

Feed testing *See* Feeds—Analysis

Feed the Children (Organization)

Feeding the hungry with surplus food [L. Jones] il por *Christ Today* 31:54 O 2 '87

Feedback (Biology) *See* Biological control systems

Feedback (Psychology)

See also

Biofeedback training

Giving—and getting—feedback [excerpt from The art of managing people] P. L. Hunsaker and A. J. Alessandra. il *Work Woman* 12:30+ Ap '87

Feeders (Birds) *See* Bird feeders

Feeding, Tube *See* Tube feeding

Feeding of plants *See* Plants—Nutrition

Feedlots

See also

Cattle feedlots

Swine feedlots

Feeds

See also

Forage plants

Silage

Analysis

Rusitec the cow [rumen simulation as part of project to analyse different feedstuffs] il *Courier* 40:26 Mr '87

Carbohydrate content

Nutrient balance revs up dairy cows [soluble carbohydrate] J. R. Borcherding. il *Success Farm* 85:36 S '87

Contamination

From tainted feed to mothers' milk [heptachlor contamination] D. Farley. il *FDA Consum* 21:38-40 Mr '87

Corn

Cheap corn makes cheap Holsteins competitive. *Success Farm* 85 no6:B17 Mr '87

Fat content

Added fat can help save calves. *Success Farm* 85:44 N '87

Product report: Megalac [protected fat for cows] J. R. Borcherding and D. Wanner. il *Success Farm* 85:54 N '87

Grain

Put grain in stocker calves. G. Johnston. il *Success Farm* 85:7 My '87

Medicated feed

See also

Antibiotic feed supplements

Nitrogen content

Manage NPN to boost or hold dairy profits [nonprotein nitrogen] *Success Farm* 85:D8 My '87

Selenium content

Should you add selenium to your dairy rations? *Success Farm* 85:D6 My '87

Soybeans

Bean "soup" for bossy. J. R. Borcherding. il *Success Farm* 85:38-9 N '87

Feeding hogs whole beans may beat soybean meal. *Success Farm* 85 no3:18T F '87

Feeling Fine Programs (Firm)

Random House Audio tries self-help with a health series [coproduced by A. Ulene's production firm] il *Publ Wkly* 231:39-40 My 1 '87

Feelings *See* Emotions
Feerst, Irwin
about
Feerst in close call. J. Walsh. por *Science* 235:26 Ja 2 '87
Fees, Bank *See* Banks and banking—Service charges; Investment banking—Service charges
Fees, Immigration *See* Immigration and emigration—Right of entry fees
Fees, Legal *See* Lawyers—Salaries, fees, etc.
Feet *See* Foot
Fegley, Randall
A cardinal who spoke truth to power. *Christ Century* 104:325-6 Ap 8 '87
Fehren, Henry
[Column] *See* issues of U.S. Catholic
Feiffer, Jules
about
Little murders [drama] Reviews
N Y 20:108 My 25 '87. J. Simon
New Yorker 63:87-8 My 18 '87. E. Oliver
Feigen, Richard
about
A mystery buyer plucks van Gogh's buds for a record sum [interview] M. Small. il por *People Wkly* 27:55-7 Ap 20 '87
Feigenbaum, Mitchell
about
Mr. Chaos. A. Rosenfeld. por *N Y* 20:26 My 18 '87
Feigner, Eddie
about
Pitcher perfect. J. Eppinger. il por *50 Plus* 27:56-7+ Ag '87
Feijoada *See* Cooking, Brazilian
Fein, Elaine
Kidnapped! il pors *Ladies Home J* 104:46+ Je '87
(ed) *See* Garcia, Carmen. "Help! My baby is drowning!"
Fein, Esther B.
The current state of affairs. *Mademoiselle* 93:247+ Ag '87
Turning KIDS off drugs. il *N Y Times Mag* p26-32 My 24 '87
Feinberg, Andrew
Blown away by Black Monday. il por *N Y Times Mag* p38-9+ D 20 '87
Feinberg, Henry
about
E.T.'s "phone home" inventor speaks. S. Morris. il por *Omni* 9:140-1 Ap '87
Feinberg, Lisa
about
Adwoman of the mountain. J. Seabury. il por *N Y* 20:22 Mr 16 '87
Feinberg, Mortimer R.
Crash course in crisis management. il *Work Woman* 12:24+ Ja '87
Feinberg, Susan
Wharton by the sea. il *Wash Mon* 19:29-30+ O '87
Feinglass, Joe
Next, the McDRG. il *Progressive* 51:28 Ja '87
Feininger, Andreas, 1906-
about
Meet the masters. F. Cameron. il *Petersens Photogr Mag* 15:38-40 Mr '87
Feinstein, Dianne
about
Feinstein looks beyond San Francisco. por *Newsweek* 110:59 N 2 '87
Feinstein, John
Back from the brink. il pors *Sport Mag* 78:29-30+ D '87
about
'A season on the brink' is the season's surprise #1 bestseller. D. Masello. il pors *Publ Wkly* 231:28-30 Mr 27 '87
Feinstein, Michael
about
Cabaret: 's marvelous. S. Drucker. il por *Vogue* 177:124 F '87
Rock may tumble and punk may crumble, but Michael Feinstein insists old songs are here to stay. J. Stark. il pors *People Wkly* 27:126-7+ My 4 '87
"Wanna sing a show tune . . .". G. Clarke. il por *Time* 129:91 My 4 '87
Feinstein, Neil J.
about
The gay market has put this CPA on the fast Track. P. Finch. il por *Bus Week* p58 Ap 27 '87
Feirstein, Bruce
Breaking up without falling apart. *Harpers Bazaar* 120:80-1+ Ja '87

Top 10 turnoffs. *Harpers Bazaar* 120:306+ S '87
Feit, Edward
Gary Milek. il *Am Artist* 51:64-9+ O '87
James Harrington. il *Am Artist* 51:42-7 Jl '87
Feiveson, Harold A.
(jt. auth) *See* Albright, David, and Feiveson, Harold A.
Feiveson, Harold A., and others
A low-threshold test ban is feasible. bibl f il *Science* 238:455-9 O 23 '87
Fela, 1938-
about
Fela. D. Fricke. il por *Roll Stone* p14 Ja 15 '87
Fela. G. Santoro. il pors *Down Beat* 54:52 Mr '87
Felber, Edith
Decorating by the book. il por *Publ Wkly* 232:76 Ag 14 '87
Feld, Eliot
about
Embraced waltzes [ballet] Reviews
N Y 20:108 O 19 '87. T. Tobias
Reviews:
Performances at the Joyce Theater, New York City. S. Greco. *Dance Mag* 61:82-3 N '87
Performances at the Joyce Theater, New York City. O. Stuart. *Dance Mag* 61:44-5+ Ap '87
Feld, Kenneth Jeffrey, 1948-
about
Ladies and gentlemen, presenting—Kenneth Feld. M. E. Recio. il por *Bus Week* p76+ Je 8 '87
Feld Ballet
Abiding passions [performance of Embraced waltzes at the Joyce Theater] T. Tobias. il *N Y* 20:108-9 O 19 '87
The lonely crowd [spring season at the Joyce Theater, New York City] T. Tobias. il *N Y* 20:73-4 Mr 23 '87
Reviews:
Performances at the Joyce Theater, New York City. S. Greco. *Dance Mag* 61:82-3 N '87
Performances at the Joyce Theater, New York City. O. Stuart. *Dance Mag* 61:44-5+ Ap '87
Felder, Leonard
A double perspective: publishers & authors. il *Publ Wkly* 232:23-4 Ag 28 '87
Driven crazy by advice? il *Parents* 62:94-6+ My '87
How to make peace (not war) with a difficult mother-in-law. il *Redbook* 168:104-5+ Ap '87
Ten ways to make your articles sparkle. *Writer* 100:14-16 D '87
Felder, Raoul
about
Divide & conquer: an interview with divorce lawyer Raoul Felder. M. Willens. *Harpers Bazaar* 120:141+ Ag '87
Feldinger, Frank
(jt. auth) *See* Weinhouse, Beth, and Feldinger, Frank
Feldman, Corey
about
The Lost Boys: behind the scenes [interview] il pors *Teen* 31:49+ Jl '87
Feldman, Gayle
Anatomy of an acquisition (I). il *Publ Wkly* 231:19-27 Je 26 '87
Anatomy of an acquisition (II). il *Publ Wkly* 232:17-23 Jl 3 '87
The widening world of travel books. il *Publ Wkly* 231:31-2+ F 13 '87
Feldman, Hervey Allen
about
Service starts with the man at the top. B. Saporito and M. J. Williams. il pors *Fortune* 116:108 D 7 '87
Feldman, Jim
The Queen of Soul's reigning passions. por *Harpers Bazaar* 120:138+ Ag '87
Feldman, Laura
Hands On Science . . . hands on fun. il *Child Today* 16:21-4 S/O '87
Feldman, Linda
One man's family. il pors *McCalls* 115:18-22 D '87
The stars who make Christmas special. il pors *McCalls* 115:90+ D '87
The unlikeliest movie star. il pors *McCalls* 115:162+ N '87
Feldman, Martin L.
Why the First Amendment is not incompatible with national security interests [address, January 14, 1987] *Vital Speeches Day* 53:394-8 Ap 15 '87

Feldman, Trude B.
Three Thanksgivings: the saga of Robert McFarlane. il pors *McCalls* 115:22+ N '87
Feldschuh, Joseph, 1935-
about
Seeing red. S. N. Chakravarty. il por *Forbes* 139:76+ Je 1 '87
Feldstein, Martin S.
Correcting the trade deficit. bibl f *Foreign Aff* 65:795-806 Spr '87
about
'Another 15 to 20 percent' drop [interview] por *U S News World Rep* 102:43 Mr 9 '87
Felipe II, King of Spain, 1527-1598 *See* Philip II, King of Spain, 1527-1598
Felix, Norm, and others
Combining categorical program services can make a major difference. *Phi Delta Kappan* 68:787-8 Je '87
Felker, Clay
about
Return of the native. *Time* 129:62 Je 1 '87
Fell, Derek
How southern gardens grow. il map *Travel Holiday* 167:44-9 Mr '87
Feller, Gordon
(jt. auth) *See* Sommer, Mark, and Feller, Gordon
Fellheimer, Alan
about
'Nice guys don't get paid'. il por *Bus Week* p110 S 21 '87
Felling of trees *See* Tree felling
Fellman, Bruce
Researchers climb inside of the fire to tweak the flame. bibl (p229) il *Smithsonian* 18:70-2+ O '87
Fellner, Eric
about
The Brit pack. R. Nicolson. il pors *Vogue* 177:80 D '87
Fellowships *See* Scholarships and fellowships
Felt, Irving Mitchell, 1910-
about
Divorce, Dominican style. L. Saunders. il por *Forbes* 140:79 D 28 '87
Felt making *See* Felting
Felting
Sheep on your feet [slippers from wool batting] il *Sunset* 179:132+ N '87
Felton, Elise
A greenhouse in the Midwest. il *Flower Gard* 31:16-17 O/N '87
Feltsman, Vladimir
about
88 keys to the city. K. Ames. il pors *Newsweek* 110:78-9 N 23 '87
A symbol takes the stage. M. Walsh. il por *Time* 130:86 N 23 '87
Feminine beauty *See* Beauty, Personal
Feminine hygiene products
The toxic shock puzzle [tampon absorbency] D. Todd. il *Macleans* 100:8 S 21 '87
Women are lining up for Lore Harp's Le Funelle. P. Finch. il por *Bus Week* p80 Je 8 '87
Women take a stand in public restrooms [Le Funelle] *Prevention* 39:12 F '87
Labeling
Tampon absorbency, not material, increases TSS risk. *FDA Consum* 21:2 N '87
Femininity (Psychology)
Femininity: do you buy it? K. Madden. il *Vogue* 177:444-6 Mr '87
La gamine: fun and flirty. il *Harpers Bazaar* 120:86+ Ap '87
Feminism
See also
Ecofeminism
Feminist literary criticism
Feminists for Life of America
Press and feminism
Anatomy and destiny [medical school] P. Klass. *Ms* 16:66+ Jl/Ag '87
The chalice and the blade: an interview with Riane Eisler. F. P. Hosken. *Humanist* 47:26-30+ Jl/Ag '87
Daughter/mother. A. Sheedy. il pors *Ms* 16:158-9 Jl/Ag '87
The "F" word. C. R. Stimpson. *Ms* 16:80+ Jl/Ag '87
Feminist update. C. Kocol. See issues of The Humanist beginning September/October 1986
The feminization of the American left. J. Nuechterlein. *Commentary* 84:43-8 N '87
Growing girls and grandmothers [Fort Wayne Feminists] M. K. Blakely. il por *Ms* 15:12+ Je '87

How optimistic are American women? [results of poll] il *Ms* 16:172-4+ Jl/Ag '87
Humanism and the second wave of feminism. G. Steinem. il por *Humanist* 47:11-15+ My/Je '87
If moral decay is the question, is a feminist ethic the answer? G. Steinem. il *Ms* 16:57-9+ S '87
The impact of the women's movement(s) on the family: a father's perspective. E. Marciniak. *America* 156:194-6 Mr 7 '87
Liberty, equality, sexuality. A. D. Bloom. *Commentary* 83:24-30 Ap '87
Looking to the future. G. Steinem. *Ms* 16:55-7 Jl/Ag '87
My gloves are off, sisters [women's movement and racism] M. A. Gillespie. por *Ms* 15:19-20 Ap '87
The next wave [feminism and working class women] B. Ehrenreich. il *Ms* 16:166-8+ Jl/Ag '87
An officer and a feminist. J. M. Dubik. por *Newsweek* 109:8-9 Ap 27 '87
Preserving values in a changing world [views of B. Friedan] il por *USA Today (Periodical)* 116:2-3 Ag '87
Real prolifers defend women, too [with readers' comments] J. Ball. *U S Cathol* 52:16-21 Ag '87
Suburban classic [sharing the tasks of married life] L. Garis. il por *Ms* 16:142+ Jl/Ag '87
Taking charge of change: how the new role definitions for women are created by women. J. Kagan. *Work Woman* 12:53-4 Ag '87
What women want now [cover story; special section; with editorial comment by Kevin Doyle] il *Macleans* 100:2, 42-4+ N 16 '87
When a good word takes on a negative meaning. T. K. Daley. por *U S News World Rep* 102:9 Ja 12 '87
When women fight for equality, says Warren Farrell, fairness to men may be one of the casualties [interview] L. Powell. il pors *People Wkly* 27:49-50+ Je 15 '87
Whip me, beat me and while you're at it cancel my N.O.W. membership: feminists war against each other over pornography. A. Levine and K. Currie. *Wash Mon* 19:17-21 Je '87
Women in America: how equal today? [cover story; special issue] il map *Sch Update* 119:3-14+ My 18 '87
"You've got a long way to go, baby": a conversation about the women's movement with Ruth Hubbard. M. Davidson. por *USA Today (Periodical)* 116:92-5 S '87
Conferences
See also
National Women's Political Caucus
History
Resisting amnesia [excerpt from address, February 1983] A. Rich. *Ms* 15:66-7 Mr '87
Language question
See Sex discrimination in language
Periodicals
A feminist reader's guide. D. Cole. *Ms* 16:73 O '87
Feminism and religion *See* Women and religion
Feminism and the press *See* Press and feminism
Feminism in literature
Kissing off Snow White. J. D. Zipes. *N Y Times Book Rev* 92:32 Mr 22 '87
Margaret Atwood's testaments: resisting the Gilead within. J. K. Larson. *Christ Century* 104:496-8 My 20-27 '87
Feminism in motion pictures
A feminist fairy tale [E. Beckman's Cinderella] V. Dika. il *Art Am* 75:31-3 Ap '87
A young filmmaker with a sense of purpose [L. Barrett's Business as usual] J. M. Wall. *Christ Century* 104:739-40 S 9-16 '87
Feminist literary criticism
Literary feminism comes of age. E. Kolbert. il por *N Y Times Mag* p110+ D 6 '87
Feminist literature
See also
Booksellers and bookselling—Feminist literature
Feminist poetry
Bibliography
Fighting back in four languages [series entitled The defiant muse] D. Ackerman. il *N Y Times Book Rev* 92:38-9 My 3 '87
Feminists for Life of America
The new pro-life rebels [pro-life feminism] M. Gallagher. *Natl Rev* 39:37-9 F 27 '87
Femmes fatales in opera
The feared woman [Samson et Dalila] J. Kestner. il *Opera News* 51:34-7+ Ap 11 '87

Fencerows *See* Field borders
Fences
> *See also*
> Hedges
> Snow fences

3 wood fences. il *Workbench* 43:32-7 Jl/Ag '87
10 tips make fence building easier. R. F. Jordan. il *Home Mech* 83:55-6 My '87
Build a fence that's a feature. il *South Living* 22:96+ Ap '87
First-class fence [board-and-lattice fence and moon gate] E. Thompson and E. Thompson. il *Pop Mech* 164:98-102+ Je '87
Iron fences from plain to fancy. il *Better Homes Gard* 65:66 Ap '87
Lattice screen also opens [carport and parking area] il *South Living* 22:189 N '87
Modular fence built in the workshop. il *Sunset* 178:120 Mr '87
Panels for spa privacy and for a changing room. il *Sunset* 179:102 Jl '87
Planter fences and pergolas. A. W. Lees. il *Pop Sci* 231:72-4 Ag '87
Trellis and screen for front-yard privacy. il *Sunset* 179:138-9 O '87
> History

Good fences. A. O. Boulton. il *Am Herit* 38:90-5 F/Mr '87
Fences, Electric
Build fence right to get a powerful zzzap. B. Eftink and F. Buckingham. il *Success Farm* 85:50 S '87
Successful farming tests the imported fencers. B. Eftink and F. Buckingham. il *Success Farm* 85:48-9 S '87
Fences [drama] See Wilson, August
Fencing
Getting her point across [C. Bilodeaux] D. Stathoplos. il pors *Sports Illus* 66:54-6 Mr 9 '87
Fenders (Motorcycles) *See* Motorcycles—Fenders
Fendick, Patty
> *about*

Woman to watch: Patty Fendick. il por *Women's Sports Fitness* 9:84 S '87
Feng shui
How to keep the dragons happy [use in Hong Kong architecture] H. G. Chua-Eoan. il *Time* 129:44 Je 22 '87
Fénix (Musical group)
Hot jazz from the banks of the River Plate. M. Holston. il *Américas* 39:57-60 S/O '87
Fenn, Donna
The rediscovery of local pizzazz. il *Work Woman* 12:66-8+ Jl '87
Fennel salads *See* Salads
Fenner, Frank, 1914-
Can smallpox return? il *World Health* p18-21 Ag/S '87
Fentanyl
Doctors who use drugs. J. Pekkanen. il *Good Housekeep* 205:198-9+ S '87
Fenton, Lois
> *about*

How to dress with style: a guide for the fifty plus man [interview] il *50 Plus* 27:48-51 Mr '87
Fenway Park (Boston, Mass.)
The Wall's inside story [scoreboard] E. M. Swift. il *Sports Illus* 67:48-50 Jl 6 '87
Fenwick, Ben C.
The plot to kill Washington. il por *Am Hist Illus* 21:8-12 F '87
Fenyo, Jean-Pierre
> *about*

Answers. *New Yorker* 63:18-19 Ag 17 '87
Fenyvesi, Charles
Where our roots are. por *Rodale's Org Gard* 34:102-3 S '87
Feral animals *See* Wildlife
Feral goats *See* Goats, Wild
Ferber, Edith
> *about*

McCall's goes to a party: lunch in the country. C. Rossant. il pors *McCalls* 145:115-16+ Mr '87
FERC *See* United States. Federal Energy Regulatory Commission
Ferchat, Robert A.
Productivity in a customer vein [address, February 23, 1987] *Vital Speeches Day* 53:602-5 Jl 15 '87
Fergus, Charles
A barrier island interlude. il maps *Ctry J* 14:21-5 Je '87
A bear of America. il *Ctry J* 14:43-7+ O '87
Empty days: a journal of two weeks afield. il *Ctry J* 14:64-9 D '87

The tracking snow. il *Ctry J* 14:32-7 F '87
Wild jams and jellies. il *Ctry J* 14:56-9 Ag '87
Ferguson, Charles H.
> *about*

The Japanese strategy for computer supremacy [interview] N. Gall. il por *Forbes* 139:76+ F 9 '87
Ferguson, Charles W.
Unforgettable DeWitt Wallace. il pors *Read Dig* 130:177-80+ F '87
Ferguson, Dan
Painting with flash. il *Petersens Photogr Mag* 16:72-3 My '87
Ferguson, Edward W., and others
Tornadoes: fewest fatalities on record. il maps *Weatherwise* 40:28-35 F '87
Ferguson, Henry N.
Take out some marriage insurance. il *Read Dig* 130:213-14+ My '87
Ferguson, Ronald
> *about*

When the critics get tough, Fergie's major defender, her dad, rides to the rescue [cover story; interview] F. Hauptfuhrer. il pors *People Wkly* 28:100-3 S 21 '87
Ferguson, Sarah See Sarah, Duchess of York, 1959-
Ferguson, Sybil
> *about*

Pounds to dollars. P. F. Stewart. il por *Ladies Home J* 104:150 O '87
Ferguson, Thomas, 1949-
Kirk's cant. *Nation* 244:385 Mr 28 '87
Ferguson, Tom, 1943-
The best bet yet for worried smokers [excerpt from The smoker's book of health] il *Prevention* 39:74-80 Je '87
Fergusson, Francis, 1904-1986
> *about*

Francis Fergusson, 1904-1986. J. McCormick. *Am Sch* 56:557-64 Aut '87
Fermat's theorem
Closing in on Fermat's last theorem. *Sci News* 131:397 Je 20 '87
Progress on Fermat's famous math problem. G. Kolata. il *Science* 235:1572-3 Mr 27 '87
Fermenta AB
A golden boy who lost his luster [R. El Sayed] P. Sherrid. il por *U S News World Rep* 103:41 Jl 27 '87
Scandal in Sweden: how the Fermenta dream turned sour. J. Kapstein. il por *Bus Week* p68-9 Je 8 '87
Fermentation
> *See also*
> Glycolysis

Fermi (Enrico) Award *See* Enrico Fermi Award
Fernández, Adelfa
The doyenne of Brazilian skies. il por *Américas* 39:54-5 Ja/F '87
Tegucigalpa: a taste of colonial times. il *Américas* 39:38-43 N/D '87
Fernandez, Julio *See* Larraz, Julio, 1944-
Fernandez, Louis
> *about*

Cutting the golden years down to a few months. C. Power. il por *Bus Week* p114-15 Jl 20 '87
Fernández Larios, Armando
> *about*

Confession of a 'good soldier'. M. R. Meyer. il por *Newsweek* 109:43 F 16 '87
Derailing Pinochet. J. Dinges and S. Landau. il *Nation* 244:280-2 Mr 7 '87
Ferns
Electrophoretic evidence for genetic diploidy in the bracken fern (Pteridium aquilinum). P. G. Wolf and others. bibl f il *Science* 236:947-9 My 22 '87
Ferns for the West: these get by with less water. il *Sunset* 178:260-1 My '87
When ferns get in trouble. il *Sunset* 178:180-1 F '87
Ferorelli, Enrico
In the glare of history. il *Life* 10:110-16+ O '87
Ferra, Joan Miró *See* Miró, Joan, 1893-1983
Ferragamo, Wanda
> *about*

Winning by a foot. N. J. Perry. il por *Fortune* 116:137 O 26 '87
Ferragamo (Salvatore) SpA *See* Salvatore Ferragamo SpA
Ferranti plc
Ferranti plans to merge with U.S. defense company. *Aviat Week Space Technol* 127:28 S 28 '87
Ferrar, Ann
The Bangles. il *Stereo Rev* 52:85-7 Ja '87

Ferrara, Jerry L.
Looking ahead. il *Natl Wildl* 25:10-11 O/N '87
Why vultures make good neighbors [photographs] il *Natl Wildl* 25:16-21 Je/Jl '87
Ferrara, Mike
Preventive maintenance. See issues of Home Mechanix beginning November 1985
Ferrari, Enzo, 1898-
about
"Just a country boy with a vision". D. Sherman. il *Car Driv* 33:9 S '87
Life after Enzo. P. Windsor. il pors *Car Driv* 32:179+ My '87
Maranello revisited. L. C. Crane. il *Road Track* 39:114+ S '87
Ferrari, Piero Lardi
about
Life after Enzo. P. Windsor. il pors *Car Driv* 32:179+ My '87
Ferrari (Automobile) *See* Sports cars
Ferrari SpA Esercizio Fabbriche Automobili e Corse
"Just a country boy with a vision" [E. Ferrari] D. Sherman. il *Car Driv* 33:9 S '87
Life after Enzo [P. L. Ferrari] P. Windsor. il pors *Car Driv* 32:179+ My '87
Maranello revisited. L. C. Crane. il *Road Track* 39:114+ S '87
Red cars rising [Ferrari factories in Modena and Maranello] D. Sherman. il *Car Driv* 33:93-5+ Ag '87
Ferraro, Geraldine A.
No celibates, please. il por *Life* 10:72 Ag '87
Ferraro, Susan
Inspired by quilts and samplers. il por *Americana* 15:53-7 Mr/Ap '87
Ferraro, Terry
Orchid mania. il *Flower Gard* 31:30-2+ O/N '87
Ferrary, Jeannette
Loving Brillat-Savarin: a tale of a tasteful affair. por *N Y Times Book Rev* 92:51+ My 31 '87
Ferreira, José R.
The need to know. il *World Health* p7-8 O '87
Ferrell, Frank
about
An evening with Trevor's dad. E. S. Vaughn. il pors *Christ Today* 31:12-13 F 20 '87
Ferrell, Nancy
The Tombstone Twins: lights at the top of the world. il map *Sea Front* 33:344-51 S/O '87
Ferrell, Sarah
Christmas in Bethlehem. il *Saturday Evening Post* 259:66-70 D '87
Ferrell, Trevor
about
An evening with Trevor's dad. E. S. Vaughn. il pors *Christ Today* 31:12-13 F 20 '87
Ferrets
Fertile ferret? [capture of last known black-footed ferret living in the wild] il *Nat Hist* 96:6-7 My '87
Anecdotes, facetiae, satire, etc.
Yet another true study of mankind [black-footed ferrets] R. Blount. il *Atlantic* 259:34 Ap '87
Ferretti, Fred
Canton. il *Gourmet* 47:56-63+ My '87
Cheesemaking in Parma. il *Gourmet* 47:74-9+ O '87
A gourmet at large. See issues of Gourmet beginning January 1985
The great American meat loaf. il *50 Plus* 27:46-9 Jl '87
Turn over a new leaf. il *50 Plus* 27:74-7 Mr '87
Ferri, Alessandra
about
Ferri tales can come true: Giselle goes to the movies [cover story] J. Gruen. il pors *Dance Mag* 61:36-43 O '87
Petites: short & sexy. pors *Harpers Bazaar* 120:400-3 S '87
Ferri, Roger C., 1949-
about
A pastoral pavilion. C. Amery. il *House Gard* 159:182-9+ My '87
Ferrieri, Anna Castelli *See* Castelli Ferrieri, Anna
Ferrieri, Giuliano
Death by choice. *World Press Rev* 34:51 D '87
Ferries
A B.C. tourism gamble [refitting Victoria-Seattle ferries with gambling casinos] il *Macleans* 100:29 Ap 20 '87
Crossings. S. B. Wright. il *Americana* 15:55-8 Jl/Ag '87
Floating the Hudson: Big Apple commuters get mellow. G. Langer. il *Sierra* 72:12 N/D '87

India's backwater highways [Malabar Coast] K. Brueckmann and D. Brueckmann. il map *Oceans* 20:24-9 Ja/F '87
Relaxing on Norfork Lake. il *South Living* 22:35 Ag '87
Riding the waves to work. P. Nulty. il *Fortune* 116:100-4 O 26 '87
This summer, one more way to get to Victoria by water. il *Sunset* 179:34-5 Ag '87
Accidents
Death in the North Sea [Herald of Free Enterprise ferry] N. Cooper. il map *Newsweek* 109:38 Mr 16 '87
A fading tragedy [Herald of Free Enterprise] P. Lewis. il *Macleans* 100:8 N 9 '87
Heroism—and horror [Herald of Free Enterprise] M. McIver. il *Macleans* 100:54-5 Mr 23 '87
Identity crisis [forensics used to identify victims of English Channel ferry disaster] J. Lowenstein. il *Oceans* 20:72 N/D '87
A question of stability [Herald of Free Enterprise] J. Lowenstein. il *Oceans* 20:72 Jl/Ag '87
Tragedy in the harbor [Herald of Free Enterprise sinks] J. Bierman. il *Macleans* 100:26-7 Mr 16 '87
A tragic end for day trippers [British Channel ferry, Herald of Free Enterprise, capsizes] M. S. Serrill. il *Time* 129:52 Mr 16 '87
Ferris, Charles D.
Should Congress approve the Fairness Doctrine? [excerpts from testimony, March 18, 1987] *Congr Dig* 66:250+ O '87
Ferris, Jean Léon Gérôme, 1863-1930
Scenes from the life of Washington. il *Am Hist Illus* 21:22-31 F '87
about
J.L.G. Ferris. B. J. Mitnick. il por *Am Hist Illus* 21:14-21 F '87
Ferris, Richard J., 1936-
about
Allegis: is a name change enough for UAL? J. E. Ellis. il por *Bus Week* p54-5+ Mr 2 '87
Even if Allegis wins, the victory could be pyrrhic. J. E. Ellis. por *Bus Week* p37 Je 15 '87
How Dick Ferris blew it. K. Labich. il por *Fortune* 116:42-4+ Jl 6 '87
Investors' breakup of Allegis prompts Ferris resignation. *Aviat Week Space Technol* 126:82 Je 15 '87
One man's dream comes down to earth. C. P. Work and H. Wells. il por *U S News World Rep* 102:44-5 Je 22 '87
Stopping a Ferris wheel. D. Pauly. il por *Newsweek* 109:42-3 Je 22 '87
The unraveling of an idea. J. E. Ellis and C. Hawkins. il por *Bus Week* p42-3 Je 22 '87
Ferris, Timothy
Where are we going? il *Sky Telesc* 73:486-90 My '87
The year the warning lights flashed on. il *Life* 10:67-8+ Ja '87
Ferrite radio filters *See* Radio filters
Ferritin
Identification of the iron-responsive element for the translational regulation of human ferritin mRNA. M. W. Hentze and others. bibl f il *Science* 238:1570-3 D 11 '87
Ferrous carbonate *See* Iron carbonates
Ferrum College. Blue Ridge Institute *See* Blue Ridge Institute
Ferry, Bryan
about
Rock's phantom of the paradox. L. Robinson. por *Vogue* 177:108 Ag '87
The sweet smell of Sussex. J. Bowes-Lyon. il por *House Gard* 159:188-95 N '87
Fertile Crescent *See* Mesopotamia
Fertility (Biology)
See also
Artificial insemination, Human
Conception
Infertility
Fertility control *See* Birth control
Fertility drugs
See also
Danazol
Factrel
Pergonal
Fertilization (Artificial insemination) *See* Artificial insemination, Human
Fertilization (Biology)
See also
Conjugation (Biology)
Ova
Spermatozoa

Fertilization (Biology)—*cont.*

The biology and chemistry of fertilization. P. M. Wassarman. bibl f il *Science* 235:553-60 Ja 30 '87

Fertilization in vitro

And baby makes four: for the first time a surrogate bears a child genetically not her own. B. Johnson. il por *People Wkly* 27:95-6+ My 4 '87

British government rekindles debate on embryo research. D. Dickson. *Science* 238:1348 D 4 '87

"Easier than selling soap" [in vitro fertilization clinics] L. Gubernick. il *Forbes* 139:112+ F 9 '87

The grueling baby chase. J. Seligmann. il *Newsweek* 110:78-9+ N 30 '87

"I had in vitro quadruplets"; ed. by Ann Schrader. D. Schock. il por *Redbook* 170:41+ D '87

The miracle baby [frozen embryo in vitro fertilization] B. Weinhouse and F. Feldinger. il *Ladies Home J* 104:104+ Ap '87

The private pain of infertility. G. Davis. il por *N Y Times Mag* p106+ D 6 '87

Anecdotes, facetiae, satire, etc.

In the name of progress. R. Baker. il *N Y Times Mag* p18 My 3 '87

Ethical aspects

Ethics in embryo [Harper's forum; cover story] *Harpers* 275:37-47 S '87

Fertilization of plants

See also
    Pollen

Aerodynamics of wind pollination. K. J. Niklas. bibl (p116) il *Sci Am* 257:90-5 Jl '87

Deceit and corruption in the blueberry patch [flower mimicry by mummy berry fungus (Monilinia)] S. W. T. Batra. il *Nat Hist* 96:56-9 Ag '87

The mysterious magic of pollination [work of Karl Niklas] C. Reiter. il *Natl Wildl* 25:14-17 Ag/S '87

Fertilizer industry

Turmoil in the fertilizer industry [cover story; special section] il *Success Farm* 85 no5:15-21 Mr '87

Marketing

Dealers fight over fewer farmers, less acres. M. Holmberg. il *Success Farm* 85 no5:20-1 Mr '87

Fertilizers and manures

See also
    Compost
    Humus
    Mulching

Add fertilizer, subtract herbicide [nitrogen for soybeans] M. Holmberg. il *Success Farm* 85 no1:26P Ja '87

Fertilizer strategies for short-term leases. M. Holmberg. il *Success Farm* 85 no3:18Q F '87

Fertilizing with rocks [work of Ward Chesworth in Tanzania] S. Strauss. il *Technol Rev* 90:11-12 Ap '87

Getting controlled-release fertilizers to work as they're supposed to. il *Sunset* 178:260 Ap '87

One man's fertilizer [cover story] J. C. Page. il *Ctry J* 14:33-7 Ap '87

Time to fertilize the garden. L. C. Askey. il *South Living* 22:76 Mr '87

Analysis

Match fertilizer placement to soil type. R. Fee. il *Success Farm* 85 no5:26T Mr '87

On-the-go nitrate tester. M. Holmberg. il *Success Farm* 85:43 O '87

Take proper credit for manure's fertilizer value. *Success Farm* 85 no5:26P Mr '87

Handling

10 ways to fertilize ridges. M. Holmberg. il *Success Farm* 85:18AJ-18AK Ap '87

Anhydrous on drill, but seed feels no pain [no-till wheat] M. Holmberg. il *Success Farm* 85 no1:30 Ja '87

Bend, but don't break, starter placement [fertilizer placement for corn] R. Fee. il *Success Farm* 85 no4:18E F '87

Herbicide in anhydrous loses company push [Sutan and Eradicane] R. Fee. il *Success Farm* 85 no1:26AL Ja '87

'Incorporate' chemicals in no-till [herbicide impregnated on dry bulk fertilizer] R. Fee. il *Success Farm* 85 no1:26Z Ja '87

Liquid starter easier—can you afford it? Dry starter cheaper—can you handle it? R. Fee. il *Success Farm* 85:14-15 My '87

Spike starter with extra nitrogen. R. Fee. il *Success Farm* 85:18Y Ap '87

Split decision on split nitrogen. R. Fee. il *Success Farm* 85 no3:F1 F '87

They read the leaves to target fertilizer [DRIS analysis] M. Holmberg. il *Success Farm* 85 no3:18AH F '87

Injurious effects

Hazards of the game [golf courses] J. Edmondson. il *Audubon* 89:24-8+ N '87

Prices

Fertilizer prices could rise despite soft demand. *Success Farm* 85 no5:10 Mr '87

Fertilizer prices headed up. R. Fee. il *Success Farm* 85:56 O '87

Oversupply drives prices down. R. Fee. il *Success Farm* 85 no5:16-17 Mr '87

Ferullo, Joseph

Flacking in the fields of the Lord. il pors *Channels* 7:45-8 Mr '87

Fescue

Meadow and decks . . . easy-maintenance and naturally handsome [unmowed creeping red fescue] il *Sunset* 179:222-3 O '87

Feshbach, Herman

A meeting with Sakharov [interview] il pors *Phys Today* 40:7+ Ap '87

Small systems: when does thermodynamics apply? il *Phys Today* 40:9+ N '87

Feshbach, Joseph

about

This bull sees Japanese cash driving up the Dow to 3500. R. McNatt. il por *Money* 16:186 O '87

Festa, Susan

Autumn adventures. il *Women's Sports Fitness* 9:92-3 S '87

How exercise can K-O your period. il *Mademoiselle* 93:120 Ag '87

That time of month: when menstrual cramps hit, will exercise help? il *Women's Sports Fitness* 9:29-31 Ag '87

A triple triumph: taking on the triathlon challenge. il *Work Woman* 12:130+ Je '87

Upper-body work out. il *Women's Sports Fitness* 9:22-6 Jl '87

Le Festival (New York, N.Y.: Restaurant) *See* New York (N.Y.)—Restaurants, nightclubs, bars, etc.

Festival of Festivals (Toronto, Ont.) *See* Motion picture festivals—Ontario

Festivals

See also
    Carnival (Pre-Lenten festival)
    Dance festivals
    Drama festivals
    Literary festivals
    Motion picture festivals
    Music festivals
    Television festivals

Apple picking time. D. J. Williamson. il *Americana* 15:54-7+ S/O '87

It's festival time! [national parks] L. Tuttle. il *Natl Parks* 61:14-15+ Jl/Ag '87

Of ice and men [winter festivals re-create old-time ice harvests] K. D. Irvine. il *Americana* 14:15-16+ Ja/F '87

International aspects

Summer festival fun! il *Essence* 17:23+ Ap '87

Azores

Whaling in the Azores [reenactment during Sea Week] R. B. Silverman. il *Sea Front* 33:174-82 My/Je '87

Barbados

Crop Over: more than a big party [cover story] T. Best. il *Américas* 39:16-21 Jl/Ag '87

California

See also
    Forestville (Calif.)—Festivals

Canada

Celebrations of summer. il *Macleans* 100:36-9 Jl 13 '87

Chile

"Running Christ against the bandits" [horsemen carry on Easter tradition] C. Caviedes. il *Nat Hist* 96:44-53 My '87

Florida

See also
    Fort Lauderdale (Fla.)—Festivals

Georgia

Foliage and festivals in the Georgia mountains. G. D. Ford. il *South Living* 22:10-12 O '87

Guatemala

See also
    Santiago (Guatemala)—Festivals

Indiana

See also
    Indiana Black Expo
    Indianapolis (Ind.)—Festivals

Festivals—cont.

Italy

See also
Palio di Siena (Italy)

Maryland

See also
Easton (Md.)—Festivals

Massachusetts

See also
Worcester (Mass.)—Festivals
Bach and knolls in the Berkshires. P. Harris and D. Lyon. il *Travel Holiday* 167:38+ My '87

Michigan

See also
Holland (Mich.)—Festivals

New Jersey

See also
Hollybush Festival

New York (State)

See also
Artpark (Lewiston, N.Y.)
Brooklyn (New York, N.Y.)—Festivals
New York (N.Y.)—Festivals
Next Wave Festival
PepsiCo Summerfare
Queens (New York, N.Y.)—Festivals

Pennsylvania

See also
Kutztown (Pa.)—Festivals

Peru

Return of the Pleiades [festival of Qoyllur Rit'i] R. Randall. il *Nat Hist* 96:42-53 Je '87

Québec (Province)

See also
Québec (Québec)—Festivals

Scotland

Mary Queen of Scots: a tragedy in four cities. P. M. Prince. il *Travel Holiday* 167:54-9 Ap '87

Tennessee

See also
Chattanooga (Tenn.)—Festivals

Texas

See also
Austin (Tex.)—Festivals
San Antonio Festival

Virginia

See also
Norfolk (Va.)—Festivals
Preserving mountain ways [Blue Ridge Folklife Festival] il *South Living* 22:20 O '87

Fetal growth See Fetus—Growth
Fetal tissue

Transplantation

The amazing new brain surgery for Parkinson's disease. E. Kiester. il *50 Plus* 27:24-6+ O '87
Cell grafts proceed, value uncertain [fetal brain cell transplants for Parkinson's disease] R. Weiss. *Sci News* 132:341 N 28 '87
Dramatic results with brain grafts [treatment of Parkinson's disease] R. Lewin. il *Science* 237:245-7 Jl 17 '87
Fetal tissue transplants: a technique raising hope—and controversy. A. Bard and S. Baker. il *Bus Week* p116+ D 7 '87
The flesh peddlers. *Progressive* 51:9-10 O '87
Help from the unborn [cell implants from aborted fetuses] J. Levine. il *Time* 129:62 Ja 12 '87
Human fetal-cell transplants planned [Parkinson's disease research] R. Weiss. *Sci News* 132:22 Jl 11 '87
Should medicine use the unborn? M. Clark. il *Newsweek* 110:62-3 S 14 '87
Steps toward a brave new world [treating neural disorders with brain implants of fetal nerve tissue and adrenal gland tissue] L. Jaroff. il *Time* 130:56-7 Jl 13 '87
Les fêtes d'Hébé [opera] See Rameau, Jean Philippe
Fetoprotein
Diversity of alpha-fetoprotein gene expression in mice is generated by a combination of separate enhancer elements. R. E. Hammer and others. bibl f il *Science* 235:53-8 Ja 2 '87
Raf, a trans-acting locus, regulates the α-fetoprotein gene in a cell-autonomous manner. T. F. Vogt and others. bibl f il *Science* 236:301-3 Ap 17 '87
Screening for neural tube defects. P. A. Hillard. il *Parents* 62:194+ S '87
FETs (Field-effect transistors) See Transistors
Fetter, Steve
Would a test ban strengthen SDI? il *Bull At Sci* 43:40-1 N '87

Fettner, Ann Giudici
The AIDS scare: answers to frightening questions. *Redbook* 168:28-30+ Ap '87
Fettucine cooking See Cooking—Pasta
Fetus
See also
Amnion
Fetoprotein
Maternal-fetal exchange
Prenatal influences
Umbilical cord
Cellular localization of somatomedin (insulin-like growth factor) messenger RNA in the human fetus. V. K. M. Han and others. bibl f il *Science* 236:193-7 Ap 10 '87
Eat right, stay off your feet—or go to jail [proposed measures protecting fetal rights at the expense of the mother] M. Takas. *Vogue* 177:148 My '87
A matter of neglect [fetal rights vs. maternal rights] J. Bermel. il *Parents* 62:335-6+ N '87
The ordeal of Pamela Rae Stewart [charged with irresponsible prenatal care] A. Bonavoglia. il pors *Ms* 16:92-5+ Jl/Ag '87
Policing pregnancy [views on forced obstetrical procedures] *Sci Am* 257:26+ Ag '87

Brain

See Brain

Diseases
Diagnosis

See also
Neural tube—Diseases—Diagnosis
Perfect people? [cover story] A. Virshup. il *N Y* 20:26-34 Jl 27 '87
Prenatal tests and where to get them. il *U S News World Rep* 102:70 My 25 '87
Today's prenatal testing. B. D. Shephard. *McCalls* 114:88+ S '87
Women's medical tests: what your doctor may not tell you. P. Gadsby. il *Good Housekeep* 205:239-40 N '87

Therapy

Retroviruses and mouse embryos: a rapid model for neurovirulence and transplacental antiviral therapy. A. H. Sharpe and others. bibl f il *Science* 236:1671-4 Je 26 '87

Growth

Is the baby growing normally? P. A. Hillard. il *Parents* 62:252+ N '87

Surgery

3 children who needed a medical miracle [kidney surgery]; ed. by Sara Nelson. D. Belanger. il *Redbook* 168:111+ F '87
Fetus, Death of
See also
Abortion
Miscarriage
Stillbirth
Fetus, Effect of hormones on the
Prenatal 'sex change' for a leaner ewe [research by John Klindt] *Sci News* 131:361 Je 6 '87
Feudalism

Great Britain

The Lord of Sark may not have serfs, but his pigeon rights are heir-tight [M. Beaumont] J. Cooper. il pors *People Wkly* 28:89-91 Jl 27 '87
Feuds
"Friend by day, enemy by night" [blood feuds in Thull, Pakistan] R. L. Keiser. il *Nat Hist* 96:8+ N '87
Feuerstein, Phyllis A.
Exercise—or how the other half lives. il *Curr Health 2* 13:10-11 Mr '87
High tech diagnosis: from X-rays to MRI. il *Curr Health 2* 14:26-7 N '87
Prejudice. il *Curr Health 2* 13:28-9 Ap '87
Fever
See also
Typhoid fever
Fevers: friend or foe? J. Haley. il *Saturday Evening Post* 259:64-6 Mr '87
Fever thermometers See Thermometers, Clinical
FHA See Future Homemakers of America; United States. Farmers Home Administration; United States. Federal Housing Administration
Fialco, Diane De Lena
about
The case against Brian Spencer. P. Dexter. il *Sports Illus* 66:98-102+ My 11 '87
A hockey player's victory in court. M. Gray. il pors *Macleans* 100:46-7 O 26 '87

Fialkov, Vladimir

about

Scientist Vladimir Fialkov focuses on the future of a unique natural wonder: crystalline Lake Baikal. S. K. Reed. il pors *People Wkly* 27:121+ Ap 6 '87

Fiat SpA

Fiat's unsung Roman general [C. Romiti] R. I. Kirkland, Jr. il por *Fortune* 115:64 Ja 5 '87

Ford bids again, Fiat gets the nod [Fiat outbids Ford for Alfa Romeo] P. Lienert. *Road Track* 38:100 F '87

Hot wheels [chief executive V. Ghidella] T. Pouschine. il por *Forbes* 140:232 N 30 '87

Steering to new records [C. Romiti] R. I. Kirkland, Jr. il por *Fortune* 116:48 Ag 3 '87

Fiber crafts *See* Textile crafts

Fiber in diet

See also

　Cooking—Grain

Delicious high-fiber breakfasts. J. B. Hurley. il *Prevention* 39:82-4+ F '87

A guide to dietary fiber and your health. il *Prevention* 39:34-6+ N '87

Know your oats! S. C. Finn. il *50 Plus* 27:62-6 D '87

New hope for those with diverticular disease. E. Weck. il *FDA Consum* 21:23-5 Jl/Ag '87

Selling high-fiber cereals. il *FDA Consum* 21:6 S '87

Serious breakfast. P. Dranov. il *Health* 19:57-8+ Mr '87

Sleuthing to prevent cancer [skin tags help identify persons at risk for colon polyps] C. SerVaas. il *Saturday Evening Post* 259:98+ Jl/Ag '87

Untangling the fiber story. J. Silberner. il *U S News World Rep* 103:71 N 30 '87

Fiber optics

See also

　Amplifiers—Optical equipment

　Compact disc players—Optical equipment

　Guided missiles—Optical equipment

　Optical switching

Fiber-optic feeding frenzy [telephone cables attacked by sharks] *Time* 129:77 Je 22 '87

Light-headed: optical links. D. Ranada. il *High Fidel* 37:13 N '87

Light makes the perfect wire. H. Friedman. il *Radio-Electron* 58:31+ O '87

London calling, on a beam of light [telephone cables under the Atlantic Ocean] S. Koepp. map *Time* 129:52 Ja 19 '87

Marines' remotely operated device will use aerial fiber-optic link. il *Aviat Week Space Technol* 126:73 F 2 '87

Optical-fiber gyro. D. Scott. il *Pop Sci* 230:25 Je '87

Optical fibers are taking over telecommunications. A. J. Zuckerman. il map *Pop Sci* 231:70-4 O '87

Optical materials. A. M. Glass. bibl f il *Science* 235:1003-9 F 27 '87

Satellites seen as strong optical fiber competitors. *Aviat Week Space Technol* 126:127 Mr 9 '87

Why the shark bites [underwater telephone cables] B. D. Stutz. *Nat Hist* 96:94+ N '87

Fiber optics industry

See also

　US Sprint Communications Inc.

Jeno Paulucci's dream: bring fiber optics home [residential phones for Heathrow, Fla.] S. Ticer. il por *Bus Week* p34-5 S 21 '87

Fiber reinforced concrete *See* Concrete, Reinforced

Fiberglass

See also

　Certain-Teed Corp.

　Owens-Corning Fiberglas Corp.

Fiberglass boats *See* Boats and boating—Materials

Fibers

See also

　Carbon fibers

　Kenaf

Fibich, Sylvia, and Yulsman, Tom

Modern midwifery: new childbirth options. *McCalls* 114:92-3 S '87

Fibrinogen

The adenovirus major late transcription factor activates the rat γ-fibrinogen promoter. L. A. Chodosh and others. bibl f il *Science* 238:684-8 O 30 '87

Interaction of a liver-specific nuclear factor with the fibrinogen and α_1-antitrypsin promoters. G. Courtois and others. bibl f il *Science* 238:688-92 O 30 '87

Fibrinolysin

α_2-antiplasmin Enschede: alanine insertion and abolition of plasmin inhibitory activity. W. E. Holmes and others. bibl f il *Science* 238:209-11 O 9 '87

Fibrinolysis

See also

　Plasminogen

Fibroblast growth factors *See* Growth regulators

Fibroblasts

Clonal gene therapy: transplanted mouse fibroblast clones express human α1-antitrypsin gene in vivo. R. I. Garver, Jr. and others. bibl f il *Science* 237:762-4 Ag 14 '87

The CML-specific P210 *bcr/abl* protein, unlike v-*abl*, does not transform NIH/3T3 fibroblasts. G. Q. Daley and others. bibl f il *Science* 237:532-5 Jl 31 '87

Frequency dependence of electric field modulation of fibroblast protein synthesis. K. J. McLeod and others. bibl f il *Science* 236:1465-9 Je 12 '87

Future 'patchwork' cure for hemophilia? D. D. Edwards. *Sci News* 131:168 Mr 14 '87

Genetic reconstitution of functional acetylcholine receptor channels in mouse fibroblasts. T. Claudio and others. bibl f il *Science* 238:1688-94 D 18 '87

Implantation of genetically engineered fibroblasts into mice: implications for gene therapy. R. F. Selden and others. bibl f il *Science* 236:714-18 My 8 '87

Oncogenes in radioresistant, noncancerous skin fibroblasts from a cancer-prone family. E. H. Chang and others. bibl f il *Science* 237:1036-9 Ag 28 '87

Transformation of rat fibroblasts by FSV rapidly increases glucose transporter gene transcription [Fujinami sarcoma virus] M. J. Birnbaum and others. bibl f il *Science* 235:1495-8 Mr 20 '87

Fibrocystic breast disease *See* Breast—Diseases

Fibroid tumors

Therapy

"Reversible menopause" may help some women who have endometriosis or fibroid tumors [use of gonadotropin releasing hormone] *Prevention* 39:62-3 O '87

Fibromyalgia *See* Fibrositis

Fibrosis, Cystic *See* Cystic fibrosis

Fibrositis

Fibromyalgia. P. Gadsby. il *Good Housekeep* 205:263-4 S '87

Fichman, Niv

about

Blue snake [film] Reviews

　Dance Mag 61:74 Ja '87. J. Gruen

Fichter, Allison

We passed this way again. il *South Living* 22:76 Ag '87

Fichter, Joseph H.

Parishes for Anglican usage. *America* 157:354-7 N 14 '87

FICO *See* Financing Corporation (U.S.)

Fiction

See also

　American fiction

　Best sellers

　Black fiction

　Canadian fiction

　Characters in literature

　Computer novels

　Detective and mystery stories

　Dime novels

　English fiction

　Fantasies, Literary

　Graphic novels

　Historical fiction

　Horror tales

　Hungarian fiction

　Italian fiction

　Lincoln, Abraham, 1809-1865—Fiction

　Publishers and publishing—Fiction

　Realism in literature

　Religion in literature

　Romance fiction

　Russian fiction

　Science fiction

　United States—History—Civil War, 1861-1865—Fiction

　Western stories

　Women in literature

　World War, 1939-1945—Fiction

　Young adults' literature

Commercial fiction on tape. A. Postman. il *Publ Wkly* 232:27-30+ S 4 '87

In pursuit of the ultimate fiction. J. Kaplan. il *N Y Times Book Rev* 92:1+ Ap 19 '87

Fiction—cont.

The library of nonexistent classics. C. Ozick. il *N Y Times Book Rev* 92:12 Ap 12 '87

The sun never sets on the English novel [authors of many nations writing in English] M. Gorra. il *N Y Times Book Rev* 92:1+ Jl 19 '87

Where orphans can still become heiresses [relationship between the novel and biography] C. Ozick. il *N Y Times Book Rev* 92:13 Mr 8 '87

Word-for-word [audio tapes] J. Zinsser. il *Publ Wkly* 231:52+ F 20 '87

Authorship

Always a storyteller. M. H. Clark. *Writer* 100:9-11 Ag '87

Answers to questions on fiction writing. S. Sheldon. il *Writer* 100:9-11 Ap '87

Beyond the first novel. J. Dolce. il *Harpers Bazaar* 120:108+ Ag '87

"Commercial" vs. "literary"—the artificial debate. J. M. Auel. il *Writer* 100:9-12+ O '87

Getting your novel started in ten days. G. Gunn. *Writer* 100:11-13 F '87

Good novelists, bad citizens. C. Ozick. il *N Y Times Book Rev* 92:13 F 15 '87

The hidden censor. D. Lefer. *Writer* 100:7-10 My '87

How I write. G. Godwin. il *Writer* 100:17-18 O '87

On being a writer. V. S. Naipaul. il *N Y Rev Books* 34:7 Ap 23 '87

Pop fiction for smart girls. R. Lawrence. il por *N Y Times Mag* p20-1 Jl 5 '87

The professional response. S. Sheldon. *Writer* 100:6 O '87

The reigning king of literature [interview with S. Bellow] A. P. Sanoff. il por *U S News World Rep* 103:52-3 S 7 '87

The Scheherazade factor [interview with J. Barth] A. P. Sanoff. il por *U S News World Rep* 103:55 Ag 31 '87

Tarot cards catch the eye of a master writer [interview with M. Norman] A. P. Sanoff. por *U S News World Rep* 102:78 Je 8 '87

The uses of autobiography. G. Godwin. *Writer* 100:7-9+ Mr '87

A woman writer treads on male turf [interview with M. Piercy] A. P. Sanoff. por *U S News World Rep* 102:74 My 18 '87

'Writers have a third eye' [interview with P. Roth] A. P. Sanoff. il pors *U S News World Rep* 102:61-2 F 2 '87

Anecdotes, facetiae, satire, etc.

The author. D. Barthelme. *New Yorker* 63:27 Je 15 '87

Bibliography

For whom the blurbs toll: the most likely to be talked about this month. C. E. Rinzler. il *Vogue* 177:475-6 S '87

Narration

The light at the end of the novel; tr. by Leigh Hafrey. P. Schneider. il *N Y Times Book Rev* 92:1+ Jl 26 '87

Setting

Crime in every hamlet. M. Stasio. il *N Y Times Book Rev* 92:1+ Ag 2 '87

On location. J. Markus. il *Writer* 100:21-3 Je '87

A sense of place. M. Elmblad. *Writer* 100:22-4 O '87

Single works

See also

Short stories

See name of author for full entry

After my divorce. French, Marilyn, 1929-

Arrest me. Hirson, Denis

The captains. Dickey, James

The ceremony of farewell. Naipaul, V. S. (Vidiadhar Surajprasad), 1932-

A clockwork orange: the missing chapter. Burgess, Anthony, 1917-

Dry your smile. Morgan, Robin

Fine things. Steel, Danielle

The gamble. Spencer, LaVyrle

A game of dots. Grunwald, Lisa

The girl from Rockaway. Eisenstadt, Jill

Golden urchin. Brent, Madeleine

Hard luck. Dorris, Michael

High society. Trent, Dan

Hollywood casting. Fisher, Carrie

Intimate enemies. Rivers, Caryl

Jacob's ladder. Williams, John Alfred, 1925-

Jaws—the revenge. Searls, Hank

Legacy. Michener, James A. (James Albert), 1907-

Love's own dream. Cookson, Catherine

The making of the president. Vidal, Gore, 1925-

Mama. McMillan, Terry

Memoirs of an invisible man. Saint, H. F. (Harry F.)

The more evil monster. Shelley, Mary Wollstonecraft, 1797-1851

Paris-on-Thames. Huysmans, J.-K. (Joris-Karl), 1848-1907

The point. Barth, John

The prince of tides. Conroy, Pat

Risks of love. Bloom, Patrice

The silk vendetta. Holt, Victoria, 1906-

The slipper. Wilde, Jennifer

Stories and histories. Winterson, Jeanette

Stranger on the beach. Johnston, Velda

Surviving the seasons. Kupfer, Fern

A Tidewater morning. Styron, William, 1925-

Together for life. Michener, James A. (James Albert), 1907-

A touch of magic. Myers, M. Ruth

Style

See Style, Literary

Technique

See also

Characterization

Detective and mystery stories—Technique

Dialogue

Historical fiction—Technique

Plots (Drama, novel, etc.)

Short story

How beautiful was Helen of Troy? What Homer never told us [descriptions of characters' appearance] A. Krystal. il *N Y Times Book Rev* 92:3 Jl 12 '87

Howells as anti-novelist. J. Updike. *New Yorker* 63:78-88 Jl 13 '87

It was a lovely year for a bookstore [novelists' sentence writing techniques] A. Broyard. il *N Y Times Book Rev* 92:12 My 17 '87

Let fiction change your life. L. S. Schwartz. *Writer* 100:14-17 N '87

A matter of life or death: finding a dynamic problem for your story. P. A. Whitney. il *Writer* 100:7-9+ Jl '87

The truth, the whole truth, may be anything *but* the truth. J. T. Hospital. *Writer* 100:19-21 Ap '87

Using images in fiction. M. J. Gerber. *Writer* 100:15-18 Ja '87

Writing a novel. B. Granger. il *Writer* 100:10-12 Jl '87

Fiction and motion pictures *See* Motion picture adaptations; Motion pictures and literature

Fiction in periodicals and newspapers

Rag time [small press literary magazines] J. Queenan. *New Repub* 196:13-14 Ap 6 '87

Writing the short love story. I. Stewart. *Writer* 100:16-18+ Mr '87

Fictitious places *See* Geographical myths

Ficus

See also

Fig trees

Fiddler, Ileen

30 super scholarships. *Seventeen* 46:120-1+ Ja '87

Fiddlers

Fiddling [Old Fiddlers' Convention in Galax, Va.] W. White. *New Yorker* 63:74+ Jl 20 '87

Fidelity Bank, N.A.

From teaching nun to bank president [R. Greco] M. Rowland. il por *Work Woman* 12:60 D '87

Fidelity Freedom Fund

Fidelity's cover boy [M. Kassen] D. Machan. il por *Forbes* 139:229-30 My 18 '87

Fidelity Magellan Fund

Lynch: loading up with 'outrageous bargains'. L. Helm. il por *Bus Week* p99 N 23 '87

Peter Lynch. L. Therrien. il por *Bus Week* Sp Issue:261 Ap 17 '87

The see-sawing Dow doesn't scare Peter Lynch. G. G. Marcial. por *Bus Week* p108 O 26 '87

Fidelity Management & Research Co.

Egad, chaps! It's a Yankee discount broker [in London] L. Therrien. il *Bus Week* p97 F 16 '87

Selling the best—and most—mutual funds [E. C. Johnson] S. Smith. il por *Fortune* 115:85 Ja 5 '87

Supermarketeer of the fund industry. M. Schiffres. il *U S News World Rep* 102:54-5 F 16 '87

Tips from America's best income investor [B. Johnstone] J. E. Goodman. il por *Money* 16:81-4 Ja '87

Fidelity Select-Health Care Fund

Still prescribing drug stocks [interview with W. J. Hayes] A. E. Serwer. il por *Fortune* 115:112 F 16 '87

Fiduccia, Peter

about

Breaking the rules for deer. K. Etling. il *Outdoor Life* 180:68-9+ O '87

Fiedler, Fred Edward
When to lead, when to stand back. il *Psychol Today* 21:26-7 S '87

Fiedler, Ralph
about
Something passing in the night. G. L. Verschuur. il *Astronomy* 15:26-31 D '87

Fiel, Maxine Lucille
Starcast. See issues of Mademoiselle

Field, Leslie
about
The family jewels. R. Koenig. por *N Y* 20:40 O 19 '87

Field, Marshall, V
about
Divided we stand. P. Newcomb. il pors *Forbes* 140 Sp Issue:68-9 O 26 '87

Field, Michael
'Revolutionizing' a middle-class society. il *World Press Rev* 34:19-20 My '87

Field, Ron
about
Twenty years later . . . Ron Field revisits Cabaret. K. Grubb. il *Dance Mag* 61:66-7 O '87

Field, Sally
about
Sally Field: having the time of her life [cover story] E. Sherman. il pors *Ladies Home J* 104:70+ S '87
Sally Field, superstar [excerpt] J. Bonderoff. il pors *McCalls* 115:96-8+ O '87

Field, Ted
about
Divided we stand. P. Newcomb. il pors *Forbes* 140 Sp Issue:68-9 O 26 '87

Field, Tiffany
about
The play's the thing. R. J. Trotter. bibl (p63) il pors *Psychol Today* 21:26-34 Ja '87

Field athletics *See* Track and field athletics

Field borders
A case for hedgerows. P. Koepke. il *Rodale's Org Gard* 34:79-80 S '87

Field cameras *See* Cameras

Field-effect transistors *See* Transistors

Field experiments (Agriculture)
See also
Corn—Field experiments
Soybeans—Field experiments
Do your own variety trials. D. S. Wechsler. il por *Rodale's Org Gard* 34:61-4 F '87

Field glasses *See* Binoculars

Field guides *See* Nature literature

Field theory (Physics)
See also
Superstring theories (Physics)
Asymptotic freedom [adaptation of address, April 1986] D. J. Gross. il *Phys Today* 40:39-44 Ja '87
To the Big Bang and beyond. S. Odenwald. il *Astronomy* 15:90-5 My '87

Field work (Teacher training)
A look at field experiences for preservice teachers in the arts. B. L. Bennett. *Des Arts Educ* 89:12-13 S/O '87

Fieldhouse, Richard W.
Nuclear weapons at sea. bibl f il *Bull At Sci* 43:19-23 S '87

Fielding, Ellen Wilson
Career change. il por *Christ Today* 31:26-8 D 11 '87

Fielding, Eric
The United States wins Prague Quadrennial. il *Theatre Crafts* 21:32-3+ O '87

Fields, Debbi
Just once I wanted to hear that maybe I was different, individual, that I had something of my own to offer [excerpt from One smart cookie] il pors *Glamour* 85:122+ S '87

Fields, Kim
about
Kim Fields keeps busy with her TV career and college classes [cover story] A. Collier. il pors *Jet* 72:56-8 Ag 31 '87
Kim Fields sues ex-agent in a contract dispute. *Jet* 72:56 Ap 27 '87
Kim Fields sues ex-agent in a contract dispute [reprint from April 27, 1987 issue] *Jet* 72:24 My 11 '87

Fields, Richard
about
Richard Fields: catching his own rising star. il por *Bus Week* p59 Ag 17 '87

Fields, Shelby
about
Black doctor sentenced to life for death of white woman patient in Georgia. il por *Jet* 73:33 O 26 '87
Hold Georgia physician in death of white patient. *Jet* 72:4 My 11 '87

Fields, W. C., 1879-1946
about
Close encounters with W. C. Fields [excerpt from Days of wine and moguls] E. Freeman. il pors *Saturday Evening Post* 259:36-9 D '87

Fields, Magnetic *See* Magnetic fields

Fierce attachments [dance] See Dance reviews—Single works

Fiero (Automobile) *See* Sports cars

Fierstein, Harvey
about
Safe sex [drama] Reviews
N Y il 20:66+ Ap 20 '87. J. Simon
Nation 244:656+ My 16 '87. T. M. Disch
New Yorker 63:75 Ap 20 '87. E. Oliver
Vogue il por 177:44+ Je '87. D. DeNicolo

Fifth Avenue (New York, N.Y.)
Spring walk. *New Yorker* 63:32 My 11 '87

Fifth force (Physics)
The fifth force: pulling both ways. D. E. Thomsen. il *Sci News* 132:135 Ag 29 '87
Force of a different color. G. Greenwell. il *Sci Am* 257:26+ D '87
Gone with the wind? [work of Ephraim Fischbach and others] *Sci Am* 256:66-7 Ja '87
Intrepid filmmaker braves Greenland ice cap with an expedition searching for mysterious fifth force of the universe. C. R. Barnett. il *Smithsonian* 18:40+ N '87
May the force be with you [work of E. Fischbach] B. Schechter. il por *Omni* 9:36-8+ Mr '87
New clues to the fifth force and its source. D. E. Thomsen. *Sci News* 132:212 O 3 '87

Fifties (Decade) *See* Nineteen hundred and fifties

Fig trees
Grow figs anywhere. L. Reich. *Flower Gard* 31:29 F/Mr '87

Figes, Eva
about
PW interviews. M. Field. por *Publ Wkly* 231:56-7 Ja 16 '87

Figgie International Inc.
Figgie relives the go-go years. G. G. Marcial. *Bus Week* p132 Je 22 '87

Fighter pilots *See* Air pilots

Fighter planes *See* Airplanes, Military

Fighting *See* Boxing

Fighting (Psychology)
See also
Quarrels

Fighting among animals See Animals—Habits and behavior

Figs
See also
Cooking—Fruit

Figurative art
Exhibitions
Image in line [exhibit of drawings, lithographs and etchings by British figurative artists at Bernard Jacobson Gallery, New York City] J. Higgins. il *Art News* 86:166+ My '87

Figure, Human *See* Body, Human

Figure skating
Competitions
All that glittered was gold [U.S. Figure Skating Championships] E. M. Swift. il *Sports Illus* 66:63-5 F 16 '87
A championship in pure gold [B. Orser] il por *Macleans* 100:20-1 D 28 '87
Cool on ice [D. Thomas] A. Engeler. por *Vogue* 177:102+ Ag '87
Debi Thomas: on the cutting edge. J. Kaufman. il pors *Seventeen* 46:258-9+ Mr '87
Debi Thomas: skater extraordinaire. M. Kort. pors *Ms* 15:32-3 F '87
Dull blades [compulsories may be eliminated] M. Friedlander. il *Women's Sports Fitness* 9:68 N '87
Fire on ice [K. Witt and D. Thomas] E. Greenspan. il pors *Women's Sports Fitness* 9:22-5+ Mr '87
Guts and gold [Olympic gold medalists T. Albright and S. Hamilton] W. Bingham. il pors *Sports Illus* 67:57+ O 19 '87
Previewing the Games [Skate Canada] J. Howse. il *Macleans* 100:50-1 N 9 '87
Sweet victory [B. Orser wins World Figure Skating Championships] D. Jenish. il por *Macleans* 100:31 Mr 23 '87

Figure skating—Competitions—_cont._
Thou swell, thou Witt-y [world championships] E. M. Swift. il pors *Sports Illus* 66:20-3 Mr 23 '87
A track for all seasons [Calgary Olympic Oval] H. Quinn. il *Macleans* 100:44-5 O 5 '87
Woman to watch: Cindy Bortz [15 year old skater] M. Friedlander. il por *Women's Sports Fitness* 9:18 F '87

Figures, Michael A.
about
Black lawyer forces KKK to pay $7 million for lynching black, 19. T. S. Moore. il pors *Jet* 71:6-8 Mr 9 '87

Figures of speech
See also
Metaphor

Figurines
Art deco bronze and ivory figures [cover story] S. Jones. il *Antiques Collect Hobbies* 92:24-8 Ag '87
Game figurines [board and table games] R. R. Radcliff. il *Antiques Collect Hobbies* 92:32-3 D '87
Itty Bitty monster hits [animal figurines from United Design Corporation] J. Culpepper and S. Dark. il pors *Nations Bus* 75:58 Jl '87
The Staffordshire tithe pig group [figural grouping] S. Bagdade and A. Bagdade. il *Antiques Collect Hobbies* 92:27 Ap '87

Fiji
See also
Cruising—Fiji
Military assistance, American—Fiji
Nurses and nursing—Study and teaching—Fiji
Foreign relations
United States
See United States—Foreign relations—Fiji
Politics and government
The big chill settles over paradise [military coup] H. G. Chua-Eoan. il map *Time* 129:49 My 25 '87
The fight in Fiji [questions about U.S. involvement in coup] W. H. Schaap. *Nation* 244:707 My 30 '87
Methodists involved in Fiji coup. D. C. White. *Christ Century* 104:548-9 Je 17-24 '87
Now they'll do it their way [military coup fuels racial tensions] J. D. Reed. il *Time* 129:44 Je 1 '87
Of Fiji, race, and all that. B. Crozier. *Natl Rev* 39:26+ D 4 '87
A squall in the South Pacific. F. Willey. il map *Newsweek* 109:31 My 25 '87
Was the U.S. behind it? [Fiji coup] J. Wypijewski. il *Nation* 245:117-18+ Ag 15-22 '87
What's it all about, AAFLI? [discussion of August 15-22, 1987 article, Was the U.S. behind it?] J. Wypijewski. *Nation* 245:666+ D 5 '87
Race relations
See also
Church and race relations—Fiji
Now they'll do it their way [military coup fuels racial tensions] J. D. Reed. il *Time* 129:44 Je 1 '87
Of Fiji, race, and all that. B. Crozier. *Natl Rev* 39:26+ D 4 '87
Religious institutions and affairs
See also
Church and race relations—Fiji
Methodist Church—Fiji

Fiji Theater Company
Reviews:
Performances of Angels of Swedenborg at the Brooklyn Academy of Music and Kindness at La Mama E.T.C. S. Sommer. il *Dance Mag* 61:93-5 Ap '87

Fila pastry *See* Pastry
Filariasis
See also
Onchocerciasis
Filbert trees
Curly filbert won't grow straight. il *South Living* 22:77 Mr '87
Nuts for a hedge. J. Ruttle. il *Rodale's Org Gard* 34:56-7 O '87
File organization (Computers)
See also
Data structures (Computer science)
Sorting (Computers)
Better batch files through assembly language. W. J. Claff. bibl il *Byte* 12 no12 Sp Issue:159-60+ '87
A flexible data base [FileMaker Plus] J. Bell. il *Pers Comput* 11:234 Je '87
A link between operating systems [MacLinkPlus] A. C. Hixson. il *Pers Comput* 11:152 Ag '87
Multiuser programming. F. D. Davis. *Byte* 12:177-80+ Jl '87

PC software that helps you think. A. Field. il *Bus Week* p142 N 2 '87
Reconcilable differences: data transfer between mismatched disk formats. R. Cook. il *Pers Comput* 11:143+ D '87
Serious filing [RapidFile] C. O'Malley. *Pers Comput* 11:160 Jl '87
Transferring PFS files. R. Wallace. *Pers Comput* 11:197 Mr '87
Word processing file conversion [Word for Word] B. Sillery. il *Pers Comput* 11:156 Mr '87
Files, Recipe *See* Recipe boxes, files, etc.
Files and rasps
Using files (III). R. Capotosto. il *Pop Mech* 164:14 Ja '87
Filing systems
See also
Household records
Recipe boxes, files, etc.
Tape recordings—Filing systems
Filipino American business enterprises
Road to riches: cars for immigrants [auto dealership owned by E. Reodica] J. Foote. il por *Newsweek* 110:48 S 7 '87
Filipinos
United States
America: the 'great fish trap'. J. A. Chua. por *U S News World Rep* 103:16 O 5 '87
La fille mal gardée [ballet] *See* Ballet reviews—Single works
Filler, Martin, 1948-
"21" plus. il *House Gard* 159:24+ S '87
Aulenti assoluta. il pors *House Gard* 159:134-41+ Je '87
Chelsea chaste. il *House Gard* 159:156-61+ N '87
Dr. Freud's last dream. il *House Gard* 159:176-81+ F '87
Dresser's success. il *House Gard* 159:32+ N '87
Eminent domain. il *House Gard* 159:162-9+ Ap '87
Eye of his times. il *Archit Rec* 175:108-19 mid-S '87
Growing pains. il *Art Am* 75:14-19 Jl '87
The house as art [cover story] il por *House Gard* 159:152-61+ O '87
Individualist interiors. il por *House Gard* 159:64+ Mr '87
L.A. elevation. il *House Gard* 159:86-9+ Ja '87
Le Corbusier's true colors. il por *House Gard* 159:174-81+ My '87
London assurance. il *House Gard* 159:90-3+ Ja '87
The master builder. il *N Y Rev Books* 34:30-4 Ja 29 '87
Modern remastered. il *House Gard* 159:136-43+ Ja '87
A quiet place for art. il *House Gard* 159:74+ Jl '87
A shrine to wine. il *House Gard* 159:154-7+ S '87
Soane country. il por *House Gard* 159:172-9+ N '87
Thoroughly modern master. il *N Y Rev Books* 34:49-50+ D 17 '87
A visual wisdom. il *House Gard* 159:174-7+ Je '87
Fillers (in newspapers) *See* Newspaper fillers
Fillin-Yeh, Susan
Charles Sheeler's American interiors. bibl f il *Antiques* 131:828-37 Ap '87
Filling (Earthwork)
Environmental aspects
Are landfills a major threat to climate? [source of atmospheric methane; study by Paul J. Crutzen and H. G. Bingemer] J. Raloff. *Sci News* 131:150 Mr 7 '87
Filling materials
A new repair system stops wood rot [Minwax High Performance Wood Hardener and Filler] R. N. Hoffman. il *Workbench* 43:65 Jl/Ag '87
Fillings, Dental *See* Dental materials
Film *See* Motion pictures
Film adaptations *See* Motion picture adaptations
Film Arts Ltd.
A catalyst for Canadian film [D. Haig] A. Gould. il por *Macleans* 100:62 Mr 30 '87
Film audiences *See* Motion picture audiences
Film editing *See* Motion pictures—Editing
Film festivals *See* Motion picture festivals
Film Finances, Ltd.
Lights! Camera! Completion bond! R. Grover. il por *Bus Week* p50 Ag 24 '87
Film scripts *See* Motion picture scripts
Film speeds *See* Photography—Exposure
Film-to-video transfer system
Be a copycat with Sima's CopyKit. K. Geller-Shinn. il *Petersens Photogr Mag* 15:18 Ja '87
Converting home movies to video. J. Cohen. il *Consum Res Mag* 70:32-4 Jl '87

Film-to-video transfer system—*cont.*

Tamron Fotovix: the great slide to video transfer. D. Brooks. il *Petersens Photogr Mag* 15:66-7 Ja '87

Filming Othello [film] See Motion picture reviews—Single works

Films

See also
Photography—Films
Soap bubbles and films
Thin films

The microstructure of high-critical current superconducting films. P. Chaudhari and others. bibl f il *Science* 238:342-4 O 16 '87

Sticky threadlike substances that tend to draw themselves out into bead arrays. J. Walker. il *Sci Am* 257:108-11 S '87

Filmwriting See Motion picture authorship

Filofax plc

The little black book becomes a mania. M. Maremont. il por *Bus Week* p82 Ap 20 '87

Filters and filtration

See also
Air filters
Automobile engines—Filters
Light filters
Radio filters
Water filters and filtration
Water reuse

Fimrite, Ron

The A's new Stew can do. il pors *Sports Illus* 67:69-70 O 5 '87

Battered Birds flying high. il *Sports Illus* 66:38-41 My 18 '87

The battle of his life. il pors *Sports Illus* 67:72-80 Ag 24 '87

A Californian's lament: the Raiders and Lakers are not laid-back, thank you. il por *Sports Illus* 66:108 Je 1 '87

Facing the sad truth. il por *Sports Illus* 66:96 Mr 9 '87

Gussied up for the game. il por *Sports Illus* 67:116 N 2 '87

It was more than just a game. il *Sports Illus* 67 Sp Issue:106-10+ N 18 '87

It won't be an Indian summer. il *Sports Illus* 66:28-30+ Je 29 '87

Let's just play ball. por *Sports Illus* 66:154 Ap 6 '87

Nile Kinnick. il pors *Sports Illus* 67:112-24 Ag 31 '87

No.1 in his field. il pors *Sports Illus* 67:60-9 S 28 '87

No wonder he's hot. il pors *Sports Illus* 66:92-6+ Ja 12 '87

Of heroes, hellions and homer hankies. il *Sports Illus* 67:14-17 D 28 '87-Ja 4 '88

Padre with a passion. il pors *Sports Illus* 66:52-4+ My 4 '87

Pow! Wow! il pors *Sports Illus* 66:74-6+ Ap 6 '87

Reggie: an appreciation. il por *Sports Illus* 67:98 O 5 '87

Toronto's big brass Bell. il pors *Sports Illus* 67:24-6+ S 7 '87

Up, down and up again. il *Sports Illus* 66:42-6+ Ja 26 '87

Finance

See also
Asset-backed financing
Banks and banking
Bonds
Bonds, Government
Capital
Cash management
Church finance
Commerce
Credit
Debt
Debts, Public
Default (Finance)
Deflation (Finance)
Federal Reserve System (U.S.)
Financial institutions
Hedging (Finance)
Inflation (Finance)
Interest (Economics)
Investment trusts
Investments
Liquidity (Economics)
Money
Money markets
Municipal finance
Securities
Speculation

Stock exchanges
Stocks
Swap financing
Taxation
Television broadcasting—Financial programs
United States—Appropriations and expenditures
United States—Economic conditions
United States. Dept. of the Treasury
See also subhead Finance under various subjects

Figures of the week. See issues of Business Week through January 18, 1988

Finance. See issues of Business Week

Observations. A. Bladen. See occasional issues of Forbes

Terminology

The words of Wall Street. D. O. Relin. il *Sch Update* 120:15 D 18 '87

British Columbia

See also
Stock exchanges—Vancouver exchange

Touching the right-wing bases [M. Couvelier unveils new budget] P. C. Newman. il por *Macleans* 100:48 Mr 23 '87

California

Lotus Land isn't what it used to be [declining services] S. L. Hawkins. il *U S News World Rep* 103:23-4 O 19 '87

Canada

See also
Banks and banking—Canada
Budget—Canada
Canada—Appropriations and expenditures
Securities—Canada
Stock exchanges—Toronto exchange

There are no sacred trusts when you're broke [address, March 26, 1987] N. J. Patterson. *Vital Speeches Day* 53:484-7 Je 1 '87

Developing countries

See also
Loans, Bank—Developing countries
Loans, Foreign—Developing countries

France

See also
Securities—France
Stock exchanges—Paris exchange

Germany (West)

See also
Stock exchanges—Frankfurt exchange

Great Britain

See also
Bank of England
Securities—Great Britain
Stock exchanges—London exchange

Hong Kong

See also
Stock exchanges—Hong Kong exchange

Japan

See also
Securities—Japan
Stock exchanges—Tokyo exchange

How Japan is beating the profit squeeze [zaitech financing] A. Borrus. il *Bus Week* p60-1 My 11 '87

Japan Inc.'s new face [cover story; special section] il *Macleans* 100:22-8+ N 30 '87

Japan writes a new definition of zaitech: 'investor beware' [speculation] B. Buell. *Bus Week* p45 S 21 '87

Massachusetts

See also
Massachusetts. Industrial Finance Agency

Mexico

See also
Stock exchanges—Mexico exchange

Now, it's dollars crossing the Rio Grande in reverse migration. K. R. Sheets. *U S News World Rep* 102:45 Je 15 '87

Norway

See also
Securities—Norway

Ontario

An election budget. S. Aikenhead. il *Macleans* 100:11 Je 1 '87

Québec (Province)

Taking stock of the QSSP [Quebec Stock Savings Plan] B. Wallace. il *Macleans* 100:30 N 23 '87

Saskatchewan

Devine's tough talk. T. Tedesco. *Macleans* 100:47 Mr 23 '87

Hard times budget. D. Eisler. il *Macleans* 100:14-15 Je 22 '87

Singapore

See also
Stock exchanges—Singapore exchange

Finance—*cont.*

Texas

Clear as MUD [defaults of municipal utility district bonds] W. P. Barrett. il *Forbes* 139:96-8 Je 15 '87

West Virginia

Economic paralysis could stop Arch Moore cold [gubernatorial race] M. Rothman. il por *Bus Week* p86+ N 30 '87

Western Europe

See also
Securities—Western Europe

Finance, International

See also
Balance of payments
Banks and banking, International
Capital movements
Debts, External
Development banks
Eurobond market
Foreign exchange
Inflation (Finance)
International Finance Corporation
International Monetary Fund
Iranian-Iraqi War, 1980- —Economic aspects
Loans, Foreign
Money—International aspects
Paris Club
World Bank

All eyes on the U.S. Y. Messarovitch. *World Press Rev* 34:25-6 N '87

Finance and free trade. G. P. Brockway. il *New Leader* 70:10-11 F 9-23 '87

Financial markets [address, June 9, 1987] A. M. Solomon. *Vital Speeches Day* 53:725-9 S 15 '87

The global funny money game. H. M. Wachtel. il *Nation* 245:784-6+ D 26 '87-Ja 2 '88

A global new deal. G. Soros. il *N Y Rev Books* 34:52-3 Ag 13 '87

International financial reform [address, May 18, 1987] A. T. Lambert. *Vital Speeches Day* 53:689-91 S 1 '87

Our changing capital markets [address, April 30, 1987] D. B. Marron. *Vital Speeches Day* 53:586-8 Jl 15 '87

The perils of trading money for money. Y. Messarovitch. *World Press Rev* 34:46-7 Jl '87

Talk—and fear—of a recession. M. Blondet. il *World Press Rev* 34:24-5 N '87

Finance, Personal

See also
Aged—Economic conditions
Artists—Economic conditions
Bankruptcy
Black women—Economic conditions
Blacks—Economic conditions
Budget, Household
Children—Cost of raising
Credit
Credit counseling
Debt
Divorcees—Economic conditions
Estate planning
Farm women—Economic conditions
Financial statements
Home economics
Investments
Loans, Personal
Money—Psychological aspects
Presidential candidates—Economic conditions
Purchasing, Household
Saving and savings
Single people—Economic conditions
Single women—Economic conditions
Thrift
Wealth
Widows—Economic conditions
Women—Economic conditions
Youth—Economic conditions

1987 & beyond [special issue] il *Changing Times* 41:27-47+ Ja '87

After the crash [cover story; special section] il *Money* 16:74-80+ D '87

Americans and their money: 1987 [survey] W. C. Banks. il *Money* 16:211-12+ N '87

Building family wealth [cover story; special section] il *Money* 16:52-6+ O '87

[Column] J. B. Quinn. See occasional issues of Newsweek

Family finance. T. Tilling. See issues of Parents beginning July 1986

Home finances. H. Porter. See issues of The Family Handyman beginning September 1986

It's your money. R. Brady. See issues of Nation's Business beginning September 1983

Life at the edge (I). il *Consum Rep* 52:375-8 Je '87

Life at the edge (II). il *Consum Rep* 52:436-9 Jl '87

Life at the edge (III). il *Consum Rep* 52:504-7 Ag '87

Living high vs. living smart [Jordan and Gaston families] S. Seixas. il *Money* 16:128-32+ O '87

Marrying your money personalities [excerpt from The working woman financial advisor] B. Siverd. il *Work Woman* 12:78+ My '87

Model portfolio. See issues of Money beginning April 1983

Money. M. Daly. See issues of Better Homes and Gardens

Money anniversary issue. il *Money* Sp Issue:8-9+ Fall '87

Money helps. See issues of Money

Money management: 5 mistakes you don't have to make. D. J. Drucker. il por *Changing Times* 41:27-8+ Ag '87

Money news. K. Barrett and R. Greene. See issues of Ladies' Home Journal beginning March 1983

The Money readers' poll. C. Rubenstein. il *Money* 16:194-7 F '87

Money savers. il *Read Dig* 130:175-6 Mr '87

Money talks. R. Blodgett. See issues of McCall's

More for your money. B. G. Quint. See issues of Glamour

One family's finances. See issues of Money

Personal affairs. W. G. Flanagan. See issues of Forbes

Personal business. D. H. Dunn. See issues of Business Week

A question of money. See occasional issues of Consumer Reports beginning June 1983

$$$$-saver: money-gram. See issues of Good Housekeeping

Sizing up your finances [cover story; special section] il *U S News World Rep* 102:52-8+ Je 8 '87

Taking affairs into your own hands. il *U S News World Rep* 102:48 F 23 '87

Test your financial IQ [quiz] K. Barrett and R. Greene. il *Ladies Home J* 104:50+ N '87

Two paychecks: yours, mine, or ours? T. Segal. il *Bus Week* p116-17 Je 1 '87

Your money. G. W. Weinstein. See issues of Good Housekeeping

Your money and your life. L. Stains. See issues of Prevention (Emmaus, Pa.) beginning February 1987

Study and teaching

Do you really want to be rich? [mail order finance courses] M. Schiffres. il *Changing Times* 41:73-4+ O '87

Finance Committee *See* United States. Congress. Senate. Committee on Finance

Finance companies

See also
Commercial Credit Company
First Money Stores Corporation
General Motors Acceptance Corp.
Household International, Inc.
Leucadia National Corp.
Loan Depot Corporation
Money brokers

Acquisitions and mergers

Sanford Weill [takeover of Commercial Credit] C. S. Eklund. il por *Bus Week* Sp Issue:230 Ap 17 '87

Financial Accounting Standards Board

The death of universal life? L. Jereski and T. Pouschine. il *Forbes* 139:96 Ap 6 '87

Invisible debt [accounting treatment of unconsolidated subsidiaries] L. Jereski. il *Forbes* 139:68 F 9 '87

Victory at last? [inflation accounting] J. Andresky. il *Forbes* 139:65-6 Je 1 '87

Financial analysts *See* Investment advisers

Financial consultants *See* Investment advisers

Financial controls (Accounting) *See* Auditing—Internal control

Financial Corp. of America

Going once, going twice . . . [W. Popejoy's plan] T. Carson. il por *Bus Week* p102 O 5 '87

One deal away from being Mr. Megathrift [A. M. Frank of First Nationwide wants Financial Corp. of America] J. B. Levine. il por *Bus Week* p103-4 O 26 '87

Psst! Wanna buy the big daddy of thrifts? [Federal Home Loan Bank Board looking for a buyer] T. Carson. *Bus Week* p36 Mr 30 '87

Snake eyes again for Fincorp. J. A. Conway. il *Forbes* 140:10 Jl 27 '87

There may be a buyer for FCA. T. Carson. *Bus Week* p38-9 Je 8 '87

Financial futures *See* Interest rate futures
Financial institutions
  See also
    American Financial Corp.
    Banks and banking
    Black brokers
    Brokers
    Finance companies
    Insurance companies
    Investment trusts
    Savings and loan associations
    Savings banks
    Thrift institutions
The money game will get brutal [1990s] G. Hector.
  il *Fortune* 115:42-4 F 2 '87
        Acquisitions and mergers
A fight over Baldwin's ghost [Leucadia goes after
  PHLCorp] C. S. Eklund. il *Bus Week* p72 Mr 30
  '87
Kinder-Care may stick to its sitting. D. Foust. il por
  Bus Week p36 Jl 13 '87
Monarch buys its own insurance policy [acquisition of
  BankAmerica's investment management subsidiaries]
  K. H. Hammonds. il *Bus Week* p93+ S 7 '87
        International aspects
It won't stop with the Shearson deal [Nippon Life
  Insurance buys stake in Shearson Lehman Brothers]
  W. Glasgall and T. Aritake. il *Bus Week* p36 Ap
  6 '87
PaineWebber gets a little insurance from Japan [18%
  stake bought by Yasuda Mutual Life Insurance] C.
  Farrell. il *Bus Week* p118 D 14 '87
Picking up the pieces [Metropolitan Life's purchase offer
  for Principal Group's assets] J. Howse. il *Macleans*
  100:26-7 Ag 31 '87
Reckoning for a broker [First National Bank of Chicago
  considers purchasing stake in Wood Gundy] T. Tedesco.
  il *Macleans* 100:37 D 7 '87
Rising Sun on Wall Street: how Japanese money and
  firms are moving in. D. Burstein. il *N Y* 20:32-8
  Mr 2 '87
            Canada
A megamerger in the works [Wood Gundy and Royal
  Bank of Canada] P. C. Newman. il *Macleans* 100:46
  My 4 '87
        Investments
See Institutional investments
        Laws and regulations
            Canada
Banking on new business. D. Jenish. il *Macleans* 100:24-5
  Ag 31 '87
Making them do it his way [finance minister T. Hockin]
  P. C. Newman. il por *Macleans* 100:29 Ag 31 '87
Regulating deregulation. T. Fennell. il *Macleans* 100:36-7
  O 12 '87
            Peru
The bankers' hero [M. Vargas Llosa leads opposition
  to A. García Perez's efforts to nationalize financial
  institutions] A. Cockburn. *Nation* 245:402 O 17 '87
Judging García [nationalizing financial institutions] L.
  Rogers. il *World Press Rev* 34:46 O '87
Mario meets Crazy Horse [M. Vargas Llosa leads opposi-
  tion to government takeover] H. G. Chua-Eoan. il
  Time 130:30 S 7 '87
Peru's bad boy is starting to look like a desperate man
  [A. García Perez moves to nationalize financial
  institutions] J. Ryser. il por *Bus Week* p55 Ag 17
  '87
        Canada
  See also
    Central Capital Corporation
    Counsel Corporation
    First City Financial Corporation
    Laurentian Group Corporation
    Principal Group Ltd.
        Japan
The tidal wave that's sweeping international finance.
  B. Buell and others. il *Bus Week* p56-7 Jl 13 '87
        Pacific region
Bill Simon goes treasure-hunting in the Pacific. T. Carson
  and C. Debes. il por *Bus Week* p84-6 Mr 9 '87
William Simon's Pacific overtures. L. J. Davis. il pors
  N Y Times Mag p14-17+ D 27 '87
Financial institutions, International
  See also
    Banks and banking, International
    Development banks
    International Monetary Fund
    World Bank

Financial planners *See* Investment advisers
Financial post (Canada)
A new voice for business [Toronto Sun Publishing buys
  the Financial post] P. Best. il *Macleans* 100:37-8 O
  12 '87
Partners for the Post [Financial post venture by Toronto
  Sun Publishing to include London's Financial times]
  P. Best. por *Macleans* 100:40 O 19 '87
Financial printing industry *See* Printing industry
Financial Security Assurance
He does it with mirrors [J. Lopp] J. R. Hayes. il por
  Forbes 140:112-13 Ag 10 '87
Financial services
  See also
    American Express Co.
    American Financial Corp.
    Baldwin-United Corp.
    Brokers
    Computers—Financial services use
    Dean Witter Reynolds Inc.
    Disclosure Information Group
    Dreyfus Corp.
    Dun & Bradstreet Corp.
    First City Financial Corporation
    First Nationwide Financial Corp.
    Goldman, Sachs & Co.
    Gulf & Western, Inc.
    IDS Financial Services Inc.
    Investment advisers
    Merrill Lynch & Co., Inc.
    Primerica Corp.
    Sears, Roebuck and Co.
    Tax consultants
    Trade unions—Financial services
    Transamerica Corp.
    Visa International Inc.
Financial products of 1987: heavy hype, light returns.
  il *Money* 16:11 D '87
Financial services. M. Schifrin. il *Forbes* 139:126+ Ja
  12 '87
The money game will get brutal [1990s] G. Hector.
  il *Fortune* 115:42-4 F 2 '87
Financial statements
  See also
    Congressmen—Financial disclosure
    Corporation reports
    Public officers—Financial disclosure
    Securities—Prospectuses
Ready . . . set . . . go! Get organized. il *Changing
  Times* 41:63-5 Ja '87
So how am I doing? How to find out [use of income
  statements and balance sheets in personal finance]
  il *U S News World Rep* 102:54-5 Je 8 '87
Unreal accounting [operating earnings on income
  statements] S. N. Chakravarty. il *Forbes* 140:74+ N
  16 '87
Financial times
Partners for the Post [Financial post venture by Toronto
  Sun Publishing to include London's Financial times]
  P. Best. por *Macleans* 100:40 O 19 '87
Financing Corporation (U.S.)
Bonds away at the Bank Board. V. Cahan. *Bus Week*
  p102 O 5 '87
Finch, Chris
            about
Chris Finch, Madonna's high-stepping sidekick who's
  also a Penn pal. K. Hubbard. il por *People Wkly*
  28:106-7 Ag 17 '87
Finch, Christopher, 1939-
Art: European watercolors: luminous washes by
  nineteenth-century painters. il *Archit Dig* 44:140-5 S
  '87
Finch, Robert, 1943-
Bank swallows. il *Ctry J* 14:76-80 My '87
Fincher, Jack, 1930-
A gathering of legends. il *Read Dig* 131:49-53 Jl '87
El Jefe is building a desert 'ark' to keep zebras and
  other equids afloat. bibl (p184) il pors *Smithsonian*
  18:138-42+ My '87
The many faces of Audrey Anne Wilder. il *Read Dig*
  130:36-8+ Ap '87
"Operation Rx" sting. il *Read Dig* 131:36-41 S '87
Remembering a special student. il por *Read Dig*
  131:149-54 O '87
Finches
Finches fight greenhouse pests. R. L. Kohl. il *Rodale's
  Org Gard* 34:42-3+ Ag '87
In Brazil, bird songs aren't just cheap trills. M. Levinson.
  il *Int Wildl* 17:48-53 S/O '87

Finches—*cont.*
Natural selection: bird seeds of change [research by Peter R. Grant and H. Lisle Gibbs] R. Monastersky. il *Sci News* 131:373-4 Je 13 '87
Finder, Joseph
A male secretary. il *N Y Times Mag* p68 F 22 '87
Findlay Flint Glass Company
The Findlay Flint Glass Company. J. S. Measell. il *Antiques Collect Hobbies* 91:18-19 Ja '87
Findlen, Barbara
Gay marriage: lifting the bans. il *Ms* 15:29 F '87
Fine, John C.
Saint-Pierre Bay: Mont Pelée's underwater graveyard. il *Sea Front* 33:288-95 Jl/Ag '87
Fine, Larry, 1950-
In tune with the right piano [excerpt from The piano book; cover story] il *Consum Res Mag* 70:11-15 S '87
Fine, Michael
about
Wolfe and Fine form mass market company. pors *Publ Wkly* 231:20 My 22 '87
Fine, Ralph Adam, 1941-
"Plea bargaining should be abolished" [condensed from Escape of the guilty] il *Read Dig* 131:233-4+ N '87
Fines (Penalties)
See also
Tax penalties
Traffic tickets
Finger, Bill
History for sale. il *Americana* 15:50-4 My/Je '87
Finger, Harold B.
Celebrating 30 years of nuclear energy. il *USA Today (Periodical)* 116:52-4 N '87
Nuclear reactions [discussion of December 1986 article, First word] *Omni* 9:15 Ap '87
Finger joints *See* Joints (Carpentry)
Finger Lakes Community College *See* Community College of the Finger Lakes
Finger Lakes region (N.Y.)
See also
Geology—Finger Lakes region (N.Y.)
Description and travel
New York's Finger Lakes. D. Gallo. il *Travel Holiday* 168:44-9 Jl '87
Fingernail biting *See* Nail biting
Fingernail manicuring *See* Manicuring
Fingernails *See* Nails (Anatomy)
Fingerprints
Can fingerprints be clues to disease? P. Gadsby. il *Good Housekeep* 204:275 My '87
Fingerprinting only black males in town sparks tension, fear [Homestead, Pa.] L. Ransom. il *Jet* 72:12-14+ S 21 '87
Homestead NAACP chided on fingerprint support. il *Jet* 73:7 S 28 '87
The search for a rapist [blacks asked to submit to fingerprinting in Homestead, Pa.] il *Newsweek* 110:42 S 14 '87
Trying to trace a rapist [fingerprinting of blacks in Homestead, Pa.] F. Trippett. il *Time* 130:28 S 14 '87
Fingerprints, DNA *See* DNA fingerprints
Finishes and finishing
See also
Furniture—Finishes and finishing
Isabel O'Neil Foundation for the Art of the Painted Finish
Wood—Finishes and finishing
Finishing sanders *See* Sanding and sanding equipment
Finite element method
ANSYS-PC/Linear and MSC/pal 2. N. Baran. il *Byte* 12:205-6+ N '87
Fink, Donald E.
Editorial. See issues of Aviation Week & Space Technology beginning October 28, 1985
Fink, Ida
A scrap of time [story]; tr. by Madeline G. Levine and Francine Prose. *New Yorker* 63:32-4 My 25 '87
Fink, Leslie
What a day it was! il *Women's Sports Fitness* 9:75-6 My '87
Fink, Robert A.
Drought: sure signs in Merkle, Texas [poem] *Ctry J* 14:62 Ag '87
Fink (Term)
Goons and ginks and company finks. W. Safire. il *N Y Times Mag* p18+ N 1 '87

Finkel, Bernie
about
Obituary
Road Track il por 38:38 F '87. J. Dinkel
Finkel, Donald
Joy ride [poem] *New Repub* 196:47 F 9 '87
This is where I draw the line [poem] *New Repub* 196:40 Ap 13 '87
Finkelson, Allen
about
Two lawyers turning Cravath into a force in takeovers. M. Frons. pors *Bus Week* p103 Ja 26 '87
Finkelstein, Edward S., 1925-
about
The year's best sale at Macy's: itself. A. Dunkin. il por *Bus Week* p136-7 Ja 12 '87
Finkelstein, Michael O.
A shared fate. *Nation* 244:599 My 9 '87
Finkielstain, Jacobo
about
Closely watched banks: one that got away. F. A. Miller and R. A. Kessler. il por *Bus Week* p108 O 19 '87
Finland
See also
Country estates—Finland
Helsinki (Finland)
Music—Finland
Public health—Finland
Description and travel
Five days in Finland at the age of fifty-five. J. Updike. *New Yorker* 63:86-8+ S 28 '87
Land of 'green winter'—and epic heroes. A. Hamilton. il *World Press Rev* 34:62 My '87
Religious institutions and affairs
See also
Monasteries—Finland
Orthodox Eastern Church—Finland
Finlay, Ian Hamilton, 1925-
about
Neoclassical rearmament. C. Gintz. il *Art Am* 75:110-17 F '87
Finley, Mitch
The last thing teens need is birth control [with readers' comments] *U S Cathol* 52:14-19 Ap '87
My children's father: a self-portrait for Father's Day. *America* 156:499-500 Je 20-27 '87
Real Christians pray every day [with readers' comments] *U S Cathol* 52:14-19 F '87
Stop patting us laypeople on the head [with readers' comments] *U S Cathol* 52:13-19 Jl '87
Finley, Robert B., Jr.
The value of research collections. *BioScience* 37:92 F '87
Finley, Kumble, Wagner, Heine, Underberg, Manley, Myerson & Casey
And now stay tuned for N.Y. law. L. J. Tell. il *Bus Week* p38 S 21 '87
Breaking up. A. A. Lappen. il *Forbes* 140:8 D 14 '87
Fall of a rainmaker [S. Kumble] D. Fanning. il por *Forbes* 139:68+ Je 1 '87
Finn, Charles Albert
about
The new bayonet stabs, slices and even dices, thanks to Mickey Finn. il por *People Wkly* 27:79 Ja 5 '87
Finn, Chester E., 1944-
A call for radical changes in educational delivery. *Educ Dig* 52:2-5 Ja '87
about
'What do our 17-year-olds know?' assesses the failure of American high school education. *Publ Wkly* 232:134 S 18 '87
Finn, Neil
about
Take heart from Neil Finn's Crowded House. E. Miller. il por *Seventeen* 46:80-1 Jl '87
Finn, Susan Calvert
about
A life in nutrition. B. Lindeman. il por *50 Plus* 27:6 My '87
Finn, Thomas D'Arcy
about
Exit of the spy master. H. Mackenzie. por *Macleans* 100:25 S 21 '87
Finn, Huckleberry (Fictional character) *See* Huckleberry Finn (Fictional character)
Finnegan, William
Getting the story (I). *New Yorker* 63:31-4+ Jl 13 '87
Getting the story (II). *New Yorker* 63:40-2+ Jl 20 '87

Finney, Albert
about
'The opportunity to live several lives' [interview] A. P. Sanoff. por *U S News World Rep* 103:63 D 14 '87
Finney, Nikky
On wings made of gauze [poem] *Essence* 17:120 Ap '87
Finnish baths *See* Sauna
Finnish house decoration *See* House decoration, Finnish
Finster, Howard
about
So outside he's in, Howard Finster paints what he sees—visions of angels, devils and Elvis. D. Van Biema. il pors *People Wkly* 28:109+ Jl 6 '87
Finta, Imre
about
Accusations of war crimes. M. Gray. *Macleans* 100:31 D 21 '87
La finta giardiniera [opera] *See* Mozart, Wolfgang Amadeus, 1756-1791
Fiords *See* Fjords
Fiori, Pamela
Travel & leisure. il *Writer* 100:30-1 Ap '87
Fire
See also
Combustion
Flames
Spontaneous human combustion
Fire [drama] *See* Ledoux, Paul
Fire alarms
See also
Fire detectors
Ella hits high note and trips fire alarm [E. Fitzgerald] il por *Jet* 72:22 Mr 30 '87
Fire ant stings *See* Insect bites and stings
Fire companies *See* Fire departments
Fire departments
See also
Firefighters
Gaithersburg (Md.)—Firefighters
New York (N.Y.)—Firefighters
Where there's smoke, there's a fire drill! [volunteer firemen] R. Fee. il *Success Farm* 85:56K N '87
Fire detectors
Alarming wallpaper [fire sensing vinyl wall coverings introduced by B. F. Goodrich] il *Prevention* 39:14 Mr '87
How to properly install and test smoke detectors. il *Workbench* 43:53 Ja/F '87
Optical fire spotter [Room Sentry] D. Petraglia. il *Pop Sci* 230:65 Ap '87
Toxic gas and smoke alarm [Ultralert System] R. A. Marcus. il *Pop Sci* 231:44 O '87
Fire drills
Where there's smoke, there's a fire drill! [volunteer firemen] R. Fee. il *Success Farm* 85:56K N '87
Fire ecology
See also
Forest fires—Controlled fires
Fire engines
Testing
Bringing up the rear [riding tillerman on hook and ladder] J. Miller. il *Car Driv* 33:96-7+ D '87
Fire escapes
How to escape a fire. S. L. Englebardt. *Read Dig* 131:163-4+ Ag '87
A net plus for safety, Ralph Baker's Life Chute may save lives in high-rise fires. J. Calio. il por *People Wkly* 28:107-8 Jl 13 '87
Pet survival tips: critical steps for families and pets. V. Webster. *Better Homes Gard* 65:83 Ap '87
Fire extinction
See also
Firefighters
Equipment
See also
Fire engines
Fire extinguishers
Fire sprinklers
Fire extinguishers
Halon provides extinguishing gains [aircraft] il *Aviat Week Space Technol* 126:137 F 9 '87
Fire insurance *See* Insurance, Fire
Fire Island (N.Y.)
See also
Architecture, Domestic—Fire Island (N.Y.)
Fire Island National Seashore (N.Y.)
Forest in the dunes [Sunken Forest] M. J. Mooney. il map *Sea Front* 33:120-7 Mr/Ap '87

Fire making
Light my fire. *Consum Res Mag* 70:16 Je '87
Fire prevention
See also
Airplanes—Fires and fire prevention
Airplanes, Jet—Fires and fire prevention
Automobiles—Fires and fire prevention
Boats and boating—Fires and fire prevention
Fire departments
Forest fires—Prevention and control
Houses—Fires and fire prevention
Lightning protection
Skyscrapers—Fires and fire prevention
Textile fabrics, Fireproof
Fire! New ways to prevent it. G. Kolata. il *Science* 235:281-2 Ja 16 '87
Holiday safety. M. S. Dolan. *Consum Res Mag* 70:2 D '87
Research
See Fire research
Fire rescues *See* Rescue work
Fire research
Chemistry of molecular growth processes in flames. K. C. Smyth and J. H. Miller. bibl f il *Science* 236:1540-6 Je 19 '87
Radical dangers up in smoke [preventing free radical damage to fire victims; research by Thomas M. Lachocki and others] S. Weisburd. *Sci News* 132:169 S 12 '87
Researchers climb inside of the fire to tweak the flame. B. Fellman. bibl (p229) il *Smithsonian* 18:70-2+ O '87
Fire resisting materials
See also
Textile fabrics, Fireproof
Fire safety
Fire safety trailer in Walnut Creek. il *Sunset* 179:124 O '87
Fire sprinklers
Bringing fire sprinklers into the home. S. Budiansky. il *U S News World Rep* 103:82 O 19 '87
Fire testing *See* Fire research
Fire trucks *See* Fire engines
Firearms
See also
Air guns
Cartridges
Gunstocks
Machine guns
Pistols
Rifles
Shotguns
The charge of the green brigade [new guns from Remington] B. Brister. il *Field Stream* 91:99-101 Mr '87
Confessions of a gun swapper. J. Bashline. il *Field Stream* 92:74+ Jl '87
New guns for 1987. J. Carmichel. il *Outdoor Life* 180:80-1+ Jl '87
Sons of guns [love of guns in Texas] W. Saletan. *New Repub* 196:11-13 Mr 2 '87
Collectors and collecting
Romantic relics of the wild, wild West. R. W. King. il *Bus Week* p88-9 F 2 '87
Decoration
A canvas of steel [wildlife gun engravings] R. L. Wilson and E. R. Ricciuti. il *Audubon* 89:100-9 N '87
Exhibitions
SHOT '87: an embarrassment of riches [Shooting, Hunting, and Outdoor Trade Show] B. Brister. il *Field Stream* 91:91-2+ Ap '87
History
The good old stuff. J. Bashline. il *Field Stream* 92:64+ S '87
Laws and regulations
Battle over the plastic gun. G. Hackett. il *Newsweek* 109:31 Je 1 '87
Crime and the Constitution [gun control] D. O. Relin and C. Lawrence. il *Sch Update* 120:10-11 D 4 '87
Endangered tradition. D. E. Petzal. See issues of Field & Stream beginning March 1985
Florida's new crop of pistol packers [gun controls lifted] T. Gest. il *U S News World Rep* 103:16 O 12 '87
A lethal lucky charm [Florida gun laws] M. McIver. il *Macleans* 100:59-60 O 12 '87
Local gun controls bite the dust [Florida] T. Gest. il *U S News World Rep* 102:14-15 My 25 '87
The NRA is right [need to ban handguns] J. Sugarmann. il *Wash Mon* 19:11-15 Je '87
Pistol packers [Florida] C. Garcia. il *Time* 130:28 S 28 '87

Firearms—Laws and regulations—cont.
Prentice Rasheed jabs Florida's new gun law. il por *Jet* 73:18 O 19 '87
Singer Wilson Pickett convicted of gun charge. il por *Jet* 72:56 Jl 20 '87
Wyatt Earp comes to the Sunshine State [Florida gun law] *Newsweek* 110:42 O 12 '87
Security measures
Firearms security. J. Elder. il *Field Stream* 92:78 D '87
Sights
Fore-and-aft scope mounting. J. Carmichel. il *Outdoor Life* 180:42-3 D '87
High-class glass. D. E. Petzal. il *Field Stream* 92:82+ Jl '87
The latest and best riflescopes. J. Carmichel. il *Outdoor Life* 179:20+ My '87
Makeshift marksmanship. N. Strung. *Field Stream* 92:113 N '87
Out of sight, out of luck. B. Woods. il *Mother Earth News* 107:96-8 S/O '87
Sighting in made easy [adjusting the scope by holding rifle in a vise] T. Clauss. il *Outdoor Life* 179:112 Ja '87
Firearms industry
See also
Remington Arms Co., Inc.
Smith & Wesson
Acquisitions and mergers
International aspects
A raider's new world [G. Hutchings' bid for Smith & Wesson] M. Maremont. il por *Bus Week* p49-50 Je 15 '87
Fireballs *See* Meteors
Firefighters
See also
Cooking by firefighters
Gaithersburg (Md.)—Firefighters
New York (N.Y.)—Firefighters
Inferno on the interstate [fireman J. P. Sullivan saves five victims of traffic accident] S. Kelly. il *Read Dig* 130:106-11 Ja '87
A just war [fighting forest fire in northern Calif.] J. D. Hull. il *Time* 130:23-4+ O 26 '87
Nutrition
With hydraulic skillets and enormous toasters, OK's caterers feed the fight against forest fires [feeding firefighters in the West] M. Grant. il *People Wkly* 28:47-8 S 21 '87
Ukraine
An eyewitness to disaster, Soviet fireman Leonid Telyatnikov recounts the horror of Chernobyl. D. Grogan. il por *People Wkly* 28:57-8+ O 5 '87
Fireflea sexual behavior *See* Sexual behavior—Crustaceans
Firefleas *See* Ostracods
Fireflies
Southern lights. H. Middleton. il *South Living* 22:22+ Ag '87
Fireman's Fund Insurance Company
Most improved. il *Forbes* 139:155 Ja 12 '87
Fireplace alcoves *See* Alcoves
Fireplaces
See also
Chimneys
Mantels
10 most-often asked questions about fireplaces. J. Gaynor. il *Home Mech* 83:66+ S '87
Arizona firebox sculpture [cover story] il *Sunset* 178:128-9 Mr '87
Fired with efficiency. S. Maviglio. bibl il *Home Mech* 83:60-2+ S '87
Fireplace facelift. N. Cooper. il *Home Mech* 83:48-9 D '87
Fireplace hearth: update it with new tile! [ceramic tile] D. Kassler. il *Workbench* 43:88-9 Ja/F '87
Fireplace hides its history. il *South Living* 22:189 Ap '87
Fireplace without a chimney; Replace that rusty fireplace liner. A. C. West. il *Pop Sci* 231:46 O '87
Foolproof fireplace construction [Thermal Energy Storage Systems fireplaces] S. Maviglio. il *Home Mech* 83:52+ N '87
Habits of the hearth: symbolism and style meet at the fireplace. M. Hampton. il *House Gard* 159:42-3+ Ja '87
The hearth is a marble triangle. il *Sunset* 178:81 Ja '87
The hearth that's more. il *Sunset* 178:172 My '87
Homemade brick hearth for a wood stove. J. Collins. il *Workbench* 43:56-9 N/D '87

Keep the home fires burning—safely. S. J. Forbis. il *Read Dig* 131:105-8 D '87
New fireplace saves space. il *South Living* 22:172-3 Mr '87
Open hearth surgery. A. Rooze. il *Fam Handyman* 37:12 N '87
Today's ceramic tiles warm the hearth. il *Better Homes Gard* 65:27 O '87
Equipment
Burning sensations [product picks from the Wood Heating Alliance Show] S. Maviglio. il *Home Mech* 83:56-9 S '87
Safety devices and measures
How to use your fireplace and woodburning stove—safely. A. Arnott. il *McCalls* 114:103 F '87
Fireproof textiles *See* Textile fabrics, Fireproof
Fires
See also
Airplanes—Fires and fire prevention
Airplanes, Jet—Fires and fire prevention
Airplanes, Military—Fires and fire prevention
Arson
Automobiles—Fires and fire prevention
Boats and boating—Fires and fire prevention
Burning of land
Fire prevention
Forest fires
Hotels, motels, etc.—Fires and fire prevention
Houses—Fires and fire prevention
Libraries—Fires and fire prevention
Museums—Fires and fire prevention
Skyscrapers—Fires and fire prevention
Subways—Fires and fire prevention
Tires, Automobile—Fires and fire prevention
Rescue work
See Rescue work
Fireside Books
Fireside signs Spike Lee to two-book contract. *Publ Wkly* 231:59 Je 12 '87
Firestone, Harvey Samuel, 1868-1938
about
The U.S. Business Hall of Fame. A. M. Louis. il por *Fortune* 115:106 Ap 13 '87
Firestone, Roy
about
Cable's Mr. Capable. W. Taaffe. il por *Sports Illus* 66:77 F 23 '87
Firestone Tire & Rubber Co.
John Nevin rescued Firestone—his way. Z. Schiller. il por *Bus Week* p96+ My 11 '87
Rubber revelations [visit to Firestone's International Technical Center in Rome] T. Assenza. il *Car Driv* 33:22 Ag '87
A tiremaker lags. S. Koepp. il *Time* 129:48 F 16 '87
Firewood storage *See* Woodbins, racks, etc.
Fireworks
Accidents
Fireworks: don't let safety go up in smoke. il *Curr Health 2* 13:24-5 My '87
Photographs and photography
Fireworks! D. Wilhelm. il *Petersens Photogr Mag* 16:22-3 Jl '87
Firing of clergymen *See* Clergy—Dismissal
Firing of employees *See* Employees—Dismissal
Firing of executives *See* Black executives—Dismissal; Executives—Dismissal
Firing of public officers *See* Public officers—Dismissal
Firing of teachers *See* Teachers—Dismissal
Firing of women executives *See* Women executives—Dismissal
Firing ranges *See* Shooting ranges
Firmage, Charles K.
Art discoveries and resurrections. See issues of Antiques & Collecting Hobbies beginning July 1987
Firmin, Robert L.
about
IPOs: now only the best and the brightest need apply. K. H. Hammonds. il *Bus Week* p37-8 N 30 '87
First aid for animals
See also
Hunting dogs—Care
Emergency care for pets. P. Spencer. il *Better Homes Gard* 65:42+ Ag '87
First aid for pets. D. McRae and M. Smith. il *FDA Consum* 21:24-7 Je '87
First aid in illness and injury
See also
Ambulance service
Burns and scalds
Heimlich maneuver
Red Cross

First aid in illness and injury—See also—*cont.*
Resuscitation
Common injuries and what to do about them. D. Sobel. il *Good Housekeep* 204:91-4 Mr '87
Emergency! Take first-aid action. R. Mason. il *Teen* 31:48+ Mr '87
First aid & safety. See issues of Current Health 2
Four first-aid moves that could save your life. J. Meade. il *Prevention* 39:27-8+ Ja '87
Fundamental first aid for the hunter. S. Netherby. il *Field Stream* 92:86+ N '87
Redbook's first-aid guide for summer. il *Redbook* 169:125-8 Je '87
Rx for pain: RICE. D. M. Podolsky. *Good Housekeep* 204:112 My '87
Summer first-aid guide [excerpt from The healthy traveler] B. Weinhouse. *Ladies Home J* 104:34+ Je '87
The summer "ouch" book. il *Good Housekeep* 205:67+ Jl '87
Summer safety & first aid. C. L. Carney. il *Parents* 62:96-8+ Jl '87

First aid kits *See* Medical equipment
First American Bank & Trust (North Palm Beach, Fla.)
Cool deal [stock price] T. Jaffe. *Forbes* 140:310 S 7 '87
First Bank System Inc.
Take this art and . . . [visual arts program] J. Herzfeld. il *Art News* 86:12+ Ap '87
First Boston Corp.
A deal that would get Allegheny out of the spotlight [leveraged buyout] M. Rothman and G. L. Miles. il *Bus Week* p34 Mr 23 '87
How the spike in interest rates snagged First Boston [Treasury bond options] D. Zigas. *Bus Week* p30-1 Je 29 '87
First Capital Holdings Corp.
Instant tycoon [R. Weingarten, chairman] J. Heins. il por *Forbes* 139:38+ Mr 23 '87
First City Bancorporation of Texas, Inc.
A billion-dollar bailout, Texas style [A. R. Abboud takeover] K. R. Sheets. il por *U S News World Rep* 103:54 S 21 '87
Bob Abboud is back in banking—but what a bank [taking over First City with help from the FDIC] T. Vogel. il por *Bus Week* p30 S 21 '87
Here comes the cavalry [A. R. Abboud takeover] G. Bock. il por *Time* 130:52 S 21 '87
A new Abboud? N. J. Perry. il por *Fortune* 116:192 O 12 '87
First City Financial Corporation
Belzbergs on the prowl. T. Fennell. il *Macleans* 100:32 Je 29 '87
First Committee (United Nations) *See* United Nations. Political and Security Committee
First day covers (Philately) *See* Covers (Philately)
First days of school *See* School children—Adjustment
The first Eden: the Mediterranean world and man [television program] See Television program reviews—Single works
First editions *See* Rare books
First Executive Corp.
Fred Carr buys some insurance [ICH acquires greater share of First Executive Corp.] T. Carson. *Bus Week* p36 O 26 '87
First frontier [television program] See Television program reviews—Single works
First Interstate Bancorp
The man who would be boss at BankAmerica [J. Pinola] R. E. Norton. il pors *Fortune* 115:88-90+ F 16 '87
Suddenly, First Interstate looks a whole lot slimmer. T. Carson. il por *Bus Week* p126 N 9 '87
Who needs BankAmerica? Not Joe Pinola. T. Carson. il por *Bus Week* p46 F 23 '87
First Investors Corp.
Door-to-door funds. M. Schifrin and L. R. Walbert. il *Forbes* 140:156+ S 21 '87
First Jersey Securities, Inc.
Trying not to be a second First Jersey [sale of retail brokerage to be named Sherwood Investors] C. Welles. il por *Bus Week* p44 Ja 12 '87
First Ladies *See* Presidents—Wives
First Money Stores Corporation
Cashing in on money stores. T. Gallant-Stokes. il *Black Enterp* 17:17 My '87
First National Bank of Chicago
Career makeover: from secretary to assistant vice president [S. Coe's career] il por *Glamour* 85:84+ Ja '87
Reckoning for a broker [considers purchasing stake in Wood Gundy] T. Tedesco. il *Macleans* 100:37 D 7 '87

First Nations Financial Project
America's new entrepreneurs [cover story] R. J. Margolis. por *New Leader* 70:11-12 N 30 '87
First Nationwide Financial Corp.
One deal away from being Mr. Megathrift [A. M. Frank of First Nationwide wants Financial Corp. of America] J. B. Levine. il por *Bus Week* p103-4 O 26 '87
First Nationwide Savings, A Federal Savings & Loan Assoc.
Attention, savers! K Mart wants you. J. B. Levine. il *Bus Week* p81-2 Ja 19 '87
First Pennsylvania Corp.
Junk bond substitute? [stock price] T. Jaffe. *Forbes* 139:182 Mr 23 '87
First person singular [television program] See Television program reviews—Single works
First Union Corp.
How 'Fast Eddie' is pulling First Union out ahead [E. Crutchfield] S. Ticer. il por *Bus Week* p142+ Mr 23 '87
This gorilla can putt. J. Willoughby. *Forbes* 140:154 O 19 '87
Firstrust Savings Bank
How to steal an S&L—legally [Green family buyout] B. D. Fromson. il *Fortune* 116:57-8+ O 12 '87
Firtel, Richard A.
(jt. auth) See Gomer, Richard H., and Firtel, Richard A.
Fisch, Arline
Goldsmiths of Veneto. il *Am Craft* 47:36-41+ D '87/Ja '88
Fischbach, Ephraim
about
May the force be with you. B. Schechter. il por *Omni* 9:36-8+ Mr '87
Fischbach Corporation
Every man for himself [V. Posner buys controlling block of APL Corp. from NVF Co.] A. Sloan. il por *Forbes* 139:37-8 Je 29 '87
Victor reverts to type [V. Posner] J. A. Conway. por *Forbes* 139:8 Mr 9 '87
Fischell, Rosalind
Chine de commande. il *House Gard* 159:70+ D '87
Fischer, Arlene
"An accident destroyed my face". il pors *Redbook* 169:36+ O '87
Babies in pain. il *Redbook* 169:124-5+ O '87
"I never thought it could happen to me". il *Redbook* 169:120-2+ Je '87
Rape strikes the suburbs. il *Read Dig* 131:59-62 S '87
Surgery: always get a second opinion. *Redbook* 168:94-5+ Ja '87
What is your body trying to tell you? *Redbook* 168:89-91+ Mr '87
Fischer, Eric A., and Petersen, Chris W.
The evolution of sexual patterns in the seabasses. bibl f il *BioScience* 37:482-9 Jl/Ag '87
Fischer, Frederick J.
Graduation-contingent student aid: fighting the high costs of dropping out. il *Change* 19:40-7 N/D '87
Fischer, Karl
about
Profiting in the third world. il por *U S News World Rep* 102:61-2 My 11 '87
Fischer, Raymond L.
Suffer the little children: the FCC does it again. il *USA Today (Periodical)* 115:84-6 Ja '87
To be or not to be commercial?—That is the question. *USA Today (Periodical)* 116:89-91 S '87
Fischer, Theodore
How to ask for a raise—and get it! A 7-point plan for talking to the boss. *McCalls* 114:122 Ja '87
Your child's college education: how to afford the cost. il *McCalls* 114:21+ Ap '87
Fischer-Dieskau, Dietrich, 1925-
about
Lieder evenings worth remembering . . . P. Moor. il por *High Fidel* 37:61-2 Je '87
Fischl, Eric
about
Eric Fischl at Mary Boone. S. Tillim. il *Art Am* 75:214-15 Ap '87
The four brushmen of the apocalypse. L. Hirschberg. il pors *Esquire* 107:76-84+ Mr '87
Fischler, Stan
Chico Resch. il por *Sport Mag* 78:94-5 D '87
Fischli, Peter, 1952-
about
Masters of the glum "eureka!". C. Ratcliff. il *Art Am* 75:98-101 Ja '87

Fischman, Joshua
  Type A on trial. bibl (p64) il *Psychol Today* 21:42-4+
    F '87
  (jt. auth) See Chance, Paul, and Fischman, Joshua
Fise, Mary Ellen R.
  (jt. auth) See Gillis, Jack, and Fise, Mary Ellen R.
Fish, Allan See Marioni, Tom, 1937-
Fish, Hamilton, III
          about
  Change and continuity. *Nation* 245:73 Ag 1-8 '87
  The Fish family feud. M. Kaus. il pors *Newsweek* 110:18
    Ag 24 '87
Fish, Hamilton, 1888-
          about
  The Fish family feud. M. Kaus. il pors *Newsweek* 110:18
    Ag 24 '87
Fish, O. A.
  The day Challenger exploded. il *Read Dig* 130:67-9 Ja
    '87
Fish, Ray
  Medical technology in the 21st century. il *Radio-Electron*
    58:112-14 My '87
Fish, Shirley
          about
  The long agony of Shirley Fish. G. Bennett. il por
    McCalls 114:148-50 Ap '87
Fish
      See also
    Aquariums
    Cannibalism—Fish
    Coelacanths
    Electric organs in fish
    Eye—Fish
    Fisheries
    Hearing—Fish
    Nervous system—Fish
    Vision—Fish
      See also names of fish
  The strange case of the freshwater marine fishes. D.
    Perrine. il *Sea Front* 33:114-19 Mr/Ap '87
          Breeding
      See also
    Fish culture
          Classification
  Hatracks and theories [L. Agassiz's Research on fossil
    fishes] S. J. Gould. il *Nat Hist* 96:12+ Mr '87
          Coloration
    See Color of fish
          Contamination
    See Fish contamination
          Diseases and pests
  Clownfish larvae with sickle cells [work of Louis
    Leibovitz] *Sea Front* 33:223-4 My/Je '87
  Propagation in cell culture of the dinoflagellate
    Amyloodinium, an ectoparasite of marine fishes. E.
    J. Noga. bibl f il *Science* 236:1302-4 Je 5 '87
          Ecology
      See also
    Fish populations
          Food and feeding
  Fewer barnacles [rockfish prey on barnacle larvae in
    California kelp forest; research by Steven D. Gaines
    and Jonathan Roughgarden] *Sea Front* 33:384-5 S/O
    '87
  Fish in offshore kelp forests affect recruitment to intertidal
    barnacle populations [rockfish] S. D. Gaines and J.
    Roughgarden. bibl f il *Science* 235:479-81 Ja 23 '87
  A major food web component in the Orinoco River
    channel: evidence from planktivorous electric fishes.
    J. G. Lundberg and others. bibl f il *Science* 237:81-3
    Jl 3 '87
  Wind speed and mortality rate of a marine fish, the
    northern anchovy (Engraulis mordax). R. M. Peterman
    and M. J. Bradford. bibl f il *Science* 235:354-6 Ja
    16 '87
          Habits and behavior
      See also
    Sexual behavior—Fish
          Larvae
      See Larvae
          Migration
      See also
    Salmon
          Reproduction
      See also
    Spawning
  The evolution of sexual patterns in the seabasses. E.
    A. Fischer and C. W. Petersen. bibl f il *BioScience*
    37:482-9 Jl/Ag '87

          Antarctic regions
  Sensory tuning of lateral line receptors in Antarctic fish
    to the movements of planktonic prey [teleosts] J. C.
    Montgomery and J. A. Macdonald. bibl f il *Science*
    235:195-6 Ja 9 '87
      Great Barrier Reef (Australia)
  Super grouper. il map *Natl Geogr World* 145:34-5 S
    '87
          Hawaii
  Deep questions about shallow seas [diversity of species]
    K. E. F. Watt. il *Nat Hist* 96:60-5 Jl '87
Fish, Deep sea
      See also
    Tuna fish
Fish, Dressing of
  Fast field dressing. N. Strung. il *Field Stream* 92:156
    My '87
  Fish: the ultimate health food. J. Murray. il *Outdoor
    Life* 179:106-8+ My '87
Fish, Effect of temperature on
  Bass in the brrrrrrrr. L. Stout. il *Outdoor Life* 180:88-9+
    N '87
  Death on the Miramichi [heat wave endangers salmon]
    K. Harley. il *Macleans* 100:41 Ag 3 '87
  Finding the comfort zone [how water temperature affects
    saltwater fishing] B. Stearns. il *Field Stream* 92:91+
    Je '87
  Hey, Pisces, what's your latitude? [silversides; research
    by David O. Conover and Stephen W. Heins] *Sci
    News* 131:232 Ap 11 '87
  Smallies in the swelter [small mouth bass fishing] K.
    Etling. il *Outdoor Life* 179:60-1+ Je '87
  Test tank for fast fish [researching body temperature
    regulation and swimming dynamics of warm-blooded
    albacore tuna] *Oceans* 20:5 My/Je '87
Fish, Extinct
  Facing up to a backwards fossil [work of David K.
    Elliott] *Sci News* 132:47 Jl 18 '87
  A reassessment of Astraspis desiderata, the oldest North
    American vertebrate. D. K. Elliott. bibl f il *Science*
    237:190-2 Jl 10 '87
Fish, Fossil
  Facing up to a backwards fossil [work of David K.
    Elliott] *Sci News* 132:47 Jl 18 '87
  Hatracks and theories [L. Agassiz's Research on fossil
    fishes] S. J. Gould. il *Nat Hist* 96:12+ Mr '87
  A reassessment of Astraspis desiderata, the oldest North
    American vertebrate. D. K. Elliott. bibl f il *Science*
    237:190-2 Jl 10 '87
Fish, Raw
      See also
    Sushi
Fish and Game Dept. (Calif.) *See* California. Dept. of
    Fish and Game
Fish and Wildlife Service (U.S.) *See* U.S. Fish and Wildlife
    Service
Fish as food
      See also
    Caviar
    Cooking—Fish
    Scombroid poisoning
    Surimi
  As Americans start to eat fish that once were thrown
    back, things look good for the men who go to sea
    to catch them. J. P. Wiley, Jr. *Smithsonian* 18:36+
    My '87
  Fish: the ultimate health food. J. Murray. il *Outdoor
    Life* 179:106-8+ My '87
  A fishy tale that's true. B. Hayton. il *Curr Health 2*
    13:14-16 Mr '87
  From our kitchen to yours. K. Adams. *South Living*
    22:213 Ap '87
  Low triglycerides native to fish eaters. il *Prevention*
    39:9 My '87
  Mackerel works miracles with blood pressure. il *Prevention*
    39:14 Jl '87
          Contamination
    See Fish contamination
Fish contamination
  PCB-polluted fishes cause seal decline [Waddenzee,
    Netherlands] *Sea Front* 33:305-6 Jl/Ag '87
  Should we beware the gourmet grouper? [ciguatera] D.
    M. Schwartz. il *Int Wildl* 17:36-7 N/D '87
  Star-Kist's revival [reopening of St. Andrews, N.B. plant]
    T. Fennell. il *Macleans* 100:34 S 28 '87
  Troubled waters [contaminated fish from Santa Monica
    Bay] S. Pritikin. il *Sierra* 72:16 Ja/F '87
  Warning: the Friday night fish fry may be hazardous
    to your health [pollution of Wisconsin's Fox River
    and Green Bay by waste from the Fort Howard Paper
    Co.] M. Hudson. il maps *Audubon* 89:24-6+ Jl '87

Fish cooking *See* Cooking—Fish
Fish culture
      See also
      Shellfish culture
Adoption [Bronx sixth graders learn about Hudson River Striped Bass Hatchery] *New Yorker* 62:31-2 F 9 '87
Farming your pond for profit. il *Success Farm* 85 no4:20 F '87
Frankenstein's fish. T. Williams. il *Audubon* 89:74-7 S '87
Grandpa and the kid [working at a fish hatchery] D. Sisson. il *Field Stream* 92:81+ My '87
No mud for the new catfish. L. Shapiro. il *Newsweek* 109:53 Je 29 '87
Return of the leaper [Atlantic salmon] M. Rosenthal. il *Ctry J* 14:30-5 Jl '87
                              History
Aquaculture in ancient Hawaii. B. A. Costa-Pierce. bibl f il maps *BioScience* 37:320-31 My '87
                     Great Lakes region
The lake trout returns to Lake Ontario. J. E. Marsden. il *Conservationist* 41:10-13 My/Je '87
                              Hawaii
Aquaculture in ancient Hawaii. B. A. Costa-Pierce. bibl f il maps *BioScience* 37:320-31 My '87
                              Norway
Salmon-farming success in Norway. E. S. Iversen and J. Z. Iversen. il map *Sea Front* 33:354-61 S/O '87
Fish farming *See* Fish culture
Fish genetics
Frankenstein's fish. T. Williams. il *Audubon* 89:74-7 S '87
Fish hatcheries *See* Fish culture
Fish hooks *See* Fishhooks
Fish in art
                           Exhibitions
Big fish, big pond [J. Borofsky's sculpture Fish with ruby eye hanging in Cathedral of St. John the Divine] S. Staggs. il *Art News* 86:17-18 My '87
Fish industry
      See also
      Shellfish industry
      Star-Kist Foods, Inc.
                     Export-import trade
Fish story [Japan's rising importation of U.S. tuna] P. Fuhrman. il *Forbes* 140:38-9 Ag 10 '87
                              Canada
      See also
      National Sea Products Ltd.
                              Japan
Fish story [Japan's rising importation of U.S. tuna] P. Fuhrman. il *Forbes* 140:38-9 Ag 10 '87
Fish industry workers
      See also
      United Seafood Workers, Smoked Fish and Cannery Union
Fish markets
      See also
      Fulton Fish Market
Fish trip [Corlears School makes field trip to De Martino's Fish Market in New York City] *New Yorker* 62:25 Ja 12 '87
Fish window [F. Lara's window displays at the Citarella Fish Company in Manhattan] *New Yorker* 63:23-5 Jl 6 '87
                              Japan
A gourmet at large [Tokyo's Tsukiji market] F. Ferretti. il *Gourmet* 48:44+ Je '87
Fish nets *See* Fishing nets
Fish oil
Fish: food for a healthy heart. H. Garrison. il *Parents* 62:92-4+ Ja '87
Fish for the heart. J. Lowenstein. il *Oceans* 20:72 Mr/Ap '87
Fish oil: a new arthritis tamer? M. Mihalik. *Prevention* 39:30-2 Mr '87
Fish oil helps prevent tumor spread [research by Debra Szeluga and others] *Prevention* 39:6+ O '87
Fish oil prevents insulin resistance induced by high-fat feeding in rats. L. H. Storlien and others. bibl f il *Science* 237:885-8 Ag 21 '87
Fish oil slows plaque deposits. *Prevention* 39:100-1 Ap '87
A fish (oil) story? J. Silberner. *Sci News* 131:89 F 7 '87
A healthy change of heart [fish oil protects heart from damage during attack; research by Carl Hock] il *Prevention* 39:8 Ag '87
The omega factor. K. Freifeld. il *Health* 19:78 F '87

Surf 'n turf [cattle injected with fish oil to produce meat with less saturated fat] M. Mintzer. il *Health* 19:15 S '87
Fish oil supplements
Fish oil and cholesterol: a megadose of hype? T. Monmaney. il *Newsweek* 109:67-8 Ap 13 '87
Fish-oil capsules: good for your heart? C. Schaeffer. il *Changing Times* 41:14 My '87
Fish oil takes a dive? [research by William S. Harris] *Sci News* 132:342 N 28 '87
Three "half truths" about health. il *Glamour* 85:406 S '87
Fish packing industry *See* Fish industry
Fish populations
Where have all the billfish gone? B. Waitzkin. il *Mot Boat Sail* 160:44-5+ O '87
Fish processing industry *See* Fish industry
Fish protection
Editorial [barbless fishing hooks] D. Barnes. il *Field Stream* 92:7 My '87
New conservation ideas [role of aquariums] D. G. Gordon. il *Oceans* 20:59 N/D '87
Fish sandwiches *See* Sandwiches
Fish sounds
Not-so-silent sea [excerpt from Blues] J. Hersey. il *Harpers* 274:30-1 My '87
Fish soups *See* Chowder; Soups
Fish stew *See* Stew
Fish stores *See* Fish markets
Fishburn, Janet F.
Seminary, ministry and social responsibility. *Christ Century* 104:100-2 F 4-11 '87
Fishel, Elizabeth
Baby makes three. il *Parents* 62:73-6+ S '87
Transforming your kitchen. il *Parents* 62:62+ Ap '87
Fisher, Amanda G., and others
The *sor* gene of HIV-1 is required for efficient virus transmission in vitro. bibl f il *Science* 237:888-93 Ag 21 '87
Fisher, Andrew
Germany's 'international' producer. *World Press Rev* 34:58 Ap '87
Fisher, Arthur
Science newsfront. See issues of Popular Science
What's new in photography. See alternate issues of Popular Science beginning January 1986
Fisher, Candia
                              about
Manhattan still life. J. Giovannini. il *House Gard* 159:178-83+ Je '87
Fisher, Carl A.
                              about
Baltimore priest 1st black bishop for West Coast. por *Jet* 71:36 Ja 26 '87
Fisher, Carrie
Hollywood casting [fiction] il pors *Redbook* 169:42+ Jl '87
                              about
Carrie Fisher's Postcards from the edge: Princess Leia lands in a drug clinic. C. Krupp. il por *Glamour* 85:206+ Ag '87
High times. E. G. Carter. por *Vogue* 177:186+ Ag '87
In an impressive literary debut Carrie Fisher sends sardonic Postcards from the edge. J. Jerome. il pors *People Wkly* 28:68-70 S 7 '87
Fisher, Donald
                              about
He fell out with father. il por *U S News World Rep* 103:56-7 Jl 6 '87
The supermen of specialty stores. S. Smith. il por *Fortune* 116:142-3 O 12 '87
Fisher, Francis Dummer
Higher education circa 2005. il *Change* 19:40-5 Ja/F '87
Fisher, Hans, 1928-
Nutrition in your life. See issues of Prevention (Emmaus, Pa.) beginning January 1987
Fisher, Harrison
                              about
The greatest moments in a girl's life. C. E. Rinzler. il *Am Herit* 38:34-5 F/Mr '87
Fisher, Helen E.
The four-year itch: do divorce patterns reflect our evolutionary heritage? il *Nat Hist* 96:22+ O '87
Fisher, Herman, d. 1985
                              about
Accident victim's son, 2, awarded nearly $1.7 million. pors *Jet* 72:36 Ag 17 '87
Fisher, Joel, 1947-
                              about
Joel Fisher. M. Poirier. il *Art News* 86:171-2 O '87

Fisher, Kenneth L.
Growth stocks. See issues of Forbes beginning July 16, 1984
Fisher, M. F. K. (Mary Frances Kennedy), 1908-
about
Loving Brillat-Savarin: a tale of a tasteful affair. J. Ferrary. por *N Y Times Book Rev* 92:51+ My 31 '87
With bold pen and fork. M. Sheraton. il por *Time* 129:67 Ja 26 '87
Fisher, Mary Frances Kennedy See Fisher, M. F. K. (Mary Frances Kennedy), 1908-
Fisher, Mel
about
A fabulous lady from Spain [cover story] R. A. Green. il por *Antiques Collect Hobbies* 92:30-4 My '87
Fisher, Philip A.
about
Maybe it's 1928 again [interview] T. Jaffe. por *Forbes* 140:126+ N 30 '87
A talk with Philip Fisher. T. Jaffe. *Forbes* 140:41+ O 19 '87
What we can learn from Phil Fisher. W. E. Buffett. il por *Forbes* 140:40 O 19 '87
Fisher, Robert
about
Groucho: a life in revue [drama] Reviews
Dance Mag il 61:89 Ja '87. K. Grubb
Fisher, Ronne
about
Out of sight. C. Vogel. il *N Y Times Mag* p58-62 Je 14 '87
Fisher, Sethard
Black Americans need their own agenda [with discussion] il por *Cent Mag* 20:25-36 My/Je '87
Fisher, Terry Louise
about
Terry Louise Fisher: how she dreamed up the women of "L.A. law". M. Kort. por *Ms* 15:38-9+ Je '87
Fisher, V. Carol
Five basics for glorious chrysanthemums. il *Flower Gard* 31:72-3 Ap/My '87
Fisher, William
Romania in the age of *glasnost*. il *New Leader* 70:11-13 Je 29 '87
Fisher, William L.
Can the U.S. oil and gas resource base support sustained production? bibl f il *Science* 236:1631-6 Je 26 '87
Oil and gas discovery rates [discussion of June 26, 1987 article, Can the U.S. oil and gas resource base support sustained production?] *Science* 238:878-9 N 13 '87
Fisher Island (Fla.)
Fortress Fisher. W. G. Flanagan. il map *Forbes* 140:232+ D 14 '87
Fisheries
See also
Fish culture
Fishermen
Poaching
Reefs, Artificial
Shellfish fisheries
United States. National Marine Fisheries Service
As Americans start to eat fish that once were thrown back, things look good for the men who go to sea to catch them. J. P. Wiley, Jr. *Smithsonian* 18:36+ My '87
Immiscible investigators: oceanographers, meteorologists, and fishery scientists. W. S. Wooster. *BioScience* 37:728-30 N '87
Oil and fishing industries negotiate: mediation and scientific issues [conflicts arising off California coast] G. W. Cormick and A. Knaster. bibl il *Environment* 28:6-15+ D '86
The round haul [Penobscot Bay herring fishery; excerpt from Amaretto] J. Upton. il *Oceans* 20:8-17 Ja/F '87
Salmon make a comeback, but what's ahead? il *Sunset* 179:220 S '87
Saltwort meadows needed by fishes [Florida salt marshes; research by Grant Gilmore and others] il *Sea Front* 33:461-3 N/D '87
Standoff at Oregon Inlet [Army Corps of Engineers proposal to build jetties at Cape Hatteras, N.C.] L. S. Bates. il *Oceans* 20:5-6 Mr/Ap '87
International aspects
Heating up the cod war [Newfoundland angry over Franco-Canadian fishing agreement] C. Barrett. il *Macleans* 100:12-13 F 23 '87
Nothing fishy about new tuna treaty [U.S. and the Pacific region] D. G. Knibb. il *Oceans* 20:6-7 Jl/Ag '87
Rites of the fishermen [Newfoundland fishermen angered at agreement with France] M. Clark. il map *Macleans* 100:12 F 9 '87

South Pacific regional fisheries treaty signed [State Dept. statement, April 2, 1987] *Dep State Bull* 87:82 Je '87
Why men fish. W. McCloskey. il *Int Wildl* 17:34-40 Mr/Ap '87
Laws and regulations
See Fishery laws and regulations
Management
A case study in interstate cooperation [Atlantic Coast summer flounder] G. C. Colvin. il *Conservationist* 42:18 S/O '87
Managing New York's marine fishery. G. C. Colvin. il *Conservationist* 42:10-17 S/O '87
Squeteague: New York's saltwater trout [weakfish management program] A. M. Weber. il *Conservationist* 42:20-3 S/O '87
Australia
Australia's southern seas. R. Ellis. il map *Natl Geogr* 171:286-319 Mr '87
Canada
Heating up the cod war [Newfoundland angry over Franco-Canadian fishing agreement] C. Barrett. il *Macleans* 100:12-13 F 23 '87
Rites of the fishermen [Newfoundland fishermen angered at agreement with France] M. Clark. il map *Macleans* 100:12 F 9 '87
Seal-salmon controversy escalates in B.C. [harbor seals] B. Obee. il *Oceans* 20:8-9 S/O '87
Gulf of Mexico
House approvals. *Sea Front* 33:381 S/O '87
The perils of popularity [redfish] L. Lohmeier. il *Oceans* 20:8-13 My/Je '87
Kalymnos (Greece: Island)
Sponge divers of Kalymnos. T. Zappa. *World Press Rev* 34:57-8 Ja '87
Philippines
A deadly business [Philippine divers collect venomous snakes for snakeskin trade; with photographs] H. Hall. il *Int Wildl* 17:12-15 Jl/Ag '87
Staying afloat: subsistence fishery in the Philippines. S. M. Tejada. il map *Oceans* 20:46-53 Ja/F '87
Fishermen
See also
Trade unions—Fishermen
It's the people. N. Strung. il *Field Stream* 92:50+ Je '87
"Snitty" [R. Sizemore] K. McCafferty. il *Field Stream* 91:44+ Ja '87
Those wild tuna guys [objections by crew to placing women observers aboard tuna fishing boats] *Harpers* 274:19-20 Je '87
Why men fish. W. McCloskey. il *Int Wildl* 17:34-40 Mr/Ap '87
Anecdotes, facetiae, satire, etc.
Out of sync [continual failure to meet fishing partners] P. F. McManus. il *Outdoor Life* 180:144+ Jl '87
Why bad stuff happens to fishermen. M. F. Pfaff. il *Field Stream* 91:47-9 Mr '87
Psychology
Big success from little signs [alertness when fishing] B. Stearns. il *Field Stream* 92:115-16 My '87
Time to quit. N. Strung. il *Field Stream* 92:54+ D '87
What if? G. Hill. il *Field Stream* 91:32+ Ja '87
Fishery laws and regulations
See also
California. Dept. of Fish and Game
Poaching
Fishy politics. L. Williamson. il *Outdoor Life* 179:28+ Ap '87
Of salmon and sovereignty [trial of Yakima leader D. Sohappy for illegally selling fish] J. Rosenberg. *Christ Century* 104:428-9 My 6 '87
Scotland
A small misunderstanding [interest in salmon spawning on Scotland's Endrick River] R. Holland. il *Audubon* 89:62-3 S '87
Fishes See Fish
Fisheye lenses See Lenses, Photographic
Fishfinders (Depth indicators) See Depth indicators
Fishhooks
The cutting edge. J. Gibbs. il *Outdoor Life* 179:36+ F '87
Editorial [barbless fishing hooks] D. Barnes. il *Field Stream* 92:7 My '87
Sharp and to the point. P. B. Wright. il *Mot Boat Sail* 160:92+ N '87
Weed-proofing hooks and lures. N. Strung. il *Field Stream* 92:116 Jl '87

Fishing

See also
Bait
Bass fishing
Billfish fishing
Casting (Fishing)
Catfish fishing
Char fishing
Crappie fishing
Dapping (Fishing)
Eskimos—Fishing
Fisheries
Fishermen
Grayling fishing
Indians of North America—Fishing
Mullet fishing
Muskellunge fishing
Panfish fishing
Pickerel fishing
Pike fishing
Prickleback fishing
Reefs, Artificial
Salmon fishing
Salt water fishing
Sturgeon fishing
Sunfish fishing
Tarpon fishing
Trawls and trawling
Trout fishing
Walleye fishing
Women in fishing

An angler reborn. S. Trammel. il *Outdoor Life* 179:66-7+
Ap '87
A beginner's guide to fishing. B. Woods. il *Mother Earth
News* 105:68-75 My/Je '87
Charting for fishing success. N. Rothery. il map *Outdoor
Life* 179:62-4+ Ja '87
Editorial [sport fishing] D. Barnes. il *Field Stream* 92:5
Jl '87
Fishing. P. Barrett. See issues of Field & Stream beginning
February 1984
Fishing. J. Gibbs. See issues of Outdoor Life
Secret spots. J. Barsness. il *Field Stream* 91:76-7 Ap
'87
Solunar tables. See issues of Field & Stream
Stalking small streams. J. Bashline. il *Field Stream* 92:72+
Je '87
To catch a fish [fishing from a cruiser] S. Stapleton.
il *Mot Boat Sail* 159:118 Ap '87
Tricks that make fish strike. K. Schultz. il *Field Stream*
92:42+ N '87
Troublesome trifles [reprint from April 1964 issue] T.
Trueblood. il *Field Stream* 92:30+ O '87

Anecdotes, facetiae, satire, etc.

Beaten. N. Strung. il *Field Stream* 92:27-8 Ag '87
Letter to my boss. P. F. McManus. il *Outdoor Life*
180:168+ N '87
Paths of enlightenment. J. Kulpa. il *Field Stream* 92:39-40
Jl '87
Struck with luck. P. F. McManus. il *Outdoor Life* 180:158+
O '87
Why later is better. J. Bashline. il *Field Stream* 92:36+
D '87

Bibliography

Books & comments. See occasional issues of Field &
Stream beginning April 1985

Competitions

Beat bass at their own game [suggestions from BASS
Masters Classic competitors] L. Cribb. il *Outdoor Life*
179:64-5+ Mr '87
Big boy blues ['87 Bertram-Hatteras Shootout] C. Davis.
il *Mot Boat Sail* 159:48-51+ Je '87
Big event, small fish [1987 BASS Masters Classic] J.
Skorupa. il *Pop Mech* 164:25+ D '87
Competition angling. G. Reiger. il *Field Stream* 92:14+
D '87
Hidden Treasure [Treasure Cay Billfish Championship]
J. Clemans. il *Mot Boat Sail* 160:46-9+ O '87
Holy Mackerel [Arthur Smith King Mackerel Tournament,
Myrtle Beach, S.C.] C. Davis. il *Mot Boat Sail* 159:54-6
Ja '87
Shakeout in big-money tournament fishing [walleye] J.
Skorupa. il *Pop Mech* 164:19-20 O '87
Tuna alley [Cat Cay Tuna Tournament] B. Waitzkin.
il *Mot Boat Sail* 160:34-7+ S '87

Equipment

See also
Depth indicators
Electronics in fishing
Fishing nets
Fishing tackle

Better ways to gaff gamefish. B. Stearns. il *Field Stream*
91:91+ F '87
Build a troll-aid. N. Strung. il *Field Stream* 92:123
Je '87
What's new. See issues of Outdoor Life

Ethical aspects

Editorial. D. Barnes. il *Field Stream* 91:7 Ja '87
The good, the bad and the in-between. S. Mulak. il
Outdoor Life 180:122+ O '87

History

Editorial ["the good old days"] D. Barnes. *Field Stream*
92:8 Je '87
Good enough [nostalgia for fishing with grandfather]
G. Hill. il *Field Stream* 92:20 Je '87

International aspects

Global hotspots. P. B. Wright. il map *Mot Boat Sail*
160:50-1+ O '87

Laws and regulations

See Fishery laws and regulations

Noise

Shhhh! [how noise affects fishing] A. H. Putnam. il
Field Stream 92:34+ Je '87

Photographs and photography

Fishing isn't a sport, it's a calling [cover story] il *Oceans*
20:34-43 Jl/Ag '87

Study and teaching

Schools for fly-fishers. J. I. Merritt. il *Money* 16:67-8+
Jl '87
Untangling the mysteries of fly-fishing. M. N. Vamos.
il *Bus Week* p170-1 S 14 '87

Alaska

A bear in camp [Alaskan brown bear]; ed. by Larry
Mueller. B. Herron. il *Outdoor Life* 180:80-1+ N '87
Divots & shadows [Bristol Bay watershed float trip]
L. B. Aiuppy. il *Field Stream* 91:54-5+ F '87
Fishing with the right stuff [fishing with C. Yeager]
J. Zumbo. il por *Outdoor Life* 179:64-5+ Ap '87
The ultimate estuary [salmon fishing in Karluk Lagoon]
B. Stearns. il *Field Stream* 92:100+ Jl '87

Bahamas

Big boy blues ['87 Bertram-Hatteras Shootout] C. Davis.
il *Mot Boat Sail* 159:48-51+ Je '87
Hidden Treasure [Treasure Cay Billfish Championship]
J. Clemans. il *Mot Boat Sail* 160:46-9+ O '87

British Columbia

Hot springs. E. Iglauer. *New Yorker* 63:62-9 Jl 6 '87
Salmon: by land, sea, or air. J. Bashline. il *Field Stream*
91:46+ Ap '87

California

Floating and fishing the big rivers [Sacramento River]
S. Netherby. il *Field Stream* 92:97+ Jl '87
Landlubber largemouths [technique of J. Burkett] D.
Bartholomew. il por *Outdoor Life* 180:70-1+ Jl '87
Poke-poling for the homely but delicious monkeyface
prickleback. il *Sunset* 179:56 S '87

Canada

Fishing across Canada. *Field Stream* 91:80+ Mr '87

Florida

All roads lead to Florida fishing. il *South Living* 22:18
Je '87
The fishing story [Key West] il *Travel Holiday* 167:42
Ja '87
The promised land [largemouth bass fishing in the
Everglades] P. Kaminsky. il *Field Stream* 92:62-3+
N '87

Great Lakes region

Lessons from a little stream [Reefer Creek] J. Kulpa.
il *Field Stream* 91:43+ Mr '87

Hawaii

Tag lines and other Hawaiian legends. P. B. Wright.
il *Mot Boat Sail* 160:84+ D '87

Iceland

Icelandic snowmobiling and ice-fishing adventure. S.
Netherby. *Field Stream* 91:98 Ja '87

Idaho

The second spring [trout fishing] P. Barrett. il *Field
Stream* 92:78+ Jl '87

Long Island (N.Y.)

The end of the season [fishing excursion in bad weather]
P. A. Janssen. il *Mot Boat Sail* 160:9 D '87

Louisiana

A state's scheme to rig the reefs [Louisiana Rigs-to-Reefs
project] C. R. Cotton. il *Sierra* 72:19 Jl/Ag '87

Maine

Bring bass bugs, just in case [smallmouth bass] P. Barrett.
il *Field Stream* 92:107-8+ My '87

Manitoba

Fishing in God's country [God's Lake] P. Barrett. il
Field Stream 91:86+ Ap '87
Manitoba grayling. J. Reynolds. il *Field Stream* 92:41-3
Je '87

Fishing—Manitoba—cont.

Manitoba river walleyes. K. Schultz. il map *Field Stream* 92:49+ O '87

Minnesota

The day of the walleyes. P. Kaminsky. il *Field Stream* 91:68-9+ Mr '87

Montana

Casting about in Montana [float fishing trips for trout run by the Nature Conservancy] V. Klinkenborg. il *Esquire* 107:31+ My '87

Float to wild trout. E. A. Bauer. il *Outdoor Life* 180:58-9+ Ag '87

New Brunswick

Death on the Miramichi [heat wave endangers salmon] K. Harley. il *Macleans* 100:41 Ag 3 '87

New York (State)

Brook trout—an appreciation. J. Rowen. il *Conservationist* 42:36-41 Jl/Ag '87

Cleaner waters pay off in better fishing. L. Smith and E. Stegemann. il *Conservationist* 41:6-15 Mr/Ap '87

Finding your own secret fishing hole. L. J. Ellman. il *Conservationist* 41:16-19 Mr/Ap '87

In the hush of the night [fishing on Long Lake in the 1930's] V. Engels. il *Conservationist* 41:14-17 My/Je '87

Landowners and sportsmen united [Dept. of Environmental Conservation cooperative program allowing public to hunt or fish on private lands] J. Major. il *Conservationist* 41:42-5 Ja/F '87

Pray for rain [trout fishing] J. MacGregor. il *Field Stream* 92:46-7+ Ag '87

New Zealand

Gourmet holidays: trout fishing in New Zealand. P. J. Wade. il maps *Gourmet* 47:54-9+ Ap '87

Northwest Territories

The lady in pink [Arctic char] C. Gammon. il *Sports Illus* 67:54-8 Ag 24 '87

NWT means no wimpy trout. P. Barrett. il *Field Stream* 91:73+ Ja '87

Nova Scotia

Cinderella brown trout. J. Gibbs. il *Outdoor Life* 180:76-7+ Jl '87

Ohio

Cross Creek. K. McCafferty. il *Field Stream* 91:60-1+ Mr '87

Okefenokee Swamp (Ga. and Fla.)

Canoeing and fishing the Okefenokee Swamp. S. Netherby. il *Field Stream* 91:76+ Ja '87

Ozark Mountains region

Home by dark-thirty [Ozark smallmouth bass] P. Kaminsky. il *Field Stream* 91:58-9+ Ja '87

Pacific Northwest

Big river walleyes [Columbia River] J. Gibbs. il *Outdoor Life* 179:100-1+ My '87

Québec (Province)

In a tizzy over tommy cod [ice fishing for spawning tommycod in Ste.-Anne River] S. Homer. il *Int Wildl* 17:18-24 Ja/F '87

South Carolina

Holy Mackerel [Arthur Smith King Mackerel Tournament, Myrtle Beach] C. Davis. il *Mot Boat Sail* 159:54-6 Ja '87

Soviet Union

White nights, Red faces [U.S. anglers in Soviet Union] C. Gammon. il *Sports Illus* 67:76-8+ O 26 '87

Tennessee

Nighttime smallmouths. M. Hicks. il por *Outdoor Life* 180:78-9+ Jl '87

United States

See Fishing

Venezuela

Viva Venezuela [billfish fishing] J. Clemans. il *Mot Boat Sail* 159:42-5+ Ja '87

Washington (State)

Fun with "alligators" on the Columbia River [sturgeon] P. Barrett. il *Field Stream* 91:82+ F '87

Western States

The clean-living cutthroat. J. Barsness. il *Field Stream* 92:84-5+ My '87

The downward progression [unorthodox flies and tactics for trout fishing] G. Webster. il *Field Stream* 92:68-9+ Je '87

High-country cutthroats. S. Netherby. il *Field Stream* 92:134 S '87

Fishing, Winter

Back on the ice. J. Gierach. il *Field Stream* 91:66-7+ Ja '87

Cranking in the cold [crankbait for bass] L. Larsen. il *Outdoor Life* 179:52-3+ Ja '87

Icelandic snowmobiling and ice-fishing adventure. S. Netherby. *Field Stream* 91:98 Ja '87

In a tizzy over tommy cod [ice fishing for spawning tommycod in Quebec's Ste.-Anne River] S. Homer. il *Int Wildl* 17:18-24 Ja/F '87

Fishing boats

Moving up afloat [top of the line sportfishermen] B. McKeown. il *Outdoor Life* 180:48+ Jl '87

Newest afloat for '87. B. McKeown. il *Outdoor Life* 179:26+ F '87

Chartering

See Fishing boats—Leasing and renting

Design

Running the flats [Scooter high-speed fishing platform] T. H. Cole. il *Pop Mech* 164:32 My '87

Engines

See Motor boat engines

Equipment

Fit out for fun afloat. B. McKeown. il *Outdoor Life* 179:46+ Ap '87

Leasing and renting

Say goodby to the office [J. Courbier's charter business] S. Stapleton. il por *Mot Boat Sail* 159:44-7+ My '87

Maintenance and repair

Fixing up for fishing. B. McKeown. il *Outdoor Life* 179:82+ My '87

Prices

A boat for every budget. J. Clemans. il *Mot Boat Sail* 160:52-5+ O '87

Safety devices and measures

Wild eyes and roostertails. K. Schultz. il *Field Stream* 92:70-1 Jl '87

Speed

Wild eyes and roostertails. K. Schultz. il *Field Stream* 92:70-1 Jl '87

Testing

Bulletproof [Runaway 36] J. Clemans. il *Mot Boat Sail* 160:38-41+ Ag '87

Family fishing [Whaler 27 Full Cabin, Black Fin 32, Ocean 48 Super Sport, Hatteras 41 Convertible and Viking 48 Convertible] C. Davis and others. il *Mot Boat Sail* 160:38-43+ O '87

Flawless fifty [Bertram Convertible] J. Clemans. il *Mot Boat Sail* 160:56-9+ S '87

High-flying Huckins [Kirkline 60] B. Waitzkin. il *Mot Boat Sail* 159:62-5+ Ap '87

Jumbo jet [Lydia 90] J. Clemans. il *Mot Boat Sail* 160:48-53+ Jl '87

Trojan goes fishing [10.8 meter and 12 meter convertibles] B. Waitzkin. il *Mot Boat Sail* 159:50-3+ Mr '87

Fishing by birds *See* Birds—Food and feeding

Fishing clothes *See* Clothing and dress—Sports clothes

Fishing flies *See* Fishing lures, flies, etc.

Fishing guides *See* Guides

Fishing industry *See* Fisheries

Fishing lines *See* Fishing tackle

Fishing literature

Anecdotes, facetiae, satire, etc.

The exploding fish. T. Leeson. il *Field Stream* 91:49-50+ Ja '87

Fishing lures, flies, etc.

See also

Casting (Fishing)

Back to bugging bass. J. Dean. il *Outdoor Life* 179:87-9+ My '87

Bassic strategy for pike. T. Mandile. il *Outdoor Life* 179:62-3+ Je '87

Blessed are the weak [use of floating/shallow-diving plug for bass] C. Hauptman. il *Field Stream* 92:56-7 S '87

Bring bass bugs, just in case [smallmouth bass in Maine] P. Barrett. il *Field Stream* 92:107-8+ My '87

Caddisflies: the go-anywhere, fish-anytime patterns. D. Hughes. il *Field Stream* 91:70-1+ Mr '87

Casting for a better bait [Swimming Snake Worms designed by W. Davidson] D. Young. il por *South Living* 22:138 My '87

Confessions of a chicken chaser [fly tying] J. Dean. il *Field Stream* 91:37+ Ap '87

Cranking in the cold [crankbait for bass] L. Larsen. il *Outdoor Life* 179:52-3+ Ja '87

The downward progression [unorthodox flies and tactics for trout fishing in Western States] G. Webster. il *Field Stream* 92:68-9+ Je '87

Fishing the non-hatch [dry flies for trout] R. L. Henry. il *Field Stream* 92:64-5+ Jl '87

Floating worms for finicky bass [largemouth] J. Arrington. il *Outdoor Life* 180:52-3+ D '87

A fly called the Thor. P. Barrett. il *Field Stream* 92:75+ Je '87

The flylures. J. Gibbs. il *Outdoor Life* 180:104-5+ S '87

Fishing lures, flies, etc.—cont.
Follow the bouncing fly [trout fishing] L. M. Wright. il *Field Stream* 92:52-3+ D '87
Going deep [getting lures deep for tarpon] B. Stearns. il *Field Stream* 92:78-9 Ag '87
Hairy monsters. J. Gibbs. il *Outdoor Life* 179:66-7+ Je '87
How to pick a plastic worm. C. Hauptman. il *Field Stream* 92:42-3+ D '87
In the hush of the night [fishing on Long Lake in the 1930's] V. Engels. il *Conservationist* 41:14-17 My/Je '87
Live baits & lures. A. H. Putnam. il *Field Stream* 92:97+ My '87
The minis: big medicine for bass [fishing jigs] J. Gibbs. il *Outdoor Life* 179:24+ Ap '87
Muddling with minis [Muddler Minnows] J. Gibbs. il *Outdoor Life* 179:34+ Je '87
Nail 'em in neutral [neutrally buoyant crankbaits] J. Murray. il *Outdoor Life* 180:62-3+ Ag '87
New lows with new crankbaits. J. Gibbs. il *Outdoor Life* 179:28+ Ja '87
A new wiggle for plastic worms. R. G. Brown. il *Field Stream* 91:144 Mr '87
Pumping silver [dodger and flasher spoons] J. Gibbs. il *Outdoor Life* 179:28+ Mr '87
A salmon delights in gaudy colors [cover story; with editorial comment by Les Line] T. Rosenbauer. il *Audubon* 89:4, 64-73 S '87
Salty snacks for sweet bass [saltwater lures] J. Gibbs. il *Outdoor Life* 180:46+ O '87
Siren song of the slim minnow. J. Doggett. il *Field Stream* 91:69+ Ap '87
Spinning a stream. G. Webster. il *Field Stream* 92:93+ My '87
Tradition unbound [salmon anglers] J. Bashline. il *Field Stream* 91:68+ Ja '87
Tricks with lures. K. Schultz. il *Field Stream* 92:70-1 Je '87
Weed-proofing hooks and lures. N. Strung. il *Field Stream* 92:116 Jl '87
Wet flies up, dry flies down. J. Bashline. il *Field Stream* 92:60+ My '87
Why not try a dragonfly? C. Hauptman. il *Field Stream* 92:64-5+ Je '87
Collectors and collecting
Lured in. J. A. Trachtenberg. il *Forbes* 140:290-1+ N 16 '87
Storage
The all-in-one fly box. D. Hughes. il *Field Stream* 91:106 Ap '87
Fishing nets
Net gain [use of cast nets for mullet] G. Norman. il *Oceans* 20:56 N/D '87
Netting a solution [fur seals killed by entanglement] L. Williamson. il *Outdoor Life* 180:38+ Jl '87
Fishing poles *See* Fishing tackle
Fishing reels *See* Fishing tackle
Fishing rods *See* Fishing tackle
Fishing tackle
  See also
  Fishhooks
  Fishing lures, flies, etc.
An angler's lament. H. Middleton. il *South Living* 22:34+ F '87
Bobbers on the rebound. J. Gibbs. bibl il *Outdoor Life* 180:44+ N '87
Double duty [fly tackle for trout works for panfish] C. Hauptman. il *Field Stream* 92:48-9+ Ag '87
Follow the bouncing fly [trout fishing] L. M. Wright. il *Field Stream* 92:52-3+ D '87
The half-foot advantage [fly rods] P. Barrett. il *Field Stream* 92:57-9 D '87
Innovative new fishing tackle '87. K. Schultz. il *Field Stream* 91:71+ Ja '87
An irreverent look at leaders. P. Barrett. il *Field Stream* 91:95-6+ Mr '87
The light-tackle advantage. K. Schultz. il *Field Stream* 92:32+ Ag '87
A matter of inches [leaders that stretch] P. B. Wright. il *Mot Boat Sail* 160:92 O '87
The problems of fly fishing deep [trout] P. Barrett. il *Field Stream* 92:70+ N '87
Profiles [bamboo rod maker R. J. Kusse] C. P. Crow. *New Yorker* 63:34-8+ Je 22 '87
The reel thing. G. Hill. il *Field Stream* 91:12+ F '87
Tag lines and other Hawaiian legends. P. B. Wright. il *Mot Boat Sail* 160:84+ D '87
Things you should know about fishing line. K. Schultz. *Field Stream* 92:108 Je '87

Thread on the water [light tackle] A. J. McClane. il *Field Stream* 92:54+ Ag '87
Trends in tackle. J. Gibbs. il *Outdoor Life* 179:72-5 Mr '87
History
The good old stuff. J. Bashline. il *Field Stream* 92:64+ S '87
Storage
An all-season tackle bag. B. Stearns. il *Field Stream* 91:110 Ap '87
Fishing tournaments *See* Fishing—Competitions
Fishing trophies
Trophies [with editorial comment by Duncan Barnes] N. Strung. *Field Stream* 92:7, 44+ S '87
Fishman, Katharine Davis
All in good time. il *N Y* 20:66-71 N 23 '87
American High: at Seward Park, the melting pot still bubbles. il *N Y* 20:78-80+ Mr 2 '87
Fishworms *See* Earthworms
Fisk, Carol Fraser
Commissioner's corner. See issues of Aging beginning no348 1985
Fisk, Lennard
  about
Outlook for space science: conversations with Burt Edelson and Lennard Fisk. M. Freeman; T. Reichhardt. pors *Space World* X-11-287:26-31 N '87
Fisk University
Bill and Camille Cosby make $1.3 million gift to aid Fisk University. *Jet* 71:52 Ja 12 '87
Fisk bounces back. M. Marshall. il *Ebony* 42:33-4+ My '87
Fisk president tells meaning of the Cosbys' gift of $1.3 million. il por *Jet* 71:16 Ja 19 '87
Untold story—real reason the Cosbys gave Fisk $1.3 million. il por *Jet* 71:14-15 F 9 '87
Fissinger, Laura
Good night, insomnia. il *Seventeen* 46:182+ Mr '87
A real-life supermom: Meredith Baxter Birney. il pors *McCalls* 114:75-7 Ag '87
The rock report. il *Seventeen* 46:45 Jl '87
Fission, Nuclear *See* Nuclear fission
Fission-track dating *See* Radioactive dating
Fissures (Geology) *See* Faults (Geology)
Fitch, David
Curran and dissent: the case for the Holy See. il *America* 156:341-3+ Ap 25 '87
Fitch, James Marston, 1909-
  about
To save the world we built [interview] S. Rattner. il *Am Herit* 38:84-91 Ap '87
Fitch, Richard D.
Antique radios. See issues of Radio-Electronics beginning February 1985
Fitness *See* Physical fitness
Fitt, William K.
(jt. auth) See Heslinga, Gerald A., and Fitt, William K.
Fitts, C. Austin, 1950-
  about
The wonder woman of muni bonds. A. Bianco. il por *Bus Week* p112-13 F 23 '87
Fitz, Earle L.
  about
Earle Fitz's Bible blitz. R. Clapp. il por *Christ Today* 31:14-15 Ap 17 '87
Fitz-Gerald, Desmond John Villiers, 1937-
Castletown, County Kildare. il *House Gard* 159:184-96+ Mr '87
Fitzgerald, Charles R.
Thinking like Christopher. il *Parents* 62:102-4 Ap '87
Fitzgerald, Edmund B.
  about
How Northern Telecom is riding out the storm. J. J. Keller. il por *Bus Week* p84-5 Ja 26 '87
Fitzgerald, Ella
  about
Ella Fitzgerald wows fans at Hollywood Bowl concert. por *Jet* 72:25 Ag 24 '87
Ella hits high note and trips fire alarm. il por *Jet* 72:22 Mr 30 '87
Fitzgerald, Bearden get president's Medal of Arts. il por *Jet* 72:52 Jl 6 '87
Fitzgerald, F. Scott (Francis Scott), 1896-1940
  about
F. Scott Fitzgerald's little drinking problem. J. M. Irwin. *Am Sch* 56:415+ Summ '87
The Gatsby gamble. S. Flatow. il *Horizon* 30:60-2 O '87
Reminiscing in Great Gatsbyland. J. Kern. il *Travel Holiday* 168:28+ O '87

Fitzgerald, F. Scott (Francis Scott), 1896-1940—about— *cont.*

The room where Scott died. S. Graham. il por *N Y Times Mag* p20-1 Jl 26 '87

FitzGerald, Frances, 1940-

Architecture: Ian Athfield: a residence for vintners in Hawkes Bay, New Zealand. il por *Archit Dig* 44:78-83 Ja '87

Charge of the lightweight brigade. il map *Roll Stone* p46-8+ O 22 '87

Reagan's band of true believers. il *N Y Times Mag* p36-9+ My 10 '87

Fitzgerald, Francis Scott Key *See* Fitzgerald, F. Scott (Francis Scott), 1896-1940

Fitzgerald, Jim, d. 1987

about

When Jim Fitzgerald was killed, racing lost its grand old man, and Paul Newman lost a friend. il pors *People Wkly* 28:122-3 N 23 '87

FitzGerald, Karen

Campus report: is there a drinker in the house? il *Ms* 15:30 F '87

Making reader-friendly books. il *Ms* 15:34 Je '87

(jt. auth) See Bray, Rosemary L., and FitzGerald, Karen

Fitzgerald, Randy

The case of the poisoned wildlife refuge. il por *Read Dig* 131:133-7 O '87

A painless way to slash the deficit. *Read Dig* 130:79-82 Mr '87

Fitzgerald family

about

Birth of a dynasty [excerpts from The Fitzgeralds and the Kennedys] D. K. Goodwin. il pors *People Wkly* 27:54-6+ Ja 26 '87

Fitzmyer, Joseph A.

The Dead Sea scrolls and the Bible: after forty years. il *America* 157:300-3 O 31 '87

Fitzpatrick, Catherine A.

(tr) See Orlov, Yuri. My life in exile

Fitzpatrick, David

The bad news hits home. por *Newsweek* 109:8 Mr 23 '87

Fitzpatrick, Donovan

My first jump. il *Read Dig* 130:29-30+ Mr '87

Fitzpatrick, Jean Grasso

Can your marriage survive your diet? il *Parents* 62:58-62 Ja '87

"I want to be alone" [with editorial comment by Elizabeth Crow] il *Parents* 62:8, 77-80 My '87

Fitzpatrick, Joseph P.

A tale of two cities. *America* 157:4-5 Jl 4-11 '87

Fitzpatrick, Richard Dunne

about

All in the name of science, Houston's Richard Fitzpatrick goes flat out for NASA—in bed. B. Stewart. il pors *People Wkly* 28:59-60 D 21 '87

Fitzpatrick, Robert J.

about

Hi-ho! Hi-ho! Culture high and low. il por *Harpers Bazaar* 120:210 S '87

Fitzpatrick, Sean K.

about

Those heartbeat ads are a hit in the heartland. C. Dugas. il *Bus Week* p107 F 23 '87

Fiut, Aleksander

Separate nations: poetry and the people [excerpt from Conversations with Czeslaw Milosz]; tr. by Richard Lourie. il *N Y Times Book Rev* 92:3+ O 11 '87

Five owls (Periodical)

New ventures in the Snow State. K. O. Fakih. *Publ Wkly* 231:102-3 F 27 '87

The five rings [dance] See Dance reviews—Single works

Fixed base operators (Aviation) *See* Airplane service stations

Fixed rate mortgages *See* Mortgages

Fizdale, Robert

about

Composition for two: Robert Fizdale and Arthur Gold's city residence. M. M. Thomas. il pors *Archit Dig* 44:212-15+ N '87

Fizzell, Robert L.

Inside a school of choice. il *Phi Delta Kappan* 68:758-60 Je '87

Fjermedal, Grant

The Blade runner blues. *Omni* 9:78 Ja '87

Online junkies. il *Omni* 9:22+ Jl '87

When robots rule the world. il *Omni* 10:24 N '87

Fjords

Turbidity current activity in a British Columbia fjord. D. B. Prior and others. bibl f il map *Science* 237:1330-3 S 11 '87

Flach, Ken

The flag first! il *World Tennis* 35:49+ O '87

about

It's doubles or nothing. R. Sullivan. il pors *Sports Illus* 67:60+ Ag 10 '87

Flagell, Eugene G.

Easy ways to retire the debt. por *Newsweek* 109:8 Ja 26 '87

Flagellates

See also

Dinoflagellates

Trypanosomes

Flagler, Henry Morrison, 1830-1913

about

Flagler built this Florida church. il *South Living* 22:50 N '87

Legacies. M. Granetz. *New Repub* 197:42 O 5 '87

Flagon's Wine Bar & Bistro (New Orleans, La.) *See* New Orleans (La.)—Restaurants, nightclubs, bars, etc.

Flagpoles

Bedford, Texas runs the flag out of town, causing a flap. K. Demaret. il por *People Wkly* 27:53-4 My 11 '87

Flags of convenience *See* Ships—Registration and transfer; Tankers—Registration and transfer

Flagstaffs *See* Flagpoles

Flaherty, Francis J.

A record that speaks for itself. il *Commonweal* 114:477-80 S 11 '87

Flaherty, William

Sloth: fools rush in. il *U S Cathol* 52:8-10 Ag '87

Who says bingo is for losers? *U S Cathol* 52:40 Ja '87

Flahive, Peg

The duration [poem] *America* 156:82 Ja 31 '87

Flake, Carol

Betting too big on the blood. *Harpers* 274:58-9 My '87

Flake, Floyd H.

about

This congressman preaches in church every Sunday [interview] por *Christ Today* 31:58-9 Mr 20 '87

Flake, Stanley Anthony

about

126 pounds lighter through diet, prayer and hard work. il pors *Ebony* 42:70+ S '87

Flame retardant textiles *See* Textile fabrics, Fireproof

Flamenco

See also

Ballet Español de Yoko Komatsubara

Duende [videotapes] D. Towers. il *Dance Mag* 61:76-7 Ja '87

Flamenco puro. M. Aloff. *Dance Mag* 61:55+ Mr '87

Flamenco puro [guitar festival in Belgium] D. Gordon. il *Down Beat* 54:12 Jl '87

Reviews:

Cumbre Flamenca in Madrid. L. Kumin. *Dance Mag* 61:34-5 Ja '87

Flames

Fanning flames in space [research by Felix J. Weinberg and F. B. Carleton] I. Peterson. *Sci News* 132:389 D 19-26 '87

Flamingo Stakes *See* Horse racing

Flamingos

Keeping flamingos under his wing [work of J. Nixon on Great Inagua, Bahamas] B. Krist. il por *Int Wildl* 17:46-51 Ja/F '87

Pink flamingos. il *Natl Geogr World* 142:16-21 Je '87

Photographs and photography

In the pink. R. Caputo. il *Nat Hist* 96:104-5 O '87

Flanagan, Sue Morrow

A roar of tearing metal. *Read Dig* 130:145 Ja '87

Flanagan, William G.

Personal affairs. See issues of Forbes

Flank steak cooking *See* Cooking—Meat

Flannery, Brian P., and others

Three-dimensional X-ray microtomography. bibl f il *Science* 237:1439-44 S 18 '87

Flannery, Merle

Learning to become a nation of artists. *Educ Dig* 52:24-6 My '87

Flaps (Airplane) *See* Airplanes, Jet—Flaps; Airplanes, Military—Flaps

Flares, Solar *See* Solar flares

Flashing (Buildings) *See* Waterproofing

Flashing (Photography) *See* Photography—Processing

Flashing (Sewing)

Flashing? It's a 16th-century look for a stocking, pillowcase, or vest. il *Sunset* 179:118+ D '87

Flashing lights *See* Electric lamps, Flashing
Flashlight photography *See* Photography, Flashlight
Flashlights
 See also
  Rayovac Corporation
 Halbach's "astroflash" [gravity-operated flashlight] E. A. Halbach. il *Sky Telesc* 74:90-1 Jl '87
 Rechargeable lanterns and flashlights. il *Consum Rep* 52:234-7 D '87
 Rechargeable lights. il *Consum Rep* 52:303-6 My '87
Flasks *See* Bottles
Flat earth theory
 Anecdotes, facetiae, satire, etc.
 Last word. D. Christopher. por *Omni* 10:178 D '87
Flat panel information display systems *See* Information display systems
Flat-screen information display *See* Information display systems
Flat-screen television receivers *See* Television receivers
Flatbush (New York, N.Y.)
 Flatbush: touches of the Dutch and turn-of-the-century grandeur. P. Tyre. il map *N Y* 20:64-6 My 4 '87
Flatow, Sheryl
 Double play [cover story] il pors *Opera News* 51:10-13+ Je '87
 The Gatsby gamble. il *Horizon* 30:60-2 O '87
 Risky business. il *Opera News* 51:18-20+ My '87
 Sisters: Debbie Allen and Phylicia Rashad. il pors *McCalls* 114:90-5 Jl '87
 Taylor-made design. il *Theatre Crafts* 21:24-5+ Ja '87
Flats, etc. (Horticulture)
 A simpler way with seedlings [making soil blocks] N. Woodin. il *Rodale's Org Gard* 34:74-9 Mr '87
 Wired for warmth [bottom heating devices for starting seeds indoors] P. H. Johnson. il *Rodale's Org Gard* 34:68-73 Ja '87
Flattery *See* Praise
Flatulence
 The digestive discomfort of gas. R. W. Miller. il *FDA Consum* 21:32-4 Ap '87
 Relief is just a mint away [peppermint oil for excess stomach gas; work of Thomas L. Kun] il *Prevention* 39:14 My '87
Flavin, Christopher
 Electricity in the developing world [cover story] bibl f il *Environment* 29:12-15+ Ap '87
 The future of nuclear power: seeking new energy sources. *Current* 298:24-9 D '87
 Nuclear power's burdened future. bibl f il *Bull At Sci* 43:26-31 Jl/Ag '87
 Revising the nuclear dream. il *USA Today (Periodical)* 116:60-2 Jl '87
Flavor
 The flavor factor [dieting; research by Susan Schiffman] D. Tonnessen. il *Health* 19:8 Ag '87
Flavoring essences
 See also
  Vanilla
Flea markets
 Anecdotes, facetiae, satire, etc.
 The gospel according to Ermel. R. Cone. il *Antiques Collect Hobbies* 92:35-6 My '87
 Photographs and photography
 Country flea markets. S. Bullaty and A. Lomeo. il *Ctry J* 14:54-7 Jl '87
Fleas
 Needed: one fleabag [Susan Wade builds artificial dog for flea research] il *U S News World Rep* 102:64 Je 1 '87
 Control
 Natural flea control. D. Downs. il *Mother Earth News* 106:29+ Jl/Ag '87
Die Fledermaus [operetta] See Strauss, Johann, 1825-1899
Fleece *See* Wool
Fleece, Agricultural *See* Plants—Protection
Fleet Street (London, England)
 "The whole thing is breaking up". R. Morais. il *Forbes* 139:148+ My 18 '87
Fleetwood, Blake
 From the people who brought you the Twinkie defense: the ride of the expert witness industry. il *Wash Mon* 19:33-7 Je '87
Fleetwood Mac (Musical group)
 Fleetwood Mac [concert at the Capital Centre, Maryland] D. Wild. il *Roll Stone* p17 D 3 '87
 Fleetwood Mac shimmers back. J. Pareles. il *Roll Stone* p51-2 My 7 '87
 Lindsey Buckingham leaves Fleetwood Mac. J. Ressner. *Roll Stone* p15+ S 24 '87
 New Fleetwood Mac album due. D. Wild. *Roll Stone* p30 Mr 26 '87

Rockers: then & now. il pors *Teen* 31:62-3 O '87
 Talking about each other: the women of Fleetwood Mac. C. Krupp. por *Glamour* 85:302 S '87
Fleischer, Ernest
 about
 The hedgeaholic. J. Willoughby. il por *Forbes* 140:180+ N 16 '87
Fleischer, Leonore
 Sales & bargains. See issues of New York
 Talk of the trade. See issues of Publishers Weekly
Fleischner, Eva
 Learning from history. *Commonweal* 114:167-8 Mr 27 '87
Fleit, Linda H.
 Overselling technology on campus. *Educ Dig* 53:19-21 N '87
Fleming, Anne Taylor
 Elizabeth Taylor: act II. pors *Vogue* 177:434-41+ O '87
 Our fascination with Baby M. il por *N Y Times Mag* p32-6+ Mr 29 '87
Fleming, Dan B.
 Teaching the great issues of the future. il por *Futurist* 21:27-8 Ja/F '87
 (jt. auth) See Cortés, Carlos E., and Fleming, Dan B.
Fleming, Dan B., and Hunt, Thomas C., 1930-
 The world as seen by students in Accelerated Christian Education schools [with reply by Ronald E. Johnson] bibl f il *Phi Delta Kappan* 68:518-23 Mr '87
Fleming, John
 A passion for history. il *House Gard* 159:122-5+ Mr '87
Fleming, Michael, and Manvell, Roger, 1909-1987
 Through a lens, darkly. il *Psychol Today* 21:26-30+ Jl '87
Fleming, Robert
 Carver Federal carves out its market niche. il por *Black Enterp* 17:214-16+ Je '87
Fleming, Thomas J., 1927-
 The big leak. il por *Am Herit* 38:64-71 D '87
 The Civil War and American destiny. il *Natl Rev* 39:48+ N 6 '87
 Countdown to a miracle: the making of our Constitution. il *Read Dig* 131:132-40+ S '87
 Office romance [story] il *Good Housekeep* 205:152-3 N '87
Flemming, Nicholas, and Redknap, Mark
 Plunging into the past. il *Courier* 40:4-7 N '87
Flesch, Hugo
 Les neues. *Nation* 245:174 Ag 29 '87
Fletcher, George P.
 Goetz on trial. bibl f il *N Y Rev Books* 34:22-4+ Ap 23 '87
Fletcher, James C.
 Space [address, October 12, 1987] *Vital Speeches Day* 54:66-8 N 15 '87
 Terradreaming [excerpts from remarks, March 25, 1987] por *Space World* X-7-283:36 Jl '87
 United States space program [address, June 24, 1987] *Vital Speeches Day* 53:642-4 Ag 15 '87
 about
 Interview. A. R. Oberg. il por *Omni* 10:120-2+ D '87
Fletcher, Janet
 Examining the library market. il *Publ Wkly* 232:15 Ag 14 '87
Fletcher, John, 1579-1625
 about
 The tamer tamed [drama] Reviews
 Nation 245:458-9 O 24 '87. T. M. Disch
Fletcher, Ralph
 Why your school board needs you. il *Parents* 62:78+ O '87
Fletcher, Sheila
 Sailing to the edge of the world. il *Hist Today* 37:10-11 S '87
Fleur de Lys (San Francisco, Calif.: Restaurant) *See* San Francisco (Calif.)—Restaurants, nightclubs, bars, etc.
Fleur de Lys Automobile Manufacturing, Ltd.
 Fleur de Lys Newark. D. Nye. il *Road Track* 38:71+ Mr '87
Flexibility (Physiology)
 How flexible should you be? E. Smith. il *Women's Sports Fitness* 9:10 S '87
Flexible manufacturing systems
 Getting man and machine to live happily ever after. J. Hoerr. il *Bus Week* p61-2 Ap 20 '87
 Will corporate America become more flexible? G. Bakoulis. *Work Woman* 12:25+ O '87

Flexible spending accounts See Fringe benefits

Flexner, Stuart Berg
about
All the words that are fit to print—and some that aren't—fill the hefty new Random House dictionary. E. Levin. il por *People Wkly* 28:167-9 N 23 '87

Flextime
Flextime: turning absence into presence. H. Hall. il *Psychol Today* 21:32 O '87

Flieger, Ken
Testing in 'real people'. il *FDA Consum* 21:10-12+ N '87

Flier, Jeffrey S., and others
Elevated levels of glucose transport and transporter messenger RNA are induced by *ras* or *src* oncogenes. bibl f il *Science* 235:1492-5 Mr 20 '87
Severely impaired adipsin expression in genetic and acquired obesity. bibl f il *Science* 237:405-8 Jl 24 '87

Flies
See also
Blackflies
Dragonflies
Drosophila
Fruit flies
Houseflies
Maggots
White flies
The surprising genetics of bottlenecked flies [research by Edwin Bryant and others] R. Lewin. *Science* 235:1325-7 Mr 13 '87

Control
How to build a fly trap that really works [horn flies] il *Success Farm* 85:41B Je '87
Winning the battle against those wily flies. il *Sunset* 179:72-3 Jl '87

Flies, Artificial See Fishing lures, flies, etc.

Flies as carriers of infection
See also
Onchocerciasis

Flight
See also
Gliding and soaring
Anecdotes, facetiae, satire, etc.
Diary of a flying man. R. Cohen. *New Yorker* 63:34-5 S 21 '87
Physiological aspects
See Aviation—Physiological aspects

Flight, Interplanetary See Space flight

Flight attendants See Airlines—Flight attendants

Flight control systems (Computer systems) See Computers—Aviation use

Flight crews See Airplane crews

Flight Dynamics, Inc.
Flight Dynamics prepares to test wind shear guidance with HUD [holographic head-up display] il *Aviat Week Space Technol* 126:107+ Ja 12 '87

Flight Dynamics Laboratory (U.S.) See Air Force Flight Dynamics Laboratory (U.S.)

Flight instructors See Aviation—Study and teaching

Flight International Group, Inc.
Contractor expands inventory for airborne threat training. B. M. Greeley, Jr. il *Aviat Week Space Technol* 127:139+ O 12 '87
Flight International will provide USAF electronic warfare training [use of corporate jets] *Aviat Week Space Technol* 126:101 Je 1 '87
Putting the right stuff to work in business [chairman D. G. Matthews] P. Finch. il por *Bus Week* p105 Mr 23 '87

Flight planning (Computer systems) See Computers—Aviation use

Flight recorders
Corporate operators increase use of CVRs [cockpit voice recorders] *Aviat Week Space Technol* 127:117 S 28 '87
Midair collision builds pressure for CVRs in commuter aircraft [cockpit voice recorders] *Aviat Week Space Technol* 126:32 Ja 26 '87
New modular system monitors engine, airframe parameters automatically [digital flight data acquisition unit] K. J. Stein. il *Aviat Week Space Technol* 126:99+ Mr 30 '87
Safety Board urges mandatory use of FDR/CVRs in commuter transports [flight data and cockpit voice recorders] E. H. Phillips. il *Aviat Week Space Technol* 127:73-5 Ag 31 '87

Flight service stations See United States. Federal Aviation Administration—Flight service stations

Flight simulators
See also
Air Force Flight Test Center (U.S.)
FlightSafety International, Inc.
SimuFlite Training International, Inc.
Space flight simulators
Air Force to evaluate on-board EW simulator [electronic warfare] il *Aviat Week Space Technol* 126:48-9+ F 16 '87
Boeing evaluating new control laws in 7J7 advanced-technology simulator [fly-by-wire control system] B. D. Nordwall. il *Aviat Week Space Technol* 126:54-6+ Je 29 '87
Crew systems lab offers rapid feedback on cockpit concepts [Northrop Corp.] il *Aviat Week Space Technol* 127:98-9+ N 23 '87
Descent into disaster [SimuFlite's microburst simulator profile] J. M. McClellan. *Flying* 114:100-1 Ag '87
Enhanced simulators aid development of engineering, man/machine interfaces [helicopter simulators] il *Aviat Week Space Technol* 126:56-8 Ja 19 '87
Human factors research key element of LHX design. il *Aviat Week Space Technol* 126:118-19+ Ja 19 '87
Latter-day Load Star [C-5 Galaxy] R. L. Collins. il *Flying* 114:17-18 Mr '87
Lufthansa, Swissair introduce full-simulator pilot training [Futura] K. F. Mordoff. il *Aviat Week Space Technol* 127:38-9+ Ag 10 '87
Military Airlift Command will transition to C-130 flight crew training system. K. J. Stein. il *Aviat Week Space Technol* 127:109-10 Jl 6 '87
Multipilot air-to-air combat evaluated in Northrop simulator. M. A. Dornheim. il *Aviat Week Space Technol* 127:64-5+ N 30 '87
NASA/Army upgrading simulation facilities at Ames [helicopters] il *Aviat Week Space Technol* 126:57 Ja 19 '87
New Boeing facility will play key role in ATF competition [advanced tactical fighter] *Aviat Week Space Technol* 126:89+ Ja 26 '87
Northrop upgrades simulator center to bolster ATF program effort [advanced tactical fighter] M. A. Dornheim. il *Aviat Week Space Technol* 127:95-8 N 23 '87
SAC stresses air crew training to defeat Soviet defenses. B. M. Greeley, Jr. il *Aviat Week Space Technol* 126:72-3+ F 9 '87
Simulators. E. Weiner. *Flying* 114:78 F '87
Snake dance. P. Bradley. il *Flying* 114:12 O '87
United conducts total training of MAC C-5 crews. il *Aviat Week Space Technol* 127:112 Jl 6 '87
Virtual Prototyping System speeds evaluation of cockpit configurations. il *Aviat Week Space Technol* 127:81+ D 7 '87

Flight training See Aviation—Study and teaching

FlightSafety International, Inc.
Still flying high. J. A. Conway. por *Forbes* 139:8 Je 15 '87

Flindt, Flemming
about
Phaedra [ballet] Reviews
Dance Mag 61:25 O '87. J. Neal
Swan Lake [ballet] Reviews
Dance Mag 61:29+ Mr '87. J. Neal

Flint, Harrison L. (Harrison Leigh), 1929-
Bird cherries [excerpt from The country journal book of hardy trees and shrubs] il *Ctry J* 14:6-7 Ag '87

Flint, Richard, and Flint, Shirley
Curing curly top. il map *Rodale's Org Gard* 34:70-3 Ag '87

Flint, Shirley
(jt. auth) See Flint, Richard, and Flint, Shirley

Flint (Mich.)
Economic conditions
In Flint, tough times last [General Motors pulls out] M. Moore. il *Nation* 244:753-6 Je 6 '87
Race relations
Flint blacks angered by youth's 'suicide' probe [death of J. Carter] L. Ransom. il pors *Jet* 72:51-3 Ag 24 '87

Flint Hills (Kan. and Okla.)
See also
Osage Hills (Okla.)

Flip-flops (Circuits) See Multivibrators

FLIR (Foward-looking infrared) sensors See Detectors, Infrared

Flirting
A flirting lesson. L. Darling. *Mademoiselle* 93:155 Ag '87
How to be a flirt [views of Beverly Palmer] *USA Today (Periodical)* 116:10 N '87

Flirting—*cont.*

Men who flirt and run. il *Glamour* 85:96 Ag '87

The new come-on: 6 steps get you fit to flirt. il *Mademoiselle* 93:222-5 N '87

Anecdotes, facetiae, satire, etc.

The new flirt. M. Dowd. il *N Y Times Mag* p18 Mr 1 '87

Flo Hyman Memorial Award

Flo Hyman Sports Award brings Martina to tears. *Jet* 71:5 F 23 '87

Float (Banking) *See* Banks and banking—Float

Float fishing *See* Fishing

Float trips *See* River trips

Floating-point arithmetic

The state of numerics [floating-point coprocessors] S. S. Fried. il *Byte* 12 no12 Sp Issue:115-18+ '87

Floating prisons *See* Prison ships

Floats, Parade *See* Parade floats

Flom, Edward L.

Stop, look and listen [address, May 6, 1987] *Vital Speeches Day* 53:594-6 Jl 15 '87

Flood, James F., and others

Modulation of memory processing by cholecystokinin: dependence on the vagus nerve. bibl f il *Science* 236:832-4 My 15 '87

Flood prevention and control

    See also

    Atchafalaya River (La.)—Regulation

    Dams

    Great Salt Lake (Utah)—Regulation

    Mississippi River—Regulation

The Army's giant swampbuster [proposed draining of Yazoo Backwater Swamp, Miss.] J. McCafferty. il *Sierra* 72:84-5 Jl/Ag '87

Will the river stay 'way from their door? [1937 Ohio River flood and current prevention efforts] J. G. Mitchell. il *Audubon* 89:28-32+ My '87

Italy

Venice is shrinking. M. Rossi. *World Press Rev* 34:58 Ja '87

Floods

Floods: the nation's primary weather hazard. D. H. Hickcox. *Focus* 37:29-30 Spr '87

In the United States—flash floods and drought [1986] D. Le Comte. il *Weatherwise* 40:12-16 F '87

History

Will the river stay 'way from their door? [1937 Ohio River flood and current prevention efforts] J. G. Mitchell. il *Audubon* 89:28-32+ My '87

Illinois

An Illinois policeman puts his job on the line by rushing to the aid of his family [C. Launius] il por *People Wkly* 28:59 O 19 '87

United States

    See Floods

Utah

A greater Salt Lake. P. Barnes-Svarney. il map *Earth Sci* 39:22-3 Wint '86

Floor cleaning appliances

    See also

    Vacuum cleaners

Floor coverings

    See also

    Rugs and carpets

Color your floors bright [stenciled doormat and painted floor cloth] V. Hahn. il *Parents* 62:147-8+ Ag '87

Floor lamps *See* Electric lamps

Floor painting and decoration

Faux rugs for fun. il *South Living* 22:90 Ag '87

Painted floors. D. L. Caringer. il *Better Homes Gard* 65:40-1 Ag '87

Floor skylights *See* Skylights

Floor tile laying *See* Tile laying

Floorcloths *See* Floor coverings

Flooring

3 great wood floors. H. Wicks. il *Home Mech* 83:28-32+ D '87

Options in kitchen flooring. il *South Living* 22:128 O '87

This parquet has a new twist. il *South Living* 22:160 My '87

Flooring, Plastic

Waxing eloquent [vinyl] *Changing Times* 41:17-18 Ja '87

Floors

    See also

    Floor coverings

Focus on floors. M. D. Glass. il *Ladies Home J* 104:98-103 Ag '87

Care

    See Floors—Maintenance and repair

Finishes and finishing

Refinish your floors without sanding. J. White. il *Fam Handyman* 37:52-6 N '87

Refinishing wood floors. B. Vila. il *Pop Mech* 164:14+ Mr '87

Sanding a hardwood floor. A. Rooze. il *Fam Handyman* 37:46-51 N '87

Maintenance and repair

Hardwood floor care. *Better Homes Gard* 65:225 N '87

Squeaky floors: causes, cures. G. Branson and C. J. De Groote. il *Fam Handyman* 37:34-8+ N '87

Floppy disk memory (Computers) *See* Computers—Memory systems

Flora, Desert *See* Desert flora

Flora (Ill.)

Prisons and reformatories

Illinois town supports theory of black appellate judge: crime does pay. *Jet* 72:22 Je 8 '87

Floral decoration *See* Flower arrangement

Floral painting *See* Flowers in art

Floral print fabrics *See* Textile fabrics

Florence, Heather Grant

Controlling ideas. *Society* 24:19-21 Jl/Ag '87

Florence, Ronald

The optimum boat. See issues of Motor Boating & Sailing beginning June 1986

Florence (Italy)

Churches (Buildings)

    See also

    Santa Maria del Carmine (Church: Florence, Italy)

Music

    See also

    Opera—Italy

Stores

Artisans of Florence. A. M. Zwack. il *Gourmet* 47:50-5+ Jl '87

Florence bazaar. G. Whitmore. il *Harpers Bazaar* 120:74 Jl '87

Flores, Alberto

(jt. auth) See Otterstetter, Horst, and Flores, Alberto

Flores, Lito Tejada- *See* Tejada-Flores, Lito

Flores Labra, Carlos Fernando

    about

From prison to a software fortune. il por *Fortune* 115:132 Je 8 '87

Florescue, Barry

    about

Why didn't they pay him to stay home? B. Leonard. il por *Forbes* 139:120-1 Je 15 '87

Floriculture *See* Flower gardens and gardening

Florida

    See also

    Abortion clinics—Florida

    Arts—Florida

    Beaches—Florida

    Birds—Florida

    Birth control clinics—Florida

    Booksellers and bookselling—Florida

    Child welfare—Florida

    Courts—Florida

    Criminal justice, Administration of—Florida

    Environmental policy—Florida

    Everglades (Fla.)

    Fisher Island (Fla.)

    Fishing—Florida

    Fortification—Florida

    Game laws—Florida

    Health resorts, watering places, etc.—Florida

    Historic houses, sites, etc.—Florida

    Kissimmee River (Fla.)

    Law—Florida

    Manatee County (Fla.)

    Medical care—Florida

    Motion picture festivals—Florida

    Okefenokee Swamp (Ga. and Fla.)

    Radon pollution—Florida

    Sales tax—Florida

    Sea Islands

    Shore protection—Florida

    Wildlife conservation—Florida

    Wildlife sanctuaries—Florida

Description and travel

The best things in Florida are free! S. Birnbaum. il *Good Housekeep* 204:54+ F '87

Economic conditions

Growing pains in the Sunshine State. A. L. Taylor, III. il *Fortune* 116:40-2+ Ag 17 '87

Florida—*cont.*
Fisheries
See Fisheries
Industries
See also
Citrus fruit industry
Fruit industry
Motion picture industry
Real estate business
Politics and government
Florida's rookie governor is stuck in a slump [B. Martinez] G. DeGeorge. il por *Bus Week* p174+ O 12 '87
NAACP criticizes Florida Gov. Martinez on hiring. *Jet* 72:29 Ap 13 '87
Florida. Dept. of Health and Rehabilitative Services
The empty crib [deaf parents struggle to retain custody of child; case of S. Timmons] L. A. Walker. il por *Ladies Home J* 104:76+ Mr '87
Florida A & M University
The class of 1987. il *Ebony* 42:116-18+ Ag '87
Florida Agricultural and Mechanical University *See* Florida A & M University
Florida Keys (Fla.)
See also
Birds—Florida Keys (Fla.)
Key West (Fla.)
Resorts—Florida Keys (Fla.)
Wildlife conservation—Florida Keys (Fla.)
Photographs and photography
Use your camera to unlock the beauty of the Florida Keys. C. Purcell and A. Purcell. il *Pop Photogr* 94:30+ Jl '87
Florida panthers *See* Pumas
Florin, Peter, 1921-
about
President of the forty-second session. il pors *UN Chron* 24:9 N '87
Florio, James J.
Should Congress adopt the House-passed "Gephardt Amendment"? [excerpts from debate, April 29, 1987] *Congr Dig* 66:176+ Je/Jl '87
Florists
See also
Melridge, Inc.
Florman, Samuel C.
[Column] *See* occasional issues of Technology Review
Flosi, James V.
about
Does the Church have good news for divorced Catholics? [cover story; interview] il por *U S Cathol* 52:6-13 My '87
Flounders
A case study in interstate cooperation [Atlantic Coast summer flounder] G. C. Colvin. il *Conservationist* 42:18 S/O '87
Flour
No-calorie substitute for flour. J. Raloff. *Sci News* 131:251 Ap 18 '87
Flour mills
See also
Jewel Evans Family Foods
Flow of air *See* Air flow
Flow of fluids *See* Fluid dynamics
Flower, Joe
Secrets of the masters. il *Esquire* 107:128-9+ My '87
Flower arrangement
Best in bloom. M. Webb. il *Harpers Bazaar* 121:56+ D '87
The flowers are the show [use of clear vases] L. C. Askey. il *South Living* 22:60-1 N '87
A fresh look at arrangements. L. C. Askey. il *South Living* 22:42+ Jl '87
A gift of roses—make it last! R. Haskell. il *Flower Gard* 31:8 F/Mr '87
How to make cut daffodils last longer. il *Sunset* 178:194 Mr '87
A place for roses: the inimitable world of Ned and Marlo Phillips. M. Peppiatt. il por *Archit Dig* 44:206-11 N '87
These are Sunset's Monday morning bouquets. il *Sunset* 179:74-5 Jl '87
Flower boxes, planters, etc.
Brake drum planter. K. Haugaard. il *Pop Mech* 164:57 Je '87
Building your own windowbox. il *Home Mech* 83:51 Je '87
Dress up a planter with tile. J. Drako. il *Workbench* 43:62-3 My/Je '87
Is this the ultimate living Christmas tree container? It disassembles. It has wheels. il *Sunset* 179:192+ D '87

A long happy life for a wooden container. il *Sunset* 178:196-7 Mr '87
Planter fences and pergolas. A. W. Lees. il *Pop Sci* 231:72-4 Ag '87
A smart solution for a stark deck. il *South Living* 22:45 Jl '87
Their deck has bloom built in. il *Sunset* 178:78-9 Mr '87
Two looks for this large planter. il *South Living* 22:168-9 Mr '87
Very big boxes for hillside flowers, vegetables. il *Sunset* 179:92 Ag '87
Window boxes to brighten every sill. J. A. McKeon. il *Better Homes Gard* 65:128-31 Ap '87
Flower exhibits
The Chelsea Flower Show. J. Ruttle. il *Rodale's Org Gard* 34:22-3+ Ap '87
Dates of the big flower shows for 1987. *Flower Gard* 31:14 F/Mr '87
Garden events [title varies] *See* issues of Sunset (Central edition)
In Philadelphia: a flower show. G. Jaynes. il *Time* 129:14-16 Ap 6 '87
The New York Flower Show and Uncle Sam Umbrella Shop. H. Bridges. il *Gourmet* 47:42+ Mr '87
On the calendar. *See* issues of Flower and Garden
Southern garden events. *See* issues of Southern Living
Flower gardens and gardening
See also
Biennials (Plants)
Perennials (Plants)
Shade gardens and gardening
Wildflower gardens and gardening
Celebrate the bicentennial: create a Constitution garden. A. Reilly. il *Flower Gard* 31:80-1 Ap/My '87
Cut-your-own bouquets [flowers as a cash crop] E. E. Ogden. il *Rodale's Org Gard* 34:81-2+ Ja '87
Four-season showoffs. il *Sunset* 179:108-11 N '87
Grow your own cut flowers from seed. D. A. Jimerson. il *Better Homes Gard* 65:45-53 My '87
Summer flowers for the long haul. il *Sunset* 178:120-1 My '87
Tough guys grow petunias. S. Brewer. il *50 Plus* 27:28-31 My '87
Welcome butterflies. D. A. Jimerson. il *Better Homes Gard* 65:104-7 Mr '87
Anecdotes, facetiae, satire, etc.
Flowers of evil: ask Charles Baudelaire. F. Gannon. il por *Atlantic* 260:44 S '87
Alabama
Beautiful flowers from humble beginnings. il *South Living* 22:94-5 Mr '87
Georgia
Dan's garden: a journal in flowers [cover story] L. C. Askey. il *South Living* 22:124-7 Ap '87
Pennsylvania
Fields of color [J. Thouron's flower gardens in the Brandywine Valley] D. M. Stone. il *House Gard* 159:68-77+ Ag '87
A riot of roses [rose garden of Dr. Joseph Kassab] C. Vogel. il *N Y Times Mag* p52-3 My 24 '87
Flower painting *See* Flowers in art
Flower pot holders
See also
Cachepots
Flower shows *See* Flower exhibits
Flower stands *See* Plant stands, flower stands, etc.
Flowering trees
See also
Cherry trees
Golden rain trees
Flowers, Pam
about
Dog-sledder goes it alone. N. Klouda. il por *Women's Sports Fitness* 9:20 Mr '87
Flowers
See also
Biennials (Plants)
Bulbs
Perennials (Plants)
Wildflowers
See also names of flowers
Fertilization
See Fertilization of plants
Marketing
Cut-your-own bouquets [flowers as a cash crop] E. E. Ogden. il *Rodale's Org Gard* 34:81-2+ Ja '87
Photographs and photography
Floral derangement [work of A. G. Richards] N. Guccione. il *Omni* 10:100-5 D '87

Flowers—Photographs and photography—*cont.*
Francesco Scavullo: flower photographer. F. Scavullo. por *Saturday Evening Post* 259:47-9 Jl/Ag '87
Light of spring. J. Shaw. il por *Pop Photogr* 94:38-45 My '87
Symbol, a single flower: an exercise in point of view by students of photography at Art Center College of Design. B. Hurter. il *Petersens Photogr Mag* 16:36-8 Ag '87

Varieties
New plants. il *Flower Gard* 32:21-8+ D '87/Ja '88
New varieties for your garden. il *Rodale's Org Gard* 34:34-7+ Ja '87

Flowers, Artificial
See also
Glass flowers
How petals from the sea form these fragile blossoms [seashell flowers by J. Manoff] G. B. Ruh. il por *Smithsonian* 17:106-10 Ja '87

Flowers, Forcing of *See* Forcing (Plants)
Flowers, Glass *See* Glass flowers
Flowers as food
See also
Cooking—Flowers
Salad days. B. Kafka. il *Vogue* 177:208 My '87
West Coast petal pushers Jay and Pamela North foster a flowering culinary fad. N. Geeslin. il pors *People Wkly* 28:95+ Ag 17 '87

Flowers in art
See also
Wildflowers in art
Botanical illustration [prints] S. J. Zietz. il *Antiques* 131:600-13 Mr '87
A remarkable book from the 'greatest painter of flowers' [Knopf/Callaway publication of Georgia O'Keeffe: one hundred flowers] W. Goldstein. il *Publ Wkly* 232:27+ S 11 '87
An unabashedly sensual approach to a genteel genre [Georgia O'Keeffe's works] il *Newsweek* 110:74-5 N 9 '87
The watercolor page. S. E. Bader. il por *Am Artist* 51:58-63 F '87
The watercolor page. S. M. Rasmussen. il por *Am Artist* 51:42-5+ My '87

Flowers in house decoration *See* Plants in house decoration
Flowers in opera
A Puccini bouquet: in his works the composer cultivated floral imagery. K. Stern. il por *Opera News* 51:14-16 Ja 17 '87

Floyd, Nathaniel M.
about
An expert finds that bullies and their victims are linked in a strange, unconscious courtship [interview] E. Levin. il por *People Wkly* 27:143-4+ Ap 13 '87

Flu *See* Influenza
Flu viruses *See* Influenza viruses
Fluid dynamics
See also
Laminar flow
Magnetohydrodynamics
Bedform alignment in directionally varying flows [cover story] D. M. Rubin and R. E. Hunter. bibl f il *Science* 237:276-8 Jl 17 '87
Fluid dynamics. *Phys Today* 40:S34-S36 Ja '87
A numerical laboratory [computer simulation] K.-H. A. Winkler and others. bibl f il *Phys Today* 40:28-37 O '87
Quantitative three-dimensional optical tomographic imaging of supersonic flows. G. W. Faris and R. L. Byer. bibl f il *Science* 238:1700-2 D 18 '87
Sticky threadlike substances that tend to draw themselves out into bead arrays. J. Walker. il *Sci Am* 257:108-11 S '87
Time-resolved three-dimensional concentration measurements in a gas jet. B. Yip and others. bibl f il *Science* 235:1209-11 Mr 6 '87
Why a fluid flows faster when the tube is pinched. J. Walker. il *Sci Am* 257:104-7 Jl '87

Fluids
See also
Fluid dynamics
Liquids
Solvents
Fluid interfaces, including fractal flows, can be studied in a Hele-Shaw cell. J. Walker. il *Sci Am* 257:134-6+ N '87

Flukes *See* Trematodes
Fluor Corp.
After the frying pan, what? M. Beauchamp. il por *Forbes* 139:60+ Mr 9 '87

Fluorescence
See also
Mössbauer effect

Physiological effects
See Light—Physiological effects
Fluorescence, Photography of *See* Ultraviolet photography
Fluorescent indicators in biological research
Cellular and subcellular heterogeneity of $[Ca^{2+}]_i$ in single heart cells revealed by fura-2. W. G. Wier and others. bibl f il *Science* 235:325-8 Ja 16 '87
Fluorescence properties of calmodulin-binding peptides reflect alpha-helical periodicity. K. T. O'Neil and others. bibl f il *Science* 236:1454-6 Je 12 '87
Nerve terminal remodeling visualized in living mice by repeated examination of the same neuron. D. Purves and others. bibl f il *Science* 238:1122-6 N 20 '87
A system for rapid DNA sequencing with fluorescent chain-terminating dideoxynucleotides. J. M. Prober and others. bibl f il *Science* 238:336-41 O 16 '87
Tumor promoters halt cell-cell 'talk' [research by John Holland] J. Raloff. *Sci News* 131:230-1 Ap 11 '87

Fluorescent lighting *See* Lighting, Fluorescent
Fluorides
See also
Sulfur fluorides
Fluoride: not just for teeth. E. T. Becker. il *Women's Sports Fitness* 9:14 Jl '87

Fluorocarbons
See also
Chlorofluorocarbons
Polyvinylidene fluoride

Fly, Richard, and others
Why the Reagan era won't end in 1989. il por *Bus Week* p33 Jl 13 '87

Fly ash *See* Ashes
Fly-by-wire systems *See* Computers—Aviation use
Fly casting *See* Casting (Fishing)
Fly control *See* Flies—Control
Fly fishing *See* Casting (Fishing)
Fly-ins *See* Aviation—Exhibitions
Fly rods *See* Fishing tackle
Fly tackle *See* Fishing tackle
Fly tying *See* Fishing lures, flies, etc.
Flygare, Thomas J.
De jure. See issues of Phi Delta Kappan
Flying, Fear of *See* Fear of flying
Flying (Periodical)
60th anniversary issue [cover story; special issue; with editorial comment by Richard L. Collins] il *Flying* 114:2+ S '87
Flying boats *See* Airplanes, Amphibious; Seaplanes
Flying Karamazov Brothers
Juggling the Bard [The comedy of errors] L. Sauvage. *New Leader* 70:20-1 Je 29 '87
Robert Brustein on theater [The comedy of errors] R. Brustein. *New Repub* 197:28 Jl 6 '87
Tenpins aloft, forsooth [The comedy of errors] W. A. Henry. il *Time* 129:70 Je 15 '87
Theater [The comedy of errors] T. M. Disch. *Nation* 245:31-2 Jl 4-11 '87
The theatre [The comedy of errors] E. Oliver. *New Yorker* 63:72 Je 15 '87
Up in the air [performance of The comedy of errors] J. Simon. il *N Y* 20:91 Je 15 '87
Flying observatories *See* Airplanes in astronomy
Flying reptiles *See* Pterosaurs
Flying saucers *See* UFOs
Flying schools *See* Aviation—Study and teaching
Flynn, Don
"Please ackuse me . . . ". il *Seventeen* 46:178 S '87
Flynn, John
about
Best seller [film] Reviews
Macleans 100:58 O 5 '87. L. O'Toole
Newsweek 110:84 O 5 '87. D. Ansen
Time 130:85 O 12 '87
Flynn, Richard M.
The utility industry [address, March 9-11, 1987] *Vital Speeches Day* 53:463-5 My 15 '87
Flynn, Sydney
My mother's cookbook. il por *McCalls* 114:47+ My '87
Flynt, Althea, d. 1987
about
Her death ends the improbable love match of porn merchants Althea and Larry Flynt. M. Green. il pors *People Wkly* 28:32-4+ Jl 20 '87

Flynt, Larry
    about
  Her death ends the improbable love match of porn merchants Althea and Larry Flynt. M. Green. il pors *People Wkly* 28:32-4+ Jl 20 '87
  Jerry Falwell vs. Larry Flynt. A. Press. il pors *Newsweek* 110:76 D 14 '87
FM *See* Radio frequency modulation
FM receivers *See* Radio receivers
FMLN *See* Farabundo Martí National Liberation Front
FNMA *See* Federal National Mortgage Association
Fo, Dario
    about
  Almost by chance a woman: Elizabeth [drama] Reviews *Nation* 244:860-2 Je 20 '87. T. M. Disch
Foam insulation *See* Insulation (Heat)
Foam plastic houses *See* Plastic houses
Foams
  Foam structures with a negative Poisson's ratio. R. Lakes. bibl f il *Science* 235:1038-40 F 27 '87
  Putting the squeeze on foam [research by Roderic Lakes] I. Peterson. il *Sci News* 131:166 Mr 14 '87
  Squeeze me [work of Roderic S. Lakes] *Sci Am* 256:62+ My '87
Focus groups (Market research)
  Listening, the old-fashioned way. J. A. Trachtenberg. il *Forbes* 140:202+ O 5 '87
Focusing *See* Photography—Focusing
Focusing attachment for telescopes *See* Telescopes—Equipment
Fodor, Joe
  Last word. il *Omni* 10:182 O '87
Foegen, J. H.
  The menace of high-tech employment. il por *Futurist* 21:38-40 S/O '87
Foerster, Richard
  Halley's comet [poem] *Nation* 244:620 My 9 '87
Fog
    See also
  Aviation—Fog hazards
Fog, Artificial
  Fog . . . foggier . . . foggiest [machines and fluids] A. Brightman. il *Theatre Crafts* 21:28-9+ Mr '87
FOG-M (Fiber optic guided missiles) *See* Guided missiles—Optical equipment
Fog signals
  Fog songs [cover story] E. De Wire. il *Sea Front* 33:164-73 My/Je '87
Fogarty, John T.
  And now, the good news. il *World Tennis* 34:64 Mr '87
Fogden, Patricia
  War & passion. il *Int Wildl* 17:12-17 Ja/F '87
Fogelman, Avron
    about
  Needy kids, perpetual aid. por *Time* 130:70 N 30 '87
Fogerty, John
    about
  Fogerty plays Creedence songs at vets benefit. A. DeCurtis. il por *Roll Stone* p14 Ag 13 '87
  John Fogerty [interview] J. Henke. por *Roll Stone* p146-8+ N 5-D 10 '87
FOIA (Freedom of Information Act) *See* Freedom of information
Foisy, Ruth
    about
  A desperate search for a second life. M. Jacobbi and R. Wright. il pors *McCalls* 114:127-9 Je '87
Fokker BV
  Ansett Airlines prepares Fokker 50 for start of service in November. K. F. Mordoff. il *Aviat Week Space Technol* 127:49-50 S 28 '87
  Fokker, MBB agree to study future cooperation. *Aviat Week Space Technol* 127:30 O 19 '87
  German airline begins service with Fokker 50 transport. il *Aviat Week Space Technol* 127:36-7 S 7 '87
  Manufacturer preparing to deliver first Fokker 50 to Ansett. il *Aviat Week Space Technol* 126:299 Je 15 '87
Folates *See* Folic acid
Folding boats *See* Boats and boating
Folding cameras *See* Cameras
Folding chairs *See* Chairs
Folding ladders *See* Ladders
Folding of clothes
  Folding [art of folding sweaters at a Benetton store in Manhattan] *New Yorker* 63:30-1 My 25 '87

Folding screens *See* Screens (Furniture)
Folding tables *See* Tables
Folds (Geology)
  All shook up: Los Angeles earthquake reveals new signposts of seismic danger [research by Thomas L. Davis] J. Horgan. il *Sci Am* 257:18+ D '87
Foley, James
    about
  Who's that girl [film] Reviews
    Macleans il 100:50 Ag 24 '87. N. Jennings
    New Repub 197:25 S 7 '87. S. Kauffmann
    People Wkly il 28:6 Ag 24 '87. R. Novak
    Roll Stone il p23 S 24 '87. J. Rosenbluth
Foley, James D., 1942-
  Interfaces for advanced computing [cover story] bibl (p183-4) il *Sci Am* 257:126-30+ O '87
Foley, John
    about
  Flacking in the fields of the Lord. J. Ferullo. il pors *Channels* 7:45-8 Mr '87
Foley, Raymond
    about
  "Any jerk can publish a magazine". F. Meeks. il por *Forbes* 140:394+ Jl 13 '87
Foley, Suzanne
  Eleanor Moty [cover story] il por *Am Craft* 47:34-9+ Je/Jl '87
Foley, Tricia
  Fuel for thought [excerpt from Having tea] il *Work Woman* 12:142-3+ S '87
Folger Shakespeare Library
  Shakespeare lives at the Folger. M. Severy. il *Natl Geogr* 171:244-59 F '87
Folic acid
  Vitamin C helps keep gums healthy; Folate may help, too. *Prevention* 39:79 F '87
Folk art
    See also
  Cigar store Indians
  Olsen, Barbara
  Phillips, Ammi
  Roybal, Maximiliano
  Santos (Art)
  Young, Susan
  Folk art [American folk art; cover story; special section] bibl il *Antiques* 132:438-9, 514-59 S '87
  Whirligigs and whimsies: enchanting folk art you can build. J. Williams and J. Severson. il *Better Homes Gard* 65:102-4+ My '87
  Young America [condensation] J. Lipman and others. il *Read Dig* 131:163-7 Jl '87
    Collectors and collecting
  Folk tales: of baseballs and weathervanes in Washington, D.C. [J. and J. Wallach's collection] C. T. Buckley. il pors *Archit Dig* 44:62-7+ Jl '87
  Living with antiques:
    A New England folk art collection. S. Klein and S. Rotenstreich. il *Antiques* 132:538-45 S '87
  Peter H. Tillou's American flair. C. D. B. Bryan. il por *Archit Dig* 44:64+ Je '87
    Exhibitions
    See also
  Metropolitan Museum of Art (New York, N.Y.). American Wing
  Museum of American Folk Art
  American folk art [exhibit entitled American folk art: a sampling from northern California collections] S. B. Sherrill. il *Antiques* 131:96+ Ja '87
  American folk art [traveling exhibition entitled An American sampler: folk art from the Shelburne Museum] S. B. Sherrill. il *Antiques* 132:986 N '87
  The art of mingei at Kuromatsu. H. Junker. il por *Archit Dig* 44:98+ My '87
  Folk art treasures at San Francisco's Mexican Museum. il *Sunset* 178:12 F '87
  A joyous art [Peruvian folk art; exhibit at the OAS Museum of Modern Art of Latin America in Washington] V. G. Stoddart. il *Américas* 39:57 Jl/Ag '87
  Museum accessions [collection of Herbert Waide Hemphill Jr. acquired by the National Museum of American Art] E. H. Gustafson. il *Antiques* 132:438-9+ S '87
  New, Mexican folk art gallery in Texas [San Antonio Museum of Art] *Américas* 39:58 Ja/F '87
  Taking to the road [An American sampler: folk art from the Shelburne Museum] J. Newcombe. il *Americana* 15:26-31 N/D '87

Folk art in the home *See* Art in the home
Folk Festival (Kutztown, Pa.) *See* Kutztown (Pa.)—Festivals
Folk festivals *See* Festivals
Folk lore *See* Folklore
Folk medicine
> *See also*
> Home remedies
> Medicine men
Folk music
> *See also*
> Compact discs—Folk music
> Phonograph records—Folk music
Folk music, American
> *See also*
> Country music
Folk music, Russian
> Janna Bichevskaya is Russia's most popular balladeer—and sounds just like Joan Baez. S. K. Reed. il pors *People Wkly* 27:76+ Ap 6 '87
Folk poetry, Arabic
> Bedouin blues [Egyptian Bedouin poetry] L. Abu-Lughod. il *Nat Hist* 96:24-33 Jl '87
Folk poetry, Brazilian
> Clothesline literature [folhetos] C. Pisa. il *Courier* 39:26-8 D '86
Folk songs, Swiss
> The ranz des vaches. G. Métraux. il *Courier* 40:32-3 F '87
Folk tales *See* Folklore
Folkes, Neisha
> Fashionably fit! il *Essence* 18:22 S '87
Folkl, Joseph
> *about*
> Joe Folkl remembers. G. Morgenson. por *Forbes* 140:304 N 16 '87
Folklife Festival (Va.) *See* Festivals—Virginia
Folklore
> *See also*
> Automobile lore
> Weather lore
> Wolves in religion, folklore, etc.
> August House starts American folklore series this fall. *Publ Wkly* 231:60+ Je 12 '87
> **United States**
> *See* Folklore
Folklore and children
> *See also*
> Fairy tales
Folkman, Judah, and Klagsbrun, Michael
> Angiogenic factors. bibl f il *Science* 235:442-7 Ja 23 '87
Folks, Thomas, and others
> Cytokine-induced expression of HIV-1 in a chronically infected promonocyte cell line. bibl f il *Science* 238:800-2 N 6 '87
Folkways Records
> This man captured the true sounds of a whole world [M. Asch] T. Scherman. il pors *Smithsonian* 18:110-12+ Ag '87
Follett, R. F. (Ronald F.), 1939-
> (jt. auth) See Power, J. F., and Follett, R. F. (Ronald F.), 1939-
Follett, Ronald F. *See* Follett, R. F. (Ronald F.), 1939-
Follicle-stimulating hormone *See* Gonadotropins
Follies (Architecture)
> Alpine undercurrents: the subterranean poolhouse of a mountain chalet [decorated by Tessa Kennedy] E. Lambert. il *Archit Dig* 44:96-9 Ja '87
Follows, Megan
> *about*
> Anne of Green Gables grows up [cover story; special section; with editorial comment by Kevin Doyle] il pors *Macleans* 100:2, 46-8+ D 7 '87
Foltz, Peter J.
> U.S. needs comprehensive plan to restore air traffic control. por *Aviat Week Space Technol* 127:81 O 5 '87
Fomon, Robert M., 1925-
> *about*
> The fall of the House of Hutton. S. Bartlett. il pors *Bus Week* p98-9+ D 21 '87
Fonar Corp.
> The inventor [R. Damadian] K. McAuliffe. il por *U S News World Rep* 102:66 Ja 26 '87
Fonda, Jane, 1937-
> Sending a daughter to college. il pors *Ladies Home J* 104:22+ Ja '87
> *about*
> The fitness queen. J. Kaplan. il *Vogue* 177:417+ N '87
> Jane Fonda & Tom Hayden [interview] D. Sheff. pors *Roll Stone* p123-4+ N 5-D 10 '87

Jane Fonda: from Barbarella . . . to barbells. S. Levin. il pors *Women's Sports Fitness* 9:24-8 D '87
Fondues
> Serve your guests a "two-jewel" dinner . . . Asian fondue and soup. il *Sunset* 178:214+ Ap '87
Fong, Bobby
> Commonplaces about teaching: second thoughts. il *Change* 19:28-34 Jl/Ag '87
Fons-Kruger, Valerie
> *about*
> The longest honeymoon. J. Mills. il pors map *Women's Sports Fitness* 9:80-4+ Mr '87
Fontaine, André
> Gorbachev's détente. *World Press Rev* 34:10-11 Je '87
Fontaine, Douglas
> Should the "Minimum Wage Restoration Act of 1987" be approved? [excerpts from testimony, July 23, 1987] *Congr Dig* 66:205+ Ag/S '87
Fontaine, Richard
> *about*
> A three-way approach puts Rich Fontaine's new fund on top. R. A. Lynch. il por *Money* 16:210 F '87
Fontaine, Roger W.
> U.S. policies in Central America: choices on Nicaragua. *Current* 291:34-40 Mr/Ap '87
Fontana, Lucio, 1899-1968
> *about*
> Fontana's post-Dada operatics. H. Cotter. il *Art Am* 75:80-5 Mr '87
Fonyo, Steve
> *about*
> Setbacks along the way. R. Laver. il por *Macleans* 100:42 Mr 30 '87
Food
> *See also*
> Appetite
> Breakfasts
> Convenience foods
> Cooking
> Diet
> Digestion
> Dinners and dining
> Eating
> Fasting
> Fish as food
> Flowers as food
> Frankfurters
> Gastronomy
> Insects as food
> Irradiated food
> Man, Prehistoric—Food
> Menus
> Nutrition
> Oysters as food
> Proteins
> Rice
> Salads
> Sandwiches
> Sausage
> School lunches
> Seaweed as food
> Space flight—Food problems
> Spreads (Food)
> Vitamins
> Comfort food says "I love you". H. Garrison. il *Parents* 62:111-16+ F '87
> Country medicine. H. H. Price. il *Gourmet* 47:58+ O '87
> Diet and cavities: the good news. D. Webb. *McCalls* 114:114 F '87
> Fed up to here [trendy food] L. Wells. il *N Y Times Mag* p133-4 D 6 '87
> Food for thought. B. T. Hunter. See issues of Consumers' Research Magazine
> Food in Vogue. B. Kafka. See issues of Vogue beginning September 1983
> Future foods. L. Lippincott. il *Women's Sports Fitness* 9:20 N '87
> The healthy gourmet foods of summer. J. B. Hurley. il *Prevention* 39:44+ Je '87
> The "lite rite" diet. R. Winter. il *Harpers Bazaar* 120:166-7+ Ap '87
> Mighty mouth [food and oral hygiene] S. Baker. il *Health* 19:55-6 Ja '87
> A potpourri of consumers' questions about food. M. Segal. il *FDA Consum* 21:30-2 N '87
> Ten best and worst things to eat in the car. P. Bedard. il *Car Driv* 32:69 Ja '87
> What's new for American families in '87. il *Better Homes Gard* 65:18 Ja '87

Food—*cont.*

Why don't we eat bugs? They're too expensive [views of Marvin Harris] il *Discover* 8:6+ Ap '87

Analysis and chemistry

See also

Food additives

Canning and preserving

See Canning and preserving

Coloring matter

See Coloring matter in cosmetics, food, etc.

Conferences

Odd and unusual tastes [conference at Saint Anthony's College, Oxford, England] R. Sokolov. il *Nat Hist* 96:104-7 N '87

Talking Turkey [International Food Congress] R. Sokolov. il *Nat Hist* 96:92-5 Mr '87

Contamination

See Food contamination

Cooling

Food care in camp. T. Thomas. *Field Stream* 92:54-5 Jl '87

Drying

See also

Vegetables—Drying

Long-lasting snacks: dried vegetables, fruit, yogurt. il *Sunset* 178:196+ My '87

Exhibitions

Fancy is as fancy does [Fancy Food and Confection Show] M. Sheraton. il *Time* 130:70 Jl 27 '87

Fun with food [exhibit at Ontario Science Centre] il *Natl Geogr World* 140:25-7 Ap '87

Meals in store for the future [trade show at Chicago's McCormick Place] L. Shapiro. il *Newsweek* 109:66-7 Je 15 '87

Taste of Texas [food show in Manhattan] *New Yorker* 63:32 S 28 '87

Fat content

Digging into low-fat foods. il *Newsweek* 109:57 Je 29 '87

Eating smart. il *Glamour* 85:316-17 My '87

Fast fat finder. il *Curr Health 2* 13:15 Mr '87

Fat and the cholesterol connection. il *Glamour* 85:310-13 O '87

Fat facts to live by. il *Glamour* 85:262-5 F '87

The Fat Point System: a winning thinning strategy. D. Eller. il *Mademoiselle* 93:248 My '87

Fat: the food that makes you fat. K. Keller. il *Mademoiselle* 93:290 Mr '87

For cattle, the svelte look is in [lower fat beef] S. D. Atchison. il *Bus Week* p154-5 N 30 '87

High-carb diets questioned [theory of Gerald Reaven] G. Kolata. *Science* 235:164 Ja 9 '87

How fat is your salad? B. Hayton. il *Curr Health 2* 14:16 S '87

An introduction to fats and cholesterol. il *FDA Consum* 21:12 F '87

Prime choices [eating red meat] G. Bakoulis. il *Health* 19:49-51 Je '87

Snake oil [dietary fats] E. R. Shell. il *Atlantic* 260:74-5 Ag '87

Surf 'n turf [cattle injected with fish oil to produce meat with less saturated fat] M. Mintzer. il *Health* 19:15 S '87

Trimming the fat. J. Omark. il *Women's Sports Fitness* 9:14+ S '87

When being a vegetable doesn't mean a thing [fatty acids in certain oils] B. Horn. por *U S News World Rep* 102:6 Mr 23 '87

Which fat is worst? *Prevention* 39:18 D '87

Your diet: good fat, bad fat. J. S. Stern. *Vogue* 177:448 F '87

History

Columbus's biggest discovery. R. Sokolov. il *Nat Hist* 96:66-7 Ag '87

Labeling

Can "lite" foods help you lose? D. Longobardi. il *Mademoiselle* 93:112 My '87

Cutting cholesterol? Look to the label. C. Lecos. il *FDA Consum* 21:8-13 F '87

Deciphering food labels. il *Prevention* 39:46 F '87

A guide to food labels. *Good Housekeep* 204:203 Mr '87

Health claims about food: boon or bane? B. T. Hunter. il *Consum Res Mag* 70:8-9 N '87

Health claims on food labels. *Consum Res Mag* 70:17 Jl '87

Labeling proposals: how useful? [cholesterol content] B. T. Hunter. *Consum Res Mag* 70:8 Mr '87

"Light" on the label: what does it mean? L. Hoppe. il *Better Homes Gard* 65:40 My '87

Making food labels readable. T. Hunter. il *Consum Res Mag* 70:8-9 D '87

Selling nutrition: should food packages carry health messages? il *FDA Consum* 21:22-5 N '87

What "lite" and "lean" don't always mean [convenience foods] il *USA Today (Periodical)* 115:3 F '87

When being a vegetable doesn't mean a thing [fatty acids in certain oils] B. Horn. por *U S News World Rep* 102:6 Mr 23 '87

Marketing

See Food industry—Marketing

New sources

See Food supply—New sources

Packaging

See also

Food, Canned

Food pouches

Food wraps

Hey, Ma, what's in the microwave? M. J. Pitzer. il *Bus Week* p68+ N 30 '87

Preservation

See Food preservation and preservatives

Prices

See also

Meat—Prices

Religious aspects

Feasting on herbs in the midst of love: a conversation with Jeff Smith. P. P. Allen. por *Christ Century* 104:1087-90 D 2 '87

Social aspects

The spice of life: food and culture [cover story; special issue; with editorial comment by Edouard Glissant] il *Courier* 40:3-34 My '87

Storage

Keeping your food fresh. S. Burstein. il *Work Woman* 12:170 My '87

Summer food safety tips. F. E. Young and K. J. Skinner. il *FDA Consum* 21:16-19 Je '87

Terminology

Chewing on words. B. Miller. il *N Y Times Mag* p10+ Jl 19 '87

Food, Canned

See also

Cooking—Canned food

Campbell's primordial soup: spontaneous generation: a danger in canned foods? F. Schmugge. *Harpers* 274:18 My '87

Food, Dried

See also

Cooking—Dried food

Food—Drying

Food, Effect of radiation on *See* Irradiated food

Food, Frozen

See also

Fruit, Frozen

Ice cream, ices, etc.

Potatoes, Frozen

Turkeys, Frozen

The bun also rises with freeze-hearty yeast. S. Weisburd. *Sci News* 132:9 Jl 4 '87

From our kitchen to yours. K. Adams. *South Living* 22:210 My '87

Like Chinese food? Our taste testers rate Chinese-style entrées. il *Glamour* 85:270 F '87

Food, Irradiated *See* Irradiated food

Food, Organic

See also

Cooking—Organic food

China's health food tradition. L. Ruifen. il *Courier* 40:24-7 My '87

Clean greens. D. Meeker. il *Health* 19:43-4+ Ag '87

Food that can save your life. R. Rodale. il *Prevention* 39:17-18+ Ag '87

Q & A food. See issues of Rodale's Organic Gardening through February 1987

Food, Raw

The pros and cons of eating food in the raw. N. Malkin. il *Mademoiselle* 93:278+ N '87

Food, Smoked

Up in smoke. S. Bashline. il *Field Stream* 91:24+ F '87

What about right-in-the-oven smoking? il *Sunset* 178:138-41 Mr '87

Food, Synthetic *See* Food substitutes

Food, Wild

See also

Plants, Edible

Food additives

See also

Coloring matter in cosmetics, food, etc.

Sulfites

Food additives—*cont.*

The additives debate. J. Schmid. *Vogue* 177:405+ O '87

All natural? [frozen fruit bars] B. T. Hunter. il *Consum Res Mag* 70:8-9 Ap '87

Food that can kill [cover story; special section; with editorial comment by Kevin Doyle] R. Corelli. il *Macleans* 100:2, 26-31+ Ap 27 '87

Food adulteration *See* Food contamination

Food allergy

See also

Lactose intolerance

Food allergies [excerpt from No more cravings] D. Hunt. *Essence* 17:15-16+ Mr '87

Medical disputes you should know about [views of S. Berger] G. Williams. *Ladies Home J* 104:56+ Mr '87

Food and Agriculture Organization of the United Nations

Crop substitution: a tactic to reduce drug supply. il *UN Chron* 24:xix My '87

FAO 'food summit' adopts four-prong strategy for African agricultural recovery. *UN Chron* 23:94 N '86

FAO heads international campaign to avert locust and grasshopper outbreaks and save Africa's crops. il *UN Chron* 23:92-3 N '86

FAO reports locust infestations continue, harvests better in Africa. il *UN Chron* 24:74 My '87

The politics of food [re-election of E. Saouma] H. Mackenzie. il por *Macleans* 100:25 N 23 '87

Swift action to save the world's forests and woodlands urged by FAO expert task force. il *UN Chron* 22:105-6 N/D '85

Twenty-third conference of the FAO adopts pesticide code, food security compact. il *UN Chron* 23:61 Ja '86

Food and Drug Administration (U.S.) *See* United States. Food and Drug Administration

Food and drug interactions in the body *See* Drugs—Physiological effects

Food Animal Concerns Trust

Bullish on calves and sheep [J. Snyder, broker and farmer] H. Zelinsky. il por *Ms* 15:23 Ap '87

For discriminating shoppers. W. Shipman. il *Ctry J* 14:15-16 Ap '87

Food as gifts

Christmas giftbook. il *Good Housekeep* 205:70+ N '87

Delicious gifts from your kitchen. il *Good Housekeep* 205:154-64+ N '87

Delicious summer gifts. il *South Living* 22:138-9 Jl '87

Fancy foods by mail. il *Consum Rep* 52:715-18 N '87

Foods for holiday giving. il *Gourmet* 47:84-5+ D '87

Gifts from the kitchen. C. Rossant. il *McCalls* 115:110+ N '87

The giveaway gourmet. il *Mademoiselle* 93:274-6 N '87

In the spirit of giving [Christmas gifts] C. Lyons. il *Ebony* 43:110-12+ D '87

Last-minute holiday gifts. K. S. White. il *McCalls* 114:82-4+ Ja '87

Mail-order morsels: good tastes to go. L. W. Eckhardt. *Harpers Bazaar* 121:137-8+ D '87

Postable treats [Christmas gifts] il *Gourmet* 47:96-7 D '87

Present the best. il *Redbook* 170:120-4+ N '87

Season's eatings. il *Seventeen* 46:122-3+ D '87

Spirited fruit [Christmas gifts] il *Sunset* 179:130 D '87

Food buying *See* Purchasing, Household

Food canneries *See* Canneries

Food chains (Ecology)

Bacteria: link or sink? [discussion of May 16, 1986 article, Bacterioplankton: a sink for carbon in a coastal marine plankton community] H. W. Ducklow and others. *Science* 235:88-9 Ja 2 '87

Environmental correlates of food chain length. F. Briand and J. E. Cohen. bibl f il *Science* 238:956-60 N 13 '87

A major food web component in the Orinoco River channel: evidence from planktivorous electric fishes. J. G. Lundberg and others. bibl f il *Science* 237:81-3 Jl 3 '87

Saltwort meadows needed by fishes [Florida salt marshes; research by Grant Gilmore and others] il *Sea Front* 33:461-3 N/D '87

Food coloring matter *See* Coloring matter in cosmetics, food, etc.

Food contamination

See also

Apples—Contamination

Chocolate—Contamination

Fish contamination

Food inspection

Meat contamination

Milk contamination

Pasta—Contamination

Potatoes—Contamination

Poultry contamination

Rapeseed oil—Contamination

Shellfish contamination

Breaking the 'circle of poison' [pesticide residues] P. H. Johnson. il *Rodale's Org Gard* 34:52-63 Ap '87

Food phobias. C. Tevis. il *Success Farm* 85 no2:18H-18I Ja '87

Food safety [cover story; special issue] il *World Health* p2-23 Mr '87

Food that can kill [cover story; special section; with editorial comment by Kevin Doyle] R. Corelli. il *Macleans* 100:2, 26-31+ Ap 27 '87

Food that can save your life. R. Rodale. il *Prevention* 39:17-18+ Ag '87

Garden gate [National Academy of Sciences report on pesticide residues] S. O. Daniels. il *Rodale's Org Gard* 34:4 Ag '87

How safe are the pesticides on food? [EPA's testing process] P. Durner. il *Rodale's Org Gard* 34:69-76 Je '87

How safe is your food? [cancer threat from pesticides] K. McAuliffe. il *U S News World Rep* 103:70-2 N 16 '87

Moth-proof [contamination at Asia Trading Company in St. Louis] il *FDA Consum* 21:30 My '87

Mouse gavotte [Forrest City Grocery Company cited for insanitary conditions] il *FDA Consum* 21:43 F '87

NAS reports on pathogens in poultry . . . and pesticides in food. *Sci News* 131:361 Je 6 '87

Pasta al pesticidio, with a side of salmonella. M. Katz. il *Sierra* 72:16-17 S/O '87

Pesticide protection [California markets test produce] J. Adler. il *Newsweek* 110:69+ N 9 '87

Regulating pesticides in food [National Academy of Sciences report] L. Tangley. il *BioScience* 37:452-6 Jl/Ag '87

Smite the mites [insect contamination of Oriental foods] il *FDA Consum* 21:39 Je '87

Snack attacks. *FDA Consum* 21:31-2 O '87

Will your dinner make you sick? K. McAuliffe. il *U S News World Rep* 103:73 N 16 '87

Food cravings *See* Eating—Psychological aspects

Food critics and criticism

America the bountiful—best eating guides. B. Kafka. il *Vogue* 177:133-4 Je '87

Can you trust restaurant reviews? il *Glamour* 85:332 N '87

Getting rich on dinner [Zagat restaurant survey] L. Shapiro. il pors *Newsweek* 110:60 D 21 '87

In a gastronomic grudge match, a seasoned contender from Italy taunts the Times's top taster [feud between B. Miller and H. Cipriani over reviews of restaurants named Bellini and Harry Cipriani] A. Richman. il por *People Wkly* 28:67-8 D 7 '87

In the world according to the Zagats, everyone's a critic. K. Johnson. il pors *People Wkly* 28:52-4 Jl 6 '87

Food cutters, presses, etc.

See also

Pastry cutters

Food decoration *See* Cooking—Garnishes; Cooking, Ornamental

Food distribution *See* Food industry—Marketing

Food for children *See* Children—Nutrition

Food for infants *See* Infants—Nutrition

Food for the Poor (Organization)

Père Mahfood's Food for the Poor. A. Rodriguez-Soto. *America* 156:153-4 F 21 '87

Food freezers *See* Freezers

Food habits *See* Eating

Food handling

Don't lose your stuffing. J. Storm. *Women's Sports Fitness* 9:18 D '87

Food safety [cover story; special issue] il *World Health* p2-23 Mr '87

Foodborne illness: a growing problem. B. T. Hunter. il *Consum Res Mag* 70:11-14 F '87

From our kitchen to yours. K. Adams. il *South Living* 22:167 S '87

Is this food safe to eat? P. Von Nostitz. il *Parents* 62:204+ Ag '87

Kitchen alert: the right way to store and prepare food. B. L. G. Morgan. il *Ladies Home J* 104:50+ Ap '87

Summer food safety tips. F. E. Young and K. J. Skinner. il *FDA Consum* 21:16-19 Je '87

Food in art
Tell the tooth! Dr. Joe Daugherty's rock repast may look filling, but it's a real jawbreaker [converting rocks into fake food] il por *People Wkly* 27:123 My 25 '87

Exhibitions
Mixed marriage [Honeymoon project by A. Miralda] C. Peck. il *Art News* 86:15-16 Mr '87

Food industry
See also
Agricultural industries
American Natural Foods, Inc.
Beech-Nut Nutrition Corp.
Blanchard & Blanchard & Son Ltd.
Borden, Inc.
C. F. Mueller & Co.
Campbell Soup Company
Candy industry
Castle & Cooke, Inc.
Collective labor agreements—Food industry
ConAgra, Inc.
CPC International Inc.
Fish industry
Fruit industry
General Foods Corp.
General Host Corp.
General Mills, Inc.
Golden Valley Microwave Foods Inc.
Goya Foods, Inc.
Hershey Foods Corp.
J. M. Smucker Co.
Jewel Evans Family Foods
Kellogg Co.
Kraft Inc.
Kroger Co.
Lance, Inc.
Nabisco Brands, Inc.
Pepsico, Inc.
Pet Incorporated
Pillsbury Co.
Poultry industry
Procter & Gamble Co.
Quaker Oats Co.
Sara Lee Corp.
Sarabeth's Kitchen
Shellfish industry
Sorrell Ridge (Firm)
Staley Continental Inc.
Tomsun Foods International Inc.
Watsonville Canning and Frozen Food Company
Women in the food industry

Acquisitions and mergers
Adviser beware: cooked books may burn you, too [investment bankers face fraud charges in CPC International's suit against McKesson and Morgan Stanley over sale of C. F. Mueller] L. J. Tell. il *Bus Week* p58+ O 26 '87
Did Drexel bully takeover candidates? [suit brought by Staley Continental] C. Welles. *Bus Week* p43-4 Mr 9 '87
How ConAgra grew big—and now, beefy [acquisition of Monfort] M. Ivey. il por *Bus Week* p87-8 My 18 '87
Will Philip Morris nibble at Hershey? G. G. Marcial. *Bus Week* p106 O 5 '87

International aspects
Buying into the big time [R. Lewis's TLC Group purchases BCI International Food Company] J. M. Horowitz. il por *Time* 130:42 Ag 24 '87
Canada's Labatt has just one way to grow: south. E. B. Terry. il por *Bus Week* p70 N 9 '87
Reg Lewis hits the big time—and takes it in stride [acquisition of BCI International Food Co.] P. Finch. il por *Bus Week* p27+ Ag 24 '87
Reginald Lewis cuts the big deal [cover story; with editorial comment by Earl G. Graves] A. Edmond, Jr. il pors *Black Enterp* 18:9, 42-6 N '87
TLC deal signals new era for black business [acquisition of Beatrice International] K. D. Thompson. por *Black Enterp* 18:21-2 O '87

Advertising
Health claims about food: boon or bane? B. T. Hunter. il *Consum Res Mag* 70:8-9 N '87
"Real food" stages a comeback. A. Toufexis. il *Time* 130:61 O 12 '87
A sizzling food fight [high cholesterol products push nutrition in ads] A. Miller. il *Newsweek* 109:56 Ap 20 '87
Tricks of the trade [food stylist P. Winters] B. Kanner. il por *N Y* 20:18+ N 2 '87

Export-import trade
Beware of imported foods. C. Lecos. il *Consum Res Mag* 70:15-17 F '87
Smite the mites [insect contamination of Oriental foods] il *FDA Consum* 21:39 Je '87

Finance
The big brands are back in style. K. Dreyfack. il *Bus Week* p74 Ja 12 '87
Food processors. J. Novack. il *Forbes* 139:134-5+ Ja 12 '87

Laws and regulations
See Food laws and regulations

Management
Cashing in on food and drink [billionaires] B. Saporito. il por *Fortune* 116:152-3 O 12 '87

Marketing
Handmade muffins [gourmet foods] J. Clements. il *Forbes* 140:99+ D 28 '87
Hey, Ma, what's in the microwave? M. J. Pitzer. il *Bus Week* p68+ N 30 '87
Marketing's new look [Campbell Soup's move to regionalization] C. Dugas. il *Bus Week* p64-9 Ja 26 '87
Take the high ground [Pet Inc.] J. Flint. il *Forbes* 139:228+ Je 15 '87

Securities
Microwave food: a hot investment idea? T. Segal. *Bus Week* p104 Mr 30 '87

Great Britain
See also
Allied-Lyons plc

Scotland
See also
Baxters of Speyside Ltd.

Switzerland
See also
Nestle SA

Food industry workers
See also
Strikes—Food industry workers

Food inspection
Avoiding sick chicks [Chik Chek test for salmonella bacteria] M. Kemp. il *Discover* 8:20 O '87
Beware of imported foods. C. Lecos. il *Consum Res Mag* 70:15-17 F '87
A close watch on U.S. borders to keep the world's bugs out. E. Larson. bibl (p154) *Smithsonian* 18:106-8+ Je '87; il
Looking out for food safety. il *Sunset* 179:272 N '87

Canada
Dining-room detectives [Health Protection Branch] il *Macleans* 100:34+ Ap 27 '87

Food laws and regulations
See also
Food inspection
United States. Food and Drug Administration
Regulating pesticides: the "Delaney paradox". C. Norman. il *Science* 236:1054-5 My 29 '87

International aspects
Watchdog! [Codex Alimentarius Commission standards] V. Abramov. il *World Health* p23 Mr '87

Food Lion Inc.
That roar you hear is Food Lion. R. W. Anderson. il *Bus Week* p65-6 Ag 24 '87

Food literature

Anecdotes, facetiae, satire, etc.
Serving up a new slice of news [food as news] C. Gordon. il *Macleans* 100:10 D 28 '87

Authorship
Loving Brillat-Savarin: a tale of a tasteful affair [work of M. F. K. Fisher] J. Ferrary. por *N Y Times Book Rev* 92:51+ My 31 '87

Food mail order business *See* Mail order business

Food mixes
See also
Cake mixes
Cornbread mix offers possibilities. il *South Living* 22:119 Ag '87

Food plants *See* Plants, Edible

Food poisoning
See also
Salmonellosis
Scombroid poisoning
Don't lose your stuffing. J. Storm. *Women's Sports Fitness* 9:18 D '87
Food-borne diarrhea. B. T. Hunter. il *Consum Res Mag* 70:8-9 Jl '87
Food safety [cover story; special issue] il *World Health* p2-23 Mr '87
Foodborne illness: a growing problem. B. T. Hunter. il *Consum Res Mag* 70:11-14 F '87

Food poisoning—*cont.*

From our kitchen to yours. K. Adams. il *South Living* 22:167 S '87

Handle with care: this bird can make you sick [turkey cooking] *Consum Rep* 52:602 O '87

Is this food safe to eat? P. Von Nostitz. il *Parents* 62:204+ Ag '87

Kitchen alert: the right way to store and prepare food. B. L. G. Morgan. il *Ladies Home J* 104:50+ Ap '87

Spain's deadly elixir [toxic industrial rapeseed oil poisoning case] il *Macleans* 100:35 Ap 13 '87

Spin-off from space travel [hazard analysis critical control point in preventing food associated diarrheal diseases] S. Michanie and F. L. Bryan. il *World Health* p26-7 Ag/S '87

Summer food safety tips. F. E. Young and K. J. Skinner. il *FDA Consum* 21:16-19 Je '87

Will your dinner make you sick? K. McAuliffe. il *U S News World Rep* 103:73 N 16 '87

Food policy *See* Nutrition policy

Food pouches

'Sous-vide' cooking: haute cuisine in a pouch? J. B. Levine. il *Bus Week* p104-5 Jl 13 '87

Food preservation and preservatives

See also

Canning and preserving

Food—Cooling

Food—Drying

Sulfites

Promising sulfite alternatives [research by Gerald M. Sapers] *Sci News* 132:63 Jl 25 '87

Food processing industry *See* Food industry

Food processors (Appliances)

Food processors. il *Consum Rep* 52:668-75 N '87

Food relief *See* Relief work

Food research

See also

Food supply—New sources

Human Nutrition Research Center (U.S.)

Awards

See also

General Foods World Food Prize

Food safety *See* Food inspection

Food sanitation *See* Food handling

Food sensitiveness *See* Food allergy

Food service

See also

Airlines—Food service

Caterers and catering

Hospitals—Food service

Kitchen Privileges (Firm)

Restaurants

Rock concerts—Food service

Rykoff-Sexton Inc.

Sightseeing boats—Food service

Staley Continental Inc.

TW Services Inc.

Food slicers

Super slicer. il *McCalls* 114:121-2 S '87

Food spoilage

See also

Food contamination

Food inspection

How much do you know about food safety? [quiz] il *Glamour* 85:296 Ag '87

Food store signs

On display [S. Jenkins, maker of signs used at Fairway food market in Manhattan] *New Yorker* 63:37-8 D 7 '87

Food stores

See also

Fairway Fruits & Vegetables (New York, N.Y.)

La Villita Tortillas (Firm)

Sarabeth's Kitchen

Southland Corp.

Supermarkets

The Christmas table [New York City] *New Yorker* 63:84+ D 21 '87

When you're truly in dire knead, line up at the Cheese Board with Berkeley's well-bread upper crust. il *People Wkly* 27:78-9 F 23 '87

Sanitation

Beware of imported foods. C. Lecos. il *Consum Res Mag* 70:15-17 F '87

Food stylists

Tricks of the trade [P. Winters] B. Kanner. il por *N Y* 20:18+ N 2 '87

Food substitutes

No-calorie substitute for flour. J. Raloff. *Sci News* 131:251 Ap 18 '87

Food supply

See also

Crop yields

Famines

Grain supply

Production, Agricultural

World Food Council

World Food Day

International aspects

See also

Food and Agriculture Organization of the United Nations

Does more food mean less famine? A. Smith. il *Esquire* 108:55-6 Jl '87

First word [feeding the world] L. Ruppe. il *Omni* 9:6 Je '87

Food for all—the 'Paris appeal' [universal free access to basic foodstuffs] Y. Coutsocheras. il *Courier* 40:34 O '87

World food. P. H. Abelson. *Science* 236:9 Ap 3 '87

New sources

Food security: a technological alternative: biotechnology can convert biomass into a stable food supply. M. H. Rogoff and S. L. Rawlins. bibl il *BioScience* 37:800-7 D '87

Krill: food of the future? S. Nicol. il *Sea Front* 33:12-17 Ja/F '87

Africa

A grain revolution: the impact of imported rice on millet-based African civilizations. T. Ndoye and M. M'Baye. il *Courier* 40:8-9 My '87

The snack that crawls [mopane worm caterpillars eaten as food] H. Brandon. il *Int Wildl* 17:16-21 Mr/Ap '87

Canada

Food that can kill [cover story; special section; with editorial comment by Kevin Doyle] R. Corelli. il *Macleans* 100:2, 26-31+ Ap 27 '87

China

Setting a full table [improvement in farm production chronicled by S. H. Witter and others] G. Garelik. il *Time* 130:55 O 12 '87

Developing countries

See also

Educational Concerns for Hunger Organization

World Food Council

Eastern Europe

"Food revolution" threatens communism [consumer demands for a better diet; views of Robert Deutsch] il *USA Today (Periodical)* 115:11 Ap '87

Soviet Union

"Food revolution" threatens communism [consumer demands for a better diet; views of Robert Deutsch] il *USA Today (Periodical)* 115:11 Ap '87

Tropics

Nights—and days—of the iguana [captive-breeding project in Panama; work of D. Werner] J. P. Cohn. il por *Américas* 39:34-9 Jl/Ag '87

Food waste disposers *See* Refuse disposers

Food wraps

It's a wrap [plastic that breathes] D. Pine. il *Health* 19:17 N '87

Foodmaker, Inc.

No more junk in the box. E. Paris. il por *Forbes* 140:136+ N 16 '87

Foose, Robert James, 1938-

The watercolor page. il por *Am Artist* 51:56-9+ O '87

Foot

See also

Heel bone

Abnormalities

See also

Syndaktylia

Care and hygiene

See also

Podiatry

The agony of de-feet [tennis players] J. E. McNerney. il *World Tennis* 34:8-9 F '87

Feet be sexy & happy. D. Longstreet. il *Good Housekeep* 204:102 My '87

Feet: sometimes fleet, seldom neat, often beat. J. Lewis. il *Curr Health 2* 13:28-9 My '87

Foot problems? Here's real help. H. Twidale. il *Good Housekeep* 205:207 Jl '87

Foot revivers. *Vogue* 177:46 Ag '87

Lady fingers (& toes). il *Mademoiselle* 93:124-7 Jl '87

No more hot, smelly feet! S. Young. il *Glamour* 85:14 Jl '87

Pedicures: new rules. il *Vogue* 177:38 Ap '87

Prom-perfect. il *Seventeen* 46:112 Mr '87

Self-care for your feet. il *Prevention* 39:34-6+ Mr '87

Foot—Care and hygiene—*cont.*

Sound footing. L. Wells. il *N Y Times Mag* p32 Ag 9 '87

When your feet feel good, you feel good. P. Von Nostitz. il *Parents* 62:216+ S '87

Diseases

See also
Athlete's foot (Disease)

Diagnosis

May the force be with you [force platform] D. Tonnessen. *Health* 19:20-1 Mr '87

Surgery

Tune in to your feet and head off serious problems. il *Prevention* 39:131-2 Mr '87

Wounds and injuries

Foot locker [toe lock] D. Tonnessen. il *Health* 19:21 My '87

Prevention's the best medicine [tennis injuries] J. E. McNerney. il *World Tennis* 35:16-17 Jl '87

Foot bridges *See* Bridges, Foot

Football

See also
Football players
Irish football

Equipment

Tackling football injuries [high school safety] M. Conroy. il *Better Homes Gard* 65:43 S '87

Football, College

See also
Football coaches
Football players
Football records

All-South 1987 [special section] il *South Living* 22:81+ S '87

Another border war [Oklahoma defeats Texas] R. Telander. il *Sports Illus* 67:24-9 O 19 '87

Bad Tidings from 'Bama [fans protest hiring of coach B. Curry] R. Reilly. por *Sports Illus* 66:78 Ja 19 '87

Baker Field [Columbia vs. Lehigh] *New Yorker* 63:37-8 N 16 '87

The Big Red's bigger bite [Cornell defeats Penn] F. Lidz. il *Sports Illus* 67:48+ S 28 '87

Black QBs led eight teams to bowl game appearances. *Jet* 71:54 Ja 19 '87

Black quarterbacks get nod at major colleges in upcoming bowl games. il *Jet* 73:46-7 D 7 '87

Boom and doom [Oklahoma defeats Nebraska; cover story] R. Telander. il *Sports Illus* 67:20-5 N 30 '87

The bowl of bowls [Penn State beats Miami in the Fiesta Bowl] T. Callahan. il *Time* 129:68 Ja 12 '87

A bull's-eye for a new Archer [LSU defeats Texas A & M] H. Hersch. il *Sports Illus* 67:26-8+ S 14 '87

The 'Canes were very able [Miami defeats Florida State; cover story] R. Telander. il *Sports Illus* 67:28-30+ O 12 '87

Carried away in Syracuse. T. Callahan. il *Time* 130:86 N 16 '87

College football. See issues of Sports Illustrated published during the college football season beginning September 15, 1986

College football '87 [special issue] il *Sports Illus* 67:22-32+ Ag 31 '87

College football preview '87. M. Francesa. il *Sport Mag* 78:26-7+ S '87

The Crimson is in the clover [Harvard beats Yale for Ivy League championship] J. Lieber. il *Sports Illus* 67:26-7 N 30 '87

CSU kicks off season dedicated to Paul Robeson. por *Jet* 72:53 S 14 '87

Dashing debut by the Vols [Tennessee vs. Iowa in the Kickoff Classic] D. S. Looney. il *Sports Illus* 67:22-3 S 7 '87

The Emperor of Arkansas [F. Broyles, athletic director of the University of Arkansas] D. Whitford. il pors *Sport Mag* 78:68-73 Ja '87

Football feuds—on the field and off. K. Rappoport. il *Saturday Evening Post* 259:24+ N '87

Guts, brains and glory [Penn State defeats Miami in Fiesta Bowl] R. Reilly. il *Sports Illus* 66:12-17 Ja 12 '87

Hail, Columbia, where losing isn't everything, it's the only thing—just ask the fans. J. Friedman. il *People Wkly* 28:110-11 O 19 '87

Head man [coach E. Russell of Georgia Southern] D. S. Looney. il pors *Sports Illus* 67:98-100+ Ag 31 '87

A high time for the Huskers [Nebraska defeats UCLA] R. Telander. il *Sports Illus* 67:62-5 S 21 '87

Holy smokes! 'Bama is back [Alabama defeats Penn State] H. Hersch. il *Sports Illus* 67:66-7 S 21 '87

Hoosier Big Ten favorite now? [Indiana defeats Minnesota] H. Hersch. il *Sports Illus* 67:74-5 O 26 '87

Mississippi Valley coach leads FB exodus to Ark. [A. Cooley] por *Jet* 71:50 Ja 12 '87

The not-so Big Eight [domination by Oklahoma and Nebraska; cover story] D. S. Looney. il *Sports Illus* 67:20-5 N 16 '87

Notre Dame is golden again. E. M. Swift. il *Sports Illus* 67:26-8+ N 9 '87

The Orange has the juice [Syracuse defeats Penn State] P. Putnam. il *Sports Illus* 67:70-2 O 26 '87

A pair extraordinaire [T. Ellis and S. Sharpe lead South Carolina over North Carolina State] D. S. Looney. il *Sports Illus* 67:100+ N 9 '87

Pouring on the orange crush [Clemson defeats Georgia] R. Wiley. il *Sports Illus* 67:30-3 S 28 '87

Resurrection at Notre Dame. G. Norman. il por *Sport Mag* 78:26-8+ O '87

Spartan results for Indiana [Michigan State beats Hoosiers] D. S. Looney. il *Sports Illus* 67:22-4+ N 23 '87

Starting out from Zip [University of Akron under coach G. Faust] P. Putnam. il por *Sports Illus* 67:33 N 9 '87

A stranger in the family [new Alabama coach B. Curry] D. Whitford. il pors *Sport Mag* 78:45+ S '87

Sweet-toothed Tigers [Auburn defeats Alabama] M. Bishop. il *Sports Illus* 67:40 D 7 '87

They're fit to be tied in the SEC [top Southeastern Conference teams in tie games] H. Hersch and B. Newman. il *Sports Illus* 67:30-2+ O 5 '87

Time to play Foote ball? [president Tad Foote striving for excellence in academics at football power Miami] R. Sullivan. il *Sports Illus* 67:58-60+ D 21 '87

USC rose to the occasion [victory over UCLA earns Rose Bowl bid] R. Wiley. il *Sports Illus* 67:28-30+ N 30 '87

Winning the Penn State way [Fiesta Bowl win over Miami] P. Axthelm. il *Newsweek* 109:48 Ja 12 '87

You're barely better in '87 [Miami defeats Notre Dame] R. Wiley. il *Sports Illus* 67:36-8+ D 7 '87

Advertising

Some vintage advertising [use of Bartles and Jaymes takeoffs to promote Iowa State football program] il *Sports Illus* 67:18 O 12 '87

Awards

Time to air it out [Heisman Trophy candidates] il por *Sports Illus* 67:33 S 14 '87

Ethical aspects

Agents of turmoil [N. Walters and L. Bloom accused of wooing blue chip athletes with cash] C. Neff. il pors *Sports Illus* 67:34-40+ Ag 3 '87

Agents of violence? [dealings of N. Walters and L. Bloom] B. Selcraig. il por *Sports Illus* 66:25 Ap 6 '87

Bosworth faces the music [casualty of the NCAA's steroid crackdown] C. Neff. il pors *Sports Illus* 66:20-2+ Ja 5 '87

Dallas station refuses to flinch as it topples a gridiron power [WFAA takes on SMU scandal] D. Holder. il *Channels* 7:13 My '87

"Death" to S.M.U. football. *Time* 129:72 Mr 9 '87

The draft resistance [NFL supplemental draft will include college players kicked off teams] D. S. Looney. il *Sports Illus* 67:19 Ag 31 '87

Howard U. battles NCAA over grid playoff snub. *Jet* 73:50 D 14 '87

Is there life after football? [Southern Methodist University] P. Applebome. il *N Y Times Mag* p73-4+ O 4 '87

More football madness [firing of Ohio State coach Earle Bruce and lowering of admission standards at Columbia] J. Kirshenbaum. il por *Sports Illus* 67:110 N 30 '87

Payoff, hike! [Gov. W. Clements' involvement in illegal payments to football players at SMU] E. Magnuson. il *Time* 129:34 Mr 16 '87

Playing for pay in Texas [Gov. W. Clements admits involvement in SMU football scandal] T. E. Johnson. por *Newsweek* 109:32 Mr 16 '87

Shame on you, SMU [NCAA suspends program] R. Sullivan and C. Neff. il *Sports Illus* 66:18-21+ Mr 9 '87

SMU [program suspended] S. Bayless. il *Sport Mag* 78:98 D '87

SMU football is called for illegal motion. il *Newsweek* 109:55 Mr 9 '87

A star flunks his test [B. Bosworth found using steroids] P. Axthelm. il por *Newsweek* 109:48-9 Ja 5 '87

Trouble in Tennessee [with editorial comment by Neil Cohen] J. D. Miller and D. Whitford. il *Sport Mag* 78:6, 68-73+ N '87

Football, College—*cont.*

Halftime

'Mr. Black Magic' singer Billy Daniels serenades Orange Bowl. il pors *Jet* 71:55-6 Ja 19 '87

History

A game worth playing: college football taught this ex-player lasting lessons [playing for Northwestern University in 1971] R. Telander. por *Sports Illus* 67:130 Ag 31 '87

George Gipp: "One for the Gipper!". J. Gustaitis. por *Am Hist Illus* 22:40-1 N '87

Nile Kinnick [Iowa's 1939 Heisman winner who died in World War II] R. Fimrite. il pors *Sports Illus* 67:112-24 Ag 31 '87

Organization and administration

College grid playoff: just a matter of time. L. Wheeler. il *Sport Mag* 78:13 Ja '87

Now playing: how to save college football [playoff proposal] N. Cohen. *Sport Mag* 78:8 Ap '87

Photographs and photography

Shooting football [cover story] B. Fox. il *Petersens Photogr Mag* 16:60-3 O '87

Polls

How the polls really work. B. Condor. il *Sport Mag* 78:41-3+ Ja '87

Recruiting

See also
National High School Football Recruiting Service

The fall roundup [persuasive hostesses help recruit top prospects] A. Wolff. il *Sports Illus* 67:46-50+ Ag 31 '87

A week in the life of a college recruiter [Duke's T. Limbaugh] D. Whitford. il pors *Sport Mag* 78:76-80+ Mr '87

Rules

Eleven is a big fat crowd [case for using fewer players] F. Deford. il *Sports Illus* 67 Sp Issue:42-5 S 9 '87

Television broadcasting

See Television broadcasting—Sports

Tickets

The old college try. D. Davidson. il *Sport Mag* 78:85 O '87

Football, High school

See also
Football coaches
Football players

Accidents and injuries

Remembering a special student [Hampton (Iowa) High School seniors' deeds in memory of S. Varrelman] J. Fincher. il por *Read Dig* 131:149-54 O '87

Tackling football injuries. M. Conroy. il *Better Homes Gard* 65:43 S '87

Religious aspects

U.S. judge rules prayer before a game is illegal. *Jet* 71:6 Mr 2 '87

Football, Professional

See also
Arena football
Collective bargaining—Football, Professional
Football coaches
Football players
National Football League
Pro Football Hall of Fame
Strikes—Football players
United States Football League

The 1987 pro football preview [cover story] il *Sport Mag* 78:28-32+ Ag '87

Assault on Mount Landry [Dallas' losing season] P. Zimmerman. il por *Sports Illus* 67:40-3 D 21 '87

A belated Christmas gift [Redskins vs. Rams in NFC wild card playoff] E. M. Swift. il *Sports Illus* 66:16-17 Ja 5 '87

Black QBs' face-off: first in NFL in 5 years. por *Jet* 73:46 O 5 '87

Break up the Colts! [improved Indianapolis obtains E. Dickerson; cover story] A. Murphy. il *Sports Illus* 67:18-23 N 9 '87

The Broncos busted 'em [playoff victory over Patriots] B. Newman. il *Sports Illus* 66:29-31 Ja 12 '87

The Broncos were boffo [Denver vs. Seattle; cover story] R. Reilly. il *Sports Illus* 67:26-8+ S 21 '87

Charge! [San Diego's strong start] P. Zimmerman. il pors *Sports Illus* 67:14-19 N 23 '87

Cut, cut, snip, snip. The Turk comes a-calling [man who informs players that they have been released from the team] M. Zwonitzer. il *Sport Mag* 78:92 N '87

Deep-sixing the Niners [Giants' victory in playoffs] P. Zimmerman. il *Sports Illus* 66:22-4 Ja 12 '87

Dickerson trade shifts NFL balance of power. il *Jet* 73:50 N 30 '87

Don't take me out to the football game [football vs. baseball] B. G. Harrison. *Mademoiselle* 93:108 F '87

Full steam ahead [49ers defeat Chiefs in Hall of Fame game] R. Wiley. il *Sports Illus* 67:18-21 Ag 17 '87

Getting there the hard way [Denver defeats Cleveland in AFC championship game] R. Telander. il *Sports Illus* 66:14-20 Ja 19 '87

A Giants man, all the way [coach B. Parcells] J. Kaplan. il pors *N Y Times Mag* p28-30+ S 6 '87

Grin and bear it, Giants [Bears defeat Giants] P. Zimmerman. il *Sports Illus* 67:34-6+ S 21 '87

Hey, it's heavenly [Saints beat Steelers to assure winning record] P. Zimmerman. il *Sports Illus* 67:20-3 D 7 '87

Just a breeze for the Giants [victory over Redskins in NFC championship game] P. Zimmerman. il *Sports Illus* 66:21-4+ Ja 19 '87

Miracles of the Midway [J. McMahon leads Bears to three come-from-behind wins] P. Zimmerman. il *Sports Illus* 67:28-30+ N 16 '87

New formation: odd man out [aftermath of strike] T. Callahan. il *Time* 130:86 N 9 '87

The new specialists [special teams] J. D. Miller. il *Sport Mag* 78:45-6 O '87

Pro football '87. il *Sports Illus* 67 Sp Issue:14-26+ S 9 '87

Reading is fun-damental [how a quarterback reads a defense] J. McMahon. il por *Sport Mag* 78:22-3 Ja '87

Reprieve for the Browns [victory over Jets in playoffs] E. M. Swift. il *Sports Illus* 66:26-9 Ja 12 '87

Season for no reason. R. Reilly. il *Sports Illus* 67:44-6+ N 30 '87

Shuffling off to hibernation [Redskins vs. Bears in playoff] R. Telander. il *Sports Illus* 66:18-21 Ja 12 '87

Sizzling rivals [Broncos vs. Rams in preseason game] R. Reilly. il *Sports Illus* 67:14-17 S 7 '87

Sports [New York Giants coach B. Parcells] E. Pooley. il por *N Y* 20:136-7 S 21 '87

Staring down his rowdy ruffians, Chicago coach Mike Ditka prods the Bears to the Super Bowl. J. Friedman. il pors *People Wkly* 27:66-7+ Ja 5 '87

Success story of the year [Cleveland Browns] T. Callahan. il *Time* 129:66 Ja 5 '87

Tough as nails [Cleveland defeats Pittsburgh] J. Lieber. il *Sports Illus* 67:14-21 S 28 '87

Troubled times in Titletown [relationship between Green Bay, Wis. and its Packers] F. Deford. il *Sports Illus* 66:70-4+ My 25 '87

True blue: from Giants to supermen. E. Pooley. il *N Y* 20:26-34 Ja 26 '87

Waiting for the whistle. P. Axthelm. il *Newsweek* 110:72-3 S 14 '87

Wake-up call for the Jets [victory over Kansas City in AFC wild card playoff] P. Zimmerman. il *Sports Illus* 66:12-15 Ja 5 '87

Welcome back to the NFL [season in wake of strike] P. Zimmerman. il *Sports Illus* 67:62-3 O 26 '87

Welcome home, guys—maybe [Redskins defeat Jets] R. Reilly. il *Sports Illus* 67:42-4+ N 2 '87

Accidents and injuries

Fast comeback for a quarterback with a bad back [return of J. Montana after spinal disk surgery] il *Discover* 8:14 Ja '87

Man down on the field [D. Dawson attempts comeback after Achilles injury] J. D. Miller. il *Sport Mag* 78:102 Ag '87

Sic transit McMahon: the cheering has stopped for the NFL's bad boy—now he's rich, famous and hurt. J. Friedman. il pors *People Wkly* 27:46-8 Ja 19 '87

So little gain for the pain. R. Mix. il *Sports Illus* 67:54-6+ O 19 '87

Antitrust cases

NFL owners may have fumbled away their victory. A. Bernstein. il *Bus Week* p162 N 2 '87

Awards

Martin wins NFL award for spirit of service. por *Jet* 72:50 Jl 20 '87

Bibliography

Football: the new must-read. J. Millman. il *Sport Mag* 78:85-6 F '87

Sports books due in wake of America's Cup and Super Bowl. *Publ Wkly* 231:82-3 Mr 6 '87

Draft

The 1987 first round preview. J. D. Miller. *Sport Mag* 78:70-1 My '87

Dr. Z charts the '87 draft. P. Zimmerman. il *Sports Illus* 66:56-7 Ap 27 '87

Dr. Z sums up the draft. P. Zimmerman. il *Sports Illus* 66:24 My 11 '87

Draft day. *New Yorker* 63:33-5 My 11 '87

Football, Professional—Draft—*cont.*

The draft resistance [NFL supplemental draft will include college players kicked off teams] D. S. Looney. il *Sports Illus* 67:19 Ag 31 '87

Grambling biggest black college winner in draft, but black QBs left out. il *Jet* 72:46 My 18 '87

"Play me—or trade me" [NFL draft compared to impending merger rules] S. Blotnick. il *Forbes* 140:176 Jl 27 '87

Too much NFL testing [pre-draft evaluations of college players] D. S. Looney. il por *Sports Illus* 66:120 My 11 '87

Unbending Bo sticks with baseball despite Raiders [B. Jackson drafted] por *Jet* 72:47 My 18 '87

Economic aspects

And now for the real Superbowl [views of G. Klein on professional football TV contracts] J. A. Trachtenberg. il por *Forbes* 139:122 F 9 '87

Black day for the CFL [Montreal Alouettes go out of business] H. Quinn. *Macleans* 100:21 Jl 6 '87

Taking a hike to Jacksonville? [bid tempts Houston's Oilers] T. Vogel. il *Bus Week* p36 S 21 '87

This Bud's not for you [Oilers owner B. Adams nixes move to Jacksonville] F. Deford. il pors *Sports Illus* 67:67-8+ N 2 '87

Why the football Cardinals are singing the St. Louis blues. J. E. Ellis. il *Bus Week* p44 D 21 '87

Anecdotes, facetiae, satire, etc.

The talk of the town [Irwindale, Calif., home-to-be of the Raiders] R. Reilly. por *Sports Illus* 67:84 S 14 '87

Ethical aspects

Drug free Bronco feels good, chats with Hollywood [C. Kay] *Jet* 71:46 F 16 '87

LT: living on the edge [football player's cocaine use; excerpt; cover story] L. Taylor and D. Falkner. il pors *Sport Mag* 78:68-72+ S '87

NFL MVP Taylor reveals trap of drugs caught him. por *Jet* 72:51 Ap 6 '87

Raiders' star Robinson facing Calif. drug charge [J. Robinson] por *Jet* 72:50 Ag 10 '87

Tony Elliott: just back from the dead, a too well-traveled NFL star bears witness to a chilling drug odyssey. W. Plummer. il pors *People Wkly* 27:81-4+ Ja 5 '87

History

Football's fat man [playing in the 1950's] A. J. Donovan. il pors *People Wkly* 28:79-80+ N 9 '87

The greatest game never played [1958 NFL championship; excerpt from Fatso] A. J. Donovan. il *Sport Mag* 78:53-5 Jl '87

Present at the creation: professional football in the twenties. E. L. Cuneo. *Am Sch* 56:487-501 Aut '87

Up, down and up again [the Giants] R. Fimrite. il *Sports Illus* 66:42-6+ Ja 26 '87

Officiating

Don't play it again: the NFL should do away with the instant replay. J. McCallum. por *Sports Illus* 67 Sp Issue:130 S 9 '87

Will instant replay trip the ref? [Super Bowl XXI] M. Moran. il *N Y Times Mag* p24-30+ Ja 25 '87

Organization and administration

See also

National Football League

United States Football League

Al Davis: on the move again? [Los Angeles Raiders] il por *Bus Week* p34 Ag 10 '87

Al the bad [L.A. Raiders owner A. Davis] M. Lupica. il por *Esquire* 108:75-6+ O '87

Black NFL executives plan job finders dept. *Jet* 72:50 Ag 24 '87

Ex-NFL star Bubba Smith wants to own Balt. team. por *Jet* 72:46 Ag 24 '87

NFL appoints black to monitor minority hiring [D. Cornwell] *Jet* 73:46 O 12 '87

Payton pursues pioneer plan to become NFL owner. il por *Jet* 72:52 Je 1 '87

Payton says he may be first owner/coach/player. por *Jet* 72:48 Je 29 '87

Payton's agent could pose a problem with NFL plans [plans to own team could be hindered by conduct of P. Holmes] *Jet* 72:50 Jl 13 '87

Photographs and photography

Shooting football [cover story] B. Fox. il *Petersens Photogr Mag* 16:60-3 O '87

A week of Sundays [Denver playing at Mile High Stadium] J. McDonough. il *Sport Mag* 78:36-45 F '87

Public opinion

Results: the Sport football poll. il *Sport Mag* 78:16 N '87

Statistics

Missing numbers. K. Lamb. il *Sport Mag* 78:48-9 N '87

Super Bowl

Elway and the Giant way [Giants vs. Broncos] T. Callahan. il *Time* 129:74 Ja 26 '87

A fan's further notes [Giants vs. Broncos] F. Exley. il pors *Esquire* 107:150-2 Je '87

Killer Giants. P. Zimmerman. il *Sports Illus* 66:14-22+ F 2 '87

My blue heaven [celebration of Giants' victory at the Meadowlands] il *N Y* 20:34-5 F 9 '87

Super Bowl countdown. A. Finlayson. il *Macleans* 100:39 Ja 26 '87

Super Bowl XXI [preview of Giants-Broncos game; special section] il *Sports Illus* 66:22-6+ Ja 26 '87

Super Sundays of the rich and famous. il *Sport Mag* 78:51 F '87

Super upset: the Broncos will win. P. Axthelm. il *Newsweek* 109:79-80 Ja 26 '87

To all the men in blue hats [Giants' fans] R. Rosenblatt. il *Sports Illus* 66:30-1 F 2 '87

Will instant replay trip the ref? M. Moran. il *N Y Times Mag* p24-30+ Ja 25 '87

Your Super Bowl home companion [symposium] il *Sport Mag* 78:33-47+ F '87

Economic aspects

And now the Super Bowl lineup: Seiko, McDonald's, Pepsi . . . [TV ads] C. Dugas. il *Bus Week* p35 F 2 '87

History

Super Bowl. M. Heisler. il *Sports Illus* 66:35+ Ja 12 '87

The whole game in their hands [J. Smith drops pass in game XIII and J. O'Brien kicks winning field goal in game V] D. Whitford. il por *Sport Mag* 78:25-8 F '87

Television broadcasting

See Television broadcasting—Sports

Canada

See also

Canadian Football League

Black day for the CFL [Montreal Alouettes go out of business] H. Quinn. *Macleans* 100:21 Jl 6 '87

Anecdotes, facetiae, satire, etc.

Sometimes they shoot heroes. A. Fotheringham. il *Macleans* 100:56 Jl 6 '87

Football coaches

See also

Archer, Mike

Bruce, Earle

Casem, Marino

Cooley, Archie

Curry, Bill

Ditka, Mike, 1939-

Faust, Gerry

Harrison, Bob

Hayes, Woody

Holtz, Lou

Hoskins, Joe

Landry, Tom

Madden, John

Parcells, Bill

Robinson, Eddie

Robinson, John

Russell, Erk

Washington, Otis

Coaching beyond the record [southern high school coaches Leon McCoy, Greg Sherwood, and Wayman Creel] D. Young. il *South Living* 22:82+ O '87

Harry Edwards hints at college sports boycott. *Jet* 73:51 O 26 '87

NFL 49ers produce plan to promote black coaches. *Jet* 72:46 Je 15 '87

NFL training camp aids black college coaches. *Jet* 72:50 S 21 '87

Rozelle says black coach is an NFL owners' problem. *Jet* 72:46 Jl 20 '87

Shamefully lily-white: NFL head-coach opening? Blacks need not apply. R. Telander. il por *Sports Illus* 66:80 F 23 '87

Who will be the first black head coach in NFL? W. Leavy. il *Ebony* 42:36+ Ja '87

Dismissal

Detroit football coach files $10 million job suit [high school coach J. Hoskins] *Jet* 71:46 Mr 9 '87

Ex-Southern grid coach gets $50,000 settlement [O. Washington] *Jet* 72:46 Ap 6 '87

Football fans

To all the men in blue hats [Giants' fans at the Super Bowl] R. Rosenblatt. il *Sports Illus* 66:30-1 F 2 '87

Football players

See also

Andersen, Morten
Anderson, Gary
Andrews, William
Bailey, Johnny
Banks, Gene
Bavaro, Mark
Bethea, Elvin Lamonte
Bethea, Larry
Bosworth, Brian
Brock, Lou, Jr.
Brown, Jim, 1936-
Brown, Tim
Cade, Mossy
Campbell, Earl
Carpenter, Cris
Carson, Harry, 1953-
Carter, Cris
Chandler, Chris
Cherico, Tony
Christensen, Todd
Collier, Reggie
Cunningham, Randall
Davis, Jimmie
Dawson, Doug
DeBerg, Steve
DeForest, Joe
Dickerson, Eric
Dierdorf, Dan
Dudek, Joe
Elliott, Tony
Ellis, Todd
Elway, John
Esiason, Boomer
Evans, Vince
Fouts, Dan
Gastineau, Mark
Gault, Willie
Giftopoulos, Pete
Green, Tim
Greene, Joe
Harrah, Dennis
Hill, Jim
Hill, Tony
Holieway, Jamelle
Igwebuike, Donald
Jackson, Bo
Jackson, Earnest
Jackson, Kenny
Kay, Clarence
Kelly, Jim
Kinnick, Nile, 1919?-1943
Lockbaum, Gordie
Lofton, James
Malone, Mark, 1958-
Manley, Dexter
Martin, George
Mayes, Rueben
McCallum, Napoleon
McConkey, Phil, 1957-
McMahon, Jim
McPherson, Don
Meggyesy, Dave
Miller, Chris
Montana, Joe
Morgan, Stanley
National Football League Players Association
Nehemiah, Renaldo, 1959-
O'Brien, Jim
Okoye, Christian
Palmer, Paul
Paris, Bubba
Payton, Walter, 1954-
Pearson, Drew
Perez, Mike
Perry, William
Rice, Jerry
Richards, David
Rives, Chip
Robinson, Jerry
Rodgers, Johnny, 1951-
Sample, Johnny
Sharpe, Sterling
Simms, Phil, 1955-
Smith, Bubba
Smith, Emmitt
Smith, Jackie L., 1940-
Snow, Carlos
Spielman, Chris
Steinkuhler, Dean

Strikes—Football players
Sullivan, Mark
Taylor, Lawrence
Testaverde, Vinny
Toon, Al
Torri, Dave
Upshaw, Gene
Warfield, Paul
Waters, Bob
White, Lorenzo
Williams, Doug
Williams, Jimmy
Williams, Reggie

Adidas 1986 All-American high school football team. il *Sch Update* 119:28 My 18 '87

The best and the brightest [unsung college players who are also good students] E. M. Swift. il *Sports Illus* 67:40-5 Ag 31 '87

Black QBs led eight teams to bowl game appearances. *Jet* 71:54 Ja 19 '87

Black quarterbacks get nod at major colleges in upcoming bowl games. il *Jet* 73:46-7 D 7 '87

Brutal face-off [pro centers and noseguards] P. Zimmerman. il *Sports Illus* 67 Sp Issue:32-41 S 9 '87

Chicago's weighty issue [quarterback trouble for the Bears; cover story] R. Telander. il pors *Sports Illus* 67:28-32+ Ag 24 '87

Grambling biggest black college winner in draft, but black QBs left out. il *Jet* 72:46 My 18 '87

The living daylights [top players discuss the art of hitting] M. Kiefer. il *Sport Mag* 78:28-32+ Ag '87

Rating the quarterbacks [pros] D. Levine. il *Sport Mag* 78:21-9 Ja '87

A season for leaders [quarterbacks] P. Axthelm. il *Newsweek* 110:100 D 7 '87

The secondary is primary in K.C. P. Zimmerman. il *Sports Illus* 67 Sp Issue:118-22 S 9 '87

Switching signals [black quarterbacks in college football] B. McDermott. il *Life* 10:43+ N '87

These Bills stack up [Buffalo's defensive players] R. Reilly. il *Sports Illus* 67:66-7+ D 7 '87

What I learned in school today [sitting in on a class taken by football players at the University of Michigan] S. Shuger. il *Sport Mag* 78:60-1 O '87

Accidents and injuries

See Football, High school—Accidents and injuries; Football, Professional—Accidents and injuries

Awards

See Football, College—Awards; Football, Professional—Awards

Health and hygiene

The battle of his life [Lou Gehrig's disease hits B. Waters and other former San Francisco 49ers] R. Fimrite. il pors *Sports Illus* 67:72-80 Ag 24 '87

Cowboys start AIDS tests; entire team disease free. il *Jet* 72:46 Ag 17 '87

An incurable killer strikes three ex-49ers, and an anguished victim doubts it's a coincidence [B. Waters, victim of Lou Gehrig's disease] D. Grogan. il por *People Wkly* 27:94-5 F 9 '87

Probing a mysterious "cluster" [three former San Francisco football players develop amyotrophic lateral sclerosis] C. Wallis. il *Time* 129:70 F 23 '87

Names

Anecdotes, facetiae, satire, etc.

Of many things. G. W. Hunt. *America* 156:inside cover Ja 17 '87

Photographs and photography

Better to receive [bumper crop of college pass catchers] il *Sports Illus* 67:22-9 Ag 31 '87

Salaries, pensions, etc.

See also

Collective bargaining—Football, Professional

The cost of a free agent [NFL strike] A. Wilson-Smith. *Macleans* 100:48 O 5 '87

Ex-Bears' QB Evans sues USFL for $1.3 million pay. por *Jet* 71:49 F 2 '87

Football's millionaires [black players] il *Ebony* 43:132+ N '87

Jack be nimble: a day in the life of an agent [J. Mills] D. S. Looney. il por *Sports Illus* 67:100-1 O 19 '87

NFL owners may have fumbled away their victory. A. Bernstein. il *Bus Week* p162 N 2 '87

Once again, time out for the fans [strike issue of free agency] A. P. Sanoff. il *U S News World Rep* 103:30-1 O 5 '87

The penalties for delay of game [free agency issue] T. Callahan. il *Time* 130:59-60 O 5 '87

USFL Blitz ordered to pay QB Evans $1.6 million [V. Evans] por *Jet* 72:50 Ap 27 '87

Football players—Salaries, pensions, etc.—_cont._
Why the owners can't scuttle free agents. J. Hoerr. il
Bus Week p42 O 5 '87
Football records
The toothless Lions [Columbia breaks consecutive loss
record] H. Hersch. il *Sports Illus* 67:70-1 O 19 '87
Football video games *See* Video games
Foote, Horton
about
The Widow Claire [drama] Reviews
N Y 20:50 Ja 5 '87. J. Simon
Foote, Shelby
The letters in perspective. *Am Herit* 38:28 Jl/Ag '87
about
Telling how it was. G. C. Ward. il *Am Herit* 38:14+
D '87
Foote, Timothy
After more than two centuries, this may be Mr. Madison's
year. bibl (p186) il pors *Smithsonian* 18:76-82+ S '87
The ids of March. il *Atlantic* 259:14+ Mr '87
Footwear
See also
Running shoes
Tennis shoes
Walking shoes
The art of walking. il *Harpers Bazaar* 120:300-3 Mr
'87
Booting up for action. B. McKeown. il *Outdoor Life*
180:70-4 Ag '87
The evening "jewel" of the season may well be a shoe:
chic, heeled, wholly charming. il *Vogue* 177:372 O
'87
Fancy footwork: exercise shoes in the '80s. T. Osborne.
il *Curr Health 2* 13:19-21 Ap '87
How to buy a comfortable pair of heels. il *Glamour*
85:202 O '87
The latest, greatest aerobics shoes. T. Brunick. il *Women's
Sports Fitness* 9:34-6 D '87
New sport designs afoot [specialty shoes] J. Skorupa.
il *Pop Mech* 164:12+ Jl '87
Once upon a shoe . . . a maker of magic: Roger Vivier.
J. J. Buck. il por *Vogue* 177:292-7+ D '87
Prom-perfect. il *Seventeen* 46:112 Mr '87
Sheep on your feet [slippers from wool batting] il *Sunset*
179:132+ N '87
Shoes for warm weather [men] R. La Ferla. il *N Y
Times Mag* p60 Je 21 '87
Shoes: names of the game. il *Vogue* 177:262+ Ag '87
Sneak peeks. il *Teen* 31:74-5 Mr '87
The sneaker. J. Berendt. il *Esquire* 107:26+ My '87
Sneaks preview: your 1987 wardrobe. J. Capouya. il
Sport Mag 78:86 F '87
Sports shoe dynamics: messages from down-under. il
Teen 31:50 Ag '87
Super shoes '87 [sports shoes; special section] M. Kort.
il *Women's Sports Fitness* 9:29+ Mr '87
These shoes coddle your feet—and your career [men's
dress shoes] S. Woolley. il *Bus Week* p140 N 23
'87

Anecdotes, facetiae, satire, etc.
Cruel shoes [women's shoes] J. Miller. il *Ms* 16:54 S
'87
Sneaker chic. J. A. Cox. il *Read Dig* 130:17-18 Je '87
Care
A care and repair guide for shoes. J. Jurnovoy and
D. Jenness. il *Mademoiselle* 93:182 My '87
Exhibitions
In Vivier's shoes [exhibition at Musée des Arts la Mode,
Paris] P. McColl. il *N Y Times Mag* p36 D 27 '87
Manufacture
See Shoe industry
Footwear, Aerobics *See* Aerobics—Equipment
Forage plants
See also
Arrowhead Country Forage Council
Hay
Millet
Flexible forages. il *Success Farm* 85 no6:B3-B6+ Mr
'87
Foraging for edible plants *See* Plants, Edible
Foraging theory, Optimal *See* Optimal foraging theory
Forbes, Bertie Charles
Business ethics, immigrants' treatment—70 years ago
and now. il por *Forbes* 140:33-4 Jl 13 '87
Forbes, Elizabeth
Portrait of a lady. por *Opera News* 52:38-9 N '87
Forbes, Leslie
Of truffles and lavender. il *House Gard* 159:42+ S '87
The renaissance of English cookery. il *House Gard*
159:124+ N '87

Strong breads, dark sweets. il *House Gard* 159:88+ D
'87
Forbes, Malcolm S., Jr.
Fact and comment II. See issues of Forbes
Forbes, Malcolm Stevenson
The art of motorcycle touring. il pors *Pop Mech* 164:90-4+
Je '87
Fact and comment. See issues of Forbes
about
Cosmopolitan talks to Malcolm Forbes. M. Willens.
Forbes 139:18 Ap 20 '87
The great Amazonian expedition. C. T. Buckley. il pors
map *Forbes* 140:193-8+ O 19 '87
The Highlander: aboard Malcolm Forbes' remarkable
yacht. C. T. Buckley. il por *Archit Dig* 44:100-9+
Ja '87
Ich bin ein ballooner. B. Conrad, III. il map *Forbes*
140:116-20+ Ag 24 '87
Malcolm Forbes's ultra-bash boasted French fizz and
prom queen named Liz. T. Cunneff. il por *People
Wkly* 27:97-9 Je 15 '87
A swellegant party. K. Ames. il por *Newsweek* 109:57
Je 8 '87
What's up with Malcolm Forbes. N. Mayersohn. il *Pop
Mech* 164:94 Je '87
Forbes, Walter A.
about
How Comp-U-Card hooks home shoppers. R. Mitchell.
il por *Bus Week* p73-4 My 18 '87
Forbes (Periodical)
Creative destruction [70th anniversary issue; cover story;
special issue] il *Forbes* 140:49-51 Jl 13 '87
Flashbacks. D. A. Saunders. See issues of Forbes
'Forbes': Springsteen is rock's top earner. F. Goodman.
Roll Stone p21 O 22 '87
Secret of a success [Forbes business psychologist S.
Blotnick exposed as a fraud] por *Time* 130:61 Ag
3 '87
Forbes four hundred *See* Rich
Forbis, Steven J.
Keep the home fires burning—safely. il *Read Dig*
131:105-8 D '87
Force and energy
See also
Fifth force (Physics)
Quantum theory
Sixth force (Physics)
Forcing (Plants)
Flowers all winter long. T. James. il *Ladies Home J*
104:92+ N '87
Forcing bulbs: an easy fall project that yields winter
cheer. il *Glamour* 85:96 S '87
Spring bulbs indoors. R. Keller. il *Rodale's Org Gard*
34:14-15 N '87
Winter blooms. J. Glattstein. il *Home Mech* 83:74+
O '87
Ford, Betty
The day my family saved my life [excerpt from Betty];
ed. by Chris Chase. il pors *Good Housekeep* 204:132-3+
F '87
about
Betty Ford's brave mission. E. Sherman. il pors *Ladies
Home J* 104:80+ Je '87
Frank as ever, former First Lady Betty Ford describes
her harrowing years of addiction. A. Chambers. il
pors *People Wkly* 27:88-9+ Mr 9 '87
Ford, Charlotte
Etiquette: doing it right. See issues of McCall's beginning
January 1987
Yasmin Khan: my mother, Rita Hayworth. il pors
McCalls 114:138-9+ My '87
Ford, Corey, 1902-1969
Fish dry and vote wet! il *50 Plus* 27:62-4 Je '87
Ford, Cristina
about
Cristina [excerpt from The Fords] P. Collier and D.
Horowitz. il pors *Good Housekeep* 205:58+ O '87
Ford, Daniel
I skied Killington in March, April, May, and June.
il *Skiing* 39:45-9 Spr '87
Ford, Gerald R., 1913-
Gerald Ford on flying high today and paying tomorrow.
il por *Life* 10:28-9 O '87
about
The Ford years. F. Barnes. *New Repub* 196:7-9 My
25 '87
Often, momentum can lead to a bad arms treaty [inter-
view] D. Frost. por *U S News World Rep* 103:33
D 7 '87

Ford, Harold, 1945-
about
Ford doing fine after suffering chest pains. il por *Jet* 72:14 My 25 '87
Gag order lifted in Harold Ford fraud case. por *Jet* 73:39 O 26 '87
Memphis churches back Rep. Ford with $100,000. il por *Jet* 72:7 Je 15 '87
Rep. Ford gets backing for new welfare reform bill. por *Jet* 72:36 Ap 20 '87
Rep. Ford indicted and says he will fight charges. por *Jet* 72:4 My 11 '87

Ford, Harrison
about
The special chemistry of Harrison Ford and Peter Weir. J. Powell. il por *Glamour* 85:132 Ja '87

Ford, Henry, 1863-1947
about
Two giant U.S. business efforts that failed in Brazil. M. S. Forbes. il *Forbes* 140:18-19 O 19 '87

Ford, Henry, 1917-1987
about
Cristina [excerpt from The Fords] P. Collier and D. Horowitz. il pors *Good Housekeep* 205:58+ O '87
Obituary
Jet il pors 73:12-13 O 19 '87
Time il por 130:56 O 12 '87. J. S. DeMott

Ford, John
The girl with the gift [story] il *Redbook* 170:58-61 N '87

Ford, Kathleen, 1945-
The Ryans [story] il *U S Cathol* 52:32-7 Ag '87

Ford, Richard, 1944-
Children [story] *New Yorker* 63:25-34+ Ag 3 '87
Montaigne's invitation to the past: a historic residence in Natchez, Mississippi. il por *Archit Dig* 44:114-17+ Jl '87
My mother, in memory. il *Harpers* 275:44-57 Ag '87
Optimists [story] *New Yorker* 63:28-36 Mr 30 '87

Ford, Rita
about
Music boxes and Maxilla & Mandible. H. Bridges. il *Gourmet* 47:28+ S '87

Ford, Tyrone
about
Former Reagan boy hero, 13, returns home from 'streetlife'. il por *Jet* 72:27 Ag 3 '87

Ford, William Clay, Jr.
about
The scion also rises. R. Morais. il por *Forbes* 139:282 Ja 12 '87

Ford (Henry) Museum and Greenfield Village *See* Henry Ford Museum and Greenfield Village

Ford (Rita), Inc. *See* Rita Ford, Inc.

Ford Aerospace & Communications Corp.
Battle management definition advances at Ford Aerospace. *Aviat Week Space Technol* 127:19 N 30 '87

Ford family
about
Holidays—and centuries—come and go, but for the faithful Fords, it's semper Fidelia's fruitcake. il *People Wkly* 28:133 N 30 '87

Ford Foundation
A case history of one foundation's philanthropy [Contemporary Music Project] R. J. Werner. *Des Arts Educ* 88:19-22 Mr/Ap '87

Ford Ice Driving School (Steamboat Springs, Colo.) *See* Automobile driving—Study and teaching

Ford International Automotive Operations. Ford of Europe Inc.
Ford bids again, Fiat gets the nod [Fiat outbids Ford for Alfa Romeo] P. Lienert. *Road Track* 38:100 F '87
A hit in Europe, but a miss in the states [Merkur] J. B. Treece. il *Bus Week* p81 S 28 '87
Somebody does it better [Ford and GM cars made in Europe] M. Keller. il *Mot Trend* 39:102 Ja '87

Ford Motor Co.
1987 Man of the Year [chairman D. E. Petersen] il por *Mot Trend* 39:43 F '87
The automotive world of the 21st century. D. E. Petersen. il *Radio-Electron* 58:91-5 My '87
Can Ford stay on top? [cover story] J. B. Treece. il pors *Bus Week* p78-82+ S 28 '87
Cash flow in the fast lane [Ford buys Aston Martin] T. Tedesco. il *Macleans* 100:39 S 21 '87
Continuing education for blue-collar workers [UAW-Ford Employee Development and Training Program] P. H. Abelson. *Science* 238:875 N 13 '87
A different sort of victory for the UAW. *Newsweek* 110:65 S 28 '87

Ford chasing women. il *Mot Trend* 39:38 Ag '87
The Ford dilemma: go for glory? il *Forbes* 140:35-6 D 28 '87
Ford-UAW contract bolsters job security. il *Mon Labor Rev* 110:31-3 N '87
A Ford vehicle doomed to stall at General Motors [UAW contract] J. A. Seamonds. il *U S News World Rep* 103:16 S 28 '87
Ford's Bruce Blythe has a big blank check—and a mission. J. B. Treece. il por *Bus Week* p79+ D 21 '87
Ford's warranty commitment. M. J. Schultz. *Pop Mech* 164:24+ S '87
GM may be off the hook: the Ford talks leave plenty of loopholes. A. Bernstein and W. Zellner. il *Bus Week* p26-7 S 28 '87
The happiest man at Ford. G. Baxter. il *Car Driv* 32:23 Mr '87
Have you driven an Aston Martin lately? [Ford agrees to buy Aston Martin Lagonda] il *Newsweek* 110:64 S 21 '87
How Ford became #1 [cover story; with editorial comment by Robert E. Petersen] il *Mot Trend* 39 no12 Sp Issue:4, 6-7+ '87
How IBM wooed Ford into a more meaningful relationship. W. J. Hampton. il por *Bus Week* p87 Mr 30 '87
Is anybody out there listening? [market research techniques] R. Ceppos. il *Car Driv* 33:24-5 O '87
Is Textron in Ford's future? The pros think so. G. G. Marcial. il *Bus Week* p61 Jl 27 '87
Miscellaneous ramblings [open letter to CEO D. Petersen] J. Dinkel. il *Road Track* 39:37-9 O '87
Most improved. il *Forbes* 139:71 Ja 12 '87
One down, tougher one to go [UAW settles with Ford] J. Castro. il *Time* 130:52 S 28 '87
The poor boy who outearned GM [D. Petersen] A. L. Taylor, III. il por *Fortune* 116:28-9 Ag 3 '87
The scion also rises [W. C. Ford Jr.] R. Morais. il por *Forbes* 139:282 Ja 12 '87
The shape of Ford's success [designer J. Telnack; cover story] P. Patton. il pors *N Y Times Mag* p18-22+ My 24 '87
Smiling fender to fender [UAW contract] W. Zellner and A. Bernstein. il *Bus Week* p39 O 5 '87
The stylist who put Ford out in front [J. Telnack] A. L. Taylor, III. il por *Fortune* 115:78+ Ja 5 '87
The U.S.: team at the top of no. 2 [D. E. Petersen and H. A. Poling] il pors *Fortune* 116:82 N 9 '87
The UAW sees a smoother road at Ford. W. Zellner. il *Bus Week* p125+ S 14 '87
What Ford can afford [argument for cutting car prices to fight imports] P. A. London. *New Repub* 196:16+ Je 8 '87
What's good for America. J. Flint. il *Forbes* 140:173-6+ Jl 13 '87
Why black workers may say 'thanks, but no thanks' to Ford [partial worker ownership of Samcor] S. Mufson. il *Bus Week* p47 Jl 6 '87
Yamaha to build Ford V6. D. McCosh. il *Pop Sci* 231:14 S '87

Ford Motor Co. of Canada Limited
Death sentences from America [Ford of Canada ordered to drop Canadian advertising agencies] P. C. Newman. il *Macleans* 100:39 O 5 '87

Ford of Europe Inc. *See* Ford International Automotive Operations. Ford of Europe Inc.

Fordlandia Plantation *See* Plantations—Brazil

Forecasting
See also
Agricultural forecasting
Business forecasting
Economic forecasting
Educational forecasting
Nineteen hundred and eighty-eight
Nineteen hundred and nineties
Political forecasting
Population forecasting
Social forecasting
Stocks—Price forecasting
Technological forecasting
Twenty-first century
Two thousand (Year)
Two thousand one (Year)
Two thousand seven (Year)
Two thousand seventeen (Year)
Weather forecasting
World Future Society
Early warning. See issues of World Press Review
First word [future law] F. L. Bailey. il *Omni* 9:4 Ap '87

Forecasting—*cont.*

Future histories: a new approach to scenarios [SIGMA computer simulation] W. L. Renfro. il por *Futurist* 21:38-41 Mr/Ap '87

Outlook '88 and beyond. il *Futurist* 21:53-60 N/D '87

Siskel on Ebert—Ebert on Siskel [interview] *Omni* 9:52+ Je '87

Tomorrow in brief. See issues of The Futurist

Tomorrow: newsletter. See issues of U.S. News & World Report

Foreclosure

Buying a foreclosed home. *U S News World Rep* 103:85 O 5 '87

Fighting to stave off foreclosure, farmer Garth Conlan ends up taking his bank to the cleaners. D. Grogan. il por *People Wkly* 28:50-2 Ag 10 '87

A second mortgage that turned into a first-class nightmare [Richard D. Price family] D. Cook. il *Bus Week* p68 F 9 '87

Foreign accents *See* Accents
Foreign adoption *See* Adoption and adopted children
Foreign agents *See* Foreign propagandists
Foreign automobiles *See* Automobiles, Foreign
Foreign Buildings Office (U.S.) *See* United States. Foreign Buildings Office
Foreign cooking *See* Cooking, International
Foreign correspondents

See also

Aikman, David, 1944-

Afghanistan

See also

Afghanistan—Russian invasion, 1979- —Reporters and reporting

China

A reporter's odyssey in unseen China. J. F. Burns. il map *N Y Times Mag* p29-31+ F 8 '87

Czechoslovakia

Falling for a Warsaw Pact dame [British journalist's experiences] J. Simpson. il *Harpers* 274:58-62 Je '87

Developing countries

Coups and earthquakes only. S. Kassam. *World Press Rev* 34:64 S '87

Great Britain

Di's brother: new man on the beat [Viscount Althorp to report on British matters for the Today show] D. Waggoner. il pors *People Wkly* 27:22-5 Mr 2 '87

Greece

See also

Greece—History—Civil War, 1944-1949—Reporters and reporting

Israel

See also

Israel-Arab Wars, 1967- —Reporters and reporting

Middle East

See also

Iranian-Iraqi War, 1980- —Reporters and reporting

South Africa

A correspondent's farewell to Johannesburg. S. Mufson. il *Bus Week* p56 Je 8 '87

A farewell to South Africa. A. Cowell. il *N Y Times Mag* p36-9+ Ja 25 '87

Soviet Union

See also

Daniloff-Zakharov espionage case, 1986

Better slow than sorry [attitudes of foreign press towards M. Gorbachev] T. Griffith. il *Time* 129:83 My 4 '87

A close-up look at *glasnost* [CBS special Seven days in May] J. Alter. il *Newsweek* 109:62 Je 29 '87

A Soviet assessment [evaluating an American journalist's views]; tr. by Gretchen Trimble. D. Biryukov. il por *U S News World Rep* 103:54 O 19 '87

The USSR and the press. P. Taubman. *Current* 291:28-33 Mr/Ap '87

Foreign Corrupt Practices Act of 1977

Am I my brother's keeper? D. Fanning. il *Forbes* 139:66 My 4 '87

Foreign debts *See* Debts, External

Foreign exchange

See also

Balance of payments
Capital movements
Eurobond market
International Monetary Fund
Money markets

Crisis and reform [address, November 13, 1986] C. F. Bergsten. *Vital Speeches Day* 53:281-8 F 15 '87

Currency 'target zones': still little more than talk. K. Pennar. il *Bus Week* p41 Mr 9 '87

The dollar: No, garçon, I ordered a Big Mac, not a cognac [tables] il *Money* 16:40 Ap '87

Finance ministers meet on exchange rates [statement, February 22, 1987] *Dep State Bull* 87:31-2 Ap '87

The gnomes behind the dollar's fall. P. Sherrid. il *U S News World Rep* 102:43-4 F 16 '87

How far the dollar goes in far-flung places. D. H. Dunn. il *Bus Week* p149 O 19 '87

Imposing order on a global economy [Group of 7 meeting in Washington] il *Macleans* 100:30 Ap 20 '87

One way to win high marks from future historians [new international monetary system] M. S. Forbes, Jr. il *Forbes* 139:25 Ap 6 '87

The Paris pact may not buoy the dollar for long [February 1987 meeting] B. Riemer and others. il *Bus Week* p40-1 Mr 9 '87

Playing for a fall [investment outlook in light of falling dollar] E. A. Finn, Jr. il *Forbes* 139:98-101 F 23 '87

The search for a new exchange-rate regime. J. Williamson. bibl f il *Science* 237:489-93 Jl 31 '87

Supporting the dollar [Group of Five meeting in Paris] A. Finlayson. *Macleans* 100:38 Mr 9 '87

Taming the wild buck [Group of Five intervention] M. R. Meyer. il *Newsweek* 109:53 Mr 2 '87

Twin deficits and the G-7 [Paris accord] il *Natl Rev* 39:19-20 Ap 24 '87

Foreign exchange brokers

'I think I'm going to make money'. P. Sherrid. il *U S News World Rep* 102:44 F 16 '87

To be franc, currency trader Steve Peras has a yen to make sure the buck doesn't stop here. E. Levin. il por *People Wkly* 27:95-6 F 16 '87

Ethical aspects

Can Volkswagen pull itself out of the mud? [currency fraud charges] R. Ingersoll. il por *Bus Week* p60-1 Je 22 '87

Computer fraud at VW [foreign exchange fraud] P. Lewis. il *Macleans* 100:32 Mr 30 '87

A currency scandal adds to VW's woes. J. E. Pluenneke. *Bus Week* p54+ Mr 23 '87

Foreign exchange options

Check your options [Swiss francs] S. W. Angrist. il *Forbes* 139:125 Ap 20 '87

Foreign Intelligence Advisory Board (U.S.) *See* United States. President's Foreign Intelligence Advisory Board

Foreign Intelligence Press

Spying on the spooks pays off for a publisher [J. P. Quirk] M. Frons. il por *Bus Week* p107 My 11 '87

Foreign language booksellers *See* Booksellers and bookselling—Foreign language books

Foreign languages *See* Language and languages

Foreign loans *See* Loans, Foreign

Foreign missions *See* Missions

Foreign news

See also

Greece—History—Civil War, 1944-1949—Reporters and reporting

Iranian-Iraqi War, 1980— —Reporters and reporting

Lebanon hostage cases, 1984- —Reporters and reporting

Libyan-American conflict, 1986—Reporters and reporting

Reagan-Gorbachev summit conference, 1987—Reporters and reporting

Stark (Warship)—Iraqi missile attack, 1987—Reporters and reporting

Beat the devil [reporting on death of B. E. Linder] A. Cockburn. *Nation* 244:636-7 My 16 '87

Cover-up at 'The New York review' [criticism of R. Leiken's reports from Nicaragua by Tony Jenkins] A. Cockburn. *Nation* 245:9 Jl 4-11 '87

Shamed [R. Leiken's reporting on Nicaragua criticized by Tony Jenkins] A. Cockburn. *Nation* 245:79 Ag 1-8 '87

The war that no one can cover [reporting on the Nicaraguan contras] J. Borrell. il *Time* 129:60 F 16 '87

Anecdotes, facetiae, satire, etc.

Snap books [books by big-name authors about their brief experiences in foreign countries] M. Massing. *New Repub* 196:21+ My 4 '87

Foreign opinion of the United States *See* United States—Foreign opinion

Foreign population *See* Immigrants

Foreign propagandists

United States

Advice for sale. D. M. Levy. *Foreign Policy* 67:64-86 Summ '87

How 'Japan, Inc.' pleads its case in Washington. J. L. Sheler. *U S News World Rep* 102:22 My 4 '87

Samurais for hire [Toshiba lobbying Congress] G. Witkin. il *U S News World Rep* 103:50 O 5 '87

Foreign propagandists—United States—*cont.*
Why "foreign agents" seek friends in Congress. P. M. Jones. il *Sch Update* 119:20-1 Ja 12 '87
Foreign relations *See* International relations
Foreign Relations Committee *See* United States. Congress. Senate. Committee on Foreign Relations
Foreign rights (Books) *See* Copyright
Foreign Service (U.S.) *See* United States. Dept. of State. Foreign Service
Foreign station wagons *See* Station wagons, Foreign
Foreign stock funds *See* Investment trusts
Foreign stocks *See* Stocks
Foreign students

Great Britain
The last diploma he got was in high school, but Ed Gorman, 69, is setting his cap on a masters from Oxford [American student] il por *People Wkly* 27:58 Ap 20 '87
Oxford's U.S. rowers jump ship, leaving the varsity without all its oars in the water. W. Plummer. il *People Wkly* 27:38+ F 23 '87

United States
Among the seven pillars of wisdom [blind East Indian student at Pomona College] V. Mehta. *New Yorker* 63:34-6+ Ag 24 '87
At the gates of California [blind student applies for college admission in 1952] V. Mehta. *New Yorker* 63:82-97 My 11 '87
Diplomats in our backyard. M. D. Rentz. por *Newsweek* 109:10 F 16 '87
Even Communists like capitalist justice [Chinese students study law in the U.S.] J. Adler. il *Newsweek* 110:74 O 19 '87
Foreign students: a valuable link. il *Change* 19:39-43 Jl/Ag '87
Foreign students under fire. J. N. Baker. il *Newsweek* 110:73-4 O 19 '87
Foreigners in science [report from the National Science Foundation] C. Holden. il *Science* 237:970 Ag 28 '87
I stopped my daughter's wedding [plans for bogus marriage to foreign student] R. Bode. il pors *Good Housekeep* 204:106+ Mr '87
The impact of foreign graduate students on engineering education in the United States. E. G. Barber and R. P. Morgan. bibl f il *Science* 236:33-7 Ap 3 '87
Out of South Africa [black exchange student, Mvelase] J. Levine. il pors *N Y Times Mag* p81+ S 20 '87
Robert Brown oversees the enrollment of Mandela's daughter at Boston Univ. il por *Jet* 72:28 Je 8 '87
Thinking about home [reaction of Chinese students in the U.S. to student protests in China] il *Time* 129:45 F 2 '87
You can't go home again, MBA-san [Japanese business students] il *Fortune* 116:9 Ag 3 '87
Foreign study
See also
Student exchange programs
Foreign subsidiaries *See* Corporations, International
Foreign trade *See* Export-import trade
Foreign trade regulation
See also
General Agreement on Tariffs and Trade
Foreign travel *See* Travel
Foreign trucks *See* Trucks, Foreign
Foreign workers *See* Alien labor
Foreigner (Musical group)
Foreigner set to release new album. F. Goodman. *Roll Stone* p15 D 3 '87
Foreman, George

about
Ebony update: George Foreman. N. O. Unger. il pors *Ebony* 42:92+ Je '87
Ex-champ Foreman a real heavyweight in comeback. por *Jet* 71:50 F 9 '87
Foreman nixes Arizona for heavyweight bout. il por *Jet* 73:51 N 16 '87
Foreman to keep busy after easy comeback win. por *Jet* 72:46 Mr 30 '87
Foremost Corp. of America
First and Foremost. T. Jaffe. *Forbes* 140:269 D 14 '87
Foremost-McKesson, Inc. *See* McKesson Corp.
Forensic anthropology
Bones of contention [Rembrandt] A. Steacy. por *Macleans* 100:66-7 D 7 '87
Finding the children [identifying Argentine missing children through genetic testing] B. Beckwith. il *Ms* 16:88 S '87
Forensic experts aid Philippine search for disappeared. K. Hannibal. il *Science* 235:535-6 Ja 30 '87
Identifying Argentina's 'disappeared'. S. G. Michaud. il *N Y Times Mag* p18-21+ D 27 '87

Identity crisis [forensics used to identify victims of English Channel ferry disaster] J. Lowenstein. il *Oceans* 20:72 N/D '87
Forensic criminology *See* Criminal investigation
Forensic illustration
A new way to find missing children [drawings that simulate the way children would look today] J. Hope. il *Good Housekeep* 204:50+ Mr '87
Forensic medicine *See* Medical jurisprudence
Forensic psychiatry
Trials of an expert witness [conflict arising from being asked to testify in defense of accused war criminal J. Demjanjuk] E. F. Loftus. por *Newsweek* 109:10-11 Je 29 '87
Forest, Jim
Christ meets Stalin in Soviet-made film. *Christ Century* 104:676-7 Ag 12-19 '87
Forest clearcutting *See* Clearcutting
Forest conservation
See also
Forest fires—Prevention and control
International Year of the Forest, 1985
Forests [Environmental Quality Index] il *Natl Wildl* 25:38 F/Mr '87
Forest crown canopy
The canopy raft [balloons in forest ecology research] il *Courier* 40:25-6 O '87
Down to the treetops by balloon [exploring the tropical forest canopy; work of Francis Halle and others] il map *Natl Geogr World* 146:13-19 O '87
End of the old-growth canopy [destruction of Pacific Northwest forests endangers spotted owls] L. Tuttle. il *Natl Parks* 61:16-21 My/Je '87
Out on a limb [exploring the tropical forest canopy by hot air balloon; work of Francis Halle and others] K. Brower. il *Omni* 9:56-64+ Ap '87
Forest ecology
See also
Deforestation
Forest crown canopy
Forest fires—Controlled fires
Growing a forest from scratch [Guanacaste National Park re-created tropical dry forest in Costa Rica; work of Daniel H. Janzen] E. C. Wolf. il por *Futurist* 21:41-2 Jl/Ag '87
In virgin forest [Hutcheson Memorial Forest] *New Yorker* 63:21-3 Jl 6 '87
Kuna Indians: building a bright future [preservation of virgin rain forest] N. Myers. il map *Int Wildl* 17:18-24 Jl/Ag '87
Trees of the trembling earth [southern beech forest of Chile] T. T. Veblen. il *Nat Hist* 96:42-7 S '87
Forest fallow cultivation *See* Shifting cultivation
Forest fauna
See also
Birds
Owls
Secret life of a forest. G. H. Harrison. il *Natl Wildl* 25:30-1 Je/Jl '87
Forest fire fighting *See* Forest fires—Prevention and control
Forest fires
Fire out of China [Daxing'anling forest] il *Time* 129:45 Je 1 '87
A just war [fighting forest fire in northern Calif.] J. D. Hull. il *Time* 130:23-4+ O 26 '87
The summer Montana burned [1984] R. Heim, Jr. il map *Weatherwise* 40:184-7 Jl/Ag '87
With hydraulic skillets and enormous toasters, OK's caterers feed the fight against forest fires [feeding firefighters in the West] M. Grant. il *People Wkly* 28:47-8 S 21 '87
Controlled fires
Born of fire [prescribed burning for sequoia groves] W. C. Tweed. il *Natl Parks* 61:22-7+ Ja/F '87
Ping-pong bombs [balls filled with chemicals used to ignite fires] *Discover* 8:8+ N '87
Western fires add to prescribed burning data. il *Natl Parks* 61:13 N/D '87
You only choke twice [southern Calif. forest fire smoke contains automobile exhaust] il *Discover* 8:6+ O '87
Prevention and control
From dragon slayers. T. Emonds. il *Mother Earth News* 107:80-3+ S/O '87
Forest frogs *See* Frogs
Forest management
See also
Clearcutting
Forest conservation
Forest fires—Controlled fires
United States. Forest Service

Forest management—*cont.*
Congress should investigate Forest Service violations [with editorial comment by George T. Frampton] il *Wilderness* 50:2-3 Summ '87
The lopsided ledger [management of the national forests] L. Williamson. il *Outdoor Life* 179:18+ Ja '87
Forest planting
See also
Reforestation
Forest policy *See* Forest management
Forest products industry
See also
Bohemia Inc.
Georgia-Pacific Corp.
International Paper Co.
Louisiana-Pacific Corp.
Lumber industry
Wood pulp industry
Finance
Reams of profits for the paper business. J. B. Levine. il *Bus Week* p87 Ja 12 '87
Forest products workers
Peonage in the pines [migrant Mexican forest workers] J. Juffer. il *Progressive* 51:24-7 N '87
Forest rangers
New York (State)
See also
New York State Ranger School (Wanakena, N.Y.)
Forest regeneration *See* Forest reproduction
Forest reproduction
Dynamic ecosystem consequences of tree birth and death patterns [computer models] H. H. Shugart. bibl il *BioScience* 37:596-602 S '87
Forest reproduction, Artificial *See* Reforestation
Forest Service (U.S.) *See* United States. Forest Service
Forest workers *See* Foresters
Foresters
See also
Society of American Foresters
Awards
Foresters receive awards [presented by the Society of American Foresters] *BioScience* 37:163 F '87
Forestier-Walker, Katherine
China lights a 'Spark'. il *World Press Rev* 34:46-7 Ag '87
Forestry *See* Forests and forestry
Forestry education
See also
New York State Ranger School (Wanakena, N.Y.)
Is woodland management for you? [home study course] D. J. Decker. il *Conservationist* 41:38-41 Ja/F '87
Forests, National *See* National forests
Forests and forestry
See also
Computers—Forestry use
Forest conservation
Forest fires
Foresters
Lumber industry
Lumbering
National forests
Rain forests
Reforestation
Society of American Foresters
Trees
United States. Forest Service
Woodlots
US forested wetlands: 1940-1980 [Forest Service surveys] Y. Abernethy and R. E. Turner. bibl il maps *BioScience* 37:721-7 N '87
Study and teaching
See Forestry education
Atlantic States
The forest decline enigma. D. Hinrichsen. il *BioScience* 37:542-6 S '87
California
Root rot turns back the clock on the Yosemite Valley [trees destroyed by fungus Fomes annosus] il *Discover* 8:10+ Ja '87
Central Europe
The forest decline enigma. D. Hinrichsen. il *BioScience* 37:542-6 S '87
China
Fire out of China [Daxing'anling forest] il *Time* 129:45 Je 1 '87
Costa Rica
Growing a forest from scratch [Guanacaste National Park re-created tropical dry forest; work of Daniel H. Janzen] E. C. Wolf. il por *Futurist* 21:41-2 Jl/Ag '87

Europe
Acid rain in Europe [cover story; special section; with editorial comment by Leen Hordijk] il f il maps *Environment* 29:inside cover, 4-15+ N '87
Germany (West)
Green devolution. il map *Natl Parks* 61:17 S/O '87
Mexico
Guarding the monarch's kingdom [plan to protect butterfly's wintering grounds; cover story] S. Sullivan. il map *Int Wildl* 17:4-11 N/D '87
Nepal
Is Nepal going bald? T. Kerasote. il map *Audubon* 89:28-30+ S '87
New Jersey
In virgin forest [Hutcheson Memorial Forest] *New Yorker* 63:21-3 Jl 6 '87
New York (State)
Caulked boots and white water [Adirondack logging in the 19th and early 20th centuries] D. Wharton. il *Conservationist* 41:38-43 Mr/Ap '87
North Carolina
Forests are dying but is acid rain really to blame? [research by Robert I. Bruck] J. R. Luoma. il map *Audubon* 89:36-8+ Mr '87
Pacific Northwest
End of the old-growth canopy [destruction of Pacific Northwest forests endangers spotted owls] L. Tuttle. il *Natl Parks* 61:16-21 My/Je '87
Preserving old-growth forests [spotted owl controversy] D. B. Edelson. bibl f il *Environment* 29:3-5 O '87
Public dismay over private cuts [clearcutting by Plum Creek Timber Company on private land] J. Sher. il *Sierra* 72:83-4 Mr/Ap '87
The shrinking province of the primeval [cover story] K. Ervin. il map *Sierra* 72:38-45 Jl/Ag '87
Threat to the spotted owl [destruction of Pacific Northwest forests] L. Burnham. il *Sci Am* 257:34+ O '87
Queen Charlotte Islands (B.C.)
The South Moresby war [Haida Indians protest logging] M. Gee. il *Macleans* 100:12 Jl 6 '87
Switzerland
Avalanche! S. Cashen. il *Int Wildl* 17:36-7 My/Je '87
Forestville (Calif.)
Festivals
Heidi had an itch to be festival queen [Poison Oak Festival, Forestville, Calif.] il *Audubon* 89:20 N '87
Forever Lulu [film] *See* Motion picture reviews—Single works
Forgery
See also
Art—Forgeries
Counterfeits and counterfeiting
Bogus documents now on sale—$25 and up [immigration documents] S. L. Hawkins. il *U S News World Rep* 102:26 Ja 19 '87
Forgetfulness *See* Memory
Forgiveness
Fallen leaders are not "damaged goods". R. W. Dingman. il por *Christ Today* 31:12 D 11 '87
Forgive and you will be forgiven. G. G. Seibert. *America* 157:119 Ag 29-S 5 '87
Forgiving all his trespasses. D. Heyn. *Mademoiselle* 93:176 Ap '87
I'll never forgive you! A. Penney. il *Ladies Home J* 104:42+ Mr '87
The road to restoration: how should the church treat its fallen leaders? [cover story] K. S. Kantzer. il *Christ Today* 31:19-22 N 20 '87
When to forgive a friend and when to forget her. J. Kaufman. il *Seventeen* 46:250-1+ Mr '87
When to hold a grudge. M. A. Kellogg. il *Glamour* 85:165+ F '87
Form letters
Developing good form [customized form letters] C. O'Malley. il *Pers Comput* 11:99-102+ My '87
Formaldehyde
EPA indicts formaldehyde, 7 years later. E. Marshall. *Science* 236:381 Ap 24 '87
Formic acid
100 trillion ants drop acid [research by Thomas Graedel] il *Discover* 8:8 S '87
Ants and the atmosphere: no picnic [research by Thomas Graedel] R. Monastersky. *Sci News* 131:345 My 30 '87
Forms, blanks, etc.
See also
Tax returns

Forms, Dress *See* Dress forms
Forms of address
Ms. conceptions [impact of courtesy titles; study by Kenneth Dion] J. A. Natale. il *Psychol Today* 21:20 D '87
Fornax (Constellation) *See* Constellations
Fornay, Alfred
Beauty '87: new look for the New Year. il *Ebony* 42:110-12+ Ja '87
Fornora, Anne
Guy Coheleach—artist and hunter [cover story] il *Conservationist* 42:26-33 N/D '87
Fornos, Werner
The moral implications of our population policy. il por *Humanist* 47:30-2 Ja/F '87
Forrest, Michael
Collecting French clocks. il *Antiques Collect Hobbies* 91:24-8 F '87
The eighteenth-century French print. il *Antiques Collect Hobbies* 92:58-60 Je '87
Forrestal, Robert P.
The economic outlook for 1987 and beyond [address, January 5, 1987] *Vital Speeches Day* 53:273-7 F 15 '87
Forrester, A. Theodore
about
Obituary
Phys Today por 40:113-14 N '87. E. Gerjuoy
Forrester, Frank H.
Tsunami! il *Weatherwise* 40:84-9 Ap '87
Forrester, Joel
Nightclub nightmares: a musician's view. *Down Beat* 54:52-3 My '87
Forrester, Maureen
about
In the vanguard for the arts. il por *Macleans* 100:22-3 D 28 '87
Forscher, Marty
about
From the other side of the camera: a talk with Marty Forscher. A. Goldsmith. il por *Pop Photogr* 94:26 Jl '87
Forskolin
Forskolin and phorbol esters reduce the same potassium conductance of mouse neurons in culture. D. S. Grega and others. bibl f il *Science* 235:345-8 Ja 16 '87
Forssell, Eva
(jt. auth) *See* Forssell, Jeff, and Forssell, Eva
Forssell, Jeff, and Forssell, Eva
Life after Chernobyl. il pors *Mother Earth News* 105:94-8+ My/Je '87
Forstall, Lionel
Life in remedial English: learning about teaching and learning. *Phi Delta Kappan* 68:796-7 Je '87
Forster, Ron
about
Ron Forster bikes off—way off—the beaten track. il por *People Wkly* 27:91 Je 22 '87
Forsterite
Phonon density of states and specific heat of forsterite, Mg_2SiO_4. K. R. Rao and others. bibl f il *Science* 236:64-5 Ap 3 '87
Forsthoffer, J. P.
A cultural momentum. il *Horizon* 30:41-7 D '87
Forstmann-Leff Associates
Today's rejects, tomorrow's buys [strategy of W. F. Harnisch] G. G. Marcial. *Bus Week* p120 My 18 '87
Forstmann Little & Company
Behind the scenes at a leveraged buyout [Sybron Corp.] E. Spragins. il *Bus Week* p120-2 Jl 20 '87
Forstmann Little: going fast by going slow. E. Spragins. il *Bus Week* p76-8 Ja 26 '87
Forsyth, Bill
about
Housekeeping [film] Reviews
Macleans 100:67 D 14 '87. L. O'Toole
New Yorker 63:147-9 D 14 '87. P. Kael
Newsweek 110:89 D 7 '87. J. Kroll
Time il 130:101 N 23 '87. R. Schickel
Vogue il 177:72 D '87. M. Haskell
Forsyth, Frederick, 1938-
about
Britain's shy spymaster at work. *World Press Rev* 34:61 My '87
Forsythe, William
about
Choreographing the unexpected. H. Brubach. por *Vogue* 177:70 Jl '87

Fort-Brescia, Bernardo
about
Bernardo Fort-Brescia and Laurinda Spear: the iconoclasts. B. Dumaine. il pors *Fortune* 115:152-3 Je 22 '87
Fort Gibson Military Park (Okla.) *See* Fortification—Oklahoma
Fort Howard Paper Co.
Warning: the Friday night fish fry may be hazardous to your health [pollution of Wisconsin's Fox River and Green Bay] M. Hudson. il maps *Audubon* 89:24-6+ Jl '87
Fort Lauderdale (Fla.)
Child welfare
Johnny Carson's son must pay support for black child who was living on welfare. il por *Jet* 72:52-3 Ap 13 '87
Festivals
Art along the boulevard [Las Olas Art Festival] il *South Living* 22:44 Mr '87
Historic houses, sites, etc.
A visit with the Stranahans. il *South Living* 22:45 O '87
Fort Meyers (Fla.)
Historic houses, sites, etc.
See also
Edison Winter Home and Museum (Fort Myers, Fla.)
Fort Morgan Museum (Gulf Shores, Ala.)
Remembering the bay's battles. il *South Living* 22:27-8 N '87
Fort Mose (Fla.) *See* Fortification—Florida
Fort Smith (Ark.)
Historic houses, sites, etc.
Touring the Belle Grove Historic District. il *South Living* 22:24+ Mr '87
Fort Valley (Ga.)
Criminal justice, Administration of
Black doctor sentenced to life for death of white woman patient in Georgia [V. D. Mallory] il por *Jet* 73:33 O 26 '87
Hold Georgia physician in death of white patient [V. D. Mallory held in murder of S. Fields] *Jet* 72:4 My 11 '87
Fort Wayne (Ind.)
Social conditions
Growing girls and grandmothers [Fort Wayne Feminists] M. K. Blakely. il por *Ms* 15:12+ Je '87
Fort Wilderness (Orlando, Fla.: Resort) *See* Resorts—Florida
Fort Worth (Tex.)
Education
Fort Worth, Texas: a high school that helps teenage mothers shape new lives [New Lives Center] L. Chandler. il *Sch Update* 119:24 Mr 23 '87
Gardens and gardening
See also
Water Gardens (Fort Worth, Tex.)
Historic houses, sites, etc.
A classic courthouse [Tarrant County Courthouse] il *South Living* 22:59 N '87
Forth (Computer language)
Stack machines and compiler design: the Novix CPU's FORTH instruction set and the design of a C compiler. D. L. Miller. bibl il *Byte* 12:177-8+ Ap '87
Forti, Simone, 1935-
about
Reviews:
S. Forti and D. Zambrano at the Ethnic Folk Arts Center, New York City. C. Hardy. *Dance Mag* 61:40-1 Ap '87
Fortier, Edmund
Touring the stellar cycle. il *Astronomy* 15:49-53 Mr '87
Fortification
Alabama
See also
Fort Morgan Museum (Gulf Shores, Ala.)
Caribbean region
Securing the Spanish Main [cover story] W. Houk. il map *Américas* 39:8-13+ My/Je '87
Florida
Holding the fort [Fort Mose excavations] il map *Sci Am* 257:18-19 Ag '87
Scientists explore site of first free U.S. blacks [Fort Mose] *Jet* 71:25 F 16 '87
Haiti
Haiti's majestic monuments [Citadelle Laferriére and Sans Souci Palace] R. Bishop. il *Américas* 39:2-7+ Ja/F '87

Fortification—Haiti—*cont.*
'We will confound the calumniators of our race . .
. ' [Citadelle and Sans Souci Palace of H. Christophe]
F. Maclean. il por map *Smithsonian* 18:160-6+ O
'87

India
Explore the forts of a fabled land. V. Fass. il *Horizon*
30:26-7 Mr '87

Northern Ireland
Conchobor's Ulster [Navan Fort] D. Byrne. il *Hist Today*
37:5-6 F '87

Oklahoma
Outpost guards Oklahoma history [Fort Gibson Military
Park] il *South Living* 22:20 Ja '87

West Virginia
Life in a pioneer fort [Pricketts Fort] C. Griffith. il
South Living 22:26+ Jl '87

Fortino, Denise
Can exercise cure PMS? il *Women's Sports Fitness* 9:44-7
N '87
Famous diets that don't work. *Harpers Bazaar* 120:94+
O '87

Fortney, David L.
These kids mean business. il *Read Dig* 130:147-50+
F '87

Fortran (Computer language)
Lahey Personal Fortran 77. N. Baran. *Byte* 12:97-8 D
'87
Three Fortran 77 compilers. D. W. Burleigh. il *Byte*
12:187-8+ N '87

Forts *See* Fortification
Fortune, Marie M.
Saying no to the Klan. *Christ Century* 104:958-9 N
4 '87

Fortune 500 *See* Corporations—Directories
Fortune telling
See also
Astrology

Fortuyn/O'Brien (Group)
Fortuyn/O'Brien: Luhring, Augustine & Hodes. E. Hayt-
Atkins. il *Art News* 86:159-60 D '87

Forverts (Newspaper) *See* Jewish daily forward
Forward, Gordon
                    about
Forward's march. L. M. Keefe. il por *Forbes* 139:104-5
Ap 20 '87

Forward, Robert L.
                    about
Fast Forward: a conversation with Robert L. Forward.
R. M. Powers. il por *Space World* X-1-277:30-6 Ja
'87
Putting the science in science fiction. M. J. Mackowski.
il por *Space World* X-1-277:32-3 Ja '87

Forward, Susan
                    about
Blueprints for survival and change. A. Steacy. por
Macleans 100:42 Je 22 '87
Counselor to the women men hate, Susan Forward is
still looking for love. K. McMurran. il pors *People
Wkly* 27:71-2+ Ap 27 '87
Smart women—and men—read this one. L. Shapiro.
il por *Newsweek* 109:65 Je 1 '87

Forward area air defense *See* Air defenses
Forward-looking infrared sensors *See* Detectors, Infrared
Forwarding companies *See* Freight forwarders
Fosback, Norman G.
                    about
Go for the aggressive funds. A. E. Serwer. il por *Fortune*
115:116 Ap 13 '87

Fosle, Art
                    about
He has no truck with unemployment, so when Art Fosle
needed a job, he didn't spin his wheels. il por *People
Wkly* 27:64 My 11 '87

Fosse, Bob
                    about
Obituary
    Dance Mag il por 61:82-3 D '87. K. Grubb
    Jet il pors 73:18 O 12 '87
    People Wkly il por 28:87 O 12 '87
    Time il por 130:80 O 5 '87. W. A. Henry

Fossel, Peter V.
Design and lay a flagstone walk. il *Americana* 15:63-5
My/Je '87
Let your house breathe. il *Ctry J* 14:35-9 N '87
The pollution within. il *Ctry J* 14:44-9 S '87

Fossey, Dian
                    about
I didn't kill Dian. She was my friend; ed. by Beverly
Trainer and Gina Maranto. W. McGuire. il pors maps
Discover 8:28-32+ F '87

PW interviews [biographer F. Mowat] B. Slopen. por
Publ Wkly 232:79-80 O 2 '87
Fossil bones *See* Paleontology
Fossil hoaxes *See* Hoaxes
Fossil man *See* Man, Prehistoric
Fossil microorganisms *See* Micropaleontology
Fossil plants *See* Paleobotany
Fossils *See* Paleontology
Fossils, State *See* State fossils
Fossils, Trace *See* Trace fossils
Foster, Bill
                    about
The Wildcats' great hope. A. H. Malcolm. il por *N
Y Times Mag* p38-9+ Mr 1 '87
Foster, Clare
The Sandinista heritage. il *Hist Today* 37:5-8 Ap '87
Foster, Darryl
                    about
N.Y. sax player labeled criminal in Daily news in case
of mistaken identity. il por *Jet* 72:38 My 11 '87
Foster, Greg
                    about
Rude hello for an old foe. K. Moore. il pors *Sports
Illus* 66:16-17 Ja 26 '87
Foster, Jaclyn
                    about
Twins attend reunion of once-frail babies. il pors *Jet*
72:32 Je 29 '87
Foster, James
                    about
A summertime fix for football fans. L. Therrien. il *Bus
Week* p50 Ag 3 '87
Foster, Jodie
                    about
Educating Jodie [interview] S. Peters. il pors *Life* 10:80-2
S '87
Jodie Foster: this petite blonde packs a lot of pow!
C. Krupp. por *Glamour* 85:230 O '87
The prime of Miss Jodie Foster. D. Maychick. il pors
Mademoiselle 93:144 S '87
Foster, Judy
(jt. auth) See Porter, Kay, and Foster, Judy
Foster, Lauren
                    about
Twins attend reunion of once-frail babies. il pors *Jet*
72:32 Je 29 '87
Foster, Louis W.
                    about
If you own a Porsche, don't bother applying. T. Carson.
il por *Bus Week* p61 Ag 10 '87
Foster, Norm, 1949-
                    about
My darling Judith [drama] Reviews
    Macleans 100:70 O 19 '87. K. Harley
Foster, Norman, 1935-
                    about
City of the future. W. Feaver. il *Art News* 86:44 Mr
'87
Exhibition report: New architecture: Foster, Rogers, Stir-
ling. H. Aldersey-Williams. *Archit Rec* 175:73+ Mr
'87
Foster, Pamela
                    about
Assault charges dropped against Harvard's Loury. pors
Jet 72:25 S 7 '87
Harvard prof charged with beating up live-in lover.
il pors *Jet* 72:24-5 Je 29 '87
Foster, Richard J.
The good life. il por *Christ Today* 31:20-4 D 11 '87
Foster, Stephen Collins, 1826-1864
                    about
Commemorating an anniversary that never was. E.
Rochette. il *Antiques Collect Hobbies* 92:74-5 Mr '87
"Dear friends and gentle hearts". A. Thompson. il pors
Am Hist Illus 22:44-9 Ap '87
Foster, Tabatha, 1984-
                    about
Girl, 3, fights odds after multiple organ transplant. il
por *Jet* 73:8 N 16 '87
Kentucky tot hospitalized three years goes home. il por
Jet 72:36 Jl 13 '87
Foster, Tony
Sierran souvenirs. il *Sierra* 72:55-60 N/D '87
Foster, William E.
                    about
Mixed blessings. K. K. Wiegner. il por *Forbes* 140:70+
S 21 '87
Foster (L. B.) Co. *See* L. B. Foster Co.
Foster Grandparent Program (U.S.)
Foster grandparents go inside prison walls. E. Sklar and
C. M. Carlson. il *Aging* no356:20-3 '87

Foster Grandparent Program (U.S.)—cont.
Three generations of love [Foster Grandparents work in child care center for teenage parents in Detroit, Mich.] N. Walls. il *Aging* no355:2-5 '87
Foster home care
Don't forget them after Christmas [children in need all year-round] H. Smith. por *U S News World Rep* 103:5 D 21 '87
Fostering prejudice [policy prohibiting homosexuals from being foster parents in Mass.] W. F. Schulz, Jr. il *Progressive* 51:15 Ja '87
Kaleidoscope's Youth Development Program: a last chance for youth "aging out" of foster care. S. M. Stehno. il *Child Today* 16:29-33 S/O '87
Specialized foster care: families as treatment resources [Saint Louis, Mo.] S. S. Stepleton. il *Child Today* 16:27-31 Mr/Ap '87
The tears—and rage—of a foster mother; ed. by Barbara Hanson Pierce. B. Rex. il por *Redbook* 169:34+ Jl '87

Religious life
Church, state and foster-care children [New York State] H. J. Byrne. *America* 157:38-41 Jl 18-25 '87

Taxation
Foster children bring tax benefits, too. *Black Enterp* 17:30 Jl '87
Foster home care for the aged
A very special home for the elderly [A. and M. Coleman's home in Springfield, Or.] L. Stone and L. Snyder-Stone. il *McCalls* 114:68-9 Jl '87
Foster Medical Corp.
Anyhow, it was nice while it lasted. G. Morgenson. il por *Forbes* 139:50+ Ja 12 '87
Fothergill, Robert
about
Detaining Mr. Trotsky [drama] Reviews
Macleans 100:70 N 9 '87. J. Bemrose
Fotheringham, Allan, 1932-
Church and state sex scandals. *World Press Rev* 34:32-3 Jl '87
Column. See issues of Maclean's
Foucault, Jean Bernard Léon, 1819-1868
about
Perfecting the modern reflector. W. Tobin. il por *Sky Telesc* 74:358-9 O '87
Fouce, Frank, Jr.
about
The feud that toppled a TV empire. G. Critser. il pors *Channels* 7:24-31 Ja '87
Foulkes, Richard
about
His time horizon is long [interview] M. McFadden. il por *Fortune* 115:20 Ja 5 '87
Foundation for the Community of Artists
Alone together: The Foundation for the Community of Artists. J. Jevnikar. il *Am Artist* 51:14+ Ja '87
Foundation garments
See also
Brassieres
Foundation planting See Landscape gardening
Foundations, Charitable and educational
See also
Americares Foundation
Dia Art Foundation
Dr. Lacey Kirk Williams Educational Trust
Ford Foundation
Heritage Foundation (Washington, D.C.)
I Have a Dream Foundation
International Oceanographic Foundation
Isabel O'Neil Foundation for the Art of the Painted Finish
John D. and Catherine T. MacArthur Foundation
Landmark Foundation
Lois Young-Thomas Scholarship and Leadership Guild
Moody Foundation
Sunbow Foundation
Women's Sports Foundation
Establishing a local education foundation. W. B. Nesbit. *Educ Dig* 52:21-3 My '87
Giving it away [views of C. Merrill] B. Leonard. il por *Forbes* 140 Sp Issue:380+ O 26 '87
Philanthropy: blessing or barrier? [patronage of arts education; special issue] *Des Arts Educ* 88:2-32+ Mr/Ap '87

Taxation
You don't have to be a Ford to start a foundation. D. H. Dunn. il *Bus Week* p140 N 23 '87
Canada
See also
Calmeadow Charitable Foundation

Italy
See also
Rossini Foundation
Soviet Union
See also
Soviet Cultural Foundation
Sweden
See also
Nobel Foundation
Foundations (Building)
Add-on foundations. G. Branson and C. J. De Groote. il *Fam Handyman* 37:60-1+ Mr '87
Fast foundations [concrete block foundation] R. Day. il *Pop Sci* 230:72-3 My '87
Foundations (Cosmetics) See Cosmetics
Founders, Corporate See Entrepreneurs
Founding Fathers
Editorial. W. Garrett. *Antiques* 132:775 O '87
Foundermania breaks out in the Senate. J. Weisberg. il *Newsweek* 110:14 Ag 24 '87
The Founding Fathers. il *Life* 10:51-2+ Fall '87
Foundries
See also
Hoka Hey Foundry
Fountain, Reggie
about
108 in the shade. P. A. Janssen. il por *Mot Boat Sail* 160:11 Jl '87
Full throttle, damn the shorts. R. L. Stern. il por *Forbes* 139:80-1 Je 1 '87
A stock sinks. A. A. Lappen. il por *Forbes* 140:8 D 28 '87
Fountain Powerboats Industries
108 in the shade [R. Fountain] P. A. Janssen. il por *Mot Boat Sail* 160:11 Jl '87
Full throttle, damn the shorts. R. L. Stern. il por *Forbes* 139:80-1 Je 1 '87
A stock sinks. A. A. Lappen. il por *Forbes* 140:8 D 28 '87
Fountain Restaurant (Philadelphia, Pa.) See Philadelphia (Pa.)—Restaurants, nightclubs, bars, etc.
Fountains
Splashing oasis just inside this Fresno front entry. il *Sunset* 179:158 Jl '87
Three-tiered brick fountain turns the corner [garden fountain] il *Sunset* 179:98 S '87
Four saints in three acts [opera] See Thomson, Virgil, 1896-
Four Seasons (New York, N.Y.: Restaurant) See New York (N.Y.)—Restaurants, nightclubs, bars, etc.
Four Seasons Partnership
A handshake for all seasons [partnership between B. Gaudio and F. Valli] C. P. Alexander. il pors *Time* 129:54 My 11 '87
Four wheel drive vehicles
See also
Automobiles—Four wheel drive
Automobiles, Foreign—Four wheel drive
Sports cars—Four wheel drive
Station wagons—Four wheel drive
Station wagons, Foreign—Four wheel drive
Tractors—Four wheel drive
Trucks—Four wheel drive
'88 sport/utility [cover story; special section] il *Pop Mech* 164:79+ S '87
Big-league 4x4s. T. Opre. il *Outdoor Life* 180:68-9+ Ag '87
Buy two, they're cheap [advertising the Suzuki Samurai] J. Flint. il *Forbes* 140:193+ N 2 '87
Panther Stampede. A. Hope. il *Car Driv* 33:33 O '87
Trip the two-track. T. Opre. il *Outdoor Life* 179:52+ My '87
Remodeled vehicles
On the road again [Motor trend Bronco II] il *Mot Trend* 39:112-13 Je '87
Testing
1987 Nissan Pathfinder. M. Brockman. il *Mot Trend* 39:73-5 Mr '87
Bog-cogs slog on. D. Scott. il *Pop Sci* 230:14 F '87
Bronco XL Sport. M. Brockman. il *Mot Trend* 39 no12 Sp Issue:60-3 '87
Chevy S-10 Blazer. R. James. il *Ctry J* 14:69-71 S '87
Dodge Dakota 4x4. D. C. Ross. il *Mot Trend* 39:96+ My '87
Dodge Raider. R. Ceppos. il *Car Driv* 32:131-2 Je '87
The Dodge Raider. B. Kilpatrick. il *Field Stream* 91:108 Ap '87
Ford Bronco. W. Hampton. il *Ctry J* 14:63-5 Jl '87
Four-wheelers from afar. J. Edgerton. il *Money* 16:62-4+ Ap '87

Four wheel drive vehicles—Testing—*cont.*
Isuzu Trooper II. M. Anson. il *Mot Trend* 39:64+ Jl '87
It's not a 4x4. It's a 4x4 [Range Rover] J. Skorupa. il *Pop Mech* 164:94-7 S '87
Lamborghini LM002. B. W. Yates. il *Car Driv* 33:78-82 O '87
Mazda 4x4 LX Cab-plus. M. Brockman. il *Mot Trend* 39:85-6 My '87
Mitsubishi Montero. W. Hampton. il *Ctry J* 14:62-4 Mr '87
The pick of the 4WD's [for the skier] R. Homan. il *Skiing* 40:243-7+ O '87
Putting Raider to the test [Dodge Raider] T. Opre. il *Outdoor Life* 180:40+ N '87
Range Rover. M. Anson. il *Mot Trend* 39:78+ Ap '87
Range Rover. T. Assenza. il *Car Driv* 32:78-9+ Je '87
Range Rover. R. James. il *Ctry J* 14:77-9 N '87
Range Rover. T. West. il *Road Track* 39:67-9 N '87
Range Rover over here. J. Lamm. il *Road Track* 38:78+ Mr '87
Sports/utility stampede. B. Hartford. il *Pop Mech* 164:12 F '87
Suzuki's little warrior [Samurai] il *Fam Handyman* 37:66-7 D '87
Toyota 4Runner. M. Brockman. il *Mot Trend* 39:65-6 Ja '87
Upscale Rover [Range Rover] T. Opre. il *Outdoor Life* 180:28+ O '87

Four wheel steering (Automobiles) *See* Automobiles—Steering gear; Automobiles, Foreign—Steering gear; Sports cars—Steering gear

Fourcade, Vincent
about
Entertaining. W. P. Rayner and C. Rayner. il *Vogue* 177:222 Ap '87

Fouret, Birgitta
about
Moulin refuge. C. de Liagre. il por *House Gard* 159:138-47+ Ap '87
Objects of affection. J. J. Buck. il pors *Vogue* 177:400-7+ N '87

Fourie, Johan
about
Track's longest-running win streak. il por *Sports Illus* 67:16 Jl 27 '87

Fourier, Charles, 1772-1837
about
Keep your compassion, give me your madness. A. Broyard. il *N Y Times Book Rev* 92:12 Je 21 '87

Fourier transformation
Fourier transformation. *Sci Am* 257:26+ Jl '87

Fournet, Jean, 1913-
about
Fournet—à la française. A. Ulrich. il por *Opera News* 51:38-9+ Ap 11 '87

Fourth Committee (United Nations) *See* United Nations. Decolonization Committee

Fourth dimension *See* Hyperspace

The fourth protocol [film] *See* Motion picture reviews—Single works

Fourth world movement
Ill at ease in the fourth world. K. Sale. il *Nation* 245:592-4 N 21 '87

Fouts, Dan
about
Blood, grit and years. P. Korn. il pors *Sport Mag* 78:36-8+ O '87
Charge! P. Zimmerman. il pors *Sports Illus* 67:14-19 N 23 '87

Fow, Mark
about
One patient's experience with interferon [interview] R. W. Miller. por *FDA Consum* 21:11 Ap '87

Fowl shooting *See* Game bird shooting; Water bird shooting

Fowler, Brad
about
360° panorama assemblages [interview] F. Cameron. il *Petersens Photogr Mag* 15:22-5 Mr '87

Fowler, Frances C.
The French experience with public aid to private schools. bibl f *Phi Delta Kappan* 68:356-9 Ja '87

Fowler, J. S., and others
Mapping human brain monoamine oxidase A and B with ¹¹-labeled suicide inactivators and PET. bibl f il *Science* 235:481-5 Ja 23 '87

Fowler, Jacqueline
about
Kentucky teacher hits The wall with Pink Floyd. T. J. Flygare. il *Phi Delta Kappan* 69:237-8 N '87

Fowler, Mark S.
about
Life after Fowler. J. L. Swerdlow. il *Channels* 7:14 Mr '87

Fowler, Orson Squire, 1809-1887
about
Orson Fowler: foursquare pioneer in the progressive tradition. J. Gustaitis. il *Am Hist Illus* 21:44-5 Ja '87

Fowles, Donald
Captain's log. il *Aging* no356:44-inside back cover '87
The use of community services. il *Aging* no355:36-inside back cover '87

Fowles, John, 1926-
In a mess. il por *Archit Dig* 44:24+ Je '87

Fowlie, Alfred H., Jr.
Unitarians. il por *Cent Mag* 20:15-17 S/O '87

Fowlie, Wallace, 1908-
Remembering Jacques Maritain. *Am Sch* 56:355-66 Summ '87

Fox, Bill
Shooting football [cover story] il *Petersens Photogr Mag* 16:60-3 O '87

Fox, David
about
Father of the bride. J. Adler. il pors *Esquire* 107:170-2+ Je '87

Fox, Gary R.
about
That's a lot of bullion. F. Greve. il *50 Plus* 27:18-19 Jl '87

Fox, Geoffrey C., and Messina, P. C. (Paul C.), 1943-
Advanced computer architectures. bibl (p183) il *Sci Am* 257:66-74 O '87

Fox, Glenn, and others
Balancing basic and applied science: the case of agricultural research. bibl f il *BioScience* 37:507-9 Jl/Ag '87

Fox, James, 1945-
Rendezvous in Mali. il *House Gard* 159:94+ S '87

Fox, Marisa
New-tech contraception. il *Health* 19:30-3 F '87

Fox, Michael J.
about
Coping with the "cute" factor. R. Corliss. il pors *Time* 129:97 My 4 '87
Little big guy: Michael J. Fox. il pors *McCalls* 114:70 Ag '87
Little big man [cover story] A. Richman. il pors *People Wkly* 27:86-8+ Ap 20 '87
Michael J. Fox [excerpt from The Michael J. Fox scrapbook] M. Kasbah. il pors *Good Housekeep* 205:50+ Ag '87
Michael J. Fox bares his talent. S. Bolotin. por *Vogue* 177:86F F '87
Michael J. Fox: his success is no secret. M. L. Baer. por *Teen* 31:55 Je '87
Michael J. Fox: TV's favorite son is short of stature but long on talent. S. Granger. por *Ladies Home J* 104:112+ Ap '87
Michael J. Fox unwinds. M. Morrison. il pors *Roll Stone* p30-2+ Mr 12 '87
The star has risen [special section; with editorial comment by Kevin Doyle] B. D. Johnson. il pors *Macleans* 100:2, 40-6 F 9 '87
The straight men: Michael J. Fox, Huey Lewis, Tom Cruise. C. Krupp. il pors *Glamour* 85:250 Ap '87
Trading places. S. Pond. il pors *Roll Stone* p25-6 Ja 15 '87
Why Helen Slater won't be out-foxed. D. Maychick. il pors *Mademoiselle* 93:72 My '87

Fox, Michael R.
Perspectives in risk [address, June 1987] *Vital Speeches Day* 53:730-2 S 15 '87

Fox, Michael W., 1937-
Pet life. See issues of McCall's beginning March 1986

Fox, Richard Wightman, 1945-
The liberal ethic and the spirit of Protestantism [cover story; with discussion] il por *Cent Mag* 20:4-14 S/O '87

Fox, Robin Lane *See* Lane Fox, Robin

Fox, Samantha
about
If cheesecake could sing, it might sound like Sam Fox, topless model-turned-rocker. il pors *People Wkly* 27:89-90 Ja 12 '87

Fox Broadcasting Company
At Fox, the quarry is teenagers. W. A. Henry. il *Channels* 7:65 Jl/Ag '87
A different brand of entertainment. D. Fanning. il *Forbes* 140:49+ N 30 '87

Fox Broadcasting Company—*cont.*

Fox and the hounds [Cable News Network's reporting]
L. Brown. il *Channels* 7:18 Ja '87

The Fox trot ends for Joan Rivers. J. Friedman. il
pors *People Wkly* 27:28-31 Je 1 '87

Fox's new network goes after the baby boomers. R.
Grover. *Bus Week* p41+ Ap 6 '87

"Hey, gang, let's put on a show". A. B. Block. il *Forbes*
139:140+ Ap 6 '87

The revolution will not be televised: Fox on the fritz.
C. Schine. il *Vogue* 177:64 Jl '87

Room for one more? R. Zoglin. il *Time* 129:74 Ap
6 '87

Rupert Murdoch. R. Grover. il por *Bus Week* Sp Issue:246
Ap 17 '87

Rupert Murdoch, can we talk? R. Grover. il por *Bus
Week* p50 Je 1 '87

Tally-ho, Rupert [interview with R. Murdoch] M. Brown
and R. Buck. il pors *Channels* 7:70-1 Ja '87

Fox Inc.

L.A.'s eclectic entertainment executive [B. Mutchnick]
J. Giambanco. il pors *Work Woman* 12:128+ Ap '87

Storming television's toll bridge [interview with B. Diller]
P. E. Bauer. il *Channels* 7:70-1 S '87

Fox-Lockert, Lucía

Amorous fantasies. por *Américas* 39:38-41 Ja/F '87

Fox River (Wis.)

Warning: the Friday night fish fry may be hazardous
to your health [pollution by waste from the Fort
Howard Paper Co.] M. Hudson. il maps *Audubon*
89:24-6+ Jl '87

Foxboro Company

Setting up shop in China: three paths to success. D.
J. Yang. il *Bus Week* p74 O 19 '87

Foxes

The fox next door [red fox] D. Petersen. il map *Mother
Earth News* 107:104+ S/O '87

Living is tough for the desert fox [San Joaquin kit
fox] D. Holing. il *Natl Wildl* 25:14-17 Ap/My '87

The red fox. R. A. Carey. il *Ctry J* 14:56-61 S '87

What it means to be a fox [red foxes in Saskatchewan]
J. D. Henry. il *Int Wildl* 17:12-16 N/D '87

Foxfire [television program] See Television program
reviews—Single works

Foxgloves

Foxgloves are worth remembering. il *South Living* 22:78
My '87

Foxx, Redd

about

A comedic look at the black middle class. W. Leavy.
il pors *Ebony* 42:68+ Ag '87

Redd Foxx does prison benefits in memory of his ex-con
brother. il pors *Jet* 72:56-7 Mr 30 '87

Redd Foxx makes first film-for-TV 'Ghost of a chance'
[cover story] A. Collier. il pors *Jet* 72:56-7 My 11
'87

Foyers See Halls

Fractals

Beauty and profundity: the Mandelbrot set and a flock
of its cousins called Julia. A. K. Dewdney. il *Sci
Am* 257:140-5 N '87

Chaos, strange attractors, and fractal basin boundaries
in nonlinear dynamics. C. Grebogi and others. bibl
f il *Science* 238:632-8 O 30 '87

Creating fractals. W. A. McWorter and J. M. Tazelaar.
bibl il *Byte* 12:123-8+ Ag '87

Fluid interfaces, including fractal flows, can be studied
in a Hele-Shaw cell. J. Walker. il *Sci Am* 257:134-6+
N '87

Fractal fairy tales. B. Schechter. il *Omni* 10:86-91 O
'87

Fractal growth. L. M. Sander. bibl (p128) il *Sci Am*
256:94-100 Ja '87

Fractals: magical fun or revolutionary science? D. E.
Thomsen. il *Sci News* 131:184 Mr 21 '87

Mimicking mountains. T. Jeffery. il *Byte* 12:337-8+ D
'87

Packing it in [image compression; work of Michael F.
Barnsley and others; cover story] I. Peterson. il *Sci
News* 131:283-5 My 2 '87

The shapes of random walks. J. Rudnick and G. Gaspari.
bibl f il *Science* 237:384-9 Jl 24 '87

Unmashing chaos [work of Mitchell Feigenbaum and
others] il *Sci Am* 256:61-2 F '87

Fractions

Fractions as fun [board games] il *Sunset* 179:125-6 O
'87

Fracture mechanics

See also
Glass—Fracture

Fractures

Get 'hip' with vitamin C [avoiding hip fractures]
Prevention 39:8 Jl '87

Going through the motions [continuous passive motion
devices aid in fracture healing; work of Robert Salter]
R. Boling. *Health* 19:21 D '87

'I think it's broken'. L. Crawford. il *Work Woman*
12:150+ Ap '87

A little estrogen, fewer broken hips [osteoporosis] il
Newsweek 110:99 N 16 '87

Love and hate on one leg [leg fractured in traffic accident]
K. Bonnell. il por *Glamour* 85:73-4 O '87

The pain that won't go away [epidemic of stress fractures
in professional basketball] R. Demak. il *Sports Illus*
66:60-2+ Ap 27 '87

Treating the mind, risking the body [drugs linked to
hip fractures; study by Wayne A. Ray and others]
Sci News 131:122 F 21 '87

Fragile X syndrome

The fragile X site in somatic cell hybrids: an approach
for molecular cloning of fragile sites [cover story]
S. T. Warren and others. bibl f il *Science* 237:420-3
Jl 24 '87

Tracing fragile X syndrome. J. Murphy. il *Time* 129:78
Mr 16 '87

Fragments of a Greek trilogy [drama] See Serban, Andrei

Fragrance See Perfumes

Fragrant plants See Plants, Fragrant

Fraleigh, Sue

She found a career when she lost 80 pounds; ed. by
Maria Mihalik. il por *Prevention* 39:60-2+ N '87

Frames for pictures See Picture frames and framing

Frames for windows See Windows

Framing (Building)

Basic framing techniques. C. J. De Groote. il *Fam
Handyman* 37:52-3+ Ap '87

Need more room? Build a dormer. G. Branson and
C. J. De Groote. il *Fam Handyman* 37:62-3+ Jl/Ag
'87

Framingham (Mass.)

Public health

Take part, take heart [Heart Study] A. Hollister. il *Life*
10:56-8+ F '87

França, Jose-Augusto

The stately heritage of Portuguese baroque. il *Courier*
40:27-9 S '87

France, Randal D.

Psychosomatic illness: is it all in your head? por *McCalls*
114:81 Ap '87

France

See also
AIDS (Disease)—France
Alps
Americans—France
Annecy (France)
Anti-nuclear movement—France
Anti-Semitism—France
Antique dealers—France
Architecture—France
Architecture, Domestic—France
Argentines—France
Art and state—France
Automobile racing—France
Automobile rallies—France
Aviation and state—France
Blacks—France
Bordeaux (France)
Brittany (France)
Burgundy (France)
Castles—France
Cévennes Biosphere Reserve and National Park
(France)
Chinese—France
Christmas—France
Cognac (France)
College education and state—France
Country estates—France
Dance—France
Dance festivals—France
Deauville (France)
Easter—France
Ermenonville (France)
Espionage, Russian—France
French
Gardens and gardening—France
Grasse (France)
Great Britain—Diplomatic and consular service—
France
Grenoble (France)
Health resorts, watering places, etc.—France
Historic houses, sites, etc.—France

France—See also—*cont.*
Information storage and retrieval systems—France
Intelligence service—France
Investment banking—France
Investments, Canadian—France
Investments, French
Investments, Italian—France
Investments, Swedish—France
Islands—France
Jura Mountains (France and Switzerland)
Languedoc (France)
Marseilles (France)
Mont Blanc (France and Italy)
Motion pictures—France
Music festivals—France
Narcotics trade—France
Nobility—France
Nuclear power plants—France
Opera—France
Paris (France)
Passports—France
Pessac (France)
Pigeon postal service—France
Planetariums—France
Poissy (France)
Portuguese—France
Private schools—France
Privatization—France
Provence (France)
Public health—France
Real estate investment—France
Resorts—France
Restaurants—France
Saint-Paul-de-Vence (France)
Science—France
Sculpture gardens and parks—France
Securities—France
Skis and skiing—France
Stone Age—France
Strikes—France
Strikes—Railroad workers—France
Student protests, demonstrations, etc.—France
Television advertising—France
Television broadcasting—France
Television laws and regulations—France
Terrorism—France
Toulon (France)
United Nations—France
Val d'Isère (France)
War crime trials—France
Wildlife conservation—France

Air Force
See also
Patrouille de France (Flight squadron)
Airex 87 tests French Air Force in chemical, EW environments. J. M. Lenorovitz. *Aviat Week Space Technol* 126:70-1 Mr 16 '87
French Air Force will receive improved Mirage 2000 fighters. *Aviat Week Space Technol* 126:71 Mr 16 '87

Antiquities
The Madrague de Giens wreck [Roman freighter off coast of France] A. Tchernia. il *Courier* 40:11 N '87

Army
Forces in Lebanon
Council members ask urgent measures for UNIFIL security [Shiites clash with French troops] *UN Chron* 23:58 N '86
Security Council condemns attacks against UNIFIL as 'criminal', calls for end to 'any military presence' unacceptable to Lebanon [Shiites clash with French troops] il *UN Chron* 23:59-62 N '86

Colonies
See also
French Polynesia
New Caledonia

Commerce
Canada
Quebec's French connection [book imports] J. Poulin. il *Publ Wkly* 232:24 N 13 '87
United States
See United States—Commerce—France

Cultural relations
United States
See United States—Cultural relations—France

Defenses
See also
Airplanes, Military—France
Airplanes, Military transport—France
France—Air Force
Guided missiles, French

A European deterrent? B. Crozier. *Natl Rev* 39:24 Jl 31 '87

Description and travel
See also
Automobile touring—France

Economic policy
Chirac's chance to remake France may be slipping away. F. J. Comes and J. Rossant. por *Bus Week* p44-5 Mr 30 '87

Foreign relations
See also
Military assistance, French
The president of France speaks out [interview with F. Mitterrand] M. S. Forbes. il pors *Forbes* 140:22-3+ D 28 '87

Canada
See also
Mitterrand, François, 1916—Visit to Canada, 1987
Heating up the cod war [Newfoundland angry over Franco-Canadian fishing agreement] C. Barrett. il *Macleans* 100:12-13 F 23 '87
The new embassy wars [Quebec and Ottawa jockey for position in relations with France] A. Wilson-Smith. *Macleans* 100:14 Ap 27 '87
Rites of the fishermen [Newfoundland fishermen angered at agreement with France] M. Clark. il map *Macleans* 100:12 F 9 '87

Comoros
Sovereignty of Comoros over island of Mayotte reaffirmed by Assembly. *UN Chron* 24:82 F '87

Great Britain
See Great Britain—Foreign relations—France

Iran
See also
Iran—Diplomatic and consular service—France
A costly exchange [suspected Iranian terrorist freed following release of French hostages in Lebanon] R. Laver. il *Macleans* 100:31 D 14 '87
Embassy standoff. C. D. Van De Stadt. il *World Press Rev* 34:36 S '87
France's change of heart could turn the tide against Iran. F. J. Comes. il *Bus Week* p45 Ag 3 '87
A French terrorist-for-hostage deal? [Iranian terror suspect set free after two French hostages in Lebanon were freed] il *Newsweek* 110:61 D 14 '87
Furtive swap [suspected Iranian terrorist set free by France and French hostages released by Iran] *Time* 130:51 D 14 '87
Showdown on Embassy Row [France and Iran sever diplomatic ties] J. Greenwald. il *Time* 130:46 Jl 27 '87
A showdown with Teheran. H. Anderson. il *Newsweek* 110:28-30 Jl 27 '87

Japan—History
Diplomats under surveillance [Japanese official mission to France in 1862; excerpt from Autobiography] F. Yukichi. il *Courier* 40:27-8 Ap '87

Quebec (Province)
The new embassy wars [Quebec and Ottawa jockey for position in relations with France] A. Wilson-Smith. *Macleans* 100:14 Ap 27 '87

United States
See United States—Foreign relations—France

History
Louis XI, 1461-1483
A patriot for whom? The treason of Saint-Pol, 1474-75. S. H. Cuttler. bibl f il *Hist Today* 37:43-8 Ja '87

Revolution, 1789-1799
See also
Jacobins
An American's attempt to rescue Lafayette [rescue attempt by F. Huger; cover story] A. L. Levin. il por *Am Hist Illus* 22:16-20+ O '87
Counter-revolution? Toulon, 1793. W. S. Cormack and M. Sydenham. bibl il *Hist Today* 37:49-55 O '87

Third Republic, 1870-1940—Bibliography
The Third Republic. J. F. McMillan. il *Hist Today* 37:50-2 Je '87

German occupation, 1940-1945
Barbie and the children [roundup of the children of Izieu] *Newsweek* 109:44 Je 15 '87
The Barbie file [cover story] T. Morgan. il pors *N Y Times Mag* p18-24+ My 10 '87
The children of Izieu. il *N Y Times Mag* p26-7 Ag 2 '87
Letter from Europe [K. Barbie trial] J. Kramer. *New Yorker* 63:130-6+ O 12 '87
Shame and punishment [M. Ophuls' documentary on K. Barbie] J. J. Buck. il pors *Vogue* 177:392-3+ N '87

France—cont.

Industries

See also
Aerospace industries—France
Air France
Art trade—France
Bakers and bakeries—France
Bénédictine SA
Bénéteau (Firm)
Brokers—France
Chanel (Firm)
Château Haut-Brion (Firm)
Christian Dior (Firm)
Clothing industry—France
Compagnie Européenne de Publication
Compagnie Générale de Constructions Téléphoniques
Compagnie Générale d'Électricité
Corporations—Acquisitions and mergers—France
Crouzet (Firm)
Dassault Breguet Aviation (Avions Marcel)
Elf Aquitaine
Generale Occidentale SA
Groupe Bernard Tapie
Groupe Financière Agache
House of Hermès (Firm)
Jean Patou (Firm)
Key Independent System
Librairie Arthème Fayard
Louis Vuitton (Firm)
Matra SA
Michelin et Cie
Moët Hennessy
Munitions—France
Perfume industry—France
Peugeot SA
Pierre Balmain (Firm)
Publishers and publishing—France
Renault (Regie Nationale des Usines Renault)
Rhone-Poulenc SA
Rossignol Production (Skis)
Rothschild & Associates Bank
SOCATA
Source Perrier SA
Television industry—France
Thomson-C S F
Thomson SA
TOTAL-Compagnie Française des Pétroles
Wine industry—France

Kings and rulers

See also
Napoleon I, Emperor of the French, 1769-1821

Languages

See also
French language in France

Military policy

France weighing value of political autonomy against trend toward defense cooperation. *Aviat Week Space Technol* 127:129+ O 12 '87

Navy

McDonnell Douglas offers F/A-18 for French Navy's carrier air fleet. J. D. Morrocco. *Aviat Week Space Technol* 127:33-5 S 7 '87

Politics and government

See also
Conservatism—France
Greenpeace bombing incident, 1985
Political campaigns—France
Political candidates—France
The future of cohabitation in France [J. Chirac and F. Mitterrand] J. Valls-Russell. il *New Leader* 70:3-4 Mr 9 '87
Liberté, egalité, chaos. J. Bonfante. il por *Time* 129:36-7 Ja 19 '87
The perils of power sharing [with interview with J. Chirac] W. R. Doerner. il pors *Time* 129:43-4 Ap 6 '87
The summer of French discontent. J. Valls-Russell. il *New Leader* 70:8-9 S 21 '87
A talk with Chirac: privatization was 'a psychological revolution'. S. B. Shepard and others. *Bus Week* p45 Mr 30 '87

Population

See also
Haitians—France

Race relations

Fanning French fears [presidential candidate J.-M. Le Pen] R. Bernstein. il por *N Y Times Mag* p50+ O 4 '87
Of Fiji, race, and all that. B. Crozier. *Natl Rev* 39:26+ D 4 '87

Religious institutions and affairs

See also
Catholic Church—France
John Paul II, Pope, 1920—Visit to France, 1986

Social history

Conflict in continuity in 17th-century France. R. Mettam. bibl il *Hist Today* 37:30-5 F '87

Social life and customs

Anecdotes, facetiae, satire, etc.

Learning one's letters from Mme. la Comtesse. R. Chelminski. il *Smithsonian* 18:212 D '87

Territories and possessions

See also
Mayotte Island

France and the United States

See also
United States—History—Revolution, 1775-1783—French participation

Frances, Mary
The domestic silly food person speaks out. il *Teen* 31:20 S '87

Francesa, Mike
College football preview '87. il *Sport Mag* 78:26-7+ S '87

Franchise system
See also
Automobile dealers—Chain and franchise operations
Hotels, motels, etc.—Chain and franchise operations
Interior decorators—Chain and franchise operations
Printing industry—Chain and franchise operations
Pyramid selling operations
Restaurants—Chain and franchise operations
Buying a franchise? Here's what you should look out for. A. Goldstein. *Work Woman* 12:52+ F '87
Converting to a franchise. R. Hotch. il *Nations Bus* 75:28-30+ Je '87
Finding the franchise formula for success [Black enterprise Franchise 50; cover story; special section; with editorial comment by Earl G. Graves] il *Black Enterp* 18:9, 50-2+ S '87
The franchise route. il *Nations Bus* 75:20 Mr '87
Franchises: buying a piece of the action. P. Plawin. il *Changing Times* 41:81-5 S '87
Franchising: business services. B. Gatty. il *Nations Bus* 75:38-40 Mr '87
Franchising education. R. Hotch. il *Nations Bus* 75:30-1 Ap '87
Franchising fever. J. Castro. il *Time* 130:36-8 Ag 31 '87
Franchising: find that niche. R. Hotch and M. Whittemore. il *Nations Bus* 75:35-6+ F '87
The long road to franchising your business. R. R. Roha. il *Changing Times* 41:94-6+ Ja '87
Taking the franchise route [special section] il *Nations Bus* 75:33-8+ O '87
You don't have to be an expert to run a franchise. P. Plawin. *Changing Times* 41:80+ Ag '87

Francis, Debbie
about
Attention, shoppers: check out the wedding special in aisle 2! L. Tielis. il pors *People Wkly* 28:143-5 O 26 '87

Francis, Diane
[Column] See alternate issues of Maclean's beginning May 4, 1987

Francis, John
about
'Silent man' gets master's; more studies at U. of Pa. *Jet* 71:24 Ja 26 '87

Francis, Peter, and Self, Stephen
Collapsing volcanoes. bibl (p136) il *Sci Am* 256:90-7 Je '87

Francis, Samuel T.
Activist, strategist. *Natl Rev* 39:38-9 S 11 '87

Francis Marion National Forest (S.C.)
Little Wambaw Swamp, South Carolina. R. H. Mohlenbrock. il map *Nat Hist* 96:68-70 Ag '87

Franciscans
Banjo and guitar picker John Michael Talbot gave up rock for a new role as a musical monk. C. A. Azizian. il pors *People Wkly* 27:145-6 Je 8 '87
Death and resurrection in Matiguás [death of Franciscan brother T. Zavaleta in Nicaragua] E. Rivera. *America* 157:261-2 O 24 '87
From songs of protest to hymns of praise [J. M. Talbot] L. K. Cook. por *Christ Century* 104:279-80+ Mr 18-25 '87

Francisco, Maranda
about
The miracle of Maranda. E. Sherman. il pors *Ladies Home J* 104:48+ N '87

Franklin, William L.
My two decades with America's camels [cover story] il *Int Wildl* 17:34-43 S/O '87
Franklin County (N.C.)
Historic houses, sites, etc.
Under thin disguise: an 18th-century original [home of Patty Person Taylor restored by Michael and Donna Goswick] E. Wood. il *South Living* 22:204+ N '87
Franklin Expedition (1845)
Canned food sealed icemen's fate [lead poisoning cited] il *Hist Today* 37:3 O '87
Franklin Institute (Philadelphia, Pa.)
Franklin Institute honors eight physicists. il *Phys Today* 40:101-2+ Ap '87
Franklin Institute honors seven physicists with 1987 awards. il *Phys Today* 40:139-40 O '87
Franklin Resources, Inc.
Why Franklin is looking beyond mutual funds. J. B. Levine. il por *Bus Week* p101 S 21 '87
Franklin Savings Association
The hedgeaholic [E. Fleischer] J. Willoughby. il por *Forbes* 140:180+ N 16 '87
Frankovich, Victoria L.
about
Vicki Frankovich. C. Doudna. por *Ms* 15:74-6+ Ja '87
Frank's Place [television program] See Television program reviews—Single works
Frank's Trattoria (New York, N.Y.) See New York (N.Y.)—Restaurants, nightclubs, bars, etc.
Frantz, Douglas
The unraveling of Dennis Levine. il *Esquire* 108:160-4+ S '87
Franz Marc Museum (Kochel, Germany)
Murnau and Kochel: where the Blue Rider was born. J. Dornberg. il pors *Art News* 86:77-8+ D '87
Franza, August
Does "What works" work in the classroom? *Educ Dig* 52:10-13 F '87
Franzen, Bill
Driving [story] *Harpers* 274:36 Je '87
Franzese, Michael
about
Quitting the Mafia. E. Barnes and W. Shebar. il pors *Life* 10:108-9+ D '87
Franzmeier, Stephen A.
The art of vacationing. il *Nations Bus* 75:83+ My '87
Frappat, Pierre
Grenoble, France's high-powered mountain city. il *Courier* 40:16-17 F '87
Fraser, Alan
Vodka: that old white magic. il *Vogue* 177:328 Mr '87
Fraser, Antonia, 1932-
about
PW interviews. R. Herbert. por *Publ Wkly* 231:104-5 Je 19 '87
Fraser, C. Gerald
Charlayne Hunter-Gault: from front line to firing line. il pors *Essence* 17:40-2+ Mr '87
Fraser, Debra
about
Dieting with Debbie. P. A. Taylor. por *Essence* 17:109 Ap '87
Fraser, Derek
Joseph Chamberlain and the municipal ideal. bibl il por *Hist Today* 37:33-9 Ap '87
Fraser, Donald William Russell
about
Khashoggi's connections. D. Jenish. il por *Macleans* 100:34-6 Ja 19 '87
Fraser, Kennedy
Profiles [M. Rothschild] il *New Yorker* 63:45-8+ O 19 '87
Fraser, Matthew
Beineix wages cinematic 'war'. por *World Press Rev* 34:61 Mr '87
Fraser, Scott E., and others
Selective disruption of gap junctional communication interferes with a patterning process in hydra. bibl f il *Science* 237:49-55 Jl 3 '87
Frashier, Gary
about
Techno-blinders. A. A. Lappen. il pors *Forbes* 140:104+ D 28 '87
Fraternidade Descendencia Americana
In Brazil: echoes from the Confederacy [descendants of Americans who fled the South after the Civil War] M. Kepp. il *Time* 130:14 N 16 '87

Fraternities See College fraternities
Fratianno, Jimmy, 1913-
about
Once a hit man, now a stoolie, Jimmy 'the Weasel' Fratianno says the feds owe him a living [interview] J. Wadler. il pors *People Wkly* 28:38-40 D 21 '87
Fraud
See also
Advertising ethics
Airplane industry—Ethical aspects
Appraisers—Ethical aspects
Audio equipment stores—Ethical aspects
Automobile industry—Ethical aspects
Automobile mechanics (Persons)—Professional ethics
Automobile sales personnel—Professional ethics
Automobiles—Leasing and renting—Ethical aspects
Avionics industry—Ethical aspects
Banks and banking—Ethical aspects
Brokers—Ethical aspects
Cancer research—Ethical aspects
Checks, Fraudulent
Cleaning services—Ethical aspects
Commodity brokers—Ethical aspects
Compact discs—Unauthorized recording
Computer crimes
Computer industry—Ethical aspects
Contractors—Ethical aspects
Counterfeits and counterfeiting
Credit card crimes
Digital audio tape recorders and recording—Unauthorized recording
Drug industry—Ethical aspects
Foreign exchange brokers—Ethical aspects
Health maintenance organizations—Ethical aspects
Hoaxes
Insurance crimes
Job applications—Ethical aspects
Mail fraud
Mortgage brokers—Ethical aspects
Notaries—Ethical aspects
Nursing homes—Ethical aspects
Petroleum industry—Ethical aspects
Pharmaceutical research—Ethical aspects
Phonograph record industry—Ethical aspects
Phonograph records—Unauthorized recording
Photographic industry—Ethical aspects
Politics, Corruption in
Psychiatric research—Ethical aspects
Psychological research—Ethical aspects
Quacks and quackery
Research—Ethical aspects
Tape recordings—Unauthorized recording
Tax evasion
Telephone crimes
Television equipment industry—Ethical aspects
Ticket selling—Ethical aspects
Tourist trade—Ethical aspects
Videotapes—Unauthorized use
The 8(a) follies [minority set-asides] il *Fortune* 115:17-18 F 2 '87
The Assad connection [Eurobond frauds masterminded by H. Zubaidi] R. Morais. il *Forbes* 139:32-3 Je 15 '87
The big chill [M. Zolp's self-cooling can scam] J. Crudele. il *N Y* 20:19+ Ag 24 '87
The con man [FBI informer M. Raymond] M. A. Farber. il por *N Y Times Mag* p34+ Je 21 '87
A concerned Christian goes the Second Mile [J. A. Peterson's effort to refund investors bilked in bankrupt nursing home fraud] *Christ Today* 31:47-8 F 6 '87
Confessions of a heat merchant [bucket shop investment scams] W. G. Flanagan. il *Forbes* 140:190+ S 21 '87
Côte de Fraud [boiler room scam operators in Orange County, Calif.] M. Beauchamp. il *Forbes* 140:32-3 N 2 '87
Crime wave [securities crime; cover story] R. L. Stern and M. Schifrin. il *Forbes* 139:67-70 Je 29 '87
Dial-a-dupe on Con Man's Coast [boiler room phone scams in Orange County, Calif.] P. Cary. il *U S News World Rep* 103:62-3 D 21 '87
Downfall of a schemer [W. Player's role in Toronto real estate fraud scandal] P. Best. il por *Macleans* 100:32 Jl 20 '87
Faith, hope, and chicanery [mismanaged and fraudulent charities] J. Wark and G. Marx. il *Wash Mon* 18:25-31 Ja '87
The Fat Man: the life and high times of Irwin Schiff [cover story] M. Daly. il pors *N Y* 20:46-61 O 19 '87

Fraud—*cont.*

Fleecing the flock [faith healer P. Popoff debunked by J. Randi; with editorial comment by Paul Hoffman] J. Tierney. il pors *Discover* 8:50-4+ N '87

Free enterprise rushes to fill a delicate need [mail order urine samples circumvent drug testing regulations] D. Collins. il *U S News World Rep* 102:10 F 23 '87

A good deed that pays. *Consum Rep* 52:329 Je '87

Green thumbs: the PIK and Roll and other scams from the farm belt. J. L. Pasley. il *Wash Mon* 19:11-14+ S '87

The hustler's best friend: you [investment fraud] D. N. Dreman. il *Forbes* 139:105 Ja 26 '87

In Galveston, Moody's blues [investigation of Moody Foundation fraud] G. Hackett. il por *Newsweek* 109:33 F 2 '87

J. R. McConnell: the ballad of a Texas tornado. T. Vogel. il por *Bus Week* p80+ N 9 '87

Letter from Europe [A. Verdiglione's psychoanalysis scam in Milan] J. Kramer. *New Yorker* 63:88+ Je 8 '87

"The most corrupt person" [fabricating fraudulent Soviet orders for goods made by Dayco; case of E. Reich] N. J. Perry. por *Fortune* 116:93 Ag 17 '87

The mysterious fall of a star [former Intelsat chief R. Colino convicted of fraud] J. S. DeMott. il por *Time* 130:51 O 5 '87

A nest-egg deal that turned rotten [investment fraud charges against Elliott Enterprises] P. Engardio. il por *Bus Week* p98 Ap 27 '87

The net at last? [investment fraud practiced by J. P. Galanis] J. A. Conway. il *Forbes* 139:8 My 18 '87

Pied Piper to the truly rich [C. Atkins indicted for tax evasion and securities fraud] F. Ungeheuer. il por *Time* 129:52 Ap 6 '87

Poison lures at the end of the line [investment fraud by phone] J. Rachlin. il *U S News World Rep* 103:47 Jl 20 '87

The return of the blacklist [Justice Department's use of suspension orders against government contractors] D. Fanning. il *Forbes* 139:84 Ap 6 '87

Revisions to fraud statute aid suit against Raytheon. *Aviat Week Space Technol* 127:27 N 9 '87

Sidney Poitier and others linked to tax shelter scam [case against C. Atkins] *Jet* 72:14 Ap 13 '87

Telefraud: they've got your number [boiler room investment scams] il *Consum Rep* 52:289-93 My '87

That's a lot of bullion [G. R. Fox convicted of investment fraud] F. Greve. il *50 Plus* 27:18-19 Jl '87

Wall Street's prime-time crime drama [tax evasion and securities fraud charges against C. Atkins] D. Pauly. il por *Newsweek* 109:44 Ap 6 '87

Wrong number! [boiler room scams] P. Glastris. *Read Dig* 130:161-4 Je '87

Yale takes action against psychiatrists for financial improprieties. C. Holden. *Science* 238:745 N 6 '87

Fraunces Tavern Museum

The Fraunces Tavern Museum. H. Bridges. il *Gourmet* 48:40+ Je '87

Frawley, Brian

about

The Pope's foot soldiers. J. Buckley. il pors *U S News World Rep* 103:60-4+ S 21 '87

Frayn, Michael

about

Wild honey [drama] Reviews

N Y il 20:49-50 Ja 5 '87. J. Simon
Theatre Crafts il 21:26-7+ Ja '87. M. Sommers
Time il 129:79 Ja 5 '87. W. A. Henry

Frazer, Lance

A constitution for 2087. il *Space World* X-5-281:32-4 My '87

Frazier, Duncan

Edge of the Arctic [cover story] il *Natl Parks* 61:18-23 N/D '87

Frazier, Edward Franklin, 1894-1962

A world of make-believe: 1955 [excerpt from *Black bourgeoisie*] *Harpers* 274:44 F '87

Frazier, Ian

Brandy by firelight. *New Yorker* 63:37 D 21 '87

The last segment. *New Yorker* 63:23-4 Jl 13 '87

Where the bodies are buried. il *Atlantic* 259:26 Je '87

Frazier, Jim

about

UFO update. J. Clark. il *Omni* 9:89 F '87

Frazier, Kendrick

about

UFO update. J. Clark. il *Omni* 9:89 F '87

Frazier, Regina Jollivette

Speaking out: is the black middle class blowing it? . . . No! por *Ebony* 42:89-90 Ag '87

Frazier, Ruth

about

"Mother-in-chief" with a mission. J. Page. il por *McCalls* 114:138 S '87

Frazier, Walt, 1945-

about

Walt Frazier feels great becoming an NBA legend. por *Jet* 71:49 Mr 2 '87

Frears, Stephen, 1931-

about

Gritty Brit. H. Kennedy. il por *Film Comment* 23:15-17 Mr/Ap '87

Prick up your ears [film] Reviews

Macleans il 100:48 My 18 '87. L. O'Toole
N Y il 20:76+ Ap 20 '87. D. Denby
N Y Rev Books il 34:3-4 S 24 '87. G. Annan
Nation 244:618-19 My 9 '87. T. Rafferty
Natl Rev 39:52-4 My 22 '87. J. Simon
New Repub 196:28-9 Ap 20 '87. S. Kauffmann
New Yorker 63:128+ My 4 '87. P. Kael
Newsweek il 109:89 Ap 20 '87. D. Ansen
People Wkly 27:8 My 4 '87. P. Travers
Time il 129:76 Ap 20 '87. R. Corliss
Vogue il 177:70 Ap '87. M. Haskell

Sammy and Rosie get laid [film] Reviews

Macleans 100:71 N 16 '87. P. Hluchy
N Y il 20:114+ N 9 '87. D. Denby
Nation 245:606-8 N 21 '87. T. Rafferty
New Repub 197:24-6 N 30 '87. S. Kauffmann
New Yorker 63:140-2+ N 16 '87. P. Kael
Newsweek 110:77 N 9 '87. D. Ansen
Time il 130:91 N 9 '87. R. Corliss
Vogue il 177:74 D '87. M. Haskell

Sex, violence, & gratuitous social comment. F. Simon. por *Vogue* 177:70+ Ap '87

Fred Alger Management Inc.

Fred Alger is high on the 'one-world' economy. G. G. Marcial. il por *Bus Week* p83 Ja 19 '87

Live and learn [failed ad campaign] D. Machan. il por *Forbes* 140:135 S 7 '87

Fred Harvey Company

How good food and Harvey 'skirts' won the West. J. A. Cox. il *Smithsonian* 18:130-4+ S '87

Freddy (Fictional character)

Fan club organized for Walter Brooks's 'Freddy' books. J. Roginski. il *Publ Wkly* 231:105 F 27 '87

Frederick R. Weisman Museum

Same story, second verse [plans for converting Greystone Mansion into museum are abandoned] A. Decker. *Art News* 86:198 Ja '87

Frederick Warne & Co. Ltd.

Brightening up Beatrix [work of J. Taylor in republishing books by B. Potter] K. O. Fakih. il pors *Publ Wkly* 232:25-6 S 25 '87

Updated Beatrix Potter brews a storm in Britain. J. Taylor. il *Publ Wkly* 232:26 O 30 '87

Frederick's of Hollywood Bra Museum

Touring the Bra Museum. C. Leerhsen. il *Newsweek* 110:103 D 7 '87

Fredman, Irwin F.

The presidential follies. il *Am Herit* 38:38-43 S/O '87

Fredrickson, Donald S.

about

Fredrickson takes leave from Hughes. B. J. Culliton. por *Science* 236:510 My 1 '87

Fredrickson's bitter end at Hughes. B. J. Culliton. il por *Science* 236:1417-18 Je 12 '87

Free, Micki

about

Micki Free says he likes his wife's sexy image. pors *Jet* 72:59 Ag 24 '87

Free, World B.

about

It's a brave new World. J. McCallum. il por *Sports Illus* 67:78 D 14 '87

Free agents (Athletes) *See* Athletes—Salaries, pensions, etc.

Free agents (Baseball players) *See* Baseball players—Salaries, pensions, etc.

Free agents (Basketball players) *See* Basketball players—Salaries, pensions, etc.

Free agents (Football players) *See* Football players—Salaries, pensions, etc.

Free electron lasers *See* Lasers

Free energy

Free energy calculations by computer simulation. P. A. Bash and others. bibl f il *Science* 236:564-8 My 1 '87

Free enterprise

See also

Competition

Free enterprise—*cont.*
200 and going strong [U.S. Constitution] il *Nations Bus* 75:49-50 Jl '87
The free enterprise system [address, February 11, 1987] V. Jordan. *Vital Speeches Day* 53:466-8 My 15 '87
The ghost of Adam Smith. R. J. Samuelson. il *Newsweek* 109:54 F 9 '87
How 200 words created our framework for free enterprise. T. Osborne. il *Sch Update* 120:19-20 S 4 '87
Ideological backlash. Y. Guihannec. il *World Press Rev* 34:17 D '87
Lewis F. Powell, Jr.: his warning brought a new era of business activism. il por *Nations Bus* 75:66 Ag '87
Liberty to all [address, June 22, 1987] W. E. Simon. *Vital Speeches Day* 54:7-11 O 15 '87
Of markets and myths. R. B. Reich. *Commentary* 83:38-42 F '87
On the problem of America's policy myopia [address, October 22, 1986] E. H. Crane. *Vital Speeches Day* 53:184-8 Ja 1 '87
Why business is at a loss in a free market. R. Kuttner. *Bus Week* p18 S 28 '87
Free Flight (Musical group)
Free Flight. S. Yanow. il *Down Beat* 54:20-2 My '87
Free press *See* Freedom of the press
Free radicals *See* Radicals (Chemistry)
Free speech *See* Freedom of speech
Free trade and protection
      See also
   Balance of trade
   General Agreement on Tariffs and Trade
   Mercantile system
   Tariff
   United States—Commercial policy
Free trade is no free lunch. W. R. Hawkins. *Natl Rev* 39:38-9 Ag 28 '87
Guidance from a classic: the centennial of Henry George's Protection or free trade [address, November 13, 1986] C. L. Harriss. *Vital Speeches Day* 53:171-3 Ja 1 '87
'New protectionism' to fit the times. R. H. Bork, Jr. il *U S News World Rep* 102:44-5 Ap 6 '87
Free will and determinism
      See also
   Election (Theology)
Freed, James Ingo, 1930-
      about
A go-ahead for "bad manners". K. Andersen. il por *Time* 129:65 Je 29 '87
Freed, Lynn
Useful Zulu phrases. il *Harpers* 274:26-8 My '87
Freedman, James O.
      about
"Civility" for Dartmouth. por *Time* 129:85 Ap 27 '87
Freedman, Jerrold
      about
Native son [film] Reviews
   Essence il 17:40-2+ Ap '87. B. Allen
   Macleans 100:18 Ja 5 '87. L. O'Toole
   Ms il 15:15-17 Mr '87. S. McHenry
   People Wkly il 27:8 Ja 19 '87. S. Haller
Freedman, Jill
Ireland [excerpt from A time that was] il *People Wkly* 28:124-5+ N 2 '87
Freedman, Lawrence
Caution and doubt in Europe. il *World Press Rev* 34:15-16 N '87
Patience should pay off. il *World Press Rev* 34:15-16 O '87
Freedman, Rita Jackaway
Looking good: the double standard [excerpt from Beauty bound] *Vogue* 177:357+ Ap '87
Freedman, Samuel G.
Blues breaker. il pors *Roll Stone* p91-2+ S 24 '87
John Sayles's labor of love. il pors *Roll Stone* p27-8 O 8 '87
Leaving his imprint on Broadway. il pors *N Y Times Mag* p38+ N 22 '87
Murder hits home. il *N Y Times Mag* p20+ My 31 '87
A voice from the streets. il pors *N Y Times Mag* p36+ Mr 15 '87
The world of their fathers. il *Roll Stone* p86-8+ Mr 26 '87
Freedom *See* Liberty
Freedom and Peace (Organization)
Between issues. *New Leader* 70:2 Ap 6 '87
WiPing Poland into shape. F. Michalski. il *Nation* 244:680-2 My 23 '87

Freedom National Bank of New York
Tab Buford resigns from Freedom National Bank. por *Jet* 71:7 F 23 '87
Freedom Newspapers, Inc.
A family feud that could break a newspaper chain. R. Neff. il por *Bus Week* p38 F 16 '87
Rifts in a press empire. M. Gray. *Macleans* 100:47 Mr 9 '87
Freedom of information
      See also
   Classified information
   Executive privilege (Government information)
   Government and the press
   Journalistic ethics
   Science, Freedom of
Behind the lines in the information war [former Justice Dept. attorney Q. Shea's work with Freedom of Information Act appeals] D. A. Demac. il *Progressive* 51:32 My '87
Closing the file [Tower Commission records placed beyond reach of Freedom of Information Act] *Nation* 245:4 Jl 4-11 '87
Information: important issue for '88 [cover story] H. I. Schiller. *Nation* 245:1+ Jl 4-11 '87
The national guards. D. Goldberg. il *Omni* 9:44-6+ My '87

          Soviet Union
Future shock in Moscow. A. Toffler. *Cent Mag* 20:59-60 S/O '87
Freedom of Information Act *See* Freedom of information
Freedom of religion *See* Religious liberty
Freedom of science *See* Science, Freedom of
Freedom of speech
      See also
   Freedom of the press
   Libel and slander
Black woman's 'murder wish' for Reagan is free speech, Supreme Court says [case of A. M. Jackson] il por *Jet* 72:30 Jl 13 '87
Bork v. the First. J. Kalven. *Nation* 245:269-70 S 19 '87
Free speech and the 'bleacher creatures' [Tiger Stadium's efforts to curb fans' bad behavior] il *Newsweek* 110:38 S 21 '87
Free speech in the Catholic Church [address, December 19, 1986] R. P. McBrien. *Vital Speeches Day* 53:237-40 F 1 '87
Just shut up and shop [shopping centers impose bans on public discourse; with editorial comment by Erwin Knoll] K. Peck. il *Progressive* 51:4, 23-5 O '87
Kentucky teacher hits The wall with Pink Floyd [J. Fowler fights dismissal for showing R-rated movie] T. J. Flygare. il *Phi Delta Kappan* 69:237-8 N '87
Learned Hand and the great train ride. F. R. Kellogg. *Am Sch* 56:471-86 Aut '87
On the way to the forum [forum analysis] K. Peck. il *Progressive* 51:28-9 F '87
A sophist's theory of free speech [views of R. H. Bork] G. Marzorati. *Harpers* 275:62-3 S '87
A sort of memoir [M. Dukakis and free speech] P. Green. *Nation* 245:158-60+ Ag 29 '87
Turned on? Turn it off: switching channels may be one cure for the contagion of porn. R. Corliss. il *Time* 130:72-3 Jl 6 '87
Who are the 'moderates'? [ACLU objects to Detroit Tigers' attempt to curb fans' vulgarity] G. F. Will. il *Newsweek* 110:100 O 12 '87
Freedom of teaching *See* Academic freedom
Freedom of the press
      See also
   Government and the press
   Libel and slander
A brief on the freedom of the press [address, November 25, 1986] M. Cuomo. *Vital Speeches Day* 53:265-9 F 15 '87
Freedom under attack around the world. il *World Press Rev* 34:44-8 F '87
Jousts without winners: after a flurry of major libel cases, no one has much to crow about. W. A. Henry. il *Time* 130:68-70 Jl 6 '87
Students should have freedom of the press, too! D. Fuchs. por *Seventeen* 46:182 S '87
Freedom Savings & Loan Association
Booby trap [S. Zell's investment] R. King, Jr. *Forbes* 140:48 N 30 '87
Freedom's journal *See* Black press—History
Freelance writing *See* Periodical articles
Freeman, Bradford
      about
Sharp shoppers. M. Fritz. il por *Forbes* 140:236 N 30 '87

Freeman, Castle, Jr.
Homemade beer. il *Ctry J* 14:68-73 Mr '87
Freeman, Charles W.
The human rights dimension in Africa [address, November 6, 1986] *Dep State Bull* 87:42-5 F '87
Freeman, Derek
about
Letters [discussion of November 1986 article, Untrashing Margaret Mead] *Sci Am* 256:6 F '87
Freeman, Everett
Close encounters with W. C. Fields [excerpt from Days of wine and moguls] il pors *Saturday Evening Post* 259:36-9 D '87
Freeman, Fred
about
Lunar fantasies. R. Miller and F. C. Durant. il *Omni* 9:50-5 F '87
Freeman, John W.
Records. See issues of Opera News
Roberta Alexander. por *Stereo Rev* 52:113 My '87
Sharing the music [interview with J. Wustman] il pors *Opera News* 52:16-18+ Jl '87
Freeman, Mark
Paradise beyond road's end. il *Sierra* 72:64-7 S/O '87
Freeman, Marsha
Tomorrow's rockets: a conversation with Franklin Chang-Diaz. il pors *Space World* X-9-285:14-16 S '87
Freeman, Orville L.
America's agricultural future. il por *Futurist* 21:15-17 S/O '87
Freeman, Robert
Where are we, and where do we go from here? *Des Arts Educ* 88:29-32 Jl/Ag '87
Freeman, Robert M.
about
John Weinberg. A. Bianco. por *Bus Week* Sp Issue:224 Ap 17 '87
The ordeal of Bob Freeman. R. B. Stolley. il pors *Fortune* 115:66-8+ My 25 '87
Freeman, Sally
A few snapshots, a few regrets. il *Parents* 62:100-1 Jl '87
Freeman Tilden Award for the Outstanding Interpreter of the Year *See* National parks and reserves—Employees—Awards
Freestyle skiing competitions *See* Skis and skiing—Competitions
Freeways *See* Express highways
Freezers
Prefab root cellar [from old freezer] M. Bubel and N. Bubel. il *Mother Earth News* 107:22 S/O '87
Alarms
Prevent freezer disasters. S. Milius. il *Rodale's Org Gard* 34:50-1 Jl '87
Freezing
See also
Cryobiology
Food, Frozen
Ice
Water pipes—Freezing
Freezing. A. D. J. Haymet. bibl f il *Science* 236:1076-80 My 29 '87
Freezing of human bodies *See* Cryonics
Freidin, Gregory
Gorbo's other woman. *New Repub* 197:15-16 D 28 '87
Freifeld, Karen
Consuming interest. See issues of Health (New York, N.Y.) beginning July 1984
Freight airplanes *See* Airplanes, Freight
Freight and freightage
See also
Air freight service
Shipping
Trucking
Freight forwarders
Antitrust cases
A freight-rate inquiry [price fixing inquiry in Canada] A. Walmsley. *Macleans* 100:43 Je 1 '87
Canada
A freight-rate inquiry [price fixing inquiry] A. Walmsley. *Macleans* 100:43 Je 1 '87
Freight rates
See also
Trucking—Rates
A freight-rate inquiry [price fixing inquiry in Canada] A. Walmsley. *Macleans* 100:43 Je 1 '87
Freight vessels *See* Freighters
Freighters
See also
Columbia Star (Ship)
Container ships

Tankers
History
A boy at sea [memories of life aboard a Pacific lumber schooner in 1915] R. B. Hope. il por *Am Hist Illus* 21:14-18 Ja '87
Freiherr, Gregory
Naming names. il por *Space World* X-8-284:31-3 Ag '87
Freiligrath, Ferdinand, 1810-1876
about
Remembering the uprising [address, June 17, 1987; with introd. by Timothy Garton Ash] F. R. Stern. il por *N Y Rev Books* 34:14-16+ D 3 '87
Freiman, Jane
Brunch. il *N Y* 20:66-8+ Je 29-Jl 6 '87
Holiday entertaining [cover story] il *N Y* 20:55-70+ O 26 '87
Summer entertaining [cover story] il *N Y* 20:34-52+ My 18 '87
Where the foodies go. il *N Y* 20:86-9 My 4 '87
Freire, Paulo, 1921-
about
A tribute to Paulo Freire. *Courier* 39:46 D '86
Frel, Jiří
about
Getty 'improprieties' attract IRS scrutiny. A. Decker. *Art News* 86:31-2 My '87
Frell, Ellen
A country Christmas. il *Mother Earth News* 108:84-6 N/D '87
Fremantle (Australia)
Description
Captains and kangaroos [America's Cup] P. J. O'Rourke. il *Roll Stone* p60-2+ Ap 9 '87
Frémont, Jessie Benton, 1824-1902
about
Jessie Benton Frémont. P. Herr. il pors *Am Hist Illus* 22:18, 20-9+ S '87
Frémont, John Charles, 1813-1890
about
Jessie Benton Frémont. P. Herr. il pors *Am Hist Illus* 22:18, 20-9+ S '87
French, A. P. (Anthony Philip), 1920-
The PSSC course in retrospect [discussion of September 1986 article, Setting new directions in physics teaching: PSSC thirty years later] *Phys Today* 40:11+ Ap '87
French, Anthony Philip *See* French, A. P. (Anthony Philip), 1920-
French, Marilyn, 1929-
After my divorce [fiction] il *Ladies Home J* 104:82+ O '87
French, Roberta
about
Woven in Oaxaca. R. C. Toll and M.-P. Toll. il *House Gard* 159:102+ My '87
French, William
A Soviet poet's praise for freedom. il *World Press Rev* 34:61 Je '87
French
Lebanon
A costly exchange [suspected Iranian terrorist freed following release of French hostages in Lebanon] R. Laver. il *Macleans* 100:31 D 14 '87
A French terrorist-for-hostage deal? [Iranian terror suspect set free after two French hostages in Lebanon were freed] il *Newsweek* 110:61 D 14 '87
Furtive swap [suspected Iranian terrorist set free by France and French hostages released by Iran] *Time* 130:51 D 14 '87
Mali
History
Into the heart of Africa [visit to Timbuktu in the 1820s; excerpt from Journal d'un voyage à Temboctou et à Jenné] R. Caillé. il *Courier* 40:35-6 Ap '87
Tahiti
History
Island fling [French traveler's description of 1903-4 Tahitian ceremony; excerpt from Journal des îles] V. Segalen. il *Courier* 40:23 Ap '87
Tibet
History
A visit to the regent of Tibet [mid-19th century; excerpt from Souvenirs d'un voyage dans la Tartarie et le Thibet] E.-R. Huc. il por *Courier* 40:25 Ap '87
French and Indian War, 1755-1763 *See* United States—History—French and Indian War, 1755-1763

French architecture *See* Architecture, French
French art *See* Art, French
French artificial satellites *See* Artificial satellites, French
French bread *See* Bread
French Canada *See* Québec (Province)
French Canadians
　　　See also
　　Acadians
　　　　　　Health and hygiene
Tracking a genetic error [familial hypercholesterolemia] B. Wallace. *Macleans* 100:58 S 28 '87
French chefs, Women *See* Women cooks
French communications satellites *See* Communications satellites, French
French cooking *See* Cooking, French
French decorative arts *See* Decoration and ornament
French furniture *See* Furniture, French
French Grand Prix *See* Automobile racing—France
French Guiana
　　　See also
　　Rain forests—French Guiana
　　Space centers—French Guiana
French helicopters *See* Helicopters
French house decoration *See* House decoration, French
French Institute for Research into the Exploitation of the Sea *See* Institut Français de Recherche pour l'Exploitation de la Mer
French jewelry *See* Jewelry, French
French language
　　　　　　Conferences
Concerns at the summit [meeting of francophone nations in Quebec City] M. Rose. il *Macleans* 100:24 S 7 '87
Speaking with one tongue [La Francophonie conference in Quebec] M. Rose. il *Macleans* 100:8-9 S 14 '87
Troubles of a tongue *en crise* [Quebec summit] W. R. Doerner. il *Time* 130:49 S 14 '87
French language in France
　　　　　　History
Conflict in continuity in 17th-century France. R. Mettam. bibl il *Hist Today* 37:30-5 F '87
French language question in Canada *See* Canada—Languages
French language question in New Brunswick *See* New Brunswick—Languages
French language question in Québec (Province) *See* Québec (Province)—Languages
French literature
　　　　Anecdotes, facetiae, satire, etc.
Total immersion: Henry James and mineral waters [effect of new Paris water bar] A. Broyard. il *N Y Times Book Rev* 92:10 Ja 4 '87
French military assistance *See* Military assistance, French
French music *See* Music, French
French opera *See* Opera, French
French Polynesia
　　　See also
　　New Caledonia
　　　　　Description and travel
The other side of paradise. N. H. Belcher. il maps *Travel Holiday* 168:54-9+ Ag '87
French pottery *See* Pottery, French
French prints *See* Prints
French Revolution *See* France—History—Revolution, 1789-1799
French spaceplane *See* Spaceplane, French
French terrorists *See* Terrorists, French
French West Indian cooking *See* Cooking, West Indian
French wines *See* Wine
Frenchboro (Me.)
Search for a sea change. L. Wainwright. il *Life* 10:22 N '87
　　　　　Photographs and photography
An island of rare hospitality. R. Howard. il *People Wkly* 27:96-9 Ap 20 '87
Freni, Mirella
　　　　　　about
Testa dura. M. Krauss. il por *Opera News* 52:33-4 O '87
Frenk, Julio
Mexico faces the challenge. il *World Health* p20-3 Ap '87
Frenkiel, François N., 1910-1986
　　　　　　about
Obituary
　　Phys Today por 40:123-4 F '87. R. J. Emrich
Frense, Amina
Winnie Mandela [interview] il por *Ms* 15:82-3+ Ja '87
Frensley, William R.
Gallium arsenide transistors. bibl (p116) il *Sci Am* 257:80-7 Ag '87

Frenzel, Bill
Should Congress adopt the House-passed "Gephardt Amendment"? [excerpts from debate, April 29, 1987] *Congr Dig* 66:177+ Je/Jl '87
Frequency allocation, Television *See* Television frequency allocation
Frequency changers
New life for old car radios (II) [deluxe shortwave converter] G. McClellan. il *Radio-Electron* 58:50-2 Je '87
Frequency domain optical storage *See* Optical storage devices
Frequency modulation, Radio *See* Radio frequency modulation
Frequency modulation receivers *See* Radio receivers
Frequency response (Electric engineering)
Clearing the cobwebs. J. D. Hirsch. il *Stereo Rev* 52:24+ S '87
The joys of equalization. L. Klein. il *High Fidel* 37:62-5+ N '87
Music and meters. R. Long. il *High Fidel* 37:16 My '87
The perfect match [tape's characteristics must match the deck's] P. W. Mitchell. il *High Fidel* 37:44-6 F '87
Those pesky curves. R. Long. il *High Fidel* 37:22 Mr '87
Frequent flier programs
An affinity for flying [affinity credit cards cosponsored by airlines and banks] G. Eichler. il *Esquire* 108:82 O '87
Changing the rules in midair. B. Bauer. il *U S News World Rep* 103:58-60 Ag 24 '87
Credit cards that say: 'fly me'. T. Segal. il *Bus Week* p139 N 23 '87
Frequent crying [rule changes] il *Time* 129:75 My 4 '87
The frequent-flier flap. E. Williams. il *Newsweek* 109:40 My 4 '87
Get your reward! G. Stoller. il *Essence* 17:22 Mr '87
Pan Am, American continue negotiations [joint frequent-flier program] *Aviat Week Space Technol* 127:54 Ag 3 '87
Frequent guest programs
Picking up a suite deal. G. Eichler. il *Esquire* 107:34 F '87
Frère, Paul
Letter from Europe. See issues of Road & Track through December 1987
Fresco Ristorante (Glendale, Calif.) *See* Glendale (Calif.)—Restaurants, nightclubs, bars, etc.
Frescobaldi family
　　　　　　about
A charmed life. G. Y. Dryansky. il *Vogue* 177:446-53+ O '87
Frescoes
　　　　Conservation and restoration
Art historian James Beck urges the Vatican to clean up its act, not Michelangelo's frescoes [interview] H. Shapiro. il por *People Wkly* 27:69+ Mr 30 '87
Controversy over the Sistine ceiling. J. Dillenberger. *Christ Century* 104:708-9 Ag 26-S 2 '87
Crown moves up Sistine Chapel video [documentary on restoration of Michelangelo's frescoes] il *Publ Wkly* 231:32 Mr 27 '87
Dispelling clouds [restoration of Sistine Chapel frescoes] J. Gardner. *Commonweal* 114:599-601 O 23 '87
He didn't paint by the numbers, but he's getting digitized now [Michelangelo's Sistine Chapel frescoes] il *Discover* 8:8 My '87
Michelangelo rediscovered [Sistine Chapel; cover story] M. K. Talley, Jr. il *Art News* 86:159-70 Summ '87
Out of grime, a domain of light [restoration in the Sistine Chapel] R. Hughes. il *Time* 129:86-7 Ap 27 '87
Recovering Michelangelo's true colors. J. Arias. *World Press Rev* 34:60 Ap '87
Storm over the Sistine ceiling. J. Pope-Hennessy. il *N Y Rev Books* 34:16+ O 8 '87
True colors [restoration of frescoes in the Brancacci Chapel in the church of Santa Maria del Carmine, Florence, Italy] G. Armstrong. il *Art News* 86:39+ Mr '87
Frese, Paul F.
We're on the right track in saving wildflowers. il *Flower Gard* 31:40-3+ Ag/S '87
Fresh water ecology
　　　See also
　　Pond ecology
Autumn's hidden harvest [carbon in fallen leaves as energy source for stream creatures] R. H. Boyle. il *Natl Wildl* 25:4-9 O/N '87

Fresh water ecology—*cont.*
Getting the drift [behavioral drift of aquatic insects] P. Schullery. il *Ctry J* 14:66-9 Ag '87
Getting the edge on bass. C. Hauptman. il *Field Stream* 92:88-90 My '87
Lake Baikal. il *Courier* 40:30-1 O '87
A major food web component in the Orinoco River channel: evidence from planktivorous electric fishes. J. G. Lundberg and others. bibl f il *Science* 237:81-3 Jl 3 '87

Freshmen, College *See* College students

Le Fresne (Author, France: Castle) *See* Castles—France

Freud
On the salt. il *Cycle* 38:50-3 Ap '87

Freud, Emma
about
Chat show host Emma Freud, Sigmund's great-granddaughter, gets the lowdown by lying down. M. Neill. il pors *People Wkly* 28:155-6 D 7 '87

Freud, Lucian
about
Art. K. Larson. *N Y* 20:109 N 2 '87
Lucian Freud: Hirshhorn Museum. N. Grimes. por *Art News* 86:164 D '87
On Lucian Freud. R. Hughes. il *N Y Rev Books* 34:54-9 Ag 13 '87
A reasonable definition of love. W. Feaver. il *Archit Dig* 44:34+ Jl '87
The unblinking eye. M. Stevens. il *New Repub* 197:30-3 N 9 '87

Freud, Sigmund, 1856-1939
about
Ardent adaptationism [discussion of February 1987 article, Freudian slip] S. J. Gould. il *Nat Hist* 96:4+ Ap '87
Dr. Freud's last dream. M. Filler. il *House Gard* 159:176-81+ F '87
Freudian slip. S. J. Gould. *Nat Hist* 96:14+ F '87
Freud's phylogenetic fantasy. S. J. Gould. *Nat Hist* 96:10+ D '87
J'appelle un chat un chat. J. Malcolm. *New Yorker* 63:84-92+ Ap 20 '87

Freud (Sigmund) Museum (London, England) *See* Sigmund Freud Museum (London, England)

Freudenberger, Herbert J.
Today's troubled men. bibl (p63) il *Psychol Today* 21:46-7 D '87

Freudenheim, Betty
Interlacing: the elemental fabric. il *Am Craft* 47:42-9 Ap/My '87

Freudianism *See* Psychoanalysis

Freund, Charles Paul
The zeitgeist checklist. See issues of The New Republic beginning September 8, 1986

Freundlich, Peter
The crime of the tooth. *Harpers* 275:65-8 S '87
Gazing into Bergdorf's window. *Harpers* 275:73-6 D '87

Freundlich Books
Freundlich Books bankrupt, to be liquidated. *Publ Wkly* 232:11 O 23 '87

Frey, Jane
about
Jane Frey. B. S. Goldman. il por *Am Artist* 51:44-9 S '87

Frey, Karen
The watercolor page. il por *Am Artist* 51:61 Je '87

Fri, Robert W.
New directions for oil policy. bibl f il *Environment* 29:16-20+ Je '87

Friar, Jerome
White patriots. il *Society* 25:87-93 N/D '87

Fricke, David
Live! Twenty concerts that changed rock & roll [cover story; special section] il *Roll Stone* p44-6 Je 4 '87
Paul Simon's amazing Graceland tour [cover story] il pors *Roll Stone* p42-4+ Jl 2 '87
Pink Floyd: the inside story [cover story] il *Roll Stone* p44-6+ N 19 '87
Robyn in wonderland. il por *Roll Stone* p17 Ja 29 '87

Friderich, Nicole
Learning to live. il *Courier* 40:5-6 Jl '87

Fridman, Klavdia
about
Notes and comment. *New Yorker* 63:29-30 S 21 '87

Fried, Eliot
about
A pair of prescient winners. P. Nulty. il pors *Fortune* 116 Sp Issue:176-9 Fall '87

Shearson Lehman Brothers [interview] il por *Fortune* 116 Sp Issue:186-7 Fall '87

Fried, Eunice, 1933-
The connoisseur's coolers. il *Harpers Bazaar* 120:108+ My '87
The trail of the snail. il *Harpers Bazaar* 120:166+ Mr '87
Wine. See issues of Black Enterprise

Fried chicken *See* Cooking—Poultry

Friedan, Betty
about
Preserving values in a changing world. il por *USA Today (Periodical)* 116:2-3 Ag '87

Frieda's Finest/Produce Specialties, Inc.
The Princess of Produce [F. Caplan] P. F. Stewart. il por *Ladies Home J* 104:156 O '87

Friedland, Robert M.
about
A gold miner helps Pickens chip away at Newmont. S. D. Atchison. il por *Bus Week* p36 Ag 31 '87

Friedlander, Carolee
about
Everything the Duchess of Windsor touched has turned to gold (plated), thanks to Carolee Friedlander. il por *People Wkly* 27:137 My 11 '87

Friedlander, Gerhart
(jt. auth) See Weneser, Joseph, and Friedlander, Gerhart

Friedlander, Gerhart, and Weneser, Joseph
Solar neutrinos: experimental approaches. bibl f il *Science* 235:760-5 F 13 '87

Friedlander, Steven
Competing couples. il *Health* 19:38-40 N '87
His four biggest health fears. il *Health* 19:34-6 N '87

Friedman, Barry
about
Imprints of the avant-garde—Barry Friedman. A. Berman. il por *Archit Dig* 44:114+ N '87

Friedman, Benjamin M.
New directions in the relation between public and private debt. bibl f il *Science* 236:397-403 Ap 24 '87

Friedman, Dick
The interview as mating ritual. il *Work Woman* 12:106-8 Ap '87

Friedman, Elizabeth
about
Breaking codes was this couple's lifetime career. J. R. Chiles. bibl (p154) il pors *Smithsonian* 18:128-30+ Je '87

Friedman, Herb
Communications corner. See issues of Radio-Electronics

Friedman, Ken
about
Claptrap [drama] Reviews
N Y il 20:68 Je 22 '87. J. Simon
New Yorker 63:68 Je 29 '87. M. Kramer

Friedman, Kinky, 1944-
about
It's elementary: shooting from the lip, cocky Kinky Friedman has a talent for music and mysteries. A. Chambers. il pors *People Wkly* 28:117-18+ N 9 '87

Friedman, Milton, 1912-
1929 and 1987: the differences. *Natl Rev* 39:50 N 20 '87

Friedman, Nancy
"Why don't I enjoy sex more?". *Read Dig* 130:141-4 Ap '87

Friedman, Richard Elliott
about
Who wrote the first five books of the Bible? A. P. Sanoff. il por *U S News World Rep* 103:52-3 Ag 24 '87

Friedman, Sara Ann
Celebrating the wild mushroom [excerpt] bibl il *Mother Earth News* 104:76-83 Mr/Ap '87

Friedman, Sharon M., and others
Reporting on radon: the role of local newspapers. *Environment* 29:4-5+ Mr '87

Friedman, Sonya
Psychologist's journal. See issues of Ladies' Home Journal beginning September 1983
about
On the sunny side of 50, pop psychologist Sonya Friedman has legs as talk cable's new queen. S. Toepfer. il pors *People Wkly* 28:75-6 N 16 '87

Friedman, Steve, 1946-
about
Behind the McTelevision show. N. J. Perry. il pors *Fortune* 116:122 S 28 '87

Friedman, Thomas L.
The focus on Israel. il *N Y Times Mag* p14-19+ F 1 '87

Friedman, Thomas L.—*cont.*
My neighbor, my enemy. il *N Y Times Mag* p14-19+ Jl 5 '87

Friedman, William Frederick, 1891-1969
about
Breaking codes was this couple's lifetime career. J. R. Chiles. bibl (p154) il pors *Smithsonian* 18:128-30+ Je '87

Friedman (Barry) Ltd. *See* Barry Friedman Ltd.

Friedmann, E. Imre, and Weed, Rebecca
Microbial trace-fossil formation, biogenous, and abiotic weathering in the Antarctic cold desert. bibl f il *Science* 236:703-5 My 8 '87

Friedmann, Robert, and others
Changing how society views children. il *Child Today* 16:10-14 Jl/Ag '87

Friedrich, Dick
County blocks bomb exercise. *Progressive* 51:16 My '87

Friedrich, Otto, 1929-
Monte Cassino: a story of death and resurrection. bibl (p163) il map *Smithsonian* 18:128-32+ Ap '87
Traveling with a sense of history. il *Am Herit* 38:29-31+ Ap '87
about
Tales of imperial Hollywood. J. Skow. il *Time* 129:74 Ja 5 '87

Friedt, Glenn
about
Forget flowers: an FTD for book fanciers. *Newsweek* 110:37 Jl 6 '87

Frieling, Thomas J.
Alms for an orbiter. il *Space World* X-2-278:29-31 F '87
The devastating delay. il *Space World* X-7-283:27-30 Jl '87

Friend, Tad
Wishing it was just the thought. il *Harpers* 275:68-9 D '87

Friendly Islands *See* Tonga

Friendly Press
'Rolling stone' history coming from Friendly Press. il *Publ Wkly* 231:251 My 15 '87

Friends of the River (Organization)
For the rivers, come hell or high water [work of M. Dubois] K. Crist. il pors *Sierra* 72:61-5 My/Je '87

Friends United Meeting *See* Society of Friends

Friendship
See also
　Pen pals
3 secrets about men that women won't keep. il *Jet* 73:34 N 16 '87
Are his friends crowding you out? C. Elflein. il *Seventeen* 46:240-1+ Mr '87
Are you too concerned with being liked? [teenagers] W. J. Rohr. *Teen* 31:22+ My '87
Best friends: why they're so special. W. J. Rohr. il *Teen* 31:24+ O '87
Best girlfriends. B. Omolade. il *Ms* 16:138-40 Jl/Ag '87
Breaking up with my out-laws. L. Mosedale. il *Glamour* 85:324 N '87
Can this friendship be saved? K. Heller. il *Mademoiselle* 93:238-9+ N '87
A case of bigamy [partnership of author and J. Falsey] J. Brand. il *N Y Times Mag* p100 My 17 '87
Children without friends. D. F. Bjorklund and B. Bjorklund. il *Parents* 62:209 My '87
The comfort of pals [men] M. M. Hunt. il *N Y Times Mag* p46 Ja 18 '87
Do ex-lovers make good friends? *Glamour* 85:120 D '87
Do men make good pals? [views of J. Bisset] L. Kleinmann. por *Health* 19:42 N '87
Do you betray a lover when you discuss your relationship with a friend? C. L. Mithers. *Glamour* 85:392 S '87
The experience gap [sexual experience influences friendships] K. McCoy. *Seventeen* 46:34+ Jl '87
Finding your heart . . . away from home [teenager-adult friendships] S. Nelson. il *Seventeen* 46:152-3+ My '87
Friendly firing: do you warn a pal about a pink slip? C. Rickey. *Mademoiselle* 93:106 Je '87
How many friends are enough? [children's social development] C. Berman. il *Parents* 62:64-6+ Ja '87
How to be your husband's best friend. C. Jabs. *McCalls* 114:40+ Ap '87
In praise of 'best friends'. B. Ehrenreich. por *Ms* 15:35-6 Ja '87
Life without lunch: fitting in friends [women] J. Giambanco. il *Work Woman* 12:51+ Jl '87
Living with a friend's love swings. C. Rickey. *Mademoiselle* 93:94 Ja '87

The long and bumpy road from lovers to just friends. S. Nelson and S. Simels. il *Glamour* 85:194-5+ Je '87
A love story, sort of. J. Gonick. il *Glamour* 85:204+ My '87
Making friends [preschoolers] L. G. Katz. il *Parents* 62:263 N '87
My son didn't have any friends. il *Good Housekeep* 205:20+ Jl '87
Sister-friends. M. A. Gillespie. il por *Ms* 16:130+ Jl/Ag '87
Sisterhood is powerful. P. Gaines-Carter. por *Essence* 18:176 My '87
Tending friendships (even when work gets in the way). L. Sorenson. il *Work Woman* 12:108-10+ O '87
Till birth do us part [women's friendships vs. motherhood] K. E. Livingston. il *Parents* 62:87-91 Mr '87
To tell (or not) on a troubled friend. P. S. Rix. il *Teen* 31:48+ My '87
The trouble with money [coming between friends] M. Jacobson. il *Esquire* 107:49-50 Ap '87
What does it mean when a friend constantly cancels plans? il *Glamour* 85:50 Ja '87
What does it say about him if you hate his friends? *Glamour* 85:184 O '87
What men can teach women—and women teach men—about friendship. L. C. Pogrebin. il *Glamour* 85:278-9+ Mr '87
What pregnant women need from friends. il *Glamour* 85:60 F '87
When beauty blooms: do friends fade? il *Teen* 31:30 Ja '87
When friends fight, should you fix it? C. Rickey. *Mademoiselle* 93:160 Ag '87
When to forgive a friend and when to forget her. J. Kaufman. il *Seventeen* 46:250-1+ Mr '87
When you disapprove of your teenager's pals. J. K. Rosemond. il *Better Homes Gard* 65:48 Ag '87
You get ahead, she gets mad. G. Blair. *Mademoiselle* 93:219 S '87
Your good friends may be bad for you. J. Jobin. il *Redbook* 168:108-9+ Mr '87
Your new path to a stronger immune system. R. Rodale. il *Prevention* 39:20-1+ S '87

Friesen, Dorothy
Human rights problems persist in the Philippines. *Christ Century* 104:348 Ap 15 '87
Leandro Alejandro: victim of militarism. *Christ Century* 104:877-8 O 14 '87
Vigilantes resurgent. il *Progressive* 51:21-3 N '87

Friesen, Gil
about
Gil Friesen [interview] S. Pond. il por *Roll Stone* p103-4+ D 17-31 '87

Fringe benefits
See also
　Bonus system
　Insurance, Health
　Profit sharing
　Retirement benefits
20 corporations that listen to women [results of survey] R. B. Will and S. D. Lydenberg. il *Ms* 16:45-52 N '87
Analyzing employers' costs for wages, salaries, and benefits. F. Nathan. bibl f il *Mon Labor Rev* 110:3-11 O '87
Benefits, buffet style. M. Allen. il *Nations Bus* 75:45-7 Ja '87
Employee benefits: know your options before you sign on. *Glamour* 85:152+ Mr '87
How companies help. S. Nelton and K. Berney. il *Nations Bus* 75:27 My '87
Motivating without money: a strokes and perks primer. S. Mernit. il *Work Woman* 12:75 D '87
Those burgeoning worker benefits. J. R. Morris. il *Nations Bus* 75:53-4 F '87
Work and family [Conference Board report entitled Corporations and families] il *Child Today* 16:3-4 Ja/F '87

Laws and regulations
The American folly of courting "Europeanization" [address, September 1, 1987] J. E. Sloan. *Vital Speeches Day* 54:29-32 O 15 '87
Hidden taxes [mandating benefits] J. Novack. il *Forbes* 140:36-7 S 21 '87
Making business pay for welfare [mandated benefits bills] B. Cohn and J. Schwartz. il por *Newsweek* 109:49 Je 15 '87
Put up the price of beans [mandated benefits policy] J. Novack and H. Banks. il *Forbes* 139:32-5 Ap 6 '87

Fringe benefits—Laws and regulations—*cont.*
Should business be forced to help bring up baby? [battle over 'mandated benefits'] M. E. Recio. il *Bus Week* p39-40 Ap 6 '87
The threat of higher benefits costs. H. Bacas. il *Nations Bus* 75:32-4 Jl '87

Taxation
Congress and the work place: tax reform and employee benefits [address, December 3, 1986] F. B. McArdle. *Vital Speeches Day* 53:215-19 Ja 15 '87
How to keep the tax man out of your nest egg. P. Besson. il *Black Enterp* 17:65-6+ Mr '87
Prospects for your perks. M. Posner. il *Changing Times* 41:77-80 Ja '87
Time to review benefits [views of Frank McArdle and Milton Pickman] J. C. Szabo. il *Nations Bus* 75:33-5 Mr '87
What the new tax law does to your benefits. W. Konrad. *Work Woman* 12:166 Ap '87
Your benefits may never be the same. D. M. Topolnicki. il *Money* 16:87-90+ Mr '87

Japan
Japan's newest perk: the corporate tomb. *Newsweek* 109:55 Mr 2 '87

The fringe dwellers [film] *See* Motion picture reviews—Single works
Fringe-toed lizards *See* Lizards

Fringed gentians
The elusive gentians [excerpt from Hal Borland's Twelve moons of the year] H. Borland. il *Audubon* 89:51 N '87

Frink, Cheryl Coggins
The million-dollar baby nobody wants. il pors *Ladies Home J* 104:48+ D '87

Fripp Island (S.C.)
See also
Architecture, Domestic—Fripp Island (S.C.)

Frisari family
about
Canta e pasta. *New Yorker* 63:27-9 Mr 23 '87

Frisbee (Game)
No romp in the park [U.S. Open Flying Disc Championships] A. Killion. il *Sports Illus* 67:99 S 21 '87

Frisell, Bill
about
Blindfold test. G. Santoro. il por *Down Beat* 54:53 Ap '87

Frishman, Elyse D.
The Hanukkah miracle. il *Good Housekeep* 205:92+ D '87

Frist, Thomas F., Jr.
about
Physician, heal thy chain. S. Ticer. *Bus Week* p52 Je 1 '87

Fritch, Jane
about
A Florida success story. M. Kane. il por *Rodale's Org Gard* 34:60-4 D '87

Fritchey, Clayton
about
Social graces in Georgetown: Polly and Clayton Fritchey's Victorian enclave. S. M. Alsop. il pors *Archit Dig* 44:188-91 O '87

Fritchey, Polly
about
Social graces in Georgetown: Polly and Clayton Fritchey's Victorian enclave. S. M. Alsop. il pors *Archit Dig* 44:188-91 O '87

Fritts, Edward Owens
Free time is not the answer. por *U S News World Rep* 102:8 Je 1 '87
Should Congress approve the Fairness Doctrine? [excerpts from testimony, April 7, 1987] *Congr Dig* 66:247+ O '87

Fritts-Richards Organ Builders (Firm)
Emulating the great age of organ building. E. Clark. il *Am Craft* 47:56-63 O/N '87

Fritz, Barbara
Oasis food. il *Prevention* 39:74-6+ Mr '87
Vegetables galore! il *Prevention* 39:74+ O '87

Frivolous suits *See* Actions and defenses

Frizon, Maud
about
Architectural digest visits: Maud Frizon. C. Aillaud. il pors *Archit Dig* 44:118-25+ Je '87

Frogdesign Inc.
Hartmut Esslinger: high tech's one-man Bauhaus. K. M. Hafner. il por *Bus Week* p59 Ag 17 '87

Frogs
See also
Toads

Fatherhood in frogdom [coqui forest frogs of Puerto Rico] D. S. Townsend. il *Nat Hist* 96:28-35 My '87
Frog went a-courtin' [gray tree frog; work of Georg M. Klump and H. Carl Gerhardt] il *Sci Am* 256:28 Je '87

Locomotion
See Animal locomotion

Ova
See Ova

Photographs and photography
Funny frog faces. il map *Natl Geogr World* 147:32-5 N '87
Jumping blues. S. Dalton. il *Nat Hist* 96:96-7 Mr '87

Sexual behavior
See Sexual behavior—Amphibia

Skin
See Skin—Amphibia

Treatment
Apples, frogs, and animal rights [Apple Computer television commercial] C. Holden. *Science* 238:1345 D 4 '87
A teen fights for frog rights, and bio may never be the same [J. Graham refuses to dissect frog in biology class in Victorville, Calif.] il por *People Wkly* 27:109 My 25 '87

Frogs, Fossil
An upper Eocene frog from the Dominican Republic and its implication for Caribbean biogeography. G. O. Poinar and D. C. Cannatella. bibl f il *Science* 237:1215-16 S 4 '87

Frohman Academy for Musical Theatre Education
Making musicals. K. Milam. il *Horizon* 30:63 Jl/Ag '87

From the hip [film] *See* Motion picture reviews—Single works

Fromer, Margot Joan, 1939-
Bone marrow transplants: from Chernobyl to cancer therapy. il *FDA Consum* 21:12-15 Ap '87

The front page [drama] *See* Hecht, Ben, 1894-1964

Front wheel drive vehicles
See also
Automobiles—Front wheel drive
Automobiles, Foreign—Front wheel drive

Front yards *See* Home grounds

Frontal cortex *See* Brain

Frontier and pioneer life
See also
Homesteads—History
Wagon trains

Western States
Jessie Benton Frémont [with editorial comment by Ed Holm] P. Herr. il pors *Am Hist Illus* 22:18, 20-9+ S '87

Fronts (Meteorology)
A Cessna to the rescue [helping Cherokee pilot land in stationary cold front] F. Anders. *Flying* 114:101 Jl '87

Photographs and photography
More about that visible cold front [discussion of July/August 1987 article, A visible cold front] L. Rummel. il *Weatherwise* 40:301-2+ D '87
A "visible" cold front. L. Rummel. il *Weatherwise* 40:183 Jl/Ag '87

Frost, David
'For me there is a double standard' [interview with J. Jackson] il por *U S News World Rep* 103:19 D 21 '87
George Bush on God, war and Ollie North [interview] il por *U S News World Rep* 103:47-8 D 14 '87
'I had a plan . . . to deal from strength' [interview with R. Reagan] il pors *U S News World Rep* 103:31-2 D 7 '87
'I love ideas, but I'm not an intellectual' [interview with J. Kemp] il por *U S News World Rep* 103:17 D 28 '87-Ja 4 '88
Iran arms deal was more serious than Watergate [interview with J. Carter] por *U S News World Rep* 103:32 D 7 '87
Often, momentum can lead to a bad arms treaty [interview with G. R. Ford] por *U S News World Rep* 103:33 D 7 '87
about
TV's David Frost quizzes the men who would be president. J. Hall. il pors *People Wkly* 28:78-80 D 7 '87

Frost, Deborah
How I spent my summer vacation: one woman's journey to fantasy bodybuilding camp. il *Women's Sports Fitness* 9:38-41 Je '87
Wild in the streets. il pors *Women's Sports Fitness* 9:33-6 My '87

Frost, Honor
How Carthage lost the sea. il maps *Nat Hist* 96:58-67 D '87
Frost, Polly
Fast forward to the past. *New Yorker* 63:26-7 Jl 6 '87
From a free-lancer's notebook. *New Yorker* 62:29-30 Ja 19 '87
Plan 10 from Zone R-3. *New Yorker* 63:28-9 Ap 13 '87
Frost, Tom
about
How NatWest plans to stretch its string of successes. R. A. Melcher. il por *Bus Week* p46 Jl 6 '87
Frost
See also
Frozen ground
Frost boils *See* Frost heaving
Frost heaving
Frost boils. K. Schlenker. il *Ctry J* 14:71-4 Ap '87
Frost protection of plants *See* Plants—Protection
Frowick, Roy Halston *See* Halston
Frozen desserts *See* Ice cream, ices, etc.
Frozen food *See* Food, Frozen
Frozen fruit *See* Fruit, Frozen
Frozen ground
See also
Frost heaving
Life upon the permafrost [Arctic] F. Bruemmer. il *Nat Hist* 96:30-9 Ap '87
Probing the permafrost [work of Arthur H. Lachenbruch and B. Vaughn Marshall] il *Sci Am* 256:62 F '87
Frozen potatoes *See* Potatoes, Frozen
Frozen turkeys *See* Turkeys, Frozen
Frozen yogurt *See* Yogurt
Fructose
Copper: what a difference sex makes [research by Meira Fields and others] J. Raloff. *Sci News* 131:70 Ja 31 '87
The frugal gourmet [television program] *See* Television program reviews—Single works
Frugality *See* Thrift
Fruit
See also
Cooking—Fruit
See also names of fruit
Better veggies ahead. L. Shapiro. il *Newsweek* 110:87-8 O 5 '87
Get fresh! [choosing ripe produce] A. Arnott. il *McCalls* 114:132+ Ag '87
Go bananas! S. C. Finn. il *50 Plus* 27:70-1+ Ag '87
Diseases and pests
See also
Fruit flies
When brown rot attacks your summer fruit. il *Sunset* 178:224 Je '87
Drying
Hanging the harvest. B. R. Rogers. il *Ctry J* 14:73-5 O '87
Home food drying. N. Bubel. bibl il *Ctry J* 14:50-5 Ag '87
Varieties
New varieties for your garden. il *Rodale's Org Gard* 34:34-7+ Ja '87
Fruit, Dried
See also
Cooking—Fruit
Prunes
Fruit, Frozen
Freeze now—enjoy later! il *Better Homes Gard* 65:34 Jl '87
Fruit butter
See also
Apple butter
Fruit butters. K. Haedrich. il *Ctry J* 14:20-3 N '87
Fruit culture
Insect control
See Insect control
Fruit desserts *See* Desserts
Fruit drinks *See* Beverages
Fruit flies
See also
Drosophila
On display: the stars of the stripes [fruit fly mimicry of jumping spider territorial display; research by Erick Greene and others] il *Discover* 8:9-10 My '87
A sheep in wolf's clothing: tephritid flies mimic spider predators. M. H. Mather and B. D. Roitberg. bibl f il *Science* 236:308-10 Ap 17 '87
A tephritid fly mimics the territorial displays of its jumping spider predators. E. Greene and others. bibl f il *Science* 236:310-12 Ap 17 '87

Why the spider did not eat the fly [jumping spider mimicry among fruit flies] S. Weisburd. il *Sci News* 131:261 Ap 25 '87
Control
The invasion of the avocado snatchers [Medfly back in California] J. Flynn. il *Bus Week* p42 S 14 '87
Medfly replay. il *Nat Hist* 96:4 Je '87
Fruit ices *See* Ice cream, ices, etc.
Fruit industry
See also
Citrus fruit industry
New Rx: try an atemoya a day [M. and K. Ellenby run Florida's largest independent tropical fruit business] L. Shapiro. il pors *Newsweek* 110:77-77A+ N 23 '87
New Zealand
The captivating kiwifruit. N. Vietmeyer. il *Natl Geogr* 171:682-8 My '87
Fruit juices
See also
Apple juice
New England Apple Products Company Inc.
Orange juice
Getting juiced [fruit-based cocktails] J. F. Mariani. il *Harpers Bazaar* 120:98+ Ag '87
Fruit of the Loom, Inc.
Look who wants to be president [executive W. Farley] B. Saporito. il pors *Fortune* 116:141+ N 23 '87
Some things are easier said than done [W. Farley] S. B. Weiner. il por *Forbes* 139 Ann Directory:56-7 Ap 27 '87
Fruit pie *See* Pie
Fruit punch *See* Punch (Beverage)
Fruit salads *See* Salads
Fruit sauces *See* Sauces
Fruit tarts *See* Tarts
Fruit trees
See also
Apple trees
Cherry trees
Citrus fruit trees
Fig trees
Persimmon trees
Plum trees
Pruning
See Pruning
Training
Espalier: sculpted fruit trees for tight spaces (I). J. Ruttle. il *Rodale's Org Gard* 34:82-5+ F '87
Espalier: sculpted fruit trees for tight spaces (II). J. Ruttle. il *Rodale's Org Gard* 34:30+ Mr '87
Fruit trees, Dwarf
Fruit trees. P. L. Spencer. *Consum Res Mag* 70:2 Mr '87
Fruitcake
Holidays—and centuries—come and go, but for the faithful Fords, it's semper Fidelia's fruitcake. il *People Wkly* 28:133 N 30 '87
Fruitlands Museums (Harvard, Mass.)
Stepping back in time. B. Golightly. il *Horizon* 30:20-1 My '87
Fruits *See* Fruit
Fruits, vegetables, etc. in decoration
Apples at Christmas. L. C. Askey. il *South Living* 22:80-1 D '87
Arrangements to suit the season [use of branches] il *South Living* 22:56+ F '87
Frustration
See also
Repression (Psychology)
Fry, C. George
about
How could the Iran-Iraq War affect Christianity? [interview] S. Mumper. il por *Christ Today* 31:46-7 N 6 '87
Fry, Charles Rahn
about
The pochoir prints of Charles Rahn Fry. J. Gruen. il por *Archit Dig* 44:94+ Ap '87
Fry, William Henry, 1813-1864
about
Leonora [opera] Reviews
New Yorker 63:94-5 Mr 9 '87. A. Porter
Frydman, Anne
(tr) *See* Dovlatov, Sergeĭ. Father
(tr) *See* Dovlatov, Sergeĭ. Uncle Leopold
Frye, Alton
Crafting a strategic compromise. *Society* 24:44-50 Jl/Ag '87
Frying
See also
Stir-frying

Frying—*cont.*
Fry, he said. J. F. Mariani. il *Mot Boat Sail* 160:24 S '87
Frymier, Jack Rimmel, 1925-
Bureaucracy and the neutering of teachers [cover story] il *Phi Delta Kappan* 69:8-14 S '87
FSH (Follicle-stimulating hormone) *See* Gonadotropins
FSLIC *See* Federal Savings and Loan Insurance Corporation
FTC *See* United States. Federal Trade Commission
Fuchs, Debbie
Students should have freedom of the press, too! por *Seventeen* 46:182 S '87
Fuchs, Klaus Emil Julius, 1911-1988
about
The conscientious spy. S. E. Toulmin. bibl f il *N Y Rev Books* 34:54-60 N 19 '87
Fuchs, Michael Joseph
about
At age 15, HBO chases the networks [interview] M. Brown. il pors *Channels* 7:78-9 O '87
Is HBO on its way to being boffo again? D. Lieberman. il por *Bus Week* p60-1 Ag 3 '87
Fuchs, Rudi
Spotlight; tr. by Beth O'Brien. il por *Art News* 86:67-8 S '87
Fuchs, Sharon
(jt. auth) See Alvarez, Elizabeth, and Fuchs, Sharon
Fudge (Term)
Oh, fudge. W. Safire. il *N Y Times Mag* p8+ F 1 '87
Fuel
See also
Airplane engines—Energy usage
Airplane engines—Fuel
Airplane engines, Jet—Energy usage
Airplane engines, Jet—Fuel
Alcohol as fuel
Automobile engines—Energy usage
Biomass energy
Coal
Diesel engines, Automotive—Energy usage
Furnaces—Energy usage
Gasoline
Motorcycle engines—Energy usage
Natural gas
Peat
Petroleum
Refuse as fuel
Wood as fuel
Conservation
See Energy conservation
Fuel, Synthetic
See also
Alcohol as fuel
Fuel cells
A better battery. il *Sci Am* 256:88-9 F '87
Energy technology in the 21st century. S. B. Kuznetsov. il *Radio-Electron* 58:107-11 My '87
Multi-fuel fuel cells. S. Ashley. il *Pop Sci* 231:94-5 N '87
New life for a cell: the ceramic solution. T. Dworetzky. il *Discover* 8:16 Jl '87
Fuel combustion *See* Combustion
Fuel conservation *See* Energy conservation
Fuel filters
See also
Automobile engines—Filters
Fuel industry *See* Energy industries
Fuel injection systems *See* Motorcycle engines—Fuel feeding
Fuel supply
See also
Agriculture—Energy usage
Airlines—Energy usage
Degree days
Electric plants—Energy usage
Gas supply
Industry—Energy usage
Petroleum supply
Fuel systems, Airplane *See* Airplane engines—Fuel feeding; Airplane engines, Jet—Fuel feeding
Fuel systems, Automobile *See* Automobile engines—Fuel feeding
Fuel systems, Motorcycle *See* Motorcycle engines—Fuel feeding
Fuel tanks
See also
Space vehicles—Fuel tanks
Fuentes, Carlos
Architecture: Ricardo Legorreta: the Los Angeles residence of Georgiana and Ricardo Montalban. il por *Archit Dig* 44:164-71+ Mr '87

The United States and Latin America [with discussion] il por *Cent Mag* 20:4-19 Ja/F '87
Who is the real threat? il *World Press Rev* 34:24-5 Ap '87
Zurbaran's theater of martyrs. il *Art News* 86:116-19 O '87
Fuentes Millán, Hugo
Just what it says [story] il *Américas* 39:48-50 Ja/F '87
Fuerst, J. S.
More than a peacemaker. il *Commonweal* 114:701-3 D 4 '87
Fugard, Athol
about
A place with the pigs [drama] Reviews
Newsweek il 109:79 Ap 13 '87. J Kroll
The road to Mecca [drama] Reviews
Time il 129:70 Je 15 '87. W. A. Henry
Fugitives from justice
See also
Escapes
Claude Dallas update. R. P. Stuart. por *Outdoor Life* 179:49 Mr '87
In Idaho: a killer becomes a mythic hero [C. Dallas] M. Riley. il por *Time* 129:10-11 Ja 26 '87
Taking a byte out of crime [Scorecard program used to track federal fugitives] E. Shannon. il *Time* 129:63 My 25 '87
Fuhr, Grant
about
Black hockey star led Oilers to 3rd NHL crown. il por *Jet* 72:47 Je 22 '87
Fuji-Hakone-Izu National Park (Japan) *See* National parks and reserves—Japan
Fuji Photo Film Co., Ltd.
Kodak fights Fuji with 'me-too' tactics. L. Helm. il *Bus Week* p138 F 23 '87
Fujitec Company
Fiasco at Fujitec [American operations] R. Simon and A. Tanzer. il *Forbes* 139:60-1 Mr 23 '87
Fujitsu Ltd.
Cold feet [Fujitsu drops bid for Fairchild] *Time* 129:52 Mr 30 '87
Fighting the chip wars: Fujitsu loses Fairchild. J. B. Copeland. il *Newsweek* 109:50 Mr 30 '87
Gaijin makes good [American N. Petersen appointed to board of directors] M. Beauchamp. il por *Forbes* 140:124 S 7 '87
The market for mainframes will never be the same [IBM-Fujitsu software copyright fight] J. W. Verity. il *Bus Week* p62 O 5 '87
What the Fairchild fiasco signals for trade policy [Fujitsu deal collapses] J. W. Wilson and S. J. Dryden. il *Bus Week* p28 Mr 30 '87
Fujiyama (Japan) *See* Mount Fuji (Japan)
Fukuoka, Masanobu
about
Farming with a future: the passing of the plow [interview] P. Stone. bibl il pors *Mother Earth News* 104:110-14+ Mr/Ap '87
Fulda, Joseph S.
State control of universities. *Cent Mag* 20:59 My/Je '87
Fulder, Stephen
Complementary medicine. il *Courier* 40:16-19 Ag '87
Fulfillment (Psychology) *See* Self realization
Fulford, Robert
about
The end of Fulford's era. D. Fetherling. *Macleans* 100:53 Jl 6 '87
Fulghum, Robert
We learned it all in kindergarten. il *Read Dig* 131:115 O '87
Fulgurite
What killed the dinosaurs? [asteroid impact theory; work of Eric Essene and Daniel Fisher] il *USA Today (Periodical)* 115:9 Je '87
Fulkerson, John F.
Biological impact and assessment: biological potentials over time [address, November 14, 1986] por *BioScience* 37:187-9 Mr '87
Full employment
Cathedrals in the desert [Western Europe] H. Banks. il *Forbes* 140:225-6+ Jl 13 '87
Jobilism, or, Is the world really flat? R. B. McKenzie. il *Forbes* 140:68-70 Jl 13 '87
Labor & the limits of the market place. *Commonweal* 114:3-4 Ja 16 '87
Making an issue of full employment. B. M. Gross. il *Nation* 244:72-5 Ja 24 '87

Full employment—*cont.*

Making the case for full employment. M. Hope and J. Young. *Christ Century* 104:715-18 Ag 26-S 2 '87

Nearing full employment. S. Dentzer and R. Thomas. il *Newsweek* 110:42 Jl 20 '87

Rethinking full employment. B. M. Gross. il *Nation* 244:44-6+ Ja 17 '87

Full Gospel Business Men's Fellowship International

Murph the Surf rides again [J. Murphy] J. Lombardi. il por *Esquire* 108:114-16+ N '87

Full metal jacket [film] See Motion picture reviews—Single works

Fuller, Buckminster *See* Fuller, R. Buckminster (Richard Buckminster), 1895-1983

Fuller, Graham

Combat rocker [interview with J. Strummer] il pors *Film Comment* 23:45-6+ Jl/Ag '87

Fuller, John Frederick Charles, 1878-1966

about

The tank and visions of future war. B. H. Reid. bibl il *Hist Today* 37:36-41 D '87

Fuller, John Grant, 1913-

Day of the killer tornadoes [condensed from Tornado watch #211] il map *Read Dig* 130:152-61+ My '87

Fuller, Peter, 1947-

The vivid imagery of Australia's artists. il *Archit Dig* 44:204+ S '87

Fuller, R. Buckminster (Richard Buckminster), 1895-1983

about

A Buckminster Fuller dictionary. E. J. Applewhite. il pors *Futurist* 21:24-8 S/O '87

The World Game at 20. M. Gabel. il por *Futurist* 21:20-3 S/O '87

Fuller, R. Steven

The gift of a Yellowstone Christmas. il *Natl Wildl* 26:4-11 D '87/Ja '88

Fuller, Thomas F.

A portable copy stand. il *Petersens Photogr Mag* 16:72-3 S '87

Fuller (H.B.) Company *See* H.B. Fuller Company

Fuller Brush Co.

Brushing up at Fuller [introducing mail order catalog and retail stores] il *Newsweek* 110:44 S 7 '87

Fuller Theological Seminary

Fuller Seminary releases study on the miraculous. il *Christ Today* 31:44-5 F 6 '87

Fullerton, Alex

about

Science at McDonald Observatory. R. Reeves. il pors *Astronomy* 15:6-17 Jl '87

Fulton, Robert, 1765-1815

about

Robert Fulton. C. O. Philip. bibl f il por *Antiques* 132:1132-9 N '87

Fulton County (Ga.)

County contracts

King helps create new minority contract office in Fulton County, Ga. [M. L. King III] por *Jet* 72:31 Jl 27 '87

Politics and government

Two Georgia commissioners indicted for extortion [A. R. Eaves and C. Williams] *Jet* 73:12 N 2 '87

Fulton Fish Market

Fishy business [Fulton Fish Market and the Mafia] A. A. Lappen. il *Forbes* 140:8 N 16 '87

Fumento, Michael

AIDS: are heterosexuals at risk? *Commentary* 84:21-7 N '87

Some dare call them . . . robber barons. il *Natl Rev* 39:32-3+ Mr 13 '87

Fumes

Control

Another antismog device? [controlling ozone by trapping vapors from gasoline refueling] il *U S News World Rep* 103:8 Ag 3 '87

EPA attacks vapor villain [reducing ozone pollution by trapping gasoline vapors emitted during refueling] *Mot Trend* 39:44 N '87

Funaro, Dilson

about

Brazil's would-be miracle worker. W. Woods. il por *Fortune* 115:68 Ja 5 '87

Functions

See also

Mappings (Mathematics)

Fund, John

(jt. auth) See Wooster, Martin, and Fund, John

Fund raising

See also

AIDS (Disease)—Fund raising

Baseball, Professional—Benefit games

Benefit performances

Campaign funds

Combined Federal Campaign (U.S.)

Dance—Benefit performances

Evangelical Council for Financial Accountability

Telethons

United Way of America

Ashe, Gibson raise funds for tennis, UNCF on yacht. il pors *Jet* 72:8 Ag 10 '87

Bake sales: it's simple to make them a success! W. Hood. il por *McCalls* 115:147 N '87

California kids say their calendar poses no skin problem, but their school officials say it's unsuitable [student venture in Gilroy] il *People Wkly* 27:59 My 18 '87

Detroit NAACP raises record $720,000 at Freedom banquet. il *Jet* 72:23 My 18 '87

Did Oral Roberts go too far? R. Frame. por *Christ Today* 31:43-5 F 20 '87

Financing the Great Commission [special section] il *Christ Today* 31:25-40 My 15 '87

God and Oral [brouhaha following O. Roberts's conversation with God about fund-raising techniques] T. C. Muck. *Christ Today* 31:17 Mr 20 '87

Holy hoaxers? [overzealous preachers giving Christian fund raisers a bad name] il *U S News World Rep* 102:10 Mr 23 '87

How to raise money for worthy causes. il *Sunset* 179:45-6 D '87

Marla Gibbs hosts gala Los Angeles fund-raiser [CHOICE] il pors *Jet* 71:58-60 Mr 2 '87

A Michigan sheriff turns the county jail into a high-rent hoosegow, causing quite a stir [Macomb County] il *People Wkly* 27:88-9 Je 1 '87

Penny-wise fund-raising [study by James M. Weyant] R. J. Moss. *Psychol Today* 21:12 Ja '87

Please pass the medaillons of veal [organizing a charity event] L. Gubernick. il *Forbes* 139:127 F 23 '87

A price tag on salvation [O. Roberts' plea] L. Black. *Macleans* 100:43 Mr 2 '87

Questioning tactics [results of Gallup poll on fund raising by evangelical groups] *Time* 129:70 Mr 30 '87

Spelling for dollars [school Spell-a-Thon] M. J. Valentine. *Phi Delta Kappan* 69:312-13 D '87

The state of Christian broadcasting. R. Frame. il *Christ Today* 31:48-50 Mr 20 '87

Thanks to a Detroit dee jay, even death hasn't stopped Elvis from turning out more Presleys [fake "daughter of Elvis Presley" certificates issued to raise funds for hospital; work of D. Purtan] il por *People Wkly* 28:45 Jl 27 '87

USArts: strategies for the 80's. See issues of Horizon (Tuscaloosa, Ala.)

What will Oral Roberts do next? M. Dobbin. il pors *U S News World Rep* 102:25 Mr 9 '87

Why do Americans distrust Christian fund raisers? L. Cryderman. il *Christ Today* 31:38 Ap 17 '87

Your money or his life [O. Roberts' plea for funds] R. N. Ostling. *Time* 129:63 Ja 26 '87

Anecdotes, facetiae, satire, etc.

Uncivil liberties. C. Trillin. *Nation* 244:840 Je 20 '87

Fund raising auctions *See* Auctions

Fund raising on airplanes

UNICEF's new trick: giving on the fly. *Newsweek* 110:43 Jl 27 '87

Fundamentalism

See also

Liberty Federation

Moral Majority

Catholic bishops address Protestant fundamentalism. *Christ Today* 31:54-5 D 11 '87

Going topless and other sins [Baptist row over Mercer University] B. Kantrowitz and A. Murr. il *Newsweek* 110:79-80 O 26 '87

Moderates and minicoups [Southern Baptist Convention] J. Carey. il *U S News World Rep* 103:16 N 23 '87

More ferment among Southern Baptists. K. A. Lawton. il *Christ Today* 31:46-7+ N 20 '87

Nine wins in a row [Southern Baptist Convention reelects A. Rogers] il por *Time* 129:57 Je 29 '87

The rise of Catholic fundamentalism. P. M. Arnold. il *America* 156:297-302 Ap 11 '87

SBC battles. *Christ Century* 104:992-3 N 11 '87

Southeastern Seminary: fundamentalists move in. W. H. Willimon. *Christ Century* 104:1020-1 N 18 '87

Swordplay in Sunday school [Southern Baptist indoctrination] R. R. Smith. por *Newsweek* 110:9 D 21 '87

Anecdotes, facetiae, satire, etc.

BSAT [Biblical Scholastic Aptitude Test] D. Halberstein. *New Repub* 197:12 S 14-21 '87

Fundamentalism—*cont.*

Bibliography

Giving God a hand. M. Gardner. il *N Y Rev Books* 34:17-18+ Ag 13 '87

Fundamentalism and public schools *See* Public schools and religion

Fundamentalists Anonymous

FA's legal task force. *Christ Century* 104:552 Je 17-24 '87

Funder, John W.

Adrenal steroids: new answers, new questions. bibl f *Science* 237:236-7 Jl 17 '87

Funderburgh, Anson

about

Anson Funderburgh. T. Schuller. il por *Down Beat* 54:46-7 Ja '87

Funds, Investment *See* Investment trusts

Funds, Pension *See* Pensions

Fundy, Bay of *See* Bay of Fundy

Funeral directors *See* Undertakers and undertaking

Funeral industry *See* Undertakers and undertaking

Funeral rites and ceremonies

Notes and comment [J. Baldwin's funeral] *New Yorker* 63:31 D 21 '87

India

See also

Suttee

Japan

Japan's newest perk: the corporate tomb. *Newsweek* 109:55 Mr 2 '87

Funes, Donald

Demographic changes: what meaning for arts education? *Des Arts Educ* 89:29-33 N/D '87

Fung, Teresa

Being Chinese in America. il por *Sch Update* 120:37 S 18 '87

Fung, Yuen-Kai T., and others

Structural evidence for the authenticity of the human retinoblastoma gene. bibl f il *Science* 236:1657-61 Je 26 '87

Fung shui *See* Feng shui

Fungal enzymes *See* Enzymes, Fungal

Fungal genetics

Meiotic recombination in yeast: alteration by multiple heterozygosities. R. H. Borts and J. E. Haber. bibl f il *Science* 237:1459-65 S 18 '87

Fungal spores

The electric life of plants gives fungal spores a charge [research by Charles M. Leach] S. Weisburd. il *Sci News* 132:53 Jl 25 '87

Fungi

See also

Lichens
Mildew
Mushrooms
Mutation—Fungi
Mycorrhiza
Neurospora
Slime molds
Truffles
Yeasts

Metabolism

Fungi: California's answer to selenium? [Kesterson National Wildlife Refuge] *Sci News* 132:8 Jl 4 '87

Toxic wastes? A little fungus may help. S. Budiansky. il *U S News World Rep* 103:85 N 9 '87

Fungi, Fossil

Fossil mycorrhizae: a case for symbiosis. S. P. Stubblefield and others. bibl f il *Science* 237:59-60 Jl 3 '87

Pulling each other through bad times [fossil mycorrhiza; research by Sara P. Stubblefield and others] *Sci News* 132:47 Jl 18 '87

Fungi, Pathogenic

See also

Candidiasis

Fungi feel their way to feast [bean rust fungi; research by Harvey C. Hoch and others] S. Weisburd. il *Sci News* 131:214 Ap 4 '87

Signaling for growth orientation and cell differentiation by surface topography in Uromyces. H. C. Hoch and others. bibl f il *Science* 235:1659-62 Mr 27 '87

Funicello, Annette

about

Frankie and Annette: back to the beach. E. Sherman. il pors *Ladies Home J* 104:48+ Jl '87

Once more onto the beach. R. Wolmuth. il pors *People Wkly* 28:24-7 Ag 10 '87

Funk, M. Christine

Mom, I want to have the baby. il por *Ladies Home J* 104:22+ N '87

Funk, Peter

It pays to enrich your word power. See issues of Reader's Digest

Funnies *See* Comic books, strips, etc.

Funny feet [musical] *See* Musicals, revues, etc.—Reviews—Single works

Funseth, Robert L.

U.S. refugee policy and programs for FY 1987 [statements, September 16 and 26, 1986] il *Dep State Bull* 86:78-81 D '86

Fuqua, Don

Defense industry and government: partners or antagonists? por *Aviat Week Space Technol* 127:133+ S 7 '87

Fuqua, J. B.

about

At 69, J.B. Fuqua still keeps 'em guessing. S. Ticer. il por *Bus Week* p82 N 23 '87

Fuqua, John Brooks *See* Fuqua, J. B.

Fuqua Industries, Inc.

At 69, J.B. Fuqua still keeps 'em guessing [selling Georgia Federal Bank] S. Ticer. il por *Bus Week* p82 N 23 '87

Fur

See also

Hides and skins

Fur bearing animals

See also

Badgers
Bobcats
Foxes
Otters
Seals (Animals)

Fur coats, wraps, etc.

A coyote coat for Lue. E. Park. il *Outdoor Life* 179:58-9+ F '87

Furs: a new beat . . . il *Vogue* 177:310-17 Ag '87

How to find a good fur coat without getting fleeced. il *Glamour* 85:154 O '87

Now's the time for thinking mink. T. Segal. il *Bus Week* p112 Ap 13 '87

Fur industry

Marketing

Hey, big spender [selling furs to women] K. Haynes. il *Work Woman* 12:48 Ja '87

Canada

Caesars of the wilderness [excerpt] P. C. Newman. il map *Macleans* 100:42-6+ O 12 '87

Canada's fur-trading empire [Hudson's Bay Company] P. C. Newman. il map *Natl Geogr* 172:192-229 Ag '87

Siberia (Soviet Union)

From the wilderness to Saks Fifth Avenue, the fur trail leads from the hunt to riches. M. Brower. il por *People Wkly* 27:98-100+ Ap 6 '87

United States

See Fur industry

Fur seals *See* Seals (Animals)

Fur trade *See* Fur industry

Furie, Sidney J.

about

Superman IV [film] Reviews

People Wkly il 28:8 Ag 10 '87. R. Novak

Furlaud, Richard M., 1923-

about

A tough act to follow. K. Hannon. il por *Forbes* 139:88+ Je 15 '87

Furling (Sails) *See* Sails

Furnaces

See also

Smelters

Frugal furnace [Dornback condensing oil furnace] D. Stover. il *Pop Sci* 231:45 O '87

Rocky V (the furnace) [electric heat storing furnace] V. E. Gilmore. il *Pop Sci* 230:77 F '87

When you should replace your furnace. L. Green. il *Home Mech* 83:44-9+ S '87

When your furnace or central air conditioner or water heater needs replacement. L. Green. il *Good Housekeep* 204:218+ Ap '87

Energy usage

High-efficiency furnaces. il *Consum Rep* 52:250-4 D '87

High-efficiency furnaces. il *Consum Rep* 52:28-33 Ja '87

Home heating: fundamentals and high-efficiency furnaces. M. Fillon. il *Workbench* 43:19-22 S/O '87

Home heating: high-efficiency furnaces and boilers. M. Fillon. il *Workbench* 43:18+ N/D '87

Furness, Frank, 1839-1912

about

The furniture of Frank Furness. W. Kaplan. bibl f il *Antiques* 131:1088-95 My '87

Furnishings, Household See Household furnishings

Furniss, Ronnie D.
(jt. auth) See Bourke, Walter, and Furniss, Ronnie D.

Furniture

See also
Armoires
Beds
Benches
Bookcases
Buffets, sideboards, etc. (Furniture)
Cabinets (Furniture)
Chairs
Chests
Computer furniture
Cupboards
Desks
Drawers
Kitchen cabinets
Kitchen furniture
Office furniture
Screens (Furniture)
Shelves and racks
Sofas
Tables
Upholstery
Veneers and veneering
Wicker furniture

100 ideas under $100. S. Coulter. il *Better Homes Gard* 65:63-90+ Jl '87
Heirlooms for the future [handmade furniture] il *South Living* 22:138+ F '87

Bibliography
A short history of furniture. J. Plumb. il *House Gard* 159:120+ Ap '87

Care
See Furniture—Maintenance and repair

Design
Comment [furniture making as art] G. Gordon. *Am Craft* 47:20 F/Mr '87
Designing women [A. Castelli Ferrieri] A. V. Anderson. il por *Ms* 16:26 D '87
Fish, frogs and furniture [designs of F. Saunders] il por *Workbench* 43:96 N/D '87
The hot seat in France belongs to brash designer Philippe Starck. N. Geeslin. il por *People Wkly* 27:95-6 Ja 26 '87
Inspiration for would-be designers [designs by D. Wiener] J. R. Provey. il por *Home Mech* 83:86-8 O '87
Making it yours, truly. T. Klenck. il *Pop Mech* 164:95-8 N '87
Modern conveniences. C. Vogel. il *N Y Times Mag* p136-7 D 6 '87
New directions in style [furniture designs of S. S. Lewis] H. Drohojowska. il por *Archit Dig* 44:252+ My '87
Scott Burton: Max Protetch. E. Heartney. il *Art News* 86:148+ D '87
Social seating [S. Burton's designs; cover story] N. Princenthal. bibl f il *Art Am* 75:130-7 Je '87

Exhibitions
Modern touches [Southern Furniture Market] C. Vogel. il *N Y Times Mag* p97 O 11 '87
Upholding traditional tastes [Southern Furniture Market] C. Vogel. il *N Y Times Mag* p66 Ap 5 '87

Finishes and finishing
A darker look for wicker. D. Hastings. il *South Living* 22:152+ S '87
How to get a fine furniture finish. A. Rooze. il *Fam Handyman* 37:21-2 N '87
New life for an old chair. il *Glamour* 85:318 Mr '87
Refinishing & preserving fine furniture heirlooms [work of John Stair] R. Lorenz. il *Fam Handyman* 37:54-7 Ja '87
Take the guesswork out of finishing furniture. il *Fam Handyman* 37:57-60 Jl/Ag '87
Think twice before you refinish. *South Living* 22:124-5 Jl '87

Maintenance and repair
Easy furniture fix-ups. J. Williams and J. Severson. il *Better Homes Gard* 65:50-2 Ap '87
A field guide to country antiques. L. Larason. il *Ctry J* 14:41-5 Mr '87

Painting
See Furniture, Painted

Prices
"North Carolina problem" [mail order furniture discounters] J. Merwin. il *Forbes* 140:41+ N 30 '87

Refinishing
See Furniture—Finishes and finishing

Furniture, American
See also
House decoration, American

Shaker furniture
A Duncan Phyfe bill and the furniture it documents [James Brinckerhoff's bill of sale] J. V. Sloane. bibl f il *Antiques* 131:1106-13 My '87
A field guide to country antiques. L. Larason. il *Ctry J* 14:41-5 Mr '87
The furniture of Frank Furness. W. Kaplan. bibl f il *Antiques* 131:1088-95 My '87
John Chipman, cabinetmaker of Salem, Massachusetts. P. A. Louis and D. R. Sack. il *Antiques* 132:1318-25 D '87
Philadelphia carving shops: Hercules Courtenay and his school. L. Beckerdite. bibl f il *Antiques* 131:1044-63 My '87

Collectors and collecting
Belter style. R. Christian. il pors *Americana* 15:46-50 S/O '87
The furniture [State Dept. Collection] H. Sack. il *Antiques* 132:160-73 Jl '87
Haunted house & garden [American Gothic furniture] A. K. Leopold. il *Vogue* 177:234 S '87
The installation of American furniture from the Kaufman Collection at the National Gallery of Art. W. A. Cooper. bibl f il *Antiques* 131:1096-1105 My '87
Living with antiques:
A collection of American neoclassical furnishings on the East Coast. A. M. Eckardt. il *Antiques* 131:858-63 Ap '87
A look at painted furniture. M. Jailer. il *Antiques Collect Hobbies* 92:32-6 Je '87
Made on the place [southern plain style furniture] P. Patton. il *Esquire* 108:41-2 O '87
Wright's furnishings [F. L. Wright] F. Donegan. il *Americana* 15:16+ My/Je '87

Exhibitions
American furniture [An Elegant assortment: the furniture of Duncan Phyfe and his contemporaries, 1800 to 1840 at the Museum of the City of New York] S. B. Sherrill. il *Antiques* 131:1176+ Je '87
The installation of American furniture from the Kaufman Collection at the National Gallery of Art. W. A. Cooper. bibl f il *Antiques* 131:1096-1105 My '87
Living with antiques:
A collection of early Delaware River Valley furnishings. E. D. Garrett. il *Antiques* 131:282-7 Ja '87
Museum accessions. E. H. Gustafson. il *Antiques* 131:980-1 My '87
The William Efner Wheelock Collection at the East Hampton Historical Society. J. A. Graybeal and P. M. Kenny. bibl f il *Antiques* 132:328-39 Ag '87

Reproductions
Classic furniture series [Lincoln corner cabinet] D. A. Warren. il *Workbench* 43:26-34 S/O '87
When you might prefer a copy to the real thing. B. Brophy. il *U S News World Rep* 102:44-5 Je 29 '87

Furniture, Bentwood See Bentwood furniture

Furniture, Built in
Build-in a video corner. M. Brett. il *Pop Sci* 231:76-7 D '87
Built-ins organize this master suite. il *South Living* 22:137 F '87
Everything's built in! [family room] il *South Living* 22:188 N '87
Fake right, go left [corner dresser] il *Sunset* 178:140 My '87
They built curves into the study. il *Sunset* 178:156 My '87

Furniture, Children's
See also
Cabinets (Furniture)
Chairs
Cradles
Cribs (Beds)
Tables

Make-believe kitchen for kids. B. A. Lewis. il *Better Homes Gard* 65:64+ Mr '87

Furniture, Doll See Doll furniture

Furniture, English

Collectors and collecting
Living with antiques:
A collection of eighteenth-century English furniture. W. Rieder. il *Antiques* 131:1314-25 Je '87
Rare and early [antique furniture collected by A. Csaky] E. Greene. il *House Gard* 159:162-7+ N '87

Exhibitions
See also
Hyde Park Antiques Ltd.
Kentshire Galleries Ltd.

Furniture, English—*cont.*

Reproductions

See also

Bombay Company

Classic furniture series [Chippendale tilt-top table] G. Derzinski. il *Workbench* 43:66-9+ N/D '87

English country [reproduction of washstand] H. Wicks. il *Home Mech* 83:64-8 Mr '87

Regency redux [T. Messel, designer of wood furniture] C. Aslet. il por *House Gard* 159:106+ N '87

Furniture, French

Collectors and collecting

Antiques: ormolu: opulent adornment for fine French furniture. M. M. Thomas. il *Archit Dig* 44:84-9+ F '87

Jean-Henri Riesener: furniture maker to royalty. A. Bahar. il por *Antiques Collect Hobbies* 92:39-42 N '87

Exhibitions

French decorative and fine arts [High Museum of Art exhibition entitled The elegance of Paris: furniture of the Second Empire] S. B. Sherrill. il *Antiques* 131:80+ Ja '87

Furniture, German

See also

Biedermeier furniture

Furniture, Gothic revival

Collectors and collecting

Haunted house & garden [American Gothic furniture] A. K. Leopold. il *Vogue* 177:234 S '87

Furniture, Italian

Exhibitions

The Milan forecast [Salone Internazionale del Mobile] C. Vogel. il *N Y Times Mag* p152-3+ S 13 '87

Milan's luxurious fare: classical strains, a gentler wit [Milan Furniture Fair] B. Plumb. il *Vogue* 177:104 Ja '87

Furniture, Metal

Collectors and collecting

Antiques: steel furniture. J. A. Cuadrado. il *Archit Dig* 44:178-83 N '87

Furniture, Middle Eastern

Collectors and collecting

Moroccan in Manhattan [apartment of Leon Amar] O. Bernier. il *House Gard* 159:164-7+ F '87

Furniture, Miniature

See also

Rugs and carpets, Miniature

The "modern style": furniture by Miren Tong. A. Bahar. il por *Antiques Collect Hobbies* 91:44-7 Ja '87

Vintage toys and Golden Oak [work of B. Burkey] A. Bahar. il por *Antiques Collect Hobbies* 92:46-9 S '87

Collectors and collecting

Doll house furnishings to be auctioned August 14 and 15 [collection of M. E. Newman] *Antiques Collect Hobbies* 92:36 Ag '87

Furniture, Modern *See* Furniture

Furniture, Outdoor

See also

Benches

Chairs

Tables

Best outdoor projects. il *Fam Handyman* 37:36-7 My/Je '87

The new iron rage [cast iron furniture] C. Vogel. il *N Y Times Mag* p102-5 My 17 '87

Outdoor living. G. D. Cook and others. il *Better Homes Gard* 65:33-43+ Je '87

Maintenance and repair

Outdoor furniture. *Better Homes Gard* 65:113 Ap '87

Furniture, Painted

See also

Isabel O'Neil Foundation for the Art of the Painted Finish

Going with the grain of tradition [decorative painting techniques; work of L. Pardon] S. Wood. il por *Home Mech* 83:62-3 Mr '87

Collectors and collecting

A look at painted furniture. M. Jailer. il *Antiques Collect Hobbies* 92:32-6 Je '87

Furniture, Prefabricated

New antiques [kit furniture] A. Rooze. il *Fam Handyman* 37:43-4+ Ap '87

Furniture, Rococo

Collectors and collecting

Belter style. R. Christian. il pors *Americana* 15:46-50 S/O '87

Furniture, Rustic

Build a stick bed. G. Campbell. il *Home Mech* 83:32 Ja '87

Cabin in the sky: a designer's retreat in the Montana Rockies [home of M. London] B. D. Colen. il por *Archit Dig* 44:132-9+ Je '87

The rustic furniture of Ernest Stowe. C. Gilborn. bibl f il *Antiques* 132:550-7 S '87

Straight sticks for some simple rustic artistry. il *Sunset* 179:127 D '87

Wild and woody [twig furniture] D. Mack. il por *Mother Earth News* 103:42-7 Ja/F '87

Furniture, Shaker *See* Shaker furniture

Furniture finishing *See* Furniture—Finishes and finishing

Furniture industry

See also

Bombay Company

History

Philadelphia carving shops: Hercules Courtenay and his school. L. Beckerdite. bibl f il *Antiques* 131:1044-63 My '87

Marketing

Fine furniture by phone—cheap. *U S News World Rep* 103:111 N 9 '87

"North Carolina problem" [mail order furniture discounters] J. Merwin. il *Forbes* 140:41+ N 30 '87

Furniture making *See* Furniture

Furniture polishes *See* Polishing materials

Furniture stores

See also

IKEA Svenska Forsaljnings AB

International Contract Furnishings (Firm)

Seaman Furniture Co., Inc.

Productivity trends in the furniture and home furnishings stores industry. A. S. Herman and J. E. Henneberger. bibl f il *Mon Labor Rev* 110:24-9 My '87

Furniture workers

Salaries, pensions, etc.

Furniture workers' wages higher under incentive systems. bibl f il *Mon Labor Rev* 110:26-7 N '87

Furosemide

A showdown at the shore: Bet Twice beat Alysheba in the Haskell at Monmouth, but Lasix lurked in the shadows. C. Gammon. il *Sports Illus* 67:36-8+ Ag 10 '87

Furriers *See* Fur industry

Furst, Alan

A coast of many moods. il map *50 Plus* 27:78-82 O '87

Gardens: glacial legacy: a multilevel landscape in British Columbia. il *Archit Dig* 44:202-7 Ap '87

Vancouver Island. il *50 Plus* 27:52-5 Ap '87

Furtwängler, Wilhelm, 1866-1954

about

The symphonic Furtwängler. W. H. Youngren. il *Atlantic* 259:77-80 Ja '87

Furukawa, Susumu

about

Will Lotus overrun Microsoft's Japanese garden? B. Buell. il por *Bus Week* p76 Ap 13 '87

Fury, Kathleen

Ask the best cat in the world. il *50 Plus* 27:84 S '87

My kitchen, my self. il por *50 Plus* 27:80 Ag '87

The sneaky woman's garden. il *50 Plus* 27:90 Je '87

This working life. See issues of Working Woman

Fusco Corporation

Fusco Corporation: the power of the personal computer [access to mainframe data] J. Blackford. il *Pers Comput* 11:135+ My '87

Fuselli, Carlo

Sight and sound: a hopeless wodge: unscrambling the international TV picture. *Opera News* 52:36+ Ag '87

Fusidic acid

"On the shelf" AIDS drug in clinical trial. D. M. Barnes. *Science* 238:276 O 16 '87

Fusion, Magnetic *See* Magnetic fusion

Fusion, Nuclear *See* Nuclear fusion

Fusion reactors *See* Nuclear reactors

Fuss, Eduardo

Worlds within worlds: a fantasy of leaves and air trapped by pond ice [photographs] il *Audubon* 89:34-9 Ja '87

Fussell, Betty Harper

Peru's sophistication. il *N Y Times Mag* p49-50 F 1 '87

Fusselle, Warner

The voices of summer [excerpt from Baseball: a laughing matter] *Sport Mag* 78:65 Jl '87

Futons

Futon sofa bed. K. Collier. il *Fam Handyman* 37:76-80 O '87

Futrell, Mary Hatwood

Restructuring teaching: a call for research. *Educ Dig* 53:2-5 S '87

Futrell, Mary Hatwood—*cont.*
about
Futrell says hiring blacks will end teacher shortage. por *Jet* 72:30 Ap 13 '87

Futter, Deborah
about
Bantam's Deborah Futter wins Tony Godwin Award. por *Publ Wkly* 231:26 F 13 '87

Future
See also
Forecasting
Nineteen hundred and eighty-eight
Nineteen hundred and nineties
Twenty-first century
Two thousand (Year)
Two thousand one (Year)
Two thousand seven (Year)
Two thousand seventeen (Year)
World Future Society
World Game
Child likes [children's images of the future; study by Ruthanne Kurth-Schai] D. Sobel. il *Omni* 10:30+ N '87
Children's visions of the future [Weekly reader survey] L. Johnson. il por *Futurist* 21:36-40 My/Je '87
Future phobia: take charge of your tomorrow. S. Glass. il *Teen* 31:58+ Jl '87
Future view. See issues of The Futurist beginning October 1984
Time travel [imagining one's future as a therapeutic tool; work of J. Hart] B. Lawren. il *Omni* 10:20+ N '87
Viewing the future as a marketable product. D. L. Johnson. il *Futurist* 21:60 Ja/F '87
Anecdotes, facetiae, satire, etc.
The New First Lady. R. Cohen. *New Yorker* 63:36-7 My 18 '87

Future Homemakers of America
Mr. President [first male national president T. Lucas] B. Greene. il por *Esquire* 107:29-30 Ja '87

Future life
See also
Eschatology
Resurrection
Why I believe there is life after death. N. V. Peale. il *Read Dig* 130:139-40 My '87

Futures *See* Commodity futures; Hedging (Finance); Interest rate futures

Futures for Children (Organization)
"Mother-in-chief" with a mission [work of R. Frazier] J. Page. il por *McCalls* 114:138 S '87

Futurist (Periodical)
Using The futurist. T. Willard. *Futurist* 21:7 Ja/F '87

Futurology *See* Forecasting

G

G, Kenny
about
Kenny G blows up the pop charts with a hot and sax-y jazz sound. il por *People Wkly* 28:47 Ag 17 '87

G., Alberto Quiroga *See* Quiroga G., Alberto

G-CSF
Upping cell counts: on clinical trial. D. D. Edwards. *Sci News* 132:396 D 19-26 '87

G. Gordon Liddy Academy of Corporate Security and Private Investigation
Where tough guys go to get tougher: Fort Liddy. D. Blum. il por *N Y* 20:64-71 Ap 13 '87

G. Heileman Brewing Co., Inc.
Heileman's Russell Cleary: brawling for breweries. M. D. Oneal. il por *Bus Week* p68+ Mr 2 '87
Is Carling Black Label worth a trip from Australia? [A. Bond's bid for G. Heileman Brewing] M. D. Oneal. il por *Bus Week* p33-4 S 21 '87

G. Jackson & Sons
Master of plaster. C. Aslet. il *House Gard* 159:204-5+ N '87

G N Associates
The birth of a business. M. Slavin. il pors *Work Woman* 12:31-3 Ag '87

G proteins
A G protein directly regulates mammalian cardiac calcium channels. A. Yatani and others. bibl f il *Science* 238:1288-92 N 27 '87

Second wind for second-messenger research: how do G proteins and external signals influence intracellular activity? C. Vaughan. il *BioScience* 37:642-6 O '87

GABA (Gamma-aminobutyric acid) *See* Aminobutyric acid

Gabel, Medard
The World Game at 20. il por *Futurist* 21:20-3 S/O '87

Gabelli, Mario
about
Famous artists. R. Phalon. il pors *Forbes* 139:102+ Je 1 '87
A Grahamite finds value in the rubble [interview] J. P. Newport, Jr. il por *Fortune* 116:212 N 23 '87
Hot wires. T. Jaffe. *Forbes* 140 Sp Issue:402 O 26 '87

Gabelli & Company
A Grahamite finds value in the rubble [interview with M. Gabelli] J. P. Newport, Jr. il por *Fortune* 116:212 N 23 '87

Gabelli Equity Trust
Famous artists [C. Allmon, M. Gabelli and M. Zweig] R. Phalon. il pors *Forbes* 139:102+ Je 1 '87

Gabelli Value Partners
A cigar-chomping venture capitalist named Francine [F. Sommer] P. Finch. por *Bus Week* p101 Jl 20 '87

Gable, Robert, and Rogers, Vincent
Taking the terror out of research. il *Phi Delta Kappan* 68:690-5 My '87

Gabler, Edna M.
Dustbusting: how they build the cleanest rooms on earth. il *Archit Rec* 175:128-33 Ap '87

Gablik, Suzi
Dream space. il *Art Am* 75:132-3+ Mr '87

Gabo, Naum, 1890-1977
about
Gabo's progeny. C. Nadelman. il por *Art News* 86:123-7 D '87

Gabriel, Peter
about
Big time. S. Pond. il pors *Roll Stone* p36-8+ Ja 29 '87
Flying solo: stars take off alone. il pors *Teen* 31:80-1 My '87
The groove carries on. J. Cocks. il por *Time* 129:80 F 2 '87

Gabriel, Trip
On the edge of greatness: Olympian Pirmin Zurbriggen [cover story] il pors *N Y Times Mag* p10-13+ D 27 '87
Rolling thunder. il *Roll Stone* p73-6 Jl 16-30 '87
Why wed? The ambivalent American bachelor. il *N Y Times Mag* p24-9+ N 15 '87

Gaby—a true story [film] *See* Motion picture reviews—Single works

Gadd Gang (Musical group)
The Gadd Gang: not just the same old stuff. G. Kalbacher. il *Down Beat* 54:16-19 O '87

Gaddafi, Muammar *See* Qaddafi, Muammar al-, 1942-

Gaddis, John Lewis
How the cold war might end. il *Atlantic* 260:88-92+ N '87

Gaddis, William, 1922-
Szyrk v. Village of Tatamount et al. *New Yorker* 63:44-50 O 12 '87
Trickle-up economics: JR goes to Washington. il *N Y Times Book Rev* 92:29 O 25 '87
about
Recognizing Gaddis. L. Auchincloss. il por *N Y Times Mag* p36+ N 15 '87

Gade, Daniel W.
Rodrigues. il maps *Focus* 37:34-5 Fall '87

Gadgets
The case for a cheap dog [folly of putting your trust in things] C. Gordon. por *Macleans* 100:39 Je 15 '87
The Revenger offers drivers a shot at life in the blast lane [inventors D. McMahan and M. Grubbs] il por *People Wkly* 28:179 D 14 '87

Gadomski, Michael P.
Aspens. il *Conservationist* 41:24-6 Ja/F '87

Gaelic football *See* Irish football

Gaelic language
Anecdotes, facetiae, satire, etc.
Exit laughing. E. Zern. il *Field Stream* 92:138 O '87

GAF Corp.
Cornering Borg-Warner. J. E. Ellis. il por *Bus Week* p39 Ap 13 '87
GAF's Heyman: the hunter could soon become the hunted. A. L. Cowan. il por *Bus Week* p74-5 Mr 2 '87

GAF Corp.—*cont.*
What changed Sam Heyman's mind about LBOs. J. A. Byrne. il por *Bus Week* p31 S 21 '87
Will GAF cash in its Borg-Warner chips—or up the ante? [leveraged buyout led by Merrill Lynch] J. E. Ellis. *Bus Week* p34-5 Ap 27 '87

Gaffney, Eugene S., and others
Modern turtle origins: the oldest known cryptodire. bibl f il *Science* 237:289-91 Jl 17 '87

Gaffney, Frank J., Jr.
SDI: incentive for arms control [with discussion] *Cent Mag* 20:33-8 S/O '87

Gaffney, James
Hagar & her sisters: precedent for conduct. il *Commonweal* 114:240-2 Ap 24 '87
Our bishops and our economy. *America* 156:44-9 Ja 24 '87

Gaffs, Fishing *See* Fishing—Equipment

Gage, Diane, and Hibsch, Marcia
Are you picking up your parents' bad habits? il *Seventeen* 46:132+ Mr '87

Gage, Joan
My mother's mystery. il pors *N Y Times Mag* p36-7+ My 17 '87

Gage, Martha, 1911-1985
about
My mother's mystery. J. Gage. il pors *N Y Times Mag* p36-7+ My 17 '87

Gage, Suzann
about
Facing the fear: help for women with AIDS. R. L. Bray. il por *Ms* 15:31 My '87

Gage Park (Ill.)
Juvenile justice, Administration of
White Ill. youth sentenced for torching black home [L. Kalafut] *Jet* 72:18 Mr 30 '87
Race relations
White Ill. youth sentenced for torching black home [L. Kalafut] *Jet* 72:18 Mr 30 '87

Gages
See also
Strain gages
Tire pressure gages
Gauges eliminate the guesswork [diesel boats] E. Dennis. il *Mot Boat Sail* 160:95-6 Ag '87

Gagliani, Oliver
about
Meet the masters. D. Brooks. il *Petersens Photogr Mag* 16:30-2 Jl '87

Gagnon, Claude
about
The kid brother [film] Reviews
Macleans il 100:60 O 19 '87. C. Bell

Gahan, Peter
about
Thou shalt not covet thy neighbor's lawn, so grab a papal sprinkler and let us spray. il pors *People Wkly* 27:123 Je 8 '87

Gai lohn *See* Chinese broccoli

Gaia hypothesis
Gaia: the life of a theory. R. Monastersky. *Sci News* 132:364 D 5 '87

Gailey, Phil
Sam Nunn's rising star. il pors *N Y Times Mag* p24-9+ Ja 4 '87

Gaillard, Slim
about
Claude Bolling/Slim Gaillard. F. Bouchard. il por *Down Beat* 54:51 Ja '87

Gaines, Charles
Landscapes of color. il por *Archit Dig* 44:44+ Je '87

Gaines, John Ryan
about
Da Vinci drawing tops 'triumphant' Gaines sale. R. W. Walker. *Art News* 86:16 Ja '87

Gaines, Lee, 1914-1987
about
Obituary
Jet il por 72:56 Ag 10 '87

Gaines, Steven D., and Roughgarden, Jonathan
Fish in offshore kelp forests affect recruitment to intertidal barnacle populations. bibl f il *Science* 235:479-81 Ja 23 '87

Gaines, William M.
about
The secret is in the repackaging. G. Slutsker. il por *Forbes* 139:230+ Je 15 '87

Gaines-Carter, Patrice
Sisterhood is powerful. por *Essence* 18:176 My '87

Gaither quintuplets *See* Quintuplets

Gaithersburg (Md.)
Firefighters
Md. fire chief reprimanded for telling a racist joke [R. J. Wilson] *Jet* 71:5 Ja 19 '87
Race relations
Md. fire chief reprimanded for telling a racist joke [R. J. Wilson] *Jet* 71:5 Ja 19 '87

Gakkyusha (Firm)
Money from misery. H. Katayama. il por *Forbes* 139:256 Je 15 '87

Galactic clusters *See* Galaxies

Galactic Resources Ltd.
A gold miner helps Pickens chip away at Newmont [R. M. Friedland cut into Ivanhoe Partners deal] S. D. Atchison. il por *Bus Week* p36 Ag 31 '87

Galactosidases
In situ detection of β-galactosidase in lenses of transgenic mice with a γ-crystallin/*lacZ* gene. D. R. Goring and others. bibl f il *Science* 235:456-8 Ja 23 '87

Galanis, John Peter
about
The net at last? J. A. Conway. il *Forbes* 139:8 My 18 '87

Galapagos Islands
See also
Birds—Galapagos Islands
Wildlife—Galapagos Islands
Description and travel
The anomalous Galápagos [cover story] F. Bavendam. il *Oceans* 20:26-35 N/D '87
Photographs and photography
A living museum. N. Farb. il map *N Y Times Mag* p40-3 Mr 29 '87

Galassi, Jonathan
Beautiful loser [poem] *Nation* 244:158 F 7 '87
(tr) *See* Montale, Eugenio, 1896-1981. Little testament
(tr) *See* Montale, Eugenio, 1896-1981. Wind and flags

Galax (Va.)
Music festivals
See Music festivals—Virginia

Galaxies
See also
Magellanic clouds
Milky Way
Nebulae
Radio sources (Astronomy)
Advanced computing for science [simulating collisions between galaxies] P. Hut and G. J. Sussman. bibl (p184) il *Sci Am* 257:144-8+ O '87
Arcs, birth and a disk in the sky [arcs of light curving around clusters of galaxies] M. D. Lemonick. il *Time* 129:59 Ja 19 '87
The biggest mystery in the cosmos [luminous arcs between galaxies; work of Roger Lynds] B. Weber. il *N Y Times Mag* p70 Jl 19 '87
Birth announcements [disk of particles around Beta Pictoris; possible new radio galaxy 3C 326.1; luminous arcs encircling distant galaxies] *Sci Am* 256:60+ Mr '87
Bright infrared galaxies. il *Sky Telesc* 73:29-30 Ja '87
Cosmic mergers [work of A. Toomre] S. J. Nadis. il *Omni* 9:24+ Ag '87
Dark shadows among the galaxies [Malin 1] D. E. Thomsen. il *Sci News* 131:308 My 16 '87
Deep-sky wonders. W. S. Houston. See issues of Sky and Telescope
Discovering M31's spiral shape. G. H. de Vaucouleurs. il por *Sky Telesc* 74:595-8 D '87
The formation of galaxies. J. Silk. bibl il *Phys Today* 40:28-35 Ap '87
Gas jet seen projecting from Seyfert Galaxy [Markarian 315; work of John W. MacKenty] *Astronomy* 15:84-5 Ja '87
Giant galactic arcs [research by Roger Lynds and Vahe Petrosian] L. J. Robinson. il *Sky Telesc* 73:379 Ap '87
Globular clusters in the Coma cluster of galaxies [CCD observations by William E. Harris] il *Sky Telesc* 74:346-7 O '87
How do spiral galaxies spiral? [cover story] N. Comins and L. A. Marschall. il *Astronomy* 15:6-23 D '87
Is that all there is? [edge of the visible universe; research by J. Anthony Tyson and Patrick Seitzer] il *Discover* 8:10+ S '87
The large-scale structure of the universe gets larger—maybe [research by R. Brent Tully] M. M. Waldrop. il *Science* 238:894 N 13 '87
Large warp detected in spiral galaxy [NGC-4013 in Ursa Major] *Astronomy* 15:92-3 N '87

Galaxies—*cont.*

The long voyage from home [cover story] R. P. Burruss. il por *Futurist* 21:29-33 S/O '87

Luminous arcs discovered between galaxies [galactic clusters; research by Roger Lynds and Vahe Petrosian] D. E. Thomsen. il *Sci News* 131:36 Ja 17 '87

Luminous arcs dwarf the galaxies [research by Roger Lynds and Vahe Petrosian] M. M. Waldrop. il *Science* 235:631-2 F 6 '87

M-87: describing the indescribable [cover story] J. Kanipe. il *Astronomy* 15:6-13 My '87

M101, the Ursa Major spiral. J. Corder. il *Sky Telesc* 73:678-9 Je '87

Markarian 348: a tidally disturbed Seyfert galaxy [cover story] S. M. Simkin and others. bibl f il *Science* 235:1367-70 Mr 13 '87

Massive, dark galaxy found in void [Malin 1] *Astronomy* 15:75-6 S '87

Massive objects in galactic nuclei may be black holes. P. H. Andersen. bibl il *Phys Today* 40:22 O '87

Matter flow from a Seyfert nucleus [work of Jean W. Goad and John S. Gallagher] *Sci News* 132:254 O 17 '87

NGC-262 found to be the largest isolated galaxy. il *Astronomy* 15:74 Je '87

Observing spring galaxies with binoculars. C. Crossen. il *Astronomy* 15:62-7 My '87

Polar-ring galaxies. il *Sky Telesc* 74:459-60 N '87

Polar-ring galaxies yield cosmological insights. *Astronomy* 15:87+ O '87

Ring around a gravitational lens [luminous arcs between galaxies; work of Vahe Petrosian and Roger Lynds] D. E. Thomsen. *Sci News* 132:326 N 21 '87

Ring around the galaxy [polar ring galaxies] K. Hartley. il *Sci News* 132:282-3 O 31 '87

Secrets of galaxy clusters. D. H. Smith. il *Sky Telesc* 73:377-8 Ap '87

Signs of black holes [work of Douglas Richstone and Alan Dressler] A. Fisher. il *Pop Sci* 231:14+ N '87

Spirals from order and chaos. D. H. Smith. il *Sky Telesc* 74:136-8 Ag '87

Strings that blow bubbles in the cosmos. D. E. Thomsen. *Sci News* 131:22 Ja 10 '87

Tracing M81's spiral arms. M. Kaufman. il *Sky Telesc* 73:135-7 F '87

What's in the Bootes void? [work of Robert P. Kirshner and others] il *Sky Telesc* 74:232-3 S '87

A young dwarf galaxy . . . and a giant [Haro 2 and Malin 1] il *Sky Telesc* 74:122-4 Ag '87

Evolution

The young Virgo Cluster? il *Sky Telesc* 74:578 D '87

Motion in line of sight

Are we all in the grip of a Great Attractor? M. M. Waldrop. il *Science* 237:1296-7 S 11 '87

The Great Attractor [research by Alan Dressler] il *Sky Telesc* 74:119-20 Ag '87

Heavenly drifters. M. Bartusiak. il *Omni* 9:22 My '87

The large-scale streaming of galaxies. A. Dressler. bibl (p120) il *Sci Am* 257:46-54 S '87

Large-scale structure, streaming and galaxy formation. P. H. Andersen. bibl il *Phys Today* 40:19-21 O '87

Ripples in the universal Hubble flow. P. H. Andersen. il *Phys Today* 40:17-19 O '87

Where are we going? T. Ferris. il *Sky Telesc* 73:486-90 My '87

Photographs and photography

Shooting galaxies from the suburbs. C. Gibbons. il *Astronomy* 15:42-7 F '87

Six-meter views of M33. D. H. Smith. il *Sky Telesc* 74:140-1 Ag '87

Radial velocity

See Galaxies—Motion in line of sight

Spectra and spectroscopy

Black holes: coming to a galaxy near you. il *Discover* 8:10 O '87

Bright infrared galaxies may be young quasars. il *Astronomy* 15:78-9 Ap '87

Cosmic collisions [IRAS data] S. P. Maran. *Nat Hist* 96:22+ Ag '87

The giant arcs are gravitational mirages [theory of Roger Lynds and Vahe Petrosian] M. M. Waldrop. il *Science* 238:1351-2 D 4 '87

Hearts of darkness: evidence grows that black holes lurk at the center of galaxies. J. Horgan. il *Sci Am* 257:30+ O '87

The most distant "normal" galaxy [work of S. G. Djorgovski] il *Sky Telesc* 73:365-6 Ap '87

Quantized galaxy redshifts. W. G. Tifft and W. J. Cocke. il *Sky Telesc* 73:19-21 Ja '87

Quasars in the making? [link with infrared galaxies; research by David B. Sanders and others] il *Sky Telesc* 74:577-8 D '87

Star formation and IRAS galaxies. D. A. Allen. il *Sky Telesc* 73:372-4 Ap '87

Warm infrared galaxy discovered behind SMC [work of Jay Frogel and Jonathan H. Elias] *Astronomy* 15:65-6 Ag '87

Galbaugh, Glen

Excludable from justice. *America* 156:315-16 Ap 18 '87

Galbraith, Evan

Softening up the Germans. il *Natl Rev* 39:34-5 My 22 '87

Galbraith, John Kenneth, 1908-

The 1929 parallel. il *Atlantic* 259:62-6 Ja '87

Can the Russians reform? *Harpers* 274:52-5 Je '87

Radical, teacher, technician. *Natl Rev* 39:34-5 S 11 '87

Wild about Harry. il por *Wash Mon* 19:44-5 Je '87

about

First encounters. E. Sorel and N. C. Sorel. il *Atlantic* 259:61 My '87

Galdikas, Birutė

about

Interview. D. Lessem. por *Omni* 9:76-8+ Jl '87

Gale, George

Do we need opera? *World Press Rev* 34:60 S '87

Gale, Iain, and Irvine, Susan

A welcoming home [excerpt from Laura Ashley style] il *Redbook* 170:83-9 N '87

Gale, Katherine

In praise of marriage. por *Essence* 17:135 F '87

Gale, Robert Peter

about

A battle against deadly dust. C. Gorman. il por *Time* 130:66 N 16 '87

Chernobyl's high cost [interview] J. Bennett. il por *Macleans* 100:6-8 Jl 6 '87

Interview. M. C. Smith. il pors *Omni* 10:110-12+ O '87

Gale, William

about

William Gale & Son, New York silversmiths. R. A. Green. il *Antiques Collect Hobbies* 91:18-20 F '87

Galeano, Eduardo H., 1940-

The Americas: enlightenment and enterprise [excerpt from Memory of fire]; tr. by Cedric Belfrage. *Harpers* 274:24+ F '87

Galeener-Moore, Laverne, 1930-

about

The skeleton in the courthouse. C. E. Kraft. il *Antiques Collect Hobbies* 92:68-71 S '87

Galeev, Albert A.

(jt. auth) See Sagdeyev, Roald Zinnurovich, and Galeev, Albert A.

Galef, David

Incident in the park. il *N Y Times Mag* p56 F 8 '87

Galella, Ron

about

Paparazzo. D. K. Mano. *Natl Rev* 39:60-1 Mr 13 '87

Galen, Michele

Nowhere to run from radon. il *Nation* 244:180-2 F 14 '87

Galena (Ill.)

Historic houses, sites, etc.

A river town that thrives on its history. P. T. Reynolds. il *Americana* 14:56-60 Ja/F '87

Galerie 360

King's Road ransom. V. Becker. il pors *House Gard* 159:76+ My '87

Galerie Schmit

French virtuosity at Galerie Schmit. J. A. Cuadrado. il por *Archit Dig* 44:86+ Je '87

Galesi, Francesco

about

Francesco Galesi isn't used to losing. P. Finch. il por *Bus Week* p114 My 4 '87

Galette *See* Pastry

Galiano, Henry

about

Music boxes and Maxilla & Mandible. H. Bridges. il *Gourmet* 47:28+ S '87

Galiber, Yetta W.

about

Yetta Galiber: Christmas every day of the year. il pors *Ebony* 43:27-30 D '87

Galie, Larry

about

Guarding the till at LTV. M. Kuntz. il por *Forbes* 139:90 Ja 26 '87

Galileo flights to Jupiter *See* Space flight to Jupiter

Gallagher, Hugh Gregory

about

A stirring passage from the horseback era to the TV age [interview] M. Dubrow. il *People Wkly* 27:32-3 Mr 23 '87

Gallagher, Jack *See* Gallagher, John P.

Gallagher, John P.

about

A special interest in Dome. P. C. Newman. il por *Macleans* 100:48 Ap 27 '87

Gallagher, Joseph

The 'silence' of Pius XII: again. il *America* 156:279-81 Ap 4 '87

Gallagher, Lawrence J., and Lowe, Wendy

10 retreats for the restless. il *Esquire* 107 Summ Traveler:T30-T37 Ap '87

Gallagher, Maggie

For want of a nail. il *Natl Rev* 39:32+ N 20 '87

Here comes the judge. *Natl Rev* 39:33+ D 18 '87

Maggie in Ollieland. il *Natl Rev* 39:42+ N 6 '87

The new pro-life rebels. *Natl Rev* 39:37-9 F 27 '87

What men really want. *Natl Rev* 39:39-40 My 22 '87

Womb to let. il *Natl Rev* 39:27-30 Ap 24 '87

Gallagher, Michael

Looking north at a world of self. *America* 157:82-3 Ag 15-22 '87

Sidestepping The challenge of peace. il *Commonweal* 114:9-13 Ja 16 '87

about

Living in sin with nuclear arms. J. M. Wall. *Christ Century* 104:155-6 F 18 '87

Gallagher, Michael

"Am I old enough to be a parent?"; ed. by Kate Manning. il por *Redbook* 169:34+ My '87

Gallagher, Michael S.

The future (?) of legal services for the poor. il *America* 156:395-6 My 16 '87

Gallagher, Tess

"And you ate an apple, and I ate a pear". il *Seventeen* 46:97-9 D '87

about

Love, literature and solitude link mutually admiring authors Raymond Carver and Tess Gallagher. A. Chambers. il pors *People Wkly* 28:81-2+ N 23 '87

Gallagher, Winifred

"Boy, could I use a . . ." (a) drink, (b) pill, (c) joint. If you filled in the blank you could be a preaddict. *Mademoiselle* 93:210-11+ O '87

High anxiety. il *Roll Stone* p34-5+ Mr 12 '87

To the manner born. il *Roll Stone* p56+ N 19 '87

Gallant, Mavis

Déclassé [story] il *Mademoiselle* 93:116+ F '87

Dédé [story] *New Yorker* 62:28-34 Ja 5 '87

Let it pass [story] *New Yorker* 63:38-50+ My 18 '87

about

An interview with Mavis Gallant. P. H. Samway. *America* 156:485-7 Je 13 '87

Gallant-Stokes, Trudy

Venturing out on your own. il *Black Enterp* 17:49-52 Ja '87

Gallas, Despina

about

A black prince of the church. G. Clifford. il pors *People Wkly* 28:30-5 S 28 '87

Gallati, Barbara Dayer

The watercolors of John La Farge. bibl f il *Antiques* 132:1290-301 D '87

Gallbladder

See also

Bile acids and salts

Diseases

See also

Gallstones

Gallego, Julian

An art of gilt and pathos. il *Courier* 40:14-17 S '87

Gallen, John J., and Lopresti, James J.

Penance in crisis. *America* 157:217-22 O 10 '87

Galleries and museums, Art *See* Art galleries and museums

Gallery of Texas History

Listening to Texas history. il *South Living* 22:60 Ap '87

Galles, Gary M.

The power of positive procrastination. *Read Dig* 131:9-10 Ag '87

Gallese, Liz Roman

"I don't want to work anymore": the new career dropouts. il *Mademoiselle* 93:268-9+ Mr '87

Galleys (Boat kitchens) *See* Boats and boating—Galleys

Galleys (Ships)

See also

Triremes

Gallico, Paul, 1897-

The awful secret of Monsieur Bonneval [story] il *Read Dig* 130:143-6 My '87

"I love ya, baby" [story] il *50 Plus* 27:70-1+ Jl '87

Gallie, Daniel R., and others

In vivo uncoating and efficient expression of foreign mRNAs packaged in TMV-like particles. bibl f il *Science* 236:1122-4 My 29 '87

Gallier House (New Orleans, La.) *See* New Orleans (La.)—Historic houses, sites, etc.

Gallium arsenide

Ballistic electrons in semiconductors. M. Heiblum and L. F. Eastman. il *Sci Am* 256:102-11 F '87

Chemical coat helps semiconductor prospects. A. L. Robinson. il *Science* 238:27-9 O 2 '87

Gallium arsenide transistors. W. R. Frensley. bibl (p116) il *Sci Am* 257:80-7 Ag '87

ITT Avionics focuses on EW production with investment in GaAs technology. il *Aviat Week Space Technol* 126:98+ F 16 '87

ITT invests $20 million to obtain gallium-arsenide MMIC benefits. il *Aviat Week Space Technol* 126:111-13 F 16 '87

Light switch [work of André Mysyrowicz and others] *Sci Am* 256:74-5 Mr '87

Speeding to a gallium arsenide record. il *Sci News* 131:25 Ja 10 '87

Gallman, Vanessa

Holidays and single moms. il *Essence* 18:102 D '87

Gallo, Diane

New York's Finger Lakes. il *Travel Holiday* 168:44-9 Jl '87

Gallo, Giuseppe, 1954-

about

Giuseppe Gallo at Sperone Westwater. H. Cotter. il *Art Am* 75:188 My '87

Gallo, Miguel Mujica *See* Mujica Gallo, Miguel

Gallo, Nick

Adolescence: challenges of the teen years [cover story] il *Curr Health 2* 14:3-9 O '87

Cosmetic surgery today. il *Better Homes Gard* 65:94+ Ap '87

Gallo, Paul

about

Speed lighting: Paul Gallo prefers the fast track [cover story] A. M. Hale. il por *Theatre Crafts* 21:34-9+ Ap '87

Gallo, Robert C.

The AIDS virus. bibl (p128) il map *Sci Am* 256:46-56 Ja '87

First word. por *Omni* 10:10 D '87

about

Gallo gets itchy feet, looks to academe. W. Booth. *Science* 238:1223 N 27 '87

Marketing an AIDS expert. R. Rhein, Jr. and M. Maremont. *Bus Week* p38+ D 14 '87

Maxwell may back Gallo. B. J. Culliton. *Science* 238:1643 D 18 '87

Gallo (E. & J.) Winery *See* E. & J. Gallo Winery

Gallo Institute (Proposed)

Marketing an AIDS expert. R. Rhein, Jr. and M. Maremont. *Bus Week* p38+ D 14 '87

Galloway, David

From Bankfurt to Frankfurt: a cash & carry renaissance. il *Art Am* 75:152-9 S '87

The perils of public sculpture. il *Art Am* 75:37-9+ D '87

Report from Germany. il *Art Am* 75:31-5+ Je '87

Galloway, James N., and others

Acid rain: China, United States, and a remote area. bibl f il maps *Science* 236:1559-62 Je 19 '87

Galloway cattle *See* Cattle

Gallstones

Nutritional aspects

Rapid weight loss may cause gallstones [research by Jay Marks] *Prevention* 39:23 My '87

Therapy

Gallstone lithotripsy. C. SerVaas. il *Saturday Evening Post* 259:100+ Ap '87

Getting rid of gallstones. C. Schaeffer. *Changing Times* 41:22+ N '87

Lithotriptor therapy coming of age. *Sci News* 132:187 S 19 '87

Gallup, Alec

(jt. auth) See Gallup, George, 1930-, and Gallup, Alec

Gallup, Alec, and Clark, David L. (David Louis), 1929-
The 19th annual Gallup poll of the public's attitudes toward the public schools. *Phi Delta Kappan* 69:17-30 S '87

Gallup, George, 1930-, and Gallup, Alec
What successful people have in common [condensed from The great American success story] *Read Dig* 130:110-12 Je '87

Galtung, Johan
The real Star Wars threat. *Nation* 244:248-50 F 28 '87

Galveston (Tex.)
Architecture
Turning toward the water [remodeled ranch-style house on Lake Madeline] E. Wood. il *South Living* 22:66-8 Jl '87
Historic houses, sites, etc.
Galveston revival: Victorian gems amid castles of sand. C. Barrington. il *Travel Holiday* 168:54-9 D '87

Galvin, Brendan
An American naturalist writes to a Londoner, 1758 [poem] *New Yorker* 63:38 My 25 '87
The patience of white birches [poem] *New Yorker* 63:36 Mr 16 '87

Galvin, Robert W.
The power of information [address, June 15, 1987] *Vital Speeches Day* 53:647-9 Ag 15 '87

Gambel's quail shooting See Quail shooting

Gambia
See also
National parks and reserves—Gambia

Gamble, Edward, and Koch, Christof
The dynamics of free calcium in dendritic spines in response to repetitive synaptic input. bibl f il *Science* 236:1311-15 Je 5 '87

Gamble, Willie, Jr.
about
Georgia murder conviction overturned: black jurors struck for racial reasons. *Jet* 72:40 Ag 3 '87

Gambler's Book Shop (Las Vegas, Nev.) See Booksellers and bookselling—Nevada

Gambling
See also
Bingo
Horse race betting
Lotteries
Poker (Game)
Steve Wynn on high rollers. D. Seligman. il pors *Fortune* 115:116 Mr 2 '87
Laws and regulations
Las Vegas North: buying chips from the Chippewa [Vegas Kewadin casino in Mich.] J. A. Seamonds. il *U S News World Rep* 102:31 F 9 '87
Moral and religious aspects
Lottery foes target public policy [proposed Indiana state lottery] B. L. Rohrig. *Christ Century* 104:396-7 Ap 29 '87
The myth of the money tree [state lotteries] C. W. Colson. il *Christ Today* 31:64 Jl 10 '87
Psychological aspects
My cousin, the gambler. K. L. Adelman. *Read Dig* 131:84-8 D '87
My husband is irresponsible. L. Werner. il *Ladies Home J* 104:12+ N '87
Taxation
Taxing a gambler's loss [Canadian embezzler B. Molony] D. Jenish. il por *Macleans* 100:34+ D 14 '87
Canada
A B.C. tourism gamble [refitting Victoria-Seattle ferries with gambling casinos] il *Macleans* 100:29 Ap 20 '87
Great Britain
Anecdotes, facetiae, satire, etc.
Against all odds [betting on the election] D. Seligman. il *Fortune* 116:101-2 Jl 20 '87
United States
See Gambling

Gambling casinos See Casinos

Gambling literature
See also
Booksellers and bookselling—Gambling literature

Gambling machines
Oaklander wins $1 mil. on Reno slot machine [P. Anderson] il por *Jet* 72:52 S 21 '87

Gambling machines industry
See also
Bally Manufacturing Corp.
International Game Technology

Gamboa, Diane
about
Diane Gamboa. L. Goldman. il *Art News* 86:52+ My '87

Gamboni, Dario, 1955-
about
Art vandals: why do they do it? J. Dornberg. il por *Art News* 86:102-9 Mr '87

Gambrell, Jamey
Art capital of the third coast. il *Art Am* 75:186-203 Ap '87
Five from Spain. il pors *Art Am* 75:160-71 S '87
Texas: state of the art. il *Art Am* 75:114-31+ Mr '87

Game
See also
Cooking—Game
Hunting
Transportation
Easy game sled [use of mini-boggans] N. Strung. *Field Stream* 92:110 O '87

Game, Dressing of
Fast field dressing. N. Strung. il *Field Stream* 92:156 My '87
The way to quality venison [field dressing] M. Stickney. il *Conservationist* 42:44-7 N/D '87

Game bird shooting
See also
Duck shooting
Goose shooting
Grouse shooting
Mourning dove shooting
Partridge shooting
Pheasant shooting
Pigeon shooting
Quail shooting
Water bird shooting
Woodcock shooting
The new game in Africa [Botswana] J. F. Walker. il *Forbes* 139:94+ Ap 20 '87
Routine matters [upland bird hunting] C. Michaels. il *Field Stream* 92:54-5+ O '87

Game birds
See also
Water birds

Game calls See Animal calling

Game guns See Shotguns

Game laws
See also
Game wardens
Poaching
Wildlife Legislative Fund of America
Are we managing the outdoors to death? N. Strung. il *Field Stream* 91:58-9+ F '87
Ducks and disaster. G. Reiger. il *Field Stream* 92:14+ O '87
Refuge hunting: perverse use or logical harvest? M. Satchell. il *U S News World Rep* 102:26 Ja 12 '87
California
See also
California. Dept. of Fish and Game
Lions—mountain or mounted? [California cougar] K. Glass. il *Sierra* 72:12-13 Jl/Ag '87
Florida
Endangered species? Load the shotgun! [K. Ghumman accused of shooting red cockaded woodpeckers] R. L. Di Silvestro. il *Audubon* 89:12 S '87

Game preserves
See also
Shooting preserves
Kenya
Facing Mount Kenya and Kilimanjaro, too. F. D. Brown. il *Black Enterp* 17:66-7 Ap '87
Rhythms of survival [Masai Mara Game Preserve] W. Eddy. il map *Natl Parks* 61:21-3 S/O '87

Game protection See Wildlife conservation

Game shows See Television broadcasting—Game shows

Game theory
See also
Simulation games in education
The game of chicken may lead to nuclear war [views of Steven Brams and Marc Kilgour] il *Discover* 8:10 Ap '87

Game wardens
A warden's story [Audubon Warden R. Chandler of Kissimmee Prairie Sanctuary] F. Graham. il pors *Audubon* 89:105-21 Mr '87

Games
See also
APBA Pro League Baseball Game
Billiards
Bingo
Checkers (Game)
Chess
Croquet
Darts (Game)

Games—See also—*cont.*
  Dominoes
  Educational games
  Frisbee (Game)
  Go (Game)
  Hacky Sack (Game)
  Lazer Tag (Game)
  Management games
  Play
  Puzzles
  Rotisserie League Baseball
  Skill cranes (Games)
  Solarquest (Game)
  Spinjammer (Game)
  Strat-O-Matic Baseball (Game)
  Toy and game industry
  Video games
  War games
  Word games
  World Game
8 silly little games (and why they're so important) [playing with baby] C. Medvescek. il *Parents* 62:92-4+ Je '87
Games children play. D. F. Bjorklund and B. Bjorklund. il *Parents* 62:164 Je '87
Ready, set, learn! 10 games to grow on [cover story] R. Seaman. il *Parents* 62:84-6+ Jl '87
Games, Mathematical *See* Mathematical recreations
Games, Theory of *See* Game theory
Games in art
Game figurines [board and table games] R. R. Radcliff. il *Antiques Collect Hobbies* 92:32-3 D '87
Gametchu, Bahiru
Glucocorticoid receptor-like antigen in lymphoma cell membranes: correlation to cell lysis. bibl f il *Science* 236:456-61 Ap 24 '87
Gametes
    See also
    Spermatozoa
Gametrics Ltd.
Choosing baby's gender [research by Ronald Ericsson and Allan Abramovitch] N. Underwood. *Macleans* 100:66 N 9 '87
Gamma ray astronomy
Extragalactic gamma-ray bursters? [views of Bohdan Paczynski] *Sky Telesc* 74:9-10 Jl '87
Gamma-ray bursters might be as distant as quasars [views of Bohdan Paczynski] *Astronomy* 15:83-4 Ja '87
A gamma-ray pinhole camera. W. J. Wild. il *Sky Telesc* 74:126-7 Ag '87
Getting vibes from cosmic strings [research by Arif Babul and others] *Sci News* 131:345 My 30 '87
A hint of gamma rays; Blank about Mont Blanc [supernova 1987A] D. E. Thomsen. *Sci News* 132:286 O 31 '87
New class of celestial bursters [Soft Gamma Repeater 1806-20] *Sci News* 132:219 O 3 '87
Two gamma-ray sources and ancient guest stars. Z.-R. Wang. bibl f il *Science* 235:1485-6 Mr 20 '87
Very high energy gamma-ray binary stars. R. C. Lamb and T. C. Weekes. bibl f il *Science* 238:1528-34 D 11 '87
Gammon, Bryan
Evoking an era. il *Petersens Photogr Mag* 15:42-3 Ja '87
Gammon, Clive
Boning up for a battle. il pors *Sports Illus* 66:46-9 Mr 2 '87
The lady in pink. il *Sports Illus* 67:54-8 Ag 24 '87
One real honey of a dandy. il pors *Sports Illus* 66:58+ My 4 '87
A showdown at the shore: Bet Twice beat Alysheba in the Haskell at Monmouth, but Lasix lurked in the shadows. il *Sports Illus* 67:36-8+ Ag 10 '87
Toe-to-toe for the title. il *Sports Illus* 66:54 Je 22 '87
Tuning up for Tyson. il pors *Sports Illus* 67:48-50+ D 14 '87
White nights, Red faces. il *Sports Illus* 67:76-8+ O 26 '87
Gammons, Peter
The best money can buy. il *Sports Illus* 67:30-2+ D 14 '87
Billy the Kid rides again. il pors *Sports Illus* 67:18-19 Ag 3 '87
Birds on the wing [cover story] il *Sports Illus* 67:22-7 O 5 '87
The Bucs don't stop here. il *Sports Illus* 67:22-4 S 28 '87
Close to a clincher. il *Sports Illus* 67:22-5 S 21 '87
Game 6. il *Sports Illus* 66:110-14+ Ap 6 '87

Inside baseball. See issues of Sports Illustrated published during the baseball season beginning April 14, 1986
Lefty's last stand. il por *Sports Illus* 66:48-9 Mr 30 '87
Look what Santa brought. il *Sports Illus* 67:64-5 D 21 '87
A man who can't say no. il pors *Sports Illus* 67:16-17 D 21 '87
Midseason baseball report with statistical analysis by Bill James. il *Sports Illus* 67:26-34 Jl 20 '87
More than a media Darling. il pors *Sports Illus* 66:56-8+ Ap 6 '87
O.K., drop that emery board. il *Sports Illus* 67:34-7 Ag 17 '87
Oh, for those glory days of yesteryear. il *Sports Illus* 67:42-4+ Ag 10 '87
Out! il *Sports Illus* 67:20-5 O 12 '87
Playing hardball. por *Sports Illus* 66:108 Ja 12 '87
Replete with Bronx cheer. il *Sports Illus* 67:24-5 Jl 13 '87
Return of the Royal nonesuch. il pors *Sports Illus* 66:28-9 Je 8 '87
Septembers to remember. il *Sports Illus* 67:40-3+ S 14 '87
To know 'em is to fear 'em. il *Sports Illus* 66:24-6+ Je 22 '87
A tough day at the office. il pors *Sports Illus* 67:42-4 Jl 6 '87
Twin wins [cover story] il *Sports Illus* 67:46-53 O 26 '87
What a win for the Twins [cover story] il *Sports Illus* 67:40-2+ O 19 '87
What ever happened to the strike zone? il *Sports Illus* 66:36-40+ Ap 6 '87
Will Bo be a hit or a miss? il pors *Sports Illus* 66:36-8 My 4 '87
(ed) See Jackson, Reggie. "We have a serious problem that isn't going away"
Gamson, Annabelle
        about
Close encounters. T. Tobias. il *N Y* 20:84-5 F 16 '87
Gance, Abel
        about
Napoleon [film] Reviews
    Stereo Rev il 52:111 Mr '87. S. Simels
Gandhi, Mahatma, 1869-1948
        Anecdotes, facetiae, satire, etc.
Gandhi's girls. A. Levine. il pors *Wash Mon* 19:25-7 Jl/Ag '87
Gandhi, Mohandas Karamchand *See* Gandhi, Mahatma, 1869-1948
Gandhi, Rajiv, 1944-
        about
End of an enchanted honeymoon. E. W. Desmond. il por *Time* 129:40 Ap 6 '87
For Gandhi, everything turns sour. M. Satchell. il por *U S News World Rep* 102:34-5 Ap 6 '87
Gandhi at midterm. P. H. Kreisberg. *Foreign Aff* 65:1055-76 Summ '87
Gandhi under the gun. D. D'Monte. il *New Leader* 70:8-10 Je 29 '87
Letter from New Delhi. V. Mehta. il *New Yorker* 62:52+ Ja 19 '87
No longer Mr. Clean. por *Time* 130:20 Ag 10 '87
Rajiv Gandhi stumbles. H. Anderson. il por *Newsweek* 109:38 F 23 '87
Rajiv Gandhi's honeymoon is over. K. Thapar. il por *World Press Rev* 34:40-1 Je '87
Shades of a cover-up. il por *Macleans* 100:22-3 Ap 20 '87
Singh a song of discord. F. Willey. il por *Newsweek* 110:28 Ag 3 '87
'Such a dance of death'. F. Willey. il *Newsweek* 110:34 Jl 20 '87
"We don't have the bomb" [interview] P. Gupte. il pors *Forbes* 139:156+ My 18 '87
Gandolfo, Carol
        about
Instant success . . . ! [cover story] J. Gray. il *Petersens Photogr Mag* 15:28-9+ Mr '87
Gandy, Joan W., and Gandy, Thomas H.
Steamboats on the Mississippi. il *Am Hist Illus* 22:36-49 Mr '87
Gandy, Thomas H.
(jt. auth) See Gandy, Joan W., and Gandy, Thomas H.
Ganglia *See* Nerve cells
Ganglion cells *See* Nerve cells
Gangs
    See also
    Westies (Gang)

Gangs—*cont.*

Dealing with youth gangs in the schools. D. Stover. *Educ Dig* 52:30-3 F '87

The Insane Dragons meet the Unknown Vice Lords [Youth for Christ's work with gangs in Chicago] G. Lewis. il *Christ Today* 31:10+ N 20 '87

L.A. law: gangs and crack. G. Hackett and M. A. Lerner. il *Newsweek* 109:35-6 Ap 27 '87

Life and death with the gangs [Los Angeles] J. D. Hull. il *Time* 130:21-2 Ag 24 '87

Canada

Young and merciless [Chinese gangs in Vancouver] J. O'Hara. il *Macleans* 100:59 O 26 '87

Gangsters *See* Mafia; Organized crime

Gann, Paul

about

Stand up to AIDS. M. G. Stoddard. il pors *Saturday Evening Post* 259:54-5 S '87

Gannett Co., Inc.

Gatsby with a typewriter [A. Neuharth] D. Hutchins. il por *Fortune* 115:92 Ja 5 '87

Grant's back & Gannett's got him [deal with G. Tinker] J. Baker. il por *Channels* 7:40-3 Jl/Ag '87

The growing gets tougher. S. N. Chakravarty. il pors *Forbes* 139:68+ Je 15 '87

Ingram launches retail print ad campaign. A. Symons. *Publ Wkly* 232:35 Jl 10 '87

Invasion of the Gannettoids. P. Weiss. il *New Repub* 196:18-20+ F 2 '87

Gannon, Frank

Bret, like, brainstorms [excerpt from Vanna Karenina] *Harpers* 275:35-6 D '87

Flowers of evil: ask Charles Baudelaire. il por *Atlantic* 260:44 S '87

Her way. *New Yorker* 62:24 Ja 5 '87

I know what I'm doing [excerpt from Yo, Poe] *Harpers* 274:28+ My '87

Gannon, Kathy

Caught in the cross fire. il *Progressive* 51:14 Ja '87

Gannon, Robert

Going star-crazy. il *Earth Sci* 40:16-17 Fall '87

Ganoe, William H.

Letter from Brighton. il *Space World* X-12-288:21-6 D '87

Payloads. See issues of Space World beginning June 1987

Gans, Jonathan B.

Out-island builder. il map *Mother Earth News* 104:48-55 Mr/Ap '87

Gants, Bob

A necessary response. il *Consum Res Mag* 70:15-17 My '87

Gantt, Harvey

about

Gantt seeks third term as Charlotte, N.C., mayor. il por *Jet* 72:32 Jl 20 '87

Gap, Inc.

Bridging the Gap. J. Sherman. il *Work Woman* 12:58 Je '87

Correcting the Gap. T. Jaffe. *Forbes* 140:246 N 2 '87

Exploring a new Hemisphere. J. B. Copeland. il *Newsweek* 110:57 S 14 '87

Falling into the Gap [stock declines rapidly] N. R. Gibbs. il *Time* 130:54 O 5 '87

He fell out with father [D. Fisher] il por *U S News World Rep* 103:56-7 Jl 6 '87

Most improved. il *Forbes* 139:207 Ja 12 '87

Put the zipper on the back. H. Rudnitsky. il por *Forbes* 139:89-90 Je 29 '87

Shock of the news [analysts overestimate earnings] J. Crudele. il *N Y* 20:19 O 5 '87

Win one, lose one. A. A. Lappen. il *Forbes* 140:8 O 19 '87

Gap junctions *See* Junctions (Physiology)

Garage doors

Deep doors add to design. il *South Living* 22:121 Je '87

Weatherstrip garage door. G. Branson. il *Fam Handyman* 37:54 F '87

Control

Genie Genius garage door opener. B. Gould. il *Workbench* 43:18-19 Mr/Ap '87

Maintenance and repair

6 steps to keep garage doors rolling. A. W. Lees. *Pop Sci* 230:84 Ap '87

Replace a worn garage door. J. Drako. il *Workbench* 43:85-6 Mr/Ap '87

Windows

Interference patterns on garage door windows. C. F. Bohren. il *Weatherwise* 40:266-70 O '87

Garage sales

Anecdotes, facetiae, satire, etc.

Sale of goods. M. Kenyon. il *Gourmet* 47:122+ N '87

Garages

Basic framing techniques. C. J. De Groote. il *Fam Handyman* 37:52-3+ Ap '87

Side-wall storage in narrow garage. il *Sunset* 178:152+ My '87

Garages, Municipal

Pier 40: a remembrance [closing of Manhattan parking garage built on unsound pier] *New Yorker* 63:31-2 S 14 '87

Garages, Remodeled

Garden office . . . it was an old single-car garage. il *Sunset* 178:184 Ap '87

Great garage makeover [bedroom/sitting room] S. Wood. il *McCalls* 114:62-4 Ap '87

Turn a garage into living space (I). D. A. Warren. il *Fam Handyman* 37:29-35 Ja '87

Turn a garage into living space (II). D. A. Warren. il *Fam Handyman* 37:27-32+ F '87

Turning garage into home office without banishing the car. il *Sunset* 178:56-7 Ja '87

Garasich, John

about

How to choose a pool and someone to build it [interview] R. Cogan. il por *Fam Handyman* 37:76-7 My/Je '87

Garavani, Valentino *See* Valentino

Garbage *See* Refuse and refuse disposal

Garbage as fuel *See* Refuse as fuel

Garbage barges *See* Barges

Garbage cans *See* Refuse containers

Garbage containers *See* Refuse containers

Garbage disposers *See* Refuse disposers

Garbage trucks *See* Refuse trucks

Garber, Angie

about

On the land for good. R. Wilkins. il pors *Christ Today* 31:12-13 Je 12 '87

Garber, Fern

A lawyer tells women what they should know about divorce. *Good Housekeep* 205:64+ Jl '87

Garber, Steve

Going first class on the Titanic. il por *Christ Today* 31:25-7 N 20 '87

Garber, Terri

about

Lean and leggy [cover story] L. Kleinmann. il pors *Health* 19:50-3 Ag '87

Garbus, Martin, 1934-

Crime and publishing. il *Publ Wkly* 232:20-2 D 4 '87

Garcia, Andy

about

Andy Garcia, a gunslinger on the right side of The Untouchables, who turns out to be a hit, man. M. Neill. il pors *People Wkly* 28:93-4 Ag 3 '87

Untouchable Andy. E. Pooley. il por *N Y* 20:24 Je 15 '87

Garcia, Carmen

"Help! My baby is drowning!"; ed. by Elaine Fein. il por *Redbook* 169:26+ Je '87

García, Cristián Godoy- *See* Godoy-García, Cristián

Garcia, Jerry

about

Jerry Garcia. il por *People Wkly* 28:72-3 D 28 '87-Ja 4 '88

García, Joaquín Torres- *See* Torres-García, Joaquín, 1874-1949

García-Barrio, Constance

Desktop banking. il *Essence* 18:138 My '87

García-España, Felipe

(jt. auth) See Massey, Douglas S., and García-España, Felipe

García Márquez, Gabriel, 1928-

Cuba libre, sans Coke. *World Press Rev* 34:34 N '87

García Pérez, Alan

about

The bankers' hero. A. Cockburn. *Nation* 245:402 O 17 '87

Debt, democracy and terrorism in Peru. D. P. Werlich. bibl f *Curr Hist* 86:29-32+ Ja '87

Judging García. L. Rogers. il *World Press Rev* 34:46 O '87

Peru's bad boy is starting to look like a desperate man. J. Ryser. il por *Bus Week* p55 Ag 17 '87

Shining Path burns with a hotter flame. B. Durr. il *U S News World Rep* 102:35 My 25 '87

Garcia Ruiz, Jesus F.

'Let the days come in'. il *Courier* 40:7 Ag '87

Gardaz, Emile

Pilgrims of the southern cross. *Courier* 39:8 D '86

Gardels, Nathan
(jt. auth) See Luczywo, Helena, and Gardels, Nathan
Garden borders
Wildflowers for a sunny border. H. R. Phillips. il *Rodale's Org Gard* 34:72-7+ My '87
Garden carts See Carts
Garden catalogs See Catalogs, Seed and plant
Garden centers (Retail trade)
Make the most of your garden center. J. Burnett. il *Rodale's Org Gard* 34:23-7 Jl '87
Garden design
See also
Landscape gardening
Art: gardens by design. S. Drummond. il *Archit Dig* 44:164-9+ Ap '87
Garden equipment
See also
Garden hose
Hoes
Lawn equipment
Tractors
Don't bag 'em, bale 'em! [leaf baler] L. A. Lowe. il *Rodale's Org Gard* 34:69-71 S '87
Feeding a garden shredder. J. Burnett. il *Rodale's Org Gard* 34:22+ S '87
Finding the best equipment. S. O. Daniels. il *Rodale's Org Gard* 34:7 S '87
The finer points of tool buying. R. Engman. il *Flower Gard* 31:10-12 O/N '87
Garden tools. R. Kimber. il *Ctry J* 14:8-10 Ap '87
Machines in the garden. M. Ferrara. il *Home Mech* 83:52-6 Ap '87
Practical or just pretty, these gift ideas help give a garden its character. il *Sunset* 179:183-4 D '87
Seeds 'n' greetings [gardening gifts] J. Burnett. il *Rodale's Org Gard* 34:77-81 D '87
Tools for the toughest garden jobs. il *Sunset* 179:247-8 N '87
Well equipped. J. Ruttle. See issues of Rodale's Organic Gardening beginning May 1986 through July 1987
What's new for your lawn and garden. T. O. Bakke. See occasional issues of Popular Science beginning June 1986
Yard power. il *Pop Mech* 164:101-2+ Ag '87
Maintenance and repair
See also
National Equipment Servicing Dealers Association
He keeps a barrel for cleaning tools. il *Sunset* 179:218 O '87
Important advice [storing gasoline-powered tools] il *Flower Gard* 31:38 O/N '87
Storage
See also
Sheds
Garden storage concealed in the side yard. il *Sunset* 178:174 F '87
Testing
Get ready for fall. il *Workbench* 43:60-1 S/O '87
Leaf Eater makes cleanup fun [Vornado Leaf Eater] il *Rodale's Org Gard* 34:23 S '87
Small and lightweight: a new trend in equipment. il *Flower Gard* 31:38-9 Je/Jl '87
Garden exhibits
Garden events [title varies] See issues of Sunset (Central edition)
On the calendar. See issues of Flower and Garden
Southern garden events. See issues of Southern Living
Garden follies (Architecture) See Follies (Architecture)
Garden fountains See Fountains
Garden gates See Gates
Garden gloves See Gloves
Garden hose
Click-together, hose-end devices. il *Flower Gard* 31:48 Ap/My '87
Long, thin buckets. R. Kimber. il *Ctry J* 14:61-2 Jl '87
Garden houses, shelters, etc.
See also
Arbors
Pergolas
Sheds
Tea houses
All-year garden pavilion in Albuquerque. il *Sunset* 178:182-3 Ap '87
Behind the lattice: the garden's work and storage place. il *Sunset* 179:144 S '87
Canvas top for a garden gazebo. il *Sunset* 178:170 My '87
A gazebo of your own. L. Hyde and L. Hyde, Jr. il *Ctry J* 14:21-6 Ag '87

Outbuilding on a budget [converted kennel] D. Wotruba. il *Workbench* 43:40-2 Mr/Ap '87
Ready for dinner on top of the spa [Los Angeles gazebo] il *Sunset* 178:133 Je '87
Summer fun in a gazebo. il *Workbench* 43:42-6 Jl/Ag '87
Garden literature
See also
Gardens and gardening—Bibliography
Publishers and publishing—Garden literature
Gardening for love [southern market bulletins; excerpt] E. Lawrence. bibl il por *Rodale's Org Gard* 34:28-31 O '87
Authorship
Garden writers, classic and contemporary [E. Lawrence and F. Rushing] B. Summer. *Publ Wkly* 231:40 Mr 20 '87
'I've never seen a dazzling rose': the bossy approach to garden writing [work of D. G. Hessayon] I. Shenker. il por *N Y Times Book Rev* 92:15 My 31 '87
Garden markets See Farmers' markets
The garden of earthly delights [drama] See Clarke, Martha, 1944?-
Garden of Eden See Eden
Garden pesticides See Pesticides
Garden pools
Building a garden pond using fiberglass. il *Sunset* 178:134+ Ap '87
A manmade pond with natural beauty. il *South Living* 22:62 S '87
Garden records
Garden gate. S. O. Daniels. il *Rodale's Org Gard* 34:6 F '87
Garden rooms
From glass house to our house: three centuries of indoor/outdoor rooms in a new book to inform, inspire [Living under glass] B. Plumb. il *Vogue* 177:218 Ap '87
A minor miracle in lattice. il *Sunset* 178:112-13 My '87
Garden sheds See Sheds
Garden steps
How to build durable, compatible garden steps. B. A. Branson. il *Flower Gard* 31:56 Je/Jl '87
Steps solved the problem. il *South Living* 22:55 Ag '87
Garden symphylans
Control
Symphilid solutions. S. Solomon. il *Rodale's Org Gard* 34:80+ O '87
Garden therapy See Gardens and gardening—Therapeutic use
Garden tours
Garden Week in Charlottesville. T. Weeks. il *Gourmet* 47:66-71 Ap '87
Garden tractors See Tractors
Garden walks See Walks (Paths)
Garden walls
Put color where you want it with wall planters. T. E. Eltzroth. il *Flower Gard* 31:28+ Ap/My '87
What can a window do for a garden wall? il *Sunset* 179:76-7 Jl '87
Gardeners
Regeneration gardener. See issues of Rodale's Organic Gardening beginning January 1987
Health and hygiene
Allergies? There's no reason why you can't garden. K. Wilson. il *Rodale's Org Gard* 34:21-4 Ag '87
Gardening See Gardens and gardening
Gardening as a profession See Horticulture as a profession
Gardens and gardening
See also
Aged—Gardens and gardening
America the Beautiful Fund
Botanical gardens
Bulbs
Catalogs, Seed and plant
Cold frames
Container gardens and gardening
Fertilizers and manures
Flats, etc. (Horticulture)
Flower gardens and gardening
Garden centers (Retail trade)
Grafting
Greenhouses
Handicapped—Gardens and gardening
Hedges
Herbs
High-altitude gardens and gardening
Hillside gardens and gardening
Hydroponics
Landscape gardening

Gardens and gardening—See also—*cont.*
Lawns
Meadow gardening
Miniature gardens and gardening
Mulching
Organic gardens and gardening
Plant propagation
Plants—Protection
Pruning
Sculpture gardens and parks
Seeding
Seeds
Shade gardens and gardening
Shrubs
Spraying and dusting
Telephone in gardening
Tillage
Vegetable gardens and gardening
Watering of gardens, lawns, etc.
Weeds
Wildflower gardens and gardening
Window gardens and gardening
Calendar. See issues of Rodale's Organic Gardening through July 1987
Constitution gardening. W. Shipman. il *Ctry J* 14:14 Ap '87
Dr. Ellen's gardening tips. E. Henke. *Good Housekeep* 204:225-6 Ap '87
Easy does it ideas. See issues of Flower and Garden
Garden American. F. McGourty. por *Rodale's Org Gard* 34:111-12 D '87
Garden gate [projects linked with the Constitution's bicentennial] S. O. Daniels. il *Rodale's Org Gard* 34:6 Mr '87
Garden uses for old tires. G. Abraham and K. Abraham. il *Flower Gard* 31:32 Je/Jl '87
Gardener's log. See issues of Better Homes and Gardens
Gardening in small spaces [garden of Sarah and Virginia Weatherly] D. A. Jimerson. il *Better Homes Gard* 65:92-5 F '87
Gardening with your regional editor. See issues of Flower and Garden
Gardens to visit [public gardens in the U.S.] il *Flower Gard* 31:24-30+ Ag/S '87
Getting the most from your garden. E. Henke. il *Saturday Evening Post* 259:96+ S '87
Great moments in gardening. R. Rodale. il *Rodale's Org Gard* 34:18-20 Je '87
In our own back yard. J. P. Baumgardt. See issues of Flower and Garden
It's what's happening . . . See issues of Flower and Garden
Letters to our garden editors [questions and answers] See issues of Southern Living
The loafer's garden. B. Keating. il *50 Plus* 27:104+ Ap '87
[Month] in your garden. See issues of Sunset (Central edition)
[Month] notes. See issues of Flower and Garden
Our picks for '87: the best new flowers and vegetables. D. A. Jimerson and J. A. McKeon. il *Better Homes Gard* 65:41-5 Ja '87
The seasons of the garden. G. Williams and P. Williams. See issues of The Mother Earth News beginning July/August 1985
Test garden update [raised beds] D. A. Jimerson and J. A. McKeon. il *Better Homes Gard* 65:34 Ja '87
What's new for American families in '87. il *Better Homes Gard* 65:22 Ja '87
Where our roots are. C. Fenyvesi. por *Rodale's Org Gard* 34:102-3 S '87

Anecdotes, facetiae, satire, etc.
The sneaky woman's garden. K. Fury. il *50 Plus* 27:90 Je '87

Bibliography
Books for gardeners. il *Flower Gard* 31:64-6 O/N '87
Gardening. A. Lacy. il *N Y Times Book Rev* 92:32+ D 6 '87
Gardening. A. Lacy. il *N Y Times Book Rev* 92:14 My 31 '87
Gardening books. P. Hagan. il *Americana* 15:51-3 Jl/Ag '87
Summer bounty. H. Mitchell. il *House Gard* 159:46+ Ag '87

Equipment
See Garden equipment
Exhibitions
See Garden exhibits
History
Down the garden path to history; The search for authenticity [preservation of America's horticultural heritage] M. Horn; C. Fenyvesi. il *U S News World Rep* 102:60-1 Je 1 '87
Insect control
See Insect control
Lighting
The magic of night lighting. R. Mabes. il *Flower Gard* 31:52-4+ Ap/My '87
Night lights [work of Artistic Lighting] S. M. L. Aronson. il *House Gard* 159:56+ F '87
Pest control
See Pest control
Photographs and photography
Great gardens! M. D. Glass. il *Ladies Home J* 104:100-5 Jl '87
Soil preparation
See also
Humus
Study and teaching
See also
School gardens and gardening
Aids and devices
See also
Videotapes—Gardening use
Therapeutic use
Why gardening is good for your health. J. Meade. il *Prevention* 39:59-64 Ja '87
Alabama
See also
Bellingrath Gardens
British Columbia
See also
Vancouver (B.C.)—Gardens and gardening
Gardens: glacial legacy: a multilevel landscape in British Columbia [created by Bill and Anne Peters] A. Furst. il *Archit Dig* 44:202-7 Ap '87
California
See also
Long Beach (Calif.)—Gardens and gardening
San Francisco (Calif.)—Gardens and gardening
Gardening in winter. K. R. Gessert. il *Rodale's Org Gard* 34:49-53 N '87
Connecticut
Cultivating romance [J. Saladino's garden] E. Greene. il *House Gard* 159:166-73+ My '87
Garden generosity [M. Ley's garden] S. Eddison. il *House Gard* 159:142-7+ Je '87
Reshaping a corner of Connecticut [R. Page designs garden for G. Stutz] K. Whiteside. il *House Gard* 159:152-5+ Jl '87
Florida
See also
Jacksonville (Fla.)—Gardens and gardening
New Port Richey (Fla.)—Gardens and gardening
Walt Disney World (Fla.)—Gardens and gardening
France
See also
Deauville (France)—Gardens and gardening
Green architecture [La Mormaire] F. Champin. il *House Gard* 159:162-71+ Mr '87
Georgia
See also
Atlanta (Ga.)—Gardens and gardening
Great Britain
December at Great Dixter [excerpt from The year at Great Dixter] C. Lloyd. il *Archit Dig* 44:84+ D '87
Fantasy bestowed on form [gardens at Shute House] A. Tree. il *House Gard* 159:190-7+ Ap '87
The flowering hayfield. M. Rothschild. il por *Archit Dig* 44:24+ Ja '87
The force of nature [East Anglian garden] G. Greer. il por *House Gard* 159:66+ N '87
Garden American. F. McGourty. por *Rodale's Org Gard* 34:111-12 D '87
Rare species [G. S. Thomas, overseer of the gardens of the National Trust] H. Mitchell. il por *House Gard* 159:56+ O '87
The sweet smell of Sussex [rock star B. Ferry's garden] J. Bowes-Lyon. il por *House Gard* 159:188-95 N '87
Transatlantic transplant [influence of American designer L. Roper] J. Brown. il por *House Gard* 159:90+ Je '87
Italy
See also
Bellagio (Italy)—Gardens and gardening

Gardens and gardening—Italy—*cont.*
Gardens: plotting an alpine cliffhanger: the Bagatti Valsecchi villa above Lake Como. M. Spark. il por *Archit Dig* 44:124-9+ F '87
Villar Perosa. M. Agnelli. il *House Gard* 159:144-53+ S '87

Long Island (N.Y.)
Down the garden path [F. Niven's garden] C. Vogel. il *N Y Times Mag* p68-71 Je 28 '87
A painter's garden. R. Dash. il *House Gard* 159:100-11 Ag '87

Louisiana
See also
Baton Rouge (La.)—Gardens and gardening

Maine
Gardens: enhancing the Maine aspect. S. M. Alsop. il por *Archit Dig* 44:172-7 Mr '87

Maryland
See also
Baltimore (Md.)—Gardens and gardening

Morocco
See also
Marrakesh (Morocco)—Gardens and gardening

New Jersey
See also
Cherry Hill (N.J.)—Gardens and gardening
North Plainfield (N.J.)—Gardens and gardening
Gardens: autumn fields [W. Chandoha's garden] C. Kittredge. il por *Archit Dig* 44:170-5 S '87

New Mexico
Gardening the Zuni way [waffle gardens help beat the heat] C. A. Doherty. il *Rodale's Org Gard* 34:62-4 Ag '87

New York (State)
See also
Old Westbury Gardens
A garden heritage [estate called the Meadows] U. G. Dietz. il *House Gard* 159:176-9+ S '87

North Carolina
The garden is their delight [small walled garden] il *South Living* 22:64 N '87
Wing Haven [garden and bird sanctuary of E. Clarkson] K. Whiteside. il *House Gard* 159:166-73+ Je '87

Oregon
See also
Portland (Or.)—Gardens and gardening
Oregon Eden. J. W. S. Platt. il *House Gard* 159:142-9+ F '87

Pennsylvania
Gardens: Dans la Forêt: Japanese inspiration in Pennsylvania [designed by Hiroshi Makita for Jack Miller] E. B. Steiner. il *Archit Dig* 44:118-23+ Jl '87

Southern States
See also
Southern Garden History Society
How southern gardens grow. D. Fell. il map *Travel Holiday* 167:44-9 Mr '87
The southern garden. See issues of Southern Living

Soviet Union
Home gardens in the Soviet Union. K. R. Gessert. il *Rodale's Org Gard* 34:57-8+ Mr '87

Spain
See also
Alhambra (Granada, Spain)—Gardens
Generalife (Granada, Spain)—Gardens

Texas
See also
Houston (Tex.)—Gardens and gardening

United States
See Gardens and gardening

Virginia
See also
Monticello (Va.: Estate)—Gardens
Williamsburg (Va.)—Gardens and gardening
Garden Week in Charlottesville [Historic Garden Week throughout Virginia] T. Weeks. il *Gourmet* 47:66-71 Ap '87

Western States
Just in case it's another dry winter. il *Sunset* 179:210 O '87

Wisconsin
See also
Madison (Wis.)—Gardens and gardening

Gardens and gardening, Colonial
Re-creating a seventeenth-century garden [Whipple House, Ipswich, Mass.] A. Leighton. il *House Gard* 159:20+ Jl '87

Gardens and gardening, English
Create an English country garden [views of M. Inabnit] A. Davis. il por *Home Mech* 83:60-1 Je '87

Fields of color [J. Thouron's flower gardens in the Brandywine Valley] D. M. Stone. il *House Gard* 159:68-77+ Ag '87

Gardens and gardening, Japanese
See also
Bonsai
Gardens: Dans la Forêt: Japanese inspiration in Pennsylvania [designed by Hiroshi Makita for Jack Miller] E. B. Steiner. il *Archit Dig* 44:118-23+ Jl '87
A Japanese garden in Jacksonville. il *South Living* 22:92 Ap '87

Gardens and gardening in art
Art: gardens by design. S. Drummond. il *Archit Dig* 44:164-9+ Ap '87

Gardens of stone [film] See Motion picture reviews—Single works

Gardiner, John Eliot
about
Gardiner's magnificent Bach Passion. S. Lincoln. por *Stereo Rev* 52:81 Jl '87

Gardiner, John Rolfe
Game farm [story] *New Yorker* 63:36-42 S 21 '87
World after dark [story] *New Yorker* 62:28-34 Ja 26 '87

Gardiner, Peter R., and others
Identification and isolation of a variant surface glycoprotein from Trypanosoma vivax. bibl f il *Science* 235:774-7 F 13 '87

Gardiner, Rockie
Horoscope. See issues of Vogue beginning July 1984

Gardner, Arlene
about
Maybe it's not the freezer of Turin, but Arlene Gardner says she sees Jesus on her G.E. il por *People Wkly* 27:80 Je 29 '87
A modern miracle. il *Esquire* 108:159-61 D '87

Gardner, David P.
The Pacific century. *Science* 237:233 Jl 17 '87

Gardner, Denise C.
about
Real-estate management made easy. J. Wechsler. il por *Work Woman* 12:70+ My '87

Gardner, Gary
about
Soft Sheen president-CEO elected new AHBAI chair. por *Jet* 73:25 O 12 '87

Gardner, James
Dispelling clouds. *Commonweal* 114:599-601 O 23 '87
Picasso's motif. *Commentary* 83:56-9 My '87
A pleasant walk through. il *Commonweal* 114:356+ Je 5 '87

Gardner, James C.
Three lessons for living [adaptation of address, May 24, 1986] il *Read Dig* 130:185-7 Mr '87

Gardner, Janet
Answers at last? il *Nation* 244:460-2 Ap 11 '87

Gardner, Jermaine
about
Blind boy, 3, learns to play 50 songs on piano. D. M. Cheers. il pors *Jet* 72:22-3 My 25 '87
Blind piano player, 3, visits Stevie Wonder. il pors *Jet* 72:18 Je 22 '87
Blind piano prodigy, age 4, gets free facial surgery. il por *Jet* 72:24 S 14 '87
Blind since birth and barely 4, Jermaine Gardner happily hits all the right keys—and heartstrings. K. Hubbard. il pors *People Wkly* 27:53+ Je 22 '87

Gardner, Martin, 1914-
Giving God a hand. il *N Y Rev Books* 34:17-18+ Ag 13 '87
Isness is her business. il *N Y Rev Books* 34:16-19 Ap 9 '87

Gardner, Paul
Auction signals: how to bid like an insider. il *Art News* 86:101-5 F '87
The envelope, please . . . Who deserves more time in the spotlight? Who should be hooked off the stage? The experts cast their votes. il *Art News* 86:167-71 N '87
The old master. il por *Art News* 86:120-3 S '87
SoHo: downtown boomtown. il *Art News* 86:128-33 Mr '87

Garelik, Glenn
about
Our man in Kazakhstan. G. L. Rogin. por *Discover* 8:4 Je '87

Garet, Jedd
about
Jedd Garet: Galerie Lelong. N. Grimes. il *Art News* 86:148 D '87

Garfield, James A., 1831-1881
Collectibles
Garfield memorial tumbler. M. Wollett and B. Wollett. il *Antiques Collect Hobbies* 92:53 S '87
Garfield, Johanna
How cousins enrich our lives. il *Read Dig* 130:80-2 Ap '87
Garfield, Kim
Good heavens, Shirley! por *Ladies Home J* 104:31+ O '87
Garfinkel, Irwin
about
Wisconsin's child-support experiment. R. J. Margolis. il *New Leader* 70:14-16 O 19 '87
Gargalli, Claire
about
Two very different first ladies of finance. N. J. Perry. il pors *Fortune* 116:191 O 12 '87
Gargan, Edward A.
China's cultural crackdown. il *N Y Times Mag* p24-6+ Jl 12 '87
Garí, Enrique Sacerio- *See* Sacerio-Garí, Enrique
Garine, Igor de
Food, culture and society. il *Courier* 40:4-7 My '87
Garis, Leslie
Didion & Dunne: the rewards of a literary marriage. il pors *N Y Times Mag* p18-24+ F 8 '87
Staying home in the '80s. *Vogue* 177:336+ Ap '87
Suburban classic. il por *Ms* 16:142+ Jl/Ag '87
Garisto, Robert
about
Isaac Newton goofed, and it took student Robert Garisto to get to the core of the matter. R. Wolmuth. il por *People Wkly* 27:43 Je 29 '87
New superhero at Sigma Xi. il por *Time* 129:77 Je 22 '87
Garland, Anne Witte
Food that's, like, totally rad. il *Sierra* 72:20-3 My/Je '87
Garland, Lillian
about
Garland's bouquet. A. Wilentz. il por *Time* 129:14-15 Ja 26 '87
A new family issue. A. Press. il por *Newsweek* 109:22-4 Ja 26 '87
Supreme Court gives motherhood its legal due. B. Brophy. il por *U S News World Rep* 102:12 Ja 26 '87
Garland, Michael
Balancing interests in art and illustration. il *Am Artist* 51:54-9+ Ja '87
Garland, Phyl
Wole Soyinka: Nobel laureate. il pors *Ebony* 42:141-2+ Ap '87
Garland, Robert
Greek geriatrics. bibl il *Hist Today* 37:12-18 S '87
Garland, Suzanne
Warm up to cold-weather workouts. il *Prevention* 39:68+ D '87
Garlic
See also
Cooking—Herbs and spices
Can garlic lick cancer? [study by Tariq Abdullah] M. S. Boyd. il *Health* 19:13 Ag '87
Garlic boosts natural killer cell action [research by Tariq Abdullah] il *Prevention* 39:6 Ag '87
Garlic you plant only once [J. Capriotti's method of growing elephant garlic] L. Korn. il pors *Rodale's Org Gard* 34:91-2 Ap '87
Odorless garlic lowers blood fats [research by Benjamin Lau and others] *Prevention* 39:8+ S '87
Triple-size but less potent . . . elephant garlic. il *Sunset* 179:251 N '87
Garmaise, Freda
Brazen blonde. il por *Ms* 16:30+ N '87
Shoulder high! or What Joan Crawford knew. il *Ms* 16:50 S '87
Garmelow Manor (Staffordshire, England: Historic house) *See* Historic houses, sites, etc.—Great Britain
Garment, Leonard
The guns of Watergate. *Commentary* 83:15-23 Ap '87
Garment, Suzanne
Can the media be reformed? *Commentary* 84:37-43 Ag '87
Gary Hart and the press: can the media be reformed? *Current* 298:11-17 D '87
Journalistic ethics [discussion of August 1987 article, Can the media be reformed?] *Commentary* 84:2+ D '87

Garment industry *See* Clothing industry
Garment workers
Salaries, pensions, etc.
Industrial homework and sweatshops [address, July 20, 1987] J. Mazur. *Vital Speeches Day* 53:701-2 S 1 '87
Let's sock it to the women again [home labor] C. Kocol. il *Humanist* 47:35 N/D '87
Garmisch-Partenkirchen Olympics, 1936 *See* Olympic Games—1936—Winter Olympics
Garn, Jake
about
A father's special gift of love. M. F. Hoyt. il por *Good Housekeep* 204:74+ F '87
Garnets
Direct observation of dissociated dislocations in garnet. F. M. Allen and others. bibl f il *Science* 238:1695-7 D 18 '87
Garnishes in cooking *See* Cooking—Garnishes
Garofalo, Joe
Developing metacognition for school mathematics. *Educ Dig* 53:48-9 D '87
Garon, Claude F.
(jt. auth) *See* Barbour, Alan G., and Garon, Claude F.
Garr, Doug
Pluto the planetoid. il *Omni* 9:25 Jl '87
What's on the tube? Videos to go. il *Sport Mag* 78:91+ Mr '87
Garr, Teri
about
What gets Teri Garr going? L. Kleinmann. por *Health* 19:58 F '87
Garrard, Leslie
(jt. auth) *See* Chevannes, Paul, and Garrard, Leslie
Garraty, John Arthur, 1920-
101 more things every college graduate should know about American history. il *Am Herit* 38:49-53+ D '87
Garreau, Daniel
about
Frenchy and the Persians. C. Trillin. *New Yorker* 63:44+ Je 29 '87
Garrett, David A.
about
Indianapolis principal axed after playing 'Klan' tune. *Jet* 71:21 F 23 '87
Garrett, Elisabeth Donaghy
A collection of early Delaware River Valley furnishings. il *Antiques* 131:282-7 Ja '87
Garrett, Kenny
about
Kenny Garrett. G. Kalbacher. il por *Down Beat* 54:47-8 Ag '87
Garrett, Laura Coti
Chew the drumstick slowly. il *World Tennis* 35:44-6 D '87
Fan fare. il *World Tennis* 35:45-6 S '87
Garrett, Siedah
about
Bad luck has Michael Jackson's new protégée, singer Siedah Garrett, looking like a shore thing. il por *People Wkly* 28:165 N 23 '87
Garrett, Terry
about
Calif. 'Big Spin' winner pleads guilty to theft. *Jet* 71:36 Ja 12 '87
Garrett, Wendell
Editorial. *See* issues of Antiques
Garrett, Wilbur E.
George Washington's Patowmack Canal. il maps *Natl Geogr* 171:716-53 Je '87
Garrett Corporation
Garrett ATF3: outgrowing its growing pains. J. M. McClellan. il *Flying* 114:38+ Ap '87
Garrett tests new ATF-3 seal to correct oil leak problems. *Aviat Week Space Technol* 126:26-7 Je 22 '87
Just in time—American-style [Garrett turbochargers made in Japan] G. Bronson. il *Forbes* 139:132+ Mr 9 '87
Garrison, Deborah Gottlieb
What we hear toward morning [poem] *New Yorker* 62:38 F 16 '87
Garrison, Peter
Aftermath. *See* issues of Flying
Technicalities. *See* alternate issues of Flying beginning March 1985
Garrison, Peter
Technotherapy. il *Omni* 10:162 D '87

Garrison, Zina
about
Black tennis stars winning big bucks but snubbed for commercials. pors *Jet* 72:48 Jl 20 '87
Winning is only half the battle. M. Witherell. il pors *World Tennis* 34:38-41+ My '87
Zina Garrison cracks tennis' $1 million club. il por *Jet* 73:46 O 26 '87
Garrity, John
Revving up in Motown [cover story] il *Sports Illus* 67:22-5 Ag 17 '87
Streak City. il *Sports Illus* 67:14-17 Ag 3 '87
Garrow, David J., 1953-
about
That old, rugged cross. J. E. White. il por *Time* 129:24 Ja 19 '87
Garside, Steve
about
The perfect ski. C. Leocha. il *Esquire* 108:35-6 D '87
Garson, Sascha
The sound and fury of mania. por *Newsweek* 109:10 Ap 13 '87
Garter snakes *See* Snakes
Garth Fagan's Bucket Dance Theatre
Dancing:
Performances at the Joyce Theater. A. Croce. *New Yorker* 63:102-3 D 21 '87
Out on a limb. E. Kendall. il *Vogue* 177:120 N '87
Woman's work [performances at the Joyce Theater, New York City] T. Tobias. il *N Y* 20:108-9 N 23 '87
Garthoff, Raymond L.
Cuba: even dicier than we knew. il *Newsweek* 110:34 O 26 '87
Refocusing the SDI debate. il *Bull At Sci* 43:44-50 S '87
Garton Ash, Timothy
From World War to cold war. bibl f il *N Y Rev Books* 34:44-50 Je 11 '87
In the Churchill museum. bibl f il *N Y Rev Books* 34:22-7 My 7 '87
Garver, Robert I., Jr., and others
Clonal gene therapy: transplanted mouse fibroblast clones express human α1-antitrypsin gene in vivo. bibl f il *Science* 237:762-4 Ag 14 '87
Garvey, John
Anger: let me call you @#&*! il *U S Cathol* 52:14-15 Ag '87
Of several minds. See alternate issues of Commonweal
Garvey, Linda
The body barometer. il *Health* 19:80-2+ Je '87
Garvey, Marcus, 1887-1940
about
November issue of Ebony remembers Marcus Garvey. il por *Jet* 73:37 N 16 '87
Rangel urges Congress to clear record of Garvey. *Jet* 72:22 Ap 20 '87
Remembering Marcus Garvey. il pors *Ebony* 43:138+ N '87
Rousing. *New Yorker* 63:22-4 Ag 31 '87
Garvey, Steve
about
Mr. Consistency. B. Phillips. il por *Sch Update* 120:24-5 O 16 '87
Garwin, Richard
An SDI defense: a Maginot Line in space [with discussion] il por *Cent Mag* 20:45-53 N/D '87
Garwood, Patricia, and Hajcak, Frank
5 wrong reasons to have sex [excerpt from Hidden bedroom partners] il *Glamour* 85:250-1+ Ag '87
Gary, Willie
about
The lawyer who wins $100 million damage suits. C. Whitaker. il pors *Ebony* 42:127-30+ O '87
Gary (Ind.)
Politics and government
Former campaign manager of Richard Hatcher ousts him as mayor of Gary, Ind. [T. Barnes] il por *Jet* 72:15 My 25 '87
Garzarelli, Elaine
about
The newest seer now predicts a bear market rally (what a relief!). G. Anrig, Jr. il por *Money* 16:232 D '87
GAS *See* Glass Art Society
Gas, Gastrointestinal *See* Flatulence
Gas, Natural *See* Natural gas
Gas and oil engines
See also
Automobile engines
Briggs & Stratton Corp.
Motor boat engines
Motorcycle engines

Truck engines
Ignition
Microchip ignition for yard machines [Power-Start module] E. F. Lindsley. il *Pop Sci* 230:113 Je '87
Gas barbecue grills *See* Barbecue grills
Gas centrifuge uranium enrichment *See* Uranium metallurgy
Gas companies *See* Gas utilities
Gas detectors
See also
Carbon monoxide detectors
Oxygen detectors
Toxic gas and smoke alarm [Ultralert System] R. A. Marcus. il *Pop Sci* 231:44 O '87
Gas heating
Gas heat does double duty [Unicore integrated heating system] D. Stover. il *Pop Sci* 231:40 O '87
Gas hypersensitized film *See* Photography—Films
Gas industry
See also
Airgas, Inc.
Coastal Corporation
Gas utilities
Hondo Oil & Gas Company
Panhandle Eastern Corporation
Seagull Energy Corp.
TransAmerican Natural Gas Corporation
Acquisitions and mergers
Jack Stanley's 30-year oil feud is sizzling [Coastal Corp's O. Wyatt stages hostile takeover of TransAmerican Natural Gas in bankruptcy court] J. R. Norman. il *Bus Week* p58-9 Ap 13 '87
Life is a gas [acquisitions by Airgas, Inc.] R. Simon. il por *Forbes* 140:114+ D 14 '87
Export-import trade
Gas for the lamps of Seoul? [Alaskan gas] L. Minard. map *Forbes* 139:34-5 Mr 23 '87
Finance
Guess which fuel is looking hot. P. Nulty. il map *Fortune* 115:94-6+ Je 8 '87
Natural gas. L. M. Keefe. il *Forbes* 139:164-5+ Ja 12 '87
Securities
Natural gas stocks begin to burn brighter. J. Mendes. il *Fortune* 116:99 Ag 31 '87
Canada
See also
Dome Petroleum Ltd.
Inter-City Gas Corp.
Manitoba Consumers Gas Corporation
Gas laws and regulations
See also
Natural gas—Prices
Pipeline companies—Laws and regulations
Gas leases *See* Oil and gas leases
Gas mileage, Automobile *See* Automobile engines—Energy usage; Diesel engines, Automotive—Energy usage
Gas mileage, Motorcycle *See* Motorcycle engines—Energy usage
Gas pipeline companies *See* Pipeline companies
Gas pipelines
See also
Pipeline companies
Environmental aspects
Blue flame, black gunk [PCB-laced oil buried along Texas Eastern's pipelines] J. Egginton. il map *Audubon* 89:106-12 S '87
Cleanup target: 10,000 miles of toxic soup [PCBs dumped along Texas Eastern pipeline] map *U S News World Rep* 103:16 N 23 '87
Mopping up the PCB mess [problem at Texas Eastern] J. Castro. il *Time* 130:50 N 23 '87
Alaska
Gas for the lamps of Seoul? L. Minard. map *Forbes* 139:34-5 Mr 23 '87
Gas policy *See* Natural gas—Prices
Gas prices *See* Natural gas—Prices
Gas rates *See* Gas utilities—Rates; Natural gas—Prices
Gas stations *See* Airplane service stations; Automobile service stations
Gas stoves *See* Stoves
Gas supply
Can the U.S. oil and gas resource base support sustained production? W. L. Fisher. bibl f il *Science* 236:1631-6 Je 26 '87
Oil and gas discovery rates [discussion of June 26, 1987 article, Can the U.S. oil and gas resource base support sustained production?] W. L. Fisher. *Science* 238:878-9 N 13 '87

Gas turbines, Aircraft See Airplane engines, Jet
Gas turbines, Automotive
Turbine turn-on [Chevrolet Express] D. McCosh. il *Pop Sci* 230:38-40 Ap '87
Gas utilities
Natural gas. L. M. Keefe. il *Forbes* 139:164-5+ Ja 12 '87

Rates
How to make everyone unhappy [gas pipeline take-or-pay contracts] L. M. Keefe. il *Forbes* 140:40-1 Ag 10 '87

Great Britain
See also
British Gas plc
Gasconade Farm
Gasconade Farm: where apprentice farmers learn their trade. J. Thorndike. il *Ctry J* 14:27-30+ Ag '87
Gases
See also
Atmosphere
Hydrogen
Methane
Oxygen
Plasma (Ionized gases)
Gas-phase polymerization: ultraslow chemistry. H. Reiss. bibl f il *Science* 238:1368-73 D 4 '87
Time-resolved three-dimensional concentration measurements in a gas jet. B. Yip and others. bibl f il *Science* 235:1209-11 Mr 6 '87
Trace gases: potential impacts on ozone and temperature. *Environment* 29:40 Ja/F '87

Physiological effects
See also
Decompression (Physiology)
Gases, Asphyxiating and poisonous See Poisonous gases
Gash, Joe See Granger, Bill
Gasohol See Alcohol as fuel
Gasoline
Tanking up on biomass gas [research at the Solar Energy Research Institute] J. Raloff. *Sci News* 131:265 Ap 25 '87
What you can do about bad fuel [cover story] G. Williams. il *Home Mech* 83:76-9 Je '87

Lead content
EPA tests confirm lack of lead in gas damages engines. *Success Farm* 85:37 Ag '87
Gas pains [boats] B. Stearns. il *Field Stream* 92:89-90 O '87
How to buy and use lead additives. D. Mowitz. il *Success Farm* 85 no3:F4 F '87
Is there life after lead? S. F. Brown. il *Pop Sci* 231:92+ O '87
Life after lead [Ethyl Corp.] K. Hannon. il *Forbes* 139:65 My 18 '87

Octane rating
Knock, knock. M. S. Dolan. il *Consum Res Mag* 70:2 N '87
Octane and knock. D. Owen. il *Atlantic* 260:53-60 Ag '87
Who's minding the fuel pump? il *Consum Rep* 52:7 Ja '87

Prices
Cost of living: in Prague, one person steers, another pushes. il *Money* 16:32 Jl '87
It's comeback time for $1-a-gallon gasoline and OPEC. K. R. Sheets. *U S News World Rep* 102:36 Je 29 '87

Taxation
Making crime pay [gasoline bootlegging] J. Cook. il *Forbes* 140:56+ Jl 27 '87
Oil slick. *New Repub* 196:7-9 Ap 13 '87
Gasoline-alcohol fuels See Alcohol as fuel
Gasoline cans
A hazardous fuel can [Pumper] il *Consum Rep* 52:5 Ja '87
Gasoline consumption, Automobile See Automobile engines—Energy usage
Gasoline consumption, Motorcycle See Motorcycle engines—Energy usage
Gasoline fumes See Fumes
Gasoline stations See Airplane service stations; Automobile service stations
Gaspari, George
(jt. auth) See Rudnick, Joseph, and Gaspari, George
Gass, William H., 1924-
A failing grade for the present tense. il *N Y Times Book Rev* 92:1+ O 11 '87
Goodness knows nothing of beauty: on the distance between morality and art. il *Harpers* 274:37-44 Ap '87
A visit with Yevtushenko. *Harpers* 274:36+ Ja '87

Gasté, Lou Lou
about
More than Feelings. il por *Time* 130:37 Ag 10 '87
Gastineau, Mark
about
Dodging eggs and insults, N.Y. Jet Mark Gastineau lines up against his old union and his team. A. Richman. il por *People Wkly* 28:50-2 O 12 '87
The life of a $725,000 scab. B. Saporito. il por *Fortune* 116:91-2+ O 26 '87
Gaston, A. G.
about
Full speed ahead at 94. F. White, III. il pors *Ebony* 42:52-4+ Je '87
Gaston, Anthony J.
Seabird citadels of the Arctic. il *Nat Hist* 96:54-9 Ap '87
Gaston (A. G.) Enterprises See A. G. Gaston Enterprises
Gastric ulcers See Peptic ulcers
Gastrointestinal diseases See Digestive system—Diseases
Gastrointestinal gas See Flatulence
Gastrointestinal tract See Digestive system
Gastronomy
See also
La Chaîne des Rôtisseurs
Food critics and criticism
A gourmet at large. F. Ferretti. See issues of Gourmet beginning January 1985
Tasting the bitter and the sweet. M. Sheraton. il *Time* 129:68 Ja 5 '87
With bold pen and fork [M. F. K. Fisher] M. Sheraton. il por *Time* 129:67 Ja 26 '87
With two best-sellers, a hot show and a happy home, frugal gourmet Jeff Smith is cooking on all burners. N. Geeslin. il pors *People Wkly* 27:101-2 F 23 '87
Gastropods
See also
Sea slugs
Slugs
Snails

Food and feeding
See Mollusks—Food and feeding
Gatchev, Georgii D.
Baroque in the Slav countries. il *Courier* 40:46 S '87
The gate [film] See Motion picture reviews—Single works
Gate latches See Latches
Gates, Anita
Big bucks, baby—get wise to the ways to rise. *Mademoiselle* 93:154-5 F '87
If you're so powerful, how come you're fetching coffee? *Mademoiselle* 93:256-7+ N '87
If you're so smart . . . how come you're working for that salary? il *Mademoiselle* 93:238-9+ Ag '87
Gates, Charles Cassius
about
Charlie Gates gives up the glitz. S. D. Atchison. il por *Bus Week* p104 My 11 '87
Gates, Phyllis
My husband, Rock Hudson [excerpt] pors *Ladies Home J* 104:70-1+ Jl '87
Gates, Robert M.
The CIA and American foreign policy. bibl f *Foreign Aff* 66:215-30 Wint '87/'88
about
Bob Gates will have to bring the CIA in from the cold. E. Clark. por *Bus Week* p43 F 16 '87
Casey's well-groomed successor. N. Traver. il por *Time* 129:22-3 F 16 '87
Spies out in the cold. J. McLaughlin. *Natl Rev* 39:24 Mr 13 '87
Gates, William H.
Balancing chips and operating systems. por *Pers Comput* 11:242 O '87
about
Bill Gates on: a platform for the next 10 years [cover story; interview] S. R. Reed. il pors *Pers Comput* 11:74-5+ My '87
The billion-dollar whiz kid [cover story] R. Brandt. il pors *Bus Week* p68-72+ Ap 13 '87
A computer jock's $550-million jackpot. B. Uttal. il por *Fortune* 115:84-5 Ja 5 '87
A quartet of high-tech pioneers. B. O'Reilly. il pors *Fortune* 116:148-9 O 12 '87
Self-made billionaire. il por *U S News World Rep* 103:48-9 Jl 6 '87
Gates
See also
City gates
2 great garden gates. il *Home Mech* 83:50+ My '87

Gates (Logic circuits) *See* Logic circuits
Gates Corporation
Back to the knitting. M. Kirk. il *Forbes* 140:154 D 14 '87
Charlie Gates gives up the glitz. S. D. Atchison. il por *Bus Week* p104 My 11 '87
Gates Learjet Corp.
Former Gates Learjet employees are assembling Avanti sections. il *Aviat Week Space Technol* 127:78 S 28 '87
Gates Learjet unveils Model 31, Model 55C jets. *Aviat Week Space Technol* 127:21 O 5 '87
Gates Rubber Co.
Gates Rubber: the push for standards [personal computer access to mainframe data] J. Blackford. il *Pers Comput* 11:132-3 My '87
Miscellaneous ramblings [aftermarket fan belts] J. Dinkel. il *Road Track* 39:31 S '87
Gateway Medical Systems Inc.
A hospital 'savior' goes on the critical list. D. Foust. il por *Bus Week* p58 S 7 '87
Gatewood, J. M., and others
Sequence-specific packaging of DNA in human sperm chromatin. bibl f il *Science* 236:962-4 My 22 '87
Gatherers and hunters *See* Hunters and gatherers
A gathering of old men [television program] *See* Television program reviews—Single works
Gati, Charles
Gorbachev and Eastern Europe. *Foreign Aff* 65:958-75 Summ '87
GATT *See* General Agreement on Tariffs and Trade
Gatti, Claudio
'A map is worth 10,000 words'. *World Press Rev* 34:54 Ag '87
Gattuso, James L.
The liability crisis isn't over yet. il map *Consum Res Mag* 70:15-19 O '87
Gatwick Airport *See* London (England)—Airports
Gaubert, Thomas Merrill, 1939-
about
An S&L whodunit where everyone's a suspect. J. Weber, Jr. il por *Bus Week* p96-8 Jl 13 '87
Gaubiac, Yves
A World Congress on Copyright Teaching. il *Courier* 40:34 Jl '87
Gaucher's disease
Gene defect located for Gaucher's disease [research by Shoji Tsuji and others] B. Bower. *Sci News* 131:167-8 Mr 14 '87
New understanding of Gaucher's disease [research by Edward Ginns and others] G. Kolata. *Science* 235:1328 Mr 13 '87
Gaudio, Bob
about
A handshake for all seasons. C. P. Alexander. il pors *Time* 129:54 My 11 '87
Gauges *See* Gages
Gault, Charlayne Hunter- *See* Hunter-Gault, Charlayne
Gault, Willie
about
Barred from track again, Gault settles on football. por *Jet* 72:48 Ap 20 '87
Willie Gault adds speed to his swift lifestyle. *Jet* 71:51 F 16 '87
Gaultier, Jean-Paul
about
The defiant ones. D. Drier. il pors *Art Am* 75:47-9+ S '87
Modern contrasts: more/less. il pors *Vogue* 177:432-43 Mr '87
Gaupp, Peter
Haiti: a year after 'Baby Doc'. il *World Press Rev* 34:26-8 Ap '87
Gautreau's (New Orleans, La.: Restaurant) *See* New Orleans (La.)—Restaurants, nightclubs, bars, etc.
Gavenas, Mary Lisa
Flexibility & fine fabrics: Jess Goldstein's costume designs. il por *Theatre Crafts* 21:18-21+ F '87
Gavian, Sarah
(jt. auth) See Mellor, John Williams, 1928-, and Gavian, Sarah
Gavin, Renée
Derek's herd. il por *Ctry J* 14:21-5 Jl '87
Gavin, William F.
Cultural failure: the American preoccupation. *Current* 293:16-19 Je '87
Gavitt, Dave
about
Free throw. R. Koselka. il por *Forbes* 139:162+ My 4 '87

Gavrilov, Andrei
about
Musical events. A. Porter. *New Yorker* 62:99 Ja 12 '87
Gay, Alberta
about
Obituary
Jet il por 72:57 My 25 '87
Gay, Ruth
A spa in Germany. *Am Sch* 56:549-56 Aut '87
Gay Games
The death of an athlete [Gay Games organizer, T. Waddell, dies of AIDS] D. Schaap. il *Sports Illus* 67:26-8+ Jl 27 '87
Notes and comment [T. Waddell v. USOC over restrictions on use of term Olympics] *New Yorker* 63:19-20 Ag 24 '87
Gay/Lesbian Pride Parade (New York, N.Y.) *See* New York (N.Y.)—Parades
Gay rights *See* Homosexuality
Gayle, Jackie
about
Jackie Gayle shows his mettle as an actor in Tin men. L. Armstrong. il pors *People Wkly* 27:65-6 Ap 13 '87
Gaylin, Jody
100% successful birthday parties. il *Parents* 62:70-2 Ja '87
Protecting children's innocence [with editorial comment by Elizabeth Crow] il *Parents* 62:6, 88+ O '87
The trouble with Emily. il *Parents* 62:54+ Mr '87
TV cold turkey. il *Parents* 62:102-4 S '87
When a young mother dies. *Ladies Home J* 104:78+ F '87
Gaylord, William G., d. 1985
about
Odyssey by the bay: the San Francisco peregrinations of Herb Caen. H. Caen. il por *Archit Dig* 44:68-71+ Jl '87
Gaylord (New York, N.Y.: Restaurant) *See* New York (N.Y.)—Restaurants, nightclubs, bars, etc.
Gaynor, Elizabeth, 1946-
A dacha in Finland [excerpt from Scandinavia] il *House Gard* 159:86-93+ Ag '87
Gaynor, John
Home Q&A. See issues of Home Mechanix beginning January 1985
Gayton, Tony
about
Athens, Ga. [film] Reviews
Roll Stone p27 Ap 23 '87. A. DeCurtis
Gaza Strip territorial question *See* Israel-Arab Wars, 1967-—Territorial questions
Gazebos *See* Garden houses, shelters, etc.
Gazehounds
The wind-splitters. L. Mueller. il por *Outdoor Life* 180:22+ D '87
Gazelle hunting
Gazelle killing in Stone Age Syria [emergence of agriculture at Tell Abu Hureyra] A. J. Legge and P. A. Rowley-Conwy. il map *Sci Am* 257:88-95 Ag '87
Letters [discussion of August 1987 article, Gazelle killing in Stone Age Syria] A. J. Legge and P. A. Rowley-Conwy. *Sci Am* 257:8+ N '87
Gazenko, Oleg G.
Travelling light: coping with weightlessness in space. il *Courier* 40:12-13 Je '87
GE *See* General Electric Co.
GE Fanuc Automation Corporation
Japan's robot king wins again. G. Bylinsky. il pors *Fortune* 115:53-4+ My 25 '87
Geannette, Mark
Resurrector of wrecks. il pors *Oceans* 20:36-41 N/D '87
Gearing
See also
Motorcycles—Gearing
Algebra and the differential gear. A. Bass. il *Technol Rev* 90:56 Ap '87
Geary, Anthony
about
Whatever happened to Luke? L. Z. Tilden. il pors *Mademoiselle* 93:80 Ag '87
Gebbie, Kristine M.
about
Fresh troops for president's AIDS panel. W. Booth. pors *Science* 238:1034 N 20 '87
Gebhart, Fred
Our new tax law—what's in it for you? il *Read Dig* 130:81-4 F '87

Gechtoff, Sonia, 1926-
about
Sonia Gechtoff: Gruenebaum. G. Henry. il *Art News* 86:152 D '87
Geduld, Harry M.
Film review. See issues of The Humanist
Geese
See also
Cooking—Poultry
Geese, Wild
Shooting
See Goose shooting
Treatment
Killing Canada geese. M. McIver. il *Macleans* 100:58 O 12 '87
Geese Company
In Massachusetts: theater therapy [including prisoners in performances] D. Brand. il *Time* 130:12+ N 9 '87
Geffen, Alice M.
(jt. auth) See Berglie, Carole, and Geffen, Alice M.
Gehret, Jeanne B.
Respite care: help goes both ways. *Christ Century* 104:76-7 Ja 28 '87
Gehrig, Henry Louis *See* Gehrig, Lou, 1903-1941
Gehrig, Lou, 1903-1941
about
Just a Pipp of a legend. B. Anderson. il pors *Sports Illus* 66:78-82+ Je 29 '87
Gehrig's disease *See* Amyotrophic lateral sclerosis
Gehring, Walter J.
Homeo boxes in the study of development. bibl f il *Science* 236:1245-52 Je 5 '87
Gehrke, Craig
(jt. auth) See Anderson, Michael, and Gehrke, Craig
Gehry, Frank
about
The house as art [cover story] M. Filler. il por *House Gard* 159:152-61+ O '87
A man who made architecture an art of the unexpected. M. Webb. bibl (p162) il por *Smithsonian* 18:48-54+ Ap '87
Geigis, Deborah
Starstruck. il *Glamour* 85:100+ Mr '87
When the town pizza parlor shut down. il *Glamour* 85:278+ S '87
Geisel, Theodor Seuss, 1904- *See* Seuss, Dr.
Geisler, Alex
about
What do Live from the Met and Family ties have in common? il pors *Bus Week* p71 Ag 31 '87
Geist, William
The Rolling stone interview: Woody Allen [cover story] il pors *Roll Stone* p38-40+ Ap 9 '87
Gel electrophoresis *See* Electrophoresis
Gelada baboons *See* Baboons
Gelatt, Roland, 1920-1986
about
Obituary
High Fidel por 37:7 F '87. S. Fleming
Gelb, Barbara
about
At last Carlotta O'Neill, Eugene's feisty widow, takes stage center in a play by Barbara Gelb. L. Rozen. il por *People Wkly* 27:61-2+ Mr 23 '87
My Gene [drama] Reviews
N Y il 20:56-7 F 9 '87. J. Simon
Vogue il 177:38 Ja '87. V. Radin
Gelb, Norman
Anomalous Berlin. il *New Leader* 70:8-9 Ja 12-26 '87
Britain's opposition regroups. il por *New Leader* 70:6-7 S 7 '87
British trade union blues. il *New Leader* 70:6-7 O 5 '87
Europe's decoupling anxiety. il *New Leader* 70:7-8 Ap 20 '87
Kinnock on the defensive. il *New Leader* 70:8-9 Mr 23 '87
Love and hate across the Atlantic. il *New Leader* 70:3-4 N 30 '87
Thatcher on dangerous ground. il *New Leader* 70:5-6 N 2 '87
Thatcher's third term target. il *New Leader* 70:6-7 Je 29 '87
Geldermalsen (Ship)
The shipwrecked remainders of Europe's china boom. C. R. Boxer. il *Hist Today* 37:45-8 Ap '87
Geldermann Inc.
A make-or-break move into financial futures. J. N. Frank. il por *Bus Week* p114 F 23 '87

Geldof, Bob
about
The heart of rock & roll. D. Fricke. por *Roll Stone* p83+ F 12 '87
Gelernter, David
Programming for advanced computing. bibl (p183) il *Sci Am* 257:90-6+ O '87
Gelfand, Marvin
The Street. il map *Am Herit* 38:53-6+ N '87
Gell-Mann, Murray, 1929-
First word. il *Omni* 9:8 F '87
Geller, Simon
about
The invincible voice of Cape Ann. R. J. Bidinotto. il por *Read Dig* 131:201-2+ O '87
Geller, Uri, 1946-
about
A Twilight Zone defense? D. Gates. il por *Newsweek* 109:5 My 11 '87
Geller-Shinn, Karen
Compacts in action. See issues of Petersen's Photographic Magazine beginning July 1985 through October 1987
Tools of the trade. See issues of Petersen's Photographic Magazine
Gellhorn, Alfred
(jt. auth) See Bryant, John H., and Gellhorn, Alfred
Gels *See* Colloids
Gem smuggling *See* Smuggling
Gemant Award
Morrison is first recipient of AIP's Gemant Award. por *Phys Today* 40:58 Je '87
Nominations urgently sought for Gemant Award. *Phys Today* 40:73 Ja '87
Gemberling, Stephen
about
Painting a world. E. Greene. il por *House Gard* 159:40+ D '87
Gemfibrozil
The battle of the lipoproteins [Helsinki study shows gemfibrozil lowers LDL levels while raising HDL levels] C. Gorman. il *Time* 130:68 N 23 '87
More good news about 'good cholesterol' [gemfibrozil increases HDL levels] *U S News World Rep* 103:14 N 23 '87
A powerful tonic for Warner-Lambert [anticholesterol drug Lopid] L. Baum. il por *Bus Week* p144+ N 30 '87
Gemignani, Paul
about
Double play [cover story] S. Flatow. il pors *Opera News* 51:10-13+ Je '87
Geminiani, Francesco, 1687-1762
about
Musical events:
F. Geminiani's The enchanted forest. A. Porter. *New Yorker* 63:92 My 25 '87
Gems
See also
Crown jewels
Diamonds
Jewelry
Rubies
Sapphires
GenCorp Inc.
GenCorp feels the pincers [Wagner & Brown-AFG team] T. Carson and Z. Schiller. *Bus Week* p33-4 Mr 30 '87
Will GenCorp bow out of broadcasting—or be pushed? [FCC decision threatens RKO's licenses] D. Lieberman and others. il *Bus Week* p25 Ag 24 '87
Gender determination *See* Sex determination and control
Gender differences *See* Sex differences
Gene amplification
Breast cancer: *neu* clue [work of Dennis J. Slamon and others] *Sci Am* 256:71+ Mr '87
Detection of minimal residual cells carrying the t(14;18) by DNA sequence amplification. M.-S. Lee and others. bibl f il *Science* 237:175-8 Jl 10 '87
*erb*B-2 is a potent oncogene when overexpressed in NIH/3T3 cells. P. P. Di Fiore and others. bibl f il *Science* 237:178-82 Jl 10 '87
Genetic clue to cancer prognosis [breast cancer] J. Silberner. *Sci News* 131:46 Ja 17 '87
Human breast cancer: correlation of relapse and survival with amplification of the HER-2/*neu* oncogene. D. J. Slamon and others. bibl f il *Science* 235:177-82 Ja 9 '87
Identification of an amplified, highly expressed gene in a human glioma. K. W. Kinzler and others. bibl f il *Science* 236:70-3 Ap 3 '87

Gene amplification—*cont.*
Oncogenes give breast cancer prognosis [research by Dennis J. Slamon and others] G. Kolata. *Science* 235:160-1 Ja 9 '87

Gene banks *See* Germplasm resources
Gene cloning *See* Clones (Biology)
Gene expression *See* Genetic regulation
Gene mapping *See* Chromosome mapping
Gene position in chromosomes *See* Locus (Genes)
Gene probes
Disease diagnosis by recombinant DNA methods. C. T. Caskey. bibl f il *Science* 236:1223-9 Je 5 '87
Localization of amyloid β protein messenger RNA in brains from patients with Alzheimer's disease. S. Bahmanyar and others. bibl f il *Science* 237:77-80 Jl 3 '87
A new probe for the diagnosis of myotonic muscular dystrophy. R. J. Bartlett and others. bibl f il *Science* 235:1648-50 Mr 27 '87

Gene repression *See* Genetic regulation
Gene resources *See* Germplasm resources
Gene splicing research *See* Genetic research
Gene therapy
Better animal models for genetic defects [technique developed by Mario R. Capecchi and Kirk R. Thomas] S. Eisenberg. *Sci News* 132:327 N 21 '87
Clonal gene therapy: transplanted mouse fibroblast clones express human α1-antitrypsin gene in vivo. R. I. Garver, Jr. and others. bibl f il *Science* 237:762-4 Ag 14 '87
Future 'patchwork' cure for hemophilia? D. D. Edwards. *Sci News* 131:168 Mr 14 '87
Gene therapy takes aim at liver, lungs. R. Weiss. *Sci News* 132:119 Ag 22 '87
The good news—and the bad—about gene therapy prospects. *Science* 236:29-30 Ap 3 '87
Implantation of genetically engineered fibroblasts into mice: implications for gene therapy. R. F. Selden and others. bibl f il *Science* 236:714-18 My 8 '87
New avenues for LNS gene transfer. K. Hartley. *Sci News* 131:390 Je 20 '87
The next stage: gene therapy. A. Virshup. *N Y* 20:30 Jl 27 '87
Shiverless deportment [gene surgery for mice lacking myelin basic protein; work of Leroy E. Hood] il *Sci Am* 256:64 My '87

Ethical aspects
The growing danger from gene-spliced hormones. T. H. Murray. il *Discover* 8:88+ F '87

Gene transfer
See also
Gene therapy
Biotech's bid to build a better mouse [transferring human genes into mice to make human proteins] R. Rhein, Jr. il *Bus Week* p102 N 9 '87
Construction of a novel oncogene based on synthetic sequences encoding epidermal growth factor. D. F. Stern and others. bibl f il *Science* 235:321-4 Ja 16 '87
Epidermal growth factor-dependent transformation by a human EGF receptor proto-oncogene. T. J. Velu and others. bibl f il *Science* 238:1408-10 D 4 '87
Gene transfer in cereals. E. C. Cocking and M. R. Davey. bibl f *Science* 236:1259-62 Je 5 '87
Gene transfer in corn. D. D. Edwards. *Sci News* 131:37 Ja 17 '87
Gene transfer in crop improvement. R. M. Goodman and others. bibl f il *Science* 236:48-54 Ap 3 '87
Genetic ablation: targeted expression of a toxin gene causes microphthalmia in transgenic mice. M. L. Breitman and others. bibl f il *Science* 238:1563-5 D 11 '87
Ingrained genes. *Sci Am* 256:68 Mr '87
Manipulating milk in mammals [betalactoglobulin gene in mice; research by J. Paul Simons and others] R. Weiss. *Sci News* 132:84 Ag 8 '87
Progress toward engineering monocots. L. Tangley. *BioScience* 37:462 Jl/Ag '87
Shotgun approach to genetic engineering [work of Theodore M. Klein and others] J. Raloff. *Sci News* 131:310 My 16 '87
Shotgun marriage [use of microprojectiles for delivering nucleic acids into living plant cells; work of Theodore M. Klein and others] il *Sci Am* 257:23-4 Jl '87
Stable integration and expression of a bacterial gene in the mosquito Anopheles gambiae. L. H. Miller and others. bibl f il *Science* 237:779-81 Ag 14 '87
Strange bedfellows. P. B. Moses. il *BioScience* 37:6-10 Ja '87

The *tat* gene of human T-lymphotropic virus type 1 induces mesenchymal tumors in transgenic mice. M. Nerenberg and others. bibl f il *Science* 237:1324-9 S 11 '87
Tissue-specific expression of functionally rearranged λ1 Ig gene in a retrovirus vector. R. D. Cone and others. bibl f il *Science* 236:954-7 My 22 '87
Transformation by oncogenes encoding protein kinases induces the metastatic phenotype. S. E. Egan and others. bibl f il *Science* 238:202-5 O 9 '87
A transgenic mouse model for human neurofibromatosis. S. H. Hinrichs and others. bibl f il *Science* 237:1340-3 S 11 '87
Transgenic plants as tools to study the molecular organization of plant genes. J. St. Schell. bibl f *Science* 237:1176-83 S 4 '87

Genealogical catalogs *See* Catalogs, Genealogical
Genealogy
See also
L.W. Anderson Genealogical Library
Registers of births, etc.
The genealogy craze. il *World Press Rev* 34:30-1 N '87
Korean-Americans: the early migration. C. E. Kraft. il *Antiques Collect Hobbies* 92:80-4 Ap '87
So you want to climb your family tree. S. Woolley. il *Bus Week* p156-7 N 30 '87

Anecdotes, facetiae, satire, etc.
The skeleton in the courthouse [work of L. Galeener-Moore] C. E. Kraft. il *Antiques Collect Hobbies* 92:68-71 S '87

Genentech, Inc.
Birth of a blockbuster: how Genentech delivered the goods [FDA approves TPA] J. O. Hamilton. il *Bus Week* p138-40+ N 30 '87
Companies vie over new heart drug [Genentech vs. Wellcome] M. Sun. il *Science* 237:120-2 Jl 10 '87
FDA puts new heart drug on hold. M. Sun. il *Science* 237:16-18 Jl 3 '87
Genentech sues FDA on growth hormone. M. Crawford. il *Science* 235:1454-5 Mr 20 '87
Genentech takes a tumble [FDA's adverse ruling on TPA] D. Pauly. il *Newsweek* 109:48 Je 15 '87
Genentech takes another hit [Britain rejects TPA patent] J. O. Hamilton and M. Maremont. *Bus Week* p75 Jl 20 '87
The man who could make biotechnology profitable—at last [R. A. Swanson] G. Bylinsky. il por *Fortune* 115:101 Ja 5 '87
A nasty shock for Genentech [FDA rejects TPA] J. O. Hamilton and R. Rhein, Jr. *Bus Week* p37 Je 15 '87
Picking up the pieces at Genentech [FDA denies marketing approval for TPA] G. Bylinsky. il *Fortune* 116:60-1 Jl 6 '87
Robert Swanson. J. O. Hamilton. il por *Bus Week* Sp Issue:242 Ap 17 '87
Ruling on heart drug may boost research [British court's TPA patent ruling] M. Sun. il *Science* 237:244 Jl 17 '87

General Agreement on Tariffs and Trade
Attacking farm subsidies. D. Jenish. il *Macleans* 100:30 Jl 20 '87
Counting the cost of protectionism [ruling against Canadian beer and wine tariffs] M. Janigan. il *Macleans* 100:14 N 23 '87
A crossroads in U.S. trade policy [address, May 4, 1987] R. K. Shelp. *Vital Speeches Day* 53:618-21 Ag 1 '87
More equitable rules for international trade. L. C. Thurow. il *Technol Rev* 90:22+ F/Mr '87
Rising above trade rivalry [BizNet teleconference on U.S.-Japanese trade] il *Nations Bus* 75:45-6 Ap '87
Trade is key to economic growth, GATT told. *UN Chron* 23:106 N '86
A worldwide glut of food. M. Drohan. il *Macleans* 100:37-8 N 9 '87

General aviation *See* Aviation
General aviation industry *See* Airplane industry
General Aviation Manufacturers Association
GAMA looks ahead. E. Weiner. *Flying* 114:101 Ap '87
General Cinema Corporation
The new show at Neiman-Marcus. J. P. Newport, Jr. il por *Fortune* 115:103-4+ Ap 27 '87
General Development Corp.
This developer is on solid ground. J. M. Laderman. il *Bus Week* p100 Ap 27 '87
General Dynamics Corp.
Beggs and General Dynamics cleared of fraud [Divad gun case] I. Goodwin. *Phys Today* 40 pt1:53 Ag '87

General Dynamics Corp.—cont.

A defense case may break [witnesses get immunity in General Dynamics ship probe] S. Payne. *Bus Week* p40+ Mr 23 '87

General Dynamics, Beggs cleared of fraud charges [Divad contract] *Aviat Week Space Technol* 126:25-6 Je 29 '87

General Dynamics begins tests in new anechoic chamber [cover story] C. A. Shifrin. *Aviat Week Space Technol* 127:51-2 O 19 '87

The General Dynamics case sets a bad precedent [Justice Dept. decides not to seek indictment] P. Dwyer and S. Payne. il *Bus Week* p41 Je 8 '87

General Dynamics cites launch candidates for Atlas G/Centaur. il *Aviat Week Space Technol* 126:25 Mr 23 '87

General Dynamics considers ways to advance F-16 agility. C. A. Shifrin. *Aviat Week Space Technol* 126:120-1+ F 16 '87

General Dynamics proposes F-16 upgrade for 1990s [Agile Falcon] J. D. Morrocco. il *Aviat Week Space Technol* 127:22-3 Ag 3 '87

Indictment of Beggs dropped [Divad gun fraud case] E. Marshall. *Science* 237:21 Jl 3 '87

Japan's defense agency selects F-16 as basis for FS-X aircraft. *Aviat Week Space Technol* 127:22-3 O 26 '87

Justice Dept.'s broadax [dismissal of indictment in Divad gun case] D. E. Fink. *Aviat Week Space Technol* 127:9 Jl 13 '87

Probe scuttled [Justice Dept. drops inquiry] *Time* 129:51 Je 1 '87

Tadiran-General Dynamics team will compete as second-source for Army Sincgars radios. *Aviat Week Space Technol* 127:28 Jl 13 '87

Union vote ends General Dynamics strike. *Aviat Week Space Technol* 127:29 Ag 17 '87

Who's counting? [Justice Dept. abandons Divad gun fraud case] W. Biddle. *Nation* 245:148-9 Ag 29 '87

General Dynamics Corp. Electric Boat Division

Torpedoing free speech [ordinance to regulate anti-nuclear protests in Groton, Conn.] S. Burkholder. il *Progressive* 51:15-16 My '87

General education *See* Liberal education

General Electric Co.

7J7 delay could erode GE's position in ultrahigh bypass development. il *Aviat Week Space Technol* 127:28-9 Ag 31 '87

A $78 million check from GE [settlement of suit over failed Zimmer nuclear plant] Z. Schiller. *Bus Week* p64 D 7 '87

And then there was one [sale of consumer electronics division to Thomson SA] J. B. Copeland. il *Newsweek* 110:36 Ag 3 '87

Are TVs still in GE's big picture? K. Dreyfack. il *Bus Week* p37 My 2 '87

A contrast in styles on Wall Street [Kidder parent GE] il *Fortune* 115:8 Je 8 '87

GE/Martin selected to provide ATF electro-optic sensor [YF-22A advanced tactical fighter] *Aviat Week Space Technol* 126:73 Je 15 '87

GE boosting CF6-80C2 production to meet order backlog. il *Aviat Week Space Technol* 126:56 Ap 6 '87

GE cannot meet Army air defense test deadline [forward-area air defense system] *Aviat Week Space Technol* 126:30 Ja 19 '87

GE examines technical challenges to ducted UHB engine development [ultrahigh bypass turbine engine concepts] *Aviat Week Space Technol* 126:31-2 F 2 '87

GE gift-wraps a landmark lab [donating the David Sarnoff Research Center to SRI International] O. Port. il *Bus Week* p35 F 16 '87

GE is pulling out the stops at home [new line of refrigerators] Z. Schiller. il *Bus Week* p94 N 2 '87

GE produces family of VHSIC-like operational chips for aerospace [very high speed integrated circuits] P. J. Klass. il *Aviat Week Space Technol* 126:88-9 Ja 26 '87

GE suspends engine shipments to correct inspection failure. *Aviat Week Space Technol* 126:32 Ap 13 '87

GE, Turbo-Union allowed to rebid on EFA interim engine [European fighter aircraft program] *Aviat Week Space Technol* 126:24 F 23 '87

GE will build UDF production version, nears end of demonstrator test program [GE36 unducted fan engine] K. F. Mordoff. il *Aviat Week Space Technol* 126:28-9 F 2 '87

General Eclectic. E. A. Finn, Jr. il *Forbes* 139:74-8+ Mr 23 '87

General Electric and Boeing analyze data following initial UDF flight tests [unducted fan] *Aviat Week Space Technol* 126:67 Ap 13 '87

General Electric develops quieter UDF propeller blade configuration; production engine work under way [unducted fan] *Aviat Week Space Technol* 126:34-5 My 25 '87

General Electric is stalking big game again. J. R. Norman. il por *Bus Week* p112-13 Mr 16 '87

General Electric will expand collaborative engine programs. il *Aviat Week Space Technol* 126:30-1 Je 22 '87

GE's gamble on American-made TVs. P. Petre. il *Fortune* 116:50-2+ Jl 6 '87

Jack Welch: how good a manager? [cover story] R. Mitchell. il pors *Bus Week* p92-6+ D 14 '87

Japan's robot king wins again [joint venture with Fanuc] G. Bylinsky. il pors *Fortune* 115:53-4+ My 25 '87

John Welch. R. W. King. il por *Bus Week* Sp Issue:240 Ap 17 '87

Jumping Jack strikes again [J. Welch sells NBC Radio Network and consumer electronic division] P. Elmer-Dewitt. il *Time* 130:44 Ag 3 '87

Kidder does a $25 million deal with Giuliani [GE tries to limit damage from insider trading] *Newsweek* 109:49 Je 15 '87

Labor and management [address, September 18, 1986] F. P. Doyle. *Vital Speeches Day* 53:293-5 Mr 1 '87

Lockheed, GE run ultrahigh bypass engine prototypes in ground tests. il *Aviat Week Space Technol* 126:46-7 Ap 27 '87

The man who brought GE to life [J. Welch] P. Petre. por *Fortune* 115:76-7 Ja 5 '87

McDonnell Douglas resumes flight tests with GE UDF engine [unducted fan engine] *Aviat Week Space Technol* 127:35 N 2 '87

McDonnell Douglas UHB demonstrator flies with GE unducted fan engine [ultrahigh bypass ratio engine] M. A. Dornheim. il *Aviat Week Space Technol* 126:32-4 My 25 '87

No. 2 UDF engine prototype will fly on MD-80 by June [unducted fan ultrahigh bypass engine] il *Aviat Week Space Technol* 126:58+ Ap 13 '87

No more shooting for the moon [impact of medical costs on technology] R. Greene. il *Forbes* 140:221-2 D 14 '87

A nuclear cloud hangs over GE's reputation [flawed plant designs and responsibility for cost overruns] D. Cook. il *Bus Week* p32 Je 15 '87

Overnight, Thomson has the stuff to take on the titans [purchase of GE's consumer electronics business] T. Peterson. il *Bus Week* p36-7 Ag 10 '87

A push for 'quick justice' has GE squirming [summary trial in suit over Zimmer nuclear plant] Z. Schiller. *Bus Week* p31-2 S 21 '87

Rolls, GE propose engine versions to power A330. *Aviat Week Space Technol* 126:36 Mr 30 '87

Sanders-GE team forms INEWS management structure [integrated electronic warfare system] *Aviat Week Space Technol* 126:78 F 16 '87

Strong demand prompts increase in CF6, CFM56 engine production. J. M. Lenorovitz. *Aviat Week Space Technol* 127:35-6 N 9 '87

A sweet swap for GE and Thomson. *Fortune* 116:8 Ag 17 '87

Turning on the juice [J. F. Welch] P. Petre. il por *Fortune* 116:31 Ag 3 '87

UHB demonstrator aircraft continues unducted fan tests [GE UDF engine] il *Aviat Week Space Technol* 127:81 O 26 '87

What makes giant GE keep on growing? J. Egan. il *U S News World Rep* 103:48-9 N 23 '87

Why GE is cleaning house at Kidder [trying to limit damage from insider trading scandal] J. R. Norman. il *Bus Week* p45 Je 1 '87

General Electric Co. Management Development Institute

GE's training camp: an 'Outward Bound' for managers. J. H. Dobrzynski. il *Bus Week* p98 D 14 '87

General Electric Company plc

GEC completes purchase of Lear Siegler units. *Aviat Week Space Technol* 127:125 O 12 '87

General Felt Industries, Inc.

The sour smell of success [M. S. Cogan] G. Slutsker. il pors *Forbes* 139:54-5 Ja 26 '87

General Foods Corp.

Life in the outside lane [A. M. Shaver] D. Machan. il pors *Forbes* 140:220+ O 5 '87

General Foods Corp. Maxwell House Division

Maxwell House serves up a yuppie brew [Private Collection gourmet line] A. Dunkin. il *Bus Week* p62 Mr 2 '87

General Foods World Food Prize
Scientists: their rewards and humanity [awarded to M. S. Swaminathan] R. D. Havener. *Science* 237:1281 S 11 '87
General Host Corp.
Hidden value. T. Jaffe. il *Forbes* 139:126 Ap 20 '87
General Instrument Corp.
The General [General Instrument buys Video Cipher from M/A-Com] A. B. Block. il *Forbes* 139:38-9 Je 29 '87
General Mills, Inc.
Bantam, General Mills schedule audio promotion. il *Publ Wkly* 232:69-70 O 9 '87
Food fight! [General Mills to challenge Quaker Oats with Total Oatmeal] S. B. Weiner. il *Forbes* 140:86+ Jl 27 '87
Most improved. il *Forbes* 139:134 Ja 12 '87
General Motors Acceptance Corp.
Will a spinoff rev up GM? G. G. Marcial. *Bus Week* p100 F 16 '87
General Motors Corp.
The $750 million muzzle [R. Smith forces H. R. Perot out at GM] D. Sherman. il *Car Driv* 32:7 Mr '87
A billionaire for the common man [H. R. Perot] B. O'Reilly. il por *Fortune* 115:47 Ja 5 '87
Bumps ahead for a car guy [R. C. Stempel] A. L. Taylor, III. il por *Fortune* 116:105-6+ S 28 '87
Can GM afford this deal? *Newsweek* 110:63 O 19 '87
Can Roy Roberts rebuild the GM machine? [cover story] K. D. Thompson. il pors *Black Enterp* 18:57-60+ D '87
Catalysts of genius, dealers in hope [address, October 14, 1986] L. E. Reuss. *Vital Speeches Day* 53:173-6 Ja 1 '87
Detroit [H. R. Perot ousted] P. Lienert. il pors *Road Track* 38:110 Mr '87
Does GM rate shelf space? [views of J. D. Power on superdealers] M. Beauchamp. il por *Forbes* 139:144 F 23 '87
The engineer who aims to tune up GM [R. C. Stempel named president] J. B. Treece. il por *Bus Week* p38 Je 8 '87
Fiddling with figures while sales drop. J. Flint and L. Jereski. il *Forbes* 140:32-5 Ag 24 '87
A Ford vehicle doomed to stall at General Motors [UAW contract] J. A. Seamonds. il *U S News World Rep* 103:16 S 28 '87
General Motors in reverse. B. Powell. il *Newsweek* 110:42-3 S 7 '87
General Motors' little engine that could [Quad 4] W. J. Hampton. il *Bus Week* p88-9 Ag 3 '87
General Motors' new uphill course. J. A. Seamonds. il *U S News World Rep* 103:9 O 19 '87
General Motors: what went wrong. W. J. Hampton and J. R. Norman. il *Bus Week* p102-8+ Mr 16 '87
GM flexes its 1988 muscle. P. Lienert. il *Road Track* 39:126+ N '87
GM maps massive cutbacks. P. Lienert. *Road Track* 38:100+ F '87
GM may be off the hook: the Ford talks leave plenty of loopholes. A. Bernstein and W. Zellner. il *Bus Week* p26-7 S 28 '87
GM: the bonus days are over [scrapping bonuses in favor of stock option plan] J. Schwartz. il *Newsweek* 109:53 Ap 27 '87
GM wants to use Soviet launchers. E. Marshall. *Science* 238:23 O 2 '87
GM's 1988 prices are lower—in a way. J. B. Treece. il *Bus Week* p41-2 O 12 '87
GM's bootstrap battle: the factory-floor view [E. Schaefer brings team management to Van Nuys plant] A. Gabor. il por *U S News World Rep* 103:52-3 S 21 '87
GM's late-starting trumpeter [E. W. Johnson] N. J. Perry. il por *Fortune* 116:137 O 26 '87
GM's new cars for the nineties. P. Lienert. il *Road Track* 39:94+ S '87
GM's new luxury cars: why they're not selling. R. Mitchell. il *Bus Week* p94+ Ja 19 '87
GM's not-so-radical proposal [productivity of each plant to determine wage increases and job security] *Fortune* 116:10 S 14 '87
How G.M. bought itself a lemon [tracing the Electronic Data Systems acquisition] M. M. Thomas. il *Nation* 244:108-9 Ja 31 '87
How GM and the UAW kept from butting heads. W. Zellner. il *Bus Week* p32 O 26 '87
In Flint, tough times last. M. Moore. il *Nation* 244:753-6 Je 6 '87
It's no fun running no. 1 when you're taking heat [R. B. Smith] A. L. Taylor, III. il por *Fortune* 116:26-7 Ag 3 '87

It's time for a tune-up at GM [new president R. C. Stempel] J. B. Treece. il por *Bus Week* p22-3 S 7 '87
Linden [GM assembly plant for Chevrolet Beretta and Corsica in N.J.] R. Ceppos. il *Car Driv* 32:37 F '87
Lotus: living with the General. P. Bingham. il *Mot Trend* 39:48-51 F '87
The NUMMI experience [joint venture between Toyota and General Motors] M. Keller. il *Mot Trend* 39:126-7 Mr '87
Revenge of the tin men [management obscures product] A. Girdler. il *Road Track* 38:32 Ag '87
Roger Smith. W. J. Hampton. il por *Bus Week* Sp Issue:232 Ap 17 '87
Roy Roberts gets top personnel post at GM. por *Jet* 72:27 Ap 27 '87
The shadow of Mr. Sloan. il pors *Forbes* 139:10-11 Ja 26 '87
Slippery roads for GM. D. Jenish. il *Macleans* 100:36-8 F 23 '87
Somebody does it better [Ford and GM cars made in Europe] M. Keller. il *Mot Trend* 39:102 Ja '87
Sprint's chance to gallop [contract to supply network services to GM] J. J. Keller. il *Bus Week* p33 Je 15 '87
To be continued [serial television ads] B. Kanner. il *N Y* 20:14+ F 2 '87
A troubleshooter moves in at flabby GM [R. C. Stempel appointed president] K. R. Sheets. *U S News World Rep* 102:45 Je 8 '87
A view from the shop floor. J. K. Adamson. por *Newsweek* 109:8-9 F 9 '87
What the Auto Workers are up against. A. Bernstein. il *Bus Week* p83-4 Ap 27 '87
What's good for America. J. Flint. il *Forbes* 140:173-6+ Jl 13 '87
Will a spinoff rev up GM? [General Motors Acceptance Corp.] G. G. Marcial. *Bus Week* p100 F 16 '87
You don't lose 'em all [buyout of H. R. Perot] C. Siler. il por *Forbes* 140:34 Ag 10 '87
General Motors Corp. Buick Motor Division *See* Buick Motor Division
General Motors Corp. Cadillac Motor Car Division *See* Cadillac Motor Car Division
General Motors Corp. Chevrolet Motor Division *See* Chevrolet Motor Division
General Motors Corp. Saturn Corporation *See* Saturn Corporation
General Motors Egypt S.A.E.
GM's grand design in Egypt may be a mirage. B. Slavin. il *Bus Week* p46 Mr 30 '87
General Motors of Canada Ltd.
Keeping the assembly line rolling [government aid keeps plant in Boisbriand, Que. open] il *Macleans* 100:10 Ap 13 '87
Slippery roads for GM. D. Jenish. il *Macleans* 100:36-8 F 23 '87
General practitioners *See* Physicians
General Sciences Corp.
A stock 'for your mother'? G. G. Marcial. *Bus Week* p108 O 26 '87
General Services Administration *See* United States. General Services Administration
General stores
See also
Casey's General Stores Inc.
General Telephone & Electronics Corporation
See also
GTE Corp.
General Tire & Rubber Co. *See* GenCorp Inc.
Generale Occidentale SA
Sir Jimmy pulls the plug on his French connection [J. Goldsmith sells out stake in Générale Occidentale to Compagnie Générale d'Electricité] J. Rossant. il por *Bus Week* p24 Ag 10 '87
Generalife (Granada, Spain)
Gardens
Poetry in water. R. Lane Fox. il *House Gard* 159:104-15+ Ja '87
Generals
See also
Gorden, Fred
Powell, Colin L.
Randolph, Bernard P.
Rogers, Bernard W.
Generation, Spontaneous *See* Spontaneous generation
Generation gap
Before you lambast this generation [address, October 19, 1987] B. H. Alexander. *Vital Speeches Day* 54:70-2 N 15 '87

Generation gap—*cont.*

Deathbed politics: Medicare and the baby boom generation. P. Longman. *New Repub* 196:18-20 Mr 30 '87

The growing claims of the aged. D. Cohen. por *Macleans* 100:7 Mr 2 '87

I like Bruce Springsteen! R. Coles. il *50 Plus* 27:84 My '87

Midlife music [40 yr. old can't keep up with contemporary rock] M. Goldensohn. il *N Y Times Mag* p48 Je 21 '87

The patrimony society [cover story] R. Kuttner. *New Repub* 196:18-21 My 11 '87

The Ten Commandments of an aging society [address, November 6, 1987] R. D. Lamm. *Vital Speeches Day* 54:133-9 D 15 '87

The war between the generations. L. Smith. il *Fortune* 116:78-80+ Jl 20 '87

Generation gap in literature

The generation gap: from Persephone to Portnoy. E. Lenz. il *N Y Times Book Rev* 92:1+ Ag 30 '87

Generative organs *See* Reproductive organs

Generators, Electric *See* Electric generators

Generators, Random number *See* Random number generators

Generators, Signal *See* Signal generators

Generic drug industry *See* Drug industry

Generic drug laws and regulations *See* Drug laws and regulations

Generic drugs *See* Drugs

Generix Drug Corporation

Playing hide and seek with FDA. R. C. Thompson. il *FDA Consum* 21:36-7 Ap '87

Genes

> *See also*
> Genomes
> Linkage (Genetics)
> Transposons

Cloning of genomic and complementary DNA from Shaker, a putative potassium channel gene from Drosophila. D. M. Papazian and others. bibl f il *Science* 237:749-53 Ag 14 '87

Clustering of genes dispensable for growth in culture in the S component of the HSV-1 genome. R. Longnecker and B. Roizman. bibl f il *Science* 236:573-6 My 1 '87

Identification of a family of muscarinic acetylcholine receptor genes. T. I. Bonner and others. bibl f il *Science* 237:527-32 Jl 31 '87

On the rescue gene and the origin of species [work of Michael Ashburner and Pierre Hutter] *Discover* 8:6-7 Ag '87

Programmed gene rearrangements altering gene expression. P. Borst and D. R. Greaves. bibl f il *Science* 235:658-67 F 6 '87

Rapid identification of nonessential genes of herpes simplex virus type 1 by Tn5 mutagenesis. P. C. Weber and others. bibl f il *Science* 236:576-9 My 1 '87

Ruth Kavenoff liked what she saw in her microscope, so she's putting genes and germs on her T-shirts. il por *People Wkly* 28:133 N 9 '87

Two mammalian genes transcribed from opposite strands of the same DNA locus. J. P. Adelman and others. bibl f il *Science* 235:1514-17 Mr 20 '87

Genesis (Musical group)

Genesis [performance in Chapel Hill, N.C.] P. Puterbaugh. il *Roll Stone* p18 Ap 9 '87

Genesis wraps up smash tour. D. Browne. *Roll Stone* p21+ Jl 16-30 '87

Genet, Philippe

Japan, the armsmaker. *World Press Rev* 34:52-3 O '87

Genetic code

> *See also*
> Amino acid sequence
> Genetic transcription

Agencies vie over human genome project. L. Roberts. il *Science* 237:486-8 Jl 31 '87

Apolipoprotein B-48 is the product of a messenger RNA with an organ-specific in-frame stop codon. S.-H. Chen and others. bibl f il *Science* 238:363-6 O 16 '87

Biology's awesome challenge: breaking the code of life. il *Fortune* 116:89 O 26 '87

Blood clot agent's genes are read [tissue factor; work of Ronald Bach and others] *Sci News* 132:104 Ag 15 '87

Contemplating the human genome [sequencing project] J. L. Fox. il *BioScience* 37:457-60 Jl/Ag '87

Developmental control gene sequenced [fruit flies; work of Gerald Rubin and others] J. L. Marx. *Science* 236:26-7 Ap 3 '87

E.T. may look like us [research by Cyril Ponnamperuma] il *USA Today (Periodical)* 115:16 Je '87

erg, a human *ets*-related gene on chromosome 21: alternative splicing, polyadenylation, and translation. V. N. Rao and others. bibl f il *Science* 237:635-9 Ag 7 '87

First human genome map completed. R. Weiss. *Sci News* 132:245 O 17 '87

Flap arises over genetic map. L. Roberts. il *Science* 238:750-2 N 6 '87

Geneshot [sequencing the human genome; views of Charles P. DeLisi] *Sci Am* 256:58-9 My '87

The genome initiative. S. Begley. il *Newsweek* 110:58-60 Ag 31 '87

The genome project. R. Kanigel. il por *N Y Times Mag* p44+ D 13 '87

A grand plan to map the gene code [W. Gilbert's Genome Corp.] A. Beam. il por *Bus Week* p116-17 Ap 27 '87

Hereditary highway map: assessing the toll [genome map] R. Weiss. *Sci News* 132:101 Ag 15 '87

Homeo boxes in the study of development. W. J. Gehring. bibl f il *Science* 236:1245-52 Je 5 '87

Homeo domain of the yeast repressor α2 is a sequence-specific DNA-binding domain but is not sufficient for repression. M. N. Hall and A. D. Johnson. bibl f il *Science* 237:1007-12 Ag 28 '87

Human cancer gene sequenced [retinoblastoma; work of Wen-Hwa Lee and others] G. Kolata. *Science* 235:1323 Mr 13 '87

Human genetic map: worth the effort? D. D. Edwards. *Sci News* 131:134 F 28 '87

Human genome: questions of cost. L. Roberts. il *Science* 237:1411-12 S 18 '87

Human lipoprotein lipase complementary DNA sequence. K. L. Wion and others. bibl f il *Science* 235:1638-41 Mr 27 '87

Human retinoblastoma susceptibility gene: cloning, identification, and sequence. W.-H. Lee and others. bibl f il *Science* 235:1394-9 Mr 13 '87

Interview [L. E. Hood, developer of automated DNA sequencer] J. Davis. il por *Omni* 10:116-18+ N '87

Japanese super-sequencer poised to roll. R. Lewin. *Science* 236:31 Ap 3 '87

Lens crystallins may be moonlighting [determination of nucleotide sequence for mole rat crystallin gene; work of Wiljan Hendriks and others] *Sci News* 132:104 Ag 15 '87

National Academy looks at human genome project, sees progress. R. Lewin. *Science* 235:747-8 F 13 '87

New sequencers to take on the genome. L. Roberts. il *Science* 238:271-3 O 16 '87

Opening new frontiers in molecular biology [automated DNA sequencer] T. Dworetzky. il *Discover* 8:14-15 Mr '87

Politics of the genome. R. Lewin. *Science* 235:1453 Mr 20 '87

Reading frame selection and transfer RNA anticodon loop stacking. J. F. Curran and M. Yarus. bibl f il *Science* 238:1545-50 D 11 '87

Reading the human blueprint. K. McAuliffe. il *U S News World Rep* 103:92+ D 28 '87-Ja 4 '88

Sequence of a probable potassium channel component encoded at Shaker locus of Drosophila. B. L. Tempel and others. bibl f il *Science* 237:770-5 Ag 14 '87

Sequencing the human genome. D. E. Koshland, Jr. *Science* 236:505 My 1 '87

Sevenless, a cell-specific homeotic gene of Drosophila, encodes a putative transmembrane receptor with a tyrosine kinase domain. E. Hafen and others. bibl f il *Science* 236:55-63 Ap 3 '87

Structurally divergent human T cell receptor γ proteins encoded by distinct Cγ genes. M. S. Krangel and others. bibl f il *Science* 237:64-7 Jl 3 '87

A system for rapid DNA sequencing with fluorescent chain-terminating dideoxynucleotides. J. M. Prober and others. bibl f il *Science* 238:336-41 O 16 '87

Variable occurrence of the *nrd*B intron in the T-even phages suggests intron mobility. J. Pedersen-Lane and M. Belfort. bibl f il *Science* 237:182-4 Jl 10 '87

Who owns the human genome? L. Roberts. il *Science* 237:358-61 Jl 24 '87

Genetic counseling

Better babies. R. Lewis. il *Health* 19:23-4+ Mr '87

"Will the baby be okay?". C. Schaeffer. il *Changing Times* 41:97-103 Mr '87

Genetic diseases *See* Heredity of disease
Genetic engineering (Plants) *See* Plant genetics
Genetic engineering industry *See* Genetic research industry
Genetic engineering research *See* Genetic research
Genetic mapping *See* Chromosome mapping
Genetic polymorphism *See* Polymorphism (Biology)
Genetic regulation

Allelic exclusion in transgenic mice that express the membrane form of immunoglobulin μ. M. C. Nussenzweig and others. bibl f il *Science* 236:816-19 My 15 '87

Antisense RNA inactivation of myosin heavy chain gene expression in Dictyostelium discoideum [cover story] D. A. Knecht and W. F. Loomis. bibl f il *Science* 236:1081-6 My 29 '87

The approaching era of the tumor suppressor genes. G. Klein. bibl f *Science* 238:1539-45 D 11 '87

A cell-cycle constraint on the regulation of gene expression by platelet-derived growth factor. B. J. Rollins and others. bibl f il *Science* 238:1269-71 N 27 '87

CH₃ips off the old genetic block [DNA methylation] D. D. Edwards. *Sci News* 132:36 Jl 18 '87

A chicken transferrin gene in transgenic mice escapes X-chromosome inactivation. M. A. Goldman and others. bibl f il *Science* 236:593-5 My 1 '87

Control protein for AIDS virus identified [research by Gary Nabel and David Baltimore] J. L. Marx. il *Science* 236:393 Ag 24 '87

Cytokine-induced expression of HIV-1 in a chronically infected promonocyte cell line. T. Folks and others. bibl f il *Science* 238:800-2 N 6 '87

Differential expression of c-*myb* mRNA in murine B lymphomas by a block to transcription elongation. T. P. Bender and others. bibl f il *Science* 237:1473-6 S 18 '87

Diversity of alpha-fetoprotein gene expression in mice is generated by a combination of separate enhancer elements. R. E. Hammer and others. bibl f il *Science* 235:53-8 Ja 2 '87

Expression and processing of the AIDS virus reverse transcriptase in Escherichia coli. W. G. Farmerie and others. bibl f il *Science* 236:305-8 Ap 17 '87

Expression and properties of two types of protein kinase C: alternative splicing from a single gene. Y. Ono and others. bibl f il *Science* 236:1116-20 My 29 '87

Expression of an exogenous growth hormone gene by transplantable human epidermal cells. J. R. Morgan and others. bibl f il *Science* 237:1476-9 S 18 '87

Expression of the multidrug-resistant gene in hepatocarcinogenesis and regenerating rat liver. S. S. Thorgeirsson and others. bibl f il *Science* 236:1120-2 My 29 '87

The *fos* gene as "master switch". J. L. Marx. bibl il *Science* 237:854-6 Ag 21 '87

Genetic reconstitution of functional acetylcholine receptor channels in mouse fibroblasts. T. Claudio and others. bibl f il *Science* 238:1688-94 D 18 '87

Glowing tobacco [gene tagging with luciferase] A. Fisher. il *Pop Sci* 230:8 Ap '87

Glucocorticoid receptor mutants that define a small region sufficient for enhancer activation. R. Miesfeld and others. bibl f il *Science* 236:423-7 Ap 24 '87

Growth switch [cell division gene of yeast; work of Melanie G. Lee and Paul Nurse] *Sci Am* 257:23 Jl '87

Homeo domain of the yeast repressor α2 is a sequence-specific DNA-binding domain but is not sufficient for repression. M. N. Hall and A. D. Johnson. bibl f il *Science* 237:1007-12 Ag 28 '87

Human CSF-1: molecular cloning and expression of 4-kb cDNA encoding the human urinary protein. G. G. Wong and others. bibl f il *Science* 235:1504-8 Mr 20 '87

Identification by cell fusion of gene sequences that interact with positive trans-acting factors. T. Lufkin and C. Bancroft. bibl f il *Science* 237:283-6 Jl 17 '87

The inheritance of epigenetic defects. R. Holliday. bibl f il *Science* 238:163-70 O 9 '87

Interaction of a liver-specific nuclear factor with the fibrinogen and α₁-antitrypsin promoters. G. Courtois and others. bibl f il *Science* 238:688-92 O 30 '87

Introduction of a normal human chromosome 11 into a Wilms' tumor cell line controls its tumorigenic expression. B. E. Weissman and others. bibl f il *Science* 236:175-80 Ap 10 '87

Lighting up [gene tagging with luciferase] il *Sci Am* 256:60-2 Ja '87

The lords of the flies. S. Brownlee. il *Discover* 8:26-9+ Ap '87

Mapping patterns of c-*fos* expression in the central nervous system after seizure. J. I. Morgan and others. bibl f il *Science* 237:192-7 Jl 10 '87

Metalloregulator DNA-binding protein encoded by the *mer*R gene: isolation and characterization. T. O'Halloran and C. Walsh. bibl f il *Science* 235:211-14 Ja 9 '87

Methylation gives mom/dad distinction [DNA methylation] *BioScience* 37:651 O '87

The mitochondrial genotype can influence nuclear gene expression in yeast. V. S. Parikh and others. bibl f il *Science* 235:576-80 Ja 30 '87

Molecular events guide embryonic development. D. M. Barnes. il *Science* 238:893-4 N 13 '87

A nerve growth factor-induced gene encodes a possible transcriptional regulatory factor. J. Milbrandt. bibl f il *Science* 238:797-9 N 6 '87

Peptide turn-on for the ACh receptor gene [research by Jean-Pierre Changeux and others] D. M. Barnes. *Science* 238:1652-3 D 18 '87

Post-transcriptional control of class I MHC mRNA expression in adenovirus 12-transformed cells. R. T. M. J. Vaessen and others. bibl f il *Science* 235:1486-8 Mr 20 '87

'Precancer' gene localized in embryo, sperm [int-1 expression] il *Sci News* 132:68 Ag 1 '87

Programmed gene rearrangements altering gene expression. P. Borst and D. R. Greaves. bibl f il *Science* 235:658-67 F 6 '87

A promoter with an internal regulatory domain is part of the origin of replication in BPV-1 [bovine papilloma virus] A. Stenlund and others. bibl f il *Science* 236:1666-71 Je 26 '87

Raf, a trans-acting locus, regulates the α-fetoprotein gene in a cell-autonomous manner. T. F. Vogt and others. bibl f il *Science* 236:301-3 Ap 17 '87

Region-specific expression of two mouse homeo box genes. M. F. Utset and others. bibl f il *Science* 235:1379-82 Mr 13 '87

Regulation in vitro of metallothionein gene binding factors. C. Seguin and D. H. Hamer. bibl f il *Science* 235:1383-7 Mr 13 '87

Regulation of *bcl*-2 proto-oncogene expression during normal human lymphocyte proliferation. J. C. Reed and others. bibl f il *Science* 236:1295-9 Je 5 '87

Regulation of inducible and tissue-specific gene expression. T. Maniatis and others. bibl f il *Science* 236:1237-45 Je 5 '87

Severely impaired adipsin expression in genetic and acquired obesity. J. S. Flier and others. bibl f il *Science* 237:405-8 Jl 24 '87

Site-specific nick in the T-DNA border sequence as a result of Agrobacterium vir gene expression. K. Wang and others. bibl f il *Science* 235:587-91 Ja 30 '87

Stable integration and expression of a bacterial gene in the mosquito Anopheles gambiae. L. H. Miller and others. bibl f il *Science* 237:779-81 Ag 14 '87

Tissue distribution and developmental expression of the messenger RNA encoding angiogenin. H. L. Weiner and others. bibl f il *Science* 237:280-2 Jl 17 '87

Tissue-specific expression of functionally rearranged λ1 Ig gene through a retrovirus vector. R. D. Cone and others. bibl f il *Science* 236:954-7 My 22 '87

Xenopus oocytes injected with rat uterine RNA express very slowly activating potassium currents. M. B. Boyle and others. bibl f il *Science* 235:1221-4 Mr 6 '87

Genetic research

1987 guide to biotechnology products and instruments [with editorial comment] S. S. Roberts. *Science* 235 pt2:G4, G23+ F 27 '87

Battling illness with body proteins. M. Murray. il *Sci News* 131:42-5 Ja 17 '87

Body doubles [engineering of healing proteins] J. Kluger. il *Omni* 9:48-50+ Ag '87

Cracking the mold [gene targeting and anti-sense techniques used in Dictyostelium myosin research] *Sci Am* 257:26 Ag '87

Disruption of the Dictyostelium myosin heavy chain gene by homologous recombination. A. De Lozanne and J. A. Spudich. bibl f il *Science* 236:1086-91 My 29 '87

Freeing hemophiliacs from the risk of AIDS [synthetic clotting factor offers hope] R. Rhein, Jr. and L. Therrien. il *Bus Week* p38 Ap 13 '87

Frontiers in recombinant DNA [special issue; with editorial comment by Daniel E. Koshland, Jr.] *Science* 236:1157, 1223-68 Je 5 '87

Genetic recombination. F. W. Stahl. il *Sci Am* 256:90-101 F '87

Insect viruses invade biotechnology [baculoviruses] B. R. Jasny. il *Science* 238:1653 D 18 '87

Medicines from the body. C. P. Weinstock. il *FDA Consum* 21:6-10 Ap '87

Genetic research—*cont.*

Probing gene action during development [special section] il *Science* 236:29-31 Ap 3 '87

Splicing of messenger RNA precursors. P. A. Sharp. bibl f il *Science* 235:766-71 F 13 '87

Environmental aspects

Altered bacteria released [frost preventing bacteria] *Sci News* 131:277 My 2 '87

Assessing the risks of microbial release. J. L. Marx. bibl il *Science* 237:1413-17 S 18 '87

Biological impact and assessment: biological potentials over time [address, November 14, 1986] J. F. Fulkerson. por *BioScience* 37:187-9 Mr '87

Biotech tests given go-ahead, look-see. *Sci News* 131:122 F 21 '87

BioTechnica tests EPA review process [field test of Rhizobium bacteria] M. Crawford. *Science* 235:840 F 20 '87

Bozeman chain saw massacre [G. A. Strobel's Dutch elm disease experiment] W. E. Brock. il pors *Discover* 8:78-82+ N '87

California field test goes forward [Frostban bacteria] M. Crawford. il *Science* 236:511 My 1 '87

The case for qualifying "case by case". H. I. Miller. *Science* 236:133 Ap 10 '87

Down on the farm: genetic engineering meets ecology. D. Pimentel. il *Technol Rev* 90:24-30 Ja '87

Engineered bacteria released [preventing frost damage] L. Tangley. *BioScience* 37:461 Jl/Ag '87

Europe splits over gene regulation. D. Dickson. *Science* 238:18-19 O 2 '87

Gene-altered hog vaccine causes stir for USDA [Omnivac pseudorabies vaccine] *Success Farm* 85 no6:18AZ Mr '87

Ice minus and jobs minus. D. E. Koshland, Jr. *Science* 236:761 My 15 '87

The importance of being blue [South Carolina experiment attempts to track genetically altered Pseudomonas in soil] M. D. Lemonick. il *Time* 130:82-3 N 9 '87

Montana State's troublesome elms [G. Strobel illegally injects diseased trees with genetically altered bacteria] M. D. Lemonick. il por *Time* 130:67 S 14 '87

MSU faults Strobel for Dutch elm test. L. Roberts. *Science* 237:1286 S 11 '87

New biotechnologies [address, December 12, 1986] P. W. Huber. *Vital Speeches Day* 53:369-71 Ap 1 '87

New questions in Strobel case [field test of Dutch elm disease] L. Roberts. *Science* 237:1097-8 S 4 '87

NIH finds Argentine experiment did not break U.S. biotechnology rules. M. Crawford. *Science* 235:276 Ja 16 '87

One potato patch that is making genetic history [test of genetically engineered Ice-minus bacteria at Tulelake, Calif.] S. S. Hall. il *Smithsonian* 18:125-6+ Ag '87

Policy forum. F. E. Sharples; B. D. Davis. *Science* 235:1329-35 Mr 13 '87

Researcher flouts gene-splicing rules [G. Strobel's Dutch elm disease experiment] M. Crawford. *Science* 237:838-9 Ag 21 '87

Tubers, berries and bugs [bacteria designed to inhibit frost formation sprayed on plants] P. Elmer-Dewitt. il *Time* 129:63 My 11 '87

Ethical aspects

Gene of the week. R. Bazell. *New Repub* 196:13-14 Mr 23 '87

Perfect people? [cover story] A. Virshup. il *N Y* 20:26-34 Jl 27 '87

Should Christians oppose genetic engineering? W. A. Durbin, Jr. il *Christ Today* 31:54-5 S 4 '87

Laws and regulations

See also

Biotechnology Science Coordinating Council (U.S.)

Biotech lawsuits filed, regs amended. D. D. Edwards. *Sci News* 131:87 F 7 '87

Biotechnology and the regulation hydra. P. W. Huber. il *Technol Rev* 90:57-60+ N/D '87

Court rejects Rifkin in biotech cases. M. Crawford. *Science* 235:159 Ja 9 '87

Harvesting the fruits of biotechnology. F. E. Young. il *FDA Consum* 21:2-3 S '87

Ice minus and jobs minus. D. E. Koshland, Jr. *Science* 236:761 My 15 '87

The making of a monster. il *U S News World Rep* 103:10 Ag 31 '87

RAC recommends easing some recombinant DNA guidelines. M. Crawford. *Science* 235:740-1 F 13 '87

Germany (West)

. . . German moratorium urged. D. Dickson. *Science* 235:741 F 13 '87

Patents

Animal patent debate heats up. R. Weiss. *Sci News* 132:69-70 Ag 1 '87

Animals can now be patented. L. Tangley. *BioScience* 37:461-2 Jl/Ag '87

Biotech in court. A. S. Moffat. il *Technol Rev* 90:16+ Ag/S '87

Controversy over animal patents. A. L. Spitler. *BioScience* 37:652 O '87

Genetic engineering and the Patent Office. J. G. Sheldon and D. L. Anderson. *BioScience* 37:679-81 O '87

If it moves, patent it [animals produced by biotechnology] *Sci News* 131:263 Ap 25 '87

Man-beast: patent pending. il *U S News World Rep* 102:18 Ap 27 '87

Of judges, genes and genetic engineers. R. Weiss. il *Sci News* 132:124-5 Ag 22 '87

OTA: property right, donor consent factors cloud "gifts" of human tissue. M. Crawford. *Science* 235:1564 Mr 27 '87

Patenting animals. G. Vincent. il *Success Farm* 85:64 Ag '87

Religious groups join animal patent battle. M. Crawford. *Science* 237:480-1 Jl 31 '87

Selling a pound of flesh [biotech use of patients' cell lines] J. Schwartz. il *Newsweek* 109:55 Ap 20 '87

Should animals be patented? C. Wallis. il *Time* 129:110 My 4 '87

Should man make beast? T. Monmaney. il *Newsweek* 109:64 My 4 '87

Who owns human tissues and cells? [report by the Office of Technology Assessment] L. Tangley. *BioScience* 37:376-8 Je '87

Who owns the human genome? L. Roberts. il *Science* 237:358-61 Jl 24 '87

Great Britain

Companies vie over new heart drug [Genentech vs. Wellcome] M. Sun. il *Science* 237:120-2 Jl 10 '87

Genentech takes another hit [Britain rejects TPA patent] J. O. Hamilton and M. Maremont. *Bus Week* p75 Jl 20 '87

Ruling on heart drug may boost research [British court's TPA patent ruling] M. Sun. il *Science* 237:244 Jl 17 '87

Plants

See Plant genetics

Public opinion

Mixed views on biotech [Office of Technology Assessment survey] M. Crawford. *Science* 236:1179 Je 5 '87

Argentina

NIH finds Argentine experiment did not break U.S. biotechnology rules. M. Crawford. *Science* 235:276 Ja 16 '87

Developing countries

Biotechnology, agriculture and development [cover story; special issue; with editorial comment by Edouard Glissant] il *Courier* 40:3-34 Mr '87

Japan

Japanese super-sequencer poised to roll. R. Lewin. *Science* 236:31 Ap 3 '87

Western Europe

Europe splits over gene regulation. D. Dickson. *Science* 238:18-19 O 2 '87

Genetic research industry

See also

Amgen (Firm)

Applied Microbiology Inc.

Bio-Technology General Corp.

Biotechnica International Inc.

Celgene Corporation

Centocor, Inc.

Cetus Corporation

Collaborative Research, Inc.

Genentech, Inc.

Genex Corp.

Genome Corporation

Integrated Genetics, Inc.

MicroGeneSys Inc.

Monsanto Company

Thermedics Inc.

Acquisitions and mergers

The big boys are joining the biotech party. S. Gannes. il *Fortune* 116:58-60+ Jl 6 '87

Cyanamid is bullish on a cure for sick cows [acquiring stake in Applied Microbiology's protein for mastitis] G. G. Marcial. il *Bus Week* p136 My 11 '87

Finance

Designer proteins: the next boom in biotech. M. Bluestone. il *Bus Week* p94+ Ap 13 '87

Here come the bionic piglets. G. Bylinsky. il *Fortune* 116:74-6+ O 26 '87

Genetic research industry—*cont.*
International aspects
Profiting from biotechnology. *World Press Rev* 34:48 Ap '87
Laws and regulations
See Genetic research—Laws and regulations
Management
Striking it rich in biotech [scientist-founders] S. Gannes. il *Fortune* 116:131-2+ N 9 '87
Securities
Biotechnology's stock market blues. M. Crawford. il *Science* 238:1503-4 D 11 '87
Super stocks for tomorrow: biotech [cover story] M. C. Paulson. il *Changing Times* 41:24-30+ Je '87
Will biotech's boom go bust? J. J. Curran. il *Fortune* 116:101-2 Jl 6 '87
Canada
See also
Quadra Logic Technologies Inc.
Sweden
See also
Fermenta AB
Genetic screening
Gene of the week. R. Bazell. *New Repub* 196:13-14 Mr 23 '87
Genes that predict disease. K. McAuliffe. il *Read Dig* 131:17-18+ S '87
Perfect people? [cover story] A. Virshup. il *N Y* 20:26-34 Jl 27 '87
Predicting diseases [cover story] K. McAuliffe. il *U S News World Rep* 102:64-9 My 25 '87
"Will the baby be okay?". C. Schaeffer. il *Changing Times* 41:97-103 Mr '87
Genetic toxicology
An excuse for workplace hazard [fetal protection policies discriminate against women] C. Marshall. il *Nation* 244:532-4 Ap 25 '87
Gauging the value of carcinogen assays. J. Raloff. *Sci News* 131:343 My 30 '87
The genetic effect. C. Marshall. *Vogue* 177:404+ O '87
The poisoned womb [views of John Elkington] *Futurist* 21:55 My/Je '87
Prediction of chemical carcinogenicity in rodents from in vitro genetic toxicity assays. R. W. Tennant and others. bibl f il *Science* 236:933-41 My 22 '87
Genetic transcription
Activation of adenovirus promoters by the adenovirus E1A protein in cell-free extracts. R. Spangler and others. bibl f il *Science* 237:1044-6 Ag 28 '87
The adenovirus major late transcription factor activates the rat γ-fibrinogen promoter. L. A. Chodosh and others. bibl f il *Science* 238:684-8 O 30 '87
HTLV *x* gene mutants exhibit novel transcriptional regulatory phenotypes. W. Wachsman and others. bibl f il *Science* 235:674-7 F 6 '87
Human proto-oncogene c-*jun* encodes a DNA binding protein with structural and functional properties of transcription factor AP-1. D. Bohmann and others. bibl f il *Science* 238:1386-92 D 4 '87
Multiple global regulators control HIS4 transcription in yeast. K. T. Arndt and others. bibl f il *Science* 237:874-80 Ag 21 '87
Oncogenes and transcriptional control. H. E. Varmus. bibl f *Science* 238:1337-9 D 4 '87
Protein-binding sites in Ig gene enhancers determine transcriptional activity and inducibility. M. Lenardo and others. bibl f il *Science* 236:1573-7 Je 19 '87
Recombinant fragment of protein kinase inhibitor blocks cyclic AMP-dependent gene transcription. J. R. Grove and others. bibl f il *Science* 238:530-3 O 23 '87
Reverse transcription. H. E. Varmus. bibl (p120) il *Sci Am* 257:56-9+ S '87
Transcriptional regulation in the yeast life cycle. K. Nasmyth and D. Shore. bibl f il *Science* 237:1162-70 S 4 '87
Genetic transformation *See* Gene transfer
Genetic variation *See* Variation (Biology)
Genetics
See also
Adaptation (Biology)
AIDS (Disease)—Genetic aspects
Alcoholics and alcoholism—Genetic aspects
Alzheimer's disease—Genetic aspects
Animal genetics
Behavioral genetics
Cancer—Genetic aspects
Chromosomes
Clones (Biology)
Crossing over (Genetics)
Depression, Mental—Genetic aspects
Diabetes—Genetic aspects

Fish genetics
Fungal genetics
Germplasm resources
Heart—Diseases—Genetic aspects
Heredity and environment
Heredity of disease
Homozygosis
Immunogenetics
Linkage (Genetics)
Microbial genetics
Molecular genetics
Monoclonal antibodies
Mosaics (Biology)
Muscular dystrophy—Genetic aspects
Mutation
Natural selection
Obesity—Genetic aspects
Personality—Genetic aspects
Plant genetics
Population genetics
Variation (Biology)
Research
See Genetic research
Genetics, Comparative
The ancestry of the giant panda [molecular analysis; cover story] S. J. O'Brien. il map *Sci Am* 257:102-7 N '87
Conservation of the Duchenne muscular dystrophy gene in mice and humans. E. P. Hoffman and others. bibl f il *Science* 238:347-50 O 16 '87
My close cousin the chimpanzee. R. Lewin. il *Science* 238:273-5 O 16 '87
Phylogenetic relations of humans and African apes from DNA sequences in the ψη-globin region. M. M. Miyamoto and others. bibl f il *Science* 238:369-73 O 16 '87
Tics in the tocks of molecular clocks. I. Amato. il *Sci News* 131:74-5 Ja 31 '87
Genetics and environment *See* Heredity and environment
Geneva (Switzerland)
Hotels, motels, etc.
Aristocratic Bergues. T. Kreiter. il *Saturday Evening Post* 259:90-1 Mr '87
Music
See also
Opera—Switzerland
Geneva Auto Show *See* Automobiles—Exhibitions
Geneva Business Services, Inc.
Sell now. J. Heins. il por *Forbes* 139 Ann Directory:124+ Ap 27 '87
Genevie, Louis E.
about
Happy Mother's Day [interview] B. Johnson. il pors *People Wkly* 27:57-8+ My 11 '87
Genevie, Louis E., and Margolies, Eva
How women feel about "helpful" husbands & how children affect a marriage [excerpts from The motherhood report] *Good Housekeep* 204:188-9+ My '87
The motherhood report [excerpts] il *Good Housekeep* 204:73-6 Ap '87
Genex Corp.
Techno-blinders. A. A. Lappen. il pors *Forbes* 140:104+ D 28 '87
Geng, Veronica
Hands up. *New Yorker* 63:29 Mr 2 '87
My and Ed's peace proposals. *New Yorker* 63:74 S 7 '87
Pat Robertson's catalog essay for a new exhibition of paintings by David Salle. *N Y Rev Books* 34:34 N 19 '87
Poll. *New Yorker* 63:21 Ag 3 '87
Genie Awards
People: the Genie Awards. Y. Cox. il *Macleans* 100:44-5 Mr 30 '87
Genital herpesviruses *See* Herpesviruses
Genitals *See* Reproductive organs
Genius
See also
Children, Gifted
Genoa (Italy)
Music
See also
Opera—Italy
Genome Corporation
The genome project. R. Kanigel. il por *N Y Times Mag* p44+ D 13 '87
A grand plan to map the gene code. A. Beam. il por *Bus Week* p116-17 Ap 27 '87
Genomes
Agencies vie over human genome project. L. Roberts. il *Science* 237:486-8 Jl 31 '87

Genomes—*cont.*

Biology's awesome challenge: breaking the code of life. il *Fortune* 116:89 O 26 '87

Contemplating the human genome [sequencing project] J. L. Fox. il *BioScience* 37:457-60 Jl/Ag '87

First human genome map completed. R. Weiss. *Sci News* 132:245 O 17 '87

Flap arises over genetic map. L. Roberts. il *Science* 238:750-2 N 6 '87

Geneshot [sequencing the human genome; views of Charles P. DeLisi] *Sci Am* 256:58-9 My '87

The genome initiative. S. Begley. il *Newsweek* 110:58-60 Ag 31 '87

Hereditary highway map: assessing the toll [genome map] R. Weiss. *Sci News* 132:101 Ag 15 '87

Human genetic map: worth the effort? D. D. Edwards. *Sci News* 131:134 F 28 '87

Human genome: questions of cost. L. Roberts. il *Science* 237:1411-12 S 18 '87

National Academy looks at human genome project, sees progress. R. Lewin. *Science* 235:747-8 F 13 '87

New sequencers to take on the genome. L. Roberts. il *Science* 238:271-3 O 16 '87

A physical map of the Escherichia coli K12 genome. C. L. Smith and others. bibl f il *Science* 236:1448-53 Je 12 '87

Politics of the genome. R. Lewin. *Science* 235:1453 Mr 20 '87

Sequencing the human genome. D. E. Koshland, Jr. *Science* 236:505 My 1 '87

Who owns the human genome? L. Roberts. il *Science* 237:358-61 Jl 24 '87

Gentians, Fringed *See* Fringed gentians

Les gentilhommes [ballet] *See* Ballet reviews—Single works

Gentlemen's quarterly

20 things a 30-year-old regular guy should know. B. Barol. il *Newsweek* 109:82 Je 22 '87

Gentling, Scott

about

Twins Scott and Stuart Gentling sell off a high-priced Audubon and give wing to their own bird book. M. Vespa. il pors *People Wkly* 27:117-18 Je 15 '87

Gentling, Stuart

about

Twins Scott and Stuart Gentling sell off a high-priced Audubon and give wing to their own bird book. M. Vespa. il pors *People Wkly* 27:117-18 Je 15 '87

Gentrification

The gentrification of Harlem. M. Mittelstaedt. *World Press Rev* 34:44 Ap '87

Gentry, Ric

Charismatic Clint. il pors *McCalls* 114:136+ Je '87

Konchalovsky: the force of nature. il por *Theatre Crafts* 21:63-6 Mr '87

Gentry, Roger L.

Seals and their kin [cover story] il supp (folded map) *Natl Geogr* 171:474-501 Ap '87

Genuine Parts Company

Grease monkey's dream. K. Hannon. il por *Forbes* 140:193 N 30 '87

GEO [television program] *See* Television program reviews—Single works

Geo. A. Hormel & Co.

And this little pig processor does nicely. R. Simon. il por *Forbes* 139:93 F 23 '87

Local lunch meat makes good, and Austin, Minnesota pays homage with a fond 'Play it again, Spam'. il *People Wkly* 28:53 Jl 20 '87

Geochemistry

See also

Biogeochemical cycles

Biogeochemistry

Geochronology *See* Geological time

Geodesic domes

Homes of foam [cover story] V. E. Gilmore. il *Pop Sci* 230:78-81+ Mr '87

Geodesy

See also

National Geodetic Survey (U.S.)

Geodetic surveying *See* Surveying

Geoghegan, Thomas

Mobbed. *New Repub* 197:11-12 N 16 '87

Geographers

The rewards of travel. J. Crane. *Focus* 36:1 Wint '86

Geographical distribution of animals and plants

See also

Animal introduction

Plant introduction

Can only evapotranspiration make a tree? [variation in biodiversity by locale; research by David J. Currie and Viviane Paquin] map *Sci News* 132:215 O 3 '87

The ecology of biological invasions. H. A. Mooney and J. A. Drake. bibl f il maps *Environment* 29:10-15+ Je '87

Gene flow and the geographic structure of natural populations. M. Slatkin. bibl f il *Science* 236:787-92 My 15 '87

Heritability at the species level: analysis of geographic ranges of Cretaceous mollusks. D. Jablonski. bibl f il *Science* 238:360-3 O 16 '87

Species richness: a geographic approach to protecting future biological diversity [cover story] J. M. Scott and others. bibl f il map *BioScience* 37:782-8 D '87

Stress physiology and the distribution of plants. C. B. Osmond and others. bibl f il *BioScience* 37:38-48 Ja '87

Geographical myths

The potency of myth [special section] il *Courier* 40:8-10 Ap '87

Geographical names *See* Names, Geographical

Geographical perception

Place maps [regional distortions in map drawing by college freshman; study by Thomas F. Saarinen] C. Simon. maps *Psychol Today* 21:15 N '87

Geography

See also

Bible—Geography

Geographers

Medical geography

National Geographic Society (U.S.)

The Focus quiz. il *Focus* 37:1+ Summ '87

Gee-whiz geography. il maps *Natl Geogr World* 145:12-13 S '87

Test your GQ (geography quotient). E. Kunes. il *Seventeen* 46:117 N '87

Geography, Historical

See also

Maps, Early

Geography, Political *See* Geopolitics

Geological climate *See* Paleoclimatology

Geological physics *See* Geophysics

Geological research

See also

Antarctic research

Geological Survey (U.S.)

Turf battle over federal responsibility for groundwater. A. L. Spitler. *BioScience* 37:317 My '87

Geological Survey of Canada

Out of the past [founder W. E. Logan] S. S. Doria and J. J. Doria. *Earth Sci* 39:29 Wint '86

Geological surveys

See also

Geological Survey (U.S.)

Geological Survey of Canada

Geological time

See also

Radioactive dating

A substantial bias in nonparametric tests for periodicity in geophysical data. S. M. Stigler and M. J. Wagner. bibl f il *Science* 238:940-5 N 13 '87

Geologists

See also

Women geologists

Geology

See also

Caves

Computers—Geological use

Continental drift

Drilling and boring (Earth and rocks)

Earthquakes

Erosion

Faults (Geology)

Folds (Geology)

Geological Survey (U.S.)

Geological time

Holography—Geological use

Landslides

Lunar geology

Mars (Planet)—Geology

Minerals

Mountains

Ocean bottom

Ore deposits

Petroleum—Geology

Rocks

Sand

Sedimentation and deposition

Subduction (Geology)

Geology—See also—*cont.*
   Submarine geology
   Subsidences (Earth movements)
   Tomography—Geological use
   Tors
   Venus (Planet)—Geology
   Volcanoes
   Weathering
All is flux [hot spots; research by Peter Molnar and Joann Stock] R. Kunzig. *Sci Am* 257:24+ S '87
Delving deep into the Indian past [ocean hot spots] R. Monastersky. map *Sci News* 132:56 Jl 25 '87
Direct measurements confirm plate tectonics [very long baseline interferometry] R. A. Kerr. il *Science* 236:1425-6 Je 12 '87
Do tectonic plates drive themselves? R. A. Kerr. *Science* 236:1426 Je 12 '87
Geoquiz. J. V. O'Connor. See issues of Earth Science beginning Summer 1985
Geoquiz [tectonic plates] il map *Earth Sci* 40:22 Fall '87
Salt tectonics. C. J. Talbot and M. P. A. Jackson. bibl (p116) il *Sci Am* 257:70-9 Ag '87
Set adrift by wandering hotspots [cover story] R. Monastersky. il map *Sci News* 132:250-2 O 17 '87

Conferences
Calendar. See issues of Earth Science
Old and new geology meet in Phoenix [special section] R. A. Kerr. il *Science* 238:890-1 N 13 '87

Maps
Books & maps. See issues of Earth Science

Terminology
Geoquiz. J. V. O'Connor. il *Earth Sci* 40:26 Summ '87

Amazon River Valley
Fluvial perturbance in the western Amazon basin: regulation by long-term sub-Andean tectonics. M. E. Räsänen and others. bibl f il map *Science* 238:1398-401 D 4 '87

Arizona
   See also
   Grand Canyon (Ariz.)
Slowly sinking in the West [subsidence] F. Turner. il *Wilderness* 51:47-50 Fall '87

Asia
Making the world's roof. R. A. Kerr. *Science* 236:911 My 22 '87

Australia
Horizontal plate motion: a key allocyclic factor in the evolution of the Great Barrier Reef. P. J. Davies and others. bibl f il map *Science* 238:1697-700 D 18 '87
Solar records set in stone. il *Sky Telesc* 73:153-4 F '87

Bahamas
Sand castles from the past: Bahamian stromatolites discovered [cover story] E. A. Shinn. il map *Sea Front* 33:334-43 S/O '87

California
Earthquakes are giving little warning [crustal deformation] *Science* 235:165-6 Ja 9 '87
Is the San Andreas weak at heart? R. A. Kerr. il *Science* 236:388-9 Ap 24 '87
New evidence on the state of stress of the San Andreas fault system. M. D. Zoback and others. bibl f il maps *Science* 238:1105-11 N 20 '87

Canada
   See also
   Geological Survey of Canada

Cape Cod (Mass.)
Unique satellite image shows geology of Cape Cod. il *Earth Sci* 39:7-8 Wint '86

Finger Lakes region (N.Y.)
Living near a glacial oddity. P. Barnes-Svarney. il *Conservationist* 41:22-5 Mr/Ap '87

Illinois
Garden of the Gods, Illinois. R. H. Mohlenbrock. il map *Nat Hist* 96:66-8 Je '87

Manitoba
Adventure in Manitoba. S. M. Marcus. il *Earth Sci* 40:21-3 Summ '87

Maryland
Soldiers Delight. S. Newcomb. il map *Earth Sci* 40:24-5 Summ '87

Middle Atlantic States
   See also
   Reading Prong

New Mexico
Slowly sinking in the West [subsidence] F. Turner. il *Wilderness* 51:47-50 Fall '87

North America
Pollen and spores date origin of rift basins from Texas to Nova Scotia as early late Triassic. A. Traverse. bibl f il map *Science* 236:1469-72 Je 12 '87
Unlocking the amazing mystery of our continent. R. Schiller. il map *Read Dig* 131:152-6+ S '87

Ohio
   See also
   Cleveland (Ohio)—Geology

Oregon
Travels of an ancient reef. G. D. Stanley, Jr. il maps *Nat Hist* 96:36-43 N '87

Southeast Asia
Review of 'geological risks' in ESCAP urban areas planned. *UN Chron* 23:22 Ja '86

Tibet
Geologic evolution of northern Tibet: results of an expedition to Ulugh Muztagh. P. H. Molnar and others. bibl f il maps *Science* 235:299-305 Ja 16 '87

Geology, Economic
   See also
   Mines and mineral resources
Geology, Stratigraphic
   See also
   Paleontology
Chronology of fluctuating sea levels since the Triassic. B. U. Haq and others. bibl f il *Science* 235:1156-67 Mr 6 '87
Sea cycle clock [seismic stratigraphy; work of Peter R. Vail and others] S. Weisburd. il *Sci News* 131:154-5 Mr 7 '87

Cretaceous
Asteroid impact gets more support [research by Bruce Bohor and others] R. A. Kerr. bibl il *Science* 236:666-8 My 8 '87
A big splash in the Pacific [work of Frank Kyte and others] map *Sky Telesc* 74:12 Jl '87
End-Cretaceous mass extinction event: argument for terrestrial causation. A. Hallam. bibl f il *Science* 238:1237-42 N 27 '87
Extinction upon impact? [research by Bruce F. Bohor and others] R. Monastersky. il *Sci News* 131:309-10 My 16 '87
Point of impact: Manson, Iowa? R. Monastersky. *Sci News* 132:396 D 19-26 '87
Searching land and sea for the dinosaur killer. R. A. Kerr. il *Science* 237:856-7 Ag 21 '87
Shock of impact [shocked quartz as evidence of asteroid impact with earth; work of Bruce F. Bohor and others] *Sci Am* 257:22-3 Jl '87
Shocked quartz in the Cretaceous-Tertiary boundary clays: evidence for a global distribution. B. F. Bohor and others. bibl f il map *Science* 236:705-9 My 8 '87
Volcanoes and extinctions: round two [theory of Vincent E. Courtillot and Stanley Cisowski] S. Weisburd. il map *Sci News* 131:248-50 Ap 18 '87
Who killed the dinosaurs? [impact-generated extinction theory] *Space World* X-8-284:9 Ag '87

Precambrian
Solar records set in stone [Australian study] il *Sky Telesc* 73:153-4 F '87

Triassic
Travels of an ancient reef. G. D. Stanley, Jr. il maps *Nat Hist* 96:36-43 N '87
Geology, Structural *See* Geology
Geomagnetism *See* Magnetism, Terrestrial
Geometry
   See also
   Angles
   Fractals
   Transformations (Mathematics)

Study and teaching
   Anecdotes, facetiae, satire, etc.
Up from Euclid. D. Seligman. il *Fortune* 116:187 S 28 '87
Geophagia *See* Pica (Pathology)
Geophysics
   See also
   American Geophysical Union
   Earth—Internal structure
   Magnetism, Terrestrial
   Seismometers and seismometry
Geophysics. *Phys Today* 40:S37-S42 Ja '87
A geophysics potpourri in San Francisco [special section] R. A. Kerr. il *Science* 235:433-5 Ja 23 '87

Awards
American Geophysical Union honored eight in 1986. il *Phys Today* 40:83-4+ Je '87

Conferences
Geophysics smorgasbord was spread in Baltimore [special section] R. A. Kerr. il *Science* 236:1425-7 Je 12 '87

Geopolitics

Economic imbalances and world politics. C. F. Bergsten. bibl f *Foreign Aff* 65:770-94 Spr '87

The U.S.-Soviet conflict: concert through decompression. G. Liska. *Current* 289:32-40 Ja '87

Will the cold war fade away? W. Isaacson. il *Time* 130:40-2+ Jl 27 '87

George V, King of Great Britain, 1865-1936
about

Was the king murdered? K. Slack. *Christ Century* 104:6-7 Ja 7-14 '87

George, B.
about

One of each, please. B. Barol. il pors *Newsweek* 109:54-5 Ap 6 '87

George, Henry, 1839-1897
about

Guidance from a classic: the centennial of Henry George's Protection or free trade [address, November 13, 1986] C. L. Harriss. *Vital Speeches Day* 53:171-3 Ja 1 '87

George, Nelson

Cameo! il *Essence* 18:54-5+ Jl '87

George, T. J. S.

Vietnam: time to change course. il *World Press Rev* 34:29+ F '87

George Banta Company, Inc.

Banta to print 85 titles for Brazil's Distribuidora. J. P. Frank. *Publ Wkly* 231:24 Ja 23 '87

George C. Marshall Institute

Pro-SDI panel forecasts $121-billion antimissile costs, excluding research. *Aviat Week Space Technol* 126:133 F 9 '87

George C. Marshall Space Flight Center

Last of the rocket team: a conversation with Georg von Tiesenhausen. F. I. Ordway. il por *Space World* X-6-282:29-32 Je '87

George Eastman House International Museum of Photography *See* International Museum of Photography at George Eastman House

George M. Low Center for Industrial Innovation

In the Northeast. G. Anderson. il *Archit Rec* 175:90-5 Jl '87

George Washington Bridge (N.Y. and N.J.)

Goodbye, old paint. B. Weber. il *N Y Times Mag* p94 S 27 '87

George Washington National Forest (Va. and W. Va.)

Blackie's Hollow, Virginia. R. H. Mohlenbrock. il map *Nat Hist* 96:70-2 Jl '87

Georgetown (Washington, D.C.)

Social graces in Georgetown: Polly and Clayton Fritchey's Victorian enclave. S. M. Alsop. il pors *Archit Dig* 44:188-91 O '87

Georgetown University

Geek House [Right House, a conservatives-only group house] C. Lane. *New Repub* 196:16-17 Ja 5-12 '87

Georgia

See also
Architecture, Domestic—Georgia
Botanical gardens—Georgia
Brooks County (Ga.)
Criminal justice, Administration of—Georgia
Drama festivals—Georgia
Educational laws and regulations—Georgia
Festivals—Georgia
Flower gardens and gardening—Georgia
Fulton County (Ga.)
Gwinnett County (Ga.)
Historic houses, sites, etc.—Georgia
Medical care—Georgia
Okefenokee Swamp (Ga. and Fla.)
Resorts—Georgia
Sea Islands
Stone Mountain Memorial (Ga.)
Taxation—Georgia

Description and travel

The enchanted land [Georgia coast] H. Middleton. il map *South Living* 22:76-81 F '87

Legislature

Black Georgia politician helps kill betting bill [Charles Walker] *Jet* 71:4 F 16 '87

Politics and government

See also
Georgia—Legislature

Georgia Federal Bank, FSB

At 69, J.B. Fuqua still keeps 'em guessing [selling Georgia Federal Bank] S. Ticer. il por *Bus Week* p82 N 23 '87

Georgia-Pacific Corp.

Ear to the ground. D. Henry. il *Forbes* 140:71 O 19 '87

Most improved. il *Forbes* 139:205 Ja 12 '87

Georgia Power Co.

Denied promotion, woman shoots supervisors and kills self in Atlanta [suicide of M. Dansby] *Jet* 72:25 My 18 '87

Whispering hope [suicide of M. Dansby, woman denied promotion] R. Weems. il *Ms* 16:40-1 D '87

Georgia Satellites (Musical group)

After a shaky lift-off the Georgia Satellites are sitting on top of the world. S. Dougherty. il *People Wkly* 27:45-6 Je 1 '87

Bands hitting the headlines. il por *Teen* 31:55 My '87

Georgia Satellites. M. McCormick. il *Roll Stone* p16 Ja 29 '87

Georgian Group

Articles of association: the Georgian Group. il *Hist Today* 37:62 Jl '87

Georgian house decoration *See* House decoration, Georgian

Georgian period *See* Great Britain—History—1714-1837

Georgopoulos, Apostolos P., and others

Neuronal coding and robotics [discussion of September 26, 1986 article, Neuronal population coding of movement direction] *Science* 237:300-1 Jl 17 '87

GeoSpectra Corporation

Business as usual . . . but not with the Soviets? [GeoSpectra hesitant to handle Soviet satellite photographs] *Space World* X-12-288:7-8 D '87

Geostationary operational environmental satellites *See* Artificial satellites—Meteorological use

Geothermal energy *See* Geothermal resources

Geothermal measurements *See* Earth temperature

Geothermal resources

See also
Hot springs

Central America

Drilling for cheap, hot power. W. J. Cook. il *U S News World Rep* 102:82 Mr 16 '87

Great Britain

Hot dry rock: problems, promise [projects in Cornwall, England and Fenton Hill, N.M.] R. A. Kerr. il *Science* 238:1226-8 N 27 '87

New Mexico

Hot dry rock: problems, promise [projects in Cornwall, England and Fenton Hill, N.M.] R. A. Kerr. il *Science* 238:1226-8 N 27 '87

Geotropism

See also
Seeds, Effect of weightlessness on

Apogeotropic roots in an Amazon rain forest. R. L. Sanford. bibl f il *Science* 235:1062-4 F 27 '87

When growing down isn't good enough [apogeotropic roots; study by Robert L. Sanford, Jr.] *Sci News* 131:188 Mr 21 '87

Gephardt, Richard A.

Should Congress adopt the House-passed "Gephardt Amendment"? [excerpts from debate, April 29, 1987] *Congr Dig* 66:174+ Je/Jl '87
about

An Eagle Scout from Missouri wins peers' praise. D. Chu. il por *People Wkly* 27:40-1 Ap 13 '87

Gephardt rides in. *Nation* 244:67-8 Ja 24 '87

Gephardt's inside moves. M. Kondracke. il *New Repub* 196:20-2 Je 1 '87

The high jumper from St. Louis. J. S. DeMott. il por *Time* 129:42 Mr 9 '87

Howdy, I'm Dick Gephardt—trade warrior. D. Harbrecht. il por *Bus Week* p98-9 My 4 '87

Inside Gephardt's PACscam [cover story] D. Corn. il *Nation* 244:559+ My 2 '87

Letter from Washington. Cato. *Natl Rev* 39:11 Je 5 '87

Neo-Gephardt. J. J. Pitney, Jr. *New Repub* 197:13-14 D 14 '87

Planning a secret-poll scam. M. Duffy. il por *Time* 130:27 N 23 '87

Political battles over trade wars. W. Shapiro. il pors *Time* 129:24 My 4 '87

Young man in a hurry. M. Duffy. il pors *Time* 130:26+ N 30 '87

Geraniums

Geraniums are on a roll! T. Marston. il *Flower Gard* 31:10+ F/Mr '87

Overwinter geraniums. H. Barnett. il *Rodale's Org Gard* 34:22-3 O '87

Gérard de Nerval *See* Nerval, Gérard de, 1808-1855

Geraty, Virginia Mixson
about

Special words, special lady. D. Young. il por *South Living* 22:146 Mr '87

Gerber, Eduard A., 1907-1986
about
Obituary
    Phys Today 40:124+ F '87. A. Ballato
Gerber, Merrill Joan
Hold tight, my love [story] il *Redbook* 168:60+
    Ap '87
Using images in fiction. *Writer* 100:15-18 Ja '87
Gere, Richard, and Thurman, Robert A. F.
Spirit in exile: the Dalai Lama pleads for the Tibetan
    people. il por *Roll Stone* p68-9 D 3 '87
Gergley, Lisa Bellini- *See* Bellini-Gergley, Lisa
Gerhart, Mary
Saviors, myths, & sacred heroes. il *Commonweal*
    114:250-1 Ap 24 '87
Women, religion, & utopia. *Commonweal* 114:682-3 N
    20 '87
Geriatrics *See* Aged—Care and hygiene; Aged—Medical
    care
Geringer, Dan
Pex sell tix [cover story] il pors *Sports Illus* 67:80-4+
    D 7 '87
Queen of the surf. il pors *Sports Illus* 67:60-3 Jl 27
    '87
Germ plasm resources *See* Germplasm resources
German art *See* Art, German
German communications satellites *See* Communications
    satellites, German
German cooking *See* Cooking, German
German Grand Prix *See* Automobile racing—Germany
    (West)
German historians *See* Historians, German
German Hygiene Museum (Dresden, Germany) *See* Deut-
    sches Hygiene-Museum (Dresden, Germany)
German photographers *See* Photographers, German
German pottery *See* Pottery, German
German reunification question
Deutschland uber allies. C. Layne. *New Repub* 197:12-14
    S 28 '87
Germany: a snapshot. E. von Kuehnelt-Leddihn. *Natl
    Rev* 39:46 D 4 '87
Germany: East meets West. A. Nagorski. il *Newsweek*
    110:50 S 14 '87
Remembering the uprising [address, June 17, 1987; with
    introd. by Timothy Garton Ash] F. R. Stern. il por
    N Y Rev Books 34:14-16+ D 3 '87
Two Germanys: edging closer? [with interview with E.
    Honecker] D. Stanglin and V. Pope. il *U S News
    World Rep* 102:33-5 Ja 12 '87
West Germany's old demons. D. C. Marsh. il *World
    Press Rev* 34:22-4 S '87
German scientists *See* Scientists, German
German sculpture *See* Sculpture, German
German war criminals *See* World War, 1939-1945—War
    criminals
German Wine Academy
Uncorking secrets of the vine: Germany's Wine Academy.
    W. Gisslen. il *Travel Holiday* 168:72-7 Jl '87
German wines *See* Wine
Germanium
Altering atomic structures [use of scanning tunneling
    microscope] T. H. Cole. il *Pop Mech* 164:10 S '87
Germans
Canada
Canada's Nazi presence [war criminals] M. Drohan. il
    Macleans 100:38-9 My 25 '87
A safe haven no longer [Canadian government agrees
    to track down and prosecute Nazi war criminals] M.
    Drohan. il *Macleans* 100:14-15 Mr 23 '87
Soviet Union
Audacious airman [M. Rust lands in Red Square] il
    pors map *Life* 10:66-9 Ag '87
Destination Red Square [German pilot, M. Rust, lands
    small plane] B. Levin. il *Macleans* 100:24 Je 8 '87
A folk hero in the slammer [M. Rust arrested after
    landing small plane in Red Square] N. Cooper. il
    por *Newsweek* 109:36 Je 15 '87
Four years for a "fun" flight [sentencing of German
    pilot, M. Rust, for landing plane in Moscow] W.
    R. Doerner. il por *Time* 130:42 S 14 '87
Gaps in Soviet defenses? [West German, M. Rust, lands
    plane in Moscow] R. Kaylor. il *U S News World
    Rep* 102:30 Je 15 '87
A hard landing in Moscow [M. Rust sentenced to 4
    yrs. in Soviet labor camp] C. Redden. il por *Macleans*
    100:22 S 14 '87
Joyride [M. Rust's flight to Moscow] W. F. Buckley.
    Natl Rev 39:56 Jl 17 '87
Kremlin prop wash [West German, M. Rust, lands Cessna
    in Red Square] W. R. Doerner. il por *Time* 129:30-2
    Je 15 '87

Red faces in Red Square [West German, M. Rust, lands
    small plane in Moscow] N. Cooper. il por *Newsweek*
    109:36 Je 8 '87
Rust's unhappy landing [sentenced to a labor camp for
    flying small plane into Red Square] S. Seibert. il
    Newsweek 110:49 S 14 '87
Welcome to Moscow [German pilot, M. Rust, lands
    plane in Red Square] J. Greenwald. il por *Time* 129:34-5
    Je 8 '87
United States
See also
    Pennsylvania Germans
NASA's Nazis. L. Hunt. *Nation* 244:671 My 23 '87
History
Invasion of the German left [American misperception
    of Nazism] E. von Kuehnelt-Leddihn. *Natl Rev* 39:28
    S 11 '87
Germany
See also
    Artists' and authors' colonies—Germany
    Berlin (Germany)
    Concentration camps—Germany
    Germans
    Jews—Germany
    Medicine—Germany
    Opera—Germany
    Physics—Germany
Foreign opinion
American
Invasion of the German left [American misperception
    of Nazism] E. von Kuehnelt-Leddihn. *Natl Rev* 39:28
    S 11 '87
History
1618-1648
See also
    Thirty Years' War, 1618-1648
20th century
Einstein and Germany [discussion of February 1986
    article] F. R. Stern. *Phys Today* 40:15+ Jl '87
1933-1945
See also
    National socialism
1933-1945—Bibliography
Getting along with Hitler. G. A. Craig. il *N Y Rev
    Books* 34:32-5 Jl 16 '87
1933-1945—Historiography
Albert Brackmann & the Nazi adjustment of history.
    M. Burleigh. bibl il por *Hist Today* 37:42-6 Mr '87
Erasing the past? G. Hirschfeld. *Hist Today* 37:8-10
    Ag '87
The war of the German historians. G. A. Craig. il *N
    Y Rev Books* 33:16-19 Ja 15 '87
Bibliography
Paperback history. I. R. Mitchell. *Hist Today* 37:55
    F '87
Population
Deutschlands truebste Zeit: the calamity of 1648. C.
    E. Kraft. il *Antiques Collect Hobbies* 92:79-81 Je '87
Religious institutions and affairs
See also
    Catholic Church—Germany
Germany (Democratic Republic) *See* Germany (East)
Germany (East)
See also
    Berlin (Germany: East)
    Music festivals—Germany (East)
    Opera—Germany (East)
Description and travel
Where money has little currency. H. Koning. *Harpers*
    275:71-6 N '87
Economic policy
East Germany's economic model. T. A. Baylis. bibl
    f *Curr Hist* 86:377-81+ N '87
Foreign relations
See also
    Berlin question, 1945-
Germany (West)
    See Germany (West)—Foreign relations—Germany
    (East)
History
Uprising, June 1953
Remembering the uprising [address, June 17, 1987; with
    introd. by Timothy Garton Ash] F. R. Stern. il por
    N Y Rev Books 34:14-16+ D 3 '87
Bibliography
After the Reich. G. A. Craig. il *N Y Rev Books* 34:38-41
    O 8 '87
Social conditions
Inside East Germany. P. Lewis. il por *Macleans* 100:16-18
    S 14 '87

Germany (East) and the United States
See also
Student exchange programs
Germany (Federal Republic) See Germany (West)
Germany (West)
See also
Art—Germany (West)
Art and state—Germany (West)
Astronomy—Germany (West)
Automobile racing—Germany (West)
Aviation and state—Germany (West)
Baden-Baden (Germany)
Badenweiler (Germany)
Banks and banking—Germany (West)
Berlin (Germany: West)
Business and education—Germany (West)
Business management—Germany (West)
Collective bargaining—Metal industry—Germany (West)
Cost and standard of living—Germany (West)
Darmstadt (Germany)
Direct broadcast satellite services—Germany (West)
Environmental policy—Germany (West)
Essen (Germany)
Forests and forestry—Germany (West)
Frankfurt am Main (Germany)
Genetic research—Laws and regulations—Germany (West)
Grube Messel (Germany)
Hamburg (Germany)
Heidelberg (Germany)
Income tax—Germany (West)
Investments, German
Investments, Japanese—Germany (West)
Kronberg (Germany)
Military research—Germany (West)
Money—Germany (West)
Morale, National—Germany (West)
Motion picture festivals—Germany (West)
Münster (Germany)
Murnau (Germany)
Music festivals—Germany (West)
Nobility—Germany (West)
Nuclear research—Germany (West)
Opera—Germany (West)
Paleontology—Germany (West)
Publishers and publishing—Germany (West)
Radioactive pollution—Germany (West)
Refuse and refuse disposal—Germany (West)
Rhine River
Rock music—Germany (West)
Schleswig-Holstein (Germany)
Skis and skiing—Germany (West)
Taxation—Germany (West)
Terrorism—Germany (West)
Theatrical agencies and agents—Germany (West)
Trade unions—Germany (West)
Trade unions—Metal workers—Germany (West)
Armed Forces
Three European Air Forces step up training at Goose Bay. Aviat Week Space Technol 127:86 O 5 '87
Commerce
See also
Balance of trade—Germany (West)
Japan
Saying hello to BMW-san [BMW's success in exporting cars] B. Hillenbrand. il Time 129:56-7 My 25 '87
United States
See United States—Commerce—Germany (West)
Defenses
See also
Airplanes, Military—Germany (West)
Canada—Armed Forces—Forces in Germany (West)
Guided missiles, German
United States. Air Force—Forces in Germany (West)
United States. Army—Forces in Germany (West)
Achtung: too much disarmament too fast. J. Joffe. il map U S News World Rep 103:43 D 7 '87
The singular threat to the Atlantic Alliance [excerpts from address, May 28, 1987] H. Kissinger. Natl Rev 39:18-19 Jl 3 '87
To get an impactful feel for how upsetting . . . [views of F. J. Strauss on upcoming arms agreement between U.S. and Soviet Union] M. S. Forbes, Jr. il por Forbes 140:25 Ag 24 '87
Description and travel
See also
Motorcycling—Germany (West)

Economic policy
Between competitiveness and co-operation [address, March 26, 1987] O. von Lambsdorff. Vital Speeches Day 53:455-60 My 15 '87
Can Germany withstand the heat from abroad this time? J. Templeman. il Bus Week p50-1 O 5 '87
German roulette? P. Fuhrman and R. Morais. il Forbes 139:34-5 Je 1 '87
How slow will they grow? S. Nasar. il Fortune 116:67+ N 9 '87
Kohl's second term: Washington may feel a chilly breeze. F. A. Miller and J. E. Pluenneke. il por Bus Week p48 F 9 '87
The low-energy German economy. R. Morais. il Forbes 140:116+ N 2 '87
What will it take to budge Germany? W. Glasgall. il Bus Week p48-9+ N 23 '87
Why a stubborn Germany won't fire up its economy. F. A. Miller. il Bus Week p48-9 Ap 27 '87
Economic relations
What will it take to budge Germany? W. Glasgall. il Bus Week p48-9+ N 23 '87
United States
See United States—Economic relations—Germany (West)
Western Europe
Europe can't move any faster than Germany. J. Templeman. il Bus Week p50-1 Ap 6 '87
Foreign relations
Germany (East)
See also
Berlin question, 1945-
German reunification question
Honecker, Erich—Visit to Germany (West), 1987
German 'togetherness' could cause trouble for East and West. F. A. Miller. il Bus Week p41 Ap 20 '87
'The shadows of the Reich' [H. Kohl's campaign remark concerning East German concentration camps] N. Cooper. il por Newsweek 109:32 Ja 19 '87
Israel
Odyssey of remembrance [Israeli president C. Herzog visits West Germany] il por Macleans 100:21 Ap 20 '87
Poland
They couldn't hit a . . . oops! [Polish ship accidentally fires at West German ship in the Baltic Sea] il Time 129:39 Je 29 '87
Soviet Union
See Soviet Union—Foreign relations—Germany (West)
United States
See United States—Foreign relations—Germany (West)
History
Bibliography
After the Reich. G. A. Craig. il N Y Rev Books 34:38-41 O 8 '87
Industries
See also
Adam Opel AG
Aerospace industries—Germany (West)
Audi AG
BASF AG
Bayer AG
Bayerische Motoren Werke AG
Bertelsmann AG
Daimler-Benz AG
Deutsche Airbus
DLT German Domestic Airlines
Dornier GmbH
Hoechst AG
Lufthansa
Messerschmitt-Bölkow-Blohm GmbH
Motion picture industry—Germany (West)
MTU Motoren-und-Turbinen-Union
Porsche AG
Siemens AG
Textile machinery industry—Germany (West)
Thyssen AG
Trading companies—Germany (West)
Volkswagen AG
Politics and government
See also
Elections—Germany (West)
Political attitudes—Germany (West)
Political campaigns—Germany (West)
Germany: a snapshot. E. von Kuehnelt-Leddihn. Natl Rev 39:46 D 4 '87

Germany (West)—Politics and government—cont.
History
See Germany (West)—History
Germicides See Disinfection and disinfectants
Germination
Despite centuries underwater, seeds from a sunken galleon prove life begins at 365 [research by C. Malcom] il por *People Wkly* 28:59 Ag 3 '87
Germplasm resources
Anecdotes, facetiae, satire, etc.
Wanted: old genetic furniture from the planet's attic. J. Gorman. il *Discover* 8:24+ F '87
Plants
See also
Seed Savers Exchange
Conservation of traditional agroecosystems. M. L. Oldfield and J. B. Alcorn. bibl f il *BioScience* 37:199-208 Mr '87
The plant germplasm controversy [cover story; with reply by H. G. Wilkes] J. Kloppenburg, Jr. and D. L. Kleinman. bibl f il maps *BioScience* 37:190-8, 215-18 Mr '87
Save our seeds. K. Z. Peppler. il *Rodale's Org Gard* 34:38-41 D '87
Seeds of struggle: the geopolitics of genetic resources. J. Kloppenburg, Jr. and D. L. Kleinman. il map *Technol Rev* 90:46-53 F/Mr '87
SOS—save our seeds! L. Ponte. il *Read Dig* 130:118-22 Je '87
Gernsback, Hugo
about
Looking into the future. A. C. Clarke. il *Radio-Electron* 58:81-3 My '87
Gerontology
One hundred candles [interview with T. F. Williams] E. Kiester. il *50 Plus* 27:28-30 Je '87
Conferences
Adjusting to an aging population. C. Holden. il *Science* 236:772-3 My 15 '87
Course & conference calendar. See issues of Aging
Study and teaching
See also
Ethel Percy Andrus Gerontology Center
Course & conference calendar. See issues of Aging
New curriculum in gerontology for occupational therapists. L. J. Davis. il *Aging* no356:34 '87
Gerry, Elbridge, 1744-1814
about
The non-signers. C. L. Mee. pors *Am Herit* 38:78-9 S/O '87
Gerrymander
The House unrepresentative. *Natl Rev* 39:20 S 11 '87
Gersh, Martin
The best of wines. See issues of Vogue
Gershen, Howard
A consumer guide to charity: where to get more balm for your buck. il *Esquire* 108:185-6+ D '87
Gershwin, George, 1898-1937
about
"The birth of Rhapsody in blue". E. Salzman. il *Stereo Rev* 52:110 Ap '87
Gershwin. W. Livingstone. il *Stereo Rev* 52:63-6 Ag '87
Nice work if you can get it. A. Rich. il por *Newsweek* 109:70-1 Mr 16 '87
Of many things. G. W. Hunt. *America* 157:442 D 12 '87
Porgy and Bess [opera] Reviews
Opera News il 51:10-13 Mr 28 '87. G. Heymont
Shall we dance? T. Tobias. il *N Y* 20:92-3 Mr 30 '87
Gerson, Barry
about
Barry Gerson. D. Rubey. il *Art News* 86:168 My '87
Gerstenfeld, Sheldon L.
Pet set. See occasional issues of Parents
Gerth, Jeff
(jt. auth) See Tolchin, Martin, and Gerth, Jeff
Gertler, T.
The Pee-wee perplex. il pors *Roll Stone* p36-8+ F 12 '87
Gertrude, Sister
about
Sister Gertrude and the children of Karachi. L. Weber. il *Christ Century* 104:887-9 O 14 '87
Gerusky, Thomas M.
Pennsylvania: protecting the homefront. il map *Environment* 29:12+ Ja/F '87
Gervers, John H.
The NIMBY syndrome: is it inevitable? bibl f il *Environment* 29:18-20+ O '87

Gerz, Esther Shalev- See Shalev-Gerz, Esther
Gerz, Jochen, 1940-
about
Sinking feelings. M. Gibson. il *Art News* 86:105+ Summ '87
Gessert, Kate Rogers
Gardening in winter. il *Rodale's Org Gard* 34:49-53 N '87
Home gardens in the Soviet Union. il *Rodale's Org Gard* 34:57-8+ Mr '87
Getschow, George
about
Three-decades-long Texas estate feud being chronicled in Norton book. M. J. O'Brien. *Publ Wkly* 232:29 O 23 '87
Getting into history [television program] See Television program reviews—Single works
Getty, Ann
about
Places in the heart. L. Blandford. il pors *Vogue* 177:326-33+ Ag '87
Getty, Don
about
Alberta's part-time premier. J. Howse. il por *Macleans* 100:12 Mr 9 '87
Preparing for a new Senate. M. Drohan. il por *Macleans* 100:14 My 11 '87
Getty, Gordon P.
about
Funding opera: an endearing attitude. S. Von Buchau. il por *Opera News* 51:14+ Je '87
Getty, Sarah
Presbyopia [poem] *New Repub* 197:39 S 7 '87
Getty (J. Paul) Museum See J. Paul Getty Museum
Getty Center for Education in the Arts
Changing the look of art education. M. Esterow. il *Art News* 86:112-13 Ap '87
A report on discipline-based art education. D. C. Hines. *Am Artist* 51:68-9+ Ag '87
Getty Petroleum Corp.
Now Getty's a play in retailing, too. G. G. Marcial. *Bus Week* p76 Ap 20 '87
Gettysburg, Battle of, 1863
Addressing Gettysburg. A. C. Danto. il *Harpers* 275:36+ Jl '87
Gettysburg National Military Park (Pa.)
Riddle of Gettysburg's vultures. E. Daniels. il *Audubon* 89:82-4+ Ja '87
Getz, Arlene
Apartheid's troubled children. *World Press Rev* 34:34-5 D '87
Getzoff, Elizabeth D., and others
Mechanisms of antibody binding to a protein. bibl f il *Science* 235:1191-6 Mr 6 '87
Gever, Martha
Where we are now. il *Art Am* 75:43-9 Jl '87
Gevins, Alan S., and others
Human neuroelectric patterns predict performance accuracy. bibl f il *Science* 235:580-5 Ja 30 '87
Gevisser, Mark
Girls apart. *Nation* 245:463-4 O 24 '87
Gewen, Barry
Writers & writing. See occasional issues of The New Leader
Geyelin, Philip
The Reagan crisis: dreaming impossible dreams. *Foreign Aff* 65 Sp Issue:447-57 ['87]
Geysen, H. Mario, and others
Antigenicity of myohemerythrin [discussion of March 6, 1987 article, Chemistry of antibody binding to a protein] *Science* 238:1584-6 D 11 '87
Chemistry of antibody binding to a protein. bibl f il *Science* 235:1184-90 Mr 6 '87
GFCI (Ground fault circuit interrupters) See Electric circuit breakers
Ghana
See also
Homeless—Ghana
Kumasi (Ghana)
National parks and reserves—Ghana
Wildlife conservation—Ghana
History
Ghana: thirty years on. R. Rathbone. il *Hist Today* 37:5-7 Mr '87
Politics and government
Ghana's shift from radical populism. J. Kraus. *Curr Hist* 86:205-8+ My '87
Ghandour, Ali
The Middle East in the year 2000 [address, April 24, 1987] *Vital Speeches Day* 53:450-5 My 15 '87

Ghermezian family
about
Fantasyland furore [annual report by the Auditor General] M. Drohan. il *Macleans* 100:14 N 9 '87
On time in Bloomington [Ghermezian brothers complete deal to build Fashion Mall of America in Minnesota] D. Jenish. il *Macleans* 100:36 Ja 19 '87
Ghettos *See* Slums
Ghidella, Vittorio
about
Hot wheels. T. Pouschine. il por *Forbes* 140:232 N 30 '87
Ghiglieri, Michael P.
War among the chimps [cover story] il *Discover* 8:66-70+ N '87
Ghigna, Charles
Heart art [poem] il *Good Housekeep* 204:190 F '87
Summerizing [poem] *Good Housekeep* 204:154 Je '87
Ghorbanifar, Manucher
about
Double-dealing over Iran. E. Magnuson. il por *Time* 129:22+ F 2 '87
Washington diarist. C. Lane. *New Repub* 196:58 Je 8 '87
Ghost of a chance [television program] *See* Television program reviews—Single works
Ghost stories
See also
Horror tales
Ghost towns
See also
Kennecott (Alaska)
Ghosts
Ghost guide [The ghostly register, guidebook to haunted dwellings] B. Karlin. il *Omni* 10:134 D '87
Maureen Reagan meets Lincoln's ghost. il *Newsweek* 109:29 F 2 '87
That's the spirit. A. Myers. il *Travel Holiday* 168:114 O '87
GHR Energy Corp.
See also
TransAmerican Natural Gas Corporation
Ghumman, Kulbir
about
Endangered species? Load the shotgun! R. L. Di Silvestro. il *Audubon* 89:12 S '87
Giaccone, Rosetta
about
Jailed Mafia men face the wrath of Sicilian widows. il pors *People Wkly* 27:40-2+ My 18 '87
Giacconi, Riccardo
Continuing the tradition: amateur astronomers and the Space Telescope [address, August 7, 1986] il por *Astronomy* 15:24+ Ja '87
(jt. auth) *See* Brown, Robert A., and Giacconi, Riccardo
Giamatti, A. Bartlett, 1938-
about
Of Spenser, the Red Sox, and drinking in the stands. B. Welling. il por *Bus Week* p66 Ag 17 '87
Giampapa, Mark S.
The solar-stellar connection. il *Sky Telesc* 74:142-6 Ag '87
Giant clams *See* Clams
Giant Group Ltd.
What's his line? [B. Sugarman of Giant Group buys Chuck Barris Productions] A. B. Block. il por *Forbes* 139:70-1 Ja 26 '87
Giant pandas *See* Pandas
Giant stars *See* Stars, Giant
Giardia *See* Protozoa, Pathogenic
Giardiasis
The last companion you'll want on the trail. J. Silberner. il *U S News World Rep* 102:66 Je 22 '87
Giardina, Roberto
East Berlin gets a new face. il *World Press Rev* 34:59 F '87
Giarelli, Andrew
Regional report: Asia/Pacific. *See* issues of World Press Review beginning October 1986
Giasone [opera] *See* Cavalli, Pier Francesco, 1602-1676
Gibans, Nina Freedlander
about
Invading the heart of the problem [interview] B. K. Beach. bibl f *Des Arts Educ* 88:45-8 N/D '86
Gibbons, Clive
Shooting galaxies from the suburbs. il *Astronomy* 15:42-7 F '87

Gibbons, Fred
One size of software doesn't fit all. por *Pers Comput* 11:232 O '87
Gibbons, Grinling, 1648-1721
about
Homage to Grinling Gibbons. D. Esterly. il por *House Gard* 159:18+ Ja '87
Gibbons, J. Whitfield
Why do turtles live so long? [cover story] bibl f il *BioScience* 37:262-9 Ap '87
Gibbons, Kaye, 1960-
about
Is it art yet? L. Fleischer. *Publ Wkly* 231:34 My 8 '87
Gibbs, Christopher
Bennison style. il *House Gard* 159:170-7+ Ap '87
Of horse and hound. il por *House Gard* 159:76+ N '87
Gibbs, Chuck
about
The last picture by a man who loved bears. il por *Audubon* 89:16-17 Jl '87
Gibbs, Ellen Berland
Banding together. il *Channels* 7:73 Je '87
Hot number. il *Channels* 7:69 S '87
Gibbs, Fred
about
Speed briefs. P. Scott. il por *Flying* 114:70-2+ O '87
Gibbs, Gary
Zap, crackle, pop. il *Progressive* 51:22-4 S '87
Gibbs, Jerry
Fishing. *See* issues of Outdoor Life
Gibbs, Lawrence B.
about
The new chief of the IRS discusses how it, too, needs reform [interview] W. L. Updegrave. il por *Money* 16:128 F '87
Gibbs, Lee W.
We, the theologians. pors *Christ Today* 31:29-31 D 11 '87
Gibbs, Marla
about
1987 Essence Awards. A. Edwards. pors *Essence* 18:121+ My '87
Marla Gibbs hosts gala Los Angeles fund-raiser. il pors *Jet* 71:58-60 Mr 2 '87
Sex, sass and laughs keep "227" TV show a smash hit [cover story] il pors *Jet* 72:56-8 Ag 24 '87
Gibbs, Richard A., and Caskey, C. Thomas
Identification and localization of mutations at the Lesch-Nyhan locus by ribonuclease A cleavage. bibl f il *Science* 236:303-5 Ap 17 '87
Gibbs, Tony
The Cup comes back. il *New Yorker* 63:86-90+ Mr 2 '87
Gibel, Inge Lederer- *See* Lederer-Gibel, Inge
Gibney, Alex, and Thompson, Anne
Make money, not war. il *Film Comment* 23:17-18+ N/D '87
Gibson, Allan T.
about
His customers bank on service. H. Morris. il por *Nations Bus* 75:69 Ja '87
Gibson, Althea, 1927-
about
Ashe, Gibson raise funds for tennis, UNCF on yacht. il pors *Jet* 72:8 Ag 10 '87
Ex-tennis star Gibson sees herself in Martina. il pors *Jet* 72:49 Mr 30 '87
Gibson, Bob, 1935-
about
Bob Gibson fears baseball will fail to promote blacks. por *Jet* 72:50 Jl 27 '87
Gibson, Butler
about
Houston man waits in dark, kills assailant. *Jet* 72:12 Ag 24 '87
Gibson, Carol, and McWilliams, Patricia G.
Stained glass. il *Ctry J* 14:65-8 Je '87
Gibson, Debbie
about
After four years of training, singer Debbie Gibson, 16, comes Out of the blue and onto the charts. il por *People Wkly* 28:67 S 7 '87
Debbie Gibson: from out of the blue to stardom [interview] por *Teen* 31:65 N '87
The Merrick express. P. Tyre. il por *N Y* 20:22 Je 8 '87

Gibson, Derrick
about
Utah's tiny Derrick Gibson is a dervish who makes bigger tumblers bounce up and take notice. il por *People Wkly* 28:121 Jl 6 '87

Gibson, Helen
Britain goes batty over bats. il *Int Wildl* 17:42-4 N/D '87

Gibson, James William
about
From Platoon to Pan Am. R. McGough. il por *Forbes* 139:105 Ap 20 '87

Gibson, Janice T.
As they grow/1-year-olds. See issues of Parents beginning January 1984

Gibson, Mary Margaret
about
Marketing the 'lowdown on high tech'. K. Cook. il por *Work Woman* 12:74+ My '87

Gibson, Mel
about
Mel Gibson: from macho man to family man. E. Sherman. por *Ladies Home J* 104:72+ Ag '87
Mel Gibson unbuttoned. D. Maychick. por *Mademoiselle* 93:232-4 Mr '87

Gibson, Michael
The Musée d'Orsay: a new and different 19th century. il *Art News* 86:142-6 Ap '87

Gibson, Ralph
about
Meet the masters. F. Cameron. il *Petersens Photogr Mag* 15:28-30 Ja '87

Gibson, Roy
Governments must strive to make private enterprise work in space. por *Aviat Week Space Technol* 127:91-2 N 2 '87
about
British space chief quits in protest. D. Dickson. *Science* 237:719 Ag 14 '87
The model of a modern director general: a conversation with Roy Gibson. T. Furniss. il por *Space World* X-5-281:26-7 My '87
U.K. space chief resigns over funding; ESA reevaluates impact on polar platform. J. M. Lenorovitz. il *Aviat Week Space Technol* 127:26-7 Ag 10 '87

Giddings, Lon E.
It's fun to grow succulents from seeds. il *Flower Gard* 31:74-5 O/N '87

Giddins, Gary
about
Celebrating Bird. M. Bourne. il por *Down Beat* 54:63 Ap '87

Giedroyc, Jerzy
Activist, strategist. il *Natl Rev* 39:35-6 S 11 '87

Gieringer, Dale H.
Compassion vs. control: FDA investigational drug regulation. il *USA Today (Periodical)* 115:69-73 Mr '87

Gies, Doug
about
Science at McDonald Observatory. R. Reeves. il pors *Astronomy* 15:6-17 Jl '87

Gies, Jan
about
The friends of Anne Frank. il pors *U S News World Rep* 102:77 My 11 '87

Gies, Miep, 1909-
about
The friends of Anne Frank. il pors *U S News World Rep* 102:77 My 11 '87

Giese, Jo
The high-tech date. il *Ms* 16:25-7+ N '87
Of rubbers and lovers. il *Ms* 16:100 S '87
On the difficulty of asking a man to wear a condom. *Vogue* 177:227+ Je '87

Giese, N. A., and others
The role of individual cysteine residues in the structure and function of the v-*sis* gene product. bibl f il *Science* 236:1315-18 Je 5 '87

Gieseking, Hal
The travel advisor. See issues of Travel Holiday

Gifford, Frank
about
A fan's further notes. F. Exley. il pors *Esquire* 107:150-2 Je '87

Gift shops
See also
Museum stores

Gift wrapping *See* Wrapping of packages
Gifted children *See* Children, Gifted
Giftopoulos, Pete
about
Pete Giftopoulos. R. Demak. por *Sports Illus* 67:73 Ag 31 '87

Gifts
See also
Black colleges and universities—Gifts, legacies, etc.
Books as gifts
Christmas gifts
Colleges and universities—Gifts, legacies, etc.
Food as gifts
Giving
Pets as gifts
Phonograph records as gifts
Plants as gifts
Videotapes as gifts
Wedding gifts
Wrapping of packages
A Fathers' Day gift for the whole family [Grandfather remembers, a journal for personal memories] C. Loomis. il *Parents* 62:15 Je '87
Gifts: you're a wonderful giver. How well do you receive? [quiz] E. Weiner. il *Glamour* 85:20+ D '87
Graduation and Father's Day gifts he'll love. il *Glamour* 85:182 Je '87
Mother's Day—making life easier. C. Loomis. il *Parents* 62:17 My '87
Objects of affection: 5 loving gifts to craft [Valentine's Day gifts] J. Williams and J. Severson. il *Better Homes Gard* 65:98-9+ F '87
On gift-giving. W. F. Buckley. *Natl Rev* 39:55 D 31 '87
Timely treats [Father's Day] il *Harpers Bazaar* 120:36 My '87
Valentine gifts he'll continue to receive. il *Glamour* 85:48 F '87
The well-bred house gift. il *Harpers Bazaar* 120:50 Jl '87

Taxation
See also
Gifts to minors
Gifts for children
See also
Christmas gifts for children
The best birthday presents ever [kits for children] E. Berg. il *Parents* 62:102-4+ Ag '87
Gifts in business
Executive gifting. J. Krotz. il *Work Woman* 12:90-2+ D '87
Fresh ideas for office gift-giving [Christmas] M. M. Kennedy. il *Glamour* 85:108 D '87
It's time to say thank you. S. Nelton. il *Nations Bus* 75:40 N '87
When that gift just has to be first-class. L. Zinn. il *Bus Week* p151 D 7 '87
Gifts in literature
Gifts the Magi never brought: a literary quiz. A. Broyard. il *N Y Times Book Rev* 92:9 D 6 '87
Gifts to minors
Family planning. *U S News World Rep* 103:78 D 7 '87
The new ABCs of asset shifting. C. E. Trunzo. il *Money* 16:91-2 O '87
Rethinking income shifting. G. W. Padwe. *Nations Bus* 75:66 Ja '87
Saving for college: one scheme has survived [minor's Section 2503(c) trust] P. Philipps. il *Bus Week* p147 Ja 12 '87
The young and the bullish. J. Crudele. il *N Y* 20:23-4 O 12 '87
Gigase, Paul
The notion of health. il *Courier* 40:4-6 Ag '87
Gigi, Claudette
What's cooking? il *Seventeen* 46:91-2+ Mr '87
Gigli, Romeo
about
Gigli's brave new world. il *Vogue* 177:214-15 Jl '87
Gil Evans Orchestra
Gil Evans Orchestra. R. Tolleson. *Down Beat* 54:54 Jl '87
Gilbert, Avery N., and Wysocki, Charles J.
The smell results: survey. il *Natl Geogr* 172:514-25 O '87
Gilbert, Bil
In from the fields, wildflowers find a new welcome among gardeners. bibl (p162) il por *Smithsonian* 18:36-45 Ap '87
Lizards that take to the desert like ducks to water. bibl (p145) il *Smithsonian* 18:78-84+ Ag '87

Gilbert, Felix, 1905-
Venetian secrets. il *N Y Rev Books* 34:37-9 Jl 16 '87
What Ranke meant. *Am Sch* 56:393-7 Summ '87
Gilbert, Melissa
about
Melissa Gilbert . . . all grown up! N. Gittelson. il
pors *McCalls* 114:94-8 S '87
Gilbert, Neil
The unfinished business of welfare reform. *Society* 24:5-11
Mr/Ap '87
Gilbert, Roswell
about
The agony did not end for Roswell Gilbert, who killed
his wife to give her peace. L. Marx. il pors *People
Wkly* 27:30-2+ Ja 12 '87
Gilbert, Ruth
Ruth recommends. See issues of New York beginning
February 13, 1984
Gilbert, Sandra M., and Gubar, Susan, 1944-
Sex wars: not the fun kind. il *N Y Times Book Rev*
92:1+ D 27 '87
Gilbert, Steven W.
(jt. auth) See Green, Kenneth C., and Gilbert, Steven
W.
Gilbert, W. S. (William Schwenck), 1836-1911
about
HMS Pinafore [operetta] Reviews
Macleans 100:58 N 23 '87. J. Bemrose
The Mikado [operetta] Reviews
Dance Mag 61:24+ Ap '87. M. U. West
N Y il 20:133 Ap 27 '87. P. G. Davis
New Yorker 63:86 Ap 13 '87. E. Oliver
The sorcerer [operetta] Reviews
N Y il 20:133-4 Ap 27 '87. P. G. Davis
Very model records of the major Gilbert & Sullivan.
P. Kresh. il pors *High Fidel* 37:56-8 Je '87
Gilbert, Walter, 1932-
about
The genome project. R. Kanigel. il por *N Y Times
Mag* p44+ D 13 '87
A grand plan to map the gene code. A. Beam. il por
Bus Week p116-17 Ap 27 '87
Gilbert, William Schwenck See Gilbert, W. S. (William
Schwenck), 1836-1911
Gilborn, Craig
The rustic furniture of Ernest Stowe. bibl f il *Antiques*
132:550-7 S '87
Gildart, Robert C.
Big Sky ski sampler. il *Travel Holiday* 168:26-9 N '87
Next stop: Council Bluffs. *Travel Holiday* 168:106+ O
'87
Gildea, Patricia M.
(jt. auth) See Miller, George Armitage, 1920-, and Gildea,
Patricia M.
Gilder, George F., 1939-
Don't let the Grinch steal Christmas. il *Natl Rev* 39:40-4
Ap 24 '87
A loner's quest. il pors *Life* 10:62-4+ S '87
about
Christianity today talks to George Gilder. L. Neff. por
Christ Today 31:35 Mr 6 '87
Gilding
See also
Carvers and Gilders (Firm)
Reflections of gold. il *Home Mech* 83:48-50 Ja '87
Giles, Jeffrey
The selling of the young. *Natl Rev* 39:64-5 N 20 '87
Gilford, Lisa
about
At last there's something more for the pooch who has
everything (including odor)—doggie perfume. il por
People Wkly 28:117 S 21 '87
Gilia
See also
Scarlet gilia
Gill, Brendan, 1914-
American grandeur. il por *House Gard* 159:112-23+ S
'87
American simplicity. il *House Gard* 159:162-73+ O '87
In the presence of the past. il por *Archit Dig* 44:98+
N '87
The sky line. See occasional issues of The New Yorker
beginning February 23, 1987
Still here at the New Yorker. il *N Y Times Book Rev*
92:1+ O 4 '87
Gill, Mark
Addressing the student market. il por *Esquire* 108:76
D '87
Beyond the beeper. il por *Esquire* 108:94 O '87
Hotter than a pistil. il por *Esquire* 107:72 My '87
The pawn king. il por *Esquire* 108:52 Jl '87

The rise and rise of HSN. il pors *Esquire* 107:70 Ap
'87
Turning health into wealth. il por *Esquire* 108:94 S
'87
Gill, Susan
Painting from the heart. il por *Art News* 86:128-35 Ap
'87
Sue Coe's inferno [cover story] il pors *Art News* 86:110-15
O '87
Gillard, Bill
about
It walks, talks and falls asleep, and so animal lovers
must ask—is it live or is it Robopet? il *People Wkly*
28:97 D 7 '87
Gilleland, Richard A.
about
A revived Intermedics has some unexpected fans. J.
E. Davis. il por *Bus Week* p120 Ap 27 '87
Gillenkirk, Jeff
In over my head. il *America* 157:9-14 Jl 4-11 '87
Gillers, Stephen, 1943-
The Meese lie. *Nation* 244:205 F 21 '87
Gillespie, Dizzy, 1917-
about
Dizzy's clarion calls for degree in bebop. por *Jet* 72:63
Jl 13 '87
Young musicians today more talented: Dizzy says. *Jet*
71:17 Mr 2 '87
Gillespie, John Birks See Gillespie, Dizzy, 1917-
Gillespie, Marcia Ann
A different take on the ol' bump and grind. il por
Ms 16:88+ O '87
My gloves are off, sisters. por *Ms* 15:19-20 Ap '87
Sister-friends. il por *Ms* 16:130+ Jl/Ag '87
Gillespie, Richard
about
Richard Hollander; Richard Gillespie. B. Westerfield.
il *Art News* 86:33-4 Mr '87
Gillet, Ed
about
Land creatures. *New Yorker* 63:30-1 S 21 '87
Gillett, George
about
George Gillett's private world [cover story] R. Buck.
il pors *Channels* 7:28-34 S '87
Gillett, Thomas R.
Surround sound. il *Stereo Rev* 52:54-8 Ap '87
Gillett Group Inc.
Clarence McKee takes helm of $365 million TV station.
por *Jet* 72:36-7 Ag 24 '87
George Gillett's private world [cover story] R. Buck.
il pors *Channels* 7:28-34 S '87
McKee, Gillett Co. buy $365 mil. Fla. TV station. por
Jet 72:6 Mr 30 '87
Gillette, Jean
Where the czars shined. il *Travel Holiday* 167:6+ F
'87
Gillette Co.
How Ron Perelman scared Gillette into shape. K. H.
Hammonds. il *Bus Week* p40-1 O 12 '87
Meet a corporate Dr. No [R. Giovacchini, vice president
of product integrity] J. Strahinich. il por *Read Dig*
130:101-4 Mr '87
New hunters may be stalking Gillette. G. G. Marcial.
Bus Week p100 F 16 '87
An unlikely savior for Gillette? [W. E. Buffett] G. G.
Marcial. *Bus Week* p188 N 16 '87
Gilley, J. Wade
College athletics reform: losing through intimidation.
Educ Dig 52:57-9 Mr '87
Gillham, C. E.
Me and that groundhog [reprint from May 1969 issue]
il *Audubon* 89:72-5 Jl '87
Gilliam, Sharon Gist
about
Sharon Gist Gilliam: the woman in charge of Chicago's
$3.8 billion budget. il pors *Ebony* 42:31-2+ Mr '87
Gilliam, T. Conrad, and others
A DNA segment encoding two genes very tightly linked
to Huntington's disease. bibl f il *Science* 238:950-2
N 13 '87
Gilliatt, Penelope
Ex libris [story] *New Yorker* 63:32-7 My 4 '87
Lingo [story] *New Yorker* 63:30-5 S 7 '87
Gillin, Frances D., and others
Encystation and expression of cyst antigens by Giardia
lamblia in vitro. bibl f il *Science* 235:1040-3 F 27
'87
Gillingham, John
Images of Ireland 1170-1600: the origins of English
imperialism. bibl il *Hist Today* 37:16-22 F '87

Gillis, Jack
The best and worst 1987 cars [excerpts from The 1987 car book] il *Good Housekeep* 205:265 S '87
Recalls: an up-to-date list. See issues of Good Housekeeping beginning May 1987
Gillis, Jack, and Fise, Mary Ellen R.
The ABC's of safe parenting. il *Good Housekeep* 205:90+ S '87
Gillman, Peter
The most savage mountain. il *World Press Rev* 34:36-7 D '87
Gillom, Jennifer
about
Racist, sexist comment by CBS sports anchors riles nation's women's groups. il por *Jet* 72:54 S 14 '87
Gillon, Iris E.
about
How Iris Gillon keeps an orchestra in her apartment. T. Thompson. il por *Bus Week* p115 O 26 '87
Gilmore, Mikal
Blues with a bullet . . . and Robert Cray holds the smoking gun [cover story] il pors *Roll Stone* p40-2+ Je 18 '87
The Madonna mystique [cover story] il pors *Roll Stone* p36-9+ S 10 '87
The new dawn of the Grateful Dead [cover story] il *Roll Stone* p46-7+ Jl 16-30 '87
Gilmore, Roger
The policy and public relations role of higher education with respect to K-12 arts education. *Des Arts Educ* 88:28-9 Ja/F '87
Gilmore, V. Elaine
What's new in tools. See issues of Popular Science
Gilpin, Laura
about
An enduring grace: the photography of Laura Gilpin. M. A. Sandweiss. il por *USA Today (Periodical)* 115:54-63 Mr '87
Gilroy (Calif.)
Education
California kids say their calendar poses no skin problem, but their school officials say it's unsuitable [student fund raising venture] il *People Wkly* 27:59 My 18 '87
High-school students make YBa$_2$Cu$_3$O$_{7-x}$ [class produces superconducting material] W. Sweet. il *Phys Today* 40:111-12 O '87
Gilstrap, Suzy
about
Against all odds: Suzy Gilstrap. M. Altman. il por *Seventeen* 46:214 Ag '87
Gilyard, Keith
Automatic natural [poem] *Essence* 17:120-1 Ap '87
Gin
Gin without the tonic. W. Grimes. il *Esquire* 108:24 Ag '87
Ginaven, Marlene
Collecting pot lids: Staffordshire Pratt ware painted by Jesse Austin. il *Antiques Collect Hobbies* 92:22-4 D '87
Gingerbread
How to make gingerbread. L. Colwin. il *Gourmet* 47:98+ D '87
Gingerbread houses, ornaments, etc. *See* Cooking, Ornamental
Gingivitis
Nutritional aspects
Vitamin C helps keep gums healthy; Folate may help, too. *Prevention* 39:79 F '87
Gingold, Alfred
Shawn with the wind. il *New Repub* 196:10-12 F 9 '87
Gingras, Christiane Bilodeau *See* Bilodeau Gingras, Christiane
Gingrasso, Susan Hughes
Dance education certification: current status and significance. bibl f *Des Arts Educ* 89:31-5 S/O '87
Gingrich, Newt
Replace social security with a stable, permanent retirement system. il *USA Today (Periodical)* 116:22-3 Jl '87
about
The right's free lunch. M. Kaus. *New Repub* 196:14 Mr 9 '87
Ginnie Mae securities *See* Mortgage bonds and notes
Ginsberg, Allen, 1926-
Velocity of money [poem] *Harpers* 274:38 Ja '87
about
The poet's pursuit: capturing dreams [interview] A. P. Sanoff. il por *U S News World Rep* 102:74 F 16 '87

Ginsberg, Bill
about
Beyond the beeper. M. Gill. il por *Esquire* 108:94 O '87
Ginsburg, Douglas H., 1946-
about
Betrayal. H. S. Scott. *New Repub* 197:12-13 D 14 '87
Exit the smoking judge. I. Austen. il por *Macleans* 100:32 N 16 '87
The Ginsburg generation. *Nation* 245:577 N 21 '87
The Ginsburg test: bad logic. C. Krauthammer. il *Time* 130:102 N 23 '87
The high hurdles between Ginsburg and the High Court. P. Dwyer. il *Bus Week* p77 N 16 '87
If at first you don't succeed . . . J. V. Lamar, Jr. il por *Time* 130:52 N 9 '87
Judging Ginsburg. *Nation* 245:543-4 N 14 '87
Law and economics: a new order in the Court? P. Dwyer. il por *Bus Week* p93+ N 16 '87
Marshall's ex-clerk tabbed for U.S. Supreme Court seat. *Jet* 73:5 N 16 '87
The new case of Douglas Ginsburg: a 'baby Bork'? T. Gest. il por *U S News World Rep* 103:15 N 9 '87
Pot & politics [cover story] A. Press. il pors *Newsweek* 110:46-52 N 16 '87
Round II. F. Barnes. *New Repub* 197:9-11 N 23 '87
Rules of the game. *New Repub* 197:4+ N 23 '87
Sins of the past. M. Hornblower. por *Time* 130:18-20 N 16 '87
Spoiling for a second round [special section] il pors *Newsweek* 110:42-3+ N 9 '87
Up in smoke: the undoing of a High Court nominee. B. Duffy and D. Baer. il por *U S News World Rep* 103:24-6 N 16 '87
Anecdotes, facetiae, satire, etc.
Just say no comment. A. Z. Posner. *New Repub* 197:10 N 30 '87
Ginsburg, Fred
Missing link: a practical guide to wireless mics. il *Theatre Crafts* 21:49-52 Ap '87
Ginsburg, Genevieve Davis
Coping with widowhood: 'who am I without my mate?' [excerpt from To live again] il por *50 Plus* 27:44-5+ Je '87
To live again: coping with widowhood [excerpt] il pors *50 Plus* 27:52+ My '87
Ginsburg, Isaac, and others
Phagocytosis of Candida albicans enhances malignant behavior of murine tumor cells. bibl f il *Science* 238:1573-5 D 11 '87
Ginsburg, Philip E.
The three lives of . . . Marie Hilley [excerpt from Poisoned blood] il pors *Good Housekeep* 205:148-9+ N '87
Ginseng
Gender modification in North American ginsengs. M. A. Schlessman. bibl f il *BioScience* 37:469-75 Jl/Ag '87
Gintz, Claude
Neoclassical rearmament. il *Art Am* 75:110-17 F '87
Giordan, Alma Roberts
A bouquet for Battista [poem] *America* 156:505 Je 20-27 '87
Giordano, Joseph
The Mafia mystique. por *U S News World Rep* 102:6 F 16 '87
Giordano's Bakery
In New Jersey: bread that casts a spell. R. Conniff. il *Time* 129:15-16 Je 8 '87
Giorgio Abetti Observatory *See* Astronomical observatories—Italy
Giotto cometary mission *See* Space flight—Cometary missions
Giovacchini, Robert
about
Meet a corporate Dr. No. J. Strahinich. il por *Read Dig* 130:101-4 Mr '87
Giovannini, Joseph
Architecture: Johannes Van Tilburg. il *Archit Dig* 44:136-42 F '87
Building his own bridges. il *House Gard* 159:112-21+ Mr '87
Manhattan still life. il *House Gard* 159:178-83+ Je '87
A matter of style. il *N Y Times Mag* p54 O 18 '87
Gipe, Robert K.
(jt. auth) See Perrin, Charles L., and Gipe, Robert K.
Gipp, George
about
George Gipp: "One for the Gipper!". J. Gustaitis. por *Am Hist Illus* 22:40-1 N '87

Gipsy moths *See* Gypsy moths
Girardin, René Louis, marquis de, 1735-1808
about
Folies de grandeur. R. M. Adams. il map *House Gard* 159:48+ Ja '87
Il Girasole (Italy: Historic house) *See* Historic houses, sites, etc.—Italy
Girdler, Allan
10/10ths. See alternate issues of Road & Track beginning May 1985
Girl Scouts of the United States of America
A diamond for the Girl Scouts [Juliette Gordon Low Birthplace] il *South Living* 22:18 Mr '87
For Juliette Gordon Low's girls, a sparkling Diamond Jublilee. J. Howard. bibl (p229) il *Smithsonian* 18:46-55 O '87
Girl Scouts celebrate seventy-five years of service. il *Am Hist Illus* 22:9 Mr '87
Uniforms
Scout's honor: the new uniform is blue. J. Miller. il *Ms* 15:58-9 Mr '87
Girlfriends and boyfriends *See* Women and men
Girls
See also
Sex differences
Health and hygiene
See also
Gynecologic examinations
Photographs and photography
Sally Mann at Marcuse Pfeiffer [12 year old girls] A. Ellenzweig. *Art Am* 75:140 Ja '87
Girls, Delinquent *See* Juvenile delinquents and delinquency
Girls apart [film] See Motion picture reviews—Single works
Girls' clubs
See also
Girl Scouts of the United States of America
Girls Clubs of America
Helping parents help their children [KID-ABILITY sexual abuse prevention program] *Child Today* 16:5 My/Je '87
Girls in art *See* Women in art
Girls' rooms *See* Children's rooms
Girls' schools *See* Private schools
Girouard, Mark, 1931-
Memories of an eccentric world. il *Archit Dig* 44:54+ Je '87
about
PW interviews. A. Smith. por *Publ Wkly* 232:55-6 D 4 '87
Girton, Brenda M.
about
Lawyer in the lobby. N. A. Williams. il por *Essence* 18:113+ Jl '87
Giselle [ballet] See Ballet reviews—Single works
Gish, Lillian, 1896?-
Lillian Gish. il por *People Wkly* 27:70-1 F 9 '87
about
Cane and Able. J. Ney. il por *Film Comment* 23:2+ Ja/F '87
Grand old Lillian Gish makes a big splash in The whales of August. B. Darrach. il pors *People Wkly* 28:70-2+ D 14 '87
Gisslen, Wayne, 1946-
Uncorking secrets of the vine: Germany's Wine Academy. il *Travel Holiday* 168:72-7 Jl '87
Gitano (Firm)
Chic for the masses. E. Pomice. il *Forbes* 139:126-7 F 23 '87
Gite, Lloyd
Creating a dream home. il *Black Enterp* 18:66-8+ O '87
Degrees of success. il *Black Enterp* 17:92-4+ F '87
Two for a fresh start. il *Black Enterp* 17:31-2+ Ja '87
Gitlin, Todd
The Lone Driver rides again. il *Progressive* 51:36-40 F '87
about
After the Ginsburg debacle, a chronicler of the sixties ponders the new politics of pot [interview] M. Wilhelm. il por *People Wkly* 28:124+ N 23 '87
Gittelson, Bernard, and Torbet, Laura
Are you a little bit psychic? [excerpt from Intangible evidence] *Redbook* 169:76+ O '87
Gittelson, Natalie
Coming back big: Sally Struthers' lucky streak. il pors *McCalls* 114:12-13+ Je '87
Family ties: the day-care center a TV show built. il *McCalls* 114:61-4 Ag '87
"He is my life". il pors *McCalls* 114:14-15+ F '87
Linda Gray: "I have more fun alone!". il pors *McCalls* 114:13+ Ja '87

Loni Anderson: matters of the heart. il pors *McCalls* 114:12-14+ My '87
Loretta Swit. il pors *McCalls* 114:10-11+ Jl '87
Melissa Gilbert . . . all grown up! il pors *McCalls* 114:94-8 S '87
Wendy Goldberg: "the most gracious hostess in town". il pors *McCalls* 114:124-6+ F '87
Gittens, Donna Latson
Managing maternity. il *Essence* 18:106+ Je '87
Gittings, John
A 'familiar struggle'. il *World Press Rev* 34:16 Mr '87
Giuliani, Rudolph W.
about
Convictions and conflict: a top cop's tale. D. Baer. il pors *U S News World Rep* 102:23-4+ Mr 23 '87
Giuliani retreats—but he's poised for a new attack. L. J. Tell. il por *Bus Week* p44 Je 1 '87
Gotcha! [cover story; interview] N. Collins. il pors *N Y* 20:28-40 My 25 '87
His way. J. Klein. il pors *N Y* 20:34+ O 26 '87
Keep your eye on Giuliani. G. F. Will. il *Newsweek* 109:84 Mr 2 '87
New York's 'Eliot Ness'. L. Black. il por *Macleans* 100:6-7 Ap 6 '87
A stumble during the waltz. B. Powell. il por *Newsweek* 109:34 My 25 '87
Giulini, Carlo Maria
about
Giulini's elegant Bruckner. D. Hall. il por *Stereo Rev* 52:150+ N '87
Giurlanda, Paul
The challenge of post-liberal theology. *Commonweal* 114:40-2 Ja 30 '87
Giustino [opera] See Vivaldi, Antonio, 1678-1741
Given names *See* Names, Personal
Givenchy, Hubert de
about
Givenchy grandeur. J. Richardson. il *House Gard* 159:218-30 Ap '87
Givens, Robin
about
If Robin Givens can jump from Harvard to Head of the class, there's no ceiling on her talent. R. Arias. il pors *People Wkly* 27:127-8 My 11 '87
Mike Tyson and Robin Givens: champ talks about their romance and his rise from street gangs to success [cover story] R. E. Johnson. il pors *Jet* 73:58-60 D 28 '87-Ja 4 '88
Robin Givens leaves Harvard Med School for Hollywood [cover story] A. Collier. il pors *Jet* 72:54-5+ Je 29 '87
Waking up rich and famous. il pors *Ebony* 42:36+ S '87
Giving
See also
Charities
Christian giving
Christmas gifts
Corporations—Charitable contributions
Gifts
Check a box, do some good [state tax checkoffs to fund worthy causes] L. Wiener. il *U S News World Rep* 103:82 O 12 '87
Fear of giving. M. Jacobson. il *Esquire* 108:61-2 D '87
From sea to shining sea [Plymouth Pride in America Road Rally in which participants depend on the generosity of strangers] M. Neill. il map *People Wkly* 28:28-33 S 21 '87
In need of an angel (I). il *People Wkly* 27:24-31 Mr 16 '87
In need of an angel (II). M. Small and B. Little. il *People Wkly* 27:94-5+ Ap 27 '87
In need of an angel (III). M. Small. il *People Wkly* 28:80-2+ N 30 '87
Isn't this what Christmas is all about? R. Rooney. il *Good Housekeep* 205:120+ D '87
"Joy comes from sharing". C. L. Player. il *McCalls* 115:133-5 D '87
Teaching children to give. B. Spock. il por *Redbook* 170:34+ D '87
Glaberson, William I., and Schwarz, Klaus W.
Quantized vortices in superfluid helium-4. bibl f il *Phys Today* 40:54-60 F '87
Glacial epochs
Domino effect invoked in Ice Age extinctions [theory of Norman Owen-Smith] R. Lewin. il *Science* 238:1509-10 D 11 '87
Forests made the world frigid? [theory of James C. G. Walker and Andrew H. Knoll] S. Weisburd. *Sci News* 131:9 Ja 3 '87

Glacial epochs—*cont.*
Ice on the world. S. W. Matthews. il maps *Natl Geogr* 171:78-103 Ja '87
Glacier National Park (Mont.)
See also
Waterton-Glacier International Peace Park (Alta. and Mont.)
The last picture by a man who loved bears [photographer C. Gibbs killed by grizzly] il por *Audubon* 89:16-17 Jl '87
Return of the western wolf. il *Nat Hist* 96:4 O '87
Summer chalets in Glacier . . . but you must plan now. il *Sunset* 178:42+ Ja '87
Glaciers
See also
Glacial epochs
Icebergs
Glaciers on the move [Hubbard and Columbia] J. L. Eliot. il map *Natl Geogr* 171:104-19 Ja '87
Hubbard glacier. P. Barnes-Svarney. il *Earth Sci* 40:20 Fall '87
Lakes and glaciers of the Alps. H. Löffler. il *Courier* 40:37-8 F '87
New maps show possible overflow of glacier lake [Hubbard Glacier] map *Earth Sci* 40:6-7 Summ '87
Shake hands with a glacier [Mount Rainier] il maps *Sunset* 179:44-8 Jl '87
Glad, John
(tr) See Voĭnovich, Vladimir, 1932-, and Zalygin, Sergei. Where glasnost has its limits
Glad Day Bookshop (Toronto, Ont.) *See* Booksellers and bookselling—Ontario
Gladiolus
The gardening secrets of a glad man [John Berens] M. C. Smith. il *Flower Gard* 31:10+ Je/Jl '87
Gladiolus thrips *See* Thrips
Gladstone, Bernard
Boatkeeper. See issues of Motor Boating & Sailing
Boatyard. See issues of Motor Boating & Sailing
Gladstone, Valerie
The birth of the classics. il *Horizon* 30:18-19 Mr '87
Gladstone, W. E. (William Ewart), 1809-1898
about
Gladstonian finance. H. C. G. Matthew. bibl il por *Hist Today* 37:41-5 Jl '87
Gladstone, William Ewart *See* Gladstone, W. E. (William Ewart), 1809-1898
Gladwell, Malcolm
Semi-tough. *New Repub* 196:9-11 My 18 '87
Gladwell, Malcolm, and Sharpe, Rochelle
Baby M winner. *New Repub* 196:15-16+ F 16 '87
Glands
See also
Bursa Fabricii
Pancreas
Prostate gland
Diseases
See also
Cystic fibrosis
Glands, Ductless *See* Endocrine glands
Glantz, Michael H.
Drought in Africa. il maps *Sci Am* 256:34-40 Je '87
Glanzelius, Anton
about
Anton Glanzelius unleashes a fierce talent in My life as a dog. il por *People Wkly* 28:82 Ag 10 '87
Glaser, Paul Michael
about
The running man [film] Reviews
People Wkly il 28:18 N 30 '87. R. Novak
Glasgow (Scotland)
City planning
A new city of culture. R. Laver. il *Macleans* 100:6 N 23 '87
Music
See also
Scottish Opera
Glasner, David
Cheap labor on campus. por *Newsweek* 110:12 N 9 '87
Glasnost (Periodical)
Glasnost vs. glasnost. C. Krauthammer. *New Repub* 197:14-15 D 28 '87
A journalistic profile in courage [publisher S. I. Grigoryants] J. Alter. il por *Newsweek* 110:37 D 14 '87
New mag in Moscow. M. Garbus. *N Y Rev Books* 34:49 Ag 13 '87
Glass, A. M.
Optical materials. bibl f il *Science* 235:1003-9 F 27 '87

Glass, Andrew J.
Why politicians don't matter on Wall Street. il *New Leader* 70:3-4 N 2 '87
Glass, Charles
Down the black hole. il pors *Roll Stone* p58-60+ D 3 '87
Kidnapping
A 'confession' under duress. por *Newsweek* 110:35 Jl 20 '87
Down the black hole. C. Glass. il pors *Roll Stone* p58-60+ D 3 '87
Escape from Beirut. W. E. Smith. il *Time* 130:24-5 Ag 31 '87
Escape in Beirut—and maybe much more. J. Wallace. il por *U S News World Rep* 103:32-3 Ag 31 '87
A kidnapped reporter's daring escape. C. Wood. il por *Macleans* 100:16 Ag 31 '87
Minority report. C. Hitchens. *Nation* 245:294 S 26 '87
Newsman Charles Glass relives his 62 days of terror as a hostage in Beirut. J. Cooper. il por *People Wkly* 28:46-7 S 7 '87
No deals. por *Time* 130:17 Jl 6 '87
No help for Glass [Syria declines to use its power in Lebanon] *Newsweek* 110:32 Jl 6 '87
Now, a hostage. por *Newsweek* 109:43 Je 29 '87
An ominous kidnapping. J. Muir. *Macleans* 100:19 Jl 6 '87
Syria: forgive and forget? B. Hewitt. il por *Newsweek* 110:31 Ag 31 '87
The taking of a journalist. il por *Time* 129:39 Je 29 '87
Terror TV—nasty little farce [coerced confession] il pors *U S News World Rep* 103:14 Jl 20 '87
Glass, Ellen
(jt. auth) See Walters, Barbara, and Glass, Ellen
Glass, Julie
Animal love. See alternate issues of Glamour beginning July 1987
What are the limits of love? il *Glamour* 85:198 S '87
Glass, Kathy
(jt. auth) See Carr, Patrick, and Glass, Kathy
Glass, Sheriann
Future phobia: take charge of your tomorrow. il *Teen* 31:58+ Jl '87
Glass
See also
Fulgurite
Glassware
Glazes and glazing (Glass)
Tektites
Vitrification
Windows
Disordered materials: a survey of amorphous solids. Y.-T. Cheng and W. L. Johnson. bibl f il *Science* 235:997-1002 F 27 '87
Fracture
The fracturing of glass. T. A. Michalske and B. C. Bunker. il *Sci Am* 257:122-9 D '87
Glass, Ornamental *See* Glassware
Glass, Stained *See* Glass painting and staining
Glass Art Society
Glass Art Society looks inward [Philadelphia conference] J. Tognini. il *Am Craft* 47:12-13+ Je/Jl '87
Glass blocks and bricks
Glass with class. L. E. Oberwager. il *Home Mech* 83:44-6+ N '87
What makes this small kitchen seem large? A curving glass-block wall. il *Sunset* 178:84-5 Ja '87
Whether transparent or translucent, glass blocks let in light, hold in heat, keep out sound, and add beauty to your home. il *Sunset* 179:90-1 Jl '87
Glass blowing and working
An everyday luxury [work of S. Pearce] N. F. Weber. il *House Gard* 159:76+ F '87
Glass cleaners *See* Cleaning compositions
Glass construction
Compilation of sloping-glass codes shows regional differences. J. Trewhitt. il *Archit Rec* 175:37 O '87
From glass house to our house: three centuries of indoor/outdoor rooms in a new book to inform, inspire [Living under glass] B. Plumb. il *Vogue* 177:218 Ap '87
Glass container industry *See* Container industry
Glass containers
Administration Building powder jar [1893 Columbian Exposition] M. Wollett and B. Wollett. il *Antiques Collect Hobbies* 92:30 Je '87
Glass doors *See* Doors
Glass etching
One-of-a-kind glass gifts . . . with easy chemical etching. il *Sunset* 179:95-6 D '87

Glass fibers, Optical See Fiber optics
Glass flowers
Collectors and collecting
Forever flowers of glass and magic [Harvard's Ware Collection of Blaschka Glass Models] L. Ware. il *Audubon* 89:96-109 My '87
Glass industry
>*See also*
>AFG Industries, Inc.
>Anchor Glass Container Corp.
>Anchor Hocking Corp.
>PPG Industries, Inc.
>Steuben Glass
History
>*See also*
>Findlay Flint Glass Company
Ireland
>*See also*
>Waterford Glass Group plc
The glass menagerie [film] See Motion picture reviews—Single works
Glass painting and staining
Less is Moorish [New York City apartment with prominent stained glass window] M. Bethany. il *N Y* 20:82-4 N 16 '87
President and Mrs. McKinley portraits [reverse glass painting] M. Wollett and B. Wollett. il por *Antiques Collect Hobbies* 91:37 F '87
Stained glass. C. Gibson and P. G. McWilliams. il *Ctry J* 14:65-8 Je '87
Stained glass for the home. C. Zusy. bibl f il *Antiques* 131:848-57 Ap '87
Threatened light sources [church stained glass windows by Charles J. Connick Studio] M. E. Marty. *Christ Century* 104:295 Mr 18-25 '87
Glass sculpture
The Corning Museum of Glass [acquisition of Innerland, Steuben glass sculpture by E. Hilton] il *Antiques Collect Hobbies* 91:56-7 Ja '87
David Huchthausen: controlled fragments [cover story] R. Silberman. il por *Am Craft* 47:54-9 Ag/S '87
Exhibitions
At the Renwick: Dan Dailey. K. M. Burke. il *Smithsonian* 18:158+ Je '87
Glass-Steagall Act See Banks and banking—Laws and regulations
Glass Tiger (Musical group)
Rock wrap up. il por *Teen* 31:58 Mr '87
Glass vases See Vases
Glasser, Selma
Puns and parodies pay off. *Writer* 100:19-20+ Je '87
Glasser, William, 1925-
>*about*
The key to improving schools: an interview with William Glasser. P. B. Gough. il *Phi Delta Kappan* 68:656-62 My '87
Glasses (Spectacles) See Eyeglasses
Glassie, John H.
Joel Jaecks. il por *Am Artist* 51:34-9 S '87
Glassware
>*See also*
>Biedermeier glassware
>Bottles
>Glass Art Society
>Glass etching
>Glass sculpture
>Lampwork (Paperweights)
>Sandblasting
>Vases
An everyday luxury [work of S. Pearce] N. F. Weber. il *House Gard* 159:76+ F '87
Splendid glass. C. Vogel. il *N Y Times Mag* p40-1 Jl 5 '87
Collectors and collecting
>*See also*
>American Cut Glass Association
American historical glass. M. Wollett and B. Wollett. See issues of Antiques & Collecting Hobbies beginning March 1985
American historical glass. M. Wollett and B. Wollett. See issues of Hobbies through February 1985
Charles Tuthill: a legend in cut and intaglio glass. B. Boggess and L. Boggess. il *Antiques Collect Hobbies* 92:14-18 Ap '87
The Findlay Flint Glass Company. J. S. Measell. il *Antiques Collect Hobbies* 91:18-19 Ja '87
Glass of the 80s [The Saxe Collection: contemporary American and European glass at the American Craft Museum] R. Kehlmann. il pors *Am Craft* 47:32-9 Ap/My '87

In a glass house. M. Schafer. il *House Gard* 159:112-21 F '87
Exhibitions
The Corning Museum of Glass [Glass of the Caesars exhibition] il *Antiques Collect Hobbies* 92:52 Ap '87
Glass [Frederick Carder: portrait of a glassmaker at the Walters Art Gallery, Baltimore] S. B. Sherrill. il *Antiques* 131:352+ F '87
Glass of the 80s [The Saxe Collection: contemporary American and European glass at the American Craft Museum] R. Kehlmann. il pors *Am Craft* 47:32-9 Ap/My '87
The Rockwell Museum [Carder's Carder exhibition] il *Antiques Collect Hobbies* 92:53 Ag '87
Photographs and photography
Shooting glass. L. B. MacArthur. il *Petersens Photogr Mag* 16:72-3 O '87
Glastris, Paul
Frank Fat's napkin: how the trial lawyers (and the doctors!) sold out to the tobacco companies. il *Wash Mon* 19:19-25 D '87
The freest enterprise. *Wash Mon* 19:51-4 F '87
Inside tax reform. *Wash Mon* 19:52-6 Je '87
The powers that shouldn't be: five Washington insiders the next Democratic president shouldn't hire [cover story] pors *Wash Mon* 19:39-46+ O '87
Warning: the Surgeon General may be good for your health. por *Wash Mon* 19:13-16+ Mr '87
Wrong number! *Read Dig* 130:161-4 Je '87
Glattstein, Judy
Little bulbs give lots of color. il *Flower Gard* 31:32-4+ Ag/S '87
Real gardeners have coldframes. il *Flower Gard* 31:44-5 O/N '87
Glavkosmos
Glavcosmos establishes prices for 'getaway special' payloads. *Aviat Week Space Technol* 127:27 O 12 '87
Glaxo Holdings plc
Can Glaxo strike it rich again? R. A. Melcher. *Bus Week* p48 Mr 2 '87
Glazer, Steven A.
Here's one way to deal with clients' unpaid bills. *Archit Rec* 175:39 Mr '87
Glazes and glazing (Glass)
How to reglaze windows. R. Capotosto. il *Pop Mech* 164:121-2 S '87
Replacement windows [low-emissivity glass] M. Brett. il *Pop Sci* 230:60-2 My '87
Understanding glazing—and the new "low-e" windowpane. il *Sunset* 179:72 Ag '87
Understanding low-E glass. J. Vara. il *Ctry J* 14:32-3 Mr '87
Gleason, Jackie
>*about*
Obituary
>*Jet* il pors 72:60-1 Jl 13 '87
>*Macleans* 100:54 Jl 6 '87. P. Young
>*Natl Rev* 39:19 Jl 31 '87
>*Newsweek* il pors 110:49 Jl 6 '87. J. Adler
>*People Wkly* il pors 28:94-100 Jl 13 '87. B. Darrach
>*Time* por 130:19 Jl 6 '87. R. Zoglin
Gleason, Michie
>*about*
Summer heat [film] Reviews
>*People Wkly* il 27:12 Je 15 '87. R. Novak
Glechoma hederacea See Ground ivy
Gleeson, Day
>*about*
Day Gleeson and Dennis Thomas at A & P. T. Cokes. il *Art Am* 75:139-40 Ja '87
Gleick, James
An electrifying discovery. *Read Dig* 131:131 Jl '87
In the trenches of science. il *N Y Times Mag* p28-31+ Ag 16 '87
New images of chaos that are stirring a science revolution. bibl (p205) il *Smithsonian* 18:122-4+ D '87
Science on the track of God. il *N Y Times Mag* p22-3 Ja 4 '87
Glen, John
>*about*
The living daylights [film] Reviews
>*Humanist* il 47:43 N/D '87. H. M. Geduld
>*Macleans* il 100:49 Ag 3 '87. L. O'Toole
>*N Y* il 20:54 Ag 10 '87. D. Denby
>*People Wkly* 28:8 Ag 31 '87. R. Novak
>*Time* il 130:55 Ag 10 '87. R. Corliss

Glen Canyon Dam *See* Dams
Glenconner, Colin Christopher Paget Tennant, 3rd Baron
about
Caribbean folly: Lord Glenconner's villa on Mustique. Suzy. il *Archit Dig* 44:132-9 S '87
Glendale (Ariz.)
Education
Collecting for fun, education, and the Arizona Kidney Foundation [Glendale American School] E. Walker. *Phi Delta Kappan* 68:402-3 Ja '87
Glendale (Calif.)
Courts
L.A. NAACP wants judge fired for 'nigger' slur [removal of D. Calabro] *Jet* 72:12 S 14 '87
Education
Role-playing in class: casting counts [friction caused by simulation game] *Newsweek* 110:76 D 14 '87
Race relations
L.A. NAACP wants judge fired for 'nigger' slur [removal of D. Calabro] *Jet* 72:12 S 14 '87
Restaurants, nightclubs, bars, etc.
Spécialités de la maison:
Fresco Ristorante. il *Gourmet* 48:32+ Je '87
Glendale Industries
Home-based business—a moving experience [W. Lazar revives Glendale Industries] L. L. Small. il pors *Ms* 16:76+ S '87
Glendon, Mary Ann, 1938-
about
Mary Ann Glendon: "We have let our love of individual liberty trump everything else, such as our sense of community" [interview] M. Asnes. il por *Vogue* 177:238+ N '87
Glenn, Charles L.
Curriculum in the public schools: can compromise be reached? il *Christ Century* 104:441-3 My 6 '87
The new common school. il *Phi Delta Kappan* 69:290-4 D '87
Other sides to the textbook controversy [discusssion of May 6, 1987 article, Curriculum in the public schools: can compromise be reached?] il *Christ Century* 104:631-2 Jl 15-22 '87
Textbook controversies: a 'disaster for public schools'? bibl f *Phi Delta Kappan* 68:451-5 F '87
Glenn, Jerome C.
Conscious technology: uniting the technocrat and the mystic. *Futurist* 21:60 My/Je '87
Glenn, John, 1921-
about
Glenn asks Reagan to halt Pakistan aid pending review of nuclear programs. M. Crawford. por *Science* 235:1321 Mr 13 '87
John Glenn anniversary. *Space World* X-4-280:37 Ap '87
Glenn, Karen
Guide to your child's health. il *McCalls* 114:43-6 Ag '87
Headaches. il *Seventeen* 46:270-1+ Mr '87
Glennan, Keith
about
Ike's nightmare is upon us. H. Sidey. il por *Time* 130:24 S 14 '87
Glennie, John R.
Should the "Minimum Wage Restoration Act of 1987" be approved? [excerpts from testimony, July 23, 1987] *Congr Dig* 66:221+ Ag/S '87
Glenville, Peter
about
Custom of the country. J. Richardson. il por *House Gard* 159:146-56 Ag '87
Glerum, Jay O.
Retrofitting the sixties: rigging & rigging control. il *Theatre Crafts* 21:26-7+ F '87
Gless, Sharon
about
Sharon Gless & Tyne Daly. M. Gordon. il pors *Ms* 15:40-1+ Ja '87
Gleysteen, William H., Jr., and Romberg, Alan D.
Korea: Asian paradox. *Foreign Aff* 65:1037-54 Summ '87
Glick, J. Leslie
about
Techno-blinders. A. A. Lappen. il pors *Forbes* 140:104+ D 28 '87
Glick, Peter
Help, at a distance. *Psychol Today* 21:66-7 F '87
Stars in our eyes. il *Psychol Today* 21:6-7 Ag '87
Glickman, Carl D.
Good and/or effective schools: what do we want? bibl f il *Phi Delta Kappan* 68:622-4 Ap '87

Unlocking school reform: uncertainty as a condition of professionalism. bibl f il *Phi Delta Kappan* 69:120-2 O '87
Glickman, Marshall
Money and freedom. il *N Y Times Mag* p62 Ap 26 '87
Glicksman, Marlaine
Hanif Kureishi. por *Roll Stone* p33-4 N 19 '87
Highway 61 revisited [interview with R. Frank] il pors *Film Comment* 23:32-9 Jl/Ag '87
Hotel 'Heaven' [interview] il *Film Comment* 23:32-7 Mr/Ap '87
Whoopi's blue eyes. *Harpers* 274:29 Ja '87
Gliders (Aviation)
See also
Gliding and soaring
Gliding and soaring
Hanging around over Rio. C. Purcell. il *Américas* 39:46-9 S/O '87
Hanging out. G. Bowen. il *Flying* 114:72+ My '87
New wings for women. H. Casabona. il *Women's Sports Fitness* 9:46 O '87
On limber wings. E. Weiner. il *Flying* 114:64-6 My '87
Gliedman, John
Is the pact too little, too late? il *Nation* 245:376-80 O 10 '87
Glimmerglass Opera Theater
Musical events:
Alice Busch Opera Theatre, new opera house in Cooperstown, N.Y. A. Porter. *New Yorker* 63:72-4 Jl 13 '87
Summer night's dream. W. D. West. il *Opera News* 51:34-5 Je '87
Glin Knight *See* Fitz-Gerald, Desmond John Villiers, 1937-
Glissant, Edouard, 1928-
Baroque as a world philosophy. il *Courier* 40:18-19 S '87
(jt. auth) *See* Bouatchidzé, Gaston, and Glissant, Edouard, 1928-
Glitman, Maynard W.
INF extended session ends [statement, March 26, 1987] *Dep State Bull* 87:18 My '87
Glitz
Glitz! D. Harris. il *Vogue* 177:318-19+ D '87
The look of glitz. S. Drucker. il *Vogue* 177:320-1 D '87
Glixon, Niel
Senator Hatch questions Al Capone. il *Commonweal* 114:436 Ag 14 '87
Global Asset Management Ltd.
A confident British 'fundamentalist' [G. de Botton] R. A. Melcher. il por *Bus Week* p154-5 D 28 '87-Ja 4 '88
Global Oscillation Network Group
GONG: to see inside our sun [cover story] J. W. Harvey and others. il map *Sky Telesc* 74:470-6 N '87
Global Positioning System *See* Artificial satellites—Navigational use
Global studies *See* International education
Global Travel Publishers
African safari guide from new Florida publisher [work of M. Nolting] por *Publ Wkly* 231:60 Je 12 '87
Globe (Ariz.)
Education
The pride of Globe, Arizona [K. Zeigler's high school astronomy program] J. K. Beatty. il por *Sky Telesc* 74:192-3 Ag '87
Globesat, Inc.
Globesat designing satellite for Unisys. *Aviat Week Space Technol* 127:29 O 19 '87
Globins
See also
Haptoglobins
Globular clusters *See* Stars—Clusters
Globulins
See also
Immunoglobulins
Manipulating milk in mammals [betalactoglobulin gene in mice; research by J. Paul Simons and others] R. Weiss. *Sci News* 132:84 Ag 8 '87
Globus, Yoram
about
Is the go-go gone? M. Dougherty. il pors *Life* 10:102 Ap '87
Glogowski, Miroslaw
The mistake on Iran was 'poor execution'. il *World Press Rev* 34:30 Mr '87
Glossbrenner, Alfred
The computer as an investment tool. il *Work Woman* 12:47-8 F '87

Glosser, John L.
To S. K. [poem] *Christ Century* 104:84 Ja 28 '87
Glossolalia *See* Speaking in tongues
Gloster, Hugh M.
about
Dr. Gloster weeps as he awards Wonder last degree as president of Morehouse. il pors *Jet* 72:24 Je 8 '87
Glover, Clarence E., Jr.
about
Spirituality: an African view [interview] J. D. Simmons. por *Essence* 18:61+ D '87
Glover, Crispin
about
Crispin Glover of River's edge emerges as king of the oddballs. N. Geeslin. il pors *People Wkly* 27:74-6 Je 22 '87
Glover, Danny
about
Danny Glover, Mel Gibson team up for action in 'Lethal weapon'. C. Waldron. il pors *Jet* 72:58-60 Ap 6 '87
Danny Glover says he was never a member of the Black Panther Party. por *Jet* 72:59 Ap 20 '87
Danny Glover stars in 'Mandela' movie that tugs at heart, shocks senses [cover story] il pors *Jet* 73:58-60 O 5 '87
Glover, James, and Glover, Regina
The natural magic of Olaus Murie. il pors *Sierra* 72:69-73 S/O '87
Glover, Regina
(jt. auth) *See* Glover, James, and Glover, Regina
Gloves
See also
Baseball gloves
A concise history of the stringback driving glove. P. Egan. il *Road Track* 38:72 Je '87
Cycle Racer Gloves. il *Cycle* 38:18 O '87
Hand warmers [gloves and mittens] T. H. Cole. il *Pop Mech* 164:27 Ja '87
Hot & cold running gloves [motorcycle gloves tested by infrared camera for heat retention] P. Gordon. il *Cycle* 38:75-7+ D '87
Insects removed surgically [surgical gloves as protection against insect bites] M. Simmons. il *Field Stream* 92:111 Je '87
Leather gloves in the garden . . . what's best? il *Sunset* 178:172-3 F '87
Putting on the gloves to fight AIDS [boxing referees ordered to wear rubber gloves] il *Newsweek* 110:49 Jl 27 '87
Głowacki, Janusz
about
Hunting cockroaches [drama] Reviews
N Y 20:56+ Mr 16 '87. J. Simon
Nation 244:448 Ap 4 '87. M. Hodgson
New Leader 70:20-1 Mr 9 '87. L. Sauvage
New Yorker 63:71 Mr 16 '87. E. Oliver
Time il 129:93 Mr 16 '87. W. A. Henry
Gloxinias
Windowsill gloxinias. D. E. Stebbins. il *Rodale's Org Gard* 34:14-15 S '87
Gluck, Christoph Willibald, Ritter von, 1714-1787
about
Alceste [opera] Reviews
Opera News 51:46-7 Ap 11 '87. H. Koegler
Glucocorticoid receptors *See* Hormone receptors
Glucolysis *See* Glycolysis
Glucose metabolism *See* Carbohydrate metabolism
Glucose transport *See* Biological transport
Glue *See* Adhesives
Glue guns
The first ever cordless glue guns. R. N. Hoffman. il *Workbench* 43:28-9 Jl/Ag '87
This gun's for hire [Loctite cordless glue gun] R. Capotosto. il *Pop Mech* 164:45 O '87
Glueck, Charles J.
about
NIH moves to debar cholesterol researcher. C. Holden. por *Science* 237:718-19 Ag 14 '87
Glusman, John F.
Why I went to Jerusalem. por *Publ Wkly* 231:61 My 29 '87
Gluttony
Gluttony: love at first bite. K. Guentert. il *U S Cathol* 52:11-13 Ag '87
Glycel skin care products *See* Cosmetics
Glycerides
Low triglycerides native to fish eaters. il *Prevention* 39:9 My '87

Glycerol
Insulin rapidly increases diacylglycerol by activating de novo phosphatidic acid synthesis. R. V. Farese and others. bibl f il *Science* 236:586-9 My 1 '87
A rapid cold-hardening process in insects. R. E. Lee, Jr. and others. bibl f il *Science* 238:1415-17 D 4 '87
Rapid stimulation of diacylglycerol production in Xenopus oocytes by microinjection of H-*ras* p21. J. C. Lacal and others. bibl f il *Science* 238:533-6 O 23 '87
Glycoalkaloids *See* Alkaloids
Glycogen phosphorylase *See* Phosphorylases
Glycogenolysis *See* Carbohydrate metabolism
Glycols
Camouflaged drugs make Enzon stand out [coating enzymes with polyethylene glycol] M. Bluestone. il *Bus Week* p115-16 Ap 27 '87
Glycolysis
Glycolysis preferentially inhibits ATP-sensitive K^+ channels in isolated guinea pig cardiac myocytes. J. N. Weiss and S. T. Lamp. bibl f il *Science* 238:67-9 O 2 '87
Glycophorin
Evidence for increased somatic cell mutations at the glycophorin A locus in atomic bomb survivors. R. G. Langlois and others. bibl f il *Science* 236:445-8 Ap 24 '87
Glycoproteins
See also
Elastin
Glycophorin
Laminin
Uromodulin
Cancer's genes and chemotherapy [research with P-glycoprotein mRNA by Ira Pastan and Michael M. Gottesman] *Sci News* 131:57 Ja 24 '87
Functional regions of the envelope glycoprotein of human immunodeficiency virus type 1. M. Kowalski and others. bibl f il *Science* 237:1351-5 S 11 '87
A G1 glycoprotein epitope of La Crosse virus: a determinant of infection of Aedes triseriatus. D. R. Sundin and others. bibl f il *Science* 235:591-3 Ja 30 '87
Identification and isolation of a variant surface glycoprotein from Trypanosoma vivax. P. R. Gardiner and others. bibl f il *Science* 235:774-7 F 13 '87
Identification of human uromodulin as the Tamm-Horsfall urinary glycoprotein. D. Pennica and others. bibl f il *Science* 236:83-8 Ap 3 '87
Solo actions of AIDS virus coat. D. M. Barnes. bibl il *Science* 237:971-3 Ag 28 '87
Glycosides
See also
Ouabain
Glycosylation
Glucose and aging. A. C. Cerami and others. bibl (p128) il *Sci Am* 256:90-6 My '87
Glyndebourne Festival Opera Company
Glyndebourne/Brighton. N. Goodwin. il *Opera News* 52:43 D 5 '87
Glynn, Lenny, and Mathewson, Judith
After the fall: how Hart's workers picked up the pieces. il por *Glamour* 85:362-3+ S '87
GM *See* General Motors Corp.
GM-CSF
Beefing up the defenses [use in fighting infection in AIDS patients] il *Time* 130:69 S 14 '87
Boosting cell numbers in AIDS. D. D. Edwards. *Sci News* 132:165 S 12 '87
Cell growth factor: use with caution. R. Weiss. *Sci News* 132:375 D 12 '87
Upping cell counts: on clinical trial. D. D. Edwards. *Sci News* 132:396 D 19-26 '87
GMP *See* Guanosine monophosphate
Gnann, John W., Jr., and others
Synthetic peptide immunoassay distinguishes HIV type 1 and HIV type 2 infections. bibl f il *Science* 237:1346-9 S 11 '87
GNP *See* Gross national product
GnRH *See* Gonadotropin releasing hormone
Gnus
See also
Wildebeest
Go (Game)
An American in Tokyo shows the Japanese he's got it at Go [M. Redmond] il por *People Wkly* 28:63 Ag 24 '87
Go-karting
If you think kart racing is kid's stuff, think again [Formula K world championship held in Jacksonville, Fla.] D. Green. il *Mot Trend* 39:131-3 Mr '87

Goa (India)
Social life and customs
Endless summer of love [hippies in Goa] D. Black. il *Harpers* 274:47-52 My '87
Goals (Psychology)
Go for the goal! J. L. Lippert. il *Health* 19:40-1 My '87
Life after high school. P. S. Rix. il *Teen* 31:24+ S '87
Life as a tap dance: it only looks easy. J. Stone. *Glamour* 85:208 My '87
My greatest challenge: thirteen men discuss the obstacles they seek to surmount. P. Johnson and C. James. il *Essence* 18:58-60+ N '87
Take this dream and shove it. M. Jacobson. il *Esquire* 108:53-4 N '87
Tom Clancy: "By God, I'm going to do it.". W. Hoffer. il por *Nations Bus* 75:46-7 D '87
Where do the best goals come from? [excerpt from The human side of management] G. S. Odiorne. il *Work Woman* 12:32+ D '87
Goats
See also
Ibex
Rocky Mountain goats
Goats, Wild
Getting the author's goat [discussion of November 1986 article, Rhum deal for goats] R. I. M. Dunbar. il *Nat Hist* 96:2+ Mr '87
Gochman, Alice Rubinstein
Afternoon tea in New York. il *Gourmet* 47:92-7+ N '87
Gockley, David
about
General director David Gockley: HGO's best seller [cover story] il por *Opera News* 52:20+ O '87
God
See also
Atheism
Christianity
Creation
Faith
Trinity
Word of God (Theology)
God as woman. G. G. Seibert. *America* 157:311 O 31 '87
God isn't fair (and I'm glad He isn't). P. Yancey. il *Christ Today* 31:72 N 20 '87
The God who can't be tamed. P. Yancey. il *Christ Today* 31:72 S 18 '87
A hidden and playful God. B. C. Lane. *Christ Century* 104:812-13 S 30 '87
Humanists and talk of God. D. E. Marietta. il por *Humanist* 47:8-10+ S/O '87
I will not forget. M. K. Hellwig. *America* 156:inside back cover F 21 '87
"I've found God". Teresa, Mother. il por *Saturday Evening Post* 259:16 Jl/Ag '87
The return of the God-hypothesis. B. Durbin, Jr. il por *Christ Today* 31:22-3 Ap 3 '87
Talking about God [young children] J. Segal and Z. Segal. il *Parents* 62:208 S '87
Goodness
As God is good. M. K. Hellwig. *America* 156:inside back cover F 14 '87
Does evil have a life of its own? J. Deedy. il *U S Cathol* 52:20-5 D '87
God is no bully. G. G. Seibert. *America* 157:23 Jl 4-11 '87
Love
See Love (Theology)
Name
A matter of being, and a matter of being right. W. Wangerin. il *Christ Century* 104:591-3 Jl 1-8 '87
Providence
On providence and prayer. J. A. Keller. *Christ Century* 104:967-9 N 4 '87
Suffering
See Suffering of God
Wrath
Sleepers in the hands of an angry God. W. D. Eisenhower. il por *Christ Today* 31:26-8 Mr 20 '87
God and politics [television program] See Television program reviews—Single works
Godard, Jean Luc, 1930-
about
BlueJean-Luc Godard. H. A. Rodchenko. il *Film Comment* 23:2+ N/D '87
Hail Mary [film] Reviews
Phi Delta Kappan il 68:401-2 Ja '87. T. J. Flygare

Godber, John
about
Bouncers [drama] Reviews
Nation 245:457-8 O 24 '87. T. M. Disch
New Yorker 63:109 O 5 '87. E. Oliver
Godbey, Susan Flagg
Rambling through the English countryside. il *Prevention* 39:60-2+ Je '87
Godbold, Jake M.
Jacksonville: a rising star on Florida's northeast coast. il *USA Today (Periodical)* 115:34-42 Ja '87
Godey, Louis Antoine
about
Godey and Hale: a fashionable alliance. E. Baroody. il *Antiques Collect Hobbies* 92:34-8 N '87
Godey's lady's book (Periodical) See Godey's magazine
Godey's magazine
Godey and Hale: a fashionable alliance. E. Baroody. il *Antiques Collect Hobbies* 92:34-8 N '87
Godmilow, Jill
about
Waiting for the moon [film] Reviews
Christ Today il 31:61 Jl 10 '87. S. Ulstein
Macleans 100:48 My 18 '87. L. O'Toole
Nation 244:773-4 Je 6 '87. R. Drexler
New Repub 196:25-6 Mr 2 '87. S. Kauffmann
Godoy-García, Cristián
San Martín and the OAS. il *Américas* 39:55-6 Jl/Ag '87
Gods Lake (Man.)
Fishing in God's country. P. Barrett. il *Field Stream* 91:86+ Ap '87
Godsell, Bobby
(jt. auth) See Berger, Peter L., and Godsell, Bobby
Godsey, R. Kirby
about
Going topless and other sins. B. Kantrowitz and A. Murr. il *Newsweek* 110:79-80 O 26 '87
Godwin, Gail
How I write. il *Writer* 100:17-18 O '87
The uses of autobiography. *Writer* 100:7-9+ Mr '87
Godwin, George, 1813-1888
about
Building bridges: George Godwin and architectural journalism. R. Thorne. bibl il por *Hist Today* 37:11-17 Ag '87
Godwin, Phillip
What to do when health insurance won't pay. bibl il *Better Homes Gard* 65:72+ N '87
Godwin, Richard P.
about
Acquisition chief's successor named. *Aviat Week Space Technol* 127:30-1 S 28 '87
Acquisition czar dethroned. D. E. Fink. *Aviat Week Space Technol* 127:11 S 21 '87
Godwin decides to resign as Defense acquisition chief. J. D. Morrocco. *Aviat Week Space Technol* 127:33 S 14 '87
Godwin testifies on success of meeting challenges to acquisition decisions. *Aviat Week Space Technol* 126:106 Ap 13 '87
Pentagon formalizes charter for Defense Acquisition Office. *Aviat Week Space Technol* 126:29 F 16 '87
Weapons buying: did anyone really want reform? D. Griffiths. il por *Bus Week* p33 S 28 '87
Why the Pentagon's waste-watcher can't trim the fat. D. Griffiths. *Bus Week* p49 Je 8 '87
Godwin (Tony) Memorial Award See Editors and editing—Awards
Goebbels, Joseph, 1897-1945
about
Jottings from the Third Reich. J. Smolowe. il por *Time* 130:44 S 14 '87
Goebbels, Paul Joseph See Goebbels, Joseph, 1897-1945
Goell, Yosef
Not ready to talk. il *World Press Rev* 34:14-15 Jl '87
Goen, Susan
Washington watch. il *Ms* 16:75 D '87
GOES (Geostationary operational environmental satellites)
See Artificial satellites—Meteorological use
Goethite
In situ X-ray absorption study of surface complexes: selenium oxyanions on α-FeOOH. K. F. Hayes and others. bibl f il *Science* 238:783-6 N 6 '87
Goetz, Bernhard
Subway shooting case
Bernie Goetz goes on trial. T. Morganthau. il por *Newsweek* 109:30 My 11 '87
Cat and mouse [trial in New York City] por *Time* 129:26 My 11 '87

Goetz, Bernhard—Subway shooting case—*cont.*
Doubts about self-defence. M. Gray. il pors *Macleans* 100:45 Je 29 '87
Goetz and the future of New York. *Natl Rev* 39:19 Jl 17 '87
Goetz, at last. *Natl Rev* 39:18-20 F 13 '87
Goetz on trial. G. P. Fletcher. bibl f il *N Y Rev Books* 34:22-4+ Ap 23 '87
Goetz verdict will endanger young black males, leaders say. il por *Jet* 72:18 Jl 6 '87
Isiah & Bernhard. J. Morley. *Nation* 245:4-5 Jl 4-11 '87
New York's vigilante: victim or villain? *Newsweek* 109:31 Je 1 '87
North, Goetz, and the American audience. J. Saltzman. *USA Today (Periodical)* 116:55 N '87
"Not guilty". O. Friedrich. il por *Time* 129:10-11 Je 29 '87
Slotnick for the defense [B. I. Slotnick] P. McKillop. por *Newsweek* 109:62 My 4 '87
Subway shooter Bernhard Goetz is the latest defendant to hire the hottest legal gun in town—Barry Slotnick. K. Gross. il pors *People Wkly* 27:115-16+ My 4 '87
Subways are for shooting. *Nation* 244:871 Je 27 '87
A trial that wouldn't end. A. Press. il pors *Newsweek* 109:20-2 Je 29 '87
A verdict by their peers [views of prison inmates] R. Blecker. il *Nation* 245:334-6 O 3 '87
Whatever Bernie wants. *New Repub* 197:9-10 Jl 13-20 '87

Goetz, Joseph William
William Schickel's 'Salvation suite'. il *America* 157:304-5 O 31 '87

Goetz, Ronald
Cosmic groanings. il *Christ Century* 104:1083-7 D 2 '87

Gofen, Ethel
Minding your own blood pressure. il *Curr Health 2* 13:3-9 Mr '87

Goff, James R., Jr.
Brother Westbrook shouted, "Glory," and mother spoke in tongues. il por *Christ Today* 31:18-19 O 16 '87

Goggles
The best eyewear for your sport. il *Glamour* 85:37 Jl '87
Sport specs: play it safe! H. Platt. il *Harpers Bazaar* 120:44+ Ap '87

Gogh, Vincent van, 1853-1890
about
$40 million van Gogh brings back mixed and vivid memories. M. S. Forbes. il *Forbes* 139:20+ Je 1 '87
An artful dodger? E. C. Baig. il por *Fortune* 116:166 D 21 '87
Blue Irises and blue chips. il *Newsweek* 110:85 N 23 '87
Call him Vincent. J. Herzfeld. por *Art News* 86:15 Summ '87
Conspicuous consumer. H. Katayama. il por *Forbes* 139:252 Je 15 '87
Flower power. R. W. Walker. il *Art News* 86:31 My '87
The inner purpose of Vincent van Gogh. G. James. il *Macleans* 100:46-7 Ja 12 '87
'Irises'. *America* 157:396-7 N 28 '87
The museum without walls. W. F. Buckley. *Natl Rev* 39:60-1 My 8 '87
A mystery buyer plucks van Gogh's buds for a record sum [interview with R. Feigen] M. Small. il por *People Wkly* 27:55-7 Ap 20 '87
Of Vincent and Eanum Pig. R. Hughes. il *Time* 129:80-1 Ap 13 '87
Sizes. *New Yorker* 63:28-30 Ap 27 '87
Van Gogh in Saint-Rémy and Auvers. A. C. Danto. *Nation* 244:56-60 Ja 17 '87
Van Gogh in Saint-Remy and Auvers. R. Pickvance. il por *USA Today (Periodical)* 115:74-83 Ja '87
Van Gogh's Irises: how much? R. W. Walker. il *Art News* 86:25 N '87
Vincent van Gogh. por *People Wkly* 28:54 D 28 '87-Ja 4 '88
A visit with Vincent van Gogh. J. F. Cotter. *America* 156:50-1+ Ja 24 '87

Goiania (Brazil)
Radioactive pollution
A battle against deadly dust [R. Gale and others treat radiation victims] C. Gorman. il por *Time* 130:66 N 16 '87
A carnival of glittering poison [effects of discarded cesium-137] S. Seibert. il *Newsweek* 110:55 O 19 '87
Deadly glitter [poisoning caused by discarded cesium-137] *Time* 130:38 O 19 '87

Playing with radiation [poisoning caused by discarded cesium-137] A. Dwyer. il *Macleans* 100:44 N 2 '87
Radiation accident grips Goiânia. L. Roberts. il map *Science* 238:1028-31 N 20 '87

Going, Michael
about
Going beyond Polaroid: the artful manipulations of Michael Going. F. Cameron. il por *Petersens Photogr Mag* 15:22-4 F '87

Goizueta, Roberto C.
about
He put the kick back into Coke. T. Moore. il por *Fortune* 116:46-8+ O 26 '87

Golan, Galia
Gorbachev's Middle East strategy. bibl f *Foreign Aff* 66:41-57 Fall '87

Golan, Menahem
about
Is the go-go gone? M. Dougherty. il pors *Life* 10:102 Ap '87
Over the top [film] Reviews
Macleans il 100:52 F 23 '87. L. O'Toole
Newsweek il 109:79 F 23 '87. D. Ansen
People Wkly il 27:6 Mr 2 '87. T. Cunneff

Golan Heights Peace Force *See* United Nations—Armed Forces—Forces in the Middle East

Goland, Paul
about
Mushrooms in the mountains. J. O'Brien. il pors *Ctry J* 14:28-32 S '87

Gold, Arthur
about
Composition for two: Robert Fizdale and Arthur Gold's city residence. M. M. Thomas. il pors *Archit Dig* 44:212-15+ N '87

Gold, Gerard G.
A reform strategy for education: employer-sponsored teacher internships. il *Phi Delta Kappan* 68:384-7 Ja '87

Gold, Rozanne
Supermarkets take up the challenge. il *Work Woman* 12:177-8+ My '87

Gold
See also
Goldsmithing
Fighting acid rain with gold [use as catalyst to reduce nitrogen oxide after coal is burned for fuel; work of Arun Someshwar] *USA Today (Periodical)* 115:5-6 Je '87
A small gold-conjugated antibody label: improved resolution for electron microscopy [cover story] J. F. Hainfeld. bibl f il *Science* 236:450-3 Ap 24 '87
Prices
How good is gold? J. Mendes. il *Fortune* 116:208 N 23 '87
Keith Smith, gold's raging bull. R. A. Melcher. il por *Bus Week* p70-1 Je 22 '87
Solid gold in hard times. M. Janigan. il *Macleans* 100:33 N 2 '87
Therapeutic use
Antiarthritic gold compounds effectively quench electronically excited singlet oxygen. E. J. Corey and others. bibl f il *Science* 236:68-9 Ap 3 '87
Why does gold help arthritics? [research by Elias J. Corey and others] *Sci News* 131:264 Ap 25 '87

Gold as an investment
See also
Coins as an investment
Gold mines and mining—Securities
Buying gold you never see [gold storage accounts] S. W. Angrist. il *Forbes* 139:98 Ap 20 '87
The gold bug bites again. M. Hulbert. por *Forbes* 140:214 S 21 '87
Gold is back. J. Kosnett. il *Changing Times* 41:95-6+ S '87
Gold is still the mutual fund heavyweight champ. G. Weiss. il *Bus Week* p152-3 O 12 '87
Gold moves to the front of the mutual fund parade. J. M. Laderman. il *Bus Week* p78-9 Ap 13 '87
Gold: still the safest commodity. D. L. Dennis. il *Fortune* 116 Sp Issue:28 Fall '87
Gold's new glitter. J. A. Conway. il *Forbes* 139:8 My 18 '87
How good a hedge is gold? J. J. Curran. il *Fortune* 115:169-70 Je 22 '87
How good is gold? J. Mendes. il *Fortune* 116:208 N 23 '87
How to get the most from gold this year. R. McNatt. il *Money* 16:137-8+ Ja '87
Keith Smith, gold's raging bull. R. A. Melcher. il por *Bus Week* p70-1 Je 22 '87

Gold as an investment—*cont.*

Old-fashioned remedy. S. Lee. il *Forbes* 139:162 F 23 '87

Onward and upward [gold stocks] S. Lee. il *Forbes* 139:194 Je 1 '87

Precious way to hedge your bets. M. Schiffres. il *U S News World Rep* 102:68 Ap 27 '87

Protecting your portfolio with a gold lining. G. Weiss. il *Bus Week* p76 Jl 6 '87

REITs are looking rosy again . . . and gold is panning out [views of Bailard, Biehl & Kaiser] G. G. Marcial. *Bus. Week* p88 Ap 13 '87

The right and wrong ways to buy gold. M. Meyer. il *Money* 16:47-8+ Ag '87

Risky hedges [shares in mining companies] M. Ozanian. il *Forbes* 139:248 My 18 '87

Solid gold in hard times. M. Janigan. il *Macleans* 100:33 N 2 '87

Gold as money

Baker's plan: no glitter [gold based price index] M. McNamee. por *Bus Week* p56 O 19 '87

Golden promise [J. A. Baker's proposed commodity price index tied to gold] il *Natl Rev* 39:17-18 N 6 '87

Investors should rejoice [J. A. Baker's proposed gold based price index] M. S. Forbes, Jr. il por *Forbes* 140 Sp Issue:29 O 26 '87

Jim Baker shakes up a little gold dust [proposed commodity price index tied to gold] *Newsweek* 110:66 O 12 '87

What investors should ask of Alan Greenspan [letting gold be his guide] M. S. Forbes, Jr. il por *Forbes* 139:25 Je 29 '87

Gold Castle Records

Gold Castle's golden oldies. J. Schwartz. il por *Newsweek* 110:64 S 21 '87

Gold Coast Railroad Museum

The "Magellan" rides again. il *South Living* 22:29 Jl '87

Gold coins as an investment *See* Coins as an investment

Gold funds *See* Investment trusts

Gold Kist Inc.

Capitalist in the henhouse. D. Henry. il *Forbes* 139:37 Ja 26 '87

Gold mines and mining

See also

Grandview Resources Inc.

America's newest gold rush. P. Dworkin. il *U S News World Rep* 103:57-8 O 12 '87

Environmental aspects

Of gold fever and brown rivers [Alaska] T. Turner. il *Sierra* 72:30-3 Jl/Ag '87

Securities

Caveat emptor for investors. L. Wiener. il *U S News World Rep* 103:58 O 12 '87

Old-fashioned remedy. S. Lee. il *Forbes* 139:162 F 23 '87

Onward and upward. S. Lee. il *Forbes* 139:194 Je 1 '87

REITs are looking rosy again . . . and gold is panning out [views of Bailard, Biehl & Kaiser] G. G. Marcial. *Bus Week* p88 Ap 13 '87

Risky hedges. M. Ozanian. il *Forbes* 139:248 My 18 '87

Alaska

Of gold fever and brown rivers. T. Turner. il *Sierra* 72:30-3 Jl/Ag '87

Australia

On earth. M. Hill. *Earth Sci* 39:38 Wint '86

Reynolds hits pay dirt Down Under. G. L. Miles. il *Bus Week* p99 Jl 13 '87

Brazil

The gospel and the gold rush [Tucano Indians caught between Salesian missionaries and gold mining interests] R. N. Ostling. il *Time* 129:64 Je 1 '87

Photographs and photography

An epic struggle for gold. S. Salgado. il *N Y Times Mag* p34-41 Je 7 '87

Fragments and frames [A. Jaar's installation Frame of mind at the Grey Art Gallery] N. Princenthal. il *Art Am* 75:144-5 My '87

Gold rush to hell [A. Jaar's installation of photographs of Brazilian gold rush in New York subway station] S. Staggs. il *Art News* 86:9 F '87

California

California gold rush country. I. Ireland. il map *Road Track* 38:52-6 F '87

Cornish pumps kept California gold mines dry, but forced miners to take a strange and dangerous route to work. M. Hill. *Earth Sci* 40:38 Summ '87

Glitter and dirt [Yuba Natural Resources] A. A. Lappen. il *Forbes* 140:8 N 30 '87

Where the Gold Rush began . . . an autumn drive [Georgetown Divide] il map *Sunset* 179:12-13+ O '87

Canada

See also

Dome Mines Limited

Echo Bay Mines Ltd.

Placer Dome Inc.

Thompson Bousquet Gold Mines Ltd.

Defence of a gold mine [run on Dome Mines] D. Jenish. il *Macleans* 100:32-3 Ag 17 '87

Gold's revival in the East [Atlantic Canada] R. Surette. il *Macleans* 100:26-7 S 14 '87

Placer Dome: will it pan out? E. B. Terry. *Bus Week* p42+ S 7 '87

Nevada

There really is gold in them thar hills. H. Rudnitsky and J. Clements. il map *Forbes* 140:156+ N 30 '87

North America

Going for the gold [U.S. and Canadian companies] A. Ramirez. il *Fortune* 116:153-7 N 9 '87

Northwest Territories

Truckers brave the barren lands to supply an Arctic gold mine. J. Krakauer. il *Smithsonian* 18:128-34+ N '87

South Africa

See also

Anglo American Corp. of South Africa, Ltd.

Munk's glittering gamble [purchase of Consolidated Gold Fields stock by Barrick Resources] D. Jenish. il por *Macleans* 100:22-3 Ja 12 '87

South Dakota

More precious than gold [opposition to open pit gold mining] J. W. Wilson. il *Progressive* 51:11 N '87

United States

See Gold mines and mining

Wales

Gold in the valleys. A. Hills. il *Hist Today* 37:3-4 D '87

Western States

On earth. M. Hill. *Earth Sci* 39:38 Wint '86

Yukon Territory

Photographs and photography

Klondike scrapbook [photographs by C. and C. Kinsey] N. Bolotin. il *Am Hist Illus* 22:26-35 O '87

Gold of Peru Museum *See* Museo Oro del Peru

Gold Rush of 1849 *See* Gold mines and mining—California

Gold stocks *See* Gold mines and mining—Securities

Gold storage accounts *See* Gold as an investment

Gold work *See* Goldsmithing

Goldberg, Arthur M.

about

If at first . . . A. A. Lappen. il por *Forbes* 140:8 S 7 '87

Goldberg, Danny

about

Gold Castle's golden oldies. J. Schwartz. il por *Newsweek* 110:64 S 21 '87

Goldberg, Donald

The national guards. il *Omni* 9:44-6+ My '87

Wind of war out of Washington. *Harpers* 274:56-7 Je '87

Goldberg, Gary David

about

Family ties: the day-care center a TV show built. N. Gittelson. il *McCalls* 114:61-4 Ag '87

Goldberg, George, and Goldberg, Jeff

The progress of Bookland EAN. il *Publ Wkly* 232:51-5 O 16 '87

Goldberg, Hayden

The architecture of Charles Bulfinch on historical blue Staffordshire (II). bibl f il *Antiques* 131:434-43 F '87

Goldberg, Jeff

(jt. auth) *See* Goldberg, George, and Goldberg, Jeff

Goldberg, Joan Rachel

Crying it out. il *Health* 19:64-6 F '87

Wild livin'. il *Health* 19:51-2 Ap '87

Goldberg, Larry, 1934-

about

Goldberg can go home again. C. Trillin. *New Yorker* 63:87-92+ Ap 6 '87

Goldberg, Michael, and Handelman, David

Is Michael Jackson for real? [cover story] il pors *Roll Stone* p50-1+ S 24 '87

Goldberg, Norman

Shoptalk. *See* issues of Popular Photography through November 1987

Goldberg, Robert

Clash of the titans. il *Sport Mag* 78:56-8+ Ja '87

Serious stars: Timothy Hutton. por *Vogue* 177:482+ Mr '87

Goldberg, Vicki
The unflinching eye [cover story] il pors *N Y Times Mag* p12-18+ Jl 12 '87
Goldberg, Wendy
about
Wendy Goldberg: "the most gracious hostess in town". N. Gittelson. il pors *McCalls* 114:124-6+ F '87
Goldberg, Whoopi
about
'Fatal beauty' love scene cut; Goldberg cites racism. por *Jet* 73:63 O 5 '87
Whoopi Goldberg and Sam Elliott star in 'Fatal beauty,' a humor-laced drama [cover story] il pors *Jet* 73:58-60 N 16 '87
Whoopi Goldberg becoming sought after black actress. *Jet* 71:27 Ja 26 '87
Whoopi Goldberg makes her funniest film in 'Burglar' [cover story] il pors *Jet* 72:56-7 Ap 20 '87
Whoopi sounds off on sex, drugs, race. por *Jet* 72:24 Je 15 '87
Whoopi's blue eyes [interview with S. Lee] M. Glicksman. *Harpers* 274:29 Ja '87
Goldberger, Marvin L.
What's right, what's wrong with U.S. science? [address, March 13, 1987] *Vital Speeches Day* 53:537-40 Je 15 '87
Goldberger, Paul
Allan Greenberg's rooms in the Department of State. il *Antiques* 132:132-43 Jl '87
Architectural vigor of the summer enclave. il *Archit Dig* 44:74+ Je '87
Architecture. il *N Y Times Book Rev* 92:22+ D 6 '87
Architecture: John C. Portman, Jr. [cover story] il por *Archit Dig* 44:98-111 D '87
A new presence for craft. il *Am Craft* 47:30-2 F/Mr '87
The poetics of space. il por *Archit Dig* 44:266+ N '87
Reorienting a classic: inventive decor for a Lloyd Wright house [cover story] il por *Archit Dig* 44:108-15 Mr '87
Golde, Brigitte, and Köper, Ingeborg
The German Hygiene Museum. il *World Health* p16-17 Je '87
Golden, Diana
about
Golden Girl. P. Miller. il pors *Skiing* 40:44+ N '87
Golden, Frederic
about
A sailor with wide horizons. G. L. Rogin. il por *Discover* 8:6 Ja '87
Golden, Joy
about
The Joy of advertising. A. Miller. il por *Newsweek* 110:43 Jl 27 '87
Golden, Kristen
Dutch tribute to gay pride. *Ms* 15:32 Je '87
Golden, Mike
Frontiersman [interview with R. Wurlitzer] il por *Film Comment* 23:40-4 Jl/Ag '87
Golden, Rashunda
about
Georgia sisters indicted for their mother's murder. *Jet* 73:47 N 2 '87
Two Georgia sisters held for their mother's murder. il pors *Jet* 72:32 Ag 17 '87
Golden, Tim
Duarte's last stand. *New Repub* 196:12-14 Je 22 '87
The golden age [ballet] See Ballet reviews—Single works
The golden child [film] See Motion picture reviews—Single works
The golden cockerel [opera] See Rimsky-Korsakov, Nikolay, 1844-1908
Golden Door (Escondido, Calif.: Resort) See Health resorts, watering places, etc.—California
Golden Door diet See Diet
Golden Gate (Fla.)
Crime
A teenager's tragedy: birth and death in a Florida town [M. Clark charged with murder of her newborn child] C. Mitchell and T. Burdick. il por *Ms* 16:60-3 D '87
Golden Gate Bridge (San Francisco, Calif.)
Golden anniversary. il *Time* 129:43 My 25 '87
Golden anniversary. R. Reinhardt. il *Am Herit* 38:96-7 Ap '87
On its 50th birthday, a survivor celebrates his victory over the Golden Gate Bridge [suicide leap by K. Baldwin] W. Plummer. il pors *People Wkly* 27:110-12 My 25 '87
Spanning the Golden Gate. R. Dillon. il *Am Hist Illus* 22:34-45 My '87

Tale of two cities: did party poopers prevail? [50th anniversary celebration] W. L. Chaze. il *U S News World Rep* 102:26 My 4 '87
Photographs and photography
Birthday photographs of the Golden Gate Bridge. il *Sunset* 178:94 My '87
A Golden opportunity to celebrate. il *Life* 10:18-19 Ag '87
Golden Gate National Recreation Area (Calif.)
Holiday hikes, programs, and bird-watching at Rodeo Lagoon. il *Sunset* 179:38 D '87
The golden girls [television program] See Television program reviews—Single works
Golden Globe Awards
Cathy Tyson, Dex Gordon are Golden Globe nominees. il *Jet* 71:26 Ja 26 '87
New couples, Family ties and gushy Moonlighting love made the world of the Golden Globes go round. il *People Wkly* 27:83 F 16 '87
Golden Groove Productions
Carew "Busts loose" [T. Carew] S. Herbert. por *Black Enterp* 18:25 S '87
Golden Horn (Turkey)
See also
Marine pollution—Golden Horn (Turkey)
Golden Nugget, Inc.
For Bally, dumping Trump raises the ante [purchase of Golden Nugget in Atlantic City] M. D. Oneal. il *Bus Week* p45 Mr 9 '87
Steve Wynn on high rollers. D. Seligman. il pors *Fortune* 115:116 Mr 2 '87
Trump vs. Wynn: 'giant egos on the line'. R. Grover. il por *Bus Week* p31-2 Jl 27 '87
Zero-sum game [Bally buys Golden Nugget's Atlantic City casino] R. Phalon. il pors *Forbes* 139:110-12 Mr 23 '87
Golden Palominos (Musical group)
Music. G. Santoro. *Nation* 244:696-8 My 23 '87
Golden parachutes (Executive compensation) See Executives—Salaries, pensions, etc.
Golden rain trees
Goldenrain tree for a double feature. il *South Living* 22:46-7 Je '87
Golden shiners See Shiners (Fish)
Golden Turtle (San Francisco, Calif.: Restaurant) See San Francisco (Calif.)—Restaurants, nightclubs, bars, etc.
Golden Valley Microwave Foods Inc.
Microwave popcorn: the heat is on. M. J. Pitzer. il por *Bus Week* p52 Jl 6 '87
Pass the butter: a hot popcorn stock. G. G. Marcial. *Bus Week* p120 My 18 '87
Golden West Financial Corp.
Boring is better. J. Heins. il pors *Forbes* 140:167-8 N 16 '87
Goldenberg, Gary
Extras, extras! Which food supplements do you need? il *Mademoiselle* 93:144 Ap '87
Goldenrain trees See Golden rain trees
Goldenrod
Guerrillas of the goldenrod [ambush bugs; cover story] L. G. Mason. il *Nat Hist* 96:34-9 Ag '87
Goldensohn, Marty
Midlife music. il *N Y Times Mag* p48 Je 21 '87
Goldfarb, Alex
Testing *glasnost*: an exile visits his homeland [cover story] il pors *N Y Times Mag* p46-9+ D 6 '87
Goldfeder, Howard
International competitiveness [address, June 8, 1987] *Vital Speeches Day* 53:722-5 S 15 '87
Goldfish
Vision
See Vision—Fish
Goldfish plant See Hypocyrta
Goldfluss, Howard E.
Courtroom psychics. *Omni* 9:12 Jl '87
UFO update. il *Omni* 9:95 Je '87
Goldgaber, Dmitry, and others
Characterization and chromosomal localization of a cDNA encoding brain amyloid of Alzheimer's disease. bibl f il *Science* 235:877-80 F 20 '87
Goldin, Edwin, 1933-
about
Goldin and Romm are selected to be Congressional Fellows. pors *Phys Today* 40:79 Jl '87
Goldin, Nan, 1953-
about
The family of Nan. M. Kozloff. il pors *Art Am* 75:38-9+ N '87
Nan Goldin. E. Heartney. il por *Art News* 86:177+ Ap '87

Goldman, Betsy Schein
Families of artists coping with day-to-day problems. il *Am Artist* 51:40-5+ O '87
Jane Frey. il por *Am Artist* 51:44-9 S '87
Jim Cantrell. il por *Am Artist* 51:32-7 Jl '87
Suzanne Lemieux. il por *Am Artist* 51:64-9+ N '87
William A. Berry. il por *Am Artist* 51:68-73+ F '87
Goldman, E. S.
Way to the dump [story] il *Atlantic* 260:81-4+ D '87
Goldman, Francisco
Poetry and power in Nicaragua. il por *N Y Times Mag* p44-6+ Mr 29 '87
Goldman, Jane
How to find an apartment (seriously) [cover story] il *N Y* 20:30-8 Je 22 '87
Goldman, Marc
about
Taste of victory. M. Fritz. il por *Forbes* 139:234 My 18 '87
Goldman, Marshall I.
Can anybody fix the Soviet system? il por *U S News World Rep* 102:38-9 F 9 '87
Opening the Soviet hothouse: how far can Gorbachev go? il por *Technol Rev* 90:18+ Ja '87
The shifting balance of world power. il por *Technol Rev* 90:20-1 Ap '87
Why Reagan and Gorbachev need an arms agreement. il por *Technol Rev* 90:18+ Jl '87
Goldman, Marvin
Chernobyl: a radiobiological perspective. bibl f *Science* 238:622-3 O 30 '87
Goldman, Merle, and Wagner, Rudolf
China: intellectuals at bay. il *N Y Rev Books* 34:17-20 Mr 26 '87
Goldman, Michael A., and others
A chicken transferrin gene in transgenic mice escapes X-chromosome inactivation. bibl f il *Science* 236:593-5 My 1 '87
Goldman, Sachs & Co.
John Weinberg. A. Bianco. por *Bus Week* Sp Issue:224 Ap 17 '87
The ordeal of Bob Freeman [insider trading] R. B. Stolley. il pors *Fortune* 115:66-8+ My 25 '87
Stocks for a difficult market [interview with S. Einhorn] A. E. Serwer. il por *Fortune* 116:176 D 21 '87
Suddenly the fish get bigger [insider trading scandal; special section] il *Bus Week* p28-35 Mr 2 '87
Goldner, Kathryn Allen, and Vogel, Carole Garbuny
Pros and cons of a writing partnership. *Writer* 100:24-5 S '87
Goldoftas, Barbara
Recycling: coming of age. il *Technol Rev* 90:28-35+ N/D '87
Goldress, Jerry E.
about
The master of the 'slash and burn' school. il por *Bus Week* p114 S 21 '87
Goldrich, Laurie
The salad-bar chef. il *Work Woman* 12:94+ F '87
Goldridge Farm (Sebastopol, Calif.) See Sebastopol (Calif.)—Historic houses, sites, etc.
Goldsborough, Jennifer Faulds
Silver and gold in the diplomatic reception rooms. il *Antiques* 132:174-81 Jl '87
Goldsborough, Reid
Celebrating the Constitution. il *Americana* 15:70+ My/Je '87
Goldschmidt, Lucien, 1912-
about
Losing Lucien. G. Henry. il por *Art News* 86:16+ Mr '87
Goldschmidt (Lucien) Inc. See Lucien Goldschmidt Inc.
Goldsmith, Arthur
Panorama. See issues of Popular Photography
Goldsmith, Barbara
"We are survivors . . .". il *Ms* 16:88-9 Jl/Ag '87
Goldsmith, Bram, 1923-
about
Bank to the stars. L. Gubernick. il por *Forbes* 140:65-6 D 28 '87
Goldsmith, Del
Togetherness—suburban style [poem] *Good Housekeep* 204:247 Ap '87
Goldsmith, Sir James, 1933-
about
Goodyear seems to be getting the last laugh. Z. Schiller. il por *Bus Week* p48 Mr 9 '87
The lucky gambler. O. Friedrich. il por *Time* 130:60-2 N 23 '87

Sir Jimmy goes shopping again. G. G. Marcial. *Bus Week* p188 N 16 '87
Sir Jimmy pulls the plug on his French connection. J. Rossant. il por *Bus Week* p24 Ag 10 '87
Goldsmith, Russell
about
Republic flies again. L. Gubernick. il por *Forbes* 140:248 D 14 '87
Goldsmithing
See also
Gilding
Society of North American Goldsmiths
Castle Lizzardo [miniature gold castle designed by W. Tolliday] A. Bahar. il por *Antiques Collect Hobbies* 92:48-52 Mr '87
Exhibitions
See also
Museo Oro del Peru
Goldsmiths of Veneto [traveling exhibition entitled Italian jewelers from the Veneto region] A. Fisch. il *Am Craft* 47:36-41+ D '87/Ja '88
Goldson, Alfred
about
Doctor makes mock baby breast feeder for dads. il pors *Jet* 73:44 D 28 '87-Ja 4 '88
Goldson, Elizabeth
Are you a klutz? il *Teen* 31:56 S '87
Goldstein, Arnold
Buying a franchise? Here's what you should look out for. *Work Woman* 12:52+ F '87
Goldstein, Carl
Tiptoeing toward democracy? il *World Press Rev* 34:19-20 N '87
Goldstein, Eddie
about
Magical tools for the 1980s. H.-J. Taferner. il por *Pers Comput* 11:173+ O '87
Goldstein, Irving, 1938-
about
Comsat is forced to narrow its orbit. S. Payne. por *Bus Week* p74 Jl 20 '87
Goldstein, Jess
about
Flexibility & fine fabrics: Jess Goldstein's costume designs. M. L. Gavenas. il por *Theatre Crafts* 21:18-21+ F '87
Goldstein, Joey
about
'Have I got a story!'. D. S. Looney. il pors *Sports Illus* 66:58-60+ My 18 '87
Goldstein, Judith L.
Lifestyles of the rich and tyrannical. *Am Sch* 56:235-47 Spr '87
Goldstein, Kenneth K.
Risking all for a cure. il *50 Plus* 27:51-2 Ja '87
Goldstein, Lawrence
about
Terra incognita. T. Jaffe. il por *Forbes* 140:38-40 D 28 '87
Goldstein, Lynda
Pine-leaf penstemon. il *Flower Gard* 31:36-7 Ap/My '87
Goldstein, Marvin M.
(jt. auth) See Ploscowe, Stephen A., and Goldstein, Marvin M.
Goldstein, Melvyn C.
When brothers share a wife. il *Nat Hist* 96:38-49 Mr '87
Goldstein, Stanley P.
about
Melville's new crew aims to get back to speed. F. McCoy. il por *Bus Week* p94 Jl 13 '87
Goldstein, Susan
about
Number-crunching helps sell yuppie puppy food. S. Sherry. il por *Work Woman* 12:40-1 Ja '87
Goldstein, William
(jt. auth) See Davis, Joann, and Goldstein, William
Goldthwait, Bob
about
Bob "Bobcat" Goldthwait. E. Miller. il pors *Seventeen* 46:96+ Ap '87
Goldwin, Robert A., 1922-
The Constitution [discussion of May 1987 article, Why blacks, women & Jews are not mentioned in the Constitution] *Commentary* 84:2+ O '87
The Constitution and the people left out: a study in original intent. *Current* 295:4-10 S '87
Why blacks, women & Jews are not mentioned in the Constitution. *Commentary* 83:28-33 My '87

Goleman, Daniel

Failing to recognize bias in science. il *Technol Rev* 90:26-7 N/D '87

The mind over the body. il *N Y Times Mag* p36+ S 27 '87

Who are you kidding? bibl (p59) il *Psychol Today* 21:24-6+ Mr '87

Golf

See also
Caddies (Golf)
Miniature golf
National Negro Golf Association

Fore play: a celebration of golf the glorious. R. B. Cramer. il *Esquire* 107:99-101 Je '87

Ms. Duffer's guide to life on the links. M. B. Nelson. il *Women's Sports Fitness* 9:40-3 Jl '87

Nixon: the fairway tapes [excerpt from Slammin' Sam] S. Snead. *Harpers* 274:28 Ja '87

Anecdotes, facetiae, satire, etc.

Smothered shots. J. K. Glassman. *New Repub* 196:42 My 18 '87

Equipment

See also
Golf clubs (Sticks)

Has golf gotten too groovy? [effect of high tech equipment] J. Diaz. il *Sports Illus* 67:52-9 Ag 3 '87

History

Essence woman [golfer M. Hathaway's fight against segregation] F. Newby and R. D. Manuel. por *Essence* 17:26 F '87

Psychological aspects

Temper fugit [excerpt from Strokes of genius] T. Boswell. il *Sport Mag* 78:59-60 Jl '87

Scoring

A victory for the System [method of scoring used at the International] J. Diaz. il *Sports Illus* 67:70-1 Ag 24 '87

Study and teaching

See also
Jack Nicklaus Academy of Golf (Orlando, Fla.)

Golf and tennis schools. M. C. Lewis. il *Travel Holiday* 167:18+ Je '87

School for swingers [Jimmy Ballard Golf Workshop at Miami's Doral Hotel & Country Club] G. Waggoner. il *Esquire* 108:31-2 N '87

Taking a crash course on the links. P. Finch. il *Bus Week* p98-9 Jl 6 '87

Aids and devices

Bobby Jones shows you how to hit 'em [How I play golf video] I. Maisel. *Sports Illus* 67:101 D 21 '87

Tournaments

See also
PGA Tour Inc.

Another era, same Player [G. Player's victory in U.S. Senior Open] J. Diaz. il por *Sports Illus* 67:18-19 Jl 20 '87

At last Tom has a fling [T. Watson wins Nabisco Championships of Golf] J. Diaz. il por *Sports Illus* 67:44-5 N 9 '87

Cool customer in a hot PGA [victor L. Nelson] J. Diaz. il pors *Sports Illus* 67:28-30+ Ag 17 '87

A cup for the old world [Ryder Cup] J. Diaz. il *Sports Illus* 67:58-61 O 5 '87

Golf and glory [Muirfield, host to the British Open] S. Ballard. il *Sports Illus* 67:54-9 Jl 13 '87

Grooving on a Sunday afternoon [D. Pooley wins Memorial Tournament] J. Diaz. il pors *Sports Illus* 66:73-4 Je 8 '87

The Haig and some recent Masters. H. W. Wind. *New Yorker* 63:89-100+ My 18 '87

Has golf gotten too groovy? [effect of high tech equipment] J. Diaz. il *Sports Illus* 67:52-9 Ag 3 '87

'Like a Rembrandt' [L. Trevino hits hole in one in Skins Game] J. Diaz. il por *Sports Illus* 67:26-7 D 7 '87

Mac is back and right on track [Tournament of Champions' victor M. O'Grady] J. Diaz. il por *Sports Illus* 66:50-1 Ja 19 '87

Mayfairest of them all [B. Mayfair wins U.S. Amateur] J. Diaz. il por *Sports Illus* 67:75 S 7 '87

Mr. Chip [L. Mize wins Masters playoff] D. Granger. il por *Sport Mag* 78:10 D '87

My, oh Mize [L. Mize defeats G. Norman in sudden death Masters playoff] S. Ballard. il pors *Sports Illus* 66:36-43 Ap 20 '87

National golf group sets minority college tourney [National Negro Golf Assn.] *Jet* 72:50 Ap 27 '87

A new force in the game [L. Davies wins U.S. Women's Open] J. Diaz. il pors *Sports Illus* 67:66+ Ag 10 '87

The Olympic Club and the Open. H. W. Wind. *New Yorker* 63:47-8+ Jl 27 '87

One more time, Jack [Masters winner in 1986] J. G. Hubbell. il pors *Read Dig* 130:121-6 Ap '87

An Open and shut case [S. Simpson defeats T. Watson in U.S. Open; cover story] R. Reilly. il pors *Sports Illus* 66:20-7 Je 29 '87

Peete drops by course in time for $105G prize. por *Jet* 72:50 Ap 13 '87

PGAer Calvin Peete hosts Fla. benefit golf tourney. por *Jet* 71:49 F 23 '87

The power of Love [analysis of D. Love III's swing] J. Diaz. il pors *Sports Illus* 66:44-6+ Mr 23 '87

Shootout down at the Shore [Nabisco Dinah Shore] J. Diaz. il *Sports Illus* 66:57-8 Ap 13 '87

T.C. conquers L.A. in O.T. [Los Angeles Open] R. Reilly. il por *Sports Illus* 66:22-4+ Mr 2 '87

Taming a toothless tiger [Tournament Players Championship] S. Ballard. il *Sports Illus* 66:128-30 Ap 6 '87

Time for the Pat and Nancy show [new LPGA season] J. Diaz. il pors *Sports Illus* 66:84+ F 9 '87

Very British Open. R. Reilly. il pors *Sports Illus* 67:18-23 Jl 27 '87

A victory for the System [method of scoring used at the International] J. Diaz. il *Sports Illus* 67:70-1 Ag 24 '87

Caddies

See Caddies (Golf)

Economic aspects

Spreading the wealth [PGA commissioner D. Beman; cover story] R. Behar. il pors *Forbes* 140:74-7+ Ag 10 '87

History

Amen corner [11th, 12th and 13th holes at Augusta National, site of the Masters] D. Granger. il *Sport Mag* 78:64-5 My '87

Seven ahead, nine to go, and then . . . [A. Palmer's loss in 1966 U.S. Open] R. Reilly. il *Sports Illus* 66:62-6+ Je 15 '87

Rules

Par cut off at the knees. T. Callahan. il *Time* 129:72 Mr 9 '87

Scoring

See Golf—Scoring

Television broadcasting

See Television broadcasting—Sports

Golf carts

Golf carts 'killing' caddies and blacks on PGA tour [views of C. Peete] por *Jet* 71:46 Ja 26 '87

Golf clubs (Sticks)

See also
Pederson Custom Golf Clubs Inc.

How to become Arnold Palmer [high tech clubs designed by C. Duclos] D. Goodgame. il por *Time* 130:51 Ag 17 '87

Picking the perfect putter. D. Granger. il *Sport Mag* 78:85 My '87

Golf courses

Amen corner [11th, 12th and 13th holes at Augusta National, site of the Masters] D. Granger. il *Sport Mag* 78:64-5 My '87

The Olympic Club and the Open. H. W. Wind. *New Yorker* 63:47-8+ Jl 27 '87

Environmental aspects

Eighteen holes at the oasis [proposed development of Agua Caliente land in the Indian Canyons] O. Redwine. il *Sierra* 72:83-4 N/D '87

Hazards of the game. J. Edmondson. il *Audubon* 89:24-8+ N '87

Scotland

Golf and glory [Muirfield, host to the British Open] S. Ballard. il *Sports Illus* 67:54-9 Jl 13 '87

Unseen hands on my game [a week at Royal Dornoch] R. Reilly. il map *Sports Illus* 67:66-70+ Ag 17 '87

Golfers

See also
Azinger, Paul
Bradley, Pat
Casper, Billy
Chen, T. C.
Crampton, Bruce
Davies, Laura
Elder, Lee
Faldo, Nick
Hagen, Walter, 1892-1969
Hathaway, Maggie
Knudson, George
Lopez, Nancy, 1957-
Love, Davis, III
Mayfair, Billy
Mize, Larry
Nelson, Larry

Golfers—See also—*cont.*
Nicklaus, Jack
Norman, Greg, 1955-
O'Grady, Mac
Palmer, Arnold, 1929-
Peete, Calvin
Player, Gary
Pooley, Don
Rodriguez, Chi Chi
Sheehan, Patty
Simpson, Scott
Stewart, Payne
Terry, Ralph, 1936-
Trevino, Lee
Tway, Bob
Watson, Tom, 1949-
Golf carts 'killing' caddies and blacks on PGA tour [views of C. Peete] por *Jet* 71:46 Ja 26 '87
Psychology
See Golf—Psychological aspects

Golia, Vinny
about
Vinny Golia. T. Levi. il por *Down Beat* 54:45-6 My '87

Golin, Mark
Regenerative living. See issue of Prevention (Emmaus, Pa.) beginning January 1987

Gollust, Keith R.
about
The trio that humbled Allegis. S. P. Sherman. il pors *Fortune* 116:52-4+ Jl 20 '87

Golob, Steven
Sell abroad; you can collect. il *Nations Bus* 75:44+ N '87

Golub, Harvey
about
Golub: the workaholic telling clients to relax. M. J. Pitzer. il por *Bus Week* p98 N 23 '87

Golub, Richard
about
In the case of the bum rap song, Richard Golub courts justice for his fellow lawyers. L. Wohlfert. il por *People Wkly* 27:71+ F 2 '87

Gomer, Richard H., and Firtel, Richard A.
Cell-autonomous determination of cell-type choice in Dictyostelium development by cell-cycle phase. bibl f il *Science* 237:758-62 Ag 14 '87

Gomes, Antonio Carlos, 1836-1896
about
Salvator Rosa [opera] Reviews
N Y 20:115 My 25 '87. P. G. Davis
New Yorker 63:93 My 25 '87. A. Porter

Gomez, Alain
about
Overnight, Thomson has the stuff to take on the titans. T. Peterson. il *Bus Week* p36-7 Ag 10 '87

Gomez, Andres
about
And the surfer ate the shark. J. Diaz. il por *Sports Illus* 66:73 My 18 '87

Gomez, Edward M.
Jamaican designs. il map *Travel Holiday* 167:48-51 Ja '87

Gomez, Ronda
about
In her own image. F. Greenberg. il por *Work Woman* 12:76-7 D '87

Gómez Izquierdo, José
about
Sowing justice in Ecuador. P. R. Greene. *Christ Century* 104:910-12 O 21 '87

Gomory, Ralph E.
about
Innovation vs. invention [interview] W. J. Cook. por *U S News World Rep* 103:55 D 14 '87

Gonadotropin releasing hormone
Making antisense [work of John P. Adelman and others] *Sci Am* 256:26 Je '87
"Reversible menopause" may help some women who have endometriosis or fibroid tumors. *Prevention* 39:62-3 O '87

Gonadotropins
See also
Inhibin
Pergonal
Do you really want twins? Try yams [stimulates release of the follicle-stimulating hormone in the Yoruba tribe] il *Newsweek* 110:62 N 23 '87

Gonads
See also
Testicles

Gondolas
'Delicious! Ah! What else is like the gondola?' [Venice] D. J. Hamblin. bibl (p147) il *Smithsonian* 18:96-105 Jl '87
Gondola [ride in Central Park] *New Yorker* 63:24-5 Je 1 '87

GONG *See* Global Oscillation Network Group

Gonick, Jean, 1950-
A love story, sort of. il *Glamour* 85:204+ My '87

Gonorrhea
See also
Neisseria
Antibiotic-resistant VD on increase. *Sci News* 131:200 Mr 28 '87
Belligerent bug makes Korean debut [spectinomycin-resistant Neisseria gonorrhoeae; research by John W. Boslego and others] *Sci News* 132:94 Ag 8 '87
A new venereal threat [penicillin-resistant gonorrhea] N. Underwood. il *Macleans* 100:51 S 21 '87

Gonyaulax *See* Dinoflagellates

Gonzalez, Antonio
about
The world's oldest eatery, Casa Botin, reigns in Spain. N. Geeslin. il por *People Wkly* 28:153+ D 14 '87

González, Felipe
about
Washington could get burned by putting the heat on Madrid. J. Patterson and others. il *Bus Week* p58 N 23 '87

Gonzalez, Pancho, 1928-
Hands. il *World Tennis* 35:28-9 Je '87
Power. il *World Tennis* 34:29 Ap '87
That period of adjustment. il por *World Tennis* 35:80 Ag '87
about
Power and the fury; ed. by Neil Amdur. R. A. Gonzalez. il *World Tennis* 35:25-7 S '87

Gonzalez, Rita Agassi
Power and the fury; ed. by Neil Amdur. il *World Tennis* 35:25-7 S '87

González-Palacios, Alvar
A royal family heritage [cover story] il *House Gard* 159:162-72+ Jl '87

Gooch, Brad, 1952-
Architectural digest visits: Burt Bacharach and Carole Bayer Sager. il pors *Archit Dig* 44:128-33+ O '87

Good, Ken
about
An Amazon love story. R. Arias. il pors *People Wkly* 27:24-9 Ja 19 '87

Good, Michael F., and others
Construction of synthetic immunogen: use of new T-helper epitope on malaria circumsporozoite protein. bibl f il *Science* 235:1059-62 F 27 '87

Good, Thomas L., 1943-, and Grouws, Douglas A.
Increasing teachers' understanding of mathematical ideas through inservice training. bibl f il *Phi Delta Kappan* 68:778-83 Je '87

Good and evil
See also
Sin
Temptation
Asceticism & the evil one. J. Garvey. *Commonweal* 114:311-12 My 22 '87
Does evil have a life of its own? J. Deedy. il *U S Cathol* 52:20-5 D '87

Good and evil in motion pictures
The best film of 1986: probing the depths of evil [Blue velvet] J. M. Wall. *Christ Century* 104:7-9 Ja 7-14 '87

The good father [film] *See* Motion picture reviews—Single works

Good housekeeping (Periodical)
Articles for Good housekeeping: the whats and the how-tos. il *Writer* 100:24-5 Je '87
Editor's notebook. J. M. Carter. See issues of Good Housekeeping

Good morning, Babylon [film] *See* Motion picture reviews—Single works

Good morning, Vietnam [film] *See* Motion picture reviews—Single works

Good Samaritanism *See* Assistance in emergencies

The good wife [film] *See* Motion picture reviews—Single works

Good works (Theology)
Survivor's debt. D. A. Tate. il *N Y Times Mag* p38 Ag 30 '87

Goodall, Jackson Wallace, Jr.
about
No more junk in the box. E. Paris. il por *Forbes* 140:136+ N 16 '87

Goodall, Jane
A plea for the chimps. il *N Y Times Mag* p108-10+ My 17 '87
Goode, W. Wilson
about
A fracas in Philadelphia. il pors *U S News World Rep* 103:20 N 16 '87
Philadelphia's bare-knuckled political brawl. T. E. Johnson. il pors *Newsweek* 110:59 N 2 '87
Wilson Goode, Frank Rizzo stump for mayor's seat in Philadelphia election. *Jet* 72:12 Je 8 '87
Goodell, Michael
Housing and hope for census tract 5130. *Christ Century* 104:213-15 Mr 4 '87
Gooden, Dwight
about
Coke and a pitching ace. il por *Macleans* 100:26 Ap 13 '87
A crash landing for an ace. S. Wulf. il pors *Sports Illus* 66:32-4 Ap 13 '87
Doc. *New Yorker* 63:29-30+ Mr 23 '87
Dr. K strikes out. por *Time* 129:67 Ap 13 '87
Fla. race issue clouds Dwight Gooden arrest. il pors *Jet* 71:46-7 Ja 12 '87
Going to bat against the fear of failure. J. M. Wall. *Christ Century* 104:371-2 Ap 22 '87
The good Doctor has a bad scrape. W. Nack. il pors *Sports Illus* 66:28-30+ Ja 5 '87
Gooden looks to better days, signs for $1.5 million. il por *Jet* 71:46 Mr 9 '87
Gooden plans to wed his longtime friend. *Jet* 72:31 Jl 20 '87
Gooden sheds light on his problem with cocaine. *Jet* 72:52 Jl 13 '87
Gooden to start working back into Mets rotation. il por *Jet* 72:48 My 18 '87
Gooden's ex-fiancée nabbed en route to reconciliation. il por *Jet* 71:12 F 16 '87
In minor league debut Gooden still looks great. por *Jet* 72:49 Je 1 '87
Mets moral support may speed up Gooden's return after drug rehabilitation. il pors *Jet* 72:50 Ap 20 '87
Mets provide protection while 'Dr. K' heals himself. por *Jet* 72:46 My 25 '87
Off to a troubled start. P. Axthelm. il pors *Newsweek* 109:66-7 Ap 13 '87
Police sue Mets' Gooden, seek $3 million award. por *Jet* 73:50 O 26 '87
Say it ain't snow, Doc! Baseball hero Dwight Gooden is knocked out of the box by cocaine. J. S. Kunen. il por *People Wkly* 27:123-4 Ap 20 '87
Welcome warms Gooden as he returns to form. il por *Jet* 72:52 Je 22 '87
Goodenough, J. B.
Clearing [poem] *Ctry J* 14:55 F '87
Goodin, Suzanna
about
Now thanks to Suzanna Goodin, pets can clean the bowl—and then eat the spoon that feeds them. il por *People Wkly* 27:119 Mr 9 '87
Goodlad, John I.
A new look at core curriculum. *Educ Dig* 52:6-9 My '87
Goodman, Allan E.
Reforming U.S. intelligence. bibl f *Foreign Policy* 67:121-36 Summ '87
Goodman, Allegra
The succession [story] *Commentary* 84:45-52 S '87
Total immersion [story] *Commentary* 84:45-53 O '87
Young people [story] *Commentary* 83:59-65 Mr '87
Goodman, Amy
(jt. auth) See Dobie, Kathy, and Goodman, Amy
Goodman, Benny, 1909-1986
about
BG serenade [discography] J. McDonough. *Down Beat* 54:34 Ap '87
Goodman, Calvin J.
How artists use videocassettes. il *Am Artist* 51:58-61 Jl '87
Goodman, Catherine Chase
Putting their caring on the line. il *Aging* no355:20-1 '87
Goodman, D. W., and Houston, J. E.
Catalysis: new perspectives from surface science. bibl f il *Science* 236:403-9 Ap 24 '87
Goodman, David L.
Professor sues MIT over tenure. *Progressive* 51:13 Je '87

Goodman, Dennis
about
Thanks, Dennis. L. Gubernick. il por *Forbes* 140:126+ S 7 '87
Goodman, Ellen
"Hey, Dad, thanks for coming". il *Read Dig* 130:151-2 Ap '87
Goodman, George J. W. See Smith, Adam, 1930-
Goodman, Hirsh
Israel's opportunity. *New Repub* 196:13-15 Je 29 '87
Pretoria connection. *New Repub* 196:20-1 Ap 20 '87
Goodman, Joan
The best Bette yet. il pors *Ladies Home J* 104:30+ Je '87
The private side of Anne Bancroft. il pors *Ladies Home J* 104:72+ O '87
Goodman, June K.
The priority of K-12 arts education for state and local arts councils. *Des Arts Educ* 88:20-2 N/D '86
Goodman, Robert M., and others
Gene transfer in crop improvement. bibl f il *Science* 236:48-54 Ap 3 '87
Goodman, Robert O.
about
Ebony update: Lt. Robert O. Goodman. il pors *Ebony* 42:124+ My '87
Goodman, Sidney, 1936-
about
Sidney Goodman at Terry Dintenfass. R. G. Edelman. il *Art Am* 75:184-5 N '87
Goodman, Stephen F.
Periodontal disease: how to win the battle against tooth loss. por *McCalls* 114:119 F '87
Goodman, Susan
The fine art of taking control of your life. il *Curr Health 2* 13:3-9 Ja '87
Group dating: safety—and fun—in numbers. il *Curr Health 2* 14:12-13 D '87
The signs of life: a guide to assessing your health risks. il *Curr Health 2* 13:3-9 Ap '87
Understanding alcohol [cover story] bibl il *Curr Health 2* 14:3-9 N '87
Goodman, Walter
Albert, Fawn and Ollie. il *New Leader* 70:5-7 Jl 13-27 '87
Giving the Word. *New Leader* 70:7 Ja 12-26 '87
Glasnost and the condom. il *New Leader* 70:11-12 Mr 9 '87
Soviet specimens. il *New Leader* 70:7-8 N 2 '87
Goodness of God See God—Goodness
Goodrich, Lloyd
about
Obituary
Art News por 86:54 Summ '87. W. I. Homer
Goodrich, Mary Louise
about
Montaigne's invitation to the past: a historic residence in Natchez, Mississippi. R. Ford. il por *Archit Dig* 44:114-17+ Jl '87
Goodrich, Michael
about
For those who see the past and the future, but can't find their way to the bank, Michael Goodrich offers—himself. D. Van Biema. il pors *People Wkly* 27:113-14+ My 18 '87
Goodrich, Norma Lorre
about
In search of Camelot. A. J. S. Rayl. il *Omni* 9:24+ Mr '87
Goodspeed Opera House
Goodspeed Opera House. M. Loeffler and M. Sommers. il *Theatre Crafts* 21:32-7+ N '87
Goodstadt, Michael S.
School-based drug education: what is wrong? *Educ Dig* 52:44-7 F '87
Goodway, Martha
Phosphorus in antique iron music wire. bibl f il *Science* 236:927-32 My 22 '87
Goodwill in business
Accounting
Paper victory. L. Saunders. *Forbes* 139:78+ Mr 9 '87
Goodwin, Betty
about
The intensity of Betty Goodwin. G. James. il *Macleans* 100:53-4 Je 1 '87
Goodwin, Betty
Anjelica Huston. pors *Harpers Bazaar* 120:98, 348-51 S '87
The black advantage. *Harpers Bazaar* 120:105+ Jl '87
Daryl: film's new fit beauty. il pors *Harpers Bazaar* 120:211-13+ O '87

Goodwin, Betty—*cont.*
Let's get metaphysical. por *Roll Stone* p34-5 Ja 29 '87
You just found out he wants out. *Harpers Bazaar* 120:140+ Ag '87

Goodwin, Doris Kearns
Birth of a dynasty [excerpts from The Fitzgeralds and the Kennedys] il pors *People Wkly* 27:54-6+ Ja 26 '87

about
The Kennedy hustle. C. Peters. il *Wash Mon* 19:47-9 My '87

Goodwin, James
about
James Goodwin swings from soaps to Shakespeare. D. Hutchings. il pors *People Wkly* 28:109-10 Ag 24 '87

Goodwin, Jan
Caught in the crossfire [excerpt] il por *Ladies Home J* 104:22+ Ap '87
South African journal [with interview with C. S. King] il por *Ladies Home J* 104:74+ Ja '87

Goodyear Aerospace Corp.
Loral to acquire Goodyear Aerospace for $640 million in cash transaction. *Aviat Week Space Technol* 126:30 Ja 19 '87
Merci, Jimmy [Loral's acquisition of Goodyear Aerospace] S. N. Chakravarty. il por *Forbes* 139:114+ Je 15 '87

Goodyear Tire & Rubber Company
Back to basics. S. N. Chakravarty. il por *Forbes* 140:40-1 S 21 '87
Goodyear seems to be getting the last laugh. Z. Schiller. il por *Bus Week* p48 Mr 9 '87
Robert Mercer. Z. Schiller. il por *Bus Week* Sp Issue:266 Ap 17 '87
Terrorists in three-piece suits [address, March 3, 1987] R. E. Mercer. *Vital Speeches Day* 53:421-3 My 1 '87
Unleashing workers [competing with Japan] il *U S News World Rep* 103:44 Ag 24 '87

Goolrick, Robert M.
George Shultz, wimp. il *Wash Mon* 19:18-19 O '87

Gooneys *See* Albatrosses
Goose Bay Air Base (Canada) *See* Air bases
Goose cooking *See* Cooking—Poultry
Goose shooting
Flagging for geese [Canada geese] B. Sayler. il *Outdoor Life* 180:58-60+ D '87
The sportiest goose [snow goose] B. W. Dalrymple. il *Field Stream* 92:46-7+ D '87

GOP (Grand Old Party) *See* Republican Party (U.S.)
Gopnik, Adam
The blue room [story] *New Yorker* 63:34-8 F 23 '87
Comics and catastrophe. il *New Repub* 196:29-34 Je 22 '87

Gorbachev, Mikhail
See also
Reagan-Gorbachev summit conference, 1986
Document: the Revolution and *perestroika* [excerpts from address, November 2, 1987] *Foreign Aff* 66:410-25 Wint '87/'88
Gorbachev talks tough [excerpts from address, June 19, 1986] *Time* 129:54 Ja 5 '87
In his words [excerpt from Perestroika] il pors *U S News World Rep* 103:70-2+ N 9 '87
Nuclear disarmament [address, February 28, 1987] *Vital Speeches Day* 53:386-7 Ap 15 '87
U.S.S.R. foreign relations [address, October 1, 1987] *Vital Speeches Day* 54:130-3 D 15 '87
about
10 days that shook the Kremlin [with interview with A. Yakolev; editorial comment by Mortimer B. Zuckerman] H. Trewhitt. il por *U S News World Rep* 103:51-2, 92 N 16 '87
70 years after Lenin [cover story; special section] il pors *U S News World Rep* 103:30-42+ O 19 '87
Advantage Gorbachev. S. Sullivan. il por *Newsweek* 109:38 Mr 9 '87
Advice from the third man. S. Talbott. il pors *Time* 130:18 N 30 '87
Again, Mikhail the acrobat displays his tricks. P. R. Range. il *U S News World Rep* 103:6 Ag 3 '87
America's chance. C. W. Maynes. *Foreign Policy* 68:88-99 Fall '87
An arms tango in Moscow. A. Finlayson. il pors *Macleans* 100:18-19 Ap 27 '87
Barriers in the fast lane for Moscow. J. Trimble. il por *U S News World Rep* 102:20 F 16 '87
Better slow than sorry. T. Griffith. il *Time* 129:83 My 4 '87

Bothered, bewildered and in some cases bewitched. P. R. Range. il pors *U S News World Rep* 102:28-9 Ap 13 '87
The call to reform. W. R. Doerner. il pors *Time* 129:28-30 F 9 '87
Can anybody fix the Soviet system? M. I. Goldman. il por *U S News World Rep* 102:38-9 F 9 '87
Can Gorbachev break a 40-year deadlock with Japan? N. Gross and others. il *Bus Week* p57 O 5 '87
Captain Zero Option. C. Krauthammer. *New Repub* 196:12-14 Mr 30 '87
Caution and doubt in Europe. L. Freedman. il *World Press Rev* 34:15-16 N '87
Challenging abroad, opening up at home. J. O. Jackson. por *Time* 129:36 Ja 5 '87
Closer to an arms deal. I. Austen. *Macleans* 100:28 Ag 3 '87
Coming to terms with Gorbachev. B. Amiel. il *Macleans* 100:7 Ap 13 '87
Conspicuous by his absence. il por *Newsweek* 110:42 O 5 '87
Coping with Gorbachev. H. Trewhitt. il pors *U S News World Rep* 102:26-8 Ap 13 '87
Countering Gorbachev. M. Whitaker. il por *Newsweek* 109:32-3 F 23 '87
The curtain rises on Gorbachev's Act II. S. Bialer. il *U S News World Rep* 103:36-7 Jl 13 '87
Dealing at last [cover story; special section] il pors map *Newsweek* 109:20-8+ Ap 27 '87
A dirty word. D. Seligman. il *Fortune* 116:203 Ag 3 '87
A disarming surprise. I. Austen. *Macleans* 100:20 Ag 10 '87
Downfall of a folk hero. C. Redden. il por *Macleans* 100:21 N 23 '87
Editor Gorbo. D. Kimelman. *New Repub* 197:13-14 S 7 '87
Encounter with Gorbachev: what the smile can't hide. S. B. Shepard. por *Bus Week* p36 D 21 '87
Final reductions. M. Kondracke. *New Repub* 196:15-16 My 11 '87
From Stalin's grim legacy, new weapons for reform. D. Stanglin. il por *U S News World Rep* 103:36 Ag 10 '87
Giving better than she got. W. R. Doerner. il pors *Time* 129:50 Ap 13 '87
Glasnost: between hope and history. S. Schmemann. il *N Y Times Book Rev* 92:12-13 Ap 26 '87
Glasnost: 'There's no turning back' [interview with A. Sakharov and E. Bonner] M. B. Zuckerman. il pors *U S News World Rep* 102:31 Ap 20 '87
Gorbachev: a new foreign policy? D. K. Simes. bibl f *Foreign Aff* 65 Sp Issue:477-500 ['87]
Gorbachev and Eastern Europe. C. Gati. *Foreign Aff* 65:958-75 Summ '87
Gorbachev and 'Iragua'. B. Crozier. *Natl Rev* 39:28 F 13 '87
Gorbachev and the Jews. H. Anderson. il por *Newsweek* 109:34-5 Ap 13 '87
A Gorbachev arms offer even Europe may not refuse. B. Javetski and P. Galuszka. il por *Bus Week* p53 Ap 27 '87
The Gorbachev era [cover story; special section] il pors *Time* 130:28-34+ Jl 27 '87
Gorbachev: faster, faster. R. A. Manning. il *U S News World Rep* 102:25-6 F 23 '87
Gorbachev: going slow. R. Watson. il por *Newsweek* 110:74-6 N 16 '87
Gorbachev has planted the seeds, but will they grow? P. Galuszka and others. il por *Bus Week* p44-5 F 2 '87
Gorbachev is making a bold bid to get his reforms moving. P. Galuszka. il *Bus Week* p49 Je 29 '87
Gorbachev: no time to relax [with interview with A. Yakovlev] J. L. Galloway. il por *U S News World Rep* 102:36-8 Je 1 '87
The Gorbachev offensive. C. S. Gray. *Society* 24:38-44 Jl/Ag '87
Gorbachev on the high wire. H. Trewhitt. il por *U S News World Rep* 102:36-7 F 9 '87
Gorbachev opens the border for Jews—with good reason. J. Pearson. il *Bus Week* p28 Ap 20 '87
Gorbachev reforms declare a dividend. il *U S News World Rep* 102:12 Ap 6 '87
The Gorbachev regime after two years. J. Cracraft. bibl f *Bull At Sci* 43:31-3 My '87
Gorbachev: risking all for reform [with editorial comment by Mortimer B. Zuckerman] S. Bialer. il por *U S News World Rep* 102:50-1, 79-80 Ap 27 '87
Gorbachev tackles the Academy. R. Cornwell. *World Press Rev* 34:53 Ag '87

Gorbachev, Mikhail—about—*cont.*

Gorbachev takes a bearlike grip on the Politburo. J. Trimble. il por *U S News World Rep* 103:12-13 Jl 6 '87

Gorbachev takes on the generals. J. Trimble. il por *U S News World Rep* 102:29-30 Je 15 '87

Gorbachev the bold. P. Reddaway. bibl f il *N Y Rev Books* 34:21-5 My 28 '87

Gorbachev: the great counter-reformer; tr. by Pat Hunt and Jonathan Kozol. A. Michnik. *Harpers* 275:19-20 N '87

Gorbachev: the man with a nice smile and iron teeth. R. Evans and R. D. Novak. por *Read Dig* 131:90-5 O '87

Gorbachev: the rest of the story. M. B. Zuckerman. il *U S News World Rep* 103:84-5 D 21 '87

Gorbachev: the view from Warsaw [interview with J. Kuron] H. Luczywo and N. Gardels. *Harpers* 275:26-7 Jl '87

Gorbachev: upping the ante. M. Whitaker. il por *Newsweek* 110:28 Jl 6 '87

Gorbachev's arms control moves. J. Dean. il *Bull At Sci* 43:34-40 Je '87

Gorbachev's bottom line. P. G. Peterson. bibl f il *N Y Rev Books* 34:29-33 Je 25 '87

Gorbachev's 'courageous' reform plan [interview with A. Sakharov] por *U S News World Rep* 102:13 F 16 '87

Gorbachev's Das kapitalism. B. Javetski and J. Pearson. il por *Bus Week* p30-1 Jl 13 '87

Gorbachev's dilemma. E. H. Methvin. *Natl Rev* 39:42+ D 4 '87

Gorbachev's disillusioned intellectuals. F. Coleman. il por *Newsweek* 110:37 N 30 '87

Gorbachev's gamble. por *World Press Rev* 34:9-12+ Ap '87

Gorbachev's gamble. P. Taubman. il por *N Y Times Mag* p28-9+ Jl 19 '87

Gorbachev's Gulf game. M. Whitaker. il por *Newsweek* 110:32-3 Jl 20 '87

Gorbachev's long reach. K. Scanlon. il por map *Macleans* 100:31-2 Mr 16 '87

Gorbachev's Middle East strategy. G. Golan. bibl f *Foreign Aff* 66:41-57 Fall '87

Gorbachev's move. S. Bialer. *Foreign Policy* 68:59-87 Fall '87

Gorbachev's new challenge. por *Macleans* 100:19 Jl 6 '87

Gorbachev's next move. M. A. Evangelista. il *Harpers* 274:24+ Ja '87

Gorbachev's opposition. R. Watson. il por *Newsweek* 109:48-50 My 18 '87

Gorbachev's prairie pals. T. Jacoby. il pors *Newsweek* 109:31 Ap 6 '87

Gorbachev's profs. J. Rupnik. *New Repub* 197:10+ D 7 '87

Gorbachev's progress. *Macleans* 100:20 Mr 2 '87

Gorbachev's revolution [special section] il pors *U S News World Rep* 103:68-72+ N 9 '87

Gorbachev's Soviet Union: after two years [cover story; special issue; with editorial comment] bibl il *Nation* 244:785-6, 792-800+ Je 13 '87

Gorbachev's tomatoes. M. B. Zuckerman. il *U S News World Rep* 102:76 Ap 20 '87

Gorbachev's uncertain reformation. J. W. Hahn. il *Commonweal* 114:586-8+ O 23 '87

Gorby's new economics. *Natl Rev* 39:16-17 Jl 31 '87

A hard bargain [special section] il pors *Newsweek* 109:12-23 Ja 5 '87

Harper & Row to ship book by Gorbachev in early November. B. Levine. *Publ Wkly* 232:41-2 O 16 '87

"I am very guilty". W. R. Doerner. il pors *Time* 130:34 N 23 '87

If Gorbachev loses . . . il *Progressive* 51:9-10 My '87

The INF trap. E. V. Rostow. *New Repub* 197:16-17 Ag 24 '87

Is it reform or rhetoric? Gorbachev and the Soviet economy. E. A. Hewett. *Current* 291:21-7 Mr/Ap '87

Kissinger: how to deal with Gorbachev. H. Kissinger. il pors *Newsweek* 109:39-40+ Mr 2 '87

Lenin to the rescue. B. Crozier. *Natl Rev* 39:26 S 11 '87

The Leninist quandary. B. Crozier. *Natl Rev* 39:26+ Mr 13 '87

Lifting the veil on history. T. A. Sancton. il por *Time* 130:45+ N 16 '87

Madcap Mik. H. Hertzberg. *New Repub* 196:4 Mr 2 '87

Marching orders. R. Watson. il pors *Newsweek* 109:34-6 Je 15 '87

Mikhail Gorbachev. il por *People Wkly* 28:32-3 D 28 '87-Ja 4 '88

Mikhail Gorbachev, author [interview with S. M. Bessie] A. P. Sanoff. il por *U S News World Rep* 103:73 O 12 '87

Mikhail's year of living dangerously. J. Trimble. il por *U S News World Rep* 102:12 Mr 2 '87

The Moscow/Peking dilemma. B. Crozier. *Natl Rev* 39:26 D 18 '87

Moscow meeting—the *glasnost* menagerie. S. Frankel. il pors *Bull At Sci* 43:8-12 My '87

Moscow stalling. A. B. Ulam. *New Repub* 197:12-14 D 7 '87

Moscow's man in a hurry. J. Smolowe. il por *Time* 130:16 Jl 6 '87

Now, super-zero? G. J. Church. il pors *Time* 129:20-3 Ap 27 '87

An offer that Reagan can't refuse? J. Young. il por *Newsweek* 110:27 Ag 3 '87

One step forward. *Nation* 245:544-5 N 14 '87

Opening the Soviet hothouse: how far can Gorbachev go? M. I. Goldman. il por *Technol Rev* 90:18+ Ja '87

Orchestrating Gorbachev. P. S. Nathan. *Publ Wkly* 232:21 N 6 '87

Planning the 'second revolution'. *World Press Rev* 34:31 Mr '87

Plenty of guns, no politics for Gorbachev's generals. J. Trimble. il por *U S News World Rep* 102:32 My 11 '87

The promise—and problems—of Gorbachev's offer. B. Javetski and D. Griffiths. il por *Bus Week* p36 Mr 16 '87

A promising Soviet ploy. B. Van Voorst. por *Time* 130:18 Ag 3 '87

Red star blazes on. B. Crozier. *Natl Rev* 39:26 Ag 14 '87

Removing Gorbachev's edge. M. Svec. il *Foreign Policy* 69:148-65 Wint '87/'88

Russia: where Gorbanomics is leading. R. I. Kirkland, Jr. il por *Fortune* 116:82-4+ S 28 '87

The second revolution. C. Redden. il por *Macleans* 100:19-20+ N 9 '87

Sending a message loud and clear: no more graft. P. Galuszka. il *Bus Week* p44-5 Jl 6 '87

Skeptical satellites. J. Bugajski. *New Repub* 196:15-16 My 4 '87

Slowing down *glasnost*. C. Redden. il por *Macleans* 100:30-1 N 16 '87

The Soviet system today. P. M. Kennedy. il *Current* 296:16-26 O '87

The Soviet Union, 1987 [special issue] bibl f il map (inside back cover) *Curr Hist* 86:305-47 O '87

The Soviet Union at seventy. R. V. Daniels. il *New Leader* 70:11-13 O 19 '87

Sovieticus. S. F. Cohen. *Nation* 244:315 Mr 14 '87

States of two unions. *Nation* 244:129 F 7 '87

Straight talk. por *Time* 129:43 Je 1 '87

Thatcher on Gorbachev [cover story] C. Thatcher. il pors *Life* 10:32-4 O '87

A touch of democracy. *Newsweek* 109:42 F 9 '87

TV's week: of gab and *glasnost*. R. Zoglin. il por *Time* 130:67-8 D 14 '87

Two deal-makers. *New Repub* 197:4+ D 28 '87

U.S.-Soviet relations: testing Gorbachev's "new thinking" [address, July 1, 1987] M. H. Armacost. *Dep State Bull* 87:36-41 S '87

Was there scuffling in the Kremlin? il *Newsweek* 110:53 N 9 '87

What Gorbachev is up against. P. M. Kennedy. il *Atlantic* 259:29-38+ Je '87

What Gorbachev wants [cover story] S. Sestanovich. *New Repub* 196:20-3 My 25 '87

When to call off the cold war. C. Krauthammer. *New Repub* 197:18-21 N 16 '87

When worlds collide. J. Klein. il por *N Y* 20:35-6+ D 14 '87

Why Reagan and Gorbachev need an arms agreement. M. I. Goldman. il por *Technol Rev* 90:18+ Jl '87

The Yeltsin affair. *Natl Rev* 39:17 D 18 '87

Yeltsin walks the plank. R. Watson. por *Newsweek* 110:37 N 23 '87

Anecdotes, facetiae, satire, etc.

Notes and comment. *New Yorker* 63:33-4 D 28 '87

Visit to Czechoslovakia, 1987

Apostle of *glasnost* visits Prague. *America* 156:333 Ap 25 '87

Gorbachev: a soft sell for the satellites. F. Willey. il por *Newsweek* 109:37 Ap 20 '87

Gorbachev's Prague spring. il por *Macleans* 100:18-19 Ap 20 '87

Gorbachev, Mikhail—Visit to Czechoslovakia, 1987—*cont.*
Smiling Mike wows 'em in Prague. W. Svoboda. il por *Time* 129:40 Ap 20 '87

Visit to Romania, 1987
Glasnost on the road, to mixed review. J. L. Galloway. il por *U S News World Rep* 102:34 Je 8 '87
With friends like these . . . J. Smolowe. il por *Time* 129:36 Je 8 '87

Visit to the United States, 1987
See also
Reagan-Gorbachev summit conference, 1987

Gorbachev, Raisa Maksimovna
about
Coffee or tea? il pors *Time* 130:33 D 14 '87
Confrontation of the superwives. M. Hornblower. il pors *Time* 130:23 D 21 '87
Gorbo's other woman. G. Freidin. *New Repub* 197:15-16 D 28 '87
'Her schedule is more sensitive than his'. il por *Newsweek* 110:23 D 14 '87
Irrepressible Raisa. I. Austen. il por *Macleans* 100:28 D 21 '87
Kremlinologists play a video game. N. Cooper. il por *Newsweek* 109:35 Ap 13 '87
A new style First Lady. M. Blyth. il pors *Ladies Home J* 104:98+ S '87
Raisa and Nancy: superpower struggle. il pors *Newsweek* 110:18-19 D 21 '87
'We discuss everything'. C. Redden. il por *Macleans* 100:23 D 14 '87

Gorden, Fred
about
Fred Gorden first black commandant at West Point Academy. por *Jet* 72:4 Ag 31 '87

Gordimer, Nadine, 1923-
about
Conscious of time and place. P. Schwartz. il por *World Press Rev* 34:61 O '87
Nadine Gordimer: choosing to be a white African. C. Sternhell. il pors *Ms* 16:28+ S '87
PW interviews. M. Berkley. por *Publ Wkly* 231:80-1 Ap 10 '87
South African countdown. W. Clemons. por *Newsweek* 109:78 My 4 '87

Gordon, Alice
As rare as a day in June. il *House Gard* 159:124-33 Je '87
A château in bloom: Maryll and Bernard Lanvin's house in the Île de France. il *Vogue* 177:328-39 D '87
Flying colors. il *House Gard* 159:180-3 S '87
Little house in the mountains. il *House Gard* 159:100-3+ Ja '87
The thoroughbred way of life: houses fit for the world's noblest horses. il *House Gard* 159:148-61+ Ap '87

Gordon, Charles
The case for a cheap dog. por *Macleans* 100:39 Je 15 '87
Gloating in the locker room. por *Macleans* 100:60 O 5 '87
Golden oldies in the year 2017. por *Macleans* 100:9 Ja 12 '87
How we earn our place in the sun. por *Macleans* 100:7 F 9 '87
Paying for a good squeeze. por *Macleans* 100:7 Mr 9 '87
When summer blues turn pink. por *Macleans* 100:35 Ag 10 '87

Gordon, David, 1936-
about
Reviews:
Performances at Brooklyn Academy of Music. B. Newman. *Dance Mag* 61:29+ Ap '87

Gordon, David G.
New conservation ideas. il *Oceans* 20:59 N/D '87
What is that? il *Oceans* 20:44-9 Jl/Ag '87
Wildlife au naturel. *Travel Holiday* 168:30-1 Jl '87

Gordon, Dawn
Plug into the latest electronic trends! il *Essence* 17:85-6 Ja '87

Gordon, Dexter
about
Charm of the Duke led Gordon to be musician. *Jet* 72:62 Ag 31 '87
Dexter Gordon/New York Philharmonic. M. Bourne. *Down Beat* 54:56 S '87
Dexter Gordon, Hancock win Oscar nominations. il pors *Jet* 71:63 Mr 2 '87
Gordon detained by French police on 1967 DUI charge. por *Jet* 72:57 Jl 20 '87

Gordon, Diana R.
Varelli: in from the cold. *Nation* 244:273+ Mr 7 '87

Gordon, Elinor
Chinese export porcelain. il *Antiques* 132:182-7 Jl '87

Gordon, Glenn, 1943?-
Comment. *Am Craft* 47:20 F/Mr '87

Gordon, Ilene S.
about
Ilene Gordon: hey, what's she doing here? M. Mallory. il por *Bus Week* p76 O 26 '87

Gordon, James, 1833-1912
My hunting comrade, Pete [reprint from January 1900 issue] il *Field Stream* 91:60-1 F '87

Gordon, John E.
about
A lawyer's touch. L. Howard. il *Newsweek* 110:6 N 16 '87

Gordon, Linda
Reproductive rights for today. il *Nation* 245:230-2 S 12 '87
Shape-up. See issues of Glamour

Gordon, Mary, 1949-
"Baby M". il *Ms* 15:25-6+ Je '87
Sharon Gless & Tyne Daly. il pors *Ms* 15:40-1+ Ja '87
Violation [story] *Mademoiselle* 93:132+ My '87
about
Growing up Catholic and creative [interview] A. P. Sanoff. por *U S News World Rep* 103:74 O 5 '87

Gordon, Mary Ebbitt
Touch of evil: memories of a molested child. *Mademoiselle* 93:188+ Mr '87

Gordon, Max, 1903-
about
A lifetime in the Vanguard. J. Levenson. il por *Down Beat* 54:65 S '87

Gordon, Meryl
2 smart women, one top job: who got the VP promotion? il *Mademoiselle* 93:144-5+ Je '87
Psst! Wanna buy a station? il *Channels* 7:38-40 Ja '87

Gordon, Michael R.
Dateline Washington: INF: a hollow victory? *Foreign Policy* 68:159-79 Fall '87

Gordon, Paul
Poles: high-tech, high-toned. il *Skiing* 40:132+ S '87

Gordon, Peter
The curfew [story] *New Yorker* 63:38-44 O 19 '87

Gordon, Stuart
about
We killed 'em in Chicago. M. Brody. il por *Film Comment* 23:68-70+ Ja/F '87

Gordon, Theodore J.
Medical breakthroughs: cutting the toll of killer diseases. il por *Futurist* 21:15-17 Ja/F '87

Gordon, Walter Lockhart
about
Obituary
Macleans il por 100:36 Ap 6 '87. P. C. Newman

Gordon (David)/Pick Up Company See David Gordon/Pick Up Company

Gordon Research Conferences
Gordon Research Conferences. A. M. Cruickshank. *Science* 238:212-17 O 9 '87
Gordon Research Conferences. A. M. Cruickshank. *Science* 235:1233-60 Mr 6 '87

Gordon setters
A hunting dog's days afield. H. Middleton. il *South Living* 22:38+ D '87

Gordy, Walter, 1909-1985
about
Obituary
Phys Today 40:128+ F '87. F. C. De Lucia

Gore, Albert, Jr.
about
Al Gore hits a Democratic sore spot. T. Jacoby. il por *Newsweek* 110:33 O 26 '87
Al Gore's generation gap. E. Calonius. il por *Newsweek* 110:44 D 21 '87
A fighting Democrat. M. McDonald. il por *Macleans* 100:31-2 O 26 '87
Letter from Washington. Cato. *Natl Rev* 39:15 S 25 '87
New Hampshire diarist. M. Peretz. *New Repub* 197:43 Jl 27 '87
Nice young man. *New Repub* 196:4 Je 1 '87
Patriotic gore. J. Klein. por *N Y* 20:38+ N 16 '87
Political notes. J. McLaughlin. *Natl Rev* 39:20 Je 5 '87
The southern strategist [cover story] M. Kondracke. il *New Repub* 197:20-3 D 7 '87

Gore, Albert, Jr.—about—*cont.*

A Tennessee stalking horse. H. Fineman. il por *Newsweek* 110:40 S 14 '87

Trying to set himself apart. S. Talbott. il pors *Time* 130:17-18 O 19 '87

A Washington tale: Gore chic. T. Noah. il por *Newsweek* 109:20 F 16 '87

What (or who) makes Albert Gore run. M. E. Recio. il por *Bus Week* p45 Ap 27 '87

Whistling Dixie. pors *Time* 129:32 Ap 6 '87

Gore, Mary Elizabeth *See* Gore, Tipper, 1948-

Gore, Tipper, 1948-

about

A 'R'-rated book on Raising 'PG' kids. B. Summer. *Publ Wkly* 231:44 Ap 24 '87

Raising kids in an X-rated society. F. Barnes. *Des Arts Educ* 89:47-8 N/D '87

Tipper de doo dah. H. Hertzberg. *New Repub* 197:22-3 D 7 '87

Tipper Gore: the PMRC swings back into action. R. Love. por *Seventeen* 46:56 Jl '87

Gorelick, Kenny *See* G, Kenny

Gorge-purge syndrome *See* Bulimia

Goria, Giovanni

about

Italy gets a new government. S. F. Senigallia. por *New Leader* 70:3-4 Jl 13-27 '87

Will Italy be able to regain the high ground? W. C. Symonds. por *Bus Week* p38 Ag 10 '87

Gorillas

I didn't kill Dian. She was my friend [murder of gorilla protector D. Fossey]; ed. by Beverly Trainer and Gina Maranto. W. McGuire. il pors maps *Discover* 8:28-32+ F '87

Anecdotes, facetiae, satire, etc.

Last word. T. Runté. il *Omni* 9:142 Ap '87

Goring, D. R., and others

In situ detection of β-galactosidase in lenses of transgenic mice with a γ-crystallin/*lacZ* gene. bibl f il *Science* 235:456-8 Ja 23 '87

Gorky, Maksim, 1868-1936

about

Philistines [drama] Reviews

Nation 245:349-50 O 3 '87. T. M. Disch

Gorky, Maxim *See* Gorky, Maksim, 1868-1936

Gorman, Ed

about

The last diploma he got was in high school, but Ed Gorman, 69, is setting his cap on a masters from Oxford. il por *People Wkly* 27:58 Ap 20 '87

Gorman, Greg

A day in the life of a screen goddess. il pors *Life* 10:122-5+ Ap '87

Gorman, James, 1949-

Light elements. *See* issues of Discover beginning May 1985

Gorman, Kevin

(jt. auth) *See* Redling, Edward T., and Gorman, Kevin

Gorman, Marion

Chef's skills. *See* issues of Rodale's Organic Gardening through February 1987

Low-calorie okra! il *Rodale's Org Gard* 34:42-4+ Jl '87

Gormican, John

(jt. auth) *See* Wettstein, Mike, Jr., and Gormican, John

Gornick, Michael

about

Creepshow 2 [film] Reviews

People Wkly il 27:10 My 25 '87. R. Novak

Gornick, Vivian

Fierce attachments [excerpts] il por *Ms* 15:52-4+ Je '87

The world and our mothers. il *N Y Times Book Rev* 92:1+ N 22 '87

Gorra, Michael

The sun never sets on the English novel. il *N Y Times Book Rev* 92:1+ Jl 19 '87

Gorris, Marleen

about

Broken mirrors [film] Reviews

New Repub 196:26-7 Mr 16 '87. S. Kauffmann

Gortari, Carlos Salinas de *See* Salinas de Gortari, Carlos

The gospel at Colonus [musical] *See* Musicals, revues, etc.—Reviews—Single works

Gospel music

See also

Christian contemporary music

Phonograph records—Gospel music

Shirley Caesar belts the gospel according to God and Grammy. K. Hubbard. il pors *People Wkly* 28:85-6 N 9 '87

Goss-Custard, John

Hard times on mussel beach. il *Nat Hist* 96:64-71 Mr '87

Gossip

See also

Rumor

Gossip: why we love it. S. Nelson. il *Seventeen* 46:140-1 O '87

How to make the grapevine work for you [excerpt from Managing people at work desk guide] T. L. Quick. *Work Woman* 12:23 S '87

Intelligencer. J. Kasindorf. *See* issues of New York beginning August 19, 1985

New-wave gossip [Hollywood Kids] R. Alleman. il *Vogue* 177:102 Ag '87

Office gossip: is your name on more lips than Chap Stick? J. Stone. *Glamour* 85:21 Ap '87

Anecdotes, facetiae, satire, etc.

You didn't hear this from me, but . . . the sexiest man alive has cooties. I. Shoales. il *Mademoiselle* 93:98-9+ Jl '87

Gosudarstvennij Universalnij Magazin (Moscow, Soviet Union) *See* GUM (Moscow, Soviet Union)

Gotham Bar and Grill (New York, N.Y.) *See* New York (N.Y.)—Restaurants, nightclubs, bars, etc.

Gotham Book Mart (New York, N.Y.) *See* Booksellers and bookselling—New York (State)

Gothic [film] *See* Motion picture reviews—Single works

Gothic art *See* Art, Gothic

Gothic revival architecture *See* Architecture, Gothic revival

Gothic revival furniture *See* Furniture, Gothic revival

Gothic revival house decoration *See* House decoration, Gothic revival

Gotlieb, Allan E.

about

The ambassador's tale. M. McDonald. il por *Macleans* 100:21 Je 8 '87

Goto, Midori *See* Midori, 1971-

Goto, Yasuo

about

Conspicuous consumer. H. Katayama. il por *Forbes* 139:252 Je 15 '87

Gott, Peter

Is your doctor over-doctoring you? il *Redbook* 169:112-13+ O '87

Gott, Peter

about

The esoteric art of splitting (and fitting) wood shingles. D. Petersen. il *Mother Earth News* 105:56-9 My/Je '87

Gottfried, Gilbert

about

Manic comic Gilbert Gottfried cops a scene—and a career boost—in Beverly Hills cop II. F. A. Bernstein. il pors *People Wkly* 28:42+ Jl 20 '87

Psycho-nebbish. J. Sherman. por *Vogue* 177:130 O '87

Gottfried, Paul

Legality, legitimacy, and Carl Schmitt. *Natl Rev* 39:52-4 Ag 28 '87

Gotti, John

about

The "Dapper Don" beats a rap. J. S. DeMott. il por *Time* 129:18 Mr 23 '87

A jury sides with 'the Dapper Don'. *Newsweek* 109:30 Mr 23 '87

Gottlieb, Annie

Fit at forty: the new "middle age". *Vogue* 177:270 O '87

How to get what you want—nicely. *McCalls* 114:54-5 Ja '87

What you write is what you are. il *McCalls* 115:175+ N '87

Gottlieb, Danny

about

Blindfold test. B. Milkowski. por *Down Beat* 54:53 Je '87

Gottlieb, Michael

about

Mannequin [film] Reviews

Macleans 100:57 Mr 9 '87. P. Young

Gottlieb, Robert Adams, 1931-

about

After Shawn. E. Diamond. il por *N Y* 20:14+ Je 8 '87

The fate of the earth. E. Diamond. il por *N Y* 20:12-13 Ja 26 '87

Fear and loathing at the New Yorker. M. Salter. il por *Macleans* 100:46 Ja 26 '87

Gottlieb to leave Knopf for New Yorker. por *Publ Wkly* 231:20 Ja 23 '87

Gottlieb, Robert Adams, 1931-—about—cont.
Shawn with the wind. A. Gingold. il *New Repub* 196:10-12
F 9 '87
The squawk of the town. J. Alter. il pors *Newsweek*
109:83 Ja 26 '87
Still here at the New Yorker. B. Gill. il *N Y Times
Book Rev* 92:1+ O 4 '87
The talk of the town. J. Kelly. il pors *Time* 129:69
Ja 26 '87

Gottlieb, William
Healing garden. See issues of Rodale's Organic Gardening
beginning August 1987

Gottovi, Sara L.
It's time to raise the minimum wage. por *Seventeen*
46:126 Ag '87

Gottschalk, Marie
Political reform in China. il *Nation* 244:677-80 My 23
'87

Goucher College
The one and only [J. Monheit, first male student] por
Time 129:68 My 18 '87

Goudinoff, Peter, and Tobias, Sheila
Arizona airhead. *New Repub* 197:15-16 O 26 '87

Gough, Pauline B.
The key to improving schools: an interview with William
Glasser. il *Phi Delta Kappan* 68:656-62 My '87

Goulart, Frances Sheridan
Hugging your way to health. il *Saturday Evening Post*
259:26+ Mr '87
Test your pet IQ. il *Saturday Evening Post* 259:32+
Ja/F '87

Gould, Beryl
Adopt an aspidistra. il *Flower Gard* 31:74 Ap/My '87
Chinese hibiscus. il *Flower Gard* 31:48+ O/N '87
Grow a goldfish in a pot. il *Flower Gard* 31:13 O/N
'87

Gould, Carol
Keeper of the flame [interview with R. E. H. Hadingham]
il pors *World Tennis* 35:46+ Jl '87

Gould, Carole
Where are the cheerleaders for a mother's daily marathon?
il *Glamour* 85:178 N '87

Gould, Cheryl
'Lines straight out of my life'. il por *Newsweek* 110:50
D 28 '87

Gould, Dick
about
Good as Gould. L.-M. Singer. il por *World Tennis* 35:41-3
D '87

Gould, Glenn, 1932-1982
about
Glenn Gould at the Metropolitan Museum. E. W. Said.
Nation 245:533-5 N 7 '87

Gould, Gordon
about
The end of a long patent fight. *Sci News* 132:349 N
28 '87
Vindicated! K. Hannon. por *Forbes* 140:35-6 D 14 '87

Gould, Irving, 1919-
about
Why did heads roll at Commodore? G. Lewis. il por
Bus Week p114 My 11 '87

Gould, James L., 1945-, and Marler, Peter
Learning by instinct. il *Sci Am* 256:74-85 Ja '87

Gould, Meredith, and Stephano, José Luis
Electrical responses of eggs to acrosomal protein similar
to those induced by sperm. bibl f il *Science* 235:1654-6
Mr 27 '87

Gould, Mitch
Probing the Phobian storehouse. por *Space World*
X-12-288:39 D '87

Gould, Stephen Jay, 1941-
Animals and us. il *N Y Rev Books* 34:20-5 Je 25 '87
Darwinism defined: the difference between fact and
theory. il *Discover* 8:64-5+ Ja '87
The lesson of the dinosaurs: evolution didn't inevitably
lead to us. il *Discover* 8:51 Mr '87
The terrifying normalcy of AIDS. il *N Y Times Mag*
p32-3 Ap 19 '87
This view of life. See issues of Natural History
The verdict on creationism. il *N Y Times Mag* p32+
Jl 19 '87
about
Stephen Jay Gould [interview] J. Tierney. il por *Roll
Stone* p38-9+ Ja 15 '87
Bibliography
The metaphor and the rock. F. J. Sulloway. il *N Y
Rev Books* 34:37-40 My 28 '87

Gould, Stephen Jay, 1941-, and others
Asymmetry of lineages and the direction of evolutionary
time. il *Science* 236:1437-41 Je 12 '87

Gould Inc.
The case for the $435 hammer [Navy contract] J. Fairhall.
Wash Mon 18:47-8+ Ja '87
Taking the pledge. S. B. Weiner. *Forbes* 139:41-2 Je
29 '87

Goulianos, Joan Rodman
(ed) See Dougan, Cindy. 3 children who needed a medical
miracle

Gourds
How the world puts gourds to work. R. Conniff. il
Int Wildl 17:18-24 My/Je '87

Gouré, Leon
Developing Soviet forces. *Society* 24:50-5 Jl/Ag '87

Gourmet food industry *See* Food industry

Gourmets *See* Food critics and criticism; Gastronomy

Gourse, Leslie
The wizard of ahs. il pors *Horizon* 30:34-7 Jl/Ag '87

Gousha, Richard P., and others
Standards are changing for school administrators. *Educ
Dig* 53:25-7 S '87

Gout
Oh, my aching toe! G. M. Kaplan. *Nations Bus* 75:68
Ja '87
So you thought gout was a thing of the past? I. Pave.
il *Bus Week* p129 O 5 '87

Gouzé, Mary Ann
To love a daughter, to love an addict. il *Ladies Home
J* 104:107-9+ S '87

Government, Resistance to
See also
Hunger strikes
Protests, demonstrations, etc.
Revolutions
Body on the line [B. Willson run over by train while
protesting against U.S. arms shipments to Central
America] B. Kessler. *Nation* 245:329 O 3 '87
Does a protester have a right to damage a missile site?
D. O. Relin. il *Sch Update* 120:32 N 20 '87
The fear of doing nothing [jailed anti-abortionist J.
Andrews] C. W. Colson. il *Christ Today* 31:72 My
15 '87
One night in the Beatty lockup [anti-nuclear protest]
L. R. Peattie. il *Commonweal* 114:140-3 Mr 13 '87
Anecdotes, facetiae, satire, etc.
Up the rebels! M. Ivins. il *Progressive* 51:28 N '87

Government accounting
Accounting and accountability [address, May 6, 1987]
D. R. Kullberg. *Vital Speeches Day* 53:606-8 Jl 15
'87
How much does Uncle Sam owe? J. C. Szabo. il *Nations
Bus* 75:42 Ag '87
How the government cooks the books. P. Longman.
Wash Mon 19:47-52 Jl/Ag '87
International aspects
Sound financial reporting by nation states [address, Sep-
tember 29, 1986] M. Egol. *Vital Speeches Day* 53:176-8
Ja 1 '87

Government advertising *See* Government publicity

Government agencies
See also
Regulatory agencies
United States—Executive departments

Government airplanes *See* Airplanes, Government

Government and agriculture *See* Agricultural administration

Government and art *See* Art and state

Government and aviation *See* Aviation and state

Government and business *See* Industry and state

Government and church *See* Church and state

Government and dance *See* Dance and state

Government and literature *See* Literature and state

Government and medicine *See* Medical policy

Government and science *See* Science and state

Government and technology *See* Technology and state

Government and the arts *See* Arts and state

Government and the press
See also
Pentagon Papers
Presidents—Press relations
Reagan, Ronald, 1911-—Press relations
Senators—Press relations
Breaking a confidence [O. North revealed as source
of government leaks to news organizations] L. Zucker-
man. il *Time* 130:61 Ag 3 '87
Can we talk? [efforts to avoid leaks from the Senate
Select Committee investigating Iran arms-contra aid
case] il *Time* 129:22 F 16 '87
D.C. mayor Barry sues U.S. Atty. over 'leak a week'.
Jet 72:5 Jl 13 '87
Eosat to mount challenge to Landsat restrictions [use
by news media] *Aviat Week Space Technol* 127:26-7
N 2 '87

Government and the press—*cont.*

Government reins on private satellites [coping with press use of photos from space] J. Eberhart. *Sci News* 132:87 Ag 8 '87

How well has press used its freedom? [views of Maynard Parker and others] *USA Today (Periodical)* 116:12-13 D '87

Leak-a-boo. M. Hosenball. *New Repub* 197:23-5 O 12 '87

Media satellite could complicate military, foreign policy activities [news gathering] *Aviat Week Space Technol* 126:22-3 Je 8 '87

Newswatch from space [cover story] J. Eberhart. *Sci News* 132:28-9 Jl 11 '87

Not available for comment. J. Saltzman. il *USA Today (Periodical)* 116:73 S '87

Purposeful leaks [congressional foreign policy leaks] *Natl Rev* 39:20 S 11 '87

Secret sharers [leaks from Congress and the Reagan administration] il *Time* 130:14+ Jl 27 '87

Space censors? [satellite photos] A. A. Lappen. il *Forbes* 140:12 S 7 '87

A spy satellite for the press? E. Marshall. il *Science* 238:1346-8 D 4 '87

Stop press! Launch satellite! J. Heckman. il *Space World* X-8-284:24-6 Ag '87

Two leaks, but by whom? [O. North's charges against Congress] il por *Newsweek* 110:16 Jl 27 '87

Why the First Amendment is not incompatible with national security interests [address, January 14, 1987] M. L. Feldman. *Vital Speeches Day* 53:394-8 Ap 15 '87

History

The big leak [U.S. war plans against Germany in 1941] T. J. Fleming. il por *Am Herit* 38:64-71 D '87

International aspects

Freedom under attack around the world. il *World Press Rev* 34:44-8 F '87

The media's new spies in the sky. C. R. Mohan. il *World Press Rev* 34:55-6 Je '87

The unfree press. *Nation* 245:435-6 O 24 '87

Canada

See also

Mulroney, Brian—Press relations

Conflicts and credibility gaps [media coverage of case against S. Stevens] G. Bain. il *Macleans* 100:52 D 21 '87

Fever in a climate of scandal [reporting on the Oerlikon affair] G. Bain. il *Macleans* 100:49 F 23 '87

Harsh lessons from an inquiry [S. Stevens affair and the press] G. Bain. il *Macleans* 100:44 Ag 24 '87

China

The revenge of the intellectuals [Humanities: theory and criticism magazine] *Newsweek* 109:36 Mr 2 '87

'Thought examination' in China. *World Press Rev* 34:59-60 Jl '87

Czechoslovakia

Falling for a Warsaw Pact dame [British journalist's experiences] J. Simpson. il *Harpers* 274:58-62 Je '87

Developing countries

Assembly calls for co-operation in a new world information and communication order. *UN Chron* 24:96-7 F '87

Great Britain

BBC says, 'No, prime minister'. R. Laver. il *Macleans* 100:45 F 16 '87

The blowup over the BBC. *Newsweek* 109:43 F 16 '87

Britain: tinker, tailor, censor, spy [government's press ban on ex-agent P. Wright's memoirs] J. N. Baker. il *Newsweek* 110:32 Ag 17 '87

How not to silence a spy [furor over P. Wright's Spycatcher] L. Zuckerman. il *Time* 130:55 Ag 17 '87

Imperial reach. D. Campbell. *Nation* 245:669-70 D 5 '87

New statesman downed by law. C. Hitchens. il *Nation* 244:217-19 F 21 '87

Spooked [controversy surrounding publication of Spycatcher by P. Wright] M. Hosenball. *New Repub* 197:13-14 Ag 31 '87

A tale of treachery [Britain's futile efforts to suppress publication of P. Wright's Spycatcher] M. McIver. por *Macleans* 100:42-3 Jl 27 '87

Tales of a spy writer [excerpts from P. Wright's controversial book Spycatcher printed in British press despite government ban] M. McIver. il por *Macleans* 100:52 My 11 '87

Israel

Israel's censored Palestinians. J. Greenberg. *World Press Rev* 34:56 My '87

Korea (South)

The news from Seoul. *Harpers* 275:13-14 Ag '87

Unchaining South Korean journalists. S. J. Ungar. il *U S News World Rep* 103:31 Ag 10 '87

Nicaragua

A bumpy road to democracy [reopening of La prensa] H. Anderson. il *Newsweek* 110:38-9 O 5 '87

How "La prensa" was silenced; tr. by Steven Blakemore. J. Chamorro. *Commentary* 83:39-44 Ja '87

Minority report. C. Hitchens. *Nation* 244:458 Ap 11 '87

"Our people cannot be silenced" [censorship of La prensa]; tr. by Steven Blakemore. J. Chamorro. *Read Dig* 130:169-70+ My '87

Playing to the crowd [discussion of April 11, 1987 article, Minority report] C. Hitchens. *Nation* 244:564-5 My 2 '87

South Africa

A farewell to South Africa. A. Cowell. il *N Y Times Mag* p36-9+ Ja 25 '87

Getting the story (I) [J. Qwelane, black reporter on the Johannesburg Star] W. Finnegan. *New Yorker* 63:31-4+ Jl 13 '87

Getting the story (II) [J. Qwelane, black reporter on the Johannesburg Star] W. Finnegan. *New Yorker* 63:40-2+ Jl 20 '87

South African clampdown. B. Shelby. il *World Press Rev* 34:43 F '87

Stiff challenge, swift reaction. W. Svoboda. il *Time* 129:38 Ja 19 '87

Soviet Union

See also

Daniloff-Zakharov espionage case, 1986

TASS (Soviet Union)

A close-up look at *glasnost* [CBS special Seven days in May] J. Alter. il *Newsweek* 109:62 Je 29 '87

Curbing *glasnost* [Y. Ligachev calls for press restraint] por *Time* 130:40 O 5 '87

Editor Gorbo. D. Kimelman. *New Repub* 197:13-14 S 7 '87

Foreign correspondents on Soviet changes. il *World Press Rev* 34:30-2 Je '87

'Glasnost' in print. L. Branson. il *World Press Rev* 34:34-5 Ag '87

Glasnost vs. glasnost. C. Krauthammer. *New Repub* 197:14-15 D 28 '87

Putting it on the line. J. Alter. il *Newsweek* 110:32+ D 14 '87

Reinventing politics in the Soviet press. R. K. Manoff. il *Progressive* 51:18 My '87

Testing *glasnost's* boundaries. D. Brand. il *Time* 130:54 S 7 '87

Troubled waters [Kremlin infighting] B. Crozier. *Natl Rev* 39:24 Ag 28 '87

The USSR and the press. P. Taubman. *Current* 291:28-33 Mr/Ap '87

United States

See Government and the press

Government auctions *See* Auctions

Government automobiles *See* Automobiles, Government

Government bonds *See* Bonds, Government

Government contracts *See* Contracts, Government

Government corporations *See* Corporations, Government

Government-developed inventions and patents *See* Patents and government-developed inventions

Government documents *See* Government publications

Government employees

See also

Black government employees

Bureaucracy

Civil service

Conflict of interests (Public office)

Congressmen—Staff

Postal employees

Presidents—Staff

Public officers

State employees

United States. Navy—Civilian employees

White House (Washington, D.C.)—Employees

Somebody has to do it [deterioration of government employees] D. Gergen. il *U S News World Rep* 102:64 Je 29 '87

Crime

Truth and reason upside down [CIA employees accused of selling rare postage stamps that were government property] J. V. Lamar, Jr. il *Time* 130:32 S 14 '87

Health and hygiene

Big John [guidelines for administering drug tests to federal workers] il *Time* 129:19 Mr 2 '87

Pissing contests [guidelines for drug testing] *Harpers* 274:19-20 My '87

Reagan administration drug testing program [federal employees] *Congr Dig* 66:131-60 My '87

Government employees—*cont.*

Legal status, laws, etc.

High Court splits on search of public employee's office [O'Connor v. Ortega] T. J. Flygare. *Phi Delta Kappan* 68:792-4 Je '87

Sworn to silence. D. A. Demac. il *Progressive* 51:29-32 My '87

Taking the Fifth [interpretation of Fifth Amendment rights concerning participants in Iran arms scandal in light of Reagan administration attack on the rights of public employees] C. Becker. *Nation* 244:101 Ja 31 '87

Pensions

See Civil service pensions

Recruiting

The C.I.A. goes back to college. J. Wiener. il *Nation* 245:719-20 D 12 '87

Salaries, allowances, etc.

See also

Public officers—Salaries, allowances, etc.

Revenge of the nerds [federal employee wages excluded from student loan collection efforts] F. Zakaria. *New Repub* 197:16-17 S 14-21 '87

Great Britain

Anecdotes, facetiae, satire, etc.

The hospital without patients [excerpt from The complete Yes, minister] J. Lynn and A. Jay. *Wash Mon* 19:41-6 Jl/Ag '87

Government entertaining

126 VIPs chosen for historic White House dinner during summit. S. Booker. il *Jet* 73:4-6+ D 28 '87-Ja 4 '88

The banquet beat [Washington, D.C.] M. Aronson. *New Repub* 196:11-12 Je 22 '87

Derby Day breakfast for 12,000! [given by Kentucky's Governor M. L. Collins] J. Siroto. il por *McCalls* 114:108-11 Ap '87

Leonard is lionized on Capitol Hill as guest of Kan. Sen. Robert Dole [boxer S. R. Leonard] il pors *Jet* 72:12 My 11 '87

Not since Jefferson dined alone [dinner at the White House for the Gorbachevs] H. Sidey. il *Time* 130:22 D 21 '87

Warwick wows Reagan, French premier, and others at White House. il por *Jet* 72:6 Ap 20 '87

China

China's removable feast [limiting state banquets] il *Newsweek* 110:53 S 14 '87

Government ethics *See* Political ethics

Government finance *See* Finance

Government helicopters *See* Helicopters, Government

Government housing projects *See* Housing projects

Government information

See also

Classified information

Computers—Government use

Executive privilege (Government information)

Freedom of information

Government and the press

Government publications

National Security Archive

Official secrets

Tax returns

Telephone—Government use

United States. National Archives and Records Administration

Government investigations

Challenging the special prosecutors [Justice Dept. takes a stand against independent investigations] D. Baer and G. Borger. il *U S News World Rep* 102:24 Mr 9 '87

Debate over special prosecutors. R. Lacayo. il *Time* 130:73 D 28 '87

Did Robert Bork bend the rules in a 1984 case? [failure to bow out of civil rights case in which a liberal group was seeking the appointment of a special prosecutor] T. Gest. il por *U S News World Rep* 103:12 Jl 20 '87

The petty inquisitors. M. Charen. il *Natl Rev* 39:36+ D 18 '87

Picking on the prosecutors [challenging the constitutionality of special prosecutors] D. Beckwith. il *Time* 129:31 Mr 9 '87

The young pol's guide to the brave new world [grueling confirmation hearings] D. Brooks. il *Natl Rev* 39:28-30+ Ap 10 '87

Government lending

See also

Black business enterprises—Federal aid

Export-Import Bank of the United States

Farm Credit System (U.S.)

Minority business enterprises—Federal aid

Savings and loan associations—Federal aid

Small business—Federal aid

United States. Small Business Administration

Going once, going twice—going nowhere fast [loan sales by federal government] R. Brady. il *Bus Week* p35 Jl 13 '87

Tough as marshmallows [collecting on outstanding loans] J. Novack. il *Forbes* 139:44 Mr 23 '87

Uncle Sam the cosigner [off-budget financing] R. Thomas. il *Newsweek* 109:50+ Je 8 '87

Uncle Sam's loan sale: low prices, no guarantees. H. Gleckman. *Bus Week* p41-2 Ja 26 '87

Government liability

See also

Insurance, Government liability

Supreme Court extends limits on suits by military personnel. M. Mecham. *Aviat Week Space Technol* 126:26 My 25 '87

Canada

Judgment of liability [reversal of personal injury damage award in M. McErlean vs. Brampton, Ont.] R. Corelli. il por *Macleans* 100:52 O 12 '87

Government loans *See* Government lending

Government National Mortgage Association securities *See* Mortgage bonds and notes

Government officials *See* Public officers

Government ownership

See also

Corporations, Government

Electric utilities—Government ownership

Privatization

Railroads and state

Peru

The bankers' hero [M. Vargas Llosa leads opposition to A. García Perez's efforts to nationalize financial institutions] A. Cockburn. *Nation* 245:402 O 17 '87

Judging García [nationalizing financial institutions] L. Rogers. il *World Press Rev* 34:46 O '87

Mario meets Crazy Horse [M. Vargas Llosa leads opposition to government takeover of financial institutions] H. G. Chua-Eoan. il *Time* 130:30 S 7 '87

Peru's bad boy is starting to look like a desperate man [A. García Perez moves to nationalize financial institutions] J. Ryser. il por *Bus Week* p55 Ag 17 '87

Government Printing Office (U.S.) *See* United States. Government Printing Office

Government publications

See also

Classified information

United States. Government Printing Office

Bibliography

Publications. See issues of Department of State Bulletin

Source material. J. A. Kreslins. See issues of Foreign Affairs beginning Fall 1986

Translations into Spanish

Resources for Hispanic and other minorities [aged] il *Aging* no355:23 '87

Government publicity

An ad agency's war with the Army [N. W. Ayer] P. Dwyer. *Bus Week* p102+ Ap 13 '87

Government records *See* Public records

Government regulation of industry *See* Industry and state

Government regulatory agencies *See* Regulatory agencies

Government secrecy *See* Classified information; Official secrets

Government service *See* Public officers

Government service contracts *See* Contracts, Government

Government spending policy *See* United States—Appropriations and expenditures

Government use of computers *See* Computers—Government use

Governors

See also

National Governors' Association

The best of state capitols. il *U S News World Rep* 103:52-3 D 21 '87

Travel

Innocents abroad [governors promoting states] *Fortune* 116:12+ N 23 '87

Gow, Anthony J., and Tucker, Walter B., III

Physical properties of sea ice discharged from Fram Strait. bibl f il map *Science* 236:436-9 Ap 24 '87

Gower, John

about

Serenity on a scrap heap of dreams. J. Barber. il por *Macleans* 100:41 Ja 26 '87

Gowin, Steve

Sound by Splet. il *Theatre Crafts* 21:71-2 F '87

Gowns, Wedding *See* Wedding clothes

Goya [opera] See Menotti, Gian Carlo, 1911-

Goya Foods, Inc.
Goya: a lot more than black beans and sofrito. F. McCoy. il *Bus Week* p137-8 D 7 '87
Goya: luz y sombra [dance] *See* Dance reviews—Single works
Goyette, Thomas
about
"Bail out, Tommy! Eject!". P. Michelmore. il *Read Dig* 130:106-11 F '87
GPA Airbus A320 (Firm)
International companies unite in A320 leasing venture. *Aviat Week Space Technol* 126:36 Ja 19 '87
GPO *See* United States. Government Printing Office
GQ (Periodical) *See* Gentlemen's quarterly
Grable, Ron
Technologue. See issues of Motor Trend
Grace, Princess of Monaco, 1929-1982
about
My romance with Grace Kelly [excerpt from In my own fashion] O. Cassini. il pors *Ladies Home J* 104:32+ S '87
Grace (Theology)
Empirical liturgy: the search for grace. A. M. Greeley. *America* 157:379-83+ N 21 '87
A meditation after Easter. D. K. Mano. *Natl Rev* 39:60 Ap 24 '87
Grace & Rothschild
State of Grace. B. Kanner. il *N Y* 20:16+ Ap 6 '87
Graceland
Amazing Graceland. V. Balfour. il pors *Life* 10:44-6+ S '87
Greetings from Graceland. B. Greene. il por *Esquire* 108:53-4+ D '87
Graco Inc.
Paint by the numbers. T. Jaffe. il *Forbes* 140 Sp Issue:402 O 26 '87
Grad, Harold, d. 1986
about
Obituary
Phys Today 40:86 Mr '87. A. A. Blank
Grade repetition (Education)
Left back a grade: how to break the news. F. Roberts. *Parents* 62:60+ Je '87
What doesn't work: explaining policies of retention in the early grades. M. L. Smith and L. A. Shepard. bibl f il *Phi Delta Kappan* 69:129-34 O '87
Grading and marking (Students)
See also
Grade repetition (Education)
Cleveland pays for its A's [Scholarship-in-Escrow Program] il *Newsweek* 110:66 Ag 31 '87
Dealing with child's low grades. il *USA Today (Periodical)* 115:11 Ap '87
Judge: get good grades or go to jail for failing [Judge P. Katic's program in Hammond, Ind.] *Jet* 73:24 D 14 '87
Grading of meat *See* Meat—Grading
Graduate Management Admission Council
Group pushes MBAs for minorities with forum tour. *Jet* 72:24 Ag 31 '87
Wanted: black M.B.A.s. M. Mallory. il *Black Enterp* 18:28 O '87
Graduate schools *See* Colleges and universities—Graduate work
Graduate students, Black *See* Black students
Graduate students, Foreign *See* Foreign students
Graduate work *See* Colleges and universities—Graduate work
Graduates, College *See* College graduates
Graduates, High school *See* High school graduates
Graduation addresses *See* Baccalaureate addresses
Graduation requirements (High school) *See* High schools—Graduation requirements
Graduations *See* Commencements
Graf, Gary R.
No business like space business. il *Space World* X-5-281:21-3 My '87
Off to see the wizard. il *Space World* X-4-280:26-9 Ap '87
Graf, Rudolf F.
(jt. auth) *See* Sheets, William, and Graf, Rudolf F.
Graf, Rudolf F., and Sheets, William
SCA/FM-stereo receiver (I) [cover story] il *Radio-Electron* 58:39-44+ Ag '87
SCA/FM-stereo receiver (II). il *Radio-Electron* 58:46+ S '87
Video effects generator (I) [cover story] il *Radio-Electron* 58:41-5+ S '87
Video effects generator (II). il *Radio-Electron* 58:48-52+ O '87

Graf, Steffi
about
Germany shows a pair of aces. T. Callahan. il pors *Time* 129:58-60 Je 29 '87
Is this Graf's championship season? S. Flink. il por *World Tennis* 34:18+ My '87
On and up with Steffi. J. Diaz. il por *Sports Illus* 67:92 N 30 '87
One step to stardom. J. Ryan. il pors *Women's Sports Fitness* 9:30-2 Je '87
Score one more for Steffi. F. Deford. il pors *Sports Illus* 66:38-42 Je 15 '87
She's no. 2 with a bullet. D. S. Looney. il pors *Sports Illus* 66:34-6+ Mr 16 '87
Steffi Graf's prime time. P. Axthelm. il por *Newsweek* 109:51 Mr 23 '87
Strokes of genius: Steffi Graf peaks for the U.S. Open. M. Stone. il pors *N Y* 20:48-52 Ag 31 '87
This little tennis star goes to market. P. R. Range. il pors *U S News World Rep* 103:46 S 7 '87
Unglaublich! R. Wetzsteon. il pors *Sport Mag* 78:35-40 D '87
Yes she can. G. M. Heldman. il pors *World Tennis* 35:18-21+ N '87
Graff, Don
Torn curtain. il *Channels* 7:68-9 Jl/Ag '87
A Washington portrait. il *Travel Holiday* 168:51-5 O '87
Graff, Harvey J.
(jt. auth) *See* Arnove, Robert F. (Robert Frederick), and Graff, Harvey J.
about
Literacy at the barricades. J. W. Tuttleton. *Commentary* 84:45-8 Jl '87
Graff, Yveta Synek
Water nymph. il *Opera News* 51:32-3 F 28 '87
Graffiti
Graffiti removal. G. Branson. il *Fam Handyman* 37:58 F '87
Miscellaneous ramblings [walls of Road & track offices] J. Dinkel. il *Road Track* 38:47-9 Je '87
Welcome to my nightmare: the graffiti of homeless youth. G. C. Luna. il *Society* 24:73-8 S/O '87
Graffman, Naomi
On the road to Biloxi. il por *N Y Times Mag* p72-5+ N 22 '87
Grafting
New grafting technique [work of Gary Meltzer and David Frybarger] D. Duchin. il *Rodale's Org Gard* 34:62-6 Ja '87
Grafting of brain tissue *See* Brain—Transplantation
Grafting of skin *See* Skin grafting
Grafton, Anthony
Portrait of Justus Lipsius. *Am Sch* 56:382-90 Summ '87
Graglia, Lino A.
A theory of power. il *Natl Rev* 39:33-6 Jl 17 '87
Graham, Benjamin
about
The father of value investing. il por *Fortune* 116 Sp Issue:48 Fall '87
A message from Ben Graham. M. Schifrin. *Forbes* 140:258 N 30 '87
Graham, Bill
about
Bill Graham reins in the creeps who kill horses for profit. D. Van Biema. il pors *People Wkly* 28:46-8 Jl 20 '87
Graham, Billy, 1918-
about
Billy Graham postpones China trip. il por *Christ Today* 31:54 O 2 '87
Under the tent with John Paul. *Time* 130:55 Jl 13 '87
"We may never go home". B. Spring. il pors *Christ Today* 31:14-15 Mr 20 '87
Graham, Bob, 1936-
about
NPCA names Sen. Graham Conservationist of Year. il por *Natl Parks* 61:36 Ja/F '87
Graham, Dale K.
From the publisher. See issues of Antiques & Collecting Hobbies beginning January 1986
From the publisher. See issues of Hobbies through December 1985
Graham, Dan, 1942-
about
Dan Graham at Marian Goodman. W. Thompson. il *Art Am* 75:153 D '87

Graham, Daniel Robert *See* Graham, Bob, 1936-
Graham, Edward, d. 1987
about
Obituary
Jet 72:18 Ap 20 '87
Graham, Frank, 1925-
Birdland. See issues of Audubon
Graham, Harrison
about
Find 7 bodies in Philly, jail tenant. *Jet* 72:18 Ag 31
'87
Graham, Janis
What's new in dentistry. *McCalls* 114:107-8+ F '87
Graham, Jenifer
about
A teen fights for frog rights, and bio may never be
the same. il por *People Wkly* 27:109 My 25 '87
Graham, John D., 1886-1961
about
John Graham: brilliant amateur? P. Brach. il *Art Am*
75:130-7 D '87
Modernism's essential eccentric. J. Perl. il *Vogue* 177:36
Je '87
Graham, Jorie, 1951-
What the end is for [poem] *New Yorker* 62:35
F 9 '87
Graham, Loren R.
Science and technology. *Nation* 244:804-8 Je 13 '87
Graham, Martha
about
Canticle for innocent comedians [dance] Reviews
N Y il 20:102 N 2 '87. T. Tobias
Celebration [dance] Reviews
N Y il 20:102-3 N 2 '87. T. Tobias
Past masters and schlockmeisters. L. A. Jacobs. *New
Leader* 70:22-3 N 2 '87
Peter Sparling: new positions. J. Gruen. il pors *Dance
Mag* 61:66-9 Ap '87
Graham, N. E., and Barnett, T. P.
Sea surface temperature, surface wind divergence, and
convection over tropical oceans. bibl f il *Science*
238:657-9 O 30 '87
Graham, Patricia Albjerg
Black teachers: a drastically scarce resource. bibl f il
Phi Delta Kappan 68:598-605 Ap '87
Graham, Robert
War is crippling Nicaragua's economy. *World Press Rev*
34:50 Jl '87
Graham, Roberta L.
The fine art of fly fishing. il *Women's Sports Fitness*
9:52-4+ My '87
Lynne Cox comes in from the cold. il *Women's Sports
Fitness* 9:12-13 N '87
Graham, Sheilah
The room where Scott died. il por *N Y Times Mag*
p20-1 Jl 26 '87
Graham, Tim
The year of the royal mess [excerpt from The royal
year; cover story] il *Good Housekeep* 205:138-41+ N
'87
Graham (Martha) Dance Company *See* Martha Graham
Dance Company
Grahm, Randall
about
Identified flying object. F. J. Prial. il por *N Y Times
Mag* p30 Ja 4 '87
Grail in opera
Who is the Grail? M. O. Lee. il *Opera News* 51:16-19
Ap 11 '87
Grain
See also
Amaranth
Cooking—Grain
Corn
Feeds—Grain
Millet
Quinoa
Rice
Wheat
Gene transfer in cereals. E. C. Cocking and M. R.
Davey. bibl f *Science* 236:1259-62 Je 5 '87
Progress toward engineering monocots. L. Tangley.
BioScience 37:462 Jl/Ag '87
Diseases and pests
They'll bug you this summer. B. Freese. il *Success Farm*
85:34C Je '87
Drying
See also
Grain dryers
Drying. il *Success Farm* 85:16 Ag '87

Handling
See Grain handling
Harvesting
Would your grain pass our test? [cover story; special
section] D. Mowitz and C. Finck. il *Success Farm*
85:11-17 Ag '87
Marketing
PIK and Roll: you sell, buy; then sell again. *Success
Farm* 85:62F O '87
Program guides you through marketing blizzard [Grain
Marketing Advisor expert system] *Success Farm* 85
no6:18AX Mr '87
Prices
See also
Agricultural administration
Farmers shouldn't count their chickens quite yet. J.
N. Frank. il *Bus Week* p61 My 25 '87
Flat markets? Look again. G. Johnston. il *Success Farm*
85:7 N '87
Storage
See also
Bins
1.7 billion bushels without a home. G. Johnston and
D. Mowitz. il *Success Farm* 85:32-3 Je '87
Spoilage threatens sea of grain. D. Mowitz. il *Success
Farm* 85:18O My '87
Storage. il *Success Farm* 85:17 Ag '87
Yield
For Moscow, a harvest of good news. D. Stanglin and
J. Trimble. il *U S News World Rep* 103:79 S 28
'87
Grain alcohol as fuel *See* Alcohol as fuel
Grain bins *See* Bins
Grain cooperatives *See* Agriculture, Cooperative
Grain dryers
Energy usage
Machinery. D. Mowitz and C. Finck. il *Success Farm*
85:7 Ag '87
Grain futures *See* Commodity futures
Grain handling
Go-go grain carts. D. Mowitz. il *Success Farm* 85:62N
O '87
Up, up and away with grain. D. Mowitz. il *Success
Farm* 85:62D-62E O '87
Would your grain pass our test? [cover story; special
section] D. Mowitz and C. Finck. il *Success Farm*
85:11-17 Ag '87
Grain in photography *See* Photography—Grain
Grain supply
Use it or lose it. C. Siler. il *Forbes* 140:80+ D 14
'87
Grain trade
See also
Rice—Export-import trade
Wheat trade
Export increases rely on developing markets. T. White.
il *Success Farm* 85 no4:7 F '87
How U.S. farmers rate in world competition. D. Ohrtman.
il *Success Farm* 85:10-13 Ap '87
Graining
Going with the grain of tradition [decorative painting
techniques; work of L. Pardon] S. Wood. il por *Home
Mech* 83:62-3 Mr '87
Grambling State University
Howard, Grambling get fed. funds for anti drug plans.
Jet 73:32 N 2 '87
Sugar Ray Leonard, an Eddie Robinson fan, gifts $250G's
to Grambling. il pors *Jet* 72:50 Jl 13 '87
Graminae *See* Grasses
Gramm, Lou
about
Lou Gramm: nothing but the truth [interview] por *Teen*
31:78 Ag '87
Gramm, Phil, 1942-
Should the Boren Amendment approach to curtailing
PAC's be adopted? [excerpts from debate, August 11,
1986] *Congr Dig* 66:57+ F '87
about
The battle-ax of the republic. P. Magnusson. il por
Bus Week p78-9 Ag 31 '87
A Texas tornado hits the Senate. E. H. Methvin. il
por *Read Dig* 130:17-18+ Ap '87
Gramm, William Philip *See* Gramm, Phil, 1942-
Gramm-Rudman bill *See* Budget
Grammar
See also
Sentences (Grammar)
Grammy Awards
Anita Baker leads parade of black Grammy winners.
il por *Jet* 71:55-6 Mr 16 '87

Grammy Awards—*cont.*
Gripes about the Grammys. J. Pareles. il *Mademoiselle* 93:78+ F '87
Groovin' at the Grammys: rock sparks '87 awards. M. Coleman. il *Roll Stone* p10-11 Ap 9 '87
Marsalis, Jackson get big votes for Grammys. *Jet* 71:59 Ja 26 '87
Gran Teatre del Liceu *See* Opera—Spain
Graña, César
The bullfight and Spanish national decadence. *Society* 24:33-7 Jl/Ag '87
Granada (Spain)

Historic houses, sites, etc.
See also
　Alhambra (Granada, Spain)
　Generalife (Granada, Spain)
Grand Canyon (Ariz.)
See also
　Colorado River (Colo.-Mexico)
Grand walking at the Grand Canyon. S. Zarrow. il *Prevention* 39:44-6+ My '87
What's new in the ol' Grand? [cover story] R. Monastersky. il map *Sci News* 132:392-5 D 19-26 '87
Grand Canyon National Park (Ariz.)
NTSB cites air tour rules in canyon crash [airliner-helicopter crash, June 18, 1986] *Aviat Week Space Technol* 126:40 Mr 30 '87
Overflight bill includes flight-free zones. *Natl Parks* 61:38 My/Je '87
Overflight rules not tough enough. *Natl Parks* 61:46-8 Mr/Ap '87
Grand Central Art Galleries Educational Association
New educational association promotes realist art. il *Am Artist* 51:90 Ag '87
Grand Champions Resort Development Corporation
A new racquet [C. Pasarell] E. Paris. il por *Forbes* 139:144-5 F 23 '87
Grand Hotel (Mackinac Island, Mich.) *See* Hotels, motels, etc.—Mackinac Island (Mich.)
Grand jury
The high price of indictment [problems of public officials] T. Gest and D. Baer. il *U S News World Rep* 102:23-4 Je 8 '87
Grand Mesa (Colo.)
Grand Mesa, Colorado. R. H. Mohlenbrock. il map *Nat Hist* 96:14-16 My '87
Grand Motors (Firm)
Road to riches: cars for immigrants. J. Foote. il por *Newsweek* 110:48 S 7 '87
Grand Palace (Petrodvorets, Soviet Union) *See* Palaces—Soviet Union
Grand Prix racing *See* Automobile racing; Motorcycle racing
Grand Teton National Park (Wyo.)
BuRec gives up plan to mine in Grand Teton [reconstruction of the Jackson Lake Dam] il *Natl Parks* 61:35 Jl/Ag '87
The Yellowstone Complex. B. G. Norton. il map *Wilderness* 50:26-30 Spr '87
Grandchamp, Gail
about
Woman boxer sues AAU to get amateur status. il por *Jet* 72:49 Jl 20 '87
Grande, Rutilio, 1928-1977
about
A torch held on high. J. R. Brockman. *America* 156:214-16+ Mr 14 '87
Grande Bretagne (Athens, Greece: Hotel) *See* Athens (Greece)—Hotels, motels, etc.
Grandfathers *See* Grandparents
Grandmothers *See* Grandparents
Grandmothers of the Plaza de Mayo (Organization)
Finding the children [identifying Argentine missing children through genetic testing] B. Beckwith. il *Ms* 16:88 S '87
Fingerprints on file: the search for missing children. J. B. Elshtain. il *Commonweal* 114:229-30 Ap 24 '87
Grandparents
See also
　Foster Grandparent Program (U.S.)
America's grandmother fixation [use of term to define women] S. W. Olds. il *Ms* 15:104 Ja '87
A Fathers' Day gift for the whole family [Grandfather remembers, a journal for personal memories] C. Loomis. il *Parents* 62:15 Je '87
Fighting to see the grandkids they love. F. Greve. *50 Plus* 27:18-20 Ap '87
Good enough [nostalgia for fishing with grandfather] G. Hill. il *Field Stream* 92:20 Je '87
A grandmother too soon! [mothers of pregnant teenagers] C. Berman. il *McCalls* 114:84-6 My '87

A grandmother's love. L. J. Aron; B. W. DuBois. il *McCalls* 115:70+ N '87
Grandpa and the kid. D. Sisson. See alternate issues of Field & Stream beginning September 1983
My parents, my children. R. Coles. il *50 Plus* 27:100 F '87
"Nana, I can't visit you". B. Lindeman. il *50 Plus* 27:4 Jl '87
Popularity contest [results of poll on sources of pleasure or satisfaction] J. Queenan. *New Repub* 196:14-15 Mr 23 '87
Roommates [grandfather] M. Apple. il *N Y Times Mag* p68 My 3 '87
Thoroughly modern grandparents. il *USA Today (Periodical)* 115:6-7 My '87
Visit with my grandmother [excerpt from Domestic affairs] J. Maynard. il pors *Ladies Home J* 104:42+ Ap '87

Anecdotes, facetiae, satire, etc.
In the name of progress. R. Baker. il *N Y Times Mag* p18 My 3 '87
What's in a name, Moonbeam? P. F. McManus. il *Outdoor Life* 179:130+ Ap '87

Photographs and photography
Pride & joy. il *50 Plus* 27:50-4 D '87
Les Grands Ballets Canadiens
Montreal troupes light birthday candles at 15 and 30. K. Greenaway. il *Dance Mag* 61:14 N '87
Grandview Resources Inc.
Is there gold in this here hill? G. G. Marcial. *Bus Week* p114 Je 1 '87
Grandy, Fred
about
Iowans have a Grandy Old Party as their G.O.P. Gopher takes a bride in a blizzard. il por *People Wkly* 27:99 Ap 13 '87
Granetz, Marc
Legacies. *New Repub* 197:42 O 5 '87
Granger, Bill
Writing a novel. il *Writer* 100:10-12 Jl '87
Granger, Michele
about
Almost untouchable. H. Hersch. il pors *Sports Illus* 67:24 Ag 24 '87
Faster than a speeding bullet. M. Kort. il por *Ms* 16:90 N '87
Woman to watch: Michele Granger. por *Women's Sports Fitness* 9:25 My '87
Granger, Susan
Jimmy Stewart: It's a wonderful life. il pors *Ladies Home J* 104:142-3+ D '87
Michael J. Fox: TV's favorite son is short of stature but long on talent. por *Ladies Home J* 104:112+ Ap '87
Granite
Granite: real thing and fool-the-eye [kitchen countertops] il *Sunset* 179:112-14+ N '87
Graniteville Co.
Three sparkling turnarounds: can this really be Victor Posner? P. Engardio. il por *Bus Week* p56-7 Jl 27 '87
Grann, Phyllis, 1937-
about
Peter Israel leaves Putnam; Phyllis Grann becomes CEO. pors *Publ Wkly* 232:15 Ag 28 '87
Grannis, Eric
Man of the hour. *Nation* 244:635 My 16 '87
Grant, Cary, 1904-1986
about
Cary Grant [excerpt] W. G. Harris. il pors *Good Housekeep* 205:189-91+ S '87
Cary Grant: "I've lived my life". J. Robinson. il pors *Redbook* 168:28+ Mr '87
Obituary
　Film Comment por 23:78 Ja/F '87. R. Corliss
　Forbes il por 139:25 Ja 12 '87. M. S. Forbes
Poor little rich girl: the tragic story of the real Barbara Hutton. il pors *Redbook* 170:106-11+ D '87
Grant, Charity
Sarabeth Eason [interview] il pors *Ms* 15:60-1+ Ja '87
Grant, Daniel
Art for barter: a cultural currency. *Am Artist* 51:S12+ N '87
Art laws: a handshake, yes, but what are my rights? *Am Artist* 51:16+ My '87
Boxes full of art history. *Am Artist* 51:10+ S '87
Families: the ultimate support system for artists. *Am Artist* 51:70+ O '87
Is there recognition after death? *Am Artist* 51:70-3 Jl '87
Liability insurance for artists. *Am Artist* 51:66-7 Jl '87

Grant, Daniel—*cont.*
The special problems faced by children of famous artists. *Am Artist* 51:76+ O '87
A study in art investment. il *Consum Res Mag* 70:23-5 Ja '87
The unknown soldiers of the art world. *Am Artist* 51:12+ D '87
When artists change styles. *Am Artist* 51:22+ D '87
Grant, Gilbert S.
Paint chips and albatross chicks. il *Sea Front* 33:270-2 Jl/Ag '87
Grant, Gwendolyn Goldsby
Just between us. See issues of Essence beginning May 1983
Grant, Harvey
about
A couple of Grants-in-aid. K. Hannon. il pors *Sports Illus* 66:153 F 9 '87
Grant, Horace
about
A couple of Grants-in-aid. K. Hannon. il pors *Sports Illus* 66:153 F 9 '87
Grant, James
about
Calling credit into question [interview] A. E. Serwer. il por *Fortune* 116:104 Jl 6 '87
Grant, James
(ed) See Rice, Donna. Donna Rice tells her story
Grant, James P., 1922-
about
Lessons for UNICEF. P. Valley. il por *World Press Rev* 34:53-4 Mr '87
One million children with a chance to live [interview] J. Ling. il *World Health* p10-12 Ja/F '87
Grant, John A., and Schultz, Peter H.
Possible tornado-like tracks on Mars. bibl f il maps *Science* 237:883-5 Ag 21 '87
Grant, Jonathan, and Bathmann, Ulrich V.
Swept away: resuspension of bacterial mats regulates benthic-pelagic exchange of sulfur. bibl f il *Science* 236:1472-4 Je 12 '87
Grant, Lee
about
Grant opportunities. L. Rosenberg. por *Harpers Bazaar* 120:139+ Ag '87
Grant, Marcus, and Khan, Inayat
Drug abuse—a call to action. il *World Health* p29 My '87
Grant, Milt
about
Milt Grant's fall: the moral. J. Baker. il *Channels* 7:15 F '87
Grant, Priscilla
Sexual ethics. See issues of Glamour through March 1987
Why women cheat. il *Glamour* 85:148-9+ Jl '87
Grant, Roberta
Why smart men still want dumb women. il *Ladies Home J* 104:78+ S '87
Women and the new midlife crisis. il *Ladies Home J* 104:87-9+ Ag '87
Women: where we are today. *Ladies Home J* 104:94-5+ Mr '87
(ed) See Kennedy, Kristina. Baby on set
Grant, Ulysses S. (Ulysses Simpson), 1822-1885
about
Meeting at the McLean House. R. G. Wilson. il pors *Am Hist Illus* 22:46-9 S '87
Notes and comment [pleading the Fifth during last year in office] *New Yorker* 63:21 Je 22 '87
Grant Broadcasting System Inc.
Milt Grant's fall: the moral. J. Baker. il *Channels* 7:15 F '87
Grants, Research *See* Research grants
Grants-in-aid
AAP endorses Senate bill to change educational block grants. H. Fields. *Publ Wkly* 232:20 Ag 14 '87
An uneasy peace. K. A. Hamblen. bibl f *Des Arts Educ* 88:23-7 Mr/Ap '87
Grant's interest rate observer (Newsletter) *See* Investment newsletters
Granulation, Stellar *See* Stars—Granulation
Granulocyte colony-stimulating factor *See* G-CSF
Granulocyte-macrophage colony-stimulating factor *See* GM-CSF
Granville, Joseph Ensign, 1923-
about
It's a hit and miss business. il por *U S News World Rep* 103:84 S 28 '87

Grape boycott *See* Boycott
Grapefruits
Grapefruit hybrid that needs no sugar: 'Oroblanco'. il *Sunset* 178:236-7 Ap '87
Grapefruit pectin reduces cholesterol [research by James Cerda] *Sci News* 132:63 Jl 25 '87
Grapes
See also
Cooking—Fruit
Raisins
Viticulture
Wine making
Diseases and pests
Stealing from thieves [use of copper sulfate in Bordeaux vineyards] F. J. Prial. il *N Y Times Mag* p74 Mr 15 '87
Graphic arts
See also
Book design
Corchia Woliner Associates
Drawing
Drypoint
Graphic Designers (Firm)
Lithography
Prints
Graphic Designers (Firm)
A Mac on every drafting table [K. Shafton's use of computers] P. Honan. il por *Pers Comput* 11:185+ O '87
Graphic methods
Publish and prosper [E. Tufte's The visual display of quantitative information] W. Baldwin. il por *Forbes* 139:121-3 My 18 '87
Graphic novels
See also
Publishers and publishing—Graphic novels
Graphic novels: comics, magazines, or books? G. Beahm. por *Publ Wkly* 232:22 N 6 '87
Graphics, Computer *See* Computer graphics
Graphics Press
Publish and prosper [E. Tufte's The visual display of quantitative information] W. Baldwin. il por *Forbes* 139:121-3 My 18 '87
Graphite
Graphite intercalation compounds [Japanese research] H. Kamimura. bibl il *Phys Today* 40:64-71 D '87
Graphite drawing *See* Drawing
Graphology
Graphology: the write stuff? [study by Gershon Ben-Shakhar] J. Fischman. il *Psychol Today* 21:11 Jl '87
What you write is what you are. A. Gottlieb. il *McCalls* 115:175+ N '87
Graphophones *See* Phonograph
Graphs *See* Graphic methods
Grass *See* Grasses
Grass burning *See* Burning of land
Grass seed *See* Grasses—Seed
Grasse (France)
Description
The essence of Grasse. T. Skari. il *Life* 10:66-8 N '87
Grasses
See also
Bamboo
Fescue
Grazing
Lawns
Millet
Seed
Big demand spurs grass seed harvest this year. *Success Farm* 85:43 Je '87
Tomorrow's good lawns are in the bag today (literally!). A. Reilly. il *Flower Gard* 31:18-19 Ag/S '87
Grasshoppers
Control
FAO heads international campaign to avert locust and grasshopper outbreaks and save Africa's crops. il *UN Chron* 23:92-3 N '86
FAO reports locust infestations continue, harvests better in Africa. il *UN Chron* 24:74 My '87
Photographs and photography
A real drag. A. Bannister. il *Nat Hist* 96:86-7 Jl '87
Grasshoppers in art
Weaves of grass [Hong Kong craftsman Chan Chong Chi makes grasshopper figures out of grass] B. B. Ryan. il pors *Travel Holiday* 167:34-6 Mr '87
Grassland ecology *See* Prairie ecology
Grateful Dead (Musical group)
Bill Kreutzmann/Mickey Hart: Rhythm Devils. C. Vaughan. il pors *Down Beat* 11:23-5 N '87

Grateful Dead (Musical group)—*cont.*

Bob Dylan and the Grateful Dead [concert at Giants Stadium] D. Browne. il por *Roll Stone* p22-3 S 10 '87

Dead ahead. E. F. Cone. il *Forbes* 140:8 D 14 '87

The Dead and Dylan [New Jersey concert] *New Yorker* 63:24-5 Jl 27 '87

The Dead live on. D. Goldman. il *Sch Update* 120:23 N 20 '87

Jerry Garcia. il por *People Wkly* 28:72-3 D 28 '87-Ja 4 '88

The new dawn of the Grateful Dead [cover story] M. Gilmore. il *Roll Stone* p46-7+ Jl 16-30 '87

"We're a straight business now". A. D. Frank and E. F. Cone. il *Forbes* 139:43 My 18 '87

Gratings, Diffraction *See* Diffraction gratings

Gratitude

Happy thankstaking: how to handle gratitude. J. Stone. *Glamour* 85:156 N '87

Gratton, Michel

about

An unflattering portrait of Mulroney. M. Rose. il por *Macleans* 100:17 S 28 '87

Gratuities *See* Tipping

Grau, Georges E., and others

Tumor necrosis factor (cachectin) as an essential mediator in murine cerebral malaria. bibl f il *Science* 237:1210-12 S 4 '87

Graubard, Katherine, and Hartline, Daniel K.

Full-wave rectification from a mixed electrical-chemical synapse. bibl f il *Science* 237:535-7 Jl 31 '87

Grave robberies *See* Body snatching

Graves, David

Stretch out to shape up. il *Harpers Bazaar* 120:168-71+ My '87

Graves, Earl G. (Earl Gilbert), 1935-

Publisher's page. See issues of Black Enterprise

about

'Salute to Greatness' program honors Black enterprise publisher. il pors *Jet* 71:4-6+ F 9 '87

Graves, Michael, 1934-

about

Architecture: Michael Graves. C. Jencks. il por *Archit Dig* 44:138-45+ My '87

The Graves of wrath. D. Ketcham. il *Vogue* 177:110 Ap '87

In the living room of Michael Graves. il por *Esquire* 108:102-3 N '87

A shrine to wine. M. Filler. il *House Gard* 159:154-7+ S '87

Graves, Nancy, 1940-

about

Forms of fantasy. C. McGuigan. il pors *N Y Times Mag* p62-4+ D 6 '87

Graves *See* Tombs

Gravestones *See* Sepulchral monuments

Gravitation *See* Gravity and gravitation

Gravitational constant *See* Physical constants

Gravitational lens effect *See* Gravity and gravitation

Gravity and gravitation

See also
Falling bodies
Fifth force (Physics)
Quantum gravity
Relativity (Physics)
Sixth force (Physics)
Weightlessness

Borehole measurement of the Newtonian gravitational constant. A. T. Hsui. bibl f il map *Science* 237:881-3 Ag 21 '87

Gathering cosmic string [gravitational lens; work of Lennox L. Cowie and Esther M. Hu] *Sci Am* 257:19 Ag '87

The giant arcs are gravitational mirages [theory of Roger Lynds and Vahe Petrosian] M. M. Waldrop. il *Science* 238:1351-2 D 4 '87

Gravitationally lensed giant galaxy [3C-324 radio galaxy] il *Sky Telesc* 73:482-3 My '87

Gravity waves: a progress report. V. Trimble. il *Sky Telesc* 74:364-9 O '87

A matter of gravity and the SSC. D. E. Thomsen. *Sci News* 132:315 N 14 '87

Newton vindicated—Einstein, too! il *Sky Telesc* 73:484-5 My '87

The quest for gravity waves. il *Astronomy* 15:18 O '87

Ring around a gravitational lens [luminous arcs between galaxies; work of Vahe Petrosian and Roger Lynds] D. E. Thomsen. *Sci News* 132:326 N 21 '87

Star formation in W49A: gravitational collapse of the molecular cloud core toward a ring of massive stars. W. J. Welch and others. bibl f il *Science* 238:1550-5 D 11 '87

Measurement

Balances and gravimetric equipment. *Science* 235 pt2:G31-G33 F 27 '87

Geophysics on the fifth force's trail. S. Weisburd. *Sci News* 131:6 Ja 3 '87

Gravitational wave observatories. A. D. Jeffries and others. il *Sci Am* 256:50-6+ Je '87

Intimations of gravity waves. D. E. Thomsen. *Sci News* 131:8 Ja 3 '87

Letters [discussion of June 1987 article, Gravitational wave observatories] A. D. Jeffries and others. *Sci Am* 257:8-9 D '87

Resonant-mass detectors of gravitational radiation [cover story] P. F. Michelson and others. bibl f il *Science* 237:150-7 Jl 10 '87

A satellite triangle for gravity waves. D. E. Thomsen. *Sci News* 131:24 Ja 10 '87

Physiological effects

See also
Geotropism

Canadians investigate pilot's loss of consciousness prior to F-20A crash [May 14, 1985] *Aviat Week Space Technol* 126:75+ Mr 23 '87

Safety Board urges pilot training in G-induced loss of consciousness [crash of F-20A prototype at Goose Bay, Labrador, May 14, 1985] il *Aviat Week Space Technol* 126:103-4 Mr 30 '87

Snakes under pressure [circulatory system adapts to the demands of gravity; cover story] H. B. Lillywhite. il *Nat Hist* 96:58-67 N '87

What do you suppose B-forces make? [high ratio of daughters to sons in fighter pilots exposed to high G-forces; research by Bertis Little] *Sci News* 132:377 D 12 '87

Gravity waves *See* Gravity and gravitation

Gray, Arthur, Jr.

about

A hot seer sees the Dow at 3000. G. G. Marcial. *Bus Week* p62 Ag 10 '87

Gray, Colin S.

The Gorbachev offensive. *Society* 24:38-44 Jl/Ag '87

Gray, Eileen, 1879-1976

about

Eileen Gray: in the vanguard of twentieth-century design. A. Berman. il por *Archit Dig* 44:62+ My '87

Gray, Ellen, and Coolen, Peter

How do kids really feel about being home alone? bibl f il *Child Today* 16:30-2 Jl/Ag '87

Gray, Francine du Plessix

In Quiberon, a pleasure spa. *Vogue* 177:180+ D '87

Gray, J. W., and others

High-speed chromosome sorting. bibl f il *Science* 238:323-9 O 16 '87

Gray, Jeffrey

Escuintla [poem] *Atlantic* 260:79 Jl '87

Gray, Jim

Instant success . . . ! [cover story] il *Petersens Photogr Mag* 15:28-9+ Mr '87

Gray, Linda

about

Linda Gray: "I have more fun alone!". N. Gittelson. il pors *McCalls* 114:13+ Ja '87

Linda Gray interview [cover story] D. Brooks. il pors *Petersens Photogr Mag* 16:49-50+ N '87

Linda Gray: "Why isn't life fair?". T. Reinhold. il pors *Redbook* 169:16+ My '87

Gray, Patricia Bellew

Tobacco goes on trial. *Read Dig* 131:225-6+ O '87

Gray, Robert H.

How does philanthropy value arts education? *Des Arts Educ* 88:6-11 Mr/Ap '87

Gray, Robert Reed

Aviation safety: fact or fiction [cover story] il *Technol Rev* 90:32-40 Ag/S '87

Gray, Simon James Holliday, 1936-

about

The common pursuit [drama] Reviews *Commonweal* 114:18-19 Ja 16 '87. G. Weales

Gray, Spalding, 1942?-

The haul of fame. il por *Roll Stone* p30-1+ My 21 '87

House for sale: why I hate where I live. il *House Gard* 159:134-5+ Ja '87

The stately dogs of England. il *House Gard* 159:142+ N '87

Gray, Spalding, 1942?—*cont.*
about
Not one to table a discussion, Spalding Gray delivers a real talkie to movie audiences. K. Hubbard. il pors *People Wkly* 27:87-8 Ap 13 '87
Somebody to talk about. M. Simpson. il pors *N Y Times Mag* p40+ Mr 8 '87

Gray, Todd, 1954-
The power of profile. il *Petersens Photogr Mag* 16:36-7 Je '87

Gray, William H., III
about
Bill Gray can't lose in the budget battle. D. Harbrecht. il por *Bus Week* p25-6 S 7 '87
Congressman Gray puts together first trillion dollar budget in history of U.S. S. Booker. il pors *Jet* 72:12-13 Jl 13 '87
Gray calls on Reagan to help S. African detainees. por *Jet* 72:12 Ag 31 '87
Gray likely appointed to powerful post in Congress. por *Jet* 72:17 Ag 17 '87
Gray pushes for sanctions against Ethiopia atrocity. *Jet* 73:4 O 12 '87
Gray works to save fed. programs cut by Reagan. *Jet* 71:4 Mr 9 '87
The many shades of Gray. N. J. Perry. il por *Fortune* 116:159-60 N 9 '87

Gray market (Export-import trade)
New protection for goods in the gray market [American Warranty Co.] il *Consum Rep* 52:525 S '87
Sight and sound: buyer beware! [audio equipment] H. Fantel. *Opera News* 51:44 Je '87

Gray whales *See* Whales

Graybar Electric Co., Inc.
Staying aloof. J. R. Hayes. il *Forbes* 140:152 D 14 '87

Graybeal, Jay A., and Kenny, Peter M.
The William Efner Wheelock Collection at the East Hampton Historical Society. bibl f il *Antiques* 132:328-39 Ag '87

Graybeal, Sidney N., and Krepon, Michael, 1946-
The limitations of on-site inspection [cover story] il *Bull At Sci* 43:22-6 D '87

Graybill, Christopher
Last word. il *Omni* 9:114 Ja '87
Last word. por *Omni* 10:178 N '87

Grayer, Jeff
about
The unknown Cyclone. J. Garrity. il por *Sports Illus* 67:86 D 21 '87

Grayling fishing
Manitoba grayling. J. Reynolds. il *Field Stream* 92:41-3 Je '87

Grayson, Andrew Jackson, 1818-1869
about
Back from oblivion. F. Graham. il map *Audubon* 89:20-4+ S '87

Grayson, Donald K.
Death by natural causes. il *Nat Hist* 96:8+ My '87

Grayson, John N.
about
Black businessman charges conspiracy behind losses. il por *Jet* 71:15 Mr 23 '87

Grazier, Debbie
about
"A faith healer gave us our child". J. Grazier. il pors *McCalls* 115:164-6 O '87

Grazier, Jack
"A faith healer gave us our child". il pors *McCalls* 115:164-6 O '87
A tornado took away his world. il pors *McCalls* 114:130-2 Je '87

Grazing
See also
Forage plants
Sheep herding
Head 'em up, move 'em out [controlled grazing] *Success Farm* 85:B3 My '87
In New Mexico: desert healer [work of A. Savory] G. Ehrlich. il por *Time* 130:10-11 D 7 '87

Grazing lands *See* Livestock ranges

Great Abaco Island (Bahamas)
Description and travel
Islands in time. V. Haagen. il map *Oceans* 20:50-5 My/Je '87

Great Adventure (Jackson, N.J.) *See* Amusement parks
Great American Race (Rally) *See* Motor vehicle rallies
Great American Salvage Company
In New York: salvaged pieces. J. D. Reed. il *Time* 130:12-14 D 21 '87

Great Atlantic & Pacific Tea Company, Inc.
Just how good is the Great A&P? B. Saporito. il por *Fortune* 115:92-3 Mr 16 '87

Great Barrier Reef (Australia)
See also
Fish—Great Barrier Reef (Australia)
Horizontal plate motion: a key allocyclic factor in the evolution of the Great Barrier Reef. P. J. Davies and others. bibl f il map *Science* 238:1697-700 D 18 '87
The largest, grandest coral reef in the world. il map *Sunset* 179:77-8+ N '87

Great Basin National Park (Nev.)
A Basin of beauty. T. Morganthau. il map *Newsweek* 110:16-17 Ag 24 '87
The Great Basin is a lonely place for a national park. D. D. Jackson. bibl (p269) il *Smithsonian* 18:68-74+ N '87
Our newest national park, Nevada's Great Basin. il map *Sunset* 178:42+ My '87
Stalagmites and stunning vistas. J. Willwerth. il *Time* 130:46 Ag 24 '87

Great Britain
See also
AIDS (Disease)—Great Britain
Airports—Great Britain
Americans—Great Britain
Animal experimentation—Protests, demonstrations, etc.—Great Britain
Anti-nuclear movement—Great Britain
Anti-Semitism—Great Britain
Antique dealers—Great Britain
Architecture—Great Britain
Archives—Great Britain
Art—Great Britain
Arts—Great Britain
Astronomical observatories—Great Britain
Astronomy—Great Britain
Automobile racing—Great Britain
Aviation and state—Great Britain
Birds—Great Britain
Boat rallies—Great Britain
Bonds, Government—Great Britain
Books and reading—Great Britain
Booksellers and bookselling—Great Britain
British
Canadians—Great Britain
Catalogs, Union—Great Britain
Cellular radio—Great Britain
Christmas—Great Britain
College education and state—Great Britain
Colleges and universities—Great Britain
Commonwealth of Nations
Country estates—Great Britain
Country life—Great Britain
Cricket (Sport)—Great Britain
Cultural property—Protection—Great Britain
Do-it-yourself work—Great Britain
Education—Great Britain
Espionage, Czech—Great Britain
Espionage, Russian—Great Britain
Feudalism—Great Britain
Foreign correspondents—Great Britain
Foreign students—Great Britain
Gambling—Great Britain
Gardens and gardening—Great Britain
Genetic research—Patents—Great Britain
Geothermal resources—Great Britain
Government and the press—Great Britain
Government employees—Great Britain
Historic houses, sites, etc.—Great Britain
Horse racing—Great Britain
Hospitals—Great Britain
Immigration and emigration—Great Britain
Income tax—Great Britain
Indians (East Indian)—Great Britain
Intelligence service—Great Britain
Investments, American—Great Britain
Investments, British
Investments, Canadian—Great Britain
Investments, Swiss—Great Britain
Jews—Great Britain
Journalism—Great Britain
Knights and knighthood—Great Britain
Labyrinths—Great Britain
Libraries—Great Britain
Lighthouses—Great Britain
Medical research—Great Britain
Military research—Great Britain
Minorities—Great Britain
Money—Great Britain

Great Britain—See also—*cont.*
Motion pictures—Great Britain
Motorcycle racing—Great Britain
Music—Great Britain
Music festivals—Great Britain
National Trust (Great Britain)
Nobility—Great Britain
Northern Ireland
Nuclear power plants—Great Britain
Occult sciences—Great Britain
Opera—Great Britain
Paleontology—Great Britain
Parapsychology—Great Britain
Periodicals—Great Britain
Physics—Great Britain
Police—Great Britain
Poll tax—Great Britain
Press and politics—Great Britain
Privatization—Great Britain
Radio broadcasting—Great Britain
Radioactive waste disposal—Great Britain
Real estate investment—Great Britain
Research—Great Britain
Roads—Great Britain
Rock music—Great Britain
Science—Great Britain
Science and state—Great Britain
Sculpture gardens and parks—Great Britain
Securities—Great Britain
Securities—Laws and regulations—Great Britain
Soccer, Professional—Great Britain
Social classes—Great Britain
Space research—Great Britain
Speedways—Great Britain
Strikes—Great Britain
Suicide—Great Britain
Television broadcasting—Great Britain
Trade unions—Great Britain
Trade unions—Servicemen—Great Britain
Unemployment—Great Britain
Veterinary hospitals—Great Britain
Villages—Great Britain
Wales
Wildlife conservation—Great Britain
Wildlife management—Great Britain
Women—Great Britain
Zoos—Great Britain

Anecdotes, facetiae, satire, etc.
Oh to be in England—and bored. A. Fotheringham. il *Macleans* 100:64 D 21 '87

Antiquities
See also
Stonehenge (England)
Roads to ruins [destruction of archeological sites by road crews] K. Nurse. il *Hist Today* 37:2 Mr '87

Armed Forces
Appropriations and expenditures
Britain will reduce real-term defense spending through 1988. D. A. Brown. *Aviat Week Space Technol* 126:32-3 My 11 '87

Climate
Rainy day blues and whites. M. Reed. il *Weatherwise* 40:262-3 O '87

Colonies
See also
United States—History—Colonial period, ca. 1600-1775
Bermuda
Commonwealth of Nations
Falkland Islands
Great Britain. Empire Marketing Board
Hong Kong

Commerce
South Africa
Britain's assault on the Commonwealth [Britain refuses to agree to wider sanctions against South Africa] H. Mackenzie. il *Macleans* 100:24-5 O 26 '87
United States
See United States—Commerce—Great Britain

Commercial policy
See also
Great Britain. Empire Marketing Board

Defenses
See also
Airplanes, Military—Great Britain
Great Britain. Royal Air Force
Guided missiles, British
A European deterrent? B. Crozier. *Natl Rev* 39:24 Jl 31 '87
If Labour wins. W. B. Messmer. *Foreign Policy* 67:137-53 Summ '87

Labor's defense [interview with N. Kinnock] J. Lloyd and P. Kellner. *World Press Rev* 34:15-16 My '87
A Labour Britain, NATO and the bomb. D. Healey. *Foreign Aff* 65:716-29 Spr '87
Thunder over Britain. W. F. Buckley. *Natl Rev* 39:62-3 Ap 24 '87

Description and travel
See also
Cycling—Great Britain
London ramblings. M. S. Forbes. il *Forbes* 139:18 Ja 26 '87
Rambling through the English countryside. S. F. Godbey. il *Prevention* 39:60-2+ Je '87
The Royal Windsor Horse Show. S. Wilding. il *Gourmet* 47:60-5+ Ap '87

Diplomatic and consular service
France
Paris in the thirties: some letters home. V. Lawford. il por *Archit Dig* 44:210+ Mr '87

Economic conditions
Anecdotes, facetiae, satire, etc.
Talk about a buyout! [leveraged buyout for all of Britain] B. Stein. il *N Y Times Mag* p50+ Mr 1 '87

Economic history
Gladstonian finance. H. C. G. Matthew. bibl il por *Hist Today* 37:41-5 Jl '87
Imperial images: the Empire Marketing Board, 1926-32. D. Meredith. bibl f il *Hist Today* 37:30-6 Ja '87
Is the U.S. going the way of Britain? K. Pennar. il *Bus Week* p64-6 Ap 20 '87

Economic policy
A jolly good show for the economy. R. A. Melcher. il *Bus Week* p47 F 16 '87
Thatcher after the crash: carry on, then. R. A. Melcher. il *Bus Week* p80-1 N 16 '87
Thatcher's capitalist revolution [cover story] H. Raines. il pors *N Y Times Mag* p16-19+ My 31 '87
Thatcher's revolution: act III. R. A. Melcher. il por *Bus Week* p72-4 My 25 '87
What Maggie has wrought. R. I. Kirkland, Jr. il pors *Fortune* 115:91-2 Je 8 '87

Foreign opinion
German
Ernst Lissauer and the Hymn of hate [WWI anti-English propaganda poem by German-Jewish poet] C. C. Aronsfeld. bibl il por *Hist Today* 37:48-50 D '87

Foreign relations
See also
Espionage, British
Mrs. Thatcher's election prospects [interview with R. Pennant-Rea] A. Balk. il por *World Press Rev* 34:30-3 Ja '87

Anti-Communist measures
The democracy syndrome, cont'd. B. Crozier. *Natl Rev* 39:26 Je 19 '87
Staunch allies? [comparing Soviet support of allies to U.S. and British policies] B. Crozier. *Natl Rev* 39:26 Ap 24 '87
Argentina
Assembly asks Argentina and United Kingdom to initiate negotiations on Falklands (Malvinas). *UN Chron* 24:81 F '87
Call for negotiations for peaceful, definitive resolution of Falklands (Malvinas) issue. map *UN Chron* 23:8-10 Ja '86
Argentina—History
A cold war: Britain, Argentina and Antarctica. P. J. Beck. bibl il maps *Hist Today* 37:16-23 Je '87
Australia
Australia's nuclear graveyard [British nuclear tests in the outback during the 1950s and 1960s] R. Milliken. il map *Bull At Sci* 43:38-44 Ap '87
China
Direct elections in Hong Kong? Not if Beijing can help it. D. J. Yang. il *Bus Week* p62 Mr 16 '87
Future shock in Hong Kong. J. Morris. il *N Y Times Mag* p48-51+ O 25 '87
Hong Kong: a colony eyes Chinese rule. L. Hopping. il *Sch Update* 119:10-11 Ap 6 '87
France
See also
Great Britain—Diplomatic and consular service—France
France—History
Counter-revolution? Toulon, 1793. W. S. Cormack and M. Sydenham. bibl il *Hist Today* 37:49-55 O '87
Ireland
The empire's last nervous twitch [Anglo-Irish cooperation] C. C. Mann. *Commonweal* 114:562-5 O 9 '87

Great Britain—Foreign relations—Ireland—*cont.*
Ireland—History
Images of Ireland 1170-1600: the origins of English imperialism. J. Gillingham. bibl il *Hist Today* 37:16-22 F '87
Soviet Union
See also
Thatcher, Margaret—Visit to the Soviet Union, 1987
United States
See United States—Foreign relations—Great Britain
History
Roman period, 55 B.C.-449 A.D.—Bibliography
Roman Britain. R. J. A. Wilson. il *Hist Today* 37:47-51 Ag '87
Anglo-Saxon period, 449-1066—Bibliography
Paperback history. M. Budny. *Hist Today* 37:60 O '87
Plantagenets, 1154-1399
An Age of Chivalry [Age of Chivalry: art in Plantagenet England 1200-1400 at the Royal Academy; cover story; special issue] il *Hist Today* 37:2-57 N '87
Wars of the Roses, 1455-1485
Stoke Field's last stand [500th anniversary of the Battle of Stoke Field] N. Bainbridge. il map *Hist Today* 37:2-3 Je '87
Tudors, 1485-1603
See also
Great Britain—History—Elizabethan period, 1558-1603
Estates, degrees and sorts in Tudor and Stuart England. K. Wrightson. bibl f il *Hist Today* 37:17-22 Ja '87
Tudors, 1485-1603—Bibliography
Paperback history. S. Adams. *Hist Today* 37:57 My '87
Henry VIII, 1509-1547
Power and the early-Tudor courtier's house [excerpt from The early Tudor country house] M. Howard. bibl il por *Hist Today* 37:44-50 My '87
Privy secrets: Henry VIII and the Lords of the Council [cover story] D. Starkey. bibl il pors *Hist Today* 37:23-31 Ag '87
Elizabethan period, 1558-1603
A patriot for whom? Stanley, York and Elizabeth's Catholics [1587 defection of key officers in the Netherlands] S. Adams. bibl il *Hist Today* 37:46-50 Jl '87
16th century
See also
Great Britain—History—Tudors, 1485-1603
Stuarts, 1603-1714
Estates, degrees and sorts in Tudor and Stuart England. K. Wrightson. bibl f il *Hist Today* 37:17-22 Ja '87
Stuarts, 1603-1714—Bibliography
The century of revolution. L. Stone. il *N Y Rev Books* 34:38-43 F 26 '87
Civil War, 1642-1649
Signs & wonders & the English Civil War. C. Durston. bibl il *Hist Today* 37:22-8 O '87
Puritan Revolution, 1642-1660—Bibliography
The century of revolution. L. Stone. il *N Y Rev Books* 34:38-43 F 26 '87
Puritan Revolution, 1642-1660—Historiography
Clarendon and the Great Rebellion. R. Ollard. bibl il por *Hist Today* 37:47-52 S '87
Charles II, 1660-1685
A tale of two Cliffords. R. Hutton. il por *Hist Today* 37:8-9 Jl '87
1714-1837
From rank to class: innovation in Georgian England. P. Corfield. bibl il *Hist Today* 37:36-42 F '87
1760-1789
See also
United States—History—Revolution, 1775-1783
1800-1837
See also
United States—History—War of 1812
Victorian period, 1837-1901
See Victorian period
20th century
See also
World War, 1939-1945—Campaigns and battles—Great Britain
World War, 1939-1945—Great Britain
Anthony Eden & the decline of Britain. O. Harries. *Commentary* 83:34-43 Je '87
1945-
Demythologising Nye Bevan. J. Campbell. bibl il pors *Hist Today* 37:13-18 Ap '87
Writing our own history [contribution of H. Dalton's political diary and others to British post-war history] T. Benn. il pors *Hist Today* 37:9-12 Ap '87

Sources
Writing our own history [contribution of H. Dalton's political diary and others to British post-war history] T. Benn. il pors *Hist Today* 37:9-12 Ap '87
Study and teaching
History and controversy in the classroom. J. Slater. il *Hist Today* 37:6-7 Ja '87
Not waving, but drowning. *Hist Today* 37:2-3 Jl '87
History, Naval
See also
Bounty Mutiny, 1789
Jane's fighting ships [J. Austen's brother] P. Honan. bibl il pors *Hist Today* 37:40-6 Ag '87
Industries
See also
A G B Research plc
Advertising agencies—Great Britain
Aerospace industries—Great Britain
Airlines—Acquisitions and mergers—Great Britain
Airlines—Great Britain
Airship Industries, Ltd.
Allied-Lyons plc
Art trade—Great Britain
Associated Book Publishers plc
B E T plc
Banks and banking—Acquisitions and mergers—Great Britain
Blue Arrow plc
British Aerospace plc
British Caledonian Airways Ltd.
British Caledonian Group plc
British Gas plc
British Petroleum Co. plc
British Telecom plc
Britoil plc
Brokers—Great Britain
Cambrian & General Securities
Carvers and Gilders (Firm)
Computer industry—Great Britain
Corporations—Acquisitions and mergers—Great Britain
Courtaulds plc
F. H. Tomkins plc
Ferranti plc
Film Finances, Ltd.
Filofax plc
Fleur de Lys Automobile Manufacturing, Ltd.
G. Jackson & Sons
General Electric Company plc
Glaxo Holdings plc
Group Lotus Car Companies Ltd.
Guinness plc
Hanson Trust plc
Hill Samuel Group plc, London
ICI Fibres (Firm)
Imperial Chemical Industries plc
Insituform Group Ltd.
Investment advisers—Great Britain
Investment trusts—Great Britain
Lloyd's of London
London European Airways
Marconi Co. Ltd.
Motion picture industry—Great Britain
Motorcycle industry—Great Britain
Munitions—Great Britain
National Westminster Bank plc
Newspaper publishers and publishing—Great Britain
Panmure Gordon & Company
Pearson plc
Pentos plc
Petroleum industry—Acquisitions and mergers—Great Britain
Plessey Co. plc
Publishers and publishing—Acquisitions and mergers—Great Britain
Publishers and publishing—Great Britain
R. Twining & Co. Ltd.
Reed International plc
Rolls-Royce Ltd.
Rolls-Royce Motors Ltd.
S.G. Warburg Group plc
Saatchi & Saatchi Company plc
Smiths Industries plc
Tailors—Great Britain
Television industry—Great Britain
Walker Books Ltd.
Wedgwood plc
Wellcome Foundation Ltd.
Westland plc
Woolworth Holdings plc
WPP Group plc

Great Britain—cont.

Intellectual life
See also
Bloomsbury group

Kings and rulers
See also
Elizabeth II, Queen of Great Britain, 1926-
George V, King of Great Britain, 1865-1936
Great Britain—Royal family
Victoria, Queen of Great Britain, 1819-1901
Kings, queens and lovers. T. Suddon. il *Macleans* 100:36 N 9 '87

Languages
See also
English language in Great Britain

Moral conditions
See also
Prostitution—Great Britain

Nationalism
See also
Britannia (British national symbol)
John Bull (British national symbol)
The quest for Englishness [nationalism in English society during the Victorian period] P. Rich. bibl il *Hist Today* 37:24-30 Je '87

Politics and government
See also
Conservatism—Great Britain
Conservative Party (Great Britain)
Elections—Great Britain
Great Britain. Constitution
Labour Party (Great Britain)
Liberal Party (Great Britain)
Official secrets—Great Britain
Political campaigns—Great Britain
Social Democratic Party (Great Britain)
Socialism—Great Britain
Television and politics—Great Britain
Elections loom in Thatcher's future. K. Slack. *Christ Century* 104:183-4 F 25 '87
Kohl on a roll [British prospects in light of German election] W. Laqueur. *New Repub* 196:17-18 Mr 2 '87
Maggie Thatcher: "She's all backbone". D. Reed. por *Read Dig* 131:213-14+ N '87
Mrs. Thatcher's election prospects [interview with R. Pennant-Rea] A. Balk. il por *World Press Rev* 34:30-3 Ja '87
A search for 'respect'. R. Laver. il por *Macleans* 100:30 Mr 9 '87
Sugar bowls and election fever. M. S. Serrill. il *Time* 129:43 Mr 30 '87
Tea with Margaret Thatcher. J. Goodwin. *Ladies Home J* 104:135+ N '87
Thatcher is looking more like a three-time winner. R. A. Melcher. il *Bus Week* p53 Ap 13 '87
Thatcher pushes ahead [cover story; special section] il *World Press Rev* 34:11-16 My '87
'U.S. motivation is benign, but often misguided' [interview with D. Trelford] J. R. Moskin. por *World Press Rev* 34:27-8 N '87
"We are building a property-owning democracy" [interview with M. Thatcher] C. Ogden and F. Melville. il *Time* 129:38 Je 22 '87
What Maggie hath wrought. R. Knight and others. il pors *U S News World Rep* 102:30-2 Ap 6 '87

Anecdotes, facetiae, satire, etc.
The hospital without patients [excerpt from The complete Yes, minister] J. Lynn and A. Jay. *Wash Mon* 19:41-6 Jl/Ag '87

Popular culture
Terminal culture? "The British Edge" [exhibition at Boston's Institute of Contemporary Art] P. H. Smith. il *Art Am* 75:36-9+ S '87

Religious institutions and affairs
See also
Catholics—Great Britain
Church of England
House churches—Great Britain
Mormons and Mormonism—Great Britain
Dissidents in an age of faith? Wyclif and the Lollards. J. Catto. bibl il *Hist Today* 37:46-52 N '87
London letter. K. Slack. See occasional issues of The Christian Century through October 28, 1987

History
See also
Reformation
Boy into bishop: a festive role-reversal. N. Mackenzie. bibl il *Hist Today* 37:10-16 D '87
Signs & wonders & the English Civil War. C. Durston. bibl il *Hist Today* 37:22-8 O '87

Royal family
See also
Andrew, Prince, Duke of York, 1960-
Anne, Princess, daughter of Elizabeth II, Queen of Great Britain, 1950-
Charles, Prince of Wales, 1948-
Diana, Princess of Wales, 1961-
Edward, Prince of Great Britain, 1964-
Elizabeth II, Queen of Great Britain, 1926-
Henry, Prince of Great Britain, 1984-
Philip, Prince, consort of Elizabeth II, Queen of Great Britain, 1921-
Sarah, Duchess of York, 1959-
William, Prince of Great Britain, 1982-
All in the family [severely retarded Bowes-Lyon sisters, relatives of the royal family, secretly institutionalized in Great Britain] il *Time* 129:45 Ap 20 '87
Ambassadors from the realm of fairy tale [Windsors] P. Iyer. il *Time* 129:80 Je 15 '87
The big bang [press coverage] S. Hoggart. *New Repub* 197:11-12 N 23 '87
'Fabulous Fergie' [cover story; special section; with editorial comment by Kevin Doyle] il pors *Macleans* 100:2, 26-30+ Jl 27 '87
Fergie, Britain's clown princes and an all-star celeb cast turn joustabouts for charity. il *People Wkly* 28:32-3 Jl 6 '87
A royal family secret [confinement of Queen Mother's nieces to a mental institution] il *Macleans* 100:24 Ap 20 '87
The royal family tree: 1819-1987. il *Life* 10:36-7 S '87
The royal family's gothic shocker [Queen Mother's nieces locked in mental hospital] N. Cooper. il *Newsweek* 109:49 Ap 20 '87
A royal scandal [cover story; special section; with editorial comment by Kevin Doyle] il pors *Macleans* 100:2, 30-4+ N 9 '87
There'll always be an England [mock medieval tourney for charity] il *Newsweek* 109:73 Je 29 '87
What ho! The Windsors! [mock conflict staged for charity] G. D. Garcia. il *Time* 129:68-9 Je 29 '87
When in doubt, run the Royals. L. Zuckerman. il pors *Time* 130:52 Jl 13 '87
The year of the royal mess [excerpt from The royal year; cover story] T. Graham. il *Good Housekeep* 205:138-41+ N '87

Social history
Wet-nursing boom in England explored [research by Valerie Fildes] G. Kolata. il *Science* 235:745-7 F 13 '87

Social life and customs
See also
Sloane Rangers

Social policy
Now the other Britain needs Thatcher's attention. R. A. Melcher. il por *Bus Week* p43 Je 29 '87
Thatcher's third term target. N. Gelb. il *New Leader* 70:6-7 Je 29 '87

Great Britain. Army

Crimes and misdemeanors
Brutality in Britain's barracks. *Newsweek* 110:83 N 16 '87

Great Britain. Army. Australian and New Zealand Army Corps
Condoms to the rescue: New Zealand's Ettie Rout "made vice safe" in World War I. J. Tolerton. il pors *Ms* 15:28-30 My '87

Great Britain. Civil Aviation Authority
CAA chief backs move by small carriers to prevent British Airways/BCal merger; British Caledonian downplays impact of merger on competitors. D. A. Brown. *Aviat Week Space Technol* 127:56-7 Ag 3 '87

Great Britain. Constitution
Kingdom of unwritten rules. D. Brand. il *Time* 130:95-6 Jl 6 '87

Great Britain. Empire Marketing Board
Imperial images: the Empire Marketing Board, 1926-32. D. Meredith. bibl f il *Hist Today* 37:30-6 Ja '87

Great Britain. King's Council *See* Great Britain. Privy Council

Great Britain. National Portrait Gallery *See* National Portrait Gallery (Great Britain)

Great Britain. National Space Center *See* National Space Center (Great Britain)

Great Britain. Navy *See* Great Britain. Royal Navy

Great Britain. Parliament. House of Commons
Blacks in Parliament. D. J. Dent. il *Black Enterp* 18:22 S '87
First 3 blacks elected to British Parliament. il *Jet* 72:36 Jl 6 '87

Great Britain. Parliament. House of Lords
Britain: Lords a-leaping. N. Cooper. il *Newsweek* 110:46 N 30 '87
Great Britain. Privy Council
Privy secrets: Henry VIII and the Lords of the Council [cover story] D. Starkey. bibl il pors *Hist Today* 37:23-31 Ag '87
Great Britain. Royal Air Force
Three European Air Forces step up training at Goose Bay. *Aviat Week Space Technol* 127:86 O 5 '87
Great Britain. Royal Court Theatre *See* Royal Court Theatre
Great Britain. Royal Navy
    Forces in the Persian Gulf region
Warnings at sea. I. Mather. il *Macleans* 100:32 S 21 '87
Great Britain. Society for Psychical Research *See* Society for Psychical Research (Great Britain)
Great Britain and France
    See also
      English Channel tunnel
Great Britain and Germany
    See also
      Great Britain—Foreign opinion—German
Great Britain and Spain
    See also
      Spain—Foreign opinion—British
Great Britain and the United States
    See also
      United States—Foreign opinion—British
Great Britain-Canada air agreements *See* Aviation—International aspects
Great Britain-Soviet Union air agreements *See* Aviation—International aspects
Great Britain-United States air agreements *See* Aviation—International aspects
Great Central Valley (Calif.) *See* Central Valley (Calif.)
Great Depression *See* Business depression, 1929-1939
Great Dixter (Sussex, England: Country estate) *See* Country estates—Great Britain
The great Gatsby [ballet] See Ballet reviews—Single works
Great gray owls *See* Owls
Great horned owls *See* Owls
Great Kennebec River Whatever Race *See* Boat racing
Great Lakes
    See also
      Lake Michigan
      Water pollution—Great Lakes
Great Lakes: the 'monster' on Chicago's shore [rising water levels] M. Bosc. il *U S News World Rep* 102:25 Ja 12 '87
The Great Lakes' troubled waters. C. E. Cobb. il supp (folded map) maps *Natl Geogr* 172:2-31 Jl '87
The Greater Lakes. S. Begley. il map *Newsweek* 109:76-7 Mr 16 '87
High water and rising fear. A. Steacy. il *Macleans* 100:44 Ja 19 '87
The rise and fall of the Great Lakes. I. Peterson. *Sci News* 131:133 F 28 '87
Great Lakes region
    See also
      Air pollution—Great Lakes region
      Fishing—Great Lakes region
      Shipping—Great Lakes region
    Industries
    See also
      Fish culture—Great Lakes region
Great men and women
    See also
      Founding Fathers
      Heroes and heroines
      Leadership
Great Peace March, 1986
Diane Clark: the mayor of Peace City. P. Skalka. il pors *McCalls* 114:134 Ap '87
One small step. W. Greider. il *Roll Stone* p29-30 Ja 15 '87
The Peace March presses on. L. Lindeman. il *50 Plus* 27:22+ F '87
Still on the road for peace [elderly veterans of the Great Peace March continue to be involved] L. Lindeman. il *50 Plus* 27:20-2 Je '87
    Photographs and photography
By the time I get to Davenport. K. McEwen. il *U S Cathol* 52:34-9 F '87
A peace march starts a photographer's career [J. Share] H. Chapnick. il por *Pop Photogr* 94:20 My '87
Putting their cause on the line. L. Gomez. il *Life* 10:90-5 Ja '87
Great Plains Software, Inc.
Plains seeking. K. Berney. il por *Nations Bus* 75:77 O '87

Great Salt Lake (Utah)
A greater Salt Lake. P. Barnes-Svarney. il map *Earth Sci* 39:22-3 Wint '86
    Regulation
Lake pumper [West Desert Pumping Project] G. Davis. il *Pop Sci* 231:68-70 S '87
Great Smoky Mountains National Park (N.C. and Tenn.)
Bill advocates wilderness for majority of Smokies. *Natl Parks* 61:38 S/O '87
Southern Appalachian forests. B. G. Norton. il map *Wilderness* 50:23-4 Spr '87
Great Society *See* United States—Social policy
Great Western Financial Corp.
How playing it safe worked for Great Western. T. Carson. il por *Bus Week* p70 S 7 '87
Greater London Enterprise Board
London's technology networks. S. Gordon. il *Technol Rev* 90:12-13 O '87
Greater Yellowstone *See* Yellowstone National Park region
Greaves, D. R.
(jt. auth) See Borst, Piet, and Greaves, D. R.
Greb, Harry, 1894-1926
    about
The Sugar Ray of his day. J. Harvey. il por *Sports Illus* 66:83 Mr 30 '87
Grebenschikov, Boris
    about
Aquarium's leader rises to the surface. N. Traver. il por *People Wkly* 27:51 Ap 6 '87
Grebogi, Celso, and others
Chaos, strange attractors, and fractal basin boundaries in nonlinear dynamics. bibl f il *Science* 238:632-8 O 30 '87
Grecco, Richard J.
'Eternal peace lasts only until the next war'. *America* 156:509-11 Je 20-27 '87
Greco, Rosemarie B.
    about
From teaching nun to bank president. M. Rowland. il por *Work Woman* 12:60 D '87
Greco, El *See* El Greco, 1541-1614
Greece
    See also
      Aegean Islands
      Aged—Greece
      Architecture, Domestic—Greece
      Athens (Greece)
      Thera (Greece: Island)
      Women—Greece
    Antiquities
    See also
      Acropolis (Athens, Greece)
      Parthenon (Athens, Greece)
Odyssey: dig on Ithaca seeks the dwelling of Homer's famed wanderer [work of Sarantis Symeonoglou] J. Horgan. il *Sci Am* 257:18+ N '87
    Defenses
    See also
      United States—Armed Forces—Forces in Greece
    Description and travel
Greek expectations. D. Mungen and D. G. Salter. il *Essence* 18:20+ Ag '87
    Foreign relations
      Cyprus
    See Cyprus
      Turkey
Storm clouds over the Aegean. J. Bierman. il map *Macleans* 100:26-7 Ap 6 '87
      United States
    See United States—Foreign relations—Greece
    History
      Peloponnesian War, 431-404 B.C.
A patriot for whom? Alcibiades of Athens. P. Cartledge. bibl il por *Hist Today* 37:15-19 O '87
      Civil War, 1944-1949—Reporters and reporting
Secret history. A. Cockburn. *Nation* 244:70-1 Ja 24 '87
      Bibliography
Paperback history. R. Stoneman. *Hist Today* 37:57 S '87
      Historiography
The father of it all. J. Griffin. il *N Y Rev Books* 34:11-12+ Ap 9 '87
    History, Naval
An Athenian legend sails the Aegean once more [trireme replica] L. Rosellini. il *U S News World Rep* 103:54-5 Ag 17 '87
The Athenian trireme. P. Lipke. il *Oceans* 20:8-10 N/D '87
The glory that was Greece [replica of trireme] A. Toufexis. il *Time* 130:73 Ag 17 '87

Greece—History, Naval—*cont.*
Rho, rho, rho, your boat [trireme replica] il *Discover* 8:8 N '87

Politics and government

Margarita Papandreou [interview] C. Dreifus. il *Progressive* 51:21-4 D '87

While Andreas Papandreou, Greece's prime minister, dallies with a dame, all *hellas* is breaking loose [affair with D. Liani] il pors *People Wkly* 28:62 O 26 '87

Greed *See* Avarice

Greek Americans
Sample Greek culture in Tarpon Springs. C. Griffith. il *South Living* 22:36+ Ag '87

Greek islands *See* Aegean Islands

Greek language

Study and teaching
Anecdotes, facetiae, satire, etc.
Greek: who needs it? K. Byrne. il *America* 156:52-4 Ja 24 '87

Greek Orthodox Church *See* Orthodox Eastern Church

Greek poetry
See also
Epic poetry, Greek

Greek revival architecture *See* Architecture, Greek revival

Greek Village Festival (Queens, N.Y.) *See* Queens (New York, N.Y.)—Festivals

Greeks

United States
See also
Greek Americans

Greeley, Andrew M., 1928-
Community as social capital: James S. Coleman on Catholic schools. *America* 157:110-12 Ag 29-S 5 '87
Empirical liturgy: the search for grace. *America* 157:379-83+ N 21 '87
Who reads book reviews anyway? por *Publ Wkly* 231:78 Ap 10 '87
Why Catholics stay in the Church [cover story] il *America* 157:54-7+ Ag 1-8 '87

about
In defense of book critics. J. Bass. por *Publ Wkly* 231:48 My 8 '87
Little shop of horrors [cover story] M. Z. Stange. il por *Commonweal* 114:412-17 Jl 17 '87
Little shop of horrors [discussion of July 17, 1987 article] M. Z. Stange. *Commonweal* 114:546+ O 9 '87

Greeley, Ronald
Release of juvenile water on Mars: estimated amounts and timing associated with volcanism. bibl f il *Science* 236:1653-4 Je 26 '87

Greeley County (Kan.)

Description and travel
The simplest of counties. B. Wallach. il *Focus* 37:18-21 Summ '87

Green, Alvar J.

about
The pack leader still acts 'like a hungry rat'. J. B. Levine. il por *Bus Week* p84 My 25 '87

Green, Anthony
Philadelphia: the city that gave us a nation. il *Natl Parks* 61:24-9 Mr/Ap '87

Green, Bill, 1929-
Policies on global warming and ozone depletion. *Environment* 29:5+ Ap '87

Green, Bill
In-circuit digital IC tester (I). il *Radio-Electron* 58:43-8 N '87
In-circuit digital IC tester (II). il *Radio-Electron* 58:55-8 D '87

Green, Ernest

about
Ebony update: Ernest Green. il pors *Ebony* 43:72+ D '87

Green, Freddie

about
Obituary
Jet il por 71:5 Mr 16 '87

Green, Frederick C.

about
Ombudsman of child abuse. il pors *Ebony* 42:82+ F '87
Six things parents should never say to their children. por *Jet* 73:14+ N 30 '87

Green, Gerald
Brownsville. il *N Y* 20:102-3 D 21-28 '87

Green, Jaki Shelton, 1953-
A birthday tribute III [poem] *Essence* 18:137 D '87
Eva I [poem] *Essence* 17:122 Mr '87

Green, Jesse
An every-afternoon affair [story] il *Mademoiselle* 93:128+ Ag '87

Green, Jimmy

about
Deaf mute cleared of murdering Ala. woman. *Jet* 73:36 O 19 '87

Green, Judith H.

about
Inside stories: author Judith Green's Park Avenue residence. J. Kornbluth. il por *Archit Dig* 44:134-9+ D '87

Green, Kenneth C., and Gilbert, Steven W.
Software piracy. il *Change* 19:46-9 Ja/F '87

Green, Lilias
There's a protozoan in that painting. il *BioScience* 37:181-5 Mr '87

Green, Michelle
Bewitched, bothered and Bisset. por *Harpers Bazaar* 120:205+ Ap '87

Green, Peter
Roofing: synthesizing design and craftsmanship. il *Archit Rec* 175:136-41 F '87

Green, Philip, 1932-
A sort of memoir. *Nation* 245:158-60+ Ag 29 '87

Green, Richard C., Jr.

about
Building a powerhouse, one utility at a time. M. Ivey. il por *Bus Week* p81 F 2 '87

Green, Robert Alan
A fabulous lady from Spain [cover story] il por *Antiques Collect Hobbies* 92:30-4 My '87
William Gale & Son, New York silversmiths. il *Antiques Collect Hobbies* 91:18-20 F '87

Green, S. William (Sedgwick William) *See* Green, Bill, 1929-

Green, Sara
The eyes and ears have it in DC. il *Theatre Crafts* 21:41+ Ap '87

Green, Seth

about
Zowie! Comics and Radio days make Seth Green a little Woody. il por *People Wkly* 27:115 Ap 20 '87

Green, Tim

about
'I will be ostracized'. J. Lieber. il por *Sports Illus* 67:61 O 26 '87

Green, Verna

about
Topping the charts. J. Chenault. il *Essence* 17:90+ Ja '87

Green, Vincent S.
The wrong way home [poem] *Ctry J* 14:79 Ap '87

Green, Walter

about
How to run a really good meeting [interview] por *U S News World Rep* 103:80 O 12 '87

Green Bay (Wis.)

Sports
Troubled times in Titletown [relationship between Green Bay, Wis. and its Packers] F. Deford. il *Sports Illus* 66:70-4+ My 25 '87

Water pollution
Warning: the Friday night fish fry may be hazardous to your health [pollution by waste from the Fort Howard Paper Co.] M. Hudson. il maps *Audubon* 89:24-6+ Jl '87

Green belts *See* Greenbelts

Green Berets *See* United States. Army. Special Forces

Green Briar Nursing Home (Kendall, Fla.) *See* Nursing homes

Green family

about
How to steal an S&L—legally. B. D. Fromson. il *Fortune* 116:57-8+ O 12 '87

Green Mountain Herbs, Ltd.
The eternal promoter [W. A. Kilpatrick] A. A. Lappen. il por *Forbes* 140:8 Ag 10 '87
The never-say-die promoter [W. Kilpatrick] J. A. Conway. por *Forbes* 139:8 Ap 6 '87
The promoter who never quits [tax shelter operator W. A. Kilpatrick] A. A. Lappen. il por *Forbes* 139:60-1 F 9 '87

Green Party (U.S.)
Local issues fuel activism. il *U S News World Rep* 103:31 Ag 31 '87
Organic platform in 1988? S. O. Daniels. il *Rodale's Org Gard* 34:7 N '87

Green Party (Western Europe)
The flowering of the Greens in Europe. D. Stanglin. il *U S News World Rep* 103:30-1 Ag 31 '87
Green revolution *See* Agriculture—Developing countries
Greenbelts
Greenways: keeping the outdoors great. il *Futurist* 21:51 Jl/Ag '87
A network of green corridors, threading its way through city and countryside, is proposed by a presidential commission. J. P. Wiley, Jr. il *Smithsonian* 18:26+ Jl '87
Greenberg, Alan C.
about
Ace may be the Street's top card. B. Hetzer. il por *Fortune* 115:94 Ja 5 '87
"Just a simple customers' man from Oklahoma". D. Machan. il por *Forbes* 140:118+ S 7 '87
Greenberg, Alfred H.
Skier-at-large. See issues of Skiing beginning November 1986
Greenberg, Allan
The diplomatic reception rooms of Edward Vason Jones. bibl f il *Antiques* 132:122-31 Jl '87
about
Allan Greenberg's rooms in the Department of State. P. Goldberger. il *Antiques* 132:132-43 Jl '87
Greenberg, Arnold C.
about
Coleco: out of the Cabbage Patch and into the fire. S. Benway. il por *Bus Week* p54 Mr 30 '87
Greenberg, Clement, 1909-
about
Clement Greenberg—the critic and his artists. S. Schwartz. *Am Sch* 56:535-45 Aut '87
Criticism and culture, or Greenberg's doubt. S. Tillim. *Art Am* 75:122-7+ My '87
The idea of tradition in American art criticism. H. Kramer. *Am Sch* 56:319-27 Summ '87
Greenberg, D. A.
Modeling tidal power. il maps *Sci Am* 257:128-128C+ N '87
Greenberg, Daniel S.
Can chicken-coop inventors help us win? il *U S News World Rep* 103:42 Jl 27 '87
The club that breeds success. il *U S News World Rep* 102:44-5 Ap 20 '87
The government bends to AIDS victims' pleas. il *U S News World Rep* 102:76 Mr 23 '87
A hidden cost of military research: less national security. il *Discover* 8:94+ Ja '87
Publish or perish—or fake it. il *U S News World Rep* 102:72-3 Je 8 '87
Greenberg, Emanuel
(jt. auth) See Greenberg, Madeline, and Greenberg, Emanuel
Greenberg, Jerald
(jt. auth) See Mark, Melvin M., and Greenberg, Jerald
Greenberg, Joel
Israel's censored Palestinians. *World Press Rev* 34:56 My '87
Greenberg, Madeline, and Greenberg, Emanuel
Food. See issues of 50 Plus beginning May 1983
Greenberg, Pearl, 1927-
Expanding the domain of arts education. bibl f *Des Arts Educ* 88:39-40 Ja/F '87
Greenberg, Richard
about
The maderati [drama] Reviews
N Y 20:111-12 Mr 2 '87. J. Simon
New Yorker 63:76 Mr 2 '87. E. Oliver
Greenberger, Ellen, and Steinberg, Laurence D., 1952-
Bypassing the unpaid work of growing up: teens with jobs. *Educ Dig* 53:29-31 O '87
Greene, Bob
1964 [excerpt from Be true to your school] il por *Esquire* 107:86-90+ F '87
American beat. See issues of Esquire
Greene, Elaine
Beacon Hill spirit. il *House Gard* 159:154-61 Mr '87
Country in the capital. il *House Gard* 159:168-75 F '87
The country set. il *House Gard* 159:162-9 D '87
Cultivating romance. il *House Gard* 159:166-73+ My '87
A decorating eye. il *House Gard* 159:148-55+ Je '87
The English channel. il pors *House Gard* 159:32+ Jl '87
Fabulous fakery. il *House Gard* 159:134-43 S '87
For ever England. il por *House Gard* 159:198-203 My '87
Image makers. il pors *House Gard* 159:180-7 N '87

New style in the Old South. il *House Gard* 159:140-5+ Jl '87
A New York of one's own: Mario Buatta furnishes a pied-à-terre on Fifth Avenue. il *House Gard* 159:204-9 Ap '87
Old World white. il *House Gard* 159:94-9 Ja '87
Painting a world. il por *House Gard* 159:40+ D '87
Rare and early. il *House Gard* 159:162-7+ N '87
A subtle palette. il por *House Gard* 159:122-9+ F '87
Textile tending. il por *House Gard* 159:87-8+ Mr '87
Where opposites attract. il *House Gard* 159:144-9+ Ja '87
Greene, Ellen
about
Critics agree with the man-eating plant in Little shop of horrors: Ellen Greene is delicious. D. Hutchings. il pors *People Wkly* 27:43-4 Ja 12 '87
Greene, Erick, and others
A tephritid fly mimics the territorial displays of its jumping spider predators. bibl f il *Science* 236:310-12 Ap 17 '87
Greene, Gael
Adding up the new '21'. il *N Y* 20:40-7 Je 1 '87
Ask Gael: where our critic tells her friends to eat. il *N Y* 20:20-6+ Ja 5 '87
The Box Tree Hotel: Augustin Paege's opulent setting in Turtle Bay. il por *Archit Dig* 44:170-7 N '87
Castle in the air: a family lodge above Aspen. il *Archit Dig* 44:136-9+ Ag '87
The French evolution. il *N Y* 20:50-5 Mr 23 '87
In the nabes. il *N Y* 20:62-5 S 14 '87
The insatiable critic. See occasional issues of New York
Le Pavillon. il *N Y* 20:86 D 21-28 '87
True West. il *N Y* 20:44-6+ Jl 27 '87
Greene, Harold H.
about
More heat for Judge Greene. il por *Fortune* 116:9+ O 12 '87
Greene, Janice L.
Emilia-Romagna: Italy's best-kept vacation secret. il *Black Enterp* 18:90-1 S '87
Greene, Joe
about
Mean Joe Greene back to work for NFL Steelers. por *Jet* 71:51 Mr 16 '87
Greene, Joe
about
Not gunmen, but smarties. B. Dolan. il por *Time* 129:85 Ap 27 '87
Greene, Lawrence J.
Making kids smarter. il *Parents* 62:94-8+ D '87
Greene, Lorne, 1915-1987
about
Obituary
Macleans il pors 100:42-3 S 21 '87. P. Young
People Wkly por 28:36-7 S 28 '87
Greene, Melissa Fay
All the hours of the night: the recollections of a country midwife. il pors *Ctry J* 14:58-63 N '87
No rms, jungle vu. il *Atlantic* 260:62-8+ D '87
Greene, Pat Ryan
Sowing justice in Ecuador. *Christ Century* 104:910-12 O 21 '87
Greene, Preston
Ethnic politics American style. *America* 157:28+ Jl 18-25 '87
Greene, Ralph C.
Personal autonomy and public health: an ethical imperative for preventing disease. il por *Humanist* 47:6-9 Jl/Ag '87
Greene, Randy
Does it have to hurt to punish your kids? il *U S Cathol* 52:24-31 N '87
Yours, mine, and ours: can stepfamilies ever blend? il *U S Cathol* 52:31-7 Jl '87
Greene, Richard
I'm a new father who takes his role seriously: why doesn't anyone else? il *Glamour* 85:94 Je '87
(jt. auth) See Barrett, Katherine, and Greene, Richard
Greene, Richard T.
about
Carver Federal carves out its market niche. R. Fleming. il por *Black Enterp* 17:214-16+ Je '87
Greene (Stephen) Press *See* Stephen Greene Press
Greenfield, Ellen J.
Rate your home: how safe is it? [excerpt from House dangerous] *Redbook* 168:117-18 Mr '87
Greenfield, Jerry
about
Cold comfort. D. C. Craig. il pors *Life* 10:58-9 S '87

Greenfield, Larry, and others
Mutations in diphtheria toxin separate binding from entry and amplify immunotoxin selectivity. bibl f il *Science* 238:536-9 O 23 '87

Greenfield, Meg
[Column] See occasional issues of Newsweek

Greenfield-Sanders, Timothy
about
Eye of the beholder. S. Edelson. il por *N Y* 20:36 Ap 27 '87

Greenfield Village *See* Henry Ford Museum and Greenfield Village

Greenhalgh, Susan, and Bongaarts, John, 1945-
China's population program [discussion of March 6, 1987 article, Fertility policy in China: future options] *Science* 238:1025-6 N 20 '87
Fertility policy in China: future options. bibl f il *Science* 235:1167-72 Mr 6 '87

Greenhouse effect
The biggest chill. W. S. Broecker. il maps *Nat Hist* 96:74-80+ O '87
Climate modeling [cover story] S. H. Schneider. il *Sci Am* 256:72-8+ My '87
Congress considers global climate change. N. Bell. *BioScience* 37:258 Ap '87
Evidence that the world's climate may be changing irreversibly has not yet resulted in any coordinated response. R. M. Adams. il *Smithsonian* 18:12 Ag '87
Forecast for disaster. R. H. Boyle. il *Sports Illus* 67:78-84+ N 16 '87
A future danger: hothouse hurricanes? [work of Kerry Emanuel] il *Discover* 8:10+ Je '87
Greenhouse effect study [joint US/China agreement] *Sea Front* 33:463-4 N/D '87
The heat is on [cover story] M. D. Lemonick. il *Time* 130:58-63+ O 19 '87
Hothouse futures? [research by Irving M. Mintzer] il *Futurist* 21:43-4 N/D '87
How much drying from a greenhouse warming? [views of Thomas Karl] R. A. Kerr. *Science* 235:435 Ja 23 '87
An icy warning of a global warming? [icebergs separate from Antarctic ice sheet] map *Newsweek* 110:65 D 28 '87
Life, the great chemistry experiment [State of the earth 1987] S. Postel. il *Nat Hist* 96:41-8 Ap '87
More violent hurricanes? [caused by warmer climate; views of Kerry Emanuel] *Time* 129:69 Ap 20 '87
Ozone and global warming: what to do? S. Weisburd. *Sci News* 131:86 F 7 '87
Policies on global warming and ozone depletion. B. Green. *Environment* 29:5+ Ap '87
Precipitation fluctuations over Northern Hemisphere land areas since the mid-19th century. R. S. Bradley and others. bibl f il maps *Science* 237:171-5 Jl 10 '87
Probing the permafrost [work of Arthur H. Lachenbruch and B. Vaughn Marshall] il *Sci Am* 256:62 F '87
Report on reports: the carbon dioxide debate: reports from SCOPE and DOE. A. B. Pittock. bibl *Environment* 29:25-30 Ja/F '87
Trace gases: potential impacts on ozone and temperature. *Environment* 29:40 Ja/F '87
Vapor lock [air bubbles in Antarctic ice record carbon dioxide and climate] T. Beardsley. *Sci Am* 257:32 D '87
Will species die out as the earth heats up? T. A. Lewis. il *Int Wildl* 17:18-21 N/D '87

Greenhouses
See also
Cold frames
Garden rooms
A garden in the window [window greenhouse] il *Mother Earth News* 108:65 N/D '87
Great greenhouse add-ons [expanding apartment space] il *McCalls* 114:90-3+ Ag '87
A greenhouse in the Midwest. E. Felton. il *Flower Gard* 31:16-17 O/N '87
Greenhouse or sunroom? il *Flower Gard* 31:18-24 O/N '87
Plain and fancy [Albemarle Conservatory, Charlottesville, Va.] M. Gaskie. il *Archit Rec* 175:106-9 Ja '87
They added a two-story greenhouse room. il *Sunset* 178:155 Ap '87
This heated greenhouse uses no gas or electricity [solar greenhouse] il *Sunset* 179:227 O '87
Insect control
See Insect control

Greening, Jim
Pipeline. See issues of Cycle

Greenland
See also
Aviation—Greenland
Ice—Greenland

Greenland Sea *See* Norwegian Sea

Greenleaf, Christopher, and Hirsch, Julian D.
Car stereo. See alternate issues of Stereo Review

Greenly, Mike
Getting "non-techs" on-line: tomorrow's easier computers. il *Futurist* 21:60 Jl/Ag '87
Interactive journalism and computer networking: exploring a new medium. il pors *Futurist* 21:12-16 Mr/Ap '87

Greenmail
Are USG's walls crumbling? [Desert Partners bid] J. E. Ellis. il *Bus Week* p59 O 19 '87
Back to business [effects of R. Perelman's raid on CPC International] J. Cook. il por *Forbes* 140:40-1 O 5 '87
The greenmail factor [Belzberg family accused of attempting to greenmail GTE] L. Black. il *Macleans* 100:67 F 2 '87
Natalie Koether: the lady is a raider. P. Finch. il por *Bus Week* p118-19 F 23 '87
Trump vs. Wynn: 'giant egos on the line' [Golden Nugget stock] R. Grover. il por *Bus Week* p31-2 Jl 27 '87
What color is your mail? [Salomon Brothers pays greenmail to Minerals & Resources Corp.] A. Sloan. il *Forbes* 140:36-7 O 19 '87

Greenmarkets *See* Farmers' markets

Greenough, Sarah, 1951-
The letters of Georgia O'Keeffe. bibl f il por *Antiques* 132:1110-17 N '87

Greenpeace bombing incident, 1985
Secretary-General mediates successfully in 'Rainbow Warrior' affair; France, New Zealand to abide by ruling. *UN Chron* 23:75 N '86

Greenpeace Foundation
The zeal of disapproval. M. H. Brown. il por *Oceans* 20:36-41 My/Je '87

Greens, Edible
See also
Burnet
Celtuce
Cooking—Vegetables
Herbs
Lettuce
Designer greens. C. Idone. il *Harpers Bazaar* 120:48+ Ag '87
How to grow exotic salad greens. il *Consum Res Mag* 70:28-9 My '87
Mesclun of Nice is really just mixed salad greens. Here's how to grow it. il *Sunset* 179:215 O '87

Greensboro (N.C.)
Police
First black police chief in Greensboro, N.C. is used to being a first [S. Daughtry] por *Jet* 72:12 Ap 13 '87

Greenspan, Alan
about
Act I at Alan Greenspan's Fed. por *Newsweek* 110:56 S 14 '87
Alan Greenspan is headed for a quiet honeymoon. M. McNamee. il por *Bus Week* p27 Ag 3 '87
A delicate balance. S. Koepp. il *Time* 130:32-3 Ag 10 '87
Exit Volcker, enter Greenspan. *Natl Rev* 39:17+ Jl 3 '87
Forecasting's dim prognosis. S. Dentzer and R. Thomas. il por *Newsweek* 110:42 Jl 27 '87
Greenspan isn't a Volcker clone. L. Smith. il pors *Fortune* 116:34-6 Jl 6 '87
Greenspan's big test. il por *Time* 130:29 N 2 '87
Greenspan's debut draws raves. J. C. Szabo. il por *Nations Bus* 75:9-10 O '87
How does the Street spell relief? G-r-e-e-n-s-p-a-n. S. Weiss. il por *Bus Week* p122-3 Je 22 '87
An inflation fighter steps down. I. Austen. il pors *Macleans* 100:34-5 Je 15 '87
Is Alan Greenspan really such a hero? S. Zucker. por *Bus Week* p35 D 14 '87
The Jim and Alan show: will the markets buy it? T. Morganthau. il pors *Newsweek* 110:18-19 N 2 '87
The new Mr. Dollar [cover story; special section] il pors *Time* 129:46-53 Je 15 '87
One plus one plus one equals zero. D. Machan. il por *Forbes* 139:58+ Ap 20 '87
Reagan's man at the Fed [special section] il pors *Newsweek* 109:16-20+ Je 15 '87
The rising risk of recession. J. Egan. il pors *U S News World Rep* 102:47+ Je 15 '87

Greenspan, Alan—about—*cont.*
The task ahead for Alan Greenspan. T. May, Jr. il *Fortune* 116:49+ Ag 17 '87
Testing time for Greenspan. J. Egan. il por *U S News World Rep* 103:49-50 S 21 '87
What investors should ask of Alan Greenspan. M. S. Forbes, Jr. il por *Forbes* 139:25 Je 29 '87
What's in store at the Fed [cover story; special section] il pors *Bus Week* p26-30 Je 15 '87
Why Greenspan is bullish [cover story] S. Nasar. il pors *Fortune* 116:28-32+ O 26 '87

Anecdotes, facetiae, satire, etc.
And now, the Fed letters. pors *U S News World Rep* 103:43 Jl 27 '87

Greenspan, Edward L.
about
A vocal opponent [interview] M. Janigan. il por *Macleans* 100:10 Mr 16 '87

Greenspan, Edward L., and Jonas, George, 1935-
The case for the defence [excerpt from Greenspan] il pors *Macleans* 100:48-50+ O 19 '87

Greenspan, Emily
A consumer's guide to over-the-counter tests. il *Ms* 15:60+ Je '87
Fire on ice. il pors *Women's Sports Fitness* 9:22-5+ Mr '87

Greenspan O'Neil Associates
One plus one plus one equals zero. D. Machan. il por *Forbes* 139:58+ Ap 20 '87

Greenstreet, Bob
Integration of law and practice into the curriculum. il por *Archit Rec* 175:43 Mr '87

Greenville (Miss.)
Police
First black police chief hired in Greenville, Miss. [M. Wynn] por *Jet* 72:10 Ag 31 '87

Greenwald, Gerald
about
Chrysler's conundrum. S. Flack. il por *Forbes* 139:104 Ap 20 '87

Greenwich (Conn.)
Architecture
Domestic arts [Shope House] G. Anderson. il *Archit Rec* 175:80-5 mid-Ap '87
Part and parcel [former chauffeur's barn at Conyer's Manor] C. Vogel. il *N Y Times Mag* p58-60 Ap 19 '87

Historic houses, sites, etc.
Back country Greenwich [English decoration by S. Parish for H. De Kwiatkowski] S. M. L. Aronson. il *House Gard* 159:132-9+ Ag '87

Social life and customs
Connecticut Yankees court the Yorks [visit of Prince Andrew and Sarah; cover story] L. Rozen. il pors *People Wkly* 28:96-7+ S 21 '87

Greenwich Village (New York, N.Y.)
Answers [J.-P. Fenyo, the Free Advice Man of Greenwich Village] *New Yorker* 63:18-19 Ag 17 '87
The East Village: rebels and immigrants in the land of the Stuyvesants. A. Virshup. il map *N Y* 20:54-6 My 4 '87
A forest grows in Manhattan [A. Sonfist's Time Landscape] P. Hagan. il *Sierra* 72:16+ Mr/Ap '87
The fun's over: the East Village scene gets burned by success. A. Virshup. il *N Y* 20:48-50+ Je 22 '87
Moonlighting [astronomer T. Hoffman offers passersby a look through a telescope] J. Stone. il *Discover* 8:93-5 O '87
The place of the past: growing up in Greenwich Village. I. C. Kuhn. il *Gourmet* 47:78-80+ Ap '87
There goes the neighborhood: gangs of yuppies move onto the turf of New York's Hells Angels [East Village] J. S. Kunen. il *People Wkly* 28:119-20+ S 7 '87
The West Village: artists' outposts, ancient mariners, and the meat of the city. E. Hopkins. il map *N Y* 20:82-4 My 4 '87

Greenwood, Bruce
about
Racial mishap sparks buy boycott in Isola, Miss. *Jet* 73:32 N 2 '87

Greenwood, Gail
I was a teacher, but my son couldn't learn. il *Work Woman* 12:180+ N '87

Greenwood (Miss.)
Race relations
Miss. councilman seeks aid after KKK threats [D. Jordan] il por *Jet* 71:6 Mr 23 '87

Greer, Germaine, 1939-
The force of nature. il por *House Gard* 159:66+ N '87

Greer, Rebecca
Woman's day. il *Writer* 100:31 Ap '87

Greeting card industry
See also
Hallmark Cards, Inc.
L'Image Graphics

Greeting cards
See also
Christmas cards
Valentines
Contemporary greeting cards: more than hearts and flowers [selling photographs to greeting card companies] G. Schaub. il *Pop Photogr* 94:21 Mr '87
Here they are! The top winning cards in the 1987 Mother's Day contest! il *Good Housekeep* 204:36+ My '87
Photo cards: personalized messages handcrafted from your photo files. H. Katin. il *Petersens Photogr Mag* 16:82-3 Je '87
Postal photography [mailable photo greetings] L. Nielsen. il *Petersens Photogr Mag* 15:70-1 Ap '87

Grega, Debra S., and others
Forskolin and phorbol esters reduce the same potassium conductance of mouse neurons in culture. bibl f il *Science* 235:345-8 Ja 16 '87

Greger, Debora, 1949-
Snow White and Rose Red [poem] *New Yorker* 63:42 D 21 '87

Gregerson, Linda
The bad physician [poem] *Atlantic* 259:67 Ja '87

Gregg, Judd
Is the administration approach to federal employee drug testing sound? [excerpts from debate, September 17, 1986] *Congr Dig* 66:148 My '87

Gregg, Randy
about
Edmonton's Rx for D. A. Murphy. il pors *Sports Illus* 66:42-4 My 25 '87

Grego, Daniel
The trembling [poem] *America* 157:83 Ag 15-22 '87

Gregor, Arthur, 1923-
Mozartian [poem] *Nation* 244:896 Je 27 '87

Gregor, Katherine
Just getting started. il pors *Art News* 86:59-60+ N '87

Gregory, André
about
Andre Gregory: scene stealer. R. Kramer. por *Harpers Bazaar* 120:124+ Ap '87

Gregory, B. L.
Solid state technology in the 21st century. il *Radio-Electron* 58:97-8 My '87

Gregory, Dick
about
730-lb. man trying Dick Gregory's formula to aid in weight loss. il pors *Jet* 72:52 My 4 '87
After 27 years in his bedroom, 1,200-lb. Walter Hudson decides to take a load off. W. Plummer. il pors *People Wkly* 28:60-1 O 26 '87
A comedic look at the black middle class. W. Leavy. il pors *Ebony* 42:68+ Ag '87
Dick Gregory launches new enterprise with Slim-Safe Bahamian Diet. il por *Jet* 72:16 Mr 30 '87
Dick Gregory starts workshops, seminars to market formulas. por *Jet* 72:16 Ap 6 '87
Dick Gregory thrilled with response to new company, diet formulas. por *Jet* 72:16 Ap 13 '87
Gregory comes to rescue of 1,000-pound Walter Hudson. il pors *Jet* 73:17-18 N 9 '87

Gregory, Richard Claxton *See* Gregory, Dick

Greider, William
The heart of everything that is. il *Roll Stone* p37-8+ My 7 '87
National affairs. See issues of Rolling Stone
The price of money (I). *New Yorker* 63:54-6+ N 9 '87
The price of money (II). *New Yorker* 63:68-72+ N 16 '87
The price of money (III). *New Yorker* 63:49-50+ N 23 '87
about
Money gods. R. Hornik. il por *Time* 130:50-1 D 7 '87

Greif, Judith
All about headaches. il *N Y* 20:56-8+ Mr 9 '87

Greiner, John W., and others
Recombinant interferon enhances monoclonal antibody-targeting of carcinoma lesions in vivo. bibl f il *Science* 235:895-8 F 20 '87

Grenada
See also
Calypso music—Grenada
Music and state—Grenada

Grenada—See also—*cont.*
Trials—Grenada
Description and travel
Cowboys and West Indians. D. A. Rose. il *Esquire* 107:20+ F '87
Grenada revisited: better than ever. A. Ponsford. il *World Press Rev* 34:63 F '87
Industries
See also
Spice industry—Grenada
Invasion, 1983
One U.S. invasion later . . . C. Garcia. il *Time* 130:43 N 23 '87
Yesterday's revolution [trial of M. Bishop's murderers] B. Shacochis. il *Harpers* 275:41-4+ O '87
Politics and government
One U.S. invasion later . . . C. Garcia. il *Time* 130:43 N 23 '87
Some fell slow and some fell fast [trial of M. Bishop's murderers] G. Wagner. *Natl Rev* 39:32-3 Je 5 '87
Yesterday's revolution [trial of M. Bishop's murderers] B. Shacochis. il *Harpers* 275:41-4+ O '87
Grenier, Jeannine E.
Legislative alert: what we want from the 100th Congress. il *Ms* 15:24 Ap '87
Grenoble (France)
Galleries and museums
See also
Centre National d'Art Contemporain (Grenoble, France)
Population
Grenoble, France's high-powered mountain city. P. Frappat. il *Courier* 40:16-17 F '87
Grenoble Olympics, 1968 *See* Olympic Games—1968—Winter Olympics
Grensing, Lin
Employee 'relations'. il *Essence* 17:105+ F '87
Grenz, Stanley, 1950-
Pannenberg on Marxism: insights and generalizations. *Christ Century* 104:824-6 S 30 '87
What is sex for? il por *Christ Today* 31:22-3 Je 12 '87
Greschner, Ron
about
Carol and her big lug. E. M. Swift. il pors *Sports Illus* 66:88-91+ F 9 '87
Gress, Edmund
Fleeing to Canada. *Commonweal* 114:164-6 Mr 27 '87
Gretzky, Wayne
about
Hot shots on ice [cover story] A. Murphy. il por *Sports Illus* 66:26-9 Je 1 '87
A superstar's amazing year. por *Macleans* 100:14-15 D 28 '87
Grevatt, Marge
Everybody came but 'Larry'. il *Nation* 245:228-9 S 12 '87
Grey, Jennifer
about
Hotchacha. J. Sherman. por *Vogue* 177:70 Ag '87
Jennifer Grey (Joel's baby and Matthew Broderick's lady) turns up the heat in Dirty dancing. D. Hutchings. il pors *People Wkly* 28:47-8 S 14 '87
Greyhound Corp.
All aboard [Greyhound to buy Trailways] il *Time* 129:46 Je 29 '87
Can Greyhound leave the dog days behind? S. Toy. il por *Bus Week* p72+ Je 8 '87
First black president of Greyhound's Western Division reveals plans [V. Brown] il pors *Jet* 72:38-9 Je 29 '87
How an ace mechanic wants to fix Greyhound Lines [takeover by F. W. Currey's investor group] J. Hurlock. *Bus Week* p45-6 Ja 12 '87
Leave the driving to Fred Currey [plan for fusing Greyhound and Trailways] J. Weber, Jr. il por *Bus Week* p62-3 Ag 24 '87
Trying to put Greyhound back on its feet [sale of bus line] il *Newsweek* 109:40 Ja 5 '87
Unhappy Trails [to acquire Trailways] *Newsweek* 109:49 Je 29 '87
Greyhound Leasing & Financial Corp.
Equipment leasing faces trial by tax reform. G. Weiss. il *Bus Week* p114-15 Ja 12 '87
Grice, Ayesha Jihada
Sign time. See issues of Essence
Grief
See also
Church work with the bereaved

Bereavement: reeling in the years [mourning process after a sudden loss; study by Camille B. Wortman and others] B. Bower. *Sci News* 131:84 F 7 '87
How to cope with grief. il *Ebony* 42:86B+ Jl '87
In memory of David Koop [excerpt from Sometimes mountains move] C. E. Koop and E. Koop. il pors *Saturday Evening Post* 259:62-3+ N '87
My mother's cookbook [discovery of cookbook prompts memories of recently deceased mother] S. Flynn. il por *McCalls* 114:47+ My '87
Stillbirth. P. A. Hillard. il *Parents* 62:142+ Jl '87
The tears of God [N. Wolterstorff's Lament for a son] M. E. Marty. *Christ Century* 104:607 Jl 1-8 '87
What's in a name? [death of a son] W. T. Hanlon. *America* 157:317-18 N 7 '87
When a child dies [parents' grief] R. J. Knapp. il *Psychol Today* 21:60-3+ Jl '87
When I was grieving [letters from friends provide comfort after death of premature infant] A. P. Murphy. il *Glamour* 85:302 My '87
When my wife's mother died, the loss tore us apart. N. Dillon. *Glamour* 85:234+ Mr '87
Where there's a will: from anger to action [M. Jackson-Randolph's life after losing her children in a fire] B. M. Campbell. il pors *Essence* 18:57-8+ D '87
Griffey, Ken, Jr.
about
Griffey Jr. looks like a chip off the old block. il por *Jet* 72:46 Je 22 '87
Griffin, Anthony
about
Charges of racism. L. Van Dusen. il *Macleans* 100:14+ N 30 '87
Griffin, David
A birth control vaccine. il *World Health* p25-7 N '87
Griffin, Jasper
The father of it all. il *N Y Rev Books* 34:11-12+ Ap 9 '87
Griffin, Larry
Sport. See issues of Car and Driver
Griffin, Marvin W., Jr.
about
Are we there yet? E. F. Cone. il por *Forbes* 139:110+ Mr 9 '87
Promises, promises. J. A. Conway. il por *Forbes* 139 Ann Directory:10+ Ap 27 '87
Griffin, Merv, 1925-
about
The millionaire who made Vanna White a star. V. Scott. il pors *Good Housekeep* 204:66+ My '87
Griffin, William
Religious books. See occasional issues of Publishers Weekly beginning July 29, 1983
Religious publishing. See occasional issues of Publishers Weekly beginning July 18, 1986
Griffith, Aline *See* Aline, Countess of Romanones
Griffith, Bill *See* Granger, Bill
Griffith, George
about
Light as a feather. D. Wallace. il por *Mot Boat Sail* 159:54-6+ Mr '87
Griffith, George V.
Setting things right in school. por *Newsweek* 110:16-17 S 21 '87
Griffith, Linda Lewis, 1953-, and Pine, Devera
Making time to work out. *Women's Sports Fitness* 9:28-33 S '87
Griffith, Mark Winston
Say, brother. por *Essence* 18:10 S '87
Griffith, Nanci
about
The queen of folkabilly. P. Nelson. por *Roll Stone* p20 My 7 '87
Griffith, Thomas
Newswatch. See issues of Time
Griffiths, Franklyn
"New thinking" in the Kremlin. bibl f *Bull At Sci* 43:20-4 Ap '87
Grigg, William
The thalidomide tragedy—25 years ago. il *FDA Consum* 21:14-17 F '87
Warming to the idea: heat research may help hearts, kidneys, and man's best friend. il por *FDA Consum* 21:25-7 My '87
Griggs, Shirley A.
(jt. auth) See Berkson, Jerrold, and Griggs, Shirley A.
Griggs, Steve
Steve Lacy's solo on Skippy—a soprano saxophone transcription. il *Down Beat* 54:60-2 D '87

Grigorovich, IŪrii Nikolaevich, 1927-
about
Back from the USSR: Bolshoi blockbuster [cover story] M. E. Willis. il *Dance Mag* 61:34-8 Jl '87
Bolshoi intrigue. L. Shapiro. il *Newsweek* 110:47 Jl 6 '87
Bolshoi lords aleaping. M. Duffy. il *Time* 130:74-5 Jl 27 '87
Giselle [ballet] Reviews
    N Y il 20:50-1 Ag 3 '87. T. Tobias
The golden age [ballet] Reviews
    Art Am il 75:30-1+ N '87. J. R. Acocella
    N Y 20:52 Jl 20 '87. T. Tobias
    New Leader 70:22-3 Ag 10-24 '87. L. A. Jacobs
    New Yorker 63:61 Jl 27 '87. A. Croce
The next great leap: measuring the Bolshoi. D. McDonagh. *Commonweal* 114:499-500 S 11 '87
Raymonda [ballet] Reviews
    N Y il 20:50-1 Ag 3 '87. T. Tobias
    New Yorker 63:61-2 Jl 27 '87. A. Croce
Skirting controversy at home, the Bolshoi's Yuri Grigorovich brings his dancers to the U.S. il por *People Wkly* 28:40-2 Jl 27 '87
The Soviet dance theater of Yuri Grigorovich. N. Alovert. il por *Dance Mag* 61:39-42 D '87
Yuri Grigorovich: an appreciation. N. Alovert. il por *Dance Mag* 61:44-7 Jl '87

Grigoryants, Sergei I.
about
A journalistic profile in courage. J. Alter. il por *Newsweek* 110:37 D 14 '87
New mag in Moscow. M. Garbus. *N Y Rev Books* 34:49 Ag 13 '87

Griliches, Zvi, 1930-
R&D and productivity: measurement issues and econometric results. bibl f il *Science* 237:31-5 Jl 3 '87

Grilling *See* Barbecue cooking
Grillner, Sten
(jt. auth) See Buchanan, James T., and Grillner, Sten
Grillo, Jean Bergantini
Loughlin's lament. il por *Channels* 7:66-7 Jl/Ag '87
Grills, Barbecue *See* Barbecue grills
Grimes, John A.
Are the media shortchanging organized labor? *Mon Labor Rev* 110:53-4 Ag '87
Grimes, Martha
Seeing around curves. *Writer* 100:11-13+ S '87
about
The terribly English mysteries of Martha Grimes are a welcome addition to the pub-lic domain. A. Chambers. il pors *People Wkly* 27:64+ F 2 '87
Grimes, William
The best of the West Indies. il *Esquire* 107:46 Je '87
Canadian draft picks. il *Esquire* 107:34 Ap '87
Gin without the tonic. il *Esquire* 108:24 Ag '87
Grand Andalusians. il *Esquire* 108:44 O '87
Licorice shtick. il *Esquire* 108:54 S '87
Muscat ramble. il *Esquire* 107:34 My '87
The one-man wine bar. il *Esquire* 107:34 Mr '87
Slow fizz. il *Esquire* 108:44+ D '87
Grimm, Mary
Book of dreams [story] *New Yorker* 63:29-33 Je 22 '87
Grimm, Michele, and Grimm, Tom
Travel in focus. See alternate issues of Travel Holiday
Grimm, Tom
(jt. auth) See Grimm, Michele, and Grimm, Tom
Grindelwald (Switzerland)
Swiss twins. K. Castle. il map *Travel Holiday* 168:36-43 O '87
Grinding machines
A new grind [Delta grinder] H. Wicks. il *Home Mech* 83:20 O '87
Grindy, Robert
More about magnesium [interview with M. Seelig] il por *Saturday Evening Post* 259:50-3+ Jl/Ag '87
Grinnell, George Bird, 1849-1938
about
A man called Bird. J. G. Mitchell. il pors map *Audubon* 89:81-104 Mr '87
Grinspoon, David H.
Was Venus wet? Deuterium reconsidered. bibl f il *Science* 238:1702-4 D 18 '87
Griot musicians *See* Musicians, African
Gripen airplanes *See* Airplanes, Military—Sweden
Gris, Charles Édouard Jeanneret- *See* Le Corbusier, 1887-1965
Grisanti, Mary Lee
The man without a country. il pors *N Y* 20:38-43 Ja 12 '87

Griscom, Thomas
about
White House split. L. Howard. il por *Newsweek* 110:3 Jl 13 '87
Grissom, Gus, 1926-1967
about
ISO: Liberty Bell. T. Reichhardt. il por *Space World* X-1-277:25-8 Ja '87
Gristina, Anthony G.
Biomaterial-centered infection: microbial adhesion versus tissue integration. bibl f il *Science* 237:1588-95 S 25 '87
Griswold, Gary K.
Religion: an obstacle to a better world? il por *Humanist* 47:18-19+ Mr/Ap '87
Griswold, Jerry
Confessions of a bibliophile. *Writer* 100:5-6 My '87
Pollyanna, ex-bubblehead. *N Y Times Book Rev* 92:51 O 25 '87
Grits cooking *See* Cooking—Grain
Grizzly bears *See* Bears
Grobel, Lawrence
about
Huston family portrait announced by Scribners for spring 1989. il por *Publ Wkly* 232:75 O 2 '87
Grobman, Susan
Child of divorce. il *USA Today (Periodical)* 116:40-2 Jl '87
Grocery shopping *See* Purchasing, Household
Grocery trade
See also
    Computers—Grocery trade use
    Food Lion Inc.
    Food stores
    Great Atlantic & Pacific Tea Company, Inc.
    Kroger Co.
    Safeway Stores, Inc.
    Southland Corp.
    Supermarkets
    Vons Grocery Co.
    West Point Market
    Wetterau Incorporated
                    Finance
Food distributors. R. King, Jr. il *Forbes* 139:130+ Ja 12 '87
Grodinsky, Caroline, and Stüwe, Michael
With lots of help, alpine ibex return to their mountains. il *Smithsonian* 18:68-72+ D '87
Groening, Matt
25th New York, New York, Film Festival. il *Film Comment* 23:56-7 S/O '87
about
A doodle god makes good. J. Foote. il por *Newsweek* 110:70+ S 28 '87
Groff, Patrick
The maturing of phonics instruction. *Educ Dig* 52:42-4 Ja '87
Groh, Carol A.
about
The birth of a business. M. Slavin. il pors *Work Woman* 12:31-3 Ag '87
Gronseth, Charlotte M.
Christmas [poem] il *Christ Century* 104:1161 D 23-30 '87
Grooming for women *See* Beauty, Personal
Grooming of dogs *See* Dogs—Care
Grooms, Red
about
Corn-pone cubism, red-neck deco. R. Hughes. il *Time* 130:78 S 21 '87
Portraits of the artists. H. Cotter. il *Art Am* 75:154-7 N '87
Red Grooms. A. C. Danto. *Nation* 245:242-5 S 12 '87
Red Grooms. M. Wade. il por *Horizon* 30:12-16 Jl/Ag '87
Red Grooms's ghost riders take Manhattan on a joyride. H. Shapiro. il pors *People Wkly* 28:106-8 O 5 '87
Groover, Jan, 1943-
about
Jan Groover: melancholy modernist. M. Kozloff. il *Art Am* 75:144-7 Je '87
Gropp, Lou
The editor's page. See issues of House & Garden
Gross, Alexander L.
about
Running shoes make a leap into the space age. K. Dreyfack. il por *Bus Week* p70 Ja 19 '87
Gross, Barbara Rudd
about
Barbara Rudd Gross, Ebony account exec, new advertising group prexy. por *Jet* 72:30 Je 15 '87

Gross, Bertram Myron, 1912-
Making an issue of full employment. il *Nation* 244:72-5 Ja 24 '87
Rethinking full employment. il *Nation* 244:44-6+ Ja 17 '87

Gross, David J.
Asymptotic freedom [adaptation of address, April 1986] il *Phys Today* 40:39-44 Ja '87

Gross, Harold T.
(jt. auth) See Weinstein, Bernard L., and Gross, Harold T.

Gross, Leonard H.
What your husband is afraid to tell you. il *Redbook* 168:76-7+ F '87

Gross national product
Can America compete? [growth crisis; cover story; special section] il *Bus Week* p44-9+ Ap 20 '87
Don't buy predictions of a growth spurt. V. Brownstein. il *Fortune* 115:61+ Mr 16 '87
GNP will take a hit from lagging auto output . . . and even the Japanese are feeling the crunch. G. Koretz. il *Bus Week* p14 Je 29 '87
A handicapper's guide to Reaganomics. A. S. Blinder. il *Bus Week* p18 F 9 '87
How slow will they grow? [West Germany and Japan] S. Nasar. il *Fortune* 116:67+ N 9 '87
Revisionist thoughts on growth. H. Banks. *Forbes* 139:33 Ja 12 '87
Slow growth ahead. J. C. Szabo. il *Nations Bus* 75:10+ Jl '87
The trade gap is a symptom. Low growth is the disease. N. Jonas. il *Bus Week* p40 Ja 26 '87

Grossberger, Lewis
Reagan tells all. il *Roll Stone* p43-5 Jl 16-30 '87
This is the article about Garry Shandling's show. il por *Roll Stone* p41-2 F 26 '87

Grossblatt, Robert
Designer's notebook. See issues of Radio-Electronics beginning March 1984
The drawing board. See issues of Radio-Electronics

Grossen, Françoise, 1943-
about
A living journal: Francoise Grossen. W. Seelig. il *Am Craft* 47:34-7 O/N '87

Grosser, Maurice, 1903-1986
about
Maurice Grosser at Fischbach. L. Campbell. il *Art Am* 75:159-60 Je '87

Grosskurth, Phyllis
The woman who broke away. il *N Y Rev Books* 34:14-17 N 5 '87

Grossman, Florence
Spring sewing [poem] *Nation* 245:464 O 24 '87
Still life [poem] *Nation* 244:545 Ap 25 '87
Weather radio [poem] *Nation* 245:427 O 17 '87

Grossman, Larry
about
Turning up the heat. S. Aikenhead. il por *Macleans* 100:8-9 Ag 31 '87

Grossman, Lawrence K.
about
Friends in high places. B. Yagoda. il pors *Channels* 7:54-61 Ja '87

Grossman, M. Gary
about
Meet the men who invented vibrating bedroom slippers. P. Finch. il pors *Bus Week* p91 N 9 '87

Grossman, Walter S.
about
'Betting on the genius' of Henley's chairman. G. G. Marcial. il por *Bus Week* p118 N 23 '87

Grossmann, John
A prairie dog companion. il pors *Audubon* 89:52-4+ Mr '87
(ed) See Brandon, Dale. Chad's dad

Grossman's Inc.
Grossman's new look may be more than just a facade. J. M. Laderman. *Bus Week* p96 Je 15 '87

Grotberg, Edith H., and others
Changing childrearing practices in Sudan: an early stimulation demonstration program. bibl f il *Child Today* 16:26-9 Ja/F '87

Grothe, Mardy
about
How to deal with an unbearable boss [interview] il por *U S News World Rep* 102:56 Ja 19 '87
Problem bosses: they come in all sizes, shapes and styles—and everybody thinks that he's got one [interview] T. Cunneff. il pors *People Wkly* 27:95-6+ Je 8 '87

Groton (Conn.)
Protests, demonstrations, etc.
Torpedoing free speech [ordinance to regulate anti-nuclear protests] S. Burkholder. il *Progressive* 51:15-16 My '87

Groucho: a life in revue [drama] See Marx, Arthur
Ground beef See Beef
Ground beef cooking See Cooking—Meat
Ground coupled heat pumps See Heat pumps
Ground cover plants
See also
Sedum
Sun roses
Carpet the garden with flowers. il *South Living* 22:86-7 Ap '87
Dwarf bamboo for ground cover that's different. J. W. Waddick. il *Flower Gard* 31:34+ F/Mr '87
Ground covers. T. Martin. il *Ctry J* 14:52-7 My '87
Pavers and plants add a soft touch. il *South Living* 22:70-1 N '87

Ground crews, Aviation See Airplane mechanics (Persons)
Ground fault circuit interrupters See Electric circuit breakers
Ground ivy
Ground ivy: one mean weed. L. C. Askey. il *South Living* 22:56 O '87
Ground meat cooking See Cooking—Meat
Ground squirrels
A squirrel in its desert world [cover story] il map *Natl Geogr World* 143:3-5 Jl '87
Ground stations (Communications satellites) See Communications satellites—Ground stations
Ground Wave Emergency Network system See Radio, Military
Groundhogs See Woodchucks
Groundnuts
Help rediscover an American vegetable: apios. J. A. Duke. il *Rodale's Org Gard* 34:98-101 Ja '87
Groundwater pollution See Water pollution
Group counseling
See also
Self help groups
Group homes for children
Bringing lives up to par [golfer P. Sheehan's sponsorship of home for teenage girls] J. Diaz. il pors *Sports Illus* 67:28-9 D 21 '87
Group legal services See Prepaid legal services
Group Lotus Car Companies Ltd.
The legacy [founder C. Chapman] C. Fox. il pors *Car Driv* 32:101-5 Je '87
Little leaks from Lotus. P. Lienert. *Road Track* 38:98 My '87
Lotus: living with the General. P. Bingham. il *Mot Trend* 39:48-51 F '87
Group medical practice
See also
Katonah Medical Group
Why your family doctor is a group. M. Fay. il *N Y Times Mag* p16-20+ Je 7 '87
Group portraits, Photographic See Photography—Portraits
Group practice in medicine See Group medical practice
Group psychotherapy
See also
Family psychotherapy
Group relations training
See also
Esalen Institute
Group Research Inc.
Fanatics beware. C. Hitchens. *Nation* 244:529 Ap 25 '87
Group W Productions
Making a new Merv [Group W grooms W. Shriner] B. Yagoda. il pors *Channels* 7:46-50 F '87
Group work in education
The art of collaborative learning. K. A. Bruffee. il *Change* 19:42-7 Mr/Ap '87
It's hard to get left out of a pair [work of D. W. and R. T. Johnson] A. Kohn. bibl (p62) il pors *Psychol Today* 21:52-7 O '87
The key to improving schools: an interview with William Glasser. P. B. Gough. il *Phi Delta Kappan* 68:656-62 My '87
A teacher's view on cooperative learning. R. A. Smith. il *Phi Delta Kappan* 68:663-6 My '87
Group work in industry See Team work in industry
Groupe Bernard Tapie
'Seduction' is name of the game [founder B. Tapie] P. Sherrid. il por *U S News World Rep* 103:39-40 Jl 27 '87
Groupe Financière Agache
The marriage of high finance and high fashion. F. J. Comes. il por *Bus Week* p59 F 23 '87

Groupers

Super grouper [Great Barrier Reef] il map *Natl Geogr World* 145:34-5 S '87

Groups, Self help *See* Self help groups

Groups (Sociology)

See also

Elite (Social sciences)

Peer groups

Cliques: what they're really about. il *Teen* 31:96-7 Ap '87

Groupthink, rethink: speaking up—even against the majority. B. L. Stern. *Vogue* 177:360-1 D '87

Groups (Special interest) *See* Special interest groups

Grouse

See also

Ptarmigans

Grouse shooting

One-on-one grouse. S. D. Carpenteri. il *Field Stream* 92:26+ O '87

Prairie bird [sharptail grouse] J. Barsness. il *Field Stream* 92:31+ D '87

Where do you find Mr. Ruff? J. McCue. il *Outdoor Life* 180:84-5+ N '87

Grout, William

Inside Skiing. See issues of Skiing beginning September 1986

Grouws, Douglas A.

(jt. auth) *See* Good, Thomas L., 1943-, and Grouws, Douglas A.

Grove, Andrew S.

Managing people and their computers. por *Pers Comput* 11:228 O '87

about

Andrew Grove. J. W. Wilson. il por *Bus Week* Sp Issue:252 Ap 17 '87

Can Andy Grove practice what he preaches? J. W. Wilson. il por *Bus Week* p68-9 Mr 16 '87

Grove, J. Russell, and others

Recombinant fragment of protein kinase inhibitor blocks cyclic AMP-dependent gene transcription. bibl f il *Science* 238:530-3 O 23 '87

Grove, Noel

Air: an atmosphere of uncertainty. il map *Natl Geogr* 171:502-37 Ap '87

A tunnel through time. il supp (folded map) maps *Natl Geogr* 171:216-43 F '87

Grove Press, Inc.

Weidenfeld and Grove: a flying start. C. T. Anthony. il *Publ Wkly* 232:15-18 S 4 '87

Groves, David

Drug tests in the workplace: are they reliable? *McCalls* 114:155 My '87

Eight ways to total-body fitness. il *Work Woman* 12:134+ Je '87

Update on herpes. *McCalls* 115:95-6 N '87

Growth

See also

Brain—Growth

Growth regulators

Mammary glands—Growth

Maturation (Biology)

Maturity

Morphogenesis

Nerve cells—Growth

Regeneration (Biology)

Opioids moonlighting in cell growth? D. D. Edwards. *Sci News* 131:230 Ap 11 '87

Mollusks

The age of the nautilus [work of Neil H. Landman] *Oceans* 20:5-6 N/D '87

Plants

See also

Geotropism

Growth regulators—Plants

Tree rings

Growth, Economic *See* Economic development

Growth factors *See* Growth regulators

Growth hormone *See* Pituitary hormones

Growth hormone, Synthetic *See* Pituitary hormones, Synthetic

Growth of children *See* Children—Growth and development

Growth of cities and towns *See* Cities and towns—Growth

Growth regulators

See also

Angiogenin

Colony-stimulating factors

Epidermal growth factor

Erythropoietin

G-CSF

GM-CSF

Interleukin

Mitogens

Nerve growth factor

Neuroleukin

Pituitary hormones

Somatomedins

Accelerated healing of incisional wounds in rats induced by transforming growth factor-β. T. A. Mustoe and others. bibl f il *Science* 237:1333-6 S 11 '87

Angiogenesis research comes of age. J. L. Marx. il *Science* 237:23-4 Jl 3 '87

Angiogenic factors. J. Folkman and M. Klagsbrun. bibl f il *Science* 235:442-7 Ja 23 '87

A cell-cycle constraint on the regulation of gene expression by platelet-derived growth factor. B. J. Rollins and others. bibl f il *Science* 238:1269-71 N 27 '87

Chemical identification of a tumor-derived angiogenic factor. F. C. Kull, Jr. and others. bibl f il *Science* 236:843-5 My 15 '87

Clinical promise with new hormones [hematologic growth factors] G. Kolata. il *Science* 236:517-19 My 1 '87

Epithelial wound healing enhanced by transforming growth factor-α and vaccinia growth factor. G. S. Schultz and others. bibl f il *Science* 235:350-2 Ja 16 '87

erbB-2 is a potent oncogene when overexpressed in NIH/3T3 cells. P. P. Di Fiore and others. bibl f il *Science* 237:178-82 Jl 10 '87

Human CSF-1: molecular cloning and expression of 4-kb cDNA encoding the human urinary protein. G. G. Wong and others. bibl f il *Science* 235:1504-8 Mr 20 '87

Immune boosters [hematologic growth factors; cover story] G. Kolata. il *Discover* 8:68-72+ S '87

Lymphotoxin is an important T cell-derived growth factor for human B cells. J. H. Kehrl and others. bibl f il *Science* 238:1144-6 N 20 '87

Molecular cloning and expression of a human B-cell growth factor gene in Escherichia coli. S. Sharma and others. bibl f il *Science* 235:1489-92 Mr 20 '87

The molecular control of blood cell development. L. Sachs. bibl f il *Science* 238:1374-9 D 4 '87

New family of growth factor genes identified [fibroblast growth factors] J. L. Marx. il *Science* 237:602-3 Ag 7 '87

New tumor factor may disrupt calcium levels [development of hypercalcemia in cancer patients] D. M. Barnes. bibl il *Science* 237:363-4 Jl 24 '87

Opioids moonlighting in cell growth? D. D. Edwards. *Sci News* 131:230 Ap 11 '87

A parathyroid hormone-related protein implicated in malignant hypercalcemia: cloning and expression. L. J. Suva and others. bibl f il *Science* 237:893-6 Ag 21 '87

Reversible inhibition of mammary gland growth by transforming growth factor-β. G. B. Silberstein and C. W. Daniel. bibl f il *Science* 237:291-3 Jl 17 '87

The role of individual cysteine residues in the structure and function of the v-*sis* gene product [platelet-derived growth factor] N. A. Giese and others. bibl f il *Science* 236:1315-18 Je 5 '87

Stimulating recovery. T. Beardsley. *Sci Am* 257:30+ N '87

Microorganisms

Clathrin requirement for normal growth of yeast. S. K. Lemmon and E. W. Jones. bibl f il *Science* 238:504-9 O 23 '87

Plants

See also

Daminozide

Hormones, Plant

Unlocking plants' secret potential [use of triethylamine DCPTA] J. Raloff. *Sci News* 131:265 Ap 25 '87

Growth Stock Outlook, Inc.

Famous artists [C. Allmon, M. Gabelli and M. Zweig] R. Phalon. il pors *Forbes* 139:102+ Je 1 '87

Growth stocks *See* Stocks

Grubb, Kevin

Broadway and beyond. See issues of Dance Magazine

Grubbs, Michael

about

The Revenger offers drivers a shot at life in the blast lane. il por *People Wkly* 28:179 D 14 '87

Grube Messel (Germany)

Dumping on science [plan to use fossil rich site as a garbage dump] P. Shipman. il map *Discover* 8:60-6 D '87

Gruber, Michael

(jt. auth) *See* Russell, Milton, and Gruber, Michael

Gruen, John

Antiques: companions for flowers. il *Archit Dig* 44:186-91 Ap '87

Gruen, John—*cont.*

Architectural digest visits: Beverly Sills. il pors *Archit Dig* 44:184-9 N '87

The ascent of Apolio: mounting Olympus. il *Dance Mag* 61:156-65 Je '87

A beckoning stillness. il por *Archit Dig* 44:40+ F '87

Coloratura: old world living in a New York apartment. il *Archit Dig* 44:166-9 O '87

Controlled frenzy. il por *Art News* 86:116-20 Mr '87

East Side story. il *Archit Dig* 44:92-5 Jl '87

Ferri tales can come true: Giselle goes to the movies [cover story] il pors *Dance Mag* 61:36-43 O '87

Formal details. il *Archit Dig* 44:186-92 D '87

The geometry of nature and the nature of geometry. il pors *Art News* 86:86-92 F '87

George Sugarman's maximal, musical sculpture. il por *Art News* 86:138-43 Ja '87

Martins talks back: Peter's perspectives [cover story] il pors *Dance Mag* 61:38-42 N '87

The Met's Jane Hermann: offstage assoluta. il por *Dance Mag* 61:48-51 Jl '87

Paean to glamour: dramatic formality for an Italianate villa in Beverly Hills. il *Archit Dig* 44:102-7 S '87

Peter Sparling: new positions. il pors *Dance Mag* 61:66-9 Ap '87

The pochoir prints of Charles Rahn Fry. il por *Archit Dig* 44:94+ Ap '87

Robert Mangold: 'a maker of images—nothing more and nothing less'. il pors *Art News* 86:132-8 Summ '87

Suggesting a plausible fantasy. il por *Archit Dig* 44:154+ Jl '87

Gruen Marketing Corporation

Swatch watching. K. Murray. il por *Forbes* 140:88+ O 19 '87

Gruenebaum, Thomas

about

Late bloomer. S. Staggs. il por *Art News* 86:11-12 Ap '87

Thomas Gruenebaum at Ingber. L. Campbell. il *Art Am* 75:224 Ap '87

Gruenerwald, William

about

El Jefe is building a desert 'ark' to keep zebras and other equids afloat. J. Fincher. bibl (p184) il pors *Smithsonian* 18:138-42+ My '87

Grueninger, Walter F.

Recorded music in review. See issues of Consumers' Research Magazine

Grumman Corp.

Congressional, Navy leaders back Grumman A-6F at roll-out. il *Aviat Week Space Technol* 127:31 Ag 10 '87

Grumman A-6F design stresses aircraft maintenance, survivability. il *Aviat Week Space Technol* 127:74-5 N 16 '87

Grumman gets a slap in the face from the Navy [F-14 contract] D. Griffiths. *Bus Week* p45 Ap 13 '87

Grumman refining naval multimission RPV concept [shipborne, vertical takeoff and landing remotely piloted vehicle] S. W. Kandebo. il *Aviat Week Space Technol* 126:117-18+ My 11 '87

Navy opts to cut F-14D buy, will compete F-14A update. D. M. North. *Aviat Week Space Technol* 126:18-20 Mr 30 '87

Navy's emphasis on ATA threatens A-6F funding. D. M. North. *Aviat Week Space Technol* 127:20-1 O 26 '87

New Grumman facility advances F-14D avionics integration. K. J. Stein. il *Aviat Week Space Technol* 127:141+ S 7 '87

Grünbaum, Adolf

The place of secular humanism [address, May 7, 1987] *Vital Speeches Day* 54:42-7 N 1 '87

Grundberg, Andy

Photography. il *N Y Times Book Rev* 92:20-1 D 6 '87

Grundy, Kenneth W.

South Africa: coercion and demands for change. bibl f *Curr Hist* 86:197-200+ My '87

Grunebaum, Ernest

about

So you thought you'd seen the last of tax straddles. D. Zigas. il por *Bus Week* p90 Je 15 '87

Gruneich, Kevin

PW Index underperformed. il *Publ Wkly* 231:36 Ja 9 '87

Gruner, Sol M.

Time-resolved X-ray diffraction of biological materials. bibl f il *Science* 238:305-12 O 16 '87

Gruntal Financial Corporation

Gruntal & Co. [interview with A. Rosenfeld] il por *Fortune* 116 Sp Issue:180-1 Fall '87

Grunwald, Lisa

E.G. Smith, sockmeister. il pors *Esquire* 107:F41+ Mr '87

A game of dots [fiction] il *Esquire* 108:76-81 Ag '87

Grushkin, Paul

Art rock [excerpt from The art of rock] il *Roll Stone* p71-5 S 24 '87

Gruson, Lindsey

Martini redux. il *N Y Times Mag* p56 Ag 30 '87

Sailing into port. il *N Y Times Mag* p50 S 27 '87

Select company. il *N Y Times Mag* p46 F 1 '87

(jt. auth) See Hubner, John, and Gruson, Lindsey

Grutman, Norman Roy

about

The Bakkers vs. the hired gun. G. Carroll. il por *Newsweek* 110:61-2 S 7 '87

GSA *See* United States. General Services Administration

Gstaad (Switzerland)

Swiss twins. K. Castle. il map *Travel Holiday* 168:36-43 O '87

GTE Corp.

Can GTE keep foiling the raiders? J. R. Norman. il por *Bus Week* p100-1 Ap 6 '87

The greenmail factor [Belzberg family accused of attempting to greenmail GTE] L. Black. il *Macleans* 100:67 F 2 '87

GTE adapts off-the-shelf hardware to improve command and control [WWMCCS Information System] W. H. Gregory. il *Aviat Week Space Technol* 126:73+ F 23 '87

GTE transmits messages by bouncing voice signals off meteor trails. J. C. Lowndes. il *Aviat Week Space Technol* 126:80-1 Ja 26 '87

GTE Sprint Communications

See also

US Sprint Communications Inc.

Gtech Corporation

Can Gtech keep winning at the lottery? [designing and installing state lottery systems] L. Helm. il *Bus Week* p93-4 My 18 '87

GTG Entertainment (Firm)

Behind the McTelevision show. N. J. Perry. il pors *Fortune* 116:122 S 28 '87

Grant's back & Gannett's got him. J. Baker. il por *Channels* 7:40-3 Jl/Ag '87

How CBS landed Grant Tinker. M. Brown. il por *Channels* 7:26 Ap '87

Starting over [G. Tinker; cover story] D. K. Shah. il pors *N Y Times Mag* p26-9+ O 25 '87

Tinker's CBS deal. A. D. Frank. il por *Forbes* 140:184+ O 19 '87

GTP *See* Guanosine triphosphate

Guadalupe Island (Mexico)

Description and travel

Guadalupe. G. Y. Jennings. il *Oceans* 20:40-5+ S/O '87

Guam

See also

Public health—Guam

Guan Guangmei

about

Cabbages and capitalists. D. Elliott. il por *Newsweek* 110:37 Jl 20 '87

Guanacaste National Park (Costa Rica) *See* National parks and reserves—Costa Rica

Guanacos *See* Llamas

Guanethidine

The gold standard [guanethidine to treat rheumatoid arthritis] J. R. Goldberg. *Health* 19:26-7 Je '87

Guangdong Province (China)

In China, the buck starts here. N. D. Kristof. il map *N Y Times Mag* p40-2+ D 20 '87

Guangzhou (China)

Description

Canton. F. Ferretti. il *Gourmet* 47:56-63+ My '87

Guanosine diphosphate

A cytoplasmic protein stimulates normal N-*ras* p21 GTPase, but does not affect oncogenic mutants. M. Trahey and F. McCormick. bibl f il *Science* 238:542-5 O 23 '87

Guanosine monophosphate

Divalent cations directly affect the conductance of excised patches of rod photoreceptor membrane. J. H. Stern and others. bibl f il *Science* 236:1674-8 Je 26 '87

The molecules of visual excitation. L. Stryer. bibl (p116) il *Sci Am* 257:42-50 Jl '87

Guanosine triphosphate
See also
G proteins
The α subunit of the GTP binding protein G$_k$ opens atrial potassium channels. J. Codina and others. bibl f il *Science* 236:442-5 Ap 24 '87
A cytoplasmic protein stimulates normal N-*ras* p21 GTPase, but does not affect oncogenic mutants. M. Trahey and F. McCormick. bibl f il *Science* 238:542-5 O 23 '87
Direct activation of mammalian atrial muscarinic potassium channels by GTP regulatory protein G$_k$. A. Yatani and others. bibl f il *Science* 235:207-11 Ja 9 '87

Guanylate cyclase See Enzymes
Guaranty See Warranty
Guaranty, Treaties of See Treaties of guaranty
Guardian and ward
See also
Custody of children
Parent and child (Law)
Choosing a guardian who cares. R. Micheli. il *Money* 16:54 O '87
Life after Ozzie & Harriet [custody battle for S. Nelson; cover story] B. Darrach. il pors *People Wkly* 28:40-5 S 7 '87
Who will get our child? J. H. Sousa. il *Parents* 62:72+ D '87
Who's guarding the guardians? [elderly] M. Sinclair. il *50 Plus* 27:12+ D '87

Guardian Angels (Organization)
Citizen crime-fighters: do they help or hurt police efforts? il *Sch Update* 120:12-13 D 4 '87
Why are there Angels in the Dells? [Wisconsin] il *Newsweek* 110:21 Ag 24 '87

Guardian Mutual Fund, Inc.
A value seeker says there's plenty left [interview with K. Simons] A. E. Serwer. il por *Fortune* 116:200 Ag 3 '87

Guardrails See Roads—Guard fences
Guards
Guard hailed by police fired by bank; gets a better job and pay raise [J. Massey of Wells Fargo Bank, San Francisco] *Jet* 72:12 Mr 30 '87

Guatelli, Roberto
about
After five centuries, a devoted modeler gives shape to genius. J. P. Wiley, Jr. bibl (p145) il por *Smithsonian* 18:90-5 Ag '87

Guatemala
See also
Antigua (Guatemala)
Indians of Central America—Guatemala
Political prisoners—Guatemala
Santiago (Guatemala)
Trade unions—Guatemala
Antiquities
See also
El Mirador site (Guatemala)
Description and travel
The travel bargain of the Americas. J. W. Michaels. il map *Forbes* 139:158+ Ap 6 '87
Foreign relations
United States
See United States—Foreign relations—Guatemala
History
Photographs and photography
A portrait of change [excerpt from Eadweard Muybridge in Guatemala, 1875] E. B. Burns. il *Américas* 39:26-33 Jl/Ag '87
Politics and government
Giving democracy a chance [President V. Cerezo Arévalo] J. Moody. il por *Time* 129:45 Ap 20 '87
Going it alone. J. A. Briggs. il *Forbes* 139:172-4 My 18 '87
Guatemala. L. Hopping. il *Sch Update* 119:14-15 Mr 9 '87
Guatemala's transition toward democracy. *Dep State Bull* 87:84-6 F '87
The happy birds move on [Guatemalan Indian refugees flee to Mexico] R. J. Stout. il *Christ Century* 104:222-3 Mr 4 '87
Religious institutions and affairs
See also
Catholic Church—Guatemala
Pentecostal churches—Guatemala

Guatemalan refugees See Refugees, Guatemalan
Guayabera shirts See Shirts
Guaymas (Tiburon, Calif.: Restaurant) See Tiburon (Calif.)—Restaurants, nightclubs, bars, etc.

Gubar, Susan, 1944-
(jt. auth) See Gilbert, Sandra M., and Gubar, Susan, 1944-
Gubernski, Yuri, and Litvinov, Nikolai
Space around the houses matters too. il *World Health* p23-5 Jl '87
Gucci Group
Can an outsider fill Aldo Gucci's loafers? [M. Martellini] K. Wolman. il por *Bus Week* p52 N 30 '87
Guccione, Bob, 1930-
about
Guccione's unlikely new conquest. D. Lieberman. il por *Bus Week* p40 N 23 '87
Guccione, Nina
Floral derangement. il *Omni* 10:100-5 D '87
Patently absurd. il *Omni* 10:100-5+ N '87
Gucwa, David
about
The elephant as artist. J. Ehmann. il *Natl Wildl* 25:26-8 F/Mr '87
An elephant who draws pictures. J. Ehmann. il por *Read Dig* 131:96-9 O '87
Gudmundson, Lowell
Costa Rica's Arias at midterm. bibl f *Curr Hist* 86:417-20+ D '87
Gudorf, Christine
Indigenous moral problems in Peru. *America* 157:270-3 O 24 '87
Guentert, Kenneth
Gluttony: love at first bite. il *U S Cathol* 52:11-13 Ag '87
Sunday Mass: what we've lost, what we've gained. *U S Cathol* 52:34-7 Je '87
Guerra, Francisco
about
Swine's way. B. Lawren. il *Omni* 9:18 Ja '87
Guerra, Ruy
about
Malandro's opera [film] Reviews
Américas 39:60-1 S/O '87. J. Mosier
Guerra de Macedo, Carlyle
The challenges ahead. il *World Health* p26-9 O '87
Guerrier, Jude
about
12-year-old boy awarded $28 million for burns in fire that killed mother. D. M. Cheers. il pors *Jet* 73:20-1 D 28 '87-Ja 4 '88
Guerrillas
Angola
See also
National Union for the Total Independence of Angola
El Salvador
See also
Farabundo Martí National Liberation Front
Ethiopia
See also
Eritrean People's Liberation Front
Kampuchea
See also
Khmer Rouge
Latin America
Guerrillas who came in from the cold [restoration of democracy in Uruguay, Argentina, and Brazil] C. A. Robbins. il *U S News World Rep* 102:33-4 My 11 '87
Mozambique
See also
Mozambique National Resistance Movement
Peru
See also
Sendero Luminoso (Guerrilla group)
Philippines
See also
New People's Army (Philippines)
Uganda
See also
Holy Spirit Movement (Uganda)
Guess?, Inc.
Does Guess have a friend in the IRS? [Guess vs. Jordache] R. Behar. il map *Forbes* 140:146-50+ N 16 '87
The IRS mess [corruption charges surrounding Guess, Inc. feud with Jordache] R. Behar. il *Forbes* 140:8 N 30 '87
Guest, Anthony Haden- See Haden-Guest, Anthony
Guest, Christopher
about
Take a wild Guest . . . V. Radin. il por *Vogue* 177:82 F '87
Guest, Robert H.
Mega mergers [address, September 7, 1987] *Vital Speeches Day* 54:20-2 O 15 '87

Guest houses

The house as art [F. Gehry's Winton guesthouse in Minnesota; cover story] M. Filler. il por *House Gard* 159:152-61+ O '87

Guest ranches *See* Ranches

Guest rooms

The pleasure of your company. M. Hampton. il *House Gard* 159:22+ Ag '87

Raise the floor. A. W. Lees. il *Pop Sci* 231:82-5 S '87

Guests

See also
Entertaining
Hospitality

How to handle a parent's visit [excerpt from Do your parents drive you crazy?] J. Dight. il *Glamour* 85:153-4 N '87

Make the most of a party even if you're not a party person. il *Glamour* 85:56 D '87

Party panic: ten tips to get you through the night. L. Werner. il *Ladies Home J* 104:70+ D '87

The sleep-over. P. Theroux. il *Parents* 62:64+ Je '87

Anecdotes, facetiae, satire, etc.

How to survive the party when he's the world's worst guest. B.-J. Raphael. *Glamour* 85:32 F '87

Guevara, Che *See* Guevara, Ernesto, 1928-1967

Guevara, Ernesto, 1928-1967

about

Remembering Che. G. Black. *Nation* 245:401+ O 17 '87

Guggenheim, Marguerite *See* Guggenheim, Peggy, 1898-1979

Guggenheim, Peggy, 1898-1979

about

Heir heads. K. Larson. il *N Y* 20:94-5 Mr 30 '87

Guggenheim (Solomon R.) Museum *See* Solomon R. Guggenheim Museum

Guida, Lou

about

Here's to Mack the Knife. D. S. Looney. il por *Sports Illus* 67:63-4 Ag 17 '87

Guidance *See* Counseling

Guidance, Vocational *See* Vocational guidance

Guidance counseling, Educational *See* Educational counseling

Guidance counselors, Educational *See* Educational counselors

Guide (Computer program) *See* Hypertext

Guide dogs

Two eyes named Aston. G. Clark. il *McCalls* 114:64-5 S '87

Guidebooks

See also
Booksellers and bookselling—Guidebooks
Publishers and publishing—Guidebooks

Bringing color to the dreary world of travel guidebooks [H. Hoefer's Insight guides] C. Purcell. il *Pop Photogr* 94:24-5 F '87

A good travel guide is easy to find. L. Hazelton. *Black Enterp* 17:35 Mr '87

Bibliography

America the bountiful—best eating guides. B. Kafka. il *Vogue* 177:133-4 Je '87

A guide to the guides. R. Bongartz. il *Publ Wkly* 231:46-8+ F 13 '87

National Park Service Handbooks [with editorial comment by Ed Holm] il *Am Hist Illus* 22:4, 10-11 O '87

A path to the best travel guide. B. Bauer. il *U S News World Rep* 103:77-8 S 14 '87

Shopping by the book. D. P. Marshall. il *Travel Holiday* 168:16-17 S '87

Guided missile bases

See also
Titan II Missile Museum (Ariz.)

Air Force plans to issue RFPs for rail-based MX development [request for proposals] B. A. Smith. il *Aviat Week Space Technol* 126:18-19 Ap 6 '87

Boeing wins contract to design MX rail-garrison basing system. B. A. Smith. *Aviat Week Space Technol* 127:21 S 21 '87

Italian RPV wins $16-million bid for NATO missile range service [Mirach 100/Mizar remotely piloted vehicle] J. M. Lenorovitz. il *Aviat Week Space Technol* 126:52-3 F 23 '87

Reagan will pursue rail-based MX, full-scale Midgetman development. J. D. Morrocco. il *Aviat Week Space Technol* 126:20-1 Ja 5 '87

USAF plans single launch control facility for first small ICBM force. B. A. Smith. il *Aviat Week Space Technol* 126:47-8 My 18 '87

Crews

The keys to Kingdom Come [Minuteman missile crews based at Malmstrom Air Force Base, Montana] D. Quammen. il *Roll Stone* p60-2+ Je 18 '87

Guided missile industries

See also
General Dynamics Corp.
McDonnell Douglas Corp.
Raytheon Co.
Williams International

Export-import trade

Administration cancels missile sale; Congress critical of Middle East policy [proposed sale of 1,600 Maverick antitank missiles to Saudi Arabia] M. Mecham. *Aviat Week Space Technol* 126:70-1 Je 15 '87

A busy swarm of Stingers. N. Cooper. il *Newsweek* 110:44 N 23 '87

Congress moves to block sale of Mavericks to Saudis. M. Mecham. *Aviat Week Space Technol* 126:23-4 Je 8 '87

Seven nations curb nuclear weapon launch system exports [Missile Technology Control Regime] D. M. North. *Aviat Week Space Technol* 126:28-9 Ap 20 '87

What's the Chinese word for chutzpah? [sale of missiles to Iran] *Newsweek* 110:59 N 9 '87

International aspects

Missile manufacturers stress tailoring of current systems [Paris Air Show] S. W. Kandebo. il *Aviat Week Space Technol* 126:85+ Je 29 '87

RAM program achieves successes following near cancellation [multinational XIM-116A rolling airframe missile] M. A. Dornheim. il *Aviat Week Space Technol* 126:57-9+ Je 22 '87

Seven nations near accord on modular standoff weapons. il *Aviat Week Space Technol* 126:27 Je 22 '87

Quality control

GAO warns Congress of flaws that may cause missiles to fail [Navy missile systems] *Aviat Week Space Technol* 127:34-5 S 28 '87

Brazil

See also
Orbita Aerospace Systems (Firm)

France

See also
Matra SA

Western Europe

NATO armaments programs hinge on technology transfer benefits. M. A. Dornheim. il *Aviat Week Space Technol* 126:220-2+ Je 15 '87

Guided missiles

A busy swarm of Stingers. N. Cooper. il *Newsweek* 110:44 N 23 '87

Accidents and explosions

GAO warns Congress of flaws that may cause missiles to fail [Navy missile systems] *Aviat Week Space Technol* 127:34-5 S 28 '87

Anecdotes, facetiae, satire, etc.

Hot tub astronomy: a fire on the moon [bright light in sky over California caused by missile misfiring] B. Mosier. il *Astronomy* 15:26+ Ap '87

Control

See also
Inertial guidance systems

Costs

Acquisition Board endorses low-rate AMRAAM production [advanced medium-range air-to-air missile] *Aviat Week Space Technol* 126:24 Je 8 '87

Air Force defends MX management as Northrop is charged with fraud. M. Mecham. *Aviat Week Space Technol* 127:16-18 Ag 31 '87

Air Force refers Northrop investigation to U.S. Attorney; Late IMUs delay scheduled MX deployment [inertial measurement units] B. A. Smith. *Aviat Week Space Technol* 126:72 Je 15 '87

Defense official challenges continuing SICBM development [F. C. Ikle's views on Midgetman] J. D. Morrocco. *Aviat Week Space Technol* 126:18-19 Mr 16 '87

Guidance unit shortage keeps 8 MXs off alert [Northrop contract] M. Mecham. *Aviat Week Space Technol* 127:22-3 Jl 6 '87

House weighs major cuts for combat aircraft, missiles. *Aviat Week Space Technol* 127:32-3 O 19 '87

Northrop boosts IMU deliveries, expects to meet schedule in March [inertial measurement units for MX intercontinental ballistic missile] B. A. Smith. il *Aviat Week Space Technol* 127:31-2 S 7 '87

Reagan will pursue rail-based MX, full-scale Midgetman development. J. D. Morrocco. il *Aviat Week Space Technol* 126:20-1 Ja 5 '87

Guided missiles—Costs—*cont.*

Reduced tactical weapons budget cuts purchases, dampens new starts. M. A. Dornheim. il *Aviat Week Space Technol* 126:237-8+ Mr 9 '87

Revisions to fraud statute aid suit against Raytheon. *Aviat Week Space Technol* 127:27 N 9 '87

Science board seeks new MX test procedures, affirms IMU reliability. M. Mecham. *Aviat Week Space Technol* 127:32-3 N 2 '87

Senate committee drops small ICBM in favor of rail-garrison MX [Appropriations Committee] *Aviat Week Space Technol* 127:26 D 7 '87

Trouble for the triad [deficiencies in MX guidance systems] J. Barry. il *Newsweek* 110:17-18 S 7 '87

USAF probes Northrop's MX program purchases. *Aviat Week Space Technol* 126:27 Je 1 '87

USAF withholds MX progress payments from Northrop. *Aviat Week Space Technol* 126:23 Ap 13 '87

Deactivation

Swords into plowshares [dismantling Titan II missiles] W. S. Malone and others. il *Life* 10:26-30+ N '87

Defenses

See also

North American Aerospace Defense Command
Radar defense networks
Railguns
Strategic Defense Initiative
United States. Air Force. Space Command

Air Force, Marine Corps study C-130 missile defense systems. D. Hughes. il *Aviat Week Space Technol* 127:89+ Ag 24 '87

Allies approach agreement on joint ATM programs [antitactical missile] J. D. Morrocco. *Aviat Week Space Technol* 126:18-20 Je 29 '87

Army missile test demonstrates FLAGE guidance [flexible lightweight agile guided experiment] J. D. Morrocco. il *Aviat Week Space Technol* 126:22-3 Je 1 '87

Army to test off-the-shelf systems for use in theater missile defense. *Aviat Week Space Technol* 126:20-1 Je 29 '87

ATBM—a solution in search of a problem. B. Morel. bibl f *Bull At Sci* 43:39-41 My '87

Defense Dept. panel to coordinate ICBM penetration aid R&D [Ballistic Missile Technology Coordination panel] J. D. Morrocco. *Aviat Week Space Technol* 126:25-6 Mr 30 '87

A dispute over Soviet ABM plans. C. Norman. *Science* 235:524-6 Ja 30 '87

The empire strikes back [proposed Dept. of the Defense Force] R. C. Kirkwood. *Natl Rev* 39:41 Jl 17 '87

Pentagon will develop defense against Soviet tactical missiles [antitactical ballistic missile defense] J. D. Morrocco. *Aviat Week Space Technol* 126:22 Ja 19 '87

Slow progress may delay decision on antitactical missile. J. D. Morrocco. *Aviat Week Space Technol* 127:26-7 N 23 '87

Soviet strategic defense technology. E. Stubbs. bibl f il map *Bull At Sci* 43:14-19 Ap '87

Soviets' newest threat [prompts West to develop antitactical ballistic missile system] W. J. Cook. il *U S News World Rep* 102:30 Mr 16 '87

A tactical defense initiative for Western Europe? I. H. Daalder. bibl f il *Bull At Sci* 43:34-9 My '87

Towed expendable RF decoy to defeat classified threats. *Aviat Week Space Technol* 127:23 S 21 '87

Triumph at Pad 17 [successful test of ICBM defense system] R. K. Bennett. il *Read Dig* 131:59-64 Jl '87

Design

Army limits pedestal-mounted Stinger competition to two rivals. *Aviat Week Space Technol* 126:30 My 4 '87

Army modifies TOW missile to counter recent advances in Soviet reactive armor. *Aviat Week Space Technol* 127:23 Jl 27 '87

Boeing Aerospace wins contract to provide LOS-R Stinger system [line of sight-rear component of the Army's forward area air defense system] C. A. Shifrin. il *Aviat Week Space Technol* 127:25-6 Ag 31 '87

Martin Marietta ADATS wins Army air defense competition [Anti-Tank Air Defense System] J. D. Morrocco. il *Aviat Week Space Technol* 127:26-7 D 7 '87

Missile manufacturers stress tailoring of current systems [Paris Air Show] S. W. Kandebo. il *Aviat Week Space Technol* 126:85+ Je 29 '87

Raytheon wins contracts for Stinger, Sparrow missiles. *Aviat Week Space Technol* 127:29 O 5 '87

Seven nations near accord on modular standoff weapons. il *Aviat Week Space Technol* 126:27 Je 22 '87

Disarmament

See Disarmament; Strategic Arms Limitation Talks; Strategic Arms Reduction Talks

Launchers

See Guided missiles—Propulsion systems

Launching from airplanes

Acquisition Board endorses low-rate AMRAAM production [advanced medium-range air-to-air missile] *Aviat Week Space Technol* 126:24 Je 8 '87

AIM-120A AMRAAM passes key congressional test [advanced medium-range air-to-air missile] *Aviat Week Space Technol* 126:31 My 11 '87

Britain, France to assess joint development of cruise missile. *Aviat Week Space Technol* 127:25 D 21 '87

British Aerospace delays missile program [air-launched antiradiation missile] *Aviat Week Space Technol* 127:23 S 21 '87

F-14 crew fires at Iranian jet to defend Navy Gulf patrol. B. M. Greeley, Jr. il *Aviat Week Space Technol* 127:22-3 Ag 17 '87

Initial Penguin Mk. 3 production under way for joint test program. D. A. Brown. il *Aviat Week Space Technol* 126:140-1+ F 9 '87

Navy, Air Force plan HARM upgrade to extend missile life through 1990s. il *Aviat Week Space Technol* 126:101+ F 9 '87

Navy will request proposals for advanced interdiction weapon. J. D. Morrocco. *Aviat Week Space Technol* 126:71-2 My 4 '87

One missile's lessons [costs of advanced medium-range air-to-air missile] R. J. Shapiro. il *U S News World Rep* 103:33 S 28 '87

Two AMRAAMs fail to hit targets [advanced medium-range air-to-air missiles] *Aviat Week Space Technol* 127:26 Jl 13 '87

Launching from helicopters

Army tests air-to-air Stinger missile prior to installation on OH-58C/Ds. il *Aviat Week Space Technol* 126:114-15 Ja 19 '87

Sea Eagle missile evaluated on Indian, Chilean aircraft [antiship missile] il *Aviat Week Space Technol* 126:159 Je 15 '87

Launching from ships

Evolving cruise missile upgrades stress versatility, flexibility [sea-launched Tomahawk cruise missile] S. W. Kandebo. il *Aviat Week Space Technol* 127:103+ N 23 '87

RAM program achieves successes following near cancellation [multinational XIM-116A rolling airframe missile] M. A. Dornheim. il *Aviat Week Space Technol* 126:57-9+ Je 22 '87

Raytheon wins contract to design new version of Standard Missile. D. Hughes. il *Aviat Week Space Technol* 127:24-5 Ag 17 '87

Upgrading Stark: will it prevent a tragedy? il *Pop Mech* 164:115 O '87

Launching from submarines

Navy launches first advanced Trident missile. *Aviat Week Space Technol* 126:29 Ja 19 '87

Skirting human error: the Navy's missile launch system. G. E. Marsh. *Bull At Sci* 43:38 Ja/F '87

Sub-launched Tomahawk destroys bunker. il map *Aviat Week Space Technol* 127:24-5 S 14 '87

Launching sites

See Guided missile bases

Optical equipment

Army will seek bids for fiber-optics guided missile. il *Aviat Week Space Technol* 127:20-1 O 19 '87

A missile that sees over hills [fiber optic guided missile] S. Budiansky. *Science* 236:138 Ap 10 '87

Propulsion systems

SDI watch [fast burn ICBM boosters] *Natl Rev* 39:17 Mr 13 '87

USAF, Aerojet revive concept of integrated rocket stages. R. G. O'Lone. il *Aviat Week Space Technol* 126:37-8 Ap 27 '87

Radar equipment

Aerojet develops missile radome cooling technique for SDIO. *Aviat Week Space Technol* 127:76 Ag 17 '87

Army missile test demonstrates FLAGE guidance [flexible lightweight agile guided experiment] J. D. Morrocco. il *Aviat Week Space Technol* 126:22-3 Je 1 '87

The missile that waits [Tacit Rainbow anti-radar cruise missiles] S. F. Brown. il *Pop Sci* 231:69 O '87

Specifications

International missiles [tables] il *Aviat Week Space Technol* 126:172-3 Mr 9 '87

Soviet missiles [tables] il *Aviat Week Space Technol* 126:174-5 Mr 9 '87

U.S. missiles [tables] il *Aviat Week Space Technol* 126:170-1 Mr 9 '87

Guided missiles—*cont.*

Testing

See also

White Sands Missile Range (N.M.)

Air defense leaders emerge from live-fire trials; Contenders for Army mobile air defense system near completion of tests at White Sands Range. il *Aviat Week Space Technol* 127:18-19 O 19 '87

Army air defense candidates score six hits in 15 attempts. J. D. Morrocco. *Aviat Week Space Technol* 127:24-5 S 21 '87

Army tests air-to-air Stinger missile prior to installation on OH-58C/Ds. il *Aviat Week Space Technol* 126:114-15 Ja 19 '87

Army tests line-of-sight air defense systems [forward area air defense system] C. A. Shifrin. *Aviat Week Space Technol* 127:20-2 Jl 6 '87

Army will begin ADATS field testing in 1989. *Aviat Week Space Technol* 127:24 D 21 '87

Navy launches first advanced Trident missile. *Aviat Week Space Technol* 126:29 Ja 19 '87

Patriot missile with new fuze, warhead tested against another Patriot target. il *Aviat Week Space Technol* 127:28-9 N 16 '87

RAM program achieves successes following near cancellation [multinational XIM-116A rolling airframe missile] M. A. Dornheim. il *Aviat Week Space Technol* 126:57-9+ Je 22 '87

U.S., Israel to test Arrow antitactical missile. *Aviat Week Space Technol* 127:26-7 D 21 '87

Suspension

Ban missile flight testing. S. Plous. *Nation* 244:219-20 F 21 '87

Tracking

Boost-phase requirements lead sensor development program. il *Aviat Week Space Technol* 127:54-5 N 23 '87

SDI National Test Facility to aid in recording ICBM signature data. il *Aviat Week Space Technol* 126:39 Ap 27 '87

Guided missiles, British

Britain, France to assess joint development of cruise missile. *Aviat Week Space Technol* 127:25 D 21 '87

British Aerospace delays missile program [air-launched antiradiation missile] *Aviat Week Space Technol* 127:23 S 21 '87

British Aerospace developing Rapier 2000 missile system. il *Aviat Week Space Technol* 126:143 F 9 '87

Short Brothers pushes Starstreak for U.S. Army air defense. D. A. Brown. il *Aviat Week Space Technol* 126:68-9 Ap 6 '87

Guided missiles, Chinese

China tailors exhibit to pursue military, commuter aircraft markets [Paris Air Show] il *Aviat Week Space Technol* 126:25-6 Je 22 '87

Chinese facility combines capabilities to produce Long March boosters, ICBMs. C. Covault. il *Aviat Week Space Technol* 127:50-3 Jl 27 '87

Guided missiles, European

About-face on arms [Soviet strategy] *World Press Rev* 34:10-12 Ap '87

Allies approach agreement on joint ATM programs [antitactical missile] J. D. Morrocco. *Aviat Week Space Technol* 126:18-20 Je 29 '87

Allies weigh new deployments to offset proposed INF cuts. J. D. Morrocco. *Aviat Week Space Technol* 126:18-19 My 18 '87

April's spy scare [Soviet espionage and the INF proposals] D. Schorr. il *New Leader* 70:3-4 Ap 20 '87

Arms control: 'the fix is in' [missiles in Europe] R. Watson. il *Newsweek* 109:28-30 My 4 '87

An arms offer is accepted [eliminating medium-range missiles in Europe; with interview with M. Kampelman] M. Satchell. il *U S News World Rep* 102:26-7 Mr 16 '87

Arms talks [cover story; special section] il *World Press Rev* 34:9-15 Je '87

An arms tango in Moscow [G. P. Shultz meets with M. Gorbachev] A. Finlayson. il pors *Macleans* 100:18-19 Ap 27 '87

Battle of the bean counters [effect of zero option proposal on NATO and Warsaw Pact forces] C. Redman. il map *Time* 129:33-4 Je 15 '87

Before we cheer [comparison between impending INF Treaty and the nuclear test ban treaty of 1963] S. H. Day, Jr. *Progressive* 51:14-15 N '87

Benefits of an INF agreement [response to R. M. Nixon and H. Kissinger] G. P. Shultz. *Dep State Bull* 87:17-18 Jl '87

Bombs away [INF deal] *New Repub* 197:7-8 O 12 '87

'Breakthrough' on arms control [intermediate range nuclear forces in Europe] R. Watson. il *Newsweek* 109:36-7 Mr 16 '87

Can NATO survive an arms deal? [views of B. W. Rogers] J. Keegan. il *U S News World Rep* 103:30 Jl 27 '87

Captain Zero Option [Gorbachev's latest proposal concerning European INF forces] C. Krauthammer. *New Repub* 196:12-14 Mr 30 '87

The complexities of nuclear diplomacy [INF proposals] R. J. Bresler. il *USA Today (Periodical)* 116:7 Jl '87

Dateline Washington: INF: a hollow victory? M. R. Gordon. *Foreign Policy* 68:159-79 Fall '87

Dealing at last [M. Gorbachev's offer to cut back Euromissiles; cover story; special section] il pors map *Newsweek* 109:20-8+ Ap 27 '87

Disarmament is no bargain. M. S. Forbes, Jr. il *Forbes* 139:33 My 18 '87

Disarming [INF agreement; cover story; special section] il *World Press Rev* 34:11-18 N '87

Euromissile pact may affect NATO's conventional/high-technology balance. J. D. Morrocco. il map *Aviat Week Space Technol* 126:122+ Je 15 '87

Europe's decoupling anxiety [disarmament proposals frighten Western European leaders] N. Gelb. il *New Leader* 70:7-8 Ap 20 '87

Europe's security dilemmas. C. Bertram. *Foreign Aff* 65:942-57 Summ '87

Final reductions [Soviet Euromissile proposal] M. Kondracke. *New Repub* 196:15-16 My 11 '87

Future missile cuts would force NATO to improve conventional arms planning. *Aviat Week Space Technol* 126:212-14 Je 15 '87

Generals can be right [B. Rogers on proposed INF Treaty] W. F. Buckley. *Natl Rev* 39:56 Jl 31 '87

A Gorbachev arms offer even Europe may not refuse. B. Javetski and P. Galuszka. il por *Bus Week* p53 Ap 27 '87

Gorbachev's long reach [proposal to eliminate intermediate range nuclear missiles in Europe] K. Scanlon. il por map *Macleans* 100:31-2 Mr 16 '87

Happy birthday, flexible response [NATO nuclear strategy] W. M. Arkin. *Bull At Sci* 43:5-6 D '87

The harm is done [treaty arranged by Reagan-Shultz to remove intermediate nuclear weapons from Europe] W. F. Buckley. *Natl Rev* 39:66 N 20 '87

If Gorbachev loses . . . [intermediate range missiles] il *Progressive* 51:9-10 My '87

In defense of the zero option [eliminating medium-range missiles] R. N. Perle. il *U S News World Rep* 102:36-7 My 25 '87

INF deal faces conservative opposition. L. V. Sigal. il *Bull At Sci* 43:14-16 My '87

The INF trap [Gorbachev's gambit] E. V. Rostow. *New Repub* 197:16-17 Ag 24 '87

An interview with Richard Nixon [views on zero option proposal] J. F. Stacks and S. Talbott. il por *Time* 129:23 My 4 '87

Kissinger: a new era for NATO. H. Kissinger. il *Newsweek* 110:57-8+ O 12 '87

Kissinger and INF. il *Natl Rev* 39:17 N 6 '87

Let's make a deal [removal of medium-range missiles from Europe] J. Smolowe. il map *Time* 129:38-9 Mr 16 '87

Looking this gift horse in the mouth [Soviet INF proposal] W. F. Buckley. *Natl Rev* 39:60 Ap 10 '87

Memo to the Senate [views of B. Rogers on INF deal] *Natl Rev* 39:15 Jl 17 '87

Missile pact edges closer. C. Norman. il *Science* 236:378-9 Ap 24 '87

The missile treaty is only a 3% solution. B. Javetski and D. Griffiths. il *Bus Week* p24 S 7 '87

NATO armaments programs hinge on technology transfer benefits. M. A. Dornheim. il *Aviat Week Space Technol* 126:220-2+ Je 15 '87

NATO defense ministers back INF agreement. B. A. Smith. *Aviat Week Space Technol* 127:26-7 N 9 '87

NATO looks for arms control loopholes [prospect of an INF accord] D. Charles. il *Bull At Sci* 43:7-12 S '87

NATO planning group to discuss post-INF tactical nuclear strategy. J. D. Morrocco. *Aviat Week Space Technol* 127:125+ O 12 '87

Nearing a deal on Euromissiles. H. Trewhitt. il por *U S News World Rep* 102:48-9 Ap 27 '87

The need for nuclear arms [interview with B. W. Rogers] R. Knight. por *U S News World Rep* 102:22-3 Je 22 '87

Negotiations on Intermediate-range Nuclear Forces. il *Dep State Bull* 87:24-7 S '87

Guided missiles, European—*cont.*

Nervous about nuclear security [NATO allies object to possible removal of INF missiles] C. Redman. il *Time* 129:37 My 11 '87

Nitty-gritty time for arms control. P. R. Range. il map *U S News World Rep* 102:44-5 Mr 30 '87

North Atlantic Council meets in Iceland [texts of final communique and news conference, June 12, 1987] G. P. Shultz. *Dep State Bull* 87:59-63 Ag '87

Now, super-zero? [M. Gorbachev's proposal to NATO] G. J. Church. il pors *Time* 129:20-3 Ap 27 '87

Nuclear disarmament [address, February 28, 1987] M. Gorbachev. *Vital Speeches Day* 53:386-7 Ap 15 '87

The Ogarkov factor [Soviet arms control proposals linked to views of N. Ogarkov] B. Crozier. *Natl Rev* 39:22 Je 5 '87

One way to arms-control unity: twist allied arms. P. Hassner. il *U S News World Rep* 102:24-5 Je 22 '87

The opiate of arms control. G. F. Will. il *Newsweek* 109:86 Ap 27 '87

Peacedrunk [INF Treaty] W. F. Buckley. *Natl Rev* 39:71 O 23 '87

Post-Moscow blues [Soviet INF proposal] W. F. Buckley. *Natl Rev* 39:57 My 22 '87

The problem: the other guy says 'yes' [INF talks; with editorial comment by Mortimer B. Zuckerman] H. Trewhitt. il *U S News World Rep* 102:41, 78 My 4 '87

The proposed Euromissile agreement: an important step toward nuclear sanity [INF agreement] R. E. Powaski. *America* 157:183-4+ O 3 '87

The proposed treaty [Soviet INF proposal] *Natl Rev* 39:13-15 My 22 '87

Protocol and peace [J. Reston's comments on proposed INF Treaty] W. F. Buckley. *Natl Rev* 39:54 Je 5 '87

Reagan & Gorbachev: arms-control breakthrough? [cover story; special issue] il map *Sch Update* 120:4-10+ N 20 '87

Reagan's no suicide [defense of Reagan's Euromissile disarmament stance] W. A. Rusher. *Natl Rev* 39:36 Je 5 '87

Reagan's suicide pact [Soviet INF proposals; cover story; special section] il *Natl Rev* 39:27-30+ My 22 '87

Rejecting the suicide pact [opposition to proposed INF agreement] *Natl Rev* 39:12-13 Je 5 '87

A reply to Nixon and Kissinger [defense of zero option proposal] G. P. Shultz. il por *Time* 129:40 My 18 '87

The road to zero. S. Talbott. il *Time* 130:18-21+ D 14 '87

Rocky road to INF accord. M. Krepon. il *Bull At Sci* 43:3-4 S '87

The saver? [latest Soviet zero option proposal] M. Kramer. il *N Y* 20:14-15 Mr 30 '87

Secretary's trip to Helsinki, Moscow, and Brussels. G. P. Shultz. il por *Dep State Bull* 87:12-24 Je '87

Senate leadership warns president against 'rushing' into Euromissile pact. P. Mann. *Aviat Week Space Technol* 126:40-1 Ap 27 '87

Shevardnadze schmooze [U.S.-Soviet agreement in principle on INF forces] F. Barnes. *New Repub* 197:10+ O 19 '87

A tactical defense initiative for Western Europe? I. H. Daalder. bibl f il *Bull At Sci* 43:34-9 My '87

A thunderclap [proposal that all nuclear missiles be removed from European soil] E. von Kuehnelt-Leddihn. *Natl Rev* 39:44 Jl 17 '87

To ratify or not to ratify? [outlook for Senate ratification of proposed arms control deal with the Soviets] J. McLaughlin. *Natl Rev* 39:28 S 25 '87

To win the peace [Russian offer on Euromissiles sets stage for peace movement] *Nation* 244:561-2 My 2 '87

Two ways to zero. *Natl Rev* 39:15-16 Jl 3 '87

The uneasy nuclear balance [Soviet offers to reduce the number of nuclear missiles deployed in Europe] D. E. Fink. *Aviat Week Space Technol* 126:25 Ap 27 '87

The wary warlords [views of Joint Chiefs on Euromissile treaty] D. Gates. il *Newsweek* 109:5 My 11 '87

'A way out of the nuclear dilemma' [INF talks] *America* 156:393-4 My 16 '87

Why an INF agreement makes sense [address, May 1, 1987] K. L. Adelman. *Vital Speeches Day* 53:514-18 Je 15 '87

Why arms talks unnerve NATO. J. Keegan. il *U S News World Rep* 102:28-30 Ap 20 '87

Yalta II [implications of Soviet Union's zero option INF proposal] J. Morley. *New Repub* 196:14-15 Mr 30 '87

Zero option II [latest Soviet proposal] *Natl Rev* 39:16-17 Mr 27 '87

The 'zero option'—a Western idea. H. Schmidt. il *World Press Rev* 34:28-30 Jl '87

Zero plus zero [options for nuclear-arms cuts in Europe] *Natl Rev* 39:15 Je 19 '87

Guided missiles, French

Britain, France to assess joint development of cruise missile. *Aviat Week Space Technol* 127:25 D 21 '87

France keeps option open on missile contractor choice. *Aviat Week Space Technol* 126:107 F 9 '87

French missile line includes national, international efforts. *Aviat Week Space Technol* 126:221 Je 15 '87

Guided missiles, German

Cruisin' for a bruisin' [INF reductions expose the Germans] J. Joffe. *New Repub* 197:17-18 O 5 '87

East-West missile deal: Helmut Kohl feels the heat. D. Stanglin. il por *U S News World Rep* 102:13 Je 1 '87

Germany's decision on proposed INF reductions [statement, June 4, 1987] R. Reagan. *Dep State Bull* 87:50 Ag '87

Kohl is nudged, but will he budge? [INF disarmament proposal] *Newsweek* 109:39 Je 1 '87

Kohl vows to scrap Pershing 1As if U.S., Soviets agree on treaty [INF] *Aviat Week Space Technol* 127:18 Ag 31 '87

Last tango in Geneva [INF talks] B. Levin. *Macleans* 100:29-30 S 7 '87

A major sticking point [disagreement over West German Pershing IAs stalls INF pact] il *Time* 130:14 Ag 10 '87

Moscow's arms-control offer has Kohl in a corner. J. E. Pluenneke and F. Thelen. il *Bus Week* p69 My 18 '87

Much ado about zero [INF forces] *Bull At Sci* 43:2 S '87

New rules for war [H. Kohl drops objection to Soviet offer on Euromissiles] P. Lewis. il por *Macleans* 100:20-1 Je 8 '87

Off-Road Roland missile system improves West German air defense. K. F. Mordoff. il *Aviat Week Space Technol* 127:99 O 5 '87

The singular threat to the Atlantic Alliance [excerpts from address, May 28, 1987] H. Kissinger. *Natl Rev* 39:18-19 Jl 3 '87

Softening up the Germans [Soviet INF proposals] E. Galbraith. il *Natl Rev* 39:34-5 My 22 '87

To get an impactful feel for how upsetting . . . [views of F. J. Strauss on upcoming arms agreement between U.S. and Soviet Union] M. S. Forbes, Jr. il por *Forbes* 140:25 Ag 24 '87

U.S., West German concessions improve prospects for INF Treaty with Soviets. *Aviat Week Space Technol* 127:19 Ag 31 '87

West German angst [reaction to European missile proposal] il *World Press Rev* 34:11+ Je '87

West Germany to dismantle Pershing IA missiles [White House statement, August 26, 1987] *Dep State Bull* 87:49 O '87

Guided missiles, Iranian

Chin to chin in a sea of trouble [Iranian missiles hit Kuwaiti tanker sailing under U.S. flag] B. Duffy. il map *U S News World Rep* 103:25 O 26 '87

How did Iran get Stinger missiles? il *Newsweek* 110:42-3 O 26 '87

Silkworm's sting [Iranian missile attack on Kuwaiti tanker sailing under American flag] M. S. Serrill. il map *Time* 130:42-3 O 26 '87

U.S. will attack Iranian missile sites if hostile intent is evident. P. Mann. *Aviat Week Space Technol* 127:29-30 Jl 20 '87

What's the Chinese word for chutzpah? [sale of missiles to Iran] *Newsweek* 110:59 N 9 '87

Will Reagan hit back at Iran? [retaliation for missile strike against U.S.-flagged tanker] N. Cooper. il *Newsweek* 110:42-3 O 26 '87

Guided missiles, Iraqi

  See also

    Stark (Warship)—Iraqi missile attack, 1987

Guided missiles, Israeli

Battle of Jericho [Soviet objection to Israeli Jericho II missiles] *Time* 130:22 Ag 10 '87

Funding problems dampen U.S. support for Israeli Arrow missile. *Aviat Week Space Technol* 127:32 D 7 '87

U.S., Israel to test Arrow antitactical missile. *Aviat Week Space Technol* 127:26-7 D 21 '87

Guided missiles, Norwegian

Initial Penguin Mk. 3 production under way for joint test program. D. A. Brown. il *Aviat Week Space Technol* 126:140-1+ F 9 '87

Guided missiles, Russian

ATBM—a solution in search of a problem. B. Morel. bibl f *Bull At Sci* 43:39-41 My '87

Missile begets new charge [Soviet deployment of SS-24s cited as violation of SALT] *Bull At Sci* 43:2 O '87

Soviet missiles [tables] il *Aviat Week Space Technol* 126:174-5 Mr 9 '87

Soviet strategic defense technology. E. Stubbs. bibl f il map *Bull At Sci* 43:14-19 Ap '87

Soviets increase deployment of mobile ballistic, cruise missiles. B. M. Greeley, Jr. il *Aviat Week Space Technol* 126:24-5 Mr 30 '87

Guided missiles, Saudi Arabian

Administration cancels missile sale; Congress critical of Middle East policy [proposed sale of 1,600 Maverick antitank missiles to Saudi Arabia] M. Mecham. *Aviat Week Space Technol* 126:70-1 Je 15 '87

Congress moves to block sale of Mavericks to Saudis. M. Mecham. *Aviat Week Space Technol* 126:23-4 Je 8 '87

Guided projectiles *See* Projectiles

Guides

The basin [elk hunting guide] B. Brister. il *Field Stream* 92:54-5+ N '87

From woods to Roots [wilderness guide O. Stringer] D. Cumming. por *Macleans* 100:6 Ja 19 '87

My last hunter [Rocky Mountain elk hunt] M. Lapinski. il *Outdoor Life* 179:60-1+ F '87

Outfitted or on your own [fishing or hunting trip] S. Netherby. il *Field Stream* 91:103+ Mr '87

Guiding of telescopes *See* Telescopes—Control

Guidon, Niède

Cliff notes. il map *Nat Hist* 96:6+ Ag '87

Guidry, Jacqueline M.

Our breakfast club. il *Parents* 62:84+ D '87

Guidry, Lori L.

City vs. rural environment: which is healthier? il *Curr Health 2* 14:24-5 S '87

Guihannec, Yves

Ideological backlash. il *World Press Rev* 34:17 D '87

Guilford Mills, Inc.

What makes a survivor? M. Kuntz. il por *Forbes* 139:77 Ja 26 '87

Guillaud, Jacqueline

about

Paris calling. C. de Liagre. il pors *N Y* 20:24 F 16 '87

Guillaud, Maurice

about

Paris calling. C. de Liagre. il pors *N Y* 20:24 F 16 '87

Guillet, Jean-Gerard, and others

Immunological self, nonself discrimination. bibl f il *Science* 235:865-70 F 20 '87

Guilt

Feeling guilty. E. Crow. il *Parents* 62:8 Ag '87

The great manipulator. M. Larkin. bibl il *Health* 19:65-6+ Ja '87

The guilt that drives working mothers crazy. B. J. Berg. il *Ms* 15:56-9+ My '87

Guilty ourselves [juror guilt; research by Lawrence A. Fehr] D. Schechter. *Psychol Today* 21:20 O '87

Your child is in the hospital, and you're blanketed by guilt. P. Klass. il *Discover* 8:20+ Ja '87

Guinan, James, 1932?-

about

Can the closeout king unload its woes? S. Phillips. il por *Bus Week* p94 D 7 '87

Guinness, Alec

about

Gray ghost. D. Thomson. il pors *Film Comment* 23:26+ Mr/Ap '87

Guinness plc

Bank Leu's new brouhaha. J. Templeman. il *Bus Week* p50 F 2 '87

Britain's business elite takes a fall. P. Sherrid. il *U S News World Rep* 102:47-8 F 2 '87

Britain's own Boesky case. R. I. Kirkland, Jr. il por *Fortune* 115:85-6 F 16 '87

A consulting firm too hot to handle? [Bain & Co.] N. J. Perry. il *Fortune* 115:91-2+ Ap 27 '87

Downfall of a titan [E. W. Saunders' role in Guinness securities scandal] T. Fennell. il por *Macleans* 100:28 My 25 '87

Fearing that "muck will stick" [Guinness stock trading scandal] S. Holmes. il *Time* 129:61 Mr 9 '87

The Guinness affair gets curiouser and curiouser [role of M. Riklis and sale of Schenley to Guinness] M. Maremont. *Bus Week* p59-60 My 25 '87

Guinness' new boss starts plugging the holes [A. M. Tennant] M. Maremont. il por *Bus Week* p51 O 5 '87

How Guinness suddenly fell from grace. R. A. Melcher and M. Maremont. il pors *Bus Week* p44-6 F 9 '87

Look who may take a fall in the Guinness scandal. M. Maremont. por *Bus Week* p48 O 26 '87

The questions surrounding Guinness' U.S. connection [Washington lawyer T. J. Ward] P. Dwyer and M. Maremont. il por *Bus Week* p36-7 Ap 27 '87

Scandal at Guinness. R. Laver. il *Macleans* 100:62 F 2 '87

The scandal at Guinness: will the chief fall? [insider trading charges] M. Maremont and R. A. Melcher. il por *Bus Week* p52 Ja 19 '87

Guiraut, Denis Hautin- *See* Hautin-Guiraut, Denis

Guirlinger, Austin

about

The lord of modular. E. Schmuckler. il por *Forbes* 140:208+ D 14 '87

Guitar

Study and teaching

Aids and devices

Guitar 101 [guitar instructional videos] B. Milkowski. *Down Beat* 54:57 O '87

Guitar music

See also

Phonograph records—Guitar music

Videotapes—Guitar music

Flamenco puro [guitar festival in Belgium] D. Gordon. il *Down Beat* 54:12 Jl '87

Martinique guitar fest [Seventh International Guitar Festival] D. Gordon. il *Down Beat* 54:12 Mr '87

Steve Morse's The whistle—a guitar transcription. J. Dennison. il *Down Beat* 54:59 Ap '87

Terje Rypdal's The curse—a guitar transcription. J. Dennison. il *Down Beat* 54:56 O '87

Guitarists

See also

Alomar, Carlos

Barbosa-Lima, Carlos

Bernsen, Randy

Carew-Reid, Lloyd

Cray, Robert

Eubanks, Kevin

Frisell, Bill

Funderburgh, Anson

Henderson, Scott

Leitch, Peter

McLaughlin, John

Morse, Steve

Parkening, Christopher, 1947-

Paul, Les, 1915-

Robillard, Duke

Ruffner, Mason

Rypdal, Terje, 1947-

Scofield, John

Segovia, Andrés, 1893-1987

Stern, Leni

Stern, Mike

Stewart, Jimmy

Sumlin, Hubert

Torn, David

Guitarists, Handicapped

After years of hard traveling, mountain maestro Doc Watson looks to find some easy pickin' at last. R. Wolmuth. il pors *People Wkly* 28:57-8+ Ag 10 '87

Guiton, Bonnie

about

From welfare roll to White House payroll. R. L. Haywood. il pors *Jet* 72:6-8 Ag 31 '87

Gulags *See* Concentration camps—Soviet Union

Gulf & Western, Inc.

Can a tough boss mellow? [M. Davis] M. J. Williams. il pors *Fortune* 116:105+ D 21 '87

Gulf & Western: from grab bag to lean, mean, marketing machine. D. Lieberman. il *Bus Week* p152-3+ S 14 '87

Gulf & Western Industries, Inc.

See also

Gulf & Western, Inc.

Gulf Canada Limited

The Reichmann touch: facing the toughest test yet. E. B. Terry. il *Bus Week* p96-7+ Mr 23 '87

Gulf of California (Mexico)

Blazing the charter trail in Baja. B. Duke and S. Duke. il *Mot Boat Sail* 160:56-9+ Ag '87

Gulf of California (Mexico)—*cont.*
Photographs and photography
Return to the Sea of Cortez: following in the wake of John Steinbeck. P. Skinner. il map *Petersens Photogr Mag* 15:36-40 F '87

Gulf of Maine
Modeling tidal power [tidal power dam in the Bay of Fundy would raise tide levels in the Gulf of Maine] D. A. Greenberg. il maps *Sci Am* 257:128-128C+ N '87

Gulf of Mexico
See also
Fisheries—Gulf of Mexico
Petroleum—Gulf of Mexico

Gulf of Sidra incident, 1986 *See* Libyan-American conflict, 1986

Gulf Shores (Ala.)
Galleries and museums
See also
Fort Morgan Museum (Gulf Shores, Ala.)

Gulf States (U.S.)
Description and travel
The Gulf Coast. G. S. Bush. il map *Better Homes Gard* 65:144+ F '87

Gulfport (Miss.)
Libraries
See also
L.W. Anderson Genealogical Library

Gulfstream Aerospace Corp.
Air Force exploits speed, range of Gulfstream C-20 in VIP role. P. Proctor. il *Aviat Week Space Technol* 126:74-5 Je 8 '87
Manufacturer investigating modified Gulfstream 4s as Navy P-3 follow-on. P. Proctor. il *Aviat Week Space Technol* 126:94-5 Ap 13 '87
Why Gulfstream's rivals are gazing up in envy. S. Ticer. il por *Bus Week* p66+ F 16 '87

Gulick, John Thomas, 1832-1923
about
The process whereby species originate [cover story] H. L. Carson. bibl il por *BioScience* 37:715-20 N '87

Gullah dialect
Old-time talk we still de talkem here! P. Jones-Jackson. il *Natl Geogr* 172:744 D '87
Special words, special lady [V. M. Geraty] D. Young. il por *South Living* 22:146 Mr '87

Gullans International (Firm)
A leg up [showroom at International Design Center] C. K. Gandee. il *Archit Rec* 175:106-9 My '87

Gullatt, David E.
How to help students in reading mathematics. *Educ Dig* 52:40-1 Ja '87

GUM (Moscow, Soviet Union)
Red Square chic. G. Perrelli and E. Regazzoni. il *World Press Rev* 34:19-20 Ap '87

Gum chewing *See* Chewing gum

Gumbel, Bryant, 1948-
about
Gumbel to become NBC's Seoul man for Olympics. por *Jet* 72:46 Jl 20 '87
Today's man: the double-edged charm of Bryant Gumbel. S. Weller. il pors *McCalls* 114:69-71+ Je '87

Gumbiner, Anthony Joseph
about
A 'rescue finance' team takes on banking. D. Cook. il por *Bus Week* p120 Mr 16 '87

Gumbo *See* Cooking, Creole

Gump, Jean
about
Bonded by love and conscience, the Gumps of Morton Grove accept prison. D. Chu. il pors *People Wkly* 28:163-4+ D 14 '87

Gump, Joseph
about
Bonded by love and conscience, the Gumps of Morton Grove accept prison. D. Chu. il pors *People Wkly* 28:163-4+ D 14 '87

Gums
Getting a grip on gum damage [proper grip on toothbrush] il *Prevention* 39:12 D '87
Diseases
See also
Dental plaque
Gingivitis
The battle in your mouth. L. S. Senz. il *Saturday Evening Post* 259:22-3+ Mr '87
Periodontal disease: how to win the battle against tooth loss. S. F. Goodman. por *McCalls* 114:119 F '87
Rx for healthy gums: preventing periodontal disease. L. Lamberg. *Better Homes Gard* 65:75 Mr '87

Therapy
New approach to treating gum disease [antibiotic therapy] *Sci News* 132:268 O 24 '87

Gums and resins, Fossil
See also
Amber

Gun control legislation *See* Firearms—Laws and regulations
Gun engraving *See* Firearms—Decoration
Gun sights *See* Firearms—Sights
Gun stocks *See* Gunstocks

Gunderson, J. H., and others
Structurally distinct, stage-specific ribosomes occur in Plasmodium. bibl f il *Science* 238:933-7 N 13 '87

Gunmakers *See* Firearms industry

Gunn, Genni
Getting your novel started in ten days. *Writer* 100:11-13 F '87

Gunnerson, Ronnie
Parents also have rights. por *Newsweek* 109:10-11 Mr 2 '87

Gunning, Richard
Increased numbers of ion channels promoted by an intracellular second messenger. bibl f il *Science* 235:80-2 Ja 2 '87

Gunrunning *See* Smuggling

Guns, Anti-aircraft
After Divad, an $11-billion plan. S. Budiansky. il *Science* 236:137-40 Ap 10 '87
Beggs and General Dynamics cleared of fraud [Divad gun case] I. Goodwin. *Phys Today* 40 pt1:53 Ag '87
General Dynamics, Beggs cleared of fraud charges [Divad contract] *Aviat Week Space Technol* 126:25-6 Je 29 '87
Indictment of Beggs dropped [General Dynamics Divad gun fraud case] E. Marshall. *Science* 237:21 Jl 3 '87
Justice Dept.'s broadax [dismissal of indictment against General Dynamics in Divad gun case] D. E. Fink. *Aviat Week Space Technol* 127:9 Jl 13 '87
Who's counting? [Justice Dept. abandons Divad gun fraud case against General Dynamics] W. Biddle. *Nation* 245:148-9 Ag 29 '87

Guns, Toy *See* Toys
Guns (Small arms) *See* Firearms; Pistols; Rifles; Shotguns
Guns as investments *See* Firearms—Collectors and collecting
Gunstock camera supports *See* Camera supports

Gunstocks
Get the oil out [oil-soaked gunstocks] R. Swartley. il *Outdoor Life* 179:56 Mr '87
Synthetic stocks are here to stay. J. Carmichel. il *Outdoor Life* 180:68+ S '87

Guo, Peixuan, and others
A small viral RNA is required for in vitro packaging of bacteriophage φ29 DNA. bibl f il *Science* 236:690-4 My 8 '87

Gupta, Bhabani Sen
An Indian view of the contras. il *World Press Rev* 34:15-16 S '87

Gupta, Chidananda Das *See* Das Gupta, Chidananda
Gupta, Nina, and others
Pay-for-knowledge compensation plans: hypotheses and survey results. bibl f il *Mon Labor Rev* 110:40-3 O '87

Gurin, Carol Duchow
Depression: is there a quick fix for this dangerous disease? il *Ms* 16:48-9+ D '87

Gurion, David Ben- *See* Ben-Gurion, David, 1886-1973
Gurlitt, Manfred, 1890-1973
about
Wozzeck [opera] Reviews
Opera News 52:62+ S '87. J. H. Sutcliffe

Gurney, A. R. (Albert Ramsdell), 1930-
about
Sweet Sue [drama] Reviews
Commonweal 114:83-4 F 13 '87. G. Weales
N Y il 20:52 Ja 19 '87. J. Simon
New Leader 70:17-18 F 9-23 '87. L. Sauvage
New Yorker 62:70-1 Ja 19 '87. B. Gill
Time il 129:77 Ja 19 '87. W. A. Henry

Gurney, Albert Ramsdell *See* Gurney, A. R. (Albert Ramsdell), 1930-
Gurney, Guy
about
Camera on deck. B. London. il por *Pop Photogr* 94:70-6 Jl '87

Gürsey, Feza
about
Gürsey receives Wigner Medal for symmetry work. por *Phys Today* 40:89 Ja '87

Gush Emunim
Israel's dangerous fundamentalists. I. S. Lustick. bibl f *Foreign Policy* 68:118-39 Fall '87

Gussow, Mel
Clarke work. il pors *N Y Times Mag* p30-4+ Ja 18 '87
Gust, Paul
about
Award of honor. R. V. Araskog. il *N Y Times Mag* p54 S 6 '87
Gustafson, Donald W., 1918-
about
The high cost of education. J. A. Conway. por *Forbes* 139:8 F 23 '87
Gustafson, Eleanor H.
Museum accessions. See occasional issues of Antiques
Gustaitis, Joseph
Babe Didrikson: America's greatest athlete? il por *Am Hist Illus* 22:34-5 Ap '87
George Gipp: "One for the Gipper!". por *Am Hist Illus* 22:40-1 N '87
Horatio Alger: creator of the American success story. por *Am Hist Illus* 22:36-7 O '87
Orson Fowler: foursquare pioneer in the progressive tradition. il *Am Hist Illus* 21:44-5 Ja '87
Gustin, Mary K.
(jt. auth) See McCracken, Gary F., and Gustin, Mary K.
Gut, Rainer Emil, 1932-
The world as seen from the vantage point of a Swiss banker [address, June 17, 1987] *Vital Speeches Day* 53:668-71 Ag 15 '87
Gutfreund, John
about
Big investors on Wall Street. pors *Fortune* 116:8 O 26 '87
Salomon and Revlon: what really happened. A. Bianco. il pors *Bus Week* p156+ O 12 '87
What's behind the profit squeeze at Salomon. A. Bianco. il por *Bus Week* p72-3 Ap 20 '87
Guthrie, Arlo, 1947-
Despite the shadow of his father's (and possibly his own) deadly disease, a folk hero celebrates life; ed. by Cable Neuhaus. il pors *People Wkly* 28:97-8+ S 7 '87
about
Native sons. *New Yorker* 63:35-6 D 21 '87
Guthrie, Patricia
Lavaland. il map *Natl Parks* 61:22-7 My/Je '87
Guthrie, Woody, 1912-1967
about
Despite the shadow of his father's (and possibly his own) deadly disease, a folk hero celebrates life; ed. by Cable Neuhaus. A. Guthrie. il pors *People Wkly* 28:97-8+ S 7 '87
Gutierrez, Sergio
about
A ring and a prayer. R. Reilly. il pors *Sports Illus* 67:88-92+ D 21 '87
Gutiérrez Menoyo, Eloy
about
In Castro's gulag. G. Volsky. il pors *N Y Times Mag* p80-2+ O 18 '87
Gutman, Nathaniel
about
Deadline [film] Reviews
New Repub 197:26 S 28 '87. S. Kauffmann
Gutmann, Henning
The bad new tax law. il *N Y Rev Books* 34:26-8 F 12 '87
The bad new tax law: an exchange [discussion of February 12, 1987 article] il *N Y Rev Books* 34:49-51 Jl 16 '87
Guttenberg, Steve
about
Meet the new "Mr. Moms" [interview] K. Henderson. il pors *Redbook* 170:44+ N '87
Steve Guttenberg graduates from Police Academy—for good. C. Passalacqua. il pors *Mademoiselle* 93:62 D '87
Who is the father of this baby? [interview] il pors *Good Housekeep* 205:106+ N '87
Gutteridge, Frank
(jt. auth) See Bankowski, Zbigniew, and Gutteridge, Frank
Gutters (Roof) See House drainage
Guy, Jasmine
about
After years of trying to fit in, actress Jasmine Guy at last finds happiness in A different world. F. A. Bernstein. il pors *People Wkly* 28:123-4 N 9 '87
Guy, Richard
about
Beyond the valley of the beautiful dolls. D. Heyn. il *Mademoiselle* 93:182+ N '87

The crowning touch of Richard Guy and Rex Holt shapes Texas teens into lovelies who just can't lose. L. Aitken. il pors *People Wkly* 27:53-4 My 4 '87
Guyana
See also
Guyanese
Technical assistance, American—Guyana
Guyanese
United States
I spy: how a Queens College student helped catch a KGB agent and set off a superpower showdown [L. Bhoge; cover story] M. Daly. il pors *N Y* 20:34-47 Ap 6 '87
Gwathmey Siegel Architects
A change of space [Manhattan apartment] C. Vogel. il *N Y Times Mag* p32-5 D 27 '87
Gwathmey Siegel & Associates: coming soon to a school near you [college building projects] il *Archit Rec* 175:53 Je '87
GWEN (Ground Wave Emergency Network) system See Radio, Military
Gwinnett County (Ga.)
Gwinnett County, Georgia. il map *Time* 129:17 Je 15 '87
Gwyn, Richard J., 1934-
Europe at 30. il *World Press Rev* 34:21-3 My '87
Fear and risk. il *World Press Rev* 34:15 Je '87
A profitable irony of the war. il *World Press Rev* 34:19-20 O '87
Gwynn, Kathy
about
A little friendly advice—at $100 an hour. por *Bus Week* p46 Mr 9 '87
Gwynne, S. C. (Samuel C.), 1953-
American bank loans line the pockets of the third world's elite. *Wash Mon* 19:51-2 O '87
Welcome to the Nassau branch! [condensed from Selling money] il *Read Dig* 130:127-30 Ap '87
about
Hookers, Jaguars, and lots of stupid loans. C. Lane. *Wash Mon* 18:55-7 Ja '87
Gwynne, Samuel C. See Gwynne, S. C. (Samuel C.), 1953-
Gylys, Julius A.
The bishops' letter, world debt and the U.S. trade deficit. il *America* 157:86-7 Ag 15-22 '87
Gym classes See Physical education and training
Gymnasiums
Threat to women's gyms [men sue for entry in San Francisco] il *Women's Sports Fitness* 9:18 Mr '87
Gymnastics
See also
Acrobats and acrobatism
Tumbling
Game and gutsy, three tiny teens limber up for the '88 Olympics [M. Marlowe, P. Mills, and K. Phillips] A. Chambers. il pors *People Wkly* 28:130-2 N 2 '87
Gymnastics for grownups. H. Heyman. il *Women's Sports Fitness* 9:60-4 S '87
Mary Lou II [K. Phillips] B. Phillips. il por *Sch Update* 119:12 Mr 23 '87
A reborn Russian, a new Nadia [World Championships] C. Neff. il *Sports Illus* 67:74+ N 2 '87
A tumble from the top [U.S. men's gymnasts lose to Soviets in the McDonald's Challenge] H. Hersch. il *Sports Illus* 66:40-1 My 4 '87
What's in the future for women's sports? [demise of gymnastics at Southwest Texas State University as an example of effects of weakened Title IX regulations] C. L. Hogan. il *Women's Sports Fitness* 9:42-7 Je '87
Study and teaching
Olympic hopes in the balance [coach B. Karolyi] B. Weber. il pors *N Y Times Mag* p58 Ag 9 '87
Gynecologic examinations
Your first gynecological exam: what to expect. K. McCoy. *Seventeen* 46:76+ Ag '87
Gynecologists and patients
Sex Rx: is your gynecologist good enough? E. Rapp. il *Mademoiselle* 93:104+ O '87
Gynecology
See also
Reproductive organs—Surgery
A gynecologist answers your most intimate questions. S. A. Kaufman. *Ladies Home J* 104:50+ Mr '87
A special ob-gyn section. il *McCalls* 114:85-8+ S '87
Gypsum wallboard See Wallboard
Gypsy moths
Control
Shenandoah NP battles against the gypsy moth. il *Natl Parks* 61:38 Jl/Ag '87

Gypsy wagons
Switzerland by gypsy wagon: a one-horsepower Jura tour.
R. E. Baronas. il *Travel Holiday* 167:52-5+ My '87

Gyroscopes
Optical-fiber gyro. D. Scott. il *Pop Sci* 230:25 Je '87
Soviets use new gyros to stabilize Mir station. J. M.
Lenorovitz. il *Aviat Week Space Technol* 127:79-80
N 2 '87

Testing
Singer targets Trilag ring laser gyros for tactical, reentry
vehicle uses. K. J. Stein. il *Aviat Week Space Technol*
126:163+ Ap 27 '87

Gyroscopic equipment
See also
Inertial guidance systems
Gyrostabilizers: steady as she goes [for cameras] R.
Attaway. il *Pop Photogr* 94:77 Jl '87

Failure
Australian panel investigates 1985 crash of IAI Westwind
[report on October 10 accident off the South Head
of Botany Bay, New South Wales] il *Aviat Week
Space Technol* 126:357-8+ Je 15 '87
Tough guy [simulated failure of attitude indicators causes
crash of Australian business jet] J. M. McClellan.
Flying 114:24+ N '87

H

H & R Block, Inc.
Bloch that IRS return. W. Hoffer. il pors *Nations Bus*
75:69-70 Mr '87
Block, Block, fizz, fizz [Alka-Seltzer and H&R Block
join advertising forces] S. D. Atchison. il *Bus Week*
p36 Mr 30 '87

H.B. Fuller Company
Fuller's worldwide strategy: think local. M. J. Pitzer.
il *Bus Week* p169 N 16 '87

H-bombs *See* Atomic bombs

H.E. "Tex" Sutton Horse Charters
This man can make a horse fly [T. Sutton] D. Young.
il pors *South Living* 22:158+ Ap '87

H. F. Holdings
Bill Simon goes treasure-hunting in the Pacific. T. Carson
and C. Debes. il por *Bus Week* p84-6 Mr 9 '87
The king of the S&L's [P. Martin] R. Thomas. il por
Newsweek 109:52-3 Mr 30 '87

H. J. Russell Construction Co., Inc.
Atlanta City Hall to get facelift; black firm helps build
new addition. il *Jet* 72:33 S 21 '87
Building up, spreading out. D. Marth. il pors *Nations
Bus* 75:58-9 Ja '87
How Herman Russell built his business . . . brick by
brick. N. McCall. il pors *Black Enterp* 17:176-80+
Je '87

H. L. Mencken House (Baltimore, Md.) *See* Baltimore
(Md.)—Historic houses, sites, etc.

H.M.K. Management Corporation
The stranger in the corner [broker H. Kirschner launches
securities scam from Greenwich office of Shearson
Lehman Brothers] D. Fanning. *Forbes* 140:37-8 O 5
'87

H₂O Swimwear Ltd.
Thanks to Lisa Lomas, this season's beautiful bodies
are making waves in H_2O. il por *People Wkly* 27:130-1
My 18 '87
These tiny swimsuits are getting enormous visibility
[L. Lomas designs] P. Finch. il por *Bus Week* p105
Mr 23 '87

Haack, Robert A.
(jt. auth) See Mattson, William J., and Haack, Robert
A.

Haacke, Hans
about
Hans Haacke. E. Heartney. il *Art News* 86:143-4 Mr
'87
Hans Haacke: unfinished business. A. C. Danto. *Nation*
244:190-5 F 14 '87
Money changes everything. K. Larson. il *N Y* 20:88+
F 16 '87

Haagen, Victor
Islands in time. il map *Oceans* 20:50-5 My/Je '87

Häagen-Dazs Company, Inc.
Building a better sundae [marketing vice president B.
Bronner] J. Sherman. il por *Work Woman* 12:48 Jl
'87
Is Haagen-Dazs trying to freeze out Ben & Jerry's?
K. H. Hammonds. il *Bus Week* p65 D 7 '87

Scooped. L. Gubernick. il por *Forbes* 139:107 Je 29
'87

Haas, Charlie
Desert sojourn. il *Esquire* 108:136-43 O '87
The myth grew, the holly wouldn't. il *People Wkly*
27:40-2+ F 9 '87
What's new in L.A.? il *Esquire* 107 Summ
Traveler:T38-T42+ Ap '87

Haas, Richard
about
Suggesting a plausible fantasy. J. Gruen. il por *Archit
Dig* 44:154+ Jl '87

Haas, Warren R.
about
Blown away by Black Monday. A. Feinberg. il por *N
Y Times Mag* p38-9+ D 20 '87

Habecker, Eugene B.
Biblical guidelines for asking and giving. il por *Christ
Today* 31:32-4 My 15 '87

Haber, Bill
about
Buying a second house in Paris. C. Styles-McLeod. il
pors *Archit Dig* 44 Archit Dig Travels:10+ O '87

Haber, Carole, 1942-
about
Buying a second house in Paris. C. Styles-McLeod. il
pors *Archit Dig* 44 Archit Dig Travels:10+ O '87

Haber, James E.
(jt. auth) See Borts, Rhona H., and Haber, James E.

Haber, Sheldon E., and others
On their own: the self-employed and others in private
business. bibl f il *Mon Labor Rev* 110:17-23 My '87

Haberle, John, 1856-1933
about
Another Haberle rediscovery. E. H. Gustafson. il *Antiques*
132:1080 N '87
Two rediscovered paintings by John Haberle. G. G.
Sill. bibl f il por *Antiques* 132:1118-21 N '87

Haberman, Martin
Alternative certification and urban schools. *Educ Dig*
52:22-5 Ja '87
What the media teach the public about education. *Educ
Dig* 53:5-7 N '87

Habermas, Ronald T.
Gray matters. il por *Christ Today* 31:23-5 Ag 7 '87

Habib, Philip Charles
Development of U.S.-Nicaragua policy [statements,
February 5, 1987] *Dep State Bull* 87:80-2 My '87

Habicht, Gail S., and others
Lyme disease. bibl (p116) il map *Sci Am* 257:78-83
Jl '87

Habitat, Animal *See* Animal ecology

Habitat for Humanity Inc.
"Every little bit . . .". S. Pacher. il *Mother Earth News*
108:45-7 N/D '87
Homes grown. M. Hammond. il *Essence* 18:30 My '87
With our own hands [excerpt from Everything to gain]
J. Carter and R. Carter. il pors *McCalls* 114:44+ Jl
'87

Habits
See also
Nail biting
Are you picking up your parents' bad habits? [teenagers]
D. Gage and M. Hibsch. il *Seventeen* 46:132+ Mr
'87
Bad habits that can ruin your health. W. Korn. il *Ladies
Home J* 104:36+ S '87
Five healthy habits that can hurt you. H. Rodale. il
Prevention 39:50-4 Ja '87
His bad habits: can you change them? Should you even
try? *Glamour* 85:12 Jl '87
How to break your man's bad habits. D. Hales. *McCalls*
114:56-7 Ja '87

Anecdotes, facetiae, satire, etc.
12 things no woman has the right to ask her man
to give up. P. Richmond. il *Glamour* 85:44+ Je '87

Habits of animals *See* Animals—Habits and behavior

Habitual criminals *See* Recidivists

Habre, Hissene
Visit of Chad president [remarks, June 19, 1987] il
por *Dep State Bull* 87:23-4 S '87

Visit to the United States, 1987
Visit of Chad president [remarks, June 19, 1987] R.
Reagan; H. Habre. il por *Dep State Bull* 87:23-4 S
'87

Hachette (Librairie)
1986 earnings show Mondadori and Hachette top their
home markets. H. R. Lottman. *Publ Wkly* 232:312
Ag 7 '87
A press giant is set to pounce [Hachette eyes U.S.
companies] F. J. Comes. *Bus Week* p54+ D 21 '87

Hack, Shelley
about
Windy City walker. L. Kleinmann. por *Health* 19:32 Ap '87
Hacker, Andrew
American apartheid. bibl f il *N Y Rev Books* 34:26-33 D 3 '87
Supermarket U. il *Fortune* 115:327+ Ap 27 '87
Hackers (Computer enthusiasts)
A confederation of hackers. J. Pournelle. *Byte* 12:267-8+ F '87
The hacker who vanished [B. Landreth] G. Hackett. il por *Newsweek* 109:22 Ja 19 '87
Hacking through NASA [penetration of Space Physics Analysis Network] W. D. Marbach. il *Newsweek* 110:38 S 28 '87
Teaching computer ethics in the schools. W. Weintraub. *Educ Dig* 52:34-5 F '87
Hackett, Kevin J., and others
A defined medium for a fastidious spiroplasma. bibl f il *Science* 237:525-7 Jl 31 '87
Hackford, Taylor
about
Chuck Berry Hail! Hail! Rock 'n' roll [film] Reviews *N Y* 20:102-3 O 19 '87. D. Denby
Hackstedde, Peter
about
Using investors' gut feelings to gauge the future. T. Carson. il por *Bus Week* p89 S 28 '87
Hacky Sack (Game)
The case of the missing creative fitness games. T. Osborne. il *Curr Health 2* 13:26-7 My '87
Hadady Corporation
Using investors' gut feelings to gauge the future [P. Hackstedde] T. Carson. il por *Bus Week* p89 S 28 '87
Hadassah Hospital (Jerusalem) *See* Jerusalem—Hospitals
Hadden, Jeffrey K.
Silence does not a statesman make. por *U S News World Rep* 102:8 Ap 13 '87
about
As the spiritual soap opera plays on, an expert assesses how Jim Bakker's fall could change television preaching [interview] J. S. Podesta. il pors *People Wkly* 27:44-6 Ap 13 '87
Haddock, Patricia
The right fit in health clubs. il *Consum Res Mag* 70:35-6 S '87
Haden, Charlie
about
Charlie Haden's search for freedom. H. Mandel. il pors *Down Beat* 54:20-3 S '87
Haden-Guest, Anthony
Calvin Klein: an obsession with perfection. il por *Harpers Bazaar* 120:178-85+ F '87
Contemporary energies at the Paula Cooper Gallery. il por *Archit Dig* 44:78+ Ap '87
Hyde Park's English cast. il por *Archit Dig* 44:282+ N '87
Hadge, Luke
After the fall. il *World Tennis* 35:26+ Jl '87
Hadid, Zaha M., 1951?-
about
Beyond the Peak. D. Dietsch. il *Archit Rec* 175:118-29 Je '87
A room of one's own. D. Dietsch. il *Archit Rec* 175:84-9 mid-S '87
Zaha Hadid at Max Protetch. J. Merkel. il *Art Am* 75:184-5 O '87
Hadingham, R. E. H. (Reginald Edward Hawke)
about
Keeper of the flame [interview] C. Gould. il pors *World Tennis* 35:46+ Jl '87
Hadingham, Reginald Edward Hawke *See* Hadingham, R. E. H. (Reginald Edward Hawke)
Hadley, Arthur T.
Back to the front. *New Repub* 197:16-18 N 16 '87
Hadrons *See* Particles (Nuclear physics)
Hadrosaurs *See* Dinosaurs
Hadson Energy Risk Management Inc.
Oilmen have a new way to cope with falling prices [energy asset insurance guarantees a price floor] T. Thompson. il *Bus Week* p74 Ag 3 '87
Haedrich, Ken
A baker's basic battery. il *Ctry J* 14:56-61 F '87
A Cajun fish story. il *Ctry J* 14:65-7 Mr '87
Cook's tour. See issues of Country Journal beginning January 1987
Grilling. il *Ctry J* 14:46-50 Je '87
Savory turnovers. il *Ctry J* 14:29-32 Ja '87
A summer feast. il *Ctry J* 14:40-3+ S '87

Thanksgiving puddings. il *Ctry J* 14:54-7 N '87
Haemisegger, Wynne
about
With a name like Wynne . . . S. Shuger. il *Women's Sports Fitness* 9:21 Ap '87
Haemophilus infections *See* Hib infections
Hafen, Bruce C.
The First Amendment and obscenity [address, November 13, 1986] *Vital Speeches Day* 53:210-12 Ja 15 '87
Hafen, Ernst, and others
Sevenless, a cell-specific homeotic gene of Drosophila, encodes a putative transmembrane receptor with a tyrosine kinase domain. bibl f il *Science* 236:55-63 Ap 3 '87
Hafrey, Leigh
(tr) See Schneider, Peter, 1940-. The light at the end of the novel
Håfström, Jan, 1937-
about
Jan Håfström. H. Cotter. il *Art News* 86:132 S '87
Haft family
about
The Hafts may mean it. M. J. Pitzer. il *Bus Week* p37 O 5 '87
The most feared family in retailing. B. Saporito. il *Fortune* 115:65-6+ Je 22 '87
Will Dart bag a grocer this time? [Supermarkets General] T. Ichniowski. *Bus Week* p35-6 Mr 23 '87
Hagan, Patti
Gardening books. il *Americana* 15:51-3 Jl/Ag '87
Hagan, Richard
about
Old-time seltzer in new-fangled bottles. J. O. Hamilton. il por *Bus Week* p164 S 14 '87
Hagedorn, Terry
about
Everybody in this picture is named Miller or Yoder except for one poor guy. D. Van Biema. il por *People Wkly* 27:46-8 Mr 30 '87
Hagen, Walter, 1892-1969
about
The Haig and some recent Masters. H. W. Wind. *New Yorker* 63:89-100+ My 18 '87
Hager, Rachel
How to take care of what you own. il *Ladies Home J* 104:67-8+ F '87
Hagerman, Heidi
Can a state require public schools to allow a moment of silence? il por *Christ Today* 31:52 N 20 '87
Haggin, B. H. (Bernard H.), 1900-1987
about
Obituary
New Repub 197:41-2 Jl 6 '87. W. H. Pritchard
Haggin, Bernard H. *See* Haggin, B. H. (Bernard H.), 1900-1987
Haggling (Shopping)
A guide to the fine art of haggling. B. Bauer. il *U S News World Rep* 103:57-8 S 7 '87
Hagin, Barbara
Just out. See issues of Popular Photography beginning February 1987
Pro tips. See issues of Popular Photography beginning November 1987
Hagler, Bertha
about
Hagler ordered out of his home for domestic dispute. il pors *Jet* 72:30 Jl 20 '87
Wife's demand for Hagler to be treated for drugs disputed by her attorney. *Jet* 72:18 Jl 20 '87
Hagler, Marvin
about
Boxing's angry man. P. Berger. il pors *N Y Times Mag* p34-6+ Mr 22 '87
Clash of the opposites. P. Axthelm. pors *Newsweek* 109:52 Ap 6 '87
Comeback for the ages. W. Nack. il pors *Sports Illus* 66:18-25 Ap 13 '87
'Everything I did worked'. W. Nack. il pors *Sports Illus* 66:50-2+ Ap 20 '87
Family feuding behind bad press on him, Hagler says. il por *Jet* 72:12 Jl 27 '87
Hagler belted by new loss—a champ no more. *Jet* 72:47 My 11 '87
Hagler hasn't retired yet, he's busy counting money. *Jet* 72:46 Je 15 '87
Hagler ordered out of his home for domestic dispute. il pors *Jet* 72:30 Jl 20 '87
Hagler retires to privacy, decision forces rematch. por *Jet* 72:50 Ap 27 '87
Hagler vs. Leonard: the seniors tour. M. Katz. il pors *Sport Mag* 78:76-82 Ap '87

Hagler, Marvin—about—*cont.*
The illusion of victory: another view of the Leonard-Hagler decision. H. McIlvanney. il por *Sports Illus* 66:120 Ap 20 '87
Leonard adds new tactic in preparing for Hagler. il por *Jet* 71:46 F 23 '87
Leonard banks on a decision while Hagler mulls a murder and Hearns wants a double KO. pors *Jet* 72:50 Ap 6 '87
'Let the world know I'm O.K.'. W. Nack. il pors *Sports Illus* 67:34-7 S 28 '87
Notes and comment. *New Yorker* 63:25-6 Ap 20 '87
One will be made whole. R. Reilly. il pors *Sports Illus* 66:58-64+ Mr 30 '87
Prediction. W. Nack. il pors *Sports Illus* 66:70-2+ Mr 30 '87
Sugar Ray Leonard says he has a plan for Hagler. il pors *Jet* 71:47 Ja 12 '87
Sugar Ray Leonard scores upset, joins history's greatest. il pors *Jet* 72:51 Ap 20 '87
Sugar Ray Leonard: why I am fighting again [cover story] N. O. Unger. il *Ebony* 42:92-4+ Ap '87
Sugar's sweet comeback. il pors *People Wkly* 27:40-1 Ap 20 '87
Sugar's sweetest confection. P. Axthelm. il pors *Newsweek* 109:71 Ap 20 '87
A super finish to a SuperFight. il pors *Macleans* 100:46 Ap 20 '87
Too moving to be mayhem. T. Callahan. il pors *Time* 129:62 Ap 20 '87
Wife's demand for Hagler to be treated for drugs disputed by her attorney. *Jet* 72:18 Jl 20 '87
Photographs and photography
Dream fight. J. McDonough. il pors *Sport Mag* 78:56-63 D '87
Hagman, Larry
about
My son, Larry Hagman. E. Sirkin. il pors *Good Housekeep* 205:111+ Jl '87
Hagstrum, Paul D., Jr.
about
They've got one-stop shopping for vacation homes. P. Houston. il pors *Bus Week* p75 Ag 10 '87
Hague, Frank, 1876-1956
about
Boss. *New Yorker* 63:22-4 Je 15 '87
Hague (Netherlands)
City hall
Design awards/competitions: competition for a new city hall in The Hague, Holland. T. Metz. il *Archit Rec* 175:54-5 Ap '87
Richard Meier, abroad and at home [commission for a new city hall] T. Metz. il *Archit Rec* 175:51 Jl '87
Hahn, Andrew
Reaching out to America's dropouts: what to do? [cover story] il *Phi Delta Kappan* 69:256-63 D '87
Hahn, Carl H.
about
Can Volkswagen pull itself out of the mud? R. Ingersoll. il por *Bus Week* p60-1 Je 22 '87
A speed demon hits a slippery patch. L. S. Richman. il por *Fortune* 116:41 Ag 3 '87
Hahn, Jeffrey W.
Gorbachev's uncertain reformation. il *Commonweal* 114:586-8+ O 23 '87
Hahn, Jessica
about
Baring body and soul. il pors *People Wkly* 28:32-7 O 5 '87
Donna Fawn Hahn. pors *People Wkly* 28:62-3 D 28 '87-Ja 4 '88
The follies of 1987 [special section] il *World Press Rev* 34:32-4 Jl '87
Hahn bares her soul, etc. G. Hackett. il pors *Newsweek* 110:43 O 12 '87
New Bakker charge. K. L. Woodward. il por *Newsweek* 109:6 Ap 13 '87
The new seductress. N. Scovell. il pors *Mademoiselle* 93:244-7 N '87
On the springboard of notoriety. F. Trippett. il pors *Time* 130:64-5 O 12 '87
Hahn, Vera
Living with antiques. il *Parents* 62:134-6+ F '87
Haida Indians
Agreeing to a new park. J. Barber. *Macleans* 100:35 Jl 20 '87
Canada's Queen Charlotte Islands: homeland of the Haida. M. Johnston. il map *Natl Geogr* 172:102-27 Jl '87
The salvation of a homeland [leader M. Richardson] il por *Macleans* 100:32-3 D 28 '87

The South Moresby war [protest logging on Queen Charlotte Islands] M. Gee. il *Macleans* 100:12 Jl 6 '87
Haig, Alexander Meigs, 1924-
Equitable arms control [address, February 19, 1987] *Vital Speeches Day* 53:387-90 Ap 15 '87
about
Out of control. F. Barnes. il *New Repub* 196:13-15 My 4 '87
A quixotic four-star foray. L. I. Barrett. il por *Time* 129:32 Ap 6 '87
Why Haig threw his helmet into White House ring. J. M. Hildreth. il por *U S News World Rep* 102:22 Ap 6 '87
Haig, Don
about
A catalyst for Canadian film. A. Gould. il por *Macleans* 100:62 Mr 30 '87
Haigh, Katy
about
Child of silence: retrieved from the shadow-world of autism, Katy finds her voice. J. Mason. il pors *Life* 10:84-9 S '87
Haight, Matt
A garden varmint trap. il por *Mother Earth News* 106:34+ Jl/Ag '87
Haiku
Concision, perception, awareness—haiku. C. Van den Heuvel. il *N Y Times Book Rev* 92:1+ Mr 29 '87
James Luguri's haiku. J. E. McEntyre. *Christ Century* 104:486-8 My 20-27 '87
Hail Mary [film] See Motion picture reviews—Single works
Haim, Corey
about
Corey Haim. E. Miller. por *Seventeen* 46:106 S '87
The Lost Boys: behind the scenes [interview] il pors *Teen* 31:49+ Jl '87
Haimovitz, Matt
A classical education. il por *N Y* 20:26 N 23 '87
about
Teenage prodigy Matt Haimovitz coaxes big trills from his cello. il por *People Wkly* 28:103 Ag 17 '87
Haines, Peter
(ed) See Swinson, Ginny. How I (and the taxman) won $27,000 in prizes on Wheel of fortune!
Haines, Randa
about
Children of a lesser god [film] Reviews
USA Today (Periodical) il 115:96-7 Ja '87. K. R. Hey
Haines, William
High explosives. il *Flying* 114:108-9 Jl '87
Haines (Alaska)
Art
Artists prefer Haines. S. Eppenbach. il map *Travel Holiday* 168:48-53 D '87
Hainfeld, James F.
A small gold-conjugated antibody label: improved resolution for electron microscopy [cover story] bibl f il *Science* 236:450-3 Ap 24 '87
Hainsworth, Geoffrey B.
Indonesia's economic downswing and political reforms. bibl f *Curr Hist* 86:172-5+ Ap '87
Hair, Jay D.
NWF takes up call for natural resources protection. *Environment* 29:9-10 My '87
"We the people . . . " [excerpts from address, March 1987] il *Natl Wildl* 25:25-6 Je/Jl '87
Hair
See also
Baldness
Beards
Dandruff
Eyebrows
Hairstyling
Wigs
All-American all-out blondes [special section] il *Harpers Bazaar* 120:164-179+ Ap '87
Reds: turn on the heat [special section] il *Harpers Bazaar* 120:108-11+ Jl '87
Care
Dry skin, limp hair: fight-back winter beauty strategies. il *Mademoiselle* 93:16 F '87
Essentials for black hair and skin: what's new, what's tried and true. il *Glamour* 85:38 Ap '87
Eye on beauty [interview with Wanakee] M. Garth-Taylor. pors *Essence* 17:30+ Ja '87
Great solutions for frizzy, limp, sun-baked summer hair. il *Glamour* 85:170-3 Jl '87
Hair care 87! il *Essence* 17:60-1+ Ja '87

Hair—Care—cont.

Hair care now! [interview with O. L. Benson] M. Garth-Taylor. por *Essence* 18:50 S '87

Hair frenzy fix-up. C. Duhé. il *Harpers Bazaar* 120:110-13+ Ja '87

Hair, glorious hair. J. L. Lippert. il *Health* 19:58-60+ My '87

Hair now. See issues of Vogue

Hair on the light side [care of blond hair] il *Teen* 31:84-5 Je '87

Hair perfection. il *Harpers Bazaar* 120:108+ Je '87

Hair Q & A. *Vogue* 177:180 Ag '87

The healthy-hair diet. il *Mademoiselle* 93:38 Ag '87

Help for summer hair. P. Kripke. il *Work Woman* 12:94 Mr '87

High-speed hair treats. il *Harpers Bazaar* 121:30 N '87

Make the most of your hair! il *McCalls* 115:41-6 N '87

My shoulder-length hair is oily and dull even though I wash it daily. il *Prevention* 39:63-4 Ag '87

Rich, lustrous hair. P. L. Kjellberg. il *Harpers Bazaar* 120:220-1+ O '87

Summer hair. il *Good Housekeep* 204:82 My '87

Summerizing your hair—wilt-proof looks, foolproof care. il *Mademoiselle* 93:24 Jl '87

Take the tress test. il *Teen* 31:73+ Mr '87

Dyeing and bleaching

After-dark daring dos . . . comb-in color! il *Mademoiselle* 93:28 D '87

The blond leading the blond [celebrities] M. Musto. il *Mademoiselle* 93:44 Je '87

Brazen blonde. F. Garmaise. il por *Ms* 16:30+ N '87

Color '87: hot shots. il *Vogue* 177:384-99 O '87

The coloring advantage. S. Riddles. il *Harpers Bazaar* 120:18+ Ag '87

Get rich quick: a glow-up guide for hair [highlighting] il *Mademoiselle* 93:174-7 F '87

Hair coloring: going from good to better. P. Kripke. il *Work Woman* 12:140-3 N '87

Haircolor '87: the new enhancers [special section] il *Vogue* 177:414-21+ F '87

Lowlighting. M. Fox. il *Health* 19:54-7 Jl '87

The new blondes—going pro. il *Harpers Bazaar* 120:176-9+ Ap '87

To live and dye [haircolor market] B. Kanner. il *N Y* 20:14+ F 23 '87

Your redhead beauty guide. S. Riddles. *Harpers Bazaar* 120:109+ Jl '87

Anecdotes, facetiae, satire, etc.

'Therapist dyed, sessions canceled'. R. E. Lovett. il *Smithsonian* 18:152 Ag '87

Removal

Hair problems: too much, too little. P. Gadsby and H. Twidale. *Good Housekeep* 204:216 Je '87

Take it off: a hair-removal guide. il *Mademoiselle* 93:18 Je '87

Hair analysis

Hair analysis: what it can and cannot tell you. il *Glamour* 85:327+ O '87

Hair care products

See also

Baldness remedies

Shampoos

Body builders . . . [conditioners] il *Harpers Bazaar* 120:38+ Ag '87

Give your hair deep-down help. il *Redbook* 169:86-9 Jl '87

Hair body builders [for men] il *Harpers Bazaar* 120:34 My '87

Hair: high-speed revivers. il *Harpers Bazaar* 120:104 F '87

Hair signals: style and something more . . . S. Lord. il *Vogue* 177:182-3+ Jl '87

The new daring delights. il *Harpers Bazaar* 120:404-7+ S '87

What comes in a bottle (and battles buildup)? il *Mademoiselle* 93:46 O '87

Packaging

Revlon must change package similar to Soft Sheen's. *Jet* 73:18 O 19 '87

Hair care products industry

See also

Dudley Products, Inc.

Johnson Products Company, Inc.

Lamaur Inc.

Soft Sheen Products

Acquisitions and mergers

An acid test for antitakeover laws [Minnesota law could help Alberto-Culver land Lamaur] M. J. Pitzer. il *Bus Week* p31 S 28 '87

Advertising

To live and dye [haircolor market] B. Kanner. il *N Y* 20:14+ F 23 '87

Marketing

The battle of the curls [American Health and Beauty Aids Institute objects to Revlon racist statement about black consumers and black hair care manufacturers] K. Smikle. *Black Enterp* 17:18 Ja '87

A gaffe at Revlon has the black community seething [disparaging black-owned hair-care companies] C. Dugas and K. Dreyfack. il *Bus Week* p36-7 F 9 '87

Splitting hairs. L. Wells. il *N Y Times Mag* p76 O 18 '87

Hair cells of the cochlea *See* Labyrinth (Ear)

Hair coloring *See* Hair—Dyeing and bleaching

Hair conditioners *See* Hair care products

Hair dryers

Safety devices and measures

New hair dryer reduces risk of electric shock [Sunbeam Perfect Safe Idea] il *Consum Rep* 52:269 My '87

Hair restorers *See* Baldness remedies

Haircutting *See* Hairstyling

Hairdressers *See* Hairstylists

Hairpieces *See* Wigs

Hairston, Deborah W.

Meeting the challenges of family finances [cover story] il *Black Enterp* 17:40-4+ Jl '87

Hairstyling

See also

Hairstylists

16-hour hair. G. Bakoulis. il *Work Woman* 12:114 S '87

20 newest hairdos [modeled by actresses] il *Good Housekeep* 205:112-19+ Jl '87

25 prettiest hairdos for spring [modeled by TV stars] il *Good Housekeep* 204:114-23+ Mr '87

America's five top hair dressers show 25 super new styles. il *McCalls* 145:42-7 Mr '87

Back to the future beauty [reinterpreting legendary actresses' hairstyles] L. M. Cybul. il *Good Housekeep* 204:126-31+ F '87

Beat the heat hair. il *Teen* 31:102-3 My '87

Beauty '87: new look for the New Year. A. Fornay. il *Ebony* 42:110-12+ Ja '87

Beauty in a new light. il *Vogue* 177:774-81 S '87

Bows & bands & braids [modeled by Connie Sellecca] il *Redbook* 168:10 Mr '87

Cherchez la femme! [Paris fashions] il *Essence* 18:90-5 O '87

The cut of the year. il *Mademoiselle* 93:140-3 Ja '87

Cuts that count. il *Seventeen* 46:308-13 Ag '87

Dear beauty editor. il *Teen* 31:113-4+ Ag '87

'Do's that outdo! il *Teen* 31:70-1 Ap '87

Easy-care hair. L. Wells. il *N Y Times Mag* p54 My 31 '87

Eye on beauty. il *Essence* 17:35-6 Mr '87

Facing up to fall. L. Wells. il *N Y Times Mag* p100-4 S 20 '87

Fall hair news. il *Glamour* 85:352-7 S '87

Fall signals: the clothes, the hair, the look. il *Vogue* 177:168-83+ Jl '87

Forecast! [black women] il *Essence* 18:48+ My '87

Getting rid of growing pains. il *Seventeen* 46:54 Ja '87

Go wild! Be sleek! The two new views of evening hair. il *Mademoiselle* 93:240-3 N '87

Growing short hair long: 7 ways to make it easier, even enjoyable. il *Glamour* 85:300-1 My '87

Growing your hair? How to get through the "in-between" phase—beautifully! C. Straley. il *Parents* 62:34 Mr '87

Hair/makeup: the active edge. il *Vogue* 177:290-3 Ag '87

Hair duos. il *Teen* 31:78-80 D '87

Hair, glorious hair. J. L. Lippert. il *Health* 19:58-60+ My '87

Hair guide: perfect cut, perfect perm. il *Good Housekeep* 204:104-7 Je '87

Hair headaches. il *Teen* 31:78-9 F '87

Hair line. See issues of Mademoiselle

Hair magic! Tricks for your tresses. il *Teen* 31:74-5 F '87

Hair news. See issues of Essence

Hair now. See issues of Vogue

Hair: the mood continues . . . [black women] il *Essence* 18:76-81 N '87

Hair: the new romance. il *Seventeen* 46:244-9 Mr '87

Hair today, change tomorrow? *Vogue* 177:166-7 Jl '87

Hairstyles of the rich & famous. il *Ladies Home J* 104:128-31+ Ap '87

Holiday hair dare. il *Harpers Bazaar* 121:42 D '87

Hairstyling—*cont.*

A home perm: could it be the solution to your hair problems? il *Glamour* 85:28 My '87

Hotshot holiday hair. il *Harpers Bazaar* 121:204-9+ N '87

The impact of a new year. il *Vogue* 177:140-3 Ja '87

In-style hints on cuts and care for straight hair. il *Redbook* 169:10 S '87

The kindest cuts—do's that reshape your face. il *Mademoiselle* 93:60 Ap '87

Love-me do's: affairs of the hair for spring. il *Mademoiselle* 93:222-5 Mr '87

Making waves: the new perms break with tradition. il *Mademoiselle* 93:198-201 Ap '87

The mane event. il *Seventeen* 46:101-2 My '87

A matter of style [men's haircuts] J. Giovannini. il *N Y Times Mag* p54 O 18 '87

The modern requirement that improves texture, enhances style. il *Vogue* 177:421+ F '87

The naked neck—the new erogenous zone. il *Mademoiselle* 93:52 Mr '87

Natural hair: a style report. B. Brandon and M. Garth-Taylor. il *Essence* 17:60-6+ Ap '87

The new bangs: on the cutting edge. il *Mademoiselle* 93:30 My '87

The new hair, the new makeup. il *Mademoiselle* 93:204-11 My '87

A new mood! [black women] il *Essence* 18:70-5 S '87

New-twist ponytails. il *Glamour* 85:202-5 Je '87

The new wave [pincurls] il *Vogue* 177:136 D '87

New waves. C. Straley. il *Parents* 62:146-8+ Ap '87

New waves: the latest movement in perms. il *Seventeen* 46:77-8 Ja '87

New wispy bangs: a plus for almost any hairstyle. il *Glamour* 85:85 O '87

Newest hairdos from around the world. il *Good Housekeep* 205:48+ S '87

One-night strands: summer's sexiest party hair. il *Harpers Bazaar* 120:84-5 Jl '87

The panic-proof makeover: three stages to sensational. il *Mademoiselle* 93:48 O '87

Party hair & party flair. il *Teen* 31:82-3 N '87

Perfect haircut. See occasional issues of Glamour

Perfect perms! C. Straley. il *Parents* 62:161-4 O '87

"Please do something with my hair!". il *Redbook* 169:96-9 Je '87

Premiere hair. il *Mademoiselle* 93:272-5 S '87

Salon watch. il *Essence* 18:46+ O '87

Shades of evening. L. Wells. il *N Y Times Mag* p66 N 15 '87

Smooth news. il *Mademoiselle* 93:188-91 Ag '87

Soft new styles to update short hair. il *Glamour* 85:292-7 N '87

Staying droop-proof; Spin-perm to the groove. il *Seventeen* 46:60 Ag '87

Summer beauty's point of view [black women] il *Essence* 18:80-5 Jl '87

Summer cuts! il *Essence* 18:43 Jl '87

Summer hair makeovers. C. Straley. il *Parents* 62:142-4 Ag '87

Take your hair to new heights—the perfect perm. il *Mademoiselle* 93:36 F '87

Three lengths of hair: the tips, tricks, '87 differences. il *Vogue* 177:210 N '87

Tips from a tonsorial tout [barber M. Pitts' analysis of candidates' hairstyles] H. Sidey. il por *Time* 129:25 F 16 '87

The trend that didn't take [elaborate Parisian styling] L. Wells. il *N Y Times Mag* p34 Ja 11 '87

Two carefree cuts for 24-hour style. il *Glamour* 85:174-5 Jl '87

Unforgettable faces [makeup and hairstyles that reinterpret film stars' legendary looks] il pors *Seventeen* 46:120-5 F '87

The ups & downs of hairstyling. il *Teen* 31:76-7 Mr '87

What's new? Bangs! il *Redbook* 168:120-3 Mr '87

Why did my last permanent wave turn out spotty? *Prevention* 39:80-1 My '87

Wild & free: the curl advantage. il *Harpers Bazaar* 120:168-71+ Ap '87

Woman fired for cornrows sues Hyatt hotel in Virginia [C. Tatum] il por *Jet* 73:36 O 19 '87

Yes, long hair can go to work. il *Mademoiselle* 93:30 D '87

Your best look for '87. il *Glamour* 85:160-5 Ja '87

Equipment

See also
Hair dryers

Style revival: classic tools make newsy dos. il *Mademoiselle* 93:46 N '87

Tools that take your hair anywhere. il *Mademoiselle* 93:36 Ja '87

History

Hair [influence of rock singers] il *Roll Stone* p117 Ap 23 '87

Psychological aspects

Roots of discontent. L. J. Nonkin. *Vogue* 177:332+ S '87

Hairstyling salons *See* Beauty shops

Hairstylists

Mane man Anthony Morrocco works on moon time to deliver the kindest cut of all. il por *People Wkly* 28:113 Jl 13 '87

New York artist Terry Niedzialek specializes in turban blight. il por *People Wkly* 27:47 Ja 12 '87

Thanks to Denise McAdam, Fergie always turns up tressed for success. il por *People Wkly* 28:30-1 Jl 20 '87

Anecdotes, facetiae, satire, etc.

Time loves a haircut [former baseball player B. Carbo] B. Cardoso. *Harpers* 274:68-9 Ap '87

Hairy-cell leukemia *See* Leukemia

Haiti

See also
AIDS (Disease)—Haiti
Art—Haiti
Fortification—Haiti
Haitians
Investments, Haitian
Military assistance, American—Haiti
Palaces—Haiti
Relief work—Haiti
Riots—Haiti
Terrorism—Haiti

Antiquities

See also
La Navidad (Haiti)

Commerce

United States

See United States—Commerce—Haiti

Description and travel

Haiti: against all odds. C. E. Cobb. il supp (folded map) maps *Natl Geogr* 172:644-71 N '87

Foreign relations

United States

See United States—Foreign relations—Haiti

History

Revolution, 1791-1804

Haiti's majestic monuments [Citadelle Laferriére and Sans Souci Palace] R. Bishop. il *Américas* 39:2-7+ Ja/F '87

'We will confound the calumniators of our race . . .' [Citadelle and Sans Souci Palace of H. Christophe] F. Maclean. il por map *Smithsonian* 18:160-6+ O '87

Politics and government

See also
Elections—Haiti
Haiti. Constitution
Political campaigns—Haiti
Politics, Corruption in—Haiti

Death in the streets. M. Nichols. il *Macleans* 100:19 Ag 10 '87

Exhilaration to disenchantment. D. Hautin-Guiraut. *World Press Rev* 34:28 Ap '87

Haiti: a bump in the road to democracy. *Newsweek* 110:37 Jl 13 '87

Haiti: a year after 'Baby Doc'. P. Gaupp. il *World Press Rev* 34:26-8 Ap '87

Haiti: against all odds. C. E. Cobb. il supp (folded map) maps *Natl Geogr* 172:644-71 N '87

Haiti: the new violence. M. Massing. il *N Y Rev Books* 34:45-52 D 3 '87

In the eye of Haiti's hurricane. C. Cleaver. il *New Leader* 70:5-7 S 21 '87

An island between seasons. B. Shacochis. il *Harpers* 274:57-60+ F '87

Limping toward democracy. J. Smolowe. il *Time* 129:42 F 16 '87

Pondering chaos. *Commonweal* 114:517-18 S 25 '87

Promoting democracy in Haiti. R. N. Holwill. map *Dep State Bull* 87:60-2 O '87

A rumbling in the belly of the beast. A. Wilentz. il *Time* 130:34-6 O 19 '87

The struggle for a democratic Haiti. M. D. Danner. il *N Y Times Mag* p38-42+ Je 21 '87

Religious institutions and affairs

See also
Church and social problems—Haiti

Haiti. Constitution
Miracle in Haiti [ratification] *Nation* 244:527-8 Ap 25 '87
White for victory [new constitution approved] *Macleans* 100:20 Ap 13 '87
A 'yes' for democracy: constitutional plebiscite. L. Compa. il *Commonweal* 114:262-3 My 8 '87
Haitian dance *See* Dance, Haitian
Haitian painting *See* Painting, Haitian
Haitians

France
What's up, Baby Doc? il por *Time* 129:42 F 16 '87
United States
Political activities
Haitian sets self afire in protest of nation's strife [A. Thurel] *Jet* 72:4 S 21 '87
Hajcak, Frank
(jt. auth) See Garwood, Patricia, and Hajcak, Frank
Hakim, Albert, 1936-
about
The "Belly Button" file. M. McDonald. il pors *Macleans* 100:26 Je 15 '87
A big bonus for "Belly Button". J. V. Lamar, Jr. il pors *Time* 129:18-19 Je 15 '87
Hot on the Iran money trail. T. Morganthau. il por *Newsweek* 109:24-5 My 4 '87
North: felon or fall guy? T. Morganthau. il pors *Newsweek* 109:28+ Je 15 '87
Week 5: the strangest tales yet. M. Healy. il por *U S News World Rep* 102:20-1 Je 15 '87
Hakone (Japan)
Hotels, motels, etc.
In the realm of the sensuous [Matsu-no Chaya] I. Buruma. il *House Gard* 159:170-3+ D '87
Hakonen, Pertti, and Lounasmaa, Olli V.
Vortices in rotating superfluid He³. bibl f il *Phys Today* 40:70-8 F '87
Hal Riney & Partners
America's hottest adman [H. Riney] F. Kessler. il por *Fortune* 115:110-11 Ja 5 '87
Hal Roach Studios Inc.
Hal Roach rides again. A. B. Block. il *Forbes* 139:56-7 F 9 '87
Halaby, Lisa *See* Nur el Hussein, Queen, consort of Hussein, King of Jordan
Halamandaris, Bill
about
The growing Halamandaris empire. R. Rosenblatt. il pors *50 Plus* 27:14-17 Jl '87
Halamandaris, Val
about
The growing Halamandaris empire. R. Rosenblatt. il pors *50 Plus* 27:14-17 Jl '87
Halard, Michelle
about
A spontaneous charm. C. de Liagre. il por *House Gard* 159:126-33+ D '87
Halard, Yves
about
A spontaneous charm. C. de Liagre. il por *House Gard* 159:126-33+ D '87
Halas, George Stanley, 1895-1983
about
The U.S. Business Hall of Fame. A. M. Louis. il por *Fortune* 115:106 Ap 13 '87
Halavais, Richard
about
Inventor proposes locator system using one geosynchronous satellite. il *Aviat Week Space Technol* 126:89+ Je 22 '87
Halberstam, David, 1934-
The fitness-goers. il por *Vogue* 177:234-5+ Jl '87
The stuff dreams are made of. il pors *Sports Illus* 66:38-40+ Je 29 '87
about
Putting the brakes on the Orient Express. J. M. Fallows. *Wash Mon* 19:39-45 Ap '87
Halberstein, Dan
The basketball championship of Lebanon [chart] il *New Repub* 197:11 Jl 27 '87
BSAT. *New Repub* 197:12 S 14-21 '87
Reflagging: the secret NSC agenda. il *New Repub* 197:11 Ag 24 '87
Halbo, Sverre
Our lives are here and now [poem]; tr. by Peter Bilton. *Humanist* 47:28 My/Je '87
Halbouty, Michel Thomas, 1909-
Give the people light [address, June 9, 1987] *Vital Speeches Day* 53:653-5 Ag 15 '87

The petroleum industry at its crossroads [address, February 19, 1987] *Vital Speeches Day* 53:381-4 Ap 1 '87
Halbur (Iowa)
Economic conditions
Is there oil in Iowa? C. O'Connor. il *Newsweek* 109:26 Je 22 '87
Hale, Alan
Observing the elusive Comet Wilson. il *Astronomy* 15:79-81 Ja '87
Hale, Ellen
Crossing paths with a snake. il map *FDA Consum* 21:14-19 Jl/Ag '87
Good nutrition for your growing child. il *FDA Consum* 21:20-7 Ap '87
Hale, John P.
Where he started & where he stands. *Commonweal* 114:47-51 Ja 30 '87
Hale, Judson D.
Unforgettable Uncle Robb [condensed from The education of a Yankee] il por *Read Dig* 131:87-8+ N '87
Hale, Sarah Josepha
about
Godey and Hale: a fashionable alliance. E. Baroody. il *Antiques Collect Hobbies* 92:34-8 N '87
Haleakala National Park (Hawaii)
Haleakala National Park [excerpt from Haleakala] J. Mack. il *Natl Parks* 61:46-7 Ja/F '87
Hales, Dianne
50 ways to get to sleep [excerpt from How to sleep like a baby, wake up refreshed and get more out of life] il *Good Housekeep* 204:179+ My '87
Can you small talk? (Women who can have better marriages). *Redbook* 169:166-7+ S '87
How to break your man's bad habits. *McCalls* 114:56-7 Ja '87
How to say you're sorry. *McCalls* 115:22+ O '87
Hypnosis: could it help you? *McCalls* 114:14 Ag '87
The lowdown on PMS. *Seventeen* 46:116-17 Ja '87
When baby makes three. il *McCalls* 115:54+ N '87
Halévy, Ludovic, 1834-1908
Breaking the rules; tr. by Clarence H. Russell. il *Opera News* 51:36-7+ Mr 14 '87
Haley, Alex
about
Alex Haley's hideaway. H. J. Massaquoi. il pors *Ebony* 42:52-4+ S '87
Reagan puts black progress on hold, Alex Haley says. por *Jet* 72:29 Ap 27 '87
Haley, Gail E.
about
Gail Haley never grew up. J. T. Black. il pors *South Living* 22:105 Jl '87
Haley, Jim
Fevers: friend or foe? il *Saturday Evening Post* 259:64-6 Mr '87
Half, Robert
Checking references? Here are ten tough questions to ask. *Work Woman* 12:21 F '87
Half dollar coins *See* Coins
Half Moon Street [film] See Motion picture reviews—Single works
Halftime (Football games) *See* Football, College—Halftime
Halfway houses for the aged
A bridge between hospital and home [Halfway to Health housing program] L. A. Poppleton and R. Cornman. il *Aging* no355:12-13 [14-15] '87
Halifax (N.S.)
Religious institutions and affairs
In search of tradition [Buddhist community] C. Wood. il por *Macleans* 100:15+ My 4 '87
Theater
See also
Neptune Theatre
Hall, Adrian
about
All the king's men [drama] Reviews
New Repub 196:25-7 My 25 '87. R. Brustein
Hall, Alan
about
The stage manager: Off-Broadway or on, the buck stops here. R. Conniff. il pors *Smithsonian* 17:92-4+ F '87
Hall, Alice J.
James Madison: architect of the Constitution. il pors supp (folded map) map *Natl Geogr* 172:340-69 S '87
Hall, Arsenio
about
Arsenio Hall makes it big on late night TV talk show. il pors *Jet* 73:58-9 N 9 '87

Hall, Barbara
The artists-in-schools concept and curriculum-based instruction: what relationship? *Des Arts Educ* 88:40-1 N/D '86
News coverage of arts and arts education. *Des Arts Educ* 88:10-12 Jl/Ag '87

Hall, Carol
Local TV stalks print clients. il *Channels* 7:46-8 N '87

Hall, Conrad, 1927-
about
Connie's comeback. L. Klady. il por *Film Comment* 23:6-8 Mr/Ap '87

Hall, Craig, 1950-
about
The once and future fat cat. L. M. Keefe. por *Forbes* 139:106 Je 29 '87

Hall, Dave
about
"Operation Rx" sting. J. Fincher. il *Read Dig* 131:36-41 S '87

Hall, David
Fugitive color [photographs] il *Oceans* 20:30-5 My/Je '87

Hall, Deidre
about
The lives of Deidre Hall fans, made bleak by her absence from the soaps, get a new lease on Our house. J. Pearlman. il pors *People Wkly* 28:65-6+ D 14 '87

Hall, Donald, 1928-
Mr. Wakeville on Interstate 90 [poem] *Nation* 245:497 O 31 '87
Old roses and birdsong. il *Harpers* 275:35-41 Ag '87
Prophecy [poem] *Harpers* 275:38+ N '87
A sister on the tracks [poem] *Nation* 245:497 O 31 '87
about
The Lenore Marshall Prize. R. Pinsky. *Nation* 245:496-8 O 31 '87

Hall, Elizabeth
All in the family. il pors *Psychol Today* 21:54-8+ N '87
China's only child. bibl (p68) il *Psychol Today* 21:44-7 Jl '87

Hall, Fawn
about
The ballad of Fawn and Arturo [cover story] J. Morley. il *Nation* 245:397+ O 17 '87
Blossoms of American springtime. F. Bruning. por *Macleans* 100:9 Jl 6 '87
Donna Fawn Hahn. pors *People Wkly* 28:62-3 D 28 '87-Ja 4 '88
Fawn Hall, Ollie's ally and shredder, wows the Hill. M. Green. il por *People Wkly* 27:32-3 Je 22 '87
The follies of 1987 [special section] il *World Press Rev* 34:32-4 Jl '87
The new seductress. N. Scovell. il pors *Mademoiselle* 93:244-7 N '87
Ollie's angel. pors *Time* 129:36 Mr 9 '87
On the springboard of notoriety. F. Trippett. il pors *Time* 130:64-5 O 12 '87
Shredded policies, arrogant attitudes. E. Magnuson. il por *Time* 129:21-2 Je 22 '87
A small-town girl lands in the spotlight. G. Hackett. por *Newsweek* 109:30 Je 15 '87
The story of Fawn Hall, all-American secretary. J. Adler. il pors *Newsweek* 109:36-7 Mr 9 '87
The women in North's life. W. Lowther. il pors *Macleans* 100:19 Jl 20 '87

Hall, Howard
A deadly business [with photographs] il *Int Wildl* 17:12-15 Jl/Ag '87

Hall, Jerry
about
Mick's girlfriend is jailed after receiving a surprise package. por *People Wkly* 27:96 F 9 '87

Hall, Judith Vidal- *See* Vidal-Hall, Judith

Hall, Kevin Peter
about
Kevin Peter Hall, whose Predator performance is, yes, towering. il pors *People Wkly* 28:89+ Jl 13 '87

Hall, Michael N., and Johnson, Alexander D.
Homeo domain of the yeast repressor α2 is a sequence-specific DNA-binding domain but is not sufficient for repression. bibl f il *Science* 237:1007-12 Ag 28 '87

Hall, Peter E.
Quest for an ideal. il *World Health* p13-15 N '87

Hall, Phyllis A.
All our lonely children. por *Newsweek* 110:12 O 12 '87

Hall, Ristene
"I had to shape up my life"; ed. by Teresa Jordan. il pors *Redbook* 169:54+ S '87

Hall, Robert F., 1906-
The bugs of autumn. il *Conservationist* 42:48 S/O '87

Hall, Roy S.
Inside a Texas tornado [reprint from June 1951 issue] *Weatherwise* 40:72-5 Ap '87

Hall, Sandi
Little progress for Mexico's women. *World Press Rev* 34:53-4 My '87

Hall, Stephen S.
One potato patch that is making genetic history. il *Smithsonian* 18:125-6+ Ag '87

Hall, Tony P.
about
Calling for a commission on values in public education. *Christ Today* 31:43-4 S 18 '87

Hall, W. G.
(jt. auth) See Kucharski, David, and Hall, W. G.

Hall-Evans, Jo Ann
Hope [poem] *Essence* 17:131 Ap '87

Hall Financial Group
The once and future fat cat [workout specialist C. Hall] L. M. Keefe. por *Forbes* 139:106 Je 29 '87

Hall of Fame for U.S. Business Leadership *See* Halls of fame

Hallam, Anthony
End-Cretaceous mass extinction event: argument for terrestrial causation. bibl f il *Science* 238:1237-42 N 27 '87

Haller, Grant
about
Shades of luck. S. Piperato. il por *Pop Photogr* 94:72-3 Je '87

Haller, John M.
Stubs, knobs and bulges. il *Flower Gard* 31:14 Ap/My '87

Halley, Edmond, 1656-1742
about
Newton's Principia: a retrospective. G. E. Christianson. il por *Sky Telesc* 74:18-20 Jl '87

Halley, Peter, 1953-
about
The artist as cynic. J. Masheck. *New Leader* 70:22-3 Je 29 '87
Neo-geo: art's computer hum. M. Stevens. il *Newsweek* 110:119 N 16 '87

Halley's comet
See also
International Halley Watch
Space flight—Cometary missions
Anatomy of a comet [cover story; special issue] il *Sky Telesc* 73:236+ Mr '87
A child's perspective of Halley's comet. B. Johnston. il *Astronomy* 15:24+ F '87
The eye's view of Comet Halley. C. S. Morris. il *Astronomy* 15:90-6 Ja '87
Halley revisited. D. M. Ludlum. *Ctry J* 14:24 My '87
Halley's legacy. il *Sci Am* 256:62 F '87
Japanese data center in Australia [NEC Halley's Comet Observation Center] S. J. O'Meara. il *Sky Telesc* 73:201-3 F '87
Observing Comet Halley's near-nucleus features. S. M. Larson and D. H. Levy. il *Astronomy* 15:90-5 S '87
Search for the primitive [cover story] R. Berry. il *Astronomy* 15:6-22 Je '87
Anecdotes, facetiae, satire, etc.
'How much is that comet?'. R. J. Nemiroff. il *Astronomy* 15:30 F '87
Conferences
Halley in Heidelberg, planets in Paris. R. Berry. il *Astronomy* 15:24+ Mr '87
Photographs and photography
The IHW island network [International Halley Watch] M. B. Niedner, Jr. and W. Liller. il *Sky Telesc* 73:258-63 Mr '87
Processed images detail comet's surface [Giotto probe] il *Aviat Week Space Technol* 127:60-1 Jl 27 '87
'A tell-tale tail'. R. F. Burns. *Astronomy* 15:30 Je '87
To catch a child's imagination [Halley's comet project aboard the Kuiper Airborne Observatory] J. H. Nicholson. il *Sky Telesc* 74:303-5 S '87
Visitor from outer space. il *Life* 10:98-100 Ja '87
Spectra and spectroscopy
Halley's whiskers: first space polymer detected [work of Walter F. Huebner] J. Eberhart. il *Sci News* 132:100 Ag 15 '87
Polymer found in Comet Halley. il *Astronomy* 15:94 D '87

Halley's comet—Spectra and spectroscopy—*cont.*
Sampling the stuff of a comet [dust in Halley's coma] R. Knacke. il *Sky Telesc* 73:246-50 Mr '87
Halliday, E. M.
The boss was a hustler or, How I got my Bible. *N Y Times Book Rev* 92:20 D 13 '87
Halliday, Fred
Where the Soviets stand. *World Press Rev* 34:18-19 O '87
Hallman, Bruce
Evangelical politicians defeat themselves. il por *Christ Today* 31:12 N 6 '87
Hallmark Cards, Inc.
　　See also
　　Kaleidoscope (Program)
The feud that toppled a TV empire [Spanish International Communications Corp. sold to Hallmark Cards] G. Critser. il pors *Channels* 7:24-31 Ja '87
A Hallmark expression [Visitors Center in Kansas City] F. Warnecke. *Travel Holiday* 168:16-17 D '87
Hallmark Hall of Fame. R. Buck. il *Channels* 7:47-8 O '87
How Hallmark goes about being low-cost producer [interview with I. O. Hockaday] il por *Fortune* 115:31 My 25 '87
Hallmark Hall of Fame [television program] See Television program reviews—Single works
Halloween
Come Halloween, pumpkin carver Hugh McMahon has no trouble scaring up famous faces. V. R. Peterson. il por *People Wkly* 28:143-4 N 2 '87
Let's face Halloween with a trick or two! [cover story] il *Natl Geogr World* 146:3-5 O '87
Lunch bag luminarias for some Halloween magic. il *Sunset* 179:108 O '87
The scream scene [special section] il *Seventeen* 46:106-7 O '87
When they're too young to trick or treat. C. Loomis. il *Parents* 62:13 O '87
While demons howl, folks in a Florida nursing home scare kids every witch way but loose [Green Briar Nursing Home in Kendall] il *People Wkly* 28:98 N 2 '87
Halloween cookies See Cookies
Halloween cooking
Halloween treats. il *McCalls* 115:149-50 O '87
Marzipan menagerie. il *Sunset* 179:180-1 O '87
Treat your friends to a Halloween buffet. il *South Living* 22:174-5 O '87
Halloween costumes See Costume
Halloween masks See Masks
Hallowell, Christopher
Fathers and sons [excerpt from Father to the man] il *Glamour* 85:68+ Je '87
Ordinary medicines can have extraordinary side effects. il *Redbook* 169:132-4+ My '87
Hallowell, Edward
How teachers can cope with greater demands. *Educ Dig* 52:20-3 Ap '87
Halls
Arches and columns make an open hallway. il *South Living* 22:164 My '87
Bringing the front door forward . . . with a new skylighted entry hall. il *Sunset* 178:115 F '87
A good first impression [foyers] C. Engle. il *South Living* 22:142-3+ S '87
Grand entrances. il *Glamour* 85:336-9 Ap '87
Halls of fame
　　See also
　　Black Filmmakers Hall of Fame
　　Black Press Hall of Fame
　　Publishing Hall of Fame
　　Rock & Roll Hall of Fame
The U.S. Business Hall of Fame. A. M. Louis. il *Fortune* 115:102-7 Ap 13 '87
Hallström, Lasse
　　about
My life as a dog [film] Reviews
　　Commonweal 114:420 Jl 17 '87. T. O'Brien
　　Macleans 100:51 Je 15 '87. L. O'Toole
　　N Y il 20:70 My 11 '87. D. Denby
　　Natl Rev 39:56 Je 19 '87. J. Simon
　　New Repub 196:24 My 25 '87. S. Kauffmann
　　People Wkly 28:6 Ag 24 '87. S. Haller
　　Vogue il 177:32 Je '87. M. Haskell
Hallucinogenic drugs
　　See also
　　LSD

Hallwood Group Inc.
A 'rescue finance' team takes on banking [Hallwood Group takes on BancTexas Group] D. Cook. il por *Bus Week* p120 Mr 16 '87
Halmi (Robert), Inc. See Robert Halmi, Inc.
Halogen electric lamps See Electric lamps, Halogen
Halon fire extinguishers See Fire extinguishers
Halothane
Genetic analysis of halothane sensitivity in Caenorhabditis elegans. M. M. Sedensky and P. M. Meneely. bibl f il *Science* 236:952-4 My 22 '87
Halper, Barry
　　about
One fan's tribute to baseball greats—and almost-greats [cover story] R. W. Creamer. il por *Smithsonian* 18:102-6+ Ap '87
Halperin, Marj
Find out what it's worth. il *Americana* 15:14+ S/O '87
Halperin, Morton H.
The case against covert action [cover story] *Nation* 244:345+ Mr 21 '87
Halpern, Daniel, 1945-
　　about
Ecco—selling beyond the 'core' audience. J. Barbato. *Publ Wkly* 232:39 D 18 '87
Halpern, Sue M.
RU-486: the unpregnancy pill. il *Ms* 15:56+ Ap '87
Halpert, Felicia E.
Blazing racquets! The day the legends met. il *Women's Sports Fitness* 9:64 Jl '87
Play ball! bibl il *Women's Sports Fitness* 9:30-5 Jl '87
What turns girls on to sports? il *Women's Sports Fitness* 9:98-9 S '87
Halsted, Hank
Boat handling. See issues of Motor Boating & Sailing
Halston
　　about
The prisoner of Seventh Avenue: how Halston lost the right to his own name. L. Belkin. il pors *N Y Times Mag* p16-22+ Mr 15 '87
Halston Enterprises
The prisoner of Seventh Avenue: how Halston lost the right to his own name. L. Belkin. il pors *N Y Times Mag* p16-22+ Mr 15 '87
Halton, Mark R.
Israel enjoys silent airwaves. il *Christ Century* 104:1111-12 D 9 '87
Ham, Keith See Bhaktipada
Ham
　　See also
　　Cooking—Meat
The great Christmas ham: a report from Southside Virginia. R. Wilson. il *Ctry J* 14:33-8 Ja '87
Hamadei, Mohammed Ali
　　about
The big fish and the rule of law. il por *Newsweek* 109:34 Ja 26 '87
No deals. por *Time* 130:17 Jl 6 '87
Wanted for murder and air piracy. W. Svoboda. il *Time* 129:29 Ja 26 '87
West Germany to prosecute terrorist [White House statement, June 24, 1987] *Dep State Bull* 87:85 Ag '87
The West reels in 'a big fish' at last. il *U S News World Rep* 102:14 Ja 26 '87
Hamakawa, Yoshihiro
Photovoltaic power [cover story] il *Sci Am* 256:86-92 Ap '87
Hamann, Henry Paul
　　about
Hanged on his own gallows. M. E. Marty. *Christ Century* 104:1127 D 9 '87
Hamblen, Karen A.
An uneasy peace. bibl f *Des Arts Educ* 88:23-7 Mr/Ap '87
Hambletonian (Race) See Harness racing
Hamblett, Beatrice
Computerography. *Dance Mag* 61:86-7 Ja '87
Hamblin, Dora Jane, 1920-
'Delicious! Ah! What else is like the gondola?'. bibl (p147) il *Smithsonian* 18:96-105 Jl '87
For Rome, riches and glory in an outpost of empire. bibl (p270) il map *Smithsonian* 18:100-4+ N '87
Has the Garden of Eden been located at last? bibl (p184) il map *Smithsonian* 18:127-35 My '87
Hambrecht & Quist Incorporated
A high-tech repairman who 'can fix anything' [Q. T. Wiles] il por *Bus Week* p111 S 21 '87
How H&Q picks the Apples of tomorrow. G. G. Marcial. il *Bus Week* p76 Ap 20 '87

Hamburg (Germany)
          Art
Loony Luna Luna: this antic amusement park will raise your artbeat. J. Fayard. il *Life* 10:76-9 S '87
       Monuments, statues, etc.
Sinking feelings [Monument against fascism, war and violence by J. Gerz and E. Shalev-Gerz] M. Gibson. il *Art News* 86:105+ Summ '87

Hamburger, Philip
Lighted by Matisse. *New Yorker* 63:61-5 Ag 10 '87

Hamburger fast food restaurants See Drive-in restaurants; Fast food restaurants

Hamburger Hill [film] See Motion picture reviews—Single works

Hamburgers See Cooking—Meat

Hamby, Robert E., Jr.
       about
Multimedia's maverick. J. Baker. por *Channels* 7:55 Je '87

Hamer, Dean H.
(jt. auth) See Seguin, Carl, and Hamer, Dean H.

Hamil, Ralph E.
The arrival of the 5-billionth human. il por *Futurist* 21:36-7 Jl/Ag '87

Hamill, Pete
The New York we've lost. il *N Y* 20:61-5 D 21-28 '87
The secret city. il *N Y* 20:38-41 My 4 '87
When summers were free. il *Read Dig* 131:72-4 Jl '87

Hamilton, Alex, 1930-
Land of 'green winter'—and epic heroes. il *World Press Rev* 34:62 My '87

Hamilton, Carol
Esau's birthright [poem] *Christ Century* 104:661 Jl 29-Ag 5 '87
Isaac [poem] *Christ Century* 104:396 Ap 29 '87
Salt bread [poem] *Christ Century* 104:325 Ap 8 '87
Window [poem] *Christ Century* 104:308 Ap 1 '87

Hamilton, Carrie, 1964-
       about
"My mom saved my life". A. W. Petrucelli. pors *Redbook* 170:108-9+ N '87

Hamilton, George
       about
The Breakaway: a seagoing scenario for George Hamilton. I. Borger. il por *Archit Dig* 44:86-9 Ag '87

Hamilton, Ian, 1938-
       about
AAP and seven authors ask to join Random House in Salinger appeal. H. Fields. *Publ Wkly* 232:11 S 25 '87
AAP files amicus brief for Random House in appeal of Salinger decision. M. Yen. *Publ Wkly* 231:90 F 27 '87
Holden Caulfield goes to law school. A. Delbanco. *New Repub* 196:27-8+ Mr 9 '87
Random House seeks review of Salinger decision. M. Yen. *Publ Wkly* 231:24 F 13 '87
Return to sender. por *Time* 129:62 F 9 '87
Salinger and 'The bell jar': what do they mean to publishers? C. E. Rinzler. il *Publ Wkly* 231:20-2 Ap 24 '87
The Salinger file. P. Hoban. il pors *N Y* 20:36-42 Je 15 '87
Whose mail is it, anyway? A. Press. il pors *Newsweek* 109:58 F 9 '87
Whose words are they, anyway? D. Margolick. il *N Y Times Book Rev* 92:1+ N 1 '87

Hamilton, Juan
       about
The $70 million battle over Georgia O'Keeffe's will. S. D. Atchison. il pors *Bus Week* p44 Ja 26 '87
The battle over Georgia O'Keeffe's multimillion-dollar legacy. A. Decker. il pors *Art News* 86:120-7 Ap '87

Hamilton, Lee H.
       about
Rules of the game: does Congress have the guts to go one-on-one with Reagan? W. Greider. il *Roll Stone* p37-9 Je 18 '87

Hamilton, Linda
       about
Maybe King Kong lives isn't the greatest movie ever made, but don't try to palm it off on Linda Hamilton. J. Stark. il pors *People Wkly* 27:88-90 Ja 19 '87

Hamilton, Martha
       about
The new and improved Martha Hamilton. il pors *Ebony* 43:84-6+ N '87

Hamilton, Scott
       about
Guts and gold. W. Bingham. il pors *Sports Illus* 67:57+ O 19 '87

Hamilton, Seena
       about
Easter Bowl: through her eyes. C. Shmerler. il por *World Tennis* 34:24+ Ap '87

Hamilton, William, 1939-
Adrift on the Amazon. il *House Gard* 159:64+ F '87

Hamilton (Ont.)
       Harbor
In search of a safe harbor. M. Ritts. il *Macleans* 100:6+ My 18 '87
       Water pollution
In search of a safe harbor. M. Ritts. il *Macleans* 100:6+ My 18 '87

Hamilton-Finlay, Ian See Finlay, Ian Hamilton, 1925-

Hamilton Island (Australia)
Paradise found [owner K. Williams] N. Rabinowitz. il pors *Mot Boat Sail* 160:54-7+ D '87

Hamilton Standard Division See United Technologies Corp. Hamilton Standard Division

Hamlin, Harry
       about
Last of the great romantics [cover story] L. Rozen. il pors *People Wkly* 27:82-4+ Mr 30 '87
Wild about Harry. E. Sherman. pors *Ladies Home J* 104:70+ Ag '87

Hamm, Rod
Egg thieves of Playa Grande. il map *Sea Front* 33:27-33 Ja/F '87

Hamman, Robert
       about
Making it in big-time bridge. T. Buckley. il pors *N Y Times Mag* p22-5+ Jl 26 '87

Hammarskjöld, Dag, 1905-1961
       about
25th anniversary of Dag Hammarskjöld's death observed. il *UN Chron* 23:12 N '86

Hammer, Armand, 1898-
Entries in a détente diary. il pors *Life* 10:40-1+ Ja '87
Profiles in realpolitik. il *Newsweek* 109:79+ Ap 20 '87
       about
A geriatric who won't slow down. B. O'Reilly. il por *Fortune* 116:58 Ag 3 '87

Hammer, Charles
The door SDI won't shut. il *Wash Mon* 19:21-4 Mr '87

Hammer, Robert E., and others
Diversity of alpha-fetoprotein gene expression in mice is generated by a combination of separate enhancer elements. bibl f il *Science* 235:53-8 Ja 2 '87

Hammerman, Bernard
       about
Fantasy in blue. B. Weber. il por *N Y Times Mag* p102 O 25 '87

Hammerman Bros. Inc.
Fantasy in blue [platinum, diamond and sapphire necklace] B. Weber. il por *N Y Times Mag* p102 O 25 '87

Hammers
       Prices
The case for the $435 hammer [Navy contract] J. Fairhall. *Wash Mon* 18:47-8+ Ja '87

Hammocks
Sleeping on air. R. Kimber. il *Ctry J* 14:64-5 Ag '87

Hammond, C. M.
As they said in the Writer in 1887 . . . [reprint of April 1887 article] *Writer* 100:1 S '87
How to make writing pay [reprint of October 1887 article] *Writer* 100:18 O '87

Hammond, Harry
Build a heated dew cap for less than $10. il *Astronomy* 15:72-4 N '87

Hammond, John, 1910-1987
       about
Obituary
    Down Beat il por 54:11 O '87. J. McDonough
    High Fidel 37:71 N '87. R. C. Walls
    Jet il por 72:55 Jl 27 '87
    New Yorker 63:90-2 Ag 31 '87. W. Balliett
    Roll Stone il pors p23+ Ag 27 '87. M. Goldberg

Hammond, Linda Darling- See Darling-Hammond, Linda, 1951-

Hammond, Mary Stewart
Cosmetics [poem] *New Yorker* 63:38-9 S 28 '87
Grandmother's rug [poem] *New Yorker* 63:40-1 My 4 '87

Hammond, Robert
Insured success. il *Pop Photogr* 94:66-7 Ag '87

Hammond, William C., III
Why 'big books' are essential. por *Publ Wkly* 232:26 Jl 31 '87

Hammond (Ind.)
Juvenile justice, Administration of
Judge: get good grades or go to jail for failing [Judge P. Katic's program] *Jet* 73:24 D 14 '87

Hammons, George J.
about
Black appointed racing commissioner in Arkansas. *Jet* 71:17 F 16 '87

Hamner, Clay
about
How to win friends and enrich people. S. B. Weiner. il por *Forbes* 140:196+ D 14 '87

Hamnett, Katharine
about
Been there, seen that, done that. J. Cocks. il por *Time* 129:88-9 Mr 16 '87
Katharine Hamnett: "It's nice to have statements that say both 'money' and 'protest'". M. Blonsky. il pors *Vogue* 177:464+ S '87

Hampel, Robert L.
(jt. auth) See Farrar, Eleanor, and Hampel, Robert L.

Hampsten, Andy
about
A wheeler, but no dealer. A. Wolff. il pors *Sports Illus* 66:58+ Je 29 '87

Hampton, Christopher, 1946-
about
Les liaisons dangereuses [drama] Reviews
America 157:88+ Ag 15-22 '87. G. G. Seibert
N Y il 20:105-7 My 18 '87. J. Simon
N Y Rev Books il 34:28-9 Ag 13 '87. L. Sante
Nation 244:694 My 23 '87. M. Hodgson
New Leader 70:20-1 Jl 1-15 '87. L. Sauvage
New Repub 196:26+ Je 15 '87. R. Brustein
New Yorker 63:80 My 11 '87. E. Oliver
Newsweek il 109:81 My 11 '87. J. Kroll
Theatre Crafts il 21:27-31+ Ag/S '87. M. Sommers
Time il 129:82 My 11 '87. W. A. Henry
Vogue il 177:90 Ap '87. V. Radin

Hampton, Henry
about
Eyes on the prize. J. Rosen. il por *Channels* 7:48-50 O '87

Hampton, Lionel
about
The Univ. of Idaho honors Hampton with Music School. por *Jet* 71:22 F 23 '87

Hampton, Mark
The classical villa restated. il *House Gard* 159:114-23 Je '87
On decorating. See issues of House & Garden beginning October 1984

Hampton, Wally
Travel-protect your film. il *Petersens Photogr Mag* 16:24+ O '87

Hampton, William
Jeep Cherokee. il *Ctry J* 14:69-71 Ja '87
Mitsubishi Montero. il *Ctry J* 14:62-4 Mr '87
On and off the road. See alternate issues of Country Journal beginning January 1987 through July 1987
Volkswagen Vanagon Syncro. il *Ctry J* 14:67-8 My '87

Hampton (Iowa)
Education
Remembering a special student [Hampton (Iowa) High School seniors' deeds in memory of S. Varrelman] J. Fincher. il por *Read Dig* 131:149-54 O '87

Hampton (Lionel) School of Music See University of Idaho. Lionel Hampton School of Music

Hampton Court Palace (London, England)
Hampton Court Palace. D. Starkey. il *Hist Today* 37:62-3 O '87

Hampton National Historic Site (Towson, Md.)
Hampton's Georgian charm. il *South Living* 22:30+ D '87

Hampton University
The richest black school. D. C. Lyons. il *Ebony* 43:52+ D '87

Hamptons (Long Island, N.Y.) See Long Island (N.Y.)

Han, Victor K. M., and others
Cellular localization of somatomedin (insulin-like growth factor) messenger RNA in the human fetus. bibl f il *Science* 236:193-7 Ap 10 '87

Hanauer, Amy B.
Give my regards to Jersey. por *Seventeen* 46:80-1 My '87

Hanauer, Cathi
An American in Vienna: Aerin Lauder. pors *Seventeen* 46:118+ S '87

Oldest, youngest, middle, or only: what your birth order says about you. il *Seventeen* 46:106-7+ Ja '87
The Seventeen honor roll: most likely to succeed. il *Seventeen* 46:210-13 S '87

Hanauer, Gary
Death by stress? il *Omni* 9:22+ Ag '87
'My favorite subject is gardening!'. il *Rodale's Org Gard* 34:42+ Ap '87

Hanc, John
The abdominal showmen. il *Sport Mag* 78:81+ O '87

Hancock, Herbie, 1940-
about
Dexter Gordon, Hancock win Oscar nominations. il pors *Jet* 71:63 Mr 2 '87
Herbie Hancock. E. Levin. il pors *People Wkly* 27:66+ Ja 19 '87
Herbie Hancock: walking the tightrope between jazz and pop. L. Norment. il pors *Ebony* 42:132+ Mr '87
Oscar was a 'stunning' award for Herbie Hancock. il por *Jet* 72:58-9 Ap 20 '87

Hancock, John
about
Weeds [film] Reviews
Macleans il 100:52 N 2 '87. L. O'Toole
New Yorker 63:136-7 N 2 '87. P. Kael
Newsweek 110:109 N 16 '87. D. Ansen
People Wkly il 28:14 O 26 '87. R. Novak

Hand, Douglas
Keeping an ear on orcas. il *Oceans* 20:10-19+ Jl/Ag '87

Hand, Learned, 1872-1961
about
Learned Hand and the great train ride. F. R. Kellogg. *Am Sch* 56:471-86 Aut '87

Hand
See also
Manicuring

Abnormalities
See also
Syndaktylia

Care
Handle with care: a complete package for healthier hands and nails. P. Boyer. il *Prevention* 39:44+ Mr '87
The newest beauty asset: hands & nails. il *Glamour* 85:364-9 S '87

Hand tools See Tools

Handbags
Cachet & carry. il *Harpers Bazaar* 120:42 Mr '87
Charm: in the bag . . . [R. Pellegrino designs] il por *Vogue* 177:346 O '87
In the bag: what you carry, and how you carry it, is as important as what you wear. J. Mattera. il *Glamour* 85:102 Je '87
Judith Leiber's customers are left holding the bag. B. Johnson. il por *People Wkly* 27:117-18 Ap 20 '87

Handball
See also
Racquetball

Handedness See Left- and right-handedness

Handel, George Frideric, 1685-1759
about
Acis and Galatea [oratorio] Reviews
New Yorker 63:112 S 14 '87. A. Porter
Alcina [opera] Reviews
New Yorker 63:60 Jl 6 '87. A. Porter
Athalia [oratorio] Reviews
New Yorker 63:137-8 My 4 '87. A. Porter
Esther [oratorio] Reviews
New Yorker 63:72 Mr 16 '87. A. Porter
Israel in Egypt [oratorio] Reviews
New Yorker 63:137-9 N 23 '87. A. Porter
Joshua [oratorio] Reviews
New Yorker 63:75-6 Je 15 '87. A. Porter
Saul [oratorio] Reviews
New Yorker 63:75-6 Je 15 '87. A. Porter
New Yorker 63:72-3 Mr 16 '87. A. Porter
Tolomeo [opera] Reviews
New Yorker 63:134+ My 4 '87. A. Porter

Handel & Haydn Society
Handel, Haydn & Hogwood. W. Livingstone. por *Stereo Rev* 52:53-5 Mr '87
Musical events:
Athalia. A. Porter. *New Yorker* 63:137-8 My 4 '87

Handelman, David
Are four Heads better than one? il por *Roll Stone* p34-6+ Ja 15 '87
The aristobrats: they're young, they're rich, they're oh-so-shallow (could you be one of them?). il *Mademoiselle* 93:230-1+ Ap '87
Local heroes. il pors *Roll Stone* p68-70+ O 22 '87

Handelman, David—*cont.*
New York doll. por *N Y* 20:74-6 Mr 2 '87
(jt. auth) See Goldberg, Michael, and Handelman, David
Handey, Jack
Stunned. *New Yorker* 63:33 Ap 27 '87
Handgun Control, Inc.
Mrs. Brady's letter. D. E. Petzal. *Field Stream* 91:31
Ap '87
Handgun control legislation See Firearms—Laws and regulations
Handguns See Firearms
Handicapped
See also
Actors and actresses, Handicapped
Amputees
Architecture and the handicapped
Artists, Handicapped
Blind
Cerebral palsy
Children, Handicapped
Choreographers, Handicapped
Dancers, Handicapped
Deaf
Deaf-mutes
Farmers, Handicapped
Guitarists, Handicapped
Mentally handicapped
Mentally handicapped children
Mothers, Handicapped
Museum workers, Handicapped
Paralytics
Parents of the handicapped
Photographers, Handicapped
Physicians, Handicapped
Pianists, Handicapped
Scientists, Handicapped
Seamen, Handicapped
Theater and the handicapped
Theatrical directors, Handicapped
United Nations Decade of Disabled Persons, 1983-1992
Visually handicapped
Agencies on Aging can serve developmentally disabled
older adults. T. Rose. il *Aging* no356:32-3 '87
Disabled, not different [quiz] G. Dardick. il *Seventeen*
46:145 S '87
Our largest minority: Americans with handicaps [special
section] B. Davidson. il *McCalls* 114:61-8 S '87
"To help the handicapped, talk to them". I. Perlman.
il por *Glamour* 85:64 Mr '87
Civil rights
See also
National Council on Independent Living
Disability power. B. Davidson. il *McCalls* 114:64 S '87
Education
Society and the disabled. il *Courier* 40:29 Jl '87
Employment
AIDS: a job-rights victory [Supreme Court decision]
G. Witkin. il *U S News World Rep* 102:10-11 Mr
16 '87
Handicap rights [Supreme Court extends rights to those
with contagious diseases] R. Lacayo. il *Time* 129:66
Mr 16 '87
Handicapped thinkers [Supreme Court decision] D. Seligman. *Fortune* 115:110 Ap 13 '87
On unwarranted fears [Supreme Court confers privileged
victim status on individuals with contagious diseases]
America 156:266-7 Ap 4 '87
Supreme Court holds that contagious diseases are handicaps. T. J. Flygare. *Phi Delta Kappan* 68:705-6 My
'87
A victory for AIDS victims [Supreme Court decision]
A. Press. il *Newsweek* 109:33 Mr 16 '87
Your Constitution: is disease a legal handicap? D.
Pawelek. *Sch Update* 119:12 Ap 20 '87
Equipment
See also
Computers and the handicapped
Wheelchairs
Help for the handicapped [ABLENET control device
designed by Lee Hallgren] il *USA Today (Periodical)*
115:15 Je '87
Family relationships
See also
Parents of the handicapped
Gardens and gardening
Gardening saved his life [amputee J. G. Wilson] P.
H. Johnson. il por *Rodale's Org Gard* 34:60-4 My
'87

Psychology
A day on wheels. C. A. Davis. *Progressive* 51:34 N
'87
Recreation
See also
Camps for the handicapped
Religious life
See also
Church work with the handicapped
Sexual behavior
The disabled and sexual disappointment [study by Carol
Gill] *USA Today (Periodical)* 116:10 N '87
Sports
See also
Special Olympics
The end of an odyssey [wheelchair athlete R. Hansen]
M. Gray. il por *Macleans* 100:46+ Je 1 '87
A hero comes home [wheelchair athlete R. Hansen;
cover story; special section] il pors map *Macleans*
100:34-40+ Mr 30 '87
Paraplegic Rick Hansen proves a wheelchair is no handicap with a 25,000-mile marathon. W. Plummer. il
pors *People Wkly* 27:36-8+ Ap 27 '87
That great Abbott switch [University of Michigan pitcher
who has only one hand] H. Hersch. il pors *Sports
Illus* 66:28-9 My 25 '87
That wheeling feeling [wheelchair racers in the Boston
Marathon] C. Neff. il por *Sports Illus* 66:96 My 4
'87
Canada
Daily obstacles of the disabled. J. Barber. il *Macleans*
100:40 Mr 30 '87
Handicapped and animals
See also
Guide dogs
A boy who climbed the marigold [P. Burkarth's participation in horseback riding program for the handicapped]
A. Jones. il pors *Read Dig* 130:96-100 F '87
Monkeys with helping hands [capuchin monkeys aid
quadriplegics: work of M. J. Willard] J. T. MacFadyen.
il por *Read Dig* 131:38-43 Ag '87
The triumph of Mikko Mayeda [multiple sclerosis victim
becomes a competitive equestrian] V. Scott. il por
Good Housekeep 204:40 Mr '87
Handicapped and the theater See Theater and the handicapped
Handicapped in literature
Books your children will enjoy and learn from. C. W.
Levy. *McCalls* 114:68 S '87
Handicapped in motion pictures
"Are all cripples bad guys?". B. Davidson. *McCalls*
114:67-8 S '87
Distorted view of disabled [views of Paul K. Longmore]
il *USA Today (Periodical)* 115:6-7 Ap '87
Handicapped in television
Distorted view of disabled [views of Paul K. Longmore]
il *USA Today (Periodical)* 115:6-7 Ap '87
Handicapping of race horses See Horse race betting
Handicraft See Arts and crafts
Handler, Joshua
Waging submarine warfare. bibl f il *Bull At Sci* 43:40-3
S '87
Handler, Lowell
about
Two pros overcome handicaps for successful careers.
H. Chapnick. il pors *Pop Photogr* 94:20 F '87
Handler, Sharon J.
about
A case for the unconventional. J. Giambanco. il pors
Work Woman 12:80+ F '87
Handlin, Oscar, 1915-
Libraries and learning. *Am Sch* 56:205-18 Spr '87
Handling of food See Food handling
Handman, Edward
"Don't forget to eat!". *Read Dig* 131:23-4 Jl '87
Hands Across America, 1986
'We are the world' tune, Hands Across America net
$82.5 million for needy. *Jet* 72:58 Ap 13 '87
Hands-On-Science Outreach Program
Hands On Science . . . hands on fun. L. Feldman.
il *Child Today* 16:21-4 S/O '87
Handwarmers (Clothing)
Easy-to-make handwarmer tube. P.-M. Zanetti. il *Field
Stream* 92:41 N '87
ThermoPak—heat at the press of a button. R. M. Koolish.
il *Sky Telesc* 74:602 D '87
Handwriting See Penmanship
Handwriting analysis See Graphology
Haney, Daniel Q.
Getting to the heart of lobster love. il por *Natl Wildl*
25:18-21 Ap/My '87

Hanford Reservation (Wash.)
DOE shuts N-reactor for safety repairs but fears persist. I. Goodwin. il *Phys Today* 40:63-4 F '87
End game for the N reactor? [Hanford reactor] E. Marshall. il *Science* 235:17-18 Ja 2 '87
Energy Department blurs line between civilian, military reactors [plan to convert Unit One of the Washington Public Power Supply System to weapons purposes] M. M. Hoenig. bibl f *Bull At Sci* 43:25-7 Je '87
Hanford's radioactive tumbleweed. E. Marshall. il *Science* 236:1616-20 Je 26 '87
Plutonium blues in Hanford [reactor temporarily closed] O. Friedrich. il *Time* 129:22 Ja 12 '87
Hang gliding *See* Gliding and soaring
Hanging
Execution of ANC member deplored and condemned [B. Moloise] por *UN Chron* 22:14 N/D '85
Hanging of pictures *See* Pictures—Hanging
Hanging plants
Hanging baskets even in winter. il *Sunset* 179:208 O '87
Hanging gardens. T. Dudley. il *Ctry J* 14:60-3 D '87
Hangings, Wall *See* Wall hangings
Hangouts
Teen hot spots. il *Teen* 31:38+ O '87
Hangovers *See* Alcohol—Physiological effects
Hanks, David A., and Toher, Jennifer
Donald Deskey's decorative designs. bibl f il *Antiques* 131:838-45 Ap '87
Hanks, Stephen
The comeback trail. il *Esquire* 107:35-6 Ja '87
Hanks, Tom
about
How to look like a page out of Esquire [cover story] A. MacWeeney. il pors *Esquire* 107:F49-F55 Mr '87
Tom Hanks: funny, frank and fancy-free. por *Ladies Home J* 104:113+ Ap '87
Hanley, Catherine
Bake sale best-sellers [excerpt from Blue ribbon winners] il *Ladies Home J* 104:134-5+ O '87
Hanley, Rochelle M., and others
Functional analysis of a complementary DNA for the 50-kilodalton subunit of calmodulin kinase II. bibl f il *Science* 237:293-7 Jl 17 '87
Hanley, William Lee, 1940-
about
'You can't yank the rug out' [interview] pors *Channels* 7:62-3 Mr '87
Hanlon, Brendan
After tax reform, what? il *Theatre Crafts* 21:12 Ja '87
The code is dead! Long live the code! il *Theatre Crafts* 21:12+ Mr '87
Hanlon, Roger T.
Traditional squid fishing in the Azores. il *Sea Front* 33:34-41 Ja/F '87
Hanlon, William T.
What's in a name? *America* 157:317-18 N 7 '87
Hann, Marlys
about
Little house in the mountains. A. Gordon. il *House Gard* 159:100-3+ Ja '87
Hanna-Barbera Productions, Inc.
Joe Barbera. D. Diehl. il pors *People Wkly* 27:69+ Mr 16 '87
Hannah, Daryl
about
Daryl: film's new fit beauty. B. Goodwin. il pors *Harpers Bazaar* 120:211-13+ O '87
People are talking about . . . il por *Vogue* 177:216-17 Jl '87
Young at heart. P. Herbst. por *N Y* 20:24 Je 22 '87
Hannah, Lee
Changes underway at the World Bank. *BioScience* 37:186 Mr '87
Endangered Species Act: uncertain prospects in 100th Congress. *BioScience* 37:16 Ja '87
A turning point for environmentally sound development. *BioScience* 37:464 Jl/Ag '87
Hannah and her sisters [film] *See* Motion picture reviews—Single works
Hannay, Richard (Fictional character) *See* Richard Hannay (Fictional character)
Hannibal, Joseph T.
Building beasts. il *Earth Sci* 39:20-1 Wint '86
Hannibal, Joseph T., and Schmidt, Mark T.
The geology of art: Cleveland Museum of Art has walls and sculptures made of rock, and sidewalks made of skeletons [cover story] il *Earth Sci* 40:12-15 Summ '87

Hanniya, Akram
A death in Palestine [story]; tr. by Shirley Eber. *Harpers* 274:29-31 Ap '87
Hannon, Kent
A couple of Grants-in-aid. il pors *Sports Illus* 66:153 F 9 '87
Hannun, Yusuf A., and Bell, Robert Maurice, 1944-
Lysosphingolipids inhibit protein kinase C: implications for the sphingolipidoses. bibl f il *Science* 235:670-4 F 6 '87
The Hanoi Hilton [film] *See* Motion picture reviews—Single works
Hanover (N.H.)
Galleries and museums
See also
Hood Museum of Art
Hansberry, Lorraine, 1930-1965
about
A raisin in the sun [drama] Reviews
Jet il 72:59 Ap 27 '87
Work in progress: the definitive Lorraine Hansberry. R. L. Bray. pors *Ms* 15:31 F '87
Hansen, C. B.
Unforgettable Omar Bradley. il por *Read Dig* 131:118-24 Ag '87
Hansen, Dale
about
Daring to tackle the home team. W. Taaffe. il por *Sports Illus* 66:22 Mr 9 '87
Hansen, Diana Williams
Microwave cooking for kids. il *Ladies Home J* 104:66+ S '87
Hansen, George Vernon
about
Free George Hansen? D. Klinghoffer. *Natl Rev* 39:41 Ag 14 '87
Hansen, Joy
about
Joy is back. J. Mills. por *Women's Sports Fitness* 9:46 O '87
Hansen, Rick
about
The end of an odyssey. M. Gray. il por *Macleans* 100:46+ Je 1 '87
A hero comes home [cover story; special section] il pors map *Macleans* 100:34-40+ Mr 30 '87
Paraplegic Rick Hansen proves a wheelchair is no handicap with a 25,000-mile marathon. W. Plummer. il pors *People Wkly* 27:36-8+ Ap 27 '87
Hansen's disease *See* Leprosy
Hanslick, Eduard, 1825-1904
about
A critic's nightmare. S. W. Shrader. por *Opera News* 51:20-1 Ja 3 '87
Hanson, Curtis
about
The bedroom window [film] Reviews
Glamour 85:225-6 Mr '87. J. G. Boyum
Macleans 100:56 Ja 19 '87. L. O'Toole
N Y 20:57 F 2 '87. D. Denby
New Yorker 62:94-5 F 9 '87. P. Kael
People Wkly il 27:14 Ja 26 '87. P. Travers
Time il 129:76+ F 16 '87. R. Corliss
Hanson, Dennis G.
Some plain dealing pays off. il *Sierra* 72:20-2 Ja/F '87
The tide is turning for old beacons adrift at land's end [cover story] bibl (p145) il *Smithsonian* 18:98-106+ Ag '87
Hanson, Marla
about
Marla Hanson: "All of a sudden I'm on the 'in' list for parties. I sit next to Bianca Jagger at dinner". R. O'Connor. por *Vogue* 177:438+ S '87
Model Marla Hanson, showing the face of courage to a jury, helps convict the thug who maimed her. J. Wadler. il pors *People Wkly* 27:38-40+ Ja 5 '87
Hanson, Peter G. (Peter George), 1947-
about
Turning stress into profits. D. Francis. por *Macleans* 100:9 Je 1 '87
Hanson, Philip
Soviet industrial espionage. bibl f il *Bull At Sci* 43:25-9 Ap '87
Hanson, Sherry B.
Fitness facts and fables. *McCalls* 114:76 F '87
Hanson Trust plc
Beware the Romeo raider [Sir G. White] C. Knowlton. il por *Fortune* 115:42 Ja 5 '87

Hanson Trust plc—*cont.*
  Hanson and Kidde: a marriage made in low tech; A portrait of the raider as respected industrialist. L. Baum and R. A. Melcher. il *Bus Week* p36-7 Ag 17 '87
  Time to stop ignoring Hanson? G. G. Marcial. *Bus Week* p132 Je 22 '87
Hanssen, Kirsten
about
  Racing sleek. S. Rubin. il pors *Women's Sports Fitness* 9:38-41 O '87
Hanukkah
  The December dilemma [gentile-Jewish marriages face Christmas and Hanukkah] B. Kantrowitz. il *Newsweek* 110:56 D 28 '87
  The Hanukkah miracle. E. D. Frishman. il *Good Housekeep* 205:92+ D '87
  Happy Hanukkah from the Boresow family. J. Taylor. il *Better Homes Gard* 65:87-92 D '87
Hanukkah cooking *See* Cooking, Jewish
Hanzek, Michael J., and Waddell, Charles L.
  Painting with light. il *Petersens Photogr Mag* 16:72-3 D '87
Hanzel Galleries
  S.R.O. at Hanzel Galleries April art & antique auction. il *Antiques Collect Hobbies* 92:50-1 Je '87
Hapgood, Fred
  Let there be life. il *Omni* 9:40-2+ Ap '87
  The prodigious soybean [cover story] il map *Natl Geogr* 172:66-91 Jl '87
  Roden's eye. il por *Atlantic* 260:46-52 Ag '87
  Viruses emerge as a new key for unlocking life's mysteries [cover story] bibl (p270) il *Smithsonian* 18:116-27 N '87
Happiness
See also
  Pleasure
  Are you afraid to be happy? K. Shanor. il *Ladies Home J* 104:108+ Ap '87
  Cheer up! Happiness is something anyone can find. S. Jeffers. *Redbook* 169:160-1+ S '87
  Is happiness good for your health? C. Tavris. *Vogue* 177:178 Mr '87
  Keep a happiness calendar. J. Culhane. il *Read Dig* 130:63-6 Ja '87
  Marriage on the rocks [decrease in marital happiness; research by Norval D. Glenn and Charles Weaver] N. D. Glenn. il *Psychol Today* 21:20-1 O '87
  Mother as joymonger. P. Theroux. il *Parents* 62:55-7 D '87
  The pursuit of happiness. Publius. il *New Leader* 70:12-13 O 5 '87
Happy days [drama] *See* Beckett, Samuel, 1906-
Haptoglobins
  Salt-sensitive genes [research by Judy Z. Miller] V. DeBenedette. *Health* 19:23 My '87
Haq, Bilal U., and others
  Chronology of fluctuating sea levels since the Triassic. bibl f il *Science* 235:1156-67 Mr 6 '87
Har-lev, Raphael
about
  "We were overweight". M. Fritz. il por *Forbes* 140:226 O 5 '87
Hara, Koichi
about
  Le style Japonesque. R. Castile. il por *House Gard* 159:28+ Je '87
Harassment
See also
  Sexual harassment
Haraszti, Miklós, 1945-
  The dialectics of dissent [excerpt from The velvet prison] *Harpers* 275:28+ D '87
  The seduction of censorship [excerpt from The velvet prison] *New Repub* 197:32-4+ N 23 '87
Harayda, Janice
  Beating the rejection blues. *Writer* 100:21-3 S '87
  How to be happily single [excerpt from The joy of being single] *Essence* 18:61-2 O '87
  It's time people stopped putting down yuppies. il *Glamour* 85:40 O '87
  Lights! Camera! Action! por *Publ Wkly* 231:78 Ja 16 '87
Harb, Joseph A.
  How to survive a tax audit. il *Consum Res Mag* 70:21-3 Mr '87
Harbison, John
about
  Musical events:
    Performance of J. Harbison's The flight into Egypt. A. Porter. *New Yorker* 63:86-7 Je 8 '87

New life for the invalid. M. Walsh. il por *Time* 129:71 Je 1 '87
Harbor seals *See* Seals (Animals)
Harbors
See also
  Boston (Mass.)—Harbor
  Condominiums (Boat docking)
  Hamilton (Ont.)—Harbor
  New York (N.Y.)—Harbor
  Ports
  Saint-Pierre (Martinique)—Harbor
  San Francisco (Calif.)—Harbor
Harcombe, P. A.
  Tree life tables. bibl il *BioScience* 37:557-68 S '87
Harcourt, LaRue
about
  'At times you flat cry': how LaRue Harcourt's baseball player clients were driven to tears. A. Keteyian. il *Sports Illus* 67:90-1 O 19 '87
Harcourt, Michael
about
  A moderate takes over. J. O'Hara. *Macleans* 100:16 Ap 27 '87
Harcourt Brace Jovanovich, Inc.
  Battle of the book barons [R. Maxwell's bid] R. Henkoff. il por *Newsweek* 109:46 Je 1 '87
  A British press lord goes global [R. Maxwell seeks takeover] P. Sherrid. il por *U S News World Rep* 102:49-50 Je 1 '87
  A costly save at Harcourt [antitakeover measures against R. Maxwell's bid] P. Engardio. *Bus Week* p42 Je 8 '87
  Falling off a limb at Harcourt [Salomon and Mutual Shares lost on convertible bond gamble] D. Zigas. por *Bus Week* p32 Jl 6 '87
  HBJ filing with SEC outlines austerity plans. *Publ Wkly* 232:17 Ag 28 '87
  HBJ has $70 million quarterly loss, plans to sell magazine unit. il *Publ Wkly* 232:11 S 4 '87
  HBJ rejects Maxwell's $1.7 billion bid. il por *Publ Wkly* 231:18 My 29 '87
  HBJ sells units to Edgell group for $334.1 million. C. Reid. *Publ Wkly* 232:11 N 27 '87
  HBJ shows the leveraged deal is alive and well [R. L. Edgell acquires magazine unit] G. DeGeorge. *Bus Week* p36-7 N 30 '87
  How Harcourt plans to keep the wolf away [junk bonds] G. DeGeorge. *Bus Week* p40+ S 14 '87
  Jovanovich charges Maxwell is 'unfit' [takeover controversy; with interview with R. Maxwell] M. Reuter. *Publ Wkly* 231:13-14 Je 5 '87
  Jovanovich sees nothing friendly in Maxwell's bid. P. Engardio. il por *Bus Week* p47 Je 1 '87
  Judge backs Harcourt in ruling on debentures. *Publ Wkly* 232:12 Jl 3 '87
  Maxwell sues to block HBJ's $3 billion plan. *Publ Wkly* 231:23 Je 12 '87
  Most improved. il *Forbes* 139:99 Ja 12 '87
Hard boiled eggs *See* Cooking—Eggs
A hard day's night [film] *See* Motion picture reviews—Single works
Hard disk memory (Computers) *See* Computers—Memory systems
Hard of hearing *See* Deaf; Deafness
Hard Rock (Firm)
  Sour notes for Hard Rock Cafe [American depositary receipts] G. G. Marcial. *Bus Week* p72 Ap 6 '87
Hard Rock Cafe (New York, N.Y.) *See* New York (N.Y.)—Restaurants, nightclubs, bars, etc.
Hard times [drama] *See* Jeffreys, Stephen
Hardee's Food Systems, Inc.
  Hardee's: the bigger it grows, the hungrier it gets. D. Foust. il por *Bus Week* p106 My 4 '87
Hardenbergh, Chalmers
  The other negotiations. il *Bull At Sci* 43:48-9 Mr '87
  The other negotiations. *Bull At Sci* 43:52-3 S '87
Hardenbergia
  Quick and colorful climber. il *Sunset* 178:179 F '87
Hardening of the arteries *See* Arteriosclerosis
Hardesty, Michael
about
  Michael Hardesty at Germans van Eck. S. Westfall. il *Art Am* 75:121-2 Jl '87
Hardiman, Joseph R.
about
  Hardiman could be just what the NASD needs. V. Cahan. *Bus Week* p32 Jl 6 '87
Hardin, Garrett James, 1915-
  How many creatures? [discussion of October 1986 article, Cultural carrying capacity: a biological approach to human problems] *BioScience* 37:246-7 Ap '87

Harding, Dave
From beyond the horizon. il *Conservationist* 41:20-1
Mr/Ap '87
Harding, Randy
about
Manhattan or bust. J. Paris. il pors *Read Dig* 131:5-6+
Jl '87
Hardison, Bethann
about
Bethann: then and now. R. Hartman. pors *Essence*
17:42-3+ Ja '87
Hardoy, Jorge Enrique
Governments come and go . . . the community abides.
il *World Health* p26-7 Jl '87
Hardware
See also
Bolts and nuts
Fasteners
Hinges
Nails
Rivets and riveting
Screws
Waxman Industries, Inc.
A touch of brass [making custom hardware] W. E. Burton.
il *Pop Mech* 164:82-5 Mr '87
Hardware stores
See also
Home improvement centers
Hallelujah! All hail the hardware store! G. Martin. il
Esquire 107:120-2 Je '87
Hardwick, Elizabeth
The fictions of America. il *N Y Rev Books* 34:12+ Je
25 '87
The heart of the seasons [cover story] il *House Gard*
159:122-31+ My '87
Hardwood flooring *See* Flooring
Hardy, Douglas
Writers discuss their craft, and censorship, at PEN panel
in Boston. *Publ Wkly* 232:43 D 25 '87
Hardy, Larry W., and others
Atomic structure of thymidylate synthase: target for
rational drug design. bibl f il *Science* 235:448-55 Ja
23 '87
Hardy, Oliver, 1892-1957
about
Laurel and Hardy in the big house. D. M. Kimmel.
il pors *Film Comment* 23:2+ Jl/Ag '87
Hardy, Richard R., and others
Rheumatoid factor secretion from human Leu-1⁺ B cells.
bibl f il *Science* 236:81-3 Ap 3 '87
Hardy, Thomas, 1840-1928
The oxen [poem] *America* 157:474 D 19 '87
Hare, Nathan, 1934-
Speaking out: is the black middle class blowing it? .
. . Yes! por *Ebony* 42:85-6 Ag '87
Hare Krishna consciousness movement *See* Krishna con-
sciousness movement
Hares
See also
Rabbits
Leaping lepus. B. D. Stutz. il *Nat Hist* 96:46-9 F '87
Sexual behavior
See Sexual behavior—Animals
Hareven, Tamara K.
Divorce, Chinese style. il *Atlantic* 259:70-6 Ap '87
Haring, Bernard *See* Häring, Bernhard, 1912-
Häring, Bernhard, 1912-
Moral theologian under attack: Saint Alphonsus Liguori.
America 156:362-6 My 2 '87
Harkison, Judy
'A chorus of groans,' notes Sherlock Holmes. il
Smithsonian 18:196 S '87
Harkness, Robert P.
(jt. auth) See Wheeler, J. Craig, and Harkness, Robert
P.
Harlem (New York, N.Y.)
See also
Apollo Theatre (New York, N.Y.)
Harlem Opera House (New York, N.Y.)
Best intentions: Edmund Perry's path from Harlem to
Exeter to death on a street in Morningside Heights
[excerpt] R. S. Anson. il pors map *N Y* 20:30-45
My 11 '87
Brief encounter [discussing the plight of Harlem with
white man on Manhattan's East Side] J. M. McConnell.
il *America* 157:101 Ag 29-S 5 '87
A dream come true [followup on students of P.S. 121
in East Harlem helped by E. M. Lang] M. deC. Hinds.
il por *N Y Times Mag* p32-6 Ap 26 '87
The gentrification of Harlem. M. Mittelstaedt. *World
Press Rev* 34:44 Ap '87

Harlem hospitality [focus of month long celebration]
P. A. Taylor. il *Essence* 18:18+ O '87
Hospital gets facelift [North General Hospital] M. Scott.
Black Enterp 18:20 N '87
Sugar Hill: a citadel of style and echoes of an earlier
America. P. Blauner. il map *N Y* 20:90-2 My 4 '87
Harlem Dance Theatre *See* Dance Theatre of Harlem
Harlem Globetrotters
1st female Globetrotter quits in contract flap [L. Woodard]
il pors *Jet* 73:48 N 16 '87
Ex-Globetrotters balk at 'slave labor,' form own basketball
team. *Jet* 71:46 F 9 '87
Globetrotter stooge for a day [playing for the Washington
Generals against the Globetrotters] J. Coplon. il *Sport
Mag* 78:84 Je '87
Trotters quietly sign their 2nd woman player [J. White]
il por *Jet* 71:48 Ja 19 '87
Harlem Opera House (New York, N.Y.)
The Harlem Opera House. *New Yorker* 63:20-1 Je 29
'87
Harlem renaissance
Exhibitions
Born again [Harlem renaissance: art of black America]
K. Larson. il *N Y* 20:74-5 Mr 16 '87
Harlem in the Jazz Age [Studio Museum exhibit] il
N Y Times Mag p32-3 F 8 '87
Harlem renaissance: art of black America [exhibit at
the Studio Museum of Harlem] F. Tyler. il *Art News*
86:191 O '87
Harlem revisited during Black History Month [special
programs at American Museum of Natural History]
Jet 71:28 F 9 '87
Harleman, Patricia McGarry
about
Love the outfit, Mrs. Harleman, but your kids want
to just die. D. Grogan. il pors *People Wkly* 28:141-3
O 12 '87
Harlev, Rafi *See* Har-lev, Raphael
Harley-Davidson Motor Co., Inc.
Harley back in gear. J. A. Conway. il *Forbes* 139:8
Ap 20 '87
Harley-Davidson: ready to ride on its own [asking to
end import restraints against Japan] *Newsweek* 109:50
Mr 30 '87
That vroom you hear is Harley [stock price] G. G.
Marcial. *Bus Week* p78 Ag 17 '87
Why Milwaukee won't die [Japanese motorcycles imitate
Harleys] il *Cycle* 38:35-7+ Je '87
Harling, Robert, 1910-
about
Steel magnolias [drama] Reviews
N Y 20:94 Ap 6 '87. J. Simon
Nation 244:481 Ap 11 '87. T. M. Disch
New Yorker 63:63 Ag 17 '87. E. Oliver
Harlow, Nora
Madness in the family. il *Redbook* 169:130-1+ My '87
(ed) See Abel, Gene G. The child abuser: how can
you spot him?
HARM missiles *See* Guided missiles—Launching from
airplanes
Harman, Susan M.
about
Susan Harman: an instinct for high-tech success. P. Finch.
por *Bus Week* p81 F 9 '87
Harmless, William
Night casting: Epiphany in Galilee [poem] *America*
156:365 My 2 '87
Harmon, Kitty
Peter Miller Books: where design professionals go to
shop. il pors *Publ Wkly* 231:56-8 F 20 '87
Harmon, Mark
about
Dawber hits the Mark! F. A. Bernstein. il pors *People
Wkly* 27:44-6+ Mr 2 '87
Life after Ozzie & Harriet [cover story] B. Darrach.
il pors *People Wkly* 28:40-5 S 7 '87
Mark Harmon. por *Seventeen* 46:164 Ag '87
Mark Harmon hates being a hunk. D. Maychick. il
pors *Mademoiselle* 93:72 Ag '87
Harmonia Mundi (Firm)
What are the French doing in Frisco? [recording Handel's
Arias for Senesino] P. Moor. il *High Fidel* 37:62 Ap
'87
Harmonic analysis
The tide at Tarawa [computer program] D. W. Olson.
il map *Sky Telesc* 74:526-8 N '87
Harmonic Convergence
The end of the world (again). B. Barol. il map *Newsweek*
110:70-1 Ag 17 '87
Hum if you love the Mayans. J. Friedman. il *People
Wkly* 28:26-9 Ag 31 '87

Harmonic Convergence—*cont.*
A New Age dawning. M. Smilgis. il *Time* 130:63 Ag 31 '87

Harmonica players
See also
Chrisley, John

Harmony
See also
Melody
Musical intervals and scales
Take the 'A' strain: a hearing test. D. Wilhite. il *Down Beat* 54:60-1 Je '87

Harness racing
But Jate, why so late? [Meadowlands Pace] D. Stathoplos. il *Sports Illus* 67:69-70 Jl 27 '87
In Florida: sweet charity [George Plimpton Celebrity Challenge Cup Harness Race in Pompano Beach, Fla.] P. Jordan. il *Time* 129:9+ Ap 13 '87
Economic aspects
Here's to Mack the Knife [Hambletonian winner Mack Lobell and owner L. Guida] D. S. Looney. il por *Sports Illus* 67:63-4 Ag 17 '87
Ethical aspects
Shame at Yonkers [drivers suspended in suspected fixed race] S. Wulf. il *Sports Illus* 67:11 D 14 '87

Harney, John
The music of lost hours [poem] *New Yorker* 63:40 Mr 16 '87

Harnisch, William F.
about
Today's rejects, tomorrow's buys. G. G. Marcial. *Bus Week* p120 My 18 '87

Harnoy, Ofra
about
Making music with passion. il por *Macleans* 100:12-13 D 28 '87

Harold Washington College
Chicago city college renamed to honor late mayor Harold Washington. il por *Jet* 73:32 D 21 '87

Harp, Lore
about
Women are lining up for Lore Harp's Le Funelle. P. Finch. il por *Bus Week* p80 Je 8 '87

Harper, Charles Michael
about
How ConAgra grew big—and now, beefy. M. Ivey. il por *Bus Week* p87-8 My 18 '87

Harper, Edward
All eyes on her. il *N Y Times Mag* p40 My 24 '87

Harper, Judith A.
Preventive preschool programming that works. il *Phi Delta Kappan* 69:81-2 S '87

Harper, Maribeth
New directions in telecommunications. il *Nations Bus* 75:38-40 Ap '87

Harper, Marjory
'A family affair': colonising New Kincardineshire. bibl il map *Hist Today* 37:42-8 O '87

Harper, Nan
Lawrence: a cultural palette. il *Horizon* 30:24-30+ S '87

Harper, Suzanne
Twins. il *Seventeen* 46:122-3+ Je '87

Harper, Valerie
about
Suing the bosses who bounced her, a bitter Valerie Harper fights to save her reputation. D. Hutchings. il pors *People Wkly* 28:46-8 O 19 '87

Harper & Row Publishers, Inc.
Burlingame to have imprint at Harper; Shinker is publisher. il pors *Publ Wkly* 232:14-15 O 16 '87
Citizen Murdoch makes his mark in books and television. D. Pauly. il por *Newsweek* 109:47+ Ap 13 '87
Harper & Row gets $190 million offer from private investor [T. L. Cross] M. Reuter. il por *Publ Wkly* 231:10 Mr 20 '87
Harper & Row purchases Caedmon. il *Publ Wkly* 231:52+ Je 5 '87
Harper & Row revamps; 50 jobs to be lost. M. Reuter. il *Publ Wkly* 232:12 Jl 10 '87
Harper & Row studies HBJ, Cross takeover bids. *Publ Wkly* 231:13 Mr 27 '87
Harper & Row to ship book by Gorbachev in early November. B. Levine. *Publ Wkly* 232:41-2 O 16 '87
Harper, San Francisco: experienced at weathering change [religious division] L. See. *Publ Wkly* 232:49 Jl 31 '87
Mikhail Gorbachev, author [interview with S. M. Bessie] A. P. Sanoff. il por *U S News World Rep* 103:73 O 12 '87

Murdoch to sell half of Harper & Row to Collins, to become co-chairman. J. Mutter and V. Menkes. *Publ Wkly* 232:70 S 18 '87
Offbeat auction [L. Erdich's dissatisfaction with Bantam leads to acquisition of rights to Tracks by Harper & Row] P. S. Nathan. *Publ Wkly* 232:40 N 13 '87
Orchestrating Gorbachev [foreign rights to M. Gorbachev's book Perestroika] P. S. Nathan. *Publ Wkly* 232:21 N 6 '87
Penta files breach of contract suit against Harper & Row. *Publ Wkly* 232:25 Jl 17 '87
Rupert Murdoch to acquire Harper & Row for $65 a share. M. Reuter. il por *Publ Wkly* 231:16-17 Ap 10 '87
Thomas and 13 others leave Harper & Row [reorganization in wake of takeover by News Corporation Ltd.] M. Reuter. il *Publ Wkly* 231:21-2 My 29 '87
The word according to Roget [Roget's international thesaurus] R. A. Carter. *Publ Wkly* 232:36 O 2 '87
The year of the "LRFO": Let's Read-and-Find-Out books in the '80s. K. O. Fakih. il *Publ Wkly* 231:38-9 Ja 23 '87

Harper's (Periodical)
Happy anniversary [third anniversary of redesign] L. H. Lapham. *Harpers* 274:10-11 Mr '87

Harper's bazaar (Periodical)
Bazaar's best and brightest. il *Harpers Bazaar* 121:226-9 N '87

Harpsichord
Phosphorus in antique iron music wire. M. Goodway. bibl f il *Science* 236:927-32 My 22 '87
The well-tempered clavier [use of phosphorus alloy in harpsichord strings; research by Martha Goodway] il *Sci Am* 257:20+ Ag '87

Harragan, Betty Lehan
Dear Betty Harragan. See issues of Working Woman
Work wise. See issues of Mademoiselle

Harrah, Dennis
about
Biggest change in town. R. Reilly. il pors *Sports Illus* 67 Sp Issue:76-8+ S 9 '87

Harrell, Lorraine
Widow [poem] *Essence* 18:110 Je '87

Harrier airplanes See Airplanes, Military

Harries, Owen
Anthony Eden & the decline of Britain. *Commentary* 83:34-43 Je '87

Harrigan, Anthony
The challenge of the future [address, September 22, 1987] *Vital Speeches Day* 54:109-11 D 1 '87

Harrigan, Kathryn Rudie
about
Endgame strategy [interview] J. Willoughby. il por *Forbes* 140:181-2 Jl 13 '87

Harriman, Pamela
about
The lady has a Midas touch. E. Thomas. il pors *Newsweek* 109:32-3 Je 15 '87
Mango Bay: Pamela Harriman's residence on Barbados. W. Walton. il por *Archit Dig* 44:84-9 Ja '87

Harrington, Blair
Rock out: learn to scale new heights. il *Women's Sports Fitness* 9:94-5 S '87

Harrington, Daniel J.
Books on the Bible [cover story] *America* 157:431-7 D 5 '87
A new paradigm for Paul. il *America* 157:290-3 O 31 '87

Harrington, Fred H.
The man who cries wolf. il *Nat Hist* 96:22+ F '87

Harrington, James
about
James Harrington. E. Feit. il *Am Artist* 51:42-7 Jl '87

Harrington, Ollie
The last days of Richard Wright. il pors *Ebony* 42:58-60+ Mr '87

Harrington, Sheila, 1953-
The watercolor page. il por *Am Artist* 51:48-51+ Ap '87

Harris, Alice Kessler- See Kessler-Harris, Alice

Harris, Dale
A civilized intuition. il por *Archit Dig* 44:148-55 N '87
Full cycle. il *Opera News* 51:12-14+ F 28 '87
Glitz! il *Vogue* 177:318-19+ D '87
Hamptons homestead: the D. Ronald Daniels' converted barn. il *Archit Dig* 44:158-63 Je '87
Rien de trop. por *Opera News* 51:10-11+ My '87
The Tiffany touch: a wealth of riches. il *Harpers Bazaar* 120:206+ S '87

Harris, Dick
(ed) See Morrison, Martha. My 17 years as a drug addict
Harris, James, III See Jam, Jimmy
Harris, Jay
Books on Jews and Judaism. *America* 157:163-4+ S 26 '87
Harris, Jean (Jean Struven)
about
The lady killer: should Jean Harris go free? B. G. Harrison. *Mademoiselle* 93:164 Ag '87
Harris, Jeffrey E.
The AIDS epidemic: looking into the 1990s. il *Technol Rev* 90:58-64 Jl '87
Harris, Jesse
about
Harris is youngest judge ever appointed in Okla. por *Jet* 71:27 Ja 19 '87
Harris, Jessica B.
Crafted by Indian hands. il *Horizon* 30:22-3 Mr '87
Highbrow nightlife. il *Black Enterp* 17:39-40 My '87
A taste of the islands: spicy, sweet and savory. il *Black Enterp* 17:47-8 My '87
Harris, Jordan
about
Virgin's odd couple. S. Pond. pors *Roll Stone* p22+ Ap 9 '87
Harris, Lis
Brother sun, sister moon. *New Yorker* 63:80-92+ Ap 27 '87
Harris, Mary Jane
about
The Italian baroque paintings of Morton and Mary Jane Harris. C. Ratcliff. il por *Archit Dig* 44:50+ My '87
Harris, Mel
about
Yuppie babies, beaus and tales of woe on thirtysomething plunk a responsive chord for Mel Harris. T. Gold. il pors *People Wkly* 28:55-6+ O 26 '87
Harris, Monica
about
Gooden plans to wed his longtime friend. *Jet* 72:31 Jl 20 '87
Harris, Morton B.
about
The Italian baroque paintings of Morton and Mary Jane Harris. C. Ratcliff. il por *Archit Dig* 44:50+ My '87
Harris, Myles
Tourists in hell [excerpt from Breakfast in hell] *Harpers* 274:28-31 F '87
Harris, Patricia, and Lyon, David
Bach and knolls in the Berkshires. il *Travel Holiday* 167:38+ My '87
Harris, Polly Lee
about
D.C. mayor's mother-in-law pleads guilty to arson. *Jet* 72:8 Jl 13 '87
Harris, R. H.
about
Mamas and papas. M. Jefferson. il pors *Vogue* 177:100 O '87
Harris, Richard
about
Stepping out [drama] Reviews
N Y il 20:63 Ja 26 '87. J. Simon
New Yorker 62:69 Ja 26 '87. B. Gill
Harris, Richard, 1926-1987
The other day (as culled from the New York "Times" of August 9th). *New Yorker* 63:90-2+ S 21 '87
Suffering toward the White House. *New Yorker* 63:65-6+ Ag 3 '87
about
Obituary
New Yorker 63:120 S 21 '87
Harris, Robert S.
Sensational star traces. il *Petersens Photogr Mag* 16:62-5+ N '87
Harris, Sheryl
Beat the messy room rap. il *Teen* 31:26+ N '87
Harris, Susan
about
Gilded girl. il pors *Vogue* 177:362 O '87
Harris, Tracy
about
Manager, trainer, father, Patterson guides his son. il pors *Jet* 71:52 Mr 2 '87
Harris, Warren G.
Cary Grant [excerpt] il pors *Good Housekeep* 205:189-91+ S '87

Harris, William
about
Saviors of an island church. B. MacAndrew. il *Macleans* 100:43 N 2 '87
Harris, William
Making Malcolm. il pors *Theatre Crafts* 21:73-4 F '87
Harris, William Hamilton, 1944-
The black labor movement and the fight for social advance. *Mon Labor Rev* 110:37-8 Ag '87
Harris Corp.
Harris chief warns of economic chaos if manufacturing continues overseas move [views of J. A. Boyd] E. H. Kolcum. *Aviat Week Space Technol* 127:89 S 14 '87
Harris Corp. offering digital map generator for airborne operations. E. H. Kolcum. il *Aviat Week Space Technol* 126:84-5+ Mr 16 '87
Why Harris has to make it outside the Pentagon. G. DeGeorge. il por *Bus Week* p138-9 N 2 '87
Harris-Smith, Shirley A., d. 1987
about
Pregnant woman found hanged in N.Y. jail cell; angry blacks ask probe. *Jet* 72:8 Jl 13 '87
Harrison, Barbara Grizzuti
The private eye. See issues of Mademoiselle
Something in the way he works . . . why we have an eye for the driven guy. il *Mademoiselle* 93:262-3+ S '87
Spiritual glitz. *Ms* 16:72+ Jl/Ag '87
Harrison, Bob
about
New football league tabs black head coach for D.C. *Jet* 72:51 Je 8 '87
Harrison, Brian Howard
'Kindness and reason': William Lovett and education. bibl il por *Hist Today* 37:14-22 Mr '87
Harrison, George
about
After five years of musical silence, Beatle emeritus George Harrison comes out singing on Cloud nine. S. Dougherty. il pors *People Wkly* 28:62-4 O 19 '87
George Harrison [interview] A. DeCurtis. por *Roll Stone* p47-8+ N 5-D 10 '87
George Harrison gets back [cover story] A. DeCurtis. pors *Roll Stone* p36-8+ O 22 '87
New LP from George Harrison. A. DeCurtis. il por *Roll Stone* p11 Ag 13 '87
The quiet Beatle goes public. M. A. Lerner. il por *Newsweek* 110:92 O 26 '87
Harrison, Jenilee
about
Reggie Jackson mum on rumor of wedding to blonde 'Dallas' star. pors *Jet* 71:53 Ja 26 '87
Harrison, Jim, 1937-
Night walking. il *Roll Stone* p91+ Mr 26 '87
Harrison, Selig S.
Dateline South Korea: a divided Seoul. bibl f *Foreign Policy* 67:154-75 Summ '87
Harrison/Erickson (Firm)
Bonnie Erickson: graduating from Sesame Street. P. Finch. il por *Bus Week* p81 F 9 '87
Harriss, C. Lowell
Guidance from a classic: the centennial of Henry George's Protection or free trade [address, November 13, 1986] *Vital Speeches Day* 53:171-3 Ja 1 '87
Harriss, Joseph A.
The newest quilt fad seems to be going like crazy [cover story] bibl (p184) il *Smithsonian* 18:114-16+ My '87
Harrodsburg (Ky.)
          Historic houses, sites, etc.
See also
Shaker Village of Pleasant Hill (Harrodsburg, Ky.)
Harrowsmith (Periodical)
Harrowsmith's leader cuts his roots [J. Lawrence sells out to Telemedia] A. Shortell. il por *Macleans* 100:30 Mr 30 '87
Harry, Jackee See Jackee
HARRY (Dance company)
Reviews:
Performances at the Joyce Theater, New York City. S. Sommer. *Dance Mag* 61:38-9 Ap '87
Harry and the Hendersons [film] See Motion picture reviews—Single works
Harry Cipriani (New York, N.Y.: Restaurant) *See* New York (N.Y.)—Restaurants, nightclubs, bars, etc.
Harry N. Abrams, Inc.
Abrams celebrates National Geographic 1988 centennial. il *Publ Wkly* 231:51 My 29 '87
Harry's Bar and American Grill (San Francisco, Calif.) *See* San Francisco (Calif.)—Restaurants, nightclubs, bars, etc.

Hart, Evelyn

about

A dream of a dancer. P. Hluchy. il por *Macleans* 100:52 Mr 9 '87

Hart, Gary, 1936-

about

After sticking with a troubled marriage, Lee Hart watches a dream die. M. Green. il pors *People Wkly* 27:38-40 My 25 '87

After the fall: how Hart's workers picked up the pieces. L. Glynn and J. Mathewson. il por *Glamour* 85:362-3+ S '87

All smiles [cover story] F. Barnes. il *New Repub* 196:17-20 My 18 '87

Are the sex lives of all politicians now fair game? A. P. Sanoff. il por *U S News World Rep* 102:12 Je 15 '87

Boston diarist. H. Hertzberg. *New Repub* 196:42 Je 15 '87

A bubble of summer madness. M. Kaus. il por *Newsweek* 110:18 Ag 31 '87

A change of Hart [special section] J. Alter. il pors *Newsweek* 110:12-18 D 28 '87

Chronicle of a ruinous affair. M. Green. il pors *People Wkly* 27:104-8 Je 15 '87

Donna Rice tells her story; ed. by James Grant. D. Rice. il *Life* 10:82-6+ Jl '87

Donna Rice: 'the woman in question'. A. Richman. il pors *People Wkly* 27:32-7 My 18 '87

Fall from grace [cover story; special section] il pors *Time* 129:16-20+ My 18 '87

Femme is fatal. B. Ehrenreich and J. O'Reilly. *New Repub* 196:15-16 Je 1 '87

Gary Hart. il por *People Wkly* 28:36-7 D 28 '87-Ja 4 '88

Gary Hart: a candidate in search of himself. H. Fineman. il pors *Newsweek* 109:25-7 Ap 13 '87

The Gary Hart affair: the media's role. J. B. Judis. *Current* 297:28-32 N '87

Gary Hart and Joe Biden: a surfeit of behavior. *America* 157:203 O 10 '87

Gary Hart: just what the Democrats don't need. L. Walczak and R. Fly. por *Bus Week* p85 D 28 '87-Ja 4 '88

Gary Hart slips a joker into the Democratic deck. il pors *U S News World Rep* 103:11-12 D 28 '87-Ja 4 '88

Gary Hart: the elusive front-runner [cover story] E. J. Dionne, Jr. il pors *N Y Times Mag* p28-34+ My 3 '87

Gary Hart's snakebit debut. il *U S News World Rep* 102:17 Ap 27 '87

Gary Hart's ticking debt bomb. K. T. Walsh. il por *U S News World Rep* 102:25 Ap 6 '87

Gary-kari—& after. *Commonweal* 114:307-9 My 22 '87

The ghost of Gary past [cover story] W. Shapiro. il pors *Time* 130:14-20 D 28 '87

Gotta have Hart. J. E. Oberg. *Natl Rev* 39:40 Jl 17 '87

Hart murmurs. por *Time* 130:20 Ag 31 '87

The Hart poll. V. S. Navasky. *Nation* 245:112-13 Ag 15-22 '87

Hart's campaign: from high road to low. *Newsweek* 109:34 Ap 27 '87

Hart's problem & ours. W. F. Buckley. *Natl Rev* 39:55 Je 5 '87

Here comes Gary, again. M. Kaus. il por *Newsweek* 109:26 Je 29 '87

Infidelity. *Nation* 244:633-4 My 16 '87

Just what is he up to? W. Shapiro. il por *Time* 130:29 S 21 '87

Kennedy going on Nixon. L. Morrow. il *Time* 129:90 My 18 '87

A little spice for the tapioca. G. Witkin. il pors *U S News World Rep* 103:14 S 21 '87

The loneliest long-distance runner. W. Shapiro. il por *Time* 129:31 Ap 27 '87

The loss of Hart. *New Repub* 196:9-11 Je 1 '87

Memo to: Gary Hart from: National review. *Natl Rev* 39:17-18 Mr 27 '87

A message from the party pros: save your breath, Gary. R. Fly and P. Magnusson. por *Bus Week* p37 S 7 '87

Monkey Business Inc. il *Newsweek* 109:48 Je 29 '87

The mourning after. F. Trippett. il *Time* 129:34 My 25 '87

A new Hart show. A. Kopkind. *Nation* 245:775-6 D 26 '87-Ja 2 '88

New morality, new journalism. *Natl Rev* 39:15 Je 5 '87

New photos behind the fall. il pors *Newsweek* 109:22 Je 8 '87

No longer Gary Hart's spokesman, Kevin Sweeney ponders his fate while waiting tables at Lily's. R. Arias. il pors *People Wkly* 28:103+ N 9 '87

Notes and comment. *New Yorker* 63:27 My 25 '87

Notes on a brief campaign. P. Tauber. il *N Y Times Mag* p48-50+ My 31 '87

Now after Hart, the questions [cover story; special section] il pors *U S News World Rep* 102:18-25 My 18 '87

Now the Democrats have a pack of front-runners. R. Fly and D. Harbrecht. por *Bus Week* p61 My 18 '87

Of many things. G. W. Hunt. *America* 156:inside cover My 23 '87

On the zipper beat. *New Repub* 196:4+ My 25 '87

Political battles over trade wars. W. Shapiro. il pors *Time* 129:24 My 4 '87

Politics: a change of Hart. C. O'Connor. il por *Newsweek* 109:27 F 23 '87

Preaching & practice. D. R. Carlin, Jr. *Commonweal* 114:342-3 Je 5 '87

The press, the process, and Gary Hart [address, May 29, 1987] O. C. Henkel. *Vital Speeches Day* 53:697-700 S 1 '87

Private lives and public people. M. McDonald. il por *Macleans* 100:28-9 S 21 '87

Private lives, public values. M. Greenfield. il *Newsweek* 109:92 My 18 '87

Private sex and public exposure. G. Bain. il *Macleans* 100:48 My 25 '87

The public and the private Gary Hart. J. M. Wall. *Christ Century* 104:483-4 My 20-27 '87

Pumping policy [cover story] M. Kondracke. *New Repub* 196:13-14+ My 18 '87

The return of Gary Hart. I. Austen. il por *Macleans* 100:42 D 28 '87

The same old questions about a new candidacy. K. T. Walsh. il pors *U S News World Rep* 102:22-3 Ap 20 '87

Sex, privacy and journalism. T. Griffith. il por *Time* 129:90 Je 8 '87

Should the press play vice cop? [cover story] N. Von Hoffman. *Nation* 244:835+ Je 20 '87

Sluicegate. H. Hertzberg. *New Repub* 196:11-12 Je 1 '87

The sting of scandal [cover story; special section; with editorial comment by Kevin Doyle] il pors *Macleans* 100:2, 24-8+ My 18 '87

The sudden fall of Gary Hart [cover story; special section] il pors *Newsweek* 109:22-8+ My 18 '87

A visitation of phantoms. M. Kaus. il pors *Newsweek* 110:32-3 S 21 '87

Why it hurts: the murky worlds of Hart and Secord raise painful questions about what America expects of its leaders and institutions. R. Stengel. il *Time* 129:14-15 My 18 '87

Winning hearts through minds. R. Stengel. il por *Time* 129:24-5 F 16 '87

X-rated politicians: going public with private lies. B. G. Harrison. *Mademoiselle* 93:234 S '87

Anecdotes, facetiae, satire, etc.

A truly Hart-stopping chickadee. A. Fotheringham. il *Macleans* 100:56 My 18 '87

Hart, Jeffrey

How dark a horse? *Natl Rev* 39:16 Ag 28 '87

The ivory foxhole. See occasional issues of National Review beginning September 26, 1986

The New York intellectuals & the socialist legacy. *Natl Rev* 39:58+ S 11 '87

Hart, Joe

about

Time travel. B. Lawren. il *Omni* 10:20+ N '87

Hart, Kathleen

Is mother's milk safe? Dioxin climbs to the top of the food chain. il *Progressive* 51:32-4 Mr '87

Hart, Lee

about

After sticking with a troubled marriage, Lee Hart watches a dream die. M. Green. il pors *People Wkly* 27:38-40 My 25 '87

'I'd have told her to leave the jerk'. il por *Newsweek* 110:16 D 28 '87

Lee Hart's ordeal. C. O'Connor. il por *Newsweek* 109:31 My 18 '87

Lee: "It was hell". M. Hornblower. il por *Time* 130:19 D 28 '87

Hart, Mary

about

Beyond meat and potatoes. L. Kleinmann. por *Health* 19:40 Jl '87

Hart, Mary—about—cont.
Entertainment tonight hides Mary Hart's gams, and it's one leg-pull her fans could do without. J. Ash. il pors *People Wkly* 28:103-4 S 7 '87
Hart, Mickey
about
Bill Kreutzmann/Mickey Hart: Rhythm Devils. C. Vaughan. il pors *Down Beat* 11:23-5 N '87
Hart, Rose Mary
I can no longer remain a bystander. il *Commonweal* 114:556-7 O 9 '87
Hart Mountain National Antelope Refuge (Or.) *See* Wildlife sanctuaries—Oregon
Hartcher, Peter
Absentee fathers. il *World Press Rev* 34:59 O '87
Hartford, Bill
Imports. See issues of Popular Mechanics
Hartford (Conn.)
Galleries and museums
See also
Wadsworth Atheneum
Historic houses, sites, etc.
See also
Mark Twain Memorial (Hartford, Conn.)
Politics and government
New England's 1st black mayor to step down at end of his third term [T. L. Milner] por *Jet* 72:29 Ag 10 '87
Hartford Ballet
Reviews:
Winter season in Hartford. M. S. Gaylin. *Dance Mag* 61:78+ S '87
Harth, E., and others
The inversion of sensory processing by feedback pathways: a model of visual cognitive functions. bibl f il *Science* 237:184-7 Jl 10 '87
Hartle, Anthony E.
Reflections on war. por *Humanist* 47:41-2 Ja/F '87
Hartley, Craig H.
A remote camera trigger for under $5! il *Petersens Photogr Mag* 15:68-70 F '87
Hartley, John T., Jr.
about
Why Harris has to make it outside the Pentagon. G. DeGeorge. il por *Bus Week* p138-9 N 2 '87
Hartley, Mariette
about
17 hours with Mariette Hartley. L. Eisenberg. il pors *Good Housekeep* 204:180-1+ My '87
Hartline, Daniel K.
(jt. auth) See Graubard, Katherine, and Hartline, Daniel K.
Hartman, Arthur
about
'Preventable'—in hindsight [interview] por *U S News World Rep* 102:38 Ap 27 '87
Washington diarist. L. Wieseltier. *New Repub* 196:42 My 11 '87
'We're in an entirely new era' [interview] por *U S News World Rep* 102:39 F 2 '87
Hartman, Elizabeth, d. 1987
about
Elizabeth Hartman. M. Ryan. il pors *People Wkly* 28:135-7+ S 7 '87
Hartman, Terri
Do you see yourself as others do? il *Teen* 31:16+ Mr '87
Great hometown adventures. il *Teen* 31:28+ Je '87
Lying: how much is too much? il *Teen* 31:34+ S '87
Hartmarx Corporation
A new cut for the gray flannel. S. B. Weiner. il *Forbes* 140:61+ D 28 '87
A retailored Hartmarx still needs some altering. M. D. Oneal. il *Bus Week* p109 Mr 9 '87
Hartnett, Robert C., 1904-1987
about
Obituary
America 156:63 Ja 31 '87
Hartray, John F., 1930-
about
The apprentice system: should it make a comeback? M. F. Schmertz. *Archit Rec* 175:9 N '87
Hartsfield International Airport *See* Atlanta (Ga.)—Airports
Hartt, Frederick, 1914-
about
A model for David? J. Tully. il *Art News* 86:53-4 Summ '87
Hartt, Stanley
about
The rise of the man behind the budget. B. Wallace. il por *Macleans* 100:10 Mr 2 '87

Hartung, William D.
Nations vie for arms markets. bibl f il *Bull At Sci* 43:27-35 D '87
The Reagan revival of arms deals. bibl f il *Bull At Sci* 43:20-5 Jl/Ag '87
Hartwell, George
Dolphin talk [interview with D. Reiss] *Oceans* 20:62-3 Mr/Ap '87
Hartwell, Leland H.
(jt. auth) See Koshland, Douglas, and Hartwell, Leland H.
Hartz Mountain Corporation
From birdseed to the Meadowlands [L. Stern] N. J. Perry. il por *Fortune* 116:122 S 28 '87
Hartzell, Stephen H.
(jt. auth) See Heaton, Thomas H., and Hartzell, Stephen H.
Hartzmark, Gini
Skin. il *Ms* 15:74+ Ap '87
Harvard (Mass.)
Galleries and museums
See also
Fruitlands Museums (Harvard, Mass.)
Harvard Business School *See* Harvard University. Graduate School of Business Administration
Harvard law review
The tyranny of beauty [Adam Cohen's article on facial discrimination] *New Repub* 197:4 O 12 '87
Harvard Law School
Black Harvard professor protests tenure policy [views of D. Bell] *Jet* 72:28 Je 29 '87
Harvard University
And you thought Harvard was only keen on Keynes [economist R. Barro appointed to faculty] N. Jonas. il por *Bus Week* p78+ S 7 '87
The CIA-Harvard controversy over secrecy. T. A. Idinopulos. il *USA Today (Periodical)* 115:38-40 My '87
Harvard to the rescue [divestiture of portfolio in South Africa; candidates for overseer] W. F. Buckley. *Natl Rev* 39:58 Jl 3 '87
Longhorns 8, Crimson 4 [endowments] W. P. Barrett. il *Forbes* 140:116+ O 19 '87
The quality of the university today: an exchange at Harvard [address, October 1986] W. J. Bennett; D. C. Bok. *Current* 291:4-11 Mr/Ap '87
Tainted money: the ethics and rhetoric of divestment [colleges and business] R. L. Payton. il *Change* 19:55-60 My/Je '87
Harvard University. American Repertory Theatre
Disorientation as an art form. W. A. Henry. il *Time* 129:75 Ja 12 '87
Harvard University. Botanical Museum
Forever flowers of glass and magic [Ware Collection of Blaschka Glass Models] L. Ware. il *Audubon* 89:96-109 My '87
Harvard University. Dumbarton Oaks *See* Dumbarton Oaks
Harvard University. Graduate School of Business Administration
Banking on ethics [J. S. R. Shad's endowment for business ethics studies] *Time* 129:79 Ap 13 '87
Business is his business [black professor J. I. Cash] il pors *Ebony* 42:31-3+ O '87
Ethics 101: can the good guys win? [J. S. R. Shad funds business ethics program] B. Brophy. il por *U S News World Rep* 102:54 Ap 13 '87
Ethics for greedheads. F. Zakaria. *New Repub* 197:18+ O 19 '87
Gatsby at the B school [use of fiction in business ethics course] R. Coles. *N Y Times Book Rev* 92:1+ O 25 '87
Harvard's $30 million windfall for ethics 101 [J. S. R. Shad's gift] J. A. Byrne. por *Bus Week* p40 Ap 13 '87
Harvard's capitalist experiment [Jeffrey L. Cruikshank's A delicate experiment] P. Baida. il *Am Herit* 38:20-1 D '87
New debate about Harvard Business School [cover story] W. Kiechel, III. il *Fortune* 116:34-6+ N 9 '87
Shad the lawgiver [J. S. R. Shad's gift] D. Seligman. il *Fortune* 115:154 My 11 '87
A teacher who made a difference [G. F. Doriot] P. Fuhrman. il por *Forbes* 140:362+ Jl 13 '87
Harvard University. Graduate School of Design
Architectural education: what kinds do practicing architects want? [professional development courses] W. S. Saunders. por *Archit Rec* 175:45 Jl '87
Harvard University. Hasty Pudding Club *See* Hasty Pudding Club

Harvard University. John Fitzgerald Kennedy School of Government *See* John Fitzgerald Kennedy School of Government

Harvest festivals *See* Festivals

Harvesting

See also
  Corn—Harvesting
  Grain—Harvesting

Harvesting machinery

Amphibious combine. C. Finck. il *Success Farm* 85:56H N '87

Combines: bigger on the inside. C. Finck. il *Success Farm* 85:14-17 S '87

'Flight simulator' helps you learn to pilot combine [Deere's HarvesTrainer] D. Mowitz. il *Success Farm* 85:18 Ag '87

Harvey, Andrew, 1952-

Infidelity: Italian (and Russian) style. il pors *Vogue* 177:442-3+ O '87

Journey to Pagan. il *House Gard* 159:72+ Mr '87

Harvey, Carol

How to make every bite count. il *Women's Sports Fitness* 9:12 My '87

Harvey, Cynthia

about

Harvey's Royal stint: "like Fonteyn in overdrive". S. Greco. il por *Dance Mag* 61:4 Mr '87

Harvey, Donald

about

Lethal doses. por *Time* 130:17 Ag 24 '87

Harvey, Fred

about

How good food and Harvey 'skirts' won the West. J. A. Cox. il *Smithsonian* 18:130-4+ S '87

Harvey, James R.

about

Stalking Transamerica. E. Paris. il por *Forbes* 140:55 S 21 '87

Harvey, John

The Sugar Ray of his day. il por *Sports Illus* 66:83 Mr 30 '87

Harvey, John Collins

Diagnosing the Vatican 'Instruction'. *Commonweal* 114:238-9 Ap 24 '87

Harvey, John W., and others

GONG: to see inside our sun [cover story] il map *Sky Telesc* 74:470-6 N '87

Harvey, Jonathan, 1939-

about

Musical events:
  American premiere of J. Harvey's Bhakti. A. Porter. *New Yorker* 63:121 D 14 '87

Harvey, Paul, 1918-

More of Paul Harvey's Rest of the story [condensation]; ed. by Paul Aurandt. il *Read Dig* 130:17-18+ F '87

"Sold! to the young man in shorts". il *Read Dig* 131:265-6 N '87

Harvey, Stephen

25th New York Film Festival. il *Film Comment* 23:60+ N/D '87

Harvey, William B.

An ebony view of the ivory power: memories of a black faculty member. *Change* 19:46-9 My/Je '87

Harvey (Fred) Company *See* Fred Harvey Company

Harvey (Ill.)

Employees

Harvey, Ill., woman sues township for $900,000 [employment discrimination suit brought by C. Ladner] *Jet* 72:8 S 7 '87

Harwell, Christine C.

(jt. auth) See Harwell, Mark A., and Harwell, Christine C.

Harwell, Mark A., and Harwell, Christine C.

Updating the "nuclear winter" debate. *Bull At Sci* 43:42-4 O '87

Harwood, Linda

about

Winning at beauty. il pors *Teen* 31:74-7 Jl '87

Harwood, Michael

Through the eye of the beholder. il *Nat Hist* 96:24-9 D '87

Harwood, Richard T.

Wisdom from the well. il *Mother Earth News* 108:8+ N/D '87

Harwood, Suzanne P.

Full moons and white men. il *Ms* 16:103 O '87

Hary, David, and others

The Asyst software for scientific computing. bibl f il *Science* 236:1128-32 My 29 '87

Hasbro Inc.

Marketing [views of Hasbro vice president S. Schwartz] *New Yorker* 63:28-9 F 23 '87

Haseltine, Robert W.

Perils of a new minimum wage. il *USA Today (Periodical)* 116:21 Jl '87

Hash House Harriers (Organization)

Games runners play. J. Cohen. il *Women's Sports Fitness* 9:70-1 My '87

Hashemi, Mehdi

about

An execution in Tehran. K. Scanlon and C. Jerome. il por *Macleans* 100:32 O 12 '87

Hashing (Computer science)

Look it up faster with hashing. J. C. Snader. bibl il *Byte* 12:128-30+ Ja '87

Hasidism

'Farbrengen' my baby back home [cablecast of Lubavitcher gatherings] M. Pally. il por *Film Comment* 23:75-7 My/Je '87

Haskell, Francis, 1928-

The artist and the museum. il *N Y Rev Books* 34:38-42 D 3 '87

Haskell, Molly

People are talking about . . . movies. See issues of Vogue

Haskins, Clemette

about

Clemette Haskins breaks dad's mark at W. Kentucky. il por *Jet* 72:46 Ap 6 '87

Hassan bin Talal, Crown Prince of Jordan

about

A voice of hope and moderation [interview] H. Mackenzie. il por *Macleans* 100:21 Je 22 '87

Hassanal Bolkiah, Sultan of Brunei, 1946-

about

Brunei's free-spending sultan of oil. L. Kraar. il pors *Fortune* 116:132-3 O 12 '87

His $10 million contra-bution got lost, but to the Sultan of Brunei it was (sigh) only money. M. Wilhelm. il pors *People Wkly* 27:32-3 Je 1 '87

Hasse, Margaret, 1950-

Local arts councils as advocates. *Des Arts Educ* 88:42-4 N/D '86

Hassner, Pierre

One way to arms-control unity: twist allied arms. il *U S News World Rep* 102:24-5 Je 22 '87

Hassrick, Peter H.

Painting the American frontier [excerpt from American frontier life] il *Nat Hist* 96:36-41 My '87

Hastings, Alcee L.

about

A brief for impeachment. il por *U S News World Rep* 102:9 Mr 30 '87

Hastings: critics are motivated by racism. por *Jet* 71:29 F 16 '87

Judge fights impeachment. L. Brown. il por *Black Enterp* 18:18 Ag '87

Judge Hastings faces congressional hearing on charges of bribery. por *Jet* 73:6+ N 2 '87

Hasty Pudding Club

Baryshnikov a strong but silent Man of the Year. D. Cox. por *Dance Mag* 61:7 My '87

Hat pins *See* Hatpins

Hata, Shingo, and others

Identification of putative human T cell receptor δ complementary DNA clones. bibl f il *Science* 238:678-82 O 30 '87

Hatch, Orrin G.

Anecdotes, facetiae, satire, etc.

Senator Hatch questions Al Capone. N. Glixon. il *Commonweal* 114:436 Ag 14 '87

Hatch, Peter J., 1949-

about

In Mr. Jefferson's garden. P. L. Hudson. il por *Americana* 14:50-5 Ja/F '87

Hatch, Robert W.

about

Putting the yeast back into profits. R. Simon. il por *Forbes* 139:62+ F 9 '87

Hatcher, Barbara

Let yourself go! [adaptation of address, December 19, 1986] *Read Dig* 131:169-70 N '87

Living with abandon! [address, December 19, 1986] *Vital Speeches Day* 53:296-7 Mr 1 '87

Hatcher, Billy

about

Astros' Hatcher uses bat of teammate; later ejected because it was corked. por *Jet* 72:46 S 21 '87

Hatcher, Peter
Confronting the problem. il *World Press Rev* 34:13-15 Ag '87
Hatcheries *See* Fish culture
Hatch's #7 (Denver, Colo.: Bookstore) *See* Booksellers and bookselling—Colorado
Hate
See also
Misogyny
Hate mail
Poison-pen mail [anti-gay form letters] *Harpers* 275:16+ S '87
Hatfield, Densie Webb
Nutrition/fitness. See issues of McCall's beginning March 1986
Hatfield, Richard B.
about
Clean sweep [cover story; special section; with editorial comment by Kevin Doyle] il pors *Macleans* 100:2, 14-16+ O 26 '87
Hatfield's toughest fight. K. Harley. il por *Macleans* 100:13 S 14 '87
A very political mistress. A. Fotheringham. il *Macleans* 100:64 N 2 '87
Hatfield, Ted
about
Double-barreled beauty. G. Norman. il *Esquire* 108:43-4 S '87
Hathaway, Maggie
about
Essence woman. F. Newby and R. D. Manuel. por *Essence* 17:26 F '87
Hathaway, Rufus, 1770-1822
about
Rufus Hathaway, artist and physician. L. Valentine and N. F. Little. bibl f il *Antiques* 131:628-41 Mr '87
Hatpins
Collectors and collecting
In praise of pins [collection of L. Baker] D. Reed. il por *Americana* 15:30-4 My/Je '87
Hats
See also
Hatpins
Straw hats
Bolivia's crowning glory [regional styles of hats] K. Hickman. il *Américas* 39:22-5+ Jl/Ag '87
The cowboy hat. J. Berendt. il *Esquire* 107:16+ F '87
The homburg. J. Berendt. il *Esquire* 107:32+ Ap '87
Milliner for an unknown planet, Phillipe Ruise tests the limits of weird. C. Ruskin. il por *People Wkly* 27:100-2 Je 15 '87
My mother's Easter hat. J. Monninger. il *Glamour* 85:108+ Ap '87
Purses & plumage. il *Harpers Bazaar* 121:52 D '87
Hatsopoulos, G. N. (George N.)
about
Serendipity. W. Baldwin. il por *Forbes* 140:274+ N 16 '87
Hatsopoulos, George N. *See* Hatsopoulos, G. N. (George N.)
Hatteras Lighthouse *See* Lighthouses
Hattin, Battle of, 1187
Saladin's triumph over the crusader states: the Battle of Hattin, 1187 [cover story] N. Housley. bibl il map *Hist Today* 37:17-23 Jl '87
Hattori Seiko Co. Ltd.
A tough sell? [Seiko's Jean Lassale Swiss watch] K. Murray. il *Forbes* 139:137-8 Mr 9 '87
Hauerwas, Stanley, 1940-
about
The challenge of post-liberal theology. P. Giurlanda. *Commonweal* 114:40-2 Ja 30 '87
Haugan, Mark P., and Will, Clifford M., 1946-
Modern tests of special relativity. il *Phys Today* 40:69-76 My '87
Haugen, Greg
about
Local boy makes good. P. Putnam. il pors *Sports Illus* 66:59 Je 15 '87
Haughey, Charles
about
Hollow victory. por *Time* 129:31 Mr 2 '87
Ireland's right-wing rut. K. Jacobsen. il *New Leader* 70:5-6 Jl 1-15 '87
The Irish Houdini. R. Laver. il por *Macleans* 100:17 Mr 2 '87
Haughey, John C.
Civilizing work. *America* 156:382-4 My 9 '87
Haught, John F.
Is human life only chemistry? *Current* 294:4-7 Jl/Ag '87

Haun, Harry
Oscar's firsts, mosts, and onlys. il *Horizon* 30:11-12 Ap '87
Swoosie [cover story] il pors *Horizon* 30:33-5 Je '87
Haunted houses *See* Ghosts
Haupt (Enid A.) Garden (Washington, D.C.) *See* Enid A. Haupt Garden (Washington, D.C.)
Hauptmann, Bruno Richard
about
The case that will not close. F. Russell. bibl f il por *N Y Rev Books* 34:4+ N 5 '87
Hause, Irene
(jt. auth) *See* Neveux, Michael, and Hause, Irene
Hauser, Ernest O., 1910-
Unforgettable Marc Chagall. il pors *Read Dig* 130:180-7 Je '87
Hauser, Thomas
You and the law. See issues of McCall's
Haustov, Vladimir
about
Stuffs from the steppes. D. M. Lisi. il pors *House Gard* 159:58+ D '87
Haut-Brion Château (Firm) *See* Château Haut-Brion (Firm)
Haut Dog (Firm)
With a new line of suits, formal wear and even (ruff!) lingerie, any hound can put on the dog. il *People Wkly* 28:73 O 5 '87
Hautin-Guiraut, Denis
Exhilaration to disenchantment. *World Press Rev* 34:28 Ap '87
Havana (N.D.)
In North Dakota: the town that wouldn't die. G. Jaynes. il *Time* 129:12-13 Je 15 '87
Havana Biennial
Report from Havana. bibl f il *Art Am* 75:21-3+ Mr '87
Have I got a girl for you! [musical] *See* Musicals, revues, etc.—Reviews—Single works
Havel, Václav
about
The Czechs' defiant playwright. M. Winn. il por *N Y Times Mag* p78-82+ O 25 '87
The regime within [interview]; tr. by A. G. Brain. E. Blair. *Harpers* 274:24+ Je '87
Search for the human dimension [interview] E. Blair. il por *World Press Rev* 34:24-5 My '87
Havemann, Ernst
The exiles [story] il *Atlantic* 260:103-6 N '87
A farm at Raraba [story] il *Atlantic* 259:56-60 Ja '87
My father's son [story] il *Atlantic* 259:48-52 Je '87
Haven, Susan Perkis
Are you at a turning point? *Glamour* 85:168+ N '87
Let's bring back the bad old rules of love. il *Glamour* 85:206 Mr '87
Havener, Robert D.
Scientists: their rewards and humanity. *Science* 237:1281 S 11 '87
Haverhill (Mass.)
Crime
Exercising her right to madness, accused killer Gena Spero poses a legal problem without a solution [pleading insanity] J. S. Kunen. il pors *People Wkly* 28:115-16+ O 5 '87
Havertown (Pa.)
Religious institutions and affairs
The Pope's foot soldiers [B. Frawley and R. Dlugos, parish priests; cover story] J. Buckley. il pors *U S News World Rep* 103:60-4+ S 21 '87
Havill, Eric
Inside the storm. il *Ctry J* 14:40-6 Ag '87
Hawaii
See also
Arts and crafts—Hawaii
Astronomical observatories—Hawaii
Beaches—Hawaii
Birds—Hawaii
Earthquakes—Hawaii
Ecology—Hawaii
Fish—Hawaii
Fishing—Hawaii
Haleakala National Park (Hawaii)
Insects—Hawaii
Kauai (Hawaii)
Kilauea (Hawaii)
Loihi (Hawaii)
Maui (Hawaii)
Molokai (Hawaii)
Motion picture festivals—Hawaii
Resorts—Hawaii

Hawaii—See also—*cont.*
  Restaurants—Hawaii
Industries
See also
Alexander & Baldwin, Inc.
Amfac, Inc.
Castle & Cooke, Inc.
Construction industry—Hawaii
Fish culture—Hawaii
Small business—Hawaii
Social life and customs
See also
Hula (Dance)
The aloha spirit of enterprise. S. Nelton. il *Nations Bus* 75:6 Ag '87

Hawaii in motion pictures
Lights, camera, aloha! On location in Hawaii. A. Satterfield. il map *Travel Holiday* 168:36-41 Ag '87
Hawaii International Film Festival *See* Motion picture festivals—Hawaii
Hawaii Opera Theatre
Honolulu. H. Driver. *Opera News* 52:40 Ag '87
Hawaiian cooking *See* Cooking, Hawaiian
Hawaiian Islands *See* Hawaii
Hawaiian shirts *See* Shirts
Hawes, Elizabeth, 1903-1971
about
Early feminist fashion. B. Berch. il por *Ms* 15:26 Mr '87
Hawes, John H.
Improving the balance of conventional forces in Europe [address, March 27, 1987] *Dep State Bull* 87:18-21 Jl '87
Hawk, Cynthia
about
Mich. mom flees crime, is stopped by racism. *Jet* 72:16 Ag 3 '87
Hawk, Tony
about
Teenager Tony Hawk soars above everybody in the scary sport of skateboarding. B. Manning. il pors *People Wkly* 27:48-9 Mr 23 '87
Hawke, Robert J. L. (Robert James Lee), 1929-
about
Hawke's sweeping victory. P. Kopvillem. il por *Macleans* 100:25 Jl 20 '87
Hawken, Paul
about
A 'New Age' look at business [interview] P. Dworkin. por *U S News World Rep* 103:51 N 30 '87
Hawkes, G. W.
At the walls of Jericho [story] il *Atlantic* 260:79-82 O '87
Hawkes, Melanie
about
Roving the deep. il por map *Natl Geogr World* 144:6-11 Ag '87
Hawkeye Bancorporation
Back from the brink. C. Siler. il por *Forbes* 140:8 Ag 24 '87
Hawking, S. W. (Stephen W.)
Stephen Hawking on the arrows: excerpts from a timely lecture. il por *Discover* 8:70-1 F '87
about
Genius unbound. R. Morais. il por *Forbes* 139:142 Mr 23 '87
'He loves life'. L. Fleischer. *Publ Wkly* 232:56 O 16 '87
Hawking, Stephen W. *See* Hawking, S. W. (Stephen W.)
Hawkins, Erick
about
Reviews:
  Performances at the Joyce Theater, New York City. C. Hardy. *Dance Mag* 61:40-2 F '87
Hawkins, Hersey
about
He won his case on a higher court. J. Garrity. il por *Sports Illus* 67 Sp Issue:91 N 18 '87
Hawkins, Paula
Is the administration approach to federal employee drug testing sound? [excerpts from address, September 25, 1986] *Congr Dig* 66:138+ My '87
Hawkins, Ted, 1936-
about
Hell and back. K. Loder. il por *Roll Stone* p30+ Jl 16-30 '87
Hawkins, Trip *See* Hawkins, William M.
Hawkins, William J.
Electronics newsfront. See issues of Popular Science beginning February 1986
What's new in electronics. See issues of Popular Science

Hawkins, William M.
How CD-I will change our use of computers. por *Pers Comput* 11:246 O '87
about
Trip Hawkins wants to be the Walt Disney of software. R. Brandt. il por *Bus Week* p134 N 9 '87
Hawkins, William R.
Free trade is no free lunch. *Natl Rev* 39:38-9 Ag 28 '87
Hawkins (Erick) Dance Company *See* Erick Hawkins Dance Company
Hawks
See also
Ospreys
Photographs and photography
One picture . . . [red-shouldered hawk and garter snake] J. McDonald. il *Audubon* 89:80-1 Ja '87
Hawley, Anne
Improving the cultural climate. *Des Arts Educ* 88:15-16 N/D '86
Hawley, Richard A.
Schoolchildren and drugs: the fancy that has not passed. il *Phi Delta Kappan* 68:K1-K8 My '87
Hawley, V. Guy
Training rural-based nurses. il *World Health* p12-15 My '87
Hawley, William A., and others
Aedes albopictus in North America: probable introduction in used tires from northern Asia. bibl f il *Science* 236:1114-16 My 29 '87
Hawley Group, Inc.
The British raider who sneaked up on ADT [M. Ashcroft] M. Maremont. il por *Bus Week* p33+ Ag 31 '87
Cleaning up. A. A. Lappen. il por *Forbes* 139:118 Je 15 '87
Haws, Buck
The gamecockers' call to arms. *Harpers* 275:34 O '87
Hawthorne, Sophia Amelia Peabody, 1811-1871
about
Three sisters who showed the way. M. Marshall. il pors *Am Herit* 38:58-63+ S/O '87
Hay, James M.
The public face of the chemical industry [address, November 11, 1986] *Vital Speeches Day* 53:178-80 Ja 1 '87
Hay, John, 1915-
about
Closely watched terns. J. Page. il *Oceans* 20:65 N/D '87
Hay
The best forage grower in Indiana [David Forgey] J. R. Borcherding. il *Success Farm* 85:56-7 Ag '87
Drying
Mat-maker speeds hay drying. *Success Farm* 85:66G S '87
Harvesting
See Hay handling
Preservation and preservatives
How to pick and use hay desiccants and preservatives. J. R. Borcherding. il *Success Farm* 85:70B Ag '87
Prices
Record production drives down hay prices. *Success Farm* 85 no3:18AJ F '87
Hay fever
Ah-choo! C. Schaeffer. *Changing Times* 41:16 O '87
Hay handling
Making hay. J. D. Randolph. il *Ctry J* 14:4-5 Je '87
Equipment
See also
Baling machinery
Hay making *See* Hay handling
Hayakawa, S. I.
Why English should be our official language. *Educ Dig* 52:36-7 My '87
Hayashi, Chikara
Ultrafine particles. bibl il *Phys Today* 40:44-51 D '87
Haydée, Marcia
about
The sleeping beauty [ballet] Reviews
  Dance Mag il 61:20 Ag '87. H. Koegler
Hayden, Bruce P.
(jt. auth) See Michaels, Patrick J., and Hayden, Bruce P.
Hayden, J. G.
Superintendent-school board conflict: working it out. *Educ Dig* 52:11-13 Ap '87
Hayden, Tom
about
Jane Fonda & Tom Hayden [interview] D. Sheff. pors *Roll Stone* p123-4+ N 5-D 10 '87

Haydn, Joseph, 1732-1809
about
Haydn seekers. P. G. Davis. il *N Y* 20:125 My 4 '87
Haydn, Lili
about
Lili and Lotus. il pors *Teen* 31:60 D '87
Hayes, Charles
about
What makes a survivor? M. Kuntz. il por *Forbes* 139:77 Ja 26 '87
Hayes, Colleen Ballard
Blue and Gray Virginia: commemorating battles of a nation divided. il map *Travel Holiday* 167:52-5+ Je '87
Kangaroo Island. il *Travel Holiday* 168:26-9 S '87
Washington and Lincoln slept here. il maps *Travel Holiday* 167:46-50 F '87
Hayes, David
about
Overloaded. *New Yorker* 62:28-31 F 9 '87
Hayes, Del
Acid trip. il *Flying* 114:99 Je '87
Hayes, Isaac
about
A conversation with . . . Isaac Hayes. J. Simmons. por *Essence* 18:33 Jl '87
Isaac Hayes talks about his third comeback. il pors *Jet* 71:22-3 Mr 9 '87
Hayes, Jack
Air cleaners: the inside story. il *Saturday Evening Post* 259:30-1 Ja/F '87
Blowing away the ceiling fan myths. il *Saturday Evening Post* 259:28-9 S '87
Exercise for homebodies. il *Saturday Evening Post* 259:26 Jl/Ag '87
Furnaces go underground. il *Saturday Evening Post* 259:28+ D '87
Home, secure home. il *Saturday Evening Post* 259:30+ Ap '87
New ceilings: looking up. il *Saturday Evening Post* 259:32 My/Je '87
The race for inner space. il *Saturday Evening Post* 259:30-1 Mr '87
Warming up to heat pumps. il *Saturday Evening Post* 259:20 N '87
Window with a view to the future. il *Saturday Evening Post* 259:28+ O '87
Hayes, Kim F., 1953-, and others
In situ X-ray absorption study of surface complexes: selenium oxyanions on α-FeOOH. bibl f il *Science* 238:783-6 N 6 '87
Hayes, Mary Cartledge- *See* Cartledge-Hayes, Mary
Hayes, Mike
about
Mike Hayes learns that tuition is just common cents. il por *People Wkly* 28:154 N 16 '87
Plea for pennies turns up $14,000 for college student attending U. of Illinois. *Jet* 73:24 O 26 '87
Hayes, Peter, 1953-, and others
Korean tripwire. *Nation* 245:256-7 S 19 '87
Hayes, William J.
about
Still prescribing drug stocks [interview] A. E. Serwer. il por *Fortune* 115:112 F 16 '87
Hayes, Woody
about
Obituary
Sports Illus il 66:94 Mr 23 '87. R. Telander
Haying *See* Hay handling
Hayman, Francis, 1708-1776
about
British painting. S. B. Sherrill. il *Antiques* 131:746 Ap '87
Haymet, A. D. J.
Freezing. bibl f il *Science* 236:1076-80 My 29 '87
Haymon, Alan
about
Eddie Murphy's dad and black promoter now book comedian's concert tour. il pors *Jet* 73:28-30 O 19 '87
Haynes, Gary
Where elephants die. il *Nat Hist* 96:28-33 Je '87
Haynes, Henry D., 1920-1971
See also
Homer and Jethro
Haynes, Lloyd, 1934-1986
about
Despite cancer, Haynes played his ABC soap role. por *Jet* 71:61 F 2 '87
Obituary
Jet il por 71:18 Ja 19 '87

Haynes, Wesley
Windows: techniques for restoration and replacement. il *Archit Rec* 175:150-65 Je '87
Haynes Environmental Systems, Inc.
Haynes offers PC-based weather, flight plan system [WeatherStar satellite information system] *Aviat Week Space Technol* 126:100 My 25 '87
Hays, Carole Shorenstein *See* Shorenstein Hays, Carole
Hays, Charlotte
'And the greatest of these is social justice'. *Natl Rev* 39:36+ D 31 '87
Hays, Daniel
about
Passage at Cape Horn. A. Smith. il pors *Esquire* 107:88-90+ Mr '87
Hays, David
about
Passage at Cape Horn. A. Smith. il pors *Esquire* 107:88-90+ Mr '87
Hayton, Bea
A fishy tale that's true. il *Curr Health 2* 13:14-16 Mr '87
Food foolers and other little-known facts about food. il *Curr Health 2* 13:24-7 Ja '87
Keeping stress at bay the nutritious way. il *Curr Health 2* 14:16-19 O '87
Salad bars: as good as they look? il *Curr Health 2* 14:14-16 S '87
Hayward, Brooke
It's all relative. *Harpers Bazaar* 121:126-7+ D '87
Thomas and Nan Kempner in New York: evolution of a Park Avenue apartment. il por *Archit Dig* 44:166-71+ My '87
about
California in focus. D. Thomson. il por *House Gard* 159:140-5+ Ag '87
Hayward, T.
(jt. auth) See Craig, H., and Hayward, T.
Hayworth, Rita, 1918-1987
about
Honoring her stricken mother, Rita Hayworth, Yasmin Khan stages a dazzling benefit. il pors *People Wkly* 27:36-7 My 25 '87
Obituary
Time por 129:76 My 25 '87. G. Clarke
Remembering Rita [cover story] il pors *People Wkly* 27:72-6+ Je 1 '87
Yasmin Khan: my mother, Rita Hayworth. C. Ford. il pors *McCalls* 114:138-9+ My '87
Hazan, Marcella
about
La professoressa della cucina. C. Hemphill. il por *House Gard* 159:24+ My '87
Hazardous substances
See also
Asbestos
Chemicals
Poisons and poisoning
Accidents and explosions
See also
Rhine River chemical spills, 1986
Airborne toxic releases: are communities prepared? S. L. Cutter. bibl f il map *Environment* 29:12-17+ Jl/Ag '87
Disposal
See also
Citizen's Clearinghouse for Hazardous Wastes, Inc.
Love Canal case
Radioactive waste disposal
Trade waste—Disposal
Waste disposal in the ocean
Before you throw it out, read this! [household products] S. Berkman. il *Good Housekeep* 204:254 Ap '87
Decontaminating federal facilities: the case of the Rocky Mountain Arsenal [with editorial comment by Wallace N. Quintrell] K. B. Wiley and S. L. Rhodes. bibl f il maps *Environment* 29:2-3, 16-20+ Ap '87
The greening of DOE. E. Marshall. *Science* 235:1315 Mr 13 '87
The homes that stopped polluting. S. Milius. il *Rodale's Org Gard* 34:28-32 Jl '87
Poisons in your home: a disposal dilemma. A. Schwartz. il *Audubon* 89:12-16 My '87
What to do with our waste. W. D. Marbach. il *Newsweek* 110:51-2 Jl 27 '87
Laws and regulations
Environmental crime: putting offenders behind bars. D. Wann. bibl f il *Environment* 29:5+ O '87
The export of U.S. toxic wastes [cover story] A. Porterfield and D. Weir. il *Nation* 245:325+ O 3 '87

Hazardous substances—Disposal—Laws and regulations
—cont.
A nasty scrap over toxic household waste. J. O. Hamilton
and M. Bluestone. il *Bus Week* p35-6 S 21 '87
Export-import trade
The export of U.S. toxic wastes [cover story] A. Porterfield
and D. Weir. il *Nation* 245:325+ O 3 '87
Labeling
A nasty scrap over toxic household waste. J. O. Hamilton
and M. Bluestone. il *Bus Week* p35-6 S 21 '87
Haze
Air pollution by particles. R. W. Shaw. bibl (p116)
il *Sci Am* 257:96-103 Ag '87
Hazelnut trees *See* Filbert trees
Hazelton, Lynette
Buying to rent. il *Black Enterp* 18:85-6+ O '87
Philadelphia: a big city with small-town appeal. il *Black
Enterp* 17:71-2+ My '87
Securing the home front while you're away. il *Black
Enterp* 17:91 Jl '87
Hazelton, Nika
Delectations. See occasional issues of National Review
Hazelwood (Mo.)
Education
A civics lesson at Hazelwood East [principal of high
school censors student newspaper; Supreme Court case]
S. Visser. il *Nation* 245:441-2 O 24 '87
From Hazelwood to the High Court [principal of high
school deletes articles from school newspaper] M. A.
Uhlig. il *N Y Times Mag* p100-7 S 13 '87
Hazle, Albert J.
Colorado: the legacy of uranium mining. il *Environment*
29:13+ Ja/F '87
Hazzard, Shirley, 1931-
The place to be [story] *New Yorker* 63:26-36+ Je
29 '87
HBO *See* Home Box Office
HDLs (High density lipoproteins) *See* Lipoproteins
HDM Worldwide (Firm)
Japan is getting too small for Dentsu. T. Holden and
A. Dunkin. il *Bus Week* p62+ O 26 '87
HDTV *See* High definition television
He-Man (Fictional character)
Although lacking a movie deal, the Wadsworths (He-
and She-) find they still have the power. D. Van
Biema. il pors *People Wkly* 27:87+ My 4 '87
Head, James, and Crumpler, L. S.
Evidence for divergent plate-boundary characteristics and
crustal spreading on Venus. bibl f il maps *Science*
238:1380-5 D 4 '87
Head
See also
Craniometry
Face
Wounds and injuries
Hard knocks [head injuries of inner city children; work
of George E. Locke and others] *Sci Am* 256:30 Je
'87
Real trouble ahead [hit in head with mattock] J. McClin-
tock. il *N Y Times Mag* p40 Ag 9 '87
Head in art
See also
Portrait painting
Head Start Project (U.S.) *See* Project Head Start (U.S.)
Head tax *See* Poll tax
Head tax (Airline passengers) *See* Air travel—Taxation
Head-up display systems *See* Air navigation—Aids and
devices
Headache
All about headaches. J. Greif. il *N Y* 20:56-8+ Mr 9
'87
Beating headaches cold [study by Seymour Diamond]
J.-B. Shoemaker. il *Health* 19:21 Ja '87
Best remedies for your special kind of headache. G.
Maleskey. *Prevention* 39:65-7 Ag '87
Doctors close in on the mechanisms behind headache
[migraine] E. Kiester. il *Smithsonian* 18:175-6+ D '87
Headache relief hitched to marital therapy [work of
Ranjan Roy] *Prevention* 39:32 Ap '87
Headaches. K. Glenn. il *Seventeen* 46:270-1+ Mr '87
Headaches [cover story] M. Clark. bibl il *Newsweek*
110:76-82 D 7 '87
Headaches [cover story] L. Stanwood. il *Curr Health*
2 13:3-9 My '87
How to outsmart a headache. L. F. McCarthy. il
Mademoiselle 93:116+ Mr '87
Just another swallow away [doses for tension headache]
F. Lunzer. il *Forbes* 139:224 My 18 '87
Music hath charms to soothe a throbbing head [migraine
treatment; research by Janet Lapp] P. Chance. il *Psychol
Today* 21:14 F '87

Now here's a real headache for lovers [sex-induced
headaches] il *Discover* 8:12+ F '87
Penetrating the mystery of migraine. B. Clayman. il
Nations Bus 75:71-2 Jl '87
Postexercise headaches. P. Ennis. il *Women's Sports
Fitness* 9:14 Ag '87
Treating tension headaches. M. J. Porcelli. il *Essence*
18:12+ My '87
When two aspirin aren't enough [headache clinics] P.
Angiolillo. il *Bus Week* p94 Ap 20 '87
Women's headaches can be cured with sex. *Jet* 73:35
N 16 '87
Nutritional aspects
Forbidden foods. S. Baker. il *Health* 19:55-6 My '87
Headboards *See* Beds
Headgear
See also
Hats
Headhunters, Corporate *See* Executive search consultants
Headington (England)
Architecture
Listen, if there are flying fish, there are bound to be
accidents [B. Heine sticks shark sculpture into roof
of his home] il por *People Wkly* 27:66 Mr 2 '87
Headlam, Stewart Duckworth, 1847-1924
about
Stewart Headlam and the Christian Socialists. E. Norman.
bibl il por *Hist Today* 37:27-32 Ap '87
Headlights, Automobile *See* Automobiles—Lighting
Headlines, Newspaper *See* Newspapers—Headlines
Headphones
Beyer DT 990 headphones. J. D. Hirsch. il *Stereo Rev*
52:48+ My '87
Headphone sound. I. Masters. *Stereo Rev* 52:18 Ag '87
Headphones. R. Hodges. il *Stereo Rev* 52:74-8 D '87
A headset of the times [pilots] E. Weiner. il *Flying*
114:74-6 D '87
Sounds of silence [Telex ProAir 2000E] R. L. Collins.
il *Flying* 114:93 Je '87
Headroom, Max (Fictional character) *See* Max Headroom
(Fictional character)
Heads of state
See also
Prime ministers
Official residences
See Official residences
Wives
Gorbo's other woman [role of Soviet leader's wife] G.
Freidin. *New Repub* 197:15-16 D 28 '87
Headsets *See* Headphones
Healey, Denis
A Labour Britain, NATO and the bomb. *Foreign Aff*
65:716-29 Spr '87
Healey, William V.
A note to health-care policy makers. *America* 156:435-6
My 30 '87
Healing
See also
Wound healing
On the mend with arginine. H. Fisher. *Prevention* 39:98+
O '87
Healing, Divine *See* Faith cure
Health
See also
Computers—Medical use
Diet
Environmental health
Exercise
Holistic medicine
Housing and health
Longevity
Medicine
Mental health
Nutrition
Physical fitness
Public health
Relaxation
Sickness
Sleep
See also subheads Care and hygiene; Health and
hygiene under classes of persons or ethnic groups
25 tips for good health and great looks [condensed from
How to become a healthier, prettier you] M. E. Pink-
ham. il *Read Dig* 130:112-14 Ja '87
365 tips for a year of health. L. Eisenberg. il *Good
Housekeep* 204:77-80+ Ja '87
The best tips from America's best health centers. il
Prevention 39:34-6+ D '87
Checkups. See issues of Health (New York, N.Y.)

Health—*cont.*

Detox your body [excerpt from Living health] H. Diamond and M. Diamond. pors *Redbook* 169:84-5+ Jl '87

Five healthy habits that can hurt you. H. Rodale. il *Prevention* 39:50-4 Ja '87

Future youth: how to regenerate your energy [excerpt; with editorial comment by Mark Bricklin] C. Keough. il *Prevention* 39:57, 102+ Jl '87

Health. D. Kaercher. See issues of Better Homes and Gardens

Health. M. Weber. See issues of Vogue

Health and safety risk analyses: information for better decisions. L. B. Lave. bibl f *Science* 236:291-5 Ap 17 '87

Health focus. See issues of Glamour

Health's 1987 annual report [special section] G. Bakoulis. il *Health* 19:25-9+ D '87

The healthy parent. P. Von Nostitz. See issues of Parents beginning January 1987 through September 1987

How to keep your stomach from growling and other things no one else ever tells you. L. Jay. il *Ladies Home J* 104:34+ Ja '87

Just ask us . . . [questions and answers] See issues of Current Health 2

Medical mailbox. C. SerVaas. See issues of The Saturday Evening Post

Medicine and health [cover story; special issue] il *Courier* 40:3-34 Ag '87

Metaphysical hints and tips: how to find health in the strangest places. R. Rodale. il *Prevention* 39:23-5 D '87

A question of health. See issues of Consumer Reports

Regenerative living. M. Golin. See issue of Prevention (Emmaus, Pa.) beginning January 1987

What's new for American families in '87. il *Better Homes Gard* 65:27 Ja '87

Your 10 toughest health questions. M. Mihalik. *Prevention* 39:24+ O '87

Bibliography

Mind/body/health. il *N Y Times Book Rev* 92:34-5 Ap 5 '87

Periodicals

See also

Health (Periodical)

Health (Periodical)

As we see it. H. Herman. See occasional issues of Health (New York, N.Y.)

Health and housing *See* Housing and health

Health and Human Services Dept. (U.S.) *See* United States. Dept. of Health and Human Services

Health and religion *See* Medicine and religion

Health and weather *See* Weather—Mental and physiological effects

Health care *See* Medical care

Health care costs *See* Medical care—Costs

Health care industry *See* Medical care industry

Health care policy *See* Medical policy

Health centers *See* Health facilities

Health clinics *See* Health facilities

Health clubs

See also

Exer-Dance Fitness Center (Butte, Mont.)

LivingWell Inc.

YMCA

All in the family [RiverPlace Athletic Club, Portland, Or.] D. Dietsch. il *Archit Rec* 175:100-5 Ag '87

Beware of fitness club contracts. M. Engel. il *Glamour* 85:92 Ag '87

Know when to jump ship: warning signs of a dying health club. R. B. Taylor. il *Women's Sports Fitness* 9:14 Ag '87

Panting by the numbers [computerized scoring allows members of FitLab health club to compete against each other] M. Maran. *Women's Sports Fitness* 9:54 Jl '87

Picking a place to shape up. H. Edleson. il *Changing Times* 41:51+ Ag '87

Revving up [high tech equipment] L. Wells. *N Y Times Mag* p58 F 15 '87

The right fit in health clubs. P. Haddock. il *Consum Res Mag* 70:35-6 S '87

A wait that's worth the wait [airport health clubs] G. Eichler. il *Esquire* 108:80 S '87

Wash & sweat [Clean & Lean, laundromat-fitness center in Visa, Calif.] *Time* 130:94 N 16 '87

You don't need a great body at L.A.'s cushiest health club, but a big name and fat wallet help [Sports Club/LA] S. K. Reed. il pors *People Wkly* 28:113-14 N 30 '87

Health Communications Inc.

A big bestseller helps a small company grow. D. Masello. il *Publ Wkly* 231:47-8 Ap 17 '87

Health Concepts IV Inc.

The pros say 'yes' to a rehab clinic. G. G. Marcial. *Bus Week* p61 Ag 31 '87

Health education

See also

Health workers—Training

Nutrition education

Physical education and training

AIDS instruction: a troubling test for educators. K. McCormick. *Educ Dig* 53:56-9 S '87

Kids ask about AIDS. P. Krantz. *Better Homes Gard* 65:96+ O '87

Self-management skills and student health practices. R. Petosa. *Educ Dig* 52:56-9 Ja '87

International aspects

Ignorance means risk [health education in food safety] M. Abdussalam. il *World Health* p5-7 Mr '87

Mexico

Children-power in Mexico [immunization program] L. Taylor. il *World Health* p24-5 Ja/F '87

Health examinations *See* Physical examinations

Health facilities

See also

Abortion clinics

Alternative pregnancy centers

Birth control clinics

Group medical practice

Hospitals

Medical laboratories

Mental health centers

Mobile health facilities

TME, Inc.

Trauma care units

Day surgery. F. Lunzer. il *Forbes* 140:105+ Ag 10 '87

"Easier than selling soap" [in vitro fertilization clinics] L. Gubernick. il *Forbes* 139:112+ F 9 '87

New for women: one-stop health care. M. Weber. *Vogue* 177:150+ F '87

Pain centers. S. Levin. *McCalls* 115:80-1 O '87

Total care at the Ms. Mayo clinics [women's health clinics] A. Toufexis. il *Time* 129:86 My 4 '87

When two aspirin aren't enough [headache clinics] P. Angiolillo. il *Bus Week* p94 Ap 20 '87

Administration

Issues for school clinics. L. Edwards and N. Brent. *Educ Dig* 53:52-5 N '87

Architecture

Beyond the hospital: building for a healthier future. G. J. Mann. il por *Futurist* 21:9-10+ Ja/F '87

California

See also

Concord (Calif.)—Health facilities

San Francisco (Calif.)—Health facilities

Florida

See also

Saint Petersburg (Fla.)—Health facilities

Missouri

See also

Saint Louis (Mo.)—Health facilities

New York (State)

See also

Brooklyn (New York, N.Y.)—Health facilities

Ontario

See also

Toronto (Ont.)—Health facilities

Texas

See also

Dallas (Tex.)—Health facilities

Health food *See* Food, Organic

Health food cooking *See* Cooking—Organic food

Health fraud *See* Quacks and quackery

Health insurance *See* Insurance, Health

Health maintenance organizations

See also

International Medical Centers Inc.

Maxicare Health Plans, Inc.

United Healthcare Corp.

Health care in America [address, December 4-5, 1986] F. E. Samuel, Jr. *Vital Speeches Day* 53:335-7 Mr 15 '87

The HMO option: is it best for your health care? B. G. Quint. il *Glamour* 85:120 Ja '87

HMO: the three letters that are revolutionizing health care. M. J. Pitzer. il *Bus Week* p94-6+ Mr 2 '87

How not to control medical costs [gatekeeping] C. M. Lindsay. il por *Fortune* 116:105-6 Jl 6 '87

Health maintenance organizations—*cont.*
In a doctor's wallet [fee for service vs. HMO payment system] R. A. Berenson. *New Repub* 196:11-13 My 18 '87
Second thoughts on HMOs. C. Schaeffer. il *Changing Times* 41:33-4+ My '87
Should you join an HMO? D. S. Stroetzel and D. Stroetzel. *Read Dig* 131:91-5 Ag '87
Strong medicine for health bills [companies bargaining for better deals] S. Gannes. il *Fortune* 115:70-2+ Ap 13 '87

Ethical aspects
The company that has HMOs sick with worry [International Medical Centers Inc.] G. DeGeorge. il *Bus Week* p52 My 11 '87

Securities
HMOs may be moving into the recovery room [views of M. M. LeConey] G. G. Marcial. por *Bus Week* p124 Je 8 '87

Health Management Assoc.
Healthy profits. M. Fritz. il por *Forbes* 140:454 Jl 13 '87

Health news *See* Medical news
Health newsletters *See* Newsletters
Health Protection Branch (Canada) *See* Canada. Health Protection Branch
Health research *See* Medical research
Health resorts, watering places, etc.
See also
Pritikin Longevity Centers
Elite retreats. il *Harpers Bazaar* 120:126+ Ag '87
The hot new '90s spas. D. Schefer. *Vogue* 177:348+ D '87
I learn the secret of the spas. R. Rodale. il *Prevention* 39:20-2+ Mr '87
In search of the perfect spa. S. Lord. *Vogue* 177:349+ D '87
Inside the super spas [with Golden Door diet plan] L. J. Johnson. il *Ladies Home J* 104:96-101+ My '87
Slim chance! New-season shapeup. S. F. Buckmaster. il *Harpers Bazaar* 120:186-7 F '87
Spa spree in your own home. il *Harpers Bazaar* 120:94+ S '87
Spa vacations for two. il *Glamour* 85:288-91 O '87
Spas for the fit life. S. Lord. il *Vogue* 177:372-3+ Ap '87
Time-sparing spas. il *Harpers Bazaar* 120:154 Mr '87
A well-planned retreat. G. Leatherman and P. Porter. il *Women's Sports Fitness* 9:77 N '87

International aspects
Allure of the sea: spa secrets. il *Harpers Bazaar* 120:224-7+ O '87
Spa sprint [short programs] S. Lord. il *Vogue* 177:358+ Ag '87

Arkansas
See also
Eureka Springs (Ark.)

Brazil
Spa in paradise: Búzios, Brazil, the newest "active" getaway. R. Alleman. il *Vogue* 177:224+ O '87

California
Behind the Golden Door. A. Gross. *Vogue* 177:422+ F '87
Fine tuning at the spa [C. Brinkley shaping up at Cal-a-Vie in Vista] C. Tuhy. il pors *Life* 10:68-71+ F '87
To renew muscles, revive spirits: Cal-a-Vie, California's newest spa. il *Vogue* 177:130 My '87
Wellness for the well-heeled [La Costa's Center for Lifestyle Management] G. Waggoner. il *Esquire* 107:55 Je '87

Florida
The beauty principle [T. C. Johns at Safety Harbor Spa and Fitness Center] B. Brandon and others. il pors *Essence* 18:50-7 Je '87
Exercising options in Florida [Y. Rubio, public relations director of Safety Harbor Spa] J. Giambanco. il pors *Work Woman* 12:105-6+ Je '87

France
The great escape [Bobet Biarritz spa] J. J. Buck. *Vogue* 177:262+ S '87
In Quiberon, a pleasure spa [thalassotherapy] F. du P. Gray. *Vogue* 177:180+ D '87

Germany (West)
See also
Baden-Baden (Germany)
Badenweiler (Germany)

Italy
Spa Italian style [Bagni de Lucca] A. Alvarez. il *House Gard* 159:74+ O '87

Jamaica
Jamaica: the weekend cure [Sans Souci] A. Gross. il *Vogue* 177:224+ D '87

Saint Martin
Last man at a spa [La Samanna] F. Eberstadt. *Vogue* 177:186+ Mr '87

Health workers
See also
Hospital employees
Midwives
Nurses and nursing
Ophthalmic assistants
Meet the members of today's health-care team. E. Granfort. *McCalls* 114:146 Jl '87

Health and hygiene
AIDS infects health workers. *Sci News* 131:326 My 23 '87
Changing the rules [contraction of AIDS by three health workers] *Time* 129:59 Je 1 '87
Courage, Doc [C. E. Koop reprimands health professionals who refuse to treat AIDS patients] por *Time* 130:57 S 21 '87
Dangerous leaks in AIDS lab [laboratory workers infected] *Discover* 8:14+ D '87
Misplaced fears over new AIDS cases. K. McAuliffe. il *U S News World Rep* 102:58 Je 1 '87
A new worry for health-care workers [contact with AIDS-contaminated blood] J. Seligmann. il *Newsweek* 109:55 Je 1 '87
An unexplained AIDS infection [medical laboratory worker infected] *Newsweek* 110:63 S 14 '87
Workers and blood: call for caution. S. Weisburd. *Sci News* 131:341 My 30 '87

Legal status, laws, etc.
Who oversees health-care workers? M. Engel. il *50 Plus* 27:14-16 S '87

Salaries, pensions, etc.
Occupational pay structure in nursing and personal care facilities. il *Mon Labor Rev* 110:41-2 Jl '87

Supply and demand
Great expectations [health manpower out of balance; cover story; special issue] il *World Health* p3-29 Ap '87

Training
Meeting health needs. A. R. Al-Awadi. il *World Health* p28-9 Ag/S '87
Training respite workers for Alzheimer's families. L. Middleton. il *Aging* no356:24-6 '87

Healthsouth (Firm)
Turning health into wealth. M. Gill. il por *Esquire* 108:94 S '87

Healy, Catherine
Fashion with a flair. il *Américas* 39:2-7 My/Je '87

Healy, Jane M.
Helping your child with homework [excerpt from Your child's growing mind] il *Good Housekeep* 205:114 S '87

Heaney, Seamus
Brodsky's Nobel: what the applause was about. por *N Y Times Book Rev* 92:1+ N 8 '87
In memoriam: Robert Fitzgerald [poem] *N Y Rev Books* 34:9 D 17 '87
An open letter [poem] *Harpers* 274:39-40 Mr '87

Heard, Lonear Windham
about
McQueen of the Golden Arches. L. Gite. il pors *Black Enterp* 18:64-6+ S '87

Hearing
See also
Deafness
Ear
Ear, Artificial
Echolocation (Physiology)
Psychoacoustics
Speech perception
Hearing problems—the danger signals [infants] C. Loomis. il *Parents* 62:15 Je '87
Key notes on the mind [neuropsychology of music] T. Monmaney. il *Omni* 9:44-6+ Ja '87

Animals
Auditory pathways to the frontal cortex of the mustache bat, Pteronotus parnellii. J. B. Kobler and others. bibl f il *Science* 236:824-6 My 15 '87

Fish
Shhhh! [how noise affects fishing] A. H. Putnam. il *Field Stream* 92:34+ Je '87

Rodents
A link between the brains of mice and men [research by Günter Ehret] il *Discover* 8:10+ Ap '87
Mice get an earful from left brain [research by Günter Ehret] B. Bower. *Sci News* 131:69 Ja 31 '87

Hearing aids

Baby boomers face hearing aid future. il *USA Today (Periodical)* 115:5 F '87

Sweet music for the deaf. M. Clark. il *Newsweek* 110:73 N 9 '87

Hearing loss *See* Deafness

Hearing protectors *See* Ear—Protection

Hearn, John Wayne

about

Family business: murder would settle it, and Debra Banister knew who to ask. J. Wadler. il pors *People Wkly* 28:57-8+ Jl 6 '87

Hearne, John, 1926-

about

The puzzle for Caribbean writers. N. Faria. *World Press Rev* 34:62 Ja '87

Hearns, Thomas

about

Fourth title for Thomas. R. Wiley. il pors *Sports Illus* 67:34-6 N 9 '87

Hearns sees 'Iron Mike' in his boxing future. *Jet* 73:48 O 12 '87

'Hit Man' Hearns ready to capture third title. *Jet* 71:53 Mr 9 '87

'Hit Man' Hearns ready to make boxing history. por *Jet* 72:48 S 21 '87

Leonard banks on a decision while Hagler mulls a murder and Hearns wants a double KO. pors *Jet* 72:50 Ap 6 '87

Record fourth title win sets Hearns atop boxing. il pors *Jet* 73:46 N 16 '87

Hearon, Shelby, 1931-

The season of secrecy. *Harpers Bazaar* 121:127+ D '87

about

PW interviews. B. Levine. por *Publ Wkly* 231:56-7 Ap 3 '87

Hearst, William Randolph, 1863-1951

about

California Xanadu. A. Cockburn. il pors *House Gard* 159:222-30+ O '87

Hearst Corporation

Citizens rich [cover story] W. P. Barrett. il pors *Forbes* 140:141-3+ D 14 '87

The empire strikes back. E. Diamond. il *N Y* 20:16+ Ap 13 '87

The selling of Esquire. J. Alter. il *Newsweek* 109:80 F 16 '87

Spurning a father's advice [centennial anniversary] J. Kelly. il *Time* 129:62-3 Je 1 '87

Hearst-San Simeon State Historical Monument (Calif.)

California Xanadu [San Simeon designer J. Morgan] A. Cockburn. il pors *House Gard* 159:222-30+ O '87

Heart

See also

Atrial natriuretic factor

Contraction

See Heart—Muscle—Contraction

Diseases

See also

Arteriosclerosis

Cardiacs

Black doctors have higher rate of heart disease. *Jet* 72:36 Ap 13 '87

Boosting the odds of beating a heart attack. F. Lunzer. il *Forbes* 140:214+ O 5 '87

A child for Christmas [cardiac N. Claar risks pregnancy] W. Barnhill. il pors *Good Housekeep* 205:66+ D '87

Exercise O.K. for many with angina [research by Mayer M. Bassan] il *Prevention* 39:15 Je '87

Happy to be here: how I survived a heart attack. J. Karras. il por *Better Homes Gard* 65:68+ N '87

A heart attack prompts a veteran broadcaster to clean up his off-the-air act. L. King. il pors *People Wkly* 27:75-6+ My 11 '87

Heart beat [recent research] *Sci Am* 256:71-2 Ja '87

Murmurs of the heart [mitral valve prolapse] P. M. Barrier. il *Nations Bus* 75:82 D '87

Silent heart disease: who's at risk? Why? M. Castleman. il *Redbook* 169:118-19+ My '87

Warning signs from your heart [mitral valve prolapse] il *Redbook* 168:12+ Mr '87

What to know about chest pains. P. Gadsby. il *Good Housekeep* 204:278 My '87

Anecdotes, facetiae, satire, etc.

A day at the beach. G. Wolff. il *Esquire* 108:254-6+ D '87

Causes

See also

Arteriosclerosis—Causes

Cocaine can damage the heart [work of Henry Tazelaar] *USA Today (Periodical)* 115:6-7 F '87

Cocaine cardiology: problems, mysteries [research by Jeffrey M. Isner and others] J. Silberner. *Sci News* 131:69 Ja 31 '87

Female trouble [menopause-heart disease link] *Sci Am* 257:24+ Jl '87

One more reason to stay in bed [morning heart attacks and blood platelet aggregation; research by Geoffrey Tofler and others] *Discover* 8:6+ O '87

Safe supinity [platelet aggregation and morning heart attacks; research by Geoffrey H. Tofler and others] *Sci News* 131:409 Je 27 '87

Smoking raises female heart attack risk [research by Walter C. Willett and others] S. Eisenberg. *Sci News* 132:341 N 28 '87

Diagnosis

See also

Electrocardiography

Take a test for heart disease [excerpt from Health risks] E. J. Howard. il *U S News World Rep* 103:64-5 Ag 17 '87

These pictures could save your life [imaging devices] R. Brandt. il *Bus Week* p112-13 Jl 13 '87

A tube that could be a killer [cardiac catheterization] *U S News World Rep* 103:65 N 23 '87

Watch Q-Med as it stalks a silent killer [portable EKG machine to detect silent ischemia] G. G. Marcial. il *Bus Week* p88 Ap 13 '87

Genetic aspects

Family ties and heart disease [research by Roger R. Williams and others] J. Silberner. *Sci News* 131:85 F 7 '87

Mortality

Another up/down side of trimming the fat. D. D. Edwards. *Sci News* 131:261-2 Ap 25 '87

Avoiding the morning danger zone [work of Stefan N. Willich] il *Prevention* 39:16 Ag '87

Death by stress? [sudden cardiac arrest; research by Robert Eliot] G. Hanauer. il *Omni* 9:22+ Ag '87

Medical breakthroughs: cutting the toll of killer diseases. T. J. Gordon. il por *Futurist* 21:15-17 Ja/F '87

New sickle cell trait raises risk for blacks [risk of sudden death during strenuous exercise] *Jet* 73:14 N 2 '87

Sickle-cell alert [risk of sudden death during strenuous exercise] *Time* 130:61 O 5 '87

Sudden death tied to sickle-cell trait [risks of strenuous exercise] D. D. Edwards. *Sci News* 132:197 S 26 '87

Nutritional aspects

See also

Arteriosclerosis—Nutritional aspects

Cholesterol

The American Heart Association's guide to healthy eating. il *Prevention* 39:34-6+ F '87

Copper: what a difference sex makes [research by Meira Fields and others] J. Raloff. *Sci News* 131:70 Ja 31 '87

Eat healthy—and love it! D. A. Cooley and C. E. Moore. il *Redbook* 169:101-5 O '87

Fish: food for a healthy heart. H. Garrison. il *Parents* 62:92-4+ Ja '87

Fish for the heart. J. Lowenstein. il *Oceans* 20:72 Mr/Ap '87

Fish oil and cholesterol: a megadose of hype? [diet supplements] T. Monmaney. il *Newsweek* 109:67-8 Ap 13 '87

Fish-oil capsules: good for your heart? C. Schaeffer. il *Changing Times* 41:14 My '87

Fish oil slows plaque deposits. *Prevention* 39:100-1 Ap '87

A fish (oil) story? J. Silberner. *Sci News* 131:89 F 7 '87

Fish oil takes a dive? [research by William S. Harris] *Sci News* 132:342 N 28 '87

Good-for-your-heart dishes. J. Nash. il *Essence* 17:82 Ja '87

A healthy change of heart [fish oil protects heart from damage during attack; research by Carl Hock] il *Prevention* 39:8 Ag '87

High-carb diets questioned [theory of Gerald Reaven] G. Kolata. *Science* 235:164 Ja 9 '87

Low triglycerides native to fish eaters. il *Prevention* 39:9 My '87

Magnesium deficiency linked to heart disorders [work of Robert Rude and Elizabeth Ryzen] *USA Today (Periodical)* 115:4-5 F '87

Magnesium stops heart arrhythmias. *Prevention* 39:13 N '87

More about magnesium [interview with M. Seelig] R. Grindy. il por *Saturday Evening Post* 259:50-3+ Jl/Ag '87

Heart—Diseases—Nutritional aspects—*cont.*

Myocardial failure in cats associated with low plasma taurine: a reversible cardiomyopathy [cover story] P. D. Pion and others. bibl f il *Science* 237:764-8 Ag 14 '87

Niacin for the heart. G. Maleskey. *Prevention* 39:28-31 Jl '87

No fat advantage in meatless meals? [research by Bonnie Worthington-Roberts] il *Prevention* 39:8 N '87

The omega factor [fish oil] K. Freifeld. il *Health* 19:78 F '87

Planning a diet for a healthy heart [cover story] C. Lecos. il *FDA Consum* 21:29-36 Mr '87

Pritikin gets respect. M. S. Balter. il *Health* 19:67-8+ Je '87

Score another one for the Mediterranean diet. *Prevention* 39:57 My '87

Snake oil [dietary fats] E. R. Shell. il *Atlantic* 260:74-5 Ag '87

Your diet: good fat, bad fat. J. S. Stern. *Vogue* 177:448 F '87

Prevention

Crimes of the heart [Phone-In Program of Marvin Mordkoff] B. Prescott. il *Health* 19:23 S '87

How to keep your heart healthy. E. Royte. il *Mademoiselle* 93:90 F '87

Looking for shortcuts to a healthy heart. J. Silberner. il *U S News World Rep* 103:111-12 D 28 '87-Ja 4 '88

A low-fat meal, a little wine—and hold the smokes. J. Carey and J. Silberner. il *U S News World Rep* 103:57-8 Ag 17 '87

A 'PIP' of a heart program [Phone-In Program of Marvin Mordkoff] il *Prevention* 39:16 Ap '87

Take part, take heart [Framingham, Mass. Heart Study] A. Hollister. il *Life* 10:56-8+ F '87

Psychological aspects

Competitive women risk heart attacks [findings of Carl Thoresen] il *USA Today (Periodical)* 116:8 S '87

The hardy heart [research by Richard J. Contrada] C. Wood. *Psychol Today* 21:22 Ja '87

Healthy denial [helping bypass patients to improve health; research by David G. Folks and Arthur M. Freeman] L. Crawford. il *Psychol Today* 21:24 O '87

Heart disease and job stress [study by Robert Karasek] il *USA Today (Periodical)* 115:5 F '87

Mind games taken to heart [post-operative cardiac patients at Children's Hospital in San Diego] N. Benford and D. Gage. il *Health* 19:25 N '87

Patient knows best [predicting heart attack recovery; study by Dan Bar-On] M. Roberts. *Psychol Today* 21:10 Je '87

Smile your way to a longer life [work of Meyer Friedman] L. Vaughn. il *Prevention* 39:87-90+ Ag '87

Stress and the silent heart attack [research by Leisa J. Freeman and others] M. Roberts. *Psychol Today* 21:7 Ag '87

Type A on trial. J. Fischman. bibl (p64) il *Psychol Today* 21:42-4+ F '87

Therapy

See also
Defibrillators
TPA (Drug)

Bypass breakthrough [University of Southern California study on lowering cholesterol through diet and drugs] il *Time* 129:52 Je 29 '87

Can heart diseases be reversed? [study by D. Ornish] D. Grady. il pors *Discover* 8:54-6+ Mr '87

A celebration of walking—and life [cardiac rehabilitation program at Duke University] T. Shealey. il *Prevention* 39:102-4 Ap '87

Diet, drugs slow heart-felt 'insults' [lowering cholesterol; University of Southern California study] D. D. Edwards. il *Sci News* 131:407 Je 27 '87

Drug may protect brains of heart attack victims [use of MK-801 to limit neuronal injury after ischemia] D. M. Barnes. il *Science* 235:632-3 F 6 '87

Help's arrived for heart-attack victims [TPA] S. Findlay. il *U S News World Rep* 103:109-11 D 28 '87-Ja 4 '88

Killer cholesterol: the news is good [study by University of Southern California] il *U S News World Rep* 102:11 Je 29 '87

One for the heart [University of Southern California study on lowering cholesterol through diet and drugs] T. Monmaney. il *Newsweek* 109:56-7 Je 29 '87

Study bolsters case against cholesterol [University of Southern California research] L. Roberts. il *Science* 237:28-9 Jl 3 '87

Innervation

Direct activation of mammalian atrial muscarinic potassium channels by GTP regulatory protein G_k. A. Yatani and others. bibl f il *Science* 235:207-11 Ja 9 '87

Metabolism

A G protein directly regulates mammalian cardiac calcium channels. A. Yatani and others. bibl f il *Science* 238:1288-92 N 27 '87

Glycolysis preferentially inhibits ATP-sensitive K^+ channels in isolated guinea pig cardiac myocytes. J. N. Weiss and S. T. Lamp. bibl f il *Science* 238:67-9 O 2 '87

Sodium-calcium exchange in heart: membrane currents and changes in $[Ca^{2+}]i$. L. Barcenas-Ruiz and others. bibl f il *Science* 238:1720-2 D 18 '87

Muscle

The α subunit of the GTP binding protein G_k opens atrial potassium channels. J. Codina and others. bibl f il *Science* 236:442-5 Ap 24 '87

Cellular and subcellular heterogeneity of $[Ca^{2+}]_i$ in single heart cells revealed by fura-2. W. G. Wier and others. bibl f il *Science* 235:325-8 Ja 16 '87

Contraction

Effect of membrane potential changes on the calcium transient in single rat cardiac muscle cells. M. B. Cannell and others. bibl f il *Science* 238:1419-23 D 4 '87

Surgery

See also
Cardiac catheterization

An angel from Tennessee [G. Williams brings medical aid to Ethiopia and 14 yr. old Tefera to the U.S. for heart surgery] J. L. McCoy. il pors *McCalls* 114:132-4 Je '87

Bypass heart damage with vitamin E [free radical formation; research by Nicholas Cavarocchi] *Prevention* 39:11 O '87

Experts predict phase-out of heart bypass. *50 Plus* 27:22-3 Je '87

Healthy denial [helping bypass patients to improve health; research by David G. Folks and Arthur M. Freeman] L. Crawford. il *Psychol Today* 21:24 O '87

Leapin' lizards! This doc zaps hearts [laser canalization; work of M. Mirhoseini] J. Langone. il por *Discover* 8:56-8+ Ag '87

Profiles: Denton A. Cooley, M.D. R. Conniff. il pors *Archit Dig* 44:194-201+ My '87

Skeletal muscle as the potential power source for a cardiovascular pump: assessment in vivo. M. A. Acker and others. bibl f il *Science* 236:324-7 Ap 17 '87

Transplantation

The CEO who got a new heart [restored health of MCI head W. McGowan] W. J. Cook. il pors *U S News World Rep* 103:60-2+ O 19 '87

Heart to heart: can a chimp transplant save human life? [research conducted at Columbia Presbyterian Medical Center, N.Y.] N. Taylor. il *N Y* 20:44-8 Jl 13 '87

The hearts of the matter [domino donors at Johns Hopkins Hospital] C. Wallis. il *Time* 129:60 My 25 '87

Parting MCI's veil of secrecy [secrecy surrounding president W. G. McGowan's heart transplant surgery] J. J. Keller. *Bus Week* p54 My 18 '87

Racing for life [5-month-old A. Dela Peña gets new heart] J. Korman. il pors *N Y Times Mag* p62-4+ S 20 '87

A second chance [heart-lung transplant recipient C. Bilodeau Gingras] L. Van Dusen. il por *Macleans* 100:44 N 23 '87

A second chance at life. D. Chandler and M. Chandler. il pors *People Wkly* 27:124-7+ Je 8 '87

Suffering and joy [anencephalic baby as heart donor] A. Steacy. il *Macleans* 100:40-1 N 23 '87

Transplant by the numbers [heart transplants and Medicare] R. Rosenblatt. *50 Plus* 27:19 O '87

Heart, Artificial

The heart that failed [Jarvik] E. Kiester. il *50 Plus* 27:28-31 F '87

Shiley ends sale of heart valve. *FDA Consum* 21:2 F '87

Heart (Musical group)

Rockers: then & now. il pors *Teen* 31:62-3 O '87

Heart attacks See Heart—Diseases

Heart beat

See also
Electrocardiography
Pacemaker, Artificial (Heart)

Heart beat—*cont.*

Attacks real, not imaginary [panic attacks verified by increased heart rates; Stanford University School of Medicine study] il *USA Today (Periodical)* 115:12-13 Ap '87

Smoke and stress: a double whammy [effect on heart rate; research by Kenneth A. Perkins] G. Lowe. *Psychol Today* 21:19 My '87

Vital signs [radar detection of heartbeat and breathing] *Sci Am* 256:69-70 Ja '87

Defibrillators
See Defibrillators

Heart catheterization *See* Cardiac catheterization
Heart diseases *See* Heart—Diseases
Heart Institute Research Centre

'The consummate surgeon' [director general W. Keon] P. Gessell. il por *Macleans* 100:42 N 23 '87

Heart muscle *See* Heart—Muscle
Heart patients *See* Cardiacs
Heart rate *See* Heart beat
Heart research

See also
National Heart, Lung, and Blood Institute (U.S.)

Drew U. medical study focuses on 75 twins. il *Jet* 72:36 Ap 13 '87

Ethical aspects
Integrity of research papers questioned [study by Walter W. Stewart and Ned Feder] B. J. Culliton. *Science* 235:422-3 Ja 23 '87

A long-disputed paper goes to press [Walter W. Stewart's and Ned Feder's critical study of publications by J. Darsee and coauthors] M. Murray. il *Sci News* 131:52-3 Ja 24 '87

NIH finally resolves 7-year dispute [case of J. S. Borer] C. Holden. *Science* 238:151 O 9 '87

A soap opera for science [study by Walter Stewart and Ned Feder] D. E. Chubin. bibl f *BioScience* 37:259-61 Ap '87

Federal aid
Duke's heart center in bureaucratic jam. M. Basgall. *Science* 238:882-3 N 13 '87

Canada
See also
Heart Institute Research Centre

Heart valves, Artificial *See* Heart, Artificial
Heartbreak Ridge [film] *See* Motion picture reviews—Single works
Heartburn

Extinguishing heartburn. F. Lunzer. *Forbes* 140:296 N 16 '87

Hearths *See* Fireplaces
Heartney, Eleanor

The hot new cool art: simulationism. il *Art News* 86:130-7 Ja '87

How wide is the gender gap? il *Art News* 86:139-45 Summ '87

Sighted in Münster. il *Art Am* 75:140-3+ S '87

Hearts of fire [film] *See* Motion picture reviews—Single works

Heat

See also
Calorimeters and calorimetry
Hot weather
Specific heat
Thermodynamics
Thermography

Convection
Convection theory vindicated [work of Kwing Chan and Sabatino Sofia] *Sky Telesc* 73:603 Je '87

Validity tests of the mixing-length theory of deep convection. K. L. Chan and S. Sofia. bibl f il *Science* 235:465-7 Ja 23 '87

Physiological effects
Beating the heat. C. Hanauer. *Seventeen* 46:59 Jl '87

Heat up to heal faster [use of hot packs to heal stubborn wounds] *Prevention* 39:9 Jl '87

Warming to the idea: heat research may help hearts, kidneys, and man's best friend [work of P. Ruggera] W. Grigg. il por *FDA Consum* 21:25-7 My '87

Radiation and absorption
Helium loss, tectonics, and the terrestrial heat budget. E. R. Oxburgh and R. K. O'Nions. bibl f il map *Science* 237:1583-8 S 25 '87

Transmission
See also
Heat exchangers

Heat [film] *See* Motion picture reviews—Single works
Heat engines

Demons, engines and the second law. C. H. Bennett. bibl (p150-1) il *Sci Am* 257:108-16 N '87

Heat exchangers

Heat exchangers [swine houses] B. Freese. il *Success Farm* 85:H5 Ap '87

The pollution within [use of heat recovery ventilator] P. V. Fossel. il *Ctry J* 14:44-9 S '87

Heat Moon, William Least *See* Least Heat Moon, William
Heat pipes

Cool savings for muggy climates [heat pipe enhanced air conditioner] V. E. Gilmore. il *Pop Sci* 231:30 N '87

Heat production (Biology) *See* Temperature, Animal and human
Heat pump water heaters *See* Water heaters
Heat pumps

Furnaces go underground. J. Hayes. il *Saturday Evening Post* 259:28+ D '87

Ground-source heat pump—still a smart buy? J. Horst. il *Pop Sci* 231:38+ O '87

New heat pump matches speed to load [Carrier Infinity] J. Hume. il *Pop Sci* 231:46 O '87

Warming up to heat pumps. J. Hayes. il *Saturday Evening Post* 259:20 N '87

Heat radiation *See* Heat—Radiation and absorption
Heat reflectors *See* Reflectors (Heat)
Heat regulators *See* Thermostats
Heat shields (Artificial satellites) *See* Artificial satellites—Shielding (Heat)
Heat shock proteins *See* Proteins
Heat storage

Heat-storing walls [Heat Soak] N. J. Freundlich. il *Pop Sci* 231:98 S '87

Rocky V (the furnace) [electric heat storing furnace] V. E. Gilmore. il *Pop Sci* 230:77 F '87

ThermoPak—heat at the press of a button. R. M. Koolish. il *Sky Telesc* 74:602 D '87

Heat transfer images *See* Thermography
Heaters

See also
Water heaters

Safety devices and measures
Portable heater safety. il *Better Homes Gard* 65:113 N '87

Vigilant heater [Arvin Alert portable electric heater] A. C. West. il *Pop Sci* 231:22 N '87

Warming up to safe heating. T. M. Scanlon. *Consum Res Mag* 70:32-3 F '87

Heath, Aloise Buckley

The true sprit of Christmas. il *Natl Rev* 39:27-9 D 31 '87

Heath, Craig

Shuttered windows. *Humanist* 47:27-8 N/D '87

Heath, Shirley Brice

Where is the crisis in American literacy? *Educ Dig* 52:18-19 F '87

Heath, Shirley Brice, and McLaughlin, Milbrey Wallin, 1941-

A child resource policy beyond school and family. *Educ Dig* 53:19-21 O '87

A child resource policy: moving beyond dependence on school and family [cover story] bibl f il *Phi Delta Kappan* 68:576-80 Ap '87

Let's not throw out the baby with the bath water [discussion of April 1987 article, A child resource policy: moving beyond dependence on school and family] bibl f *Phi Delta Kappan* 68:784-6 Je '87

Heathenism *See* Paganism
Heathers

Growing Grandma's heather bed. J. Howard. il *Ctry J* 14:48-51 D '87

Heathrow (Fla.)

Jeno Paulucci's dream: bring fiber optics home [residential phones] S. Ticer. il por *Bus Week* p34-5 S 21 '87

Heating

See also
Boilers
Chimneys
Degree days
Fireplaces
Furnaces
Gas heating
Insulation (Heat)
Solar heating
Stoves
Thermostats
Wood as fuel
Wood stoves

Heating equipment

See also
Boilers
Furnaces
Heat pumps

Heating equipment—See also—*cont.*
     Radiators
     Stoves
     Wood stoves
     Home heating product review [special section] il *Pop Sci* 231:38+ O '87
Heaton, Thomas H., and Hartzell, Stephen H.
     Earthquake hazards on the Cascadia subduction zone. bibl f il maps *Science* 236:162-8 Ap 10 '87
Heaven [film] See Motion picture reviews—Single works
Heaven in mass media
     The last resort: "heaven . . .". C. Medwick. il *Vogue* 177:313+ My '87
Heaven on earth [television program] See Television program reviews—Single works
Heavy metal music *See* Rock music
Heavy water *See* Deuterium oxide
Heberlein, Thomas A.
     Stalking the predator: a profile of the American hunter [cover story] bibl f il *Environment* 29:6-11+ S '87
Hebert, Pierre
                    about
     Roz Newman forms a multi-national alliance. E. Zimmer. il por *Dance Mag* 61:4 F '87
Hebrew literature
                    Translations
          See also
               Institute for the Translation of Hebrew Literature Ltd.
Hebrew manuscripts, Biblical *See* Bible—Manuscripts, Hebrew
Hebrew National Kosher Foods, Inc.
     83 plus 17 [new advertising theme] *New Yorker* 63:35 O 19 '87
Hebrides (Scotland)
          See also
               Barra Island (Scotland)
               Historic houses, sites, etc.—Hebrides (Scotland)
Hechinger, Grace
     Education. See issues of Glamour
Hecht, Annabel
     Know the right way to take your medicines. il *FDA Consum* 21:22-4 My '87
Hecht, Annabel, and Janssen, Wallace F.
     Diet drug danger déjà vu. il *FDA Consum* 21:22-7 F '87
Hecht, Ben, 1894-1964
                    about
     The front page [drama] Reviews
          Nation 244:24-5 Ja 10 '87. M. Hodgson
          New Repub 196:25-6 Ja 5-12 '87. R. Brustein
Hecht, Chic
                    about
     Letter from Washington. Cato. *Natl Rev* 39:15 O 23 '87
Hecht, Jeff
     Planet stalkers. il *Omni* 10:34 N '87
Heckert, Richard Edwin
                    about
     A boss like Reagan. P. Sellers. il por *Fortune* 116:36-7 Ag 3 '87
Heckman, Joanne
     Ready, set, GOES: weather eyes for the 21st century. il maps *Space World* X-7-283:23-6 Jl '87
     Stop press! Launch satellite! il *Space World* X-8-284:24-6 Ag '87
     Tomorrow's weather: looking further ahead. il por *Futurist* 21:27-9 Mr/Ap '87
Heckscher, Morrison H.
     Mount Cuba in Delaware. il *Antiques* 131:1078-87 My '87
Hedden, Roger
                    about
     Bodies, rest, and motion [drama] Reviews
          N Y 20:50 Ja 5 '87. J. Simon
Hedden-Sellman, Zelda
     Cyclothymia: when mood swings are serious. il *McCalls* 114:87 Ag '87
Hedgehogs
                    Care
     Driver, spare that hedgehog [St. Tiggywinkle's clinic in Aylesbury, England] il *Time* 130:38 N 23 '87
Hedgerows *See* Field borders
Hedges
     Nuts for a hedge [filberts] J. Ruttle. il *Rodale's Org Gard* 34:56-7 O '87
                    Pruning
          See Pruning
Hedging (Finance)
          See also
               Portfolio insurance (Securities)

A cattle plan your banker will like. G. Johnston. *Success Farm* 85:7 S '87
Fancy stuff [funds with sophisticated option strategies and the market crash] W. Baldwin. il *Forbes* 140:185 N 30 '87
Four ways to hedge your gains. J. E. Goodman. *Money* 16:47 O '87
The hedgeaholic [E. Fleischer of Franklin Savings Association] J. Willoughby. il por *Forbes* 140:180+ N 16 '87
Hedging against the dollar [bond and equity funds] J. A. Conway. il *Forbes* 139:8 Je 15 '87
How to hedge against rising mortgage rates. J. N. Frank. *Bus Week* p142 My 4 '87
The newest pitch: funds that use the big boys' hedges. S. Weiss. il *Bus Week* p65 F 23 '87
The synthetic hedge: reducing market risk [corn] G. Vincent. il *Success Farm* 85 no6:5 Mr '87
Where these fund managers go, you follow [hedge funds] D. P. Wiener. il *U S News World Rep* 103:50-1 Jl 13 '87
Hedin, Diane
     Expanding the use of cross-age/peer tutoring. *Educ Dig* 53:39-41 D '87
Hedlund, Dennis
                    about
     A rock 'n' roller with a class act in videos. P. Finch. il por *Bus Week* p80 Je 8 '87
Hedonism
     Decadence à la mode. J. I. Packer. il *Christ Today* 31:13 O 2 '87
     Going first class on the Titanic. S. Garber. il por *Christ Today* 31:25-7 N 20 '87
Hedrick, L. R.
     Agnostic. See Harbor seal. por *Publ Wkly* 231:29 My 1 '87
Heel bone
                    Wounds and injuries
     When heels are hurting. D. Parsinnen. il *Women's Sports Fitness* 9:22 D '87
Heffernan, Maryclare J.
     Simple celebrations [story] il *Ladies Home J* 104:88+ F '87
Hefley, Joel Maurice
     Should Congress adopt the House-passed "Gephardt Amendment"? [excerpts from debate, April 29, 1987] *Congr Dig* 66:189+ Je/Jl '87
Hefner, Christie
     The Meese Commission: sex, violence, and censorship. il por *Humanist* 47:25-9+ Ja/F '87
Hehir, J. Bryan
     Church/world watch. See occasional issues of Commonweal
     Morality and foreign policy: a sketch of the issues. il *America* 156:64-8 Ja 31 '87
Heiblum, Mordehai, and Eastman, Lester F.
     Ballistic electrons in semiconductors. il *Sci Am* 256:102-11 F '87
Heidelberg (Germany)
                    Dance
     Reviews:
          J. Kresnik's dance group at the Municipal Theater. H. Koegler. *Dance Mag* 61:23+ O '87
                    Description
     Heidelberg. S. Wilding. il *Gourmet* 47:48-53+ Ja '87
Heidemann, Mandy
                    about
     Mandy goes to Moscow. M. J. Mackowski. il por *Space World* X-2-278:34-5 F '87
Heider, Franz, and others
     Magnetic properties of hydrothermally recrystallized magnetite crystals. bibl f il *Science* 236:1287-90 Je 5 '87
Heidnik, Gary
                    about
     Black women report of sex, torture, murder at hands of white Philadelphia 'bishop'. il por *Jet* 72:6-7 Ap 13 '87
     House of horrors. por *Time* 129:34 Ap 6 '87
     A little house of horrors. T. E. Johnson. il por *Newsweek* 109:29 Ap 6 '87
     Philadelphia's house of horrors. il *U S News World Rep* 102:11 Ap 6 '87
Heidrick & Struggles, Inc.
     Hero hunter [G. R. Roche] N. J. Perry. il por *Fortune* 116:160+ N 9 '87
Heiferman, Marvin, and Kismaric, Carol
     Getting close to Gotham. il *Art News* 86:106-11 S '87
Heifers
     Calve heifers, then market them [single-calf heifer system] B. Eftink. il *Success Farm* 85:16-17 O '87

Heifetz, Jascha, 1901-1987
about
Obituary
Time il por 130:71 D 21 '87. M. Walsh
U S News World Rep il pors 103:16 D 21 '87.
M. Horn
Heifetz, Jeanne
Crossing the border. *Glamour* 85:174+ Ap '87
Height of man *See* Stature
Heil, Andrea
Has the backlash had a sobering effect? il *Seventeen* 46:162-3+ My '87
Heilbroner, Robert L.
Hard times. *New Yorker* 63:96-8+ S 14 '87
Heilbrun, Carolyn G., 1926-
The case of the missing woman. il *Ms* 16:76+ O '87
Heileman (G.) Brewing Co., Inc. *See* G. Heileman Brewing Co., Inc.
Heilman, Joan Rattner
The miraculous story of a coma survivor. il por *Redbook* 169:90-1+ Jl '87
Heilmeier, George
The future of artificial intelligence. il *Radio-Electron* 58:85-90 My '87
Heim, Richard, Jr.
The summer Montana burned. il map *Weatherwise* 40:184-7 Jl/Ag '87
Heimaey (Iceland)
See also
Birds—Heimaey (Iceland)
Heimel, Cynthia
about
What makes single girls tingle. D. Maychick. il por *Mademoiselle* 93:38 Je '87
Heimlich maneuver
Heimlich hug and other help for kids. C. Schaeffer. *Changing Times* 41:18 Mr '87
Heine, Bill
about
Listen, if there are flying fish, there are bound to be accidents. il por *People Wkly* 27:66 Mr 2 '87
Heinecken, Robert, 1931-
about
Robert Heinecken at the Art Institute. A. Slaton. il *Art Am* 75:165-6 D '87
Heineman (Dannie) Prize *See* Physics—Awards
Heinemann, H. Erich
Time for the Fed to tighten. il *Fortune* 115:129-30+ My 25 '87
Heiney, P. A., and others
Disorder in Al-Li-Cu and Al-Mn-Si icosahedral alloys. bibl f il *Science* 238:660-3 O 30 '87
Heinrich, Bernd
Thermoregulation in winter moths. bibl (p128) il *Sci Am* 256:104-11 Mr '87
Heinrichs, Jay
Risky business. il *Natl Wildl* 25:12-15 Je/Jl '87
Heins, Marjorie
The clearing of Vanessa Redgrave. il *Nation* 245:713-15 D 12 '87
Heinz, H. John *See* Heinz, John, III
Heinz, Henry John, 1908-1987
about
Obituary
Natl Rev 39:19-20 Mr 27 '87. W. F. Buckley
Heinz, John, III
International trade [address, January 13, 1987] *Vital Speeches Day* 53:277-9 F 15 '87
Heirs *See* Inheritance
Heisler, Gregory
about
Black-dot diffusion helps capture a subject's character. B. Hagin. il por *Pop Photogr* 94:68 D '87
Heisler, Mark
Super Bowl. il *Sports Illus* 66:35+ Ja 12 '87
Heisman Trophy *See* Football, College—Awards
Held, Al, 1928-
about
Al Held at Robert Miller. S. Tillim. il *Art Am* 75:182-3 My '87
Heavy traffic. K. Larson. il *N Y* 20:70 Mr 23 '87
Heldmaier, Gerhard
(jt. auth) See Southwick, Edward E., and Heldmaier, Gerhard
Heldman, Gladys M.
Singles to doubles. il *World Tennis* 34:34 Ap '87
Yes she can. il pors *World Tennis* 35:18-21+ N '87
about
12 who mattered. C. Shmerler. il por *World Tennis* 35:64 N '87

Heldt, Barbara
The burden of caring. *Nation* 244:820-4 Je 13 '87
Helfand, David, 1950-
Bang: the supernova of 1987. bibl il *Phys Today* 40 pt1:24-32 Ag '87
Helferich, Gerard
Facts on File. *Writer* 100:44 D '87
Helgesen, Sally
On your own. See issues of Glamour through January 1987
What I learned about love on the silver screen. il *Glamour* 85:192 Ja '87
Why would a woman peel off her clothes and pose nude for Playboy? Three women tell their stories. il *Glamour* 85:218-19+ Je '87
Helianthemum *See* Sun roses
Helicopter airlines
See also
Manhattan Helicopter Tours
Omniflight Helicopter Services, Inc.
U.S. Jet
Shuttle service
Agency suspends Omniflight scheduled services in New York [FAA] *Aviat Week Space Technol* 126:37 Je 8 '87
Helicopter Association International
Helicopter show reflects slow worldwide sales [Helicopter Assn. International meeting and industry exposition] P. Proctor. il *Aviat Week Space Technol* 126:76-7 Mr 16 '87
Helicopter engines
International firms to compete for procurement of 800 engines. il *Aviat Week Space Technol* 126:74-5 Ja 19 '87
Military helicopter needs spur investment by U.S. engine makers. il *Aviat Week Space Technol* 126:73 Ja 19 '87
Defects
Avco Lycoming seeks solutions to LT101 reliability problems. P. Proctor. *Aviat Week Space Technol* 126:61-2 My 25 '87
Design
Army may reengine UH-1H if LHX is delayed further. B. M. Greeley, Jr. *Aviat Week Space Technol* 127:32 S 14 '87
Italy, West Germany examine upgrading Allison engines. *Aviat Week Space Technol* 126:72 F 23 '87
P&W, Williams joint venture for helicopter engine work. il *Aviat Week Space Technol* 127:33 N 2 '87
Rolls-Royce plans to join MTM390 engine program [French and German program] *Aviat Week Space Technol* 127:29 Ag 10 '87
Helicopter industry
See also
Bell Helicopter Textron Inc.
Boeing Co. Boeing Vertol Company (Div.)
McDonnell Douglas Helicopter Company
Orlando Helicopter Airways
Schweizer Aircraft Corp.
Sikorsky Aircraft
Strikes—Helicopter industry
Export-import trade
Helicopter show reflects slow worldwide sales [Helicopter Assn. International meeting and industry exposition] P. Proctor. il *Aviat Week Space Technol* 126:76-7 Mr 16 '87
International firms to compete for procurement of 800 engines. il *Aviat Week Space Technol* 126:74-5 Ja 19 '87
Italy, West Germany examine upgrading Allison engines. *Aviat Week Space Technol* 126:72 F 23 '87
Japan to purchase foreign aircraft to ease balance of trade [helicopter imports] *Aviat Week Space Technol* 127:22 Jl 6 '87
U.S. commercial helicopter shipments. il *Aviat Week Space Technol* 126:51 Ap 20 '87
Westland, Sikorsky export helicopters for military roles. il *Aviat Week Space Technol* 126:136 Ap 27 '87
Finance
Military helicopter needs spur investment by U.S. engine makers. il *Aviat Week Space Technol* 126:73 Ja 19 '87
International aspects
See also
Helicopter Association International
Helicopter displays at Paris focus on military requirements [Paris Air Show] K. F. Mordoff. il *Aviat Week Space Technol* 126:75-6 Je 29 '87
Rotorcraft technology update [special section; with editorial comment by Donald E. Fink] il *Aviat Week Space Technol* 126:11, 45-51+ Ja 19 '87

Helicopter industry—International aspects—*cont.*
U.S., Europe face decisions on new combat helicopter programs. R. R. Ropelewski. *Aviat Week Space Technol* 126:105 Mr 9 '87

Suits and claims
Supreme Court weighs liability in military contractor suit [Boyle vs. Sikorsky over helicopter crash] M. Mecham. il *Aviat Week Space Technol* 127:81-2 O 26 '87

Canada
Bell shifts assembly of light helicopters to Canadian facility. il *Aviat Week Space Technol* 126:77-8 Mr 16 '87

France
See also
Aerospatiale. Helicopter Division

Great Britain
See also
Westland plc

Italy
See also
Agusta SpA

Soviet Union
Soviets developing advanced aircraft to upgrade civil, military air fleets [Paris Air Show] il *Aviat Week Space Technol* 126:20-2 Je 22 '87

Western Europe
See also
European Helicopter Industries
Design requirement set for European Tonal helicopter. il *Aviat Week Space Technol* 126:78-9 Ja 19 '87
NATO NH-90 helicopter program enters one-year definition phase. K. F. Mordoff. il *Aviat Week Space Technol* 127:28 Jl 20 '87

Helicopter pilots

Psychology
Human factors research key element of LHX design. il *Aviat Week Space Technol* 126:118-19+ Ja 19 '87

Training
See Aviation—Study and teaching
Helicopter shuttle service *See* Helicopter airlines—Shuttle service
Helicopter simulators *See* Flight simulators
Helicopters

Accidents
Supreme Court extends limits on suits by military personnel. M. Mecham. *Aviat Week Space Technol* 126:26 My 25 '87
Supreme Court weighs liability in military contractor suit [Boyle vs. Sikorsky] M. Mecham. il *Aviat Week Space Technol* 127:81-2 O 26 '87

Armaments
Sikorsky Aircraft assesses new H-76 armament pylon. il *Aviat Week Space Technol* 126:49 Mr 23 '87
UH-60A tested with Volcano multiple delivery mine system. il *Aviat Week Space Technol* 126:73 Mr 2 '87

Blades
See Helicopters—Rotors
Business use
See Helicopters in business
Cockpits
ARTI researchers assess feasibility of varied single-pilot operations. il *Aviat Week Space Technol* 126:61+ Ja 19 '87
Fighter, helicopter test pilots challenge cockpit design concepts. W. B. Scott. *Aviat Week Space Technol* 127:65+ N 16 '87

Control
See also
Computers—Aviation use
Costs
Senators urge Army to keep helicopter production lines open. *Aviat Week Space Technol* 126:23 Mr 23 '87
Design
Advanced technology prompts reevaluation of helicopter design. *Aviat Week Space Technol* 126:252 Mr 9 '87
Cal Poly students attempting human-powered helicopter flight. il *Aviat Week Space Technol* 127:77 D 21 '87
Manufacturer details configurations of Navy/Coast Guard SH-60F derivatives. S. W. Kandebo. il *Aviat Week Space Technol* 126:96-7 My 18 '87
Rotorcraft technology update [special section; with editorial comment by Donald E. Fink] il *Aviat Week Space Technol* 126:11, 45-51+ Ja 19 '87
Soviets develop lightweight helicopter for civil operations [Mi-34] il *Aviat Week Space Technol* 126:31 Ap 13 '87

Electronic equipment
See also
Computers—Aviation use

Aerospatiale adding rotor, avionics improvements to its product line. il *Aviat Week Space Technol* 126:101+ Ja 19 '87
AH-64A Apaches represent blend of electronic, airframe technologies. W. B. Scott. il *Aviat Week Space Technol* 127:72-3+ Jl 20 '87
McDonnell Douglas to propose Apache target handoff system. *Aviat Week Space Technol* 127:22 O 19 '87

Engines
See Helicopter engines
Frames
MBB focuses on airframes, rotors for the PAH-2, NH-90. il *Aviat Week Space Technol* 126:111-12 Ja 19 '87
MBB to test composite helicopter airframe. K. F. Mordoff. il *Aviat Week Space Technol* 127:87 Ag 3 '87
History
Civilizing the helicopter: upwardly mobile. M. Phelps. il *Flying* 114:128 S '87
Hydraulic equipment
Army will shield UH-60 hydraulics against EMI [electromagnetic interference] *Aviat Week Space Technol* 127:29 N 23 '87

Manufacture
See Helicopter industry
Materials
Bell pushes for broader application of composites to helicopter structures. il *Aviat Week Space Technol* 126:95-6 Ja 19 '87
MBB to test composite helicopter airframe. K. F. Mordoff. il *Aviat Week Space Technol* 127:87 Ag 3 '87
Use of lighter materials to reduce helicopter life-cycle costs. il *Aviat Week Space Technol* 126:75+ Ja 19 '87

Military use
See also
Anti-helicopter weapons
Helicopters—Armaments
Agusta A129 marks European entry into 1990s combat helicopter design. R. R. Ropelewski. il *Aviat Week Space Technol* 126:50-1+ Je 8 '87
AH-1T Cobra attack helicopters deploy with Persian Gulf force. il *Aviat Week Space Technol* 127:42-3 O 19 '87
AH-64A Apaches represent blend of electronic, airframe technologies. W. B. Scott. il *Aviat Week Space Technol* 127:72-3+ Jl 20 '87
Anglo-Italian EH101 prototype expanding envelope in early flights. D. A. Brown. il *Aviat Week Space Technol* 127:111 N 23 '87
Apache helicopter will begin flights to explore agility. il *Aviat Week Space Technol* 126:24-5 Mr 2 '87
Army again changes LHX acquisition plan. *Aviat Week Space Technol* 126:24-5 Ap 20 '87
Army analysis of LHX program cites strengths of tilt-rotor. B. M. Greeley, Jr. *Aviat Week Space Technol* 126:22-3 Mr 23 '87
Army developing helicopter derivatives for special operations missions. S. W. Kandebo. il *Aviat Week Space Technol* 127:47+ D 14 '87
Army may reengine UH-1H if LHX is delayed further. B. M. Greeley, Jr. *Aviat Week Space Technol* 127:32 S 14 '87
Army seeks additional AH-64, UH-60 helicopters. il *Aviat Week Space Technol* 126:27 Mr 16 '87
Army's analysis of LHX helicopters will omit close air support issue. *Aviat Week Space Technol* 126:18 F 16 '87
Black Hawk helicopters assist Tibetan military operations. il *Aviat Week Space Technol* 127:104+ O 19 '87
Brazilian Army to buy 260 helicopters for airmobile battalions. *Aviat Week Space Technol* 127:47 Ag 17 '87
Conflicting requirements stymie German/French PAH-2 project. *Aviat Week Space Technol* 126:80-1 Ja 19 '87
Defense Board to review LHX prior to full-scale development. B. M. Greeley, Jr. *Aviat Week Space Technol* 126:22-3 F 9 '87
EH 101 helicopter favored in Canadian bid. il *Aviat Week Space Technol* 127:28-9 Ag 10 '87
EH101 helicopter rolled out; British to order utility version. D. A. Brown. il *Aviat Week Space Technol* 126:30 Ap 13 '87
Fighter, helicopter test pilots challenge cockpit design concepts. W. B. Scott. *Aviat Week Space Technol* 127:65+ N 16 '87
Flight restrictions lifted for most Marine Corps CH-53Es [transmission problems] *Aviat Week Space Technol* 127:28-9 Jl 13 '87

Helicopters—Military use—cont.

France, Germany agree on common specifications for combat helicopter [PAH-2 program] il *Aviat Week Space Technol* 126:61-2 Ap 6 '87

France, Germany authorize combat helicopter development [PAH-2/HAP/HAC-3G] J. M. Lenorovitz and K. F. Mordoff. il *Aviat Week Space Technol* 127:20-2 Jl 27 '87

French, West Germans consider combining helicopter versions. *Aviat Week Space Technol* 126:27 F 23 '87

Germany backs development of PAH-2 combat helicopter. K. F. Mordoff. *Aviat Week Space Technol* 127:28-9 N 16 '87

Helicopter displays at Paris focus on military requirements [Paris Air Show] K. F. Mordoff. il *Aviat Week Space Technol* 126:75-6 Je 29 '87

Joint development complications delay first flight of EH-101. *Aviat Week Space Technol* 127:25 S 14 '87

Manufacturer details configurations of Navy/Coast Guard SH-60F derivatives. S. W. Kandebo. il *Aviat Week Space Technol* 126:96-7 My 18 '87

McDonnell Douglas studies updated maritime AH-64A Apache derivative. il *Aviat Week Space Technol* 126:26-7 Ap 6 '87

McDonnell Douglas to propose Apache target handoff system. *Aviat Week Space Technol* 127:22 O 19 '87

Military aircraft: how much high tech is enough? D. Griffiths. il *Bus Week* p76+ My 11 '87

NATO NH-90 helicopter program enters one-year definition phase. K. F. Mordoff. il *Aviat Week Space Technol* 127:28 Jl 20 '87

Navy antisubmarine warfare helicopter makes first flight [Navy/Sikorsky SH-60F] il *Aviat Week Space Technol* 126:57 Ap 6 '87

Navy deploys helicopters to counter Gulf mine threat [Sikorsky RH-53D Sea Stallion] M. Mecham. *Aviat Week Space Technol* 127:25-6 Ag 3 '87

Navy restricts Sikorsky helicopter flights [defect in the transmission gear] *Aviat Week Space Technol* 126:27 F 23 '87

The 'Night Stalkers': death in the dark [Army helicopters locate Iranian minelayer in Persian Gulf] S. Seibert. *Newsweek* 110:26-7 O 5 '87

Orlando helicopter will modify H-19/S-55s into 'Hind look-alikes'. il *Aviat Week Space Technol* 127:53 Ag 10 '87

The ritual of the sub hunt [Sikorsky SH-3H Sea King] D. Powers. il *Flying* 114:56-8+ Ap '87

Rolls-Royce plans to join MTM390 engine program [French and German program] *Aviat Week Space Technol* 127:29 Ag 10 '87

Salvaging the LHX. D. E. Fink. *Aviat Week Space Technol* 126:11 Mr 30 '87

Senators urge Army to keep helicopter production lines open. *Aviat Week Space Technol* 126:23 Mr 23 '87

Sikorsky/Navy program to prolong service life of SH-3 helicopter. il *Aviat Week Space Technol* 126:100-1 My 18 '87

Soviet helicopters perform medical, reconnaissance missions in Nicaragua. il *Aviat Week Space Technol* 127:16-17 Ag 31 '87

Supreme Court weighs liability in military contractor suit [Boyle vs. Sikorsky over helicopter crash] M. Mecham. il *Aviat Week Space Technol* 127:81-2 O 26 '87

Two firms vie for new Canadian helicopter program [E. H. Industries' EH101 and Aerospatiale's AS332 Mk. 2 Super Puma] il *Aviat Week Space Technol* 126:28-9 Je 22 '87

U.S., Europe face decisions on new combat helicopter programs. R. R. Ropelewski. *Aviat Week Space Technol* 126:105 Mr 9 '87

Westland, Sikorsky export helicopters for military roles. il *Aviat Week Space Technol* 126:136 Ap 27 '87

Noise

Helicopters at Mesa Verde cause run-in with Utes. il *Natl Parks* 61:8 N/D '87

Radar equipment

Army's R&D plan stresses development of passive interferometry detectors. *Aviat Week Space Technol* 126:113 F 9 '87

Millimeter-wave radar may enhance safety of helicopter flights. *Aviat Week Space Technol* 127:103 Jl 6 '87

Rotors

Aerospatiale adding rotor, avionics improvements to its product line. il *Aviat Week Space Technol* 126:101+ Ja 19 '87

Bell Helicopter flying second-generation version of model 680 research rotor. il *Aviat Week Space Technol* 126:81+ Ja 19 '87

Designer proposes helicopter pressure jet rotor system to Army [work of Merrill M. Keller] *Aviat Week Space Technol* 126:122 Ja 19 '87

Look! No tail rotor! Notar. N. Moll. il *Flying* 114:30-1+ N '87

McDonnell to include no-tail rotor concept in future designs [Notar] *Aviat Week Space Technol* 127:90 Jl 6 '87

Single-rotor helicopter [Notar] N. J. Freundlich. il *Pop Sci* 231:52+ O '87

Specifications

International rotary wing aircraft [tables] il *Aviat Week Space Technol* 126:142-3 Mr 9 '87

U.S. rotary wing aircraft [tables] il *Aviat Week Space Technol* 126:144 Mr 9 '87

Stability and stabilizers

Army modifies UH-60s to cut electromagnetic interference in controls. *Aviat Week Space Technol* 127:27-8 N 16 '87

Testing

Aerospatiale testing modified version of AS 332 Super Puma. *Aviat Week Space Technol* 126:27 Mr 16 '87

Agusta A129 marks European entry into 1990s combat helicopter design. R. R. Ropelewski. il *Aviat Week Space Technol* 126:50-1+ Je 8 '87

AH-64A Apaches represent blend of electronic, airframe technologies. W. B. Scott. il *Aviat Week Space Technol* 127:72-3+ Jl 20 '87

Anglo-Italian EH-101s are being readied for flight testing. *Aviat Week Space Technol* 126:79 Ja 19 '87

Anglo-Italian EH101 prototype expanding envelope in early flights. D. A. Brown. il *Aviat Week Space Technol* 127:111 N 23 '87

Apache helicopter will begin flights to explore agility. il *Aviat Week Space Technol* 126:24-5 Mr 2 '87

Boeing Vertol Model 360 helicopter to undergo performance, stability tests [cover story] il *Aviat Week Space Technol* 127:143 Jl 13 '87

Helicopter flight maneuvers demonstrate aircraft versatility [Paris Air Show] il *Aviat Week Space Technol* 127:107 Jl 6 '87

Joint development complications delay first flight of EH-101. *Aviat Week Space Technol* 127:25 S 14 '87

Look! No tail rotor! Notar. N. Moll. il *Flying* 114:30-1+ N '87

Navy antisubmarine warfare helicopter makes first flight [Navy/Sikorsky SH-60F] il *Aviat Week Space Technol* 126:57 Ap 6 '87

Schweizer will fly turbine helicopter before year-end [Model 330 Sky Knight] P. Proctor. il *Aviat Week Space Technol* 127:69 Jl 20 '87

Transmission

Defects

Flight restrictions lifted for most Marine Corps CH-53Es. *Aviat Week Space Technol* 127:28-9 Jl 13 '87

Navy restricts Sikorsky helicopter flights. *Aviat Week Space Technol* 126:27 F 23 '87

Helicopters, Government

FAA reports frequent violations of airspace over Reagan's ranch [near midair collision, August 13, 1987] map *Aviat Week Space Technol* 127:24-5 Ag 24 '87

Helicopters, Jet

Hot-air chopper [Voljet air pressure jet copter] F. Mackerodt. il *Pop Mech* 164:82-4 F '87

Helicopters, Military *See* Helicopters—Military use

Helicopters, Remodeled

Orlando helicopter will modify H-19/S-55s into 'Hind look-alikes'. il *Aviat Week Space Technol* 127:53 Ag 10 '87

Helicopters in business

The rotary club. B. Kallen. il *Forbes* 140 Sp Issue:366-7 O 26 '87

Helicopters in medical care

Aeromedical aircraft accidents register sharp increase in 1987. P. Proctor. *Aviat Week Space Technol* 127:55+ Jl 13 '87

Charter company expanding medevac operations with BK. 117 fleet. P. Proctor. il *Aviat Week Space Technol* 126:83+ Ja 26 '87

The speed of Life [BK117 LifeStar EMS helicopter] N. Moll. il *Flying* 114:50-4+ Ap '87

Helicopters in rescue work

Flying with the Coasties [Coast Guard] S. Wilkinson. il *Oceans* 20:12-19 N/D '87

Helicopters in skiing

First tracks in the Gothics [British Columbia] J. Skow. il *Skiing* 40:224-9+ S '87

The ultimate ski adventure. P. Oliver. il *Skiing* 40:114 O '87

Helioseismology
See also
Global Oscillation Network Group
Exciting solar oscillations [work of Ken Libbrecht] il *Sky Telesc* 73:276 Mr '87
Heliosphere
Hunting for the heliosphere [research by William R. Webber] il *Sky Telesc* 74:578-9 D '87
Heliothis See Bollworms
Heliports
Heliport planning, development gain from pressures of fixed-wing traffic. P. Proctor. map *Aviat Week Space Technol* 126:59+ Mr 2 '87
Success of tilt-rotor service will require special heliports. il *Aviat Week Space Technol* 127:115-16 N 9 '87
Helitzer, Melvin
about
This course is a joke. N. Karlen. il por *Roll Stone* p106+ S 24 '87
Helium
Helium loss, tectonics, and the terrestrial heat budget. E. R. Oxburgh and R. K. O'Nions. bibl f il map *Science* 237:1583-8 S 25 '87
Helium-rich supernovas. J. C. Wheeler and R. P. Harkness. bibl (p150) il *Sci Am* 257:50-8 N '87
Partners for a noble element [work of Gernot Frenking and others] *Sci News* 132:334 N 21 '87
Isotopes
Helium-3 and helium-4 [special issue; with introd. by Russell J. Donnelly] bibl f il *Phys Today* 40:23+ F '87
Reserves
Dismantling the helium empire [Bureau of Mines' operations] M. Crawford. il *Science* 237:238-40 Jl 17 '87
Helium, Liquid
See also
Superfluidity
Electrons and ions at the helium surface. A. J. Dahm and W. F. Vinen. bibl f il *Phys Today* 40:43-50 F '87
Quantized vortices in superfluid helium-4. W. I. Glaberson and K. W. Schwarz. bibl f il *Phys Today* 40:54-60 F '87
Vortices in rotating superfluid He[3]. P. Hakonen and O. V. Lounasmaa. bibl f il *Phys Today* 40:70-8 F '87
Helium, Solid
Novel magnetic properties of solid helium-3. M. C. Cross and D. D. Osheroff. bibl f il *Phys Today* 40:34-41 F '87
The surface of crystalline helium-4. H. J. Maris and A. F. Andreev. bibl f il *Phys Today* 40:25-30 F '87
Hell Canyon (S.D.)
Trouble in Hell Canyon [Indians oppose Honeywell's proposed munitions testing site] T. E. Johnson. il *Newsweek* 110:30 S 28 '87
Helleberg, Marilyn M.
My father's song [condensed from God's best for you] il *Read Dig* 131:53-6 S '87
Hellebores
The hellebores: a perennial surprise. L. C. Askey. il *South Living* 22:48-50 F '87
Plant hellebores to herald springtime. K. Piper. il *Flower Gard* 32:58-61 D '87/Ja '88
Hellemans, Alexander
New directions for encyclopedias. il *Publ Wkly* 232:40+ O 2 '87
Heller, André
about
Aiming high, André Heller floats the U.S. a fantastic loan. K. Hubbard. il por *People Wkly* 28:90-1 S 28 '87
Heller, Anne Conover
Is there a man in your man's life? What every girl should know about the bisexual guy. *Mademoiselle* 93:134-5+ Jl '87
Jennifer Levin and Robert Chambers: a walk with love and death. il pors *Mademoiselle* 93:145-7+ Ja '87
A new rash of measles. *Redbook* 169:30 Jl '87
Heller, H. Robert, 1940-
U.S. exporters need first-rate global banking networks. il *Bus Week* p20 Je 8 '87
Heller, Joseph
about
Catch-2: author Joe Heller remarries; this time it's the nurse who brought him back to health. K. Gross. il pors *People Wkly* 27:42+ Ap 27 '87
Heller, Karen
Can this friendship be saved? il *Mademoiselle* 93:238-9+ N '87

Class makes a comeback: the return of the lady. il *Mademoiselle* 93:214-15+ My '87
Is he husband material or a boyfriend kind of guy? il *Mademoiselle* 93:162-3+ O '87
Heller, Peter
A little tatter of sky [story] *Harpers* 275:28+ Ag '87
Heller, Walter W.
about
Obituary
Time il por 129:46 Je 29 '87. G. J. Church
Hellerstein, David
Men in the eighties: multiplying roles: the next stage. il *Ms* 16:48-50 O '87
Hellman, Lillian, 1906-1984
about
Making up the truth. G. C. Ward. il *Am Herit* 38:18+ S/O '87
Hellman, Peter
The little airplane that could. il *Discover* 8:78-87 F '87
Street smart. il por *N Y* 20:48-53 N 23 '87
about
A way with words—and music. G. L. Rogin. il por *Discover* 8:4 F '87
Hello again [film] See Motion picture reviews—Single works
Hello Kitty (Fictional character)
Mickey Mouse, meet Hello Kitty. M. Beauchamp and H. Katayama. il por *Forbes* 139:68+ My 18 '87
Hell's Angels
There goes the neighborhood: gangs of yuppies move onto the turf of New York's Hells Angels [East Village] J. S. Kunen. il *People Wkly* 28:119-20+ S 7 '87
Hellwig, Monika K.
The Word. See issues of America beginning June 23-30, 1984 through June 20-27, 1987
Helmberger, Marshall
Farmers plow up Pentagon's budget. *Progressive* 51:15-16 Mr '87
Strategic Air Command bombs out. il *Progressive* 51:11-12 Ag '87
Helmets
Bendix, Israeli firm demonstrate high-accuracy helmet sight. il *Aviat Week Space Technol* 127:148 Ag 10 '87
Helmet sunglasses [for motorcyclists] il *Cycle* 38:39 N '87
Video helmet [LCD display on astronauts' visors] M. Costello. il *Omni* 9:103 Ja '87
Helms, Chet
about
Artists sue over posters: San Francisco battle focuses on rights to psychedelic artwork from the sixties. M. Goldberg. *Roll Stone* p29 Ap 23 '87
Helms, Jesse A.
about
Coming soon: the odd couple. T. Noah and E. Clift. il pors *Newsweek* 109:28 F 2 '87
The discreet charms of a demogogue. G. Epps. bibl f il *N Y Rev Books* 34:31-5 My 7 '87
Jess and Les. por *Time* 129:25 F 2 '87
Lessons from the fringe. T. Branch. *Wash Mon* 19:56-8 F '87
Helms, Richard
about
Deep in the Bear's den. H. Sidey. il por *Time* 129:14 Je 29 '87
Helmsley, Harry B., 1909-
about
Tax troubles hound Gotham hotel queen Leona Helmsley, whom subjects call a royal pain. K. McMurran. il pors *People Wkly* 27:32-5 Ja 5 '87
Helmsley, Leona
about
Tax troubles hound Gotham hotel queen Leona Helmsley, whom subjects call a royal pain. K. McMurran. il pors *People Wkly* 27:32-5 Ja 5 '87
Helmut Newton's illustrated (Periodical)
Mr. Peepers's nights: dangerous liaisons. il por *N Y* 20:23-4 Ap 6 '87
Heloise
The Heloise helpline for all your household problems. See issues of Good Housekeeping beginning November 1983
Help! [film] See Motion picture reviews—Single works
Help wanted advertising See Advertising, Classified
Helping behavior
See also
Assistance in emergencies
Favors

Helping behavior—*cont.*
Help, at a distance [effect of distance and personal space] P. Glick. *Psychol Today* 21:66-7 F '87
Your new path to a stronger immune system. R. Rodale. il *Prevention* 39:20-1+ S '87
Helping Hands (Organization)
Someone to share the hurt. C. L. O'Shea. il por *Read Dig* 131:67-71 S '87
Helplessness (Psychology)
Stop blaming yourself [linking explanatory style with learned helplessness, depression, and illness; research by M. E. P. Seligman] R. J. Trotter. bibl (p64) il pors *Psychol Today* 21:30-2+ F '87
Stressed out: learned helplessness in rats sheds light on human depression. E. Collins. *Sci Am* 257:30 N '87
Helsinki (Finland)
　　Restaurants, nightclubs, bars, etc.
Northern light [K. Blomstedt's redesign of Bulevardia restaurant; cover story] P. M. Sachner. il *Archit Rec* 175:120-5 Ag '87
Helsinki Human Rights Day
Helsinki Human Rights Day, 1987 [proclamation, July 31, 1987] R. Reagan. *Dep State Bull* 87:37 O '87
Hemangiomas *See* Tumors (Benign)
Hematopoiesis *See* Blood cells—Growth
Hembree, Diana
(jt. auth) *See* Beers, David, and Hembree, Diana
Hemdale Film Corporation
The battle for Platoon [video rights] J. Vitale. il *Channels* 7:59 O '87
A jungle war over the 'Platoon' video. il *Newsweek* 110:56 N 23 '87
Lights, camera, lawyers! [battle over video rights to Platoon] W. Harris. il *Forbes* 140:33 Ag 10 '87
What's the point? [dispute over distribution of profits from Platoon] il *Fortune* 116:9 N 23 '87
Hemerocallis *See* Daylilies
Hemerythrin
Antigenicity of myohemerythrin [discussion of March 6, 1987 article, Chemistry of antibody binding to a protein] H. M. Geysen and others. *Science* 238:1584-6 D 11 '87
Chemistry of antibody binding to a protein [myohemerythrin] H. M. Geysen and others. bibl f il *Science* 235:1184-90 Mr 6 '87
Mechanisms of antibody binding to a protein [myohemerythrin] E. D. Getzoff and others. bibl f il *Science* 235:1191-6 Mr 6 '87
Hemet (Calif.)
　　Description
Some like it hot! [retirees] S. Angel. il *50 Plus* 27:54-8 Je '87
Hemingway, Ernest, 1899-1961
Pamplona in July [excerpt from Dateline Toronto] il *50 Plus* 27:50-4 Jl '87
A train trip [story] il *Esquire* 108:162-4+ D '87
　　about
Hemingway's Miró. S. Staggs. il *Art News* 86:12 D '87
Pressure under grace. F. C. Crews. bibl f il por *N Y Rev Books* 34:30-7 Ag 13 '87
'Pressure under grace': an exchange [discussion of August 13, 1987 article] F. C. Crews. il *N Y Rev Books* 34:59-60 O 22 '87
Where's Papa? B. P. Solomon. *New Repub* 196:30-4 Mr 9 '87
Hemingway, Hadley
　　about
Brenda Frazier biographer turns to Hadley Hemingway. W. Goldstein. *Publ Wkly* 232:79-80 Ag 14 '87
Heminway, John Hylan, 1944-
An African bird makes its move around the world. bibl (p183) il map *Smithsonian* 18:60-6+ My '87
Despite long odds, mighty herds still plunge across the Serengeti. bibl (p143) il *Smithsonian* 17:50-6+ F '87
Hemisphere (Firm)
Exploring a new Hemisphere. J. B. Copeland. il *Newsweek* 110:57 S 14 '87
Hemispherectomy *See* Brain—Surgery
Hemispheric dominance *See* Laterality
Hemley, R. J., and others
Laser techniques in high-pressure geophysics. bibl f il *Science* 237:605-12 Ag 7 '87
Hemmeter, Christopher
　　about
Designer of all he surveys, Hawaii's Chris Hemmeter leis on the luxury to embellish his visions of paradise. M. Neill. il pors *People Wkly* 28:92-4 O 19 '87
Peacocks, geysers, marble stallions—Mr. Mega-Resort strikes again. J. B. Levine. il por *Bus Week* p64-5 Mr 30 '87

Hemmings, Peter
　　about
Opera's turn. A. Rich. il por *Opera News* 52:16-18+ D 5 '87
Hemodialysis equipment
Reuse of kidney dialysis equipment. *FDA Consum* 21:2 Mr '87
Hemoglobin
　　See also
　　Blood boosting
Blood imbalance detected in SIDS victims. J. Greenberg. *Sci News* 131:292 My 9 '87
Crib death clue [hemoglobin F] N. Eurman. il *Health* 19:25 N '87
Delay time of hemoglobin S polymerization prevents most cells from sickling in vivo. A. Mozzarelli and others. bibl f il *Science* 237:500-6 Jl 31 '87
Hemophilia
　　Therapy
Freeing hemophiliacs from the risk of AIDS [synthetic clotting factor offers hope] R. Rhein, Jr. and L. Therrien. il *Bus Week* p38 Ap 13 '87
Future 'patchwork' cure for hemophilia? D. D. Edwards. *Sci News* 131:168 My 14 '87
Hemophilus infections *See* Hib infections
Hemorrhage
　　See also
　　Brain—Hemorrhage
　　Nosebleed
Plaque hemorrhage linked to stroke [use of computer tomography to scan carotid arteries; research by Antonio Culebras and others] S. Weisburd. il *Sci News* 131:167 Mr 14 '87
Postpartum hemorrhage. P. A. Hillard. il *Parents* 62:104+ Ja '87
Hemorrhoid Clinics of America
Hemorrhoid treatment to go. *Prevention* 39:140 Ja '87
Hemp
　　See also
　　Kenaf
　　Marijuana
Hempe, A. Henry, and Decker, William
Child-custody issues and the schools. *Educ Dig* 53:50-1 O '87
Hempel, Amy
William Wegman: the artist and his dog. il pors *N Y Times Mag* p40-2+ N 29 '87
Hempen, Hal
　　about
Hal Hempen's All-American dream. J. Schuster. il *Sport Mag* 78:90 S '87
Hemphill, Christopher
La professoressa della cucina. il por *House Gard* 159:24+ My '87
Hemptinne, Marc de, 1902-1986
　　about
Obituary
　　Phys Today 40:93 Ja '87. J. Deutsch
Hemstreet, Robert M.
Religious humanism meets scientific atheism. il por *Humanist* 47:5-7+ Ja/F '87
Henbest, Nigel
Misreading the stars. il *World Press Rev* 34:55 S '87
Henderiks, Joy
　　about
French connection. il pors *Vogue* 177:156 Jl '87
Henderson, Bruce B.
The kids who saved a dying town. il *Read Dig* 131:42-6 S '87
Henderson, Denys H.
　　about
A busy body bent on doing better. R. I. Kirkland, Jr. il por *Fortune* 116:60 Ag 3 '87
Henderson, Donald A.
The lessons learnt. il por *World Health* p8-11 Ag/S '87
Henderson, Doug
Nutrition and the athlete [cover story] il *FDA Consum* 21:18-21 My '87
Henderson, Joe
　　about
Joe Henderson's solo on Song for my father—a tenor saxophone transcription. J. T. Cohen. il *Down Beat* 54:58-9 S '87
Henderson, Kathy, 1954-
Mama Mia! "My daughter has a gift with children" [interview with M. O'Sullivan] il pors *Redbook* 169:50+ S '87
Meet the new "Mr. Moms" [interviews with T. Selleck, T. Danson, and S. Guttenberg] il pors *Redbook* 170:44+ N '87

Henderson, Kathy, 1954—cont.
"Ms. Dipesto, you look fabulous!" [interview] il pors
Redbook 168:18+ Mr '87
Tactics for living with your teen. il McCalls 115:63-5
N '87

Henderson, Mark
about
Panmure Gordon & Co. [interview] il por Fortune 116
Sp Issue:182-3 Fall '87

Henderson, Mary, Lady
In the Chalk Hills: Sir Nicholas and Lady Henderson's
West Country cottages. il pors Archit Dig 44:184-7+
Je '87

Henderson, Sir Nicholas
about
In the Chalk Hills: Sir Nicholas and Lady Henderson's
West Country cottages. M. Henderson, Lady. il pors
Archit Dig 44:184-7+ Je '87

Henderson, Phil
about
The old college try—again. A. Wolf. il por Sports Illus
67 Sp Issue:72 N 18 '87

Henderson, Ralph H.
EPI: "shots" that save lives. il World Health p4-6 Ja/F
'87

Henderson, Scott
about
Scott Henderson. B. Milkowski. il por Down Beat 54:42-3
My '87

Hendricks, Paula
Condoms: a straight girl's best friend. il Ms 16:98+
S '87

Hendrix, Jimi
about
Jimi Hendrix and the Band of Gypsys: The Fillmore
East, New York City, December 31st, 1969, and January
1st, 1970. D. Fricke. il pors Roll Stone p71-2 Je
4 '87

Hendry, Bruce, 1942-
about
The 'pugnacious bulldog' fighting for Kaiser Steel. M.
J. Pitzer. il por Bus Week p72-3 F 16 '87

Henjum, Mark G.
(jt. auth) See Bull, Evelyn L., and Henjum, Mark G.

Henke, Ellen
Celebrating the rose. il Saturday Evening Post 259:46-7
Jl/Ag '87
Deck your halls with houseplants. il Saturday Evening
Post 259:84-5+ D '87
Dr. Ellen's gardening tips. Good Housekeep 204:225-6
Ap '87
Getting the most from your garden. il Saturday Evening
Post 259:96+ S '87
Perennial beauty. il Saturday Evening Post 259:94-5 My/Je
'87
Putting your bulbs to bed. il Saturday Evening Post
259:34-5+ O '87
Shortcuts to a healthy lawn. il Saturday Evening Post
259:96-7 Ap '87

Henkel, Oliver C.
The press, the process, and Gary Hart [address, May
29, 1987] Vital Speeches Day 53:697-700 S 1 '87

Henkin, Louis
Foreign affairs and the Constitution. bibl f Foreign Aff
66:284-310 Wint '87/'88

Henley, Beth
about
Crimes of the heart writer Beth Henley talks about
Sissy, Diane and Jessica. C. Krupp. il por Glamour
85:134 Ja '87
The eccentric genius of "Crimes of the heart". M. Rochlin.
il por Ms 15:12+ F '87
The Lucky Spot [drama] Reviews
N Y 20:83-4 My 11 '87. J. Simon
New Yorker 63:80-1 My 11 '87. E. Oliver

Henley, Don
about
Don Henley [interview] M. Gilmore. por Roll Stone
p287-91 N 5-D 10 '87

Henley, F. Milene
Coming back to life. il pors Ladies Home J 104:34+
Jl '87
Good, better, best. il pors Work Woman 12:86-9 D
'87

Henley, Martin, 1943-
Something is missing from the education reform movement. il Phi Delta Kappan 69:284-5 D '87

Henley Group Inc.
'Betting on the genius' of Henley's chairman [stock picker
W. S. Grossman bets on M. Dingman] G. G. Marcial.
il por Bus Week p118 N 23 '87

Mike Dingman tunes 'em up, turns 'em around, spins
'em off. S. Toy. il por Bus Week p90-2+ O 5 '87
Santa Fe's pursuers may have to settle for pieces. S.
Toy. il Bus Week p74 D 28 '87-Ja 4 '88
Trying to turn Henley into more than 'assets and a
dream'. L. Baum. il por Bus Week p80 F 2 '87
The turnaround king investors love. B. Dumaine. il
por Fortune 115:66 Ja 5 '87

Hennayake, Shantha K., and Duncan, James S.
A disputed homeland. il map Focus 37:20-7 Spr '87

Hennepin County (Minn.)
Child welfare
Are home based services effective? A public child welfare
agency's experiment. P. AuClaire and I. M. Schwartz.
il Child Today 16:6-9 My/Je '87

Hennessy, Edward L., Jr.
about
Small payoffs from big deals. P. Nulty. il por Fortune
116:139+ D 7 '87
Will all that restructuring ever pay off for Ed Hennessy's
Allied? J. H. Dobrzynski. il por Bus Week p78-80
F 2 '87

Hennessy, John
about
New capitals for raising capital? [interview] R. Morais.
por Forbes 139:64 Mr 9 '87

Hennessy, John Pope- See Pope-Hennessy, John

Henning, W., and others
Calcium-41 concentration in terrestrial materials:
prospects for dating of Pleistocene samples. bibl f
il Science 236:725-7 My 8 '87

Henri Bendel Inc.
The battle of Bendel's [takeover by L. Wexner] J. Korn-
bluth. il pors N Y 20:26-33 F 23 '87
Buster of Bendel's [doorman] G. Stutz. il N Y 20:68
D 21-28 '87

Henry VIII, King of England, 1491-1547
about
Privy secrets: Henry VIII and the Lords of the Council
[cover story] D. Starkey. bibl il pors Hist Today
37:23-31 Ag '87
Whatever happened to the English Reformation? G.
Redworth. bibl il Hist Today 37:29-36 O '87

Henry, Prince of Great Britain, 1984-
about
Harry, His Royal Shyness, assumes his rightful role
as a Cygnet at big brother Wills's old school. il por
People Wkly 28:127 O 5 '87
No conquering William, Harry is Britain's bashful birthday boy. il pors People Wkly 28:147-9 S 14 '87

Henry, Carl F. H., 1913-
An eye on the cradle. il por Christ Today 31:26-7 N
6 '87
about
Lost momentum [interview] B. Spring. il por Christ
Today 31:30-2 S 4 '87

Henry, Gerrit
Dark poetry [cover story] il pors Art News 86:104-11
Ap '87

Henry, J. David, 1945-
What it means to be a fox. il Int Wildl 17:12-16 N/D
'87

Henry, James S.
Brazil says: nuts. New Repub 197:25+ O 12 '87
Dance of debt isn't over yet. il U S News World Rep
103:39-41 Ag 31 '87
Three cheers for Citicorp's initiative. il U S News World
Rep 102:48 Je 1 '87

Henry, Michael
A true test or a trivia game? por Newsweek 109:10-11
Je 22 '87

Henry, William A., 1950-
George Will among the polysyllables. il por Esquire
107:87-92 Ja '87
Private eye. See issues of Channels (New York, N.Y.:
1986)

Henry Ford Museum and Greenfield Village
Henry Ford Museum & Greenfield Village [The
automobile in American life exhibit] il Antiques Collect
Hobbies 92:47-8 Jl '87

Henry Holt and Company
Fayard and Holt settle dispute over world rights to
Walesa autobio. W. Goldstein. il pors Publ Wkly
232:23-4 Jl 31 '87

Henry IV, part 1 [drama] See Shakespeare, William,
1564-1616

Henry Threadgill Sextett
Henry Threadgill Sextett. L. Birnbaum. Down Beat 54:56
Je '87

Henson, Ahnahkaq
about
Eskimo son of explorer Matthew Henson dies in Greenland of cancer. pors *Jet* 72:12 Jl 27 '87
Matthew Henson's Eskimo son comes to U.S. for a reunion with relatives. il pors *Jet* 72:6 Je 15 '87
Henson, Jim
about
Post-Muppet Primitives. B. Weber. il por *N Y Times Mag* p78 Ag 16 '87
Henson, Matthew Alexander, 1866-1955
about
The Eskimo offspring of Matthew Henson. S. A. Counter. il pors *Ebony* 42:50+ Ja '87
Eskimo son of explorer Matthew Henson dies in Greenland of cancer. pors *Jet* 72:12 Jl 27 '87
Explorers' Eskimo offspring visit America. il *Ebony* 42:84+ S '87
Matthew Henson will be reburied in Arlington. por *Jet* 73:26 N 23 '87
Matthew Henson's Eskimo son comes to U.S. for a reunion with relatives. il pors *Jet* 72:6 Je 15 '87
No slouches at breaking the ice, polar explorers Peary and Henson each left behind a son in the Arctic. C. Neuhaus. il pors *People Wkly* 27:41-2 Je 1 '87
Hentoff, Nat
Birdland. il *N Y* 20:92 D 21-28 '87
Indigenous music. See issues of The Progressive
Profiles (I) [Cardinal J. J. O'Connor] por *New Yorker* 63:59-76 Mr 23 '87
Profiles (II) [Cardinal J. J. O'Connor] il *New Yorker* 63:37-8+ Mr 30 '87
Hentze, Matthias W., and others
Identification of the iron-responsive element for the translational regulation of human ferritin mRNA. bibl f il *Science* 238:1570-3 D 11 '87
Henze, Hans Werner, 1926-
about
Musical events:
　H. W. Henze's Seventh symphony. A. Porter. *New Yorker* 63:134+ N 23 '87
The other side of the churchyard wall. I. Strasfogel. il pors *Opera News* 51:30-2+ My '87
Heparin
Heparin promotes the inactivation of antithrombin by neutrophil elastase. R. E. Jordan and others. bibl f il *Science* 237:777-9 Ag 14 '87
Hepatic encephalopathy *See* Reye's syndrome
Hepatitis
Vaccines and vaccination
Oral vaccine sought for hepatitis B. R. Weiss. *Sci News* 132:39 Jl 18 '87
Hepatitis viruses
Proteolytic self-cleavage of hepatitis B virus core protein may generate serum e antigen. R. H. Miller. bibl f il *Science* 236:722-5 My 8 '87
Hepatology
See also
Sammy Davis Jr. National Liver Institute
Hepburn, Katharine, 1909-
The making of The African Queen [excerpts] il pors *Ladies Home J* 104:77-80+ N '87
'The making of "The African Queen"' [excerpts] il por *Newsweek* 110:53-5 Ag 31 '87
Secrets of vitality. por *Saturday Evening Post* 259:26 S '87
about
Kate [cover story] P. Battelle. il pors *Ladies Home J* 104:124-5+ O '87
Kate [cover story] T. Mathews. il pors *Newsweek* 110:48-52 Ag 31 '87
Three neighbors. T. Capote. il pors *Esquire* 108:223-4 D '87
Unforgettable faces [makeup and hairstyles that reinterpret legendary looks] il pors *Seventeen* 46:120-5 F '87
Heppenheimer, T. A., 1947-
Journey to the center of the earth. il map *Discover* 8:86-90+ N '87
Heptachlor
From tainted feed to mothers' milk. D. Farley. il *FDA Consum* 21:38-40 Mr '87
Heptathlon
Is she the greatest of them all? [J. Joyner] P. Freeman. il pors *Women's Sports Fitness* 9:38-42+ Ja '87
On top of the worlds [J. Joyner-Kersee wins heptathlon and long jump at World Track and Field Championships; cover story] K. Moore. il pors *Sports Illus* 67:18-23 S 14 '87
Ties that bind [J. Joyner-Kersee and brother A. Joyner] K. Moore. il pors *Sports Illus* 66:76-80+ Ap 27 '87

Herald of Free Enterprise (Ferry) *See* Ferries
Herald Square (New York, N.Y.)
Into the valley of death? [Abraham & Straus opens] J. Flint. il *Forbes* 140:160 O 19 '87
Herb gardens *See* Herbs
Herb tea *See* Tea (Beverage)
Herb vinegar *See* Vinegar
Herb wreaths *See* Wreaths
Herber, Harold L., and Nelson-Herber, Joan
Helping students become independent learners. *Educ Dig* 53:12-15 D '87
Herber, Joan Nelson- *See* Nelson-Herber, Joan
Herbert, Rosemary
Arthur Thornhill looks back on 39 years at Little, Brown. il por *Publ Wkly* 231:18+ F 6 '87
The building of a dictionary: how Robert Burchfield devoted 29 years to the 'OED supplement'. il por *Publ Wkly* 232:38-9 O 2 '87
Hubbard awards, three years old, find sanction. il *Publ Wkly* 231:22 My 22 '87
Herbert, Solomon
The business of show biz. il por *Essence* 18:116+ S '87
Selling the home advantage. il pors *Black Enterp* 18:90-2 O '87
Herbert, Victor
about
Naughty Marietta [operetta] Reviews
N Y 20:134 Ap 27 '87. P. G. Davis
Herbert, Zbigniew
Mass for the imprisoned [poem]; tr. by Michael March and Jaroslaw Anders. *N Y Rev Books* 33:15 Ja 15 '87
Herbicide spraying equipment *See* Spraying equipment
Herbicides
See also
Agent Orange
Double-barrel loads for weed battle; Command is back! B. Freese. il *Success Farm* 85 no1:22-3 Ja '87
Killing weeds with daylight [aminolaevulinic acid] *Success Farm* 85 no3:20 F '87
Weed control in lawns and other turf. il *Consum Res Mag* 70:16-18+ Ap '87
Handling
Blown-on weed control. D. Mowitz. il *Success Farm* 85 no5:26J Mr '87
Herbicide in anhydrous loses company push [Sutan and Eradicane] R. Fee. il *Success Farm* 85 no1:26AL Ja '87
'Incorporate' chemicals in no-till [herbicide impregnated on dry bulk fertilizer] R. Fee. il *Success Farm* 85 no1:26Z Ja '87
'Ole eyeball' gets infrared view of weed problems [Soilection Systems of Soil Teq, Inc.] il *Success Farm* 85 no2:18P Ja '87
Injurious effects
Scepter carryover stunts cotton and corn. *Success Farm* 85:62 S '87
See no evil [EPA approval of Sonar herbicide based on incomplete data] T. Turner. *Mother Earth News* 106:114-15 Jl/Ag '87
Weed killer [Monsanto's Roundup] A. L. Kimery. il *Progressive* 51:20-1 Jl '87
Prices
Herbicide prices wilt under competitive stress. B. Freese. il *Success Farm* 85 no6:18A Mr '87
Herbicides on sale! B. Freese. il *Success Farm* 85 no1:19 Ja '87
Herbig-Haro objects
A Herbig-Haro object unmasked [cosmic jets of HH34] *Sky Telesc* 73:30-1 Ja '87
Herbivores
Domino effect invoked in Ice Age extinctions [theory of Norman Owen-Smith] R. Lewin. il *Science* 238:1509-10 D 11 '87
Herbivory in rocks and the weathering of a desert [impact of lichen feeding by snails] M. Shachak and others. bibl f il *Science* 236:1098-9 My 29 '87
Large herbivore foraging and ecological hierarchies. R. L. Senft and others. bibl il *BioScience* 37:789-95+ D '87
On the benefits of being eaten [herbivory benefits plants; research by Ken Paige and Thomas Whitham] R. Lewin. il *Science* 236:519-20 My 1 '87
Snails dine at desert dust depot [research by Clive G. Jones and others] K. Hartley. il *Sci News* 131:373 Je 13 '87
Herbs
See also
Burnet
Chamomile

Herbs—See also—*cont.*
Chives
Cooking—Herbs and spices
Costmary
Garlic
Ginseng
Overbrook Herb Farm (Lansdale, Pa.)
Sweet cicely
Thyme
A choice of barbecue herbs. il *Sunset* 178:206 Ap '87
"The formality of the French, the loose, spilly quality of the English" [Portland, Or. garden] il *Sunset* 178:207 Je '87
Herbal renewal. J. Sherman. il *Work Woman* 12:83 O '87
Herbs handy to the back door [Jodie Slaymaker's Nashville herb garden] il *South Living* 22:55 Je '87
Herbs with a view [windowsill culture] T. James. il *50 Plus* 27:38-40+ Ag '87
Japanese herbs: easy to use, easy to grow. il *Sunset* 179:62-4, 156 Ag '87
Standout southern herbs. L. Hutson. il *Rodale's Org Gard* 34:81-6 S '87
Try these novel uses for surplus herbs. K. Kraft and P. Kraft. il *Flower Gard* 32:46-7 D '87/Ja '88
Herbs, Medicinal *See* Botany, Medical
Herbst, Peter
Cafe au Go Go. il *N Y* 20:81 D 21-28 '87
Hercules Aerospace Company
Hercules prepares for INF verification inspections. il *Aviat Week Space Technol* 127:23-4 D 14 '87
New Hercules plant to cut solid rocket cost. il *Aviat Week Space Technol* 126:117 Ap 27 '87
Herding behavior of animals *See* Animals—Habits and behavior
Herding of sheep *See* Sheep herding
Hereafter *See* Future life
Heredity
See also
Chromosomes
Clones (Biology)
Genes
Hybridization
Linkage (Genetics)
Natural selection
Variation (Biology)
Heredity and environment
The eerie world of reunited twins [Minnesota study] C. M. Rosen. il *Discover* 8:36-42+ S '87
Exploring the traits of twins [study by the Minnesota Center for Twin and Adoption Research] J. Leo. il *Time* 129:63 Ja 12 '87
Genes and behavior: a twin legacy [Minnesota study by Thomas J. Bouchard] C. Holden. il *Psychol Today* 21:18-19 S '87
The genetics of personality. C. Holden. il *Science* 237:598-601 Ag 7 '87
Growing up: Del and Rey, Johnny and Jimmy [experiments carried out on twins in the early 1930's] il *Sci Am* 257:30-2 Jl '87
Letters [discussion of November 1986 article, Untrashing Margaret Mead] *Sci Am* 256:6 F '87
Nature, nurture, and behavior. D. E. Koshland, Jr. *Science* 235:1445 Mr 20 '87
Sins and twins. R. Bazell. *New Repub* 197:17-18 D 21 '87
To the manner born [study of twins] W. Gallagher. il *Roll Stone* p56+ N 19 '87
Heredity of disease
See also
AIDS (Disease)—Genetic aspects
Alcoholics and alcoholism—Genetic aspects
ALD (Disease)
Alzheimer's disease—Genetic aspects
Bloom's syndrome
Cancer—Genetic aspects
Cystic fibrosis
Demyelination—Genetic aspects
Depression, Mental—Genetic aspects
Diabetes—Genetic aspects
Down syndrome
Fragile X syndrome
Gaucher's disease
Gene probes
Gene therapy
Genetic counseling
Genetic screening
Heart—Diseases—Genetic aspects
Hemophilia
Huntington's disease
Hypercholesteremia

Hypertension—Genetic aspects
Lesch-Nyhan syndrome
Leukemia—Genetic aspects
Muscular dystrophy—Genetic aspects
Neural tube—Diseases
Neurofibromatosis
Sickle cell anemia
Syndaktylia
Better animal models for genetic defects [technique developed by Mario R. Capecchi and Kirk R. Thomas] S. Eisenberg. *Sci News* 132:327 N 21 '87
Genetic promise [restriction fragment length polymorphism mapping] *Sci Am* 257:30-1 Ag '87
Homozygosity mapping: a way to map human recessive traits with the DNA of inbred children. E. S. Lander and D. Botstein. bibl f il *Science* 236:1567-70 Je 19 '87
The inheritance of epigenetic defects. R. Holliday. bibl f il *Science* 238:163-70 O 9 '87
Molecular genetics: applications to the clinical neurosciences [linkage analysis with restriction fragment length polymorphisms] J. B. Martin. bibl f il *Science* 238:765-72 N 6 '87
Herenton, Willie W.
about
Memphis educator named Atlanta superintendent. por *Jet* 73:22 N 9 '87
Heresy
See also
Catholic Church. Congregation for the Doctrine of the Faith
Dissidents in an age of faith? Wyclif and the Lollards. J. Catto. bibl il *Hist Today* 37:46-52 N '87
Hering, Doris
about
Dance Magazine Awards 1987. il pors *Dance Mag* 61:44-6 F '87
Heritage, Protection of *See* Cultural property—Protection
Heritage Communications, Inc.
Starting over in Dallas. C. Capuzzi. il *Channels* 7:23-4 Jl/Ag '87
The unimportance of being earners. J. Baker. il map *Channels* 7:51-6 Mr '87
Heritage Foundation (Washington, D.C.)
The Heritage Foundation goes abroad [activities in Great Britain; cover story] il *Nation* 244:747+ Je 6 '87
Heritage USA (N.C.)
God's country. G. C. Wescott. il *Life* 10:84-7 Ag '87
Herken, Gregg, 1947-
The earthly origins of Star Wars [cover story] bibl f il *Bull At Sci* 43:20-8 O '87
Herling, Gustav, 1919-
about
Houses of the dead. F. Eberstadt. *Commentary* 83:43-7 F '87
Herling-Grudzinski, Gustav *See* Herling, Gustav, 1919-
Herman, David
about
'They used to call me McEnroe'. P. M. Coan. il *World Tennis* 34:20-1 My '87
Herman, Hank
As we see it. See occasional issues of Health (New York, N.Y.)
Herman, Jan K., and Barger, M. Susan
The moon on a silver plate. il *Astronomy* 15:98-103 O '87
Herman, Pee-wee
about
Harlequin. K. Leishman. il *Atlantic* 259:20-2 My '87
The Pee-wee perplex. T. Gertler. il pors *Roll Stone* p36-8+ F 12 '87
Pee-wee, the E.T. of comedy. C. Schine. il por *Vogue* 177:114+ F '87
The weird world of Pee-wee. H. F. Waters. il pors *Newsweek* 109:83-4 My 18 '87
Herman, Steven A., and Coffin, John M.
Efficient packaging of readthrough RNA in ALV: implications for oncogene transduction. bibl f il *Science* 236:845-8 My 15 '87
Herman Miller, Inc.
Lone star [Dallas showroom] C. K. Gandee. il *Archit Rec* 175:110-15 My '87
Hermann, Eric
Yurts! il *Sierra* 72:51-4 N/D '87
Hermann, Jane
about
The Met's Jane Hermann: offstage assoluta. J. Gruen. il por *Dance Mag* 61:48-51 Jl '87
Hermann, Loretta
(jt. auth) See Hermann, Phil, and Hermann, Loretta

Hermann, Phil, and Hermann, Loretta
Wild about wildlife. il *Petersens Photogr Mag* 15:28-31 Ap '87
Hermann-Grima House (New Orleans, La.) *See* New Orleans (La.)—Historic houses, sites, etc.
Hermeneutics
Hermen eutic's original intent [derivation of term] W. Safire. il *N Y Times Mag* p10+ S 6 '87
Hermès, Jean-Louis Dumas- *See* Dumas-Hermès, Jean-Louis
Hermes, Joan Garvey
Kids deserve better than perfect parents. *U S Cathol* 52:38-40 Mr '87
Hermès (Firm) *See* House of Hermès (Firm)
Hermes (Space vehicle) *See* Spaceplane, French
Hermeto
about
Hermeto. H. Mandel. il por *Down Beat* 54:15 Ap '87
Hermits
Facing eviction from his Boston hovel, hermit Bill Britt pleads there's no place like home. C. Neuhaus. il pors *People Wkly* 27:61-2 Ap 13 '87
Hernandez, Keith, 1953-
about
First love. C. Wolff. il pors *Sport Mag* 78:51-5 Je '87
Hernandez-Claire, José
about
Into the looking glass. S. Piperato. il *Pop Photogr* 94:46-9 Mr '87
Herndon, David
TV hoops: technical foul. il *Sport Mag* 78:66-7 F '87
Herniated disks *See* Spine—Abnormalities
Herodotus
about
The father of it all. J. Griffin. il *N Y Rev Books* 34:11-12+ Ap 9 '87
Herodotus's theory of how the pyramids were built gets a lift. il *Discover* 8:8-9 Je '87
Heroes and heroines
See also
  Courage
Alice Walker, Coretta King most outstanding: poll [World almanac poll] il *Jet* 71:27 Ja 19 '87
Cosby named top hero in World almanac poll. *Jet* 71:52 Ja 12 '87
Democracy and its heroes. J. R. Silber. *Current* 294:16-19 Jl/Ag '87
'Fridge' Perry is tops, say U.S. teens. *Jet* 71:32 Ja 19 '87
Heroes for today. il *Read Dig* 130:17-18+ My '87
Heroes for today. il *Read Dig* 130:179-80+ Mr '87
Heroes for today. il *Read Dig* 131:225-6+ N '87
Heroes for today. il *Read Dig* 131:110-12 S '87
Heroes for today. il *Read Dig* 131:88-90 Jl '87
Heroes, past and present [cover story; special section] il *Newsweek* 110:52-6+ Jl 6 '87
Heroic proportions [most admired men and women polls; study by Tom W. Smith] A. H. Rosenfeld. il *Psychol Today* 21:15 Jl '87
Look who won our most admired women and men polls. il *Good Housekeep* 204:48 Ja '87
Oliver North joins ranks with Paul Revere, Betsy Ross and other idols of dubious distinction. il *People Wkly* 27:64+ Ja 12 '87
Heroin
Boy George comes clean—and tries to come back—after heroin addiction and his pals' drug deaths. L. S. Healy. il pors *People Wkly* 28:92-3+ Ag 24 '87
More problems for Boy George. M. Goldberg. *Roll Stone* p13 Ja 15 '87
Mr. Clean: Boy George straightens up his act. M. Goldberg. il pors *Roll Stone* p87-8+ O 8 '87
The new panic in Needle Park: AIDS. T. Morganthau. il *Newsweek* 109:63 Ap 13 '87
To love a daughter, to love an addict. M. A. Gouzé. il *Ladies Home J* 104:107-9+ S '87
Laws and regulations
See Narcotics laws and regulations
Therapeutic use
Quickly. Death is going on [treating terminal cancer] W. F. Buckley. *Natl Rev* 39:63 N 6 '87
Relieving cancer pain. J. Dahl and D. Joranson. il *World Health* p28-9 N '87
Heroin trade *See* Narcotics trade
Heroines *See* Heroes and heroines
Heroism *See* Courage
Heron, Echo
"Don't let my baby die!" [excerpt from Intensive care] il por *Redbook* 168:122-4+ Ap '87
Emergency room nurse [excerpt from Intensive care] il *Glamour* 85:330-1+ Ap '87

Herons
See also
  Egrets
Photographs and photography
Cast master [bait fishing by green-backed herons of Suizenji Park, Kumamoto, Japan] H. Higuchi. il *Nat Hist* 96:40-3 Ag '87
Herpesviruses
See also
  Cytomegalovirus
  Epstein-Barr virus
Clustering of genes dispensable for growth in culture in the S component of the HSV-1 genome. R. Longnecker and B. Roizman. bibl f il *Science* 236:573-6 My 1 '87
Herpes latency makes 'anti-sense'. D. D. Edwards. *Sci News* 132:356 D 5 '87
The herpes nobody knows. E. Rapp. il *Mademoiselle* 93:80 Ja '87
Herpes virus linked to 'love bite' on neck. *Jet* 73:28 S 28 '87
Herpes virus transplanted with organs? [genital herpesvirus in contaminated organs; research by Jesse L. Goodman] D. D. Edwards. *Sci News* 132:255 O 17 '87
Rapid identification of nonessential genes of herpes simplex virus type 1 by Tn5 mutagenesis. P. C. Weber and others. bibl f il *Science* 236:576-9 My 1 '87
RNA complementary to a herpesvirus α gene mRNA is prominent in latently infected neurons. J. G. Stevens and others. bibl f il *Science* 235:1056-9 F 27 '87
Update on herpes. D. Groves. *McCalls* 115:95-6 N '87
The virus that never goes away. P. Gadsby. il *Good Housekeep* 205:202-3 Jl '87
Immunological aspects
Worried sick: hassles and herpes [research by Susan Kennedy and others] R. Weiss. *Sci News* 132:360 D 5 '87
Legal aspects
The cost of kissing and not telling [negligence suits] D. Brand. il *Time* 129:78 Je 8 '87
Therapy
New OTC takes the hurt out of herpes [InterVir ointment] *Prevention* 39:12 Ja '87
Herr, Pamela
Jessie Benton Frémont [with editorial comment by Ed Holm] il pors *Am Hist Illus* 22:18, 20-9+ S '87
Herrera, Carolina
about
An evening with Carolina and Reinaldo Herrera: strong opinions, European style. W. P. Rayner and C. Rayner. il pors *Vogue* 177:342 Mr '87
Reinaldo and Carolina Herrera in Manhattan. C. T. Buckley. il pors *Archit Dig* 44:128-35+ Ap '87
Herrera, Reinaldo
about
An evening with Carolina and Reinaldo Herrera: strong opinions, European style. W. P. Rayner and C. Rayner. il pors *Vogue* 177:342 Mr '87
Reinaldo and Carolina Herrera in Manhattan. C. T. Buckley. il pors *Archit Dig* 44:128-35+ Ap '87
Herrera, Roberto Diaz *See* Diaz Herrera, Roberto
Herrhausen, Alfred
about
The banker behind the shakeup at Daimler-Benz. R. Ingersoll and R. Brady. il pors *Bus Week* p36-7 Jl 27 '87
Herrick, Bruce R.
Curbing abuses in computer modeling. il *Technol Rev* 90:24-5 O '87
Herrick & Feinstein
The law of increasing returns. R. Thompson. il *Nations Bus* 75:47 Ap '87
Herring, Milena
Busman's holiday in Rome. il *Publ Wkly* 232:47 Ag 21 '87
Herring fisheries (Commercial) *See* Fisheries
Herrington, John S., 1939-
IEA governing board meets in Paris [statement and text of final communique, May 11, 1987] *Dep State Bull* 87:47-51 Jl '87
Herriot, James
Bonny's big day [excerpt] il *Redbook* 169:62 S '87
Herrlinger, Paul David
about
Hey Wall Street, wanna buy the Brooklyn Bridge? G. Weiss. il por *Bus Week* p31 Jl 6 '87
Hersch, Hank
Anchors aweigh. il por *Sports Illus* 67:22 Jl 6 '87
Best krewe in the bayou. il *Sports Illus* 66:59 Mr 9 '87

Hersch, Hank—*cont.*
A bull's-eye for a new Archer. il *Sports Illus* 67:26-8+ S 14 '87
The Cardinal rules.' il *Sports Illus* 66:60-1 Je 15 '87
High-flying household. il *Sports Illus* 66:44-6+ Je 22 '87
Holy smokes! 'Bama is back. il *Sports Illus* 67:66-7 S 21 '87
Hoosier Big Ten favorite now? il *Sports Illus* 67:74-5 O 26 '87
It's war out there! [cover story] il *Sports Illus* 67:14-17 Jl 20 '87
Miles from nowhere. il *Sports Illus* 66:78-82+ F 16 '87
Number one at the gun. il pors *Sports Illus* 66:64+ My 18 '87
One rip-roaring family affair. il pors *Sports Illus* 66:26-8+ Mr 9 '87
Pete has 'em seeing Red. il *Sports Illus* 67:24-7 Ag 10 '87
A short (but sweet) story. il pors *Sports Illus* 67:20-1 Jl 20 '87
Texas pooled its talent. il *Sports Illus* 66:60 F 2 '87
A Texas waltz in Tennessee. il *Sports Illus* 67:44-6+ D 21 '87
That great Abbott switch. il pors *Sports Illus* 66:28-9 My 25 '87
A tumble from the top. il *Sports Illus* 66:40-1 My 4 '87

Hersch, Hank, and Newman, Bruce
They're fit to be tied in the SEC. il *Sports Illus* 67:30-2+ O 5 '87

Hersch, Patricia
Superstation super mess. il *Channels* 7:45-6 Ja '87

Herschbach, Dudley R., 1932-
about
Herschbach, Lee and Polanyi receive 1986 Chemistry Nobel. P. H. Andersen. il pors *Phys Today* 40:17-20 Mr '87

Hersey, Brook
In praise of fly-by-night romances. il *Glamour* 85:302 O '87

Hersey, John, 1914-
Asymmetry. *New Yorker* 63:36-40+ S 7 '87
Jimmy Yen: crusader for mankind. il por *Read Dig* 131:138-45+ O '87
My summer job with Sinclair Lewis. il pors *N Y Times Book Rev* 92:1+ My 10 '87
Not-so-silent sea [excerpt from Blues] il *Harpers* 274:30-1 My '87
The terrorist [story] il *Esquire* 108:114-15+ Ag '87

Hersh, Seymour M.
Target Qaddafi. il *N Y Times Mag* p16-22+ F 22 '87
Who's in charge here? il por *N Y Times Mag* p34-5+ N 22 '87

Hershey, Barbara
about
Barbara Hershey. Seriously. il pors *Esquire* 107:91-3 My '87
Serious stars: Barbara Hershey. T. Rafferty. por *Vogue* 177:483+ Mr '87

Hershey, Jacqueline A.
How schools sabotage a creative work force. il *Bus Week* p16 Jl 13 '87

Hershey Foods Corp.
The high-profit candy habit. J. Novack. il *Forbes* 139:76 Je 29 '87
Will Philip Morris nibble at Hershey? G. G. Marcial. *Bus Week* p106 O 5 '87

Hershkovits, David
Taking direct action. pors *Harpers Bazaar* 121:144-5 N '87

Hershkowitz, Allen
Burning trash: how it could work [cover story] il *Technol Rev* 90:26-34 Jl '87

Herskowitz, Joel
about
A doctor's new popcorn diet makes excess pounds go poof. P. Brawley. il por *People Wkly* 27:137-8 Je 8 '87

Herskowitz, Michael
(ed) See Davis, Bette, 1908-. Bette Davis talks back!

Herst, Herman, Jr.
Philately. See issues of Antiques & Collecting Hobbies beginning March 1985
Philately. See issues of Hobbies through February 1985
"What is the worth of a unique historic rarity?". il *Forbes* 139:26 Mr 9 '87

Hertzberg, Arthur
Glasnost and the Jews. il *N Y Rev Books* 34:20-3 O 22 '87
Israel: the tragedy of victory. il *N Y Rev Books* 34:12-18 My 28 '87

Hertzberg, Hendrik
Let's get representative. *New Repub* 196:15-18 Je 29 '87

Hervey, Ramon
about
Ex-Miss America Vanessa Williams weds her publicist. pors *Jet* 71:14 Ja 19 '87
Vanessa Williams and hubby have baby girl. il pors *Jet* 72:28 Jl 20 '87
Vanessa Williams and husband Ramon Hervey hold L.A. reception. il pors *Jet* 71:57 Mr 16 '87
Vanessa Williams and Ramon Hervey take marriage vows. A. Collier. il pors *Jet* 71:54-7 F 2 '87

Herzberg, Osnat, and Moult, John
Bacterial resistance to β-lactam antibiotics: crystal structure of β-lactamase from Staphylococcus aureus PC1 at 2.5 Å resolution. bibl f il *Science* 236:694-701 My 8 '87

Herzog, Chaim, 1918-
about
Odyssey of remembrance. il por *Macleans* 100:21 Ap 20 '87

Herzog, Whitey
about
Angling to win the Rat race. S. Wulf. il pors *Sports Illus* 67:72+ Jl 6 '87

Hesburgh, Theodore Martin
about
Father Hesburgh retires. *America* 156:433 My 30 '87
First in his class. *Commonweal* 114:341-2 Je 5 '87
His trumpet was never uncertain. E. Bowen. il por *Time* 129:68+ My 18 '87
Notre Dame's 'Father Ted' bids farewell. K. L. Woodward. por *Newsweek* 109:75+ My 11 '87
Of many things. G. W. Hunt. *America* 156:inside cover My 30 '87

Hesketh, Lady Christian
Reflections on a venerable British tradition. il por *Archit Dig* 44:98+ Je '87

Heskett, James L.
Thank heaven for the service sector. il *Bus Week* p22 Ja 26 '87

Heslin, Jo-Ann, and Natow, Annette B.
Cut it out! il *Redbook* 169:65-9 Jl '87
The perfect salad. il *Redbook* 169:79-82 Je '87

Heslinga, Gerald A., and Fitt, William K.
The domestication of reef-dwelling clams [cover story] il *BioScience* 37:332-9 My '87

Hess, Allen K., 1945-
The self-imposed death sentence. bibl (p56) il *Psychol Today* 21:50-3 Je '87

Hess, John L.
Malthus then and now. il *Nation* 244:496-500 Ap 18 '87
The necrophiles. *Nation* 244:37-8 Ja 17 '87

Hess, Leon
about
Leon Hess: can the bottom-of-the-barrel oil baron get back on top? J. R. Norman. il por *Bus Week* p50-1+ Je 29 '87

Hess, Moses, 1812-1875
about
A light unto the nations? R. R. Wisse. *Commentary* 84:30-5 D '87

Hess, Rudolf, 1894-1987
about
Obituary
    Life il pors 10:40-2 O '87
    Macleans il pors 100:18 Ag 31 '87. A. Bilski
    Natl Rev 39:21 S 11 '87
    Newsweek il por 110:39 Ag 31 '87. A. Nagorski
    Time il pors 130:31 Ag 31 '87. J. Greenwald
    U S News World Rep il por 103:13 Ag 31 '87. M. Satchell

Hess, Stephen
Being newsworthy. *Society* 24:39-47 Ja/F '87

Hessayon, D. G. (David Gerald), 1928-
about
'I've never seen a dazzling rose': the bossy approach to garden writing. I. Shenker. il por *N Y Times Book Rev* 92:15 My 31 '87

Hessayon, David Gerald See Hessayon, D. G. (David Gerald), 1928-

Hesse, Georgia
Daybreak on the Pacific. il *Travel Holiday* 167:91-2+ Ap '87

Hesse, Georgia—*cont.*
A lost dynasty revealed. il *Travel Holiday* 167:24-7 Ja '87

Hesse, Martha O., 1942-
about
Public sector pragmatist. L. M. Keefe. il por *Forbes* 139:283+ Ja 12 '87

Hesseman, Howard
about
Once a druggie, he nearly flunked out, but a reformed Howard Hesseman goes straight to the Head of the class. F. A. Bernstein. il pors *People Wkly* 27:75-6+ Ja 19 '87

Hession, Catherine, and others
Uromodulin (Tamm-Horsfall glycoprotein): a renal ligand for lymphokines. bibl f il *Science* 237:1479-84 S 18 '87

Hester, Wilhelm
about
Puget Sound: the maritime world of Wilhelm Hester. R. A. Weinstein. il *Am Hist Illus* 21:20-35 Ja '87

Heston, Ty B.
Living history: the horseshoe crab. bibl il *Sea Front* 33:195-9 My/Je '87

Hetch Hetchy Water Supply Project
A shocker from Hodel [proposal to tear down O'Shaugnessy Dam in Yosemite National Park] T. Turner. il *Mother Earth News* 108:130-1 N/D '87
Undamming Hetch Hetchy [proposal by D. P. Hodel] C. Pope. il *Sierra* 72:34-8 N/D '87

Hettrick, Jane Schatkin
about
Salieri at Rider. K. Richardson. il *High Fidel* 37:56 Mr '87

Heublein, George R.
about
Hotter than a pistil. M. Gill. il por *Esquire* 107:72 My '87
Planting the seeds of a blossoming business. M. J. Parks. il por *Bus Week* p82 Je 1 '87

Heublein, Inc.
Heublein: getting remote offices in touch [personal computer access to mainframe data] J. Blackford. *Pers Comput* 11:137+ My '87

Heuristic programming
Heuristic algorithms [special section] il *Byte* 12:147-52+ O '87

Hewes, Havelock
Major league nightmares. il *Sport Mag* 78:79-81 Ag '87

Hewett, Edward A.
Is it reform or rhetoric? Gorbachev and the Soviet economy. *Current* 291:21-7 Mr/Ap '87
Reforming the economy. *Nation* 244:802-4 Je 13 '87

Hewitt, Christopher
(tr) See Cassian, Nina. Four poems

Hewitt, Glenn
Bound by freedom [discussion of September 23, 1987 article, Victimized by justice] *Christ Century* 104:1022-3 N 18 '87
Victimized by justice. *Christ Century* 104:780-1 S 23 '87

Hewitt, Mark A.
William Adams Delano and the Muttontown enclave. bibl f il *Antiques* 132:316-27 Ag '87

Hewitt, William F.
Manhattan highway plan resurfaces. il *Sierra* 72:23-4+ My/Je '87

Hewitt family
about
The moving spirits of Ringwood Manor. R. Lynes. il *Archit Dig* 44:27+ Jl '87

Hewlett, William R.
about
A quartet of high-tech pioneers. B. O'Reilly. il pors *Fortune* 116:148-9 O 12 '87

Hewlett-Packard Co.
Hewlett-Packard may have come up with a winner [RISC technology] R. Brandt. il *Bus Week* p48 Je 1 '87
Making the short list again. K. K. Wiegner. il *Forbes* 139:124+ Je 15 '87

Hewson, Paul *See* Bono

Hey, Kenneth R.
Films. See alternate issues of USA Today (Periodical) through March 1987
The reel world. See alternate issues of USA Today (Periodical) beginning May 1987

Heydon Hall (Norfolk, England) *See* Historic houses, sites, etc.—Great Britain

Heyen, William, 1940-
Until the next time [poem] *America* 157:265 O 24 '87

Heyerdahl, Thor
about
Profiles: Thor Heyerdahl. D. H. Minassian. il pors *Archit Dig* 44:102-9 F '87

Heyman, Abigail
about
Abigail Heyman reaps the rewards of being a stay-at-home. H. Chapnick. il por *Pop Photogr* 94:32 Ag '87

Heyman, Harriet
Gymnastics for grownups. il *Women's Sports Fitness* 9:60-4 S '87

Heyman, Ira Michael
Trapped in an 'athletics arms race'. por *U S News World Rep* 103:7 Jl 20 '87

Heyman, Samuel J.
about
Cornering Borg-Warner. J. E. Ellis. il por *Bus Week* p39 Ap 13 '87
GAF's Heyman: the hunter could soon become the hunted. A. L. Cowan. il por *Bus Week* p74-5 Mr 2 '87
What changed Sam Heyman's mind about LBOs. J. A. Byrne. il por *Bus Week* p31 S 21 '87
Will GAF cash in its Borg-Warner chips—or up the ante? J. E. Ellis. *Bus Week* p34-5 Ap 27 '87

Heymont, George
Ego intact. il pors *Opera News* 52:38+ D 5 '87
Having a ball. il *Saturday Evening Post* 259:38-9+ N '87
In it together. il *Opera News* 51:10-13 Mr 28 '87
Music director John DeMain: the real thing. il por *Opera News* 52:22 O '87
A painful process [cover story] il *Opera News* 52:12-15 N '87

Heyn, Dalma
American Bandstand's Dick Clark . . . not the boy next door. il pors *McCalls* 114:115-17 Ja '87
Beyond the valley of the beautiful dolls. il *Mademoiselle* 93:182+ N '87
The big, bad buy—shopping addiction: the nice girl's vice. il *Mademoiselle* 93:198-9+ Ag '87
The fine art of worrying. *Seventeen* 46:158+ S '87
How's your body vision? When thin women see fat. il *Mademoiselle* 93:212-13+ Ap '87
The intelligent woman's guide to sex. See issues of Mademoiselle beginning December 1986
It happened one date. il *Mademoiselle* 93:158-67 D '87
When divorce is not the answer. *McCalls* 114:28+ Ag '87
Why seven magazines pretend you don't exist. il *50 Plus* 27:38-41 Mr '87

Heyward, Andy
about
Babe in Toyland. P. E. Bauer. il pors *Channels* 7:48-51 Jl/Ag '87

HGH (Human growth hormone) *See* Pituitary hormones
HGH (Human growth hormone), Synthetic *See* Pituitary hormones, Synthetic
HHS *See* United States. Dept. of Health and Human Services
Hi-fi sound systems *See* Audio systems
Hi Hopes (Musical group)
Along with crippling retardation, Doris Walker finds in her students a baffling paradox—genius. M. Neill. il pors *People Wkly* 28:159-61 D 14 '87

Hiatt, Howard H.
Health care bites the bullet. *Bull At Sci* 43:7-8 Je '87
about
Sick about America's health care [interview] K. McAuliffe. por *U S News World Rep* 102:64 Je 15 '87

Hiatt, John
about
Family man. S. Hochman. il por *Roll Stone* p25 S 10 '87

Hib infections
Vaccines and vaccination
Immunizing babies against a viral killer. *Newsweek* 110:93 O 12 '87
New vaccine aids infants. R. Weiss. *Sci News* 132:198-9 S 26 '87

Hibbard, Lyndon S., and others
Three-dimensional representation and analysis of brain energy metabolism. bibl f il *Science* 236:1641-6 Je 26 '87

Hibbs, John B., Jr., and others
Macrophage cytotoxicity: role for L-arginine deiminase and imino nitrogen oxidation to nitrite. bibl f il *Science* 235:473-6 Ja 23 '87
Hibernation
The big sleep. A. Pistorius. il *Ctry J* 14:45-9 Ja '87
Hibiscus
See also
Chinese hibiscus
Hawaii, stand back [Hibiscus moscheutos] il *Sunset* 178:226 Je '87
Hibiscus cannabinus *See* Kenaf
Hibsch, Marcia
(jt. auth) *See* Gage, Diane, and Hibsch, Marcia
Hick, John
about
Hick rejected. *Christ Century* 104:304-5 Ap 1 '87
Hickcox, David H.
America's hurricane threat. *Focus* 37:36 Fall '87
Extreme fluctuations characterize recent winters. *Focus* 36:31-2 Wint '86
Floods: the nation's primary weather hazard. *Focus* 37:29-30 Spr '87
The nation's hottest temperature. *Focus* 37:31 Summ '87
Temperature extremes. il *Weatherwise* 40:38-40 F '87
Trends in oil imports. *Focus* 37:33 Spr '87
Hickey, John R.
(jt. auth) *See* Wolff, Charles L., and Hickey, John R.
Hickeys
Herpes virus linked to 'love bite' on neck. *Jet* 73:28 S 28 '87
Hickman, Elnor B. G.
about
Black woman new prexy for Ill. secretary group. por *Jet* 72:30 Je 15 '87
Hickman, Katie
Bolivia's crowning glory. il *Américas* 39:22-5+ Jl/Ag '87
Hickoff, Stephen
Here [poem] *Ctry J* 14:83 O '87
In the hardware store [poem] *Ctry J* 14:69 Jl '87
Hicks, Alan
In search of wintering bats. *Conservationist* 41:14-17+ Ja/F '87
Hicks, David, 1929-
about
The classical villa restated. M. Hampton. il *House Gard* 159:114-23 Je '87
Hicks, John W.
Red crabs on the march on Christmas Island. il map *Natl Geogr* 172:822-31 D '87
Hidden treasure *See* Treasure trove
Hides and skins
Export-import trade
A deadly business [Philippine divers collect venomous snakes for snakeskin trade; with photographs] H. Hall. il *Int Wildl* 17:12-15 Jl/Ag '87
Hiebert, Murray
A new gerontocracy. *World Press Rev* 34:30 F '87
Hielscher, Almut
Arabs vs. settlers in the Gaza Strip. *World Press Rev* 34:56-7 Ja '87
Hieroglyphics, Maya *See* Mayas—Writing
Hiestand, Emily
Likewise [poem] *Atlantic* 259:78 F '87
These are for your consideration [poem] *Atlantic* 259:51 Je '87
Higby, Sha Sha
about
Aiming for the mind's eye: Sha Sha Higby's costume sculptures. M. Weisang. il *Theatre Crafts* 21:42-3+ Ap '87
Higdon, Hal
about
Snow job. B. Lindeman. il *50 Plus* 27:6 F '87
Higgins, David, and Eicher, David J.
The secret world of dark nebulae. il *Astronomy* 15:46-51 S '87
Higgins, George G.
Malachi Martin's The Jesuits: an appraisal. il *America* 156:229-31+ Mr 21 '87
The women's challenge. *America* 156:3-6 Ja 3-10 '87
Higgins, Judith
Britain's 'new generation'. il *Art News* 86:118-22 D '87
Pousette-Dart's windows into the unknowing. il por *Art News* 86:108-16 Ja '87
Higgins, Mary D.
Just a bowl of cherries. il *Ladies Home J* 104:94-5+ Je '87

Higgins, Sean
about
Signed, sealed and sorry. A. Keteyian and A. Wolff. il por *Sports Illus* 66:24-6 F 23 '87
Higgins, William J.
about
Why one phone is stirring up the Big Board. J. M. Laderman. il por *Bus Week* p123 Jl 20 '87
High, Johnny, d. 1987
about
Drug scandal witness dies, Phoenix case loses steam. por *Jet* 72:47 Jl 6 '87
High altitude, Influence of *See* Altitude, Influence of
High-altitude gardens and gardening
How three bountiful Colorado gardens solved mountain problems. il *Sunset* 178:264-5 My '87
High altitude sickness *See* Mountain sickness
High blood pressure *See* Hypertension
High chairs *See* Chairs
High Commissioner for Refugees *See* United Nations. High Commissioner for Refugees
High country news
Saga of a High country newsman [T. Bell] G. O'Gara. por *Sierra* 72:72-7 Mr/Ap '87
High definition television
Coming: sharper TV. J. Free. il *Pop Sci* 230:72-5+ Ja '87
Crystal clear TV. R. Coorsh. il *Consum Res Mag* 70:4 F '87
High-definition DBS. B. Cooper, Jr. il *Radio-Electron* 58:62-3 Jl '87
High definition TV. J. Bernard. il *Radio-Electron* 58:48-51 Ag '87
High-definition's spectrum needs spur TV broadcasters to action [UHF vs. radio spectrum] S. Behrens. il *Channels* 7:16 Ap '87
In case you tuned in late [new features] P. Elmer-Dewitt. il *Time* 130:59 D 21 '87
Is HDTV the key to an international standard? B. Cooper, Jr. il map *Radio-Electron* 58:28-9+ Ag '87
Mick meets HDTV [recording M. Jagger's Let's work] P. Hoban. il pors *N Y* 20:31 Ag 24 '87
Seeing the future. D. Ranada. il *High Fidel* 37:22 Ag '87
Suddenly, TV's overhaul gets priority treatment. S. Behrens. il *Channels* 7 Sp Issue:90 D '87
Television makers are dreaming of a wide crispness. F. Seghers. il *Bus Week* p108-9 D 21 '87
High density lipoproteins *See* Lipoproteins
High energy physics *See* Nuclear physics
High fiber diet *See* Fiber in diet
High fidelity (Periodical)
Front lines. W. Tynan. See issues of High Fidelity (New York, N.Y.) through January 1987
High Fidelity International Record Critics Awards *See* Phonograph records—Awards
High jumping
A man of bars and measures [D. Nordquist] R. Wiley. il pors *Sports Illus* 66:50+ Je 15 '87
High jumping records
Sneaking up on the eight-foot barrier [P. Sjoberg] por *Newsweek* 110:49 Jl 13 '87
Sweden's new royal highness [P. Sjöberg sets world record] K. Moore. il por *Sports Illus* 67:26-7 Jl 13 '87
High Plains (U.S.)
See also
Irrigation—High Plains (U.S.)
High pressure (Science)
Central heating [estimating temperature of the earth's core from the melting point of iron at immense pressure] *Sci Am* 256:25-6 Je '87
Earth's most abundant mineral [perovskite; research by Elise Knittle and Raymond Jeanloz] S. Weisburd. *Sci News* 131:103 F 14 '87
First X-ray pattern of hydrogen solid [work of Russell Hemley and others] *Sci News* 131:201 Mr 28 '87
Glasnost comes to Soviet physics [misdirection of high-pressure physics research] A. L. Robinson. il *Science* 236:671-2 My 8 '87
High-temperature cubic boron nitride P-N junction diode made at high pressure. O. Mishima and others. bibl f il *Science* 238:181-3 O 9 '87
How hot is the heart of the earth? [research by Quentin Williams and others] S. Weisburd. *Sci News* 131:245 Ap 18 '87
Laser techniques in high-pressure geophysics. R. J. Hemley and others. bibl f il *Science* 237:605-12 Ag 7 '87
The melting curve of iron to 250 gigapascals: a constraint on the temperature at earth's center. Q. Williams and others. bibl f il *Science* 236:181-2 Ap 10 '87

High pressure (Science)—*cont.*
Putting the heat on new semiconductors [cubic boron nitride diode; work of Osamu Mishima and others] I. Peterson. *Sci News* 132:247 O 17 '87
Synthesis and equation of state of (Mg,Fe)SiO₃ perovskite to over 100 gigapascals. E. Knittle and R. Jeanloz. bibl f il *Science* 235:668-70 F 6 '87
High pressure washers *See* Pressure washers
High school and college cooperation *See* Educational cooperation
High school athletes *See* Athletes
High school athletics *See* School athletics
High school dropouts *See* Dropouts
High school graduates
Life after high school. P. S. Rix. il *Teen* 31:24+ S '87
Speech for a high school graduate [father's advice to daughter] R. Rosenblatt. il *Time* 129:72 Je 29 '87
High school journalism *See* College and school journalism
High school proms *See* Proms (Dances)
High school reunions
Ex-bank thief Delbert Dunmire busts loose with a classy high school reunion in the Bahamas. R. Arias. il pors *People Wkly* 28:30-1 Ag 31 '87
High school students
See also
High school graduates
Student activities
Teenage pregnancy
1964 [excerpt from Be true to your school] B. Greene. il por *Esquire* 107:86-90+ F '87
The high-schooler's informational IQ test [proposal for test as requirement for teenage driver's license] W. F. Buckley. *Natl Rev* 39:57 Jl 17 '87
The Seventeen honor roll: most likely to succeed. C. Hanauer. il *Seventeen* 46:210-13 S '87
Adjustment
Heading into high school. J. P. Comer. il *Parents* 62:201 Ag '87
Anecdotes, facetiae, satire, etc.
Youthful ambitions. R. Baker. il *N Y Times Mag* p16 Je 14 '87
Attitudes
America's future teaching force: predictions and recommendations [survey of seniors] R. E. Kemper and J. N. Mangieri. bibl f *Phi Delta Kappan* 68:393-5 Ja '87
An eye on the future [results of survey of seniors] J. G. Bachman. il *Psychol Today* 21:6+ Jl '87
High school seniors react to their teachers and their schools. D. L. Clark. il *Phi Delta Kappan* 68:503-9 Mr '87
Intergenerational understanding in the middle school [attitudes towards aged] J. Berkson and S. A. Griggs. *Educ Dig* 52:30-2 Ap '87
Awards
See also
Scholastic Awards
Civil rights
See Students—Civil rights
Grading
See Grading and marking (Students)
Political activities
How Update readers stand on top issues. J. Ferber. *Sch Update* 119:22-3 Ja 12 '87
Lawmakers—not lawbreakers [seventh graders from Sandwich, Mass. lobby for tougher cigarette sales law] C. Lowrance. il *Good Housekeep* 204:96 Mr '87
Students who focus debate on U.S.-Soviet relations. il *Sch Update* 120:16-17 N 20 '87
Psychology
Holding on to student enthusiasm. S. G. Sava. *Educ Dig* 52:28-31 Mr '87
Sexual behavior
See Youth—Sexual behavior
Volunteer service
See Volunteer service
High school students, Gifted
See also
North Carolina School of Science and Mathematics
No mistake, these five kids have all the answers: they scored perfect 1600s on their SAT exams. M. Small. il *People Wkly* 27:63-4+ Je 8 '87
State residential high schools for mathematically talented youth. J. C. Stanley. bibl f il *Phi Delta Kappan* 68:770-3 Je '87
High school students and drugs *See* Drugs and youth
High school yearbooks
See also
Video yearbooks

Racial slur in yearbook, sparks Mass. school probe [Taunton High School] *Jet* 72:16 Je 15 '87
Collectors and collecting
If your school's most (or least) likely succeeded, hang on to that mildewed yearbook—it's golden [collector W. A. Day] il *People Wkly* 27:110-11 Je 1 '87
High schools
See also
Catholic schools
Cincinnati Academy of Physical Education
Education, Secondary
North Carolina School of Science and Mathematics
Cool schools [special section] il *Seventeen* 46:140-1 S '87
The deep structure of schooling. B. B. Tye. il *Phi Delta Kappan* 69:281-4 D '87
High schools that work [inner-city schools] R. E. McKinney. il *Ebony* 43:34+ N '87
Social services in American high schools. E. Farrar and R. L. Hampel. il *Phi Delta Kappan* 69:297-303 D '87
Awards
Successful secondary schools [study of Secondary School Recognition Program winners; excerpt from The search for successful secondary schools] T. B. Corcoran and B. L. Wilson. *Educ Dig* 53:22-4 S '87
Birth control clinics
See Birth control clinics
Curriculum
See also
Biology—Study and teaching
History—Study and teaching
Literature—Study and teaching
Mathematics—Study and teaching
Physics—Study and teaching
Theater—Study and teaching
Thought and thinking—Study and teaching
Vocational-technical education
Desegregation
See Public schools—Desegregation
Graduation requirements
See also
International baccalaureate
Courses and test scores yield mixed results. G. W. Bracey. il *Phi Delta Kappan* 68:397-8 Ja '87
A true test or a trivia game? [Maryland's citizenship test] M. Henry. por *Newsweek* 109:10-11 Je 22 '87
Medical care
See also
Birth control clinics
Race relations
Racial slur in yearbook, sparks Mass. school probe [Taunton High School] *Jet* 72:16 Je 15 '87
High schools and business *See* Business and education
High schools and religion *See* Public schools and religion
High season [film] See Motion picture reviews—Single works
High Sierras *See* Sierra Nevada Mountains (Calif. and Nev.)
High society *See* Upper classes
High-speed antiradiation missiles *See* Guided missiles—Launching from airplanes
High speed photography *See* Photography, High speed
High tech *See* Technology
High tech industries *See* Computer industry; Electronic industries
High temperatures
High-temperature cubic boron nitride P-N junction diode made at high pressure. O. Mishima and others. bibl f il *Science* 238:181-3 O 9 '87
Putting the heat on new semiconductors [cubic boron nitride diode; work of Osamu Mishima and others] I. Peterson. *Sci News* 132:247 O 17 '87
High wire walking
Profiles [P. Petit] G. Kinkhead. *New Yorker* 63:35-8+ Je 15 '87
Higher education *See* College education; Colleges and universities; Community and junior colleges
Highgate Cemetery (London, England)
Tales of Highgate. T. D. Mathews. il *House Gard* 159:86+ Ap '87
Highland Park (N.J.)
Crime
Murder hits home [murder of school principal W. H. Donahue] S. G. Freedman. il *N Y Times Mag* p20+ My 31 '87
Highlanders of Vietnam *See* Montagnards (Vietnamese people)

Highlands (Scotland)
History
'Having and holding': the Highland land war of the 1880s. I. C. Bradley. bibl il *Hist Today* 37:23-8 D '87
Highlighting (Hair coloring) *See* Hair—Dyeing and bleaching
Highrise buildings *See* Skyscrapers
Highstein, Jene, 1942-
about
Jene Highstein at La Jolla Museum of Contemporary Art. R. L. Pincus. *Art Am* 75:189 My '87
Highway, Tomson
about
The rez sisters [drama] Reviews
Macleans il 100:69 O 19 '87. D. Taylor
Highway construction *See* Highway engineering
Highway engineering
Minority claims in state contracts being probed [road construction in Illinois] *Jet* 73:32 N 2 '87
Highway patrol *See* Police
Highways *See* Express highways; Roads
Higuchi, Hiroyoshi
Cast master. il *Nat Hist* 96:40-3 Ag '87
Hijacking of airplanes *See* Airplane hijacking
Hiking
See also
Backpacks and backpacking
Trails
High on llamas: you do the walking, they'll do the work. E. McGrath. il *Women's Sports Fitness* 9:20-3 Ag '87
The last companion you'll want on the trail [giardiasis] J. Silberner. il *U S News World Rep* 102:66 Je 22 '87
Take a walk on the wild side. S. Zarrow. il *Prevention* 39:82+ My '87
International aspects
Off the beaten path [hiking tours] N. Henderson. il *Changing Times* 41:52-6+ My '87
Photographs and photography
A shot in the park. M. Grimm and T. Grimm. il *Travel Holiday* 167:27-9 My '87
Nepal
Trekking in Nepal. R. W. Cox. il map *Travel Holiday* 167:42-7+ My '87
Hilbert, Betsy
How to stop being so tough on yourself. il *Ladies Home J* 104:70+ My '87
Hildago-Diaz, Leonel
about
Excludable from justice. G. Galbaugh. *America* 156:315-16 Ap 18 '87
Hileman, Jim
(jt. auth) *See* Baker, DeWitt C., and Hileman, Jim
Hilger, Wolfgang
about
A CEO as cheerleader. L. S. Richman. por *Fortune* 116:52 Ag 3 '87
Hill, Calvin
about
Ex-NFL star Hill joins Orioles bd. of directors. por *Jet* 72:48 Ag 10 '87
Hill, Gene
Hill country. See issues of Field & Stream
Hill, George
A book of revelations. *World Press Rev* 34:55 D '87
Hill, Jacqueline
about
Black and white cops duel in lovers' quarrel; he is critical and she is dead. *Jet* 73:8 N 2 '87
Hill, Janet
about
Former Army Secretary and woman scientist try to change baseball image. il pors *Jet* 73:50-1 N 9 '87
Hill, Jim
about
Ex-gridder Hill moves to ABC after CBS stint. por *Jet* 72:23 Ag 10 '87
Hill, Jon
about
Executive toque. por *Time* 130:64 Ag 31 '87
Hill, Kent R.
about
Is there a link between Christianity and democracy? [interview] il por *Christ Today* 31:42 S 18 '87
Hill, Kirk
about
Manhattan or bust. J. Paris. il pors *Read Dig* 131:5-6+ Jl '87

Hill, Lewis, 1924-
Pruning fruit trees [excerpt from Pruning simplified] il *Mother Earth News* 103:51-5 Ja/F '87
Hill, Lewis, 1924-, and Hill, Nancy
A rogues gallery of garden pests: how to control common pests in the vegetable garden. il *Ctry J* 14:35-9 Ag '87
Hill, Mary, 1923-
On earth. See issues of Earth Science
Hill, Nancy
(jt. auth) *See* Hill, Lewis, 1924-, and Hill, Nancy
Hill, Nolanda
about
How Hill got leveled. D. Holder. il por *Channels* 7:42-4 Ja '87
Hill, Norman
Forging a partnership between blacks and unions. *Mon Labor Rev* 110:38-9 Ag '87
Hill, Richard
about
Foot and Falconetti are TV's most popular penguin pitchmen, and it serves them right. il por *People Wkly* 28:50 Ag 24 '87
Hill, Robert Bernard, 1938-
The black middle class defined. il por *Ebony* 42:30+ Ag '87
Hill, Tony
about
Cowboys axe receiver Tony Hill over weight. por *Jet* 72:50 Ag 10 '87
Hill, Walter, 1942-
about
Extreme prejudice [film] Reviews
Macleans il 100:58 My 4 '87. L. O'Toole
N Y 20:70+ My 11 '87. D. Denby
Newsweek il 109:75 My 4 '87. D. Ansen
People Wkly il 27:10 My 11 '87. R. Novak
Time il 129:97 My 4 '87. R. Schickel
Hill & Wang, Inc.
Wasserman named publisher of Noonday Press, Hill and Wang. por *Publ Wkly* 232:12 S 11 '87
Hill Broadcasting Inc.
How Hill got leveled. D. Holder. il por *Channels* 7:42-4 Ja '87
Hill farming
See also
Walsers
Hill Samuel Group plc, London
The big cheese in London banking could be Swiss [Union Bank of Switzerland's proposed buyout of Hill Samuel Group plc] J. Templeman. il *Bus Week* p37 Jl 27 '87
Hill Street Blues [television program] *See* Television program reviews—Single works
Hill Top Research, Inc.
Thelma Williams' daredevil nose probes the pungent secrets of America's toes. R. Arias. il por *People Wkly* 28:164-5 S 7 '87
Hillard, Paula Adams
As they grow/pregnancy and birth. See issues of Parents
Hillegass, Cliff
about
Fast food for thought. N. Atkins. il por *Roll Stone* p110-12+ Mr 26 '87
Hiller, Arthur
about
Outrageous fortune [film] Reviews
Commonweal 114:182 Mr 27 '87. T. O'Brien
Macleans 100:47 F 9 '87. L. O'Toole
N Y 20:96 F 9 '87. D. Denby
New Leader 70:23 Ap 6 '87. J. Gardner
New Repub 196:24 Mr 2 '87. S. Kauffmann
New Yorker 63:112-13 F 23 '87. P. Kael
Newsweek il 109:76 Ja 26 '87. D. Ansen
People Wkly 27:10 F 16 '87. P. Travers
Time il 129:73 F 2 '87. R. Corliss
Hiller, Stanley, Jr.
about
Why the Baker-Hughes merger almost didn't happen. C. S. Eklund and T. Vogel. il pors *Bus Week* p110-11 My 11 '87
Hillerman, Tony
The reader as partner. *Writer* 100:14-16 O '87
Hillesum, Etty, 1914-1943
about
Letters from 'The Kingdom of Night'. L. S. Cunningham. il *Commonweal* 114:316-18 My 22 '87

Hilley, Audrey Marie
about
The three lives of . . . Marie Hilley [excerpt from Poisoned blood] P. E. Ginsburg. il pors *Good Housekeep* 205:148-9+ N '87
Hillhouse, Ruth, and La Rosa, Suzanne
Think smart. See issues of McCall's beginning November 1986
Hillila, Bernhard
Persistent suitor [poem] il *America* 157:480 D 19 '87
Hillis, Burton
Man next door. See issues of Better Homes and Gardens
Hillis, Daniel
The Connection Machine. il *Sci Am* 256:108-15 Je '87
Hillman, Eugene
Military duty and moral scruple. il *America* 157:185+ O 3 '87
Hillman, Gracia M.
about
Gracia Hillman pilots voter group for political victories across nation. S. Booker. il por *Jet* 71:12-13 Ja 26 '87
Hills, Patricia
John Singer Sargent: style and sensibility. il por *USA Today (Periodical)* 115:77-83 Mr '87
Hillside architecture
Architecture: Michael Graves [home of Thomas and Ingrid Plocek in New Jersey] C. Jencks. il por *Archit Dig* 44:138-45+ My '87
Classical allusions: a hillside pavilion in Greece [designed by Hugh Newell Jacobsen] C. Aillaud. il *Archit Dig* 44:72-7 Jl '87
Earth sheltered: blending with nature on the Costa Brava [home designed by F. J. Barba] N. Shrady. il *Archit Dig* 44:90-5 Ja '87
Hot tub and decks for a steep slope. il *Sunset* 179:97 Ag '87
The villa transformer [Schwartz/Fiekowsky weekend house, West Stockbridge, Mass.] C. K. Gandee. il *Archit Rec* 175:114-21 mid-Ap '87
Hillside gardens and gardening
A hillside garden to fit a family. il *South Living* 22:88-90 Mr '87
Very big boxes for hillside flowers, vegetables. il *Sunset* 179:92 Ag '87
Hilt, James, 1947-
Professionals must adjust their fees. il *Christ Today* 31:30 F 6 '87
Hiltermann, Joost R.
Force for change in the West Bank. il *Nation* 245:338-40 O 3 '87
Hilton, Alison
Russian painting at the dawn of modernism. il *Art News* 86:110-15 Mr '87
Hilton, Davey
about
Fighting is in his blood. W. Nack. il pors *Sports Illus* 67:58-61+ N 16 '87
Hilton, Eric, 1937-
about
The Corning Museum of Glass. il *Antiques Collect Hobbies* 91:56-7 Ja '87
Hilton, Isabel
A British view of the contras. il *World Press Rev* 34:17 S '87
Hilton, Joni Winn
Keeping up with the Joneses. il *Parents* 62:86-8+ Je '87
Hilton, Margaret, and Straw, Ronnie
Cooperative training in telecommunications: case studies. bibl f *Mon Labor Rev* 110:32-6 My '87
Hilton, Matthew
about
Canada's new lord of the ring. D. Burke. il por *Macleans* 100:26 Jl 13 '87
Fighting is in his blood. W. Nack. il pors *Sports Illus* 67:58-61+ N 16 '87
Hilton & Towers (Chicago, Ill.: Hotel) *See* Chicago (Ill.)—Hotels, motels, etc.
Hilton Head Island (S.C.)
Description and travel
A Hilton Head footnote. R. W. Cox. il *Travel Holiday* 168:24-6 Ag '87
Hilton Hotels Corp.
Will a buyer check in to Hilton? G. G. Marcial. *Bus Week* p148 Mr 23 '87
Hilton International Co.
Can UAL and its Hilton wing fly in formation? J. E. Ellis. il *Bus Week* p45 Ja 12 '87

Himalaya Mountains
See also
Mount Everest (China and Nepal)
A hope for the Himalayas and its people. il *Environment* 29:10-11 Ap '87
'Mount Everest is a junk pile' [Himalayan pollution] S. Begley. il *Newsweek* 110:104-5 N 16 '87
Himalayan climbs *See* Mountaineering
Himes, Kenneth R.
Single-issue politics and the Church. *America* 156:377-81 My 9 '87
Himmelman, Peter
about
Psychic success story. D. Wild. por *Roll Stone* p20 Ap 9 '87
Hinckley, John, Jr.
about
Hinckley's hope. por *Time* 129:29 Ap 20 '87
Hindenburg (Airship)
Zep blows up. P. Bradley. il *Flying* 114:12 S '87
Hinderas, Natalie, 1927-1987
about
Obituary
Jet por 72:4 Ag 10 '87
Hinderstein, Rina
In the dough. il *Mother Earth News* 108:30 N/D '87
Hinds, David
(jt. auth) See Reed, Paul, 1956-, and Hinds, David
Hinds, Michael deCourcy
A dream come true. il por *N Y Times Mag* p32-6 Ap 26 '87
Hinduism
See also
Catholic Church—Relations—Hinduism
Converts from Hinduism
Yoga
Rites and ceremonies
See also
Suttee
United States
Hinduism in America. R. B. Williams. *Christ Century* 104:247-9 Mr 11 '87
Hinduism and Christianity *See* Christianity and other religions
Hinduja Brothers
about
The world is their bazaar [cover story] P. Gupte. il *Forbes* 140:85-90+ D 28 '87
Hindus
Hell on wheels [Sikh extremists murder Hindu bus travelers] il *Time* 130:50 Jl 20 '87
'Such a dance of death' [Sikh attacks against Hindus] F. Willey. il *Newsweek* 110:34 Jl 20 '87
Converts to Christianity
See Converts from Hinduism
Hines, Diane Casella
David Jenks. il pors *Am Artist* 51:54-9+ S '87
A report on discipline-based art education. *Am Artist* 51:68-9+ Ag '87
Hines, Thomas S.
Configuration for a canyon. il *Archit Dig* 44:166-9+ S '87
Hinges
Invisible hinges [Roto-Hinge] P. McCafferty. il *Pop Sci* 231:99 S '87
Hinrichs, Steven H., and others
A transgenic mouse model for human neurofibromatosis. bibl f il *Science* 237:1340-3 S 11 '87
Hinrichs, W., and others
An amylose antiparallel double helix at atomic resolution. bibl f il *Science* 238:205-8 O 9 '87
Hinrichsen, Don
The forest decline enigma. il *BioScience* 37:542-6 S '87
In Krakow even the buildings dissolve. il *Int Wildl* 17:12-15 Mr/Ap '87
Hinson, David
about
Heeding a gospel of measured growth. J. E. Ellis. il por *Bus Week* p62 S 21 '87
Hinton, Milt, 1910-
about
Milt Hinton at Parsons. P. Karmel. il *Art Am* 75:140 Ja '87
Hip exercises *See* Exercise
Hip joint
Get 'hip' with vitamin C [avoiding hip fractures] *Prevention* 39:8 Jl '87
A little estrogen, fewer broken hips [osteoporosis] il *Newsweek* 110:99 N 16 '87

Hip joint—*cont.*
Treating the mind, risking the body [drugs linked to hip fractures; study by Wayne A. Ray and others] *Sci News* 131:122 F 21 '87

Tomography
See Tomography—Medical use

Hip joint, Artificial
Her joints are jumping [artificial hip recipient B. Benson] P. Spencer. il *pors* 50 Plus 27:44-50 Ja '87
The personal you: hip, hip, hooray! [hip replacement surgery for dancers] M. Horosko. il *Dance Mag* 61:60-1 D '87

Hippies
See also
Children of hippies
The graying of Aquarius. J. Adler. il *Newsweek* 109:56-8 Mr 30 '87

India
Endless summer of love [Goa] D. Black. il *Harpers* 274:47-52 My '87

Hippocampal neurons *See* Nerve cells
Hippocampus (Brain) *See* Brain
Hippopotamus
Michel Jutras doesn't win any trophies for cleaning hippo teeth, but he does get plenty of plaque. il *por People Wkly* 27:123 Je 15 '87
Move over, Felix and Oscar, move way over—these two are a really heavy-duty odd couple [elephant and hippo living together at Cincinnati Zoo] il *People Wkly* 28:116 D 21 '87

Hipps, Bob
about
Everyman's farm . . . one man's struggle. T. Krautwurst. il *pors Mother Earth News* 108:114-17 N/D '87

Hipps, Carol B.
You'll look up to tithonia. il *Flower Gard* 31:69+ Ap/My '87

Hipson, Bill
about
OCO's symbolic victory. H. Quinn. il *por Macleans* 100:40 Je 8 '87

Hirai, Hisamaru, and others
A novel putative tyrosine kinase receptor encoded by the *eph* gene. bibl f il *Science* 238:1717-20 D 18 '87

Hiram Walker Resources Ltd.
The $1.2-million sales pitch [corporate junket sponsored by Allied-Lyons to highlight stake in Hiram Walker] D. Francis. *por Macleans* 100:9 Je 29 '87

Hiraoka, Yasushi, and others
The use of a charge-coupled device for quantitative optical microscopy of biological structures. bibl f il *Science* 238:36-41 O 2 '87

Hirdt, Peter
Would you trade this man? [cover story] il *Sport Mag* 78:41 Ap '87

Hiro, Dilip
Oil, the Gulf and the Iranians. *Nation* 245:261-3 S 19 '87

Hirohito, Emperor of Japan, 1901-
about
An emperor and a gentleman. M. Clugston. il *por Macleans* 100:32-3 N 30 '87

Hiroshi, Koichibara
Tomatomation: Japan's high-tech food factories. il *Courier* 40:17-19 Mr '87

Hiroshige (Andō Hiroshige), 1797-1858
about
Views of Edo: high and low. K. Varnedoe. il *Art Am* 75:98-105 Jl '87

Hiroshima (Japan)
Bombardment, 1945
A-bomb radiation doses reassessed. R. Weiss. *Sci News* 132:263 O 24 '87
Atomic bomb doses reassessed. L. Roberts. il *Science* 238:1649-51 D 18 '87
Baseball at ground zero [Hiroshima Stadium built near epicenter of nuclear explosion] G. Mitchell. il *Progressive* 51:20-1 Ag '87
Evidence for increased somatic cell mutations at the glycophorin A locus in atomic bomb survivors. R. G. Langlois and others. bibl f il *Science* 236:445-8 Ap 24 '87
Hiroshima, mon amour. il *Natl Rev* 39:18-19 S 11 '87

Hiroshima Stadium (Japan)
Baseball at ground zero. G. Mitchell. il *Progressive* 51:20-1 Ag '87

Hirsch, Edward
Evening star [poem] *Nation* 244:408 Mr 28 '87
Homage to O'Keeffe [poem] *New Repub* 196:36 Ja 5-12 '87

Infertility [poem] *New Repub* 197:32 N 9 '87
Hirsch, Eric Donald
Cultural literacy: what every American needs to know [condensation] *Read Dig* 131:79-83 D '87
about
Are student heads full of emptiness? E. Bowen. il *Time* 130:56-7 Ag 17 '87
A cathode ray tube is. J. Coyne. il *Glamour* 85:118+ Ag '87
The Department of Factual Verification. H. Kenner. *Natl Rev* 39:37-8+ O 9 '87
A dunce cap for America. D. Gates. il *Newsweek* 109:72-4 Ap 20 '87
If you can read this, says E.D. Hirsch, you may still be illiterate [interview] J. Cramer. il *por People Wkly* 28:69-71+ Ag 10 '87
Literacy at the barricades. J. W. Tuttleton. *Commentary* 84:45-8 Jl '87

Hirsch, Julian D.
Technical talk. See issues of Stereo Review
(jt. auth) See Greenleaf, Christopher, and Hirsch, Julian D.

Hirsch, Julian D., and Stark, Craig
Equipment test reports. See issues of Stereo Review
Hirsch, Martin S., and Kaplan, Joan C.
Antiviral therapy. il *Sci Am* 256:76-85 Ap '87
Hirsch, Richard, 1941-
about
Rise and fall and rise. B. Leonard. il *por Forbes* 139:98-9 F 9 '87

Hirsch, Robert L.
Impending energy crisis? [discussion of March 20, 1987 article, Impending United States energy crisis] *Science* 236:763-5 My 15 '87
Impending United States energy crisis. bibl f il *Science* 235:1467-73 Mr 20 '87

Hirschberg, Lynn
10 'perfect 10' men. il *Harpers Bazaar* 120:64+ My '87
The four brushmen of the apocalypse. il *pors Esquire* 107:76-84+ Mr '87
The man who turns on America. il *pors Roll Stone* p59-60+ O 22 '87
Personal style: the new moods of beauty. il *Harpers Bazaar* 120:147+ F '87

Hirschel, J. David
(jt. auth) See Lab, Steven P., and Hirschel, J. David
Hirschfeld, Gerhard, 1946-
Erasing the past? *Hist Today* 37:8-10 Ag '87
Hirschfeld, Robert M. A.
Clinical depression: when the blues won't go away. *por McCalls* 145:88 Mr '87
Hirschfield, Robert
Hospice: caring at life's edge. *Christ Century* 104:159 F 18 '87
Manhattan's Martinique. *Commonweal* 114:71-2 F 13 '87
The Martinique Hotel: housing the homeless. *America* 156:90-1 F 7 '87
Hirschhorn, Joel S.
(jt. auth) See Oldenburg, Kirsten U., and Hirschhorn, Joel S.

Hirshberg, Gerald
about
Miscellaneous ramblings. J. Dinkel. il *Road Track* 38:33-4 Ja '87

Hirshey, Gerri
Meet the new Bond. il *por Roll Stone* p37-9 Jl 16-30 '87
Reincarnation? Channeling? Hell, no, I won't go! il *Glamour* 85:72 D '87
Twenty years of rock & roll style. il *Roll Stone* p97-100+ Ap 23 '87

Hirson, Denis
Arrest me [fiction] *Harpers* 275:25-6 O '87
Hispanic American art *See* Art, Hispanic American
Hispanic American market
Learning to say 'buy' in Spanish [ad agency Sosa & Associates] D. Graff. il *Channels* 7:17 S '87
Madison Avenue's big Latin beat. S. Brown. il *Time* 130:57 Jl 20 '87

Hispanic Americans
For Latinos, a growing divide. D. Whitman. il *U S News World Rep* 103:47-9 Ag 10 '87
The next underclass? L. Chavez. *New Repub* 197:12-13 Ag 3 '87
Resources for Hispanic and other minorities [aged] il *Aging* no355:23 '87

Hispanic Americans—*cont.*

Education

Making a robot out of rubbish [CHICO project for Hispanic students sponsored by University of Maryland] il *Natl Geogr World* 141:25-9 My '87

Health and hygiene

The changing face of AIDS. R. Stengel. il *Time* 130:12-14 Ag 17 '87

The uneven odds: minorities are afflicted with AIDS in significantly disproportionate numbers. A. Levine. il *U S News World Rep* 103:31-3 Ag 17 '87

Religious life

Ministry and vocations: going back to the drawing board. A. F. Deck. *America* 156:212-13+ Mr 14 '87

Papa do preach [state of Hispanic Catholicism] A. Sullivan. *New Repub* 197:13-14+ O 5 '87

Hispanic Americans in motion pictures

Hispanic Hollywood. J. Foote. il *Newsweek* 110:66-7 Ag 17 '87

Hispanic Americans in television

Blacks better portrayed on TV than Hispanics: study. *Jet* 72:23 Jl 20 '87

Hiss, Tony

Experiencing places (I). *New Yorker* 63:45-9+ Je 22 '87

Experiencing places (II). *New Yorker* 63:73-80+ Je 29 '87

Histamine

See also

Scombroid poisoning

Histamine receptors *See* Chemoreceptors

Histocompatibility *See* Immunological tolerance

Histocompatibility antigens *See* Antigens and antibodies

Histocompatibility complex *See* Major histocompatibility complex

Histones

Identification of the human U7 snRNP as one of several factors involved in the 3′ end maturation of histone premessenger RNA's. K. L. Mowry and J. A. Steitz. bibl f il *Science* 238:1682-7 D 18 '87

Protein-DNA interactions in vivo upstream of a cell cycle-regulated human H4 histone gene. U. Pauli and others. bibl f il *Science* 236:1308-11 Je 5 '87

Historians, American

American history is falling down. B. A. Weisberger. il *Am Herit* 38:26-32 F/Mr '87

The (non) teaching of American history: U.S. history is falling down. B. A. Weisberger. *Current* 293:20-7 Je '87

Historians, English

See also

Burke, Edmund, 1729?-1797

Clarendon, Edward Hyde, 1st Earl of, 1609-1674

Davies, Norman

Ensor, R. C. K., 1877-1958

May we borrow your historians? [U.S. universities' recruitment of English professors] M. Kishlansky. il *Hist Today* 37:6-7 Je '87

Historians, German

See also

Brackmann, Albert, 1871-1952

Ranke, Leopold von, 1795-1886

Erasing the past? G. Hirschfeld. *Hist Today* 37:8-10 Ag '87

The war of the German historians. G. A. Craig. il *N Y Rev Books* 33:16-19 Ja 15 '87

Historians, Greek

See also

Herodotus

Historic Deerfield, Inc.

Glimpse into the past. M. Wade. il *Horizon* 30:42 N '87

Historic farms *See* Agricultural museums

Historic house museums *See* Historic houses, sites, etc.

Historic houses, sites, etc.

See also

Castles

Fortification

Houses, Restored

Memorials

Official residences

Palaces

Plantations

Ranches

Villages, Restored

After tax reform, historic rehabs can still pay off. B. Hitchings. il *Bus Week* p123 Ap 6 '87

Building a cozy tax shelter with historic rehabs [real estate limited partnership] T. Segal. il *Bus Week* p118 S 7 '87

Dolls and toys at home for Christmas. M. Jailer. il *Antiques Collect Hobbies* 92:34-8 D '87

Historic houses, landmarks, and museums. See issues of Antiques

Preserving the past. il *Futurist* 21:40-1 Ja/F '87

Rediscover America [cover story; special issue; with editorial comment by Timothy C. Forbes] il *Am Herit* 38:6-7, 29-31+ Ap '87

Spiffing up the urban heritage [downtown areas; cover story] K. Anderson. il *Time* 130:72-6+ N 23 '87

Take a "novel" vacation! [visiting literary landmarks in the U.S.] S. Birnbaum. il *Good Housekeep* 205:44+ Jl '87

Alabama

See also

Huntsville (Ala.)—Historic houses, sites, etc.

Arkansas

See also

Fort Smith (Ark.)—Historic houses, sites, etc.

Belgium

See also

Brussels (Belgium)—Historic houses, sites, etc.

California

See also

Beverly Hills (Calif.)—Historic houses, sites, etc.

Hearst-San Simeon State Historical Monument (Calif.)

Hollywood (Calif.)—Historic houses, sites, etc.

Los Angeles (Calif.)—Historic houses, sites, etc.

Piedmont (Calif.)—Historic houses, sites, etc.

Salinas (Calif.)—Historic houses, sites, etc.

San Francisco (Calif.)—Historic houses, sites, etc.

San Jose (Calif.)—Historic houses, sites, etc.

Scotty's Castle (Calif.)

Sebastopol (Calif.)—Historic houses, sites, etc.

Yorba Linda (Calif.)—Historic houses, sites, etc.

Caribbean region

See also

Fortification—Caribbean region

Connecticut

See also

Greenwich (Conn.)—Historic houses, sites, etc.

Litchfield (Conn.)—Historic houses, sites, etc.

Litchfield County (Conn.)—Historic houses, sites, etc.

Mystic Seaport Museum

Blass country [designer's 1779 house] C. T. Buckley. il *House Gard* 159:132-43+ My '87

Colonial contours: traditional lines for a Connecticut farmhouse [decorated by Thomas Britt] C. D. B. Bryan. il *Archit Dig* 44:102-7 Jl '87

A Housatonic holiday [Housatonic Railroad's excursion] C. La VO. il *Travel Holiday* 168:30+ S '87

Playing to a full house [guest cottage in Connecticut decorated by B. Blass] C. Vogel. il *N Y Times Mag* p51-3 Ag 9 '87

Delaware

See also

Kent County (Del.)—Historic houses, sites, etc.

Wilmington (Del.)—Historic houses, sites, etc.

Egypt

See also

Cairo (Egypt)—Historic houses, sites, etc.

Florida

See also

Fort Lauderdale (Fla.)—Historic houses, sites, etc.

Fortification—Florida

Saint Augustine (Fla.)—Historic houses, sites, etc.

Tranquilla: an Italianate palazzo on Biscayne Bay [home of C. and M. Candib, decorated by Valerian S. Rybar and Jean-François Daigré; cover story] J. Taylor. il pors *Archit Dig* 44:148-55 Ap '87

France

See also

Ermenonville (France)—Historic houses, sites, etc.

Poissy (France)—Historic houses, sites, etc.

Historic houses: Le Corbusier's cabanon. T. Benton. il *Archit Dig* 44:146-51+ D '87

Georgia

See also

Savannah (Ga.)—Historic houses, sites, etc.

American grandeur [restoration of Georgia mansion by W. N. Banks] B. Gill. il por *House Gard* 159:112-23+ S '87

Germany (West)

See also

Darmstadt (Germany)—Historic houses, sites, etc.

Kronberg (Germany)—Historic houses, sites, etc.

Murnau (Germany)—Historic houses, sites, etc.

Great Britain

See also

Chelsea (London, England)—Historic houses, sites, etc.

Historic houses, sites, etc.—Great Britain—See also—*cont.*

Clarendon Park (Wiltshire, England)—Historic houses, sites, etc.
Derbyshire (England)—Historic houses, sites, etc.
East Stoke (England)—Historic houses, sites, etc.
Georgian Group
Hull (England)—Historic houses, sites, etc.
London (England)—Historic houses, sites, etc.
Twickenham (London, England)—Historic houses, sites, etc.

50 rooms with a view [Holker Hall, estate of G. and H. Cavendish] R. Billington. il pors *Vogue* 177:314-21+ My '87
At Deene Park: the Brudenell family estate in Northamptonshire. E. Lambert. il *Archit Dig* 44:110-15+ Ja '87
Badminton House: the Duke and Duchess of Beaufort in Avon. A. Somerset. il *Archit Dig* 44:48-55+ Jl '87
Blickling Hall, Norfolk. J. Maddison. il *Antiques* 131:1280-7 Je '87
British architecture [Robert Adam and Kedleston Hall at the Cooper-Hewitt] S. B. Sherrill. il *Antiques* 131:1170+ Je '87
A comfortable perfection [Biddick] A. Lambton. il *House Gard* 159:146-55 N '87
Educating the eye in England. M. Hampton. il *House Gard* 159:90+ N '87
Fantasy bestowed on form [gardens at Shute House] A. Tree. il *House Gard* 159:190-7+ Ap '87
Image makers [Garmelow Manor, home of A. and P. Machin] E. Greene. il pors *House Gard* 159:180-7 N '87
The Oriental porcelains at Burghley House, Lincolnshire, England [Cecil family collection] G. Lang. il *Antiques* 131:236-47 Ja '87
Painting Petworth [tradition of artists portraying stately English home] M. Egremont. il *House Gard* 159:116+ N '87
Partners with the past: Lady Anne and Michael Tree at Shute House. A. Tree. il *Archit Dig* 44:168-73 Je '87
The past mastered [Ironbridge Institute's course in heritage management] T. Aldous. *Hist Today* 37:4-5 My '87
Power and the early-Tudor courtier's house [excerpt from The early Tudor country house] M. Howard. bibl il por *Hist Today* 37:44-50 My '87
Reflections on a venerable British tradition [dower houses] Lady C. Hesketh. il por *Archit Dig* 44:98+ Je '87
To the manor reborn [Heydon Hall renovated by David Mlinaric] C. Vogel. il *N Y Times Mag* p80-4 N 22 '87
Wild gaming [private zoo at Howletts, country home of J. Aspinall] B. Masters. il por *House Gard* 159:222-5+ N '87

Guatemala
See also
Antigua (Guatemala)—Historic houses, sites, etc.

Hebrides (Scotland)
Old renewed in the Western Isles. A. Hills. il *Hist Today* 37:7-8 O '87

Illinois
See also
Chicago (Ill.)—Historic houses, sites, etc.
Galena (Ill.)—Historic houses, sites, etc.

India
See also
Fortification—India

Indiana
See also
Indianapolis (Ind.)—Historic houses, sites, etc.

Iowa
See also
Eldon (Iowa)—Historic houses, sites, etc.

Italy
See also
Trieste (Italy)—Historic houses, sites, etc.
The house that turns to the sun [Il Girasole, built in the 1930s by A. Invernizzi] T. Williams. il *House Gard* 159:150-7+ F '87

Japan
Japan's balance of past and present. A. Hills. il *Hist Today* 37:4-5 F '87

Kansas
See also
Lawrence (Kan.)—Historic houses, sites, etc.

Kentucky
See also
Bardstown (Ky.)—Historic houses, sites, etc.
Lexington (Ky.)—Historic houses, sites, etc.
Stanford (Ky.)—Historic houses, sites, etc.

Korea (South)
Revaluing South Korea's heritage. A. Hills. il *Hist Today* 37:3-4 Ap '87

Louisiana
See also
New Orleans (La.)—Historic houses, sites, etc.

Maine
Maine light: the summer house of Mr. and Mrs. Douglas Auchincloss. S. M. Alsop. il *Archit Dig* 44:188-95 Je '87

Maryland
See also
Baltimore (Md.)—Historic houses, sites, etc.

Massachusetts
See also
Boston (Mass.)—Historic houses, sites, etc.
Duxbury (Mass.)—Historic houses, sites, etc.
Edgartown (Mass.)—Historic houses, sites, etc.
Historic Deerfield, Inc.
Ipswich (Mass.)—Historic houses, sites, etc.
Manchester (Mass.)—Historic houses, sites, etc.
Trustees of Reservations (Mass.)
The Berkshires: hills of heaven. J. Colihan. il *Am Herit* 38:26+ My/Je '87

Michigan
See also
Marshall (Mich.)—Historic houses, sites, etc.

Mississippi
See also
Natchez (Miss.)—Historic houses, sites, etc.
Oxford (Miss.)—Historic houses, sites, etc.

Morocco
See also
Essaouira (Morocco)—Historic houses, sites, etc.
Tangier (Morocco)—Historic houses, sites, etc.

Mount Desert Island (Me.)
Hanging in there [International Style house] C. Vogel. il *N Y Times Mag* p72-3 Ag 16 '87

Nantucket (Mass.)
Pure Nantucket [H. N. Jacobsen remodels E. Voorhees' 1757 house] J. Chancellor. il *House Gard* 159:78-85+ Ag '87

New England
As rare as a day in June [18th century stone country house owned by a fashion designer] A. Gordon. il *House Gard* 159:124-33 Je '87
The barn builder [R. Babcock] B. Trebilcock. il pors *Ctry J* 14:34-40 Mr '87

New Hampshire
See also
Temple (N.H.)—Historic houses, sites, etc.

New Jersey
See also
Edison National Historic Site
Ringwood (N.J.)—Historic houses, sites, etc.

New Mexico
See also
Santa Fe (N.M.)—Historic houses, sites, etc.
Taos (N.M.)—Historic houses, sites, etc.

New York (State)
See also
Cape Vincent (N.Y.)—Historic houses, sites, etc.
Mohonk Mountain House
Muttontown (N.Y.)—Historic houses, sites, etc.
New York (N.Y.)—Historic houses, sites, etc.
Old Westbury Gardens
Sagaponack (N.Y.)—Historic houses, sites, etc.
Saratoga National Historical Park (N.Y.)
Staten Island (New York, N.Y.)—Historic houses, sites, etc.
Great houses along the Hudson. F. Allen. il *Am Herit* 38:28+ S/O '87
New York's famous and historic trees. C. Wiedemann. il *Conservationist* 41:32-7 Mr/Ap '87
Sylvan cider mill: Jean and Harcourt Amory's Westchester Hills restoration. S. M. L. Aronson. il *Archit Dig* 44:204-8+ Je '87

North Carolina
See also
Asheville (N.C.)—Historic houses, sites, etc.
Franklin County (N.C.)—Historic houses, sites, etc.
Historic Preservation Foundation of North Carolina
Everyman's farm . . . one man's struggle [fight to turn Overhome into a museum] T. Krautwurst. il pors *Mother Earth News* 108:114-17 N/D '87

Northern Ireland
See also
Fortification—Northern Ireland

Oklahoma
See also
Fortification—Oklahoma

Historic houses, sites, etc.—*cont.*
Ontario
See also
Kingston (Ont.)—Historic houses, sites, etc.
Pennsylvania
See also
Philadelphia (Pa.)—Historic houses, sites, etc.
Valley Forge National Historical Park (Pa.)
Portugal
Portugal's manor houses [guest accommodations] C. Barrington. il map *Travel Holiday* 168:48-53 N '87
Queensland (Australia)
Nindooinbah House [1850s homestead] P. Hockey. il *House Gard* 159:150-60 Ja '87
Rhode Island
See also
Newport (R.I.)—Historic houses, sites, etc.
Sandbar Island (Me.)
Autumn on Sandbar Island: Dr. Lee Salk's retreat in Maine. C. T. Buckley. il por *Archit Dig* 44:134-9 O '87
Scotland
Mary Queen of Scots: a tragedy in four cities. P. M. Prince. il *Travel Holiday* 167:54-9 Ap '87
Singapore
Singapore's token conservation. A. Hills. il *Hist Today* 37:3-4 Mr '87
South Carolina
See also
Charleston (S.C.)—Historic houses, sites, etc.
Columbia (S.C.)—Historic houses, sites, etc.
Southern States
Historic architecture teaches preservation. il *South Living* 22:92 O '87
Sweden
See also
Sundborn (Sweden)—Historic houses, sites, etc.
Tennessee
See also
Piney Flats (Tenn.)—Historic houses, sites, etc.
Texas
See also
Fort Worth (Tex.)—Historic houses, sites, etc.
Galveston (Tex.)—Historic houses, sites, etc.
Independence (Tex.)—Historic houses, sites, etc.
San Antonio (Tex.)—Historic houses, sites, etc.
United States
See Historic houses, sites, etc.
Virgin Islands of the United States
The U.S. Virgin Islands: another reason. J. Colihan. il *Am Herit* 38:20+ Jl/Ag '87
Virginia
See also
Appomattox Court House National Historical Park (Va.)
Fairfax County (Va.)—Historic houses, sites, etc.
Williamsburg (Va.)
Blue and Gray Virginia: commemorating battles of a nation divided. C. B. Hayes. il map *Travel Holiday* 167:52-5+ Je '87
Blue Ridge variation: augmenting a house in the Virginia horse country [Queen Anne farmhouse addition by O'Neil & Manion] J. S. Wamsley. il *Archit Dig* 44:176-9 Ap '87
A stately duel in Virginia [homes of the participants and excerpts from the constitutional ratification debate of 1788] D. G. Kinney. il *Life* 10:66-74 Fall '87
Wales
Gold in the valleys. A. Hills. il *Hist Today* 37:3-4 D '87
Welsh comfort [Cruglas, ancestral home of the Lisburnes] D. Briers. il *House Gard* 159:112-19+ Ag '87
Washington (D.C.)
See Washington (D.C.)—Historic houses, sites, etc.
Washington (State)
A well-rounded barn. M. Hofferber. il *Ctry J* 14:42-6 F '87
West Virginia
See also
Fortification—West Virginia
Historic Preservation Foundation of North Carolina
History for sale. B. Finger. il *Americana* 15:50-4 My/Je '87
Historic sites *See* Historic houses, sites, etc.
Historic trees *See* Trees, Historic
Historical art *See* History in art
Historical chronology *See* Chronology, Historical
Historical fiction
Authorship
Lincoln: fiction & fact [interview with W. Safire] A. M. Schlesinger. il pors *Am Herit* 38:84-9 D '87

A modern vote for Abraham Lincoln [interview with W. Safire] A. P. Sanoff. il por *U S News World Rep* 103:57 Ag 24 '87
Old and novel. G. Jennings. il *N Y Times Mag* p16+ N 29 '87
The rise and fall of the American empire [interview with G. Vidal] A. P. Sanoff. por *U S News World Rep* 103:62 Jl 13 '87
William Safire talks about 'Freedom,' his new novel. T. Todd. por *Publ Wkly* 231:49-50 My 29 '87
Technique
Some problems for the historical novelist. L. McBain. *Writer* 100:24-7 Ag '87
Writing the un-historical novel. G. Jennings. il *Writer* 100:7-10+ S '87
Historical literature
See also
Historical fiction
History—Bibliography
Publishers and publishing—Historical literature
Historical Maritime Group of New England
Quest for shipwrecks. C. Lowrance. il *Oceans* 20:50-4+ Jl/Ag '87
Historical novels *See* Historical fiction
Historical research
The historian: 'a wrestler with the angel'. D. J. Boorstin. il *N Y Times Book Rev* 92:1+ S 20 '87
Historical societies
See also
American Antiquarian Society
Chester County Historical Society
Chicago Historical Society
East Hampton Historical Society
There's a historical society in every western state, and you can join. il *Sunset* 179:54-5+ D '87
Historiography
See also
Great Britain—History—Puritan Revolution, 1642-1660—Historiography
Soviet Union—History—Revolution, 1917-1921—Historiography
Germany—History—1933-1945—Historiography
Greece—History—Historiography
Holocaust, Jewish (1939-1945)—Historiography
Ireland—History—Historiography
Jews—Poland—History—Historiography
Lincoln, Abraham, 1809-1865—Historiography
Mary, Queen of Scots, 1542-1587—Historiography
Reformation—Historiography
Soviet Union—History—Historiography
Trade unions—Great Britain—History—Historiography
Women—History—Historiography
The historian: 'a wrestler with the angel'. D. J. Boorstin. il *N Y Times Book Rev* 92:1+ S 20 '87
History without letters [trend towards electronic communication reduces sources for historians] W. Isaacson. il *Time* 130:65-6 Ag 31 '87
What Ranke meant. F. Gilbert. *Am Sch* 56:393-7 Summ '87
History
See also
Church history
Civilization
Current events
Heroes and heroines
Historical fiction
Literature and history
Oral history
Progress
Radio and history
Television and history
See also subhead History under various subjects
Outside history [America] L. Weschler. *Harpers* 274:16-18 Ja '87
Anecdotes, facetiae, satire, etc.
More of Paul Harvey's Rest of the story [condensation]; ed. by Paul Aurandt. P. Harvey. il *Read Dig* 130:17-18+ F '87
Bibliography
Book reviews. See issues of History Today
Historiography
See Historiography
Psychological aspects
Time machine psychology [M. E. P. Seligman's study of explanatory styles] il *Psychol Today* 21:36-7 F '87
Research
See Historical research
Sources
See also
Archives

History—Sources—See also—*cont.*
  Statesmen—Correspondence
Study and teaching
  See also
  United States—History—Study and teaching
  Vietnamese War, 1957-1975—Study and teaching
A creative approach to learning [high school history teacher J. Ause in Buffalo, Minn.] C. Orange. por *Progressive* 51:12 N '87
Have our kids lost their past? [National Endowment for the Humanities study] J. N. Baker. il *Newsweek* 110:60-1 S 7 '87
History and controversy in the classroom. J. Slater. il *Hist Today* 37:6-7 Ja '87
Not waving, but drowning [teaching of history in British colleges] *Hist Today* 37:2-3 Jl '87
A shortsighted vision [National Endowment for the Humanities study] D. R. Carlin, Jr. *Commonweal* 114:615-16 N 6 '87
Tot sociology: grade school history. D. Ravitch. *Current* 298:4-10 D '87
Tot sociology: or What happened to history in the grade schools. D. Ravitch. *Am Sch* 56:343-54 Summ '87
TV: show business or education? J. Yardley. *Des Arts Educ* 88:46-7 Jl/Ag '87
'What do our 17-year-olds know?' assesses the failure of American high school education. *Publ Wkly* 232:134 S 18 '87
What happened to history in the grade schools? D. Ravitch. *Educ Dig* 53:7-9 O '87
Textbooks
  See also
  United States—History—Textbooks
History and literature *See* Literature and history
History and radio *See* Radio and history
History in art
  J.L.G. Ferris. B. J. Mitnick. il por *Am Hist Illus* 21:14-21 F '87
Exhibitions
Shrinking history [Morality tales: history painting in the 1980s at NYU's Grey Art Gallery] K. Larson. il *N Y* 20:101-2 O 5 '87
History in motion pictures
  History for rent [fiction films with historical settings] G. C. Ward. il *Am Herit* 38:16+ Ap '87
  Nostalgia and dis-history. K. R. Hey. *USA Today (Periodical)* 116:93 N '87
Hit men *See* Murder
Hitachi, Ltd.
  The mountain priest [K. Mita] F. H. Katayama. il por *Fortune* 116:42 Ag 3 '87
Hitchcock, Alfred, 1899-1980
  about
  The ghost of Alfred Hitchcock. R. Corliss. il *Time* 129:76+ F 16 '87
Hitchcock, Robyn
  about
  Robyn in wonderland. D. Fricke. il por *Roll Stone* p17 Ja 29 '87
Hitchens, Christopher
  Blabscam: TV's rigged political talk shows. *Harpers* 274:75-6 Mr '87
  Britain in the South Pacific. il *Harpers Bazaar* 120:264+ S '87
  It dare not speak its name: fear and self-loathing on the gay right. *Harpers* 275:70-2 Ag '87
  Minority report. See issues of The Nation
  New statesman downed by law. il *Nation* 244:217-19 F 21 '87
Hitchner, Earle
  Fanfare for the common editor. por *Publ Wkly* 232:40 S 4 '87
Hite, Shere
  about
  Back off, buddy [cover story] C. Wallis. il *Time* 130:68-73 O 12 '87
  If feminist Shere Hite thinks women are so miserable, how come she's so happy with her husband? R. Sanders. il pors *People Wkly* 28:60-2 D 7 '87
  Men aren't her only problem. B. Barol. il por *Newsweek* 110:76 N 23 '87
  Tapping a mine of female discontent. M. McIver. il por *Macleans* 100:44-5 O 19 '87
Hitler, Adolf, 1889-1945
  about
  Jottings from the Third Reich. J. Smolowe. il por *Time* 130:44 S 14 '87
Bibliography
Getting along with Hitler. G. A. Craig. il *N Y Rev Books* 34:32-5 Jl 16 '87

Hitschler, Tony
  about
  A cellar of stocks now ripe for buying. G. G. Marcial. il por *Bus Week* p114 D 7 '87
Hitt, Jack
  And now, for something completely cheap. il *Harpers* 275:58-9 N '87
  What did Noah do with the manure? and other burning questions of creation science. il *Wash Mon* 19:25-8 F '87
Hitzelburger, Bobby
  about
  Ex-champ Ernie Terrell training Foreman's foe. *Jet* 71:50 Mr 2 '87
HIV viruses
  Activation of the HIV-1 LTR by T cell mitogens and the trans-activator protein of HTLV-I. M. Siekevitz and others. bibl f il *Science* 238:1575-8 D 11 '87
  The AIDS debate: call it a draw [conflict between French and U.S. researchers resolved] *Newsweek* 109:64 Ap 13 '87
  AIDS patent dispute settled. D. M. Barnes. *Science* 236:17 Ap 3 '87
  AIDS researchers debate danger of HIV-2. D. D. Edwards. *Sci News* 131:151 Mr 7 '87
  The AIDS virus. R. C. Gallo. bibl (p128) il map *Sci Am* 256:46-56 Ja '87
  The AIDS virus—well known but a mystery. J. L. Marx. il *Science* 236:390-2 Ap 24 '87
  Blocking of HIV-1 infectivity by a soluble, secreted form of the CD4 antigen. D. H. Smith and others. bibl f il *Science* 238:1704-7 D 18 '87
  Characterization and clinical association of antibody inhibitory to HIV reverse transcriptase activity. J. Laurence and others. bibl f il *Science* 235:1501-4 Mr 20 '87
  'Competition' cause of AIDS dementia? [work of Mark E. Gurney and others] D. D. Edwards. *Sci News* 132:150-1 S 5 '87
  Control protein for AIDS virus identified [research by Gary Nabel and David Baltimore] J. L. Marx. il *Science* 236:393 Ap 24 '87
  Cytokine-induced expression of HIV-1 in a chronically infected promonocyte cell line. T. Folks and others. bibl f il *Science* 238:800-2 N 6 '87
  Cytokines alter AIDS virus production [research by Anthony Fauci and Thomas Folks] D. M. Barnes. il *Science* 236:1627 Je 26 '87
  Expression and processing of the AIDS virus reverse transcriptase in Escherichia coli. W. G. Farmerie and others. bibl f il *Science* 236:305-8 Ap 17 '87
  Expression of the art/trs protein of HIV and study of its role in viral envelope synthesis. D. M. Knight and others. bibl f il *Science* 236:837-40 My 15 '87
  The frustrating fight against AIDS. J. Schecter. il *Technol Rev* 90:65 Jl '87
  Functional interaction and partial homology between human immunodeficiency virus and neuroleukin [cause of AIDS dementia] M. R. Lee and others. bibl f il *Science* 237:1047-51 Ag 28 '87
  Functional regions of the envelope glycoprotein of human immunodeficiency virus type 1. M. Kowalski and others. bibl f il *Science* 237:1351-5 S 11 '87
  Human T-lymphotropic virus type 4 and the human immunodeficiency virus in West Africa. P. J. Kanki and others. bibl f il *Science* 236:827-31 My 15 '87
  Hybrid particle mimics AIDS virus [retrotransposons] D. D. Edwards. *Sci News* 132:151 S 5 '87
  Isolation of a T-lymphotropic virus from domestic cats with an immunodeficiency-like syndrome. N. C. Pedersen and others. bibl f il *Science* 235:790-3 F 13 '87
  Marketing an AIDS expert [R. Gallo] R. Rhein, Jr. and M. Maremont. *Bus Week* p38+ D 14 '87
  New virus, growth factor found for AIDS [research by Robert C. Gallo and others] D. D. Edwards. *Sci News* 131:356 Je 6 '87
  One AIDS problem or two? [Africa] D. Dickson. *Science* 238:606 O 30 '87
  Probing the AIDS virus and its relatives [special section] J. L. Marx. il *Science* 236:1523-5 Je 19 '87
  Solo actions of AIDS virus coat. D. M. Barnes. bibl il *Science* 237:971-3 Ag 28 '87
  The *sor* gene of HIV-1 is required for efficient virus transmission in vitro. A. G. Fisher and others. bibl f il *Science* 237:888-93 Ag 21 '87
  The source of AIDS. J. C. Peck. *Futurist* 21:12-13 N/D '87
  Stopping sperm may block AIDS [virus penetration of HLA-DR tagged cells; research by Ellyn Ashida and Virginia Scofield] *Discover* 8:11+ O '87

HIV viruses—*cont.*
Synthetic peptide immunoassay distinguishes HIV type 1 and HIV type 2 infections. J. W. Gnann, Jr. and others. bibl f il *Science* 237:1346-9 S 11 '87
Yalta of AIDS [agreement between French and American researchers] *Time* 129:57 Ap 13 '87
HLA (Human leukocyte antigens) *See* Antigens and antibodies
Hmong refugees *See* Refugees, Laotian
HMOs *See* Health maintenance organizations
HMS Pinafore [operetta] See Sullivan, Sir Arthur, 1842-1900
Ho, Stanley
about
Macau's casino king gets set to play with Beijing. M. Shao. il por *Bus Week* p98-9 Ja 19 '87
Hoadley, Walter E.
The hidden issues facing America [address, January 6, 1987] *Vital Speeches Day* 53:270-3 F 15 '87
Hoagland, Edward
Christmases past. *Nation* 245:776-7 D 26 '87-Ja 2 '88
Summer skunks. *Nation* 245:149 Ag 29 '87
Up with spring. *Nation* 244:751 Je 6 '87
Hoang, Nhu Tran
about
Twelve years out of Vietnam, Air Force cadet Hoang Nhu Tran discovers the sky's the limit. R. Arias. il pors *People Wkly* 27:45-6 Je 15 '87
Hoarseness
Hoarseness: when to worry. il *Good Housekeep* 204:255 Ap '87
Hoaxes
Bird hoax [Archaeopteryx] I. Smullen. il *Omni* 9:100 My '87
Feathers still fly in row over fossil bird [Archaeopteryx debate] D. Dickson. il *Science* 238:475-6 O 23 '87
Hey Wall Street, wanna buy the Brooklyn Bridge? [takeover hoax surrounding Dayton Hudson shows market's vulnerability to rumor] G. Weiss. il por *Bus Week* p31 Jl 6 '87
UFO update [circles of flattened grain in southern England fields possibly a hoax; research by Paul Fuller and Terence Meaden] J. Randles. il *Omni* 10:141 O '87
Hoban, Phoebe
Only in 'Amerika': the mini-series everyone loves to hate. il *N Y* 20:36-41 Ja 26 '87
The Salinger file. il pors *N Y* 20:36-42 Je 15 '87
Star tech. See issues of New York beginning September 24, 1984
Hobbes, Thomas, 1588-1679
about
Locke meets Hobbes at Iran-contra hearings. J. M. Wall. *Christ Century* 104:643-4 Jl 29-Ag 5 '87
Hobbie, Lawrence, and others
Restoration of LDL receptor activity in mutant cells by intercellular junctional communication. bibl f il *Science* 235:69-73 Ja 2 '87
Hobbies
See also
Collectors and collecting
Bibliography
Book reviews. See issues of Hobbies through February 1985
Hobbs, Charles R.
Thirteen ways to procrastinate efficiently and gain control of your time. *Work Woman* 12:96-7 O '87
Hobbs, Lyndall
about
Back to the beach [film] Reviews
Macleans 100:51 Ag 17 '87. L. O'Toole
Hobbs, Mark
about
Mrs. Hunt's Rainwater. L. Gubernick. por *Forbes* 140:108 Ag 24 '87
Hoberman, J.
(jt. auth) See Das Gupta, Chidananda, and Hoberman, J.
Hoboes *See* Homeless
Hobsbawm, E. J. (Eric J.), 1917-
The jazz comeback. il *N Y Rev Books* 34:11-14 F 12 '87
Slyest of the foxes. bibl f il *N Y Rev Books* 34:3-4+ N 19 '87
Hobsbawm, Eric J. *See* Hobsbawm, E. J. (Eric J.), 1917-
Hobson, Cindy Graff
Fairfax County: a legacy of arts. il *Horizon* 30:24-30+ Jl/Ag '87
Hoch, Harvey C., and others
Signaling for growth orientation and cell differentiation by surface topography in Uromyces. bibl f il *Science* 235:1659-62 Mr 27 '87

Hochbaum, H. Albert (Hans Albert), 1911-
about
How Leopold learned to think like a mountain. C. Meine. *Wilderness* 51:57-8+ Wint '87
Hochbaum, Hans Albert *See* Hochbaum, H. Albert (Hans Albert), 1911-
Hochberg, David
Turning highway rights into wrongs. por *U S News World Rep* 103:6 N 30 '87
Hochfield, Sylvia
Rembrandt: the unvarnished truth? [cover story] il pors *Art News* 86:102-11 D '87
Soviet art: new freedom, new directions. il *Art News* 86:102-7 O '87
Thoroughly modern Met. il *Art News* 86:112-17 F '87
Hochman, Gail
about
Agent Gail Hochman's role in the ascent of 'Presumed innocent'. A. O'Malley. il por *Publ Wkly* 231:35-6 Ap 3 '87
Hockaday, Irvine O.
about
How Hallmark goes about being low-cost producer [interview] il por *Fortune* 115:31 My 25 '87
Hockey, Patrick
Nindooinbah House. il *House Gard* 159:150-60 Ja '87
Hockey
See also
Hockey players
Phenomena, comment and notes. J. P. Wiley, Jr. il *Smithsonian* 18:30+ D '87
Playing for lunch money [Team USA against Soviets] A. Murphy. il *Sports Illus* 67:50-2+ D 21 '87
Ethical aspects
A hockey fight that cost a medal [Canadians fight Soviets at the world junior hockey championship in Czechoslovakia] M. Janigan. il *Macleans* 100:50 Ja 19 '87
There was no penalty on the play [violence in Canadian amateur hockey] A. Fotheringham. il *Macleans* 100:60 Mr 16 '87
Tournaments
The battle for hockey supremacy [Canada Cup] H. Quinn. il *Macleans* 100:48 S 7 '87
The Bear bit the Badger [Soviets defeat Team USA in Canada Cup competition] A. Murphy. il *Sports Illus* 67:24-5 S 14 '87
Détente on ice [NHL All-stars vs. Soviets' best] E. M. Swift. il *Sports Illus* 66:12-19 F 23 '87
An exhilarating Rendez-Vous [highlights of NHL-Soviet hockey games at Quebec City festival] H. Quinn. il *Macleans* 100:50-1 F 23 '87
Getting their act together [Canada Cup] H. Quinn. il *Macleans* 100:47 S 14 '87
A multimillion-dollar Rendezvous [NHL All-stars vs. Soviet national team highlights Rendez-Vous 87 festival in Quebec] H. Quinn. il *Macleans* 100:30-1 F 9 '87
Notes and comment [American journalists ignore Canada Cup] *New Yorker* 63:27-8 S 28 '87
O Canada Cup: a rousing finale [Canada defeats Soviet Union] A. Murphy. il *Sports Illus* 67:12 S 28 '87
Playing two for the show [Canada and Soviet Union in Canada Cup finals] A. Murphy. il *Sports Illus* 67:74+ S 21 '87
A rocky road to the 1988 Olympics [Canadian national team's poor showing in Calgary Cup competition] H. Quinn. il *Macleans* 100:44-5 Ja 12 '87
Team Canada: greatest show on ice [Canada Cup] H. Quinn. il *Macleans* 100:51 S 28 '87
A tenacious will for winning [Rendez-Vous 87 organizer M. Aubut] il por *Macleans* 100:30-1 D 28 '87
Two finalists worthy of the Cup [Canada Cup] H. Quinn. il *Macleans* 100:46 S 21 '87
History
The miracle upsets [U.S. Olympic team in 1960 and 1980] W. Bingham. il *Sports Illus* 67:47+ S 21 '87
Hockey, College
Tournaments
The Sioux came through [T. Hrkac leads North Dakota to the NCAA title] P. Putnam. il *Sports Illus* 66:132+ Ap 6 '87
Hockey, Professional
See also
National Hockey League
The 1987-88 NHL preview. il *Sport Mag* 78:49-52+ O '87
The Battle of Quebec [Montreal and Quebec meet in the playoffs] A. Murphy. il *Sports Illus* 66:20-5 My 4 '87
A bloody mess [Calgary Flames vs. Edmonton Oilers] A. Murphy. il *Sports Illus* 66:24-6+ Mr 30 '87

Hockey, Professional—*cont.*

Capital punishment [Islanders beat Capitals in overtime playoff game] A. Murphy. il *Sports Illus* 66:26-8+ Ap 27 '87

The Cup runneth overlong [NHL playoffs] E. M. Swift. il por *Sports Illus* 66:88 Ap 13 '87

Edgy from lack of Coffey [Edmonton Oilers off to so-so start without star defenseman] A. Murphy. il *Sports Illus* 67:26-7 N 16 '87

Having a Devil of a time [New Jersey] A. Murphy. il *Sports Illus* 67:20-1 N 23 '87

Hot shots on ice [Oilers vs. Flyers in Stanley Cup finals; cover story] A. Murphy. il por *Sports Illus* 66:26-9 Je 1 '87

How they bore us in the Norris [NHL's sorriest division] E. M. Swift. il *Sports Illus* 66:36-9 Ja 19 '87

Little by little . . . [Winnipeg Jets] R. Davis. il *Sports Illus* 66:54-5 Mr 2 '87

Make way for Hartford. A. Murphy. il *Sports Illus* 66:69-70 Mr 23 '87

New model in Motown [Red Wings coach J. Demers] A. Murphy. il pors *Sports Illus* 66:30-2 Mr 16 '87

NHL preview: off and hackin' [special section] il *Sports Illus* 67:88-92+ O 12 '87

Overovertime [Patrick Division semifinal between the New York Islanders and the Washington Caps] C. Warner. il *Sport Mag* 78:13 D '87

Party time in Edmonton [Oilers defeat Flyers for Stanley Cup] A. Murphy. il *Sports Illus* 66:22-5 Je 8 '87

The Penguins are percolating [acquisition of P. Coffey] E. M. Swift. il por *Sports Illus* 67:20-1 D 14 '87

A series with punch [Flyers vs. Rangers in playoffs] A. Murphy. il *Sports Illus* 66:82+ Ap 20 '87

The shooter and the stopper [Philadelphia Flyers vs. Montreal Canadiens in Stanley Cup semifinals] A. Murphy. il *Sports Illus* 66:42-3 My 18 '87

Sympathy for the devil [Philadelphia Flyers coach M. Keenan] P. Fichtenbaum. il pors *Sport Mag* 78:59-63 My '87

The test of champions [Oilers vs. Flyers in Stanley Cup finals] H. Quinn. il *Macleans* 100:36 Je 1 '87

Those low-flying Flyers. A. Murphy. il *Sports Illus* 67:44-6+ D 7 '87

Three sevens on one roll [playoffs] E. M. Swift. il *Sports Illus* 66:34-6+ My 11 '87

The triumph of skill: by beating Philly, the Oilers struck a blow for finesse. E. M. Swift. il por *Sports Illus* 66:96 Je 8 '87

A view to a kill [sportswriter views game from ice level] P. Fichtenbaum. il *Sport Mag* 78:86 Ja '87

Accidents and injuries

Of tragedy and triumph [4 players on Swift Current Bronco hockey team killed in bus accident in Canada] R. Corelli. il *Macleans* 100:48-50+ Mr 30 '87

Economic aspects

John Ziegler's spectacular save: the NHL. B. Welling. il por *Bus Week* p110 My 18 '87

Ethical aspects

Hockey as a cause [three Montreal Canadiens accused of sexual misconduct with minors] H. Quinn. il *Macleans* 100:50-1 Ap 27 '87

The lowdown on a high-sticking [Flyer D. Brown injures Rangers' T. Sandstrom] il por *Sports Illus* 67:16 N 9 '87

The NHL isn't so tough [gratuitous violence] E. M. Swift. il por *Sports Illus* 67:122 O 12 '87

The NHL's alcohol problem. R. Friedman. il *Sport Mag* 78:13 N '87

Organization and administration

See also
National Hockey League

Beers with [interview with New York Rangers general manager P. Esposito] P. Fichtenbaum. il por *Sport Mag* 78:19-21 N '87

Refereeing

Whistling a new tune [referee P. Stewart] M. Bishop. il pors *Sports Illus* 67:72-4+ N 30 '87

Hockey coaches

See also
Demers, Jacques, 1944-
Keenan, Mike

Hockey players

See also
Bourne, Bob
Bourque, Ray, 1960-
Brown, Dave
Carson, Jim
Coffey, Paul
Dionne, Marcel
Fuhr, Grant
Greschner, Ron

Gretzky, Wayne
Hrkac, Tony
Hull, Brett
Jarvis, Doug
Kluzak, Gord
Kyte, Jim
Lemieux, Mario
Poddubny, Walt
Robitaille, Luc
Sandstrom, Tomas
Spencer, Brian
Turgeon, Pierre

Hockey's big brother act [Sutter brothers] J. Mills. il *N Y Times Mag* p64-5+ Mr 29 '87

Accidents and injuries

See Hockey, Professional—Accidents and injuries

Hockfield, Susan

A mab to a unique cerebellar neuron generated by immunosuppression and rapid immunization. bibl f il *Science* 237:67-70 Jl 3 '87

Monoclonal antibodies as phylogenetic labels [discussion of July 3, 1987 article, A mab to a unique cerebellar neuron generated by immunosuppression and rapid immunization] *Science* 238:1730-1 D 18 '87

Hockin, Tom

about

Making them do it his way. P. C. Newman. il por *Macleans* 100:29 Ag 31 '87

Hockney, David

about

Drawing with a camera. S. Piperato. il por *Pop Photogr* 94:50-5 S '87

A fairy-tale Wagner in L.A. J. Huck. il por *Newsweek* 110:73 D 21 '87

Hodel, Donald Paul, 1935-

about

The national view [interview] R. A. Taylor. por *U S News World Rep* 103:51 Ag 31 '87

A shocker from Hodel. T. Turner. il *Mother Earth News* 108:130-1 N/D '87

The twilight ozone. H. Klingeman. *Natl Rev* 39:40-1 Ag 14 '87

Undamming Hetch Hetchy. C. Pope. il *Sierra* 72:34-8 N/D '87

Worse than Watt. *New Repub* 197:7-9 Jl 6 '87

Hodenfield, Chris

Gin-soaked boy [cover story; interview with C. Bukowski] il pors *Film Comment* 23:53-4+ Jl/Ag '87

Hodes, Art

about

Art for Art's sake [discography] J. Sohmer. il *Down Beat* 54:40-1 Je '87

Hodes, Stuart

State arts councils: what educational role? A personal review. *Des Arts Educ* 88:11-14 N/D '86

Hodge, A. Trevor

Latin rises again. *World Press Rev* 34:57 N '87

Hodge, Helena Norberg- *See* Norberg-Hodge, Helena

Hodge, Marie

(jt. auth) *See* Blyskal, Jeff, and Hodge, Marie

Hodge, Marie, and Blyskal, Jeff

How to sell your home yourself. il *Read Dig* 130:89-93 Mr '87

Hodges, Mike

about

A prayer for the dying [film] Reviews
Macleans 100:59 S 21 '87. L. O'Toole
New Repub 197:26-7 S 28 '87. S. Kauffmann
People Wkly 28:10 O 5 '87. R. Novak

Hodges, Ralph

The high end. *See* issues of Stereo Review beginning June 1984

Hodgins, Patty

Bird-watching basics. bibl il *Better Homes Gard* 65:222+ N '87

Lessons that pets can teach your children and how pets help kids grow. il *Better Homes Gard* 65:181+ My '87

Hodgins, William

about

Boston uncommon. D. Roberts. il *Archit Dig* 44:156-9 S '87

Mistaken identity. C. Vogel. il *N Y Times Mag* p36-40 Ag 23 '87

Old World white. E. Greene. il *House Gard* 159:94-9 Ja '87

Hodgkin, Howard, 1932-

about

The texture of a dream. D. Sylvester. il por *Archit Dig* 44:54+ Mr '87

Hodgkin's disease
Hodgkin's disease: a can-win battle. A. Brown. il *Curr Health 2* 13:28-9 Mr '87
A survivor's bout with cancer [W. Traber] M. Maran. il por *Sch Update* 119:4-5 Ap 20 '87
Therapy
When pain is the only choice [bone marrow transplant for Hodgkin's patient] E. Rosenthal. il *Discover* 8:24 D '87

Hodgson, Bryan
North Dakota: tough times on the prairie. il map *Natl Geogr* 171:320-47 Mr '87

Hodgson, Moira
PepsiCo Summerfare. *Nation* 245:208-10 S 5 '87

Hodler, Ferdinand, 1853-1918
about
Ferdinand Hodler: landscapes: National Academy of Design. M. Moorman. il *Art News* 86:156 D '87
Spanish inquisition. K. Larson. il *N Y* 20:96-7 O 12 '87

Hodsoll, Frank, 1938-
The unity and diversity of the Americas. *Américas* 39:52-3 Ja/F '87

Hodson, Millicent
about
Dancing:
    M. Hodson's reconstruction of Le sacre du printemps. A. Croce. *New Yorker* 63:140-2+ N 23 '87
In search of Sacre. J. R. Acocella. il *Dance Mag* 61:44-8 N '87

Hoechst AG
A CEO as cheerleader [W. Hilger] L. S. Richman. por *Fortune* 116:52 Ag 3 '87

Hoefer, Hans
about
Bringing color to the dreary world of travel guidebooks. C. Purcell. il *Pop Photogr* 94:24-5 F '87

Hoekema, David A.
The price of pacifism [discussion of October 22, 1986 article, A practical Christian pacifism] *Christ Century* 104:20-2 Ja 7-14 '87

Hoenig, Milton M.
Energy Department blurs line between civilian, military reactors. bibl f *Bull At Sci* 43:25-7 Je '87

Hoenig, Stuart A., 1928-
about
All stuck up, no way to go. S. Budiansky. il *U S News World Rep* 103:62 Jl 20 '87

Hoerburger, Rob
Singing a new Toon. il pors *Sport Mag* 78:41-7 N '87

Hoes
In search of the perfect hoe. il *Mother Earth News* 106:108-9 Jl/Ag '87

Hofer, Evelyn
about
A procession of wonders. J. Perl. il *Vogue* 177:86 D '87

Hofer, Stephen F.
Pre-war television sets: today's collectible. il *Antiques Collect Hobbies* 92:79-80 My '87

Hoff, Lew
about
An impression on business. P. M. Fielding. il por *Nations Bus* 75:66 F '87

Hoff, Richard Chandler, 1945-
Techniques of drawing: Richard C. Hoff. il por *Am Artist* 51:64-7 S '87

Hoffa, Harlan
Research as caring skepticism. *Des Arts Educ* 88:5-9 My/Je '87

Hoffer, William
(ed) See Mahmoody, Betty. Not without my daughter

Hofferber, Michael
The Duchess of Oldenburg and other edible antiques. il *Ctry J* 14:68-71 O '87
A well-rounded barn. il *Ctry J* 14:42-6 F '87

Hoffman, Abbie
Closing argument. *Nation* 244:562-3 My 2 '87
The future is yours (still) [closing remarks to jury, April 15, 1987] *Harpers* 275:21+ Jl '87
Reefer madness. *Nation* 245:580-1 N 21 '87
about
Amy Carter and Abbie Hoffman win acquittal, but they want to keep the C.I.A. on trial. F. A. Bernstein. il pors *People Wkly* 27:57-8+ My 4 '87
On trial: cheers and jeers for Amy Carter. por *Newsweek* 109:33 Ap 20 '87

Hoffman, Carl
Marvels of the marketplace. *Travel Holiday* 167:118 Ap '87

Hoffman, Charles D.
(jt. auth) See Teyber, Edward, and Hoffman, Charles D.

Hoffman, Dustin, 1937-
about
Dustin on Warren [cover story] S. Allison. il pors *Life* 10:62-5+ My '87
On the road to Ishtar [cover story] B. Darrach. il pors *People Wkly* 27:102-4+ My 25 '87
The road to 'Ishtar'. D. Blum. il pors *N Y* 20:34-43 Mr 16 '87

Hoffman, Eric P., and others
Conservation of the Duchenne muscular dystrophy gene in mice and humans. bibl f il *Science* 238:347-50 O 16 '87

Hoffman, Jeffrey A.
Astronaut's diary [excerpt] il *Omni* 10:32+ O '87

Hoffman, Mary Virginia
about
Style of a lifetime. M. McDougall. il *House Gard* 159:178-83+ Mr '87

Hoffman, Nan
Indianapolis: a climate of progress. il *Horizon* 30:25-30+ Je '87

Hoffman, Paul
A chess player realizes the game controls his life. bibl (p147) il *Smithsonian* 18:129-30+ Jl '87
Ciphernauts. il *Omni* 9:26+ My '87
From the editor. See issues of Discover beginning September 1987
The man who loves only numbers. il por *Atlantic* 260:60-8+ N '87
Triskaidekaphobia can strike when you're most expecting it. il *Smithsonian* 17:122-4+ F '87

Hoffman, Stephen L., and others
Naturally acquired antibodies to sporozoites do not prevent malaria: vaccine development implications. bibl f il *Science* 237:639-42 Ag 7 '87

Hoffman, Tony
about
Moonlighting. J. Stone. il *Discover* 8:93-5 O '87

Hoffman, William M.
about
As is [drama] Reviews
    Nation 244:656 My 16 '87. T. M. Disch

Hoffmann, Paul
about
Hidden gems in a high market [interview] A. E. Serwer. il por *Fortune* 115:126 My 25 '87

Hoffmann, Peter
(jt. auth) See Maudlin-Jeronimo, John M., and Hoffmann, Peter

Hoffmann, Robert S.
about
Around the Mall and beyond. E. Park. il por *Smithsonian* 18:18+ Jl '87

Hoffmann, Stanley
Reagan's underworld. bibl f il *N Y Rev Books* 34:9-13 My 7 '87

Hoffmann-La Roche Inc.
Corporate child care: playpens in the boardroom or productivity investment? L. Silverman. il *USA Today (Periodical)* 115:67-9 My '87

Hoffs, Susanna
about
A Bangle bares all in a teen flick directed by her mom. T. Gold. il pors *People Wkly* 27:46-7 Je 8 '87

Hoffs, Tamar
about
A Bangle bares all in a teen flick directed by her mom. T. Gold. il pors *People Wkly* 27:46-7 Je 8 '87

Hofmann, Ed
'Thieves' at the auto shop. por *Newsweek* 110:10-11 S 28 '87

Hofmann, Hans, 1880-1966
about
The sweet singer of modernism. B. Berkson. il *Art Am* 75:138-43 Je '87

Hofmann, Mark
about
A Latter-Day forger. A. Wilentz. il por *Time* 129:32 F 2 '87

Hofmannsthal, Hugo von, 1874-1929
about
A luminous carousel. G. R. Marek. il pors *Opera News* 51:14-17 F 14 '87

Hofsiss, Jack
Paralyzed after a near-fatal accident, director Jack Hofsiss stages a dramatic comeback; ed. by Bonnie Johnson. il pors *People Wkly* 28:131-2+ S 14 '87

Hofstadter, Dan
A life hardly less romantic and turbulent than his novels. bibl (p163) il pors *Smithsonian* 18:74-80+ Ap '87
Profiles [A. Arikha] il *New Yorker* 63:37-40+ Je 1 '87
Profiles [R. Diebenkorn] il *New Yorker* 63:54-5+ S 7 '87

Hog contracts *See* Contracts, Agricultural
Hog houses *See* Swine houses
Hog Island (Me.)
See also
Camps—Hog Island (Me.)
Hogan, Barbara, and Kadlecek, Mary
Five pounds a day. il *Conservationist* 41:18-25 My/Je '87
Hogan, Candace Lyle
What's in the future for women's sports? il *Women's Sports Fitness* 9:42-7 Je '87
Hogan, John P.
Uprooting Duvalierism. *Commonweal* 114:518-19 S 25 '87
Hogan, Mary Barbera- *See* Barbera-Hogan, Mary
Hogan, Paul, 1941?-
about
Paul Hogan. E. Sherman. por *Ladies Home J* 104:82 My '87
Hogan, Ruth
Techniques for making white-line woodblock prints. il *Am Artist* 51:62-5 D '87
Hoge, James F.
about
The 'News' news. E. Diamond. il por *N Y* 20:19+ F 16 '87
On Gramercy Park: the New York apartment of Sharon and James Hoge. S. K. Hoge. il por *Archit Dig* 44:56-61+ Jl '87
Hoge, Sharon King
On Gramercy Park: the New York apartment of Sharon and James Hoge. il por *Archit Dig* 44:56-61+ Jl '87
Hogg, Christopher A.
about
Turning around an old industry. il por *U S News World Rep* 102:62-3 My 11 '87
Hoggart, Simon, 1946-
Among the Star Warriors. *World Press Rev* 34:20 Mr '87
The big bang. *New Repub* 197:11-12 N 23 '87
Hogge, Allison, and Musick, Greg
Audubon essay winners. il *Audubon* 89:104-5 S '87
Hogle, James M., and others
The structure of poliovirus. bibl (p128) il *Sci Am* 256:42-9 Mr '87
Hogs *See* Swine
Hogue, William P.
My beard and I. il *Glamour* 85:230 Je '87
Hogwood, Christopher
about
Handel, Haydn & Hogwood. W. Livingstone. por *Stereo Rev* 52:53-5 Mr '87
Hogwood's Beethoven. R. Freed. por *Stereo Rev* 52:99 Mr '87
Hohenthal, Karl *See* May, Karl Friedrich, 1842-1912
Hohenwald (Tenn.)
Stores
The town that transforms junk into treasure. G. Witkin. il *U S News World Rep* 102:22 Mr 16 '87
Hohler, Robert T., 1951-
The death and life of Christa McAuliffe [excerpt from I touch the future] il pors *Good Housekeep* 204:90-3+ Ja '87
"I touch the future . . . " [condensation] il pors *Read Dig* 130:78-85 Je '87
Hohlfelder, Robert L.
Herod the Great's city on the sea. il maps *Natl Geogr* 171:260-79 F '87
Hoiles, Harry
about
A family feud that could break a newspaper chain. R. Neff. il por *Bus Week* p38 F 16 '87
Rifts in a press empire. M. Gray. *Macleans* 100:47 Mr 9 '87
Hoiles family
about
A family feud that could break a newspaper chain. R. Neff. il por *Bus Week* p38 F 16 '87
Rifts in a press empire. M. Gray. *Macleans* 100:47 Mr 9 '87
Hoisting equipment
These shop hoists roost in the rafters [farm shops] C. Finck. il *Success Farm* 85 no6:18AJ Mr '87

Rigging
Don't be a sucker—rig for safety [mounting a production of Barnum] R. Libbon. il *Theatre Crafts* 21:32-3+ Ja '87
Retrofitting the sixties: rigging & rigging control. J. O. Glerum. il *Theatre Crafts* 21:26-7+ F '87
Hoka Hey Foundry
Building a foundry for fine art [W. Cowan] L. Thomas. il por *South Living* 22:162 Ap '87
Hoke, John
Oh, it's so nice to have a sloth around the house. il *Smithsonian* 18:88-92+ Ap '87
Holahan, Dennis John Drew
about
Loretta Swit. N. Gittelson. il pors *McCalls* 114:10-11+ Jl '87
Holbert, Al
about
Daytona do. J. Rusz. il *Road Track* 38:118-20+ My '87
They burned up the track. S. Moses. il *Sports Illus* 66:72-3 F 9 '87
Holbrook, James J.
Biology's answer to toxic dumps. *Sierra* 72:24-5+ Ja/F '87
Holby, Grethe Barrett
about
Grethe Holby: high-spirited style . . . L. J. Nonkin. il pors *Vogue* 177:294-9 Ag '87
Holck, Susan
Cancer and the pill. il *World Health* p18-19 N '87
Holcomb, Betty
Hospital hype: competition for patients spurs a marketing blitz. il *N Y* 20:30-5 Ag 3 '87
House rules for care-givers. il *Parents* 62:56+ My '87
Where's mommy? The great debate over the effects of day care. il *N Y* 20:72-8+ Ap 13 '87
Holcomb, Donald F., and others
New approaches to introductory physics. *Phys Today* 40:87 My '87
Holden, Anthony, 1947-
Man in a gilded cage [cover story] il pors *Life* 10:32-5 S '87
Holden, Barry
about
Sculpture takes off from O'Hare. S. Taylor. il *Art News* 86:13-14 S '87
Holden, Constance
Artificial intelligence: the rational optimist. *Current* 293:36-40 Je '87
Creativity and the troubled mind. il *Psychol Today* 21:9-10 Ap '87
Genes and behavior: a twin legacy. il *Psychol Today* 21:18-19 S '87
Holden, Stephen
Bogosian's voices. il por *N Y Times Mag* p34-5+ My 24 '87
Holder, Dennis
From medical breakthrough to health-care tool. il por *Work Woman* 12:69-70 My '87
How Hill got leveled. il por *Channels* 7:42-4 Ja '87
Keeping the bankers at bay. il por *Channels* 7:55-6 My '87
Staying up when your industry's down. il pors *Work Woman* 12:45-6 My '87
Holding companies
See also
Bank holding companies
Holding devices (Machine work)
See also
Chucks (Machine work)
Clamps
Jigs (Tools)
Vises
Simple hold-down for your table saw. A. J. Hand. il *Pop Sci* 230:98 My '87
Holguin, José
about
Lieutenant Holguin's final mission. J. P. Blank. il *Read Dig* 130:83-8 Ap '87
Holiday Corp.
Attack on pornography misses the mark [National Federation for Decency calls on Holiday Inn to remove "pornographic movies" from its motels] J. M. Wall. *Christ Century* 104:811-12 S 30 '87
Holiday entertaining *See* Entertaining
Holiday Inns, Inc.
See also
Holiday Corp.

Holiday parties *See* Christmas entertaining
Holidays
> *See also*
> Christmas
> Festivals
> Halloween
> Kwanzaa
> Labor Day
> Martin Luther King Day
> New Year
> Thanksgiving Day
> Vacations
> Valentine's Day

7 strategies: how to eat, drink and be merry—without blowing your diet! S. S. Lang. il *McCalls* 114:99 Ja '87
Count your calories now, feast later. I. Pave. il *Bus Week* p154 D 7 '87
Death takes a holiday [holiday suicide patterns; study by David P. Phillips and John S. Wills] J. Folkenberg. *Psychol Today* 21:22 N '87
Holiday temptations: how to keep your shape and your sanity through all the eating. L. Gordon. il *Glamour* 85:44+ D '87
The new rules and new roles at family holiday get-togethers. il *Glamour* 85:99 N '87

Anecdotes, facetiae, satire, etc.
Aunt Lucy's country cure [holiday stress] J. Taylor. il *Mother Earth News* 108:144 N/D '87

Holieway, Jamelle
> *about*
Jamelle Holieway. J. Garrity. il por *Sports Illus* 67:63 Ag 31 '87

Holing, Dwight
Living is tough for the desert fox. il *Natl Wildl* 25:14-17 Ap/My '87
Lizard and the links. il map *Audubon* 89:38-42+ N '87

Holistic medicine
Complementary medicine. S. Fulder. il *Courier* 40:16-19 Ag '87
'Holistic' medicine: no longer hocus-pocus. D. Edleman. il *Bus Week* p125 My 4 '87
A new prescription: mind over malady. R. Wechsler. il *Discover* 8:50-3+ F '87

Holker Hall (Lancashire, England) *See* Historic houses, sites, etc.—Great Britain
Holl, Steven, 1947-
> *about*
Magnificent obsession. K. D. Stein. il *Archit Rec* 175:90-101 mid-S '87

Holl (Steven), Architects *See* Steven Holl, Architects
Holladay, Wilhelmina Cole, 1922-
> *about*
To bravos and boos, a daring Wilhelmina Holladay brings women a museum they can call their own. H. Shapiro. il por *People Wkly* 27:113-15 Ap 27 '87
The women's museum—a house is not a home? il *Ms* 16:24 S '87

Holland, Anne L.
> *about*
Staying up when your industry's down. D. Holder. il pors *Work Woman* 12:45-6 My '87
Holland, Bernard
A new and awful silence. il *Harpers* 275:70-1 Jl '87
Holland, Dave
> *about*
Dave Holland Big Band. G. Kalbacher. *Down Beat* 54:57 S '87
Holland, Endesha Ida Mae
Granny midwives: portrait of a timeless profession. il pors *Ms* 15:48-51+ Je '87
Holland, Julia
(jt. auth) See O'Brien, Margaret, and Holland, Julia
Holland, Robert
A bird in the hand. il *Natl Wildl* 25:42-3 F/Mr '87
The duel. il *Audubon* 89:60-1 N '87
A small misunderstanding. il *Audubon* 89:62-3 S '87
Too many mallards. il *Audubon* 89:64-7 Ja '87
Holland, Spencer H.
Positive primary education for young black males. *Educ Dig* 53:56-8 N '87
Holland, Tom, 1936-
> *about*
Controlled frenzy. J. Gruen. il por *Art News* 86:116-20 Mr '87
Holland, William R., and McWilliams, James C.
Computer modeling in physical oceanography from the global circulation to turbulence. bibl f il *Phys Today* 40:51-7 O '87

Holland (Mich.)
> **Festivals**
Holland, Michigan [Tulip Time] W. T. Anderson. il *Saturday Evening Post* 259:82-4 My/Je '87
Holland & Knight
$1.1 mil. suit filed by athletes in Fla. land deal [legal malpractice against Holland & Knight] *Jet* 72:50 Je 8 '87
Hollandaise sauce *See* Sauces
Hollandale (Miss.)
> **Politics and government**
Black woman wins mayor's race in Hollandale, Miss. [H. Perkins] *Jet* 72:8 My 4 '87
Hollander, Jean
Correct blinking [poem] *Am Sch* 56:367-8 Summ '87
Hollander, John
By the sound [poem] *N Y Rev Books* 34:30 Ap 9 '87
Elemental colloquy [poem] *New Repub* 196:34 Mr 30 '87
Leland Bell: gesture and trope. il *Art Am* 75:112-19 Jl '87
Lines for a simple computer to sort out [poem] *New Repub* 196:34 Mr 30 '87
Hollander, Richard
> *about*
Richard Hollander; Richard Gillespie. B. Westerfield. il *Art News* 86:33-4 Mr '87
Hollandsworth, Skip
She's stealing the heart of Texas. il pors *Women's Sports Fitness* 9:49-51+ F '87
Hollenbach, David
AIDS education: the moral substance. *America* 157:493-4 D 26 '87
Holley, James G., III
> *about*
Portsmouth, Va., mayor is cited in hate mail scandal. *Jet* 72:4 Ag 3 '87
Holley, Marietta, 1836-1926
> *about*
"The Samantha stories". D. E. Matter and R. M. Matter. il *Antiques Collect Hobbies* 91:48-50 Ja '87
Holliday, R. (Robin)
The inheritance of epigenetic defects. bibl f il *Science* 238:163-70 O 9 '87
Holliday, Robin *See* Holliday, R. (Robin)
Hollinger, Inc.
Black and white and read all over [C. Black] T. Fennell. il por *Macleans* 100:32-3 Je 15 '87
Hollings, Ernest F., 1922-
Should Congress approve the Fairness Doctrine? [excerpts from debate, April 21, 1987] *Congr Dig* 66:234+ O '87
Should the proposed Product Liability Reform Act be approved? [excerpts from debate, September 17, 1986] *Congr Dig* 66:11+ Ja '87
Hollingsworth, Helen Partello- *See* Partello-Hollingsworth, Helen
Hollis, Michael
> *about*
The $90 million dream: the rise and fall of Michael Hollis. C. Whitaker. il pors *Ebony* 43:188-90+ N '87
The crash of Air Atlanta. R. Witherspoon. il por *Black Enterp* 17:59-60 Je '87
Hollis, Peter B.
> *about*
Gremlins are eating up the profits at Ames. J. R. Norman. il por *Bus Week* p132-3 O 19 '87
Hollister, Paul
Natural wonders: the lampwork of Paul J. Stankard. il *Am Craft* 47:36-43 F/Mr '87
Hollister, William
A wild turkey for Thanksgiving. il *Conservationist* 42:2-9 S/O '87
Hollister (Calif.)
> **Riots**
Forty hours in Hollister [legendary riots during 1947 motorcycle rally] J. Dorrance. il *Cycle* 38:50-4+ Ag '87
Holloway, Glenna
The ages of rock [poem] *McCalls* 114:124 Ja '87
A word about the artist [poem] *America* 157:8 Jl 4-11 '87
Holloway, James
Bugged pitot. il *Flying* 114:104 D '87
Holly
Dwarf Burford won't grow up. il *South Living* 22:62 D '87

Holly Farms Poultry Industries
They're fencing beak to beak [ready-to-eat chicken products] M. Sheraton. il *Time* 130:76 S 28 '87
Holly Springs (Miss.)
Galleries and museums
See also
Kate Freeman Clark Art Gallery
Holly Sugar Corp.
Arb makes good [M. Buchsbaum's Holly Sugar Corp. attracts Shamrock Holdings] P. Berman and C. Brown. por *Forbes* 139:152 Je 1 '87
Sweetening the pot at Holly Sugar [bid by Brookehill Equities] M. Ivey. il *Bus Week* p34 Je 29 '87
Hollybush Festival
Musical events:
Performance of Prokofiev's The love of three oranges. A. Porter. *New Yorker* 63:63-5 Ag 24 '87
Hollywood (Calif.)
See also
Walk of Fame (Hollywood, Calif.)
Anniversaries, etc.
100 years of Hollywood [cover story: special section; with editorial comment by Franklin Cameron] il *Petersens Photogr Mag* 16:4, 16-21 S '87
100 years of Hollywood [special section] il *People Wkly* 27:25-31+ F 9 '87
Hollywood hits 100 [cover story; special section; with editorial comment by Kevin Doyle] il *Macleans* 100:2, 32-9 Je 8 '87
Hollywood turns 100: Tinseltown glitters again. P. L. Brosnan. il *Travel Holiday* 168:42-7 Ag '87
Hooray for Hollywood. G. Hackett. il *Newsweek* 109:24-5 F 16 '87
The stars shine at the shrine as Hollywood wishes itself a happy 100th birthday. il *People Wkly* 27:40-1 My 11 '87
Architecture
California in focus [F. Scarfiotti's Hollywood home decorated by B. Hayward] D. Thomson. il por *House Gard* 159:140-5+ Ag '87
Sutherland's folly. D. Sutherland. il por *House Gard* 159:184-9+ Je '87
Description
Hollywood turns 100: Tinseltown glitters again. P. L. Brosnan. il *Travel Holiday* 168:42-7 Ag '87
Where is Hollywood? We can help you find it. il map *Sunset* 179:70+ N '87
Galleries and museums
See also
Frederick's of Hollywood Bra Museum
Historic houses, sites, etc.
Castillo del Lago. R. Reed. il *House Gard* 159:204-14 My '87
Historic houses: Cecil B. De Mille: family scenario for a Hollywood legend. M. Webb. il por *Archit Dig* 44:144-53+ Mr '87
Industries
See also
Motion picture industry
Television industry
Moral conditions
David Brunson [deterioration of city] D. Brunson. il por *People Wkly* 27:55 F 9 '87
Restaurants, nightclubs, bars, etc.
Spécialités de la maison:
Columbia Bar & Grill. C. Bates. il *Gourmet* 47:36+ F '87
Social history
Scandals. il *People Wkly* 27:50-2 F 9 '87
Social life and customs
For glamour and good food on Oscar night, Hollywood's top drawer opts for Swifty's. il *People Wkly* 27:42-3 Ap 13 '87
Hollywood blacklisting period *See* Blacklisting
Hollywood Cemetery (Richmond, Va.) *See* Richmond (Va.)—Cemeteries
Hollywood Kids
New-wave gossip. R. Alleman. il *Vogue* 177:102 Ag '87
Hollywood on Location (Firm)
Hollywood on Location. I. Silden. *Travel Holiday* 168:35 Ag '87
Hollywood shuffle [film] See Motion picture reviews—Single works
Hollywood Way (Firm)
The Hollywood Way. S. Flack. por *Forbes* 139:174+ Je 1 '87
Hollywood's favorite heavy: businessmen on prime time TV [television program] See Television program reviews—Single works

Holm, John Cecil, 1904-1981
about
Three men on a horse [drama] Reviews
Macleans 100:50 S 21 '87. J. Bemrose
Holm, Pat
A deer-proof garden. il *Rodale's Org Gard* 34:31-3 D '87
Holm, Peter
I married Alexis. il *Harpers* 275:17-20 Ag '87
about
Daytime's steamy new soap. G. Clarke. il pors *Time* 130:68 Ag 3 '87
Divorcing for dollars [cover story] E. Hoover and D. Lindeman. il pors *People Wkly* 28:40-2+ Ag 10 '87
The gorge also rises. L. Fleischer. *Publ Wkly* 232:153 S 18 '87
Anecdotes, facetiae, satire, etc.
Imaginary interview: Peter Holm. G. W. S. Trow. *New Yorker* 63:25 Ag 24 '87
Holmes, Allen
Meeting of NATO's Special Consultative Group [statement, December 10, 1986] *Dep State Bull* 87:46 Mr '87
Holmes, Alvin A.
about
Ala. cabinet member and governor apologize for racial, ethnic slurs. por *Jet* 72:32 Jl 20 '87
Holmes, Bradley P.
about
Bradley Holmes is slated for FCC seat by Reagan. por *Jet* 73:10 D 7 '87
Holmes, Larry
about
Ex-champ Larry Holmes turns grandfather at 37. por *Jet* 73:48 S 28 '87
Fight judge files a suit against ex-champ Holmes. por *Jet* 72:50 Je 8 '87
Holmes to sing at Sands before Spinks' big bout. *Jet* 72:52 Je 15 '87
Larry Holmes agrees to fight Mike Tyson in '88. *Jet* 73:48 O 26 '87
Holmes, Linda
The insurance crisis. *Ms* 15:74 Je '87
Holmes, Marjorie, 1910-
about
Writer Marjorie Holmes celebrates a marriage made in heaven and set to words and music in Pittsburgh. K. McMurran. il pors *People Wkly* 28:115-16+ N 2 '87
Holmes, Oliver Wendell, 1841-1935
about
Learned Hand and the great train ride. F. R. Kellogg. *Am Sch* 56:471-86 Aut '87
Holmes, Paul
about
Payton's agent could pose a problem with NFL plans. *Jet* 72:50 Jl 13 '87
Holmes, Richard
about
Nuclear healing. J. Gruber. il por *Black Enterp* 18:24 O '87
Holmes, Stephen, 1948-
The professor of smashing. *New Repub* 197:30-8 O 19 '87
Holmes, W. E., and others
α_2-antiplasmin Enschede: alanine insertion and abolition of plasmin inhibitory activity. bibl f il *Science* 238:209-11 O 9 '87
Holmes, Sherlock (Fictional character) *See* Sherlock Holmes (Fictional character)
Holmes à Court, Robert
about
Holmes a Court's fortunes are sinking Down Under. C. Debes. il por *Bus Week* p142-4 D 7 '87
Is Holmes a Court trying to lasso Texaco? T. Thompson. il por *Bus Week* p59 Jl 27 '87
Jaws: the Australian. J. Castro. il por *Time* 130:53 Jl 27 '87
The raiders Down Under may be down and out. C. Debes. il por *Bus Week* p55 N 9 '87
Stalker of wounded game. T. Jaffe. il por *Forbes* 139:38+ Je 15 '87
Stalking Texaco. *Time* 129:52 Je 1 '87
Will Aussie raider deliver coup de grace to crippled Texaco? K. R. Sheets. *U S News World Rep* 102:43 Je 1 '87
Will he, or won't he? Australia keeps Texaco on edge. K. R. Sheets. *U S News World Rep* 103:37 Jl 27 '87

Holmstrom, David
Ice cream at noon [story] il por *McCalls* 114:97-8 Ag '87
Sourdough. il *Americana* 15:40-3 S/O '87
Holocaust, Jewish (1939-1945)
See also
Warsaw (Poland)—History—Uprising of 1943
Children of Holocaust survivors
World War, 1939-1945—War criminals
The Auschwitz Carmel [controversy over convent at Auschwitz] *America* 156:206 Mr 14 '87
Barbie and the children [roundup of the children of Izieu, France] *Newsweek* 109:44 Je 15 '87
Blessed Edith Stein. *America* 156:354-5 My 2 '87
Breaking the silence [K. Barbie and role of the Catholic Church] K. McCaffrey. il *Commonweal* 114:418-20 Jl 17 '87
The children of Izieu. il *N Y Times Mag* p26-7 Ag 2 '87
The death doctors [Nazi doctors] N. Ascherson. il *N Y Rev Books* 34:29-34 My 28 '87
Edith Stein's early years. J. W. Donohue. *America* 156:7-9+ Ja 3-10 '87
Europe faces its Nazi past. S. Sullivan. il pors *Newsweek* 109:34-6 Ap 20 '87
The friends of Anne Frank [J. and M. Gies, couple who sheltered Frank family during the Holocaust] il pors *U S News World Rep* 102:77 My 11 '87
Le Pen against the 'immigrant lobby'. por *Newsweek* 110:38 S 28 '87
Learning from history [Carmelite convent at Auschwitz] E. Fleischner. *Commonweal* 114:167-8 Mr 27 '87
Letter from Europe [K. Barbie trial] J. Kramer. *New Yorker* 63:130-6+ O 12 '87
A martyr of Auschwitz [E. Stein] S. M. Batzdorff. por *N Y Times Mag* p52-5+ Ap 12 '87
O'Connor's critics misconstrue terms [Cardinal O'Connor's comments on the Holocaust] J. M. Wall. *Christ Century* 104:75-6 Ja 28 '87
Odyssey of remembrance [Israeli president C. Herzog visits West Germany] il por *Macleans* 100:21 Ap 20 '87
Office politics [Cardinal O'Connor's visit to Israel] *New Repub* 196:9 Ja 26 '87
One teacher's prejudice [J. Israeli urges New Brunswick to take action against anti-Semitic school teacher M. Ross] K. Harley. il pors *Macleans* 100:17 Ap 27 '87
The Pope's letter [Holocaust letter marred by recent meeting with K. Waldheim] W. F. Buckley. *Natl Rev* 39:64-5 S 25 '87
The priests of Dachau. W. J. O'Malley. il *America* 157:351-3 N 14 '87
Remembering Liane, age six [L. Krochmal, victim of K. Barbie] G. F. Will. il por *Newsweek* 109:80 My 25 '87
Saintly passions [Jews protest beatification of E. Stein, also known as Teresa Benedicta of the Cross] D. Brand. por *Time* 129:82-3 My 4 '87
'The shadows of the Reich' [H. Kohl's campaign remark concerning East German concentration camps] N. Cooper. il por *Newsweek* 109:32 Ja 19 '87
Shameful silence [myth of silence of Pius XII] *Natl Rev* 39:17 F 13 '87
Shoah: enough already? [Christian resistance to dishonestly polemical uses of the Holocaust] R. J. Neuhaus. *Natl Rev* 39:38 Je 5 '87
The 'silence' of Pius XII: again. J. Gallagher. il *America* 156:279-81 Ap 4 '87

Caricatures and cartoons
Comics and catastrophe [A. Spiegelman's Maus] A. Gopnik. il *New Repub* 196:29-34 Je 22 '87
Mauschwitz [excerpt from Maus, part II] A. Spiegelman. il *Esquire* 107:67-9+ Mr '87

Exhibitions
Hope and despair through refugees' eyes [Bitter hope: from Holocaust to haven; exhibit at the New York State Museum] il *USA Today (Periodical)* 115:50-9 Ja '87

Historiography
The war of the German historians. G. A. Craig. il *N Y Rev Books* 33:16-19 Ja 15 '87
When historians judge their own [historian N. Davies sues Stanford University over denial of professorship because of his views on Jews] J. Wiener. il *Nation* 245:584-6+ N 21 '87

Memorials
See also
U.S. Holocaust Memorial Museum
Personal narratives
Beyond judgment; tr. by Raymond Rosenthal. P. Levi. il *N Y Rev Books* 34:10+ D 17 '87

Reporters and reporting
War and remembrance [A. M. Rosenthal's column comparing the Holocaust to the Iran arms scandal] L. Wieseltier. *New Repub* 196:50 F 9 '87
Holocaust, Jewish (1939-1945), in art
Anselm Kiefer: a call to memory. S. H. Madoff. il por *Art News* 86:125-30 O '87
Broken continuities: Night and White crucifixion [M. Chagall and E. Wiesel; cover story] K. A. Plank. il por *Christ Century* 104:963-6 N 4 '87
Holocaust, Jewish (1939-1945), in drama
British traditions [controversy surrounding J. Allen's play Perdition] A. Cockburn. *Nation* 245:187 S 5 '87
Foul play [controversy surrounding production of J. Allen's Perdition by the Royal Court Theatre] D. Pryce-Jones. *New Repub* 196:15-17 Mr 2 '87
Holocaust, Jewish (1939-1945), in literature
Books on the Holocaust. M. Saperstein. *America* 157:385-9 N 21 '87
Broken continuities: Night and White crucifixion [M. Chagall and E. Wiesel; cover story] K. A. Plank. il por *Christ Century* 104:963-6 N 4 '87
Letters from 'The Kingdom of Night' [E. Hillesum's diary, An interrupted life] L. S. Cunningham. il *Commonweal* 114:316-18 My 22 '87
Light, darkness and bridges in Norway [E. Wiesel's acceptance of Nobel Peace Prize] R. M. Brown. *Christ Century* 104:5-6 Ja 7-14 '87
Holocaust, Jewish (1939-1945), in motion pictures
Shame and punishment [M. Ophuls' documentary on K. Barbie] J. J. Buck. il pors *Vogue* 177:392-3+ N '87

Holograms *See* Holography
Holography
See also
Museum of Holography (New York, N.Y.)
Demonstration of X-ray holography with an X-ray laser. J. E. Trebes and others. bibl f il *Science* 238:517-19 O 23 '87
Flight Dynamics prepares to test wind shear guidance with HUD [holographic head-up display] il *Aviat Week Space Technol* 126:107+ Ja 12 '87
Hologram: new dimension for X-rays. S. Weisburd. *Sci News* 132:279 O 31 '87
Holograms for books—a hit and a miss. il *Publ Wkly* 231:58-60 Je 5 '87
Picosecond holographic-grating spectroscopy. D. A. Wiersma and K. Duppen. bibl f il *Science* 237:1147-54 S 4 '87
X-ray holograms at improved resolution: a study of zymogen granules. M. Howells and others. bibl f il *Science* 238:514-17 O 23 '87
Geological use
Stressed-out holograms [study of earthquake producing stresses] R. Monastersky. il *Sci News* 132:396 D 19-26 '87
Holstein, Howard M.
A gentle genius of the guitar. il pors *Américas* 39:50-3 Jl/Ag '87
Holstein cattle *See* Cattle
Holston, Mark
Hot jazz from the banks of the River Plate. il *Américas* 39:57-60 S/O '87
Hot sounds from a cool group. il *Américas* 39:56-8 Mr/Ap '87
Holt, Donald A.
Agricultural R&D [discussion of September 18, 1987 article, A competitive R&D strategy for U.S. agriculture] *Science* 238:1493-5 D 11 '87
A competitive R&D strategy for U.S. agriculture. bibl f *Science* 237:1401-2 S 18 '87
Holt, Henry
As they said in the Writer in 1887 . . . [reprint of June 1887 article] *Writer* 100:1 Je '87
Holt, Patricia
What everyone should know about 'The Year of the Reader'. il *Publ Wkly* 231:36-7 My 29 '87
Holt, Rex
about
Beyond the valley of the beautiful dolls. D. Heyn. il *Mademoiselle* 93:182+ N '87
The crowning touch of Richard Guy and Rex Holt shapes Texas teens into lovelies who just can't lose. L. Aitken. il pors *People Wkly* 27:53-4 My 4 '87
Holt, Sam
about
A yogurt named Zack's. D. Marth. il por *Nations Bus* 75:52 Ag '87

Holt, Stephen
about
The casting of Kevin Christian [drama] Reviews *Nation* 244:775-6 Je 6 '87. T. M. Disch
Holt, Victoria, 1906-
The silk vendetta [fiction] il por *Good Housekeep* 205:203-6+ O '87
Holt (Henry) and Company *See* Henry Holt and Company
Holtsville (N.Y.)
Description
00501. *New Yorker* 62:27-8 F 2 '87
Holtz, Lou
about
Notre Dame is golden again. E. M. Swift. il *Sports Illus* 67:26-8+ N 9 '87
Resurrection at Notre Dame. G. Norman. il por *Sport Mag* 78:26-8+ O '87
Holtzman, Seymour, 1935-
about
Swatch watching. K. Murray. il por *Forbes* 140:88+ O 19 '87
Holusha, John
A modern coach. il *N Y Times Mag* p46 My 10 '87
Holwill, Richard N.
Promoting democracy in Haiti. map *Dep State Bull* 87:60-2 O '87
Holy family *See* Jesus Christ—Family
Holy Ghost *See* Holy Spirit
Holy Ghosts [drama] *See* Linney, Romulus, 1930-
Holy Grail in opera *See* Grail in opera
Holy Land
See also
Bethlehem
Antiquities
See Bible—Antiquities
Holy Shroud
C-14 dating for Shroud of Turin? J. Raloff. *Sci News* 131:265 Ap 25 '87
Shroud dating isn't ironed out. *Sci News* 132:302 N 7 '87
Tempting providence with the Turin Shroud? C. Chippindale. il *Hist Today* 37:5-6 S '87
Holy Spirit
See also
Pentecost
Pentecostalism
Trinity
To be your advocate. M. K. Hellwig. *America* 156:inside back cover My 16 '87
Holy Spirit Movement (Uganda)
Alice's army on the march [followers of A. Lakwena] M. A. Fitzgerald. il por *Macleans* 100:24 N 2 '87
Goodbye, Mama Alice [rebel leader] W. R. Doerner. il por *Time* 130:38 N 23 '87
Holy Thursday *See* Maundy Thursday
Holy Week
See also
Maundy Thursday
Holyfield, Evander
about
Holyfield stops Ocasio, setting up Qawi rematch. *Jet* 72:46 S 7 '87
Tuning up for Tyson. C. Gammon. il pors *Sports Illus* 67:48-50+ D 14 '87
Holzel, Tom
about
Mallory's camera. J. Taylor. il por *Omni* 9:90 F '87
Holzer, Harold
"Her thunders shook the mighty deep". il *Am Hist Illus* 22:24-31 N '87
Philadelphia, 1787. il *Am Hist Illus* 22:20-5 My '87
Holzer, Harold, and Neely, Mark E., Jr.
Picturing the Constitution. il *Am Hist Illus* 22:30-5 S '87
Holzer, Joseph E.
Keeping a rein on returns. por *Publ Wkly* 232:428 Ag 7 '87
Hom, Ken
Let them eat pastry. il *N Y Times Mag* p55-6 D 20 '87
Homan, Richard
The pick of the 4WD's. il *Skiing* 40:243-7+ O '87
Homans, John
Making old '21' young. il *N Y Times Mag* p42-3+ F 15 '87
Homans, Mary
about
Gardens: enhancing the Maine aspect. S. M. Alsop. il por *Archit Dig* 44:172-7 Mr '87

Home
See also
Christmas gifts for the home
Family
Editor's letter [survey on the state of the American home] G. Havens. *Fam Handyman* 37:2 O '87
Home to Jericho [excerpts] H. Shuptrine. il *South Living* 22:88-91 O '87
Summer reading: House, Home and Home mechanix [books by Tracy Kidder and Witold Rybczynski] J. R. Provey. il *Home Mech* 83:6 Ag '87
Home accidents *See* Accidents
Home and the school *See* School and the home
The home and the world [film] *See* Motion picture reviews—Single works
Home bars *See* Bars for the home
Home Box Office
At age 15, HBO chases the networks [interview with M. Fuchs] M. Brown. il pors *Channels* 7:78-9 O '87
Is HBO on its way to being boffo again? D. Lieberman. il por *Bus Week* p60-1 Ag 3 '87
Home building *See* House construction
Home building industry *See* Construction industry
Home-built airplanes *See* Airplanes, Home-built
Home-built automobiles *See* Automobiles, Home-built
Home buying *See* House buying
Home care services
See also
Clinical Homecare Corporation
Foster home care
National Association for Home Care
New England Critical Care
Respite care
Are home based services effective? A public child welfare agency's experiment [Hennepin County, Minn.] P. AuClaire and I. M. Schwartz. il *Child Today* 16:6-9 My/Je '87
Are you taking care of someone who is sick or elderly? Help may be ahead for you. M. Engel. il *Glamour* 85:50+ My '87
Death in the mountains [terminal home care for old man] J. Smoot. il *South Living* 22:100 N '87
Family based services [special issue] il *Child Today* 15:4-32 N/D '86
Getting hospital-quality care at home. D. B. Moskowitz. il *Bus Week* p121 Mr 9 '87
New options for the aging. M. Loeb. il *Saturday Evening Post* 259:112 O '87
Training respite workers for Alzheimer's families. L. Middleton. il *Aging* no356:24-6 '87
Laws and regulations
Who oversees health-care workers? M. Engel. il *50 Plus* 27:14-16 S '87
Home computers *See* Computers—Home use
Home construction *See* House construction
Home cooling *See* Cooling
Home decoration *See* House decoration
Home Depot, Inc.
Do-it-yourself debacle. L. M. Keefe. il por *Forbes* 139:48 My 4 '87
Home economics
See also
American Home Economics Association
Budget, Household
Cooking
Entertaining
Finance, Personal
Food
Future Homemakers of America
Homemakers
Household employees
Household records
Houses—Maintenance and repair
Laundry
Purchasing, Household
Storage in the home
The Heloise helpline for all your household problems. Heloise. See issues of Good Housekeeping beginning November 1983
Home news. A. Arnott. See issues of McCall's beginning March 1986
Kitchen to kitchen. See issues of Rodale's Organic Gardening beginning September 1985 through February 1987
Why men won't help with housework [excerpt from Sexual static] M. H. Shaevitz. il *Ladies Home J* 104:76+ Je '87
History
"Labor saving" means more work. R. S. Cowan. il *Read Dig* 131:181-4 D '87

Home economics—History—cont.

Less work for mother? R. S. Cowan. il *Am Herit* 38:68-70+ S/O '87

What did women do? [Domestic Skills Program at Old Salem; with editorial comment by Sandra Wilmot] R. Mashburn. il *Americana* 15:4, 49-52 Mr/Ap '87

Home education

An overview of home instruction. P. M. Lines. il *Phi Delta Kappan* 68:510-17 Mr '87

Teaching your kids at home. N. Henderson. il *Changing Times* 41:83-7 Mr '87

Home electronics

    See also

    Audio systems

    Audio-visual equipment

    Children's electronics

    Compact disc interactive

    Compact disc players

    Compact discs

    Phonograph

    Radio receivers

    Tape recorders and recording

    Television equipment

    Television receivers

    Video equipment

    Videodiscs

    Videotape recorders and recording

    Videotapes

Behind the buzzwords in home entertainment. S. Woolley. il *Bus Week* p150-1 Je 8 '87

Better pictures, higher fi [special section] il *U S News World Rep* 103:92-4+ N 9 '87

Black enterprise guide to home entertainment [special section] S. Miller. il *Black Enterp* 18:81-8 S '87

Digital dilemmas. W. C. Banks and G. Hedberg. il *Money* 16:183-4+ D '87

Electronic review. J. Cohen. il *Consum Res Mag* 70:19-22 F '87

Gifts they won't expect. D. Moreau. il *Changing Times* 41:74-7 N '87

High-tech toys for homebodies. T. Segal. il *Bus Week* p150-1 D 7 '87

New tech. C. Begole. See occasional issues of Glamour

Plug into the latest electronic trends! D. Gordon. il *Essence* 17:85-6 Ja '87

A review of coming electronics. J. Cohen. il *Consum Res Mag* 70:24-6 O '87

Technology special [special section] il *Roll Stone* p69-70+ Je 18 '87

That's entertainment! [special section] il *Pop Sci* 231:39-42+ N '87

Watts for Christmas. P. Hoban. il *N Y* 20:30+ D 14 '87

Exhibitions

    See also

    Consumer Electronics Show

Home energy conservation *See* Energy conservation

Home environment allergy *See* Allergy

Home equity conversion

Betting against the house. M. Hodge. il *50 Plus* 27:52-5 Mr '87

Borrowing against your home: tax-free home-equity loans. R. Hillhouse and S. La Rosa. il *McCalls* 114:95 My '87

Borrowing on the house—the temptations, the risks. G. Williams. *Vogue* 177:142+ F '87

Bridge loans: when you're between homes. T. Tilling. il *Parents* 62:54 Je '87

Bridging the house gap. L. Scheer and W. G. Flanagan. il *Forbes* 140:176 O 19 '87

Home equity: a tender trap? D. Pauly. il *Newsweek* 109:46-7 Mr 9 '87

Home equity credit: banking on your home [cover story] J. Anthony. il *Consum Res Mag* 70:11-14 Ag '87

Home equity credit: friend or foe? H. Porter. *Fam Handyman* 37:14+ O '87

The home equity gold rush. S. Bartlett. il *Bus Week* p64-8+ F 9 '87

Home-equity loans: promises and pitfalls. G. Malott. il *Better Homes Gard* 65:34+ My '87

Home equity's big costs. P. Tai. il *Money* 16:172 Ap '87

Home is where the debt is. G. M. Bock. il *Time* 129:62 Je 8 '87

The love affair with home equity loans: not so hot after all? G. Koretz. il *Bus Week* p30 Mr 9 '87

A mortgage that pays you [reverse mortgages] B. Thompson. il *Changing Times* 41:67+ Jl '87

The pros and cons of home equity loans. W. L. Updegrave. il *Pop Mech* 164:133-5 Jl '87

Reverse mortgages: the new way to use home equity. M. Hodge. il *50 Plus* 27:32-5 Jl '87

Second thoughts on second mortgages. B. Weberman. il *Forbes* 140:42 O 5 '87

The selling of home equity, 1987. *Consum Rep* 52:654 N '87

Should you hock your house? S. Bartlett. il *Read Dig* 130:86-8 Je '87

Sizing up home-equity deals. H. J. Lehman. il *Changing Times* 41:31-2+ F '87

Thinking of your house as a cash cow. C. P. Work. il *U S News World Rep* 102:56-7 Je 8 '87

Turning your house into a credit card. A. McGrath. il *U S News World Rep* 102:49-50 Mr 9 '87

Your guide to home equities. J. B. Quinn. il *Newsweek* 110:39 Jl 6 '87

Home fire prevention *See* Houses—Fires and fire prevention

Home freezers *See* Freezers

Home furnishings *See* Household furnishings

Home grounds

    See also

    Landscape gardening

    Lawns

    Playgrounds, Home

Planting for wildlife [backyard habitat; work of Michael and Carol Gunther] R. Haskell. il *Flower Gard* 31:48-50 Ag/S '87

Equipment

Best outdoor projects [cover story; with editorial comment by Gary Havens] A. Rooze. il *Fam Handyman* 37:2, 29-32+ My/Je '87

Home improvement centers

    See also

    Home Depot, Inc.

    K Mart Corp.

    Pay N Pak Stores, Inc.

Productivity trends in the furniture and home furnishings stores industry. A. S. Herman and J. E. Henneberger. bibl f il *Mon Labor Rev* 110:24-9 My '87

Home improvement contractors *See* Contractors

Home improvement contracts *See* Contracts

Home improvements *See* Houses—Maintenance and repair; Houses, Remodeled

Home industries *See* Cottage industries

Home information storage and retrieval systems *See* Information storage and retrieval systems

Home inspection *See* Building inspection

Home insurance *See* Insurance, Homeowners'

Home labor

    See also

    Cottage industries

    Telecommuting

Industrial homework and sweatshops [address, July 20, 1987] J. Mazur. *Vital Speeches Day* 53:701-2 S 1 '87

Is "homework" the answer? J. Walsh. il *Ms* 16:124-5+ Jl/Ag '87

Let's sock it to the women again. C. Kocol. il *Humanist* 47:35 N/D '87

Staying home is paying off. J. Castro. il *Time* 130:112-13 O 26 '87

Home libraries *See* Libraries, Private

Home Loan Bank Board *See* United States. Federal Home Loan Bank Board

Home mechanix (Periodical)

D-I-Y Analyzer: what it means to you. J. R. Provey. il *Home Mech* 83:6 Ap '87

We listen! J. R. Provey. il *Home Mech* 83:4 Je '87

Home medical test equipment *See* Medical equipment

Home mortgages *See* Mortgages

Home of Franklin Delano Roosevelt National Historic Site (N.Y.)

The house at Hyde Park. G. C. Ward. il pors *Am Herit* 38:41-6+ Ap '87

Home office deductions *See* Income tax—Deductions

Home offices

At-home professionalism [P. Tagliarino's office] P. Kripke. il por *Work Woman* 12:106-7 Mr '87

The complete home office. R. R. Roha. il *Changing Times* 41:105-6+ D '87

Garden office . . . it was an old single-car garage. il *Sunset* 178:184 Ap '87

Home office. C. O'Malley. See issues of Personal Computing beginning July 1987

Turning garage into home office without banishing the car. il *Sunset* 178:56-7 Ja '87

The well-equipped home office. C. Begole. il *Better Homes Gard* 65:37-9 Ap '87

Home Owners Federal Savings & Loan Assn.

Home Owners has the key to growth. G. G. Marcial. *Bus Week* p76 F 9 '87

Home owners' warranty *See* Warranty
Home ownership
    See also
      Home equity conversion
      House buying
      Insurance, Mortgage
      Mortgages
Should you sell your empty nest? L. Stains. il *Prevention* 39:62-4 My '87
    Anecdotes, facetiae, satire, etc.
House for sale: why I hate where I live. S. Gray. il *House Gard* 159:134-5+ Ja '87
Home playgrounds *See* Playgrounds, Home
Home remedies
Folklore remedies. L. Lamberg. il *Better Homes Gard* 65:92+ O '87
Home rule, Municipal *See* Municipal home rule
Home runs (Baseball)
Don't blame the rabbit [explosion of home runs in the majors] D. Seligman. il *Fortune* 115:165-6 Je 22 '87
Is it all in the ball? [home run explosion in the majors] T. N. Dawidoff. il *Sports Illus* 66:44 Je 1 '87
It's a routine . . . home run. T. Callahan. il *Time* 130:72 Jl 13 '87
Rabbit ball: whodunit? F. Deford. por *Sports Illus* 67:94 Jl 27 '87
    Records
    See Baseball records
Home safety devices and measures *See* Accidents—Prevention
Home selling *See* House selling
Home shopping, Electronic *See* Electronic shopping
Home Shopping Network Inc.
A 'bear raid' at Home Shopping? G. G. Marcial. *Bus Week* p80 Mr 2 '87
Fabulous fads that fizzled? G. Morgenson. il *Forbes* 139:40+ F 23 '87
Home Shopping Network's credibility gap. G. DeGeorge. il *Bus Week* p45-6 O 12 '87
Now you can call a 'video broker'. G. G. Marcial. *Bus Week* p108 S 21 '87
One home for two home shoppers? [Home Shopping Network's bid for COMB and its Cable Value Network] G. DeGeorge. *Bus Week* p34-5 F 2 '87
Reaching the top: risk and reward. C. Capuzzi. il *Channels* 7:29 Je '87
The rise and rise of HSN [partners R. Speer and L. Paxon] M. Gill. il pors *Esquire* 107:70 Ap '87
Viewers start tuning out Home Shopping. G. DeGeorge. il *Bus Week* p30 Mr 30 '87
A visit to 'The Home Shopping Club'. M. Wilkins. il *Film Comment* 23:70-2+ Mr/Ap '87
Where are you, Mr. Cheslock? J. A. Conway. il *Forbes* 139:10 Mr 23 '87
Home storage *See* Storage in the home
Home study courses *See* Correspondence schools and courses
Home swimming pools *See* Swimming pools, Home
Home tennis courts *See* Tennis courts
Home warranty *See* Warranty
Home water conservation *See* Water conservation
Home workshops *See* Workshops
Homeier, Richard
Low-cost spectacles. il *World Health* p18-19 My '87
Homelands policy (South Africa) *See* Apartheid
Homeless
    See also
      Comic Relief (Project)
      Refugee children
      Runaways
The $37,000 slum [New York City's system for housing its homeless] C. Coulson. *New Repub* 196:15-16 Ja 19 '87
At issue: freedom for the irrational [institutionalizing the homeless mentally ill] R. Stengel. il *Time* 130:88 S 14 '87
Atlanta mayor wears disguise and feels hurt of the homeless [A. Young] T. S. Moore. il pors *Jet* 71:22-4 Mr 16 '87
A capital solution. il *U S News World Rep* 102:10 F 9 '87
"Caring from the heart" [teaching children to help the homeless] S. Lapinski. il *Ladies Home J* 104:26+ Mr '87
The coming of the 'couch people'. D. Whitman. il *U S News World Rep* 103:19-21 Ag 3 '87
Crazy in the streets [deinstitutionalized mentally ill] P. S. Appelbaum. *Commentary* 83:34-9 My '87
Crazy in the streets: the policy of deinstitutionalization. P. S. Appelbaum. *Current* 296:4-10 O '87

Death of a homeless man [Boston] S. R. Sanders. il *Progressive* 51:50 Mr '87
Down and out in L.A. [not-quite-homeless forced to live in garages, automobiles, etc.] F. Trippett. il *Time* 129:23 Je 22 '87
Down and out in the 'Path Hotel' [living in a tunnel under Manhattan] D. Whitman. il *U S News World Rep* 102:69-71 Mr 23 '87
An evening with Trevor's dad [work with the homeless of Philadelphia by T. and F. Ferrell] E. S. Vaughn. il pors *Christ Today* 31:12-13 F 20 '87
Families of the street [study by Kay Young McChesney] il *USA Today (Periodical)* 115:8 My '87
A family down and out [Brand family of Kansas City, Mo.] P. King. il *Newsweek* 109:44-6 Ja 12 '87
Forcing the mentally ill to get help [rounding up the homeless] D. Gelman. il *Newsweek* 110:47-8 N 9 '87
Helping and hating the homeless. P. Marin. il *Harpers* 274:39-44+ Ja '87
The homeless. M. Magnet. il *Fortune* 116:170-2+ N 23 '87
The homeless: a mental-health debate. H. Hall. il *Psychol Today* 21:65 F '87
Homeless families: how they got that way [study by Kay Young McChesney] *Society* 25:4 N/D '87
Homeless in New York. D. K. Mano. *Natl Rev* 39:64-5+ O 9 '87
A homeless Vietnam veteran's unhappy story of high hopes and misfortune [Jesse Moses] L. Cohler. *Sch Update* 119:8-9 Mr 23 '87
How the homeless bought a Rolls for Cornelius Pitts [running Washington, D.C. welfare hotel] M. Szegedy-Maszak. il por *Wash Mon* 19:11-15 Jl/Ag '87
Inhuman rights [U.S. forces U.N. to omit footage of New York City's homeless from documentary] *Nation* 244:36-7 Ja 17 '87
Is a San Francisco architect's plan to put the homeless in boxes humane or heartless? [D. MacDonald's city sleepers] il por *People Wkly* 28:95 Ag 31 '87
Little house on the prairie ["cabin" built by homeless family in New York City] P. Weber. il *N Y* 20:40 D 14 '87
Manhattan's Martinique [hotel for homeless families] R. Hirschfield. *Commonweal* 114:71-2 F 13 '87
The Martinique Hotel: housing the homeless. R. Hirschfield. *America* 156:90-1 F 7 '87
Matthew Weaver: helping the down-and-out in L.A. [food relief] C. Lapin. por *Seventeen* 46:111 O '87
The mayor is right [New York City program to hospitalize mentally ill homeless people] *America* 157:396 N 28 '87
No good applied social research goes unpunished. P. H. Rossi. *Society* 25:73+ N/D '87
Notes and comment [volunteer shelter for the homeless at Ansche Chesed Synagogue in Manhattan] *New Yorker* 63:27-8 S 14 '87
The omnipotence scandal. D. E. Koshland, Jr. *Science* 238:1335 D 4 '87
Slow descent into hell [Philadelphia] J. D. Hull. il *Time* 129:26-7+ F 2 '87
Street people [discussion of May 1987 article, Crazy in the streets] P. S. Appelbaum. *Commentary* 84:14-16+ S '87
Toward a national policy to end homelessness. M. Leland. il *America* 156:69-71 Ja 31 '87
Under the boardwalk [Atlantic City, N.J.] B. Jacobs. il *Progressive* 51:20-2 O '87
A week in the life of a homeless family. A. Fadiman. il *Life* 10:30-6+ D '87
When I was homeless, you sat in your La-Z-Boy. R. E. Burns. *U S Cathol* 52:2 Ap '87
Where do the homeless come from? [rent control] W. Tucker. il *Natl Rev* 39:32+ S 25 '87
Where's the help for the homeless? F. D. Brown. il *Black Enterp* 18:27 Ag '87
Why are they homeless? P. Marcuse. il *Nation* 244:426+ Ap 4 '87
    History
Memories of the road [Depression era hobo life] D. Mansfield. il por *Am Hist Illus* 21:34-41 F '87
    International aspects
    See also
      International Year of Shelter for the Homeless, 1987
Shelter for the homeless [cover story; special issue] il *World Health* p2-27 Jl '87
    Political activities
Black solons camp out in D.C. streets for needy. il *Jet* 71:32 Mr 23 '87
    Statistics
How many homeless? *Natl Rev* 39:34 S 25 '87

Homeless—Statistics—_cont._
The urban homeless: estimating composition and size [Chicago study] P. H. Rossi and others. bibl f il _Science_ 235:1336-41 Mr 13 '87

Canada
The search for a future [with editorial comment by Kevin Doyle] M. Nichols. il _Macleans_ 100:2, 34-43 F 16 '87
Serenity on a scrap heap of dreams [failed Toronto industrialist J. Gower] J. Barber. il por _Macleans_ 100:41 Ja 26 '87

Ghana
Where eight share one room. K. Adarkwa. il _World Health_ p20-1 Jl '87

Homeless and the press
Hitting bottom. D. Seligman. _Fortune_ 115:17 F 2 '87

Homeless as actors and actresses
Their home is the streets, but the play's the thing for L.A.'s down-but-not-out skid row players. M. Small. il por _People Wkly_ 28:127-8+ D 7 '87

Homeless children
See also
Covenant House (New York, N.Y.)
Against all odds [Jackson children living at Brooklyn Arms welfare hotel] B. Campbell. il _N Y_ 20:68-74+ N 16 '87
The children of the homeless. M. Dobbin. il _U S News World Rep_ 103:20-1 Ag 3 '87
Homeless children [study by Child Welfare League of America] il _Child Today_ 16:2 My/Je '87
Welcome to my nightmare: the graffiti of homeless youth. G. C. Luna. il _Society_ 24:73-8 S/O '87
Where Christmas never comes [children in New York shelters and hotels] M. Small. il _People Wkly_ 28:50-60 D 14 '87

Homeless in television
Reduced and abandoned [Kate & Allie episode] J. Leonard. il _N Y_ 20:115 O 19 '87

Homeless women
Down and out—but determined [J. Brown, homeless woman deemed mentally ill by New York City] M. Hornblower. il _Time_ 130:29 N 23 '87
Ex-fashion model Ivy Nicholson hits the skids. il pors _People Wkly_ 27:37 F 16 '87
Posing as a bag lady, housewife Beulah Lund finds fear and love in the homeless netherworld [Washington, D.C.] R. Arias. il pors _People Wkly_ 27:32-4+ F 16 '87
Two kinds of thanks [evening at a shelter] E. Bence. il por _Christ Today_ 31:34 Ja 16 '87

Homeliness
The tyranny of beauty [Adam Cohen's article on facial discrimination in Harvard law review] _New Repub_ 197:4 O 12 '87

Anecdotes, facetiae, satire, etc.
Ugly rights. D. Seligman. _Fortune_ 116:95-6 Ag 31 '87

Homemakers
See also
Clothing and dress—Homemakers
Future Homemakers of America
Mothers Are Women (Organization)
Different kinds of mothering [homemakers vs. working moms] L. Harris. il _Parents_ 62:59-60+ Jl '87
Home-grown kids need a full-time mom. W. Metts, Jr. il por _Christ Today_ 31:12 Mr 6 '87
Homemaker dads. R. B. McCall. il _Parents_ 62:232 Ap '87
"Labor saving" means more work. R. S. Cowan. il _Read Dig_ 131:181-4 D '87
Less work for mother? R. S. Cowan. il _Am Herit_ 38:68-70+ S/O '87
The return of the housewife [special section] il _Vogue_ 177:334-9+ Ap '87
The toughest choice [career vs. staying home] M. D. Leonard. il por _Ladies Home J_ 104:22+ O '87
"What's a smart woman like you doing at home?" [search for child care; excerpt] L. Burton. il _Read Dig_ 131:29-30+ O '87
Why I'm at home. E. Berg. il _Parents_ 62:122-3 Ap '87

Homemaking _See_ Home economics
Homeopathy
Homeopathic remedies. il _Consum Rep_ 52:60-2 Ja '87
Homeowners' insurance _See_ Insurance, Homeowners'
Homer
about
The heroic women of Greek epic. M. R. Lefkowitz. _Am Sch_ 56:503-18 Aut '87
Odyssey: dig on Ithaca seeks the dwelling of Homer's famed wanderer. J. Horgan. il _Sci Am_ 257:18+ N '87

Homer, Stephen
In a tizzy over tommy cod. il _Int Wildl_ 17:18-24 Ja/F '87

Homer and Jethro
about
Homer and Jethro. S. M. Stroff. il _Antiques Collect Hobbies_ 92:50-2 Ag '87

Homes, Institutional
See also
Big Oak Boys Ranch (Ala.)
Boys Town (Neb.)
Group homes for children
Nursing homes
Orphans and orphanages
Rawhide Boys Ranch

Homesickness
Looking homeward. M. Blumenthal. il _N Y Times Mag_ p78 Je 14 '87

Homestead (Pa.)
Crime
Fingerprinting only black males in town sparks tension, fear. L. Ransom. il _Jet_ 72:12-14+ S 21 '87
Homestead NAACP chided on fingerprint support. il _Jet_ 73:7 S 28 '87
The search for a rapist [blacks asked to submit to fingerprinting] il _Newsweek_ 110:42 S 14 '87
Trying to trace a rapist [fingerprinting of blacks] F. Trippett. il _Time_ 130:28 S 14 '87

Homesteads
Learning to homestead [Malachite Small Farm School, Colo.] S. Voynick. il _Ctry J_ 14:60 Ja '87
History
Bibliography
Book notes [women homesteaders] J. Long. _Nation_ 244:371-4 Mr 21 '87
Maine
An island of rare hospitality [Frenchboro, Me. offer of free homesteads] R. Howard. il _People Wkly_ 27:96-9 Ap 20 '87
New Mexico
In New Mexico: a family lives in its own world [Oest family] J. Ackermann-Blount. il _Time_ 130:12-13 O 5 '87

Homework
Coping with the ways students cope with homework. T. N. Turner. _Educ Dig_ 52:32-5 Ja '87
Helping your child with homework [excerpt from Your child's growing mind] J. M. Healy. il _Good Housekeep_ 205:114 S '87
The homework blues. D. Elkind. il _Parents_ 62:214 S '87
Television viewing and homework [study by the National Assessment of Education Progress] il _Consum Res Mag_ 70:36 Ag '87

Homeworkers _See_ Home labor
Homicide _See_ Murder
Homilies _See_ Sermons
Homing pigeons _See_ Pigeons
Hominids _See_ Man, Prehistoric
Hominy
See also
Cooking—Grain
Homma, Yoshiaki
about
Rug merchant. E. F. Cone. il por _Forbes_ 140:57+ Ag 24 '87
Hommel, Carolyn L.
(jt. auth) See Carey, Cathy, and Hommel, Carolyn L.
Homology (Biology)
Clathrin light chains LCA and LCB are similar, polymorphic, and share repeated heptad motifs. T. Kirchhausen and others. bibl f il _Science_ 236:320-4 Ap 17 '87
'Competition' cause of AIDS dementia? [work of Mark E. Gurney and others] D. D. Edwards. _Sci News_ 132:150-1 S 5 '87
Dorsal, an embryonic polarity gene in Drosophila, is homologous to the vertebrate proto-oncogene, c-rel. R. Steward. bibl f il _Science_ 238:692-4 O 30 '87
Double-duty proteins [research by Graeme Wistow and Joram Piatigorsky] _Sci News_ 131:409 Je 27 '87
Functional interaction and partial homology between human immunodeficiency virus and neuroleukin [cause of AIDS dementia] M. R. Lee and others. bibl f il _Science_ 237:1047-51 Ag 28 '87
Gene makeup a surprise [apolipoprotein(a) and plasminogen] D. M. Barnes. _Science_ 238:1513 D 11 '87
Homeo domain of the yeast repressor α2 is a sequence-specific DNA-binding domain but is not sufficient for repression. M. N. Hall and A. D. Johnson. bibl f il _Science_ 237:1007-12 Ag 28 '87

Homology (Biology)—*cont.*

Identification of putative human T cell receptor δ complementary DNA clones. S. Hata and others. bibl f il *Science* 238:678-82 O 30 '87

A novel thyroid hormone receptor encoded by a cDNA clone from a human testis library. D. Benbrook and M. Pfahl. bibl f il *Science* 238:788-91 N 6 '87

Recruitment of enzymes as lens structural proteins. G. Wistow and J. Piatigorsky. bibl f il *Science* 236:1554-6 Je 19 '87

A sea urchin gene encodes a polypeptide homologous to epidermal growth factor. D. A. Hursh and others. bibl f il *Science* 237:1487-90 S 18 '87

Similarity of cruzin, an inhibitor of Trypanosoma cruzi neuraminidase, to high-density lipoprotein. R. P. Prioli and others. bibl f il *Science* 238:1417-19 D 4 '87

When does homology mean something else? R. Lewin. *Science* 237:1570 S 25 '87

Homosexual literature

See also

Booksellers and bookselling—Homosexual literature

The universal voice of gay writers. M. Denneny. por *Publ Wkly* 232:48 Jl 3 '87

Homosexual market

The gay market has put this CPA on the fast Track [N. J. Feinstein owner of chain of gay nightclubs Tracks International] P. Finch. il por *Bus Week* p58 Ap 27 '87

Homosexuality

See also

Bisexuality

Children of homosexuals

Gay Games

Lesbianism

Parents of homosexuals

Sodomy

AIDS and the sexual counter-revolution. *Natl Rev* 39:19 Jl 3 '87

AIDS: are heterosexuals at risk? M. Fumento. *Commentary* 84:21-7 N '87

Anonymous sex. H. Klingeman. *Natl Rev* 39:42-3 Je 19 '87

Another muzzle for AIDS education? [Congress attacks comic book aimed at homosexuals] W. Booth. *Science* 238:1036 N 20 '87

An attack on gay rights [news of E. Schreyer in Manitoba] *Macleans* 100:11 Jl 27 '87

Backlash? W. F. Buckley. *Natl Rev* 39:66-7 N 20 '87

Carol Lynn Pearson pens a moving memoir on her gay husband's death from AIDS. K. McMurran. il pors *People Wkly* 27:91+ F 2 '87

The Columbus of AIDS [G. Dugas named Patient Zero] *Natl Rev* 39:19 N 6 '87

Death of a conservative [T. Dolan] J. Alter. il *Newsweek* 109:23 Ja 12 '87

The death of an athlete [Gay Games organizer, T. Waddell, dies of AIDS] D. Schaap. il *Sports Illus* 67:26-8+ Jl 27 '87

Epidemics and civil rights [AIDS] D. E. Koshland, Jr. *Science* 235:729 F 13 '87

Extremism on campus: symbols of hate, symbols of hope [collegiate gay baiting] E. D. Howard. il *Christ Century* 104:625-7 Jl 15-22 '87

Fear of death and disease [AIDS in Canada] A. Finlayson. il *Macleans* 100:34-5 Ja 12 '87

For a new coalition [National March for Lesbian and Gay Rights in Washington, D.C.] *Nation* 245:433 O 24 '87

Fostering prejudice [policy prohibiting homosexuals from being foster parents in Mass.] W. F. Schulz, Jr. il *Progressive* 51:15 Ja '87

From Dolan to da Vinci. A. Cockburn. *Nation* 244:135 F 7 '87

Gay marriage: lifting the bans. B. Findlen. il *Ms* 15:29 F '87

Gays: a family phenomenon? [study by Richard Pillard and James Weinrich] J. Meer. *Psychol Today* 21:66-7 Ap '87

Getting honest. D. G. Phelps. il *N Y Times Mag* p53 Mr 15 '87

Have gays taken over Yale? J. Adler. il *Newsweek* 110:96 O 12 '87

Homosexuality: an effeminate beginning? [study by Richard Green] J. Meer. il *Psychol Today* 21:66 Ap '87

Inventing the homosexual. M. A. Rosenberg. *Commentary* 84:36-40 D '87

Is Yale now colored mauve? [gay and lesbian presence] J. Hart. *Natl Rev* 39:30 O 9 '87

It dare not speak its name: fear and self-loathing on the gay right. C. Hitchens. *Harpers* 275:70-2 Ag '87

More gay-bashing [congressional amendment to appropriations bill that will hamstring safer sex education programs aimed at gays] *Nation* 245:473 O 31 '87

My husband, Rock Hudson [excerpt] P. Gates. pors *Ladies Home J* 104:70-1+ Jl '87

My husband was gay. il *Good Housekeep* 204:24+ Ja '87

Needs of gay students for acceptance and support [high schoolers] G. J. Krysiak. *Educ Dig* 53:44-7 D '87

Notes and comment [Gay/Lesbian Pride Parade in New York City] *New Yorker* 63:17-18 Jl 13 '87

On tour with Rock Hudson [promoting Rock Hudson, his story] S. Davidson. il *N Y Times Mag* p54+ My 3 '87

One couple's finances: paying AIDS' cruel cost [Rick Atkins and Phil Hastings] S. Seixas. il *Money* 16:89-90+ Jl '87

Poison-pen mail [anti-gay form letters] *Harpers* 275:16+ S '87

Sexual destinies [work of G. Dörner] L. Murray. il *Omni* 9:100-2+ Ap '87

Show opening in New Haven [homosexuality at Yale] J. Hart. *Natl Rev* 39:26 N 20 '87

This is what you thought: 59% disapprove of gay couples adopting children [results of survey] *Glamour* 85:63 Ja '87

Those were the gays. R. Blow. *New Repub* 197:14-16 N 2 '87

Anecdotes, facetiae, satire, etc.

The Shakespeare number [Belles lettres magazine studies the question, Was Shakespeare gay?] C. Simmons. *Nation* 244:291-5 Mr 7 '87

History

'Commanding the heart': Edward Carpenter and friends. S. Rowbotham. bibl il pors *Hist Today* 37:41-6 S '87

Dutch tribute to gay pride [Amsterdam monument to homosexuals killed during Nazi regime] K. Golden. *Ms* 15:32 Je '87

The gay decades. F. Rich. il *Esquire* 108:87-92+ N '87

Homosexuality and Christianity

See also

Church work with homosexuals

Dignity (Organization)

Homosexuals Anonymous Fellowship Services

Ordination of homosexuals

Universal Fellowship of Metropolitan Community Churches

Eros between men [discussion of December 26, 1986 article, Gay rights/gay plight] S. Elred. *Commonweal* 114:300-3 My 8 '87

Gays in the clergy. K. L. Woodward. il *Newsweek* 109:58-60 F 23 '87

His fundamentalist mother and his father's gay lover square off over custody of young Brian Batey. M. Brower. il pors *People Wkly* 28:112-14 N 9 '87

Homosexuality & the priesthood. R. P. McBrien. *Commonweal* 114:380-3 Je 19 '87

Homosexuality & the priesthood [discussion of June 19, 1987 article] R. P. McBrien. *Commonweal* 114:493-7 S 11 '87

Homosexuality: challenging the church to grow. J. J. McNeill. il *Christ Century* 104:242-6 Mr 11 '87

Homosexuals and the churches. E. Tivnan. il *N Y Times Mag* p84-6+ O 11 '87

McNeill on the church and gays [discussion of March 11, 1987 article, Homosexuality: challenging the church to grow] J. J. McNeill. *Christ Century* 104:443-4+ My 6 '87

Tragic confusion [homosexual clergy] *Natl Rev* 39:21 Mr 13 '87

What about the homosexual? T. Stafford. il *Christ Today* 31:28 O 2 '87

Wisconsin boys ranch says no to hiring homosexuals [Rawhide Boys Ranch] W. North. il *Christ Today* 31:48 Mr 6 '87

Homosexuality in art

Exhibitions

Where we are now [Homo video at the New Museum in New York] M. Gever. il *Art Am* 75:43-9 Jl '87

Homosexuality in mass media

The gay decades. F. Rich. il *Esquire* 108:87-92+ N '87

Homosexuality in motion pictures

On the set [making of Maurice] V. Radin. il *Vogue* 177:62+ My '87

Partners and friends for 26 years, James Ivory and Ismail Merchant film a hotly debated gay love story [adaptation of E. M. Forster's Maurice] J. Stark. il pors *People Wkly* 28:119-22 O 26 '87

Homosexuality in motion pictures—*cont.*
A queer kind of film [Lesbian and Gay Experimental Film Festival in New York City] J. Stuart. *Film Comment* 23:4+ N/D '87

Homosexuality in television
That certain subject. W. A. Henry. il *Channels* 7:43-5 Ap '87

Homosexuals Anonymous Fellowship Services
Leading ex-gay figure resigns counseling post [C. Cook] R. Frame. il *Christ Today* 31:57 Mr 6 '87

Homotopy
Twists of space [visualization of the Romboy homotopy; cover story] I. Peterson. il *Sci News* 132:264-6 O 24 '87

Homozygosis
Homozygosity mapping: a way to map human recessive traits with the DNA of inbred children. E. S. Lander and D. Botstein. bibl f il *Science* 236:1567-70 Je 19 '87
Reduction to homozygosity of genes on chromosome 11 in human breast neoplasia. I. U. Ali and others. bibl f il *Science* 238:185-8 O 9 '87

Honan, Park
Jane's fighting ships. bibl il pors *Hist Today* 37:40-6 Ag '87

Honasan, Gregorio
about
The impatience of being 'Gringo'. il por *Newsweek* 110:28 S 7 '87
Inside the rebel camp. M. Liu. il pors *Newsweek* 110:40-2 S 21 '87
Manila's threatening new storm. L. Neumann. il por *Macleans* 100:21 S 14 '87
Roundup of an elusive renegade. H. G. Chua-Eoan. il *Time* 130:48 D 21 '87
Seizing a most wanted man. M. Liu. il por *Newsweek* 110:48 D 21 '87

Honda (Automobile) *See* Automobiles, Foreign; Sports cars

Honda Motor Co., Ltd
Culture shock [T. Chino transferred back to Toyko] A. Tanzer. il por *Forbes* 140:196+ S 21 '87
Honda is turning red, white, and blue [second U.S. plant] W. J. Holstein and J. B. Treece. il *Bus Week* p38 O 5 '87
Honda: made in the U.S.A. J. B. Copeland. il *Newsweek* 109:42 Ja 19 '87
A hot American car may hit Japan: the Honda [strong yen could prompt Japanese carmakers to reexport from the U.S.] W. J. Hampton and others. il *Bus Week* p50 Ja 26 '87
Japan: hands on at Honda [president T. Kume] F. H. Katayama. il por *Fortune* 116:88 N 9 '87
"Nobody likes us except the consumer". J. Flint. il *Forbes* 140:56-7+ O 19 '87
Nothing is forever [Honda Britain Racing disbands] J. Greening. il *Cycle* 38:21 Mr '87
The winning difference [address, April 7, 1987] S. Irimajiri. *Vital Speeches Day* 53:650-2 Ag 15 '87

Hondo Oil & Gas Company
Robert Anderson is shaking up the oil patch again [merging Hondo into Pauley] J. Flynn. il por *Bus Week* p39 Ag 17 '87

Honduran refugees *See* Refugees, Honduran

Honduras
See also
Christmas—Honduras
Military assistance, American—Honduras
Tegucigalpa (Honduras)
Antiquities
See also
Copán (Ancient city)
Commerce
United States
See United States—Commerce—Honduras
Defenses
See also
Airplanes, Military—Honduras
United States—Armed Forces—Forces in Honduras
Foreign relations
Nicaragua
The comforts of 10 Lemp Alley [refugees, contras and U.S. soldiers in Honduras] M. McDonald. il *Macleans* 100:22-4 F 23 '87
Contradiction. W. Greider. il *Roll Stone* p32+ F 12 '87
Nicaragua asks for World Court to consider cases against Costa Rica and Honduras. *UN Chron* 23:88 N '86
Odd man out [role of Honduras] J. Eldridge. *America* 157:348-9 N 14 '87

Security Council considers Nicaraguan complaint of 'serious incidents' in Central America. il *UN Chron* 24:64 F '87
United States
See United States—Foreign relations—Honduras
Politics and government
The Honduran dilemma. R. Millet. bibl f *Curr Hist* 86:409-12+ D '87
Honduras. E. Bibb. *Sch Update* 119:12-13 Mr 9 '87
In over my head. J. Gillenkirk. il *America* 157:9-14 Jl 4-11 '87

Honecker, Erich
about
'Ample opportunities' for arms pact [interview] R. Knight. il por *U S News World Rep* 102:34-5 Ja 12 '87
Visit to Germany (West), 1987
Bridging two Germanies. R. Laver. il por *Macleans* 100:30 S 21 '87
An East-West milestone. M. Frankland. *World Press Rev* 34:24 S '87
Germany: East meets West. A. Nagorski. il *Newsweek* 110:50 S 14 '87
The hidden agendas in Honecker's trip to Bonn. F. Thelen and B. Javetski. il *Bus Week* p47 S 7 '87
A historic German visit. H. Wetzel. il *Macleans* 100:19 S 14 '87
Homecoming for a serious boy. W. R. Doerner. pors *Time* 130:31 S 7 '87
Honecker's historic journey home. J. L. Galloway. il *U S News World Rep* 103:40-1 S 14 '87
Inside East Germany. P. Lewis. il por *Macleans* 100:16-18 S 14 '87
Little Man vs. Big Man. W. R. Doerner. il pors *Time* 130:45 S 21 '87
Reporters and reporting
After Honecker. C. D. Van De Stadt. il *World Press Rev* 34:40 N '87

Honesdale (Pa.)
Crime
Pennsylvania gothic [death of K. Umstadter in alcohol-related traffic accident results in her brother's murdering of driver] G. Hackett. il por *Newsweek* 110:27 Ag 17 '87
Primed to kill, an angry young man shoots his dead sister's boyfriend, leaving two families in ruins [T. Umstadter kills G. Evans] J. Hammer. il *People Wkly* 28:159-60+ N 16 '87

Honesty
See also
Cheating in school work
Integrity
Are you an honest woman? [quiz] E. Kunes. il *Seventeen* 46:91 Ja '87
Driving along minding his business, Melvin Kiser ran into $2 million—then he did the unthinkable [returned money that fell out of armored car] M. Dougherty. il pors *People Wkly* 28:75-6 N 30 '87
Honesty: look them in the eye and smile [research by George Rotter and Naomi Rotter] P. Chance. *Psychol Today* 21:23 S '87
A nation of liars? [special section] M. McLoughlin. il *U S News World Rep* 102:54-61 F 23 '87
On honesty and self-deception: 'you are the man'. L. Steffen. *Christ Century* 104:403-5 Ap 29 '87
Truth or consequences: what U.S. Catholic readers admit about their everyday honesty. T. Unsworth. il *U S Cathol* 52:6-17 Mr '87

Honey, Martha
(jt. auth) *See* Avirgan, Tony, and Honey, Martha

Honey, Martha, and Avirgan, Tony
Leaning on Arias. *Nation* 245:220-1 S 12 '87

Honey
See also
Bee culture
Bees

Honey Island Swamp (La.)
Louisiana's Honey Island Swamp. il *South Living* 22:34+ My '87

Honeybees *See* Bees

Honeyghan, Lloyd
about
Boxer wins award for his fight vs. apartheid. por *Jet* 72:48 Je 8 '87
Champ refuses to fight South African, junks belt. il por *Jet* 71:46 Ja 26 '87
One real honey of a dandy. C. Gammon. il pors *Sports Illus* 66:58+ My 4 '87

Honeymoon resorts *See* Resorts
Honeywell Bull Inc.
Can a turnaround wizard make Honeywell Bull work? [J. Stern] T. Peterson. il por *Bus Week* p84-5 Ap 20 '87
Honeywell Inc.
Buying health care in the new era of medicine [address, April 28, 1987] E. W. Spencer. *Vital Speeches Day* 53:713-16 S 15 '87
New infrared line scanner to enter Air Force service [Honeywell AN/AAD-5B] il *Aviat Week Space Technol* 127:108 S 7 '87
Trouble in Hell Canyon [Indians oppose proposed munitions testing site in South Dakota] T. E. Johnson. il *Newsweek* 110:30 S 28 '87
The turmoil in aerospace could boost Honeywell. G. G. Marcial. il *Bus Week* p62 Ag 10 '87
Hong Kong
See also
    Architecture—Hong Kong
    Arts and crafts—Hong Kong
    Dance festivals—Hong Kong
    Horse race betting—Hong Kong
    Immigration and emigration—Hong Kong
    Investments, Hong Kong
    Investments, Japanese—Hong Kong
    Organized crime—Hong Kong
    Shopping and shoppers—Hong Kong
    Youth—Hong Kong
Description and travel
Future shock in Hong Kong. J. Morris. il *N Y Times Mag* p48-51+ O 25 '87
On the road in China. P. Plawin. il *Changing Times* 41:89-92+ D '87
Economic conditions
Debating the future of the colony. T. Fennell. il *Macleans* 100:30-1 Ag 17 '87
Hong Kong: a colony eyes Chinese rule. L. Hopping. il *Sch Update* 119:10-11 Ap 6 '87
Industries
See also
    Dragon Airlines Ltd.
    Jardine Matheson & Co., Ltd.
Politics and government
Direct elections in Hong Kong? Not if Beijing can help it. D. J. Yang. il *Bus Week* p62 Mr 16 '87
Future shock in Hong Kong. J. Morris. il *N Y Times Mag* p48-51+ O 25 '87
Hong Kong and Macao: two colonies. il *Sch Update* 120:28 S 18 '87
Hong Kong and Shanghai Banking Corporation *See* Hongkong and Shanghai Banking Corporation
Hong Kong Dance Company
Reviews:
    Collection of new works entitled Femme fatale. D. Ries. il *Dance Mag* 61:73 D '87
    Performances at the Asian Arts Festival. D. Ries. *Dance Mag* 61:91 Ap '87
Hong Kong Stock Exchange *See* Stock exchanges—Hong Kong exchange
Hongkong and Shanghai Banking Corporation
Banking on greatness [Canadian operations] P. C. Newman. il por *Macleans* 100:32 Ap 13 '87
Honig, Marvin
about
What a way to start. D. Machan. il por *Forbes* 140:448 Jl 13 '87
Honkala (Finland: Country estate) *See* Country estates—Finland
Honolulu (Hawaii)
Music
See also
    Hawaii Opera Theatre
Waikiki Beach
See Waikiki Beach (Honolulu, Hawaii)
Honorary degrees *See* Degrees, Honorary
Hood, Ann
At war with Amy [story] il por *McCalls* 114:152+ S '87
Hood, Kit
about
Singing the puberty blues. P. Hluchy. il *Macleans* 100:54 Ja 19 '87
Hood, Leroy E.
about
Interview. J. Davis. il por *Omni* 10:116-18+ N '87
Hood, Wilma
Bake sales: it's simple to make them a success! il por *McCalls* 115:147 N '87

Hood Museum of Art
Good neighbors [architect C. Moore] K. Norment and C. Giuliano. il *Art News* 86:51-2 Ja '87
Hood River (Or.)
Sports
A boardhead's paradise. J. N. Baker. il *Newsweek* 110:59 Ag 24 '87
Hood River Conservation Project
Conservation pays: insulating the future. C. Nichols. il *Technol Rev* 90:14-15 Jl '87
Hoofed animals *See* Ungulates
Hoogland, John L.
about
A prairie dog companion. J. Grossmann. il pors *Audubon* 89:52-4+ Mr '87
Hook, Harold S.
about
Harold Hook's magnificent machine. W. P. Barrett. il por *Forbes* 140:48+ O 19 '87
Hook, Janet
Catastrophic insurance for all. il *Wash Mon* 19:37-40 F '87
Hook, Sidney, 1902-
Radical, teacher, technician. il *Natl Rev* 39:32-3 S 11 '87
about
The importance of Sidney Hook. H. Kramer. *Commentary* 84:17-24 Ag '87
More at home than out of step. E. A. Shils. *Am Sch* 56:577-80+ Aut '87
Philosophy & faith [discussion of August 1987 article, The importance of Sidney Hook] H. Kramer. *Commentary* 84:2+ N '87
Hooley, Mace
(jt. auth) *See* Reeves, Robert, and Hooley, Mace
Hooliganism (Term)
Uncivil liberties. C. Trillin. il *Nation* 245:330 O 3 '87
Hooper, Joseph
Anatomy of a sticker price. il *Esquire* 108:167-71 O '87
Mexico City. il *Esquire* 107 Summ Traveler:T8+ Ap '87
Montreal. il *Esquire* 107 Summ Traveler:T5-T6 Ap '87
Where the tasting never stops. il *Esquire* 108:51+ S '87
Hooper, Michael S.
Cry Haiti. *Nation* 245:740-1 D 19 '87
Hooper, Stix
about
Drummer Stix Hooper heads the L.A. chapter of NARAS. por *Jet* 72:57 S 21 '87
Hooperman [television program] *See* Television program reviews—Single works
Hoosiers [film] *See* Motion picture reviews—Single works
Hooters (Musical group)
The Hooters' Philly fans wonder when the rest of the world will face the music and give a hoot. S. Dougherty. il *People Wkly* 28:106-8 N 9 '87
Hoover, Gary E.
about
Selling books, Texas style. J. Schwartz. il por *Newsweek* 110:63 O 26 '87
Hoover, Herbert, 1874-1964
about
The Hoover test. H. Evans. il *U S News World Rep* 103:76 N 30 '87
Hoover, J. Edgar (John Edgar), 1895-1972
about
The Sunday school fascist. T. Branch. *Wash Mon* 19:46-8 Ap '87
Hoover, John Edgar *See* Hoover, J. Edgar (John Edgar), 1895-1972
Hoover, Paul, 1946-
Demonstration [story] *New Yorker* 63:40-6 O 5 '87
Hoover, Ron
about
Ron Hoover at Graham. S. Kalil. il *Art Am* 75:142-3 Ja '87
Hope, Bob, 1903-
about
Bob Hope: thanks for the memories. C. Adams. il por *Ladies Home J* 104:40+ D '87
The stars who make Christmas special. L. Feldman. il pors *McCalls* 115:90+ D '87
Hope, Catherine
Dumped: how I survived the first six months. il por *Glamour* 85:236+ Ap '87
Hope, Jack
A new way to find missing children. il *Good Housekeep* 204:50+ Mr '87

Hope, Jack—*cont.*
New York's Chautauqua County. il map *Mother Earth News* 108:48-55 N/D '87
(ed) See Eaton, Eileen. The wisest decision I ever made
Hope, Jonathan
about
Golden threads. S. M. L. Aronson. il por *House Gard* 159:20+ O '87
Hope, Marjorie, and Young, James, 1916-
Making the case for full employment. *Christ Century* 104:715-18 Ag 26-S 2 '87
Who cares for the mentally ill? il *Nation* 245:782-4 D 26 '87-Ja 2 '88
Hope, Robert B.
A boy at sea. il por *Am Hist Illus* 21:14-18 Ja '87
Hope, Samuel
Media and arts education policy. *Des Arts Educ* 88:20-8 Jl/Ag '87
Hope
A living hope. M. K. Hellwig. *America* 156:inside back cover Ap 18 '87
Sober hope: some themes in Protestant theology today. G. Fackre. *Christ Century* 104:790-2 S 23 '87
Hope and glory [film] See Motion picture reviews—Single works
Hope University
They all have high hopes [arts education of mentally retarded] E. M. Reingold. il por *Time* 129:61 Mr 2 '87
Hopewell, Joan
Motown's other mogul. il por *Channels* 7:38-9 S '87
Hopfield, John J.
(jt. auth) See Tank, David W., and Hopfield, John J.
Hopfield, John J., and Tank, David W.
Computing with neural networks [discussion of August 8, 1986 article, Computing with neural circuits: a model] bibl f il *Science* 235:1226-9 Mr 6 '87
Hopi Indians
Indian land, white greed [Navajo-Hopi relocation issue] T. Johnson. il *Nation* 245:15-18 Jl 4-11 '87
The land of the Navajo and the Hopi [cover story] il maps *Sunset* 178:96-109 My '87
Hopkins, Ellen
Behind the soapy scenes of 'One life to live': endless loves. il *N Y* 20:70-2+ My 18 '87
Blacks at the top: torn between two worlds. il *N Y* 20:20-31 Ja 19 '87
Club Lit: reading groups of the rich and famous. il *N Y* 20:32-5 Jl 20 '87
How often do you think about sex? *Mademoiselle* 93:124-5+ Ja '87
Love: the fervid quest for the 'L' word. il *N Y* 20:32-6+ Je 29-Jl 6 '87
The sound of music. il *N Y* 20:54-7 N 23 '87
The West Village: artists' outposts, ancient mariners, and the meat of the city. il map *N Y* 20:82-4 My 4 '87
Hopkins, Harry Lloyd, 1890-1946
about
Wild about Harry. J. K. Galbraith. il por *Wash Mon* 19:44-5 Je '87
Hopkins, Mark
Beijing plays coy with Moscow. il *New Leader* 70:8-9 Ag 10-24 '87
China hits the clutch. por *New Leader* 70:3-4 Ja 12-26 '87
China passes the torch. por *New Leader* 70:5-6 N 30 '87
China's last emperor. il *New Leader* 70:7-10 O 19 '87
Waiting for October in China. il *New Leader* 70:3-4 Ap 6 '87
Writing in China. il *New Leader* 70:27-8 My 4-18 '87
Hopkins, Mary
Eye care for the summer. il *Consum Res Mag* 70:11-14 Je '87
(ed) See Copulos, Milton. Can Chernobyl happen here?
Hoppe, Arthur Watterson
Just be patient. il *Read Dig* 130:139-40 Je '87
Hopper, D. H.
If Luther were sitting in the end zone. *Christ Century* 104:781-2 S 23 '87
Hopper, Dennis
Uncommon images [photographs] il pors *People Wkly* 27:124-7 Ap 13 '87
about
An easy rider's lens. D. Davis. il *Newsweek* 109:83 Je 8 '87
Hopper's return from the edge. R. Stayton. por *Harpers Bazaar* 120:381+ S '87

Hopping John See Cooking, American
Hopson, Dennis
about
Dennis, the Buckeye menace. A. Murphy. il por *Sports Illus* 66:81 F 9 '87
Hopson, Janet L.
Boys will be boys, girls will be . . . bibl (p67) il *Psychol Today* 21:60-6 Ag '87
Horan, Hillary
The first good-bye [story] il *Redbook* 169:29-30 Ag '87
Horatio Alger Association of Distinguished Americans
Famous Amos among ten rags-to-riches inductees. por *Jet* 72:6 Mr 30 '87
Hord, Earl
about
Top two U.S. airports headed by black execs. pors *Jet* 72:8 Je 22 '87
Horel, Lisa
Developing partnerships between families and service providers in rural Vermont. il *Child Today* 16:17-19 Ja/F '87
Horenstein, Henry, and O'Neil, Elaine
High contrast. il *Pop Photogr* 94:56-61 Jl '87
Horford, Tito
about
The dawn of Tito Horford. J. Capouya. il pors *Sport Mag* 78:50-5 Ja '87
Horgan, John
Hearts of darkness: evidence grows that black holes lurk at the center of galaxies. il *Sci Am* 257:30+ O '87
Höricke, Friedrich
about
If feminist Shere Hite thinks women are so miserable, how come she's so happy with her husband? R. Sanders. il pors *People Wkly* 28:60-2 D 7 '87
Horiuchi, Noboru, and others
Similarity of synthetic peptide from human tumor to parathyroid hormone in vivo and in vitro. bibl f il *Science* 238:1566-8 D 11 '87
Horizon (Periodical)
Arts exchange. See issues of Horizon (Tuscaloosa, Ala.) beginning May 1986
Hormats, Robert D.
about
We better keep them happy [interview] A. D. Frank. il por *Forbes* 140:37-8 N 30 '87
Hormel (Geo. A.) & Co. See Geo. A. Hormel & Co.
Hormone receptors
See also
Chemoreceptors
Adrenal steroids: new answers, new questions [mineralocorticoids and glucocorticoids] J. W. Funder. bibl f *Science* 237:236-7 Jl 17 '87
After insulin binds. O. M. Rosen. bibl f il *Science* 237:1452-8 S 18 '87
A chimeric, ligan-binding v-erbB/EGF receptor retains transforming potential. H. Riedel and others. bibl f il *Science* 236:197-200 Ap 10 '87
Cloning of human mineralocorticoid receptor complementary DNA: structural and functional kinship with the glucocorticoid receptor. J. L. Arriza and others. bibl f il *Science* 237:268-75 Jl 17 '87
Decreased TRH receptor mRNA activity precedes homologous downregulation: assay in oocytes. Y. Oron and others. bibl f il *Science* 238:1406-8 D 4 '87
Epidermal growth factor-dependent transformation by a human EGF receptor proto-oncogene. T. J. Velu and others. bibl f il *Science* 238:1408-10 D 4 '87
Glucocorticoid receptor mutants that define a small region sufficient for enhancer activation. R. Miesfeld and others. bibl f il *Science* 236:423-7 Ap 24 '87
The glucocorticoid receptor protein binds to transfer RNA. M. Ali and W. V. Vedeckis. bibl f il *Science* 235:467-70 Ja 23 '87
Identification of a novel thyroid hormone receptor expressed in the mammalian central nervous system. C. C. Thompson and others. bibl f il *Science* 237:1610-14 S 25 '87
New leads in osteoporosis [estrogen receptors in osteoblasts; research by B. Lawrence Riggs and others] D. M. Barnes. *Science* 236:915 My 22 '87
A novel thyroid hormone receptor encoded by a cDNA clone from a human testis library. D. Benbrook and M. Pfahl. bibl f il *Science* 238:788-91 N 6 '87
Hormones
See also
ACTH
Cholecystokinin
Corticosterone

Hormones—See also—*cont.*
   Endocrine glands
   Epidermal growth factor
   Erythropoietin
   Fetus, Effect of hormones on the
   Hydrocortisone
   Hypothalamic hormones
   Insulin
   Juvenile hormones
   Melatonin
   Parathyroid hormone
   Pheromones
   Pituitary hormone releasing factors
   Pituitary hormones
   Prostaglandins
   Somatomedins
   Steroids
   Stilbestrols
   Thyrotropin releasing factor
   Vasoactive intestinal polypeptide
   Vasopressin
The hormone mysteries: what we know now. E. Switzer. *Vogue* 177:236+ Mr '87
A new wave of enzymes for cleaving prohormones. J. L. Marx. il *Science* 235:285-6 Ja 16 '87
A user's guide to hormones. M. Clark and D. Gelman. il *Newsweek* 109:50-6+ Ja 12 '87

Hormones, Plant
Plant hormone: key to ozone toxicity? [research by Horst Mehlhorn and Alan R. Wellburn] J. Raloff. *Sci News* 131:357-8 Je 6 '87

Hormones, Sex
   See also
   Estrogens
   Gonadotropins
   Testosterone
Boys will be boys, girls will be . . . [spotted hyenas may help answer questions about gender and aggression in humans] J. L. Hopson. bibl (p67) il *Psychol Today* 21:60-6 Ag '87

Hormones, Synthetic
   See also
   Pituitary hormones, Synthetic

Horn, Bernard
When being a vegetable doesn't mean a thing. por *U S News World Rep* 102:6 Mr 23 '87

Horn, Jack C.
Bigger pay for better work. il *Psychol Today* 21:54-7 Jl '87

Horn, Jack C., and Meer, Jeff
The vintage years. bibl (p95) il *Psychol Today* 21:76-7+ My '87

Horn, Karen
   about
Peripatetic banker. D. Machan. il por *Forbes* 139:170+ Je 1 '87
Two very different first ladies of finance. N. J. Perry. il pors *Fortune* 116:191 O 12 '87

Horn, Linda
   about
Return to romance: Linda and Steve Horn's Manhattan penthouse. S. M. L. Aronson. il por *Archit Dig* 44:122-7+ O '87

Horn, Richard
Fab '50s: the now look. il *Harpers Bazaar* 120:274-7+ Mr '87

Horn, Robert C.
Soviet policy in East Asia. bibl f *Curr Hist* 86:321-4+ O '87

Horn, William Pierce
   about
Disputed territory. R. Cahn and P. Cahn. il *Natl Parks* 61:28-33 My/Je '87
Fuel for an Arctic controversy. L. Williamson. il *Outdoor Life* 179:42+ Mr '87
Takeover at the Park Service. R. Cahn. *Natl Parks* 61:53 Mr/Ap '87

Horn & Hardart Co.
The Automat [New York City] N. Simon. il *N Y* 20:66-7 D 21-28 '87
Why didn't they pay him to stay home? [Bojangles' stores mismanaged by B. Florescue] B. Leonard. il por *Forbes* 139:120-1 Je 15 '87

Horn of Africa *See* East Africa

Hornaday, Ann
Executive assistants—is there power behind the throne? il *Ms* 16:28+ O '87
Rape prevention: Du Pont's model program. il *Ms* 15:31 Je '87

Hornbeck, David W.
   about
New president of school chiefs outlines plan to focus on at-risk youth. *Phi Delta Kappan* 68:407 Ja '87

Hornberger, H. Richard
   about
M*A*S*H's Maine man. C. E. Lincoln. il pors *50 Plus* 27:42+ Mr '87

Horne, Alistair
Macmillan remembered. il *Natl Rev* 39:44-6 Ja 30 '87

Horne, Jennifer F. M.
(jt. auth) See Short, Lester L., and Horne, Jennifer F. M.

Horne, Lena
   about
Lena Horne and daughter receive achievement awards. *Jet* 72:57 Je 8 '87
Lena Horne receives ASCAP's top award. il por *Jet* 72:62 Ap 6 '87

Horne, Vanessa
Chile's impending choice. *Natl Rev* 39:40 Ag 28 '87

Horne family
   about
That Horne thing. C. Kramer. il *McCalls* 145:50-4 Mr '87

Horned lizards *See* Lizards
Horned owls *See* Owls
Horner, Bob
   about
A new kind of Orient Express. A. Wolff. il por *Sports Illus* 66:28-9 My 18 '87

Horney, Karen, 1885-1952
   about
The woman who broke away. P. Grosskurth. il *N Y Rev Books* 34:14-17 N 5 '87

Hornibrook, Ettie A. *See* Rout, Ettie A.

Horns

                Animals
   See also
   Antlers
The rhino's fatal flaw [horn trade in Africa and Asia] P. Jackson. il maps *Int Wildl* 17:4-11 Ja/F '87

Horns, Automobile *See* Automobile horns

Hornsby, Bruce
   about
Bands hitting the headlines. il por *Teen* 31:55 My '87
Rock & roll's other Bruce. S. Pond. il por *Roll Stone* p16 F 12 '87

Hornsby (Bruce) and the Range (Musical group) *See* Bruce Hornsby and the Range (Musical group)

Horoscopes *See* Astrology

Horosko, Marian
Changes in ballet and modern dance techniques: crossovers/fallouts. il *Dance Mag* 61:168-71 Je '87
Education. See issues of Dance Magazine
The personal you. See issues of Dance Magazine
Technique: Plisetskaya teaches. il pors *Dance Mag* 61:54-6 O '87

Horowitz, Amity Kaye
Adventures: kids in the capital. il *Publ Wkly* 231:144-5 My 15 '87

Horowitz, David, 1939-
(jt. auth) See Collier, Peter, and Horowitz, David, 1939-

Horowitz, David, 1939-, and Collier, Peter
The Dellums record [discussion of January 1987 article, Another "low dishonest decade" on the left] *Commentary* 84:2-3+ Jl '87

Horowitz, Irving Louis
Disenthralling sociology. bibl f *Society* 24:48-55 Ja/F '87
Disenthralling sociology [discussion of January/February 1987 article] *Society* 24:3-5 Jl/Ag '87
Looking backward and lurching forward. *Society* 25:9-12 N/D '87
The unraveling of the Reagan presidency. il *New Leader* 69:5-7 D 29 '86
When freedom to read suffers. por *Publ Wkly* 232:38 Jl 17 '87

Horowitz, Joy
Mysteries from a novelist nun. il por *N Y Times Mag* p34-5 Ag 30 '87
A new light in the sky. il *N Y Times Mag* p52+ Mr 29 '87

Horowitz, Murray M.
Campus fashions: what today's college students are wearing. il *USA Today (Periodical)* 115:64-8 Mr '87

Horowitz, Vladimir, 1904-
   about
Applause! Applause! P. G. Davis. il por *N Y* 20:53-4 Ja 12 '87

Horowitz, Vladimir, 1904—about—*cont.*
Vlad tidings from Milan. E. Greenfield. il pors *High Fidel* 37:58-9 S '87
Horris, Lamar, d. 1987
about
Machine gunman, high on crack, pumps 26 fatal bullets into boy, 3. il por *Jet* 73:36 D 7 '87
Horror films *See* Motion pictures—Horror films
Horror tales
See also
Booksellers and bookselling—Horror tales
Tape recordings—Horror tales
The big chiller. G. Stade. *Nation* 244:258-62 F 28 '87
Dark thoughts from Dark Carnival [opinion of Larry Mori] S. Sherman. *Publ Wkly* 232:26 D 4 '87
Authorship
Horror fiction: exploring the dark side. W. F. Nolan. *Writer* 100:20-3 D '87
Horror of horrors. G. Masterton. *Writer* 100:15-18+ Ag '87
How IT happened. S. King. il *Writer* 100:14-15 Ap '87
Meet the new (Stephen) King of horror, Briton Clive Barker. A. Chambers. il pors *People Wkly* 27:87-8 Je 15 '87
Hors d'oeuvres *See* Appetizers
Horse auctions *See* Auctions
Horse breeding *See* Horses—Breeding
Horse Cavalry Association (U.S.) *See* U.S. Horse Cavalry Association
Horse farms *See* Horses—Breeding
Horse race betting
By the numbers [handicapper L. Ragozin] J. Coplon. por *New Yorker* 63:56+ D 21 '87
Get warm to the Form [learning to handicap] J. Rolfe. il *Sport Mag* 78:91+ Jl '87
Laws and regulations
Black Georgia politician helps kill betting bill [Charles Walker] *Jet* 71:4 F 16 '87
Hong Kong
A $40 million day at the races. D. J. Yang. il *Bus Week* p160 Mr 23 '87
Horse racing
See also
Arkansas Racing Commission
Harness racing
Horse race betting
Horses, Race
Race tracks
Robots—Horse racing use
Battling for her place [woman jockey V. Aragon] P. Dexter. il pors *Sports Illus* 66:48-52 F 23 '87
Busting out for a cool million [Bet Twice wins Belmont Stakes] W. Nack. il *Sports Illus* 66:26-8+ Je 15 '87
Catch a rising star [Chart The Stars wins the San Felipe] B. Anderson. il *Sports Illus* 66:46 Mr 30 '87
Classic fit for an old Shoe [Bill Shoemaker rides Ferdinand to win in Breeders' Cup] W. Nack. il *Sports Illus* 67:36-8+ N 30 '87
Days of wine and bloody noses [Alysheba wins Kentucky Derby] T. Callahan. il *Time* 129:91 My 11 '87
The Derby as a prizefight [Kentucky Derby won by Alysheba] P. Axthelm. il *Newsweek* 109:68 My 11 '87
Doing battle with the Demon [Kentucky Derby preview] W. Nack. il por *Sports Illus* 66:42-4+ My 4 '87
A dud in the mud [Java Gold wins Travers] W. Nack. il *Sports Illus* 67:14-15 Ag 31 '87
Good to the last drop [Java Gold wins Marlboro Cup] D. Stathoplos. il *Sports Illus* 67:56-7 S 28 '87
The greatest two minutes in sports [1986 Kentucky Derby] J. Culhane. il *Read Dig* 130:236-8+ My '87
Gulch's Wood, but the Demon could. D. Stathoplos. il *Sports Illus* 66:36-7 Ap 27 '87
The hands have it: jockey Chris McCarron and Alysheba grab for racing's Triple Crown. il pors *People Wkly* 27:48-50 Je 8 '87
The home stretch [trainer J. Van Berg and Alysheba] J. Rolfe. il pors *Sport Mag* 78:49-50+ D '87
The long run for the roses [history of Demons Begone, early favorite to win the Kentucky Derby] L. Rosellini. il *U S News World Rep* 102:64-5 My 4 '87
Make way for superbug [apprentice jockey K. Desormeaux] D. Stathoplos. il por *Sports Illus* 67:91 Jl 13 '87
Muddy track, hopeless long shots . . . it's a living [M. Venezia, long-time jockey at Aqueduct] J. Rolfe. il *Sport Mag* 78:98 Mr '87
Our Triple Crown tout service. M. Smith. il *Sport Mag* 78:79-80 Je '87

Racing's reining queen [J. Krone] P. Axthelm. il por *Newsweek* 110:61 D 28 '87
Reunited, the Iacoccas celebrated the ups at Churchill Downs [celebrities at the Kentucky Derby] il *People Wkly* 27:51-2 My 18 '87
The son shines bright [Alysheba wins Kentucky Derby] W. Nack. il *Sports Illus* 66:26-31 My 11 '87
A stake in the future [Talinum's victory in the Flamingo Stakes] D. Stathoplos. il *Sports Illus* 66:70-1 Mr 9 '87
This is no joyride [Tevis Cup, 100-mile cross country race] D. Stathoplos. il map *Sports Illus* 67:50-3 S 14 '87
Three to get ready and . . . [Kentucky Derby preps] D. Stathoplos. il *Sports Illus* 66:26-8+ Ap 13 '87
Triple Crown showdown [J. Van Berg's Alysheba vs. W. Stephens' Gone West in the Belmont] P. Axthelm. il pors *Newsweek* 109:86+ Je 8 '87
Two down, now the Crown [Alysheba wins the Preakness] W. Nack. il *Sports Illus* 66:30-2+ My 25 '87
Uncrowned prince of the Triple Crown [jockey J. Santos] J. Rolfe and P. Demartini. il pors *Sport Mag* 78:63+ Je '87
A woman of substance [jockey J. Krone] G. Maranto. il pors *Sports Illus* 67:62+ Ag 24 '87
Woman to watch: Vicky Aragon. O. Young. il por *Women's Sports Fitness* 9:54 Je '87
Ethical aspects
New Triple Crown threat [medication given to race horses] J. Rolfe. il *Sport Mag* 78:16 Je '87
A showdown at the shore: Bet Twice beat Alysheba in the Haskell at Monmouth, but Lasix lurked in the shadows. C. Gammon. il *Sports Illus* 67:36-8+ Ag 10 '87
Periodicals
See also
Daily racing form
Great Britain
Chasers [steeplechases at Ascot] B. Barich. *New Yorker* 63:78-83 Mr 23 '87
Princess Anne clears a new hurdle: the steeplechase. J. Cooper. il pors *People Wkly* 27:36-7 Mr 30 '87
Hong Kong
See also
Royal Hong Kong Jockey Club
Italy
See also
Palio di Siena (Italy)
Horse shows
The Royal Windsor Horse Show. S. Wilding. il *Gourmet* 47:60-5+ Ap '87
Horse stables *See* Barns and stables
Horse trainers
See also
Lukas, D. Wayne
Stephens, Woody
Van Berg, Jack, 1936-
Horseback riding *See* Horsemanship
Horseback trips
Exploring Bryce Canyon's high country on horseback. il *Sunset* 179:60 Jl '87
Horseback camping [British Columbia] il map *Natl Geogr World* 141:7-13 My '87
How to plan a Sierra horsepack trip. il maps *Sunset* 178:78-80, 98-103 Ap '87
Toward happier trails. J. Zumbo. il *Outdoor Life* 180:70+ N '87
Photographs and photography
A shot in the park. M. Grimm and T. Grimm. il *Travel Holiday* 167:27-9 My '87
Horsebeans *See* Beans
Horsehead (Nebula) *See* Nebulae
Horseless carriages *See* Automobiles, Antique
Horsemanship
See also
Polo
A boy who climbed the marigold [P. Burkarth's participation in horseback riding program for the handicapped] A. Jones. il pors *Read Dig* 130:96-100 F '87
The bridle path [Central Park] M. Korda. il *N Y* 20:100-1 D 21-28 '87
Calgary's world classic [Spruce Meadows Masters Show Jumping Tournament] J. Howse. il *Macleans* 100:19 S 28 '87
How I found the child in me I thought was lost forever. C. Thompson. il *Glamour* 85:178 Jl '87
"Running Christ against the bandits" [horsemen carry on Easter tradition in Chile] C. Caviedes. il *Nat Hist* 96:44-53 My '87

Horsemanship—*cont.*

The triumph of Mikko Mayeda [multiple sclerosis victim becomes a competitive equestrian] V. Scott. il por *Good Housekeep* 204:40 Mr '87

Horsepower (Mechanics)

Engine performance: the dyno room [motorcycle engines] K. Cameron. il *Cycle* 38:72-5+ Ag '87

Torque and horsepower. R. Grable. il *Mot Trend* 39:106-7 S '87

Working under pressure [power loss represented by pressure on the undersides of descending pistons] K. Cameron. il *Cycle* 38:15 Je '87

Horses

See also
Police horses

Bonny's big day [excerpt] J. Herriot. il *Redbook* 169:62 S '87

Breeding

Betting too big on the blood [catalog entry for thoroughbred horse at Keeneland Selected Yearling Sale] C. Flake. *Harpers* 274:58-9 My '87

Building a winning horse with biotech [embryo transfer used on Grand Prix jumpers] S. Budiansky. il *U S News World Rep* 103:63 N 2 '87

For a real day at the races, buy a horse. D. Cook. il *Bus Week* p162-3 My 11 '87

High-tech horses [embryo transplants] J. Horgan. il *Sci Am* 257:29-31 S '87

Old foes, new race [breeding stallions Alydar and Affirmed at Calumet Farm] W. Nack. il *Sports Illus* 66:44-6+ Je 8 '87

Post time? [investing in thoroughbred horses] K. Hannon. il *Forbes* 140:74+ O 5 '87

Training

See also
Horses, Wild—Training

Treatment

Bill Graham reins in the creeps who kill horses for profit. D. Van Biema. il pors *People Wkly* 28:46-8 Jl 20 '87

Horses, Draft

The Suffolk punch [cover story] J. Page. il *Mother Earth News* 106:72-9 Jl/Ag '87

Horses, Fossil

Life's little joke [evolution] S. J. Gould. il *Nat Hist* 96:16+ Ap '87

Horses, Miniature

Little horse, big deal—protestors cry 'There goes the neighborhood' [P. Fairchild fights to keep her miniature horse in Thousand Oaks, Calif.] il pors *People Wkly* 27:96-7 Je 1 '87

Horses, Race

A high-stakes dream [Look To The Top] B. Weber. il por *N Y Times Mag* p62 Ag 2 '87

In the groove at long last [champion sprinter Groovy] W. Nack. il *Sports Illus* 67:50-3 O 19 '87

The long run for the roses [history of Demons Begone, early favorite to win the Kentucky Derby] L. Rosellini. il *U S News World Rep* 102:64-5 My 4 '87

Air transport

See also
H.E. "Tex" Sutton Horse Charters

Auctions

See Auctions

Barns and stables

See Barns and stables

Breeding

See Horses—Breeding

Handicapping

See Horse race betting

Horses, Wild

The final roundup for America's wild horses? M. Satchell. il *U S News World Rep* 102:68-9 Mr 2 '87

Tracking down mustangs. il map *Sunset* 178:46+ F '87

Training

These cowboys are convicts [taming wild mustangs at Colorado State Penitentiary] J. Willwerth. il *Time* 130:20 Ag 31 '87

Horses in art

The art of Count Bernard de Clavière d'Hust. C. Styles-McLeod. il *Archit Dig* 44:208-15+ My '87

Exhibitions

Susan Rothenberg. J. Bell. il *Art News* 86:147 My '87

Horseshoe crabs

Birds of a feather feed together [feeding on horseshoe crab eggs by migrating shore birds at Delaware Bay] W. P. Carty. il *Américas* 39:28-33+ S/O '87

Diving for horseshoe crabs. il *Natl Geogr World* 141:20-3 My '87

Living history: the horseshoe crab. T. B. Heston. bibl il *Sea Front* 33:195-9 My/Je '87

Horsford, Anna Maria

about
Showstopper: Anna Maria Horsford. P. Johnson. por *Essence* 18:25 Jl '87

Horst, Mark

Worship's focus: seeking the face of God. *Christ Century* 104:991-2 N 11 '87

Horszowski, Mieczyslaw

about
Horszowski: honest, vital authority. R. Freed. il por *Stereo Rev* 52:88+ S '87

Horticultural exhibitions *See* Garden exhibits

Horticultural societies

See also
Southern Garden History Society

Horticulturalists

See also
Dirr, Michael

A living encyclopedia of southern California horticulture [work of panel of garden experts] il *Sunset* 178:196 F '87

Horticulture

See also
Forcing (Plants)
Gardens and gardening
Greenhouses
Vegetable gardens and gardening

The forum: your questions answered. See issues of Flower and Garden

Horticulture as a profession

Horticulture: not just a hobby. G. Hechinger. il *Glamour* 85:314 Ag '87

Turning your green thumb into a new career [cover story] S. Brewer. il *50 Plus* 27:27-31 O '87

Horticulture therapy *See* Gardens and gardening—Therapeutic use

Horton, Andrew

Black like Mich. il por *Film Comment* 23:8-9 Mr/Ap '87

Horton, Earle

about
Flying high with Church's Chicken. il pors *Ebony* 42:72+ Jl '87

Horton, James C., and Bicak, Charles J.

Modeling for biologists. bibl il *BioScience* 37:808-9 D '87

Horton, Mark

The Swahili corridor. il maps *Sci Am* 257:86-8+ S '87

Horton, Thomas R.

The old management magic [address, October 5, 1987] *Vital Speeches Day* 54:111-13 D 1 '87

Horton, Yogi, d. 1987

about
Luther Vandross' drummer killed in 17-story leap. il por *Jet* 72:53 Je 29 '87

Horton Plaza (San Diego, Calif.: Shopping center) *See* San Diego (Calif.)—Stores

Horvath, Tibor

about
Two decades of ultimate dialogue. D. J. Leigh. *America* 157:504-5 D 26 '87

Horvitz Enterprises

The ultimate family feud. L. Gubernick and R. King, Jr. il *Forbes* 139:80-1 Je 29 '87

Horvitz family

about
The ultimate family feud. L. Gubernick and R. King, Jr. il *Forbes* 139:80-1 Je 29 '87

Horwitz, Simi

Healthy stress: the energy boost. *Harpers Bazaar* 120:204+ Mr '87

Hosang, Ulric

about
$3 million lotto win 'numbs' Queens man. il por *Jet* 72:24 Ag 24 '87

Hose

See also
Automobile engines—Hoses
Garden hose

Hosea, Book of *See* Bible. O.T. Hosea

Hosenball, Mark

Autopen presidency. *New Repub* 196:16-18 My 11 '87

The culture of lying [cover story] *New Repub* 197:16-18 Jl 13-20 '87

The Khashoggi memo. *New Repub* 196:14+ F 2 '87

Leak-a-boo. *New Repub* 197:23-5 O 12 '87

Spooked. *New Repub* 197:13-14 Ag 31 '87

(jt. auth) See Isikoff, Michael, and Hosenball, Mark

Hosiery

Baby Steps are the socks of choice for toddlers who don't want to hit the skids early [marketed by V. Reisman and R. Lerner] il *People Wkly* 28:183 N 16 '87

I dreamed I saved a swimmer in my Maidenform pantyhose [protection from jellyfish] S. Brownlee. il *Discover* 8:52 Ag '87

Panty hose. il *Consum Rep* 52:177-80 D '87

Panty hose: born to run? il *Consum Rep* 52:49-52 Ja '87

Hosiery industry

See also

E. G. Smith Color Socks (Firm)

Nancy Atkins, Inc.

Hosken, Fran P., 1919-

The chalice and the blade: an interview with Riane Eisler. *Humanist* 47:26-30+ Jl/Ag '87

Hosking, Leslie

about

Commodity exchange. S. W. Angrist. il por *Forbes* 140:126 S 7 '87

Hoskins, Bob, 1942-

about

Cockney charisma. W. Boyd. il pors *N Y Times Mag* p52+ D 6 '87

Hoskins, Joe

about

Detroit football coach files $10 million job suit. *Jet* 71:46 Mr 9 '87

Hospices

New York (State)

Hospice: caring at life's edge [Cabrini Hospice in Manhattan] R. Hirschfield. *Christ Century* 104:159 F 18 '87

Hospital, Janette Turner, 1942-

The truth, the whole truth, may be anything *but* the truth. *Writer* 100:19-21 Ap '87

Hospital care

See also

Children—Hospital care

Children—Preparation for hospital and medical care

Infants, Newborn—Hospital care

Intensive care units

Malpractice

Monitoring (Medical care)

Costs

See also

AIDS (Disease)—Costs

Higher hospital costs. *Futurist* 21:50-1 Mr/Ap '87

Next, the McDRG [diagnostic related groups] J. Feinglass. il *Progressive* 51:28 Ja '87

The rising cost of health care: what it means to the nation, the elderly, and you [cover story; special issue] il *Sch Update* 119:2-12+ Ap 20 '87

Your money or your life. P. Downs. il *Progressive* 51:24-8 Ja '87

Hospital Corp. of America

HCA may breathe new life into ESOPs. G. Weiss. il *Bus Week* p94 Je 15 '87

Physician, heal thy chain [plan to sell Hospital Corp. of America hospitals to employee-owned company] S. Ticer. *Bus Week* p52 Je 1 '87

Hospital employees

Salaries, pensions, etc.

Hospital occupational pay in 23 metropolitan areas. bibl f il *Mon Labor Rev* 110:43-5 O '87

Hospital equipment industry

See also

Baxter Travenol Laboratories Inc.

Hospital interns See Interns (Medicine)

Hospital management industry

See also

American Medical International, Inc.

Gateway Medical Systems Inc.

Health Management Assoc.

Hospital Corp. of America

Humana Inc

National Healthcare, Inc.

Health. M. Fritz. il *Forbes* 139:140+ Ja 12 '87

Prognosis: empty beds and falling profits. J. O. Hamilton. il *Bus Week* p102 Ja 12 '87

Your money or your life. P. Downs. il *Progressive* 51:24-8 Ja '87

Hospital of the University of Pennsylvania See University of Pennsylvania. Hospital

Hospital patient representatives

See also

Black hospital patient representatives

Patient reps: the Rx for hospital hassles. I. Pave. il *Bus Week* p164 Je 22 '87

She cares [H. Blanchard] por *Essence* 18:12 Ag '87

Hospital patients

A friend's in the hospital: how to show you care. il *Glamour* 85:101 My '87

Civil rights

See also

Hospital patient representatives

Psychology

Patients' best friend [pet room at the Swedish American Hospital in Rockford, Ill.] il *Prevention* 39:8 Ap '87

Psychiatric 'stretch' in the hospital [research by George Fulop and others] *Sci News* 132:94 Ag 8 '87

Visitors

See Hospitals—Visitors

Hospital pharmacies See Hospitals—Pharmaceutical services

Hospital ships

See also

Americares Foundation

Hospitality

See also

Entertaining

Guests

Gift of new life. M. K. Hellwig. *America* 156:inside back cover Je 20-27 '87

Hospitals

See also

Children—Hospitals

Collective labor agreements—Hospitals

Hospices

Hospital care

Nursing homes

Veterinary hospitals

Administration

See also

Hospital management industry

The new hospital [views of Russell C. Coile] *Futurist* 21:11 Ja/F '87

Advertising

Hospital hype: competition for patients spurs a marketing blitz [New York City] B. Holcomb. il *N Y* 20:30-5 Ag 3 '87

Hospitals learn the hard sell. S. Koepp. il *Time* 129:56 Ja 12 '87

Architecture

Indigenous high-tech [Aga Khan University Hospital and Medical College, Karachi, Pakistan; cover story] M. F. Schmertz. il *Archit Rec* 175:136-49 My '87

The picture of health [with introd. by Margaret Gaskie] il *Archit Rec* 175:101-15 O '87

An unexpected surprise [C. Vandenhove's design for the Centre Hospitalier Universitaire au Sart Tilman, Liège, Belgium] G. Bekaert. il *Archit Rec* 175:126-35 Jl '87

Conservation and restoration

First aid for hospitals [restoration plans in Great Britain] il *Hist Today* 37:4-5 S '87

Diagnostic services

Hospital vampires? [ordering excessive blood tests] *Prevention* 39:8+ Ag '87

Emergency services

See also

Trauma care units

Emergency room nurse [excerpt from Intensive care] E. Heron. il *Glamour* 85:330-1+ Ap '87

Then I had this day that was one rape after another [pediatric emergency room] P. Klass. il *Discover* 8:18+ Jl '87

Wheezer in the E.R.: musings on a cookbook admission [asthmatic children] P. Klass. il *Discover* 8:18+ Ap '87

Employees

See Hospital employees

Federal aid

A grim outlook for hospitals [government might limit Medicare capital cost payouts] G. Weiss. il *Bus Week* p126+ My 11 '87

Finance

Doctored diagnosis? [nonprofit hospitals; views of Regina E. Herzlinger and William S. Krasker] *Sci Am* 256:28-9 Je '87

Food service

A heart-healthy proving ground [Chez Eddy at Houston's Methodist Hospital] *Prevention* 39:50-1+ F '87

Intensive care units

See Intensive care units

Management and regulation

See Hospitals—Administration

Marketing

Marketing [address, April 3, 1987] D. McDonald. *Vital Speeches Day* 53:566-72 Jl 1 '87

Hospitals—*cont.*
Maternity care
No money, no vacancy! [patient dumping] L. David and I. David. *Health* 19:64 Ag '87
Pharmaceutical services
How do drugs become 'the ones hospitals use most?'. il *Consum Rep* 52:329 Je '87
Regulation
See Hospitals—Administration
Securities
A grim outlook for hospitals [government might limit Medicare capital cost payouts] G. Weiss. il *Bus Week* p126+ My 11 '87
Visitors
Bedside etiquette. S. Whitman. il *Seventeen* 46:102 Je '87
Georgia
See also
Atlanta (Ga.)—Hospitals
Great Britain
First aid for hospitals [restoration plans] il *Hist Today* 37:4-5 S '87
Illinois
See also
Chicago (Ill.)—Hospitals
Rockford (Ill.)—Hospitals
Israel
See also
Jerusalem—Hospitals
Massachusetts
See also
Newburyport (Mass.)—Hospitals
Michigan
See also
Detroit (Mich.)—Hospitals
Mount Pleasant (Mich.)—Hospitals
New York (State)
See also
New York (N.Y.)—Hospitals
West Islip (N.Y.)—Hospitals
Re-examining the 36-hour day [proposal to reform residents' training] C. Wallis. il *Time* 130:54-5 Ag 31 '87
Ohio
See also
Cincinnati (Ohio)—Hospitals
Ontario
See also
Ottawa (Ont.)—Hospitals
Pennsylvania
See also
Pittsburgh (Pa.)—Hospitals
Saudi Arabia
See also
Riyadh (Saudi Arabia)—Hospitals
Soviet Union
See also
Moscow (Soviet Union)—Hospitals
Texas
See also
Athens (Tex.)—Hospitals
Houston (Tex.)—Hospitals
Hospitals, Children's *See* Children—Hospitals
Hospitals, Military
See also
United States. Veterans Administration—Hospitals
Hospitals, Psychiatric
Commitment laws
See Mentally ill—Civil rights
Massachusetts
'Titicut follies': an asylum with a past [Bridgewater State Hospital] il *Newsweek* 110:57 Jl 20 '87
New York (State)
Saying 'no' to psychiatry [patient rights activist G. Ebert vs. Willard Psychiatric Center, Ithaca] M. Schultz. il por *Progressive* 51:17 F '87
Washington (D.C.)
Hinckley's hope [government blocks one day leave for J. Hinckley from St. Elizabeths Hospital] por *Time* 129:29 Ap 20 '87
Host, Michel
about
International front. H. R. Lottman. *Publ Wkly* 231:167 F 27 '87
Host-guest complexes (Chemistry)
Chemistry in the image of biology [molecular recognition research] R. Lewin. il pors *Science* 238:611-12 O 30 '87
Nobel prizes: chemistry. J. Horgan. *Sci Am* 257:46 D '87

Host International, Inc.
Blacks fly with Marriott [concessionary business at Tampa International Airport] R. Baker. il *Black Enterp* 17:22 Ap '87
Host-parasite relationships
Looking for Mr. Goodbird [relationship between garish plumage and parasite resistance; research by Andrew Read] il *Discover* 8:8 O '87
One giant leap for aphid-kind [escape-response behavior of parasitized aphids; research by Murdoch K. McAllister and Bernard D. Roitberg] *Sci News* 132:158 S 5 '87
Thyca: underarm and underfoot [starfish parasite] T. Bratcher. il *Sea Front* 33:286-7 Jl/Ag '87
Vertical distribution of an estuarine snail altered by a parasite. L. A. Curtis. bibl f il *Science* 235:1509-11 Mr 20 '87
Hostages
See also
Beirut airplane hijacking, 1985
Iranian seizure of United States embassy, 1979-1981
Lebanon hostage cases, 1984-
Please don't hurt me! [woman taken hostage after Texas prison break] R. Williams. il por *Ladies Home J* 104:18+ S '87
Taking hostages, a crime as old as money and power, has often paid off. il *People Wkly* 27:110-11 F 23 '87
Anecdotes, facetiae, satire, etc.
Last word [Teddy Rescue, the hostage negotiator talking bear] M. Wilkins. il *Omni* 9:134 Je '87
Religious life
The role of prayer in gaining the release of hostages. K. A. Lawton. il *Christ Today* 31:34-6 S 18 '87
Hostels *See* Hotels, motels, etc.
Hostess gifts *See* Gifts
Hostility (Psychology)
See also
Anger
Don't be a victim of hostility—his or your own. il *Glamour* 85:97 N '87
Hot air balloons *See* Balloons
Hot dogs (Meat) *See* Frankfurters
Hot drinks *See* Beverages
Hot flashes (Menopause) *See* Menopause
Hot lines, Information *See* Telephone in counseling; Telephone in medical care; Telephone information service
Hot lines, Toll-free *See* Toll-free telephone service
Hot pursuit [film] *See* Motion picture reviews—Single works
Hot spots (Geology) *See* Geology
Hot springs
Deep-sea hydrocarbon seep communities: evidence for energy and nutritional carbon sources. J. M. Brooks and others. bibl f il *Science* 238:1138-42 N 20 '87
Hot springs [British Columbia] E. Iglauer. *New Yorker* 63:62-9 Jl 6 '87
Large warm spot in the Pacific [megaplume discovered by Edward T. Baker] *Sci News* 132:238 O 10 '87
Megaplume, a really big undersea find [hydrothermal plume; work of Edward Baker and Gary Massoth] il map *Discover* 8:7+ F '87
Ocean hot springs similar around globe. R. A. Kerr. il *Science* 235:435 Ja 23 '87
Symbiosis in the deep sea [sulfide based ecosystem at hydrothermal vents] J. J. Childress and others. il *Sci Am* 256:114-20 My '87
Hot toddies *See* Alcoholic beverages
Hot tubs
Panels for spa privacy and for a changing room. il *Sunset* 179:102 Jl '87
Sanitation
Are there bugs in the tub? J. Venturino. il *Women's Sports Fitness* 9:17 D '87
Little tub of horrors: pools and hot tubs can make you sick. J. C. Johnson. il *Mademoiselle* 93:74 Je '87
Hot water heaters *See* Water heaters
Hot water supply
See also
Water heaters
Hot weather
See also
Droughts
Summer
Summer simmer index
The nation's hottest temperature. D. H. Hickcox. *Focus* 37:31 Summ '87
Mental and physiological effects
Heat wave. D. Starr. il *Natl Wildl* 25:22-4 Ag/S '87

Hot weather—Mental and physiological effects—*cont.*

Playing it cool: the inside story on beating the heat. G. Bakoulis. il *Work Woman* 12:120+ Je '87

Summer power: diet and exercise for hot times. J. M. Toal. il *Mademoiselle* 93:54+ Jl '87

Hotel and Restaurant Employees and Bartenders International Union *See* Hotel Employees and Restaurant Employees International Union

Hotel charges *See* Hotels, motels, etc.—Rates

Hotel decoration

　　See also

　　Art in hotels, motels, etc.

The Box Tree Hotel: Augustin Paege's opulent setting in Turtle Bay [New York City] G. Greene. il por *Archit Dig* 44:170-7 N '87

Contemporary caravansary: the Hotel Tichka in Marrakesh [decorated by Bill Willis] L. Dennis. il *Archit Dig* 44:52-9+ Ja '87

Sheet style! [sheets used in decoration at Mainstay Inn, Cape May, N.J.] S. Wood and E. Young. il *McCalls* 114:70-3+ My '87

Wyck Hill House: a country hotel in the Cotswolds. J. Lees-Milne. il *Archit Dig* 44:128-33 D '87

Hotel des Bergues (Geneva, Switzerland) *See* Geneva (Switzerland)—Hotels, motels, etc.

Hotel dining rooms *See* Restaurants

Hôtel Drouot (Paris, France)

Paris journal. C. P. Reynolds. il *Gourmet* 47:36+ O '87

Hotel Employees and Restaurant Employees International Union

Solidarity lives among hotel workers [Local 2 in San Francisco] P. Somlo. il *Progressive* 51:15 Mr '87

Hotel Grande Bretagne (Athens, Greece) *See* Athens (Greece)—Hotels, motels, etc.

Hotel Group of America

A hotel of one's own [Y. Lembi-Detert partnered with father] M. Dowie. il por *Ms* 16:38-9 D '87

Hotel Investors Trust

An off-beat REIT's alluring prospects. A. E. Serwer. il *Fortune* 115:114-15 Ap 13 '87

Hotel management

　　See also

　　Hotel Group of America

　　Women in hotel management

The butler does it [S. Bromley, manager of the Clift Hotel in San Francisco] P. Tyre. il por *N Y* 20:14 Ag 3 '87

Drawing a bead on a new dream: having helped two sons to become world-class biathletes, a couple now address their own future [Jim and Betty Schreiner to run a bed-and-breakfast business] S. Seixas. il *Money* 16:182-4 F '87

So you want to be an innkeeper . . . L. J. Gallagher. il *Esquire* 108:74 N '87

Hotel Tichka (Marrakesh, Morocco) *See* Marrakesh (Morocco)—Hotels, motels, etc.

Hotel workers

　　See also

　　Bellhops

　　Concierges

　　Hotel Employees and Restaurant Employees International Union

Hotels, motels, etc.

　　See also

　　Bed and breakfast accommodations

　　Resorts

　　Underwater hotels, motels, etc.

　　Welfare hotels

Charming country inns for a fall weekend getaway. il *Glamour* 85:318+ S '87

Hotel check list: 10 things to remember. *Glamour* 85:89 Mr '87

Travelers' respite [park hostels] T. Stroll. il *Natl Parks* 61:14-15 My/Je '87

Architecture

Climate as context [Bay Island Hotel, Port Blair, India] M. F. Schmertz. il *Archit Rec* 175:114-19 Ag '87

A slice of history [addition to Sylvia Hotel, Vancouver, B.C.] P. M. Sachner. il *Archit Rec* 175:108-11 N '87

Chain and franchise operations

　　See also

　　Days Inns Corp.

　　Hilton Hotels Corp.

　　Hilton International Co.

　　Holiday Corp.

　　Hyatt Corp.

　　Marriott Corporation

　　Ramada Inc.

　　Resorts International Inc.

　　UAL Inc.

Hey, little spender, have these motels got a deal for you. T. Ichniowski. il *Bus Week* p63 N 2 '87

Hotel and motel chains. il *Consum Rep* 52:301-5 D '87

Decoration

　　See Hotel decoration

Fires and fire prevention

Death in a towering inferno [Dupont Plaza hotel in San Juan, Puerto Rico] B. Levin. il *Macleans* 100:16-19 Ja 12 '87

In the wake of a tragic hotel fire, disaster attorneys seek compensation for the victims—and for themselves [Dupont Plaza in San Juan, Puerto Rico] J. S. Kunen. il pors *People Wkly* 27:36-8 Ja 26 '87

"A New Year we'll never forget" [Dupont Plaza, San Juan] A. Wilentz. il map *Time* 129:19-20 Ja 12 '87

San Juan's towering inferno [Dupont Plaza hotel] G. Hackett. il *Newsweek* 109:24 Ja 12 '87

Tactics to make a safe exit from a flaming hotel. T. Segal. il *Bus Week* p108 Ja 26 '87

International aspects

The hotel hit parade. W. G. Flanagan. il *Forbes* 140:218 O 5 '87

Management

　　See Hotel management

Marketing

　　See also

　　Frequent guest programs

Choice and confusion [segmentation] S. Shane. *Travel Holiday* 167:22 Mr '87

Rates

　　See also

　　Frequent guest programs

Hey, little spender, have these motels got a deal for you. T. Ichniowski. il *Bus Week* p63 N 2 '87

Lodging for less. H. Gieseking. il *Travel Holiday* 168:75-6 Ag '87

Low-cost family vacation lodgings. K. Kiefer. il *Better Homes Gard* 65:22+ Je '87

Restaurants

　　See Restaurants

Services

The executive suite goes traveling. J. Castro. il *Time* 129:55 Mr 30 '87

Fast food and fast lodging. R. Simon. il *Forbes* 139:78-9 Ja 26 '87

Lifted lexicons [dictionaries at San Francisco's Stanford Court] *Time* 129:87 Ap 6 '87

Those magicians at the desk [concierges] M. Smilgis. il *Time* 130:68 D 28 '87

Alberta

　　See also

　　Calgary (Alta.)—Hotels, motels, etc.

Arkansas

　　See also

　　Eureka Springs (Ark.)—Hotels, motels, etc.

Atlantic States

Weekend vacations [country inns] J. Cecil and M. W. Robbins. il *N Y* 20:58-64+ Ap 27 '87

Austria

　　See also

　　Vienna (Austria)—Hotels, motels, etc.

Bahamas

　　See also

　　Nassau (Bahamas)—Hotels, motels, etc.

Bermuda

The Bermuda Collection [cottage colonies] A. S. Blask. *Travel Holiday* 168:30-3 N '87

British Columbia

　　See also

　　Vancouver (B.C.)—Hotels, motels, etc.

A Canadian Christmas feast: bringing out the British [hotels offering special medieval Christmas feasts] A. Satterfield. il *Travel Holiday* 168:66-9 N '87

California

　　See also

　　San Francisco (Calif.)—Hotels, motels, etc.

Canada

　　See also

　　Delta Hotels Ltd.

Caribbean region

How to take care of business at your Caribbean retreat. E. D. Smith. *Black Enterp* 17:43 Mr '87

Florida

　　See also

　　Miami Beach (Fla.)—Hotels, motels, etc.

France

　　See also

　　Saint-Paul-de-Vence (France)—Hotels, motels, etc.

Arranging a stay in a French chateau. il *Sunset* 178:52-3 Mr '87

Hotels, motels, etc.—*cont.*

Georgia

See also

Savannah (Ga.)—Hotels, motels, etc.

Great Britain

See also

London (England)—Hotels, motels, etc.

Wyck Hill House: a country hotel in the Cotswolds. J. Lees-Milne. il *Archit Dig* 44:128-33 D '87

Greece

See also

Athens (Greece)—Hotels, motels, etc.

Illinois

See also

Chicago (Ill.)—Hotels, motels, etc.

India

See also

Port Blair (India)—Hotels, motels, etc.

Italy

See also

Como (Italy)—Hotels, motels, etc.

Taormina (Italy)—Hotels, motels, etc.

Venice (Italy)—Hotels, motels, etc.

Jamaica

Jamaica Inn: Caribbean idyll. L. M. Stewart. il *Harpers Bazaar* 120:139 My '87

Japan

See also

Hakone (Japan)—Hotels, motels, etc.

Tokyo (Japan)—Hotels, motels, etc.

Ryokan: the Japanese inn. A. M. Stinchecum. il map *Travel Holiday* 168:60-5 N '87

Mackinac Island (Mich.)

100 years later, the Grand Hotel still boasts the biggest front porch in America [owner R. D. Musser] K. Gross. il por *People Wkly* 28:80-1 Ag 3 '87

Grand cruise: Mackinac Island's Grand Hotel provides an elegant setting for a weekend on the new extended bridge Cruisers 42. D. Fales. il *Mot Boat Sail* 160:46-9+ D '87

The grandest [Grand Hotel; cover story] J. Mason. il map *Americana* 15:26-32 Jl/Ag '87

Simply Grand [Grand Hotel] M. G. Stoddard. il *Saturday Evening Post* 259:92-4 Mr '87

Mexico

Life among Mexico's ruins: ancient cities, modern inns. D. A. Thomas. il map *Travel Holiday* 167:51-5+ F '87

Morocco

See also

Marrakesh (Morocco)—Hotels, motels, etc.

New England

Joining the inn crowd. T. Mulligan. il *50 Plus* 27:44-8 Ag '87

New York (State)

See also

Bolton Landing (N.Y.)—Hotels, motels, etc.

New York (N.Y.)—Hotels, motels, etc.

New Zealand

The friendly farms of New Zealand [accommodations for tourists] il *Sunset* 178:46 Ap '87

Kiwi gothic: Grant Wood farmstays in New Zealand [farmers who invite travelers into their homes] D. P. Marshall. il map *Travel Holiday* 168:42-7 N '87

North Carolina

A ring of welcome around Asheville. il map *South Living* 22:14-15 Ag '87

Pennsylvania

Pennsylvania's inn places: Bucks County bed & breakfast. M. M. Mason. il *Travel Holiday* 168:54-9 N '87

Portugal

Portugal's manor houses [guest accommodations] C. Barrington. il map *Travel Holiday* 168:48-53 N '87

Puerto Rico

See also

San Juan (Puerto Rico)—Hotels, motels, etc.

South Carolina

See also

Charleston (S.C.)—Hotels, motels, etc.

Soviet Union

Trump lands in Red Square [proposed luxury hotels] J. Barnathan. il por *Newsweek* 110:41 Jl 20 '87

Sweden

See also

Stockholm (Sweden)—Hotels, motels, etc.

Switzerland

See also

Geneva (Switzerland)—Hotels, motels, etc.

Tennessee

See also

Memphis (Tenn.)—Hotels, motels, etc.

Washington (D.C.)

See Washington (D.C.)—Hotels, motels, etc.

Western Europe

"Welcomed at your convenience". B. Kallen. il *Forbes* 139:149+ My 4 '87

Hothouses *See* Greenhouses

Houckgeest, Gerard, ca. 1600-1661

about

The pleasure of the image. S. Sontag. il *Art Am* 75:122-31 N '87

Houghland, Kenneth

Pentecostals and NCC begin dialogue. *Christ Century* 104:87-9 Ja 28 '87

Houghton, R. A.

Terrestrial metabolism and atmospheric CO_2 concentrations. bibl il *BioScience* 37:672-8 O '87

Houghton Mifflin Co.

Collins autobio inspires sound track. S. Bolle. *Publ Wkly* 232:50 O 16 '87

HM spends $600G for book on West Pt. Class of '66 [R. Atkinson's The long gray line] *Publ Wkly* 231:37 My 8 '87

Houghton Mifflin, Brilliance collaborate on two audio lines. *Publ Wkly* 231:42+ My 8 '87

Houk, Kathe

On the road again [interview with D. Christensen] il por *Space World* X-12-288:29 D '87

Houk, Walter

Securing the Spanish Main [cover story] il map *Américas* 39:8-13+ My/Je '87

Hounds

See also

Mountain curs

The dog who came to stay [condensation] H. Borland. il *Read Dig* 130:123-30+ Je '87

First aid for hounds. L. Mueller. il *Outdoor Life* 179:40+ F '87

Hound music and a very big bear [record black bear in Arizona] F. Peters. il *Outdoor Life* 179:94-5+ My '87

The hour of the star [film] *See* Motion picture reviews—Single works

Hours of labor

See also

Flextime

Overtime

Employment, hours, and earnings data from establishment surveys. See issues of Monthly Labor Review

How can she stop working seventy-hour weeks? il *Glamour* 85:152 Mr '87

Like 60-hour weeks? Try your own business. il *Bus Week* p75 Ag 10 '87

Stealing time: the subtlest theft. *Nations Bus* 75:23 Je '87

Teachers' hours, bankers' hours? [research by Brad Chissom] G. W. Bracey. il *Phi Delta Kappan* 69:73-4 S '87

Workers shun shorter workweek [Bureau of Labor Statistics study] il *Futurist* 21:43 Ja/F '87

Japan

Why Tokyo is tinkering with the treadmill. L. Armstrong. il *Bus Week* p45+ S 28 '87

Housatonic Railroad Company

A Housatonic holiday [excursion] C. La VO. il *Travel Holiday* 168:30+ S '87

Housatonic River (Conn. and Mass.)

Sunken PCBs taint the Housatonic. J. Fahys. il *Sierra* 72:85 Jl/Ag '87

House, Amelia Blossom

Hills [poem] *Essence* 18:138 D '87

House, Christopher

about

Working with music, muscle and motion. P. Hluchy. pors *Macleans* 100:54 Mr 9 '87

House, Colin, and Kemp, Bruce E.

Protein kinase C contains a pseudosubstrate prototype in its regulatory domain. bibl f il *Science* 238:1726-8 D 18 '87

House & garden (Periodical)

The editor's page. L. Gropp. See issues of House & Garden

House & Garden Design Awards [special section] il *House Gard* 159:140-61+ O '87

Keeping up with the Joneses. J. Conant. il *Newsweek* 110:64 S 7 '87

House arrest [drama] *See* Bozzone, Bill

House building *See* House construction

House building industry *See* Construction industry

House buying

See also

House selling

House buying—See also—*cont.*

Housing—Costs
Housing finance
Insurance, Mortgage
Mortgages

Bargain for that house like a pro. il *Changing Times* 41:45-6+ My '87

Building the assets you live in [special section] il *Money* 16:70-4+ Je '87

Buying a foreclosed home. *U S News World Rep* 103:85 O 5 '87

Buying a second house in Paris [experience of B. and C. Haber] C. Styles-McLeod. il pors *Archit Dig* 44 Archit Dig Travels:10+ O '87

The great American trade-up. C. Skrzycki. il *U S News World Rep* 102:48-9 Ap 13 '87

Here's a win-win deal: buy your folks' house. G. Weiss. il *Bus Week* p110-11 Je 15 '87

Home-buying strategies. B. A. Lewis. il *Better Homes Gard* 65:132-7 Ap '87

Home economics. S. Kennedy. il *Black Enterp* 18:55-6+ O '87

If you can buy, you should. A. McGrath. il *U S News World Rep* 103:58-9 Ag 3 '87

A place in the sun [vacation homes] C. Luckey. *Changing Times* 41:14 Ap '87

Who represents the home buyer? *South Living* 22:172 My '87

Anecdotes, facetiae, satire, etc.

On buying a house. M. Jones. il *South Living* 22:138 S '87

House churches

Great Britain

Great Britain's alternative churches. G. C. Bennett. il *Christ Today* 31:56+ O 16 '87

House cleaning

Easy ways to tackle your 6 least-favorite chores. il *Good Housekeep* 204:132 My '87

Secrets of the speed cleaners [excerpts from Speed cleaning] J. Campbell. il *Redbook* 168:114-15+ Ap '87

Anecdotes, facetiae, satire, etc.

Clean for a day. G. Martin. il *Esquire* 107:40 Mr '87

House construction

See also

Houses, Prefabricated

Breaking ground [P. Noel builds his dream house] L. Brown. il por *Black Enterp* 18:76-8+ O '87

Build-it-yourself! The big-savings way into your own vacation home [special section] P. S. Gelfman. il *Fam Handyman* 37:42+ Ja '87

Choice not chance [home designed and built for Ira Friedlander by Hadi Clements] il *Mother Earth News* 106:50-3 Jl/Ag '87

Mr. Davis builds his dream house [Owner-Built Housing Program] P. Skalka. il por *Read Dig* 131:100-4 S '87

Out-island builder [Eleuthera stone house] J. B. Gans. il map *Mother Earth News* 104:48-55 Mr/Ap '87

Owner-built solar home [cover story] J. Bogart. il *Workbench* 43:20-2+ Mr/Ap '87

Professional advisor. See issues of Home Mechanix beginning July 1985

Summer reading: House, Home and Home mechanix [books by Tracy Kidder and Witold Rybczynski] J. R. Provey. il *Home Mech* 83:6 Ag '87

"We built it ourselves!". il *McCalls* 114:53-60+ F '87

Working with the pros: architect, designer/builder, contractor. G. D. Cook. il *Better Homes Gard* 65:126-31 My '87

Warranty

See Warranty

House construction industry *See* Construction industry

House decoration

See also

Antiques
Apartments
Art in the home
Bathrooms
Bedrooms
Blinds
Bowls in house decoration
Children's rooms
Chintz
Christmas decorations
Color in house decoration
Crystals in house decoration
Curtains and draperies
Dens (Rooms)
Dining alcoves, etc.
Display of antiques, art objects, etc.
Drawing rooms
Electric lamps
Family rooms
Fireplaces
Floor coverings
Flowers, Artificial
Fruits, vegetables, etc. in decoration
Guest rooms
Household furnishings
Houses, Remodeled
Interior decorators
Kitchens
Living rooms
Mantels
Mirrors
Paneling
Pictures—Hanging
Plants in house decoration
Recreation rooms
Rooms
Rugs and carpets
Screens (Furniture)
Sheets
Shelves and racks
Shutters
Slipcovers
Spa rooms
Table decoration
Textile fabrics
Upholstery
Wall coverings
Wall hangings
Wallpaper and wallpapering
Walls
Window shades
Windows

6-page portfolio of celebrity homes. M. Fiore. il *Good Housekeep* 204:94-9 Ja '87

6 quick, low-cost decorating projects. N. Cooper. il *Home Mech* 83:48-51 D '87

8-page portfolio of celebrity homes. M. Fiore. il *Good Housekeep* 205:108-15+ Ag '87

Affordable redecorating: three room redos—on a budget! D. L. Caringer and R. E. Dittmer. il *Better Homes Gard* 65:33-9 N '87

American grandeur [restoration of Georgia mansion by W. N. Banks] B. Gill. il por *House Gard* 159:112-23+ S '87

Architectural digest visits: Baron and Baroness Guy de Rothschild: the evolution of the chalet at Ferrières [decorated by François Catroux] C. Aillaud. il pors *Archit Dig* 44:208-18+ Ap '87

Architectural digest visits: Burt Bacharach and Carole Bayer Sager [Bel-Air home decorated by Waldo Fernandez] B. Gooch. il pors *Archit Dig* 44:128-33+ O '87

Architectural digest visits: Dinah Shore [Malibu beach house decorated by Val Arnold] B. D. Colen. il por *Archit Dig* 44:158-63+ D '87

As rare as a day in June [18th century stone country house owned by a fashion designer] A. Gordon. il *House Gard* 159:124-33 Je '87

Australian classic: the Robin and Peter Briggs house near Perth [decorated by Annalaura Angeletti] C. Aillaud. il por *Archit Dig* 44:116-23 F '87

Bay Area spirit. M. Schafer. il *House Gard* 159:184-9 O '87

Beacon Hill spirit [Honora Haley Hillier redecorates Beacon Hill row house] E. Greene. il *House Gard* 159:154-61 Mr '87

Bellagio House: the David Murdock estate in Bel-Air. M. M. Thomas. il por *Archit Dig* 44:52-61 F '87

Breaking boundaries. il *South Living* 22:113 D '87

Brillig on the wave: island aerie of Nancy and Henry Luce III [summer house off Connecticut shore] C. T. Buckley. il pors *Archit Dig* 44:180-3+ My '87

California crafted [architect C. Howard transforms M. Palevsky's Beverly Hills house] il *House Gard* 159:182-9 Ap '87

California in focus [F. Scarfiotti's Hollywood home decorated by B. Hayward] D. Thomson. il por *House Gard* 159:140-5+ Ag '87

Choose your own style. S. Ross. il *Fam Handyman* 37:43-6+ My/Je '87

A civilized intuition [Manhattan townhouse owned and designed by J. P. Molyneux] D. Harris. il por *Archit Dig* 44:148-55 N '87

Classical cool [M. and A. Ertegun's Manhattan town house] S. M. L. Aronson. il por *House Gard* 159:100-11+ Mr '87

The classical villa restated [D. Hicks's design for Vila Verde in Portugal] M. Hampton. il *House Gard* 159:114-23 Je '87

House decoration—*cont.*

Colors and light fixtures are the key. il *South Living* 22:176+ Ap '87

Cottage by the sea: Maria Tallchief and Henry D. Paschen on Martha's Vineyard [home decorated by Bruce Gregga] J. Allen. il *Archit Dig* 44:170-5+ O '87

Country comforts in a brand-new American barn. il *Good Housekeep* 204:126-31 Mr '87

Country goes elegant! il *Redbook* 168:69-75 F '87

Country house in town: a designer's residence on the Thames [Lindsey House, home of J. Stefanidis] E. Lambert. il por *Archit Dig* 44:110-17+ My '87

Country houses [cover story; special issue] il *Archit Dig* 44:108-208+ Je '87

Country in the capital [Mark Hampton aids in decoration of house in Kalorama section of Washington, D.C.] E. Greene. il *House Gard* 159:168-75 F '87

The country set [William Diamond revives shingle style for Westchester, N.Y. house] E. Greene. il *House Gard* 159:162-9 D '87

Country style today [excerpt from Better homes and gardens country style] R. E. Jaffin. il *Better Homes Gard* 65:58 F '87

Country with style [eighteenth century homes in Litchfield, Conn.] M. D. Glass. il *Ladies Home J* 104:136-41 O '87

A cozy Victorian cottage. il *Redbook* 168:110-15 Mr '87

Decorating. S. Wood. See issues of McCall's beginning May 1986

A decorating eye [remodeled carriage house of Kaaren Parker Gray] E. Greene. il *House Gard* 159:148-55+ Je '87

Decorating scruples [collaboration with designer J. Axelrod on California house] J. Krantz. il por *House Gard* 159:208-17+ O '87

Decoration for a dynasty [19th century Tripcovich-Banfield house redecorated by Emilio Carcano] W. Weaver. il *House Gard* 159:100-11+ F '87

Dressing up a dream house. il *McCalls* 114:54-60 F '87

Elements of country: four simple ingredients spell success! D. L. Caringer. il *Better Homes Gard* 65:109 My '87

The fine points of placement [room arrangement] M. Hampton. il *House Gard* 159:24+ Mr '87

Forever Ashley [Brussels house] H. Montgomery-Massingberd. il *House Gard* 159:158-65+ S '87

A fresh new look. M. D. Glass. il *Ladies Home J* 104:104-9 My '87

Gentleman's quarters: James Rogers' Beaux-Arts townhouse in Manhattan [decorated by Keith Irvine] J. Taylor. il *Archit Dig* 44:76-83 F '87

Givenchy grandeur [Paris home] J. Richardson. il *House Gard* 159:218-30 Ap '87

Graceful details: classical lines in a designer's Los Angeles villa [L. Cataffo] H. Drohojowska. il *Archit Dig* 44:66-71 Ag '87

House's style is their own [Wilson, N.C. house] E. Wood. il *South Living* 22:144-6 My '87

How could you paint your bedroom red? [out-of-the-ordinary decorating] M. D. Glass. il *Ladies Home J* 104:124-7 Ap '87

Ideas to bring home [decorating a manufactured house] il *Redbook* 169:132-7 O '87

In the light of the Bay [M. Taylor decorates Wilsey house in San Francisco] L. H. Bucklin. il por *House Gard* 159:124-33+ S '87

Laurie Mallet's walls may not have ears, but they do have chairs, tables, boots and an overcoat. il por *People Wkly* 28:123-5 Jl 6 '87

Let nature help you decorate. C. Engle. il *South Living* 22:170 Mr '87

The most romantic house in Hollywood [Jane Seymour's house] M. Fiore. il *Good Housekeep* 204:120-3 F '87

New finishes for a dramatic change. il *South Living* 22:180 My '87

A new look American home. S. Wood and E. Young. il *McCalls* 114:38-41 Jl '87

On Riverside Drive [townhouse designed by D. Laurance] M. M. Thomas. il por *Archit Dig* 44:156-63 N '87

Opposite attractions [J. Levin's Bel-Air house decorated by Donna Livingston] L. Bernikow. il *Archit Dig* 44:176-81 O '87

Piece-by-piece decorating. D. L. Caringer and R. E. Dittmer. il *Better Homes Gard* 65:74-9 Je '87

Playing to a full house [guest cottage in Connecticut decorated by B. Blass] C. Vogel. il *N Y Times Mag* p51-3 Ag 9 '87

Portrait of a lady [Mary Ann Tsao residence] D. Brenner. il *Archit Rec* 175:156-61 mid-S '87

The quality of white. M. Hampton. il *House Gard* 159:44+ Jl '87

Rare and early [antique furniture collected by A. Csaky] E. Greene. il *House Gard* 159:162-7+ N '87

Reader of the year: decorating. il *McCalls* 115:50+ O '87

Reinaldo and Carolina Herrera in Manhattan [brownstone decorated by Robert Metzger] C. T. Buckley. il pors *Archit Dig* 44:128-35+ Ap '87

Ruffles and flourishes. M. D. Glass. il *Ladies Home J* 104:114-18 Mr '87

Second nature [Ron Mann decorates Napa Valley vacation home] M. Schafer. il *House Gard* 159:156-61 Jl '87

Social graces in Georgetown: Polly and Clayton Fritchey's Victorian enclave. S. M. Alsop. il pors *Archit Dig* 44:188-91 O '87

Still-life decorating [views of S. Scull] J. R. Provey. il por *Home Mech* 83:66-7 Ja '87

Style of a lifetime [M. V. Hoffman's Georgetown house] M. McDougall. il *House Gard* 159:178-83+ Mr '87

A subtle palette [A. Julian's Connecticut home] E. Greene. il por *House Gard* 159:122-9+ F '87

Summer coolers. il *Glamour* 85:306-8+ My '87

A tale of two brownstones: the New York residence of Annabel and Mike Nichols [decorated by Rendell Fernandez] A. Nichols. il *Archit Dig* 44:96-101+ F '87

Texas formality [contemporary Houston home decorated by Steve Chase] M. Ennis. il *Archit Dig* 44:170-5 Ap '87

A tower in Tuscany [home of G. and B. von Rezzori] B. Chatwin. il *House Gard* 159:78-85+ Ja '87

Traditional comforts on the Sound: a welcoming Connecticut residence [decorated by Arthur E. Smith] L. Bernikow. il *Archit Dig* 44:70-5 F '87

Virtues of nuance [Dallas home decorated by K. Alaton] M. Ennis. il *Archit Dig* 44:62-9 F '87

A visit to the Carters' home in Plains, Georgia. C. Varney. il pors *Good Housekeep* 204:110-13+ Je '87

A welcoming home [excerpt from Laura Ashley style] I. Gale and S. Irvine. il *Redbook* 170:83-9 N '87

Welsh comfort [Cruglas, ancestral home of the Lisburnes] D. Briers. il *House Gard* 159:112-19+ Ag '87

What's new for American families in '87. il *Better Homes Gard* 65:20 Ja '87

Your place: what's new, neat, worth a try. See issues of Glamour beginning June 1985

Exhibitions

In the Baldwin tradition [exhibition at Luten Clarey Stern showroom] C. Vogel. il por *N Y Times Mag* p89-91 My 3 '87

Periodicals

See also

House & garden (Periodical)

Keeping up with the Joneses. J. Conant. il *Newsweek* 110:64 S 7 '87

House decoration, American

See also

Furniture, American

American heritage: Yankee art, western vistas [home of E. and L. Lauder] F. Stanfill. il pors *Vogue* 177:340-7+ Ap '87

American primitive. il *Fam Handyman* 37:58-61 My/Je '87

Colonial contours: traditional lines for a Connecticut farmhouse [decorated by Thomas Britt] C. D. B. Bryan. il *Archit Dig* 44:102-7 Jl '87

The country life [three historic farmhouses] il *Redbook* 169:191-6 S '87

Lessons in simplicity [work of H. Partello-Hollingsworth] C. D. B. Bryan. il por *Archit Dig* 44:92+ O '87

Out of the woods [East Hampton house built and decorated by Noel Jeffrey] S. Slesin. il *N Y Times Mag* p58-9 Jl 19 '87

Rejuvenating a Connecticut parsonage: a designer's Litchfield County colonial [home of H. Partello-Hollingsworth] R. Conniff. il *Archit Dig* 44:108-17+ Je '87

A road less traveled: New York country haven of Marilynn and Ivan Karp. J. Kornbluth. il *Archit Dig* 44:196-203+ Je '87

Southwest rhythms: restoring a Sante Fe adobe [home of M. Mahaffey] L. Bernikow. il por *Archit Dig* 44:130-5 F '87

House decoration, Chinese

Images of contemporary China. I. M. Elliott. il por *Archit Dig* 44:166+ Ja '87

House decoration, Colonial and early American *See* House decoration, American

House decoration, English

50 rooms with a view [Holker Hall, estate of G. and H. Cavendish] R. Billington. il pors *Vogue* 177:314-21+ My '87

Back country Greenwich [English decoration by S. Parish for H. De Kwiatkowski] S. M. L. Aronson. il *House Gard* 159:132-9+ Ag '87

English country. il *Fam Handyman* 37:44-6+ My/Je '87

An English import: country style for a Tudor revival house in Maryland [home of Lawrence and Judith Burman, decorated by Anthony P. Browne] S. M. Alsop. il *Archit Dig* 44:184-7+ My '87

English transfer [decoration of Manhattan apartment by C. Cleaver] T. Brown. il *House Gard* 159:196-203 N '87

For ever England [H. Nye's Manhattan duplex] E. Greene. il por *House Gard* 159:198-203 My '87

From old England to New England. J. Richardson. il *House Gard* 159:214-21+ My '87

A living scrapbook [M. Buatta's rendition of English country style in apartment designed for Cathy Hardwick] C. Vogel. il *N Y Times Mag* p34-7 S 6 '87

A mix of two country styles. L. Joyner. il *South Living* 22:112-13 Jl '87

Partners with the past: Lady Anne and Michael Tree at Shute House. A. Tree. il *Archit Dig* 44:168-73 Je '87

A style of one's own: a new home furnishings collection inspired by the work of the Bloomsbury group. B. Plumb. il *Vogue* 177:278 F '87

To the manor reborn [Heydon Hall renovated by David Mlinaric] C. Vogel. il *N Y Times Mag* p80-4 N 22 '87

House decoration, Exterior

See also

Christmas decorations, Outdoor

House decoration, Finnish

A dacha in Finland [Honkala, summer home of the Gullichsen family; excerpt from Scandinavia] E. Gaynor. il *House Gard* 159:86-93+ Ag '87

House decoration, French

Allure in the grand manner [J. T. de la Chaume's French-style apartment in Manhattan] J. Kornbluth. il por *House Gard* 159:152-9+ D '87

Fabulous fakery [R. L. Neas uses trompe l'oeil to create French atmosphere in Long Island cottage] E. Greene. il *House Gard* 159:134-43 S '87

A formal balance: cosmopolitan influences in a Toronto setting [home of George and Saundra Mann decorated by Robert Dirstein] D. Lasker. il *Archit Dig* 44:90-5 F '87

Setting the stage: Baroness Philippine de Rothschild in Paris. C. Aillaud. il por *Archit Dig* 44:98-101 Ag '87

House decoration, Georgian

Sound choice: a Georgian revival estate on Long Island's North Shore [decorated by Georgina Fairholme] J. Kornbluth. il *Archit Dig* 44:190-5 Mr '87

House decoration, Gothic revival

The Gothic revival library at the Metropolitan Museum of Art. A. Peck. il *Antiques* 131:824-7 Ap '87

A Gothic tale [L. B. Anderson's New York townhouse] E. Lebow. il *House Gard* 159:190-7+ My '87

Of time and place [Gothic revival library in the Metropolitan Museum of Art] C. Vogel. il *N Y Times Mag* p50-1 F 15 '87

House decoration, International

A Vienna success [R. S. and J. C. Lauder decorate ambassador's residence] T. Lessing. il por *House Gard* 159:100-5+ Jl '87

House decoration, Italian

A charmed life [Palazzo Frescobaldi in Florence] G. Y. Dryansky. il *Vogue* 177:446-53+ O '87

The cool retreat in Venice [home of L. Biagiotti] il por *Vogue* 177:766-73 S '87

Dressing dreams: costumier Umberto Tirelli's residences in Rome and Capri. C. Aillaud. il por *Archit Dig* 44:140-5 O '87

Paean to glamour: dramatic formality for an Italianate villa in Beverly Hills [decorated by Illya Hendrix and Thomas Allardyce] J. Gruen. il *Archit Dig* 44:102-7 S '87

Traces of the future's past: Nicola Trussardi's palazzo in Bergamo. G. Y. Dryansky. il por *Archit Dig* 44:152-9 My '87

Tranquilla: an Italianate palazzo on Biscayne Bay [home of C. and M. Candib, decorated by Valerian S. Rybar and Jean-François Daigré; cover story] J. Taylor. il pors *Archit Dig* 44:148-55 Ap '87

House decoration, Jamaican

Jamaican cadence: Rose Marie Bogley's cottage above Montego Bay. J. S. Wamsley. il *Archit Dig* 44:202-7 My '87

House decoration, Japanese

Japanese style. S. Slesin. il *N Y Times Mag* p54-6 Ag 2 '87

Pacific orientation [Lapham house in Pebble Beach, Calif.] M. Schafer. il por *House Gard* 159:160-5+ My '87

Reorienting a classic: inventive decor for a Lloyd Wright house [Los Angeles home of designer M. London; cover story] P. Goldberger. il por *Archit Dig* 44:108-15 Mr '87

House decoration, Mexican

Custom of the country [P. Glenville's house in San Miguel de Allende] J. Richardson. il por *House Gard* 159:146-56 Ag '87

House decoration, Oriental

International style: Oriental touch for Mexico City [interior design by Jay Spectre] P. Warner. il *Archit Dig* 44:84-91 Jl '87

Orientalist opulence in Belgravia: the London residence of Princess Firyal of Jordan [decorated by R. Mongiardino] G. Y. Dryansky. il *Archit Dig* 44:216-20 My '87

House decoration, Portuguese

Courting pleasure in Portugal [C. Pereira, owner of Azinhal estate] il *Vogue* 177:488-95 Mr '87

House decoration, Renaissance revival

On Russian Hill: transforming a 1920s San Francisco residence [decorated by Robert Hutchinson] J. D. Houston. il *Archit Dig* 44:116-21 S '87

House decoration, Scandinavian

Scandinavian country. il *Fam Handyman* 37:50+ My/Je '87

House decoration, Spanish American

Casa de las Mil Flores: Harold and Matilda Stream in Guatemala. C. T. Buckley. il *Archit Dig* 44:108-15 Ag '87

House decoration, Victorian

A clearing-house for Victorian crafts [Artistic License craft guild; cover story] N. R. Day. il *Americana* 15:36-41 Mr/Ap '87

House Democratic Caucus (U.S.)

Bill Gray can't lose in the budget battle. D. Harbrecht. il por *Bus Week* p25-6 S 7 '87

Gray likely appointed to powerful post in Congress. por *Jet* 72:17 Ag 17 '87

House drainage

Downspouts and gutters: how to keep them in good repair. il *Better Homes Gard* 65:114 Ap '87

A drainage problem becomes an asset [manmade creek and drainage swale] il *South Living* 22:96 My '87

Gutters and downspouts] J. Vara. il *Ctry J* 14:19-20 Je '87

How to install vinyl gutters. J. Truini. il *Pop Mech* 164:131-4 Mr '87

In the gutter. C. Goosen. il *Mother Earth News* 108:118-19 N/D '87

Plastic gutters. G. Branson. il *Fam Handyman* 37:50 F '87

House expansion *See* Houses, Remodeled

House guests *See* Guests

House husbands *See* Homemakers

House inspection *See* Building inspection

House insulation *See* Insulation (Heat)

House lighting *See* Lighting

House models

See also

Doll houses

Make a model before you build. J. Glattstein. il *Home Mech* 83:48 Jl '87

House museums *See* Historic houses, sites, etc.

House of Assembly (South Africa) *See* South Africa. Parliament. House of Assembly

House of Commons (Canada) *See* Canada. Parliament. House of Commons

House of Commons (Great Britain) *See* Great Britain. Parliament. House of Commons

House of games [film] *See* Motion picture reviews—Single works

House of Hermès (Firm)

Hermès. C. P. Reynolds. il *Gourmet* 47:42-7+ F '87

House of Lords (Great Britain) *See* Great Britain. Parliament. House of Lords

House of Pennathur (Firm)

Shamianas, anyone? P. Gupte. il pors *Forbes* 140:190+ O 5 '87

House of Representatives (U.S.) *See* United States. Congress. House

House of Rothschild

about

The movie version [insider information as handled in movie The House of Rothschild] D. Seligman. il *Fortune* 115:27-8 F 16 '87

House organs

Anecdotes, facetiae, satire, etc.

Mr. Curmudgeon's company news. K. Fury. il *Work Woman* 12:120 Ja '87

House paint *See* Paint

House painting

Both house and door get full-toned premium color. S. Ross. il *Fam Handyman* 37:34-6 Ap '87

Exterior paint: problems and cures. il *Consum Res Mag* 70:29-33 Ag '87

Four steps to a good paint job. *Consum Rep* 52:366 Je '87

Get along, old paint. A. McGrath. *U S News World Rep* 103:69 Ag 17 '87

Paint problems. B. Vila. il *Pop Mech* 164:16+ Ap '87

Painting tips from the White House. B. Kneemiller. il *Workbench* 43:88-90 Mr/Ap '87

The possibilities of paint. M. Schultz. il *Good Housekeep* 204:193-5+ Ap '87

Special effects: how to use paint to create eye-catching, inexpensive home furnishings. S. Wood. il *Home Mech* 83:44-50 Ja '87

What you really need to know about house paint and painting. il *Sunset* 179:80-6 S '87

Whole house painting manual. G. Branson. il *Fam Handyman* 37:29-32+ Mr '87

House plans *See* Architecture, Domestic—Designs and plans

House plants

See also

Aspidistra

Begonias

Christmas cactus

Ferns

Garden rooms

Gloxinias

Hanging plants

Orchids

Plants in house decoration

Schefflera

5 hardy houseplants for winter. il *Glamour* 85:47 Ja '87

Deck your halls with houseplants. E. Henke. il *Saturday Evening Post* 259:84-5+ D '87

Don't leave houseplants in the cold. il *South Living* 22:55 F '87

Easy maintenance house plants. G. Taloumis. il *Flower Gard* 31:40-2 O/N '87

The five best bloomers. J. Rapp. il *Redbook* 169:72-3+ Ag '87

Flowers all winter long. T. James. il *Ladies Home J* 104:92+ N '87

Good news about houseplants. L. B. Trigg. il *South Living* 22:42-4 Ja '87

The hottest houseplants. K. Wilson. il *Rodale's Org Gard* 34:68+ D '87

Houseplants. L. M. O'Boyle. il *Mother Earth News* 108:56-9 N/D '87

Houseplants with child appeal. L. J. Brown. il *Good Housekeep* 205:253 O '87

January's blossoms [flowering houseplants] T. Martin. il *Ctry J* 14:39-44 Ja '87

Plants from the table [indoor fruit and nut trees] J. Rapp. il *Redbook* 168:102-5 F '87

Anecdotes, facetiae, satire, etc.

My life in a greenhouse. M. G. Stoddard. il *Saturday Evening Post* 259:64-5 N '87

Training

See Plants—Training

House prices *See* Housing—Costs

House protection

See also

Alarms

Burglary protection

House purchasing *See* House buying

House selling

25 quick fix-ups that help sell a house. P. S. Gelfman. il *Fam Handyman* 37:77-80 Ap '87

Building the assets you live in [special section] il *Money* 16:70-4+ Je '87

How to sell your home yourself. M. Hodge and J. Blyskal. il *Read Dig* 130:89-93 Mr '87

Money trees [landscaping enhances property values; views of Duane Durgee] il *USA Today (Periodical)* 116:7-8 D '87

Sell-it-yourself takes work but saves thousands. H. Porter. *Fam Handyman* 37:20+ Ap '87

Selling a house? The IRS is watching. il *Consum Rep* 52:508-9 Ag '87

Signs of the times—sale by owner. J. A. Seamonds. il *U S News World Rep* 102:43 Je 29 '87

Trade down without tripping up [avoiding taxation on house sale profits] K. McCormally. il *Changing Times* 41:20 O '87

House sparrows *See* Sparrows

House to house selling *See* Door-to-door selling

House ventilation *See* Ventilation

House wiring *See* Electric wire and wiring

Housecleaning *See* House cleaning

Houseflies

Control

Another way to get rid of houseflies? It's biological [use of parasitic wasps] il *Sunset* 178:204-5 Je '87

Household accidents *See* Accidents

Household animals *See* Domestic animals

Household appliances

See also

Clothes dryers

Dishwashers

Freezers

Household appliances industry

Irons

Kitchen utensils and appliances

Vacuum cleaners

Washing machines

"Labor saving" means more work. R. S. Cowan. il *Read Dig* 131:181-4 D '87

Less work for mother? R. S. Cowan. il *Am Herit* 38:68-70+ S/O '87

Anecdotes, facetiae, satire, etc.

The good old days [technology taking over household appliances] L. W. Strick. il *Good Housekeep* 205:82+ Ag '87

Control

Home appliances [need for home-bus standard] A. Kleiman. il *Radio-Electron* 58:12 Ja '87

Energy usage

Buy your next appliance from your utility and you may just get a rebate! H. Porter. *Fam Handyman* 37:8 N '87

Inefficient at best [with reply by B. Gants] D. Bandow. il *Consum Res Mag* 70:14-17 My '87

Life-cycle costing. T. Sahagian. il *Workbench* 43:17 Jl/Ag '87

Maintenance and repair

Appliance clinic. S. Toth. See issues of Popular Mechanics

Appliance repair [questions and answers] C. Maxwell. See issues of The Family Handyman beginning February 1985

How to take care of what you own. R. Hager. il *Ladies Home J* 104:67-8+ F '87

Safety devices and measures

Are your appliances safe? T. Sahagian. il *Home Mech* 83:70-3 Ag '87

Household appliances industry

See also

Magic Chef, Inc.

Maytag Co.

Newell Co.

Rubbermaid Incorporated

Townecraft (Firm)

Welbilt Corp.

Acquisitions and mergers

Maytag's new girth will test its marketing muscle [Magic Chef acquisition] K. Deveny. il *Bus Week* p68+ F 16 '87

International aspects

On the verge of a world war in white goods. Z. Schiller and J. Kapstein. il *Bus Week* p91+ N 2 '87

Directories

Where to buy appliance parts. C. Maxwell. See issues of The Family Handyman beginning February 1986

Finance

Consumer products. R. Koselka. il *Forbes* 139:114-15 Ja 12 '87

Quality control

Appliance repairmen are getting lonelier. Z. Schiller. il *Bus Week* p139-40 Je 8 '87

Household budget *See* Budget, Household

Household chemical disposal *See* Hazardous substances—Disposal

Household chores, Children's *See* Children's chores

Household cleaning preparations *See* Cleaning compositions

Household employees

See also

Butlers

White House (Washington, D.C.)—Employees

Household employees—*cont.*
Beyond baby-sitting: an au pair primer. S. Johnson. il *Work Woman* 12:49-50 Ag '87
Now that illegal aliens are out, au pairs are in. D. B. Moskowitz. il *Bus Week* p148 Ja 12 '87
South Africa
Useful Zulu phrases [managing servants in South Africa] L. Freed. il *Harpers* 274:26-8 My '87
Household energy conservation *See* Energy conservation
Household environment allergy *See* Allergy
Household Finance Corporation *See* Household International, Inc.
Household furnishings
   See also
    Christmas gifts for the home
    Electric lamps
    Mirrors
    Packing of household furnishings
100 ideas under $100. S. Coulter. il *Better Homes Gard* 65:63-90+ Jl '87
Finishing touches: decorating with favorite accessories. D. L. Caringer and R. E. Dittmer. il *Better Homes Gard* 65:119-27 Ap '87
Instant decorating. D. L. Caringer and R. E. Dittmer. il *Better Homes Gard* 65:108-15+ Mr '87
Post office incorporated into design [window with mailboxes and collection organizer] il *South Living* 22:188 Ap '87
Collectors and collecting
Wright's furnishings [F. L. Wright] F. Donegan. il *Americana* 15:16+ My/Je '87
Design
Designer cheek [New York City shops] J. Dolce. il *Harpers Bazaar* 120:210+ Mr '87
Going public [J. Spectre] C. Vogel. il por *N Y Times Mag* p64-5 Mr 22 '87
Household furnishings, Moving of *See* Moving
Household furnishings industry
Acquisitions and mergers
Still expanding [Newell Co. acquisition of Anchor Hocking] A. A. Lappen. il *Forbes* 140:8 O 19 '87
Finance
Consumer products. R. Koselka. il *Forbes* 139:114-15 Ja 12 '87
Marketing
   See also
    Home improvement centers
Household International, Inc.
Happy ending. S. B. Weiner. il *Forbes* 140:73 Ag 10 '87
Household inventories *See* Household records
Household management *See* Home economics
Household mechanics *See* Houses—Maintenance and repair
Household pest control
   See also
    Termites—Control
Household pests
   See also
    Fleas
Household purchasing *See* Purchasing, Household
Household records
Insured success [videotape inventory] R. Hammond. il *Pop Photogr* 94:66-7 Ag '87
Keeping important papers. *Essence* 18:112 N '87
Household timers *See* Timing devices
Househusbands *See* Homemakers
Housekeeping *See* Home economics
Housekeeping [film] See Motion picture reviews—Single works
Houses
   See also
    Architecture, Domestic
    City houses
    Condominiums
    Cottages
    Doll houses
    Farmhouses
    Guest houses
    Home ownership
    Log cabins, houses, etc.
    Plastic houses
    Pool houses
    Ranch houses
    Stone houses
    Storage in the home
    Two family houses
    Vacation houses
Hidden wonders of your house [condensed from The secret house] D. Bodanis. *Read Dig* 130:126-8 F '87

They say a man's home is his castle, but David Bodanis' Secret house reveals the creepy truth. il pors *People Wkly* 27:133-5 Ap 20 '87
Air pollution
See Air pollution
Automation
See Computers—Home use
Cooling
See Cooling
Environmental engineering
See Environmental engineering (Buildings)
Finance
See Housing finance
Fires and fire prevention
After the smoke clears. D. Moreau. il *Changing Times* 41:65-70 F '87
Make your plans now toward home fire safety. A. W. Lees. *Pop Sci* 230:78 My '87
Where there's a will: from anger to action [M. Jackson-Randolph's life after losing her children in a fire] B. M. Campbell. il pors *Essence* 18:57-8+ D '87
Leasing and renting
Here's a win-win deal: buy your folks' house. G. Weiss. il *Bus Week* p110-11 Je 15 '87
Tenants, anyone? E. Schnurr. il *Work Woman* 12:167+ N '87
Maintenance and repair
   See also
    Insulation (Heat)
    Plumbing
    Waterproofing
25 quick fix-ups that help sell a house. P. S. Gelfman. il *Fam Handyman* 37:77-80 Ap '87
Around the house. See issues of Southern Living
Ask Handyman. G. Branson. See isssues of The Family Handyman beginning January 1987
Good housekeeping's American home improvement guide '87 [special section] il *Good Housekeep* 204:187-8+ Ap '87
Handy hints. See issues of The Family Handyman
Home & shop improvements. M. Thompson. See issues of The Family Handyman beginning September 1986
Home improvement guide [special section] il *Pop Mech* 164:109-14+ Ap '87
Home mechanix picks: 14 great home products. il *Home Mech* 83:10+ Ag '87
Home Q&A. J. Gaynor. See issues of Home Mechanix beginning January 1985
Homeowners' clinic. N. Becker. See issues of Popular Mechanics beginning June 1984
The housesmith. J. Vara. See issues of Country Journal beginning October 1986
Housewrighting without headaches. B. Purlin. il *Mother Earth News* 106:66-9 Jl/Ag '87
Improve your home [special section] il *Pop Sci* 231:75-86+ S '87
Old house restoration. B. Vila. See issues of Popular Mechanics beginning May 1986
Products. il *Workbench* 43:38-9 Jl/Ag '87
Projects and products for spring spruce-ups [special section] il *Pop Sci* 230:59-74+ Ap '87
Tips, tools, and techniques. See occasional issues of Better Homes and Gardens
What's new in home improvement. S. Ashley. See issues of Popular Science beginning May 1986
Whole house repair manual [cover story; special section] G. Branson. il *Fam Handyman* 37:64+ O '87
Whole house repair manual [special section] G. Branson. il *Fam Handyman* 37:49-50+ F '87
Whole house repair manual [special section] G. Branson. il *Fam Handyman* 37:79-80+ My/Je '87
Workbench solver. See issues of Workbench beginning May/June 1987
Your home: like it or not, every house is a fixer-upper. il *Money* 16:36 Ap '87
Models
See House models
Prices
See Housing—Costs
Radon pollution
See Radon pollution
Ventilation
See Ventilation
Warranty
See Warranty
Houses, Earth sheltered
Earth sheltered: blending with nature on the Costa Brava [home designed by F. J. Barba] N. Shrady. il *Archit Dig* 44:90-5 Ja '87
Underground oaks. D. Schoonmaker. il *Mother Earth News* 108:24 N/D '87

Houses, Foam plastic *See* Plastic houses
Houses, Historic *See* Historic houses, sites, etc.
Houses, Lakeside *See* Lakeside architecture
Houses, Miniature *See* House models
Houses, Model *See* Model houses

Houses, Octagonal

Cushmans: a house built to overlook the ocean [Hat Island, Wash.] P. S. Gelfman. il *Fam Handyman* 37:45 Ja '87

Orson Fowler: foursquare pioneer in the progressive tradition. J. Gustaitis. il *Am Hist Illus* 21:44-5 Ja '87

Houses, Prefabricated

A buyer-manufacturer partnership [precut from Miles Homes] R. Barnhart. il *Home Mech* 83:26-7 My '87

The disposable home: here today, junk tomorrow. E. S. Cornish. il *Futurist* 21:2+ S/O '87

Ideas to bring home [decorating a manufactured house] il *Redbook* 169:132-7 O '87

Mailing away for a house. L. J. Gallagher. il *Esquire* 108:84 S '87

Material advantages [Deck House post-and-beam panelized construction system] R. Barnhart. il *Home Mech* 83:54-5 Mr '87

The pre-fab alternative. *Black Enterp* 18:80 O '87

Two-story colonial in 30 days! [Penn Lyons home] R. Barnhart. il *Home Mech* 83:64-5 O '87

Houses, Remodeled

Addition settles into the garden [Richmond, Va. house] il *South Living* 22:166 Mr '87

Adobe blowup [Ron Robles remodels Santa Fe house] G. Winkel. il *House Gard* 159:122-5 Ja '87

American Wood Council 1986 Remodeling Awards. il *Archit Rec* 175:56-7 Ap '87

Before remodeling, they dug back into the house's roots [Craftsman era house in Piedmont, Calif.] il *Sunset* 179:118+ O '87

Blue Ridge variation: augmenting a house in the Virginia horse country [Queen Anne farmhouse addition by O'Neil & Manion] J. S. Wamsley. il *Archit Dig* 44:176-9 Ap '87

Building a barn house [home of John Eusden] B. Trebilcock. il *Ctry J* 14:38-9 Mr '87

Building on the past [remodeled Provençal farmhouse of C. Confino-Addor] C. de Liagre. il *House Gard* 159:124-31+ Ag '87

Can you tell where they added a second story? il *Sunset* 178:110 Je '87

The ceiling now goes from 8 to 18 feet. il *Sunset* 179:95 S '87

Cottage charm in Florida. il *South Living* 22:112 Je '87

Creating a dream home. L. Gite. il *Black Enterp* 18:66-8+ O '87

Down with three walls, up with a glass roof. il *Sunset* 178:146 Ap '87

Every inch counts in this under-the-old-house addition. il *Sunset* 178:158+ Ap '87

For more light and drama, they "bashed" through the ceiling. il *Sunset* 179:88-9 Jl '87

Front entry bump-out. il *Better Homes Gard* 65:40 Ap '87

Gallery and river room add views [Jacksonville, Fla. house] C. Engle. il *South Living* 22:82-4 Ja '87

Gallery improves traffic flow. il *South Living* 22:152-3 My '87

Good housekeeping's American home improvement guide '87 [special section] il *Good Housekeep* 204:187-8+ Ap '87

Greenery and a weeping wall in the middle of their house. il *Sunset* 178:168 Ap '87

Hamptons homestead: the D. Ronald Daniels' converted barn. D. Harris. il *Archit Dig* 44:158-63 Je '87

Home for a new generation. E. Wood. il *South Living* 22:132+ F '87

Home improvement contest winners. il *Better Homes Gard* 65:129-41 N '87

Home improvements that are money in the bank. M. C. Thomsett. il *Home Mech* 83:44-6 Ag '87

House conversion reaps cash rewards [rental apartment] H. Porter. *Fam Handyman* 37:18+ My/Je '87

In the shadow of Clarendon House [living in converted stables] B. Neil. il por *House Gard* 159:230-8 N '87

Informal living inside and out [Florida house] il *South Living* 22:127 Jl '87

Instead of a too-hot greenhouse, three levels of living space. il *Sunset* 178:130 My '87

Keeping home expense records for the tax man. T. Tilling. *Parents* 62:52 Jl '87

Local real estate agent best bet for rating dollar value of home improvements. H. Porter. *Fam Handyman* 37:12+ S '87

The makeover: when it pays to remodel. D. Harris. il *Money* 16:93-4+ Je '87

Making home fix-up pay [reducing taxable profit on home sale] L. Wiener. il *U S News World Rep* 103:53 Jl 13 '87

A masterful makeover [Connecticut house] il *Ladies Home J* 104:142-9 N '87

Metal tie rods opened up this ranch house. il *Sunset* 178:144 My '87

Mews of the day [converted stable in Knightsbridge, London by John Stefanidis] J. Brittain. il *House Gard* 159:226-9 N '87

Mistaken identity [converted carriage house of W. Hodgins in Manchester, Mass.] C. Vogel. il *N Y Times Mag* p36-40 Ag 23 '87

New third story and three decks take 36 years off its age. il *Sunset* 178:116+ Je '87

Next-door neighbors stay put and remodel [Souter and Collins families] B. A. Lewis. il *Better Homes Gard* 65:65-9 Je '87

Old house restoration. B. Vila. See issues of Popular Mechanics beginning May 1986

Old World white [W. Hodgin's remodeled carriage house in Manchester-by-the-Sea, Mass.] E. Greene. il *House Gard* 159:94-9 Ja '87

Part and parcel [former chauffeur's barn at Conyer's Manor, Greenwich, Conn.] C. Vogel. il *N Y Times Mag* p58-60 Ap 19 '87

Passive solar: add the space you want and save energy, too! G. G. Butler. il *Better Homes Gard* 65:116-19 Mr '87

Planning begins with professional help. *South Living* 22:118-19 Je '87

Professional advisor. See issues of Home Mechanix beginning July 1985

Pure Nantucket [H. N. Jacobsen remodels E. Voorhees' 1757 house in Nantucket] J. Chancellor. il *House Gard* 159:78-85+ Ag '87

Raise high the ranch roof. A. W. Lees. il *Pop Sci* 231:66-9+ Jl '87

Reach for the sun. T. O. Bakke. il *Pop Sci* 230:76-9+ Je '87

Remodel an A-frame? It's a challenge; Another A-frame answer: built-ins and plaster. il *Sunset* 178:108-9 Mr '87

Remodeling to muffle the sound of the San Diego Freeway. il *Sunset* 179:94+ Jl '87

The renovation rage in Canadian homes. M. Gray. il *Macleans* 100:42-3 N 2 '87

Roof-to-rafter openness inside a small 1920s house. il *Sunset* 178:132 Ap '87

Same house, new face [Winter Park, Fla.] il *South Living* 22:208-9 N '87

A separate space [creating an apartment in your home] R. Barnhart. il *Home Mech* 83:38-42 Ja '87

Start-to-finish room addition. G. D. Cook. il *Better Homes Gard* 65:43-7 Ap '87

Stretching back gave them a master suite and big, sheltered deck. il *Sunset* 179:104-5 Jl '87

Sutherland's folly [remodeling of Hollywood house] D. Sutherland. il por *House Gard* 159:184-9+ Je '87

Sylvan cider mill: Jean and Harcourt Amory's Westchester Hills restoration. S. M. L. Aronson. il *Archit Dig* 44:204-8+ Je '87

A tale of two brownstones: the New York residence of Annabel and Mike Nichols [decorated by Rendell Fernandez] A. Nichols. il *Archit Dig* 44:96-101+ F '87

They cut into the roof for a new top-floor bedroom. il *Sunset* 178:102 F '87

They pushed out the back, linked indoors to a wide deck [Berkeley bungalow] il *Sunset* 179:101 Jl '87

They put the skeleton on the outside. il *Sunset* 179:98-9 Ag '87

Turning toward the water [ranch-style house on Lake Madeline] E. Wood. il *South Living* 22:66-8 Jl '87

Two ways to build a back room. A. W. Lees. il *Pop Sci* 231:103-7 N '87

Whole house remodeling: room by room: what we did, what it cost. B. A. Lewis. il *Better Homes Gard* 65:117-25 My '87

With two add-ons, the owners can enjoy the view. il *Sunset* 179:157 N '87

Working with the pros: architect, designer/builder, contractor. G. D. Cook. il *Better Homes Gard* 65:126-31 My '87

Houses, Remodeled—*cont.*
Anecdotes, facetiae, satire, etc.
From the editor [failed home improvement projects] G. Havens. *Fam Handyman* 37:2 F '87
Houses, Restored
See also
Historic houses, sites, etc.
Finding materials for a restoration [interview with P. Poore] S. Romeo. il por *Home Mech* 83:22+ Je '87
Homes: an artless Victorian makes a perfect refuge [Long Island summer home of Chuck and Martha Baker] M. Bethany. il *N Y* 20:84-8 Je 29-Jl 6 '87
Rejuvenating a Connecticut parsonage: a designer's Litchfield County colonial [home of H. Partello-Hollingsworth] R. Conniff. il *Archit Dig* 44:108-17+ Je '87
Renovation: one woman's story. il *Glamour* 85:286-8 Ag '87
Under thin disguise: an 18th-century original [home of Patty Person Taylor restored by Michael and Donna Goswick] E. Wood. il *South Living* 22:204+ N '87
Houses, Rotating
The house that turns to the sun [Il Girasole, built in the 1930s by A. Invernizzi] T. Williams. il *House Gard* 159:150-7+ F '87
Houses, Round
People who live in globe houses [project designed by Dries Kreijkamp in the Netherlands] il *Pop Mech* 164:79 Jl '87
Houses, Seashore *See* Beach architecture
Houses, Solar *See* Solar houses
Houses, Tree *See* Tree houses
Houses, Underground *See* Houses, Earth sheltered
Houses, Wood *See* Wood houses
Housewares *See* Household appliances
Housewives *See* Homemakers
Housework *See* Home economics
Housing
See also
Aged—Housing
Black women—Housing
Blacks—Housing
Celebrities—Housing
Cluster housing
College students—Housing
Condominiums
Congregate housing
Construction industry
Discrimination in housing
Gentrification
Housing projects
Local Initiatives Support Corporation
Poor—Housing
Rich—Housing
Single people—Housing
Widows—Housing
Building from the bottom up [community-based groups building low cost housing] J. Hull. il *Time* 129:22-3 F 9 '87
Too long at the party [career of Levittown developer W. Levitt] L. Gubernick. il por *Forbes* 139:40 My 4 '87
What's new for American families in '87. il *Better Homes Gard* 65:17 Ja '87
Costs
Best bets for housing. J. Knudsen. il *Changing Times* 41:18+ N '87
The high cost of housing. C. Vogel. *N Y Times Mag* p38 Je 28 '87
Houses: couples making $4 an hour can buy one. il *Money* 16:42 Mr '87
Housing affordability index. il *Consum Res Mag* 70:33 Ap '87
The new bottom line. H. J. Lehman. il *Changing Times* 41:121-4 Ja '87
The new vise on the middle class [housing crunch] R. Eisenberg. il *Money* 16:48-9 S '87
Pricking the housing balloon. il *U S News World Rep* 103:43+ N 9 '87
What, no pool in the foyer? [luxury housing market] J. Castro. il *Time* 130:50-2 S 21 '87
Federal aid
See also
Federal National Mortgage Association
Housing projects
Housing vouchers
National Housing Partnership
Rent subsidies
United States. Dept. of Housing and Urban Development

A blueprint for affordable housing. R. Kuttner. il *Bus Week* p18 Ag 31 '87
Raise the roof. *America* 157:469 D 19 '87
Shelter skelter. *New Repub* 196:7-8 My 11 '87
Finance
See Housing finance
Health aspects
See Housing and health
International aspects
See also
United Nations. Commission on Human Settlements
Atlantic States
Buy the beloved country: finding an affordable retreat [within striking distance of New York City] M. W. Robbins. il *N Y* 20:48-56+ My 25 '87
California
See also
Blackhawk (Calif.)—Housing
Los Angeles (Calif.)—Housing
Malibu (Calif.)—Housing
San Francisco (Calif.)—Housing
Canada
The renovation rage in Canadian homes. M. Gray. il *Macleans* 100:42-3 N 2 '87
Return of the low rates [mortgages] D. Jenish. il *Macleans* 100:27 F 9 '87
Caribbean region
Beating winter in a home away from home [villa and private home rentals] B. Bauer. il *U S News World Rep* 102:58-9 F 9 '87
Connecticut
See also
Bridgeport (Conn.)—Housing
France
See also
Paris (France)—Housing
Pessac (France)—Housing
Georgia
See also
Atlanta (Ga.)—Housing
Ghana
See also
Kumasi (Ghana)—Housing
Maryland
See also
Baltimore (Md.)—Housing
Massachusetts
See also
Marshfield (Mass.)—Housing
Mexico
See also
Acapulco (Mexico)—Housing
New York (State)
See. also
New York (N.Y.)—Housing
Pennsylvania
See also
Pittsburgh (Pa.)—Housing
Philippines
See also
Manila (Philippines)—Housing
South Africa
The "graying" of a nation [integration of neighborhoods] W. R. Doerner. il *Time* 130:38 N 30 '87
Soviet Union
Pierce takes U.S. group on tour of Soviet Union. por *Jet* 73:4 O 26 '87
Space around the houses matters too. Y. Gubernski and N. Litvinov. il *World Health* p23-5 Jl '87
Tennessee
See also
Memphis (Tenn.)—Housing
Texas
See also
Dallas (Tex.)—Housing
Houston (Tex.)—Housing
Bush's covenants [G. Bush's stand on civil rights and restrictive housing covenants] D. Robb. *Nation* 245:616-17 N 28 '87
How housing woes in Texas affect the national picture. G. Koretz. il *Bus Week* p34 F 23 '87
Virginia
See also
Falls Church (Va.)—Housing
Richmond (Va.)—Housing
Washington (D.C.)
See Washington (D.C.)—Housing
Washington (State)
See also
Seattle (Wash.)—Housing

Housing and health
Shelter for the homeless [cover story; special issue] il *World Health* p2-27 Jl '87
Housing and Urban Development Dept. (U.S.) *See* United States. Dept. of Housing and Urban Development
Housing authority bonds *See* Bonds, Housing authority
Housing bonds *See* Mortgage bonds and notes
Housing construction industry *See* Construction industry
Housing finance
See also
Bonds, Housing authority
Home equity conversion
Housing—Costs
Information storage and retrieval systems—Real estate use
Mortgage banks
Mortgages
United States. Federal Home Loan Bank Board
Home finances. H. Porter. See issues of The Family Handyman beginning September 1986
Housing laws and regulations
See also
Building inspection
Discrimination in housing
Housing vouchers
Rent laws
Housing projects
See also
Dallas (Tex.)—Housing
Habitat for Humanity Inc.
Housing solutions sought as federal subsidy agreements run out [projects that owners will have option of taking onto open market] J. Trewhitt. il *Archit Rec* 175:35 O '87
A new squeeze on housing: publicly assisted projects are imperiled. S. Dentzer. il *Newsweek* 110:48-9 Ag 10 '87
Up from public housing [tenant management] M. Wooster and J. Fund. il *Read Dig* 131:139-43 Jl '87
Netherlands
People who live in globe houses [project designed by Dries Kreijkamp] il *Pop Mech* 164:79 Jl '87
Housing vouchers
Freedom of choice. il *Time* 129:23 F 9 '87
Squeezing the poor [uselessness of vouchers in cities with rent control] *Natl Rev* 39:41 S 25 '87
Housley, Norman
Saladin's triumph over the crusader states: the Battle of Hattin, 1187 [cover story] bibl il map *Hist Today* 37:17-23 Jl '87
Housman, A. E. (Alfred Edward), 1859-1936
about
First encounters. E. Sorel and N. C. Sorel. il *Atlantic* 260:83 Jl '87
Housman, Alfred Edward *See* Housman, A. E. (Alfred Edward), 1859-1936
Houston, J. E.
(jt. auth) *See* Goodman, D. W., and Houston, J. E.
Houston, James D.
On Russian Hill: transforming a 1920s San Francisco residence. il *Archit Dig* 44:116-21 S '87
Houston, Kevin
about
All that he can be. B. Newman. il pors *Sports Illus* 66:30-1 Ja 19 '87
Houston, Margaret Moffette Lea, 1819-1867
about
The conquest of Sam Houston. C. P. Waldrop. il pors *Am Hist Illus* 21:36-43 Ja '87
Houston, Samuel, 1793-1863
about
The conquest of Sam Houston. C. P. Waldrop. il pors *Am Hist Illus* 21:36-43 Ja '87
Houston, W. Robert
Lessons for teacher education from corporate practice. bibl f il *Phi Delta Kappan* 68:388-92 Ja '87
Houston, Walter Scott
Deep-sky wonders. See issues of Sky and Telescope
about
Dean of the deep sky turns 75. D. Di Cicco. il pors *Sky Telesc* 73:566-9 My '87
Houston, Whitney
about
The prom queen of soul. R. Corliss. il pors *Time* 130:58-9+ Jl 13 '87
Rock's supergirl stars. pors *Teen* 31:58 O '87
The selling of Whitney Houston. C. McGuigan. il pors *Newsweek* 110:58-9 Jl 13 '87
Whitney Houston a hit at Italian music show. *Jet* 71:63 F 23 '87

Whitney Houston: can her new album and new tour top the first? [cover story] A. Collier. il pors *Jet* 72:58-9 Jl 6 '87
Whitney Houston hits jackpot with new album. *Jet* 72:62 Jl 27 '87
Whitney Houston: why success won't go to her head. A. Collier. il pors *Jet* 71:58-9 F 16 '87
Whitney plays it safe. V. Aletti. il por *Roll Stone* p49-51 Ag 13 '87
Who's the greatest? [cover story] W. Leavy. il pors *Ebony* 42:140+ O '87
Houston (Mrs. Sam) House (Independence, Tex.) *See* Independence (Tex.)—Historic houses, sites, etc.
Houston (Tex.)
Architecture
Texas formality [contemporary Houston home decorated by Steve Chase] M. Ennis. il *Archit Dig* 44:170-5 Ap '87
Art
Art capital of the third coast. J. Gambrell. il *Art Am* 75:186-203 Ap '87
Banks
See also
Unitedbank-Houston
Bridges
A man and his bridge [K. Farris' McKee Street Bridge Park] K. Gregor. il por *Art News* 86:11 Ap '87
Crime
Houston man waits in dark, kills assailant [B. Gibson slays man who had robbed him of his social security money] *Jet* 72:12 Ag 24 '87
Description
Houston. G. Asher. il *Gourmet* 47:66-73+ O '87
On location in . . . Houston. il *Seventeen* 46:172 Ag '87
Economic conditions
The silver lining in Houston [low cost of living] W. P. Barrett. il *Forbes* 140:174+ O 19 '87
Galleries and museums
See also
De Menil Collection (Houston, Tex.)
Gallery of Texas History
Museum of Fine Arts (Houston, Tex.)
Gardens and gardening
A new look for an old garden. il *South Living* 22:92-3 My '87
Hospitals
See also
Texas Medical Center (Houston, Tex.)
A heart-healthy proving ground [Chez Eddy at Methodist Hospital] *Prevention* 39:50-1+ F '87
Housing
Six bites from one apple [R. Campo sells Houston condo investors on desyndication deal] W. P. Barrett. il por *Forbes* 140:88+ S 7 '87
Industries
Wildcatters in the laboratory [medical technology ventures in Houston] T. Mack. il *Forbes* 140:258+ N 16 '87
Music
See also
Houston Grand Opera Association
Music festivals
See Music festivals—Texas
Parks and playgrounds
A man and his bridge [K. Farris' McKee Street Bridge Park] K. Gregor. il por *Art News* 86:11 Ap '87
Police
Houston police chief receives NOBLE award [L. P. Brown] *Jet* 72:40 Ag 3 '87
Politics and government
Kathy Whitmire. M. Ivins. il pors *Work Woman* 12:120-2+ Mr '87
Religious institutions and affairs
Houston Catholics must refrain from sex to have gala church wedding. *Jet* 73:33 N 16 '87
A plan for Catholic marriages [penalty for cohabitation] K. L. Woodward. il *Newsweek* 110:73 D 14 '87
Social life and customs
Why Jerry Moore left River Oaks [Houston millionaire craves social esteem] E. F. Cone. il pors *Forbes* 140 Sp Issue:102+ O 26 '87
Theater
See also
A.D. Players
Houston (Tex.). Wortham Theater Center *See* Wortham Theater Center
Houston Grand Opera Association
Can do [Wortham Theater Center; special section] G. Schmidgall. il *Opera News* 52:12-16+ O '87

Houston Grand Opera Association—*cont.*
Musical events:
J. Adams' Nixon in China. A. Porter. *New Yorker* 63:124+ N 30 '87
Nixon—the opera [Nixon in China] P. G. Davis. il *N Y* 20:102+ N 9 '87
Stagecraft as soulcraft [Nixon in China] M. Walsh. il *Time* 130:110 N 9 '87

Houston Industries Incorporated
Houston power company invests in Space Services, Inc. *Aviat Week Space Technol* 126:59 F 23 '87

Houston Livestock Show and Rodeo *See* Rodeos

Houston-Montgomery, Beauregard
A hipster's holidaze. il *Harpers Bazaar* 121:64+ D '87

Houston Symphony Orchestra
Musical events:
Houston Symphony's series of fanfares. A. Porter. *New Yorker* 63:71-3 Ja 20 '87

Hovercraft *See* Air cushion vehicles

How-to videotapes *See* Videotapes—Educational use

Howard, Bion
What's in an energy efficient home. il *Consum Res Mag* 70:11-15 Mr '87

Howard, Charles H., III
about
Requiem for a heavyweight. L. Jereski. il *Forbes* 140:152 N 30 '87

Howard, Coy
about
California crafted. il *House Gard* 159:182-9 Ap '87

Howard, Elliott J.
Take a test for heart disease [excerpt from Health risks] il *U S News World Rep* 103:64-5 Ag 17 '87

Howard, Evan Drake
Extremism on campus: symbols of hate, symbols of hope. il *Christ Century* 104:625-7 Jl 15-22 '87

Howard, George
about
George Howard: in the groove. Z. Stewart. il por *Down Beat* 54:24-6 My '87

Howard, Henrietta *See* Suffolk, Henrietta Hobart Howard, Countess of, 1681-1767

Howard, James J.
about
Fast talk. R. Ceppos. il *Car Driv* 33:26-7 Jl '87

Howard, Jane
For Juliette Gordon Low's girls, a sparkling Diamond Jubilee. bibl (p229) il *Smithsonian* 18:46-55 O '87

Howard, Jerry
Growing Grandma's heather bed. il *Ctry J* 14:48-51 D '87

Howard, John A. (John Addison), 1921-
Higher education [address, September 8, 1987] *Vital Speeches Day* 54:13-17 O 15 '87
Resurrecting common sense [address, December 17, 1986] *Vital Speeches Day* 53:240-2 F 1 '87

Howard, Maurice
Power and the early-Tudor courtier's house [excerpt from The early Tudor country house] bibl il por *Hist Today* 37:44-50 My '87

Howard, Richard
An island of rare hospitality [photographs] il *People Wkly* 27:96-9 Ap 20 '87

Howard, Richard, 1929-
My dinner with Imelda. *Harpers* 275:29-30+ O '87
(tr) *See* Cocteau, Jean, 1889-1963. Witness at the free-for-all

Howard, Richard A.
Accompaniment: an invitation. *America* 157:455-7 D 12 '87

Howard, Susan
about
Life after "Dallas" [cover story] H. G. Miller. il pors *Saturday Evening Post* 259:60-3 O '87

Howard, William R.
about
Friendly guy, unfriendly skies. N. J. Perry. il por *Fortune* 116:122 S 14 '87
United's pilots are inching closer to a coup. J. E. Ellis. il por *Bus Week* p32-3 Ag 31 '87
United's pilots get a captain and cash. *Newsweek* 110:32 Ag 24 '87

Howard (E.) & Company *See* E. Howard & Company

Howard Beach case
A bitter bite of the Big Apple. D. Collins. il *U S News World Rep* 102:24 Ja 12 '87
Black vs. white in Howard Beach. R. Stengel. il *Time* 129:48 Ja 5 '87
The Hitler continuum. *Natl Rev* 39:20-1 Ja 30 '87
Howard Beach: an angry tide. T. E. Johnson. il *Newsweek* 109:25 Ja 12 '87

Howard Beach rumbles. J. Bierman. il *Macleans* 100:20 Ja 12 '87
Inside Howard Beach. J. Rieder. *New Repub* 196:17-19 F 9 '87
The legal circus. E. Breindel. *New Repub* 196:20-2 F 9 '87
Mean streets in Howard Beach. T. E. Johnson. il *Newsweek* 109:24-5 Ja 5 '87
On the Beach [J. L. Jackson's comments] *New Repub* 196:8 F 23 '87
Racial tension lingers in New York City after attack on three blacks. il *Jet* 71:12-13 Ja 12 '87
Racism on the rise. R. Dennis. il *Black Enterp* 17:17 Ap '87
The search for racism. W. F. Buckley. il *Natl Rev* 39:71 Ja 30 '87
The signal from Howard Beach. *America* 156:61 Ja 31 '87
Survivor of racial attack in N.Y. wants special probe [C. Sandiford] il por *Jet* 71:4 Ja 19 '87
Twelve are indicted in Howard Beach. *Newsweek* 109:29 F 23 '87
Victims of hatred and bad luck. F. Bruning. por *Macleans* 100:9 Ja 19 '87

Reporters and reporting
Howard Beach: the use and abuse of race. J. Sobran. il *Natl Rev* 39:28-30+ Mr 27 '87

Howard Clock Products, Inc.
Made in the U.S.A. R. Koselka. il pors *Forbes* 139:80-1+ Je 15 '87

Howard Hughes Medical Institute
Choppin takes reins at Howard Hughes. B. J. Culliton. il por *Science* 237:1406-7 S 18 '87
Fredrickson takes leave from Hughes. B. J. Culliton. por *Science* 236:510 My 1 '87
Fredrickson's bitter end at Hughes. B. J. Culliton. il por *Science* 236:1417-18 Je 12 '87
Howard Hughes moves into science education. B. J. Culliton. il *Science* 238:150 O 9 '87
Hughes settles with IRS. B. J. Culliton. il *Science* 235:1318 Mr 13 '87
Perpich to head new Hughes program. B. J. Culliton. por *Science* 236:141 Ap 10 '87
Scientific philanthropy. T. Beardsley. *Sci Am* 257:22+ D '87

Howard University
Camille Cosby delivers Howard graduation address; receives honorary degree. il por *Jet* 72:24 Je 1 '87
Howard, Grambling get fed. funds for anti drug plans. *Jet* 73:32 N 2 '87
Howard U. battles NCAA over grid playoff snub. *Jet* 73:50 D 14 '87
Singer Paul Simon strikes sour chord with students at Howard U. over album [Graceland] *Jet* 71:59 F 2 '87

Howard University. School of Divinity
New HU Divinity School named for Benjamin E. Mays gets $750,000 Lilly Award. *Jet* 72:30 My 18 '87

Howard W. Sams & Co.
Sams & Co.: publishing for the hi-tech market. T. Unsworth. *Publ Wkly* 231:32 Je 12 '87

Howatch, Susan
about
PW interviews. A. Smith. por *Publ Wkly* 232:67-8 O 16 '87

Howdy Doody (Puppet)
I remember Howdy; ed. by Cable Neuhaus. B. Smith. il pors *People Wkly* 28:149-50+ N 30 '87
Kowabunga! Staging a '50s-style freckled face-off, Milwaukee tells America it's Howdy Doody time again. il *People Wkly* 28:72-3 Jl 20 '87

The Howdy Doody show [television program] *See* Television program reviews—Single works

Howe, Irving
Justice for Leskov. il *N Y Rev Books* 34:32-6 Ap 23 '87
Socialism and sensibility. *New Repub* 197:38-42 O 26 '87

Howe, John
about
Driven to perfection. P. Bedard. il pors *Esquire* 107:109-10 Je '87

Howe, Jonathan
about
Crossroads [interview] E. Weiner. il pors *Flying* 114:82-4+ N '87

Howe, Lucy
The religious climate under *glasnost* [cover story] il *Christ Century* 104:883-5 O 14 '87

Howe, Tina
about
Coastal disturbances [drama] Reviews
Nation 244:25-6 Ja 10 '87. M. Hodgson
New Repub 196:26-7 Ja 5-12 '87. R. Brustein
Howell, J. Andreas
The challenge of space surveillance. il *Sky Telesc*
73:584-6+ Je '87
Howell, John M.
Early farming in northwestern Europe. il map *Sci Am*
257:118-24+ N '87
Howell, Ron
20 years of theatrical excellence. il pors *Ebony* 42:92+
Mr '87
New York: the good, the bad and the ugly. il *Black
Enterp* 17:294-6+ Je '87
Howells, Malcolm, and others
X-ray holograms at improved resolution: a study of
zymogen granules. bibl f il *Science* 238:514-17 O 23
'87
Howells, William Dean, 1837-1920
about
First encounters. E. Sorel and N. C. Sorel. il *Atlantic*
260:101 N '87
Howells as anti-novelist. J. Updike. *New Yorker* 63:78-88
Jl 13 '87
Howes, Terence
about
The chase for leftover fortunes. D. Francis. il *Macleans*
100:5 Jl 27 '87
Howletts (England: Historic house) *See* Historic houses,
sites, etc.—Great Britain
Howser, Dick, 1936-1987
about
Facing the sad truth. R. Fimrite. il por *Sports Illus*
66:96 Mr 9 '87
Hoy, Anne H.
Art circles: portrait photographs from ARTnews, 1905-
1986. il *Art News* 86:93-100 F '87
Hoyas *See* Wax plants
Hoyle, John R., and Johnson, Glenn Ross
The 21st-century professor. il pors *Futurist* 21:26-7 N/D
'87
Hoyo, José Azcona *See* Azcona Hoyo, José
Hoyt, Mary Finch
Amy Carter faces life. il pors *Good Housekeep* 205:143+
O '87
A father's special gift of love. il por *Good Housekeep*
204:74+ F '87
I learned to "think" stress away—and so can you. il
pors *Good Housekeep* 204:50+ Je '87
Hoyt, Richard, 1941-
about
Richard Hoyt's outrageous thrillers are quite a trip.
M. Donovan. il pors *People Wkly* 28:58-60 Ag 31
'87
Hoyt, Wade
Freewheeling. See issues of Popular Mechanics beginning
January 1986
HP Books
HP Books to try audio under Knight-Ridder imprint
this spring [birth and childcare audiocassettes] il *Publ
Wkly* 231:70 F 13 '87
HPV *See* Human papilloma virus
HPVs (Human powered vehicles) *See* Human powered
vehicles
Hrkac, Tony
about
The Sioux came through. P. Putnam. il *Sports Illus*
66:132+ Ap 6 '87
Hsu, Hsin-liang
about
A dissident turned back. J. Motavalli. il por *Progressive*
51:14-15 F '87
Hsu, Ti-Shan
about
Ti Shan Hsu at Castelli and Pat Hearn. H. Cotter.
il *Art Am* 75:173 S '87
Hsüan-tsang, ca. 596-664
How Buddhism came to Karnasuvarna [excerpt from
Records of the western regions of the great T'ang
dynasty] il *Courier* 40:24 Ap '87
Hsui, Albert T.
Borehole measurement of the Newtonian gravitational
constant. bibl f il map *Science* 237:881-3 Ag 21 '87
HTLV viruses
See also
HIV viruses
AIDS's cancerous cousin. M. Clark. il por map *Newsweek*
109:73 Je 8 '87

HTLV-I-associated B-cell CLL: indirect role for retrovirus
in leukemogenesis [chronic lymphocytic leukemia] D.
L. Mann and others. bibl f il *Science* 236:1103-6
My 29 '87
HTLV-V: a new human retrovirus isolated in a Tac-
negative T cell lymphoma/leukemia. V. Manzari and
others. bibl f il *Science* 238:1581-3 D 11 '87
HTLV *x* gene mutants exhibit novel transcriptional
regulatory phenotypes. W. Wachsman and others. bibl
f il *Science* 235:674-7 F 6 '87
Leukemia virus linked to nerve disease [HTLV-I] J.
L. Marx. bibl il *Science* 236:1059-61 My 29 '87
New human retrovirus [HTLV-V] *Sci News* 132:391 D
19-26 '87
The *tat* gene of human T-lymphotropic virus type 1
induces mesenchymal tumors in transgenic mice. M.
Nerenberg and others. bibl f il *Science* 237:1324-9
S 11 '87
A transgenic mouse model for human neurofibromatosis.
S. H. Hinrichs and others. bibl f il *Science* 237:1340-3
S 11 '87
U3 sequences from HTLV-I and -II LTRs confer p*x*
protein response to a murine leukemia virus LTR.
H. Kitado and others. bibl f il *Science* 235:901-4
F 20 '87
Hu, Yao-pang, 1915- *See* Hu Yaobang, 1915-
Hu Yaobang, 1915-
about
China [cover story; special section] il *World Press Rev*
34:11-16 Mr '87
China drops the copilot. R. Watson. il por *Newsweek*
109:30-1 Ja 26 '87
China hits the clutch. M. Hopkins. por *New Leader*
70:3-4 Ja 12-26 '87
China's reform consumes one of its creators. M. Lord.
il por *U S News World Rep* 102:34 Ja 26 '87
Deng cracks down. J. Smolowe. il por *Time* 129:24-5
Ja 26 '87
The end of a beginning. M. Janigan. il por *Macleans*
100:24 Ja 26 '87
Hu's not on first. F. Schurmann. *Nation* 244:100-1 Ja
31 '87
HUAC *See* United States. Congress. House. Committee
on Un-American Activities
Huandacareo (Mexico)
Economic conditions
Sad return of the prodigal sons [Mexicans returning
to Huandacareo as result of new immigration law]
J. Moody. il *Time* 129:52 My 18 '87
Huang, E.
(jt. auth) *See* Bassett, W. A., and Huang, E.
Huang, H. T., and Yang, Pei
The ancient cultured citrus ant: a tropical ant is used
to control insect pests in southern China. bibl il map
BioScience 37:665-71 O '87
Huang, Y.-L., and Moriarty-Schieven, G. H.
A revisit to the guest star of A.D. 185. bibl f il *Science*
235:59-60 Ja 2 '87
Hubbard, John, 1931-
about
John Hubbard at the Yale Center for British Art. J.
Hollander. il *Art Am* 75:140-1 Ja '87
Hubbard, L. Ron (La Fayette Ron), 1911-1986
about
A defeat for Scientology. D. Todd. *Macleans* 100:54
D 14 '87
Hubbard awards, three years old, find sanction. R.
Herbert. il *Publ Wkly* 231:22 My 22 '87
Hubbard, La Fayette Ron *See* Hubbard, L. Ron (La Fayette
Ron), 1911-1986
Hubbard, Randall D., 1935-
about
What makes Dee Hubbard run after companies. T.
Carson. il por *Bus Week* p56 Ap 27 '87
Hubbard, Ruth, 1924-
about
"You've got a long way to go, baby": a conversation
about the women's movement with Ruth Hubbard.
M. Davidson. por *USA Today (Periodical)* 116:92-5
S '87
Hubbard Glacier (Alaska) *See* Glaciers
Hubbell, John G.
The iron courage of Joni Dunn. il pors *Read Dig*
130:39-44 Ja '87
Mike Benge and his marvelous tree. il por *Read Dig*
131:103-7 Ag '87
One more time, Jack. il pors *Read Dig* 130:121-6 Ap
'87
"Why my babies?". il *Read Dig* 131:117-22 N '87
Hubbell, Sue
Bugs. il *New Yorker* 63:79-82+ D 28 '87

Hubble constant
Ripples in the universal Hubble flow. P. H. Andersen. il *Phys Today* 40:17-19 O '87
Hubble Space Telescope (Satellite) *See* Artificial satellites—Astronomical use
Huber, Jane Park

about

A trendy voice. R. J. Stanislaw. il por *Christ Today* 31:72 S 4 '87
Huber, Peter W.
Biotechnology and the regulation hydra. il *Technol Rev* 90:57-60+ N/D '87
Injury litigation and liability insurance dynamics. bibl f il *Science* 238:31-6 O 2 '87
Liability insurance and litigation [discussion of October 2, 1987 article, Injury litigation and liability insurance dynamics] *Science* 238:1635-7 D 18 '87
New biotechnologies [address, December 12, 1986] *Vital Speeches Day* 53:369-71 Ap 1 '87
Who will protect us from our protectors? il *Forbes* 140:56+ Jl 13 '87
Hubert H. Humphrey Metrodome (Minneapolis, Minn.)
No bad hops with Wally [W. McNeil, top beer seller at Metrodome baseball games] F. Lidz. il pors *Sports Illus* 67:54+ Jl 6 '87
Hubner, John, and Gruson, Lindsey
Dial om for murder. il pors *Roll Stone* p53-4+ Ap 9 '87
Huc, Evariste-Régis, 1813-1860
A visit to the regent of Tibet [excerpt from Souvenirs d'un voyage dans la Tartarie et le Thibet] il por *Courier* 40:25 Ap '87
Huchthausen, David R.

about

David Huchthausen: controlled fragments [cover story] R. Silberman. il por *Am Craft* 47:54-9 Ag/S '87
Huck Finn (Fictional character) *See* Huckleberry Finn (Fictional character)
Huckleberry Finn (Fictional character)
Anecdotes, facetiae, satire, etc.
Notes and comment [Huck Finn at school during the summer] *New Yorker* 63:27 O 26 '87
Hucknall, Mick

about

Simply Red's Mick Hucknall. E. Miller. il pors *Seventeen* 46:89-90+ S '87
HUD *See* United States. Dept. of Housing and Urban Development
HUD (Head-up display) systems *See* Air navigation—Aids and devices
Hudgins, Andrew
Child on the marsh [poem] *Nation* 245:532 N 7 '87
Grandmother's spit [poem] *Atlantic* 260:40 Ag '87
Hudlin, Reginald

about

The Hudlin brothers. N. George. pors *Essence* 18:32 S '87
Hudlin, Warrington

about

The Hudlin brothers. N. George. pors *Essence* 18:32 S '87
Hudson, Edith Baumann- *See* Baumann-Hudson, Edith
Hudson, Helen
A daughter's duty [story] il *Redbook* 169:31-2+ Ag '87
Hudson, Lillian

about

Essence woman. B. Taylor. il por *Essence* 17:30 Mr '87
Hudson, Marc, 1947-
Warning: the Friday night fish fry may be hazardous to your health. il maps *Audubon* 89:24-6+ Jl '87
Hudson, Patricia L.
In Mr. Jefferson's garden. il por *Americana* 14:50-5 Ja/F '87
Hudson, Rock, 1925-1985

about

My husband, Rock Hudson [excerpt] P. Gates. pors *Ladies Home J* 104:70-1+ Jl '87
On tour with Rock Hudson. S. Davidson. il *N Y Times Mag* p54+ My 3 '87
Hudson, Walter

about

After 27 years in his bedroom, 1,200-lb. Walter Hudson decides to take a load off. W. Plummer. il pors *People Wkly* 28:60-1 O 26 '87
Gregory comes to rescue of 1,000-pound Walter Hudson. il pors *Jet* 73:17-18 N 9 '87

Inability to get up, go to mother's funeral, gives 700-pounder will to diet. R. L. Haywood. il pors *Jet* 73:54-6 O 5 '87
Hudson, William, III

about

13-year-old conducts wedding like veteran. il por *Jet* 71:29 Mr 16 '87
13-year-old preacher talks about love, sex, sin and forgiveness. T. S. Moore. il pors *Jet* 72:14-16 Je 29 '87
In Chicago, God's word often comes out of the mouth of a mere babe—the Rev. William Hudson III, 13. D. Grogan. il pors *People Wkly* 28:102+ Ag 24 '87
Hudson Hills Press Inc.
Revising the history of impressionism [publication of Charles F. Stuckey's Berthe Morisot] il *Publ Wkly* 232:29-30 S 11 '87
Hudson River (N.Y. and N.J.)
Adoption [Bronx sixth graders learn about Hudson River Striped Bass Hatchery] *New Yorker* 62:31-2 F 9 '87
The riverkeeper [J. Cronin, monitor] A. Wilkinson. il *New Yorker* 63:49-50+ My 11 '87
Bridges

See also

George Washington Bridge (N.Y. and N.J.)
Hudson River School
Exhibitions
American sublime [American paradise: the world of the Hudson River School] R. Atkins. il *Horizon* 30:36-9 S '87
Echoes [American paradise at the Metropolitan Museum of Art] J. Furth. il *Life* 10:56-60 O '87
Hudson River bracketed [American paradise: the world of the Hudson River School at the Metropolitan Museum of Art] K. Larson. il *N Y* 20:106-7 N 23 '87
The Hudson River School. A. C. Danto. *Nation* 245:530-3 N 7 '87
Hudson River School featured at the Metropolitan Museum of Art in New York. il *Antiques Collect Hobbies* 92:16-17 N '87
Realism and idealism in Hudson River School painting [exhibition entitled American paradise at the Metropolitan Museum of Art] O. Rodriguez Roque. bibl f il *Antiques* 132:1096-109 N '87
The search for paradise lost. C. McGuigan. il *Newsweek* 110:82-3 O 12 '87
Hudson River Valley (N.Y. and N.J.)
Description and travel
Great houses along the Hudson. F. Allen. il *Am Herit* 38:28+ S/O '87
Jaunts: follow the Hudson back to a better age. B. Costikyan. il *N Y* 20:48-52+ Je 29-Jl 6 '87
Photographs and photography
Echoes [D. Waugh's landscape photographs] J. Furth. il *Life* 10:56-60 O '87
Hudson's Bay Co.
Caesars of the wilderness [excerpt] P. C. Newman. il map *Macleans* 100:42-6+ O 12 '87
Canada's fur-trading empire. P. C. Newman. il map *Natl Geogr* 172:192-229 Ag '87
The Nor'westers' revenge [sells off Northern Stores] P. C. Newman. il *Macleans* 100:42 My 11 '87
Retreat from the frontier [sale of northern outlets] A. Walmsley. il *Macleans* 100:26-7 F 16 '87
Huebner, Albert L.
Worker safety comes under attack. *Progressive* 51:11-12 Jl '87
Huebner, W. F. (Walter F.), 1928-
First polymer in space identified in Comet Halley. bibl f il *Science* 237:628-30 Ag 7 '87
Huebner, Walter F. *See* Huebner, W. F. (Walter F.), 1928-
Huey Lewis and the News (Musical group)
Huey Lewis & rock's last taboo. R. Wolmuth. il pors *People Wkly* 27:38-40+ Ja 19 '87
Hufford, Larry
Stop all military aid now! *America* 156:146-7 F 21 '87
Huffy Corporation
Easy rider. K. Hannon. il por *Forbes* 140:304-5 N 16 '87
Huge, Jurgan Frederick, 1809-1878

about

Jurgan Frederick Huge. J. Lipman. bibl f il *Antiques* 132:496, 546-9 S '87
Hugel, Charles E.

about

From dirt to glamour and mixed reviews. R. McGough. il por *Forbes* 139:112+ Mr 23 '87
What smoke screen? N. J. Perry. il por *Fortune* 116:137-8 O 26 '87

Huger, Francis, 1773-1855
about
An American's attempt to rescue Lafayette [cover story] A. L. Levin. il por *Am Hist Illus* 22:16-20+ O '87
Hugging *See* Embracing
Hugh L. Dryden Flight Research Center
The Dryden Flight Research Facility. H. A. Butowsky. il *Space World* X-8-284:34-5 Ag '87
X-men [X-29 test pilots] E. Weiner. il *Flying* 114:38-40+ Ja '87
Hughes, Allen
about
Art for the outdoorsman. H. Middleton. il por *South Living* 22:100+ Je '87
Hughes, David W.
A mysterious woodcut. il *Sky Telesc* 74:252 S '87
Hughes, Holly, 1951-
about
Holly Hughes. S. R. Goldberg. il *Art News* 86:164+ My '87
Hughes, Jim
about
Reviews:
J. Hughes and R. de Lara present Contrapuntos program as part of Theater Frontiers series. L. Kumin. *Dance Mag* 61:100 My '87
Hughes, John
about
Voyage around the Horn. il por *Macleans* 100:27 Ap 13 '87
Hughes, John
about
Planes, trains and automobiles [film] Reviews
Macleans 100:67 D 14 '87. L. O'Toole
N Y il 20:152 D 7 '87. D. Denby
People Wkly il 28:14 D 14 '87. P. Travers
Time il 130:104 N 30 '87. R. Schickel
Some kind of wonderful [film] Reviews
Newsweek 109:72 Mr 16 '87. D. Ansen
Hughes, Kathleen
For God's sake, pray for favors. *U S Cathol* 52:35-6 Ja '87
Hughes, Patrick E.
The blizzard of '88. il *Weatherwise* 40:312-14+ D '87
Hurricanes haunt our history. il *Weatherwise* 40:134-40 Je '87
Hughes, Revella, d. 1987
about
Obituary
Jet por 73:17 N 16 '87
Hughes, Robert
Architecture: Richard Meier [cover story] il *Archit Dig* 44:152-9+ O '87
The artist as entrepreneur [cover story] *New Repub* 197:24-5+ D 14 '87
On Lucian Freud. il *N Y Rev Books* 34:54-9 Ag 13 '87
about
Living a truth. por *Art News* 86:9 Ja '87
Robert Hughes: the art of bushwhacking the bourgeoisie [interview] M. Blonsky. por *Vogue* 177:212-13+ Ja '87
The shock of the Hughes. R. Koenig. il pors *N Y* 20:30-5 Ja 5 '87
Hughes, Robert W.
about
Keeping the bankers at bay. D. Holder. il por *Channels* 7:55-6 My '87
Hughes, William J., 1932-
Should Congress adopt the House-passed "Gephardt Amendment"? [excerpts from debate, April 29, 1987] *Congr Dig* 66:181+ Je/Jl '87
Hughes (Howard) Medical Institute *See* Howard Hughes Medical Institute
Hughes Aircraft Co.
Hughes APG-70 radar provides enhanced F-15 combat capabilities. W. B. Scott. il *Aviat Week Space Technol* 126:95+ My 25 '87
Hughes develops HS 601 communications satellite. *Aviat Week Space Technol* 127:29 O 19 '87
Hughes focuses on new market ventures with its HS 601 communications satellite. B. A. Smith. il *Aviat Week Space Technol* 127:67+ O 26 '87
Hughes group wins ATF avionics contract [advanced tactical fighter] *Aviat Week Space Technol* 127:32 Ag 3 '87
Hughes hybrid radar will improve F-14D tracking/shootdown capability. W. B. Scott. il *Aviat Week Space Technol* 127:85+ N 16 '87
Hughes to build direct broadcast satellites. *Aviat Week Space Technol* 126:21 Je 8 '87

McDonnell Douglas receives firm commercial Delta launch orders [Hughes Aircraft to purchase for launch of British Satellite Broadcasting spacecraft] *Aviat Week Space Technol* 127:24 Jl 20 '87
Hughes Helicopters, Inc.
See also
McDonnell Douglas Helicopter Company
Hughes Mining Company
The platinum rush of 1987 is on. S. D. Atchison. il *Bus Week* p67 S 7 '87
Hughes Tool Company
Why the Baker-Hughes merger almost didn't happen. C. S. Eklund and T. Vogel. il pors *Bus Week* p110-11 My 11 '87
Hugo, Victor, 1802-1885
about
A life hardly less romantic and turbulent than his novels. D. Hofstadter. bibl (p163) il pors *Smithsonian* 18:74-80+ Ap '87
Hui, Dou
A skeptical look at initiatives. il *Bull At Sci* 43:35-6 Mr '87
Huke, Robert E.
Letter from Manila. *Focus* 37:33 Summ '87
Hula (Dance)
In praise of the goddess Pele. J. Skow. il *Time* 130:67 Ag 24 '87
Hull, Brett
about
Skating in a shadow. M. Alberstat. il por *Macleans* 100:45 Ja 12 '87
Hull, John
about
The misadventures of El Patrón. J. V. Lamar, Jr. il por *Time* 130:31-2 N 16 '87
Hull (England)
Historic houses, sites, etc.
Restoring Hull's medieval past [Beverley Gate] S. Barclay. il *Hist Today* 37:4-5 Jl '87
Human behavior *See* Behavior (Psychology)
Human beings *See* Man
Human bites *See* Bites, Human
Human body *See* Body, Human
Human capital *See* Man—Economic value
Human cold storage *See* Cryonics
Human combustion, Spontaneous *See* Spontaneous human combustion
Human Development Services Office (U.S.) *See* United States. Office of Human Development Services
Human ecology
See also
Biosphere II
Deep ecology
Gaia hypothesis
Indians of North America—Influence on nature
Man—Influence of environment
Man—Influence on nature
Man and the Biosphere Programme
Quality of life
United Nations Conference on the Human Environment
Back from the abyss [excerpt from Earth] A. H. Ehrlich and P. R. Ehrlich. il *Sierra* 72:54-60 Mr/Ap '87
Ecology of modern humans [views of Robert Foley] R. Lewin. *Science* 237:1295 S 11 '87
Now (I think) I understand the ecologists better. J. Simon. il por *Futurist* 21:18-19 S/O '87
Report on reports: Our common future. I. Burton. bibl f *Environment* 29:25-9 Je '87
Social traps and environmental policy. R. Costanza. bibl f il *BioScience* 37:407-12 Je '87
The world's most polymorphic species. W. R. Catton. bibl f il *BioScience* 37:413-19 Je '87
Human embryo *See* Fetus
Human error *See* Errors
Human experimentation *See* Medical research—Experimentation on man; Pharmaceutical research—Experimentation on man; Psychiatric research—Experimentation on man; Psychological research—Experimentation on man
Human figure in art
See also
Anatomy, Artistic
Nude in art
Portrait drawing
Portrait painting
Portraits
Women in art
David Park: facing Eden. B. Berkson. bibl f il *Art Am* 75:164-71+ O '87

Human figure in art—*cont.*
Exhibitions
Figures in the Golden Anniversary National Art Exhibition [with introd. by Kenneth W. Marlow] il *Am Artist* 51:62-5 Je '87
Le Corbusier secret. E. Beck. il *Art News* 86:163 S '87
Human growth hormone *See* Pituitary hormones
Human growth hormone, Synthetic *See* Pituitary hormones, Synthetic
Human immunodeficiency viruses *See* HIV viruses
Human information processing
    See also
    Neural network computers
Answering autobiographical questions: the impact of memory and inference on surveys. N. M. Bradburn and others. bibl f il *Science* 236:157-61 Ap 10 '87
Artificial intelligence: the rational optimist [H. A. Simon] C. Holden. *Current* 293:36-40 Je '87
The cognitive unconscious. J. F. Kihlstrom. bibl f *Science* 237:1445-52 S 18 '87
Human neuroelectric patterns predict performance accuracy. A. S. Gevins and others. bibl f il *Science* 235:580-5 Ja 30 '87
Windows on the mind [work of A. S. Gevins] E. Smith. il *Omni* 9:92-6 My '87
The workings of working memory. M. M. Waldrop. il *Science* 237:1564-7 S 25 '87
Your mindless brain [views of M. L. Minsky] P. Hoffman. il *Discover* 8:84-5+ S '87
Human League (Musical group)
No matter the question, music's the answer. Ask the Human League's Philip Oakey. E. Miller. il por *Seventeen* 46:66-7 My '87
Human leukocyte antigens *See* Antigens and antibodies
Human locomotion
    See also
    Running
    Walking
Human mechanics *See* Biomechanics
Human milk *See* Milk, Human
Human Nutrition Research Center (U.S.)
For nutrition research, women in Grand Forks, North Dakota are licking their plates clean. J. Friedman. il *People Wkly* 27:109-10+ Ap 20 '87
Human papilloma virus
The next sex epidemic [a cause of cervical cancer] S. Downie. il *Mademoiselle* 93:154 N '87
A sexually transmitted cancer virus [views of D. Norman Dahm on importance of Pap tests] C. SerVaas. il *Saturday Evening Post* 259:104-5 My/Je '87
Human powered aircraft
    See also
    Daedalus Project
88-pound pedal plane [Michelob Light Eagle] S. Ashley. il *Pop Sci* 230:70-3+ F '87
Cal Poly students attempting human-powered helicopter flight. il *Aviat Week Space Technol* 127:77 D 21 '87
Human powered vehicles
The new fastest way to get through the water [Flying Fish II, human powered boat] S. Morris. il *Omni* 9:111-12 Ja '87
Human relations
    See also
    Brotherhood of man
    Caring
    Child-adult relationship
    Communication—Social aspects
    Conversation
    Courtesy
    Criticism, Personal
    Dependency (Psychology)
    Embracing
    Friendship
    Helping behavior
    Interpersonal attraction
    Intimacy
    Jealousy
    Life skills
    Loneliness
    Love
    Marriage
    Married couples
    Monogamy
    Neighbors
    Parent-child relationship
    Personal space
    Popularity
    Praise
    Prejudice
    Quarrels

    Rejection (Psychology)
    Revenge
    Romance
    Sensitivity
    Sympathy
    Toleration
    Touch
    Women and men
The best gift we can give ["being there"] K. O'Connor. il *Read Dig* 130:61-2+ My '87
The human dimension of data-based decision making [interview with Newman Walker] D. B. Strother. il por *Phi Delta Kappan* 68:470-3 F '87
Make yourself available! M. E. Marty. *Read Dig* 131:179-80 O '87
Seeing connections. K. Kolenda. il *Humanist* 47:43 My/Je '87
Study and teaching
    See also
    Esalen Institute
Human rights *See* Civil rights
Human Rights Commission (United Nations) *See* United Nations. Commission on Human Rights
Human Rights Committee (United Nations) *See* United Nations. Human Rights Committee
Human T cell leukemia viruses *See* HTLV viruses
Humana Inc
David Jones. K. Deveny. il por *Bus Week* Sp Issue:271 Ap 17 '87
Harsh reality. G. Morgenson. il *Forbes* 139:48 Je 15 '87
The performance took a beating, the paychecks didn't [D. A. Jones] J. E. Davis and K. Deveny. il pors *Bus Week* p54 My 4 '87
Humanism
    See also
    Christianity and humanism
    Philosophical anthropology
Dora who? [D. Russell; adaptation of address, June 1987] B. Earles. il pors *Humanist* 47:17-19+ N/D '87
Humanism and the second wave of feminism. G. Steinem. il por *Humanist* 47:11-15+ My/Je '87
The humanist. L. L. Morain. *Humanist* 47:2 Mr/Ap '87
A humanist alternative to A.A.'s twelve steps. B. F. Skinner. *Humanist* 47:5 Jl/Ag '87
The humanist family and moral education. D. Carroll. por *Humanist* 47:35-6 Mr/Ap '87
Humanists and traditional moral values. L. Hyman. por *Humanist* 47:29+ Mr/Ap '87
Humanists versus religiosity in the Boy Scouts. D. Carroll. por *Humanist* 47:37 N/D '87
Looking back. *Humanist* 47:29-30 N/D '87
The place of secular humanism [address, May 7, 1987] A. Grünbaum. *Vital Speeches Day* 54:42-7 N 1 '87
Polish humanist in a Communist world: Stanislaw Ossowski. J. Mucha. *Society* 24:70-7 My/Je '87
Revising the Copernican revolution. K. Kolenda. por *Humanist* 47:41-2 Mr/Ap '87
Sir Julian Huxley: a memoir. C. Lamont. *Humanist* 47:27-8+ My/Je '87
Sixth annual North American Essay Contest [special section] il *Humanist* 47:14-22+ Mr/Ap '87
The well-rounded humanist. D. Carroll. il por *Humanist* 47:35-6 Jl/Ag '87
Humanism and Christianity *See* Christianity and humanism
Humanism in literature
Humanism in literature. See issues of The Humanist
Margaret Atwood [address] M. Atwood. il *Humanist* 47:5-7+ S/O '87
Humanism in poetry
Wallace Stevens: poet of the secular imagination. D. Lawson. *Humanist* 47:35-6 My/Je '87
Humanist (Periodical)
Looking back. *Humanist* 47:29-30 N/D '87
Humanities
    See also
    Science and the humanities
Study and teaching
    See also
    Science and the humanities—Study and teaching
Better than rubies [High School for the Humanities, New York City] J. W. Donohue. il *America* 157:319-26 N 7 '87
Curriculum changes spark debate at MIT. W. Booth. il *Science* 236:1515-16 Je 19 '87
Escape into esthetics. J. J. Pelikan. *Cent Mag* 20:57-8 Ja/F '87
Humanities: theory and criticism (Periodical)
The revenge of the intellectuals. *Newsweek* 109:36 Mr 2 '87

Humanity
Search for the human dimension [interview with V. Havel] E. Blair. il por *World Press Rev* 34:24-5 My '87

Humboldt, Alexander, Freiherr von, 1769-1859
The swimming postman. il *Courier* 40:14 Ap '87

Humboldt, Friedrich Wilhelm Heinrich Alexander *See* Humboldt, Alexander, Freiherr von, 1769-1859

Humboldt County (Calif.)
            Crime
Getting straight [marijuana growers] M. Beauchamp. il *Forbes* 139:92+ Je 1 '87

Humboldt Redwoods State Park (Calif.) *See* California—Parks and reserves

Hume, Frederick R.
Advancements in the application of computers to scientific research. *Science* 235 pt2:G54+ F 27 '87

Hume, Paul
            about
"Equally bizarre, but somewhat different". M. S. Forbes. *Forbes* 140:18-19 Ag 10 '87
Here's how the Washington post was scooped on Truman's letter. M. S. Forbes. il *Forbes* 139:18 Je 29 '87

Humidifiers
Install a humidifier. G. Branson. il *Fam Handyman* 37:70-1 O '87
            Maintenance and repair
Humidifier on the blink. J. R. Provey. il *Home Mech* 83:8 Ja '87

Humidity
            See also
Condensation (Meteorology)
Hot weather
Summer simmer index

Humidity meters *See* Moisture meters

Hummel, Don, 1907-
            about
Smokey would never believe this. A. Chase. *Wash Mon* 19:45-6+ N '87

Humor
            See also
Knock-knock jokes
Laughter
Limericks
Phonograph records—Comedy records
Puns and punning
Radio broadcasting—Comedy programs
Comic culture [special section] il *Seventeen* 46:112-13 N '87
Ethnic jokes may cost N.J. workers their jobs [Long Branch, N.J.] *Jet* 71:14 Mr 23 '87
Meet Mr. Bigot: how to nix his nasty jokes. G. Blair. *Mademoiselle* 93:204 N '87
Mother told jokes [condensed from An American childhood] A. Dillard. il *Read Dig* 131:122-5 O '87
The perils of the good life [Jewish American princess jokes] F. Bruning. por *Macleans* 100:13 O 5 '87
Smile if you want to find this funny [research by Fritz Strack] *Discover* 8:18-19 N '87
Tell me another one [ethnic joke etiquette] *New Repub* 196:4 Je 29 '87
What makes kids laugh? D. F. Bjorklund and B. Bjorklund. il *Parents* 62:132-4+ O '87
            Anecdotes, facetiae, satire, etc.
Last word. C. Graybill. por *Omni* 10:178 N '87
            Authorship
The comic bad men of English letters. M. Bradbury. il *N Y Times Book Rev* 92:15 Mr 22 '87
Dave's kids: the twisted minds behind the Letterman show. E. Pooley. il por *N Y* 20:36-45 Ja 19 '87
Having fun writing humor. G. Perret. *Writer* 100:13-15 Mr '87
Puns and parodies pay off. S. Glasser. *Writer* 100:19-20+ Je '87
            Conferences
Laughter in the Balkans [International Biennial of Humor and Satire in the Arts in Gabrovo, Bulgaria] B. Bernstein. *New Yorker* 63:98-101+ O 26 '87

Humor, American
            Bibliography
Books about the South. C. Griffith. il *South Living* 22:78 Ag '87

Humor, Pictorial
            See also
Caricatures and cartoons
Comic books, strips, etc.
Photography, Humorous

Humor, Political *See* Politics—Anecdotes, facetiae, satire, etc.

Humor and religion *See* Religion and humor

Humor in business
Going for the jocular. S. Bing. il *Esquire* 108:86 O '87
Tension? Lock your boss in a Mason jar [humor consultants] il *Newsweek* 110:64-5 O 12 '87
The value of humor [in the workplace; views of Peter Desberg] il *USA Today (Periodical)* 115:5-6 Ap '87
What's black and blue and floats in the Monongahela River? [executives' humor] D. Machan. il *Forbes* 140:216+ N 2 '87

Humor in medicine
Hippocratic humor [letters to the New England journal of medicine] J. Schuster. il *Technol Rev* 90:14 O '87
Sick jokes. P. Klass. il *Discover* 8:30+ N '87

Humor in motion pictures
            See also
Motion pictures—Comedy films

Humor in television
            See also
Cable television—Comedy programs
Television broadcasting—Comedy programs

Humorists
            See also
Ade, George, 1866-1944
Perelman, S. J. (Sidney Joseph), 1904-1979

Humorous photography *See* Photography, Humorous

Humphrey (Hubert H.) Metrodome (Minneapolis, Minn.) *See* Hubert H. Humphrey Metrodome (Minneapolis, Minn.)

Humphreys, Curtis Judson, 1898-1986
            about
Obituary
    Phys Today por 40 pt1:84+ Ag '87. K. L. Andrew

Humphreys, Josephine
            about
PW interviews. B. Summer. por *Publ Wkly* 232:49 S 4 '87

Humphries, Valerie
            about
Catch-2: author Joe Heller remarries; this time it's the nurse who brought him back to health. K. Gross. il pors *People Wkly* 27:42+ Ap 27 '87

Humus
Undercover light 'reads' soil organic level. *Success Farm* 85:56L N '87

Hungarian fiction
The other Europeans. I. Sanders. *Nation* 245:279-82 S 19 '87

Hungarian Grand Prix *See* Automobile racing—Hungary
Hungarian partridge shooting *See* Partridge shooting

Hungaroton (Firm)
Liszt galore. B. A. Varga. il *High Fidel* 37:61 Mr '87

Hungary
            See also
Arts and state—Hungary
Automobile racing—Hungary
Censorship—Hungary
Science and state—Hungary
Taxation—Hungary
Underground literature—Hungary
            Commerce
            United States
            See United States—Commerce—Hungary
            Description and travel
In the land of the setting sun [cover story] S. Brockmann. il *America* 157:238-43 O 17 '87
            Economic policy
Can 'goulash communism' survive austerity? F. A. Miller. il por *Bus Week* p81 My 25 '87
Reform adjusts to realities. K. W. Banta. il *Time* 130:40 O 5 '87
"The Soviets are now in a very romantic period". P. Fuhrman. il *Forbes* 140:62+ D 14 '87
            Industries
            See also
Hungaroton (Firm)
Wine industry—Hungary
            Politics and government
            See also
Communist Party (Hungary)
Hungary: before the storm breaks. I. Völgyes. *Curr Hist* 86:373-6+ N '87
            Social conditions
In the land of the setting sun [cover story] S. Brockmann. il *America* 157:238-43 O 17 '87

Hungary and Poland
            Anecdotes, facetiae, satire, etc.
Hungary: a Pole's paradise? Klakson. il *World Press Rev* 34:41 Ja '87

Hunger

See also
Appetite
Famines
Feed the Children (Organization)
Food supply
Hands Across America, 1986
World Food Day
Harry Chapin is gone, but friends carry his song in their hearts. il pors *People Wkly* 28:49-50 D 21 '87
Hunger in the U.S. J. L. Brown. il *Sci Am* 256:36-41 F '87
Letters [discussion of February 1987 article, Hunger in the U.S.] J. L. Brown. *Sci Am* 256:6+ Je '87
The politics of hunger [food surplus keeps growing] W. Greider. il *Roll Stone* p34-5 Jl 2 '87
Rethinking hunger in America: adapting the Sullivan principles. N. Amidei. il *Christ Century* 104:51-4 Ja 21 '87
Top African leaders Diouf, Odhiambo hailed for fight against hunger. il pors *Jet* 73:6 O 5 '87
Hunger and church *See* Church and social problems
The hunger artist [drama] See Clarke, Martha, 1944?-
Hunger relief *See* Relief work
Hunger strikes
Fasting for life [C. Hyder's hunger strike for disarmament] J. Cott. il por *Roll Stone* p33+ My 7 '87
The hunger artists [fast by veterans protesting U.S. policy in Nicaragua] W. F. Schulz, Jr. il *Progressive* 51:14-15 Je '87
A matter of life and death [fast for disarmament; interview with C. Hyder] J. Cott. il por *Roll Stone* p48-9+ F 26 '87
Physicist Hyder fasts for peace. W. Sweet. il por *Phys Today* 40:68 Ap '87
Hungerford (Berkshire, England)

Crime
A bloody rage in rural England [M. Ryan's shooting spree] il *U S News World Rep* 103:11 Ag 31 '87
The market-day massacre. B. Levin. il *Macleans* 100:20 Ag 31 '87
They shoot only in America, don't they? [M. Ryan's killing spree] por *Newsweek* 110:34 Ag 31 '87
Wednesday, bloody Wednesday [gunman M. Ryan] C. Ogden. il *Time* 130:27 Ag 31 '87
Hungry Mind (Saint Paul, Minn.: Bookstore) *See* Booksellers and bookselling—Minnesota
Hunner, Robert J.
Defining active and reasonable efforts to preserve families. il *Child Today* 15:27-30 N/D '86
Hunnicutt, Tia

about
All-American Girl-talk. il pors *Teen* 31:46 Jl '87
Toying with success. il por *Teen* 31:68+ Ja '87
Hunsaker, Phillip L., and Alessandra, Anthony J.
Giving—and getting—feedback [excerpt from The art of managing people] il *Work Woman* 12:30+ Ap '87
Hunsucker, Robert D.

about
The performance took a beating, the paychecks didn't. J. E. Davis and K. Deveny. il pors *Bus Week* p54 My 4 '87
Hunt, Carla
Puebla and Cholula. il *Travel Holiday* 167:23-4+ Ap '87
Hunt, Douglas, 1930-
Food allergies [excerpt from No more cravings] *Essence* 17:15-16+ Mr '87
Hunt, George W., 1937-
America and theological education [address] *America* 157:6-8 Jl 4-11 '87
Of many things. See issues of America beginning July 7-14, 1984
Hunt, Gerald L.
Miracle nutrient? il *Omni* 9:24 F '87
Hunt, Joe

about
The Billionaire Boy—and the missing body. por *Newsweek* 109:61 My 4 '87
Murder and intrigue California-style. M. Gray. por *Macleans* 100:44 F 16 '87
Hunt, Linda
NASA's Nazis. *Nation* 244:671 My 23 '87
Hunt, Marilyn
Antony Tudor: master provocateur. il pors *Dance Mag* 61:36-41 My '87
Argentina's golden boy Julio Bocca. il pors *Dance Mag* 61:60-1 Mr '87
Jens-Jacob Worsaae sets a sparkling stage: designing the light fantastic. il por *Dance Mag* 61:48-52 Ap '87
More than make-believe. il *Dance Mag* 61:58-60 O '87

On edge [cover story] il pors *Dance Mag* 61:43-7 S '87
Paris Opéra Ballet at the Met: compagnie de cristal. il *Dance Mag* 61:50-5 Ja '87
Suki Schorer takes the mystery out of mastery: caring. il pors *Dance Mag* 61:54-7 F '87
Trials by Fire. il pors *Dance Mag* 61:42-5 My '87
Hunt, Morton M., 1920-
The comfort of pals. il *N Y Times Mag* p46 Ja 18 '87
A common-sense guide to health insurance. il *N Y Times Mag* p46-50+ My 3 '87
Navigating the therapy maze. il *N Y Times Mag* p28-31+ Ag 30 '87
Was man meant to fly? il *N Y Times Mag* p42-4+ N 1 '87
What the new divorce laws are doing to women. il *Good Housekeep* 205:64+ Jl '87
Hunt, Peter

about
Assassination [film] Reviews
People Wkly 27:16 F 2 '87. I. Hellman
Hunt, Richard Morris, 1827-1895

about
The golden age of Newport. A. Pryce-Jones. il *House Gard* 159:190-7+ Je '87
Hunt, Thomas C., 1930-
(jt. auth) See Fleming, Dan B., and Hunt, Thomas C., 1930-
Hunt, William Lanier
Reflowering Dixie. por *Rodale's Org Gard* 34:95-6 N '87
Hunt family

about
Battling a billion-dollar debt [cover story] J. A. Jenkins. il *N Y Times Mag* p24-9+ S 27 '87
Fighting to rescue the family fortune. H. J. Steinbreder. il *Fortune* 115:53 Ja 5 '87
It's white-knuckle time for the Hunts. T. Mason. il *Bus Week* p29 Mr 30 '87
The worst investors of our time. L. Luciano. il *Money* Sp Issue:38 Fall '87
Hunter, Alberta, ca. 1895-1984

about
Blues singer Alberta Hunter: the forgotten years [excerpt from Alberta Hunter]; ed. by Gerald Cook. F. C. Taylor. por *Ms* 15:46-8+ Mr '87
Hunter, Beatrice Trum
Food for thought. See issues of Consumers' Research Magazine
Hunter, Donnell
When it stopped singing [poem] *America* 157:293 O 31 '87
Hunter, Duncan L.

about
Two in Congress debate U.S. defense [interview] J. Martin. pors *Sch Update* 119:22 F 23 '87
Hunter, Frances Gardner, 1916-

about
"A faith healer gave us our child". J. Grazier. il pors *McCalls* 115:164-6 O '87
Hunter, Holly

about
Five foot two, how she grew. D. Ansen. il pors *Newsweek* 110:46-7 D 28 '87
Hey, man, it's Holly Hunter! E. Pooley. il pors *N Y* 20:70-4 D 14 '87
Holly Hunter takes Hollywood. R. Corliss. il pors *Time* 130:75 D 21 '87
Hunter, J. Robert
Should the financing of U.S. catastrophic health care emphasize private insurance methods? [excerpts from testimony, February 17, 1987] *Congr Dig* 66:123+ Ap '87
Hunter, James Davison, 1955-

about
Christianity today talks to James Davison Hunter. D. Neff and B. Spring. por *Christ Today* 31:64-5 N 20 '87
Hunter, Kevin

about
Wire Train's hippie conductor. M. Goldberg. il por *Roll Stone* p38 Mr 26 '87
Hunter, Mark
The beat goes off: how technology has gummed up rock's grooves. il *Harpers* 274:53-7 My '87
Hunter, Nan

about
Who should take the test for HIV and why? [interview] L. Kravitz. il pors *Sch Update* 120:21 O 16 '87

Hunter, Paula
about
Reviews:
P. Hunter at Merce Cunningham Studio, New York City. M. Aloff. *Dance Mag* 61:38-9 Ja '87
Hunter, Ralph E.
(jt. auth) See Rubin, David M., and Hunter, Ralph E.
Hunter, Robert E.
The Reagan administration and the Middle East. *Curr Hist* 86:49-52+ F '87
Hunter, Robert O.
about
Hunter and Nelson named to DOE posts. I. Goodwin. *Phys Today* 40 pt1:53 Ag '87
Hunter, Shireen T.
After the Ayatollah. *Foreign Policy* 66:77-97 Spr '87
Hunter, Teola P.
about
Black woman speaker pro tempore of Michigan House. por *Jet* 71:22 Ja 12 '87
Hunter, Tim
about
River's edge [film] Reviews
Film Comment il 23:70-1 Jl/Ag '87. G. Smith
Glamour 85:153-4 Je '87. J. G. Boyum
Macleans il 100:48 Je 8 '87. L. O'Toole
Mademoiselle il 93:80 Ag '87. R. Rosenbaum
Ms il 16:26 S '87. J. Barthel
N Y il 20:90+ My 18 '87. D. Denby
Natl Rev 39:55-6 Je 19 '87. J. Simon
New Repub 196:26-7 Je 8 '87. S. Kauffmann
New Yorker 63:78-9 Je 15 '87. P. Kael
Newsweek il 109:69 Je 1 '87. D. Ansen
People Wkly il 27:8 Je 1 '87. P. Travers
Roll Stone il p43-4 Ap 23 '87. D. Edelstein
Time il 129:73 Je 1 '87. R. Schickel
Hunter-Gault, Charlayne
Washington confidential: an interview with Tip O'Neill. por *Vogue* 177:756-7+ S '87
about
Charlayne Hunter-Gault: from front line to firing line. C. G. Fraser. il pors *Essence* 17:40-2+ Mr '87
Hunters
See also
Farmer-hunter relations
Stalking the predator: a profile of the American hunter [cover story] T. A. Heberlein. bibl f il *Environment* 29:6-11+ S '87
Health and hygiene
Are you tough enough to hunt elk? J. Zumbo. il *Outdoor Life* 180:94-5+ N '87
Fundamental first aid for the hunter. S. Netherby. il *Field Stream* 92:86+ N '87
Skin deep. E. D. Thomas. il *Outdoor Life* 180:14+ D '87
Super-C for hunters and dogs [preventing muscle soreness] L. Mueller. il *Outdoor Life* 180:76+ S '87
Psychology
Alone. G. Hill. il *Field Stream* 91:14+ Mr '87
A hunter's story. J. Barsness. il *Field Stream* 91:66-7 Mr '87
Just talkin'. J. Barsness. il *Field Stream* 92:23-5 Ag '87
Time to quit. N. Strung. il *Field Stream* 92:54+ D '87
What if? G. Hill. il *Field Stream* 91:32+ Ja '87
Vision
See Vision
Hunters and gatherers
Gazelle killing in Stone Age Syria [emergence of agriculture at Tell Abu Hureyra] A. J. Legge and P. A. Rowley-Conwy. il map *Sci Am* 257:88-95 Ag '87
Hunter-gatherers of the tropical forest. L. Palade. il maps *Courier* 40:20-2 Je '87
Letters [discussion of August 1987 article, Gazelle killing in Stone Age Syria] A. J. Legge and P. A. Rowley-Conwy. *Sci Am* 257:8+ N '87
The worst mistake in the history of the human race. J. M. Diamond. il *Discover* 8:64-6 My '87
Hunters Books (Firm)
40 to lose jobs when Hunters in Westwood, Beverly Hills close. L. See. *Publ Wkly* 232:23 D 25 '87
Hunthausen, Raymond G.
about
Hunthausen reinstated. *Christ Century* 104:522 Je 3-10 '87
Hunthausen restored. *Commonweal* 114:372-3 Je 19 '87
Panel probe in Seattle. *Christ Century* 104:215 Mr 4 '87

Hunting
See also
Bear hunting
Bobcat hunting
Buffalo hunting
Caribou hunting
Coyote hunting
Decoys (Hunting)
Deer hunting
Duck shooting
Elk hunting
Eskimos—Hunting
Farmer-hunter relations
Game, Dressing of
Game laws
Gazelle hunting
Goose shooting
Grouse shooting
Hunting dogs
Hunting with bow and arrow
Leopard hunting
Moose hunting
Mourning dove shooting
Partridge shooting
Pheasant shooting
Pigeon shooting
Poaching
Pronghorn hunting
Quail shooting
Rabbit hunting
Sealing
Squirrel hunting
Tiger hunting
Turkey hunting
Water bird shooting
Whaling
Woodcock shooting
Grandpa and the kid. D. Sisson. See alternate issues of Field & Stream beginning September 1983
Licking big game [finding big game at mineral licks] G. P. Michiel. il *Outdoor Life* 179:98-9+ My '87
Of vanishing birds and dogs—and neckties. R. M. Cera. il *Conservationist* 42:22-5 N/D '87
Secret spots. J. Barsness. il *Field Stream* 91:76-7 Ap '87
Solunar tables. See issues of Field & Stream
Stalking the predator: a profile of the American hunter [cover story] T. A. Heberlein. bibl f il *Environment* 29:6-11+ S '87
Toward happier trails. J. Zumbo. il *Outdoor Life* 180:70+ N '87
Troublesome trifles [reprint from April 1964 issue] T. Trueblood. il *Field Stream* 92:30+ O '87
The way of the snail [slow motion tactics in big game hunting] H. Buck. il *Field Stream* 92:58-9+ O '87
Accidents and injuries
Sit tight for turkeys. D. Painter. il *Field Stream* 92:82-3 My '87
A thin disguise [life of a farmer imitated by author] R. Rhodes. il *N Y Times Mag* p62 Jl 19 '87
Anecdotes, facetiae, satire, etc.
Beaten. N. Strung. il *Field Stream* 92:27-8 Ag '87
How to shoot ducks. E. Zern. il *Field Stream* 92:148 N '87
A month of Sundays [young hunters] A. Liere. il *Field Stream* 92:21+ D '87
Why later is better. J. Bashline. il *Field Stream* 92:36+ D '87
Bibliography
Books & comments. See occasional issues of Field & Stream beginning April 1985
Equipment
See also
Blinds (Camouflage)
Boat seats for bucks. C. Slovensky. il *Outdoor Life* 180:136-7 O '87
Bowhunting gear. D. Petersen. il *Mother Earth News* 108:60-4 N/D '87
Gone in a flash [game spooked by reflective hunting gear] B. McRae. il *Field Stream* 92:68-9+ Jl '87
The stuff that counts. B. Brister. il *Field Stream* 92:75-8 N '87
What's new. See issues of Outdoor Life
Ethical aspects
Editorial. D. Barnes. il *Field Stream* 91:7 Ja '87
The good, the bad and the in-between. S. Mulak. il *Outdoor Life* 180:122+ O '87
The quality of mercy. K. McCafferty. il *Field Stream* 92:40+ O '87

Hunting—*cont.*

Fees

Restoring New York's wildlife [Pittman-Robertson program] L. DeGraff and J. Dell. il *Conservationist* 42:2-11+ N/D '87

History

Editorial ["the good old days"] D. Barnes. *Field Stream* 92:8 Je '87

Noise

Quiet clothes make the man [quiet hunting clothes] T. Huggler. il *Outdoor Life* 180:84-6+ Jl '87

Safety devices and measures

See also

Camouflage (Hunting)

It could happen to you [safety for turkey hunters] W. H. Gross. il *Outdoor Life* 179:64-5+ Je '87

Orange helps bring 'em back alive. R. Deigh. il *U S News World Rep* 103:70 D 14 '87

Storm conditions

Dismal day gobblers. K. Etling. il *Outdoor Life* 179:62-3+ Mr '87

Study and teaching

Teach your children well [lack of shooting ranges] L. Williamson. il *Outdoor Life* 180:82+ S '87

Africa

A lesson from Africa. G. Hill. il *Field Stream* 92:13 Jl '87

Alaska

Dangerous game, dangerous country [Kodiak brown bear; cover story] T. Dawson. il *Field Stream* 92:39-41+ Ag '87

Arizona

Hound music and a very big bear [record black bear] F. Peters. il *Outdoor Life* 179:94-5+ My '87

Legend of the Gambel [quail] B. Tarrant. il *Field Stream* 92:148+ My '87

Botswana

The new game in Africa. J. F. Walker. il *Forbes* 139:94+ Ap 20 '87

California

A beginning [boy's quail hunt in California] B. Kahn. il *Field Stream* 91:64-5 Ja '87

India

Jim Corbett: the reluctant executioner. G. C. Ward. il por maps *Audubon* 89:44-9+ Jl '87

Indiana

Thunder gobbler. T. Weddle. il *Outdoor Life* 180:70-1+ O '87

Kansas

In search of the perfect dove hunt. M. Pearce. il *Outdoor Life* 180:66-7+ Ag '87

Labrador (Nfld.)

Four-of-a-kind caribou. H. L. Lawrence. il *Outdoor Life* 179:68-9+ Mr '87

Maryland

Flagging for geese [Canada geese] B. Sayler. il *Outdoor Life* 180:58-60+ D '87

Mexico

Treasure of Tamaulipas [whitewing doves] W. L. Bourne. il *Field Stream* 92:58-9+ S '87

Missouri

Dismal day gobblers. K. Etling. il *Outdoor Life* 179:62-3+ Mr '87

Great day in the morning [quail hunting] J. M. Vance. il *Field Stream* 92:14+ Jl '87

The sporting life 'ADAPTs' their farm [John and Mary Jo Rouse farm] J. Walter. il *Success Farm* 85 no4:27 F '87

Montana

Blood brothers [pronghorn hunting] K. McCafferty. il *Field Stream* 92:44-5 D '87

Burdensome bison [Yellowstone] J. Robbins. il *Audubon* 89:24+ Ja '87

A morning under the Missions [duck shooting with stepson] J. Barsness. il *Field Stream* 92:44+ Je '87

A week with the wapiti. J. Barsness. il *Field Stream* 92:64-5+ N '87

Where the elk are. S. Curtis. il *Field Stream* 92:56-7+ O '87

New York (State)

1986 Big Buck Club winners. il *Conservationist* 42:46-7 S/O '87

Breaking the rules for deer [hunter P. Fiduccia] K. Etling. il *Outdoor Life* 180:68-9+ O '87

Landowners and sportsmen united [Dept. of Environmental Conservation cooperative program allowing public to hunt or fish on private lands] J. Major. il *Conservationist* 41:42-5 Ja/F '87

A wild turkey for Thanksgiving. W. Hollister. il *Conservationist* 42:2-9 S/O '87

Oregon

Grandpa and the kid [jumpshooting end of season ducks on the Umpqua River with a Chesapeake Bay retriever] D. Sisson. il *Field Stream* 91:49+ F '87

Pacific Northwest

The other kind of elk [Roosevelt elk] N. Nelson. il *Field Stream* 92:54-5+ S '87

Pennsylvania

Empty days: a journal of two weeks afield. C. Fergus. il *Ctry J* 14:64-9 D '87

Québec (Province)

Four-of-a-kind caribou. H. L. Lawrence. il *Outdoor Life* 179:68-9+ Mr '87

Rocky Mountains region

Muleys where you want them. S. Curtis. il *Outdoor Life* 180:98-9+ S '87

My last hunter [Rocky Mountain elk hunt] M. Lapinski. il *Outdoor Life* 179:60-1+ F '87

Pattern for elk. D. Dobie. il *Outdoor Life* 180:64-5+ O '87

Scotland

Public vs. private hunting [stag stalking] G. Reiger. *Field Stream* 91:38+ Mr '87

Siberia (Soviet Union)

From the wilderness to Saks Fifth Avenue, the fur trail leads from the hunt to riches. M. Brower. il por *People Wkly* 27:98-100+ Ap 6 '87

South Dakota

Roosters within reach [cock pheasants] J. Murray. il *Outdoor Life* 180:78-9+ O '87

United States

See Hunting

Utah

Hard time mule deer. S. Curtis. il *Outdoor Life* 180:78-9+ N '87

Vermont

A deer to believe in. H. F. Blaisdell. il *Read Dig* 131:25-6+ N '87

Western States

Approach to antelope. B. Journey. il *Outdoor Life* 180:92-3+ S '87

Bucks at the edge [mule deer] W. L. Prothero. il *Field Stream* 92:46+ N '87

Hunt the locked-up places. J. Zumbo. il *Outdoor Life* 180:90-1+ N '87

Wyoming

The basin. B. Brister. il *Field Stream* 92:54-5+ N '87

What price, hunting? [privatization of wildlife and public lands access] L. Williamson. il *Outdoor Life* 180:38+ Ag '87

Zambia

African notes [big game hunting] D. E. Petzal. il *Field Stream* 92:60+ D '87

Hunting by animals *See* Predation (Biology)

Hunting clothes *See* Clothing and dress—Sports clothes

Hunting cockroaches [drama] *See* Głowacki, Janusz

Hunting dogs

See also

Beagles (Dogs)

English setters

Hounds

Retrievers

Attack of the midnight screamer. W. J. Buchanan. il *Read Dig* 130:169-70+ Ap '87

Brag dogs. S. Guion. il *Outdoor Life* 179:66-7+ Mr '87

Dog days. G. Hill. il *Field Stream* 92:13+ My '87

Gun dogs. B. Tarrant. See issues of Field & Stream

How to pick a sporting pup. J. Walter. il *Success Farm* 85:23 O '87

Hunting dogs. L. Mueller. See issues of Outdoor Life

Of vanishing birds and dogs—and neckties. R. M. Cera. il *Conservationist* 42:22-5 N/D '87

Care

Buying an older dog. B. Tarrant. il *Field Stream* 92:127-8 Je '87

First aid for hounds. L. Mueller. il *Outdoor Life* 179:40+ F '87

Handling heat [conditioning hunting dogs for hot weather] B. Tarrant. il *Field Stream* 92:130+ Jl '87

Super-C for hunters and dogs [preventing muscle soreness] L. Mueller. il *Outdoor Life* 180:76+ S '87

A warm welcome for newborn pups. L. Mueller. il *Outdoor Life* 179:41+ Ap '87

Training

The 90-second heel [methods of S. Rafe] L. Mueller. il pors *Outdoor Life* 180:59+ N '87

The basics of bird dog training (I). B. Tarrant. il *Field Stream* 91:134+ F '87

The basics of bird dog training (II). B. Tarrant. il *Field Stream* 91:105-6 Mr '87

Hunting dogs—Training—cont.
The basics of bird dog training (III). B. Tarrant. il *Field Stream* 91:134+ Ap '87
Cable training for retrievers. L. Mueller. il *Outdoor Life* 179:126+ My '87
Fetch on faith and cripples first [M. Kellogg's methods of training for retrievers] L. Mueller. il por *Outdoor Life* 180:44-5 Ag '87
Grandpa and the kid. D. Sisson. il *Field Stream* 92:51+ S '87
How to be top dog [training methods of S. C. Rafe] L. Mueller. il *Outdoor Life* 180:102-3+ S '87
Instant underwater retriever training [Labrador retrievers] L. Mueller. il *Outdoor Life* 179:24-6 Ja '87
Kellogg's "arm extenders" [use of a slingshot in training dogs] L. Mueller. il pors *Outdoor Life* 180:52+ Jl '87
Looking good. B. Tarrant. il *Field Stream* 91:89-91 Ja '87
Making retrievers seaworthy. B. Tarrant. il *Field Stream* 92:174+ S '87
Retriever scent training. L. Mueller. il *Outdoor Life* 179:52+ Mr '87
Teaching pup to charge. B. Tarrant. il *Field Stream* 92:124+ O '87
The way the wind blows. B. Tarrant. il *Field Stream* 92:115+ N '87

Laws and regulations
Ban on dog training? [Anti-Live Animal Lure Act of 1987] R. Herzberg. *Outdoor Life* 180:152 S '87
Hunting guides *See* Guides
Hunting handwarmers *See* Handwarmers (Clothing)
Hunting in art
L.L. Bean vs. the preppified pooch [artist W. Spitzmiller's suit against L. L. Bean's doctoring of hunting scene on catalog cover] il por *Newsweek* 109:53 Mr 16 '87
Of horse and hound [G. Nevill, dealer in hunting art] C. Gibbs. il por *House Gard* 159:76+ N '87
A sporting tradition [cover story] J. Madson. il *Natl Wildl* 25:48-57 O/N '87
Hunting knives *See* Knives
Hunting laws *See* Game laws
Hunting records
The grand deer slammer [bowhunter B. Long] T. Stienstra. il por *Outdoor Life* 179:54-5+ Ja '87
Hound music and a very big bear [record black bear in Arizona] F. Peters. il *Outdoor Life* 179:94-5+ My '87
Hunting rifles *See* Rifles
Hunting season laws *See* Game laws
Hunting stands *See* Hunting—Equipment
Hunting trophies
1986 Big Buck Club winners. il *Conservationist* 42:46-7 S/O '87
Editorial [whitetail trophy deer] D. Barnes. *Field Stream* 92:7 Ag '87
Four-of-a-kind caribou [Quebec and Labrador] H. L. Lawrence. il *Outdoor Life* 179:68-9+ Mr '87
A tale of two bucks [C. Van Lith and B. Kontras take trophy whitetail deer with bow and arrow] J. Murray and M. Pearce. il pors *Outdoor Life* 180:68-9+ Jl '87
Trophies [with editorial comment by Duncan Barnes] N. Strung. *Field Stream* 92:7, 44+ S '87
Watch a trail to take a trophy [deer] W. L. Prothero. il *Outdoor Life* 180:72-3+ Jl '87
Hunting with bow and arrow
100 deer with a bow [C. Yates] J. E. Phillips. il *Outdoor Life* 179:52-3+ F '87
Bowbag a gobbler. J. E. Churchill. il *Outdoor Life* 179:90-1+ My '87
Bowhunting gear. D. Petersen. il *Mother Earth News* 108:60-4 N/D '87
Don't bugle up a grizzly bear [bowhunting bugling bull elk] B. McRae. il *Outdoor Life* 179:54-5+ Ap '87
The grand deer slammer [bowhunter B. Long] T. Stienstra. il por *Outdoor Life* 179:54-5+ Ja '87
A tale of two bucks [C. Van Lith and B. Kontras take trophy whitetail deer] J. Murray and M. Pearce. il pors *Outdoor Life* 180:68-9+ Jl '87
Without a trace [art of camouflage in bowhunting for deer] G. Helgeland. il *Field Stream* 91:56-7+ F '87
Huntingdon, Selina Shirley, Countess of, 1707-1791
about
Lady Huntingdon's chapel. T. Aldous. il por *Hist Today* 37:2-3 Ag '87
Huntington, Roger
1988 Detroit model review. il *Consum Res Mag* 70:11-13 N '87

Huntington, Samuel P.
about
Academy rejects Huntington nomination. E. Marshall. por *Science* 236:661-2 My 8 '87
Blood lust in academia. F. Zakaria. *New Repub* 197:16-18 Jl 27 '87
The posse stops a "softie". E. Bowen. il *Time* 129:76-7 My 11 '87
Scholars bite Mad Dog. *Nation* 244:595 My 9 '87
Soft sciences are often harder than hard sciences. J. M. Diamond. il *Discover* 8:34-5+ Ag '87
Huntington's disease
Animals yield clues to Huntington's disease [possibly caused by quinolinic acid] J. L. Marx. il *Science* 238:1510-11 D 11 '87
Despite the shadow of his father's (and possibly his own) deadly disease, a folk hero celebrates life; ed. by Cable Neuhaus. A. Guthrie. il pors *People Wkly* 28:97-8+ S 7 '87
A DNA segment encoding two genes very tightly linked to Huntington's disease. T. C. Gilliam and others. bibl f il *Science* 238:950-2 N 13 '87
Huntington's marker. *Sci News* 132:343 N 28 '87
New clue [effect of quinolinic acid on brain cells in Huntington's disease; work of Dennis Choi and others] *USA Today (Periodical)* 115:9 F '87
The ticking of a time bomb in the genes [cover story] D. Grady. il *Discover* 8:26-8+ Je '87
Therapy
New tissue eases Huntington's disease [work of Paul R. Sanberg and others] J. Greenberg and B. Bower. *Sci News* 131:328 My 23 '87
Huntley, Robert Edward Royall, 1929-
about
Best Products: trying to put pizzazz back in the showroom. T. Smart. il por *Bus Week* p39-40 Mr 16 '87
Huntsville (Ala.)
Historic houses, sites, etc.
Have an old-fashioned Huntsville Christmas. J. T. Black. il *South Living* 22:10-11+ D '87
Industries
Star Wars fell on Alabama [profits from Strategic Defense Initiative] D. Charles. il *Nation* 245:748-50 D 19 '87
Huong
about
Alaskan marine life and the Eskimo—through art. B. Rush and H. Lebelson. il por *Sea Front* 33:84-9 Mr/Ap '87
Hurd, Thacher
about
Thacher Hurd: a talent in his own right. D. E. Roback. il por *Publ Wkly* 231:33+ Ja 23 '87
Hurdelsh, Mark
Pennsylvania: small scale strip mining [poem] *America* 156:71 Ja 31 '87
Hurdle racing
Ed Moses looks forward to new streak after loss. il pors *Jet* 72:51 Je 22 '87
Moses wins, Nehemiah falls at track meet in England. *Jet* 72:46 Ag 17 '87
Nehemiah hopes surgery will improve his comeback. *Jet* 71:50 Mr 9 '87
Nehemiah ready for U.S. debut against Olympians. por *Jet* 71:49 Ja 19 '87
The reign ended in Spain [E. Moses' loss in the 400 hurdles] P. Butcher. il pors *Sports Illus* 66:34-5 Je 15 '87
Rude hello for an old foe [G. Foster vs. R. Nehemiah in the Sunkist Invitational high hurdles] K. Moore. il pors *Sports Illus* 66:16-17 Ja 26 '87
Hurford, Daphne
Lucky, plucky Becky Sinkler. il por *50 Plus* 27:50+ Ag '87
Hurley, Andrew
(tr) See Valladares, Armando. Against all hope: the prison memoirs of Armando Valladares
Hurley, Dan
A sound mind in an unsound body. bibl (p67) il *Psychol Today* 21:34-8+ Ag '87
Hurley, James, d. 1987
'I'm dying—AIDS is your problem now'. por *Newsweek* 110:38-9 Ag 10 '87
Hurley, Judith Benn
Asparagus . . . with a light touch. il *Rodale's Org Gard* 34:86-9 Ap '87
Delicious high-fiber breakfasts. il *Prevention* 39:82-4+ F '87
Feasting on healthy appetizers. il *Prevention* 39:40+ Ap '87
Have an Italian-style picnic. il *Prevention* 39:60+ Jl '87

Hurley, Judith Benn—*cont.*

The healthy gourmet foods of summer. il *Prevention* 39:44+ Je '87

Healthy microwaving. See issues of Prevention (Emmaus, Pa.) beginning January 1987

How to get more health from your food. il *Prevention* 39:57-8+ D '87

Paste tomatoes. il *Rodale's Org Gard* 34:38+ Ag '87

Pepper pleasures. il *Rodale's Org Gard* 34:40-2+ Je '87

Poultry: go from good to great. il *Prevention* 39:66-8+ My '87

Semiwild game. il *Prevention* 39:90-2+ N '87

Summer microwaving. il *Prevention* 39:50-2+ Ag '87

Sundried tomatoes. il *Rodale's Org Gard* 34:47 Ag '87

Hurrell, George

about

In the Hurrell style. M. Raboy. il *Petersens Photogr Mag* 16:20-1 S '87

Hurricanes

See also

Cyclones

National Hurricane Center

America's hurricane threat. D. H. Hickcox. *Focus* 37:36 Fall '87

Atlantic hurricane season [1986] M. B. Lawrence. il map *Weatherwise* 40:21-4 F '87

Flying into the eye of a hurricane [cover story] J. M. Masters. il *Weatherwise* 40:128-33 Je '87

A future danger: hothouse hurricanes? [work of Kerry Emanuel] il *Discover* 8:10+ Je '87

The human dimension in hurricane forecasting. M. Clary. il *Weatherwise* 40:197-9 Jl/Ag '87

Hurricane dangers increase as coastal cities grow. *Earth Sci* 40:5 Fall '87

Hurricanes haunt our history. P. E. Hughes. il *Weatherwise* 40:134-40 Je '87

More violent hurricanes? [caused by warmer climate; views of Kerry Emanuel] *Time* 129:69 Ap 20 '87

Hursh, Deborah A., and others

A sea urchin gene encodes a polypeptide homologous to epidermal growth factor. bibl f il *Science* 237:1487-90 S 18 '87

Hurst, Lynda

Today's baby-boomers, tomorrow's elderly. *World Press Rev* 34:26-8 Ag '87

Hurst, Mary Ann

(tr) See Ding Ling. The silent speech of love

Hurt, Frances Hallam

The dog with nine lives. il *Read Dig* 130:115-18 Ja '87

Hurt, Henry

From the jaws of death. il *Read Dig* 130:116-20 Ap '87

The heart of Canton, Ohio. *Read Dig* 130:49-52 Mr '87

Little Boy Blue of Chester, Nebraska. *Read Dig* 131:73-8 D '87

Seeds that grow hope. il *Read Dig* 130:19-22+ Mr '87

Hurtado, Gerry *See* Skatemaster Tate

Hurtado, Miguel de la Madrid *See* Madrid Hurtado, Miguel de la

Hurter, Bill

One to one. See issues of Petersen's Photographic Magazine

Hurwitz, Charles E.

about

Razing the giant redwoods. P. Abramson. il por *Newsweek* 110:38 Jl 6 '87

A takeover artist who's turning redwoods into quick cash. J. R. Norman. il por *Bus Week* p64-5 F 2 '87

Hurwitz, David

Domesticating digital. il *High Fidel* 37:62-4+ O '87

Midprice CDs are here. il *High Fidel* 37:73-4 D '87

Hurwitz, Marty

about

The man they love to hate. J. Traub. il pors *Channels* 7:66-70 Je '87

Husain, Jory

about

Class acts: guys who make the grade. M. L. Baer. il pors *Teen* 31:59-60 N '87

Husák, Gustáv

about

A new face, an old policy in Prague. il por *Newsweek* 110:27 D 28 '87

A reluctant reformer bows out. W. R. Doerner. il por *Time* 130:34 D 28 '87

Husarska, Anna

Midsummer Leningrad dreams. il *New Leader* 70:8-9 S 7 '87

Publishing in Poland. il *New Leader* 69:21-4 D 1-15 '86

A talk with Joseph Brodsky [interview] *New Leader* 70:8-11 D 14 '87

Husayn, Ṣaddām *See* Hussein, Ṣaddām

Husband and wife *See* Marriage; Married couples

Husband and wife quarrels *See* Quarrels

Husbands

See also

Adultery

Divorce

Marriage

Married couples

Separation (Law)

Wife abuse

How to break your man's bad habits. D. Hales. *McCalls* 114:56-7 Ja '87

How to live with a difficult man. A. Van der Meer. *Redbook* 169:104-5+ My '87

My husband couldn't tell the truth. il *Good Housekeep* 205:22+ N '87

My husband was gay. il *Good Housekeep* 204:24+ Ja '87

My husband was never on time. il *Good Housekeep* 204:26+ F '87

Stranger in my house [retired husband] H. Sampson. il *Read Dig* 130:9-10 Ap '87

Support thy wife [good husbands help make good mothers] R. B. McCall. il *Parents* 62:168 Jl '87

Why men won't help with housework [excerpt from Sexual static] M. H. Shaevitz. il *Ladies Home J* 104:76+ Je '87

Employment

A profile of husbands in today's labor market. H. Hayghe and S. E. Haugen. bibl f il *Mon Labor Rev* 110:12-17 O '87

Huse, Robert J.

about

'I want him crucified'. G. Hackett. il por *Newsweek* 110:36 O 5 '87

Hüsker Dü (Musical group)

Hüsker Dü. G. Santoro. il *Down Beat* 54:14 Ap '87

Hüsker Dü tells the hard truth. D. Fricke. il *Roll Stone* p131-3 Mr 26 '87

Husky Oil Ltd.

Putting out the welcome mat [takeover of Husky Oil by Li Ka-shing] D. Francis. por *Macleans* 100:9 My 18 '87

Hussein, King of Jordan, 1935-

about

Hussein's game. S. Reed. *Nation* 244:839-40 Je 20 '87

Jordan's malaise. M. C. Wilson. bibl f *Curr Hist* 86:73-6+ F '87

Homes

Architectural digest visits: King Hussein and Queen Noor of Jordan [beach house on Gulf of Aqaba] G. Y. Dryansky. il pors *Archit Dig* 44:68-77+ Ja '87

Hussein, Ibrahim

about

Kenyan wins NY Marathon, points to '88 Olympics. il por *Jet* 73:51 N 23 '87

New look in the long run. C. Neff. il pors *Sports Illus* 67:24-5 N 9 '87

Hussein, Ṣaddām

about

Iraq's no-win, no-lose war? J. Barnes. il por *U S News World Rep* 103:38-9 O 12 '87

Hust, Bernard de Clavière d' *See* Clavière d'Hust, Bernard de, Count

Hustad, Donald P.

Let's not just praise the Lord. il por *Christ Today* 31:28-31 N 6 '87

Hustler (Periodical)

Author and publisher groups make filings in two Supreme Court cases [libel suit brought against Hustler magazine by J. Falwell] H. Fields. *Publ Wkly* 232:12 S 4 '87

'Emotional distress' briefs to High Court [Hustler vs. J. Falwell] il *Publ Wkly* 232:13 Jl 17 '87

High Court queries leave outcome of 'Hustler'-Falwell case uncertain. H. Fields. *Publ Wkly* 232:15 D 18 '87

Jerry Falwell vs. Larry Flynt [emotional distress suit goes to Supreme Court] A. Press. il pors *Newsweek* 110:76 D 14 '87

Huston, Anjelica

about

Anjelica [interview] B. Walker. il por *Film Comment* 23:24-6 S/O '87

Anjelica Huston. B. Goodwin. pors *Harpers Bazaar* 120:98, 348-51 S '87

Huston, Anjelica—about—*cont.*
Anjelica Huston sheds her princess past. D. Maychick. por *Mademoiselle* 93:92 Ap '87
What is it about Anjelica Huston? We asked nine men to comment. il pors *Esquire* 108:182-5 S '87
Huston, John, 1906-1987
about
The African Queen [film] Reviews
Ladies Home J il pors 104:77-80+ N '87. K. Hepburn
Newsweek il 110:53-5 Ag 31 '87. K. Hepburn
An American portrait: director John Huston. S. De Santis. il por *Pop Mech* 164:82 Ja '87
The dead [film] Reviews
Commonweal 114:748-9 D 18 '87. T. O'Brien
Macleans 100:66 D 14 '87. L. O'Toole
New Repub 197:26-8 D 21 '87. S. Kauffmann
New Yorker 63:144+ D 14 '87. P. Kael
Newsweek il 110:68 D 21 '87. D. Ansen
Huston [cover story] W. Schulz-Keil. il pors *Film Comment* 23:18-23 S/O '87
John Huston: Hollywood's giant. J. Culhane. il pors *Read Dig* 131:136-43 N '87
John Huston raises The dead. M. Walsh. il pors *Time* 129:92-3 Mr 16 '87
Obituary
Macleans 100:63 S 7 '87. P. Hluchy
Nation 245:259 S 19 '87. A. Cockburn
Natl Rev 39:21-2 O 9 '87. J. Simon
Newsweek por 110:71 S 7 '87. D. Ansen
People Wkly il pors 28:40-1 S 14 '87. P. Travers
Time por 130:64 S 7 '87. R. Schickel
Huston family
about
Huston family portrait announced by Scribners for spring 1989. il por *Publ Wkly* 232:75 O 2 '87
Hut, Piet, 1952-, and Sussman, Gerald Jay
Advanced computing for science. bibl (p184) il *Sci Am* 257:144-8+ O '87
Hutches (Furniture) *See* Cabinets (Furniture)
Hutcheson Memorial Forest (N.J.) *See* Forests and forestry—New Jersey
Hutchings, Gregory
about
A raider's new world. M. Maremont. il por *Bus Week* p49-50 Je 15 '87
Hutchins, Carleen Maley
about
Fiddling with the future. T. Rothman and A. Mereson. il pors *Discover* 8:58-64+ S '87
Hutchins (Robert Maynard) Center for the Study of Democratic Institutions *See* Robert Maynard Hutchins Center for the Study of Democratic Institutions
Hutchinson, Earl R.
To kill a messenger [address, April 16, 1987] *Vital Speeches Day* 53:572-6 Jl 1 '87
Hutchinson, Janet R.
Progress towards change: the National Resource Center on Family Based Services. *Child Today* 15:6-7 N/D '86
Hutchinson, Robert
about
Shock of the past: ancient objects accent a visionary San Francisco design. J. Chatfield-Taylor. il *Archit Dig* 44:116-27 Ap '87
Hutchinson, Robert J.
Transforming the sea wind. il *Oceans* 20:12-19 S/O '87
Hutchinson, Thomas
about
With Thomas Hutchinson's marvelous ERICA, a flick of an eye brings help to the helpless. L. Albrecht. il por *People Wkly* 28:85-6 Jl 20 '87
Hutchinson (Kan.)
Galleries and museums
See also
Kansas Cosmosphere and Space Center
Hutchinson River Parkway (N.Y.) *See* Express highways—New York (State)
Huth, Tom
The greener grass of Calvin Peete. il pors *Esquire* 107:108-12+ F '87
Huts
See also
Yurts
Hutton, Barbara
about
The Farrah Fawcett/Barbara Hutton connection [interview with F. Fawcett and L. Persky] M. J. Bandler. il pors *McCalls* 115:186-8 N '87
Poor little rich girl: the tragic story of the real Barbara Hutton. il pors *Redbook* 170:106-11+ D '87

Hutton, Candace Perry
Schoenhut's wooden animals. il *Antiques Collect Hobbies* 92:40-2+ Ag '87
Hutton, Ray
AC Ace. il *Car Driv* 32:33 Mr '87
Hutton, Ronald
A tale of two Cliffords. il por *Hist Today* 37:8-9 Jl '87
Hutton, Timothy
about
Serious stars: Timothy Hutton. R. Goldberg. por *Vogue* 177:482+ Mr '87
Hutton, Will, 1950-
Toward a trade war. *World Press Rev* 34:19 Ag '87
Hutton (E. F.) Group Inc. *See* E. F. Hutton Group Inc.
Hutzler, Heinz
about
A patient card player's picks [interview] J. P. Newport, Jr. il por *Fortune* 116:176 N 9 '87
Huxley, Julian, 1887-1975
about
Sir Julian Huxley: a memoir. C. Lamont. *Humanist* 47:27-8+ My/Je '87
Huxley, Thomas Henry, 1825-1895
about
Life's little joke. S. J. Gould. il *Nat Hist* 96:16+ Ap '87
Huyghe, Patrick
Wheels of light, sea of fire. il *Oceans* 20:20-5 N/D '87
Huysmans, J.-K. (Joris-Karl), 1848-1907
Paris-on-Thames [fiction] il *Courier* 40:33 Ap '87
Huysmans, Joris-Karl *See* Huysmans, J.-K. (Joris-Karl), 1848-1907
Hwa, Terrence L.
about
Hwa is the recipient of the 1986 Apker Award. il por *Phys Today* 40:95 Ja '87
Hwange National Park (Zimbabwe) *See* National parks and reserves—Zimbabwe
Hyacinths
Hyacinths are hard to resist. S. Bender. il *South Living* 22:122-3 Mr '87
Hyacinths, Water *See* Water hyacinths
Hyades Cluster *See* Stars—Clusters
Hyaline membrane disease *See* Respiratory distress syndrome
Hyatt, Carole
about
Why smart people fail [interview] il por *U S News World Rep* 102:55 Ap 6 '87
Hyatt, Ralph
When you need psychotherapy. il *USA Today (Periodical)* 116:84-6 N '87
Hyatt Corp.
Glitzy resorts and suburban hotels: Hyatt breaks new ground. J. E. Ellis. il por *Bus Week* p100-1 My 4 '87
Woman fired for cornrows sues Hyatt hotel in Virginia [C. Tatum] il por *Jet* 73:36 O 19 '87
Hybridization
See also
Cell hybridization
Dysgenesis
Plants—Breeding
Wheat—Hybrids
Hybrids for the year 2000. R. G. Butenko and Z. B. Shamina. il *Courier* 40:20-1 Mr '87
Hyde, Dayton O., 1925-
Don Coyote [condensation] il *Read Dig* 130:70-8+ Mr '87
Hyde, Edward *See* Clarendon, Edward Hyde, 1st Earl of, 1609-1674
Hyde, Henry J.
Iran/contra: reality and unreality. *Natl Rev* 39:19-20 D 4 '87
about
Spying on Henry Hyde at Mass. C. W. Colson. il *Christ Today* 31:80 N 6 '87
U.S. foreign aid: virtue or vice? [interview] P. M. Jones. pors *Sch Update* 119:26 F 23 '87
Hyde, Lewis, and Hyde, Lewis, Jr.
A gazebo of your own. il *Ctry J* 14:21-6 Ag '87
Hyde, Lewis, Jr.
(jt. auth) See Hyde, Lewis, and Hyde, Lewis, Jr.
Hyde Park (N.Y.)
Historic houses, sites, etc.
See also
Home of Franklin Delano Roosevelt National Historic Site (N.Y.)

Hyde Park Antiques Ltd.
Hyde Park's English cast. A. Haden-Guest. il por *Archit Dig* 44:282+ N '87

Hyder, Charles
about
Fasting for life. J. Cott. il por *Roll Stone* p33+ My 7 '87
A matter of life and death [interview] J. Cott. il por *Roll Stone* p48-9+ F 26 '87
Physicist Hyder fasts for peace. W. Sweet. il por *Phys Today* 40:68 Ap '87

Hydra (Constellation) *See* Constellations

Hydra (Zoology)
Selective disruption of gap junctional communication interferes with a patterning process in hydra. S. E. Fraser and others. bibl f il *Science* 237:49-55 Jl 3 '87

Hydra-Fitness Industries, Inc.
A coach who got back in the game [J. D. Brentham] N. L. Croft. il por *Nations Bus* 75:51-2 Ag '87

Hydraulic engineering
See also
Channels (Hydraulic engineering)
Wings beneath the bay [vortex foils tested in San Francisco Bay] *Oceans* 20:3 Mr/Ap '87

Hydraulic equipment
See also
Helicopters—Hydraulic equipment

Hydraulic rams
Hydraulic ram system. il *Workbench* 43:69-71 Mr/Ap '87

Hydraulic tools
Seawater hydraulics. *Sea Front* 33:384 S/O '87

Hydrocarbons
See also
Olefins
Chemistry of molecular growth processes in flames. K. C. Smyth and J. H. Miller. bibl f il *Science* 236:1540-6 Je 19 '87
Fingerprinting the mean bees [Africanized bees; research by Dave Carlson and Barry Lavine] *Sci News* 131:218 Ap 4 '87
Interstellar polycyclic aromatic hydrocarbons and carbon in interplanetary dust particles and meteorites. L. J. Allamandola and others. bibl f il *Science* 237:56-9 Jl 3 '87
An invariance in the isoheptanes of petroleum. F. D. Mango. bibl f il *Science* 237:514-17 Jl 31 '87
Organic matter on asteroid 130 Elektra. D. P. Cruikshank and R. H. Brown. bibl f il *Science* 238:183-4 O 9 '87

Hydrochloric acid
Reviving an old route to chlorine [work of Sidney W. Benson and Mohammed Hisham] *Sci News* 132:121 Ag 22 '87

Hydrocortisone
Highs and woes of runners' hormones [elevated ACTH and cortisol levels] D. D. Edwards. *Sci News* 131:325 My 23 '87
Reactions to alcohol: cortisol clues [research by Marc A. Schuckit] B. Bower. *Sci News* 132:324 N 21 '87

Hydrodynamics
See also
Drops
Magnetohydrodynamics
Turbulence
Viscosity
Water hammer

Hydroelectric dams *See* Dams

Hydroelectric plants
See also
Consolidated Hydro Inc.
Environmental aspects
Tapping lakes in Norway: clean but risky energy. il *Environment* 28:23 D '86
Norway
Tapping lakes in Norway: clean but risky energy. il *Environment* 28:23 D '86

Hydroelectric power
See also
Tide power
Wave power
Export-import trade
Whose power to which people? [B. C. Hydro's plans for hydroelectric dam for export on the Peace River] J. Baker. il *Sierra* 72:22-4 Ja/F '87

Hydrofoils
Testing
High-flying hydrofoil [Hercules, Navy PHM-2] D. Wallace. il *Mot Boat Sail* 160:32-5+ D '87

Hydrogen
Evaluation of intrinsic binding energy from a hydrogen bonding group in an enzyme inhibitor. P. A. Bartlett and C. K. Marlowe. bibl f il *Science* 235:569-71 Ja 30 '87
First X-ray pattern of hydrogen solid [work of Russell Hemley and others] *Sci News* 131:201 Mr 28 '87
Structures of two thermolysin-inhibitor complexes that differ by a single hydrogen bond. D. E. Tronrud and others. bibl f il *Science* 235:571-4 Ja 30 '87
Isotopes
See also
Deuterium
Tritium
Spectra and spectroscopy
Exploring the Lyman-alpha forest [work of Wallace L. W. Sargent] M. M. Waldrop. *Science* 235:284 Ja 16 '87
Probing the early universe with quasar light [Lyman alpha forest] B. M. Schwarzschild. bibl f il *Phys Today* 40:17-20 N '87

Hydrogen, Interstellar *See* Matter, Interstellar

Hydrogen bombs *See* Atomic bombs

Hydrogen chloride *See* Hydrochloric acid

Hydrogen ion concentration
See also
Soil acidity
Acid rain monitor. W. D. Scott. il *Radio-Electron* 58:48-9+ Ap '87

Hydrogen sulfide
Chemical energy fuels ecosystems [gutless clam able to oxidize and get energy directly from sulfides] il *Sea Front* 33:62-4 Ja/F '87

Hydrolases
Macrophage cytotoxicity: role for L-arginine deiminase and imino nitrogen oxidation to nitrite. J. B. Hibbs, Jr. and others. bibl f il *Science* 235:473-6 Ja 23 '87

Hydrolysis
Abzymes [catalytic antibodies] *Sci Am* 256:84-5 F '87
Actin polymerization and ATP hydrolysis. E. D. Korn and others. bibl f il *Science* 238:638-44 O 30 '87

Hydroponics
Tomatomation: Japan's high-tech food factories. K. Hiroshi. il *Courier* 40:17-19 Mr '87

Hydroquinones
A predator plant's chemical radar [research by David Lynn and others] S. Weisburd. *Sci News* 132:190 S 19 '87

Hydrotherapy
See also
Thalassotherapy

Hydrothermal vents *See* Hot springs

Hydroxytryptamine *See* Serotonin

Hydrozoa
See also
By-the-wind sailor (Hydrozoa)

Hyenas
Sexual behavior
See Sexual behavior—Animals

Hygiene
See also
Disinfection and disinfectants

Hyland, William G., 1929-
Reagan-Gorbachev III. *Foreign Aff* 66:7-21 Fall '87

Hylton, Richard D.
How high the bull? il *Black Enterp* 18:49-50+ N '87

Hyman, B. D. (Barbara Davis)
about
Bette Davis talks back! [excerpt from This 'n that]; ed. by Michael Herskowitz. B. Davis. il pors *Redbook* 168:34+ Ap '87

Hyman, Barbara Davis *See* Hyman, B. D. (Barbara Davis)

Hyman, Gabby
Self made man. il pors *Horizon* 30:14-16 Mr '87

Hyman, Irwin A.
Punitiveness and public policy: child abuse in American schools. il *USA Today (Periodical)* 116:44-7 S '87

Hyman, Lawrence
Humanists and traditional moral values. por *Humanist* 47:29+ Mr/Ap '87

Hyman (Flo) Memorial Award *See* Flo Hyman Memorial Award

Hymenoptera bites and stings *See* Insect bites and stings

Hymes, Donna
Alcoholism: yes, it can happen to you. il *Curr Health 2* 13:18-21 F '87
Marijuana update: new reasons to "keep off the grass". il *Curr Health 2* 13:18-21 Mr '87
Over-the-counter drugs: handle with care! il *Curr Health 2* 13:14-15 Ja '87

Hymes, James L., 1913-
Public school for four-year-olds. *Educ Dig* 53:47-9 O '87

Hymnals *See* Hymns

Hymns
See also
Gospel music
An apology for the hymn [Catholic Church] J. P. Swain. *America* 156:421-3 My 23 '87
Hymnal completed [United Methodist Hymnal Revision Committee] *Christ Century* 104:993 N 11 '87
Let's not just praise the Lord. D. P. Hustad. il por *Christ Today* 31:28-31 N 6 '87
A trendy voice [J. P. Huber's A singing faith] R. J. Stanislaw. il por *Christ Today* 31:72 S 4 '87
Anecdotes, facetiae, satire, etc.
Bulletins. M. E. Marty. *Christ Century* 104:903 O 14 '87

Hynd, Ronald
about
The merry widow [ballet] Reviews
Dance Mag il 61:62-7 Mr '87. M. Crabb

Hynde, Chrissie
about
The Chrissie Hynde story: sex & drugs & rock 'n' roll & politics & motherhood & vegetables. R. Wolmuth. il pors *People Wkly* 27:68+ Mr 23 '87

Hynes, John, III
about
Home field advantage. B. Leonard. il por *Forbes* 139:91-2 Ja 26 '87

Hynninen, Jorma
about
The Finnish line [interview] G. Jellinek. il pors *Opera News* 51:32-3 Ja 31 '87

Hyperactivity
See also
Attention deficit disorder
Nutritional aspects
The hyperactive breakfast [research by C. Keith Connors and others] B. Bower. *Sci News* 132:168 S 12 '87
Hyperactivity: no go for amino acid [research by Alan J. Zametkin and others] *Sci News* 131:376 Je 13 '87

Hyperbaric oxygenation
A tornado took away his world [coma victim R. Snyder treated with hyperbaric oxygenation] J. Grazier. il pors *McCalls* 114:130-2 Je '87

Hypercalcemia
New tumor factor may disrupt calcium levels [development in cancer patients] D. M. Barnes. bibl il *Science* 237:363-4 Jl 24 '87
A parathyroid hormone-related protein implicated in malignant hypercalcemia: cloning and expression. L. J. Suva and others. bibl f il *Science* 237:893-6 Ag 21 '87
Parathyroid hormone-related protein of malignancy: active synthetic fragments. B. E. Kemp and others. bibl f il *Science* 238:1568-70 D 11 '87
Similarity of synthetic peptide from human tumor to parathyroid hormone in vivo and in vitro. N. Horiuchi and others. bibl f il *Science* 238:1566-8 D 11 '87

HyperCard (Computer program)
Hyper-excitement at Apple. M. Rogers. il *Newsweek* 110:45 Ag 31 '87
HyperCard. G. Williams. il *Byte* 12:109-10+ D '87
Hyping the Mac. S. R. Reed. il *Pers Comput* 11:38 S '87
Planting seeds at Apple. R. A. Shaffer. il *Pers Comput* 11:55 N '87
Populist programming. C. Strehlo. il *Pers Comput* 11:268+ D '87
Two programs bundled with 1-megabyte Macs [MultiFinder and HyperCard] G. Williams and T. Thompson. il *Byte* 12:45 S '87

Hypercharge (Physics) *See* Fifth force (Physics)

Hypercholesteremia
Tracking a genetic error [among French Canadians] B. Wallace. *Macleans* 100:58 S 28 '87

Hyperkinesis *See* Hyperactivity

Hypersensitivity *See* Allergy

Hypersensitized film *See* Photography—Films

Hypersonics
Advanced fuel systems crucial to high-speed transport progress. P. Proctor. il *Aviat Week Space Technol* 126:45+ F 9 '87
Maching birds. N. Moll. il *Flying* 114:148+ S '87
Students propose interior designs for hypersonic travel [Art Center College of Design in Pasadena, Calif.] il *Aviat Week Space Technol* 126:328 Je 15 '87

X-30 research narrowing hypersonic design options [National Aerospace Plane] C. Covault. il *Aviat Week Space Technol* 126:32-3 Ap 27 '87

Hyperspace
Dimensions. G. Williams. il *Omni* 9:52-4+ My '87

Hypertension
Better control of hypertension has reduced stroke deaths [report by Centers for Disease Control] *FDA Consum* 21:2 Jl/Ag '87
Black M.D.'s convene in Atlanta on hypertension. il *Jet* 72:16 Ap 13 '87
Blinding stress [central serous chorioretinopathy; research by Gary S. Gelber and Howard Schatz] P. Chance. *Psychol Today* 21:22-3 Jl '87
Eye of the (emotional) storm [central serous chorioretinopathy; research by Gary S. Gelber and Howard Schatz] *Sci News* 131:40 Ja 17 '87
Hypertension, hostility, and race [study by Neil Schneiderman] *USA Today (Periodical)* 115:9 My '87
Minding your own blood pressure. E. Gofen. il *Curr Health 2* 13:3-9 Mr '87
Pregnancy hypertension marker found. *Sci News* 131:344 My 30 '87
Smooth muscle-mediated connective tissue remodeling in pulmonary hypertension. R. P. Mecham and others. bibl f il *Science* 237:423-6 Jl 24 '87
Suppressing anger a fatal flaw [work of Mara Julius] *Prevention* 39:16 My '87
Genetic aspects
Salt-sensitive genes [research by Judy Z. Miller] V. DeBenedette. *Health* 19:23 My '87
Nutritional aspects
See also
Low sodium cooking
Blood pressure bows to tryptophan. *Prevention* 39:17-18 D '87
Calcium/blood-pressure link confirmed. il *Prevention* 39:6+ Mr '87
Calcium may take the pressure off pregnancy. *Prevention* 39:10 F '87
Mackerel works miracles with blood pressure. il *Prevention* 39:14 Jl '87
Shaking the salt habit. C. Schaeffer. il *Changing Times* 41:20 S '87
The sodium-hypertension connection [cover story] J. Schein. il *Consum Res Mag* 70:11-14+ O '87
Your best blood-pressure news in years. G. Maleskey. *Prevention* 39:24+ N '87
Therapy
Getting the drop on blood pressure. B. Bower. *Sci News* 131:405 Je 27 '87
High blood pressure: drugless treatment? D. D. Edwards. *Sci News* 131:181 Mr 21 '87
High blood pressure: what helps besides drugs? *Consum Rep* 52:315 My '87
Hypertension: a bitter pill to swallow [research by Sydney H. Croog] Y. Baskin. il *Psychol Today* 21:12 F '87
Lowering pressure as a fountain of youth? [research by Aram V. Chobanian] J. Silberner. *Sci News* 131:89 F 7 '87
Pedaling down the pressure. il *Prevention* 39:6 O '87
Reducing hypertension: the role of drugs. J. Schein. il *Consum Res Mag* 70:31-3 N '87

Hypertext
Another odd lot [Guide system for the Macintosh] E. Shapiro. *Byte* 12:301+ Ap '87
The big link [T. H. Nelson's Xanadu system] S. Ditlea. il *Omni* 9:16+ S '87
Guide. W. R. Hershey. *Byte* 12:244-6 O '87
On the road to Xanadu. T. H. Nelson. *Pers Comput* 11:170 D '87
Product of the month: Guide. B. F. Webster. *Byte* 12:292+ Ap '87
What you need to know about hypertext. P. Saffo. il *Pers Comput* 11:166-7+ D '87

Hyperthermia *See* Heat—Physiological effects

Hypnotism
Hypnosis may be hazardous [study by Frank MacHovec] P. Knight. *Psychol Today* 21:20-1 Ja '87
Diet use
Losing weight through hypnosis. M. P. Scott. il *Better Homes Gard* 65:84+ O '87
Therapeutic use
Battle of the binge [tool against bulimia] J. Slothower. il *Health* 19:19+ O '87
A biobehavioral approach to managing childhood asthma. D. P. Kohen. bibl f il *Child Today* 16:6-10 Mr/Ap '87
Hypnosis: could it help you? D. Hales. *McCalls* 114:14 Ag '87

Hypnotism—Therapeutic use—*cont.*
Hypnosis: it could help you be calmer or pain-free. il *Glamour* 85:61 Je '87
Hypnosis power: tranceforming. P. Nicoll. il *Harpers Bazaar* 120:184+ Mr '87
Repeat after me: some hard facts about hypnosis. M. Starkman. il *Vogue* 177:112+ S '87
Hypocrisy
A toast to hypocrisy. E. Janko. por *Newsweek* 109:6 Ja 5 '87
Hypocyrta
Grow a goldfish in a pot. B. Gould. il *Flower Gard* 31:13 O/N '87
Hypodermic syringes *See* Syringes
Hypothalamic hormones
  See also
  Pituitary hormone releasing factors
  Thyrotropin releasing factor
A new prosomatostatin-derived peptide reveals a pattern for prohormone cleavage at monobasic sites. R. Benoit and others. bibl f il *Science* 238:1126-9 N 20 '87
Hypothalamus
Borrowed time [transplantation of suprachiasmatic nuclei restores circadian rhythm in hamsters] *Sci Am* 256:84 F '87
Thyroid hormone regulates TRH biosynthesis in the paraventricular nucleus of the rat hypothalamus. T. P. Segerson and others. bibl f il *Science* 238:78-80 O 2 '87
Hypothermia
The deadliest kind of cold. S. Begley. il *Newsweek* 109:63 Mr 9 '87
Hypothermia: a springtime hazard. T. O'Toole and J. O'Toole. il *Saturday Evening Post* 259:60-2 My/Je '87
Hypothermia and the elderly. *FDA Consum* 21:34-5 F '87
Hypothermia, the chilling killer. S. L. Englebardt. *Read Dig* 131:160-2 D '87
Non-invasive treatment for hypothermia. *Sea Front* 33:307-8 Jl/Ag '87
Hypres Inc.
He's walking tall where IBM wouldn't tread. O. Port. il por *Bus Week* p124 My 4 '87
Hyslop, Peter H. St George- *See* St George-Hyslop, Peter H.
Hysterectomy
Change of life. P. Dranov. il *N Y* 20:70-6 O 19 '87
Surgery women should think about twice. A. Mereson. *McCalls* 114:139-40 Jl '87
Hyundai (Automobile) *See* Automobiles, Foreign
Hyundai Electronics Industry Co., Ltd.
Hyundai computers are stuck in the slow lane. G. Lewis. il *Bus Week* p50 Je 15 '87
Hyundai Group
A patriarch relaxes his control [Chung Ju Yung] il por *Newsweek* 110:26-7 Ag 31 '87
Sputtering back to life [Hyundai strike settled; others continue] H. G. Chua-Eoan. il *Time* 130:30 Ag 31 '87
Hyundai Motor Co. Ltd.
Hyundai tries to pass the Japanese. H. Becker. *World Press Rev* 34:47+ My '87
The road most traveled. S. B. Weiner. il *Forbes* 140:60+ O 19 '87

I

I am yours [drama] See Thompson, Judith, 1939-
I.C.H. Corp.
Fred Carr buys some insurance [ICH acquires greater share of First Executive Corp.] T. Carson. *Bus Week* p36 O 26 '87
ICH Corp.'s ascent from nowhere. C. J. Loomis. il por *Fortune* 115:50-2+ Ap 13 '87
I Have a Dream Foundation
For a host of philanthropists inspired by a common dream, charity begins at school. M. Brower. il *People Wkly* 28:74-6+ O 5 '87
I lived, but . . . [film] See Motion picture reviews—Single works
Iacocca, Lee A.
In order to [address, August 10, 1987] *Vital Speeches Day* 53:745-8 O 1 '87
  about
The blockbustering of Lee Iacocca. P. Wyden. il *N Y Times Book Rev* 92:1+ S 13 '87

Iacocca: 'Did we screw up? You bet'. *Newsweek* 110:42 Jl 13 '87
Living as a legend. A. L. Taylor, III. il por *Fortune* 116:43 Ag 3 '87
Power romance. F. A. Bernstein. il pors *People Wkly* 27:100-2 F 2 '87
Iacocca, Lia
  about
Pooling the Iacocca talent, Lee makes Lia head of his winery. il pors *People Wkly* 28:85 S 14 '87
Iaconetti, Joan
Seven delegating mistakes—and how to avoid them. *Work Woman* 12:24+ Jl '87
Iacono, Michael J., and Blanchard, Duncan C.
Soap bubble meteorology. il *Weatherwise* 40:141-2 Je '87
IAEA *See* International Atomic Energy Agency
IAM *See* International Association of Machinists and Aerospace Workers
Iannone, Carol
The fiction we deserve. *Commentary* 83:60-2 Je '87
Minimalist fiction [discussion of June 1987 article, The fiction we deserve] *Commentary* 84:14-15+ O '87
Post-counterculture tristesse. *Commentary* 83:57-61 F '87
Toni Morrison's career. *Commentary* 84:59-63 D '87
IATA *See* International Air Transport Association
Iatrogenic diseases
Is your doctor over-doctoring you? P. Gott. il *Redbook* 169:112-13+ O '87
IATSE *See* International Alliance of Theatrical Stage Employees and Moving Picture Machine Operators of the U.S. and Canada
Iberis *See* Candytuft
Ibex
With lots of help, alpine ibex return to their mountains. C. Grodinsky and M. Stüwe. il *Smithsonian* 18:68-72+ D '87
IBM *See* International Business Machines Corp.
Ibn Battuta, 1304-1377
The obedience due to princesses [excerpt from Rihla] il *Courier* 40:34-5 Ap '87
IBP, Inc.
Hog heaven or hell [community opposition to proposed IBP plant in Manchester, Iowa] C. Isenhart. il *Progressive* 51:13 O '87
IBS Publishing (Firm)
The need to self-publish AIDS books [work of B. Moffatt] L. See. *Publ Wkly* 232:56 Ag 28 '87
IC Industries, Inc.
Why IC is uncoupling itself from the past. K. Deveny. il por *Bus Week* p120+ O 12 '87
IC testers *See* Testing equipment
Icahn, Carl C.
  about
The battle for USX: Icahn retreats for now. *Newsweek* 109:42 Ja 19 '87
Carl Icahn deals himself in. J. R. Norman. il por *Bus Week* p38 D 14 '87
Carl Icahn is at it again. C. Hawkins. *Bus Week* p42+ Mr 16 '87
Carl Icahn may soon be back in the raiding business. C. Hawkins and C. Power. *Bus Week* p29-30 Ag 3 '87
For Carl Icahn, the flight path never ends. por *Newsweek* 109:50 Mr 16 '87
How USAir cut Icahn out. S. Payne. il por *Bus Week* p35 Mr 23 '87
Icahn proposes merger that could make TWA a private company. *Aviat Week Space Technol* 127:32 Jl 27 '87
Icahn thickens the Texaco plot. *Newsweek* 110:66 D 7 '87
Icahn's juggle: TWA, USX, SEC. C. J. Loomis. il por *Fortune* 115:81-2 My 11 '87
Let 'Icahn do your work for you'. G. G. Marcial. *Bus Week* p106 D 21 '87
The raider who kept TWA flying. J. Nielsen. il por *Fortune* 115:63 Ja 5 '87
Standing up to Carl Icahn. C. Friday and J. Schwartz. il *Newsweek* 109:54 Ap 13 '87
The takeover game: many were forced to punt. C. Hawkins and others. il por *Bus Week* p53 N 2 '87
Taking over the controls. pors *Time* 130:43 Ag 3 '87
Waterloo at USX. J. Castro. il por *Time* 129:51 Ja 19 '87
ICAO *See* International Civil Aviation Organization
ICBI *See* International Council on Biblical Inerrancy
ICBM (Intercontinental ballistic missiles) *See* Guided missiles

Ice

See also
Glaciers
Icebergs
The surface composition of Charon: tentative identification of water ice. R. L. Marcialis and others. bibl f il *Science* 237:1349-51 S 11 '87

Harvesting

See Ice harvesting

Manufacture

See also
Beverley Ice Company

Photographs and photography

First freeze. D. L. Johnson. il *Petersens Photogr Mag* 16:36-8 O '87
Ice. R. Lovell. il *Ctry J* 14:43-7 D '87

Therapeutic use

Beating headaches cold [study by Seymour Diamond] J.-B. Shoemaker. il *Health* 19:21 Ja '87

Greenland

Frozen fire [study of volcanic aerosols in Greenland ice cores] il *Earth Sci* 40:14-16 Spr '87
Greenland's cosmic dust deposits [work of Michel Maurette and others] il *Sky Telesc* 73:367-8 Ap '87
Intrepid filmmaker braves Greenland ice cap with an expedition searching for mysterious fifth force of the universe. C. R. Barnett. il *Smithsonian* 18:40+ N '87
Radioactive cesium from the Chernobyl accident in the Greenland ice sheet. C. I. Davidson and others. bibl f maps *Science* 237:633-4 Ag 7 '87
Taking a vacuum to extraterrestrial dust [work of Michel Maurette and others] R. Monastersky. *Sci News* 132:133 Ag 29 '87

Polar regions

Arctic seas that never freeze [polynyas] M. J. Dunbar. il map *Nat Hist* 96:50-3 Ap '87
Huge ice cube in Antarctic waters. il *Sci News* 132:311 N 14 '87
Ice-edge eddies in the Fram Strait marginal ice zone. O. M. Johannessen and others. bibl f il maps *Science* 236:427-9 Ap 24 '87
Ice on the world. S. W. Matthews. il maps *Natl Geogr* 171:78-103 Ja '87
Ice traces of catastrophe: Chernobyl . . . and the ancient volcano Thera. *Sci News* 132:121 Ag 22 '87
An icy warning of a global warming? [icebergs separate from Antarctic ice sheet] map *Newsweek* 110:65 D 28 '87
Mesoscale oceanographic processes beneath the ice of Fram Strait. T. O. Manley and others. bibl f il maps *Science* 236:432-4 Ap 24 '87
Ocean dynamics and acoustic fluctuations in the Fram Strait marginal ice zone. I. Dyer and others. bibl f il *Science* 236:435-6 Ap 24 '87
On the edge between water and ice [Marginal Ice Zone Experiment] R. Monastersky. il *Sci News* 131:280 My 2 '87
Physical properties of sea ice discharged from Fram Strait. A. J. Gow and W. B. Tucker, III. bibl f il map *Science* 236:436-9 Ap 24 '87
Remote sensing of the Fram Strait marginal ice zone. R. A. Shuchman and others. bibl f il *Science* 236:429-31 Ap 24 '87
Vapor lock [air bubbles in Antarctic ice record carbon dioxide and climate] T. Beardsley. *Sci Am* 257:32 D '87

Ice, Interstellar *See* Matter, Interstellar
Ice Age man *See* Man, Prehistoric
Ice Age man in literature *See* Man, Prehistoric, in literature
Ice ages *See* Glacial epochs
Ice and snow building *See* Building, Ice and snow
Ice breaking vessels

Seeking new salvation [Versatile Corp. seeks Canadian government contract to build Polar 8 icebreaker] J. O'Hara. il *Macleans* 100:36 Mr 16 '87

Ice climbing *See* Snow and ice climbing
Ice cream cones

Scoop-and-serve dunce cones. il *Sunset* 179:195 N '87

Ice cream, ices, etc.

See also
Milkshakes
Chocolate log, raspberry wreath . . . you "sculpt" ice cream. il *Sunset* 179:146-7 D '87
Desserts for melting days. C. Idone. il *N Y Times Mag* p59-60 Ag 16 '87
Fruits and herbs for summer sorbets. il *Sunset* 178:184 Je '87
Ice cream bar exam. A. Richman. il *People Wkly* 28:94-8 Ag 10 '87
Ice-cream desserts. K. Haedrich. il *Ctry J* 14:14-17 Ag '87

Ice cream for adults [sundaes] A. Deane. il *Work Woman* 12:72-4 Ag '87
The latest scoop [frozen desserts] K. Freifeld. il *Health* 19:8 My '87
Peaches and cream [Lillo de Domenico's double dolce] B. Costikyan. il *N Y* 20:57 Ag 17 '87
Raspberry sorbet. il *Good Housekeep* 204:96 Je '87
Smooth and sinfully rich . . . white chocolate tartufo. il *Sunset* 179:164 N '87
Summer and ice [sorbets] C. Claiborne and P. Franey. il *N Y Times Mag* p63-4 Je 7 '87
Summer freezer pleasers—sorbets & ices. H. Garrison. il *Parents* 62:154-6+ Ag '87
Sweet tooth diet: the latest scoop. C. A. Pearce. il *Harpers Bazaar* 120:62+ Jl '87

Labeling

All natural? [frozen fruit bars] B. T. Hunter. il *Consum Res Mag* 70:8-9 Ap '87

Ice cream, ices, etc. in music

Anecdotes, facetiae, satire, etc.

Ice-cream music [pianist supplying mood music for corporate reception featuring ice cream] D. Asher. il *Harpers* 274:68-71 Je '87

Ice cream industry

See also
Ben & Jerry's Homemade Inc.
Häagen-Dazs Company, Inc.
Hot growth in a cold market. B. Rudolph. il *Time* 129:47 Je 29 '87

Antitrust cases

Is Haagen-Dazs trying to freeze out Ben & Jerry's? K. H. Hammonds. il *Bus Week* p65 D 7 '87

Marketing

Dessert [D. Braff promoting frozen desserts] *New Yorker* 63:21-3 Jl 27 '87

Ice cream makers

Ice-cream makers. il *Consum Rep* 52:50-4 D '87
The latest scoop on ice-cream makers. T. Segal and C. Tuzzolino. il *Bus Week* p121 Ag 17 '87

Ice cream toppings

The best dessert in the world. il *Redbook* 169:112-13 Je '87
It's yogurt—not ice cream. il *South Living* 22:138-9 Je '87

Ice fishing *See* Fishing, Winter
Ice harvesting

Of ice and men [winter festivals re-create old-time ice harvests] K. D. Irvine. il *Americana* 14:15-16+ Ja/F '87

Ice hazards in automobile driving *See* Automobile driving—Winter driving
Ice hazards in aviation *See* Aviation—Ice hazards
Ice hockey *See* Hockey
Ice on rivers, lakes, etc.

Ice magic. J. W. Miller. il *Read Dig* 130:43-6 F '87

Photographs and photography

Worlds within worlds: a fantasy of leaves and air trapped by pond ice. E. Fuss. il *Audubon* 89:34-9 Ja '87

Ice palaces

The magic chill of ice palaces still beckons us. F. Anderes and A. Agranoff. bibl (p131) il *Smithsonian* 17:62-9 Ja '87

Ice racing, Automobile *See* Automobile racing
Ice sailing *See* Ice surfing
Ice shows

Torvill & Dean: so nice on ice. D. Chase. il pors *Saturday Evening Post* 259:48-9+ Ja/F '87

Benefit performances

Fighting drugs on ice [Torvill and Dean benefit for N. Reagan's anti-drug crusade] P. SerVaas. il pors *Saturday Evening Post* 259:50 Ja/F '87

Ice skating

See also
Figure skating
Ice shows
Speed skating
Making kids great skaters. C. Loomis. il *Parents* 62:286 N '87

Ice skating rinks

A track for all seasons [Calgary Olympic Oval] H. Quinn. il *Macleans* 100:44-5 O 5 '87

Equipment

You're an old smoothie [history of the Zamboni machine] L. Montville. il pors *Sports Illus* 66:38-40+ Mr 30 '87

Ice storms

A memorable Easter ice storm [Illinois, 1978] M. Reed. il *Weatherwise* 40:78-83 Ap '87

Ice surfing

Fire on ice. E. Olsen. il *Mot Boat Sail* 159:50-3+ Ja '87

Ice surfing—*cont.*

Steel on ice. K. Robberson. il *Pop Mech* 164:71-3 F '87

Icebergs

Huge ice cube in Antarctic waters. il *Sci News* 132:311 N 14 '87

An icy warning of a global warming? [icebergs separate from Antarctic ice sheet] map *Newsweek* 110:65 D 28 '87

The Titanic's legacy to safety. R. L. Scheina. il *Sea Front* 33:200-9 My/Je '87

Icebreakers *See* Ice breaking vessels

Iceland

See also

Fishing—Iceland

Snowmobiles and snowmobiling—Iceland

Surtsey (Iceland)

Women—Iceland

Civilization

A nonesuch people. B. Leithauser. il *Atlantic* 260:32-4+ S '87

Culture

See Iceland—Civilization

Description and travel

Iceland: life under the glaciers. L. E. Levathes. il maps *Natl Geogr* 171:184-215 F '87

Two days in Reykjavík is not enough. J. Edgar. il *Ms* 16:37 D '87

Industries

See also

Whaling—Iceland

Politics and government

See also

Political parties—Iceland

Iceland summit, 1986 *See* Reagan-Gorbachev summit conference, 1986

Ices *See* Ice cream, ices, etc.

Ichthyosaurs *See* Reptiles, Fossil

ICI *See* Imperial Chemical Industries plc

ICI Fibres (Firm)

Synthesizing success. C. Brown. il por *Forbes* 139:179 Je 1 '87

ICM *See* International Creative Management (Firm)

ICN Pharmaceuticals, Inc.

Risky business on AIDS [experience with ribavirin] J. Crudele. il *N Y* 20:16+ Ap 27 '87

Icons

The icons of old Russia. A. Bahar. il *Antiques Collect Hobbies* 92:24-8 My '87

The scientist who makes icons weep [S. Carlson] il por *Newsweek* 110:79 O 26 '87

ICs *See* Integrated circuits

Idaho

See also

Crime and criminals—Idaho

Fishing—Idaho

National forests—Idaho

Public lands—Idaho

Ranches—Idaho

Salmon River (Idaho)

Teton Valley (Idaho)

Wilderness areas—Idaho

IDCNY *See* International Design Center New York

Ideal states *See* Utopias

Idealism

Pursue not just the material [address, May 7, 1987] A. M. Schindler. *Vital Speeches Day* 53:659-60 Ag 15 '87

Tempering the old idealism [Maclean's/Decima poll] C. Wood. il *Macleans* 100:36-7 Ja 5 '87

Ideas

See also

Creativity

Ideas in business

Creativity and enterprise [address, June 1, 1987] A. W. Elliott. *Vital Speeches Day* 53:637-40 Ag 1 '87

How to think like an innovator. D. Waitley and R. B. Tucker. il *Futurist* 21:9-15 My/Je '87

Office politics: when to push for your point of view—and when not to. *Glamour* 85:172 S '87

People behind the wonders [condensed from Breakthroughs!] J. M. Ketteringham and R. P. Nayak. il *Read Dig* 131:134-8 Jl '87

Tapping your creativity [advice for business people from Michael Ray and Rochelle Myers] H. Bacas. il *Nations Bus* 75:48 Mr '87

Identical twins *See* Twins

Identification

See also

Cows—Identification

DNA fingerprints

Fingerprints

Forensic anthropology

Warships—Identification

Identification cards, tags, etc.

See also

Medical identification

Identity (Psychology)

See also

Blacks—Race identity

The road well-taken: why you rely on past tactics to confront the present. B. L. Stern. *Vogue* 177:444 F '87

Your child's cultural identity. J. Segal and Z. Segal. il *Parents* 62:154 Jl '87

Idinopulos, Thomas A.

The CIA-Harvard controversy over secrecy. il *USA Today (Periodical)* 115:38-40 My '87

(jt. auth) *See* Eldar, Yishai, and Idinopulos, Thomas A.

Idiot savants *See* Savant syndrome

Iditarod Trail Sled Dog Race *See* Dog racing

Idleness

Television: idle comfort [study by Robert W. Kubey] J. Goetz. il *Psychol Today* 21:10 Je '87

Idler (Periodical)

Attacking the left's sacred cows [Canada Council refuses grant] B. Amiel. il *Macleans* 100:9 D 7 '87

Idol, Billy

about

Billy Idol. A. DeCurtis. il por *Roll Stone* p21 Je 4 '87

Flying solo: stars take off alone. il pors *Teen* 31:80-1 My '87

He went three years between albums, but Billy Idol's idyll was neither idle nor ideal. L. Russell. il pors *People Wkly* 27:39-40 Ja 12 '87

Idone, Christopher

Designer greens. il *Harpers Bazaar* 120:48+ Ag '87

Desserts for melting days. il *N Y Times Mag* p59-60 Ag 16 '87

about

Salad days. L. Wells. il *N Y Times Mag* p65-6 Je 28 '87

IDS Financial Services Inc.

Golub: the workaholic telling clients to relax. M. J. Pitzer. il por *Bus Week* p98 N 23 '87

IEA *See* International Energy Agency

IEEE *See* Institute of Electrical and Electronics Engineers

IFALPA *See* International Federation of Airline Pilots Associations

IFOAM *See* International Federation of Organic Agriculture Movements

IFR flying *See* Aviation—Instrument flying

IFREMER *See* Institut Français de Recherche pour l'Exploitation de la Mer

IGBP *See* International Geosphere-Biosphere Program

IGFs (Insulin-like growth factors) *See* Somatomedins

Igiebor, Nosa

The Soviets' new look. *World Press Rev* 34:9-10 Ap '87

Iglauer, Bruce

about

Our blues. J. W. Poses. il *High Fidel* 37:84-5 D '87

Iglauer, Edith

Hot springs. *New Yorker* 63:62-9 Jl 6 '87

Iglesias, Cristina, 1956-

about

Five from Spain. J. Gambrell. il pors *Art Am* 75:160-71 S '87

Iglesias, Timothy

CUF and dissent: a case study in religious conservatism. *America* 156:303-7 Ap 11 '87

Ignatieff, Michael

Family photo albums [excerpt from The Russian album] *Harpers* 274:27-8 Je '87

Ignatieff family

about

Family photo albums [excerpt from The Russian album] M. Ignatieff. *Harpers* 274:27-8 Je '87

Ignatius, David, 1950-

about

The spy as a modern Everyman [interview] A. P. Sanoff. por *U S News World Rep* 103:69 D 7 '87

Ignatius, Michael J., and others

Lipoprotein uptake by neuronal growth cones in vitro. bibl f il *Science* 236:959-62 My 22 '87

Igneous rocks *See* Rocks, Igneous
Ignition, Gas and oil *See* Gas and oil engines—Ignition
Ignorance
Anecdotes, facetiae, satire, etc.
Relevant ignorance. R. Baker. il *N Y Times Mag* p10
    Jl 12 '87
Iguanas
Breeding
Nights—and days—of the iguana [captive-breeding project
    in Panama; work of D. Werner] J. P. Cohn. il por
    Américas 39:34-9 Jl/Ag '87
Igwebuike, Donald
about
NFL's lone black kicker recalls a bigger 'Fridge'. pors
    Jet 71:51 Ja 12 '87
IHW *See* International Halley Watch
IIASA *See* International Institute for Applied Systems
    Analysis
Iida, Yotaro
about
The romantic of heavy industry. F. H. Katayama. il
    por *Fortune* 116:54 Ag 3 '87
IKEA Svenska Forsaljnings AB
The store that runs on a wrench. J. S. DeMott. il
    Time 130:54 Jl 27 '87
Ikerd, Cheri
about
Suing over a transparent bikini, Cheri Ikerd made the
    judge see right through her argument. il por *People
    Wkly* 28:113 Ag 24 '87
Iklé, Fred Charles
about
Defense official challenges continuing SICBM develop-
    ment. J. D. Morrocco. *Aviat Week Space Technol*
    126:18-19 Mr 16 '87
IKOY Partnership
Heavy metal [three buildings in Canada] P. M. Sachner.
    il *Archit Rec* 175:126-35 My '87
Ikummaq, Theo
about
A feel for living. B. Wallace. il por *Macleans* 100:24
    My 11 '87
Ileitis, Regional *See* Regional ileitis
Ilex *See* Holly
Ill *See* Sick
I'll take Manhattan [television program] *See* Television
    program reviews—Single works
Illegal aliens *See* Aliens
Illegal literature *See* Underground literature
Illegitimacy
See also
Paternity
Illinois
See also
Abortion clinics—Illinois
Agriculture—Illinois
Banks and banking—Illinois
Booksellers and bookselling—Illinois
Child welfare—Illinois
Du Page County (Ill.)
Environmental movement—Illinois
Express highways—Illinois
Floods—Illinois
Geology—Illinois
Motion picture festivals—Illinois
Music festivals—Illinois
Opera—Illinois
Wetlands—Illinois
Climate
A memorable Easter ice storm [1978] M. Reed. il
    Weatherwise 40:78-83 Ap '87
Moral conditions
Obscenity test challenged in U.S. Supreme Court [intent
    of Miller test questioned in Pope v. Illinois] H. Fields.
    Publ Wkly 231:10 Mr 13 '87
Supreme Court fine-tunes third part of 'Miller' test [Pope
    v. Illinois] *Publ Wkly* 231:20 My 22 '87
Illinois Central Gulf RR. Co.
Why IC is uncoupling itself from the past. K. Deveny.
    il por *Bus Week* p120+ O 12 '87
Illinois Functional Programming (Computer language)
Illinois Functional Programming: a tutorial. A. D.
    Robison. il *Byte* 12:114-16+ F '87
Illiteracy
See also
International Literacy Day
Literacy education
"I've kept my secret for too long"; ed. by Deidre Sullivan.
    S. Budz. il por *Redbook* 169:61-3 O '87
Literacy [cover story; special section] il *Phi Delta Kappan*
    69:184-206 N '87

Where is the crisis in American literacy? S. B. Heath.
    Educ Dig 52:18-19 F '87
Illness *See* Sickness
Illumination *See* Lighting
Illumination of books and manuscripts
Devotions & delights: the illuminated books of Gothic
    England. J. Backhouse. bibl il *Hist Today* 37:25-31
    N '87
Illusions, Optical *See* Optical illusions
Illustrated books
See also
Booksellers and bookselling—Illustrated books
Picture books
Picture books for children
Bibliography
Illustrated gift books. il *Publ Wkly* 232:32+ S 11 '87
Illustration
See also
Forensic illustration
Balancing interests in art and illustration. M. Garland.
    il *Am Artist* 51:54-9+ Ja '87
Flying starts: new faces of 1987 [children's books] D.
    E. Roback; K. O. Fakih. il *Publ Wkly* 232:36-8+ D
    25 '87
Illustrator Boris Diodorov gives a winning Russian accent
    to a bear called 'Vinni-Pukh'. J. W. Seymore. il por
    People Wkly 27:52-4 Ap 6 '87
PW interviews [J. Burningham and H. Oxenbury] M.
    Field. il pors *Publ Wkly* 232:168-9 Jl 24 '87
William Steig at 80 [children's book illustrator] D. Allen-
    der. il por *Publ Wkly* 232:116-18 Jl 24 '87
Words & pictures: the right order [children's literature;
    adaptation of address] R. Wells. por *Publ Wkly* 231:146
    F 27 '87
Censorship
For art's sake [letters to the Progressive commenting
    on illustrations] E. Knoll. *Progressive* 51:4 N '87
Exhibitions
Master Eagle hosts seventh Original art exhibit [children's
    books] *Publ Wkly* 231:39 Ja 23 '87
Illustrators
See also
Berry, William A., 1933-
Davis, Paul, 1938-
Diodorov, Boris
Fisher, Harrison
Hurd, Thacher
Larsson, Carl Olof, 1853-1919
Minor, Wendell
ILO *See* International Labour Organisation
ILWU *See* International Longshoremen's and
    Warehousemen's Union
Image, Body *See* Body image
Image consultants
Creating the right impression. L. Wells. il *N Y Times
    Mag* p56 Mr 22 '87
Crossing the magic threshold [creating a look of affluence
    and self-assurance] J. Ciabattari. il *Work Woman*
    12:94-7+ Je '87
Image processing
See also
Thermography
Tomography
AT&T's TrueVision image processing system. R. Tinney.
    Byte 12:215-17 Mr '87
Build a gray-scale video digitizer (I). S. Ciarcia. il *Byte*
    12:95-106 My '87
Build a gray-scale video digitizer (II). S. Ciarcia. il *Byte*
    12:129-38 Je '87
Designing a raster-image processor. J. Barrett and K.
    Reistroffer. il *Byte* 12:171-4+ My '87
Digital disinformation. S. Ditlea. il *Omni* 9:26 F '87
Electronic imaging today [special section] il *Pop Photogr*
    94:68-73 S '87
ESP: image of the future [electronic still photography]
    S. A. Booth. il *Pop Mech* 164:16+ F '87
Image processing [cover story; special section] il *Byte*
    12:140-1+ Mr '87
The important things about photography will not change
    [video still cameras] N. Rothschild. il *Pop Photogr*
    94:10 Ja '87
Is it real or is it Scitex? I. Chithelen. il *Forbes* 140:110-11
    S 7 '87
Kodak electronic photos [still video systems] S. A. Booth.
    il *Pop Mech* 164:40 O '87
Looking into metal specimens [Mossbauer imaging; work
    of Stephen J. Norton] *Sci News* 132:361 D 5 '87
Packing it in [image compression; work of Michael F.
    Barnsley and others; cover story] I. Peterson. il *Sci
    News* 131:283-5 My 2 '87

Image processing—*cont.*

Polaroid Palette Computer Image Recorder. S. Drafahl. il *Petersens Photogr Mag* 16:48-51 My '87

Reading pictures into your computer [Princeton Graphic Systems LS-300] R. Lockwood. il *Pers Comput* 11:240 Je '87

Scanning images into your computer [Microtek MS-300A] J. Bell. il *Pers Comput* 11:158 Mr '87

Using the ImageWise video digitizer (I). S. Ciarcia. il *Byte* 12:113-19 Jl '87

Using the ImageWise video digitizer (II). S. Ciarcia. il *Byte* 12:117-21 Ag '87

A video data base [PicturePower] R. Lockwood. il *Pers Comput* 11:178 Jl '87

Art use

Digital image processing in art conservation [secrets of the Mona Lisa] J. F. Asmus. bibl il *Byte* 12:151-60+ Mr '87

Unmasking a 'Mona Lisa' coverup [work of John F. Asmus] I. Peterson. *Sci News* 131:152 Mr 7 '87

Astronomical use

CCD images of supernova remnants. il *Sky Telesc* 73:27 Ja '87

Ferret: an image processor. C. Harris. il *Byte* 12:317-18+ D '87

A gamma-ray pinhole camera. W. J. Wild. il *Sky Telesc* 74:126-7 Ag '87

Globular clusters in the Coma cluster of galaxies [CCD observations by William E. Harris] il *Sky Telesc* 74:346-7 O '87

Sky on a chip: the fabulous CCD. J. Janesick and M. Blouke. il *Sky Telesc* 74:238-42 S '87

Stars and spikes [finding stellar diffraction patterns for different telescope types; computer program] R. W. Sinnott. il *Sky Telesc* 74:294-6 S '87

Aviation use

Technical survey: tactical airborne reconnaissance [cover story; special section] il *Aviat Week Space Technol* 127:68-9+ S 7 '87

Earth sciences use

Geologist's hammer is joined by spectrometers [work of Gregg Vane] R. A. Kerr. *Science* 236:1625 Je 26 '87

Medical use

See also
Radiography, Medical

The better to see you with. R. Greene. il *Forbes* 140:222 D 14 '87

From outer space to the inner man. il *Byte* 12:146 Mr '87

High tech diagnosis: from X-rays to MRI. P. A. Feuerstein. il *Curr Health 2* 14:26-7 N '87

Medicine's new vision. H. Sochurek. il *Natl Geogr* 171:2-41 Ja '87

Medicine's new wonder machines. H. Sochurek. il *Read Dig* 130:193-8 My '87

These pictures could save your life. R. Brandt. il *Bus Week* p112-13 Jl 13 '87

Religious use

The Vatican goes to Hell [ancient texts recreated by computer imaging] E. Stone. il *Omni* 9:24 S '87

Space flight use

JPL alters Voyager 2 controls to improve imaging of Neptune [Jet Propulsion Laboratory] *Aviat Week Space Technol* 127:131 Ag 10 '87

Probing space by camera: the development of image processing at NASA's Jet Propulsion Laboratory. K. Sheldon. il *Byte* 12:143-8 Mr '87

Imagery techniques in fiction *See* Fiction—Technique

Images, Mental *See* Images and imagery (Psychology)

Images and imagery (Psychology)

See also
Visualization

Animal gender benders [animal-gender associations; study by Steven Lash and James Polyson] il *Psychol Today* 21:8 D '87

A biobehavioral approach to managing childhood asthma. D. P. Kohen. bibl f il *Child Today* 16:6-10 Mr/Ap '87

"Positive thinking"—why it works [views of Bernie Zilbergeld and Arnold Lazarus] C. Tavris. *Vogue* 177:124 My '87

Imagination

See also
Creativity
Fantasy
Images and imagery (Psychology)

The me I didn't know [pretending to be someone else as a way to self improvement; research by Robert Hartley] P. Chance. *Psychol Today* 21:20 Ja '87

The reader as partner. T. Hillerman. *Writer* 100:14-16 O '87

Using imagination in plotting. J. Aiken. *Writer* 100:7-10+ D '87

Imagination in children

See also
Children's fantasies

Let's pretend. P. Theroux. il *Parents* 62:66+ My '87

Imaging systems *See* Image processing

Imamura, Shohei

about

The pornographers [film] Reviews

New Repub 196:25-6 Je 15 '87. S. Kauffmann

Iman

about

From Africa with love. R. D. Manuel. pors *Essence* 18:38+ My '87

Imberman, Fred

about

An English accent at Kentshire. D. Rosenthal. il pors *Archit Dig* 44:78+ Mr '87

The English channel. E. Greene. il pors *House Gard* 159:32+ Jl '87

Imbert, Enrique Anderson

Toward a universal language. *Américas* 39:54-5 Jl/Ag '87

Imbimbo, Tony

Just smashing! il *Women's Sports Fitness* 9:45-7 Ap '87

Imes, Birney

about

Delta blues. S. Piperato. il *Pop Photogr* 94:60-5 O '87

IMF *See* International Monetary Fund

IMG International Management Group

And one who prospered: with agents' help, ex-outfielder Garry Maddox made a fortune. J. Lieber. il por *Sports Illus* 67:96 O 19 '87

Mark McCormack does everything but play the game. D. Cook and others. il por *Bus Week* p52-3 Ag 31 '87

Imhoff, Gary, and Bikales, Gerda

The battle over preserving the English language. il *USA Today (Periodical)* 115:63-5 Ja '87

Immigrant labor *See* Alien labor

Immigrants

See also
Aliens
Asians—United States
British—United States
Canadians—United States
Chinese—United States
Cubans—United States
Europeans—United States
Filipinos—United States
Germans—United States
Guyanese—United States
Haitians—United States
Indians (East Indian)—United States
Indochinese—United States
Irish—United States
Japanese—United States
Kampucheans—United States
Latin Americans—United States
Legal assistance to immigrants
Mexicans—United States
Nicaraguans—United States
Russians—United States
Salvadorans—United States
Senegalese—United States
South Africans—United States
Thais—United States
United States. Immigration and Naturalization Service
Vietnamese—United States

The economic consequences of immigration. G. J. Borjas and M. Tienda. bibl f il *Science* 235:645-51 F 6 '87

Attitudes

Unleashed. S. Blotnick. il *Forbes* 139:108 Ja 26 '87

Brazil

See also
Americans—Brazil

Canada

See also
Chinese—Canada
Indians (East Indian)—Canada
Scots—Canada
Tamils—Canada
Turks—Canada

France

See also
Haitians—France

Immigrants—France—See also—cont.
Portuguese—France
Great Britain
See also
Indians (East Indian)—Great Britain
Turkey
See also
Iranians—Turkey
United States
See Immigrants
Western Europe
No foreigners needed here. X. Mellish. *Progressive* 51:14-15 My '87

Immigration and emigration
See also
Alien labor
Aliens
Asylum, Right of
Deportation
Legal assistance to immigrants
McCarran-Walter Act
Refugees
United States. Immigration and Naturalization Service

Along the Salvadoran pipeline. R. Symanski. il map *Focus* 36:2-11 Wint '86
Can the trek to El Norte be curbed? [enforcing new immigration law; special section] il *U S News World Rep* 102:22-6 Ja 19 '87
The challenge of immigration. F. Peña. il *USA Today (Periodical)* 115:60-2 Ja '87
A chance to leave the sweatshop behind [program to legalize undocumented aliens begins] D. deF. Whitman. il *U S News World Rep* 102:18 My 11 '87
Churches band together to help register undocumented aliens. R. Frame. il *Christ Today* 31:34-5 Jl 10 '87
Coming soon: crackdown on hiring illegal aliens [Immigration Reform and Control Act of 1986] R. Thompson. il *Nations Bus* 75:32-4+ Ap '87
Confusion on both sides of the border [amnesty and illegal aliens] A. Bernstein and others. il *Bus Week* p68-9 Jl 20 '87
FY 1988 assistance requests for migration and refugees [statement, March 26, 1987] J. Moore. *Dep State Bull* 87:83-4 Je '87
I stopped my daughter's wedding [plans for bogus marriage to foreign student] R. Bode. il pors *Good Housekeep* 204:106+ Mr '87
Immigration: bordering on the absurd [new law and hiring of illegal aliens] D. Whitman. il *U S News World Rep* 103:25-6 S 14 '87
Immigration law: when the best minds in Washington . . . [regulations for companies] K. R. Sheets. *U S News World Rep* 102:39 Mr 9 '87
Immigration reform II. *New Repub* 196:7-8 Mr 30 '87
The impact of Simpson-Rodino [Salvadorans] P. Shiras. *Commonweal* 114:276-7 My 8 '87
The jittery 'other illegals' [European-born aliens] T. Morganthau. il *Newsweek* 110:35-6 O 5 '87
Moral borders. M. Kondracke. *New Repub* 197:12-15 N 23 '87
New law won't stop illegals' influx [immigration reform law; views of David Heer] *USA Today (Periodical)* 115:7 Ap '87
A new statute of liberty. T. Bethell. *Natl Rev* 39:38+ D 18 '87
No aliens, lots of paperwork [Immigration Reform and Control Act] H. Bacas. il *Nations Bus* 75:26+ N '87
Out of the shadows [Immigration Reform and Control Act of 1986] R. Stengel. il *Time* 129:14-17 My 4 '87
Perspectives on U.S. refugee programs [address, June 11, 1987; statement June 30, 1987] J. Moore. *Dep State Bull* 87:54-8 S '87
Proposed refugee admissions for FY 1988 [statement, September 23, 1987] J. Moore. il *Dep State Bull* 87:47-52 N '87
Quietly keeping them out: the dark side of immigration reform. A. J. Estrada. il *Harpers* 275:42-3 Ag '87
Reform breeds its own crisis: how the new immigration law affects employers. M. E. Recio. il *Bus Week* p26-7 Mr 30 '87
Refugees and foreign policy: immediate needs and durable solutions [address, April 6, 1987] J. Moore. *Dep State Bull* 87:70-4 Jl '87
Rotten shame [immigration reform creates shortage of migrant farm workers] S. Koepp. il *Time* 129:49 Je 22 '87
Sad return of the prodigal sons [Mexicans returning to Huandacareo as result of new immigration law] J. Moody. il *Time* 129:52 My 18 '87

The social process of international migration [Mexican migration to the U.S.] D. S. Massey and F. García-España. bibl f il *Science* 237:733-8 Ag 14 '87
Twice blest [bill to allow Salvadoran refugees to remain in U.S.] *America* 157:76 Ag 15-22 '87
U.S. refugee policy and programs for FY 1987 [statements, September 16 and 26, 1986] J. Moore; R. L. Funseth. il *Dep State Bull* 86:78-81 D '86
U.S. should consider open borders [views of Annelise Anderson] il *USA Today (Periodical)* 115:7 Ap '87
The uneasy amnesty. *America* 156:413 My 23 '87
We need more people. M. S. Forbes, Jr. il *Forbes* 139:25 F 9 '87
What every manager must know about the new immigration law. J. Sherman. *Work Woman* 12:17-18+ Jl '87
Wooing the migrant farmer [growers' campaign to explain Immigration Reform and Control Act] J. B. Copeland. il *Newsweek* 109:47 Je 29 '87
Your papers, please [instructions for employer compliance with Immigration Reform Act] E. Knoll. *Progressive* 51:4 My '87

History
Business ethics, immigrants' treatment—70 years ago and now. B. C. Forbes. il por *Forbes* 140:33-4 Jl 13 '87

Right of entry fees
Why not let immigrants pay for speedy entry? G. S. Becker. il *Bus Week* p20 Mr 2 '87

Canada
Charlesville's big boom [East Indian refugee landing site generates tourist trade] B. Hatfield. il *Macleans* 100:8 O 5 '87
Closing the door [Central American refugees] A. Dwyer. *Nation* 244:384-5 Mr 28 '87
Drawing a harder line on migrants [Sikhs] M. Janigan. il *Macleans* 100:10+ Ag 10 '87
Fleeing to Canada [Central American refugees] E. Gress. *Commonweal* 114:164-6 Mr 27 '87
A harrowing story [Sikhs] M. Janigan. il *Macleans* 100:10-11 Ag 17 '87
Immigrants in an uneasy wait [refugees turned back at Canadian border] B. Wallace. il *Macleans* 100:8-10 Mr 9 '87
New policy, new protests. M. Rose. il *Macleans* 100:14-16 My 18 '87
The newest boat people [Sikhs' voyage to Nova Scotia; special section] il *Macleans* 100:6-10 Jl 27 '87
Ottawa shuts the gate [refugees] M. Gee. il *Macleans* 100:12 Mr 2 '87
The Peter Mansbridge syndrome [talented Canadians opting to leave Canada] C. Gordon. il *Macleans* 100:52 N 30 '87
Saying no [refugee policy; cover story; special section] il map *Macleans* 100:8-17 Ag 24 '87
A wary welcome for a human cargo [Sikhs] M. Janigan. il *Macleans* 100:18-19 Ag 3 '87
We say hello [refugees in Nova Scotia] il *Time* 130:47 Jl 27 '87

Great Britain
May we borrow your historians? [U.S. universities' recruitment of English humanities professors] M. Kishlansky. il *Hist Today* 37:6-7 Je '87

Hong Kong
Refugees in Hong Kong [Vietnamese] M. H. Kelleher. *America* 157:84-5 Ag 15-22 '87

Ireland
A fresh Irish wave laps U.S. shores. B. Duffy and R. Knight. il *U S News World Rep* 102:15 Mr 2 '87

Israel
Escape to uncertainty [Ethiopian Jews who have settled in Israel] N. Morris. il *Macleans* 100:6-7 Je 22 '87
Going home to Israel. I. Lederer-Gibel. *Christ Century* 104:162-4 F 18 '87
The humanitarian side of the Reagan administration: the rescue of Ethiopian Jews. M. Bard and H. M. Lenhoff. *Humanist* 47:25-6+ N/D '87
Israel's new conversion crisis [case of S. Miller] R. N. Ostling. il por *Time* 129:75 Ja 19 '87
Secret exodus: the story of Operation Moses [excerpt] C. Safran. il *Read Dig* 130:96-104+ Ja '87

Latin America
More Latin migrants. il *Futurist* 21:45 Ja/F '87

Mexico
The happy birds move on [Guatemalan Indian refugees flee to Mexico] R. J. Stout. il *Christ Century* 104:222-3 Mr 4 '87

Pakistan
Caught in the cross fire [Afghan refugees] K. Gannon. il *Progressive* 51:14 Ja '87

Immigration and emigration—*cont.*

Philippines

America: the 'great fish trap'. J. A. Chua. por *U S News World Rep* 103:16 O 5 '87

Portugal

In the absence of men [male emigration] C. B. Brettell. il *Nat Hist* 96:52-61 F '87

Soviet Union

Between issues [oppression of Soviet Jews] *New Leader* 70:2 O 19 '87

Doctor with a mission [G. Batist presses Soviet authorities to release refusenik patients with cancer] L. Van Dusen. il por *Macleans* 100:49-50 My 18 '87

Friends and enemies [march for Soviet Jewish emigration in Washington, D.C.] M. Walzer. *New Repub* 197:13-14 D 28 '87

Gorbachev and the Jews. H. Anderson. il por *Newsweek* 109:34-5 Ap 13 '87

Gorbachev opens the border for Jews—with good reason [trying to win support of U.S. Jews for relaxation of the Jackson-Vanik trade terms] J. Pearson. il *Bus Week* p28 Ap 20 '87

Hemming in the Kremlin [Jewish immigration policy] il *U S News World Rep* 103:25 D 21 '87

The long hard road to Moscow [émigrés return home from U.S.] J. Smolowe. il *Time* 129:47 Ja 12 '87

Moscow cracks the gates [Jewish emigrants] W. R. Doerner. il *Time* 130:74 N 9 '87

My American dream. V. V. Tokarev. il *Newsweek* 110:49 D 14 '87

New deal for Soviet Jews? T. Jacoby. il *Newsweek* 110:8 N 2 '87

Notes and comment [K. Fridman and her Jewish refusenik parents] *New Yorker* 63:29-30 S 21 '87

The return of the prodigal Russians [émigrés return after living in the U.S.] *Newsweek* 109:31 Ja 12 '87

Some refuseniks see no *glasnost*. J. Walsh. *Science* 237:356-7 Jl 24 '87

The Soviet gate opens—a bit. D. Stanglin. il *U S News World Rep* 102:37-8 Je 22 '87

The struggle to settle [refuseniks and returnees] C. Redden. il *Macleans* 100:33 Ja 19 '87

Will *glasnost* reunite Soviet-American couples? E. A. Condon. por *U S News World Rep* 102:10 Mr 2 '87

Thailand

The last bus [attempt to resettle Thailand's Hmong refugees in the U.S.] D. A. Ranard. il *Atlantic* 260:26-8+ O '87

Waiting in a cruel limbo [Cambodian refugees in Thailand camps] B. Barber. il *Macleans* 100:15-16 Ag 24 '87

United States

See Immigration and emigration

Western Europe

Europe closes the doors. R. Laver. il *Macleans* 100:13 Ag 24 '87

Migration and Western Europe: the old world turning new. G. Therborn. bibl f il *Science* 237:1183-8 S 4 '87

Immigration and Naturalization Service (U.S.) *See* United States. Immigration and Naturalization Service

Immigration Reform and Control Act *See* Immigration and emigration

Immortality

See also

Future life

Reincarnation

Anecdotes, facetiae, satire, etc.

Immortality and risk assessment. D. E. Koshland, Jr. *Science* 236:241 Ap 17 '87

Immune deficiency diseases *See* Immunologic diseases

Immunities and privileges *See* Privileges and immunities

Immunity

See also

Allergy

Antigens and antibodies

Cancer—Immunological aspects

Cattle—Diseases and pests—Vaccines and vaccination

Complements (Immunity)

Herpesviruses—Immunological aspects

Monoclonal antibodies

Neuroimmunology

Phagocytes and phagocytosis

Pregnancy—Immunological aspects

Psychoneuroimmunology

Transfer factor

Vaccines and vaccination

The aging of immunity [research by Steven J. Schleifer and others] J. Greenberg and B. Bower. *Sci News* 131:328 My 23 '87

Frontiers in immunology [special issue; with editorial comment by Daniel E. Koshland, Jr.] *Science* 238:1023, 1065-104 N 20 '87

Get a zing out of zinc. *Prevention* 39:8 D '87

Histocompatibility restriction explained [antigens] J. L. Marx. il *Science* 235:843-4 F 20 '87

Immunological self, nonself discrimination. J.-G. Guillet and others. bibl f il *Science* 235:865-70 F 20 '87

Maximize your immune system. D. Ostreicher and D. Klein. *McCalls* 115:79-80 O '87

New clues to the immune system [photophoresis treatment of lymphatic cancer and immunologic function of skin] S. Squire. il por *N Y Times Mag* p32-3+ F 1 '87

Raise your immunity level. W. Gottlieb. il *Rodale's Org Gard* 34:14+ D '87

Vitamin B_6 may put more fight in immune system. *Prevention* 39:113-14 S '87

The wars within us. P. Jaret. il *Read Dig* 130:164-6+ Ja '87

Why vitamin A may fight infections [research by Susan Smith and Colleen Hayes] *Sci News* 132:46 Jl 18 '87

Immunity (Exemption) *See* Privileges and immunities

Immunity (Plants) *See* Plants—Disease and pest resistance

Immunization *See* Vaccines and vaccination

Immunoassay

Synthetic peptide immunoassay distinguishes HIV type 1 and HIV type 2 infections. J. W. Gnann, Jr. and others. bibl f il *Science* 237:1346-9 S 11 '87

Immunochemistry

A mab to a unique cerebellar neuron generated by immunosuppression and rapid immunization. S. Hockfield. bibl f il *Science* 237:67-70 Jl 3 '87

Monoclonal antibodies as phylogenetic labels [discussion of July 3, 1987 article, A mab to a unique cerebellar neuron generated by immunosuppression and rapid immunization] S. Hockfield. *Science* 238:1730-1 D 18 '87

A small gold-conjugated antibody label: improved resolution for electron microscopy [cover story] J. F. Hainfeld. bibl f il *Science* 236:450-3 Ap 24 '87

Immunogenetics

See also

Major histocompatibility complex

Antibody research garners Nobel Prize [work of S. Tonagawa] J. L. Marx. il por *Science* 238:484-5 O 23 '87

The basis for the immunoregulatory role of macrophages and other accessory cells. E. R. Unanue and P. M. Allen. bibl f il *Science* 236:551-7 My 1 '87

Development of the primary antibody repertoire. F. W. Alt and others. bibl f il *Science* 238:1079-87 N 20 '87

Early restriction of the human antibody repertoire. H. W. Schroeder, Jr. and others. bibl f il *Science* 238:791-3 N 6 '87

Finding the children [identifying Argentine missing children through genetic testing] B. Beckwith. il *Ms* 16:88 S '87

Germline organization of the murine T cell receptor β-chain genes. H. S. Chou and others. bibl f il *Science* 238:545-8 O 23 '87

Hard chargers find the keys to glory [S. Tonegawa and other Nobel Prize science winners] S. Budiansky. il por *U S News World Rep* 103:12-13 O 26 '87

Immunochemical proof that a novel rearranging gene encodes the T cell receptor δ subunit. H. Band and others. bibl f il *Science* 238:682-4 O 30 '87

Killer cells, MHC: factors in AIDS? D. D. Edwards. *Sci News* 132:52 Jl 25 '87

Measuring the human T cell receptor γ-chain. W. M. Strauss and others. bibl f il *Science* 237:1217-19 S 4 '87

Medicine, chemistry, physics Nobels announced [S. Tonegawa and others] S. Eisenberg. il por *Sci News* 132:244 O 17 '87

Molecular diversity of the human T-gamma constant region genes. P. G. Pelicci and others. bibl f il *Science* 237:1051-5 Ag 28 '87

New insights into antigen recognition. P. Marrack. *Science* 235:1311-13 Mr 13 '87

Nobel prizes: physiology or medicine. K. Wright. *Sci Am* 257:45-6 D '87

Post-transcriptional control of class I MHC mRNA expression in adenovirus 12-transformed cells. R. T. M. J. Vaessen and others. bibl f il *Science* 235:1486-8 Mr 20 '87

Structurally divergent human T cell receptor γ proteins encoded by distinct Cγ genes. M. S. Krangel and others. bibl f il *Science* 237:64-7 Jl 3 '87

Immunogenetics—*cont.*

The T cell receptor. P. Marrack and J. Kappler. bibl f il *Science* 238:1073-9 N 20 '87

The T cell receptor family is growing. J. L. Marx. bibl il *Science* 236:1187-8 Je 5 '87

Immunoglobulins

Allelic exclusion in transgenic mice that express the membrane form of immunoglobulin μ. M. C. Nussenzweig and others. bibl f il *Science* 236:816-19 My 15 '87

Allergy alert [immunoglobulin E blood test for children] C. Bushnell. il *Health* 19:15 Ja '87

The chicken B cell compartment. J.-C. Weill and C.-A. Reynaud. bibl f il *Science* 238:1094-8 N 20 '87

Detecting allergy-prone children [immunoglobulin E blood test] *USA Today (Periodical)* 115:12 F '87

Development of the primary antibody repertoire. F. W. Alt and others. bibl f il *Science* 238:1079-87 N 20 '87

Human lymphocytes making rheumatoid factor and antibody to ssDNA belong to Leu-1+ B-cell subset. P. Casali and others. bibl f il *Science* 236:77-81 Ap 3 '87

The immunoglobulin octanucleotide: independent activity and selective interaction with enhancers. T. G. Parslow and others. bibl f il *Science* 235:1498-1501 Mr 20 '87

Interferon-γ and B cell stimulatory factor-1 reciprocally regulate Ig isotype production. C. M. Snapper and W. E. Paul. bibl f il *Science* 236:944-7 My 22 '87

Protein-binding sites in Ig gene enhancers determine transcriptional activity and inducibility. M. Lenardo and others. bibl f il *Science* 236:1573-7 Je 19 '87

Rheumatoid factor secretion from human Leu-1+ B cells. R. R. Hardy and others. bibl f il *Science* 236:81-3 Ap 3 '87

Two pairs of recombination signals are sufficient to cause immunoglobulin V-(D)-J joining. S. Akira and others. bibl f il *Science* 238:1134-8 N 20 '87

Immunologic diseases

See also
AIDS (Disease)
Allergy
Lupus erythematosus
Sjögren's syndrome

Autoimmunity may cause infertility [research by Norbert Gleicher and others] R. Weiss. *Sci News* 132:52-3 Jl 25 '87

Autoreactive epitope defined as the anticodon region of alanine transfer RNA. C. C. Bunn and M. B. Mathews. bibl f il *Science* 238:1116-19 N 20 '87

Human lymphocytes making rheumatoid factor and antibody to ssDNA belong to Leu-1+ B-cell subset. P. Casali and others. bibl f il *Science* 236:77-81 Ap 3 '87

Organ-resident, nonlymphoid cells suppress proliferation of autoimmune T-helper lymphocytes. R. R. Caspi and others. bibl f il *Science* 237:1029-32 Ag 28 '87

Rheumatoid factor secretion from human Leu-1+ B cells. R. R. Hardy and others. bibl f il *Science* 236:81-3 Ap 3 '87

Therapy

See also
Institute for Immunological Disorders

Immunological tolerance

Leukemic cells rehabilitated in rats [research by Joaquin J. Jimenez and Adel A. Yunis] R. Weiss. *Sci News* 132:357 D 5 '87

A mab to a unique cerebellar neuron generated by immunosuppression and rapid immunization. S. Hockfield. bibl f il *Science* 237:67-70 Jl 3 '87

Monoclonal antibodies as phylogenetic labels [discussion of July 3, 1987 article, A mab to a unique cerebellar neuron generated by immunosuppression and rapid immunization] S. Hockfield. *Science* 238:1730-1 D 18 '87

New transplant findings fit like a glove [research by Elaine Reed and others] R. Weiss. *Sci News* 131:375 Je 13 '87

Noninvasive transplant-rejection test? *Sci News* 131:282 My 2 '87

Thalidomide: is there a silver lining? [graft-versus-host disease; research by Georgia B. Vogelsang] D. D. Edwards. *Sci News* 131:198 Mr 28 '87

Tolerance induced by thymic epithelial grafts in birds. H. Ohki and others. bibl f il *Science* 237:1032-5 Ag 28 '87

Tumor cell rejection through terminal cell differentiation [leukemia cells] J. J. Jimenez and A. A. Yunis. bibl f il *Science* 238:1278-80 N 27 '87

Immunology *See* Immunity

Immunopathology *See* Immunologic diseases

Immunosuppression *See* Immunological tolerance

Immunosuppressive agents

See also
Cyclosporin
Uromodulin

Immunotherapy

See also
Arthritis—Therapy
Cancer—Therapy
Diabetes—Therapy
Lymphatic system—Cancer—Therapy

Immunotoxins *See* Toxins and antitoxins

Imo Delaval Inc.

A 'mundane' stock may go into orbit. G. G. Marcial. *Bus Week* p76 Ap 20 '87

Impac '88

What (or who) makes Albert Gore run. M. E. Recio. il por *Bus Week* p45 Ap 27 '87

Impeachments

A brief for impeachment [case of Judge A. Hastings of Florida] il por *U S News World Rep* 102:9 Mr 30 '87

Hastings: critics are motivated by racism [ethics charges against Florida judge] por *Jet* 71:29 F 16 '87

Judge fights impeachment [A. L. Hastings] L. Brown. il por *Black Enterp* 18:18 Ag '87

Judge Hastings faces congressional hearing on charges of bribery. por *Jet* 73:6+ N 2 '87

Imperial Chemical Industries plc

A busy body bent on doing better [D. H. Henderson] R. I. Kirkland, Jr. il por *Fortune* 116:60 Ag 3 '87

Imperialism

Images of Ireland 1170-1600: the origins of English imperialism. J. Gillingham. bibl il *Hist Today* 37:16-22 F '87

The white peril [G. Vidal's comments on decline of U.S. and rise of Japan] J. M. Fallows. il *Atlantic* 259:18+ My '87

Impersonation

The me I didn't know [pretending to be someone else as a way to self improvement; research by Robert Hartley] P. Chance. *Psychol Today* 21:20 Ja '87

Some like it hot [M. Monroe impersonator A. Lorre] B. Greene. il pors *Esquire* 108:59-60+ O '87

Impersonators, Female

See also
Trockadero Gloxinia Ballet Company

Implants, Breast *See* Surgery, Plastic

Implants, Cochlear *See* Ear, Artificial

Implements, utensils, etc.

See also
Bone implements and weapons
Kitchen utensils and appliances
Stone implements and weapons
Tools

Import companies *See* Trading companies

Import trade *See* Export-import trade

The importance of being earnest [drama] *See* Wilde, Oscar, 1854-1900

Impostor phenomenon *See* Fear of success

Impostors and imposture

See also
Quacks and quackery

Impotence

Dealing with impotence. R. Blaun. il *N Y* 20:50-8 Mr 30 '87

Impotence is more treatable than you think. T. Carson. il *Bus Week* p106 Ja 19 '87

Impregnation, Artificial *See* Artificial insemination, Human

Impresarios

See also
Theatrical agencies and agents

Impressionism (Art)

See also
Ecole de Rouen

Berthe Morisot's experimental techniques and impressionist style. W. P. Scott. il *Am Artist* 51:42-7 D '87

Joseph Moure's California impressionist paintings [collector] I. Borger. il por *Archit Dig* 44:86+ Mr '87

Exhibitions

The heart of the seasons [American impressionist paintings from the Terra Museum; cover story] E. Hardwick. il *House Gard* 159:122-31+ My '87

Impressions (Periodical)

Impressions of Alabama. il *Horizon* 30:57-8 D '87

Imprisonment See Prisons

Improvisation (Music)

Large-scale jazz [influence of D. Ellington and trend towards composition] F. Davis. il *Atlantic* 260:76-7 Ag '87

In fact (Periodical)

Eye witness [editor G. Seldes] E. Knoll. *Progressive* 51:4 Je '87

In God we trust (Motto) See Mottoes

In-laws

See also
Mothers-in-law
Sons-in-law

In love and war [television program] See Television program reviews—Single works

In memory of . . . [ballet] See Ballet reviews—Single works

In service education (College teachers) See College teachers—Education in service

In service education (Teachers) See Teachers—Education in service

In-store advertising See Supermarkets—In-store advertising

In the mood [film] See Motion picture reviews—Single works

In the shadow of the wind [film] See Motion picture reviews—Single works

In the upper room [dance] See Dance reviews—Single works

In vitro fertilization See Fertilization in vitro

Inaba, Seiuemon

about

Japan's robot king wins again. G. Bylinsky. il pors *Fortune* 115:53-4+ My 25 '87

Inabnit, Mark

about

Create an English country garden. A. Davis. il por *Home Mech* 83:60-1 Je '87

Inaugurations

See also
Presidents—Inaugurations

Inbreeding

Homozygosity mapping: a way to map human recessive traits with the DNA of inbred children. E. S. Lander and D. Botstein. bibl f il *Science* 236:1567-70 Je 19 '87

Rescuing uniparental embryos: new possibilites for animal breeding. il *BioScience* 37:381 Je '87

Incarnation

January in the body. B. L. Rohrig. *Christ Century* 104:77-8 Ja 28 '87

Incas

Antiquities

See also
Machu Picchu (Peru)

Incentives in education

Cleveland pays for its A's [Scholarship-in-Escrow Program] il *Newsweek* 110:66 Ag 31 '87

The prizes of first grade [incentive program at Lincoln School, Caldwell, Idaho] P. Skreslet. por *Newsweek* 110:8 N 30 '87

Top-grade perks for teens [program at DuSable High School, Chicago] M. Oshin. il *Essence* 18:38 Je '87

Incentives in industry

See also
Bonus system
Profit sharing

Bigger pay for better work [results of survey] J. C. Horn. il *Psychol Today* 21:54-7 Jl '87

Getting top performance from your sales force. H. Waldrop. il *Work Woman* 12:56 D '87

Incer, Jaime

Nature's red-hot caldrons. il *Américas* 39:18-25 Ja/F '87

Incest

Beauty queen is the alleged victim of father's incest [D. Keating] por *Jet* 72:12 Ag 10 '87

Brutal treatment, vicious deeds [C. Pierson and other abused children who murder their parents] J. D. Hull. il por *Time* 130:68 O 19 '87

Daughter alleges father sired his own grandkids [case of Rev. L. Elliott] il por *Jet* 72:16+ Ag 31 '87

In Massachusetts, an ugly battle for a little girl [child abuse charges in custody case of N. LaLonde] G. Hackett. il por *Newsweek* 110:41 O 19 '87

Texas preacher guilty of siring 12 of his grandkids [L. Elliott] il por *Jet* 73:16 D 7 '87

"We have a problem" [daughter molested by father] J. Marks. il *Parents* 62:70+ My '87

Incineration and incinerators

Burning trash: how it could work [cover story] A. Hershkowitz. il *Technol Rev* 90:26-34 Jl '87

Citizens douse a hazardous burn [plan to incinerate PCBs at University of North Dakota's Energy Research Center] J. Hamilton. il *Sierra* 72:88-9 N/D '87

Garbage in, garbage out [waste-to-energy incinerators] C. Mann. il *Sierra* 72:20+ S/O '87

Garbage: to burn or not to burn? T. Davis. il *Technol Rev* 90:19 F/Mr '87

Keeping dioxins down in the dumps. I. Peterson. *Sci News* 132:118-19 Ag 22 '87

Model studies of polychlorinated dibenzo-p-dioxin formation during municipal refuse incineration [fly ash] F. W. Karasek and L. C. Dickson. bibl f il *Science* 237:754-6 Ag 14 '87

Inclusion bodies See Cells—Inclusions

Income

See also
Gross national product
Minimum wage
Retirement income
Wealth

Changes in the distribution of American family incomes, 1947 to 1984. F. S. Levy. bibl f il *Science* 236:923-7 My 22 '87

The golden mean [income distribution] G. P. Brockway. il *New Leader* 70:15-16 N 2 '87

How to win an election bet [income growth figures favor the Democrats] J. Crudele. il *N Y* 20:16 N 16 '87

Incomes are up—and not a minute too soon. W. B. Franklin and J. C. Cooper. il *Bus Week* p37-8 My 11 '87

Inequality in America: where do we stand? G. T. Burtless. il *Current* 297:4-10 N '87

Living well on less. P. E. Godwin. il *Changing Times* 41:26-30+ Mr '87

The skewing of America: disparities in wealth and income. R. D. Pasquariello. il *Christ Century* 104:164-6 F 18 '87

Slow wage growth means more sag in sales. W. B. Franklin and J. C. Cooper. il *Bus Week* p23-4 F 9 '87

A surge in inequality [international competition and the feminization of poverty are distorting the distribution of income] L. C. Thurow. bibl (p128) il *Sci Am* 256:30-7 My '87

Third world income just can't catch up [report by Organization for Economic Cooperation & Development] G. Koretz. il *Bus Week* p21 F 9 '87

Income investments See Investments

Income statements See Financial statements

Income tax

See also
Aged—Taxation
Americans—Foreign countries—Taxation
Artists—Taxation
Blacks—Taxation
Business entertaining—Taxation
Business travel—Taxation
Children—Taxation
Computers—Tax return use
Corporations—Taxation
Dancers—Taxation
Divorcees—Taxation
Employees as stockholders—Taxation
Entertainers—Taxation
Estimated tax
Farmers—Taxation
Fringe benefits—Taxation
Interest (Economics)—Taxation
Investments—Taxation
Master limited partnership—Taxation
Pensions—Taxation
Rent—Taxation
Rich—Taxation
Self employed—Taxation
Social security—Taxation
Tax evasion
Tax refunds
Tax shelters
United States. Internal Revenue Service
Withholding tax
Women—Taxation

10 year-end tax saving tips! S. Kess and B. Weltman. il *Good Housekeep* 205:246 N '87

11th-hour moves that boomerang. L. Wiener. il *U S News World Rep* 102:56 Ja 26 '87

The 12 tax tips of Christmas. A. E. Serwer. il *Fortune* 116:175 D 21 '87

1987 taxes—worse than you think. H. Banks. *Forbes* 139:27 Mr 23 '87

Income tax—*cont.*

The bad new tax law. H. Gutmann. il *N Y Rev Books* 34:26-8 F 12 '87

The bad new tax law: an exchange [discussion of February 12, 1987 article] H. Gutmann. il *N Y Rev Books* 34:49-51 Jl 16 '87

Battling the tax steamroller. J. C. Szabo. il *Nations Bus* 75:12 Ag '87

Beyond tax populism. R. Darman. *Society* 24:35-8 S/O '87

Coping with the new tax law. K. J. Artis. il *Saturday Evening Post* 259:112 Ap '87

Down with taxes [cover story] L. Wiener. il *U S News World Rep* 103:73-6+ D 7 '87

Education [effect of new tax laws on dance-related activities] M. Horosko. bibl il *Dance Mag* 61:107-9 Ja '87

Facing up to the most dreaded tax [alternative minimum tax] C. Yang. il *Bus Week* p132-3 D 21 '87

For high incomes, less escape [alternative minimum tax] L. Wiener. il *U S News World Rep* 103:62 Ag 3 '87

How to save at least $500 on your '87 taxes. H. Wheelwright. *Money* 16:215 Mr '87

Inside tax reform [work of J. H. Birnbaum and A. S. Murray] P. Glastris. *Wash Mon* 19:52-6 Je '87

Just when you thought you were safe . . . [tax reform booby traps] K. McCormally. il *Changing Times* 41:102-7 O '87

Lessons from a neighbor [tax reform] I. Austen. il *Macleans* 100:39 Je 29 '87

Loopholes at large. R. S. McIntyre. *New Repub* 196:12+ Je 15 '87

Money and taxes. J. A. Schnepper. il *USA Today (Periodical)* 115:69 Ja '87

More answers to taxing questions. K. McCormally. il *Changing Times* 41:57-60 Ap '87

New House Speaker Wright's awfully wrong turn [postponing promised tax reduction] M. S. Forbes. *Forbes* 139:17 Ja 26 '87

The new tax facts. J. Malveaux. il *Essence* 17:94+ Ja '87

Noteworthy anniversary; noteworthy man [J. Kemp] M. S. Forbes, Jr. il por *Forbes* 140:25 Ag 10 '87

Of deficits and taxes. G. P. Brockway. *New Leader* 70:14-15 O 5 '87

Our new tax law—what's in it for you? F. Gebhart. il *Read Dig* 130:81-4 F '87

Plan now for next Apr. 15. B. Hitchings. *Bus Week* p157 My 18 '87

Play it again, Uncle Sam. K. McCormally. il *Changing Times* 41:107-8+ Ja '87

Populism and tax reform. R. Darman. il *USA Today (Periodical)* 116:29-31 S '87

Rich man's populist [views of J. Kemp] R. S. McIntyre. *New Repub* 196:16-17 Mr 23 '87

Simplifying the simplification. L. Wiener. il *U S News World Rep* 103:78 S 14 '87

The smart taxpayer's guide. L. Wiener. il *U S News World Rep* 102:50-1+ Mr 2 '87

Surprise! The unexpected results of the new tax law . . . and how you can benefit from them [cover story; special section] il *Money* 16:52-6+ S '87

The tax-cut voodoo lives on. H. Banks. *Forbes* 140:33 Jl 27 '87

The tax reform lie. J. A. Schnepper. il *USA Today (Periodical)* 115:17 My '87

Tax-saving moves you'd better make soon. K. McCormally. il *Changing Times* 41:78-9+ D '87

Taxes: fairness first [tax reform and cheating; study by Amitai Etzioni] V. Bozzi. *Psychol Today* 21:12 Ap '87

Timely answers to taxing questions. K. McCormally. il *Changing Times* 41:35-6+ My '87

Understanding the new tax law [with editorial comment by M. Stanton Evans] il *Consum Res Mag* 70:3, 18-22 Ja '87

Washington's odd couple shakes up taxes [B. Packwood and D. Rostenkowski] A. R. Dowd. il pors *Fortune* 115:40-1 Ja 5 '87

Welcome to year one of tax reform [special section] il *Money* 16:67-74+ F '87

Who'll win with the tax law. T. Minsky. il *Esquire* 107:44 F '87

Year-end tax strategies. M. Daly. il *Better Homes Gard* 65:96+ N '87

Year-end tax tips. C. Poole. il *Forbes* 140:60+ N 30 '87

You and your 1040: how women fare under the new tax law. E. Card. il *Ms* 15:68+ F '87

Your '86 return: how to avoid expensive mistakes. B. G. Quint. *Glamour* 85:180+ Mr '87

Your best tax strategy for 1988. M. Schiffres. il *U S News World Rep* 102:64 Mr 2 '87

Your taxes: up or down? il *Consum Rep* 52:164-71 Mr '87

Anecdotes, facetiae, satire, etc.

Taxing times. R. Baker. il *N Y Times Mag* p16 Ap 19 '87

Auditing

See Tax auditing

Bibliography

A guide to the tax guides. G. Anrig, Jr. il *Money* 16:157-8+ F '87

Words to file by: those new tax guides. D. H. Dunn. il *Bus Week* p104 F 9 '87

Collection

See Tax collection

Deductions

See also
Depletion allowances

Are losses still deductible? [casualty losses] P. D. Lawrence. il *Esquire* 108:50 Jl '87

Black groups miss out on boom in donations spurred by tax reform. *Jet* 71:33 Ja 26 '87

The delicate art of donating art. T. Segal. il *Bus Week* p167 Je 22 '87

Easy-to-miss deductions: they add up. S. Weiss. *Bus Week* p103 Mr 30 '87

Family planning. *U S News World Rep* 103:78 D 7 '87

The fine art of donating fine art. L. Wiener. il *U S News World Rep* 103:104 S 28 '87

Getty 'improprieties' attract IRS scrutiny [investigation into donations of works of art to the J. Paul Getty Museum] A. Decker. *Art News* 86:31-2 My '87

Giving to charity without giving to Uncle Sam. C. Yang. il *Bus Week* p184 O 12 '87

Home is where the job is. L. Wiener. il *U S News World Rep* 103:63 Ag 24 '87

The new keys to home-office deductions. P. Philipps. il *Bus Week* p100 Jl 6 '87

Profiting from losses. L. Wiener. il *U S News World Rep* 102:56 Ap 13 '87

Real estate deals that help ol' alma mater—and you. D. B. Moskowitz. il *Bus Week* p126 O 26 '87

Take my yacht. Please! [charitable deduction] W. G. Flanagan and L. Scheer. il *Forbes* 140:114-15 D 28 '87

Taking deductions. G. Anrig, Jr. *Money* 16:239-40 N '87

Tax breaks for a Picasso. M. Malone. il *Newsweek* 109:39-40 Ja 5 '87

Unlock deductions. il *U S News World Rep* 103:75-6 D 7 '87

Unsure about a deduction? Run it by the IRS. S. Woolley. il *Bus Week* p117 S 7 '87

Your 1986 return: what's new on the 1040 and what you can still do to reduce your tax bill. *Money* 16:114 F '87

History

Original sins. L. Saunders. il *Forbes* 140:286-7+ Jl 13 '87

When Uncle Sam's tax bite was a nibble. M. Lefkowitz. il *Nations Bus* 75:36 S '87

Records

See Tax records

Returns

See Tax returns

Canada

See also
Canada. Revenue Canada

Cautious reform [special section] il *Macleans* 100:34-41 Je 29 '87

Gentle persuasion for the rich. D. Francis. por *Macleans* 100:7 Je 15 '87

A major assault on the tax laws. P. C. Newman. il *Macleans* 100:30 Je 8 '87

The new shape of tax reform. P. C. Newman. il *Macleans* 100:38 Je 22 '87

Stranded on the road to reform. D. Francis. por *Macleans* 100:5 Jl 13 '87

Tinkering with tax reform [J. Playfair's views] P. C. Newman. il por *Macleans* 100:42 Je 29 '87

Waiting for tax reform. M. Drohan. il por *Macleans* 100:8-9 Mr 2 '87

Germany (West)

Going over like a lead zeppelin [tax reform] J. Templeman. il *Bus Week* p47 O 26 '87

West Germany. *Bus Week* p61 Mr 9 '87

Income tax—*cont.*

Great Britain

Whose crazy idea was this? L. Saunders. il por *Forbes* 140:290 Jl 13 '87

New York (State)

The continuing success of Return a Gift to Wildlife [tax checkoff] S. Keeler. il *Conservationist* 41:2-5 Mr/Ap '87

United States

See Income tax

Income tax, State *See* Taxation, State
Income tax consultants *See* Tax consultants
Income tax credits *See* Tax credits
Incontinence, Urinary *See* Urine—Incontinence
Incubation, Mental *See* Problem solving
Incubators (Entrepreneurship)

Can chicken-coop inventors help us win? D. S. Greenberg. il *U S News World Rep* 103:42 Jl 27 '87

Indentured servants

United States

Orphaned and lost. A. McCarthy. *Commonweal* 114:407-8 Jl 17 '87

Independence, Personal *See* Self reliance
Independence (Aircraft carrier)

Photographs and photography

A flattop is born again. T. Moore. il *Fortune* 116:100-5 S 14 '87

Independence (Tex.)

Historic houses, sites, etc.

A reminder of Sam Houston [Mrs. Sam Houston House] il *South Living* 22:32 F '87

Independence National Historical Park (Pa.)

Philadelphia: the city that gave us a nation. A. Green. il *Natl Parks* 61:24-9 Mr/Ap '87

Independent (Newspaper: Great Britain)

Fleet Street's shake-out. R. Laver. il *Macleans* 100:38-40 O 19 '87

Independent American Savings & Loan Association

An S&L whodunit where everyone's a suspect. J. Weber, Jr. il por *Bus Week* p96-8 Jl 13 '87

Independent Federation of Flight Attendants

Back to work [TWA ordered to reinstate former strikers] D. Bensman. *Nation* 244:875 Je 27 '87

Standing up to Carl Icahn. C. Friday and J. Schwartz. il *Newsweek* 109:54 Ap 13 '87

Vicki Frankovich [Independent Federation of Flight Attendants' strike against TWA] C. Doudna. por *Ms* 15:74-6+ Ja '87

Independent International Commission on Health Research for Development

New look at health in developing nations. J. Walsh. il *Science* 238:746 N 6 '87

Independent motion picture industry *See* Motion picture industry
Independent regulatory commissions *See* Regulatory agencies
Independent television stations *See* Television stations
Index funds

Bank introduces indexed investing. R. Brady. il *Nations Bus* 75:85-6 My '87

Index funds: getting more bond for the buck. G. Weiss. il *Bus Week* p104 S 21 '87

These funds want to tie the averages [Vanguard's new Bond Market Fund and Quantitative Portfolios] C. S. Eklund. il por *Bus Week* p80 Ja 19 '87

When keeping up with the averages is better than average. J. M. Laderman. il *Bus Week* p114-15 Je 8 '87

Index linking (Economics) *See* Indexation (Economics)
Index numbers (Economics)

See also

Indexation (Economics)
Price indexes

Indexation (Economics)

See also

Cost of living adjustments
Index funds

A pension breakthrough [Chrysler Canada agrees to index pensions against inflation] D. Jenish. il *Macleans* 100:32-3 S 28 '87

Indexes

Agnostic. See Harbor seal. L. R. Hedrick. por *Publ Wkly* 231:29 My 1 '87

Indexes, Environmental *See* Environment—Statistics
Indexing

See also

Computers—Indexing use

India

See also

Americans—India
Arts—India
Arts and crafts—India
Astronomical observatories—India

Bhopal poisonous gas disaster, India, 1984
Bidar (India)
Birds—India
Bombay (India)
Chandigarh (India)
Chinese—India
College education and state—India
Divorce—India
Education—India
Environmental movement—India
Environmental policy—India
Goa (India)
Hippies—India
Hunting—India
Indians (East Indian)
Investments, American—India
Ladakh
Malabar Coast (India)
Medical care—India
Motion pictures—India
National parks and reserves—India
New Delhi (India)
Palaces—India
Pharmaceutical research—India
Poor—India
Port Blair (India)
Prostitution—India
Public health—India
Punjab (India)
Volcanoes—India
Waterways—India
Wildlife—India
Wildlife conservation—India

Army

Forces in Sri Lanka

The battle for Jaffna [Indian troops mount assault on Tamil stronghold] T. A. Sancton. il *Time* 130:52 O 26 '87

The long agony of a city under siege [Indian troops fight Tamil rebels in Jaffna] B. Barber. il map *Macleans* 100:22-3 N 2 '87

An orgy of killing. K. Scanlon. il *Macleans* 100:34-5 O 19 '87

The siege of Jaffna. N. Cooper. il map *Newsweek* 110:67 N 2 '87

The siege of Jaffna. K. Scanlon. il map *Macleans* 100:33 O 26 '87

Sri Lanka: a nation disintegrates [cover story] S. R. Weisman. il map *N Y Times Mag* p34-8+ D 13 '87

Sri Lanka: a reluctant slaughter [Indian troops move against Tamils] *Newsweek* 110:49 O 26 '87

Wrong side, wrong war, for India [fighting between Indian troops and Tamil rebels] W. A. Taylor. il *U S News World Rep* 103:38 O 26 '87

Commerce

United States

See United States—Commerce—India

Defenses

See also

Fortification—India

India, Pakistan racing to be last [nuclear weapons] R. V. R. Chandrasekhar Rao. il *Bull At Sci* 43:32-4 N '87

Description and travel

A fortnight in India. T. McNally. *Horizon* 30:2 S '87

Reflections of India [special section] il *Horizon* 30:17-30+ Mr '87

Economic policy

Assessing development costs in India [cover story] R. Sharma. bibl f il *Environment* 29:6-11+ Ap '87

Foreign relations

China

See China—Foreign relations—India

Pakistan

Blood and ice at 20,000 ft. [battle in the Siachen Glacier region] il *Time* 130:45 O 12 '87

India and Pakistan: brothers and enemies. S. K. Mehera. map *World Press Rev* 34:32-4 S '87

India, Pakistan racing to be last [nuclear weapons] R. V. R. Chandrasekhar Rao. il *Bull At Sci* 43:32-4 N '87

Sri Lanka

Bearing gifts [Indian support of Tamil rebels] *Time* 129:40 Je 15 '87

Behind the haste in Sri Lanka. G. Jain. *World Press Rev* 34:49 O '87

Giving peace a chance: India and Sri Lanka forge a Tamil compromise. F. Willey. il *Newsweek* 110:43 Ag 10 '87

India—Foreign relations—Sri Lanka—cont.
If this is peace . . . [agreement signed by India and Sri Lanka] E. W. Desmond. il map *Time* 130:18-20 Ag 10 '87
Mother India intervenes [Air Force drops food to Tamils] R. Nordland. il *Newsweek* 109:38 Je 15 '87
Peace flexes its muscle [Tamil rebels surrender arms in Sri Lanka] H. G. Chua-Eoan. il *Time* 130:42 Ag 17 '87
Row over the airdrop [Indian airdrop of relief supplies to Tamils] A. Bilski. il *Macleans* 100:27 Je 15 '87
Taming the Tigers [Tamils] M. Ispahani. *New Repub* 197:14+ Jl 27 '87
A troubled peace plan. K. Hall. il *Macleans* 100:20 Ag 10 '87
Yes, politics makes strange bedfellows [India's help in subduing Tamil rebels] W. A. Taylor. il *U S News World Rep* 103:8 Ag 10 '87
United States
See United States—Foreign relations—India
History
1500-1765
See also
Mogul Empire
18th century
A patriot for whom? Yusuf Khan: conflicts of loyalty in eighteenth-century India. A. Bakshian. il map *Hist Today* 37:40-4 Ap '87
1947-
The killing fields . . . and streets and trains and buses. S. Kogelfranz. il *World Press Rev* 34:22-3 N '87
Bibliography
Paperback history. F. Robinson. *Hist Today* 37:57 Jl '87
Industries
See also
Air India
Art trade—India
Computer industry—India
Diamond industry—India
Motion picture industry—India
Soft drink industry—India
Tata Sons Ltd.
Languages
See also
English language in India
Native peoples
See also
Tamils
Photographs and photography
Your first trip to India. P. Slaughter. il *Petersens Photogr Mag* 16:26-31 D '87
Politics and government
See also
Elections—India
Politics, Corruption in—India
For Gandhi, everything turns sour. M. Satchell. il por *U S News World Rep* 102:34-5 Ap 6 '87
Gandhi at midterm. P. H. Kreisberg. *Foreign Aff* 65:1055-76 Summ '87
Gandhi under the gun. D. D'Monte. il *New Leader* 70:8-10 Je 29 '87
The killing fields . . . and streets and trains and buses. S. Kogelfranz. il *World Press Rev* 34:22-3 N '87
Letter from New Delhi. V. Mehta. il *New Yorker* 62:52+ Ja 19 '87
No longer Mr. Clean [R. Gandhi] por *Time* 130:20 Ag 10 '87
Passage to democracy. *New Repub* 197:7-9 S 7 '87
Pols of India [actor-politicians M. G. Ramachandran and N. T. Ramo Rao] C. Das Gupta and J. Hoberman. il pors *Film Comment* 23:20-4 My/Je '87
Rajiv Gandhi stumbles. H. Anderson. il por *Newsweek* 109:38 F 23 '87
Rajiv Gandhi's honeymoon is over. K. Thapar. il por *World Press Rev* 34:40-1 Je '87
'Such a dance of death' [Sikh attacks against Hindus] F. Willey. il *Newsweek* 110:34 Jl 20 '87
"We don't have the bomb" [interview with R. Gandhi] P. Gupte. il pors *Forbes* 139:156+ My 18 '87
Religious institutions and affairs
See also
Buddhism—India
Catholic Church—India
Church and social problems—India
Church of South India
Hinduism
Jains—India
Social conditions
See also
Sexual behavior—India

India and the United States
See also
United States—Foreign opinion—Indian (East Indian)
Indian art (American) *See* Indians of North America—Art
Indian art (East Indian) *See* Art, Indian (East Indian)
Indian artifacts (American) *See* Indians of North America—Antiquities
Indian blankets, rugs, etc. (American)
Modern Navajo rugs: subtle in all but price. S. D. Atchison. il *Bus Week* p118 S 7 '87
Indian Canyons (Calif.)
Eighteen holes at the oasis [proposed development of Agua Caliente land in the Indian Canyons] O. Redwine. il *Sierra* 72:83-4 N/D '87
Indian cooking (East Indian) *See* Cooking, Indian (East Indian)
Indian corn *See* Corn
Indian dance (East Indian) *See* Dance, Indian (East Indian)
Indian drama (East Indian)
Drama that endures. V. Gladstone. il *Horizon* 30:28-9 Mr '87
Indian languages (American) *See* Indians (American)—Languages
Indian Market (Santa Fe, N.M.)
Indian art at its best . . . in Santa Fe, August 22 and 23. il *Sunset* 179:12-13 Ag '87
Indian Ocean
See also
Cruising—Indian Ocean
United Nations. Ad Hoc Committee on the Indian Ocean
Delving deep into the Indian past [hot spots] R. Monastersky. map *Sci News* 132:56 Jl 25 '87
Drill ship probes Indian Ocean mysteries. K. Riedel. il *Oceans* 20:6-7 S/O '87
Indian relics (American) *See* Indians of North America—Antiquities
Indian reservations (American) *See* Indians of North America—Reservations
Indian River (P.E.I.)
Churches (Buildings)
Saviors of an island church [St. Mary's Roman Catholic Church] B. MacAndrew. il *Macleans* 100:43 N 2 '87
Indian rugs (American) *See* Indian blankets, rugs, etc. (American)
Indian students (East Indian) in the United States *See* Foreign students—United States
Indian theater (American) *See* Theater, Indian (American)
Indian weaving (American) *See* Weaving
Indiana
See also
Agriculture—Indiana
Booksellers and bookselling—Indiana
Hunting—Indiana
Juvenile justice, Administration of—Indiana
Moral conditions
High Court asked to rule on RICO bookstore case [adult bookstore] *Publ Wkly* 232:10 N 13 '87
Politics and government
Lottery foes target public policy [proposed state lottery] B. L. Rohrig. *Christ Century* 104:396-7 Ap 29 '87
Indiana Black Expo
Black stars highlight the 17th Indiana Black Expo, the state's biggest ever. il *Jet* 72:58+ Ag 3 '87
Indiana Black Expo. il *Ebony* 43:76+ N '87
Indiana Repertory Theatre
Drama with determination. B. Golightly. il *Horizon* 30:19 Je '87
Indiana University, Bloomington
Education and values [address, October 12, 1987] T. Ehrlich. *Vital Speeches Day* 54:106-9 D 1 '87
Indiana University, Bloomington. School of Music
Keepers of the flame [opera teachers V. Zeani and N. Rossi-Lemeni] C. Battaglia. il pors *Opera News* 52:28-30+ N '87
Indiana University of Pennsylvania. Benjamin E. Mays Academy of Scholars *See* Benjamin E. Mays Academy of Scholars
Indiana University Opera Theatre
Musical events:
Rimsky-Korsakov's Czar Saltan. A. Porter. *New Yorker* 63:107-8 My 18 '87
Indianapolis (Ind.)
Airports
Air express growth creates night rush at Midwest center. J. Ott. il *Aviat Week Space Technol* 126:37+ F 23 '87
Art
Individual aesthetics. il *Horizon* 30:20-1 Je '87

Indianapolis (Ind.)—*cont.*

Arts
Indianapolis [special section] il *Horizon* 30:17-30+ Je '87

Auditoriums, convention facilities, etc.
Indianapolis becomes new center for black conventions. il *Black Enterp* 17:82 Jl '87

Blacks
Indianapolis [special section] il *Black Enterp* 17:67+ Jl '87

Description
Indianapolis [special section] il *Horizon* 30:17-30+ Je '87

Indianapolis: a born-again Hoosier diamond in the rust. D. D. Jackson. bibl (p153) il *Smithsonian* 18:70-6+ Je '87

Indianapolis: city on the rebound. L. E. Levathes. il map *Natl Geogr* 172:230-59 Ag '87

This year in Indianapolis [site of Pam American Games] il *Américas* 39:62-3 Jl/Ag '87

Economic conditions
Indianapolis: a born-again Hoosier diamond in the rust. D. D. Jackson. bibl (p153) il *Smithsonian* 18:70-6+ Je '87

Indianapolis: city on the rebound. L. E. Levathes. il map *Natl Geogr* 172:230-59 Ag '87

Education
After-school discussion helps problem students [program at Central High School] W. Bourke and R. D. Furniss. il *Phi Delta Kappan* 69:241-2 N '87

Indianapolis principal axed after playing 'Klan' tune [case of D. A. Garrett] *Jet* 71:21 F 23 '87

Festivals
Indiana Senator Lugar hosts Fitness Festival. il por *Jet* 72:29 Jl 6 '87

Galleries and museums
See also
Children's Museum of Indianapolis
Indianapolis Museum of Art

Historic houses, sites, etc.
A heritage rediscovered [black heritage] il *Black Enterp* 17:84 Jl '87

Police
Police questioned in Indianapolis homicide [suspicious suicide of Michael Taylor] *Jet* 73:46 N 2 '87

Race relations
Indianapolis principal axed after playing 'Klan' tune [case of D. A. Garrett] *Jet* 71:21 F 23 '87

Sports
Cashing in in the cornfields [amateur sports center] G. Witkin. il *U S News World Rep* 103:21 Ag 10 '87

Theater
See also
Circle Theatre (Indianapolis, Ind.)
Indiana Repertory Theatre

Indianapolis 500 *See* Automobile racing

Indianapolis Museum of Art
One of the oldest museums in the country constantly updates its image. M. Wade. il *Horizon* 30:17-18 Je '87

Indianapolis Symphony Orchestra
Sizing up the symphony. B. Golightly. il *Horizon* 30:22-3 Je '87

Indians (American)
See also
Alcohol and Indians (American)
Indians of Central America
Indians of North America
Indians of South America
Indians of the West Indies
Paleo-Indians

Antiquities
See also
Paleo-Indians

Languages
Speaking in many tongues. R. Lewin. *Science* 238:1232 N 27 '87

Voices from the past [clues to New World migrations from study of Indian languages] M. Ruhlen. map *Nat Hist* 96:6+ Mr '87

Indians (American) in art
See also
Cigar store Indians
Howard Terpning. M. E. Stegmaier. il por *Am Artist* 51:66-71+ D '87

Indians (East Indian)
See also
Hindus
Sikhs

Canada
A shattered dream [excerpt from The sorrow and the terror: the haunting legacy of the Air India tragedy] C. Blaise and B. Mukherjee. il pors *Macleans* 100:42-5 My 25 '87

Great Britain
History
An Indian poet visits an English parson [summer of 1912; excerpt from A Tagore reader] Sir R. Tagore. il por *Courier* 40:32 Ap '87

United States
Religious life
Hinduism in America. R. B. Williams. *Christ Century* 104:247-9 Mr 11 '87

Indians of Central America
See also
Cuna Indians
Mayas

Guatemala
The happy birds move on [Guatemalan Indian refugees flee to Mexico] R. J. Stout. il *Christ Century* 104:222-3 Mr 4 '87

Indians of Mexico
See also
Aztecs
Zapotec Indians

Antiquities
See Yucatan (Mexico: State)—Antiquities

Weaving
See Weaving

Indians of North America
See also
Alcohol and Indians (American)
Cahuilla Indians
Chippewa Indians
Cree Indians
Dakota Indians
Eskimos
Haida Indians
Hopi Indians
Iroquois Indians
Kutenai Indians
Navaho Indians
Passamaquoddy Indians
Penobscot Indians
Pima Indians
Pueblo Indians
Salish Indians
Siksika Indians
Ute Indians
Yakima Indians
Zuñi Indians

Agriculture
Gardening the Zuni way [waffle gardens help beat the heat] C. A. Doherty. il *Rodale's Org Gard* 34:62-4 Ag '87

Antiquities
See also
Alabama—Antiquities
Chaco Culture National Historical Park (N.M.)
Pacific Northwest—Antiquities

Recent discussions with Indian leaders have raised questions about repatriation of skeletal remains and sacred objects. R. M. Adams. il *Smithsonian* 18:12 N '87

Violating history [American archeological sites] J. Robbins. il *Natl Parks* 61:26-31 Jl/Ag '87

We have an obligation to return the Indian skeletal remains in our collections to tribal descendants. R. M. Adams. *Smithsonian* 18:12 My '87

Art
See also
Indian Market (Santa Fe, N.M.)
Totem poles

Echoes of a shaman's song: artifacts and ethics in the Northwest. J. Magnuson. il *Christ Century* 104:406-8 Ap 29 '87

Collectors and collecting
American Fabergé. A. Matthews. il *Forbes* 140:213-14 O 5 '87

Exhibitions
See also
Millicent Rogers Museum (Taos, N.M.)

At the Renwick, American traditions [Lost and found traditions: native American art 1965-1985] K. M. Burke. il *Smithsonian* 18:236 O '87

Culture and conflict [Calgary's Olympic Arts Festival] P. Young. il *Macleans* 100:52+ N 9 '87

Children
See also
Futures for Children (Organization)

Indians of North America—*cont.*

Civil rights

Tasting bitter failure [failure to find a way of entrenching native self-government in the Canadian Constitution] P. Gessell. il *Macleans* 100:21-2 Ap 6 '87

Claims

See also
Indians of North America—Land tenure

Dental care

Head Start combats baby bottle tooth decay. M. G. Phillips and P. E. Stubbs. il *Child Today* 16:25-8 S/O '87

Education

See also
Futures for Children (Organization)

An enthusiasm to learn through video [Santo Domingo Indian children] B. Atencio. *Phi Delta Kappan* 68:632-3 Ap '87

Guiding minority students into adulthood [Yukon-Koyukuk School District Postsecondary Counselor Program] J. Kleinfeld. il *Phi Delta Kappan* 68:553-4 Mr '87

Fishing

Of salmon and sovereignty [trial of Yakima leader D. Sohappy for illegally selling fish] J. Rosenberg. *Christ Century* 104:428-9 My 6 '87

Government relations

See also
Indians of North America—Land tenure
Indians of North America—Reservations
Indians of North America—Water rights

Adrift in their own land. il *Time* 130:89 Jl 6 '87

An awkward visit [South African ambassador to Canada G. Babb invited to Peguis Indian reservation] D. Smith. il por *Macleans* 100:20 Mr 23 '87

On the reservation: America's apartheid [cover story] T. Williams. il *Natl Rev* 39:28-30 My 8 '87

The Sioux reject nuclear waste [Cheyenne River Sioux reservation] J. W. Wilson. *Progressive* 51:11-12 S '87

Industries

See also
First Nations Financial Project
Indian blankets, rugs, etc. (American)
Tribal Assets Management

Chairman of the tribe [P. MacDonald of the Navahos] J. Cook. il por *Forbes* 139:238+ My 18 '87

Help wanted—work, not handouts. J. Cook. il *Forbes* 139:68-71 My 4 '87

Las Vegas North: buying chips from the Chippewa [Vegas Kewadin casino in Mich.] J. A. Seamonds. il *U S News World Rep* 102:31 F 9 '87

Suddenly Peter MacDonald is business' best friend. S. D. Atchison. il por *Bus Week* p64 Ag 10 '87

Influence on nature

The Salish-Kootenai comeback [environmental management of reservation lands] J. Bruggers. il *Sierra* 72:22-3+ Jl/Ag '87

Land tenure

See also
Cowboy and Indian Alliance

Forest Service steps on Blackfeet [struggling to save sacred land in Lewis and Clark National Forest] J. Bruggers. il *Progressive* 51:14 Ap '87

Give it back to the Indians? [P. Stevens leads Sioux claim to the Black Hills] T. Jacoby. il pors *Newsweek* 110:47 D 7 '87

The heart of everything that is [Sioux Indians battle for return of the Black Hills] W. Greider. il *Roll Stone* p37-8+ My 7 '87

Indian land, white greed [Navajo-Hopi relocation issue] T. Johnson. il *Nation* 245:15-18 Jl 4-11 '87

A people's last stand [Lubicon Albertan band] J. Howse. il *Macleans* 100:20 N 16 '87

Wilderness and worship—or wells? [Lewis and Clark National Forest Plan vs. Blackfeet Indians] M. Kantor. il *Sierra* 72:67-8 My/Je '87

Legal status, laws, etc.

See Indians of North America—Government relations

Medicine

Saved by the Indians [scurvy antidote given to French explorers; excerpt from Voyages au Canada] J. Cartier. il *Courier* 40:12 Ap '87

Museums

See also
Southwest Museum (Los Angeles, Calif.)
Sun House Museum (Ukiah, Calif.)

Photographs and photography

Environmental portrait. E. A. Johnson. il *Petersens Photogr Mag* 16:62-3 Jl '87

Religion and mythology

See also
Totem poles

Affirming native spirituality: a call to justice [cover story] J. Magnuson. il *Christ Century* 104:1114-17 D 9 '87

Andrews's sisters. R. M. Staubs. il por *Omni* 10:28 O '87

Cutting through a sacred forest [Ojo power line and sacred sites in the Jemez Mountains, N.M.] D. Gibson. il *Sierra* 72:135-6 Ja/F '87

Echoes of a shaman's song: artifacts and ethics in the Northwest. J. Magnuson. il *Christ Century* 104:406-8 Ap 29 '87

Forest Service steps on Blackfeet [struggling to save sacred land in Lewis and Clark National Forest] J. Bruggers. il *Progressive* 51:14 Ap '87

On the land for good [Navajo missionary A. Garber] R. Wilkins. il pors *Christ Today* 31:12-13 Je 12 '87

Sun dances, corn pollen, & the cross [Native American Catholics] C. Vecsey. il *Commonweal* 114:345-51 Je 5 '87

Wilderness and worship—or wells? [Lewis and Clark National Forest Plan vs. Blackfeet Indians] M. Kantor. il *Sierra* 72:67-8 My/Je '87

Reservations

The land of the Navajo and the Hopi [cover story] il maps *Sunset* 178:96-109 My '87

On the reservation: America's apartheid [cover story] T. Williams. il *Natl Rev* 39:28-30 My 8 '87

Seeking a new direction [violence and drug abuse plague Cree Indian reserve of Shamattawa, Man.] C. Barrett. il *Macleans* 100:24 F 2 '87

Schools

See Indians of North America—Education

Sculpture

See also
Totem poles

Securities

Smoke signals [brokers promote tax free municipals] M. Schifrin. il *Forbes* 139:42+ Je 15 '87

Social conditions

See also
Indians of North America—Reservations

Suicide

See Suicide

Theater

See Theater, Indian (American)

Wars

See also
United States—History—French and Indian War, 1755-1763

Water rights

The Winters Doctrine. *Wilderness* 51:37 Fall '87

Weaving

See Weaving

Women

One day in August. R. E. Parrott. *Christ Century* 104:679-80 Ag 12-19 '87

Photographs and photography

The Americanization of Indian girls [exhibit at the Voorhees Zimmerli Art Museum at Rutgers University] M. N. Powers. il *Society* 24:83-6 Ja/F '87

Alaska

Guiding minority students into adulthood [Yukon-Koyukuk School District Postsecondary Counselor Program] J. Kleinfeld. il *Phi Delta Kappan* 68:553-4 Mr '87

Canada

See also
Cree Indians
Shuswap Indians

An awkward visit [South African ambassador to Canada G. Babb invited to Peguis Indian reservation] D. Smith. il por *Macleans* 100:20 Mr 23 '87

Legends on the stage [native theater] D. Taylor. il *Macleans* 100:69 O 19 '87

Saved by the Indians [scurvy antidote given to French explorers; excerpt from Voyages au Canada] J. Cartier. il *Courier* 40:12 Ap '87

Tasting bitter failure [failure to find a way of entrenching native self-government in the Constitution] P. Gessell. il *Macleans* 100:21-2 Ap 6 '87

Indians of North America in art *See* Indians (American) in art

Indians of South America

See also
Yanoama Indians

Antiquities

See also
Chile—Antiquities

Indians of South America—Antiquities—See also—*cont.*
Ciudad Perdida (Colombia)
Colombia—Antiquities
Costume and adornment
Bolivia's crowning glory [regional styles of hats] K. Hickman. il *Américas* 39:22-5+ Jl/Ag '87
Government relations
An imperilled people [Brazil's Yanoama endangered by Amazonian development] B. Levin. il map *Macleans* 100:26-7 Je 29 '87
Languages
See also
Aymara language
Medicine
See also
Medicine men
Religion and mythology
Return of the Pleiades [festival of Qoyllur Rit'i in Peru] R. Randall. il *Nat Hist* 96:42-53 Je '87
Sowing justice in Ecuador [liberation theology practitioners L. Proaño and J. Gómez Izquierdo] P. R. Greene. *Christ Century* 104:910-12 O 21 '87
Sports
The fiesta in the town of ghosts [ritual fistfight in Bolivian Andes] G. Smith. il *Sports Illus* 67:76-80+ O 5 '87
Bolivia
Bolivia's crowning glory [regional styles of hats] K. Hickman. il *Américas* 39:22-5+ Jl/Ag '87
The fiesta in the town of ghosts [ritual fistfight in Andes] G. Smith. il *Sports Illus* 67:76-80+ O 5 '87
Brazil
See also
Tucano Indians
Anthropologists turn advocates for the Brazilian Indians. G. Kolata. il *Science* 236:1183-7 Je 5 '87
An imperilled people [Yanoama endangered by Amazonian development] B. Levin. il map *Macleans* 100:26-7 Je 29 '87
Chile
By the banks of the Chinchihuapi. T. D. Dillehay. il map *Nat Hist* 96:8+ Ap '87
Ecuador
Sowing justice in Ecuador [liberation theology practitioners L. Proaño and J. Gómez Izquierdo] P. R. Greene. *Christ Century* 104:910-12 O 21 '87
Peru
Return of the Pleiades [festival of Qoyllur Rit'i] R. Randall. il *Nat Hist* 96:42-53 Je '87
Suriname
See also
Trio Indians
Indians of the West Indies
Health and hygiene
Swine's way [swine flu as cause of Indian deaths after arrival of Columbus; views of F. Guerra] B. Lawren. il *Omni* 9:18 Ja '87
Indicators, Economic *See* Economic indicators
Indigestion *See* Dyspepsia
Indigo
A blue future for Mexican indigo. G. N. Ross. il *Américas* 39:40-6 Jl/Ag '87
Individual differences
See also
Sex differences
Making the world safe for difference. R. J. Neuhaus. *Natl Rev* 39:24 N 20 '87
Individual liberty *See* Liberty
Individual retirement accounts
10 ways to put that IRA to work. J. Rachlin. il *U S News World Rep* 102:53 Ap 20 '87
Building a cycle-proof IRA. A. Rock. il *Money* 16:66-8+ Mr '87
The duel for your IRA. J. B. Quinn. il *Newsweek* 109:55 Mr 30 '87
An early tally of the last-minute dash for IRAs . . . and a startling view of their effect on saving. G. Koretz. il *Bus Week* p22 Je 15 '87
Five smart moves on your IRA. M. Schiffres. il *U S News World Rep* 102:50 F 23 '87
Good-bye, IRA. W. G. Flanagan. il *Forbes* 139:152 My 4 '87
An IRA for 1987 still may pay. B. Hitchings. *Bus Week* p150 Mr 16 '87
The IRA lives! New moves for a new era. W. L. Updegrave. il *Money* 16:58+ Mr '87
IRA payouts: use 'em or lose 'em. K. McCormally. il *Changing Times* 41:99-102 D '87
IRAs still lovely. M. Zall. il *Success Farm* 85:F4 My '87
IRAs—still a good investment. B. M. Stephens. *Black Enterp* 17:322+ Je '87

Is it time to retire your IRA? D. R. Katz. il *Esquire* 107:61-2 Ap '87
Last call for IRAs. K. McCormally. il *Changing Times* 41:33-4+ Ap '87
Penalties for early IRA withdrawal. T. Tilling. *Parents* 62:51 N '87
Possible penalties for switching IRA accounts. T. Tilling. *Parents* 62:46 S '87
Rolling with new rollover rules [rolling over pension money into an IRA] A. Rock. *Money* 16:74-5 Mr '87
Savings: where to do your last-minute IRA shopping. il *Money* 16:43 F '87
Should you open an IRA this year? M. Asnes. *Vogue* 177:200 Mr '87
Should you open an IRA this year? B. G. Quint. *Glamour* 85:86+ Je '87
Taxing days of change for IRAs. B. Rudolph. il *Time* 129:58 Ap 27 '87
Why you need two IRAs. M. Rowland. il *Work Woman* 12:34 F '87
Will IRAs survive tax reform? J. Bodnar. *Changing Times* 41:9 S '87
Your IRA: still a good deal? *Consum Rep* 52:12-15 Ja '87
Advertising
Whatever happened to the IRA ad blitz? S. Weiss. il *Bus Week* p85 Ap 13 '87
Individualism
Decadence American style [responding to R. N. Bellah's *Habits of the heart*] K. S. Kantzer. il *Christ Today* 31:12-13 Ag 7 '87
Individualism vs. liberal arts education [address, September 8, 1987] R. L. Spaeth. *Vital Speeches Day* 54:22-6 O 15 '87
Individuality
See also
Personality
Self
Lost in the crowd [group size and composition can affect behavior; research by Brian Mullen] J. Goetz. il *Psychol Today* 21:60 Je '87
Indochina
See also
Indochinese
Kampuchea
Laos
Vietnam
Indochinese
United States
Trouble for America's 'model' minority. D. Whitman. il *U S News World Rep* 102:18-19 F 23 '87
Mortality
Sudden refugee death. *Nat Hist* 96:4+ O '87
Indoctrination
See also
Brainwashing
Cultural control [with discussion] L. Nader. il por *Cent Mag* 20:50-9 Mr/Ap '87
Indonesia
See also
Bonds, Government—Indonesia
Loans, Foreign—Indonesia
Ocean thermal power plants—Indonesia
Economic policy
Indonesia: a poor, populous nation struggling to develop. L. Hopping. il *Sch Update* 119:13 Ap 6 '87
Indonesia's economic downswing and political reforms. G. B. Hainsworth. bibl f *Curr Hist* 86:172-5+ Ap '87
Industries
See also
Airplane industry—Indonesia
Shipping—Indonesia
Politics and government
See also
Political campaigns—Indonesia
Invisible Indonesia. D. K. Emmerson. bibl f map *Foreign Aff* 66:368-87 Wint '87/'88
Indonesian cooking *See* Cooking, Indonesian
Indonesian Environmental Forum
WALHI: the Indonesian Environmental Forum. T. Wickham. *Environment* 29:2-4 S '87
Indonesian praus *See* Praus (Boats)
Indoor gardens and gardening
See also
Greenhouses
House plants
Miniature gardens and gardening

Indoor lacrosse (Professional) *See* Lacrosse, Professional
Indoor pollution *See* Air pollution
Indoor pollution, Radon *See* Radon pollution
Indoor rowing *See* Rowing, Indoor
Indoor soccer (Professional) *See* Soccer, Professional
Induction coils
Collecting early electro-medical apparatuses. F. Polansky.
il *Antiques Collect Hobbies* 92:61-2+ D '87
Industrial accidents
See also
Bhopal poisonous gas disaster, India, 1984
Insurance, Workers' compensation
Mine accidents and explosions
Motion picture production and direction—Accidents
Nuclear power plants—Accidents and explosions
Deaths in industry, 1985: BLS survey findings. D. M.
Cotter and J. Macon. il *Mon Labor Rev* 110:45-7
Ap '87
Prevention
See Occupational health and safety
Industrial arts
See also
Engineering
Industrial Bank of Japan, Ltd.
Nice moves for a big kid. J. Heins. il *Forbes* 140:134+
S 21 '87
Industrial buildings
See also
Factories
Industrial capacity
The smokestacks steam again. H. J. Steinbreder. il *Fortune*
116:47-8 D 21 '87
Industrial democracy *See* Participative management
Industrial design *See* Design, Industrial
Industrial development bonds *See* Bonds, Industrial development
Industrial Development Organization *See* United Nations.
Industrial Development Organization
Industrial discipline *See* Labor discipline
Industrial diseases *See* Occupational health and safety
Industrial diversification *See* Diversification in industry
Industrial education *See* Vocational-technical education
Industrial engineering *See* Engineering
Industrial entertaining *See* Business entertaining
Industrial equipment industry
See also
Hughes Tool Company
Machinery industry
Petroleum equipment industry
Finance
Heavy equipment. B. Stavro. il *Forbes* 139:146-7 Ja
12 '87
Securities
The big revival in milltown. P. Nulty. il *Fortune* 116:173+
D 7 '87
Cautious calls in capital equipment. A. E. Serwer. il
Fortune 115:172 Je 22 '87
Companies that refused to rust. J. Egan. il *U S News*
World Rep 103:50 Jl 27 '87
Industrial equipment leases
The new attraction in leasing. B. Gatty and M. I. Finney.
il *Nations Bus* 75:50-3 Mr '87
Taxation
Equipment leasing faces trial by tax reform. G. Weiss.
il *Bus Week* p114-15 Ja 12 '87
Lease loophole preserves investment tax credit. C. Finck.
il *Success Farm* 85:18T My '87
Limited partnerships that like tax reform. A. E. Serwer.
il *Fortune* 116:102 Ag 17 '87
Industrial Equity Pacific Ltd.
Market letter writer makes good [R. Brierley] T. Jaffe.
il *Forbes* 139:32-4 F 23 '87
Ron Brierley is king of the middle of the road. C.
Debes. por *Bus Week* p78+ S 21 '87
Industrial espionage *See* Business intelligence
Industrial ethics *See* Business ethics
Industrial expansion
See also
Capital investments
How to manage a growing company. H. Waldrop. il
Work Woman 12:39-42 Ap '87
Keeping up in the fast lane. N. L. Croft. il *Nations*
Bus 75:24-6 Jl '87
Where owners go astray. H. McCrum. il *Work Woman*
12:48 Je '87
Industrial feeding
See also
OK's Company
Industrial films *See* Motion pictures in industry
Industrial Finance Agency (Mass.) *See* Massachusetts. Industrial Finance Agency

Industrial forecasting *See* Business forecasting
Industrial innovations *See* Technological innovations
Industrial laws and regulations
See also
Labor laws and regulations
Industrial Light and Magic (Studio)
Reel illusions. T. G. Smith. il *Omni* 9:70-9 Je '87
Industrial location *See* Location in business and industry
Industrial management *See* Business management
Industrial microbiology
It's a dirty job. G. Greenwell. *Sci Am* 257:47-8 O '87
Molasses and microbes mix to sustain oil flow in Oklahoma. *Earth Sci* 40:7-8 Summ '87
Roughnecks [use of bacteria in petroleum production]
Sci Am 256:60+ My '87
Industrial photography *See* Photography in industry
Industrial policy *See* Industry and state
Industrial productivity *See* Productivity, Industrial
Industrial psychology *See* Psychology, Industrial
Industrial purchasing *See* Purchasing, Industrial
Industrial relations
See also
Church and labor
Collective bargaining
Collective labor agreements
Communication in management
Employee ownership
Layoffs
Participative management
Productivity, Industrial
Strikes
Team work in industry
United States—Labor policy
United States. National Labor Relations Board
Developments in industrial relations. G. Ruben. See
issues of Monthly Labor Review
Enterprise and double cross [excerpt from Tales of a
new America] R. B. Reich. *Wash Mon* 18:13-19 Ja
'87
Japan and the U.S.: the economics of equity. R. S.
Bachelder. *Christ Century* 104:719-23 Ag 26-S 2 '87
Labor and management [address, September 18, 1986]
F. P. Doyle. *Vital Speeches Day* 53:293-5 Mr 1 '87
A Labor Day warning. A. H. Raskin. por *Newsweek*
110:7 S 7 '87
Labor-management scene in 1986 reflects continuing
difficulties. G. Ruben. il *Mon Labor Rev* 110:37-48
Ja '87
Robert Reich takes on Rambo [Tales of a new America]
T. J. Peters. *Wash Mon* 19:51-6 Mr '87
Italy
Italian labor relations: a system in transition. T. Treu.
Mon Labor Rev 110:37-9 Mr '87
Japan
Japan and the U.S.: the economics of equity. R. S.
Bachelder. *Christ Century* 104:719-23 Ag 26-S 2 '87
Industrial research
See also
Arthur D. Little, Inc.
AT&T Bell Labs
Aviation research
David Sarnoff Research Center
Electronics research
Fire research
Genetic research industry
George M. Low Center for Industrial Innovation
Hill Top Research, Inc.
Industrial Technology Institute
Inventions
Products, New
Technological innovations
America's R&D performance: a mixed review. il *Bus*
Week p59 Ap 20 '87
Despite cuts, basic research survives and revives at Exxon.
W. Sweet. il *Phys Today* 40:59-60 Jl '87
The pedagogy of competition. M. L. Weidenbaum. *Society*
25:46-54 N/D '87
Federal aid
Broader R&D role sought for Commerce. M. Crawford.
il *Science* 237:19 Jl 3 '87
U.S. must understand the link between R&D and the
economy. R. S. Ames. por *Aviat Week Space Technol*
127:149-50 O 12 '87
Finance
Corporations are putting less into research. G. Koretz.
il *Bus Week* p18 Ag 10 '87
Limited partnerships for those who love long shots
[research and development limited partnerships] G.
Weiss. *Bus Week* p180 Jl 20 '87
Research spending is building up to a letdown. S. Siwolop.
il *Bus Week* p139-40 Je 22 '87

Industrial research—Finance—*cont.*
Statistics
R&D scoreboard. il *Bus Week* p141+ Je 22 '87
Switzerland
IBM's Zurich Lab is "flower" in Europe. D. Dickson. il *Science* 237:125-6 Jl 10 '87
Industrial revenue bonds *See* Bonds, Industrial development
Industrial revolution

United States
Exhibitions
New exhibit at Smithsonian [Engines of change: the American Industrial revolution, 1790-1860] il *Am Hist Illus* 21:8-9 Ja '87
Industrial robots *See* Robots—Industrial use
Industrial safety *See* Occupational health and safety
Industrial secrets *See* Trade secrets
Industrial suppliers *See* Industrial equipment industry
Industrial Technology Institute
In the Middle West. G. Anderson. il *Archit Rec* 175:96-9 Jl '87
Industrial waste *See* Trade waste
Industrial waste disposal *See* Trade waste—Disposal
Industrie Pininfarina SpA
"A delicate subject" [Cadillac Allante designed by Pininfarina rather than by GM Design Staff] R. Hutton. il *Car Driv* 32:85 Mr '87
Pininfarina heads for the U.S. in a Caddy [Allante] W. C. Symonds. il por *Bus Week* p58-9 F 9 '87
Industry
See also
Big business
Computers—Industrial use
Corporations
Home labor
Lasers—Industrial use
Location in business and industry
Productivity, Industrial
Rural industries
Science and industry
Small business
Standardization
Trusts, Industrial
Ultrasonic waves—Industrial use
See also subhead Industries under names of countries, states, cities, etc.
Elderly services programs
The graying of America spawns a new crisis. S. B. Garland. il *Bus Week* p60+ Ag 17 '87
Energy usage
Saving energy. R. D. Roslansky. il *Nations Bus* 75:40 Ja '87
History
See also
Industrial revolution
Location
See Location in business and industry
Physical fitness programs
Executives & health leaders: how to get your people walking! M. Bricklin. il *Prevention* 39:92 Ap '87
Fitness in the workplace [address, February 18, 1987] C. Latham. *Vital Speeches Day* 53:446-8 My 1 '87
Linking employee fitness programs to lower medical costs and absenteeism. *Mon Labor Rev* 110:27-8 N '87
Working out at work. L. Villarosa. il *Essence* 17:106+ Mr '87
Security measures
See also
Employee theft
G. Gordon Liddy Academy of Corporate Security and Private Investigation
Industry, Nationalization of *See* Government ownership
Industry and art *See* Art and industry
Industry and convict labor *See* Convict labor
Industry and day care *See* Day care and industry
Industry and education *See* Business and education
Industry and state
See also
Aerospace industries—Federal aid
Airplane industry—Federal aid
Black business enterprises—Federal aid
Business—Political aspects
Chemicals—Laws and regulations
Construction industry—Federal aid
Contracts, Government
Corporations, Government
Economic conversion
Electric utilities—Laws and regulations
Factories—Shutdowns—Laws and regulations
Free enterprise
Full employment

Government ownership
Industrial research—Federal aid
Insurance law
Labor laws and regulations
Massachusetts. Industrial Finance Agency
Mercantile system
Military-industrial complex
Minority business enterprises—Federal aid
Pesticides—Laws and regulations
Privatization
Railroads and state
Regulatory agencies
Small business—Laws and regulations
Strip mining—Laws and regulations
Tobacco industry—Federal aid
Transportation—Laws and regulations
U.S. Consumer Product Safety Commission
United States—Labor policy
United States. Federal Trade Commission
United States. Occupational Safety and Health Administration
United States. Small Business Administration
Wage-price policy
An advocate for competitiveness. A. Holzinger. il *Nations Bus* 75:12 Mr '87
Bush business [G. Bush courting Business Roundtable] *Nation* 244:420-1 Ap 4 '87
Business can't bank on Judge Kennedy's vote. P. Dwyer. il por *Bus Week* p33 N 30 '87
Can we make U.S. industry competitive again? H. A. Poling. il *USA Today (Periodical)* 116:22-4 N '87
Competing for political gain on competitiveness. K. R. Sheets. il *U S News World Rep* 102:42 Mr 2 '87
Competitive confusion. R. J. Samuelson. il *Newsweek* 109:39 Ja 26 '87
"Competitiveness" bill goes to Congress [Trade, Employment, and Productivity Act of 1987] M. Crawford. *Science* 235:967 F 27 '87
The competitiveness craze [cover story] R. Kuttner. *New Repub* 197:22+ N 2 '87
The 'competitiveness' craze: a new name, an old idea. C. Welles. il *Bus Week* p31 Ja 19 '87
The competitiveness problem [address, September 14, 1987] G. M. Keller. *Vital Speeches Day* 54:61-4 N 1 '87
Congressional alert. See issues of Nation's Business
Deadlock at the Court [business cases before the Supreme Court] P. Dwyer. il *Bus Week* p36-7 O 12 '87
Deregulation disaffection [re-regulation trend] *Natl Rev* 39:18-19 Ag 28 '87
Don't let the Grinch steal Christmas. G. F. Gilder. il *Natl Rev* 39:40-4 Ap 24 '87
The great debate inside Robert Bork [business rulings and writings] P. Dwyer. il por *Bus Week* p34-5 S 14 '87
Hope or hyperbole? High tech and economic development. E. J. Malecki. il *Technol Rev* 90:44-51 O '87
How nit-picking regulations get that way [excerpt from Tales of a new America] R. B. Reich. *Harpers* 274:18+ F '87
How to keep mature industries innovative [cover story] C. F. Sabel and others. il *Technol Rev* 90:26-35 Ap '87
Innocents abroad [governors promoting states] *Fortune* 116:12+ N 23 '87
International competitiveness [address, June 8, 1987] H. Goldfeder. *Vital Speeches Day* 53:722-5 S 15 '87
Japanese challenge—American response [address, March 5, 1987] P. Cannon. *Vital Speeches Day* 53:503-9 Je 1 '87
Jesse Jackson urges big businesses to 'reinvest in America'. il pors *Jet* 72:4+ S 7 '87
Keeping business at home [state economic development programs] M. Leepson. il *Nations Bus* 75:67-70 My '87
Lewis F. Powell, Jr.: his warning brought a new era of business activism. il por *Nations Bus* 75:66 Ag '87
A liberal gets rich yet keeps the faith [I. Magaziner] P. Petre. il pors *Fortune* 116:69-72 Ag 31 '87
The myth of a post-industrial economy. S. S. Cohen and J. Zysman. il *Technol Rev* 90:54-60+ F/Mr '87
National economic competitiveness [Ohio's Thomas Edison Program; address, February 6, 1987] C. M. Coburn. *Vital Speeches Day* 53:478-80 My 15 '87
Of markets and myths. R. B. Reich. *Commentary* 83:38-42 F '87
Politics & policy. See issues of Fortune beginning March 5, 1984
The quest for the '88 issue [competitiveness] L. Martz. il *Newsweek* 109:14-16 Ja 19 '87

Industry and state—*cont.*

Re-regulation rag. *New Repub* 196:5-7 My 18 '87

A risky tack for Democrats [antibusiness sentiment] S. H. Wildstrom. *Bus Week* p71 Jl 20 '87

Rolling back regulation: a debate rages over how much freedom should be given to industry. S. Koepp. il *Time* 130:50-2 Jl 6 '87

Time to end corporate welfare. J. A. Courter. *Read Dig* 130:35-40 Je '87

Unbinding Gulliver [address, April 9, 1987] R. A. Voell. *Vital Speeches Day* 53:661-5 Ag 15 '87

The United States-Japan economic Olympics [address, December 11-12, 1986] R. A. Morse. *Vital Speeches Day* 53:409-11 Ap 15 '87

Washington roundup. See issues of Nation's Business beginning September 1985

What can America sell? *New Repub* 196:5-7 My 25 '87

What Congress is pushing now. A. C. Isgrò. il *Fortune* 115:99+ My 11 '87

International aspects

To form a more perfect union [call for international restraint on global corporations; with editorial comment] Publius. *New Leader* 70:2, 11-12 Jl 13-27 '87

Brazil

Up the river [Manaus] E. A. Finn, Jr. il map *Forbes* 140:102+ N 2 '87

Canada

See also
Atlantic Canada Opportunities Agency
Canada. Dept. of Regional Industrial Expansion
Canada Development Investment Corporation
Corporations, Government—Canada

Disappointment and delight [U.S.-Canada trade accord] D. Jenish. il *Macleans* 100:20-2 O 19 '87

Keeping the assembly line rolling [government aid keeps GM plant in Boisbriand, Que. open] il *Macleans* 100:10 Ap 13 '87

New money, old refrains. S. MacLeod. por *Macleans* 100:52 Ag 31 '87

Rebellion in the West. M. Janigan. il *Macleans* 100:12+ Mr 30 '87

Ireland

Lessons from Ireland. K. K. Wiegner. il *Forbes* 140:37-8+ S 7 '87

Israel

The enemy within [interview with D. Doron] P. Brimelow. il por *Forbes* 140:54+ D 28 '87

Italy

Italy gets set to vote on its future. W. C. Symonds and K. Wolman. il *Bus Week* p52-3 Je 8 '87

Japan

A storm gathers in Japan [address, June 15, 1987] K. Ohmae. *Vital Speeches Day* 53:729-30 S 15 '87

Korea (South)

Chaebols' end? *Forbes* 140:104 O 5 '87

Korea grows up. A. Tanzer. il *Forbes* 140:90+ N 16 '87

Seoul puts big business on a shorter leash. L. Nakarmi. il *Bus Week* p51 Ag 17 '87

Philippines

Andres Soriano's battle for San Miguel. M. Shao. il por *Bus Week* p54 S 28 '87

South Africa

An Afrikaans insider questions the system [industrialist J. Rupert] S. Mufson. il por *Bus Week* p80+ My 18 '87

Spain

Look out for the Spanish bulls. A. Zagorin. il *Time* 129:51 Ja 26 '87

Sweden

As Stockholm lays siege to Nobel . . . [arms smuggling charges] J. Kapstein. il *Bus Week* p46 S 21 '87

United States

See Industry and state

Venezuela

Trust me [views of C. A. Perez] L. Gubernick. il por *Forbes* 139:152 Mr 9 '87

Industry and the arts *See* Arts and industry

Industry and the church *See* Church and industry

Industry and the environment

See also
Chemical plants—Environmental aspects
Coal industry—Environmental aspects
Electric plants—Environmental aspects
Electronic industries—Environmental aspects
Emission reduction credits
Gas pipelines—Environmental aspects
Gold mines and mining—Environmental aspects
Hydroelectric plants—Environmental aspects
Insurance, Pollution liability

Oil shale industry—Environmental aspects
Paper mills—Environmental aspects
Petroleum industry—Environmental aspects
Resorts—Environmental aspects
Smelters—Environmental aspects
Tourist trade—Environmental aspects
Trade waste—Disposal
Uranium industry—Environmental aspects

Industry and the environment [address, October 30, 1987] G. M. Keller. *Vital Speeches Day* 54:154-7 D 15 '87

Paying the piper [letting industry pay the costs of damaging the environment] G. Reiger. *Field Stream* 92:15-16+ My '87

Belize

In Belize, Coke goes better [Coca-Cola vs. rain forest] D. Voelker. il map *Sierra* 72:12 S/O '87

Developing countries

The lessons of Bhopal. F. M. Bordewich. il *Atlantic* 259:30-3 Mr '87

United States

See Industry and the environment

Industry and weather

See also
Degree days
Winter cities

On the continent, growth is in the deep freeze [Western Europe] J. Templeman. il *Bus Week* p46 F 2 '87

Industry in art

Landscapes of power [paintings of C. Sheeler] J. Colihan. il por *Am Herit* 38:86-91 N '87

Inerrancy (Biblical) *See* Bible—Evidence, authority, etc.

Inert substances

Bug-spray alert [potentially poisonous inert substances] W. Kistner and A. Porterfield. il *Technol Rev* 90:10+ My/Je '87

Inertial guidance systems

Air Force defends MX management as Northrop is charged with fraud. M. Mecham. *Aviat Week Space Technol* 127:16-18 Ag 31 '87

Air Force refers Northrop investigation to U.S. Attorney; Late IMUs delay scheduled MX deployment [inertial measurement units] B. A. Smith. *Aviat Week Space Technol* 126:72 Je 15 '87

Guidance unit shortage keeps 8 MXs off alert [Northrop contract] M. Mecham. *Aviat Week Space Technol* 127:22-3 Jl 6 '87

Northrop boosts IMU deliveries, expects to meet schedule in March [inertial measurement units for MX intercontinental ballistic missile] B. A. Smith. il *Aviat Week Space Technol* 127:31-2 S 7 '87

Science board seeks new MX test procedures, affirms IMU reliability. M. Mecham. *Aviat Week Space Technol* 127:32-3 N 2 '87

Trouble for the triad [deficiencies in MX guidance systems] J. Barry. il *Newsweek* 110:17-18 S 7 '87

Stands, tables, etc.

Company to demonstrate two-axis inertial navigation test stand. il *Aviat Week Space Technol* 126:239 Je 15 '87

Inertial upper stage (Launch vehicle) *See* Space vehicles—Propulsion systems

INF (Intermediate Nuclear Force) reduction *See* Disarmament

Infancy of animals *See* Animals, Infancy of

Infant learning *See* Infants—Growth and development

Infant mortality

See also
Stillbirth
Sudden infant death syndrome

. . . and in the U.S. [black infants] J. Gruber. *Black Enterp* 17:16 My '87

Black infant mortality risks studied. *Sci News* 132:218 O 3 '87

Children on the frontline [Southern Africa] M. A. Fortune. il *Black Enterp* 17:16 My '87

Dying young: infant mortality in the United States. G. M. Anderson. il *America* 157:498-500+ D 26 '87

Edelman raps U.S. high black infant death rate [M. Edelman] por *Jet* 71:9 F 23 '87

Firms, officials indicted over unsafe infants' drug [premature babies given vitamin E supplement E-Ferol] *FDA Consum* 21:4 O '87

How we can save our babies [prenatal care] L. David and I. David. il *Health* 19:29-31+ Ag '87

Preventing child mortality [Child survival: risks and the road to health report] il *Futurist* 21:41 N/D '87

When I was grieving [letters from friends provide comfort after death of premature infant] A. P. Murphy. il *Glamour* 85:302 My '87

Infant psychology
See also
Parent-child relationship
Play
Baby face-off: the roots of attraction [study by Judith H. Langlois and others] B. Bower. *Sci News* 131:310 My 16 '87
Baby research comes of age. *Psychol Today* 21:46-7 My '87
Beauty is in the eye of the baby [infants prefer attractive faces; research by Judith H. Langlois] H. Hall. il *Psychol Today* 21:12 Ag '87
Bringing up baby: emotion's early role [research by Jeannette M. Haviland and Mary Lelwica] B. Bower. *Sci News* 131:104 F 14 '87
Is day care bad for babies? C. Wallis. il *Time* 129:63 Je 22 '87
Sugar babies and clucking mommies [newborns; research by Elliott Blass] il *Discover* 8:10 N '87
What babies know, and noises parents make [newborns; research by Elliott Blass] G. Kolata. *Science* 237:726 Ag 14 '87
You've come a long way, baby. R. J. Trotter. bibl (p94) il *Psychol Today* 21:34-6+ My '87
You've come a long way, baby. R. J. Trotter. *Current* 295:11-16 S '87

Infanticide *See* Murder
Infants
See also
Fetus
Play
Accidents
See Accidents
Birth defects
See Birth defects
Brain
See Brain
Care and hygiene
See also
Infants—Medical care
Infants—Nutrition
Baby, it's cold outside. K. Karlsrud and D. Schultz. il *Parents* 62:256 N '87
A boost for low-weight babies. *Sci News* 132:46 Jl 18 '87
"If you ask me . . .". K. Karlsrud and D. Schultz. il *Parents* 62:146 Jl '87
Meeting infant care needs [reports from National Center for Clinical Infant Programs] il *Child Today* 16:2-4 Jl/Ag '87
Room with view: no adults [baby tender designed by Stephen Ledoux and Carl Cheney] P. Chance. il *Psychol Today* 21:14 Ap '87
Crying
26 ways to comfort a crying baby. L. MacCallum. il *Glamour* 85:226+ Ag '87
Carry on: a cure for chronic crying [research by Urs A. Hunziker and Ronald G. Barr] H. Hall. il *Psychol Today* 21:10 Ja '87
No language but a cry. M. Roberts. il *Psychol Today* 21:57-8 Je '87
Why is the baby crying? K. Karlsrud and D. Schultz. il *Parents* 62:188 Ag '87
Day care
See Day care
Diseases
See also
Allergy
Colic
Diarrhea
Equipment
See also
Bundle of Convenience (Firm)
Cribs (Beds)
Buying safe for your baby. C. G. Dawson. il *Consum Res Mag* 70:33-4 S '87
Exhibitions
'Generations': a family album [exhibit at International Gallery] D. M. Bolz. il *Smithsonian* 18:276 N '87
Food and feeding
See Infants—Nutrition
Growth and development
See also
Infant psychology
As they grow/birth to 1 year. K. Karlsrud and D. Schultz. See issues of Parents beginning March 1987
Games babies play [research by Hildy S. Ross and Susan P. Lollis] J. Fischman. il *Psychol Today* 21:14 O '87

Growing up: Del and Rey, Johnny and Jimmy [experiments carried out on twins in the early 1930's] il *Sci Am* 257:30-2 Jl '87
Lead in utero: low-level danger [effect on mental development in first two years of life; research by David Bellinger and others] B. Bower. *Sci News* 131:277 My 2 '87
Leaden development [lead in the womb and mental development; study by David Bellinger] J. Rubin. il *Psychol Today* 21:13 S '87
No threshold to lead's learning effect. J. Raloff. *Sci News* 131:374 Je 13 '87
The play's the thing [importance of parental interaction with child; research by T. Field] R. J. Trotter. bibl (p63) il pors *Psychol Today* 21:26-34 Ja '87
"Stuck on you!" [effects of maternal-infant attachment] N. S. Schwartzberg. il *Parents* 62:100-2+ O '87
You've come a long way, baby. R. J. Trotter. bibl (p94) il *Psychol Today* 21:34-6+ My '87
You've come a long way, baby. R. J. Trotter. *Current* 295:11-16 S '87
Hearing
See Hearing
Language
See Children—Language
Medical care
First-year doctor visits. K. Karlsrud and D. Schultz. il *Parents* 62:190 Ap '87
Nutrition
See also
Baby bottles
Breast feeding
Milk, Human
Wet nurses
Baby fat [study by Douglas S. Lewis and others] J. Silberner. *Sci News* 131:73 Ja 31 '87
Beech-Nut indicted over phony juice. il *FDA Consum* 21:4 F '87
For babies, fat's not so bad [dangers of putting infants on a diet] J. Silberner. il *U S News World Rep* 103:75 S 14 '87
Mama knows best. P. L. Spencer. *Consum Res Mag* 70:2 F '87
Nutri-myth [views of Mary Story and Judith E. Brown] P. McCarthy. il *Psychol Today* 21:58-9 Je '87
Psychology
See Infant psychology
Sleep
See Sleep
Surgery
Racing for life [5-month-old A. Dela Peña gets new heart] J. Korman. il pors *N Y Times Mag* p62-4+ S 20 '87
Suffering and joy [anencephalic baby as heart donor] A. Steacy. il *Macleans* 100:40-1 N 23 '87
Infants, Newborn
See also
Fetus
As they grow/birth to 1 year. K. Karlsrud and D. Schultz. See issues of Parents beginning March 1987
Irritable rule for breast-fed babies [research by Janet A. DiPietro and others] *Sci News* 132:94 Ag 8 '87
Maternal scents [mothers most likely to recognize newborns by smell] E. Comte. *Health* 19:26 N '87
Birth defects
See Birth defects
Diseases
See also
Respiratory distress syndrome
Diagnosis
Panel urges newborn sickle cell screening. G. Kolata. *Science* 236:259-60 Ap 17 '87
Hospital care
See also
Baby Doe rules
Hospitals—Maternity care
Firms, officials indicted over unsafe infants' drug [premature babies given vitamin E supplement E-Ferol] *FDA Consum* 21:4 O '87
Neonatal resuscitation. P. A. Hillard. il *Parents* 62:150+ Je '87
Psychology
See Infant psychology
Surgery
Babies in pain [surgery without painkillers] A. Fischer. il *Redbook* 169:124-5+ O '87
Weight
See Birth weight
Infants, Premature
See also
Respiratory distress syndrome

Influenza—*cont.*

The geography of influenza. G. F. Pyle and K. D. Patterson. il maps *Focus* 37:16-23 Fall '87

Is "Thucydides syndrome" back? [toxic shock as complication of flu] C. Wallis. il *Time* 129:62 Mr 30 '87

New mean team: flu and toxic shock. *Sci News* 131:169 Mr 14 '87

Swine's way [swine flu as cause of Indian deaths after arrival of Columbus; views of F. Guerra] B. Lawren. il *Omni* 9:18 Ja '87

Vaccines and vaccination

Flu shot season approaches. *FDA Consum* 21:4 O '87

Shouldn't you get immunized? P. Spencer. il *50 Plus* 27:16+ O '87

Influenza viruses

Selective inactivation of influenza C esterase: a probe for detecting 9-O-acetylated sialic acids. E. A. Muchmore and A. P. Varki. bibl f il *Science* 236:1293-5 Je 5 '87

Viral exposure boosts schizophrenia risk [research by Sarnoff A. Mednick and others] B. Bower. *Sci News* 132:180 S 19 '87

Infomart (Dallas, Tex.: Trade mart)

The soft sell and the Crystal Palace. L. M. Keefe. il *Forbes* 139:130-1 Je 15 '87

Informants *See* Informers

Information, Classified *See* Classified information

Information, Communication of *See* Communication; Telecommunication

Information, Freedom of *See* Freedom of information

Information centers (Data processing)

How to use your company's information center. A. Oshins. *Work Woman* 12:23+ F '87

Systems matchmaking [Information Center for Client Computing at Portland General Electric] R. Dalton. il *Pers Comput* 11:75-6+ N '87

Information Committee (United Nations) *See* United Nations. Committee on Information

Information display systems

See also

Airplanes—Electronic equipment

Airplanes, Jet—Electronic equipment

Space vehicles—Electronic equipment

Build the GT180 color graphics board (III). S. Ciarcia. il *Byte* 12:85-92 Ja '87

Compute anywhere with PCs to go [LCD portables] W. J. Hawkins. il *Pop Sci* 230:88-90 F '87

Data structures in a bit-mapped text editor: how Carnegie-Mellon University displays text on the IBM RT PC. W. J. Hansen. il *Byte* 12:183-4+ Ja '87

Displays for small sizes. *BioScience* 37:353 My '87

EGA times 12 [enhanced graphics adapter boards] C. H. Pappas and W. H. Murray. il *Byte* 12:313-14+ Ja '87

Hercules discovers color graphics [InColor Card] A. C. Hixson. il *Pers Comput* 11:162 Jl '87

Hercules Graphics Card Plus. il *Radio-Electron* 58 ComputerDigest:85+ Ap '87

Managing VDT safety and comfort. H. McCandless. *Work Woman* 12:20+ Jl '87

The many splendors of VGA [IBM's video graphics array] J. Blackford. il *Pers Comput* 11:279-80 S '87

The Micro Clipper Graphics subsystem. C. D. Weston. il *Byte* 12:257-8+ S '87

Microtip TV [flat-screen display] N. J. Freundlich. il *Pop Sci* 231:60-1+ Ag '87

A multi-display board from NEC [GB-1 graphics board] P. Honan. il *Pers Comput* 11:208 My '87

A new touch [InfoWindow touch-screen] W. J. Hawkins. il *Pop Sci* 230:14+ Mr '87

A 'super' EGA standard [Vega Deluxe "Super" EGA high-resolution graphics board] il *Pers Comput* 11:29-30 Je '87

Teaching old screens new tricks: create fancy screen displays for your homegrown programs. M. J. Sorens. il *Byte* 12:129-33 S '87

Today's high resolution standards: EGA & VGA. P. Honan. il *Pers Comput* 11:119+ D '87

Tseng Labs' EVA/480 [enhanced graphics adapter card] il *Radio-Electron* 58 ComputerDigest:135-6 My '87

VDT comfort. M. S. Dolan. *Consum Res Mag* 70:2 Ag '87

Vector-to-raster algorithms. D. Pountain. *Byte* 12:177-8+ S '87

VGA arrives for PCs [VGA Extra board] P. Honan. il *Pers Comput* 11:260 D '87

The writer's support group. C. O'Malley. il *Pers Comput* 11:51-2+ My '87

Information managers

More room at the top [chief information officers] L. M. Keefe. il *Forbes* 139:102+ Je 29 '87

Information processing, Human *See* Human information processing

Information Resources Inc.

Nielsen boosts its ratings. A. Dunkin. il *Bus Week* p40 S 14 '87

Information services

See also

Art—Information services

Disclosure Information Group

Investments—Information services

Medicine—Information services

Small business—Information services

Telephone information service

Toll-free telephone service

United States. National Technical Information Service

White House Conference on Library and Information Services

Women—Sports—Information services

Losing the future to the past [effects of information revolution on entrepreneurism] M. Pastin. il por *Nations Bus* 75:4 F '87

The power of information [address, June 15, 1987] R. W. Galvin. *Vital Speeches Day* 53:647-9 Ag 15 '87

Taxation

A science tax on information? *Sci News* 131:57 Ja 24 '87

Information storage and retrieval systems

See also

Boston CitiNet

Computers

Hypertext

Offices—Automation

Text processing (Computer science)

Trintex Inc.

U.S. Videotel Inc.

Word processors and processing

Are you ready for Pacific Bell's 'wonder phone'? [Project Victoria] il *U S News World Rep* 102:61 Mr 30 '87

Customized newspaper [X Press] T. Onosko. *Omni* 9:103 Ja '87

Info gridlock [U.S. lagging in videotex due to breakup of AT&T] *New Repub* 196:4 Ja 26 '87

Modem madness: telecommunications at a crossroads. S. Shulman. il *Technol Rev* 90:8 Jl '87

A new kind of censorship? [narrowing focus of information intake] E. Dyson. il *Forbes* 140:107 D 28 '87

People still don't know just what they're missing [videotex] G. H. Arlen. il *Channels* 7 Sp Issue:123 D '87

Personal bibliographic databases. R. E. Wachtel. bibl f il *Science* 235:1093-6 F 27 '87

Suddenly, videotex is finding an audience. il *Bus Week* p92+ O 19 '87

Tapping into computer services. M. S. Matthews. il *Consum Res Mag* 70:11-17 Ja '87

What's new in on-line services. R. Lockwood. il *Pers Comput* 11:151-3+ Je '87

'You'll see alliances you won't believe'. F. Seghers. il *Bus Week* p99 D 7 '87

Aged

The AgeLine database. M. Eccles. *Aging* no355:23-5 '87

Architectural use

Using your micro to specify [with editorial comment by Mildred F. Schmertz] S. S. Ross. il *Archit Rec* 175:9, 134-7 S '87

Art use

A brand-new way to organize fine art [J. Creiger's Omnivex, Inc. computerized videodisc art catalog] A. Oshins. il por *Work Woman* 12:66+ My '87

Clever, and it's art [Omnivex Network] il *Pers Comput* 11:257 Jl '87

Astronomical use

CompuServe information service; Computer bulletin-board systems (BBS's). il *Sky Telesc* 74 Sky Telesc Handb:18-21 S '87

Aviation use

Datalog flight planner. J. M. McClellan. *Flying* 114:94 Mr '87

Harris Corp. offering digital map generator for airborne operations. E. H. Kolcum. il *Aviat Week Space Technol* 126:84-5+ Mr 16 '87

Banking use

See also

Systematics, Inc.

Desktop banking. C. García-Barrio. il *Essence* 18:138 My '87

Biological use

Electrophoresis and large-scale databases. N. G. Anderson. bibl f *Science* 235 pt2:G65 F 27 '87

Information storage and retrieval systems — Biological use—*cont.*

New database for AIDS research. D. M. Barnes. *Science* 235:634 F 6 '87

Boating use

Computer taps to databases. J. H. Rhodes. il *Mot Boat Sail* 159:68+ Ap '87

Botanical use

TAXACOM, an online service for systematic botany. R. H. Zander. il *BioScience* 37:616-18 S '87

Business travel use

Now, the 'paperless' expense account. S. Gelfond. il *Bus Week* p106 S 7 '87

Business use

See also

Information centers (Data processing)

Dun & Bradstreet's overheard Dialog [access to Dun's Financial Records] *Newsweek* 110:39 D 28 '87

An inside look at a LAN data archive system [Becton Dickinson system] M. W. Perry. il *Byte* 12:169-70+ Jl '87

On-line contacts. H. Fersko-Weiss. il *Pers Comput* 11:83-5+ Ja '87

People tracking [specialized data bases] S. Diamond. il *Pers Comput* 11:133-5+ D '87

Strategic connections [personal computers and mainframe data] J. Blackford. il *Pers Comput* 11:131-3+ My '87

Dance use

High tech hiring links dancers and troupes [Dansource] L. Dally. il *Dance Mag* 61:14 Ja '87

Ecological use

Society links national decision makers with expert ecologists [Ecological Information Network] *BioScience* 37:85 Ja '87

Educational use

See also

National Geographic Kids Network

Perfect match [MVP Athletic Network links women athletes with scholarships] il *Women's Sports Fitness* 9:58 F '87

ScholarNet: the beginning of a world academic community. R. W. Slatta. il por *Futurist* 21:17-19 Mr/Ap '87

Employment use

Pounding the pavement by computer. D. H. Dunn. il *Bus Week* p166 My 11 '87

Encyclopedias

Would you believe Encyclopedia Electronica? R. R. Roha. il *Changing Times* 41:49+ Jl '87

Insurance use

See also

Insurance Information Inc.

SelectQuote Insurance Services

Insurance on simpler terms [term insurance information services] B. Kallen. il *Forbes* 140:108+ Ag 10 '87

A new way to price term life. *Money* 16:14 S '87

Investment use

See also

Telerate, Inc.

The computer as an investment tool. A. Glossbrenner. il *Work Woman* 12:47-8 F '87

Desk-top investing aids. M. O'Brien. il *Nations Bus* 75:45-6 Mr '87

How's the Dow? Check it on your PC [stock quote services and software] B. Hitchings. il *Bus Week* p105 Ja 26 '87

New tools for the armchair investor. B. Kallen. il *Forbes* 139:150 Mr 23 '87

Thrive without a broker. R. Cullen. il *Pers Comput* 11:91-5+ Ap '87

Venturing abroad [data bases tracking foreign stocks] il *Forbes* 139:112 Ap 20 '87

What's new in software for investors. A. Kupfer. il *Fortune* 116 Sp Issue:233+ Fall '87

Laws and regulations

The telecommunications jungle. D. Caruso. il *Pers Comput* 11:89-90 Je '87

Management

See also

Communications software

Ashton-Tate: a high hurdle for a front-runner [creating new software for 80386 machines] R. Neff. il *Bus Week* p85-6 Ja 26 '87

Benchmarking dBASE III Plus compilers [Quicksilver, Clipper, and FoxBase] M. Rubel. il *Byte* 12:277-81 S '87

Connectivity. M. Liskin. See issues of Personal Computing beginning July 1987

Dac Easy data base [Dac Easy Base] A. C. Hixson. il *Pers Comput* 11:200 My '87

The data base alternative [maintaining a mailing list] C. O'Malley. il *Pers Comput* 11:103 My '87

Data base management. M. Liskin. See issues of Personal Computing beginning June 1987

Database managers. C. Spezzano. il *Byte* 12 Sp Issue:77-88 Summ '87

Finders keepers [Dragnet text-retrieval program] A. C. Hixson. il *Pers Comput* 11:184+ Ap '87

A flexible data base [FileMaker Plus] J. Bell. il *Pers Comput* 11:234 Je '87

Flexible, not muscular [Reflex] C. Spencer. il *Pers Comput* 11:147 F '87

Hall-Comsec's Wiretap, Hayes' Transet 1000, Disc Instruments' µLynx Trackball, and Finot Group's Keep Track. il *Radio-Electron* 58 ComputerDigest:92 Ap '87

The Intelligent Assistant [Q&A's natural-language interface] G. G. Hendrix and B. A. Walter. il *Byte* 12:251-2+ D '87

Intelligent databases. C. D. S. Moss. il *Byte* 12:97-8+ Ja '87

Into the 4th Dimension [relational database manager] E. Shapiro. il *Byte* 12:269-70+ O '87

A link between operating systems [MacLinkPlus] A. C. Hixson. il *Pers Comput* 11:152 Ag '87

Linking all the company data: we're not there yet. R. Brandt. il *Bus Week* p151 My 11 '87

Mac heats up DB market [dBase Mac] J. Bell. il *Pers Comput* 11:40 D '87

Maximizing the power in data base programs. C. O'Malley. il *Pers Comput* 11:147-9+ N '87

The network-model DBMS. D. Kruglinski. il *Byte* 12 Sp Issue:25-6+ Summ '87

The output side of data bases. C. O'Malley. *Pers Comput* 11:89+ Jl '87

PC software that helps you think. A. Field. il *Bus Week* p142 N 2 '87

Q&A. J. Pournelle. *Byte* 12:294-6+ S '87

Q&A 2.0. P. R. Robinson. *Byte* 12:249-51 My '87

R:base System V [relational database management system] S. Cobb. *Byte* 12:255-7 Ap '87

Serious filing [RapidFile] C. O'Malley. *Pers Comput* 11:160 Jl '87

Some like it Hot; some may not [DOS application management utilities] S. Makrias. il *Pers Comput* 11:164 Ja '87

Super searcher [Fast Data Finder designed by Kwang-I Yu] J. Schefter. il *Pop Sci* 231:60-1 D '87

Toward a shared data base. T. Badgett. il *Pers Comput* 11:111+ O '87

Two network managers [Lanscope and LANWatch] il *Byte* 12:70 D '87

A video data base [PicturePower] R. Lockwood. il *Pers Comput* 11:178 Jl '87

WordCruncher [text indexing and retrieval program] R. Rabinovitz. *Byte* 12:216+ N '87

Yes, but what does it do? A guide to a new software generation. J. Schwartz. il *Newsweek* 110:68 D 14 '87

Zoomracks II. T. Sperry. il *Byte* 12:272+ Je '87

Medical use

Does your computer know how sick you are? [diagnostic system DXplain] *Newsweek* 110:47 Jl 13 '87

When your doctor needs to know—fast [MEDLINE] M. E. DeBakey. il *Read Dig* 131:110-13 Jl '87

Meteorological use

Haynes offers PC-based weather, flight plan system [WeatherStar satellite information system] *Aviat Week Space Technol* 126:100 My 25 '87

Photographic use

Ultimate slide management [SlideScribe System] K. Geller-Shinn. il *Petersens Photogr Mag* 15:20 Mr '87

Political use

Fresh-baked political wisdom [Presidential Campaign Hotline compendium of political news and analysis] M. Kaus. il *Newsweek* 110:83 N 2 '87

Publishing use

Facts on File offers database that contains author contracts. *Publ Wkly* 232:12 S 11 '87

Purchasing use

See Electronic shopping

Rates

Data companies are mad as hell at the FCC. F. Seghers. il *Bus Week* p60+ O 19 '87

The hidden peril of electronic publishing. P. Lemmons. *Byte* 12:6 F '87

Real estate use

See also

Vacation Properties Network

Computerized mortgage shopping: a lack of interest. P. E. Godwin. il *Changing Times* 41:20 Je '87

Information storage and retrieval systems—*cont.*
Scientific use
Death of a data directive. R. Chalk. il *Technol Rev* 90:13-14 Jl '87

Information please. *Courier* 40:24 O '87

Making waves: Poindexter sails into scientific databases. I. Goodwin. por *Phys Today* 40:51-2 Ja '87

SDIO offers unclassified spinoff program [database describing technology developed under SDI sponsorship] *Aviat Week Space Technol* 127:84 N 23 '87

What is federal policy on scientific communication? D. R. Corson. *Phys Today* 40:144 Ja '87
Search strategies
See On line searching
Security measures
Coming: the big chill? [restrictions on unclassified data; cover story] J. Raloff. il *Sci News* 131:314-17 My 16 '87

In rough waters, White House cancels controls on databases. I. Goodwin. *Phys Today* 40:66 My '87

Making waves: Poindexter sails into scientific databases. I. Goodwin. por *Phys Today* 40:51-2 Ja '87

Security on-line. P. Honan. *Pers Comput* 11:107 Ja '87

Tapping new secrets [government initiatives to control database information] M. McIver. il *Macleans* 100:60-1 S 28 '87

What is federal policy on scientific communication? D. R. Corson. *Phys Today* 40:144 Ja '87
Space flight use
Hacking through NASA [penetration of Space Physics Analysis Network] W. D. Marbach. il *Newsweek* 110:38 S 28 '87

Langley develops optical technique for storing satellite data [Earth Radiation Budget Experiment satellites] *Aviat Week Space Technol* 127:145 Ag 10 '87
Sports use
See also
Sports News Network
Stock exchange use
See Information storage and retrieval systems—Investment use
Developing countries
The electronic Peace Corps. D. H. Rothman. *Natl Rev* 39:43-4 Mr 27 '87
France
The sexy computer [Minitel system] J. De Lacy. il *Atlantic* 260:18+ Jl '87

Will Minitel play deep in the heart of Texas? [U.S. Videotel] J. E. Davis. il por *Bus Week* p94 O 19 '87

Information theory
Information theory. R. Bharath. bibl il *Byte* 12:291-2+ D '87

Information theory in psychology
See also
Human information processing

Informed consent (Medical law)
California
Full disclosure: the California informed-consent law [designed to protect prospective hysterectomy patients] P. Dranov. *N Y* 20:75 O 19 '87

Informers
See also
Whistle blowing (Public interest)
The con man [FBI informer M. Raymond] M. A. Farber. il por *N Y Times Mag* p34+ Je 21 '87

Once a hit man, now a stoolie, Jimmy 'the Weasel' Fratianno says the feds owe him a living [interview] J. Wadler. il pors *People Wkly* 28:38-40 D 21 '87

The sins of the father: a mobster's past shadows his sons' football stardom [S. Polisi] N. Taylor. il *N Y* 20:42-4+ Ja 26 '87

Squeal [tax informers] L. Saunders. il *Forbes* 139:62-3 My 4 '87

Infrared astronomy
Bright infrared galaxies. il *Sky Telesc* 73:29-30 Ja '87

Bright infrared galaxies may be young quasars. il *Astronomy* 15:78-9 Ap '87

Dust clouds detected around six nearby stars [study by Dana Backman and others] *Astronomy* 15:75+ My '87

Getting the picture in the infrared. D. E. Thomsen. il *Sci News* 131:295 My 9 '87

Imagery comes to infrared astronomy [infrared array detector] M. M. Waldrop. il *Science* 236:1525-6 Je 19 '87

Laying bare Venus' dark secrets [infrared observations with the Anglo-Australian Telescope] D. A. Allen. il *Sky Telesc* 74:350-3 O '87

Observing Halley from 41,000 feet [Kuiper Airborne Observatory and Lear Jet Observatory] H. Campins and H. A. Weaver. *Sky Telesc* 73:251 Mr '87

Quasars in the making? [link with infrared galaxies; research by David B. Sanders and others] il *Sky Telesc* 74:577-8 D '87

Seeing red. il *Discover* 8:18 N '87

Warm infrared galaxy discovered behind SMC [work of Jay Frogel and Jonathan H. Elias] *Astronomy* 15:65-6 Ag '87

Infrared Astronomy Satellite *See* Artificial satellites—Astronomical use

Infrared communications
Build a trainable infrared master controller. S. Ciarcia. il *Byte* 12:113-23 Mr '87

Build an infrared remote controller. S. Ciarcia. il *Byte* 12:101-10 F '87

Infrared detectors *See* Detectors, Infrared

Infrared equipment
A DTMF receiver [dual tone multi-frequency receiver] R. Grossblatt. il *Radio-Electron* 58:82-3 Mr '87

SMT project: I-R remote on a keychain [surface-mount technology] F. M. Mims. il *Radio-Electron* 58:77-9 N '87

Infrared interferometers *See* Interferometers and interferometry

Infrared thermography *See* Thermography

Infrastructure *See* Public works

Infringement of copyright *See* Copyright infringement

Infringement of patents *See* Patent infringement

Ing, Dean
Prix de lune. il *Omni* 9:52-5 Jl '87

Ing. C. Olivetti & Co., SpA
AT&T may be ready to cut its losses in computers [Olivetti to join in a spinoff] J. J. Keller. il *Bus Week* p30 Jl 6 '87

Dealmaker De Benedetti [cover story] W. C. Symonds. il pors *Bus Week* p42-7 Ag 24 '87

More rabbits, please, Signor De Benedetti [linkup with AT&T] S. Solomon. por *Forbes* 139:114+ Mr 9 '87

Olivetti's global deal maker [C. De Benedetti] P. C. Newman. il por *Macleans* 100:51 N 30 '87

Ingber, Dina
Staying safe: the smart woman's guide to self-defense. il pors *McCalls* 145:138+ Mr '87

Ingersoll, Andrew P.
Uranus. il *Sci Am* 256:38-45 Ja '87

Ingersoll, Ralph, II
about
A quixotic father's acquisitive son. P. Berman. il por *Forbes* 140:8 O 5 '87

Ingersoll Publications Company
A quixotic father's acquisitive son [R. Ingersoll II] P. Berman. il por *Forbes* 140:8 O 5 '87

Ingham, Curtis
Are the SATs unfair? il *Seventeen* 46:142-3+ O '87

Ingle, David J.
Color vision and the retinex theory [discussion of February 8, 1985 article, The goldfish as a retinex animal] il *Science* 238:1731-2 D 18 '87

Inglenooks *See* Alcoves

Ingram, Bertha Lee
about
Bertha's triumph. P. Jordan. il *Read Dig* 131:55-9 Ag '87

Ingram Book Company
Ingram launches retail print ad campaign [project with Gannett newspapers] A. Symons. *Publ Wkly* 232:35 Jl 10 '87

Ingredient labeling of food *See* Food—Labeling

Ingwerson, Donald W.
(jt. auth) See Schlechty, Phillip C., and Ingwerson, Donald W.

Inheritance
See also
Estate planning
Estates, Decedents'
Probate law and practice
Wills
If life hands you a silver spoon—gild it [billionaires] B. Dumaine. il por *Fortune* 116:160-1 O 12 '87

Keeping it in the family: should kids inherit fortunes? R. I. Kirkland, Jr. *Current* 289:16-20 Ja '87

The patrimony society [cover story] R. Kuttner. *New Repub* 196:18-21 My 11 '87

Inheritance of diseases *See* Heredity of disease

Inheritance tax
Angel of death loophole [proposal to tax capital gains at death] *New Repub* 197:4 Jl 13-20 '87

Inheritance tax—*cont.*

Constitutional wrongs [upcoming Supreme Court case challenging Congress' attempt to overrule and impose estate taxes retroactively] L. Saunders. il *Forbes* 140:154 S 21 '87

For the quick, a $20 billion estate tax loophole. P. Philipps. il *Bus Week* p152 F 23 '87

Gentle persuasion for the rich [Canada] D. Francis. por *Macleans* 100:7 Je 15 '87

Keeping it in the family. C. Hutton. il *Fortune* 116 Sp Issue:111-12+ Fall '87

Of capital, taxes, and death. D. R. Katz. il *Esquire* 107:55-6 Mr '87

Of death and taxes [putting life insurance into an irrevocable trust] L. R. Walbert. il *Forbes* 140:460 Jl 13 '87

Worth less than the sum of its parts? G. W. Padwe. il *Nations Bus* 75:75 N '87

Inhibin

Localization, secretion, and action of inhibin in human placenta. F. Petraglia and others. bibl f il *Science* 237:187-9 Jl 10 '87

Inhibition

See also
Repression (Psychology)

Inhibition of enzymes *See* Enzymes—Inactivation
Inhibitors, Enzyme *See* Enzymes—Inactivation
Initial public offerings (Stock) *See* Stocks—Marketing
Initiation rites

The R.C.I.A. misunderstood? [Catholic Church's Rite of Christian Initiation of Adults] R. A. Duffy. il *America* 156:385+ My 9 '87

Initiative and referendum *See* Referendum
Injuries

See also
Exercise—Accidents and injuries
First aid in illness and injury
Foot—Wounds and injuries
Heel bone—Wounds and injuries
Industrial accidents
Knee—Wounds and injuries
Leg—Wounds and injuries
Muscle—Wounds and injuries
Teeth—Wounds and injuries
Traumatism

Injuries (Law) *See* Damages
Injustice

Feelings of injustice. D. F. Bjorklund and B. Bjorklund. il *Parents* 62:202 D '87

Ink

See also
Printing ink
Conductive inks and adhesives. F. M. Mims. il *Radio-Electron* 58:81-4 N '87

Ink blot test *See* Rorschach test
Ink drawing *See* Pen drawing
Ink-jet printers (Computers) *See* Computers—Print-out equipment
Inkatha movement (South Africa)

The chief [G. Buthelezi] M. Massing. bibl f il por *N Y Rev Books* 34:15-22 F 12 '87

The future of South Africa [address, November 24, 1986] G. M. Buthelezi. *Vital Speeches Day* 53:194-6 Ja 15 '87

Inkster (Mich.)

Police
Three police killed in shootout near Detroit. il *Jet* 72:8 Jl 27 '87

Inkwells and inkstands

Centennial inkwell [1876] M. Wollett and B. Wollett. il *Antiques Collect Hobbies* 92:27 Jl '87

Ceramic inkwells: pottery gems from the past. K. McConnell. bibl il *Antiques Collect Hobbies* 92:28-31 S '87

Inland navigation

See also
River trips

Inland Steel Industries, Inc.

Want it painted? We'll paint it. C. Siler. il *Forbes* 140:142+ N 16 '87

INMARSAT *See* International Maritime Satellite Organization
Inn, Frank

about
Unleashed by Hollywood, the star of Benji the hunted has tongues wagging all over America. J. Jarvis. il por *People Wkly* 28:78-80 Jl 20 '87

Inner city education *See* Education, Urban
Innerspace [film] *See* Motion picture reviews—Single works

Innerst, Mark, 1958?-

about
Mark Innerst at Curt Marcus. H. Cotter. il *Art Am* 75:142-3 F '87

Innervation of the brain *See* Brain—Innervation
Innervation of the eye *See* Eye—Innervation
Innervation of the heart *See* Heart—Innervation
Innocence (Psychology)

The loss of innocence [7 year olds] D. F. Bjorklund and B. Bjorklund. il *Parents* 62:210 S '87

Protecting children's innocence [with editorial comment by Elizabeth Crow] J. Gaylin. il *Parents* 62:6, 88+ O '87

Innovations, Agricultural *See* Agricultural innovations
Innovations, Technological *See* Technological innovations
Innovations & Development Inc.

Meet the men who invented vibrating bedroom slippers. P. Finch. il por *Bus Week* p91 N 9 '87

Inns *See* Hotels, motels, etc.
Inoculation *See* Vaccines and vaccination
Inositol

See also
Phosphatidylinositol

Inoue, Kazuo

about
I lived, but . . . [film] Reviews
New Repub 196:24-6 Ap 13 '87. S. Kauffmann

Inouye, Daniel K.

Should Congress approve the Fairness Doctrine? [excerpts from statement, March 18, 1987] *Congr Dig* 66:240+ O '87

INPO *See* Institute of Nuclear Power Operations (U.S.)
Insane

Legal status, laws, etc.
See Insanity—Jurisprudence

Insane, Criminal and dangerous

See also
Forensic psychiatry
Insanity—Jurisprudence
Advances reported in predicting violence [study by Antonio Convit and others] J. Greenberg. *Sci News* 131:324-5 My 23 '87

Insanity

Jurisprudence
See also
Forensic psychiatry
Mentally ill—Civil rights
Exercising her right to madness, accused killer Gena Spero poses a legal problem without a solution [pleading insanity] J. S. Kunen. il pors *People Wkly* 28:115-16+ O 5 '87

Insanity and art *See* Art and mental illness
Insanity in literature *See* Mental illness in literature
Inscriptions

See also
Epitaphs
Tablets, Ancient

Inscriptions, Maya *See* Mayas—Writing
Insect baits and repellents

Bug off: how to keep mosquitoes away. il *Glamour* 85:39 Jl '87

Debugging yourself. R. Kimber. il *Ctry J* 14:14-15 My '87

Insect repellents. il *Consum Rep* 52:423-6 Jl '87

Insect repellents. il *Consum Rep* 52:199-202 D '87

Insect bites and stings

Hymenoptera: small and considered dangerous. il *Curr Health 2* 13:26-7 Ap '87

Insects removed surgically [surgical gloves as protection against insect bites] M. Simmons. il *Field Stream* 92:111 Je '87

Not an ant-idote [effectiveness of meat tenderizer in treating fire ant stings] *Sci News* 131:374 Je 13 '87

Summertime blues. H. Middleton. il *South Living* 22:26+ Je '87

Anecdotes, facetiae, satire, etc.
Love at first bite. R. Winter. il *Field Stream* 92:29-31 Je '87

Insect communication

Bat predation and its influence on calling behavior in neotropical katydids. J. J. Belwood and G. Morris. bibl f il *Science* 238:64-7 O 2 '87

Driven batty, katydids change tune [influence of predator bats; research by J. J. Belwood and G. Morris] R. Weiss. *Sci News* 132:231 O 10 '87

Insect contamination of food *See* Food contamination
Insect control

See also
Airplanes in insect control
Armyworms—Control
Bacillus thuringiensis

Insect control—See also—*cont.*
　Beetles—Control
　Bollworms—Control
　Borers (Insects)—Control
　Cockroaches—Control
　Corn rootworms—Control
　Cutworms—Control
　Earwigs—Control
　Fleas—Control
　Flies—Control
　Fruit flies—Control
　Grasshoppers—Control
　Gypsy moths—Control
　Houseflies—Control
　Pest control services
　Pesticides
　Springtails—Control
　Termites—Control
　Thrips—Control
　White flies—Control
The ancient cultured citrus ant: a tropical ant is used to control insect pests in southern China. H. T. Huang and P. Yang. bibl il map *BioScience* 37:665-71 O '87
Attracting beneficial garden insects. N. Bubel. il *Ctry J* 14:6-8 Je '87
Bug eat bug. P. L. Spencer. *Consum Res Mag* 70:2 My '87
Bugs bite the dust on bitter pill [use of parasitic nematodes as biological controls] *Sci News* 132:377 D 12 '87
Bugs vs. bugs [work of Jeffrey Aldrich] *USA Today (Periodical)* 115:8 Je '87
Finches fight greenhouse pests. R. L. Kohl. il *Rodale's Org Gard* 34:42-3+ Ag '87
New strategy for an ongoing battle: "integrated pest management". il *Sunset* 178:212 Mr '87
New war against pests. T. H. Cole. il *Pop Mech* 164:10 S '87
Painless pest control. J. Burnett. il *Rodale's Org Gard* 34:53-9 Ag '87
Pest-proof your home. A. Arnott. il *McCalls* 114:37 Jl '87
A rogues gallery of garden pests: how to control common pests in the vegetable garden. L. Hill and N. Hill. il *Ctry J* 14:35-9 Ag '87
Safe ways to banish bugs. H. Twidale. il *Good Housekeep* 204:216 Je '87
'Tis the season to be buggèd. S. Budiansky. il *U S News World Rep* 103:61 Ag 24 '87
Weed & insect control issue [special section] il *Success Farm* 85 no1:19-26+ Ja '87
Your organic bug-free garden. R. Rodale. il *Rodale's Org Gard* 34:22-4 Ja '87
　　　　Biological control
　　See Insect control
Insect eating by birds See Birds—Food and feeding
Insect introduction
Aedes albopictus in North America: probable introduction in used tires from northern Asia. W. A. Hawley and others. bibl f il *Science* 236:1114-16 My 29 '87
Hold that tiger: a very tiresome pursuit [probable introduction of Asian tiger mosquitoes in used tires from northern Asia; research by Paul Reiter] il map *Discover* 8:8-9 Ag '87
Unwelcome immigrant: the Asian cockroach. il *Discover* 8:10 Mr '87
Insect populations
　　See also
　Population genetics—Insects
Insect sex attractants
　　See also
　Pheromones—Insects
Insect societies See Insects—Habits and behavior
Insect sounds
　　See also
　Insect communication
Insect viruses See Viruses, Insect
Insecticide handling See Pesticides—Handling
Insecticide spraying equipment See Spraying equipment
Insecticides See Pesticides
Insectivorous birds See Birds—Food and feeding
Insects
　　See also
　Age—Insects
　Aviation—Insect hazards
　Cuticle—Insects
　Embryology—Insects
　Eye—Insects
　Pheromones—Insects

　　See also names of insects
The bugs of autumn. R. F. Hall. il *Conservationist* 42:48 S/O '87
　　　Anecdotes, facetiae, satire, etc.
Bug slaying and other minor chivalries for the man of the eighties. V. Klinkenborg. il *Glamour* 85:390 S '87
　　　Collection and preservation
The North Borneo Expedition of 1981 [college students collect samples of agricultural pests] C. Alexander. map *New Yorker* 63:39-44+ S 14 '87
　　　　　Coloration
　　See Color of insects
　　　　　Control
　　See Insect control
　　　　　Development
Developmental control gene sequenced [fruit flies; work of Gerald Rubin and others] J. L. Marx. *Science* 236:26-7 Ap 3 '87
Oncogene linked to fruit-fly development [research by Roel Nusse and others] J. L. Marx. bibl il *Science* 238:160-1 O 9 '87
Sevenless, a cell-specific homeotic gene of Drosophila, encodes a putative transmembrane receptor with a tyrosine kinase domain. E. Hafen and others. bibl f il *Science* 236:55-63 Ap 3 '87
　　　　　Eggs
Parasitic wasps keep on ticking [research by Jonathan M. Schmidt and J. J. B. Smith] R. Weiss. *Sci News* 132:134 Ag 29 '87
Short interval time measurement by a parasitoid wasp. J. M. Schmidt and J. J. B. Smith. bibl f il *Science* 237:903-5 Ag 21 '87
　　　　Food and feeding
　　See also
　Insects, Predatory
Insects that mark host plants. B. D. Roitberg and R. J. Prokopy. il *BioScience* 37:400-6 Je '87
Punching holes in a sticky defense [insect vein-cutting behavior counters plant latex defenses; research by David E. Dussourd and Thomas Eisner] D. D. Edwards. il *Sci News* 132:134 Ag 29 '87
The role of drought in outbreaks of plant-eating insects. W. J. Mattson and R. A. Haack. bibl f il *BioScience* 37:110-18 F '87
Vein-cutting behavior: insect counterploy to the latex defense of plants. D. E. Dussourd and T. Eisner. bibl f il *Science* 237:898-901 Ag 21 '87
　　　　Habits and behavior
　　See also
　Insect communication
　Sexual behavior—Insects
Ant wars. H. Topoff. il *Nat Hist* 96:62-6+ Ja '87
The body snatchers [western slave-making ants] H. Topoff. il *Natl Wildl* 25:33 O/N '87
One giant leap for aphid-kind [escape-response behavior of parasitized aphids; research by Murdoch K. McAllister and Bernard D. Roitberg] *Sci News* 132:158 S 5 '87
Temperature control in honey bee colonies [social cooperation] E. E. Southwick and G. Heldmaier. bibl f il *BioScience* 37:395-9 Je '87
　　　　　Host plants
　　See Insects—Food and feeding
　　　　　Metabolism
Chemistry of pheromone and hormone metabolism in insects. G. D. Prestwich. bibl f il *Science* 237:999-1006 Ag 28 '87
　　　　　Reproduction
Insects that mark host plants. B. D. Roitberg and R. J. Prokopy. il *BioScience* 37:400-6 Je '87
Labile sex ratios in wasps and bees. J. H. Werren. bibl f il *BioScience* 37:498-506 Jl/Ag '87
　　　　　Hawaii
Bugs versus stars? [Mauna Kea observatories] S. Wong. il *Technol Rev* 90:13-14 N/D '87
Insects, Aquatic
Autumn's hidden harvest [carbon in fallen leaves as energy source for stream creatures] R. H. Boyle. il *Natl Wildl* 25:4-9 O/N '87
Getting the drift [behavioral drift] P. Schullery. il *Ctry J* 14:66-9 Ag '87
Insects, Effect of temperature on
A rapid cold-hardening process in insects. R. E. Lee, Jr. and others. bibl f il *Science* 238:1415-17 D 4 '87
Thermoregulation in winter moths. B. Heinrich. bibl (p128) il *Sci Am* 256:104-11 Mr '87
Insects, Predatory
Bugs vs. bugs [work of Jeffrey Aldrich] *USA Today (Periodical)* 115:8 Je '87

Insects, Predatory—*cont.*
On display: the stars of the stripes [fruit fly mimicry of jumping spider territorial display; research by Erick Greene and others] il *Discover* 8:9-10 My '87
A sheep in wolf's clothing: tephritid flies mimic spider predators. M. H. Mather and B. D. Roitberg. bibl f il *Science* 236:308-10 Ap 17 '87
A tephritid fly mimics the territorial displays of its jumping spider predators. E. Greene and others. bibl f il *Science* 236:310-12 Ap 17 '87
Why the spider did not eat the fly [jumping spider mimicry among fruit flies] S. Weisburd. il *Sci News* 131:261 Ap 25 '87

Insects, Stinging
See also
Ambush bugs
Insect bites and stings

Insects as carriers of infection
See also
Mosquitoes as carriers of infection
Ticks as carriers of infection
AIDS and insects. K. Leishman. il *Atlantic* 260:56-66+ S '87
Deceit and corruption in the blueberry patch [flower mimicry by mummy berry fungus (Monilinia)] S. W. T. Batra. il *Nat Hist* 96:56-9 Ag '87

Insects as food
The snack that crawls [mopane worm caterpillars eaten as food in Africa] H. Brandon. il *Int Wildl* 17:16-21 Mr/Ap '87

Insects in art
See also
Bees in art
Grasshoppers in art
Bugs. S. Hubbell. il *New Yorker* 63:79-82+ D 28 '87

Insecurity (Psychology) *See* Security and insecurity (Psychology)

Insel, Barbara
The making of a top manager. il *Work Woman* 12:105-8+ My '87

Insemination, Artificial *See* Artificial insemination, Human
Inservice education (College teachers) *See* College teachers—Education in service
Inservice education (Teachers) *See* Teachers—Education in service

Insider trading
Back in the spotlight [I. Boesky] F. Ungeheuer. il por *Time* 130:55 D 21 '87
The Boesky scandal. il *World Press Rev* 34:22 Ja '87
The Boesky touch. T. C. Muck. il *Christ Today* 31:14-15 Mr 6 '87
Boesky's sentence: who will be next? il por *Newsweek* 110:36 D 28 '87
Britain's own Boesky case [Guinness affair] R. I. Kirkland, Jr. il por *Fortune* 115:85-6 F 16 '87
The British connection [insider trading scandals hit Merrill Lynch] A. Miller. il por *Newsweek* 109:39 Mr 23 '87
Buy-outs on Wall Street [merger activity rises in spite of insider trading scandal] L. Black. il *Macleans* 100:29 Mr 30 '87
The buzz on Wall Street [rumors surround the insider trading scandal] B. Powell. *Newsweek* 109:49 Mr 9 '87
C.E.O.s take on their investment bankers [insider trading scandal could lead to lower fees] S. P. Sherman. il *Fortune* 115:57-8+ Ap 27 '87
A contrast in styles on Wall Street [Kidder parent GE] il *Fortune* 115:8 Je 8 '87
Crackdown on Bay Street [Ontario Securities Commission probe] T. Tedesco. il *Macleans* 100:22-3 Jl 13 '87
Crime and punishment [I. Boesky sentenced] T. Tedesco. *Macleans* 100:43 D 28 '87
Crook of the year [I. Boesky] G. Kinkead. il por *Fortune* 115:48-9 Ja 5 '87
Downfall of a titan [E. W. Saunders' role in Guinness securities scandal] T. Fennell. il por *Macleans* 100:28 My 25 '87
Drexel in the cross hairs [SEC investigation] B. Powell and C. Friday. il *Newsweek* 109:48 F 16 '87
Easy consciences on Wall Street. J. M. Wall. *Christ Century* 104:179-80 F 25 '87
Ethics and the investment industry [Notre Dame conference] T. C. Widner. *America* 157:444-5 D 12 '87
Explosive questions about trading [Ontario Securities Commission investigation] A. Walmsley. il *Macleans* 100:33 Jl 20 '87
The fallout from Wall Street's Greedgate. il *Fortune* 115:8 Mr 16 '87
Fearing that "muck will stick" [Guinness stock trading scandal] S. Holmes. il *Time* 129:61 Mr 9 '87

From pinstripes to prison stripes. S. Koepp. il *Time* 129:48-9 Mr 2 '87
Getting even with Ivan & company. D. Baer. il *U S News World Rep* 102:46 Mr 2 '87
Giuliani retreats—but he's poised for a new attack. L. J. Tell. il por *Bus Week* p44 Je 1 '87
The grin is gone, but arbitrageur Boesky still sings. K. R. Sheets. il por *U S News World Rep* 102:45 My 4 '87
The Guinness affair gets curiouser and curiouser [role of M. Riklis and sale of Schenley to Guinness] M. Maremont. *Bus Week* p59-60 My 25 '87
Handcuffs on Wall Street [with interview with F. Joseph] D. Baer. il *U S News World Rep* 102:38-9 F 23 '87
How Guinness suddenly fell from grace. R. A. Melcher and M. Maremont. il pors *Bus Week* p44-6 F 9 '87
Illegal insider trading [address, October 17, 1986] J. H. Sturc. *Vital Speeches Day* 53:404-9 Ap 15 '87
Insider report. See issues of Money beginning September 1986 through January 1987
The insider scandal travels abroad [charges against N. Vaskevitch and D. Sofer] S. Koepp. il por *Time* 129:51 Mr 23 '87
Insider trading: business as usual. G. Weiss and C. Power. il *Bus Week* p20-1 Ag 24 '87
The insider-trading dragnet is stretching across the globe. J. Templeman and W. Glasgall. il *Bus Week* p50-1 Mr 23 '87
Insider trading: the High Court hasn't ended the confusion. C. Yang. il por *Bus Week* p34 N 30 '87
Insider trading's victims [investors rush to court] B. Powell and C. Friday. il *Newsweek* 109:40-1 Ap 6 '87
The insiders. *Natl Rev* 39:20 Mr 13 '87
It isn't greed alone. S. Blotnick. il *Forbes* 139:178 Mr 23 '87
Ivan Boesky's final deal. il por *U S News World Rep* 103:13 D 28 '87-Ja 4 '88
Ivan Boesky's latest deal: a guilty plea. il por *Newsweek* 109:45 My 4 '87
John Weinberg [Goldman, Sachs partner R. M. Freeman charged] A. Bianco. por *Bus Week* Sp Issue:224 Ap 17 '87
Keep your eye on Giuliani. G. F. Will. il *Newsweek* 109:84 Mr 2 '87
Kidder does a $25 million deal with Giuliani [GE tries to limit damage from insider trading] *Newsweek* 109:49 Je 15 '87
The lawyers to call when there's heat on the Street [attorneys who battle for accused insider traders] G. Weiss. il *Bus Week* p58+ Ap 6 '87
Look who may take a fall in the Guinness scandal. M. Maremont. por *Bus Week* p48 O 26 '87
Making punishment fit white-collar crime. L. J. Tell. il *Bus Week* p84-5 Je 15 '87
Maybe we just need a dictionary [proposals for an insider-trading definition] *Fortune* 116:14 S 14 '87
The Memotec affair [insider trading scandal] B. Wallace. il *Macleans* 100:38 O 5 '87
Money managing in a bell jar. M. M. Thomas. il *Nation* 244:318-20 Mr 14 '87
The movie version [insider information as handled in movie The House of Rothschild] D. Seligman. il *Fortune* 115:27-8 F 16 '87
New arrests on Wall Street [arrest of M. A. Siegel and others] D. Pauly. il por *Newsweek* 109:48-50 F 23 '87
No news is bad news [quicker corporate disclosure to discourage insider trading] J. Crudele. il *N Y* 20:20-1 Je 8 '87
Now Drexel Burnham is fighting on two fronts [SEC allegations] C. Welles. il por *Bus Week* p90-3+ F 16 '87
Of loose lips and stock tips [Supreme Court upholds conviction of R. F. Winans] J. Castro. il por *Time* 130:63 N 30 '87
The ordeal of Bob Freeman. R. B. Stolley. il pors *Fortune* 115:66-8+ My 25 '87
The other scandal. *New Repub* 196:6 Mr 23 '87
Outsider's guide to insider moves. M. C. Paulson. bibl il *Changing Times* 41:89-92 O '87
The paranoid life of arbitragers. J. Fierman. il *Fortune* 116:97+ N 9 '87
Picking up the pieces [career moves by P. Thayer] W. P. Barrett. il por *Forbes* 140:113 Ag 10 '87
The price of Ivan Boesky's greed. C. Friday. il por *Newsweek* 110:51 D 21 '87
The questions surrounding Guinness' U.S. connection [Washington lawyer T. J. Ward] P. Dwyer and M. Maremont. il por *Bus Week* p36-7 Ap 27 '87

Insider trading—*cont.*

A raid on Wall Street [informant M. A. Siegel and arrest of three investment bankers] G. Russell. il por *Time* 129:64-6 F 23 '87

Recent deals show less inside trading. K. R. Sheets. il *U S News World Rep* 102:47 Mr 23 '87

Rivals refuse to be out on a limb with Drexel Burnham. C. P. Work. il *U S News World Rep* 102:41 Ap 6 '87

Roundup on Wall Street. T. Fennell. il *Macleans* 100:39 F 23 '87

Scandal at Guinness. R. Laver. il *Macleans* 100:62 F 2 '87

The scandal at Guinness: will the chief fall? M. Maremont and R. A. Melcher. il por *Bus Week* p52 Ja 19 '87

Scary times on Wall Street. R. Brady. il *Nations Bus* 75:63-4 F '87

The SEC isn't clearing up anything. G. Weiss. il *Bus Week* p22 Ag 24 '87

The SEC's busy crimebuster [G. Lynch] F. Rice. il por *Fortune* 115:51 Ja 5 '87

The Securities Act of 1988? P. Fuhrman. il *Forbes* 139:40-1 Mr 9 '87

The seduction of Ilan [I. Reich] A. Smith. il *Esquire* 107:75-6 My '87

Smoke signals? [Cherokee Group] T. Jaffe. *Forbes* 139:267 My 18 '87

'Spin control' on Wall Street. J. Reed. il *U S News World Rep* 102:46 Ap 20 '87

Stale dope [insider trades reported late to the SEC] J. Novack. *Forbes* 140:180 N 2 '87

Stocks: the inside story. J. B. Quinn. il *Newsweek* 109:54 Mr 16 '87

A stumble during the waltz [government drops charges against Robert Freeman, Timothy Tabor and Richard Wigton] B. Powell. il por *Newsweek* 109:34 My 25 '87

Suddenly the fish get bigger [scandal touches Kidder, Peabody and Goldman, Sachs; special section] il *Bus Week* p28-35 Mr 2 '87

This is what you thought: 79% think many Wall Streeters break the law [results of survey] *Glamour* 85:129 My '87

Tracing Ivan's deals, Ivan's money. P. Sherrid; A. Gabor. por *U S News World Rep* 102:47 F 2 '87

Trading places [I. Boesky sentenced] por *Time* 130:63 D 28 '87

The unraveling of Dennis Levine. D. Frantz. il *Esquire* 108:160-4+ S '87

The Wall Street dragnet hits a legal snag. K. R. Sheets. il *U S News World Rep* 102:45 My 25 '87

Wall Street poker. D. Seligman. il *Fortune* 115:99-100 Mr 30 '87

Wall Street weak [new network business shows] J. F. Berry. il *Channels* 7:60-1 Mr '87

Wall Street's top cop [U.S. Attorney C. M. Carberry] il pors *Newsweek* 109:48-50 Mr 2 '87

Were Drexel and Boesky in cahoots? J. Egan and D. Baer. il por *U S News World Rep* 102:45 F 16 '87

What is insider trading? An answer may be on the way. V. Cahan. il *Bus Week* p28 Je 29 '87

What the Boesky scandal means to you and your money [takeover stocks] J. Edgerton. il *Money* 16:64-7 Ja '87

Where the scam faltered [D. B. Levine] D. Hutchins. por *Fortune* 115:49-50 Ja 5 '87

Why GE is cleaning house at Kidder [trying to limit damage from insider trading scandal] J. R. Norman. il *Bus Week* p45 Je 1 '87

Wrangling over the booty from insider trading. C. Yang. il *Bus Week* p158+ O 12 '87

Anecdotes, facetiae, satire, etc.

Uncivil liberties. C. Trillin. il *Nation* 244:352 Mr 21 '87

Wall Street's dark humor. L. Black. il *Macleans* 100:40 My 11 '87

Insight Personnel Agency of New York Inc.

"I pray for cash and it comes in". S. Caminiti. il por *Fortune* 115:46 Ap 27 '87

Insignia

See also

Emblems

Insituform Group Ltd.

Fixing the pipes. J. Novack. il *Forbes* 140:70 Ag 24 '87

Insituform of North America, Inc.

Fixing the pipes. J. Novack. il *Forbes* 140:70 Ag 24 '87

Inslaw (Firm)

The InJustice of it all [Dept. of Justice found guilty of stealing computer program from Inslaw] il *Time* 130:52 O 12 '87

Insomnia

50 ways to get to sleep [excerpt from How to sleep like a baby, wake up refreshed and get more out of life] D. Hales. il *Good Housekeep* 204:179+ My '87

Combating chronic insomnia [views of Richard M. Coleman] il *USA Today (Periodical)* 115:6 F '87

Good night, insomnia. L. Fissinger. il *Seventeen* 46:182+ Mr '87

"I can't get to sleep!". J. Viorst. il *Redbook* 169:124-5+ My '87

Stalking a good night's sleep. il *Consum Rep* 52:136-8 Mr '87

Inspection

See also

Airplanes, Military—Inspection

Building inspection

Disarmament—Inspection

Food inspection

Instant Medical Tests (Firm)

Doc-in-a-drugstore. M. H. Coppess. il *Health* 19:28 N '87

Instant print photography *See* Photography—Processing

Instant replay (Sports)

Curse of the camera [TV replays can go too far] R. Reilly. por *Sports Illus* 66:85 Mr 2 '87

Don't play it again: the NFL should do away with the instant replay. J. McCallum. por *Sports Illus* 67 Sp Issue:130 S 9 '87

Will instant replay trip the ref? [Super Bowl XXI] M. Moran. il *N Y Times Mag* p24-30+ Ja 25 '87

Instinct

Learning by instinct. J. L. Gould and P. Marler. il *Sci Am* 256:74-85 Ja '87

Institut Français de Recherche pour l'Exploitation de la Mer

Down to the great ship [Titanic] W. F. Buckley. il por *N Y Times Mag* p40-1+ O 18 '87

Reminders of a tragedy [Titanic] B. Wallace. il *Macleans* 100:58 N 9 '87

Tempest over the Titanic. M. D. Lemonick. il *Time* 130:56 Ag 3 '87

Treasure quest in a tomb [salvage mission to the Titanic] A. Steacy. *Macleans* 100:42 Ag 3 '87

Institut Pasteur (Paris, France)

The AIDS debate: call it a draw [conflict between French and U.S. researchers resolved] *Newsweek* 109:64 Ap 13 '87

AIDS patent dispute settled. D. M. Barnes. *Science* 236:17 Ap 3 '87

Yalta of AIDS [agreement between French and American researchers] *Time* 129:57 Ap 13 '87

Institute for Immunological Disorders

Houston facility wages a war against AIDS [work of D. G. Moreschi] E. Fudge. *Christ Today* 31:52+ Mr 6 '87

Institute for Independent Education

Escape to freedom [independent schools; address, March 6, 1987] J. D. Ratteray. *Vital Speeches Day* 53:497-8 Je 1 '87

Institute for Industrial Reconstruction (Italy) *See* Istituto per la Ricostruzione Industriale

Institute for Journalism Education

Group urges more minority managers in newsrooms. *Jet* 72:24 My 4 '87

Institute for the History of Ancient Civilizations (China)

The search for a common heritage through the study of ancient civilizations has become a truly international effort. R. M. Adams. il *Smithsonian* 18:10 D '87

Institute for the Study of Drug Dependence

Information on drug abuse. *World Health* p5 Je '87

Institute for the Translation of Hebrew Literature Ltd.

Out of Hebrew. il *Publ Wkly* 231:28-9 F 20 '87

Institute for Theoretical Physics (Minn.)

Minnesota establishes a new physics theory institute. W. Sweet. il *Phys Today* 40:99-100 F '87

Institute of Electrical and Electronics Engineers

Feerst in close call. J. Walsh. por *Science* 235:26 Ja 2 '87

Institute of Medicine (U.S.)

IOM elects new members. *Science* 236:1422 Je 12 '87

Institute of Nuclear Power Operations (U.S.)

Holes in the U.S. nuclear safety net. D. Utroska. bibl f il *Bull At Sci* 43:36-40 Jl/Ag '87

Institute on Religion and Democracy
Is there a link between Christianity and democracy? [interview with K. R. Hill] il por *Christ Today* 31:42 S 18 '87

Institutional investments
   See also
   Banks and banking—Trust departments
   Workout investments
The battle for corporate control [cover story] B. Nussbaum and J. H. Dobrzynski. il *Bus Week* p102-9 My 18 '87
The big portfolios. S. Lee. See issues of Forbes beginning July 2, 1984
The Forbes/TUCS institutional portfolio report. S. Kichen. il *Forbes* 139:156-7 F 23 '87
The Forbes/TUCS institutional portfolio report. S. Kichen. il *Forbes* 140:126-7 Ag 24 '87
The Forbes/TUCS institutional portfolio report. S. Kichen. il *Forbes* 139:251-2 My 18 '87
How top money managers do it [cover story] J. P. Newport, Jr. il *Fortune* 116:28-33+ Jl 20 '87
The markets: some 'heavy tinkering' ahead [inadequacy of market makers in coping with trading by large institutional investors] C. Welles. il *Bus Week* p40+ N 9 '87
Money managers after the crash. J. P. Newport, Jr. il *Fortune* 116:71-2 D 7 '87
Shareholders aren't just rolling over anymore. C. Power. il *Bus Week* p32-3 Ap 27 '87

Institutional Revolutionary Party (Mexico)
Continuity for Mexico [C. Salinas de Gortari] A. Landaburu. por *World Press Rev* 34:25 D '87
The fickle finger of a president [M. de la Madrid to pick successor] J. Contreras. il *Newsweek* 109:35 Ja 12 '87
For De la Madrid, it's almost like being reelected [hand picked heir C. Salinas de Gortari] S. Baker. il por *Bus Week* p78-9 O 19 '87
Let us now await the hidden one [possible PRI presidential candidates] J. Smolowe. il *Time* 129:34 Mr 23 '87
The machine and the tiger. M. Kondracke. *New Repub* 196:16-21 F 23 '87
Mexico chooses a new president [C. Salinas de Gortari] por *Newsweek* 110:52 O 12 '87
Mexico: the presidential problem. A. Aguilar Zinser. bibl f *Foreign Policy* 69:40-60 Wint '87/'88
Mexico's precarious balancing act. S. Baker and E. Weiner. il por *Bus Week* p54-5 S 14 '87
Mexico's race is on. P. Chapman. *World Press Rev* 34:45 Ja '87
A political split in Mexico [dissension in PRI over president's selection of candidate] J. Contreras. il *Newsweek* 110:32 Jl 6 '87
A professor's pupil makes good [P.R.I. candidate C. Salinas de Gortari] J. Smolowe. por *Time* 130:37 O 19 '87
Why De la Madrid's successor won't be another De la Madrid. S. Baker. por *Bus Week* p65 My 11 '87

Institutions, Financial *See* Financial institutions
Institutions, Nonprofit *See* Nonprofit institutions
Institutions, Research *See* Research institutions
Instruction *See* College teaching; Education; Teaching
Instruction sets (Computers)
   See also
   Reduced instruction set computers
Instruction set strategies [cover story; special section] il *Byte* 12:141-6+ Ap '87
Microcoded versus hard-wired control. P. Koopman. il *Byte* 12:235-42 Ja '87
Instructional media *See* Audio-visual instruction
Instructional technology *See* Educational technology
Instructors, College *See* College teachers
Instrument flying *See* Aviation—Instrument flying
Instrument panels
   See also
   Airplanes—Instrument panels
   Automobiles—Dashboards
Instrumental ensembles
   See also
   Cantata Singers and Ensemble
   Clarion Music Society
   Concert Royal
   Mannes Camerata
   New York Woodwind Quintet
   Parnassus (Instrumental ensemble)
   Speculum Musicae (Musical group)
Instrumental music
   See also
   Chamber music
   Guitar music
   Saxophone music

Instrumentation amplifiers *See* Amplifiers
Instruments
   See also
   Musical instruments
   Scientific equipment
Insulating materials *See* Insulation (Heat)
Insulating window film *See* Windows
Insulating window shades *See* Window shades
Insulation (Heat)
   See also
   Clothing, Cold weather
   Reflectors (Heat)
   Space vehicles—Insulation
   Space vehicles—Propulsion systems—Insulation
   Weatherproofing
Does your home need more insulation? il *Consum Res Mag* 70:17-21 D '87
Don't shingle on top of foam board. E. R. C. Capulong. *Pop Sci* 231:104 S '87
Insulate! R. Barnhart. il *Home Mech* 83:56-60+ Ja '87
Product reports 1988. il *Archit Rec* 175:51-3+ D '87
Re-roofing? Add insulation. K. L. Herrington. il *Pop Sci* 231:68-9 Ag '87
Winter prep. M. S. Dolan. *Consum Res Mag* 70:2 N '87
Insulation (Sound) *See* Soundproofing
Insulin
Fish oil prevents insulin resistance induced by high-fat feeding in rats. L. H. Storlien and others. bibl f il *Science* 237:885-8 Ag 21 '87
High-carb diets questioned [theory of Gerald Reaven] G. Kolata. *Science* 235:164 Ja 9 '87
Insulin rapidly increases diacylglycerol by activating de novo phosphatidic acid synthesis. R. V. Farese and others. bibl f il *Science* 236:586-9 My 1 '87
ras p21 as a potential mediator of insulin action in Xenopus oocytes. L. J. Korn and others. bibl f il *Science* 236:840-3 My 15 '87
Insulin-like growth factors *See* Somatomedins
Insulin receptors *See* Hormone receptors
Insull, Samuel, 1859-1938
        about
"Do it big, Sammy". P. Fuhrman. il pors *Forbes* 140:278-80 Jl 13 '87
Insults, Verbal *See* Invective
Insurance
   See also
   Information storage and retrieval systems—Insurance use
        Cancellation
When your time is up. P. D. Lawrence. il *Esquire* 108:80 N '87
        Laws and regulations
   See Insurance law
        Rates and tables
The hot air in "no-load" insurance. M. Brill. il *Changing Times* 41:89-92 Ap '87
Saving $500—the easy way. P. D. Lawrence. il *Esquire* 108:90 S '87
        Self insurance
        Accounting
The naked truth. L. Jereski. il *Forbes* 139:86+ My 18 '87
Insurance, Art
Liability insurance for artists. D. Grant. *Am Artist* 51:66-7 Jl '87
A policy for your Pollock. P. D. Lawrence. il *Esquire* 107:46 Ja '87
Insurance, Automobile
Car insurance: cut the cost of your coverage. M. C. Paulson. il *Changing Times* 41:59-62 My '87
Car insurance: is it ever smart not to file a claim? M. Daly. il *Better Homes Gard* 65:91+ S '87
Car insurance: picking the policy. M. C. Paulson. il *Changing Times* 41:62 F '87
Combined policies fizzle out. H. Porter. *Fam Handyman* 37:22+ F '87
Cracking down on a costly car-rental option [collision waivers] C. Brown. il *Bus Week* p135 N 30 '87
Cutting your car-insurance costs. A. Arnott. il *McCalls* 115:170 N '87
Facts about auto insurance. il *Consum Res Mag* 70:35-7 Jl '87
A freeze on insurance [Ontario auto insurance] S. Aikenhead. *Macleans* 100:14 My 4 '87
In a crash, bigger is better [report by the Highway Loss Data Institute] il *U S News World Rep* 103:106 S 28 '87
Insurance in the fast lane [luxury or sports cars] B. Kallen. il *Forbes* 139:276+ Ja 12 '87

Insurance, Automobile—*cont.*
Rental-car insurance: don't get taken for a ride. T. Segal. *Bus Week* p106 Ja 19 '87
The safest cars, the least costly cars [report by the Highway Loss Data Institute] il *Consum Res Mag* 70:14-17 N '87

Insurance, Aviation
Air fare arbitrage [cancellation insurance] M. Fritz. il *Forbes* 139:152 Mr 23 '87
For safety's sake: indemnify air traffic control manufacturers. R. H. Jones. *Aviat Week Space Technol* 127:11 Jl 20 '87
Insurance companies spur increase in pilot training. P. Proctor. *Aviat Week Space Technol* 126:82-3 My 4 '87
Wing ding [airplane rental insurance] P. Bradley. il *Flying* 114:10 Mr '87

Insurance, Bank account *See* Bank accounts—Insurance
Insurance, Casualty *See* Insurance, Property and casualty
Insurance, Certificates of deposit *See* Certificates of deposit—Insurance

Insurance, Computer
See also
SunGard Data Systems (Firm)

Insurance, Disability
Employer-sponsored long-term disability insurance. D. Hill. bibl f il *Mon Labor Rev* 110:16-22 Jl '87
The tangle of disability claims [D. McTaggart suing Crown Life for disability benefits] D. Francis. il *Macleans* 100:11 D 14 '87

Insurance, Drug *See* Insurance, Pharmaceutical services
Insurance, Employees' health *See* Insurance, Health

Insurance, Energy asset
Oilmen have a new way to cope with falling prices [energy asset insurance guarantees a price floor] T. Thompson. il *Bus Week* p74 Ag 3 '87

Insurance, Environmental impairment liability *See* Insurance, Pollution liability

Insurance, Fire
After the smoke clears. D. Moreau. il *Changing Times* 41:65-70 F '87

Insurance, Government liability
For safety's sake: indemnify air traffic control manufacturers. R. H. Jones. *Aviat Week Space Technol* 127:11 Jl 20 '87

Insurance, Health
See also
Civilian Health and Medical Program of the Uniformed Services
Health maintenance organizations
Insurance, Disability
Insurance, Mental health
Insurance, Nursing home care
Insurance, Pharmaceutical services
Kaiser-Permanente Medical Care Program
Medicare
Aging in America: wealth and the elderly. R. England. *Current* 294:26-9 Jl/Ag '87
AIDS: testing insurance. J. B. Quinn. il *Newsweek* 109:55 Je 8 '87
Are the elderly overinsured? [medigap insurance] A. R. Dennon. il *Consum Res Mag* 70:16-19 Mr '87
Beyond Medicare [catastrophic illness] il *Newsweek* 109:3 Ja 5 '87
A burden too heavy to bear [cost of AIDS] G. Bock. il *Time* 130:39 Ag 31 '87
Buying health care in the new era of medicine [address, April 28, 1987] E. W. Spencer. *Vital Speeches Day* 53:713-16 S 15 '87
Catastrophic costs and the poor [views of Leon Wyszewianski] *USA Today (Periodical)* 115:3 Ap '87
Catastrophic coverage. R. Coorsh. *Consum Res Mag* 70:4 D '87
Catastrophic health care may be flat on its back. S. B. Garland. *Bus Week* p45 Jl 13 '87
Catastrophic health insurance. *Congr Dig* 66:97-128 Ap '87
Catastrophic-illness insurance: not if, but when. M. A. Pollock and R. Fly. il *Bus Week* p46-7 Ja 12 '87
Catastrophic insurance for all. J. Hook. il *Wash Mon* 19:37-40 F '87
Checking up on your health insurance. M. Loeb. il *Saturday Evening Post* 259:30 Jl/Ag '87
A common-sense guide to health insurance. M. M. Hunt. il *N Y Times Mag* p46-50+ My 3 '87
Congress wakes up to Medicare reform [catastrophic care] C. Murphy. il *50 Plus* 27:26-9 Ap '87
The crisis in health benefits. S. B. Garland. il *Bus Week* p36 Je 15 '87
Dr. Bowen's catastrophic insurance is bad medicine. il *Consum Res Mag* 70:30-3 Je '87

Employer-sponsored health insurance for retirees: the need and the cost. *Mon Labor Rev* 110:38 My '87
Fighting back. K. Freifeld. il *Health* 19:78 Mr '87
The financial agony of long-term illness. A. McGrath. il *U S News World Rep* 102:53-5 F 9 '87
Health-care bandwagon gets rolling [catastrophic illness insurance] G. Borger. il *U S News World Rep* 102:22-3 Mr 2 '87
Health insurance: covering the bills. M. C. Paulson. il *Changing Times* 41:60 F '87
Health insurance loss: the case of the displaced worker. M. Podgursky and P. Swaim. bibl f il *Mon Labor Rev* 110:30-3 Ap '87
Here's how to cut your health insurance costs. *Success Farm* 85:52 N '87
Kennedy's health plan will pit business against business. S. B. Garland. il por *Bus Week* p62 My 25 '87
Mandatory insurance? [bill to provide workers with a minimum policy] R. Coorsh. *Consum Res Mag* 70:4 Jl '87
Medical care and pauperization. G. P. Brockway. *New Leader* 70:11-12 D 28 '87
National health insurance: an idea whose time has come back. R. Kuttner. il *Bus Week* p14 Ag 3 '87
No socialized medicine now [catastrophic illness legislation] J. McLaughlin. *Natl Rev* 39:24 S 11 '87
Packing a policy [proper medical coverage before going abroad] E. S. Orzac. *Travel Holiday* 167:32-3+ F '87
Paring insurance costs without paring benefits [employee benefits] P. Plawin. *Changing Times* 41:102-3 F '87
Peace of mind [catastrophic illness] *America* 156:185 Mr 7 '87
Preparing for the worst. M. Pollick. il *Nations Bus* 75:28+ O '87
Profiting from the medigap [TV ads for health insurance] G. P. Brockway. *New Leader* 70:11-12 Ap 20 '87
Reagan joins the catastrophic care bandwagon. A. McGrath. il *U S News World Rep* 102:8 F 23 '87
The real health care catastrophe: more than 30 million uninsured. V. Cahan. il *Bus Week* p29 F 9 '87
Risk and reality: the AIDS crisis and insurance [address, July 14, 1987] D. R. Ross. *Vital Speeches Day* 53:681-4 S 1 '87
An Rx for catastrophe [O. R. Bowen's proposal] O. Friedrich. il por *Time* 129:38-9 Ja 5 '87
Shopping for major medical. P. D. Lawrence. il *Esquire* 108:74 D '87
Sick about America's health care [interview with H. Hiatt] K. McAuliffe. por *U S News World Rep* 102:64 Je 15 '87
Sick retirees could kill your company. J. Nielsen. il *Fortune* 115:98-9 Mr 2 '87
The silent killer [accounting treatment of employee health benefits] L. Jereski. il *Forbes* 139:112 F 23 '87
The staggering price of AIDS. L. J. Lord. il *U S News World Rep* 102:16-18 Je 15 '87
Strong medicine for health bills [companies bargaining for better deals] S. Gannes. il *Fortune* 115:70-2+ Ap 13 '87
Taking the pulse of your health plan. C. E. Trunzo. il *Money* 16:137-8+ O '87
The threat of higher benefits costs. H. Bacas. il *Nations Bus* 75:32-4 Jl '87
Unfunded, nonregulated, miscalculated [retiree health benefits] C. Murphy. il *50 Plus* 27:14+ O '87
Unhealthy insurance [bill to require employers to buy health insurance for all workers and their families] *Natl Rev* 39:18 My 22 '87
What to do when health insurance won't pay. P. Godwin. bibl il *Better Homes Gard* 65:72+ N '87
What you need to know to protect your life's savings. P. Martin. bibl il *50 Plus* 27:32-40+ O '87
Women's health insurance: old problems, new programs [medical services for low income women] D. Lipson. *Ms* 15:24 Mr '87

Taxation
Health insurance: Democrats borrow a line from Reagan [treating Medicare benefits as taxable income] S. B. Garland. il *Bus Week* p43 My 4 '87
More benefits in store for part-timers. J. Bodnar. *Changing Times* 41:11 N '87

Canada
See also
Medicare—Canada

Insurance, Homeowners'
Are you covered if someone gets hurt at your house? M. Daly. il *Better Homes Gard* 65:85-6+ My '87
Combined policies fizzle out. H. Porter. *Fam Handyman* 37:22+ F '87
What coverage doesn't cover [special-form insurance] P. D. Lawrence. il *Esquire* 107:70 My '87

Insurance, Legal services *See* Prepaid legal services
Insurance, Liability

See also

Insurance, Automobile
Insurance, Aviation
Insurance, Government liability
Insurance, Homeowners'
Insurance, Malpractice liability
Insurance, Nuclear hazards
Insurance, Pollution liability
Insurance, Space flight

Architects' responsibility versus the liability crisis. *Archit Rec* 175:35+ Mr '87
The crisis is over—but insurance will never be the same. C. Farrell. il *Bus Week* p122-3 My 25 '87
How the insurance crisis will affect your summer vacation. M. Engel. il *Glamour* 85:48+ Jl '87
Injury litigation and liability insurance dynamics. P. W. Huber. bibl f il *Science* 238:31-6 O 2 '87
Lawsuit insurance. W. C. Banks. *Money* 16:70 O '87
Liability insurance and litigation [discussion of October 2, 1987 article, Injury litigation and liability insurance dynamics] P. W. Huber. *Science* 238:1635-7 D 18 '87
Liability insurance for artists. D. Grant. *Am Artist* 51:66-7 Jl '87
Liability insurance: is the time right for captives? [architects' needs] J. Trewhitt. il *Archit Rec* 175:47 Ag '87
Solving the liability crisis. B. Gatty. il *Nations Bus* 75:39-40+ Je '87

Canada
Judgment of liability [reversal of personal injury damage award in M. McErlean vs. Brampton, Ont.] R. Corelli. il por *Macleans* 100:52 O 12 '87

Insurance, Life

See also

Annuities

The death of universal life? [accounting standards] L. Jereski and T. Pouschine. il *Forbes* 139:96 Ap 6 '87
"Guaranteed" life insurance: who needs it? M. Rowland. il *50 Plus* 27:12+ N '87
The hot air in "no-load" insurance. M. Brill. il *Changing Times* 41:89-92 Ap '87
How much life insurance do you need? *Read Dig* 131:120-3 D '87
Insurance on simpler terms [term insurance information services] B. Kallen. il *Forbes* 140:108+ Ag 10 '87
Insurance that you can bank on now [single-premium variable life insurance] L. Wiener. il *U S News World Rep* 103:73 D 21 '87
Insure the parent, not the child, even when the policy is a college fund. R. A. Lynch. il *Money* 16:51 Ja '87
Investing in the dark [life insurance and interest rates] L. R. Walbert. *Forbes* 140:157 N 2 '87
Life insurance as an investment. D. M. Topolnicki. il *Good Housekeep* 205:266 S '87
Life insurance as investment. J. Anthony. *Consum Res Mag* 70:22-4 N '87
Life insurance: should your protection double as an investment? [special section] il *Money* 16:140-2+ Mr '87
Locking up safe returns in annuities or insurance. M. Harris. il *Money* 16:124-5 D '87
Low-cost life insurance: finding the best deals by phone. *Better Homes Gard* 65:52 N '87
A new policy on life [universal II] P. D. Lawrence. il *Esquire* 107:65 Mr '87
A new way to price term life [information services] *Money* 16:14 S '87
Policies so hot they almost sell themselves [single premium products] R. W. King. il *Bus Week* p172 D 28 '87-Ja 4 '88
Retirement for life [buying life insurance through a Keogh] P. D. Lawrence. il *Esquire* 108:46 Ag '87
Risk and reality: the AIDS crisis and insurance [address, July 14, 1987] D. R. Ross. *Vital Speeches Day* 53:681-4 S 1 '87
Switching your policy. T. Tilling. il *Parents* 62:62+ Mr '87
Tough new rules for life insurance [tests for AIDS in Canada] C. Wood. il *Macleans* 100:45 My 18 '87
Updating your life insurance. H. R. Kennedy. *U S News World Rep* 103:65 S 7 '87
What's under the rock? [high-yield insurance products financed with junk bonds] B. Kallen. il *Forbes* 139:134-5 F 23 '87

Policy loans
The insurance loan dilemma. L. R. Walbert. il *Forbes* 139:112 Je 29 '87

Taxation
Costly zeros [life insurance wrapped around Treasury zeros] B. Weberman. il *Forbes* 140:131 D 28 '87
Insurance: how tax reform makes it more appealing. B. Hitchings. il *Bus Week* p118-19 F 16 '87
The insurance loan dilemma. L. R. Walbert. il *Forbes* 139:112 Je 29 '87
Life after taxes. P. D. Lawrence. il *Esquire* 107:42 F '87
More benefits in store for part-timers. J. Bodnar. *Changing Times* 41:11 N '87
Of death and taxes [putting life insurance into an irrevocable trust] L. R. Walbert. il *Forbes* 140:460 Jl 13 '87
Tax reform adds luster to life insurance. L. A. Smith. il *Black Enterp* 17:93-4 Je '87
Your life as a tax shelter. R. Eisenberg. il *Money* 16:153-4+ Mr '87

Insurance, Malpractice liability
In Florida, everybody loses. R. Goudreau. *50 Plus* 27:18 S '87
Medicine today and tomorrow [address, April 13, 1987] J. Coury. *Vital Speeches Day* 53:621-4 Ag 1 '87
Insurance, Medical *See* Insurance, Health
Insurance, Mental health
Mental health benefits financed by employers. A. Blostin. bibl f il *Mon Labor Rev* 110:23-7 Jl '87
Insurance, Mortgage
FHA mortgages: pros and cons. T. Tilling. *Parents* 62:47-8 My '87
Insurance refund packaged in red tape [FHA mortgage insurance] H. Porter. il *Fam Handyman* 37:12 S '87
News on the home front. J. A. Conway. il *Forbes* 139:8 Je 1 '87
Why you need mortgage insurance. M. C. Thomsett. il *Home Mech* 83:70 Mr '87
Insurance, Motion picture
Lights! Camera! Completion bond! R. Grover. il por *Bus Week* p50 Ag 24 '87
Insurance, Motorcycle
Totalled or not: no easy answer [totalling vs. repairing Honda 600 Hurricane] T. Carrithers. il *Cycle* 38:47-9 N '87
Insurance, Municipal bond *See* Municipal bonds—Insurance
Insurance, Nuclear hazards
Price tag for Price-Anderson Act. K. Hartley. *Sci News* 132:70 Ag 1 '87
Insurance, Nursing home care
Easing the pain of nursing home bills. I. Pave. il *Bus Week* p142 My 4 '87
Insurance for long-term care. C. Schaeffer. il *Changing Times* 41:113-15+ Ja '87
Long-term care: a political time bomb. S. B. Garland and R. Fly. il *Bus Week* p40 N 30 '87
Nursing home insurance. R. Coorsh. il *Consum Res Mag* 70:4 N '87
Nursing home insurance. M. Daly. il *Better Homes Gard* 65:27-8 Mr '87
Nursing home insurance. C. Kitch. il *Good Housekeep* 204:207 F '87
What you need to know to protect your life's savings. P. Martin. bibl il *50 Plus* 27:32-40+ O '87
Insurance, Pharmaceutical services

See also

PCS, Inc.

The generic drug industry: an overview [address, October 8, 1987] M. Zeiger. *Vital Speeches Day* 54:142-7 D 15 '87
Insurance, Physicians' liability *See* Insurance, Malpractice liability
Insurance, Pollution liability
An asbestos decision that's hazardous to insurers' health [California court sticks them with $2 billion tab for claims] R. Brandt. *Bus Week* p33-4 Je 15 '87
Environmental impairment liability insurance [discussion of January/February 1987 article, Gridlock in environmental insurance: the failure of EIL coverage] H. Kunreuther. il *Environment* 29:2-3 My '87
Gridlock in environmental insurance: the failure of EIL coverage [environmental impairment liability] H. Kunreuther. bibl il *Environment* 29:18-20+ Ja/F '87
Life after death [after asbestos claims litigation scares off insurers, Acmat Corp. forms own company to write liability policies] B. Leonard. il por *Forbes* 139:132-3 My 4 '87
The toxic waste battle is boiling over [Westinghouse's court fight with insurers] M. Schroeder. il *Bus Week* p73-4 Ag 3 '87
Insurance, Prescription *See* Insurance, Pharmaceutical services

Insurance, Property and casualty
   See also
     Insurance, Automobile
     Insurance, Homeowners'
     Insurance, Motorcycle
   Insurers should get just what they need: a dull year.
   C. Farrell. *Bus Week* p109 Ja 12 '87
Insurance, Psychiatric *See* Insurance, Mental health
Insurance, Savings bank life *See* Savings banks—Insurance
Insurance, School
   The crisis in athletics. F. Roberts. *Parents* 62:50+ My
   '87
Insurance, Social *See* Social security
Insurance, Space flight
   Insurance companies defend higher pricing policy [satel-
   lites] *Aviat Week Space Technol* 127:61 S 7 '87
   McDonnell Douglas receives firm commercial Delta
   launch orders [Hughes Aircraft to purchase for launch
   of British Satellite Broadcasting spacecraft] *Aviat Week
   Space Technol* 127:24 Jl 20 '87
   Satellite owners reenter insurance market [communica-
   tions satellites] *Aviat Week Space Technol* 126:78-9
   Ja 26 '87
   Soviets will offer space launch insurance at competitive
   prices. *Aviat Week Space Technol* 127:138-9 S 28
   '87
Insurance, Trade waste disposal *See* Insurance, Pollution
   liability
Insurance, Travelers'
   Covering the globe-trotter. P. D. Lawrence. il *Esquire*
   108:88 O '87
   Hedging against a trip that goes awry. I. Pave. il *Bus
   Week* p117 Je 1 '87
   Insure to be sure. H. Gieseking. *Travel Holiday* 168:79-81
   Jl '87
   Travel injuries abroad—who's responsible? H. Gieseking.
   Travel Holiday 167:71-2 Je '87
   When you have to cancel. B. Bauer. il *U S News World
   Rep* 103:80-1 O 5 '87
   When you're on the go. P. D. Lawrence. il *Esquire*
   107:68 Ap '87
Insurance, Unemployment
   Changes in unemployment insurance legislation during
   1986. D. Runner. *Mon Labor Rev* 110:21-4 F '87
   Unemployment insurance data. See issues of Monthly
   Labor Review
   Unemployment pay may be denied jobless new moms
   [women on maternity leave who don't return] *Jet*
   71:25 Mr 23 '87
                  Canada
   Deciding on nothing. M. Clark. *Macleans* 100:14 My
   25 '87
Insurance, Weather
   Ready for a rainy day. il *Fortune* 116:12 O 12 '87
Insurance, Workers' compensation
   Workers' compensation: 1986 state enactments. L. C.
   Tinsley. il *Mon Labor Rev* 110:67-71 Ja '87
   The worsening ills of workers' comp. R. W. King. il
   Bus Week p46 O 12 '87
Insurance agents
   See also
     Assured Enterprises
Insurance brokers
   See also
     Alexander & Alexander Services Inc.
     Marsh & McLennan Cos. Inc.
Insurance companies
   See also
     20th Century Insurance Company
     American General Corp.
     Bankers Life & Casualty Co.
     Black insurance companies
     Equitable Life Assurance Society of the United States
     Fireman's Fund Insurance Company
     Leucadia National Corp.
     Metropolitan Life Insurance Co.
     Mutual Life Insurance Co. of New York
     Phoenix Mutual Life Insurance Co.
     Pre-Paid Legal Services, Inc.
     Prudential Insurance Co. of America
     Reliance Group Holdings, Inc.
     St. Paul Companies, Inc.
     Travelers Corp.
     United Coastal Insurance
     Universal Life Insurance Company
                Accounting
   The big easy [asset valuation] J. Andresky. il *Forbes*
   140:142 N 2 '87
   The death of universal life? L. Jereski and T. Pouschine.
   il *Forbes* 139:96 Ap 6 '87

Investing in the dark [life insurance and interest rates]
   L. R. Walbert. *Forbes* 140:157 N 2 '87
            Acquisitions and mergers
Fred Carr buys some insurance [ICH acquires greater
   share of First Executive Corp.] T. Carson. *Bus Week*
   p36 O 26 '87
St. Paul may be doing too well [Alleghany's stake] M.
   J. Pitzer. il *Bus Week* p41-2 D 21 '87
World's largest up & comer [Xerox's acquisition of Crum
   & Forster] H. Rudnitsky. il *Forbes* 139:78+ My 18
   '87
            International aspects
An insurer gets eyed from abroad [Farmers Group Inc.]
   G. G. Marcial. *Bus Week* p112 O 19 '87
            Advertising
Profiting from the medigap [TV ads for health insurance]
   G. P. Brockway. *New Leader* 70:11-12 Ap 20 '87
            Antitrust cases
Insurers warm up for an all-out brawl in Washington.
   P. Dwyer. *Bus Week* p49+ F 23 '87
            Captive companies
Liability insurance: is the time right for captives? [ar-
   chitects' needs] J. Trewhitt. il *Archit Rec* 175:47 Ag
   '87
            Finance
The crisis is over—but insurance will never be the
   same. C. Farrell. il *Bus Week* p122-3 My 25 '87
The damage is mounting in property and casualty. R.
   W. King. il *Bus Week* p32 Ag 10 '87
Insurance. J. R. Adams. il *Forbes* 139:154-5 Ja 12 '87
Insurers should get just what they need: a dull year
   [property and casualty industry] C. Farrell. *Bus Week*
   p109 Ja 12 '87
            History
Insuring a growing country. R. W. Vinson. il *Nations
   Bus* 75:89+ S '87
            Laws and regulations
   See Insurance law
            Management
Harold Hook's magnificent machine [American General]
   W. P. Barrett. il por *Forbes* 140:48+ O 19 '87
            Securities
Insurers that can tough it out. A. E. Serwer. il *Fortune*
   116:190 O 26 '87
Insurers that specialize in profits. A. E. Serwer. *Fortune*
   115:110 F 2 '87
Why 'big uglies' are beautiful to contrarians. C. Farrell.
   il *Bus Week* p110 Je 29 '87
            Taxation
Fresh-start blues [tax credit for property-casualty insurers]
   J. Andresky. il *Forbes* 140:212 D 14 '87
Standing firm on tax reform [Canada] M. Drohan. il
   Macleans 100:28 S 14 '87
            Canada
   See also
     Crown Life Insurance Co.
Standing firm on tax reform. M. Drohan. il *Macleans*
   100:28 S 14 '87
Tough new rules for life insurance [tests for AIDS]
   C. Wood. il *Macleans* 100:45 My 18 '87
            Great Britain
   See also
     Lloyd's of London
            Japan
   See also
     Asahi Mutual Life Insurance Company
     Nippon Life Insurance Co.
     Yasuda Fire & Marine Insurance Co. Ltd.
     Yasuda Mutual Life Insurance Company
Insurance crimes
Bill Graham reins in the creeps who kill horses for
   profit. D. Van Biema. il pors *People Wkly* 28:46-8
   Jl 20 '87
Cracking down on a costly car-rental option [collision
   waivers] C. Brown. il *Bus Week* p135 N 30 '87
Frenchy and the Persians [N. Sakhai and H. Mahboubian
   mastermind New York City theft of Near Eastern
   antiquities for insurance recovery] C. Trillin. *New
   Yorker* 63:44+ Je 29 '87
Insurance exchanges
   See also
     Lloyd's of London
Insurance holding companies
   See also
     Capital Holding Corp.
     Crum and Forster
     Farmers Group Inc.
     First Executive Corp.
     Foremost Corp. of America
     I.C.H. Corp.
     Monarch Capital Corp.

Insurance holding companies—See also—*cont.*
W. R. Berkley Corp.
Insurance Information Inc.
Insurance on simpler terms. B. Kallen. il *Forbes* 140:108+ Ag 10 '87
Insurance law
Damage control [Supreme Court to decide on damages awarded in suit against Bankers Life] D. Fanning. il *Forbes* 139:84 Je 29 '87
The damage is mounting in property and casualty. R. W. King. il *Bus Week* p32 Ag 10 '87
California
An asbestos decision that's hazardous to insurers' health [court sticks them with $2 billion tab for claims] R. Brandt. *Bus Week* p33-4 Je 15 '87
Canada
The tangle of disability claims [D. McTaggart suing Crown Life for disability benefits] D. Francis. il *Macleans* 100:11 D 14 '87
New York (State)
Insurance agents attack New York's savings bank life insurance. *Consum Rep* 52:331 Je '87
Ontario
A freeze on insurance [auto insurance] S. Aikenhead. *Macleans* 100:14 My 4 '87
Insurance premiums *See* Insurance—Rates and tables
Insurance rates *See* Insurance—Rates and tables
Insurance stocks *See* Insurance companies—Securities
Insurrections *See* Revolutions
Intan, Princess of Malaysia
about
The untold story of black ambassador who weds Asian princess. S. Booker. il pors *Jet* 73:12+ O 12 '87
Intangible assets
Taxation
Making intangibles real tax advantages. G. W. Padwe. il *Nations Bus* 75:86 My '87
Integrated amplifiers *See* Amplifiers
Integrated circuit testers *See* Testing equipment
Integrated circuits
See also
Charge coupled devices (Electronics)
Copyright—Integrated circuits
Josephson junctions
Logic circuits
Memory cards
Microprocessors
Microwave integrated circuits
Random access memory
Read only memory
Reduced instruction set computers
Surface mounting (Electronics)
Transistors
Chip nerves [reconnecting nerve fibers; work of Morton Grosser and Joseph M. Rosen] J. I. Mattill. il *Technol Rev* 90:15 O '87
Ciarcia's circuit cellar. S. Ciarcia. See issues of Byte
Controller chips add more zip to SCSI [small computer system interface] *Byte* 12:14 N '87
Fast times in silicon circuits. I. Peterson. il *Sci News* 132:20 Jl 11 '87
Good connections? It's in the chips [reconnecting nerve fibers; work of Joseph M. Rosen and Morton Grosser] D. D. Edwards. il *Sci News* 131:86 F 7 '87
How to design oscillator circuits (VII) [CMOS oscillators] J. J. Carr. il *Radio-Electron* 58:65-6+ Ja '87
Making mighty chips. il *Natl Geogr World* 139:12-17 Mr '87
Repair shop [reconnecting nerve fibers] O. Davies. il *Omni* 10:140 N '87
A simple CMOS oscillator. R. Grossblatt. il *Radio-Electron* 58:96 F '87
Solid state technology in the 21st century. B. L. Gregory. il *Radio-Electron* 58:97-8 My '87
Speeding to a gallium arsenide record. il *Sci News* 131:25 Ja 10 '87
Tone generator IC's. R. F. Scott. il *Radio-Electron* 58:80-1 Ap '87
VHSIC demonstrates significant benefits in performing signal processing functions [use in Flir imagery] *Aviat Week Space Technol* 127:98-9 S 7 '87
Defects
Butterfly catcher [gettering process for crystalline silicon] G. Greenwell. il *Sci Am* 257:28-9 S '87
Magic butterfly cleans up chips [gettering process for crystalline silicon] J. Raloff. il *Sci News* 132:55 Jl 25 '87
Design
A bang-bang IC [CMOS controller] R. F. Scott. il *Radio-Electron* 58:124-5 N '87

CAD for building chips: silicon compilers and the automated building of VLSI circuits. S. Trimberger and J. Rowson. il *Byte* 12:217-18+ Je '87
Chips for advanced computing. J. D. Meindl. il *Sci Am* 257:78-84+ O '87
Collective computation in neuronlike circuits. D. W. Tank and J. J. Hopfield. il *Sci Am* 257:104-8+ D '87
Computing with neural networks [discussion of August 8, 1986 article, Computing with neural circuits: a model] J. J. Hopfield and D. W. Tank. bibl f il *Science* 235:1226-9 Mr 6 '87
Do-it-yourself chips get easier [circuit design machines] O. Port. *Bus Week* p92 Mr 30 '87
The evolution of VHSIC. R. Grossblatt. il *Radio-Electron* 58:59-62 Mr '87
GE produces family of VHSIC-like operational chips for aerospace [very high speed integrated circuits] P. J. Klass. il *Aviat Week Space Technol* 126:88-9 Ja 26 '87
Mosaic Systems develops circuit board with electrically programmable network [wafer scale integration technique] il *Aviat Week Space Technol* 126:81 Ap 6 '87
Non-volatile memory IC's. R. Grossblatt. il *Radio-Electron* 58:60-3 O '87
Working with flip-flops. R. Marston. il *Radio-Electron* 58:64-9 Je '87
Energy usage
A battery backup for CMOS-based circuits. R. Grossblatt. il *Radio-Electron* 58:79 Ap '87
Manufacture
See Electronic industries
Prices
The truce in the chip war may be temporary [U.S.-Japan] J. W. Wilson. *Bus Week* p46-7 F 23 '87
Integrated circuits, Effect of radiation on
Travelling robot to work in radiation-hardened IC lab [Sandia National Laboratories] *Radio-Electron* 58:4 N '87
Integrated Genetics, Inc.
Biotech's bid to build a better mouse. R. Rhein, Jr. il *Bus Week* p102 N 9 '87
Integrated marketing *See* Marketing
Integrated optics
See also
Fiber optics
Optical data processing
Integrated pest management *See* Insect control
Integrated Resources, Inc.
Outflanked, outmaneuvered [Integrated Resources vs. Cohen Brothers Realty over 666 5th Ave., New York City] H. Rudnitsky. il *Forbes* 140:343-4 Jl 13 '87
Integrated services digital network
New developments in computer and communications technologies [address, March 31, 1987] J. S. Mayo. *Vital Speeches Day* 53:499-503 Je 1 '87
Integrated software *See* Computer programming
Integration in education *See* Colleges and universities—Desegregation; Public schools—Desegregation
Integrity
Integrity and trust [address, January 21, 1987] P. Dawkins. *Vital Speeches Day* 53:344-7 Mr 15 '87
Intel Corp.
Andrew Grove. J. W. Wilson. il por *Bus Week* Sp Issue:252 Ap 17 '87
Can Andy Grove practice what he preaches? J. W. Wilson. il por *Bus Week* p68-9 Mr 16 '87
Intel and Sequent kiss and make up [80386 microprocessors] J. W. Wilson. il *Bus Week* p120 My 25 '87
Intellect *See* Mind
Intellectual development of children *See* Children—Growth and development
Intellectual development of infants *See* Infants—Growth and development
Intellectual liberty
See also
Academic freedom
Censorship
Science, Freedom of
Intellectual property
Invisible property [bankruptcy proceedings and rights to intellectual property] D. Fanning. il *Forbes* 139:104 Mr 23 '87
Protecting against patent piracy. D. DeConcini. il *USA Today (Periodical)* 116:25-6 N '87
Sue 'em? Or love 'em? E. Dyson. il *Forbes* 140:307 S 7 '87
When the going gets tough, the tough go to court [chipmakers wage intellectual property battles] K. K. Wiegner. il *Forbes* 140:36-7 D 28 '87

Intellectuals and intellectual life
　See also
　　Boston (Mass.)—Intellectual life
　　China—Intellectual life
　　Israel—Intellectual life
　　Jews—Intellectual life
　　Key West (Fla.)—Intellectual life
　　London (England)—Intellectual life
　　New York (N.Y.)—Intellectual life
　　Paris (France)—Intellectual life
　　Poland—Intellectual life
　　Soviet Union—Intellectual life
　　United States—Intellectual life
The intellectual's dilemma in the modern world. R. Bendix. *Society* 25:63-4+ N/D '87

History
　See also
　　Bloomsbury group
　　　Bibliography
Paperback history [twelfth and thirteenth centuries] H. Lawrence. *Hist Today* 37:57 Mr '87

Intelligence
　See also
　　Age and intelligence
　　Intelligence tests
　　Mind
Bright, average, or slow? N. S. Schwartzberg. il *Parents* 62:106-8+ My '87
Bright people not always good leaders [views of Fred Fielder] *USA Today (Periodical)* 116:12 D '87
Early signs of school age IQ. G. Kolata. il *Science* 236:774-5 My 15 '87
Making kids smarter. L. J. Greene. il *Parents* 62:94-8+ D '87
The prejudice of height [link between intelligence and height in children; research by Darrell Wilson] S. Vandershaf. *Psychol Today* 21:14 Mr '87

Blacks
Battling the IQ-test ban [M. Amaya contests California ruling that bars black students from taking IQ tests] J. N. Baker. il por *Newsweek* 110:53 Jl 27 '87
Intelligence, Animal *See* Animal intelligence
Intelligence, Artificial *See* Artificial intelligence
Intelligence, Business *See* Business intelligence
Intelligence, Military *See* Military intelligence
Intelligence, Select Committee on *See* United States. Congress. House. Select Committee on Intelligence
Intelligence quotient *See* Intelligence tests
Intelligence service
　See also
　　United States. Army. Counter Intelligence Corps
　　United States. Central Intelligence Agency
　　United States. Defense Intelligence Agency
　　United States. Federal Bureau of Investigation
　　United States. Naval Security and Investigative Command
　　United States. President's Foreign Intelligence Advisory Board
Echoes of Watergate [break-ins and surveillance campaign against critics of U.S. Central American policy] B. Levin. il *Macleans* 100:22+ F 16 '87
The national security bureaucracy [address, February 6, 1987] J. F. Sieberling. *Vital Speeches Day* 53:362-5 Ap 1 '87
The real cause of Irangate. K. E. Sharpe. bibl f *Foreign Policy* 68:19-41 Fall '87
Reforming U.S. intelligence. A. E. Goodman. bibl f *Foreign Policy* 67:121-36 Summ '87
Terrorism and intelligence [address, May 26, 1987] L. P. Bremer, III. *Vital Speeches Day* 53:578-81 Jl 15 '87

Canada
　See also
　　Canadian Security Intelligence Service
　　Royal Canadian Mounted Police

Cuba
Spilled beans [defection of Cuban intelligence chief F. Aspillaga Lombard] K. M. Pierce. il *Time* 130:17 Ag 24 '87

France
　See also
　　Greenpeace bombing incident, 1985
Down among the backwoodsmen. R. Alan. *New Leader* 70:8-9 O 5 '87

Great Britain
Britain: tinker, tailor, censor, spy [government's press ban on ex-agent P. Wright's memoirs] J. N. Baker. il *Newsweek* 110:32 Ag 17 '87

British official suggests ousting Viking board to stop 'Spycatcher' [effort to prevent U.S. publication of book by P. Wright] V. Menkes. *Publ Wkly* 232:311 Ag 7 '87
Down among the backwoodsmen. R. Alan. *New Leader* 70:8-9 O 5 '87
Former British P.M. Harold Wilson is unimpressed by claims that the CIA sought his downfall. F. Hauptfuhrer. il pors *People Wkly* 28:91-2+ D 21 '87
How not to silence a spy [furor over P. Wright's Spycatcher] L. Zuckerman. il *Time* 130:55 Ag 17 '87
Mining the spy world. R. Alan. il *New Leader* 70:9-11 N 16 '87
Minority report [P. Wright's Spycatcher] C. Hitchens. *Nation* 245:223 S 12 '87
Spooked [controversy surrounding publication of Spycatcher by P. Wright] M. Hosenball. *New Repub* 197:13-14 Ag 31 '87
The 'Spycatcher' secrets [excerpt] P. Wright. il por *Macleans* 100:38-40 Ag 3 '87
A tale of treachery [Britain's futile efforts to suppress publication of P. Wright's Spycatcher] M. McIver. por *Macleans* 100:42-3 Jl 27 '87
Tales of a spy writer [excerpts from P. Wright's controversial book Spycatcher printed in British press despite government ban] M. McIver. il por *Macleans* 100:52 My 11 '87

Israel
　See also
　　Israel. Mossad
　United States
　See Intelligence service
Intelligence tests
　See also
　　Aptitude tests
Battling the IQ-test ban [M. Amaya contests California ruling that bars black students from taking IQ tests] J. N. Baker. il por *Newsweek* 110:53 Jl 27 '87
Brainstorms [IQ tests as job performance predictor; findings reported in the Journal of vocational behavior] D. Seligman. *Fortune* 116:206+ Ag 3 '87
Getting smart about IQ. A. Levine. il *U S News World Rep* 103:53-5 N 23 '87
Good grades for day-care [IQ tests and infant-mother bond; studies by Margaret Burchinal] R. J. Moss. il *Psychol Today* 21:20 F '87
IQ's generation gap. B. Bower. *Sci News* 132:108-9 Ag 15 '87
Older and wiser? [Everyday Problem-Solving Inventory intelligence test; research by Steven W. Cornelius and Avshalom Caspi] A. H. Rosenfeld. *Psychol Today* 21:20 N '87
There's more to success than IQ. J. Segal and Z. Segal. il *Parents* 62:118 Ja '87
Intelsat *See* International Telecommunications Satellite Organization
Intelsat satellites *See* Communications satellites
Intensive care units
Critical care nurses. S. Wilding. il *Good Housekeep* 204:136+ My '87
Inter-City Gas Corp.
Heating up the gas wars [Manitoba purchases supply network belonging to Inter-City Gas Corp.] D. Smith. il *Macleans* 100:37 Je 22 '87
Inter-Varsity Christian Fellowship
A call to transform the marketplace [conference called Marketplace '86] L. Lau. *Christ Today* 31:41+ F 6 '87
Gordon MacDonald leaves the helm of InterVarsity. il por *Christ Today* 31:38-9 Jl 10 '87
Mission possible [Urbana student missionary conferences] H. Smith. *Christ Today* 31:15 D 11 '87
Interactive computer periodicals
Magazine on floppy disk [New Aladdin] il *Futurist* 21:48 Jl/Ag '87
Interactive computer systems
Interfaces for advanced computing [cover story] J. D. Foley. bibl (p183-4) il *Sci Am* 257:126-30+ O '87
The potential for interactive technology. A. M. Bork. *Byte* 12:201-2+ F '87
Interactive fiction *See* Computer novels
Interactive toys *See* Toys
Interactive video
Business use
Videos are starring in more and more training programs. R. Neff. il *Bus Week* p108-10 S 7 '87
Educational use
How children learn words. G. A. Miller and P. M. Gildea. il *Sci Am* 257:94-9 S '87

Interactive video—*cont.*
Retail trade use
Birth of a salesman: how video is revving up retailing. L. Therrien. il *Bus Week* p109 S 7 '87
Intercalation compounds
Graphite intercalation compounds [Japanese research] H. Kamimura. bibl il *Phys Today* 40:64-71 D '87
Intercellular junctions *See* Junctions (Physiology)
Interchangeable mechanisms
Eli Whitney's other talent [myth of invention of interchangeable parts] P. Baida. il *Am Herit* 38:22-3 My/Je '87
Intercollegiate athletics *See* College athletics
Intercom systems
Nine-station intercom. D. Morrison. il *Radio-Electron* 58:57-60 Ja '87
Retrofitting the sixties: rethinking your intercom system. R. Long. il *Theatre Crafts* 21:84-7 D '87
Talk is cheap [PS Engineering's Aerocom] M. Phelps. il *Flying* 114:98 Ap '87
Intercoms *See* Intercom systems
Intercontinental ballistic missiles *See* Guided missiles
Intercourse, Sexual *See* Sexual behavior
Intercristo (Organization)
Suit challenges Christian employment service practices. R. Frame. *Christ Today* 31:48 Ap 3 '87
Intercropping *See* Companion crops
Intercultural education
Family differences. D. F. Bjorklund and B. Bjorklund. il *Parents* 62:198 Ag '87
What is an American education? R. Rodriguez. *Des Arts Educ* 89:44-6 N/D '87
Intercultural marriage *See* Interracial marriage
Intercultural research
Faces of emotion: social or innate? [research by Ross Buck and Wan-Cheng Teng] B. Bower. *Sci News* 132:150 S 5 '87
Just married—but will it last? [anthropologist Helen Fisher's cross cultural study] K. McAuliffe. il *U S News World Rep* 102:68-9 Je 8 '87
The search for a common heritage through the study of ancient civilizations has become a truly international effort. R. M. Adams. il *Smithsonian* 18:10 D '87
Teaching selflessness in a selfish society. T. J. Lasley. bibl f il *Phi Delta Kappan* 68:674-8 My '87
Interdependence *See* Dependency (Psychology)
Interdisciplinary studies *See* Correlation (Education)
Interest (Economics)
See also
Bank accounts—Interest (Economics)
Credit cards—Interest (Economics)
Federal Reserve System (U.S.)
Interest rate futures
Investments
Mortgages
Act I at Alan Greenspan's Fed [increase in discount rate] por *Newsweek* 110:56 S 14 '87
Back in sync? [Treasury bond yields and price-earnings ratios] E. A. Finn, Jr. *Forbes* 140:34-5 N 16 '87
A bad case of nerves [April's market jolts] S. Bartlett. il *Bus Week* p30-2 Ap 27 '87
The bears aren't in charge—yet. G. Weiss and J. M. Laderman. il *Bus Week* p109 Je 1 '87
Borrowing: better deals for banks' best customers. il *Money* 16:28 D '87
Borrowing: high rates are getting still higher. il *Money* 16:30 O '87
Borrowing: rates are so high there's no place to go up. il *Money* 16:30 Jl '87
Borrowing: some rates drop as the public shifts to equity loans. il *Money* 16:41 Je '87
The bull market takes a hit [effect of rising rates] J. M. Laderman. il *Bus Week* p143 S 14 '87
The Bundesbank edges closer to a rate cut. J. Templeman. il *Bus Week* p59 Je 1 '87
The Bundesbank's hardliner has a change of heart [H. Schlesinger willing to cut interest rates] B. Riemer. il por *Bus Week* p32 D 14 '87
A case of bottom-line blues [banks raise the prime rate and reclassify loans to Brazil as nonperforming] B. Rudolph. il *Time* 129:63 Ap 13 '87
Construction-economy update: rising interest rates won't help the short-term outlook. G. A. Christie. il *Archit Rec* 175:37+ S '87
Coping with the markets [April jitters] B. Powell. il *Newsweek* 109:54 Ap 27 '87
A crash diet for an overweight economy [Bank of England hikes interest rates] R. A. Melcher. il *Bus Week* p34-5 Ag 24 '87
Equilibrium ahead for interest rates. T. May, Jr. il *Fortune* 115:63+ Mr 30 '87

Expecting the Fed to ease? Don't hold your breath. B. Reimer. il *Bus Week* p30 F 16 '87
The Fed sees trouble if the deficits diverge. K. Pennar. il *Bus Week* p80 Mr 30 '87
Guarding against a 24% decline. M. Sivy. il *Money* 16:51-2 Jl '87
The higher and higher cost of borrowing. R. H. Bork, Jr. il *U S News World Rep* 102:57-8 My 18 '87
Higher interest rates: just what a bloated deficit doesn't need. G. Koretz. il *Bus Week* p18 Jl 6 '87
How the bond market is forcing the Fed's hand. S. Bartlett. il *Bus Week* p42 My 11 '87
In Japan we (must) trust [Japanese investments in U.S. Treasuries affect interest rates] E. A. Finn, Jr. il *Forbes* 140:32-4 S 21 '87
Interest rates are calling the tune for the economy. W. B. Franklin and J. C. Cooper. *Bus Week* p27 Jl 13 '87
Interest rates: edging down. T. May, Jr. il *Fortune* 116:47+ D 7 '87
Interest rates have nowhere to go but up. S. Bartlett. il *Bus Week* p142-3 S 14 '87
Interest rates—the deceptive calm. H. Banks. *Forbes* 140:27 O 5 '87
Investing in the dark [life insurance and interest rates] L. R. Walbert. *Forbes* 140:157 N 2 '87
An investor the U.S. can't afford to lose [Japan in Treasury bond market] W. Glasgall. il *Bus Week* p32 My 4 '87
A jolt from the banks [higher prime rate] B. Riemer. il *Bus Week* p32-3 Ap 13 '87
Long-term rates are on the march. J. C. Cooper. il *Bus Week* p33-4 O 12 '87
Mr. Volcker: higher interest is the last thing we need. A. S. Blinder. il *Bus Week* p30 Je 1 '87
An optimist with a different twist [interview with D. A. Levine] G. Slutsker. il por *Forbes* 139:54+ My 18 '87
The rate shift that's handcuffing the Fed [views of Mickey D. Levy] G. Koretz. il *Bus Week* p16 Ap 20 '87
Riding the rate curve [Provident National Bank] B. Weberman. il *Forbes* 140 Sp Issue:395 O 26 '87
Rising interest rates dim economic prospects. P. E. Kidd. il *Archit Rec* 175:43 Je '87
Slump in dollar's value clouds interest-rate outlook. P. E. Kidd. il *Archit Rec* 175:41 Mr '87
Stop procrastinating on interest rates. H. Banks. *Forbes* 139:27 F 9 '87
A storm in the markets. il *Macleans* 100:28-9 Ap 13 '87
A time to stay calm. H. Banks. il *Forbes* 139:29+ Je 1 '87
Time to tighten. *Natl Rev* 39:15-16 Je 5 '87
Two messages Washington should send to the world [raising the discount rate and meaningful deficit reduction] H. Gleckman and B. Riemer. il *Bus Week* p45 My 11 '87
Ways to dodge those interest-rate swings. il *Changing Times* 41:65 D '87
Weaving a dollar crisis out of whole cloth [weak dollar] P. C. Roberts. il *Bus Week* p31 F 23 '87
What interest rates mean to consumers. J. Malveaux. il *Essence* 18:120 S '87
Which way for rates? J. C. Szabo. il *Nations Bus* 75:10 Je '87
Why higher rates won't clobber consumer spending. G. Koretz. il *Bus Week* p17 S 7 '87
Why steeper interest rates won't stunt growth. B. Riemer. il *Bus Week* p48 My 18 '87
Will tighter money really help? Nudging up rates may not be enough to stem inflation fears. M. McNamee. il *Bus Week* p28-9 S 21 '87
Taxation
Deduction canceled for lack of interest. G. W. Padwe. il *Nations Bus* 75:88 O '87
How to get Americans to sock away a bit more. B. Nussbaum. il *Bus Week* p86 Ap 13 '87
Paperwork burden grows. *Nations Bus* 75:102-3 S '87
When tax reform clobbers small business [interest rates may soar on industrial development bond loans] L. Helm. il *Bus Week* p41 My 4 '87
Interest groups *See* Special interest groups
Interest rate futures
A make-or-break move into financial futures [Geldermann Inc.] J. N. Frank. il por *Bus Week* p114 F 23 '87
The wave of the futures may be good ol' commodities. M. E. Kreca. il *Bus Week* p164+ D 28 '87-Ja 4 '88
Interest rate options
How the spike in interest rates snagged First Boston [Treasury bond options] D. Zigas. *Bus Week* p30-1 Je 29 '87

Interest rate options—*cont.*
How to hedge against rising mortgage rates. J. N. Frank. *Bus Week* p142 My 4 '87
Interest rates *See* Interest (Economics)
Interfaces
Probing interfaces involving liquids. A. L. Robinson. *Science* 236:150-1 Ap 10 '87
Interfaces (Computers) *See* Computers—Input-output equipment
Interfaith marriage
The December dilemma [gentile-Jewish marriages face Christmas and Hanukkah] B. Kantrowitz. il *Newsweek* 110:56 D 28 '87
Interference (Light)
Interference patterns on garage door windows. C. F. Bohren. il *Weatherwise* 40:266-70 O '87
Interference (Radar) *See* Radar interference
Interference (Radio) *See* Radio interference
Interferometers and interferometry
Army's R&D plan stresses development of passive interferometry detectors. *Aviat Week Space Technol* 126:113 F 9 '87
Astrometric interferometer successful. *Sci News* 131:345 My 30 '87
Astronomers seek high resolution. P. H. Andersen. bibl f il *Phys Today* 40:19-23 Je '87
At the diffraction limit [use of speckle interferometry with the Multiple Mirror Telescope] il *Sky Telesc* 74:236 S '87
Centennial of the Michelson-Morley experiment [cover story; special issue] bibl f il pors *Phys Today* 40:23-30+ My '87
Direct measurements confirm plate tectonics [very long baseline interferometry] R. A. Kerr. il *Science* 236:1425-6 Je 12 '87
Families of giant stars [use of speckle interferometry] *Sky Telesc* 73:25-6 Ja '87
The Fourier tachometer. il *Sky Telesc* 74:476 N '87
Infrared telescopes take to the road [Berkeley mobile infrared interferometer] il *Sky Telesc* 74:575-6 D '87
Interferometer measures angular diameter of Sirius [amplitude technique used by John Davis and William J. Tango] *Astronomy* 15:78-9 F '87
More than just a spot: facing an asteroid at last [speckle interferometer images of Vesta; work of Jack Drummond and others] J. Eberhart. il *Sci News* 132:343 N 28 '87
Speckled Vesta [use of speckle interferometer] il *Sky Telesc* 73:598 Je '87
Taking the measure of the stars [optical interferometry] D. E. Thomsen. *Sci News* 131:10-11 Ja 3 '87
Interferon
Human β_2 interferon and B-cell differentiation factor BSF-2 are identical. P. B. Sehgal and others. bibl f *Science* 235:731-2 F 13 '87
Interferon-γ and B cell stimulatory factor-1 reciprocally regulate Ig isotype production. C. M. Snapper and W. E. Paul. bibl f il *Science* 236:944-7 My 22 '87
One patient's experience with interferon [interview with M. Fow] R. W. Miller. por *FDA Consum* 21:11 Ap '87
Recombinant interferon enhances monoclonal antibody-targeting of carcinoma lesions in vivo. J. W. Greiner and others. bibl f il *Science* 235:895-8 F 20 '87
Intergalactic clouds *See* Matter, Interstellar
Intergalactic flight *See* Space flight
Intergovernmental Committee on Science and Technology for Development *See* United Nations. Intergovernmental Committee on Science and Technology for Development
Intergovernmental fiscal relations
See also
Grants-in-aid
Intergovernmental tax relations
National change and the regional conundrum. B. L. Weinstein and H. T. Gross. *Society* 25:55-61 N/D '87
Intergovernmental tax relations
Watch out for 'little brother' [federal-state cooperation in tax collection] L. Wiener. il *U S News World Rep* 103:47 Jl 27 '87
Interior decoration
See also
Apartments
Apartments, Remodeled
Art in the home
Boat decoration
Feng shui
G N Associates
Hotel decoration
House decoration

Office decoration
Restaurant decoration
Store decoration
Design. M. Bethany. See issues of New York beginning February 20, 1984
Individualist interiors [work of A. Buchsbaum] M. Filler. il por *House Gard* 159:64+ Mr '87
What works: priceless tips from the super-decorators [cover story] M. Bethany. il *N Y* 20:36-58+ Ap 13 '87
What's modern now [cover story] M. Bethany. il *N Y* 20:48-73 S 28 '87
Awards
House & Garden Design Awards [special section] il *House Gard* 159:140-61+ O '87
Record Interiors 1987 [cover story; special issue; with introd. by Charles K. Gandee] il *Archit Rec* 175:83-161 mid-S '87
Exhibitions
See also
West Week
Interior decorators
See also
Axelrod, Joan
Bennison, Geoffrey
Blomstedt, Kaisa
Buatta, Mario, 1935-
Cataffo, Louis
Cleaver, Chester
Crosetti, Ronald
Denning, Robert
Designer Referral Service, Inc.
Deskey, Donald
Doboujinsky, Rostislav
D'Urso, Joe, 1943-
Dwork, Melvin
Ertegun, Mica
Fourcade, Vincent
Hicks, David, 1929-
Hodgins, William
Laurance, David
Lewis, Sally Sirkin
London, Mimi
Machado, Anthony
Marino, Peter
Molyneux, Juan Pablo
Mongiardino, Renzo
Naggar, Patrick
Neas, Richard Lowell
Parish, Sister
Pfister, Charles, 1940-
Pierrepont, Nancy
Pinto Coelho, Duarte
Saladino, John
Scull, Sudi
Spectre, Jay
Stefanidis, John
Taylor, Michael
Choosing and using an interior designer: more than a matter of style. S. Ballen. il *Money* 16:221 D '87
Chain and franchise operations
Sprucing up with decorating franchises. D. Shipley. il *Nations Bus* 75:40-1 Ag '87
Vanguards of design, '80s-style [decorators operating out of minivans] M. Smilgis. il *Time* 130:88 O 5 '87
Interior Dept. (U.S.) *See* United States. Dept. of the Interior
Interior designers *See* Interior decorators
Interiors, Photography of *See* Photography—Interiors
Interiors in art *See* Rooms in art
Interleaf Inc.
Desktop publishing challenges. R. A. Shaffer. il *Pers Comput* 11:59 D '87
Interleukin
The anticancer company expands [Biotherapeutics] G. Bylinsky. il *Fortune* 116:121+ N 23 '87
Betting that Cetus will soar again. G. G. Marcial. il *Bus Week* p117 Ja 12 '87
Cancer M.D.'s clash over interleukin therapy [work of Steven A. Rosenberg] M. Bloom. il por *Science* 235:154-5 Ja 9 '87
Corticotropin-releasing factor-producing neurons in the rat activated by interleukin-1. F. Berkenbosch and others. bibl f il *Science* 238:524-6 O 23 '87
Downregulation of L3T4+ cytotoxic T lymphocytes by interleukin-2. C. C.-Y. Shih and R. L. Truitt. bibl f il *Science* 238:344-7 O 16 '87
The end of the beginning? [adoptive immunotherapy] D. Thompson. il *Time* 129:59 Ap 20 '87
The IL-2 receptor β chain (p70): role in mediating signals for LAK, NK, and proliferative activities. J. P. Siegel and others. bibl f il *Science* 238:75-8 O 2 '87

Interleukin—*cont.*

Interferon-γ and B cell stimulatory factor-1 reciprocally regulate Ig isotype production. C. M. Snapper and W. E. Paul. bibl f il *Science* 236:944-7 My 22 '87

Interleukin-1 stimulates the secretion of hypothalamic corticotropin-releasing factor. R. M. Sapolsky and others. bibl f il *Science* 238:522-4 O 23 '87

Interleukin-1's secret message to ACTH. D. D. Edwards. *Sci News* 132:277 O 31 '87

Interleukin-2: an encouraging study [cancer immunotherapy] por *Newsweek* 109:74 Ap 20 '87

Lyme disease. G. S. Habicht and others. bibl (p116) il map *Sci Am* 257:78-83 Jl '87

Psychiatric side-effects of interleukin-2 [research by Kirk D. Denicoff and others] R. Weiss. *Sci News* 132:196 S 26 '87

The regulation of ACTH secretion by IL-1. M. D. Lumpkin. bibl f *Science* 238:452-4 O 23 '87

Release of multiple hormones by a direct action of interleukin-1 on pituitary cells. E. W. Bernton and others. bibl f il *Science* 238:519-21 O 23 '87

Three-dimensional structure of interleukin-2. B. J. Brandhuber and others. bibl f il *Science* 238:1707-9 D 18 '87

Interlochen Center for the Arts

Camp for creativity. L. Rubinstein. *Horizon* 30:48 Je '87

Intermarriage *See* Interfaith marriage

Intermarriage, Racial *See* Interracial marriage

Intermediate Nuclear Force reduction *See* Disarmament

Intermedics Inc.

A revived Intermedics has some unexpected fans. J. E. Davis. il por *Bus Week* p120 Ap 27 '87

Intermodal transportation

If it isn't profitable, don't do it [CSX Corp. strategy] J. Cook. il por *Forbes* 140:54+ N 30 '87

Internal auditing *See* Auditing—Internal control

Internal migration *See* Migration, Internal

Internal Revenue Service (U.S.) *See* United States. Internal Revenue Service

Internal security

See also

Anti-Communist movements

United States. Congress. House. Committee on Un-American Activities

United States. Federal Bureau of Investigation

United States. Readiness Command

The national security bureaucracy [address, February 6, 1987] J. F. Sieberling. *Vital Speeches Day* 53:362-5 Ap 1 '87

The real cause of Irangate. K. E. Sharpe. bibl f *Foreign Policy* 68:19-41 Fall '87

Secret government. E. Knoll. *Progressive* 51:4 S '87

Why the First Amendment is not incompatible with national security interests [address, January 14, 1987] M. L. Feldman. *Vital Speeches Day* 53:394-8 Ap 15 '87

Why the secrets slip out [cover story] M. Satchell. il *U S News World Rep* 102:20-2 Je 1 '87

Soviet Union

See also

KGB

InterNation (Consortium)

What is InterNation? *Nation* 244:751+ Je 6 '87

International Aero Engines

Airbus expecting delivery delays for A320s powered by V2500 engine. J. M. Lenorovitz. *Aviat Week Space Technol* 127:32-3 D 14 '87

Airbus Industrie to offer International Aero Engines SuperFan on proposed A340. J. M. Lenorovitz. *Aviat Week Space Technol* 126:33 Ja 5 '87

Boeing will consider alternative to unducted fan for twin-aisle 7J7 [IAE V2500 SuperFan] R. G. O'Lone. il *Aviat Week Space Technol* 126:31-2 Ja 26 '87

Engine makers examine IAE to avoid pitfalls in collaborative efforts [V2500 SuperFan development problems] S. W. Kandebo. *Aviat Week Space Technol* 126:245-6 Je 15 '87

IAE board cancels development of V2500 SuperFan version; International Aero Engines' decision on V2500 SuperFan raises questions, controversy. D. A. Brown. *Aviat Week Space Technol* 126:34-6 Ap 13 '87

IAE delays V2500 certification to develop new components. *Aviat Week Space Technol* 126:31 My 25 '87

IAE V2500 engine enters critical development period. S. W. Kandebo. il *Aviat Week Space Technol* 127:33-4 D 14 '87

International Aero Engines seeks solutions to V2500 development problems; IAE details V2500 turbofan test program. S. W. Kandebo. il *Aviat Week Space Technol* 126:88-9 Ap 13 '87

Japanese study partners' sales, support techniques. *Aviat Week Space Technol* 127:49-50 S 21 '87

Lufthansa delays decision on retaining IAE V2500. il *Aviat Week Space Technol* 127:36 N 9 '87

Lufthansa reevaluates V2500 as powerplant for A320 fleet. *Aviat Week Space Technol* 126:30 My 25 '87

Pratt & Whitney expands role in V2500 compressor work; Rolls-Royce retains lead in IAE V2500 cold-section development. *Aviat Week Space Technol* 126:32-3 Mr 16 '87

Why Pratt & Whitney is sputtering. R. W. King and F. J. Comes. il *Bus Week* p24 Ap 20 '87

International Air Transport Association

Competitive airline market spurs IATA to develop new services. C. A. Shifrin. *Aviat Week Space Technol* 127:45-6 N 16 '87

IATA faults fee increases, new restrictions on noise. C. A. Shifrin. *Aviat Week Space Technol* 127:37 N 2 '87

International Alliance of Theatrical Stage Employees and Moving Picture Machine Operators of the U.S. and Canada

Union shopping. A. B. Block. il *Forbes* 139:106+ Je 15 '87

International American Homes Inc.

Looking to build an empire—again [R. H. Winnerman] S. Benway. il por *Bus Week* p114 Jl 20 '87

International Association of Crime Writers

Crime: a new East-West dialogue [meeting in Yalta] L. See. il *Publ Wkly* 232:25 O 16 '87

My week with Oleg 1: writers, detectives and the caviar Mafia [executive committee meeting] R. L. Simon. il *N Y Times Book Rev* 92:11 S 13 '87

International Association of Machinists and Aerospace Workers

Air Canada resumes flights after reaching pact with union. *Aviat Week Space Technol* 127:38 D 21 '87

Grounding Air Canada [strike] C. Barrett. il *Macleans* 100:15 D 7 '87

It's that time at Eastern. P. Engardio. il *Bus Week* p33 F 2 '87

Judge blocks transfer of Eastern workers. *Aviat Week Space Technol* 127:31 Jl 13 '87

Northwest suit charges nine with organizing job slowdown. *Aviat Week Space Technol* 127:34 S 21 '87

Not-so-friendly skies [Air Canada strike] D. Jenish. il *Macleans* 100:31 D 21 '87

Returning to the air [Air Canada strike ends] L. Van Dusen. il *Macleans* 100:49 D 28 '87

Standing up to Carl Icahn. C. Friday and J. Schwartz. il *Newsweek* 109:54 Ap 13 '87

Strike forces Air Canada to halt flight operations. *Aviat Week Space Technol* 127:35 D 7 '87

Union vote ends General Dynamics strike. *Aviat Week Space Technol* 127:29 Ag 17 '87

Why Eastern is backing off from a union showdown. P. Engardio. il *Bus Week* p108-9 O 12 '87

International Astronautical Federation

British refusal to boost space funding threatens European Space Agency unity. *Aviat Week Space Technol* 127:26-7 O 19 '87

Letter from Brighton. W. H. Ganoe. il *Space World* X-12-288:21-6 D '87

Report from the IAF. F. I. Ordway. *Space World* X-12-288 Space Advocate:2 D '87

U.S., Europeans debate long-term space goals. D. A. Brown. il *Aviat Week Space Technol* 127:77+ O 26 '87

International Astronomical Union

Amateurs triumph in Paris [colloquium celebrating the 100th anniversary of the Société Astronomique de France] S. J. O'Meara. il *Sky Telesc* 74:481-3 N '87

International Atomic Energy Agency

Assembly affirms confidence in IAEA, urges co-operation regarding peaceful uses of nuclear energy. *UN Chron* 23:10 Ja '86

Assembly urges co-operation with IAEA to promote peaceful use of nuclear energy. il *UN Chron* 24:83-5 F '87

Harnessing the peaceful atom: past performance and future challenges [address, March 23, 1987] R. T. Kennedy. *Dep State Bull* 87:76-80 Je '87

IAEA asked to consider measures to ensure Israel does not attack 'peaceful nuclear facilities' [General Assembly resolution prompted by Israel's attack on the Tammuz nuclear reactor in Iraq] *UN Chron* 23:11 Ja '86

IAEA conventions on nuclear safety provide for co-operation in wake of nuclear accident. il *UN Chron* 23:74 N '86

IAEA General Conference marks 30th anniversary. *UN Chron* 24:51 N '87

International Atomic Energy Agency—*cont.*
Peaceful uses of nuclear energy increasing worldwide. *UN Chron* 24:12 Ag '87
Three conventions on nuclear safety now in force. *UN Chron* 24:52 My '87
U.S. reconfirms support for IAEA [statement, November 11, 1986] R. T. Kennedy. *Dep State Bull* 87:86-7 Ja '87
International Azalea Festival (Norfolk, Va.) *See* Norfolk (Va.)—Festivals
International baccalaureate
High school graduation, international style. M. G. Bruce. il *Phi Delta Kappan* 69:79-81 S '87
International balance of payments *See* Balance of payments
International Bank for Reconstruction and Development *See* World Bank
International banking *See* Banks and banking, International
International Basketball Association
Hey, shorty, wanna play ball? A. Beam. il por *Bus Week* p82 Mr 2 '87
International Beauty Show
Beauty [show at the Javits Center] *New Yorker* 63:25-6 Mr 30 '87
International Biennial of Tapestry *See* Tapestry—Exhibitions
International Black Toy Manufacturers Association
Black toys make inroads. M. Mallory. il *Black Enterp* 18:32 D '87
International book fairs *See* Book fairs
International Brotherhood of Teamsters, Chauffeurs, Warehousemen and Helpers of America
The AFL-CIO: a tougher team with the Teamsters. A. Bernstein and S. B. Garland. il *Bus Week* p110 N 9 '87
AFL-CIO's strange bedfellows [Teamsters seek readmission] *U S News World Rep* 103:13 N 2 '87
Breaking the Teamsters [government prosecution through RICO statute] J. Schwartz. il *Newsweek* 109:43 Je 22 '87
How Teamsters high command may be unhorsed [use of RICO statute] W. L. Chaze. il *U S News World Rep* 102:12-13 Je 22 '87
Letter from Washington [Justice Dept. to pursue case against J. Presser] Cato. *Natl Rev* 39:13 Jl 31 '87
Long haul to democracy [Teamsters back in AFL-CIO] *Nation* 245:505 N 7 '87
Mobbed [Teamsters readmitted to the AFL-CIO] T. Geoghegan. *New Repub* 197:11-12 N 16 '87
Organized crime and the Teamsters. L. Black. il *Macleans* 100:44 Je 29 '87
The Teamsters rumble back. B. Cohn. il *Newsweek* 110:54 N 30 '87
Teamsters' vote clears path for USAir's acquisition of PSA. C. Preble. il *Aviat Week Space Technol* 126:41 My 25 '87
Why not try union democracy? [racketeering suit] J. Connolly. il *Nation* 245:192-4+ S 5 '87
International Business Machines Corp.
All-around achiever [IBM executive J. Donald's commitment to helping young people] J. Sands. il por *Essence* 18:102+ Je '87
Big Blue still has a bad case of the blahs. G. Lewis. il *Bus Week* p39 Ja 26 '87
The billion-dollar whiz kid [W. Gates gets IBM to endorse Microsoft operating system; cover story] R. Brandt. il pors *Bus Week* p68-72+ Ap 13 '87
Childhood's end? [Personal System/2] E. Dyson. il *Forbes* 139:257 My 18 '87
Danish modern [Software and Publications Center in Allerød, Denmark] P. M. Sachner. il *Archit Rec* 175:134-41 O '87
'Day of the living clones,' starring IBM [unveiling of new line called Personal System/2] C. P. Work. il *U S News World Rep* 102:41 Ap 13 '87
Down but not out at IBM. A. Walmsley. il *Macleans* 100:24-5 F 9 '87
'The first sign of spring' for IBM and its rivals. G. Lewis. il *Bus Week* p35-6 Ap 27 '87
The greatest capitalist in history [cover story] T. J. Watson, Jr. il pors *Fortune* 116:24-32+ Ag 31 '87
High-tech tariffs boomerang on the U.S. G. Lewis. il *Bus Week* p26-7 S 7 '87
How IBM hopes to skin the copycats [new lineup of PCs] G. Lewis. il *Bus Week* p40 Ap 6 '87
IBM adopts PostScript. *Pers Comput* 11:27-8 My '87
IBM and Tandy turn up the heat [personal computers] il *Fortune* 116:12 Ag 31 '87
IBM, clonebuster. P. Nulty. il *Fortune* 115:225 Ap 27 '87

The IBM-DEC wars: it's 'the year of the customer'. A. Beam and G. Lewis. il *Bus Week* p86-8 Mr 30 '87
IBM Host computer system operational at Boston center [FAA air traffic control system] *Aviat Week Space Technol* 127:56 O 26 '87
IBM: not so fearsome [support for concept of an open system] R. A. Shaffer. il *Pers Comput* 11:39 Jl '87
IBM squares off against DEC [midrange office computers] il *Fortune* 116:8 Jl 20 '87
IBM tries another remedy [launching new mainframes and an improved laptop] G. M. Bock. *Bus Week* p32-3 F 9 '87
IBM unveils the sons of PC. W. D. Marbach. il *Newsweek* 109:61 Ap 13 '87
IBM's Big Blues: a legend tries to remake itself. C. J. Loomis. il *Fortune* 115:34-6+ Ja 19 '87
IBM's new family of personal computers taps greater power and compatibility [Personal System/2] S. Miller. il *Black Enterp* 17:90 Je '87
IBM's new systems: what do you do now? [cover story; special section; with editorial comment by Fred Abatemarco] il *Pers Comput* 11:5, 94-7+ Je '87
IBM's software 'road map': a magic carpet to the future? [Systems Application Architecture] G. Lewis. il *Bus Week* p159 My 11 '87
IBM's steady plod on the turnaround trail. J. W. Verity. *Bus Week* p33-4 O 26 '87
IBM's Zurich Lab is "flower" in Europe. D. Dickson. il *Science* 237:125-6 Jl 10 '87
Inside IBM's PS/2 line. J. Blackford. il *Pers Comput* 11:245-6+ Jl '87
Inside the IBM PCs [cover story; with editorial comment by G. Michael Vose] bibl il *Byte* 12 no12 Sp Issue:6+ '87
Into the wild blue yonder [Personal System/2] P. Elmer-Dewitt. il *Time* 129:68 Ap 13 '87
Intriguing tales from the early days of the PS/2. P. Lemmons. il *Byte* 12:6 Ag '87
Invincible IBM? Not today, as it faces still more setbacks. F. W. Frailey. *U S News World Rep* 102:45 F 2 '87
John Akers. R. Mitchell. il por *Bus Week* Sp Issue:210 Ap 17 '87
Just when IBM was roaring back in Japan . . . A. Borrus. il por *Bus Week* p70-1 F 2 '87
The knockoffs head for a knockdown fight with IBM. K. M. Hafner. il *Bus Week* p112-13 D 21 '87
Letting the sun shine in [J. Akers] N. J. Perry. por *Fortune* 116:29 Ag 3 '87
Lotus' dream-come-true: a sweet deal with IBM [1-2-3/M spreadsheet] A. Field and A. Beam. il *Bus Week* p116 My 25 '87
The many splendors of VGA [video graphics array] J. Blackford. il *Pers Comput* 11:279-80 S '87
The market for mainframes will never be the same [IBM-Fujitsu software copyright fight] J. W. Verity. il *Bus Week* p62 O 5 '87
Mixed blessings [Stratus Computer's marketing arrangement with IBM] K. K. Wiegner. il por *Forbes* 140:70+ S 21 '87
An optical memory that can be wiped clean. E. T. Smith. il *Bus Week* p56+ Je 15 '87
Software plays hardball [Apple's proposed programming company and IBM's deal with Lotus] *Time* 129:52 My 11 '87
Stalking the corporate buyer [new series of personal computers] R. A. Shaffer. il *Pers Comput* 11:45 Ag '87
The submicron era may belong to the Japanese [dynamic random access memory chips] O. Port. il *Bus Week* p98 Mr 16 '87
Super PC [IBM Personal System/2] W. J. Hawkins. il *Pop Sci* 230:34-6 Je '87
A survival manual for the new PC's. W. J. Cook. il *U S News World Rep* 102:50 Ap 20 '87
The verdict on IBM's System/2: clonemakers are still in the game. G. Lewis. il *Bus Week* p118+ My 4 '87
The wall comes tumbling down [IBM and Apple personal computers] P. Elmer-Dewitt. il *Time* 129:68 F 2 '87
What has IBM got that other stocks don't? J. W. Verity. il *Bus Week* p182 N 16 '87
Who's afraid of IBM? [Compaq Computer; cover story] J. E. Davis. il por *Bus Week* p68-72+ Je 29 '87
International Center for Development Policy
Why Meese spoke [E. Meese's "surprise" announcement of diversion of funds from Iran arms sale] D. Lindorff. *Nation* 244:349 Mr 21 '87

International Churchill Society
Churchill envy. A. Sullivan. il *New Repub* 197:14-16 D 7 '87
International Civil Airports Association
Forum urges initiation of joint efforts to expand airport, airway capacity. K. F. Mordoff. *Aviat Week Space Technol* 127:49+ O 12 '87
International Civil Aviation Organization
U.S. payment shortfall threatens cutback in ICAO operations. J. Ott. *Aviat Week Space Technol* 127:43 N 2 '87
International Coffee Agreement
Coffee growers are in for lots of sleepless nights. G. Weiss. il *Bus Week* p67 F 2 '87
International commercial policy *See* Commercial policy
International commodity control *See* Commodity control
International competition *See* Competition
International Conference for the Immediate Independence of Namibia
Comprehensive study outlines post-independence national development strategies for Namibia. il *UN Chron* 23:34-5 N '86
International Conference for Independence of Namibia calls for mandatory sanctions against South Africa. il map *UN Chron* 23:21-32 N '86
International Conference on Drug Abuse and Illicit Trafficking
Assembly adopts three texts on issues to combat drug abuse and illicit trafficking. il *UN Chron* 24:110-12 F '87
Draft declaration on drug control priorities recommended for adoption by world drug conference. il *UN Chron* 24:45 My '87
Drug abuse—a call to action. M. Grant and I. Khan. il *World Health* p29 My '87
International Conference on Drug Abuse and Illicit Trafficking [special section] il *UN Chron* 24:i-xxxii My '87
International drug conference calls for 'vigorous action' against drug abuse, illicit trafficking. il *UN Chron* 24:6-9 Ag '87
UN narcotics conference meets in Vienna [statement, message, and text of declaration, June 15-26, 1987] E. Meese; R. Reagan. *Dep State Bull* 87:77-80 S '87
International Conference on the Relationship between Disarmament and Development
International commitment to reallocate military expenditures for development reaffirmed. il *UN Chron* 24:23-8 N '87
It's guns or butter, says UN conference. H. A. Jack. *Christ Century* 104:878-9 O 14 '87
International conferences
See also
Commonwealth of Nations—Conferences
Conference on Confidence and Security-Building Measures and Disarmament in Europe
Conference on Security and Cooperation in Europe
Economic conferences
Organization of Petroleum Exporting Countries—Conferences
Reagan-Gorbachev summit conference, 1986
Reagan-Gorbachev summit conference, 1987
Non-aligned at Harare call for sanctions [call for convening of the Security Council to impose sanctions against South Africa] *UN Chron* 23:46 N '86
Sanctions and survival [South Africa and the 1986 nonaligned nations conference] R. Shaplen. il *New Yorker* 62:74-80+ F 2 '87
Third world nations meet [non-aligned summit] K. Crooks. *Black Enterp* 17:17 Ja '87
International Contract Furnishings (Firm)
A little bit timeless [showroom designed by M. Botta] P. M. Sachner. il *Archit Rec* 175:124-9 mid-S '87
International Controls Corp.
If at first . . . [owner and chairman A. M. Goldberg] A. A. Lappen. il por *Forbes* 140:8 S 7 '87
International cooking *See* Cooking, International
International cooperation
See also
Alliances
ANZUS Council
ASEAN
Declaration of the Principles of International Cultural Co-operation
International education
International organization
North Atlantic Treaty Organization
United Nations
Warsaw Treaty Organization
Is the international community a myth? R. J. Dupuy. il *Courier* 40:4-8 Ja '87

"What a legacy for our children!" [interview with S. Aga Khan] P. Gupte. il por *Forbes* 139:100+ Je 15 '87
International corporations *See* Corporations, International
International Council of Scientific Unions. International Astronomical Union *See* International Astronomical Union
International Council on Biblical Inerrancy
Christian organization runs its course, according to plan. il *Christ Today* 31:42+ N 6 '87
For once we knew when to quit. K. S. Kantzer. il *Christ Today* 31:11 N 6 '87
Inerrancy Council searches for unity on tough issues. R. Frame. il *Christ Today* 31:38-9 F 6 '87
Problems inerrancy doesn't solve. K. S. Kantzer. il *Christ Today* 31:14-15 F 20 '87
International Court of Justice
Fortieth anniversary message: 'developing the rule of law' [excerpts from address, October 25, 1985] N. Singh. *UN Chron* 22:101 N/D '85
Nicaragua [statement, November 3, 1986] H. S. Okun. *Dep State Bull* 87:82-4 Ja '87
Nicaragua asks for World Court to consider cases against Costa Rica and Honduras. *UN Chron* 23:88 N '86
Security Council does not adopt text calling for compliance with International Court ruling regarding Nicaraguan case. il *UN Chron* 24:62-3 F '87
Security Council does not adopt text calling for full compliance with International Court ruling in case of 'military and paramilitary activities in and against Nicaragua'. il *UN Chron* 23:83-8 N '86
The United States vs. the World Court [report of the Independent Commission on Respect for International Law] *Cent Mag* 20:59-62 My/Je '87
World Court news. il *UN Chron* 24:81 My '87
World Court news. il *UN Chron* 24:77 Ag '87
International courts
See also
International Court of Justice
International Creative Management (Firm)
The man they love to hate [agent M. Hurwitz] J. Traub. il pors *Channels* 7:66-70 Je '87
International date line
Notes and comment. *New Yorker* 63:39-40 N 9 '87
International Day for the Elimination of Racial Discrimination
Special meetings mark 27th anniversary of Sharpeville massacre. il *UN Chron* 24:26-7 My '87
International Day of Solidarity with the Palestinian People
Palestine Solidarity Day observed on 29 November. *UN Chron* 23:6 Ja '86
International Day of Solidarity with the Struggle of Women of South Africa and Namibia
Day of Solidarity with South African and Namibian Women observed. il *UN Chron* 23:36 N '86
International Day of Solidarity with the Struggling Peoples of South Africa
Soweto Day ceremony held on 16 June, marking eleventh anniversary of massacre. *UN Chron* 24:25 Ag '87
International debts *See* Debts, External
International Design Center New York
A leg up [Gullans International showroom] C. K. Gandee. il *Archit Rec* 175:106-9 My '87
International Drinking Water Supply and Sanitation Decade, 1981-1990
Water, source of life [Latin America] H. Otterstetter and A. Flores. il *World Health* p11-13 O '87
International economic policy *See* Economic policy
International education
See also
International baccalaureate
Language and languages—Study and teaching
Nuclear weapons—Study and teaching—International aspects
Peace studies
Student exchange programs
International schools for international people. M. G. Bruce. *Phi Delta Kappan* 68:707-8 My '87
New Children's Museum gallery celebrates global themes [Passport to the World gallery] P. Rowe. il *Child Today* 16:14-17 My/Je '87
International educational exchanges *See* Educational exchanges
International Energy Agency
IEA governing board meets in Paris [statement and text of final communique, May 11, 1987] J. S. Herrington. *Dep State Bull* 87:47-51 Jl '87
International Federation of Airline Pilots Associations
Pilot ownership concept takes several forms at world carriers. *Aviat Week Space Technol* 126:49+ My 11 '87

International Federation of Organic Agriculture Movements
International Federation of Organic Agriculture Movements (IFOAM) conference. L. Korn. *Rodale's Org Gard* 34:28+ F '87
International finance *See* Finance, International
International Finance Corporation
IFC investments surpass $1 billion for first time. *UN Chron* 23:106 N '86
International Forum for a Nuclear-Free World
From Russia with hope. B. Kaufman. il por *50 Plus* 27:29-31 Jl '87
Moscow calling. K. V. Heuvel. *Nation* 244:277 Mr 7 '87
Moscow meeting—the *glasnost* menagerie. S. Frankel. il pors *Bull At Sci* 43:8-12 My '87
Physicists report progress at Moscow disarmament forum. W. Sweet. il *Phys Today* 40:67-70 Ap '87
A U.S. scientist addresses Gorbachev [address, February 16, 1987] F. Von Hippel. *Bull At Sci* 43:12-13 My '87
Wooing the West. J. Greenwald. il *Time* 129:22-4 Mr 2 '87
Yoko Ono attends Soviet peace parley. A. DeCurtis. il pors *Roll Stone* p14 Ap 9 '87
International Game Technology
Want to improve your hand? Try this casino stock. G. G. Marcial. il *Bus Week* p132 Je 22 '87
International Geosphere-Biosphere Program
The 1987 State of the world describes a planet crossing thresholds. A global science effort will look for some answers. J. P. Wiley, Jr. il *Smithsonian* 18:28+ Ap '87
Global questions. *Sci Am* 256:22+ Je '87
Global science [discussion of October 1986 article, Mission to planet earth] T. F. Malone. *Environment* 29:3-4 Mr '87
International group will study earth as a system. *Earth Sci* 40:6-7 Fall '87
International Halley Watch
The IHW island network. M. B. Niedner, Jr. and W. Liller. il *Sky Telesc* 73:258-63 Mr '87
Inside the IHW: the amateurs [interview with S. J. Edberg] A. MacRobert. il por *Sky Telesc* 73:264-5 Mr '87
Inside the IHW: the professionals [interview with R. Newburn and J. Rahe] J. K. Beatty. pors *Sky Telesc* 73:256-7 Mr '87
International Harvester Co.
See also
Navistar International Corporation
International herald tribune
The Paris Tribune at one hundred. R. Reeves. il *Am Herit* 38:114-19 N '87
International house decoration *See* House decoration, International
International Institute for Applied Systems Analysis
National security and the environment. W. C. Clark. bibl *Environment* 29:inside cover+ Je '87
Security Council blocks NSF grant to IIASA. C. Norman. il *Science* 236:514-15 My 1 '87
International Labour Organisation
50 to 200 million children under 15 are in world's work force, ILO says [developing countries] il *UN Chron* 23:116 N '86
ILO governing body focuses on standards, worker safety and budget. *UN Chron* 24:80 My '87
ILO prepares new standards on employment, social security, construction safety. il *UN Chron* 24:75-6 Ag '87
International law
See also
Airspace (International law)
Asylum, Right of
Embargo
International Court of Justice
Maritime law
Passports
Sanctions (International law)
Slave trade
Territorial waters
United Nations. Legal Committee
Coping with terrorism. C. C. O'Brien. il por *Cent Mag* 20:45-9 Mr/Ap '87
George Shultz's feisty lawyer [A. Sofaer, State Dept. legal adviser] B. Van Voorst. por *Time* 129:31 Ap 6 '87
Minority report [views of State Dept. legal adviser A. D. Sofaer] C. Hitchens. *Nation* 244:103 Ja 31 '87
International Law Commission (United Nations) *See* United Nations. International Law Commission

International Lease Finance Corporation
Fear of leasing? [stock price] T. Jaffe. *Forbes* 140:246-7 O 5 '87
Leasing company selects CFM56-5 to power A320s. *Aviat Week Space Technol* 126:33 Ap 6 '87
International Literacy Day
Four prizes awarded on International Literacy Day. *UN Chron* 23:20 N '86
International loans *See* Loans, Foreign
International Longshoremen's and Warehousemen's Union
Losing jobs by trying to save them [New York harbor] J. Cook. il *Forbes* 139:56+ Je 1 '87
International Management Group *See* IMG International Management Group
International Maritime Satellite Organization
FAA plans Inmarsat satellite surveillance of oceanic routes. P. J. Klass. *Aviat Week Space Technol* 127:47+ D 7 '87
FCC proposes plan to offer competitive air-to-ground links. *Aviat Week Space Technol* 126:36 My 4 '87
International Medical Centers Inc.
The company that has HMOs sick with worry. G. DeGeorge. il *Bus Week* p52 My 11 '87
International Monetary Fund
Debt and the dollar: the markets are making all the rules. W. Glasgall and M. McNamee. il *Bus Week* p57 O 12 '87
The dollar gets no respect [meeting of the World Bank and the International Monetary Fund] A. Zagorin. il *Time* 129:53 Ap 20 '87
Imposing order on a global economy [meeting in Washington] il *Macleans* 100:30 Ap 20 '87
Michel Camdessus is making the IMF less of a Scrooge. M. McNamee. il *Bus Week* p36-7 O 5 '87
They won't feel like partying at the IMF meetings [pressure to halt dollar's slide] M. McNamee. il *Bus Week* p36 S 28 '87
International Museum of Photography at George Eastman House
Two American museums provide new homes for old cameras. E. S. Lothrop. il *Pop Photogr* 94:28 Ag '87
International Narcotics Control Board
Drug abuse and trafficking on the increase worldwide, with links to international crime and finance. il *UN Chron* 24:viii-xiii My '87
International news *See* Foreign news
International Oceanographic Foundation
Sea winds. See issues of Sea Frontiers beginning January/ February 1986
International Olympic Committee
Goodbye, olive wreaths; hello, riches and reality. W. O. Johnson. il *Sports Illus* 66:168+ F 9 '87
Olympic veteran becomes 1st black woman on IOC [A. DeFrantz] por *Jet* 71:51 F 9 '87
International organization
Causes of war and causes of peace [address, February 12, 1987] F. A. Rodgers. *Vital Speeches Day* 53:375-9 Ap 1 '87
To form a more perfect union [call for international restraint on global corporations; with editorial comment] Publius. *New Leader* 70:2, 11-12 Jl 13-27 '87
International Organization of Scenographers, Theatre Architects and Technicians
Amsterdam OISTAT conference. R. Long. *Theatre Crafts* 21:24 N '87
International Paper Co.
International Paper: being chased? G. G. Marcial. *Bus Week* p114 D 7 '87
The long wait [capital spending strategy] D. Henry. il *Forbes* 139:66-7 Je 15 '87
The strikers strike out [scabs replace paper mill workers] M. Satchell. il *U S News World Rep* 103:41-2 O 26 '87
International PEN Club *See* PEN
International Physicians for the Prevention of Nuclear War
Asymmetry [meeting in Moscow] J. Hersey. *New Yorker* 63:36-40+ S 7 '87
International Physics Group *See* American Physical Society. International Physics Group
International Physics Olympiad
Romanians outdo US and Soviets in Physics Olympiad. W. Sweet. il *Phys Today* 40:75 S '87
International Playthings, Inc.
When the boss leads the way [T. Kiesewetter's use of computers] F. Abatemarco. il por *Pers Comput* 11:152-3 O '87
International Recovery, Inc.
The sleuth who snoops for sloops. B. Rice. il por *50 Plus* 27:76-8+ Je '87

International Red Cross See Red Cross
International relations
    See also
       Alliances
       Balance of power
       Council on Foreign Relations
       Diplomacy
       Disarmament
       Geopolitics
       Imperialism
       International conferences
       International cooperation
       International law
       International organization
       Militarism
       Monroe Doctrine
       Peace
       Treaties of guaranty
       United Nations
       War
       World politics
Chronology 1986. S. Robertson. *Foreign Aff* 65 Sp Issue:653-96 ['87]
From illusions to norms in international relations. K. W. Thompson. *Society* 25:15-20 N/D '87
International outlook. See issues of Business Week
On the road. *Natl Rev* 39:18 My 8 '87
The president of France speaks out [interview with F. Mitterrand] M. S. Forbes. il pors *Forbes* 140:22-3+ D 28 '87
Words and deeds in foreign policy. K. W. Thompson. *Society* 24:24-8 My/Je '87
         Bibliography
Recent books on international relations. L. E. Despard. See issues of Foreign Affairs
Source material. J. A. Kreslins. See issues of Foreign Affairs beginning Fall 1986
International security
    See also
       Disarmament
       Peace
       Peace studies
       United Nations. Political and Security Committee
International Seminar on the Future of Mankind and Cooperation Among Religions
Cooperation among world religions. R. L. Shinn. *America* 156:482-4 Je 13 '87
International Signal & Control Group, plc
Ferranti plans to merge with U.S. defense company. *Aviat Week Space Technol* 127:28 S 28 '87
International Society for Krishna Consciousness See Krishna consciousness movement
International Space University
Higher education. D. Stewart. il *Omni* 10:26+ N '87
International Space Year, 1992
Forum participants urge joint ventures during International Space Year. *Aviat Week Space Technol* 127:25 O 12 '87
International Space Year spurs plans for multinational activities. *Aviat Week Space Technol* 127:70-1 N 2 '87
International Stamp Exchange Corporation
Beware the stamp man [M. Rousso] J. Clements. il por *Forbes* 139:232+ My 18 '87
International Standard Book Numbers
    See also
       Bookland EAN system
International studies See International education
International Telecommunications Satellite Organization
Martin signs contract to launch Intelsat 6 satellites on Titan 3s. *Aviat Week Space Technol* 127:22 Ag 17 '87
Matra wins Telecom 2 contest, resolves constraints on TRW for Intelsat bid. *Aviat Week Space Technol* 127:24-5 N 30 '87
The mysterious fall of a star [former Intelsat chief R. Colino convicted of fraud] J. S. DeMott. il por *Time* 130:51 O 5 '87
International Telephone and Telegraph Corporation See ITT Corporation
International Tennis Hall of Fame
Hall of Fame deserves the best [B. Borg's decision not to attend induction ceremonies] S. Flink. il por *World Tennis* 35:22+ Jl '87
International Theatrical Arts Society
Texas producer puts dance at top of his list [T. Adams] E. Elam. *Dance Mag* 61:16-17 Mr '87
International Thomson Organisation Ltd.
Thomson to sell general publishing units of ABP conglomerate. V. Menkes. *Publ Wkly* 232:16 O 2 '87

International Tin Council
Bankers beware. R. Morais. il *Forbes* 139 Ann Directory:63 Ap 27 '87
International travel See Travel
International trusteeships
    See also
       United Nations. Trusteeship Council
International Ultraviolet Explorer (Satellite) See Artificial satellites—Astronomical use
International Union for Conservation of Nature and Natural Resources
International defense. H. Eidsvik. il *Natl Parks* 61:12-13 S/O '87
International Union of Pure and Applied Physics
IUPAP and Corporate Associates meet in Washington. W. Sweet. il *Phys Today* 40:76-7 D '87
International Union of United Automobile, Aerospace and Agricultural Implement Workers of America See United Automobile, Aerospace and Agricultural Implement Workers of America
International Whaling Commission
Research whaling on the table [Iceland] J. Walsh. *Science* 237:481 Jl 31 '87
International Wildlife Coalition
Whales off the Faeroe Islands. L. Lockett. por *Newsweek* 110:11 N 23 '87
International Year of Peace, 1986
Report on International Year of Peace [Secretary-General's report] il *UN Chron* 23:16 N '86
International Year of Shelter for the Homeless, 1987
Decent shelter for all . . . J. Pérez de Cuellar. *UN Chron* 24:inside cover Ag '87
International Year of Shelter for the Homeless (1987) [cover story; symposium] il *UN Chron* 24:48-55 Ag '87
Investing in human beings [interview with R. Premadasa] il por *World Health* p2-5 Jl '87
The world's homeless millions. il *Courier* 40:18-19 Ja '87
International Year of the Forest, 1985
Swift action to save the world's forests and woodlands urged by FAO expert task force. il *UN Chron* 22:105-6 N/D '85
International Youth Year, 1985
The 38th floor [excerpts from statement, November 13, 1985] J. Pérez de Cuellar. il *UN Chron* 23:2+ Ja '86
Global strategy for youth endorsed at conclusion of World Conference on International Youth Year (1985). il *UN Chron* 23:23-6 Ja '86
Youth in the 1980s [special section] il *UN Chron* 23:27-42 Ja '86
Internav Ltd.
A future in smart boxes. il por *Macleans* 100:40 Ap 20 '87
Internment camps See Concentration camps
Internment of Japanese Americans, 1942-1945 See Japanese Americans—Evacuation and relocation, 1942-1945
Interns (Business)
Internships: for undergraduates and career changers. G. Hechinger. il *Glamour* 85:342-3 N '87
A reform strategy for education: employer-sponsored teacher internships. G. G. Gold. il *Phi Delta Kappan* 68:384-7 Ja '87
Summer intern program places students in industry [physics] il *Phys Today* 40:93 S '87
Interns (Education) See Student teachers
Interns (Medicine)
Don't ask for whom the beeper beeps, it beeps for thee. P. Klass. il *Discover* 8:16-18 Je '87
Re-examining the 36-hour day [New York State proposal to reform residents' training] C. Wallis. il *Time* 130:54-5 Ag 31 '87
What I know now that I didn't know a year ago. P. Klass. il *Discover* 8:18+ Ag '87
Interns (Physics) See Physics—Study and teaching
Interpersonal attraction
When opposites attract. L. S. Dumas. il *Health* 19:35-9+ S '87
Interpersonal communication See Communication—Social aspects
Interpersonal relations See Human relations
Interplanetary dust See Matter, Interstellar
Interplanetary flight See Space flight
Interplanting See Companion crops
Interpreters (Computer programs)
Four C language interpreters [Run/C, Run/C Professional, C-terp, and Instant-C] J. Unger. il *Byte* 12:245-8+ Je '87

Interracial adoption *See* Adoption and adopted children
Interracial dating
Guess who's coming to dinner now? [black women and white men] D. Tucker. il *Essence* 17:45-6+ Ap '87
Minn. Bible College jock says he was expelled for dating white girl there [case of C. Addison of Pillsbury Baptist Bible College] il por *Jet* 72:14 My 11 '87
Probe interracial dating policy at Bible College [Pillsbury Baptist Bible College] *Jet* 71:21 F 23 '87
Interracial marriage
See also
Children of interracial parents
Atlanta probes murder mystery of black wife of white millionaire [murder of L. M. Sullivan] D. M. Cheers. il pors *Jet* 72:24-7 My 25 '87
Guess who's coming to dinner now? [black women and white men] D. Tucker. il *Essence* 17:45-6+ Ap '87
Interracial couple in N.Y. get damages from landlord. *Jet* 72:29 My 4 '87
Interracial couple in Richmond, Va. fight to overcome racism [J. and M. Wicker] il pors *Jet* 73:52-5 D 28 '87-Ja 4 '88
Mississippi repeals ban on interracial marriages. il *Jet* 73:18 N 23 '87
Mixed marriage 67 years ago has 3 generations of mixed descendants [descendants of Joseph Dixon and Emily Ashford] J. Collins. il *Jet* 71:14-16 F 16 '87
Nephew of S. African envoy weds 'colored' [nephew of Piet Koornhof] *Jet* 72:12 Jl 6 '87
Retarded couple face the new year with a baby boy [R. and D. Thornton] pors *Jet* 71:8 Ja 12 '87
U.S. Rep. Major Owens fights ex-wife on charges of race bias, back alimony. il pors *Jet* 73:16-17 N 2 '87
The untold story of black ambassador who weds Asian princess [R. D. Palmer weds Princess Intan in Mauritius] S. Booker. il pors *Jet* 73:12+ O 12 '87
What makes love last [Caucasian-Japanese marriage of J. and M. Michener] S. Arnout. il pors *McCalls* 114:166+ F '87
Interrogation, Police *See* Police questioning
Interspecies communication *See* Animal communication
Interstate Bakeries Corporation
Putting the yeast back into profits. R. Simon. il por *Forbes* 139:62+ F 9 '87
Interstate Book Manufacturers Inc.
Krueger buys Nelson's Interstate Book Mfrs. *Publ Wkly* 231:54 Je 19 '87
Interstate commerce
The expanding economic vista [commerce clause of the Constitution] R. B. Reich. il *N Y Times Mag* p52-4+ S 13 '87
Canada
Trade tangles at home. M. Drohan. il *Macleans* 100:20 Ap 6 '87
Interstate highway system *See* Express highways
Interstellar bubbles *See* Nebulae
Interstellar communication
Bob Dixon: still waiting for a long distance call [SETI scientist at Ohio State University] M. J. Mackowski. il por *Space World* X-8-284:17-20 Ag '87
E.T., phone NASA [SETI project] S. Vogel. il *Discover* 8:78-9 O '87
Laser clones [views of J. D. G. Rather] B. Lawren. il *Omni* 9:24 Ja '87
Space [address, October 12, 1987] J. C. Fletcher. *Vital Speeches Day* 54:66-8 N 15 '87
Where are the extraterrestrials hiding? S. Shostak. il *Saturday Evening Post* 259:62-5 S '87
Interstellar flight *See* Space flight
Interstellar matter *See* Matter, Interstellar
Interstitial cystitis *See* Cystitis
Intertidal ecology
Energy for life among the waves [research by Egbert G. Leigh, Jr. and others] I. Peterson. *Sci News* 131:183 Mr 21 '87
Fewer barnacles [rockfish prey on barnacle larvae in California kelp forest; research by Steven D. Gaines and Jonathan Roughgarden] *Sea Front* 33:384-5 S/O '87
Fish in offshore kelp forests affect recruitment to intertidal barnacle populations [rockfish] S. D. Gaines and J. Roughgarden. bibl f il *Science* 235:479-81 Ja 23 '87
Life thrives under breaking ocean waves [research by Egbert Leigh and others] R. Lewin. il *Science* 235:1465-6 Mr 20 '87
Intervals (Music) *See* Musical intervals and scales
Intervening sequences (Genetics) *See* Genetic code
Interviewing
See also
Employment interviewing

Scoop du jour [interview with N. Collins] L. Smith. il por *Vogue* 177:352-3+ Ap '87
Intestines
See also
Colon (Anatomy)
Diseases
See also
Colitis
Constipation
Diarrhea
Diverticular disease
Regional ileitis
Short bowel syndrome
Microbiology
Feeling sleepy? Shhh! Bacteria at work. il *Discover* 8:12 Ap '87
Intimacy
See also
Embracing
Kissing
Dance with an intimate stranger [interview with H. G. Lerner] C. Tavris. *Vogue* 177:44 D '87
Fear of intimacy: not for men only [excerpt from Women men love/women men leave] C. Cowan and M. Kinder. il *Glamour* 85:96+ O '87
How to keep your love alive: playing for keeps [excerpts from Intimate play] W. Betcher. il *Glamour* 85:250-2+ F '87
Intimacy: how to get it; how to give it. R. Masello. *Glamour* 85:158-9+ Ja '87
Intimacy: our latest sexual fantasy. T. Stafford. il *Christ Today* 31:21-7 Ja 16 '87
Special survey results: 26,000 women reveal the secrets of intimacy. C. Rubenstein and C. Tavris. il *Redbook* 169:147-9+ S '87
Why can't we be closer? [excerpt from I love you] D. S. Viscott. il *Health* 19:44-6+ O '87
Intiman Theatre (Seattle, Wash.)
Intiman playhouse at Seattle Center. K. Marchese. il *Theatre Crafts* 21:46-7+ D '87
Intimate contact [television program] See Television program reviews—Single works
Into the light [musical] See Musicals, revues, etc.—Reviews—Single works
Into the woods [musical] See Musicals, revues, etc.—Reviews—Single works
Intolerance *See* Prejudice
Intoxication *See* Alcoholics and alcoholism
Intracoastal Waterway
Southern comfort [visiting Charleston, S.C. via the Intracoastal Waterway in a Grand Banks 42 motor yacht] J. Clemans. il *Mot Boat Sail* 159:42-5+ Mr '87
Intracranial bleeding *See* Brain—Hemorrhage
Intrauterine devices *See* Contraceptives
Intravenous therapy
See also
New England Critical Care
Equipment
Unsterile IVs [sets imported by D.R.O. Medical Product, Inc.] *FDA Consum* 21:35-6 S '87
Introduction of animals *See* Animal introduction
Introduction of birds *See* Bird introduction
Introduction of insects *See* Insect introduction
Introduction of plants *See* Plant introduction
Introns *See* Genetic code
Introversion and extroversion
Converging character [interactions between introverts and extraverts; study by Avril Thorne] P. Chance. il *Psychol Today* 21:22-3 D '87
Intrusion alarm systems *See* Alarms
Inuits *See* Eskimos
Invasion of privacy *See* Privacy, Right of
Invective
Fighting words: the shame of name-calling. D. Heyn. *Mademoiselle* 93:120 D '87
The gentle art of the resounding put-down. J. Epstein. *Am Sch* 56:311-18 Summ '87
Six things parents should never say to their children [verbal abuse] por *Jet* 73:14+ N 30 '87
Inventions
See also
Inventors
Patents
Patents and government-developed inventions
Technological innovations
United States. Patent and Trademark Office
Mishaps that mothered invention. B. Gatty. il *Nations Bus* 75:58-9 F '87
People behind the wonders [condensed from Breakthroughs!] J. M. Ketteringham and R. P. Nayak. il *Read Dig* 131:134-8 Jl '87

Inventions—*cont.*

Competitions

E.T.'s "phone home" inventor speaks [creative contraption competition] S. Morris. il por *Omni* 9:140-1 Ap '87

Little wizards [children] A. A. Lappen. il *Forbes* 139:156-7 Ap 6 '87

Anecdotes, facetiae, satire, etc.

My wacky idea! il *Natl Geogr World* 139:24-5 Mr '87

Inventories

Bulging inventories must be cut. H. Banks. il *Forbes* 139:27 Je 15 '87

Inventories: no sweat. V. Brownstein. il *Fortune* 115:40 My 25 '87

Taxation

Impractical capacity [practical capacity method of valuation for tax purposes] L. Saunders. il *Forbes* 140:64-5 Jl 27 '87

New inventory rules. G. W. Padwe. *Nations Bus* 75:62 F '87

Inventories, Household *See* Household records

Inventors

See also
Children as inventors
Inventions
Kurzweil, Raymond
Rabinow, Jacob

Anecdotes, facetiae, satire, etc.

A family of firsts. P. Volk. il *N Y Times Mag* p70-1 O 4 '87

Inventory control *See* Inventories

Invernizzi, Angelo

about
The house that turns to the sun. T. Williams. il *House Gard* 159:150-7+ F '87

Invertase

Many random sequences functionally replace the secretion signal sequence of yeast invertase. C. A. Kaiser and others. bibl f il *Science* 235:312-17 Ja 16 '87

Invertebrates

See also
Echinoderms
Nervous system—Invertebrates

Invertebrates, Fossil

The emergence of animals. M. A. S. McMenamin. bibl (p128) il map *Sci Am* 256:94-102 Ap '87

Inverters, Electric *See* Electric current inverters

Investcorp *See* Arabian Investment Banking Corporation

Investigations, Government *See* Government investigations

Investment advisers

See also
Ariel Capital Management Inc.
Ashland Management Inc.
Atalanta Sosnoff Capital Corp.
Bailard, Biehl & Kaiser
Banks and banking—Trust departments
Batterymarch Financial Management
Bessemer Group, Inc.
Brandywine Asset Management
Brokers
Cashman Farrell & Associates
Claremont Economics Institute
Clemente Capital Inc.
Comstock Partners
Concord Capital Management
Criterion Group Inc.
Delfi American Corporation
Delphi Management Inc.
Disciplined Investment Advisors Inc.
Fidelity Management & Research Co.
Forstmann-Leff Associates
Forstmann Little & Company
Frank Russell Company
Fred Alger Management Inc.
Greenspan O'Neil Associates
Growth Stock Outlook, Inc.
Laidlaw Capital Management Inc.
Manning & Napier Advisors Inc.
Montrose Capital Corporation
Newell Associates
Riordan Freeman & Spogli
Rosenberg Institutional Equity Management
Rosewood Financial (Firm)
Snyder Capital Management (Firm)
Steinhardt Partners
Stovall/Twenty-First Advisers Inc.
Tweedy, Browne Inc.
United Asset Management Corporation
Value Line Inc.
Wellington Management Company
Welsh, Carson, Anderson & Stowe
Women investment advisers

Working Assets Funding Service

The best financial planners. R. Eisenberg and W. Lubetkin. il *Money* Sp Issue:139-40+ Fall '87

The best money managers. W. L. Updegrave and L. Shea. il *Money* Sp Issue:163-4+ Fall '87

Cheapskates in a pricey stock market [value investing] B. D. Fromson. il *Fortune* 116 Sp Issue:41-2+ Fall '87

The decline of the superstar [cover story] A. Bianco. il *Bus Week* p90-6+ Ag 17 '87

Eight to watch in '87. il *Money* 16:58-62 Ja '87

Fidelity's cover boy [M. Kassen] D. Machan. il por *Forbes* 139:229-30 My 18 '87

Five stellar advisers tell (almost) all. A. B. Fisher. il *Fortune* 116 Sp Issue:205+ Fall '87

Gurus who called the crash—or fell on their faces. P. Finch and M. Frons. il *Bus Week* p124-6+ N 30 '87

How top money managers do it [cover story] J. P. Newport, Jr. il *Fortune* 116:28-33+ Jl 20 '87

Is your adviser as sharp as you think? J. Kosnett. il *Changing Times* 41:37-8+ F '87

It's a hit and miss business [forecaster J. E. Granville] il por *U S News World Rep* 103:84 S 28 '87

Making sense of the weather map [analysis of leading industries] D. P. Wiener and E. Pomice. il *U S News World Rep* 103:80 D 28 '87-Ja 4 '88

Money managing in a bell jar. M. M. Thomas. il *Nation* 244:318-20 Mr 14 '87

Money profile. See issues of Money

My wife, the Comtesse [M. Sosnoff] D. Machan. il por *Forbes* 139 Ann Directory:119-20 Ap 27 '87

Pros for small portfolios. A. McGrath. il *U S News World Rep* 103:67-8+ S 14 '87

Rating the new market timers [money managers timing the market with mutual funds] J. Edgerton. il *Money* 16:117-20+ Mr '87

The ratings game pinches the beguiling gurus of get-rich TV. il *Money* 16:13-14 Ja '87

Reader beware [newsletter writers turned portfolio managers] R. Simon. il *Forbes* 140:113+ N 16 '87

Sages of Wall Street. L. Luciano and R. Micheli. il *Money* 16:120-5 Je '87

The schizoid life of the media analyst. J. F. Berry. il *Channels* 7:62-8 F '87

The stock analysts. J. Rothchild. il *Wash Mon* 19:10-14+ O '87

Their own money. J. Crudele. il *N Y* 20:20+ S 14 '87

They've got your money in their hands [mutual fund managers] J. Rachlin. il *U S News World Rep* 102:59-62 F 16 '87

Time for a heart-to-heart with a planner? T. Segal. il *Bus Week* p140-1 N 9 '87

Trading by proxy [commodity trading advisers] S. W. Angrist. il *Forbes* 140:306 S 7 '87

Wall Street's hottest hands. D. Machan. il *Forbes* 139:86-8 Ja 26 '87

Watching the bull through a technician's eyes [technical analysts] J. M. Laderman. il *Bus Week* p88-9 S 28 '87

What we can learn from Phil Fisher. W. E. Buffett. il por *Forbes* 140:40 O 19 '87

Where the pros put their money. M. Schiffres. il *U S News World Rep* 102:50-3 Ap 6 '87

Acquisitions and mergers

Norton Reamer collects money management firms. A. Beam. il por *Bus Week* p114 My 18 '87

Securities

Are fund management stocks cheap? R. McGough. il *Forbes* 140:156+ S 7 '87

Canada

See also
Barnes Investor Relations Ltd.

Great Britain

See also
Global Asset Management Ltd.

Bubble and squeak. R. McGough. *Forbes* 140:161 S 7 '87

Scotland

The best investors may be Scottish. S. Tully. il *Fortune* 116:58-60 Ag 31 '87

Investment annuities *See* Annuities

Investment banking

See also
Bankers Trust Company
Bear, Stearns & Co. Inc.
Black investment banking
Blackstone Group
Citicorp Investment Bank Ltd.

Investment banking—See also—*cont.*

    Continental Illinois National Bank & Trust Co. of Chicago
    D. H. Blair & Co., Inc.
    Dillon Read & Co. Inc.
    Drexel Burnham Lambert Incorporated
    E.M. Warburg, Pincus & Co., Inc.
    First Boston Corp.
    Goldman, Sachs & Co.
    Hallwood Group Inc.
    J. P. Morgan & Co. Incorporated
    Kidder, Peabody & Co., Incorporated
    Kohlberg Kravis Roberts & Co.
    L.F. Rothschild Holdings Inc.
    Mason Best Company
    Merrill Lynch & Co., Inc.
    Merrill Lynch Capital Markets
    Morgan Stanley and Company
    Over-the-counter securities markets
    PaineWebber Group Inc.
    Robertson, Colman & Stephens
    Salomon Inc.
    Shearson Lehman Brothers Inc.
    Small business investment companies
    Smith Barney, Harris Upham & Co. Incorporated
    Stephens Inc.
    Wesray Capital Corporation
    Women in investment banking

The big chill on Wall Street. A. Bianco. il *Bus Week* p54-7 D 7 '87

Deals of the year. D. P. Wiener. il *Fortune* 115:68-72+ F 2 '87

The decline of the superstar [cover story] A. Bianco. il *Bus Week* p90-6+ Ag 17 '87

'Down with M.B.A.'s!' [effect of stock market crash] J. Taylor. il *N Y* 20:34-7 N 2 '87

Everybody's doing it, doing it [hostile takeover game] A. Sloan. il *Forbes* 139:32 Ap 20 '87

Going to investment banking 'boot camp' with Midland's Marines. A. Beam. *Bus Week* p82 Ap 6 '87

Hardball on Wall Street [R. A. Minicucci; cover story] J. Sterngold. il pors *N Y Times Mag* p22-7+ Ag 16 '87

It's back to the basics for your friendly broker. D. P. Wiener. il *U S News World Rep* 103:62-3 N 16 '87

A jolt for Wall St.'s whiz kids [wave of layoffs] B. Powell and C. Friday. il *Newsweek* 110:55-6+ O 26 '87

Look who's charging into the merger business [big banks] S. Bartlett. il *Bus Week* p44 Mr 9 '87

Making oodles of boodle [Financial world list of top money earners] il *Time* 129:49 Je 22 '87

Scarlett O'Hara comes to Wall Street [scramble over leveraged buyout financing] R. L. Stern and E. F. Cone. il *Forbes* 140:37-8+ S 21 '87

This year's MBAs are staying off the Street. L. Helm. il *Bus Week* p40 D 14 '87

Upheaval ahead on Wall Street. R. E. Norton. il *Fortune* 116:68-9+ S 14 '87

Wall Street craving for capital. A. Bianco. il *Bus Week* p34-5 Ap 6 '87

Wall Street is solid—but very nervous. A. Bianco. il *Bus Week* p110 Ja 12 '87

Wall Street's hottest hands. D. Machan. il *Forbes* 139:86-8 Ja 26 '87

Wall Street's new austerity [special section] il *Bus Week* p28-31 O 26 '87

Wall Street's outrageous fortunes. A. Smith. il *Esquire* 107:73-4 Ap '87

When bad things happen to rich people [layoffs on Wall Street] D. Bleeker. *New Repub* 197:17-18 N 23 '87

Accounting

Merrill's loss: why the numbers keep changing [trading fiasco in mortgage-backed securities] E. Spragins. il *Bus Week* p72 Ag 3 '87

Acquisitions and mergers

Big investors on Wall Street [sparring over Salomon Inc.] pors *Fortune* 116:8 O 26 '87

Salomon and Revlon: what really happened. A. Bianco. il pors *Bus Week* p156+ O 12 '87

What color is your mail? [Salomon Brothers pays greenmail to Minerals & Resources Corp.] A. Sloan. il *Forbes* 140:36-7 O 19 '87

A white knight saves Salomon [W. Buffett outflanks R. Perelman] B. Powell. il por *Newsweek* 110:66 O 12 '87

White-knight time on Wall Street [W. Buffett saves Salomon Brothers from corporate raider R. Perelman] J. Egan. il pors *U S News World Rep* 103:60 O 12 '87

Western Europe

The big cheese in London banking could be Swiss [Union Bank of Switzerland's proposed buyout of Hill Samuel Group plc] J. Templeman. il *Bus Week* p37 Jl 27 '87

Anecdotes, facetiae, satire, etc.

Secrets of his success. R. B. Reich. il *N Y Times Mag* p94-5 My 3 '87

Ethical aspects

Adviser beware: cooked books may burn you, too [investment bankers face fraud charges in CPC International's suit against McKesson and Morgan Stanley over sale of C. F. Mueller] L. J. Tell. il *Bus Week* p58+ O 26 '87

Bank Leu's new brouhaha [Guinness spillover] J. Templeman. il *Bus Week* p50 F 2 '87

A big crack in the 'Chinese wall' [arbitrage coexisting with investment banking] C. Welles. il *Bus Week* p33 Mr 2 '87

C.E.O.s take on their investment bankers [insider trading scandal could lead to lower fees] S. P. Sherman. il *Fortune* 115:57-8+ Ap 27 '87

The case against Drexel: will the government come up short? C. Welles. il por *Bus Week* p56-60 Ag 10 '87

Corporate clients feel seduced and abandoned. J. A. Byrne. il *Bus Week* p34 Mr 2 '87

Did Drexel bully takeover candidates? [suit brought by Staley Continental] C. Welles. *Bus Week* p43-4 Mr 9 '87

Ethics and the investment industry [Notre Dame conference] T. C. Widner. *America* 157:444-5 D 12 '87

Have ethics disappeared from Wall Street? R. S. Bachelder. il *Christ Century* 104:628-30 Jl 15-22 '87

The other scandal. *New Repub* 196:6 Mr 23 '87

Press relations

Why Mike Milken is suddenly taking himself public. C. Welles. il pors *Bus Week* p27-8 S 7 '87

Service charges

C.E.O.s take on their investment bankers [insider trading scandal could lead to lower fees] S. P. Sherman. il *Fortune* 115:57-8+ Ap 27 '87

Investment banking takes a new—and risky—turn [bridge loans] C. Farrell. il *Bus Week* p92+ Je 15 '87

Canada

Countdown to an open market. T. Fennell. il *Macleans* 100:38-9 Je 1 '87

Regulating deregulation. T. Fennell. il *Macleans* 100:36-7 O 12 '87

East Asia

East meets Little Rock [Stephens Inc. joint ventures] S. W. Angrist. il por *Forbes* 139:168+ Ap 6 '87

France

    See also
    Rothschild & Associates Bank

Now, the Bourse is in the game for real [le Big Bang] J. Rossant. il *Bus Week* p88 Jl 20 '87

Germany (West)

    See also
    Deutsche Bank AG

Great Britain

    See also
    Credit Suisse First Boston Ltd.
    Hill Samuel Group plc, London
    S.G. Warburg Group plc

Big Bang babies [English bankers working for American banks in London] M. Lewis. *New Repub* 196:17-18 Ja 5-12 '87

Big bust [Big Bang aftermath] R. L. Stern and D. Henry. il *Forbes* 140:64-5 Ag 24 '87

The City of London wanted competition—but not this much. R. A. Melcher. il *Bus Week* p37 Ag 10 '87

Japan

    See also
    Nomura Securities Co. Ltd.

Can Japan work the Street? B. Powell. il *Newsweek* 110:60 O 19 '87

Deregulation: a two-way street. B. Buell. *Bus Week* p62 Je 22 '87

The hesitant money machine. J. Dreyfuss. il *Fortune* 115:38-9+ Mr 30 '87

Japanese takeover artists are learning fast. B. Buell. il *Bus Week* p40-1 Ag 3 '87

Switzerland

    See also
    Bank Leu AG

Investment banking in motion pictures

The platoon of pros who helped out on Wall Street. C. Welles. il por *Bus Week* p38-9 D 21 '87

A view from the trenches [Wall Street] S. Rattner. il *Newsweek* 110:80 D 14 '87

Wall Street's gutter ethics [movie Wall Street] P. C. Newman. il *Macleans* 100:46 D 28 '87

Investment clubs

The club that makes you rich and happy. M. Rowland. il *Work Woman* 12:72-5+ Je '87

Investment clubs. J. W. Merline. il *Consum Res Mag* 70:38 Ag '87

Little guys who beat the market. M. McFadden. il *Fortune* 115:101-2+ F 2 '87

Investment companies *See* Investment trusts

Investment dealers' digest

Lawyer, writer, activist, millionaire [T. L. Cross] A. Kupfer. il por *Fortune* 115:62 Ja 5 '87

Investment fraud *See* Fraud

Investment newsletters

Ace analyst Robert Prechter says when skirts rise, so does the stock market—no bull [Elliott Wave theorist newsletter] L. Aitken. il pors *People Wkly* 27:42-4 My 11 '87

The acid test. M. Hulbert. il *Forbes* 140:320 N 16 '87

Après nous le déluge. M. Hulbert. il *Forbes* 140:242 N 2 '87

Bear? Or bull? [Dow Theory] M. Hulbert. il *Forbes* 140:256 N 30 '87

Calling credit into question [interview with J. Grant of Grant's interest rate observer] A. E. Serwer. il por *Fortune* 116:104 Jl 6 '87

The champion market forecaster [R. Prechter's Elliott Wave theorist] M. A. Elliott. il por *Fortune* 115:75 Ja 5 '87

Chartists [R. Prechter's Elliott Wave theorist] J. K. Glassman. *New Repub* 196:8-10 Ap 6 '87

Go for the aggressive funds [interview with N. G. Fosback of Mutual fund forecaster] A. E. Serwer. il por *Fortune* 115:116 Ap 13 '87

The gold bug bites again. M. Hulbert. por *Forbes* 140:214 S 21 '87

The guru who saw a 2000 Dow [R. Prechter's Elliott Wave theorist newsletter] A. Miller. il por *Newsweek* 109:40+ Ja 19 '87

Half the picture [bond market predictions] M. Hulbert. il *Forbes* 140:140 D 28 '87

How healthy is the bull? M. Hulbert. por *Forbes* 140:308 S 7 '87

How to find top small stocks before the big guys do [OTC insight, newsletter edited by L. G. Navallier] L. Laurence. il por *Money* 16:216 Mr '87

Mailbox mavens [commodity trading investment letters] S. W. Angrist. il *Forbes* 139:168 F 23 '87

A market Prophet who ignores profits [interview with PSR prophet editor M. Brill] A. E. Serwer. il por *Fortune* 116:106 Ag 17 '87

More is not better [switching of mutual funds] M. Hulbert. il *Forbes* 140:216 O 19 '87

Mr. Convertibles [A. S. Lyons of Value Line convertibles] P. Brimelow. por *Forbes* 139:109 My 18 '87

Of wizards and soothsayers. D. N. Dreman. il *Forbes* 139:180 My 4 '87

Popularity doesn't pay [investment letters' favorite mutual funds] M. Hulbert. por *Forbes* 140:132 Ag 10 '87

Rating the newsletters. C. Leinster. il *Fortune* 116 Sp Issue:225+ Fall '87

Reader beware [newsletter writers build portfolio managers] R. Simon. il *Forbes* 140:113+ N 16 '87

Regressing to the mean? [A. Frank's picks for Prudent speculator] M. Hulbert. il *Forbes* 140:262 D 14 '87

The stock market catches a big wave [R. Prechter's Elliott Wave theorist] il por *Discover* 8:12 Mr '87

The ultimate newsletter [Personal portfolio manager] *Money* 16:14 O '87

Where to get good investment advice. J. McNulty. il *Work Woman* 12:122-4 My '87

Who needs a one-way ticket? [market timing letters] M. Hulbert. il *Forbes* 140:244 O 5 '87

Investment tax credit

After tax reform, historic rehabs can still pay off. B. Hitchings. il *Bus Week* p123 Ap 6 '87

Hitch 22 [tax credits intended to draw investment into housing for the poor] J. Novack. il *Forbes* 139:54 F 9 '87

Lease loophole preserves investment tax credit. C. Finck. il *Success Farm* 85:18T My '87

Want a tax shelter—and a good conscience? [tax credits for investing in housing for the poor] C. Yang. *Bus Week* p130 O 5 '87

Investment trusts

  See also

  Alliance Technology Fund

  Americus Shareowner Service Corporation

  Bancroft Convertible Fund, Inc.

  Cash management accounts

  College Retirement Equities Fund

  Commodity funds

  Common Fund

  Constellation Growth Fund

  Decision/Capital Fund Inc.

  Dimensional Fund Advisors

  Dreyfus Capital Value Fund

  Dreyfus Corp.

  Fairmont Fund

  Fidelity Freedom Fund

  Fidelity Magellan Fund

  Fidelity Management & Research Co.

  Fidelity Select-Health Care Fund

  First Investors Corp.

  Franklin Resources, Inc.

  Gabelli Equity Trust

  Growth Stock Outlook, Inc.

  Guardian Mutual Fund, Inc.

  Index funds

  Lehman Opportunity (Firm)

  M. D. Sass Institutional Arbitrage Partners

  Massachusetts Financial Emerging Growth Trust

  Medical Technology Fund

  Miller & Schroeder's Municipal Investors Trust of America

  Mutual Shares Corp.

  Neuberger & Berman Money Market Plus

  Northeast Investors Growth Fund

  Pacific Horizon Aggressive Growth Mutual Fund

  Pennsylvania Mutual Fund

  Petroleum investment trusts

  Quantum Fund

  Real estate investment trusts

  Selected American Shares, Inc.

  Small business investment companies

  Stranger Partnership Fund

  T. Rowe Price Capital Appreciation Fund

  T. Rowe Price New Era Fund Inc.

  T. Rowe Price New Horizons Mutual Fund Inc.

  Tocqueville Fund

  Tudor Fund

  Vanguard Group Inc.

  Vanguard World-U.S. Growth Fund

  Weingarten Equity Fund, Inc.

  Windsor Fund

  World International Growth Portfolio

  Wright Investors' Service

  Yes Fund

  Zweig Fund

1987 annual fund survey [cover story; special section] il *Forbes* 140:133-7+ S 7 '87

Bear-market protection? [funds offering portfolio insurance] J. B. Quinn. il *Newsweek* 109:43 My 25 '87

The best funds over the past five years. T. Paré. il *Fortune* 116 Sp Issue:52 Fall '87

The best mutual funds: here are the pros' choices for the next decade. L. N. Vreeland. il *Money* Sp Issue:65-70+ Fall '87

Best ways to buy foreign stocks. R. Micheli. il *Money* 16:75+ My '87

Bond mutual funds. il *Consum Rep* 52:280-90 D '87

A bond voyage to high yields [foreign bond mutual funds] G. Anrig, Jr. il *Money* 16:129-30+ My '87

Bonds away! Getting off the canvas after the market's shocking KO [bond funds] B. Hager and others. il *Money* 16:26-7 Je '87

Building a worry-free portfolio of mutual funds [cover story; special section] il *Money* 16:92-4+ Ag '87

Bully for bond funds. J. Kosnett. il *Changing Times* 41:47-8+ Mr '87

Chasing yield [closed-end bond funds] D. Henry. il *Forbes* 139:262 Je 15 '87

Choosing a mutual fund: what you should know. L. Marsa. il *Black Enterp* 18:31-3 N '87

A close look at closed-end funds. il *Changing Times* 41:87-8+ My '87

Closed-end funds: keep your eyes open. T. Segal. il *Bus Week* p171 S 14 '87

Closed-end mutual funds can be a bargain. S. Rowe. il *Black Enterp* 18:31-2 Ag '87

Do your homework before stashing that cash [money market mutual funds] F. A. Miller. il *Bus Week* p170 D 28 '87-Ja 4 '88

Investment trusts—*cont.*

Down, but hardly out [fund companies and the crash] R. Simon. il *Forbes* 140:81 N 30 '87

The end of innocence in mutual funds. E. Schurenberg. il *Money* 16:126-8+ D '87

End of the comfort factor [effect of stock market crash] N. R. Gibbs. il *Time* 130:60 N 16 '87

The exclusive Money rankings. il *Money* 16:181-2+ My '87

The exclusive Money rankings. il *Money* 16:159-65+ N '87

Fair-weather genius [speculative mania in mutual funds] K. L. Fisher. il *Forbes* 140:304 S 7 '87

Fixed-income mutual funds. il *Consum Rep* 52:570-9 S '87

For mutual funds, the best of times and the worst of times. S. Weiss. il *Bus Week* p66-7 Jl 6 '87

Fund watch. See issues of Money

The fund way to invest abroad. *Fortune* 116 Sp Issue:78 Fall '87

The funds. See issues of Forbes

Funds that have it both ways [dual-purpose funds] A. L. Cowan. il *Bus Week* p92 Mr 9 '87

Getting the most from mutual funds [Mutual fund scoreboard; special section] J. M. Laderman. il *Bus Week* p64-7+ F 23 '87

Go for the aggressive funds [interview with N. G. Fosback of Mutual fund forecaster] A. E. Serwer. il por *Fortune* 115:116 Ap 13 '87

Gold is still the mutual fund heavyweight champ. G. Weiss. il *Bus Week* p152-3 O 12 '87

Gold moves to the front of the mutual fund parade. J. M. Laderman. il *Bus Week* p78-9 Ap 13 '87

Gold rush [subculture of individuals, small businesses and bureaucracies has sprung up around mutual fund business] M. Kuntz. il *Forbes* 139 Ann Directory:75-6+ Ap 27 '87

Government minus [misrepresentation of government bond fund yields] B. Weberman. il *Forbes* 139:117 Ap 20 '87

A guide to mutual funds [cover story] il *Consum Rep* 52:352-64 Je '87

The hassle-less road to investing abroad. P. M. Scherschel. il *U S News World Rep* 102:56-7 My 11 '87

Hedging against the dollar [bond and equity funds] J. A. Conway. il *Forbes* 139:8 Je 15 '87

How cheap is cheap enough? [closed-end funds] C. Farrell. il *Bus Week* p180 N 16 '87

How put options prop up mutual funds. P. Nulty. il *Fortune* 116:174-5 D 21 '87

How risky are bonds? M. Kuntz and D. Pardee. il *Forbes* 139:168 Mr 23 '87

How to hold a bond fund's feet to the fire. E. Schurenberg. il *Money* 16:113-15+ Ja '87

How to pick the next fund hits [cover story; special section] il *Money* 16:34-8+ My '87

Investing: good way to begin. H. Twidale. il *Good Housekeep* 204:215 Je '87

Investor bites sleeping dog [changing from closed-end to open-end status] R. Phalon. il *Forbes* 140:178-9 O 5 '87

Keep it simple [ratings of 400 funds] W. Baldwin. il *Forbes* 139:128-30+ F 9 '87

Leery of land? Try mutual funds. M. Zall. *Success Farm* 85:66 S '87

Leveraging your mutual funds. B. Kallen. il *Forbes* 139:161-2 Ap 6 '87

Looking for an encore in mutual funds. M. Schiffres. il *U S News World Rep* 102:52-3 Ap 20 '87

Making the most of the bond debacle. D. Zigas. il *Bus Week* p202-3 N 2 '87

Megafunds: what have they done for you lately? M. Schiffres. il *Changing Times* 41:103-6+ N '87

Money funds: higher yields lure billions from savvy savers. il *Money* 16:30 Jl '87

Mutual fund daze [special section] il *U S News World Rep* 102:52-62 F 16 '87

Mutual-fund madness. P. Wang and D. Pauly. il *Newsweek* 110:40-1 Ag 31 '87

Mutual fund mayhem may not be over [stock market crash] L. Helm. il *Bus Week* p42-3 N 9 '87

Mutual fund update. See issues of Changing Times beginning June 1987

Mutual funds: how to figure your real return. J. Bodnar. il *Changing Times* 41:69-70 Ap '87

Mutual funds that have outpaced the bull. J. Rachlin. il *U S News World Rep* 103:58-60 Ag 31 '87

Mutual funds that thrive on risk [sector funds] M. Schiffres. il *U S News World Rep* 102:60 Mr 16 '87

Mutual funds: what a party [cover story] J. Kosnett. il *Changing Times* 41:24-34+ O '87

A new plate with bearish fare [post-crash strategies] il *U S News World Rep* 103:34+ N 9 '87

New ways to pick winners [cover story; special section] il *Money* 16:48-53+ N '87

No exit [rash of closed-end investment trusts as harbinger of market crash] L. Jereski. il *Forbes* 139:170 Mr 23 '87

No place to hide [hyping of bond fund yields] J. B. Quinn. il *Newsweek* 109:62 My 11 '87

Patience, sir [closed-end bond funds] B. Weberman. il *Forbes* 140:235 N 2 '87

Places for investors to park their profits [money market deposit accounts and money market mutual funds] M. J. Williams. il *Fortune* 116:127 S 28 '87

Play those sexy sectors with care. C. A. Fried. il *Money* 16:75-7+ Ap '87

Playing the closed-ends. J. B. Quinn. il *Newsweek* 110:65 Ag 17 '87

Playing the market a sector at a time. J. M. Laderman. il *Bus Week* p122-3 Ap 6 '87

Popularity doesn't pay [investment letters' favorite mutual funds] M. Hulbert. por *Forbes* 140:132 Ag 10 '87

Portfolio monitor. See issues of Changing Times beginning June 1987

The privilege of paying more [minimum investments] J. R. Hayes. il *Forbes* 140:206 S 21 '87

A question of principle: can do-gooders do well? [ethical funds] J. Rachlin. il *U S News World Rep* 102:50-1 Ja 26 '87

Rating the new market timers [money managers timing the market with mutual funds] J. Edgerton. il *Money* 16:117-20+ Mr '87

Reader beware [newsletter writers turned portfolio managers] R. Simon. il *Forbes* 140:113+ N 16 '87

Rx for stock market shock. J. P. Newport, Jr. il *Fortune* 116:169+ N 9 '87

The savvy way to buy closed-end funds. M. Meyer. il *Money* 16:153-4+ S '87

A second look at load funds. il *Consum Rep* 52:512-15 Ag '87

Sector funds: how to get a piece of the action [cover story] J. Kosnett. il *Changing Times* 41:26-32 My '87

Seek funds that give growth plus income. A. Rock. il *Money* 16:95-6+ Ja '87

Sizing up those single-state munis [municipal bond funds] C. A. Fried. il *Money* 16:105-6+ O '87

Steady-course mutual funds. L. N. Vreeland. il *Money* 16:52+ Mr '87

The still-booming bond funds. J. A. Conway. il *Forbes* 139:8 F 9 '87

Stock mutual funds. il *Consum Rep* 52:267-80 D '87

Switching mutual funds. M. Rowland. il *Work Woman* 12:60+ N '87

Ten all-star funds for all seasons. E. Schurenberg. il *Money* 16:111-12+ Je '87

That closed-end feeling. J. Rachlin. il *U S News World Rep* 103:83 O 12 '87

These investors take a stand. L. Stern. il *Changing Times* 41:134-6 N '87

True-blue, Simon-pure no-load mutual funds. A. E. Serwer. il *Fortune* 115:19 Ja 5 '87

The unlikely kings of IPOs [closed-end funds] G. Weiss. il *Bus Week* p60 Jl 27 '87

Wall Street's laggards. S. Weiss. il *Bus Week* p34-5 Ja 26 '87

What the doctor ordered: medical mutual funds. T. Segal. il *Bus Week* p96 Ag 3 '87

What to do about the bond bust: timely answers to help mutual fund investors rethink their strategies. il *Money* 16:68-9 Je '87

What to do when bond funds fall. J. M. Laderman. il *Bus Week* p140-1 My 4 '87

When the house always wins [performance of mutual funds operated by largest national brokerage houses] W. L. Updegrave. il *Money* 16:97-100 Jl '87

Where these fund managers go, you follow [hedge funds] D. P. Wiener. il *U S News World Rep* 103:50-1 Jl 13 '87

Which funds lost the least? [stock market crash] L. R. Walbert. il *Forbes* 140:36-7 N 16 '87

Why muni bond funds got massacred. D. Zigas. il *Bus Week* p108 Je 1 '87

Why this is 1929 all over again. M. M. Thomas. *Nation* 244:641-2+ My 16 '87

You'll find a few nuggets in the mutual fund rubble. G. Weiss. il *Bus Week* p160-1 D 28 '87-Ja 4 '88

Acquisitions and mergers

Leave it to T. Boone's son to sniff out a bargain [race for closed-end funds] W. Glasgall. il por *Bus Week* p113-14 Mr 16 '87

Investment trusts—Acquisitions and mergers—*cont.*
International aspects
$11 for a $10 bill? [M. B. Javett's bid for Bancroft Convertible] R. Phalon. il *Forbes* 139:99 Ja 26 '87
Distressed merchandise [Cambrian & General Securities] R. Phalon. por *Forbes* 139:180 Ap 6 '87

Advertising
The honor system. B. Weberman. il *Forbes* 140:255 D 14 '87
Live and learn [failed ad campaign by Fred Alger Mgt.] D. Machan. il por *Forbes* 140:135 S 7 '87
Mutual fund ads: only the hype is '100% guaranteed!' [bond funds] T. Segal. *Bus Week* p92 Ag 24 '87

Customer relations
Busy signals [customers' inability to get through to brokers and funds on toll free numbers during the crash] M. Schifrin. il *Forbes* 140:38+ N 16 '87

Directors
Nice work if you can get it. *Forbes* 140:137 S 7 '87

Dollar cost averaging
How some funds turn the best investing strategy into a bum deal. C. A. Fried and L. N. Vreeland. il *Money* 16:35-6+ S '87

Laws and regulations
The SEC's Kathryn McGrath keeps mutual funds in line. L. N. Vreeland. il por *Money* 16:160 Jl '87

Management fees
At last, a way to compare loads and fees. il *Money* 16:37 My '87
Find the hidden fee. *Consum Rep* 52:357 Je '87
The long trail [fund companies paying brokers an annual commission] R. Simon. il *Forbes* 140:204 S 21 '87
Mutual funds: finding the hidden fees. B. G. Quint. *Glamour* 85:196 Jl '87
Now there's more to fees than meets the eye. V. Cahan. il *Bus Week* p67 F 23 '87
Steal this trade [free riding on money management advice] R. McGough. il *Forbes* 139:49 Ja 12 '87
A tax on income you never see. E. Schurenberg. il *Money* 16:81-2+ S '87

Marketing
Dispassionate advice [conflict of interests arising from brokers sales of mutual funds] J. Heins. il *Forbes* 139:160+ Mr 9 '87
Go for gray, forget the pickup trucks. L. Saunders. il *Forbes* 140:134-5 S 7 '87

Taxation
Attention, swappers [trade-in time for funds] G. Weiss. il *Bus Week* p180 N 16 '87
Fund havens. R. Phalon. il *Forbes* 140:140+ S 7 '87
Mutual funds' 'phantom' cash. C. Yang. *Bus Week* p104 O 26 '87
Seven tax tips. W. Baldwin. il *Forbes* 140:154+ S 7 '87
State muni bond funds: coming your way? [triple-tax-exempts] B. Hitchings. *Bus Week* p124 Ap 6 '87
A tax on income you never see. E. Schurenberg. il *Money* 16:81-2+ S '87
Where tax reform hits mutual funds. P. Philipps. il *Bus Week* p106 Mr 30 '87
Why funds disincorporate. J. R. Hayes. il *Forbes* 139:250 My 18 '87

Great Britain
See also
Cambrian & General Securities
Templeton, Galbraith & Hansberger Ltd.
Bubble and squeak. R. McGough. *Forbes* 140:161 S 7 '87

Japan
See also
Japan Fund, Inc.

Korea (South)
See also
Korea Fund Inc.

Pacific region
The exotic East: land of the rising funds. T. Segal. il *Bus Week* p116-17 Jl 13 '87

Investments
See also
American Association of Individual Investors
Annuities
Art as an investment
Black brokers
Bondholders
Bonds
Bonds, Government
Brokers
Calculators—Investment use
Capital investments
Coins as an investment
Colleges and universities—Investments

Computers—Investment use
Dividends
Firearms—Collectors and collecting
Gold as an investment
Hedging (Finance)
Information storage and retrieval systems—Investment use
Institutional investments
Interest (Economics)
Investment clubs
Investment newsletters
Investment trusts
Joint ventures
Mortgage bonds and notes
Platinum as an investment
Postage stamps as an investment
Precious metals as an investment
Real estate investment
Saving and savings
Securities
Silver as an investment
Small business investment companies
Speculation
Stockholders
Stocks
Television broadcasting—Financial programs
Venture capital
Wine as an investment
Workout investments
10 great ways to invest for income [cover story; special section] il *Money* 16:59-64+ Je '87
The 1988 investor's guide. il *Fortune* 116 Sp Issue:8-9+ Fall '87
About investing. V. VanCaspel. il *Saturday Evening Post* 259:112 Mr '87
About investing. V. VanCaspel. il *Saturday Evening Post* 259:30+ My/Je '87
After the crash [cover story; special section] il *Money* 16:74-80+ D '87
Answering your financial questions. V. VanCaspel. il *Saturday Evening Post* 259:12+ S '87
Answering your financial questions. V. VanCaspel. il *Saturday Evening Post* 259:16+ D '87
The best investors of our time [M. Steinhardt, A. Rock and W. E. Buffett] il pors *Money* Sp Issue:32-6+ Fall '87
The best ways to invest your next $1,000 [cover story; special section] il *Money* 16:54-60+ Jl '87
Betting on the buck. M. Schiffres. il *Changing Times* 41:48-50 S '87
Black enterprise annual money management issue [special issue; with editorial comment by Earl G. Graves] il *Black Enterp* 18:9, 48-50+ O '87
Building up an investment portfolio. D. Lamaute. il *Black Enterp* 17:35-6 F '87
Common sense investing [collectibles] M. Thorne. *Antiques Collect Hobbies* 92:51-2 S '87
The contrarian. D. N. Dreman. See alternate issues of *Forbes*
Coups and calamities of investment year 1986. il *Money* 16:13 F '87
Cutting risks in risky times. J. B. Quinn. il *Newsweek* 110:47 Ag 31 '87
Don't climb off the bull yet. J. J. Curran. il *Fortune* 116:195-6+ Ag 3 '87
Five ways to protect your money. J. B. Quinn. il *Newsweek* 110:52-3 O 26 '87
Frenzy feeds frenzy [G. Soros' The alchemy of finance] R. Phalon. por *Forbes* 139:44-5 My 18 '87
Getting rich by only half trying. D. N. Dreman. il *Forbes* 140 Sp Issue:396 O 26 '87
Getting the best of the bear [cover story; special section] il *U S News World Rep* 103:33-4+ N 9 '87
The good times roll on for investors [midyear investment outlook; cover story; special section] il *Bus Week* p56-62+ Jl 6 '87
Great investment portfolios [cover story] D. M. Kehrer. il *Changing Times* 41:24-36 S '87
Guarding your hard-won wealth. R. Eisenberg. il *Money* 16:62-4+ O '87
How to find a safe haven—and when to get back in. J. B. Quinn. il *Newsweek* 110:39-40 N 2 '87
How to handle a windfall. J. Crudele. il *N Y* 20:10-11 Ag 3 '87
How to invest $1,000. B. G. Quint. il *Glamour* 85:186+ N '87
Investing $1,000: here's how to get started. G. G. Burger. il *McCalls* 114:133-4 Ag '87
Investing: dollar sinks the markets like a pair of cement shoes. il *Money* 16:42 Je '87

Investments—*cont.*

Investing for a brighter future [excerpt from 50 plus guide to retirement investing] W. W. David. il *50 Plus* 27:68+ Mr '87

Investment tips for income-seekers. J. Bodnar. *Changing Times* 41:7 My '87

Investments: a funny thing happened on the way to 3000. il *Money* 16:32 D '87

Investments: a stronger dollar lifts stocks and bonds. il *Money* 16:28 Ag '87

Investments: can the stock market dodge another bullet? il *Money* 16:34 Jl '87

Investments: does the bull market have nine lives? il *Money* 16:32 O '87

Investments: hope triumphs over real rate increases. il *Money* 16:30 My '87

Investments: lost in a dark cloud of interest-rate worries. il *Money* 16:28 N '87

Investments: no doubt about it—that's no bull, it's a gorilla. il *Money* 16:40 Mr '87

Investments: rising on a tide of worldwide liquidity. il *Money* 16:30 S '87

Investments: the market shrugs off the Boesky-Iran bomb-shells. il *Money* 16:42 Ja '87

Investments: who says Wall Street doesn't have a sole? il *Money* 16:38 Ap '87

Investments: why 1986 was the year of the blue chip. il *Money* 16:52 F '87

Investor's scorecard [special section] P. Tai. il *Money* Sp Issue:12-14+ Fall '87

"It's just not fair" [investing in collectibles] S. Blotnick. il *Forbes* 139:302-3 Ja 12 '87

Making your money grow. V. VanCaspel. *Saturday Evening Post* 259:34+ N '87

Markets & investments. See issues of Business Week

The master money manager [views of G. Soros] D. R. Katz. il por *Esquire* 108:67-8 D '87

Model portfolio. See issues of Money beginning April 1983

Money managers after the crash. J. P. Newport, Jr. il *Fortune* 116:71-2 D 7 '87

Money profile. See issues of Money

New kick in the bull market. J. J. Curran. il *Fortune* 115:157-8+ My 11 '87

On your money. See issues of Changing Times beginning August 1983 through May 1987

Out of harm's way: girding for inflation. J. Crudele. il *N Y* 20:22 Je 1 '87

Personal investing. See issues of Fortune

Playing for a fall [investment outlook in light of falling dollar] E. A. Finn, Jr. il *Forbes* 139:98-101 F 23 '87

Portfolio monitor. See issues of Changing Times beginning June 1987

Protecting your nest egg: a long-term strategy. J. B. Quinn. il *Newsweek* 110:40-1 N 9 '87

Rich for life [special section] il *Work Woman* 12:31-4+ F '87

The six best ways to invest in 1987 [special section] il *Money* 16:54-62+ Ja '87

Smart investments for savvy money managers [special section] il *Black Enterp* 17:319-20+ Je '87

Solid investments you can get your hands around [tangible assets] B. Bauer. il *U S News World Rep* 103:106 D 28 '87-Ja 4 '88

Taking the plunge: how to start investing [cover story] J. Kosnett. il *Changing Times* 41:22-6+ Ap '87

That rare thing, an investment book worth reading [views of M. Talley] R. Brady. il por *Nations Bus* 75:76 N '87

Their own money. J. Crudele. il *N Y* 20:20+ S 14 '87

To win, be willing to make mistakes [interview with M. D. Talley] il por *U S News World Rep* 103:58 Ag 10 '87

To win, play by the rules [interview with A. P. Tobias] por *U S News World Rep* 103:86 N 16 '87

Trivial pursuits: investing for fun in the toys and kitsch of the fabulous '50s. H. Wheelwright. il *Money* 16:65-6+ D '87

Wall Street letter. See issues of Money through December 1987

The watchword after Bloody Monday: diversify. D. Zigas. *Bus Week* p142 N 9 '87

What you can do with $1,000. L. Wiener. il *U S News World Rep* 103:78-80 O 19 '87

What's ahead for 1987: investing. il *Changing Times* 41:57-61 Ja '87

What's new? A profusion of smart investment moves. M. Asnes. *Vogue* 177:66 Ja '87

Where to invest in 1988 [cover story; special section] il *Bus Week* p95-9+ D 28 '87-Ja 4 '88

Where to put your money now. J. Rachlin and L. Wiener. il *U S News World Rep* 103:100-1+ D 28 '87-Ja 4 '88

Where to put your rainy day funds. S. Rowe. il *Black Enterp* 17:87-9 Jl '87

Would you panic if your stock took a dive? J. Rachlin. il *U S News World Rep* 102:60-1 Je 8 '87

Your new game plan [after the stock market crash] J. Rachlin and A. McGrath. il *U S News World Rep* 103:25-6+ N 2 '87

Bibliography

Blue-chip books for investors. J. Kosnett. il *Changing Times* 41:69+ D '87

In a changing market, put stock in a good library. J. Rachlin. il *U S News World Rep* 103:85-6 N 16 '87

Information services

Where to get great investment advice for free. B. Hager. il *Money* 16:131-2+ S '87

Psychological aspects

Are you the type who really goes for it? J. M. Laderman. il *Bus Week* p138 D 28 '87-Ja 4 '88

Expert advice on how to cope with economic anxiety. C. Friday. il *Newsweek* 109:20-1 My 4 '87

Insights. S. Blotnick. See issues of Forbes beginning July 28, 1986

Social aspects

See also

Community Reinvestment Act of 1977

Give your dollars a political spin. A. T. Marlin and others. il *Nation* 244:75-6+ Ja 24 '87

Laura Scher: doing good business helps good causes. M. Mallory. il por *Bus Week* p76 O 26 '87

A question of principle: can do-gooders do well? J. Rachlin. il *U S News World Rep* 102:50-1 Ja 26 '87

Realizing happy returns, even if they're small [investing in community development loan funds] J. Rachlin. il *U S News World Rep* 103:68 N 30 '87

Reaping high returns from social investments. B. Robson. il *Black Enterp* 18:86-8+ D '87

These investors take a stand. L. Stern. il *Changing Times* 41:134-6 N '87

Study and teaching

Do you really want to be rich? [mail order finance courses] M. Schiffres. il *Changing Times* 41:73-4+ O '87

Inner-city students are bullish on investing [Washington, D.C.] P. Rowe. il *Child Today* 16:22-6 My/Je '87

Taxation

How seven pros are shifting gears. P. A. Dreyfus and L. N. Vreeland. il *Money* 16:72-4+ F '87

Investment angles. il *U S News World Rep* 103:76+ D 7 '87

Investments that can save you taxes. il *Money* 16:135-6+ F '87

Look on the bright side: Uncle Sam is simplifying your decisions. C. Yang. il *Bus Week* p107 D 28 '87-Ja 4 '88

Moneywise. il *Harpers Bazaar* 120:40+ Ja '87

Surprise! The unexpected results of the new tax law . . . and how you can benefit from them [cover story; special section] il *Money* 16:52-6+ S '87

Tax reform changes investment strategies. M. Zall. *Success Farm* 85 no6:19 Mr '87

Timing losses and gains. G. Anrig, Jr. *Money* 16:239 N '87

Tips for holding down your taxes. R. E. Norton. il *Fortune* 116 Sp Issue:93-4+ Fall '87

Using your new money freedom. M. Rowland. il *Work Woman* 12:31-4 F '87

Your investment strategy after tax reform. J. C. Szabo. il *Nations Bus* 75:26-8 Ap '87

Terminology

A global investor's lexicon. il *Money* 16:137 My '87

Investments, American

American competitiveness is healthier than it looks. P. C. Roberts. il *Bus Week* p18 Jl 13 '87

Are you ready to go global? [foreign stocks] J. Mendes. il *Fortune* 116 Sp Issue:71-2+ Fall '87

Buying abroad [foreign stock funds] R. Addis. il *Forbes* 140:142+ S 7 '87

The global money game [cover story; special section] il map *U S News World Rep* 102:49-54+ My 11 '87

Going global [special section] il *Money* 16:50-2+ My '87

Innocent victims [multinational corporations getting caught in trap set for tax haven abusers] L. Saunders. il *Forbes* 140:64+ O 5 '87

Investments, American—*cont.*

Strong currencies signal hot spots for trading. B. Riemer. il *Bus Week* p148-50 D 28 '87-Ja 4 '88

There are still some bargains left in foreign stocks. J. Templeman. il *Bus Week* p62 Jl 6 '87

Trading on foreign soil. D. R. Katz. il *Esquire* 107:39-40 Ja '87

Venturing abroad [data bases tracking foreign stocks] il *Forbes* 139:112 Ap 20 '87

Where your bucks should stop over there [foreign securities] P. A. Dreyfus. il *Money* 16:131-2+ Ja '87

Why U.S. companies don't always win friends abroad. P. M. Jones. il *Sch Update* 120:31-2 O 2 '87

Yankee, stay home. B. Weberman. il *Forbes* 140:127 Ag 10 '87

You don't have to be a giant to score big overseas. il *Bus Week* p62-3 Ap 13 '87

Australia

Head Down Under for double-digit bond yields. T. Segal. *Bus Week* p126 S 21 '87

Reynolds hits pay dirt Down Under [gold] G. L. Miles. il *Bus Week* p99 Jl 13 '87

Barbados

The case of a Chicago electronics company [relocation of assembly operations] *Focus* 37:4 Summ '87

Belize

Fishing in muddy waters. W. P. Barrett. il *Forbes* 139:128+ My 4 '87

In Belize, Coke goes better [Coca-Cola vs. rain forest] D. Voelker. il map *Sierra* 72:12 S/O '87

Brazil

Bungling in Brazil. N. Gall. il *Forbes* 140:39-40 Jl 27 '87

Two giant U.S. business efforts that failed in Brazil [H. Ford's Fordlandia and D. Ludwig's Jari Project] M. S. Forbes. il *Forbes* 140:18-19 O 19 '87

Canada

Americanization of a high-flyer [DeHavilland Aircraft of Canada since the Boeing takeover] P. C. Newman. il *Macleans* 100:42 F 23 '87

Amoco becomes bolder [bid for Dome] C. Siler. il *Forbes* 140:88 N 2 '87

Bell shifts assembly of light helicopters to Canadian facility. il *Aviat Week Space Technol* 126:77-8 Mr 16 '87

Canada trade talks may end 'fire sales' of U.S. subsidiaries. H. Fields. *Publ Wkly* 232:12-13 O 23 '87

Death sentences from America [Ford of Canada ordered to drop Canadian advertising agencies] P. C. Newman. il *Macleans* 100:39 O 5 '87

Dome's day of reckoning [creditors disappointed with Amoco Canada bid] T. Tedesco. il *Macleans* 100:29 My 25 '87

Dome's deepening saga [proposed sale of Dome to Amoco Canada Petroleum Co. Ltd.] D. Jenish. il *Macleans* 100:26 Jl 6 '87

Dome's last deal [bid by Amoco Canada; cover story; special section; with editorial comment by Kevin Doyle] il *Macleans* 100:2, 34-42 My 4 '87

Dome's light at the end of the tunnel [Amoco raises its takeover offer] D. Jenish. il *Macleans* 100:50 N 30 '87

Dome's lingering drama [agreement with Amoco Canada Petroleum] T. Tedesco. il *Macleans* 100:40 My 18 '87

A free trade advance. D. Jenish. il *Macleans* 100:38-9 My 18 '87

Open for business, up for sale. A. Fotheringham. il *Macleans* 100:56 Je 1 '87

The ownership issue [Canada-U.S. free trade negotiations] D. Jenish. il *Macleans* 100:40+ Je 1 '87

Picking up the pieces [Metropolitan Life's purchase offer for Principal Group's assets] J. Howse. il *Macleans* 100:26-7 Ag 31 '87

Reckoning for a broker [First National Bank of Chicago considers purchasing stake in Wood Gundy] T. Tedesco. il *Macleans* 100:37 D 7 '87

A threat to the public interest [loss to Canada of Dome to Amoco] P. C. Newman. il *Macleans* 100:31 Jl 6 '87

Caribbean region

See also

Caribbean Basin Initiative, 1983-

China

The China bubble bursts. L. Kraar. il *Fortune* 116:86-9 Jl 6 '87

McDonnell Douglas grabs a piece of China's sky. D. J. Yang. il *Bus Week* p35 Ag 17 '87

The next 'Asian miracle' may be under way—in China. D. J. Yang. il *Bus Week* p144-5 N 2 '87

Setting up shop in China: three paths to success [PPG, Reebok and Foxboro] D. J. Yang. il *Bus Week* p74 O 19 '87

Egypt

GM's grand design in Egypt may be a mirage. B. Slavin. il *Bus Week* p46 Mr 30 '87

Great Britain

Big Bang babies [English bankers working for American banks in London] M. Lewis. *New Repub* 196:17-18 Ja 5-12 '87

Cash flow in the fast lane [Ford buys Aston Martin] T. Tedesco. il *Macleans* 100:39 S 21 '87

Egad, chaps! It's a Yankee discount broker [Fidelity Management in London] L. Therrien. il *Bus Week* p97 F 16 '87

Gary Klesch is no innocent abroad. S. Miller. il por *Bus Week* p144 S 14 '87

Have you driven an Aston Martin lately? [Ford agrees to buy Aston Martin Lagonda] il *Newsweek* 110:64 S 21 '87

Lotus: living with the General. P. Bingham. il *Mot Trend* 39:48-51 F '87

India

The mouse that roared at Pepsi [Double-Cola] S. Tefft. il *Bus Week* p42 S 7 '87

Ireland

How Citicorp landed in an Irish stew [trading gaffe in Dublin] R. A. Melcher. *Bus Week* p40-1 D 21 '87

Lessons from Ireland. K. K. Wiegner. il *Forbes* 140:37-8+ S 7 '87

Italy

Tooling into the luxury market in a Lamborghini [Chrysler's deal] W. C. Symonds. il *Bus Week* p45+ My 4 '87

Japan

Avon calling—at the Tokyo Exchange [selling 40% of Japanese subsidiary to the Japanese] T. Holden. il *Bus Week* p116 D 14 '87

Deregulation: a two-way street. B. Buell. *Bus Week* p62 Je 22 '87

How to beat the Japanese at home. J. Dreyfuss. il *Fortune* 116:80-3 Ag 31 '87

How to beat the Japanese: five U.S. companies rise to the challenge [cover story; special section] C. P. Work and others. il *U S News World Rep* 103:38-45 Ag 24 '87

How to say frenzy in Japanese. A. Rock. il *Money* 16:211-12 Je '87

In Tokyo, U.S. firms are slugging it out [brokers] B. Buell. il *Bus Week* p90 S 7 '87

Just in time—American-style [Garrett turbochargers made in Japan] G. Bronson. il *Forbes* 139:132+ Mr 9 '87

Just when IBM was roaring back in Japan . . . A. Borrus. il por *Bus Week* p70-1 F 2 '87

Sitting tight in Japan [interview with L. Biehl] A. E. Serwer. il por *Fortune* 115:306 Ap 27 '87

Soon, Citicorp 'branches' could be all over Japan [sharing automated teller machines with Dai-Ichi Kangyo] J. B. Treece. *Bus Week* p82 Ja 19 '87

Straw in the wind? [A. Sieg, president of Kodak Japan] A. Tanzer. il por *Forbes* 139:122-3 F 9 '87

Time to go easy on Japanese stocks? J. P. Newport, Jr. il *Fortune* 116:97-8 Ag 31 '87

Korea (South)

Playing politics [volatility of share price of the Korea Fund] P. Fuhrman. il *Forbes* 140:51 Ag 24 '87

Latin America

See also

ACCION International

Mexico

Going south to cut costs. H. Eason. il *Nations Bus* 75:24 F '87

Made in U.S.A./Mexico: a new industrial partnership. E. C. Conkling. map *Focus* 36:32-3 Wint '86

The Mexican connection [U.S. auto factories] P. Lyons. *Car Driv* 32:69 Mr '87

The rise of gringo capitalism [U.S. companies in the border zones] J. B. Copeland. il *Newsweek* 109:40-1 Ja 5 '87

Where the dollar still buys a hot property [Acapulco] A. Bard. il *Bus Week* p180 My 25 '87

Yankee! Welcome to Mexico! J. Castro. il *Time* 129:51 Je 1 '87

Northern Ireland

Why Irish eyes frown at U.S. help [pressure to open jobs in American firms to Ulster Catholics] P. Sherrid. il *U S News World Rep* 103:32 Ag 24 '87

Pacific region

Bill Simon goes treasure-hunting in the Pacific. T. Carson and C. Debes. il por *Bus Week* p84-6 Mr 9 '87

Investments, American—Pacific region—*cont.*
William Simon's Pacific overtures. L. J. Davis. il pors *N Y Times Mag* p14-17+ D 27 '87

Saudi Arabia
Arabian slights. il *Fortune* 115:7-8 Ja 5 '87

South Africa
The business of fighting apartheid. M. Massing. il *Atlantic* 259:26-32 F '87
Citicorp pulls out. A. Edmond, Jr. *Black Enterp* 18:22 S '87
Commandments without Moses [L. Sullivan, author of Sullivan principles, demands withdrawal of U.S. firms] W. E. Smith. il por *Time* 129:34 Je 15 '87
Cutting ties to a troubled land [impact of U.S. corporate pullout] B. Rudolph. il *Time* 129:44-5 Je 29 '87
Dow and South Africa [address, April 11, 1987] R. K. Long. *Vital Speeches Day* 53:520-4 Je 15 '87
Exxon becomes 87th U.S. firm to quit S. Africa. *Jet* 71:4 Ja 19 '87
Exxon pulls the plug [sale of South African holdings] T. Fennell. il *Macleans* 100:27 Ja 12 '87
Harvard to the rescue [divestiture of portfolio in South Africa; candidates for overseer] W. F. Buckley. *Natl Rev* 39:58 Jl 3 '87
If Coke has its way, blacks will soon own 'the real thing' [bid to sell off stake in South African bottler] S. Mufson. il *Bus Week* p56 Mr 23 '87
McGraw-Hill to sell South Africa branch. *Publ Wkly* 231:10 Mr 13 '87
Methodists will cut some stocks linked to S. Africa. *Jet* 72:14 S 14 '87
Out of South Africa. J. M. Woods. *Essence* 17:30 Mr '87
Out of South Africa: divestment hits a snag [Baltimore ordinance requiring public pension funds to sell stocks challenged] E. Weiner and L. J. Tell. il *Bus Week* p53 Jl 6 '87
Pull out of S. Africa in 9 months, Sullivan urges. por *Jet* 72:4 Je 22 '87
Shell game [Shell Oil accused of using former church leader James Armstrong to neutralize religious opposition to Shell's South African activities] *Christ Century* 104:937 O 28 '87
South Africa: why Leon Sullivan gave up his 'principles'. R. A. Manning. il por *U S News World Rep* 102:10-11 Je 15 '87
South African disinvestment: social responsibility for the long haul. K. Bean. il por *Humanist* 47:28-9+ S/O '87
'Sullivan principles' deadline draws near. por *Jet* 71:14 Ja 12 '87
Sullivan says divest [Rev. L. Sullivan] F. D. Brown and D. C. Ruffin. il por *Black Enterp* 18:17 Ag '87
Sullivan's principles [call for disinvestment] L. Waldorf. *New Repub* 197:14-16 S 7 '87
Tainted money: the ethics and rhetoric of divestment [colleges and business] R. L. Payton. il *Change* 19:55-60 My/Je '87
The U.S. and apartheid. L. H. Sullivan; P. Duignan. *Current* 297:11-17 N '87
When freedom to read suffers [implications of decisions of McGraw-Hill and other publishing firms to terminate their South African operations] I. L. Horowitz. por *Publ Wkly* 232:38 Jl 17 '87
Why black workers may say 'thanks, but no thanks' to Ford [partial worker ownership of Samcor] S. Mufson. il *Bus Week* p47 Jl 6 '87
Yale anti-apartheid protest. il *Jet* 72:15 Je 15 '87

Southeast Asia
Seagate goes East—and comes back a winner. R. Brandt. il por *Bus Week* p94 Mr 16 '87

Soviet Union
Trump lands in Red Square [proposed luxury hotels] J. Barnathan. il por *Newsweek* 110:41 Jl 20 '87
The twain are meeting—and cutting deals [U.S.-Soviet joint ventures] R. W. King and P. Galuszka. il *Bus Week* p88 D 7 '87

Spain
Spain: Europe's sun belt. H. Eason. map *Nations Bus* 75:28 Mr '87

Venezuela
Trust me [views of C. A. Perez] L. Gubernick. il por *Forbes* 139:152 Mr 9 '87

Virgin Islands of the United States
The Caribbean Basin Initiative [address, October 1, 1987] A. A. Farrelly. *Vital Speeches Day* 54:68-70 N 15 '87

Investments, Arab
United States
The boys from Bahrain [Arabian Investment Banking Corp.] R. Morais. il por *Forbes* 140:181 O 5 '87

Investments, Argentine
United States
Closely watched banks: one that got away [Central National Bank of New York] F. A. Miller and R. A. Kessler. il por *Bus Week* p108 O 19 '87

Investments, Australian
Canada
Carling goes Australian [takeover by Elders IXL Ltd.] T. Tedesco. il *Macleans* 100:36 Mr 9 '87

United States
Ansett's stock purchase will place foreign stake in America West at 20%. M. A. Dornheim. il map *Aviat Week Space Technol* 127:41-2+ Jl 20 '87
A drum, a drum, Renouf doth come [raid on Benequity Holdings] H. Rudnitsky. il *Forbes* 139:146+ My 18 '87
Is Carling Black Label worth a trip from Australia? [A. Bond's bid for G. Heileman Brewing] M. D. Oneal. il por *Bus Week* p33-4 S 21 '87
Is Holmes a Court trying to lasso Texaco? T. Thompson. il por *Bus Week* p59 Jl 27 '87
Jaws: the Australian [accumulation of Texaco stock by R. Holmes à Court] J. Castro. il por *Time* 130:53 Jl 27 '87
Stalker of wounded game [R. Holmes à Court's interest in Texaco stock] T. Jaffe. il por *Forbes* 139:38+ Je 15 '87
Stalking Texaco [stock purchase by R. Holmes à Court] *Time* 129:52 Je 1 '87
Will Aussie raider deliver coup de grace to crippled Texaco? [plans of R. Holmes à Court] K. R. Sheets. *U S News World Rep* 102:43 Je 1 '87
Will he, or won't he? Australia keeps Texaco on edge [R. Holmes à Court plans to boost holdings] K. R. Sheets. *U S News World Rep* 103:37 Jl 27 '87

Investments, British
Canada
The $1.2-million sales pitch [corporate junket sponsored by Allied-Lyons to highlight stake in Hiram Walker] D. Francis. por *Macleans* 100:9 Je 29 '87
An oil-patch marriage [British Gas buys major stake in Bow Valley Industries] J. Howse. il *Macleans* 100:33 Ag 17 '87

South Africa
A study in disinvestment [Barclays Bank leaves South Africa] C. Wolman. *World Press Rev* 34:54 O '87

United States
And Madison Avenue thought, 'it can't happen here' [J. Walter Thompson gets bid from WPP Group] M. N. Vamos and R. A. Melcher. il *Bus Week* p48 Je 22 '87
Bare knuckles on Madison Avenue [Saatchi & Saatchi takeover of Ted Bates] A. Kleiner. il por *N Y Times Mag* p34-9+ N 8 '87
Battle of the book barons [R. Maxwell's bid for Harcourt Brace Jovanovich] R. Henkoff. il por *Newsweek* 109:46 Je 1 '87
A British press lord goes global [R. Maxwell seeks takeover of Harcourt Brace Jovanovich] P. Sherrid. il por *U S News World Rep* 102:49-50 Je 1 '87
The British raider who sneaked up on ADT [M. Ashcroft] M. Maremont. il por *Bus Week* p33+ Ag 31 '87
Buying American [British invasion of U.S. advertising industry] B. Kanner. il *N Y* 20:20-1 Ag 10 '87
A costly save at Harcourt [antitakeover measures against R. Maxwell's bid] P. Engardio. *Bus Week* p42 Je 8 '87
GEC completes purchase of Lear Siegler units. *Aviat Week Space Technol* 127:125 O 12 '87
Hang on, Madison Avenue, Martin Sorrell isn't finished [WPP Group acquires J. Walter Thompson] R. A. Melcher and M. N. Vamos. il por *Bus Week* p80-1 Jl 13 '87
Hanson and Kidde: a marriage made in low tech; A portrait of the raider as respected industrialist. L. Baum and R. A. Melcher. il *Bus Week* p36-7 Ag 17 '87
Jovanovich sees nothing friendly in Maxwell's bid. P. Engardio. il por *Bus Week* p47 Je 1 '87
Lear Siegler sells subsidiary companies to Smiths Industries. *Aviat Week Space Technol* 127:32 Ag 3 '87
Plessey's new face in the U.S. [Stromberg-Carlson purchase in 1982] J. J. Keller. il *Bus Week* p32 Ap 20 '87
A raider's new world [G. Hutchings' bid for Smith & Wesson] M. Maremont. il por *Bus Week* p49-50 Je 15 '87
Trading places [Longman Group U.S.A.] M. Schifrin. il por *Forbes* 139:56-7 Je 29 '87

Investments, British—United States—*cont.*
A whiz kid bids for Manpower [A. Berry's Blue Arrow plc] M. D. Oneal and R. A. Melcher. il por *Bus Week* p37-8 Ag 17 '87
Why BP is going all out for all of Standard Oil. S. Miller. il *Bus Week* p50 Ap 13 '87

Investments, Canadian

Brazil
The lure of southern money. A. Shortell. il *Macleans* 100:26-7 Ja 19 '87

East Asia
Laurentian's Asian campaign. P. C. Newman. il por *Macleans* 100:24 Jl 13 '87

France
A fashionable Canadian connection [Paris fashion house of Pierre Balmain] B. Janssen. il por *Macleans* 100:37 N 16 '87

Great Britain
Capital developments [Reichmann's take over London's Canary Wharf project] D. Jenish. il *Macleans* 100:28-9 Ag 24 '87

Siberia (Soviet Union)
Power's new Siberian connection [pulp operation to be constructed by Power Corp. of Canada] P. C. Newman. il por *Macleans* 100:44 Je 1 '87

South Africa
Munk's glittering gamble [purchase of Consolidated Gold Fields stock by Barrick Resources] D. Jenish. il por *Macleans* 100:22-3 Ja 12 '87

United States
Burlington almost invited Edelman to attack [bid by A. B. Edelman and Dominion Textile] D. Foust. il por *Bus Week* p69 F 2 '87
Campeau's cash squeeze [R. Campeau's takeover of Allied Stores] T. Fennell. il por *Macleans* 100:26 Mr 2 '87
Canada's Labatt has just one way to grow: south. E. B. Terry. il por *Bus Week* p70 N 9 '87
Dominion's unraveling bid [bid for Burlington Industries] D. Foust. *Bus Week* p49-50 Je 1 '87
The greenmail factor [Belzberg family accused of attempting to greenmail GTE] L. Black. il *Macleans* 100:67 F 2 '87
Is Campeau in over his head at Allied Stores? D. Cook. il *Bus Week* p52-3 F 9 '87
On time in Bloomington [Ghermezian brothers complete deal to build Fashion Mall of America in Minnesota] D. Jenish. il *Macleans* 100:36 Ja 19 '87

Investments, Church *See* Church finance

Investments, European

United States
Europeans increase acquisition of U.S. firms [aerospace] *Aviat Week Space Technol* 127:30-1 Ag 10 '87
Taking the sting out of the plunging dollar [European companies exporting from U.S. subsidiaries] B. Riemer and F. J. Comes. il *Bus Week* p72-3 D 7 '87

Investments, Foreign
See also
Black business enterprises—International aspects
Business—International aspects
Corporations, International
Debts, External

Brazil
Up the river [Manaus] E. A. Finn, Jr. il map *Forbes* 140:102+ N 2 '87

Canada
Making them do it his way [finance minister T. Hockin] P. C. Newman. il por *Macleans* 100:29 Ag 31 '87
The new debate about takeovers. D. Jenish. il *Macleans* 100:38-9 My 4 '87

China
See also
China International Trust and Investment Corporation
Economic reforms may have begun a long march backward. D. J. Yang and R. T. Grieves. il *Bus Week* p54-5 Mr 16 '87

Developing countries
An offer the third world can't refuse. J. Berger. il *Bus Week* p65 Je 29 '87

Philippines
Aquino needs a new miracle. L. Kraar. il por *Fortune* 116:90-2+ S 14 '87
Foreign money runs scared. L. Reaves. *Bus Week* p54 O 5 '87

South Africa
Apartheid: a study in black and white [role of transnational corporations] il *UN Chron* 22:26-8 N/D '85
'End apartheid by 1 January 1987', Panel of Eminent Persons asks; details world programme for action by TNCs. il *UN Chron* 22:18-20 N/D '85

Fifty-two witnesses present testimony during four days of hearings [role of transnational corporations] il *UN Chron* 22:21-5 N/D '85

Soviet Union
Comrade capitalists, come make money in the Soviet Union. K. R. Sheets. il *U S News World Rep* 102:39 Ja 19 '87
Ivan starts learning the capitalist ropes [joint ventures] R. Lewald. il *Bus Week* p154 N 2 '87
Letting Western business in. P. Galuszka and others. *Bus Week* p40 Ap 20 '87
Western business may get a piece of *perestroika*. P. Galuszka and others. il *Bus Week* p70 D 28 '87-Ja 4 '88

Spain
Look out for the Spanish bulls. A. Zagorin. il *Time* 129:51 Ja 26 '87

United States
The 100 largest foreign investments in the U.S. il *Forbes* 140:146-50 Jl 27 '87
Advertising dollars from abroad pouring into U.S. television. M. Schrage. il *Channels* 7:13 Jl/Ag '87
America on the auction block. C. Skrzycki. il *U S News World Rep* 102:56-8 Mr 30 '87
And now the bill comes due [U.S. foreign debt] B. Nussbaum. il *Bus Week* p160-1+ N 16 '87
The buying of America. il *World Press Rev* 34:16-18 Je '87
The corporate immigrants [cover story] H. Eason. il *Nations Bus* 75:12-14+ Ap '87
The economic black hole [U.S. trade deficit and foreign debt] L. C. Thurow and L. D. Tyson. bibl f *Foreign Policy* 67:3-21 Summ '87
Flag-waving foreigners [investing in stock market] S. Lee. il *Forbes* 140:236 N 2 '87
For sale: America [cover story] S. Koepp. il *Time* 130:52-6+ S 14 '87
Foreign investors outstrip U.S. [university-industry complex] W. Biddle. *Science* 237:354 Jl 24 '87
Foreign money, U.S. fears. M. Tolchin and S. Tolchin. il *N Y Times Mag* p63-4+ D 13 '87
The growing foreign role in U.S. policy. K. N. Johnson. il por *Fortune* 116:36-8 Jl 6 '87
Innocents abroad [governors promoting states] *Fortune* 116:12+ N 23 '87
The local rush to attract foreign money. P. M. Jones. il *Sch Update* 119:6-7 Ja 26 '87
Looking at Japan's stock market through Japanese eyes . . . casts light on Wall Street's raging bull. G. Koretz. il *Bus Week* p26 S 14 '87
New capitals for raising capital? [interview with J. Hennessy] R. Morais. por *Forbes* 139:64 Mr 9 '87
Raiders of the cheap buck [foreign raiders after the crash] D. Pauly. il *Newsweek* 110:51 N 30 '87
The U.S. gets foreign aid [Treasury bond sale] J. B. Copeland. il *Newsweek* 109:58 My 18 '87
Why the dollar could head south again . . . and send the economy into recession next year [U.S. as debtor nation] G. Koretz. il *Bus Week* p20 Jl 13 '87

Investments, French

United States
Aerospatiale Helicopter plans to diversify U.S. facility. *Aviat Week Space Technol* 126:78 Mr 16 '87
And then there was one [GE sells consumer electronics division to Thomson SA] J. B. Copeland. il *Newsweek* 110:36 Ag 3 '87
Can Beneteau fill its sails in the U.S. boat market? M. Resener. il por *Bus Week* p75 Ag 17 '87
Champagne's California twist [French wine makers in the Napa Valley] G. C. Lubenow and A. Miller. il *Newsweek* 110:40 Ag 24 '87
Is KIS beating a retreat from the U.S.? C. Gaffney. il *Bus Week* p58 Mr 16 '87
Overnight, Thomson has the stuff to take on the titans [purchase of GE's consumer electronics business] T. Peterson. il *Bus Week* p36-7 Ag 10 '87
Perrier's unquenchable U.S. thirst [acquiring Arrowhead Drinking Water Co.] J. Rossant. *Bus Week* p46 Je 29 '87
A press giant is set to pounce [Hachette eyes U.S. companies] F. J. Comes. *Bus Week* p54+ D 21 '87
A sweet swap for GE and Thomson. *Fortune* 116:8 Ag 17 '87

Investments, German

United States
Bertelsmann's U.S. invasion may be just beginning. J. E. Pluenneke. il *Bus Week* p72-3 Ag 10 '87

Investments, Haitian

United States
Judge: $115,000 Duvalier aide's condo in Miami belongs to Haiti Republic. *Jet* 71:6 Mr 2 '87

Investments, Hong Kong

Debating the future of the colony. T. Fennell. il *Macleans* 100:30-1 Ag 17 '87

Canada

Banking on greatness [Canadian operations of Hongkong and Shanghai Banking Corporation] P. C. Newman. il por *Macleans* 100:32 Ap 13 '87

Putting out the welcome mat [takeover of Husky Oil by Li Ka-shing] D. Francis. por *Macleans* 100:9 My 18 '87

Rich and powerful [Li Ka-shing; cover story; special section; with editorial comment by Kevin Doyle] il *Macleans* 100:2, 24-31 Ag 17 '87

China

The man who envisions a New Jersey Turnpike in China [G. Wu] L. Kraar. il por *Fortune* 116:89 Jl 6 '87

United States

Jardine's giant step from Hong Kong to Wall Street [stake in Bear Stearns] D. J. Yang and others. il por *Bus Week* p39-40 O 12 '87

Investments, Irish

United States

An Irishman feasts on American trees [M. Smurfit] K. Labich. il por *Fortune* 116:62-4+ Jl 20 '87

Investments, Italian

France

An Italian chipmaker shows the way [SGS's merger with Thomson] W. C. Symonds. il por *Bus Week* p134+ My 25 '87

Western Europe

Conglomeration Italian style [C. De Benedetti's empire] S. Solomon. il por *Forbes* 139:36-8 Mr 23 '87

Investments, Japanese

Japan Inc.'s new face [cover story; special section] il *Macleans* 100:22-8+ N 30 '87

Canada

The Japanese go shopping. *Macleans* 100:25 N 30 '87

A Pacific future for the taking [views of P. Barter] P. C. Newman. il por *Macleans* 100:37 Ap 6 '87

Germany (West)

The Japanese are firing up Frankfurt. J. E. Pluenneke. il *Bus Week* p40 Ap 20 '87

Hong Kong

By the time China takes over, Japan may own the joint. M. Shao. *Bus Week* p76+ My 25 '87

Mexico

The Far East goes south [Japanese factories] J. Contreras. il *Newsweek* 109:46 Je 22 '87

How to mix sake and tequila. K. K. Wiegner. il *Forbes* 139:48+ Mr 23 '87

Mexico looks better and better to Japan. S. Baker. il *Bus Week* p58 Je 8 '87

Tokyo opens a southern trade route [factories in Mexico] S. L. Hawkins. il map *U S News World Rep* 103:40+ Ag 3 '87

Taiwan

End run [Japanese automakers in Taiwan] A. Tanzer. il *Forbes* 139:52 My 4 '87

United States

Asian fat cats are betting big on Vegas. R. Grover. il *Bus Week* p24 Ag 24 '87

Bridgestone may try an end run around the yen [construction of U.S. plant to make car tires] Z. Schiller and J. B. Treece. il *Bus Week* p31 F 2 '87

Can Japan work the Street? B. Powell. il *Newsweek* 110:60 O 19 '87

Carmakers are doing their dreaming in California [American and Japanese design studios in California] S. Toy. il *Bus Week* p50+ Mr 30 '87

Chipping away at Silicon Valley. R. H. Bork, Jr. il *U S News World Rep* 102:58 Mr 30 '87

Cold feet [Fujitsu drops bid for Fairchild] *Time* 129:52 Mr 30 '87

Comparative disadvantage [Japanese brokers] P. Fuhrman. il *Forbes* 139:144 My 18 '87

The 'crash of '88' scenario. M. Meyer. il *Newsweek* 110:49-50 N 23 '87

Damn the dollar, full speed ahead. M. Tharp. il *U S News World Rep* 103:50-1 D 14 '87

Deregulation: a two-way street. B. Buell. *Bus Week* p62 Je 22 '87

Fiasco at Fujitec. R. Simon and A. Tanzer. il *Forbes* 139:60-1 Mr 23 '87

Fighting the chip wars: Fujitsu loses Fairchild. J. B. Copeland. il *Newsweek* 109:50 Mr 30 '87

Hell camp, Malibu-style [Kanrisha Yosei management training center] R. Phalon. il *Forbes* 140:110+ D 28 '87

Honda is turning red, white, and blue [second U.S. plant] W. J. Holstein and J. B. Treece. il *Bus Week* p38 O 5 '87

Honda: made in the U.S.A. J. B. Copeland. il *Newsweek* 109:42 Ja 19 '87

A hot American car may hit Japan: the Honda [strong yen could prompt Japanese carmakers to reexport from the U.S.] W. J. Hampton and others. il *Bus Week* p50 Ja 26 '87

I'll take Manhattan—and Waikiki [Japanese investors in American real estate] J. Castro. il *Time* 129:62 Mr 9 '87

In Japan, using 'logic and emotion' [investment specialist S. Kaneko] B. Buell. il por *Bus Week* p155 D 28 '87-Ja 4 '88

In Japan we (must) trust [Japanese investments in U.S. Treasuries affect interest rates] E. A. Finn, Jr. il *Forbes* 140:32-4 S 21 '87

An investor the U.S. can't afford to lose [Japan in Treasury bond market] W. Glasgall. il *Bus Week* p32 My 4 '87

It won't stop with the Shearson deal [Nippon Life Insurance buys stake in Shearson Lehman Brothers] W. Glasgall and T. Aritake. il *Bus Week* p36 Ap 6 '87

Japan is winning friends in the Rust Belt [midwesterners becoming less protectionist as a result of Japanese auto plant locations] W. J. Holstein. il *Bus Week* p54 O 19 '87

Japan on Wall Street [cover story] W. Glasgall. il *Bus Week* p82-6+ S 7 '87

The Japanese are elbowing into Chicago's futures pits. J. N. Frank. il *Bus Week* p106-7 Je 1 '87

The Japanese are here to stay. D. Harris and A. Rock. il *Money* 16:140-2+ My '87

The Japanese buying binge [U.S. real estate] L. S. Richman. il *Fortune* 116:77+ D 7 '87

Japanese takeover artists are learning fast. B. Buell. il *Bus Week* p40-1 Ag 3 '87

Japan's newest import: U.S. equities. P. Fuhrman. il *Forbes* 139:43 Ja 12 '87

Kabuki theater on Wall Street. J. Egan. il *U S News World Rep* 103:41-2 Ag 17 '87

Life at Nissan: paradise lost? [UAW's new drive to unionize Smyrna, Tenn. plant] B. Turque and J. B. Copeland. il *Newsweek* 110:50 Ag 10 '87

Maybe this time . . . [Detroit hangs on against imports and immigrant autos] J. Flint. il *Forbes* 140:34 S 7 '87

More than a yen [Nomura Securities buys interest in Eastdil Realty] J. Willoughby. il por *Forbes* 139:122 F 9 '87

Nissan, Tennessee [poor treatment of workers at Smyrna plant; cover story] J. Junkerman. il *Progressive* 51:16-18+ Je '87

No place like home [Nippon Life Insurance Co.] J. Heins. il *Forbes* 140:104 N 16 '87

"Nobody likes us except the consumer" [Honda] J. Flint. il *Forbes* 140:56-7+ O 19 '87

The Rising Sun on U.S. real estate. il *Technol Rev* 90:80 Ag/S '87

Rising Sun on Wall Street: how Japanese money and firms are moving in. D. Burstein. il *N Y* 20:32-8 Mr 2 '87

The sayonara scenario: worry over a Japanese pullout. J. Crudele. il *N Y* 20:37 S 21 '87

The sin of 'smelling Japanese' [trying to build a more American image] A. Miller. il *Newsweek* 109:55 Ap 27 '87

Small world [Sanyo Securities buys stake in Spear Financial Services] J. Heins. il *Forbes* 139:159+ My 4 '87

A solid gold record deal [Sony acquires CBS Records] D. Lieberman and W. J. Holstein. il *Bus Week* p36 N 30 '87

This bull sees Japanese cash driving up the Dow to 3500 [views of J. Feshbach] R. McNatt. il por *Money* 16:186 O '87

U.S. parts makers just won't say 'Uncle'. J. B. Treece. il *Bus Week* p76+ Ag 10 '87

We better keep them happy [interview with R. D. Hormats] A. D. Frank. il por *Forbes* 140:37-8 N 30 '87

We'll send you VCRs—you send us stocks. M. Beauchamp and J. Heins. il *Forbes* 140:60-2 Ag 10 '87

What the Fairchild fiasco signals for trade policy [Fujitsu deal collapses] J. W. Wilson and S. J. Dryden. il *Bus Week* p28 Mr 30 '87

Where the jobs are [special section] il *Newsweek* 109:42-8 F 2 '87

Investments, Japanese—United States—*cont.*
Why banks fear Congress' help [trade bill restrictions on Japanese banks and brokers in the U.S.] M. McNamee. il *Bus Week* p35 S 14 '87
Working for the Japanese [Bridgestone Tire Co.'s factory in Tenn.] il *Time* 130:60 S 14 '87
The yen to spend [Japanese dumping of U.S. equity sends Dow down] P. Fuhrman. *Forbes* 139:126 Ap 20 '87
Your next boss may be Japanese. B. Powell. il *Read Dig* 130:141-4 Je '87
Investments, Korean
United States
Korea's newest export: management style. L. Baum. il *Bus Week* p66 Ja 19 '87
Investments, New Zealand
United States
Market letter writer makes good [R. Brierley] T. Jaffe. il *Forbes* 139:32-4 F 23 '87
Ron Brierley is king of the middle of the road. C. Debes. por *Bus Week* p78+ S 21 '87
Investments, Scottish
The best investors may be Scottish. S. Tully. il *Fortune* 116:58-60 Ag 31 '87
Investments, Swedish
France
The Swedes give AT&T, and the U.S., painful black eyes [L. M. Ericsson captures piece of Compagnie Générale de Constructions Téléphoniques] T. Peterson and F. J. Comes. il *Bus Week* p44-5 My 4 '87
United States
The store that runs on a wrench [IKEA] J. S. DeMott. il *Time* 130:54 Jl 27 '87
Investments, Swiss
Great Britain
The big cheese in London banking could be Swiss [Union Bank of Switzerland's proposed buyout of Hill Samuel Group plc] J. Templeman. il *Bus Week* p37 Jl 27 '87
United States
Know when to fold them [G. MacDougal sells Mark Controls to Swiss investors] J. Flint. il por *Forbes* 140:124 D 28 '87
A promise comes of age [Ciba-Geigy takes over Spectra-Physics] R. Addis. il *Forbes* 140:8 Ag 24 '87
Investments, Taiwanese
United States
The bank of what? [Bank of Canton of California] P. Fuhrman. il *Forbes* 139:38+ Ap 6 '87
Investor owned hospitals *See* Hospital management industry
Investors *See* Bondholders; Investments; Stockholders
Investor's daily
Look who's nipping at the Wall Street journal. S. Toy. il por *Bus Week* p121-2+ D 21 '87
Inwood, Kirby
about
Aftermath of a romance. R. Corelli. il pors *Macleans* 100:58 S 28 '87
Io (Satellite) *See* Jupiter (Planet)—Satellites
IOC *See* International Olympic Committee
Iodine in the body
Painful breasts may benefit from iodine [fibrocystic breast disease; research by Bernard A. Eskin and William R. Ghent] il *Prevention* 39:12 Ap '87
Ion transport *See* Biological transport
Ionization
See also
Hydrogen ion concentration
Ionization of gases
See also
Plasma (Ionized gases)
Ionosphere *See* Atmosphere, Upper
Ions
See also
Ammonium
Plasma (Ionized gases)
Dianion stabilization by $(M(C_5(CH_3)_5)_2)^+$: theoretical evidence for a localized ring in $(DDQ)^{2-}$. J. S. Miller and D. A. Dixon. bibl f il *Science* 235:871-3 F 20 '87
Some halfway steps give scientists a look at a quantum leap. il *Discover* 8:9 Ja '87
Physiological effects
Divalent cations directly affect the conductance of excised patches of rod photoreceptor membrane. J. H. Stern and others. bibl f il *Science* 236:1674-8 Je 26 '87
When negative is positive [effect of negative ions on athletic performance] J. Venturino. il *Women's Sports Fitness* 9:55 Ap '87

Iooss, Walter, Jr.
about
Meet the masters. F. Cameron. il *Petersens Photogr Mag* 16:16-19+ O '87
Iosso, Chris
Denominational moves raise questions. *Christ Century* 104:484-6 My 20-27 '87
Iovine, Jimmy
about
Rock elves from Sting to Springsteen give the Special Olympics A very Special Christmas. M. Green. il por *People Wkly* 28:157-9 N 2 '87
Iovine, John
Piezoelectric plastic film. il *Radio-Electron* 58:57-8+ Mr '87
Iovine, Julie V.
"Die Revision der Moderne": postmodernism on display at Williams College. il *Archit Rec* 175:91 Je '87
Iowa
See also
Agriculture—Iowa
Education—Iowa
Medical care—Iowa
Organic farming—Iowa
Economic conditions
Watering the Iowa economy [Iowa Caucus] il *Fortune* 116:8 Ag 3 '87
Industries
See also
Petroleum industry
Politics and government
See also
Caucuses—Iowa
Iowa Beef Processors, Inc.
See also
IBP, Inc.
Iowa Center for the Book *See* University of Iowa. Iowa Center for the Book
Ipomopsis aggregata *See* Scarlet gilia
Ipswich (Mass.)
Historic houses, sites, etc.
Early American pleasures [Whipple House] K. Whiteside. il *House Gard* 159:110-19+ Jl '87
Re-creating a seventeenth-century garden [Whipple House] A. Leighton. il *House Gard* 159:20+ Jl '87
IQ Foundation (Firm)
Trying to profit from child's play. J. Alexander. il por *Money* 16:162-4 F '87
IQ tests *See* Intelligence tests
Iquitos (Peru)
Markets
Risky business [Peruvian Amazon markets] C. Padoch. il *Nat Hist* 96:56-65 O '87
IRA *See* Irish Republican Army
Iran
See also
Americans—Iran
Canadians—Iran
Civil rights—Iran
Middle classes—Iran
Military service, Compulsory—Iran
Munitions—Iran
Nuclear power plants—Iran
Political prisoners—Iran
Religious liberty—Iran
Tehran (Iran)
United Nations—Iran
Air Force
Shortages, lack of experience cripple Iranian Air Force. P. Proctor. *Aviat Week Space Technol* 126:25-6 F 23 '87
Commerce
See also
Iranian-Iraqi War, 1980- —Economic aspects
China
See China—Commerce—Iran
Israel
See also
Iran-contra affair—Israeli participation
Italy
'Irangate' unfolds in Italy [arms smuggling charges against F. Borletti] W. C. Symonds. *Bus Week* p46 S 21 '87
Sweden
Rhetoric and reality in the Iranian arms trade. P. Gupte. il por *Forbes* 140:32-5 O 19 '87
Western Europe
Europe's arms pipeline to Iran. K. R. Timmerman. *Nation* 245:47-8+ Jl 18-25 '87
Everybody's doing it [arms sales] G. Russell. il *Time* 129:31 Mr 16 '87

Iran—Commerce—Western Europe—*cont.*

A profitable irony of the war [Western Europe as supplier of arms to Iran] R. J. Gwyn. il *World Press Rev* 34:19-20 O '87

Rhetoric and reality in the Iranian arms trade. P. Gupte. il por *Forbes* 140:32-5 O 19 '87

The shame of the game [European arms sales to Iran] E. Clift. il *Newsweek* 110:44 S 21 '87

Defenses

See also

Guided missiles, Iranian

Diplomatic and consular service

France

Embassy standoff. C. D. Van De Stadt. il *World Press Rev* 34:36 S '87

Showdown on Embassy Row [France and Iran sever diplomatic ties] J. Greenwald. il *Time* 130:46 Jl 27 '87

A showdown with Teheran. H. Anderson. il *Newsweek* 110:28-30 Jl 27 '87

Economic conditions

Living with war and revolution. W. E. Smith. il *Time* 130:32-4 Ag 17 '87

Foreign relations

At war on all fronts [cover story; special section] il pors *Time* 130:22-6+ Ag 17 '87

Coping with Khomeini. H. Trewhitt. il *U S News World Rep* 103:25-7 Ag 3 '87

Iran's quest for superpower status. G. Sick. bibl f *Foreign Aff* 65:697-715 Spr '87

The method in Iran's seeming madness. C. Dickey. il *Newsweek* 110:26 Ag 3 '87

Spreading the faith. B. Levin. il *Macleans* 100:14-17 Jl 27 '87

France

See France—Foreign relations—Iran

Iraq

See also

Iranian-Iraqi War, 1980-

Israel

See also

Iran-contra affair—Israeli participation

Saudi Arabia

Confronting the 'monster' [Saudi Arabia clashes with Iran] T. Clifton. il *Newsweek* 110:36 S 7 '87

Soviet Union

See Soviet Union—Foreign relations—Iran

Syria

Assad and his allies: irreconcilable differences? C. Dickey. bibl f *Foreign Aff* 66:58-76 Fall '87

United States

See United States—Foreign relations—Iran

Politics and government

See also

Iranian seizure of United States embassy, 1979-1981

After the Ayatollah. S. T. Hunter. *Foreign Policy* 66:77-97 Spr '87

At war on all fronts [cover story; special section] il pors *Time* 130:22-6+ Ag 17 '87

Institutionalizing the new order in Iran. S. Akhavi. bibl f *Curr Hist* 86:53-6+ F '87

Iran: a mullah for all seasons [Rafsanjani] T. Stanger. por *Newsweek* 109:35 F 16 '87

Iran looks beyond Khomeini. R. Wright. il *Nation* 244:129+ F 7 '87

Iran: scuffling in the wheelhouse. J. L. Galloway. il *U S News World Rep* 103:40 O 12 '87

Iran's smiling powerbroker [Rafsanjani] R. Wright. por *New Leader* 70:5-7 Ja 12-26 '87

Islamic terrorism: a growing peril [interview with A. Taheri] D. Bombardier. il *World Press Rev* 34:17-19 My '87

Khomeini's Iran: a case study of hatred toward the U.S. L. Hopping. il *Sch Update* 120:27-8 O 2 '87

Meantime, back in Tehran [possible successors to Khomeini] W. E. Smith. il *Time* 129:36-7 Ja 12 '87

Religious institutions and affairs

See also

Muslims—Iran

Social conditions

Living among the believers. F. A. Reed. il *Macleans* 100:14-15 Jl 27 '87

Living with war and revolution. W. E. Smith. il *Time* 130:32-4 Ag 17 '87

'Revolutionizing' a middle-class society. M. Field. il *World Press Rev* 34:19-20 My '87

Iran and Afghanistan

How did Iran get Stinger missiles? [missiles sent by U.S. to Afghan resistance] il *Newsweek* 110:42-3 O 26 '87

Iran arms-contra aid case *See* Iran-contra affair

Iran-contra affair

Arms-for-hostages deal: dogging the money trail. S. Emerson. il *U S News World Rep* 102:21 F 16 '87

The arms scandal [special section] il *World Press Rev* 34:11-16 F '87

Ash Wednesday: 'going forward' [R. Reagan's response to the Tower Commission report] *America* 156:226 Mr 21 '87

Assessing the damage. M. Greenfield. il *Newsweek* 109:76 Mr 9 '87

An autopsy. T. Draper. bibl f il *N Y Rev Books* 34:67-77 D 17 '87

The Ayatollah's big sting [cover story; with editorial comment by Mortimer B. Zuckerman] il pors maps *U S News World Rep* 102:18-24, 82 Mr 30 '87

The ballad of Fawn and Arturo [F. Hall and A. Cruz Jr.; cover story] J. Morley. il *Nation* 245:397+ O 17 '87

Beat the devil. A. Cockburn. *Nation* 244:6-7 Ja 10 '87

Behind all the President's woes. J. Bierman. il *Macleans* 100:20-1 Ja 26 '87

Beltway bandits. D. Corn and J. Morley. *Nation* 245:188 S 5 '87

Brain dead. F. Barnes. *New Repub* 196:10-11 Ja 19 '87

Break point [special section] il *Newsweek* 109:18-25 F 23 '87

Breaking up is hard to do [G. P. Shultz testifies that channels to Iran remained open after scandal was made public] por *Time* 129:22 F 2 '87

Bring back war. H. Fairlie. *New Repub* 197:16-17 Ag 10-17 '87

The Bush connection [G. Bush; cover story] A. Nairn. il *Progressive* 51:19-23 My '87

Calm in the eye of the storm [J. Poindexter] il por *Time* 129:29 Ap 6 '87

Can he recover? [Tower Commission report; special section] il pors *Time* 129:20-4+ Mr 9 '87

Can 'Operation Comeback' work? K. T. Walsh. il por *U S News World Rep* 102:18-20 Ja 26 '87

Cap on top [C. Weinberger counters the Tower Commission report] F. Barnes. il *New Repub* 196:13-15 Ap 20 '87

Carterized [Reagan administration domestic legislative proposals floundering in wake of Iran arms scandal] F. Barnes. *New Repub* 196:14-15 Mr 16 '87

The case against covert action [cover story] M. H. Halperin. *Nation* 244:345+ Mr 21 '87

The case against glee [R. Reagan's decline] M. Kondracke. *New Repub* 196:16-17 Ja 26 '87

The case for the prosecution. W. F. Buckley. *Natl Rev* 39:70-1 Ja 30 '87

Charge of the lightweight brigade. F. FitzGerald. il map *Roll Stone* p46-8+ O 22 '87

The CIA's 'cowboys': out of control? [disclosures by G. P. Shultz] L. Martz. il por *Newsweek* 109:22-4 F 2 '87

Closing the file [Tower Commission records placed beyond reach of Freedom of Information Act] *Nation* 245:4 Jl 4-11 '87

The colonels' coup [involvement of military officers] F. Zakaria. *New Repub* 197:15 Jl 13-20 '87

Commagate [Roosevelt's illegal sale of destroyers to Great Britain in 1940 compared to Iran-contra scandal] D. Seligman. *Fortune* 116:217+ O 12 '87

Congress's case. J. V. Lamar, Jr. il *Time* 129:29 Ap 20 '87

A 'contra' democracy? [memo to Oliver North] R. W. Owen. *Harpers* 275:19-20 O '87

The contras after Iranamok. *New Repub* 196:7-9 Je 29 '87

Covert action and national policy: beyond North and Poindexter. R. J. Bresler. il *USA Today (Periodical)* 115:6-7 Mr '87

Covert loophole [executive order authorizes privatization of covert operations] I. F. Stone. *Nation* 245:184-5 S 5 '87

Covert operations: play by the rules. M. Kramer. il *U S News World Rep* 103:15-16 Jl 20 '87

Crisis of confidence. M. McDonald. il *Macleans* 100:31 Ja 19 '87

A critic's view of Reagan's tussles with the truth [interview with J. D. Barber] D. Grogan. il *People Wkly* 27:40-2 Mr 9 '87

The culture of lying [cover story] M. Hosenball. *New Repub* 197:16-18 Jl 13-20 '87

Damage control [Tower Commission report] R. Fly and others. il por *Bus Week* p38-9 Mr 9 '87

Iran-contra affair—*cont.*

Damning with faint praise [Tower Commission report; special section; with editorial comment by David Gergen] il pors *U S News World Rep* 102:14-24, 68 Mr 9 '87

Daniel Ellsberg [interview] D. Sheff. il por *Roll Stone* p221-2+ N 5-D 10 '87

Dateline Washington: Gipperdämmerung. D. McManus. *Foreign Policy* 66:156-72 Spr '87

Dateline Washington: the conservative crackup. S. Blumenthal. *Foreign Policy* 69:166-88 Wint '87/'88

Deeper and deeper. B. Duffy. il *U S News World Rep* 102:18-19 Mr 2 '87

Déjà vu all over again [contragate and Watergate] *Nation* 245:665 D 5 '87

Democracy and Colonel North. L. Wieseltier. *New Repub* 196:22-5 Ja 26 '87

Double-dealing over Iran [relationship of arms dealer M. Ghorbanifar to the CIA] E. Magnuson. il por *Time* 129:22+ F 2 '87

Escape from Iranscam: Bush's campaign gets a boost. R. Fly. por *Bus Week* p47 Ag 17 '87

The establishment steps in. H. Sidey. il *Time* 129:26 Mr 23 '87

Even Reagan was somber [Tower panel investigation] H. Sidey. il *Time* 129:26 F 23 '87

Facing the strains. L. Martz. il *Newsweek* 109:18-21 Ja 12 '87

Fade to black [provisional nature of American presidency] L. H. Lapham. *Harpers* 274:8+ My '87

A failure to communicate [R. Reagan] C. J. Matthews. il por *U S News World Rep* 102:27 Ja 26 '87

The fall of an American junta. T. Draper. bibl f il *N Y Rev Books* 34:45-57 O 22 '87

Fifth Amendment patriots. *New Repub* 196:4 Ja 5-12 '87

For Reagan, it will be a state of the presidency address. R. Fly. por *Bus Week* p47 Ja 26 '87

Foreign policy crossroads [special section] il *World Press Rev* 34:11-16+ Ja '87

Four men in North's safe: the uses of intellectuals [Elie Wiesel, Joachim Maitre, Max Singer and Michael Ledeen] A. Cockburn. *Nation* 244:350-1+ Mr 21 '87

Full medal jackoff: what ever happened with Oliver North? R. Corliss. *Film Comment* 23:16 S/O '87

Getting high on secrecy. M. Greenfield. il *Newsweek* 109:82 F 23 '87

Gipperdämmerung? Cui bono? [effect of scandal on 1988 presidential race] *Natl Rev* 39:19-20 Ja 30 '87

Going nowhere fast. L. Martz. il por *Newsweek* 109:24-5 F 9 '87

Gorbachev and 'Iragua'. B. Crozier. *Natl Rev* 39:28 F 13 '87

Government by plumbers. *Progressive* 51:9-10 Ja '87

A growing, dreamy detachment [R. Reagan's behavior] C. O'Connor. il por *Newsweek* 109:26 Ja 5 '87

A guide to Iran/contra theories [cover story] D. Corn and J. Morley. *Nation* 245:73+ Ag 1-8 '87

Gulliver's travails. H. Sidey. il *Time* 129:18 Ja 12 '87

The guns of Watergate. L. Garment. *Commentary* 83:15-23 Ap '87

Hanging Ollie out to dry [O. North as scapegoat] T. Morganthau. il por *Newsweek* 109:16-17 Ja 19 '87

The hard road ahead on the comeback trail [special section; with editorial comment by Mortimer B. Zuckerman] il pors *U S News World Rep* 102:16-20, 88 Mr 16 '87

The high costs of scandal. I. Austen. il *Macleans* 100:28 F 23 '87

A hostage-swap headache for Bush. *U S News World Rep* 103:13 D 28 '87-Ja 4 '88

Hot on the Iran money trail. T. Morganthau. il por *Newsweek* 109:24-5 My 4 '87

How the drug czar got away [Drug Enforcement Administration botches case against Colombian J. L. Ochoa Vasquez] M. A. Lee. il *Nation* 245:189-92 S 5 '87

Hysteria's hidden agendas. *Natl Rev* 39:16-18 Mr 13 '87

The I.S.A. behind the N.S.C. [Intelligence Support Activity] M. Perry. il *Nation* 244:33+ Ja 17 '87

Im---ch Reagan? *Commonweal* 114:339-41 Je 5 '87

The imperial temptation: Reagan's presidency succumbs. A. M. Schlesinger. *New Repub* 196:17 Mr 16 '87

Independent counsel to investigate arms sales to Iran [address, December 2, 1986] R. Reagan. *Dep State Bull* 87:6 Mr '87

The ins and outs of the scandal. M. Healy. il *U S News World Rep* 102:32 Je 22 '87

Inside Ollie's mind [O. L. North] E. Alterman. il *New Repub* 196:12-15 F 16 '87

Into the vacuum stepped Ollie North [U.S. needs a bureaucracy on the European model to counteract reliance on the military] J. Keegan. por *U S News World Rep* 103:14 Ag 31 '87

The Iran/arms control connection [R. Perle's efforts to damage existing arms control agreements] M. Krepon. il *Bull At Sci* 43:9-10 Mr '87

Iran and the GOP. J. McLaughlin. *Natl Rev* 39:24 My 22 '87

Iran and U.S. policy [statement; with text of question and answer session, December 8, 1986] G. P. Shultz. *Dep State Bull* 87:22-33 F '87

Iran arms and contra aid controversy [address, March 4, 1987] R. Reagan. *Dep State Bull* 87:1-2 My '87

Iran arms deal was more serious than Watergate [interview with J. Carter] D. Frost. por *U S News World Rep* 103:32 D 7 '87

The Iran arms scandal, says a historian, shows how the power of myth can cloud a president's mind [interview with R. Slotkin] D. Van Biema. il pors *People Wkly* 27:97-8+ Ja 19 '87

The Iran-contra affair [address, August 12, 1987] R. Reagan. *Vital Speeches Day* 53:674-6 S 1 '87

Iran-contra controversy and president's goals [excerpts from address, August 12, 1987] R. Reagan. *Dep State Bull* 87:4-5 O '87

The Iran-contra scandal. T. Rothenberg. il *Sch Update* 119:10 F 23 '87

The Iran coverup [special section] il *Newsweek* 109:20-7 Mr 2 '87

Iran games [special section] il *Natl Rev* 39:34-8+ Ja 30 '87

Iranamok and OPEC. P. J. Sloyan. *New Repub* 197:19-21 N 9 '87

Iranian arms and contra aid [address, March 6, 1987] A. Cox. *Vital Speeches Day* 53:531-3 Je 15 '87

Iranscam: the real meaning of Oliver North. il pors *Ms* 15:24-7 My '87

Iranscam: will Reagan's answer man be allowed to answer? [D. M. Abshire] B. Javetski and others. *Bus Week* p55 Ja 12 '87

Iranscam's grim tidings. J. V. Lamar, Jr. il *Time* 129:40+ Ja 5 '87

Iranscam's near tragedy [R. McFarlane attempts suicide] G. J. Church. il por *Time* 129:25 F 23 '87

Is Reagan lying? W. F. Buckley. *Natl Rev* 39:56-7 Jl 31 '87

Is there life after Tower? [Tower Commission report] B. Crozier. *Natl Rev* 39:26 Ap 10 '87

It isn't over. M. Kramer. il *N Y* 20:16+ Mr 23 '87

The Katzenjammer Falcon: an elaborate government sting gets fouled up in Reagan's Iranscam. J. Traub. il por *N Y* 20:36-42 F 9 '87

The Khashoggi memo. M. Hosenball. *New Repub* 196:14+ F 2 '87

The king is hostage. T. E. Arnold. il *Natl Rev* 39:34-6+ Ap 10 '87

Learning from our theater of the absurd. J. M. Wall. *Christ Century* 104:299 Ap 1 '87

Learning from Reagan's debacle [applying Iran arms scandal mistakes to business management] A. R. Dowd. il por *Fortune* 115:169-72 Ap 27 '87

Leaving bad enough alone. M. Kempton. il *N Y Rev Books* 34:45 Ja 29 '87

Lessons for the president. D. Schorr. por *New Leader* 70:3-4 Ag 10-24 '87

Lessons of the Iran-contra affair [symposium] il *Read Dig* 130:72-7 Je '87

Letter from Washington. E. Drew. *New Yorker* 63:111-19 Mr 30 '87

Letter from Washington. E. Drew. *New Yorker* 62:95-102+ F 16 '87

Letter from Washington [D. Regan resigns] Cato. *Natl Rev* 39:14 Mr 27 '87

A lone ranger or just a good soldier? [involvement of O. L. North] R. Stengel. por *Time* 129:35 Ja 5 '87

The lonesome drifter [R. Reagan] W. Greider. il *Roll Stone* p25-6 Mr 12 '87

The long road back [special section] il pors *Newsweek* 109:18-22 Mr 16 '87

Making book on Oliver North. S. Meredith. *Harpers* 274:54-5 Mr '87

A man of many faces [O. L. North; cover story] D. Friend. il pors *Life* 10:12-17 Ag '87

McFarlane's folly. D. Schorr. *New Leader* 70:3-4 F 9-23 '87

A memo to Reagan [alleged harassment of contra critic J. Terrell by O. North and staff] il pors *Newsweek* 110:7 S 21 '87

Iran-contra affair—*cont.*

Mercenary with a cause [J. Terrell turns from contra mercenary to contra whistleblower] B. Connie and D. Bernstein. *Progressive* 51:13 Ag '87

Minority report [linking Iranian hostage case to contragate] C. Hitchens. *Nation* 245:582 N 21 '87

Minority report [possible link between Iranian hostage case and contragate] C. Hitchens. *Nation* 245:440 O 24 '87

Minority report [possible link between Iranian hostage case and contragate] C. Hitchens. *Nation* 245:80 Ag 1-8 '87

Minority report [possible link between Iranian hostage case and contragate] C. Hitchens. *Nation* 245:7 Jl 4-11 '87

Minority report [possible link between Iranian hostage case and contragate] C. Hitchens. *Nation* 244:842 Je 20 '87

Minority report [Tower Commission report] C. Hitchens. *Nation* 244:314 Mr 14 '87

The misadventures of El Patrón [involvement of contra supporter J. Hull] J. V. Lamar, Jr. il por *Time* 130:31-2 N 16 '87

Missing link? [Danish freighter used to carry profits diverted from the Iran arms sale] il *Newsweek* 109:7 Mr 23 '87

The mistake on Iran was 'poor execution' [Polish view] M. Glogowski. il *World Press Rev* 34:30 Mr '87

Mixed blessing [Senate report] J. V. Lamar, Jr. il *Time* 129:16-17 Ja 19 '87

Morsels of the tangled truth [Senate Intelligence Committee report] il *U S News World Rep* 102:11 F 9 '87

The murky world of weapons dealers. G. J. Church. il *Time* 129:26-9 Ja 19 '87

Must governments deal in deceit? C. W. Colson. il *Christ Today* 31:66 F 6 '87

Must reading [chronology published by S. Armstrong] il por *Time* 129:29 Je 1 '87

Nancy: no pardons [opposition to pardoning O. North and J. Poindexter] L. Howard. por *Newsweek* 110:7 N 30 '87

A nation in decline? B. W. Tuchman. il *N Y Times Mag* p52+ S 20 '87

Never give up [effect on R. Reagan] H. Sidey. il pors *Time* 130:14-15 Ag 24 '87

New doubts about Meese and the contra inquiry. L. Martz. il por *Newsweek* 109:29-30 Ap 20 '87

News conference of March 19, 1987. R. Reagan. *Dep State Bull* 87:2-6 My '87

The Nicaragua dilemma. *Natl Rev* 39:17-18 D 18 '87

No confidence [call for no confidence in presidency mechanism in wake of Iran arms scandal] M. Kaus. *New Repub* 196:15-16 Mr 23 '87

No pardon [presidential pardon for O. North and J. Poindexter] *New Repub* 197:7-9 D 28 '87

Notes and comment. *New Yorker* 62:21 Ja 26 '87

Notes and comment [missing forty million dollars] *New Yorker* 63:25-6 F 23 '87

Notes and comment [Tower Commission report] *New Yorker* 63:25-6 Mr 9 '87

Notes and comment [war powers aspect of the Constitution and aid to the contras] *New Yorker* 63:23-4 Je 1 '87

Of many things. G. W. Hunt. *America* 156:inside cover Ja 31 '87

The old boys' role in the Iran-contra affair [cronies of E. P. Wilson] P. Cary. il pors *U S News World Rep* 103:16-17 Ag 10 '87

Oliver North. il por *People Wkly* 28:38-9 D 28 '87-Ja 4 '88

Oliver North's strange recruits. P. Maas. il *N Y Times Mag* p20-2+ Ja 18 '87

Oliver's twists [O. North] N. Atkins. il *Roll Stone* p65-6+ Jl 16-30 '87

Ollie's blueprint. J. Morley. *New Repub* 196:16-18 My 25 '87

On tempering hilarity with restraint. *America* 156:89-90 F 7 '87

One down and a few more to go [criminal charges brought against C. Channell, fund raiser for the contras] D. Baer. il por *U S News World Rep* 102:17 My 11 '87

Out in the cold [covert operations directed by W. J. Casey] *Time* 130:20 S 7 '87

Pardon? [discussion of presidential pardon for J. Poindexter and O. North] F. Barnes. *New Repub* 196:13-15 Ja 5-12 '87

Pardon my Spanish [presidential pardon for J. Poindexter and O. North] R. Paulson. *New Repub* 197:4+ Ag 10-17 '87

Perot's private probes. G. J. Church. il por *Time* 129:18 My 4 '87

Persian diversion. M. Ivins. il *Progressive* 51:17 Ja '87

Personal politics. J. C. Alexander. *New Repub* 196:12-13 Ap 6 '87

Picking the lesser of two evils. B. Duffy. il *U S News World Rep* 102:10-11 Ja 19 '87

"A picture of real disarray" [Senate Intelligence Committee report] J. V. Lamar, Jr. il *Time* 129:19-20 F 9 '87

Placing truth above loyalty, John Tower delivers a tough verdict on Reagan's men. M. Wilhelm. il por *People Wkly* 27:38-9 Mr 9 '87

The politics of empire [Reagan presidency] N. Birnbaum. il *Nation* 244:9-12 Ja 10 '87

The presidency and the power of suggestion. J. M. Wall. *Christ Century* 104:43 Ja 21 '87

Presidential blessings [Bible inscribed by R. Reagan delivered to Iranians] il *Time* 129:37 F 9 '87

The president's performance [news conference] M. McDonald. il por *Macleans* 100:20-1 Mr 30 '87

President's response to the Tower Commission report [address, March 4, 1987] R. Reagan. *Vital Speeches Day* 53:322-4 Mr 15 '87

Pride and power [Tower Commission report; special section; with editorial comment by Kevin Doyle] il pors *Macleans* 100:2, 16-22+ Mr 9 '87

Process, not people [Tower Commission report] il *Progressive* 51:8-9 Ap '87

Putting a bad business behind him? [G. Bush] K. T. Walsh. il por *U S News World Rep* 103:27 S 21 '87

Reagan breaks his fall [new arms proposal and H. Baker made chief of staff] R. Fly and others. il pors *Bus Week* p34-5 Mr 16 '87

The Reagan crisis: dreaming impossible dreams. P. Geyelin. *Foreign Aff* 65 Sp Issue:447-57 ['87]

Reagan: what next? *Natl Rev* 39:15-16 Mr 27 '87

Reagan's band of true believers. F. FitzGerald. il *N Y Times Mag* p36-9+ My 10 '87

Reagan's de facto détente. D. Schorr. il *New Leader* 70:3-4 S 21 '87

Reagan's dirty trick. W. Greider. il *Roll Stone* p31-2+ Ja 29 '87

Reagan's failure [Tower Commission findings; special section] il pors *Newsweek* 109:16-23+ Mr 9 '87

Reagan's junta. T. Draper. bibl f il *N Y Rev Books* 34:5+ Ja 29 '87

Reagan's junta [discussion of January 29, 1987 article] T. Draper. *N Y Rev Books* 34:47-8 Ap 23 '87

Reagan's public relations offensive. M. McDonald. il por *Macleans* 100:28-9 Mr 16 '87

Reagan's underworld. S. Hoffmann. bibl f il *N Y Rev Books* 34:9-13 My 7 '87

The real cause of Irangate. K. E. Sharpe. bibl f *Foreign Policy* 68:19-41 Fall '87

Reality? Just say no [R. Reagan's denial syndrome] G. Sheehy. *New Repub* 196:16-18 Mr 30 '87

Regan bashing. T. Morganthau. il por *Newsweek* 109:18-19 F 16 '87

Resign, Ed Meese. il *New Repub* 197:7-9 N 9 '87

Responding to the failures of government. B. Spring. il *Christ Today* 31:57+ My 15 '87

Reykjavik and revelations: a turn of the tide? J. R. Schlesinger. *Foreign Aff* 65 Sp Issue:426-46 ['87]

The rise of the American junta. T. Draper. bibl f il *N Y Rev Books* 34:47-58 O 8 '87

Rules governing covert operations [ACLU report Covert operations and the democratic process: the implications of the Iran-contra affair] *Cent Mag* 20:57-8 N/D '87

The scandal that Reagan cannot kill. I. Austen. il por *Macleans* 100:26 Ag 24 '87

Scorpions, worms, and Iranian missiles. P. Yancey. il *Christ Today* 31:72 Mr 20 '87

A secret arms network's ever expanding cast. S. Emerson. il maps *U S News World Rep* 103:30-1 N 16 '87

The secret team behind contragate. P. D. Scott. il *Nation* 244:97+ Ja 31 '87

The secret warriors tell their story [American pilots making airdrops over Nicaragua] E. Calonius. il *Newsweek* 109:26-8 F 9 '87

Secretary praises AID and comments on Iran [remarks, November 25, 1986] G. P. Shultz. *Dep State Bull* 87:23 Ja '87

Secretary's interview on "Meet the press" [interview with G. P. Shultz; transcript of program, January 18, 1987] *Dep State Bull* 87:20-3 Mr '87

Selective conservatism. *Commonweal* 114:371-2 Je 19 '87

Sending in the clowns. L. H. Lapham. *Harpers* 274:8+ F '87

Iran-contra affair—*cont.*

A shadow government. *Commonweal* 114:99-100 F 27 '87

Shaking off a shadow [G. Bush] M. McDonald. il por *Macleans* 100:28 S 7 '87

The shrug market [stock market's reaction] J. K. Glassman. *New Repub* 196:15-16 Ja 5-12 '87

Sifting the debris. il *Progressive* 51:9-10 F '87

Silent witness: William Casey, Iranscam's mystery man, will tell no tales. E. Barnes and M. Dubrow. il pors *Life* 10:28-31 S '87

The smoking gun fallacy [question of Reagan's personal knowledge] *New Repub* 197:4+ Jl 6 '87

A star turn for the Gipper. J. L. Sheler. il por *U S News World Rep* 102:8 Mr 30 '87

State of the scandal. M. Kramer. il *N Y* 20:20-1 F 2 '87

Story of a consummate bureaucrat [F. Carlucci; cover story] J. Morley. *Nation* 245:737+ D 19 '87

The stuff of patriotism [O. L. North and what makes a patriot] H. Evans. il *U S News World Rep* 103:66 Ag 10 '87

Taking the Fifth [interpretation of Fifth Amendment rights concerning participants in Iran arms scandal in light of Reagan administration attack on the rights of public employees] C. Becker. *Nation* 244:101 Ja 31 '87

Ten myths about the Reagan debacle. W. Safire. il pors *N Y Times Mag* p20-6+ Mr 22 '87

This is Watergate. *New Repub* 196:7 Mr 16 '87

Too good to trust. R. Clapp. *Christ Today* 31:15 F 20 '87

Tower Commission report: the day the spinning stopped. *America* 156:205 Mr 14 '87

The Tower of Babel [Tower Commission report] W. Greider. il *Roll Stone* p55-6 Ap 23 '87

Tower of judgment [pending report by the Tower Commission] G. J. Church. il *Time* 129:12-16 Mr 2 '87

Tracking Oliver North. L. Gomez and P. Meyer. il pors *Life* 10:30-4+ My '87

Trying a comeback [R. Reagan; special section] il pors *Time* 129:18-20+ Mr 16 '87

U.S. initiative to Iran [special section] *Dep State Bull* 87:65-75 Ja '87

The unraveling of the Reagan presidency. I. L. Horowitz. il *New Leader* 69:5-7 D 29 '86

Washington diarist [involvement of M. Ledeen and M. Ghorbanifar] C. Lane. *New Repub* 196:58 Je 8 '87

Washington notebook. D. Schorr. il *New Leader* 70:3-4 Mr 23 '87

A Washington power trip to the edge and back [R. McFarlane's suicide attempt] S. Powell. il por *U S News World Rep* 102:11 F 23 '87

Wayward ship [Danish freighter used by O. North to ship weapons to the contras] il *Time* 129:17 Mr 2 '87

Well, he survived [R. Reagan answers questions at press conference] G. J. Church. il pors *Time* 129:20-3 Mr 30 '87

What North might have wrought [cover story] P. Kornbluh. il *Nation* 244:871+ Je 27 '87

What Washington should worry about. J. M. Fallows. il *U S News World Rep* 102:37 Ja 12 '87

When men act like boys. M. Greenfield. il *Newsweek* 109:76 Je 1 '87

When secrecy meets democracy. C. Krauthammer. il *Read Dig* 130:116-18 F '87

White House outlaws [Tower Commission report] *New Repub* 196:7-8 Mr 23 '87

The White House secrets. M. McDonald. il *Macleans* 100:14-15 Mr 2 '87

Why Iranscam won't keep Congress from aiding the contras. D. Harbrecht and S. J. Dryden. *Bus Week* p57 Je 22 '87

Why Meese spoke [E. Meese's "surprise" announcement of diversion of funds] D. Lindorff. *Nation* 244:349 Mr 21 '87

Would you believe . . . Iranian moderates? [politicization of intelligence; cover story] M. McDonald. *Wash Mon* 19:39-45+ Mr '87

Anecdotes, facetiae, satire, etc.

Baloney hero [O. North] P. J. O'Rourke. il *Roll Stone* p34-5 S 10 '87

Creepy work in the basement. A. Fotheringham. il *Macleans* 100:56 Ja 26 '87

The Gipper's changing gait. A. Fotheringham. il *Macleans* 100:56 Je 8 '87

Giving the Word [gift of the Bible to Iran's "moderates"] W. Goodman. *New Leader* 70:7 Ja 12-26 '87

Grab the salt. M. Ivins. il *Progressive* 51:28 S '87

Iran-'contra' nostalgia quiz. P. Slansky. *New Repub* 197:24-5 Ag 31 '87

Iran-contra quiz. P. Slansky. *New Repub* 196:7-9 My 18 '87

May your best friend fail, too. A. Fotheringham. il *Macleans* 100:60 Mr 9 '87

Oh, dear me. R. Baker. il *N Y Times Mag* p12 Ja 4 '87

True North. T. Southern. *Nation* 245:41-2 Jl 18-25 '87

Uncivil liberties. C. Trillin. *Nation* 244:38 Ja 17 '87

Uncivil liberties. C. Trillin. *Nation* 244:242 F 28 '87

Canadian participation

The Canada connection; Threats behind the disclosure. M. McDonald. il por *Macleans* 100:22-5 Ag 3 '87

The swami connection [Shri Chandra Swami Maharaj] M. McDonald. il por *Macleans* 100:26+ N 9 '87

The swami of Iranamok [Shri Chandra Swami Maharaj; cover story] M. Isikoff and M. Hosenball. *New Repub* 197:21-3 N 9 '87

Caricatures and cartoons

The world in cartoons. il *World Press Rev* 34:34-5 F '87

Computer tapes

Can a system keep a secret? P. Elmer-Dewitt. il *Time* 129:68-9 Ap 6 '87

The computer that kept secrets. *Newsweek* 109:20 F 23 '87

Congressional hearings

Abrams on the hot seat. T. Jacoby. il por *Newsweek* 109:18-19 Je 8 '87

Albert, Fawn and Ollie. W. Goodman. il *New Leader* 70:5-7 Jl 13-27 '87

Another blow for Ed Meese [committee report] T. Jacoby. il por *Newsweek* 110:24-5 N 30 '87

The art of the plausible. M. Greenfield. il *Newsweek* 110:64 Ag 10 '87

Awaiting the admiral [J. M. Poindexter] M. Healy and K. T. Walsh. il por *U S News World Rep* 103:26-7 Jl 13 '87

Beat the devil [testimony of O. North] A. Cockburn. *Nation* 245:78 Ag 1-8 '87

The "Belly Button" file [A. Hakim's testimony] M. McDonald. il pors *Macleans* 100:26 Je 15 '87

A big bonus for "Belly Button" [testimony of A. Hakim] J. V. Lamar, Jr. il pors *Time* 129:18-19 Je 15 '87

The big hearings. *Natl Rev* 39:14-15 Je 5 '87

The big ones that got away. D. Corn. il *Nation* 245:152-4 Ag 29 '87

Blossoms of American springtime [role of F. Hall] F. Bruning. por *Macleans* 100:9 Jl 6 '87

The book on Iranamok [committee report] *New Repub* 197:7-8 D 14 '87

'The buck stops here' [J. M. Poindexter's testimony] M. McDonald. il por *Macleans* 100:12-13 Jl 27 '87

But what laws were broken? G. J. Church. il *Time* 129:24-6 Je 1 '87

By a thread [future of E. Abrams] F. Barnes. *New Repub* 197:11-13 Jl 13-20 '87

Can North be believed? E. Magnuson. il por *Time* 130:12 Jl 6 '87

Charging up Capitol Hill [testimony of O. North; cover story; special section] il pors *Time* 130:12-18+ Jl 20 '87

Constructing scandal. J. C. Alexander. *New Repub* 196:18+ Je 8 '87

The contra fight on Capitol Hill. H. Anderson. il *Newsweek* 109:36 Je 1 '87

Covert no more? [CIA and Iran-contra] J. McLaughlin. *Natl Rev* 39:22 Ag 28 '87

Curtain call. H. Fairlie. *New Repub* 197:16-19 S 7 '87

Dirty tricks again? [activities of G. A. Robinette] L. Howard. il por *Newsweek* 110:6 Jl 6 '87

Down a sinkhole [testimony of R. W. Owen] M. Kempton. *N Y Rev Books* 34:53-4 Je 25 '87

Drugs and contras. *Nation* 244:786-7 Je 13 '87

An edge of anger [testimony of G. Shultz; special section] il pors *Time* 130:12-17 Ag 3 '87

Elliott Abrams must now face the music on Nicaragua, and Congress is calling the tune. W. Plummer. por *People Wkly* 27:44-5 Je 8 '87

The emperor's new clothes. il *Progressive* 51:7-8 Jl '87

Encore! [call for additional hearings on contra aid] *Commonweal* 114:435-7 Ag 14 '87

Examining the loose ends in the Iran-contra affair [forthcoming report] P. Cary. il *U S News World Rep* 103:22-3 O 26 '87

Exeunt omnes. *Natl Rev* 39:14-15 Ag 28 '87

The fall of a hero [O. L. North] M. McDonald. *Macleans* 100:20-1 Je 8 '87

Fawn Hall, Ollie's ally and shredder, wows the Hill. M. Green. il por *People Wkly* 27:32-3 Je 22 '87

Iran-contra affair—Congressional hearings—*cont.*

The final witness [R. Reagan] *Nation* 245:109 Ag 15-22 '87

Finally, the scandal front and center. B. Duffy. il *U S News World Rep* 102:23-4 My 4 '87

For Reagan, a bit of relief [J. Poindexter's testimony; special section] il por *U S News World Rep* 103:14-21 Jl 27 '87

Gavel to grovel: why the hearings failed [cover story] il *Progressive* 51:14-18 S '87

Giving truth a bad name. M. Greenfield. il *Newsweek* 110:64 Jl 27 '87

The good soldier [testimony of R. McFarlane] J. V. Lamar, Jr. il pors map *Time* 129:30-1+ My 25 '87

Halfway—and a hatful of trouble ahead. B. Duffy. il *U S News World Rep* 102:31 Je 22 '87

Hear no evil. C. Schine. il *Vogue* 177:114 Ag '87

The hearings [cover story; special section] il *World Press Rev* 34:11-18 S '87

The hearings, and after. *Natl Rev* 39:17-18 Ag 14 '87

Here comes the prosecutor [report issued] E. Magnuson. il *Time* 130:17 N 30 '87

Hero or outlaw? [O. L. North; cover story; special section; with editorial comment by Kevin Doyle] il pors *Macleans* 100:2, 14-21 Jl 20 '87

A hero's mission [O. L. North] M. Kempton. il *N Y Rev Books* 34:13 Ag 13 '87

Hints of conspiracy [special section] il *Time* 129:10-16+ My 11 '87

How much damage? [Reagan's credibility] L. Walczak and others. il por *Bus Week* p24-5 Jl 27 '87

Implausible deniability. M. B. Zuckerman. il *U S News World Rep* 103:68 Ag 3 '87

Iran/contra: reality and unreality. H. J. Hyde. *Natl Rev* 39:19-20 D 4 '87

Iran-contra hearings. il *World Press Rev* 34:9 Jl '87

The Iran-contra hearings halfway. D. Schorr. il *New Leader* 70:3-4 Jl 1-15 '87

Irangate's hallowed hearing room. il *Life* 10:12-13 Jl '87

'It was my idea' [R. C. McFarlane's testimony] L. Martz. il pors *Newsweek* 109:16-19 My 25 '87

"It's very difficult to accept". J. V. Lamar, Jr. il pors *Time* 130:11 Ag 10 '87

Just wondering [testimony of Poindexter and Shultz] W. F. Buckley. *Natl Rev* 39:58-9 Ag 28 '87

Keeping up his guard [O. North refuses to testify in closed session] F. Trippett. il por *Time* 129:14+ Je 29 '87

Letter from Washington. Cato. *Natl Rev* 39:14 Ag 14 '87

Letter from Washington. E. Drew. *New Yorker* 63:75-6+ Je 22 '87

Letter from Washington [testimony of O. North and J. Poindexter] E. Drew. *New Yorker* 63:71-89 Ag 31 '87

Limits of American 'glasnost'. J. Steele. il *World Press Rev* 34:64 Ag '87

Locke meets Hobbes at Iran-contra hearings. J. M. Wall. *Christ Century* 104:643-4 Jl 29-Ag 5 '87

Lying in State [testimony of E. Abrams] *Nation* 244:835 Je 20 '87

The man asking Iranscam's tough questions [lawyer A. L. Liman] C. Knowlton. il pors *Fortune* 115:76-9+ Je 8 '87

The man who ran the show [testimony of R. Secord] G. J. Church. il pors *Time* 129:34-6 My 18 '87

Minority report. C. Hitchens. *Nation* 244:673 My 23 '87

Muffled report. *Nation* 245:615-16 N 28 '87

North: felon or fall guy? [testimony of A. Hakim] T. Morganthau. il pors *Newsweek* 109:28+ Je 15 '87

Not with a bang [scheduled testimony of O. North; cover story; special section] il pors *Newsweek* 110:14-21 Jl 13 '87

Not yet a potted plant [damage to R. Reagan's credibility] E. Magnuson. il pors *Time* 130:12-13 Ag 10 '87

Notes and comment. *New Yorker* 63:31 My 18 '87

Notes and comment [O. L. North's testimony] *New Yorker* 63:19-20 Jl 20 '87

Notes and comment [question of presidential responsibility for actions of staff] *New Yorker* 63:21 Jl 27 '87

Of many things [O. L. North's testimony] G. W. Hunt. *America* 157:50 Ag 1-8 '87

Oliver's twist [cover story; special section] B. Duffy. il pors *U S News World Rep* 103:18-22+ Jl 20 '87

Ollie takes the Hill [cover story; special section] il pors *Newsweek* 110:12-22+ Jl 20 '87

Ollie's turn [O. L. North scheduled to testify; cover story; special section] il pors *Time* 130:22-6+ Jl 13 '87

On being full of passionate intensity. *America* 156:494 Je 20-27 '87

On with the show. *Natl Rev* 39:15 My 22 '87

Passing the buck [testmony of J. Poindexter; special section] il pors *Time* 130:8-14+ Jl 27 '87

A patriot—or a profiteer? [R. V. Secord] L. Martz. il por *Newsweek* 109:38-40+ My 18 '87

Patriots pursuing profits. E. Magnuson. il por *Time* 129:24-5 Je 8 '87

A portrait of 'chaos'. M. McDonald. il *Macleans* 100:16-17 Ag 10 '87

Pressing North [more questions for O. L. North] J. Garvey. *Commonweal* 114:437-8 Ag 14 '87

The price of not 'breaking faith'. M. McDonald. il por *Macleans* 100:16-17 My 25 '87

The Pro-American Activities Committee. *Natl Rev* 39:16-17 Jl 3 '87

Profiteers and loons [lack of moral outrage] M. Ivins. il *Progressive* 51:28 Jl '87

Questions for the colonel [O. L. North] il por *U S News World Rep* 103:26-7 Jl 13 '87

Reagan's secret government. *New Repub* 196:7-9 Je 1 '87

Report card. D. Corn. *Nation* 245:668-9 D 5 '87

The rewards of watching. L. Wainwright. il *Life* 10:120 O '87

Round one of the hearings. *America* 156:433-4 My 30 '87

Rules of the game: does Congress have the guts to go one-on-one with Reagan? [views of L. Hamilton] W. Greider. il *Roll Stone* p37-9 Je 18 '87

A 'sad and sordid' story [R. Secord's testimony] I. Austen. il por *Macleans* 100:18-19 My 18 '87

Saving covert action from Ollie North. *New Repub* 197:5-7 Ag 3 '87

Scowcroft's concerns. H. Sidey. il *Time* 129:17 My 4 '87

See no evil, hear no evil, speak no evil [O. L. North, J. M. Poindexter, and U.S. foreign policy] M. Kramer. il *U S News World Rep* 103:12 Jl 27 '87

Shredded policies, arrogant attitudes. E. Magnuson. il por *Time* 129:21-2 Je 22 '87

Shultz takes the stand. M. McDonald. il por *Macleans* 100:28 Ag 3 '87

Shultz's long war [special section] il pors *Newsweek* 110:14-19 Ag 3 '87

Silent partners. *Nation* 244:747 Je 6 '87

A simmering scandal's opening act. B. Duffy. il *U S News World Rep* 102:27-8 My 18 '87

A small-town girl lands in the spotlight [F. Hall] G. Hackett. por *Newsweek* 109:30 Je 15 '87

The stalwarts retreat. T. Jacoby and R. Parry. il *Newsweek* 109:20-1 Je 22 '87

A stand-up guy's disquieting tales [testimony of G. Shultz] M. Healy. il por *U S News World Rep* 103:18 Ag 3 '87

Still no smoking gun [special section] il *Newsweek* 110:12-16 Ag 10 '87

Stokes lectures Col. North, nation on law and America. il pors *Jet* 72:28-9 Ag 3 '87

Stones unturned. *Nation* 245:75-6 Ag 1-8 '87

The story so far. D. Corn. *Nation* 244:874-5 Je 27 '87

The summer of 1987. *Foreign Aff* 66:1-6 Fall '87

Taking blame [testimony of J. Poindexter; special section] il por *Newsweek* 110:14-19 Jl 27 '87

Taking the stand [J. Singlaub] T. Brewster. il pors *Life* 10:28-32 Ag '87

Talk show [testimony of J. Singlaub] *Nation* 244:750-1 Je 6 '87

The tangled web. *Nation* 245:39-40 Jl 18-25 '87

Television's blinding power [O. L. North's testimony; cover story] M. McLoughlin. il pors *U S News World Rep* 103:18-21 Jl 27 '87

Time of trial [special section] il por *Newsweek* 109:16-23+ My 11 '87

A troubling midsummer mystery [conflicting evidence] B. Duffy. il *U S News World Rep* 103:14-15 Ag 10 '87

Turning to Teheran. *Nation* 245:1 Jl 4-11 '87

TV's new maxiseries: they don't make hearings like they used to. L. Wainwright. il *Life* 10:22 Jl '87

Uncovering the cover-up [testimony of Charles Cooper] T. Morganthau. il *Newsweek* 110:19 Jl 6 '87

The untouchables [testimony of O. North and J. Poindexter] J. Klein. il por *N Y* 20:12-13 Jl 27 '87

The 'wall around the president' is beginning to crumble. P. Dwyer. il *Bus Week* p71 My 25 '87

Iran-contra affair—Congressional hearings—*cont.*

Washington circus. *America* 157:51 Ag 1-8 '87

Water torture [White House method of coping with the hearings] F. Barnes. *New Repub* 196:11-12 Je 8 '87

Week 2: more troubling questions [R. McFarlane's testimony] B. Duffy. il por *U S News World Rep* 102:24-5 My 25 '87

Week 3: a Marine's problems multiply. M. Healy and K. T. Walsh. il *U S News World Rep* 102:19 Je 1 '87

Week 4: the other figures emerge [E. Abrams' testimony] J. P. Shapiro. il por *U S News World Rep* 102:21 Je 8 '87

Week 5: the strangest tales yet [testimony of A. Hakim] M. Healy. il por *U S News World Rep* 102:20-1 Je 15 '87

What do we know? When did we know it? W. F. Buckley. *Natl Rev* 39:56-7 Jl 17 '87

What the president should have known [committee report] M. McDonald. il *Macleans* 100:34-7+ N 30 '87

What will Ollie say—and when? D. Baer and M. Healy. il por *U S News World Rep* 102:23-4 Je 29 '87

Where the buck finally stops [report issued] H. Gorey. il *Time* 130:19 N 23 '87

Who will believe Oliver North? M. Healy. il por *U S News World Rep* 103:12-13 Jl 6 '87

Zeal without understanding: reflections on Rambo and Oliver North. R. Jewett. il *Christ Century* 104:753-6 S 9-16 '87

Anecdotes, facetiae, satire, etc.

Reagan tells all. L. Grossberger. il *Roll Stone* p43-5 Jl 16-30 '87

Senator Hatch questions Al Capone. N. Glixon. il *Commonweal* 114:436 Ag 14 '87

Uncivil liberties. C. Trillin. *Nation* 244:840 Je 20 '87

Photographs and photography

In the glare of history. E. Ferorelli. il *Life* 10:110-16+ O '87

Egyptian participation

Dreams of the Great Satan [A. Khashoggi's statements alleging a U.S. assassination plot against Khomeini and an Egyptian involvement in Iranscam] A. Cockburn. *Nation* 245:186 S 5 '87

Israeli participation

Back to the beginning in the Iran-contra affair. S. Emerson. il *U S News World Rep* 102:20-2 Je 29 '87

'Iranblame'—a tiff among friends. J. M. Hildreth and J. L. Sheler. il *U S News World Rep* 102:21 Ja 26 '87

Israel: showdown. *Newsweek* 109:6 Ja 26 '87

Israelamok [Iranamok and the Pollard affair] *New Repub* 196:9 Mr 30 '87

Israel's end of the Iran affair. S. Emerson. il *U S News World Rep* 102:20 Ap 13 '87

Triple trouble in Israel [with editorial comment] E. Salpeter. il *New Leader* 70:2, 5-7 Mr 23 '87

Anecdotes, facetiae, satire, etc.

So who's confused? M. Nesvisky. *World Press Rev* 34:16 F '87

Legal aspects

Black judge dismisses two suits in Iran arms case [B. D. Parker] por *Jet* 72:4 Mr 30 '87

Crime, the Constitution, and the Iran-contra affair. L. G. Crovitz. *Commentary* 84:23-30 O '87

Issues of law and ethics. *Time* 129:16 Mr 2 '87

A new legal defense: Ollie made me do it. T. Jacoby. il *Newsweek* 110:24-5 N 30 '87

Public opinion

Advantage Gorbachev. S. Sullivan. il por *Newsweek* 109:38 Mr 9 '87

Assessing the performance. il *Time* 130:15 Jl 20 '87

The cynic route. W. Schneider. *New Repub* 196:12-13 Ja 19 '87

A distinct sense of unease [results of survey] il *U S News World Rep* 103:22-3 Jl 13 '87

Erosion of U.S. power [effect of scandal in Europe] J. Amalric. il *World Press Rev* 34:12-13 F '87

Everybody came but 'Larry' [Oliver North Day in Philmont, N.Y.] M. Grevatt. il *Nation* 245:228-9 S 12 '87

How they see it in Arkansas. il *Time* 130:16-17 Ag 3 '87

Iranscam couldn't happen there [European reaction] J. Bonfante. il *Time* 129:36 Ja 26 '87

Landscape with trolls [O. L. North] L. H. Lapham. *Harpers* 275:6-8 S '87

The making of a folk hero [O. L. North] C. W. Colson. il *Christ Today* 31:80 S 4 '87

A Newsweek poll: shielding others. il *Newsweek* 110:18 Jl 20 '87

Next step for North? [proposing a political career for O. North] W. F. Buckley. *Natl Rev* 39:55 Ag 14 '87

North displays talent for television politics. J. M. Wall. il *Christ Century* 104:611-12 Jl 15-22 '87

Ollie? Golly! [O. North] T. Lencz. *Natl Rev* 39:40 Ag 14 '87

Ollie North and the trajectory of fame. C. Krauthammer. il *Time* 130:76 Jl 27 '87

Ollie North, the movie. D. Denby. il *New Repub* 197:7-9 Ag 3 '87

Ollie-oop! B. Darrach. il pors *People Wkly* 28:32-7 Jl 27 '87

One-third say Reagan should consider resigning. il *Newsweek* 109:21 Mr 9 '87

The paradox of North's popularity [O. L. North] J. Morley. il *Nation* 245:122-5 Ag 15-22 '87

'Platoon' and Iranamok. *New Repub* 196:4+ Mr 9 '87

A simple turn of the fates [views of Bloomington, Minn. residents] H. Rainie. il *U S News World Rep* 103:24 Jl 20 '87

Street sign [B. Breeden arrested for stealing street sign named to honor J. Poindexter in Odon, Indiana] *Progressive* 51:4 Ag '87

Anecdotes, facetiae, satire, etc.

Maggie in Ollieland [O. North Day in Philmont, New York] M. Gallagher. il *Natl Rev* 39:42+ N 6 '87

Reporters and reporting

Afterglow: all the president's men [post Tower Commission report press conference] A. Cockburn. *Nation* 244:422-3 Ap 4 '87

Beat the devil. A. Cockburn. *Nation* 244:278-9 Mr 7 '87

Blaming the customer. T. Griffith. il *Time* 129:65 Mr 30 '87

Can we talk? [efforts to avoid leaks from the Senate Select Committee] il *Time* 129:22 F 16 '87

CBS News with Dan Rather [distortions on Nicaragua] W. F. Buckley. *Natl Rev* 39:54-5 Je 5 '87

Comment on the crisis. il *World Press Rev* 34:14-15 Ja '87

Inside dopes [press treatment of O. L. North] J. L. Pasley. *New Repub* 196:14-16 F 23 '87

Irangate: stereotypes as side effects [stereotyping the Reagans harms women and the elderly] L.-M. Delloff. *Christ Century* 104:263-4 Mr 18-25 '87

Killing the messenger. M. Ivins. il *Progressive* 51:18 Mr '87

Ollie's gang [lack of reporting on O. North's secret teams in Nicaragua] A. Cockburn. *Nation* 245:115 Ag 15-22 '87

Other comment on the affair. *World Press Rev* 34:18 S '87

The power and the story [interview with W. Pincus] L. Hirschberg. por *Roll Stone* p45-6+ My 21 '87

Reagan and Hegel. A. Cockburn. *Nation* 244:709 My 30 '87

The real heroes of contra-gate [reporters B. Barger and R. Parry] J. Morley and T. Rosenberg. il pors *Roll Stone* p48-50+ S 10 '87

Secord agent [use of FBI to investigate journalists suing Gen. Secord] *Nation* 245:40-1 Jl 18-25 '87

War and remembrance [A. M. Rosenthal's column comparing the Holocaust to the Iran arms scandal] L. Wieseltier. *New Repub* 196:50 F 9 '87

When sources get immunity [press treatment of O. North] J. Alter. il *Newsweek* 109:54 Ja 19 '87

The White House crisis. il *World Press Rev* 34:7-8 Ap '87

Anecdotes, facetiae, satire, etc.

Welcome to the seven o'clock news. W. F. Buckley. *Natl Rev* 39:58 Ag 28 '87

South African participation

Contra-gate: a black issue. R. Knight. por *Essence* 18:144 Je '87

South Africa link. D. Corn. *Nation* 245:221-2 S 12 '87

Special prosecutor

And now for the hard part. D. Baer. il por *U S News World Rep* 103:35 Ag 17 '87

And offstage, the legal drama begins to unfold. il *Newsweek* 109:26 My 11 '87

'Big shoe' delayed. il por *Newsweek* 110:6 Ag 31 '87

But was it a crime? K. M. Pierce. il *Time* 130:14 Jl 27 '87

Conspiracy theories [basis of criminal prosecutions] il *Time* 129:33 My 25 '87

Have brief, will travel [L. E. Walsh] S. Lichtman. il *New Repub* 197:14-16 Ag 24 '87

One deliberate step at a time, a prosecutor builds his case [L. E. Walsh] J. Friedman. il por *People Wkly* 28:58-9 D 7 '87

Iran-contra affair—Special prosecutor—*cont.*

A passel of new trouble from a posse of lawyers [L. E. Walsh and staff] D. Baer and M. Healy. il por *U S News World Rep* 102:19-20 Je 15 '87

Preparing for the real story. I. Austen. il *Macleans* 100:34-5 N 30 '87

Prosecutor in a cocoon. il por *Newsweek* 110:17 Jl 27 '87

Timing tiff [Senate Select Committee and L. Walsh clash over granting immunity to J. Poindexter and O. North] *Time* 129:26 Mr 23 '87

Walsh makes his move. P. Shenon. il por *N Y Times Mag* p46-7+ O 25 '87

Walsh vs. Congress [granting immunity] T. Morganthau. il pors *Newsweek* 109:24+ Mr 23 '87

What will they say—and when? [tussle over who gets immunity] M. Healy. il pors *U S News World Rep* 102:20 Mr 23 '87

Terminology

Between issues. *New Leader* 69:2 D 29 '86

Bravo Zulu! W. Safire. il *N Y Times Mag* p18+ Mr 29 '87

Finding's losings. W. Safire. il *N Y Times Mag* p10+ Ja 25 '87

Glossary of a scandal. W. Safire. il *N Y Times Mag* p12+ Ag 16 '87

The gruntled employee. W. Safire. il *N Y Times Mag* p12+ Ap 5 '87

Miss Feasance of 1987. W. Safire. *N Y Times Mag* p6+ Mr 15 '87

Nine yards to imbroglio. W. Safire. il *N Y Times Mag* p8 Ja 4 '87

Notional timeline. W. Safire. *N Y Times Mag* p10+ F 22 '87

Teed off over teed up. W. Safire. il *N Y Times Mag* p10+ Ap 19 '87

Thisgate? Or is it Thatscam? M. Greenfield. il *Newsweek* 109:86 Ja 26 '87

Anecdotes, facetiae, satire, etc.

Iranamok. *New Repub* 196:9-10 Ja 5-12 '87

Wiretaps

The White House tapes, again. A. Nairn. il *Progressive* 51:20-3 Ap '87

Iranian crisis, 1979-1981 *See* Iranian seizure of United States embassy, 1979-1981

Iranian-Iraqi War, 1980-

See also

Stark (Warship)—Iraqi missile attack, 1987

As diplomats bog down, war heats up. J. Barnes. il *U S News World Rep* 102:45 F 9 '87

At war on all fronts [cover story; special section] il pors *Time* 130:22-6+ Ag 17 '87

Back Iraq. D. Pipes and L. Mylroie. *New Repub* 196:14-15 Ap 27 '87

Breaking the Persian Gulf stalemate. B. Cerha. il *World Press Rev* 34:21-3 Mr '87

Death in the Garden of Eden. B. Levin. il map *Macleans* 100:18-19 Ja 26 '87

Eyewitness at the front. R. Laver. il *Macleans* 100:14-15 F 9 '87

How to beat the draft in Teheran? Flee to Turkey. J. P. Shapiro. il map *U S News World Rep* 102:30 F 23 '87

'I want to see Iraq crushed'. T. Stanger. il *Newsweek* 109:37+ F 9 '87

Iran: scuffling in the wheelhouse. J. L. Galloway. il *U S News World Rep* 103:40 O 12 '87

Iran strikes on two fronts. W. E. Smith. il *Time* 129:26+ Ja 26 '87

Iran tightens the noose. R. Watson. il *Newsweek* 109:36 F 2 '87

Iraq and the war with Iran. F. W. Axelgard. bibl f *Curr Hist* 86:57-60+ F '87

Iraq's no-win, no-lose war? J. Barnes. il por *U S News World Rep* 103:38-9 O 12 '87

Kurds locked in one more losing war? J. Barnes. il map *U S News World Rep* 103:55 N 9 '87

Kuwait rolls the dice for high stakes. J. Barnes. il *U S News World Rep* 103:30 Ag 3 '87

Kuwait shies away from confronting Iran [interview with S. N. al-Sabah] L. Lief. il *U S News World Rep* 103:40 N 2 '87

Life among the smoldering ruins [effect on port of Basra] D. Fischer. il map *Time* 129:47 Mr 30 '87

The long siege of Basra. N. Traver. il *Time* 129:40 F 2 '87

Meantime, back in Tehran. W. E. Smith. il *Time* 129:36-7 Ja 12 '87

The Persian Gulf: stakes and risks [statement, May 29, 1987] R. W. Murphy. *Dep State Bull* 87:64-7 Jl '87

Prelude to a 'final offensive'? M. Whitaker. il map *Newsweek* 109:33 Ja 26 '87

'Profound concern' over Iran-Iraq situation expressed by Security Council members. *UN Chron* 24:69 F '87

Rage in the marshlands. P. Kopvillem. il *Macleans* 100:28-9 F 2 '87

The real stakes in the Persian Gulf. R. N. Perle. il *U S News World Rep* 103:26+ O 26 '87

Secretary-General calls for moratorium by Iran and Iraq on attacks on civilian areas. *UN Chron* 23:77-8 N '86

Secretary-General's 26 November report on Iran-Iraq. *UN Chron* 24:68-9 F '87

Security Council members condemn use of chemical weapons in Iran-Iraq conflict. *UN Chron* 24:33-4 Ag '87

Seeking eternal bliss in battle. S. Allis. il *Time* 129:52 My 25 '87

U.S. interests in the Persian Gulf [statement, January 27, 1987] G. P. Shultz. *Dep State Bull* 87:19-20 Mr '87

The view from the Mustansiriyah. M. Viorst. map *New Yorker* 63:76-96 O 19 '87

While Iran attacks, the world dithers. P. R. Range. il *U S News World Rep* 102:35 Ja 26 '87

Who started the war? N. M. Renfrew. *Foreign Policy* 66:98-108 Spr '87

You decide the U.S. response to a crisis. L. Kravitz. map *Sch Update* 119:14 F 23 '87

Aerial operations

Shortages, lack of experience cripple Iranian Air Force. P. Proctor. *Aviat Week Space Technol* 126:25-6 F 23 '87

Economic aspects

American hubris: from Truman to the Persian Gulf. T. Draper. bibl f il *N Y Rev Books* 34:40-8 Jl 16 '87

America's Gulf minuet [protection of shipping lanes] W. L. Chaze. il *U S News World Rep* 102:18-19 Je 8 '87

Back to the bullets [Iraq launches a new tanker war] M. S. Serrill. il *Time* 130:38-9 S 14 '87

A balance sheet in the Gulf. N. Cooper. il *Newsweek* 110:59 N 9 '87

A battle for sea lanes [renewed attacks on shipping] R. Laver. il *Macleans* 100:20 S 14 '87

Buildup in the Gulf [U.S. commitment to keep shipping lanes open; special section] il map *Newsweek* 109:32-5 Je 8 '87

Collision course? [U.S. flags to protect Kuwaiti oil tankers in Persian Gulf] L. Howard. il *Newsweek* 109:5 My 25 '87

Crisis in the Gulf: waiting for the other shoe to drop. J. L. Galloway. il *U S News World Rep* 103:38 Jl 13 '87

The dangers of taking sides [U.S. reflagging decision] L. C. Wilson. *USA Today (Periodical)* 116:47 N '87

Democrats cite risk in Kuwaiti reflagging [report by Democratic Study Group] P. Mann. *Aviat Week Space Technol* 126:33 Je 22 '87

Escort service for the Gulf [U.S. plans to keep shipping lanes open] J. V. Lamar, Jr. il *Time* 129:23 Je 8 '87

Europe's arms pipeline to Iran. K. R. Timmerman. *Nation* 245:47-8+ Jl 18-25 '87

Everybody's doing it [European arms sales to Iran] G. Russell. il *Time* 129:31 Mr 16 '87

Go it alone in the Gulf [U.S. protection of shipping lanes] M. Kramer. il *U S News World Rep* 102:20 Je 8 '87

The good life in the Persian Gulf. D. Kirk. il *New Leader* 70:3-5 S 7 '87

Guerrilla war on the water. C. Dickey. il map *Newsweek* 109:41 Je 15 '87

The Gulf [cover story; special section] il *World Press Rev* 34:13-16+ O '87

The Gulf war—among friends [United States protects shipping lanes] J. L. Galloway. il map *U S News World Rep* 102:26-8 Je 15 '87

Gulf—or abyss? [U.S. commitment to protect shipping lanes] I. F. Stone. *Nation* 244:838-9 Je 20 '87

High drama in the Persian Gulf. R. Evans and R. D. Novak. il map *Read Dig* 131:133-6 D '87

How to defend the Gulf [U.S. to protect neutral shipping] *New Repub* 196:7-9 Je 22 '87

If necessary, a superpower acts alone [U.S. decision to protect shipping lanes] C. Krauthammer. il map *Time* 129:83-4 Je 22 '87

In the Gulf, nowhere to hide. R. Watson. il map *Newsweek* 110:44-5 S 14 '87

Iranian-Iraqi War, 1980——Economic aspects—*cont.*
Oil, the Gulf and the Iranians. D. Hiro. *Nation* 245:261-3 S 19 '87
Patrolling the Gulf [U.S. commitment] *Natl Rev* 39:15+ Jl 17 '87
The Persian Gulf: where U.S. policy is adrift. D. Griffiths. il *Bus Week* p41 Je 15 '87
Piloting the camel [U.S. reflagging commitment to Kuwait] M. B. Zuckerman. il *U S News World Rep* 103:76 Jl 6 '87
Pitfalls and promises in the Persian Gulf powder keg. J. L. Galloway. il *U S News World Rep* 102:18-19 Je 29 '87
Prevailing in the Gulf [US forces as sign of power] D. Gergen. il *U S News World Rep* 103:84 S 14 '87
Profiteering on the Iran-Iraq War. M. Brzoska. bibl f il *Bull At Sci* 43:42-5 Je '87
Protecting allied security [European ships] il *Macleans* 100:27 O 5 '87
Pseudo-crisis in the Persian Gulf [U.S. to defend free shipping] *Natl Rev* 39:20-1 Jl 3 '87
Reflagging folly [U.S. plan to flag Kuwaiti ships and reinforce American military presence] N. Safran. *New Repub* 197:10-11 Ag 3 '87
Rhetoric and reality in the Iranian arms trade. P. Gupte. il por *Forbes* 140:32-5 O 19 '87
Rough seas and new names [Kuwaiti tankers flying under American flag] J. V. Lamar, Jr. il map *Time* 129:13 Je 29 '87
The shame of the game [European arms sales to Iran] E. Clift. il *Newsweek* 110:44 S 21 '87
Ship attacks boom: so do the profits. J. Barnes. il *U S News World Rep* 103:38 S 14 '87
Square one again in the Gulf [Iraq resumes tanker attacks] W. L. Chaze. il map *U S News World Rep* 103:35-6 S 14 '87
Stoking the Gulf fires [Iraq resumes tanker attacks] R. Laver. il *Macleans* 100:27 S 7 '87
Supersap [U.S. effort to protect access to Persian Gulf oil results in price rise] *New Repub* 197:4 Ag 31 '87
Troubled waters [European and Japanese dependence on oil from the Persian Gulf] il *Time* 129:22 Je 1 '87
U.S. policy in the Persian Gulf and Kuwaiti reflagging [statement, June 16, 1987] M. H. Armacost. *Dep State Bull* 87:78-81 Ag '87
Undertow from the Gulf. W. Glasgall. il *Bus Week* p32-4 Ag 17 '87
Up Shiites creek [U.S. commitment] W. Greider. il *Roll Stone* p32+ O 22 '87
When the Gulf coughs, the oil market shivers. W. J. Cook. il map *U S News World Rep* 103:20-1 Ag 17 '87
Who arms Iran? Almost everyone. W. L. Chaze. il *U S News World Rep* 103:26-8 Ag 31 '87
Who needs the Gulf, anyway? [oil pipelines] M. Gart. map *Time* 130:27 Ag 24 '87
Why Reagan pulled his punch in the Persian Gulf [retaliating against Iran for missile attack on a U.S.-flagged tanker] B. Javetski and D. Griffiths. il *Bus Week* p161 N 2 '87
Why we are uneasy [U.S. commitment to protect shipping lanes] *America* 156:473 Je 13 '87
Moral and religious aspects
How could the Iran-Iraq War affect Christianity? [interview with C. G. Fry] S. Mumper. il por *Christ Today* 31:46-7 N 6 '87
Peace and mediation
Can Moscow play peacemaker in the Persian Gulf War? P. Galuszka. il *Bus Week* p45 Ag 31 '87
Iran-Iraq War [statements, January 23 and February 25, 1987] R. Reagan. *Dep State Bull* 87:52 Ap '87
Meeting with Arab League delegation [remarks, May 7, 1987] G. P. Shultz. il por *Dep State Bull* 87:63 Jl '87
Questions from the Persian Gulf. *America* 157:316 N 7 '87
Secretary-General discusses 'outline plan' during trip to Teheran, Baghdad. il pors *UN Chron* 24:16-18 N '87
Secretary-General suggests Security Council ministerial-level meeting to explore Iran-Iraq situation. il *UN Chron* 24:12-14 My '87
Secretary Shultz attends UN General Assembly [texts of news conferences, September 21-October 1, 1987] G. P. Shultz. *Dep State Bull* 87:52-60 N '87
Security Council again calls for immediate cease-fire, cessation of all hostilities, withdrawal of forces to international boundaries without delay. map *UN Chron* 24:66-8 F '87

Security Council calls for cease-fire in Iran-Iraq War [statements; with text of resolution, July 20, 1987] G. P. Shultz; R. Reagan. *Dep State Bull* 87:75-7 S '87
Security Council demands immediate cease-fire as first step towards negotiated settlement of Iran-Iraq War. il *UN Chron* 24:19-22 N '87
Where interests converge [U.S.-Soviet interest in ending Iranian-Iraqi War] M. J. Gart. il *Time* 130:14 O 19 '87
Reporters and reporting
The Gulf. il *World Press Rev* 34:6-7 D '87
The Gulf. il *World Press Rev* 34:7 N '87
The Persian Gulf. il *World Press Rev* 34:8-9 S '87
Russian participation
The broader picture. B. Crozier. *Natl Rev* 39:28+ N 6 '87
Can Moscow play peacemaker in the Persian Gulf War? P. Galuszka. il *Bus Week* p45 Ag 31 '87
Where the Soviets stand. F. Halliday. *World Press Rev* 34:18-19 O '87
Saudi Arabian participation
Administration to cite Saudi involvement in Gulf as justification for arms sale. M. Mecham. *Aviat Week Space Technol* 127:31 Ag 24 '87
No flinching in the kingdom. W. L. Chaze. il *U S News World Rep* 103:26-8 Ag 24 '87
Simmering about the Saudis [U.S. wants support in the Persian Gulf] H. Anderson. il *Newsweek* 109:40 Je 15 '87
Tornado attack. *Newsweek* 110:51 O 12 '87
Washington is protecting much more than Kuwaiti tankers. B. Javetski and others. il *Bus Week* p89 Jl 20 '87
Secret service
Faking the red menace [Reagan administration's invention of a Soviet threat to Iran] *Nation* 244:65 Ja 24 '87
Anecdotes, facetiae, satire, etc.
Poindexter file [disinformation supplied to Iran and Iraq concerning Soviet threat] R. R. Lingeman. *Nation* 244:68-9 Ja 24 '87
Iranian postage stamps *See* Postage stamps
Iranian propaganda *See* Propaganda, Iranian
Iranian refugees *See* Refugees, Iranian
Iranian seizure of United States embassy, 1979-1981
Minority report [linking Iranian hostage case to contragate] C. Hitchens. *Nation* 245:582 N 21 '87
Minority report [possible link between Iranian hostage case and contragate] C. Hitchens. *Nation* 245:440 O 24 '87
Minority report [possible link between Iranian hostage case and contragate] C. Hitchens. *Nation* 245:80 Ag 1-8 '87
Minority report [possible link between Iranian hostage case and contragate] C. Hitchens. *Nation* 245:7 Jl 4-11 '87
Minority report [possible link between Iranian hostage case and contragate] C. Hitchens. *Nation* 244:842 Je 20 '87
Iranian terrorists *See* Terrorists, Iranian
Iranians
Turkey
How to beat the draft in Teheran? Flee to Turkey. J. P. Shapiro. il map *U S News World Rep* 102:30 F 23 '87
Refugees from Iran. R. Laver. il *Macleans* 100:29-30 F 2 '87
Iraq
See also
Al-Kūfah (Iraq)
Baghdad (Iraq)
Basra (Iraq)
Iranian-Iraqi War, 1980-
Nuclear power plants—Iraq
United Nations—Iraq
Antiquities
See also
Babylon (Ancient city)
Commerce
See also
Iranian-Iraqi War, 1980- —Economic aspects
Description and travel
The view from the Mustansiriyah. M. Viorst. map *New Yorker* 63:76-96 O 19 '87
Foreign relations
Israel
IAEA asked to consider measures to ensure Israel does not attack 'peaceful nuclear facilities' [General Assembly resolution prompted by Israel's attack on the Tammuz nuclear reactor in Iraq] *UN Chron* 23:11 Ja '86

Iraq—Foreign relations—*cont.*
United States
See United States—Foreign relations—Iraq
History
The view from the Mustansiriyah. M. Viorst. map *New Yorker* 63:92+ O 12 '87
Politics and government
Iraq and the war with Iran. F. W. Axelgard. bibl f *Curr Hist* 86:57-60+ F '87
Iraq's no-win, no-lose war? J. Barnes. il por *U S News World Rep* 103:38-9 O 12 '87
Religious institutions and affairs
See also
Muslims—Iraq
IRAs *See* Individual retirement accounts
IRAS (Infrared Astronomy Satellite) *See* Artificial satellites—Astronomical use
IRD *See* Institute on Religion and Democracy
Ireland, Doug
France. *Nation* 244:464-6 Ap 11 '87
Ireland, Jill
A battle with breast cancer puts a star's life into focus. il pors *People Wkly* 27:57-8+ Mr 16 '87
Life wish [excerpt] il *Ladies Home J* 104:53-6+ Ja '87
Ireland, Patrick
about
View points. C. Ratcliff. il *Art Am* 75:96-103 Mr '87
Ireland
See also
Bantry (Ireland)
Country estates—Ireland
Dublin (Ireland)
Immigration and emigration—Ireland
Industry and state—Ireland
Investments, American—Ireland
Investments, Irish
Irish
Northern Ireland
Real estate investment—Ireland
Description and travel
Our Regency rental [summer house] A. Emmet. il *House Gard* 159:52+ Jl '87
Economic policy
After the Irish elections. T. P. O'Mahony. *America* 156:267-8 Ap 4 '87
Economic agendas. P. Kirby. *Commonweal* 114:136-7 Mr 13 '87
Ireland's right-wing rut. K. Jacobsen. il *New Leader* 70:5-6 Jl 1-15 '87
Foreign relations
Great Britain
See Great Britain—Foreign relations—Ireland
Northern Ireland
See also
Irish unification question
History
When Irish skies are frowning. R. J. Margolis. il *New Leader* 70:15-16 S 7 '87
To 1603
Images of Ireland 1170-1600: the origins of English imperialism. J. Gillingham. bibl il *Hist Today* 37:16-22 F '87
Historiography
Irish studies and myth history. A. Laurence. il *Hist Today* 37:8-9 D '87
Industries
See also
Jefferson Smurfit Group Ltd.
Waterford Glass Group plc
Languages
See also
Gaelic language
Photographs and photography
Ireland [excerpt from A time that was] J. Freedman. il *People Wkly* 28:124-5+ N 2 '87
Politics and government
See also
Elections—Ireland
Study and teaching
See Irish studies
Union (Proposed)
See Irish unification question
Ireland, Northern *See* Northern Ireland
IRI (Firm) *See* Istituto per la Ricostruzione Industriale
Iridium
Beyond the K-T boundary. R. A. Kerr. *Science* 236:667 My 8 '87
Big splash from an ancient fall [Montagnais crater off Nova Scotia coast] R. Monastersky. *Sci News* 131:404 Je 27 '87

A big splash in the Pacific [work of Frank Kyte and others] map *Sky Telesc* 74:12 Jl '87
Mass extinctions caused by large bolide impacts [adaptation of address, December 11, 1986; cover story] L. W. Alvarez. bibl f il *Phys Today* 40:24-33 Jl '87
Where have all the dinos gone? [work of L. Alvarez] il *U S News World Rep* 103:67 Jl 6 '87
Irimajiri, Shoichiro
The winning difference [address, April 7, 1987] *Vital Speeches Day* 53:650-2 Ag 15 '87
Irion, Mary Jean
In extremadura [poem] *Christ Century* 104:748 S 9-16 '87
O boy [poem] *Christ Century* 104:846 O 7 '87
Irises
Arilbred irises. W. A. Shear. il *Flower Gard* 31:46-7 Je/Jl '87
Integrate ravishing irises [cover story] P. Byers. il *Flower Gard* 31:44-5+ Je/Jl '87
Irish
United States
See also
Irish Americans
A fresh Irish wave laps U.S. shores. B. Duffy and R. Knight. il *U S News World Rep* 102:15 Mr 2 '87
Irish Americans
See also
NORAID
Of many things. G. W. Hunt. *America* 156:inside cover Mr 21 '87
Irish bagpipe *See* Bagpipe
Irish football
The rugged sport of Irish football . . . in San Francisco. il *Sunset* 178:90 My '87
Irish Northern Aid Committee *See* NORAID
Irish Republican Army
The carnage in Enniskillen. G. C. Lubenow. il *Newsweek* 110:42 N 23 '87
The empire's last nervous twitch [Anglo-Irish cooperation] C. C. Mann. *Commonweal* 114:562-5 O 9 '87
An Ulster blast heard in Boston [Enniskillen bombing] M. Satchell. il *U S News World Rep* 103:14 N 23 '87
Irish studies
Irish studies and myth history. A. Laurence. il *Hist Today* 37:8-9 D '87
Irish terrorists *See* Terrorists, Irish
Irish unification question
Belfast: the allure of the 'troubles' [excerpt from Living with war] S. Belfrage. *Harpers* 275:27+ O '87
The empire's last nervous twitch [Anglo-Irish cooperation] C. C. Mann. *Commonweal* 114:562-5 O 9 '87
In Belfast, war is a way of life [excerpt from Living with war] S. Belfrage. il *Nation* 245:156-8 Ag 29 '87
Irkutsk (Soviet Union)
Social life and customs
For Scotty and Lida Sclocchini, a unique superpower detente begins at home in Irkutsk. J. W. Seymore. il pors *People Wkly* 27:42+ Ap 6 '87
Iron
See also
Cast iron
Bacterial methanogenesis and growth from CO_2 with elemental iron as the sole source of electrons. L. Daniels and others. bibl f il *Science* 237:509-11 Jl 31 '87
Central heating [estimating temperature of the earth's core from the melting point of iron at immense pressure] *Sci Am* 256:25-6 Je '87
How hot is the heart of the earth? [research by Quentin Williams and others] S. Weisburd. *Sci News* 131:245 Ap 18 '87
Making a meal of iron [role of methanogens in biocorrosion; work of Lacy Daniels and others] *Sci News* 132:104 Ag 15 '87
Mechanism of the body-centered cubic-hexagonal close-packed phase transition in iron. W. A. Bassett and E. Huang. bibl f il *Science* 238:780-3 N 6 '87
The melting curve of iron to 250 gigapascals: a constraint on the temperature at earth's center. Q. Williams and others. bibl f il *Science* 236:181-2 Ap 10 '87
Iron beds *See* Beds
Iron carbonates
A rusty path to life's origin [effect of ultraviolet rays on ferrous carbonate; work of Gustaf Arrhenius] I. Peterson. *Sci News* 131:152 Mr 7 '87
Iron deficiency anemia *See* Anemia
Iron fences *See* Fences
Iron Horse Vineyards
A symphony in every bottle. M. Gersh. *Vogue* 177:204 Ag '87

Iron in the body
See also
Anemia
Ferritin
Iron: how to get enough in your diet. L. Hoppe. il *Better Homes Gard* 65:34 F '87
Juvenile delinquents lack iron. *Prevention* 39:9 F '87
Three "half truths" about health. il *Glamour* 85:406 S '87

Iron industry
See also
Cleveland-Cliffs, Inc.
Securities
Dilution control [stockholders vs. management over share value at Cleveland-Cliffs Inc.] P. Fuhrman. il *Forbes* 140:174 O 5 '87

Iron ores
See also
Magnetite

Ironbridge Institute
The past mastered [course in heritage management] T. Aldous. *Hist Today* 37:4-5 My '87

Irons
Steam irons. il *Consum Rep* 52:172-7 Mr '87
Steam irons. il *Consum Rep* 52:64-8 D '87
Travel irons & steamers. il *Consum Rep* 52:279-81 My '87
Travel irons and steamers. il *Consum Rep* 52:68-71 D '87

Ironside, William Edmund, Baron of, 1880-1959
about
John Buchan's Richard Hannay. G. Powell. bibl il pors map *Hist Today* 37:32-9 Ag '87
Ironweed [film] See Motion picture reviews—Single works
Iroquois Indians
"The fire that never dies". H. Arden. il map *Natl Geogr* 172:370-403 S '87

Irradiated food
Food irradiation. B. Chinsman. il *World Health* p10-11 Mr '87
Food that's, like, totally rad. A. W. Garland. il *Sierra* 72:20-3 My/Je '87
Food wars: diet and irradiation. M. Moynihan. *Vogue* 177:405+ O '87
The gamma-ray gourmet: scientists cook up tests for irradiated food. R. Weiss. il *Sci News* 132:398-9 D 19-26 '87
Irradiated fruits & vegetables. B. T. Hunter. il *Consum Res Mag* 70:8-9 O '87
No fried food in New Jersey [anti-irradiation activists] K. Terry. *Progressive* 51:25 S '87
Why is D.O.E. for food irradiation? [justifying the extraction of plutonium from commercial nuclear wastes for use in nuclear weapons] K. Terry. il *Nation* 244:142+ F 7 '87
Zap, crackle, pop. G. Gibbs. il *Progressive* 51:22-4 S '87
Zapped at the grocery store. E. T. Becker. il *Women's Sports Fitness* 9:85 Mr '87

Irrationalism (Philosophy)
How to deal with countries gone mad. C. Krauthammer. il *Time* 130:82 S 21 '87

Irreligion
The deadly sin [unbelief] P. De Vries. il por *Christ Today* 31:22-4 My 15 '87

Irrigation
See also
Watering of gardens, lawns, etc.
Environmental aspects
The case of the poisoned wildlife refuge [J. Claus discovers selenium at Kesterson National Wildlife Refuge] R. Fitzgerald. il por *Read Dig* 131:133-7 O '87
Fowl play [selenium pollution at Kesterson National Wildlife Refuge] C. Caufield. il *Omni* 9:22+ Je '87
Kesterson: an unsolvable problem? [environmental impact of drainage from federally serviced irrigation districts] K. E. Claus. bibl f *Environment* 29:4-5 Jl/Ag '87
Alberta
From desert to oasis [Bassano Dam] J. Howse. il *Macleans* 100:9-10 S 21 '87
Colorado
Dryland farmers say no to water [farmers sue Bureau of Reclamation over Dolores River Project] J. Price. il *Progressive* 51:11 Jl '87
High Plains (U.S.)
The Great American aquifer [Ogallala] C. E. Little. il *Wilderness* 51:43-7 Fall '87
Nebraska
The land that corn farmers forgot. J. Walter. il *Success Farm* 85 no3:18K F '87

Western States
The function of aridity. W. E. Stegner. il *Wilderness* 51:14-18 Fall '87
Wisconsin
How they protect their groundwater. B. Freese. il *Success Farm* 85:12-13 S '87

Irrigation equipment
Water works [installing a drip irrigation system] J. Burnett. il *Rodale's Org Gard* 34:62-72 O '87
IRS *See* United States. Internal Revenue Service
IRS informers *See* Informers

Irvin, John
about
Hamburger Hill [film] Reviews
Macleans 100:54 S 14 '87. L. O'Toole
N Y il 20:108-9+ S 14 '87. D. Denby
New Repub 197:32-3 S 14-21 '87. S. Kauffmann
New Yorker 63:97-8 S 7 '87. P. Kael
Newsweek il 110:83 S 14 '87. J. Kroll
People Wkly il 28:14 S 14 '87. R. Novak
Irvine, Kathleen Doe
Of ice and men. il *Americana* 14:15-16+ Ja/F '87
Irvine, Susan
(jt. auth) See Gale, Iain, and Irvine, Susan
Irvine (Calif.)
Restaurants, nightclubs, bars, etc.
Spécialités de la maison:
Prego. C. Bates. il *Gourmet* 47:20+ S '87
Irvine Co.
Owning Irvine, Calif., isn't what it used to be [D. Bren] J. Flynn. il por *Bus Week* p80+ Mr 9 '87
Irving, Amy
about
The private lives of star moms [excerpt from Starring mothers] J. Barber. il pors *McCalls* 114:57+ My '87
Irving, Candace G.
about
When toys mean business. J. Giambanco. il pors *Work Woman* 12:133-4+ My '87
Irving, David John Cawdell, 1938-
about
British author 'vindicated' by new edition of '67 book. *Publ Wkly* 232:24-5 S 4 '87
Irving, Kenneth Colin
about
Irving's taxing battle. C. Wood. il por *Macleans* 100:34 Ag 3 '87
Irving, William N.
New dates from old bones. map *Nat Hist* 96:8+ F '87
Irving Trust Co.
Is Irving worth the wait? [Bank of New York bids for Irving Trust] F. A. Miller. il *Bus Week* p162 O 12 '87
Irwin, Bill
about
The regard of flight [drama] Reviews
New Yorker 63:73 Ap 27 '87. E. Oliver
Irwin, John Rice
about
John Rice Irwin's gift of the past. D. Young. il pors *South Living* 22:92+ D '87
Irwin, Julie M.
F. Scott Fitzgerald's little drinking problem. *Am Sch* 56:415+ Summ '87
Irwin, Mark
America [poem] *Nation* 244:332 Mr 14 '87
Irwindale (Calif.)
Sports
Anecdotes, facetiae, satire, etc.
The talk of the town [home-to-be of the Raiders] R. Reilly. por *Sports Illus* 67:84 S 14 '87
Isaac, William M.
about
Fence jumper. E. Giltenan. il por *Forbes* 140:224 O 5 '87
Isaacman, Allen F.
Mozambique and the regional conflict in Southern Africa. bibl f *Curr Hist* 86:213-16+ My '87
Isaacs, Jeremy
about
Channel 4. il por *Channels* 7:55 O '87
Isaacs, John D.
Arms control in the new Congress. il *Bull At Sci* 43:4-5 Ja/F '87
Congress tries again on arms control. il *Bull At Sci* 43:3-4 Je '87
The fall and rise of Les Aspin. il por *Bull At Sci* 43:4-5 Ap '87
Senate infighting on treaty. il *Bull At Sci* 43:3-4 N '87

Isaacs, John D.—*cont.*
Senate minority could imperil treaty. il *Bull At Sci* 43:5-6 S '87
Isaacs, Susan
Why everyone hates "friendly advice". il *Parents* 62:89-93 D '87
Isaacs, Susan, and Soares, Cecilia
Animal magnetism. il *Parents* 62:92-6+ Mr '87
Isaacs, Susan, 1943-
about
Uncompromising positions. M. Jefferson. il por *Vogue* 177:90 O '87
Isaak, Chris
about
Chris Isaak. G. Santoro. il por *Down Beat* 54:14 S '87
Retro cool. M. Goldberg. il por *Roll Stone* p55-6+ My 21 '87
Isabel O'Neil Foundation for the Art of the Painted Finish
Isabel O'Neil and the Art of the Painted Finish. S. Wilding. il *Gourmet* 47:76-9+ My '87
Isadora Duncan Dance Awards
Bay Area's 3rd "Izzies" are bestowed. J. Ross. il *Dance Mag* 61:8 Ag '87
Isamu Noguchi Garden Museum
Metaphors for the world. R. Tracy. il por *Archit Dig* 44:72+ O '87
Ischemia, Cerebral *See* Cerebrovascular disease
Ischemia, Myocardial *See* Heart—Diseases
ISDN *See* Integrated services digital network
Isenhart, Charles
Hog heaven or hell. il *Progressive* 51:13 O '87
Two Iowa farmers sow the seeds of change. il pors *Sierra* 72:79-82 N/D '87
Isermann, Jim
about
Jim Isermann at Patty Aande. D. Cooper. il *Art Am* 75:191 My '87
Ish, Jefferson G., d. 1987
about
Obituary
Jet 71:18 Ja 26 '87
Ishi Wilderness (Calif.) *See* Wilderness areas—California
Ishige, Naomichi
(Table) manners makyth man. il *Courier* 40:18-21 My '87
Ishiwara, Jun
about
Einstein and Michelson-Morley [discussion of August 1982 article, How I created the theory of relativity] A. I. Miller. bibl f il *Phys Today* 40:9+ My '87
Ishizuka, Masahiko
'The real cause' of the U.S. trade deficit. *World Press Rev* 34:45 Mr '87
Ishler, Richard E., and Leslie, E. C.
Bridging the gap between a public school system and a university. *Phi Delta Kappan* 68:615-16 Ap '87
Ishtar [film] *See* Motion picture reviews—Single works
Isikoff, Michael
Twice poisoned. *Wash Mon* 19:49-50 D '87
Isikoff, Michael, and Hosenball, Mark
The swami of Iranamok [cover story] *New Repub* 197:21-3 N 9 '87
Islam
See also
Bahaism
Mecca (Saudi Arabia)
Muslims
Is there an Islamic fundamentalism? W. Shepard. *Christ Century* 104:85-7 Ja 28 '87
Islamic terrorism: a growing peril [interview with A. Taheri] D. Bombardier. il *World Press Rev* 34:17-19 My '87
Militant Islam gains ground. R. Wright. il *Nation* 244:675-7 My 23 '87
Moslem radicals: idealism and intolerance [views of Richard Dekmejian] il *USA Today (Periodical)* 115:14 Ap '87
Spreading the faith [Iran] B. Levin. il *Macleans* 100:14-17 Jl 27 '87
Islam and Christianity *See* Christianity and other religions
Islam and science
Beeping the faith [Prayer Times Clock and international lunar date line calculations for Moslem travelers] map *Sci Am* 256:74 Mr '87
Islamic architecture *See* Architecture, Islamic
Islamic cooking *See* Cooking, Islamic
Island ecology
Complex dynamics link islands' predators [research by Thomas Schoener and David Spiller] R. Lewin. *Science* 236:917 My 22 '87

Effect of lizards on spider populations: manipulative reconstruction of a natural experiment. T. W. Schoener and D. A. Spiller. bibl f il *Science* 236:949-52 My 22 '87
Islands at risk. il *Courier* 40:20-3 O '87
Island life *See* Islands
Island Records
Chris Blackwell's Island life. J. Milward. il por *N Y* 20:43 D 7 '87
Islands
See also
Barrier islands
Magical American islands. S. Birnbaum. il *Good Housekeep* 204:64+ Ap '87
Canada
Reminders of man's mortality. A. Fotheringham. il *Macleans* 100:64 S 7 '87
France
Gourmet holidays: France's Atlantic islands. D. Beal. il map *Gourmet* 47:50-5+ Ag '87
Islands, Artificial *See* Artificial islands
Islands of the Pacific
See also
Oceania
Pacific Islands (Trust territory)
Isle of Rum (Scotland)
See also
Wildlife—Isle of Rum (Scotland)
Isle Royale National Park (Mich.)
Surrender on Lake Superior. C. Buhl. il *Travel Holiday* 168:56-9+ Jl '87
Isleta (N.M.)
Politics and government
Verna Williamson [Pueblo leader] R. Brown. il por *Ms* 16:102+ Jl/Ag '87
Islets of Langerhans *See* Pancreas
Islip (N.Y.)
Sanitary affairs
Don't be a litterbarge [various cities turn away barge filled with garbage] J. V. Lamar, Jr. il map *Time* 129:26 My 4 '87
The good news barge [garbage barge Mobro] M. W. Robbins. il *Oceans* 20:2 Jl/Ag '87
Isoelectric focusing
Ultra-sensitive blood test is a new anti-crime weapon. R. Layne. *Pop Sci* 230:104 Ap '87
Isola (Miss.)
Race relations
Racial mishap sparks buy boycott in Isola, Miss. [treatment of B. Greenwood by police sparks boycott] *Jet* 73:32 N 2 '87
Isolation (Social) *See* Social isolation
Isolationism (U.S.) *See* United States—Foreign relations
Isomerases
The visual cycle operates via an isomerase acting on all-trans retinol in the pigment epithelium. C. D. Bridges and R. A. Alvarez. bibl f il *Science* 236:1678-80 Je 26 '87
Isomers and isomerism
An invariance in the isoheptanes of petroleum. F. D. Mango. bibl f il *Science* 237:514-17 Jl 31 '87
Isopods
See also
Pillbugs
Sowbugs
Isotopes
See also
Calcium—Isotopes
Carbon—Isotopes
Cesium—Isotopes
Helium—Isotopes
Lead—Isotopes
Osmium—Isotopes
Oxygen—Isotopes
Radioactive tracers
Rhenium—Isotopes
Stable isotopes. W. W. Dickinson. il *Earth Sci* 40:19-20 Summ '87
Isozaki, Arata
Builders of promise: seven Japanese architects worth watching. il *House Gard* 159:28+ Ja '87
about
The Japanese are coming (again). K.-H. Krüger. il *World Press Rev* 34:59 Ap '87
L.A. elevation. M. Filler. il *House Gard* 159:86-9+ Ja '87
The L.A. Museum of Contemporary Art: what's in a name? H. Muschamp. il *Archit Rec* 175:83+ My '87
Ispahani, Mahnaz
The perils of Pakistan. *New Repub* 196:19-21+ Mr 16 '87

Ispahani, Mahnaz—*cont.*
Taming the Tigers. *New Repub* 197:14+ Jl 27 '87
Israel, Peter
about
Peter Israel leaves Putnam; Phyllis Grann becomes CEO.
pors *Publ Wkly* 232:15 Ag 28 '87
Israel, Robert
about
An English accent at Kentshire. D. Rosenthal. il pors
Archit Dig 44:78+ Mr '87
The English channel. E. Greene. il pors *House Gard*
159:32+ Jl '87
Israel
See also
Agriculture—Israel
Airplane service stations—Israel
Aviation and state—Israel
Catholic Church—Relations (Diplomatic)—Israel
Collective bargaining—Airlines—Israel
Education—Israel
Espionage, American—Israel
Government and the press—Israel
Immigration and emigration—Israel
Industry and state—Israel
Jews—Israel
Kibbutzim
Military assistance, American—Israel
Military assistance, Israeli
Military research—Israel
Negev (Israel)
Neve Shalom (Israel)
Political prisoners—Israel
Privatization—Israel
Red Sea
Rock music—Israel
Strikes—Television news—Israel
Terrorism—Israel
Trials—Israel
United Nations—Israel
War crime trials—Israel
Youth—Israel
Air Force
Israeli Air Force to decide on F-4 conversion by next
year [Super Phantom] D. A. Brown. il *Aviat Week
Space Technol* 126:65-6 Je 22 '87
Antiquities
See also
Caesarea (Ancient city)
Armed Forces
Appropriations and expenditures
Arms and the budget in Israel. E. Salpeter. il *New Leader*
70:5-6 F 9-23 '87
Commerce
Arab countries
Japan's Israel problem [Japan's compliance with Arab
economic boycott of Israel] H. Stanislawski. *New Repub*
196:11-12 Mr 9 '87
Japan
Japan's Israel problem [Japan's compliance with Arab
economic boycott of Israel] H. Stanislawski. *New Repub*
196:11-12 Mr 9 '87
South Africa
Pretoria connection [Israeli arms sales] H. Goodman.
New Repub 196:20-1 Ap 20 '87
Triple trouble in Israel [with editorial comment] E.
Salpeter. il *New Leader* 70:2, 5-7 Mr 23 '87
United States
See United States—Commerce—Israel
Defenses
See also
Airplanes, Military—Israel
Guided missiles, Israeli
Israel—Air Force
Remotely piloted vehicles—Israel
A case of treason [trial of M. Vanunu] A. Bilski. il
por *Macleans* 100:25 S 14 '87
Israel's nuclear ambiguity. A. Cohen and B. Frankel.
Current 294:34-8 Jl/Ag '87
Israel's nuclear ambiguity. A. Cohen and B. Frankel.
bibl f il *Bull At Sci* 43:15-19 My '87
Minority report [case of M. Vanunu] C. Hitchens. *Nation*
244:387 Mr 28 '87
A right to disobedience? [trial of M. Vanunu] S. Seibert.
il por *Newsweek* 110:41 S 7 '87
Economic policy
See also
Budget—Israel
Israel Center for Social and Economic Progress
Israel looks inward. E. Salpeter. *New Leader* 69:3-4 D
29 '86

Israel without television. E. Salpeter. il *New Leader*
70:7-8 N 30 '87
Israel's right turn is working. L. S. Richman. il *Fortune*
115:98-100+ F 16 '87
National pride vs. economics. R. Rosenberg. il *U S
News World Rep* 103:36 Ag 31 '87
Foreign opinion
The focus on Israel. T. L. Friedman. il *N Y Times
Mag* p14-19+ F 1 '87
American
See also
American Israel Public Affairs Committee
Brothers with blood in their eyes [views of U.S. Jewish
leaders on J. Pollard case] W. E. Smith. il *Time*
129:40 Mr 30 '87
Double identity [attachment of American Jews to Israel]
New Repub 196:4 Ap 6 '87
The spy who came between friends [J. Pollard case]
M. Satchell. il por *U S News World Rep* 102:32-3
Mr 30 '87
Strains in the family [Pollard case sets off spat between
U.S. Jews and Israel] M. Whitaker. il por *Newsweek*
109:32-4 Mr 30 '87
Foreign relations
See also
Espionage, Israeli
Byzantine bedfellows. Y. Karny. *New Repub* 196:23-5
F 2 '87
'Nothing to hide' [interview with Y. Shamir] il por
U S News World Rep 102:16 F 23 '87
Arab countries
See Jewish-Arab relations
Germany (West)
See Germany (West)—Foreign relations—Israel
Iraq
See Iraq—Foreign relations—Israel
Soviet Union
See Soviet Union—Foreign relations—Israel
Tunisia
Security Council 'vigorously' condemns Israeli 'aggression'
against Tunisian territory. il *UN Chron* 22:3-6 N/D
'85
United States
See United States—Foreign relations—Israel
History
See also
Zionism
History and the body politic in Israel. D. Ashkenazy.
il *Christ Century* 104:822-3 S 30 '87
Israel: the tragedy of victory. A. Hertzberg. il *N Y
Rev Books* 34:12-18 My 28 '87
Israel's providential men. P. Johnson. *Commentary*
84:60-3 O '87
The Kissinger covenant and other reasons Israel is in
trouble [excerpt from Sands of sorrow; cover story]
M. Viorst. por map *Wash Mon* 19:23-9+ Je '87
Industries
See also
Aerospace industries—Israel
El Al Israel Airlines Ltd.
Electro-optics Industries, Ltd.
Israel Aircraft Industries Ltd.
Publishers and publishing—Israel
Tadiran Israel Electronics Industries Ltd.
Intellectual life
Israel's alienated intellectuals. E. Rothstein. *Commentary*
83:53-7 F '87
Politics and government
See also
Gush Emunim
Political attitudes—Israel
Press and politics—Israel
Destined for a dogfight [confrontation between S. Peres
and Y. Shamir over possible peace conference] W.
E. Smith. il pors *Time* 129:39 My 11 '87
Face-off in Israel [growing mutual hostility over inter-
national Middle East peace conference; cover story]
E. Salpeter. il *New Leader* 70:5-6 Ap 20 '87
The focus on Israel. T. L. Friedman. il *N Y Times
Mag* p14-19+ F 1 '87
A government at war over peace [S. Peres's proposal
for an international peace conference] B. Levin. il
pors *Macleans* 100:18 My 25 '87
A house divided [secular vs. Orthodox Jews] T. A.
Sancton. il *Time* 130:34-5 O 12 '87
Israel [cover story; special section] il *World Press Rev*
34:11-21 Jl '87
Israel: a case of tired blood. T. Jacoby. il *Newsweek*
109:38 Ap 13 '87
Israel: at war with itself [Mideast peace plan] M. J.
Kubic. il pors *Newsweek* 109:30 My 25 '87

Israel—Politics and government—*cont.*

Israel: the Peres era and its legacy. S. W. Lewis. *Foreign Aff* 65 Sp Issue:582-610 ['87]

Israel without television. E. Salpeter. il *New Leader* 70:7-8 N 30 '87

Israel's year of transition. B. Reich. bibl f *Curr Hist* 86:69-72+ F '87

Letter from Israel. A. Elon. *New Yorker* 63:33-8+ Jl 27 '87

Peace-talks plan: push comes to shove in Israel. il *U S News World Rep* 102:16 My 25 '87

The politics of secrecy and silence. Y. Marcus. il *Newsweek* 109:33 Mr 30 '87

Sagging spirits. J. Smolowe. il *Time* 129:34-6 Ap 20 '87

So much for national unity [coalition government threatened by prospect of international peace conference] il por *Time* 129:50 My 25 '87

Population
See also
Circassians—Israel

Religious institutions and affairs
See also
Christians—Israel
Evangelistic work—Israel
Seeing Israel in full perspective. J. M. Wall. *Christ Century* 104:515-17 Je 3-10 '87

Social conditions
Israel: a house divided? R. R. Wisse. *Commentary* 84:33-8 S '87

Letter to a new Israeli. R. R. Wisse. *Commentary* 83:44-9 Je '87

A light unto the nations? R. R. Wisse. *Commentary* 84:30-5 D '87

Territorial expansion
See also
Israel-Arab Wars, 1967- —Territorial questions

Israel. Mossad
Decline of the superspies. il *Time* 129:32 Mr 23 '87
Minority report [case of M. Vanunu] C. Hitchens. *Nation* 244:387 Mr 28 '87

Israel. Shin Bet
Decline of the superspies. il *Time* 129:32 Mr 23 '87

A pileup of scandals in Israel [government reports on the Pollard case and role of Shin Bet in I. Napsu's imprisonment] N. Cooper. il por *Newsweek* 109:42 Je 8 '87

A scandal in the ranks [I. Napsu's claims against Shin Bet arouses Circassian community] E. Silver. *Macleans* 100:28+ My 4 '87

Security on trial [J. Pollard and I. Napsu cases] B. Levin. il por *Macleans* 100:22 Je 8 '87

Thrice rebuked [cases of J. Pollard and I. Napsu] il por *Time* 129:40 Je 8 '87

Torture in Israel [counterterrorist torture] *New Repub* 197:7 N 23 '87

Israel Aircraft Industries Ltd.
Funding problems dampen U.S. support for Israeli Arrow missile. *Aviat Week Space Technol* 127:32 D 7 '87

Israel Aircraft Industries displays F-4E Super Phantom conversion [Paris Air Show] il *Aviat Week Space Technol* 126:92-3 Je 29 '87

Israel developing 707-based surveillance platform [Phalcon] il *Aviat Week Space Technol* 126:175 Je 15 '87

Israel plans to complete third Lavi prototype. *Aviat Week Space Technol* 127:27-8 S 28 '87

Israel renews debate on Lavi development. D. E. Fink. *Aviat Week Space Technol* 126:18-19 Je 1 '87

Israelis petition FAA for repair station rule exemption. *Aviat Week Space Technol* 126:31 Mr 30 '87

Lavi termination [special section; with editorial comment by Donald E. Fink] il *Aviat Week Space Technol* 127:15, 22-5 S 7 '87

Israel and the United States
See also
Israel—Foreign opinion—American

Israel-Arab relations *See* Jewish-Arab relations
Israel-Arab Wars, 1967-
The cost of self-deception [classified documents argue that G. A. Nasser's generals led him into Six Day War] il por *U S News World Rep* 102:36 Je 8 '87

Israel's great victory [Six Day War; cover story] M. Walzer. il *New Repub* 196:22-3+ Je 8 '87

A just war remembered [Six Day War] G. F. Will. il *Newsweek* 109:90 Je 8 '87

Six-Day War: a victory that changed the Mideast map. J. Keegan. il *U S News World Rep* 102:35-6 Je 8 '87

The Six-Day War and Jewish power. *New Repub* 196:7-8+ Je 8 '87

Occupied territories
See Israel-Arab Wars, 1967- —Territorial questions
Peace and mediation
See also
Israel-Arab Wars, 1967- —Territorial questions
United Nations—Armed Forces—Forces in the Middle East

Reporters and reporting
Twenty years on. A. Cockburn. *Nation* 245:45 Jl 18-25 '87

Territorial questions
See also
International Day of Solidarity with the Palestinian People
Palestine Center for Non-Violent Resistance
United Nations—Armed Forces—Forces in the Middle East
United Nations. Committee on the Exercise of the Inalienable Rights of the Palestinian People
Arab vs. Arab over Palestine. D. Pipes. *Commentary* 84:17-25 Jl '87

Arabs vs. settlers in the Gaza Strip. A. Hielscher. *World Press Rev* 34:56-7 Ja '87

Arafat makes another comeback. S. Reed. il *Nation* 244:137-41 F 7 '87

Arafat's answer. *New Repub* 196:9 My 4 '87

Assembly adopts seven resolutions on Middle East and Palestine issues; calls for comprehensive settlement under UN auspices. il *UN Chron* 24:48-50 F '87

Assembly says Israeli breaches of Geneva Convention constitute 'war crimes'. *UN Chron* 24:54-5 F '87

Beyond zero-sum thinking in the Arab-Israeli struggle. R. A. Eckardt. il *Christ Century* 104:1143-5 D 16 '87

Bitterness in Bethlehem [West Bank violence] J. Bierman. il *Macleans* 100:10+ Ja 5 '87

Conference call [meeting of the Palestine National Council in Algiers] *Nation* 244:670-1 My 23 '87

Days of rage in the territories [Israeli troops crack down on Arab rioters] M. S. Serrill. il *Time* 130:32 D 28 '87

Destined for a dogfight [confrontation between S. Peres and Y. Shamir over possible peace conference] W. E. Smith. il pors *Time* 129:39 My 11 '87

Edward Said: an exile's exile [interview] M. Stevenson. il *Progressive* 51:30-4 F '87

Ending the 20-year war. M. Viorst. il *Newsweek* 109:10 Je 15 '87

Face-off in Israel [growing mutual hostility over international Middle East peace conference; cover story] E. Salpeter. il *New Leader* 70:5-6 Ap 20 '87

Fallen state [implications of the Lavi fiasco] A. Kenan. *Nation* 245:293 S 26 '87

Force for change in the West Bank [Palestinian labor movement] J. R. Hiltermann. il *Nation* 245:338-40 O 3 '87

A government at war over peace [S. Peres's proposal for an international peace conference] B. Levin. il pors *Macleans* 100:18 My 25 '87

Hussein's game [willingness to enter peace negotiations with Israel independent of the P.L.O.] S. Reed. *Nation* 244:839-40 Je 20 '87

In defense of West Bank settlement [interview with Y. Ben-Shlomo] *Harpers* 275:18-20 S '87

Interpreting Palestine. E. W. Said. *Harpers* 274:19-22 Mr '87

An interview with Yasser Arafat (I). S. MacLeod. bibl f il *N Y Rev Books* 34:36-40 Je 11 '87

An interview with [Yasser] Arafat (II). S. MacLeod. bibl f il pors *N Y Rev Books* 34:41-5 Je 25 '87

Invisible Palestinians: ideology and reality in Israel. R. R. Ruether. il *Christ Century* 104:587-91 Jl 1-8 '87

Is 'peace' at hand? [proposed conference to settle West Bank question] M. Kramer. il *U S News World Rep* 102:14 Je 29 '87

Israel. *Bus Week* p69 Je 22 '87

Israel [cover story; special section] il *World Press Rev* 34:11-21 Jl '87

Israel and the Palestinian question: 1987. K. J. Kelly. *America* 156:424-6 My 23 '87

Israel: at war with itself [peace plan] M. J. Kubic. il pors *Newsweek* 109:30 My 25 '87

Israel: the tragedy of victory. A. Hertzberg. il *N Y Rev Books* 34:12-18 My 28 '87

An Israeli and an Arab tour for peace [views of M. Peled] J. M. Wall. *Christ Century* 104:427-8 My 6 '87

Israel's angry peace [cover story; special section; with editorial comment by Kevin Doyle] il map *Macleans* 100:2, 22-8+ Je 1 '87

Israel-Arab Wars, 1967—Territorial questions—*cont.*
Israel's dangerous fundamentalists [Gush Emunim] I. S. Lustick. bibl f *Foreign Policy* 68:118-39 Fall '87
Israel's opportunity. H. Goodman. *New Repub* 196:13-15 Je 29 '87
The Kissinger covenant and other reasons Israel is in trouble [excerpt from Sands of sorrow; cover story] M. Viorst. por map *Wash Mon* 19:23-9+ Je '87
A land that history forgot [Gaza] J. McGeary. il *Time* 130:40 N 30 '87
Letter from Israel. A. Elon. *New Yorker* 63:33-8+ Jl 27 '87
Letter from Israel. A. Kenan. *Nation* 245:581 N 21 '87
The Middle East in the year 2000 [address, April 24, 1987] A. Ghandour. *Vital Speeches Day* 53:450-5 My 15 '87
Middle East: time for negotiations. J. Carter. il por *Time* 129:38-9 Ap 20 '87
The Mideast: crying wolf? [S. Peres' proposed peace conference] N. Cooper. il por *Newsweek* 109:54-5 My 18 '87
Militant Islam: defying Israel's control [violence in the West Bank and Gaza] J. Barnes. il *U S News World Rep* 103:39 O 26 '87
My neighbor, my enemy. T. L. Friedman. il *N Y Times Mag* p14-19+ Jl 5 '87
Myths about Palestinians. K. Christison. bibl f *Foreign Policy* 66:109-27 Spr '87
A new-breed Palestinian. A. Deming. il *Newsweek* 109:38 Ap 6 '87
Peace feelers. C. Charney. *World Press Rev* 34:43 O '87
Peace nix [S. Peres's proposal for an international conference on the Mideast] M. Kondracke. il *New Repub* 196:20-2 Je 8 '87
Peace-talks plan: push comes to shove in Israel. il *U S News World Rep* 102:16 My 25 '87
The Peres peace plan: battling extremism. J. M. Wall. *Christ Century* 104:931-2 O 28 '87
Pipe-dream politics on the West Bank. M. Kramer. il *U S News World Rep* 103:16 Jl 6 '87
Rumors of peace at hand [possibility of an international peace conference on the Middle East] J. Bierman. il *Macleans* 100:20-2 Ap 27 '87
Secretary-General finds increased interest in Middle East peace conference 'encouraging'. *UN Chron* 24:20 Ag '87
Security Council considers situation in Middle East, takes no action. il *UN Chron* 22:7-9 N/D '85
Security Council reaffirms that 1949 Geneva Convention applies to Israeli-occupied territories. *UN Chron* 24:56 F '87
Shut up and deal [S. Peres's proposal for an international peace conference] *New Repub* 197:7-9 O 26 '87
So much for national unity [coalition government threatened by prospect of international peace conference] il por *Time* 129:50 My 25 '87
Special Political Committee says Israel's 'grave breaches' of Geneva Convention are 'war crimes and an affront to humanity'. il *UN Chron* 23:51-3 Ja '86
The strange bedfellows [peace plan conceived by Israeli M. Amirav and Arab S. Nuseibeh] M. J. Kubic. il por *Newsweek* 110:42 O 5 '87
This land is whose land? [progress and problems since Six Day War] J. McGeary. il *Time* 129:38-9 Je 8 '87
This year in Jerusalem. J. G. Dunne. il *Esquire* 108:237-40+ D '87
Trouble in the Holy Land [violence in the West Bank and Gaza] E. Silver. il *Macleans* 100:40-1 D 28 '87
Violence in Gaza. A. Kenan. *Nation* 245:777-8 D 26 '87-Ja 2 '88
A visionary's Mideast peace plan [views of M. Benvenisti] J. M. Wall. *Christ Century* 104:459-60 My 13 '87
A voice of hope and moderation [interview with Hassan bin Talal] H. Mackenzie. il por *Macleans* 100:21 Je 22 '87
The war is over; the struggle goes on [progress and problems since Six Day War; symposium] il map *U S News World Rep* 102:37-8 Je 8 '87
'We hate the occupation' [insurrection in the Gaza Strip] R. Watson. il *Newsweek* 110:25 D 28 '87
When Israelis and Palestinians meet [meeting in Rumania, November 1986] Y. Lotan. *Nation* 244:141-2 F 7 '87
Working for peace and freedom [address, May 17, 1987] G. P. Shultz. *Dep State Bull* 87:7-10 Jl '87

Israel Ballet
Israel Ballet, the country's only classical troupe, is 20. D. Sowden. il *Dance Mag* 61:7 My '87

Israel Center for Social and Economic Progress
The enemy within [interview with D. Doron] P. Brimelow. il por *Forbes* 140:54+ D 28 '87

Israel in Egypt [oratorio] See Handel, George Frideric, 1685-1759

Israeli, Julius
about
One teacher's prejudice. K. Harley. il pors *Macleans* 100:17 Ap 27 '87

Israeli authors See Authors, Israeli

Israelson, David
Holes in the ozone accord. *World Press Rev* 34:54 N '87

Issues in science and technology (Periodical)
Academy to drop Issues quarterly. J. Walsh. *Science* 235:968 F 27 '87

Istanbul (Turkey)
Description
Visiting the city of sultans. C. Reed. il *Bus Week* p182 O 12 '87
Terrorism
See Terrorism—Turkey

Istituto per la Ricostruzione Industriale
Europe's quiet revolution [interview with R. Prodi] S. Solomon. il por *Forbes* 140:52+ D 14 '87
Lessons from a master [R. Prodi] R. I. Kirkland, Jr. il por *Fortune* 116:34-5 Ag 3 '87
Mussolini's corporate legacy. P. C. Newman. il por *Macleans* 100:31 N 23 '87
The turnaround sparking a new Italian renaissance. W. C. Symonds. il por *Bus Week* p60-1 Mr 2 '87

Istomin, Eugene, 1925-
about
On the road to Biloxi. N. Graffman. il por *N Y Times Mag* p72-5+ N 22 '87

Isuzu (Automobile) See Automobiles, Foreign

It was twenty years ago today [television program] See Television program reviews—Single works

Italian Americans
The Mafia mystique [stereotypes] J. Giordano. por *U S News World Rep* 102:6 F 16 '87
Wartime Sunday. G. Talese. il *Esquire* 107:95-8+ My '87

Italian Americans in motion pictures
Family lies. G. De Stefano. il *Film Comment* 23:22-4+ Jl/Ag '87

Italian art See Art, Italian
Italian bread See Bread
Italian fiction
The heirs of Calvino and the Eco effect. S. Perosa. il *N Y Times Book Rev* 92:1+ Ag 16 '87
Italian furniture See Furniture, Italian
Italian Grand Prix See Automobile racing—Italy
Italian house decoration See House decoration, Italian
Italian jewelry See Jewelry, Italian
Italian majolica See Majolica
Italian painting See Painting, Italian
Italian Riviera See Riviera (France and Italy)
Italian terrorists See Terrorists, Italian
Italians
United States
See also
Italian Americans

Italtel (Firm)
A failed merger blows Italy's shot at the big time [Italtel and Telettra] W. C. Symonds. il *Bus Week* p52+ N 23 '87

Italy
See also
Adriatic Sea region
Afghans—Italy
Agriculture—Italy
Americans—Italy
Architecture, Domestic—Italy
Astronomical observatories—Italy
Automobile racing—Italy
Basketball, Professional—Italy
Bellagio (Italy)
Bergamo (Italy)
Booksellers and bookselling—Italy
Business management—Italy
Canadians—Italy
Carnival (Pre-Lenten festival)—Italy
Como (Italy)
Country estates—Italy
Cultural property—Protection—Italy
Elba (Italy)
Emilia-Romagna (Italy)
Express highways—Italy
Flood prevention and control—Italy
Florence (Italy)

Italy—See also—*cont.*
　　Gardens and gardening—Italy
　　Health resorts, watering places, etc.—Italy
　　Historic houses, sites, etc.—Italy
　　Industrial relations—Italy
　　Industry and state—Italy
　　Investments, American—Italy
　　Investments, Italian
　　Jews—Italy
　　Milan (Italy)
　　Mont Blanc (France and Italy)
　　Monte Cassino (Monastery: Cassino, Italy)
　　Motion picture festivals—Italy
　　Motion pictures—Italy
　　Motorcycle racing—Italy
　　Music festivals—Italy
　　Narcotics laws and regulations—Italy
　　Opera—Italy
　　Palaces—Italy
　　Paleontology—Italy
　　Pienza (Italy)
　　Police—Italy
　　Privatization—Italy
　　Radioactive pollution—Italy
　　Riviera (France and Italy)
　　Rome (Italy)
　　Sculpture gardens and parks—Italy
　　Sicily
　　Siena (Italy)
　　Space centers—Italy
　　Sperlonga (Italy)
　　Strikes—Italy
　　Student protests, demonstrations, etc.—Italy
　　Taormina (Italy)
　　Television broadcasting—Italy
　　Terrorism—Italy
　　Trieste (Italy)
　　Tuscany (Italy)
　　Vatican City
　　Venice (Italy)

Antiquities
　　See also
　　Pompeii (Ancient city)

Commerce
Iran
　　See Iran—Commerce—Italy
Japan
YB4 and 5: the Yamaha connection [Yamaha motorcycle engines used by Bimota] B. De Prato. il *Cycle* 38:87-8 Jl '87
United States
　　See United States—Commerce—Italy

Defenses
　　See also
　　Remotely piloted vehicles—Italy

Economic conditions
　　See also
　　Underground economy—Italy
The Italian miracle begins underground. J. Algañaraz. *World Press Rev* 34:50-1 Je '87
Land of pasta and pizza spots exports and profits. J. P. Shapiro. il *U S News World Rep* 102:49 Je 8 '87

Economic policy
Will Italy be able to regain the high ground? [new prime minister G. Goria] W. C. Symonds. por *Bus Week* p38 Ag 10 '87

Foreign relations
Soviet Union
　　See Soviet Union—Foreign relations—Italy
United States
　　See United States—Foreign relations—Italy

History
　　See also
　　World War, 1939-1945—Campaigns and battles—Italy

Industries
　　See also
　　Aeritalia SpA
　　Aerospace industries—Italy
　　Agusta SpA
　　Alfa Romeo SpA
　　Alitalia SpA
　　Art trade—Italy
　　Automobile factories—Italy
　　Barilla Group
　　Benetton SpA
　　Bimota (Firm)
　　Bisiach & Carrù SpA
　　Cheese industry—Italy
　　Compagnia Finanziaria De Benedetti

　　Elettronica SpA
　　Ente Nazionale Idrocarburi
　　Ferrari SpA Esercizio Fabbriche Automobili e Corse
　　Fiat SpA
　　Gucci Group
　　Industrie Pininfarina SpA
　　Ing. C. Olivetti & Co., SpA
　　Istituto per la Ricostruzione Industriale
　　Italtel (Firm)
　　Krizia (Firm)
　　Lamborghini (Firm)
　　Mondadori Viaggi SpA
　　Rinaldo Piaggio (Firm)
　　Salvatore Ferragamo SpA
　　SGS Ates Componeti Elettronici SpA
　　Telecommunication—Acquisitions and mergers—Italy
　　Telettra Telefonia Elettronica e Radio SpA
　　Tire factories—Italy
　　Tourist trade—Italy
　　Valsella Meccanotecnica (Firm)
　　Zagato (Firm)

Navy
　　Forces in the Persian Gulf region
Italy in the Gulf. S. F. Senigallia. *New Leader* 70:3-4 O 19 '87

Photographs and photography
A procession of wonders [work of E. Hofer at the Witkin Gallery, New York City] J. Perl. il *Vogue* 177:86 D '87

Politics and government
　　See also
　　Communist Party (Italy)
　　Elections—Italy
　　Political campaigns—Italy
　　Politics, Corruption in—Italy
　　Radical Party (Italy)
　　Radicalism—Italy
Coalition politics, Italian-style. P. C. Newman. il *Macleans* 100:38 N 16 '87
Craxi leaves behind 'a new Italy'. J. Wyles. *World Press Rev* 34:37 Ap '87
Decline of the Italian left. L. Rosenthal. il *Nation* 244:878-81 Je 27 '87
Italy gets a new government [G. Goria government] S. F. Senigallia. por *New Leader* 70:3-4 Jl 13-27 '87
Italy's moot relay. S. F. Senigallia. il *New Leader* 69:8-9 D 29 '86
Italy's 'stable instability' [interview with A. Levi] J. R. Moskin. por *World Press Rev* 34:22-4 Je '87
Season of strikes and discontent. M. Johnson. il *Time* 130:35 D 7 '87

Social conditions
Changing Italy. E. von Kuehnelt-Leddihn. *Natl Rev* 39:42 Ag 14 '87
A national contempt for the law. P. C. Newman. il *Macleans* 100:40 D 7 '87

Italy and the United States
　　See also
　　United States—Foreign opinion—Italian
Itami, Juzo
　　　　　about
Tampopo [film] Reviews
　　Macleans 100:46 Ag 31 '87. C. Bell
　　New Repub 196:26 Je 1 '87. S. Kauffmann
　　New Yorker 63:101-2 Je 1 '87. P. Kael
　　Newsweek 109:71 Je 15 '87. D. Ansen
　　Time il 130:65 Ag 3 '87. R. Schickel
Itano, Wayne M.
　　(jt. auth) See Wineland, David J., and Itano, Wayne M.
Itano, Wayne M., and others
Laser spectroscopy of trapped atomic ions. bibl f il *Science* 237:612-17 Ag 7 '87
ITC *See* International Tin Council
Ithaca (N.Y.)
Politics and government
Activists take to the airwaves [production of More than the news] M. Schultz. il *Progressive* 51:13 S '87
Stores
Made in New York [M. Turback's Made-in-New York Store and Great State Wine Shop] *New Yorker* 63:36-7 D 28 '87
ITI *See* Industrial Technology Institute
It's a man's world [drama] See Mehrten, Greg
It's Garry Shandling's show [television program] See Television program reviews—Single works
ITT Corporation
George Shultz, wimp [role in antitrust case] R. M. Goolrick. il *Wash Mon* 19:18-19 O '87

ITT Corporation—*cont.*
How cleaning house may help ITT clean up. C. Power. il por *Bus Week* p64+ Mr 23 '87
ITT Avionics focuses on EW production with investment in GaAs technology [gallium-arsenide manufacturing technology] il *Aviat Week Space Technol* 126:98+ F 16 '87
ITT invests $20 million to obtain gallium-arsenide MMIC benefits. il *Aviat Week Space Technol* 126:111-13 F 16 '87
ITT uses process control methods to increase plant productivity [use of Taguchi method in electronic warfare manufacturing] B. D. Nordwall. il *Aviat Week Space Technol* 126:69+ My 11 '87
Most improved. il *Forbes* 139:106 Ja 12 '87
These buyers still think ITT is raider bait. G. G. Marcial. il *Bus Week* p88 Je 29 '87
IUD (Intrauterine devices) *See* Contraceptives
IUE (International Ultraviolet Explorer) satellite *See* Artificial satellites—Astronomical use
IUS (Inertial upper stage) launch vehicle *See* Space vehicles—Propulsion systems
Ivanhoe Partners
A gold miner helps Pickens chip away at Newmont [R. M. Friedland cut into Ivanhoe Partners deal] S. D. Atchison. il por *Bus Week* p36 Ag 31 '87
One swallow could make Pickens' summer [pursuit of Newmont Mining] J. E. Davis. il por *Bus Week* p37 S 14 '87
I've heard the mermaids singing [film] *See* Motion picture reviews—Single works
Ivermectin
An act of vision for the third world [Merck & Co.'s donation of ivermectin to treat river blindness] S. Budiansky. il *U S News World Rep* 103:14 N 2 '87
End of river blindness in sight? *Sci News* 132:287 O 31 '87
Merck donates drug for river blindness. J. Walsh. *Science* 238:610 O 30 '87
Miracle worker [Merck & Co.'s donation of ivermectin to cure river blindness in the third world] il *Time* 130:78 N 2 '87
Will livestock drug cause dung crisis? [research by Richard Wall and Les Strong] J. Raloff. *Sci News* 131:358 Je 6 '87
Iversen, Edwin S., and Iversen, Jane Z.
Salmon-farming success in Norway. il map *Sea Front* 33:354-61 S/O '87
Iversen, Jane Z.
(jt. auth) *See* Iversen, Edwin S., and Iversen, Jane Z.
Iverson, Donald D.
　　　　　　　　　about
Keeping top secrets inside the computer. M. E. Recio. il por *Bus Week* p85 My 25 '87
Iverson Technology Corporation
Keeping top secrets inside the computer. M. E. Recio. il por *Bus Week* p85 My 25 '87
IVF (in vitro fertilization) *See* Fertilization in vitro
Ivins, Molly
Kathy Whitmire. il pors *Work Woman* 12:120-2+ Mr '87
The Lege has a taxing session. il *Nation* 245:120-2 Ag 15-22 '87
Small favors. See issues of The Progressive beginning March 1986
There will always be a Texas. il *Ms* 16:82-4 Jl/Ag '87
Ivo, Lêdo
The poor in the bus depot [poem]; tr. by Amy Antin. *New Yorker* 63:44 D 14 '87
Ivory, Cornelius F., and others
Electromagnetic stabilization of weakly conducting fluids. bibl f il *Science* 238:58-61 O 2 '87
Ivory, James
　　　　　　　　　about
Maurice [film] Reviews
　Macleans 100:59 S 21 '87. L. O'Toole
　N Y il 20:136+ S 28 '87. D. Denby
　Nation 245:498-500 O 31 '87. V. Russo
　Natl Rev 39:59-60 N 6 '87. J. Simon
　New Repub 197:28 O 5 '87. S. Kauffmann
　New Yorker 63:103+ S 21 '87. P. Kael
　Newsweek il 110:76 S 21 '87. D. Ansen
　People Wkly il 28:14-15 S 28 '87. P. Travers
　Vogue il 177:62+ My '87. V. Radin
Partners and friends for 26 years, James Ivory and Ismail Merchant film a hotly debated gay love story. J. Stark. il pors *People Wkly* 28:119-22 O 26 '87
The Raj duet. D. Smith. il pors *N Y* 20:58-60+ O 5 '87
'Rarely is justice done' [interview] P. Sherrid. il por *U S News World Rep* 103:68 D 21 '87

View from Prospero's Island. G. Clarke. il pors *Time* 129:70 Ja 12 '87
Ivory figurines *See* Figurines
Ivory industry
　　　　　　　　　History
When the music in our parlors brought death to darkest Africa [19th century use of ivory for piano keys] R. Conniff. il *Audubon* 89:76-93 Jl '87
Ivory poaching *See* Poaching
Ivorybilled woodpeckers *See* Woodpeckers
Ivry, Benjamin
What time does a Chinaman go to the dentist? [poem] *New Repub* 196:38 Je 22 '87
Ivy, Ground *See* Ground ivy
Ivy poisoning *See* Poison ivy
Iwamoto, Yukihide, and others
YIGSR, a synthetic laminin pentapeptide, inhibits experimental metastasis formation. bibl f il *Science* 238:1132-4 N 20 '87
Ixing porcelain *See* Pottery, Chinese
Ixi:z (Beverly Hills, Calif.: Water bar) *See* Beverly Hills (Calif.)—Restaurants, nightclubs, bars, etc.
Izquierdo, José Gómez *See* Gómez Izquierdo, José
Izzy's Steak & Chop House (San Francisco, Calif.) *See* San Francisco (Calif.)—Restaurants, nightclubs, bars, etc.

J

J. Bildner & Sons
The price of quick riches [venture into new issues market] R. Simon. il por *Forbes* 140:112+ S 21 '87
J. C. Penney Company, Inc.
A big deal for little Beeba's. G. G. Marcial. *Bus Week* p61 Jl 27 '87
Dressed to kill. S. B. Weiner. il *Forbes* 140:95+ N 2 '87
J.E. Morgan Knitting Mills, Inc.
Branding a success [Dawson International's P. Kemp now running J.E. Morgan] L. Gubernick. por *Forbes* 139:91 Ja 26 '87
J. I. Case Company
Can a Magnum gun down a Deere? [new tractor series] D. Mowitz and C. Finck. il *Success Farm* 85:6 N '87
Program guarantees 100-percent job security. *Mon Labor Rev* 110:72-3 S '87
J. M. Smucker Co.
Of jams and a family. A. H. Malcolm. il por *N Y Times Mag* p82-3+ N 15 '87
J. P. Morgan & Co. Incorporated
First join 'em, then beat 'em. B. Weberman. il *Forbes* 139:152 F 23 '87
How J.P. Morgan keeps its ear to the ground. il *Bus Week* p81 O 5 '87
Look who's charging into the merger business. S. Bartlett. il *Bus Week* p44 Mr 9 '87
J. Paul Getty Museum
Getty 'improprieties' attract IRS scrutiny [investigation into donations of works of art] A. Decker. *Art News* 86:31-2 My '87
The poor little rich kid of art. M. Kimmelman. il *U S News World Rep* 102:70-2 Ap 27 '87
J R (Fictional character)
Trickle-up economics: JR goes to Washington. W. Gaddis. il *N Y Times Book Rev* 92:29 O 25 '87
J. Robert Scott (Firm)
New directions in style [furniture designs of S. S. Lewis] H. Drohojowska. il por *Archit Dig* 44:252+ My '87
J. Walter Thompson Company
And Madison Avenue thought, 'it can't happen here' [J. Walter Thompson gets bid from WPP Group] M. N. Vamos and R. A. Melcher. il *Bus Week* p48 Je 22 '87
Blood on the carpet: the coup that failed at J. Walter Thompson. B. Kanner. il pors *N Y* 20:36-40 F 16 '87
Don Johnston. C. Dugas. il por *Bus Week* Sp Issue:256 Ap 17 '87
Et tu, Brutus? This time Caesar won [revolt by J. O'Donnell] C. J. Loomis. il pors *Fortune* 115:54-6 Mr 2 '87
Even golden boys can tarnish [firing of J. O'Donnell] B. Rudolph. il por *Time* 129:51 F 9 '87

J. Walter Thompson Company—*cont.*

Hang on, Madison Avenue, Martin Sorrell isn't finished [WPP Group acquires J. Walter Thompson] R. A. Melcher and M. N. Vamos. il por *Bus Week* p80-1 Jl 13 '87

Turnover, not turnaround, at J. Walter Thompson [departure of B. Metter] C. Dugas. *Bus Week* p49-50 My 11 '87

J2 Communications (Firm)

Bestselling Smart cookies don't crumble comes to video. *Publ Wkly* 231:72 F 13 '87

Jaar, Alfredo

about

Fragments and frames. N. Princenthal. il *Art Am* 75:144-5 My '87

Gold rush to hell. S. Staggs. il *Art News* 86:9 F '87

Jabbar, Kareem Abdul- *See* Abdul-Jabbar, Kareem, 1947-

Jablonski, David

Heritability at the species level: analysis of geographic ranges of Cretaceous mollusks. bibl f il *Science* 238:360-3 O 16 '87

Jablow, Martha Moraghan

(jt. auth) *See* Samalin, Nancy, and Jablow, Martha Moraghan

(ed) *See* Samalin, Nancy. How to stop fighting with your kids

(ed) *See* Samalin, Nancy. "You make me so mad!"

Jabor, Arnaldo

about

Love me now or never [film] Reviews

Américas 39:59 Mr/Ap '87. J. Mosier

Jabs, Carolyn

How to be your husband's best friend. *McCalls* 114:40+ Ap '87

What your birth order explains about you. *McCalls* 114:25+ F '87

Jaccoma, Richard

Video's new image. il *Stereo Rev* 52:70-3 O '87

Jack, Homer A.

It's guns or butter, says UN conference. *Christ Century* 104:878-9 O 14 '87

A nuclear FREEZE is a SANE proposal. *Christ Century* 104:1133-5 D 16 '87

Jack and the Beanstalk (Fairy tale) *See* Fairy tales

Jack-in-the-pulpits

Sex choice and reproductive costs in Jack-in-the-pulpit. D. Policansky. bibl f il *BioScience* 37:476-81 Jl/Ag '87

Jack London State Historic Park (Calif.) *See* California—Parks and reserves

Jack Nicklaus Academy of Golf (Orlando, Fla.)

Sports schools go high tech. M. Wellemeyer. il *Fortune* 115:119-20 F 16 '87

Jack-o'-lanterns *See* Halloween

Jackalopes

A funny thing happend on the way to the taxidermist. D. Simberloff. il *Nat Hist* 96:50-5 Ag '87

Jackee

about

Jackée Harry: how her TV role is ruining her love life. A. Collier. il pors *Ebony* 42:128+ Je '87

Jackée Harry: "I'm upstaging everybody". L. Robinson. il por *Vogue* 177:64 Jl '87

Jackee Harry sheds pounds but keeps sex appeal [cover story] A. Collier. il pors *Jet* 72:60-1 Ap 13 '87

Jackee visits N.C. roots for grandmother's 103rd birthday, clan reunion. il pors *Jet* 73:46-7 D 28 '87-Ja 4 '88

Photographs and photography

Beauty and the bubbly. G. Bernstein. il por *Petersens Photogr Mag* 16:24 N '87

Fashion plus personality [photographing J. Harry for Black elegance layout] G. Bernstein. il pors *Petersens Photogr Mag* 16:18 My '87

Jackets

Blazing ahead [men's blazers] R. La Ferla. il *N Y Times Mag* p56 F 15 '87

Figure-flattering jackets. C. DiGrappa. il *Parents* 62:157-9 O '87

Harley-Davidson fringe jackets [for motorcyclists] il *Cycle* 38:93-4 Ap '87

Jacket jackpot. il *Harpers Bazaar* 120:74+ Mr '87

The jackets of the year. il *Vogue* 177:144-55 Ja '87

Lion's Hollow—the "tuxedo" of jackets [photographer's jacket] K. Geller-Shinn. il *Petersens Photogr Mag* 16:8 S '87

The motorcycle jacket [Langlitz jacket] J. Berendt. il *Esquire* 108:36 D '87

Ordering a surgical fashion strike, the Air Force reclaims its legacy in leather—the bomber jacket. il *People Wkly* 28:47 S 28 '87

Jacko

about

Australia's toothless, tactless Jacko, a jock who's energized to plug batteries—and himself. il por *People Wkly* 28:77 D 7 '87

Jacks (Fish)

Photographs and photography

Une liaison dangereuse [juvenile jacks in jellyfish tentacles] C. Newbert. il *Nat Hist* 96:88-9 S '87

Jackson, Ardith McPherson

about

Black woman's 'murder wish' for Reagan is free speech, Supreme Court says. il por *Jet* 72:30 Jl 13 '87

Jackson, Bo

about

Bo Jackson to upset K.C. Royals' minor plans. por *Jet* 72:48 Mr 30 '87

Bo Jackson's 'hobby' could be trouble says Jim Brown. pors *Jet* 72:46 Ag 3 '87

Bo's two-way stretch. J. Underwood. il pors *Life* 10:93-4+ O '87

Jackson begins career as NFL running back. por *Jet* 73:48 N 9 '87

Jackson eyes football deal; angers baseball teammates. il por *Jet* 72:53 Jl 27 '87

Royals slugger Jackson marries, hits The Coast. por *Jet* 72:6 S 21 '87

Unbending Bo sticks with baseball despite Raiders. por *Jet* 72:47 My 18 '87

Which way will you go, Bo? [cover story] R. Wiley. il pors *Sports Illus* 67:24-6+ D 14 '87

Will Bo be a hit or a miss? P. Gammons. il pors *Sports Illus* 66:36-8 My 4 '87

Jackson, Donald Dale, 1935-

Alligators are back, breeding like crazy and making a big splash. bibl (p131) il *Smithsonian* 17:36-44+ Ja '87

'The cat would never admit her mistakes'. il *Smithsonian* 17:140 Ja '87

The Great Basin is a lonely place for a national park. bibl (p269) il *Smithsonian* 18:68-74+ N '87

Indianapolis: a born-again Hoosier diamond in the rust. bibl (p153) il *Smithsonian* 18:70-6+ Je '87

It takes a 'sixth sense' to operate underneath the streets of New York. il *Smithsonian* 18:38-47 Ag '87

Of moose and men. il *Audubon* 89:94-101 Jl '87

Who can serve better, Crabs or Scorpios? il *Smithsonian* 18:162 Je '87

World's fastest literary gun: Louis L'Amour. il por *Smithsonian* 18:154-6+ My '87

Jackson, Donald Dean, 1919-1987

The short, dramatic life of the steamboat Yellow Stone. il map *Am Herit* 38:121-8 My/Je '87

Jackson, Earnest

about

Baseball is a hobby for this Jackson. J. Reynolds. il por *Sports Illus* 67:12 N 23 '87

Jackson, Gabriel

Spain. il *Nation* 244:470-1 Ap 11 '87

Jackson, Hernell, d. 1987

about

Charge two in drug probe of U-Texas cager's death. *Jet* 72:52 Je 1 '87

Jackson, J. David

The impact of special relativity on theoretical physics. bibl f il *Phys Today* 40:34-42 My '87

Jackson, James

about

Quiz sports stars after probe produces pictures. il *Jet* 72:46 Je 1 '87

Jackson, Janet, 1967-

about

Janet Jackson: 'I'm not sexy, I'm sassy . . . I date . . . and I will marry again'. R. E. Johnson. il pors *Jet* 71:54-6 Mr 2 '87

Janet Jackson: in control at last? M. Rochlin. il pors *Seventeen* 46:130-1+ Jl '87

Janet Jackson leading American Music nominations. il por *Jet* 71:57 Ja 19 '87

Janet Jackson's new look at big bash for celebs [cover story] il pors *Jet* 72:14-16 Ag 17 '87

Janet pleased with wins; Run D.M.C. shocked with loss at Music Awards show. il por *Jet* 71:60-1 F 16 '87

Let's dance! Top tunemakers. il por *Teen* 31:55 Jl '87

Who's the greatest? [cover story] W. Leavy. il pors *Ebony* 42:140+ O '87

Jackson, Jeremy B. C., 1942-, and Kaufmann, Karl W.

Diadema antillarum was not a keystone predator in cryptic reef environments. bibl f il *Science* 235:687-9 F 6 '87

Jackson, Jermaine
about
Jermaine Jackson's wife files for divorce in L.A. il pors *Jet* 73:54 N 2 '87
Jackson, Jesse L., 1941-
Jesse speaks. *New Repub* 197:16-17 Ag 3 '87
Again: character tests. il por *U S News World Rep* 103:8 O 19 '87
Again, sex and politics. C. O'Connor. il por *Newsweek* 109:33 Je 15 '87
The disorganization man. J. Weisberg. il por *Newsweek* 110:19 Ag 17 '87
Ex-manager Martin tells Jesse: stick to politics. por *Jet* 72:46 Jl 13 '87
'For me there is a double standard' [interview] D. Frost. il por *U S News World Rep* 103:19 D 21 '87
The front-runner. *Natl Rev* 39:19-20 Jl 3 '87
Hog heaven: Jesse Jackson cultivates the farm vote in Iowa. J. Klein. il por *N Y* 20:42-5 S 7 '87
Invisible man. A. Cockburn. *Nation* 244:708-9 My 30 '87
Is Jesse the great white hope? [cover story] A. Kopkind. il *Nation* 245:773+ D 26 '87-Ja 2 '88
It's official now! Jackson joins race for president of U.S. il pors *Jet* 73:6-8 O 26 '87
Its ugly head. A. Cockburn. *Nation* 245:8 Jl 4-11 '87
Jackson a top contender for U.S. president: poll. il por *Jet* 72:4-5 Ap 6 '87
Jackson gathers political clout as he prepares to seek presidential nod. il pors *Jet* 73:10+ O 5 '87
Jackson, Reagan confab suggests open door policy. il pors *Jet* 71:5-6 Mr 16 '87
Jackson sets up shop. H. Sidey. il *Time* 130:20 S 7 '87
Jackson the moderate. J. McLaughlin. *Natl Rev* 39:24 Jl 17 '87
Jackson will announce bid for presidency next month; Cosby hosts big fund-raiser. il pors *Jet* 72:24-5 S 21 '87
Jackson's challenge [cover story] S. Muwakkil. il *Progressive* 51:16-19 Jl '87
Jackson's new clout. H. Fineman. il pors *Newsweek* 110:50-1 D 14 '87
Jesse: a rare visit at home with a sudden presidential front-runner. E. Barnes. il pors *Life* 10:24-8+ Jl '87
Jesse goes country [cover story] F. Barnes. *New Repub* 197:15-20 Ag 3 '87
Jesse Jackson [interview] W. Greider. por *Roll Stone* p111-12 N 5-D 10 '87
Jesse Jackson aims for the mainstream. J. Purnick and M. Oreskes. il pors *N Y Times Mag* p28-31+ N 29 '87
Jesse Jackson and the polls. W. F. Buckley. *Natl Rev* 39:62 Je 19 '87
Jesse Jackson gaining support of all races as he explores another run for president [cover story] D. M. Cheers. il pors *Jet* 72:4-7 Je 8 '87
Jesse Jackson leads poll since Gary Hart withdrew. por *Jet* 72:4 Je 22 '87
Jesse Jackson may not have the clout of a kingmaker after all. R. Fly. il por *Bus Week* p47 D 14 '87
Jesse Jackson names campaign leaders in quest for presidency. il por *Jet* 73:4-5 N 30 '87
Jesse Jackson no. 1 Dem as Hart bows out. il por *Jet* 72:4 My 25 '87
Jesse Jackson pens new book; speaks candidly. *Jet* 72:33 My 18 '87
Jesse Jackson puts white in the rainbow. *World Press Rev* 34:64 Jl '87
Jesse Jackson reports on trip to Japan and Korea. D. M. Cheers. il pors *Jet* 71:28-32 Ja 12 '87
Jesse Jackson stands tall in first Democrats debate. D. M. Cheers. il pors *Jet* 72:4+ Jl 20 '87
Jesse Jackson takes first step toward another run for president of United States. D. M. Cheers. il pors *Jet* 72:22-5 Ap 13 '87
Jesse Jackson urges big businesses to 'reinvest in America'. il pors *Jet* 72:4+ S 7 '87
Jesse Jackson's bold run for the presidency. D. C. Ruffin. il *Black Enterp* 18:31-3 S '87
Jesse raises $250,000 in Chicago fund-raiser. il pors *Jet* 72:4+ S 14 '87
Jesse vs. the big leagues. A. Edmond, Jr. il por *Black Enterp* 17:16 Jl '87
Lessons from the fringe. T. Branch. *Wash Mon* 19:56-8 F '87
A little spice for the tapioca. G. Witkin. il pors *U S News World Rep* 103:14 S 21 '87
A new form of black politics. W. L. Chaze. il por *U S News World Rep* 102:20-1 My 25 '87

The 'new voters' find their voice [cover story] A. Kopkind. il *Nation* 245:505+ N 7 '87
Now it's Jesse Mainstream. S. Monroe and H. Fineman. il por *Newsweek* 109:22 My 25 '87
On the Beach. *New Repub* 196:8 F 23 '87
Personal factors. il por *Newsweek* 110:6 Ag 3 '87
A populist message hits home [cover story] A. Kopkind. il *Nation* 245:37+ Jl 18-25 '87
Red in the rainbow. *Natl Rev* 39:17-18 My 22 '87
Respect and respectability. R. Ajemian. il pors *Time* 130:16-17 Ag 17 '87
Running short on cash, Jesse Jackson works a glittering Harlem bash. il pors *People Wkly* 28:61 S 14 '87
University of Michigan agrees to blacks' demands; Jesse Jackson assists. *Jet* 72:5 Ap 13 '87
What to make of the 'new' Jesse [cover story] M. Kramer. il pors *U S News World Rep* 103:34-7+ N 16 '87
    Anecdotes, facetiae, satire, etc.
Announcing the obvious. R. Baker. *N Y Times Mag* p22 S 27 '87
Beseeching the Great Decider. A. Fotheringham. il *Macleans* 100:72 D 7 '87
    Bibliography
The front-runner. M. Summers. *Nation* 245:621-4+ N 28 '87
Jackson, Joe
about
Joe Jackson orchestrates a new wave. D. Wild. il por *Roll Stone* p27 Jl 16-30 '87
Orchestral Jackson. M. Peel. por *Stereo Rev* 52:106 O '87
Jackson, Kenny
about
NFL bachelors consider fine points of marriage. pors *Jet* 71:50 F 16 '87
Jackson, Margaret Weymouth
The magical geranium [story] il *Saturday Evening Post* 259:64-9+ Jl/Ag '87
Jackson, Marion E., d. 1987
about
Obituary
    Jet por 71:52 F 9 '87
Jackson, Marlon
about
Marlon Jackson: the mystery man of Jackson clan. il pors *Jet* 73:54-5 N 23 '87
Jackson, Martin P. A.
(jt. auth) See Talbot, Christopher J., and Jackson, Martin P. A.
Jackson, Michael, 1958-
about
And in Ethiopia, the cult of the Gloved One. por *Newsweek* 109:31 My 25 '87
'Bad' Michael Jackson thrills Tokyo audience during Japan tour debut. il por *Jet* 73:4+ S 28 '87
The Badder they come. J. Cocks. il pors *Time* 130:85 S 14 '87
For sale: the Gloved One's cast-off main squeeze. il por *People Wkly* 27:88 My 25 '87
Good news: 'Bad' news. D. Handelman. *Roll Stone* p11 Ag 13 '87
Is Michael Jackson for real? [cover story] M. Goldberg and D. Handelman. il pors *Roll Stone* p50-1+ S 24 '87
Jackson LP: early sales for 'Bad' are good. F. Goodman. *Roll Stone* p15 O 8 '87
Michael grows up. D. Sigerson. il por *Roll Stone* p87-8 O 22 '87
Michael Jackson: Bad; Prince: Sign o' the times. D. Wolff. *Nation* 245:728-9 D 12 '87
Michael Jackson comes back! [cover story] R. E. Johnson. il pors *Ebony* 42:142-4+ S '87
Michael Jackson conquers Japan and continues his world tour [cover story] il pors *Jet* 73:54-7 N 9 '87
Michael Jackson tells Ebony about his new solo career. il por *Jet* 72:65 S 7 '87
Michael Jackson to get about $10M for Pepsi ads. *Jet* 71:22 F 9 '87
Michael Jackson's 'Bad' album released this month. por *Jet* 72:56 Ag 10 '87
Michael Jackson's newest thriller. C. McGuigan. por *Newsweek* 110:69 Ag 3 '87
Michael's first epistle [cover story] M. Small. il pors *People Wkly* 28:102-4+ O 12 '87
The Peter Pan of song and dance. V. Ross. il pors *Macleans* 100:57-8 S 14 '87
Richie talks about friend, fellow star Michael Jackson. il pors *Jet* 71:62 F 16 '87
Simian star of a new toy line, Michael Jackson's pet, Bubbles, plays second banana to no one. il *People Wkly* 28:189 N 16 '87

Jackson, Michael, 1958—about—*cont.*
The trouble with Michael Jackson. J. Pareles. il *Mademoiselle* 93:108+ Mr '87
Unlike anyone, even himself [cover story] C. Durkee. il pors *People Wkly* 28:86-7+ S 14 '87
A way to play Michael. T. Jaffe. por *Forbes* 140:221 S 21 '87

Jackson, Millie
about
Millie Jackson to appear at N.Y.'s Carnegie Hall. por *Jet* 71:60 F 9 '87

Jackson, Peter
The rhino's fatal flaw. il maps *Int Wildl* 17:4-11 Ja/F '87

Jackson, Rebbie
about
Rebbie Jackson goes back to Gary home, talks about famous brothers, sisters. il pors *Jet* 72:58-9 S 14 '87

Jackson, Reggie
"We have a serious problem that isn't going away" [cover story]; ed. by Peter Gammons. il pors *Sports Illus* 66:40-2+ My 11 '87
about
Jackson buys California automobile dealership. por *Jet* 73:48 N 9 '87
Reggie: an appreciation. R. Fimrite. il por *Sports Illus* 67:98 O 5 '87
Reggie at sunset. D. Remnick. il pors *Esquire* 107:128-30+ Je '87
Reggie happy for chance to play just 1 more year. *Jet* 71:46 Ja 19 '87
Reggie Jackson. J. Krich. il por *Sport Mag* 78:91+ D '87
Reggie Jackson mum on rumor of wedding to blonde 'Dallas' star. pors *Jet* 71:53 Ja 26 '87
Reggie picks Winfield to go to bat for blacks. pors *Jet* 72:50 Je 15 '87
Reggie purchases stake in Nissan dealership. *Jet* 73:50 O 26 '87

Jackson, Robert J., 1936-
New views on defense. *World Press Rev* 34:45 N '87

Jackson, Tony
Search for a drug to fight AIDS. il *World Press Rev* 34:52-3 Mr '87

Jackson, Victoria
about
Saturday night live's smart tart. D. Maychick. il pors *Mademoiselle* 93:98 N '87

Jackson, Wes
about
Farming with a future: the passing of the plow [interview] P. Stone. bibl il pors *Mother Earth News* 104:110-14+ Mr/Ap '87

Jackson (G.) & Sons *See* G. Jackson & Sons

Jackson (Ga.)
Prisons and reformatories
The angel of death row [work of Rev. M. Davis] R. Chepesiuk. por *Progressive* 51:14 My '87

Jackson (Lillie Carroll) Museum *See* Lillie Carroll Jackson Museum

Jackson (Miss.)
Architecture
In the Federal tradition. L. Hallam. il *South Living* 22:98-9+ O '87
Galleries and museums
Downtown Jackson's cluster of museums. il *South Living* 22:47+ N '87

Jackson family
about
Rebbie Jackson goes back to Gary home, talks about famous brothers, sisters. il pors *Jet* 72:58-9 S 14 '87

Jackson Hole (Wyo.: Resort) *See* Resorts—Wyoming

Jackson-Randolph, Marie
about
Where there's a will: from anger to action. B. M. Campbell. il pors *Essence* 18:57-8+ D '87

Jackson State University
Jackson State, Meharry get $100,000 each from grads. *Jet* 72:25 Je 22 '87
Jackson State Univ. names white to run Opera/South [B. J. Schooley] *Jet* 72:25 Ag 31 '87

Jackson-Stops, Gervase
Figures in a landscape: sculpture in the British garden. bibl f il *Antiques* 132:782-97 O '87
Johan Zoffany and the eighteenth-century interior [cover story] bibl f il *Antiques* 131:1264-79 Je '87

Jackson-Vanik amendment *See* United States—Commercial policy

Jacksons (Musical group)
The Jacksons: U.S. tour July-December 1981. D. Fricke. il *Roll Stone* p109-10 Je 4 '87

Jacksonville (Fla.)
Arts
See also
Arts Assembly of Jacksonville, Inc.
Jacksonville [special section] il *Horizon* 30:41-7+ D '87
Description
Jacksonville [special section] il *Horizon* 30:41-7+ D '87
Galleries and museums
See also
Cummer Gallery of Art
Jacksonville Art Museum (Fla.)
Jacksonville Museum of Arts and Sciences
Gardens and gardening
A Japanese garden in Jacksonville. il *South Living* 22:92 Ap '87
Municipal improvement
Jacksonville: a rising star on Florida's northeast coast. J. M. Godbold. il *USA Today (Periodical)* 115:34-42 Ja '87
Music
See also
Jacksonville Symphony Orchestra
St. Johns River City Band
Sports
This Bud's not for you [Oilers owner B. Adams nixes move to Jacksonville] F. Deford. il pors *Sports Illus* 67:67-8+ N 2 '87
Theater
A cooperative effort. K. Simmons. il *Horizon* 30:53 D '87
Waterfront
Down by the riverside in Jacksonville. il *South Living* 22:28-9 F '87

Jacksonville Art Museum (Fla.)
Jacksonville, Florida's three museums offer a variety of culture, education, and fun. M. Wade. il *Horizon* 30:49-51 D '87

Jacksonville Museum of Arts and Sciences
Jacksonville, Florida's three museums offer a variety of culture, education, and fun. M. Wade. il *Horizon* 30:49-51 D '87

Jacksonville Symphony Orchestra
Connoisseur concerts. K. Simmons. il *Horizon* 30:54 D '87

Jacob, Glen
(jt. auth) See Jacob, Sonja, and Jacob, Glen

Jacob, John E., 1934-
Blacks and poverty. *Cent Mag* 20:55-6 Ja/F '87
A society that is just and fair [address, July 19, 1987] *Vital Speeches Day* 53:733-6 S 15 '87
about
Racism, depression peril black America, Jacob says. por *Jet* 71:4 F 2 '87

Jacob, Rahul
India's giver. il por *World Tennis* 35:56+ D '87

Jacob, Sonja, and Jacob, Glen
Motherhood's sad loss of social esteem: one couple's reaction to America's birth dearth. pors *U S News World Rep* 103:6 Ag 17 '87

Jacobbi, Marianne, 1951-
(jt. auth) See Wright, Rosalind, and Jacobbi, Marianne, 1951-

Jacobbi, Marianne, 1951-, and Wright, Rosalind
A desperate search for a second life. il pors *McCalls* 114:127-9 Je '87
How to keep your kids safe. *McCalls* 114:95-6 F '87

Jacobean lilies
Jacobean lily. W. H. Allen. il *Flower Gard* 31:60 O/N '87

Jacobi, Derek
about
I, Jacobi. V. Radin. por *Vogue* 177:134 N '87

Jacobins
Counter-revolution? Toulon, 1793. W. S. Cormack and M. Sydenham. bibl il *Hist Today* 37:49-55 O '87

Jacobs, Barry
Under the boardwalk. il *Progressive* 51:20-2 O '87

Jacobs, Barry
Beers with . . . [interview with J. Valvano] il por *Sport Mag* 78:25-6 Ap '87

Jacobs, Clare
Loving a coke addict. il *Glamour* 85:298-9+ My '87

Jacobs, Dan
Where jungle meets river. il *World Press Rev* 34:62 O '87

Jacobs, Harvey
Stardust [fiction] il *Omni* 9:44-6+ Ag '87

Jacobs, Irwin L.
about
Irv Jacobs is calling 'time out'. P. Houston. il *Bus Week* p46 Je 1 '87

Jacobs, Irwin L.—about—*cont.*
Irv Jacobs is still spooked. G. G. Marcial. *Bus Week* p136 N 30 '87
Jacobs, Laura A.
On dance. See occasional issues of The New Leader
Jacobs, Vic
about
Flipped out in Fresno. W. Taaffe. il por *Sports Illus* 67:65 Ag 3 '87
Jacob's Pillow Dance Festival
New works from Jacob's Pillow land in lower Manhattan's Triplex theater. il *Dance Mag* 61:15 Ja '87
Reviews:
1986 season. L. Garafola. il *Dance Mag* 61:22-3+ F '87
Choreography project with dancers from the New York City Ballet at Jacob's Pillow. L. Garafola. *Dance Mag* 61:74-5 D '87
Jacobsen, Hugh Newell
about
Pavilions in the sun. W. Walton. il *House Gard* 159:118-25 D '87
Pure Nantucket. J. Chancellor. il *House Gard* 159:78-85+ Ag '87
Jacobsen, Josephine
Bibliography
Eyes that do not sleep at dawn. R. Deen. *Commonweal* 114:322-3 My 22 '87
Jacobsen, Kurt
Ireland's right-wing rut. il *New Leader* 70:5-6 Jl 1-15 '87
Jacobson, Barbara
(jt. auth) See Stuart, Richard B., and Jacobson, Barbara
Jacobson, Harlan
25th New York Film Festival. il *Film Comment* 23:61-4 N/D '87
Cannes tankerous. il *Film Comment* 23:61-3 Jl/Ag '87
Montand [interview] por *Film Comment* 23:28-32 S/O '87
Prince Rob [interview with R. Reiner] il por *Film Comment* 23:58+ S/O '87
Jacobson, Marcus
(jt. auth) See Sheard, Philip, and Jacobson, Marcus
Jacobson, Mark
The baby chase. il *Esquire* 107:49-50 My '87
The birth of an optimist. il *Esquire* 108:35-6 Jl '87
Fear of giving. il *Esquire* 108:61-2 D '87
Grave new world. il *Esquire* 108:65+ S '87
Take this dream and shove it. il *Esquire* 108:53-4 N '87
The trouble with money. il *Esquire* 107:49-50 Ap '87
The way we weren't. il *Esquire* 108:65+ O '87
Jacobson, Robert
Viewpoint. See issues of Opera News through June 1986
about
Obituary
Opera News il por 52:28-9 Jl '87. J. Scovell
Jacoby, Robert E.
about
Bare knuckles on Madison Avenue. A. Kleiner. il por *N Y Times Mag* p34-9+ N 8 '87
Jacoby, Russell
Letters [discussion of September 19, 1987 article, Radicals in academia] *Nation* 245:434 O 24 '87
Radicals in academia [excerpt from The last intellectuals] il *Nation* 245:263-4+ S 19 '87
about
Where are all the young brains? E. Bowen. il por *Time* 130:70 N 30 '87
Jacoby, Susan
The baby bandwagon. il *Glamour* 85:388-9+ S '87
The fine art of social argument. il *Glamour* 85:165+ Mr '87
The indispensable art of apology. il *Read Dig* 130:133-5 Mr '87
Living with trouble that won't go away and learning how to keep it from dominating your life. il *Glamour* 85:266-7+ My '87
Jacques, Edwin
about
Where religion has disappeared. S. Mumper. il por *Christ Today* 31:50+ S 4 '87
Jade art objects
Jade: stone of heaven [cover story] F. Ward. il map *Natl Geogr* 172:282-315 S '87
Collectors and collecting
The mystique of jade. J. Choice. il *Antiques Collect Hobbies* 91:12-15+ Ja '87

Jade industry
International aspects
Jade: stone of heaven [cover story] F. Ward. il map *Natl Geogr* 172:282-315 S '87
Jaecks, Joel
about
Joel Jaecks. J. H. Glassie. il por *Am Artist* 51:34-9 S '87
Jaehne, Karen
The Brothers M-K. il por *Film Comment* 23:66-8 S/O '87
Hooker. il *Film Comment* 23:25-32 My/Je '87
Mailer's minuet. il pors *Film Comment* 23:11-17 Jl/Ag '87
Jaén Suárez, Omar
Across the isthmus. il *Américas* 39:28-35 My/Je '87
Jaffe, Dave
(jt. auth) See Coleman, Mitch, and Jaffe, Dave
Jaffe, Dennis T.
(jt. auth) See Orioli, Esther M., and Jaffe, Dennis T.
Jagger, Mick
about
The mature cool of Mick Jagger. M. Gilmore. il *Roll Stone* p113+ N 19 '87
Mick Jagger [interview] M. Gilmore. il por *Roll Stone* p30-2+ N 5-D 10 '87
Mick meets HDTV. P. Hoban. il pors *N Y* 20:31 Ag 24 '87
Jaguar (Automobile) See Automobiles, Foreign
Jaguar Cars Ltd.
See also
Jaguar plc
Jaguar plc
Jaguar revs up. B. Kanner. il *N Y* 20:23+ Ag 31 '87
Jaguar's racing renaissance. M. Cotton. il *Mot Trend* 39:105-8 O '87
The nine lives of Britain's Jaguar. J. A. Seamonds. il *U S News World Rep* 102:47-8 Mr 9 '87
Jaguars
Jaguars: why protect a killer? [work of A. Rabinowitz in Belize; cover story] J. T. Bohlen. il map *Int Wildl* 17:4-11 Mr/Ap '87
Jahn, Helmut
about
The apotheosis of the atrium. M. F. Schmertz. *Archit Rec* 175:9 My '87
Helmut Jahn: flash and fashion. B. Dumaine. il por *Fortune* 115:155+ Je 22 '87
The temple of marketing. H. Muschamp. il *New Repub* 197:25-8 O 26 '87
Jahnkow, Rick
The ballot trap. il *Progressive* 51:14-15 Ag '87
Jail suicides See Suicide
Jailbreaks See Escapes
Jailer, Mildred
Dolls. See issues of Antiques & Collecting Hobbies beginning March 1985
A look at painted furniture. il *Antiques Collect Hobbies* 92:32-6 Je '87
Toys. See issues of Antiques & Collecting Hobbies beginning November 1985
Jails See Prisons
Jain, Girilal
Behind the haste in Sri Lanka. *World Press Rev* 34:49 O '87
Jain, Madhu
Where divorce is a fate better than death. il *World Press Rev* 34:57 Mr '87
Jains
India
The big money in cheap rock [India's Jains dominate U.S. market for low-priced diamonds] P. Gupte. il *Forbes* 140:64+ Ag 10 '87
Jakes, John, 1932-
To be a writer: what does it take? *Writer* 100:9-11 Ja '87
Jakeš, Miloš
about
A new face, an old policy in Prague. il por *Newsweek* 110:27 D 28 '87
A reluctant reformer bows out. W. R. Doerner. il por *Time* 130:34 D 28 '87
Jaki, Stanley L.
Science: from the womb of religion [address, May 1987] il *Christ Century* 104:851-4 O 7 '87
about
Science & the ways to God. H. Rolston. *Commonweal* 114:313-16 My 22 '87
Jakobson, Cathryn
Are you trapped by your image? il *Seventeen* 46:204-5+ Ap '87

Jakobson, Cathryn—*cont.*

The loneliness of the long-distance lover. il *Mademoiselle* 93:178-9 F '87

Murray Hill: mansions with pedigrees from the Age of Innocence. il map *N Y* 20:42-4 My 4 '87

The return of hard to get (smart cookies don't phone first). il *Mademoiselle* 93:220-1+ Mr '87

What's a nice couple like you doing in a fight like this? Why guys and girls can't talk. il *Mademoiselle* 93:190+ N '87

Jalousie windows *See* Windows

Jam, Jimmy

about

Introducing: 'Producers of the Year' Jimmy (Jam) Harris and Terry Lewis. pors *Ebony* 42:126 Jl '87

Jam and Lewis take control. M. Goldberg. il pors *Roll Stone* p30+ Ap 23 '87

Jam *See* Jelly, jam, etc.

Jamaica

See also

Agriculture—Jamaica

Art—Jamaica

Crime and criminals—Jamaica

Health resorts, watering places, etc.—Jamaica

Hotels, motels, etc.—Jamaica

Music festivals—Jamaica

Commerce

United States

See United States—Commerce—Jamaica

Description and travel

Jamaican designs. E. M. Gomez. il map *Travel Holiday* 167:48-51 Ja '87

Economic policy

Jamaica 25: the economy. C. Channer and M. Legister. *Black Enterp* 18:22 Ag '87

Seaga plays for time in Jamaica. P. Engardio. il por *Bus Week* p41 Ap 20 '87

Industries

See also

Clothing industry—Jamaica

Politics and government

Seaga under pressure. J. C. Baker. por *Black Enterp* 17:17 Ja '87

Jamaica-America Society

Don King gets Dr. King Award in Jamaica fete. il pors *Jet* 71:36-7 F 9 '87

Jamaica Inn (Ocho Rios, Jamaica) *See* Hotels, motels, etc.—Jamaica

Jamaica Water Properties, Inc.

See also

JWP Inc.

Jamaican house decoration *See* House decoration, Jamaican

Jamaican Stock Exchange *See* Stock exchanges—Jamaican exchange

Jamail, Joseph

about

Triumph of the sore-back lawyer. T. Mack. il por *Forbes* 139:33-4 My 4 '87

James, Ardis

about

A passion for quilts—vintage & modern. R. Siegel. il pors *Am Craft* 47:49+ D '87/Ja '88

James, Charmayne

about

Roll out the barrel! When this coltish teen cuts corners, rodeo records fall. il por *People Wkly* 28:139 O 12 '87

James, Curtia

Talk is not cheap. por *Essence* 18:130 Ag '87

James, Edward, 1907-1984

about

The surreal life of Edward James. A. Cockburn. il por *House Gard* 159:198-206+ Je '87

James, Harold, 1956-

Deep red: the international debt crisis and its historical precedents. *Am Sch* 56:331-41 Summ '87

James, Henry, 1843-1916

about

The real things. G. S. Johnston. *Harpers* 274:54-5 F '87

The rivals. L. Fleischer. *Publ Wkly* 231:130 My 15 '87

Total immersion: Henry James and mineral waters. A. Broyard. il *N Y Times Book Rev* 92:10 Ja 4 '87

James, Hubert Maxwell, 1908-1986

about

Obituary

Phys Today 40:92 Je '87. G. W. Lehman

James, John, 1946-, and Schlesinger, Ibis

Are you the one for me? [excerpt] il *Glamour* 85:378-9+ S '87

James, Joyce

Playing pizzicato [poem] *Commonweal* 114:247 Ap 24 '87

Raising animals: Esther and Eve [poem] *Commonweal* 114:246-7 Ap 24 '87

James, Kay

about

Enlisting blacks in the battle against abortion [interview] por *Christ Today* 31:63+ O 2 '87

James, Paul

about

The rock revivalists. C. Bell. il por *Macleans* 100:35 Mr 2 '87

James, Rick

about

Rick James born again; wants out of Motown. il *Jet* 71:63 F 9 '87

James, Robert

about

A passion for quilts—vintage & modern. R. Siegel. il pors *Am Craft* 47:49+ D '87/Ja '88

James, Stephen

about

Roads scholar Stephen James quits life in the bus lane to shoot for a Harvard Ph.D. M. Brower. il pors *People Wkly* 27:87-8 Je 22 '87

James, Theodore

Flowers all winter long. il *Ladies Home J* 104:92+ N '87

Herbs with a view. il *50 Plus* 27:38-40+ Ag '87

James, Vanessa *See* Beauman, Sally

James (Robert and Ardis) Collection *See* Quilts and quilting—Collectors and collecting

James B. Beam Distilling Co.

Whiskey Land, USA, Booker Noe, Prop. J. E. Bradley. il pors *Esquire* 108:204-8+ S '87

James Bond (Fictional character)

Bond at 25: back to basics. C. McGuigan. il pors *Newsweek* 110:56-7 Jl 27 '87

Bond keeps up his silver streak. R. Corliss. il *Time* 130:54-5 Ag 10 '87

Favorite drinks of James Bond. J. F. Mariani. il *Mot Boat Sail* 160:30 Ag '87

Meet the new Bond [T. Dalton] G. Hirshey. il por *Roll Stone* p37-9 Jl 16-30 '87

Oh, James, don't stop. A. Burgess. il *Life* 10:114-16+ Ap '87

James E. Sullivan Award *See* Sports—Awards

James River Corp. of Virginia

One company's standards [personal computers] P. Honan. *Pers Comput* 11:100 F '87

Jameson, Donald

What Yevgeny knew. *New Repub* 196:39-41 Je 22 '87

Jameson, John

Busted. *New Repub* 196:9-10 My 25 '87

Jameson, Kenneth P.

Mortgaging a house of cards. il *Commonweal* 114:105-7 F 27 '87

Jamieson, Alexander

about

North view. G. Lovi. il *Sky Telesc* 73:175-6 F '87

Jamieson, Bob

Return to Ghana. il *Int Wildl* 17:38-41 N/D '87

Jamming of radar *See* Radar interference

Jamming of radio signals *See* Radio interference

Jammu and Kashmir (India)

See also

Ladakh

Jane Baerwald Aron Art Center

Remodeled and restored, an "art village" at Mills College. il *Sunset* 178:36 F '87

Janecky, J. Y.

The red dress [story] *Teen* 31:28+ D '87

Jane's Addiction (Musical group)

Local heroes. D. Handelman. il pors *Roll Stone* p68-70+ O 22 '87

Jane's Publishing Company Ltd.

The gentlemen of Jane's. por *World Press Rev* 34:28-30 O '87

Janesick, James, and Blouke, Morley

Sky on a chip: the fabulous CCD. il *Sky Telesc* 74:238-42 S '87

Janis, Sidney, 1896-

about

Sidney Janis waiting a year for the blue. J. James. il por *Art News* 86:85-6 D '87

Janis (Sidney) Gallery *See* Sidney Janis Gallery

Janklow, Mort

about

Mega-Mort: superagent Janklow's blockbuster life. P. Morrisroe. il pors *N Y* 20:34-40+ F 2 '87

Janko, Edward
A toast to hypocrisy. por *Newsweek* 109:6 Ja 5 '87
Jankowiak, R., and Small, G. J.
Hole-burning spectroscopy and relaxation dynamics of amorphous solids at low temperatures. bibl f il *Science* 237:618-25 Ag 7 '87
Jannaccio, Richard
The University of Wisconsin hatches toxins. il *Progressive* 51:20 N '87
Janot's (San Francisco, Calif.: Restaurant) *See* San Francisco (Calif.)—Restaurants, nightclubs, bars, etc.
Janowitz, Phyllis
Tics [poem] *New Yorker* 62:40 F 2 '87
Janowitz, Tama
Adventures in Tinseltown. il por *N Y Times Mag* p32-3+ Mr 22 '87
Off-the-street chic. *Vogue* 177:620 S '87
about
Two divine decadents. D. Lehman. il pors *Newsweek* 110:72 S 7 '87
Janssen, Peter A.
At the helm. See issues of Motor Boating & Sailing
Janssen, Wallace F.
The Constitution and the consumer: discovering the connections. il *FDA Consum* 21:8-11 S '87
(jt. auth) See Hecht, Annabel, and Janssen, Wallace F.
January
An effect-ive stock strategy [stock market in January] il *Money* 16:12 D '87
The January almanac. il *Atlantic* 259:18 Ja '87
Janus Press
Claire Van Vliet's Janus Press. W. T. Taylor. il por *Am Craft* 47:52-9+ F/Mr '87
Janz, Denis R. (Denis Raymond), 1949-
Medjugorje's miracles: faith and profit. il *Christ Century* 104:724-5 Ag 26-S 2 '87
Janzen, Daniel H.
about
Growing a forest from scratch. E. C. Wolf. il por *Futurist* 21:41-2 Jl/Ag '87
Japan
See also
Accounting—Japan
Aged—Japan
Aged market—Japan
Agricultural administration—Japan
Air traffic control—Japan
Airports—Japan
Americans—Japan
Anti-nuclear movement—Japan
Anti-Semitism—Japan
Architecture—Japan
Astronomical observatories—Japan
Astronomy—Japan
Automation—Japan
Aviation and state—Japan
Balance of payments—Japan
Banks and banking—Japan
Baseball, Professional—Japan
Bathing customs—Japan
Billionaires—Japan
Birds—Japan
Bonds, Government—Japan
Business management—Japan
Children's literature—Japan
Comic books, strips, etc.—Japan
Commodity brokers—Japan
Copyright—Japan
Credit cards—Japan
Design—Japan
Economic assistance, Japanese
Education—Japan
Employment—Japan
Factory management—Japan
Family—Japan
Finance—Japan
Financial institutions—Japan
Fish markets—Japan
Fringe benefits—Japan
Funeral rites and ceremonies—Japan
Genetic research—Japan
Hakone (Japan)
Hiroshima (Japan)
Historic houses, sites, etc.—Japan
Hotels, motels, etc.—Japan
Hours of labor—Japan
Industrial relations—Japan
Industry and state—Japan
Investment banking—Japan
Investments, American—Japan

Investments, Japanese
Japanese
Kyoto (Japan)
Labyrinths—Japan
Land values—Japan
Marketing—Japan
Middle classes—Japan
Military research—Japan
Money—Japan
Morale, National—Japan
Mount Fuji (Japan)
Music festivals—Japan
Nagasaki (Japan)
National parks and reserves—Japan
Nuclear research—Japan
Opera—Japan
Orphans and orphanages—Japan
Osaka (Japan)
Over-the-counter securities markets—Japan
Part time employment—Japan
Physics—Japan
Public relations—Japan
Quality control—Japan
Recycling (Waste, etc.)—Japan
Research—Japan
Rock music—Japan
Sales tax—Japan
Saving and savings—Japan
Science and state—Japan
Securities—Japan
Shopping and shoppers—Japan
Singles market—Japan
Space research—Japan
Technology—Japan
Technology and state—Japan
Television advertising—Japan
Television broadcasting—Japan
Tokyo (Japan)
Trade unions—Japan
Tsukuba Science City (Japan)
Unemployment—Japan
United States—Diplomatic and consular service—Japan
Volcanoes—Japan
Wedding chapels—Japan
Wildlife—Japan
Wildlife conservation—Japan
Youth—Japan
Youth market—Japan
Yuppies—Japan

Armed Forces
Japanese self-defense forces expand modernization programs. *Aviat Week Space Technol* 126:59+ My 11 '87

Appropriations and expenditures
Japan increases defense budget share by 4% in fiscal 1987. il *Aviat Week Space Technol* 126:99+ Mr 9 '87
Japanese breakthrough. *Natl Rev* 39:21 Ja 30 '87
Make 'em pay [getting America's allies to shoulder more of the burden for their own defense] M. Kondracke. *New Repub* 197:15-17 O 12 '87
Swords to plowshares . . . and back to swords [Mitsubishi Heavy Industries] A. Tanzer. il *Forbes* 139:32-3 Ja 26 '87

Commerce
See also
Balance of trade—Japan
Japan and the Pacific Rim: economic challenge to America [cover story; special issue] il *Sch Update* 119:2-24 Ap 6 '87
"Let us shake hands". N. R. Gibbs. il *Time* 130:49 O 19 '87
Germany (West)
See Germany (West)—Commerce—Japan
Israel
See Israel—Commerce—Japan
Italy
See Italy—Commerce—Japan
Persian Gulf region
Troubled waters [European and Japanese dependence on oil from the Persian Gulf] il *Time* 129:22 Je 1 '87
Why Europe and Japan won't help. F. Willey. il *Newsweek* 109:35 Je 8 '87

Japan—Commerce—*cont.*
Soviet Union
See Soviet Union—Commerce—Japan
United States
See United States—Commerce—Japan
Western Europe
The Europeans start to play a little rough [antidumping proposals] T. Peterson. il *Bus Week* p47 F 9 '87
Commercial policy
The big switch. *New Repub* 196:5-7 Je 15 '87
The Japan problem [cover story; special section] il *World Press Rev* 34:11-19 Ag '87
Japan's choices. P. F. Drucker. bibl f *Foreign Aff* 65:923-41 Summ '87
Japan's economic choices. P. F. Drucker. *Current* 296:33-40 O '87
Japan's problems with exports [interview with K. Miyazawa] B. Blohm. *World Press Rev* 34:51 Ja '87
Let Japan do the bashing [Japan's reliance on foreign pressure as mechanism to make controversial policy decisions] R. J. Samuelson. il *Newsweek* 110:52 Ag 10 '87
The trade wars. il *World Press Rev* 34:7 Je '87
The winds of trade war [with interviews with R. Strauss and K. Kato] R. H. Bork, Jr. il *U S News World Rep* 102:46-7 Ap 13 '87
Defenses
See also
Airplanes, Military—Japan
United States. Navy—Forces in Japan
Japanese self-defense forces expand modernization programs. *Aviat Week Space Technol* 126:59+ My 11 '87
The white peril [G. Vidal's comments on decline of U.S. and rise of Japan] J. M. Fallows. il *Atlantic* 259:18+ My '87
Description and travel
See also
Motorcycling—Japan
Adventures in travel. T. Assenza. il *Car Driv* 33:27 N '87
Diplomatic and consular service
United States
Diplomats [Diplomat Samurai Band] *New Yorker* 63:29-30 Ap 20 '87
Economic conditions
See also
Consumption (Economics)—Japan
Cost and standard of living—Japan
Japan—Industries
Japan looks for a brighter new year. B. Buell. il *Bus Week* p58-9 Ja 12 '87
Japan's troubled future [special section] il *Fortune* 115:21-8+ Mr 30 '87
Remaking Japan [cover story; special section] il *Bus Week* p48-58+ Jl 13 '87
A storm gathers in Japan [address, June 15, 1987] K. Ohmae. *Vital Speeches Day* 53:729-30 S 15 '87
Economic history
Japan's century of rapid progress. J. Rose. il *Sch Update* 119:16-18 Ap 6 '87
Economic policy
How slow will they grow? S. Nasar. il *Fortune* 116:67+ N 9 '87
Is Japan as rich as you think? B. Powell. il *Newsweek* 109:48-50 Je 8 '87
Japan Inc.'s new face [cover story; special section] il *Macleans* 100:22-8+ N 30 '87
Japan's choices. P. F. Drucker. bibl f *Foreign Aff* 65:923-41 Summ '87
Japan's economic choices. P. F. Drucker. *Current* 296:33-40 O '87
Japan's pump-priming won't do much for U.S. exports. B. Buell. il *Bus Week* p49 Ap 27 '87
Tax reform: the stakes don't get much higher. B. Buell. il *Bus Week* p51+ Ap 6 '87
Welcome to the hot seat, Mr. Prime Minister [N. Takeshita] A. Borrus. il por *Bus Week* p152-3 N 2 '87
Economic relations
The Japan problem [cover story; special section] il *World Press Rev* 34:11-19 Ag '87
Japan's drive to pre-eminence. R. A. Morse. *Foreign Policy* 69:3-21 Wint '87/'88
Asia
Japan is the rich neighbor everyone loves to hate. L. Kraar. il *Fortune* 115:47 Mr 30 '87

United States
See United States—Economic relations—Japan
Foreign opinion
The Japan problem [cover story; special section] il *World Press Rev* 34:11-19 Ag '87
Let Japan do the bashing [Japan's reliance on foreign pressure as mechanism to make controversial policy decisions] R. J. Samuelson. il *Newsweek* 110:52 Ag 10 '87
American
A mix of admiration, envy and anger [attitudes towards U.S. trade war with Japan] G. J. Church. il *Time* 129:38-9 Ap 13 '87
Foreign relations
Japan: the next superpower? P. Jinzhang. *World Press Rev* 34:47 N '87
China
See China—Foreign relations—Japan
France
See France—Foreign relations—Japan
Soviet Union
See Soviet Union—Foreign relations—Japan
United States
See United States—Foreign relations—Japan
Industries
See also
Aerospace industries—Japan
Agricultural industries—Japan
Airlines—Japan
Airplane industry—Japan
Aiwa Co. Ltd.
All Nippon Airways Co. Ltd.
Art Moving Center (Firm)
Art trade—Japan
Asahi Mutual Life Insurance Company
Audio equipment industry—Japan
Automobile equipment industry—Japan
Automobile industry—Japan
Bridgestone Corp.
Brokers—Japan
Canon Inc.
Ceramics—Japan
Computer industry—Japan
Corporations—Acquisitions and mergers—Japan
Dai-Ichi Kangyo Bank, Ltd.
Daihatsu Motor Co. Ltd.
Dentsu Inc.
Fanuc Ltd.
Fish industry—Japan
Fuji Photo Film Co., Ltd.
Fujitec Company
Fujitsu Ltd.
Gakkyusha (Firm)
Hattori Seiko Co. Ltd.
Hitachi, Ltd.
Honda Motor Co., Ltd
Japan Aero Engines Corporation
Kashiyama & Co., Ltd.
Kumagai Gumi Co. Ltd.
Kyocera Corporation
Lions Petroleum Company
Mail order business—Japan
Matsushita Electric Industrial Co. Ltd.
Mitsubishi Heavy Industries, Ltd.
Mitsubishi Motors Corp.
Mitsui & Co., Ltd
Morita & Company
Motorcycle industry—Japan
Munitions—Japan
NEC Corp.
Nihon Keizai Shimbun, Inc.
Nikko Securities Co. Ltd.
Nintendo Co. Ltd.
Nippon Life Insurance Co.
Nippon Telegraph & Telephone Corporation
Nissan Motor Co. Ltd.
Nomura Securities Co. Ltd.
Outplacement consultant services—Japan
Pet industries—Japan
Phonograph record industry—Japan
Sanrio Co., Ltd.
Sanyo Securities Co. Ltd.
Service industries—Japan
Shiseido Company Ltd.
Sony Corp.
Suzuki Motor Company Ltd.
Tateho Chemical Industries Co. Ltd.
Toray Industries, Inc
Toshiba Corporation
Toshiba Machine Co. Ltd.
Tourist trade—Japan

Japan—Industries—See also—cont.
Toyota Motor Corporation
Wacoal Corp.
Whaling—Japan
Yamaha Motor Co. Ltd.
Yasuda Fire & Marine Insurance Co. Ltd.
Yasuda Mutual Life Insurance Company
Yoshiya Company Ltd.
Can Japan keep its economy from hollowing out? A. Borrus. il *Bus Week* p52-5 Jl 13 '87
The challenges of success. J. Smolowe. il *Time* 129:40+ Ap 13 '87
Fear and trembling in the colossus. J. Dreyfuss. il *Fortune* 115:32-4+ Mr 30 '87
How Japan is beating the profit squeeze [zaitech financing] A. Borrus. il *Bus Week* p60-1 My 11 '87
Japan looks for a brighter new year. B. Buell. il *Bus Week* p58-9 Ja 12 '87
"Let us shake hands". N. R. Gibbs. il *Time* 130:49 O 19 '87
Now it's Japan's turn to sweat a bit. M. Lord. il *U S News World Rep* 102:42-3 Mr 9 '87
Waiting for the yen to stop pummeling profits. L. Armstrong. il *Bus Week* p58-9 Je 1 '87

Kings and rulers
See also
Hirohito, Emperor of Japan, 1901-

Languages
See also
English language in Japan

Military policy
See also
Japan—Defenses
Japan: the next superpower? P. Jinzhang. *World Press Rev* 34:47 N '87

Nationalism
The end of innocence. J. W. Dower. il *Nation* 245:224-6+ S 12 '87
A new Japanese nationalism [cover story] I. Buruma. il *N Y Times Mag* p22-7+ Ap 12 '87
Trading superstar sets future sights by its own lights. il map *U S News World Rep* 103:44-6 D 28 '87-Ja 4 '88

Politics and government
See also
Political candidates—Japan
A back-room man steps forward [N. Takeshita chosen to succeed Y. Nakasone] H. G. Chua-Eoan. il por *Time* 130:65 N 2 '87
A black-belt prime minister [N. Takeshita] A. Bilski. por *Macleans* 100:28 N 30 '87
Can Japan still afford the politics of waiting? [prime minister-designate N. Takeshita] J. Wallace. il por *U S News World Rep* 103:42-3 N 2 '87
Japan: a change of style [new prime minister N. Takeshita] il por *Newsweek* 110:66 N 2 '87
Japan turns toward home [prime minister-designate N. Takeshita] R. Shiratori. por *World Press Rev* 34:24 D '87
A talk with Japan's new P.M. [N. Takeshita] B. Martin. *Newsweek* 110:56 N 9 '87
Welcome to the hot seat, Mr. Prime Minister [N. Takeshita] A. Borrus. il por *Bus Week* p152-3 N 2 '87
A whiff of blood in the water [furor over sales tax] B. Hillenbrand. il *Time* 129:35 Mr 23 '87
Yasu, the chips are down [effect of U.S. tariffs on Y. Nakasone's popularity] H. G. Chua-Eoan. il por *Time* 129:38 Ap 27 '87

Race relations
Behind Japanese superiority. T. Terzani. il *World Press Rev* 34:27-8 Mr '87

Religious institutions and affairs
See also
Buddhism—Japan

Social conditions
The challenges of success. J. Smolowe. il *Time* 129:40+ Ap 13 '87
Divisive forces in an inbred nation. L. Smith. il *Fortune* 115:24-8 Mr 30 '87
Goodbye consensus: divisiveness in Japan. L. Smith. *Current* 294:30-3 Jl/Ag '87
The Oriental dilemma. M. Clugston. il *Macleans* 100:26-8+ N 30 '87
Remaking Japan [cover story; special section] il *Bus Week* p48-58+ Jl 13 '87

Japan. Ministry of International Trade and Industry
Bright lights, big MITI [Toshiba's sale of top-security technology to the Soviets] C. Chandler. *New Repub* 197:11-13 Ag 31 '87

Japan Aero Engines Corporation
Japanese study partners' sales, support techniques. *Aviat Week Space Technol* 127:49-50 S 21 '87

Japan Air Lines Co. Ltd.
Japan Air Lines begins four-year expansion plan. *Aviat Week Space Technol* 126:34 Mr 2 '87
Taking a flier on JAL. A. Borrus. il *Bus Week* p42 Ag 31 '87

Japan and the United States
See also
Exchanges, Literary and scientific
Japan—Foreign opinion—American
United States—Foreign opinion—Japanese
Got a '56 Chevy? You'll find a buyer in Japan. il *Newsweek* 110:63 O 26 '87

Japan Fund, Inc.
Investor bites sleeping dog [changing from closed-end to open-end status] R. Phalon. il *Forbes* 140:178-9 O 5 '87
Leave it to T. Boone's son to sniff out a bargain [race for closed-end funds] W. Glasgall. il por *Bus Week* p113-14 Mr 16 '87

Japan lobby *See* Foreign propagandists—United States

Japanese
Behind Japanese superiority. T. Terzani. il *World Press Rev* 34:27-8 Mr '87
How to win over a Japanese boss. J. B. Copeland. il *Newsweek* 109:46-8 F 2 '87
Six who will make a difference. F. H. Katayama. il *Fortune* 115:50-3 Mr 30 '87

United States
See also
Japanese Americans
I love New York, L.A., Hawaii . . . [young Japanese tourists] B. Buell. il *Bus Week* p54 Mr 23 '87
Strangers in a strange land (Miami), four Japanese baseball players find it tough getting to first base [playing for the Marlins in the minor leagues] P. Jordan. il *People Wkly* 28:46-8 Jl 13 '87

Japanese Americans
Evacuation and relocation, 1942-1945
Interned injustice. L. H. Roth. *New Repub* 197:11-12 S 28 '87
A thousand days' detention [indemnification bills] R. F. Drinan. il *America* 157:247-9 O 17 '87
The wounds of war; ed. by Susan Schindehette. N. Y. Mineta. il pors *People Wkly* 28:173-4+ D 14 '87
Your Constitution: Japanese-Americans vs. the U.S. D. Pawelek. il *Sch Update* 119:18 Ap 6 '87

Japanese art *See* Art, Japanese
Japanese artificial satellites *See* Artificial satellites, Japanese
Japanese automobiles *See* Automobiles, Foreign
Japanese cooking *See* Cooking, Japanese
Japanese executives *See* Executives
Japanese folk art *See* Folk art
Japanese gardens *See* Gardens and gardening, Japanese
Japanese house decoration *See* House decoration, Japanese
Japanese literature
See also
Children's literature—Japan
Japanese poetry
See also
Haiku
Japanese prints *See* Prints
Japanese shuttle missions *See* Space flight—Shuttle missions, Japanese
Japanese solomon's seal (Plant) *See* Solomon's seal (Plant)
Japanese space vehicles *See* Space vehicles, Japanese
Japanese spaceplane *See* Spaceplane, Japanese
Japanese students in the United States *See* Foreign students—United States
Japanesque silverware *See* Silverware
Japonesque (Firm)
Le style Japonesque [owner K. Hara] R. Castile. il por *House Gard* 159:28+ Je '87

Jarboe, E. Dean
about
'If the Dow goes to 2300, I'll be getting out again'. J. M. Laderman. il por *Bus Week* p117 D 28 '87-Ja 4 '88

Jardin des Plantes (Paris, France)
Pleasant and living. B. Roueché. il *New Yorker* 63:121-5 F 23 '87

Jardine Matheson & Co., Ltd.
Jardine's giant step from Hong Kong to Wall Street [stake in Bear Stearns] D. J. Yang and others. il por *Bus Week* p39-40 O 12 '87

Jaret, Peter
The wars within us. il *Read Dig* 130:164-6+ Ja '87

Jargon
Could you, er, say that again? [doublespeak] M. Satchell. il *U S News World Rep* 102:71 Ap 20 '87
Anecdotes, facetiae, satire, etc.
Paradigmatic metaconsciousness. M. Ivins. il *Progressive* 51:29 Je '87
Jari Plantation *See* Plantations—Brazil
Jarman, Derek, 1942-
about
Caravaggio [film] Reviews
Art Am il 75:21-3 Ja '87. L. Tillman
Jarnagin, Laura
(jt. auth) *See* Pang, Eul-Soo, and Jarnagin, Laura
Jaroslovsky, Rich
Chalk one up for the permanent government. *Wash Mon* 19:33-7 O '87
Jarreau, Al
about
Jarreau wins new fans with 'Moonlighting' tune. por *Jet* 73:18 N 16 '87
Jarrett, Keith
about
Keith Jarrett. J. Diliberto. por *Down Beat* 54:14 Ap '87
Jars, Canning *See* Canning and preserving—Equipment
Jars, Glass *See* Glass containers
Jaruzelski, Wojciech
about
From a U.S. mole: inside story of what might have been. R. Z. Chesnoff and D. Stanglin. il por *U S News World Rep* 102:32-3 Ap 20 '87
Jaruzelski walks a fine line. A. Bromke. *World Press Rev* 34:37 Je '87
Jaruzelski wins one with the end of U.S. sanctions. D. Stanglin. il por *U S News World Rep* 102:35 Mr 2 '87
Järvefelt, Göran
about
Pure and simple. G. Loney. por *Opera News* 51:18-20+ Je '87
Jarvik, Robert
about
There's nothing artificial about the way Robert Jarvik's heart beats for his brainy bride-to-be. K. McMurran. il pors *People Wkly* 28:46-50 Jl 27 '87
Jarvik-7 (Artificial heart) *See* Heart, Artificial
Jarvis, Anna
about
Granting a mother's wish. il por *South Living* 22:46 My '87
Jarvis, Doug
about
He always comes to play. B. Kravitz. il por *Sports Illus* 66:10 Ja 5 '87
Jarvis, John
about
Traveling without a map. J. Cocks. il por *Time* 130:66 D 28 '87
Jasper, Margie
Your credit-profile rights. il *Essence* 18:120 O '87
Jasper National Park (Alta.)
Canada's Jasper National Park. A. Yarrow. il *Travel Holiday* 167:24+ My '87
Jastrow, Robert, 1925-
America has five years left. *Natl Rev* 39:42-3 F 13 '87
Java (Indonesia)
See also
Theater—Java (Indonesia)
Java Sea
See also
Cruising—Java Sea
Javelin Software Corporation
IPOs: now only the best and the brightest need apply. K. H. Hammonds. il *Bus Week* p37-8 N 30 '87
Javetski, Bill, and others
Another grenade goes off under Reagan's contra strategy. il *Bus Week* p53 Mr 2 '87
Iranscam: will Reagan's answer man be allowed to answer? *Bus Week* p55 Ja 12 '87
Javett, Michael B.
about
$11 for a $10 bill? R. Phalon. il *Forbes* 139:99 Ja 26 '87
Jaworski, Adam, and others
Left-handed DNA in vivo. bibl f il *Science* 238:773-7 N 6 '87
Jaws
Abnormalities
See also
Malocclusion

Jaws the revenge [film] *See* Motion picture reviews—Single works
Jay, Antony
(jt. auth) *See* Lynn, Jonathan, 1943-, and Jay, Antony
Jay, Leslie
How to keep your stomach from growling and other things no one else ever tells you. il *Ladies Home J* 104:34+ Ja '87
Jay, Ricky
Grand illusions. il *Omni* 9:44-6+ Mr '87
about
With tales of Learned pigs & fireproof women, Ricky Jay conjures up a memorable book. J. Jerome. il por *People Wkly* 27:67+ My 11 '87
The wizard of odd. R. Tannenbaum. il por *Roll Stone* p69-70+ Ap 23 '87
Jay Peak (Vt.: Resort) *See* Resorts—Vermont
Jayewardene, Junius Richard
about
A murderous backlash. K. Hall. *Macleans* 100:21 Ag 31 '87
Narrow escape. *Time* 130:27 Ag 31 '87
Jaynes, Gerald David, and Williams, Robin M., Jr.
Challenges and opportunities. *Society* 24:3-7 Ja/F '87
Jaynes, Gregory
Over the Alps and through the shops with Dr. Ruth. il pors *Life* 10:127-8+ N '87
Jays
How do you feel about jays? il *Sunset* 179:210 S '87
The Jekyll & Hyde jay. G. H. Harrison. il *Natl Wildl* 26:42-4 D '87/Ja '88
Smart bird gets the moth! [jays learn to find camouflaged moths] il *Natl Geogr World* 143:30-1 Jl '87
Jazz concerts
Caught. *See* issues of Down Beat
Jazz festivals *See* Music festivals
Jazz groups
See also
29th Street Saxophone Quartet
American Jazz Orchestra
Charlie Watts Orchestra
Gil Evans Orchestra
Henry Threadgill Sextett
Phonograph records—Jazz music
Rainbow Band
Stan Spiro and the Townsmen Orchestra
String Trio of New York
Vibration Society (Musical group)
World Saxophone Quartet
Jazz impressions from Philadelphia [radio program] *See* Radio program reviews—Single works
Jazz music
See also
Blues music
Compact discs—Jazz music
Phonograph records—Jazz music
Radio broadcasting—Jazz music
Television broadcasting—Jazz music
Videotapes—Jazz music
Hip hangouts for the jazz lover on the road. R. Hoffman. il *Bus Week* p118 Je 1 '87
Indigenous music. N. Hentoff. *See* issues of The Progressive
Jazz. W. Balliett. *See* occasional issues of The New Yorker
Now's the time [renaissance] M. Bourne. il *Down Beat* 54:6+ Ja '87
Pro session. *See* issues of Down Beat
Reggae or not: jazz goes dread? N. Weinstein. il *Down Beat* 54:63 Mr '87
Awards
See also
Down Beat Student Music Awards
Musicfest U.S.A. Awards
35th annual International Critics Poll [with editorial comment by Art Lange] J. McDonough. il pors *Down Beat* 54:5, 20-4 Ag '87
The 52nd annual Down Beat Readers Poll [with editorial comment by Art Lange] il *Down Beat* 54:6, 20-2 D '87
Bibliography
The jazz comeback. E. J. Hobsbawm. il *N Y Rev Books* 34:11-14 F 12 '87
History
Birdland [New York City] N. Hentoff. il *N Y* 20:92 D 21-28 '87
Eddie Condon's. V. Ziegel. il por *N Y* 20:70-1 D 21-28 '87
Round midnight [movie] H. Mandel. il *Down Beat* 54:22-3 Ja '87

Jazz music—*cont.*
Periodicals
See also
Down beat (Periodical)
Psychological aspects
The ego & the I.D. A. Lange. *Down Beat* 54:6+ O
'87
Study and teaching
Dizzy's clarion calls for degree in bebop [D. Gillespie]
por *Jet* 72:63 Jl 13 '87
Learning to listen. E. Kloss. il *Down Beat* 54:56-7 Jl
'87
Linear development. E. Kloss. il *Down Beat* 11:54-5
N '87
Playercise: practice through discovery. E. Kloss. il *Down
Beat* 54:54-6 Ja '87
Practice disciplines. J. Novello. il *Down Beat* 54:53-4
Mr '87
Vermont and all that jazz [Jazz Vermont big band
workshop] W. R. Stokes. il *Travel Holiday* 168:14+
Ag '87
Wynton debuts jazz in Chicago classrooms. B. Beuttler.
il por *Down Beat* 54:12 Ja '87
Writing
Large-scale jazz [influence of D. Ellington and trend
towards composition] F. Davis. il *Atlantic* 260:76-7
Ag '87
Latin America
Rainbow comes to Latin America [Rainbow Band on
tour] J. Robbins. il *Down Beat* 54:12 My '87
Mexico
Mexico's jazz master [E. Toussaint] M. Holston. por
Américas 39:58-60 N/D '87
New York (State)
See also
New York (N.Y.)—Music
Pennsylvania
See also
Philadelphia (Pa.)—Music
Soviet Union
Jazz *glasnost.* B. Shoemaker. il *Down Beat* 54:28-9 O
'87
Vermont
Vermont and all that jazz [Jazz Vermont big band
workshop] W. R. Stokes. il *Travel Holiday* 168:14+
Ag '87
Jazz music in literature
In and out of Storyville: jazz and fiction. V. Bourjaily.
il *N Y Times Book Rev* 92:1+ D 13 '87
Jazz musicians
See also
Phonograph records—Jazz music
See also names of jazz musicians
Auditions. See issues of Down Beat beginning August
1985
Blindfold test. See issues of Down Beat
How to become a house musician [J. Spencer and K.
Sill] M. Stryker. pors *Down Beat* 54:54+ F '87
In Wynton's wake [new generation of players] J. Levenson.
Down Beat 54:6+ F '87
Nightclub nightmares: a musician's view [New York
City jazz scene] J. Forrester. *Down Beat* 54:52-3 My
'87
Profile. See issues of Down Beat
Young musicians today more talented: Dizzy says. *Jet*
71:17 Mr 2 '87
Photographs and photography
Milt Hinton at Parsons. P. Karmel. il *Art Am* 75:140
Ja '87
Jealousy
See also
Envy
Possessiveness (Psychology)
How to understand and handle jealousy and envy. il
Glamour 85:99 My '87
Jealousy with dignity. V. Klinkenborg. il *Esquire* 107:33-4
Ja '87
Slaying the green-eyed monster. A. Grice. il *Essence*
17:56-8+ F '87
Jean de Florette [film] See Motion picture reviews—Single
works
Jean-Louis
Jean-Louis. il por *People Wkly* 27:76 F 9 '87
Jean Patou (Firm)
Affordable luxury [P. Weisenfeld's marketing of Joy
perfume] R. Koselka. il por *Forbes* 139:164 My 4
'87
Jeanloz, Raymond
(jt. auth) See Knittle, Elise, and Jeanloz, Raymond
Jeanneret-Gris, Charles Édouard *See* Le Corbusier, 1887-
1965

Jeans (Clothing)
See also
Gap, Inc.
Levi Strauss & Co.
VF Corp.
Back to basic blues [women's jeans] M. Morris. il *Work
Woman* 12:55-6 Je '87
BlueJean-Luc Godard. H. A. Rodchenko. il *Film
Comment* 23:2+ N/D '87
Jeans! Rosie Vela model-turned-singer lives in them.
J. Powell. il pors *Glamour* 85:244-9 F '87
Jeantot, Philippe
about
King of the seven seas. E. M. Swift. il por *Sports Illus*
66:74-5 My 18 '87
Marathon man. P. Whittell. il pors *Mot Boat Sail*
160:56-9+ Jl '87
Jedicke, Peter
(jt. auth) See Levy, David H., 1948-, and Jedicke, Peter
Jeep automobiles
Jeep chic shifts into high. M. Smilgis. il *Time* 130:130
O 26 '87
Testing
AMC/Jeep Cherokee Limited. M. Brockman. il *Mot Trend*
39:99+ Jl '87
Jeep Cherokee. W. Hampton. il *Ctry J* 14:69-71 Ja
'87
Jeep Wagoneer Limited. A. St. Antoine. il *Car Driv*
33:125-6 Jl '87
Pick of the pickups—how much truck do you need?
[Ford F-150, Jeep Comanche, Dodge Dakota LE, and
Chevrolet Cheyenne 1500] J. Keebler. il *Pop Sci*
230:26-8+ Je '87
Road tests of pickup trucks [Dodge Dakota, Chevrolet
S-10, Ford Ranger, and Jeep Comanche] il *Consum
Rep* 52:344-51 Je '87
Son of CJ [Wrangler] J. Keebler. il *Pop Sci* 230:36+
Ja '87
Wrangler revisited. T. Opre. il *Outdoor Life* 180:34+
D '87
Jefferies, Boyd L.
about
Jefferies's fall worries more than insiders. il por *Fortune*
115:8 Ap 13 '87
Nabbing the stealth broker. B. Powell and C. Friday.
il por *Newsweek* 109:48 Mr 30 '87
Serving his clients all too well. S. Koepp. il por *Time*
129:52 Mr 30 '87
When Boyd Jefferies talks, all of Wall Street will be
listening. C. Farrell and others. il por *Bus Week* p37
Ap 6 '87
Jefferies Group Inc.
Jefferies's fall worries more than insiders. il por *Fortune*
115:8 Ap 13 '87
Nabbing the stealth broker [B. Jefferies charged] B. Powell
and C. Friday. il por *Newsweek* 109:48 Mr 30 '87
Serving his clients all too well [criminal charges against
B. Jefferies] S. Koepp. il por *Time* 129:52 Mr 30
'87
They're not giving Jefferies the cold shoulder anymore.
G. G. Marcial. il *Bus Week* p112 O 19 '87
When Boyd Jefferies talks, all of Wall Street will be
listening. C. Farrell and others. il por *Bus Week* p37
Ap 6 '87
Jeffers, Susan
Change what you can change [excerpt from Feel the
fear and do it anyway] *Redbook* 168:82-3+ F '87
Cheer up! Happiness is something anyone can find.
Redbook 169:160-1+ S '87
How to make a no-lose decision. *McCalls* 114:53-4 Ja
'87
Jefferson, Isaac, 1775-1853
about
Isaac Jefferson: the slave who remembered. B. McGinty.
il por *Am Hist Illus* 21:32-3 F '87
Jefferson, Thomas, 1743-1826
about
1787. *Am Herit* 38:30 D '87
Isaac Jefferson: the slave who remembered. B. McGinty.
il por *Am Hist Illus* 21:32-3 F '87
Jefferson's descendant becomes a living memorial. J.
Sanderson. il por *People Wkly* 27:80-1 Ja 26 '87
Homes
In Mr. Jefferson's garden. P. L. Hudson. il por *Americana*
14:50-5 Ja/F '87
Thomas Jefferson, gardener. N. Bubel. il *Ctry J* 14:11-13
Ap '87
Religion
We, the theologians. L. W. Gibbs. pors *Christ Today*
31:29-31 D 11 '87

Jefferson County (Ky.)
Education
A proposed incentive system for Jefferson County teachers [bonus point system] P. C. Schlechty and D. W. Ingwerson. il *Phi Delta Kappan* 68:585-90 Ap '87
Jefferson Smurfit Group Ltd.
An Irishman feasts on American trees [M. Smurfit] K. Labich. il por *Fortune* 116:62-4+ Jl 20 '87
Jefferson Starship (Musical group)
See also
Starship (Musical group)
Jeffrey Amherst Bookshop (Amherst, Mass.) See Booksellers and bookselling—Massachusetts
Jeffreys, Stephen
about
Hard times [drama] Reviews
New Yorker 63:69-70 Jl 20 '87. M. Kramer
Jeffries, Andrew D., and others
Gravitational wave observatories. il *Sci Am* 256:50-6+ Je '87
Letters [discussion of June 1987 article, Gravitational wave observatories] *Sci Am* 257:8-9 D '87
Jeffries, John Patrick
The master trailbuilder of Lake Tahoe. il por map *Sierra* 72:79-82 Jl/Ag '87
Jehovah's Witnesses
The right to shun [upheld by appeals court in San Francisco] *Time* 129:57 Je 29 '87
Witness stand [community objection to proposed Watchtower Society residential building in Brooklyn Heights] P. Tyre. il *N Y* 20:14-15 Mr 16 '87
Jelinek, Robert
What makes top managers different? *Work Woman* 12:109 My '87
Jellinek, George, 1919-
The Finnish line [interview with J. Hynninen] il pors *Opera News* 51:32-3 Ja 31 '87
The gold watch. il *N Y Times Mag* p42 Je 28 '87
Jelly, jam, etc.
See also
Fruit butter
J. M. Smucker Co.
Sorrell Ridge (Firm)
Low-sugar jams. A. Hirsch. il *Rodale's Org Gard* 34:46+ Je '87
Marmalade [cover story] O. Woodier. il *Americana* 14:46-9+ Ja/F '87
Preserving persimmons. il *Sunset* 179:168+ O '87
Why bother with ornamental plums? Great jam. il *Sunset* 178:194+ Je '87
Wild jams and jellies. C. Fergus. il *Ctry J* 14:56-9 Ag '87
Jellyfish
Jellyfish aren't out to get us [stings] S. Brownlee. il *Discover* 8:42-3+ Ag '87
Photographs and photography
Une liaison dangereuse [juvenile jacks in jellyfish tentacles] C. Newbert. il *Nat Hist* 96:88-9 S '87
Jemez Mountains (N.M.)
Cutting through a sacred forest [Ojo power line] D. Gibson. il *Sierra* 72:135-6 Ja/F '87
Jemison, Mae C.
about
'Be your own role model': 1st black woman astronaut. por *Jet* 72:22 Ag 17 '87
L.A. doctor named first black female astronaut. il por *Jet* 72:5 Je 22 '87
Space is her destination. il pors *Ebony* 42:93-5+ O '87
Jencks, Charles, 1939-
Architecture: Michael Graves. il por *Archit Dig* 44:138-45+ My '87
That Palladian feeling. il *House Gard* 159:160-5+ Je '87
Jencks, Harlan W.
Defending China in 1987. bibl f *Curr Hist* 86:266-9+ S '87
Jenkins, Bonnie
about
Faces of middle class America: Bonnie Jenkins is single and living in Washington D.C. il pors *Ebony* 42:146+ Ag '87
Jenkins, Brian Michael
The future course of international terrorism. il por *Futurist* 21:8-13 Jl/Ag '87
Jenkins, Ferguson, 1943-
about
The case for the defence [excerpt from Greenspan] E. L. Greenspan and G. Jonas. il pors *Macleans* 100:48-50+ O 19 '87
Ex-pitcher Jenkins named to Canadian Hall of Fame. por *Jet* 71:46 F 23 '87

Jenkins, Geraint H.
Modern Wales. il *Hist Today* 37:49-53 F '87
Jenkins, John A.
Battling a billion-dollar debt [cover story] il *N Y Times Mag* p24-9+ S 27 '87
Jenkins, John P.
about
John Jenkins is new House bill operations chief. il por *Jet* 72:4 Ag 3 '87
Jenkins, Nancy Harmon
A Christmas feast. il *N Y Times Mag* p95-6 D 13 '87
Salute to summer's end. il *N Y Times Mag* p43-4 Ag 23 '87
Jenkins, Paulie
about
Lighting to sculpt shadows. C. Eller. il *Theatre Crafts* 21:26-7+ Mr '87
Jenkins, Peter
about
New sport: go climb a tree. M. Vogel. il por *Natl Wildl* 25:36 Je/Jl '87
Jenkins, Ron
Use of X-ray methods for the study of chemical composition. *Science* 235 pt2:G169+ F 27 '87
Jenkins, Simon, 1943-
Did the Marshall Plan work too well? il *U S News World Rep* 102:13 Je 8 '87
First you slim your fat cats. il *U S News World Rep* 103:62 N 9 '87
Why sanctions are a failure. il *U S News World Rep* 103:40 S 21 '87
Jenkins, Steven
about
On display. *New Yorker* 63:37-8 D 7 '87
Jenkins, Tony
One last chance for the contras. il *Nation* 244:638-40 My 16 '87
Jenkinson, Edward B.
The significance of the decision in 'Scopes II'. bibl f *Phi Delta Kappan* 68:445-50 F '87
Jenks, David
about
David Jenks. D. C. Hines. il pors *Am Artist* 51:54-9+ S '87
Jenks, Tom
about
Where's Papa? B. P. Solomon. *New Repub* 196:30-4 Mr 9 '87
Jenks (Okla.)
Medical care
Old-timey medicine [family doctor D. Duncan] il por *South Living* 22:146 Mr '87
Jenness, David
(jt. auth) See Jurnovoy, Joyce, and Jenness, David
Jenney, Neil, 1945-
about
The good, the bad, and the ugly. K. Larson. *N Y* 20:64-5 Ap 20 '87
Landscapes of threatened beauty. K. Larson. il *Archit Dig* 44:90+ N '87
Neil Jenney at Barbara Mathes. P. Derfner. il *Art Am* 75:178-9 S '87
Jennings, Gary
Old and novel. il *N Y Times Mag* p16+ N 29 '87
Writing the un-historical novel. il *Writer* 100:7-10+ S '87
Jennings, Greg Y.
Guadalupe. il *Oceans* 20:40-5+ S/O '87
Jennings, John F.
The Sputnik of the eighties. bibl f il *Phi Delta Kappan* 69:104-9 O '87
Jennings, Peter, 1938-
about
The most trusted men in America. C. Kramer. il pors *McCalls* 114:128+ Jl '87
Up from 'Club Thirteen': the rise and rise of Peter Jennings. D. Blum. il pors *N Y* 20:50-6 N 30 '87
Jennings (La.)
Politics and government
First black mayor serves as head of Jennings, La. [W. D. Rochelle] *Jet* 72:9 Mr 30 '87
Jenny Lind Island (N.W.T.)
See also
Birds—Jenny Lind Island (N.W.T.)
Jensen, Bill, 1945-
about
Treading watercolors. J. Perl. il *Vogue* 177:74 Ap '87
Jensen, Christopher
The All-American Soap Box Derby. il *Car Driv* 33:153-4+ D '87

Jensen, Laura, 1948-
Chimes [poem] *New Yorker* 63:46 D 28 '87
Jensen, Michael C.
The takeover controversy [address, March 17, 1987] *Vital Speeches Day* 53:426-9 My 1 '87
Jensen, Oliver (Oliver Ormerod), 1914-
The high summer of Alice Austen. il pors *House Gard* 159:94-9+ Ag '87
Jepson, Robert S., Jr.
about
Buying companies the old-fashioned way. C. Siler. il por *Forbes* 140 Sp Issue:357+ O 26 '87
Jepson Corporation
Buying companies the old-fashioned way [R. S. Jepson] C. Siler. il por *Forbes* 140 Sp Issue:357+ O 26 '87
Jerez (Spain)
Foods and finos of Spain. T. Lydecker. il *Travel Holiday* 167:16+ F '87
Jerker [drama] See Chesley, Robert, 1943-
Jerome, Jim
Hero of the heartland. il pors *Life* 10:102-4 O '87
Jeronimo, John M. Maudlin- *See* Maudlin-Jeronimo, John M.
Jersey City (N.J.)
Politics and government
Boss [F. Hague, mayor and political boss] *New Yorker* 63:22-4 Je 15 '87
Jersey Devil (Firm)
In Virginia: homes with gusto. T. Brewster. il por *Time* 129:15+ Ap 27 '87
Jerusalem
Antiquities
Mystery of the buried amulet [G. Barkay discovers ancient biblical manuscripts] C. Safran. il *Read Dig* 130:95-9 Je '87
Description
This year in Jerusalem. J. G. Dunne. il *Esquire* 108:237-40+ D '87
History
Latin Kingdom, 1099-1244
Saladin's triumph over the crusader states: the Battle of Hattin, 1187 [cover story] N. Housley. bibl il map *Hist Today* 37:17-23 Jl '87
Hospitals
Curing cancer in Jerusalem [bone marrow transplantation for leukemia patients; work of Shimon Slavin at Hadassah Hospital] C. SerVaas. il *Saturday Evening Post* 259:54-9 Jl/Ag '87
Religious institutions and affairs
Rampaging rabbis [friction between secular and ultra Orthodox Jews] A. Rabinovich. *New Repub* 197:24-6 S 14-21 '87
Jerusalem artichoke pickles See Pickles and relishes
Jerusalem artichokes
Easy to grow and use (once you know how): Jerusalem artichokes. il *Sunset* 178:176 F '87
Jerusalem cherry
Jerusalem-cherries for holiday color; grow your own. R. Webber. il *Flower Gard* 31:28 O/N '87
Jerusalem International Book Fair *See* Book fairs
Jess
about
Songs of innocence. M. Auping. il *Art Am* 75:118-27+ Ja '87
Jessup, Robert
about
Robert Jessup. J. Mackin. il por *Am Artist* 51:58-63+ Ag '87
Jesuits
Malachi Martin's The Jesuits: an appraisal. G. G. Higgins. il *America* 156:229-31+ Mr 21 '87
Malachi's 'believe it or not' [views of M. Martin] *America* 156:145-6 F 21 '87
Of many things. G. G. Seibert. *America* 157:346 N 14 '87
Sweeney agonistes [case of T. Sweeney] *America* 156:413-14 My 23 '87
Sweeney responds [discussion of May 23, 1987 article, Sweeney agonistes] *America* 157:22 Jl 4-11 '87
Missions
Assassination in South Lebanon [French Jesuit A. Masse] H. Madelin. *America* 157:397-8 N 28 '87
Paraguay's mission towns. B. Wrenn. il *Travel Holiday* 168:8+ O '87
Jesus Christ
See also
Sacred Heart devotion
about
Believe it or not:
Faith in Jesus. G. McCauley. *America* 156:282 Ap 4 '87

This is God's Chosen One. M. K. Hellwig. *America* 156:inside back cover Ja 3-10 '87
Apparitions and miracles
The appearances of the risen Jesus [cover story] G. O'Collins. il *America* 156:317-20 Ap 18 '87
Maybe it's not the freezer of Turin, but Arlene Gardner says she sees Jesus on her G.E. il por *People Wkly* 27:80 Je 29 '87
A modern miracle [claims that the face of Jesus appears on A. Garner's freezer] il *Esquire* 108:159-61 D '87
Art
Photographs and photography
Photo-gloss: on Paul Strand's "Cristo with thorns". J. Masheck. bibl f il *Art Am* 75:104-13 Mr '87
Baptism
Interconnected mysteries. P. J. Ryan. *America* 157:511 D 26 '87
Crucifixion
God on the gallows [excerpt from The cross of Christ] J. R. W. Stott. il por *Christ Today* 31:28-30 Ja 16 '87
More than a symbol. L. Morris. il por *Christ Today* 31:23-5 Ap 17 '87
Why Jesus was dying to save you [interview with J. Shea] il *U S Cathol* 52:18-25 Mr '87
Art
Broken continuities: Night and White crucifixion [cover story] K. A. Plank. il por *Christ Century* 104:963-6 N 4 '87
Divinity
Scholars say historical evidence buttresses the claims of Scripture [Jesus Christ: God and man conference] W. A. Durbin, Jr. il *Christ Today* 31:55+ Ja 16 '87
Family
Graced tensions. P. J. Ryan. *America* 157:487 D 19 '87
Humanity
Scholars say historical evidence buttresses the claims of Scripture [Jesus Christ: God and man conference] W. A. Durbin, Jr. il *Christ Today* 31:55+ Ja 16 '87
Name
Solemn reverence. P. J. Ryan. *America* 157:487 D 19 '87
Nativity
See also
Epiphany
Advent meditation:
'Messy Christmas'. J. R. Wimmer. *Christ Century* 104:1132-3 D 16 '87
Birth of a king. P. J. Ryan. il *America* 157:463 D 12 '87
Christmas meditation:
The blessing and the burden. P. P. Allen. *Christ Century* 104:1169-70 D 23-30 '87
Come to Bethlehem and see! H. Fehren. *U S Cathol* 52:36-8 D '87
Interpreting Christmas. G. O'Collins. il *America* 157:470-1 D 19 '87
Parables
Lenten meditation:
The preacher and the panhandlers [parable of the Pharisee and the tax collector] J. Killinger. il *Christ Century* 104:301-2 Ap 1 '87
Passion
A meditation after Easter. D. K. Mano. *Natl Rev* 39:60 Ap 24 '87
Your King comes. M. K. Hellwig. *America* 156:inside back cover Ap 4 '87
Priesthood
Great light. M. K. Hellwig. *America* 156:inside back cover Ja 17 '87
A royal priesthood. M. K. Hellwig. *America* 156:inside back cover My 9 '87
Resurrection and Ascension
The appearances of the risen Jesus [cover story] G. O'Collins. il *America* 156:317-20 Ap 18 '87
Emmaus and back. M. K. Hellwig. *America* 156:inside back cover Ap 25 '87
Gateway to life. M. K. Hellwig. *America* 156:inside back cover My 2 '87
He has ascended. M. K. Hellwig. il *America* 156:inside back cover My 23 '87
A living hope. M. K. Hellwig. *America* 156:inside back cover Ap 18 '87
More than a symbol. L. Morris. il por *Christ Today* 31:23-5 Ap 17 '87
Where Christ is. M. K. Hellwig. *America* 156:inside back cover Ap 11 '87
Transfiguration
Jesus transfigured. M. K. Hellwig. *America* 156:inside back cover Mr 7 '87

Jesus Christ the King, Feast of
'Lovely in eyes not his'. G. G. Seibert. *America* 157:367 N 14 '87
Jesus movement
See also
Jews for Jesus movement
Jet (Periodical)
Ticker tape scholars selected for '87-'88 [students having financial trouble] il *Jet* 72:23-4 Jl 27 '87
Jet airplane engines *See* Airplane engines, Jet
Jet airplanes *See* Airplanes, Jet
Jet America Airlines Inc.
Alaska Air Group breaks up Jet America. *Aviat Week Space Technol* 127:34 Ag 24 '87
Jet Aviation (Firm)
Drive to reduce travel costs benefits flight service firms. il *Aviat Week Space Technol* 127:92-4 S 28 '87
Jet boat engines *See* Motor boat engines
Jet boats
Testing
Get set for jets. B. McKeown. il *Outdoor Life* 179:38+ Je '87
Jet Capital Corporation
Lorenzo turns to terra firma. por *Bus Week* p34 S 7 '87
Jet fuel *See* Airplane engines, Jet—Fuel
Jet helicopters *See* Helicopters, Jet
Jet lag
Hamster jet lag: running it off [research by Nicholas Mrosovsky and Peggy A. Salmon] B. Bower. *Sci News* 132:358 D 5 '87
Lag time [participation in study testing effectiveness of triazolam in treating jet lag] K. Lautman. il *Omni* 9:16 Ja '87
Traveling through time [benefits of outdoor light] M. DuHamel. il *Women's Sports Fitness* 9:17 D '87
You don't have to give in to jet lag. J. O. Hamilton. il *Bus Week* p126 O 26 '87
Jet propulsion
See also
Guided missiles—Propulsion systems
Jet Propulsion Laboratory (U.S.)
Down to earth. M. Beauchamp. il *Forbes* 139:74+ Je 15 '87
JPL alters Voyager 2 controls to improve imaging of Neptune. *Aviat Week Space Technol* 127:131 Ag 10 '87
Probing space by camera: the development of image processing at NASA's Jet Propulsion Laboratory. K. Sheldon. il *Byte* 12:143-8 Mr '87
Jet skis and skiing
Jet Ski's big brother [Kawasaki 650] J. Skorupa. il *Pop Mech* 164:12 Jl '87
Yamaha's new water sleds. T. H. Cole. il *Pop Mech* 164:40 Mr '87
Jet stream
All about the jet stream. T. Schlatter. il *Weatherwise* 40:50-2 F '87
Jet trainers *See* Airplanes, Training
Jet transports *See* Airplanes, Jet
Jetfoils *See* Hydrofoils
Jethro Tull (Musical group)
Tull test: resorting to knavery. J. Rosenbluth. il por *Roll Stone* p16 N 19 '87
Jets (Musical group)
The Jets take off! J. A. Baggett. il *Sch Update* 120:12-13 O 16 '87
Jetstream International Airlines
Suburban turbine. M. Phelps. il *Flying* 114:40-5 My '87
Jett, Joan
about
Trading places. S. Pond. il pors *Roll Stone* p25-6 Ja 15 '87
Jetties
Standoff at Oregon Inlet [Army Corps of Engineers proposal to build jetties at Cape Hatteras, N.C.] L. S. Bates. il *Oceans* 20:5-6 Mr/Ap '87
Jevnikar, Jana
Marketing art: the basics. *Am Artist* 51:68-9 Jl '87
The Jew of Malta [drama] *See* Marlow, Christopher, 1564-1593
Jewel Evans Family Foods
Flour power: mixing pleasure with business. H. G. Miller. il por *Saturday Evening Post* 259:48-9+ Ap '87
Jewelers
See also
Clodagh, Ross & Williams Inc.
Hammerman Bros. Inc.
Moty, Eleanor
National Jewelers Exchange

Tiffany & Co.
Town & Country Jewelry Mfg. Co.
Twycross, Stephen, ca. 1745-ca. 1822
Una Donna, Ltd.
Jeweled artistry. R. La Ferla. il *N Y Times Mag* p86-7 N 22 '87
Marketing
See Jewelry—Marketing
The jeweller's shop [film] *See* Motion picture reviews—Single works
Jewelry
See also
Bracelets
Brooches
Goldsmithing
Jewelers
Necklaces
Another Papp sparkles [designer T. Papp] S. Mieses. il por *N Y* 20:14 Ja 5 '87
Artful jewels [designs of T. Binns] il por *Vogue* 177:280 Ap '87
Bauble, bauble and toil give two designing sisters the magic touch [creations of K. and L. Mandelbaum] K. Hubbard. il pors *People Wkly* 27:153 Je 8 '87
Baubling along . . . rage for rocks. J. Wilson. il *Harpers Bazaar* 120:142+ O '87
Clearly different [jewelry designed by T. Chow] il *Vogue* 177:334-7 Ag '87
Designing woman [A. Kramer] I. Ross. il por *N Y* 20:32 O 12 '87
Everything the Duchess of Windsor touched has turned to gold (plated), thanks to Carolee Friedlander. il por *People Wkly* 27:137 My 11 '87
Fashion jewelry flash. il *Teen* 31:94-5 N '87
The finishing touches. L. Washer. il *Work Woman* 12:108 D '87
Jewelry designer Robert Lee Morris sinks his claws into heavy metal. B. Johnson. il por *People Wkly* 27:121-2+ My 11 '87
Knocking off a royal jewel collection [costume copies of Duchess of Windsor's jewels] il *Newsweek* 110:59 S 14 '87
Tone Vigeland. J. Evans. il por *Am Craft* 47:24-31 Ap/My '87
What's precious now? [artist-designed jewelry] A. K. Leopold. il *Vogue* 177:464-5+ O '87
Collectors and collecting
Rings on his fingers [men's estate jewelry] S. Berkman. il *Esquire* 107:15-16 F '87
When secondhand is first choice [estate jewelry] B. Brophy. il *U S News World Rep* 102:57-9 My 4 '87
Exhibitions
A glimpse of beauty past and present [Eye of the beholder exhibition at the Royal Ontario Museum] il *Macleans* 100:50-1 Ap 13 '87
Romancing the stone [Modern jewelry: New design at San Francisco Museum of Modern Art] K. Simmons. il *Horizon* 30:37-8 D '87
Marketing
Jewelers woo the working woman. S. Caminiti. il *Fortune* 115:71-2 Je 8 '87
Prices
Selling your heirloom gems. J. H. Dobrzynski. il *Bus Week* p141 My 4 '87
Theft
Jewelry valued at $25,000 is stolen from Alice Bond. por *Jet* 72:36 Ag 10 '87
Jewelry, African
Designs on our cultural legacy [designs by Heru Ankh-Ra Semahj] K. J. Halliburton. il por *Essence* 18:42 N '87
Jewelry, British
See also
Crown jewels
Federal Bostonians and their London jeweler, Stephen Twycross. M. G. Fales. bibl f il *Antiques* 131:642-9 Mr '87
Jewels of Windsor [Duchess of Windsor's jewels] C. Vogel. il pors *N Y Times Mag* p34-6+ F 8 '87
Knocking off a royal jewel collection [costume copies of Duchess of Windsor's jewels] il *Newsweek* 110:59 S 14 '87
Mr. Peepers: more and more and more—the Windsor jewels. il pors *N Y* 20:27-8 Mr 30 '87
A multifaceted, rock-solid romance [Duchess of Windsor's jewels] il por *Newsweek* 109:83 Mr 30 '87
Of Vincent and Eanum Pig [auctions of van Gogh's Sunflowers and the Duchess of Windsor's jewelry] R. Hughes. il *Time* 129:80-1 Ap 13 '87

Jewelry, British—*cont.*
Queen of diamonds [E. Taylor's purchase at auction of the Duchess of Windsor's gems] B. Darrach. il pors *People Wkly* 27:28-33 Ap 27 '87

Jewelry, French

Exhibitions
The jewelry of René Lalique [exhibition at Goldsmiths' Hall, London] G. C. Munn. il *Antiques* 131:1288-91 Je '87

Jewelry, Italian

Exhibitions
Goldsmiths of Veneto [traveling exhibition entitled Italian jewelers from the Veneto region] A. Fisch. il *Am Craft* 47:36-41+ D '87/Ja '88

Jewelry auctions *See* Auctions
Jewelry boxes, cases, etc.
2 jewelry cases. il *Workbench* 43:39-44 N/D '87
Jewelry making *See* Jewelry
Jewelry smuggling *See* Smuggling
Jewels *See* Jewelry
Jewels, Crown *See* Crown jewels
Jewett, Robert
Zeal without understanding: reflections on Rambo and Oliver North. il *Christ Century* 104:753-6 S 9-16 '87

Jewish-Arab relations
See also
Israel-Arab Wars, 1967-
Palestine Center for Non-Violent Resistance
Arab walls, reflecting change; tr. by Yael Lotan. A. Shammas. *Harpers* 275:30+ N '87
Arabs vs. settlers in the Gaza Strip. A. Hielscher. *World Press Rev* 34:56-7 Ja '87
Beyond zero-sum thinking in the Arab-Israeli struggle. R. A. Eckardt. il *Christ Century* 104:1143-5 D 16 '87
Invisible Palestinians: ideology and reality in Israel. R. R. Ruether. il *Christ Century* 104:587-91 Jl 1-8 '87
Israel's angry peace [cover story; special section; with editorial comment by Kevin Doyle] il map *Macleans* 100:2, 22-8+ Je 1 '87
Letter from Israel. A. Kenan. *Nation* 245:581 N 21 '87
Middle East oasis of hope [Jewish and Arab families run the School for Peace in Neve Shalom, Israel] L. Press. *Macleans* 100:8 F 16 '87
My neighbor, my enemy. T. L. Friedman. il *N Y Times Mag* p14-19+ Jl 5 '87
The strange bedfellows [peace plan conceived by Israeli M. Amirav and Arab S. Nuseibeh] M. J. Kubic. il por *Newsweek* 110:42 O 5 '87
Water from the rock [Jewish-Arab cooperation at the School for Peace in Neve Shalom, Israel] *Commonweal* 114:198 Ap 10 '87

Jewish-Arab Wars, 1967- *See* Israel-Arab Wars, 1967-
Jewish baseball players *See* Baseball players
Jewish children
Barbie and the children [roundup of the children of Izieu, France] *Newsweek* 109:44 Je 15 '87
The children of Izieu. il *N Y Times Mag* p26-7 Ag 2 '87

Jewish Christians *See* Converts from Judaism
Jewish Community Museum (San Francisco, Calif.)
Raising the harvest home [Sukkah] il *Archit Rec* 175:100-3 F '87

Jewish converts *See* Converts, Jewish
Jewish cooking *See* Cooking, Jewish
Jewish daily forward
Looking back to the 'Forward'. G. Tyler. il *New Leader* 70:9-10 Ap 20 '87

Jewish dance *See* Dance, Jewish
Jewish Family Services (Baltimore, Md.)
Rose finally unpacked her belongings [Wallace H. Campbell & Co. and Jewish Family Services team up to run high-rise apartment for the elderly in Baltimore, Md.] J. B. Kurland and G. E. J. Lipsitz. il *Aging* no355:6-9 '87

Jewish-gentile marriage *See* Interfaith marriage
Jewish Historical Museum (Amsterdam, Netherlands)
Preserving the treasures of Jewish culture. R. Z. Chesnoff. il *U S News World Rep* 102:76-7 My 11 '87

Jewish identity *See* Jews—Identity
Jewish law
Liberalism & the Hebrew prophets. J. S. Auerbach. *Commentary* 84:58-60 Ag '87

Jewish literature (American) *See* American literature—Jewish authors
Jewish museums
See also
Jewish Community Museum (San Francisco, Calif.)
Jewish Historical Museum (Amsterdam, Netherlands)

Jewish National Fund
Talk about gelt trips! With only a tin cup, Sylvia Orzoff, 77, has begged $2 million for charity. il por *People Wkly* 27:91 Je 1 '87

Jewish newspapers
See also
Jewish daily forward
Jewish sects
See also
Hasidism
Jewish studies
Ethnic studies: the coming crisis: the case of "Jewish studies". J. Neusner. il *Change* 19:8-10 Jl/Ag '87
Jewish women
See also
National Council of Jewish Women
Going public as a Jew. L. C. Pogrebin. *Ms* 16:76-7+ Jl/Ag '87

Anecdotes, facetiae, satire, etc.
The perils of the good life [Jewish American princess jokes] F. Bruning. por *Macleans* 100:13 O 5 '87

Jewison, Norman

about
Moonstruck [film] Reviews
Macleans 100:65 D 14 '87. L. O'Toole
Newsweek 110:69 D 21 '87. D. Ansen

Jews
See also
Anti-Semitism
Hasidism

Bibliography
Books on Jews and Judaism. J. Harris. *America* 157:163-4+ S 26 '87

Converts to Christianity
See Converts from Judaism

Emigration from the Soviet Union
See Immigration and emigration—Soviet Union

History
See also
Holocaust, Jewish (1939-1945)
Pagans, Christians, Jews. C. Raphael. *Commentary* 84:39-44 O '87
PW interviews [book by P. Johnson] M. Field. il por *Publ Wkly* 231:50-1 My 1 '87

Identity
Israel's new conversion crisis [case of S. Miller] R. N. Ostling. il por *Time* 129:75 Ja 19 '87

Intellectual life
The New York (Jewish) intellectuals. R. R. Wisse. *Commentary* 84:28-38 N '87

Nationalism
See also
Jews—Identity
Zionism

Persecutions
See also
Holocaust, Jewish (1939-1945)

Political activities
Modern ideologies & the Jews. A. Besançon. *Commentary* 83:41-5 Mr '87

Psychology
See also
Jews—Identity
An open door [Pesach Tikvah, mental health center serving the Orthodox community in Williamsburg, Brooklyn] J. Meer. *Psychol Today* 21:17 Ap '87

Religion
See Judaism

Rites and ceremonies
See also
Hanukkah
Passover
Sukkoth

Austria

History
Austria reviews claims on looted art [artworks confiscated under the Nazi regime] A. Decker. *Art News* 86:37-8 F '87
A slow process [claims proceedings for Austrian-held artworks confiscated under the Nazi regime] A. Decker. il *Art News* 86:71-2 O '87

Ethiopia
Escape to uncertainty [Ethiopian Jews who have settled in Israel] N. Morris. il *Macleans* 100:6-7 Je 22 '87
The humanitarian side of the Reagan administration: the rescue of Ethiopian Jews. M. Bard and H. M. Lenhoff. *Humanist* 47:25-6+ N/D '87
Secret exodus: the story of Operation Moses [excerpt] C. Safran. il *Read Dig* 130:96-104+ Ja '87

Jews—*cont.*

Europe
History

Modern ideologies & the Jews. A. Besançon. *Commentary* 83:41-5 Mr '87

Germany

Ernst Lissauer and the Hymn of hate [WWI anti-English propaganda poem by German-Jewish poet] C. C. Aronsfeld. bibl il por *Hist Today* 37:48-50 D '87

Great Britain
History

East Enders recalled [Celebration of the Jewish East End] il *Hist Today* 37:61-2 My '87

Israel

Going home to Israel. I. Lederer-Gibel. *Christ Century* 104:162-4 F 18 '87

A house divided [secular vs. Orthodox Jews] T. A. Sancton. il *Time* 130:34-5 O 12 '87

Israel: a house divided? R. R. Wisse. *Commentary* 84:33-8 S '87

Letter to a new Israeli. R. R. Wisse. *Commentary* 83:44-9 Je '87

A light unto the nations? R. R. Wisse. *Commentary* 84:30-5 D '87

Rampaging rabbis [friction between secular and ultra Orthodox Jews in Jerusalem] A. Rabinovich. *New Repub* 197:24-6 S 14-21 '87

Italy
History

My mother's conversion. D. V. Segre. *Commentary* 83:27-37 F '87

Netherlands
History

The friends of Anne Frank [J. and M. Gies, couple who sheltered Frank family during the Holocaust] il pors *U S News World Rep* 102:77 My 11 '87

Letters from 'The Kingdom of Night' [E. Hillesum's diary, An interrupted life] L. S. Cunningham. il *Commonweal* 114:316-18 My 22 '87

See also
Zionism

Palestine

Poland

Poland's 'Jewish problem' [interview with M. Edelman] *Harpers* 275:21-2 Ag '87

Reviving Judaica—without Jews—in Poland. J. B. Miller. il *Christ Century* 104:916-17 O 21 '87
History

The curious case of Marek Edelman [last leader of the Warsaw Ghetto uprising remaining in Poland] L. S. Dawidowicz. *Commentary* 83:66-9 Mr '87

Poland's Jewish ghosts. R. R. Wisse. *Commentary* 83:25-33 Ja '87

Poles and Jews [discussion of January 1987 article, Poland's Jewish ghosts] R. R. Wisse. *Commentary* 83:2+ My '87

Poles and Jews [discussion of March 1987 article, The curious case of Marek Edelman] L. S. Dawidowicz. *Commentary* 84:2-4+ Ag '87
History—Historiography

When historians judge their own [historian N. Davies sues Stanford University over denial of professorship because of his views on Jews] J. Wiener. il *Nation* 245:584-6+ N 21 '87

Soviet Union

Among the refuseniks. W. Ruby. il *World Press Rev* 34:56 S '87

Between issues. *New Leader* 70:2 O 19 '87

'Exodus' in samizdat: still popular and still subversive. E. McDowell. il *N Y Times Book Rev* 92:13 Ap 26 '87

Freedom for a refusenik [interview with I. Begun] il por *Macleans* 100:6+ Ap 27 '87

Glasnost and the Jews. A. Hertzberg. il *N Y Rev Books* 34:20-3 O 22 '87

Gorbachev and the Jews. H. Anderson. il por *Newsweek* 109:34-5 Ap 13 '87

New deal for Soviet Jews? T. Jacoby. il *Newsweek* 110:8 N 2 '87

The systematic repression of Soviet Jews [address, September 28, 1986] R. Pilon. *Dep State Bull* 86:67-70 D '86

Testing *glasnost*: an exile visits his homeland [cover story] A. Goldfarb. il pors *N Y Times Mag* p46-9+ D 6 '87

Will *'glasnost'* reach the Jews? N. Levin. *Commonweal* 114:596-9 O 23 '87

Emigration

See Immigration and emigration—Soviet Union
Photographs and photography

The indomitable human spirit [work of B. Pfeffer] P. Gardner. il por *Art News* 86:13 Mr '87

Spain
History

Spain's returning Jews. C. C. Aronsfeld. bibl il *Hist Today* 37:38-43 Je '87

Turkey

The Istanbul synagogue massacre: an investigation. J. Miller. il *N Y Times Mag* p14-20+ Ja 4 '87

United States

Invoking America: a Gitche Gumee memoir [adaptation of address] H. Yglesias. il *N Y Times Book Rev* 92:1+ Jl 5 '87
History

Conservative Judaism [discussion of December 1986 article, The Judaism born in America] H. Singer. *Commentary* 83:6-8+ Ap '87

The Constitution [discussion of May 1987 article, Why blacks, women & Jews are not mentioned in the Constitution] R. A. Goldwin. *Commentary* 84:2+ O '87

The Constitution and the people left out: a study in original intent. R. A. Goldwin. *Current* 295:4-10 S '87

Why blacks, women & Jews are not mentioned in the Constitution. R. A. Goldwin. *Commentary* 83:28-33 My '87

Political activities

See also
American Israel Public Affairs Committee

Brothers with blood in their eyes [views of U.S. Jewish leaders on J. Pollard case] W. E. Smith. il *Time* 129:40 Mr 30 '87

Double identity [attachment of American Jews to Israel] *New Repub* 196:4 Ap 6 '87

Ethnic politics American style. P. Greene. *America* 157:28+ Jl 18-25 '87

Friends and enemies [march for Soviet Jewish emigration in Washington, D.C.] M. Walzer. *New Repub* 197:13-14 D 28 '87

Gorbachev opens the border for Jews—with good reason [trying to win support of U.S. Jews for relaxation of the Jackson-Vanik trade terms] J. Pearson. il *Bus Week* p28 Ap 20 '87

The kosher majority [Orthodoxy and political conservatism] D. Feder. *Natl Rev* 39:40+ Ap 10 '87

The Peres peace plan: battling extremism. J. M. Wall. *Christ Century* 104:931-2 O 28 '87

The spy who came between friends [J. Pollard case] M. Satchell. il por *U S News World Rep* 102:32-3 Mr 30 '87

Strains in the family [Pollard case sets off spat between U.S. Jews and Israel] M. Whitaker. il por *Newsweek* 109:32-4 Mr 30 '87

Jews and blacks

Black-Jewish coalition. J. Kaufman. *Cent Mag* 20:54-5+ N/D '87

Jews and Christians *See* Christianity and other religions
Jews and Protestants *See* Christianity and other religions
Jews for Jesus movement

Can Christians hand out gospel tracts in airports? [Supreme Court case involving Jews for Jesus at Los Angeles International Airport] B. Spring. il *Christ Today* 31:43-4 Ap 3 '87

Jews for Jesus ministers settle out of court [suit against UCLA for prohibiting distribution of religious literature on campus] B. Bird. il *Christ Today* 31:46 Mr 6 '87

Jews in art

The Scroll [R. Weisberg's drawing to be exhibited at Hebrew Union College] *New Yorker* 63:36-7 N 23 '87

Jews in literature
See also
American literature—Jewish authors
Holocaust, Jewish (1939-1945), in literature

Jews in motion pictures

Class clowns [W. Allen's Radio days and R. Townsend's Hollywood shuffle] A. White. il *Film Comment* 23:11-14 Mr/Ap '87

Jezek, Zdenek

In the aftermath of "target zero". il *World Health* p4-7 Ag/S '87

JFK International Airport *See* New York (N.Y.)—Airports

Jhabvala, Ruth Prawer

about

The teeming imagination of novelist Ruth Prawer Jhabvala is her window on a world she avoids. H. Shapiro. il pors *People Wkly* 28:48-50+ S 28 '87

When East meets West. L. Shapiro. il por *Newsweek* 110:62 Ag 24 '87

Jigs (Fishing) *See* Fishing lures, flies, etc.

Jigs (Tools)

Dialing for dowel joints [doweling jig] R. Capotosto. il *Pop Mech* 164:45 O '87

Finger joints . . . a nifty new jig. T. H. Jones. il *Pop Sci* 230:98-100 F '87

Guides, jigs and accessories that let you do more with your circular saw. R. J. DeCristoforo. il *Home Mech* 83:60-2+ Jl '87

Pictures locator. K. Oberrecht. il *Pop Mech* 164:150 O '87

Jigsaw puzzles

Competitions

Jigsaws don't puzzle a champ like Ohio's Donna Klett. il por *People Wkly* 28:137 S 14 '87

Jilk, Bruce A.

Designing schools for changing needs. *Educ Dig* 53:12-13 N '87

Jillette, Penn

See also

Penn & Teller

Jim Walter Corp.

Why Jim Walter is ripe for the picking [bid by Kohlberg Kravis Roberts & Co.] P. Engardio. il *Bus Week* p31+ Ag 3 '87

Jimenez, Joaquin J., and Yunis, Adel A.

Tumor cell rejection through terminal cell differentiation. bibl f il *Science* 238:1278-80 N 27 '87

Jimmy Carter National Historic Site

House bill proposes Carter Historic Site. *Natl Parks* 61:12-13 N/D '87

A presidential theme park in Plains? il *Newsweek* 110:42 O 19 '87

Jingles, Advertising *See* Advertising jingles

Jinks, Tobia

about

Judge drops case against mom who fed sons on train. *Jet* 72:24 S 14 '87

Miami mom jailed for feeding 'hungry' sons. il por *Jet* 72:55 S 7 '87

Jinzhang, Peng

Japan: the next superpower? *World Press Rev* 34:47 N '87

JMB Realty Trust

The Second City duo building a first-class colossus. J. N. Frank. il pors *Bus Week* p100 O 5 '87

Joaquin, Nick M.

Reflections on the potato. il *Courier* 40:14-15 My '87

Job absenteeism *See* Absenteeism

Job accidents *See* Industrial accidents

Job analysis

See also

Job descriptions

Job evaluation

Job applications

See also

Employment interviewing

Employment references

4-step plan to land a job long distance. M. M. Kennedy. il *Glamour* 85:158+ O '87

7 dos and don'ts for a winning résumé. M. M. Kennedy. il *Glamour* 85:130 Ag '87

Crying in your beer, eighties style [rejection letters] J. Sherman. *Work Woman* 12:27-8 My '87

A guide to job hunting. B. Nivens. il *Essence* 18:100 Ag '87

He has no truck with unemployment, so when Art Fosle needed a job, he didn't spin his wheels. il por *People Wkly* 27:64 My 11 '87

How to answer a want ad and make them want you. il *Glamour* 85:112 D '87

How to decide which job to take [excerpt from Getting to the right job] S. Cohen and P. Colina. il *Glamour* 85:132 Ag '87

How to write a winning résumé. B. Nivens. il *Essence* 18:114 N '87

Job hunting in the work jungle [cover story; special section] il *Work Woman* 12:95-7+ Ap '87

Job hunting? Let's go to the videotape. T. Segal. il *Bus Week* p114 Je 15 '87

Jobs for new college grads. P. Plawin. il *Changing Times* 41:43-6+ F '87

Looking for that first job. P. Plawin. *Changing Times* 41:78+ Ag '87

One little résumé—and how it grew. H. Rubin. *Work Woman* 12:100-2+ Ap '87

Pounding the pavement by computer. D. H. Dunn. il *Bus Week* p166 My 11 '87

The tales of four hunters. R. B. Stolley. il *Fortune* 115:31-4 Mr 2 '87

Toe stubbers for job hunters. P. Plawin. *Changing Times* 41:100-1 F '87

Video résumés: sharpening the competitive edge [dancers] E. Warshawski. il *Dance Mag* 61:40-1 Mr '87

Will smoking hinder you in a job search? il *Glamour* 85:110 D '87

Anecdotes, facetiae, satire, etc.

Almost Jeeves [hunting for a job as butler in the Hamptons] M. Kenyon. il *Gourmet* 47:64+ Jl '87

Ethical aspects

A tissue of lies. il *Fortune* 116:12 N 9 '87

Job aptitude tests *See* Aptitude tests

Job attendance

See also

Absenteeism

Flextime

Hours of labor

Job creating programs *See* Unemployment—Relief measures

Job descriptions

Bait and switch, corporate-style [excerpt from The human side of management] G. S. Odiorne. *Work Woman* 12:50+ My '87

Job discrimination *See* Discrimination in employment

Job diseases *See* Occupational health and safety

Job evaluation

How to make '87 your best year ever. il *Glamour* 85:80 Ja '87

Job hopping *See* Labor turnover

Job hunting *See* Job applications

Job interviews *See* Employment interviewing

Job mobility *See* Occupational mobility

Job performance appraisal *See* Employees—Rating; Women executives—Rating

Job performance standards *See* Performance standards

Job placement guidance *See* Vocational guidance

Job satisfaction

Career plateaus: how to handle the inevitable [interview with J. Bardwick] L. Mosedale. *Glamour* 85:218 F '87

Catch-28 [young women disillusioned in work could endanger future job opportunities for women] L. J. Nonkin. il *Work Woman* 12:118-20+ My '87

Five career ruts you can't afford. E. LaPlante. *Work Woman* 12:59 N '87

Managing nine critical career turning points [results of survey] J. Ciabattari. il *Work Woman* 12:87-90+ O '87

Second careers. S. Blotnick. il *Forbes* 139:150-1 F 9 '87

Job security

Job security: a healthy bonus [survey by Karl W. Kuhnert] M. Schanback. il *Psychol Today* 21:16 My '87

Program guarantees 100-percent job security. *Mon Labor Rev* 110:72-3 S '87

The UAW sees a smoother road at Ford. W. Zellner. il *Bus Week* p125+ S 14 '87

Job stress

Crossover dreams [black women in a white corporate world] A. Edwards. *Essence* 17:45+ Mr '87

A cure for stress? [business stress management programs] P. Wang. il *Newsweek* 110:64-5 O 12 '87

Dear Betty Harragan [burnout experienced by woman radio station manager] B. L. Harragan. il *Work Woman* 12:24+ Ag '87

Healthy stress: the energy boost. S. Horwitz. *Harpers Bazaar* 120:204+ Mr '87

Heart disease and job stress [study by Robert Karasek] il *USA Today (Periodical)* 115:5 F '87

I couldn't learn to use a computer at work. il *Good Housekeep* 204:28+ Je '87

The kind of stress managers know best. J. Ciabattari. il *Work Woman* 12:125-8+ S '87

Managing your way out of office stress. J. Ciabattari. il *Work Woman* 12:110-12 My '87

Stress hits black profs harder than whites, study. *Jet* 72:5 Mr 30 '87

Stress test [pilots] P. Garrison. il *Flying* 114:54-7 Je '87

Stressbusters. P. A. Jones. il *Black Enterp* 17:106 F '87

What happens when the boss is a baboon [study by Anthony Coelho] il *Discover* 8:12-13 Je '87

Job stress—*cont.*
When the balls come tumbling down [managing stress in junior tennis] J. E. Loehr. il *World Tennis* 35:14+ S '87
Job tenure *See* Labor turnover
Job titles *See* Job descriptions
Job training *See* Employees—Training; Unemployment—Relief measures; Vocational-technical education
Job transfers *See* Executives—Transfer; Women executives—Transfer
Jobin, Judith
Your good friends may be bad for you. il *Redbook* 168:108-9+ Mr '87
Jobs, Steven
about
Next from Steve Jobs. il por *U S News World Rep* 102:49 Ja 26 '87
Odyssey: John Sculley and the saga of the Macintosh (I) [excerpt from *Odyssey*] J. Sculley. il *Pers Comput* 11:182-5+ N '87
Odyssey: John Sculley and the saga of the Macintosh (II) [excerpt from *Odyssey*] J. Sculley. il *Pers Comput* 11:201-3+ D '87
Perot and Jobs: who's Next? M. Rogers. il pors *Newsweek* 109:48 F 9 '87
Ross Perot turns into an angel for Steve Jobs. K. M. Hafner. il pors *Bus Week* p32 F 9 '87
Sculley's lessons from inside Apple [excerpt from *Odyssey*] J. Sculley. il pors *Fortune* 116:108-11+ S 14 '87
Steven Jobs. K. M. Hafner. il por *Bus Week* Sp Issue:245 Ap 17 '87
Jobs *See* Employment; Occupations
Jockey International, Inc.
Meet the presidents: Donna Steigerwaldt. C. P. Andersen. il por *Good Housekeep* 205:64+ Ag '87
Jockeys
See also
Aragon, Vicky
Cordero, Angel
Custom Jockeys' Apparel (Firm)
Desormeaux, Kent
Krone, Julie
McCarron, Chris
Piggott, Lester, 1935-
Santos, Jose
Shoemaker, Willie, 1931-
Venezia, Mike
Jodice, Mimmo
about
Poetic reflection. S. Piperato. il por *Pop Photogr* 94:70-1 Ja '87
Joe Turner's come and gone [drama] *See* Wilson, August
Joel, Billy, 1949-
about
Billy Joel's Russian roadshow. M. R. Benson. il pors *Roll Stone* p16 S 24 '87
Joffe, Josef
Achtung: too much disarmament too fast. il map *U S News World Rep* 103:43 D 7 '87
Cruisin' for a bruisin'. *New Repub* 197:17-18 O 5 '87
Joffé, Roland
about
The mission [film] Reviews
USA Today (Periodical) il 115:94-5 Ja '87. K. R. Hey
Joffrey, Robert
about
In touch with tradition [cover story] R. Philp. il *Dance Mag* 61:HC4-HC5 D '87
Sacre: the Joffrey connection. R. Philp. il *Dance Mag* 61:49-51 N '87
Joffrey Ballet
Ashton and anniversaries [revival of La fille mal gardée] J. R. Acocella. il *Dance Mag* 61:56-9 Mr '87
Bringing back a debacle [reconstruction of Nijinsky's Le sacre du printemps] M. Duffy. il *Time* 130:97 N 16 '87
In touch with tradition [production of The Nutcracker; cover story] R. Philp. il *Dance Mag* 61:HC4-HC5 D '87
A legendary 'Rite' returns [Nijinsky's Le sacre du printemps] L. Shapiro. il *Newsweek* 110:109 N 16 '87
The Nijinsky legacy [Le sacre du printemps] L. A. Jacobs. il *New Leader* 70:22-3 N 30 '87
Re-riting spring. B. Howard. il *Theatre Crafts* 21:15 D '87
Reviews:
Performance of Clowns in Chicago. A. Barzel. *Dance Mag* 61:26+ N '87
Sacre: the Joffrey connection. R. Philp. il *Dance Mag* 61:49-51 N '87

Something wild [reconstruction of Nijinsky's Le sacre du printemps] L. Friedman. il *Vogue* 177:114 N '87
Speak, memory [reconstruction of Nijinsky's Le sacre du printemps] T. Tobias. il *N Y* 20:100 N 16 '87
Summerspace at Watch Hill [1962 and 1963] R. Philp. il *Dance Mag* 61:46-9 O '87
Jogging *See* Running
Johann Wanner (Firm)
A Swiss Christmas tree shop. L. Langseth-Christensen. il *Gourmet* 47:78-81+ D '87
Johannesburg (South Africa)
Newspapers
See also
Star (Johannesburg, South Africa: Newspaper)
Theater
Black actor stars in S. African 'Othello' [J. Kani] il por *Jet* 73:22 O 5 '87
Johannessen, O. M., and others
Ice-edge eddies in the Fram Strait marginal ice zone. bibl f il maps *Science* 236:427-9 Ap 24 '87
Johansen, Bruce E. (Bruce Elliott), 1950-
Readers take on one-paper town. il *Progressive* 51:16 Ap '87
SAC sergeant says no to spy flights. il por *Progressive* 51:12 O '87
Johansen, H. William
Coralline algae: pink plants of the seafloor. il *Sea Front* 33:438-43 N/D '87
Johansen, Karen
Teen to teen. See issues of 'Teen beginning March 1987 through December 1987
about
On a winning streak. il pors *Teen* 31:100-1 Ag '87
Sporting a winning look. il pors *Teen* 31:68-9 F '87
John, E. R., and others
Do 15 million cat neurons mediate the memory of a circle and a star? [discussion of September 12, 1986 article, Double-labeled metabolic maps of memory] *Science* 238:1586-8 D 11 '87
John, Elton
about
Elton John: The Troubadour, Los Angeles, August 25th-30th, 1970. D. Fricke. il pors *Roll Stone* p77+ Je 4 '87
John and the missus [film] *See* Motion picture reviews—Single works
John Blair & Company
The new order at Blair. J. F. Berry. il por *Channels* 7:53-6 Ap '87
Rosenfield to the rescue [J. H. Rosenfield] R. Buck. il por *Channels* 7:14 Jl/Ag '87
John Bull (British national symbol)
John Bull's family arises. P. Mellini and R. T. Matthews. bibl il *Hist Today* 37:17-23 My '87
John D. and Catherine T. MacArthur Foundation
MacArthur Foundation grants to combat deforestation. il *BioScience* 37:236 Mr '87
STSers win MacArthurs. *Sci News* 131:390 Je 20 '87
John F. Kennedy Center Honors *See* Kennedy Center Honors
John F. Kennedy International Airport *See* New York (N.Y.)—Airports
John F. Kennedy Space Center
Kennedy lightning program yielding data to increase safety in launches. il *Aviat Week Space Technol* 127:70-1 D 7 '87
Kennedy moves ahead with plans for wet countdown demonstration test [space shuttle] *Aviat Week Space Technol* 126:110 My 11 '87
Kennedy refining shuttle processing to resolve pre-accident shortcomings. E. H. Kolcum. *Aviat Week Space Technol* 126:77 Ja 26 '87
NASA modifying shuttle launch pad for safety, efficiency. E. H. Kolcum. *Aviat Week Space Technol* 127:76 D 7 '87
Shuttle processing resumes after 18-month hiatus. E. H. Kolcum. *Aviat Week Space Technol* 127:29 Ag 3 '87
Space shuttle program managers concerned about staffing levels for three-orbiter processing. *Aviat Week Space Technol* 127:75 D 21 '87
A year later [effects of Challenger disaster] B. Dickey. il *Space World* X-1-277:14-17 Ja '87
John Fitzgerald Kennedy School of Government
Harvard title for sale? [offer to donor C. C. Dickson] por *Newsweek* 110:24 N 23 '87
John Herron Art Institute
See also
Indianapolis Museum of Art

John Howe West Inc.
Driven to perfection. P. Bedard. il pors *Esquire* 107:109-10 Je '87
John Labatt Limited
Canada's Labatt has just one way to grow: south. E. B. Terry. il por *Bus Week* p70 N 9 '87
John Paul II, Pope, 1920-

about

The art of papal finesse [meeting with Jewish leaders] K. L. Woodward. il *Newsweek* 110:64 S 14 '87
An historic Rome meeting. il *America* 157:124 S 12-19 '87
The invitation. *Newsweek* 109:43 Je 29 '87
Jews dismayed by Pope. *Christ Century* 104:586 Jl 1-8 '87
John Paul clears the air [summit with Jewish leaders] R. N. Ostling. il por *Time* 130:66 S 14 '87
John Paul II: the universal Pole. M. Maneli. *Humanist* 47:26-7+ S/O '87
John Paul: the view from home; ed. by Linda Marx. W. Bayer. il pors *People Wkly* 28:118-20 S 14 '87
John Paul's feisty flock [cover story] R. N. Ostling. il por *Time* 130:46-51 S 7 '87
Kurt Waldheim's Roman holiday. il pors *U S News World Rep* 103:14 Jl 6 '87
Long time no See [terminology in papal communiqué issued after meeting with Jewish leaders] W. Safire. il *N Y Times Mag* p34+ S 20 '87
Man beneath the mitre. M. McIver. il pors *Macleans* 100:36-7 S 14 '87
Mr. Waldheim visits the Vatican. *America* 157:27 Jl 18-25 '87
One must bear witness. M. B. Zuckerman. il *U S News World Rep* 103:66 Jl 13 '87
Our brother the Pope [discussion of November 7, 1986 article, The Pope, our brother] W. M. Shea. *Commonweal* 114:34+ Ja 30 '87
A papal writ with mass appeal. P. Young. il *Macleans* 100:50 Ag 31 '87
The pariah and the Pope. pors *Time* 130:16 Jl 6 '87
The Pope and the pariah. K. L. Woodward. pors *Newsweek* 110:45 Jl 6 '87
Pope John Paul II and freedom. M. Negri. por *Humanist* 47:23-5+ S/O '87
The Pope's letter. W. F. Buckley. *Natl Rev* 39:64-5 S 25 '87
The Pope's precedent. S. Masterman. pors *Macleans* 100:29 Je 29 '87
A reception and a snub. A. Bilski. *Macleans* 100:20 Jl 6 '87
'Redemptoris Mater' [Marian encyclical] T. H. Stahel. *America* 156:353-4 My 2 '87
Seeing Waldheim. *Commonweal* 114:405-6 Jl 17 '87
Special delivery from the Pope. R. Lacayo. il *Time* 130:53 Ag 31 '87
Under the tent with John Paul. *Time* 130:55 Jl 13 '87

Travel

The peripatetic Pope: papal visits are a mixed blessing. P. Collins. il *Commonweal* 114:484-7 S 11 '87
The traveling Pontiff. il por *Newsweek* 110:28 S 21 '87

Visit to Chile, 1987

Bearer of unwelcome tidings. W. Svoboda. il por *Time* 129:47 Ap 13 '87
Business as usual: life after the Pope's visit. V. M. Bouvier. il *Commonweal* 114:373-5 Je 19 '87
A fraternal broadside. il por *Macleans* 100:22 Ap 13 '87
Human rights and the Pope's visit to Chile. R. F. Drinan. *America* 156:227-8 Mr 21 '87
In Chile, all sides angle for a nod from the Pope. M. Santini. il por *U S News World Rep* 102:38 Ap 6 '87
'Only fifty yards away'. *America* 156:313 Ap 18 '87
The Pontiff's even hand: blessing for all in Chile. C. A. Robbins. il pors *U S News World Rep* 102:33 Ap 13 '87
The Pope's battalions. F. Willey. il por *Newsweek* 109:37 Ap 13 '87
The Pope's new weapon. P. Yancey. il *Christ Today* 31:56 Ag 7 '87

Visit to France, 1986

In the one Spirit [video of visit to Taizé] *America* 156:453 Je 6 '87

Visit to Latin America, 1987

Quelling the fire of 'liberation theology'. R. A. Manning. il *U S News World Rep* 102:48-9 Mr 30 '87

Visit to Poland, 1987

The Pope goes home. A. Bilski. il por *Macleans* 100:19 Je 22 '87

The Pope in Poland. *Christ Century* 104:585-6 Jl 1-8 '87
The Pope in Poland. *Natl Rev* 39:20 Jl 17 '87
A prayer for Solidarity's heirs. W. R. Doerner. il por *Time* 129:39 Je 22 '87
The return of the native. F. Willey. il *Newsweek* 109:44 Je 15 '87

Visit to the United States, 1987

America's Catholics: what the Pope will encounter. W. Bole. il por *Christ Today* 31:58-9+ S 4 '87
Cheer up, John Paul II. M. Kempton. il *N Y Rev Books* 34:58 O 22 '87
A gay witness to Pope John Paul II [Universal Fellowship of Metropolitan Community Churches] N. L. Wilson. *Christ Century* 104:845-6 O 7 '87
Get ready, "The Pope is coming". R. Slater. il por map *Time* 130:52-3 S 7 '87
The good Pope and the stern Pope. M. E. Marty. *Christ Century* 104:876-7 O 14 '87
"I come as a pilgrim". R. N. Ostling. il pors *Time* 130:60-2+ S 21 '87
If I had five minutes with the Pope [views of 10 prominent American Catholics; cover story] il *America* 157:126-32+ S 12-19 '87
John Paul draws the line. R. N. Ostling. il pors *Time* 130:44-6 S 28 '87
John Paul: how he's changing the Church [cover story] K. L. Woodward. il pors *Newsweek* 110:22-9 S 21 '87
John Paul's hard line. K. L. Woodward. il pors *Newsweek* 110:40-1 S 28 '87
John Paul's restless Catholics [cover story; special section; with editorial comment by Kevin Doyle] il pors *Macleans* 100:2, 32-8+ S 14 '87
John Paul's U.S. roadshow. K. L. Woodward. il por *Newsweek* 110:44-5 Ag 24 '87
No joint worship [absence of Lutheran Church—Missouri Synod from ecumenical service in South Carolina] *Christ Century* 104:848 O 7 '87
Of many things [video entitled March 25: a day in the life of Catholic laity in America to be shown to the Pope] J. W. Donohue. *America* 157:122 S 12-19 '87
On tour with the Pope. A. E. Cober. il *Roll Stone* p85-9 N 19 '87
Papa do preach [state of Hispanic Catholicism] A. Sullivan. *New Repub* 197:13-14+ O 5 '87
Papal metaphysics. I. F. Stone. *Nation* 245:292-3 S 26 '87
The papal visit. *Commonweal* 114:468-9 S 11 '87
A pilgrim's progress. J. Buckley. il pors *U S News World Rep* 103:58-9 S 21 '87
A pilgrim's provocative message. J. P. Shapiro and J. Carey. il por *U S News World Rep* 103:30-1 S 28 '87
The Pope and the bishops: 'telling it like it is'. *America* 157:179-80 O 3 '87
The Pope and the colleges. *America* 157:180 O 3 '87
The Pope and the Jews. I. Austen. il por *Macleans* 100:44 S 21 '87
Pope blasts U.S. racism; urges Church to continue fight for black equality. il por *Jet* 73:4 S 28 '87
The Pope in America. *Natl Rev* 39:18-20 O 9 '87
The Pope in America. J. Carey. il por map *U S News World Rep* 103:58-60 S 14 '87
The Pope in the U.S. il *Christ Century* 104:816-17 S 30 '87
Pope John-Paul's historic meeting with black bishops. il por *Jet* 73:24 N 9 '87
The Pope rediscovers America [special section] S. K. Reed. il pors *People Wkly* 28:112-15+ S 14 '87
The Pope's call to holiness. J. J. O'Connor, Cardinal. il pors *Saturday Evening Post* 259:56-9 D '87
Pope's visit costly. *Christ Century* 104:681 Ag 12-19 '87
The Pope's visit to San Antonio. T. H. Stahel. *America* 157:147-9 S 26 '87
Reflections on the Pope's visit [cover story] J. A. O'Hare. il *America* 157:375-8 N 21 '87
A stormy papal visit. R. Corelli. il por *Macleans* 100:54 S 28 '87
'To be American and Catholic'. J. W. Malone. il por *U S News World Rep* 103:61 S 14 '87
The uses of spectacle. A. McCarthy. il *Commonweal* 114:472-3 S 11 '87

Collectibles

No, nothing's sacred: a popepourri of the tour's papalphernalia. il por *People Wkly* 28:117 S 14 '87
The selling of the Pope, American style. il por *Newsweek* 109:49 Je 29 '87

John Paul II, Pope, 1920——Visit to the United States, 1987——*cont.*

Reporters and reporting

Murray Kempton on the papal visit. *America* 157:204 O '87

The Pope came to South Carolina: unfortunately, so did the Yankee press. D. Moniz. il por *Wash Mon* 19:28-9 D '87

Johns, Gary, 1946-

The great escape. bibl (p62) il *Psychol Today* 21:30-1+ O '87

Johns, Jasper

about

Jasper Johns: a seasonal lull. S. H. Madoff. il *Art News* 86:158 My '87

Jasper Johns: the seasons. B. Rose. il por *Vogue* 177:192-9+ Ja '87

The School of Bloomingdale's. M. Stevens. *New Repub* 196:25-8 My 18 '87

Tracking the shadow [cover story] J. Johnston. bibl f il *Art Am* 75:128-43 O '87

Johns, Tracy Camila

about

The beauty principle. B. Brandon and others. il pors *Essence* 18:50-7 Je '87

Johns Hopkins University

Who says lucre is filthy? J. Novack. il *Forbes* 140:177+ N 30 '87

Johnson, Albert M., 1872-1948

about

Scotty's Castle [excerpt] S. W. Paher. il *Natl Parks* 61:46-7 S/O '87

Johnson, Alexander D.

(jt. auth) See Hall, Michael N., and Johnson, Alexander D.

Johnson, Arthur H., and others

The authors reply. bibl f il *Environment* 29:4-5 Je '87

Johnson, Ben

about

'Missourian' daily gets 1st black managing editor. *Jet* 72:40 S 7 '87

Johnson, Ben

about

Bravos for a Roman candle. K. Moore. il por *Sports Illus* 67:18-21 S 7 '87

Bursting from the shadows. K. Moore. il pors *Sports Illus* 67:94-8+ N 30 '87

Head winds and scandals. H. Quinn. *Macleans* 100:39 Ag 31 '87

It was the best of times. H. Quinn. il por *Macleans* 100:46 S 14 '87

Johnson, Beverly

about

Model makeup now! B. Brandon and M. Garth-Taylor. il pors *Essence* 17:58-9 Ja '87

Johnson, Bill

about

Uphill in the downhill. W. O. Johnson. il pors *Sports Illus* 67:66-8+ D 21 '87

Johnson, Bill

about

Bill Johnson hired as Detroit news editorialist. *Jet* 72:32 Jl 6 '87

Johnson, Bryan R., 1956-

Let's eat Chinese tonight. il *Am Herit* 38:98-103+ D '87

Johnson, Chalmers

The Pacific Basin's challenge to America: myth and reality. il *USA Today (Periodical)* 115:20-4 Mr '87

Johnson, Charles B.

about

Why Franklin is looking beyond mutual funds. J. B. Levine. il por *Bus Week* p101 S 21 '87

Johnson, Claudia Alta Taylor *See* Johnson, Lady Bird, 1912-

Johnson, Clyde L., Sr.

about

Convicted Va. minister quits council, churches. por *Jet* 72:6 Ag 24 '87

Minister/councilman's rape conviction still stuns his church, city. D. M. Cheers. il por *Jet* 72:16-17 Jl 13 '87

Minister/lawmaker may get 161 years in prison for rape, sexual battery. il por *Jet* 72:4-6 Je 29 '87

Petersburg, Va. pastor charged with alleged sexual abuse of 6 girls. *Jet* 72:10 Je 15 '87

Va. minister convicted of sex crimes gets 120 years. por *Jet* 73:51 O 5 '87

Johnson, Connie Young- *See* Young-Johnson, Connie

Johnson, Darryl L.

First freeze. il *Petersens Photogr Mag* 16:36-8 O '87

Johnson, Dave

Open-face felling. il *Ctry J* 14:24-7 N '87

Johnson, David M.

about

Thanks, Dad. B. Leonard. il por *Forbes* 140:53-4+ Ag 10 '87

Johnson, David W., 1940-

about

It's hard to get left out of a pair. A. Kohn. bibl (p62) il pors *Psychol Today* 21:52-7 O '87

Johnson, Dennis L.

Viewing the future as a marketable product. il *Futurist* 21:60 Ja/F '87

Johnson, Don

about

Don Johnson tames the Mississippi [cover story] P. Whittell. il pors *Mot Boat Sail* 160:34-7+ N '87

A wedding belle gives Miami spice [cover story] R. Sanders. il pors *People Wkly* 28:132-7 N 23 '87

Johnson, Donnaree

about

Against all odds. R. Arias. il pors *People Wkly* 28:32-42+ O 26 '87

Johnson, Earvin, 1959-

about

Magic Johnson. il pors *People Wkly* 28:64-5 D 28 '87-Ja 4 '88

Magic Johnson didn't have to hunt for a role model. il por *Jet* 71:36 F 2 '87

Magic offers his fans membership in a family. por *Jet* 72:51 Ap 6 '87

The Magic touch. A. Ward. il pors *N Y Times Mag* p66-8+ D 6 '87

'Save up,' says Magic, as NBA strike looms. *Jet* 73:48 N 2 '87

The stuff dreams are made of. D. Halberstam. il pors *Sports Illus* 66:38-40+ Je 29 '87

Johnson, Edward Crosby, III

about

Selling the best—and most—mutual funds. S. Smith. il por *Fortune* 115:85 Ja 5 '87

Johnson, Elmer W., 1932-

about

GM's late-starting trumpeter. N. J. Perry. il por *Fortune* 116:137 O 26 '87

Johnson, Eric A.

Environmental portrait. il *Petersens Photogr Mag* 16:62-3 Jl '87

Johnson, Eunice W.

about

Mrs. Eunice W. Johnson returns for Talladega to give reunion address. il pors *Jet* 72:14-16 Ag 24 '87

Mrs. Eunice W. Johnson, Warren Bacon reign at regal Carnaval. il pors *Jet* 72:33 S 7 '87

Johnson, F. Ross

about

Handy guy with a razor. B. Saporito. il por *Fortune* 116:53 Ag 3 '87

A knack for ending up on top. M. McComas. il por *Fortune* 115:108 Ja 5 '87

RJR Nabisco may cut down on tobacco. G. G. Marcial. il *Bus Week* p116 F 23 '87

Ross Johnson. S. Ticer. por *Bus Week* Sp Issue:222 Ap 17 '87

Johnson, Fridolf

Richard Pantell. il *Am Artist* 51:64-7+ F '87

Johnson, George, 1952-

Memory: learning how it works [cover story] il por *N Y Times Mag* p16-21+ Ag 9 '87

Johnson, George E.

about

A healthy paranoia. J. Parr. il por *Forbes* 139:124+ Mr 9 '87

Johnson, Gus

about

Obituary

Jet por 72:47 My 18 '87

Sports Illus il 66:100 My 18 '87. F. Deford

Johnson, Hillary

Journey into fear: the growing nightmare of Epstein-Barr virus (I). il *Roll Stone* p56-8+ Jl 16-30 '87

Journey into fear: the growing nightmare of Epstein-Barr virus (II). il *Roll Stone* p42-4+ Ag 13 '87

Johnson, Howard, 1960-

about

Three men on a roll. F. Lidz. il pors *Sports Illus* 67:40-2+ Ag 24 '87

Johnson, Jim

about

'In my mind I know I'm going to be a star'. L. Rosellini. il pors *U S News World Rep* 102:58-9 Je 15 '87

Johnson, Jodi
about
Two mothers for Laura. R. Distelheim. il pors *McCalls* 114:135-7 S '87
Johnson, Joe
about
A tough day at the office. P. Gammons. il pors *Sports Illus* 67:42-4 Jl 6 '87
Johnson, John
about
Johnson: network TV is still white man's club. *Jet* 72:23 Ag 10 '87
Johnson, John H.
about
Doing business John Johnson's way [interview; cover story] D. T. Dingle. il pors *Black Enterp* 17:150-2+ Je '87
John H. Johnson among honorees inducted into Black Press Hall of Fame. il por *Jet* 73:14-15 N 23 '87
John H. Johnson among the ten inducted into Publishing Hall of Fame. il pors *Jet* 73:12+ D 21 '87
John H. Johnson named 'Entrepreneur of Decade,' JPC top black business. il pors *Jet* 72:6-9+ My 25 '87
Miller Brewing Co. honors publisher John H. Johnson. il pors *Jet* 71:5 F 16 '87
Publisher John H. Johnson accepts lifetime achievement award from black journalists. il por *Jet* 72:16 S 14 '87
Words that give us strength. C. T. Rowan. il pors *Read Dig* 130:49-50+ Ap '87
Johnson, Joshua, 1765-1830
about
Joshua Johnson. C. J. Weekley. bibl f il *Antiques* 132:524-37 S '87
Johnson, Joyce, 1935-
Launching day, 1962 [story] *New Yorker* 63:30-5 Ap 13 '87
Johnson, Julia Claiborne
Little tub of horrors: pools and hot tubs can make you sick. il *Mademoiselle* 93:74 Je '87
News for women only: the cholesterol connection. *Mademoiselle* 93:146 Ap '87
Test your breasts (a new self-exam is getting good grades). il *Mademoiselle* 93:150 N '87
Johnson, Keith N.
The growing foreign role in U.S. policy. il por *Fortune* 116:36-8 Jl 6 '87
Johnson, Kenneth
(jt. auth) See Machlis, Gary E., and Johnson, Kenneth
Johnson, Kirk R.
(jt. auth) See Nelson, C. Hans, and Johnson, Kirk R.
Johnson, Lady Bird, 1912-
about
In from the fields, wildflowers find a new welcome among gardeners. B. Gilbert. bibl (p162) il por *Smithsonian* 18:36-45 Ap '87
Johnson, Leonard William, d. 1987
about
Obituary
Jet por 72:52 S 7 '87
Johnson, Linda E. See Rice, Linda Johnson
Johnson, Lyndon B. (Lyndon Baines), 1908-1973
about
LBJ's 'mistress' signs with Contemporary. il por *Publ Wkly* 232:42-3 O 16 '87
LBJ's way of explaining things. il pors *Psychol Today* 21:39 F '87
Lyndon Baines Johnson, an American original. il pors *People Wkly* 27:34-9 F 2 '87
Taming the NSC. J. P. Roche. *Natl Rev* 39:40-2 Mr 27 '87
Was LBJ's final secret a son? M. Brower. il pors *People Wkly* 28:30-5 Ag 3 '87
Johnson, Lynell
Children's visions of the future. il por *Futurist* 21:36-40 My/Je '87
Johnson, Magic See Johnson, Earvin, 1959-
Johnson, Marilyn
Eau no, eau yes. il *Esquire* 107:F20+ Mr '87
Return to suburbia. il *Glamour* 85:72+ Mr '87
Johnson, Marques, 1956-
about
Clippers star agrees to surgery after pay stops. por *Jet* 72:46 Ap 13 '87
Johnson, Nicholas L.
1986: very good year for Soviets. il *Space World* X-10-286:14-17 O '87
Johnson, Norman J., d. 1987
about
Obituary
Jet por 71:24 Ja 26 '87

Johnson, Paul, 1928-
Israel's providential men. *Commentary* 84:60-3 O '87
about
The age of media democracy [interview] A. P. Sanoff. por *U S News World Rep* 102:68 Je 22 '87
PW interviews. M. Field. il por *Publ Wkly* 231:50-1 My 1 '87
Johnson, Paul G.
Lutherans and liturgy [discussion of July 29-August 5, 1987 article, Making a real return to church possible] *Christ Century* 104:794-6 S 23 '87
Making a real return to church possible. il *Christ Century* 104:656-9 Jl 29-Ag 5 '87
Johnson, Phillip
Fecund mysteries. il *Wilderness* 50:37-44+ Summ '87
Johnson, Pierre Marc, 1946-
about
The PQ in turmoil. B. Wallace. il pors *Macleans* 100:8-10 N 23 '87
Under a shadow. B. Wallace. il por *Macleans* 100:16 N 16 '87
Johnson, Ralph
about
Ralph Johnson: the regionalist. B. Dumaine. il por *Fortune* 115:159-60 Je 22 '87
Johnson, Ray, 1926-
about
Ray Johnson discovers his past crimes do pay after all. M. Neill. il pors *People Wkly* 28:155-7 S 7 '87
Johnson, Robert E.
Behind the scenes with Bill Cosby. il pors *Ebony* 42:160+ F '87
Michael Jackson comes back! [cover story] il pors *Ebony* 42:142-4+ S '87
about
Reception at JPC honors author of Bill Cosby book. il pors *Jet* 72:59-60 My 18 '87
Johnson, Robert T.
about
It's hard to get left out of a pair. A. Kohn. bibl (p62) il pors *Psychol Today* 21:52-7 O '87
Johnson, Roger W.
about
One-stop shopping for IBM copycats. J. Flynn. il por *Bus Week* p76+ Ag 24 '87
Johnson, Ronald E.
ACE responds. *Phi Delta Kappan* 68:520-1 Mr '87
Johnson, Samuel, 1709-1784
about
Dr. Johnson's open house. J. Atlas. il por *House Gard* 159:12+ D '87
Johnson, Sharon
In good company: workday weight-loss support systems. il *Work Woman* 12:100+ F '87
Johnson, Susan
Jump to it! il *Women's Sports Fitness* 9:34-8 Ag '87
Johnson, Susan Moore, and Nelson, Niall C. W.
Teaching reform in an active voice. bibl f il *Phi Delta Kappan* 68:591-8 Ap '87
Johnson, Timothy J.
Mr. Pat's magical ride [story] il *Redbook* 170:168+ D '87
Johnson, Torrence V., and others
The moons of Uranus. il *Sci Am* 256:48-60 Ap '87
Johnson, Trebbe
Indian land, white greed. il *Nation* 245:15-18 Jl 4-11 '87
Johnson, W. R. (Walter Ralph), 1933-
Octavian in Alexandria [poem] *Am Sch* 56:247 Spr '87
Johnson, Walter Ralph See Johnson, W. R. (Walter Ralph), 1933-
Johnson, William L.
(jt. auth) See Cheng, Yang-Tse, and Johnson, William L.
Johnson, William Oscar
G'day, Aussie Joe! il pors *Sports Illus* 66:56+ My 25 '87
Goodbye, olive wreaths; hello, riches and reality. il *Sports Illus* 66:168+ F 9 '87
Look lively, lubbers, it's the America's Cup. il *Sports Illus* 66:74 Ja 19 '87
Polishing up the old Cup: the Australians have brought new luster to a sailing classic. por *Sports Illus* 66:80 F 2 '87
A strange and resolute calm. il *Sports Illus* 66:38-40+ Je 8 '87
Swish went the Swiss. il *Sports Illus* 66:26-30 F 16 '87
Uphill in the downhill. il pors *Sports Illus* 67:66-8+ D 21 '87

Johnson, William Oscar—*cont.*
A vote for South Korea: it's too soon to push the panic button over the Seoul Olympics. por *Sports Illus* 67:94 Jl 13 '87
Z-man is a real he-man. il pors *Sports Illus* 66:42-3 Mr 23 '87
Johnson (S. C.) & Son, Inc. *See* S. C. Johnson & Son, Inc.
Johnson Products Company, Inc.
A healthy paranoia. J. Parr. il por *Forbes* 139:124+ Mr 9 '87
Johnson Publishing Company, Inc.
Backstage [L. J. Rice appointed president] il por *Ebony* 42:26 S '87
Doing business John Johnson's way [interview; cover story] D. T. Dingle. il pors *Black Enterp* 17:150-2+ Je '87
John H. Johnson named 'Entrepreneur of Decade,' JPC top black business. il pors *Jet* 72:6-9+ My 25 '87
Johnson Publishing Company names two vice presidents [Treka Owens and Raj Shah] il *Jet* 71:16 Ja 12 '87
Linda Johnson Rice gets MBA, named president of Johnson Publishing Co. il por *Jet* 72:6+ Jl 6 '87
A nice graduation present: Johnson Publishing [L. J. Rice takes the helm] L. Therrien. por *Bus Week* p40 Jl 13 '87
Reception at JPC honors author of Bill Cosby book [R. E. Johnson] il pors *Jet* 72:59-60 My 18 '87
Johnson Space Center *See* Lyndon B. Johnson Space Center
Johnston, A. J.
Women fight sexual assault. il *Progressive* 51:12-13 S '87
Johnston, Denis, and Rudney, Gabriel
Characteristics of workers in nonprofit organizations. bibl f il *Mon Labor Rev* 110:28-33 Jl '87
Johnston, Don
about
Blood on the carpet: the coup that failed at J. Walter Thompson. B. Kanner. il pors *N Y* 20:36-40 F 16 '87
Don Johnston. C. Dugas. il por *Bus Week* Sp Issue:256 Ap 17 '87
Et tu, Brutus? This time Caesar won. C. J. Loomis. il pors *Fortune* 115:54-6 Mr 2 '87
Turnover, not turnaround, at J. Walter Thompson. C. Dugas. *Bus Week* p49-50 My 11 '87
Johnston, Gene
Hogs. See issues of Successful Farming through May 1987
Johnston, George Sim
The real things. *Harpers* 274:54-5 F '87
Johnston, Jill
Jigs, japes and Joyce. il *Art Am* 75:102-5 Ja '87
Tracking the shadow [cover story] bibl f il *Art Am* 75:128-43 O '87
Walking into art. il map *Art Am* 75:160-9 Ap '87
Johnston, John
about
Saga of a speed upgrade. C. Spencer. il *Pers Comput* 11:79 Ja '87
Johnston, Joshua *See* Johnson, Joshua, 1765-1830
Johnston, M. J. S., and Mueller, R. J.
Seismomagnetic observation during the 8 July 1986 magnitude 5.9 North Palm Springs earthquake. bibl f il maps *Science* 237:1201-3 S 4 '87
Johnston, Margaret
Juvenile articles that sell. *Writer* 100:28-9 S '87
Johnston, Moira
Canada's Queen Charlotte Islands: homeland of the Haida. il map *Natl Geogr* 172:102-27 Jl '87
Johnston, Shawn Adair
The mind of a molester. bibl (p64) il *Psychol Today* 21:60-3 F '87
Johnston, Stella
Nuclear medicine [poem] *New Repub* 196:32 My 25 '87
Johnston, Velda
Stranger on the beach [fiction] il por *Good Housekeep* 205:211-14+ N '87
Johnstone, C. Bruce
about
Tips from America's best income investor. J. E. Goodman. il por *Money* 16:81-4 Ja '87
Joinery *See* Joints (Carpentry)
Joint Center for Political Studies (U.S.)
Task force offers answers for problems facing blacks. *Jet* 72:9 Mr 30 '87
Joint Chiefs of Staff (U.S.) *See* United States. Joint Chiefs of Staff

Joint ownership
See also
Condominiums
Farmers who machine themselves to the times [joint ownership of equipment] C. Finck. il *Success Farm* 85:18BA Ap '87
Joint tenancy *See* Joint ownership
Joint ventures
Comrade capitalists, come make money in the Soviet Union. K. R. Sheets. il *U S News World Rep* 102:39 Ja 19 '87
Ivan starts learning the capitalist ropes. R. Lewald. il *Bus Week* p154 N 2 '87
Joint ventures or associations; do they work? [architectural firms] J. Falick. il *Archit Rec* 175:29 Ja '87
Letting Western business in [Soviet Union] P. Galuszka and others. *Bus Week* p40 Ap 20 '87
Making deals that won't give technology away. R. Neff. il *Bus Week* p62-3 Ap 20 '87
The twain are meeting—and cutting deals [U.S.-Soviet joint ventures] R. W. King and P. Galuszka. il *Bus Week* p88 D 7 '87
Western business may get a piece of *perestroika*. P. Galuszka and others. il *Bus Week* p70 D 28 '87-Ja 4 '88
Joints
See also
Hip joint
Knee
Ligaments
Shoulder

Diseases
See also
Arthritis
Joints, Artificial
See also
Hip joint, Artificial
Knee, Artificial
Designer bones—computers prescribe the prosthesis. S. F. Brown. il *Pop Sci* 230:89 Je '87
Joints (Carpentry)
Biscuit joinery. J. Gaynor. il *Home Mech* 83:126 O '87
Dado decisions. R. N. Hoffman. il *Workbench* 43:14 My/Je '87
Dialing for dowel joints. R. Capotosto. il *Pop Mech* 164:45 O '87
The dovetail's first cousin—the box joint. H. Wicks. il *Home Mech* 83:16 Ja '87
Edge-joining with dowels. H. Wicks. il *Home Mech* 83:20 N '87
Finger joints. C. Wedlake and T. H. Jones. il *Pop Sci* 230:98-100 F '87
Mortise-and-tenon joints. R. Capotosto. il *Pop Mech* 164:21 Mr '87
A pro's tips for making dowel joints. T. H. Jones. il *Pop Sci* 230:116 F '87
Shop basics: simple woodworking joints. il *Workbench* 43:77-9 Ja/F '87
Using dowel pins. R. Capotosto. il *Pop Mech* 164:40 D '87
Joints (Engineering)
See also
Fasteners
Jokes *See* Humor
Jokes, Knock-knock *See* Knock-knock jokes
Jokes, Practical *See* Practical jokes
Joke's on You!, Inc.
Essence woman [founder T. Moore] M. Scott. il por *Essence* 18:30 Jl '87
Jolly, Alison
Madagascar: a world apart. il maps *Natl Geogr* 171:148-83 F '87
Jolly, Wanda
In defense of the sun. il *Sky Telesc* 73:356 Ap '87
Jonas, George, 1935-
(jt. auth) *See* Greenspan, Edward L., and Jonas, George, 1935-
about
Paying homage to a best friend. B. Amiel. il *Macleans* 100:9 My 25 '87
Jonas, Gerald
Electronically yours [poem] *Atlantic* 260:88 O '87
Science fiction. il *N Y Times Book Rev* 92:30 Mr 8 '87
Science fiction. *N Y Times Book Rev* 92:29 Ap 26 '87
Science fiction. il *N Y Times Book Rev* 92:25 Ag 2 '87
Science fiction. il *N Y Times Book Rev* 92:18-19 Je 7 '87

Jonas, Gerald—*cont.*
Science fiction. il *N Y Times Book Rev* 92:18 D 20
'87
Science fiction. il *N Y Times Book Rev* 92:36 O 18
'87
Jonas, Joan
about
Joan Jonas at the Performing Garage. C. Little. il *Art
Am* 75:179-80 S '87
Jonas, R. Stevan
(jt. auth) See Blumberg, Arthur, 1923-, and Jonas, R.
Stevan
Jonathon Apples Plus Company
Reviews:
Performances at the Bessie Schönberg Theater, New
York City. C. Hardy. *Dance Mag* 61:20 Ja '87
Jones, Alan Pryce- *See* Pryce-Jones, Alan, 1908-
Jones, Amy
about
Maid to order [film] Reviews
Glamour 85:199-200 Ag '87. J. G. Boyum
People Wkly il 28:12 Ag 3 '87. R. Novak
Jones, Andrew
A boy who climbed the marigold. il pors *Read Dig*
130:96-100 F '87
Jones, Arthur A.
about
Aching back? Arthur Jones says he has the answer.
M. Frons. il por *Bus Week* p59+ D 14 '87
Jones, Bill T.
about
The animal trilogy [dance] Reviews
Dance Mag 61:23-4 Jl '87. C. Hardy
N Y il 20:47 Ja 5 '87. T. Tobias
Jones, Bobby, 1902-1971
about
Bobby Jones shows you how to hit 'em. I. Maisel.
Sports Illus 67:101 D 21 '87
Jones, Brenda
about
The sound of a miracle. T. Rademacher. il pors *Seventeen*
46:96-8 My '87
Jones, Caroline
about
Jones opens new agency. por *Black Enterp* 17:24 F
'87
Jones, Cathy
about
Cold war of the sexes. P. Hluchy. por *Macleans* 100:47
Mr 2 '87
Jones, Cleve
about
Notes and comment. *New Yorker* 63:31-2 O 5 '87
Taking up needles and thread to honor the dead helps
AIDS survivors patch up their lives. C. Ruskin. il
por *People Wkly* 28:42-4+ O 12 '87
Jones, David A.
about
David Jones. K. Deveny. il por *Bus Week* Sp Issue:271
Ap 17 '87
The performance took a beating, the paychecks didn't.
J. E. Davis and K. Deveny. il pors *Bus Week* p54
My 4 '87
Jones, David Hugh, 1934-
about
84 Charing Cross Road [film] Reviews
Christ Today 31:61 Jl 10 '87. S. Ulstein
Glamour 85:244 Ap '87. J. G. Boyum
Ms il 15:35 Ap '87. L. Stone
N Y il 20:100+ Mr 2 '87. D. Denby
New Repub 196:24 F 23 '87. S. Kauffmann
Newsweek 109:72 F 16 '87. D. Ansen
People Wkly 27:12+ Mr 30 '87. T. Cunneff
Time il 129:74+ Mr 2 '87. R. Corliss
Jones, David Pryce- *See* Pryce-Jones, David
Jones, David R.
The two faces of Soviet military power. bibl f *Curr
Hist* 86:313-16+ O '87
Jones, Dezie Woods- *See* Woods-Jones, Dezie
Jones, Edith Irby
about
Scholarship fund honors Dr. Edith Irby Jones. *Jet* 72:12
Jl 20 '87
Jones, Edward Vason, 1909-1980
about
The diplomatic reception rooms of Edward Vason Jones.
A. Greenberg. bibl f il *Antiques* 132:122-31 Jl '87
Jones, Elizabeth W.
(jt. auth) See Lemmon, Sandra K., and Jones, Elizabeth
W.

Jones, Evan, 1915-
The American scene. il *Gourmet* 47:62+ F '87
Jones, Gary Aston- *See* Aston-Jones, Gary
Jones, George
about
Black Chicagoan awarded $800,000 for false arrest. *Jet*
72:5 Mr 30 '87
Jones, Grace
about
Grace Jones 'slugs' press agent, paper says. *Jet* 71:63
F 23 '87
Jones, Gregory M.
about
Philadelphia In the black. W. J. Dawkins. il pors *Black
Enterp* 17:66 Je '87
Jones, Harold B., d. 1987
about
Obituary
Jet por 73:17 N 16 '87
Jones, Howard
about
Howard Jones sings about things you want to think
about. E. Miller. por *Seventeen* 46:68+ Je '87
Jones, Irmarie
Create a Christmas fantasy. il por *Ctry J* 14:41-2 D
'87
Jones, James Earl
about
'Fences,' Jones, grab top Tonys for drama. il pors *Jet*
72:54 Je 22 '87
Jones, Jill
about
Prince's intriguing women [cover story] L. Norment.
il pors *Ebony* 43:162-3+ N '87
Jones, Judy
Rate your shape. il *Redbook* 168:88-93 F '87
Jones, Kathi
about
For better, for worse. K. Casey. il *Ladies Home J*
104:89-91+ My '87
Jones, Kimberly
(jt. auth) See Churchill, Robert, and Jones, Kimberly
Jones, Landon Y., 1943-
Editor's notes. See issues of Money beginning June 1986
Jones, Larry
about
Feeding the hungry with surplus food. il por *Christ
Today* 31:54 O 2 '87
Jones, LeRoi *See* Baraka, Imamu Amiri, 1934-
Jones, Linda D., and others
A novel mode of arbovirus transmission involving a
nonviremic host. bibl f il *Science* 237:775-7 Ag 14
'87
Jones, Malcolm, 1952-
Moralist of the South. il por *N Y Times Mag* p42+
Mr 22 '87
Jones, Marnie
Writing great-grandfather's biography. *Am Sch* 56:519-34
Aut '87
Jones, Mary Lou
(jt. auth) See Swartz, Steven L., and Jones, Mary Lou
Jones, Melvin
On buying a house. il *South Living* 22:138 S '87
Jones, Pat
Astronauts discover new planet! il *Space World*
X-3-279:18-20 Mr '87
Jones, Patricia A.
The good life in St. Maarten and St. Eustatius. il *Black
Enterp* 17:67-8 Ja '87
Jones, Paul Tudor, II
about
Hot commodity. D. Machan. il por *Forbes* 139:282 Ja
12 '87
Jones, Richard Herbert
For safety's sake: indemnify air traffic control manufac-
turers. *Aviat Week Space Technol* 127:11 Jl 20 '87
Jones, Robert, 1934-
Writing the troubling truth. il *Commonweal* 114:501-4
S 11 '87
Jones, Robert F.
Street smart in Motown. il pors *Sports Illus* 66:68-9
Je 29 '87
Jones, Rodney, 1950-
One of the citizens [poem] il *Atlantic* 260:44 Ag
'87
Jones, S. Guernsey
How deep are your convictions? [address, March 17,
1987] *Vital Speeches Day* 53:492-4 Je 1 '87

Jones, Samuel M. (Samuel Milton), 1846-1904
about
Writing great-grandfather's biography. M. Jones. *Am Sch* 56:519-34 Aut '87
Jones, Sean M. Lynn- *See* Lynn-Jones, Sean M.
Jones, Simon
Art deco bronze and ivory figures [cover story] il *Antiques Collect Hobbies* 92:24-8 Ag '87
Art nouveau Meissen emerges from long neglect. il *Antiques Collect Hobbies* 91:11-14 F '87
Chelsea porcelain: 1745-69. il *Antiques Collect Hobbies* 92:18-22 Je '87
Jones, Sonia
It all began with Daisy [condensation] il *Read Dig* 131:82-90+ Ag '87
Jones, Spike, 1911-1965
about
Oh my aching ear! The (bang!) music of Spike (splat!) Jones is revived by a new (tweet!) band of merry makers. M. Shaughnessy. il pors *People Wkly* 27:77+ My 4 '87
Jones, Stephen, 1954-
Attic attitudes: Leighton and aesthetic philosophy. bibl il *Hist Today* 37:31-7 Je '87
Jones, Steven E.
(jt. auth) *See* Rafelski, Johann, and Jones, Steven E.
Jones, Terry, 1942-
about
Personal services [film] Reviews
Macleans 100:56 O 12 '87. L. O'Toole
Ms 15:21-2 My '87. A. B. Snitow
N Y 20:95-6 Je 1 '87. D. Denby
New Repub 196:27 My 4 '87. S. Kauffmann
New Yorker 63:84 My 18 '87. P. Kael
People Wkly 28:12 Jl 27 '87. T. Cunneff
Jones, Thad
about
35th annual International Critics Poll [with editorial comment by Art Lange] J. McDonough. il pors *Down Beat* 54:5, 20-4 Ag '87
Jones, Thomas J.
about
Obituary
America 157:495-7 D 26 '87. J. W. Donohue
Jones, Tommy, d. 1986
about
For better, for worse. K. Casey. il *Ladies Home J* 104:89-91+ My '87
Jones, Tony Armstrong- *See* Snowdon, Antony Armstrong-Jones, Earl of, 1930-
Jones, Willie James
about
Willie Jones becomes second black sheriff in Georgia. *Jet* 71:31 Mr 23 '87
Jones (Bill T.)/Arnie Zane & Company *See* Bill T. Jones/Arnie Zane & Company
Jones (Edward D.) & Company *See* Edward D. Jones & Company
Jones Transfer Co.
Gary White leads biggest U.S. minority trucking firm. *Jet* 72:36 S 7 '87
Jong, Erica
Is there life after being a good girl? *Glamour* 85:268-9+ Ag '87
Is there sexy after 40? *Vogue* 177:304-5 My '87
Jonkel, Charles
about
Making bad bears into good bears could spare bears. G. Laycock. il *Audubon* 89:22-4+ Mr '87
Jonquieres, Guy de
Europe still fails the challenge. por *World Press Rev* 34:46-7 My '87
'Privatization' becomes a global byword. *World Press Rev* 34:50 F '87
Jonquieres, Guy de, and Kaletsky, Anatole
Can American industry make it? il *World Press Rev* 34:22-6 Jl '87
Joplin, Janis, 1943-1970
about
Unreleased Janis Joplin recording surfaces. S. Weitzman. *Roll Stone* p24 N 19 '87
Joranson, David
(jt. auth) *See* Dahl, June, and Joranson, David
Jordache Enterprises Inc.
Does Guess have a friend in the IRS? [Guess vs. Jordache] R. Behar. il map *Forbes* 140:146-50+ N 16 '87
The IRS mess [corruption charges surrounding Guess, Inc. feud with Jordache] R. Behar. il *Forbes* 140:8 N 30 '87

Jordan, Bob
about
Bob Jordan: tops in news and health. il pors *Ebony* 42:145-6+ F '87
Jordan, Clyde
about
E. St. Louis mayor wins 3rd term, but spectre of dead man may mar victory. il por *Jet* 72:38 Ag 24 '87
East St. Louis mayor in dispute over election. *Jet* 72:29 Ap 13 '87
Jordan, David
Editor's letter. *See* issues of Better Homes and Gardens beginning November 1984
Jordan, David
about
Miss. councilman seeks aid after KKK threats. il por *Jet* 71:6 Mr 23 '87
Jordan, June, 1936-
'Don't you talk about my mama!' [adaptation of address, 1987] *Essence* 18:53+ D '87
Jordan, Michael
about
'Air' Jordan rates high marks in men's fashion. por *Jet* 71:29 F 23 '87
Author, producer plan film debut for Jordan. *Jet* 71:52 F 9 '87
How to stop Michael Jordan. J. Capouya. il pors *Sport Mag* 78:40-2+ Mr '87
In an orbit all his own. C. Kirkpatrick. il pors *Sports Illus* 67:82-6+ N 9 '87
Jordan scores a point, encourages kids to read. il por *Jet* 72:48 Je 15 '87
Jordan's scoring success overshadows his talents. *Jet* 72:50 My 25 '87
Jordan's Wilson deal nets him $1 million. por *Jet* 73:50 O 26 '87
Michael Jordan's life at the top. P. Axthelm. il pors *Newsweek* 109:46-8 Ja 5 '87
Michael Jordan's secret engagement hard to keep. il por *Jet* 71:30 Mr 16 '87
Michael the magnificent. B. Phillips. por *Sch Update* 119:14 Ap 20 '87
Survey says nation's kids favor Bulls' Jordan, Bears. *Jet* 72:50 Ap 13 '87
Jordan, Pat
Bertha's triumph. il *Read Dig* 131:55-9 Ag '87
Kid K. il pors *Sports Illus* 66:82-6+ Je 1 '87
Tom Seaver. il por *Sport Mag* 78:95-7 D '87
Jordan, Phyllis
A true test of power. *Black Enterp* 17:59 Ap '87
Jordan, Robert E., and others
Heparin promotes the inactivation of antithrombin by neutrophil elastase. bibl f il *Science* 237:777-9 Ag 14 '87
Jordan, Robert Paul
New Zealand: the last utopia? il map *Natl Geogr* 171:654-81 My '87
Jordan, Teresa
(ed) *See* Hall, Ristene. "I had to shape up my life"
Jordan, Vernon
The free enterprise system [address, February 11, 1987] *Vital Speeches Day* 53:466-8 My 15 '87
about
Vernon Jordan named to board of Revlon. por *Jet* 73:39 O 26 '87
Jordan
See also
Architecture, Domestic—Jordan
Antiquities, Roman
For Rome, riches and glory in an outpost of empire. D. J. Hamblin. bibl (p270) il map *Smithsonian* 18:100-4+ N '87
Foreign relations
Middle East
Hussein's game [willingness to enter peace negotiations with Israel independent of the P.L.O.] S. Reed. *Nation* 244:839-40 Je 20 '87
A voice of hope and moderation [interview with Hassan bin Talal] H. Mackenzie. il por *Macleans* 100:21 Je 22 '87
Israeli occupation, 1967-
See Israel-Arab Wars, 1967- —Territorial questions
Politics and government
Jordan's malaise. M. C. Wilson. bibl f *Curr Hist* 86:73-6+ F '87
Jorde, Paula
Microcomputers and the pro-innovation bias. *Educ Dig* 52:36-9 F '87
Jorgensen, Bernadette
"I'm allergic to my family"; ed. by Barbara Yost. il por *Redbook* 168:42+ Ap '87

Jorgensen, Gordon D.
about
The future is wow! N. Amdur. por *World Tennis* 34:6 Mr '87

Jorling, Thomas Cash
about
DEC welcomes new commissioner. por *Conservationist* 42:49 S/O '87

Jorre, John De St. *See* De St. Jorre, John

Jorstad, Eric
Zimbabwe's 'situation' and prayers for unity. *Christ Century* 104:710-11 Ag 26-S 2 '87

José Limón Dance Company *See* Limón Dance Company

Joselit, David
Portugal: the younger generation. il *Art Am* 75:19-21+ S '87
Wrinkles in time. il *Art Am* 75:106-11+ Jl '87

Joseph, Frederick H.
about
The case against Drexel: will the government come up short? C. Welles. il por *Bus Week* p56-60 Ag 10 '87
Frederick Joseph. A. Bianco. por *Bus Week* Sp Issue:212 Ap 17 '87
'An outrageous violation' of fairness [interview] il por *U S News World Rep* 102:39 F 23 '87

Joseph, Robert
about
How to survive in advertising. D. Machan. il por *Forbes* 140:446+ Jl 13 '87

Josephson, Marvin
about
One plus one plus one equals zero. D. Machan. il por *Forbes* 139:58+ Ap 20 '87

Josephson, Matthew, 1899-1978
about
A robber historian. M. Klein. il *Forbes* 140 Sp Issue:46+ O 26 '87

Josephson, Paul
Early years of Soviet nuclear physics. bibl f il *Bull At Sci* 43:36-9 D '87

Josephson International Inc.
One plus one plus one equals zero [M. Josephson's attempt to diversify into financial services through Greenspan O'Neil Associates] D. Machan. il por *Forbes* 139:58+ Ap 20 '87

Josephson junctions
He's walking tall where IBM wouldn't tread [S. Faris' Josephson junction oscilloscope] O. Port. il por *Bus Week* p124 My 4 '87

Joshua [oratorio] *See* Handel, George Frideric, 1685-1759

Jourdenais, Fernand
about
A Tory who refuses to toe the line. M. Clark. il por *Macleans* 100:18 N 2 '87

Journalism
See also
Cable television—News
College and school journalism
Communications satellites—Journalistic use
Computers—Journalistic use
Crime and the press
Editors and editing
Environmental news
Foreign news
Freedom of the press
Government and the press
Interviewing
Journalistic ethics
Libel and slander
News
Newsletters
Newspaper court reporting
Newspapers
Periodical articles
Periodicals
Press
Radio broadcasting—News
Sports journalism
Television broadcasting—News
Terrorism and the press
Wine journalism
Effective nonfiction writing: seven C's plus one. D. Ranly. *Writer* 100:19-21+ Ja '87
Public affairs journalism. A. Ross. *Cent Mag* 20:33-5 Mr/Ap '87
Should ski writers ski? A. H. Greenberg. il *Skiing* 39:28+ Ja '87
When Frank Sinatra had a cold: a reflection on the cause of today's common journalism. G. Talese. il pors *Esquire* 108:161-6 N '87

Awards
See also
National Magazine Awards (U.S.)
Pulitzer prizes
Klein Award. *Mon Labor Rev* 110:2 Mr '87
USA today wins peace award [Olive Branch Award] *USA Today (Periodical)* 116:4 Ag '87
Social aspects
See also
Muckraking
The press and the public discourse [cover story; with discussion] J. W. Carey. il por *Cent Mag* 20:4-32 Mr/Ap '87
Study and teaching
See also
Institute for Journalism Education
Pakistan
J-school for Afghan rebels [Boston University project in Pakistan] E. Salholz. il *Newsweek* 109:75-6 Mr 30 '87
Canada
Media watch. G. Bain. See occasional issues of Maclean's
Developing countries
Assembly calls for co-operation in a new world information and communication order. *UN Chron* 24:96-7 F '87
Coups and earthquakes only. S. Kassam. *World Press Rev* 34:64 S '87
Great Britain
The big bang [coverage of British royal family] S. Hoggart. *New Repub* 197:11-12 N 23 '87
Canadian shield at the Palace [royal family media relations officer V. Chapman] il por *Macleans* 100:29 Jl 27 '87
Royals bashing: a blood sport? [speculation about Charles and Diana] M. Smilgis. il pors *Time* 130:94-5 N 9 '87
When in doubt, run the Royals. L. Zuckerman. il pors *Time* 130:52 Jl 13 '87
United States
See Journalism

Journalism, Automotive
Famous last words [concluding paragraphs of motorcycle road tests] C. Hodenfield. il *Cycle* 38:41-3 S '87

Journalism, Educational
News coverage of arts and arts education. B. Hall. *Des Arts Educ* 88:10-12 Jl/Ag '87

Journalism, Labor
Are the media shortchanging organized labor? J. A. Grimes. *Mon Labor Rev* 110:53-4 Ag '87
The vanishing labor beat. J.-A. Mort. il *Nation* 245:588-90 N 21 '87

Journalism, Military
See also
World War, 1939-1945—Reporters and reporting

Journalism, Religious
See also
Church and the press
John Paul II, Pope, 1920-—Visit to the United States, 1987—Reporters and reporting
My editorial governor. M. E. Marty. *Christ Century* 104:671 Jl 29-Ag 5 '87
A plague, not a war: the religious press confronts itself through AIDS. G. G. Seibert. *America* 157:260-1 O 24 '87

Journalism, Scientific
The culture of science journalism. D. Nelkin. bibl *Society* 24:17-25 S/O '87
He's the wisest of wise guys [C. Adams, author of syndicated column The straight dope] E. Dolnick. il por *Discover* 8:82-4+ Ja '87
How to teach (and learn) astronomy? Write a column! M. S. Smith. il *Astronomy* 15:26+ F '87
Is a yawn really contagious? [syndicated science column, The straight dope, by C. Adams] E. Dolnick. il *Read Dig* 131:99-102 Jl '87
Journalism is subject of Ethics Group meeting. A. Crumpton. *Science* 237:84 Jl 3 '87
Science sections in U.S. newspapers increase dramatically in past 2 years. B. J. Culliton. *Science* 235:429 Ja 23 '87

Journalism, Trade union *See* Journalism, Labor

Journalist (Taiwan: Periodical)
A new voice is heard [interview with A. Chiang] D. R. Shanor. il por *World Press Rev* 34:21 N '87

Journalistic ethics
See also
Confidential communications—Press
Can the media be reformed? S. Garment. *Commentary* 84:37-43 Ag '87

Journalistic ethics—*cont.*

Can the press tell the truth? D. McDonald. il por *Cent Mag* 20:19-32 S/O '87

Gary Hart and the press: can the media be reformed? S. Garment. *Current* 298:11-17 D '87

Journalistic ethics [discussion of August 1987 article, Can the media be reformed?] S. Garment. *Commentary* 84:2+ D '87

To kill a messenger [address, April 16, 1987] E. R. Hutchinson. *Vital Speeches Day* 53:572-6 Jl 1 '87

Journalistic photography *See* Photography, Journalistic

Journalists

See also

Black journalists
Children as journalists
Foreign correspondents
Strikes—Television news
See also names of journalists

Friends in high places [M. Frankel, L. Grossman, R. Wald and R. Arledge of Columbia's Class of 1952] B. Yagoda. il pors *Channels* 7:54-61 Ja '87

Journals *See* Periodicals

Journals, Personal *See* Diaries

Jovanovich, William, 1920-

about

A costly save at Harcourt. P. Engardio. *Bus Week* p42 Je 8 '87

Jovanovich charges Maxwell is 'unfit'. M. Reuter. *Publ Wkly* 231:13-14 Je 5 '87

Jovanovich sees nothing friendly in Maxwell's bid. P. Engardio. il por *Bus Week* p47 Je 1 '87

Joy, William

Workstations blaze the trail for PCs. por *Pers Comput* 11:234 O '87

Joy

A magic I almost missed [sharing a joyful moment with a child] A. Lindstrom. il *Read Dig* 130:71-2 Ap '87

Joy Radio, Inc.

The Joy of advertising. A. Miller. il por *Newsweek* 110:43 Jl 27 '87

Joy Street Books

A familiar list with a new name: Joy Street. il *Publ Wkly* 231:28 Ap 24 '87

Joyce, Alisa

China takes the reformist road. il *Nation* 245:752-4 D 19 '87

Joyce, Bruce R., and Showers, Beverly

The power of schooling. bibl f il *Phi Delta Kappan* 68:352-5 Ja '87

Joyce, Diane

about

The Supreme Court puts the mike in Diane Joyce's hands, giving feminists a major victory. W. Plummer. il pors *People Wkly* 27:49-50+ Ap 13 '87

Joyce, James, 1882-1941

about

Wakers of the world, unite! You have nothing to lose but your theory. B. Maddox. il *N Y Times Book Rev* 92:20 Ag 16 '87

Anecdotes, facetiae, satire, etc.

Writer write-off. *Nation* 245:255-6 S 19 '87

Joyner, Al

about

Ties that bind. K. Moore. il pors *Sports Illus* 66:76-80+ Ap 27 '87

Joyner, Gail Tusan

about

Leading legal eagles. L. Norment. il pors *Ebony* 42:112+ F '87

Joyner, Gordon L.

about

Leading legal eagles. L. Norment. il pors *Ebony* 42:112+ F '87

Joyner, John E.

about

Black doctors elect Joyner head of NMA. por *Jet* 72:25 Ag 24 '87

Joyner-Kersee, Jackie

about

A double with trouble. C. Neff. il por *Sports Illus* 66:69 My 25 '87

Is she the greatest of them all? P. Freeman. il pors *Women's Sports Fitness* 9:38-42+ Ja '87

Jackie Joyner-Kersee to coach UCLA female cagers. il por *Jet* 73:48 O 19 '87

Joyner-Kersee's record leads U.S. Pan Am team. il por *Jet* 72:50+ Ag 31 '87

On top of the worlds [cover story] K. Moore. il pors *Sports Illus* 67:18-23 S 14 '87

Sullivan Award winner Jackie Joyner-Kersee is best amateur athlete. il por *Jet* 71:46 Mr 16 '87

Ties that bind. K. Moore. il pors *Sports Illus* 66:76-80+ Ap 27 '87

Jozwiak, Thomas L.

Electronic Xmas tree. il *Radio-Electron* 58:47-8+ D '87

JPL *See* Jet Propulsion Laboratory (U.S.)

Judaism

See also

Catholic Church—Relations—Judaism
Converts from Judaism
Hanukkah
Jews
Mysticism—Judaism
Passover
Sukkoth
Zionism

Conservative Judaism [discussion of December 1986 article, The Judaism born in America] H. Singer. *Commentary* 83:6-8+ Ap '87

Is messianism good for the Jews? J. Katz. *Commentary* 83:31-6 Ap '87

The kosher majority [Orthodoxy and political conservatism] D. Feder. *Natl Rev* 39:40+ Ap 10 '87

An open door [Pesach Tikvah, mental health center serving the Orthodox community in Williamsburg, Brooklyn] J. Meer. *Psychol Today* 21:17 Ap '87

Religious freedom for all: a Jewish perspective. S. Rabinove. il *USA Today (Periodical)* 116:32-5 N '87

Bibliography

Books on Jews and Judaism. J. Harris. *America* 157:163-4+ S 26 '87

Judaism and Christianity *See* Christianity and other religions

Judas Iscariot

about

Lenten meditation:
Judas as patron saint. R. Goetz. *Christ Century* 104:262-3 Mr 18-25 '87

Judd, Denis, 1938-

Paperback history. *Hist Today* 37:55 Je '87

Judd, O'Dean P.

about

Judd appointed SDI chief scientist at a time of program uncertainties. I. Goodwin. il por *Phys Today* 40:59-60 D '87

Judds (Musical group)

Family ties. L. Fissinger. il *Roll Stone* p18+ Jl 2 '87

The Judds: from blue grass to pure gold [interview] M. L. Baer. il *Teen* 31:47 D '87

Judge, Bruce

about

Bruce Judge: Simon's kindred spirit from Down Under. C. Debes. por *Bus Week* p86 Mr 9 '87

Judges

See also

Bork, Robert H., 1927-
Brennan, William J., Jr.
Drugs and judges
Frankfurter, Felix, 1882-1965
Ginsburg, Douglas H., 1946-
Hand, Learned, 1872-1961
Judicial ethics
Judicial power
Justice, William Wayne
Katic, Peter
Kennedy, Anthony M.
Marshall, Thurgood
Powell, Lewis F., Jr.
Turner, Jack
United States. Supreme Court

Appointment, qualifications, tenure, etc.

Biden Star Chamber? [creation of all-Democratic screening panel for Reagan judicial nominees] M. Fumento. *Natl Rev* 39:30 Mr 13 '87

The Constitution, the courts, and judicial competence. M. Cuomo. por *USA Today (Periodical)* 116:34-6 Jl '87

Jimmy Carter's judges [excerpt from The judges war] G. P. Smith, II. il *Natl Rev* 39:44+ O 23 '87

The Meese factor: packing the lower courts. I. Silver. *Commonweal* 114:102 F 27 '87

New judicial activists [conservatives] H. Schwartz. il *Nation* 244:361-2 Mr 21 '87

Picking federal judges: color-blind or blind to blacks. D. C. Ruffin. il *Black Enterp* 17:25 Ap '87

Reagan's Chicago farm team [law and economics training at University of Chicago Law School] J. McCormick. il *Newsweek* 110:46 N 9 '87

Reagan's court revolution comes up short. D. Whitman. il *U S News World Rep* 102:27-8 F 2 '87

Judges—Appointment, qualifications, tenure, etc.—*cont.*
Rolling back the Constitution [nomination of B. H. Siegan to U.S. Court of Appeals] H. Schwartz. il *Nation* 245:13-15 Jl 4-11 '87
Ronald Reagan and the Supremes. V. S. Navasky. il *Esquire* 107:77-80+ Ap '87
The trials and tribulations of getting to court. T. Gest. il *U S News World Rep* 103:12 N 2 '87

Impeachment
See Impeachments

Salaries, allowances, etc.
Justice for judges. M. B. Zuckerman. il *U S News World Rep* 102:68 Ja 19 '87

Judges and judging (Sports) *See* Sports officiating
Judgment Day
Will you be in the hot seat on Judgment Day? J. Deedy. il *U S Cathol* 52:6-12 Jl '87
Judgments
See also
Summary proceedings
Judice, Charles N.
Communications in 2001—the third age of video. il *Radio-Electron* 58:102-5 My '87
Judicial error *See* Justice, Miscarriage of
Judicial ethics
And in Vermont . . . [5 high court judges accused of misconduct] *Time* 129:72 F 23 '87
The best justice money can buy [Texas] W. P. Barrett. il *Forbes* 139:122+ Je 1 '87
A brief for impeachment [case of Judge A. Hastings of Florida] il por *U S News World Rep* 102:9 Mr 30 '87
Did Robert Bork bend the rules in a 1984 case? [failure to bow out of civil rights case in which a liberal group was seeking the appointment of a special prosecutor] T. Gest. il por *U S News World Rep* 103:12 Jl 20 '87
Hastings: critics are motivated by racism [ethics charges against Florida judge] por *Jet* 71:29 F 16 '87
Judge fights impeachment [A. L. Hastings] L. Brown. il por *Black Enterp* 18:18 Ag '87
Judge Hastings faces congressional hearing on charges of bribery. por *Jet* 73:6+ N 2 '87
More of the same [judges in Texas] W. P. Barrett. il *Forbes* 140:8 S 7 '87
Philadelphia takes a fall [suspension of 15 judges] E. Bowen. il *Time* 129:72 F 23 '87
There ought to be a law [sexist rulings and remarks in courts] K. Burkett. il *Ms* 16:74 D '87
Unorthodox behavior [Nova Scotia family court judge R. J. White] G. Emerson. il *Macleans* 100:17 Je 8 '87
Judicial power
See also
Judicial review
The blessings of liberty [judicial authority and due process] A. Press. il *Newsweek* 109:66-7 My 25 '87
The Constitution and the Court: could Meese be right? S. Levinson. *Current* 292:32-5 My '87
Government by lawyers & judges. W. Berns. *Commentary* 83:17-24 Je '87
Judicial imperialism [cover story; special section] il *Forbes* 139:109-12+ Je 1 '87
Judicial review [discussion of June 1987 article, Government by lawyers & judges] W. Berns. *Commentary* 84:6+ N '87
Power to the people [9th and 10th Amendments] W. B. Reynolds. il *N Y Times Mag* p116-18+ S 13 '87
What am I? A potted plant? [strict constructionism] R. A. Posner. *New Repub* 197:23-5 S 28 '87
What hope for the courts? [23rd national meeting of the Philadelphia Society] L. Bridges. *Natl Rev* 39:36-7+ Ag 28 '87
Judicial review
The final say. L. H. Tribe. il *N Y Times Mag* p68-70+ S 13 '87
John Marshall and the evolution of judicial review. D. G. Stephenson, Jr. il por *USA Today (Periodical)* 116:37-9 Jl '87
Judiciary *See* Courts; Judges; Judicial power
Judiciary Committee (Senate) *See* United States. Congress. Senate. Committee on the Judiciary
Judis, John B.
Apocalypse now and then. *New Repub* 197:29-30+ Ag 31 '87
The CIA & the legacy of William Casey. il *Commonweal* 114:752-6 D 18 '87
The Gary Hart affair: the media's role. *Current* 297:28-32 N '87
Mister Ed. *New Repub* 196:16-19 Ap 27 '87
Mister Ed: William Bennett. *Educ Dig* 53:36-8 D '87

The mouse that roars. *New Repub* 197:23-5 Ag 3 '87
White House vigilante. *New Repub* 196:17-18+ Ja 26 '87
Judy, Richard
about
"We enterprised it". J. Parr. il por *Forbes* 140:298+ N 16 '87
Judywhite
No more goo: advice to the lovestruck. il *Seventeen* 46:114 Ap '87
Juffer, Jane
Peonage in the pines. il *Progressive* 51:24-7 N '87
Reprieves from the war zone. il *Progressive* 51:11 D '87
Jugendstil *See* Art nouveau
Jugglers and juggling
See also
Flying Karamazov Brothers
Joggling—the whole-body workout. S. Morris. il *Omni* 9:136-7 My '87
Jugs *See* Pitchers (Pottery, glass, etc.)
Juice, Apple *See* Apple juice
Juice, Orange *See* Orange juice
Juices, Fruit *See* Fruit juices
Juigalpa (Nicaragua)
Notes and comment [Ann Arbor, Mich. donates garbage truck to sister city] *New Yorker* 63:15-16 Ag 17 '87
Juilliard American Opera Center
Trivial pursuits [Amelia goes to the ball and Tamu-tamu] P. G. Davis. il *N Y* 20:64+ My 11 '87
Juilliard String Quartet
Haydn seekers [The seven last words of Christ] P. G. Davis. il *N Y* 20:125 My 4 '87
Jujamcyn Theaters
I've got the horse right here: producer Rocco Landesman's big Broadway gamble. E. Pooley. il pors *N Y* 20:74-6+ S 28 '87
Juju music
Talking drums and juju joy [E. Obey] S. Bergman. il pors *Christ Today* 31:10-11 Ag 7 '87
Jules' Undersea Lodge (Fla.) *See* Underwater hotels, motels, etc.
Julian, Alexander
about
A subtle palette. E. Greene. il por *House Gard* 159:122-9+ F '87
Julian, Cecile
When chickens and chips fly. *Travel Holiday* 167:102 F '87
Juliette Gordon Low Birthplace (Savannah, Ga.) *See* Savannah (Ga.)—Historic houses, sites, etc.
July
The July almanac. il *Atlantic* 260:14 Jl '87
Jump rope *See* Rope jumping
Jumpers (Horses) *See* Horses
Jumping
See also
High jumping
Hurdle racing
Long jumping
Ski jumping
Triple jumping
Jumping (Horsemanship) *See* Horsemanship
Jumping by animals *See* Animal locomotion
Jumping genes *See* Transposons
Jumping rope *See* Rope jumping
Junatanov, Johnny
about
Life with father was nasty, brutish and scary, so Johnny Junatanov tried to have him murdered—repeatedly. A. Richman. il pors *People Wkly* 27:83+ Ja 19 '87
Junctions (Physiology)
Carbon tetrachloride at hepatotoxic levels blocks reversibly gap junctions between rat hepatocytes. J. C. Sáez and others. bibl f il *Science* 236:967-9 My 22 '87
Expression of functional cell-cell channels from cloned rat liver gap junction complementary DNA. G. Dahl and others. bibl f il *Science* 236:1290-3 Je 5 '87
Quantal release of transmitter is not associated with channel opening on the neuronal membrane [neuromuscular junction] S. H. Young and I. Chow. bibl f il *Science* 238:1712-13 D 18 '87
Restoration of LDL receptor activity in mutant cells by intercellular junctional communication. L. Hobbie and others. bibl f il *Science* 235:69-73 Ja 2 '87
Selective disruption of gap junctional communication interferes with a patterning process in hydra. S. E. Fraser and others. bibl f il *Science* 237:49-55 Jl 3 '87

June
The June almanac. il *Atlantic* 259:12 Je '87
Jungle *See* Rain forests
Junior Achievement
These kids mean business. D. L. Fortney. il *Read Dig* 130:147-50+ F '87
Junior colleges *See* Community and junior colleges
Junior high school students *See* High school students
Junior Olympics
The Junior Olympics: something for everyone. B. Phillips. *Sch Update* 119:2 F 23 '87
Junior tennis players *See* Tennis players
Junior tennis tournaments *See* Tennis—Tournaments
Junk
Rural sprawl: of junked cars and spent refrigerators. P. G. Quinnett. il *Ctry J* 14:68-71 N '87
Junk bonds
A better grade of junk [Levi Strauss issue] M. Schifrin. *Forbes* 140:258 N 30 '87
The case against Drexel: will the government come up short? C. Welles. il por *Bus Week* p56-60 Ag 10 '87
A chat with Michael Milken. A. Sloan. il por *Forbes* 140:248+ Jl 13 '87
Clarence Dillon: using other people's money. L. Jereski. il por *Forbes* 140:270+ Jl 13 '87
The coming defaults in junk bonds. F. S. Worthy. il *Fortune* 115:26-32+ Mr 16 '87
Despite everything, junk bonds are here to stay. C. Farrell. il *Bus Week* p92-3 F 16 '87
Drexel in the cross hairs [SEC investigation] B. Powell and C. Friday. il *Newsweek* 109:48 F 16 '87
Drexel's clients are rallying 'round Milken. C. Welles. il *Bus Week* p74 Ap 20 '87
Examine the motives of junk-bond critics. W. J. Carney. il *Bus Week* p18 Mr 30 '87
High yield, high risk [aftermath of 1984 Dart Drug leveraged buyout] P. Berman. il *Forbes* 140:38 Ag 24 '87
How Harcourt plans to keep the wolf away. G. DeGeorge. *Bus Week* p40+ S 14 '87
Is 'junk' still worth buying? J. B. Quinn. il *Newsweek* 110:70 D 7 '87
A junk-bond belly flop [Thompson family leveraged buyout of Southland] J. Weber, Jr. *Bus Week* p35 N 23 '87
Junk bonds finally face the acid test. C. Farrell. il *Bus Week* p64 N 16 '87
Low quality, high potential. B. Weberman. il *Forbes* 140:237 O 5 '87
Never-never money [PIK, or payment in kind, bonds] B. Weberman. il *Forbes* 139:265 Je 15 '87
Now Drexel Burnham is fighting on two fronts [SEC allegations] C. Welles. il por *Bus Week* p90-3+ F 16 '87
One man's junk. B. Weberman. il *Forbes* 139:173 Mr 23 '87
A recession might hit junk-bond issuers right between the eyes. G. Koretz. il *Bus Week* p24 Jl 20 '87
A record turnout for Drexel's junk-bond bash [conference in Beverly Hills] A. Bianco. il por *Bus Week* p80 Ap 13 '87
'Spin control' on Wall Street. J. Reed. il *U S News World Rep* 102:46 Ap 20 '87
Surprise! The insider trading scandal has not made junk bond funds any riskier. C. A. Fried. *Money* 16:29 Ja '87
The thrift that junk bonds built [Columbia Savings & Loan] T. Carson. il por *Bus Week* p86 Je 29 '87
Trying times for junk bonds. F. S. Worthy. il *Fortune* 116:59-60 D 7 '87
Were Drexel and Boesky in cahoots? J. Egan and D. Baer. il por *U S News World Rep* 102:45 F 16 '87
What's under the rock? [high-yield insurance products financed with junk bonds] B. Kallen. il *Forbes* 139:134-5 F 23 '87
The wonder woman of muni bonds [C. A. Fitts of Dillon, Read] A. Bianco. il por *Bus Week* p112-13 F 23 '87
Rating
Junkyard analyst [P. Maffei] J. Willoughby. il por *Forbes* 140:230+ N 2 '87
Junker, Howard
The art of mingei at Kuromatsu. il por *Archit Dig* 44:98+ My '87
A versatile retreat: designer's Lake Tahoe apartment. il *Archit Dig* 44:132-7 Mr '87
Junker, Jake
about
Indian: on the road again. E. Borin. il pors *Cycle* 38:68-72+ S '87

Junkerman, John
Nissan, Tennessee [cover story] il *Progressive* 51:16-18+ Je '87
Junkyards, Airplane *See* Airplane junkyards
Junkyards, Automobile *See* Automobile junkyards
Junkyards, Motorcycle *See* Motorcycle junkyards
Junkyards, Ship *See* Ship junkyards
Juno Awards
The stars of music. B. D. Johnson. il *Macleans* 100:62 N 16 '87
Junor, Penny
How far will these girls go? il pors *McCalls* 115:14-16+ N '87
Jupiter (Planet)
See also
Space flight to Jupiter
Jupiter's best show in twelve years [cover story] J. Olivarez. il *Astronomy* 15:64-70 N '87
Atmosphere
Jupiter's Great Red Spot. A. MacRobert. il *Sky Telesc* 74:513 N '87
Photographs and photography
High-resolution views of Mars and Jupiter [work of Jean Dragesco] il *Sky Telesc* 73:680-1 Je '87
Satellites
See also
Life on Europa (Satellite)
The Jupiter-Io connection: an Alfvén engine in space. J. W. Belcher. bibl f il *Science* 238:170-6 O 9 '87
Tales from Io. *Sky Telesc* 73:485 My '87
Timing eclipses of Jupiter's moons. J. E. Westfall. il *Sky Telesc* 74:634-6 D '87
Atmosphere
Eclipse measurements of Io's sodium atmosphere. N. M. Schneider and others. bibl f il *Science* 238:55-8 O 2 '87
Jura Mountains (France and Switzerland)
Switzerland by gypsy wagon: a one-horsepower Jura tour. R. E. Baronas. il *Travel Holiday* 167:52-5+ My '87
Variations on a Grand Traverse [ski trip] A. Pospisil. il *Skiing* 40:161-4+ N '87
Jurassic period *See* Paleontology—Jurassic
Jurgens, Lois
about
A tale of two Minnesota mothers: one seeks the truth behind their son's death, the other stands accused. D. Chu. il pors *People Wkly* 27:28-31 Mr 2 '87
Jurisdiction
See also
Privileges and immunities
Jurisdiction, Territorial
See also
Antarctic regions—Territorial claims
Jurisprudence
See also
Insanity—Jurisprudence
Medical jurisprudence
Jurnovoy, Joyce, and Jenness, David
A care and repair guide for shoes. il *Mademoiselle* 93:182 My '87
Jury, Carol
about
Two mothers for Laura. R. Distelheim. il pors *McCalls* 114:135-7 S '87
Jury
See also
Grand jury
Mock jury
Can justice be deaf, too? [deaf jurors] G. Carroll. il *Newsweek* 109:69 Mr 2 '87
From jury selection to verdict—in hours [summary jury trials] L. J. Tell. il *Bus Week* p48 S 7 '87
Georgia murder conviction overturned: black jurors struck for racial reasons [case of W. Gamble] *Jet* 72:40 Ag 3 '87
Guilty ourselves [juror guilt; research by Lawrence A. Fehr] D. Schechter. *Psychol Today* 21:20 O '87
Jury-duty journal. D. K. Mano. *Natl Rev* 39:65+ N 20 '87
Jury selection series cited by Marshall wins an award [Dallas morning news series on jury discrimination] *Jet* 72:23 Jl 20 '87
Never to be accused of rushing to judgment, a jury goes home after a trying 44 months [Monsanto dioxin-spill suit] M. Green. il *People Wkly* 28:48-50 N 9 '87
A profitable game: judge and tell [jury members cashing in on celebrated cases] T. Gest. il *U S News World Rep* 103:52-3 Ag 17 '87

Jury—cont.

Puzzling evidence [pretrial publicity and juries; study by Roger W. Davis] S. Walton. il *Psychol Today* 21:10 Ag '87

Should a priest serve on a jury? V. A. Lapomarda. il *America* 156:495-6 Je 20-27 '87

Supreme Court rule may give new trials to blacks [blacks convicted by all white juries] *Jet* 71:6 F 2 '87

Jury duty *See* Jury

Just, Ward S.

about

PW interviews. H. R. Lottman. por *Publ Wkly* 231:67-8 Mr 13 '87

Just June

about

Black female comedienne 'Just' makes 'em laugh. il pors *Jet* 72:36-7 Ag 31 '87

Just Say No (Organization)

Just Say No. J. Wilkie. il *Good Housekeep* 204:64+ Ja '87

Just war doctrine

A just-war theory for abortion. F. F. Church. *Christ Century* 104:733-4 Ag 26-S 2 '87

Justice, William Wayne

about

The eyes of Justice are on Texas. il por *Newsweek* 109:55 Ja 19 '87

Justice

See also
Equality before the law
Injustice
Religion and justice

Evening the score [society's concepts of justice reflected in sports] M. M. Mark and J. Greenberg. bibl (p63) il *Psychol Today* 21:44-50 Ja '87

The free enterprise system [address, February 11, 1987] V. Jordan. *Vital Speeches Day* 53:466-8 My 15 '87

John XXIII and the hand grenade [views of H. Arkes] R. J. Neuhaus. *Natl Rev* 39:51 S 25 '87

The pursuit of happiness. Publius. il *New Leader* 70:12-13 O 5 '87

Justice, Administration of

See also
Actions and defenses
Arbitration and award
Courts
Criminal justice, Administration of
Due process of law
Judges
Jury
Justice, Miscarriage of
Juvenile justice, Administration of
Legal procedure
Political prisoners
Public prosecutors
Searches and seizures
Summary proceedings
United States. Dept. of Justice

Justice, Miscarriage of

Abuse in the name of protecting children [guarding against false accusations] R. L. Emans. bibl f il *Phi Delta Kappan* 68:740-3 Je '87

Abuse in the name of protecting children [guarding against false accusations] R. L. Emans. *Educ Dig* 53:36-9 N '87

Alabama man cleared of murder 15 years later [case of B. J. Leaster] il por *Jet* 71:26 Ja 19 '87

Black Chicagoan awarded $800,000 for false arrest [G. Jones] *Jet* 72:5 Mr 30 '87

Black wins case against Pennsylvania state police; will receive $485,000 [case of black policeman R. Clanagan] *Jet* 72:38 My 11 '87

Court orders new trial for Steven Linscott. il por *Christ Today* 31:68+ S 4 '87

Deathbed confession frees Del. black after 12 years [case of W. Cammile] il por *Jet* 72:16 Jl 6 '87

Etta Smith's inspiration cost her four days in jail [vision of victim's body in Pacoima section of Los Angeles] J. Kelley. il por *People Wkly* 27:33 My 25 '87

Exploring an injustice [inquiry into Sydney, N.S. murder conviction of D. Marshall] M. Gee. *Macleans* 100:29 O 19 '87

Innocent man's eight-year prison ordeal [case of N. Walker in New Jersey] W. Leavy. il pors *Ebony* 42:86+ Mr '87

N.Y. sax player labeled criminal in Daily news in case of mistaken identity [case of D. Foster] il por *Jet* 72:38 My 11 '87

NFL Falcons' star sues Ga. police for $400,000 [W. Andrews] *Jet* 72:50 Jl 27 '87

Sexual abuse or abuse of justice? [false accusations] R. Lacayo. il *Time* 129:49 My 11 '87

Strange and contradictory testimony [testimony of R. N. Ebsary at inquiry into Sydney, N.S. murder conviction of D. Marshall] M. Gee. il pors *Macleans* 100:23 S 21 '87

That's outrageous! M. Royko. il *Read Dig* 130:74-8 F '87

A vision of murder [S. Linscott tried for murder on basis of dream] M. Green. il pors *People Wkly* 27:30-2 My 25 '87

Justice Dept. (U.S.) *See* United States. Dept. of Justice

Justices *See* Judges

Justices, Supreme Court *See* United States. Supreme Court

Justis, Jeff

Glacier greaser. il map *Flying* 114:109-10 F '87

Justiz, Manuel J., and Kameen, Marilyn C.

Business offers a hand to education. bibl f il *Phi Delta Kappan* 68:379-83 Ja '87

JustLife (Organization)

With the religious right in disarray, two groups consider new opportunities [with interview with R. J. Sider] B. Spring. il por *Christ Today* 31:46, 48 Jl 10 '87

Jute

See also
Kenaf

Jutra, Claude, 1930-1987

about

Obituary
Macleans il por 100:57 My 4 '87. B. D. Johnson

Jutras, Michel

about

Michel Jutras doesn't win any trophies for cleaning hippo teeth, but he does get plenty of plaque. il por *People Wkly* 27:123 Je 15 '87

Juvenile delinquents and delinquency

See also
Gangs
Juvenile justice, Administration of
School violence

Bitter memories of murder [movie River's edge recalls murder and coverup by Milpitas, Calif. teens] P. Abramson. il *Newsweek* 109:25 Je 22 '87

A boy and his dog in hell [illegal dog fighting with pit bull terriers in Philadelphia] M. Sager. il *Roll Stone* p36-7+ Jl 2 '87

Georgia sisters indicted for their mother's murder [R. Golden and M. Collier] *Jet* 73:47 N 2 '87

Hidden histories on death row [neurological disorders and homicidal behavior; study of death row juveniles by Dorothy Otnow Lewis] *Sci News* 132:287 O 31 '87

Just for kicks [vandalism] J. Brondfield. il *Read Dig* 131:33-7 Ag '87

Murder in mind [neurological disorders and homicidal behavior; study of death row juveniles by Dorothy Otnow Lewis] J. Meer. *Psychol Today* 21:62 Mr '87

Two Georgia sisters held for their mother's murder [M. Collier and R. Golden held in murder of Frances Golden] il pors *Jet* 72:32 Ag 17 '87

West Memphis youth shot by friend watching gun commercial on television [Andre McGee shot] *Jet* 73:46 N 2 '87

Nutrition

Juvenile delinquents lack iron. *Prevention* 39:9 F '87

Juvenile hormones

Chemistry of pheromone and hormone metabolism in insects. G. D. Prestwich. bibl f il *Science* 237:999-1006 Ag 28 '87

Identification of a juvenile hormone-like compound in a crustacean. H. Laufer and others. bibl f il *Science* 235:202-5 Ja 9 '87

Juvenile justice, Administration of

Kids, crime and punishment. T. Gest. il *U S News World Rep* 103:50-1 Ag 24 '87

Canada

Flaws in new laws for the young. J. Bennett. il *Macleans* 100:44 S 7 '87

Illinois

See also
Gage Park (Ill.)—Juvenile justice, Administration of

Indiana

See also
Hammond (Ind.)—Juvenile justice, Administration of

Countdown to the electric chair [18-year-old killer P. Cooper] F. Bruning. por *Macleans* 100:13 O 26 '87

Indiana killer, Italian martyr [Italians show support for juvenile killer P. Cooper] G. Hackett. il por *Newsweek* 110:37 S 21 '87

Juvenile literature *See* Children's literature
JVC Jazz Festival *See* Music festivals—New York (State)
JWP Inc.
If at first you don't succeed. J. Cook. il por *Forbes* 139:61-2 Je 29 '87

K

K Mart Corp.
Attention, savers! K Mart wants you [linkup with First Nationwide] J. B. Levine. il *Bus Week* p81-2 Ja 19 '87
K Mart to Santa: ho, ho, ho-hum. W. Zellner. il *Bus Week* p60-1 D 7 '87
Nickels and dimes no more [strategies of chairman B. Fauber] J. A. Seamonds. il por *U S News World Rep* 102:42 Je 29 '87

K2 Mountain (Pakistan)
After all is said and done, will Everest still be number one? [Navstar satellite altitude measurement; work of George Wallerstein] J. Krakauer. bibl (p231) il map *Smithsonian* 18:176-8+ O '87
Can you top this? [abstract quality of mountain's height] M. W. Browne. il *N Y Times Mag* p50 Je 14 '87
Everest toppled [Navstar satellite altitude measurement; work of George Wallerstein] il *Sky Telesc* 74:121 Ag '87
King of the mountains [Navstar satellite measurements prove Everest is higher than K2] il *Time* 130:75 N 2 '87
The most savage mountain. P. Gillman. il *World Press Rev* 34:36-7 D '87
Pique over peaks: K2 versus Everest [use of Navstar satellite to determine height] J. Kluger. il *Discover* 8:16 O '87

Kaaterskill Falls (N.Y.)
Searching for Kaaterskill Falls. N. Bliven. il *New Yorker* 63:43-58 Ag 3 '87

Kabat, Donald, and McMahon, Lynn
Step-by-step guidance for improving your operations. il *Work Woman* 12:46-7 S '87

Kabobs
Create a kabob! il *Better Homes Gard* 65:92 Je '87

The Kabuki [ballet] *See* Ballet reviews—Single works

Kadanoff, Leo P.
From neutrinos to quasiparticles. por *Phys Today* 40 pt1:7+ Ag '87
On complexity. il por *Phys Today* 40:7+ Mr '87

Kádár, János, 1912-
about
Can 'goulash communism' survive austerity? F. A. Miller. il por *Bus Week* p81 My 25 '87

Kaddafi, Muammar *See* Qaddafi, Muammar al-, 1942-

Kadlecek, Mary
Toxics in a great river—putting the pieces together. il *Conservationist* 42:34-9 N/D '87
(jt. auth) *See* Hogan, Barbara, and Kadlecek, Mary

Kadohata, Cynthia
Jack's girl [story] *New Yorker* 63:44-50 D 7 '87
Marigolds [story] *New Yorker* 62:36-9 F 9 '87

Kael, Pauline
The current cinema. See issues of The New Yorker

Kaercher, Dan
Health. See issues of Better Homes and Gardens

Käferstein, Fritz, and Sims, Jacqueline
Food safety—a worldwide public health issue. il *World Health* p3-4 Mr '87

Kafka, Barbara
Food in Vogue. See issues of Vogue beginning September 1983
Great American cakes. il *Gourmet* 47:88-9+ D '87
No place like home. il *N Y Times Mag* p25-6 D 27 '87
The old new wave. il *N Y Times Mag* p41-2 Ag 2 '87
Winds of the Antilles. il *N Y Times Mag* p61-2 F 15 '87
about
Microwaving goes big time. L. Shapiro. il por *Newsweek* 110:79 O 12 '87

Kagan, Daniel
This diet could be your last: but not for the reasons you think. *Mademoiselle* 93:262-3+ Mr '87

Kagan, Donald
Preventing World War III [discussion of March 1987 article, World War I, World War II, World War III] *Commentary* 83:2+ Je '87

World War I, World War II, World War III. *Commentary* 83:21-40 Mr '87

Kagan, Y. Y., and Knopoff, L.
Statistical short-term earthquake prediction. bibl f il *Science* 236:1563-7 Je 19 '87

Kagarlitsky, Boris
about
Cats and bears: practicing left politics in the Soviet Union [interview] A. Cockburn. *Nation* 245:706-7 D 12 '87
The left in the Soviet Union: the politics of *perestroika* [interview] A. Cockburn. *Nation* 245:672-3 D 5 '87
The Soviet new left [interview] A. Cockburn. *Nation* 245:618-19 N 28 '87

Kagle, Arlene
Kiss kiss/pow pow! The love/hate rhythms of a romance. il *Mademoiselle* 93:202-3+ My '87

Kagnoff, Martin F.
(jt. auth) *See* Omary, M. Bishr, and Kagnoff, Martin F.

Kahl, M. P. (Marvin Philip), 1934-
The royal spoonbill. il map *Natl Geogr* 171:280-4 F '87

Kahl, Marvin Philip *See* Kahl, M. P. (Marvin Philip), 1934-

Kahn, Carol
On ice. il *Health* 19:70-2+ Mr '87

Kahn, E. J. (Ely Jacques), 1916-
Coble and tenk. *New Yorker* 63:103-4+ My 11 '87
A friend on their side. *New Yorker* 62:72-7 Ja 19 '87
Hazards involved. *New Yorker* 63:64-70 Ag 17 '87
Profiles [D. O. Andreas] por *New Yorker* 62:41-2+ F 16 '87
Profiles [H. Suzman] por *New Yorker* 63:50-1+ Ap 20 '87
about
E. J. Kahn book about 'New Yorker' to be published by Stephen Greene. *Publ Wkly* 232:76 O 2 '87

Kahn, Ely Jacques *See* Kahn, E. J. (Ely Jacques), 1916-

Kahn, Herbert
Photographic masterpieces from a midwestern bank. il *USA Today (Periodical)* 115:42-53 My '87

Kahn, Joan
Editor to writer. *Writer* 100:12-13+ Ap '87

Kahn, Leo
about
Ballpoint pens "R" Us. B. Leonard. il por *Forbes* 139:172 Ap 6 '87

Kahn, Philippe
TSR: an acronym worthy of amnesia. por *Pers Comput* 11:238 O '87
about
The maverick. D. Garfinkel. il pors *Pers Comput* 11:118-21+ Mr '87

Kahn, Robert E.
Networks for advanced computing. bibl (p184) il *Sci Am* 257:136-43 O '87

Kahn, Robert Louis, 1918-
(jt. auth) *See* Rowe, John W. (John Wallis), 1944-, and Kahn, Robert Louis, 1918-

Kahn, Ronald N.
Desperately seeking supernovae [cover story] il *Sky Telesc* 73:594-7 Je '87
Letters. *Sky Telesc* 74:229-30 S '87

Kahn, Roy
Slum community saves itself. *Ms* 15:32 Je '87

Kahn, Wolf, 1927-
about
Landscapes of color. C. Gaines. il por *Archit Dig* 44:44+ Je '87

Kain, Karen
about
Kain is able. M. Crabb. il pors *Dance Mag* 61:68-9 Mr '87

Kaiser, Chris A., and others
Many random sequences functionally replace the secretion signal sequence of yeast invertase. bibl f il *Science* 235:312-17 Ja 16 '87

Kaiser, Edgar, Jr.
about
High adventure in the bank trade. P. C. Newman. il por *Macleans* 100:38 Ja 26 '87

Kaiser Aerospace & Electronics Corp.
Analyzing the Mac numbers [finance director D. Branton's use of computer] C. O'Malley. il por *Pers Comput* 11:179+ O '87

Kaiser-Permanente Medical Care Program
Kaiser Foundation in California settles. *Mon Labor Rev* 110:56-7 Je '87

Kaiser Steel Corp.
The 'pugnacious bulldog' fighting for Kaiser Steel [B. Hendry] M. J. Pitzer. il por *Bus Week* p72-3 F 16 '87

Kaku, Michio, and Axelrod, Daniel
Off with their heads: how Zbigniew Brzezinski hawked the doctrine of nuclear decapitation. il *Progressive* 51:29-31 Ja '87

Kaku, Michio, and Trainer, Jennifer
Super cyclotron. il *Omni* 9:20 F '87

Kakutani, Michiko
Our woman of letters. il pors *N Y Times Mag* p60-1+ Mr 29 '87

Kalachnikoff, Nadine
about
The dinner party as theater—feasts for the spirit and the senses. C. Rayner. il por *Vogue* 177:288 F '87

Kalafut, Larry
about
White Ill. youth sentenced for torching black home. *Jet* 72:18 Mr 30 '87

Kalalau Trail (Kauai, Hawaii) *See* Trails—Kauai (Hawaii)

Kalamarides, Ruth I., and others
Lateral isotopic discontinuity in the lower crust: an example from Antarctica. bibl f il maps *Science* 237:1192-5 S 4 '87

Kalb, Jon
about
Gossip and peer review at NSF. E. Marshall. *Science* 238:1502 D 11 '87

Kalbacher, Gene
The Gadd Gang: not just the same old stuff. il *Down Beat* 54:16-19 O '87
Sadao Watanabe's bop/pop chops. il pors *Down Beat* 54:19-21 Ja '87

Kaleidoscope, Inc.
Kaleidoscope's Youth Development Program: a last chance for youth "aging out" of foster care. S. M. Stehno. il *Child Today* 16:29-33 S/O '87

Kaleidoscope (Program)
Kaleidoscope mirrors children's perspective on art. P. Rowe. il *Child Today* 16:20-5 Ja/F '87

Kaler, James B.
The B stars: beacons of the skies. il *Sky Telesc* 74:147-50 Ag '87
The spectacular O stars. il *Sky Telesc* 74:464-9 N '87
The temperate F stars. il *Sky Telesc* 73:131-4 F '87
White Sirian stars: class A. il *Sky Telesc* 73:491-4 My '87

Kalergis, Mary Motley
Mothers talk about mothering [excerpt from Mother: a collective portrait] il *Ladies Home J* 104:43-4+ My '87

Kales, Emily Fox
Dieting to bulimia. il *Psychol Today* 21:18 D '87

Kaletsky, Anatole
(jt. auth) See Jonquieres, Guy de, and Kaletsky, Anatole

Kalich, Timothy
What's in a smell? il *Atlantic* 260:34+ O '87

Kalikstein, Kalman, 1929-1987
about
Obituary
Phys Today 40:106+ D '87. B. Kramer

Kalishman, Norton, and others
Involving children and youth in community projects. bibl f il *Child Today* 16:23-6 Mr/Ap '87

Kalman, Tibor
about
A boy's guide to chaos. H. Aldersey-Williams. il por *N Y* 20:24 My 11 '87

Kalona (Iowa)
Population
Everybody in this picture is named Miller or Yoder except for one poor guy [postmaster T. Hagedorn's problem with family names] D. Van Biema. il por *People Wkly* 27:46-8 Mr 30 '87

Kalven, Jamie
Bork v. the First. *Nation* 245:269-70 S 19 '87
U.S. visa policy: the machinery of exclusion [cover story; with editorial comment] bibl f il *Bull At Sci* 43:2, 21-30 My '87

Kalymnos (Greece: Island)
See also
Fisheries—Kalymnos (Greece: Island)

Kamber, Victor
TV news as political kingmaker. por *U S News World Rep* 102:8 Je 15 '87

Kambic, Robert
Catholics and natural family planning: tradition or innovation? *America* 157:244-6+ O 17 '87

Kameen, Marilyn C.
(jt. auth) See Justiz, Manuel J., and Kameen, Marilyn C.

Kamen, Gloria
Writing biographies for children. *Writer* 100:19-21 Mr '87

Kamen, Nick
about
Singer Nick Kamen, who launched his career with his pants down. il pors *People Wkly* 27:59-60 Je 1 '87

Kamen, Robert
(jt. auth) See Clark, Steven C., and Kamen, Robert

Kamenetz, Rodger, 1950-
Daniel da Volterra, "the breeches-maker," on Michelangelo's last judgment [poem] *New Repub* 197:40 Jl 6 '87

Kamimura, Hiroshi
Graphite intercalation compounds. bibl il *Phys Today* 40:64-71 D '87

Kaminsky, Howard
about
After the un-Random showdown. M. Reuter. il pors *Publ Wkly* 232:11 O 30 '87
Joni Evans replaces Kaminsky at Random. *Publ Wkly* 232:11 O 23 '87
The rumble at Random House. J. Alter. il pors *Newsweek* 110:62 O 26 '87

Kamisar, Yale
Drugs, AIDS and the threat to privacy. il *N Y Times Mag* p108-10+ S 13 '87

Kamm, Henry
A broken country. il *N Y Times Mag* p96+ S 20 '87

Kampelman, Max M., 1920-
Nuclear and space arms talks close round seven [statement, March 6, 1987] *Dep State Bull* 87:18 My '87
Nuclear and space arms talks close round six [statement, November 12, 1986] *Dep State Bull* 87:41-2 Ja '87
Nuclear and space arms talks open round eight [statement, May 4, 1987] *Dep State Bull* 87:26 Jl '87
about
'Getting down to zero' [interview] D. Stanglin. il por *U S News World Rep* 102:26-7 Mr 16 '87

Kampuchea
See also
Kampucheans
United Nations—Kampuchea
Foreign relations
Vietnam
Assembly endorses four principal components of a settlement to the situation in Kampuchea. il *UN Chron* 23:15-17 Ja '86
Assembly endorses four principal components of settlement of situation in Kampuchea. il *UN Chron* 24:79-80 F '87
Beyond the killing fields. M. Kelly. *America* 156:172-3 F 28 '87
The Cambodian issue [statement, March 11, 1987] J. C. Monjo. *Dep State Bull* 87:29-30 My '87
Sihanouk's 'open door'. F. Willey. il por *Newsweek* 110:56 D 14 '87
Situation in Cambodia [statement, October 20, 1986; with text of General Assembly resolution] V. A. Walters. *Dep State Bull* 87:80-2 Ja '87
Stalemate in Cambodia. E. Becker. bibl f *Curr Hist* 86:156-9+ Ap '87
History
Civil War, 1970-1975
Cambodia [discussion of April 1987 article, Pol Pot in retrospect] A. Puddington. *Commentary* 84:14-15 Ag '87
Pol Pot in retrospect. A. Puddington. *Commentary* 83:49-54 Ap '87
Politics and government
Sihanouk's 'open door'. F. Willey. il por *Newsweek* 110:56 D 14 '87
Stalemate in Cambodia. E. Becker. bibl f *Curr Hist* 86:156-9+ Ap '87
Social conditions
A broken country. H. Kamm. il *N Y Times Mag* p96+ S 20 '87

Kampuchean refugees *See* Refugees, Kampuchean

Kampucheans
United States
If I can make it there, I'll make it anywhere [New York City] B. Doyle. il *U S Cathol* 52:26-33 D '87
Religious life
One refugee's story: "sometimes I'm okay" [Thay Sam] B. R. Thompson. por *Christ Today* 31:26 F 20 '87

Kan, Yue-Sai

about

Guess what they watch in China on Sunday nights? D. J. Yang. il por *Bus Week* p91 Ja 19 '87

Helping East meet West via TV, America's Yue-Sai Kan has become the most famous woman in China. S. K. Reed. il pors *People Wkly* 27:123-4 My 18 '87

Kanakis, Louis

Getting clear on diamonds. il *Consum Res Mag* 70:20-2 Jl '87

Kandel, Bethany

Offbeat offerings. il *Travel Holiday* 167:6-7+ Ja '87

Kandell, Leslie

An angel's way . . . il por *Opera News* 51:8-10 Ja 31 '87

Kandinsky, Wassily, 1866-1944

about

Murnau and Kochel: where the Blue Rider was born. J. Dornberg. il pors *Art News* 86:77-8+ D '87

Kane, Joe

Mother Nature's army. il *Esquire* 107:98-102+ F '87

Kane, Mitchell, 1946-

about

Mitchell Kane at Robbin Lockett. M. Bonesteel. il *Art Am* 75:231 Ap '87

Kane, Paul

Rock Creek Cemetery: Washington, D.C. [poem] *New Repub* 197:32 Ag 24 '87

Kane, Pearl

Public or independent schools: does where you teach make a difference? il *Phi Delta Kappan* 69:286-9 D '87

Kane, Tim D.

Detroit—lean and mean or fat and foolish? il *USA Today (Periodical)* 116:37 S '87

Kane, Tommy

about

Raising Kane at Syracuse University. D. Burke. il por *Macleans* 100:47 N 23 '87

Kaneko, Seiichi

about

In Japan, using 'logic and emotion'. B. Buell. il por *Bus Week* p155 D 28 '87-Ja 4 '88

Kanfer, Stefan

Rejoicing in rituals. il *Read Dig* 131:131-2 O '87

about

'Time' will tell. por *Publ Wkly* 231:26-7 Ap 10 '87

Kangaroo [film] See Motion picture reviews—Single works

Kangaroo Island (Australia)

Description and travel

Kangaroo Island. C. B. Hayes. il *Travel Holiday* 168:26-9 S '87

Kangaroos U.S.A. Inc.

Running shoes make a leap into the space age [Dynacoil shoes designed by space suit developer A. L. Gross] K. Dreyfack. il por *Bus Week* p70 Ja 19 '87

Kangas, Matthew

The embodiment of ingenuity. bibl f il *Am Craft* 47:46-53 Ag/S '87

Kani, John

about

Black actor stars in S. African 'Othello'. il por *Jet* 73:22 O 5 '87

Kanievska, Marek

about

Less than zero [film] Reviews

N Y il 20:104-5 N 23 '87. D. Denby

Newsweek il 110:108 N 16 '87. D. Ansen

People Wkly 28:14 D 14 '87. S. Haller

Vogue il 177:76 N '87. B. Roe

Kanigel, Robert

The genome project. il por *N Y Times Mag* p44+ D 13 '87

One man's mousetraps. il por *N Y Times Mag* p48+ My 17 '87

Kanipe, Jeff

M-87: describing the indescribable [cover story] il *Astronomy* 15:6-13 My '87

Kanki, Phyllis J., and others

Human T-lymphotropic virus type 4 and the human immunodeficiency virus in West Africa. bibl f il *Science* 236:827-31 My 15 '87

Kanner, Bernice

The admissions-go-round: private school fever. il *N Y* 20:40-6 N 23 '87

Blood on the carpet: the coup that failed at J. Walter Thompson. il pors *N Y* 20:36-40 F 16 '87

On Madison Avenue. See issues of New York

Kanrisha Yosei

Hell camp, Malibu-style. R. Phalon. il *Forbes* 140:110+ D 28 '87

Kansai International Airport See Osaka (Japan)—Airports

Kansas

See also

Crime and criminals—Kansas

Greeley County (Kan.)

Hunting—Kansas

Paleontology—Kansas

Kansas City (Mo.)

Education

Can a judge raise taxes? [R. G. Clark's attempt to end school segregation by ordering tax increases] J. Seligmann. il por *Newsweek* 110:98 O 12 '87

Kansas judge raises taxes to desegregate schools [Russell Clark] *Jet* 73:22 O 19 '87

Poor

A family down and out [Brand family] P. King. il *Newsweek* 109:44-6 Ja 12 '87

Social conditions

Cupcake Land. R. Rhodes. il *Harpers* 275:51-7 N '87

Social life and customs

Goldberg can go home again. C. Trillin. *New Yorker* 63:87-92+ Ap 6 '87

Taxation

Can a judge raise taxes? [R. G. Clark's attempt to end school segregation by ordering tax increases] J. Seligmann. il por *Newsweek* 110:98 O 12 '87

Kansas judge raises taxes to desegregate schools [Russell Clark] *Jet* 73:22 O 19 '87

Kansas City Southern Industries, Inc.

Just when Kansas City Southern was ready to pounce . . . [hostile bid led by H. Kaskel] M. Ivey and C. Hawkins. *Bus Week* p26-7 Ag 24 '87

Kansas Cosmosphere and Space Center

Restoring America's space treasures. J. R. Vacca. il *Space World* X-8-284:10-13 Ag '87

Kantor, Kenneth L.

"I can make you an awesome deal": real-life devious speaker selling practices. il *High Fidel* 37:42-4+ Je '87

Kantor, Michael

Firewood gathering hits a snag. il *Sierra* 72:24+ Mr/Ap '87

Heavy metal on tap. il *Sierra* 72:18-20 N/D '87

Kanwar, Roop

about

Fire and faith. *Time* 130:41 S 28 '87

Kao-hsiung (Taiwan)

Monuments, statues, etc.

The New Statue of Liberty [E. Neizvestny commissioned to create colossal statue] *New Yorker* 63:21-2 Jl 13 '87

Kapferer, Jean-Noël

about

Psst! Wait till you hear this. J. Leo. il *Time* 129:76 Mr 16 '87

Kapikian, Catherine

about

A seminary's artist in residence: Cathy Kapikian's fabric of faith. L.-M. Delloff. il *Christ Century* 104:267-71 Mr 18-25 '87

Kaplan, Amy

Why your body doesn't want to work out. il *Mademoiselle* 93:76 Je '87

Kaplan, Bruce L.

about

Got the postcrash blues? A bullion dealer may have the cure. T. Segal. il por *Bus Week* p180-1 D 28 '87-Ja 4 '88

Kaplan, Gary M.

Oh, my aching toe! *Nations Bus* 75:68 Ja '87

Kaplan, H. J.

Remembering Vietnam. *Commentary* 84:13-29 D '87

Requiem for the "establishment". *Commentary* 83:37-48 Ap '87

"The wise men" [discussion of April 1987 article, Requiem for the establishment] *Commentary* 84:10-12 Jl '87

Kaplan, Helen Singer, 1929-

Are you lying in bed? por *Redbook* 169:14 Je '87

The underrated power of scent. il por *Redbook* 169:38+ My '87

"We always make love the same way". por *Redbook* 169:48 O '87

about

A warning to women on AIDS. J. Seligmann. il por *Newsweek* 110:72 Ag 31 '87

Kaplan, James

The Dreyfuss affair [cover story] il pors *Esquire* 108:144-8+ N '87

Kaplan, James—*cont.*
Everything is North/Ann Bancroft. il por *Vogue* 177:452-3+ Mr '87
A Giants man, all the way. il pors *N Y Times Mag* p28-30+ S 6 '87
Kaplan, Janice
How old is your body? Beat-the-clock strategies. il *Mademoiselle* 93:92+ Je '87
Why walk? il *Vogue* 177:240-2+ Je '87
Kaplan, Jeremiah
about
Kaplan joins Simon & Schuster as special adviser to Snyder. pors *Publ Wkly* 231:16 Ja 16 '87
Kaplan moves to new post of S & S president. il por *Publ Wkly* 232:10 S 25 '87
Macmillan and Kaplan sue each other over pay. J. Mutter. *Publ Wkly* 232:15 Ag 28 '87
Kaplan, Jim
It's a dream come true. il por *Sports Illus* 67:95 O 5 '87
The triple. il *Sport Mag* 78:52-5+ S '87
Kaplan, Joan C.
(jt. auth) See Hirsch, Martin S., and Kaplan, Joan C.
Kaplan, Jonathan
about
Project X [film] Reviews
  Glamour il 85:153 Je '87. J. G. Boyum
  Macleans il 100:62 Ap 27 '87. L. O'Toole
  Newsweek il 109:75 My 4 '87. D. Ansen
  People Wkly 27:12 Je 15 '87. S. Haller
  Time il 129:97 My 4 '87. R. Corliss
Kaplan, Justin
In pursuit of the ultimate fiction. il *N Y Times Book Rev* 92:1+ Ap 19 '87
Kaplan, Michael
Getting a good rep. il *Roll Stone* p115-16+ Mr 26 '87
Kaplan, Robert D.
The Afghan bunker. *New Repub* 197:18-19 D 28 '87
Out of Africa. *New Repub* 197:12-13 Jl 6 '87
Sons of devils. il *Atlantic* 260:38-41+ N '87
Starting over. il *Atlantic* 259:18-21+ Ap '87
Kaplan, Sheila
AASCU's clarion call to state colleges and universities. il *Change* 19:48-51+ Mr/Ap '87
Kaplan, Wendy
The furniture of Frank Furness. bibl f il *Antiques* 131:1088-95 My '87
Kaplowitz, Jane
about
Jane Kaplowitz at Jason McCoy. C. Little. il *Art Am* 75:174 S '87
Kappen, Thomas Risse- *See* Risse-Kappen, Thomas
Kappler, John
(jt. auth) See Marrack, Philippa, and Kappler, John
Kappner, Augusta Souza
about
City Univ. of N.Y. gets 1st black woman prexy. por *Jet* 73:22 N 9 '87
Kaprio, Leo A.
An element of primary care. il *World Health* p18 Ja/F '87
Karachi (Pakistan)
Hospitals
See also
Aga Khan University Hospital and Medical College
Poor
Sister Gertrude and the children of Karachi. L. Weber. il *Christ Century* 104:887-9 O 14 '87
Karadžić, Vuk Stefanović, 1787-1864
about
Vuk Stefanović Karadžić: profile of a great scholar. il por *Courier* 40:32-3 Jl '87
Karagianis, Maria
(ed) See Smith, Charles. "The children I could never forget"
Karaim, Reed
What do Cory Aquino, cocaine addicts, and American consumers have in common? They are all victims of the U.S. sugar program. *Wash Mon* 19:17-21 N '87
Karakoram Range
See also
K2 Mountain (Pakistan)
The road to Shangri-La. G. A. Rowell. il map *Int Wildl* 17:40-5 Ja/F '87
Karamazov Brothers *See* Flying Karamazov Brothers
Karami, Rashid
Assassination
Murder from the inside. J. Muir. *Macleans* 100:27 !ɔ 15 '87

Karan, Donna
about
Modern contrasts: more/less. il pors *Vogue* 177:432-43 Mr '87
Soft and sensual: Karan's cachet. il *Harpers Bazaar* 120:114-17 Je '87
Karanja, Kangugi
about
K.K. Karanja: young chess champ on a mission. U. J. Rivers. il pors *Ebony* 42:54+ F '87
Karaokes
Starmaker machinery [Panasonic RQ-84 Karaoke-Songmate] M. Coleman. il *Roll Stone* p73+ Je 18 '87
Under the boardwalk [Sing a Song Studio in Greenwich Village where amateur singers can make music tapes] *New Yorker* 63:26-7 Je 1 '87
Karasek, Francis W., 1919-, and Dickson, L. C.
Model studies of polychlorinated dibenzo-*p*-dioxin formation during municipal refuse incineration. bibl f il *Science* 237:754-6 Ag 14 '87
Karasik, Judy
Emily Dickinson: the movie. il *N Y Times Book Rev* 92:25 F 1 '87
Karate
See also
Aerobikata
Brick breaker [American expert E. A. Brown] D. E. Miller. il *Atlantic* 259:79-81 Ap '87
Eight champs headline Atlanta's Karatemania II. *Jet* 72:51 Ap 27 '87
Karatemania II features four world title fights. *Jet* 72:46 Ap 13 '87
Those terrific karate kids. L. Schnurnberger. il *Parents* 62:150-4 N '87
Karban, Richard, and others
Induced resistance and interspecific competition between spider mites and a vascular wilt fungus. bibl f il *Science* 235:678-80 F 6 '87
KARE (Minneapolis-Saint Paul, Minn.: Television station)
See Television stations
Karetnikova, Inga
The Sandinistas' favorite poet. il *Natl Rev* 39:40-2 My 8 '87
Karlen, Neal
Gin, sin, and floozies. il *Esquire* 108:46 S '87
The poker game: what is it about cards that turns sensitive New Men into Neanderthals? il *Glamour* 85:68+ S '87
This course is a joke. il por *Roll Stone* p106+ S 24 '87
Karlitz, Howard S.
How working with women has made my life better. il por *Work Woman* 12:100-1+ Jl '87
Karlsrud, Katherine, and Schultz, Dodi
As they grow/birth to 1 year. See issues of Parents beginning March 1987
Karmarkar, Narendra
about
Karmarkar's algorithm. A. A. Rockett and J. C. Stevenson. il *Byte* 12:146-52+ S '87
The startling discovery Bell Labs kept in the shadows. W. G. Wild, Jr. and O. Port. por *Bus Week* p69+ S 21 '87
Karns, Larry R., and others
Cloning of complementary DNA for GAP-43, a neuronal growth-related protein. bibl f il *Science* 236:597-600 My 1 '87
Karny, Yo'av
Byzantine bedfellows. *New Repub* 196:23-5 F 2 '87
Karoff, Barbara
Caribbean forecast: cool times, hot tastes. il *Work Woman* 12:130-2+ Mr '87
Karolyi, Bela
about
Olympic hopes in the balance. B. Weber. il pors *N Y Times Mag* p58 Ag 9 '87
Karp, Craig
Afghanistan: seven years of Soviet occupation. il maps *Dep State Bull* 87:1-21 F '87
Karp, Irwin
Let's look much harder at mergers. por *Publ Wkly* 231:46 Ap 17 '87
Karp, Ivan C., 1926-
about
A road less traveled: New York country haven of Marilynn and Ivan Karp. J. Kornbluth. il *Archit Dig* 44:196-203+ Je '87

Karp, Marilynn Gelfman
about
A road less traveled: New York country haven of Marilynn and Ivan Karp. J. Kornbluth. il *Archit Dig* 44:196-203+ Je '87
Karp, Vickie
Glass [poem] *New Yorker* 63:36 Mr 2 '87
Karpatkin, Rhoda H.
Memo to members. See issues of Consumer Reports
Karplus, Martin
Molecular dynamics simulations of proteins. bibl f il *Phys Today* 40:68-72 O '87
(jt. auth) See Elber, R., and Karplus, Martin
Karpov, Anatoly, 1951-
about
Duel of two minds. F. Lidz. il pors *Sports Illus* 67:60-3 D 7 '87
Grand mastery. *Newsweek* 110:29 D 28 '87
Virtuoso performance in Seville. J. D. Reed. il pors *Time* 130:70 D 28 '87
Karr, Bernard
about
Hyde Park's English cast. A. Haden-Guest. il por *Archit Dig* 44:282+ N '87
Karr, Jeff
Exotic excess. il *Mot Trend* 39:96-9 F '87
Karras, John
Happy to be here: how I survived a heart attack. il por *Better Homes Gard* 65:68+ N '87
Karren, Howard
You must remember this. il *N Y* 20:60-3 My 4 '87
Karriem, Jaleelah
Just a few laughs, some fun nothing serious [poem] *Essence* 18:134 O '87
Kart, Larry
Down Mobley's way. il por *Down Beat* 54:61 F '87
Kartes Video Communications, Inc.
Kartes licenses Peanuts from sister company [arrangement with United Media for home video rights] il *Publ Wkly* 231:50+ Ap 24 '87
Karting *See* Go-karting
Kasayulie, Willie
about
Willie Kasayulie: guardian of the promised land. A. Fadiman. il pors *Life* 10:17-18 F '87
Kasbah, Mimi
Michael J. Fox [excerpt from The Michael J. Fox scrapbook] il pors *Good Housekeep* 205:50+ Ag '87
Kasem, Jean
about
Playing dumb, Jean Kasem gives a brassy tint to The Tortellis. M. A. Norbom. il pors *People Wkly* 27:89-90+ Mr 16 '87
Kashiwa, Hank
Circuit training. il *Skiing* 40:48 S '87
Follow the leader to learn the line. il *Skiing* 40:23 O '87
Handling the ice. il *Skiing* 39:32 Ja '87
Mental imagery and position at the gate. il por *Skiing* 40:166 D '87
A pre-race checklist. *Skiing* 40:48+ N '87
Racing drills to sharpen your skills. il *Skiing* 39:26 Spr '87
Taking advantage of ruts. il *Skiing* 39:41 F '87
Kashiwagi, Yusuke
Japan's expanding role [address, September 25, 1987] *Vital Speeches Day* 54:79-83 N 15 '87
Kashiyama & Co., Ltd.
Brooks Brothers, beware! H. Katayama. por *Forbes* 139:173 Ap 6 '87
Kasid, U., and others
The *raf* oncogene is associated with a radiation-resistant human laryngeal cancer. bibl f il *Science* 237:1039-41 Ag 28 '87
Kasindorf, Jeanie
Dick and Joni. il pors *N Y* 20:60-4+ D 14 '87
Intelligencer. See issues of New York beginning August 19, 1985
Kaske, Karlheinz
about
Gentle leader of a sluggish Goliath. L. S. Richman. il por *Fortune* 116:45 Ag 3 '87
Siemens über alles. R. Morais. il por *Forbes* 140:366+ Jl 13 '87
Kaskel, Howard
about
Just when Kansas City Southern was ready to pounce . . . M. Ivey and C. Hawkins. *Bus Week* p26-7 Ag 24 '87

Kasparov, Gary
about
Duel of two minds. F. Lidz. il pors *Sports Illus* 67:60-3 D 7 '87
Grand mastery. *Newsweek* 110:29 D 28 '87
Virtuoso performance in Seville. J. D. Reed. il pors *Time* 130:70 D 28 '87
Kasparyan, Yuri
about
From L.A. to Russia with love: promoter Joanna Stingray says 'Da' to her Soviet rocker. il pors *People Wkly* 28:68-70 N 30 '87
Kassam, Shiraz
Coups and earthquakes only. *World Press Rev* 34:64 S '87
Kassebaum, Nancy Landon
about
Our two women in the Senate: influential and respected. M. Engel. por *Glamour* 85:50+ My '87
Kassen, Michael
about
Fidelity's cover boy. D. Machan. il por *Forbes* 139:229-30 My 18 '87
Kasten, Barbara
about
Barbara Kasten. E. Heartney. il *Art News* 86:140+ S '87
Kasten, Robert W.
Should the proposed Product Liability Reform Act be approved? [excerpts from debate, September 17, 1986] *Congr Dig* 66:18+ Ja '87
Kastner, John
about
Among sisters of crime. P. Hluchy. il por *Macleans* 100:54-5 Ja 12 '87
Kastner, Joseph
It was a big day for 'Big Jule'—and me. il *Smithsonian* 18:154 Jl '87
Katahn, Martin
Your body blueprint—born to be fat? il *Mademoiselle* 93:337+ S '87
Katahn, Martin, and Katahn, Terri
All new rotation diet dishes. il *Redbook* 169:108-13+ My '87
Katahn, Terri
(jt. auth) See Katahn, Martin, and Katahn, Terri
Kate & Allie [television program] See Television program reviews—Single works
Kate Freeman Clark Art Gallery
Rediscovering a forgotten painter. il por *South Living* 22:38 Mr '87
Kathmandu (Nepal)
Description
At the crossroads of Kathmandu. D. H. Chadwick. il maps *Natl Geogr* 172:32-65 Jl '87
Katic, Peter
about
Judge: get good grades or go to jail for failing. *Jet* 73:24 D 14 '87
Katin, Hedy
Photo cards: personalized messages handcrafted from your photo files. il *Petersens Photogr Mag* 16:82-3 Je '87
Kato, Koichi
about
What to do about America [interview] por *U S News World Rep* 102:46-7 Ap 13 '87
Katohda, Junko
about
Junko Katohda: mixing East and West in Japan. J. O'Connor. il por *Sch Update* 119:4 Ap 6 '87
Katonah (N.Y.)
Health facilities
See also
Katonah Medical Group
Katonah Medical Group
Why your family doctor is a group. M. Fay. il *N Y Times Mag* p16-20+ Je 7 '87
Kattke, Kevin
about
How a Macy's engineer and his pals became rogue American agents. N. M. Renfrew and P. Blauner. il pors *N Y* 20:102-4+ D 7 '87
Katydids
Bat predation and its influence on calling behavior in neotropical katydids. J. J. Belwood and G. Morris. bibl f il *Science* 238:64-7 O 2 '87
Driven batty, katydids change tune [influence of predator bats; research by J. J. Belwood and G. Morris] R. Weiss. *Sci News* 132:231 O 10 '87

Katz, Alex, 1927-
about
Psyching out Katz. G. Henry. il pors *Art News* 86:23 Summ '87
Taylor-made design. S. Flatow. il *Theatre Crafts* 21:24-5+ Ja '87

Katz, Arthur M.
about
When to call the exterminator [interview] P. Easton. il por *Home Mech* 83:14-15 Ap '87

Katz, Barbara Myerson
Are you raising a yuppie-puppy? il *Parents* 62:74-6 Ja '87

Katz, Donald R.
Meet the prince of penny stocks: Meyer Blinder. il por *Fortune* 115:108-10+ Ja 19 '87

Katz, Herbert
about
A new agent and a new publisher for June Flaum Singer. *Publ Wkly* 232:24 Jl 31 '87

Katz, Jacob
Is messianism good for the Jews? *Commentary* 83:31-6 Ap '87
about
Wagner as anti-Semite. S. Lipman. *Commentary* 83:57-60 Ja '87

Katz, James Everett
Telecommunications and computers: whither privacy policy? *Society* 25:81-6 N/D '87

Katz, Jonathan
State arts agencies: a resource for the arts and education. *Des Arts Educ* 88:6-10 N/D '86

Katz, Lilian G.
As they grow/3 and 4. See issues of Parents

Katz, Lillian Vernon
about
The treasure of her company. M. I. Finney. il por *Nations Bus* 75:73-4 F '87

Katz, Michael
Hagler vs. Leonard: the seniors tour. il pors *Sport Mag* 78:76-82 Ap '87

Katz, Morris, 1932-
about
Instant art. *New Yorker* 63:23-4 Je 29 '87

Katz, Richard, 1937-
Make believers. il *Omni* 10:126-8+ N '87

Katz, Ruth J.
Beribbon a tree. il *Redbook* 170:79-81 D '87
Dressed to thrill. il *Redbook* 169:16+ O '87

Katz, Solomon H.
about
History with gusto. il *Time* 129:57 Ap 6 '87

Katz-Leavy, Judith, and others
Meeting the mental health needs of severely emotionally disturbed minority children and adolescents: a national perspective. il *Child Today* 16:10-14 S/O '87

Katzenberger, Ruth
Try codonanthe. il *Flower Gard* 32:54 D '87/Ja '88

Katzman, John
about
"This isn't school". B. Kallen. il por *Forbes* 140:246+ N 16 '87

Kauai (Hawaii)
See also
Birds—Kauai (Hawaii)
Trails—Kauai (Hawaii)
Wildlife sanctuaries—Kauai (Hawaii)
Description and travel
Kauai in bloom. R. Ariyoshi. il map *Travel Holiday* 168:42-9 S '87

Kauffman, Bill
Don't underrate isolationism. il *Nation* 244:758-60 Je 6 '87

Kauffman, Janet, 1945-
Where I'd quit [story] *New Yorker* 62:30-1 F 16 '87

Kauffmann, Stanley, 1916-
Album of the Knopfs. *Am Sch* 56:371-81 Summ '87
Stanley Kauffmann on films. See issues of The New Republic

Kaufman, Bel
From Russia with hope. il por *50 Plus* 27:29-31 Jl '87

Kaufman, David
AIDS: the creative response [cover story; with editorial comment by Gray D. Boone] il *Horizon* 30:2, 13-20 N '87
Denby on dance. il pors *Horizon* 30:38-40 Jl/Ag '87
Love and death. il pors *Horizon* 30:38-40 My '87
Les miz. il *Horizon* 30:37-9 Mr '87

Kaufman, George G.
Are worries about bank failures justified? il *USA Today (Periodical)* 115:43-6 Ja '87

Kaufman, Irving R.
The creative process and libel. il *N Y Times Mag* p28-30+ Ap 5 '87

Kaufman, Jackie
Car smarts: how to handle any emergency. il *Seventeen* 46:120+ Mr '87

Kaufman, Joanne
This can't be love (because I feel so good). il *Glamour* 85:310 Mr '87
When to forgive a friend and when to forget her. il *Seventeen* 46:250-1+ Mr '87
Why I like being competitive and why I'd like to stop. il *Glamour* 85:124+ N '87
Why I never want to be a celebrity. il *Glamour* 85:68 Ap '87

Kaufman, Jonathan
Black-Jewish coalition. *Cent Mag* 20:54-5+ N/D '87

Kaufman, Len
Baseball camps: where big league dreams come true. il *Travel Holiday* 167:48-51 My '87

Kaufman, Lynne
Change of heart [story] il *Good Housekeep* 205:40+ Ag '87

Kaufman, Margo
Working out with R2-D2. il *Women's Sports Fitness* 9:100 S '87

Kaufman, Michael T.
Poland's plucky activist. il por *N Y Times Mag* p38+ Ap 26 '87
The sons of communism. il pors *N Y Times Mag* p50+ Mr 8 '87

Kaufman, Michele
Tracing M81's spiral arms. il *Sky Telesc* 73:135-7 F '87

Kaufman, Phillip
about
It's cold out there. M. Beauchamp. il por *Forbes* 139:60+ F 23 '87

Kaufman, Sherwin A.
A gynecologist answers your most intimate questions. *Ladies Home J* 104:50+ Mr '87

Kaufman, Victor
about
At Columbia, things might go better with Tri-Star. R. Grover. il por *Bus Week* p74-5 N 30 '87

Kaufmann, Elizabeth
Race to the top of the world: who will be the first American woman to reach the summit of Mount Everest? il *Women's Sports Fitness* 9:22-6 O '87

Kaufmann, Karl W.
(jt. auth) See Jackson, Jeremy B. C., 1942-, and Kaufmann, Karl W.

Kaunda, Kenneth D. (Kenneth David), 1924-
about
Zambia president reveals cause of son's death: AIDS. por *Jet* 73:14 N 2 '87
Visit to the United States, 1987
Zambia president Kaunda urges Reagan to support efforts to end apartheid. il pors *Jet* 73:4 N 2 '87

Kavan, Jan
Prague's kamikaze icebreakers. il *Nation* 244:78-82 Ja 24 '87

Kavenoff, Ruth
about
Ruth Kavenoff liked what she saw in her microscope, so she's putting genes and germs on her T-shirts. il por *People Wkly* 28:133 N 9 '87

Kavkazian (New York, N.Y.: Restaurant) *See* New York (N.Y.)—Restaurants, nightclubs, bars, etc.

Kawabata, Shinichi
about
Money from misery. H. Katayama. il por *Forbes* 139:256 Je 15 '87

Kawakubo, Rei
about
Another world of style . . . Rei Kawakubo [interview] E. Klensch. il por *Vogue* 177:306-9+ Ag '87
Designing women. D. Drier. il pors *Art Am* 75:21-3 My '87
'The monk' and 'the nun'. J. Conant. il pors *Newsweek* 109:80 F 2 '87

Kawaler, Steven D., and Winget, Donald E.
White dwarfs: fossil stars. il *Sky Telesc* 74:132-5 Ag '87

Kawasaki, Guy
The next generation of business software. por *Pers Comput* 11:244 O '87

Kawasaki syndrome
. . . and a disease seeking its raison d'être. D. D. Edwards. *Sci News* 132:246 O 17 '87

Kay, Alan
about
Pied Piper of the computer. F. Rose. il por *N Y Times Mag* p56+ N 8 '87

Kay, Clarence
about
Drug free Bronco feels good, chats with Hollywood. *Jet* 71:46 F 16 '87

Kay, Jane Holtz
The architecture of Charles Moore: 1949-1986. *Nation* 244:27-8 Ja 10 '87

Kay, John
about
Computing is just a song. C. Bermant. il por *Pers Comput* 11:182-3 O '87

Kay, Richard S.
Letting 'We the people' speak [cover story] il *New Leader* 70:8-10 Jl 13-27 '87

Kay, Robert, and others
Duplication of CaMV 35S promoter sequences creates a strong enhancer for plant genes. bibl f il *Science* 236:1299-302 Je 5 '87

Kay, Suzanne
about
Diahann Carroll & Suzanne Kay. pors *Teen* 31:48 D '87
Star mothers & daughters. pors *Harpers Bazaar* 120:129+ Ag '87

Kayaks and kayaking
See also
Running rapids
Skijaks
Float yourself a holiday. D. Moreau. il *Changing Times* 41:105-7 Mr '87
Kayak tours of Monterey Bay. il *Sunset* 179:31 S '87
Land creatures [E. Gillet kayaks across Pacific Ocean] *New Yorker* 63:30-1 S 21 '87
Sea kayaking: a water-lover's workout. Y. Pepin. il *Women's Sports Fitness* 9:60-1 Je '87

Kaye, Danny
about
Belafonte succeeds Kaye as UNICEF ambassador. pors *Jet* 71:30 Mr 23 '87
Obituary
Macleans il por 100:59 Mr 16 '87. P. Young
Newsweek por 109:80 Mr 16 '87. B. Barol
Time il pors 129:90 Mr 16 '87. W. A. Henry

Kaye, Donald
Infectious diseases; ed. by Maxine Abrams. *Good Housekeep* 204:69-72 F '87

Kaye, Nora
about
Nora Kaye on Nora Kaye: character and caring [interview] B. Newman. il pors *Dance Mag* 61:54-9 S '87
Obituary
Dance Mag il por 61:32 My '87. W. Como
Dance Mag 61:24-5 My '87. G. Parks
Dance Mag pors 61:24-5 My '87. P. W. Manchester

Kaye, Richard
1987: Miami's year in the literary limelight. il pors *Publ Wkly* 232:46-7 N 13 '87

Kaye, Tony
The birth dearth. *New Repub* 196:20-3 Ja 19 '87

Kayne, Sheryl
A diary's best medicine. il *Parents* 62:85-6+ N '87

Kazakhstan (Soviet Union)
See also
Alma-Ata (Soviet Union)
Politics and government
The 'glasnost' test. R. Pipes. *New Repub* 196:16-17 F 2 '87
Meanwhile, back in the Kazakh SSR . . . A. J. Motyl. *New Leader* 70:9 F 9-23 '87
What really happened in Alma-Ata [minority riots] J. O. Jackson. il map *Time* 129:25 Mr 2 '87

Kazakov, Yakob
about
A master painter and his aging collective bring life and color back to the Catherine Palace. S. K. Reed. il pors *People Wkly* 27:92-4+ Ap 6 '87

Kazanjian, Dodie
Animal magnetism. il *House Gard* 159:166-71+ S '87
Daniel J. Terra. il por *House Gard* 159:46+ My '87

Kazas, Tom
Arkansas stencilers. il pors *Americana* 15:35-9 My/Je '87

Kazin, Alfred, 1915-
Mencken and the great American boob. il *N Y Rev Books* 34:8-11 F 26 '87
Southwestward: the great American space. il map *Am Herit* 38:52-61 Ap '87
A walker in the city—again. il *N Y* 20:32-5 Ja 19 '87
Where would Emerson find his scholar now? [adaptation of address, June 1987] il *Am Herit* 38:93-6 D '87

KBA Partners
Richard Black is back—this time as a startup star. P. Finch. il por *Bus Week* p118-19 Ap 6 '87

KC-10 airplanes *See* Tank airplanes
KC-135 airplanes *See* Tank airplanes
KCBS (Los Angeles, Calif.: Television station) *See* Television stations

KCET magazine
Stay tuned. M. Beauchamp. il por *Forbes* 140:189 O 19 '87

KCR Technology, Inc.
A giant-killer in printers? G. G. Marcial. *Bus Week* p116 F 23 '87

Kean, Thomas H.
Rescuing the urban poor. il *USA Today (Periodical)* 116:72-5 N '87
Time to deliver. il *Change* 19:10-11 S/O '87

Keanan, Staci
about
For Staci Keanan of TV's My two dads, Hollywood can be a two-faced town. A. Blessing. il pors *People Wkly* 28:153-4+ N 23 '87

Keane, George
about
How an educated guess is paying off for George Keane. G. G. Marcial. il por *Bus Week* p106 D 21 '87
Shotgun approach. R. Phalon. il por *Forbes* 139:132+ Je 15 '87

Keane, Noel P., 1938-
about
Baby M winner. M. Gladwell and R. Sharpe. *New Repub* 196:15-16+ F 16 '87
Childless couples seeking surrogate mothers call Michigan lawyer Noel Keane—he delivers. J. S. Kunen. il pors *People Wkly* 27:93+ Mr 30 '87

Kearfott Laboratories
Singer targets Trilag ring laser gyros for tactical, reentry vehicle uses. K. J. Stein. il *Aviat Week Space Technol* 126:163+ Ap 27 '87

Kearney, Kathleen
Make custom dress forms. il *Theatre Crafts* 21:96-8 N '87

Kearns, David Todd, 1930-
The United States educational system [address, October 26, 1987] *Vital Speeches Day* 54:150-3 D 15 '87
about
Culture shock at Xerox. J. A. Byrne. il por *Bus Week* p106+ Je 22 '87

Keasler, John
about
Hounded by woes, Miamians beg for more of Ryan the Advice Dog. il por *People Wkly* 28:113 O 19 '87

Keate, James Stuart, d. 1987
about
Obituary
Macleans il por 100:46 Mr 16 '87. M. McIver

Keating, Charles H., Jr.
about
Charles Keating: feeling the heat in Phoenix. K. Kelly. il por *Bus Week* p80 Ag 31 '87

Keating, Desiree
about
Beauty queen is the alleged victim of father's incest. por *Jet* 72:12 Ag 10 '87

Keating, Norman Emanuel
about
Beauty queen is the alleged victim of father's incest. por *Jet* 72:12 Ag 10 '87

Keaton, Diane
about
Diane Keaton chucks her powerhouse corporate job in Baby boom. C. Krupp. il *Glamour* 85:256+ N '87

Heaven [film] Reviews
Christ Century 104:600 Jl 1-8 '87. D. Peerman
Newsweek il por 109:79 Ap 27 '87. D. Ansen
People Wkly 27:10 My 11 '87. P. Travers
Time 129:79 Ap 27 '87. R. Corliss
Hotel 'Heaven' [interview] M. Glicksman. il *Film Comment* 23:32-7 Mr/Ap '87
Knockin' on heaven's door. D. Edelstein. por *Roll Stone* p23-4+ My 7 '87

Keay, Douglas
Andrew and "Fergie": royalty's happiest, most unusual marriage [cover story] il pors *Good Housekeep* 204:130-1+ Ap '87

Kebabs *See* Kabobs

Kedleston Hall (Derbyshire, England) *See* Historic houses, sites, etc.—Great Britain

Keebler, Jack
What's new for your car. See issues of Popular Science

Keefauver, John
Alice in W-4 land. *Natl Rev* 39:30 Je 5 '87
Jaws XIV—a shark-eating man. *Natl Rev* 39:40 N 20 '87

Keefe, Ann
Don't let your travel agent take you for a ride. il *50 Plus* 27:56-7 O '87
Napoleonic New York. *Travel Holiday* 167:32-4 Je '87
Ten trusty tips for packing light. il *50 Plus* 27:78+ Mr '87

Keefe, Sheila

about
Tombs and inner temples. D. Neff. il por *Christ Today* 31:72 O 2 '87

Keefer, David K., and others
Real-time landslide warning during heavy rainfall. bibl f il map *Science* 238:921-5 N 13 '87

Keegan, Carol
How union members and nonmembers view the role of unions. *Mon Labor Rev* 110:50-1 Ag '87

Keegan, John, 1934-
Can NATO survive an arms deal? il *U S News World Rep* 103:30 Jl 27 '87
The ghosts of Waterloo. il *World Press Rev* 34:29-31 Ag '87
Is South Africa invulnerable? il map *U S News World Rep* 102:30-3 Mr 23 '87

Keegan, Lucy
The sunburn survival guide. il *Mademoiselle* 93:62 Jl '87

Keegan, Paul
Evan Parker: the breath and breadth of the saxophone. il pors *Down Beat* 54:26-8 Ap '87

Keeler, Shaun
The continuing success of Return a Gift to Wildlife. il *Conservationist* 41:2-5 Mr/Ap '87

Keeler, Ward
Shadow world of the Javanese. il *Nat Hist* 96:68-72+ N '87

Keely, Jane
Speaker for the house. See issues of Good Housekeeping

Keenan, Mike

about
Sympathy for the devil. P. Fichtenbaum. il pors *Sport Mag* 78:59-63 My '87

Keeneland (Lexington, Ky.: Race track) *See* Race tracks

Keeneland yearling sales *See* Auctions

Keeping track [film] See Motion picture reviews—Single works

Keeps, David A.
Christy Turlington. pors *Harpers Bazaar* 120:260, 368-71 S '87
Downtown's darling goes mainstream. il por *Harpers Bazaar* 120:208-9+ Ap '87

Keepsakes *See* Souvenirs (Keepsakes)

Keersmaeker, Anne Teresa de

about
Elena's aria [dance] Reviews
  N Y il 20:108 N 23 '87. T. Tobias
  New Leader 70:23 N 30 '87. L. A. Jacobs
Rosas danst Rosas [dance] Reviews
  Dance Mag 61:36-7 Ap '87. N. V. Dalva

Keeton, Kathy
First word. por *Omni* 10:6 O '87
Interview [E. Willmot] il por *Omni* 9:80-2+ Je '87

Keeton, Sharron
I lost 117 lbs. and won back my husband; ed. by Barbara Raymond. il pors *Good Housekeep* 204:96+ Ap '87

Keevil, N. B., Jr.

about
An ambitious venture in Alaska. P. C. Newman. il por *Macleans* 100:34 Ag 24 '87

Kefauver Committee *See* United States. Congress. Senate. Special Committee to Investigate Organized Crime in Interstate Commerce

Kegley, Charles W., and Wittkopf, Eugene R., 1943-
The two faces of the Reagan administration's foreign policy approach. il *USA Today (Periodical)* 115:10-15 Ja '87

Kehlmann, Robert
Consummate connoisseur. il por *Am Craft* 47:50-5 O/N '87

Glass of the 80s. il pors *Am Craft* 47:32-9 Ap/My '87

Kehrl, John H., and others
Lymphotoxin is an important T cell-derived growth factor for human B cells. bibl f il *Science* 238:1144-6 N 20 '87

Keiffer, Elisabeth
Making friends in the family. il *Read Dig* 130:77-80 Ja '87

Keil, Wieland Schulz- *See* Schulz-Keil, Wieland

Keillor, Garrison
Christmas in Lake Wobegon [story] il *Saturday Evening Post* 259:60-3 D '87
Garrison Keillor. il por *People Wkly* 28:82-3 D 28 '87-Ja 4 '88
Hollywood in the fifties. *New Yorker* 63:40-1 N 16 '87
How to write a personal letter. il por *Read Dig* 131:129-31 N '87
Leaving home [story] il *Atlantic* 260:47-53 S '87
Your book saved my life, Mister. *New Yorker* 63:40-1 D 28 '87

about
Farewell to Lake Wobegon. W. Kling. pors *U S News World Rep* 102:10 Je 22 '87
Garrison Keillor and culture Protestantism. D. Heim. *Christ Century* 104:517-19 Je 3-10 '87
Goodbye to Lake Wobegon. E. Levin. il pors *People Wkly* 28:34-7 O 12 '87
Leaving Lake Wobegon. J. Skow. il pors *Time* 129:64-5 Je 29 '87
Leaving the shores of Lake Wobegon. D. E. Roback. il por *Publ Wkly* 232:34-5 Ag 21 '87
A lost 'Companion'. D. Galant. il *N Y* 20:25 Je 15 '87
A shy person says so long. B. Barol. il por *Newsweek* 109:65-6 Je 15 '87
Sola gratia in Lake Wobegon [cover story] W. L. Miller. il por *Christ Century* 104:526-8 Je 3-10 '87
What now, Wobegon? B. Barol. il pors *Newsweek* 110:82-3 O 5 '87

Keino, Kip

about
'They're all my children'. F. Lidz. il pors *Sports Illus* 67:24-5 D 21 '87

Keiser, R. Lincoln
"Friend by day, enemy by night". il *Nat Hist* 96:8+ N '87

Keiter, Samuel C.
Whose aviation policy is this? por *Aviat Week Space Technol* 126:117+ My 18 '87

Keith, Charles H.
Slow transport of tubulin in the neurites of differentiated PC 12 cells. bibl f il *Science* 235:337-9 Ja 16 '87

Keith, Damon

about
Federal judge Damon Keith honored by Mich. governor for 20 years on bench. il pors *Jet* 73:14 D 21 '87
Federal judge Damon Keith hosts bicentennial banquet for nation's Constitution. il pors *Jet* 71:32-3 Mr 2 '87

Keith, Leroy

about
Dr. Leroy Keith elected new Morehouse president. por *Jet* 72:7 My 11 '87

Keith, Nancy

about
Entertaining. W. P. Rayner and C. Rayner. il *Vogue* 177:500+ S '87
Reflections of my many lives. il *House Gard* 159:66-77+ Ja '87

Keith, Slim *See* Keith, Nancy

Keith, Susan
Report on reports: Ground water quality protection: state and local strategies. *Environment* 29:25-7 My '87

Keker, John

about
A passel of new trouble from a posse of lawyers. D. Baer and M. Healy. il por *U S News World Rep* 102:19-20 Je 15 '87

Kelleher, Herbert David

about
Where 'frill' is a four-letter word. J. Weber, Jr. il por *Bus Week* p58+ S 21 '87

Kelleher, Matthew H.
Refugees in Hong Kong. *America* 157:84-5 Ag 15-22 '87

Keller, Bernard J.
Harvard 8/9/85 [poem] *Essence* 18:140 N '87

Keller, Bill
Russia's restless youth [cover story] il *N Y Times Mag* p14-19+ Jl 26 '87
Sakharov's list. il por *N Y Times Mag* p34-7+ F 15 '87

Keller, Dale
about
An Asian mystique: Dale and Patricia Keller's New York apartment. L. Bernikow. il pors *Archit Dig* 44:94-101 S '87

Keller, George M.
The competitiveness problem [address, September 14, 1987] *Vital Speeches Day* 54:61-4 N 1 '87
Industry and the environment [address, October 30, 1987] *Vital Speeches Day* 54:154-7 D 15 '87
The new energy challenge [address, February 3, 1987] *Vital Speeches Day* 53:314-17 Mr 1 '87
about
Still smiling over Gulf. B. O'Reilly. il por *Fortune* 116:40-1 Ag 3 '87

Keller, Jack
about
Trading tips from a poker player turned options pro. il por *Money* 16:242 N '87

Keller, Jack A.
On providence and prayer. *Christ Century* 104:967-9 N 4 '87

Keller, Mary Page
about
That bubbly soap charmer Mary Page Keller gets into beefing up Duet's TV ratings. F. A. Bernstein. il pors *People Wkly* 27:59-60 Je 29 '87

Keller, Maryann
Streetwise. See issues of Motor Trend beginning September 1986

Keller, Patricia
about
An Asian mystique: Dale and Patricia Keller's New York apartment. L. Bernikow. il pors *Archit Dig* 44:94-101 S '87

Keller, Scott A.
Making the most of time. *Writer* 100:22-3 Jl '87

Keller, T. L.
about
The next small step. S. Ditlea. il *Omni* 10:22 D '87

Keller, Thomas F.
The trade crisis begins at home. por *U S News World Rep* 103:8 Ag 31 '87

Kellerman, Sally
about
Sally Kellerman gets real. R. Alleman. por *Vogue* 177:100 Mr '87

Kellett, Ken
about
On the wings of yesterday. D. Young. il pors *South Living* 22:125-6 F '87

Kelley, Kitty
The first Mrs. Sinatra [excerpt from His way] il pors *Ladies Home J* 104:72-3+ Jl '87
Only the rich will write. por *Newsweek* 110:7 Ag 24 '87
Anecdotes, facetiae, satire, etc.
Her way. F. Gannon. *New Yorker* 62:24 Ja 5 '87

Kelley, Michael, 1954?-
about
Mike Kelley at Artists Space. K. O'Dell. *Art Am* 75:184 My '87

Kelley, Thomas B.
about
This moneyman isn't yelling 'sell'. G. G. Marcial. *Bus Week* p98 S 28 '87

Kellner, Peter
(jt. auth) See Lloyd, John, 1946-, and Kellner, Peter

Kellogg, Frederic Rogers
Learned Hand and the great train ride. *Am Sch* 56:471-86 Aut '87

Kellogg, Mary Alice
The new rules for on-the-job manners. il *Glamour* 85:120+ Ap '87
Short-term therapies. il *Harpers Bazaar* 120:78+ F '87
When to hold a grudge. il *Glamour* 85:165+ F '87
Your first, his second. *Harpers Bazaar* 120:138-9+ Jl '87

Kellogg, Mayo
about
Fetch on faith and cripples first. L. Mueller. il por *Outdoor Life* 180:44-5 Ag '87
Kellogg's "arm extenders". L. Mueller. il pors *Outdoor Life* 180:52+ Jl '87

Kellogg Co.
The health craze has Kellogg feeling G-r-r-reat. R. Mitchell. il *Bus Week* p52-3 Mr 30 '87

Kellwood Co.
Most improved. il *Forbes* 139:69 Ja 12 '87

Kelly, Brigit Pegeen, 1951-
about
Poetic license. J. B. Newman. il por *Horizon* 30:39-40 N '87

Kelly, Ellsworth, 1923-
about
Outdoor abstractions. J. Russell. il por *House Gard* 159:182-5+ F '87

Kelly, Eugene W.
Private prayer in the schools. *Educ Dig* 53:34-5 S '87

Kelly, Grace *See* Grace, Princess of Monaco, 1929-1982

Kelly, James R.
AIDS and the death penalty as consistency tests for the prolife movement. *America* 157:151-5 S 26 '87
Does the RENEW program renew? *America* 156:197-9 Mr 7 '87
Numbers versus principles: moral realism and teen-age pregnancies. *America* 156:130-6 F 14 '87

Kelly, Jim
about
Beers with [interview] J. Price. il pors *Sport Mag* 78:23-5 O '87

Kelly, John
about
Pass the blutwurst, bitte (The Egon Schiele story) [drama]
Reviews
Art News por 86:13+ Mr '87. M. E. Haus
Vogue il 177:140 Mr '87. J. Hobhouse

Kelly, John
Who's cool today—and who isn't. por *U S News World Rep* 102:9 Ap 20 '87

Kelly, John, 1945-
(jt. auth) See Sanger, Sirgay, and Kelly, John, 1945-

Kelly, Kate, 1950-
Alone on the highway. il *Parents* 62:66+ Ag '87
(ed) See Eisenberg, Ronni. What-to-do checklist before the baby arrives
(ed) See Eisenberg, Ronni. Where to find more time for yourself

Kelly, Kevin J.
Israel and the Palestinian question: 1987. *America* 156:424-6 My 23 '87

Kelly, Lynne
Perspiration: track down no-sweat solutions. il *Teen* 31:32+ My '87

Kelly, Michael
Beyond the killing fields. *America* 156:172-3 F 28 '87

Kelly, Michael E.
about
From the '60s with care. J. A. Seamonds. il *U S News World Rep* 102:50 Je 1 '87

Kelly, Patrick
about
In Paris, his slinky dresses have made Mississippi-born designer Patrick Kelly the new king of cling. B. Johnson. il pors *People Wkly* 27:111-12+ Je 15 '87

Kelly, Rex
Speakers and the bottom line [address, August 7, 1987] *Vital Speeches Day* 54:47-50 N 1 '87

Kelly, Richard
about
Bearish on stocks, bullish on bonds [interview] B. Weberman. *Forbes* 140:54+ N 16 '87

Kelly, Roberta House
The box. il *South Living* 22:82 D '87

Kelly, Sheldon
19 hours in "Devil's Icebox". il *Read Dig* 131:60-6 Ag '87
Burning alive! il *Read Dig* 131:95-9 S '87
Inferno on the interstate. il *Read Dig* 130:106-11 Ja '87
"Where are my children?". il *Read Dig* 130:151-2+ Je '87

Kelman, Judith
Boys, toys . . . joys. il *McCalls* 115:63-4 D '87
Can't read, write or add: the secret hell of millions of Americans. il *Glamour* 85:142+ Ap '87
My Aunt Rosie. il por *Good Housekeep* 204:120 Ap '87

Kelp
Fewer barnacles [rockfish prey on barnacle larvae in California kelp forest; research by Steven D. Gaines and Jonathan Roughgarden] *Sea Front* 33:384-5 S/O '87

Kelp—*cont.*
Fish in offshore kelp forests affect recruitment to intertidal barnacle populations [rockfish] S. D. Gaines and J. Roughgarden. bibl f il *Science* 235:479-81 Ja 23 '87

Kelton, Elmer, 1926-
Writing realistic Western fiction. il *Writer* 100:11-13 My '87

Kemble, Edwin Crawford, 1889-1984
about
Obituary
Phys Today por 40:97-9 S '87. S. H. Beer

Kemp, Bruce E.
(jt. auth) See House, Colin, and Kemp, Bruce E.

Kemp, Bruce E., and others
Parathyroid hormone-related protein of malignancy: active synthetic fragments. bibl f il *Science* 238:1568-70 D 11 '87

Kemp, Jack
Arms control perverted. il *Natl Rev* 39:30+ My 22 '87
about
Aide to Kemp dismissed for making racial slurs. *Jet* 73:37 S 28 '87
Can Jack Kemp quarterback the country? F. Lynn. il pors *50 Plus* 27:62-4+ F '87
Can Kemp do it? J. Wanniski. il *Natl Rev* 39:28-31 Ag 14 '87
A congressman who would be president [interview] por *Christ Today* 31:40 Ap 3 '87
The ex-quarterback's quest. A. Plattner. il por *U S News World Rep* 102:22-3 Ap 20 '87
From gridiron to campaign trail. M. McDonald. il pors *Macleans* 100:26+ N 16 '87
How Kemp may harden the GOP line on Star Wars. D. Griffiths and B. Javetski. *Bus Week* p71 My 25 '87
'I love ideas, but I'm not an intellectual' [interview] D. Frost. il por *U S News World Rep* 103:17 D 28 '87-Ja 4 '88
Is Jack Kemp fumbling his presidential bid? R. Fly. il por *Bus Week* p90+ Ap 13 '87
Is Jack Kemp Mr. Right? M. Dowd. il pors *N Y Times Mag* p18-21+ Je 28 '87
Kemp and the cons. F. Barnes. *New Repub* 197:10+ D 28 '87
Kemp for president? *Natl Rev* 39:19 Ag 14 '87
Kemp in New Hampshire. *Natl Rev* 39:19 Mr 13 '87
Kemp in the blocks. *Natl Rev* 39:15-16 D 18 '87
Kemp's fourth down. L. Howard. por *Newsweek* 110:7 O 26 '87
Kemp's surprising victory. L. Schiffren. *Natl Rev* 39:37+ Ap 10 '87
Letter from Washington. Cato. *Natl Rev* 39:15 My 8 '87
Noteworthy anniversary; noteworthy man. M. S. Forbes, Jr. il por *Forbes* 140:25 Ag 10 '87
The prospects for quarterback Kemp. J. McLaughlin. *Natl Rev* 39:26 O 9 '87
The quarterback of supply side. A. Stanley. il por *Time* 129:25-6 Ap 13 '87
Republican dirty tricks. F. Barnes. *New Repub* 197:18+ Jl 27 '87
Rich man's populist. R. S. McIntyre. *New Repub* 196:16-17 Mr 23 '87
Tacking further to the right. L. I. Barrett. il por *Time* 129:19 Mr 2 '87
Anecdotes, facetiae, satire, etc.
Man of the hour. E. Grannis. *Nation* 244:635 My 16 '87

Kemp, Jan
about
Jan Kemp. C. Reece. il por *Ms* 15:44+ Ja '87

Kemp, John R., 1945-
Henry Casselli. il por *Am Artist* 51:48-53+ Ag '87

Kemp, Philip
about
Branding a success. L. Gubernick. por *Forbes* 139:91 Ja 26 '87

Kemp Balloons (Firm)
Giving parades a lift [cover story] il *Natl Geogr World* 140:6-9 Ap '87

Kemper, Richard E., and Mangieri, John N.
America's future teaching force: predictions and recommendations. bibl f *Phi Delta Kappan* 68:393-5 Ja '87

Kempler, Daniel, and Van Lancker, Diana
The right turn of phrase. il *Psychol Today* 21:20+ Ap '87

Kempner, Nan
about
Thomas and Nan Kempner in New York: evolution of a Park Avenue apartment. B. Hayward. il por *Archit Dig* 44:166-71+ My '87

Kemp's ridley turtles *See* Turtles

Kempton, Beverly Gary
Classic tales of captains and castles . . . and corporations. il *Work Woman* 12:102-5+ O '87
The executive woman's guide to headhunters. il *Work Woman* 12:110-12+ Ap '87
To check or not to check. il *Work Woman* 12:45-6 Mr '87

Kempton, Murray
The appointment of death. il *N Y Rev Books* 34:40 My 28 '87
Casey and Woodward: who used whom? il *N Y Rev Books* 34:61 N 5 '87
Cheer up, John Paul II. il *N Y Rev Books* 34:58 O 22 '87
The contract for 'Baby M'. il *N Y Rev Books* 34:44 Ap 9 '87
Down a sinkhole. *N Y Rev Books* 34:53-4 Je 25 '87
A hero's mission. il *N Y Rev Books* 34:13 Ag 13 '87
Leaving bad enough alone. il *N Y Rev Books* 34:45 Ja 29 '87
Pienza: the reward of patience. il *House Gard* 159:74+ D '87
The price of peace. *N Y Rev Books* 34:46 S 24 '87
about
Murray Kempton on the papal visit. *America* 157:204 O 10 '87

Kempton-Smith, Debbi
Horoscope. See issues of Seventeen beginning March 1985

Kenaf
What's tall, tough and read all over? [use as a pulp supply] *Sci News* 132:72 Ag 1 '87

Kenan, Amos
Fallen state. *Nation* 245:293 S 26 '87
Letter from Israel. *Nation* 245:581 N 21 '87
Violence in Gaza. *Nation* 245:777-8 D 26 '87-Ja 2 '88

Kendall, Donald McIntosh, 1921-
about
The U.S. Business Hall of Fame. A. M. Louis. por *Fortune* 115:103 Ap 13 '87

Kendall, Frances
about
306 solutions to a baffling problem. B. W. Nelan. il pors *Time* 129:36 Mr 23 '87

Kendall, Jerry T.
about
Picking up the pieces at Paradyne. G. DeGeorge. il por *Bus Week* p102 Ap 6 '87

Kendavis Industries International Inc.
The Davis boys won't go down without one more fight [T. C. and K. Davis] T. Vogel. il pors *Bus Week* p108-9+ My 25 '87

Kendrick, K. M., and Baldwin, B. A.
Cells in temporal cortex of conscious sheep can respond preferentially to the sight of faces. bibl f il *Science* 236:448-50 Ap 24 '87

Keneally, Thomas
In Eritrea. il map *N Y Times Mag* p42-4+ S 27 '87

Kenez, Peter
Gorbashow and the flicks. il *New Leader* 70:10-12 Ap 6 '87

Kenison, Katrina
about
Editor Katrina Kenison of Ticknor & Fields. G. Blooston. il por *Publ Wkly* 231:64+ F 13 '87

Kennan, George Frost, 1904-
Containment then and now. *Foreign Aff* 65:885-90 Spr '87
The mission in Moscow. por *Newsweek* 110:7 Jl 13 '87
The sources of Soviet conduct [reprint of July 1947 article] *Foreign Aff* 65:852-68 Spr '87
"X" on containment, 1947. *Bull At Sci* 43:16 N '87
about
The cold war. W. Lippmann. *Foreign Aff* 65:869-84 Spr '87

Kennard, John
Scene at the ballpark [photographs] il *Americana* 15:45-9 My/Je '87

Kenneally, Joyce A.
Microwave cooking tips. See issues of Good Housekeeping beginning October 1985

Kennecott (Alaska)
History
Kennecott's boom and bust. R. Churchill and K. Jones. il *Focus* 37:1-5 Fall '87

Kennecott Mine (Alaska) *See* Copper mines and mining—Alaska

Kennedy, Anthony M.
about
Business can't bank on Judge Kennedy's vote. P. Dwyer. il por *Bus Week* p33 N 30 '87
A conservative's conservative? il por *U S News World Rep* 103:24 N 23 '87
Far more judicious. G. J. Church. il por *Time* 130:16-18 N 23 '87
From Bork to Kennedy. R. M. Dworkin. bibl f il *N Y Rev Books* 34:36+ D 17 '87
Here comes the judge. M. Gallagher. *Natl Rev* 39:33+ D 18 '87
Hey, look Kennedy over. *Nation* 245:773 D 26 '87-Ja 2 '88
The justice-to-be whom nobody really knows. T. Gest. il por *U S News World Rep* 103:48 D 14 '87
Kennedy for the Court. A. Press. il por *Newsweek* 110:21 N 23 '87
Next up, a confirmable conservative? il por *Newsweek* 110:51 N 16 '87
The other Kennedy. *Natl Rev* 39:13-14 D 31 '87
A time for panic. *Natl Rev* 39:17-18 D 4 '87

Kennedy, Bruce R.
about
Alaska Air: is it California dreamin'? J. B. Levine. il por *Bus Week* p150 N 30 '87

Kennedy, Caroline
about
Caroline Kennedy at 30. L. David. il pors *McCalls* 114:14-15+ S '87

Kennedy, Cora Wright
Tools & techniques. See issues of Popular Photography

Kennedy, Daniel
After all these years [story] il *Redbook* 168:48+ Ap '87

Kennedy, David M.
What's new at the zoo? il *Technol Rev* 90:66-73 Ap '87

Kennedy, Donald
The public and the university [address, February 17, 1987] *Vital Speeches Day* 53:412-14 Ap 15 '87

Kennedy, Edward Moore, 1932-
Should the "Minimum Wage Restoration Act of 1987" be approved? [excerpts from address, March 25, 1987] *Congr Dig* 66:200+ Ag/S '87
about
Black thought, black talk. W. F. Buckley. *Natl Rev* 39:54-5 Ag 14 '87
Edward Kennedy [interview] W. Greider. il por *Roll Stone* p99-100 N 5-D 10 '87
Hamalot. H. Fairlie. il *New Repub* 197:17-18 O 19 '87
Kennedy's health plan will pit business against business. S. B. Garland. il por *Bus Week* p62 My 25 '87
A liberal's waiting game. G. F. Will. il *Newsweek* 109:82 Mr 16 '87
Making business pay for welfare. B. Cohn and J. Schwartz. il por *Newsweek* 109:49 Je 15 '87
The old frontier. J. Klein. il por *N Y* 20:26+ O 19 '87
The prince of hacks. *Natl Rev* 39:15-16 Jl 31 '87
Sen. Ted Kennedy helps trim the fat on Capitol Hill by shedding his generous girth. il por *People Wkly* 27:100 Ap 13 '87
Treating Teddy unFairlie [discussion of October 19, 1987 article, Hamalot] H. Fairlie. *New Repub* 197:4+ N 16 '87

Kennedy, Ethel
about
Profiles: Ethel Kennedy. il pors *Archit Dig* 44:72-9+ Ag '87

Kennedy, Frances H.
Missing pieces. il *Natl Parks* 61:30-3 S/O '87

Kennedy, Harlan
Edinburgh at 40. il *Film Comment* 23:7-8 Ja/F '87
Gritty Brit. il por *Film Comment* 23:15-17 Mr/Ap '87
It's the dinosaur show. *Film Comment* 23:77+ N/D '87
Soviet spring. il *Film Comment* 23:34-6 My/Je '87
Tarkovsky. il por *Film Comment* 23:44-6 My/Je '87
A tent in Venice. *Film Comment* 23:70+ N/D '87
Wall-eyed. il *Film Comment* 23:2+ My/Je '87
Whither Britain? il *Film Comment* 23:50-1 Ja/F '87

Kennedy, James Cox
about
Big decisions. L. Gubernick. il por *Forbes* 140:222 N 2 '87

Kennedy, James H.
Whistling Dixie in Brazil. il *Américas* 39:26-31 Ja/F '87

Kennedy, John F. (John Fitzgerald), 1917-1963
about
Class reunion: Kennedy's men relive the Cuban Missile Crisis [cover story] J. A. Lukas. il *N Y Times Mag* p22-7+ Ag 30 '87
Dressing for Camelot [excerpt from In my own fashion; cover story] O. Cassini. il pors *People Wkly* 28:66-8+ Ag 24 '87
Jack Kennedy's private side. *Newsweek* 109:22 Je 8 '87
Re-evaluating the Kennedys. A. P. Sanoff. il por *U S News World Rep* 102:68 My 4 '87
Upstairs at the White House. H. Sidey. il por *Time* 129:20 My 18 '87
Photographs and photography
Cocktails at Camelot [45th birthday celebration, 1962] C. Stoughton. il pors *Life* 10:66-7+ Je '87

Kennedy, Joseph P., 1888-1969
about
Birth of a dynasty [excerpts from The Fitzgeralds and the Kennedys] D. K. Goodwin. il pors *People Wkly* 27:54-6+ Ja 26 '87

Kennedy, Joseph Patrick, II
about
Couples. M. Orth. il pors *Vogue* 177:384-5 F '87

Kennedy, Kristina
Baby on set; ed. by Roberta Grant. il pors *Ladies Home J* 104:61-2+ Je '87

Kennedy, Marilyn Moats, 1943-
Feeling bored and restless? How to stay fresh on the job. il *Glamour* 85:216-18+ F '87
Job strategies. See issues of Glamour

Kennedy, Maurice
about
A conversation with Maurice Kennedy. C. Movalli. il *Am Artist* 51:74-9+ N '87

Kennedy, Nigel
about
Pop virtuoso. L. Valdes. il por *Vogue* 177:106 N '87

Kennedy, Paul M., 1945-
The (relative) decline of America [cover story] il *Atlantic* 260:29-34+ Ag '87
The Soviet system today. il *Current* 296:16-26 O '87
The U.S. as world leader: the (relative) decline of America. il *Current* 298:30-8 D '87
What Gorbachev is up against. il *Atlantic* 259:29-38+ Je '87
about
Of many things. G. W. Hunt. *America* 157:98 Ag 29-S 5 '87

Kennedy, Richard T.
Harnessing the peaceful atom: past performance and future challenges [address, March 23, 1987] *Dep State Bull* 87:76-80 Je '87
U.S. reconfirms support for IAEA [statement, November 11, 1986] *Dep State Bull* 87:86-7 Ja '87

Kennedy, Robert D.
Strategic planning [address, March 18, 1987] *Vital Speeches Day* 53:624-7 Ag 1 '87

Kennedy, Roger G.
Walking the federal triangle. il *Good Housekeep* 205:108-9 O '87
about
Keeper of the Attic. M. Durham. il pors *Americana* 15:43-8 N/D '87

Kennedy, Rose Fitzgerald, 1890-
about
Birth of a dynasty [excerpts from The Fitzgeralds and the Kennedys] D. K. Goodwin. il pors *People Wkly* 27:54-6+ Ja 26 '87

Kennedy, Shawn
Home economics. il *Black Enterp* 18:55-6+ O '87
Meeting the demand for comprehensive coverage. il *Black Enterp* 17:223-4+ Je '87

Kennedy, Sheila
about
Couples. M. Orth. il pors *Vogue* 177:384-5 F '87

Kennedy, Ted *See* Kennedy, Edward Moore, 1932-

Kennedy, William, 1928-
Be reasonable—unless you're a writer. il *N Y Times Book Rev* 92:3 Ja 25 '87
about
Man of Ironweed. J. Parini. il por *Horizon* 30:35-6 D '87

Kennedy, X. J.
Making a name in poetry, or, How did Emily Dickinson do it? *Writer* 100:18-21+ N '87

Kennedy (John Fitzgerald) School of Government *See* John Fitzgerald Kennedy School of Government

Kennedy Center Honors
Sammy Davis among five Kennedy Center honorees. *Jet* 73:60 O 12 '87

Kennedy Center Honors—*cont.*
Sammy Davis gets Kennedy Center Honor for Christmas. il por *Jet* 73:55 D 28 '87-Ja 4 '88

Kennedy family

about

Birth of a dynasty [excerpts from The Fitzgeralds and the Kennedys] D. K. Goodwin. il pors *People Wkly* 27:54-6+ Ja 26 '87

The Kennedy hustle [work of D. K. Goodwin] C. Peters. il *Wash Mon* 19:47-9 My '87

Re-evaluating the Kennedys. A. P. Sanoff. il por *U S News World Rep* 102:68 My 4 '87

Those spunky Kennedy women. C. Kramer. il *McCalls* 115:28+ O '87

Kennedy International Airport *See* New York (N.Y.)—Airports

Kennedy Space Center *See* John F. Kennedy Space Center

Kennels
Under the stairs, a dog den. il *Sunset* 178:121 Je '87

Kenner, Hugh
The Department of Factual Verification. *Natl Rev* 39:37-8+ O 9 '87

Kenner Parker Toys Inc.
Can Monopoly find happiness in Spiderman's arms? [bid from New World Pictures] K. H. Hammonds. il *Bus Week* p34 Ag 3 '87

High drama from the folks who brought you Godzilla '85 [New World's play for Kenner] R. Grover. il pors *Bus Week* p30 S 7 '87

Is Tonka toying with trouble? [acquisition of Kenner Parker toys] G. G. Marcial. *Bus Week* p165 O 12 '87

Kenney, Asta M.
Teen pregnancy: an issue for schools [cover story; with editorial comment by Robert W. Cole] bibl f il *Phi Delta Kappan* 68:722, 728-36 Je '87

Kenney, Edward
Watching the whales [cover story] il *Conservationist* 42:24-31 S/O '87

Kenney, James J.
Best bites for '87. il *World Tennis* 34:36-7 Ja '87
Smart eats. il *World Tennis* 34:42-5 Mr '87

Kenny, Peter M.
(jt. auth) See Graybeal, Jay A., and Kenny, Peter M.

Kenny G *See* G, Kenny

Kent, Debra
Baby divorcée. il *Mademoiselle* 93:206-7+ Ap '87
The incredible shrinking couple! Therapy for the commitment-shy. il *Mademoiselle* 93:302-3+ S '87
It's 1987. Do you know where your love life is? *Mademoiselle* 93:138-9+ F '87

Kent, J. W.
When looking good is not enough. por *U S News World Rep* 102:5 My 11 '87

Kent, Julie

about

Lovers leap: behind the scenes with Baryshnikov. H. Brubach. il pors *Vogue* 177:220-3+ Jl '87

Petites: short & sexy. pors *Harpers Bazaar* 120:400-3 S '87

Teen ballerina Julie Kent is Baryshnikov's new leading lady. il por *People Wkly* 28:100 N 30 '87

Kent, Kate Peck
Navajo weaving: centuries of change. bibl il *Am Craft* 47:34-8+ Ag/S '87

Kent, Rachel B., and others
Ouabain resistance conferred by expression of the cDNA for a murine Na⁺,K⁺-ATPase α subunit. bibl f il *Science* 237:901-3 Ag 21 '87

Kent County (Del.)

Historic houses, sites, etc.

John Dickinson's Poplar Hall, Kent County, Delaware. J. A. H. Sweeney. il *Antiques* 132:820-7 O '87

Kentshire Galleries Ltd.
An English accent at Kentshire. D. Rosenthal. il pors *Archit Dig* 44:78+ Mr '87

The English channel. E. Greene. il pors *House Gard* 159:32+ Jl '87

Kentucky

See also

Big South Fork National River and Recreation Area (Tenn. and Ky.)
Botanical gardens—Kentucky
Caves—Kentucky
Child welfare—Kentucky
Jefferson County (Ky.)
Lincoln County (Ky.)
Music festivals—Kentucky

Description and travel

Kentucky Bluegrass [cover story] K. B. Raitz. il map *Focus* 37:6-11 Fall '87

Politics and government

John Y. Brown Jr. is down and out in Kentucky [loses bid for gubernatorial nomination] *Newsweek* 109:20 Je 8 '87

Kentucky Botanical Gardens *See* Botanical gardens—Kentucky

Kentucky Derby *See* Horse racing

Kentucky Opera
Musical events:
Rimsky-Korsakov's The golden cockerel. A. Porter. *New Yorker* 63:108-9 My 18 '87

Kentucky quilts *See* Quilts and quilting

Kenworthy, Eldon
United States policy in Central America. bibl f *Curr Hist* 86:401-4+ D '87

Kenya

See also

Birth control—Kenya
Civil rights—Kenya
Drug abuse—Kenya
Ecology—Kenya
Education—Kenya
Game preserves—Kenya
Nairobi (Kenya)
National parks and reserves—Kenya
Orphans and orphanages—Kenya
Paleontology—Kenya
Public health—Kenya
Television broadcasting—Kenya
Wildlife management—Kenya

Antiquities

The Swahili corridor [Shanga excavations] M. Horton. il maps *Sci Am* 257:86-8+ S '87

Description and travel

Facing Mount Kenya and Kilimanjaro, too. F. D. Brown. il *Black Enterp* 17:66-7 Ap '87

Out of Africa: an affordable safari. il *Glamour* 85:186+ F '87

Native peoples

See also
Masai (African people)
Turkana (African people)

Politics and government

Kenya: the dissolution of democracy. M. Maren. bibl f *Curr Hist* 86:209-12+ My '87

Moi? Yes, Moi. *World Press Rev* 34:41 My '87

The plot that never was [questionable memo implicates American missionaries in plot to overthrow Kenyan government] M. Hornblower. il por *Time* 130:37 N 30 '87

Religious institutions and affairs

See also
Missions—Kenya

Kenyon, Jean
Lighthouse Reef: a Caribbean atoll. il map *Sea Front* 33:428-37 N/D '87

Kenyon, Michael
Almost Jeeves. il *Gourmet* 47:64+ Jl '87
Not quite Escoffier. il *Gourmet* 47:68+ Ag '87
Sale of goods. il *Gourmet* 47:122+ N '87

Kenyon, Nicholas, 1951-
Rattling the strings. il por *World Press Rev* 34:58-9 D '87
Vintage debut. il pors *Opera News* 51:24+ Mr 28 '87

Keogh plans
Retirement for life [buying life insurance through a Keogh] P. D. Lawrence. il *Esquire* 108:46 Ag '87

Keon, Wilbert

about

'The consummate surgeon'. P. Gessell. il por *Macleans* 100:42 N 23 '87

Keough, Carol
Future youth: how to regenerate your energy [excerpt; with editorial comment by Mark Bricklin] il *Prevention* 39:57, 102+ Jl '87

Kepler's equation *See* Orbits

Keppler, Herbert
Keppler's SLR world. See issues of Popular Photography beginning September 1987

KEPROM (Keyed-access erasable programmable read-only memory) *See* Read only memory

Kerasote, Ted
Is Nepal going bald? il map *Audubon* 89:28-30+ S '87

Keratotomy, Radial *See* Cornea—Surgery

Kerchiefs *See* Scarves

Keresty, Nancy Atkins

about

Socks with soul: Nancy Atkins, Inc. J. Ciabattari. il por *Work Woman* 12:136-7 N '87

Kerkorian, Kirk
about
Can Kerkorian breathe new life into the old lion? R. Grover. il *Bus Week* p33 N 23 '87
Doing the Hollywood shuffle. M. Beauchamp. il por *Forbes* 140:35-6 O 19 '87
A high roller moves in on Pan Am. R. Grover. il por *Bus Week* p30-3 N 23 '87
Pan American council examines takeover, restructure plan. J. Ott. *Aviat Week Space Technol* 127:34 O 19 '87
Welcome aboard. The champagne is on ice. S. Toy. il por *Bus Week* p61-2 Ja 19 '87
Will it be Kerkorian to the rescue at Pan Am? C. Hawkins and R. Grover. il *Bus Week* p57-8 O 19 '87

Kern, George C., 1926-
about
A top law firm feels the heat. C. Friday. *Newsweek* 110:40-1 Jl 13 '87
When companies talk turkey, investors should be told. V. Cahan. il *Bus Week* p100 Jl 13 '87

Kern, John
Reminiscing in Great Gatsbyland. il *Travel Holiday* 168:28+ O '87

Kernan, Henry S.
My 40 years in a woodlot. il *Conservationist* 42:36-41 S/O '87

Kerosene oil lamps *See* Lamps

Kerr, Arnold D., and Pipes, R. Byron
Why we need hands-on engineering education. il *Technol Rev* 90:36-42 O '87

Kerr, Chester
The Kerr report: one more time. *Publ Wkly* 231:19-22 Je 5 '87

Kerr, Clark, 1911-
about
Clark Kerr: the masterbuilder at 75 [cover story] A. Levine. il pors *Change* 19:12-27+ Mr/Ap '87

Kerr, Steve
about
Darling of the desert. B. Anderson. il por *Sports Illus* 67:91 D 14 '87

Kerr-McGee Corp.
Making fertilizer from what? [conversion of radioactive waste to fertilizer at Sequoyah Falls plant, Okla.] M. D. Lemonick. il *Time* 130:79 N 30 '87

Kerry, John Forbes, 1943-
Should the Boren Amendment approach to curtailing PAC's be adopted? [excerpts from debate, August 11 and 12, 1986] *Congr Dig* 66:58+ F '87

Kersee, Jackie Joyner- *See* Joyner-Kersee, Jackie

Kertes, Tom
Can't anybody coach these guys? il pors *Sport Mag* 78:53-4+ F '87
V is for Final IV. il *Sport Mag* 78:84-5+ Ap '87
What's on draft. il *Sport Mag* 78:77-8+ Jl '87

Kertess, Klaus
Dancing with Carmen. il pors *Art Am* 75:180-5+ Ap '87
In nature's shadow. il *Art Am* 75:57-9 S '87
The mad potter of Biloxi. il por *House Gard* 159:104+ Je '87

Kertész, André
about
Photography. V. Goldberg. il *N Y* 20:80-1 S 21 '87

Kesler, Steven
about
Doubts about self-defence. M. Gray. il pors *Macleans* 100:45 Je 29 '87
Fear, arms and a verdict. M. Gray. il por *Macleans* 100:48 Jl 6 '87

Kessler, Brad
Body on the line. *Nation* 245:329 O 3 '87

Kessler, Richard J.
How Aquino can recoup [cover story] il *New Leader* 70:3-5 O 5 '87
Making the Constitution work [cover story] por *New Leader* 70:8-10 Mr 9 '87

Kessler-Harris, Alice
Trade unions mirror society in conflict between collectivism and individualism. bibl f *Mon Labor Rev* 110:32-6 Ag '87
Without a history . . . [excerpt from address] *Ms* 16:84-5 N '87
about
Differences and inequality [interview] D. Tell. *Society* 24:10-16 S/O '87

Kester, John G.
Too many lawyers? il *Read Dig* 130:153-4+ Ap '87

Kesterson National Wildlife Refuge *See* Wildlife sanctuaries—California

Kestigian, Mark C.
Hard work, vintage rewards. il *Travel Holiday* 167:24-7 F '87

Kestner, Joseph
Reign of pleasure. il *Opera News* 51:16-19+ F 28 '87

Ketchikan (Alaska)
Description
Ketchikan's three big totem collections . . . easy to get to. il *Sunset* 179:40-1 Ag '87

Ketelsen, James L.
about
Plowing different fields. P. Nulty. il por *Fortune* 116:62+ Ag 3 '87

Keteyian, Armen
Dark clouds over Sun country. il *Sports Illus* 66:24-5 Ap 27 '87

Keteyian, Armen, and Wolff, Alexander
Signed, sealed and sorry. il por *Sports Illus* 66:24-6 F 23 '87

Ketteringham, John M., and Nayak, Ranganath P.
People behind the wonders [condensed from Breakthroughs!] il *Read Dig* 131:134-8 Jl '87

Kettler, David, and others
Is a science of politics possible?: The view from Mannheim. *Society* 24:76-82 Mr/Ap '87

Keur Massar (Senegal)
Easing leprosy's pain. M. Rose. il por *Macleans* 100:6+ Mr 30 '87

Kevles, Barbara
The great weight-machine workout. il *Mademoiselle* 93:110 O '87
How to beat the yeast beast. il *Mademoiselle* 93:58 Jl '87

Key, Francis Scott, 1779-1843
about
The banner yet waves [condensed from Star of wonder] D. M. Epstein. il *Read Dig* 131:114-16 Jl '87

Key deer *See* Deer

Key Independent System
Is KIS beating a retreat from the U.S.? C. Gaffney. il *Bus Week* p58 Mr 16 '87

Key Porter Books Ltd.
A defeat for Scientology [Canadian publication of Russell Miller's biography of L. R. Hubbard allowed] D. Todd. *Macleans* 100:54 D 14 '87

Key West (Fla.)
Description
Key West. S. Shane. il *Travel Holiday* 167:38-43+ Ja '87

Intellectual life
Key West's literary lure draws the public too. B. Summer. *Publ Wkly* 231:55 Ja 16 '87

Keyboard instruments
See also
Piano
Don Preston: synthesizer from Apocalypse now to Zappa. J. Woodard. il por *Down Beat* 54:25-7 Ag '87
Music is alive with the sound of high tech. T. Thompson. il *Bus Week* p114-16 O 26 '87
Not for listeners only (I). C. J. Esse. il *High Fidel* 37:14+ O '87
One-man band [electronic keyboards] F. Vizard. il *Pop Mech* 164:106-8 Ap '87
The sound of a new machine [electronic keyboards] W. C. Banks. il *Money* 16:174-6+ Ap '87

Keyboards
From keypress to scan code [IBM keyboards] J. Holtzman. il *Radio-Electron* 58 ComputerDigest:70-3 Jl '87
Keyboard medley. il *Radio-Electron* 58 ComputerDigest:67-9 Jl '87
Macros [keyboard enhancers] P. Honan. il *Pers Comput* 11:77-81+ F '87
Mnemonic macros [Jot RAM-resident macro creator] R. Lockwood. il *Pers Comput* 11:148 Ag '87
Working with surplus keyboards. R. Grossblatt. il *Radio-Electron* 58 ComputerDigest:74-7 Jl '87
History
The panda's thumb of technology [history of QWERTY keyboard] S. J. Gould. il *Nat Hist* 96:14+ Ja '87

Keyes, Alan
FY 1988 assistance requests for organizations and programs [statement, April 1, 1987] *Dep State Bull* 87:88-91 Je '87
about
Alan Keyes resigns State Dept. post; charges racism. por *Jet* 73:4 O 5 '87

Keyes, Ralph
One nation and a vegetable. il *Good Housekeep* 204:76+ Je '87

Keynes, John Maynard, 1883-1946
about
Economist, speculator, bon vivant. E. A. Finn, Jr. il
Forbes 139:100-1 F 23 '87
First encounters. E. Sorel and N. C. Sorel. il *Atlantic*
259:61 My '87
The newest name in economics: John Maynard Keynes.
N. Jonas and J. Berger. *Bus Week* p42 Ja 12 '87
Keynesian economics *See* Economics
Keynote Records (Firm)
Sounding the Keynote. J. McDonough. *Down Beat* 54:28
Ja '87
Keys, Randolph
about
The Eagles' mooving force. F. Lidz. il por *Sports Illus*
67 Sp Issue:80 N 18 '87
Keys *See* Locks and keys
Keys, Florida (Fla.) *See* Florida Keys (Fla.)
Keystone (Colo.: Resort) *See* Resorts—Colorado
Keysville (Ga.)
Politics and government
Who will rule Keysville? T. E. Johnson. il *Newsweek*
110:24 S 7 '87
Race relations
Who will rule Keysville? T. E. Johnson. il *Newsweek*
110:24 S 7 '87
KGB
See also
Daniloff-Zakharov espionage case, 1986
The KGB admits a mistake [dismissal of senior officer
over arrest of Ukrainian journalist] il *Newsweek* 109:32
Ja 19 '87
The KGB gets spanked [officer dismissed over arrest
of Ukrainian journalist] il *Time* 129:43 Ja 19 '87
Kremlinologists play a video game [tape of R. Gorbachev]
N. Cooper. il por *Newsweek* 109:35 Ap 13 '87
The threat from a failed system [address, June 8, 1987]
M. Tugwell. *Vital Speeches Day* 53:645-7 Ag 15 '87
Anecdotes, facetiae, satire, etc.
The *glasnost* drapes. R. Baker. il *N Y Times Mag* p30
O 4 '87
Khadafy, Moammar *See* Qaddafi, Muammar al-, 1942-
Khadivi, H. John
about
Turning the mattress into a fortress. T. Dworetzky. il
Discover 8:22 S '87
Khan, Inayat
(jt. auth) *See* Grant, Marcus, and Khan, Inayat
Khan, Mohammad Yusuf *See* Yusuf Khan
Khan, Sadruddin Aga *See* Aga Khan, Sadruddin, Prince,
1933-
Khan, Yasmin
about
Honoring her stricken mother, Rita Hayworth, Yasmin
Khan stages a dazzling benefit. il pors *People Wkly*
27:36-7 My 25 '87
Remembering Rita [cover story] il pors *People Wkly*
27:72-6+ Je 1 '87
Yasmin Khan: my mother, Rita Hayworth. C. Ford.
il pors *McCalls* 114:138-9+ My '87
Khanna, Jitendra
(jt. auth) *See* Shah, Iqbal, and Khanna, Jitendra
Khashoggi, Adnan
about
Big man on campus. C. McCarthy. *Nation* 244:252-4
F 28 '87
Dreams of the Great Satan. A. Cockburn. *Nation* 245:186
S 5 '87
Hounded by bad debts, bad deals and angry creditors,
Adnan Khashoggi defends his dwindling empire. M.
Green. il pors *People Wkly* 27:113-14 F 9 '87
The Khashoggi memo. M. Hosenball. *New Repub* 196:14+
F 2 '87
Khashoggi's connections. D. Jenish. il por *Macleans*
100:34-6 Ja 19 '87
Khashoggi's high-flying realm. R. Stengel. il pors *Time*
129:30-4 Ja 19 '87
A super Saudi's shifting fortunes. A. Gabor. il pors
U S News World Rep 102:48-50 Ja 12 '87
Khlebnikov, Velimir, 1885-1922
about
Zangezi [drama] Reviews
Art Am il 75:25+ My '87. P. Clothier
Khmer Rouge
Cambodia [discussion of April 1987 article, Pol Pot
in retrospect] A. Puddington. *Commentary* 84:14-15
Ag '87
Pol Pot in retrospect. A. Puddington. *Commentary*
83:49-54 Ap '87

Khomeini, Ruhollah
about
At war on all fronts [cover story; special section] il
pors *Time* 130:22-6+ Ag 17 '87
The Ayatollah's big sting [cover story; with editorial
comment by Mortimer B. Zuckerman] il pors maps
U S News World Rep 102:18-24, 82 Mr 30 '87
Coping with Khomeini. H. Trewhitt. il *U S News World
Rep* 103:25-7 Ag 3 '87
Dreams of the Great Satan. A. Cockburn. *Nation* 245:186
S 5 '87
Institutionalizing the new order in Iran. S. Akhavi. bibl
f *Curr Hist* 86:53-6+ F '87
Iran looks beyond Khomeini. R. Wright. il *Nation*
244:129+ F 7 '87
Khomeini's Iran: a case study of hatred toward the
U.S. L. Hopping. il *Sch Update* 120:27-8 O 2 '87
Anecdotes, facetiae, satire, etc.
Hard sell. T. C. Boyle. *Harpers* 275:17-20 D '87
Khosla, Vinod
about
Finding the ultimate thrill. il por *Fortune* 116:91 Ag
17 '87
Khun Sa
about
Reign of an opium warlord. M. Satchell. il por *U S
News World Rep* 102:33 My 4 '87
Kibbe, David
Metamorphosis [excerpt] il *Ladies Home J* 104:126-33
O '87
about
Even if you look like the Pentagon, make-over man
David Kibbe claims he can bring out the beauty
within. K. Hubbard. il pors *People Wkly* 28:113+
O 26 '87
Kibbutzim
Finance
High Marx, low Marx. H. Kestin. il *Forbes* 139:35-6
Ja 26 '87
The kid brother [film] *See* Motion picture reviews—Single
works
Kidd, Billy
Kidd's page. *See* issues of Skiing beginning September
1984
Kidd, Phillip E.
Adjusting to tax reform will slow real growth in the
first half of the year. il *Archit Rec* 175:31 Ja '87
Finance: improvement in trade renews our real growth.
il *Archit Rec* 175:44 Ag '87
Rising interest rates dim economic prospects. il *Archit
Rec* 175:43 Je '87
Slump in dollar's value clouds interest-rate outlook. il
Archit Rec 175:41 Mr '87
Kidd, Randy
Animal birthdays. il *Mother Earth News* 104:36-9 Mr/Ap
'87
Animal emergencies. il *Mother Earth News* 103:26 Ja/F
'87
Exercising your pet. il *Mother Earth News* 105:34+ My/Je
'87
Kidde Inc.
Hanson and Kidde: a marriage made in low tech; A
portrait of the raider as respected industrialist. L.
Baum and R. A. Melcher. il *Bus Week* p36-7 Ag
17 '87
Kidder, Peabody & Co., Incorporated
A contrast in styles on Wall Street [Kidder parent GE]
il *Fortune* 115:8 Je 8 '87
Kidder does a $25 million deal with Giuliani [GE tries
to limit damage from insider trading] *Newsweek* 109:49
Je 15 '87
Suddenly the fish get bigger [insider trading scandal;
special section] il *Bus Week* p28-35 Mr 2 '87
Where Kidder's brokers bet [secondary stocks] G. G.
Marcial. *Bus Week* p78 Ag 3 '87
Why GE is cleaning house at Kidder [trying to limit
damage from insider trading scandal] J. R. Norman.
il *Bus Week* p45 Je 1 '87
Kiddieporn *See* Pornography
Kiddoo, Forbes
about
Who says no man is an island? Builder Forbes Kiddoo
is surrounded on all sides by water and curiosity.
M. Dougherty. il por *People Wkly* 28:50-2 Ag 31
'87
Kidnapping
See also
Buckley, William—Kidnapping
Choi, Un Hui—Kidnapping
Febres Cordero, León, 1931——Kidnapping
Glass, Charles—Kidnapping

Kidnapping—See also—*cont.*
    Lindbergh, Charles, Jr.—Kidnapping
    Popieluszko, Jerzy—Murder case
    Shin, Sang Ok—Kidnapping
    Small, Stephen, d. 1987—Kidnapping
    Steen, Alann—Kidnapping
    Swenson, Kari—Kidnapping
    Thate, Jeremiah—Kidnapping
    Washington, Alicia—Kidnapping
    Weir, Benjamin—Kidnapping
    Worthington, Phillip, b. 1986—Kidnapping
Kidney stones

Therapy
Kidney-stone surgery one day may pass. N. Brown. il *Nations Bus* 75:74 N '87
Shattering kidney stones [lithotripsy] P. Gadsby and L. J. Brown. il *Good Housekeep* 204:212 Je '87
Kidneys
    See also
    Adrenal glands
    Urine
Direct demonstration of macula densa-mediated renin secretion. O. Skøtt and J. P. Briggs. bibl f il *Science* 237:1618-20 S 25 '87
Doctor's notes [discussion of May 1987 article, What's shaped like a bean and acts like a screen?] K. B. Taylor. por *50 Plus* 27:6 Ag '87
Physiological role of silent receptors of atrial natriuretic factor. T. Maack and others. bibl f il *Science* 238:675-8 O 30 '87
Uromodulin (Tamm-Horsfall glycoprotein): a renal ligand for lymphokines. C. Hession and others. bibl f il *Science* 237:1479-84 S 18 '87
What's shaped like a bean and acts like a screen? K. B. Taylor. il *50 Plus* 27:80+ My '87

Cancer
Genetic aspects
Introduction of a normal human chromosome 11 into a Wilms' tumor cell line controls its tumorigenic expression. B. E. Weissman and others. bibl f il *Science* 236:175-80 Ap 10 '87

Transplantation
A desperate search for a second life [adoptee A. Sferrino gets kidney from natural mother] M. Jacobbi and R. Wright. il pors *McCalls* 114:127-9 Je '87
A father's special gift of love [J. Garn donates kidney to diabetic daughter] M. F. Hoyt. il por *Good Housekeep* 204:74+ F '87
New transplant findings fit like a glove [research by Elaine Reed and others] R. Weiss. *Sci News* 131:375 Je 13 '87
Kids like these [television program] See Television program reviews—Single works
KIDS of Bergen County (Program)
Turning KIDS off drugs. E. B. Fein. il *N Y Times Mag* p26-32 My 24 '87
Kidwell, Beatrice Ann
"Sergeant Mom". il por *Ladies Home J* 104:16+ Ja '87
Kiechel, Walter, III
Office hours. See alternate issues of Fortune
Kiefer, Anselm, 1945-
    about
Anselm Kiefer. N. Grimes. il *Art News* 86:127-8 S '87
Anselm Kiefer. R. Atkins. il *Horizon* 30:12-16 D '87
Anselm Kiefer: a call to memory. S. H. Madoff. il por *Art News* 86:125-30 O '87
Germany's master in the making. R. Hughes. il por *Time* 130:72-3 D 21 '87
The good earth. K. Larson. il *N Y* 20:91-2 Je 1 '87
Kiefer's heart of darkness. C. Ratcliff. il *Harpers Bazaar* 121:160-1+ D '87
Kiefer, Michael
The living daylights. il *Sport Mag* 78:28-32+ Ag '87
Kiel, David L.
The many uses of Carlton Hill. il *Conservationist* 42:16-21 N/D '87
Kielley, James E.
    about
A specialist slips into big-league consulting. J. A. Byrne. il por *Bus Week* p73+ Jl 27 '87
Kiely, Eugene
    about
Eugene Kiely itches to find heirs to wads of scratch. J. Kaufman. il pors *People Wkly* 28:89+ N 16 '87
Kienle, Jürgen, and others
Tsunamis generated by eruptions from Mount St. Augustine volcano, Alaska [cover story] il maps *Science* 236:1442-7 Je 12 '87

Kierkegaard, Søren, 1813-1855
    about
Of many things. G. W. Hunt. *America* 156:inside cover My 23 '87
Kieschnick, William F., Jr.
    about
From oil to oils. G. Buchalter. il por *Forbes* 139:283 Ja 12 '87
Kiesewetter, Ted
    about
When the boss leads the way. F. Abatemarco. il por *Pers Comput* 11:152-3 O '87
Kiesler, Frederick
    about
Frederick Kiesler at Alfred Kren and Jason McCoy. P. Derfner. il *Art Am* 75:136-7 Mr '87
Kiesling, Stephen
A roundup of fitness guides. il *50 Plus* 27:66-7 Ja '87
Walk-shape yourself. il *Good Housekeep* 204:100 My '87
Kiester, Edwin
Doctors close in on the mechanisms behind headache. il *Smithsonian* 18:175-6+ D '87
Kiewit (Peter) Sons, Inc. See Peter Kiewit Sons, Inc.
Kihlstrom, John F.
The cognitive unconscious. bibl f *Science* 237:1445-52 S 18 '87
Kilauea (Hawaii)
Celebration on a volcano. *Sci News* 131:53 Ja 24 '87
Kilauea National Wildlife Refuge (Kauai, Hawaii) See Wildlife sanctuaries—Kauai (Hawaii)
Kildoyle, Pat
    about
Think twice before turning up your nose at Alfin. G. G. Marcial. il *Bus Week* p98 S 28 '87
Kile, Donna Leigh- See Leigh-Kile, Donna
Kiley, John
Yes [poem] il *Natl Rev* 39:39 Ap 24 '87
Kilgour, David
    about
A dissident is shut out. por *Macleans* 100:13 Ap 20 '87
Kilgour, Vajra
A Christmas card in Tibet. por *Newsweek* 110:7 D 28 '87
Kilimnik, Karel
'Reagan people only'. *Progressive* 51:11 S '87
Killeen (Tex.)
Religious institutions and affairs
Black Methodist minister heads white Texas church [J. D. Phillips of St. Andrew's United Methodist Church in Killeen] por *Jet* 72:22 Jl 13 '87
Killens, John Oliver, 1916-1987
    about
Obituary
    Jet por 73:16 N 16 '87
Killer bees See Bees
Killer cells See Lymphocytes
Killer whales
Into the world of orcas. A. Morton. il *Int Wildl* 17:12-17 S/O '87
Keeping an ear on orcas. D. Hand. il *Oceans* 20:10-19+ Jl/Ag '87
Killer whales: playful giants. il *Natl Geogr World* 140:10-15 Ap '87
Killgallon, Martin L.
    about
Etch a future. G. Slutsker. il por *Forbes* 139:72 Mr 23 '87
Killinger, D. K. (Dennis K.), 1945-, and Menyuk, Norman
Laser remote sensing of the atmosphere. bibl f il *Science* 235:37-45 Ja 2 '87
Killinger, Dennis K. See Killinger, D. K. (Dennis K.), 1945-
Killinger, John
The preacher and the panhandlers. il *Christ Century* 104:301-2 Ap 1 '87
Killington (Vt.: Resort) See Resorts—Vermont
Killion, Ann
No romp in the park. il *Sports Illus* 67:99 S 21 '87
Killip, Chris, 1946-
Skinheads of Newcastle [photographs] il *Society* 24:84-6 Jl/Ag '87
Killy, Jean Claude, 1943-
    about
Killy the instructor. A. H. Greenberg. *Skiing* 39:42 F '87
Kilmer, Joyce, 1886-1918
    about
Joyce Kilmer: soldier and poet. B. McGinty. por *Am Hist Illus* 22:46-7 My '87

Kilmer, Val
about
Val Kilmer: he's getting serious. G. Hollobaugh. il pors *Teen* 31:41 Ja '87
Kilns
Solar kiln [solar heated lumber drying kiln] R. W. Rice. il *Workbench* 43:6+ Ja/F '87
Kilpatrick, Bill
Vehicles. See issues of Field & Stream
Kilpatrick, James J., 1920-
A country sage looks back. il por *Nations Bus* 75:50-1 S '87
Kilpatrick, Terry
Trivia trek. il *Natl Parks* 61:22-3+ Jl/Ag '87
Kilpatrick, William A.
about
The eternal promoter. A. A. Lappen. il por *Forbes* 140:8 Ag 10 '87
The never-say-die promoter. J. A. Conway. por *Forbes* 139:8 Ap 6 '87
The promoter who never quits. A. A. Lappen. il por *Forbes* 139:60-1 F 9 '87
Kilworth, Garry
Paper moon [fiction] il *Omni* 9:60-2+ Ja '87
Kim, Chong Il See Kim, Jong Il
Kim, Dae Jung
about
Kim out, Kim out, whoever you are. H. G. Chua-Eoan. il pors *Time* 130:36 O 12 '87
Kim vs. Kim. il por *Time* 130:74 N 9 '87
Korea: shame & chauvinism. I. Buruma. bibl f il *N Y Rev Books* 34:21-6 Ja 29 '87
Rebels without a pause. J. Greenwald. il pors *Time* 129:27 Je 29 '87
Will he or won't he? il por *Time* 130:45 S 21 '87
Kim, Duk-Soo
about
Playing for God. L. Cryderman. por *Christ Today* 31:42 N 20 '87
Kim, Il Sung, 1912-
about
Inside the land of the 'Great Leader'. Y. Layma. por *World Press Rev* 34:27-9 Ja '87
Kim, Jong Il
about
Kidnapped by Beloved Leader Comrade. D. Reed. il *Read Dig* 130:105-12 Mr '87
Kim, Jong Pil
about
Korean politics: Kim for a day. B. Martin. il por *Newsweek* 110:51 O 12 '87
Kim, Woo-Choong
about
Korea's export king. L. Kraar. il por *Fortune* 115:74 Ja 5 '87
The master of joint ventures. il por *U S News World Rep* 102:61 My 11 '87
Kim, Young Sam
about
Kim out, Kim out, whoever you are. H. G. Chua-Eoan. il pors *Time* 130:36 O 12 '87
Kim vs. Kim. il por *Time* 130:74 N 9 '87
Rebels without a pause. J. Greenwald. il pors *Time* 129:27 Je 29 '87
"Tomorrow will be different" [interview] B. Hillenbrand and S. Chang. il por *Time* 130:37 Jl 13 '87
Kimball, Penn
about
Vindication for a blacklist victim. D. Gates. il por *Newsweek* 110:8 S 28 '87
Kimball, Roger
Beyond abstract art? *Commentary* 83:53-8 Mr '87
Hugh Stubbins and the life of architecture. il *Archit Rec* 175:61+ Ap '87
Keep politics out of art. *Art News* 86:174 S '87
Le Corbusier at 100: conversations on his legacy. il *Archit Rec* 175:83+ N '87
Kimber, Robert
Big drops and standing waves. il *Ctry J* 14:36-41 Je '87
Hubris in the hills. il *Ctry J* 14:52-6 Mr '87
Made for the country. See issues of Country Journal beginning October 1986
Kimberly-Clark of Canada, Ltd.
Showdown over pollution [paper mill on Lake Superior ordered to install pollution controls] S. Aikenhead. il *Macleans* 100:81 F 2 '87
Kimbrell, W. Duke
about
The fast track isn't always the best track. P. Berman. il por *Forbes* 140:60+ N 2 '87

Kimbrough, Ann
Making the tough transition to financial independence. il *Black Enterp* 17:203-4+ Je '87
Kimelman, Donald
Editor Gorbo. *New Repub* 197:13-14 S 7 '87
Kimery, Anthony L.
Weed killer. il *Progressive* 51:20-1 Jl '87
Kimes, Beverly Rae
The dawn of speed. il *Am Herit* 38:92-4+ N '87
Kimmel, Daniel M.
The Bingo Long traveling all-star industrialists. il por *Film Comment* 23:41-3 Ja/F '87
Laurel and Hardy in the big house. il pors *Film Comment* 23:2+ Jl/Ag '87
Kimmel, Michael S.
Real man redux. bibl (p68) il pors *Psychol Today* 21:48-52 Jl '87
Kimmelman, Benedict B.
The example of Private Slovik. il pors *Am Herit* 38:97-104 S/O '87
Kimmins Industrial Services Corp.
Demolition demon. B. Leonard. il por *Forbes* 139:61-2 Ap 20 '87
Kimura, Chūta, 1917-
about
Art. A. C. Danto. *Nation* 245:29-30 Jl 4-11 '87
Kimura, Motoharu
Reflections of a Japanese physicist. il pors *Bull At Sci* 43:7-10 N '87
Kimura, Tschuta See Kimura, Chūta, 1917-
Kimweli, David
about
The plot that never was. M. Hornblower. il por *Time* 130:37 N 30 '87
Kin recognition
Batmom's daily nightmare [Mexican free-tailed bat maternity colonies] G. F. McCracken and M. K. Gustin. il map *Nat Hist* 96:66-73 O '87
Kinases
See also
Streptokinase
Expression and properties of two types of protein kinase C: alternative splicing from a single gene. Y. Ono and others. bibl f il *Science* 236:1116-20 My 29 '87
Functional analysis of a complementary DNA for the 50-kilodalton subunit of calmodulin kinase II. R. M. Hanley and others. bibl f il *Science* 237:293-7 Jl 17 '87
Neuronal pp60$^{c\text{-}src}$ contains a six-amino acid insertion relative to its non-neuronal counterpart. R. Martinez and others. bibl f il *Science* 237:411-15 Jl 24 '87
A novel putative tyrosine kinase receptor encoded by the *eph* gene. H. Hirai and others. bibl f il *Science* 238:1717-20 D 18 '87
Protein kinase C contains a pseudosubstrate prototope in its regulatory domain. C. House and B. E. Kemp. bibl f il *Science* 238:1726-8 D 18 '87
Transformation by oncogenes encoding protein kinases induces the metastatic phenotype. S. E. Egan and others. bibl f il *Science* 238:202-5 O 9 '87
Unique forms of the *abl* tyrosine kinase distinguish Ph¹-positive CML Ph¹-positive ALL. S. S. Clark and others. bibl f il *Science* 235:85-8 Ja 2 '87
Inactivation
Lysosphingolipids inhibit protein kinase C: implications for the sphingolipidoses. Y. A. Hannun and R. M. Bell. bibl f il *Science* 235:670-4 F 6 '87
Recombinant fragment of protein kinase inhibitor blocks cyclic AMP-dependent gene transcription. J. R. Grove and others. bibl f il *Science* 238:530-3 O 23 '87
Kincade, William H.
Future force planning. *Society* 24:55-60 Jl/Ag '87
Kind, Christian
A new era in arms control. *World Press Rev* 34:13 N '87
Kinder, Gary
about
UFO update. B. Lawren. il *Omni* 9:95 Jl '87
Kinder, Melvyn
(jt. auth) See Cowan, Connell, and Kinder, Melvyn
Kinder-Care Learning Centers Inc.
Kinder-Care may stick to its sitting. D. Foust. il por *Bus Week* p36 Jl 13 '87
Kinderberry Hill (Firm)
Day care with dinner-to-go. L. Washer. il *Work Woman* 12:122 S '87
Kindergarten
See also
Montessori method of education
The big grind in kindergarten. B. Kantrowitz. il *Newsweek* 110:55 Ag 10 '87

Kindergarten—*cont.*
Children of China. M. H. Lystad. bibl f il *Child Today* 16:20-2 Mr/Ap '87
Cutting it in kindergarten. *Harpers* 275:24 N '87
Getting a jump on schooling. G. W. Bracey. il *Phi Delta Kappan* 68:546 Mr '87
The just-missed-kindergarten blues. F. Roberts. il *Parents* 62:48 Ja '87
Kindergarten all day? M. E. Peskin. *Educ Dig* 52:17-19 Mr '87
Kindergarten in America: five major trends. S. L. Robinson. *Phi Delta Kappan* 68:529-30 Mr '87
Kindergarten: ready or not? F. Roberts. *Parents* 62:54+ Ag '87
A national cutoff date for entering kindergarten. R. Lofthouse. *Educ Dig* 53:44-5 N '87
Kindleberger, Charles P.
Fun reading for bankers. il *Forbes* 140:292+ Jl 13 '87
Kindleberger, Charles Poor, 1910-
about
The big lesson from 'the other crash' [interview] il *U S News World Rep* 103:32-3 N 2 '87
Kindness [dance] See Dance reviews—Single works
Kiner, David
about
Skijak zealot David Kiner has big feet, a dream and at least one oar in the water. il *People Wkly* 28:65 Jl 27 '87
Kinesiology See Biomechanics
Kinetic art
See also
Kinetic sculpture
Kinetic kill vehicles
High endoatmospheric defense interceptor [SDI weapon] il *Aviat Week Space Technol* 127:75+ N 23 '87
Latest ABM ploy—old is new [dispute over legality of kinetic weapons] T. K. Longstreth. il *Bull At Sci* 43:3-4 D '87
Martin studies space-based KKV concept. il *Aviat Week Space Technol* 127:20 Ag 31 '87
Opponents focus on kinetic-kill research, ABM Treaty violations [SDI] *Aviat Week Space Technol* 127:84+ N 23 '87
Rockwell to test space-based missile interceptor for SDI. M. A. Dornheim. il *Aviat Week Space Technol* 127:81+ S 14 '87
SDIO forging flight test plans for controversial weapons concepts. il *Aviat Week Space Technol* 127:57+ N 23 '87
SDIO on verge of producing kinetic kill vehicle. *Aviat Week Space Technol* 126:24 F 9 '87
Star Wars: the dream diminished [ERIS and HEDI interceptor systems] W. Biddle. il *Discover* 8:26-30+ Jl '87
Kinetic sculpture
Sculpture funhouse [audiokinetic sculptor G. Rhoads] R. Kostelanetz. il por *N Y Times Mag* p28-31 My 31 '87
King, Barbara
about
1987 Essence Awards. A. Edwards. pors *Essence* 18:121+ My '87
King, Bernard
about
A King eyes a court comeback. B. Newman. il por *Sports Illus* 66:32-3 Mr 30 '87
Knicks' King may return even for season's end. por *Jet* 72:48 Ap 6 '87
King, Billie Jean
about
12 who mattered: Billie Jean. M. Witherell. il pors *World Tennis* 35:54 Jl '87
King, Charlotte
We're black yuppies. Which world do we belong in? il *Glamour* 85:78 My '87
King, Charmaine
about
Seams right! R. D. Manuel. il por *Essence* 18:42 Ag '87
King, Coretta Scott, 1927-
about
Mrs. King approves release of official MLK sculpture. il *Jet* 71:57 F 9 '87
South African journal [interview] J. Goodwin. il por *Ladies Home J* 104:74+ Ja '87
King, Dexter
about
Dexter King says 'tone' promotes racist actions. por *Jet* 72:33 Je 1 '87

King, Don, 1929-
about
Don King gets Dr. King Award in Jamaica fete. il pors *Jet* 71:36-7 F 9 '87
Fighters sue Don King for $35 million in damages. *Jet* 72:40 Je 1 '87
King, Dorothy E.
Lollypop kiss [poem] *Essence* 17:122 Ap '87
King, Florence
Ripping Clio's bodice—the chronicles of a sweet savage hack. il *N Y Times Book Rev* 92:27+ My 3 '87
King, Frank
about
An Olympian booster. J. Howse. il por *Macleans* 100:33 Mr 23 '87
King, Jay
about
Club Nouveau Svengali Jay King boasts a platinum hit and a double-platinum ego. S. Dougherty. il pors *People Wkly* 27:109-10 Ap 27 '87
King, Judi Brown
about
Reaching out to the kids. K. Moore. il pors *Sports Illus* 67:18-19 D 21 '87
King, Larry, 1933-
A heart attack prompts a veteran broadcaster to clean up his off-the-air act. il pors *People Wkly* 27:75-6+ My 11 '87
King, Martin Luther, 1929-1968
See also
Martin Luther King Day
I have a dream [excerpts from address, 1963] *Cent Mag* 20:24 N/D '87
about
All mixed up on Martin Luther King. W. F. Buckley. *Natl Rev* 39:62 F 27 '87
Anchorage's King snub may imperil Olympic bid. *Jet* 73:48 O 26 '87
Book series on King's life slated for 1990: Mrs. King. *Jet* 72:22 Ap 27 '87
Casket on steps evokes apology from judge who denounced King's memory. *Jet* 71:4 F 16 '87
Dr. King. *Natl Rev* 39:20+ F 13 '87
The dreams of Martin Luther King. C. V. Woodward. bibl f il pors *N Y Rev Books* 33:3+ Ja 15 '87
The King family: keepers of the dream. L. Norment. il por *Ebony* 42:25-6+ Ja '87
King family reveals how they keep 'dream' alive in Jan. Ebony. il *Jet* 71:37 Ja 19 '87
The King to come [adaptation of address, January 19, 1987] B. Rustin. *New Repub* 196:19-21 Mr 9 '87
Martin Luther King's inner spiritual church. M. E. Marty. por *Christ Century* 104:44 Ja 21 '87
San Diego street named after King changed: blacks protest, urge boycott. il *Jet* 73:52 N 30 '87
Skinner chides youths' ignorance of King legacy. il pors *Jet* 71:16 F 9 '87
That old, rugged cross. J. E. White. il por *Time* 129:24 Ja 19 '87

Archives
UC Press to publish King papers. *Publ Wkly* 231:38 My 8 '87
Bibliography
A select list of books on the dream and the dreamer. *Ebony* 42:20 Ja '87
Statues, portraits, etc.
Alphas move to erect King memorial in D.C. [Alpha Phi Alpha] *Jet* 71:28 F 9 '87
Mrs. King approves release of official MLK sculpture. il *Jet* 71:57 F 9 '87
King, Martin Luther, 1958?-
about
King helps create new minority contract office in Fulton County, Ga. por *Jet* 72:31 Jl 27 '87
King, Michael
Finding capital in the tax reform era. il *Black Enterp* 17:60-5 Ap '87
Making a case for choosing a black law firm. il *Black Enterp* 17:133-6+ F '87
To sell or not to sell . . . il *Black Enterp* 17:287-8+ Je '87
King, Michael A., 1954-
Prowlers, prayers and a dream. *Christ Century* 104:959-60 N 4 '87
King, Nancy
Bring class back to the classroom. *Des Arts Educ* 89:8-11 N/D '87
King, Norman, 1926-
Oprah [excerpt from Everybody loves Oprah!] il pors *Good Housekeep* 205:107+ Ag '87

King, Patricia, 1941-
Do you work for a jerk? il *Ladies Home J* 104:52+
My '87
King, Richard V.
about
No free samples. J. Willoughby. il por *Forbes* 140:165
S 7 '87
King, Stephen, 1947-
'Ever et raw meat?' and other weird questions. il *N
Y Times Book Rev* 92:7 D 6 '87
How IT happened. il *Writer* 100:14-15 Ap '87
What's scaring Stephen King. il por *Omni* 9:16 F '87
King, Susan Bennett
about
Susan King: a stone thrower who moved into a glass
house. M. Mallory. il por *Bus Week* p59 Ag 17 '87
King, William
about
Commodores' King arrested in L.A. investment scheme.
por *Jet* 72:12 Ap 13 '87
King, William Dickey, 1925-
about
William King at Dintenfass. E. Heartney. *Art Am* 75:160
Je '87
**King (Martin Luther Jr.) Center for Nonviolent Social
Change** *See* Martin Luther King, Jr. Center for Nonvio-
lent Social Change
King (Martin Luther Jr.) Scholarship *See* Scholarships
and fellowships
King and His Court (Softball team)
Pitcher perfect [E. Feigner] J. Eppinger. il por *50 Plus*
27:56-7+ Ag '87
King Crimson (Musical group)
King Crimson. K. Richardson. il *High Fidel* 37:83-4+
O '87
King family
about
The King family: keepers of the dream. L. Norment.
il por *Ebony* 42:25-6+ Ja '87
King family reveals how they keep 'dream' alive in
Jan. Ebony. il *Jet* 71:37 Ja 19 '87
King Khaled Eye Specialist Hospital (Riyadh, Saudi Arabia)
See Riyadh (Saudi Arabia)—Hospitals
King Kong (Fictional character)
Kong is back . . . [construction of mechanical King
Kong for Universal Studios tour] il *Natl Geogr World*
137:9-15 Ja '87
King Kong lives [film] See Motion picture reviews—Single
works
King Radio Corp.
Off-the-shelf civil components improve nontactical
avionics [commercial equipment in military aircraft]
K. J. Stein. il *Aviat Week Space Technol* 126:87+
My 4 '87
King salmon fishing *See* Salmon fishing
King World Productions, Inc.
The once and future King World. T. Jaffe. il *Forbes*
139:154 F 9 '87
Kingdom, Gerry
A perfect 10: the world's best beaches. il *Travel Holiday*
167:40-5+ F '87
Kingdom of God
In a peaceable Kingdom. M. K. Hellwig. *America*
156:inside back cover Je 20-27 '87
Jesus and the Kingdom of God. M. Borg. *Christ Century*
104:378-80 Ap 22 '87
The Kingdom of God and discernment. W. A. Barry.
America 157:156-9 S 26 '87
The truth about consequences. R. Brow. il por *Christ
Today* 31:33-4 Ap 17 '87
Kingfishers
See also
Kookaburras
King's Council (Great Britain) *See* Great Britain. Privy
Council
Kings River (Calif.)
The Kings up close: focus on a threatened river. T.
Palmer. *Sierra* 72:43 Ja/F '87
Kings River Canyon (Calif.)
The long fight for Kings Canyon [proposed Rodgers
Crossing dam site] P. Carr and K. Glass. il maps
Sierra 72:38-44 Ja/F '87
Kingsborough, Donald D.
about
Top gun in the toy business. A. Ramirez. il pors *Fortune*
115:88-90+ Mr 2 '87
Kingsbury, David T.
about
Document links NSF official to biotech firm. M. Craw-
ford. *Science* 238:742 N 6 '87

NSF official's finances probed by Justice. M. Crawford.
por *Science* 238:478 O 23 '87
Kingsley, Mary Henrietta, 1862-1900
about
West Africa's Mary Kingsley. D. Birkett. bibl il pors
Hist Today 37:10-16 My '87
Kingston, Tim
The unhealthy profits of AZT. il *Nation* 245:408-9 O
17 '87
Kingston (Ont.)
Historic houses, sites, etc.
On foot in old Kingston, Ontario. D. Lasker. il *Travel
Holiday* 167:20-3 Ja '87
Prisons and reformatories
Among sisters of crime [J. Kastner's documentary Prison
mother, prison daughter] P. Hluchy. il por *Macleans*
100:54-5 Ja 12 '87
Kinkaid, Frank
Spell it M-A-D-R-I-D. il *Opera News* 51:50-1 My '87
Kinkhead, Gwen
Profiles [P. Petit] *New Yorker* 63:35-8+ Je 15 '87
Kinks (Musical group)
Ray Davies. M. Small. il pors *People Wkly* 28:86-8+
Jl 6 '87
Kinley, David
A global search yields affordable water. il *UN Chron*
24:71-2 Ag '87
Kinley, Peter, 1926-
about
Peter Kinley. J. Higgins. il *Art News* 86:177 Ap '87
Kinnear, James W., 1928-
about
Paying the price for Getty. P. Nulty. il por *Fortune*
116:34 Ag 3 '87
Texaco skids on an oil slick. W. J. Cook. il *U S News
World Rep* 102:45 Mr 9 '87
Kinney, David
about
Focus on photography books. B. Teague. il por *Publ
Wkly* 232:50-2 Jl 31 '87
Kinnick, Nile, 1919?-1943
about
Nile Kinnick. R. Fimrite. il pors *Sports Illus* 67:112-24
Ag 31 '87
Kinnock, Neil
about
Britain's opposition regroups. N. Gelb. il por *New Leader*
70:6-7 S 7 '87
A case of plagiarized passion? *Newsweek* 110:35 S 21
'87
Headed for the finish line. C. Ogden. il por *Time* 129:39
Je 15 '87
In the telly's eye: an American-style British campaign.
R. Knight. il pors *U S News World Rep* 102:10-11
Je 15 '87
Kinnock on the defensive. N. Gelb. il *New Leader* 70:8-9
Mr 23 '87
Labor's defense [interview] J. Lloyd and P. Kellner.
World Press Rev 34:15-16 My '87
Neil in the 'lion's den'. M. White. il *World Press Rev*
34:13-14 My '87
Kino, Eusebio Francisco, 1644-1711
about
On the 300-year-old trail of Father Kino. il map *Sunset*
179:52+ O '87
Kinsella, W. P.
Distances [story] il *Sport Mag* 78:66-8+ Jl '87
The great flap copy letdown. por *Publ Wkly* 231:54
Ap 3 '87
Kinsey, Clarence
about
Klondike scrapbook. N. Bolotin. il *Am Hist Illus* 22:26-35
O '87
Kinsey, Clarke
about
Klondike scrapbook. N. Bolotin. il *Am Hist Illus* 22:26-35
O '87
Kinsley, Michael
TRB from Washington. See issues of The New Republic
beginning April 25, 1983
about
I like Mike. J. Rowe. *Wash Mon* 19:50-3 D '87
Kinsolving, Susan
The jellyfish [poem] *Nation* 245:138 Ag 15-22 '87
Kinzer, Stephen
Stranded by politics and war: Nicaragua's loved, neglected
poet. por *N Y Times Book Rev* 92:3 Ja 18 '87
Kinzler, Kenneth W., and others
Identification of an amplified, highly expres[sed]
in a human glioma. bibl f il *Science*
3 '87

Kiosks, Video (Retail trade) See Electronic shopping
Kipnis, David
(jt. auth) See Schmidt, Stuart, and Kipnis, David
Kippenhahn, Rudolf, 1926-
Light from the depths of time. il *Sky Telesc* 73:140-2
F '87
Kipper, Harry
about
Marriage Vegas-style. D. Worrell. il por *Time* 129:69
Mr 2 '87
Kiraly, Karch, 1961?-
about
The sultan of spike. P. Richmond. il pors *Roll Stone*
p87+ Jl 16-30 '87
Kirby, Cecil
about
Taking the pulse of crime. A. O'Malley. por *Publ Wkly*
231:71-2 F 6 '87
Kirby, Peadar
Economic agendas. *Commonweal* 114:136-7 Mr 13 '87
Kirby, Randy
about
They may seem driven, but pupils of commercial king
Randy Kirby would settle for 30 seconds of work.
K. Hubbard. il pors *People Wkly* 28:173-6 N 30 '87
Kirby, Sam
Exhibits. See issues of American Artist
Joseph B. O'Sickey. il pors *Am Artist* 51:60-5+ Ja '87
Kirby, W. N.
(jt. auth) See Popham, W. James, and Kirby, W. N.
Kirchhausen, T., and others
Clathrin light chains LCA and LCB are similar, polymor-
phic, and share repeated heptad motifs. bibl f il *Science*
236:320-4 Ap 17 '87
Kirchner, Bill
about
Bill Kirchner. G. Kalbacher. il por *Down Beat* 54:54-5
Je '87
Kirchwey, Karl
Bells above Bretaye [poem] *New Yorker* 63:32 Je
22 '87
Museum of Holography [poem] *New Repub* 197:32
D 21 '87
Kirdar, Nemir
about
The boys from Bahrain. R. Morais. il por *Forbes* 140:181
O 5 '87
Kirili, Alain, 1946-
about
Rewriting sculpture. C. Nadelman. il por *Art News*
86:120-7 My '87
Kirk, Donald
The good life in the Persian Gulf. il *New Leader* 70:3-5
S 7 '87
Olympian hurdle in Korea. il *New Leader* 70:3-5 Je
29 '87
Rallying the body politic [cover story] il *New Leader*
70:5-7 Mr 9 '87
Kirk, Paul
about
Kirk's cant. T. Ferguson. *Nation* 244:385 Mr 28 '87
Kirk, Russell
Lost souls: a meditation. il *Natl Rev* 39:30-2 D 31
'87
Kirk, Susanne
Charles Scribner's Sons. *Writer* 100:24-5 Jl '87
Kirkjian, Tim
Send more Ripkens. pors *Sport Mag* 78:57 Ap '87
Kirkland, Gelsey
Malicious Misha [excerpt from Dancing on my grave];
ed. by Greg Lawrence. il pors *Ladies Home J* 104:74+
Jl '87
Kirkland, Lane
Reversing America's decline in international trade. il
USA Today (Periodical) 115:25-7 Mr '87
Should the "Minimum Wage Restoration Act of 1987"
be approved? [excerpts from testimony, July 23, 1987]
Congr Dig 66:202+ Ag/S '87
Kirklan ichard I., Jr.
in the family: should kids inherit fortunes?
289:16-20 Ja '87
ruce C., and others
detection of DNA from a nonculturable
genic mycoplasma-like organism. bibl f il
197-200 O 9 '87
uture. por *Sports Illus* 67 Sp Issue:116
n campus. il pors *Sports Illus* 66:32-5
pors *Sports Illus* 67:21 Jl 6 '87

Count Dracula. il pors *Sports Illus* 66:60-4+ Je 22 '87
A ferocious game of family feud. il *Sports Illus* 66:74-6+
F 9 '87
Good old violence. por *Sports Illus* 66:66 Ja 5 '87
The heat is on. il *Sports Illus* 66:14-17 Mr 16 '87
In an orbit all his own. il pors *Sports Illus* 67:82-6+
N 9 '87
Indiana, by a whisker. il *Sports Illus* 66:20-1 Mr 30
'87
The master of midair. il *Sports Illus* 66:80-1 My 4
'87
Maybe Pitt is it. il por *Sports Illus* 66:20-2+ F 16 '87
More teletrash, please. por *Sports Illus* 67:78 S 7 '87
Please don't pick us no. 1. il *Sports Illus* 67 Sp Issue:54-6+
N 18 '87
Raising the roof. il *Sports Illus* 67:16-19 D 14 '87
Seems like everyone has a shot this year. il *Sports
Illus* 66:36-8+ Mr 2 '87
A slip on poll mountain. il *Sports Illus* 66:18-20 Ja
26 '87
Smart and super. il *Sports Illus* 66:30-5 Ap 6 '87
Smash acts on centre court. il pors *Sports Illus* 67:28-30+
Jl 13 '87
A terrible omission. por *Sports Illus* 66:74 Mr 16 '87
They're jumping for joy. il pors *Sports Illus* 67 Sp
Issue:20-3+ N 18 '87
A touch of class. il pors *Sports Illus* 67:40-2+ D 14
'87
A wild new Cats' meow. il pors *Sports Illus* 66:18-19
Ja 5 '87
Kirkpatrick, Jean
about
Finding A.A. too male-oriented, Jean Kirkpatrick heads
a movement to aid women alcoholics. S. K. Reed.
il por *People Wkly* 27:101-3 Je 29 '87
Kirkpatrick, Jeane J., 1926-
Lessons of the Iran-contra affair. por *Read Dig* 130:72-3
Je '87
about
Farewell, and hail. *Natl Rev* 39:20-1 N 20 '87
Mrs. Kirkpatrick visits Managua. W. F. Buckley. *Natl
Rev* 39:67 N 20 '87
Anecdotes, facetiae, satire, etc.
I dream of Jeanie. G. F. Will. il *Newsweek* 109:82
F 2 '87
Kirkwood, R. Cort
Jim Wright makes it the old-fashioned way [cover story]
il por *Natl Rev* 39:36-7+ O 23 '87
Kirov Ballet
The beautiful and the damned [performances in Glass-
boro, N.J.] T. Tobias. il *N Y* 20:78-9 Je 8 '87
Kirschbaum, Les
When customers don't pay. il *Nations Bus* 75:24+ Je
'87
Kirschenbaum, Carol
Was I molested? The gray area of sexual abuse.
Mademoiselle 93:188+ Mr '87
Women: the new white-collar criminals. *Glamour*
85:306-7+ Mr '87
Kirschner, Herbert
about
The stranger in the corner. D. Fanning. *Forbes* 140:37-8
O 5 '87
Kirshenbaum, Jerry
More football madness. il por *Sports Illus* 67:110 N
30 '87
Kirshenbaum & Bond
Hot copy. B. Kanner. il *N Y* 20:19+ O 12 '87
Kirst, Michael W.
about
Bridging the gap between policy and research [interview]
D. B. Strother. il por *Phi Delta Kappan* 69:161-4
O '87
Kirstein, David M.
(jt. auth) See Bailey, Elizabeth E., and Kirstein, David
M.
Kirstein, Lincoln, 1907-
Drawn to the past. il por *House Gard* 159:168-71+ N
'87
Memoir through objects. il *House Gard* 159:116-21+
Ja '87
Kirtland, Robert
Authority and academic freedom. *America* 156:348-9
Ap 25 '87
Kirwan, Jack D.
The soap merchants. *Space World* X-11-287 Space
Advocate:6-7 N '87

KIS *See* Key Independent System
Kiser, Melvin
about
Driving along minding his business, Melvin Kiser ran into $2 million—then he did the unthinkable. M. Dougherty. il pors *People Wkly* 28:75-6 N 30 '87
Kishlansky, Mark
May we borrow your historians? il *Hist Today* 37:6-7 Je '87
Kismaric, Carol
(jt. auth) *See* Heiferman, Marvin, and Kismaric, Carol
Kissimmee Prairie Sanctuary (Fla.) *See* Bird sanctuaries—Florida
Kissimmee River (Fla.)
The "sewer ditch" undone [dismantling the Kissimmee River channel] F. Graham. il maps *Audubon* 89:114-15 Mr '87
Kissing
The New Year's kiss. E. Prager. il *Seventeen* 46:65 D '87
Kissinger, Henry, 1923-
The dangers ahead. il por *Newsweek* 110:34-6+ D 21 '87
Kissinger: a new era for NATO. il *Newsweek* 110:57-8+ O 12 '87
Kissinger: how to deal with Gorbachev. il pors *Newsweek* 109:39-40+ Mr 2 '87
The singular threat to the Atlantic Alliance [excerpts from address, May 28, 1987] *Natl Rev* 39:18-19 Jl 3 '87
(jt. auth) *See* Nixon, Richard M. (Richard Milhous), 1913-, and Kissinger, Henry, 1923-
about
Benefits of an INF agreement. G. P. Shultz. *Dep State Bull* 87:17-18 Jl '87
Kissinger and INF. il *Natl Rev* 39:17 N 6 '87
Kissinger and the 'dirty war'. M. Andersen. il *Nation* 245:477-80 O 31 '87
The Kissinger covenant and other reasons Israel is in trouble [excerpt from Sands of sorrow; cover story] M. Viorst. por map *Wash Mon* 19:23-9+ Je '87
Protocol and peace. W. F. Buckley. *Natl Rev* 39:54 Je 5 '87
A reply to Nixon and Kissinger. G. P. Shultz. il por *Time* 129:40 My 18 '87
Kissinger Commission *See* National Bipartisan Commission on Central America (U.S.)
Kistler, Darci
about
Solo flights. T. Tobias. il *N Y* 20:84-5 D 14 '87
Kit cars *See* Automobiles, Home-built
Kit clocks *See* Clocks
Kit foxes *See* Foxes
Kit furniture *See* Furniture, Prefabricated
Kit houses *See* Houses, Prefabricated
Kitado, Haruo, and others
U3 sequences from HTLV-I and -II LTRs confer px protein response to a murine leukemia virus LTR. bibl f il *Science* 235:901-4 F 20 '87
Kitchen, Lawrence O., 1923-
about
Trying to make Lockheed over—before a raider does. S. Toy. il *Bus Week* p38 Jl 13 '87
Kitchen cabinets
Cabinet face-lifts. il *Better Homes Gard* 65:72 Ap '87
Cabinets—for storage and style. il *South Living* 22:144+ O '87
Cure for messy cabinets [pullout trays] R. N. Hoffman. il *Workbench* 43:79 My/Je '87
Kitchen face lift. M. Morris. il *Home Mech* 83:40-2 Jl '87
Kitchen installation guide. A. Rooze. il *Fam Handyman* 37:58-60+ S '87
Kitchen carts *See* Carts
Kitchen furniture
See also
Kitchen cabinets
Angled island works for this kitchen. il *South Living* 22:176 My '87
Build a double-duty island from prefinished cabinets. G. Branson. il *Fam Handyman* 37:104-5 My/Je '87
Countertop choices. il *South Living* 22:152+ O '87
Countertop upkeep. il *Better Homes Gard* 65:28 O '87
Fixes for scorched countertops. *Workbench* 43:14 S/O '87
Granite: real thing and fool-the-eye [kitchen countertops] il *Sunset* 179:112-14+ N '87
Make-believe kitchen for kids. B. A. Lewis. il *Better Homes Gard* 65:64+ Mr '87
Turn a Victorian store counter into a kitchen island. S. Ross. il *Fam Handyman* 37:28+ N '87

A Y-shaped counter was the answer. il *Sunset* 179:112 O '87
Kitchen garbage disposers *See* Refuse disposers
Kitchen Privileges (Firm)
Someone's in the kitchen with Barry. F. Odabas-Geldiay. il por *Nations Bus* 75:48 Ap '87
Kitchen ranges *See* Stoves
Kitchen sinks *See* Sinks
Kitchen storage *See* Storage in the home
Kitchen towels *See* Towels
Kitchen utensils and appliances
See also
Blenders (Appliances)
Can openers
Coffee pots, percolators, etc.
Dishwashers
Food processors (Appliances)
Food slicers
Ice cream makers
Microwave cookware
Microwave ovens
Pastry cutters
Stoves
Toasters
Towncraft (Firm)
The 18 essential tools of a good kitchen. C. Rossant. il *McCalls* 114:112+ S '87
A baker's basic battery. K. Haedrich. il *Ctry J* 14:56-61 F '87
Cook-and-serve skillet set [cast iron] il *McCalls* 114:149-50+ F '87
High-tech timesavers for your kitchen. T. Perry. *Work Woman* 12:158 My '87
Make your kitchen a dieter's dream. D. Tkac. il *Prevention* 39:30-2+ D '87
Pots and pans. il *Consum Rep* 52:467-74 Ag '87
Pots and pans. il *Consum Rep* 52:37-42 D '87
Timesavers, funmakers: star-quality kitchen toys for cooks. A. Arnott. il *Work Woman* 12:172+ My '87
Toaster ovens and toaster-oven/broilers. il *Consum Rep* 52:58-60 D '87
Turkey roasting kit. il *McCalls* 115:153+ O '87
Turn a rolling pin. E. Waltner. il *Workbench* 43:62-4 Mr/Ap '87
Care
Copper cookware: proper care is essential. il *Better Homes Gard* 65:113 My '87
Collectors and collecting
Collectible kitchenware. K. M. McClinton. il *Antiques Collect Hobbies* 92:13-16 My '87
Maintenance and repair
From our kitchen to yours. K. Adams. *South Living* 22:144-5 Je '87
Storage
Saturday morning kitchen improvements. A. Rooze. il *Fam Handyman* 37:60+ D '87
Kitchen utensils and appliances industry *See* Household appliances industry
Kitchens
See also
Dining alcoves, etc.
8 great-idea kitchens. il *Good Housekeep* 205:192-6+ S '87
All it took was an extra 60 square feet. il *Sunset* 179:80 Ag '87
Better homes and gardens builds a state of the art kitchen. G. D. Cook. il *Better Homes Gard* 65:100-3 F '87
Big, bright kitchen replaces small, dark rooms. il *Sunset* 179:161 N '87
Classy corridor kitchens. G. D. Cook. il *Better Homes Gard* 65:98-101 Ja '87
A crane, a roof cutout, spiral stairs . . . the Lawsons got a tall airy kitchen. il *Sunset* 179:146 N '87
Design brings outdoors in. il *South Living* 22:178 Mr '87
Detailing updates remodeled kitchen. il *South Living* 22:190-1 Ap '87
Get a kitchen that works for you [cover story] S. Ross. il *Fam Handyman* 37:35-9+ S '87
The gilt-edged comeback of the kitchen [remodeling costs] B. Bauer. il *U S News World Rep* 102:64-5 Mr 30 '87
Great chefs, great kitchens [workspaces and favorite recipes of Debbi Fields, Pierre Franey, and Martha Stewart] M. D. Glass. il *Ladies Home J* 104:124-9+ S '87
Heart-of-the-home kitchens. D. Freedman. il *Better Homes Gard* 65:124-7 O '87
The inside story of re-shaping a kitchen. il *Glamour* 85:196-9 Ja '87

Kitchens—*cont.*

Kitchen installation guide. A. Rooze. il *Fam Handyman* 37:58-60+ S '87

Kitchen kudos. E. Thompson and E. Thompson. il *Pop Mech* 164:76-80+ O '87

Kitchen management [special section] il *Work Woman* 12:145+ My '87

Kitchen models of efficiency. il *Sunset* 178:80-5 F '87

A kitchen transformed. il *South Living* 22:118 Jl '87

Kitchens! Kitchens! Kitchens! il *Good Housekeep* 204:132-7 Ap '87

Light and height open small kitchen. il *South Living* 22:95 Ag '87

Remodel small spaces. P. Pederson. il *Workbench* 43:8-9+ My/Je '87

Remove walls, open the ceiling in this Santa Barbara 70-year-old? It took a new beam system. il *Sunset* 178:124 Je '87

Room partition gives them efficient work space, family dining. il *Sunset* 178:110-11 Mr '87

Scandinavian country. il *Fam Handyman* 37:50+ My/Je '87

Simple changes with a wheelchair in mind. il *Sunset* 179:150 S '87

The southern home [special section] il *South Living* 22:103+ O '87

A spiffed-up kitchen in the same old space. J. S. Norman. il *Better Homes Gard* 65:54 Ag '87

Sunny kitchen looks like a garden. C. Engle. il *South Living* 22:130-1 F '87

Transforming your kitchen. E. Fishel. il *Parents* 62:62+ Ap '87

A two-cook kitchen [kitchen of Helen and Harry Som] B. A. Lewis. il *Better Homes Gard* 65:80-3 Je '87

Warm, cozy—and spacious, too. il *South Living* 22:104-5 D '87

What makes this small kitchen seem large? A curving glass-block wall. il *Sunset* 178:84-5 Ja '87

Anecdotes, facetiae, satire, etc.

My kitchen, my self. K. Fury. il por *50 Plus* 27:80 Ag '87

Bibliography

Kitchen remodeling how-to-do-it information. D. Chermak. *Fam Handyman* 37:88 Mr '87

Lighting

See Lighting

Kitchens, Outdoor

She does all of her canning in a special harvest kitchen. il *Sunset* 179:142 Ag '87

Kitchenware *See* Kitchen utensils and appliances

Kites

Fishing the sky. R. Kimber. il *Ctry J* 14:18-21 Mr '87

The pride that flies [giant kites of Santiago, Guatemala] M. Cavallaro. il *Américas* 39:14-19 My/Je '87

Kith and kin [dance] *See* Dance reviews—Single works

Kitman, Marvin

On television. See occasional issues of The New Leader

about

Between issues. *New Leader* 70:2 D 28 '87

Kits, Medical *See* Medical equipment

Kits, Pregnancy *See* Pregnancy—Signs and diagnosis

Kitsch

Corn, glorious corn. R. Lynes. il *Archit Dig* 44:42+ Mr '87

Kitt, Michael T.

Sculpting the moon. il *Astronomy* 15:82-7 F '87

Kittredge, Carola

Gardens: autumn fields. il por *Archit Dig* 44:170-5 S '87

Kittredge, William

Redneck secrets [excerpt from Owning it all] *Harpers* 275:34-8 O '87

Kittrell, Suzanne

about

Arkansas stencilers. T. Kazas. il pors *Americana* 15:35-9 My/Je '87

Kitty Litter *See* Cat litter

Kitzinger, Sheila

Your baby, your way [excerpt] il *Glamour* 85:50+ Ag '87

Kiwak, Marnie

Photo tours. *Petersens Photogr Mag* 16:66+ N '87

Winter workshops. il *Petersens Photogr Mag* 16:47-8 D '87

Kiwi fruit

See also

Cooking—Fruit

The captivating kiwifruit. N. Vietmeyer. il *Natl Geogr* 171:682-8 My '87

Kiwi control. il *Sunset* 178:112-13 Ja '87

Kiwi fruit goes mainstream. il *Better Homes Gard* 65:90 Mr '87

Kjellberg, Penny Landsman

Rich, lustrous hair. il *Harpers Bazaar* 120:220-1+ O '87

KKK *See* Ku Klux Klan

Klady, Leonard

Connie's comeback. il por *Film Comment* 23:6-8 Mr/Ap '87

Klagsbrun, Michael

(jt. auth) See Folkman, Judah, and Klagsbrun, Michael

Klakson

Hungary: a Pole's paradise? il *World Press Rev* 34:41 Ja '87

Klander, Sharon

Telling mother [poem] *New Repub* 197:32 O 19 '87

Klapper, Zina

Syndies' title bout. il *Channels* 7:51 F '87

Klare, Michael T., 1942-

about

Be your own peacemaker. S. H. Day, Jr. il *Progressive* 51:17-18 Ap '87

Klarsfeld, Beate

about

'Because I am not Jewish but German' [interview] R. Z. Chesnoff. por *U S News World Rep* 102:36 My 18 '87

Klass, Perri, 1958-

Anatomy and destiny. *Ms* 16:66+ Jl/Ag '87

Dying in character: the myth of the impish chuckle. il *Discover* 8:20+ F '87

Turning my words against me. *N Y Times Book Rev* 92:1+ Ap 5 '87

Vital signs. See issues of Discover beginning April 1985

Klavan, Ellen

All through the night? Not quite. il *Parents* 62:80-4 F '87

Improving your child's day care. il *Parents* 62:68+ N '87

The risky world of licensing. il *Publ Wkly* 231:97-100 F 27 '87

Klawans, Stuart

The small time. *Nation* 244:407-9 Mr 28 '87

The small time. *Nation* 244:654-6 My 16 '87

The small time. *Nation* 244:263-4+ F 28 '87

The small time. *Nation* 245:422-5 O 17 '87

about

Covering alternative writing. J. Barbato. *Publ Wkly* 232:56 N 27 '87

Klay, William Earle

How are Japanese unions responding to microelectronics-based automation? bibl f *Mon Labor Rev* 110:39-40 Mr '87

Klee, Paul, 1879-1940

about

Art. A. C. Danto. *Nation* 244:441-5 Ap 4 '87

Feats of Klee. J. Perl. il por *Vogue* 177:106 F '87

Focus on feats of Klee. C. Ratcliff. il *Harpers Bazaar* 120:198-99+ F '87

Klee: for discerning buyers only. R. W. Walker. *Art News* 86:22 Ap '87

Klee time. S. H. Madoff. il por *Art News* 86:104-9 My '87

A riddle within a mystery inside an enigma: Klee. R. Wernick. bibl (p144) il *Smithsonian* 17:64-6+ F '87

Signs and symbols. K. Larson. il *N Y* 20:96+ Mr 2 '87

A whimsical fun house. C. McGuigan. il *Newsweek* 109:70-1 F 16 '87

Kleiman, Dena

She took the AIDS test. il *N Y Times Mag* p22-3+ Jl 5 '87

(ed) See Peterson, Claudia. "What has happened is incredible"

Klein, Albert

about

The man, the myth, the mileage! Californian Albert Klein motors his 1963 Beetle one million miles. N. Geeslin. il pors *People Wkly* 28:40+ Ag 3 '87

Klein, Anne

Boost your pedal power. il *Women's Sports Fitness* 9:56 Ag '87

Klein, Calvin

about

Calvin: a leaner luxury. il *Harpers Bazaar* 120:384-9 S '87

Calvin Klein: an obsession with perfection. A. Haden-Guest. il por *Harpers Bazaar* 120:178-85+ F '87

Klein, Diane

(jt. auth) See Ostreicher, David, and Klein, Diane

Klein, Frederick C.
Al Campanis. il por *Sport Mag* 78:97-8 D '87
Klein, Gene
about
And now for the real Superbowl. J. A. Trachtenberg.
il por *Forbes* 139:122 F 9 '87
Klein, Georg *See* Klein, George, 1925-
Klein, George, 1925-
The approaching era of the tumor suppressor genes.
bibl f *Science* 238:1539-45 D 11 '87
Klein, Gérard
Hide and seek [fiction] *Omni* 9:56+ Je '87
Klein, Joe, 1946-
Hog heaven: Jesse Jackson cultivates the farm vote in
Iowa. il por *N Y* 20:42-5 S 7 '87
Is Paul Simon another McGovern? No, but he may
be another Reagan. il pors *N Y* 20:50-4 D 7 '87
Koch agonistes. il pors *N Y* 20:28-32 Jl 13 '87
The Polo Grounds. il *N Y* 20:80-1 D 21-28 '87
Ready for the Duke? [cover story] il pors *N Y* 20:24-31
Ag 17 '87
Ronald Wilson Hoover? il por *N Y* 20:40-3 N 2 '87
about
Between the lines. pors *N Y* 20:9 Jl 13 '87
Klein, Larry
Audio update. See issues of Radio-Electronics beginning
January 1987
Crosstalk. See issues of High Fidelity (New York, N.Y.)
beginning March 1987
Klein, Marty
The 10 commonest questions about sex. *McCalls* 114:122+
Jl '87
"The trouble is—you've changed". il *Parents* 62:71-4
Jl '87
Klein, Maury, 1939-
A robber historian. il *Forbes* 140 Sp Issue:46+ O 26
'87
Klein, Norma, 1938-
15 great books for the teenagers in the family. *Ms*
16:160 Jl/Ag '87
Klein, Pat
about
Pat Klein at Stephen Wirtz. M. Levy. *Art Am* 75:229+
Ap '87
Klein, Susan, 1944-, and Rotenstreich, Susan
A New England folk art collection. il *Antiques* 132:538-45
S '87
Klein, Todd
Angela Lansbury: solving Sunday night blues. il pors
Saturday Evening Post 259:42-5 Ja/F '87
Oh, Vanna! [cover story] il pors *Saturday Evening Post*
259:42-3+ My/Je '87
Tom Selleck: what's next? il pors *Saturday Evening
Post* 259:50-1+ Mr '87
Klein, William, 1928-
about
Come on, baby, do the locomotion. R. Lacayo. il *Time*
129:78 Mr 9 '87
Klein (Calvin) Industries *See* Calvin Klein Industries
Klein (Lawrence R.) Award *See* Journalism—Awards
Kleiner, Art
Bare knuckles on Madison Avenue. il por *N Y Times
Mag* p34-9+ N 8 '87
Kleinfeld, Judith
Guiding minority students into adulthood. il *Phi Delta
Kappan* 68:553-4 Mr '87
Kleinman, Daniel Lee
(jt. auth) See Kloppenburg, Jack, Jr., and Kleinman,
Daniel Lee
Kleinschmidt, Andreas, and others
Blockade of "NMDA" receptors disrupts experience-
dependent plasticity of kitten striate cortex. bibl f
il *Science* 238:355-8 O 16 '87
Kleinschrod, Walter A.
By land? By air? By sea? il *Work Woman* 12:82+ N
'87
Kleinzahler, August
Pinned [poem] *Harpers* 274:30 F '87
Klemens, Michael
about
Suburban "hotbeds of sexual diversity". B. D. Stutz.
il *Nat Hist* 96:80-3 S '87
Klement, Vera, 1929-
about
Vera Klement. C. Moser. il *Art News* 86:60+ Summ
'87
Klensch, Elsa
Another world of style . . . Rei Kawakubo [interview]
il por *Vogue* 177:306-9+ Ag '87
Susie Tompkins: the spirit in Esprit [interview] il por
Vogue 177:344-7+ Ag '87

Klesch, Gary
about
Gary Klesch is no innocent abroad. S. Miller. il por
Bus Week p144 S 14 '87
Klett, Donna
about
Jigsaws don't puzzle a champ like Ohio's Donna Klett.
il por *People Wkly* 28:137 S 14 '87
Kleypas, Lisa
about
. . . Lisa Kleypas, new Wellesley grad, beauty queen
(gasp!) and successful romance novelist. S. K. Reed.
il pors *People Wkly* 28:139-40 N 16 '87
Kligman, Ruth
about
Ruth Kligman at E. M. Donahue. C. Ratcliff. il *Art
Am* 75:136-7 Ja '87
Klimov, Elem
about
Come and see [film] Reviews
N Y 20:64 F 23 '87. D. Denby
Klimpke, Alan
about
Alan Klimpke's career as a singer is running hot and
cold. il por *People Wkly* 28:79 N 30 '87
Klindt, Steven
about
Joining a winner. E. Beck. il *Horizon* 30:15 Ap '87
Kline, David
How to lose the coke war. il *Atlantic* 259:22-7 My
'87
Kline, George L.
(tr) See Brodsky, Joseph, 1940-. Eclogue V: summer
Kline, Roger A.
Special vegetables. il *Ctry J* 14:28-32 Ap '87
about
General Kline's secret army. J. Cook. il pors *Ctry J*
14:36-41 Jl '87
Kling, George W.
Seasonal mixing and catastrophic degassing in tropical
lakes, Cameroon, West Africa. bibl f il *Science*
237:1022-4 Ag 28 '87
Kling, George W., and others
The 1986 Lake Nyos gas disaster in Cameroon, West
Africa [cover story] bibl f il maps *Science* 236:169-75
Ap 10 '87
Kling, William
Farewell to Lake Wobegon. pors *U S News World Rep*
102:10 Je 22 '87
Klingeman, Henry
Angry and stupid. *Natl Rev* 39:41-2 O 9 '87
Anonymous sex. *Natl Rev* 39:42-3 Je 19 '87
Klinger, Eric, 1933-
The power of daydreams. bibl (p62) il *Psychol Today*
21:36-9+ O '87
Klingholz, Reiner
The march of AIDS. *World Press Rev* 34:56-7 F '87
Klinkenborg, Verlyn
Bug slaying and other minor chivalries for the man
of the eighties. il *Glamour* 85:390 S '87
Casting about in Montana. il *Esquire* 107:31+ My '87
Jealousy with dignity. il *Esquire* 107:33-4 Ja '87
Me and my Z. il *Esquire* 107:41-2 Je '87
A shotgun education. il *Esquire* 107:36 Ap '87
Klipsch, Paul
about
The mighty Klipschorn. R. Hodges. il *Stereo Rev* 52:216
N '87
Kliŭchevskiĭ, V. O. (Vasiliĭ Osipovich), 1841-1911
about
Klyuchevsky and the course of Russian history. P. Dukes.
il por *Hist Today* 37:51-4 Jl '87
Kliŭchevskiĭ, Vasiliĭ Osipovich *See* Kliŭchevskiĭ, V. O.
(Vasiliĭ Osipovich), 1841-1911
KLM Royal Dutch Airlines
KLM gains Orlando gateway over U.S. carriers' protests.
Aviat Week Space Technol 127:44 Ag 3 '87
U.S. airlines oppose KLM service to Orlando. *Aviat
Week Space Technol* 126:42 My 11 '87
Kloppenburg, Jack, Jr., and Kleinman, Daniel Lee
The plant germplasm controversy [cover story; with reply
by H. G. Wilkes] bibl f il maps *BioScience* 37:190-8,
215-18 Mr '87
Seeds of struggle: the geopolitics of genetic resources.
il map *Technol Rev* 90:46-53 F/Mr '87
Klose, Robert T.
The joys of science. por *Newsweek* 110:14-15 O 26
'87
Kloss, Eric
Learning to listen. il *Down Beat* 54:56-7 Jl '87
Linear development. il *Down Beat* 11:54-5 N '87

Kloss, Eric—*cont.*
Playercise: practice through discovery. il *Down Beat* 54:54-6 Ja '87
Kloss, Lynn W.
Strange pool-fellows. il *Travel Holiday* 167:8+ Ap '87
Klossowski, Michel Balthazar *See* Balthus, 1908-
Kluender, Keith R., and others
Japanese quail can learn phonetic categories. bibl f il *Science* 237:1195-7 S 4 '87
Kluge, John Werner
about
Minorities get $25 million boost from Columbia gift. *Jet* 72:32 My 18 '87
Kluger, Bruce
The night I proposed. il *Glamour* 85:90 D '87
Kluger, Jeffrey
Body doubles. il *Omni* 9:48-50+ Ag '87
Kluger, Marilyn
Carl Larsson's home—a Swedish legacy. il *Gourmet* 47:56-9+ Jl '87
Klugt, Cornelius van der
about
A competitor who smells gunpowder. S. Tully. il por *Fortune* 116:43-4 Ag 3 '87
Kluwer NV
Kluwer battles Elsevier's hostile takeover attempt. H. R. Lottman. *Publ Wkly* 232:15 Jl 10 '87
Kluzak, Gord
about
Just what the doctor ordered. J. Falla. il pors *Sports Illus* 67:91-2 O 26 '87
Kmecl, Matjaž
The Alpine culture of Slovenia. il *Courier* 40:18+ F '87
KMET (Los Angeles, Calif.: Radio station) *See* Radio stations
KMOV (Saint Louis, Mo.: Television station) *See* Television stations
Knacke, Roger
Sampling the stuff of a comet. il *Sky Telesc* 73:246-50 Mr '87
Knapp, Cleon
about
Stay tuned. M. Beauchamp. il por *Forbes* 140:189 O 19 '87
Knapp, Ronald J.
When a child dies. il *Psychol Today* 21:60-3+ Jl '87
Knapp Communications Corp.
Stay tuned. M. Beauchamp. il por *Forbes* 140:189 O 19 '87
Knapweed
Control
The scourge of the spurge. L. Williamson. il *Outdoor Life* 180:66+ N '87
Knaster, Alana
(jt. auth) *See* Cormick, Gerald W., and Knaster, Alana
Knauss, John A.
NSC and Ocean Drilling. *Environment* 29:2-3 Jl/Ag '87
Knecht, David A., and Loomis, William F.
Antisense RNA inactivation of myosin heavy chain gene expression in Dictyostelium discoideum [cover story] bibl f il *Science* 236:1081-6 My 29 '87
Knee
Surgery
The bender mender [knee replacement surgery; work of C. S. Ranawat] S. Shapiro. il *Discover* 8:22-3 O '87
Mending knees [arthroscopy] P. Gadsby and L. J. Brown. il *Good Housekeep* 204:212 Je '87
Transplantation
Gamble against uncertain odds. C. Gorman. il *Time* 130:60-1 D 7 '87
Wounds and injuries
Acupuncture and me [injury treated with Chinese herbal tea and acupuncture] S. R. Brady. il por *Good Housekeep* 205:58+ Ag '87
Avoiding knee injuries. V. A. Moss and J. A. Webster. il *Nations Bus* 75:43-4 Je '87
Good knees: how to take care of your most precious joint. R. McGuire. il *Women's Sports Fitness* 9:46-9 D '87
Heal your aching knee. H. Rodale. il *Prevention* 39:88+ Jl '87
How to avoid cyclist's knee. L. Rogak. il *Women's Sports Fitness* 9:11-12 Je '87
A King eyes a court comeback [New York Knicks basketball player B. King] B. Newman. il por *Sports Illus* 66:32-3 Mr 30 '87
Weak in the knees? [patellar chondromalacia] J. Ullyot. il *Women's Sports Fitness* 9:19 Ag '87

Knee, Artificial
The bender mender [knee replacement surgery; work of C. S. Ranawat] S. Shapiro. il *Discover* 8:22-3 O '87
Building a better knee [Kennedy ligament augmentation device] R. Lewis. il *Health* 19:18 D '87
Knee pads
Eisner Knee Preservor [for motorcyclists] il *Cycle* 38:28 Mr '87
Knepper, Mike, 1943-
Cars women want: a driving force. *Harpers Bazaar* 120:174+ S '87
Driving well is the best revenge. il *50 Plus* 27:30-3+ N '87
Foreign bodies. il *Harpers Bazaar* 120:132+ F '87
How to test drive a new car. il *Better Homes Gard* 65:180-1 Ap '87
The New-Age family cars. il *Better Homes Gard* 65:48+ N '87
Knibb, David G.
Nothing fishy about new tuna treaty. il *Oceans* 20:6-7 Jl/Ag '87
Knick, Dennis
about
To animals, Dennis Knick is Johann Sebastian Bark, maybe even Moo-zart. J. Kaufman. il pors *People Wkly* 28:153-4 N 2 '87
Knievel, Evel
about
Two American heroes. C. Hodenfield. il *Cycle* 38:14 F '87
The knife [musical] *See* Musicals, revues, etc.—Reviews—Single works
Knife sharpening *See* Sharpeners and sharpening
Knife sheaths *See* Sheaths
Knight, Bobby
about
Back from the brink. J. Feinstein. il pors *Sport Mag* 78:29-30+ D '87
College basketball's Knight-errant. T. Callahan. pors *Time* 129:67-8 Ap 13 '87
Indiana coach Knight has no sympathy for Bias; 'He was so cool'. *Jet* 72:46 Ag 3 '87
'A season on the brink' is the season's surprise #1 bestseller. D. Masello. il pors *Publ Wkly* 231:28-30 Mr 27 '87
Knight, David M., and others
Expression of the art/trs protein of HIV and study of its role in viral envelope synthesis. bibl f il *Science* 236:837-40 My 15 '87
Knight, Frank
Rare and protected [cover story] bibl il *Conservationist* 41:2-9 My/Je '87
Knight, J. Z. (Judy Zebra)
about
Channelers. K. Lowry. il por *Omni* 10:46-8+ O '87
Knight, Judy Zebra *See* Knight, J. Z. (Judy Zebra)
Knight, Philip H.
about
Looking for that strong finish. J. Heins. il por *Forbes* 139:74-5 My 4 '87
Knight, Richard, Jr.
about
Breakthrough in Dallas. il pors *Ebony* 42:120+ Ap '87
First black city manager appointed in Dallas, Tex. *Jet* 71:13 Ja 12 '87
A new man heads Dallas. R. Witherspoon. il por *Black Enterp* 17:15 Mr '87
Knight, Robert
Contra-gate: a black issue. por *Essence* 18:144 Je '87
Knight of Glin *See* Fitz-Gerald, Desmond John Villiers, 1937-
Knight-Ridder Inc.
Hot chain nixes wingo, buscapades—nabs Pulitzers, big bucks. M. Cooper. *Wash Mon* 19:17-22 S '87
Knight-Ridder's profits aren't making any news. P. Engardio. il *Bus Week* p70-1 N 23 '87
Knights and knighthood
Great Britain
Knightly codes and piety. J. Vale and M. Vale. bibl il *Hist Today* 37:12-17 N '87
Knights Ferry (Calif.)
Description
Paddling and poking around gold rush Knights Ferry. il *Sunset* 178:52-4 My '87
Knippers, Edward
about
Gruesome images, signs of hope. D. Neff. il por *Christ Today* 31:63-4 Mr 6 '87

Knit goods
Getting your money's worth from knits. il *Glamour* 85:128 Mr '87
Knit dressing: the summer solution. il *Ladies Home J* 104:38 Je '87

Knitting
Easy to knit! Summer blues [sweaters] il *Good Housekeep* 204:114-17+ Je '87
Look what kids can knit! J. Williams and J. Severson. il *Better Homes Gard* 65:100-1 N '87
Make our sweetheart sweaters. il *Good Housekeep* 204:134-7+ F '87
The new denim-look crew. il *Redbook* 169:89-90 My '87
Quick-to-knit sweaters. J. Williams and J. Severson. il *Better Homes Gard* 65:62-3 Ja '87
Take a sweater and make it sparkle. il *Good Housekeep* 205:144-7+ O '87

Terminology
A glossary of knit terms. *Outdoor Life* 180:138 N '87

Knittle, Elise, and Jeanloz, Raymond
Synthesis and equation of state of $(Mg,Fe)SiO_3$ perovskite to over 100 gigapascals. bibl f il *Science* 235:668-70 F 6 '87

Knitwear *See* Knit goods

Knives
Knives: the cutter's choice. V. T. Sparano. il *Outdoor Life* 180:98-100+ N '87
Sharpen up [utility knives] B. Winter. il *Pop Mech* 164:90-3 Ap '87

Knize, Perri
Slouching towards Stowe. il *Skiing* 40:58-9 D '87

Knock, Engine *See* Automobile engines—Detonation

Knock-knock jokes
Don't knock knock-knocks! P. Dickson. *Read Dig* 130:21-2 Ja '87

Knoll, Erwin
Memo. See issues of The Progressive

Knopf, Alfred
about
Album of the Knopfs. S. Kauffmann. *Am Sch* 56:371-81 Summ '87
S & S buys bio of Knopf by Peter Prescott. *Publ Wkly* 231:87 F 27 '87

Knopf, Blanche W.
about
Album of the Knopfs. S. Kauffmann. *Am Sch* 56:371-81 Summ '87

Knopf (Alfred A.) Inc. *See* Alfred A. Knopf, Inc.

Knopoff, L.
(jt. auth) See Kagan, Y. Y., and Knopoff, L.

Knots and splices
Cherry stems [how to tie a cherry stem into a knot inside your mouth] *New Yorker* 63:27 Je 1 '87
Simplified knots for sportsmen. N. Strung. il *Field Stream* 92:64 Ag '87

Anecdotes, facetiae, satire, etc.
A knotty problem. A. Liere. *Field Stream* 92:35+ S '87
Tying one on. P. F. McManus. il *Outdoor Life* 180:168+ S '87

Knowledge
See also
Facts
Freedom of information
Ignorance
Science

Knowledge, Theory of
See also
Cognition
Common sense
Perception
Reality
Subjectivity
Truth

Knowledge-based pay *See* Skill-based pay

Knowles, Jeremy R.
Tinkering with enzymes: what are we learning? bibl f il *Science* 236:1252-8 Je 5 '87

Knowlton, Richard L.
about
And this little pig processor does nicely. R. Simon. il por *Forbes* 139:93 F 23 '87

Knowlton, Winthrop
Supporting the arts—whose responsibility? *Des Arts Educ* 88:36-42 Mr/Ap '87

Knox, Bernard MacGregor Walker
The Spanish tragedy. il *N Y Rev Books* 34:21-8 Mr 26 '87

'The Spanish tragedy': an exchange [discussion of March 26, 1987 article] il *N Y Rev Books* 34:52-3 Je 25 '87

Knuckleball pitching *See* Pitching (Baseball)

Knudson, George
about
A detour on the Seniors trail. H. Quinn. por *Macleans* 100:21 Jl 6 '87

Knussen, Oliver, 1952-
about
Where the Wild Things are [opera] Reviews *N Y* il 20:83 N 30 '87. P. G. Davis

Knutson, Roger M.
about
When you hear a splat, reach for Roger Knutson's Flattened fauna. il por *People Wkly* 28:105 Ag 17 '87

Kobayashi, Masakazu, 1944-
about
America's challenge. H. Katayama. il por *Forbes* 140:452+ Jl 13 '87

Kobilka, B. K., and others
Cloning, sequencing, and expression of the gene coding for the human platelet α_2-adrenergic receptor. bibl f il *Science* 238:650-6 O 30 '87

Koblenz, Jay
Auto dealers shift into maximum overdrive. il *Black Enterp* 17:245-6+ Je '87

Koblenzer, Caroline
about
Life and work at the same address. F. Greenberg. il por *Work Woman* 12:92-3 Ap '87

Kobler, James B., and others
Auditory pathways to the frontal cortex of the mustache bat, Pteronotus parnellii. bibl f il *Science* 236:824-6 My 15 '87

Kobler, John
about
Citing copyright infringement, judge halts Stravinsky biography. J. Mutter. *Publ Wkly* 232:14 Ag 21 '87

Koblinsky, Sally A., and Phillips, Margaret G.
Special "cooking friends" add spice to Head Start nutrition programs. il *Child Today* 16:26-9 Jl/Ag '87

Kobren, Abraham
The future of dentistry. il *McCalls* 114:116 F '87

Koch, Bill
First cousins: V1 and marathon. il *Skiing* 40:50 O '87
For steep uphills: the diagonal V. il *Skiing* 40:40 N '87
Jump, shoot, ski . . . win. il por *Skiing* 40:42+ S '87
Switching. il *Skiing* 40:227 D '87

Koch, Christof
(jt. auth) See Gamble, Edward, and Koch, Christof
(jt. auth) See Poggio, Tomaso, and Koch, Christof

Koch, Ed, 1924-
about
Around City Hall. A. Logan. See occasional issues of The New Yorker
But does God get 15%? L. Fleischer. *Publ Wkly* 232:48 S 4 '87
Koch agonistes. J. Klein. il pors *N Y* 20:28-32 Jl 13 '87
The Koch-Newfield letters [discussion of April 4, 1987 article, Mayor Daley is alive and well in N.Y.C.] J. Newfield. *Nation* 245:2+ Jl 4-11 '87
Koch to Trump to Koch: drop dead. J. R. Norman. il por *Bus Week* p98-9 Jl 20 '87
Mayor and pig. *New Yorker* 63:16-18 Ag 10 '87
Mayor Daley is alive and well in N.Y.C. [cover story] J. Newfield. il *Nation* 244:417+ Ap 4 '87
Troubled times for Hizzoner. B. Angelo. il por *Time* 130:21-2+ N 30 '87
Wisenheimer's disease. J. Klein. il por *N Y* 20:26+ Ag 24 '87

Anecdotes, facetiae, satire, etc.
Not-Kochisms. *Harpers* 274:16 F '87

Koch, H. William, 1925-
about
H. William Koch and AIP. F. Seitz and others. *Phys Today* 40:144 Ap '87

Koch, Jim
about
Brewing American. S. W. Angrist. il por *Forbes* 139:172 Ap 6 '87

Koch, Richard
about
Boston CitiNet is boffo. K. H. Hammonds. il por *Bus Week* p92+ O 19 '87

Kochis, S. Timothy
about
Of debt and taxes [interview] C. Weiner. il por *Money* 16:71-2+ S '87
Kocol, Cleo
Feminist update. See issues of The Humanist beginning September/October 1986
Our flawed and glorious Constitution. por *Humanist* 47:37-8 My/Je '87
Kocsis, Zoltán, 1952-
about
The phenomenon Kocsis. B. A. Varga. il pors *High Fidel* 37:71-2 Ja '87
Kodak Company *See* Eastman Kodak Co.
Kodo (Musical group)
Kodo, Japan's samurai rhythm kings, play the power drum song. il *People Wkly* 27:115 Mr 30 '87
Koehler, Philip G., and Patterson, Richard S.
The Asian roach invasion. il *Nat Hist* 96:28+ N '87
Koehler, Wallace C., 1920-1986
about
Obituary
Phys Today por 40:90 Ja '87. R. M. Moon, Jr.
Koelling, William F.
Sales reps or service reps: what do architects need from them? il por *Archit Rec* 175:16-17 D '87
Koelreuteria *See* Golden rain trees
Koen, Karleen
about
Through a glass darkly emerges the portrait of Karleen Koen, a successful first-time novelist. H. Shapiro. il pors *People Wkly* 27:97-9 F 23 '87
Koenig, Helmut
Dutch treat. il map *Travel Holiday* 168:48-53+ Ag '87
Europe '87: continental savings. il *Travel Holiday* 167:59-60+ Mr '87
Koenig, Rhoda
The shock of the Hughes. il pors *N Y* 20:30-5 Ja 5 '87
Koenig, Richard E.
The new Lutheran Church: the gift of Augustana [cover story] il *Christ Century* 104:555-8 Je 17-24 '87
Koeppen climate classification system *See* Climate—Classification
Koester, Stephen
about
Hold me tight. T. Tobias. il *N Y* 20:81-2 N 30 '87
Koether, Natalie I.
about
Natalie Koether: the lady is a raider. P. Finch. il por *Bus Week* p118-19 F 23 '87
Koevenig, James L.
The watercolor page. il por *Am Artist* 51:59 Je '87
Kofler, Linda L.
The class of '87 [cover story] il *Space World* X-11-287:9-13 N '87
Koford, Judy
(jt. auth) *See* Barney, Joanne, and Koford, Judy
Kogan, Marcela
The deep currents of nostalgia. il *Américas* 39:26-31 Mr/Ap '87
Stormy adventures of the spirit. il pors *Américas* 39:8-13 N/D '87
Kogan, Richard Jay, 1941-
about
Devour thy tail. G. Bronson. il pors *Forbes* 140:85+ N 2 '87
Kogelfranz, Siegfried
The killing fields . . . and streets and trains and buses. il *World Press Rev* 34:22-3 N '87
Kogelnik, H. D., 1932-
about
Kogelnik is elected 1987 vice president of OSA. por *Phys Today* 40:73-4 Ja '87
Kohák, Erazim V.
Nuclear power's Faustian bargain. *Harpers* 274:15-16+ My '87
Kohen, Daniel P.
A biobehavioral approach to managing childhood asthma. bibl f il *Child Today* 16:6-10 Mr/Ap '87
Kohl, Helmut, 1930-
Visit of West German Chancellor Kohl [remarks and joint statement, October 21, 1986] *Dep State Bull* 87:54-6 Ja '87
about
Campaigning with a free conscience. R. Laver. il por *Macleans* 100:22-3 Ja 26 '87
Candidate for a confident time. M. S. Serrill. il por *Time* 129:32 Ja 26 '87

East-West missile deal: Helmut Kohl feels the heat. D. Stanglin. il por *U S News World Rep* 102:13 Je 1 '87
Germany's Chancellor Kohl isn't charisma-less. M. S. Forbes. il por *Forbes* 140:17 Ag 24 '87
Homecoming for a serious boy. W. R. Doerner. pors *Time* 130:31 S 7 '87
Kohl by default. N. Birnbaum. *Nation* 244:69 Ja 24 '87
Kohl is nudged, but will he budge? *Newsweek* 109:39 Je 1 '87
Kohl on a roll. W. Laqueur. *New Repub* 196:17-18 Mr 2 '87
Kohl vows to scrap Pershing 1As if U.S., Soviets agree on treaty. *Aviat Week Space Technol* 127:18 Ag 31 '87
Kohl's second term: Washington may feel a chilly breeze. F. A. Miller and J. E. Pluenneke. il por *Bus Week* p48 F 9 '87
Little Man vs. Big Man. W. R. Doerner. il pors *Time* 130:45 S 21 '87
Moscow's arms-control offer has Kohl in a corner. J. E. Pluenneke and F. Thelen. il *Bus Week* p69 My 18 '87
New rules for war. P. Lewis. il por *Macleans* 100:20-1 Je 8 '87
'The shadows of the Reich'. N. Cooper. il por *Newsweek* 109:32 Ja 19 '87
The strange appeal of Helmut Kohl. J. E. Pluenneke and F. A. Miller. il por *Bus Week* p48-9 Ja 26 '87
Visit to the United States, 1986
Visit of West German Chancellor Kohl [remarks and joint statement, October 21, 1986] R. Reagan; H. Kohl. *Dep State Bull* 87:54-6 Ja '87
Kohl, Herbert R.
What teen suicide means. il *Nation* 244:603-4+ My 9 '87
Kohl, Robert L.
Finches fight greenhouse pests. il *Rodale's Org Gard* 34:42-3+ Ag '87
Kohlberg, Lawrence, 1927-1987
(jt. auth) *See* Power, Clark, and Kohlberg, Lawrence, 1927-1987
about
A question of morality. J. R. Snarey. il *Psychol Today* 21:6+ Je '87
Kohlberg Kravis Roberts & Co.
Thank you, Kohlberg Kravis [L. B. Foster Co.'s experiences after leveraged buyout] J. Clements. il *Forbes* 140:38+ N 2 '87
Why Jim Walter is ripe for the picking. P. Engardio. il *Bus Week* p31+ Ag 3 '87
Kohlhase, Charles E.
Aiming for Neptune. il *Astronomy* 15:6-15 N '87
Kohn, Alfie
Art for art's sake. il pors *Psychol Today* 21:52-7 S '87
Cooperation over competition: how to succeed. *Current* 289:21-4 Ja '87
It's hard to get left out of a pair. bibl (p62) il pors *Psychol Today* 21:52-7 O '87
Shattered innocence. bibl (p64) il *Psychol Today* 21:54-8 F '87
Kohn Pedersen Fox Associates, PC
Five by KPF [office buildings] G. Anderson. il *Archit Rec* 175:126-35 F '87
Kohout, Pavel
about
1984 [drama] Reviews
N Y il 20:46 Ag 3 '87. J. Simon
Nation 245:133-4 Ag 15-22 '87. T. M. Disch
New Repub 197:27-8 Ag 31 '87. R. Brustein
New Yorker 63:59-60 Ag 3 '87. M. Kramer
Kojak: the price of justice [television program] *See* Television program reviews—Single works
Kokkos, Yannis
about
Greek-born designer decorates Paris stage. E. Lampert. il *Theatre Crafts* 21:18 N '87
Kokomo (Ind.)
Education
An AIDS patient's fight for life [R. White] M. Nichols. il por *Sch Update* 119:4 Ap 20 '87
Kokoschka, Oskar, 1886-1980
about
Art. A. C. Danto. *Nation* 244:156-8 F 7 '87
Artist of angst. C. E. Schorske. il *N Y Rev Books* 33:20-2 Ja 15 '87
Expressionism's wobble of pain. J. Hobhouse. il *Newsweek* 109:70-1 F 9 '87

Kokoschka, Oskar, 1886-1980—about—*cont.*
A new view of Kokoschka. R. Bass. il por *Art News* 86:106-11 F '87
Kołakowski, Leszek
about
Absolutes and my grandfather's Aunt Sarah [discussion of September 7, 1987 article, A talk with Leszek Kolakowski] M. Mihajlov. *New Leader* 70:19-20 D 14 '87
A talk with Leszek Kolakowski [cover story; interview] M. Mihajlov. *New Leader* 70:10-12 S 7 '87
Kolata, Gina
Are the horrors of cannibalism fact—or fiction? il por *Smithsonian* 17:150-2+ Mr '87
Immune boosters [cover story] il *Discover* 8:68-72+ S '87
The sad legacy of the Dalkon Shield. *N Y Times Mag* p120 D 6 '87
Kolberg, William H., 1926-
Jobs without people and people without jobs: the coming mismatch in the information society. il *USA Today (Periodical)* 116:18-20 Jl '87
Kolbert, Elizabeth
Literary feminism comes of age. il por *N Y Times Mag* p110+ D 6 '87
Kolderie, Ted
What do we mean by "privatization"? *Society* 24:46-51 S/O '87
Kolenda, Konstantin
Revising the Copernican revolution. por *Humanist* 47:41-2 Mr/Ap '87
Seeing connections. il *Humanist* 47:43 My/Je '87
Kolesnichenko, T.
Communist view: Ollie is Rambo. *World Press Rev* 34:13-14 S '87
Kollek, Amos
about
Forever Lulu [film] Reviews
Commonweal 114:319-20 My 22 '87. T. O'Brien
People Wkly il 27:8 My 4 '87. R. Novak
Kollsman Instrument Co.
Page Avjet, Kollsman completing design for Boeing 727 flight deck conversion. E. H. Kolcum. *Aviat Week Space Technol* 127:52+ S 28 '87
Kolson, Rob
The case of the popular economist. D. Seligman. il *Fortune* 116:166 N 9 '87
Kom Tang (New York, N.Y.: Restaurant) *See* New York (N.Y.)—Restaurants, nightclubs, bars, etc.
Koma
about
New moon stories [dance] Reviews
Dance Mag 61:26-8 Ap '87. C. Hardy
New Leader 69:19 D 29 '86. L. A. Jacobs
Komanecky, Michael
The screens and screen designs of Donald Deskey. bibl f il *Antiques* 131:1064-77 My '87
Komar, Vitali, 1943-
about
Nobody's fools. R. B. Woodward. il pors *Art News* 86:172-8 N '87
Komatsu, Koh
about
A Japanese survivor leads the charge on world banking. J. Dreyfuss. por *Fortune* 115:60-1 Ja 5 '87
Komatsubara, Yoko
about
Goya: luz y sombra [dance] Reviews
Dance Mag 61:75+ Ap '87. L. Kumin
Kometani, Foumiko
about
Portnoy-san's complaints. J. Adler. il por *Newsweek* 109:72+ My 25 '87
Komonchak, Joseph A.
Issues behind the Curran case. *Commonweal* 114:43-7 Ja 30 '87
Komoski, Bill, 1954-
about
Bill Komoski at Baskerville + Watson. J. Rian. *Art Am* 75:220 Ap '87
Konchalovsky, Andrei
about
The Brothers M-K. K. Jaehne. il por *Film Comment* 23:66-8 S/O '87
Duet for one [film] Reviews
Commonweal 114:83 F 13 '87. T. O'Brien
Macleans il 100:46 Mr 2 '87. L. O'Toole
People Wkly il 27:16 F 2 '87. P. Travers
Time il 129:74+ Mr 2 '87. R. Corliss

Konchalovsky: the force of nature. R. Gentry. il por *Theatre Crafts* 21:63-6 Mr '87
Kondracke, Morton
Cool Hand Duke [cover story] *New Repub* 197:17-18+ Ag 31 '87
Gephardt's inside moves. il *New Repub* 196:20-2 Je 1 '87
The machine and the tiger. *New Repub* 196:16-21 F 23 '87
Pumping policy [cover story] *New Repub* 196:13-14+ My 18 '87
Seoul searching [cover story] *New Repub* 197:24-7+ Jl 27 '87
The southern strategist [cover story] il *New Repub* 197:20-3 D 7 '87
Too good for this world. *New Repub* 197:17-18+ O 26 '87
Vice President Sunbeam [cover story] il *New Repub* 196:20-3 Mr 30 '87
Where's the beef? [cover story] *New Repub* 197:16-18+ Jl 6 '87
Who wants peace? [cover story] *New Repub* 197:16-19 S 28 '87
Kongsberg Vaapenfabrikk AS
An illegal deal's noisy repercussions [Soviet deal with Toshiba and Kongsberg for milling machines to make submarine propellers] W. J. Cook. il *U S News World Rep* 102:42 Je 15 '87
A leak that could sink the U.S. lead in submarines [illegal sales to Soviet Union] J. Kapstein. il *Bus Week* p65-6 My 18 '87
Norway is selling Kongsberg's assets to 13 other firms. *Aviat Week Space Technol* 127:32 N 23 '87
Run silent, run to Moscow [sale of submarine technology to the Soviets] G. Bock. il *Time* 129:45 Je 29 '87
Such good friends: an old alliance under pressure [U.S. anger at Norway over illegal high tech sale to the Soviets] P. Sherrid. il *U S News World Rep* 103:42 O 5 '87
Welcome to Moscow on the Ginza [sale of submarine technology to the Soviets] R. N. Perle. il *U S News World Rep* 102:31-2 Je 29 '87
Koning, Frits, and others
Identification of a T3-associated γδ T cell receptor on Thy-1⁺ dendritic epidermal cell lines. bibl f il *Science* 236:834-7 My 15 '87
Koning, Hans, 1921-
Where money has little currency. *Harpers* 275:71-6 N '87
Koningsberger, Hans *See* Koning, Hans, 1921-
Konner, Linda
I was my parents' radio. il *Glamour* 85:228+ My '87
Konner, Melvin
Childbearing and age. il *N Y Times Mag* p22-3 D 27 '87
The enigmatic smile. il *Psychol Today* 21:42-4+ Mr '87
Konrád, György
'Informing on ourselves'. *Nation* 244:237+ F 28 '87
Konrad, Walecia
The luminary of luxury lingerie. il pors *Work Woman* 12:54-7 N '87
Kontras, Bill
about
A tale of two bucks. J. Murray and M. Pearce. il pors *Outdoor Life* 180:68-9+ Jl '87
Kookaburras
Around the Mall and beyond. E. Park. il *Smithsonian* 17:22+ F '87
Koon Wah Printing, Pte., Ltd.
Krueger signs intent to buy 50% of Koon Wah. *Publ Wkly* 232:44 Jl 3 '87
Koontz, Dean, 1945-
about
Best-selling novelist Dean Koontz may be a titan of terror but he's a timid type at heart. A. Chambers. il pors *People Wkly* 27:77-8 Ap 13 '87
PW interviews. L. See. il por *Publ Wkly* 232:44-5 D 18 '87
Koontz, Katy
The 10 commonest dieting downfalls. *McCalls* 114:37 My '87
L.A. law's closest couple. il pors *Health* 19:34 Je '87
Love your job! il *Health* 19:29-33 Je '87
Koop, C. Everett
Fighting student use of smokeless tobacco. *Educ Dig* 53:53-5 D '87
Non-smokers: time to clear the air. por *Read Dig* 130:110-13 Ap '87
about
Courage, Doc. por *Time* 130:57 S 21 '87

Koop, C. Everett—about—*cont.*

A dangerous silence. A. C. Lewis. il *Phi Delta Kappan* 68:348-9 Ja '87

Disowning the Surgeon General. P. Schlafly and P. Weyrich. *Harpers* 275:16-17 Ag '87

A fall from grace on the right. D. deF. Whitman. il por *U S News World Rep* 102:27-8 My 25 '87

Koop and Bennett agree to disagree. B. Barol. il pors *Newsweek* 109:64 F 16 '87

Koop makes waves in his war on AIDS. C. O'Connor. por *Newsweek* 109:31 Mr 2 '87

The missionary doctor. il por *Time* 129:22 Je 8 '87

PHS revitalization plan stirs up NIH. G. Kolata. il por *Science* 236:1055-6 My 29 '87

Surgeon General C. Everett Koop forecasts the death toll from AIDS: 170,000 Americans in just four years [interview] M. Dubrow. il por *People Wkly* 27:43-4+ Mr 16 '87

Surgeon General Koop asks for more voluntary AIDS testing [cover story] H. G. Miller. il pors *Saturday Evening Post* 259:58-61+ N '87

Warning: the Surgeon General may be good for your health. P. Glastris. por *Wash Mon* 19:13-16+ Mr '87

What our top doc prescribes on AIDS [interview] L. Kravitz. por *Sch Update* 120:10 O 16 '87

Koop, C. Everett, and Koop, Elizabeth

In memory of David Koop [excerpt from Sometimes mountains move] il pors *Saturday Evening Post* 259:62-3+ N '87

Koop, David Charles Everett

about

In memory of David Koop [excerpt from Sometimes mountains move] C. E. Koop and E. Koop. il pors *Saturday Evening Post* 259:62-3+ N '87

Koop, Elizabeth

(jt. auth) See Koop, C. Everett, and Koop, Elizabeth

Kootenai Indians *See* Kutenai Indians

Kopelson, Arnold

about

Getting respect. A. B. Block. il por *Forbes* 139:170 Ap 6 '87

Köper, Ingeborg

(jt. auth) See Golde, Brigitte, and Köper, Ingeborg

Kopkind, Andrew

Amerika: it can't happen here. *Nation* 244:165+ F 14 '87

Down and out in L.A. il *Nation* 244:309+ Mr 14 '87

Have we seen the future? [cover story] il *Nation* 244:631+ My 16 '87

Is Jesse the great white hope? [cover story] il *Nation* 245:773+ D 26 '87-Ja 2 '88

Jim Bakker's lost America. il pors *Esquire* 108:174-8+ D '87

Letters [discussion of May 16, 1987 article, Have we seen the future?] *Nation* 244:872+ Je 27 '87

The 'new voters' find their voice [cover story] il *Nation* 245:505+ N 7 '87

Paul Simon: return of the liberal [cover story] *Nation* 245:665+ D 5 '87

A populist message hits home [cover story] il *Nation* 245:37+ Jl 18-25 '87

Koppel, Ted

about

America's Q&A man [cover story] J. Alter. il pors *Newsweek* 109:50-3+ Je 15 '87

Korda, Michael, 1933-

The bridle path. il *N Y* 20:100-1 D 21-28 '87

Ten steps to success before 40. il *Read Dig* 131:111-13 D '87

Korea

History

See also

Silla (Kingdom)

Korea (North)

See also

Loans, Bank—Korea (North)

Sports—Korea (North)

Economic policy

Pulling the plug [default on foreign debt] G. Bock. il *Time* 130:43 S 7 '87

Foreign relations

Korea (South)

See Korea (South)—Foreign relations—Korea (North)

Politics and government

Inside the land of the 'Great Leader' [Kim Il Sung] Y. Layma. por *World Press Rev* 34:27-9 Ja '87

Scenes from a neighbor kingdom. il *Time* 129:30-3 Je 29 '87

Religious institutions and affairs

See also

Christians—Korea (North)

Korea (People's Republic) *See* Korea (North)

Korea (Republic) *See* Korea (South)

Korea (South)

See also

Air traffic control—Korea (South)

Business management—Korea (South)

Civil rights—Korea (South)

Copyright infringement—Korea (South)

Factory management—Korea (South)

Government and the press—Korea (South)

Historic houses, sites, etc.—Korea (South)

Industry and state—Korea (South)

Investments, American—Korea (South)

Investments, Korean

Kyŏngju (Korea)

Political prisoners—Korea (South)

Seoul (Korea)

Stadiums—Korea (South)

Strikes—Korea (South)

Student protests, demonstrations, etc.—Korea (South)

Trade unions—Korea (South)

Wages and salaries—Korea (South)

Commerce

Korea's big push has just begun. L. Kraar. il *Fortune* 115:72-6 Mr 16 '87

United States

See United States—Commerce—Korea (South)

Commercial policy

Where sanctions against Japan are really working. S. J. Dryden. il *Bus Week* p61-2 My 11 '87

Description and travel

South Korea: anticipating visitors. O. Barrot. il *World Press Rev* 34:62 Jl '87

Economic conditions

Korea's boom times are keeping rebellion at bay—so far. L. Nakarmi and J. Becker. il *Bus Week* p42-3 Je 29 '87

New worries in South Korea. H. Becker. *World Press Rev* 34:47 S '87

Will labor unrest wreck Korea's economic boom? L. Nakarmi. il *Bus Week* p40-1 Ag 31 '87

Economic policy

Hayek in reverse. *Natl Rev* 39:17 Jl 31 '87

Korea votes for economic stability [election of Roh Tae Woo] L. Nakarmi. il por *Bus Week* p69 D 28 '87-Ja 4 '88

Korea's elections: high stakes for the economy. L. Armstrong and L. Nakarmi. il *Bus Week* p50-2 D 14 '87

South Korea's days of danger. J. Dreyfuss. il *Fortune* 116:101+ O 12 '87

Foreign relations

Korea (North)

See also

Olympic Games—1988—Summer Olympics—Boycott

Disaster in the skies [bomb suspected in downing of Korean Air Lines Flight 858] A. Bilski. il *Macleans* 100:24 D 14 '87

Kidnapped by Beloved Leader Comrade [abduction and imprisonment of Shin Sang Ok and Choi Un Hui] D. Reed. il *Read Dig* 130:105-12 Mr '87

Korea: new beginnings [address, July 21, 1987] G. J. Sigur. *Dep State Bull* 87:32-4 S '87

Korean tripwire [possibility of nuclear war] P. Hayes and others. *Nation* 245:256-7 S 19 '87

The mystery of Flight 858 [North Koreans suspected of planting bomb on Korean Air Lines plane] *Time* 130:46 D 14 '87

The poisoned flight of KAL [possible North Korean involvement in bombing of Flight 858] il *U S News World Rep* 103:12 D 14 '87

U.S. urges resumption of North-South Korean talks [State Dept. statement, August 3, 1987] *Dep State Bull* 87:23 O '87

Who destroyed Korean Air 858? M. Liu. il *Newsweek* 110:61 D 14 '87

United States

See United States—Foreign relations—Korea (South)

Industries

See also

Automobile industry—Korea (South)

Daewoo Corporation

Hyundai Electronics Industry Co., Ltd.

Hyundai Group

Hyundai Motor Co. Ltd.

Samsung Group

Korea (South)—Industries—cont.

Korea's big push has just begun. L. Kraar. il *Fortune* 115:72-6 Mr 16 '87

Photographs and photography

The quirks of Korea. R. Burri. il *Life* 10:20-7 S '87

Politics and government

See also
Elections—Korea (South)
Korea (South). Constitution
Political campaigns—Korea (South)
Political candidates—Korea (South)

Amnesty for the opposition. il *Macleans* 100:24 Jl 20 '87

The battle of Seoul. B. Levin. il *Macleans* 100:16-17 Jl 6 '87

Brinkmanship in South Korea. R. Watson. il por *Newsweek* 110:26-7 Jl 6 '87

The burden of omnipotence. J. M. Fallows. il *Atlantic* 260:20-1+ O '87

A cautious victory [Chun's reforms] B. Levin. il por *Macleans* 100:16 Jl 13 '87

Chun switches signals [postponement of reform until after the Summer Olympics] F. Willey. il por *Newsweek* 109:39 Ap 27 '87

Chun's hard line can only deepen Korea's unrest. L. Nakarmi and B. Javetski. il *Bus Week* p49 Jl 6 '87

Chun's option: to crush or concede. M. Lord. il map *U S News World Rep* 102:26-8 Je 29 '87

Crisis in Korea [cover story] R. Watson. il map *Newsweek* 109:28-35 Je 29 '87

Dark days of rage. B. Levin. il *Macleans* 100:28 Je 29 '87

Dateline South Korea: a divided Seoul. S. S. Harrison. bibl f *Foreign Policy* 67:154-75 Summ '87

"Down with dictatorship". il *Time* 129:40 Je 22 '87

Hayek in reverse. *Natl Rev* 39:17 Jl 31 '87

How South Korea's Chun is trying to bypass the opposition. R. J. Dowling. il *Bus Week* p49 My 4 '87

Korea: a bloody fall term? New riots overshadow a constitutional accord. B. Martin. il *Newsweek* 110:48 S 14 '87

Korea: Asian paradox. W. H. Gleysteen, Jr. and A. D. Romberg. *Foreign Aff* 65:1037-54 Summ '87

Korea counseling. *New Repub* 197:7-9 Jl 13-20 '87

Korea divided. *Nation* 245:3-4 Jl 4-11 '87

Korea: moving quickly toward democracy [statement, September 17, 1987] W. Clark, Jr. *Dep State Bull* 87:29-31 N '87

Korea: shame & chauvinism. I. Buruma. bibl f il *N Y Rev Books* 34:21-6 Ja 29 '87

Korean politics in transition [address, February 6, 1987] G. J. Sigur. *Dep State Bull* 87:19-21 Ap '87

Korea's brave new world. M. Lord. il *U S News World Rep* 103:32-3 Jl 13 '87

Korea's 'Democratic coup' will start another scrap. L. Nakarmi. il por *Bus Week* p32 Jl 13 '87

Korea's endless surprises. T. Walkom. il *World Press Rev* 34:20-2 Ag '87

Old friends [Roh Tae Woo designated successor to Chun Doo Hwan] M. S. Serrill. il pors *Time* 129:40 Je 15 '87

Olympian hurdle in Korea. D. Kirk. il *New Leader* 70:3-5 Je 29 '87

Olympic stakes. *Natl Rev* 39:19-20 Jl 17 '87

Onslaughts of force and fury. J. Greenwald. il *Time* 129:50-1 Mr 16 '87

Out on the street [general strike] *Time* 130:33 Ag 24 '87

Rage builds in South Korea. il *U S News World Rep* 102:18 Je 22 '87

Reforms on hold. H. G. Chua-Eoan. por *Time* 129:38-9 Ap 27 '87

The Republic of Korea [address, September 22, 1987] R. H. Myers. *Vital Speeches Day* 54:72-6 N 15 '87

Seoul searching [cover story] M. Kondracke. *New Repub* 197:24-7+ Jl 27 '87

South Korea: a mini-Japan troubled by growing unrest. L. Hopping. il *Sch Update* 119:9 Ap 6 '87

South Korea's 'miracle' week. M. Whitaker. il por *Newsweek* 110:26-8 Jl 13 '87

A strange and resolute calm [climate before the Olympic Games] W. O. Johnson. il *Sports Illus* 66:38-40+ Je 8 '87

The struggle gains its martyr [death of student protester] W. R. Doerner. il *Time* 130:43 Jl 20 '87

A successor in his own image [Roh Tae Woo chosen to succeed Chun Doo Hwan] B. Levin. il por *Macleans* 100:18 Jl 6 '87

Suddenly, a new day [party chairman Roh Tae Woo endorses reforms; with interview] W. R. Doerner. il pors *Time* 130:34-7 Jl 13 '87

Talk and fight [Chun Doo Hwan makes concessions to opposition] W. R. Doerner. il por *Time* 130:14-15 Jl 6 '87

Terror in the streets. P. McGill. il *Macleans* 100:18-19 Je 22 '87

Tradition and change at war [government of Chun Doo Hwan] W. L. Chaze. il por *U S News World Rep* 103:31-2 Jl 6 '87

Two steps forward, one back: free elections are scheduled and new violence breaks out. J. Greenwald. il *Time* 130:41 S 14 '87

Under siege [cover story; special section] il map *Time* 129:20-4+ Je 29 '87

An unlikely champion of South Korean democracy [Roh Tae Woo] L. Nakarmi. por *Bus Week* p62 S 14 '87

A volcano of unrest. W. R. Doerner. il *Time* 129:46-7 My 25 '87

A vote for South Korea: it's too soon to push the panic button over the Seoul Olympics. W. O. Johnson. por *Sports Illus* 67:94 Jl 13 '87

Why is South Korea afraid of democracy? il *World Press Rev* 34:25-7 Je '87

Will he or won't he? [Kim Dae Jung visits his native Cholla region] il por *Time* 130:45 S 21 '87

Years of dictatorship, days of destruction. F. Willey. il *Newsweek* 109:32+ Je 22 '87

Religious institutions and affairs

See also
Christians—Korea (South)
Church and state—Korea (South)
Missions—Korea (South)
Pentecostal churches—Korea (South)
Protestant churches—Korea (South)

Korea (South). Constitution

Korea: a bloody fall term? New riots overshadow a constitutional accord. B. Martin. il *Newsweek* 110:48 S 14 '87

Two steps forward, one back: free elections are scheduled and new violence breaks out. J. Greenwald. il *Time* 130:41 S 14 '87

Korea Fund Inc.

Playing politics [volatility of share price] P. Fuhrman. il *Forbes* 140:51 Ag 24 '87

Korean Air Lines Flight 007 disaster, 1983

Questions that won't go away [excerpt from KAL 007: the cover-up; cover story] D. E. Pearson. *Nation* 245:181+ S 5 '87

Korean Americans

Korean-Americans: the early migration. C. E. Kraft. il *Antiques Collect Hobbies* 92:80-4 Ap '87

Taking a chance in a new country [U. Lee] L. H. Whitson. il por *Nations Bus* 75:59 Mr '87

Korean executives *See* Executives

Korean pottery *See* Pottery, Korean

Korean War, 1950-1953

American participation

Rehearsal for a disaster [views of Max Hastings] P. McGrath. il *Newsweek* 110:47 N 30 '87

Koreans

United States

See also
Korean Americans

Korfball

A Dutch treat of a game. il *Sports Illus* 66:16 Ap 13 '87

Korman, Joshua

Racing for life. il pors *N Y Times Mag* p62-4+ S 20 '87

Korn, Edward D., and others

Actin polymerization and ATP hydrolysis. bibl f il *Science* 238:638-44 O 30 '87

Korn, Larry

Garlic you plant only once. il pors *Rodale's Org Gard* 34:91-2 Ap '87

Raising American truffles. il *Rodale's Org Gard* 34:24+ O '87

Korn, Laurence Jay, and others

ras p21 as a potential mediator of insulin action in Xenopus oocytes. bibl f il *Science* 236:840-3 My 15 '87

Korn, Lester B.

about

Old order changes. H. Seneker. il por *Forbes* 139:150 Mr 9 '87

Korn, Peter

Blood, grit and years. il pors *Sport Mag* 78:36-8+ O '87

Korn, Wendy

Bad habits that can ruin your health. il *Ladies Home J* 104:36+ S '87

The no-diet diet. il *Ladies Home J* 104:94+ N '87

Korn/Ferry International
Old order changes. H. Seneker. il por *Forbes* 139:150 Mr 9 '87
Kornbluh, Peter
Down the drain. *Nation* 245:452 O 24 '87
The selling of the F.D.N. il *Nation* 244:40-4 Ja 17 '87
What North might have wrought [cover story] il *Nation* 244:871+ Je 27 '87
Kornbluth, Jesse
Allure in the grand manner. il por *House Gard* 159:152-9+ D '87
Andy. il *N Y* 20:38-45+ Mr 9 '87
An antiques dealer's secret sources: Bruce Newman in Paris and England. il pors *Archit Dig* 44 Archit Dig Travels:20-31+ O '87
The battle of Bendel's. il pors *N Y* 20:26-33 F 23 '87
Dramatic license: an author's Park Avenue residence. il *Archit Dig* 44:164-9 N '87
Drawn to the masters—David Tunick. il por *Archit Dig* 44:74+ My '87
Inside stories: author Judith Green's Park Avenue residence. il por *Archit Dig* 44:134-9+ D '87
The little studio that could. il *N Y* 20:48-52+ Ap 6 '87
A road less traveled: New York country haven of Marilynn and Ivan Karp. il *Archit Dig* 44:196-203+ Je '87
Sound choice: a Georgian revival estate on Long Island's North Shore. il *Archit Dig* 44:190-5 Mr '87
The woman who beat the Klan. il pors *N Y Times Mag* p26-32+ N 1 '87
Kornheiser, Tony
Exit dunking. il pors *Sport Mag* 78:56-61 Je '87
The joy of dirt. il *Esquire* 107:145-6 Je '87
Kornienko, Nelly
Les Kurbas, founder of Ukrainian theatre. il por *Courier* 40:32-3 O '87
Korologos, Tom C.
about
An experienced man in Bork's corner. A. Press. por *Newsweek* 110:36 S 21 '87
Korsakov, Nikolay Rimsky- *See* Rimsky-Korsakov, Nikolay, 1844-1908
Korshin, Paul
(jt. auth) See McPherson, Mary Patterson, and Korshin, Paul
Kort, Michele
Aerobics and fitness. il *Women's Sports Fitness* 9:38-40+ Mr '87
Debi Thomas: skater extraordinaire. pors *Ms* 15:32-3 F '87
Domestic terrorism: on the front line at an abortion clinic. il por *Ms* 15:48-51+ My '87
Super shoes '87 [special section] il *Women's Sports Fitness* 9:29+ Mr '87
Terry Louise Fisher: how she dreamed up the women of "L.A. law". por *Ms* 15:38-9+ Je '87
Korthals-Altes, Stephen
Will the aerospace plane work? il *Technol Rev* 90:2, 42-51 Ja '87
Koryagin, Anatoly
about
Koryagin skeptical on *glasnost*. C. Holden. il por *Science* 238:476 O 23 '87
Soviet psychiatrist describes abuse. J. Greenberg and B. Bower. *Sci News* 131:328 My 23 '87
A test case. D. Satter. il por *N Y Rev Books* 34:3-4 F 12 '87
Koshiba, Masa-Toshi
Observational neutrino astrophysics. bibl il map *Phys Today* 40:38-42 D '87
Koshland, Daniel E., Jr.
(jt. auth) See Falke, Joseph J., and Koshland, Daniel E., Jr.
Koshland, Douglas, and Hartwell, Leland H.
The structure of sister minichromosome DNA before anaphase in Saccharomyces cerevisiae. bibl f il *Science* 238:1713-16 D 18 '87
Kosovo (Yugoslavia)
Yugoslavia's national question. J. H. Wolfe. il *USA Today (Periodical)* 116:51 S '87
Koss, John C., 1930-
about
Koss Corp.'s audio advantage. J. McCormick. il por *Newsweek* 110:72 O 12 '87
Out of Chapter 11, Koss makes sweet music again. L. Therrien. il por *Bus Week* p75 Ag 10 '87

Koss Corp.
Koss Corp.'s audio advantage. J. McCormick. il por *Newsweek* 110:72 O 12 '87
Out of Chapter 11, Koss makes sweet music again. L. Therrien. il por *Bus Week* p75 Ag 10 '87
Kostabi, Mark
about
The Kostabi case: whose art is it, anyway? M. Rose. il por *N Y* 20:29 S 7 '87
Kostelanetz, Richard
The other Berlin. il *House Gard* 159:50+ Je '87
Sculpture funhouse. il por *N Y Times Mag* p28-31 My 31 '87
Kostmayer, Pamela
Fed up with the demands of her husband's career, a congressman's wife drops out of the race; ed by Annette Kornblum. il pors *People Wkly* 28:71-2+ O 12 '87
Kostmayer, Peter H.
about
Fed up with the demands of her husband's career, a congressman's wife drops out of the race; ed by Annette Kornblum. P. Kostmayer. il pors *People Wkly* 28:71-2+ O 12 '87
Kotrosits, Lynn
Why we skipped nursery school. il *Parents* 62:68+ S '87
Kotsilibas-Davis, James, and Loy, Myrna
Myrna Loy: the private life of Hollywood's "perfect wife" [excerpt from Myrna Loy] il pors *Good Housekeep* 205:116-17+ Ag '87
Kott, Andrea
The lowdown on low-impact aerobics. il *Mademoiselle* 93:84 Ja '87
Kottler, Howard, 1930-
about
Howard Kottler: conceptualist and purveyor of psychosexual allusions. P. Failing. il por *Am Craft* 47:22-9 D '87/Ja '88
Koufos, Philip
about
In an Eastern Orthodox Chicago church, a weeping Madonna and Child bring throngs to pray and hope for miracles. C. Tamarkin. il *People Wkly* 27:44-5 Ja 19 '87
Kounellis, Jannis
about
Jannis Kounellis. C. Moser. *Art News* 86:61 Ja '87
Kovachevich, Thomas, 1943-
about
Thomas Kovachevich at Farideh Cadot. J. Rian. *Art Am* 75:127 Jl '87
Kovacs, Karen
The quest for change in Mexican education. bibl f *Curr Hist* 86:117-20+ Mr '87
Kovich, Robert
about
Multiple/choice crimes [dance] Reviews
N Y 20:80 Ap 6 '87. T. Tobias
Kowalski, Mark, and others
Functional regions of the envelope glycoprotein of human immunodeficiency virus type 1. bibl f il *Science* 237:1351-5 S 11 '87
Kowalski, Robert
Turkey with a twist. il *50 Plus* 27:74-6+ N '87
Kowalski, Theodore J.
The second coming of community education. *Educ Dig* 52:52-4 F '87
Koyanagi, Yoshio, and others
Dual infection of the central nervous system by AIDS viruses with distinct cellular tropisms. bibl f il *Science* 236:819-22 My 15 '87
Kozinn, Allan
No mere curiosity. il por *Opera News* 52:26+ Ag '87
Koziy, Bohdan
about
Accused: 28 years a U.S. citizen, Bohdan Koziy is suspected of killing Jews in World War II. E. Barnes. il pors *Life* 10:54-5+ My '87
Kozloff, Joyce
about
Pattern & decoration in the public eye. S. Webster. il *Art Am* 75:118-25 F '87
Kozloff, Max
The family of Nan. il pors *Art Am* 75:38-9+ N '87
Jan Groover: melancholy modernist. il *Art Am* 75:144-7 Je '87
Opaque disclosures. il *Art Am* 75:144-53+ O '87
Through Eastern eyes. il *Art Am* 75:90-7 Ja '87
Kozol, Jonathan
(tr) See Michnik, Adam. Gorbachev: the great counter-reformer

Kraatz, Harry R.
about
The dog ate his homework. J. R. Hayes. il por *Forbes* 140:186 O 19 '87
Krabloonik (Snowmass Village, Colo.: Restaurant) *See* Snowmass Village (Colo.)—Restaurants, nightclubs, bars, etc.
Kraft, Charles E.
A bonanza of catalogs. il *Antiques Collect Hobbies* 92:76-8 D '87
Deutschlands truebste Zeit: the calamity of 1648. il *Antiques Collect Hobbies* 92:79-81 Je '87
Korean-Americans: the early migration. il *Antiques Collect Hobbies* 92:80-4 Ap '87
The skeleton in the courthouse. il *Antiques Collect Hobbies* 92:68-71 S '87
Kraft, Ken, and Kraft, Pat
Try these novel uses for surplus herbs. il *Flower Gard* 32:46-7 D '87/Ja '88
Kraft, Pat
(jt. auth) See Kraft, Ken, and Kraft, Pat
Kraft, Scott
We had to find our daughter's molester. il *Read Dig* 130:147-51 My '87
Kraft Inc.
Kraft, minus some extra baggage, is picking up speed. K. Dreyfack. il por *Bus Week* p74-5 Mr 9 '87
The rumor mill is processing Kraft. G. G. Marcial. *Bus Week* p88 Je 29 '87
Kragen, Ken
about
Richie splits with Kragen after six-year management. il pors *Jet* 71:17 Mr 2 '87
Krajicek, Ed
about
In Nebraska, persistence pays off. C. Kenney. il por *50 Plus* 27:14+ D '87
Krakauer, Jon
After all is said and done, will Everest still be number one? bibl (p231) il map *Smithsonian* 18:176-8+ O '87
Truckers brave the barren lands to supply an Arctic gold mine. il *Smithsonian* 18:128-34+ N '87
Krakow (Poland)
Air pollution
In Krakow even the buildings dissolve. D. Hinrichsen. il *Int Wildl* 17:12-15 Mr/Ap '87
Kral, Jon
about
Household effects. S. Piperato. il por *Pop Photogr* 94:96-7 N '87
Kramer, A. Stanley
The short, unhappy life of the U.S. Camel Cavalry. il *Am Hist Illus* 22:52-7 Mr '87
Kramer, Angela
about
Designing woman. I. Ross. il por *N Y* 20:32 O 12 '87
Kramer, Carol
Five questions you'd like to ask Tom Selleck. il por *McCalls* 115:148+ N '87
Hot in Hollywood. il *McCalls* 114:42-3+ S '87
How to catch a star. il *McCalls* 114:85-7 F '87
Marie Osmond: starting over. il pors *McCalls* 114:14-16 Ap '87
The most trusted men in America. il pors *McCalls* 114:128+ Jl '87
That Horne thing. il *McCalls* 145:50-4 Mr '87
Those spunky Kennedy women. il *McCalls* 115:28+ O '87
Kramer, Hilton
The idea of tradition in American art criticism. *Am Sch* 56:319-27 Summ '87
The importance of Sidney Hook. *Commentary* 84:17-24 Ag '87
Philosophy & faith [discussion of August 1987 article, The importance of Sidney Hook] *Commentary* 84:2+ N '87
about
Lowdown. L. Wieseltier. *New Repub* 197:42 N 16 '87
Kramer, Jack, 1921-
Holding/breaking serve. il *World Tennis* 34:32 Ap '87
about
12 who mattered. S. Flink. por *World Tennis* 35:55 D '87
Racket man. B. Greene. il por *Esquire* 108:35-7 Ag '87
Kramer, Jane
Letter from Europe. See occasional issues of The New Yorker

Letter from the Elysian Fields. *New Yorker* 63:40-2+ Mr 2 '87
The rules of the game. il *House Gard* 159:86+ O '87
Kramer, Linda
Worldclass mom [cover story] il pors *Women's Sports Fitness* 9:28-31 Ap '87
Kramer, Mark, 1944-
A new romance. il *N Y Times Mag* p71 Ag 16 '87
Kramer, Michael
[Column] See issues of U.S. News & World Report beginning May 18, 1987
The national interest. See issues of New York through March 30, 1987
Kramer, Mimi, 1957-
The theatre. See issues of The New Yorker beginning June 8, 1987
Undressed for success. il *Vogue* 177:218-19+ Jl '87
Kramer, Richard
Andre Gregory: scene stealer. por *Harpers Bazaar* 120:124+ Ap '87
Kramer, Stanley, 1913-
about
The wild one [film] Reviews
　Cycle il 38:55 Ag '87. J. Dorrance
Krance, Magda
Counting the days along Lake Michigan. il *Oceans* 20:6-7+ Mr/Ap '87
Krangel, Michael S., and others
Structurally divergent human T cell receptor γ proteins encoded by distinct Cγ genes. bibl f il *Science* 237:64-7 Jl 3 '87
Krannert Center for the Performing Arts
Krannert Center for the Performing Arts. M. Sommers. il *Theatre Crafts* 21:48-9+ D '87
Krantz, Grover S.
about
Tracking the Sasquatch. S. Begley. il por *Newsweek* 110:73 S 21 '87
Krantz, Judith
Decorating scruples. il por *House Gard* 159:208-17+ O '87
Krasner, Lee, 1908-1984
about
Living a truth. por *Art News* 86:9 Ja '87
Krasner, Lenore *See* Krasner, Lee, 1908-1984
Krasnow, Stefanie
The spring training diet. il *Sport Mag* 78:93 Mr '87
Krass, Alfred C., 1936-
Growing together in spirituality: pastor and parish have a check-up. il *Christ Century* 104:311-14 Ap 1 '87
Kratt, Mary
Sunday [poem] *Christ Century* 104:102 F 4-11 '87
Kraus, Joe
For the consummate traveler. *Travel Holiday* 167:32+ Ja '87
Kraus, Jon
Ghana's shift from radical populism. *Curr Hist* 86:205-8+ My '87
Kraus, Michael
Soviet policy toward East Europe. bibl f il *Curr Hist* 86:353-6+ N '87
Krause, L. William
The next frontier of computer users. por *Pers Comput* 11:240 O '87
Krauss, Clifford
Revolution in Central America? *Foreign Aff* 65 Sp Issue:564-81 ['87]
Krauss, Melvyn
Testa dura. il por *Opera News* 52:33-4 O '87
Krauss, Rosalind
Post-history on parade. *New Repub* 196:27-30 My 25 '87
Krauthammer, Charles, 1950-
The ethics of human manufacture [cover story] *New Repub* 196:17-21 My 4 '87
Guerrilla warfare: morality and the Reagan Doctrine. *Current* 290:32-40 F '87
Let it sink [cover story] *New Repub* 197:18-23 Ag 24 '87
The price of power. *New Repub* 196:23-5 F 9 '87
When secrecy meets democracy. il *Read Dig* 130:116-18 F '87
When to call off the cold war. *New Repub* 197:18-21 N 16 '87
about
The march of power. A. Cockburn. *Nation* 244:564 My 2 '87

Kravitz, Lenny

about

Lisa Bonet marries musician Lenny "Romeo" Kravitz, son of 'The Jeffersons' TV star. il pors *Jet* 73:6 D 7 '87

Kreider, Jan F., 1942-

Alternate-energy answers. See alternate issues of Popular Science through January 1987

Energy Q & A. See issues of Popular Science beginning March 1987

Kreisberg, Paul H.

Gandhi at midterm. *Foreign Aff* 65:1055-76 Summ '87

Kreiter, Marcella S.

Crack: cheap, quick, deadly. il *Curr Health 2* 14:9-11 S '87

Fighting drugs. il *Curr Health 2* 13:12-15 Ap '87

Steroids: the stuff of synthetic supermen? il *Curr Health 2* 14:14-16 D '87

Kremer, Randall

Henri Matisse: the early years in Nice. il *USA Today (Periodical)* 115:84-7 Mr '87

Kremlinology *See* Soviet studies

Krens, Thomas

about

Art comes to the rescue. D. Davis. il por *Newsweek* 110:97 O 26 '87

Thinking big. C. Giuliano. il por *Art News* 86:35-6 S '87

Krepon, Michael, 1946-

CIA, DIA at odds over Soviet threat. *Bull At Sci* 43:6-7 My '87

High stakes in INF verification. *Bull At Sci* 43:14-16 Je '87

INF agreement in principle. il *Bull At Sci* 43:5-6 N '87

The Iran/arms control connection. il *Bull At Sci* 43:9-10 Mr '87

Rocky road to INF accord. il *Bull At Sci* 43:3-4 S '87

The Surprise Defense Initiative. il *Bull At Sci* 43:5-6 Jl/Ag '87

(jt. auth) See Graybeal, Sidney N., and Krepon, Michael, 1946-

Kresh, Paul

Very model records of the major Gilbert & Sullivan. il pors *High Fidel* 37:56-8 Je '87

Kreslins, Janice A.

Source material. See issues of Foreign Affairs beginning Fall 1986

Kresnik, Johann

about

Reviews:

J. Kresnik's dance group at the Municipal Theater. H. Koegler. *Dance Mag* 61:23+ O '87

Kress, Robert

The restful friendship of God. *America* 156:501-5 Je 20-27 '87

Kreutzmann, Bill

about

Bill Kreutzmann/Mickey Hart: Rhythm Devils. C. Vaughan. il pors *Down Beat* 11:23-5 N '87

Kreyche, Gerald F.

Crisis, crisis, who's got the crisis? il *USA Today (Periodical)* 116:98 Jl '87

Luddites and computers. il *USA Today (Periodical)* 115:98 Ja '87

The new McCarthyism. il *USA Today (Periodical)* 116:98 S '87

Platitudes and natural selection. il *USA Today (Periodical)* 115:98 My '87

Sensitivity or touchiness? *USA Today (Periodical)* 116:98 N '87

Surrogate motherhood: an ethical and moral dilemma. il *USA Today (Periodical)* 116:66-7 N '87

What's next? *USA Today (Periodical)* 115:98 Mr '87

Krich, John, 1951-

Reggie Jackson. il por *Sport Mag* 78:91+ D '87

Krieckhaus, Steve

about

Stepping out. T. Tobias. il *N Y* 20:110 Mr 2 '87

Kriegel, Leonard, 1933-

The purpose of lifting. il *N Y Times Mag* p50 Ap 12 '87

Kriegman, Mitchell

The best me possible. *New Yorker* 63:36-7 O 19 '87

Kriesberg, Joseph

Is Maine Yankee headed for the dump? *Progressive* 51:12-13 N '87

Krill

Krill: food of the future? S. Nicol. il *Sea Front* 33:12-17 Ja/F '87

Krill fisheries *See* Shellfish fisheries

Krim, Mathilde, 1926-

How not to control the AIDS epidemic [adaptation of address, June 1987] il por *Humanist* 47:14-15+ N/D '87

about

Mathilde Krim: "Across the U.S., one man in thirty is infected . . . one never knows with any man" [interview] M. Orth. il por *Vogue* 177:246+ O '87

Krisch, Alan D.

Collisions between spinning protons. bibl (p116) il *Sci Am* 257:42-50 Ag '87

Krishna consciousness movement

Dial om for murder [involvement of guru Bhaktipada in murder of S. Bryant] J. Hubner and L. Gruson. il pors *Roll Stone* p53-4+ Ap 9 '87

Krisik, John

about

Banking on a "croakie". H. Rothman. il pors *Nations Bus* 75:81 My '87

Krist, Bob

Bluefish: the most vicious fish in the sea? [photographs] il *Natl Wildl* 25:22-4 Je/Jl '87

Keeping flamingos under his wing. il por *Int Wildl* 17:46-51 Ja/F '87

Kristensen, Monica

about

Trying to cap Antarctic daredevilry. M. Satchell. il por map *U S News World Rep* 102:75 F 16 '87

Kristeva, Julia, 1941-

AIDS and Eros; tr. by Leon Roudiez. *Harpers* 275:24-5 O '87

Kristof, Nicholas D., 1959-

In China, the buck starts here. il map *N Y Times Mag* p40-2+ D 20 '87

Kristol, Irving

Don't count out conservatism. il *N Y Times Mag* p30+ Je 14 '87

Krizia (Firm)

Krizia's executive class. J. Conant. il por *Newsweek* 110:70 O 26 '87

Krobock, Richard D., d. 1987

about

The life and death of an intelligence man. M. Healy. il pors *U S News World Rep* 102:22-3 My 11 '87

Krochmal, Liane

about

Remembering Liane, age six. G. F. Will. il por *Newsweek* 109:80 My 25 '87

Kroger, Joseph J., 1934-

Artificial intelligence. il por *Futurist* 21:38-40 Jl/Ag '87

Kroger Co.

Kroger workers forgo bonus plan to save jobs. *Mon Labor Rev* 110:42-3 Mr '87

Most improved. il *Forbes* 139:131 Ja 12 '87

Krogstad, Donald J., and others

Efflux of chloroquine from Plasmodium falciparum: mechanism of chloroquine resistance. bibl f il *Science* 238:1283-5 N 27 '87

Kroh Brothers Development (Firm)

They honk when the Krohs fly by [attempt to reorganize under Chapter 11] J. Castro. il *Time* 129:56 Mr 16 '87

Kroll, Martin

A naïf vision of paradise. il por *Américas* 39:20-4 S/O '87

Kroll, Steven

Steig: nobody is grown-up. *N Y Times Book Rev* 92:26 Je 28 '87

Kromer, Lawrence F.

Nerve growth factor treatment after brain injury prevents neuronal death. bibl f il *Science* 235:214-16 Ja 9 '87

Kron, Joan

about

Hard to get. L. Fleischer. *Publ Wkly* 232:78 S 25 '87

Kronan (Ship)

Jewels from the Crown. L. Einarsson. il *Courier* 40:26-9 N '87

Kronberg (Germany)

Historic houses, sites, etc.

A Russian teahouse: memories of St. Petersburg in Germany [built in Russia and moved to Kronberg over a century ago] J. Rykwert. il *Archit Dig* 44:164-7 Je '87

Krone, Julie

about

Racing's reining queen. P. Axthelm. il por *Newsweek* 110:61 D 28 '87

A woman of substance. G. Maranto. il pors *Sports Illus* 67:62+ Ag 24 '87

Kronos Quartet
The Kronos Quartet. B. Wilcox. il *Down Beat* 54:55-7 Ap '87
Music. P. G. Davis. il *N Y* 20:86-7 S 21 '87
The new fab four. N. Tesser. il *Roll Stone* p16-17+ My 7 '87
The Zeitgeist Quartet. E. Rothstein. *New Repub* 197:29-31 O 5 '87

Kröpelin, S.
(jt. auth) See Pachur, H.-J., and Kröpelin, S.

Kropotkin, Igor
about
Obituary
Publ Wkly 231:13 Mr 20 '87

Krouse, Morton
about
Lobster lovers should thank Philly's Morty Krouse—he's singing for their supper. il por *People Wkly* 27:71 Je 1 '87

Kroy Inc.
The high cost of education. J. A. Conway. por *Forbes* 139:8 F 23 '87

Krueger, Anne
Love busters: mistakes that can wreck romance. il *McCalls* 114:65-6 Je '87
Pregnancy, PMS and menopause: no need to cramp your style. *Work Woman* 12:158+ Ap '87

Krueger (W. A.) Co. See W. A. Krueger Co.

Kruger, Barbara
about
Barbara Kruger: "You can look at Oliver North and listen to him speak and wonder how a nation doesn't know a sociopath when it sees one". L. A. Schreiber. il por *Vogue* 177:260+ O '87
Diversionary (syn)tactics. C. Squiers. il por *Art News* 86:76-85 F '87

Krüger, Karl-Heinz
The Japanese are coming (again). il *World Press Rev* 34:59 Ap '87

Kruger, Pamela
Nuclear psych-out. il *Progressive* 51:24-5 Je '87

Kruger, Valerie Fons- See Fons-Kruger, Valerie

Kruger, Verlen
about
The longest honeymoon. J. Mills. il pors map *Women's Sports Fitness* 9:80-4+ Mr '87

Krumholz, Phillip
Some scarce old safeties. il *Antiques Collect Hobbies* 91:40-3 Ja '87

Krumme, Richard
Across the editor's desk. See issues of Successful Farming

Krupat, Edward, and Kubzansky, Philip E.
Designing to deter crime. bibl (p62) il *Psychol Today* 21:58-61 O '87

Krupp, Charla
People. See issues of Glamour

Krupp family
about
And what of the Krupps? E. Giltenan. il *Forbes* 140:163 O 5 '87

Kruse, Käthe
about
Käthe Kruse: creator of the beloved classic. M. Jailer. il *Antiques Collect Hobbies* 92:36-8 Ap '87

Kruth, John
Notes from underground. il por *Progressive* 51:11 Ag '87

Kruuk, Hans
Outermost otters. il *Nat Hist* 96:34-41 Jl '87

Kryder, Mark H.
Data-storage technologies for advanced computing. il *Sci Am* 257:116-25 O '87

Krysiak, Gloria J.
Needs of gay students for acceptance and support. *Educ Dig* 53:44-7 D '87

Krystal, Arthur
How beautiful was Helen of Troy? What Homer never told us. il *N Y Times Book Rev* 92:3 Jl 12 '87
Ifs, ands, butts. il *Harpers* 274:63-7 Je '87

Kselman, John S.
The literary study of the Bible. *America* 157:297-9+ O 31 '87

KTWV (Los Angeles, Calif.: Radio station) See Radio stations

Ku Klux Klan
Bishops: joining KKK is sinful, violates teaching [Catholic bishops] *Jet* 72:29 Ap 20 '87
Black lawyer forces KKK to pay $7 million for lynching black, 19 [M. Figures work on the M. Donald case in Mobile, Ala.] T. S. Moore. il pors *Jet* 71:6-8 Mr 9 '87

Formed to terrorize the ex-slaves; Klan has a notorious past for blacks. *Jet* 71:8 Mr 9 '87
Going after the Klan [verdict in case brought by lynching victim M. Donald's family in Alabama] A. Press. il *Newsweek* 109:29 F 23 '87
Indianapolis principal axed after playing 'Klan' tune [case of D. A. Garrett] *Jet* 71:21 F 23 '87
Klan burns King photo, 1,000 react in Louisville. *Jet* 71:18 F 23 '87
Miss. councilman seeks aid after KKK threats [D. Jordan] il por *Jet* 71:6 Mr 23 '87
Mother of slain black son takes possession of KKK building won in lawsuit [mother of M. Donald] il por *Jet* 72:8 Je 8 '87
Saying no to the Klan [Rumford, Me.] M. M. Fortune. *Christ Century* 104:958-9 N 4 '87
Seeking justice for her lynched son, an Alabama mother ruins the Klan that killed him [B. M. Donald] J. S. Kunen. il pors *People Wkly* 27:55-6+ Je 8 '87
The woman who beat the Klan [B. M. Donald fights for justice for her lynched son] J. Kornbluth. il pors *N Y Times Mag* p26-32+ N 1 '87

Kubbig, Bernd W.
Will $$$$$ carry SDI forward? il *World Press Rev* 34:19-20 Mr '87

Kubrick, Stanley
about
Full metal jacket [film] Reviews
America 157:66 Ag 1-8 '87. R. A. Blake
Commonweal 114:457-8 Ag 14 '87. T. O'Brien
Macleans il por 100:55 Jl 6 '87. L. O'Toole
N Y il 20:54-5 Jl 13 '87. D. Denby
Nation 245:98-9 Ag 1-8 '87. T. Rafferty
Natl Rev 39:52-3 Ag 14 '87. J. Simon
New Repub 197:28-9 Jl 27 '87. S. Kauffmann
New Yorker 63:75-6 Jl 13 '87. P. Kael
Newsweek il 109:64-5 Je 29 '87. J. Kroll
People Wkly il 28:10 Jl 13 '87. R. Novak
Time il 129:66 Je 29 '87. R. Corliss
The Rolling stone interview: Stanley Kubrick. T. Cahill. il *Roll Stone* p29-32+ Ag 27 '87
Semper fi. R. Lacayo. il por *Film Comment* 23:11-14 S/O '87

Kubzansky, Philip E.
(jt. auth) See Krupat, Edward, and Kubzansky, Philip E.

Kucharski, David, and Hall, W. G.
New routes to early memories. bibl f il *Science* 238:786-8 N 6 '87

Kuchen See Coffee cake

Kuczynski, Pedro-Pablo
The outlook for Latin America debt. il *Foreign Aff* 66:129-49 Fall '87

Kuehnelt-Leddihn, Erik von
From the Continent. See occasional issues of National Review

Kuerten, Bruce
One-inch wonder: minimizing the visual shortcomings of video. il *Theatre Crafts* 21:103-5 My '87

Kugielski, Joseph
about
Photography guides Joseph Kugielsky along life's path. H. Chapnick. il por *Pop Photogr* 94:28 O '87

Kuhl, Christopher
The Spanish influence: a visual legacy [cover story] il *Horizon* 30:17-30+ D '87

Kuhn, Andreas
Bacteriophage M13 procoat protein inserts into the plasma membrane as a loop structure. bibl f il *Science* 238:1413-15 D 4 '87

Kuhn, Bowie
about
Bowie Kuhn: Campanis did blacks a favor. por *Jet* 72:46 Jl 27 '87

Kuhn, Irene Corbally
The place of the past: growing up in Greenwich Village. il *Gourmet* 47:78-80+ Ap '87

Kuiper Airborne Observatory See Airplanes in astronomy

Kuki, Atsuo, and Wolynes, Peter G.
Electron tunneling paths in proteins. bibl f il *Science* 236:1647-52 Je 26 '87

Kuklinski, Ryszard
about
From a U.S. mole: inside story of what might have been. R. Z. Chesnoff and D. Stanglin. il por *U S News World Rep* 102:32-3 Ap 20 '87

Kull, Frederick C., Jr., and others
Chemical identification of a tumor-derived angiogenic factor. bibl f il *Science* 236:843-5 My 15 '87

Kull, Steven
The game of perceptions in arms racing [with discussion] por *Cent Mag* 20:43-57 S/O '87
Kullberg, Duane R.
Accounting and accountability [address, May 6, 1987] *Vital Speeches Day* 53:606-8 Jl 15 '87
Kultur International Films Ltd.
A rock 'n' roller with a class act in videos [D. Hedlund] P. Finch. il por *Bus Week* p80 Je 8 '87
Kumagai Gumi Co. Ltd.
Share the profits, share the pain. A. Tanzer and M. Beauchamp. il *Forbes* 140:38+ N 30 '87
Kumasi (Ghana)
Housing
Where eight share one room. K. Adarkwa. il *World Health* p20-1 Jl '87
Kumbalek, Tom
And be merry [poem] *America* 156:129 F 14 '87
Kumble, Steven
about
Fall of a rainmaker. D. Fanning. il por *Forbes* 139:68+ Je 1 '87
Kume, Tadashi
about
Japan: hands on at Honda. F. H. Katayama. il por *Fortune* 116:88 N 9 '87
Kume, Yutaka
about
Creating a new culture. F. H. Katayama. il por *Fortune* 116:48 Ag 3 '87
Kumin, Maxine, 1925-
Creature comforts [story] il *Mademoiselle* 93:152+ Mr '87
Grappling in the central blue [poem] *Nation* 244:718 My 30 '87
Kümmel, H. (Hermann), 1922-
(jt. auth) See Bishop, Raymond F., and Kümmel, H. (Hermann), 1922-
Kümmel, Hermann *See* Kümmel, H. (Hermann), 1922-
Kummer, Corby
Cookies and wine. il *Atlantic* 259:71-3 Je '87
Designs for shopping. il *Atlantic* 259:84-5 My '87
Fast fish. il *Atlantic* 260:96-9 D '87
Fast puff pastry. il *Atlantic* 259:81-3 Ja '87
A stirring dish. il *Atlantic* 260:90-2 S '87
Kumquats
See also
Cooking—Fruit
Kuna Indians *See* Cuna Indians
Kundell, Linda
Carnegie's legacy restored. il *Travel Holiday* 167:30-2 Mr '87
Fine dining on the Hudson: the Culinary Institute of America. *Travel Holiday* 168:25+ O '87
Hotels as galleries. il *Travel Holiday* 167:56-61 Ja '87
Kunes, Ellen
Are you a leader or a follower? il *Seventeen* 46:144 Ap '87
Are you an honest woman? il *Seventeen* 46:91 Ja '87
The body vulnerable: how to strengthen your soft spots. il *Mademoiselle* 93:108 My '87
The inside story on your ovarian-cyst risk. il *Mademoiselle* 93:112 O '87
Safe sex 1987: how to make love this year. il *Mademoiselle* 93:106+ Ag '87
Were you born to be wild? il *Seventeen* 46:155 Mr '87
Küng, Hans, 1928-
about
Religions of the one God [interview] D. Toolan. *Commonweal* 114:143+ Mr 13 '87
The way forward: talking with Hans Küng [interview] D. Toolan. *Commonweal* 114:44-5 Ja 30 '87
Kunin, Claudia
Spring dreams: in pursuit of the idealized image. il *Petersens Photogr Mag* 16:40-2 My '87
Kunin, Madeleine
On political courage [excerpt from address] por *Ms* 16:84 N '87
Kunitz, Stanley, 1905-
The poet's quest for the father. il *N Y Times Book Rev* 92:1+ F 22 '87
Künkel, Reinhard, 1942-
Mystery, immensity and solitude [with photographs] il *Int Wildl* 17:44-51 Jl/Ag '87
Kunreuther, Howard
Environmental impairment liability insurance [discussion of January/February 1987 article, Gridlock in environmental insurance: the failure of EIL coverage] il *Environment* 29:2-3 My '87

Gridlock in environmental insurance: the failure of EIL coverage. bibl il *Environment* 29:18-20+ Ja/F '87
Kunsthistorisches Museum (Vienna, Austria)
A $124 million band-aid [financing package allows Kunsthistorisches Museum to install climate control equipment] F. Protzman. il *Art News* 86:39+ D '87
Dirty Dürers, empty coffers [fundraising efforts to purchase climate control system] F. Protzman. il *Art News* 86:58 S '87
Kuntz, Robert J.
Needed: a consistent, long-term policy governing technology. por *Aviat Week Space Technol* 126:155-6+ Ap 27 '87
Kunugi, Tatsuro
The strategy of humanitarian assistance. il *UN Chron* 24:54-5 My '87
Kuo, David
about
The drive to excel. A. Quindlen. il pors *N Y Times Mag* p32+ F 22 '87
Kuo family
about
When the Westinghouse Science Talent scouts dealt out their awards, they gave the Kuos a full house. M. Shaughnessy. il *People Wkly* 27:149-50 Je 8 '87
Kupersmith, Judith
about
The personal you: finding a balance. M. Horosko. il *Dance Mag* 61:52-5 Ag '87
Kuperstein, Michael, 1954-
about
Robots with a lot of nerve [cover story] I. Peterson. il *Sci News* 131:362-3 Je 6 '87
Kupfer, Fern
Surviving the seasons [fiction] il *Ladies Home J* 104:66+ Je '87
Kupferberg, Herbert
André Previn: recipient of the 1987 Mabel Mercer Award. il pors *Stereo Rev* 52:63-7 F '87
Kuppig, Christopher
Turning the tables on tours. por *Publ Wkly* 231:90 F 13 '87
Kuppin, Lawrence
about
High drama from the folks who brought you Godzilla '85. R. Grover. il pors *Bus Week* p30 S 7 '87
Kuralt, Charles, 1934-
The last brickmaker in America. il *Read Dig* 130:53-6 My '87
about
The arts, Sunday morning, and Charles Kuralt. M. Rhodes. il por *Horizon* 30:6 Je '87
Kuranda (Australia)
Description
"Crocodile" Dundee country. C. H. Crowley. il *Saturday Evening Post* 259:94 Mr '87
Kurbas, Les, 1887-1942
about
Les Kurbas, founder of Ukrainian theatre. N. Kornienko. il por *Courier* 40:32-3 O '87
Kurds
Kurds locked in one more losing war? [involvement in Iran-Iraq War] J. Barnes. il map *U S News World Rep* 103:55 N 9 '87
A remote but bitter war [Kurds vs. Turks] T. Jacoby. il map *Newsweek* 109:45 Mr 30 '87
Sons of devils. R. D. Kaplan. il *Atlantic* 260:38-41+ N '87
Kureishi, Hanif
The Buddha of suburbia [story] il *Harpers* 274:45-51 Je '87
'Sammy & Rosie' [excerpts from screenplay] il *Film Comment* 23:70-4+ S/O '87
about
Hanif Kureishi. M. Glicksman. por *Roll Stone* p33-4 N 19 '87
Kurland, Janet B., and Lipsitz, Gail E. J.
Rose finally unpacked her belongings. il *Aging* no355:6-9 '87
Kuromatsu (Firm)
The art of mingei at Kuromatsu. H. Junker. il por *Archit Dig* 44:98+ My '87
Kurón, Jacek
about
Gorbachev: the view from Warsaw [interview] H. Luczywo and N. Gardels. *Harpers* 275:26-7 Jl '87

Kurtág, György, 1926-
about
Musical events:
American premieres of works by Kurtág, Ruders and Birtwistle. A. Porter. *New Yorker* 62:96+ F 9 '87

Kurtz, Paul W., 1925-
about
Prometheus unbound. M. Berkley. il por *Publ Wkly* 231:32-4 Ja 16 '87

Kurtz, Swoosie
about
Swoosie [cover story] H. Haun. il pors *Horizon* 30:33-5 Je '87

Kuryluk, Ewa, 1946-
An interview with Irina Ratushinskaya. il por *N Y Rev Books* 34:16-20 My 7 '87

Kurys, Diane
about
Kurys makes her bed. M. Pally. il por *Film Comment* 23:84-6 S/O '87
A man in love [film] Reviews
Macleans 100:50 Ag 24 '87. L. O'Toole
N Y 20:54-5 Ag 10 '87. D. Denby

Kurzman, Dan
about
Twice poisoned. M. Isikoff. *Wash Mon* 19:49-50 D '87

Kurzweil, Allen
Dior: 40 years of triumph. il pors *Harpers Bazaar* 120:152+ S '87

Kurzweil, Raymond
about
Its master's voice. D. Lander. il por *Pop Mech* 164:69-71 O '87
Talk may be cheap, but Ray Kurzweil stands to make millions by yakking to his voice computer. L. Rozen. il pors *People Wkly* 27:113-14 Mr 9 '87

Kuschner, David
Don't fool with Mother Nature. por *Newsweek* 109:8 Je 8 '87

Kuscsik, Nina
Aging gracefully. il *Women's Sports Fitness* 9:16-21 O '87
For women only. il *Women's Sports Fitness* 9:70-1 F '87
How good runners can get close to great. il *Women's Sports Fitness* 9:62-3 Jl '87

Kushner, Harold S.
You've got to believe in something. *Redbook* 170:92-3+ D '87

Kusin, Vladimir V.
Reform and dissidence in Czechoslovakia. *Curr Hist* 86:361-4+ N '87

Kusnet, David
Labor-saving devices [cover story] il *Commonweal* 114:526-9 S 25 '87

Kuspit, Donald B. (Donald Burton), 1935-
Arnulf Rainer: self-exposures. bibl f il pors *Art Am* 75:170-9 Ap '87

Kusse, Ronald John
about
Profiles. C. P. Crow. *New Yorker* 63:34-8+ Je 22 '87

Kutchinsky, Berl
Deception and propaganda. *Society* 24:21-4 Jl/Ag '87

Kutenai Indians
The Salish-Kootenai comeback [environmental management of reservation lands] J. Bruggers. il *Sierra* 72:22-3+ Jl/Ag '87

Kuttner, Robert
A blueprint for affordable housing. il *Bus Week* p18 Ag 31 '87
The competitiveness craze [cover story] *New Repub* 197:22+ N 2 '87
The debate over new jobs is turning into mudslinging. il *Bus Week* p22 Ap 13 '87
Fat and sassy. *New Repub* 196:21-3 F 23 '87
Hoovernomics is no cure for Reaganomics. por *Bus Week* p22 N 23 '87
How the Fed can sway the fortunes of presidents. por *Bus Week* p26 D 21 '87
National health insurance: an idea whose time has come back. il *Bus Week* p14 Ag 3 '87
The patrimony society [cover story] *New Repub* 196:18-21 My 11 '87
The prospect for the summit: political gridlock. il *Bus Week* p22 Je 8 '87
Real-world trade policies are making a comeback. il *Bus Week* p18 Mr 16 '87
Selling higher taxes. *New Repub* 197:23-5 Ag 24 '87
Still more reasons to mistrust supply siders. por *Bus Week* p22 O 26 '87

There's no panacea for six years of bad policy. il *Bus Week* p28 My 11 '87
Third world debt: a flawed solution. il *Bus Week* p18 Ja 19 '87
The U.S. can't compete without a top-notch work force. il *Bus Week* p20 F 16 '87
The welfare strait. *New Repub* 197:20-1+ Jl 6 '87
Why Americans don't vote. *New Repub* 197:19-21 S 7 '87
Why business is at a loss in a free market. *Bus Week* p18 S 28 '87
Worker ownership: a commitment that's more often a con. il *Bus Week* p16 Jl 6 '87

Kutztown (Pa.)
Festivals
At the Kutztown Fair [with editorial comment by Sandra Wilmot] C. Berglie and A. M. Geffen. il map *Americana* 15:2, 33-7 Jl/Ag '87

Kutztown Folk Festival *See* Kutztown (Pa.)—Festivals

Kuwait
See also
Espionage, American—Kuwait
Foreign relations
Kuwait rolls the dice for high stakes. J. Barnes. il *U S News World Rep* 103:30 Ag 3 '87
United States
See United States—Foreign relations—Kuwait
Politics and government
Kuwait: between Iraq and a hard place. il *Time* 130:26 Ag 3 '87

Kuwait Petroleum Corporation
Dealmaker for a dynasty [A. K. Al-Sabah] S. Tully. por *Fortune* 116:64 Ag 3 '87

Kuznetsov, Stephen B.
Energy technology in the 21st century. il *Radio-Electron* 58:107-11 My '87

Kveck, Albert
about
Little big top. J. Colihan. il *Am Herit* 38:42-7 D '87

Kvennalistinn (Political party) *See* Political parties—Iceland

Kwangtung Province (China) *See* Guangdong Province (China)

Kwanzaa
The holiday spirit. S. L. Taylor. il *Essence* 18:47 D '87

Kwikscan reading system
In the beginning was the word. W. G. Flanagan. il por *Forbes* 139:100-1 Ap 20 '87
New reading system promises to increase data retention [Kwikscan New Testament] J. P. Frank. il *Publ Wkly* 232:64-5 O 16 '87

Kwitny, Jonathan
Money, drugs and the contras [cover story] il *Nation* 245:145+ Ag 29 '87
Of drugs, money and contras [discussion of August 29, 1987 article, Money, drugs and the contras] *Nation* 245:254+ S 19 '87

Kyle, Cynthia, and Walker, Lou Ann
Inspiring story ideas: a baker's dozen. *Writer* 100:5-6 N '87

Kyle, Robert C.
about
Trading places. M. Schifrin. il por *Forbes* 139:56-7 Je 29 '87

Kylián, Jiří
about
L'enfant et les sortilèges [dance] Reviews
Dance Mag 61:66-7 S '87. J. Gruen
Kylián changes keys. L. Moffett. il por *Dance Mag* 61:46-50 My '87
Reviews:
Performances at Circustheater in the Netherlands. H. Klooss. *Dance Mag* 61:70-2 Jl '87
Six dances [dance] Reviews
New Leader 70:22 Jl 13-27 '87. L. A. Jacobs

Kyocera Corporation
A cautionary tale [LaPine Technology's joint venture with Kyocera] K. K. Wiegner. il por *Forbes* 140:52-3 Ag 10 '87
Japan's newest perk: the corporate tomb. *Newsweek* 109:55 Mr 2 '87

Kyŏngju (Korea)
Antiquities
A lost dynasty revealed. G. Hesse. il *Travel Holiday* 167:24-7 Ja '87

Kyoto (Japan)
Description
Shops, temples, stairstep streets, tranquil paths . . . a walk in Kyoto's Higashiyama area. il map *Sunset* 178:80+ My '87

Kyoto (Japan)—*cont.*

Galleries and museums
See also
National Museum of Modern Art (Kyoto, Japan)

Kyte, Jim
about
A true Jet fighter. B. Newman. il pors *Sports Illus* 67:108-12 O 12 '87

KYW (Philadelphia, Pa.: Television station) *See* Television stations

L

L-5 Society
See also
National Space Society (U.S.)

L.A. law [television program] *See* Television program reviews—Single works

L. B. Foster Co.
Thank you, Kohlberg Kravis [L. B. Foster Co.'s experiences after leveraged buyout] J. Clements. il *Forbes* 140:38+ N 2 '87

L.F. Rothschild Holdings Inc.
L.F. Rothschild [interview with W. Lippman] il por *Fortune* 116 Sp Issue:184-5 Fall '87
The young turks making over L.F. Rothschild. C. Farrell. il pors *Bus Week* p58-9 Ag 31 '87

L-form substances
The significances of form. B. T. Hunter. il *Consum Res Mag* 70:8-9 Je '87

L. L. Bean, Inc.
L.L. Bean vs. the preppified pooch [artist W. Spitzmiller's suit against L. L. Bean's doctoring of hunting scene on catalog cover] il por *Newsweek* 109:53 Mr 16 '87

L. L. Cool J
about
The Cool life. M. Coleman. il por *Roll Stone* p16 O 8 '87
Rapper L.L. Cool J charged with lewdness on Ga. stage. por *Jet* 72:53 Jl 13 '87

L.M. Ericsson Telephone Co.
The Swedes give AT&T, and the U.S., painful black eyes [L. M. Ericsson captures piece of Compagnie Générale de Constructions Téléphoniques] T. Peterson and F. J. Comes. il *Bus Week* p44-5 My 4 '87

L.W. Anderson Genealogical Library
Making a place for finding the past. D. Young. il *South Living* 22:78 Ja '87

La Crosse virus *See* Bunyaviruses

La Farge, John, 1835-1910
about
First 'a marvel,' then out of fashion, a fine artist returns [cover story] H. Adams. bibl (p146) il *Smithsonian* 18:46-59 Jl '87
The watercolors of John La Farge. B. D. Gallati. bibl f il *Antiques* 132:1290-301 D '87

La Jolla (San Diego, Calif.)
Theater
See also
La Jolla Playhouse

La Jolla Playhouse
La Jolla Playhouse. A. M. Hale. il *Theatre Crafts* 21:25-31+ O '87

La Navidad (Haiti)
Searching for Columbus's lost colony. K. A. Deagan. il *Natl Geogr* 172:672-5 N '87

La Noue, Terence, 1941-
about
Terence La Noue at Emmerich. E. Heartney. il *Art Am* 75:219-20 Ap '87

La Porte (Tex.)
Architecture
The past lives at the bay [home overlooking Galveston Bay] il *South Living* 22:114-15 Je '87

La Rioja (Spain)
Description and travel
Gourmet holidays: La Rioja. P. T. Mitchell. il map *Gourmet* 47:74-9+ N '87

La Rosa, Julius
about
Profiles. W. Balliett. por *New Yorker* 63:57-8+ S 28 '87

La Rosa, Suzanne
(jt. auth) *See* Hillhouse, Ruth, and La Rosa, Suzanne

La Salle, Réné Robert Cavelier *See* La Salle, Robert Cavelier, sieur de, 1643-1687

La Salle, Robert Cavelier, sieur de, 1643-1687
about
1687. il *Am Herit* 38:108 F/Mr '87

La Salle, Roch
about
Questions about a firing. D. Burke. por *Macleans* 100:11-12 Ja 19 '87
A Tory veteran bows out. H. Mackenzie and M. Janigan. il pors *Macleans* 100:11 Mr 2 '87
Uproar over a firing. A. Wilson-Smith. por *Macleans* 100:16 Ja 26 '87

La Scala Ballet
La Scala's Patricia Neary: this lady is a champ. G. Parks. il pors *Dance Mag* 61:64-5 Ja '87

La Scala Opera *See* Opera—Italy

La Trobe-Bateman, Richard
World-class turner. il *Am Craft* 47:30-5 D '87/Ja '88

La Villita Tortillas (Firm)
A place for fresh tortillas. il *South Living* 22:32 Je '87

La VO, Carl
A Housatonic holiday. il *Travel Holiday* 168:30+ S '87
Pennsylvania's own Star of Bethlehem. *Travel Holiday* 168:14-15 D '87

Lab, Steven P., and Hirschel, J. David
Predicting crime from the weather. il pors *Futurist* 21:30-2 Mr/Ap '87

LaBastille, Anne
Adirondacks underwater [with photographs] il por *Conservationist* 42:12-15 Jl/Ag '87

LaBate, Jim
Mass production doesn't always work. por *U S News World Rep* 103:5 S 14 '87

Labatt (John) Limited *See* John Labatt Limited

LaBeef, Sleepy
about
Sleepy LaBeef. B. Beuttler. por *Down Beat* 54:14 O '87

Labels
See also
Avery International Corporation

Laber, Jeri
The Moscow Book Fair: *glasnost* has its limits. il *N Y Times Book Rev* 92:13-14 O 11 '87

Labianca, Dominick A.
Carbon monoxide: stealthy environmental pollutant. il *USA Today (Periodical)* 116:44-6 N '87

Labianca, Dominick A., and Reeves, William J.
The need for science in a core curriculum. il *USA Today (Periodical)* 115:74-6 Mr '87

Labino, Dominick, 1910-1987
about
Obituary
Am Craft il por 47:40-1 Ap/My '87. S. K. Frantz

LaBonté, C. Joseph
about
Reebok's recent blisters seem to be healing. L. Helm. il por *Bus Week* p62 Ag 3 '87

Labor
See also
Church and labor
Employment
Home labor
Hours of labor
Job satisfaction
Socialism
Strikes
Trade unions
Unemployment
Work
Labor month in review. See issues of Monthly Labor Review
The next wave [feminism and working class women] B. Ehrenreich. il *Ms* 16:166-8+ Jl/Ag '87
Attitudes
How union members and nonmembers view the role of unions. C. Keegan. *Mon Labor Rev* 110:50-1 Ag '87
Education
See also
Retraining, Occupational
Back to the basics [business and literacy] J. B. Copeland. il *Newsweek* 110:54-5 S 21 '87
'Kindness and reason': William Lovett and education [Victorian England] B. H. Harrison. bibl il por *Hist Today* 37:14-22 Mr '87
Health and hygiene
See Occupational health and safety
Periodicals
See also
Monthly labor review

Labor—*cont.*

Psychology

See Psychology, Industrial

Statistics

See also

United States. Bureau of Labor Statistics
Current labor statistics. See issues of Monthly Labor
Review

East Asia

Asia's workers are restless. M. Lord. il *U S News World
Rep* 103:51-2 S 14 '87

Labor (Obstetrics) *See* Childbirth

Labor absenteeism *See* Absenteeism

Labor agreements *See* Collective labor agreements

Labor and Human Resources Committee *See* United States.
Congress. Senate. Committee on Labor and Human
Resources

Labor and the church *See* Church and labor

Labor camps *See* Concentration camps

Labor contracts

See also

Collective labor agreements
Your new employment contract. W. Kiechel, III. il
Fortune 116:109-10 Jl 6 '87

Labor costs

See also

Automobiles—Costs
Collective labor agreements
Analyzing employers' costs for wages, salaries, and
benefits. F. Nathan. bibl f il *Mon Labor Rev* 110:3-11
O '87
Cutting costs without cutting people [cover story] B.
Saporito. il *Fortune* 115:26-32 My 25 '87
Taming the cost of the "hidden factory". H. Banks.
il *Forbes* 140:27-8 S 21 '87

International aspects

Globalization and the worldwide division of labor. H.
Shaiken. *Mon Labor Rev* 110:47 Ag '87
Why lost U.S. jobs are headed abroad. D. O. Relin.
il *Sch Update* 119:8 Ja 26 '87

Labor Day

Black serves as marshall of N.Y. Labor Day Parade
[P. J. Ottley] *Jet* 72:55 S 21 '87

Labor Dept. (U.S.) *See* United States. Dept. of Labor

Labor discipline

How to deal with bizarre employee behavior. M. Brooks.
Work Woman 12:15+ Ag '87

Labor disputes

See also

Collective bargaining
Strikes
United States. National Labor Relations Board

Labor force *See* Labor supply

Labor in advertising

Love a dodo bird [glorifying the blue collar laborer]
S. Blotnick. il *Forbes* 139:269 Je 15 '87

Labor in politics *See* Trade unions—Political activities

Labor incentives *See* Incentives in industry

Labor journalism *See* Journalism, Labor

Labor laws and regulations

See also

Boycott
Factories—Shutdowns—Laws and regulations
Hours of labor
Insurance, Workers' compensation
Minimum wage
Occupational health and safety—Laws and regulations
Picketing
United States. Congress. Senate. Committee on Labor
and Human Resources
United States. Dept. of Labor
Back to work [TWA ordered to reinstate former strikers
from the ranks of Independent Federation of Flight
Attendants] D. Bensman. *Nation* 244:875 Je 27 '87
Blocking labor's agenda. il *Nations Bus* 75:16 Ag '87
Corporate angst on Capitol Hill [opposition to pro-labor
bills by business lobby] G. Bock. il *Time* 129:48 Je
22 '87
Employers under pressure. R. R. Roha. *Changing Times*
41:84-5 Jl '87
Happy days may be here again for labor legislation.
S. B. Garland. *Bus Week* p57 Je 22 '87
Hidden taxes. J. Novack. il *Forbes* 140:36-7 S 21 '87
Industrial homework and sweatshops [address, July 20,
1987] J. Mazur. *Vital Speeches Day* 53:701-2 S 1
'87
Is "homework" the answer? J. Walsh. il *Ms* 16:124-5+
Jl/Ag '87
Labor's long winter may be coming to an end. M.
E. Recio and others. il *Bus Week* p140+ F 23 '87
Labor's looming agenda. il *Nations Bus* 75:12 N '87

Let's sock it to the women again [home labor] C. Kocol.
il *Humanist* 47:35 N/D '87
"A new era" looks like an old one. il *Nations Bus*
75:95 My '87
State labor legislation enacted in 1986. R. R. Nelson.
Mon Labor Rev 110:49-66 Ja '87
What labor's agenda could cost you. R. Thompson.
il *Nations Bus* 75:28+ My '87

British Columbia

B.C.'s low-key day of protest [general strike] J. O'Hara.
il *Macleans* 100:20-1 Je 15 '87
B.C.'s new labor wars. J. O'Hara. *Macleans* 100:18 My
11 '87

California

A lawsuit could ruin the Farmworkers' Union [damages
for violence in a 1979 strike] J. Flynn. il *Bus Week*
p42 Mr 23 '87

Canada

A strike against labor [Supreme Court of Canada's rulings
hurt labor's right to strike and bargain collectively]
il *Macleans* 100:15 Ap 20 '87

New York (State)

New York State acts to reduce plant closings. *Mon
Labor Rev* 110:39 F '87

Ontario

Legislating fair wages [controversial new pay equity
legislation] A. Walmsley. il *Macleans* 100:31-2 Jl 20
'87

Québec (Province)

Showdown in Quebec [police raids on the Confederation
of National Trade Unions] M. Rose. il *Macleans* 100:12
Je 29 '87

South Africa

Commandments without Moses [L. Sullivan, author of
Sullivan principles, demands withdrawal of U.S. firms]
W. E. Smith. il por *Time* 129:34 Je 15 '87
Pull out of S. Africa in 9 months, Sullivan urges. por
Jet 72:4 Je 22 '87
South Africa: why Leon Sullivan gave up his 'principles'.
R. A. Manning. il por *U S News World Rep* 102:10-11
Je 15 '87
'Sullivan principles' deadline draws near. por *Jet* 71:14
Ja 12 '87
Sullivan says divest [Rev. L. Sullivan] F. D. Brown
and D. C. Ruffin. il por *Black Enterp* 18:17 Ag '87
Sullivan's principles [call for disinvestment] L. Waldorf.
New Repub 197:14-16 S 7 '87

United States

See Labor laws and regulations

Wisconsin

Wisconsin boys ranch says no to hiring homosexuals
[Rawhide Boys Ranch] W. North. il *Christ Today*
31:48 Mr 6 '87

Labor leaders *See* Trade unions—Officials

Labor-management cooperation *See* Participative management

Labor-management relations *See* Industrial relations

Labor market *See* Labor supply

Labor mobility

See also

Executives—Relocation
Labor turnover
Occupational mobility
4-step plan to land a job long distance. M. M. Kennedy.
il *Glamour* 85:158+ O '87
America's new migrant workers. D. Pauly. il *Newsweek*
110:34-5 Ag 3 '87

Labor movement *See* Trade unions—History

Labor officials *See* Trade unions—Officials

Labor Party (Great Britain) *See* Labour Party (Great Britain)

Labor productivity *See* Productivity, Industrial

Labor relations *See* Industrial relations

Labor statistics *See* Employment—Statistics; Labor—
Statistics; Unemployment—Statistics

Labor Statistics Bureau (U.S.) *See* United States. Bureau
of Labor Statistics

Labor supply

See also

Aged—Employment
Alien labor
Asian Americans—Employment
Blacks—Employment
Children—Employment
College graduates—Employment
Contingent workers
Convict labor
Farm labor
Handicapped—Employment
Indentured servants
Labor mobility
Married women—Employment

Labor supply—See also—*cont.*
   Migrant labor
   Minorities—Employment
   Part time employment
   Single mothers—Employment
   Skilled labor
   Slavery
   Temporary employment
   Veterans—Employment
   White collar workers
   Widows—Employment
   Women—Employment
   Women college graduates—Employment
   Youth—Employment
An aging work force puts a drag on the economy . . . and has a hand in squelching big wage gains. G. Koretz. il *Bus Week* p17 Jl 27 '87
Behind the help-wanted signs [coexistence of labor shortages and high unemployment rates] G. J. Church. il *Time* 130:55 Jl 20 '87
The great jobs mismatch [need for skilled labor and rise in unskilled workers] R. J. Shapiro. il *U S News World Rep* 103:42-3 S 7 '87
The growth and composition of the U.S. labor force. V. M. Briggs. bibl f il *Science* 238:176-80 O 9 '87
Help wanted [cover story] A. Bernstein. il *Bus Week* p48-53 Ag 10 '87
Jobs without people and people without jobs: the coming mismatch in the information society. W. H. Kolberg. il *USA Today (Periodical)* 116:18-20 Jl '87
The labor force grows, but so do jobs. W. B. Franklin and J. C. Cooper. il *Bus Week* p39-40 Je 22 '87
Labor force projections: 1986 to 2000. H. N. Fullerton, Jr. bibl f il *Mon Labor Rev* 110:19-29 S '87
Revisions of state and local area labor force statistics. V. K. Laedlein. il *Mon Labor Rev* 110:38-41 Jl '87
The state of the workforce [address, October 6, 1987] W. E. Brock. *Vital Speeches Day* 54:37-40 N 1 '87
Where the jobs are [U.S.; special section] il *Newsweek* 109:42-8 F 2 '87
Your next boss may be Japanese. B. Powell. il *Read Dig* 130:141-4 Je '87

Mexico
The Far East goes south [Japanese factories] J. Contreras. il *Newsweek* 109:46 Je 22 '87
Going south to cut costs [U.S. firms in Mexico] H. Eason. il *Nations Bus* 75:24 F '87
How to mix sake and tequila [Japanese investment] K. K. Wiegner. il *Forbes* 139:48+ Mr 23 '87
Made in U.S.A./Mexico: a new industrial partnership. E. C. Conkling. map *Focus* 36:32-3 Wint '86
The rise of gringo capitalism [U.S. companies in the border zones] J. B. Copeland. il *Newsweek* 109:40-1 Ja 5 '87
Tokyo opens a southern trade route [Japanese factories] S. L. Hawkins. il map *U S News World Rep* 103:40+ Ag 3 '87
Yankee! Welcome to Mexico! J. Castro. il *Time* 129:51 Je 1 '87

United States
See Labor supply
Labor turnover
   See also
   Executives—Resignation
Five great ways to fight employee turnover. *Work Woman* 12:23 Je '87
Just-in-time people. S. Blotnick. il *Forbes* 140:109-10+ Jl 13 '87
Labor unions *See* Trade unions
Laboratories
   See also
   AT&T Bell Labs
   David Sarnoff Research Center
   European Molecular Biology Laboratory
   Kearfott Laboratories
   Medical laboratories
   Nuclear research laboratories
   Ortho Research Center
   Photographic laboratories
   Reading laboratories

Architecture
Looking forward [research facilities] G. Anderson. il *Archit Rec* 175:89-103 Jl '87
Minds over matter [Vollum Institute for Advanced Biomedical Research] D. Brenner. il *Archit Rec* 175:102-11 S '87

Equipment
Laboratory furniture and hardware. *Science* 235 pt2:G125 F 27 '87

Laboratories, Government
   See also
   Air Force Flight Dynamics Laboratory (U.S.)
   Argonne National Laboratory
   Brookhaven National Laboratory
   Los Alamos Scientific Laboratory
   Sandia National Laboratories
Laboratory animals
   See also
   Animal experimentation
   Chimpanzees
   Diseases—Animal models
   Frogs
Laboratory method
   See also
   Robots—Laboratory use
Laboratory workers, Medical *See* Health workers
Laborers' International Union of North America
A union in bondage to the mob. E. H. Methvin. *Read Dig* 131:171-5 N '87
Labouisse, Henry R., 1904-1987
   about
Obituary
   New Repub 196:43 Ap 27 '87. M. Peretz
Labour Party (Great Britain)
Beat the devil [Thatcher election victory] A. Cockburn. *Nation* 244:876-7 Je 27 '87
Britain's opposition regroups. N. Gelb. il por *New Leader* 70:6-7 S 7 '87
Demythologising Nye Bevan. J. Campbell. bibl il pors *Hist Today* 37:13-18 Ap '87
If Labour wins. W. B. Messmer. *Foreign Policy* 67:137-53 Summ '87
Kinnock on the defensive. N. Gelb. il *New Leader* 70:8-9 Mr 23 '87
Labor's defense [interview with N. Kinnock] J. Lloyd and P. Kellner. *World Press Rev* 34:15-16 My '87
A Labour Britain, NATO and the bomb. D. Healey. *Foreign Aff* 65:716-29 Spr '87
Neil in the 'lion's den' [N. Kinnock's U.S. visit] M. White. il *World Press Rev* 34:13-14 My '87
Thatcher's third term target. N. Gelb. il *New Leader* 70:6-7 Je 29 '87
Thunder over Britain. W. F. Buckley. *Natl Rev* 39:62-3 Ap 24 '87
The two Britains [election results] *Nation* 244:873-4 Je 27 '87
Writing our own history [contribution of H. Dalton's political diary and others to British post-war history] T. Benn. il pors *Hist Today* 37:9-12 Ap '87
Labra, Carlos Fernando Flores *See* Flores Labra, Carlos Fernando
Labrador (Nfld.)
   See also
   Hunting—Labrador (Nfld.)
Labrador retrievers *See* Retrievers
Labrecque, Thomas G., 1938-
A radical approach to banking reform [address, February 12, 1987] *Vital Speeches Day* 53:354-7 Ap 1 '87
Labrunie, Gérard *See* Nerval, Gérard de, 1808-1855
Labyrinth (Ear)
Developmental stability of the tonotopic organization of the chick's basilar papilla. G. A. Manley and others. bibl f il *Science* 237:655-6 Ag 7 '87
Inner ears and outer space [work of M. D. Ross on utricular macula cell morphology] R. Spangenburg and D. Moser. il por *Space World* X-9-285:17-20 S '87
Labyrinths

Great Britain
   See also
   Minotaur Designs (Firm)
Giant mazes. il *Natl Geogr World* 145:26-32 S '87
It is easy to get bushed when you're threading a maze. R. Wolkomir. il *Smithsonian* 18:108-12+ D '87

Japan
'You have to remember: mazes in Japan are not like mazes in England'. C. Simons. il *Smithsonian* 18:114 D '87
Lacal, Juan Carlos, and others
Rapid stimulation of diacylglycerol production in Xenopus oocytes by microinjection of H-*ras* p21. bibl f il *Science* 238:533-6 O 23 '87
Lacayo, Richard
Semper fi. il por *Film Comment* 23:11-14 S/O '87
Lacefield, Patrick
Swaggart swings through El Salvador. il por *Commonweal* 114:279-80+ My 8 '87
Time out or time's up. *Commonweal* 114:375-7 Je 19 '87

Lacey, Hugh
Domination in Latin America. *Cent Mag* 20:60-1 Mr/Ap '87

Lachenbruch, David
Video news. See issues of Radio-Electronics

LaCombe, Pierre
about
Brigadoon. T. M. Disch. il *Omni* 9:74-7 S '87

Lacquer and lacquering
When only the best will do [L. Maxym's imports of handpainted Russian lacquer boxes] R. Hotch. il por *Nations Bus* 75:78+ My '87

Lacroix, Christian
about
Christian Lacroix. il por *People Wkly* 28:50-1 D 28 '87-Ja 4 '88
Christian LaCroix genius of couture. il por *Harpers Bazaar* 120:162 Mr '87
Dancing on the lip of the volcano: Christian Lacroix's crash chic [cover story] J. Baumgold. il pors *N Y* 20:36-49 N 30 '87
Oh la la, Lacroix. J. Conant. il por *Newsweek* 110:60-1 N 9 '87
Ooh la la, Lacroix. il *Life* 10:92-3 S '87
The swagger of Christian Lacroix. C. Donovan. il pors *N Y Times Mag* p22-5+ S 6 '87
Welcome to the fresh follies. M. Duffy. il por *Time* 129:76-7 F 9 '87

Lacrosse, College
Oh brother, here comes Carolina [J. and G. Seivold] D. Brantley. il pors *Sports Illus* 66:69-70 My 4 '87
With a name like Wynne . . . [W. Haemisegger, female player on men's team at Southwestern University] S. Shuger. il *Women's Sports Fitness* 9:21 Ap '87

Lacrosse, Indoor (Professional) *See* Lacrosse, Professional
Lacrosse, Professional
Thunder on the Beltway [Eagle League: indoor box lacrosse] F. Lidz. il *Sports Illus* 66:56-7 Mr 30 '87

Lactamases
Bacterial resistance to β-lactam antibiotics: crystal structure of β-lactamase from Staphylococcus aureus PC1 at 2.5 Å resolution. O. Herzberg and J. Moult. bibl f il *Science* 236:694-701 My 8 '87

Lactation
See also
Suckling

Lactic acid
Lactic acid [substance responsible for burning sensations during exercise] J. Widman. il *Women's Sports Fitness* 9:19 N '87

Lactoglobulin *See* Globulins
Lactones
A stereospecific cyclization catalyzed by an antibody. A. D. Napper and others. bibl f il *Science* 237:1041-3 Ag 28 '87

Lactose intolerance
The lactose dilemma. C. Brining. il *Saturday Evening Post* 259:66-8 S '87

Lacy, Allen, 1935-
Gardening. il *N Y Times Book Rev* 92:14 My 31 '87
Gardening. il *N Y Times Book Rev* 92:32+ D 6 '87

Lacy, Steve
about
Steve Lacy [interview] K. Whitehead. il pors *Down Beat* 54:24-6+ D '87
Steve Lacy's solo on Skippy—a soprano saxophone transcription. S. Griggs. il *Down Beat* 54:60-2 D '87
Up a Lacy river [discography] P. Kostakis. il por *Down Beat* 54:30 My '87

Ladakh
Tibetan society bridges the future [H. Norberg-Ladakh Project] T. L. Barnett. il por *Progressive* 51:15 Ap '87
Native peoples
A beast for all seasons [yaks; photographs] B. Alexander. il map *Int Wildl* 17:44-51 My/Je '87

Ladd, Diane
about
Laura Dern & Diane Ladd. pors *Teen* 31:48 D '87

Ladd, Everett Carll
Secular and religious America. *Society* 24:63-8 Mr/Ap '87

Ladda, Justen
about
Justen Ladda at MOMA. H. Cotter. il *Art Am* 75:181-2 My '87

Ladders
Folding ladders. il *Consum Rep* 52:8-10 Ja '87
Folding ladders. il *Consum Rep* 52:231-4 D '87
Ladders: the fourth tool. D. Prestly. il *Fam Handyman* 37:50+ D '87

LADE *See* Lineas Aereas del Estado (Argentina)
Ladeco (Firm)
Chile's Ladeco using U.S. route experience as basis for expansion. il *Aviat Week Space Technol* 127:59+ Ag 31 '87

Ladies' home journal
Editor's journal. M. Blyth. See issues of Ladies' Home Journal

Ladies' rooms *See* Public comfort stations
Ladies Touring Players Association
Scuffle in the alleys. il *Women's Sports Fitness* 9:52 Je '87

Ladner, Catherine
about
Harvey, Ill., woman sues township for $900,000. *Jet* 72:8 S 7 '87

Ladner, Joyce A.
A new way to love. por *Essence* 18:140 D '87

Ladner, Richard
about
Superintendent found guilty of slander for teacher recommendation. T. J. Flygare. il *Phi Delta Kappan* 68:629-30 Ap '87

Lady and the Tramp [film] See Motion picture reviews—Single works
Lady, be good! [musical] See Musicals, revues, etc.—Reviews—Single works
Lady Day at Emerson's Bar & Grill [drama] See Robertson, Lanie
Ladybird Books Ltd.
Updated Beatrix Potter brews a storm in Britain. J. Taylor. il *Publ Wkly* 232:26 O 30 '87

Lady's slipper
Orchids indoors? il *Sunset* 178:182 F '87

Ladysmith Black Mambazo (Musical group)
Singing to the rhythm of dreams. J. Cocks. il por *Time* 130:37 Ag 10 '87

LaFalce, John J.
The third world debt crisis [address, October 29, 1986] *Vital Speeches Day* 53:162-6 Ja 1 '87

Lafayette, Gilbert de
about
Lafayette lives on as the Marquis' descendant wigs out for royalties. il por *People Wkly* 27:101 My 11 '87

Lafayette, Marie Adrienne de Noailles, marquise de, 1759-1807
about
American efforts to free Madame de Lafayette. A. L. Levin. il *Am Hist Illus* 22:22-3 O '87

Lafayette, Marie Joseph Paul Yves Roch Gilbert du Motier, marquis de, 1757-1834
about
An American's attempt to rescue Lafayette [cover story] A. L. Levin. il por *Am Hist Illus* 22:16-20+ O '87
Collectibles
America's thank you for the Statue of Liberty [Lafayette dollar] E. Rochette. il *Antiques Collect Hobbies* 92:81-2 My '87

Lafayette (New York, N.Y.: Restaurant) *See* New York (N.Y.)—Restaurants, nightclubs, bars, etc.

Lafferty, Don
about
Checker king 'Two-Ton' Tinsley jumps for joy—and victory. A. Richman. il pors *People Wkly* 28:53+ S 7 '87

LaForge, Ann E.
Monday morning at the movies. il *Work Woman* 12:50+ Je '87

Lagoon (Nebula) *See* Nebulae
Lague, Louise
How to live with a moody man. il *Glamour* 85:74+ Jl '87

Laguna Art Museum
A constant vision. K. Milam. il *Horizon* 30:55 Ja/F '87

LaHaye, Beverly
about
Powerhouse of the religious right? K. A. Lawton. il por *Christ Today* 31:34-6 N 6 '87
Watch on the right. C. Paige. por *Ms* 15:24-8 F '87

Lahr, John, 1941-
about
Love and death. D. Kaufman. il pors *Horizon* 30:38-40 My '87

Laidlaw Capital Management Inc.
This early bear is catching worms [views of W. L. Twiste] G. G. Marcial. *Bus Week* p118 N 23 '87

Laissez faire See Free enterprise

Laity

Catholic Church

See also

　Pallottine Institute for Lay Leadership and Apostolate Research

The American laity: memory, meaning and mission [adaptation of address, September 1986] D. J. O'Brien. *America* 156:189-93 Mr 7 '87

Called to broaden my horizon. J. Scheible. *Commonweal* 114:523-5 S 25 '87

Contemplation exploded in my heart. M. Mitcham. il *Commonweal* 114:474-6 S 11 '87

Counsels for the baptized. H. Brown. *Commonweal* 114:558-61 O 9 '87

God isn't finished with me yet. R. Brickley. *Commonweal* 114:410-11 Jl 17 '87

I can no longer remain a bystander. R. M. Hart. il *Commonweal* 114:556-7 O 9 '87

Lay ministers won't put priests out of business. W. F. Sullivan. *U S Cathol* 52:22-3 N '87

A letter from Rome: on the Synod of Bishops. P. R. Divarkar. *America* 157:349-50 N 14 '87

Long live the laity. H. Fehren. *U S Cathol* 52:38-40 Ap '87

Of many things [video entitled March 25: a day in the life of Catholic laity in America to be shown to the Pope] J. W. Donohue. *America* 157:122 S 12-19 '87

Prayer & the pursuit of public virtue. F. J. Macchiarola. *Commonweal* 114:440-2 Ag 14 '87

Roman holiday [synod on the laity] *Commonweal* 114:692-3 D 4 '87

Stop patting us laypeople on the head [with readers' comments] M. Finley. *U S Cathol* 52:13-19 Jl '87

Strong support for dialogue [conference entitled Faith and culture: historic moment for American Catholic laity?] *America* 156:186-7 Mr 7 '87

Vocations and the laicization of religious life. A. DiIanni. *America* 156:207-11 Mr 14 '87

What we have heard and what we will say [1987 World Synod of Bishops on The vocation and mission of the laity] J. L. May and others. *America* 157:102-4 Ag 29-S 5 '87

Why Catholics stay in the Church [cover story] A. M. Greeley. il *America* 157:54-7+ Ag 1-8 '87

Lajer-Burcharth, Ewa

Urban disturbances. bibl f il *Art Am* 75:146-53+ N '87

Lake, Carlton

Ed the collector, Jake the dentist and Beckett: a tale that ends in Texas. il *N Y Times Book Rev* 92:2 S 6 '87

Lake, George Byram

Nothing left to steal. *Natl Rev* 39:40-1 Jl 3 '87

Lake Awosting (N.Y.)

A man ahead of his time [60 years of records kept by D. Smiley] M. Winerip. il por *Natl Wildl* 25:10 F/Mr '87

Lake Baikal (Soviet Union)

Lake Baikal. il *Courier* 40:30-1 O '87

Scientist Vladimir Fialkov focuses on the future of a unique natural wonder: crystalline Lake Baikal. S. K. Reed. il pors *People Wkly* 27:121+ Ap 6 '87

Lake Cisó (Spain)

Red pond [evidence for L. Margulis' theory of evolution by symbiosis] B. Lawren. il *Omni* 9:20 Ja '87

Lake District (England)

Description and travel

Beatrix Potter country. E. Minton. il *Travel Holiday* 168:28-30 D '87

Lake ecology See Fresh water ecology

Lake fishing See Fishing

Lake Forest (Ill.)

Blacks

Mr. T chops down trees on his property; angers his neighbors in suburb. por *Jet* 72:57 Je 8 '87

Mr. T suffers backlash after tree-cutting spree. il por *Jet* 72:54 Je 15 '87

Suburb plans to legally axe Mr. T.'s tree-chopping. por *Jet* 72:33 Je 22 '87

Lake Geneva (Wis.)

Restaurants, nightclubs, bars, etc.

In Wisconsin: lip sync live, onstage tonight [contest at City Slickers] R. Conniff. il *Time* 130:10+ D 14 '87

Lake George (N.Y.)

Save the queen! C. C. Morrison. il *Conservationist* 42:6-11 Jl/Ag '87

See no evil [EPA approval of Sonar herbicide based on incomplete data] T. Turner. *Mother Earth News* 106:114-15 Jl/Ag '87

Summer at Windmill Point. M. C. Davis. il *Conservationist* 42:2-5 Jl/Ag '87

Lake houses See Lakeside architecture

Lake Manyara National Park (Tanzania) See National parks and reserves—Tanzania

Lake Michigan

By the shores of "Michigami". R. Reynolds. il *Saturday Evening Post* 259:84-5+ My/Je '87

Counting the days along Lake Michigan [eroding shoreline] M. Krance. il *Oceans* 20:6-7+ Mr/Ap '87

Lake Monoun (Cameroon)

Cameroon clouds: soda source? R. Monastersky. il *Sci News* 131:388 Je 20 '87

Lake Nyos (Cameroon)

The 1986 Lake Nyos gas disaster in Cameroon, West Africa [cover story] G. W. Kling and others. bibl f il maps *Science* 236:169-75 Ap 10 '87

Cameroon clouds: soda source? R. Monastersky. il *Sci News* 131:388 Je 20 '87

Cameroon lake: new clues, new clouds? S. Weisburd. *Sci News* 131:36-7 Ja 17 '87

A dead chief's revenge? [gas burst] H. Sigurdsson. il maps *Nat Hist* 96:44-9 Ag '87

Lake Nyos reported red and rumbling. S. Weisburd. *Sci News* 131:134 F 28 '87

Lake Nyos was rigged for disaster. R. A. Kerr. il *Science* 235:528-9 Ja 30 '87

Plumbing the depths of a lethal lake [work of George Kling] il map *Discover* 8:12 My '87

Silent death from Cameroon's killer lake. C. Stager. il map *Natl Geogr* 172:404-20 S '87

Lake Ontario (N.Y. and Ont.)

Fish culture

See Fish culture—Great Lakes region

Water pollution

See Water pollution—Great Lakes

Lake Placid (N.Y.)

Education

Summer camp and compost [Camp Treetops and North Country School] L. K. Murrow. il *Ctry J* 14:61-8 Ja '87

Religious institutions and affairs

For Kate Smith, death alone isn't grounds for burial [controversy with local Catholic Church over plans to build mausoleum] il por *People Wkly* 27:77 Je 15 '87

Lake Placid Olympics, 1980 See Olympic Games—1980— Winter Olympics

Lake Powell (Utah and Ariz.)

Lake Powell by boat . . . day or less trips. il map *Sunset* 178:58+ Ap '87

Wild West water skiing. C. Davis. il *Mot Boat Sail* 159:52-7+ F '87

Lake Superior

Water pollution

See Water pollution—Great Lakes

Lake Tahoe region (Calif. and Nev.)

See also

　Environmental policy—Lake Tahoe region (Calif. and Nev.)

　Regional planning—Lake Tahoe region (Calif. and Nev.)

　Trails—Lake Tahoe region (Calif. and Nev.)

Lake trout See Trout

Lake trout fishing See Trout fishing

Lakeland Medical Center (Athens, Tex.) See Athens (Tex.)— Hospitals

Lakes, Roderic

Foam structures with a negative Poisson's ratio. bibl f il *Science* 235:1038-40 F 27 '87

Lakes

See also

　Great Lakes

A vision of lakes. P. Steinhart. il *Audubon* 89:8+ Jl '87

Temperature

Bass in the brrrrrrrr. L. Stout. il *Outdoor Life* 180:88-9+ N '87

Arizona

Prehistoric Cameroon-style lake events [ancient crater lake; research by James D. White and Richard Fisher] R. Monastersky. *Sci News* 132:335 N 21 '87

British Columbia

See also

　Williston Lake (B.C.)

California

See also

　Mono Lake (Calif.)

Lakes—*cont.*
Cameroon
Seasonal mixing and catastrophic degassing in tropical lakes, Cameroon, West Africa. G. W. Kling. bibl f il *Science* 237:1022-4 Ag 28 '87
Europe
Lakes and glaciers of the Alps. H. Löffler. il *Courier* 40:37-8 F '87
Manitoba
See also
Gods Lake (Man.)
New York (State)
Lake acidification [effect of Big Blow of November 25, 1950 on Adirondack lakes; with reply by A. H. Johnson, D. F. Charles, and S. B. Andersen] J. E. Dobson and others. bibl f il *Environment* 29:2-5 Je '87
Photographs and photography
Adirondacks underwater [photographing acid-killed lakes] A. LaBastille. il por *Conservationist* 42:12-15 Jl/Ag '87
Saskatchewan
Canoeing Saskatchewan: Canada's watery highways. B. Wrenn. il *Travel Holiday* 168:22+ S '87
Utah
See also
Great Salt Lake (Utah)
Western States
EPA finds western lakes free of acid pollution, but vulnerable. E. Marshall. *Science* 235:423 Ja 23 '87
Lakes, Artificial
Arkansas
See also
Norfork Lake (Ark.)
Western States
See also
Lake Powell (Utah and Ariz.)
Lakeside architecture
Architecture: David Sellers [design of rustic log house on Lake Winnipesaukee, N.H.] V. J. Scully. il por *Archit Dig* 44:146-51+ Je '87
Autumn on Sandbar Island: Dr. Lee Salk's retreat in Maine. C. T. Buckley. il por *Archit Dig* 44:134-9 O '87
Kluckhuhns: a house built on a mountain lakeshore [Lake Anna, Va.] P. S. Gelfman. il *Fam Handyman* 37:47 Ja '87
Three generations under one roof [lake house in Mississippi] il *South Living* 22:122-3 Jl '87
Turning toward the water [remodeled ranch-style house on Lake Madeline] E. Wood. il *South Living* 22:66-8 Jl '87
Lakonishok, Josef
about
The 'January effect': why speculators usually have a happy New Year. C. Farrell. il por *Bus Week* p130 D 28 '87-Ja 4 '88
Lakwena, Alice *See* Mama Alice
Lal, Rattan
Managing the soils of Sub-Saharan Africa. bibl f il maps *Science* 236:1069-76 My 29 '87
Lalique, René, 1860-1945
about
The jewelry of René Lalique. G. C. Munn. il *Antiques* 131:1288-91 Je '87
LaLonde, Nicole
about
In Massachusetts, an ugly battle for a little girl. G. Hackett. il por *Newsweek* 110:41 O 19 '87
Lamas
See also
Dalai Lama XIV, 1935-
Psychic sports [practice of toumo; excerpt from Mystiques et magiciens du Tibet] A. David-Neel. il por *Courier* 40:36-7 Ap '87
Lamaur Inc.
An acid test for antitakeover laws [Minnesota law could help Alberto-Culver land Lamaur] M. J. Pitzer. il *Bus Week* p31 S 28 '87
Lamaute, Denise
Personal finance. See issues of Black Enterprise beginning March 1986
Lamb, Edward, 1902-1987
about
Obituary
Nation 244:457 Ap 11 '87
Lamb, James R., Jr.
My son, the do-gooder. por *Newsweek* 110:14-15 N 16 '87
Lamb, John M.
Roiling the arms control waters. il *Bull At Sci* 43:17-19 O '87

Lamb, Kevin
Missing numbers. il *Sport Mag* 78:48-9 N '87
Lamb, Michael E., 1953-
"Will the real 'new father' please stand up?". il *Parents* 62:77-80 Je '87
Lamb, R. C., and Weekes, Trevor C.
Very high energy gamma-ray binary stars. bibl f il *Science* 238:1528-34 D 11 '87
Lamb, Robert E.
How much security is enough? [address, January 22, 1987] *Dep State Bull* 87:27-9 My '87
Lamb, Wendy
The 10 best new picturebooks. il *Redbook* 170:24+ D '87
Why you can't talk to your parents anymore. il *Seventeen* 46:114-15 F '87
Lamb (Meat)
See also
Cooking—Meat
Lambert, Allen T.
International financial reform [address, May 18, 1987] *Vital Speeches Day* 53:689-91 S 1 '87
Lambert, Benjamin
about
More than a yen. J. Willoughby. il por *Forbes* 139:122 F 9 '87
Lambert, Christopher
about
Christopher Lambert: sexier in the movies than in his hotel room. J. Powell. por *Glamour* 85:298 S '87
Lambert, David L.
(jt. auth) See Tomkin, Jocelyn, and Lambert, David L.
Lambert, Denis-Clair
Does wealth equal health? il *Courier* 40:8-12 Ag '87
Lambert, Mary
about
Post-mod squad. G. Smith. il por *Film Comment* 23:24-9 N/D '87
Lambert, Rollins E.
Sanctions in context. *Commonweal* 114:166-7 Mr 27 '87
South Africa and its neighbors. map *America* 156:148-52 F 21 '87
Lambertson, David F.
Democracy in the Philippines [statement, September 10, 1987] *Dep State Bull* 87:27-9 N '87
U.S. policy toward Vietnam [statement, September 30, 1987] il *Dep State Bull* 87:32-3 N '87
Lamborghini (Automobile) *See* Sports cars
Lamborghini (Firm)
Survival of the fleetest [Chrysler's acquisition of AMC and Lamborghini] J. Lamm. il *Road Track* 39:118+ O '87
Tooling into the luxury market in a Lamborghini [Chrysler's deal] W. C. Symonds. il *Bus Week* p45+ My 4 '87
Lambro, Donald
How Congress creates a deficit. il *Read Dig* 131:39-40+ Jl '87
Lambsdorff, Otto von
Between competitiveness and co-operation [address, March 26, 1987] *Vital Speeches Day* 53:455-60 My 15 '87
Lambton, Antony
A comfortable perfection. il *House Gard* 159:146-55 N '87
Neoclassic beauty. il *House Gard* 159:190-9+ S '87
Lamburn, Robin
about
A mission of service to leprosy sufferers. F. Nowikowski. *Christ Century* 104:782-3 S 23 '87
Laminar flow
Speed in the groove [riblet tape invented by Michael Walsh] B. Rosenberg. il *Technol Rev* 90:10-11 N/D '87
Laminated plastics
Instant color. R. Capotosto. il *Pop Mech* 164:97-100+ My '87
Laminin
YIGSR, a synthetic laminin pentapeptide, inhibits experimental metastasis formation. Y. Iwamoto and others. bibl f il *Science* 238:1132-4 N 20 '87
Lamm, Harvey H.
about
It's tough, but it isn't doomsday. R. Phalon. il *Forbes* 139:53+ My 4 '87
Lamm, Richard D.
The Ten Commandments of an aging society [address, November 6, 1987] *Vital Speeches Day* 54:133-9 D 15 '87

Lamm, Richard D.—*cont.*
The Ten Commandments of health care. il por *Humanist* 47:16-20+ My/Je '87
We need to rethink the "unthinkable". il *USA Today (Periodical)* 116:20-1 S '87
Lamont, Corliss, 1902-
Sir Julian Huxley: a memoir. *Humanist* 47:27-8+ My/Je '87
LaMothe, William E., 1926-
about
The health craze has Kellogg feeling G-r-r-reat. R. Mitchell. il *Bus Week* p52-3 Mr 30 '87
L'Amour, Louis, 1908-
about
World's fastest literary gun: Louis L'Amour. D. D. Jackson. il por *Smithsonian* 18:154-6+ My '87
Lamp, Scott T.
(jt. auth) See Weiss, James N., and Lamp, Scott T.
Lampart, Jacob
Joanna loves Jesus [story] *Commentary* 84:44-50 Ag '87
Lampley, Jim
about
A golden boy gets axed. W. Taaffe. il *Sports Illus* 67:67 Jl 13 '87
Lampreys
Spinal cord
See Spinal cord
Lamps
See also
Electric lamps
The kerosene lamp. O. Bernier. il *Am Herit* 38:24-5 N '87
Lampwork (Paperweights)
Natural wonders: the lampwork of Paul J. Stankard [botanical lampwork] P. Hollister. il *Am Craft* 47:36-43 F/Mr '87
Lance, Inc.
Why steal your own sales? K. Hannon. il *Forbes* 139:208+ My 18 '87
Lancia (Automobile) *See* Automobiles, Foreign
Land, Edwin H.
about
Golden legend: a toast to Polaroid's 50th anniversary. N. Goldberg. il pors *Pop Photogr* 94:48+ N '87
The vindication of Edwin Land. S. N. Chakravarty. il por *Forbes* 139:83-4 My 4 '87
Land, Helen
Children having children. bibl f *Society* 24:36-40 Mr/Ap '87
Land, Leslie
American pie. il *N Y Times Mag* p33-4 Jl 5 '87
Churns for the better. il *N Y Times Mag* p53-4 F 8 '87
Land
See also
Burning of land
Public lands
Real estate business
Real property
Reclamation of land
Wetlands
Land. See occasional issues of Successful Farming
Prices
See Land values
Purchasing
See Real estate investment
Taxation
See Real property—Taxation
Land, Posting of *See* Trespass
Land buying *See* Real estate investment
Land development business *See* Real estate business
Land fills *See* Filling (Earthwork)
Land Management Bureau (U.S.) *See* United States. Bureau of Land Management
Land planning *See* Land utilization
Land reclamation *See* Reclamation of land
Land reform
Brazil
The great Brazilian land grab. A. Powers. *Commonweal* 114:288-90 My 8 '87
Land and violence in Brazil. A. Powers. *America* 156:324-6 Ap 18 '87
Philippines
Cory's broken promise. J. Collins. il *Nation* 245:549-50+ N 14 '87
Land reform: Aquino passes the buck. il *Newsweek* 110:33 Ag 3 '87
Resistance on the right. M. Liu. il *Newsweek* 110:44 Ag 10 '87

Still without land: for Filipino peasants, Aquino brings no change. W. Chapman. il *Progressive* 51:26-8 Je '87
The thin edge (II) [C. Aquino and problems of government] R. Shaplen. *New Yorker* 63:63-74+ S 28 '87
Land sales business *See* Real estate business
Land settlement
Ethiopia
Ethiopian landscapes. D. Stevens. il *Commonweal* 114:652-4 N 20 '87
Out of Africa. R. D. Kaplan. *New Repub* 197:12-13 Jl 6 '87
Saving Ethiopia from itself. D. MacKenzie. il *World Press Rev* 34:52 D '87
Land sinking *See* Subsidences (Earth movements)
Land slides *See* Landslides
Land speculation *See* Real estate investment
Land speed records
The day they broke 200 [NSU streamliner at Bonneville in 1956] P. Lyons. il *Cycle* 38:42-8 Ap '87
Flat out on the flats [Aerotech with Quad 4 engine] P. Bedard. il *Car Driv* 33:167 D '87
Project Salt Shaker [record set at Bonneville in Pontiac Aero Trans Am] S. Parker. il *Pop Mech* 164:78-81+ F '87
Land surveying *See* Surveying
Land tax *See* Real property—Taxation
Land tenure
See also
Feudalism
Homesteads—History
Indians of North America—Land tenure
Land reform
Real property
Trespass
Australia
See also
Australian aborigines—Land tenure
Scotland
'Having and holding': the Highland land war of the 1880s. I. C. Bradley. bibl il *Hist Today* 37:23-8 D '87
Land titles
See also
Deeds
Sure, it's your property, but . . . D. Moreau. il *Changing Times* 41:57-9 Ag '87
Land trusts
See also
National Park Trust
Trust for Public Land (U.S.)
Trustees of Reservations (Mass.)
Great Britain
See also
National Trust (Great Britain)
Land use *See* Land utilization
Land utilization
See also
Shore protection
Soil conservation
Top farmland's in shadow of the city. J. Walter. il *Success Farm* 85 no5:10L Mr '87
Laws and regulations
The Adirondack Park—a 2020 vision. R. Beamish. il map *Conservationist* 42:22-5 Jl/Ag '87
More on the Adirondack Park [discussion of September 1986 article, Green hills, blue lakes, and red tape] I. Nelson. il *Ctry J* 14:4+ F '87
No taking without paying [Supreme Court decision on compensation for confiscated land] A. L. Sanders. il *Time* 129:64-5 Je 22 '87
This land is my land [posting of private land] B. Trebilcock. il *Ctry J* 14:50-5 S '87
Land values
See also
Assessment
Real property—Valuation
Buy your North 40 while it's dirt-cheap [farmland] P. Houston. il *Bus Week* p92-3 Ap 20 '87
Combating modern-day feudalism: land as God's gift. W. Rybeck and R. D. Pasquariello. il *Christ Century* 104:470-2 My 13 '87
Investors pick up low-priced land [farmland] *Success Farm* 85:18BH Ap '87
More land sells, buyers pay cash, prices firm [farmland] *Success Farm* 85:19 My '87
Top farmland's in shadow of the city. J. Walter. il *Success Farm* 85 no5:10L Mr '87
Japan
Land of the Rising Billionaires [cover story] A. Tanzer. il *Forbes* 140:66-9+ Jl 27 '87

Land values—Japan—*cont.*
These prices are really insane. A. Tanzer. il *Forbes* 140:76+ D 14 '87
Landa, Lev N.
about
The Russian who makes pros out of amateurs. J. Main. il por *Fortune* 116:79 O 12 '87
Landaburu, Ander
Continuity for Mexico. por *World Press Rev* 34:25 D '87
Is it the contras' last stand? *World Press Rev* 34:41 Mr '87
Landamatic Systems Corporation
The Russian who makes pros out of amateurs [L. Landa] J. Main. il por *Fortune* 116:79 O 12 '87
Landau, Saul
(jt. auth) See Dinges, John, and Landau, Saul
Lander, Donald
about
A tough top gun. M. Clark. il por *Macleans* 100:16 O 12 '87
Lander, Eric S., and Botstein, David
Homozygosity mapping: a way to map human recessive traits with the DNA of inbred children. bibl f il *Science* 236:1567-70 Je 19 '87
Landers, Ann
Guest columnist: Ann Landers. por *Teen* 31:38 D '87
about
Dear Ann Landers: anything you can do, I can do better, write 22 dazzled but eager column hopefuls. L. Aitken. il por *People Wkly* 27:42-4+ Ap 20 '87
Looking for Miss Lonelyhearts. M. Bosc. il por *U S News World Rep* 102:13 Mr 23 '87
Mr. and Ms. Lonelyhearts. M. Bosc. il pors *U S News World Rep* 102:12 Je 15 '87
Landesman, Rocco
about
I've got the horse right here: producer Rocco Landesman's big Broadway gamble. E. Pooley. il pors *N Y* 20:74-6+ S 28 '87
Landfills *See* Filling (Earthwork)
Landi, Ann
Polonius and the book loan. por *Publ Wkly* 231:90 F 6 '87
Smart women, foolish books: can your love life be saved in ten chapters or less? *Mademoiselle* 93:180-1+ O '87
Landing areas (Air bases) *See* Air bases—Runways
Landing fees, Airport *See* Airports—Fees
Landing gear, Airplane *See* Airplanes, Jet—Landing gear
Landing of airplanes *See* Airplanes—Landing; Airplanes, Jet—Landing
Landing systems, Microwave *See* Microwave landing systems
Landis, John
about
Three amigos [film] Reviews
N Y 20:46 Ja 5 '87. D. Denby
People Wkly il 27:10+ Ja 5 '87. P. Travers
Twilight Zone: the verdict. *Time* 129:69 Je 8 '87
The 'Twilight Zone' verdict: not guilty. por *Newsweek* 109:83 Je 8 '87
Landlord and tenant
See also
Eviction
Farm tenancy
Rent
Buying to rent. L. Hazelton. il *Black Enterp* 18:85-6+ O '87
The girl in 1-A: sexual harassment hits home. A. B. Eagan. il *Mademoiselle* 93:252-3+ Ap '87
Real estate: still a hands-on affair. M. Schiffres. il *Changing Times* 41:43+ N '87
Rx for the 'Ratlord': live in your own slums [slumlord M. Avol] por *Newsweek* 110:54 Jl 27 '87
Sex for shelter: when your landlord wants more than the rent. J. Bode. il *Glamour* 85:318-19+ N '87
Slum community saves itself [efforts of single mothers to insure survival of low cost housing in Pittsburgh] R. Kahn. *Ms* 15:32 Je '87
Trials of a landlord [L.A. slumlord M. Avol] D. Seligman. il *Fortune* 116:95-6 Ag 17 '87
Up from public housing [tenant management] M. Wooster and J. Fund. il *Read Dig* 131:139-43 Jl '87
Landmark Foundation
It may be a case of the 'word-blind' leading the 'word-blind,' but Charles Drake unscrambles dyslexia. K. Gross. il pors *People Wkly* 27:105-7 Mr 30 '87
Landmark Land Company, Inc.
Just so much popcorn. E. Paris. il por *Forbes* 139:44+ Je 1 '87

Landmarks, Historic *See* Historic houses, sites, etc.
Landmarks Preservation Commission (New York, N.Y.) *See* New York (N.Y.). Landmarks Preservation Commission
Landon, Alf
about
Obituary
U S News World Rep il por 103:16 O 26 '87
Landon, Michael
about
Michael Landon: "My mother tried to stab me" [interview] T. Reinhold. il pors *Redbook* 169:59-60+ S '87
Landow, Nathan
about
What (or who) makes Albert Gore run. M. E. Recio. il por *Bus Week* p45 Ap 27 '87
Landreth, Bill, 1964-
about
The hacker who vanished. G. Hackett. il por *Newsweek* 109:22 Ja 19 '87
Landry, Tom
about
Assault on Mount Landry. P. Zimmerman. il por *Sports Illus* 67:40-3 D 21 '87
Land's edge [dance] *See* Dance reviews—Single works
Lands' End (Firm)
Steering his own course to success [G. C. Comer] S. Caminiti. il por *Fortune* 115:95 Ja 5 '87
Landsat satellites *See* Artificial satellites—Earth sciences use
Landsberg, Hans H.
Rethinking energy security: the case for coal in the United States. il *Environment* 29:18-20+ Jl/Ag '87
Landscape
Surrender to the landscape. G. Ehrlich. il *Harpers* 275:24+ S '87
Landscape architects
Do you need professional landscape help? Here is how to choose. il *Sunset* 178:248-9 Ap '87
Your own secret garden. C. Fenyvesi. il *U S News World Rep* 103:70-1 S 21 '87
Landscape architecture
See also
Follies (Architecture)
Money trees [landscaping enhances property values; views of Duane Durgee] il *USA Today (Periodical)* 116:7-8 D '87
Olmsted Heritage Landscapes Act. J. H. Kay. *Nation* 244:552-4 Ap 25 '87
Privacy, shade, and plant display on two sides. il *Sunset* 178:182-3 Mr '87
Rustic look for the entry. il *South Living* 22:52-3 Ag '87
A tropical look, Memphis style. il *South Living* 22:62-3 Je '87
Unmask hidden style at your front door [cover story] S. Ross. il *Fam Handyman* 37:27-9+ Ap '87
Landscape contractors *See* Contractors
Landscape drawing
Anita Wolff's portraits and landscapes in pastel. M. S. Schulzke. il por *Am Artist* 51:60-3+ S '87
Exhibitions
Steven Barbash. J. C. Oresman. il por *Am Artist* 51:26 F '87
Landscape ecology
Aldo Leopold—a celebration of the land ethic. J. W. Taylor. il pors *Conservationist* 42:12-15 N/D '87
How Leopold learned to think like a mountain. C. Meine. *Wilderness* 51:57-8+ Wint '87
Landscape ecology. D. L. Urban and others. bibl f il *BioScience* 37:119-27 F '87
Large herbivore foraging and ecological hierarchies. R. L. Senft and others. bibl il *BioScience* 37:789-95+ D '87
Letting Leopold down. C. E. Little. il por *Wilderness* 50:45-8 Summ '87
Painting the future [visual impact analysis used to chart changes in Sweden's landscape] il *Courier* 40:18-19 O '87
Sand County's conservation prophet [A. Leopold] D. R. Wallace. il pors *Sierra* 72:62-7 N/D '87
Landscape gardening
See also
Decks, patios, terraces, etc.
Espaliers
Garden borders
Garden steps
Ground cover plants
Hedges
Hillside gardens and gardening
Lawns

Landscape gardening—See also—*cont.*
Shrubs
Terraces (Landscape gardening)
Buying your way into Eden. J. Adler. il *Newsweek* 110:46-7 Jl 20 '87
Creative patio crafting. N. P. Pierce. il *Flower Gard* 31:16+ Ag/S '87
Days of vines and roses. M. Bethany. il *N Y* 20:58-9 Je 15 '87
Do you need professional landscape help? Here is how to choose. il *Sunset* 178:248-9 Ap '87
Fields of color [J. Thouron's flower gardens in the Brandywine Valley] D. M. Stone. il *House Gard* 159:68-77+ Ag '87
First they dug out 3 feet of their flat lot. il *Sunset* 179:152 Ag '87
Foundation planting. C. Crandall. il *Home Mech* 83:40-3 My '87
Foundation planting with a purpose. T. Steadman. il *South Living* 22:130-2 My '87
From sleepy to splendid with landscaping and paint. S. Ross. il *Fam Handyman* 37:32-3 Ap '87
Garden generosity [M. Ley's garden in Connecticut] S. Eddison. il *House Gard* 159:142-7+ Je '87
Gardens: glacial legacy: a multilevel landscape in British Columbia [created by Bill and Anne Peters] A. Furst. il *Archit Dig* 44:202-7 Ap '87
In just 425 square feet, a shady green retreat [San Francisco] il *Sunset* 179:157 O '87
Jim Taylor's self-made garden [Greensboro, N.C.] il *South Living* 22:54 Ag '87
Keeping the pool cool [planting around swimming pools] B. Damrosch. il *Esquire* 108:24 Jl '87
Landscape doctor. See issues of Rodale's Organic Gardening beginning September 1987
Landscape renovation. B. L. Appleton. il *Flower Gard* 31:64-5 Je/Jl '87
Landscaped by nature . . . or you [swimming pools] il *Sunset* 179:56-9 Ag '87
Landscaping by design [cover story] D. Kelly and L. Kelly. il *Workbench* 43:16-20 My/Je '87
Landscaping in three affordable phases. J. A. McKeon. il *Better Homes Gard* 65:102-9 S '87
Meadow and decks . . . easy-maintenance and naturally handsome [unmowed creeping red fescue] il *Sunset* 179:222-3 O '87
One design, many phases [St. Augustine, Fla.] il *South Living* 22:64 D '87
Painting the shape of the land [Tori Thomas' experiments with natural abstraction] il *House Gard* 159:178-81 Ap '87
Part open, part woodland, all wonderful! B. McDougald. il *South Living* 22:64-5 Jl '87
Removing the pool from center stage. il *South Living* 22:97 My '87
Reshaping a corner of Connecticut [R. Page designs garden for G. Stutz] K. Whiteside. il *House Gard* 159:152-5+ Jl '87
Starting over out back. il *South Living* 22:84-6 Mr '87
This entrance features a garden. il *South Living* 22:104 My '87
A time and season for water-efficient landscaping. il *Sunset* 178:236 Je '87
Unifying a garden [Little Rock, Ark.] il *South Living* 22:101 Ap '87
Using small stones to create strong effects. il *Sunset* 179:144 Ag '87
Wing Haven [garden and bird sanctuary of E. Clarkson] K. Whiteside. il *House Gard* 159:166-73+ Je '87
Your own secret garden [use of a landscape architect] C. Fenyvesi. il *U S News World Rep* 103:70-1 S 21 '87

Exhibitions
A pier full of gardens April 8-12 in San Francisco [Landscape Garden Show] il *Sunset* 178:256-7 Ap '87
What makes a garden? [Transforming the American garden: twelve new landscape designs] W. H. Adams. il *House Gard* 159:32+ Mr '87

History
Philosopher of the country house [A. J. Downing] R. Lynes. il por *Archit Dig* 44:35+ Je '87
Landscape in art
See also
Landscape drawing
Landscape painting
Landscape painting
See also
Hudson River School
Macchiaioli
Balancing interests in art and illustration. M. Garland. il *Am Artist* 51:54-9+ Ja '87

A conversation with Robert Duffy. C. Movalli. il *Am Artist* 51:54-9+ N '87
Daniel Dallmann. T. Bolt. il *Am Artist* 51:56-61 Mr '87
David Jenks. D. C. Hines. il pors *Am Artist* 51:54-9+ S '87
Harry Orlyk [cover story] M. Mathews-Berenson. il *Am Artist* 51:38-41+ Jl '87
Landscapes of color [works by W. Kahn] C. Gaines. il por *Archit Dig* 44:44+ Je '87
Places for the hungry heart [H. M. Wilson's work] M. Moorman. il por *Art News* 86:71-2 F '87
Sublime views [market for American romantic landscapes] F. Donegan. il *Americana* 15:62-4 N/D '87
Techniques of landscape painting. R. Norman. il *Am Artist* 51:54-7 Ag '87
The vivid imagery of Australia's artists. P. Fuller. il *Archit Dig* 44:204+ S '87

Exhibitions
American painting [In nature's ways: American landscape painting of the late 19th century] S. B. Sherrill. il *Antiques* 131:360+ F '87
Ferdinand Hodler: landscapes: National Academy of Design. M. Moorman. il *Art News* 86:156 D '87
Landscapes in the Golden Anniversary National Art Exhibition [with introd. by Mary Carroll Nelson] il *Am Artist* 51:46-51 Je '87
A sense of light and air in landscapes [exhibition of 19th century American landscape paintings] B. Weber. bibl f il *Am Artist* 51:40-7+ Ap '87
Landscape photography See Photography—Landscapes
Landscape protection
See also
Environmental movement
Shore protection
Wilderness areas
Landslides
Avalanche! [Switzerland] S. Cashen. il *Int Wildl* 17:36-7 My/Je '87
Real-time landslide warning during heavy rainfall. D. K. Keefer and others. bibl f il map *Science* 238:921-5 N 13 '87
Lane, Belden C.
God plays rough for love's sake. *Christ Century* 104:879-81 O 14 '87
A hidden and playful God. *Christ Century* 104:812-13 S 30 '87
Lane, Charles
Hookers, Jaguars, and lots of stupid loans. *Wash Mon* 18:55-7 Ja '87
If it's Tuesday, this must be Managua. *Wash Mon* 19:48-51 Je '87
Lane, Helen R.
(tr) See Paz, Octavio, 1914-. Edith Piaf among the pygmies
Lane, Joan Pedersen- See Pedersen-Lane, Joan
Lane, John R., 1944-
about
Eager to raise the stakes for the SFMMA. K. Regan. por *Art News* 86:32+ Ap '87
Lane College
Chambers inaugurated 8th prexy of Lane College. por *Jet* 71:40 Mr 9 '87
Lane Fox, Robin
Poetry in water. il *House Gard* 159:104-15+ Ja '87
about
Constantine's pagan triumph. P. Pettingell. *New Leader* 70:15-16 Ap 6 '87
Lanes, Jerrold
Scenes from the Macchiaioli. il *Art Am* 75:106-13 Ja '87
Laney, James T.
Education of the heart. il *Christ Today* 31:21 F 6 '87
Laney, Yolanda
about
Female coach takes over men's summer cage team. *Jet* 72:48 Jl 27 '87
Lang, Donald
about
Deaf-mute must stay in mental hospital for 1971 slaying in Chicago. *Jet* 72:17 Je 8 '87
Lang, Eugene M., 1919-
about
A dream come true. M. deC. Hinds. il por *N Y Times Mag* p32-6 Ap 26 '87
A father of innovation. R. Thompson. il pors *Nations Bus* 75:61-2 Ap '87
Lang, George, 1924-, and Lang, Jenifer Harvey
A new taste from China. il *N Y Times Mag* p49-50 Ja 25 '87

Lang, Gordon
The Oriental porcelains at Burghley House, Lincolnshire, England. il *Antiques* 131:236-47 Ja '87
Lang, Jenifer Harvey
Morel conquests. il *N Y Times Mag* p47-8 My 24 '87
(jt. auth) See Lang, George, 1924-, and Lang, Jenifer Harvey
Lang, Mary E.
(jt. auth) See Frank, Meryl, and Lang, Mary E.
Lang, Serge
about
The World Cup after Lang. A. H. Greenberg. *Skiing* 40:16 S '87
Lang, Serge, 1927-
about
Blood lust in academia. F. Zakaria. *New Repub* 197:16-18 Jl 27 '87
The posse stops a "softie". E. Bowen. il *Time* 129:76-7 My 11 '87
Soft sciences are often harder than hard sciences. J. M. Diamond. il *Discover* 8:34-5+ Ag '87
Lang, Susan S.
7 strategies: how to eat, drink and be merry—without blowing your diet! il *McCalls* 114:99 Ja '87
Langan, Marianne
Food tips to clip. See issues of McCall's beginning May 1986
Langdale, Cecily
The late watercolor/pastels of Maurice Prendergast [cover story] bibl f il *Antiques* 132:1084-95 N '87
Langdon, Philip
The automated house. il *Atlantic* 260:93-6 O '87
Romance in the rooftops. il *Atlantic* 260:85-7 Jl '87
Lange, Art
On the beat. See alternate issues of Down Beat through December 1987
Lange, David
about
Kiwis just say 'no'. J. Salzman. *Sierra* 72:32+ My/Je '87
Langerhans, Islets of See Pancreas
Langevin, Cathy
The call of the Amazon. il map *Travel Holiday* 168:60-5+ Jl '87
Langford, Gregory
about
232 pounds lost: half the size and twice as happy. il pors *Ebony* 42:60+ Ja '87
Langhart, Janet
about
Langhart is fired after refusing TV lottery job. por *Jet* 72:40 Jl 13 '87
Langlais, Bernard, 1921-1977
about
An imaginative kingdom: sculptor Bernard Langlais' Maine legacy. A. Berman. il *Archit Dig* 44:174-7+ Je '87
Langley Research Center (U.S.)
Langley develops new airflow visualization system [analysis and evaluation of vortex flap effectiveness] *Aviat Week Space Technol* 127:76-7 N 16 '87
Langley develops optical technique for storing satellite data [Earth Radiation Budget Experiment satellites] *Aviat Week Space Technol* 127:145 Ag 10 '87
NASA, Army testing composite airframe crashworthiness. E. H. Phillips. il *Aviat Week Space Technol* 127:61+ S 28 '87
Shaping the future of flight. il *Futurist* 21:51 N/D '87
Langlois, Richard G., and others
Evidence for increased somatic cell mutations at the glycophorin A locus in atomic bomb survivors. bibl f il *Science* 236:445-8 Ap 24 '87
Langseth-Christensen, Lillian
Austria's Burgenland. il map *Gourmet* 47:44-9+ Jl '87
A design for living [excerpt] il *Gourmet* 47:66+ Ag '87
Four historic Viennese hotels. il *Gourmet* 47:64-9+ Mr '87
A meister chef's legacy. il por *Gourmet* 47:80-1+ O '87
A Swiss Christmas tree shop. il *Gourmet* 47:78-81+ D '87
Langton, Simon
about
The whistle blower [film] Reviews
Macleans il 100:49 Ag 24 '87. L. O'Toole
Natl Rev 39:65-6 S 11 '87. J. Simon
New Repub 197:24 Ag 10-17 '87. S. Kauffmann
People Wkly 28:12 S 21 '87. T. Cunneff

Language, Obscene See Words, Obscene
Language and culture
You say begin, I say commence—to the victor belongs the language. R. M. Brown. il *N Y Times Book Rev* 92:13 D 20 '87
Language and education
See also
Bilingual education
Language and languages
See also
Accents
Air pilots—Language
Bilingualism
Canada—Languages
Children—Language
Chinese language
Communication
Conversation
English language
French language
Gaelic language
Greek language
Indians (American)—Languages
Latin language
Men—Language
Metaphor
Modern Language Association of America
New Brunswick—Languages
Ontario—Languages
Philology
Rhetoric
Russian language
Seamen—Language
Sex discrimination in language
Spanish language
Speech
Translators and translating
Universal language
Upper classes—Language
Zulu language
Origin
Refined speech the key to being thoroughly modern? [research by Philip Lieberman and others] R. Lewin. *Science* 236:670 My 8 '87
Philosophy
Language is smarter than we are. M. Robinson. il *N Y Times Book Rev* 92:8 Ja 11 '87
The strength of words [address, April 26, 1987] H. Taylor. *Vital Speeches Day* 53:600-2 Jl 15 '87
Political aspects
See also
Québec (Province)—Languages
Psychology
See Psycholinguistics
Sociological aspects
See Sociolinguistics
Study and teaching
See also
Phrasebooks
Learning a foreign language. H. R. Kennedy. *U S News World Rep* 103:65 Ag 31 '87
Memory boost from spaced-out learning [long-term retention of foreign languages; study by Harry P. Bahrick and Elizabeth Phelps] B. Bower. *Sci News* 131:244 Ap 18 '87
Speaking in (foreign) tongues. D. Moreau. *Changing Times* 41:41-2 Ap '87
Aids and devices
See also
Tape recordings—Language study use
Language and languages, Artificial
See also
Esperanto
Language and society See Sociolinguistics
Language development See Children—Language
Language of animals See Animal communication
Languedoc (France)
Description and travel
Gourmet holidays: the coast of Languedoc. P. T. Mitchell. il map *Gourmet* 47:60-5+ O '87
Lanier, Thomas P.
Showing emotions. por *Opera News* 51:18-19 Mr 28 '87
Lanin, Lester
about
Lester Lanin. F. Conroy. il pors *People Wkly* 28:79-80+ D 21 '87
The music man. E. F. Cone. il por *Forbes* 140 Sp Issue:382 O 26 '87

Lanin (Lester) Orchestras See Lester Lanin Orchestras
Lankford, John
  Charting the southern sky. il pors *Sky Telesc* 74:243-6
    S '87
Lannin, Joanne
  Assignment: sports. il *Women's Sports Fitness* 9:77-9+
    Mr '87
Lanoil, Georgia Witkin- See Witkin-Lanoil, Georgia
Lanois, Daniel
          about
  Daniel Lanois [interview] J. Henke. por *Roll Stone* p93-4+
    D 17-31 '87
LANs See Local area networks
Lansbury, Angela
          about
  Angela Lansbury. C. Adams. il por *Ladies Home J*
    104:38+ F '87
  Angela Lansbury: solving Sunday night blues. T. Klein.
    il pors *Saturday Evening Post* 259:42-5 Ja/F '87
  The Angela Lansbury story. B. Thomas. il pors *Good
    Housekeep* 204:132-3+ Mr '87
  Angela Lansbury takes the lead. J. Culhane. il pors
    Read Dig 130:20-2+ Je '87
Lansky, Vicki
  Nap-time strategies that work. il *Parents* 62:343-4 N
    '87
          about
  A start with babies. T. Unsworth. *Publ Wkly* 232:38
    D 11 '87
Lansner, Tom
  Ceasefire with the Communists. *World Press Rev* 34:25
    Ja '87
Lanston (Aubrey G.) & Company See Aubrey G. Lanston
  & Company
Lantern projection
          Exhibitions
  Optical amusements before movies and TV [exhibit at
    Museum of Our National Heritage] M. Jailer. il *Antiques
    Collect Hobbies* 92:46-9 Je '87
Lanterns
          See also
          Luminarias
  Old salt's lantern. C. E. Aronson. il *Workbench* 43:55-7
    Jl/Ag '87
Lantos, Robert
          about
  High drama in the world of film. B. Amiel. il *Macleans*
    100:7 S 14 '87
Lanvin, Maryll
          about
  A château in bloom: Maryll and Bernard Lanvin's house
    in the Île de France. A. Gordon. il *Vogue* 177:328-39
    D '87
Lanyi, Andrew
  How to become your broker's pet. il *Nations Bus* 75:4
    Ja '87
Laos
          See also
          Americans—Laos
          Temples—Laos
          Description and travel
  Laos. P. T. White. il maps *Natl Geogr* 171:772-95 Je
    '87
          Foreign relations
          United States
  See United States—Foreign relations—Laos
          Politics and government
  Easing the burden of socialist struggle in Laos. M. Brown.
    Curr Hist 86:152-5+ Ap '87
          Royal family
  Laotion mystery. A. Giarelli. *World Press Rev* 34:40
    S '87
Laotian refugees See Refugees, Laotian
Lap desks See Desks
Lapel pins
          Collectors and collecting
  Going for gold with Olympic pins. J. Howse. il *Macleans*
    100:56 N 9 '87
  OCO's symbolic victory [Olympic pin distributor B.
    Hipson in trademark dispute, Calgary] H. Quinn. il
    por *Macleans* 100:40 Je 8 '87
Lapham, Lewis H.
  An American fairy tale. il *Macleans* 100:20-1 Jl 20
    '87
  Notebook. See issues of Harper's
  Pride and power. il *Macleans* 100:16-17 Mr 9 '87
Lapham, Phyllis
          about
  Pacific orientation. M. Schafer. il por *House Gard*
    159:160-5+ My '87

Lapides, Morton M.
          about
  Out of his depth. M. Kuntz. il por *Forbes* 139:56-7
    F 23 '87
Lapidus, Herbert
          about
  Feet first. G. Morgenson. il por *Forbes* 140:113+ Ag
    10 '87
LaPine, Anthony
          about
  A cautionary tale. K. K. Wiegner. il por *Forbes* 140:52-3
    Ag 10 '87
LaPine Technology Corporation
  A cautionary tale [joint venture with Kyocera] K. K.
    Wiegner. il por *Forbes* 140:52-3 Ag 10 '87
Lapinski, Susan
  "Caring from the heart". il *Ladies Home J* 104:26+
    Mr '87
Lapita (Ancient people)
  Prehistoric Polynesian puzzle [origin of Lapita culture;
    cover story] B. Bower. il map *Sci News* 132:232-3
    O 10 '87
LAPL See Los Angeles Public Library
Lapland
          See also
          Lapps
          Radioactive pollution—Lapland
LaPlante, Eve
  Five career ruts you can't afford. *Work Woman* 12:59
    N '87
Lapomarda, Vincent A.
  Should a priest serve on a jury? il *America* 156:495-6
    Je 20-27 '87
Laporte, André, 1931-
          about
  Das Schloss [opera] Reviews
    Opera News il 52:46 Jl '87. D. P. Stearns
Lapps
  If you're lost, just go home. R. Rodale. il *Rodale's
    Org Gard* 34:18+ S '87
  Lapp life after Chernobyl. S. Stephens. il map *Nat Hist*
    96:32-41 D '87
Laptop computer industry See Computer industry
Laptop computers See Computers
Laqueur, Walter, 1921-
  Beyond *glasnost. Commentary* 84:63-5 O '87
  Glasnost's ghosts. *New Repub* 197:13-14 Ag 3 '87
  Kohl on a roll. *New Repub* 196:17-18 Mr 2 '87
Lar Lubovitch Dance Company
  Lar Lubovitch Dance Company [appearance at City
    Center] G. G. Seibert. *America* 156:56 Ja 24 '87
  Reviews:
    Performances at City Center, New York City. O.
      Stuart. *Dance Mag* 61:28-9 Ap '87
Lara, Fernando
          about
  Fish window. *New Yorker* 63:23-5 Jl 6 '87
Lara, Reyes de
          about
  Reviews:
    J. Hughes and R. de Lara present Contrapuntos
      program as part of Theater Frontiers series. L.
      Kumin. *Dance Mag* 61:100 My '87
Larason, Lew
  A field guide to country antiques. il *Ctry J* 14:41-5
    Mr '87
Larbey, Bob
          about
  A month of Sundays [drama] Reviews
    N Y il 20:139 Ap 27 '87. J. Simon
    New Yorker 63:73 Ap 27 '87. E. Oliver
Larceny See Stealing
Lardner, James
  The Betamax case (I). *New Yorker* 63:45-8+ Ap 6 '87
  The Betamax case (II). *New Yorker* 63:60-81 Ap 13
    '87
Laredo (Tex.)
          Buildings
  Echoes of plazas and pyramids [Cigarroa High School
    and Middle School] H. L. Smith, Jr. il *Archit Rec*
    175:88-91 S '87
Large families See Family size
Large format cameras See Cameras
Large numbers See Numbers
Large print books
          See also
          Publishers and publishing—Large print books

Largemouth bass *See* Bass
Largemouth bass fishing *See* Bass fishing
Lari, Faiyaz Ahmed
(jt. auth) See Burney, Mohammad Ilyas, and Lari, Faiyaz
Ahmed
Larios, Armando Fernández *See* Fernández Larios, Armando
Larkin, Rochelle
Philosophical Library redux. il por *Publ Wkly* 232:26-8
Ag 21 '87
Larmoth, Jeanine
Think pinks. il *House Gard* 159:44+ D '87
Larnard, Joe
about
Turn out the lighthouse, the party's over: keeper Joe
Larnard stoically awaits automation. R. Arias. il pors
People Wkly 28:86-8 S 21 '87
LaRouche, Lyndon H.
about
Bankrupt ideology. *Time* 129:80 My 4 '87
Indicted candidate. B. Levin. *Macleans* 100:18 Jl 13
'87
Larrabee, Eric
about
Of many things. G. W. Hunt. *America* 157:74 Ag 15-22
'87
Larraz, Julio, 1944-
about
Julio Larraz at Nohra Haime. D. Bourdon. il *Art Am*
75:142 Mr '87
Larrick, Nancy
Illiteracy starts too soon. bibl f il *Phi Delta Kappan*
69:184-9 N '87
Larsen, Henry A.
about
Larsen of the Northwest Passage. J. Roe. il pors map
Oceans 20:48-53+ N/D '87
Larsh, Don
A cure for excessive banking; ed. by Doug Smith. il
Skiing 40:91 N '87
Larson, Allan
(jt. auth) See Wake, David B., and Larson, Allan
Larson, Charles R.
Turning off youthful readers. por *Publ Wkly* 232:49
N 20 '87
Larson, Erik
A close watch on U.S. borders to keep the world's
bugs out. bibl (p154) *Smithsonian* 18:106-8+ Je '87;
il
Getting away with murder. il *Omni* 9:72-4+ My '87
Larson, Gary
about
Creatures from the black cartoon. P. Richmond. il por
Roll Stone p79-80+ S 24 '87
The Far side of NMNH. C. Bond. il *Smithsonian* 18:168
Ap '87
Larson, Janet Karsten
Margaret Atwood's testaments: resisting the Gilead within.
Christ Century 104:496-8 My 20-27 '87
Larson, Kay
Art. See issues of New York
Hot Pepper. il por *N Y* 20:46-8+ Je 8 '87
Landscapes of threatened beauty. il *Archit Dig* 44:90+
N '87
Up against the walls. il *N Y* 20:46-51 F 2 '87
Larson, Larry
about
Tent meeting [drama] Reviews
N Y 20:70-1 Ap 20 '87. J. Simon
Nation 244:585-6 My 2 '87. T. M. Disch
Larson, Merv
about
Merv Larson's team takes nature to the animals. B.
Reiss. il por *Smithsonian* 17:106-8+ F '87
Larson, Reed, 1950-
about
The ups and downs of teenage life. J. Fischman. il
Psychol Today 21:56-7 My '87
Larson, Rustin
October 29, 1855: variation on Thoreau's journal entry
[poem] *America* 157:248 O 17 '87
Larson, Stephen M., and Levy, David H., 1948-
Observing Comet Halley's near-nucleus features. il
Astronomy 15:90-5 S '87
Larson Company
Merv Larson's team takes nature to the animals. B.
Reiss. il por *Smithsonian* 17:106-8+ F '87
Larsson, Carl Olof, 1853-1919
about
Carl Larsson's home—a Swedish legacy. M. Kluger. il
Gourmet 47:56-9+ Jl '87

L'Art et L'Automobile Gallery
Art and the automobile. W. Hoyt. il *Pop Mech* 164:22
Ap '87
Larue, Gerald A.
Survival in the apocalyptic era. il *Humanist* 47:11-17
S/O '87
Larvae
See also
Caterpillars
Maggots
Clownfish larvae with sickle cells [work of Louis
Leibovitz] *Sea Front* 33:223-4 My/Je '87
Fewer barnacles [rockfish prey on barnacle larvae in
California kelp forest; research by Steven D. Gaines
and Jonathan Roughgarden] *Sea Front* 33:384-5 S/O
'87
Fish in offshore kelp forests affect recruitment to intertidal
barnacle populations [rockfish] S. D. Gaines and J.
Roughgarden. bibl f il *Science* 235:479-81 Ja 23 '87
Wind speed and mortality rate of a marine fish, the
northern anchovy (Engraulis mordax). R. M. Peterman
and M. J. Bradford. bibl f il *Science* 235:354-6 Ja
16 '87
Larynx
Refined speech the key to being thoroughly modern?
[research by Philip Lieberman and others] R. Lewin.
Science 236:670 My 8 '87
Cancer
Genetic aspects
The *raf* oncogene is associated with a radiation-resistant
human laryngeal cancer. U. Kasid and others. bibl
f il *Science* 237:1039-41 Ag 28 '87
Diseases
See also
Hoarseness
Las Colinas (Tex.)
Street traffic
Jammed up in Virginia, smooth sailing in Texas. W.
J. Cook. il *U S News World Rep* 103:24-5 S 7 '87
Las Olas Art Festival *See* Fort Lauderdale (Fla.)—Festivals
Las Vegas (Nev.)
Bookstores
See Booksellers and bookselling—Nevada
Hotels, motels, etc.
See also
Casinos
Poor
John 3:16 Cook has saving words for Vegas losers.
K. Hubbard. il pors *People Wkly* 27:115-16+ My 11
'87
Prisons and reformatories
Jails within a jail [Clark County Detention Center] il
Archit Rec 175:88-91 Ap '87
Restaurants, nightclubs, bars, etc.
Las Vegas dining: a sure bet. R. L. Balzer. il *Travel
Holiday* 167:18-20 Mr '87
Youth
Las Vegas teens. il *Teen* 31:36+ Ja '87
Lasansky, Jeannette
Quilts of central Pennsylvania. bibl f il *Antiques*
131:288-99 Ja '87
Lascaux murals *See* Cave drawings and paintings
Lascelles, Heidi
about
London journal. J. Bainbridge. il *Gourmet* 47:20+ F
'87
Lasch, Christopher
The children of Narcissus. *Des Arts Educ* 88:45-8 My/Je
'87
Fraternalist manifesto [excerpt from address, November
1986] *Harpers* 274:17-20 Ap '87
The paranoid presidency. *Cent Mag* 20:42-8 Jl/Ag '87
Soul of a New Age. il *Omni* 10:78-80+ O '87
Lasek, Raymond J.
(jt. auth) See Liuzzi, Francis J., and Lasek, Raymond
J.
Laser Arms (Firm)
The big chill [M. Zolp's self-cooling can scam] J. Crudele.
il *N Y* 20:19+ Ag 24 '87
Laser Author (Word processor program) *See* Word proces-
sors and processing—Programming

Laser disc players *See* Compact disc players
Laser discs *See* Compact discs
Laser discs, Video *See* Videodiscs
Laser gyroscopes *See* Gyroscopes
Laser holography *See* Holography
Laser optical disc recording *See* Optical storage devices
Laser printers *See* Computers—Print-out equipment
Laser spectroscopy *See* Spectrum analysis
Laser television projection *See* Television projection
LaserCards *See* Memory cards
Lasers
Chemical power for visible-light lasers [work of James L. Gole and others] I. Peterson. *Sci News* 132:261 O 24 '87
A free electron laser in the visible. A. L. Robinson. *Science* 236:27-8 Ap 3 '87
Free-electron lasers. T. A. Heppenheimer. il *Pop Sci* 231:63-7+ D '87
Free-electron lasers take small steps toward distant goal. B. G. Levi. il *Phys Today* 40:17-19 Je '87
Keeping it together [avoiding diffractive spreading of a laser beam; work of James Durnin and others] *Sci Am* 257:28-9 Jl '87
Lasers light the way for computer links. S. Weisburd. *Sci News* 131:408 Je 27 '87
Superlights! il *Natl Geogr World* 146:22-7 O '87
Ultrahigh-power semiconductor diode laser arrays. P. S. Cross and others. bibl f il *Science* 237:1305-9 S 11 '87

Astronomical use
Gravitational wave observatories. A. D. Jeffries and others. il *Sci Am* 256:50-6+ Je '87
Letters [discussion of June 1987 article, Gravitational wave observatories] A. D. Jeffries and others. *Sci Am* 257:8-9 D '87
A satellite triangle for gravity waves. D. E. Thomsen. *Sci News* 131:24 Ja 10 '87
Telescope tunes in to the guiding light. K. Hartley. *Sci News* 132:54 Jl 25 '87

Biological use
Demonstration of X-ray holography with an X-ray laser. J. E. Trebes and others. bibl f il *Science* 238:517-19 O 23 '87
In the light spot [optical trapping and manipulation of viruses and bacteria; work of Arthur Ashkin and Joseph M. Dziedzic] *Sci Am* 256:32 Je '87
Laser-stimulated luminescence used to measure X-ray diffraction of a contracting striated muscle. Y. Amemiya and others. bibl f il *Science* 237:164-8 Jl 10 '87
Optical trapping and manipulation of viruses and bacteria. A. Ashkin and J. M. Dziedzic. bibl f il *Science* 235:1517-20 Mr 20 '87
Tumor promoters halt cell-cell 'talk' [research by John Holland] J. Raloff. *Sci News* 131:230-1 Ap 11 '87

Chemical use
A new window onto the chemists' big bang [work of Ahmed H. Zewail and others] R. Lewin. il *Science* 238:1512-13 D 11 '87
Researchers climb inside of the fire to tweak the flame. B. Fellman. bibl (p229) il *Smithsonian* 18:70-2+ O '87
'Snapshots' of bond breaking and making [work of Ahmed H. Zewail and others] S. Weisburd. *Sci News* 132:372 D 12 '87

Communication use
Laser clones [views of J. D. G. Rather] B. Lawren. il *Omni* 9:24 Ja '87

Conferences
CLEO and IQEC in Baltimore [Conference on Lasers and Electro-optics and the International Quantum Electronics Conference] M. Marynowski. il *Phys Today* 40:62-3 Mr '87

Earth sciences use
Laser techniques in high-pressure geophysics. R. J. Hemley and others. bibl f il *Science* 237:605-12 Ag 7 '87

Industrial use
See also
Spectra-Physics, Inc.
Laser shaping of ultrahard materials [work of Stephen Copley and Michael Bass] *USA Today (Periodical)* 115:14-15 Je '87
Lasers at work. il *Pop Mech* 164:67 N '87
The powers in a beam of light [lasers by Lumonics] il *Macleans* 100:39 Ap 20 '87

Measurement use
In the blink of a laser. S. Budiansky. il *U S News World Rep* 102:68 F 2 '87

Medical use
Clogged arteries take the laser's heat—painlessly. J. Carey. il *U S News World Rep* 102:69 F 16 '87

The gentlest cut of all [gynecological laser surgery] J. Wilson. *Health* 19:57-8+ O '87
A laser to lighten the heart [vaporizing cholesterol] M. Nichols. il *Macleans* 100:45 Ag 31 '87
Laser treatment to go: outpatient uses of healing light abound [cover story] D. Farley. il *FDA Consum* 21:22-7 O '87
Lasers and heart disease [work of James M. Seeger and others in treating arteries] R. Anthony. il *Technol Rev* 90:14-15 Ap '87
Leapin' lizards! This doc zaps hearts [laser canalization; work of M. Mirhoseini] J. Langone. il por *Discover* 8:56-8+ Ag '87
Shedding light on lasers. B. Davidson. il *McCalls* 115:90+ O '87
Treating endometriosis. P. Gadsby and L. J. Brown. il *Good Housekeep* 204:213 Je '87
Unclogging arteries [use of lasers and balloons] P. Gadsby and L. J. Brown. il *Good Housekeep* 204:213 Je '87

Meteorological use
Laser remote sensing of the atmosphere [lidar systems] D. K. Killinger and N. Menyuk. bibl f il *Science* 235:37-45 Ja 2 '87

Military use
APS releases report on directed-energy weapons [special section] bibl f il *Phys Today* 40:S1-S16 My '87
Ball Aerospace will test ground-based laser element [Relay Mirror Experiment] B. A. Smith. il *Aviat Week Space Technol* 127:99+ O 19 '87
Chemical laser destroys target drone. *Aviat Week Space Technol* 127:22 O 5 '87
Debate on APS directed-energy weapons study. G. H. Canavan and others. bibl f pors *Phys Today* 40:48-53 N '87
Free electron laser success explained. A. L. Robinson. il *Science* 235:27-9 Ja 2 '87
Ground-based lasers [SDI program] il *Aviat Week Space Technol* 127:77+ N 23 '87
Martin lab halves time needed to retarget space-based laser. B. A. Smith. il *Aviat Week Space Technol* 127:28-9 S 14 '87
Martin, Lockheed, TRW win work on SDI Zenith Star laser. T. M. Foley. *Aviat Week Space Technol* 127:32-3 O 12 '87
Martin Marietta hosts Reagan SDI visit [Zenith Star laser spacecraft project] T. M. Foley. il *Aviat Week Space Technol* 127:21-2 N 30 '87
Martin Marietta selected to design potential nuclear SDI systems [nuclear-powered X-ray laser platform and nuclear hypervelocity pellet system] T. M. Foley. *Aviat Week Space Technol* 127:113-14 Ag 10 '87
Physicists assess laser lethality for ballistic missile defense role [American Physical Society] P. J. Klass. *Aviat Week Space Technol* 126:104-5 My 18 '87
Sandia develops nuclear-powered Falcon optical laser concept. T. M. Foley. *Aviat Week Space Technol* 127:24 O 19 '87
SDI attempts to zap APS directed-energy weapons report. I. Goodwin. il *Phys Today* 40:43-6 Je '87
SDI considers cluster booster to launch Zenith Star spacecraft. C. Covault. il *Aviat Week Space Technol* 127:20-1 N 30 '87
SDIO assesses energy storage for FEL defense [free electron lasers utilizing superconducting magnetic energy storage] *Aviat Week Space Technol* 126:29 Ap 6 '87
SDI's Starlab shuttle mission will test laser tracking system. *Aviat Week Space Technol* 127:25 O 19 '87
The secrets of Soviet Star Wars. W. J. Broad. il map *N Y Times Mag* p22+ Je 28 '87
Signaling subs. T. A. Heppenheimer. il *Pop Sci* 230:44-8 Ap '87
Soviet ground lasers threaten U.S. geosynchronous satellites. J. D. Morrocco. *Aviat Week Space Technol* 127:27 N 2 '87
Soviet strategic laser sites imaged by French Spot satellite. C. Covault. il *Aviat Week Space Technol* 127:26-7 O 26 '87
Space-based laser [SDI program] il *Aviat Week Space Technol* 127:80-1 N 23 '87
Stanford/TRW team demonstrates potential lethality increase of space-based free-electron lasers. *Aviat Week Space Technol* 126:23 Mr 16 '87
Star Wars in Orogrande [laser testing site] F. Gibney. il map *Newsweek* 110:42 O 19 '87
Star Wars lasers: a question of technical integrity. I. Peterson. *Sci News* 132:276 O 31 '87
Starlab to engage satellites, rockets, ground-based laser. T. M. Foley. il *Aviat Week Space Technol* 127:58-9 O 26 '87

Lasers—Military use—_cont._
Strategic defense and directed-energy weapons. C. K. N. Patel and N. Bloembergen. il map *Sci Am* 257:39-45 S '87

Mirrors
Ball Aerospace will test ground-based laser element [Relay Mirror Experiment] B. A. Smith. il *Aviat Week Space Technol* 127:99+ O 19 '87

Patents
The end of a long patent fight [case of G. Gould] *Sci News* 132:349 N 28 '87
Vindicated! [inventor G. Gould] K. Hannon. por *Forbes* 140:35-6 D 14 '87

Photographic use
See also
Holography
His classic eye catches light from the laser [K. Dexter] il por *Smithsonian* 17:118-21 F '87
Laser light on film. K. Dexter. il *Petersens Photogr Mag* 15:12-15+ Ja '87

Physics use
Bright prospects for laboratory lasers. S. Weisburd. *Sci News* 131:149 Mr 7 '87
Cooling and trapping atoms. W. D. Phillips and H. J. Metcalf. bibl (p128) il *Sci Am* 256:50-6 Mr '87
Four groups build more efficient atom traps. A. L. Robinson. il *Science* 237:26-8 Jl 3 '87
Laser cooling [cover story] D. J. Wineland and W. M. Itano. bibl f il *Phys Today* 40:34-40 Je '87
Light switch [work of André Mysyrowicz and others] *Sci Am* 256:74-5 Mr '87

Scientific use
Research applications of lasers [special issue; with editorial comment by David F. Voss] *Science* 237:573, 605-25 Ag 7 '87

Space flight use
The light stuff: laser propulsion. N. McAleer. il *Space World* X-7-283:9-11 Jl '87

Sports use
Laser bull's-eye. W. Siuru. il *Pop Sci* 231:126 N '87

Surgical use
See Lasers—Medical use
Lasers in criminal investigation, espionage, etc.
Laser listener [cover story] R. L. Pearson. il *Radio-Electron* 58:39-44 O '87
Laser listener legalities [discussion of October 1987 article, Laser listener] R. L. Pearson. il *Radio-Electron* 58:8-9 N '87

Lash, Marilyn
about
The sound of success. S. Mieses. il por *N Y* 20:22 Ap 6 '87

Lasix *See* Furosemide
Lasker, David
A formal balance: cosmopolitan influences in a Toronto setting. il *Archit Dig* 44:90-5 F '87
On foot in old Kingston, Ontario. il *Travel Holiday* 167:20-3 Ja '87

Lasker (Albert and Mary) Foundation *See* Albert and Mary Lasker Foundation
Lasker awards *See* Albert and Mary Lasker Foundation
Laskoski, Beth
Being a heavy in a skinny world. il *Seventeen* 46:336-7+ Ag '87

Lasky, Jane E.
(jt. auth) *See* Reed, David, and Lasky, Jane E.
Lasley, Thomas J.
Teaching selflessness in a selfish society. bibl f il *Phi Delta Kappan* 68:674-8 My '87

Lasorda, Tom
about
Next to his family and his beloved Dodger blue, Tommy Lasorda lives for food—and his restaurant. T. Gold. il pors *People Wkly* 28:103-4 Jl 13 '87

Lass, Matthew
about
Cushioned. *New Yorker* 62:21-2 Ja 26 '87
Lasso, Galo Plaza *See* Plaza Lasso, Galo, 1906-1987
Lasswell, Fred
about
Snuffy Smith's pappy. D. Young. il por *South Living* 22:106 Jl '87
The last bus [drama] *See* Storey, Raymond
The last emperor [film] *See* Motion picture reviews—Single works
Last Judgment *See* Judgment Day
The last straw [film] *See* Motion picture reviews—Single works
Last Supper in art
Restoring The Last Supper. il *Travel Holiday* 168:54 S '87

Laster, Howard, 1930-1986
about
Obituary
Phys Today por 40:106 D '87. A. Bardasis
Laszlo, Ervin, 1932-
about
Ervin Laszlo. B. Lawren. *Omni* 9:96 S '87
Laszlo, Pierre
Chemical reactions on clays. bibl f il *Science* 235:1473-7 Mr 20 '87
Latches
Sliding gate latch. D. Bartholomew. il *Workbench* 43:53-4 Jl/Ag '87
Latchkey children *See* Children of working parents
Late night with David Letterman [television program] *See* Television program reviews—Single works
Late nite comic [musical] *See* Musicals, revues, etc.—Reviews—Single works
The late show [television program] *See* Television program reviews—Single works
Lateness *See* Tardiness
Lateral sclerosis *See* Amyotrophic lateral sclerosis
Laterality
See also
Left- and right-handedness
Split brain
Give Randy Adamadama 40 minutes—he'll have you seeing the light [owner of Synchro-Energizer salon in California] il por *People Wkly* 28:134-5 D 14 '87
The language of the brain [cover story] B. Bower. il *Sci News* 132:40-1 Jl 18 '87
Left brain, right brain: do we educate both? S. P. Springer. *Educ Dig* 53:22-5 O '87
A link between the brains of mice and men [research by Günter Ehret] il *Discover* 8:10+ Ap '87
Mice get an earful from left brain [research by Günter Ehret] B. Bower. *Sci News* 131:69 Ja 31 '87
Old familiar voices [familiar-voice recognition] D. Van Lancker. il *Psychol Today* 21:12-13 N '87
The right turn of phrase [processing of familiar language in the brain's right hemisphere] D. Kempler and D. Van Lancker. il *Psychol Today* 21:20+ Ap '87

Anecdotes, facetiae, satire, etc.
Whose brain is it anyway? J. Gorman. il *Discover* 8:38+ N '87

Latex producing plants *See* Rubber producing plants
Latham, Colin
Fitness in the workplace [address, February 18, 1987] *Vital Speeches Day* 53:446-8 My 1 '87
Lathe chucks (Machine work) *See* Chucks (Machine work)
Lathes
See also
Turning (Machine work)
Conover 16 inch lathe set. il *Workbench* 43:50-2 Ja/F '87

Safety devices and measures
Working safely on the lathe. A. R. Gould. il *Workbench* 43:54-5 N/D '87
Lathlaen, Peggy
The teacher who dared to dream. il *Ladies Home J* 104:78+ F '87
Lathrop, Julia Clifford, 1858-1932
about
Children's Bureau 75th anniversary: 1912-1987. C. Reece. il por *Child Today* 16:4-7 S/O '87
Latin America
See also
Birth control—Latin America
Children—Latin America
Costume—Latin America
Guerrillas—Latin America
Immigration and emigration—Latin America
Jazz music—Latin America
Loans, Bank—Latin America
Medical care—Latin America
Motion pictures—Latin America
Narcotics laws and regulations—Latin America
Public health—Latin America
Rain forests—Latin America
Relief work—Latin America
Science—Latin America
South America
Water supply—Latin America
Wildlife conservation—Latin America
Women—Latin America
Regional report: Latin America. L. Rogers. *See* issues of World Press Review beginning September 1986
Trends. *See* issues of Américas

Bibliography
Book reviews. *Curr Hist* 86:125+ Mr '87
Book reviews. *Curr Hist* 86:33 Ja '87

Latin America—Bibliography—*cont.*
Books. See issues of Américas
Books on Latin America. A. A. Reding. *America* 156:252-4+ Mr 28 '87
Civilization
South of the border. E. von Kuehnelt-Leddihn. *Natl Rev* 39:28 O 9 '87
Commerce
Nicaragua
See Nicaragua—Commerce—Latin America
United States
See United States—Commerce—Latin America
Cultural relations
United States
See United States—Cultural relations—Latin America
Defenses
See also
Airplanes, Military—Latin America
Economic conditions
See also
United Nations. Economic Commission for Latin America and the Caribbean
Domination in Latin America. H. Lacey. *Cent Mag* 20:60-1 Mr/Ap '87
Economic policy
Beggaring our Latin neighbors. P. Lernoux. il *Nation* 245:709-10+ D 12 '87
The debtors' revolt is spreading in Latin America. J. Ryser and others. il *Bus Week* p88-9 D 28 '87-Ja 4 '88
Expanding freedom: a formula for growth in the Americas. E. Abrams; P. D. Taylor. il *Dep State Bull* 87:79-84 F '87
The outlook for Latin America debt. P.-P. Kuczynski. il *Foreign Aff* 66:129-49 Fall '87
Economic relations
United States
See United States—Economic relations—Latin America
Foreign relations
Brazil
See Brazil—Foreign relations—Latin America
Cuba
See Cuba—Foreign relations—Latin America
Mexico
See Mexico—Foreign relations—Latin America
United States
See United States—Foreign relations—Latin America
History
The Americas: enlightenment and enterprise [excerpt from Memory of fire]; tr. by Cedric Belfrage. E. H. Galeano. *Harpers* 274:24+ F '87
Wars of Independence, 1806-1830
Devoted wives, determined rebels. E. M. Cherpak. il *Américas* 39:32-7 Mr/Ap '87
Industries
See also
Aerospace industries—Latin America
Airlines—Latin America
Clothing industry—Latin America
Small business—Latin America
Politics and government
See also
Monroe Doctrine
Democracy in Latin America and the Caribbean: the promise and the challenge. il *Dep State Bull* 87:58-89 Mr '87
Guerrillas who came in from the cold [restoration of democracy in Uruguay, Argentina, and Brazil] C. A. Robbins. il *U S News World Rep* 102:33-4 My 11 '87
Latin America and the Caribbean: the paths to democracy [address, June 30, 1987] E. Abrams. *Dep State Bull* 87:81-5 S '87
South America, 1987 [special issue] bibl f map (inside back cover) *Curr Hist* 86:1-42 Ja '87
Strengthening Latin American democracy. A. F. Lowenthal. *Commonweal* 114:268 My 8 '87
To nurture Latin democracy [excerpt from address, March 1987] M. Vargas Llosa. *Harpers* 274:15-18 Je '87
Population
More Latin migrants. il *Futurist* 21:45 Ja/F '87
Religious institutions and affairs
See also
Catholic Church—Latin America
Church and social problems—Latin America
Evangelical churches—Latin America
Evangelistic work—Latin America

John Paul II, Pope, 1920-—Visit to Latin America, 1987
Social conditions
See also
Women—Latin America
Study and teaching
See Latin American studies
Latin America and the United States
The United States and Latin America [with discussion] C. Fuentes. il por *Cent Mag* 20:4-19 Ja/F '87
Bibliography
Books on the Americas. B. Ramsey. *America* 157:168+ S 26 '87
Latin American art *See* Art, Latin American
Latin American dance *See* Dance, Latin American
Latin American fashion designers *See* Fashion designers
Latin American music *See* Music, Latin American
Latin American photographers *See* Photographers, Latin American
Latin American studies
Learning democracy's ways [Model OAS General Assembly] C. Whelan. il *Américas* 39:50-2 S/O '87
Latin Americans
Photographs and photography
The other Americas [S. Salgado's photographs] C. Healy. il *Américas* 39:2-7 Mr/Ap '87
United States
See also
Hispanic Americans
The emigration of innocents [adoption of Latin American children] C. J. Carney. *Commonweal* 114:79-82 F 13 '87
Immigration challenge. *Society* 24:2 My/Je '87
Latin legacy in the City by the Bay. S. E. Caldwell. il *Américas* 39:44-9 N/D '87
The multiplying minority. *U S News World Rep* 103:13 S 21 '87
Latin language
Study and teaching
See also
Latin teachers
Latin rises again. A. T. Hodge. *World Press Rev* 34:57 N '87
Latin teachers
A teacher's teacher [high school Latin teacher T. Jones; cover story] J. W. Donohue. *America* 157:495-7 D 26 '87
Latinos (U.S.) *See* Hispanic Americans
Lattanzi (New York, N.Y.: Restaurant) *See* New York (N.Y.)—Restaurants, nightclubs, bars, etc.
Lattanzi family
about
Family-style: the Lattanzis have built a restaurant dynasty on anti-chic. S. Squire. il *N Y* 20:90-2+ Ag 24 '87
Latter-Day Saints *See* Mormons and Mormonism
Lattice fences *See* Fences
Latticework
A minor miracle in lattice. il *Sunset* 178:112-13 My '87
Latvia
See also
Art—Latvia
Lauda, Niki, 1949-
Niki Lauda: meine story [excerpt] il pors *Mot Trend* 39:105-8 Ja '87
Lauder, Aerin
about
An American in Vienna: Aerin Lauder. C. Hanauer. pors *Seventeen* 46:118+ S '87
Lauder, Estée
about
The best of their class. J. Fierman. il por *Fortune* 116:144-5 O 12 '87
The make-over at Estee Lauder. L. Belkin. il pors *N Y Times Mag* p32-3+ N 29 '87
Lauder, Evelyn
about
American heritage: Yankee art, western vistas. F. Stanfill. il pors *Vogue* 177:340-7+ Ap '87
Lauder, Jo Carole
about
A Vienna success. T. Lessing. il por *House Gard* 159:100-5+ Jl '87
Lauder, Leonard
about
American heritage: Yankee art, western vistas. F. Stanfill. il pors *Vogue* 177:340-7+ Ap '87
The make-over at Estee Lauder. L. Belkin. il pors *N Y Times Mag* p32-3+ N 29 '87

Lauder, Ronald S., 1944-
about
A Vienna success. T. Lessing. il por *House Gard* 159:100-5+ Jl '87
Lauer, Jeanette C., and Lauer, Robert H.
How fighting can help a marriage [excerpt from Till death do us part] il *Ladies Home J* 104:42+ Jl '87
Lauer, Robert H.
(jt. auth) See Lauer, Jeanette C., and Lauer, Robert H.
Laufer, Hans, 1929-, and others
Identification of a juvenile hormone-like compound in a crustacean. bibl f il *Science* 235:202-5 Ja 9 '87
Laugh tracks *See* Television broadcasting—Laugh tracks
Laughery, Jack
about
Hardee's: the bigger it grows, the hungrier it gets. D. Foust. il por *Bus Week* p106 My 4 '87
Laughing wild [drama] See Durang, Christopher, 1949-
Laughridge, Jamie, 1951-
Getting high on danger. *Harpers Bazaar* 120:89-90+ Jl '87
Laughter
See also
Humor
Smiles
Seriously, smile! Laughter—the new beauty attitude. il *Mademoiselle* 93:256-61 S '87
What's so funny? B. Borns. il *Seventeen* 46:112 N '87
Anecdotes, facetiae, satire, etc.
Brandy by firelight. I. Frazier. *New Yorker* 63:37 D 21 '87
Psychological aspects
It only hurts when I don't laugh [laughter as a pain killer; research by Rosemary Cogan] E. Grant. *Psychol Today* 21:21 S '87
Laugh and be well? P. Long. bibl (p62) il *Psychol Today* 21:28-9 O '87
Laugh away your troubles [views of Robert Leone] *USA Today (Periodical)* 116:10 Jl '87
Laughing matters: giggling can be good for you. il *Teen* 31:32+ F '87
Launchers for guided missiles *See* Guided missiles—Propulsion systems
Launchers for space vehicles *See* Space vehicles—Propulsion systems
Launching of space vehicles *See* Space vehicles—Launching
Launching pads, sites, etc. for space vehicles *See* Space vehicles—Launching pads, sites, etc.
Laundering of money
See also
Iran-contra affair
American bank loans line the pockets of the third world's elite [views of R. T. Naylor] S. C. Gwynne. *Wash Mon* 19:51-2 O '87
The biggest drug bust. J. A. Conway. il *Forbes* 139:8 Je 1 '87
Cashing in on ill-gotten gains [seizing proceeds derived from drug trafficking] D. Francis. il *Macleans* 100:13 N 2 '87
Laundromats
Wash & sweat [Clean & Lean, laundromat-fitness center in Visa, Calif.] *Time* 130:94 N 16 '87
Canada
Bubbles and beer mats. A. Steacy. il *Macleans* 100:62-3 S 28 '87
Laundry
Clip-out stain chart. K. Beckett. *Redbook* 169:173 S '87
How to remove the 10 worst stains from kids' clothes. il *Good Housekeep* 205:148 S '87
History
Rainy day blues and whites. M. Reed. il *Weatherwise* 40:262-3 O '87
Laundry equipment
See also
Clothes dryers
Washing machines
Laundry products
See also
Bleaching materials
Detergents
Fabric softeners
Launius, Cliff
about
An Illinois policeman puts his job on the line by rushing to the aid of his family. il por *People Wkly* 28:59 O 19 '87

Lauper, Cyndi
about
Can Cyndi Lauper bring back the headdress? C. Krupp. il por *Glamour* 85:138 Ja '87
Cyndi Lauper. D. Fricke. il por *Roll Stone* p13 F 12 '87
Cyndi Lauper flies her true colors. J. A. Baggett. por *Sch Update* 119:25 Ja 12 '87
Laura Dean Dancers and Musicians
Deanmusicdance. G. Parks. il por *Dance Mag* 61:54-5 Ap '87
Faux pas [performance of Magnetic at the Joyce Theater, New York City] T. Tobias. il *N Y* 20:137-8 Ap 27 '87
Laurance, David
about
On Riverside Drive. M. M. Thomas. il por *Archit Dig* 44:156-63 N '87
Laurel, Stan, 1890-1965
about
Laurel and Hardy in the big house. D. M. Kimmel. il pors *Film Comment* 23:2+ Jl/Ag '87
Laurel Race Course (Laurel, Md.) *See* Race tracks
Lauren, Ralph
about
Ralph Lauren's achievement. H. Brubach. il *Atlantic* 260:70-3 Ag '87
Laurence, Anne
Irish studies and myth history. il *Hist Today* 37:8-9 D '87
Laurence, Jeffrey, and others
Characterization and clinical association of antibody inhibitory to HIV reverse transcriptase activity. bibl f il *Science* 235:1501-4 Mr 20 '87
Laurence, Margaret, 1926-1987
about
Obituary
Macleans il pors 100:52-3 Ja 19 '87. T. Findley
Laurent, André
(jt. auth) See Bartolomé, Fernando, and Laurent, André
Laurentian Group Corporation
Laurentian's Asian campaign. P. C. Newman. il por *Macleans* 100:24 Jl 13 '87
Laurier [television program] See Television program reviews—Single works
Laurin, Ginette
about
Working with music, muscle and motion. P. Hluchy. pors *Macleans* 100:54 Mr 9 '87
Laurino, Maria
The battle of Bork. il por *Ms* 16:111-12 S '87
Prosecuting Jennifer Levin's killer. il pors *Ms* 16:70-2+ S '87
Laurita, Raymond E.
Let's do something about literacy now! *America* 156:455-6 Je 6 '87
Lausanne Committee for World Evangelization
Calling the next generation of Christian leaders [Singapore 87 conference] J. D. Douglas. *Christ Today* 31:39 Ag 7 '87
Lausanne group sets theme for 1989 meeting. L. Mackey. *Christ Today* 31:50 Mr 6 '87
An old-fashioned preacher [interview with T. Wang] por *Christ Today* 31:52 Mr 6 '87
Lautman, Karl
Lag time. il *Omni* 9:16 Ja '87
Lautman, Victoria
An American cache at Chicago's R. H. Love Galleries. il por *Archit Dig* 44:74+ S '87
Lauzon, Jean-Claude
about
Soul search in the dark city. B. D. Johnson. il por *Macleans* 100:50 S 28 '87
Un zoo, la nuit [film] Reviews
Macleans il 100:50 S 28 '87. B. D. Johnson
LAV viruses *See* HIV viruses
Lava
Disruption of the Mauna Loa magma system by the 1868 Hawaiian earthquake: geochemical evidence. R. I. Tilling and others. bibl f il map *Science* 235:196-9 Ja 9 '87
Lavatera *See* Tree mallows
Lave, Lester B.
Health and safety risk analyses: information for better decisions. bibl f *Science* 236:291-5 Ap 17 '87
Laventhol & Horwath
But I'm just the piano player. J. Andresky. il *Forbes* 139:56-7 My 4 '87

Laver, Rod
about
Redheads have more fun. S. Flink. il pors *World Tennis* 35:18+ S '87
Laverack, Edward
about
The beauty contest. B. Tarrant. il *Field Stream* 92:102+ Ag '87
Lavergnee, Arnauld Brejon De
The great illusionists. il *Courier* 40:30-3 S '87
Lavery, Sean
about
A dancer's nightmare. L. Leivick. il pors *N Y Times Mag* p66+ N 8 '87
Lavi airplanes *See* Airplanes, Military—Israel
Lavin, Linda
about
Alice doesn't live like this anymore. D. Mason. il pors *Vogue* 177:338-9 Ap '87
Lavin, Mark
about
Obituary
Mot Boat Sail por 159:11 Ja '87. P. A. Janssen
Law
See also
Amicus curiae
Arbitration and award
Civil rights
Compensation (Law)
Confession (Law)
Contracts
Copyright
Corporation law
Courts
Divorce
Election laws
Emotional distress (Law)
Inheritance
International law
Jury
Justice
Lawyers
Legal ethics
Legal procedure
Liability (Law)
Libel and slander
Liquor laws and regulations
Maritime law
Narcotics laws and regulations
Power of attorney
Probate law and practice
Rule of law
Television broadcasting—Trials
United States. Supreme Court
Wills
See also subheads Law; Laws and regulations; Legal status, laws, etc. under various subjects
First word [future law] F. L. Bailey. il *Omni* 9:4 Ap '87
This is the law? Yes! [antiquated laws still on the books] A. H. Berger. il *Good Housekeep* 205:243 N '87
You and the law. T. Hauser. See issues of McCall's
History
See also
Roman law
Imagine, if you will, a time without any lawyers at all. L. Casson. bibl (p230) il *Smithsonian* 18:122-4+ O '87
Philosophy
See also
Law and ethics
Religious aspects
See Religion and law
Study and teaching
See also
Law clerks
Law schools
Even Communists like capitalist justice [Chinese students study law in the U.S.] J. Adler. il *Newsweek* 110:74 O 19 '87
California
See also
Thousand Oaks (Calif.)—Ordinances
Frank Fat's napkin: how the trial lawyers (and the doctors!) sold out to the tobacco companies. P. Glastris. il *Wash Mon* 19:19-25 D '87
China
Even Communists like capitalist justice [Chinese students study law in the U.S.] J. Adler. il *Newsweek* 110:74 O 19 '87

Law and China [American expert J. A. Cohen] *New Yorker* 62:25-6 Ja 19 '87
Florida
Florida's new crop of pistol packers [gun controls lifted] T. Gest. il *U S News World Rep* 103:16 O 12 '87
A lethal lucky charm [gun laws] M. McIver. il *Macleans* 100:59-60 O 12 '87
Local gun controls bite the dust. T. Gest. il *U S News World Rep* 102:14-15 My 25 '87
Pistol packers. C. Garcia. il *Time* 130:28 S 28 '87
Prentice Rasheed jabs Florida's new gun law. il por *Jet* 73:18 O 19 '87
Wyatt Earp comes to the Sunshine State [gun law] *Newsweek* 110:42 O 12 '87
Maryland
See also
Baltimore (Md.)—Ordinances
Massachusetts
Hypocrisy [legal referral fees] D. Fanning. *Forbes* 140:83 D 14 '87
Minnesota
An acid test for antitakeover laws [law could help Alberto-Culver land Lamaur] M. J. Pitzer. il *Bus Week* p31 S 28 '87
Free gifts [anti-takeover measure influenced by Dayton Hudson's charity] J. K. Glassman. *New Repub* 197:10+ Jl 27 '87
New York (State)
See also
New York (N.Y.)—Ordinances
A fair share [N.Y. divorce ruling holds M. O'Brien's medical license to be form of property]; ed. by Micki Siegel. R. Maloney. il por *Good Housekeep* 205:54+ N '87
Texas
See also
Bedford (Tex.)—Ordinances
Attacking elderly abuse. P. Chance. il *Psychol Today* 21:24-5 S '87
United States
See Law
Virginia
Author and publisher groups make filings in two Supreme Court cases [challenge to a law on how certain books may be displayed] H. Fields. *Publ Wkly* 232:12 S 4 '87
High Court to review Va. minors access law. M. Yen. *Publ Wkly* 231:30 Mr 6 '87
Supreme Court justices quiz both sides in Virginia minors access law. H. Fields. *Publ Wkly* 232:16 N 20 '87
Law (Theology)
See also
Jewish law
Anecdotes, facetiae, satire, etc.
The law firm of Glitz, Hype, and Schmaltz. V. G. Beers. il *Christ Today* 31:13 Ap 3 '87
Law and economics
Law and economics: a new order in the Court? P. Dwyer. il por *Bus Week* p93+ N 16 '87
Reagan's Chicago farm team [law and economics training at University of Chicago Law School] J. McCormick. il *Newsweek* 110:46 N 9 '87
Law and ethics
The higher law: Bork, Burke, & moral relativism. D. R. Carlin, Jr. *Commonweal* 114:729-30 D 18 '87
Law and politics
The politicalization of America's courts [address, October 16, 1987] R. Neely. *Vital Speeches Day* 54:147-50 D 15 '87
The power of politics and the politics of power. S. M. Buchanan. por *Cent Mag* 20:4-8 Jl/Ag '87
Law and religion *See* Religion and law
Law clerks
Death row clerk [death penalty work in the Supreme Court] C. Sloan. *New Repub* 196:18+ F 16 '87
Law enforcement
See also
Computers—Police use
National Organization of Black Law Enforcement Executives
Police
Sheriffs
United States. Federal Bureau of Investigation
Law firms
See also
Black law firms
Cravath, Swaine & Moore
Finley, Kumble, Wagner, Heine, Underberg, Manley, Myerson & Casey
Herrick & Feinstein
Holland & Knight

Law firms—See also—*cont.*
Milbank, Tweed, Hadley & McCloy
Pucillo and Jaynes
Sullivan & Cromwell
United Law Network
Are storefront lawyers really a bargain? [legal clinics]
B. G. Quint. il *Glamour* 85:248+ My '87
Soon anybody may be able to own a law firm. P.
Dwyer. il *Bus Week* p42 Ja 26 '87
Tremors in the realm of giants. R. Lacayo. il *Time*
130:58-9 D 7 '87
Law of desire [film] See Motion picture reviews—Single
works
Law schools
See also
Columbia University. School of Law
Harvard Law School
University of Chicago. Law School
University of Iowa. College of Law
University of Michigan. Law School
Brains for the bar. il *U S News World Rep* 103:72-3
N 2 '87
Law societies
See also
Federalist Society
Law students
Civil rights
Trial by fire [University of Michigan law student J.
Picozzi accused of arson] T. Senger. il *Roll Stone*
p111-12+ S 24 '87
Lawford, Valentine
Paris in the thirties: some letters home. il por *Archit
Dig* 44:210+ Mr '87
Lawler, Pat
Celebration [story] il por *McCalls* 114:136+ Ap
'87
A matter of responsibility [story] il *McCalls* 114:66+
F '87
Lawless, James
Moscow "radicals" stop a nuclear plant. il por *Sierra*
72:125-30 Ja/F '87
Lawn care industry
The dangers of lawn care. J. Burnett. il *Rodale's Org
Gard* 34:24-32 N '87
Green dreams [potential problems from lawn chemicals]
J. R. Provey. il *Home Mech* 83:4 Mr '87
Look into a lawn service. il *South Living* 22:110 Ap
'87
Lawn chairs See Chairs
Lawn equipment
1987 guide to lawn care. M. Thompson. il map *Fam
Handyman* 37:48-50+ Mr '87
Blower vacs. T. O. Bakke. il *Pop Sci* 231:98-100 N
'87
Compact air broom [Homelite's HB-380 Yard Bug] D.
Chaikin. il *Home Mech* 83:89 Ja '87
Get ready for fall. il *Workbench* 43:60-1 S/O '87
Machines in the garden. M. Ferrara. il *Home Mech*
83:52-6 Ap '87
Small and lightweight: a new trend in equipment. il
Flower Gard 31:38-9 Je/Jl '87
Speed yard cleanup this fall [cover story] M. Ferrara.
il *Home Mech* 83:42-4+ O '87
What's new for your lawn and garden. T. O. Bakke.
See occasional issues of Popular Science beginning
June 1986
Yard power. il *Pop Mech* 164:101-2+ Ag '87
Maintenance and repair
See also
National Equipment Servicing Dealers Association
Safety devices and measures
Spring clean up: safety in the yard. T. M. Scanlon.
Consum Res Mag 70:25-7 My '87
Lawn mowers
1987 guide to lawn care. M. Thompson. il map *Fam
Handyman* 37:48-50+ Mr '87
External combustion [Great States hand-powered reel
mowers] *Ctry J* 14:13 My '87
You don't need 40 acres to ride a mower in style.
P. Houston. il *Bus Week* p110 Je 29 '87
Maintenance and repair
Bedding down your mower. M. Ferrara. il *Home Mech*
83:80 O '87
Keeping your mower alive. G. Buford. il *Rodale's Org
Gard* 34:66-73 Ap '87
Testing
Choosing a lawn mower. il *Consum Rep* 52:332-43 Je
'87
Electric lawn mowers. il *Consum Rep* 52:242-5 D '87
Gasoline lawn mowers. il *Consum Rep* 52:237-41 D
'87

Lawn seed *See* Grasses—Seed
Lawn sprinklers *See* Sprinklers
Lawn tractors *See* Tractors
Lawns
See also
Lawn care industry
10 steps to a healthy lawn. P. H. Johnson. il *Rodale's
Org Gard* 34:46-9 My '87
1987 guide to lawn care. M. Thompson. il map *Fam
Handyman* 37:48-50+ Mr '87
Hell no, it won't grow! Canada's Dr. Jan Weijer has
a lawn you'll have to mow only once a year. il por
People Wkly 28:39 Ag 10 '87
The perfect lawn grass? il *Sunset* 179:74-7 S '87
Shortcuts to a healthy lawn. E. Henke. il *Saturday Evening
Post* 259:96-7 Ap '87
Tomorrow's good lawns are in the bag today (literally!).
A. Reilly. il *Flower Gard* 31:18-19 Ag/S '87
Lawrance, Simon K., and others
Megabase-scale mapping of the HLA gene complex by
pulsed field gel electrophoresis. bibl f il *Science*
235:1387-90 Mr 13 '87
Lawren, Bill
(ed) See Stunkard, Albert J., 1922-. Family fat
Lawrence, D. H. (David Herbert), 1885-1930
about
The combustible Lawrence, still smoldering. A. Broyard.
il *N Y Times Book Rev* 92:14 N 8 '87
Lawrence, David Herbert See Lawrence, D. H. (David
Herbert), 1885-1930
Lawrence, Douglas P.
about
Against the odds [cover story] D. R. Squires. il pors
Black Enterp 18:48-50+ O '87
Lawrence, Elizabeth
Gardening for love [excerpt] bibl il por *Rodale's Org
Gard* 34:28-31 O '87
about
Garden writers, classic and contemporary. B. Summer.
Publ Wkly 231:40 Mr 20 '87
Lawrence, Greg
(ed) See Kirkland, Gelsey. Malicious Misha
Lawrence, Jacob
about
Bound for glory. K. Larson. il *N Y* 20:112-13 O 19
'87
Jacob Lawrence: art as seen through a people's history.
R. Wernick. bibl (p153) il por *Smithsonian* 18:56-64+
Je '87
Jacob Lawrence: Brooklyn Museum. E. Heartney. il *Art
News* 86:143 D '87
Lawrence, James
about
Harrowsmith's leader cuts his roots. A. Shortell. il por
Macleans 100:30 Mr 30 '87
Lawrence, Kathleen Rockwell
Unnatural acts and other papal indiscretions. il *Ms* 16:118
S '87
Womb for rent. *Vogue* 177:84 Jl '87
Lawrence, Melinda
Can you really trust a lab test? The scary truth. il
Glamour 85:74+ N '87
Lawrence, Miles B.
Atlantic hurricane season. il map *Weatherwise* 40:21-4
F '87
Lawrence, Rae
Pop fiction for smart girls. il por *N Y Times Mag*
p20-1 Jl 5 '87
about
Cliffie notes. S. Squire. il por *N Y* 20:24 Je 1 '87
The selling of the young. J. Giles. *Natl Rev* 39:64-5
N 20 '87
Lawrence, Robert Z., 1949-, and Litan, Robert E., 1950-
Say no to tariffs: why protectionism doesn't pay. il
Current 298:18-23 D '87
Lawrence, Sally
How to feed a beach. il *Oceans* 20:42-7 Mr/Ap '87
Lawrence (Ernest Orlando) Memorial Awards See Ernest
Orlando Lawrence Memorial Awards
Lawrence (Kan.)
Arts
See also
Lawrence Arts Center (Kan.)
Lawrence [special section] il *Horizon* 30:17-30+ S '87
Description
Lawrence [special section] il *Horizon* 30:17-30+ S '87
Historic houses, sites, etc.
Main Street city. M. Wade. il *Horizon* 30:23 S '87
Theater
See also
Seem-To-Be Players

Lawrence Arts Center (Kan.)
Enhancing the arts. B. Golightly. il *Horizon* 30:21-2 S '87
Lawrence Berkeley Laboratory
Berkeley lab marshals superconductor research in Bay Area. *Aviat Week Space Technol* 127:92 N 23 '87
Desperately seeking supernovae [cover story] R. N. Kahn. il *Sky Telesc* 73:594-7 Je '87
Letters [discussion of June 1987 article, Desperately seeking supernovae] R. N. Kahn. *Sky Telesc* 74:229-30 S '87
Lawrence R. Klein Award *See* Journalism—Awards
Laws, Rita
It's time to notice our invisible children. por *U S News World Rep* 103:4 Ag 10 '87
Laws *See* Law
Lawson, David
F.C.S. Schiller: an appreciation. *Humanist* 47:35 S/O '87
John Reed: a centenary tribute. *Humanist* 47:33-4 Mr/Ap '87
Wallace Stevens: poet of the secular imagination. *Humanist* 47:35-6 My/Je '87
Lawson, Eddie
about
YZR500: acronym for speed. D. Coe. il pors *Cycle* 38:62-4+ Jl '87
Lawson, Edward
about
This is against my rights! Three who felt wronged—and determined to battle for redress. G. Jaynes. il pors *Time* 130:40-2 Jl 6 '87
Lawson, Thomas
about
Thomas Lawson at Metro Pictures. H. Cotter. il *Art Am* 75:156 Je '87
Lawson National Distributing Company
Tapping the public market. L. Gite. il *Black Enterp* 17:63 Ap '87
Lawsuits *See* Actions and defenses
Lawton, Thomas, 1931-
about
Animal magnetism. D. Kazanjian. il *House Gard* 159:166-71+ S '87
Lawyers
See also
Belli, Melvin M., 1907-
Callahan, Michael
Clothing and dress—Lawyers
Cohen, Jerome Alan
Conflict of interests (Lawyers)
Donnelly, V. Paul
Engel, Bruce
Felder, Raoul
Golub, Richard
Grutman, Norman Roy
Janklow, Mort
Keane, Noel P., 1938-
Law clerks
Law firms
Legal ethics
Liman, Arthur L.
National Bar Association
Priests as lawyers
Public prosecutors
Reynolds, William Bradford
Rubin, Ellis
Shea, Quinlan
Slotnick, Barry Ivan
Sofaer, Abraham David, 1938-
Sullivan, Brendan V.
Tribe, Laurence H.
Vachss, Andrew H.
Vergès, Jacques
Volunteers of Legal Service
Ward, Thomas J.
Women lawyers
Best divorce lawyers in America. *Harpers Bazaar* 120:140+ Ag '87
A fear of lawyers. M. Torgov. il *N Y Times Mag* p64 N 15 '87
The lawyers to call when there's heat on the Street [attorneys who battle for accused insider traders] G. Weiss. il *Bus Week* p58+ Ap 6 '87
The new breed of patent attorney. R. Weiss. *Sci News* 132:125 Ag 22 '87
Too many lawyers? J. G. Kester. il *Read Dig* 130:153-4+ Ap '87
Wall Street's watchword: hire a watchdog [in-house legal staffs] L. J. Tell. il *Bus Week* p120+ O 5 '87

When you need a lawyer. *Good Housekeep* 204:281 My '87
Whose trial is it anyway? [defense lawyers attacking victims and prosecutors in court] R. Lacayo. il *Time* 129:62 My 25 '87
Advertising
Bring on the clowns. D. Seligman. il *Fortune* 115:120 Ja 19 '87
A decade of lawyer ads. R. R. Roha. il *Changing Times* 41:120 O '87
Malpractice
See Malpractice
Salaries, fees, etc.
See also
Prepaid legal services
Fee-busting [lawyers serving as executors and estate attorneys] D. Fanning. il *Forbes* 140:64 S 7 '87
How to keep legal fees somewhere within reason. D. H. Dunn. il *Bus Week* p91 Ag 24 '87
Hypocrisy [referral fees in Mass.] D. Fanning. *Forbes* 140:83 D 14 '87
In the wake of a tragic hotel fire, disaster attorneys seek compensation for the victims—and for themselves [Dupont Plaza in San Juan, Puerto Rico] J. S. Kunen. il pors *People Wkly* 27:36-8 Ja 26 '87
A piece of the action [Agent Orange litigation and lawyer compensation] D. Fanning. il *Forbes* 140:68 O 19 '87
Songs and music
In the case of the bum rap song, Richard Golub courts justice for his fellow lawyers. L. Wohlfert. il por *People Wkly* 27:71+ F 2 '87
Lawyers and clients
The client's bill of rights: conduct you deserve from your lawyer. W. J. Smith. *McCalls* 115:170+ N '87
Dilemma for the defense [criminal lawyer E. Rubin jailed for refusing to defend client who lied] M. A. Moore. il por *U S News World Rep* 102:24 Je 8 '87
Why I defend guilty clients. B. Winston. il *Read Dig* 130:81-4 My '87
Lawyers as authors
A lawyer courts best-sellerdom [S. Turow] J. Shear. il por *N Y Times Mag* p54-5+ Je 7 '87
PW interviews [S. Turow] W. Goldstein. por *Publ Wkly* 232:52-3 Jl 10 '87
Lawyers as boxers
Pinstripe pug: a Wall Street lawyer turns to boxing. S. N. Allen. il pors *N Y* 20:34-9 F 23 '87
Lawyers' offices
Elegant strides in the paper chase [J. Ciani] F. Greenberg. il por *Work Woman* 12:60-1 F '87
Lax, Eric
Does a working woman really need to be married? Yes. il *Work Woman* 12:61+ Ag '87
Ma Bell's revenge. il *N Y Times Mag* p2 Mr 15 '87
Laxalt, Paul
Chicken Little is wrong again [address, August 17, 1987] *Vital Speeches Day* 53:741-2 O 1 '87
Laxatives
Metamucil may move cholesterol out. *Prevention* 39:67-8 N '87
Lay, Kenneth Lee, 1942-
about
Orderly mind in a disorderly market. T. Mack. il por map *Forbes* 140:62+ S 21 '87
A trader runs amok. T. Mack. por *Forbes* 140:8 N 16 '87
Laybourne, Roxie
about
Roxie Laybourne: feather detective. R. Wolkomir. il pors *Natl Wildl* 26:20-5 D '87/Ja '88
Layer compounds *See* Intercalation compounds
Layering in plants *See* Plant propagation
Layma, Yann
Inside the land of the 'Great Leader'. por *World Press Rev* 34:27-9 Ja '87
Laymen *See* Laity
Layne, Christopher
Atlanticism without NATO. bibl f *Foreign Policy* 67:22-45 Summ '87
Deutschland uber allies. *New Repub* 197:12-14 S 28 '87
Layoffs
The bad news hits home [layoffs at CBS News] D. Fitzpatrick. por *Newsweek* 109:8 Mr 23 '87
BLS surveys mass layoffs and plant closings in 1986. L. B. Siegel. il *Mon Labor Rev* 110:39-40 O '87
Can Salomon grow by shrinking? [shutting down municipal bond unit and laying off staff] A. Bianco. il *Bus Week* p30-1 O 26 '87

Layoffs—*cont.*
Eastern-union stalemate expected to spur more layoffs. *Aviat Week Space Technol* 127:34 N 30 '87
Forced to make a fresh beginning. B. Rudolph. il *Time* 129:46 F 16 '87
How often do workers receive advance notice of layoffs? S. P. Brown. il *Mon Labor Rev* 110:13-17 Je '87
Job strategy: your company's laying off people; what should you do? il *Glamour* 85:96 Ap '87
A jolt for Wall St.'s whiz kids. B. Powell and C. Friday. il *Newsweek* 110:55-6+ O 26 '87
Rhetoric vs. real issues in the network news cutbacks. D. Lieberman. il *Bus Week* p33 Mr 30 '87
Tisch, Tisch, Tisch . . . [cutbacks at CBS News] E. Diamond. il *N Y* 20:22+ Mr 30 '87
Weak aircraft sales dictate new layoffs at Dassault-Breguet. *Aviat Week Space Technol* 127:127 O 12 '87
Welcome to the Rustbelt [cutbacks by CBS News] *New Repub* 196:4+ Mr 30 '87
When bad things happen to rich people [layoffs on Wall Street] D. Bleeker. *New Repub* 197:17-18 N 23 '87
Who gets the parachutes? J. Flint. il *Forbes* 139:38-40 Ja 12 '87
Worker dislocation report. *Mon Labor Rev* 110:2 F '87

Layton, Elizabeth
about
Elizabeth Layton: portrait of the artist as an old woman. A. Fadiman. il pors *Life* 10:21-2 Mr '87

Lazar, Irving
about
Entertaining. W. P. Rayner and C. Rayner. il pors *Vogue* 177:120+ Jl '87

Lazar, Swifty *See* Lazar, Irving

Lazar, Wendy
about
Home-based business—a moving experience. L. L. Small. il pors *Ms* 16:76+ S '87

Lazare Kaplan International Inc.
Romancing the stone. B. Kanner. il *N Y* 20:22+ N 30 '87

Lazarus, Fred, IV
Philanthropy: a limited but critical element. *Des Arts Educ* 88:30-2 Mr/Ap '87

Lazarus, Mell, 1927-
The son-in-law watcher. il *N Y Times Mag* p94 Ap 5 '87

Lazarus, Roz
about
Delicious tradition: a holiday party with a history. F. Greenberg. il pors *Work Woman* 12:94-8+ D '87

Lazer Tag (Game)
Anecdotes, facetiae, satire, etc.
Neighborhood Strategic Defense Initiative. S. Ciarcia. il *Byte* 12:109-12 Ap '87

Laziness
See also
Procrastination
Sloth: fools rush in. W. Flaherty. il *U S Cathol* 52:8-10 Ag '87

Lazy Susans
Lazy-Susan: space-saving and handy for family picnics. R. J. DeCristoforo. il *Workbench* 43:58 Jl/Ag '87

LBJ: the early years [television program] *See* Television program reviews—Single works

LC *See* Library of Congress

LCDs (Liquid crystal displays) *See* Information display systems

LDCs (Less developed countries) *See* Developing countries

LDLs (Low density lipoproteins) *See* Lipoproteins

Le Comte, Douglas
In the United States—flash floods and drought. il *Weatherwise* 40:12-16 F '87

Le Corbusier, 1887-1965
The Parthenon at dusk [excerpt from The journey to the East]; tr. by Ivan Zaknic and Nicola Pertuiset. *Harpers* 275:27-8+ Jl '87
about
Architecture. J. H. Kay. *Nation* 245:99-100 Ag 1-8 '87
Chandigarh revisited. R. Maass. il *Archit Rec* 175:72-5 Jl '87
L'esprit nouveau. M. F. Schmertz. *Archit Rec* 175:9 O '87
Historic houses: Le Corbusier's cabanon. T. Benton. il *Archit Dig* 44:146-51+ D '87
Le Corbusier as structural engineer. W. Seligmann. il *Archit Rec* 175:142-51 O '87
Le Corbusier at 100: conversations on his legacy. R. Kimball. il *Archit Rec* 175:83+ N '87
Le Corbusier secret. E. Beck. il *Art News* 86:163 S '87

Le Corbusier's Pessac: an experiment in urbanism continues. T. Matthews. il *Archit Rec* 175:87+ N '87
Le Corbusier's true colors. M. Filler. il por *House Gard* 159:174-81+ My '87
Report from Paris: no small plans. K. D. Stein. il *Archit Rec* 175:69 N '87
Bibliography
Thoroughly modern master. M. Filler. il *N Y Rev Books* 34:49-50+ D 17 '87

Le Coze, Gilbert
about
The young man and the sea. M. Cantwell. il por *Vogue* 177:236-7+ Jl '87

Le-Duc, Eugène Emmanuel Viollet- *See* Viollet-Le-Duc, Eugène Emmanuel, 1814-1879

Le Geng
about
Two young Chinese who enjoy their nation's new freedoms. J. Florcruz. il pors *Sch Update* 120:8-9 S 18 '87

Le Goascogne, Claude, and others
Neurosteroids: cytochrome P-450$_{scc}$ in rat brain. bibl f il *Science* 237:1212-15 S 4 '87

Le Grand, Alain
about
Hundred-year wonder. P. Fuhrman. il por *Forbes* 139:152 Mr 9 '87

Le Guin, Ursula K., 1929-
Daddy's big girl [fiction] il *Omni* 9:48-50+ Ja '87
Half past four [story] *New Yorker* 63:34-44+ S 28 '87
The ship ahoy [story] *New Yorker* 63:40-5 N 2 '87

Le Mans Endurance Race (Automobile race) *See* Automobile racing—France

Le Pen, Jean-Marie
about
Don't get mad, just get even. il por *Newsweek* 109:39 Je 22 '87
Fanning French fears. R. Bernstein. il por *N Y Times Mag* p50+ O 4 '87
Le Pen against the 'immigrant lobby'. por *Newsweek* 110:38 S 28 '87
New fire on the far right. W. R. Doerner. il por *Time* 129:40 Je 8 '87
Of Fiji, race, and all that. B. Crozier. *Natl Rev* 39:26+ D 4 '87
The summer of French discontent. J. Valls-Russell. il *New Leader* 70:8-9 S 21 '87

Le Pen, Pierrette
about
Don't get mad, just get even. il por *Newsweek* 109:39 Je 22 '87
Full disclosure. il *Newsweek* 109:43 Je 29 '87

Le Sieg, Theo *See* Seuss, Dr.

Lea, James F.
The president's military power under the Constitution. il *USA Today (Periodical)* 116:12-15 S '87

Leach, David G.
Hardy rhododendrons. il *Rodale's Org Gard* 34:62-6 N '87

Leach, Penelope
The first smile [excerpt from The first six months] il *Good Housekeep* 205:120 S '87

Leach, Rick
about
The case of the missing Jay. H. Quinn. por *Macleans* 100:49 S 7 '87

Leach, Robin
about
Here lies Lifestyles' Robin Leach clad in mink on a concrete beach champagne dreams within easy reach. R. Wolmuth. il pors *People Wkly* 27:46-8 F 16 '87

Lead
See also
Gasoline—Lead content
Soils—Lead content
Isotopes
What a difference the lead makes [use of lead isotope ratios to differentiate between U.S. and Canadian emissions; work of L. A. Barrie and W. T. Sturges] *Sci News* 132:204 S 26 '87

Lead based paint
Paint chips and albatross chicks [Laysan albatrosses poisoned from eating paint chips] G. S. Grant. il *Sea Front* 33:270-2 Jl/Ag '87

Lead in the body
See also
Lead poisoning

Lead paint *See* Lead based paint
Lead pencils *See* Pencils
Lead poisoning
Canned food sealed icemen's fate [lead poisoning cited in fate of the Franklin Expedition] il *Hist Today* 37:3 O '87
Ceramic teapots, pitchers recalled [Dutch pottery] il *FDA Consum* 21:6 S '87
EPA bans lead solder. il *Home Mech* 83:86 Ag '87
Getting the lead out [EPA regulations concerning lead in the water supply] *Sci News* 132:269 O 24 '87
Getting the lead out [waterfowl poisoning from lead shot] M. Rosenthal. il *Ctry J* 14:10-11 O '87
Heavy metal on tap [lead in drinking water] M. Kantor. il *Sierra* 72:18-20 N/D '87
Lead astray: the poisoning of America. M. Weisskopf. il *Discover* 8:68-74 D '87
Lead in utero: low-level danger [effect on mental development in first two years of life; research by David Bellinger and others] B. Bower. *Sci News* 131:277 My 2 '87
Lead in your drinking water? H. Manley. il map *Good Housekeep* 204:199-200 Mr '87
Leaden development [lead in the womb and mental development; study by David Bellinger] J. Rubin. il *Psychol Today* 21:13 S '87
The leaden road to ruin [excerpt from The Dean's December] S. Bellow. il *Discover* 8:76-7 D '87
No threshold to lead's learning effect. J. Raloff. *Sci News* 131:374 Je 13 '87
Paint chips and albatross chicks [Laysan albatrosses poisoned from eating paint chips] G. S. Grant. il *Sea Front* 33:270-2 Jl/Ag '87
Poison in the plumbing? [lead and water coolers] T. Monmaney. il *Newsweek* 110:56 D 21 '87
Poisoning the trumpeters [swans] P. Byrnes. il *Wilderness* 51:42-3 Wint '87
Pretty poison: lead and ceramic ware. C. Lecos. il *FDA Consum* 21:6-9 Jl/Ag '87
Steeling ourselves for the future (I) [steel shot for waterfowl] B. Brister. il *Field Stream* 92:66+ Ag '87
Steeling ourselves for the future (II) [steel shot for waterfowl] B. Brister. il *Field Stream* 92:129-30+ S '87
Trace mineral supplement also had traces of lead [Nutramin Preferred Formula Trace Minerals] *FDA Consum* 21:32 Jl/Ag '87
Water, water everywhere, but . . . [lead in drinking fountains] S. Weiss. *Sci News* 132:390-1 D 19-26 '87
Prevention
Is there lead in your home? M. Cala. il *Home Mech* 83:56-61+ O '87
Lead-base paints: update. K. Childers. *Fam Handyman* 37:68 Mr '87
Putting the lid on dangerous dinnerware [lead-glazed pottery] E. E. Goode. il *U S News World Rep* 103:56 Ag 10 '87
Still some serious questions about lead in pottery. il *Sunset* 179:168 Jl '87
Ways to get the lead out. C. Schaeffer. il *Changing Times* 41:14+ Mr '87
Lead shot *See* Shot
Lead solder *See* Solder and soldering
Leaded gasoline *See* Gasoline—Lead content
Leaders, Fishing *See* Fishing tackle
Leaders (Musical group)
The Leaders. J. Woodard. il *Down Beat* 54:14 Ja '87
Leadership
See also
Black leadership
Christian leadership
Elite (Social sciences)
Executives
Heads of state
Presidents
Women executives
The 1987 Esquire register [special section] il *Esquire* 108:95+ D '87
Are you a leader or a follower? [quiz] E. Kunes. il *Seventeen* 46:144 Ap '87
Bright people not always good leaders [views of Fred Fielder] *USA Today (Periodical)* 116:12 D '87
Management among thieves [interview with armed robber; excerpt from Bosses] J. A. Wall. *Harpers* 274:23-4 F '87
Stop, look and listen [address, May 6, 1987] E. L. Flom. *Vital Speeches Day* 53:594-6 Jl 15 '87
Wanted: leaders who can make a difference. J. Main. il *Fortune* 116:92-4+ S 28 '87
When to lead, when to stand back. F. E. Fiedler. il *Psychol Today* 21:26-7 S '87

Where America's leaders are. D. Gergen. il *U S News World Rep* 103:80 N 23 '87
Leaf balers *See* Garden equipment
Leaf blight of corn *See* Corn—Diseases and pests
Leaf blowers *See* Lawn equipment
Leaf prints *See* Leaves in art
Leaf spot
Check for leaf spot [disease that attacks photinias] il *South Living* 22:100 Ap '87
Leaflets *See* Pamphlets
Leafy spurge
Control
The scourge of the spurge. L. Williamson. il *Outdoor Life* 180:66+ N '87
League of Arab States *See* Arab League
League of Professional Theatre Training Programs
Major League players. D. Rhodes. il *Horizon* 30:49-50 Ap '87
Leahy, Thomas Francis
about
Leahy's line: sell networks' strength. L. Brown and S. Behrens. il pors *Channels* 7:62-3 Ap '87
Leakage
See also
Automobiles—Leakage
Leaks, Government *See* Government and the press
Leaning, Jennifer
Star Wars revives civil defense. il *Bull At Sci* 43:42-6 My '87
Lear, Frances
about
Leer campaign. N. J. Perry. il *Fortune* 116:159 N 9 '87
Lear, Martha Weinman
The pain of loneliness. il *N Y Times Mag* p47-8 D 20 '87
Lear, Norman
Why Johnny can't think. il *Omni* 9:30 F '87
about
A profile of Norman Lear: another pilgrim's progress. M. E. Marty. il *Christ Century* 104:55-8 Ja 21 '87
Winning one from the Gipper. A. R. Dowd. il pors *Fortune* 116:125+ N 9 '87
Lear Siegler, Inc.
GEC completes purchase of Lear Siegler units. *Aviat Week Space Technol* 127:125 O 12 '87
Lear Siegler sells subsidiary companies to Smiths Industries. *Aviat Week Space Technol* 127:32 Ag 3 '87
Learned helplessness *See* Helplessness (Psychology)
Learned institutions and societies
See also
Learned Societies Conference
Learned Societies Conference
Intelligence reports. M. Nichols. il *Macleans* 100:42+ Je 15 '87
Learning, Psychology of
See also
Animal learning
Conditioned responses
Group work in education
Learning disabilities
Memory
Students—Psychology
Associations or rules in learning language? G. Kolata. il *Science* 237:133-4 Jl 10 '87
Class before birth [fetal learning] M. Roberts. il *Psychol Today* 21:41 My '87
The early bird makes the grade [students and teachers who are most alert in the morning perform better; study by Julian Biggers] P. Chance. *Psychol Today* 21:22 O '87
Helping kids learn—their own way. L. Solórzano. il *U S News World Rep* 103:62 Ag 31 '87
Helping students become independent learners. H. L. Herber and J. Nelson-Herber. *Educ Dig* 53:12-15 D '87
How children learn words. G. A. Miller and P. M. Gildea. il *Sci Am* 257:94-9 S '87
The key to improving schools: an interview with William Glasser. P. B. Gough. il *Phi Delta Kappan* 68:656-62 My '87
Learning to learn—music. E. B. Meske. *Des Arts Educ* 89:45-8 S/O '87
Left brain, right brain: do we educate both? S. P. Springer. *Educ Dig* 53:22-5 O '87
Master of mastery [mastery learning advocate B. S. Bloom] P. Chance. bibl (p65) il pors *Psychol Today* 21:42-6 Ap '87
Music (any ol' kind) hath charm . . . G. W. Bracey. il *Phi Delta Kappan* 68:399-400 Ja '87

Learning, Psychology of—*cont.*
Robin Hood and his merry band of sigmas [examination of mastery learning by Robert Slavin] G. W. Bracey. il *Phi Delta Kappan* 69:75-6 S '87; Correction. 69:237 N '87
Teaching reasoning. R. E. Nisbett and others. bibl f il *Science* 238:625-31 O 30 '87
What we don't learn in school [informal learning] J. Fischman. *Psychol Today* 21:18 O '87

Learning and scholarship
See also
Education
Humanism
Intellectuals and intellectual life
Student achievements
Study
Wisdom
Are scholarship and technology compatible? [address, May 10, 1986] J. W. Robb. *Vital Speeches Day* 53:220-2 Ja 15 '87
Libraries and learning. O. Handlin. *Am Sch* 56:205-18 Spr '87
What do you want to know late in the twentieth century? [address, January 26, 1987] D. E. Schultz. *Vital Speeches Day* 53:366-8 Ap 1 '87

Learning disabilities
See also
Dyslexia
Can't read, write or add: the secret hell of millions of Americans. J. Kelman. il *Glamour* 85:142+ Ap '87
A personal legacy [learning problems as result of child abuse] L. Distad. bibl f il *Phi Delta Kappan* 68:744-5 Je '87
Why Josh isn't "dumb": fighting for your learning-disabled child. M. Lee. il *Ms* 15:66+ Je '87

Learning in infants *See* Infants—Growth and development
Learning technology *See* Educational technology
Learning theory *See* Learning, Psychology of
Learning vacations *See* Vacations

Lear's (Periodical)
Leer campaign [nudity in ads] N. J. Perry. il *Fortune* 116:159 N 9 '87
Sex and salesmanship [nudity in ads for Lear's magazine] A. Steacy. il *Macleans* 100:64 O 5 '87

Leary, Timothy Francis, 1920-
about
Head Coach. S. Ditlea. por *Omni* 9:23 Ap '87
Timothy Leary [interview] D. Sheff. por *Roll Stone* p226-8 N 5-D 10 '87

Lease and rental services
See also
Agricultural equipment—Leasing and renting
Airplanes—Leasing and renting
Airplanes, Business—Leasing and renting
Airplanes, Jet—Leasing and renting
Airplanes, Military—Leasing and renting
Apartments—Leasing and renting
Automobiles—Leasing and renting
Campers, Truck—Leasing and renting
Cottages—Leasing and renting
Employee leasing
Fishing boats—Leasing and renting
Greyhound Leasing & Financial Corp.
Houses—Leasing and renting
Motor boats—Leasing and renting
PHH Group Inc.
Rent-A-Center, Inc.
Ryder System, Inc.
Space stations—Leasing and renting
Tools—Leasing and renting
U-Haul International, Inc.
Vacation houses—Leasing and renting
Videotapes—Leasing and renting
Yachts and yachting—Leasing and renting
Summer rentals. il *People Wkly* 27:125-7 My 25 '87

Lease or buy decisions
To lease or not to lease. *Nations Bus* 75:52 Mr '87

Leases
See also
Eviction
Industrial equipment leases
Oil and gas leases

Least Heat Moon, William
A glass of handmade. il *Atlantic* 260:75-9+ N '87

Leaster, Bobby Joe
about
Alabama man cleared of murder 15 years later. il por *Jet* 71:26 Ja 19 '87

Leather
See also
Hides and skins

Leather garments
Dainese Lucky and Monza leathers [for motorcyclists] il *Cycle* 38:52-3+ S '87

Leather gloves *See* Gloves

Leather goods
Care
Be kind to leather. M. Maruca. il *Americana* 14:64-5 Ja/F '87

Leatherback turtles *See* Turtles

Leatherman, Glenda, and Porter, Patricia
A well-planned retreat. il *Women's Sports Fitness* 9:77 N '87

Leathers, Debbie
Campground hotline. See issues of Travel Holiday

Leatherwood, Stephen
Surf's up [photograph] il *Nat Hist* 96:76-7 Ag '87

Leavell, Walter F.
about
Leavell named prexy of Drew Med School. *Jet* 71:24 F 9 '87

Leaves
See also
Color of leaves
Autumn's hidden harvest [carbon in fallen leaves as energy source for stream creatures] R. H. Boyle. il *Natl Wildl* 25:4-9 O/N '87

Leaves in art
Homage to Grinling Gibbons [limewood carving] D. Esterly. il por *House Gard* 159:18+ Ja '87
Leaf-print pillows. il *South Living* 22:174 Ap '87

Leaves of absence
See also
Maternity leaves
Parental leaves
Paternity leaves
Sick leave
Laws and regulations
Mandated leave: small firms' nightmare. H. Bacas. il *Nations Bus* 75:32-3 Ag '87

Leavitt, David, 1961-
about
Post-counterculture tristesse. C. Iannone. *Commentary* 83:57-61 F '87

Leavy, Judith Katz- *See* Katz-Leavy, Judith

Leavy, Walter
A comedic look at the black middle class. il pors *Ebony* 42:68+ Ag '87
How athletes handle their money. il *Ebony* 42:76+ Je '87
Innocent man's eight-year prison ordeal. il pors *Ebony* 42:86+ Mr '87
Should whites adopt black children? il *Ebony* 42:76+ S '87
What's behind the resurgence of racism in America? il *Ebony* 42:132-3+ Ap '87
Who will be the first black head coach in NFL? il *Ebony* 42:36+ Ja '87
Who's the greatest? [cover story] il pors *Ebony* 42:140+ O '87

Lebacqz, Karen, 1945-
Appropriate vulnerability: a sexual ethic for singles. il *Christ Century* 104:435-8 My 6 '87
Sexuality and vulnerability [discussion of May 6, 1987 article, Appropriate vulnerability: a sexual ethic for singles] *Christ Century* 104:596-8 Jl 1-8 '87

Lebanon
See also
Americans—Lebanon
Beirut (Lebanon)
Catholic colleges and universities—Lebanon
Famines—Lebanon
French—Lebanon
Missions—Lebanon
Relief work—Lebanon
Terrorism—Lebanon
United Nations—Lebanon
United States—Diplomatic and consular service—Lebanon
Defenses
See also
France—Army—Forces in Lebanon
Syria—Armed Forces—Forces in Lebanon
United Nations—Armed Forces—Forces in Lebanon
Foreign relations
Syria
No help for Glass [Syria declines to use its power in Lebanon to free American C. Glass] *Newsweek* 110:32 Jl 6 '87

Lebanon—Foreign relations—Syria—*cont.*
Syria and Lebanon. I. Rabinovich. bibl f *Curr Hist* 86:61-4+ F '87
United States
See United States—Foreign relations—Lebanon
Politics and government
Arafat makes another comeback. S. Reed. il *Nation* 244:137-41 F 7 '87
Assad's Lebanese quagmire. R. Nordland. il *Newsweek* 109:34 Mr 2 '87
Beirut camps: is the carnival of carnage over? P. R. Range. il *U S News World Rep* 102:14 Ap 20 '87
Beirut spring [presence of Syrian troops and expected clash with PLO] *New Repub* 196:7-8 Ap 6 '87
Beirut's fragile peace. J. Muir. il *Macleans* 100:22 Mr 23 '87
Bloody battle for West Beirut. M. S. Serrill. il *Time* 129:26 Mr 2 '87
Can Syria clean up Lebanon? N. Cooper. il *Newsweek* 109:40-1 Mr 9 '87
Lebanon: a pawn in the Middle East. J. Esseff. il *USA Today (Periodical)* 115:74-7 My '87
Murder from the inside [assassination of R. Karami] J. Muir. *Macleans* 100:27 Je 15 '87
The new battle for Lebanon. J. Vidal-Hall. il *World Press Rev* 34:28-9 Je '87
Saving a city from itself [Syrians move into West Beirut] W. E. Smith. il *Time* 129:48-9 Mr 9 '87
Security Council expresses concern over continuing situation in Lebanon. il *UN Chron* 24:17 My '87
The siege of the camps [Palestinians trapped in embattled refugee camps] N. Cooper. il *Newsweek* 109:34 F 23 '87
Syria and Lebanon. I. Rabinovich. bibl f *Curr Hist* 86:61-4+ F '87
Syrian bullets impose Beirut peace—for now. P. R. Range. il pors *U S News World Rep* 102:32-3 Mr 9 '87
A war between allies. B. Levin. il *Macleans* 100:18-19 Mr 2 '87
Anecdotes, facetiae, satire, etc.
The basketball championship of Lebanon [chart] D. Halberstein. il *New Repub* 197:11 Jl 27 '87
Religious institutions and affairs
See also
Muslims—Lebanon
Lebanon hostage cases, 1984-
See also
Buckley, William—Kidnapping
Glass, Charles—Kidnapping
Iran-contra affair
Steen, Alann—Kidnapping
Weir, Benjamin—Kidnapping
Beirut's hostage-terrorist quagmire is suddenly churning. P. R. Range. il *U S News World Rep* 102:10-11 F 2 '87
Bloody Beirut—trading in lives. B. Duffy. il map *U S News World Rep* 102:24-9 F 9 '87
Churches remember U.S. hostages in Lebanon. K. Palen. il *Christ Today* 31:42 Ap 17 '87
A costly exchange [suspected Iranian terrorist freed following release of French hostages in Lebanon] R. Laver. il *Macleans* 100:31 D 14 '87
A deepening sense of frustration. J. Greenwald. il *Time* 129:36-7 F 9 '87
Escape in Beirut—and maybe much more. J. Wallace. il por *U S News World Rep* 103:32-3 Ag 31 '87
A French terrorist-for-hostage deal? [Iranian terror suspect set free after two French hostages in Lebanon were freed] il *Newsweek* 110:61 D 14 '87
A frenzy of hostage taking. M. S. Serrill. il *Time* 129:38-9 F 2 '87
Furtive swap [suspected Iranian terrorist set free by France and French hostages released by Iran] *Time* 130:51 D 14 '87
Gunboat diplomacy. W. E. Smith. il map *Time* 129:32-3 F 16 '87
Hostage to innocence. R. Steel. *New Repub* 196:4 F 23 '87
The hostages & the moral question; A strategy for hostages. W. F. Buckley. *Natl Rev* 39:62-3 Mr 13 '87
Hostages: cool it [new U.S. policy] D. Newell. il *Newsweek* 109:6 My 18 '87
Hostages in danger. B. Levin. il por *Macleans* 100:18-19 F 16 '87
Hyping the hostage crisis. F. Willey. il *Newsweek* 109:30+ F 16 '87
Iran plays the hostage game. R. Watson. il *Newsweek* 109:34-6 F 9 '87
The kidnappers strike again. S. Strasser. il *Newsweek* 109:20-2 F 2 '87

Kidnappings in Lebanon [statement, January 26, 1987] R. Reagan. *Dep State Bull* 87:51 Ap '87
The king is hostage. T. E. Arnold. il *Natl Rev* 39:34-6+ Ap 10 '87
Mixed signals in a hostages crisis. K. Scanlon. il *Macleans* 100:28 Ap 6 '87
Pawns of terror politics. B. Levin. il *Macleans* 100:16-17 F 9 '87
Stalemate in a tormented land. J. Greenwald. il *Time* 129:54-5 F 23 '87
Syria scowls at Shiites while hostages stew. J. L. Sheler. il *U S News World Rep* 103:16 Jl 13 '87
Tangled web of terror. B. Duffy. il *U S News World Rep* 102:14-16 F 23 '87
Terry Waite, a symbol of hope for hostages in the Mideast, vanishes on a mercy mission. L. Aitken. il por *People Wkly* 27:109 F 23 '87
Weir urges direct negotiations. C. W. Richard. *Christ Century* 104:324-5 Ap 8 '87
Why they hate us. S. Reed. *Nation* 244:168-9 F 14 '87
Reporters and reporting
The hostages. il *World Press Rev* 34:7 Mr '87
LeBaron, Dean
about
Is Dean LeBaron worried? A little. A. Beam. il por *Bus Week* p128 My 25 '87
LeBaron, Ervil Morerel, d. 1981
about
A hand from the grave. P. Abramson. il pors *Newsweek* 110:45 D 21 '87
Lebelson, Harry
(jt. auth) See Rush, Bette, and Lebelson, Harry
Lebensohn, Jeremy
Skill full. il *Am Craft* 47:33-5 F/Mr '87
Leblanc, Edward T.
Dime novels. il *Antiques Collect Hobbies* 92:84-6+ D '87
LeBlond, Paul H.
about
What is that? D. G. Gordon. il *Oceans* 20:44-9 Jl/Ag '87
Lebow, Barbara
about
A shayna maidel [drama] Reviews
New Yorker 63:121-2 N 30 '87. M. Kramer
LeBow, Bennett S.
about
The sad saga of Western Union's decline. A. Bianco. il pors *Bus Week* p108-10+ D 14 '87
Lebow, Edward
American ceramics now: the 27th Ceramic National. il *Am Craft* 47:26-33+ Ag/S '87
A Gothic tale. il *House Gard* 159:190-7+ My '87
In defense of Ceramic National [discussion of August/September 1987 article, American ceramics now: the 27th Ceramic National] *Am Craft* 47:24 O/N '87
John McQueen/Bellas artes. il *Am Craft* 47:88-9 O/N '87
Lebow, Richard Ned
The dangers of quick launch. bibl f il *Bull At Sci* 43:36-9 N '87
Lebow, Robert
about
Thou shalt not covet thy neighbor's lawn, so grab a papal sprinkler and let us spray. il pors *People Wkly* 27:123 Je 8 '87
LeBrecht, James
about
James LeBrecht. A. M. Hale. il por *Theatre Crafts* 21:34-5+ F '87
Lebrecht, Norman, 1948-
Muti of Milan [interview] il por *Opera News* 51:18-19+ Ja 17 '87
Lecithin
Brain boost? K. Freifeld. il *Health* 19:9-10 S '87
Leckel, John, and Robbins, Clyde
"Hard" photographs from the 19th century. il *Antiques Collect Hobbies* 92:72-5 My '87
LeClaire, Anne D.
Brothers in honor [story] il *Redbook* 169:64-9+ S '87
Brothers in honor [story] il *Redbook* 169:64-6+ O '87
Leclère, Marie-Françoise
Designing for people. il *World Press Rev* 34:60 N '87
LeCompte, Douglas
Around the world—water, water almost everywhere . . . il *Weatherwise* 40:9-11 F '87

LeCompte, Elizabeth
about
Radical cheek to cheek. L. Liebmann. pors *Vogue* 177:90 Ap '87
LeConey, Michael M.
about
HMOs may be moving into the recovery room. G. G. Marcial. por *Bus Week* p124 Je 8 '87
Leconte, Henri
about
Meet the court cutup. F. Lidz. il pors *Sports Illus* 66:54-6+ Je 1 '87
Lecos, Chris
Beware of imported foods. il *Consum Res Mag* 70:15-17 F '87
Caffeine jitters: some safety questions remain [cover story] il *FDA Consum* 21:22-7 D '87/Ja '88
Cholesterol vs. saturated fats [discussion of March 1987 article, Planning a diet for a healthy heart] il *FDA Consum* 21:5 Jl/Ag '87
Cutting cholesterol? Look to the label. il *FDA Consum* 21:8-13 F '87
Planning a diet for a healthy heart [cover story] il *FDA Consum* 21:29-36 Mr '87
Pretty poison: lead and ceramic ware. il *FDA Consum* 21:6-9 Jl/Ag '87
Risky shell game: pet turtles can infect kids. il *FDA Consum* 21:19-21 D '87/Ja '88
Still a killer: pneumonia targets the ill, the elderly. il *FDA Consum* 21:8-13 Je '87
LeCount, Gayle
about
Prairie homebuilt companions. G. Baxter. il *Flying* 114:104 My '87
Lectins
See also
Concanavalins
Lecturers and lecturing (Public speaking) *See* Public speaking
Lectures and lecturing (College teaching) *See* College teaching
LED (Light-emitting diodes) *See* Diodes
Led Zeppelin (Musical group)
Led Zeppelin: U.S. tour, December 1968-January 1969. D. Fricke. il *Roll Stone* p57+ Je 4 '87
Musician Willie Dixon satisfied out of court [copyright infringement suit] *Jet* 72:58 Mr 30 '87
Ledbetter, Eve
Kingdom of the heart [story] il *Good Housekeep* 204:100-1 Ja '87
Ledbetter, Jack
Tradition [address, September 10, 1986] *Vital Speeches Day* 53:189-90+ Ja 1 '87
Ledbetter, James
Hardguy software. *Nation* 244:150-3 F 7 '87
The sleuth in the machine. *Nation* 244:613-14 My 9 '87
Leddihn, Erik von Kuehnelt- *See* Kuehnelt-Leddihn, Erik von
Ledeen, Michael, 1941-
about
Minority report. C. Hitchens. *Nation* 244:39 Ja 17 '87
Washington diarist. C. Lane. *New Repub* 196:58 Je 8 '87
Leder, Jane Mersky
On his thirtieth birthday, my brother placed a hunting rifle in his mouth and pulled the trigger. il por *Glamour* 85:204+ N '87
Psychics at work. il *McCalls* 115:159-62 O '87
Lederer, Esther Pauline *See* Landers, Ann
Lederer-Gibel, Inge
Going home to Israel. *Christ Century* 104:162-4 F 18 '87
Lederman, Leonard L.
Science and technology policies and priorities: a comparative analysis. bibl f il *Science* 237:1125-33 S 4 '87
Ledoux, Paul
about
Fire [drama] Reviews
Macleans il 100:55 Ja 26 '87. M. Abley
Lee, Andrea, 1953-
Letter from Rome. *New Yorker* 63:133-6+ N 9 '87
Lee, Byung-Chull, d. 1987
about
Tough comeback artist. L. Kraar. por *Fortune* 116:53 Ag 3 '87
Lee, C. Y., 1917-
about
PW interviews. L. See. il por *Publ Wkly* 232:84-5 Ag 14 '87

Lee, Don L. *See* Madhubuti, Haki R.
Lee, Dwight R.
(jt. auth) See Anderson, Joan B., and Lee, Dwight R.
Lee, James F.
Prague's Smetana Museum. il *Travel Holiday* 167:84 Ja '87
Lee, Karen, and Branyon, Alaxandra
A different barbecue. il *N Y Times Mag* p59-60 Jl 12 '87
Stocking up. il *N Y Times Mag* p51-2 O 18 '87
Lee, Kuan Yew
about
The government as a matchmaker. A. Peters. il *World Press Rev* 34:58 F '87
Lee, Kyu-Ho, and others
Isolation of an olfactory cDNA: similarity to retinol-binding protein suggests a role in olfaction. bibl f il *Science* 235:1053-6 F 27 '87
Lee, Leisa
about
Career makeover: from ticket sales to corporate travel planner. il por *Glamour* 85:110 F '87
Lee, Levi
about
Tent meeting [drama] Reviews
N Y 20:70-1 Ap 20 '87. J. Simon
Nation 244:585-6 My 2 '87. T. M. Disch
Lee, Linda
(ed) See Simpson, Maylene. 3 children who needed a medical miracle
Lee, M. Owen
"Elemental, furious, wholly true". il *Opera News* 52:14-17+ D 19 '87
Who is the Grail? il *Opera News* 51:16-19 Ap 11 '87
Lee, Madeline
Why Josh isn't "dumb": fighting for your learning-disabled child. il *Ms* 15:66+ Je '87
Lee, Mark R., and others
Functional interaction and partial homology between human immunodeficiency virus and neuroleukin. bibl f il *Science* 237:1047-51 Ag 28 '87
Lee, Marshall
about
Doctor reveals sexual addiction a growing problem. T. S. Moore. il pors *Jet* 72:24-5 Mr 30 '87
Lee, Martin A.
How the drug czar got away. il *Nation* 245:189-92 S 5 '87
Lee, Milton L., and Markides, Karin E.
Chromatography with supercritical fluids. bibl f il *Science* 235:1342-7 Mr 13 '87
Lee, Ming-Sheng, and others
Detection of minimal residual cells carrying the t(14;18) by DNA sequence amplification. bibl f il *Science* 237:175-8 Jl 10 '87
Lee, Richard E., Jr., and others
A rapid cold-hardening process in insects. bibl f il *Science* 238:1415-17 D 4 '87
Lee, Robert E. (Robert Edward), 1807-1870
about
Meeting at the McLean House. R. G. Wilson. il pors *Am Hist Illus* 22:46-9 S '87
With Lee at Appomattox [cover story] E. P. Alexander. il pors map *Am Hist Illus* 22:40-5+ S '87
Lee, Ronald George, 1952-
about
Is there life after press-on nails? T. Carson. il por *Bus Week* p68 S 28 '87
Lee, Sherman E.
about
Warrant for Lee's arrest dropped. R. W. Walker. *Art News* 86:30 Summ '87
Lee, Spike
about
Fireside signs Spike Lee to two-book contract. *Publ Wkly* 231:59 Je 12 '87
'He's gotta have it'. il pors *Ebony* 42:42+ Ja '87
Spike Lee filming banned at alma mater in Atlanta. *Jet* 72:55 My 11 '87
Spike Lee wins honor for 'She's gotta have it'. por *Jet* 71:26 Ja 19 '87
Spike Lee's gotta have it. S. Mieher. il pors *N Y Times Mag* p26-9+ Ag 9 '87
Waking up rich and famous. il pors *Ebony* 42:36+ S '87
Whoopi's blue eyes [interview] M. Glicksman. *Harpers* 274:29 Ja '87
Lee, Susan, 1943-
The big portfolios. See issues of Forbes beginning July 2, 1984

Lee, Sylvia, and others
Keeping youth in school: a public-private collaboration [with reports by J. Payne and J. Smith] il *Child Today* 16:15-21 Jl/Ag '87

Lee, Ucho
about
Taking a chance in a new country. L. H. Whitson. il por *Nations Bus* 75:59 Mr '87

Lee, Valerie
Minorities in Catholic schools: why do they read better? *Educ Dig* 52:20-3 F '87

Lee, Wen-Hwa, and others
Human retinoblastoma susceptibility gene: cloning, identification, and sequence. bibl f il *Science* 235:1394-9 Mr 13 '87

Lee, Yuan T., 1936-
Molecular beam studies of elementary chemical processes [adaptation of Nobel Prize address, December 8, 1986] bibl f il *Science* 236:793-8 My 15 '87
about
Herschbach, Lee and Polanyi receive 1986 Chemistry Nobel. P. H. Andersen. il pors *Phys Today* 40:17-20 Mr '87

Lee Pharmaceuticals
Is there life after press-on nails? T. Carson. il por *Bus Week* p68 S 28 '87

Lee-Smith, Hughie
about
Hughie Lee-Smith: June Kelly. S. Kandel and E. Hayt-Atkins. il *Art News* 86:156+ D '87

Leeches
Medical use
The little suckers have made a comeback. R. Conniff. il *Discover* 8:84-6+ Ag '87
Return of the bloodsucker. P. S. Wachtel. il *Int Wildl* 17:44-6 S/O '87
The return of the bloodsuckers. M. Clark. il *Newsweek* 109:58 F 2 '87

Leeds, Dorothy
The fine art of asking smart questions [excerpt from Smart questions] il *Work Woman* 12:132-3+ N '87
Smart questions to ask to get ahead in your job [excerpts from Smart questions] il *Glamour* 85:116+ My '87

Leeds (England)
Art
'Cultivated capital' [culture and patronage of the arts in nineteenth-century Manchester and Leeds] J. Wolff and C. Arscott. bibl il *Hist Today* 37:22-8 Mr '87
Music
See also
Opera North

Leeks
Another (easier) way with leeks. D. J. Young. il *Flower Gard* 31:26-7 F/Mr '87

Leepson, Marc
Keeping business at home. il *Nations Bus* 75:67-70 My '87
Running in place—your own place. il *Nations Bus* 75:64 F '87
Taking off by the numbers. il *Nations Bus* 75:48-50 Ag '87

Lee's Enterprises, Inc.
Taking a chance in a new country [U. Lee] L. H. Whitson. il por *Nations Bus* 75:59 Mr '87

Lees-Milne, James
Wyck Hill House: a country hotel in the Cotswolds. il *Archit Dig* 44:128-33 D '87

Leesburg (Va.)
History
The dog notes of Virginia [Confederate money] E. Rochette. il *Antiques Collect Hobbies* 92:80-1 Ag '87

Leeward Islands (West Indies)
See also
Saint Barthélemy (Guadeloupe)

Lefer, Diane
The hidden censor. *Writer* 100:7-10 My '87

Lefever, Ernest W.
American churches and Vietnam [address, October 18, 1986] *Vital Speeches Day* 53:327-30 Mr 15 '87
The world crisis and American responsibility [address, March 26, 1987] *Vital Speeches Day* 53:518-20 Je 15 '87

Lefkoe, Morty
Why so many mergers fail. il por *Fortune* 116:113-14 Jl 20 '87

Lefkowitz, Mary R., 1935-
The heroic women of Greek epic. *Am Sch* 56:503-18 Aut '87

Left (Political science) *See* Communism; Liberalism; Radicalism; Socialism
Left and right (Political science) *See* Right and left (Political science)
Left- and right-handedness
Human neuroelectric patterns predict performance accuracy. A. S. Gevins and others. bibl f il *Science* 235:580-5 Ja 30 '87

Lefton, Robert Eugene, 1931-
Managing sideways. il *Work Woman* 12:34+ O '87
Leftovers *See* Cooking—Leftovers
Leg
See also
Knee
Confessions of a leg man. J. P. Davis. il *Glamour* 85:142-3 Jl '87
Entertainment tonight hides Mary Hart's gams, and it's one leg-pull her fans could do without. J. Ash. il pors *People Wkly* 28:103-4 S 7 '87
Care
Are your legs losing their looks? il *Mademoiselle* 93:16 Jl '87
Great legs! il *McCalls* 114:23-7 Ag '87
Legs! The sexy, sensory, sublime joys of legs. il *Glamour* 85:140-5 Jl '87
Wounds and injuries
Love and hate on one leg [leg fractured in traffic accident] K. Bonnell. il por *Glamour* 85:73-4 O '87
What's that leg pain? [shin splints] il *Women's Sports Fitness* 9:44 Ja '87
Leg exercises *See* Exercise
Legacies
See also
Wills
Legal aid
See also
Legal Services Corporation
Volunteers of Legal Service
Legal assistance to immigrants
See also
Proyecto Libertad
Ripping off immigrants: amnesty breeds abuses. G. Hackett. il *Newsweek* 110:21-2 S 7 '87
Legal assistance to the aged
See also
National Senior Citizens Law Center (U.S.)
My son, the do-gooder. J. R. Lamb, Jr. por *Newsweek* 110:14-15 N 16 '87
National project to help seniors with pension problems. T. Chaw. *Aging* no356:32 '87
Legal clinics *See* Law firms
Legal Committee (United Nations) *See* United Nations. Legal Committee
Legal education *See* Law—Study and teaching; Law schools
Legal ethics
See also
Conflict of interests (Lawyers)
Judicial ethics
Dilemma for the defense [criminal lawyer E. Rubin jailed for refusing to defend client who lied] M. A. Moore. il por *U S News World Rep* 102:24 Je 8 '87
Hypocrisy [referral fees in Mass.] D. Fanning. *Forbes* 140:83 D 14 '87
A lawyers' rush for judgments [Northwest Airlines crash in Detroit] T. Gest. il *U S News World Rep* 103:23 Ag 31 '87
Playing by the rules [lawyers must follow law when serving as bill collectors] D. Fanning. il *Forbes* 139:76-8 Mr 9 '87
Why I defend guilty clients. B. Winston. il *Read Dig* 130:81-4 My '87
Legal fees *See* Lawyers—Salaries, fees, etc.
Legal history *See* Law—History
Legal malpractice *See* Malpractice
Legal medicine *See* Medical jurisprudence
Legal procedure
See also
Actions and defenses
Arbitration and award
Confession (Law)
Courts martial and courts of inquiry
Due process of law
Executions and executioners
Grand jury
Jury
Mock jury
Pleas (Legal procedure)
Probate law and practice
Probation
Public prosecutors

Legal procedure—See also—cont.
  Searches and seizures
  Trials
Will counterrevolution continue? [criminal procedure and the Rehnquist Court; views of Charles Whitebread] il *USA Today (Periodical)* 116:11 Ag '87
Legal profession See Lawyers
Legal Services Corporation
The future (?) of legal services for the poor. M. S. Gallagher. il *America* 156:395-6 My 16 '87
Maximizing access to justice [address, February 12, 1987] W. C. Durant, III. *Vital Speeches Day* 53:540-4 Je 15 '87
Legasov, Valery
    about
A Soviet expert discusses Chernobyl [interview] N. Vikhlyayev. il por *Bull At Sci* 43:32-4 Jl/Ag '87
Legaux, Peter
    about
Constitution-making weather: Philadelphia, 1787. D. M. Ludlum. *Ctry J* 14:70 Jl '87
Legends
  See also
  Folklore
  Mythology
Legends, American
  See also
  Paul Bunyan (Legendary character)
Legge, Anthony J., and Rowley-Conwy, Peter A.
Gazelle killing in Stone Age Syria. il map *Sci Am* 257:88-95 Ag '87
Letters [discussion of August 1987 article, Gazelle killing in Stone Age Syria] *Sci Am* 257:8+ N '87
Legion of Honor
Knight unerring: Castelli becomes a chevalier. G. Henry. por *Art News* 86:18 Summ '87
Legionella
Hunting for Legionnaire's bacteria [study of Pittsburgh water supply] S. Weisburd. *Sci News* 132:169 S 12 '87
Legionnaires' disease
Legionnaires': old soldiers' disease hasn't faded away. il *FDA Consum* 21:14-15 Je '87
    Causes
  See also
  Legionella
Legislation
  See also
  Judicial review
  Law
  Referendum
  United States. Congress
  Veto
    Delaware
Corporate socialism [anti-takeover bill] R. J. Samuelson. il *Newsweek* 110:42 D 28 '87
Legislative bodies
  See also
  United States. Congress
    South Africa
  See also
  South Africa. Parliament
Legislative Operations Office (House) See United States. Congress. House. Office of Legislative Operations
Legislative power
  See also
  Civil supremacy over the military
Legislators
  See also
  Black legislators
  Congressmen
  Senators
  Women legislators
Lego, P. E. (Paul E.), 1930-
    about
Danforth picks his heirs. G. L. Miles and M. Rothman. *Bus Week* p26-7 Ag 10 '87
Lego, Paul E. See Lego, P. E. (Paul E.), 1930-
LEGO System AS
Lego wars: a Christmas tale [Ohio Art's Zaks vs. Lego construction toys] il *Newsweek* 110:40-1 D 28 '87
Now even Lego is going high-tech [linkage with Logo to make programmable toys] P. Angiolillo and M. Bluestone. il *Bus Week* p40 Ag 17 '87
Legorreta Vilchis, Ricardo, 1931-
    about
Architecture: Ricardo Legorreta: the Los Angeles residence of Georgiana and Ricardo Montalban. C. Fuentes. il por *Archit Dig* 44:164-71+ Mr '87

Legs See Leg
LeGuin, Ursula See Le Guin, Ursula K., 1929-
Legumes
  See also
  Beans
  Groundnuts
  Leucaena
  Lupines
  Peanuts
  Peas
  Soybeans
Dazzling! N. Vietmeyer. il *Int Wildl* 17:30-5 Jl/Ag '87
Legumes for feed and fertilizer. J. Walter. il *Success Farm* 85 no6:B6 Mr '87
Legwold, Gary
Fitness matters. il *Better Homes Gard* 65:90 O '87
Fitness matters. il *Better Homes Gard* 65:82 N '87
The good hands people. il *Sport Mag* 78:81+ N '87
Guide to a good arm. il *Sport Mag* 78:73-4 Je '87
Lehder Rivas, Carlos
    about
Breaking a drug lord. K. Scanlon. por *Macleans* 100:45 F 23 '87
Caught: cocaine's 'Mr. Big'. M. Satchell. il por *U S News World Rep* 102:12 F 16 '87
Crazy Charlie. *Nation* 244:203-5 F 21 '87
The fall of a cocaine kingpin. J. Smolowe. il por *Time* 129:37 F 16 '87
Snaring the king of coke. R. Nordland. il por *Newsweek* 109:16-18 F 16 '87
Lehigh, Scot, and Connolly, Francis J.
Duke of piety. *New Repub* 197:13-15 O 26 '87
Lehman, John F.
    about
The former Navy Secretary takes a shot at the Stark [interview] J. Barry. il por *Newsweek* 109:26 Je 1 '87
The Navy after Lehman: rough sailing ahead? D. Charles. il por *Science* 236:22-5 Ap 3 '87
'You buy carriers to protect everything else' [interview] por *U S News World Rep* 102:28 Je 15 '87
Lehman, Paul R.
Reform in music teacher education: what to do until we reach utopia. bibl f *Des Arts Educ* 89:2-11 S/O '87
Lehman, Ronald
    about
Compromise candidate. por *Newsweek* 110:4 S 14 '87
Lehman Opportunity (Firm)
Two new all-weathers. *Money* 16:39+ Jl '87
Lehmann, Hans G.
    about
The spy who loves cars. R. Hutton. il pors *Car Driv* 32:90-1+ My '87
Lehn, J.-M. (Jean-Marie)
    about
Chemistry in the image of biology. R. Lewin. il pors *Science* 238:611-12 O 30 '87
Nobel prizes: chemistry. J. Horgan. *Sci Am* 257:46 D '87
Lehn, Jean-Marie See Lehn, J.-M. (Jean-Marie)
Lehndorff, Vera
    about
Her bold looks made her a standout in the '60s, but now Veruschka paints herself into the background. M. Small. il pors *People Wkly* 27:88-90 F 16 '87
Lehrer, Merrill C.
The majesty of an ocean-going Princess. il *USA Today (Periodical)* 116:36-43 N '87
Surround sound: music and movies with dazzling realism. il *USA Today (Periodical)* 116:86-8 S '87
Video wars: the camcorder revolution. il *USA Today (Periodical)* 115:66-8 Ja '87
Lehrman, Karen
Anorexia and bulimia: causes and cures. il *Consum Res Mag* 70:29-32 S '87
Lehrman, Karen, and Pace, Jana
Day care regulation: serving children or bureaucrats? *USA Today (Periodical)* 115:63-6 My '87
Lei Yu
    about
A feather on the wind. D. Frankel. il por *N Y* 20:21 F 9 '87
Leiber, Judith
    about
Judith Leiber's customers are left holding the bag. B. Johnson. il por *People Wkly* 27:117-18 Ap 20 '87
Leiden Observatory (Netherlands) See Astronomical observatories—Netherlands

Leifer, Robert, and others
Detection of uranium from Cosmos-1402 in the stratosphere. bibl f il *Science* 238:512-14 O 23 '87
Leigh, David J.
Two decades of ultimate dialogue. *America* 157:504-5 D 26 '87
Leigh, Jennifer Jason
about
The next generation. G. Stone. il por *Vogue* 177:34 Je '87
Leigh, Pamela
Diana: why she and Charles can't agree [cover story] il pors *Ladies Home J* 104:97-9+ Jl '87
Leigh-Kile, Donna
Glimpse of the Forbidden City. il *Life* 10:36-40 Ap '87
Leight, Warren D.
Are you dinner-party paranoid? *Mademoiselle* 93:166+ Mr '87
Go away! (A guy in a bad mood means it). *Mademoiselle* 93:116 D '87
She says monogamy, he says monotony: closing the guy/girl gap. *Mademoiselle* 93:220-1+ Ap '87
Leighton, Ann, 1902?-1985
Re-creating a seventeenth-century garden. il *House Gard* 159:20+ Jl '87
Leighton, Sir Frederic, 1830-1896
about
Attic attitudes: Leighton and aesthetic philosophy. S. Jones. bibl il *Hist Today* 37:31-7 Je '87
Leiken, Robert S., 1939-
Nicaragua cliffhanger. *New Repub* 197:17-21 D 14 '87
Tangled Nicaragua: an exchange [discussion of December 5, 1985 article, The Nicaraguan tangle] il *N Y Rev Books* 34:59-61 Ag 13 '87
about
Cover-up at 'The New York review'. A. Cockburn. *Nation* 245:9 Jl 4-11 '87
Shamed. A. Cockburn. *Nation* 245:79 Ag 1-8 '87
Leishman, Katie
AIDS and insects. il *Atlantic* 260:56-66+ S '87
Harlequin. il *Atlantic* 259:20-2 My '87
Heterosexuals and AIDS. il *Atlantic* 259:39-49+ F '87
Planning ahead together. bibl il *McCalls* 114:65-7 Jl '87
Prescription: My father spent his life healing others. Now he was the patient, and I wanted to find his cure. *Glamour* 85:70+ Ja '87
Leishmania *See* Protozoa, Pathogenic
Leister, Mary
Mulberries . . . keep birds at bay. il *Rodale's Org Gard* 34:40 Mr '87
Leisure
See also
Hangouts
Hobbies
Recreation
Vacations
Leisure and recreation. A. D. Frank. il *Forbes* 139:158-9 Ja 12 '87
Use your weekends to revitalize. il *Glamour* 85:93 Ap '87
Weekends were made for regeneration. M. Golin. il *Prevention* 39:58-61 Ap '87
Leisure homes *See* Vacation houses
Leitch, Donovan, 1967-
about
Catch some rising stars. pors *Teen* 31:58 My '87
Leitch, Heather
Are you ready for Rambo aerobics? il *Women's Sports Fitness* 9:60-1 Jl '87
How to enter—and win—a competition. il *Women's Sports Fitness* 9:64 Ap '87
Leitch, Peter
about
Peter Leitch. M. Bourne. il por *Down Beat* 54:54-5 S '87
Leithauser, Brad
Light verse: dead but remarkably robust. il *N Y Times Book Rev* 92:1+ Je 7 '87
A nonesuch people. il *Atlantic* 260:32-4+ S '87
The space of one breath. *New Yorker* 63:41-2+ Mr 9 '87
Leivick, Laura
A dancer's nightmare. il pors *N Y Times Mag* p66+ N 8 '87
Lejeune, Anthony, 1928-
No slacking. *Natl Rev* 39:38 Jl 17 '87
Lekachman, Robert
Dear Doctor Lekachman . . . il *Nation* 244:250-2 F 28 '87

Dear Doctor Lekachman . . . il *Nation* 244:390-2 Mr 28 '87
Reaganomics with a human face [excerpt from Visions and nightmares] *Harpers* 274:24+ Mr '87
Leland, David
about
Wish you were here [film] Reviews
Commonweal 114:498-9 S 11 '87. T. O'Brien
Macleans il 100:56 O 12 '87. L. O'Toole
N Y il 20:54 Ag 3 '87. D. Denby
Nation 245:246-8 S 12 '87. T. Rafferty
Natl Rev 39:66-7 S 11 '87. J. Simon
New Repub 197:27 Ag 3 '87. S. Kauffmann
New Yorker 63:63-4 Jl 27 '87. P. Kael
Newsweek il 110:67 Ag 3 '87. D. Ansen
People Wkly il 28:10 Ag 17 '87. S. Haller
Vogue 177:64 Ag '87. M. Haskell
Leland, Mickey
Toward a national policy to end homelessness. il *America* 156:69-71 Ja 31 '87
LeMaistre, Charles A.
Lung cancer in perspective [address, May 10, 1987] *Vital Speeches Day* 53:564-6 Jl 1 '87
Lemann, Nancy
The trials and jubilations of Governor Edwin Edwards. il por *Esquire* 107:79-82+ My '87
Lemann, Nicholas
Breaking out of the ghetto: the origins of the underclass. *Current* 289:4-15 Ja '87
Fake masks. il *Atlantic* 260:24+ N '87
Hard times in the Big Easy. il *Atlantic* 260:16-18+ Ag '87
Magnetic attraction. *New Repub* 196:16-19 Ap 13 '87
The mirage of Miami. *New Repub* 197:37-42 N 23 '87
Lemasters, John N.
about
Contel's revolving door may soon spin again. S. Ticer and S. Payne. *Bus Week* p47 My 11 '87
Lembi-Detert, Yvonne
about
A hotel of one's own. M. Dowie. il por *Ms* 16:38-9 D '87
Lemeni, Nicola Makedon Rossi- *See* Rossi-Lemeni, Nicola Makedon, 1920-
Lemieux, Mario
about
Mario Lemieux: Pittsburgh's premier Penguin. B. Phillips. il por *Sch Update* 119:20-1 F 9 '87
Lemieux, Suzanne
about
Suzanne Lemieux. B. S. Goldman. il por *Am Artist* 51:64-9+ N '87
Lemire, Sarah
about
Sarah Lemire: creating the "Cosby" look. A. Radakovich. il pors *Seventeen* 46:87-8+ Jl '87
Lemmo, Gerard
The wings of spring [cover story] il *Conservationist* 41:26-31 Mr/Ap '87
Lemmon, Sandra K., and Jones, Elizabeth W.
Clathrin requirement for normal growth of yeast. bibl f il *Science* 238:504-9 O 23 '87
Lemna *See* Duckweeds
Lemon, Meadowlark
about
Meadowlark pens a book, but there's no lemon in it. *Jet* 72:49 Je 29 '87
Lemonick, Michael D.
Superconductors! il *Read Dig* 131:13-14+ N '87
Lemons (Automobiles) *See* Automobiles—Defects
Lemos, Peter
High-seas paradise. il *Harpers Bazaar* 120:134+ F '87
LeMoyne, James
Can the contras go on? [cover story] il map *N Y Times Mag* p32-5+ O 4 '87
about
LeMoyne's progress. A. Cockburn. *Nation* 244:423 Ap 4 '87
Lenaghan, Donna D., and Lenaghan, Michael J.
AIDS and education: the front line of prevention. il pors *Futurist* 21:17-19 N/D '87
Lenaghan, Michael J.
(jt. auth) See Lenaghan, Donna D., and Lenaghan, Michael J.
Lenard, Lane
Cancer & the mind: can you cure your own illness? *McCalls* 114:83+ Ap '87
Lenardo, Michael, and others
Protein-binding sites in Ig gene enhancers determine transcriptional activity and inducibility. bibl f il *Science* 236:1573-7 Je 19 '87

Lencioni, Angelo
about
A McDonald's coins big McMoney. J. Alexander. il *Money* 16:37+ D '87
Lend-lease operations, 1941-1945
Commagate [Roosevelt's illegal sale of destroyers to Great Britain in 1940 compared to Iran-contra scandal] D. Seligman. *Fortune* 116:217+ O 12 '87
Lendl, Ivan
Design your own diary. il *World Tennis* 34:20-1 F '87
about
Formidable forehand: a frame-by-frame look at Lendl's championship stroke. J. L. Groppel. il pors *World Tennis* 35:30-1 D '87
Ivan Lendl: master of the universe. S. Flink. il por *World Tennis* 34:56-7 F '87
Ivan Lendl: the $6 million man. D. Higdon. il por *Sport Mag* 78:32 Je '87
King without a kingdom. S. Flink. il por *World Tennis* 34:8-9 Ja '87
A letter to Lendl. S. Flink. il *World Tennis* 35:10-11 D '87
Look who's on top still. F. Deford. il por *Sports Illus* 67:44+ S 21 '87
Secrets of success. K. Cunningham. il *World Tennis* 34:18-21 F '87
Lenexa (Kan.)
Restaurants, nightclubs, bars, etc.
Show stoppers [recipes from Winds Bar and Grill] D. Welch. il *Health* 19:61-4 D '87
Lenger, Frank
about
Dreamgirls. B. Greene. il por *Esquire* 107:39-40 My '87
L'Engle, Madeleine, 1918-
Shake the universe. il *Ms* 16:182-4+ Jl/Ag '87
Length of life *See* Longevity
Length of service (Employment) *See* Labor turnover
Lengyel, Suzanne
His brilliant career. il pors *World Tennis* 35:52-4 D '87
Lenhoff, Howard M.
Is the organismic biologist an endangered species? *BioScience* 37:244 Ap '87
(jt. auth) See Bard, Mitchell, and Lenhoff, Howard M.
Lenin, Vladimir Il'ich, 1870-1924
about
Lenin to the rescue. B. Crozier. *Natl Rev* 39:26 S 11 '87
Myth and memory in Soviet society. N. Tumarkin. *Society* 24:69-72 S/O '87
Revising Lenin's legacy. F. M. Burlatskii. *Harpers* 275:27-8+ N '87
Useful idiots of the West. W. Safire. il *N Y Times Mag* p8+ Ap 12 '87
Leningrad (Soviet Union)
Description
Leningrad: the big thaw. F. Coleman. il *Newsweek* 110:10 N 9 '87
Midsummer Leningrad dreams. A. Husarska. il *New Leader* 70:8-9 S 7 '87
Where the czars shined. J. Gillette. il *Travel Holiday* 167:6+ F '87
Education
The instructors and principal at a Leningrad school challenge rigidities in Soviet education [work of F. Mikhailov] J. W. Seymore. il por *People Wkly* 27:104-7 Ap 6 '87
Palaces
See Palaces—Soviet Union
Lenman, Bruce, 1938-
The East India Company and the Emperor Aurangzeb. bibl il map *Hist Today* 37:23-9 F '87
Lennon, John, 1940-1980
about
Beatles buy-out. J. Wiener. *New Repub* 196:13-14 My 11 '87
In the shadows a killer waited. J. R. Gaines. il por *People Wkly* 27:50-2+ Mr 2 '87
John Lennon and the Plastic Ono Band: Varsity Stadium, Toronto, September 13th, 1969. D. Fricke. il por *Roll Stone* p67+ Je 4 '87
The killer takes his fall. J. R. Gaines. il por *People Wkly* 27:60-2+ Mr 9 '87
The man who shot Lennon. J. R. Gaines. il pors *People Wkly* 27:58-60+ F 23 '87
Yoko Ono [interview] D. Fricke. por *Roll Stone* p53-4 N 5-D 10 '87
Lennon, Peter
Rosi and the Italian film crisis. por *World Press Rev* 34:56 Jl '87

Leno, Jay
about
Motor mouth. C. Hodenfield. il pors *Cycle* 38:80-4 F '87
Profile (whew!) of a funny man [cover story] J. Kaufman. il pors *People Wkly* 28:134-9 N 30 '87
Photographs and photography
The background of a shot. G. Bernstein. il pors *Petersens Photogr Mag* 16:20 Jl '87
Lenore Marshall/Nation Poetry Prize *See* Poetry—Awards
Lens (Eye) *See* Crystalline lens
Lens accessories (Photography) *See* Photography—Equipment
Lenses
See also
Contact lenses
Eyeglasses
Building fun telescopes for less than $10. R. Monaghan. il *Astronomy* 15:46-9 My '87
A homemade wide-angle eyepiece [telescope] S. O. Rehnlund. il *Sky Telesc* 74:424-6 O '87
Care
Caring for optics [telescope lenses] A. MacRobert. il *Sky Telesc* 73:380-1 Ap '87
Lenses, Photographic
The 20 millimeter lens: exploring an ultrawide optic. L. Brownstein. il *Petersens Photogr Mag* 16:40-2 S '87
At close range [macro lenses; cover story] B. Hagin. il *Pop Photogr* 94:70-8 N '87
Close encounters: magnifying images with a teleconverter. N. Rothschild. il *Pop Photogr* 94:16 Ap '87
Closeup lenses: two elements are better than one. J. Shaw. il *Pop Photogr* 94:26+ S '87
A critical guide to zoom lenses. B. Schwalberg. *Pop Photogr* 94:62 My '87
Independent lenses [PMA Show] B. Hagin. il *Pop Photogr* 94:66-7 Jl '87
The long and short of it: background and focal length. J. Shaw. il *Pop Photogr* 94:36-7 Jl '87
Spherical aberration is the key to soft-focus lenses. N. Goldberg. il *Pop Photogr* 94:56+ Mr '87
Supernormal lenses [zoom lenses; cover story] S. Pollock. il *Pop Photogr* 94:54-9+ My '87
Tips on making the right lens choice for today's cameras. N. Goldberg. il *Pop Photogr* 94:80 Je '87
History
The evolution of the zoom. B. Schwalberg. il *Pop Photogr* 94:60 My '87
Fifty years of progress in camera and lens design. N. Goldberg. il *Pop Photogr* 94:16+ Ja '87
History of macro lenses. B. Schwalberg. il *Pop Photogr* 94:79 N '87
Testing
2 new Nikon AF lenses [180mm f/2.8 AF and 300mm f/2.8 AF] J. Drafahl and S. Drafahl. il *Petersens Photogr Mag* 16:44-5 Jl '87
3 more for the Maxxums: Minolta's autofocus 16mm fisheye, 20mm superwide, and 100mm macro lenses. B. Hurter and M. Stensvold. il *Petersens Photogr Mag* 15:69-71 Mr '87
3 new Sigma autofocus lenses. D. O'Neill. il *Petersens Photogr Mag* 16:40-1 Ag '87
AF Nikkor 28→85mm f/3.5-4.5. il *Pop Photogr* 94:56 O '87
Apo enlarging lenses. D. Brooks. il *Petersens Photogr Mag* 15:16-18 Ap '87
Canon EF 35→105 mm f/3.5-4.5 lens. N. Goldberg. il *Pop Photogr* 94:68-9 Jl '87
Independent autofocus. D. O'Neill. il *Petersens Photogr Mag* 16:74-6 N '87
Long shots with big cameras [telephoto lenses] D. Brooks. il *Petersens Photogr Mag* 16:24-6 Ag '87
Modern mirrors. J. A. Dickerson. il *Petersens Photogr Mag* 16:76-7 D '87
New Canon zoom. G. Lewis. il *Petersens Photogr Mag* 16:68-9 S '87
New Nikon AF lenses. J. Drafahl and S. Drafahl. il *Petersens Photogr Mag* 15:55-7 Ap '87
New Pentax soft-focus lens. J. Drafahl and S. Drafahl. il *Petersens Photogr Mag* 15:24-5 Ja '87
Nikon autofocus closeup system [SB-21 flash and 55mm macro lens] J. Drafahl and S. Drafahl. il *Petersens Photogr Mag* 16:68-70 Je '87
Olympus AF 35→70mm f/3.5-4.5 lens. il *Pop Photogr* 94:48-9 Ag '87
Pentax-F 35→70mm f/3.5-4.5 lens [zoom lens] N. Goldberg. il *Pop Photogr* 94:59 Ag '87
Rolleigon 50mm f/4, 80mm f/2.8, and 150mm f/4. N. Goldberg. il *Pop Photogr* 94:44 F '87

Lenses, Photographic—Testing—*cont.*

Sigma zooms for Maxxums. M. Stensvold. il *Petersens Photogr Mag* 15:16-17 Ja '87

Soligor 35-300mm lens. A. Stone. il *Petersens Photogr Mag* 16:46-7 Je '87

Tamron superspeed teles. B. Hurter. il *Petersens Photogr Mag* 15:16-18 F '87

Through a lens, softly. il *Pop Photogr* 94:38-45 Mr '87

Yashica AF 28→85mm F/3.5-4.5 [zoom lens] N. Goldberg. il *Pop Photogr* 94:58-9 Je '87

Zeiss Vario-Sonnar 35-70mm f/3.4 [zoom lens] N. Goldberg. il *Pop Photogr* 94:61 S '87

Lent

See also

Ash Wednesday
Easter
Maundy Thursday

Lent: with our Eyes on the prize. *America* 156:165-6 F 28 '87

Lenten meditation:

Judas as patron saint. R. Goetz. *Christ Century* 104:262-3 Mr 18-25 '87

Petitionary prayer reconsidered. C. E. Simcox. *Christ Century* 104:212-13 Mr 4 '87

The preacher and the panhandlers [parable of the Pharisee and the tax collector] J. Killinger. il *Christ Century* 104:301-2 Ap 1 '87

A question of faith. J. F. Scholer. *Christ Century* 104:237-8 Mr 11 '87

Life for all. M. K. Hellwig. *America* 156:inside back cover F 28 '87

Bibliography

Lenten reading roundup. T. H. Stahel. *America* 156:178+ F 28 '87

Lentils

See also

Cooking—Vegetables

Lentiviruses

Isolation of a T-lymphotropic virus from domestic cats with an immunodeficiency-like syndrome. N. C. Pedersen and others. bibl f il *Science* 235:790-3 F 13 '87

Lenz, Elinor

The generation gap: from Persephone to Portnoy. il *N Y Times Book Rev* 92:1+ Ag 30 '87

Leo, John

Should schools offer sex education? *Read Dig* 130:138-42 Mr '87

Leo Castelli Gallery

Leader of the pack [anniversary exhibitions] K. Larson. il *N Y* 20:110+ Mr 9 '87

The past master of pop, Leo Castelli, celebrates his 30th anniversary as art's big dealer. H. Shapiro. il pors *People Wkly* 27:41-2+ F 16 '87

Leocha, Charles

The perfect ski. il *Esquire* 108:35-6 D '87

Leonard, Bill J.

At the river: thoughts on baptism. *Christ Century* 104:813-15 S 30 '87

Leonard, Elmore, 1925-

about

Heroes of the underworld. R. Miller. il por *Macleans* 100:61 Ja 19 '87

St. Elmore's fire. M. Lupica. il por *Esquire* 107:169-71+ Ap '87

A taste for life's seamy side [interview] A. P. Sanoff. il por *U S News World Rep* 102:64 Mr 9 '87

Leonard, Graham

The tyranny of subjectivism [address, September 18, 1987] *Vital Speeches Day* 54:50-7 N 1 '87

Leonard, Jeffrey

about

Don't call him Jeff. B. Shapiro. il pors *Sport Mag* 78:82-4+ Ag '87

Three men on a roll. F. Lidz. il pors *Sports Illus* 67:40-2+ Ag 24 '87

Leonard, John

Television. See issues of New York beginning November 28, 1983

Leonard, Mary Delach

The toughest choice. il por *Ladies Home J* 104:22+ O '87

Leonard, Michael

about

Drawn to the past. L. Kirstein. il por *House Gard* 159:168-71+ N '87

Leonard, Ray Charles *See* Leonard, Sugar Ray

Leonard, Sugar Ray

about

Can Sugar Ray Leonard make a comeback? Don't even ask. J. Friedman. il pors *People Wkly* 27:58-60 Mr 30 '87

Clash of the opposites. P. Axthelm. pors *Newsweek* 109:52 Ap 6 '87

Comeback for the ages. W. Nack. il pors *Sports Illus* 66:18-25 Ap 13 '87

Concern erases risk as Leonard helps rescue tot. por *Jet* 72:46 Je 22 '87

'Everything I did worked'. W. Nack. il pors *Sports Illus* 66:50-2+ Ap 20 '87

Hagler vs. Leonard: the seniors tour. M. Katz. il pors *Sport Mag* 78:76-82 Ap '87

The illusion of victory: another view of the Leonard-Hagler decision. H. McIlvanney. il por *Sports Illus* 66:120 Ap 20 '87

Leonard adds new tactic in preparing for Hagler. il por *Jet* 71:46 F 23 '87

Leonard banks on a decision while Hagler mulls a murder and Hearns wants a double KO. pors *Jet* 72:50 Ap 6 '87

Leonard is lionized on Capitol Hill as guest of Kan. Sen. Robert Dole. il pors *Jet* 72:12 My 11 '87

Leonard rides wave of success to radio show. por *Jet* 72:48 Ag 3 '87

Notes and comment. *New Yorker* 63:25-6 Ap 20 '87

One will be made whole. R. Reilly. il pors *Sports Illus* 66:58-64+ Mr 30 '87

Prediction. W. Nack. il pors *Sports Illus* 66:70-2+ Mr 30 '87

Ray Leonard retires but won't close the door. il por *Jet* 72:46 Je 15 '87

Sugar Ray Leonard, an Eddie Robinson fan, gifts $250G's to Grambling. il pors *Jet* 72:50 Jl 13 '87

Sugar Ray Leonard says he has a plan for Hagler. il pors *Jet* 71:47 Ja 12 '87

Sugar Ray Leonard scores upset, joins history's greatest. il pors *Jet* 72:51 Ap 20 '87

Sugar Ray Leonard: why I am fighting again [cover story] N. O. Unger. il *Ebony* 42:92-4+ Ap '87

Sugar Ray retires to promote Garden bouts. por *Jet* 72:46 S 7 '87

Sugar's sweet comeback. il pors *People Wkly* 27:40-1 Ap 20 '87

Sugar's sweetest confection. P. Axthelm. il pors *Newsweek* 109:71 Ap 20 '87

A super finish to a SuperFight. il pors *Macleans* 100:46 Ap 20 '87

Sweet smell of success may keep Sugar swinging. il por *Jet* 72:48 Ap 27 '87

Tennis champ McEnroe thanks Leonard for hope. pors *Jet* 72:47 My 18 '87

Too moving to be mayhem. T. Callahan. il pors *Time* 129:62 Ap 20 '87

Photographs and photography

Dream fight. J. McDonough. il pors *Sport Mag* 78:56-63 D '87

Leonard, Terry J.

about

Death before dishonor [film] Reviews

New Leader 70:22-3 Mr 9 '87. J. Gardner

Leonard, William J.

Worship in wartime. *America* 157:58-60 Ag 1-8 '87

Leonard part 6 [film] See Motion picture reviews—Single works

Leonardo, da Vinci, 1452-1519

about

After five centuries, a devoted modeler gives shape to genius. J. P. Wiley, Jr. bibl (p145) il por *Smithsonian* 18:90-5 Ag '87

Art smart. il *Harpers Bazaar* 120:82+ My '87

Da Vinci drawing tops 'triumphant' Gaines sale. R. W. Walker. *Art News* 86:16 Ja '87

Digital image processing in art conservation. J. F. Asmus. bibl il *Byte* 12:151-60+ Mr '87

From Dolan to da Vinci. A. Cockburn. *Nation* 244:135 F 7 '87

The master builder. G. James. il *Macleans* 100:51 Ag 24 '87

The mysterious genius of Leonardo. M. Horn. il *U S News World Rep* 102:71-2 My 25 '87

Restoring The Last Supper. il *Travel Holiday* 168:54 S '87

Unmasking a 'Mona Lisa' coverup. I. Peterson. *Sci News* 131:152 Mr 7 '87

Leonhard, Wolfgang

The Bolshevik Revolution turns 70. *Foreign Aff* 66:388-409 Wint '87/'88

Leonora [opera] See Fry, William Henry, 1813-1864

Leonov, Aleksei

about

Of space walks and wolves: the incredible flight of Voskhod 2. W. W. Cook, III. il *Space World* X-1-277:11-13 Ja '87

Leopard hunting
Jim Corbett: the reluctant executioner. G. C. Ward. il por maps *Audubon* 89:44-9+ Jl '87
Leopardi, Giacomo, 1798-1837
From 'Le ricordanze' ('Memories') [poem]; tr. by John Francis Alexander Health-Stubbs. *N Y Rev Books* 34:43 Ja 29 '87
    Bibliography
The strange case of Leopardi. D. S. Carne-Ross. il *N Y Rev Books* 34:42-3 Ja 29 '87
Leopards
Coming back from the brink [removal from endangered species list] M. D. Lemonick. il *Time* 130:70 Jl 20 '87
Snow leopard. il map *Natl Geogr World* 148:8 D '87
Leopold, Aldo, 1886-1948
Earth almanac. il *Conservationist* 42:54-5 N/D '87
Farmer of the future: a conservationist [excerpt from 1939 essay] il *Success Farm* 85 no6:22-3 Mr '87
    about
Aldo Leopold—a celebration of the land ethic. J. W. Taylor. il pors *Conservationist* 42:12-15 N/D '87
How Leopold learned to think like a mountain. C. Meine. *Wilderness* 51:57-8+ Wint '87
Letting Leopold down. C. E. Little. il por *Wilderness* 50:45-8 Summ '87
Sand County's conservation prophet. D. R. Wallace. il pors *Sierra* 72:62-7 N/D '87
Leopold, Stephen
    about
Montreal's hot property market. P. C. Newman. il por *Macleans* 100:34 S 7 '87
Leopold Property Consultants Inc.
Montreal's hot property market [office space broker S. Leopold] P. C. Newman. il por *Macleans* 100:34 S 7 '87
Lepe, Manuel
    about
A naïf vision of paradise. M. Kroll. il por *Américas* 39:20-4 S/O '87
Lepers *See* Leprosy
Lepidoptera
    See also
    Butterflies
    Moths
Leppert, Mark, and others
The gene for familial polyposis coli maps to the long arm of chromosome 5. bibl f il *Science* 238:1411-13 D 4 '87
Leprosy
    See also
    Church work with leprosy patients
    Therapy
Easing leprosy's pain [Keur Massar hospital and colony in Senegal] M. Rose. il por *Macleans* 100:6+ Mr 30 '87
New drug against leprosy [clofazimine] *FDA Consum* 21:2 Mr '87
    Vaccines and vaccination
Toward a TB vaccine and a leprosy link. *Sci News* 131:264 Ap 25 '87
Lere, Mark, 1950-
    about
Mark Lere: Margo Leavin. P. Clothier. il *Art News* 86:164+ D '87
Lerman, Leo
The cookbook shelf. il *Gourmet* 47:74+ Mr '87
The cookbook shelf. il *Gourmet* 47:68+ N '87
The tiny terror: a Capote memory. il pors *Vogue* 177:762-3+ S '87
Lerman, Liz
    about
Comfort me with apples. T. Tobias. il *N Y* 20:129-30 N 9 '87
Lerman (Liz)/Exchange (Dance company) *See* Liz Lerman/Exchange (Dance company)
Lerner, Bennett
    about
Ongoing Dialogues. P. G. Davis. il *N Y* 20:82+ Ap 6 '87
Lerner, David
(jt. auth) *See* Ratner, Michael, and Lerner, David
Lerner, Eugene M.
    about
Strictly by the numbers. C. Siler. il por *Forbes* 140:184+ N 2 '87
Lerner, Harriet Goldhor
    about
Dance with an intimate stranger [interview] C. Tavris. *Vogue* 177:44 D '87

Lerner, Martin
    about
Addressing the student market. M. Gill. il por *Esquire* 108:76 D '87
Lerner, Max, 1902-
Bork's progress. *New Repub* 197:18+ S 14-21 '87
Myth America. *New Repub* 197:11-13 S 7 '87
Lerner, Rita
    about
Baby Steps are the socks of choice for toddlers who don't want to hit the skids early. il *People Wkly* 28:183 N 16 '87
Lernoux, Penny, 1940-
Beggaring our Latin neighbors. il *Nation* 245:709-10+ D 12 '87
A society torn apart by violence. il *Nation* 245:512-14+ N 7 '87
Lesbianism
    See also
    Bisexuality
AIDS: CDC report card . . . and lesbian transmission? *Sci News* 131:8 Ja 3 '87
A Methodist on trial [trial of lesbian clergywoman R. Denman in Dover, N.H.] M. Starr. il por *Newsweek* 110:62 S 7 '87
Personal politics: a lesson in straight talk [mentioning one's lesbianism in conversation] L. Van Gelder. il *Ms* 16:95 N '87
Lesbianism and Christianity *See* Homosexuality and Christianity
Lesch, Ann Mosely
A view from Khartoum. bibl f map *Foreign Aff* 65:807-26 Spr '87
Lesch-Nyhan syndrome
Identification and localization of mutations at the Lesch-Nyhan locus by ribonuclease A cleavage. R. A. Gibbs and C. T. Caskey. bibl f il *Science* 236:303-5 Ap 17 '87
New avenues for LNS gene transfer. K. Hartley. *Sci News* 131:390 Je 20 '87
Leschly, Jan
    about
His brilliant career. S. Lengyel. il pors *World Tennis* 35:52-4 D '87
Lesèvre, Lise
    about
The Barbie trial: J'accuse. F. Coleman. il pors *Newsweek* 109:41 My 11 '87
Lesions, Brain *See* Brain damage
Leskov, N. S. (Nikolaĭ Semenovich), 1831-1895
    Bibliography
Justice for Leskov. I. Howe. il *N Y Rev Books* 34:32-6 Ap 23 '87
Leskov, Nikolaĭ Semenovich *See* Leskov, N. S. (Nikolaĭ Semenovich), 1831-1895
Leslie, E. C.
(jt. auth) *See* Ishler, Richard E., and Leslie, E. C.
Lespinasse, Gaby
    about
'My angel . . . I love you in every color'. K. Ames. il por *Newsweek* 110:86 S 28 '87
Picasso's secret love. J. Richardson. il pors *House Gard* 159:174-83+ O '87
Less developed countries *See* Developing countries
Less than zero [film] *See* Motion picture reviews—Single works
Lessard, Suzannah
The issue was women. il *Newsweek* 109:32+ My 18 '87
Profiles [E. Zeisel] il *New Yorker* 63:36-40+ Ap 13 '87
Lessem, Don
Here come the killer bees. il *Int Wildl* 17:12-15 My/Je '87
History in bits and pieces: body snatcher [interview with R. W. Purcell] il *Omni* 10:82-9 D '87
Interview. por *Omni* 9:76-8+ Jl '87
Interview [F. Davidson] por *Omni* 9:80-2+ My '87
Lessing, Doris May, 1919-
The catastrophe. *New Yorker* 63:74-90+ Mr 16 '87
Womb ward [story] *New Yorker* 63:41-3 D 7 '87
    about
Narratives: the Doris Lessing standard. L. Stone. il *Ms* 16:29-30+ Jl/Ag '87
Lessing, Traudl
A Vienna success. il por *House Gard* 159:100-5+ Jl '87
Lester, Richard, 1932-
    about
Help! [film] Reviews
    Stereo Rev il 52:205 N '87. L. Meredith

Lester Lanin Orchestras
Lester Lanin. F. Conroy. il pors *People Wkly* 28:79-80+ D 21 '87
The music man. E. F. Cone. il por *Forbes* 140 Sp Issue:382 O 26 '87

Letcher, John S., Jr., and others
Stars & Stripes [cover story] il *Sci Am* 257:34-40+ Ag '87

Letelier, Orlando

Assassination
Confession of a 'good soldier' [testimony of A. Fernández Larios] M. R. Meyer. il por *Newsweek* 109:43 F 16 '87
Derailing Pinochet [A. Pinochet implicated in A. Fernandez's account of Letelier assassination] J. Dinges and S. Landau. il *Nation* 244:280-2 Mr 7 '87

Lethal weapon [film] *See* Motion picture reviews—Single works

Letter carriers *See* Postal employees

Letter holders
Mail sorter. D. Watson. il *Fam Handyman* 37:62 F '87

Letter writing *See* Letters

Lettering
See also
Kroy Inc.
Monograms

Letterman, David
about
Dave's kids: the twisted minds behind the Letterman show. E. Pooley. il por *N Y* 20:36-45 Ja 19 '87

Letters
See also
Authors—Correspondence, reminiscences, etc.
Business writing
Fan mail
Form letters
Hate mail
Love letters
Pen pals
Dear Dad [letters from celebrities to their fathers; excerpts] L. N. Cox. *Ladies Home J* 104:53 Je '87
How to write a personal letter. G. Keillor. il por *Read Dig* 131:129-31 N '87
When I was grieving [letters from friends provide comfort after death of premature infant] A. P. Murphy. il *Glamour* 85:302 My '87

Anecdotes, facetiae, satire, etc.
And in the second place . . . M. E. Marty. *Christ Century* 104:1015 N 11 '87
Learning one's letters from Mme. la Comtesse. R. Chelminski. il *Smithsonian* 18:212 D '87

Letters of recommendation
See also
Employment references
Can you be sued for letters of reference? R. S. Brown. *Educ Dig* 52:54-6 Mr '87

Letters to the editor *See* Newspapers—Letters to the editor; Periodicals—Letters to the editor

Lettuce
See also
Celtuce
For scrumptious salads, blend your lettuces. W. E. Wooldridge. il *Flower Gard* 31:79-80 F/Mr '87
Good-looking, good-tasting . . . the "new" lettuces. il *Sunset* 179:66-7 S '87
How to grow lettuce from seed. il *Sunset* 179:202 S '87
New lettuces. il *Flower Gard* 31:30+ Je/Jl '87
Sow lettuce now [use of floating row covers] K. Martin. il *Rodale's Org Gard* 34:53-4+ S '87
Year-round lettuce. M. Kane. il *Rodale's Org Gard* 34:40-5 My '87

Lettuce Leaf Restaurants
Tossing up a winner. G. Heiman. il por *Nations Bus* 75:76 D '87

Letzring, Howard
about
Howdy Letzring can make your company meetings immortal. M. Frons. il por *Bus Week* p103 Ja 26 '87

Leucadia National Corp.
A fight over Baldwin's ghost [Leucadia goes after PHLCorp] C. S. Eklund. il *Bus Week* p72 Mr 30 '87

Leucaena
Mike Benge and his marvelous tree [leucaena used to halt deforestation] J. G. Hubbell. il por *Read Dig* 131:103-7 Ag '87

Leukemia
Candlelighters: help for stricken families. D. Lund. il *Read Dig* 131:73-8 Ag '87
HTLV-I-associated B-cell CLL: indirect role for retrovirus in leukemogenesis [chronic lymphocytic leukemia] D. L. Mann and others. bibl f il *Science* 236:1103-6 My 29 '87

Causes
HTLV-V: a new human retrovirus isolated in a Tac-negative T cell lymphoma/leukemia. V. Manzari and others. bibl f il *Science* 238:1581-3 D 11 '87
In the journals [link between household pesticides and childhood leukemia] *Child Today* 16:3 S/O '87
Kids' leukemia from parents' exposures? J. Raloff. *Sci News* 132:38-9 Jl 18 '87
Magnetic fields and leukemia [power line radiation] *Newsweek* 110:56 Jl 20 '87

Genetic aspects
Fragile sites at 16q22 are not at the breakpoint of the chromosomal rearrangement in AMMoL. R. N. Simmers and others. bibl f il *Science* 236:92-4 Ap 3 '87
Relationship between the *c-myb* locus and the 6q-chromosomal aberration in leukemias and lymphomas. C. Barletta and others. bibl f il *Science* 235:1064-7 F 27 '87
Unique forms of the *abl* tyrosine kinase distinguish Ph¹-positive CML Ph¹-positive ALL. S. S. Clark and others. bibl f il *Science* 235:85-8 Ja 2 '87

Therapy
Bone marrow transplants: from Chernobyl to cancer therapy. M. J. Fromer. il *FDA Consum* 21:12-15 Ap '87
Curing cancer in Jerusalem [bone marrow transplantation for leukemia patients; work of Shimon Slavin at Hadassah Hospital] C. SerVaas. il *Saturday Evening Post* 259:54-9 Jl/Ag '87
One patient's experience with interferon [interview with M. Fow] R. W. Miller. por *FDA Consum* 21:11 Ap '87
"The sister I never knew I had saved my life" [case of C. Bracken] J. Ardmore. il por *Good Housekeep* 205:180+ S '87

Leukemia cells *See* Cancer cells

Leukemia viruses
See also
HIV viruses
HTLV viruses
A chimeric, ligan-binding v-erbB/EGF receptor retains transforming potential [avian erythroblastosis virus] H. Riedel and others. bibl f il *Science* 236:197-200 Ap 10 '87
The CML-specific P210 *bcr/abl* protein, unlike v-*abl*, does not transform NIH/3T3 fibroblasts. G. Q. Daley and others. bibl f il *Science* 237:532-5 Jl 31 '87

Leukocytes
See also
Phagocytes and phagocytosis
Chemoattractant-regulated mobilization of a novel intracellular compartment in human neutrophils. N. Borregaard and others. bibl f il *Science* 237:1204-6 S 4 '87
Cytosolic acidification as an early transductory signal of human neutrophil chemotaxis. I. Yuli and A. Oplatka. bibl f il *Science* 235:340-2 Ja 16 '87
Eosinophils cocultured with endothelial cells have increased survival and functional properties. M. E. Rothenberg and others. bibl f il *Science* 237:645-7 Ag 7 '87
Heparin promotes the inactivation of antithrombin by neutrophil elastase. R. E. Jordan and others. bibl f il *Science* 237:777-9 Ag 14 '87

Leukoplakia, Oral
Strictly speaking, watch your mouth [precursor to AIDS; research by John S. Greenspan] *Sci News* 131:135 F 28 '87

Leukotrienes
Leukotrienes and lipoxins: structures, biosynthesis, and biological effects. B. Samuelsson and others. bibl f il *Science* 237:1171-6 S 4 '87

LeVant, Simone
about
Diver just says no. A. Ferber. il por *Women's Sports Fitness* 9:25 My '87

LeVasseur, Michal
Tibet. il map *Focus* 37:34-5 Spr '87

Levathes, Louise E.
Iceland: life under the glaciers. il maps *Natl Geogr* 171:184-215 F '87
Indianapolis: city on the rebound. il map *Natl Geogr* 172:230-59 Ag '87
Mysteries of the bog. il *Natl Geogr* 171:396-420 Mr '87

Levels (Tools)
Levels. J. Truini. il *Pop Mech* 164:95-7+ Je '87

Levenson, Jeff
Arthur Blythe's creative challenge. il pors *Down Beat* 54:23-5 O '87

Levenson, Michael H. (Michael Harry), 1951-
The Nayman of Noland. il *New Repub* 197:34-7 Jl 6 '87

Leventhal, Albert Rice
Returns are born [reprint from March 10, 1975 issue] il *Publ Wkly* 232:20 N 20 '87

Leventhal, Alice Walker *See* Walker, Alice, 1944-

Leventhal, Ann Z.
Acceptance. *Writer* 100:7-8 Ag '87

Leventhal, Robert Stanley
about
The sad saga of Western Union's decline. A. Bianco. il pors *Bus Week* p108-10+ D 14 '87

Leverage (Finance)
See also
Parking (Securities)

Leveraged buyouts
7-Eleven wants out of the glare. J. Weber, Jr. il *Bus Week* p78 Jl 20 '87
Are shareholders cheated by LBOs? G. Hector. il *Fortune* 115:98-100+ Ja 19 '87
Behind the scenes at a leveraged buyout [Sybron Corp.] E. Spragins. il *Bus Week* p120-2 Jl 20 '87
'Betting on the genius' of Henley's chairman. G. G. Marcial. il por *Bus Week* p118 N 23 '87
Building a first for Canada [Onex Capital Corp.] D. Jenish. il por *Macleans* 100:22+ Jl 27 '87
Buried treasure [Du Pont discard, Vista Chemical] J. Willoughby. il *Forbes* 139:201 My 18 '87
Business 101 [T. McMillan's leveraged buyout of Frank Purcell Walnut Lumber] S. B. Weiner. il por *Forbes* 140:52 Ag 24 '87
Buying out the boss at CBS Magazines [P. Diamandis' group] D. Lieberman. il por *Bus Week* p30 Jl 27 '87
The buyout man [W. F. Farley] C. Skrzycki. il por *U S News World Rep* 102:63 Ja 26 '87
Can-do Canadian [G. Schwartz] L. Jereski. il por *Forbes* 140:124 S 7 '87
Carl Icahn may soon be back in the raiding business [taking TWA private] C. Hawkins and C. Power. *Bus Week* p29-30 Ag 3 '87
A deal that would get Allegheny out of the spotlight. M. Rothman and G. L. Miles. il *Bus Week* p34 Mr 23 '87
Did Drexel bully takeover candidates? [suit brought by Staley Continental] C. Welles. *Bus Week* p43-4 Mr 9 '87
Don't leap at these reverse LBOs [new public offerings] il *Money* 16:13 Jl '87
A fire sale at Cooper? [P. G. Montgomery's leveraged buyout scheme] J. O. Hamilton. il por *Bus Week* p37 N 23 '87
Forstmann Little: going fast by going slow. E. Spragins. il *Bus Week* p76-8 Ja 26 '87
Getting top dollar for Beatrice's leftovers. L. Therrien. il por *Bus Week* p50-1 Jl 6 '87
Going private [Southland Corp.] A. A. Lappen. il *Forbes* 140:10 Jl 27 '87
Going private: how to swing the deal of a lifetime. E. Spragins. il *Bus Week* p84-5 Ag 31 '87
The grass looks greener [venture capitalists going into leveraged buyouts] J. Heins. il *Forbes* 139:50-1 Ja 26 '87
HBJ sells units to Edgell group for $334.1 million. C. Reid. *Publ Wkly* 232:11 N 27 '87
HBJ shows the leveraged deal is alive and well [R. L. Edgell acquires magazine unit] G. DeGeorge. *Bus Week* p36-7 N 30 '87
HCA may breathe new life into ESOPs [Hospital Corp. of America] G. Weiss. il *Bus Week* p94 Je 15 '87
High yield, high risk [aftermath of 1984 Dart Drug leveraged buyout] P. Berman. il *Forbes* 140:38 Ag 24 '87
How to get in on the Safeway LBO [warrants] J. M. Laderman. *Bus Week* p100 Ap 27 '87
How to steal an S&L—legally [Green family buyout of Firstrust Saving Bank] B. D. Fromson. il *Fortune* 116:57-8+ O 12 '87
Icahn proposes merger that could make TWA a private company. *Aviat Week Space Technol* 127:32 Jl 27 '87
If you're so smart, buy it yourself. B. Kallen. il *Forbes* 139:220-1 My 18 '87

Infomaniac [R. Carson manages leveraged buyouts of information companies] L. Jereski. il por *Forbes* 140:224+ O 5 '87
A junk-bond belly flop [Thompson family leveraged buyout of Southland] J. Weber, Jr. *Bus Week* p35 N 23 '87
LBOs are taking their lumps. C. J. Loomis. il *Fortune* 116:63-4+ D 7 '87
Leaning against the wind [deals by G. Cain] J. Willoughby. il por *Forbes* 140:208+ Jl 13 '87
The little motor that couldn't [Exxon sells Reliance Electric in a leveraged buyout] J. A. Conway. il *Forbes* 139:8 F 9 '87
Need a quick billion or two? Just ask your banker [lending for mergers and LBOs] S. Bartlett. il *Bus Week* p98-9 O 26 '87
The new buyout binge. C. Friday. il *Newsweek* 110:30-1 Ag 24 '87
Peter Diamandis is finally working for himself [CBS Magazines] P. Finch. il por *Bus Week* p48 Ag 3 '87
Private thoughts. S. B. Weiner and J. Parr. il *Forbes* 140:246 N 30 '87
Scarlett O'Hara comes to Wall Street [scramble over leveraged buyout financing] R. L. Stern and E. F. Cone. il *Forbes* 140:37-8+ S 21 '87
Scholastic to go private through $84 million buyout. *Publ Wkly* 231:10 Je 26 '87
Sharp shoppers [B. Freeman specializes in leveraged buyouts of supermarkets] M. Fritz. il por *Forbes* 140:236 N 30 '87
Taking over the controls [C. Icahn plans to take TWA private] pors *Time* 130:43 Ag 3 '87
Thank you, Kohlberg Kravis [L. B. Foster Co.'s experiences after leveraged buyout] J. Clements. il *Forbes* 140:38+ N 2 '87
An unlikely savior for Gillette? [W. E. Buffett] G. G. Marcial. *Bus Week* p188 N 16 '87
Virago Press completes buyout from Random House's CBC Group. il *Publ Wkly* 232:310 Ag 7 '87
Virago quits Chatto consortium as Graham Greene enters fray [management buyout of Virago Press] V. Menkes. *Publ Wkly* 231:20 Ap 17 '87
What changed Sam Heyman's mind about LBOs [taking GAF private] J. A. Byrne. il por *Bus Week* p31 S 21 '87
Why going private didn't bring Sidney Dworkin happiness [Revco D.S. Inc.] Z. Schiller. *Bus Week* p43+ O 12 '87
Why Jim Walter is ripe for the picking [bid by Kohlberg Kravis Roberts & Co.] P. Engardio. il *Bus Week* p31+ Ag 3 '87
Will GAF cash in its Borg-Warner chips—or up the ante? [leveraged buyout led by Merrill Lynch] J. E. Ellis. *Bus Week* p34-5 Ap 27 '87
The year's best sale at Macy's: itself. A. Dunkin. il por *Bus Week* p136-7 Ja 12 '87

Anecdotes, facetiae, satire, etc.
Talk about a buyout! [leveraged buyout for all of Britain] B. Stein. il *N Y Times Mag* p50+ Mr 1 '87

Levert (Musical group)
Levert and Tease sell the sizzle. C. Rogers and M. Moore. il *Essence* 17:24 F '87
Levert follows in famed footsteps of the O'Jays. il *Jet* 73:53 N 16 '87

Lévesque, Laurence
about
Life in a Roman limbo. A. Wilson-Smith. il pors *Macleans* 100:15-16 Ja 26 '87
Triumph for two sisters. J. Barber. il pors *Macleans* 100:44 F 23 '87

Levesque, Lynn
about
Angry words in the East. M. Gee. *Macleans* 100:13 Ag 31 '87

Lévesque, Micheline
about
Life in a Roman limbo. A. Wilson-Smith. il pors *Macleans* 100:15-16 Ja 26 '87
Triumph for two sisters. J. Barber. il pors *Macleans* 100:44 F 23 '87

Lévesque, René, 1922-1987
about
Commemorated by controversy. B. Wallace. *Macleans* 100:19 N 30 '87
Obituary
Macleans il pors 100:10-12 N 16 '87
Macleans il 100:72 N 16 '87. A. Fotheringham

Levi, Arrigo
about
Italy's 'stable instability' [interview] J. R. Moskin. por *World Press Rev* 34:22-4 Je '87
Levi, Lennart
Stress in the modern world. il *Courier* 40:27-30 Je '87
Levi, Primo, 1919-1987
Beyond judgment; tr. by Raymond Rosenthal. il *N Y Rev Books* 34:10+ D 17 '87
Two poems [poem]; tr. by Gaia Servadio and A. Alvarez. *New Yorker* 63:46 O 12 '87
Weightless; tr. by Piers Spence. *Harpers* 275:38 O '87
about
Obituary
New Yorker 63:31-2 My 11 '87
Primo Levi: reconciling the man and the writer. A. Stille. por *N Y Times Book Rev* 92:5 Jl 5 '87
Levi-Montalcini, Rita, 1909-
The nerve growth factor 35 years later [address, December 8, 1986] bibl f il *Science* 237:1154-62 S 4 '87
about
The heart & mind of a genius. F. Randall. il por *Vogue* 177:480-1+ Mr '87
Levi Strauss & Co.
Back to basic blues [women's jeans] M. Morris. il *Work Woman* 12:55-6 Je '87
A better grade of junk. M. Schifrin. *Forbes* 140:258 N 30 '87
How Levi Strauss is getting the lead out of its pipeline [bar codes] J. O. Hamilton. il *Bus Week* p92 D 21 '87
Levin, Alexandra Lee
An American's attempt to rescue Lafayette [cover story] il por *Am Hist Illus* 22:16-20+ O '87
Levin, Bob
Peace process at a stalemate. *World Press Rev* 34:23-4 Ap '87
Levin, Carl
Administration wrong on ABM Treaty. il *Bull At Sci* 43:30-3 Ap '87
Should the Levin-Nunn Amendment be approved? [excerpts from address, May 14, 1987] *Congr Dig* 66:284+ N '87
Levin, Edmund
The closing of the American game. *Nation* 245:437-8+ O 24 '87
Levin, Jack
about
Opposite attractions. L. Bernikow. il *Archit Dig* 44:176-81 O '87
Levin, Jennifer Dawn, d. 1986
Murder case
Jennifer Levin and Robert Chambers: a walk with love and death. A. C. Heller. il pors *Mademoiselle* 93:145-7+ Ja '87
The people versus Robert Chambers. L. Wolfe. il pors *N Y* 20:92-9+ O 26 '87
Prosecuting Jennifer Levin's killer. M. Laurino. il pors *Ms* 16:70-2+ S '87
Levin, Michael E.
Philosophers discover the bomb. *Natl Rev* 39:34+ D 4 '87
Levin, Nora
Will 'glasnost' reach the Jews? *Commonweal* 114:596-9 O 23 '87
Levin, Rachel
about
Once-paralyzed Rachel Levin gets a fresh start in Gaby. il por *People Wkly* 28:64 D 21 '87
Levin, Susanna
The death of jogging: how to walk (not run) into shape. il *Mademoiselle* 93:60 Jl '87
Pain centers. *McCalls* 115:80-1 O '87
A skeptic's guide to walking. il *Health* 19:30-2+ Ap '87
The whole-body workout. il *Mademoiselle* 93:130 Mr '87
Levin, Wayne
A Cibachrome primer. il *Petersens Photogr Mag* 15:28-31 F '87
Levine, Art
Gandhi's girls. il pors *Wash Mon* 19:25-7 Jl/Ag '87
Levine, Art, and Currie, Kathleen
Whip me, beat me and while you're at it cancel my N.O.W. membership: feminists war against each other over pornography. *Wash Mon* 19:17-21 Je '87
Levine, Arthur
Clark Kerr: the masterbuilder at 75 [cover story] il pors *Change* 19:12-27+ Mr/Ap '87

Levine, Beth
Are you (no! not me!) boring? il *Seventeen* 46:82+ My '87
Can weather affect your mood? il *Seventeen* 46:166+ S '87
Graphic novels: the latest word in illustrated books. bibl il *Publ Wkly* 231:45-7 My 22 '87
Harper & Row to ship book by Gorbachev in early November. *Publ Wkly* 232:41-2 O 16 '87
Is writing a career for 'Grown-ups'? por *Publ Wkly* 232:23 S 4 '87
Oxford to publish 19th century black women writers series. il *Publ Wkly* 231:48-9 Je 5 '87
PAJ branches out dramatically into fiction. il *Publ Wkly* 232:28-9 N 20 '87
Unpublished work by H. L. Mencken coming from Roberts Rinehart. *Publ Wkly* 232:62 O 9 '87
Levine, Carol
The DPT dilemma. il *Parents* 62:228+ Ap '87
Levine, David
The Bucs start here. il *Sport Mag* 78:90 My '87
The pitch that ate baseball. il *Sport Mag* 78:45+ My '87
Rating the quarterbacks. il *Sport Mag* 78:21-9 Ja '87
Levine, David A.
about
An optimist with a different twist [interview] G. Slutsker. il por *Forbes* 139:54+ My 18 '87
Levine, Dennis B.
about
The seduction of Ilan. A. Smith. il *Esquire* 107:75-6 My '87
The unraveling of Dennis Levine. D. Frantz. il *Esquire* 108:160-4+ S '87
Wall Street's top cop. il pors *Newsweek* 109:48-50 Mr 2 '87
Where the scam faltered. D. Hutchins. por *Fortune* 115:49-50 Ja 5 '87
Levine, Harry, and Reinarman, Craig
What's behind 'Jar Wars'. il *Nation* 244:388-90 Mr 28 '87
Levine, James
about
Jimmy's Met. P. G. Davis. il por *N Y* 20:52-4+ Ap 20 '87
Levine, James A.
The new fatherhood. il *McCalls* 114:121-2+ Je '87
Levine, Janet
Out of South Africa. il pors *N Y Times Mag* p81+ S 20 '87
Levine, Judith
Dilemma in swaddling clothes. *Harpers* 274:47-8 Ap '87
Swearing off social drugging. *Mademoiselle* 93:276-8+ S '87
Levine, Karen
Are kids a handicap? il *Parents* 62:71+ O '87
Breast-feeding and work. il *Parents* 62:64+ D '87
Mmmmm . . . the emotional sense. il *Parents* 62:106-10 Je '87
Quality time—what's that? il *Parents* 62:76+ N '87
When your child needs help. il *Parents* 62:126-30 Ap '87
Levine, Ken
How well do you know your spouse? il *Read Dig* 131:129-31 S '87
Put yourself to the test. il *Read Dig* 130:145-6+ Je '87
Levine, Leon
about
The family feud at Family Dollar Stores. D. Foust. il *Bus Week* p32-3 S 21 '87
Levine, Lewis Elliott, 1933-
about
Guess who lost. L. M. Keefe. il por *Forbes* 140:60+ S 7 '87
Levine, Madeline G.
(tr) See Fink, Ida. A scrap of time
Levine, Mark
(jt. auth) See Pollan, Stephen M., and Levine, Mark
Levine, Mel
Should Congress adopt the House-passed "Gephardt Amendment"? [excerpts from debate, April 29, 1987] *Congr Dig* 66:183+ Je/Jl '87
Levine, Michael
about
An artist sets the stage. R. Everett-Green. il por *Macleans* 100:53 Ap 6 '87

Levine, Michael
The legacy of airline deregulation: public benefits, but new problems. por *Aviat Week Space Technol* 127:161+ N 9 '87
Levine, Philip, 1928-
Above the world [poem] *New Yorker* 63:39 N 23 '87
Buying and selling [poem] *New Yorker* 63:32 S 7 '87
On the river [poem] *New Yorker* 63:36 O 26 '87
Levine, Robert
Waiting is a power game [cover story] il *Psychol Today* 21:24-6+ Ap '87
Levine, Sarabeth
about
Foods with flair: Sarabeth's Kitchen. J. Ciabattari. il por *Work Woman* 12:134-6 N '87
Levine, Suzanne Braun
Inside Ms. See issues of Ms. beginning September 1987 through December 1987
Levine family
about
The family feud at Family Dollar Stores. D. Foust. il *Bus Week* p32-3 S 21 '87
Levinson, Barry
about
Good morning, Vietnam [film] Reviews
Time il 130:74 D 28 '87. R. Schickel
Tin men [film] Reviews
Commonweal 114:215 Ap 10 '87. T. O'Brien
Glamour il 85:217 My '87. J. G. Boyum
Macleans il 100:57 Mr 9 '87. L. O'Toole
N Y il 20:106-7 Mr 9 '87. D. Denby
Nation 244:445-6 Ap 4 '87. T. Rafferty
Natl Rev il 39:52-3 Ap 10 '87. J. Simon
New Repub 196:25-6 Mr 30 '87. S. Kauffman
New Yorker 63:82-3 Ap 6 '87. P. Kael
Newsweek il 109:78 Mr 2 '87. D. Ansen
People Wkly il 27:10 Mr 16 '87. R. Novak
Time il 129:80 Ap 6 '87. R. Corliss
Vogue 177:82 My '87. M. Haskell
Levinson, Marc
In Brazil, bird songs aren't just cheap trills. il *Int Wildl* 17:48-53 S/O '87
(jt. auth) See Aho, C. Michael, and Levinson, Marc
Levinson, Sanford, 1941-
The Constitution and the Court: could Meese be right? *Current* 292:32-5 My '87
Levinstein, Henry, 1919-1987
about
Obituary
Phys Today 40:88 Mr '87. N. Ginsberg
Levitan, Irwin B.
(jt. auth) See Lin, Stephen S., and Levitan, Irwin B.
Levitan, Sar A.
Beyond "trendy" forecasts: the next 10 years for work. il por *Futurist* 21:28-32 N/D '87
Levitas, Michael
Writers in China: how long is the leash? il *N Y Times Book Rev* 92:3+ Ag 9 '87
Levitation
See also
Acoustic levitation
Levitt, Mortimer, 1907-
about
The fabric of success. W. Hoffer. il pors *Nations Bus* 75:53+ Jl '87
Levitt, William
about
Too long at the party. L. Gubernick. il por *Forbes* 139:40 My 4 '87
Levoy, Gregg
A better mousetrap. il *N Y Times Mag* p58 Ag 23 '87
Birth controllers. il *Omni* 10:30+ O '87
Levy, Abraham
about
N.Y. woman attacks ex-judge in dispute over $482. il pors *Jet* 72:33 Ag 3 '87
Levy, Chava Willig
"Mommy, what's wrong with that lady?". il por *McCalls* 114:65-7 S '87
Levy, Daniel C.
The Mexican government's loosening grip? bibl f *Curr Hist* 86:113-16+ Mr '87
Levy, David H., 1948-
Close to home. *Space World* X-12-288:36 D '87
How to discover a comet. il *Astronomy* 15:74-7 D '87
(jt. auth) See Larson, Stephen M., and Levy, David H., 1948-

Levy, David H., 1948-, and Jedicke, Peter
Betelgeuse. il *Astronomy* 15:6-13 Ap '87
Levy, Deborah M.
Advice for sale. *Foreign Policy* 67:64-86 Summ '87
Levy, Faye
Macadamia nuts. il *Gourmet* 47:82-3+ My '87
Levy, Frank S.
Changes in the distribution of American family incomes, 1947 to 1984. bibl f il *Science* 236:923-7 My 22 '87
Lévy, Raymond
about
Hard driver at the wheel. S. Tully. por *Fortune* 116:51 Ag 3 '87
Levy (Chas.) Circulating Co. See Chas. Levy Circulating Co.
Lewandowski, Stephen
Stocking trout [poem] *Ctry J* 14:64 Mr '87
Lewis, Andrew L. See Lewis, Drew
Lewis, Andrew M.
about
Best Products: trying to put pizzazz back in the showroom. T. Smart. il por *Bus Week* p39-40 Mr 16 '87
Lewis, Anne C.
Learning to serve: high school service programs. *Educ Dig* 53:50-1 N '87
Washington news. See issues of The Education Digest beginning September 1986
Washington report. See issues of Phi Delta Kappan
Lewis, Anthony, 1927-
An ingenious structure. il *N Y Times Mag* p38-41 S 13 '87
Lewis, Billy Cache
The bells still toll for San Francisco's hills. il *Am Hist Illus* 22:36-43 Ap '87
Lewis, Brad
Boat warrior. il pors *Sport Mag* 78:43-4+ D '87
Two hours before the mast. il *Sport Mag* 78:68-9+ F '87
Lewis, Carl
about
Carl Lewis predicts calm for 1988 Seoul Olympics. por *Jet* 72:51 Mr 30 '87
Carl Lewis runs record 200 after attending dad's funeral. il por *Jet* 72:50 Je 1 '87
Carl Lewis, two musicians kick off World Peace Run. *Jet* 71:29 F 23 '87
Lewis, David L. (David Levering)
Voting in South Africa. il *Nation* 244:534+ Ap 25 '87
Lewis, Drew
about
Sweet year for a barn cleaner. P. Nulty. il por *Fortune* 115:82-3 Ja 5 '87
Lewis, Flora
Communism without Marx. il *N Y Times Mag* p44+ Je 7 '87
about
Flora Lewis: "I don't have the same power a political figure might, but I like the freedom to write what I think". J. A. Simon. por *Vogue* 177:237-8 N '87
Lewis, Frances
about
Sidney and Frances Lewis—the quest for the best in art. J. Tully. il pors *Smithsonian* 18:84-8+ N '87
Lewis, Huey
about
Huey Lewis & rock's last taboo. R. Wolmuth. il pors *People Wkly* 27:38-40+ Ja 19 '87
The straight men: Michael J. Fox, Huey Lewis, Tom Cruise. C. Krupp. il pors *Glamour* 85:250 Ap '87
Lewis, James R., and Melton, J. Gordon
Psychology and religion in court—again. *Christ Century* 104:914-16 O 21 '87
Lewis, Jan
Feet: sometimes fleet, seldom neat, often beat. il *Curr Health 2* 13:28-9 My '87
Having your sun—and a safe tan, too. il *Curr Health 2* 13:10-11 Ap '87
Tired of fatigue? il *Curr Health 2* 13:28-9 Ja '87
The two faces of makeup. il *Curr Health 2* 13:22-3 F '87
When medical treatment takes an alternate route. il *Curr Health 2* 13:22-3 Mr '87
Lewis, Jerry, 1926-
about
I stayed up with Jerry. B. Barol. il pors *Newsweek* 110:66-8 S 21 '87
Sammy Davis and Jerry Lewis star on telethon to fight muscular dystrophy [cover story] il pors *Jet* 72:60-1 S 7 '87

Lewis, Jerry, 1926-—about—*cont.*
Teaming up in the new Vegas. C. Leerhsen. pors *Newsweek* 109:83 Ap 13 '87
Lewis, Jo Ann
Georgia O'Keeffe. bibl (p270) il pors *Smithsonian* 18:154-69 N '87
Lewis, John Robert
about
Atlanta NAACP is fuming over white talk show host's calling Lewis 'Buckwheat'. il pors *Jet* 72:22 Ag 10 '87
John Lewis amends bill to aid black businesses. *Jet* 72:8 Je 22 '87
Lewis, Joy Schaleben
At home with Will Rogers. il *Travel Holiday* 168:32+ Jl '87
Talkin' M'Waukee. il *Travel Holiday* 168:25-7 D '87
Lewis, Marshall C.
Golf and tennis schools. il *Travel Holiday* 167:18+ Je '87
Lewis, Memory Elvin- *See* Elvin-Lewis, Memory
Lewis, Michael
Big Bang babies. *New Repub* 196:17-18 Ja 5-12 '87
Lewis, N. G., and others
Monitoring biosynthesis of wheat cell-wall phenyl-propanoids in situ. bibl f il *Science* 237:1344-6 S 11 '87
Lewis, Reginald F.
about
Black investor realizes mammoth 90-to-1 return. por *Jet* 72:6 Jl 27 '87
Buying into the big time. J. M. Horowitz. il por *Time* 130:42 Ag 24 '87
Reg Lewis hits the big time—and takes it in stride. P. Finch. il por *Bus Week* p27+ Ag 24 '87
Reg to riches. N. J. Perry. il por *Fortune* 116:122-3 S 14 '87
Reginald Lewis cuts the big deal [cover story; with editorial comment by Earl G. Graves] A. Edmond, Jr. il pors *Black Enterp* 18:9, 42-6 N '87
TLC deal signals new era for black business. K. D. Thompson. por *Black Enterp* 18:21-2 O '87
When Wall Street began to take blacks seriously. R. H. Bork, Jr. il por *U S News World Rep* 103:44 Ag 31 '87
Lewis, Ricki
Better babies. il *Health* 19:23-4+ Mr '87
Losing it. il *Health* 19:54-6+ Ap '87
Pap smears: a closer look. il *Health* 19:69-70+ Ap '87
Terrific teeth. il *Health* 19:74-9 Je '87
Your next child will be a: boy, girl. il *Health* 19:58-60+ Ja '87
Lewis, Sally Sirkin
about
New directions in style. H. Drohojowska. il por *Archit Dig* 44:252+ My '87
Lewis, Samuel W.
Israel: the Peres era and its legacy. *Foreign Aff* 65 Sp Issue:582-610 ['87]
about
Former diplomat becomes head of U.S. Institute of Peace. il por *Christ Today* 31:44-5+ D 11 '87
Lewis, Sara E.
Family secrets [story] il *Seventeen* 46:112-13+ Ja '87
Lewis, Sinclair, 1885-1951
about
My summer job with Sinclair Lewis. J. Hersey. il pors *N Y Times Book Rev* 92:1+ My 10 '87
Lewis, Sydney
about
Sidney and Frances Lewis—the quest for the best in art. J. Tully. il pors *Smithsonian* 18:84-8+ N '87
Lewis, Terry
about
Introducing: 'Producers of the Year' Jimmy (Jam) Harris and Terry Lewis. pors *Ebony* 42:126 Jl '87
Jam and Lewis take control. M. Goldberg. il pors *Roll Stone* p30+ Ap 23 '87
Lewis, Thomas A., 1942-
High stakes in a land of plenty [cover story; with editorial comment by Jay D. Hair] il map *Natl Wildl* 25:4-11, 28 Je/Jl '87
How did the giants die? il por *Int Wildl* 17:4-11 S/O '87
Searching for truth in alligator country. il *Natl Wildl* 25:12-19 O/N '87
Will species die out as the earth heats up? il *Int Wildl* 17:18-21 N/D '87

Lewis, Tracey P.
about
Black baseball owners sell Savannah Cardinals. il por *Jet* 73:50 D 7 '87
The only baseball boss who's young, female and black, Tracy Lewis holds the cards in Savannah. P. Jordan. il pors *People Wkly* 27:108-10 My 18 '87
Lewis, William, d. 1987
about
Obituary
Jet il por 72:50 My 25 '87
Lewis (Frances and Sydney) Collection *See* Art—Collectors and collecting
Lewis and Clark Expedition
Of prairie dogs, VCR's and Indian scouts [retracing Lewis and Clark; interview with D. Duncan] A. P. Sanoff. il por map *U S News World Rep* 103:72 Jl 6 '87
Lewis and Clark National Forest (Mont.)
Forest Service steps on Blackfeet [struggling to save sacred land] J. Bruggers. il *Progressive* 51:14 Ap '87
Wilderness and worship—or wells? [Lewis and Clark National Forest Plan vs. Blackfeet Indians] M. Kantor. il *Sierra* 72:67-8 My/Je '87
Lewis Research Center (U.S.)
Lockheed, NASA will begin propfan test assessment flights; NASA continues UHB development role [ultrahigh bypass engines] il *Aviat Week Space Technol* 126:56-8 Ap 13 '87
Lewitch, Joseph *See* Lewis, Jerry, 1926-
Lewites, Herty
about
A Sandinista holiday. M. McDonald. *Macleans* 100:6+ N 16 '87
LeWitt, Sol, 1928-
about
Burghers block the box. E. Beck. il *Art News* 86:57 S '87
Talk about lines! A guy paid $26,400 for this drawing—and then they demolished it. M. Small. il por *People Wkly* 27:43-4 My 25 '87
Lewy, Alfred J., and others
Antidepressant and circadian phase-shifting effects of light. bibl f il *Science* 235:352-4 Ja 16 '87
Lexington (Ky.)
Architecture
Courtyard opens up traditional townhouse. il *South Living* 22:162+ Mr '87
Historic houses, sites, etc.
A glimpse of the past [Fayette County Courthouse] il *South Living* 22:16 Ja '87
Markets
Lexington's timeless intersection [Lexington Festival Market] il *South Living* 22:69-70 Ap '87
Prisons and reformatories
Follow-up [Female High Security Unit to close] *Nation* 245:436 O 24 '87
The women of Lexington Prison [S. L. Rosenberg and A. Torres charge they are victims of brainwashing] W. A. Reuben and C. Norman. il *Nation* 244:881-4 Je 27 '87
Lexitel Corporation
See also
ALC Communications Corporation
Ley, Mary
about
Garden generosity. S. Eddison. il *House Gard* 159:142-7+ Je '87
Leymarie, Jean
Chalet Balthus. il por *House Gard* 159:108-17 D '87
Leys, Simon
China's new math. *New Repub* 196:13 Mr 2 '87
L'Heureux-Dubé, Claire
about
A new face on the bench. A. Wilson-Smith. il por *Macleans* 100:11 Ap 27 '87
Lhote, Henri
Oasis of art in the Sahara. il map *Natl Geogr* 172:180-91 Ag '87
Li, Ka-shing
about
Putting out the welcome mat. D. Francis. por *Macleans* 100:9 My 18 '87
Rich and powerful [cover story; special section; with editorial comment by Kevin Doyle] il *Macleans* 100:2, 24-31 Ag 17 '87
Li, Ronald
about
Ronald Li: as freewheeling as his stock exchange. M. Shao. il por *Bus Week* p76+ O 12 '87

Li Yumin
about
Banking on China. D. Fong. por *Forbes* 140:304 N 16 '87
Lia, Barry, and others
Formation of retinal ganglion cell topography during prenatal development. bibl f il *Science* 236:848-51 My 15 '87
Liability (Law)
See also
Airlines—Suits and claims
Airplane industry—Suits and claims
Asbestos industry—Suits and claims
Banks and banking—Suits and claims
Chemical industries—Suits and claims
Computer service industries—Suits and claims
Damages
Drug industry—Suits and claims
Farmers—Suits and claims
Government liability
Helicopter industry—Suits and claims
Insurance, Government liability
Insurance, Liability
Malpractice
Medical equipment industry—Suits and claims
Nuclear industry—Suits and claims
Textile machinery industry—Suits and claims
Tobacco industry—Suits and claims
Torts
Travel agencies and agents—Suits and claims
A death at work can put the boss in jail [homicide conviction against Sabine Consolidated Inc.] J. Tasini. *Bus Week* p37-8 Mr 2 '87
Enough is enough [collateral estoppel in product liability cases] D. Fanning. il *Forbes* 139:56 Ap 20 '87
The fantasy of life without risk. V. M. Earle, III. il por *Fortune* 115:113-14+ F 16 '87
In order to [address, August 10, 1987] L. A. Iacocca. *Vital Speeches Day* 53:745-8 O 1 '87
Is it safe to go back in the boardroom? [exempting directors from liability] B. Powell. il *Newsweek* 109:45-6 My 4 '87
Lawsuits: the great American plague. C. W. Colson. *Christ Today* 31:72 Mr 6 '87
The liability crisis isn't over yet. J. L. Gattuso. il map *Consum Res Mag* 70:15-19 O '87
Liability roulette. E. R. Court. por *Nations Bus* 75:4 N '87
Product liability legislation. *Congr Dig* 66:3-32 Ja '87
Walking the fine line at holiday office parties [employer liability for alcohol-related damages] L. J. Moore. il *U S News World Rep* 103:75 D 21 '87
Who will protect us from our protectors? P. W. Huber. il *Forbes* 140:56+ Jl 13 '87
Liability insurance *See* Insurance, Liability
Liagre, Christina de
Building on the past. il *House Gard* 159:124-31+ Ag '87
Moulin refuge. il por *House Gard* 159:138-47+ Ap '87
A spontaneous charm. il por *House Gard* 159:126-33+ D '87
Les liaisons dangereuses [drama] *See* Hampton, Christopher, 1946-
Liang, Heng
(jt. auth) *See* Shapiro, Judith, 1953-, and Liang, Heng
Liang, Heng, and Shapiro, Judith, 1953-
The loving penance of Hu Bo [condensed from After the nightmare] il *Read Dig* 130:104-9 Ap '87
Liani, Dimitra
about
While Andreas Papandreou, Greece's prime minister, dallies with a dame, all *hellas* is breaking loose. il pors *People Wkly* 28:62 O 26 '87
Libbey, Elizabeth
After the fact [poem] *Am Sch* 56:369-70 Summ '87
Spring and [poem] *Atlantic* 260:69 S '87
Libbon, Robert
Don't be a sucker—rig for safety. il *Theatre Crafts* 21:32-3+ Ja '87
Libel and slander
Any resemblance . . . [J. V. Anderson's libel suit against filmmakers of The bell jar] *Nation* 244:132-3 F 7 '87
Author and publisher groups make filings in two Supreme Court cases [libel suit brought against Hustler magazine by J. Falwell] H. Fields. *Publ Wkly* 232:12 S 4 '87
Author's life imitates his art [libel suit won by J. Archer in Great Britain] A. Deming. il por *Newsweek* 110:62 Ag 3 '87

Can you be sued for letters of reference? R. S. Brown. *Educ Dig* 52:54-6 Mr '87
Closing accounts on Plath's 'Bell jar' [action brought by J. V. Anderson] *Newsweek* 109:58 F 9 '87
The creative process and libel. I. R. Kaufman. il *N Y Times Mag* p28-30+ Ap 5 '87
'Emotional distress' briefs to High Court [Hustler vs. J. Falwell] il *Publ Wkly* 232:13 Jl 17 '87
Fight judge files a suit against ex-champ Holmes [F. Brunette] por *Jet* 72:50 Je 8 '87
Frisco judge dismisses Thomas libel lawsuit [suit by P. M. Thomas] por *Jet* 72:32 Je 8 '87
From book to film: a novel case of libel [J. V. Anderson sues over depiction in The bell jar movie] A. Press. il por *Newsweek* 109:63 F 2 '87
High Court queries leave outcome of 'Hustler'-Falwell case uncertain. H. Fields. *Publ Wkly* 232:15 D 18 '87
Jerry Falwell vs. Larry Flynt. A. Press. il pors *Newsweek* 110:76 D 14 '87
Jousts without winners: after a flurry of major libel cases, no one has much to crow about. W. A. Henry. il *Time* 130:68-70 Jl 6 '87
Libel in fiction to be tested in Bell jar suit [suit brought by J. V. Anderson over movie adaptation] M. Yen. *Publ Wkly* 231:290 Ja 30 '87
Masson loses libel suit against 'New Yorker,' Malcolm and Knopf. M. Colin. *Publ Wkly* 232:11 S 4 '87
The new terrorism [address, September 19, 1986] W. M. Bulger. *Vital Speeches Day* 53:430-4 My 1 '87
Of whom the Bell told [J. V. Anderson's lawsuit over character in film version of S. Plath's The bell jar] R. Lacayo. il por *Time* 129:60-1 F 9 '87
Parties settle Bell jar suit out of court [action brought by J. V. Anderson] *Publ Wkly* 231:19 F 13 '87
The press on trial [R. Adler's book on Westmoreland v. CBS and Sharon v. Time] R. M. Dworkin. bibl f il *N Y Rev Books* 34:27-37 F 26 '87
The problem of punitive damages [address, April 8, 1987] A. M. Adams. *Vital Speeches Day* 53:509-12 Je 1 '87
The revenge of the fired. J. B. Copeland. il *Newsweek* 109:46-7 F 16 '87
Salinger and 'The bell jar': what do they mean to publishers? C. E. Rinzler. il *Publ Wkly* 231:20-2 Ap 24 '87
Spare pennies [J. Archer wins libel suit against the Star] W. R. Doerner. il por *Time* 130:31-2 Ag 3 '87
Superintendent found guilty of slander for teacher recommendation [M. True v. R. Ladner] T. J. Flygare. il *Phi Delta Kappan* 68:629-30 Ap '87
Triple reverse [appeals court reverses decision in W. Tavoulareas' libel suit against the Washington post] por *Time* 129:70 Mr 23 '87
Westy's revenge [controversy over Gen. Westmoreland's libel suit against CBS leads to current network crisis; cover story] F. Barnes. *New Repub* 196:21+ Ap 6 '87

Anecdotes, facetiae, satire, etc.
I am Cinderella's stepmother and I know my rights. J. Rossner. il *N Y Times Book Rev* 92:3 Ap 19 '87
Liber (Book fair) *See* Book fairs
Liberace, 1919-1987
about
Obituary
Jet il pors 71:64-5 F 23 '87
Macleans il por 100:52 F 16 '87
Newsweek il por 109:75 F 16 '87. B. Barol
People Wkly il pors 27:24-31 F 16 '87. M. Green
Time il por 129:82 F 16 '87. W. A. Henry
Liberal arts education *See* Liberal education
Liberal-Democratic Party (Japan)
Japan [proposal for a national sales tax] *Bus Week* p53 Mr 2 '87
Nakasone: from prime minister to 'shadow shogun'? B. Buell. il *Bus Week* p83 O 19 '87
'The party gets stronger while the government gets weaker'. L. Armstrong. il *Bus Week* p58+ Jl 13 '87
The political rivals jockeying for Japan's top job. B. Buell. il *Bus Week* p36-7 Ap 20 '87
Tee time for the threesome [presidency candidates] B. Hillenbrand. il *Time* 130:38 O 19 '87
Liberal education
Eastern liberal arts colleges. il *U S News World Rep* 103:66 O 26 '87
The gamble paid off [southern liberal arts colleges] il *U S News World Rep* 103:63 O 26 '87
Getting high on study [top liberal arts colleges] il *U S News World Rep* 103:54-5 O 26 '87
The good, the true, the beautiful [M. Arnold's essay An Eton boy] J. Hart. *Natl Rev* 39:46 Mr 27 '87

Liberal education—*cont.*

Individualism vs. liberal arts education [address, September 8, 1987] R. L. Spaeth. *Vital Speeches Day* 54:22-6 O 15 '87

Project on liberal education and the sciences receives funding. B. G. Walthall. *Science* 236:610 My 1 '87

Rethinking the university: design for a new academy. F. Turner. *Current* 290:22-6 F '87

The skillful baccalaureate. G. A. Woditsch and others. il *Change* 19:48-57 N/D '87

Synchronicity and the liberal arts. D. O'Brien. *Des Arts Educ* 88:42-5 Jl/Ag '87

Teacher education and the liberal arts. E. F. Travers and S. R. Sacks. *Educ Dig* 53:9-11 D '87

Testing for eight skills [western liberal arts colleges] il *U S News World Rep* 103:62 O 26 '87

Today's university: where democracy is anarchy. A. D. Bloom. *Current* 297:22-7 N '87

Liberal Party (Canada)

All the earmarks of a Liberal sweep. K. Harley. il por *Macleans* 100:26-7 O 12 '87

The big red wave [election victory in Ontario; cover story; special section; with editorial comment by Kevin Doyle] il pors *Macleans* 100:12-14+ S 21 '87

A blow to the Liberals [byelection results] H. Mackenzie. il *Macleans* 100:16 Ag 3 '87

Clean sweep [election victory in New Brunswick; cover story; special section; with editorial comment by Kevin Doyle] il pors *Macleans* 100:2, 14-16+ O 26 '87

The end of an accord [Liberals and New Democrats in Ontario] S. Aikenhead. il *Macleans* 100:14 Jl 6 '87

The great Liberal divide. P. Gessell. il por *Macleans* 100:12 Je 8 '87

John Turner's public struggle. P. Gessell. il por *Macleans* 100:20-1 S 7 '87

A Liberal family feud [constitutional agreement] M. Rose. il *Macleans* 100:12+ My 25 '87

Ontario's power struggle [D. Peterson calls for an election] S. Aikenhead. il por *Macleans* 100:14-15 Ag 10 '87

A tide of change sweeps Ontario [D. Peterson government] S. Aikenhead. il *Macleans* 100:12-13 Ja 12 '87

Trudeau's power punch [denunciation of constitutional accord] M. Janigan. il por *Macleans* 100:10-11 Je 8 '87

Trudeau's star turn [criticism of the constitutional accord] M. Janigan. il por *Macleans* 100:14-16+ S 7 '87

Turner strikes back. P. Gessell and H. Mackenzie. il por *Macleans* 100:10-11 Ag 31 '87

Turner's counteroffensive plan [with interview] H. Mackenzie. il por *Macleans* 100:10-11 S 14 '87

Turner's troubles. M. Clark. *Macleans* 100:19 Ag 24 '87

The war among the Liberals [constitutional agreement] M. Rose. il *Macleans* 100:12-13 Je 22 '87

Liberal Party (Great Britain)

Both ends against the middle. A. Sampson. il *Newsweek* 109:30 Je 22 '87

Merger in the middle [proposed merger of the Social Democratic Party and the Liberals] R. Laver. il *Macleans* 100:22 Ag 17 '87

Liberalism

See also

Conservatism

Another "low dishonest decade" on the left. P. Collier and D. Horowitz. *Commentary* 83:17-24 Ja '87

Are America's liberals to the left of Gorbachev? P. C. Roberts. il *Bus Week* p14 S 7 '87

Black Americans need their own agenda [with discussion] S. Fisher. il por *Cent Mag* 20:25-36 My/Je '87

Bork and Bird [pro-Bork campaign contrasted with pro-Bird campaign in California] H. Meyerson. *New Repub* 197:21+ S 14-21 '87

The Dellums record [discussion of January 1987 article, Another "low dishonest decade" on the left] D. Horowitz and P. Collier. *Commentary* 84:2-3+ Jl '87

The demands of the community [with discussion] P. Selznick. por *Cent Mag* 20:33-54 Ja/F '87

Don't underrate isolationism. B. Kauffman. il *Nation* 244:758-60 Je 6 '87

Down and out in L.A. [liberal activists] A. Kopkind. il *Nation* 244:309+ Mr 14 '87

Ethnophobia, heterophobia, & liberal fascism [campus values] J. Hart. *Natl Rev* 39:46 F 13 '87

The feminization of the American left. J. Nuechterlein. *Commentary* 84:43-8 N '87

The higher law: Bork, Burke, & moral relativism. D. R. Carlin, Jr. *Commonweal* 114:729-30 D 18 '87

In demand: Wall Street's liberals. I. Ross. il *Fortune* 115:187-8+ Ap 27 '87

Is Jesse the great white hope? [cover story] A. Kopkind. il *Nation* 245:773+ D 26 '87-Ja 2 '88

Let's make a new deal. W. Greider. il *Roll Stone* p41-3 Je 4 '87

Liberalism v. reality: the ideology of Western suicide. J. Burnham. *Natl Rev* 39:39-43 S 11 '87

The liberals' mistake [with discussion] C. A. Reich. por *Cent Mag* 20:49-59 Jl/Ag '87

A liberal's waiting game [E. M. Kennedy] G. F. Will. il *Newsweek* 109:82 Mr 16 '87

The necrophiles [liberal journalists uncovering "truths" about liberalism's past] J. L. Hess. *Nation* 244:37-8 Ja 17 '87

Le nouveau canard [accusations of bigotry used as ad hominem argument by liberals] J. Sobran. *Natl Rev* 39:44-5+ F 13 '87

The performing liberal. D. K. Mano. *Natl Rev* 39:69-70 S 11 '87

Reaganomics with a human face [neoliberalism; excerpt from Visions and nightmares] R. Lekachman. *Harpers* 274:24+ Mr '87

They're back: stirrings on the left. J. Klein. il *N Y* 20:14+ Ag 31 '87

What the Soviets think about American liberals. D. D'Souza. *Natl Rev* 39:39-41+ Ag 30 '87

Anecdotes, facetiae, satire, etc.

Sympathy for the devil. M. Ivins. il *Progressive* 51:29 D '87

Periodicals

Minority report. C. Hitchens. *Nation* 244:39 Ja 17 '87

Liberalism (Religion)

Answering Pilate: truth and the postliberal church. W. H. Willimon. *Christ Century* 104:82-5 Ja 28 '87

The challenge of post-liberal theology [views of S. Hauerwas] P. Giurlanda. *Commonweal* 114:40-2 Ja 30 '87

A challenge to Willimon's postliberalism [discussion of January 28, 1987 article, Answering Pilate: truth and the postliberal church] W. H. Willimon. *Christ Century* 104:306-10 Ap 1 '87

The liberal ethic and the spirit of Protestantism [cover story; with discussion] R. W. Fox. il por *Cent Mag* 20:4-14 S/O '87

Liberalism & the Hebrew prophets. J. S. Auerbach. *Commentary* 84:58-60 Ag '87

Religion's social ladders [decline of liberal Protestant churches] R. J. Neuhaus. *Natl Rev* 39:52 O 23 '87

What can liberals and evangelicals teach each other? D. W. Shriver. il *Christ Century* 104:687-90 Ag 12-19 '87

Liberation movements, National *See* National liberation movements

Liberation theology

Christianity today talks to Michael Novak. D. Neff. por *Christ Today* 31:54-5 Jl 10 '87

Fear and political wisdom. R. J. Neuhaus. *Natl Rev* 39:48 Mr 13 '87

José Carlos Mariátegui: forgotten forerunner of liberation theology. M. Candelaria. *Christ Century* 104:885-7 O 14 '87

José María Arguedas: godfather of liberationism. S. B. Wall-Smith. *Christ Century* 104:1034-9 N 18 '87

Letter from the Elysian Fields [work of Catholic priest D. R. Santos in poor Brazilian town of Campos Elísios] J. Kramer. *New Yorker* 63:40-2+ Mr 2 '87

Liberation theology is remarkably Protestant. C. R. Padilla. il por *Christ Today* 31:12 My 15 '87

Pannenberg on Marxism: insights and generalizations. S. Grenz. *Christ Century* 104:824-6 S 30 '87

Quelling the fire of 'liberation theology'. R. A. Manning. il *U S News World Rep* 102:48-9 Mr 30 '87

Reclaiming the Catholic heritage [G. Weigel's Tranquillitas ordinis and M. Novak's Will it liberate?] A. R. Muggeridge. *Commentary* 84:39-44 S '87

Sowing justice in Ecuador [liberation theology practitioners L. Proaño and J. Gómez Izquierdo] P. R. Greene. *Christ Century* 104:910-12 O 21 '87

Liberia

See also

Economic assistance, American—Liberia

Economic policy

Liberia's new moneymen [U.S. advisers] *Newsweek* 110:81 N 16 '87

Liberman, Alvin M.

(jt. auth) *See* Whalen, D. H., and Liberman, Alvin M.

Libertarianism

See also

Christian Reconstruction movement

Liberty

See also

Civil rights

Democracy

Liberty—See also—*cont.*
    Freedom of information
    Freedom of speech
    Freedom of the press
    Religious liberty
Cultural control [with discussion] L. Nader. il por *Cent Mag* 20:50-9 Mr/Ap '87
The freedom to be free. J. D. Hair. il *Natl Wildl* 26:30 D '87/Ja '88
Liberty to all [address, June 22, 1987] W. E. Simon. *Vital Speeches Day* 54:7-11 O 15 '87
The use and abuse of liberty. T. Eastland. il por *Christ Today* 31:28-30 Jl 10 '87
Liberty Bell (Space vehicle) *See* Space vehicles
Liberty Federation
Falwell puts politics behind him—for the most part. *Christ Today* 31:53-4 D 11 '87
Goodbye to all that [J. Falwell steps down] M. Miller. por *Newsweek* 110:10 N 16 '87
A Jerry-built coalition regroups [resignation of J. Falwell] R. N. Ostling. il por *Time* 130:68-9 N 16 '87
Toll-free woes [opposition groups clogging J. Falwell's toll-free phone lines] *Time* 129:63 Ja 26 '87
Librairie Arthème Fayard
Fayard and Holt settle dispute over world rights to Walesa autobio. W. Goldstein. il pors *Publ Wkly* 232:23-4 Jl 31 '87
Librairie Hachette *See* Hachette (Librairie)
Libraries
    See also
    College libraries
    Research libraries
Shhh . . . my romance with libraries. A. Bayer. il *Seventeen* 46:48+ F '87
      Acquisitions
A new look at the library market [survey] H. Edelman and K. Muller. il *Publ Wkly* 231:30-5 My 29 '87
      Architecture
    See Library architecture
      Censorship
    See Censorship
    Fires and fire prevention
The great Los Angeles Library fire—and its happy ending. L. See. *Publ Wkly* 231:36 F 6 '87
      Periodical collections
Journal price increases [discussion of May 22, 1987 article, Libraries stunned by journal price increases] C. Holden. *Science* 238:597-8 O 30 '87
Libraries stunned by journal price increases. C. Holden. *Science* 236:908-9 My 22 '87
      Security measures
Chained libraries [chaining books] D. Byrne. il *Hist Today* 37:5-6 My '87
      Technical processes
    See also
    Books—Conservation and restoration
      California
    See also
    Los Angeles Public Library
      Great Britain
Chained libraries [chaining books] D. Byrne. il *Hist Today* 37:5-6 My '87
      New York (State)
    See also
    Troy (N.Y.)—Libraries
Libraries, College *See* College libraries
Libraries, National
    See also
    Library of Congress
    National Library of Medicine (U.S.)
Libraries, Private
All booked up. A. L. Rowse. il *House Gard* 159:54+ N '87
The Gothic revival library at the Metropolitan Museum of Art. A. Peck. il *Antiques* 131:824-7 Ap '87
Of time and place [Gothic revival library in the Metropolitan Museum of Art] C. Vogel. il *N Y Times Mag* p50-1 F 15 '87
A passion for history [J. Engelhard's collections] J. Fleming. il *House Gard* 159:122-5+ Mr '87
Voluminous obsession. C. Burden. il *House Gard* 159:126-31+ Mr '87
Libraries, University *See* College libraries
Libraries and blacks
    See also
    Schomburg Center for Research in Black Culture
Libraries and publishers
Examining the library market [forum held during American Library Association convention] J. Fletcher. il *Publ Wkly* 232:15 Ag 14 '87

The loyal librarians. J. F. Baker. *Publ Wkly* 231:18 Je 12 '87
A new look at the library market [survey] H. Edelman and K. Muller. il *Publ Wkly* 231:30-5 My 29 '87
Selling to libraries: publishers learn about a billion-dollar market. J. F. Baker. il *Publ Wkly* 232:14-15 D 18 '87
Library architecture
American Library Association/AIA 1987 Library Building Awards. il *Archit Rec* 175:78-9 N '87
Richardsonian recalls [Annenberg Library and Communications Center, Pine Manor College, Mass.] H. L. Smith, Jr. il *Archit Rec* 175:104-9 Ap '87
Library buildings *See* Library architecture
Library conferences
    See also
    White House Conference on Library and Information Services
Library of Congress
LC provides legal guidelines for Meese Commission proposals. H. Fields. *Publ Wkly* 231:20 F 20 '87
Library of Congress seeks $21 million for added staff. H. Fields. *Publ Wkly* 231:13 Mr 13 '87
New Librarian of Congress looks at books vs. technologies [J. H. Billington] H. Fields. il por *Publ Wkly* 232:16 O 16 '87
The odyssey of Daniel Boorstin [legacy of HUAC testimony; cover story] J. Wiener. il *Nation* 245:289+ S 26 '87
Library postal rates *See* Postal rates
Libration points *See* Mechanics, Celestial
Librettists
    See also
    Hofmannsthal, Hugo von, 1874-1929
Libya
    See also
    United Nations—Libya
      Antiquities
    See also
    Apollonia (Libya: Ancient city)
      Foreign relations
Pariah in the desert: the increasing isolation of Qadaffi. B. Slavin and J. P. Tarpey. por *Bus Week* p57 N 30 '87
      Australia
    See Australia—Foreign relations—Libya
      Chad
Bogged down in the desert [Libyan losses climb in war with Chad] R. Nordland. il map *Newsweek* 110:49 S 21 '87
Chad: Kaddafi on the run. F. Coleman. il map *Newsweek* 109:28 Ja 19 '87
Down and out in Faya-Largeau [Libyan troops defeated in Chad] J. Smolowe. il por map *Time* 129:42 Ap 6 '87
Libyan occupation of northern Chad [statement, November 18, 1986] H. S. Okun. *Dep State Bull* 87:87 Ja '87
Meddling in Chad. *Nation* 245:253 S 19 '87
A message for Kaddafi [U.S. steps into Chad] N. Cooper. il *Newsweek* 109:35 Ja 5 '87
Muammar's mortification [Chadian forces recapture territory] F. Willey. il map *Newsweek* 109:35 Ap 6 '87
Raiders of the armed Toyotas [successful Chadian offensive against Libya] J. Greenwald. il *Time* 130:36 S 21 '87
Security Council hears Chad complaint against Libya, takes no action. *UN Chron* 24:74 F '87
Spoils of the Saharan sands [weapons left behind by Libyans] J. Greenwald. il *Time* 129:42 Ap 27 '87
Standoff in the Sahara. B. Levin. il map *Macleans* 100:26-7 S 21 '87
War by proxy in the dunes [French air attack on Libyan forces in Chad] W. E. Smith. il *Time* 129:37 Ja 19 '87
      Oceania
Washing Libya out of their hair. H. G. Chua-Eoan. il por *Time* 129:45 Je 1 '87
      United States
    See United States—Foreign relations—Libya
    Politics and government
Libya's Qaddafi: still in command? L. Anderson. bibl f *Curr Hist* 86:65-8+ F '87
Qadhafi magic: turning defeat to verbal victory. R. Z. Chesnoff. il por *U S News World Rep* 102:31 Ap 13 '87
Libya and the United States
Gaddafi's goons [Chicago's El Rukn gang members convicted of terrorism] il *Time* 130:27 D 7 '87

Libyan-American conflict, 1986
Gaddafi plays desert phantom—staying under wraps after that American death plot. il por *People Wkly* 27:36-7 Mr 9 '87
General Assembly condemns April 1986 attack against Libyan Arab Jamahiriya. il *UN Chron* 24:73 F '87
'How I bombed Qaddafi'. il *Pop Mech* 164:110-14+ Jl '87
Libya [statement, November 19, 1986] L. Pressler. *Dep State Bull* 87:87-90 Ja '87
Libya's Qaddafi: still in command? L. Anderson. bibl f *Curr Hist* 86:65-8+ F '87
Navigation rights and the Gulf of Sidra. map *Dep State Bull* 87:69-70 F '87
Target Qaddafi. S. M. Hersh. il *N Y Times Mag* p16-22+ F 22 '87

Reporters and reporting
Inciting the Libyans [Voice of America editorials aired during the bombing of Tripoli and Benghazi] L. Alexandre. *Nation* 244:850 Je 20 '87
Libyan terrorists *See* Terrorists, Libyan
Licad, Cecile
about
Unstrung when they first met, Cecile Licad and Antonio Meneses now harmonize onstage and off. H. Shapiro. il pors *People Wkly* 27:105-6 Ap 27 '87
Lice
See also
Plant lice
Safer ways to cope with head lice [shampoos] il *Consum Rep* 52:595 O '87
Licensed product merchandising *See* Merchandising
Licenses
See also
Automobile drivers—Licenses
Motorcyclists—Licenses
Physicians—Licenses
Licenses, Television *See* Television laws and regulations
Lichens .
Herbivory in rocks and the weathering of a desert [impact of lichen feeding by snails] M. Shachak and others. bibl f il *Science* 236:1098-9 My 29 '87
Snails dine at desert dust depot [research by Clive G. Jones and others] K. Hartley. il *Sci News* 131:373 Je 13 '87
Lichine, Alexis, 1913-
about
In possession of his fortune. F. J. Prial. il por *N Y Times Mag* p58 Je 21 '87
Licht, Seymour
about
A bondholder's revenge. M. Schifrin. il por *Forbes* 140:111 Ag 24 '87
Lichtenstein, Roy, 1923-
about
The art behind the dots. D. Solomon. il por *N Y Times Mag* p42-6+ Mr 8 '87
The luck of the draw. K. Larson. il *N Y* 20:98-9 My 18 '87
Roy Lichtenstein: master of the Benday dot. E. Heartney. il *Art News* 86:210 Summ '87
Lichter, Daniel T., and Costanzo, Janice A.
How do demographic changes affect labor force participation of women? bibl f il *Mon Labor Rev* 110:23-5 N '87
Lichti, Todd
about
The right stuff—and the left. B. Anderson. il por *Sports Illus* 67 Sp Issue:85 N 18 '87
Lichtman, Allan J.
Tommy the Cork: the secret world of Washington's first modern lobbyist. il por *Wash Mon* 19:41-9 F '87
Lichtman, Louis
about
Bake sale. *New Yorker* 63:23-4 Jl 20 '87
Lick Your Chops (Firm)
Number-crunching helps sell yuppie puppy food. S. Sherry. il por *Work Woman* 12:40-1 Ja '87
Licks, Salt *See* Salt licks
Lidar *See* Optical radar
Liddy, G. Gordon
about
Where tough guys go to get tougher: Fort Liddy. D. Blum. il por *N Y* 20:64-71 Ap 13 '87
Liddy (G. Gordon) Academy of Corporate Security and Private Investigation *See* G. Gordon Liddy Academy of Corporate Security and Private Investigation
Lidsky, Lawrence M.
Safe nuclear power [cover story] *New Repub* 197:20-3 D 28 '87

Lidz, Franz
Benito finito at 34 games. il por *Sports Illus* 67:26-7 O 12 '87
The Big Red's bigger bite. il *Sports Illus* 67:48+ S 28 '87
Biggest little man. il pors *Sports Illus* 66:72-3 F 16 '87
Bulwark of the Bruins. il pors *Sports Illus* 66:36-8+ Mr 9 '87
Duel of two minds. il pors *Sports Illus* 67:60-3 D 7 '87
He's not a Stooge on the ice. il pors *Sports Illus* 67:68-71 N 16 '87
Meet the court cutup. il pors *Sports Illus* 66:54-6+ Je 1 '87
No bad hops with Wally. il pors *Sports Illus* 67:54+ Jl 6 '87
Racing to the head of his class. il pors *Sports Illus* 66:36-8 F 2 '87
The Sultans did swing. il *Sports Illus* 66:57-8 Je 22 '87
'They're all my children'. il pors *Sports Illus* 67:24-5 D 21 '87
Three men on a roll. il pors *Sports Illus* 67:40-2+ Ag 24 '87
Thunder on the Beltway. il pors *Sports Illus* 66:56-7 Mr 30 '87
Tough in so many ways. il pors *Sports Illus* 66:66-9 F 16 '87
Weavers of boxing dreams. il *Sports Illus* 67:83 Ag 3 '87
Yankee flameout in Hartford. il pors *Sports Illus* 67:20-1 Ag 3 '87
Lie detectors and detection
Lying in Congress [bill to bar testing by employers] D. Seligman. il *Fortune* 116:186+ D 7 '87
Lieber, Jill
Battlin' Buccaneer. il pors *Sports Illus* 67:50+ D 7 '87
A bruiser from Azusa. il pors *Sports Illus* 66:42-4+ Ap 27 '87
The Crimson is in the clover. il *Sports Illus* 67:26-7 N 30 '87
Great Dane in town. il pors *Sports Illus* 67:73-4+ D 21 '87
Invincible? No, just real mean. il por *Sports Illus* 66:36-8+ Ja 26 '87
'It's our strike'. il *Sports Illus* 67:46+ O 12 '87
Ready, aim . . . medal! il por *Sports Illus* 66:54-5 F 23 '87
The saint from Shiloh. il pors *Sports Illus* 67:50-2+ Ag 17 '87
A test of unity and loyalty. il *Sports Illus* 67:41-3 O 5 '87
Time to heal the wounds. il *Sports Illus* 67:86+ N 2 '87
Tough as nails. il *Sports Illus* 67:14-21 S 28 '87
Lieberman, Adrienne B.
The malpractice mess: why you should worry. il *Parents* 62:106-10+ Mr '87
Lieberman, Annette R., and Lindner, Vicki, 1944-
Why women are afraid of money [excerpt from Unbalanced accounts] il *Glamour* 85:318-19+ Ap '87
Lieberman, Nancy, 1958-
Sexism in "men-only" sports: why I'm not a victim. il por *Glamour* 85:64 Ag '87
about
One on one [interview] L. Villarosa. pors *Health* 19:30 Jl '87
Liebert, Robert E.
(jt. auth) See Pink, William T., and Liebert, Robert E.
Liebman, Dave
about
A year in the life of a sopranoist. F. Bouchard. *Down Beat* 54:36 Jl '87
Liebmann-Smith, Joan
"I had to protect Baby M" [interview with A. Abraham] il por *Redbook* 169:130-1+ O '87
Sex. il *Ms* 15:78+ Ap '87
Liebmann-Smith, Richard, 1942-
More clinical tales. *New Yorker* 63:30-1 My 4 '87
Liechtenstein
Liechtenstein: a mouse that roars. R. Z. Chesnoff. il map *U S News World Rep* 102:46-7 Je 22 '87
Liedtke, J. Hugh
about
The gambler who refused $2 billion [cover story] S. P. Sherman. il pors *Fortune* 115:50-4+ My 11 '87
Lief, Louise
(ed) See Begley, Sharon. The way we were—20,000 years ago

Liège (Belgium)

Hospitals

See also

Centre Hospitalier Universitaire au Sart Tilman (Liège, Belgium)

Liemandt, Gregory J.

about

Running room at Uccel. G. G. Marcial. por Bus Week p100 F 16 '87

Lienert, Leo

In harmony with nature. il map Courier 40:4-8 F '87

Lienert, Paul

Letter from Detroit. See issues of Road & Track through December 1987

Liens

See also

Mechanics' liens

Liepa, Andris

about

The Bolshoi in America: here's . . . Andris! W. Como. il pors Dance Mag 61:42-5 D '87

Lies See Lying

Lifar, Serge, 1905-1986

about

Obituary

Dance Mag il por 61:104-5+ Mr '87. L. Garafola

Life, Regge

about

Regge Life directs new 'Cosby show' episodes. il por Jet 72:38 Ag 31 '87

Life

See also

Conduct of life

Death

Philosophical anthropology

Quality of life

The art of living. S. L. Taylor. il por Essence 18:55 S '87

Is human life only chemistry? J. F. Haught. Current 294:4-7 Jl/Ag '87

Life flow [cover story; special section; with editorial comment] il Psychol Today 21:24-6+, 29-30+ My '87

Economic value

See Man—Economic value

Life (Biology)

See also

Biosphere

Longevity

Is the sun really necessary? S. Simon. Space World X-7-283:14 Jl '87

When life begins: embryo research. Current 292:9-10 My '87

Origin

See also

Creation

Life from outer space, or Panspermia redux [views of John Cronin] il Discover 8:10 Jl '87

A rusty path to life's origin [effect of ultraviolet rays on ferrous carbonate; work of Gustaf Arrhenius] I. Peterson. Sci News 131:152 Mr 7 '87

Life after death See Future life; Immortality

The life and loves of a she devil [television program] See Television program reviews—Single works

Life care communities

Insurance for the twilight years. J. D. Hull. il Time 129:53 Ap 6 '87

Sizing up life care. M. C. Paulson. il Changing Times 41:65-6+ My '87

Life classes [film] See Motion picture reviews—Single works

Life expectancy See Longevity

Life in hell (Comic strip) See Comic books, strips, etc.

Life insurance See Insurance, Life

Life jackets See Life preservers

Life-Link International, Inc.

Banking on a "croakie". H. Rothman. il pors Nations Bus 75:81 My '87

Life masks See Masks (Sculpture)

The life of the land [drama] See Sakamoto, Edward, 1940-

Life on Europa (Satellite)

Europa: the case for ice-bound life. R. Spangenburg and D. Moser. il Space World X-8-284:14-16 Ag '87

Life on Mars

Life search [proposed Mars Network Mission] E. Smith. il Omni 9:32 Je '87

More momentum for Mars—and Martians. J. Eberhart. Sci News 132:68-9 Ag 1 '87

Life on other planets

See also

Interstellar communication

Life on Europa (Satellite)

Life on Mars

UFOs

E.T. may look like us [research by Cyril Ponnamperuma] il USA Today (Periodical) 115:16 Je '87

Invasion of the Strieber snatchers [W. Strieber's encounters with extraterrestrial aliens] T. Cochran. il por N Y 20:26 Mr 30 '87

Looking for a few good stars [cover story] K. Croswell. il Space World X-7-283:12-15 Jl '87

Making Communion with another world [fascination with UFOs] M. Green. il pors People Wkly 27:34-9 My 11 '87

The primal fear: are we alone? F. Apsi-Ridolfo. Astronomy 15:34+ D '87

UFO update [G. Kinder's book about E. Meier's encounters with extraterrestrials] B. Lawren. il Omni 9:95 Jl '87

UFO update [W. Strieber's encounter with extraterrestrials] J. Clary. il Omni 9:111 Ap '87

What 'Communion' really said. W. Strieber. por Publ Wkly 232:72 O 2 '87

When is a true story true? [dilemma of publishing W. Strieber's Communion as nonfiction] E. B. Claflin. il por Publ Wkly 232:23-6 Ag 14 '87

Anecdotes, facetiae, satire, etc.

Extraterrestrial congress: the case of the bed-hopping aliens. Crypton, Dr. il Discover 8:104 O '87

Last word. M. Coleman and D. Jaffe. il Omni 9:138 My '87

Life preservers

PFD [personal flotation devices] P. L. Spencer. Consum Res Mag 70:2 My '87

Life saving See Rescue work

Life saving equipment

See also

Airplanes, Military—Escape devices

Life-Link International, Inc.

Life preservers

Dashboards for humans [lifesign detectors; work of Charles Lessard] D. Lampe. Pop Sci 231:33 S '87

Niagara rapids rescue [1918 breeches buoy rescue] Sea Front 33:145-6 Mr/Ap '87

Life sciences

See also

Biology

Life skills

Mastery: taking it home. G. B. Leonard. il Esquire 107:149-52 My '87

Study and teaching

Real-life learning. D. F. Bjorklund and B. Bjorklund. il Parents 62:194 Mr '87

Life span See Longevity

Life span (Animals) See Age—Animals

Life support systems (Space environment)

See also

Biosphere II

Astrocrops [Controlled Ecological Life Support System] R. Wolkomir. il Omni 9:16+ Jl '87

Seeding space [Closed Ecological Life Support System; cover story] B. Dickey. il Space World X-4-280:14-15+ Ap '87

Life with Lucy [television program] See Television program reviews—Single works

Lifeboats, life rafts, etc.

They learn to work calmly while instinct warns they're about to die [Coast Guard Motor Life Boat School] M. Parfit. il Smithsonian 18:98-102+ My '87

Lifeguards

See also

Clothing and dress—Lifeguards

Lifesat (Satellite) See Artificial satellites—Biological use

Lifestyles

Concentrating regeneration inside yourself. R. Rodale. il Prevention 39:17-21 Ap '87

If you're lost, just go home. R. Rodale. il Rodale's Org Gard 34:18+ S '87

The sacrifice buy. C. Lorenz. World Press Rev 34:50 N '87

True stories of regeneration. R. Rodale. il Prevention 39:17-18+ Jl '87

Wellness for the well-heeled [La Costa's Center for Lifestyle Management] G. Waggoner. il Esquire 107:55 Je '87

Write your regeneration resumé—and apply for a happier future. M. Golin. il Prevention 39:104+ Ja '87

Anecdotes, facetiae, satire, etc.

Me and my bed [used for sleeping and working; cover story] B. Allen. il pors Ms 16:20+ D '87

An unstyled life. R. Baker. il N Y Times Mag p10 Je 28 '87

Lifetime (Firm)
New lease on Lifetime: its latest metamorphosis may
be the best. C. Gerber. il *Channels* 7:13 O '87
Lifting and carrying
See also
Weight lifting
Lifton, Judie
I said no to drugs. il *Seventeen* 46:120-1 O '87
Ligachev, Yegor K.
about
Curbing *glasnost*. por *Time* 130:40 O 5 '87
Ligaments
Wounds and injuries
Fast comeback from injury: carbon fibers can rebuild
torn tendons. S. Reeder. *Women's Sports Fitness* 9:44-5
Ja '87
Ligaments, Artificial
Building a better knee [Kennedy ligament augmentation
device] R. Lewis. il *Health* 19:18 D '87
Ligases *See* Synthetases
Ligeti, György
about
Musical events:
Performance of Studies for piano, Book I. A. Porter.
New Yorker 63:85-6 Je 8 '87
Liggett & Myers Tobacco Company
Caveat fumator [rulings in favor of Liggett & Myers
and American Brands in product liability cases] J.
Castro. il *Time* 130:43 S 7 '87
A judicial smoke alert [pro-industry rulings in Liggett
& Myers Tobacco Co. cases] il *U S News World
Rep* 103:12 S 7 '87
Tobacco wins one in court [ruling that warning labels
on cigarettes shielded Liggett & Myers from liability
claim] D. Pauly. il *Newsweek* 110:44 S 7 '87
Liggins, Joe, d. 1987
about
Obituary
Jet por 72:18 Ag 17 '87
Light
See also
Absorption of light
Color
Diffraction
Fiber optics
Interference (Light)
Lasers
Luminescence
Photography—Light and lighting
Photons
Polarization (Light)
Reflection (Optics)
Exhibitions
Seeing the light [exhibition at New York Hall of Science]
il *Natl Geogr World* 145:6-11 S '87
Photographs and photography
See also
Reflections (Photography)
Motion light traces [time exposure] R. Barnes and T.
M. Smith. il *Petersens Photogr Mag* 15:36-7 Mr '87
Physiological effects
See also
Photoperiodism
Photoreceptors
Seasonal affective disorder
Ultraviolet rays—Physiological effects
The light factor [fluorescent lights] L. F. McCarthy. *Vogue*
177:160+ Ja '87
The light: fantastic! D. E. Zimmer. *World Press Rev*
34:55 Ap '87
A light in time [light exposure to reset biological clock;
study by Charles Czeisler] M. Roberts. il *Psychol Today*
21:22 Ja '87
Mathematics of sleep [interaction between circadian
rhythm and the sleep-wake cycle; work of Steven
Strogatz and others] S. J. Nadis. il *Technol Rev* 90:13-14
F/Mr '87
Photodynamic action [photosensitization] D. P. Valenzeno
and J. P. Pooler. bibl f il *BioScience* 37:270-6 Ap
'87
Speed
Centennial of the Michelson-Morley experiment [cover
story; special issue] bibl f il pors *Phys Today* 40:23-30+
My '87
Physics centennial [1887 Michelson-Morley experiment]
T. H. Cole. il *Pop Mech* 164:56 Jl '87
Light, Zodiacal *See* Zodiacal light
Light airplanes *See* Airplanes, Light
Light and darkness in the Bible
Great light. M. K. Hellwig. *America* 156:inside back
cover Ja 17 '87

You are the light. M. K. Hellwig. *America* 156:inside
back cover Ja 31 '87
Light boxes
Built-in light boxes for kitchen and back porch. il *Sunset*
178:166 Ap '87
Light bulbs
See also
Bulbtronics (Firm)
Casting light on the latest in bulbs. D. H. Dunn. il
Bus Week p104 F 9 '87
An illuminating guide to light bulbs. J. Seisler. il *Consum
Res Mag* 70:15-17 Ag '87
Light-bulb savers: not a bright idea [work of Alexander
Emanuel] D. Stover. *Pop Sci* 230:34 My '87
Shedding some light on long-life light bulbs [GE bulbs]
il *Consum Rep* 52:653 N '87
Advertising
Battle of the bulbs. B. Kanner. il *N Y* 20:22+ Ap 13
'87
Light bulbs in art *See* Light in art
Light communication systems
See also
Fiber optics
Infrared communications
Lasers—Communication use
Light cooking *See* Low calorie cooking
Light dimmers *See* Electric switches
Light-emitting diodes *See* Diodes
Light filters
Black-dot diffusion helps capture a subject's character
[work of G. Heisler] B. Hagin. il por *Pop Photogr*
94:68 D '87
Cokin creative filter system. K. Bloom. il *Petersens
Photogr Mag* 16:48-50 Je '87
Filter reveals fascinating solar detail [T-Scanner, H-alpha
solar filter system] D. Trombino. il *Astronomy* 15:46-7
D '87
Polarizers are for more than blue skies and reflections.
N. Rothschild. il *Pop Photogr* 94:26 Ag '87
Shades of green: using filters to previsualize your photos.
C. W. Kennedy. il *Pop Photogr* 94:36 S '87
Supafrost diffusion filters. R. Rosen. il *Petersens Photogr
Mag* 16:52-3 My '87
Light in art
See also
Sunlight in art
Neon. il *Natl Geogr World* 140:36-9 Ap '87
Neon lights the desert [New Mexico] K. Rosenberg.
il *Technol Rev* 90:14-15 F/Mr '87
A vision in high visibility, Eric Staller believes in traveling
lit [use of light bulbs] M. Small. il por *People Wkly*
28:137-9 O 19 '87
Light meters *See* Photometers and photometry
Light of day [film] *See* Motion picture reviews—Single
works
Light pollution, Outdoor *See* Lighting, Outdoor
Light production in animals and plants *See* Bioluminescence
Light rail systems
Light rail hits the West . . . again. il *Sunset* 178:58+
My '87
Trolleys—by any other name. C. Skrzycki. il *U S News
World Rep* 102:46 Ap 6 '87
Light sensitization *See* Light—Physiological effects
Light ships *See* Lightships
Light shows
Urban disturbances [work of K. Wodiczko] E. Lajer-
Burcharth. bibl f il *Art Am* 75:146-53+ N '87
Equipment
The lava light returns [Eye of the Storm] S. A. Booth.
il *Pop Mech* 164:14 S '87
Light Signatures, Inc.
What checkless society? K. K. Wiegner. il *Forbes* 140:8
S 21 '87
Light tackle *See* Fishing tackle
Light verse *See* Poetry
Lightbody, Andy
Terror-proof tourism [excerpt from The terrorism survival
guide] *Harpers* 275:24 Jl '87
Lightfoot, Gordon, 1938-
about
A troubadour's tracks into the heartland. B. D. Johnson.
il pors *Macleans* 100:52-4 Mr 16 '87
Lighthouse Reef (Belize)
Lighthouse Reef: a Caribbean atoll. J. Kenyon. il map
Sea Front 33:428-37 N/D '87
Lighthouse tenders
Turn out the lighthouse, the party's over: keeper Joe
Larnard stoically awaits automation [Boston Light]
R. Arias. il pors *People Wkly* 28:86-8 S 21 '87
Women of the lights. E. De Wire. il *Am Hist Illus*
21:42-9 F '87

Lighthouses
    See also
    Lightships
Keepers of the Hatteras light. il *South Living* 22:30 F '87
Move it or lose it [Cape Hatteras Light] O. H. Pilkey, Jr. il *Oceans* 20:23+ Mr/Ap '87
Turn out the lighthouse, the party's over: keeper Joe Larnard stoically awaits automation [Boston Light] R. Arias. il pors *People Wkly* 28:86-8 S 21 '87
Waiting for a lighthouse [Cape Henry Lighthouse] il *South Living* 22:41 S '87
    Conservation and restoration
The great lighthouse giveaway. N. Cutner. il *Life* 10:36-42 Ag '87
The tide is turning for old beacons adrift at land's end [cover story] D. G. Hanson. bibl (p145) il *Smithsonian* 18:98-106+ Ag '87
    Aleutian Islands (Alaska)
The Tombstone Twins: lights at the top of the world [Cape Sarichef and Scotch Cap on Unimak Island] N. Ferrell. il map *Sea Front* 33:344-51 S/O '87
    Great Britain
Grace Darling—the lighthouse heroine [Longstone Lighthouse] J. Mitford. il por *Archit Dig* 44:30+ S '87

Lighting
    See also
    Airport buildings—Lighting
    Automobiles—Lighting
    Candles and candleholders
    Daylight
    Discotheques—Lighting
    Electric lamps
    Light boxes
    Lighting fixtures
    Opera—Stage lighting
    Photography—Light and lighting
    Rock concerts—Stage lighting
    San Francisco Bay region (Calif.)—Lighting
    Skylights
    Theater—Stage lighting
Formed to light: thirteen projects by Gunnar Birkerts [daylighting design] D. Rastorfer. il *Archit Rec* 175:141-9 Mr '87
Improve your kitchen lighting. G. Hamilton and K. Hamilton. il *Home Mech* 83:40-2+ D '87
Kitchen lighting: a necessary variety. il *South Living* 22:130-3 O '87
    Control
    See also
    Electric switches
Installing a light timer. G. Branson. il *Fam Handyman* 37:86 My/Je '87
Mark V SM-328 professional color light controller. il *Radio-Electron* 58:35-7 D '87
Lighting, Christmas *See* Christmas decorations
Lighting, Fluorescent
Fluorescent light troubleshooting. M. Thompson. il *Fam Handyman* 37:64 N '87
    Physiological effects
    See Light—Physiological effects
Lighting, Outdoor
    See also
    Christmas decorations, Outdoor
    Gardens and gardening—Lighting
How to install outdoor lights: easier than you think! C. M. Stowers. il *Better Homes Gard* 65:78+ My '87
In the glare of the moon [threat to astronomy of light pollution] P. Ceravolo. il *Astronomy* 15:24+ My '87
Low-voltage outdoor lighting. G. D. Cook. il *Better Homes Gard* 65:50 O '87
    Control
Outdoor light controller. E. J. Holtke. il *Radio-Electron* 58:104-5 O '87
    Fixtures
    See Lighting fixtures
Lighting designers
    See also
    Artistic Lighting Inc.
    Gallo, Paul
    Jenkins, Paulie
    Meeh, Gregory
    Rigdon, Kevin
    Tipton, Jennifer
    Wechsler, Gil
Designers at work [cover story; special section] il *Theatre Crafts* 21:23-42+ My '87
Lighting fixtures
    See also
    Lanterns

Bright ideas in home security [automatic security lights] M. Morris. il *Home Mech* 83:50-1 S '87
Ceiling fixture jack. G. Branson. il *Fam Handyman* 37:66 O '87
Entry lights glow through glass-block tops. il *Sunset* 178:132 My '87
Light fixture drips water. J. Gaynor. il *Home Mech* 83:96 Mr '87
Overhead fixture jack. R. A. Hamilton. il *Home Mech* 83:77 N '87
Replace a lamp fixture. G. Branson. il *Fam Handyman* 37:84 My/Je '87
What's the buzz? [Super Beamer low-voltage track light fixture] J. R. Provey. il *Home Mech* 83:10 F '87
Lightner Museum
What I did on my summer vacation [mechanical musical instruments] B. Ault. il *Antiques Collect Hobbies* 92:62-4 O '87
Lightning
    See also
    Fulgurite
    Space flight—Lightning hazards
    Thunderstorms
Lightning: nature's terrible swift sword. J. Sedgwick. il *Read Dig* 131:23-5+ Ag '87
Lightning up in San Francisco [exhibit at the California Academy of Sciences] il *Sunset* 178:70 Mr '87
"My son was hit by lightning"; ed. by Lorene Hanley Duquin. S. Schunk. il por *Redbook* 169:17+ Ag '87
Rapid pressure changes near thunderstorms, directional lightning. T. Schlatter. il *Weatherwise* 40:99-100 Ap '87
Summer is the electric season. R. McManus. il *Sierra* 72:88-91 Jl/Ag '87
Whistling for lightning's rhythm [research by William C. Armstrong] S. Weisburd. *Sci News* 131:372 Je 13 '87
Lightning protection
Protect your home from lightning. G. Branson. il *Fam Handyman* 37:38+ Ap '87
Protection from lightning. E. Havill. il *Ctry J* 14:46 Ag '87
Lightships
Last of the lightships, in Oregon and California. il *Sunset* 178:40 Ja '87
Lightweight construction
    See also
    Tension structures
Lignin
Monitoring biosynthesis of wheat cell-wall phenyl-propanoids in situ. N. G. Lewis and others. bibl f il *Science* 237:1344-6 S 11 '87
Ligonier (Pa.)
    Architecture
A modern idyll [private residence] D. Brenner. il *Archit Rec* 175:70-9 mid-Ap '87
Liguori, Alfonso Maria de', Saint, 1696-1787
    about
Moral theologian under attack: Saint Alphonsus Liguori. B. Häring. *America* 156:362-6 My 2 '87
Lih, Lars T.
Gorbachev and the reform movement. bibl f *Curr Hist* 86:309-12+ O '87
Likens, Gene E., 1935-
(jt. auth) See Bormann, F. H., and Likens, Gene E., 1935-
Lil' Ed and the Blues Imperials (Musical group)
Lil' Ed & the Blues Imperials. D. Helland. il *Down Beat* 54:14 Jl '87
Lila Acheson Wallace Garden (Williamsburg, Va.) *See* Williamsburg (Va.)—Gardens and gardening
Lila Acheson Wallace Wing *See* Metropolitan Museum of Art (New York, N.Y.). Lila Acheson Wallace Wing
Lilies
    See also
    Calla lilies
    Daylilies
Lilies, Jacobean *See* Jacobean lilies
Lilies, Voodoo *See* Voodoo lilies
Lilla, Mark
The body politic. *New Repub* 197:14-16 S 28 '87
Lilla Hyttnäs (Sundborn, Sweden: Historic house) *See* Sundborn (Sweden)—Historic houses, sites, etc.
Liller, William, 1927-
(jt. auth) See Niedner, Malcolm B., Jr., and Liller, William, 1927-
Lillian Vernon Corporation
The treasure of her company [L. Katz] M. I. Finney. il por *Nations Bus* 75:73-4 F '87

Lillie, John M., 1937-
about
Edelman: a new Lucky strike? K. M. Hafner. il por *Bus Week* p49 F 23 '87
Lillie and Hugh Roy Cullen Sculpture Garden *See* Museum of Fine Arts (Houston, Tex.). Lillie and Hugh Roy Cullen Sculpture Garden
Lillie Carroll Jackson Museum
The Lillie Carroll Jackson Museum. W. M. T. Walls. il *Essence* 17:28 F '87
Lilly (Eli) and Company *See* Eli Lilly and Company
Lillywhite, Harvey B.
Snakes under pressure [cover story] il *Nat Hist* 96:58-67 N '87
Lily Tomlin [television program] *See* Television program reviews—Single works
Lily Tomlin: the film behind the show [film] *See* Motion picture reviews—Single works
Lima, Carlos Barbosa- *See* Barbosa-Lima, Carlos
Lima, Rafael
about
El Salvador [drama] Reviews
N Y il 20:120 O 19 '87. J. Simon
Lima (Peru)
Galleries and museums
See also
Museo Oro del Peru
L'Image Graphics
The couple with the hippest greeting cards in town [T. Barnes and W. Wilson] P. Finch. il pors *Bus Week* p80 Je 8 '87
Their season to be jolly. M. Barrier. il pors *Nations Bus* 75:75 D '87
Liman, Arthur L.
about
'I'm not a potted plant'. A. Press. il pors *Newsweek* 110:21-2 Jl 20 '87
The man asking Iranscam's tough questions. C. Knowlton. il pors *Fortune* 115:76-9+ Je 8 '87
Sparring partners. J. V. Lamar, Jr. il pors *Time* 130:23 Jl 20 '87
Limbaugh, Tommy
about
A week in the life of a college recruiter. D. Whitford. il pors *Sport Mag* 78:76-80+ Mr '87
Limericks
There was an old lady from Spain . . . B. Dubivsky. il *N Y Times Mag* p40-1 My 10 '87
Limewood carving *See* Wood carving
Limitation of arms *See* Disarmament
Limited, Inc.
The battle of Bendel's [takeover by L. Wexner] J. Kornbluth. il pors *N Y* 20:26-33 F 23 '87
Shock of the news [analysts overestimate earnings] J. Crudele. il *N Y* 20:19 O 5 '87
The Unlimited? [cover story] S. B. Weiner. il *Forbes* 139:76-80 Ap 6 '87
Win one, lose one. A. A. Lappen. il *Forbes* 140:8 O 19 '87
Limited Editions Club
Matchmakers. R. Bass. il *Art News* 86:9-10 F '87
Limited partnership
See also
Benequity Holdings, a California Limited Partnership
Boston Ventures Management Inc.
Malrite Guaranteed Broadcast Partners Limited Partnership
Master limited partnership
Mesa Limited Partnership
NV Homes L. P.
OKC Limited Partnership
Reliance Capital Group L. P.
Securities Groups
Stranger Partnership Fund
Cutting the risks in the restaurant game. T. Carson. il *Bus Week* p120-1 Ag 17 '87
Every man a venture capitalist. A. E. Serwer. il *Fortune* 116:107-8 Jl 20 '87
Getting a piece of the action through limited partnerships. D. Lamaute. *Black Enterp* 17:320+ Je '87
Hooking up to a cable-TV limited partnership. M. Ivey. il *Bus Week* p152 Je 8 '87
Limited partnerships drastically limited performance. il *Money* 16:14 D '87
Limited partnerships for those who love long shots [research and development limited partnerships] G. Weiss. *Bus Week* p180 Jl 20 '87
The next land boom [raw land syndicators] J. B. Quinn. il *Newsweek* 109:56 Mr 2 '87

Were STC's optical disks just a mirage? [suit brought by limited partnership investors against Storage Technology Corp.] M. Ivey. il *Bus Week* p67 Je 15 '87
What partnership sponsors are peddling now. *Money* 16:14 Ap '87
Acquisitions and mergers
International aspects
A drum, a drum, Renouf doth come [raid on Benequity Holdings] H. Rudnitsky. il *Forbes* 139:146+ My 18 '87
Taxation
Building a cozy tax shelter with historic rehabs [real estate limited partnership] T. Segal. il *Bus Week* p118 S 7 '87
The eternal promoter [W. A. Kilpatrick] A. A. Lappen. il por *Forbes* 140:8 Ag 10 '87
Limited partnerships that like tax reform [capital equipment leasing] A. E. Serwer. il *Fortune* 116:102 Ag 17 '87
The never-say-die promoter [tax shelter promoter W. Kilpatrick] J. A. Conway. por *Forbes* 139:8 Ap 6 '87
A 'PIG' can help with tax-shelter losses [passive income generators] B. Hitchings. *Bus Week* p94 Ap 20 '87
The promoter who never quits [tax shelter operator W. A. Kilpatrick] A. A. Lappen. il por *Forbes* 139:60-1 F 9 '87
Propping up paper losses [passive income generators] H. Wheelwright. *Money* 16:159 Jl '87
Why funds disincorporate. J. R. Hayes. il *Forbes* 139:250 My 18 '87
Limón Dance Company
Computerography [use of personal computers] B. Hamblett. *Dance Mag* 61:86-7 Ja '87
Limousine service
See also
Execucoach (Firm)
Limulus *See* Horseshoe crabs
Lin, Florence
Shanghai secrets. il *N Y Times Mag* p63-4 S 27 '87
Lin, Leslie Y.
Gaining ground zero. il *Sierra* 72:33-6 Ja/F '87
Lin, Stephen S., and Levitan, Irwin B.
Concanavalin A alters synaptic specificity between cultured Aplysia neurons. bibl f il *Science* 237:648-50 Ag 7 '87
Lin Data Corporation
Why Nashua looks even richer now [acquisition of Lin Data] G. G. Marcial. *Bus Week* p126 Jl 20 '87
Linck, Robert
about
Trapped in the wreckage of Flight 1713, Robert Linck survives to fly home again. A. Richman. il pors *People Wkly* 28:98-102 D 21 '87
Lincoln, Abraham, 1809-1865
about
The Lincoln myth. D. R. Carlin, Jr. *Commonweal* 114:72-3 F 13 '87
My father, Mr. Lincoln and me. E. Ziegler. il *Read Dig* 130:35-40 F '87
Collectibles
Lincolniana in 1986. F. J. Williams. bibl il pors *Antiques Collect Hobbies* 91:68-73 F '87
Fiction
From Nixon to Lincoln. L. Weymouth. il pors *N Y* 20:42-7 Ag 31 '87
Lincoln: fiction & fact [interview with W. Safire] A. M. Schlesinger. il pors *Am Herit* 38:84-9 D '87
A modern vote for Abraham Lincoln [interview with W. Safire] A. P. Sanoff. il por *U S News World Rep* 103:57 Ag 24 '87
Safire on Lincoln and 'Freedom'. J. Kroll. il pors *Newsweek* 110:56-7 Ag 31 '87
William Safire talks about 'Freedom,' his new novel. T. Todd. por *Publ Wkly* 231:49-50 My 29 '87
Historiography
Looking for Lincoln in the 1980's. G. S. Boritt. bibl il pors *N Y Times Book Rev* 92:1+ F 8 '87
Homes
Teaching history—alive and well [Lincoln Log Cabin project in Illinois] H. Malehorn. il *Phi Delta Kappan* 69:166-8 O '87
Washington and Lincoln slept here. C. B. Hayes. il maps *Travel Holiday* 167:46-50 F '87
Press conferences
Lincoln meets the press [imaginary conference with Lincoln's responses based on actual statements] W. Safire. il *N Y Times Mag* p28-9 Ag 23 '87
Lincoln, C. E.
In search of the second wind. il *Sport Mag* 78:87-8 Jl '87

Lincoln, Carl Eric, 1946-
M*A*S*H's Maine man. il pors *50 Plus* 27:42+ Mr '87
Lincoln (Neb.)
Moral conditions
Federal judge orders showing of controversial film [attempt to censor Hail Mary] T. J. Flygare. il *Phi Delta Kappan* 68:401-2 Ja '87
Lincoln Center for the Performing Arts. Metropolitan Opera House *See* Metropolitan Opera House (New York, N.Y.)
Lincoln County (Ky.)
Education
Kentucky teacher hits The wall with Pink Floyd [J. Fowler fights dismissal for showing R-rated movie] T. J. Flygare. il *Phi Delta Kappan* 69:237-8 N '87
Lincoln family
Photographs and photography
Lincoln's memorial: never before published, a family album of four generations. il *Life* 10:74-6+ Jl '87
Lincoln Memorial (Washington, D.C.)
An epitaph for Mr. Lincoln [inscription by R. Cortissoz] H. W. Morgan. il por *Am Herit* 38:58-63 F/Mr '87
Lincoln Property Company
Home field advantage [J. Hynes' plans for Boston Garden development] B. Leonard. il por *Forbes* 139:91-2 Ja 26 '87
Lincoln Savings & Loan Association
Charles Keating: feeling the heat in Phoenix. K. Kelly. il por *Bus Week* p80 Ag 31 '87
Lincoln University (Pa.)
Lincoln's 1st woman prexy is ready to lead school into the 21st century. *Jet* 72:12 Ap 27 '87
White charges Lincoln U. violated his civil rights [former athletic director D. A. Bennice] *Jet* 72:23 Ag 31 '87
Lincolnshire (England)
Antiquities
Nuclear prehistory [archeological finds in nuclear dump site] D. Byrne. *Hist Today* 37:3 Ag '87
Lind, William S.
about
Where are U.S. minesweepers? Out of service and out-of-date, says arms expert William Lind [interview] M. Wilhelm. il por *People Wkly* 28:30-1 Ag 24 '87
Lindbeck, George A.
about
Speaking of postliberalism. M. E. Marty. *Christ Century* 104:391 Ap 22 '87
Lindberg, Tod
The rise & fall of Roman Polanski. *Commentary* 83:61-5 Ja '87
Lindbergh, Anne
How to make believe. *Writer* 100:17-19 D '87
Lindbergh, Charles, Jr.
Kidnapping
The case that will not close. F. Russell. bibl f il por *N Y Rev Books* 34:4+ N 5 '87
Lindbergh, Charles, 1902-1974
about
Lindbergh's Spirit. P. Garrison. il por *Flying* 114:30-4 S '87
Retracing Lindy's victorious trip across the country. M. Parfit. bibl (p231) il pors map *Smithsonian* 18:200-2+ O '87
Lindbergh flight *See* Aviation—Transatlantic flights—History
Linde, Andrei
Particle physics and inflationary cosmology. bibl f il *Phys Today* 40:61-8 S '87
Lindeman, Bard
The editor's column. See issues of 50 Plus
Linden, E. von *See* May, Karl Friedrich, 1842-1912
Linden
Linden viburnum lights up autumn. il *South Living* 22:54-5 O '87
Linden automobile factory (Linden, N.J.) *See* Automobile factories
Linder, Benjamin Ernest, 1959-1987
about
Beat the devil. A. Cockburn. *Nation* 244:636-7 My 16 '87
Caught in the cross fire. il *Newsweek* 109:47 My 11 '87
The execution of Ben Linder. A. Cockburn. *Nation* 245:402-3 O 17 '87
Notes and comment. *New Yorker* 63:21-2 Je 8 '87
The sad saga of a Sandalista. J. Smolowe. il por *Time* 129:34 My 11 '87

Linder, Kate
about
Gathering no dust, Kate Linder sweeps up on TV and in the skies. J. Callan. il pors *People Wkly* 27:73-4 Je 15 '87
Linderman, Lawrence
(jt. auth) See Sills, Beverly, and Linderman, Lawrence
Lindgren, Gerry, 1946-
about
A life on the run. K. Moore. il pors *Sports Illus* 66:76-80+ My 18 '87
Lindner, Carl H.
about
How Lindner keeps his troops and investments in line. D. Cook. il por *Bus Week* p81 Ap 20 '87
Taft Broadcasting may become a Carl Lindner production. D. Cook. il por *Bus Week* p37-8 Ap 27 '87
With Lindner in charge, Penn Central is on the prowl. R. Mitchell. il *Bus Week* p80-1 Ap 20 '87
Lindner, Vicki, 1944-
(jt. auth) See Lieberman, Annette R., and Lindner, Vicki, 1944-
Lindorff, David
Why Meese spoke. *Nation* 244:349 Mr 21 '87
Lindquist, Mark
Diary of a lost weekend. il *N Y Times Mag* p48-51+ O 11 '87
Lindsay, Arto
about
Blindfold test. B. Milkowski. il por *Down Beat* 54:43 Mr '87
Lindsay, Bertha
The Shakers face their last amen; ed. by Cable Neuhaus. il pors *People Wkly* 27:78-81 Mr 2 '87
Lindsay, Cotton Mather
How not to control medical costs. il por *Fortune* 116:105-6 Jl 6 '87
Lindsay Olive Growers
Pit power [pit recycling schemes] J. K. Miller. il *Omni* 9:22 S '87
Lindstrand, Per
about
The big splashdown. N. Cooper. il pors *Newsweek* 110:37 Jl 13 '87
Lindstrom, Aletha
A magic I almost missed. il *Read Dig* 130:71-2 Ap '87
Lindvall, M. L.
The perfect Christmas pageant. il *Good Housekeep* 205:56-7 D '87
Line, Les
Etcetera. See issues of Audubon
Linear equations
See also
Simultaneous equations
Linear programming
Karmarkar's algorithm. A. A. Rockett and J. C. Stevenson. il *Byte* 12:146-52+ S '87
The startling discovery Bell Labs kept in the shadows [N. Karmarkar's algorithm] W. G. Wild, Jr. and O. Port. por *Bus Week* p69+ S 21 '87
Lineas Aereas del Estado (Argentina)
LADE pioneers air routes to southern Argentina. il *Aviat Week Space Technol* 127:62-3 Ag 31 '87
Linehan, Peter
The Cid of history and the history of The Cid. bibl il *Hist Today* 37:26-32 S '87
Linen, Household
See also
Sheets
Table linen
Towels
Linen chests *See* Chests
Linenthal, Edward T.
Moral rhetoric, moral confusion in the Star Wars debate. il *Christ Century* 104:1058-61 N 25 '87
Liners *See* Ocean liners
Lines, Patricia M.
An overview of home instruction. il *Phi Delta Kappan* 68:510-17 Mr '87
Lines, Fishing *See* Fishing tackle
Lines, Waiting *See* Queues (Waiting lines)
Ling, Jack
One million children with a chance to live [interview with J. P. Grant] il *World Health* p10-12 Ja/F '87
Lingeman, Richard R.
Poindexter file. *Nation* 244:68-9 Ja 24 '87
Lingerie *See* Underwear
Linguistics
See also
Sociolinguistics

Link, Perry
(tr) See Liu Binyan, 1925-. Delving into life—the Chinese writer's duty
Linkage (Genetics)
See also
Chromosome mapping
A DNA segment encoding two genes very tightly linked to Huntington's disease. T. C. Gilliam and others. bibl f il *Science* 238:950-2 N 13 '87
Molecular genetics: applications to the clinical neurosciences [linkage analysis with restriction fragment length polymorphisms] J. B. Martin. bibl f il *Science* 238:765-72 N 6 '87
Links (Organization)
Calif. Links group lauds superstar Ray Charles. il pors *Jet* 71:29 Mr 2 '87
Kansas City Links host 35th anniversary dinner. il *Jet* 72:38 Jl 20 '87
Linn, C. E., Jr., and others
Pheromone components and active spaces: what do moths smell and where do they smell it? bibl f il *Science* 237:650-2 Ag 7 '87
Linn, Teri Ann
about
Beauty queen Teri Ann Linn adds her Hawaiian punch to daytime's bold new soap. S. Spillman. il pors *People Wkly* 27:62-3 My 11 '87
Linnas, Karl
about
Linnas and the long war. *Natl Rev* 39:19-20 My 22 '87
The Linnas case: was justice done? N. Cooper. il por *Newsweek* 109:33-4 My 4 '87
Nazis and Communists. *New Repub* 196:4+ My 11 '87
No place to hide. il por *Time* 129:70 My 4 '87
Problems of crime and punishment. R. Lacayo. il *Time* 129:60 Ap 20 '87
Soviet firing squad awaits. por *U S News World Rep* 102:14 Ap 13 '87
Linney, Romulus, 1930-
about
April snow [drama] Reviews
New Yorker 63:69-70 Je 22 '87. M. Kramer
Holy Ghosts [drama] Reviews
N Y il 20:119 Ag 24 '87. J. Simon
Nation 245:282-4 S 19 '87. T. M. Disch
New Yorker 63:60-1 Ag 24 '87. M. Kramer
Linowes, David F.
Corporation as citizen [address, May 22, 1987] *Vital Speeches Day* 53:755-8 O 1 '87
Is the merger mania good for the nation? [address, February 19, 1987] *Vital Speeches Day* 53:423-6 My 1 '87
Lins, Harry F.
(jt. auth) See Dolan, Robert, and Lins, Harry F.
Linscott, Steven
about
Court orders new trial for Steven Linscott. il por *Christ Today* 31:68+ S 4 '87
A vision of murder. M. Green. il pors *People Wkly* 27:30-2 My 25 '87
Lint in art
In California: a palette of lint [work of S. Barron] G. Jaynes. il por *Time* 129:14 Je 1 '87
Linthicum, Kenneth J., and others
Detection of Rift Valley fever viral activity in Kenya by satellite remote sensing imagery. bibl f il maps *Science* 235:1656-9 Mr 27 '87
Lionel Hampton School of Music See University of Idaho. Lionel Hampton School of Music
Lionheart Television International
Watch out, here come more cheap imports. A. B. Block. il por *Forbes* 139:150 Mr 9 '87
Lions, Mountain See Pumas
Lions Petroleum Company
Rebel with a cause [T. Sato's campaign against rice subsidies in Japan] A. Tanzer. il por *Forbes* 139:84+ Mr 23 '87
Lip makeup See Makeup
Lip syncing
In Wisconsin: lip sync live, onstage tonight [contest at City Slickers in Lake Geneva, Wis.] R. Conniff. il *Time* 130:10+ D 14 '87
Rock-video boutiques can make you a star. M. Rogers. il *Newsweek* 110:60-1 Ag 10 '87
Anecdotes, facetiae, satire, etc.
Notes and comment. *New Yorker* 62:21-2 Ja 12 '87
Lipases
A glycan-phosphatidylinositol-specific phospholipase D in human serum. M. A. Davitz and others. bibl f il *Science* 238:81-4 O 2 '87

Human lipoprotein lipase complementary DNA sequence. K. L. Wion and others. bibl f il *Science* 235:1638-41 Mr 27 '87
Lipids
See also
Cholesterol
Glycerides
Lipoproteins
Liposomes
Lysosphingolipids
Phosphatides
Steroids
The cytoskeletal protein vinculin contains transformation-sensitive, covalently bound lipid. P. Burn and M. M. Burger. bibl f il *Science* 235:476-9 Ja 23 '87
Lipke, Paul
The Athenian trireme. il *Oceans* 20:8-10 N/D '87
Lipman, Jean, 1909-
Jurgan Frederick Huge. bibl f il *Antiques* 132:496, 546-9 S '87
Lipman, Jean, 1909-, and others
Young America [condensation] il *Read Dig* 131:163-7 Jl '87
Lipman, Samuel
Dead from Lincoln Center. *Commentary* 83:59-63 My '87
The great why of arts education [address, September 19, 1986] *Des Arts Educ* 88:20-4 Ja/F '87
Wagner as anti-Semite. *Commentary* 83:57-60 Ja '87
Lipnack, Jessica, and Stamps, Jeffrey
A network model. il pors *Futurist* 21:23-5 Jl/Ag '87
Lipoprotein receptors See Protein receptors
Lipoproteins
Apolipoprotein B-48 is the product of a messenger RNA with an organ-specific in-frame stop codon. S.-H. Chen and others. bibl f il *Science* 238:363-6 O 16 '87
Artery clogging and apo-B. J. Silberner. il *Sci News* 131:90-1 F 7 '87
The battle of the lipoproteins [Helsinki study shows gemfibrozil lowers LDL levels while raising HDL levels] C. Gorman. il *Time* 130:68 N 23 '87
Cholesterol control. B. T. Hunter. il *Consum Res Mag* 70:8-9 Mr '87
Gene makeup a surprise [apolipoprotein(a) and plasminogen] D. M. Barnes. *Science* 238:1513 D 11 '87
Life in the slow lane [research by Walker Buckalew] il *Prevention* 39:8 O '87
Lipoprotein findings may solve one riddle . . . and pose another [apolipoprotein(a)'s influence in atherosclerosis] D. D. Edwards. *Sci News* 132:311 N 14 '87
Lipoprotein uptake by neuronal growth cones in vitro. M. J. Ignatius and others. bibl f il *Science* 236:959-62 My 22 '87
More good news about 'good cholesterol' [gemfibrozil increases HDL levels] *U S News World Rep* 103:14 N 23 '87
Odorless garlic lowers blood fats [research by Benjamin Lau and others] *Prevention* 39:8+ S '87
Similarity of cruzin, an inhibitor of Trypanosoma cruzi neuraminidase, to high-density lipoprotein. R. P. Prioli and others. bibl f il *Science* 238:1417-19 D 4 '87
Up and down on the lipoprotein seesaw. D. D. Edwards. *Sci News* 132:348 N 28 '87
Walking up your HDL [study of mailmen by Timothy Cook] il *Prevention* 39:6 My '87
Liposomes
Cancer-killers from macrophages. J. Raloff. *Sci News* 131:215 Ap 4 '87
Liposomes [use in drug delivery] M. J. Ostro. il *Sci Am* 256:102-4+ Ja '87
These tiny bubbles could make a big splash. S. Siwolop and C. S. Eklund. il *Bus Week* p87-8 Jl 6 '87
Liposuction See Surgery, Plastic
Lipoxins
Leukotrienes and lipoxins: structures, biosynthesis, and biological effects. B. Samuelsson and others. bibl f il *Science* 237:1171-6 S 4 '87
Lipper, Kenneth
about
The platoon of pros who helped out on Wall Street. C. Welles. il por *Bus Week* p38-9 D 21 '87
Lippert, Barbara
Lying with a smile on Madison Avenue. il *U S News World Rep* 102:58 F 23 '87
Lippert, Del E.
about
The cellular-phone star that's burning dimmer. E. B. Terry. il por *Bus Week* p100+ D 7 '87

Lippert, Joan L.
You can make exercise fun. il *Read Dig* 131:108-10
Ag '87
Lippman, Richard E.
(jt. auth) See Tolbert, Margaret, and Lippman, Richard
E.
Lippman, William
about
L.F. Rothschild [interview] il por *Fortune* 116 Sp
Issue:184-5 Fall '87
Lippmann, Walter, 1889-1974
The cold war. *Foreign Aff* 65:869-84 Spr '87
Lips
The perfect mouth. P. Boyer. il *Prevention* 39:122-4
F '87
Pretty, sexy, kissable [excerpt from Beauty from the
inside out] D. Bihova and C. Schrader. il *Ladies
Home J* 104:100-3 F '87
Lipset, Seymour Martin
Comparing Canadian and American unions. bibl *Society*
24:60-70 Ja/F '87
The expansion of democracy [address, July 24, 1987]
Vital Speeches Day 53:748-51 O 1 '87
Lipsitz, Gail E. J.
(jt. auth) See Kurland, Janet B., and Lipsitz, Gail E.
J.
Lipsitz, George
Blue money. *Society* 24:14-15 My/Je '87
Lipsius, Justus, 1547-1606
about
Portrait of Justus Lipsius. A. Grafton. *Am Sch* 56:382-90
Summ '87
Lipske, Mike
How safe is the air inside your home? il *Natl Wildl*
25:34-9 Ap/My '87
Lipson, D. Herbert
about
Editorial freedom vs. the red suspenders. *Newsweek* 109:47
Ap 6 '87
Lipson, Inc. E. Diamond. il por *N Y* 20:28+ Ap 27
'87
Lipson, Debra
Women's health insurance: old problems, new programs.
Ms 15:24 Mr '87
Lipstick
The lowdown on lipsticks. il *Ladies Home J* 104:26
O '87
Reading lips [red lipstick] L. Wells. il *N Y Times Mag*
p53 Ja 25 '87
Lipstick application See Makeup
Liqueurs
The final course. M. Gersh. *Vogue* 177:298 O '87
Licorice shtick [sambuca] W. Grimes. il *Esquire* 108:54
S '87
New faces: some pleasant combinations of spirits and
fruits. E. Fried. il *Black Enterp* 17:92 Jl '87
Sweet new things. J. F. Mariani. il *Mot Boat Sail* 159:32
Ap '87
Liquid crystal displays See Information display systems
Liquid dietary supplements See Dietary supplements
Liquid drops See Drops
Liquid helium See Helium, Liquid
Liquid mercury telescope mirrors See Telescopes—Mirrors
Liquidation
A shareholder revolt at Telecom. B. Dumaine. il por
Fortune 115:58-60 Mr 2 '87
There's no word for Chapter 11 in Dutch. T. Vogel.
il *Bus Week* p62+ N 30 '87
Will USL join Davy Jones? [liquidation of McLean
Industries Inc.] S. Payne. *Bus Week* p30-1 Mr 30
'87
Liquidity (Economics)
Double damned. K. L. Fisher. il *Forbes* 140:238 O
5 '87
Liquidity trap [Taiwan] A. Tanzer. il *Forbes* 139:37-8
Ap 6 '87
Stay liquid to avoid hot water. il *U S News World
Rep* 103:80 O 19 '87
Taiwan's wealth crisis. M. Shao. il *Bus Week* p46-7
Ap 13 '87
Liquids
See also
Viscosity
Liquid handling. *Science* 235 pt2:G127-G134 F 27 '87
Probing interfaces involving liquids. A. L. Robinson.
Science 236:150-1 Ap 10 '87
Optical properties
See also
Sonoluminescence

Liquor
Periodicals
See also
M. Shanken Communications
Liquor industry
See also
Bacardi Corp.
Brown-Forman Distillers Corp.
Heublein, Inc.
James B. Beam Distilling Co.
National Distillers & Chemical Corp.
Schenley Industries, Inc.
Acquisitions and mergers
International aspects
The Guinness affair gets curiouser and curiouser [role
of M. Riklis and sale of Schenley to Guinness] M.
Maremont. *Bus Week* p59-60 My 25 '87
Export-import trade
Where cigarettes and spirits are still booming [Japan]
L. Armstrong. il *Bus Week* p94 S 14 '87
Marketing
In sales, liquor isn't quicker. A. Dunkin. il *Bus Week*
p120-1 Je 22 '87
Liquid assets [M. Shanken's various publications] B.
Kanner. il por *N Y* 20:37-8+ D 7 '87
Canada
See also
Hiram Walker Resources Ltd.
Seagram Company Ltd.
France
See also
Bénédictine SA
Puerto Rico
More than piña coladas: the rums of Puerto Rico. E.
Fried. il *Black Enterp* 17:45 My '87
The spirits of Puerto Rico [rum] R. L. Balzer. il *Travel
Holiday* 168:10-11+ S '87
Liquor laws and regulations
See also
Prohibition
Ontario
Nice guys can be dangerous. C. Gordon. il *Macleans*
100:48 Jl 13 '87
Pennsylvania
A drinking man's guide to Pennsylvania politics. D.
Seligman. il *Fortune* 115:18-19 F 2 '87
Soviet Union
War on Soviet alcoholism. N. Morris. il *Macleans* 100:48
Ja 19 '87
Liquor problem
See also
Alcohol—Physiological effects
Alcohol and authors
Alcohol and automobile drivers
Alcohol and boating
Alcohol and congressmen
Alcohol and employment
Alcohol and Indians (American)
Alcohol and sports
Alcohol and the aged
Alcohol and women
Alcohol and youth
Alcoholics and alcoholism
Liquor stores
Retail liquor stores experience flat trend in productivity.
J. D. York. bibl f il *Mon Labor Rev* 110:25-9 F
'87
Liquor traffic
See also
Prohibition
Liquors
See also
Brandy
Cocktails
Cooking—Liquors
Gin
Liqueurs
Rum
Vodka
Whiskey
Lisa Lisa
about
A head-to-toe new star. J. Miller. il por *Newsweek* 109:77
Je 22 '87
Lisa Lisa. E. Miller. por *Seventeen* 46:82 D '87
Lisa Lisa, on the move, tries Madonna's Latin groove.
L. Russell. il pors *People Wkly* 28:53-4 S 14 '87
Rock's supergirl stars. pors *Teen* 31:58 O '87

Lisberger, Steven
　　　about
Hot pursuit [film] Reviews
　　People Wkly 27:10 Je 8 '87. T. Cunneff
Lisboa, Antônio Francisco, 1730-1814
　　　about
The triumph of O Aleijadinho. A. C. D. S. Telles.
　　il *Courier* 40:39-41 S '87
Lisbon (Portugal)
　　　Art
Portugal: the younger generation. D. Joselit. il *Art Am*
　　75:19-21+ S '87
　　　Description
Ancient Lisbon—at old-time prices. E. Vivacqua. il *World*
　　Press Rev 34:62 Je '87
Lisburne, Shelagh, Lady
　　　about
Welsh comfort. D. Briers. il *House Gard* 159:112-19+
　　Ag '87
LISC *See* Local Initiatives Support Corporation
Lischewski, Hans-Christian
Computers: practical tips for CAD selection and manage-
　　ment. il *Archit Rec* 175:51+ Ag '87
Lish, Gordon
　　　about
Writing the troubling truth. R. Jones. il *Commonweal*
　　114:501-4 S 11 '87
Lishchenko, Viktor
Down on the farm near Coon Rapids. il *World Press*
　　Rev 34:36-7 F '87
Lisi, David M.
Stuffs from the steppes. il pors *House Gard* 159:58+
　　D '87
Liska, George
The U.S.-Soviet conflict: concert through decompression.
　　Current 289:32-40 Ja '87
Liskin, Miriam
Connectivity. See issues of Personal Computing beginning
　　July 1987
Data base management. See issues of Personal Computing
　　beginning June 1987
Tips. See issues of Personal Computing beginning January
　　1986 through May 1987
Lisp (Computer language)
Acquaint: a frame-based knowledge-development system
　　for the IBM PC. E. R. Tello. *Byte* 12:265-6+ Je '87
The chip behind TI's smart weapons [Lisp chip] T.
　　Mason. il *Bus Week* p104-6 Mr 9 '87
The GCLISP 286 Developer. E. R. Tello. il *Byte* 12:241-4
　　Ap '87
PC scheme: a lexical Lisp. W. G. Wong. il *Byte* 12:223-6
　　Mr '87
Lissauer, Ernst
　　　about
Ernst Lissauer and the Hymn of hate. C. C. Aronsfeld.
　　bibl il por *Hist Today* 37:48-50 D '87
List, Barry
Radio reviews to help the bookseller. il *Publ Wkly*
　　231:47 Ja 16 '87
Wedding fair at Bookworks. il *Publ Wkly* 232:45-6 Ag
　　21 '87
Listen for Pleasure (Firm)
Listen for Pleasure creates mid-priced line. il *Publ Wkly*
　　232:55-6 D 25 '87
Listening
Learn how to listen [skill for managers] W. Kiechel,
　　III. il *Fortune* 116:107-8 Ag 17 '87
Listen up! D. Campbell. il *Seventeen* 46:109 O '87
Listen up: be a better manager. T. Callahan. il *Work*
　　Woman 12:54 Jl '87
　　　Study and teaching
On listening. D. B. Strother. bibl f il *Phi Delta Kappan*
　　68:625-8 Ap '87
Listening devices, Electronic *See* Electronics in criminal
　　investigation, espionage, etc.
Listening devices, Laser *See* Lasers in criminal investigation,
　　espionage, etc.
Lister, George
U.S. human rights policy: origins and implementation
　　[address, May 26, 1987] *Dep State Bull* 87:73-5 Ag
　　'87
Lists, Wine *See* Wine lists
Liszt, Franz, 1811-1886
　　　about
Hit Liszt. P. G. Davis. il *N Y* 20:68+ Mr 16 '87
Liszt galore. B. A. Varga. il *High Fidel* 37:61 Mr '87
Litan, Robert E., 1950-
(jt. auth) See Lawrence, Robert Z., 1949-, and Litan,
　　Robert E., 1950-

　　　about
"I don't trust regulators" [interview] J. Novack. il por
　　Forbes 140:92+ N 2 '87
Litchfield (Conn.)
　　　Historic houses, sites, etc.
Country with style [eighteenth century homes] M. D.
　　Glass. il *Ladies Home J* 104:136-41 O '87
Litchfield County (Conn.)
　　　Historic houses, sites, etc.
Rejuvenating a Connecticut parsonage: a designer's Litch-
　　field County colonial [home of H. Partello-
　　Hollingsworth] R. Conniff. il *Archit Dig* 44:108-17+
　　Je '87
Lite food *See* Food
Literacy *See* Illiteracy; Reading
Literacy, Cultural *See* Cultural literacy
Literacy education
　　　See also
　　Dorcas Place Parent Literacy Center
　　Literacy Volunteers of America
Back to the basics [business and literacy] J. B. Copeland.
　　il *Newsweek* 110:54-5 S 21 '87
Bertha's triumph [achievements of B. L. Ingram] P.
　　Jordan. il *Read Dig* 131:55-9 Ag '87
Improving literacy level is crucial: NAEP. *Phi Delta*
　　Kappan 68:711+ My '87
Learning to be literate: reading, writing, reasoning. A.
　　N. Applebee and others. *Educ Dig* 53:6-8 D '87
Let's do something about literacy now! R. E. Laurita.
　　America 156:455-6 Je 6 '87
Literacy [cover story; special section] il *Phi Delta Kappan*
　　69:184-206 N '87
Literacy wars: a modest proposal [program to get writers
　　involved in literacy problems] P. Balla. por *Publ Wkly*
　　231:376 Ja 30 '87
Our national priority [address, February 27, 1987] L.
　　DeBakey. *Vital Speeches Day* 53:496 Je 1 '87
　　　Anecdotes, facetiae, satire, etc.
Literacy on the right. D. Seligman. il *Fortune* 116:133
　　S 14 '87
　　　Federal aid
Pell and McGraw ask for more money to fight illiteracy.
　　H. Fields. *Publ Wkly* 232:18 Ag 28 '87
　　　History
National literacy campaigns: historical and comparative
　　lessons. R. F. Arnove and H. J. Graff. bibl f il *Phi*
　　Delta Kappan 69:202-6 N '87
　　　International aspects
　　　See also
　　International Literacy Day
　　　China
Jimmy Yen: crusader for mankind. J. Hersey. il por
　　Read Dig 131:138-45+ O '87
Literacy testing *See* Reading—Testing
Literacy Volunteers of America
"I've kept my secret for too long"; ed. by Deidre Sullivan.
　　S. Budz. il por *Redbook* 169:61-3 O '87
Literary agencies and agents
　　　See also
　　Brandt & Brandt Literary Agents Inc.
　　Triad Artists, Inc.
Big time, small time: the widening gap. A. Diamant.
　　Writer 100:13-15+ Jl '87
Literary agents challenge publicity at PPA meeting. A.
　　Symons. il *Publ Wkly* 232:36 D 18 '87
Madame ambassador [M. McBride to address Soviet-
　　American Dialogue in Moscow] L. Fleischer. *Publ*
　　Wkly 232:153 S 18 '87
Mega-Mort: superagent Janklow's blockbuster life. P.
　　Morrisroe. il pors *N Y* 20:34-40+ F 2 '87
Pioneer agents who mine the Midwest. T. Unsworth.
　　Publ Wkly 231:19 My 8 '87
The truth about agents. L. Perkins. il *Publ Wkly* 231:58
　　Mr 6 '87
　　　Acquisitions and mergers
Sterling Lord and Literistic agencies merge for inter-
　　national clout. *Publ Wkly* 231:11 Mr 20 '87
　　　Great Britain
　　　See also
　　Sterling Lord Literistic Inc.
　　　Soviet Union
　　　See also
　　Soviet Union. Copyright Agency
Literary characters *See* Characters in literature
Literary clubs and societies
　　　See also
　　Book discussion groups
　　Thomas Wolfe Society
The rivals [fans of E. F. Benson and of H. James]
　　L. Fleischer. *Publ Wkly* 231:130 My 15 '87

Literary collaboration *See* Authorship—Collaboration
Literary contests *See* Literature—Competitions
Literary critics and criticism
> *See also*
> Benjamin, Walter, 1892-1940
> Book reviews and reviewing
> Deconstruction
> Feminist literary criticism
> Fergusson, Francis, 1904-1986
> Wilson, Edmund, 1895-1972

Literary London. G. Smith. *New Leader* 70:20-1 My 4-18 '87
Relax, it's only a theory [distinguishing between belief and theory] D. Donoghue. il *N Y Times Book Rev* 92:14 Mr 1 '87
Wakers of the world, unite! You have nothing to lose but your theory [various opinions of J. Joyce's Finnegans wake] B. Maddox. il *N Y Times Book Rev* 92:20 Ag 16 '87

Literary errors *See* Errors, Literary
Literary fantasies *See* Fantasies, Literary
Literary festivals

New Jersey

Melody and mystery [Geraldine R. Dodge Poetry Festival] R. J. Margolis. il *New Leader* 69:9-10 D 1-15 '86
Literary landmarks *See* Historic houses, sites, etc.
Literary periodicals *See* Literature—Periodicals
Literary prizes
> *See also*
> Carey-Thomas Awards
> National Book Awards
> National Book Critics Circle Awards
> Nobel prizes
> Poetry—Awards
> Pulitzer prizes
> Scholastic Awards
> Science fiction—Awards

International front [Prix Goncourt winner M. Host] H. R. Lottman. *Publ Wkly* 231:167 F 27 '87
Literary prizes & awards. M. E. Phelps. il *Publ Wkly* 231:31-3 Mr 13 '87
The Washington monthly 17th annual Book Award [special section] *Wash Mon* 19:38-54 Ap '87
The year's top prizes. *Publ Wkly* 231:52 Ja 9 '87
Literary recreations
> *See also*
> Rebuses

Literary research

Research tips to help you write. A. Todd. *Writer* 100:22-4+ N '87
Literary style *See* Style, Literary
Literature
> *See also*
> African literature
> Allusions
> American literature
> Anthologies
> Art and literature
> Art literature
> Astronomical literature
> Authorship
> Autobiography
> Best sellers
> Bible—Literary character
> Biography
> Books and reading
> Caribbean literature (English)
> Censorship
> Characters in literature
> Children's literature
> Computers—Literary use
> Developing countries—Literature
> Educational literature
> Fiction
> Fishing literature
> Food literature
> French literature
> Garden literature
> Homosexual literature
> Horror tales
> Literary critics and criticism
> Medical literature
> Modernism (Literature)
> New Age literature
> Nonsense literature
> Parodies
> Peace and literature
> Philology
> Plagiarism
> Poetry
> Politics and literature

> Postmodernism (Literature)
> Realism in literature
> Religious literature
> Russian literature
> Scientific literature
> Self help literature
> Symbolism in literature
> Travel literature
> Underground literature
> Young adults' literature

Awards

See Literary prizes

Competitions

> *See also*
> Poetry—Competitions
> Scholastic Awards

Prize offers. See issues of The Writer

Moral and religious aspects

> *See also*
> Religion in literature

Alternative universes: literature, ethics and the American dream. C. A. Rubino. *America* 157:332+ N 7 '87

Periodicals

> *See also*
> Caribbean writer (Periodical)
> Idler (Periodical)
> New York review of books

Literary London. G. Smith. *New Leader* 70:20-1 My 4-18 '87
Rag time [small press literary magazines] J. Queenan. *New Repub* 196:13-14 Ap 6 '87

Anecdotes, facetiae, satire, etc.

The Shakespeare number [Belles lettres magazine studies the question, Was Shakespeare gay?] C. Simmons. *Nation* 244:291-5 Mr 7 '87

Study and teaching

> *See also*
> Cliff's Notes Inc.
> English literature—Study and teaching

Have our kids lost their past? [National Endowment for the Humanities study] J. N. Baker. il *Newsweek* 110:60-1 S 7 '87
Helping literature students learn about suicide [teenagers] D.-M. Stupple. *Educ Dig* 53:56-8 D '87
A shortsighted vision [National Endowment for the Humanities study] D. R. Carlin, Jr. *Commonweal* 114:615-16 N 6 '87
What Charles knew: homage to an English teacher [Howard University teacher C. Watkins; excerpt from An apple for my teacher] H. A. Baker. pors *N Y Times Book Rev* 92:3+ Mr 22 '87
'What do our 17-year-olds know?' assesses the failure of American high school education. *Publ Wkly* 232:134 S 18 '87

Technique

> *See also*
> Fiction—Technique

Fictive techniques for nonfiction writing. K. Sale. *Writer* 100:16-18 Ap '87

Themes

> *See also*
> AIDS (Disease) literature
> Animals in literature
> Anti-Semitism in literature
> Apartheid in literature
> Australia in literature
> Automobiles in literature
> Baseball in literature
> Blacks in literature
> Boxing in literature
> Business in literature
> Capitalists and financiers in literature
> Child abuse in literature
> Children's literature—Themes
> Devil in literature
> Environment in literature
> Feminism in literature
> Generation gap in literature
> Gifts in literature
> Handicapped in literature
> Humanism in literature
> Infinite in literature
> Jazz music in literature
> Man, Prehistoric, in literature
> Mental illness in literature
> Miami (Fla.) in literature
> New England in literature
> New York (N.Y.) in literature
> Nuclear warfare in literature
> Parent-child relationship in literature
> Peru in literature

Literature—Themes—See also—*cont.*
>Politics in literature
>Reason in literature
>Religion in literature
>Slavery in literature
>Social problems in literature
>Soviet Union in literature
>Space flight in literature
>Sports in literature
>Spy stories
>Squalor in literature
>Suicide in literature
>United States in literature
>Utopias in literature
>Water in literature
>Women and men in literature
>Women in literature

Literature, Influence of
'A book can transform a life'. A. D. Bloom. il por *U S News World Rep* 103:95 S 28 '87
Chas. Levy employees describe 'books that made a difference' [contest held as part of the Year of the Reader] il *Publ Wkly* 232:12+ O 30 '87
Favorite books and how they influence [cover story] il *Christ Century* 104:490-5 My 20-27 '87
Literary talk. L. Michaels. *Harpers* 275:30+ D '87
The Scheherazade factor [interview with J. Barth] A. P. Sanoff. il por *U S News World Rep* 103:55 Ag 31 '87

Literature, Medieval
>*See also*
>Arthurian romances

Literature and art *See* Art and literature
Literature and history
History and literature [special section] bibl il map *Hist Today* 37:32-46 Ag '87
Literature and peace *See* Peace and literature
Literature and politics *See* Politics and literature
Literature and psychoanalysis *See* Psychoanalysis and literature
Literature and science
>*See also*
>Science fiction
Science and letters: God's work—and ours. C. Ozick. il *N Y Times Book Rev* 92:3+ S 27 '87
Literature and society
Post-counterculture tristesse [work of D. Leavitt and L. Moore] C. Iannone. *Commentary* 83:57-61 F '87
Responsibilities of the poet. *Harpers* 275:31-2+ Ag '87
Where is Emerson now that we need him? or, Why literature can't save us [excerpt from The renewal of literature] R. Poirier. il *N Y Times Book Rev* 92:3+ F 8 '87
Literature and state
>**China**
Delving into life—the Chinese writer's duty [excerpts from address, November 9, 1979]; tr. by Perry Link and Kyna Rubin. Liu Binyan. por *N Y Times Book Rev* 92:3+ F 22 '87
Letter from China—young writers test the limits. J. Shapiro and H. Liang. il *N Y Times Book Rev* 92:3+ Ja 11 '87
Writers in China: how long is the leash? M. Levitas. il *N Y Times Book Rev* 92:3+ Ag 9 '87
Writing in China. M. Hopkins. il *New Leader* 70:27-8 My 4-18 '87
>**Czechoslovakia**
The Czechs' defiant playwright [V. Havel] M. Winn. il por *N Y Times Mag* p78-82+ O 25 '87
>**Nicaragua**
Poetry and power in Nicaragua. F. Goldman. il por *N Y Times Mag* p44-6+ Mr 29 '87
The Sandinistas' favorite poet [V. Mayakovsky] I. Karetnikova. il *Natl Rev* 39:40-2 My 8 '87
Vice president and author [interview with S. Ramírez Mercado] A. Morales. il por *World Press Rev* 34:58 N '87
>**Philippines**
My dinner with Imelda. R. Howard. *Harpers* 275:29-30+ O '87
>**Soviet Union**
Beatniks and Bolsheviks; tr. by Bess Powell. V. P. Aksenov. *New Repub* 197:28-30+ N 30 '87
Beyond *glasnost* [A. N. Rybakov's Children of the Arbat] W. Laqueur. *Commentary* 84:63-5 O '87
A compatriot's view from the homeland [interview with A. Rybakov] D. Stanglin. il por *U S News World Rep* 103:50 Ag 17 '87
Five poems that spelled danger [I. Ratushinskaya] B. Wolfer. il *Commonweal* 114:107-11 F 27 '87

In Yulian Semyonov's thrillers the villains are CIA types—and some say the author works for the KGB. M. Brower. il pors *People Wkly* 27:81+ Ap 6 '87
An interview with Irina Ratushinskaya. E. Kuryluk. il por *N Y Rev Books* 34:16-20 My 7 '87
The Moscow Book Fair: *glasnost* has its limits. J. Laber. il *N Y Times Book Rev* 92:13-14 O 11 '87
A new candor at Issyk-Kul [U.S.-Soviet cultural exchange] A. Miller. por *Newsweek* 109:8 Ja 19 '87
A poet's view of *glasnost*; tr. by Antonina W. Bouis. A. Voznesenskii. *Nation* 244:810-12 Je 13 '87
Progress on the margin. E. von Kuehnelt-Leddihn. *Natl Rev* 39:40 D 31 '87
Reforming Soviet culture/Retrieving Soviet history. N. P. Condee and V. Padunov. il *Nation* 244:815-20 Je 13 '87
Russia's "gift" to the West [interview with I. Ratushinskaya] il por *Christ Today* 31:41 Je 12 '87
A Soviet poet's praise for freedom [A. Voznesenskii] W. French. il *World Press Rev* 34:61 Je '87
Soviet science fiction: to the present via the future. K. Rosenberg. bibl il *Technol Rev* 90:66-74 Jl '87
Tales from a time of terror [publication of A. Rybakov's Children of the Arbat] J. O. Jackson. il pors *Time* 129:45-6 Ap 27 '87
Through the *glasnost*, darkly. V. P. Aksenov. *Harpers* 274:65-7 Ap '87
What Yevgeny knew [Y. Yevtushenko's claim that the CIA helped the Soviets muzzle the writers A. Sinyavsky and I. Daniel] D. Jameson. *New Repub* 196:39-41 Je 22 '87
Yevtushenko feels a fresh wind blowing [cover story; interview] K. Vanden Heuvel. il pors *Progressive* 51:24-31 Ap '87
Literature and war *See* War and literature
Lithium
The cosmic synthesis of lithium, beryllium and boron. V. E. Viola and G. J. Mathews. il *Sci Am* 256:38-45 My '87
Lithium casts doubt on galactic history [Hyades cluster] il *Sky Telesc* 73:28 Ja '87
>**Therapeutic use**
What's in the cards for manic depression? [cover story] B. Bower. *Sci News* 131:410 Je 27 '87
Why (perhaps) lithium is doubly effective [manic depression] il *Discover* 8:12 F '87
Lithium electric batteries *See* Electric batteries
Lithography
>*See also*
>Electron beam lithography
Edge surfaces in lithographically textured molybdenum disulfide. C. B. Roxlo and others. bibl f il *Science* 235:1629-31 Mr 27 '87
Lithosphere *See* Earth—Crust
Lithotripsy
Barking bathtub's many uses. M. Weber. *Vogue* 177:284 Mr '87
Gallstone lithotripsy. C. SerVaas. il *Saturday Evening Post* 259:100+ Ap '87
Lithotriptor therapy coming of age [gallstone therapy] *Sci News* 132:187 S 19 '87
Shattering kidney stones. P. Gadsby and L. J. Brown. il *Good Housekeep* 204:212 Je '87
Lithuania
>**Photographs and photography**
"The republic of photographers" exhibits a special vitality. A. Goldsmith. il *Pop Photogr* 94:18 My '87
>**Religious institutions and affairs**
>*See also*
>Catholic Church—Lithuania
Lithuanian photographers *See* Photographers, Lithuanian
Litigation *See* Actions and defenses
Litter, Cat *See* Cat litter
Littky, Dennis
>*about*
Fighting over a principal. S. Doherty. il por *Newsweek* 109:76 My 25 '87
Little, Alastair
>*about*
London journal. J. Bainbridge. il *Gourmet* 47:36+ Ag '87
Little, Booker, 1938-1961
>*about*
A case of neglect. S. Futterman. il por *High Fidel* 37:68-9 F '87
Little, Charles E.
The challenge of Greater Yellowstone [cover story; with editorial comment by T. H. Watkins] il map *Wilderness* 51:16-56 Wint '87
The Great American aquifer. il *Wilderness* 51:43-7 Fall '87

Little, Charles E.—*cont.*
Letting Leopold down. il por *Wilderness* 50:45-8 Summ '87
Little, Malcolm *See* Malcolm X, 1925-1965
Little, Nina Fletcher
(jt. auth) See Valentine, Lanci, and Little, Nina Fletcher
Little, Robert N.

about
Obituary
Phys Today por 40:91-3 Ja '87. J. Antillón
Little, Royal, 1896-

about
Royal Little: the conglomerator. D. A. Saunders. il pors *Forbes* 140:264+ Jl 13 '87
Little, Suzanne
A literary repast for a Hungry Mind. il por *Publ Wkly* 232:41-3 N 13 '87
UMBA show reaches new high. il *Publ Wkly* 232:32-4 O 23 '87
Little, Willie

about
Blacks hit lottery for $7.5 million in New York and $2 million in Illinois. il por *Jet* 72:12 Jl 20 '87
Little (Arthur D.) Inc. *See* Arthur D. Little, Inc.
Little, Brown & Co. Inc.
Arthur Thornhill looks back on 39 years at Little, Brown. R. Herbert. il por *Publ Wkly* 231:18+ F 6 '87
Little League baseball *See* Baseball, Children's
Little murders [drama] *See* Feiffer, Jules
Little Mushroom Cafe (New York, N.Y.) *See* New York (N.Y.)—Restaurants, nightclubs, bars, etc.
Little Richard

about
Little Richard eulogizes Liberace, who also wore flamboyant stage outfits. il por *Jet* 71:64-5 F 23 '87
Little Richard sues over ownership of new hit song. por *Jet* 71:59 Mr 9 '87
Little Richard tells why he quit being a minister. il pors *Jet* 71:58-60 Ja 19 '87
Little Rock (Ark.)

Education
Ebony update: Ernest Green [central figure in 1957 desegregation case] il por *Ebony* 43:72+ D '87
Little Rock Nine return to school where violence erupted 30 years ago. W. Wofford, Jr. il *Jet* 73:14-16 N 9 '87
School named for Daisy Bates in Little Rock. il por *Jet* 72:22 S 21 '87
State's first teacher strike in Little Rock. il *Jet* 73:22 O 19 '87

Politics and government
Black woman elected mayor of Little Rock [L. Shackelford] por *Jet* 71:57 F 9 '87
Little shop of horrors [film] *See* Motion picture reviews—Single works
Little Steven *See* Van Zandt, Steve
Little Wambaw Swamp (S.C.)
Little Wambaw Swamp, South Carolina. R. H. Mohlenbrock. il map *Nat Hist* 96:68-70 Ag '87
Little White House Historic Site (Warm Springs, Ga.)
The good neighbor in Warm Springs. il *South Living* 22:22 D '87
Littlefield, Cheryl Rae

about
Cheryl Rae fell head over heels for stunt pilot Gene Littlefield, and look where it landed her. S. K. Reed. il pors *People Wkly* 28:62-4 N 9 '87
Littlefield, Gene

about
Cheryl Rae fell head over heels for stunt pilot Gene Littlefield, and look where it landed her. S. K. Reed. il pors *People Wkly* 28:62-4 N 9 '87
Littlefield, Kenneth

about
Banking on Texas. L. M. Keefe. il por *Forbes* 139:254+ Je 15 '87
Littman, Rosemary Cheris

about
Rosemary Littman has the competition licked when it comes to making uncommon cakes. il por *People Wkly* 27:101 Mr 9 '87
Litton Industries, Inc.
But the grass looked greener over there [life after restructuring] J. Heins. il *Forbes* 139 Ann Directory:54-5 Ap 27 '87
Litton, Loral to deliver F-16 warning systems. *Aviat Week Space Technol* 126:104 F 9 '87
Litton using new technologies to upgrade radar warning receivers. il *Aviat Week Space Technol* 126:91+ F 16 '87

Litvinov, Nikolai
(jt. auth) See Gubernski, Yuri, and Litvinov, Nikolai
Liu, M. E.
Enlisting [story] *Commentary* 84:41-4 Jl '87
Liu, Pin-yen *See* Liu Binyan, 1925-
Liu, Stephen Shu-Ning
August mirage [poem] *America* 157:109 Ag 29-S 5 '87
Waiting for the train [poem] *America* 157:289 O 31 '87
Liu Binyan, 1925-
Delving into life—the Chinese writer's duty [excerpts from address, November 9, 1979]; tr. by Perry Link and Kyna Rubin. por *N Y Times Book Rev* 92:3+ F 22 '87
Liu Fang

about
Two young Chinese who enjoy their nation's new freedoms. J. Florcruz. il pors *Sch Update* 120:8-9 S 18 '87
Liubimov, İÜrii *See* Lyubimov, Yuri
Liuzzi, Francis J., and Lasek, Raymond J.
Astrocytes block axonal regeneration in mammals by activating the physiological stop pathway. bibl f il *Science* 237:642-5 Ag 7 '87
Live Aid concert, 1985
Live Aid book: where's the money? D. Fricke. *Roll Stone* p25 F 26 '87
Live bait *See* Bait
Liver

See also
Bile acids and salts
Interaction of a liver-specific nuclear factor with the fibrinogen and α_1-antitrypsin promoters. G. Courtois and others. bibl f il *Science* 238:688-92 O 30 '87

Cancer
Expression of the multidrug-resistant gene in hepatocarcinogenesis and regenerating rat liver. S. S. Thorgeirsson and others. bibl f il *Science* 236:1120-2 My 29 '87

Genetic aspects
Activated oncogenes in B6C3F1 mouse liver tumors: implications for risk assessment. S. H. Reynolds and others. bibl f il *Science* 237:1309-16 S 11 '87

Surgery
Putting the freeze on liver tumors. S. Weisburd. *Sci News* 132:20-1 Jl 11 '87

Diseases

See also
Hepatitis
Reye's syndrome
Sammy Davis Jr. National Liver Institute
Carbon tetrachloride at hepatotoxic levels blocks reversibly gap junctions between rat hepatocytes. J. C. Sáez and others. bibl f il *Science* 236:967-9 My 22 '87

Transplantation
Awaiting a liver transplant, Linda Lovelace Marchiano struggles to close the book on her past. T. Kahn. il pors *People Wkly* 27:75-6 F 16 '87
Miss. tot needs transplant; parents seek financial help at PUSH in Chicago [case of Tabari Davis] *Jet* 72:4 Ag 10 '87
Nancy Ascher, M.D.: on the frontiers of medicine. M. Dowie. il por *Ms* 16:86+ N '87
People helping people [Mark Davis' liver transplant] C. SerVaas. il *Saturday Evening Post* 259:98 Ap '87
Tot gets liver thanks to help from Cosby, Jackson [case of J. Clark] por *Jet* 72:9 My 18 '87
Liver cells *See* Cells
Liver regeneration *See* Regeneration (Biology)
Livermore, Arthur H.
Up, up, and away: students will launch thousands of helium-filled balloons in nationwide experiment to learn about wind and weather [cover story] il map *Earth Sci* 40:12-13 Spr '87
Livernash, Robert
The 99th Congress: action on the environment. *Environment* 28:5+ D '86
Liversidge, Anthony
Interview [C. E. Shannon] il por *Omni* 9:60-2+ Ag '87
Livestock

See also
Cattle
Cows
Donkeys
Ducks
Horses
Poultry
Sheep
Swine

Livestock—*cont.*
Taking on livestock (I). J. Vivian. il *Mother Earth News* 104:56-61 Mr/Ap '87
Taking on livestock (II). J. Vivian. il *Mother Earth News* 105:80-4+ My/Je '87

Care
Animal birthdays. R. Kidd. il *Mother Earth News* 104:36-9 Mr/Ap '87

Diseases and pests
Will livestock drug cause dung crisis? [ivermectin; research by Richard Wall and Les Strong] J. Raloff. *Sci News* 131:358 Je 6 '87

Marketing
Marketing. See issues of Successful Farming

Treatment
See Animals—Treatment

Livestock fences, Electric *See* Fences, Electric

Livestock ranges
High noon at western haystacks [conflicts between ranchers and wild animals] S. Robertson. *Sierra* 72:28-9+ Ja/F '87
In New Mexico: desert healer [work of A. Savory] G. Ehrlich. il por *Time* 130:10-11 D 7 '87

Livestock shows
Sheep Down Under [New Zealand] *New Yorker* 63:27-9 My 4 '87

Livezey, Lois Gehr
Sexual and family violence: a growing issue for the churches [cover story] il *Christ Century* 104:938-42 O 28 '87

Living *See* Conduct of life; Life

Living, Cost and standard of *See* Cost and standard of living

Living Colours (Musical group)
Living Colours. G. Santoro. *Down Beat* 54:58 Ap '87

The living daylights [film] *See* Motion picture reviews—Single works

Living fossils
See also
Coelacanths
Stromatolites

Living rooms
See also
Drawing rooms
English country. il *Fam Handyman* 37:44-6+ My/Je '87
Finishes enrich living room. il *South Living* 22:122 Je '87
Get fresh! il *Redbook* 168:96-101 Ja '87
In the living room of Michael Graves. il por *Esquire* 108:102-3 N '87
Removing doors solves space problem. il *South Living* 22:180 Mr '87
Requiem for the parlor. R. Lynes. il *Archit Dig* 44:43+ S '87
A room of one's own [work of Z. Hadid] D. Dietsch. il *Archit Rec* 175:84-9 mid-S '87
Two peninsulas create an entertainment center. il *Sunset* 179:121 N '87

Living skills *See* Life skills

Living trusts
Planning a hassle-free legacy. D. M. Topolnicki. il *Money* 16:82-4+ O '87
Trusts you can change at will [revocable living trust] R. R. Roha. il *Changing Times* 41:141-4 N '87

Living wills
The importance of a living will. T. Hauser. il *McCalls* 114:134-5 Ag '87
Is a living will the way to go? H. R. Kennedy. *U S News World Rep* 103:65 Ag 24 '87
My father's best gift. N. P. Randall. il *Read Dig* 130:11-16 Ja '87

Livingood, John J., 1903-1986
about
Obituary
Phys Today por 40:90 Jl '87. R. Martin

Livingston, Joan
Absolutely guaranteed. il por *Nations Bus* 75:51-2 N '87

Livingston, Kathryn
Skiing in Telluride. il *Gourmet* 47:54-9+ Ja '87

Livingston, Kathryn E.
Till birth do us part. il *Parents* 62:87-91 Mr '87

Livingston, M. Stanley, 1905-1986
about
DOE bestows Fermi awards on Courant and Livingston. por *Phys Today* 40:83 Je '87
Obituary
Phys Today por 40:88+ Je '87. J. P. Blewett

Livingston, Myra Cohn
Don't cook Mother Goose. *N Y Times Book Rev* 92:20 Jl 26 '87

Livingston, William C., and others
Old and new views of solar prominences. il *Astronomy* 15:18-22 Jl '87

Livingston family
about
American historical portraits. S. B. Sherrill. il *Antiques* 131:524+ Mr '87

Livingston Manor (N.Y.: Estate) in art
Exhibitions
American historical portraits [A portrait of Livingston Manor: 1686-1850] S. B. Sherrill. il *Antiques* 131:524+ Mr '87

Livingstone, Neil C.
What Ollie North told me before he took the Fifth. *Natl Rev* 39:37-8+ Ja 30 '87

Livingstone, William
Speaking my piece. See issues of Stereo Review through April 1987
Valhalla on Thirty-fourth Street. il *Opera News* 52:14-16 Ag '87

LivingWell Inc.
So long, bench press. Thanks for the pep talk. J. E. Davis. il por *Bus Week* p72+ Ja 26 '87

Liz Claiborne, Inc.
The rag trade's reluctant revolutionary [L. Claiborne] P. Sellers. por *Fortune* 115:36-8 Ja 5 '87

Liz Lerman/Exchange (Dance company)
Comfort me with apples [L. Lerman's dances for senior performers] T. Tobias. il *N Y* 20:129-30 N 9 '87

Lizards
See also
Chameleons
Iguanas
Complex dynamics link islands' predators [research by Thomas Schoener and David Spiller] R. Lewin. *Science* 236:917 My 22 '87
Effect of lizards on spider populations: manipulative reconstruction of a natural experiment. T. W. Schoener and D. A. Spiller. bibl f il *Science* 236:949-52 My 22 '87
Lizard and the links [Coachella Valley fringe-toed lizard] D. Holing. il map *Audubon* 89:38-42+ N '87
Lizards that take to the desert like ducks to water. B. Gilbert. bibl (p145) il *Smithsonian* 18:78-84+ Ag '87
Microdragons [horned lizards] P. Schullery. il *Ctry J* 14:70-1 D '87

Sexual behavior
See Sexual behavior—Reptiles

Llamas
See also
Vicunas
Big money in small camels. C. Leerhsen. il *Newsweek* 110:70 Ag 31 '87
Heavy petting. T. Young. il *Vogue* 177:120 Ag '87
High on llamas: you do the walking, they'll do the work. E. McGrath. il *Women's Sports Fitness* 9:20-3 Ag '87
My two decades with America's camels [llamas, alpacas, guanacos and vicunas; cover story] W. L. Franklin. il *Int Wildl* 17:34-43 S/O '87

Llanda Villa (San Jose, Calif.) *See* San Jose (Calif.)—Historic houses, sites, etc.

LLC Corp.
See also
Valhi Inc.

Llewellyn, J. Bruce
about
A trailblazer's trip to the top. F. McCoy. il por *Bus Week* p129+ N 16 '87

Llosa, Mario Vargas *See* Vargas Llosa, Mario, 1936-

Lloyd, Brian
Fuel crisis. il *Flying* 114:102 Ja '87

Lloyd, Chris Evert *See* Evert, Chris

Lloyd, Christopher, 1921-
December at Great Dixter [excerpt from The year at Great Dixter] il *Archit Dig* 44:84+ D '87

Lloyd, Emily
about
Britain's Emily Lloyd breaks hearts and kayos the critics in Wish you were here. J. Stark. il pors *People Wkly* 28:43+ Ag 31 '87

Lloyd, George
about
Musical events:
Re-evaluation of G. Lloyd's symphonies. A. Porter. *New Yorker* 63:108-10 D 21 '87

Lloyd, Holly
about
Incredible journey. J. E. Loehr. il por *World Tennis* 34:16-17 Ap '87

Lloyd, John, 1946-, and Kellner, Peter
Labor's defense [interview with N. Kinnock] *World Press Rev* 34:15-16 My '87
Lloyd, Lewis
about
Rockets' pair bombed out of NBA for cocaine use. pors *Jet* 71:50 F 2 '87
Lloyd Webber, Andrew, 1948-
about
Andrew Lloyd Webber: from Superstar to Requiem [cover story; interview] D. Polkow. il por *Christ Century* 104:272-6 Mr 18-25 '87
Andrew Lloyd Webber: superstar [cover story] J. Rockwell. il pors *N Y Times Mag* p28-31+ D 20 '87
The multimillion-dollar music man. P. Young. il por *Macleans* 100:53-4 Je 8 '87
The Phantom of the Opera [musical] Reviews
Newsweek il 109:64 Mr 30 '87. J. Kroll
Starlight Express [musical] Reviews
America 156:427 My 23 '87. G. G. Seibert
Dance Mag il 61:86-7 Ap '87. K. Grubb
N Y il 20:66-8 Mr 9 '87
N Y il 20:96-7 Mr 30 '87. J. Simon
Nation 244:516 Ap 18 '87. T. M. Disch
New Leader 70:21 Ap 6 '87. L. Sauvage
New Yorker 63:93 Mr 30 '87. E. Oliver
Theatre Crafts il 21:8 Mr '87. D. F. Sisk
Time il 129:83 Mr 30 '87. W. A. Henry
U S News World Rep il 102:72-3 Mr 16 '87. M. Horn
Lloyd's Carrot Cake (Firm)
Homemade [owner L. Adams] *New Yorker* 63:26-9 Mr 9 '87
Lloyd's of London
London assurance [building designed by R. Rogers] M. Filler. il *House Gard* 159:90-3+ Ja '87
Loading of cartridges *See* Cartridges
Loan associations *See* Savings and loan associations
Loan companies *See* Finance companies
Loan Depot Corporation
The Loan Depot is ringing up some big numbers. L. Helm. il *Bus Week* p67 F 9 '87
Loans
See also
Community development loan funds
Credit
Government lending
Insurance, Life—Policy loans
Interest (Economics)
Mortgages
Loans, American
Latin America
See also
ACCION International
Loans, Bank
See also
Agricultural credit
Asset-backed financing
Bridge loans
Battling a billion-dollar debt [Hunt brothers; cover story] J. A. Jenkins. il *N Y Times Mag* p24-9+ S 27 '87
Bleak year for the banks. G. Bock. il *Time* 130:60-1 D 28 '87
How to find under $1 million [cover story] R. Thompson. il *Nations Bus* 75:14-16+ N '87
Need a quick billion or two? Just ask your banker [lending for mergers and LBOs] S. Bartlett. il *Bus Week* p98-9 O 26 '87
Oil drillers bounce back—to their lenders' doors. T. Vogel. il *Bus Week* p96 S 7 '87
Why bankers must say no. A. Sheshunoff. il por *Fortune* 115:177-8+ Je 22 '87
International aspects
Bankers beware [International Tin Council collapse] R. Morais. il *Forbes* 139 Ann Directory:63 Ap 27 '87
Deep red: the international debt crisis and its historical precedents. H. James. *Am Sch* 56:331-41 Summ '87
Hookers, Jaguars, and lots of stupid loans [views of S. C. Gwynne] C. Lane. *Wash Mon* 18:55-7 Ja '87
Argentina
A talk with Alfonsin: 'the debt cannot be paid'. J. Ryser and R. A. Kessler. por *Bus Week* p66 Je 22 '87
Bolivia
Bolivia swaps debt for conservation. J. Walsh. map *Science* 237:596-7 Ag 7 '87
Brazil
Are big-bank shares a bargain? [market reaction to Brazil's suspension of interest payments] J. Egan. *U S News World Rep* 102:68 Mr 30 '87
Bank stocks and the Brazil factor. M. McFadden. il *Fortune* 115:103-5 Mr 30 '87

The banks get tough. D. Jenish. il *Macleans* 100:28 Je 8 '87
The brave new world of swaps [Norwest Bank's dealings] P. Sherrid. il *U S News World Rep* 103:41 Ag 31 '87
Brazil and its creditors: who has more to lose? J. Ryser and W. Glasgall. il *Bus Week* p56-7 Mr 9 '87
Brazil says: nuts. J. S. Henry. *New Repub* 197:25+ O 12 '87
Brazil throws down the gauntlet [suspension of interest repayments] H. O'Shaughnessy. il *World Press Rev* 34:46-7 Ap '87
A case of bottom-line blues [banks raise the prime rate and reclassify loans to Brazil as nonperforming] B. Rudolph. il *Time* 129:63 Ap 13 '87
The debt crisis isn't Brazil's only liability. P. C. Roberts. il *Bus Week* p14 Ap 20 '87
Default, dear Brutus [Brazil unable to pay interest on foreign debt] *New Repub* 196:8+ Mr 16 '87
Dominoes in a grim game of debt [Canadian banks' reaction to Brazil's decision to suspend interest payments] P. C. Newman. il *Macleans* 100:40 Mr 16 '87
No more blood in the stone [Brazil suspends interest payments on foreign debt] G. Scott. il *Time* 129:46 Mr 2 '87
Settling Brazil's account. C. Wood. il *Macleans* 100:36 N 16 '87
Stonewalling the banks [Brazil suspends interest payments on debt] T. Fennell. il *Macleans* 100:34-5 Mr 9 '87
"This is war" [interview with M. Colasuonno] L. Minard. il por *Forbes* 139:50 Je 29 '87
Tightening up on third world loans [tying loans to environmental policy] J. De Onis. il *U S News World Rep* 103:41 O 5 '87
View from the middle [interview with A. M. da Silva] E. A. Finn, Jr. il por *Forbes* 140:60+ N 16 '87
Developing countries
Accounts receivable. P. T. Bauer. *New Repub* 196:10-12 Je 15 '87
American bank loans line the pockets of the third world's elite [views of R. T. Naylor] S. C. Gwynne. *Wash Mon* 19:51-2 O '87
Assembly reaches consensus on approach to external debt of developing countries. *UN Chron* 24:109 F '87
Bank stockholders should applaud [Citicorp's write-off of third world debt] M. S. Forbes, Jr. il *Forbes* 139:25 Je 15 '87
BankAmerica's new tight spot [reserve set aside against third world debt] J. B. Levine and S. Bartlett. il *Bus Week* p50 Je 22 '87
The banks get tough. D. Jenish. il *Macleans* 100:28 Je 8 '87
The bishops' letter, world debt and the U.S. trade deficit [pastoral letter on the economy] J. A. Gylys. il *America* 157:86-7 Ag 15-22 '87
Biting half a bullet [further write-offs of foreign loan losses by big banks] A. Sloan. il *Forbes* 140:38-9 Jl 27 '87
Citicorp breaks ranks [write-off of third world loans] S. Koepp. il *Time* 129:48-50 Je 1 '87
Citicorp faces reality—and finds it doesn't hurt [third world debt] D. Pauly. il *Newsweek* 109:42+ Je 1 '87
Dance of debt isn't over yet. J. S. Henry. il *U S News World Rep* 103:39-41 Ag 31 '87
Dealing with debt. J. Amuzegar. *Foreign Policy* 68:140-58 Fall '87
Debt and the dollar: the markets are making all the rules [meetings of the World Bank and International Monetary Fund] W. Glasgall and M. McNamee. il *Bus Week* p57 O 12 '87
Debt crisis. il *Black Enterp* 18:47 S '87
Dirty money and the debt crisis [views of T. H. Naylor] P. C. Newman. il por *Macleans* 100:39 Mr 9 '87
Hard times in store for international debtors. R. D. Hylton. il *Black Enterp* 18:19-20 S '87
How 'experts' caused the third world debt crisis. P. C. Roberts. il *Bus Week* p28 N 2 '87
How to take a $1 billion loss and look good [Citicorp write-off of third world loans] P. M. Scherschel. il *U S News World Rep* 102:46-7 Je 1 '87
John Reed's bold stroke [Citicorp's third world debt loan loss reserves; cover story] J. Fierman. il por *Fortune* 115:26-30+ Je 22 '87
A 'junk' king takes on the third world [M. R. Milken's debt crisis offensive] B. Powell and C. Friday. il por *Newsweek* 110:56 S 21 '87
Michel Camdessus is making the IMF less of a Scrooge. M. McNamee. il *Bus Week* p36-7 O 5 '87

Loans, Bank—Developing countries—*cont.*

Mortgaging a house of cards [ethics of international debt] K. P. Jameson. il *Commonweal* 114:105-7 F 27 '87

Preparing for the worst [Canadian banks and third world loans] T. Tedesco. il *Macleans* 100:32-3 Ag 3 '87

A stunner from the Citi [reserve to cushion third world loans] S. Bartlett. il por *Bus Week* p42-3 Je 1 '87

Third world debt: a flawed solution [debt-equity swaps] R. Kuttner. il *Bus Week* p18 Ja 19 '87

The third world debt crisis [address, October 29, 1986] J. J. LaFalce. *Vital Speeches Day* 53:162-6 Ja 1 '87

Three cheers for Citicorp's initiative [write-off of third world debt] J. S. Henry. il *U S News World Rep* 102:48 Je 1 '87

Welcome to the Nassau branch! [condensed from Selling money] S. C. Gwynne. il *Read Dig* 130:127-30 Ap '87

The World Bank's turn [debt quagmire] J. Egan. il *U S News World Rep* 103:54 O 12 '87

Korea (North)

Pulling the plug [default on foreign debt] G. Bock. il *Time* 130:43 S 7 '87

Latin America

Beggaring our Latin neighbors. P. Lernoux. il *Nation* 245:709-10+ D 12 '87

Best buys among banks [value adjusted for Latin debt] J. Edgerton and others. il *Money* 16:7 Jl '87

Blues south of the border. H. Eason. il *Nations Bus* 75:35-6 Jl '87

Buying debt, saving nature [offers to suspend debt payments for tropical countries which protect forests] J. B. Copeland. il *Newsweek* 110:46 Ag 31 '87

Cashing in on debt [Latin debt-to-equity swaps] T. Tedesco. il *Macleans* 100:34-5 O 5 '87

The Citi squeezes its lemons [move to clean up third world debt with debt for equity swaps] S. Bartlett. il *Bus Week* p31 Je 15 '87

Cutting the debt, saving the forest. D. Page. *Environment* 29:4-5+ S '87

The debtors' revolt is spreading in Latin America. J. Ryser and others. il *Bus Week* p88-9 D 28 '87-Ja 4 '88

Exchanging debt for conservation [debt for nature scheme] A. L. Spitler. il *BioScience* 37:781 D '87

Fast bucks in Latin loan swaps [debt-equity swaps] J. Fierman. il *Fortune* 116:91-2+ Ag 3 '87

A golden deal: debt for nature. J. D. Hair. il *Int Wildl* 17:30 S/O '87

Here comes the repo man [debt-equity swaps] W. Curtis. *Nation* 244:570+ My 2 '87

Latin America's new dance of debt. R. H. Bork, Jr. il *U S News World Rep* 102:55 Mr 16 '87

The outlook for Latin America debt. P.-P. Kuczynski. il *Foreign Aff* 66:129-49 Fall '87

There goes the neighborhood [M. Schubert's mastery of Latin loan swaps] E. A. Finn, Jr. il por *Forbes* 139:35-7 Je 29 '87

Whose debt crisis is it anyway? [U.S. as debtor compared to Latin America] P. Davidson. il *New Leader* 70:14-15 Ag 10-24 '87

Will U.S. banks do more for the LDCs? H. Banks. *Forbes* 140:27 N 2 '87

Mexico

Mexico's development crisis. J. H. Street. bibl f *Curr Hist* 86:101-4+ Mr '87

Philippines

Debt to democracy. S. C. Monsod. *New Repub* 197:16-18 D 7 '87

A new road in the Philippines spurs development [project supported by World Bank loan] L. V. Coronel. il *UN Chron* 24:66-7 Ag '87

Who's afraid of Solita Monsod? U.S. bankers, that's who [Economic Planning Minister] D. J. Yang. il por *Bus Week* p54 Ja 26 '87

South Africa

A secret bank deal with South Africa. L. Howard. il *Newsweek* 109:7 Mr 16 '87

Loans, Foreign

See also
Export-Import Bank of the United States
International Monetary Fund
World Bank

Developing countries

In debt? Ring up the Louvre [work of Paris Club in rescheduling third world debt] F. Ungeheuer. il *Time* 130:50 Jl 13 '87

Indonesia

Indonesia votes. J. Pincus. *Nation* 244:493 Ap 18 '87

Zambia

The Zambian debt dilemma: a just repayment plan. J. B. Straus, Jr. *Christ Century* 104:855-6 O 7 '87

Loans, Government *See* Government lending

Loans, Personal

See also
Boat loans
Insurance, Life—Policy loans

Borrowing: better deals for banks' best customers. il *Money* 16:28 D '87

Borrowing: high rates are getting still higher. il *Money* 16:30 O '87

Borrowing: only one out of three of us seeks the best deals. il *Money* 16:24 N '87

Borrowing: rates are so high there's no place to go up. il *Money* 16:30 Jl '87

Borrowing: some rates drop as the public shifts to equity loans. il *Money* 16:41 Je '87

How to find the best loans now. K. McCormally. il *Changing Times* 41:22-7+ F '87

A savvy borrower's shopping guide. C. E. Trunzo. il *Money* 16:161+ Ap '87

Winning the loan game: how to score points with your banker. L. Marsa. il *Black Enterp* 18:63-4+ N '87

Taxation

New rules for borrowing against retirement plans. il *Changing Times* 41:9 Mr '87

Lobbying *See* Lobbyists and lobbying

Lobbyists and lobbying

See also
Advocacy Institute
American Association of Retired Persons
American Israel Public Affairs Committee
Americans for Generational Equity
Business Executives for National Security
Business Roundtable
Chamber of Commerce of the United States of America
Children's Defense Fund (U.S.)
Citizens for Sensible Control of Acid Rain
Deaver, Michael K.—Conflict of interests case
Environmental movement
Federation of American Scientists
Foreign propagandists
Handgun Control, Inc.
Moral Majority
National Audubon Society
National Committee to Preserve Social Security and Medicare
National Rifle Association of America
Political action committees
Sierra Club
Spacecause
Wildlife Legislative Fund of America
Women lobbyists and lobbying

The aides virus [ex-congressional aides working as lobbyists] J. L. Pasley. *New Repub* 197:22+ O 19 '87

Bob Dole and the tobacco connection. D. Corn. il *Nation* 244:381+ Mr 28 '87

Corporate angst on Capitol Hill [opposition to pro-labor bills by business lobby] G. Bock. il *Time* 129:48 Je 22 '87

Guess who's not coming to brunch [Senator L. Bentsen accused of shaking down lobbyists for campaign contributions] il por *Newsweek* 109:19 F 16 '87

How do you chase a $17 billion market? With everything you've got [computer makers campaigning to win government megacontracts] F. Seghers. il *Bus Week* p120+ N 23 '87

How to win friends and influence TV [viewers lobbying networks] P. E. Bauer. il *Channels* 7:69 Ja '87

Lawmakers—not lawbreakers [seventh graders from Sandwich, Mass. lobby for tougher cigarette sales law] C. Lowrance. il *Good Housekeep* 204:96 Mr '87

Politics & policy. See issues of Fortune beginning March 5, 1984

Pricey lobbyists who do it all. A. C. Isgrò. il *Fortune* 116:74-7 Jl 20 '87

Small business and Congress [lobbying priorities] R. Thompson. il *Nations Bus* 75:9+ Mr '87

The struggle for the uncommitted [fight over R. Bork's confirmation] T. Gest. il *U S News World Rep* 103:24 Ag 24 '87

Tommy the Cork: the secret world of Washington's first modern lobbyist [T. Corcoran] A. J. Lichtman. il por *Wash Mon* 19:41-9 F '87

Tough times for tobacco lobby. A. Plattner. il *U S News World Rep* 102:17 F 23 '87

Washington's shameful revolving door [lobbying by former government officials] R. Evans and R. D. Novak. *Read Dig* 130:118-22 My '87

Lobbyists and lobbying—*cont.*
What every lobbyist should know [views of M. Pertschuk] J. L. Swerdlow. il por *Channels* 7:76 F '87

Laws and regulations
NASA apologizes for illegal lobbying to preserve budget, space station. T. M. Foley. *Aviat Week Space Technol* 127:20-1 Ag 31 '87

Canada
See also
Mothers Are Women (Organization)

Lobel, Adrianne
about
Opera on a grand scale. B. Weber. il por *N Y Times Mag* p126 O 11 '87

Lobos, Heitor Villa- *See* Villa-Lobos, Heitor

Los Lobos (Musical group)
Los Lobos: born in East L.A. M. A. Lerner. il *Newsweek* 109:76 F 23 '87
Los Lobos shake, rattle and worry. A. DeCurtis. il *Roll Stone* p51+ F 26 '87
Los Lobos: from el barrio to La bamba. D. Goldman. *Sch Update* 120:26 N 20 '87
The world of their fathers. S. G. Freedman. il *Roll Stone* p86-8+ Mr 26 '87

Lobsenz, Norman M., 1919-
Do you have a "green thumb" for marriage? *Read Dig* 130:119-22 Ja '87

Lobster fisheries *See* Shellfish fisheries

Lobsters
See also
Cooking—Shellfish
Crustacean blue genes [work of Anthony D'Agostino] il *Oceans* 20:4-5 Ja/F '87
For love of lobster. J. D. Scott. il *Read Dig* 130:91-4 Je '87
Lobster lovers should thank Philly's Morty Krouse—he's singing for their supper. il por *People Wkly* 27:71 Je 1 '87

Anecdotes, facetiae, satire, etc.
Exit laughing. E. Zern. il *Field Stream* 92:114 Ag '87

Nervous system
See Nervous system—Crustaceans

Sexual behavior
See Sexual behavior—Crustaceans

Lobue, Ange
Mayhem on the freeways. por *U S News World Rep* 103:9 S 28 '87

Lobularia maritima *See* Sweet alyssum

Local area networks
Computerizing with confidence (V). K. Berney. il *Nations Bus* 75:23-4 Mr '87
Local area networks. H.-J. Taferner. il *Pers Comput* 11:183-5+ My '87
Local area networks [cover story; special section] bibl il *Byte* 12:145-52+ Jl '87
RS-232 LANs: inexpensive office connections. C. Spencer. il *Pers Comput* 11:139-41+ Je '87
The shifting meaning of connectivity. R. J. Noorda. por *Pers Comput* 11:248 O '87
Two network managers [Lanscope and LANWatch] il *Byte* 12:70 D '87
Using the A*Star II LAN. *Byte* 12:232 Je '87
Who manages the network? [business applications] H. Fersko-Weiss. il *Pers Comput* 11:107-9+ Mr '87

Monitoring
Views on a network analyzer [Network General's Sniffer] S. Spangenberg and R. G. A. Cote. il *Byte* 12:191+ Jl '87

Standards
IEEE 802 LAN standards. il *Byte* 12:150-1 Jl '87

Local control of schools *See* School management and organization

Local finance
See also
Municipal finance

Local government
See also
Municipal incorporation

Local Initiatives Support Corporation
Priming the urban pump. J. Cook. il *Forbes* 139:62+ Mr 23 '87

Local service airlines *See* Airlines—Local service

Local taxation
See also
Assessment
Kansas City (Mo.)—Taxation
Los Angeles (Calif.)—Taxation
Montreal (Québec)—Taxation
New York (N.Y.)—Taxation
Paying the piper in the cities. *U S News World Rep* 102:14 Ja 12 '87

Local transit
See also
Bus lines
Cable railroads
Denver (Colo.)—Transit systems
Light rail systems
Los Angeles (Calif.)—Subways
Miami (Fla.)—Transit systems
New York (N.Y.)—Subways
New York (N.Y.)—Transit systems
Port Authority of New York and New Jersey
San Francisco (Calif.)—Transit systems
Seattle (Wash.)—Transit systems
Trolleys
Victoria (B.C.)—Transit systems
In transit [local transit stations; with introd. by Douglas Brenner] il *Archit Rec* 175:67 Ja '87

Panama
See also
Panama (Panama)—Transit systems

Localization of brain functions *See* Brain—Localization of functions

Locater of Missing Heirs Inc.
The chase for leftover fortunes [T. Howes' discovery of unclaimed Thompson Bousquet Gold Mines stock] D. Francis. il *Macleans* 100:5 Jl 27 '87

Location in business and industry
See also
Airplane factories—Location
Automobile factories—Location
Black business enterprises—Location
Business districts
Cattle feedlots—Location
Minority business enterprises—Location
Rural industries
Booming American cities [cover story; special section] il *Fortune* 116:30-7+ Ag 17 '87
Creative Label takes its decorative finishing closer to eastern printers [building of new plant in Martin, Tenn.] J. P. Frank. il *Publ Wkly* 231:260 My 15 '87
Cruising into the 21st century [manufacturing along Interstate 75] E. A. Finn, Jr. il map *Forbes* 140:80+ Ag 24 '87
Does it pay to move the corporate headquarters? L. Baum. il *Bus Week* p68-9 S 7 '87
East Coast redux [ports] E. A. Finn, Jr. il *Forbes* 139:162 My 18 '87
The Far East goes south [Japanese factories in Mexico] J. Contreras. il *Newsweek* 109:46 Je 22 '87
Going south to cut costs [U.S. firms in Mexico] H. Eason. il *Nations Bus* 75:24 F '87
Hope or hyperbole? High tech and economic development. E. J. Malecki. il *Technol Rev* 90:44-51 O '87
Is Texas losing its independence? [outsiders' investments] T. Mack. il *Forbes* 140:184+ D 14 '87
Keeping business at home [state economic development programs] M. Leepson. il *Nations Bus* 75:67-70 My '87
The local rush to attract foreign money. P. M. Jones. il *Sch Update* 119:6-7 Ja 26 '87
Made in U.S.A./Mexico: a new industrial partnership. E. C. Conkling. map *Focus* 36:32-3 Wint '86
National change and the regional conundrum. B. L. Weinstein and H. T. Gross. *Society* 25:55-61 N/D '87
National economic competitiveness [Ohio's Thomas Edison Program; address, February 6, 1987] C. M. Coburn. *Vital Speeches Day* 53:478-80 My 15 '87
The rediscovery of local pizzazz. D. Fenn. il *Work Woman* 12:66-8+ Jl '87
The rise of gringo capitalism [U.S. companies in the border zones] J. B. Copeland. il *Newsweek* 109:40-1 Ja 5 '87
Rocky Mountain high-tech [Colorado aerospace industries] E. Truitt. il *Space World* X-1-277:22-4 Ja '87
A tale of two cities [new segregation in Atlanta as businesses move to white suburbs leaving black workers behind] D. Beers and D. Hembree. il *Nation* 244:357-60 Mr 21 '87
Tokyo opens a southern trade route [Japanese factories in Mexico] S. L. Hawkins. il map *U S News World Rep* 103:40+ Ag 3 '87
Urban youth lose jobs to suburbs. A. F. Brimmer. il *Black Enterp* 18:45 S '87
Where to find the sunniest business climate [report by Corporation for Enterprise Development] G. Koretz. *Bus Week* p24 Ap 13 '87
Where to live—and prosper [1990s] G. Breckenfeld. il map *Fortune* 115:52-4+ F 2 '87

Location in business and industry—*cont.*
Why few ghetto factories are making it. A. Beam. il *Bus Week* p86+ F 16 '87
Why they hate New York. W. G. Flanagan. il *Forbes* 140:189 S 21 '87
Yankee! Welcome to Mexico! J. Castro. il *Time* 129:51 Je 1 '87

Locations, Motion picture *See* Motion pictures—Setting and scenery

Loch, Marilyn L.
Worcester Parian and Parian ivory porcelain of the 19th century [cover story] il *Antiques Collect Hobbies* 92:33-9 O '87

Loch Ness monster
Scotland's elusive Nessie. M. M. Mason. *Travel Holiday* 168:94 Jl '87

Lockbaum, Gordie
about
Gordie Lockbaum is offensive, then he's defensive—who says he can't have it both ways? J. Friedman. il pors *People Wkly* 28:108-10 N 2 '87

Locke, Charles Stanley, 1929-
about
Life beyond Challenger. C. Siler. por *Forbes* 140:44 S 21 '87

Locke, John, 1632-1704
about
Locke meets Hobbes at Iran-contra hearings. J. M. Wall. *Christ Century* 104:643-4 Jl 29-Ag 5 '87

Locker rooms
Assignment: sports [discrimination against women sportswriters in the men's locker rooms] J. Lannin. il *Women's Sports Fitness* 9:77-9+ Mr '87

Photographs and photography
Before the ball is tipped [University of Louisville's basketball locker room] B. Luster. il *Sport Mag* 78:60-6+ Mr '87

Lockert, Lucía Fox- *See* Fox-Lockert, Lucía

Lockett, Landon
Whales off the Faeroe Islands. por *Newsweek* 110:11 N 23 '87

Lockhart, Lettie L.
(jt. auth) *See* Wodarski, John S., and Lockhart, Lettie L.

Lockheed Corp.
Committee identifies shuttle contract issues [processing contract with Lockheed analyzed by Estess Committee] *Aviat Week Space Technol* 126:89 Mr 30 '87
Defense Dept. seeks funds to continue P-3C production. J. D. Morrocco. *Aviat Week Space Technol* 127:26 Ag 31 '87
Defense keeps tightening the screws on contractors [Lockheed reduces price of Air Force C-5B] D. Griffiths. il *Bus Week* p34 F 2 '87
Delivery of C-130s expands French military airlift capability. il *Aviat Week Space Technol* 127:29 D 14 '87
Lockheed ATF team splits responsibilities [advanced tactical fighter] *Aviat Week Space Technol* 126:29 Mr 23 '87
Lockheed developing electronic copilot in support of ATF program effort. K. J. Stein. il *Aviat Week Space Technol* 127:73+ Ag 17 '87
Lockheed developing ERIS interceptor vehicle [exoatmospheric reentry-vehicle interceptor system] il *Aviat Week Space Technol* 126:73 Mr 16 '87
Lockheed, GE run ultrahigh bypass engine prototypes in ground tests. il *Aviat Week Space Technol* 126:46-7 Ap 27 '87
Lockheed-Georgia pursues key role in Airbus projects. *Aviat Week Space Technol* 127:16 Jl 27 '87
Lockheed-Georgia seeking major role in ADI development [C-130 phased array antennas] E. H. Kolcum. il *Aviat Week Space Technol* 126:126-7 My 18 '87
Lockheed, NASA will begin propfan test assessment flights; NASA continues UHB development role [ultrahigh bypass engines] il *Aviat Week Space Technol* 126:56-8 Ap 13 '87
Lockheed prepares Altair RPV for initial test flight. S. W. Kandebo. il *Aviat Week Space Technol* 127:63-5 Jl 20 '87
Lockheed reorganizes advanced tactical fighter effort. *Aviat Week Space Technol* 127:29 D 21 '87
Lockheed to supply P-3 AEW aircraft to Customs Service. B. A. Smith. *Aviat Week Space Technol* 126:29-30 Je 8 '87
Lockheed trims $273-million from C-5B price. *Aviat Week Space Technol* 126:30 Ja 26 '87
Most improved. il *Forbes* 139:64 Ja 12 '87

NASA/Lockheed-Georgia Program continues to explore propfan noise. S. W. Kandebo. *Aviat Week Space Technol* 127:91 O 5 '87
Quality gains new emphasis after shuttle processing review. E. H. Kolcum. *Aviat Week Space Technol* 126:85+ Mr 30 '87
Questions over operational tests delay Aquila production decision. *Aviat Week Space Technol* 127:20-1 O 19 '87
Trying to make Lockheed over—before a raider does. S. Toy. il *Bus Week* p38 Jl 13 '87

Lockman-Brooks, Linda
about
Career makeover: from ticket agent to advertising director. il por *Glamour* 85:134 Ag '87

Locks and keys
See also
Automobile locks and keys
Electronic combination lock. P. Renton. il *Radio-Electron* 58:107-8+ N '87
How to install a deadbolt lock. il *Pop Mech* 164:136-7 Jl '87
How to replace a lockset. M. Henkenius. il *Pop Mech* 164:199 My '87

Exhibitions
Decorative functional metalwork [exhibit Safe and secure: keys and locks at the Cooper-Hewitt Museum] S. B. Sherrill. il *Antiques* 132:246+ Ag '87

Lockshin family
about
A Moscow mystery [family from Houston defects to Moscow] J. Fayard. il *Life* 10:42-3+ Mr '87

Locomotion
See also
Animal locomotion

Loctite Corp.
Loctite: home is where the customers are. R. W. King. il *Bus Week* p63 Ap 13 '87

Locus (Genes)
Amyloid β protein gene: cDNA, mRNA distribution, and genetic linkage near the Alzheimer locus. R. E. Tanzi and others. bibl f il *Science* 235:880-4 F 20 '87
Characterization and chromosomal localization of a cDNA encoding brain amyloid of Alzheimer's disease. D. Goldgaber and others. bibl f il *Science* 235:877-80 F 20 '87
Defect in Alzheimer's is on chromosome 21. D. M. Barnes. *Science* 235:846-7 F 20 '87
erg, a human *ets*-related gene on chromosome 21: alternative splicing, polyadenylation, and translation. V. N. Rao and others. bibl f il *Science* 237:635-9 Ag 7 '87
Gene defect located for Gaucher's disease [research by Shoji Tsuji and others] B. Bower. *Sci News* 131:167-8 Mr 14 '87
The gene for familial polyposis coli maps to the long arm of chromosome 5. M. Leppert and others. bibl f il *Science* 238:1411-13 D 4 '87
Gene for von Recklinghausen neurofibromatosis is in the pericentromeric region of chromosome 17. D. Barker and others. bibl f il *Science* 236:1100-2 My 29 '87
Gene search narrows [neurofibromatosis] R. Weiss. *Sci News* 131:359 Je 6 '87
The genetic defect causing familial Alzheimer's disease maps on chromosome 21. P. H. St George-Hyslop and others. bibl f il *Science* 235:885-90 F 20 '87
Key to Alzheimer's? [defect tracked to chromosome 21] *Sci Am* 256:68 Ap '87
Making antisense [work of John P. Adelman and others with gonadotropin releasing hormone] *Sci Am* 256:26 Je '87
Measuring the human T cell receptor γ-chain. W. M. Strauss and others. bibl f il *Science* 237:1217-19 S 4 '87
Raf, a trans-acting locus, regulates the α-fetoprotein gene in a cell-autonomous manner. T. F. Vogt and others. bibl f il *Science* 236:301-3 Ap 17 '87
Sequence of a probable potassium channel component encoded at Shaker locus of Drosophila. B. L. Tempel and others. bibl f il *Science* 237:770-5 Ag 14 '87
Three recessive loci required for insulin-dependent diabetes in nonobese diabetic mice. M. Prochazka and others. bibl f il *Science* 237:286-9 Jl 17 '87
Transposon tagging and molecular analysis of the maize regulatory locus opaque-2. R. J. Schmidt and others. bibl f il *Science* 238:960-3 N 13 '87
Two mammalian genes transcribed from opposite strands of the same DNA locus. J. P. Adelman and others. bibl f il *Science* 235:1514-17 Mr 20 '87

Locus coeruleus *See* Brain stem
Locusts *See* Grasshoppers
Locusts, Seventeen year *See* Cicadas
Loder, Kurt
  Bo Diddley [interview] il pors *Roll Stone* p76-8+ F
    12 '87
  Stardust memories [interview with D. Bowie] il pors
    Roll Stone p74-7+ Ap 23 '87
Lodges
  An Adirondack wilderness retreat [Elk Lake Lodge in
    North Hudson] D. G. Shekerjian. il *Travel Holiday*
    168:34+ N '87
  Castle in the air: a family lodge above Aspen [architecture
    by Michael Mahaffey; decorated by Steve Chase] G.
    Greene. il *Archit Dig* 44:136-9+ Ag '87
  Where the grizzlies go. L. S. Brady. il *Esquire* 107:33-4
    Mr '87
Lodi (Ohio)
                    Street traffic
  When the dinosaur hit Lodi, Ohio [overweight truck
    stopped by police] J. Paris. il *Read Dig* 130:145-8
    Ap '87
Loe, Kathleen, 1953-
                    about
  Kathleen Loe: spirit, person, place. L. Weschler. il por
    Art News 86:127-8 Summ '87
Loeb, Benjamin S., 1914-
  Amend the Constitution's treaty clause. bibl f il *Bull
    At Sci* 43:38-41 O '87
  (jt. auth) See Seaborg, Glenn T., and Loeb, Benjamin
    S., 1914-
Loeb, Deborah
                    about
  AIDS is a human disease. J. Norberg. il pors *Saturday
    Evening Post* 259:52-3 O '87
Loeb, Edward S.
                    about
  AIDS is a human disease. J. Norberg. il pors *Saturday
    Evening Post* 259:52-3 O '87
Loeb, Marshall
  Checking up on your health insurance. il *Saturday Evening
    Post* 259:30 Jl/Ag '87
  The economy of 1987—and beyond [address, January
    26, 1987] *Vital Speeches Day* 53:371-5 Ap 1 '87
  Editor's desk. See issues of Fortune beginning June 9,
    1986
  New options for the aging. il *Saturday Evening Post*
    259:112 O '87
Loeb, Nackey Scripps
                    about
  Power behind the pen. B. Wallace. il por *Macleans*
    100:6-7 O 5 '87
Loeb, William, 1905-1981
                    about
  The story that still nags at me [excerpt from Behind
    the front page] D. S. Broder. il *Wash Mon* 19:29-32+
    F '87
Loeb Drama Center (Cambridge, Mass.)
  Loeb Drama Center. B. Burns. il *Theatre Crafts* 21:40-1+
    D '87
Loehr, James E.
  The mental game. See issues of World Tennis
Loengard, John
  Cartier-Bresson. il pors *Life* 10:124-5+ D '87
  Reflections. See issues of Popular Photography beginning
    September 1987
  Talking pictures [excerpts from Pictures under discussion]
    il *Life* 10:71-2+ My '87
                    about
  Framework. S. Piperato. il por *Pop Photogr* 94:60-1
    Ag '87
Loewer, H. Peter
  A spring bulb bed. il *Rodale's Org Gard* 34:58-61 S
    '87
Loews Corporation
  Jon's room is at the top of Loews Hotels [J. M. Tisch]
    M. Frons. il por *Bus Week* p54-5 Ap 13 '87
  Most improved. il *Forbes* 139:80 Ja 12 '87
  The sons also rise in the dynasty at Loews [Tisch family]
    il *U S News World Rep* 103:54-5 Jl 6 '87
Loew's Paradise (Bronx, N.Y.) *See* Motion picture theaters
Löffler, Heinz
  Lakes and glaciers of the Alps. il *Courier* 40:37-8 F
    '87
Lofthouse, Russ
  A national cutoff date for entering kindergarten. *Educ
    Dig* 53:44-5 N '87
Lofting, Christopher
  The British Virgin Islands. il map *Travel Holiday*
    167:38-43 Mr '87

Lofton, James
                    about
  James Lofton traded to Los Angeles Raiders; assault
    trial scheduled. por *Jet* 72:46 My 4 '87
  Packer receiver Lofton faces sex assault trial. por *Jet*
    71:50 F 9 '87
  Packers win one, lose one in Green Bay sex cases.
    il pors *Jet* 72:49 Je 15 '87
Lofts, Converted *See* Apartments, Remodeled
Loftus, Elizabeth F., 1944-
  Trials of an expert witness. por *Newsweek* 109:10-11
    Je 29 '87
Log cabins, houses, etc.
  All about log houses. L. Hallam. il *South Living* 22:60-5
    Ja '87
  An Appalachian labor of love [150 year old log cabin
    forms nucleus of weekend retreat] C. Engle. il *South
    Living* 22:74-5 O '87
  Architecture: David Sellers [design of rustic log house
    on Lake Winnipesaukee, N.H.] V. J. Scully. il por
    Archit Dig 44:146-51+ Je '87
  Cabin fever. il *Redbook* 169:98-105 Jl '87
  Cabin in the sky: a designer's retreat in the Montana
    Rockies [home of M. London] B. D. Colen. il por
    Archit Dig 44:132-9+ Je '87
  Historic houses: Le Corbusier's cabanon. T. Benton.
    il *Archit Dig* 44:146-51+ D '87
Log furniture *See* Furniture, Rustic
Log splitting equipment *See* Wood cutting equipment
Logan, Andy
  Around City Hall. See occasional issues of The New
    Yorker
Logan, William, 1950-
  Political song [poem] *Harpers* 274:34 Ap '87
Logan, William Bryant
  Conquering a California hillside. il *House Gard* 159:90-9+
    Jl '87
  Heirloom vegetables. il *House Gard* 159:62+ My '87
Logan, Sir William Edmond, 1798-1875
                    about
  Out of the past. S. S. Doria and J. J. Doria. *Earth
    Sci* 39:29 Wint '86
Logan International Airport *See* Boston (Mass.)—Airports
Loggerhead turtles *See* Turtles
Logging *See* Lumbering
Logic, Symbolic and mathematical
                    See also
  Proof theory
Logic analyzers *See* Testing equipment
Logic circuits
  Computing with light beams [work of Desmond Smith
    and others] S. Budiansky. *U S News World Rep* 102:68
    F 2 '87
  Logic-gate fundamentals. R. Marston. il *Radio-Electron*
    58:50-4 Ap '87
  Programmable hardware [special section] bibl il *Byte*
    12:194-5+ Ja '87
  Working with flip-flops. R. Marston. il *Radio-Electron*
    58:64-9 Je '87
                    Design
  Defining digital circuits with Prolog. W. Clocksin. il
    Byte 12:148-9 Ag '87
  Logic-family translation. R. Grossblatt. il *Radio-Electron*
    58:30-1 Ag '87
Logic programming
  Constraint logic programming. C. Lassez. bibl il *Byte*
    12:171-2+ Ag '87
  Logic grammars [Prolog] S. Szpakowicz. bibl il *Byte*
    12:185-6+ Ag '87
  A search strategy for commonsense logic programming.
    P. V. Haley. *Byte* 12:173-5 O '87
Logica (U K) plc
  Logica will manage software definition for Columbus
    module. *Aviat Week Space Technol* 126:24 Mr 23
    '87
Logo (Computer language)
  Computers in the classroom [Project Headlight at Hen-
    nigan Elementary School, Roxbury, Mass.] A. Bass.
    il por *Technol Rev* 90:52-62+ Ap '87
  Now even Lego is going high-tech [linkage with Logo
    to make programmable toys] P. Angiolillo and M.
    Bluestone. il *Bus Week* p40 Ag 17 '87
Logos *See* Trade marks and trade names
Logs (Shooting records) *See* Shooting records
Logsdan, Tom
  Future technology [address, June 4, 1987] *Vital Speeches
    Day* 53:716-22 S 15 '87
Logue, Christopher, 1926-
  Homer's 'Iliad,' updated [poem] *Harpers* 274:25-6
    My '87

Loh, Sandra Tsing
about
Swing, Loh! Sweet chariots! A recital stops traffic in L.A. il por *People Wkly* 28:58 S 21 '87
Lohmann, Jeanne
Catching the light [poem] *America* 157:222 O 10 '87
Shaking the tree [poem] *America* 157:60 Ag 1-8 '87
Lohmann, Kenneth J., and Willows, A. O. Dennis
Lunar-modulated geomagnetic orientation by a marine mollusk. bibl f il *Science* 235:331-4 Ja 16 '87
Lohmeier, Lynne
The perils of popularity. il *Oceans* 20:8-13 My/Je '87
Loihi (Hawaii)
Birth of an island [exploration of Loihi by submarine Alvin] J. C. Borg. il map *Oceans* 20:26-33 Jl/Ag '87
Submarine crew finds volcano, minerals and exotic animals [Alvin explores Loihi] il *Earth Sci* 40:7 Fall '87
Lois, George
about
An eye for the best. E. G. Carter. il *House Gard* 159:218-21+ O '87
Lois Young-Thomas Scholarship and Leadership Guild
Md. group awards money to UMAB grad students. *Jet* 72:22 S 21 '87
Loke, Margarett
Butoh: dance of darkness. il *N Y Times Mag* p40-1+ N 1 '87
Lollards
Dissidents in an age of faith? Wyclif and the Lollards. J. Catto. bibl il *Hist Today* 37:46-52 N '87
Lomas, Lisa
about
Thanks to Lisa Lomas, this season's beautiful bodies are making waves in H₂O. il por *People Wkly* 27:130-1 My 18 '87
These tiny swimsuits are getting enormous visibility. P. Finch. il por *Bus Week* p105 Mr 23 '87
Lombard, Florentino Aspillaga *See* Aspillaga Lombard, Florentino
Lombardi, John
Murph the Surf rides again. il por *Esquire* 108:114-16+ N '87
Lombardi, Joseph L.
Moral theology and public dissent: a temporary compromise. *America* 156:100-1+ F 7 '87
Lombreglia, Ralph
Inn Essence [story] il *Atlantic* 260:46-51+ Jl '87
Lomeo, Angelo
(jt. auth) *See* Bullaty, Sonja, and Lomeo, Angelo
London, Barbara, 1946-
Camera on deck. il por *Pop Photogr* 94:70-6 Jl '87
London, Bill
Transplant in the Rockies. il *Américas* 39:38-41 My/Je '87
London, Herbert Ira
Death of the university. il por *Futurist* 21:17-22 My/Je '87
Death of the university [cover story] il *USA Today (Periodical)* 116:32-6 S '87
(jt. auth) *See* Balch, Stephen H., and London, Herbert Ira
London, Mimi
about
Cabin in the sky: a designer's retreat in the Montana Rockies. B. D. Colen. il por *Archit Dig* 44:132-9+ Je '87
Reorienting a classic: inventive decor for a Lloyd Wright house [cover story] P. Goldberger. il por *Archit Dig* 44:108-15 Mr '87
London, Oscar
Confessions of an M.D. il *Saturday Evening Post* 259:46-9+ O '87
London, Paul A.
What Ford can afford. *New Repub* 196:16+ Je 8 '87
London, Perry
Character education and clinical intervention: a paradigm shift for U.S. schools. bibl f il *Phi Delta Kappan* 68:667-73 My '87
London (England)

Airports
Crewmember with AIDS barred at Gatwick [Delta Air Lines steward] *Aviat Week Space Technol* 126:36 F 23 '87

Antiquities
Big Bang reverberations [City of London sites] K. Nurse. il *Hist Today* 37:5-6 Je '87

Rotherhithe's royal palace [excavations to uncover royal manor house and outbuildings and a Delftware factory] S. J. Evans. il *Hist Today* 37:3-4 Jl '87
Antiquities, Roman
Cross current [Garden House site] K. Nurse. il *Hist Today* 37:5 D '87

Architecture
See also
London (England)—Buildings
Beyond the Peak [work of Z. M. Hadid] D. Dietsch. il *Archit Rec* 175:118-29 Je '87
City of the future [work of Foster, Rogers, Stirling] W. Feaver. il *Art News* 86:44 Mr '87
Exhibition report: New architecture: Foster, Rogers, Stirling. H. Aldersey-Williams. *Archit Rec* 175:73+ Mr '87
Mews of the day [converted stable by John Stefanidis] J. Brittain. il *House Gard* 159:226-9 N '87
Open house [architect R. Rogers' house] D. Saatchi. il por *House Gard* 159:206-13+ N '87
Spirited composition on Chester Square: the London house of Baron and Baroness Thyssen-Bornemisza. J. J. Norwich. il por *Archit Dig* 44:104-11 O '87
Wrecking Wren's London skyline. C. Ogden. il *Time* 130:77 D 14 '87

Art
Canaletto covered the waterfront. W. Feaver. il *Art News* 86:170+ D '87
Report from London. J. McEwen. il *Art Am* 75:29-33+ Ja '87
Report from London. J. McEwen. il *Art Am* 75:30-7+ Jl '87

Banks
Big Bang babies [English bankers working for American banks] M. Lewis. *New Repub* 196:17-18 Ja 5-12 '87
Big bust [Big Bang aftermath] R. L. Stern and D. Henry. il *Forbes* 140:64-5 Ag 24 '87
The City of London wanted competition—but not this much. R. A. Melcher. il *Bus Week* p37 Ag 10 '87
"The whole thing is breaking up" [Fleet Street] R. Morais. il *Forbes* 139:148+ My 18 '87

Bookstores
See Booksellers and bookselling—Great Britain
Buildings
London assurance [Lloyd's of London building designed by R. Rogers] M. Filler. il *House Gard* 159:90-3+ Ja '87

Cemeteries
See also
Highgate Cemetery (London, England)
Description
Dinking around London [Carlsberg 'Round London Boat Marathon for inflatable dinghies] D. Wallace. il *Mot Boat Sail* 159:44-7+ Je '87
London journal. J. Bainbridge. See occasional issues of Gourmet
Anecdotes, facetiae, satire, etc.
Canadians on the beat in London. A. Fotheringham. il *Macleans* 100:60 F 16 '87
Whips and bananas in London. A. Fotheringham. il *Macleans* 100:56 F 9 '87
Docks, wharves, etc.
Capital developments [Reichmann's take over Canary Wharf project] D. Jenish. il *Macleans* 100:28-9 Ag 24 '87

Galleries and museums
See also
Dulwich Picture Gallery (London, England)
National Gallery (Great Britain)
Reminiscence Centre (London, England)
Sir John Soane's Museum (London, England)
Theatre Museum (London, England)
Report from London. J. McEwen. il *Art Am* 75:30-7+ Jl '87
Small museums of London. J. Robinson. il *Gourmet* 47:72-7+ D '87
Historic houses, sites, etc.
See also
Hampton Court Palace (London, England)
Sigmund Freud Museum (London, England)
America in London. B. Dunning. il *Am Herit* 38:76-9+ Ap '87
Dr. Johnson's open house. J. Atlas. il por *House Gard* 159:12+ D '87
Hotels, motels, etc.
Savory merriment [Christmas at London's Connaught Hotel] S. M. Dinhofer. il *Harpers Bazaar* 121:82+ D '87
Industries
See also
Greater London Enterprise Board

London (England)—*cont.*

Intellectual life
See also
Bloomsbury group
Literary London. G. Smith. *New Leader* 70:20-1 My 4-18 '87

Moral conditions
Sex and 'Madam Cyn' [cleared of managing prostitutes] N. Underwood. *Macleans* 100:48 F 23 '87

Music
See also
English National Opera
Opera—Great Britain
Royal Opera House (London, England)

Newspapers
See also
Financial times
Star (London, England: Newspaper)

Photographs and photography
Capturing London's cultural and visual diversity. C. Purcell and A. Purcell. il *Pop Photogr* 94:12 Ap '87

Popular culture
Letter from London. V. Radin. il *Vogue* 177:114+ My '87

Restaurants, nightclubs, bars, etc.
London journal [Alastair Little] J. Bainbridge. il *Gourmet* 47:36+ Ag '87
London traditions. R. L. Balzer. il *Travel Holiday* 167:16+ My '87
London's Dolphin Brasserie. J. Robinson. il *Gourmet* 47:60-1+ Ag '87
The new English cooking. F. Bissell. il *Harpers Bazaar* 120:104+ Ap '87
The pubs of central London. J. Robinson. il *Gourmet* 47:52-7+ Mr '87

Social life and customs
Mr. Peepers in London: toy boys, phantoms, other obsessions. il *N Y* 20:42-4+ O 26 '87

Stores
See also
Galerie 360
Marks & Spencer plc
Workers for Freedom (Firm)
An antiques dealer's secret sources: Bruce Newman in Paris and England. J. Kornbluth. il pors *Archit Dig* 44 Archit Dig Travels:20-31+ O '87
London bazaar. L. Nickson. il *Harpers Bazaar* 120:70+ Jl '87
Where London's architects do their shopping. il *Sunset* 179:48-48A Ag '87

Streets
See also
Fleet Street (London, England)

Subways
Escalator to an inferno. J. Smolowe. il *Time* 130:30-1 N 30 '87
Flaming horror in London's subway. A. Bilski. il *Macleans* 100:44 N 30 '87
An inferno in the London underground. il *Newsweek* 110:46 N 30 '87

Theater
See also
English Shakespeare Company
Royal Court Theatre
Royal Shakespeare Company
Theatre Museum (London, England)
Bound for the U.S.A. W. A. Henry. il *Time* 130:66-7 Ag 3 '87
Britain takes the stage. P. J. Rosenwald. il *Horizon* 30:29-31 N '87

Transit systems
See also
London (England)—Subways

Chelsea
See Chelsea (London, England)

Ealing
See Ealing (London, England)

East End
See East End (London, England)

Twickenham
See Twickenham (London, England)

London (England) fashion shows *See* Fashion shows
London (Jack) State Historic Park (Calif.) *See* California—Parks and reserves
London Book Fair *See* Book fairs
London European Airways
Privatization sparks scramble for competitive edge in England. il *Aviat Week Space Technol* 127:128+ N 9 '87

London Festival Ballet
Farther from Denmark: the two sides of Peter Schaufuss. M. E. Willis. il pors *Dance Mag* 61:56-9 D '87
London troupe highlights Hong Kong's fifteenth arts festival. D. Ries. il *Dance Mag* 61:32 Je '87
London Proms (Festival) *See* Music festivals—Great Britain
London Stock Exchange *See* Stock exchanges—London exchange
Lone, John
about
Lone star. R. Wetzsteon. il pors *N Y* 20:92-4+ D 7 '87
Lone's stardom rises in the West. *Newsweek* 110:81 N 23 '87
Lone Eagle Press
Broadening niches: multilingual children's books and movie technology guides. L. See. *Publ Wkly* 231:144 F 27 '87
Lone Star Industries, Inc.
Battling for survival in the concrete jungle [chairman J. E. Stewart] J. R. Norman. il por *Bus Week* p66-7+ S 14 '87
Lone Star Technologies Inc.
Lone Star's Howard Beasley likes trouble—but not this much trouble. T. Mason. il por *Bus Week* p54+ F 2 '87
Loneliness
All our lonely children. P. A. Hall. por *Newsweek* 110:12 O 12 '87
Lone dangers. R. E. Borgman. il *Omni* 9:24 My '87
Marriage & loneliness. C. H. Stapen. il *Parents* 62:87-91 Ag '87
The pain of loneliness. M. W. Lear. il *N Y Times Mag* p47-8 D 20 '87
Real trouble ahead. J. McClintock. il *N Y Times Mag* p40 Ag 9 '87
The road to self-reliance [lesson of boarding school] M. Norman. il *N Y Times Mag* p82 D 13 '87
The lonely passion of Judith Hearne [film] *See* Motion picture reviews—Single works
Lonetree, Clayton
about
From Russia with love and espionage. il pors *Macleans* 100:18-19 Ap 13 '87
Holes in a spy scandal. S. W. Cloud. il por *Time* 130:31 Jl 20 '87
The honey-trap spy case widens. il pors *U S News World Rep* 102:12 Ap 6 '87
A Marine and his "swallow". B. Duffy. il por *U S News World Rep* 102:25 Ja 26 '87
The Marine spy scandal: "It's a biggie". A. Wilentz. il pors *Time* 129:21-2 Ap 6 '87
The Marine traitors. *Natl Rev* 39:18 Ap 24 '87
Military justice comes to attention. R. Lacayo. il por *Time* 129:62 My 18 '87
Moonlighting in Moscow? R. Watson. il pors *Newsweek* 109:32-3 Ap 6 '87
No entry. il por *Time* 130:22 N 23 '87
Semper fie. por *Time* 129:19 Ja 26 '87
Loney, Glenn
Pure and simple. por *Opera News* 51:18-20+ Je '87
Reviving the dinosaur. il por *Opera News* 52:34-6 N '87
Long, Bob
about
The grand deer slammer. T. Stienstra. il por *Outdoor Life* 179:54-5+ Ja '87
Long, Charles D.
Ansel Adams: one with beauty. il *USA Today (Periodical)* 116:56-65 S '87
Long, Elaine
A canner's dream. il por *Rodale's Org Gard* 34:60-1 Ag '87
Long, Franklin A., 1910-
Does the SDI make good sense? [with discussion] il por *Cent Mag* 20:15-24 My/Je '87
Long, James W.
Drugs that can cause serious side effects [excerpt from The essential guide to prescription drugs] il *Good Housekeep* 204:202-3 F '87
Long, Judith
Book notes. *Nation* 244:371-4 Mr 21 '87
Long, Michael E.
What is this thing called sleep? il *Natl Geogr* 172:786-821 D '87
Long, Richard, 1945-
about
Walking into art. J. Johnston. il map *Art Am* 75:160-9 Ap '87

Long, Richard K.
Dow and South Africa [address, April 11, 1987] *Vital Speeches Day* 53:520-4 Je 15 '87

Long, Robert
Scene painting. il *Theatre Crafts* 21:44-6+ O '87

Long, Robert
Tape tracks. See issues of High Fidelity (New York, N.Y.) beginning May 1986

Long, Robert A.

about

Before the dinosaurs. B. Weber. il pors *N Y Times Mag* p66 Ag 23 '87

Long, Shelley

about

Cheers and tears: the Long goodbye. S. Haller. il pors *People Wkly* 27:44-6+ F 23 '87
The Long and the short of it. G. Stone. il por *Vogue* 177:84 F '87
Shelley Long. V. Scott. il pors *Good Housekeep* 204:89+ Ja '87
Shelley Long makes her move. E. Sherman. il pors *Ladies Home J* 104:80+ My '87
Will Shelley Long ever get a break? D. Maychick. por *Mademoiselle* 93:94 Mr '87

Long, Zelma

about

Zelma of Simi. N. Hazelton. *Natl Rev* 39:57-8 F 13 '87

Long Beach (Calif.)

Gardens and gardening

A city sanctuary [J. O'Brien's garden] K. Wilson. il por *Rodale's Org Gard* 34:18+ My '87

Long Branch (N.J.)

Employees

Ethnic jokes may cost N.J. workers their jobs. *Jet* 71:14 Mr 23 '87

Race relations

Ethnic jokes may cost N.J. workers their jobs. *Jet* 71:14 Mr 23 '87

Long Distance America Inc.
Francesco Galesi isn't used to losing. P. Finch. il por *Bus Week* p114 My 4 '87

Long distance telephone service *See* Telephone—Long distance service

Long gone [television program] See Television program reviews—Single works

Long Island (N.Y.)

See also

Architecture, Domestic—Long Island (N.Y.)
Beaches—Long Island (N.Y.)
Country estates—Long Island (N.Y.)
Fishing—Long Island (N.Y.)
Gardens and gardening—Long Island (N.Y.)

Anecdotes, facetiae, satire, etc.

Almost Jeeves [hunting for a job as butler in the Hamptons] M. Kenyon. il *Gourmet* 47:64+ Jl '87
Not quite Escoffier [summer job as a cook for a family in the Hamptons] M. Kenyon. il *Gourmet* 47:68+ Ag '87

Description and travel

Reminiscing in Great Gatsbyland. J. Kern. il *Travel Holiday* 168:28+ O '87

Industries

See also

Shellfish culture

Long Island City (N.Y.)

Buildings

A leg up [Gullans International showroom at International Design Center] C. K. Gandee. il *Archit Rec* 175:106-9 My '87

Galleries and museums

See also

Isamu Noguchi Garden Museum

Long Island Rr.
Blacks win 15-year-old suit against L.I. Railroad. *Jet* 72:36 Ag 17 '87

Long Island Sound (N.Y. and Conn.)

See also

Marine pollution—Long Island Sound (N.Y. and Conn.)

Shellfish fisheries

See Shellfish fisheries

Long johns *See* Underwear

Long jumping
On top of the worlds [J. Joyner-Kersee wins heptathlon and long jump at World Track and Field Championships; cover story] K. Moore. il pors *Sports Illus* 67:18-23 S 14 '87

Long jumping records
Giants on the earth [B. Beamon's long jump record and L. Evans' 400 meters record, set at 1968 Olympics, still stand] K. Moore. il pors *Sports Illus* 66:48-50+ Je 29 '87

Long live the lady! [film] See Motion picture reviews—Single works

Long range navigation *See* Loran

Long term care insurance *See* Insurance, Nursing home care

Longevity

See also

Aging
Centenarians
Pritikin Longevity Centers

Can you stop the aging clock? E. Kiester. il *50 Plus* 27:20-3 Ag '87
The signs of life: a guide to assessing your health risks. S. Goodman. il *Curr Health 2* 13:3-9 Ap '87
The waist span/life span link. il *Prevention* 39:12+ O '87
Why do women live longer than men? C. Holden. il *Science* 238:158-60 O 9 '87

Longevity (Animals) *See* Age—Animals

Longford, Elizabeth Harman Pakenham, Countess of, 1906-
Reflections of a biographer. *Writer* 100:20-1+ Jl '87

Longhofer, James E.

about

Who's in charge here? S. M. Hersh. il por *N Y Times Mag* p34-5+ N 22 '87

Longhorn cattle *See* Cattle

Longman, Phillip
Deathbed politics: Medicare and the baby boom generation. *New Repub* 196:18-20 Mr 30 '87
The end of the man shortage (and about time, too). il *Mademoiselle* 93:180-1+ D '87
The great train robbery. il *Wash Mon* 19:12-14+ D '87
How the government cooks the books. *Wash Mon* 19:47-52 Jl/Ag '87

Longman, Tremper, III
Reading the Bible like a book. il por *Christ Today* 31:27-8 Mr 6 '87

Longman Group U.S.A. Inc.
Trading places. M. Schifrin. il por *Forbes* 139:56-7 Je 29 '87

Longnecker, Richard, and Roizman, Bernard, 1929-
Clustering of genes dispensable for growth in culture in the S component of the HSV-1 genome. bibl f il *Science* 236:573-6 My 1 '87

Longo, Robert

about

The four brushmen of the apocalypse. L. Hirschberg. il pors *Esquire* 107:76-84+ Mr '87
Taking direct action. D. Hershkovits. pors *Harpers Bazaar* 121:144-5 N '87

Longobardi, David
Can "lite" foods help you lose? il *Mademoiselle* 93:112 My '87

Longshoremen

See also

International Longshoremen's and Warehousemen's Union

Salaries, pensions, etc.

Losing jobs by trying to save them [New York harbor] J. Cook. il *Forbes* 139:56+ Je 1 '87

Longstone Lighthouse *See* Lighthouses—Great Britain

Longstreet, Dana
Health smart. il *Harpers Bazaar* 120:44+ My '87

Longstreth, Thomas K.
Latest ABM ploy—old is new. il *Bull At Sci* 43:3-4 D '87

Lonigro, Denise

about

The girl with the silver gun. C. Siebert. il pors *Mademoiselle* 93:247-9+ Mr '87

Lonrho plc
'Tiny' Rowland: pushing 70 and pushing harder than ever. R. A. Melcher. il por *Bus Week* p70+ O 12 '87

Loo, Deryk T., and others
Extended culture of mouse embryo cells without senescence: inhibition by serum. bibl f il *Science* 236:200-2 Ap 10 '87

Look, Mary V.
Growin' in the wind. il *Rodale's Org Gard* 34:64-5 Ap '87

Loomis, Susan Herrmann
Seafood of the desert. il *N Y Times Mag* p47-8 Ag 30 '87

Loomis, William F.
(jt. auth) See Knecht, David A., and Loomis, William F.

Looney, Douglas S.
Dashing debut by the Vols. il *Sports Illus* 67:22-3 S 7 '87
'Have I got a story!'. il pors *Sports Illus* 66:58-60+ My 18 '87
Head man. il pors *Sports Illus* 67:98-100+ Ag 31 '87
Here's to Mack the Knife. il por *Sports Illus* 67:63-4 Ag 17 '87
Inside slant. il *Sports Illus* 67:58-61 Ag 31 '87
Jack be nimble: a day in the life of an agent. il por *Sports Illus* 67:100-1 O 19 '87
The most happy fella. il por *Sports Illus* 67:28-9 Jl 6 '87
The not-so Big Eight [cover story] il *Sports Illus* 67:20-5 N 16 '87
A pair extraordinaire. il *Sports Illus* 67:100+ N 9 '87
The Paz that refreshes. il pors *Sports Illus* 66:62+ Je 1 '87
Reader's digest football. il *Sports Illus* 67:22-4 Jl 20 '87
She's no. 2 with a bullet. il pors *Sports Illus* 66:34-6+ Mr 16 '87
Spartan results for Indiana. il *Sports Illus* 67:22-4+ N 23 '87
Sprinting to Calgary. il *Sports Illus* 66:166 F 9 '87
Stopped short of the magic X. il *Sports Illus* 66:36-7 Mr 30 '87
Thank you, Pete Weber. il pors *Sports Illus* 66:26-7 My 4 '87
Too much NFL testing. il por *Sports Illus* 66:120 My 11 '87
Toys for girls and boys. il pors *Sports Illus* 67:20-1 D 21 '87
Uh-oh! He's at it again. il pors *Sports Illus* 66:77-8+ My 11 '87
A very special Person. il por *Sports Illus* 66:88-9 Ja 12 '87

Loons
Listening in on the loons' tunes [work of William Barklow] S. Morton. il *Sierra* 72:14-15 My/Je '87
Spirit of the northern waters [status of common loon in upstate New York] K. E. Parker. il *Conservationist* 42:16-21 Jl/Ag '87

Loop College
See also
Harold Washington College

Looper, Kathy
about
Profiles. B. Barich. il *New Yorker* 63:51-2+ O 12 '87

Looper, Leroy
about
Profiles. B. Barich. il *New Yorker* 63:51-2+ O 12 '87

Loory, Stuart H.
New kid on the bloc: Gorbachev's reforms spill into Eastern Europe. il *Progressive* 51:21-3 Je '87

Looser, Heinrich
about
A Swiss banker's goal: just don't lose money. B. Riemer. il por *Bus Week* p154 D 28 '87-Ja 4 '88

Looting See Pillage

Loots, Barbara
In the museum [poem] *America* 156:66 Ja 31 '87

Lopatà, Sam
about
Sam Lopata, the clown prince of restaurant designers, lets nothing interfere with atmosphere. E. Levin. il pors *People Wkly* 28:103-4+ N 23 '87

Lopate, Phillip, 1943-
Waiting for the book: storms before the calm. il *N Y Times Book Rev* 92:1+ My 24 '87

Lopez, Barry
Landscapes open and closed. il map *Harpers* 275:51-8 Jl '87

Lopez, Barry Holstun, 1945-
A worldly wilderness: California Desert. il map *Natl Geogr* 171:42-77 Ja '87

Lopez, Marsha
To open the Olympics—lift this tab. il *Women's Sports Fitness* 9:68 Jl '87

Lopez, Nancy, 1957-
about
Time for the Pat and Nancy show. J. Diaz. il pors *Sports Illus* 66:84+ F 9 '87

Lopez-Barneo, Jose
(jt. auth) See Armstrong, Clay M., and Lopez-Barneo, Jose

López Guevara, Carlos Alfredo
The Panama Canal Treaties: negotiating a new order. *Américas* 39:52-3 My/Je '87

Lopez-Muñoz, Annette
The phantom interview. *New Repub* 196:11 Je 29 '87

Lopid See Gemfibrozil

Lopp, James
about
He does it with mirrors. J. R. Hayes. il por *Forbes* 140:112-13 Ag 10 '87

Lopresti, James J.
(jt. auth) See Gallen, John J., and Lopresti, James J.

LoPresto, James Charles
The geometry of space and time [cover story] il map *Astronomy* 15:6-19 O '87

Loral Corp.
Litton, Loral to deliver F-16 warning systems. *Aviat Week Space Technol* 126:104 F 9 '87
Loral to acquire Goodyear Aerospace for $640 million in cash transaction. *Aviat Week Space Technol* 126:30 Ja 19 '87
Merci, Jimmy [Loral's acquisition of Goodyear Aerospace] S. N. Chakravarty. il por *Forbes* 139:114+ Je 15 '87

Loran
1988 buyer's guide: Lorans, radars, sat navs, plotters. G. West. il *Mot Boat Sail* 160:67+ D '87
Arnav's R-30A Loran. R. L. Collins. *Flying* 114:83 O '87
Learning about Loran. D. J. Sweeney. il maps *Radio-Electron* 58:51-2+ My '87
Loran shootout. B. Mooney and D. Fales. il *Mot Boat Sail* 160:60-5 S '87
Loran's Foster home [Foster LRN-500] R. L. Collins. il *Flying* 114:102 Ap '87
New Loran ground stations will close mid-continent gap. maps *Aviat Week Space Technol* 127:120 S 28 '87
Portable Lorans [boat use] D. Fales. il *Mot Boat Sail* 159:70+ Je '87
STS has a Loran for less. J. M. McClellan. *Flying* 114:94-5 Ag '87

Lord, Frank K.
True stories. il *Parents* 62:81-2+ Ag '87

Lord, J. Dennis
Banking across state lines. il map *Focus* 37:10-15 Spr '87

Lord, M. G., 1955-
The Greek rites of exclusion. il *Nation* 245:10-13 Jl 4-11 '87

Lord, May S.
Reagan and the Disciples: a widening chasm. *Christ Century* 104:1055-6 N 25 '87

Lord & Taylor
Gearing up for the holidays [Christmas windows] B. Weber. il *N Y Times Mag* p110 N 15 '87

Lordan, Beth
The widow [story] il *Atlantic* 260:63-7 Ag '87

Lord's prayer
We dare to say 'Our Father'. L. S. Cunningham. il *Commonweal* 114:291-2 My 8 '87

Loren, Sophia, 1934-
about
Architectural digest visits: Sophia Loren. M. Peppiatt. il pors *Archit Dig* 44:116-23 Mr '87
Sophia Loren and Kirk Douglas waltz through their latest roles as Hollywood honorees. il pors *People Wkly* 27:72-3 Ja 26 '87

Lorengar, Pilar, 1928-
about
Natural instincts. P. G. Davis. il por *N Y* 20:111-12 N 16 '87

Lorentz transformations
Modern tests of special relativity. M. P. Haugan and C. M. Will. il *Phys Today* 40:69-76 My '87

Lorenz, Christopher
The sacrifice buy. *World Press Rev* 34:50 N '87

Lorenz, Konrad
about
Interview. B. Lawren. por *Omni* 9:84-6+ Ap '87
The Lizard Man. B. Chatwin. il *N Y Rev Books* 34:47-8 Ag 13 '87

Lorenzen, Lynne
about
Lynne Lorenzen, 18, wins the big one handily with 6,497 points. il por *People Wkly* 27:54 Mr 16 '87
Lynne Lorenzen: she shoots to conquer. C. Hanauer. il por *Seventeen* 46:236 Ag '87

Lorenzo, Francisco A.
about
Can this airline be saved? C. P. Work. il por *U S News World Rep* 103:37-8 Ag 3 '87

Lorenzo, Francisco A.—about—cont.
Frank Lorenzo. J. E. Davis. il por *Bus Week* Sp Issue:228 Ap 17 '87
Has Lorenzo fired the first salvo in a fare war? C. Hawkins and J. E. Ellis. *Bus Week* p37-8 S 14 '87
Is this any way to run an airline? [interview] G. Bock. il *Time* 130:55-6 N 23 '87
Lorenzo again faces problems at helm of Continental Airlines. C. A. Shifrin. il *Aviat Week Space Technol* 127:48-9+ Ag 3 '87
Lorenzo sees Continental's problems easing. *Aviat Week Space Technol* 127:41 S 28 '87
Lorenzo starts his attack. D. Pauly. il por *Newsweek* 109:49 F 2 '87
Lorenzo turns to terra firma. por *Bus Week* p34 S 7 '87
The new master of the skies. K. Labich. il por *Fortune* 115:72-3 Ja 5 '87
Plaskett replaced as Continental chief; Lorenzo takes over. *Aviat Week Space Technol* 127:32 Jl 27 '87
Taking over the controls. pors *Time* 130:43 Ag 3 '87
What it's like to work for Frank Lorenzo. J. E. Davis. il por *Bus Week* p76+ My 18 '87
Who will be Sky King? A. Miller. il pors *Newsweek* 109:54 Mr 2 '87

Anecdotes, facetiae, satire, etc.
Milking a deadbeat. R. Baker. il *N Y Times Mag* p18 O 18 '87

Lorenzo, Frank *See* Lorenzo, Francisco A.

Lorimar (Firm)
See also
Lorimar-Telepictures Corporation

Lorimar-Telepictures Corporation
The decline of Lorimar's instant empire. R. Grover. il por *Bus Week* p29 Jl 6 '87
A local kid makes good in Hollywood [M. Adelson] M. Rogers. il por *Fortune* 115:100 Ja 5 '87
Marvin Davis wants back into Tinseltown. R. Grover. por *Bus Week* p64 D 7 '87
Suing the bosses who bounced her, a bitter Valerie Harper fights to save her reputation. D. Hutchings. il pors *People Wkly* 28:46-8 O 19 '87
The world according to Lorimar-Telepictures [interview with R. Robertson] M. Brown and P. E. Bauer. il pors *Channels* 7:78-9 F '87

Loring, John
Tiffany and Company—celebrating 150 years. il *Archit Dig* 44:34+ O '87

Lorre, Arlene
about
Some like it hot. B. Greene. il pors *Esquire* 108:59-60+ O '87

Los Alamos Scientific Laboratory
Los Alamos begins work on NPB test accelerator [Neutral Particle Beam Ground Test Accelerator] T. M. Foley. il *Aviat Week Space Technol* 127:93-4+ O 19 '87
Los Alamos eyes restarting nuclear propulsion work. *Aviat Week Space Technol* 126:34 My 11 '87
No peace on the Pueblo [radioactive contamination] T. Arrandale. il *Sierra* 72:30-3 Mr/Ap '87

Los Angeles (Calif.)
Air pollution
L.A. to E.P.A.: don't hold your breath. M. Cone. il *Sierra* 72:27+ N/D '87
Airports
Board examines radar's role in Cerritos midair collision [August 31, 1986 collision] *Aviat Week Space Technol* 127:127-8+ D 14 '87
Can Christians hand out gospel tracts in airports? [Supreme Court case involving Jews for Jesus at Los Angeles International Airport] B. Spring. il *Christ Today* 31:43-4 Ap 3 '87
FAA orders expansion of Los Angeles TCA [terminal control area serving Los Angeles International Airport] map *Aviat Week Space Technol* 127:23-4 Ag 24 '87
L.A. law [expansion of terminal control area] P. Garrison. il *Flying* 114:34+ D '87
Architecture
Architectural digest visits: Robert Wagner [ranch house designed by Cliff May] J. Allen. il pors *Archit Dig* 44:124-31+ My '87
Architecture: Ricardo Legorreta: the Los Angeles residence of Georgiana and Ricardo Montalban. C. Fuentes. il por *Archit Dig* 44:164-71+ Mr '87
Art deco tour of downtown Los Angeles. il *Sunset* 179:50 S '87
Building his own bridges [B. A. Murphy's house in Santa Monica Canyon] J. Giovannini. il *House Gard* 159:112-21+ Mr '87
Collage with a view [Roger Herman House] D. Dietsch. il *Archit Rec* 175:122-7 mid-Ap '87

Configuration for a canyon [B. Phelps's Arroyo House] T. S. Hines. il *Archit Dig* 44:166-9+ S '87
Graceful details: classical lines in a designer's Los Angeles villa [L. Cataffo] H. Drohojowska. il *Archit Dig* 44:66-71 Ag '87
Art
Eight artists interviewed. H. Cotter. il *Art Am* 75:162-79+ My '87
Getting on the map. R. Hughes. il *Time* 129:78-81 Ja 12 '87
Los Angeles: the new Mecca. B. Conrad, III. il *Horizon* 30:17-30 Ja/F '87
Los Angeles: two for the show. P. Plagens. il *Art Am* 75:146-52+ My '87
Blacks
See also
Watts (Los Angeles, Calif.)
Blacks seek aid for big losses in Calif. quake. il *Jet* 73:14 N 16 '87
Los Angeles: the growing metropolis on the coast. J. Shiver. il *Black Enterp* 17:65-6+ My '87
Bookstores
See Booksellers and bookselling—California
Courts
Order judge to take 2-month leave after complaints of behavior [M. Thomas] il por *Jet* 73:36 N 30 '87
Crime
Actress suing Farrah Fawcett is attacked in Los Angeles [S. Dunson] pors *Jet* 72:26 Je 22 '87
The Billionaire Boy—and the missing body [trial of J. Hunt] por *Newsweek* 109:61 My 4 '87
Death squads invade California [threats to Salvadorans] C. Garcia. il *Time* 130:20-1 Ag 3 '87
Etta Smith's inspiration cost her four days in jail [vision of victim's body in Pacoima section] J. Kelley. il por *People Wkly* 27:33 My 25 '87
Gunfire in traffic [shooting on Los Angeles freeways] A. Steacy. il *Macleans* 100:41 Ag 17 '87
Gunplay on the freeway. M. Kaus. il *Newsweek* 110:18 Ag 10 '87
Highway to homicide [freeway shootings] F. Trippett. il *Time* 130:18 Ag 17 '87
L.A. law: gangs and crack. G. Hackett and M. A. Lerner. il *Newsweek* 109:35-6 Ap 27 '87
Life and death with the gangs. J. D. Hull. il *Time* 130:21-2 Ag 24 '87
Life with father was nasty, brutish and scary, so Johnny Junatanov tried to have him murdered—repeatedly. A. Richman. il pors *People Wkly* 27:83+ Ja 19 '87
Murder and intrigue California-style [Billionaire Boys' Club trial] M. Gray. por *Macleans* 100:44 F 16 '87
The nightmare of his mother's murder is echoed in James Ellroy's grisly new novel, The black dahlia. S. Dougherty. il pors *People Wkly* 28:122-4 D 14 '87
"Operation Rx" sting [D. Hall helps break pharmacists' prescription drug scam] J. Fincher. il *Read Dig* 131:36-41 S '87
Rambo's brothers cruise clogged expressways [freeway shootings] T. Gest. il *U S News World Rep* 103:6 Ag 10 '87
We had to find our daughter's molester. S. Kraft. il *Read Dig* 130:147-51 My '87
Description
From kitsch to classic. D. Ketcham. il map *Travel Holiday* 168:69-75 S '87
What's new in L.A.? C. Haas. il *Esquire* 107 Summ Traveler:T38-T42+ Ap '87
Education
Inching toward more school [year-round classes] J. N. Baker. il *Newsweek* 110:75-6 O 26 '87
A movie star goes to Watts to make sure the Bard gets a good rap [work of J. Agutter] K. Hubbard. il pors *People Wkly* 27:83-4 Je 29 '87
Festivals
See also
Los Angeles Festival
Finance
See also
Los Angeles (Calif.)—Taxation
Freeways
See Express highways—California
Galleries and museums
See also
Los Angeles County Museum of Art
Museum of Contemporary Art (Los Angeles, Calif.)
Southwest Museum (Los Angeles, Calif.)
Coast-to-coast. P. Clothier. il *Art News* 86:31-2 Mr '87
From kitsch to classic. D. Ketcham. il map *Travel Holiday* 168:69-75 S '87

Los Angeles (Calif.)—*cont.*
Historic houses, sites, etc.
Architectural digest visits: Burt Bacharach and Carole Bayer Sager [Bel-Air home decorated by Waldo Fernandez] B. Gooch. il pors *Archit Dig* 44:128-33+ O '87
Bellagio House: the David Murdock estate in Bel-Air. M. M. Thomas. il por *Archit Dig* 44:52-61 F '87
Reorienting a classic: inventive decor for a Lloyd Wright house [home of designer M. London; cover story] P. Goldberger. il por *Archit Dig* 44:108-15 Mr '87
Housing
Rx for the 'Ratlord': live in your own slums [slumlord M. Avol] por *Newsweek* 110:54 Jl 27 '87
Trials of a landlord [slumlord M. Avol] D. Seligman. il *Fortune* 116:95-6 Ag 17 '87
Industries
Tinseltown outgrows the movies. S. L. Hawkins. il *U S News World Rep* 102:45-6 Ja 19 '87
Libraries
See also
Los Angeles Public Library
Markets
A new generation of don't-miss markets in and around Los Angeles. il *Sunset* 179:98-101 O '87
Music
See also
Los Angeles Music Center Opera
Photographs and photography
Beyond the off-ramp [motorcycles] J. Terranova. il *Cycle* 38:72-4 Mr '87
Plazas
MOCA and more: the future of California Plaza at Bunker Hill. M. F. Schmertz. il *Archit Rec* 175:82 My '87
Police
Going it alone in the ghetto [South Central Los Angeles proposes property taxes to pay for police] J. D. Hull. il *Time* 129:22 Ap 13 '87
L.A. kills anti-crime bill that would raise taxes. *Jet* 72:8 Je 22 '87
Politics and government
Down and out in L.A. [liberal activists] A. Kopkind. il *Nation* 244:309+ Mr 14 '87
The Hollywood primary [cover story] R. Brownstein. il *New Repub* 197:19+ N 23 '87
Poor
Down and out in L.A. [not-quite-homeless forced to live in garages, automobiles, etc.] F. Trippett. il *Time* 129:23 Je 22 '87
Matthew Weaver: helping the down-and-out in L.A. [food relief] C. Lapin. por *Seventeen* 46:111 O '87
A week in the life of a homeless family. A. Fadiman. il *Life* 10:30-6+ D '87
Popular culture
Diary of a lost weekend [club scene] M. Lindquist. il *N Y Times Mag* p48-51+ O 11 '87
Population
What it was like to fear 'a knock on the door' [family of Mexicans living illegally] W. L. Chaze. il *U S News World Rep* 102:24-6 Ja 19 '87
Public health
Facing the fear: help for women with AIDS [work of S. Gage, director of the Women's AIDS Project] R. L. Bray. il por *Ms* 15:31 My '87
Hard knocks [head injuries of inner city children; work of George E. Locke and others] *Sci Am* 256:30 Je '87
Race relations
Myrlie Evers asks for protection during threat. *Jet* 72:16 Ap 6 '87
Religious institutions and affairs
Baltimore priest 1st black bishop for West Coast [C. A. Fisher] por *Jet* 71:36 Ja 26 '87
Restaurants, nightclubs, bars, etc.
Diary of a lost weekend [club scene] M. Lindquist. il *N Y Times Mag* p48-51+ O 11 '87
Next to his family and his beloved Dodger blue, Tommy Lasorda lives for food—and his restaurant. T. Gold. il pors *People Wkly* 28:103-4 Jl 13 '87
Spécialités de la maison:
    Cassis. C. Bates. il *Gourmet* 47:42+ Ag '87
    Citrus, "three for tea". C. Bates. il *Gourmet* 47:42+ D '87
    The Mandarin. C. Bates. il *Gourmet* 48:32+ Je '87
    Patout's in Westwood. C. Bates. il *Gourmet* 47:36+ F '87
    Trader Vic's, The Original Sonora Cafe, Piret's. C. Bates. il *Gourmet* 47:40+ Ap '87
To be really hip you gotta hop, because the hottest clubs these days groove on the move. il *People Wkly* 28:54-6 S 28 '87

Savings and loan associations
See also
Family Savings & Loan Association (Los Angeles, Calif.)
Schools
See Los Angeles (Calif.)—Education
Social life and customs
Adventures in Tinseltown. T. Janowitz. il por *N Y Times Mag* p32-3+ Mr 22 '87
Entertaining [L.A. hostess C. McGrath and S. Lazar's Oscar Awards party] W. P. Rayner and C. Rayner. il pors *Vogue* 177:120+ Jl '87
The Teacher and the Crows [street racing in L.A.] D. Barry. il *Car Driv* 32:109+ My '87
Sports
Who's the biggest sport in L.A.? Jerry Buss. R. Grover. il por *Bus Week* p72+ Mr 16 '87
Street traffic
Stuck inside immobile. P. Egan. il *Road Track* 38:16 My '87
Subways
Tunnel vision. T. Assenza. il *Car Driv* 32:19 F '87
Taxation
Going it alone in the ghetto [South Central Los Angeles proposes property taxes to pay for police] J. D. Hull. il *Time* 129:22 Ap 13 '87
L.A. kills anti-crime bill that would raise taxes. *Jet* 72:8 Je 22 '87
Transit systems
See also
Los Angeles (Calif.)—Subways
Water supply
Trouble ahead for exotic Mono Lake. M. Sun. il *Science* 237:716-17 Ag 14 '87
Watts
See Watts (Los Angeles, Calif.)
Los Angeles Coliseum
Al Davis: on the move again? [Los Angeles Raiders] il por *Bus Week* p34 Ag 10 '87
Los Angeles County Museum of Art
The buildings in close-up. S. Stephens. il *Art Am* 75:152-5 My '87
A gathering of fragments [Robert O. Anderson Building] M. F. Schmertz. il *Archit Rec* 175:110-19 F '87
Getting on the map. R. Hughes. il *Time* 129:78-81 Ja 12 '87
Los Angeles: two for the show. P. Plagens. il *Art Am* 75:146-52+ My '87
New face on the block. K. Norment. il *Art News* 86:23-4 F '87
The new temples of art. P. Young. il *Macleans* 100:82-3 F 2 '87
Los Angeles Festival
Hi-ho! Hi-ho! Culture high and low [mastermind R. J. Fitzpatrick] il por *Harpers Bazaar* 120:210 S '87
Los Angeles International Airport *See* Los Angeles (Calif.)—Airports
Los Angeles Music Center Opera
A fairy-tale Wagner in L.A. [D. Hockney's sets for Tristan] J. Huck. il por *Newsweek* 110:73 D 21 '87
Los Angeles. D. Perlmutter. il *Opera News* 51:35 Ja 3 '87
Los Angeles. D. Perlmutter. *Opera News* 52:52-3 D 5 '87
Opera's turn. A. Rich. il por *Opera News* 52:16-18+ D 5 '87
Los Angeles Olympics, 1984 *See* Olympic Games—1984—Summer Olympics
Los Angeles Poverty Department (Theater company)
Their home is the streets, but the play's the thing for L.A.'s down-but-not-out skid row players. M. Small. il por *People Wkly* 28:127-8+ D 7 '87
Los Angeles Public Library
The great Los Angeles Library fire—and its happy ending. L. See. *Publ Wkly* 231:36 F 6 '87
Los Angeles times book review
The great L.A. poetry battle [brouhaha over poetry policy] L. See. *Publ Wkly* 231:52 My 29 '87
Los Tecos (Organization) *See* Neo-Nazis—Mexico
Losing *See* Failure (Psychology)
Losing of articles *See* Lost articles
Loss of consciousness
See also
Coma
Lost and found art *See* Art—Missing and found works
Lost articles
The box [lost wedding gifts returned to owner after 50 years] R. H. Kelly. il *South Living* 22:82 D '87
Lost books
A woeful gallery of the world's lost masterpieces. B. Conrad. bibl (p271) il *Smithsonian* 18:239-40+ N '87

The Lost Boys [film] See Motion picture reviews—Single works

Lost children *See* Missing children

Lost empires [television program] See Television program reviews—Single works

Lost jewelry
    See also
    Jewelry—Theft

Lost money
Driving along minding his business, Melvin Kiser ran into $2 million—then he did the unthinkable [returned money that fell out of armored car] M. Dougherty. il pors *People Wkly* 28:75-6 N 30 '87

Lost persons *See* Missing persons

Lost wallets
    See also
    Wallets—Theft

Lotan, Yael
When Israelis and Palestinians meet. *Nation* 244:141-2 F 7 '87

Lotas Minard Patton McIver Inc.
The power of positive stress [S. Minard] K. Brady. il pors *Work Woman* 12:74-7 Jl '87

Lothrop, Eaton S.
Time exposure. See occasional issues of Popular Photography

Lott, Felicity, 1948-
    about
Portrait of a lady. E. Forbes. por *Opera News* 52:38-9 N '87

Lott, Trent
Lessons of the Iran-contra affair. por *Read Dig* 130:75-6 Je '87

Lotteries
    See also
    Television broadcasting—Lottery results
As drama it was a waste, but financially, Michigan's first cow-drop raffle was no flop. il *People Wkly* 28:85 Jl 6 '87
From the publisher [major magazine subscription promotional offers] D. K. Graham. *Antiques Collect Hobbies* 92:6+ O '87
Lottery foes target public policy [proposed Indiana state lottery] B. L. Rohrig. *Christ Century* 104:396-7 Ap 29 '87
The lottery luster [educational funds raised in state lotteries] C. Pipho. *Phi Delta Kappan* 69:254-5 D '87
The myth of the money tree [state lotteries] C. W. Colson. il *Christ Today* 31:64 Jl 10 '87

    Automation
Can Gtech keep winning at the lottery? [designing and installing state lottery systems] L. Helm. il *Bus Week* p93-4 My 18 '87

Lottery winners
$3 million lotto win 'numbs' Queens man [U. Hosang] il por *Jet* 72:24 Ag 24 '87
Black millionaire lottery winners party aboard ship. il *Jet* 73:16+ O 5 '87
Blacks hit lottery for $7.5 million in New York and $2 million in Illinois. il por *Jet* 72:12 Jl 20 '87
Blind D.C. woman wins $1.2 million in lottery [J. Saunders] *Jet* 71:7 Ja 19 '87
Calif. 'Big Spin' winner pleads guilty to theft [cocaine charge against T. Garrett dismissed] *Jet* 71:36 Ja 12 '87
Dream comes true for St. Louis man who won $2 million in lottery [H. Smith] il por *Jet* 72:6 S 21 '87
High school dropout strikes it rich in Calif. lottery [R. Ware] *Jet* 71:23 Ja 12 '87
Lotto winner keeps cool after winning $4 million [R. Bell of Calif.] il por *Jet* 72:40 Jl 6 '87
No longer the biggest lottery winner ever, a Chicagoan reclaims a different prize: his privacy; ed. by Civia Tamarkin. M. Wittkowski. il pors *People Wkly* 28:117-18+ N 23 '87
Shy N.Y. lotto winner claims $12 million prize after waiting 3 months [M. Richards] il por *Jet* 71:30 Mr 9 '87
Woman dies of heart attack after $1.2 million lottery win [J. Saunders] *Jet* 71:18 Mr 9 '87

Lottman, Herbert R.
International front. See occasional issues of Publishers Weekly beginning May 27, 1983

Lotus (Automobile) *See* Sports cars

Lotus Car Group Companies Ltd. *See* Group Lotus Car Companies Ltd.

Lotus Development Corporation
Both sides may win this war [spreadsheet market] A. Field. il *Bus Week* p104-5 O 19 '87

The drill instructor who made Lotus snap to attention [J. Manzi] K. H. Hammonds. il por *Bus Week* p190-2 N 16 '87
Lotus' dream-come-true: a sweet deal with IBM [1-2-3/M spreadsheet] A. Field and A. Beam. il *Bus Week* p116 My 25 '87
Lotus takes the offensive: targets 1-2-3 clones; add-in market. il *Pers Comput* 11:29-30 Mr '87
Software plays hardball [Apple's proposed programming company and IBM's deal with Lotus] *Time* 129:52 My 11 '87
Will Lotus overrun Microsoft's Japanese garden? B. Buell. il por *Bus Week* p76 Ap 13 '87

Lotus tetragonolobus *See* Winged peas

Lotz, Martin, and others
Substance P activation of rheumatoid synoviocytes: neural pathway in pathogenesis of arthritis. bibl f il *Science* 235:893-5 F 20 '87

Loudon, Jim
Let's save Mars first. il *Sky Telesc* 74:228 S '87

Loudon, John V.
Hostage in Lebanon. pors *Publ Wkly* 231:38-40 Mr 6 '87

Loudspeakers
Crossover networks. il *Radio-Electron* 58:7+ Jl '87
Heard but not seen. F. Vizard. il *Pop Mech* 164:34 Mr '87
"I can make you an awesome deal": real-life devious speaker selling practices. K. L. Kantor. il *High Fidel* 37:42-4+ Je '87
Loudspeakers. E. B. Meyer. il *High Fidel* 37:47+ S '87
The right speakers. I. Masters. il *Stereo Rev* 52:64-8 S '87
Speakers. il *Stereo Rev* 52:121-2+ F '87

    Design
Crossovers abounding. R. Hodges. il *Stereo Rev* 52:160 O '87
Heard but not seen [Bose Acoustimass speaker system] F. Vizard. il *Pop Mech* 164:35 Jl '87
Hide-and-speakers [Bose Acoustimass Speaker System] A. Fisher. il *Pop Sci* 230:102 Ap '87
Innovative speakers. F. Vizard. il *Pop Mech* 164:51-2 My '87
Loudspeakers designed for digital sound. L. Feldman. il *Pop Sci* 230:68-70 Je '87
Magnetically shielded loudspeakers. L. Klein. il *Radio-Electron* 58:83-4 O '87
The mighty Klipschorn. R. Hodges. il *Stereo Rev* 52:216 N '87
Ribbons of sound. G. Burks. il *Forbes* 140:224 N 30 '87
Speaker imaging. D. Moran. il *Stereo Rev* 52:96-9 Je '87
Speakers: the state of the art. J. D. Hirsch. il *Stereo Rev* 52:58-63 S '87
Stereo imaging. R. Hodges. il *Stereo Rev* 52:216 F '87
Stereo spatial imaging. L. Klein. il *Radio-Electron* 58:33+ N '87
Transparent images. R. Angus. il *Pop Mech* 164:104-6 D '87

    Energy usage
Powered speakers [built in amplifiers] W. Wolfe. il *Stereo Rev* 52:69-71 S '87

    Testing
3D Acoustics Cube loudspeaker. il *High Fidel* 37:36-7 Je '87
Acoustic Research TSW910 speaker system. J. D. Hirsch. il *Stereo Rev* 52:31-2+ Je '87
ADS L-990 loudspeaker. il *High Fidel* 37:24+ Je '87
Advent Maestro loudspeaker. il *High Fidel* 37:31+ N '87
Allison IC-20 loudspeaker. il *High Fidel* 37:34-5+ D '87
Altec Lansing 301 loudspeaker. il *High Fidel* 37:34+ Ap '87
Altec Lansing Model 401 speaker system. J. D. Hirsch. il *Stereo Rev* 52:53-4 F '87
American Acoustics PSW-200 powered subwoofer. il *High Fidel* 37:27+ N '87
AR TSW-410 loudspeaker. il *High Fidel* 37:31-2 Jl '87
B&W MASS car speakers. C. Greenleaf. il *Stereo Rev* 52:162+ Ja '87
Bose AM-5 speaker system. J. D. Hirsch. il *Stereo Rev* 52:62-5 Ap '87
Bose AM-5 three-piece loudspeaker system. il *High Fidel* 37:28-9 Je '87
Boston Acoustics T830 speaker system. J. D. Hirsch. il *Stereo Rev* 52:35-6 S '87
Carver's Amazing Loudspeaker. J. D. Hirsch. il *Stereo Rev* 52:18-22 D '87

Loudspeakers—Testing—*cont.*

Celestion SL700 speaker. J. D. Hirsch. il *Stereo Rev* 52:51-2+ S '87

Dahlquist M-905 speaker. J. D. Hirsch. il *Stereo Rev* 52:42+ O '87

dbx Soundfield 100 speaker system. J. D. Hirsch. il *Stereo Rev* 52:62+ Ja '87

DCM Time Frame TF-1000 speaker system. J. D. Hirsch. il *Stereo Rev* 52:67+ D '87

DCM Timeframe TF-250 loudspeaker. il *High Fidel* 37:35-6 Je '87

Design Acoustics PS-103 speaker system. J. D. Hirsch. il *Stereo Rev* 52:41-2 D '87

EPI Magnus A-12 loudspeaker. il *High Fidel* 37:52+ Ja '87

EPI T/E-280 loudspeaker. il *High Fidel* 37:35-6 S '87

EPI T/E 320 Series II speaker system. J. D. Hirsch. il *Stereo Rev* 52:31-2 Jl '87

Focus .7 high definition monitor speaker. J. D. Hirsch. il *Stereo Rev* 52:49+ Ag '87

Going pro: affordable studio monitors also work at home. B. Buontempo. il *Roll Stone* p137-8 S 24 '87

Infinity Reference Standard 8 Kappa speaker. J. D. Hirsch. il *Stereo Rev* 52:33-4 O '87

Infinity RS-7 Kappa loudspeaker. il *High Fidel* 37:35+ N '87

Jamo Compact 120 speaker. J. D. Hirsch. il *Stereo Rev* 52:81-2 N '87

Jamo Compact 90 loudspeaker. il *High Fidel* 37:41+ N '87

JBL 830 loudspeaker. il *High Fidel* 37:23+ N '87

JSE Infinite Slope Model 1 speaker. J. D. Hirsch. il *Stereo Rev* 52:35-6+ Mr '87

KEF 107 loudspeaker [discussion of November 1986 article] il *High Fidel* 37:43 F '87

KEF Model 102 loudspeaker. J. D. Hirsch. il *Stereo Rev* 52:39-40 My '87

Live vs. recorded. R. Hodges. il *Stereo Rev* 52:200 D '87

Magnat MSP 300 speaker system. J. D. Hirsch. il *Stereo Rev* 52:36+ Ag '87

Mission Model 780 Argonaut speaker. J. D. Hirsch. il *Stereo Rev* 52:30+ F '87

Paradigm 9se loudspeaker. il *High Fidel* 37:30+ Je '87

Phase Tech PC 800HO speaker system. J. D. Hisrch. il *Stereo Rev* 52:53-4 Je '87

Polk Audio SDA-1c speaker system. J. D. Hirsch. il *Stereo Rev* 52:41-2+ N '87

Siefert Research Magnum III loudspeaker. il *High Fidel* 37:27-8 Je '87

Sight and sound: mighty bantams: small speakers now deliver big. H. Fantel. il *Opera News* 52:32-3 Ag '87

Sight and sound: versatile mimics. H. Fantel. il *Opera News* 52:34-5 D 19 '87

Signet SL-100 speaker system. J. D. Hirsch. il *Stereo Rev* 52:45-6 Jl '87

Snell Type C/i loudspeaker. J. D. Hirsch. il *Stereo Rev* 52:41-2 Ap '87

Speakerlab DAS 2 speaker. J. D. Hirsch. il *Stereo Rev* 52:44-5 Mr '87

TSC Symphony 1 loudspeaker. il *High Fidel* 37:43+ N '87

Unique speaker system [Bose AM-5] C. J. Esse. il *High Fidel* 37:14+ Mr '87

Louganis, Greg
about
Diver Greg Louganis returns to dancing, his first love, before the eyes of his pal Ryan White. W. Plummer. il pors *People Wkly* 28:44-5 N 9 '87

Gaining at last on the top guy. P. Putnam. il por *Sports Illus* 66:40-1 Ap 27 '87

Loughlin, Joe
about
Loughlin's lament. J. B. Grillo. il por *Channels* 7:66-7 Jl/Ag '87

Loughlin, Lori
about
Making the big screen scene. il pors *Teen* 31:77 Ag '87

Louis XV, King of France, 1710-1774
about
Fit for a king. J. Black. por *Hist Today* 37:3 Ap '87

Louis, Errol T.
Racism on campus. *Essence* 18:53+ Ag '87

Louis, Joe, 1914-1981
about
1937. *Am Herit* 38:140 My/Je '87
TV special honors champ Louis' 50th anniversary. *Jet* 72:48 Je 22 '87

Louis, Murray
about
Black and white [dance] Reviews
N Y il 20:80 Ap 6 '87. T. Tobias
Reviews:
Performances at the Joyce Theater, New York City. K. Onoda. il *Dance Mag* 61:18-19 N '87

Louis, Peter A., and Sack, Donald R.
John Chipman, cabinetmaker of Salem, Massachusetts. il *Antiques* 132:1318-25 D '87

Louis of Luxembourg See Saint-Pol, Louis, of Luxembourg, comte de, 1418-1475

Louis Vuitton (Firm)
Moet and Vuitton: the dernier cri in chic [merger] F. J. Comes. *Bus Week* p49 Je 15 '87

Louisiana
See also
Acadians—Louisiana
Architecture, Domestic—Louisiana
Atchafalaya River (La.)
Bayous
Criminal justice, Administration of—Louisiana
Educational laws and regulations—Louisiana
Environmental policy—Louisiana
Fishing—Louisiana
Honey Island Swamp (La.)
Music festivals—Louisiana
Plantations—Louisiana
Prisons—Louisiana
Wetlands—Louisiana

Description and travel
A country called Cajun. M. Burton. il *Saturday Evening Post* 259:82-4 S '87

Do we have a swamp for you! [Louisiana Cajun country] B. Keating. il *50 Plus* 27:55-9+ Jl '87

Passing a good time on the bayou [Atchafalaya Basin] C. Maddox. il map *South Living* 22:108-15 Mr '87

Politics and government
See also
Politics, Corruption in—Louisiana
The GOP smells more than gumbo in Louisiana [governorship up for grabs] R. Fly. il por *Bus Week* p56 O 26 '87

In Louisiana: "We got the hook in 'em now, Bubba" [political organizer S. Thomas] G. Jaynes. il por *Time* 130:11 S 28 '87

Is it Edwin's last stand? [Governor E. Edwards] D. Pedersen. il por *Newsweek* 110:39 O 26 '87

Race relations
Louisiana woman losing her bid to be categorized white [S. Phipps] por *Jet* 71:36 Ja 12 '87

Louisiana Downs (Shreveport, La.: Race track) See Race tracks

Louisiana-Pacific Corp.
Respecting the law [environmental protest against Louisiana-Pacific in California] P. Steinhart. il *Audubon* 89:10+ N '87

Louisiana State Penitentiary (Angola, La.) See Prisons—Louisiana

Louisville (Ky.)
Music
See also
Kentucky Opera
Police
Black police applicants seek millions in Louisville protest. *Jet* 71:8 Mr 16 '87

Race relations
Klan burns King photo, 1,000 react in Louisville. *Jet* 71:18 F 23 '87

Religious institutions and affairs
Free office space [bids for Presbyterian Church (U.S.A.) headquarters] *Christ Century* 104:401 Ap 29 '87

Lounasmaa, Olli V.
(jt. auth) See Hakonen, Pertti, and Lounasmaa, Olli V.

Lounge Lizards (Musical group)
The Lounge Lizards. G. Santoro. il *Down Beat* 54:14 F '87

Lourie, Richard, 1940-
(tr) See Fiut, Aleksander. Separate nations: poetry and the people

Loury, Glenn C.
American blacks [discussion of January 1987 article, Who speaks for American blacks?] *Commentary* 83:2+ Ap '87

Who speaks for American blacks? *Commentary* 83:34-8 Ja '87

Why preferential admission? *Current* 296:27-9 O '87

Why preferential admission is not enough for blacks. *Educ Dig* 53:42-5 S '87

Loury, Glenn C.—*cont.*
about
Assault charges dropped against Harvard's Loury. pors *Jet* 72:25 S 7 '87
Harvard prof charged with beating up live-in lover. il pors *Jet* 72:24-5 Je 29 '87
The rise and fall of Glenn Loury. il por *Newsweek* 110:53 D 14 '87

Louv, Richard
Home sweet condo. il *Read Dig* 130:27-8+ Ap '87

Louvin Brothers (Musical group)
Rediscovered: the biggest brothers of all. il *Newsweek* 109:80 My 18 '87

Louvre Museum *See* Musée du Louvre

Louw, Leon
about
306 solutions to a baffling problem. B. W. Nelan. il pors *Time* 129:36 Mr 23 '87

Lovaas, O. Ivar
about
Saving grace. P. Chance. il *Psychol Today* 21:42-4 D '87

Lovastatin
Beyond a safe diet [Mevacor, cholesterol reducing drug] N. Underwood. il *Macleans* 100:61 Mr 23 '87
Cholesterol drug approved. *Sci News* 132:166 S 12 '87
The devil we know [Mevacor vs. niacin for reducing cholesterol] S. N. Chakravarty. il *Forbes* 140:203-4 N 2 '87
Hope for clogged arteries. S. Begley. il *Newsweek* 110:74 S 14 '87
The miracle company [Merck; cover story] J. A. Byrne. il pors *Bus Week* p84-8+ O 19 '87
New ally against heart disease. C. Gorman. il *Time* 130:69 S 14 '87
A new drug that fights cholesterol. I. Ross. il *Read Dig* 131:91-4 D '87
A new weapon in the battle against heart disease. D. Farley. il *FDA Consum* 21:26-8 N '87
A pill to cut cholesterol: hope for hearts. il *Newsweek* 109:66 Mr 2 '87

Love, Davis, III
about
The power of Love. J. Diaz. il pors *Sports Illus* 66:44-6+ Mr 23 '87

Love, Diane
about
Love at first sight. M. Bethany. il *N Y* 20:50-3 F 9 '87

Love, Howard M.
about
The best-laid plans of Howard Love . . . G. L. Miles. il por *Bus Week* p74 Ag 10 '87

Love, John M.
A cry for help [story] il *Redbook* 168:70+ Ap '87

Love, Richard H.
about
An American cache at Chicago's R. H. Love Galleries. V. Lautman. il por *Archit Dig* 44:74+ S '87

Love, Victor
about
Victor Love. B. Allen. il pors *Essence* 17:40-2+ Ap '87

Love
See also
Courtship
Crushes (Emotions)
Jealousy
Romance
And they called it puppy love [35-year reunion of former orphans results in marriage of Robert Young and Frances Neuman] D. Hurley. *50 Plus* 27:18+ F '87
Celebrities tell why they can never forget that first love. il *Jet* 71:22-4 Mr 2 '87
The dark side of love [cover story] J. S. Kunen. il *People Wkly* 28:88-90+ O 26 '87
A different kind of love triangle [views of R. J. Sternberg] M. Golin. il *Prevention* 39:80-2+ Jl '87
Does love make you anxious? C. Tavris. *Vogue* 177:154 Ag '87
Grown-up love [interview with E. Person] D. Mason. *Vogue* 177:58 O '87
Heartbreak hotel [Debora Phillips' learning vacations to deal with problems of love] D. Zevin. il *Health* 19:18 Ja '87
Hugging your way to health. F. S. Goulart. il *Saturday Evening Post* 259:26+ Mr '87
Is he falling in love? How to read the signs. *Glamour* 85:26+ N '87
Is there love after 50? K. Pickford. il *50 Plus* 27:32-4 F '87

Let love. S. L. Taylor. il *Essence* 17:49 F '87
Love: the fervid quest for the 'L' word [New York City] E. Hopkins. il *N Y* 20:32-6+ Je 29-Jl 6 '87
Loving too much [R. Norwood's Women who love too much] C. Leerhsen. il por *Newsweek* 109:52-3 Mr 9 '87
Lunching over love [excerpt from Getting better all the time] L. Carpenter. il *50 Plus* 27:28-9+ N '87
My sister is in love . . . again. J. D. Pollack. il *Seventeen* 46:196+ Mr '87
A new light on love [interview with Z. Adams] J. Simmons. il por *Essence* 18:83-4+ My '87
Newlyweds: 10 ways to make love last. L. Norment. il *Ebony* 42:146+ Je '87
No greater love [willingness of Vietnamese boy to give up his life for another during wartime] J. W. Mansur. il *Read Dig* 131:49-50 Ag '87
Scaling the heights of passion [Passionate Love Scale developed by Elaine Hatfield and Susan Sprecher] G. Lowe. il *Psychol Today* 21:10 Jl '87
Star-studded love notes. il *Teen* 31:51 S '87
Take time to love. S. L. Taylor. il *Essence* 18:47 Jl '87
This can't be love (because I feel so good). J. Kaufman. il *Glamour* 85:310 Mr '87
This just in: love is eternal [U.S. news-CNN poll] il *U S News World Rep* 102:10 F 23 '87
Three medical miracles: the medicine was love; ed. by Susan Schneider. B. S. Siegel. *Redbook* 170:84-5+ D '87
True tales of love & marriage [symposium] il *Ladies Home J* 104:44+ F '87
Why do I love you? B. Walz. il *Ladies Home J* 104:83+ Ap '87

Anecdotes, facetiae, satire, etc.
Can this be love? B.-J. Raphael. See issues of Glamour
No more goo: advice to the lovestruck. Judywhite. il *Seventeen* 46:114 Ap '87

Love, Maternal
The magic of babylove. il *Harpers Bazaar* 121:118-25 D '87
The second child. A. Quindlen. il *Ladies Home J* 104:60+ S '87
To love a daughter, to love an addict. M. A. Gouzé. il *Ladies Home J* 104:107-9+ S '87

Love (R.H.) Galleries, Inc. *See* R.H. Love Galleries, Inc.

Love (Theology)
A friend's love: why process theology matters. B. Mesle. *Christ Century* 104:622-5 Jl 15-22 '87
God plays rough for love's sake. B. C. Lane. *Christ Century* 104:879-81 O 14 '87
How prayer can strengthen your love for God [cover story; interview with W. J. Burghardt] por *U S Cathol* 52:6-13 D '87
The 'ordinary times blues'. G. G. Seibert. *America* 157:255 O 17 '87
Submitting to freedom. P. Yancey. il *Christ Today* 31:64 Je 12 '87
The ultimate lover's gift. G. G. Seibert. *America* 157:143 S 12-19 '87

Love among thieves [television program] *See* Television program reviews—Single works

Love and Rockets (Musical group)
Love and Rockets take off in America. E. Royte. il *Roll Stone* p20 My 21 '87

Love Canal case
Last stage of Love Canal cleanup. *Sci News* 132:319 N 14 '87
Love Canal: a new cleanup plan stirs old fears. T. Smart. il *Bus Week* p30 Ag 31 '87

Love in motion pictures
What I learned about love on the silver screen. S. Helgesen. il *Glamour* 85:192 Ja '87

Love letters
How to write the perfect love letter. B. L. Ascher. il *Seventeen* 46:38+ F '87

Love me now or never [film] *See* Motion picture reviews—Single works

The love of three oranges [opera] *See* Prokofiev, Sergey, 1891-1953

Lovece, Joseph A.
The impending crisis of space debris. il *Astronomy* 15:6-13 Ag '87

Lovejoy, S., and others
Functional box-counting and multiple elliptical dimensions in rain. bibl f il *Science* 235:1036-8 F 27 '87

Lovelace, Linda
about
Awaiting a liver transplant, Linda Lovelace Marchiano struggles to close the book on her past. T. Kahn. il pors *People Wkly* 27:75-6 F 16 '87

Lovelaw [television program] See Television program reviews—Single works

Loveless, Patty

about

Patty Loveless. A. Nash. il por *Stereo Rev* 52:98-9 N '87

Lovell, Jocelyn

about

Pressure to find a cure. J. Barber. il por *Macleans* 100:38-9 Mr 30 '87

Lovell, Robin

Ice [with photographs] il *Ctry J* 14:43-7 D '87

Lovelock, James

about

Gaia: the life of a theory. R. Monastersky. *Sci News* 132:364 D 5 '87

Lovenheim, Barbara

Brides at last: women over 40 who beat the odds [cover story] il *N Y* 20:20-8 Ag 3 '87

Cher: sensual, sensitive, seductive, sensational. il pors *McCalls* 115:172-6 O '87

Loventhal, Charlie

about

My demon lover [film] Reviews

People Wkly il 27:10 My 18 '87. T. Cunneff

Loverseed, Helga

Toronto's group of five: museums as varied as Canada. il *Travel Holiday* 168:44-50 O '87

Lovett, Lyle

about

Lyle Lovett. A. Nash. por *Stereo Rev* 52:128 Ja '87

Lovett, Raymond E.

'Therapist dyed, sessions canceled'. il *Smithsonian* 18:152 Ag '87

Lovett, William, 1800-1877

about

'Kindness and reason': William Lovett and education. B. H. Harrison. bibl il por *Hist Today* 37:14-22 Mr '87

Lovi, George

New charts for the deep sky. il *Sky Telesc* 73:611-13 Je '87

Rambling through the skies. See issues of Sky and Telescope

Lovins, Amory B., 1947-

about

Amory and Hunter Lovins. B. Lawren. *Omni* 9:97 S '87

By showing consumers how to save energy, Amory and Hunter Lovins put the (solar) heat on high-cost power. M. Small. il pors *People Wkly* 28:119-20+ O 19 '87

Lovins, Amory B., 1947-, and Lovins, L. Hunter, 1950-
The avoidable oil crisis. il *Atlantic* 260:22+ D '87

Lovins, L. Hunter, 1950-

(jt. auth) See Lovins, Amory B., 1947-, and Lovins, L. Hunter, 1950-

about

Amory and Hunter Lovins. B. Lawren. *Omni* 9:97 S '87

By showing consumers how to save energy, Amory and Hunter Lovins put the (solar) heat on high-cost power. M. Small. il pors *People Wkly* 28:119-20+ O 19 '87

Lovoos, Janice

The California school of watercolor. il por *Am Artist* 51:62-9+ Ap '87

Eileen Monaghan Whitaker: painting from the heart. il por *Am Artist* 51:36-41 Mr '87

Low (George M.) Center for Industrial Innovation See George M. Low Center for Industrial Innovation

Low (Juliette Gordon) Birthplace (Savannah, Ga.) See Savannah (Ga.)—Historic houses, sites, etc.

Low alcohol beer See Beer

Low calorie cooking

100 snacks under 100 calories. il *Ladies Home J* 104:130-2+ S '87

150 desserts averaging less than 200 calories a serving. il *Sunset* 179:142+ Jl '87

The active gourmet [recipes devised by triathlete E. Burt] J. Myers. il pors *Women's Sports Fitness* 9:37-9 N '87

Bayou boast [recipes from Flagon's Wine Bar & Bistro in New Orleans] M. Fox. il *Health* 19:65-6+ S '87

Christmas de-lights. F. Fabricant. *Harpers Bazaar* 121:133-4+ D '87

Comfort food. J. Torrey. il *Health* 19:48-53 Ja '87

Contemporary cuisine for a new generation. C. Lyons. il *Ebony* 42:104-6+ Ag '87

Cooking light. See issues of Southern Living

Cooking light [special section] il *South Living* 22:87+ F '87

Cut the fat! Cut the calories! il *Redbook* 169:182-5+ S '87

Dieter's delight [low calorie vegetables] P. Vargas. il *Flower Gard* 31:8+ Je/Jl '87

Fourth stars [recipes from the Fountain Restaurant in Philadelphia] M. Fox. il *Health* 19:55-6+ Je '87

Healthy, hearty low-cal dishes. J. Nash. il *Essence* 17:75-8+ Ja '87

Light & lively. C. Lyons. il *Ebony* 42:108-10+ My '87

Lighten-up lunches. il *Health* 19:29-30 Ja '87

Lite eating. See issues of McCall's beginning August 1986

Lite feast [recipes from Fio's La Fourchette in Saint Louis] J. L. Lippert. il *Health* 19:61-2+ Mr '87

The "lite rite" diet. R. Winter. il *Harpers Bazaar* 120:166-7+ Ap '87

The lite stuff. il *Seventeen* 46:134-5 Je '87

Low-calorie desserts with high appeal. il *South Living* 22:208+ Ap '87

Low-calorie soups to beat winter's chill. J. Rogers. il *Prevention* 39:66-8+ Ja '87

New recipes that will change your life! L. Hoppe. il *Better Homes Gard* 65:47-53+ Mr '87

The salad-bar chef. L. Goldrich. il *Work Woman* 12:94+ F '87

Show stoppers [recipes from Winds Bar and Grill, Lenexa, Kan.] D. Welch. il *Health* 19:61-4 D '87

Spa food at home. J. Nash. il *Essence* 18:83-8+ Je '87

Trimming your holiday recipes [cutting fat] L. Phelps. il *Better Homes Gard* 65:95 D '87

Weight Watchers winning recipes [excerpt from Weight Watchers favorite recipes] il *Redbook* 168:65-9+ Ja '87

Low calorie diet See Diet

Low density lipoproteins See Lipoproteins

Low fat cooking See Low calorie cooking

Low fat diet See Diet

Low income housing See Housing

Low power television

Chip off the old town. M. Couzens. il *Channels* 7 Sp Issue:91 D '87

Low sodium cooking

Chinese food: sensational with less salt! J. Nash. il *Essence* 18:75-8+ Ag '87

Fish is fine on your low-sodium diet. B. E. Templeton. il *South Living* 22:96+ Ja '87

Have your cake—and no salt too [research by Virginia H. Holsinger] *Sci News* 131:361 Je 6 '87

Low-salt main dishes. il *Better Homes Gard* 65:111-12 Ag '87

Low temperatures

See also

Cold

Refrigerators

Superfluidity

Frozen tools [use of deep-cryogenic processing; cover story] V. E. Gilmore. il *Pop Sci* 230:64-7+ Je '87

Helium-3 and helium-4 [special issue; with introd. by Russell J. Donnelly] bibl f il *Phys Today* 40:23+ F '87

Hole-burning spectroscopy and relaxation dynamics of amorphous solids at low temperatures. R. Jankowiak and G. J. Small. bibl f il *Science* 237:618-25 Ag 7 '87

Laser cooling [cover story] D. J. Wineland and W. M. Itano. bibl f il *Phys Today* 40:34-40 Je '87

Leo Dana: cryogenic science and technology. R. J. Donnelly. il por *Phys Today* 40:38-41+ Ap '87

Lowe, David Garrard

Sesquicentennial sparkle. il *House Gard* 159:204-7+ O '87

Lowe, Jeannette

Ted Torrey interview. il por *Flower Gard* 32:48+ D '87/Ja '88

Lowe, Lewis A.

Don't bag 'em, bale 'em! il *Rodale's Org Gard* 34:69-71 S '87

Lowe, Wendy

The company's bigger, but is it better? il pors *Work Woman* 12:45-8 Je '87

(jt. auth) See Gallagher, Lawrence J., and Lowe, Wendy

Lowe, William C.

about

IBM's Bill Lowe on: seeing beyond PC boundaries. P. E. McKie. il por *Pers Comput* 11:110-11+ Je '87

Lowell, James Russell, 1819-1891

about

First encounters. E. Sorel and N. C. Sorel. il *Atlantic* 260:101 N '87

Lowell, Robert, 1917-1977
Near the unbalanced aquarium. por *N Y Rev Books* 34:10+ Mr 12 '87

Lowell, Sondra
about
Footloose or screw loose? Sondra Lowell gives listeners all the news that's fit to tap. il por *People Wkly* 27:102-3 Ja 19 '87

Lowell (Mass.)
City planning
The dark side of a dream. G. Hackett. il *Newsweek* 110:31-2 N 30 '87

Lowenstein, Jerold
Landfall. See issues of Oceans

Lowenthal, Abraham F.
Partners in conflict. il maps *Commonweal* 114:265-72+ My 8 '87

Lower California *See* Baja California (Mexico: Peninsula)
Lower East Side (New York, N.Y.)
American High: at Seward Park, the melting pot still bubbles [high school] K. D. Fishman. il *N Y* 20:78-80+ Mr 2 '87
Palimpsests [tour led by H. Cooke] *New Yorker* 63:24-5 Ap 13 '87

Lowitz, Donald S.
Review conference held on Biological and Toxin Weapons Convention [statements, reports, and text of final declaration, September 9-26, 1986] *Dep State Bull* 86:40-7 D '86

Lowrance, Christie
Lawmakers—not lawbreakers. il *Good Housekeep* 204:96 Mr '87
Quest for shipwrecks. il *Oceans* 20:50-4+ Jl/Ag '87

Lowry, Betty
Elves [poem] *America* 157:194 O 3 '87

Lowry, Katharine
Channelers. il por *Omni* 10:46-8+ O '87

Lowry, Lois
Remembering how it was. il *Writer* 100:16-19 Jl '87

Lowy, Frank
about
"You keep your eyes and ears open". T. Jaffe. por *Forbes* 139:36 Ap 6 '87

Loy, Myrna
(jt. auth) See Kotsilibas-Davis, James, and Loy, Myrna

Loyalists, American *See* American loyalists
Loyalty
Loyalty: in a modern world, finding value in an old-fashioned concept. B. L. Stern. *Vogue* 177:530 Mr '87
"Stand by your man": the all-American romantic myth that can short-circuit moral judgment. C. L. Mithers. *Glamour* 85:326 N '87

Loyn, Richard H.
The bird that farms the dell. il *Nat Hist* 96:54-60 Je '87

LSD
Acid test [LSD and creativity; study by Oscar Janigar] R. B. Tucker. *Omni* 10:16 N '87
Timothy Leary [interview] D. Sheff. por *Roll Stone* p226-8 N 5-D 10 '87

LSI Logic Corporation
"I know I sound protectionistic" [W. Corrigan] K. K. Wiegner. il por *Forbes* 139:54+ Je 29 '87

LTV Aerospace & Defense Co.
LTV receives Air Force contract to modernize, reengine A-7Ds. C. A. Shifrin. il *Aviat Week Space Technol* 126:85+ Je 1 '87

LTV Corp.
Guarding the till at LTV [L. Galie, chairman of committee formed to represent unsecured creditors] M. Kuntz. il por *Forbes* 139:90 Ja 26 '87

Lu, Cary, 1945-
Connections. *BioScience* 37:422 Je '87

Lubaroff, Saul
Tourette's sufferers can't help but say what's on their minds—even when it hurts; ed. by Giovanna Breu. il pors *People Wkly* 27:95+ Mr 23 '87

Lubavitcher movement *See* Hasidism
Lubben, Thomas H., and others
Stop-transfer regions do not halt translocation of proteins into chloroplasts. bibl f il *Science* 238:1112-14 N 20 '87

Lubbock, Eric Reginald *See* Avebury, Eric Reginald Lubbock, 4th Baron of, 1928-
Lubbock (Tex.)
Banks
See also
American State Bank (Lubbock, Tex.)

Education
Bridging the gap between a public school system and a university [Texas Tech faculty members adopt school classes in Lubbock] R. E. Ishler and E. C. Leslie. *Phi Delta Kappan* 68:615-16 Ap '87

Lubell, Rachel
about
Whose Chagall is it, anyway? A. Decker. *Art News* 86:21 D '87

Lubetkin, Alvin Nat, 1933-
about
Endangered species? E. Paris. il por *Forbes* 139:136-7 Mr 9 '87

Lubovitch, Lar
about
Reviews:
Performances at City Center, New York City. O. Stuart. *Dance Mag* 61:28-9 Ap '87

Lubovitch (Lar) Dance Company *See* Lar Lubovitch Dance Company
Lubricants *See* Lubrication and lubricants
Lubrication and lubricants
See also
Airplanes, Jet—Lubrication and lubricants
Automobiles—Lubrication and lubricants
Motor boats—Lubrication and lubricants
Lube job [Lube PS200 invented by Harold E. Sliney] *Sci Am* 256:60 My '87

Lucas, George
about
The Force of George Lucas is now with Disney. J. B. Levine and T. Mason. il por *Bus Week* p65 Mr 9 '87
George Lucas [interview] D. Sheff. por *Roll Stone* p241-2+ N 5-D 10 '87

Lucas, Henry Lee
about
Master of cant and recant. R. Lacayo. por *Time* 129:66 Ja 12 '87

Lucas, John
about
John Lucas makes good on last chance in NBA. il por *Jet* 71:49 F 9 '87
Three strikes and he's . . . back. B. Newman. il pors *Sports Illus* 66:18-19 Mr 2 '87

Lucas, Thomas
Boys are victims of sexism, too. por *Seventeen* 46:56 Je '87
about
Mr. President. B. Greene. il por *Esquire* 107:29-30 Ja '87

Lucasfilm Ltd. Industrial Light and Magic (Studio) *See* Industrial Light and Magic (Studio)
Lucca, Papo
about
Eddie Palmieri/Hilton Ruiz/Papo Lucca. L. Birnbaum. il *Down Beat* 54:52-3 Ag '87

Lucchitta, B. K.
Recent mafic volcanism on Mars. bibl f il maps *Science* 235:565-7 Ja 30 '87

Lucci, Susan
about
Susan Lucci breaks all the rules [cover story] il pors *Redbook* 170:10 N '87

Luce, Charles Franklin, 1917-
about
You call this retirement? P. Finch. il por *Bus Week* p30 Je 29 '87

Luce, Clare Boothe, 1903-1987
about
Obituary
America 157:282 O 31 '87. J. W. Donohue
Natl Rev il por 39:20-2+ N 6 '87. W. F. Buckley
Newsweek il pors 110:43 O 19 '87
People Wkly il por 28:48 O 26 '87
Time il pors 130:22-3 O 19 '87. P. Iyer
U S News World Rep por 103:9 O 19 '87. S. Morris

Luce, Henry, III
about
Brillig on the wave: island aerie of Nancy and Henry Luce III. C. T. Buckley. il pors *Archit Dig* 44:180-3+ My '87

Luce, Nancy Bryan, d. 1987
about
Brillig on the wave: island aerie of Nancy and Henry Luce III. C. T. Buckley. il pors *Archit Dig* 44:180-3+ My '87

Luce, R. Duncan (Robert Duncan), and Narens, Louis
Measurement scales on the continuum. bibl f il *Science* 236:1527-32 Je 19 '87

Luce, Robert
As they said in the Writer in 1887 . . . [reprint of December 1887 article] il *Writer* 100:2 D '87
Luce, Robert Duncan *See* Luce, R. Duncan (Robert Duncan)
Luciano, Robert Peter
about
Devour thy tail. G. Bronson. il pors *Forbes* 140:85+ N 2 '87
Lucid dreams *See* Dreams
Lucien Goldschmidt Inc.
Losing Lucien. G. Henry. il por *Art News* 86:16+ Mr '87
Luciferase
Glowing tobacco [gene tagging with luciferase] A. Fisher. il *Pop Sci* 230:8 Ap '87
Lighting up [gene tagging with luciferase] il *Sci Am* 256:60-2 Ja '87
Lucinda Childs Dance Company
Acting aside, Childs readies troupe for NYC season. por *Dance Mag* 61:6 My '87
One for my master [performance of Calyx and other works at the Joyce Theater, New York City] T. Tobias. il *N Y* 20:64+ Je 1 '87
Luckett, Jimmy
about
Blind tour guide describes exhibits at famous museum. il pors *Jet* 72:24-5+ Ag 17 '87
The Lucky Spot [drama] *See* Henley, Beth
Lucky Stores Inc.
Edelman: a new Lucky strike? [A. Edelman's moves] K. M. Hafner. il por *Bus Week* p49 F 23 '87
Luczak, Scott
about
Since he got Connie Powers' number, long-distance operator Scott Luczak is hearing a steady aisle tone. il pors *People Wkly* 27:57 Mr 30 '87
Luczywo, Helena, and Gardels, Nathan
Gorbachev: the view from Warsaw [interview with J. Kuron] *Harpers* 275:26-7 Jl '87
Ludlam, Charles
about
Obituary
Nation 244:862-3 Je 20 '87. T. M. Disch
Ludlum, David M., 1910-
Alaskan weather. See issues of Weatherwise
Almanac. See issues of Country Journal beginning October 1986
The climythology of America. il map *Weatherwise* 40:255-9 O '87
Snowfall—below average. il *Weatherwise* 40:41-4 F '87
Weatherwatch. See issues of Weatherwise
Ludvigson, Susan
The dream of birds [poem] *Nation* 244:268 F 28 '87
Ludwig, Bob
about
An interview with Bob Ludwig. M. Dery. il por *Stereo Rev* 52:113-15 N '87
Ludwig, Daniel Keith
about
Two giant U.S. business efforts that failed in Brazil. M. S. Forbes. il *Forbes* 140:18-19 O 19 '87
Luers, Wendy W.
Open house in Prague. il pors *House Gard* 159:150-5+ My '87
Luers, William H.
The U.S. and Eastern Europe. *Foreign Aff* 65:976-94 Summ '87
Lueth, Shirley
Personally yours. *Writer* 100:25-7 O '87
Lufkin, Liz
The etiquette of eating out. il *Seventeen* 46:26+ My '87
Lufkin, Thomas, and Bancroft, Carter
Identification by cell fusion of gene sequences that interact with positive trans-acting factors. bibl f il *Science* 237:283-6 Jl 17 '87
Lufthansa
Flight crew requirements through 1999 spur Lufthansa to bolster pilot corps. il *Aviat Week Space Technol* 127:38-9 Ag 10 '87
Lufthansa advances fleet modernization with A300-600 introduction. il *Aviat Week Space Technol* 126:35 Mr 23 '87
Lufthansa delays decision on retaining IAE V2500. il *Aviat Week Space Technol* 127:36 N 9 '87
Lufthansa orders 15 A340s with V2500 SuperFan engines. *Aviat Week Space Technol* 126:34-5 Ja 26 '87
Lufthansa reevaluates V2500 as powerplant for A320 fleet. *Aviat Week Space Technol* 126:30 My 25 '87

Lufthansa rejects airline consolidation. *Aviat Week Space Technol* 126:47 F 9 '87
Lufthansa, Swissair introduce full-simulator pilot training [Futura] K. F. Mordoff. il *Aviat Week Space Technol* 127:38-9+ Ag 10 '87
Lugar, Richard G.
Promoting and protecting democracy. *Américas* 39:51 Ja/F '87
A Republican looks at foreign policy. *Foreign Aff* 66:249-62 Wint '87/'88
about
Indiana Senator Lugar hosts Fitness Festival. il por *Jet* 72:29 Jl 6 '87
Luge racing
Woman to watch: Cammy Myler. A. Osius. il por *Women's Sports Fitness* 9:70 D '87
History
Bobsleigh, luge and speed skating [U.S. Olympic competitors] W. Bingham. il *Sports Illus* 67:51+ D 14 '87
Luggage
See also
Packing of luggage
Carry-on luggage. il *Consum Rep* 52:628-33 O '87
Carry-on luggage. il *Consum Rep* 52:202-6 D '87
Great luggage getaway. il *Harpers Bazaar* 120:42 Jl '87
Lugging it in luxury. R. La Ferla. il *N Y Times Mag* p40 Ja 4 '87
Traveling in style. D. Weidner. il *Travel Holiday* 168:70-3 N '87
Luggage handling, Airline *See* Airlines—Luggage handling
Luggage industry
France
See also
Louis Vuitton (Firm)
Lughod, Lila Abu- *See* Abu-Lughod, Lila
Lugo, Joseph A., Jr.
about
Where were the cops? R. L. Stern and M. Fritz. il *Forbes* 139:60-2 Ap 6 '87
Luguri, James
about
James Luguri's haiku. J. E. McEntyre. *Christ Century* 104:486-8 My 20-27 '87
Luhrs, Warren
BOC update: dismasted in the Tasman Sea. il *Mot Boat Sail* 159:57-9+ Mr '87
Lukács, György, 1885-1971
Bibliography
The convert. I. Deak. il *N Y Rev Books* 34:39-44 Mr 12 '87
Lukacs, John, 1924-
Unexpected Philadelphia. il *Am Herit* 38:72-6+ My/Je '87
Lukas, D. Wayne
about
Doing battle with the Demon. W. Nack. il por *Sports Illus* 66:42-4+ My 4 '87
Lukas, Georg
about
Pedal, Georg, but don't look back! Something might be gainin' on ya! il por *People Wkly* 28:137 D 14 '87
Lukas, J. Anthony, 1933-
Class reunion: Kennedy's men relive the Cuban Missile Crisis [cover story] il *N Y Times Mag* p22-7+ Ag 30 '87
Lukaszewski, James E.
Corporate and private sector communications responsibility [address, October 10, 1986] *Vital Speeches Day* 53:305-10 Mr 1 '87
Luken, Thomas A.
Big-time college athletics: commercialization and corruption. il *USA Today (Periodical)* 116:64-7 Jl '87
Lukens, Meg
Seventeen's Tennis Tournament of Champions. il *Seventeen* 46:175+ Ap '87
Lull, Roderick
No dogs allowed [story] il *Saturday Evening Post* 259:42-5+ N '87
Lully, Jean Baptiste, 1632-1687
about
Atys [opera] Reviews
New Yorker 62:79-81 Ja 26 '87. A. Porter
Lulu [opera] *See* Berg, Alban, 1885-1935
Lumber
A buyer's guide to lumber. il *Mother Earth News* 106:92-3 Jl/Ag '87
Choosing and using lumber for outdoor projects. R. N. Hoffman. il *Workbench* 43:80 Jl/Ag '87

Lumber fasteners *See* Fasteners
Lumber industry
See also
Bohemia Inc.
Frank Purcell Walnut Lumber Company
Louisiana-Pacific Corp.
Pacific Lumber Co.
Plum Creek Timber Company, Inc.
WTD Industries, Inc.

Acquisitions and mergers
A takeover artist who's turning redwoods into quick cash [C. E. Hurwitz's takeover of Pacific Lumber through Maxxam Group] J. R. Norman. il por *Bus Week* p64-5 F 2 '87

Export-import trade
Nailing the consumer [Canadian lumber in the U.S.] M. Alexander and others. il *Consum Res Mag* 70:26-9 Mr '87
A new storm over trade [Canada-U.S. dispute over softwood lumber exports] M. Rose. il *Macleans* 100:10-11 Ja 12 '87
Ottawa's trade offensive [softwood lumber accord with the U.S.] M. Drohan. il por *Macleans* 100:10-11 Ja 19 '87
Talking tough on trade [U.S.-Canada softwood lumber accord; with editorial comment by Kevin Doyle] M. Drohan. il *Macleans* 100:2, 12+ Ja 26 '87

Lumbering
See also
Clearcutting
Curbing abuses in computer modeling [Forest Service's FORPLAN] B. R. Herrick. il *Technol Rev* 90:24-5 O '87
The degradation factor [timber management and watershed protection in western national forests] M. Anderson and C. Gehrke. il *Wilderness* 51:38-40 Fall '87

Competitions
Photographs and photography
Anyone seen a blue ox? [Lumberjack World Championships] J. Azel. il *Sports Illus* 67:54-9 Ag 10 '87

History
Caulked boots and white water [Adirondack logging in the 19th and early 20th centuries] D. Wharton. il *Conservationist* 41:38-43 Mr/Ap '87

Lumberjacks
Competitions
See Lumbering—Competitions

Lumet, Sidney
about
The morning after [film] Reviews
Commonweal 114:55 Ja 30 '87. T. O'Brien
Macleans 100:19-20 Ja 5 '87. L. O'Toole
Mademoiselle il 93:102+ Mr '87. R. Rosenbaum
N Y 20:45-6 Ja 5 '87. D. Denby
Natl Rev 39:56-7 F 13 '87. J. Simon
New Repub 196:24 Ja 5-12 '87. S. Kauffmann
People Wkly il 27:12 Ja 5 '87. S. Haller

Luminarias
Lunch bag luminarias for some Halloween magic. il *Sunset* 179:108 O '87

Luminescence
See also
Bioluminescence
Sonoluminescence
A flash in the crystalline pan [triboluminescence; research by Linda M. Sweeting and Arnold L. Rheingold] *Sci News* 131:360 Je 6 '87
Laser-stimulated luminescence used to measure X-ray diffraction of a contracting striated muscle. Y. Amemiya and others. bibl f il *Science* 237:164-8 Jl 10 '87

Luminous clouds *See* Noctilucent clouds
Lummer, Heinrich
about
Disco bombers. N. Birnbaum. *Nation* 244:312-13 Mr 14 '87

Lumonics Inc.
The powers in a beam of light. il *Macleans* 100:39 Ap 20 '87

Lump-sum payments *See* Wages and salaries
Lumpectomy *See* Breast—Cancer—Surgery
Lumpkin, Michael D.
The regulation of ACTH secretion by IL-1. bibl f *Science* 238:452-4 O 23 '87

Lumpkin, Michael D., and others
Arginine vasopressin as a thyrotropin-releasing hormone. bibl f il *Science* 235:1070-3 F 27 '87

Luna, G. Cajetan
Welcome to my nightmare: the graffiti of homeless youth. il *Society* 24:73-8 S/O '87

Luna Luna (Hamburg, Germany)
Loony Luna Luna: this antic amusement park will raise your artbeat. J. Fayard. il *Life* 10:76-9 S '87

Lunar bases
Destination: lunar industrial base [proposal by W. F. Mitchell] W. H. Ganoe. il *Space World* X-9-285:39 S '87
Moon base gaining support as new U.S. space goal. C. Covault. il *Aviat Week Space Technol* 126:22-4 My 11 '87
NASA forms office to study manned lunar base, Mars missions. il *Aviat Week Space Technol* 126:22-3 Je 8 '87
Ride panel will urge lunar base, earth science as new space goals. C. Covault. il *Aviat Week Space Technol* 127:16-18 Jl 13 '87
Space studies increase emphasis on manned U.S. lunar base. *Aviat Week Space Technol* 126:27 My 4 '87
A star warrior aims at the moon [L. Wood's Columbus Project] R. Spangenburg and D. Moser. il por *Space World* X-4-280:30-2 Ap '87
Support for lunar base grows among non-aerospace firms. il *Aviat Week Space Technol* 127:109-10 O 12 '87

Astronomical use
Astronomy from the moon. H. J. Smith. *Sky Telesc* 74:27 Jl '87

Lunar eclipses *See* Eclipses, Lunar
Lunar geology
See also
Moon—Surface
Tektites and lunar volcanoes. *Sky Telesc* 73:481 My '87

Lunar magnetism *See* Moon—Magnetic properties
Lunar research *See* Moon
Lunar vehicles
Design
Prix de lune [winners of the Omni moon buggy contest] D. Ing. il *Omni* 9:52-5 Jl '87

Luncheons
See also
Brunches
A day of oyster (and ancestor) worship—in South Carolina, there's nothing finer [Tony and Julie Merck of Ashe Point farm] W. P. Rayner and C. Rayner. il *Vogue* 177:212 My '87
An early fall luncheon. il *Gourmet* 47:104-10 S '87
An Easter luncheon. il *Gourmet* 47:108-14+ Ap '87
Late summer spice. F. Niven. il por *House Gard* 159:200-2 S '87
McCall's goes to a party: lunch in the country. C. Rossant. il pors *McCalls* 145:115-16+ Mr '87
Veranda luncheon. il *Gourmet* 47:70-2+ Ag '87
When things go right [preparing a birthday luncheon in Provence] P. Wells. il *N Y Times Mag* p123-4+ S 13 '87

Luncheons, Business *See* Business entertaining
Lunches
See also
Brunches
School lunches
Let's have lunch! il *South Living* 22:202-3 Ap '87
Lighten-up lunches. il *Health* 19:29-30 Ja '87
The power lunch. J. Nash. il *Essence* 18:82 Ag '87
Power lunch: eat for all-afternoon energy. il *Glamour* 85:328-9 N '87
The truth about lunch. S. M. Sims. il *Vogue* 177:449-51+ Mr '87

Lunches, Business *See* Business entertaining
Lund, Beulah
about
Posing as a bag lady, housewife Beulah Lund finds fear and love in the homeless netherworld. R. Arias. il pors *People Wkly* 27:32-4+ F 16 '87

Lund, Doris
Candlelighters: help for stricken families. il *Read Dig* 131:73-8 Ag '87

Lund, Nancy
Zachary. il por *Parents* 62:117-18+ Ag '87

Lundberg, John G., and others
A major food web component in the Orinoco River channel: evidence from planktivorous electric fishes. bibl f il *Science* 237:81-3 Jl 3 '87

Lunden, Joan
about
Joan Lunden: now she's got it all! J. Rovin. il pors *Ladies Home J* 104:62+ Ap '87

Lundquist, Barbara Reeder
Higher education and teacher preparation in music. bibl f *Des Arts Educ* 88:6-11 Ja/F '87

Lundy, Ronni
Links with Dixie. il *Esquire* 107:38+ Mr '87

Lungs
See also
Respiration
Cancer
Causes
Lung cancer and indoor air pollution in Xuan Wei, China [burning of smoky coal] J. L. Mumford and others. bibl f il map *Science* 235:217-20 Ja 9 '87
Lung cancer in perspective [address, May 10, 1987] C. A. LeMaistre. *Vital Speeches Day* 53:564-6 Jl 1 '87
Why did my sister get lung cancer? C. SerVaas. il *Saturday Evening Post* 259:56-60+ Ja/F '87
Diagnosis
Getting a lung well [sputum test called Novacyte] *Prevention* 39:12 Je '87
Genetic aspects
Cancer gene gap mapped [small cell lung cancer] *Sci News* 132:229 O 10 '87
Smoking gun? [activation of K-*ras* oncogene; research by Sjoerd Rodenhuis and others] E. Collins. *Sci Am* 257:44-5 D '87
Nutritional aspects
Diet may help prevent lung cancer. *Prevention* 39:105 Je '87
New evidence that carotene prevents cancer. *Prevention* 39:104 Ag '87
Therapy
Breath of life [radiotherapy treatment developed by Robert Sarama] S. R. Hollis. *Health* 19:76 Ja '87
Diseases
See also
Cystic fibrosis
Emphysema
Pneumonia
Respiratory distress syndrome
Tuberculosis
New clues to smog's effects on lungs. J. Raloff. *Sci News* 132:86 Ag 8 '87
Smoke screened by vitamin E. *Prevention* 39:14 F '87
Prevention
The advice is basic: don't smoke. J. Carey and J. Silberner. il *U S News World Rep* 103:63-4 Ag 17 '87
Surfactants
See Surface active substances
Transplantation
The hearts of the matter [domino donors at Johns Hopkins Hospital] C. Wallis. il *Time* 129:60 My 25 '87
I can breathe again! P. Ruff. il pors *Saturday Evening Post* 259:100-2+ D '87
New life with a new lung. C. SerVaas. il *Saturday Evening Post* 259:102+ Ap '87
A second chance [heart-lung transplant recipient C. Bilodeau Gingras] L. Van Dusen. il por *Macleans* 100:44 N 23 '87

Luo, Ming, and others
The atomic structure of Mengo virus at 3.0 Å resolution. bibl f il *Science* 235:182-91 Ja 9 '87

Luoma, Jon R.
Black duck decline: an acid rain link. il map *Audubon* 89:18-20+ My '87
Forests are dying but is acid rain really to blame? il map *Audubon* 89:36-8+ Mr '87
The state of the tiger. il map *Audubon* 89:61-3 Jl '87
Taking the heat. il *Audubon* 89:76-9 Ja '87
about
Finlandia. L. Line. il *Audubon* 89:6 Ja '87

Lüpertz, Markus, 1941-
about
Markus Lupertz. M. Poirier. il *Art News* 86:146 Mr '87

Lupica, Mike
Advantage, Mr. McEnroe? [cover story] il pors *Esquire* 108:84-8+ Jl '87
Al the bad. il por *Esquire* 108:75-6+ O '87
Full court mess. il *Esquire* 108:63-4 N '87
Golden girls. il *World Tennis* 35:40-2+ S '87
St. Elmore's fire. il por *Esquire* 107:169-71+ Ap '87
That was the year that will be. il *Esquire* 108:81-2 D '87

Lupines
Looking at the lupines. B. Pleasant. il *Rodale's Org Gard* 34:74-9 Ja '87
Lupines find sweet new markets. M. Holmberg. il *Success Farm* 85:52 O '87

Lupus (Constellation) *See* Constellations
Lupus erythematosus
Trying to unravel 'the great imitator'. K. Hartley. *Sci News* 131:396 Je 20 '87
Understanding lupus. D. L. Taylor. *Essence* 18:18+ Je '87

Lures, Fishing *See* Fishing lures, flies, etc.
Lurie, Joseph
The 'uglification' of hospitality. por *U S News World Rep* 103:8 O 12 '87
Lurie, Paul M., and Weiss, Barry D.
Computers: changing the legal rules. *Archit Rec* 175:35+ Ap '87
Lust *See* Desire
Luster, Bill
Before the ball is tipped [photographs] il *Sport Mag* 78:60-6+ Mr '87
Luster Products Inc.
Atlantan selected new 1987 S-Curl Man by Luster Products [Michael E. Jinks] il *Jet* 71:8-9 Mr 2 '87
Lusterware
Lusterware sheen resembles silversmith's art. S. Bagdade and A. Bagdade. il *Antiques Collect Hobbies* 92:37 S '87
Lustick, Ian S.
Israel's dangerous fundamentalists. bibl f *Foreign Policy* 68:118-39 Fall '87
Lustig, Bill
Man talk. il *Glamour* 85:252 F '87
Luther, Martin, 1483-1546
about
If Luther were sitting in the end zone. D. H. Hopper. *Christ Century* 104:781-2 S 23 '87
Luther, Marylou
Fashion and the stars. il *Good Housekeep* 205:80 Ag '87
Fashion and the stars. il *Good Housekeep* 205:19 Jl '87
Fashion and the stars. il *Good Housekeep* 204:21 Je '87
Fashion and the stars. il *Good Housekeep* 204:21 My '87
Fashion and the stars. il *Good Housekeep* 204:54 Ap '87
Fashion and the stars. il *Good Housekeep* 204:48 Mr '87
Fashion and the stars. il *Good Housekeep* 204:210 F '87
Fashion and the stars. il *Good Housekeep* 204:36 Ja '87
Lutheran Church
See also
Catholic Church—Relations—Lutheran Church
United States
About those Lutherans. R. J. Neuhaus. *Natl Rev* 39:43 Jl 31 '87
Chilstrom installed [bishop of newly formed Evangelical Lutheran Church in America] *Christ Century* 104:936 O 28 '87
Lutherans and liturgy [discussion of July 29-August 5, 1987 article, Making a real return to church possible] P. G. Johnson. *Christ Century* 104:794-6 S 23 '87
Making a real return to church possible. P. G. Johnson. il *Christ Century* 104:656-9 Jl 29-Ag 5 '87
Merging Lutherans: a dying and a birth [Evangelical Lutheran Church in America] J. C. Lyles. *Christ Century* 104:461-3 My 13 '87
A mightier fortress [formation of Evangelical Lutheran Church in America] il *Time* 129:60 My 11 '87
The new Lutheran Church: the gift of Augustana [Evangelical Lutheran Church in America; cover story] R. E. Koenig. il *Christ Century* 104:555-8 Je 17-24 '87
Three Lutheran denominations become one [Evangelical Lutheran Church in America] il *Christ Today* 31:55-6 Je 12 '87
Lutoslawski, Witold, 1913-
about
Musical events:
Performance of works by G. Perle and W. Lutoslawski at Tanglewood. A. Porter. *New Yorker* 63:68-9 Ag 31 '87
Lutton, Wayne
Hazardous to your health. *Natl Rev* 39:54-6 Ja 30 '87
Luttwak, Edward N.
Entering the postnuclear age. il *N Y Times Mag* p49+ Ap 5 '87
Lutwiniak, William
about
Note from the editor. S. Wilmot. il por *Americana* 15:3 My/Je '87
Lutz, Adelle
about
Stop making fashion sense. M. Mifflin. por *Vogue* 177:34 Ja '87
Lutz, John, 1939-
The long and short of it. *Writer* 100:11-13 D '87

Lutz, Robert A.
The nonsense of a "post-industrial society" [address, January 15, 1987] *Vital Speeches Day* 53:330-3 Mr 15 '87

Luxembourg
See also
Banks and banking—Luxembourg
Communications satellites, Luxembourg
Description and travel
Old castles and Old Glory: Luxembourg pays tribute to America. C. Males. il map *Travel Holiday* 168:34-41 D '87

Luxury housing *See* Housing

Lyall, Sarah
Insider's guide to D.C. careers. *Harpers Bazaar* 121:59+ N '87

Lydecker, Garrit D.
Build a drillpress. il *Theatre Crafts* 21:75 F '87

Lydecker, Toni
Foods and finos of Spain. il *Travel Holiday* 167:16+ F '87

Lydenberg, Steven D.
(jt. auth) See Will, Rosalyn B., and Lydenberg, Steven D.

Lyford Cay Club (Bahamas) *See* Resorts—Bahamas

Lying
See also
Lie detectors and detection
Giving truth a bad name [politics] M. Greenfield. il *Newsweek* 110:64 Jl 27 '87
Lying: how much is too much? T. Hartman. il *Teen* 31:34+ S '87
Making up the truth [L. Hellman and R. M. Nixon] G. C. Ward. il *Am Herit* 38:18+ S/O '87
My husband couldn't tell the truth. il *Good Housekeep* 205:22+ N '87
Reflections on bullshit. H. Frankfurt. *Harpers* 274:14-17 F '87
Telling kids the truth about lying. L. Salk. il *McCalls* 114:81 S '87
Those little white lies. J. P. Comer. il *Parents* 62:204 Ap '87
The truth about lying [views of Beverly Palmer] il *USA Today (Periodical)* 116:3-4 D '87
Why kids lie. J. Marks. il *Parents* 62:112-14 Je '87
Anecdotes, facetiae, satire, etc.
Patriotic lying. R. Baker. il *N Y Times Mag* p14 Ag 9 '87

Lyman spectrum emission *See* Hydrogen—Spectra and spectroscopy

Lyme disease
Big trouble with tiny ticks. C. Wallis. il *Time* 130:49 S 28 '87
Ecology of a new disease. J. A. Miller. il *BioScience* 37:11-15 Ja '87
Lyme disease. G. S. Habicht and others. bibl (p116) il map *Sci Am* 257:78-83 Jl '87
The spread of Lyme disease. M. Clark. il map *Newsweek* 110:54 Jl 27 '87
Ticked off. J. Ullyot. il *Women's Sports Fitness* 9:18 Jl '87

Lymphadenopathy-associated viruses *See* HIV viruses

Lymphatic system
Cancer
See also
Hodgkin's disease
Causes
HTLV-V: a new human retrovirus isolated in a Tac-negative T cell lymphoma/leukemia. V. Manzari and others. bibl f il *Science* 238:1581-3 D 11 '87
A war with hope [Vietnam vet's battle with Agent Orange-induced cancer; ed. by John Grossmann. E. Zumwalt, III. il por *Health* 19:86+ Je '87
Diagnosis
Detection of minimal residual cells carrying the t(14;18) by DNA sequence amplification. M.-S. Lee and others. bibl f il *Science* 237:175-8 Jl 10 '87
Genetic aspects
Differential expression of c-*myb* mRNA in murine B lymphomas by a block to transcription elongation. T. P. Bender and others. bibl f il *Science* 237:1473-6 S 18 '87
Mutations in the first exon are associated with altered transcription of c-*myc* in Burkitt lymphoma [chromosomal translocations] E. Cesarman and others. bibl f il *Science* 238:1272-5 N 27 '87
Regulation of *bcl*-2 proto-oncogene expression during normal human lymphocyte proliferation. J. C. Reed and others. bibl f il *Science* 236:1295-9 Je 5 '87

Relationship between the c-*myb* locus and the 6q-chromosomal aberration in leukemias and lymphomas. C. Barletta and others. bibl f il *Science* 235:1064-7 F 27 '87
Therapy
Exposing cancer to a 'light' therapy [cutaneous T-cell lymphoma] J. Silberner. *Sci News* 131:101 F 14 '87
Glucocorticoid receptor-like antigen in lymphoma cell membranes: correlation to cell lysis. B. Gametchu. bibl f il *Science* 236:456-61 Ap 24 '87
Let there be light [photopheresis to treat cutaneous T-cell lymphoma] R. Boling. *Health* 19:24 Je '87
New clues to the immune system [photophoresis treatment of lymphatic cancer and immunologic function of skin] S. Squire. il por *N Y Times Mag* p32-3+ F 1 '87
T-cell tumor elimination as a result of T-cell receptor-mediated activation. J. D. Ashwell and others. bibl f il *Science* 237:61-4 Jl 3 '87
Diseases
See also
Kawasaki syndrome

Lymphocytes
Activation of the HIV-1 LTR by T cell mitogens and the trans-activator protein of HTLV-I. M. Siekevitz and others. bibl f il *Science* 238:1575-8 D 11 '87
The basis for the immunoregulatory role of macrophages and other accessory cells. E. R. Unanue and P. M. Allen. bibl f il *Science* 236:551-7 My 1 '87
The chicken B cell compartment. J.-C. Weill and C.-A. Reynaud. bibl f il *Science* 238:1094-8 N 20 '87
Construction of synthetic immunogen: use of new T-helper epitope on malaria circumsporozoite protein. M. F. Good and others. bibl f il *Science* 235:1059-62 F 27 '87
Control protein for AIDS virus identified [research by Gary Nabel and David Baltimore] J. L. Marx. il *Science* 236:393 Ap 24 '87
Cyclic AMP-modulated potassium channels in murine B cells and their precursors. D. Choquet and others. bibl f il *Science* 235:1211-14 Mr 6 '87
Downregulation of L3T4+ cytotoxic T lymphocytes by interleukin-2. C. C.-Y. Shih and R. L. Truitt. bibl f il *Science* 238:344-7 O 16 '87
Garlic boosts natural killer cell action [research by Tariq Abdullah] il *Prevention* 39:6 Ag '87
Germline organization of the murine T cell receptor β-chain genes. H. S. Chou and others. bibl f il *Science* 238:545-8 O 23 '87
Human lymphocytes making rheumatoid factor and antibody to ssDNA belong to Leu-1+ B-cell subset. P. Casali and others. bibl f il *Science* 236:77-81 Ap 3 '87
Identification of a T3-associated γδ T cell receptor on Thy-1+ dendritic epidermal cell lines. F. Koning and others. bibl f il *Science* 236:834-7 My 15 '87
Identification of putative human T cell receptor δ complementary DNA clones. S. Hata and others. bibl f il *Science* 238:678-82 O 30 '87
Immunochemical proof that a novel rearranging gene encodes the T cell receptor δ subunit. H. Band and others. bibl f il *Science* 238:682-4 O 30 '87
Islet allograft survival after a single course of treatment of recipient with antibody to L3T4. J. A. Shizuru and others. bibl il *Science* 237:278-80 Jl 17 '87
Killer cells, MHC: factors in AIDS? D. D. Edwards. *Sci News* 132:52 Jl 25 '87
Lymphotoxin is an important T cell-derived growth factor for human B cells. J. H. Kehrl and others. bibl f il *Science* 238:1144-6 N 20 '87
Measuring the human T cell receptor γ-chain. W. M. Strauss and others. bibl f il *Science* 237:1217-19 S 4 '87
Molecular cloning and expression of a human B-cell growth factor gene in Escherichia coli. S. Sharma and others. bibl f il *Science* 235:1489-92 Mr 20 '87
Molecular diversity of the human T-gamma constant region genes. P. G. Pelicci and others. bibl f il *Science* 237:1051-5 Ag 28 '87
New insights into antigen recognition. P. Marrack. *Science* 235:1311-13 Mr 13 '87
Organ-resident, nonlymphoid cells suppress proliferation of autoimmune T-helper lymphocytes. R. R. Caspi and others. bibl f il *Science* 237:1029-32 Ag 28 '87
Regulation of *bcl*-2 proto-oncogene expression during normal human lymphocyte proliferation. J. C. Reed and others. bibl f il *Science* 236:1295-9 Je 5 '87
Rheumatoid factor secretion from human Leu-1+ B cells. R. R. Hardy and others. bibl f il *Science* 236:81-3 Ap 3 '87

Lymphocytes—*cont.*
Self-examination [major histocompatibility complex protein and T cell recognition of foreign molecules; work of Malcolm L. Gefter and others] *Sci Am* 256:65-6+ My '87
Structurally divergent human T cell receptor γ proteins encoded by distinct Cγ genes. M. S. Krangel and others. bibl f il *Science* 237:64-7 Jl 3 '87
The T cell receptor. P. Marrack and J. Kappler. bibl f il *Science* 238:1073-9 N 20 '87
The T cell receptor family is growing. J. L. Marx. bibl il *Science* 236:1187-8 Je 5 '87
T-cell tumor elimination as a result of T-cell receptor-mediated activation. J. D. Ashwell and others. bibl f il *Science* 237:61-4 Jl 3 '87
Virus-induced increases in plasma corticosterone [with reply by J. Edwin Blalock] il *Science* 238:1423-5 D 4 '87
Why vitamin A may fight infections [research by Susan Smith and Colleen Hayes] *Sci News* 132:46 Jl 18 '87

Lymphocytic leukemia *See* Leukemia
Lymphoid tissue *See* Lymphatic system
Lymphokines
See also
Interleukin
Neuroleukin
Uromodulin (Tamm-Horsfall glycoprotein): a renal ligand for lymphokines. C. Hession and others. bibl f il *Science* 237:1479-84 S 18 '87

Lymphomas *See* Lymphatic system—Cancer
Lymphotoxins *See* Toxins and antitoxins
Lynch, Beverly P., 1935-
Freedom to choose. *Society* 24:24-6 Jl/Ag '87

Lynch, Charles A.
about
Downdraft. L. Scheer. il por *Forbes* 140:196 S 21 '87

Lynch, David
about
Blue velvet [film] Reviews
Christ Century 104:7-9 Ja 7-14 '87. J. M. Wall
Progressive 51:36 Ja '87. P. Aufderheide
Dark visions on the silver screen. M. Horn. il por *U S News World Rep* 102:75 Mr 30 '87

Lynch, Gary
about
Memory: learning how it works [cover story] G. Johnson. il por *N Y Times Mag* p16-21+ Ag 9 '87

Lynch, Gary G.
about
The SEC's busy crimebuster. F. Rice. il por *Fortune* 115:51 Ja 5 '87

Lynch, Gerald W.
Cops and college. *America* 156:274-5 Ap 4 '87

Lynch, Jerry, 1942-
Mental games: ten strategies for staying motivated [excerpt from The total runner] il *Women's Sports Fitness* 9:26-8 Mr '87

Lynch, Joan D.
Love in action and contemplation. *Christ Century* 104:260-1 Mr 18-25 '87

Lynch, Kerry
about
Jump, shoot, ski . . . win. B. Koch. il por *Skiing* 40:42+ S '87

Lynch, Maureen
(ed) See Blanchard, Leslie. From drab to dazzling hair and beauty makeovers

Lynch, Michael
The next oil crisis [cover story] il *Technol Rev* 90:38-45+ N/D '87

Lynch, Peter
about
Lynch: loading up with 'outrageous bargains'. L. Helm. il por *Bus Week* p99 N 23 '87
Peter Lynch. L. Therrien. il por *Bus Week* Sp Issue:261 Ap 17 '87
The see-sawing Dow doesn't scare Peter Lynch. G. G. Marcial. por *Bus Week* p108 O 26 '87

Lynch, Timothy B.
Pat Robertson's bid: good for democracy. *Christ Century* 104:908-9 O 21 '87

Lynch, Tom, 1950-
about
Tom Lynch: Paris sketchbook. V. R. Rivers. il por *Am Artist* 51:S7-S10 N '87

Lynch, Vernon
about
Eddie Murphy's dad and black promoter now book comedian's concert tour. il pors *Jet* 73:28-30 O 19 '87

Lynch, William F., 1908-1987
about
Obituary
America 156:inside cover Ja 24 '87. G. W. Hunt
Commonweal 114:37 Ja 30 '87

Lynching
Black lawyer forces KKK to pay $7 million for lynching black, 19 [M. Figures work on the M. Donald case in Mobile, Ala.] T. S. Moore. il pors *Jet* 71:6-8 Mr 9 '87
Going after the Klan [verdict in case brought by lynching victim M. Donald's family in Alabama] A. Press. il *Newsweek* 109:29 F 23 '87
Mother of slain black son takes possession of KKK building won in lawsuit [mother of M. Donald] il por *Jet* 72:8 Je 8 '87
Seeking justice for her lynched son, an Alabama mother ruins the Klan that killed him [B. M. Donald] J. S. Kunen. il pors *People Wkly* 27:55-6+ Je 8 '87
The woman who beat the Klan [B. M. Donald fights for justice for her lynched son] J. Kornbluth. il pors *N Y Times Mag* p26-32+ N 1 '87

Lyndon B. Johnson Space Center
In charge at Mission Control: a conversation with Michele Brekke. M. Register. il por *Space World* X-4-280:33-6 Ap '87
The Lyndon B. Johnson Space Center. H. A. Butowsky. il *Space World* X-11-287:19-20 N '87

Lyne, Adrian
about
Adrian's line on sex [interview] L. Hirschberg. il por *Roll Stone* p34 N 19 '87
Fatal attraction [film] Reviews
Commonweal 114:565-6 O 9 '87. T. O'Brien
Macleans 100:58 S 21 '87. L. O'Toole
Macleans il 100:7 N 23 '87. F. Bruning
Ms il 16:78-9 D '87. L. Stone
N Y 20:116+ O 5 '87. D. Denby
Natl Rev 39:56-7 D 4 '87. J. Simon
New Repub 197:27 O 19 '87. S. Kauffmann
New Yorker 63:106-7+ O 19 '87. P. Kael
Newsweek il 110:76 S 28 '87. D. Ansen
Newsweek il 110:76-7 O 12 '87. C. McGuigan
People Wkly il 28:10 O 5 '87. P. Travers
Time il 130:69 S 28 '87. R. Schickel
Time il 130:72-6+ N 16 '87. R. Corliss

Lynes, Joseph Russell *See* Lynes, Russell, 1910-
Lynes, Russell, 1910-
1902. il *Art News* 86:154-6 N '87
Russell Lynes observes. See issues of Architectural Digest through December 1987

Lyng, Richard E.
about
Barter system has little potential, says Lyng. *Success Farm* 85:62J O '87

Lynk, Michael
Some lessons for American labor. il *Nation* 245:374-6 O 10 '87

Lynn, Catherine
Reforming America: Boston's Museum of Fine Arts offers a fresh interpretation of the Arts and crafts movement in America, 1875-1920. il *Am Craft* 47:40-9+ Je/Jl '87

Lynn, Frank
Can Jack Kemp quarterback the country? il pors *50 Plus* 27:62-4+ F '87

Lynn, Jonathan, 1943-, and Jay, Antony
The hospital without patients [excerpt from The complete Yes, minister] *Wash Mon* 19:41-6 Jl/Ag '87

Lynn, Kenneth Schuyler
The Schlesinger thesis. *Commentary* 83:46-52 Mr '87

Lynn, Stephanie
Experienced teachers share their insights. *Educ Dig* 52:16-17 F '87

Lynn-Jones, Sean M.
(jt. auth) See Davis, Tami R., and Lynn-Jones, Sean M.

Lynskey, Edward
Never once [poem] *America* 157:457 D 12 '87

Lynx Communications
Wolfe and Fine form mass market company. pors *Publ Wkly* 231:20 My 22 '87

Lynxes
See also
Bobcats

Lynyrd Skynyrd (Musical group)
Skynyrd survivors reunite. R. Malone. il *Roll Stone* p15 O 8 '87

Lyon, Bruce
Brooding on the tundra [with photographs] il *Nat Hist* 96:84-7 D '87

Lyon, David
Hey you! Make way for my technology! il *Technol Rev* 90:28-9 Ag/S '87
Once upon a time in America. il *Travel Holiday* 168:60-4 O '87
(jt. auth) See Harris, Patricia, and Lyon, David
Lyon, John Bowes- *See* Bowes-Lyon, John
Lyon Opera Ballet
Cinderella in America. J. R. Acocella. il *Art Am* 75:43-5 S '87
Lyon Opera Ballet to make U.S. bow. B. Merrill. il *Dance Mag* 61:4 Ja '87
Reviews:
    Performances at City Center, New York City. C. Hardy. il *Dance Mag* 61:28-9 My '87
Lyons, Adrian
An alliance unbalanced. *America* 157:373-4 N 21 '87
Australian bicentenary: 1988. il *America* 157:451-4 D 12 '87
Lyons, Allan S.
    about
Mr. Convertibles. P. Brimelow. por *Forbes* 139:109 My 18 '87
Lyons, Charlotte
Date with a dish. See issues of Ebony
Lyons, John
    about
Touch it, feel it, reach out and grab it. L. Fleischer. *Publ Wkly* 232:46 Jl 3 '87
Lyons, Kelly
    about
Five-year-old Rocky Lyons, son of the Jets' star, thought he could save his mom's life—and he did. R. Arias. il pors *People Wkly* 28:169-70 D 14 '87
Lyons, Nick
Forgotten skills. por *Publ Wkly* 232:48 Ag 21 '87
Lyons, Richard
Chichikov's driver [poem] *New Repub* 196:36 Je 15 '87
Lyons, Rocky
    about
Five-year-old Rocky Lyons, son of the Jets' star, thought he could save his mom's life—and he did. R. Arias. il pors *People Wkly* 28:169-70 D 14 '87
Lyons (Nick) Books *See* Nick Lyons Books
Lyric Opera of Chicago
Chicago. J. Von Rhein. il *Opera News* 51:40-1 Ap 11 '87
Chicago. J. Von Rhein. il *Opera News* 51:36-8 F 14 '87
Chicago on the air: a guide to Lyric Opera's 1987 broadcast season (I). il *Opera News* 51:25-9 My '87
Chicago on the air: a guide to Lyric Opera's 1987 broadcast season (II). il *Opera News* 51:37-42 Je '87
Lyrics (Rock music) *See* Rock music
Lyrix (Word processor program) *See* Word processors and processing—Programming
Lysergic acid diethylamide *See* LSD
Lysis
Glucocorticoid receptor-like antigen in lymphoma cell membranes: correlation to cell lysis. B. Gametchu. bibl f il *Science* 236:456-61 Ap 24 '87
Lysosphingolipids
Lysosphingolipids inhibit protein kinase C: implications for the sphingolipidoses. Y. A. Hannun and R. M. Bell. bibl f il *Science* 235:670-4 F 6 '87
Lystad, Mary H.
Children of China. bibl f il *Child Today* 16:20-2 Mr/Ap '87
Lytle, Andrew Nelson, 1902-
    about
A passionate voice. J. O. Tate. *Natl Rev* 39:52-4 Mr 13 '87
Lyubimov, Yuri
    about
Crime and punishment [drama] Reviews
    America 156:83 Ja 31 '87. G. G. Seibert
    Nation 244:231-2 F 21 '87. M. Hodgson
    New Repub 196:26-7 F 16 '87. R. Brustein
    Time il 129:76 Ja 19 '87. W. A. Henry
Director without a country. R. B. Cullen. il por *Newsweek* 109:60 Ja 19 '87
A feast in the plague-time [drama] Reviews
    Nation 245:209-10 S 5 '87. M. Hodgson
Reviving the dinosaur. G. Loney. il por *Opera News* 52:34-6 N '87

M

M & Company
A boy's guide to chaos [designer T. Kalman] H. Aldersey-Williams. il por *N Y* 20:24 My 11 '87
M-1 (Tank) *See* Tanks, Military
M-9 Multi-Purpose Bayonet *See* Bayonets
M/A-COM Inc.
The General [General Instrument buys Video Cipher from M/A-Com] A. B. Block. il *Forbes* 139:38-9 Je 29 '87
Practical descrambling [scrambling system has been breached] B. Cooper, Jr. il *Radio-Electron* 58:83-4 F '87
Videocipher has been cracked. B. Cooper, Jr. il *Radio-Electron* 58:4+ Ja '87
M. D. Sass Institutional Arbitrage Partners
Risk arbitrage for the little guy. G. G. Marcial. *Bus Week* p62 Ag 10 '87
M. Shanken Communications
Liquid assets. B. Kanner. il por *N Y* 20:37-8+ D 7 '87
M&Co (Firm) *See* M & Company
Maack, John
    about
No 1929 in sight. R. Brady. il por *Nations Bus* 75:86 O '87
Maack, Thomas, and others
Physiological role of silent receptors of atrial natriuretic factor. bibl f il *Science* 238:675-8 O 30 '87
Maas, Jane
The wild side of television advertising. il *Saturday Evening Post* 259:50-1+ S '87
Maas, Michael Eugene
    about
Racist gets prison term for harassing black family. *Jet* 72:5 Mr 30 '87
Maas, Peter, 1929-
The child custody murder. il pors *Good Housekeep* 205:154-5+ O '87
Legacy of a mother's murder. il pors *N Y Times Mag* p40-4+ Ap 12 '87
Oliver North's strange recruits. il *N Y Times Mag* p20-2+ Ja 18 '87
Winning back a child. il por *N Y Times Mag* p42+ Je 7 '87
Maass, Robert
Chandigarh revisited. il *Archit Rec* 175:72-5 Jl '87
Mabes, Robert
The magic of night lighting. il *Flower Gard* 31:52-4+ Ap/My '87
Mabley, Moms, 1897-1975
    about
Clarice Taylor calls Cosby her son on TV but finds sassier fun as Moms Mabley. T. Cunneff. il pors *People Wkly* 28:79-80 O 26 '87
Mabus, Ray
    about
Mississippi rises again. D. Winbush. il por *Time* 130:32 N 16 '87
MacAdam, Alfred J.
(tr) See Vargas Llosa, Mario, 1936-. In defense of the black market
Macadamia nuts
    See also
    Cooking—Nuts
MacAndrews & Forbes Group, Incorporated
The raider who runs Revlon [R. Perelman] A. Ramirez. il pors *Fortune* 116:56-8+ S 14 '87
Macao
    See also
    Casinos—Macao
        Industries
    See also
    Sociedade de Turismo e Diversões de Macau
        Politics and government
Macao returns to 'the motherland' [China] *Newsweek* 109:39 Ap 6 '87
Macaques *See* Monkeys
Macaroni products *See* Pasta
MacArthur, Charles, 1895-1956
    about
The front page [drama] Reviews
    Nation 244:24-5 Ja 10 '87. M. Hodgson
    New Repub 196:25-6 Ja 5-12 '87. R. Brustein
MacArthur, Lawrence B.
Shooting glass. il *Petersens Photogr Mag* 16:72-3 O '87
MacArthur (John D. and Catherine T.) Foundation *See* John D. and Catherine T. MacArthur Foundation

Macau *See* Macao
Macauley, Robert Conover
about
This Connecticut Yankee cares. T. Armbrister. il pors *Read Dig* 130:131-5 F '87
MacCallum, Lee
Your pregnancy. See issues of Glamour
MacCaskey, Michael
Time to prune roses [excerpt from Basic gardening] il *Flower Gard* 31:72-3 F/Mr '87
Macchiaioli
Exhibitions
Scenes from the Macchiaioli [The Macchiaioli: painters of Italian life, 1850-1900] J. Lanes. il *Art Am* 75:106-13 Ja '87
Macchiarola, Frank J.
Prayer & the pursuit of public virtue. *Commonweal* 114:440-2 Ag 14 '87
Maccoby, Eleanor E., 1917-
about
All in the family. E. Hall. il pors *Psychol Today* 21:54-8+ N '87
Macdonald, Brian, 1928-
about
Macdonald's many projects keep him moving from ballet to Broadway. H. M. Simpson. por *Dance Mag* 61:14+ N '87
Macdonald, Cynthia
A past-due notice [poem] *New Repub* 197:38 N 16 '87
Macdonald, Donald S.
Anecdotes, facetiae, satire, etc.
Revealing a future prime minister. A. Fotheringham. il *Macleans* 100:56 Je 22 '87
MacDonald, Donald W.
about
Is a San Francisco architect's plan to put the homeless in boxes humane or heartless? il por *People Wkly* 28:95 Ag 31 '87
MacDonald, Gordon
about
Gordon MacDonald leaves the helm of InterVarsity. il por *Christ Today* 31:38-9 Jl 10 '87
MacDonald, Jeffrey R.
about
Suit against 'Fatal vision' author is settled out of court. C. Reid. il *Publ Wkly* 232:12 D 11 '87
Macdonald, John A.
(jt. auth) See Montgomery, John C., and Macdonald, John A.
Macdonald, Peter
The Navajo Nation [address, January 13, 1987] *Vital Speeches Day* 53:342-4 Mr 15 '87
about
Chairman of the tribe. J. Cook. il por *Forbes* 139:238+ My 18 '87
Suddenly Peter MacDonald is business' best friend. S. D. Atchison. il por *Bus Week* p64 Ag 10 '87
MacDonald, Timothy L., and others
Promotion of tubulin assembly by aluminum ion in vitro. bibl f il *Science* 236:183-6 Ap 10 '87
MacDonald Dettwiler and Associates
Shooting for supremacy. il *Macleans* 100:41 Ap 20 '87
MacDougal, Gary Edward, 1936-
about
Know when to fold them. J. Flint. il por *Forbes* 140:124 D 28 '87
MacDowell, Andie
about
Andie MacDowell. S. F. Buckmaster. pors *Harpers Bazaar* 120:270, 360-3 S '87
Big joy in small packages. J. Etra. il *Harpers Bazaar* 121:122-5 D '87
Indulge [cover story; special section] K. W. Wiley. il pors *Health* 19:37-48+ D '87
Sherbet tints, ice cream dreams. il pors *Harpers Bazaar* 120:284-9 Mr '87
MacDuff, Lynn
Forever [story] il *Teen* 31:32+ Ja '87
The loser [story] *Teen* 31:88+ S '87
Mace, Mary
about
Some said Mary Mace had bats in her belfry, until she proved who made the toys in the basement. il por *People Wkly* 27:53 Ja 26 '87
Macedo, Carlyle Guerra de *See* Guerra de Macedo, Carlyle
MacFadyen, David J.
The home of the future. il *Radio-Electron* 58:115-17 My '87

MacFadyen, J. Tevere
Monkeys with helping hands. il por *Read Dig* 131:38-43 Ag '87
MacGillivray, William D.
about
Life classes [film] Reviews
Macleans 100:64 D 7 '87. S. Pedersen
MacGraw, Ali
about
Eatery-hungry Malibu laps up Ali MacGraw's new entree. il por *People Wkly* 28:50-1 N 23 '87
MacGregor, Nancy Parker
Educating arts teachers. bibl f *Des Arts Educ* 88:36-8 Ja/F '87
MacGregor, Rob
An ancient emerald city. il *Américas* 39:40-5 S/O '87
MacGregor, Rob Roy
The inevitability of death. il por *Christ Today* 31:24-6 Mr 6 '87
MacGuire, James
Scandals in Catholic Relief [cover story] il *Natl Rev* 39:26-30+ Jl 3 '87
Machado, Anesia Pinheiro *See* Pinheiro Machado, Anesia
Machado, Anthony
about
Sleight of hand. J. Chatfield-Taylor. il por *Archit Dig* 44:146-51+ My '87
Machin, Arnold
about
Image makers. E. Greene. il pors *House Gard* 159:180-7 N '87
Machin, Patricia
about
Image makers. E. Greene. il pors *House Gard* 159:180-7 N '87
Machina, Mark J.
Decision-making in the presence of risk. bibl f il *Science* 236:537-43 My 1 '87
Machine guns
Fire power [Squad Automatic Weapon] J. Bashline. il *Pop Mech* 164:67-9 S '87
Folding machine gun [ARES 9mm FMG] P. Wahl. il *Pop Sci* 231:79 Jl '87
Machine politics *See* Boss rule (Politics)
Machine sewing *See* Sewing
Machine theory
See also
Artificial intelligence
Cellular automata
Turing machines
Machine tool industry
See also
Bendix Corp.
Wedtech Corporation
Japan
See also
Fanuc Ltd.
Toshiba Machine Co. Ltd.
Machine translating
Ancient language as tool for computer age [Aymara for computerized translation; work of Ivan Guzman de Rojas] il *Futurist* 21:55 Mr/Ap '87
Getting "non-techs" on-line: tomorrow's easier computers. M. Greenly. il *Futurist* 21:60 Jl/Ag '87
Machine vision systems *See* Vision systems (Machines)
Machinery
See also
Agricultural equipment
Bearings (Machinery)
Conveying equipment
Harvesting machinery
Interchangeable mechanisms
Stands, tables, etc.
Clamshell router table. R. F. Bessmer. il *Workbench* 43:75-9 Mr/Ap '87
Finger joints: a machine you can build . . . [saw table] C. Wedlake. il *Pop Sci* 230:98-100 F '87
His table saw rolls like a garden cart. il *Sunset* 178:92 F '87
One for all [power-tool table] R. Capotosto. il *Pop Mech* 164:124-8+ Jl '87
Power base [power tool table] R. Capotosto. il *Pop Mech* 164:70-3+ S '87
Tabletop saw finds a home. J. Olivari. il *Workbench* 43:84+ S/O '87
Workshop roller extension table. D. Gustafson. il *Workbench* 43:28 My/Je '87
Machinery industry
See also
Agricultural equipment industry
Textile machinery industry

Machinery industry—*cont.*

Finance

Cost-cutting will still be the watchword. Z. Schiller. il *Bus Week* p76 Ja 12 '87

Machines *See* Machinery

Machinists

See also

International Association of Machinists and Aerospace Workers

Machlis, Gary E., and Johnson, Kenneth

Panda outposts. il map *Natl Parks* 61:14-16 S/O '87

Machu Picchu (Peru)

Raiders of the lost city. A. M. Bingham. il pors map *Am Herit* 38:54-64 Jl/Ag '87

Macintosh (Computer) *See* Computers

Mack, Dan

Wild and woody. il por *Mother Earth News* 103:42-7 Ja/F '87

Mack, Jillie

about

In a Nevada chapel, under a veil of secrecy, Tom Selleck marries his kitten from Cats. il pors *People Wkly* 28:34-5 S 21 '87

Mack, Jim

Haleakala National Park [excerpt from Haleakala] il *Natl Parks* 61:46-7 Ja/F '87

Mack, Kevin D.

about

A make-or-break move into financial futures. J. N. Frank. il por *Bus Week* p114 F 23 '87

Mack Trucks, Inc.

Mack Trucks, Auto Workers settle. *Mon Labor Rev* 110:44 Jl '87

Mackaronis, Christopher G.

about

Age bias: the uphill battle [interview] F. Greve. il por *50 Plus* 27:33-6 Mr '87

MacKenzie, Debora

Saving Ethiopia from itself. il *World Press Rev* 34:52 D '87

MacKenzie, John

about

The fourth protocol [film] Reviews

Macleans il 100:54 S 14 '87. G. Peary

New Repub 197:26 S 28 '87. S. Kauffmann

Newsweek il 110:82 S 14 '87. D. Ansen

Mackenzie, Michael

about

Control of the purse strings. M. Drohan. il por *Macleans* 100:38 Mr 16 '87

Mackenzie, Neil

Boy into bishop: a festive role-reversal. bibl il *Hist Today* 37:10-16 D '87

MacKenzie-Childs, Richard L.

about

Ceramics in Wonderland. J. Conant. il *Newsweek* 110:78 O 12 '87

MacKenzie-Childs Ltd.

Ceramics in Wonderland. J. Conant. il *Newsweek* 110:78 O 12 '87

Mackerel

Mackerel works miracles with blood pressure. il *Prevention* 39:14 Jl '87

Mackerel fishing

Competitions

See Fishing—Competitions

Mackin, Jeanne

Flowing bowl. il *Americana* 15:38-41 N/D '87

Robert Jessup. il por *Am Artist* 51:58-63+ Ag '87

Mackinac Island (Mich.)

See also

Hotels, motels, etc.—Mackinac Island (Mich.)

Mackintosh, Allan R.

The 'first computer' controversy [discussion of March 1987 article, The first electronic computer] *Phys Today* 40:13+ D '87

The first electronic computer. bibl f il pors *Phys Today* 40:25-32 Mr '87

Mackintosh, Iain

On not building for posterity. *Theatre Crafts* 21:51+ D '87

Macklem, Gayle L.

Teaching "entry" behavior to elementary schoolers. *Educ Dig* 53:40-3 N '87

Macklin, Ruth

Life & death, heart & mind [excerpt from Mortal choices] *Vogue* 177:348-9+ Ap '87

about

Medicine: the tough new questions [interview] il por *Vogue* 177:350-1+ Ap '87

Mackowski, Maura J.

Bob Dixon: still waiting for a long distance call. il por *Space World* X-8-284:17-20 Ag '87

Safety on the space station. il *Space World* X-3-279:22-4 Mr '87

MacLachlan, Kyle

about

A coupla nice kids. D. Mason. il pors *Vogue* 177:92 Mr '87

MacLaine, Shirley

about

Going even farther out on that limb. B. Kantrowitz. il pors *Newsweek* 110:46-7 Jl 27 '87

Good heavens, Shirley! K. Garfield. por *Ladies Home J* 104:31+ O '87

Isness is her business. M. Gardner. il *N Y Rev Books* 34:16-19 Ap 9 '87

Pruning time for Shirley MacLaine? C. V. Anderson. *Christ Century* 104:182-3 F 25 '87

She's having the time of her lives. por *People Wkly* 27:28-9 Ja 26 '87

Shirley's best performance. M. Harris. il por *Money* 16:160-2+ S '87

Spiritual glitz. B. G. Harrison. *Ms* 16:72+ Jl/Ag '87

Was she ever a housewife in Mesopotamia? S. Nelson. por *Glamour* 85:210 S '87

MacLaren, George

about

Front-page challenge. B. Wallace. *Macleans* 100:49 O 26 '87

Maclay, Edgar Stanton

"The most remarkable series of naval tactics and maneuvers ever known". il *Am Hist Illus* 22:16-17 N '87

Maclean, Fitzroy, 1911-

Homes of the czars. il *House Gard* 159:56+ Ap '87

Maclean, Frances

'We will confound the calumniators of our race . . . '. il por map *Smithsonian* 18:160-6+ O '87

Maclean, W. J.

about

The return of Billy Joe MacLean. C. Wood. il por *Macleans* 100:14 Mr 9 '87

Maclean's (Periodical)

From the editor's desk. K. Doyle. See issues of Maclean's beginning March 14, 1983

Injunction withdrawn [dispute over plans for special edition on Calgary Olympics] il *Macleans* 100:51 N 23 '87

An internal affair [employees strike] K. Doyle. il *Macleans* 100:2 Ap 13 '87

An Olympian struggle [Maclean's and Olympic organizers heading for confrontation in the courts over a special issue of the magazine] *Macleans* 100:59 N 9 '87

MacLennan, Hugh

about

Death on the waterfront. S. Pedersen. il por *Macleans* 100:57 N 23 '87

MacLeod, Richard P.

Have we given up on our space program? il *USA Today (Periodical)* 115:14-16 My '87

MacLeod, Scott

An interview with Yasser Arafat (I). bibl f il *N Y Rev Books* 34:36-40 Je 11 '87

An interview with [Yasser] Arafat (II). bibl f il pors *N Y Rev Books* 34:41-5 Je 25 '87

MacLeod, Stewart

An award-worthy guest column. por *Macleans* 100:52 Ag 17 '87

A different way of saying it. por *Macleans* 100:64 Mr 30 '87

It is déjà vu all over again. por *Macleans* 100:84 F 2 '87

New money, old refrains. por *Macleans* 100:52 Ag 31 '87

Speaking with fewer tongues. por *Macleans* 100:52 Ag 24 '87

A tongue in a bearded cheek. por *Macleans* 100:11 S 21 '87

When a good neighbor forgets. il *Macleans* 100:84 Ja 5 '87

MacManus, Declan Patrick Aloysius *See* Costello, Elvis

Macmillan, Harold, 1894-1986

about

Obituary

Christ Century 104:183 F 25 '87. K. Slack

Natl Rev por 39:44-6 Ja 30 '87. A. Horne

Newsweek il por 109:76 Ja 12 '87. R. Watson

Time il por 129:49 Ja 12 '87

MacMillan, Sir Kenneth
about
The sleeping beauty [ballet] Reviews
N Y il 20:76 My 11 '87. T. Tobias
New Leader 70:22 Ap 20 '87. L. A. Jacobs
New Yorker 63:88-90 My 25 '87. A. Croce
Time il 129:86 Ap 20 '87. M. Duffy
Macmillan, Inc.
Macmillan and Kaplan sue each other over pay. J.
Mutter. *Publ Wkly* 232:15 Ag 28 '87
Macmillan buys out Octopus to be sole owner of Pan
for $36.5 million. V. Menkes. *Publ Wkly* 232:15 O
2 '87
Macmillan cancels Bingham book after challenge by
family patriarch. *Publ Wkly* 232:310-11 Ag 7 '87
Macmillan to eliminate 100 back-office jobs, restructure
operations. *Publ Wkly* 232:13 D 4 '87
Macmillan's music series set new DTP standards [desktop
publishing] I. S. Berman. il *Publ Wkly* 232:38-9 N
13 '87
Upheaval at Macmillan continues; Marmur leaves. M.
Yen. *Publ Wkly* 231:20 Ja 23 '87
MacNamara, Mark
about
Much ado about pudu. J. P. Cohn. il *Int Wildl* 17:38
Ja/F '87
Macneale, Peggy
Notes for new gardeners. See issues of Flower and Garden
MacNeil, Robert, 1931-
Pigskin English. il por *Sport Mag* 78:46-7 F '87
MacNeil/Lehrer newshour [television program] See
Television program reviews—Single works
Macnow, Glen
The Erie sensation. il por *Sport Mag* 78:37-43 My '87
Macomb County (Mich.)
Prisons and reformatories
A Michigan sheriff turns the county jail into a high-rent
hoosegow, causing quite a stir. il *People Wkly* 27:88-9
Je 1 '87
MacPherson, Anne
Letter from Brazil. map *Focus* 37:29-31 Fall '87
MacQueen, Elizabeth
about
Keeping dance forever. G. Parks. il por *Dance Mag*
61:46-8 D '87
MacQuitty, Jane
Sending back wine. *World Press Rev* 34:60 Ag '87
MacRae, Allison
about
Meredith and Allison MacRae: a hard act to follow.
pors *Teen* 31:61 D '87
MacRae, Julia
about
Julia MacRae moves to Walker U.K. J. Taylor. *Publ
Wkly* 232:48 N 27 '87
MacRae, Meredith
about
Meredith and Allison MacRae: a hard act to follow.
pors *Teen* 31:61 D '87
Macrae, Norman
What works in education. il *Current* 290:14-21 F '87
Macro lenses See Lenses, Photographic
MacRobert, Alan
Backyard astronomy. See occasional issues of Sky and
Telescope beginning August 1983
Celestial calendar. See issues of Sky and Telescope
beginning October 1984
Macroengineering See Engineering
Macrophages
The basis for the immunoregulatory role of macrophages
and other accessory cells. E. R. Unanue and P. M.
Allen. bibl f il *Science* 236:551-7 My 1 '87
Cancer-killers from macrophages. J. Raloff. *Sci News*
131:215 Ap 4 '87
Macrophage cytotoxicity: role for L-arginine deiminase
and imino nitrogen oxidation to nitrite. J. B. Hibbs,
Jr. and others. bibl f il *Science* 235:473-6 Ja 23 '87
A parasite with the guts of a burglar [Leishmania; research
by David M. Mosser and Paul J. Edelson] K. Hartley.
Sci News 131:359 Je 6 '87
Macrophotography
Macro dimensional view. W. J. Watt. il *Petersens Photogr
Mag* 16:52-3 Ag '87
Macroprocessors
Beyond macro processing. W. H. Gates. il *Byte* 12 Sp
Issue:11-12+ Summ '87
Macros [keyboard enhancers] P. Honan. il *Pers Comput*
11:77-81+ F '87
Mastering macros in Lotus 1-2-3 [Macropac's 101 Macros
for Lotus 1-2-3] S. R. Reed. il *Pers Comput* 11:160
Mr '87

Mnemonic macros [Jot RAM-resident macro creator]
R. Lockwood. il *Pers Comput* 11:148 Ag '87
Macumba (Cult) See Cults—Brazil
MacWeeney, Alen
Some of her parts. il *Esquire* 107:200-3 Je '87
Macy (R. H.) & Co., Inc. See R. H. Macy & Co., Inc.
Mad (Periodical)
The secret is in the repackaging. G. Slutsker. il por
Forbes 139:230+ Je 15 '87
Madagascar
See also
Environment—Madagascar
National parks and reserves—Madagascar
Natural history—Madagascar
Civilization
Madagascar, Island of the Ancestors [exhibit at the British
Museum's Museum of Mankind] J. Mack. il *Hist Today*
37:61-2 Mr '87
Madama Butterfly [opera] See Puccini, Giacomo, 1858-1924
Madame Cyn See Payne, Cynthia
Madanes, Cloé
about
Interview with a sex therapist. L. J. Nonkin. *Vogue*
177:128 My '87
Marriage in the '80s: altered states [interview] *Vogue*
177:305+ Ag '87
Madaus, George F., and Pullin, Diana
Teacher certification tests: do they really measure what
we need to know? bibl f il *Phi Delta Kappan* 69:31-8
S '87
MADD See Mothers Against Drunk Driving
Madden, Anne
about
Anne Madden at Armstrong. T. Towle. il *Art Am*
75:149-50 F '87
Madden, John
about
Double dip for Daly City. K. Moore. il pors *Sports
Illus* 67:106-10+ O 26 '87
Endorsements: John Madden's career year? B. Condor.
il pors *Sport Mag* 78:34-5 Je '87
Madden, Patrick
Can sustainable agriculture be profitable? bibl f il
Environment 29:18-20+ My '87
Madden, Tara Roth
about
Women at war with each other. S. Nelton. il por *Nations
Bus* 75:58 N '87
Maddison, John
Blickling Hall, Norfolk. il *Antiques* 131:1280-7 Je '87
Maddox, Alton H.
about
The fire this time: two tough lawyers spur a new black
activism. P. Blauner. il pors *N Y* 20:42-7 Ap 27
'87
The legal circus. E. Breindel. *New Repub* 196:20-2 F
9 '87
Maddox, Brenda
Wakers of the world, unite! You have nothing to lose
but your theory. il *N Y Times Book Rev* 92:20 Ag
16 '87
Maddox, Garry, 1949-
about
And one who prospered: with agents' help, ex-outfielder
Garry Maddox made a fortune. J. Lieber. il por *Sports
Illus* 67:96 O 19 '87
Phils cover many bases by hiring ex-star Maddox. por
Jet 72:48 Jl 13 '87
Maddox, Robert L.
Can a state require public schools to allow a moment
of silence? il por *Christ Today* 31:52 N 20 '87
Church and state: the ramparts besieged. il *Christ Century*
104:191-2 F 25 '87
Made for television motion pictures See Television broad-
casting—Motion pictures
Made in heaven [film] See Motion picture reviews—Single
works
Madeira wine See Wine
Madelin, Alain
about
Giving French business a new message: sink or swim.
S. Tully. il por *Fortune* 115:39-40 Ja 5 '87
Madelin, Henri
Assassination in South Lebanon. *America* 157:397-8 N
28 '87
The maderati [drama] See Greenberg, Richard
Madhubuti, Haki R.
Comin strong [poem] *Essence* 18:110-11 Je '87
My brothers [poem] *Essence* 17:118 Mr '87
Safisha [poem] *Essence* 18:128 Ag '87

Madison, Deborah, and Brown, Edward Espe
The Greens cookbook. il *Gourmet* 47:74-5+ Ap '87
Madison, Deidre
My brother is an alcoholic. il *Seventeen* 46:174-5 Mr '87
Madison, James, 1751-1836
about
After more than two centuries, this may be Mr. Madison's year. T. Foote. bibl (p186) il pors *Smithsonian* 18:76-82+ S '87
Architect of a nation. H. Anderson. por *Newsweek* 109:60 My 25 '87
The father of the Constitution. M. A. Noll. por *Christ Today* 31:22 Jl 10 '87
James Madison: architect of the Constitution. A. J. Hall. il pors supp (folded map) map *Natl Geogr* 172:340-69 S '87
Religion
We, the theologians. L. W. Gibbs. pors *Christ Today* 31:29-31 D 11 '87
Madison (Ga.)
City planning
Small town grows, but keeps its charm. il *South Living* 22:180 N '87
Madison (Wis.)
Gardens and gardening
Easing the city squeeze [S. Obern's and S. Stotts' garden] K. Martin. il pors *Rodale's Org Gard* 34:78+ Ap '87
Madison Avenue (New York, N.Y.)
Here's a bit of Europe in old New York. T. Segal. il *Bus Week* p119 F 16 '87
Madison Theatre Festival *See* Drama festivals—Georgia
Madlock, Bill
about
Madlock team shopping as Dodgers release him. por *Jet* 72:47 Je 22 '87
Madness in literature *See* Mental illness in literature
Madoff, Steven Henry
Anselm Kiefer: a call to memory. il por *Art News* 86:125-30 O '87
Klee time. il por *Art News* 86:104-9 My '87
Madonna
about
Chris Finch, Madonna's high-stepping sidekick who's also a Penn pal. K. Hubbard. il por *People Wkly* 28:106-7 Ag 17 '87
Everyone said it wouldn't last . . . [cover story] J. Kaufman. il pors *People Wkly* 28:138-9+ D 14 '87
Madonna: Madison Square Garden. V. Aletti. il por *Roll Stone* p17 Ag 27 '87
The Madonna mystique [cover story] M. Gilmore. il pors *Roll Stone* p36-9+ S 10 '87
The return of a 'native' brings cheers in Italy from everyone but Madonna's family elders. il pors *People Wkly* 28:36-7 S 21 '87
The spell of pop's unstoppable siren. N. Jennings. il pors *Macleans* 100:40-1 Jl 13 '87
Who's that girl. *New Yorker* 63:23-4 Ag 24 '87
'Who's that girl' bombs. J. Rosenbluth. il por *Roll Stone* p23 S 24 '87
Who's that girl . . . Madonna! il pors *Teen* 31:61 N '87
Madonna and Child *See* Mary, Blessed Virgin, Saint—Art
Madrid (Spain)
Dance
Reviews:
J. Hughes and R. de Lara present Contrapuntos program as part of Theater Frontiers series. L. Kumin. *Dance Mag* 61:100 My '87
Description
Letter from Madrid: a view from the street. T. R. Swick. *Am Sch* 56:407-14 Summ '87
Madrid. C. Michener. il *Esquire* 107 Summ Traveler:T10 Ap '87
Music
See also
Opera—Spain
Restaurants, nightclubs, bars, etc.
Manhattan in Madrid [New Yorker restaurant] J.-P. Hayden, Jr. il *Horizon* 30:33-4 D '87
The world's oldest eatery, Casa Botin, reigns in Spain [owner A. Gonzalez] N. Geeslin. il por *People Wkly* 28:153+ D 14 '87
Madrid Hurtado, Miguel de la
about
The fickle finger of a president. J. Contreras. il *Newsweek* 109:35 Ja 12 '87
For De la Madrid, it's almost like being reelected. S. Baker. il por *Bus Week* p78-9 O 19 '87
Mexico's precarious balancing act. S. Baker and E. Weiner. il por *Bus Week* p54-5 S 14 '87

Why De la Madrid's successor won't be another De la Madrid. S. Baker. por *Bus Week* p65 My 11 '87
Madsen, Clifford K.
Research in music: science or art? bibl *Des Arts Educ* 88:10-14 My/Je '87
Madsen, Virginia
about
Following the Monroe Doctrine, sex symbol Virginia Madsen is often found lying down on the job. M. Brower. il por *People Wkly* 28:190-1 N 16 '87
Virginia Madsen. J. Nathanson. il pors *Harpers Bazaar* 120:74, 344-7 S '87
Madson, John
The oldest writing. il *Audubon* 89:62-3 Ja '87
A sporting tradition [cover story] il *Natl Wildl* 25:48-57 O/N '87
Maffei, Philip
about
Junkyard analyst. J. Willoughby. il por *Forbes* 140:230+ N 2 '87
Mafia
See also
Association of Sicilian Women Against the Mafia
Al Capone: Chicago's "untouchable" mobster. por *Am Hist Illus* 22:50-1 O '87
Breaking the Teamsters [government prosecution through RICO statute] J. Schwartz. il *Newsweek* 109:43 Je 22 '87
Busting the godfathers [Mafia dons convicted in New York City] E. Magnuson. il *Read Dig* 130:92-6 Ap '87
Capone to Kefauver: organised crime in America. M. Woodiwiss. bibl il *Hist Today* 37:8-15 Je '87
Chicago's modern mob: a home in the suburbs. J. McCormick. il *Newsweek* 109:35 My 11 '87
Cuomo and those rumors: getting to the bottom of all the 'Mob' talk [cover story] N. Pileggi. il pors *N Y* 20:44-8+ N 2 '87
The "Dapper Don" beats a rap [J. Gotti acquitted in Brooklyn] J. S. DeMott. il por *Time* 129:18 Mr 23 '87
Drawing a bead on the big-time bosses. G. Witkin. il *U S News World Rep* 102:25-6 Mr 23 '87
Fishy business [Fulton Fish Market and the Mafia] A. A. Lappen. il *Forbes* 140:8 N 16 '87
Hard time: 2,665 years in jail [Mafia trial in Sicily] il *Newsweek* 110:31 D 28 '87
Hitting back [Mafia members sentenced in Palermo] il *Time* 130:34 D 28 '87
How Teamsters high command may be unhorsed [use of RICO statute] W. L. Chaze. il *U S News World Rep* 102:12-13 Je 22 '87
How the Mafia loots JFK Airport. R. Rowan. il *Fortune* 115:54-7+ Je 22 '87
A jury sides with 'the Dapper Don' [J. Gotti trial in Brooklyn] *Newsweek* 109:30 Mr 23 '87
L.A. probe focusing on record returns. B. Haring. *Roll Stone* p11+ Ja 29 '87
The Mafia and the melting pot [cover story] J. Weisberg. il *New Repub* 197:33-4+ O 12 '87
The Mafia mystique [Italian American stereotypes] J. Giordano. por *U S News World Rep* 102:6 F 16 '87
Mobbed [Teamsters readmitted to the AFL-CIO] T. Geoghegan. *New Repub* 197:11-12 N 16 '87
Notes and comment [buying a burglar alarm after moving out of Mafia-protected neighborhood in New York City] *New Yorker* 63:21-2 Ag 31 '87
Once a hit man, now a stoolie, Jimmy 'the Weasel' Fratianno says the feds owe him a living [interview] J. Wadler. il pors *People Wkly* 28:38-40 D 21 '87
Organized crime and the Teamsters. L. Black. il *Macleans* 100:44 Je 29 '87
Pizza penance [New York City jury convicts members of smuggling drugs] il *Time* 129:34 Mr 16 '87
Quitting the Mafia [M. Franzese] E. Barnes and W. Shebar. il pors *Life* 10:108-9+ D '87
The sins of the father: a mobster's past shadows his sons' football stardom [S. Polisi] N. Taylor. il *N Y* 20:42-4+ Ja 26 '87
Taking the pulse of crime [forthcoming book about the Mafia in Canada written by T. C. Renner in collaboration with C. Kirby] A. O'Malley. por *Publ Wkly* 231:71-2 F 6 '87
Twilight of the dons [Mafia chiefs sentenced in New York City] N. Underwood. il *Macleans* 100:40 Ja 26 '87
A union in bondage to the mob [Laborers' International Union] E. H. Methvin. *Read Dig* 131:171-5 N '87
Why not try union democracy? [racketeering suit] J. Connolly. il *Nation* 245:192-4+ S 5 '87

Mafia—*cont.*
The worms in the Big Apple. J. Cook. il *Forbes* 140:102-6 S 21 '87

Magadan (Soviet Union)
Gateway to the gulag. J. O. Jackson. il *Time* 129:46 Ap 20 '87

Magasin (Grenoble, France) *See* Centre National d'Art Contemporain (Grenoble, France)

Magazine advertising *See* Advertising, Magazine

Magazine articles *See* Periodical articles

Magazine covers *See* Periodical covers

Magazine design *See* Periodical design

Magazine Development Corporation
Back-of-the-envelope philosopher [L. Solomon] D. Machan. il por *Forbes* 140:106-7 Ag 24 '87

Magazine illustration *See* Illustration

Magazine publishing *See* Publishers and publishing—Periodicals

Magazine stands, racks, etc.
Build a magazine rack. L. M. Dalsgaard. il *Home Mech* 83:16 F '87

Magaziner, Ira C.
about
A liberal gets rich yet keeps the faith. P. Petre. il pors *Fortune* 116:69-72 Ag 31 '87

Magazines *See* Periodicals

Magdalena [musical] *See* Musicals, revues, etc.—Reviews—Single works

Magellan, Ferdinand, 1480?-1521
about
Mass to the sound of gunfire [excerpt from Magellan's voyage around the world] A. Pigafetta. il *Courier* 40:11 Ap '87

Magellan flights *See* Space flight to Venus

Magellanic clouds
Magellanic "toolhouses of great merit". G. Lovi. *Sky Telesc* 73:629-30 Je '87
A simple model for neutrino cooling of the Large Magellanic Cloud supernova. D. N. Spergel and others. bibl f il *Science* 237:1471-3 S 18 '87
Supernova in the LMC. R. Berry. *Astronomy* 15:37 My '87
Supernova shines on [1987A; cover story] R. A. Schorn. il *Sky Telesc* 73:470-5 My '87
Warm infrared galaxy discovered behind SMC [work of Jay Frogel and Jonathan H. Elias] *Astronomy* 15:65-6 Ag '87

Maggio Inc.
A lawsuit could ruin the Farmworkers' Union [damages for violence in a 1979 strike] J. Flynn. il *Bus Week* p42 Mr 23 '87

Maggio Musicale (Festival) *See* Music festivals—Italy

Maggots
Flies to the rescue [maggots of Archytas marmoratus feed on corn earworms and fall armyworms; work of Robert D. Jackson] il *USA Today (Periodical)* 115:7-8 Je '87

Magi
See also
Epiphany

Magic
See also
Conjuring
Bauble, bauble and toil give two designing sisters the magic touch [jewelry creations of K. and L. Mandelbaum] K. Hubbard. il pors *People Wkly* 27:153 Je 8 '87

Magic Chef, Inc.
Maytag's new girth will test its marketing muscle [Magic Chef acquisition] K. Deveny. il *Bus Week* p68+ F 16 '87

Magicians
See also
Jay, Ricky
Penn & Teller

Magidson, Mark
about
His cups runneth over. M. Beauchamp. il por *Forbes* 139:105 Ap 20 '87

Magie, Michael L.
Patients. *Commentary* 83:48-52 F '87

Maglich, Bogdan
about
Getting nuked. P. Patton. il por *Omni* 9:82-4+ F '87

Magliozzi, Ray
about
Tuning in, tuning up. B. Barol. il pors *Newsweek* 109:68 Je 1 '87

Magliozzi, Tom
about
Tuning in, tuning up. B. Barol. il pors *Newsweek* 109:68 Je 1 '87

Magma *See* Rocks, Igneous

Magnesium in the body
Curbing magnesium deficiency in Crohn's disease. *Prevention* 39:92 Mr '87
Magnesium, a suicide-prevention mineral? *Prevention* 39:57 My '87
Magnesium deficiency linked to heart disorders [work of Robert Rude and Elizabeth Ryzen] *USA Today (Periodical)* 115:4-5 F '87
Magnesium stops heart arrhythmias. *Prevention* 39:13 N '87
More about magnesium [interview with M. Seelig] R. Grindy. il por *Saturday Evening Post* 259:50-3+ Jl/Ag '87

Magness, Bob John, 1924-
about
Making deals shrewdly. il por *U S News World Rep* 103:56-7 Jl 6 '87
Who is this guy? E. F. Cone. il por *Forbes* 139:134 Ap 6 '87

Magnet, Myron
America's underclass: what can be done? *Current* 295:17-24 S '87

Magnet schools
Magnetic attraction. N. Lemann. *New Repub* 196:16-19 Ap 13 '87
The new common school. C. L. Glenn. il *Phi Delta Kappan* 69:290-4 D '87

Magnetic [dance] *See* Dance reviews—Single works

Magnetic bearings *See* Bearings (Machinery)

Magnetic fields
Measurement
See also
Magnetoencephalography
SQUIDs (Superconducting quantum interference devices)
Magnetic properties of hydrothermally recrystallized magnetite crystals. F. Heider and others. bibl f il *Science* 236:1287-90 Je 5 '87
Physiological effects
Eastward slow, the sea slugs [research by A. O. Dennis Willows and Kenneth J. Lohmann] D. D. Edwards. *Sci News* 131:54 Ja 24 '87
Lunar-modulated geomagnetic orientation by a marine mollusk. K. J. Lohmann and A. O. D. Willows. bibl f il *Science* 235:331-4 Ja 16 '87

Magnetic fields (Astrophysics)
See also
Moon—Magnetic properties
Sun—Magnetic properties
Uranus (Planet)—Magnetic properties

Magnetic fusion
US and EC conclude fusion agreement. W. Sweet. *Phys Today* 40:56-7 Je '87
What course for U.S. fusion energy R&D? [international cooperation proposal] M. Crawford. *Science* 237:966-7 Ag 28 '87

Magnetic levitation vehicles
Is the train of the future about to pull in? S. Toy. il *Bus Week* p150 N 16 '87
Trains that can levitate. il *Time* 129:67 My 11 '87

Magnetic materials
Imitating iron's magnetism [cover story] I. Peterson. il *Sci News* 131:252-3 Ap 18 '87

Magnetic memory (Computers) *See* Computers—Memory systems

Magnetic recorders and recording *See* Tape recorders and recording

Magnetic resonance imaging
Aromatic cross-links in insect cuticle: detection by solid-state ^{13}C and ^{15}N NMR. J. Schaefer and others. bibl f il *Science* 235:1200-4 Mr 6 '87
Novel magnetic properties of solid helium-3. M. C. Cross and D. D. Osheroff. bibl f il *Phys Today* 40:34-41 F '87
Structure of a psoralen cross-linked DNA in solution by nuclear magnetic resonance. M. T. Tomic and others. bibl f il *Science* 238:1722-5 D 18 '87
Chemical use
Monitoring biosynthesis of wheat cell-wall phenylpropanoids in situ. N. G. Lewis and others. bibl f il *Science* 237:1344-6 S 11 '87
Solution of a protein crystal structure with a model obtained from NMR interproton distance restraints. A. T. Brünger and others. bibl f il *Science* 235:1049-53 F 27 '87

Magnetic resonance imaging—*cont.*
Medical use
By consensus, MRI receives high marks. *Sci News* 132:318 N 14 '87
Focusing on brain-tumor phosphates [work of Klaus Roth and others] S. Weisburd. il *Sci News* 132:375 D 12 '87
From medical breakthrough to health-care tool. D. Holder. il por *Work Woman* 12:69-70 My '87
Imaging technique passes muster. J. L. Marx. il *Science* 238:888-9 N 13 '87
The inventor [R. Damadian] K. McAuliffe. il por *U S News World Rep* 102:66 Ja 26 '87
Medical physics. il *Phys Today* 40:S42-S45 Ja '87
New technique checks brain's blood supply [projection angiography] il *Radio-Electron* 58:4 Mr '87
Saving lives with MRI. C. SerVaas. il *Saturday Evening Post* 259:54-9 Mr '87
Magnetic tape *See* Tape, Magnetic
Magnetic trains *See* Magnetic levitation vehicles
Magnetism
See also
Electromagnetism
Antiferromagnetism observed in La_2CuO_4 [research by David Johnston and others] A. L. Robinson. *Science* 236:780 My 15 '87
Magnetic engineering. R. M. White. *Phys Today* 40:89 N '87
Physiological effects
See Magnetic fields—Physiological effects
Magnetism, Lunar *See* Moon—Magnetic properties
Magnetism, Terrestrial
See also
Auroras
Polar wander
Core columns [research by David Gubbins and Jeremy Bloxham] *Sci Am* 256:67-8 Ap '87
Do asteroid impacts trigger geomagnetic reversals? [theory of Richard Muller and Donald Morris] B. M. Schwarzschild. bibl f il *Phys Today* 40:17-20 F '87
The inner earth is coming out. S. Weisburd. map *Sci News* 131:222-3 Ap 4 '87
Magnetic field reversals, polar wander, and core-mantle coupling. V. Courtillot and J. Besse. bibl f il maps *Science* 237:1140-7 S 4 '87
Quake prediction: magnetic signals? [research by Malcolm Johnston and Robert Mueller] R. Monastersky. il *Sci News* 132:167 S 12 '87
Seismomagnetic observation during the 8 July 1986 magnitude 5.9 North Palm Springs earthquake. M. J. S. Johnston and R. J. Mueller. bibl f il maps *Science* 237:1201-3 S 4 '87
Magnetite
Magnetic properties of hydrothermally recrystallized magnetite crystals. F. Heider and others. bibl f il *Science* 236:1287-90 Je 5 '87
Magnetoencephalography
Magnetoencephalography and epilepsy research. D. F. Rose and others. bibl f il *Science* 238:329-35 O 16 '87
Magnetohydrodynamics
Electromagnetic stabilization of weakly conducting fluids. C. F. Ivory and others. bibl f il *Science* 238:58-61 O 2 '87
Magnets
Will new materials stall SSC? [Superconducting Super Collider] M. Crawford. *Science* 236:247 Ap 17 '87
The magnificent rebel [film] *See* Motion picture reviews—Single works
Magnin, Ann
about
Executive quality. il por *Harpers Bazaar* 120:54+ Mr '87
Magnitudes of stars *See* Stars—Magnitudes
Magnolia Cemetery (Mobile, Ala.) *See* Mobile (Ala.)—Cemeteries
Magnuson, Ann
about
Downtown's darling goes mainstream. D. A. Keeps. il por *Harpers Bazaar* 120:208-9+ Ap '87
Give this woman a TV show! L. Liebmann. por *Vogue* 177:72+ My '87
Movin' uptown. A. Virshup. il pors *N Y* 20:46-9 Mr 30 '87
Magnuson, Ed
Busting the godfathers. il *Read Dig* 130:92-6 Ap '87
Magnuson, Jon
Affirming native spirituality: a call to justice [cover story] il *Christ Century* 104:1114-17 D 9 '87
Echoes of a shaman's song: artifacts and ethics in the Northwest. il *Christ Century* 104:406-8 Ap 29 '87

Magrane, Joe
about
Wit and wisdom of Joe Magrane. J. Schuster. il pors *Sport Mag* 78:73-4+ O '87
Maguire, Daniel C.
The Catholic legacy & abortion: a debate [transcript of debate at University of Notre Dame, February 9, 1987; with editorial comment] *Commonweal* 114:657-63+ N 20 '87
The Mahabharata [drama] *See* Brook, Peter, 1925-
Mahaffey, Michael
about
Southwest rhythms: restoring a Sante Fe adobe. L. Bernikow. il por *Archit Dig* 44:130-5 F '87
Maharaj, Chandra *See* Chandra Maharaj, Swami
Maharishi International University
The karma of capitalism. P. King and P. Wang. il *Newsweek* 110:44 Ag 3 '87
Mahathir bin Mohamad
about
Malaysia's premier jails 'hotheads' to buy time. W. A. Taylor. il por *U S News World Rep* 103:53 N 16 '87
Mahavishnu (Musical group)
Adventures in Fusionland. H. Bordowitz. il por *High Fidel* 37:87-8+ Ja '87
Mahboubian, Houshang
about
Frenchy and the Persians. C. Trillin. *New Yorker* 63:44+ Je 29 '87
Mahdesian, Linda
'It's not easy being green'. por *U S News World Rep* 103:8 N 23 '87
Mahfood, Ferdinand
about
Père Mahfood's Food for the Poor. A. Rodriguez-Soto. *America* 156:153-4 F 21 '87
Mahfood, Père *See* Mahfood, Ferdinand
Mahler, Gustav, 1860-1911
about
Bernstein's greatest hits. D. Denby. il *Vogue* 177:102 Ap '87
Mahler, Halfdan
Smallpox: never again. *World Health* p3 Ag/S '87
Mahlmann, Karsten
about
This veteran of the pits still has a soft spot for soybeans. M. E. Kreca. il por *Bus Week* p168 D 28 '87-Ja 4 '88
Mahmoody, Betty
Not without my daughter [excerpt; ed. by William Hoffer]. il por *Ladies Home J* 104:20+ Ag '87
Mahon, Denis, 1910-
about
Denis Mahon and his 'old friends'. I. Shenker. il por *Art News* 86:121-7 Mr '87
Mahon, Gigi
Manners for the eighties: how to master the daily dance of life in New York [cover story] il *N Y* 20:46-54 D 14 '87
Mahon, Kathleen A., and others
Oncogenesis of the lens in transgenic mice. bibl f il *Science* 235:1622-8 Mr 27 '87
Mahon, Robert L.
'Life is like basketball'. por *Newsweek* 109:10 F 23 '87
Mahoney, Claudia
The zest of the past. il *Americana* 15:40-4 My/Je '87
Mahoney, Paul
about
Like his father before him, a brave tugboat skipper battles wind and sea to bring great ships to port. D. Grogan. il pors *People Wkly* 28:88-9+ O 12 '87
Mahony, Devin
Coxing her way to victory. il pors *N Y Times Mag* p44+ Ap 26 '87
Maiakovsky, Vladimir *See* Mayakovsky, Vladimir, 1894-1930
Maid to order [film] *See* Motion picture reviews—Single works
Maidenform, Inc.
The mother figure of Maidenform [B. Coleman] M. Morris. il pors *Work Woman* 12:82-3+ Ap '87
Maier, Gerry
about
Always a bridesmaid. A. Walmsley. il por *Macleans* 100:42 My 4 '87
Maier, H. John, Jr.
Brazil's black magic. il *Travel Holiday* 167:100 Mr '87

Maier, Pauline, 1938-
The challenge of children's history: making it vivid, getting it right. il *N Y Times Book Rev* 92:42-3 My 17 '87
Who were we then? il *Life* 10:40 Fall '87
Maifarth, Shelly
(jt. auth) See Ballentine, Carol, and Maifarth, Shelly
Mail advertising *See* Advertising, Direct mail
Mail boxes *See* Mailboxes
Mail fraud
Did the good guys go too far? [crackdown on political corruption hamstrung by Supreme Court ruling on mail fraud] P. Dwyer. il *Bus Week* p29 Ag 31 '87
A friend on their side [work of K. R. McClelland as Postal Inspection Service consumer protection specialist] E. J. Kahn. *New Yorker* 62:72-7 Ja 19 '87
Kamasura contretemps [mail order motorcycles turn out to be mopeds] T. Carrithers. il *Cycle* 38:93-6 Ag '87
Mail order business
See also
CML Group, Inc.
Glendale Industries
Haut Dog (Firm)
L. L. Bean, Inc.
Lands' End (Firm)
Lillian Vernon Corporation
Medi-Rx America, Inc.
PC Network (Firm)
Sears, Roebuck and Co.
Sharper Image (Firm)
Spiegel, Inc.
At your service—by mail. H. Manley. il *Good Housekeep* 204:206 F '87
Avoiding mail-order mixups. S. Woolley. il *Bus Week* p152 D 7 '87
Canned house plans: well, what did you expect for $100? D. Moreau. il *Changing Times* 41:63+ Je '87
Fancy foods by mail. il *Consum Rep* 52:715-18 N '87
Free enterprise rushes to fill a delicate need [mail order urine samples circumvent drug testing regulations] D. Collins. il *U S News World Rep* 102:10 F 23 '87
Gardening by mail. J. Anderson. il por *Flower Gard* 31:40+ F/Mr '87
Mail-order companies. il *Consum Rep* 52:312-15 D '87
Mail-order companies [cover story] il *Consum Rep* 52:607-14 O '87
Mail-order morsels: good tastes to go. L. W. Eckhardt. *Harpers Bazaar* 121:137-8+ D '87
Make me a match [tableware] H. J. Lehman. il *Changing Times* 41:12 F '87
Making it in mail order. R. R. Roha. il *Changing Times* 41:129-33 N '87
"North Carolina problem" [mail order furniture discounters] J. Merwin. il *Forbes* 140:41+ N 30 '87
Postable treats [Christmas gifts] il *Gourmet* 47:96-7 D '87
Secrets to mail order success [computers] C. O'Malley. il *Pers Comput* 11:109-13+ Jl '87
Shopping by the book. D. P. Marshall. il *Travel Holiday* 167:24+ Mr '87
Anecdotes, facetiae, satire, etc.
Home-shopping Santa. M. G. Stoddard. il *Saturday Evening Post* 259:46-7 D '87
Taxation
Mail order taxes? J. W. Merline. *Consum Res Mag* 70:38 D '87
Japan
The Japanese go on a mail-order shopping spree. T. Holden. il *Bus Week* p44 S 7 '87
Mail order business fraud *See* Mail fraud
Mail order catalogs *See* Catalogs, Commercial
Mail service *See* Postal service; United States Postal Service
Mailboxes
Postal road kills. il *Ctry J* 14:21 D '87
Wooden mailbox: just like home. A. Cloud. il *Workbench* 43:59-61 Jl/Ag '87
Mailer, Norman
about
Mailer's minuet. K. Jaehne. il pors *Film Comment* 23:11-17 Jl/Ag '87
No longer such a tough guy, Norman Mailer frets over his shaky career as a filmmaker. A. Richman. il pors *People Wkly* 28:40-2 O 5 '87
Parsing a sentence. por *Time* 130:61 Jl 27 '87
Taking direct action. D. Hershkovits. pors *Harpers Bazaar* 121:144-5 N '87
Tough guys don't dance [film] Reviews
Commonweal 114:566 O 9 '87. T. O'Brien
Glamour 85:249-50 N '87. J. G. Boyum
Mademoiselle il 93:108+ N '87. R. Rosenbaum
N Y 20:138+ S 28 '87. D. Denby

New Repub 197:28-9 O 5 '87. S. Kauffmann
New Yorker 63:105-6 S 21 '87. P. Kael
Newsweek il 110:76 S 21 '87. D. Ansen
People Wkly il 28:12 O 12 '87. P. Travers
Tough guys make movie. D. Smith. il pors *N Y* 20:32-5+ Ja 12 '87
Mailing lists
See also
American List Corp.
CCX Network Inc.
The data base alternative. C. O'Malley. il *Pers Comput* 11:103 My '87
How much will you sell your name for? il *Consum Rep* 52:263 Ap '87
Maillard reaction *See* Browning
Mailmen *See* Postal employees
Mainau (Germany)
See also
Castles—Mainau (Germany)
Maine
See also
Education—Maine
Fishing—Maine
Gardens and gardening—Maine
Historic houses, sites, etc.—Maine
Homesteads—Maine
Mines and mineral resources—Maine
Monhegan Island (Me.)
Radioactive waste disposal—Laws and regulations—Maine
Resorts—Maine
Sculpture gardens and parks—Maine
Skis and skiing—Maine
Wilderness areas—Maine
Description and travel
A slice of Down East. S. H. Shetterley. il map *50 Plus* 27:70-6 O '87
Fisheries
See Fisheries
Industries
Maine: the financier's new frontier. A. Beam. il por *Bus Week* p81 Ja 19 '87
Maine, Gulf of *See* Gulf of Maine
Maine Capital Corporation
Maine: the financier's new frontier. A. Beam. il por *Bus Week* p81 Ja 19 '87
Maine in art
Exhibitions
Neil Welliver. G. Henry. il *Art News* 86:150+ My '87
Maine Yankee nuclear power plant *See* Nuclear power plants
Mainframe computers *See* Computers
Maino, Jeannette
Swimming party on the Hayfork River [poem] *America* 157:497 D 26 '87
Mainsails *See* Sails
Maiolica *See* Majolica
Maisel, Jay, 1931-
about
Traveling light: Jay Maisel's portable Mylar reflector. B. Hagin. il por *Pop Photogr* 94:56-7 N '87
Maitland, Christine
Tales of a freeway flyer or Why I left college teaching after 10 years. *Change* 19:8-9+ Ja/F '87
Maize *See* Corn
Majakowskij, Wladimir *See* Mayakovsky, Vladimir, 1894-1930
Majeau, Frank
about
Questions about a firing. D. Burke. por *Macleans* 100:11-12 Ja 19 '87
Uproar over a firing. A. Wilson-Smith. por *Macleans* 100:16 Ja 26 '87
Majestic Theater (Brooklyn, N.Y.)
Renovation [renovation for The Mahabharata] M. Sommers. il *Theatre Crafts* 21:28-31+ N '87
Majestic Theater (New York, N.Y.)
More Majestic than ever [Frederick Olsson oversees modifications to accommodate The Phantom of the Opera] B. Weber. il *N Y Times Mag* p62 S 6 '87
Majolica
Collectors and collecting
A Gubbio nuptial dish. S. Bagdade and A. Bagdade. il *Antiques Collect Hobbies* 92:41 D '87
Major, John
Landowners and sportsmen united. il *Conservationist* 41:42-5 Ja/F '87
Major, Peter F.
Tails of whales and fins, too. il *Sea Front* 33:90-6 Mr/Ap '87

Major fields of study (College students) *See* Colleges and universities—Curriculum

Major histocompatibility complex

Linking immune response genes to disease. D. M. Barnes. *Science* 237:1568 S 25 '87

Megabase-scale mapping of the HLA gene complex by pulsed field gel electrophoresis. S. K. Lawrance and others. bibl f il *Science* 235:1387-90 Mr 13 '87

The relation between major histocompatibility complex (MHC) restriction and the capacity of Ia to bind immunogenic peptides. S. Buus and others. bibl f il *Science* 235:1353-8 Mr 13 '87

Self-examination [major histocompatibility complex protein and T cell recognition of foreign molecules; work of Malcolm L. Gefter and others] *Sci Am* 256:65-6+ My '87

Structure of MHC protein solved [work of Jack Strominger and others] J. L. Marx. il *Science* 238:613-14 O 30 '87

Major Indoor Soccer League *See* Soccer, Professional

Major League Baseball Players Association

Divided they fell [views of M. Miller] D. Whitford. il por *Sport Mag* 78:84-5 Jl '87

Major Market Index *See* Stocks—Price indexes and averages

Major medical health insurance *See* Insurance, Health

Majorelle, Jacques

about

Gardens: Majorelle remembered: Yves Saint Laurent and Pierre Bergé in Marrakesh. C. Aillaud. il pors *Archit Dig* 44:160-5 O '87

Majors, Kerrick, d. 1987

about

Black Nashville youth killed by whites over $2 vase at flea market. *Jet* 72:36 Je 15 '87

Majzlin, Leonard

(jt. auth) *See* Paget, Dennis, and Majzlin, Leonard

Make-believe *See* Children's fantasies

Makeovers, Beauty *See* Beauty, Personal

Makeup

5 minutes to a perfectly polished face. il *Glamour* 85:380-1 S '87

Be your own makeup artist [views of Leah Tamburino] C. Straley. il *Parents* 62:87-90 Ja '87

Beautiful new spring makeup. il *Glamour* 85:300-3 Ap '87

Beauty '87: new look for the New Year. A. Fornay. il *Ebony* 42:110-12+ Ja '87

Beauty in a new light. il *Vogue* 177:774-81 S '87

Beauty: point by point [cosmetic pencils] il *Teen* 31:76-7 F '87

Beauty: serious business. il *Essence* 17:64-7+ Mr '87

The best spring makeup looks 1987. il *McCalls* 114:45-7 F '87

Brow power: how to shape up and make up the "new" beauty feature. il *Mademoiselle* 93:52 S '87

Cherchez la femme! [Paris fashions] il *Essence* 18:90-5 O '87

Christmas glow in gold. il *Harpers Bazaar* 121:140-3 D '87

Clear coral tints of summer. il *Harpers Bazaar* 120:166-7 My '87

Color '87: hot shots. il *Vogue* 177:384-99 O '87

Creating a lasting impression [guide to lipstick application] *Prevention* 39:128 F '87

Day-to-night makeovers. il *Harpers Bazaar* 120:30 Mr '87

Does your makeup drain you? il *Redbook* 169:156-9 S '87

The don'ts of summer. il *Redbook* 169:78-9 Jl '87

The do's of summer. il *Redbook* 169:80-1 Jl '87

Dream faces. il *Seventeen* 46:158-61 My '87

Essentials for black hair and skin: what's new, what's tried and true. il *Glamour* 85:38 Ap '87

Extra! Extra! News on eyes. il *Teen* 31:88-9 N '87

Face up to these great makeup tips! il *Teen* 31:70 S '87

Faces to fall for. il *Seventeen* 46:332-5 Ag '87

Facing up to fall. L. Wells. il *N Y Times Mag* p100-4 S 20 '87

Fall's winning looks. il *McCalls* 114:32-3 S '87

Fast makeup fixups [eye makeup] il *Harpers Bazaar* 120:36 Ap '87

First, base: beauty foundation that's better than bare. il *Mademoiselle* 93:304-7 S '87

First-rate faces. il *Teen* 31:106-15 S '87

A flawless face. il *Harpers Bazaar* 121:20 D '87

For your lips only. il *Mademoiselle* 93:134-7 F '87

Fresh start: wake up your looks. il *Harpers Bazaar* 120:24 Ja '87

From bland to all-day beautiful in 16 minutes [excerpt from New classic beauty] J. Mills. il *Good Housekeep* 205:150-1+ N '87

Get your lashes lushest. il *Mademoiselle* 93:40 Ap '87

Great eyes. il *McCalls* 114:86-7 Je '87

Great word-of-mouth news: spring lip color. il *Glamour* 85:268-71 My '87

Hair/makeup: the active edge. il *Vogue* 177:290-3 Ag '87

High contrast. il *Mademoiselle* 93:232-5 Ag '87

The impact of a new year. il *Vogue* 177:140-3 Ja '87

Learn to use blush like a pro with these easy-to-follow tips. il *Ladies Home J* 104:32 Mr '87

Let's glow to the videotape. il *Seventeen* 46:108-11 Ja '87

Make up, stand up and cheer [Team Colors makeup kits by Bonne Bell] il *Sports Illus* 67:16 S 21 '87

Makeovers! Gorgeous new looks from your own makeup. il *Glamour* 85:282-7 My '87

Makeup in a flash: nine to five. il *Harpers Bazaar* 121:26 N '87

Makeup made simple. il *Seventeen* 46:105-8 Ap '87

Makeup makeovers. il *Teen* 31:78-81 Ap '87

The makeup mistake most women make: learn to blush with style. il *Glamour* 85:284-7 Mr '87

Makeup pick-me-ups. il *Harpers Bazaar* 120:64+ F '87

Makeup: the new naturals. il *Harpers Bazaar* 120:109+ Je '87

Maximum beauty. A. Noe. *50 Plus* 27:49 S '87

Maximum-flattery fall makeup. il *Glamour* 85:284-7 O '87

Men and makeup: loving an unfinished woman. B. Weber. *Mademoiselle* 93:200 N '87

Model makeup now! [B. Johnson] B. Brandon and M. Garth-Taylor. il pors *Essence* 17:58-9 Ja '87

The new fall faces. il *Good Housekeep* 205:202-3+ S '87

The new hair, the new makeup. il *Mademoiselle* 93:204-11 My '87

A new mood! [black women] il *Essence* 18:70-5 S '87

The new "soft" eye: two looks for day, two for night. il *Mademoiselle* 93:30 Mr '87

No more tears: makeup tips for sensitive eyes. il *Mademoiselle* 93:16 My '87

Old: fall's beauty focus. S. Duff. il *Harpers Bazaar* 120:390-3+ S '87

Perfect makeup. il *Harpers Bazaar* 120:125 Ag '87

Personal elegance with the look of power. il *Work Woman* 12:106-7 O '87

Play up your eyes! C. Straley. il *Parents* 62:121-4 Je '87

Points of view [eye makeup] il *Seventeen* 46:146 N '87

Quick makeup artistry. S. F. Buckmaster. il *Harpers Bazaar* 120:114-15+ Ja '87

The seductive face. il *Harpers Bazaar* 120:200-3+ Ap '87

Shades of spring '87. *Ladies Home J* 104:28 Ap '87

Soft perfection: makeup for blondes. il *Harpers Bazaar* 120:172-3 Ap '87

Spring '87: makeup options. A. K. Leopold. il *Vogue* 177:460-1+ Mr '87

Spring beauty news. il *Good Housekeep* 204:140-3 Ap '87

Spring sheers. J. Torrey. il *Health* 19:42-3+ Mr '87

Strokes of genius [eye makeup] il *Seventeen* 46:248 Ag '87

Summer beauty's point of view [black women] il *Essence* 18:80-5 Jl '87

Summer face. il *Good Housekeep* 204:81 My '87

Summer touches. L. Wells. il *N Y Times Mag* p52 Je 14 '87

Summer's prettiest look [eye makeup] il *Redbook* 169:108-11 Je '87

Tired eyes can age you. il *Redbook* 169:120-3 O '87

The two faces of makeup. J. Lewis. il *Curr Health 2* 13:22-3 F '87

Undercover seduction. il *Harpers Bazaar* 120:252-5 O '87

Unforgettable faces [makeup and hairstyles that reinterpret film stars' legendary looks] il pors *Seventeen* 46:120-5 F '87

Wake up your makeup! il *Redbook* 169:120-3 My '87

The well-dressed face. il *Mademoiselle* 93:264-7 Mr '87

What a peach! The makeup that's just ripe. il *Mademoiselle* 93:118-21 Jl '87

What kind of beauty are you? il *Mademoiselle* 93:204-9 O '87

What you can learn from a makeup pro [tips from Joey Mills] il *Glamour* 85:30+ D '87

Makeup—*cont.*
When your looks won't go overtime—5 fast face fixers. il *Mademoiselle* 93:40 Ag '87
Word of mouth. il *Seventeen* 46:160 Mr '87
Your bare-bones beauty kit. il *Health* 19:42 D '87
Your best look for '87. il *Glamour* 85:166-7 Ja '87
Anecdotes, facetiae, satire, etc.
Tammymania! il por *People Wkly* 27:113-15 Je 22 '87
History
The history of makeup. E. Davidowitz. il *Seventeen* 46:123-4+ Mr '87
Makeup, Theatrical
Stranded: Michele Burke's friendly foreigners [science fiction film makeup] R. Seidenberg. il por *Theatre Crafts* 21:83-6 N '87
Makeup artists
See also
Burke, Michele
Get great makeup advice. il *Glamour* 85:18 Je '87
Her brilliant career [L. Rodman] il por *Seventeen* 46:88 My '87
Maki, Fumihiko, 1928-
about
Eastern diplomacy [cover story] D. Dietsch. il *Archit Rec* 175:116-27 O '87
Making Mr. Right [film] See Motion picture reviews—Single works
Makino, Clint L., and others
Intracellular topography of rhodopsin bleaching. bibl f il *Science* 238:1716-17 D 18 '87
Makofske, Mary
Planting by the stars [poem] *Rodale's Org Gard* 34:80 S '87
Malabar (Fla.)
Crime
Count Malabar [J. B. Crutchley kidnaps a woman and drinks one third of her blood] S. Baker. il por *Omni* 9:84 Ja '87
Malabar Coast (India)
Description and travel
India's backwater highways. K. Brueckmann and D. Brueckmann. il map *Oceans* 20:24-9 Ja/F '87
Malabre, Alfred L.
Living beyond our means [condensed from Beyond our means] *Read Dig* 131:123-6 N '87
about
Beyond our means. A. Bladen. il *Forbes* 140:178 Jl 27 '87
Of many things. G. W. Hunt. *America* 156:inside cover Ap 18 '87
Malandro's opera [film] See Motion picture reviews—Single works
Malanowski, Jamie
KYW's consultant coup. il *Channels* 7:22-3 S '87
Monkey-wrenching around. il *Nation* 244:568-70 My 2 '87
Malapropisms See Errors, Speech
Malaria
Tumor necrosis factor (cachectin) as an essential mediator in murine cerebral malaria. G. E. Grau and others. bibl f il *Science* 237:1210-12 S 4 '87
Prevention and control
Mankind and the mosquito [National Malaria Eradication Programme of India] R. M. Prothero. il *World Health* p18-19 Je '87
Satellites to forecast malaria hazard. il *USA Today (Periodical)* 115:6 Je '87
Travelers' advisory: malaria still threatens much of globe. E. Zamula. il *FDA Consum* 21:8-13 My '87
Therapy
Drug resistance: malaria-cancer similarity? J. Silberner. *Sci News* 131:148 Mr 7 '87
Vaccines and vaccination
Construction of synthetic immunogen: use of new T-helper epitope on malaria circumsporozoite protein. M. F. Good and others. bibl f il *Science* 235:1059-62 F 27 '87
Efficacy of murine malaria sporozoite vaccines: implications for human vaccine development. J. E. Egan and others. bibl f il *Science* 236:453-6 Ap 24 '87
Human trials begin for malaria vaccine. J. Walsh. il map *Science* 235:1319-20 Mr 13 '87
Malaria: fighting the African scourge. L. Tangley. il *BioScience* 37:94-8 F '87
Naturally acquired antibodies to sporozoites do not prevent malaria: vaccine development implications. S. L. Hoffman and others. bibl f il *Science* 237:639-42 Ag 7 '87
Parasite pacification. J. Schecter. map *Technol Rev* 90:10-11 O '87

Malarial parasites See Plasmodium (Parasite)
Malawi
See also
Medical care—Malawi
Malay, Rod
about
Magical mystery tank. C. Wood. il por *Macleans* 100:53 Jl 6 '87
Malaysia
See also
Americans—Malaysia
Electronic mail systems—Malaysia
Narcotics laws and regulations—Malaysia
Economic conditions
Malaysia: natural wealth, few industries. L. Hopping. il *Sch Update* 119:12 Ap 6 '87
Politics and government
Malaysia's premier jails 'hotheads' to buy time. W. A. Taylor. il por *U S News World Rep* 103:53 N 16 '87
The politics of ethnicity in Malaysia. G. P. Means. bibl f *Curr Hist* 86:168-71+ Ap '87
Malcolm, Andrew H., 1943-
Of jams and a family. il por *N Y Times Mag* p82-3+ N 15 '87
The Wildcats' great hope. il por *N Y Times Mag* p38-9+ Mr 1 '87
about
PW interviews. W. Goldstein. por *Publ Wkly* 231:54-5 Ap 17 '87
Malcolm, Janet
J'appelle un chat un chat. *New Yorker* 63:84-92+ Ap 20 '87
about
Masson loses libel suit against 'New Yorker,' Malcolm and Knopf. M. Colin. *Publ Wkly* 232:11 S 4 '87
Malcolm [film] See Motion picture reviews—Single works
Malcolm X, 1925-1965
The Boston Four Hundred: 1940 [excerpt from The autobiography of Malcolm X] *Harpers* 274:43 F '87
about
Remembering . . . Malcolm X. B. Shabazz. il pors *Essence* 17:61 F '87
Malcom, Corey
about
Despite centuries underwater, seeds from a sunken galleon prove life begins at 365. il por *People Wkly* 28:59 Ag 3 '87
Male nurses See Nurses and nursing
Male psychology See Masculinity (Psychology); Men—Psychology
Male secretaries See Secretaries
Male striptease
A different take on the ol' bump and grind [women watching the Chippendales striptease revue] M. A. Gillespie. il por *Ms* 16:88+ O '87
How the Chippendales survived the eighties. K. Grubb. il *Dance Mag* 61:64-5 S '87
Male teachers See Teachers
Malec, William Frank, 1940-
about
Mr. Malec versus the bureaucrats. E. A. Finn, Jr. il por *Forbes* 140:44 D 28 '87
Malecki, Edward J.
Hope or hyperbole? High tech and economic development. il *Technol Rev* 90:44-51 O '87
Malediction See Swearing
Malehorn, Hal, 1930-
Teaching history—alive and well. il *Phi Delta Kappan* 69:166-8 O '87
Males, Carolyn
Big South Fork. il *Travel Holiday* 167:12+ My '87
Big wheel, big river. il map *Travel Holiday* 168:50-5 Jl '87
Old castles and Old Glory: Luxembourg pays tribute to America. il map *Travel Holiday* 168:34-41 D '87
Maleska, Eugene T.
38 down: oops! il *N Y Times Mag* p50+ Ap 26 '87
Maley, Paul
about
Globetrotting observer Paul Maley: chasing the fleeting moment [interview] R. Reeves. il por *Astronomy* 15:40+ N '87
Malformations, Congenital See Birth defects
Mali
See also
Christmas—Mali
Droughts—Mali
French—Mali
Malians
Timbuktu (Mali)

Mali—*cont.*
Description and travel
Rendezvous in Mali. J. Fox. il *House Gard* 159:94+
S '87
Malians
United States
Out of Africa with Diane Sawyer [starving Malian boy
Mohammed Ag Albakaye adopted by C. Carter-Shotts]
M. G. Stoddard. il pors *Saturday Evening Post*
259:52-4+ Ap '87
Malibu (Calif.)
Architecture
Architectural digest visits: Dinah Shore [Malibu beach
house decorated by Val Arnold] B. D. Colen. il por
Archit Dig 44:158-63+ D '87
Architecture: Richard Meier [Malibu home of Norman
and Lisette Ackerberg; cover story] R. Hughes. il *Archit
Dig* 44:152-9+ O '87
Sea-struck living. B. Moore. il por *House Gard* 159:78+
S '87
A studied simplicity [O'Herlihy House] P. M. Sachner.
il *Archit Rec* 175:108-13 mid-Ap '87
View from Malibu: Michael and Kim McCarty in Califor-
nia. B. D. Colen. il pors *Archit Dig* 44:96-101+ Jl
'87
Galleries and museums
See also
J. Paul Getty Museum
Housing
Cute 22 acres for only $18 million—contact owner,
Barbra Streisand. il *People Wkly* 28:103 O 5 '87
Restaurants, nightclubs, bars, etc.
Eatery-hungry Malibu laps up Ali MacGraw's new entree
[Malibu Adobe] il por *People Wkly* 28:50-1 N 23
'87
Malibu Adobe (Malibu, Calif.: Restaurant) *See* Malibu
(Calif.)—Restaurants, nightclubs, bars, etc.
Malin, Amir Jacob
about
The Amir Malin story. D. Machan. il pors *Forbes*
140:178+ O 19 '87
Malin, David
In the shadow of the Horsehead [cover story] il *Sky
Telesc* 74:253-7 S '87
The splendor of Eta Carinae. il *Sky Telesc* 73:14-18
Ja '87
Malitz, Nancy
A church marriage. il por *Opera News* 51:14-16 Ja 31
'87
Maljers, F. A.
about
Pulling together a two-part company. R. I. Kirkland,
Jr. il pors *Fortune* 116:40 Ag 3 '87
Malkin, Judd D.
about
The Second City duo building a first-class colossus.
J. N. Frank. il pors *Bus Week* p100 O 5 '87
Malkovich, John
about
Acting's burning talent. por *Harpers Bazaar* 121:138
N '87
Mallard ducks *See* Ducks, Wild
Malleray, Pierre de
about
Fin de siècle fantasy. O. Bernier. il por *House Gard*
159:146-51 Jl '87
Mallet, Laurie
about
Laurie Mallet's walls may not have ears, but they do
have chairs, tables, boots and an overcoat. il por
People Wkly 28:123-5 Jl 6 '87
WilliWear partner talks about future of WilliWear. por
Jet 72:52 My 25 '87
Mallet, Victor
Stunting progress in Africa. il *World Press Rev* 34:53
S '87
Mallory, George Leigh, 1886-1924
about
Mallory's camera. J. Taylor. il por *Omni* 9:90 F '87
Mallory, Vincent Derek
about
Black doctor sentenced to life for death of white woman
patient in Georgia. il por *Jet* 73:33 O 26 '87
Hold Georgia physician in death of white patient. *Jet*
72:4 My 11 '87
Mallows, Tree *See* Tree mallows
Malloy, James
Bolivia's economic crisis. *Curr Hist* 86:9-12+ Ja '87

Malls, Shopping *See* Shopping centers
Malnutrition
See also
Deficiency diseases
Child survival: an achievable goal in hunger relief [cover
story] T. Peterson. il *Christ Century* 104:594-5 Jl 1-8
'87
A home for malnutrition [study by Gayle D. Pinchcofsky-
Devin] *Prevention* 39:68 N '87
Malnutrition, hunger—not synonymous [children] *UN
Chron* 24:67 My '87
Malocclusion
Bye-bye braces [Occlus-o-Guide, developed by Earl Berger-
sen] J. R. Goldberg. il *Health* 19:18 Ap '87
Malone, James W.
'To be American and Catholic'. il por *U S News World
Rep* 103:61 S 14 '87
Malone, John
about
Cable's biggest leaguer. B. Powell. il por *Newsweek*
109:40-1 Je 1 '87
The king of cable TV [cover story] M. Ivey. il por
Bus Week p88-92+ O 26 '87
Make way for John Malone. H. Rudnitsky and E. F.
Cone. il pors *Forbes* 139:124-6+ Ap 6 '87
Malone, Mark, 1958-
about
Open season in Pittsburgh. S. Toperoff. il pors *Sports
Illus* 67 Sp Issue:96-100+ S 9 '87
Malone, Molly
Dependent on disorder. il *Ms* 15:50+ F '87
Malone, Moses
about
Back to haunt the Sixers. J. McCallum. il pors *Sports
Illus* 66:28-9 Mr 16 '87
Moses keeps his promise on return to play Philly. il
por *Jet* 71:49 Ja 19 '87
Malone, Thomas F.
Global science [discussion of October 1986 article, Mis-
sion to planet earth] *Environment* 29:3-4 Mr '87
Malone [film] *See* Motion picture reviews—Single works
Maloney, E. S.
Notices to boatmen. See issues of Motor Boating &
Sailing
Maloney, Rita
A fair share; ed. by Micki Siegel. il por *Good Housekeep*
205:54+ N '87
Malory, Sir Thomas, 15th cent.
about
Models of kingship: Arthur in medieval romance. B.
Stone. il *Hist Today* 37:32-8 N '87
Malpede, John
about
Their home is the streets, but the play's the thing for
L.A.'s down-but-not-out skid row players. M. Small.
il por *People Wkly* 28:127-8+ D 7 '87
Malpractice
See also
Insurance, Malpractice liability
Trials (Malpractice)
$1.1 mil. suit filed by athletes in Fla. land deal [legal
malpractice against Holland & Knight] *Jet* 72:50 Je
8 '87
A case of malpractice—in market research? [Beecham
sues Yankelovich over research on new detergent]
M. Rothman. *Bus Week* p28-9 Ag 10 '87
Chicago girl, 11, wins $6 mil. settlement from hospital
[malpractice award to Vernette Eiland by Rush
Presbyterian-St. Luke's Hospital] *Jet* 72:18 Mr 30 '87
A cure for doctors who are hazardous to health. F.
Warshofsky. il *Read Dig* 130:70-4 Ja '87
Detroit couple awarded $5 mil. in hospital suit [suit
by George Hollis and wife against North Detroit
General Hospital] *Jet* 72:30 Ap 6 '87
Doctor No: when M.D. spells trouble [incompetent doc-
tors] M. Sandmaier. *Mademoiselle* 93:174+ Mr '87
Does malpractice make perfect? E. Zuckerman. *Vogue*
177:176+ My '87
A hospital stands accused [mystery surrounding A. War-
hol's death at New York Hospital] C. Wallis. il por
Time 129:64 Ap 27 '87
Kevin Porter's house calls [lawyer for hospitals in New
York City] O. Jaffe. il por *N Y* 20:20 Jl 20 '87
Let the free market end malpractice warfare [medical
malpractice] C. Farrell. il *Bus Week* p28 Ag 3 '87
The malpractice mess: why you should worry [obstetrics]
A. B. Lieberman. il *Parents* 62:106-10+ Mr '87
Malpractice suits: doctors under siege. il *Newsweek*
109:62-3 Ja 26 '87

Malpractice—*cont.*
Model portfolio [teacher Jo Anne Rosenbaum's malpractice settlement] R. McNatt. il *Money* 16:223-4 Ap '87

New York Hospital on the spot: three baffling deaths jolt a proud institution. M. Stone. il pors *N Y* 20:40-7 Je 22 '87

Quackus tyrannus. R. Greene. il *Forbes* 140:67 O 5 '87

A test for market research. A. Miller and D. Tsiantar. il *Newsweek* 110:32-3 D 28 '87

When doctors refuse to treat lawyers [obstetricians vs. women lawyers in Brunswick, Ga.] P. Cooke. il *Read Dig* 131:100-4 O '87

When the obstetrician says "no" [suits forcing physicians to drop practices] R. Sandroff. il *Health* 19:52-4+ N '87

When to sue your doctor. J. Silberner. il *U S News World Rep* 103:66-8 D 14 '87

Woman awarded $6 million after doctor/husband sewed her vagina shut [D. Crandall-Millar] *Jet* 73:12 N 23 '87

Malpractice liability insurance *See* Insurance, Malpractice liability

Malraux [ballet] *See* Ballet reviews—Single works

Malrite Guaranteed Broadcast Partners Limited Partnership
Banding together. E. B. Gibbs. il *Channels* 7:73 Je '87

Malt
See also
Penwest, Ltd.

Malta
Description and travel
The Maltese connection. S. Blow. il *House Gard* 159:56+ Ag '87

Maltas, Michael
Rock-steady trellises. il *Rodale's Org Gard* 34:56-7 My '87

Malthus, T. R. (Thomas Robert), 1766-1834
about
Malthus then and now. J. L. Hess. il *Nation* 244:496-500 Ap 18 '87

Malthus, Thomas Robert *See* Malthus, T. R. (Thomas Robert), 1766-1834

Maltin, Leonard
They're tuned in to the 'thrilling days of yesteryear'. bibl (p182) il *Smithsonian* 17:70-9 Mr '87

Malveaux, Julianne
Economics and you. See issues of Essence beginning August 1987

Malvern, Merritt
(jt. auth) *See* Malvern, Phyllis, and Malvern, Merritt

Malvern, Phyllis, and Malvern, Merritt
A visit with Ernest L. Stevens. il por *Antiques Collect Hobbies* 92:48-9+ Ag '87

Mama Alice
about
Alice's army on the march. M. A. Fitzgerald. il por *Macleans* 100:24 N 2 '87

Goodbye, Mama Alice. W. R. Doerner. il por *Time* 130:38 N 23 '87

Mama I want to sing [musical] *See* Musicals, revues, etc.—Reviews—Single works

Mamet, David
Caribbean therapy. il *Vogue* 177:298+ F '87
about
House of games [film] Reviews
Commonweal 114:703-4 D 4 '87. T. O'Brien
Glamour 85:227 O '87. J. G. Boyum
Macleans 100:63 O 26 '87. L. O'Toole
N Y il 20:101-2 O 19 '87. D. Denby
New Repub 197:22-3 N 16 '87. S. Kauffmann
People Wkly il 28:14 N 16 '87. P. Travers
Time il 130:76 O 19 '87. R. Schickel
Vogue il 177:140+ S '87. M. Haskell
Life visits David Mamet & Lindsay Crouse. D. E. Haupt. il pors *Life* 10:64-5+ O '87

Mamet plays games. por *Harpers Bazaar* 120:380+ S '87

The profane poetry of David Mamet. J. Kroll. il por *Newsweek* 110:85 O 19 '87

Mammals
See also
Bats
Marine mammals
Pinnipedia
Primates
Whales

Mammals, Fossil
Climbing adaptations in the early Eocene mammal Chriacus and the origin of Artiodactyla. K. D. Rose. bibl f il *Science* 236:314-16 Ap 17 '87

Extinctions on ice [North American land mammals and Clovis hunters; theories of Paul S. Martin and others; cover story] B. Bower. il *Sci News* 132:284-5 O 31 '87

How did the giants die? [North American land mammals and Clovis hunters; theory of P. S. Martin] T. A. Lewis. il por *Int Wildl* 17:4-11 S/O '87

Mammary glands
See also
Breast
Growth
Reversible inhibition of mammary gland growth by transforming growth factor-β. G. B. Silberstein and C. W. Daniel. bibl f il *Science* 237:291-3 Jl 17 '87

Mammography
Detecting breast cancer sooner. P. Gadsby. il *Good Housekeep* 204:201 F '87

Give mother a mammogram for Christmas. C. SerVaas. il *Saturday Evening Post* 259:90+ D '87

Good news about mammograms. S. Findlay. *U S News World Rep* 103:17 S 28 '87

Help needed [Mammobile] C. SerVaas. il *Saturday Evening Post* 259:98+ Mr '87

The lessons from Mrs. Reagan's case. M. Clark. il *Newsweek* 110:30-1 O 26 '87

Philippe Courtot: champion of mammography. il por *Saturday Evening Post* 259:16 My/Je '87

Why women don't get mammograms (And why they should). J. Willis. il *FDA Consum* 21:5-7 My '87

Mammoths
The American blitzkrieg: a mammoth undertaking [Clovis hunters] J. M. Diamond. il *Discover* 8:82-4+ Je '87

Did early North Americans mount a mammoth 'blitzkrieg'? il *Earth Sci* 40:6-7 Wint '87

The Ginsberg experiment [Clovis and pre-Clovis artifacts] D. J. Stanford. il *Nat Hist* 96:10+ S '87

Mammoth find fuels extinction debate [discovery in England] B. Bower. *Sci News* 132:372 D 12 '87

Man
See also
Anthropocentrism
Anthropology
Civilization
Creation
Ethics
Ethnology
History
Human ecology
Human relations
Humanism
Philosophical anthropology
Psychology
Our path leads upward [adaptation of address] L. C. Eiseley. il *Read Dig* 131:35-6+ N '87

Economic value
The value of a life. T. Miller. *Cent Mag* 20:62-3 Jl/Ag '87

Influence of environment
See also
Environmental health
Weather—Mental and physiological effects
Experiencing places (I) [space and environment in architecture] T. Hiss. *New Yorker* 63:45-9+ Je 22 '87

Experiencing places (II) [space and environment in architecture] T. Hiss. *New Yorker* 63:73-80+ Je 29 '87

Anecdotes, facetiae, satire, etc.
Don't fool with Mother Nature. D. Kuschner. por *Newsweek* 109:8 Je 8 '87

Influence on nature
See also
Desertification
Environmental policy
Indians of North America—Influence on nature
Man and the Biosphere Programme
Pollution
United Nations Conference on the Human Environment
As an exterminating agency, humans are comparable with any natural form of violence that has ever come along. R. M. Adams. il *Smithsonian* 18:10 S '87

Back from the abyss [excerpt from Earth] A. H. Ehrlich and P. R. Ehrlich. il *Sierra* 72:54-60 Mr/Ap '87

"Don't blame me". G. Reiger. *Field Stream* 92:14+ Ag '87

The duel. R. Holland. il *Audubon* 89:60-1 N '87

Hand of man seen in birds [tandem particle accelerator mass spectrometry used in dating; research by Storrs Olson and others] R. Lewin. *Science* 236:1522 Je 19 '87

Human population [address, June 22, 1987] M. R. Cutler. *Vital Speeches Day* 53:691-6 S 1 '87

Man—Influence on nature—*cont.*
Man-made dangers invade wildlife refuges [Stillwater National Wildlife Management Area] il *Newsweek* 109:33 Mr 16 '87
The trees fell—and so did the people. S. Budiansky. il *U S News World Rep* 102:75-6 F 9 '87
The ultimate wildlife threat [human population expansion] L. Williamson. il *Outdoor Life* 180:28+ D '87

Migrations

Blood test [clues to New World migration from genetic analysis] S. L. Zegura. il *Nat Hist* 96:8+ Jl '87
Earlier appearance of humans in New World [work of Barbara Purdy] il *USA Today (Periodical)* 115:12 Je '87
Flakes, breaks and the first Americans [controversy over date of human migration to North America] B. Bower. il *Sci News* 131:172-3 Mr 14 '87
Prehistoric Polynesian puzzle [origin of Lapita culture; cover story] B. Bower. il map *Sci News* 132:232-3 O 10 '87
Voices from the past [clues to New World migrations from study of Indian languages] M. Ruhlen. map *Nat Hist* 96:6+ Mr '87

Origin and antiquity

See Man, Prehistoric

Periodicity

See Biological rhythms

Man, Prehistoric

See also
Archeology
Bone implements and weapons
Cave drawings and paintings
Paleo-Indians
Stone implements and weapons

Africa: cradle of modern humans. R. Lewin. *Science* 237:1292-5 S 11 '87
An age-old question: why did the human lineage survive? P. Shipman. il *Discover* 8:60-4 Ap '87
Bushes all the way down: we are all products of a recent African twig [mitochondrial DNA] S. J. Gould. *Nat Hist* 96:12+ Je '87
Debate over emergence of human tooth pattern. R. Lewin. il *Science* 235:748-50 F 13 '87
Discoveries in Africa are clues to early humans [Australopithecus] il *Earth Sci* 40:8-9 Spr '87
The earliest "humans" were more like apes [Homo habilis found in Olduvai Gorge] R. Lewin. il *Science* 236:1061-3 My 29 '87
Early ancestors less human-like [work of B. Holly Smith] *USA Today (Periodical)* 115:11 Je '87
Early human skeleton apes its ancestors [Homo habilis found in Olduvai Gorge by Donald Johanson] B. Bower. il *Sci News* 131:340 My 30 '87
Family feud: enter the 'black skull' [Alan Walker's controversial discovery in Kenya] B. Bower. il *Sci News* 131:58-9 Ja 24 '87
Family ties [Homo habilis skeleton unearthed in Olduvai Gorge] il *Sci Am* 257:16+ Jl '87
Hominid evolution: a tale of two trees. B. Bower. il *Sci News* 132:7 Jl 4 '87
Hominid growth slows to an ape's pace [work of B. Holly Smith] B. Bower. *Sci News* 131:255 Ap 18 '87
Hominid headway [use of tomography to study Taung skull] B. Bower. *Sci News* 132:408-9 D 19-26 '87
Hominoid lineages and keystone clues [Robert B. Eckhardt's challenge to Todd R. Olson's nasal bone theory] B. Bower. il *Sci News* 132:71 Ag 1 '87
Lucy gets a younger sister [Homo habilis skeleton unearthed in Olduvai Gorge by Donald Johanson] A. Toufexis. il *Time* 129:63 Je 1 '87
New light on when man came down from the trees [Homo habilis skeleton discovered by Donald Johanson in Olduvai Gorge] S. Budiansky. il *U S News World Rep* 102:10-11 Je 1 '87
The origin of the modern human mind [special section] R. Lewin. il *Science* 236:668-70 My 8 '87
The prehumans: our family tree [skull related to Australopithecus boisei discovered in Kenya] P. Shipman. *Current* 290:4-8 F '87
Robust hominids: tooth and consequences [australopithecines] B. Bower. il *Sci News* 131:229 Ap 11 '87
Sizing up Neanderthals [work of Rachel Caspari at Krapina, Yugoslavia site] B. Bower. *Sci News* 131:255 Ap 18 '87
The trees fell—and so did the people. S. Budiansky. il *U S News World Rep* 102:75-6 F 9 '87
Uncovering life by an ancient lake [Olorgesailie lake basin in Kenya] B. Bower. *Sci News* 131:264 Ap 25 '87

The unmasking of mitochondrial Eve. R. Lewin. il *Science* 238:24-6 O 2 '87
The way we were—20,000 years ago [Cro-Magnon or late Ice Age man]; ed. by Louise Lief. S. Begley. il *Read Dig* 130:167-72 Mr '87
Woman of the year, 1.8 million B.C. [fossils from Olduvai Gorge, Tanzania] il *Newsweek* 109:59 Je 1 '87

Diseases

See Paleopathology

Exhibitions

The Ice Age returns [exhibit at the New York State Museum] il *Conservationist* 41:48-9 My/Je '87

Food

The 2-million-year-old meat and marrow diet resurfaces [research by Henry T. Bunn and Ellen M. Kroll] B. Bower. *Sci News* 131:7 Ja 3 '87
History with gusto [beer and prehistoric man; theory of S. Katz] il *Time* 129:57 Ap 6 '87
The myths and perturbing realities of cannibalism. P. Shipman. il *Discover* 8:70-2+ Mr '87

Man, Prehistoric, in literature

Life with Ayla and her friends: Jean Auel and the new phenomenon of Ice Age fiction. B. M. Fagan. *Sci Am* 256:132-5 Je '87

Man alive [television program] See Television program reviews—Single works
Man and nature See Man—Influence of environment; Man—Influence on nature

Man and the Biosphere Programme

Man and the Biosphere: a partnership for sustainable development [cover story; special issue] il *Courier* 40:3-30 O '87
When men and mountains meet [Alps] J. Schaller. il map *Courier* 40:9-10 F '87

Man facing southeast [film] See Motion picture reviews—Single works
A man for all seasons [drama] See Bolt, Robert
A man in love [film] See Motion picture reviews—Single works
The man who broke 1,000 chains [television program] See Television program reviews—Single works

Management

See also
Airports—Management
Art galleries and museums—Management
Arts—Management
Business management
Communication in management
Facility management
Farm management
Organization
Scheduling (Management)
School management and organization
Time management
United States. Army—Management
United States. Navy—Management
Wildlife management

Management and Budget Office (U.S.) See United States. Office of Management and Budget
Management consultants See Business consultants
Management development programs See Executives—Training

Management games

Business simulations. S. Morgenstern. il *Work Woman* 12:54+ My '87

Management of children See Children—Management and training
Managers See Executives; Women executives
Managers, Baseball See Baseball managers

Managua (Nicaragua)

Description

Letter from Managua. R. O'Connor. il *Vogue* 177:176+ Ag '87
Managua is waiting [excerpt from Where is Nicaragua?] P. Davis. il *Esquire* 107:171-4+ Mr '87
A tale of two cities. J. P. Fitzpatrick. *America* 157:4-5 Jl 4-11 '87

Photographs and photography

City on a volcano. il *Life* 10:132-7 D '87

Manalapan (N.J.: Township)

Crime

The child custody murder [battle for P. A. Taylor] P. Maas. il pors *Good Housekeep* 205:154-5+ O '87
Legacy of a mother's murder [custody battle for P. A. Taylor] P. Maas. il pors *N Y Times Mag* p40-4+ Ap 12 '87

Manas, Blanka

Unusual buttons of the past. il *Antiques Collect Hobbies* 92:60-1 O '87

Manatee County (Fla.)
Police
Psychologist with a badge [T. H. Blau] R. J. Trotter. il pors *Psychol Today* 21:26+ N '87
Manatees
Manatees, like their siren namesakes, lure us to the deep. J. P. Wiley, Jr. il *Smithsonian* 18:92-7 S '87
People, power plants, and manatees [Florida] J. E. Reynolds, III and J. R. Wilcox. il map *Sea Front* 33:263-9 Jl/Ag '87
Manaus (Brazil)
Industries
Up the river. E. A. Finn, Jr. il map *Forbes* 140:102+ N 2 '87
Mance, Lonnie
about
Chicago boy gets $2.5 mil. in injury case: his arm destroyed by electricity. por *Jet* 72:36 Jl 27 '87
Mancheski, Frederick John, 1926-
about
Service is our most important product. L. R. Walbert. il por *Forbes* 139:48+ Ap 6 '87
Manchester, William
The bloodiest battle of all. il *N Y Times Mag* p42+ Je 14 '87
A day in the life of Winston Churchill [condensed from The last lion] il pors *Read Dig* 131:156-62 O '87
The lion caged. il pors *Am Herit* 38:6-7, 65-88 F/Mr '87
Manchester (England)
Art
'Cultivated capital' [culture and patronage of the arts in nineteenth-century Manchester and Leeds] J. Wolff and C. Arscott. bibl il *Hist Today* 37:22-8 Mr '87
Manchester (Iowa)
Industries
Hog heaven or hell [community opposition to proposed IBP plant] C. Isenhart. il *Progressive* 51:13 O '87
Manchester (Mass.)
Historic houses, sites, etc.
Mistaken identity [converted carriage house of W. Hodgins] C. Vogel. il *N Y Times Mag* p36-40 Ag 23 '87
Old World white [W. Hodgin's remodeled carriage house] E. Greene. il *House Gard* 159:94-9 Ja '87
Manchester union leader (Newspaper)
Power behind the pen [N. S. Loeb] B. Wallace. il por *Macleans* 100:6-7 O 5 '87
The story that still nags at me [press coverage of E. Muskie's emotional reaction to W. Loeb's attacks in the Manchester union leader, 1972; excerpt from Behind the front page] D. S. Broder. il *Wash Mon* 19:29-32+ F '87
Mancini, Marc
M.O.B. rule. il por *Film Comment* 23:76-7 Jl/Ag '87
Video S.I.P. il *Film Comment* 23:44-9 Ja/F '87
Mancuso, Frank
about
Paramount's hot streak is untouchable—for now. R. Grover. il por *Bus Week* p153 S 14 '87
Mandabach, Caryn
about
The woman behind Cosby. D. Mason. por *Vogue* 177:206+ S '87
Mandarette (Los Angeles, Calif.: Restaurant) See Los Angeles (Calif.)—Restaurants, nightclubs, bars, etc.
Mandated benefits legislation See Fringe benefits—Laws and regulations
Mandatory retirement See Retirement
Mandel, Ernest
about
May the U.S. ban "undesirable" foreigners? S. Flack. *Sch Update* 120:35-6 O 2 '87
Mandel, Howard
Charlie Haden's search for freedom. il pors *Down Beat* 54:20-3 S '87
George Benson: strike up the band [cover story; interview] il pors *Down Beat* 54:16-19 My '87
Ornette Coleman: the color of music [cover story; interview] il pors *Down Beat* 54:16-19 Ag '87
Round midnight. il *Down Beat* 54:22-3 Ja '87
Mandel, Robert
about
Touch and go [film] Reviews
New Yorker 62:93-4 F 9 '87. P. Kael
Mandela, Nelson
about
Apartheid chic. A. White. il *Film Comment* 23:11-12+ N/D '87
Crockett heads drive for a day honoring Mandela. pors *Jet* 73:4 N 9 '87

Danny Glover stars in 'Mandela' movie that tugs at heart, shocks senses [cover story] il pors *Jet* 73:58-60 O 5 '87
Mandela: 25 years later, still a force in South Africa. *Jet* 72:6 Ag 24 '87
Robert Brown oversees the enrollment of Mandela's daughter at Boston Univ. il por *Jet* 72:28 Je 8 '87
Special Committee against Apartheid calls for release of political prisoners. il *UN Chron* 23:47 N '86
Two voices that will not be stilled. B. W. Nelan. il pors *Time* 129:37 Ja 5 '87
Mandela, Winnie
about
Two voices that will not be stilled. B. W. Nelan. il pors *Time* 129:37 Ja 5 '87
Winnie Mandela [interview] A. Frense. il por *Ms* 15:82-3+ Ja '87
Winnie one of world's 'most important women'. il por *Jet* 73:38 O 26 '87
Mandela (Mass.)
Secession move defeated. J. Ball. *Black Enterp* 17:16 Ja '87
Mandela [television program] See Television program reviews—Single works
Mandelbaum, Karen
about
Bauble, bauble and toil give two designing sisters the magic touch. K. Hubbard. il pors *People Wkly* 27:153 Je 8 '87
Mandelbaum, Lyn
about
Bauble, bauble and toil give two designing sisters the magic touch. K. Hubbard. il pors *People Wkly* 27:153 Je 8 '87
Mandelbaum, Michael
"Something is happening here". il por *Time* 129:34-5 F 16 '87
Mandelker, Jeannie
Venture magazine. il *Writer* 100:27 S '87
Mandell, Patricia
Told from the heart. il por *Americana* 15:38-40+ Jl/Ag '87
Mandelli, Mariuccia
about
Krizia's executive class. J. Conant. il por *Newsweek* 110:70 O 26 '87
Mandel'stam, Osip Yemilyevich, 1891-1938
Three poems [poem] *New Yorker* 63:40 My 18 '87
Mandlikova, Hana
Instinctively yours; ed. by Cindy Shmerler. il por *World Tennis* 34:32-3 My '87
Out of control. il por *World Tennis* 35:72 D '87
Mandoki, Luis
about
Gaby—a true story [film] Reviews
Macleans 100:67 N 30 '87. L. O'Toole
Maned wolves See Wolves
Maneli, Mieczysław
John Paul II: the universal Pole. *Humanist* 47:26-7+ S/O '87
Manella, Daniel J.
about
Faberge lands Arden: 'Now we've got mass—and class'. S. Benway. il por *Bus Week* p38-9 Ag 17 '87
Maneuvers, Military See Military maneuvers
Mangalorean cooking See Cooking, Indian (East Indian)
Mangano, Silvana
about
Infidelity: Italian (and Russian) style. A. Harvey. il pors *Vogue* 177:442-3+ O '87
Manger groups See Christmas cribs
Mangieri, John N.
(jt. auth) See Kemper, Richard E., and Mangieri, John N.
Mango, Frank D.
An invariance in the isoheptanes of petroleum. bibl f il *Science* 237:514-17 Jl 31 '87
Mangoes
Contamination
Crates of fresh poison [EDB levels in mangoes imported from Haiti] R. Caplan. *Harpers* 275:58-9 O '87
Mangold, Robert, 1937-
about
Robert Mangold: 'a maker of images—nothing more and nothing less'. J. Gruen. il pors *Art News* 86:132-8 Summ '87
Mangold, Thomas
The birth of SDI. il *World Press Rev* 34:17-19 Mr '87

Manguel, Alberto
Sweet are the uses of anthology. il *N Y Times Book Rev* 92:1+ Ag 23 '87
Mangum, Donald
Hostess [story] *New Yorker* 63:33 S 28 '87
Mangum, William
Professional page. il *Am Artist* 51:10+ Ag '87
Manhattan (Kan.)
        Education
What Living Word School doesn't have. P. F. Parsons. *Christ Today* 31:24 S 4 '87
Manhattan Beach (Calif.)
        Crime
Can the 'abused' kids be believed? [McMartin Preschool trial] T. Gest. il *U S News World Rep* 103:10 Jl 27 '87
Manhattan Community College
City Univ. of N.Y. gets 1st black woman prexy [A. S. Kappner] por *Jet* 73:22 N 9 '87
Manhattan Graphics Corporation
Rosenberg and Abbott: giant steps in desktop publishing. P. Finch. il pors *Bus Week* p81 F 9 '87
Manhattan Helicopter Tours
Big Apple choppers. M. Phelps. *Flying* 114:108 N '87
Manhattan, inc. (Periodical)
Editorial freedom vs. the red suspenders [editor J. Amsterdam quits after conflict with owner D. H. Lipson] *Newsweek* 109:47 Ap 6 '87
Lipson, Inc. E. Diamond. il por *N Y* 20:28+ Ap 27 '87
Return of the native [new editor C. Felker] *Time* 129:62 Je 1 '87
Manhattan Island (New York, N.Y.: Restaurant) *See* New York (N.Y.)—Restaurants, nightclubs, bars, etc.
Manhattan School of Music
Our favorite force of nature [B. Nilsson's master classes for opera singers] G. Schmidgall. il pors *Opera News* 52:20-2+ Jl '87
Voices of spring [performance of Chérubin] P. G. Davis. il *N Y* 20:97-8 Ap 13 '87
Manhunter [film] *See* Motion picture reviews—Single works
Maniatis, Tom, and others
Regulation of inducible and tissue-specific gene expression. bibl f il *Science* 236:1237-45 Je 5 '87
Manic depression *See* Depression, Mental
Manicotti cooking *See* Cooking—Pasta
Manicuring
Handle with care: a complete package for healthier hands and nails. P. Boyer. il *Prevention* 39:44+ Mr '87
Hands-on nail care. L. Wells. il *N Y Times Mag* p72 Je 28 '87
Knockout nails. il *Teen* 31:86-7 Je '87
Lady fingers (& toes). il *Mademoiselle* 93:124-7 Jl '87
Nails in full bloom. il *Seventeen* 46:242-3 Mr '87
Manicuring salons *See* Beauty shops
Manila (Philippines)
        Housing
"His slum, not mine". E. A. R. Ouano. il *World Health* p10-11 Jl '87
        Poor
The slum behind the Sheraton. J. DeParle. il *Wash Mon* 19:32-44 D '87
Manilow, Barry
        about
Barry Manilow: finding the time for the 'Sweet life'. W. Goldstein. por *Publ Wkly* 232:44 O 16 '87
A nice mid-life crisis. E. Levin. il pors *People Wkly* 28:40-3 N 9 '87
Manipulators (Mechanism)
Canadian MSC to provide essential station assembly, docking capability [Mobile Servicing Center] T. M. Foley. il *Aviat Week Space Technol* 126:48-50 My 25 '87
Computer-controlled robot [Armatron] J. Barbarello. il *Radio-Electron* 58 ComputerDigest:144-7 My '87
A polyurethane proboscis [artificial elephant's trunk designed by James F. Wilson and others] il *Sci Am* 256:73-4 Ap '87
Manitoba
        See also
        Birds—Manitoba
        Churchill (Man.)
        Fishing—Manitoba
        Geology—Manitoba
        Gods Lake (Man.)
        Industries
        See also
        Manitoba Consumers Gas Corporation
        Politics and government
An attack on gay rights [news of E. Schreyer] *Macleans* 100:11 Jl 27 '87

Manitoba Consumers Gas Corporation
Heating up the gas wars [Manitoba purchases supply network belonging to Inter-City Gas Corp.] D. Smith. il *Macleans* 100:37 Je 22 '87
Mankiewicz, Tom
        about
Dragnet [film] Reviews
    Macleans il 100:46 Jl 13 '87. L. O'Toole
    Newsweek il 110:60 Jl 13 '87. D. Ansen
    People Wkly il 28:10 Jl 20 '87. R. Novak
Manley, Dexter
        about
In search of trust [cover story] R. Reilly. il pors *Sports Illus* 67:84-8+ N 23 '87
Manley, unchained. C. Brennan. por *Sport Mag* 78:73-5 Ag '87
Manley, G. A., and others
Developmental stability of the tonotopic organization of the chick's basilar papilla. bibl f il *Science* 237:655-6 Ag 7 '87
Manley, John
Return technology to human hands. il *Bull At Sci* 43:7-8 D '87
Manley, Michael
        about
Seaga plays for time in Jamaica. P. Engardio. il por *Bus Week* p41 Ap 20 '87
Manley, T. O., and others
Mesoscale oceanographic processes beneath the ice of Fram Strait. bibl f il maps *Science* 236:432-4 Ap 24 '87
Mann, Charles C.
(jt. auth) *See* Blair, Gwenda, and Mann, Charles C.
(jt. auth) *See* Crease, Robert P., and Mann, Charles C.
Mann, Cuthbert Carson
The empire's last nervous twitch. *Commonweal* 114:562-5 O 9 '87
Mann, Dale
Business involvement and public school improvement (I). bibl f il *Phi Delta Kappan* 69:123-8 O '87
Business involvement and public school improvement (II). bibl f il *Phi Delta Kappan* 69:228-32 N '87
Mann, Dean L., and others
HTLV-I-associated B-cell CLL: indirect role for retrovirus in leukemogenesis. bibl f il *Science* 236:1103-6 My 29 '87
Mann, Eric
U.A.W. backs the wrong team. il *Nation* 244:171-2+ F 14 '87
Mann, George J.
Beyond the hospital: building for a healthier future. il por *Futurist* 21:9-10+ Ja/F '87
Mann, Jonathan M.
The global AIDS situation. il *World Health* p6-8 Je '87
Mann, Mary Tyler Peabody, 1806-1887
        about
Three sisters who showed the way. M. Marshall. il pors *Am Herit* 38:58-63+ S/O '87
Mann, Michael
        about
Manhunter [film] Reviews
    Christ Century 104:46-7 Ja 21 '87. M. Horst
Michael Mann [interview] L. Hirschberg. il por *Roll Stone* p163-4 D 17-31 '87
Mann, Murray Gell- *See* Gell-Mann, Murray, 1929-
Mann, Paul
Aerospace/defense executives must put their own shops in order [discussion of November 23, 1987 article, The aerospace leadership void] por *Aviat Week Space Technol* 127:61-3 D 21 '87
The aerospace leadership void [address, November 13, 1987] *Aviat Week Space Technol* 127:15 N 23 '87
Mann, Peggy
Breakthrough against cocaine. *Read Dig* 130:185-6+ Ap '87
Teen-agers and the calcium crisis. il *Saturday Evening Post* 259:68-71 Ap '87
"We're teaching our kids to use drugs". il *Read Dig* 131:106-10 N '87
Mann, Sally, 1951-
        about
Sally Mann at Marcuse Pfeiffer. A. Ellenzweig. *Art Am* 75:140 Ja '87
Mann, Terri
        about
This Mann has a mission. G. Maranto. il por *Sports Illus* 67 Sp Issue:102-3 N 18 '87

Mann, Thomas, 1875-1955
about
Pilgrimage. S. Sontag. *New Yorker* 63:38-48+ D 21 '87
Manned space flights *See* Space flight
Mannequin [film] *See* Motion picture reviews—Single works
Mannerism (Art)
Exhibitions
The magic of Medusa: European mannerisms [exhibit at Künstlerhaus in Vienna] A. Hunt. il *Art News* 86:161 S '87
Manners and customs
See also
Chivalry
Clothing and dress
Courtesy
Courtship
Dating (Social customs)
Drinking customs
Etiquette
Funeral rites and ceremonies
Holidays
Modesty
Rites and ceremonies
Tipping
Mannes Camerata
Musical events:
Giasone by P. F. Cavalli. A. Porter. il *New Yorker* 63:63 Ag 24 '87
Mannheim, Karl, 1893-1947
about
Is a science of politics possible?: The view from Mannheim. D. Kettler and others. *Society* 24:76-82 Mr/Ap '87
Manning, Dennis
about
The need for speed. P. Lyons. il *Cycle* 38:45 Ap '87
Manning, Kate
(ed) *See* Gallagher, Michael. "Am I old enough to be a parent?"
Manning, William
about
An investment that turned into a nightmare. E. T. Smith. il por *Bus Week* p102+ N 30 '87
Manning & Napier Advisors Inc.
An investment that turned into a nightmare [S. R. Ovshinsky sues W. Manning] E. T. Smith. il por *Bus Week* p102+ N 30 '87
Manning-Mims, Madeline
about
Madeline Manning-Mims elected to Sports Hall. *Jet* 73:48 S 28 '87
Mannitol
New sugar may help fat, thin alike [research by Michael DiNovi and Robert Rafka] J. Raloff. *Sci News* 131:251 Ap 18 '87
Mano, D. Keith
Colleen Dewhurst. il pors *People Wkly* 27:80-2+ Mr 9 '87
The gimlet eye. See occasional issues of National Review
Manoff, Jaqui
about
How petals from the sea form these fragile blossoms. G. B. Ruh. il por *Smithsonian* 17:106-10 Ja '87
Manoff, Robert Karl
Means and ends. *Progressive* 51:39 Mr '87
Manon [opera] *See* Massenet, Jules, 1842-1912
Manon Lescaut [opera] *See* Puccini, Giacomo, 1858-1924
Manon of the spring [film] *See* Motion picture reviews—Single works
Manpower
See also
Labor supply
Manpower, Inc.
A whiz kid bids for Manpower [A. Berry's Blue Arrow plc] M. D. Oneal and R. A. Melcher. il por *Bus Week* p37-8 Ag 17 '87
Manpower and education *See* Labor—Education
Manpowered aircraft *See* Human powered aircraft
Manpowered vehicles *See* Human powered vehicles
Mansbridge, Jane J.
Not NOW. *Nation* 244:5 Ja 10 '87
Mansbridge, Peter
about
The National's new man. P. Young. il pors *Macleans* 100:58 N 23 '87
The Peter Mansbridge syndrome. C. Gordon. il *Macleans* 100:52 N 30 '87
Mansell, Nigel
about
Minute Man(sell). R. Walker. il *Road Track* 39:144-6+ N '87

More Mansell magic. R. Walker. il por *Road Track* 38:132-4 Ja '87
Mostly Mansell. R. Walker. il *Road Track* 38:144-6+ Ag '87
Now Nelson, now Nigel. I. Ireland. il *Road Track* 39:134-8+ D '87
Williamsville. I. Ireland. il *Road Track* 39:136-8 O '87
Mansfield, Drummond
Memories of the road. il por *Am Hist Illus* 21:34-41 F '87
Mansingh, Sonal
about
Celebration of dance. K. C. Reinhart. il *Horizon* 30:30 Mr '87
Manske, Laura
Get smart! Foods and workouts that sharpen your outlook. il *Mademoiselle* 93:182 S '87
When thin isn't in (reaching the right weight doesn't always mean dieting). il *Mademoiselle* 93:114 O '87
Manson, Charles, 1934-
about
In Manson's eyes [interview] R. Healy. il pors *Life* 10:54-6 Mr '87
Mansur, John W.
No greater love. il *Read Dig* 131:49-50 Ag '87
Mantel clocks *See* Clocks
Mantels
Mail-order mantels. P. Butler and M. Butler. il *Pop Sci* 231:80-2 D '87
Manteo family
about
Chivalry lives as Mike Manteo revives knights to remember. D. Grogan. il *People Wkly* 27:52-4 Je 1 '87
Manti (Utah)
Temples
Temple on a hill [Mormon landmark] il *Americana* 15:51-3 S/O '87
Mantle, Margaret
The fine art of child appreciation. *U S Cathol* 52:30-1 S '87
In teens we trust. il *U S Cathol* 52:29-31 My '87
Mantle of the earth *See* Earth—Internal structure
Manual transmission *See* Automobiles—Transmission
Manuel, David
Teen Challenge: conquering drugs and AIDS. il *Saturday Evening Post* 259:52-5+ D '87
Manuel, Ruth
Think yourself healthy. il *Harpers Bazaar* 120:118+ F '87
Manufactured houses *See* Houses, Prefabricated
Manufacturers' agents
Suits and claims
Who'll sell what to whom? J. A. Conway. il *Forbes* 139:10 Mr 23 '87
Manufacturers Hanover Corp.
Barbara Paddock: keeping Manny Hanny ahead of the game [director of special events] P. Finch. il por *Bus Week* p91 N 9 '87
The turnaround trauma at Manufacturers Hanover. S. Bartlett. il *Bus Week* p68-70 Ag 24 '87
Manufacturing Clause (Copyright law) *See* Copyright
Manufacturing in space *See* Space processing
Manufacturing industries
See also
Industrial capacity
The basics come back. il *Fortune* 116:8 Ag 31 '87
The big revival in milltown. P. Nulty. il *Fortune* 116:173+ D 7 '87
Catching the upswing in domestic manufacturing. J. E. Goodman and W. L. Updegrave. il *Money* 16:7 Mr '87
The challenge of global competition [address, September 17, 1987] G. H. Conrades. *Vital Speeches Day* 54:125-8 D 1 '87
The challenge to U.S. competitiveness. R. M. White. *Science* 236:1041 My 29 '87
Competitiveness: getting it back. S. Nasar. il *Fortune* 115:217-18+ Ap 27 '87
Cruising into the 21st century [manufacturing along Interstate 75] E. A. Finn, Jr. il map *Forbes* 140:80+ Ag 24 '87
Engineers hear a competitive parable. W. Booth. *Science* 238:474 O 23 '87
A fan of smokestack America [interview with C. Clough] A. E. Serwer. il por *Fortune* 116:192 O 26 '87
Harris chief warns of economic chaos if manufacturing continues overseas move [views of J. A. Boyd] E. H. Kolcum. *Aviat Week Space Technol* 127:89 S 14 '87

Manufacturing industries—*cont.*

How to keep mature industries innovative [cover story] C. F. Sabel and others. il *Technol Rev* 90:26-35 Ap '87

In this corner, Uncle Sam [lower dollar helps American industry] D. Pauly. il *Newsweek* 110:61-2 D 7 '87

Making American industry competitive again [address, April 16, 1987] J. Weaver. *Vital Speeches Day* 53:560-2 Jl 1 '87

Making brawn work with brains. O. Port. il *Bus Week* p56-8+ Ap 20 '87

Manufacturing today [Canada; address, June 24, 1987] B. M. McGourty. *Vital Speeches Day* 53:752-5 O 1 '87

The myth of a post-industrial economy. S. S. Cohen and J. Zysman. il *Technol Rev* 90:54-60+ F/Mr '87

The nonsense of a "post-industrial society" [address, January 15, 1987] R. A. Lutz. *Vital Speeches Day* 53:330-3 Mr 15 '87

The obituary that should not have run. K. R. Sheets and R. F. Black. il *U S News World Rep* 103:82+ D 28 '87-Ja 4 '88

The protean corporation [cover story] S. Lee and C. Brown. il *Forbes* 140:76-9 Ag 24 '87

Revival in the Rust Belt. J. Edgerton. il *Money* 16:77-8+ Jl '87

The smokestacks won't tumble. B. Saporito. il *Fortune* 115:30-2 F 2 '87

Taming the cost of the "hidden factory". H. Banks. il *Forbes* 140:27-8 S 21 '87

Technology and global industry. P. H. Abelson. *Science* 236:1609 Je 26 '87

There's good news in the factories. K. R. Sheets. il *U S News World Rep* 103:44-5+ N 30 '87

Why manufacturing will revive. K. Pennar. il *Bus Week* p66-8 Ja 12 '87

Manure *See* Feces—Animals

Manure handling *See* Fertilizers and manures—Handling

Manures as fertilizers *See* Fertilizers and manures

Manuscript (Word processor program) *See* Word processors and processing—Programming

Manuscripts

See also

Illumination of books and manuscripts

Collectors and collecting

Getting a taste for the scribbles of history. S. Woolley. il *Bus Week* p117 S 28 '87

Exhibitions

Roads to Liberty exhibit. *Am Hist Illus* 22:14 S '87

Facsimiles

High-tech printing techniques create an 'elaborately forged' Domesday book. S. D. Bell. il *Publ Wkly* 231:50-2 Ap 17 '87

The Vatican goes to Hell [ancient texts recreated by computer imaging] E. Stone. il *Omni* 9:24 S '87

Manuscripts, American

Bill of Rights draft found [R. Sherman draft] *Am Hist Illus* 22:12 O '87

Connecticut Yankee Roger Sherman's draft of the Bill of Rights makes a surprise appearance in Washington. il por *People Wkly* 28:71 Ag 17 '87

Rights show their roots [discovery of R. Sherman's handwritten Bill of Rights draft] por *Time* 130:25 Ag 10 '87

Collectors and collecting

A passion for history [J. Engelhard's collections] J. Fleming. il *House Gard* 159:122-5+ Mr '87

Expertising

John Pierce proved that the writing on the wall was a relic [Declaration of Independence print made in 1776 in Rhode Island by Solomon Southwick] il por *People Wkly* 27:51 F 16 '87

Theft

The tale of a frog prince [arrest of C. M. Mount] M. Stevens. il por *Newsweek* 110:22 Ag 31 '87

Walking papers [C. M. Mount arrested for stealing rare historical documents] D. Seideman. il pors *Time* 130:16 Ag 31 '87

Manuscripts, English

Devotions & delights: the illuminated books of Gothic England. J. Backhouse. bibl il *Hist Today* 37:25-31 N '87

"What is the worth of a unique historic rarity?" [document signed by King Charles II] H. Herst, Jr. il *Forbes* 139:26 Mr 9 '87

Manuscripts, Hebrew

See also

Bible—Manuscripts, Hebrew

Dead Sea scrolls

Manvell, Roger, 1909-1987

(jt. auth) See Fleming, Michael, and Manvell, Roger, 1909-1987

Manwaring, Michael

about

Nouvelle cuisine for the eyes. K. Andersen. il pors *Time* 129:88-9 Je 8 '87

Many-body problem

The coupled-cluster method. R. F. Bishop and H. Kümmel. bibl f il *Phys Today* 40:52-60 Mr '87

Manzari, Vittorio, and others

HTLV-V: a new human retrovirus isolated in a Tac-negative T cell lymphoma/leukemia. bibl f il *Science* 238:1581-3 D 11 '87

Manzi, Jim P.

Revolutions don't happen overnight. por *Pers Comput* 11:223 O '87

about

The drill instructor who made Lotus snap to attention. K. H. Hammonds. il por *Bus Week* p190-2 N 16 '87

Mao, Tse-tung *See* Mao Zedong, 1893-1976

MAO (Monoamine oxidase) *See* Oxidases

Mao Zedong, 1893-1976

about

Chairman Mao Zedong. por *Sch Update* 120:26 S 18 '87

The long shadow of Mao. F. Willey. il por *Newsweek* 109:40 Mr 16 '87

Map contours *See* Contours (Cartography)

Map making, Computerized *See* Computers—Cartographic use

Mapco Inc.

Right side of the table. R. McGough. por *Forbes* 139:56 Ja 26 '87

Maple

Maple euthanasia. J. D. Randolph. il *Ctry J* 14:4+ Jl '87

Anecdotes, facetiae, satire, etc.

To kill a maple tree. A. A. Rooney. il *Saturday Evening Post* 259:66-7 Ap '87

Diseases and pests

Pancakes without maple syrup? [Quebec] J. R. Luoma. il *Audubon* 89:44 Mr '87

Sounding taps for the sugar maple. J. W. Edwards. il *Natl Wildl* 25:20 O/N '87

Maple sugar industry

Canada

Pancakes without maple syrup? [Quebec] J. R. Luoma. il *Audubon* 89:44 Mr '87

Mappings (Mathematics)

Probing the strange attractions of chaos. A. K. Dewdney. il *Sci Am* 257:108-11 Jl '87

Mapplethorpe, Robert

about

Still life in motion. C. Bush. il *Theatre Crafts* 21:32-3+ F '87

Maps

See also

Aviation charts

CD-ROM (Compact disc-Read only memory)—Maps

Computer maps

Geology—Maps

Ocean bottom—Maps

Road maps, guides, etc.

Santa Barbara County (Calif.)—Maps

United States—Maps

Vegetation maps

World maps

Maps, Astronomical *See* Astronomy—Charts, diagrams, etc.

Maps, Early

Julius Caesar and the Hereford world map. P. Wiseman. bibl il maps *Hist Today* 37:53-7 N '87

Maps, Mental *See* Geographical perception

Marable, Manning, 1950-

Black politics in crisis. il *Progressive* 51:18-23 Ja '87

Maracci, Carmelita, 1911-1987

about

Obituary

Dance Mag il pors 61:32-3 N '87. D. Perlmutter

Maramorosch, Karl

The curse of cadang-cadang. il *Nat Hist* 96:20-2 Jl '87

Maran, Stephen P.

A new generation of giant eyes gets ready to probe the universe [cover story] il *Smithsonian* 18:40-53 Je '87

Sky reporter. See occasional issues of Natural History

Maranoff, Jeff

Machine over money: a new twist on investing. il *Work Woman* 12:34+ Jl '87

Maranto, Gina
 Lady in a fast lane. il pors *Sports Illus* 67:44-7 S 28 '87
 This Mann has a mission. il por *Sports Illus* 67 Sp Issue:102-3 N 18 '87
 A woman of substance. il pors *Sports Illus* 67:62+ Ag 24 '87
Marantz Co., Inc.
 The power of prayer. J. A. Conway. por *Forbes* 139:8 Mr 9 '87
Marathon running
 Ads for ourselves [New York City Marathon]; tr. by Barry Schwabsky. J. Baudrillard. *Harpers* 275:32 O '87
 He ran a crooked 26 miles, 385 yards [Bob Prichard's analysis of New York City Marathon runners' styles] C. Neff. il *Sports Illus* 67:18 N 16 '87
 Here comes Kim! [K. Alexis] H. Herman. por *Health* 19:37+ O '87
 How good runners can get close to great. N. Kuscsik. il *Women's Sports Fitness* 9:62-3 Jl '87
 Kenyan wins NY Marathon, points to '88 Olympics [I. Hussein] il por *Jet* 73:51 N 23 '87
 Money talked, nobody walked [Boston Marathon] C. Neff. il *Sports Illus* 66:34-5 Ap 27 '87
 New look in the long run [New York City Marathon] C. Neff. il pors *Sports Illus* 67:24-5 N 9 '87
 That wheeling feeling [wheelchair racers in the Boston Marathon] C. Neff. il por *Sports Illus* 66:96 My 4 '87
 To Boston with love [people who live and toil along the Marathon course] L. Montville. il *Sports Illus* 66:94-8+ Ap 20 '87
 Woman to watch: Priscilla Welch. M. Goldberg. il por *Women's Sports Fitness* 9:18 Mr '87
  Economic aspects
 Fees cut for NYC marathoners. P. Gambaccini. il *Sport Mag* 78:16 N '87
  History
 Marathon man [M. Ernst] B. Berntsen. il por *Courier* 40:33-4 Je '87
Marberry, Craig
 Say, brother. por *Essence* 18:9 My '87
Marble
 Taking care of marble. il *Sunset* 178:160+ My '87
Marble Collectors Society of America
 Society produces video [Robert Dane: making marbles] *Antiques Collect Hobbies* 92:42 Jl '87
Marble Hill House (Twickenham, London, England) *See* Twickenham (London, England)—Historic houses, sites, etc.
Marbles (Game)
   See also
 Marble Collectors Society of America
Marc, Franz, 1880-1916
   about
 Murnau and Kochel: where the Blue Rider was born. J. Dornberg. il pors *Art News* 86:77-8+ D '87
Marc (Franz) Museum (Kochel, Germany) *See* Franz Marc Museum (Kochel, Germany)
Marcaccini, Meryl
 Let's make cheerleading a sport. il *Women's Sports Fitness* 9:78 My '87
Marceau, Marcel
   about
 Marceau founds mime institute in Midwest. M. D. Rudnicki. il por *Dance Mag* 61:8-9 Jl '87
 Speaking out from behind the mask of mime [interview] R. Z. Chesnoff. il pors *U S News World Rep* 102:62-3 F 23 '87
Marceau (Marcel) World Centre for Mime *See* Marcel Marceau World Centre for Mime
Marcel Marceau World Centre for Mime
 Marceau founds mime institute in Midwest. M. D. Rudnicki. il por *Dance Mag* 61:8-9 Jl '87
March, Michael
 (tr) *See* Herbert, Zbigniew. Mass for the imprisoned
March
 The March almanac. il *Atlantic* 259:12 Mr '87
Marchant, Sofia
 Marilyn: the legend lives on. il pors *Ladies Home J* 104:92+ Ag '87
Marching bands *See* Bands (Music)
Marchuk, G. I. (Gurii Ivanovich), 1925-
   about
 Marchuk is president of Soviet Academy. W. Sweet. *Phys Today* 40:71-2 Ja '87
Marchuk, Gurii Ivanovich *See* Marchuk, G. I. (Gurii Ivanovich), 1925-
Marcial, Gene G.
 Inside Wall Street. *See* issues of Business Week

Marcialis, Robert L., and others
 The surface composition of Charon: tentative identification of water ice. bibl f il *Science* 237:1349-51 S 11 '87
Marciano family
   about
 Does Guess have a friend in the IRS? R. Behar. il map *Forbes* 140:146-50+ N 16 '87
 The IRS mess. R. Behar. il *Forbes* 140:8 N 30 '87
Marciniak, Ed
 The impact of the women's movement(s) on the family: a father's perspective. *America* 156:194-6 Mr 7 '87
Marcinkus, Paul C.
   about
 Archbishop to appeal ruling on NAL novel. C. Reid. *Publ Wkly* 232:20 D 25 '87
 Did corruption soil Vatican's inner sanctum? J. P. Shapiro. il por *U S News World Rep* 102:10 Mr 9 '87
 Hiding behind the walls. S. Allis. il por *Time* 129:54 Mr 9 '87
 Vatican bank scandal. *Christ Century* 104:265 Mr 18-25 '87
 Vatican horror: a banking scandal widens. por *Newsweek* 109:48 Mr 9 '87
Marconi Co. Ltd.
 British set date to change Tornado radar contract. *Aviat Week Space Technol* 126:26 Ap 6 '87
 Marconi providing ECM systems for ground, air, space use [electronic countermeasures systems] il *Aviat Week Space Technol* 126:61+ F 16 '87
Marcos, Ferdinand E. (Ferdinand Edralin), 1917-
   about
 Arms for Marcos? L. Howard. il por *Newsweek* 110:5 D 21 '87
 Can Aquino break the grip of crony corruption? A. Paul. il pors *Read Dig* 131:83-7 Jl '87
 Exiled Marcos: 'We shall return' [interview] R. Z. Chesnoff. il por *U S News World Rep* 103:33 Ag 3 '87
 First Family in exile. P. S. Greenberg. il pors *Macleans* 100:23-5 Ap 27 '87
 The foiling of Ferdinand. H. Anderson. il por *Newsweek* 110:35 Jl 20 '87
 Hot on the trail of the Marcos billions. M. Shao. il pors *Bus Week* p52-3 Ag 17 '87
 Marcos at bay. F. Barnes. *New Repub* 196:9-11 Mr 2 '87
 The Marcos plot. A. Giarelli. il *World Press Rev* 34:40 S '87
 The Marcoses' moonlight sonata. S. Mydans. il pors *N Y Times Mag* p34-6+ Ap 19 '87
 Marcos's warriors: a very live threat. H. Anderson. il *Newsweek* 109:38 My 11 '87
 Please speak into the microphone. S. Tifft. il por *Time* 130:50 Jl 20 '87
 The quest for Marcos's gold. N. Cooper. il por *Newsweek* 110:33 Ag 3 '87
 Where do you hide $10 billion? Aquino wants to know. L. Kraar. por *Fortune* 116:97 S 14 '87
Marcos, Imelda
   about
 First Family in exile. P. S. Greenberg. il pors *Macleans* 100:23-5 Ap 27 '87
 Hot on the trail of the Marcos billions. M. Shao. il pors *Bus Week* p52-3 Ag 17 '87
 Lifestyles of the rich and tyrannical. J. L. Goldstein. *Am Sch* 56:235-47 Spr '87
 The Marcoses' moonlight sonata. S. Mydans. il pors *N Y Times Mag* p34-6+ Ap 19 '87
 My dinner with Imelda. R. Howard. *Harpers* 275:29-30+ O '87
Marcus, Bernard
   about
 Do-it-yourself debacle. L. M. Keefe. il por *Forbes* 139:48 My 4 '87
Marcus, James
 Tales of detection. *Nation* 245:598-9 N 21 '87
Marcus, Leonard S., 1950-
 A moon that never sets. *N Y Times Book Rev* 92:22 Ja 25 '87
Marcus, Susan M.
 Adventure in Manitoba. il *Earth Sci* 40:21-3 Summ '87
Marcus, Yoel
 The politics of secrecy and silence. il *Newsweek* 109:33 Mr 30 '87
Marcuse, Peter
 Why are they homeless? il *Nation* 244:426+ Ap 4 '87

Marden, Brice, 1938-
about
Brice Marden. M. Poirier. il *Art News* 86:201-2 Summ '87
Marder, Amy R.
Your healthy pet. See issues of Prevention (Emmaus, Pa.) beginning July 1987
Marder, Bruce
about
For stars (and crocodiles, too) Rebecca's is the hot new hangout. M. Neill. il pors *People Wkly* 28:148-9 S 7 '87
Marder, Rebecca
about
For stars (and crocodiles, too) Rebecca's is the hot new hangout. M. Neill. il pors *People Wkly* 28:148-9 S 7 '87
Mardi Gras *See* Carnival (Pre-Lenten festival)
Mardon, Deirdre
Stranded [story] il *Redbook* 169:70+ O '87
Marek, Elizabeth
A child's prison [excerpt from The children at Santa Clara] *Harpers* 274:32-4 Mr '87
about
PW interviews. J. F. Baker. il pors *Publ Wkly* 232:41-2 Jl 17 '87
Marek, George R.
Finer points. il *Opera News* 51:28+ Ja 31 '87
A luminous carousel. il pors *Opera News* 51:14-17 F 14 '87
Marek, Richard
about
PW interviews. J. F. Baker. il pors *Publ Wkly* 232:41-2 Jl 17 '87
Marell, Gail
First word. il *Omni* 9:8 My '87
Maren, Michael
Kenya: the dissolution of democracy. bibl f *Curr Hist* 86:209-12+ My '87
The right's last, best hope. il *Nation* 245:744-6 D 19 '87
Marennikova, Svetlana
Surveillance and research. il *World Health* p22-3 Ag/S '87
Marfsalov, Nikolai
about
From the wilderness to Saks Fifth Avenue, the fur trail leads from the hunt to riches. M. Brower. il por *People Wkly* 27:98-100+ Ap 6 '87
Margaret, Princess, Countess of Snowdon, 1930-
about
The misfortunes of a princess. A. Steacy. il pors *Macleans* 100:34 N 9 '87
Margaret Mead Film Festival *See* Motion picture festivals—New York (State)
Margaritondo, Giorgio, 1946-
(jt. auth) See Bauer, Robert S., and Margaritondo, Giorgio, 1946-
Margaronis, Maria
There's something happening here. *Nation* 245:757 D 19 '87
Margeotes/Fertitta & Weiss
Up the upscale. B. Kanner. il *N Y* 20:14+ Ja 26 '87
Margin buying *See* Stocks—Margin buying
Marginalia
My very own write-in campaign. V. Vaughn. por *Publ Wkly* 232:66 N 27 '87
Margolick, David
Whose words are they, anyway? il *N Y Times Book Rev* 92:1+ N 1 '87
Margolies, Eva
(jt. auth) See Genevie, Louis E., and Margolies, Eva
about
Happy Mother's Day [interview] B. Johnson. il pors *People Wkly* 27:57-8+ My 11 '87
Margolies, John
Fanciful fairways [photographs] il *Americana* 15:80-1 My/Je '87
Margolis, David I.
about
One year later, Colt is at a steady gallop. C. Power. il por *Bus Week* p134+ O 19 '87
Margolis, Esther
about
Making that first million. R. A. Carter. il pors *Publ Wkly* 231:18-20 Mr 27 '87
Margolis, Heather
about
All-American-Girl talk. por *Teen* 31:14 S '87

Margolis, Matthew
about
Bones of contention get buried in Doggy Court, where justice is tempered with mercy. il por *People Wkly* 27:135 My 11 '87
Margolis, Richard J.
America's new entrepreneurs [cover story] por *New Leader* 70:11-12 N 30 '87
The fast-care industry. il *New Leader* 70:13-14 Ja 12-26 '87
The health gift repossessed. il *New Leader* 70:13-14 Ap 6 '87
How Medicare puts the elderly on hold. *New Leader* 70:12-13 Jl 1-15 '87
Melody and mystery. il *New Leader* 69:9-10 D 1-15 '86
When Irish skies are frowning. il *New Leader* 70:15-16 S 7 '87
Wisconsin's child-support experiment. il *New Leader* 70:14-16 O 19 '87
Margolis, Susanna
Ann Bancroft. il pors *Ms* 15:71-2+ Ja '87
Margulies, Lee
Bruce Paltrow. il por *Channels* 7:26-7+ O '87
Margulis, Lynn, 1938-
(jt. auth) See Sagan, Dorion, 1959-, and Margulis, Lynn, 1938-
about
Red pond. B. Lawren. il *Omni* 9:20 Ja '87
Marian devotion *See* Mary, Blessed Virgin, Saint—Devotions
Marian Year, 1987
Protestants and the Marian Year. R. M. Brown. *Christ Century* 104:520-1 Je 3-10 '87
'Redemptoris Mater' [John Paul's Marian encyclical] T. H. Stahel. *America* 156:353-4 My 2 '87
Urgency and security in the coming Marian Year. L. S. Cunningham. il *Christ Century* 104:334-6 Ap 8 '87
Mariani, John F.
The best new bars and restaurants of 1987. il *Esquire* 108:169-72+ N '87
Getting juiced. il *Harpers Bazaar* 120:98+ Ag '87
Haute hotel tables. il *Harpers Bazaar* 121:162+ N '87
How Italians say shanks. il *Esquire* 108:56 S '87
Spirits locker. See alternate issues of Motor Boating & Sailing
Mariano, Luis, 1914-1970
about
Letter from Europe. J. Kramer. il *New Yorker* 63:66-70+ Ag 24 '87
Mariátegui, José Carlos, 1894-1930
about
José Carlos Mariátegui: forgotten forerunner of liberation theology. M. Candelaria. *Christ Century* 104:885-7 O 14 '87
Mariculture *See* Aquaculture
Marielitos *See* Cubans—United States
Marietta, Don E.
Humanists and talk of God. il por *Humanist* 47:8-10+ S/O '87
Marihuana *See* Marijuana
Marijuana
After the Ginsburg debacle, a chronicler of the sixties ponders the new politics of pot [interview with T. Gitlin] M. Wilhelm. il por *People Wkly* 28:124+ N 23 '87
Betrayal. H. S. Scott. *New Repub* 197:12-13 D 14 '87
Exit the smoking judge [D. Ginsburg] I. Austen. il por *Macleans* 100:32 N 16 '87
The Ginsburg test: bad logic. C. Krauthammer. il *Time* 130:102 N 23 '87
Marijuana update: new reasons to "keep off the grass". D. Hymes. il *Curr Health 2* 13:18-21 Mr '87
Marijuana use may cause mental problems: study. *Jet* 73:28 S 28 '87
Pot & politics [D. H. Ginsburg's Supreme Court nomination; cover story] A. Press. il pors *Newsweek* 110:46-52 N 16 '87
Sins of the past [drug use by D. Ginsburg derails Supreme Court nomination] M. Hornblower. por *Time* 130:18-20 N 16 '87
Up in smoke: the undoing of a High Court nominee [D. Ginsburg] B. Duffy and D. Baer. il por *U S News World Rep* 103:24-6 N 16 '87
Laws and regulations
Fla. man who used child for drug deal collateral jailed [case of F. W. Cook] *Jet* 71:32 F 23 '87
Getting straight [Humboldt County, Calif.] M. Beauchamp. il *Forbes* 139:92+ Je 1 '87

Marijuana—Laws and regulations—*cont.*
Jesus freak meets pothead [argument in favor of Oregon ballot initiative legalizing marijuana] *Harpers* 274:19 Ja '87

Barbados
Mick's girlfriend is jailed after receiving a surprise package [J. Hall's drug bust] por *People Wkly* 27:96 F 9 '87
Marin, Cheech
about
Born in East L.A. [film] Reviews
People Wkly il por 28:14 S 14 '87. T. Cunneff
Marin, Maguy
about
Cinderella [ballet] Reviews
Art Am il 75:43-5 S '87. J. R. Acocella
Dance Mag il 61:28-9 My '87. C. Hardy
Eden [dance] Reviews
N Y 20:129 N 9 '87. T. Tobias
New Leader 70:23 N 2 '87. L. A. Jacobs
A new face on dance. B. Haye. il *Theatre Crafts* 21:42-3+ N '87
Marin, Peter
Helping and hating the homeless. il *Harpers* 274:39-44+ Ja '87
The Weathermen, twenty years on. il *Harpers* 275:26-8 D '87
Marin County (Calif.)
The Tao of Marin County. *Harpers* 274:19-20+ Ja '87
Description and travel
Moonlighting in Marin. il *Sunset* 178:39-40 F '87
The wide-open spaces of Marin. il map *Sunset* 178:12-13 Mr '87
Marin County Community College
Bookstores
See College bookstores
Marina/Consult Corporation
Dockbroker Ed [E. J. Doherty] R. Behar. il por *Forbes* 140:166+ S 21 '87
Marina del Rey (Calif.)
Architecture
What can you do with 23 feet? il *Sunset* 179:148-9 S '87
Marinades
Pretty to look at, good to eat [marinated vegetable garnishes] S. Payne. il *South Living* 22:80-1 Je '87
Marinas
See also
Condominiums (Boat docking)
Marina/Consult Corporation
Marine accidents
See also
Boats and boating—Fires and fire prevention
Catamaran racing—Accidents and injuries
Motor boat racing—Accidents and injuries
Nuclear submarines—Accidents and explosions
Shipwrecks
Yacht racing—Accidents and injuries
Marine archeology *See* Archeology, Submarine
Marine bacteria *See* Bacteria, Marine
Marine Biological Laboratory (Woods Hole, Mass.)
Can dogfish cure diabetes? P. Raeburn. il *Natl Wildl* 26:34-9 D '87/Ja '88
Marine biology
See also
Discovery Hall Marine Biology Institute
Estuarine ecology
Marine ecology
Marine fauna
Marine pharmacology
Marine resources
Marine sediments
Plankton
Spawning
Bibliography
Reviews. See issues of Oceans
Study and teaching
Is the organismic biologist an endangered species? H. M. Lenhoff. *BioScience* 37:244 Ap '87
Marine canvas work
Boatkeeper's guide to marine fabrics. D. W. Parris. il *Mot Boat Sail* 159:76 Je '87
Marine caves
What's in a cave? [fauna in marine caves] N. Sefton. il *Sea Front* 33:404-13 N/D '87
Bahamas
In the lair of the lusca [Bahamian blue holes] R. Palmer. il *Nat Hist* 96:42-7 Ja '87

Marine charts *See* Nautical charts
Marine cooking *See* Cooking, Marine
Marine Corps (U.S.) *See* United States. Marine Corps
Marine deposits *See* Marine sediments
Marine ecology
See also
Estuarine ecology
Red tide
Can microscale chemical patches persist in the sea? Microelectrode study of marine snow, fecal pellets. A. L. Alldredge and Y. Cohen. bibl f il *Science* 235:689-91 F 6 '87
Diadema antillarum was not a keystone predator in cryptic reef environments. J. B. C. Jackson and K. W. Kaufmann. bibl f il *Science* 235:687-9 F 6 '87
New light on seaweeds [role of light harvesting pigments in depth zonation of seaweeds; cover story] M. B. Saffo. bibl il *BioScience* 37:654-64 O '87
Marine electricity *See* Boats and boating—Electric equipment
Marine electronics *See* Boats and boating—Electronic equipment
Marine engines
See also
Carburetors
Diesel engines, Marine
Motor boat engines
Engine room. T. Banse. See issues of Motor Boating & Sailing
Exhaust
Effect of ship-stack effluents on cloud reflectivity. J. A. Coakley, Jr. and others. bibl f il *Science* 237:1020-2 Ag 28 '87
Fuel
Gas pains. B. Stearns. il *Field Stream* 92:89-90 O '87
Maintenance and repair
10 gas engine lay-up tips. T. Banse. il *Mot Boat Sail* 160:86 O '87
Marine farming *See* Aquaculture
Marine fauna
See also
Bryozoa
Coral reef fauna
Corals
Echinoderms
Feces—Marine fauna
Fish
Horseshoe crabs
Marine mammals
Octopuses
Sea anemones
Sea snakes
Sponges
Starfish
Divers' dilemma [offshore rig removal vs. endangered marine species] J. S. McKinna. il *Oceans* 20:10 N/D '87
Man-made killer of the seas [plastic pollution] A. Berliant. il *U S News World Rep* 103:72 Jl 6 '87
The plastic threat to marine life. il *Sea Front* 33:464-6 N/D '87
Symbiosis in the deep sea [sulfide based ecosystem at hydrothermal vents] J. J. Childress and others. il *Sci Am* 256:114-20 My '87
Vancouver Island's undersea kaleidoscope: a diver's paradise. L. Wood. il *Sea Front* 33:97-104 Mr/Ap '87
What's in a cave? [fauna in marine caves] N. Sefton. il *Sea Front* 33:404-13 N/D '87
Food and feeding
Deep-sea hydrocarbon seep communities: evidence for energy and nutritional carbon sources. J. M. Brooks and others. bibl f il *Science* 238:1138-42 N 20 '87
Photographs and photography
Chasing rainbows in the sea. C. Newbert. il por *Natl Wildl* 25:52-9 F/Mr '87
Fugitive color. D. Hall. il *Oceans* 20:30-5 My/Je '87
Marine fauna, Effect of temperature on
Musseling in on novel cryoprotectants [research by Stephen Loomis and others] S. Weisburd. *Sci News* 132:9 Jl 4 '87
Marine fauna, Fossil
Environmental trends in extinction during the Paleozoic. J. J. Sepkoski, Jr. bibl f il *Science* 235:64-6 Ja 2 '87
Solving the extinction paradox [work of J. J. Sepkoski] *USA Today (Periodical)* 115:9-10 Je '87
Marine fauna in art
Alaskan marine life and the Eskimo—through art [work of Huong] B. Rush and H. Lebelson. il por *Sea Front* 33:84-9 Mr/Ap '87

Marine fires *See* Boats and boating—Fires and fire prevention

Marine flora
> *See also*
> Algae
> Seaweed

Marine geology *See* Submarine geology

Marine laboratories
> *See also*
> Bodega Marine Laboratory
> Marine Biological Laboratory (Woods Hole, Mass.)

Marine mammals
> *See also*
> Cetacea
> Dolphins
> Manatees
> Pinnipedia
> Seals (Animals)
> Walruses
> Whales

Laws and regulations
Comments from members [discussion of January/February 1987 article, Crow's nest] *Sea Front* 33:224-5 My/Je '87

Crow's nest. G. L. Voss. *Sea Front* 33:2-3 Ja/F '87

Training
Alysoun Seacat is number one in Nuka's heart—by a whisker. B. Rowes. il por *People Wkly* 28:110-11 Ag 10 '87

Marine meteorology *See* Meteorology, Maritime

Marine microbiology
> *See also*
> Bacteria, Marine

Marine Midland Bank, N.A.
Going to investment banking 'boot camp' with Midland's Marines. A. Beam. *Bus Week* p82 Ap 6 '87

Marine mineral resources
> *See also*
> Exclusive Economic Zone
> Ocean mining

Present at the birth of an ore deposit [Salton Sea area] R. A. Kerr. il *Science* 238:890-1 N 13 '87

Marine navigation *See* Navigation

Marine paint, Antifouling *See* Paint, Protective

Marine painting

Exhibitions
British marine painting [Masters of the sea: British marine watercolors, 1650-1930 at the Yale Center for British Art] S. B. Sherrill. il *Antiques* 131:1182 Je '87

Marine parks and reserves
Guarding Neptune's sacred grounds [Marine Sanctuary Program] M. J. Palmer. il *Sierra* 72:20+ N/D '87

Marine pharmacology
A step forward for drugs from the sea. il *Sea Front* 33:144-5 Mr/Ap '87

Will sea animals help treat cancer? S. Eisenberg. *Sci News* 132:295 N 7 '87

Marine photography
> *See also*
> Photography, Submarine

A portfolio of photography contest winners. il *Sea Front* 33:273-9 Jl/Ag '87

See a world in a grain of sand [shore photography portfolio] D. Schrader. il *Oceans* 20:24-33 Mr/Ap '87

Marine pollution
> *See also*
> Waste disposal in the ocean

How bad is ocean pollution? [views of Frederick K. Browand] il *USA Today (Periodical)* 116:13-14 Ag '87

Man-made killer of the seas [plastic pollution] A. Berliant. il *U S News World Rep* 103:72 Jl 6 '87

No safe harbor for marine life [TBT based paint and the marine environment] A. J. Mitteldorf and J. S. Weis. il *Sierra* 72:27+ S/O '87

Our befouled beaches. J. Adler. il *Newsweek* 110:50-1 Jl 27 '87

Painting with pesticides: the controversial organotin paints. S. Scott. il *Sea Front* 33:414-21 N/D '87

The plastic threat to marine life. il *Sea Front* 33:464-6 N/D '87

Troubled waters [cover story] il map *Bus Week* p88-91+ O 12 '87

Golden Horn (Turkey)
A new tune for the Golden Horn. G. L. McCurdy. il map *Sierra* 72:14-15 Mr/Ap '87

Long Island Sound (N.Y. and Conn.)
Oceans on the brink. T. H. Cole. il *Pop Mech* 164:42 D '87

An oysterman's battle to keep 'black mayonnaise' at bay [T. Backer works to clean up Long Island Sound] R. Mitchell. il *Bus Week* p98 O 12 '87

Mediterranean Sea
Cousteau's plea for the Mediterranean. J. Y. Cousteau. por *World Press Rev* 34:53 Je '87

Puget Sound (Wash.)
Turning the tide on Puget Sound's polluters. R. Brandt. il *Bus Week* p94 O 12 '87

Santa Monica Bay (Calif.)
Troubled waters [contaminated fish] S. Pritikin. il *Sierra* 72:16 Ja/F '87

Waddenzee (Netherlands)
PCB-polluted fishes cause seal decline. *Sea Front* 33:305-6 Jl/Ag '87

Marine propellers *See* Boats and boating—Propellers

Marine radar *See* Radar in navigation

Marine radiotelephone *See* Radiotelephone on ships, boats, etc.

Marine research *See* Oceanography

Marine resources
> *See also*
> Fisheries
> Marine mineral resources

Seabed materials. J. M. Broadus. bibl f il map *Science* 235:853-60 F 20 '87

Laws and regulations
Custodial politics. M. W. Robbins. il *Oceans* 20:2 My/Je '87

Marine sanctuaries *See* Marine parks and reserves

Marine sanitation devices *See* Boats and boating—Toilet facilities

Marine science *See* Oceanography

Marine sediments
> *See also*
> Ocean Drilling Program

A big splash in the Pacific [work of Frank Kyte and others] map *Sky Telesc* 74:12 Jl '87

Chronology of fluctuating sea levels since the Triassic. B. U. Haq and others. bibl f il *Science* 235:1156-67 Mr 6 '87

Natural abundances of carbon isotopes in acetate from a coastal marine sediment. N. E. Blair and others. bibl f il *Science* 236:66-8 Ap 3 '87

Refining and defending the Vail sea level curve. R. A. Kerr. il *Science* 235:1141-2 Mr 6 '87

Sea cycle clock [seismic stratigraphy; work of Peter R. Vail and others] S. Weisburd. il *Sci News* 131:154-5 Mr 7 '87

Stimulation of heterotrophic microplankton production by resuspended marine sediments. S. C. Wainright. bibl f il *Science* 238:1710-12 D 18 '87

Windfalls of dust [determining ancient wind patterns from core samples of ocean sediments] D. K. Rea. il map *Nat Hist* 96:28+ F '87

Marine toilets *See* Boats and boating—Toilet facilities

Marine turtles *See* Turtles

Marine worms
> *See also*
> Annelids

Marines (U.S.) *See* United States. Marine Corps

Marino, Peter
> *about*

Visual intrigue. S. M. L. Aronson. il pors *Archit Dig* 44:228-32+ N '87

Marion (Francis) National Forest (S.C.) *See* Francis Marion National Forest (S.C.)

Marion (Ill.)

Prisons and reformatories
The toughest prison in America [Marion Federal Penitentiary] M. Satchell. il *U S News World Rep* 103:23-4 Jl 27 '87

Marion Federal Penitentiary *See* Marion (Ill.)—Prisons and reformatories

Marionettes *See* Puppets and puppet plays

Marioni, Tom, 1937-
> *about*

Tom Marioni at Museo Italo-Americano. M. Levy. *Art Am* 75:161 Je '87

Maris, Humphrey J., and Andreev, Aleksander F.
The surface of crystalline helium-4. bibl f il *Phys Today* 40:25-30 F '87

Maris, Roger, 1934-1985
> *about*

An error for baseball: why aren't Leo Durocher and Roger Maris in the Hall? S. Wulf. il por *Sports Illus* 67:92 Ag 10 '87

Maritain, Jacques, 1882-1973
> *about*

Remembering Jacques Maritain. W. Fowlie. *Am Sch* 56:355-66 Summ '87

Marital infidelity *See* Adultery
Marital quarrels *See* Quarrels
Maritime law
> *See also*
> Boats and boating—Laws and regulations
> Convention on the Law of the Sea (1982)
> Exclusive Economic Zone
> National Oceans Policy Commission (U.S.)
> Slave trade
> Territorial waters
> United Nations. Preparatory Commission for the International Sea-Bed Authority and the International Tribunal for the Law of the Sea
The Titanic's legacy to safety. R. L. Scheina. il *Sea Front* 33:200-9 My/Je '87
> **United States**
> *See* Maritime law
Maritime meteorology *See* Meteorology, Maritime
Maritime Provinces
> **Description and travel**
Now is the season to visit these coastal retreats. S. Birnbaum. il *Good Housekeep* 204:46+ Je '87
> **Economic conditions**
> *See also*
> Atlantic Canada Opportunities Agency
Maritime Telegraph & Telephone Co., Ltd.
Fitness in the workplace [address, February 18, 1987] C. Latham. *Vital Speeches Day* 53:446-8 My 1 '87
Mark, Charles Christopher
Arts education, anyone? *Des Arts Educ* 88:17-19 N/D '86
Mark, Florine
Her 'extraordinary dream' came true; ed. by Eileen Nechas. il pors *Prevention* 39:54+ Mr '87
Mark, Mary Ellen, 1940-
> *about*
The unflinching eye. V. Goldberg. il pors *N Y Times Mag* p12-18+ Jl 12 '87
Mark, Melvin M., and Greenberg, Jerald
Evening the score. bibl (p63) il *Psychol Today* 21:44-50 Ja '87
Mark, Reuben
> *about*
The man brushing up Colgate's image. H. J. Steinbreder. il pors *Fortune* 115:106-7+ My 11 '87
Mark, Sid
> *about*
Sinatra. *New Yorker* 63:32-4 Ap 6 '87
Mark Controls Corp.
Know when to fold them [G. MacDougal sells Mark Controls to Swiss investors] J. Flint. il por *Forbes* 140:124 D 28 '87
Mark Morris Dance Group
Dance. M. Aloff. *Nation* 244:624-6 My 9 '87
Dancevision [performances on Dance in America] J. Gruen. por *Dance Mag* 61:74-5 F '87
Dancing:
> Mythologies. A. Croce. *New Yorker* 63:83-4 Je 8 '87
Morris to replace Bejart in Brussels. L. Moffett. por *Dance Mag* 61:14 D '87
Reviews:
> Performances of Stabat mater at the Brooklyn Academy of Music. J. R. Acocella. *Dance Mag* 61:35-6 Ap '87
Mark Twain Memorial (Hartford, Conn.)
The curious house that Mark built. N. A. Ruhling. il por *Antiques Collect Hobbies* 92:80-2+ Mr '87
Market bulletins (Gardening) *See* Garden literature
Market gardening *See* Truck farming
Market research
> *See also*
> A. C. Nielsen Co.
> Actmedia Inc.
> BrainReserve (Firm)
> Focus groups (Market research)
> Information Resources Inc.
> People meters (TV audience research)
> R.D. Percy & Company
> Shop'n Chek Inc.
> Single-source research (TV audience research)
> Yankelovich Clancy Shulman (Firm)
Beyond the hidden persuaders. J. A. Trachtenberg. il *Forbes* 139:134-5+ Mr 23 '87
Is anybody out there listening? [Ford's market research techniques] R. Ceppos. il *Car Driv* 33:24-5 O '87
Let the computer do it. T. Mack. il *Forbes* 140:94 Ag 10 '87
The sacrifice buy. C. Lorenz. *World Press Rev* 34:50 N '87

> **Acquisitions and mergers**
Nielsen boosts its ratings [acquisition of Information Resources Inc.] A. Dunkin. il *Bus Week* p40 S 14 '87
> **Ethical aspects**
A case of malpractice—in market research? [Beecham sues Yankelovich over research on new detergent] M. Rothman. *Bus Week* p28-9 Ag 10 '87
A test for market research. A. Miller and D. Tsiantar. il *Newsweek* 110:32-3 D 28 '87
> **Great Britain**
> *See also*
> A G B Research plc
Market share
How to take—and keep—unfair advantage. K. L. Fisher. il *Forbes* 140 Sp Issue:400 O 26 '87
The riches in market niches [fast growing companies on fringe of Fortune 500] S. Gannes. il *Fortune* 115:227-8+ Ap 27 '87
Winning the battle for market share [black entrepreneurs] B. Robson. il *Black Enterp* 17:276 Je '87
Market sweeps (Securities) *See* Street sweeps (Securities)
MarketCorp Venture Associates
The Rabbit punch [R. Wright charges Rabbit Systems and MarketCorp Venture Associates with misappropriation of trade secrets] K. Healy. il por *Forbes* 140:175-6 S 21 '87
Marketing
> *See also*
> Advertising
> Aged market
> Asian American market
> Auctions
> Blind market
> Clothing industry—Licensing agreements
> Cooperative Marketing Company
> Direct selling
> Display of merchandise
> Electronic marketing
> Franchise system
> Hispanic American market
> Homosexual market
> Mail order business
> Merchandising
> Middle age market
> Multilevel marketing
> Price policies
> Products, New
> Pyramid selling operations
> Rebates
> Roadside marketing
> Samples (Merchandising)
> Singles market
> Society for Marketing Professional Services
> Youth market
> *See also* subhead Marketing under various subjects
Do your ads need a superagency? [integrated marketing] A. Ramirez. il *Fortune* 115:81-2+ Ap 27 '87
Fiesta Ware and Tide, b'gosh [how yesterday's products get a second wind] J. Sherman. *Work Woman* 12:41 Ag '87
How to master the politics of marketing. J. Sherman. *Work Woman* 12:18+ Mr '87
Marketing's new look [Campbell Soup's move to regionalization] C. Dugas. il *Bus Week* p64-9 Ja 26 '87
The rediscovery of local pizzazz [regional marketing] D. Fenn. il *Work Woman* 12:66-8+ Jl '87
> **Japan**
The rise and rise of the Japanese yuppie. L. Armstrong and B. Buell. il *Bus Week* p54+ F 16 '87
Marketing channels
Seven strategies for gaining the competitive edge. J. M. Thompson. il *Work Woman* 12:56+ O '87
Marketing consultants
> *See also*
> BrainReserve (Firm)
Do your ads need a superagency? [integrated marketing] A. Ramirez. il *Fortune* 115:81-2+ Ap 27 '87
Marketing managers
> *See also*
> Black marketing managers
> Women marketing managers
Marketing research *See* Market research
Markets
> *See also*
> Farmers' markets
> Fish markets
> Flea markets

Markets—*cont.*
International aspects
Marvels of the marketplace. C. Hoffman. *Travel Holiday* 167:118 Ap '87
California
See also
Los Angeles (Calif.)—Markets
Japan
See also
Tokyo (Japan)—Markets
Kentucky
See also
Lexington (Ky.)—Markets
Morocco
See also
Marrakesh (Morocco)—Markets
New York (State)
See also
New York (N.Y.)—Markets
Peru
See also
Iquitos (Peru)—Markets
Markets, Black *See* Black markets
Markets, Roadside *See* Roadside marketing
Markets for authors *See* Authors and publishers
Markets for photographers *See* Photographs—Marketing
Markey, Edward J.
Should Congress approve the Fairness Doctrine? [excerpts from debate, June 3, 1987] *Congr Dig* 66:248+ O '87
about
Markey see, Markey do. M. Brown. *por Channels* 7:26 My '87
No more malarkey from Edward Markey? F. Seghers and V. Cahan. *por Bus Week* p71 N 2 '87
Markides, Karin E.
(jt. auth) See Lee, Milton L., and Markides, Karin E.
Marking (Students) *See* Grading and marking (Students)
Markkula, Mike
about
Odyssey: John Sculley and the saga of the Macintosh (I) [excerpt from Odyssey] J. Sculley. il *Pers Comput* 11:182-5+ N '87
Markle, John, d. 1987
about
Epitaph for a trader. W. P. Barrett. il *por Forbes* 140:121 D 14 '87
Markoe, Merrill
A head full of bees. il *pors Roll Stone* p31-2 Jl 2 '87
Markowitz, Marty
about
Everly Brothers. *New Yorker* 63:24-5 Ag 31 '87
Markowitz, Roberta
Today's busy woman's biggest complaint. . . "I'm too tired for sex!!". *Redbook* 170:118-19+ N '87
Marks, Bruce
about
Tales of Hans Christian Andersen [ballet] Reviews
Dance Mag il 61:52-4 N '87. I. M. Fanger
Marks, Cara Berman, and others
Mutants of bovine pancreatic trypsin inhibitor lacking cysteines 14 and 38 can fold properly. bibl f il *Science* 235:1370-3 Mr 13 '87
Marks, Dorothy Ames
A stately Willard proudly receives guests once more. il *Smithsonian* 17:78-82+ F '87
Marks, Jane
My husband is completely selfish. il *Ladies Home J* 104:10+ Jl '87
My husband is too demanding. il *Ladies Home J* 104:12+ My '87
"We have a problem". See issues of Parents beginning February 1987
Marks, Nancy S.
Citizen enforcement of environmental laws. bibl f *Environment* 29:5+ Je '87
Marks, Paul A.
about
Dr. Marks' crusade: shaking up Sloan-Kettering for a new assault on cancer [cover story] P. M. Boffey. il *pors N Y Times Mag* p26-31+ Ap 26 '87
Marks & Spencer plc
Marks & Spencer, the 'uniquely-British aunty'. I. Shenker. il *Smithsonian* 18:142-6+ N '87
Marksmen *See* Shooters (of arms)
Markus, Julia, 1939-
On location. il *Writer* 100:21-3 Je '87

Marlboro Cup (Race) *See* Horse racing
Marlboro Man (Advertising character)
Here's one tough cowboy. J. A. Trachtenberg. il *Forbes* 139:108-10 F 9 '87
Marlene [film] See Motion picture reviews—Single works
Marler, Peter
(jt. auth) See Gould, James L., 1945-, and Marler, Peter
Marley, Bob
about
Bob Marley and The Wailers: The Roxy, Los Angeles, May 26th, 1976. D. Fricke. il *pors Roll Stone* p93-4 Je 4 '87
Marlin, Alice Tepper
about
Corporate America sucks up. D. K. Mano. *Natl Rev* 39:55-7 My 8 '87
Marlin, Alice Tepper, and others
Give your dollars a political spin. il *Nation* 244:75-6+ Ja 24 '87
Marlow, Christopher, 1564-1593
about
The Jew of Malta [drama] Reviews
Nation 244:479 Ap 11 '87. T. M. Disch
Marlowe, Charles K.
(jt. auth) See Bartlett, Paul A., and Marlowe, Charles K.
Marlowe, Melissa
about
Game and gutsy, three tiny teens limber up for the '88 Olympics. A. Chambers. il *pors People Wkly* 28:130-2 N 2 '87
Marmalade *See* Jelly, jam, etc.
Marmer, Nancy
Documenta 8: the social dimension? il *Art Am* 75:128-39+ S '87
Maro, Akaji
about
The five rings [dance] Reviews
N Y 20:137-8 Ap 27 '87. T. Tobias
Marous, John C.
about
Danforth picks his heirs. G. L. Miles and M. Rothman. *Bus Week* p26-7 Ag 10 '87
Marowitz, Charles
about
Sherlock's last case [drama] Reviews
N Y il 20:60 Ag 31 '87. J. Simon
New Leader 70:22-3 S 21 '87. L. Sauvage
New Yorker 63:67 Ag 31 '87. E. Oliver
Marples, David R.
The Chernobyl disaster. bibl f *Curr Hist* 86:325-8+ O '87
Marquand, John P. (John Phillips), 1893-1960
about
Justice to John P. Marquand. T. Teachout. *Commentary* 84:54-9 O '87
Marquand, Richard
about
Hearts of fire [film] Reviews
Vogue il 177:54 Jl '87. R. O'Connor
Marquardt, Deborah
A thinly disguised message. il *Ms* 15:33 My '87
Marquesas Islands
Description and travel
To the Marquesas. J. C. Simmons. il map *Oceans* 20:20-5 Jl/Ag '87
Márquez, Gabriel García *See* García Márquez, Gabriel, 1928-
Marrack, Philippa
New insights into antigen recognition. *Science* 235:1311-13 Mr 13 '87
Marrack, Philippa, and Kappler, John
The T cell receptor. bibl f il *Science* 238:1073-9 N 20 '87
Marrakesh (Morocco)
Description
The pink oasis. J. Morris. il *Vogue* 177:228+ D '87
Galleries and museums
See also
Museum of Islamic Art (Marrakesh, Morocco)
Gardens and gardening
Gardens: Majorelle remembered: Yves Saint Laurent and Pierre Bergé in Marrakesh. C. Aillaud. il *pors Archit Dig* 44:160-5 O '87
Hotels, motels, etc.
Contemporary caravansary: the Hotel Tichka in Marrakesh [decorated by Bill Willis] L. Dennis. il *Archit Dig* 44:52-9+ Ja '87
Markets
Bargain hunting in Marrakesh. R. Riley. il *U S News World Rep* 103:58 S 7 '87

Marriage

See also

Adultery
Childlessness
Divorce
Family
Husbands
Interfaith marriage
Interracial marriage
Marriage of priests
Married couples
Married women
Monogamy
Polyandry
Polygamy
Remarriage
Separation (Law)
Weddings
Wife abuse

10 ways to keep your marriage strong [excerpt from How to honeymoon] C. Weston. il *Essence* 18:65-6+ N '87

Alcoholics: there's no place like home [difference between marriages of in-home and out-of-home drinkers; research by Nancy Jo Dunn] B. L. Benderly. *Psychol Today* 21:22 O '87

Are you neglecting your marriage? A. L. McGinnis. *Redbook* 168:86-7+ Ja '87

Baby makes three. E. Fishel. il *Parents* 62:73-6+ S '87

Black men more likely to wed than black women. *Jet* 72:36 Ap 20 '87

Can this marriage be saved? See issues of Ladies' Home Journal

Can your marriage survive your diet? J. G. Fitzpatrick. il *Parents* 62:58-62 Ja '87

Do holidays spell trouble? [effects on unhappy marriages; views of Robert L. Barker] *USA Today (Periodical)* 116:4-5 D '87

Do you have a "green thumb" for marriage? N. M. Lobsenz. *Read Dig* 130:119-22 Ja '87

Gay marriage: lifting the bans. B. Findlen. il *Ms* 15:29 F '87

Good women, bad marriages. C. Botwin and E. L. Parsons. *Redbook* 168:94-5+ F '87

Happily ever after, indeed! T. Vradenburg. il *Read Dig* 131:177-8 D '87

How to be your husband's best friend. C. Jabs. *McCalls* 114:40+ Ap '87

How to put romance back in your marriage. J. Brothers. il por *Good Housekeep* 204:117+ F '87

How to stay married [cover story] B. Kantrowitz. il *Newsweek* 110:52-7 Ag 24 '87

How to survive the stress points in your marriage. K. Stechert. il *Better Homes Gard* 65:87+ N '87

I'll never forgive you! A. Penney. il *Ladies Home J* 104:42+ Mr '87

Is your love life going down "the tube"? N. Combs. il *Read Dig* 131:146-8 O '87

Love and marriage [questions and answers] C. Deutsch. See issues of Parents

Love busters: mistakes that can wreck romance. A. Krueger. il *McCalls* 114:65-6 Je '87

Lunching over love [excerpt from Getting better all the time] L. Carpenter. il *50 Plus* 27:28-9+ N '87

Make marriage work [special section] il *Harpers Bazaar* 120:136-9+ Jl '87

Making the most of marriage. A. Kohn. il *Psychol Today* 21:6+ D '87

Marriage & loneliness. C. H. Stapen. il *Parents* 62:87-91 Ag '87

Marriage in the '80s: altered states [interview with C. Madanes] *Vogue* 177:305+ Ag '87

Marriage makes a comeback [views of Robert Lauer] *USA Today (Periodical)* 116:8 N '87

A marriage of fire and ice: a case history [excerpt from Intimate partners] M. Scarf. il *Redbook* 168:124-5+ Mr '87

Marriage on the rocks [decrease in marital happiness; research by Norval D. Glenn and Charles Weaver] N. D. Glenn. il *Psychol Today* 21:20-1 O '87

Marriage: surviving the first year [views of Fumiko Hosokawa] il *USA Today (Periodical)* 116:1-2 D '87

Marriage talk. J. Simmons. il *Essence* 18:57-8+ Jl '87

The meaning of marriage. J. McFarlane. por *Newsweek* 110:8 Ag 17 '87

My parents were risking their future. il *Good Housekeep* 205:22+ O '87

Open marriage's legacy [views of Robert Lauer] *USA Today (Periodical)* 116:2-3 D '87

Poor little rich girls [19th century American heiresses who married British nobility] C. M. Wallace. il *Forbes* 140 Sp Issue:62+ O 26 '87

Return of the shotgun wedding? [study by P. Lindsay Chase-Lansdale and Maris A. Vinovskis] P. Chance. il *Psychol Today* 21:14 S '87

Study reveals why 'shotgun weddings' last longer. il *Jet* 72:12-13 Je 1 '87

Take out some marriage insurance [praising your spouse] H. N. Ferguson. il *Read Dig* 130:213-14+ My '87

"The trouble is—you've changed". M. Klein. il *Parents* 62:71-4 Jl '87

True tales of love & marriage [symposium] il *Ladies Home J* 104:44+ F '87

The well-married manager [effect of cities on marriage] S. Blotnick. il *Forbes* 139:176-7 My 4 '87

What are you teaching your child about love & marriage? B. Spock. por *Redbook* 169:40 S '87

What couples should talk about before marriage. il *Jet* 72:14+ S 7 '87

"What makes your marriage work?" I asked [results of survey] J. Viorst. il *Redbook* 169:16-17 Je '87

When baby makes three. D. Hales. il *McCalls* 115:54+ N '87

Why husbands walk out [crisis points] J. Brothers. il *Read Dig* 131:27-8+ Jl '87

Why wed? The ambivalent American bachelor. T. Gabriel. il *N Y Times Mag* p24-9+ N 15 '87

Wise women/wonderful marriages [excerpt from Women men love/women men leave] C. Cowan and M. Kinder. *Redbook* 169:106-7+ O '87

Anecdotes, facetiae, satire, etc.

Is he marriage material? 74 sneaky ways to separate the possibilities from the deadbeats. L. Dormen and M. Zussman. il *Glamour* 85:226-7+ F '87

Stress: marriage vs. jail term. M. G. Stoddard. il *Saturday Evening Post* 259:46-7 S '87

Work marriage [relationship between people of the opposite sex who work at the same place] D. Owen. il *Atlantic* 259:22 F '87

Catholic Church

Divorced from experience. L. S. Cahill. il *Commonweal* 114:171-6 Mr 27 '87

Fidelity & faultlines. J. Garvey. *Commonweal* 114:168-9 Mr 27 '87

Houston Catholics must refrain from sex to have gala church wedding. *Jet* 73:33 N 16 '87

A plan for Catholic marriages [penalty for cohabitation in Houston] K. L. Woodward. il *Newsweek* 110:73 D 14 '87

What God has jointed together . . . B. Cooke. il *Commonweal* 114:178-82 Mr 27 '87

Religious aspects

Reconcilable differences. R. C. Roberts and E. Roberts. il pors *Christ Today* 31:17-20 Je 12 '87

Statistics

Brides at last: women over 40 who beat the odds [cover story] B. Lovenheim. il *N Y* 20:20-8 Ag 3 '87

The Census Bureau's good news for single women. M. Engel. il *Glamour* 85:276+ F '87

Here come the brides, but in what numbers? il *Discover* 8:8+ Mr '87

The marriage trap [criticism of various studies] S. Faludi. il *Ms* 16:62+ Jl/Ag '87

Why is Cupid ignoring you? [views of David M. Heer] *USA Today (Periodical)* 116:11 N '87

Mauritius

The untold story of black ambassador who weds Asian princess [R. D. Palmer weds Princess Intan] S. Booker. il pors *Jet* 73:12+ O 12 '87

United States

See Marriage

Marriage contracts

Putting love on the dotted line: do prenuptial agreements make marriages better? *Glamour* 85:64 Je '87

Spelling it out in a contract [prenuptial agreements] *Changing Times* 41:64 Ap '87

Trust-busters: the plague of prenuptial pacts. B. G. Harrison. *Mademoiselle* 93:184 Ap '87

Marriage counseling

Can Fido save this marriage? il *Prevention* 39:6 F '87

Can this marriage be saved? See issues of Ladies' Home Journal

Couples on the couch. A. Y. Napier. *Vogue* 177:386+ F '87

Couples on the couch [interviews with O. Silverstein and R. Show] *Vogue* 177:387+ F '87

Headache relief hitched to marital therapy [work of Ranjan Roy] *Prevention* 39:32 Ap '87

Marriage counseling—*cont.*
The incredible shrinking couple! Therapy for the commitment-shy [use of marriage counseling by unmarried couples] D. Kent. il *Mademoiselle* 93:302-3+ S '87

Marriage's nasty nine. C. Loomis. il *Parents* 62:15 F '87

When divorce is not the answer. D. Heyn. *McCalls* 114:28+ Ag '87

Marriage customs and rites
See also
Weddings

Pakistan
Getting to know you [arranged marriage planned by B. Bhutto and A. Zardari] il pors *Time* 130:23 Ag 10 '87

A match made in Pakistan [arranged marriage between B. Bhutto and A. Zardari] R. Nordland. il pors *Newsweek* 110:47 Ag 10 '87

Something old, something new [B. Bhutto marries A. Zardari] il pors *Newsweek* 110:31 D 28 '87

Soviet Union
Eyewitness to a Soviet wedding. B. Chambers. il *Humanist* 47:13-15+ Ja/F '87

Marriage law
See also
Marriage contracts
I stopped my daughter's wedding [plans for bogus marriage to foreign student] R. Bode. il pors *Good Housekeep* 204:106+ Mr '87

Mississippi
Mississippi repeals ban on interracial marriages. il *Jet* 73:18 N 23 '87

South Africa
Nephew of S. African envoy weds 'colored' [nephew of Piet Koornhof] *Jet* 72:12 Jl 6 '87

The marriage of Figaro [drama] See Beaumarchais, Pierre Augustin Caron de, 1732-1799

The marriage of Figaro [opera] See Mozart, Wolfgang Amadeus, 1756-1791

Marriage of priests
The church needs married priests [with readers' comments] M. O'Connell-Cahill. *U S Cathol* 52:14-19 D '87

Marriage proposals
The night I proposed. B. Kluger. il *Glamour* 85:90 D '87

Stars talk about marriage proposals [black celebrities] il *Jet* 71:56-8 F 23 '87

Married couples
See also
Dinks
The AIDS virus: "Does my husband have it? . . . If yes, do I, too? . . . I had to know". K. Winston. il *Glamour* 85:292-3+ O '87

Can you small talk? (Women who can have better marriages). D. Hales. *Redbook* 169:166-7+ S '87

Coping with a partner's depression. A. H. Rosenfeld. il *Psychol Today* 21:24 N '87

Couples: getting together, staying together, making it work [special section] il *Vogue* 177:384-93+ F '87

Do you feel like his mother or his wife? C. K. Ostrom. il *Ladies Home J* 104:100+ N '87

For better, for worse [AIDS and marriage of T. and K. Jones] K. Casey. il *Ladies Home J* 104:89-91+ My '87

From two incomes down to one [finances of Ken and Maureen Deceuster] M. Daly. il *Better Homes Gard* 65:32+ O '87

Headed for a painful breakup? Sociologist Diane Vaughan discusses the warning signs [interview] M. Wilhelm. il pors *People Wkly* 27:97-8+ Mr 2 '87

How to stay married [cover story] B. Kantrowitz. il *Newsweek* 110:52-7 Ag 24 '87

How well do you know your spouse? [quiz] K. Levine. il *Read Dig* 131:129-31 S '87

I lost 117 lbs. and won back my husband; ed. by Barbara Raymond. S. Keeton. il pors *Good Housekeep* 204:96+ Ap '87

In praise of marriage [black married couples] K. Gale. por *Essence* 17:135 F '87

The long goodbye [failing relationships; cover story] D. Vaughan. il *Psychol Today* 21:36-8+ Jl '87

My funny valentine: is living with a comedian a laugh a minute? J. Powell. il *Glamour* 85:182+ F '87

Newlyweds: 10 ways to make love last. L. Norment. il *Ebony* 42:146+ Je '87

Season of autumn-summer love [older women marrying younger men] A. Toufexis. il *Time* 130:75 N 30 '87

Suburban classic [sharing the tasks of married life] L. Garis. il por *Ms* 16:142+ Jl/Ag '87

Wedded faces [facial mimicry; study by Robert B. Zajonc] H. Hall. *Psychol Today* 21:10 D '87

When my wife's mother died, the loss tore us apart. N. Dillon. *Glamour* 85:234+ Mr '87

Anecdotes, facetiae, satire, etc.
Notes and comment. *New Yorker* 63:33-4 N 23 '87

Employment
Amour fools [directors directing their wives] A. White. il *Film Comment* 23:26-31 Ja/F '87

College daze [career and family expectations; research by Hedwin Naimark and others] E. Stark. il *Psychol Today* 21:14 N '87

Does success spoil marriage? il *Jet* 72:54-6 Ag 3 '87

Double trouble in the two-career marriage [excerpt from Successful women, angry men] B. M. Campbell. *Essence* 17:51-2+ Mr '87

Dual careers, doleful dilemmas. A. Toufexis. il *Time* 130:90 N 16 '87

Families that work [two career black couples] P. V. Pressley. il *Essence* 17:75-7+ Mr '87

Labors of love [celebrity couples] J. Etra. il *Harpers Bazaar* 120:186-7+ My '87

Marriage in the '80s [two-career couples] D. Prince. il *N Y* 20:30-8 Je 1 '87

Marrying your money personalities [excerpt from The working woman financial advisor] B. Siverd. il *Work Woman* 12:78+ My '87

My partner, my spouse. D. Machan. il *Forbes* 140:240+ D 14 '87

Pay expectations: the spouse factor [study by John Mirowsky] J. Meer. *Psychol Today* 21:11 Ap '87

Rivalry: the two-career clash. B. Wein. *Harpers Bazaar* 120:299+ Mr '87

Successful women, angry men [excerpt] B. M. Campbell. il por *Ebony* 42:38+ F '87

Two paychecks: yours, mine, or ours? T. Segal. il *Bus Week* p116-17 Je 1 '87

The two-person career on college campuses. E. Zencey. *Educ Dig* 53:56-8 O '87

Working wives, threatened husbands [interview with B. M. Campbell] il por *U S News World Rep* 102:46 F 23 '87

Quarrels
See Quarrels

Religion
See Marriage—Religious aspects

Sexual behavior
8 wrong ideas about sex: his and yours [excerpt from Super marital sex] P. Pearsall. il *Glamour* 85:216+ N '87

Danger! Marriage can make you fat [excerpt from Weight, sex and marriage] R. B. Stuart and B. Jacobson. il *Redbook* 169:92-3+ Ag '87

Dr. Ruth says: oh, grow up! R. Westheimer. il por *Redbook* 169:106-7+ My '87

Love busters [excerpt from Super marital sex] P. Pearsall. *Ladies Home J* 104:96+ O '87

Test your sex I.Q. S. S. Cohen. il *Ladies Home J* 104:58+ Ja '87

Today's busy woman's biggest complaint. . . "I'm too tired for sex!!". R. Markowitz. *Redbook* 170:118-19+ N '87

"We always make love the same way". H. S. Kaplan. por *Redbook* 169:48 O '87

What your husband is afraid to tell you. L. H. Gross. il *Redbook* 168:76-7+ F '87

Married . . . with children [television program] See Television program reviews—Single works

Married women
See also
Mothers
Brides at last: women over 40 who beat the odds [cover story] B. Lovenheim. il *N Y* 20:20-8 Ag 3 '87

Employment
See also
Mothers—Employment
Does a working woman really need to be married? No. C. E. Rinzler. il *Work Woman* 12:60+ Ag '87

Does a working woman really need to be married? Yes. E. Lax. il *Work Woman* 12:61+ Ag '87

Double trouble in the two-career marriage [excerpt from Successful women, angry men] B. M. Campbell. *Essence* 17:51-2+ Mr '87

Successful women, angry men [excerpt] B. M. Campbell. il por *Ebony* 42:38+ F '87

Working wives, threatened husbands [interview with B. M. Campbell] il por *U S News World Rep* 102:46 F 23 '87

Married women—*cont.*
Sexual behavior
See Married couples—Sexual behavior
Marriner, Neville, 1924-
about
A church marriage. N. Malitz. il por *Opera News* 51:14-16 Ja 31 '87
Marriott, B. Rodney
Fantastick voyage. il *Horizon* 30:64-5 O '87
Marriott, J. Willard, 1932-
about
It helps to have your name on the company. il por *U S News World Rep* 103:52 Jl 6 '87
Sails reefed. S. N. Chakravarty. il por *Forbes* 140:110-11+ N 30 '87
Marriott Corporation
The first name in coffee shops [Marriott's bid for Denny's] T. Ichniowski. il *Bus Week* p35-6 Je 15 '87
It helps to have your name on the company [J. W. Marriott] il por *U S News World Rep* 103:52 Jl 6 '87
Keeping youth in school: a public-private collaboration [peer mentor program for high school students sponsored by Catholic University and Marriott; with reports by J. Payne and J. Smith] S. Lee and others. il *Child Today* 16:15-21 Jl/Ag '87
Sails reefed. S. N. Chakravarty. il por *Forbes* 140:110-11+ N 30 '87
Marriott Marquis (New York, N.Y.: Hotel) *See* New York (N.Y.)—Hotels, motels, etc.
Marron, Donald B.
Our changing capital markets [address, April 30, 1987] *Vital Speeches Day* 53:586-8 Jl 15 '87
Marrow
Close encounters with an osteoclast [bone resorption] D. M. Barnes. bibl il *Science* 236:914-16 My 22 '87
Marrow suppression hampers AZT use in AIDS victims [research by Jerome Groopman and others] G. Kolata. *Science* 235:1463 Mr 20 '87
Transplantation
Bone marrow transplants: from Chernobyl to cancer therapy. M. J. Fromer. il *FDA Consum* 21:12-15 Ap '87
Chernobyl's high cost [interview with R. Gale] J. Bennett. il por *Macleans* 100:6-8 Jl 6 '87
Curing cancer in Jerusalem [bone marrow transplantation for leukemia patients; work of Shimon Slavin at Hadassah Hospital] C. SerVaas. il *Saturday Evening Post* 259:54-9 Jl/Ag '87
Interview [R. Gale] M. C. Smith. il pors *Omni* 10:110-12+ O '87
"The sister I never knew I had saved my life" [case of C. Bracken] J. Ardmore. il por *Good Housekeep* 205:180+ S '87
Thalidomide: is there a silver lining? [graft-versus-host disease; research by Georgia B. Vogelsang] D. D. Edwards. *Sci News* 131:198 Mr 28 '87
When pain is the only choice [bone marrow transplant for Hodgkin's patient] E. Rosenthal. il *Discover* 8:24 D '87
Marrow squash *See* Squashes
Marrs, Barry L.
(jt. auth) *See* Youvan, Douglas C., and Marrs, Barry L.
Mars (Planet)
See also
Life on Mars
Space flight to Mars
A case study: how to draw Mars. il *Sky Telesc* 74:605 D '87
Contamination
Let's save Mars first. J. Loudon. il *Sky Telesc* 74:228 S '87
Geology
Escape from Mars [SNC meteorites; work of John D. O'Keefe and Thomas J. Ahrens] il *Sky Telesc* 73:155 F '87
Getting Mars' rocks off [SNC meteorites; research by A. M. Vickery and H. J. Melosh] il *Discover* 8:12-13 D '87
The large crater origin of SNC meteorites. A. M. Vickery and H. J. Melosh. bibl f il *Science* 237:738-43 Ag 14 '87
Martian meteorites are arriving. R. A. Kerr. *Science* 237:721-3 Ag 14 '87
Recent mafic volcanism on Mars. B. K. Lucchitta. bibl f il maps *Science* 235:565-7 Ja 30 '87
Recent Martian volcanism indicated by new study [work of Baerbel Lucchitta] *Astronomy* 15:74-5 Je '87

Photographs and photography
High-resolution views of Mars and Jupiter [work of Jean Dragesco] il *Sky Telesc* 73:680-1 Je '87
Images. il *Sky Telesc* 73:592-3 Je '87
Space face! il *Natl Geogr World* 147:16 N '87
Satellites
Close encounter [Phobos mission] M. M. Waldrop. il *Science* 236:1428 Je 12 '87
Probing the Phobian storehouse. M. Gould. por *Space World* X-12-288:39 D '87
Soviet Phobos mission to probe moons of Mars. D. F. Robertson. il *Astronomy* 15:29-32 N '87
Surface
The changing face of Mars [evidence for water; cover story] M. W. Carroll. il *Astronomy* 15:6-22+ Mr '87
Exploring deserts [Viking images of Mars compared to the Western Desert of Egypt] T. A. Maxwell. il *Earth Sci* 39:12-14 Wint '86
In search of Martian seas. S. J. Goldman. il *Sky Telesc* 73:6 Ja '87
Possible tornado-like tracks on Mars. J. A. Grant and P. H. Schultz. bibl f il maps *Science* 237:883-5 Ag 21 '87
Release of juvenile water on Mars: estimated amounts and timing associated with volcanism. R. Greeley. bibl f il *Science* 236:1653-4 Je 26 '87
Twisters on the red planet? [research by John A. Grant and Peter H. Schultz] il *Sky Telesc* 74:579-80 D '87
Visit Mars in the off-season [possible tornadoes; research by John Grant and Peter Schultz] il *Discover* 8:10+ N '87
Watering Mars with volcanism [research by Ronald Greeley] *Sci News* 132:9 Jl 4 '87
Marsa, Linda
Brain pics. il *Omni* 9:14+ Jl '87
Hot investment strategies. il *Black Enterp* 18:95-6+ O '87
Marsalis, Branford
about
Blindfold test. L. Feather. il por *Down Beat* 54:39 My '87
The many sides of Branford Marsalis. K. Whitehead. il pors *Down Beat* 54:16-19 Mr '87
Marsalis, Wynton
about
Band-shell bop: putting the corn in cornet. D. Gates. *Newsweek* 109:69 Ap 6 '87
Wynton debuts jazz in Chicago classrooms. B. Beuttler. il por *Down Beat* 54:12 Ja '87
Wynton Marsalis. P. Johnson. il por *Essence* 18:52-3+ O '87
Wynton Marsalis: 1987 [cover story; interview] S. Crouch. il por *Down Beat* 11:16-19+ N '87
Marschall, Laurence A.
(jt. auth) *See* Comins, Neil, and Marschall, Laurence A.
Marsden, George M., 1939-
Irony of ironies: evaluating the moderns. *Christ Century* 104:359-61 Ap 15 '87
Marsden, J. Ellen
The lake trout returns to Lake Ontario. il *Conservationist* 41:10-13 My/Je '87
Marsden, Michael T.
Headlights. *See* issues of Motor Trend beginning January 1987
Marsden, Richard
about
The company wunderkind. B. Ivry. por *N Y* 20:24 My 25 '87
Marseilles (France)
Social conditions
Marseilles: a city at sea. B. Moynahan. il *World Press Rev* 34:56 Ap '87
Marsh, Clayburn
about
Burning alive! S. Kelly. il *Read Dig* 131:95-9 S '87
Marsh, Corinna
Perennial peeves [poem] *Natl Rev* 39:43 O 23 '87
Marsh, David C. (David Charles)
Beyond the spill on the Rhine. il *World Press Rev* 34:50 Ja '87
West Germany's old demons. il *World Press Rev* 34:22-4 S '87
Marsh, Gerald E.
Dangers of limited SDI. *Bull At Sci* 43:13-14 Mr '87
(jt. auth) *See* Evernden, Jack F., and Marsh, Gerald E.
Marsh, Hilary
Cystitis crisis: when a little lovesickness spells big trouble. *Mademoiselle* 93:84 F '87
First aid for bad eaters. il *Mademoiselle* 93:98 D '87

Marsh, Peter
Whose space is the space station? il *World Press Rev* 34:51 My '87
Marsh, Peter E., and Collett, Peter
Driving passion [cover story] il *Psychol Today* 21:16-18+ Je '87
Marsh, Sandy
about
'Too much money, too much time': the life and death of Sandy Marsh [cover story] P. Morrisroe. il pors *N Y* 20:42-51 S 14 '87
Marsh, Stanley
about
True grit in Amarillo. J. B. Grillo. il por *Channels* 7:74-5 O '87
Marsh & McLennan Cos. Inc.
Follow the leader. J. Andresky. il *Forbes* 139:40-1 Je 29 '87
Marsh Aviation
Flight certification tests continue on S-2 modified by Marsh Aviation. il *Aviat Week Space Technol* 126:119 F 16 '87
Marsh ecology
The salt marsh. F. C. Stuart. il *Atlantic* 260:70-6 O '87
Saltwort meadows needed by fishes [Florida salt marshes; research by Grant Gilmore and others] il *Sea Front* 33:461-3 N/D '87
Marsh plants
See also
Cattails
Saltwort
Marshak, Robert Eugene, 1916-
Time for Sakharov's global dialogue. il pors *Bull At Sci* 43:7-8 O '87
Marshall, Carolyn
An excuse for workplace hazard. il *Nation* 244:532-4 Ap 25 '87
Marshall, Catherine, 1914-1983
about
Catherine Marshall remembered. D. Schneider. il por *Saturday Evening Post* 259:55+ Ap '87
My inspiration. D. Sawyer. il pors *Saturday Evening Post* 259:50-1 Ap '87
Marshall, Donald
about
Exploring an injustice. M. Gee. *Macleans* 100:29 O 19 '87
Strange and contradictory testimony. M. Gee. il pors *Macleans* 100:23 S 21 '87
Marshall, Eliot
The little chill. *New Repub* 196:4+ F 16 '87
Marshall, George C. (George Catlett), 1880-1959
about
Marshall arts. E. Thomas. *Wash Mon* 19:54-5 Jl/Ag '87
Marshall, John, 1755-1835
about
John Marshall and the evolution of judicial review. D. G. Stephenson, Jr. il por *USA Today (Periodical)* 116:37-9 Jl '87
Marshall, Megan
Three sisters who showed the way. il pors *Am Herit* 38:58-63+ S/O '87
Marshall, Sarah Catherine Wood *See* Marshall, Catherine, 1914-1983
Marshall, Thurgood
Celebrating the Constitution: a dissent [excerpt from address, May 6, 1987] *Harpers* 275:17-19 Jl '87
The Constitution [excerpt from address, May 6, 1987] por *Essence* 18:166 S '87
Justice Thurgood Marshall on the living Constitution [excerpt from address; May 6, 1987] *Ms* 16:111 S '87
The real meaning of the Constitution bicentennial [address, May 6, 1987] il pors *Ebony* 42:62+ S '87
about
Grading the presidents. por *Newsweek* 110:33 S 21 '87
High Court backs jailing without bail; Justice Thurgood Marshall dissents. por *Jet* 72:4 Je 15 '87
Justice Marshall's minority report. T. Gest. il por *U S News World Rep* 102:12-13 My 18 '87
Marshall cites faults of Constitution at 200th year. por *Jet* 72:12 My 25 '87
Marshall hospitalized, treated for blood clot. por *Jet* 72:4 Ag 31 '87
Marshall shows for D.C. Bar tribute to Wiley Branton. il pors *Jet* 71:6-7 Ja 12 '87
Marshall will outlive 'those bastards' who want his resignation. por *Jet* 73:18 N 2 '87

Public backs Marshall in his views on Constitution. por *Jet* 72:32 Je 1 '87
Thurgood Marshall ranks Reagan last among U.S. presidents he observed. il por *Jet* 73:12-13 S 28 '87
Marshall (George C.) Institute *See* George C. Marshall Institute
Marshall (George C.) Space Flight Center *See* George C. Marshall Space Flight Center
Marshall (Lenore) Poetry Prize *See* Poetry—Awards
Marshall (Mich.)
Historic houses, sites, etc.
Marshall, Michigan. M. G. Broderick. il *House Gard* 159:128+ Ap '87
Marshall (Thurgood) Black Education Fund *See* Thurgood Marshall Black Education Fund
Marshall County (Miss.)
Politics and government
Black Miss. sheriff seeks recount, despite cross burning in front yard [B. J. Adkins] *Jet* 72:5 Ag 31 '87
Marshall Field & Company
The antique tradition of Marshall Field's [cover story] il *Antiques Collect Hobbies* 92:28-33 N '87
Marshall Islands
Politics and government
Compact of free association with Pacific Islands [text of executive order, October 16, 1986] R. Reagan. *Dep State Bull* 86:74-5 D '86
Marshall Plan
40th anniversary of the Marshall Plan [addresses, May 26 and June 1, 1987] G. P. Shultz; R. Reagan. *Dep State Bull* 87:67-72 Ag '87
Did the Marshall Plan work too well? S. Jenkins. il *U S News World Rep* 102:13 Je 8 '87
Diplomacy's splendid achievement. M. Whitaker. il *Newsweek* 109:47 Je 8 '87
Marshall arts. H. Fairlie. *New Repub* 196:7-8+ Je 15 '87
Perils of policy: the Marshall Plan only worked once. W. Pfaff. *Harpers* 274:70-2 My '87
Marshals Service (U.S.) *See* United States. Marshals Service
Marshes
See also
Bayous
Bogs
Everglades (Fla.)
Honey Island Swamp (La.)
Little Wambaw Swamp (S.C.)
Marsh ecology
Okefenokee Swamp (Ga. and Fla.)
Cattails for whitetails. J. Boatner. il *Outdoor Life* 180:48-9+ D '87
Marshfield (Mass.)
Housing
Trying to unload a 90-foot-high home is one very tall order [D. Cappelletti trying to sell observation tower] il por *People Wkly* 28:57 N 23 '87
Marshmallows
See also
Cooking—Marshmallows
Marston, Ray
Logic-gate fundamentals. il *Radio-Electron* 58:50-4 Ap '87
Using Triacs and SCR's. il *Radio-Electron* 58:64-8 S '87
Working with flip-flops. il *Radio-Electron* 58:64-9 Je '87
Working with Triacs and SCR's. il *Radio-Electron* 58:64-7+ O '87
Marston, Ted
Geraniums are on a roll! il *Flower Gard* 31:10+ F/Mr '87
Marsupials
See also
Opossums
Martel, Jay
Dog days. il *Roll Stone* p117+ Jl 16-30 '87
Sweet fifteen. *Roll Stone* p91 My 21 '87
Martellini, Maria
about
Can an outsider fill Aldo Gucci's loafers? K. Wolman. il por *Bus Week* p52 N 30 '87
Martha Graham Dance Company
Ardent songs [revival of Canticle for innocent comedians and Celebration] T. Tobias. il *N Y* 20:102-3 N 2 '87
Dance [T. Capucilli] T. Tobias. il por *N Y* 20:98-9 S 21 '87
Dancing:
Grant for preservation of Martha Graham Dance Company works. A. Croce. *New Yorker* 63:147-8 N 23 '87

Martha Graham Dance Company—*cont.*
New frontiers [City Center opening] T. Tobias. il *N Y* 20:119 O 26 '87
Past masters and schlockmeisters. L. A. Jacobs. *New Leader* 70:22-3 N 2 '87
Peter Sparling: new positions. J. Gruen. il pors *Dance Mag* 61:66-9 Ap '87
Martha's Vineyard (Mass.)
See also
Architecture, Domestic—Martha's Vineyard (Mass.)
Edgartown (Mass.)
Martí, José, 1853-1895
about
Two democrats betrayed. pors *Dep State Bull* 87:66 Mr '87
Marti, Serge
Takeover fever spreads to France. il *World Press Rev* 34:48 Mr '87
Martia, Dominic F.
Putting reading in its proper place. por *U S News World Rep* 102:6 F 9 '87
Martial arts
See also
Karate
Martin, Agnes, 1912-
about
Running on empty. M. Stevens. *New Repub* 196:25-8 Ja 19 '87
Martin, Barry
about
Take it again from the fall. A. Fadiman. il pors *Life* 10:13-14+ My '87
Martin, Billy, 1928-
about
Ex-manager Martin tells Jesse: stick to politics. por *Jet* 72:46 Jl 13 '87
Martin, Charles E., 1945-
Appalachia's art of the useful. il *Nat Hist* 96:50-9 Jl '87
Martin, Dean
about
Sammy Davis, Frank Sinatra, Dean Martin together again for historic concert tour. il pors *Jet* 73:36 D 21 '87
Martin, Dean Paul
about
Obituary
People Wkly il pors 27:128-30 Ap 13 '87. R. Arias
Martin, Eddie Owens, 1908-1986
Obituary
Am Craft il 47:96 F/Mr '87. T. Patterson
Martin, Gail
about
Stuffs from the steppes. D. M. Lisi. il pors *House Gard* 159:58+ D '87
Martin, George
about
Martin wins NFL award for spirit of service. por *Jet* 72:50 Jl 20 '87
Martin, George
about
Admen for heaven. D. Neff. il pors *Christ Today* 31:12-13 S 18 '87
Martin, George R. R.
The pear-shaped man [fiction] il *Omni* 10:62-4+ O '87
Martin, Glen
Deep colors. il *Oceans* 20:56+ Ja/F '87
Martin, Guy
The battle for Berlin. il *Esquire* 108:204-13 N '87
Clean for a day. il *Esquire* 107:40 Mr '87
Hallelujah! All hail the hardware store! il *Esquire* 107:120-2 Je '87
The tie that binds. il por *Esquire* 107:F65 Mr '87
Martin, Hank
about
Lots of toddlers dribble, but not like this big, burly hoop star, supertot Hank Martin. il pors *People Wkly* 28:120-1 S 21 '87
Martín, Ignacio Baro- *See* Martín-Baro, Ignacio
Martin, J. D.
about
Teachers can be ousted for swearing at students. *Jet* 71:23 F 23 '87
Martin, James A.
From summit to sea. il *Travel Holiday* 167:20+ F '87
Martin, John
about
Black Sparrow: the house a poet helped to build. J. Barbato. il pors *Publ Wkly* 232:26-7 O 23 '87

Martin, Joseph B.
Molecular genetics: applications to the clinical neurosciences. bibl f il *Science* 238:765-72 N 6 '87
Martin, Judith, 1938-
Miss Manners' convention etiquette. il por *Publ Wkly* 231:143 My 15 '87
Martin, Katherine
Undercover exercise. il *Ms* 15:52-5 Ap '87
Martin, Kathy
Grouse and spouse. il *Nat Hist* 96:62-9 F '87
Martin, Larry D.
(jt. auth) *See* Rothschild, Bruce, and Martin, Larry D.
Martin, Laura C.
A bit of wilderness in your own backyard. il por *Natl Wildl* 25:22-8 Ap/My '87
Martin, Lawrence
Opening the doors to disarmament. il *World Press Rev* 34:12 N '87
Martin, Leroy
about
Chicago mayor names city's second black police chief. il por *Jet* 73:5 N 16 '87
Martin, Linda B.
¡Viva Argentina! il map *Travel Holiday* 167:50-5 Mr '87
Martin, Malachi
about
Malachi Martin's The Jesuits: an appraisal. G. G. Higgins. il *America* 156:229-31+ Mr 21 '87
Malachi's 'believe it or not'. *America* 156:145-6 F 21 '87
Martin, Mary, 1913-
about
My son, Larry Hagman. E. Sirkin. il pors *Good Housekeep* 205:111+ Jl '87
Martin, Nina
VOA-Europe: message radio. *Nation* 244:848-52 Je 20 '87
Martin, Paul
Some nest eggs aren't all they're cracked up to be. il *50 Plus* 27:34-6+ N '87
What you need to know to protect your life's savings. bibl il *50 Plus* 27:32-40+ O '87
Martin, Paul S. (Paul Schultz), 1928-
Clovisia the Beautiful! *Nat Hist* 96:10+ O '87
about
How did the giants die? T. A. Lewis. il por *Int Wildl* 17:4-11 S/O '87
Martin, Preston
about
The king of the S&L's. R. Thomas. il por *Newsweek* 109:52-3 Mr 30 '87
Martin, Robert Bernard
Passion and humdrum. il *N Y Rev Books* 34:17-19 O 22 '87
Martin, Samuel K., and others
Reversal of chloroquine resistance in Plasmodium falciparum by verapamil. bibl f il *Science* 235:899-901 F 20 '87
Martin, Steve, 1945?-
about
Nose guys finish first. D. Ansen. por *Newsweek* 109:73 Je 22 '87
Sensational Steve [cover story] R. Corliss. il pors *Time* 130:50-5 Ag 24 '87
Steve Martin, seriously. D. Maychick. pors *Mademoiselle* 93:64 F '87
Martin, Tovah
Ground covers. il *Ctry J* 14:52-7 My '87
January's blossoms. il *Ctry J* 14:39-44 Ja '87
Vines for every purpose. il *Ctry J* 14:54-9 Je '87
Martin, Vaughn D.
Finding cable faults. il *Radio-Electron* 58:66-70+ Mr '87
Soldering: old techniques & new technology. il *Radio-Electron* 58:47-50 My '87
Martin, Wilbur C., d. 1987
about
Obituary
Jet 71:15 Mr 16 '87
Martin (Tenn.)
Industries
Creative Label takes its decorative finishing closer to eastern printers [building of new plant] J. P. Frank. il *Publ Wkly* 231:260 My 15 '87
Martín-Baro, Ignacio
about
Stop all military aid now! L. Hufford. *America* 156:146-7 F 21 '87

Martin Beck Theatre (New York, N.Y.)
Fe fi fo fum! Ann Slavit's boot is a ticket seller's chum [air-filled sculpture] il por *People Wkly* 28:69 D 21 '87
Martin Luther King Day
Ariz. gov. nixes King Day; Wonder snubs the state. *Jet* 71:60 F 9 '87
Arizona gov. vows to repeal King holiday [E. Mecham] *Jet* 71:37 Ja 19 '87
Arizona gov's stance on King holiday may cost state $18 million loss. *Jet* 72:36 Je 22 '87
Arizona house passes King Day legislation. *Jet* 71:4 Mr 9 '87
Arizona loses NBNA confab [National Black Nurses Association] A. Edmond, Jr. il *Black Enterp* 17:62 Je '87
Arizona observes King holiday despite repeal of state bill by governor. *Jet* 71:12 F 2 '87
Black publishers pull out of Arizona confab [protest against repeal of Martin Luther King Day] *Jet* 71:8 F 9 '87
Critics: Mecham's offer to honor Martin Luther King is unacceptable. *Jet* 72:12 Jl 6 '87
CSU honors Stevie Wonder for role in national King holiday [Central State University] il por *Jet* 71:12-13 F 9 '87
Dr. King. *Natl Rev* 39:20+ F 13 '87
Governor's stance on King holiday stirs controversy in Arizona: tempers flare. W. Wofford, Jr. il por *Jet* 73:24-6 N 2 '87
Group wants recall of Arizona Gov. Mecham; NBA cancels meeting. *Jet* 72:14 Jl 27 '87
Holiday [views of second graders] *New Yorker* 62:28-9 F 2 '87
Honor King's birthday with vote drive, says Chicago commissioner [views of J. H. Stroger] il por *Jet* 71:14 Ja 26 '87
King holiday highlights freedom here and abroad. *Jet* 71:36 Ja 19 '87
Of many things. G. W. Hunt. *America* 156:inside cover Ja 31 '87
Reagan flays racism during King observance. il por *Jet* 71:6 F 2 '87
An uneasy festival for Martin Luther King. il *Newsweek* 109:24-5 Ja 26 '87
Vandross cancels Phoenix concerts to protest Ariz. snubbing of King holiday. por *Jet* 72:53 Je 15 '87
Martin Luther King, Jr. Center for Nonviolent Social Change
'Salute to Greatness' program honors Black enterprise publisher [E. G. Graves] il pors *Jet* 71:4-6+ F 9 '87
Martin Luther King, Jr. Nonviolent Peace Prize
King Peace Prize goes to Corazon Aquino. il por *Jet* 71:8 F 2 '87
Martin Luther King, Jr. Scholarship *See* Scholarships and fellowships
Martin Marietta Corp.
British offer Ariane deployment system for use on Titan 3 [Spelda dual satellite deployment system] il *Aviat Week Space Technol* 126:32-3 Ja 12 '87
Diversity is the secret weapon. T. Smart. il *Bus Week* p36 D 14 '87
GE/Martin selected to provide ATF electro-optic sensor [YF-22A advanced tactical fighter] *Aviat Week Space Technol* 126:73 Je 15 '87
Martin converts USAF Titan 2 to launch vehicle for placing defense payloads into polar orbit. il *Aviat Week Space Technol* 127:18-19 Ag 10 '87
Martin develops simplified Flir for night-vision attack capability. *Aviat Week Space Technol* 127:101 S 21 '87
Martin evaluates bids on Titan launch adapter [Titan 3 dual satellite adapter] *Aviat Week Space Technol* 126:62-3 Je 22 '87
Martin lab halves time needed to retarget space-based laser. B. A. Smith. il *Aviat Week Space Technol* 127:28-9 S 14 '87
Martin Marietta ADATS wins Army air defense competition [Anti-Tank Air Defense System] J. D. Morrocco. il *Aviat Week Space Technol* 126:26-7 D 7 '87
Martin Marietta hosts Reagan SDI visit [Zenith Star laser spacecraft project] T. M. Foley. il *Aviat Week Space Technol* 127:21-2 N 30 '87
Martin Marietta reorganizes operations, management structure to increase competitiveness. *Aviat Week Space Technol* 127:22 Jl 13 '87
Martin Marietta selected to design potential nuclear SDI systems [nuclear-powered X-ray laser platform and nuclear hypervelocity pellet system] T. M. Foley. *Aviat Week Space Technol* 127:113-14 Ag 10 '87

Martin Marietta selects Dornier to build Titan component. *Aviat Week Space Technol* 127:27 O 19 '87
Martin pursuing 15 additional Titan launch contracts. T. M. Foley. *Aviat Week Space Technol* 126:66+ Ap 20 '87
Martin signs contract to launch Intelsat 6 satellites on Titan 3s. *Aviat Week Space Technol* 127:22 Ag 17 '87
Martin studies space-based KKV concept [kinetic kill vehicle] il *Aviat Week Space Technol* 127:20 Ag 31 '87
Martin's ALS booster design uses multiple strap-on motors [advanced launch system] B. A. Smith. il *Aviat Week Space Technol* 127:29-30 S 21 '87
Why Martin Marietta loves Mary Cunningham. T. Moore. il *Fortune* 115:66-8+ Mr 16 '87
Martínez, Bob, 1934-
about
Florida's rookie governor is stuck in a slump. G. DeGeorge. il por *Bus Week* p174+ O 12 '87
NAACP criticizes Florida Gov. Martinez on hiring. *Jet* 72:29 Ap 13 '87
Martinez, Raquel
about
Matadora in waiting. P. Clark. il por *Women's Sports Fitness* 9:54 Je '87
Martinez, Ricardo, and others
Neuronal pp60$^{c\text{-}src}$ contains a six-amino acid insertion relative to its non-neuronal counterpart. bibl f il *Science* 237:411-15 Jl 24 '87
Martini (Cocktail) *See* Cocktails
Martinique
See also
Mount Pelée (Martinique)
Music festivals—Martinique
Plantations—Martinique
Saint-Pierre (Martinique)
Martino, Donald, 1931-
about
Musical events:
Boston Symphony performs D. Martino's The white island. A. Porter. *New Yorker* 63:98+ My 11 '87
Martins, Peter
about
Ecstatic orange [ballet] Reviews
N Y 20:58 F 2 '87. T. Tobias
Les gentilhommes [ballet] Reviews
N Y il 20:64 Je 1 '87. T. Tobias
New Yorker 63:82-3 Je 8 '87. A. Croce
Martins talks back: Peter's perspectives [cover story] J. Gruen. il pors *Dance Mag* 61:38-42 N '87
Peter Martins' little nothings. M. Duffy. il por *Time* 129:77 F 2 '87
Les petits riens [ballet] Reviews
N Y 20:58 F 2 '87. T. Tobias
Martins Ferry (Ohio)
In Ohio: a town and the bard who left it [J. A. Wright] B. Morgan. il por *Time* 130:9-10 O 19 '87
Martoff, C. J.
Limits on sensitivity of large silicon bolometers for solar neutrino detection. bibl f il *Science* 237:507-9 Jl 31 '87
Marton, Eva
about
Eva Marton's vulnerable Turandot. K. Monson. por *Vogue* 177:130 Mr '87
Showing emotions. T. P. Lanier. por *Opera News* 51:18-19 Mr 28 '87
Marty, Martin E., 1928-
The Constitution and the congregation: time to celebrate. il *Christ Century* 104:523-5 Je 3-10 '87
Do Catholics take too much for granted? *America* 157:406-8+ N 28 '87
M.E.M.O. See issues of The Christian Century
Make yourself available! *Read Dig* 131:179-80 O '87
A profile of Norman Lear: another pilgrim's progress. il *Christ Century* 104:55-8 Ja 21 '87
about
I wonder what the Catholics are doing tonight [interview] por *U S Cathol* 52:20-6 Je '87
Irony of ironies: evaluating the moderns. G. M. Marsden. *Christ Century* 104:359-61 Ap 15 '87
Marty, Myron A.
Saving the soul of higher education. *Christ Century* 104:659-62 Jl 29-Ag 5 '87
Maruca, Mary
Be kind to leather. il *Americana* 14:64-5 Ja/F '87
Marui Co. Ltd.
James Baker, meet the dokushin kizoku [appeal to Japan's singles] A. Tanzer. il por *Forbes* 139:46-8 Ap 20 '87

Marvel Comics Group
The Marvel strategy [acquisition of Marvel Comics by New World Pictures] G. Critser. il *Channels* 7:24 Mr '87
Marvel Publishing (Firm)
Marvel, New World plan book-video line. il *Publ Wkly* 232:138 S 18 '87
Marvin, Lee, 1924-1987
about
Obituary
People Wkly il por 28:42 S 14 '87. B. Darrach
Marx, Arthur
about
Groucho: a life in revue [drama] Reviews
Dance Mag il 61:89 Ja '87. K. Grubb
Marx, Gary
(jt. auth) See Wark, John, and Marx, Gary
Marx, Groucho, 1891-1977
Anecdotes, facetiae, satire, etc.
A Harvard prof tells runners: on your Marx; get set; Groucho! [T. McMahon advocates jogging like Groucho] il *People Wkly* 28:85 S 21 '87
Marx, Jeffrey
(ed) See McLain, Gary. The downfall of a champion
Marx, Julius H. See Marx, Groucho, 1891-1977
Marx, Leo
Does improved technology mean progress? il *Technol Rev* 90:32-41+ Ja '87
Marx, Richard
about
Richard Marx's commercial background. S. Hochman. il por *Roll Stone* p20-1 S 24 '87
Marx, Wesley
Can strip mining clean up its act? il *Read Dig* 130:121-5 Mr '87
Marx Brothers
See also
Marx, Groucho, 1891-1977
Marxism *See* Communism
Marxism and education *See* Socialism and education
Mary, Blessed Virgin, Saint
about
Christmas meditation:
The blessing and the burden. P. P. Allen. *Christ Century* 104:1169-70 D 23-30 '87
Annunciation
Advent meditation:
Conceiving Christ first within one's heart. E. J. Bush. *Christ Century* 104:1054-5 N 25 '87
Apparitions and miracles
In an Eastern Orthodox Chicago church, a weeping Madonna and Child bring throngs to pray and hope for miracles [first sighted by Father P. Koufos at St. Nicholas Church] C. Tamarkin. il *People Wkly* 27:44-5 Ja 19 '87
Medjugorje's miracles: faith and profit. D. R. Janz. il *Christ Century* 104:724-5 Ag 26-S 2 '87
Visitations of the Virgin [Medjugorje, Yugoslavia] K. L. Woodward. il *Newsweek* 110:54-5 Jl 20 '87
Devotions
See also
Marian Year, 1987
Bring flowers of the rarest. H. Fehren. *U S Cathol* 52:59-61 Je '87
Theology
Advent meditation:
The Mary in us all. R. Goetz. *Christ Century* 104:1108-9 D 9 '87
'Redemptoris Mater' [John Paul's Marian encyclical] T. H. Stahel. *America* 156:353-4 My 2 '87
Mary, Queen of Scots, 1542-1587
about
'Gang wi' a lass'. il por *Hist Today* 37:62 Ja '87
Mary Queen of Scots: a tragedy in four cities. P. M. Prince. il *Travel Holiday* 167:54-9 Ap '87
Historiography
Much ado about nothing? K. M. Brown. il *Hist Today* 37:6-8 F '87
Mary Alice
about
On Broadway. N. A. Williams. por *Essence* 18:24 Ag '87
Mary Rose (Ship)
Evidence of a past life. N. Underwood. *Macleans* 100:54 S 7 '87
Maryland
See also
Assateague Island National Seashore (Md. and Va.)
Birds—Maryland
Camps—Maryland
Chesapeake Bay (Md. and Va.)

Colleges and universities—Maryland
Criminal justice, Administration of—Maryland
Educational laws and regulations—Maryland
Geology—Maryland
Hunting—Maryland
Music festivals—Maryland
Natural areas—Maryland
Prince Georges County (Md.)
History
Pint-sized ship of state [The Federalist, highlight of Maryland's 1788 Constitution ratification celebration] B. B. Ryan. il por *Am Hist Illus* 22:36-7+ S '87
Legislature
See also
Maryland Legislative Black Caucus
Politics and government
Barbara Mikulski [newly elected senator] L. Edmunds. por *Ms* 15:63+ Ja '87
Maryland. Motor Vehicle Administration
Vanity of vanities [allowing GOD on license plates] H. H. Morris. *Christ Century* 104:932 O 28 '87
Maryland Handel Festival *See* Music festivals—Maryland
Maryland Legislative Black Caucus
Md. Caucus to submit plan to aid black collegians. *Jet* 73:22 S 28 '87
Marzipan
Easy-to-make marzipan. il *Good Housekeep* 205:271 D '87
Marzipan menagerie. il *Sunset* 179:180-1 O '87
Marzollo, Jean
Child-care workers speak up. il *Parents* 62:114-16+ Ap '87
Making it through the holidays. il *Parents* 62:110-14 N '87
The rebus treasury [excerpt] il *Parents* 62:205-8+ N '87
Why mothers get a hard time. il *Parents* 62:103-5+ N '87
Marzorati, Gerald
Living and writing the peasant life. il pors *N Y Times Mag* p38-9+ N 29 '87
A sophist's theory of free speech. *Harpers* 275:62-3 S '87
Masai (African people)
See also
Turkana (African people)
Africa. L. Morrow. il *Time* 129:44-8+ F 23 '87
Rhythms of survival [Masai Mara Game Preserve] W. Eddy. il map *Natl Parks* 61:21-3 S/O '87
Masai Mara Game Reserve (Kenya) *See* Game preserves—Kenya
Masa's (San Francisco, Calif.: Restaurant) *See* San Francisco (Calif.)—Restaurants, nightclubs, bars, etc.
Mascaras *See* Cosmetics
Mascots
Fight, fight, fight, fight, banana slugs, banana slugs [mascot for University of California, Santa Cruz] J. Stuller. il *Audubon* 89:128-30+ Mr '87
Masculinity (Psychology)
Big boys don't cry—but why not? J. Dyer. *Seventeen* 46:56-7+ Mr '87
Boys are victims of sexism, too. T. Lucas. por *Seventeen* 46:56 Je '87
A commercial overture [sexual solicitation] B. Staples. il *N Y Times Mag* p106 S 20 '87
Don't hit a tough guy where he's tender. D. Heyn. *Mademoiselle* 93:142 O '87
Hail to the (macho) chief [desired presidential traits; study by D. Anthony Butterfield and Gary N. Powell] A. Kohn. il *Psychol Today* 21:21 D '87
I've had it with he-men. B. G. Harrison. *Mademoiselle* 93:166 My '87
The macho man behind the beard [self perception; study by Douglas Wood] V. Bozzi. il *Psychol Today* 21:20 My '87
The passions of men, 1987 [cover story; special issues; with editorial comment by Lee Eisenberg] il *Esquire* 107:29, 63+ Je '87
The poker game: what is it about cards that turns sensitive New Men into Neanderthals? N. Karlen. il *Glamour* 85:68+ S '87
Rape: the macho view [study by Donald L. Mosher and Ronald D. Anderson] P. McCarthy. *Psychol Today* 21:12 Ap '87
Real man redux [views of J. Pleck] M. S. Kimmel. bibl (p68) il pors *Psychol Today* 21:48-52 Jl '87
An ugly feeling [macho feelings while salvage diving] S. Toperoff. il *N Y Times Mag* p64 O 25 '87
Where are the sensitive men? [views of Art Bohart] il *USA Today (Periodical)* 116:1-2 Ag '87

Masekela, Hugh
about
Hugh Masekela. P. Garland. il por *Stereo Rev* 52:116 O '87
Masello, David
A big bestseller helps a small company grow. il *Publ Wkly* 231:47-8 Ap 17 '87
'A season on the brink' is the season's surprise #1 bestseller. il pors *Publ Wkly* 231:28-30 Mr 27 '87
Teaching in tongues. il *Publ Wkly* 232:31-3 Jl 10 '87
Masello, Robert
Intimacy: how to get it; how to give it. *Glamour* 85:158-9+ Ja '87
Why men cheat. il *Glamour* 85:146-7+ Jl '87
Mashburn, Rick
Molasses day. il *Ctry J* 14:57-61 O '87
What did women do? il *Americana* 15:4, 49-52 Mr/Ap '87
Masheck, Joseph
The artist as cynic. *New Leader* 70:22-3 Je 29 '87
Photo-gloss: on Paul Strand's "Cristo with thorns". bibl f il *Art Am* 75:104-13 Mr '87
Masiclat, Stephen M.
Teaching ethics. il *Phi Delta Kappan* 69:275-6 D '87
Masking (Photography) *See* Photography—Masking
Masks
See also
Dust masks
Let's face Halloween with a trick or two! [cover story] il *Natl Geogr World* 146:3-5 O '87
Make a spectacle of yourself . . . for Halloween or birthdays. il *Sunset* 179:140 O '87
Masks (Sculpture)
Mold models out of Flexwax [life masks] R. Naversen. il *Theatre Crafts* 21:104-5 O '87
Exhibitions
Magdalena Abakanowicz [exhibit at Turske & Turske, Zurich] E. Beck. il *Art News* 86:202 O '87
Maslin, Janet
Situation Commie. *New Repub* 196:25-7 F 23 '87
Masochism
See also
Sadomasochism
The parable of the cheek-turners and the cheek-smiters [feminist opposition to proposed revision of the Diagnostic and statistical manual of mental disorders] S. Boxer. il *Discover* 8:80-3 Ag '87
The politics of masochism [feminists challenge proposed revisions to Diagnostic and statistical manual of mental disorders] D. Franklin. il *Psychol Today* 21:52-7 Ja '87
Mason, Alden C., 1919-
about
Politics outlives art. L. Smallwood. il *Art News* 86:28 D '87
Mason, Bobbie Ann
La Bamba Hot Line. *New Yorker* 63:27 S 7 '87
Bumblebees [story] *New Yorker* 63:32-40 Mr 9 '87
Midnight magic [story] *New Yorker* 63:26-33 Ag 24 '87
State champions [story] il *Harpers* 274:68-72+ F '87
Mason, C. Vernon
about
The fire this time: two tough lawyers spur a new black activism. P. Blauner. il pors *N Y* 20:42-7 Ap 27 '87
The legal circus. E. Breindel. *New Repub* 196:20-2 F 9 '87
Mason, Elvis
about
The hottest merchant bank in Texas. T. Mack. il por *Forbes* 139:64+ Ap 6 '87
Mason, George, 1725-1792
about
The non-signers. C. L. Mee. pors *Am Herit* 38:78-9 S/O '87
Mason, Jackie
about
The hit of the building. R. Brustein. *New Repub* 197:27-30 O 19 '87
Jackie Mason. A. Feinstein. *Vogue* 177:134+ N '87
Rabbi's son makes good. S. Kanfer. il por *Time* 130:99 N 23 '87
A stand-up guy, still. C. Leerhsen. pors *Newsweek* 109:47 Ja 12 '87
The theatre [The world according to me!] M. Kramer. *New Yorker* 63:133-5 O 26 '87
Too much of a ham to remain a rabbi, Broadway's Jackie Mason is now the toast of the town. K. Gross. il pors *People Wkly* 27:90-1+ F 23 '87

Mason, Jill
The grandest [cover story] il map *Americana* 15:26-32 Jl/Ag '87
Mason, John Landis
about
A canner's dream. E. Long. il por *Rodale's Org Gard* 34:60-1 Ag '87
Mason, Judi Ann
about
Judi Ann Mason. P. Johnson. por *Essence* 18:27 O '87
Mason, June-Collier
about
The heroine of homegrown manufacturing. S. Wilkinson. il pors *Work Woman* 12:108-9+ N '87
Mason, Larry G.
Guerrillas of the goldenrod [cover story] il *Nat Hist* 96:34-9 Ag '87
Mason, Lisa
Arachne [fiction] il *Omni* 10:108-10+ D '87
Mason, Mary Moore
Pennsylvania's inn places: Bucks County bed & breakfast. il *Travel Holiday* 168:54-9 N '87
Scotland's elusive Nessie. *Travel Holiday* 168:94 Jl '87
Mason, Rae
Emergency! Take first-aid action. il *Teen* 31:48+ Mr '87
Mason, Timothy
about
Only you [drama] Reviews
New Yorker 63:106 D 21 '87. E. Oliver
Mason, Tommy Ray
Prison life: one convict's story. il por *Sch Update* 119:6-7 F 9 '87
Mason Best Company
The hottest merchant bank in Texas. T. Mack. il por *Forbes* 139:64+ Ap 6 '87
Mason jars *See* Canning and preserving—Equipment
Masonry
See also
Brick construction
National Concrete Masonry Association
Stone construction
Maintenance and repair
Pro tips for repairing exterior masonry. S. F. Brown. il *Pop Sci* 230:116 Je '87
Mass
See also
Altar girls
Let's take the must out of Sunday Mass [with readers' comments] T. Unsworth. *U S Cathol* 52:14-20 Ja '87
Mass to the sound of gunfire [Easter Mass in the Philippines; excerpt from Magellan's voyage around the world] A. Pigafetta. il *Courier* 40:11 Ap '87
Sunday Mass: what we've lost, what we've gained. K. Guentert. *U S Cathol* 52:34-7 Je '87
Mass (Music)
See also
Compact discs—Mass (Music)
Mass (Physics)
See also
Dark matter (Astronomy)
Stars—Mass
The bigger they are, the faster they fall [research by Barry Holstein and John Donoghue] il *Discover* 8:15-16 S '87
Neutrino mass: a positive view [work of Hong-Yee Chiu and others] D. E. Thomsen. *Sci News* 131:246 Ap 18 '87
Neutrino mass: a tritium disagreement. D. E. Thomsen. *Sci News* 131:342 My 30 '87
Mass extinction of species
Abrupt extinctions at end of Triassic [research by Paul E. Olsen and others] R. Monastersky. map *Sci News* 132:149 S 5 '87
The American blitzkrieg: a mammoth undertaking [Clovis hunters] J. M. Diamond. il *Discover* 8:82-4+ Je '87
Asteroid impact gets more support [research by Bruce Bohor and others] R. A. Kerr. bibl il *Science* 236:666-8 My 8 '87
Big splash from an ancient fall [Montagnais crater off Nova Scotia coast] R. Monastersky. *Sci News* 131:404 Je 27 '87
Death by natural causes [Pleistocene extinctions of animals may have been caused by human hunters] D. K. Grayson. il *Nat Hist* 96:8+ My '87
Did early North Americans mount a mammoth 'blitzkrieg'? il *Earth Sci* 40:6-7 Wint '87

Mass extinction of species—cont.

Domino effect invoked in Ice Age extinctions [theory of Norman Owen-Smith] R. Lewin. il *Science* 238:1509-10 D 11 '87

End-Cretaceous mass extinction event: argument for terrestrial causation. A. Hallam. bibl f il *Science* 238:1237-42 N 27 '87

Extinction upon impact? [research by Bruce F. Bohor and others] R. Monastersky. il *Sci News* 131:309-10 My 16 '87

Extinctions on ice [North American land mammals and Clovis hunters; theories of Paul S. Martin and others; cover story] B. Bower. il *Sci News* 132:284-5 O 31 '87

How did the giants die? [North American land mammals and Clovis hunters; theory of P. S. Martin] T. A. Lewis. il por *Int Wildl* 17:4-11 S/O '87

K-T mass extinctions: abrupt or what? [work of William J. Zinsmeister] R. Monastersky. *Sci News* 132:277 O 31 '87

Make no bones about it, dinosaur theory challenged [Alaskan Hadrosaur remains found by Elisabeth Brouwers and William Clemens] il *Earth Sci* 40:6 Wint '87

Mammoth find fuels extinction debate [discovery in England] B. Bower. *Sci News* 132:372 D 12 '87

Mass extinctions caused by large bolide impacts [adaptation of address, December 11, 1986; cover story] L. W. Alvarez. bibl f il *Phys Today* 40:24-33 Jl '87

New early Jurassic tetrapod assemblages constrain Triassic-Jurassic tetrapod extinction event [Nova Scotia discovery] P. E. Olsen and others. bibl f il map *Science* 237:1025-9 Ag 28 '87

Periodic mass extinctions at random [computer model developed by Michael L. McKinney] R. Monastersky. *Sci News* 132:319 N 14 '87

Point of impact: Manson, Iowa? R. Monastersky. *Sci News* 132:396 D 19-26 '87

Searching land and sea for the dinosaur killer. R. A. Kerr. il *Science* 237:856-7 Ag 21 '87

Shock of impact [shocked quartz as evidence of asteroid impact with earth; work of Bruce F. Bohor and others] *Sci Am* 257:22-3 Jl '87

Shocked quartz in the Cretaceous-Tertiary boundary clays: evidence for a global distribution. B. F. Bohor and others. bibl f il map *Science* 236:705-9 My 8 '87

Signs of Nemesis: meteors, magnetism. D. E. Thomsen. *Sci News* 131:100 F 14 '87

A substantial bias in nonparametric tests for periodicity in geophysical data. S. M. Stigler and M. J. Wagner. bibl f il *Science* 238:940-5 N 13 '87

There's a hole in the bottom of the sea [impact crater off Nova Scotia coast; research by Lubomir Jansa and Georgia Pe-Piper] map *Discover* 8:20 S '87

Today's controversy over extinction is a healthy example of what happens when varied scientific disciplines intersect. R. M. Adams. il *Smithsonian* 17:10 F '87

U.S. should take lead in preserving biological diversity. R. C. Cowen. il *Technol Rev* 90:25+ Ag/S '87

Volcanoes and extinctions: round two [theory of Vincent E. Courtillot and Stanley Cisowski] S. Weisburd. il map *Sci News* 131:248-50 Ap 18 '87

We're killing our world [address, February 14, 1987] P. H. Raven. *Vital Speeches Day* 53:472-8 My 15 '87

What killed the dinosaurs? [asteroid impact theory; work of Eric Essene and Daniel Fisher] il *USA Today (Periodical)* 115:9 Je '87

Where have all the dinos gone? [work of L. Alvarez] il *U S News World Rep* 103:67 Jl 6 '87

Who killed the dinosaurs? [impact-generated extinction theory] *Space World* X-8-284:9 Ag '87

Will species die out as the earth heats up? T. A. Lewis. il *Int Wildl* 17:18-21 N/D '87

Mass media

See also
Aged and mass media
AIDS (Disease) in mass media
Communications satellites—Journalistic use
Drugs and mass media
Heaven in mass media
Homosexuality in mass media
Journalistic ethics
Massachusetts Institute of Technology. Media Laboratory
Motion pictures
Newspapers
Periodicals
Press
Radio broadcasting
Television broadcasting

1988 field guide to the electronic environment [cover story] il *Channels* 7 Sp Issue:10-12+ D '87

Winners and sinners: media [1987] E. Diamond. il *N Y* 20:34+ D 21-28 '87

Moral and religious aspects

Shame, shame on the entertainment industry. R. M. Christenson. il *USA Today (Periodical)* 115:92-5 My '87

Political aspects

See also
Press and politics
Television and politics

Psychological aspects

The news & the bad news. C. Perlmutter. il *Prevention* 39:69-72+ N '87

Canada

Media watch. G. Bain. See occasional issues of Maclean's

United States

See Mass media

Mass media and education

What the media teach the public about education. M. Haberman. *Educ Dig* 53:5-7 N '87

Mass media and public health

Immunization: a chance for every child [promoting concept with comic books and postage stamps] il *World Health* p28-9 Mr '87

Mass media and the aged *See* Aged and mass media

Mass media and the arts

Media: what strategy? [arts education; cover story; special issue] *Des Arts Educ* 88:2-4+ Jl/Ag '87

Mass media and youth

Entertainment. C. Schine and D. Denby. See issues of McCall's beginning April 1986

How were children affected by the space shuttle disaster? G. G. Sparks. *Educ Dig* 52:55-7 F '87

Mass media in religion

See also
Radio broadcasting—Religious programs
Television broadcasting—Religious programs

Mass media industry

See also
Bonneville Media Communications
Capital Cities/ABC Inc.
Dick Clark Productions Inc.
Fox Inc.
Gulf & Western, Inc.
Hearst Corporation
Ingersoll Publications Company
John Blair & Company
MCA Inc.
MGM/UA Communications Co.
Minorities in the mass media industry
Multimedia, Inc.
Newhouse Broadcasting Corporation
Playboy Enterprises, Inc.
Price Communications Corp.
Publishers and publishing
Quantum Media, Inc.
Radio industry
Taft Broadcasting Co.
Television industry
Time Inc.
Warner Communications Inc.
Women in the mass media industry

1988 field guide to the electronic environment [cover story] il *Channels* 7 Sp Issue:10-12+ D '87

The Channels achievers [cover story; special section; with editorial comment by Les Brown] il *Channels* 7:4, 25-6+ Je '87

Communications media. A. B. Block. il *Forbes* 139:99-100 Ja 12 '87

Acquisitions and mergers

The Marvel strategy [acquisition of Marvel Comics by New World Pictures] G. Critser. il *Channels* 7:24 Mr '87

A surprise in the making. J. Baker. il *Channels* 7:59 N '87

International aspects

Citizen Murdoch makes his mark in books and television. D. Pauly. il por *Newsweek* 109:47+ Ap 13 '87

Citizen Murdoch presses for more. T. Moore. il pors *Fortune* 116:90-6 Jl 6 '87

A media magnate on a buying spree [R. Murdoch] M. Janigan. il por *Macleans* 100:40 Ja 12 '87

Rupert Murdoch. R. Grover. il por *Bus Week* Sp Issue:246 Ap 17 '87

Australia

"You keep your eyes and ears open" [Westfield Group media buys] T. Jaffe. por *Forbes* 139:36 Ap 6 '87

Mass media industry—Acquisitions and mergers—*cont.*
Canada
Agitated airwaves [Rogers Communications' offer for Selkirk Communications] P. Best. il *Macleans* 100:38 O 26 '87
Management
Why huge fortunes roll off the presses [billionaires] B. Dumaine. il por *Fortune* 116:156-7 O 12 '87
Securities
1987: for cable and radio it was a breathtaking year. M. Brown. il *Channels* 7 Sp Issue:42+ D '87
The schizoid life of the media analyst. J. F. Berry. il *Channels* 7:62-8 F '87
Canada
See also
Selkirk Communications Limited
Telemedia Inc.
Germany (West)
See also
Bertelsmann AG
Mass murder *See* Murder
Mass spectrometry *See* Spectrum analysis
Mass transit *See* Local transit
Massachusetts
See also
Arts and crafts—Massachusetts
Berkshire Hills (Mass.)
Booksellers and bookselling—Massachusetts
Cape Cod (Mass.)
Child welfare—Massachusetts
Dance festivals—Massachusetts
Education—Massachusetts
Festivals—Massachusetts
Historic houses, sites, etc.—Massachusetts
Hospitals, Psychiatric—Massachusetts
Housatonic River (Conn. and Mass.)
Law—Massachusetts
Music festivals—Massachusetts
Prisons—Massachusetts
Public welfare—Massachusetts
Taxation—Massachusetts
Unemployment—Massachusetts
Walden Pond (Mass.)
Water pollution—Massachusetts
Worcester County (Mass.)
Economic policy
The Dukakis design. J. Siegal. il *New Leader* 70:10-13 Ag 10-24 '87
Have we seen the future? [M. Dukakis' program; cover story] A. Kopkind. il *Nation* 244:631+ My 16 '87
Letters [discussion of May 16, 1987 article, Have we seen the future?] A. Kopkind. *Nation* 244:872+ Je 27 '87
Mike Dukakis has ideas—but will they travel? L. Helm. il por *Bus Week* p61 Mr 23 '87
A miracle—and the man who would take credit for it [M. Dukakis] H. Rainie. il por *U S News World Rep* 103:18-19 Ag 10 '87
A second look at an economic 'miracle' [claims of M. Dukakis] il por *Newsweek* 110:31 N 30 '87
History
See also
Boston Tea Party, 1773
Shays' Rebellion, 1786-1787
Massachusetts. Dept. of the State Treasurer. Abandoned Property Division
Eugene Kiely itches to find heirs to wads of scratch. J. Kaufman. il pors *People Wkly* 28:89+ N 16 '87
Massachusetts. Industrial Finance Agency
The unlikely hero of small-business finance [B. Carty] L. Helm. il por *Bus Week* p170 N 2 '87
Massachusetts Financial Emerging Growth Trust
Sound picks in small stocks [interview with T. Cashman] A. E. Serwer. il por *Fortune* 115:164 My 11 '87
Massachusetts Industrial Finance Agency *See* Massachusetts. Industrial Finance Agency
Massachusetts Institute of Technology
Caution: geniuses at work and play. A. Theroux. il *Read Dig* 131:215-18+ O '87
Curriculum changes spark debate at MIT. W. Booth. il *Science* 236:1515-16 Je 19 '87
Professor sues MIT over tenure [D. Noble] D. L. Goodman. *Progressive* 51:13 Je '87
Reporter: a digest of news from M.I.T. See occasional issues of Technology Review
Massachusetts Institute of Technology. Media Laboratory
Dreaming the impossible at M.I.T. P. Elmer-Dewitt. il *Time* 130:52-3 Ag 31 '87
Inventing the future. E. Dolnick. il por *N Y Times Mag* p30-3+ Ag 23 '87

Mothers of invention [excerpt from The Media Lab] S. Brand. *Omni* 9:18+ Ag '87
Massachusetts Institute of Technology. Sloan School of Management *See* Sloan School of Management
Massachusetts Museum of Contemporary Art and Architecture
Art comes to the rescue. D. Davis. il por *Newsweek* 110:97 O 26 '87
Thinking big. C. Giuliano. il por *Art News* 86:35-6 S '87
Williams College coup [G. Panza di Biumo Collection] C. Giuliano. *Art News* 86:58+ Summ '87
Massachusetts Port Authority
Massport to cut Logan traffic, foster use of reliever airports. *Aviat Week Space Technol* 127:44 S 7 '87
National groups prepare to fight plan to restrict access at Logan. D. Hughes. il *Aviat Week Space Technol* 127:34-5 D 21 '87
Operators attack plan to stem New England commuter service [plan to divert traffic from Boston's Logan Airport to reliever airports] *Aviat Week Space Technol* 127:41+ S 7 '87
Opposition grows to plan for fee increase at Logan. D. Hughes. *Aviat Week Space Technol* 127:52+ O 26 '87
Massacres
Mozambique
Massacre deep in the African bush. W. E. Smith. il map *Time* 130:28-9 Ag 3 '87
Massacre in Mozambique. S. Reiss. *Newsweek* 110:28 Ag 3 '87
Mozambique massacre. B. Shelby. *World Press Rev* 34:43 S '87
Murder in Mozambique [attack on United Methodist mission station] *Christ Century* 104:850 O 7 '87
Zimbabwe
Commune murders. *Christ Century* 104:1171 D 23-30 '87
Massacre in Matabeleland. *Macleans* 100:24 D 7 '87
A massacre's message: get out or die [attack on missionaries] il *Newsweek* 110:52 D 7 '87
Massage
See also
Chiropractic
Altered states for mind & body [Trager method] N. Amdur. il *World Tennis* 34:22+ My '87
Baby massage [preemies] il *Psychol Today* 21:34 Ja '87
Getting the massage [tennis players] B. Norris. il *World Tennis* 34:6-7 Ja '87
Lunchtime lifts. il *Harpers Bazaar* 120:150+ Mr '87
The massage break is catching on. C. Dilks. il *Nations Bus* 75:56-7 Ag '87
Massage comes out of the parlor. A. Toufexis. il *Time* 129:84-5 Mr 9 '87
Massage for the masses. M. A. D'Urso. il *Health* 19:63-4+ Ap '87
Something about Nancy Belser rubs animals the right way. il por *People Wkly* 27:121 My 18 '87
Take a massage. G. Nesmith. *Black Enterp* 17:145 F '87
Massaquoi, Hans J.
Alex Haley's hideaway. il pors *Ebony* 42:52-4+ S '87
Masse, André
about
Assassination in South Lebanon. H. Madelin. *America* 157:397-8 N 28 '87
Massenet, Jules, 1842-1912
about
Chérubin [opera] Reviews
N Y 20:97 Ap 13 '87. P. G. Davis
Manon [opera] Reviews
N Y il 20:60+ F 23 '87. P. G. Davis
New Yorker 63:104-5 Mr 2 '87. A. Porter
Opera News il 51:16-19+ F 28 '87. J. Kestner
Opera News il 51:22-4 F 28 '87
Massey, David
The tomato and I. il *Gourmet* 47:76-7+ S '87
Massey, Douglas S., and García-España, Felipe
The social process of international migration. bibl f il *Science* 237:733-8 Ag 14 '87
Massey, Jack C., 1904-
about
The U.S. Business Hall of Fame. A. M. Louis. por *Fortune* 115:105 Ap 13 '87
Massey, Jesse
about
Guard hailed by police fired by bank; gets a better job and pay raise. *Jet* 72:12 Mr 30 '87

Massey, Mike
about
If you're missing milk crates, Mike Massey will crack the case. il por *People Wkly* 28:114 S 21 '87
Massey, Ruth
Wat Phou: a miracle waiting to happen. il *UN Chron* 24:72-3 N '87
Massey, Walter E.
about
Walter E. Massey: president-elect of AAAS. N. M. Bradburn and D. Rosen. bibl f por *Science* 238:1657-8 D 18 '87
Massia, Christiane
about
Simply delicious la belle cuisine. A. Stone-Sweet. il por *Harpers Bazaar* 120:292+ S '87
Massie, Raymond G.
about
Massie, Davenport get high level Energy Dept. posts. *Jet* 72:22 Je 15 '87
Massing, Michael
The business of fighting apartheid. il *Atlantic* 259:26-32 F '87
The chief. bibl f il por *N Y Rev Books* 34:15-22 F 12 '87
Haiti: the new violence. il *N Y Rev Books* 34:45-52 D 3 '87
Snap books. *New Repub* 196:21+ My 4 '87
Trotsky's orphans. *New Repub* 196:18-20+ Je 22 '87
While Haiti burns. *New Repub* 197:14-16 N 16 '87
Massingberd, Hugh Montgomery- *See* Montgomery-Massingberd, Hugh
Massman, Bea
about
12 who mattered: teachers. P. Stites. por *World Tennis* 35:60 Ag '87
Masson, J. Moussaieff (Jeffrey Moussaieff), 1941-
about
Masson loses libel suit against 'New Yorker,' Malcolm and Knopf. M. Colin. *Publ Wkly* 232:11 S 4 '87
Masson, Jeffrey Moussaieff *See* Masson, J. Moussaieff (Jeffrey Moussaieff), 1941-
Masstor Systems Corporation
The lopsided technology company. A. A. Lappen. il por *Forbes* 140:64+ N 30 '87
Massûn, Edith
Puppets versus drugs. il *World Health* p2-5 Je '87
Mast, Coleen Kelly
Virginity regained [excerpt from Sex respect] *Harpers* 274:20-2 Ap '87
Mastectomy
A battle with breast cancer puts a star's life into focus. J. Ireland. il pors *People Wkly* 27:57-8+ Mr 16 '87
"I guess it's my turn" [N. Reagan] J. V. Lamar, Jr. por *Time* 130:36 O 26 '87
'Let's just hold hands' [N. Reagan's mastectomy; special section] il pors *Newsweek* 110:28-31 O 26 '87
Life wish [excerpt] J. Ireland. il *Ladies Home J* 104:53-6+ Ja '87
Psychological scars of breast surgery [lumpectomy vs. mastectomy; study by Lesley J. Fallowfield] P. McCarthy. *Psychol Today* 21:17 Ag '87
The Reagans' latest battle. *Macleans* 100:32 O 26 '87
Sex & the single-breasted woman. L. Dackman. *Vogue* 177:420+ S '87
Surgery women should think about twice. A. Mereson. *McCalls* 114:139-40 Jl '87
To be whole again: mastectomy treated Peggy McCann's cancer, but breast reconstruction made her well. D. E. Haupt. il pors *Life* 10:78-83+ My '87
Was this operation necessary? [N. Reagan's decision] C. Wallis. il por *Time* 130:78 N 2 '87
Words of assurance for a stricken First Lady [four celebrities tell their stories] il por *People Wkly* 28:48-50+ N 2 '87
Mastectomy reconstruction surgery *See* Surgery, Plastic
Master limited partnership
Are MLPs worth a shot? D. R. Katz. il *Esquire* 108:79-80 S '87
A new financing tool is in trouble already. E. Spragins. il *Bus Week* p84 Je 29 '87
Real estate action you can buy like stock. B. Hitchings. *Bus Week* p102 F 9 '87
Thanks a lot [rollup plans] L. R. Walbert. il *Forbes* 140:134 Ag 10 '87
Taxation
The master limited loophole. J. Egan. il *U S News World Rep* 102:63 Mr 30 '87
Mastercard International
Banking on China. D. Fong. por *Forbes* 140:304 N 16 '87

They bombed in Columbia [MasterCard's test marketing of the smart card] L. J. Moore. il *U S News World Rep* 102:50-1 F 2 '87
Masterdisk Corporation
An interview with Bob Ludwig. M. Dery. il por *Stereo Rev* 52:113-15 N '87
Masterman, Sue
Satellite TV transcends the Curtain. il *World Press Rev* 34:54 Je '87
Masters, Brian
Wild gaming. il por *House Gard* 159:222-5+ N '87
Masters, Ian
Audio Q&A. See issues of Stereo Review beginning October 1986
Masters, Jeffrey M.
Flying into the eye of a hurricane [cover story] il *Weatherwise* 40:128-33 Je '87
Masterson, Mary Stuart
about
How Mary Stuart Masterson got hot on the Hollywood grapevine. J. Powell. il pors *Glamour* 85:160+ Je '87
New York doll. D. Handelman. por *N Y* 20:74-6 Mr 2 '87
She's got what it takes. E. Miller. il pors *Seventeen* 46:61-2+ F '87
Talent: orbiting to the top. pors *Harpers Bazaar* 120:264-73 Mr '87
Masterton, Graham
Horror of horrors. *Writer* 100:15-18+ Ag '87
Mastery learning *See* Learning, Psychology of
Mastitis in cattle *See* Cattle—Diseases and pests
Mastrantonio, Mary Elizabeth
about
Cued for success. T. Young. il por *Vogue* 177:92 F '87
Mastroianni, Marcello, 1924-
about
Cary Grant, Italian style. R. Corliss. il por *Time* 130:80 O 12 '87
Infidelity: Italian (and Russian) style. A. Harvey. il pors *Vogue* 177:442-3+ O '87
Marcello Mastroianni. B. Darrach. il pors *People Wkly* 28:98-100+ D 7 '87
Still Mastroianni [cover story] C. B. Pepper. il pors *N Y Times Mag* p46-51+ S 20 '87
Masts and rigging
See also
Sails
Masturbation
Masturbation: who, what, where, when and why. R. Westen. *Glamour* 85:156+ My '87
Anecdotes, facetiae, satire, etc.
Mark Twain on the safest sex. M. Twain. *Harpers* 275:22-3 O '87
Masursky, Harold, 1922-
about
Naming names. G. Freiherr. il por *Space World* X-8-284:31-3 Ag '87
Maszak, Marianne Szegedy- *See* Szegedy-Maszak, Marianne
Match covers *See* Matchcovers
Matchcovers
Collectors and collecting
Matchbook cover collecting. D. Stewart. il *Antiques Collect Hobbies* 92:74-8 Je '87
Matches
See also
Matchcovers
Matchmaking
Matchmaking: how to offer it, ask for it. P. Grant. *Glamour* 85:312 Mr '87
Matera, Dary
(jt. auth) See De Barbin, Lucy, and Matera, Dary
about
A hot property. L. Fleischer. *Publ Wkly* 231:69 Mr 13 '87
Materialism
Gazing into Bergdorf's window. P. Freundlich. *Harpers* 275:73-6 D '87
The money society [cover story] M. Magnet. il *Fortune* 116:26-31 Jl 6 '87
The one who has the most toys when he dies, wins [life goals of college freshmen] P. Chance. il *Psychol Today* 21:54 My '87
Materials
See also
Artists' materials
Building materials
Ceramics
Magnetic materials
Raw materials

Materials—*cont.*
Learning to become a nation of artists [developing an appreciation of materials] M. Flannery. *Educ Dig* 52:24-6 My '87
Materials, Effect of radiation on
Alpha-decay-induced fracturing in zircon: the transition from the crystalline to the metamict state [cover story] B. C. Chakoumakos and others. bibl f il *Science* 236:1556-9 Je 19 '87
Materials processing in space *See* Space processing
Materials research
The age of superstuff. M. Rogers. il *Newsweek* 109:73-4 My 25 '87
Alcoa: recycling itself to become a pioneer in new materials. G. L. Miles and M. Rothman. il por *Bus Week* p56-8 F 9 '87
Alcoa restructures to enter value-added product market. S. W. Kandebo. il *Aviat Week Space Technol* 126:65-7 F 23 '87
Congress to postpone station funding if NASA constrains materials science. *Aviat Week Space Technol* 127:29 O 12 '87
The future belongs to the 'light' stuff. G. D. Wallace. il *Bus Week* p57 F 9 '87
Materials research. P. H. Abelson. *Science* 235:9 Ja 2 '87
Materials science [cover story; special issue; with editorial comment by John I. Brauman] bibl f il *Science* 235:953, 997-1035 F 27 '87
Materials scientists seek a unified voice. A. L. Robinson. *Science* 235:161-2 Ja 9 '87
The real challenge in materials engineering. T. W. Eagar. il *Technol Rev* 90:24-35 F/Mr '87
Materials Research Society
Materials Research Society meets in Boston. R. Hart and M. Marynowski. il *Phys Today* 40:57-9 N '87
Maternal behavior *See* Mothers
Maternal behavior in animals *See* Parental behavior in animals
Maternal deprivation
Quality day-care and social growth [study by Deborah Phillips and others] B. Bower. *Sci News* 132:54-5 Jl 25 '87
When a young mother dies. J. Gaylin. *Ladies Home J* 104:78+ F '87
Maternal-fetal exchange
Retroviruses and mouse embryos: a rapid model for neurovirulence and transplacental antiviral therapy. A. H. Sharpe and others. bibl f il *Science* 236:1671-4 Je 26 '87
Maternal love *See* Love, Maternal
Maternity *See* Mothers
Maternity leaves
Bargaining for time to bring up baby. B. Brophy. il *U S News World Rep* 103:62-3 Ag 24 '87
Business and pregnancy: good will is no longer good enough [Supreme Court decision] A. Bernstein. il *Bus Week* p37 F 2 '87
Court rules for women [Supreme Court on maternity leaves] J. C. Baker. *Black Enterp* 17:20 Ap '87
The family way [rulings by the Supreme Court] *Commonweal* 114:67-9 F 13 '87
Garland's bouquet [Supreme Court ruling supports pregnancy leave] A. Wilentz. il por *Time* 129:14-15 Ja 26 '87
Managing maternity. D. L. Gittens. il *Essence* 18:106+ Je '87
Maternity leaves: how managers should handle them. H. McCrum. *Work Woman* 12:18 Ja '87
A new family issue [decision by the Supreme Court] A. Press. il por *Newsweek* 109:22-4 Ja 26 '87
Pregnancy job protection upheld by Supreme Court. il *Jet* 71:5 F 2 '87
Pregnant question. *Nation* 244:97 Ja 31 '87
Supreme Court gives motherhood its legal due [L. Garland's case] B. Brophy. il por *U S News World Rep* 102:12 Ja 26 '87
Unemployment pay may be denied jobless new moms [women on maternity leave who don't return] *Jet* 71:25 Mr 23 '87
Will employers deliver more maternity leave? *Changing Times* 41:10 Ap '87
Maternity nurses *See* Nurses and nursing
Matewan [film] *See* Motion picture reviews—Single works
Mathabane, Mark
about
South African author tells of horrors of racism in new book. il pors *Jet* 72:8-9 Ag 3 '87
Mathematical ability
Asian languages aid mathematics skills [research by Irene T. Miura] B. Bower. *Sci News* 132:183 S 19 '87

Bad news about math [American students compared with others] E. Bowen. il *Time* 129:65 Ja 26 '87
Big plus for females [sports interest and math skills] J. E. Vader. por *Sports Illus* 67:100 N 23 '87
Children's math aptitude linked to mom's attitude. il *Jet* 71:39 F 9 '87
Female math anxiety on the wane. C. Holden. il *Science* 236:660-1 My 8 '87
Mathematics: a male advantage? [study by Camilla Persson Benbow] R. J. Trotter. *Psychol Today* 21:66-7 Ja '87
Mathematical analysis
See also
Finite element method
Mathematical optimization
Mathematical models
See also
AIDS (Disease)—Mathematical models
Ecological models
Evolution—Mathematical models
Game theory
Monte Carlo method
Securities—Mathematical models
Forest fires, barnacles and trickling oil [interacting particle systems; cover story] I. Peterson. il *Sci News* 132:220-3 O 3 '87
Mathematical optimization
Optimizing compilers. M. Roberts. bibl *Byte* 12:165-6+ O '87
Mathematical physics
See also
Fractals
Statistical mechanics
Computational physics [cover story; special section] bibl f il *Phys Today* 40:25-37+ O '87
Mathematical proof *See* Proof theory
Mathematical recreations
See also
Traveling salesman problem
Games. S. Morris. See issues of Omni (New York, N.Y.)
Mathematical research
Federal aid
Mathematicians and SDI: a quandary. il *Discover* 8:14 F '87
Military funding: does it add up? I. Peterson. *Sci News* 131:71 Ja 31 '87
Mathematicians
See also
Erdős, Paul, 1913-
Newton, Sir Isaac, 1642-1727
Ramanujan Aiyangar, Srinivasa, 1887-1920
Mathematics
See also
Algebra
Algorithms
Arithmetic
Calculus
Computers—Mathematical use
Equations
Fractions
Game theory
Geometry
Graphic methods
Harmonic analysis
Linear programming
Mathematical recreations
Permutations
Probabilities
Relaxation methods (Mathematics)
Transformations (Mathematics)
Philosophy
A Buckminster Fuller dictionary. E. J. Applewhite. il pors *Futurist* 21:24-8 S/O '87
Research
See Mathematical research
Study and teaching
See also
Arithmetic—Study and teaching
Calculus—Study and teaching
Geometry—Study and teaching
North Carolina School of Science and Mathematics
Developing metacognition for school mathematics. J. Garofalo. *Educ Dig* 53:48-9 D '87
Education: math and aftermath. I. Peterson. *Sci News* 131:72 Ja 31 '87
How to help students in reading mathematics. D. E. Gullatt. *Educ Dig* 52:40-1 Ja '87
Increasing teachers' understanding of mathematical ideas through inservice training. T. L. Good and D. A. Grouws. bibl f il *Phi Delta Kappan* 68:778-83 Je '87

Mathematics—Study and teaching—*cont.*
Mathematics education: a predictor of scientific competitiveness. L. A. Steen. bibl f *Science* 237:251-2+ Jl 17 '87
Points of stress in mathematics education. L. A. Steen. *Educ Dig* 52:36-9 Ja '87
State residential high schools for mathematically talented youth. J. C. Stanley. bibl f il *Phi Delta Kappan* 68:770-3 Je '87
U.S. math curriculum needs overhaul, new study says. il *Phi Delta Kappan* 68:558-9 Mr '87
Aids and devices
Let them use calculators [elementary school arithmetic] A. Ralston. il *Technol Rev* 90:30-1 Ag/S '87
Magical tools for the 1980s [math and science software created by E. Goldstein] H.-J. Taferner. il por *Pers Comput* 11:173+ O '87
Will calculators hurt math skills? F. Roberts. il *Parents* 62:50+ D '87

Matheny, Ray T.
El Mirador: an early Maya metropolis uncovered. il map *Natl Geogr* 172:316-39 S '87

Mather, Monica H., and Roitberg, Bernard D.
A sheep in wolf's clothing: tephritid flies mimic spider predators. bibl f il *Science* 236:308-10 Ap 17 '87

Matheson, Katy
Modern dance: a growing presence. il *Dance Mag* 61:151-3 Je '87

Matheu, Manuel de Falla y *See* Falla, Manuel de, 1876-1946
Mathews, Grant J.
(jt. auth) *See* Viola, Victor E., and Mathews, Grant J.

Mathews, Laura
Books. *See* issues of Glamour

Mathews, Max V., and Pierce, John Robinson, 1910-
The computer as a musical instrument. il *Sci Am* 256:126-33 F '87

Mathews, Michael B.
(jt. auth) *See* Bunn, Christopher C., and Mathews, Michael B.

Mathews, Tom Dewe
Tales of Highgate. il *House Gard* 159:86+ Ap '87

Mathews-Berenson, Margaret
Harry Orlyk [cover story] il *Am Artist* 51:38-41+ Jl '87
Reeve Schley III. il *Am Artist* 51:70-3+ N '87

Mathewson, Judith
(jt. auth) *See* Glynn, Lenny, and Mathewson, Judith

Mathias, Charles
Ordered liberty [address, July 29, 1987] *Vital Speeches Day* 53:706-10 S 15 '87

Mathieu-Faraggi, Henriette, 1915-1985
about
Obituary
Phys Today por 40:113-14 My '87. V. Gillet

Matiguás (Nicaragua)
Religious institutions and affairs
Death and resurrection in Matiguás [death of Franciscan brother T. Zavaleta] E. Rivera. *America* 157:261-2 O 24 '87

Matilija poppies
How to multiply Matilija poppies . . . challenging to very difficult. il *Sunset* 178:202-3 Je '87
Matilija poppy [cover story] il map *Sunset* 178:94-7 Je '87

Mating behavior *See* Sexual behavior
Mating calls of animals *See* Animal sounds
Matisse, Henri
about
Generic genius. J. Perl. *Vogue* 177:36 Je '87
Henri Matisse: the early years in Nice. R. Kremer. il *USA Today (Periodical)* 115:84-7 Mr '87
Lighted by Matisse. P. Hamburger. *New Yorker* 63:61-5 Ag 10 '87
Matisse: an intimate splendor. R. Shone. il pors *House Gard* 159:132-9+ Mr '87
Matisse in Nice. J. Masheck. *New Leader* 70:23 Ja 12-26 '87
Matisse's retour à l'ordre. K. Silver. bibl f il *Art Am* 75:110-23+ Je '87
Matisse's Two negresses. J. Hobhouse. il por *Art News* 86:91-2 D '87
Palette Niçoise. M. Stevens. il *New Repub* 196:28+ Mr 16 '87

Matlin, Marlee
about
Marlee Matlin. J. Etra. pors *Harpers Bazaar* 120:296-366-7 S '87
Marlee Matlin rising. pors *Esquire* 108:104-5 N '87
Personal style: the new moods of beauty. il pors *Harpers Bazaar* 120:146-53 F '87

Matlock, John F., Jr.
U.S.-Soviet relations: background and prospects [address, September 15, 1986] *Dep State Bull* 86:61-5 D '86

Matra SA
France keeps option open on missile contractor choice. *Aviat Week Space Technol* 126:107 F 9 '87
Matra wins Telecom 2 contest, resolves constraints on TRW for Intelsat bid. *Aviat Week Space Technol* 127:24-5 N 30 '87

Matrices
See also
Linear programming

Matrimony *See* Marriage
Mats, Door *See* Door mats, etc.
Mats for pictures *See* Pictures—Trimming, mounting, etc.
Matson, Tim, 1943-
New life for old ponds. il *Ctry J* 14:48-53 Jl '87

Matsu-no Chaya (Hakone, Japan: Inn) *See* Hakone (Japan)—Hotels, motels, etc.
Matsushita Electric Industrial Co. Ltd.
An optical memory that can be wiped clean. E. T. Smith. il *Bus Week* p56+ Je 15 '87
Smooth strokes from a late bloomer [A. Tanii] F. H. Katayama. il por *Fortune* 116:37 Ag 3 '87
"We do not take a short-term view". A. Tanzer. il *Forbes* 140:372+ Jl 13 '87

Mattapoisett (Mass.)
Architecture
Entire of itself [Mahoney residence] M. Gaskie. il *Archit Rec* 175:98-103 mid-Ap '87

Mattel Inc.
Another toymaker may be in play [New World Pictures to go after Mattel] G. G. Marcial. *Bus Week* p108 S 21 '87
Does Drexel have a game plan for Mattel? G. G. Marcial. il *Bus Week* p76 F 9 '87
Mattel has to play harder than ever [main shareholders, Warburg and Drexel, want a turnaround] J. Flynn. il *Bus Week* p60-1 My 25 '87
Shooting the messenger [interactive toys and TV show Captain Power and the soldiers of the future] V. Ross. il *Macleans* 100:71 O 5 '87
When toys mean business [marketing manager C. Irving] J. Giambanco. il pors *Work Woman* 12:133-4+ My '87

Matter, Darryl E., and Matter, Roxana Marie
"Little's Cross and Crown System": Sunday school awards from the early twentieth century. il *Antiques Collect Hobbies* 92:82-3 D '87
"The Samantha stories". il *Antiques Collect Hobbies* 91:48-50 Ja '87

Matter, Roxana Marie
(jt. auth) *See* Matter, Darryl E., and Matter, Roxana Marie

Matter
See also
Antimatter
Mass (Physics)
Surfaces
Condensed matter physics. *Phys Today* 40:S14-S20 Ja '87

Matter, Interstellar
See also
Dark matter (Astronomy)
Nebulae
100 trillion clouds [research by Ralph L. Fiedler and others] il *Sky Telesc* 74:121-2 Ag '87
Aging of primordial hydrogen clouds [work of Hugh S. Murdoch and others] *Sky Telesc* 74:235-6 S '87
Amino acids from space [Murchison meteorite] *Astronomy* 15:95-6 D '87
Diamonds from outer space [research by Roy Lewis] il *USA Today (Periodical)* 115:4-5 Je '87
Dust clouds detected around six nearby stars [study by Dana Backman and others] *Astronomy* 15:75+ My '87
Frosty the . . . nebula? [IRAS 09371 + 1212; work of Thierry Forveille and others] il *Sky Telesc* 74:346 O '87
Greenland's cosmic dust deposits [work of Michel Maurette and others] il *Sky Telesc* 73:367-8 Ap '87
Halley's whiskers: first space polymer detected [work of Walter F. Huebner] J. Eberhart. il *Sci News* 132:100 Ag 15 '87
Infrared cirrus [Infrared Astronomical Satellite] il *Sky Telesc* 73:601-2 Je '87
Interstellar ooze? [study of Murchison meteorite; work of Samuel Epstein and others] il *Sky Telesc* 74:233-4 S '87

Matter, Interstellar—*cont.*
Interstellar polycyclic aromatic hydrocarbons and carbon in interplanetary dust particles and meteorites. L. J. Allamandola and others. bibl f il *Science* 237:56-9 Jl 3 '87
Lambda Orionis' molecular ring [work of Ronald J. Maddalena and Mark Morris] il *Sky Telesc* 74:455 N '87
Molecular hydrogen envelopes. B. Zuckerman. il *Sky Telesc* 73:129 F '87
Occult occulters [new type of interstellar object discovered by Ralph L. Fiedler and others] *Sci Am* 257:19+ Jl '87
Oodles of 'noodles' found in galaxy [research by Ralph L. Fiedler and others] D. E. Thomsen. *Sci News* 131:247 Ap 18 '87
Oort cloud comets: blasted, bumped, and baked? [work of Alan Stern] *Sky Telesc* 74:459 N '87
Oxygen isotopes in refractory stratospheric dust particles: proof of extraterrestrial origin. K. D. McKeegan. bibl f il *Science* 237:1468-71 S 18 '87
Polymer found in Comet Halley. il *Astronomy* 15:94 D '87
Realm of the comets [Oort cloud] P. R. Weissman. il *Sky Telesc* 73:238-41 Mr '87
Refractory interplanetary dust particles. M. E. Zolensky. bibl f il *Science* 237:1466-8 S 18 '87
Sampling the stuff of a comet [dust in Halley's coma] R. Knacke. il *Sky Telesc* 73:246-50 Mr '87
Something passing in the night [Extreme Scattering Events; research by R. Fiedler] G. L. Verschuur. il *Astronomy* 15:26-31 D '87
Star dust in the sky with diamonds [research by Edward Anders and others] I. Peterson. *Sci News* 131:166 Mr 14 '87
Star formation in W49A: gravitational collapse of the molecular cloud core toward a ring of massive stars. W. J. Welch and others. bibl f il *Science* 238:1550-5 D 11 '87
Stardust on earth [interstellar diamonds] J. K. Beatty. il *Sky Telesc* 73:610 Je '87
Taking a vacuum to extraterrestrial dust [work of Michel Maurette and others] R. Monastersky. *Sci News* 132:133 Ag 29 '87
Mattera, Joanne
Clothes strategies. See issues of Glamour beginning October 1986
Mattern, Evelyn
Hunting [poem] *America* 156:199 Mr 7 '87
Matthes, William A., and Carlson, Robert V.
Why do teachers choose rural schools? *Educ Dig* 52:27-9 F '87
Matthew, H. C. G.
Gladstonian finance. bibl il por *Hist Today* 37:41-5 Jl '87
Matthew, William D.
(jt. auth) See Sandrock, Alfred W., Jr., and Matthew, William D.
Matthews, Anne
Pralines. il *Americana* 15:42-4+ Mr/Ap '87
Matthews, Christopher J.
Carnival of the candidates [cover story] il *New Repub* 197:20-5 D 21 '87
A failure to communicate. il por *U S News World Rep* 102:27 Ja 26 '87
The Old Breed strikes back. il *New Repub* 196:21-3 Mr 2 '87
Matthews, Denise *See* Vanity
Matthews, Douglas Gary, 1945-
about
Putting the right stuff to work in business. P. Finch. il por *Bus Week* p105 Mr 23 '87
Matthews, Downs
Camping out in polar bear country. il map *50 Plus* 27:44-8+ F '87
Matthews, Martin S.
Tapping into computer services. il *Consum Res Mag* 70:11-17 Ja '87
Matthews, Mike
Bluebird bungalows. il por *Mother Earth News* 104:40+ Mr/Ap '87
Matthews, Paul Taunton, d. 1987
about
Obituary
Phys Today por 40:142+ O '87. A. Salam
Matthews, Roy T.
(jt. auth) See Mellini, Peter, and Matthews, Roy T.
Matthews, Samuel W.
Ice on the world. il maps *Natl Geogr* 171:78-103 Ja '87

Matthews, Thomas
Le Corbusier's Pessac: an experiment in urbanism continues. il *Archit Rec* 175:87+ N '87
Matthews, William, 1942-
Herd of buffalo crossing the Missouri River on ice [poem] *Atlantic* 259:66 Ap '87
Matthews & Wright Inc.
How 'tax-free' are these bonds? D. Zigas. *Bus Week* p122 Ag 17 '87
Matthew's Party
Reaching baby boomers in southern California. B. Bird. il por *Christ Today* 31:45-6 Ag 7 '87
Matthies, Nina
about
A juggling act. P. Freeman. il pors *Women's Sports Fitness* 9:39-42 Ag '87
Mattingly, Don
about
A Murderers' Row of one. C. Neff. il pors *Sports Illus* 67:24-5 Jl 27 '87
Three for the record books. il por *Time* 130:62 Ag 3 '87
What's wrong with Yankee slugger Don Mattingly? George only knows, because nobody else does. J. Friedman. il pors *People Wkly* 27:79-80+ Ap 20 '87
Mattison, Alice
Bears [story] *New Yorker* 63:34-43 Mr 16 '87
Mattison, Edward M.
Shopping for instruments. il *Phys Today* 40 pt2:BG17-BG18 Ag '87
Mattole River (Calif.)
Along the Mattole, helping hands heal the watershed. il *Sierra* 72:62-3 Mr/Ap '87
Mattress industry
See also
Ohio Mattress Company
Sealy Incorporated
Acquisitions and mergers
Mattress wars [Ohio Mattress acquires Sealy] J. Andresky. il por *Forbes* 139:41 Je 15 '87
Mattresses
See also
Futons
Mattson, William J., and Haack, Robert A.
The role of drought in outbreaks of plant-eating insects. bibl f il *BioScience* 37:110-18 F '87
Matulis, Sherry
"I had no choice". il por *Redbook* 168:38+ Mr '87
Maturation (Biology)
An age-old question: why did the human lineage survive? P. Shipman. il *Discover* 8:60-4 Ap '87
Maturity
50-plussers are conservatives at heart! [mellowness of maturity] W. F. Buckley. il pors *50 Plus* 27:56-60 Mr '87
Growing up is hard to do. B. Greene. il *Esquire* 108:31-2 Jl '87
The prime of our lives. A. H. Rosenfeld and E. Stark. bibl (p94) il *Psychol Today* 21:62-4+ My '87
Rites of passage. R. M. Cohen. il *Read Dig* 131:145-6 S '87
Suddenly I'm the adult? R. M. Cohen. *Psychol Today* 21:70-1 My '87
Anecdotes, facetiae, satire, etc.
For grown-ups only. J. Viorst. il *Redbook* 169:39-40 Jl '87
Maturity, Sexual *See* Puberty
Matus, Mickey
about
A candid interview with Mickey Matus, Ford SVO marketing manager. J. Asher. il por *Mot Trend* 39 no12 Sp Issue:90-3+ '87
Mauceri, John, 1945-
about
Double play [cover story] S. Flatow. il pors *Opera News* 51:10-13+ Je '87
Maucher, Helmut
about
Stirring the coffee pot. S. Tully. il por *Fortune* 116:44 Ag 3 '87
Maudlin-Jeronimo, John M., and Hoffmann, Peter
Accreditation criteria revive some standards, tighten others. *Archit Rec* 175:33 Ja '87
Maui (Hawaii)
See also
Beaches—Maui (Hawaii)
Description and travel
Maui's very Hawaiian "up-country," less than an hour from the beaches. il map *Sunset* 179:64 O '87

Maul, Robert C.
about
Robert Maul always leaves 'em laughing. il por *Bus Week* p113 O 12 '87
Mauna Kea Observatory *See* Astronomical observatories—Hawaii
Maundy Thursday
Lenten meditation:
Maundy Thursday: Thomas's testimony. J. B. Shepherd. *Christ Century* 104:327-8 Ap 8 '87
Maupin, Armistead
about
A talk with Armistead Maupin. T. Spain. il por *Publ Wkly* 231:53-4 Mr 20 '87
Mauri Booksellers School (Venice, Italy) *See* Booksellers and bookselling—Study and teaching
Maurice [film] *See* Motion picture reviews—Single works
Maurice Bejart Ballet of the Twentieth Century
Ballet of the Twentieth Century to tour North America. il *Dance Mag* 61:16 Ja '87
Béjart mounts Malraux and The Kabuki. W. Como. il *Dance Mag* 61:84-9 My '87
Béjart's bye-bye to Brussels [move to Lausanne] L. Moffett. por *Dance Mag* 61:62 S '87
Reviews:
Performance of Malraux at the Cirque Royal in Brussels. L. Moffett. il *Dance Mag* 61:20 My '87
Premiere of Trois etudes pour Alexandre at the Théâtre Musical de Paris. L. Moffett. *Dance Mag* 61:21+ O '87
When American critics look, is "Eurotrash" all they see? D. Perlmutter. il *Dance Mag* 61:12 Jl '87
Mauritius
See also
Marriage—Mauritius
Rodrigues Island (Mauritius)
United States—Diplomatic and consular service—Mauritius
Description and travel
Mauritius rises above the dodo. E. Reyes. il *World Press Rev* 34:63 Ja '87
Maus (Comic strip) *See* Comic books, strips, etc.
Mausoleums *See* Tombs
Maverick Books
Maverick [J. R. Erickson] L. Fleischer. *Publ Wkly* 231:52 Je 26 '87
Mawby, Russell G.
University-based public service [adaptation of address, November 10, 1987] *Science* 238:1491 D 11 '87
Max Headroom (Fictional character)
Mad about M-M-Max [cover story] H. F. Waters. il *Newsweek* 109:58-62+ Ap 20 '87
Max goes mainstream. H. F. Waters. il *Newsweek* 109:55 Ap 6 '87
Max Headroom speaks the dreaded 'P-word' [Coke's new ads] S. Ticer. il *Bus Week* p40-1 Mr 16 '87
Max Headroom [television program] *See* Television program reviews—Single works
Maxicare Health Plans, Inc.
Corporate partners in a maxi-marriage [F. Wasserman and P. Anderson] C. Hutton. il pors *Fortune* 115:46 Ja 5 '87
'A time bomb is ticking at Maxicare'. J. Flynn. *Bus Week* p116 Jl 20 '87
Maxilla & Mandible (Firm)
Music boxes and Maxilla & Mandible. H. Bridges. il *Gourmet* 47:28+ S '87
Maxima Corporation
Black computer firm wins $15 million contract in Md. *Jet* 72:8 Jl 13 '87
Maxwell, Charlie
Appliance repair. See issues of The Family Handyman beginning February 1985
Where to buy appliance parts. See issues of The Family Handyman beginning February 1986
Maxwell, Daphne *See* Reid, Daphne Maxwell
Maxwell, Hamish
about
His own best customer. A. Farnham. il por *Fortune* 116:44-5 Ag 3 '87
Maxwell, Jessica
Future toys. il *Omni* 10:60-2+ D '87
Hut-one, hut-two . . . il *Esquire* 108:43-4 D '87
Maxwell, Judith
Economic forecasting [address, May 29, 1987] *Vital Speeches Day* 53:685-6 S 1 '87
Maxwell, Robert
about
Battle of the book barons. R. Henkoff. il por *Newsweek* 109:46 Je 1 '87

A British press lord goes global. P. Sherrid. il por *U S News World Rep* 102:49-50 Je 1 '87
A costly save at Harcourt. P. Engardio. *Bus Week* p42 Je 8 '87
HBJ rejects Maxwell's $1.7 billion bid. il por *Publ Wkly* 231:18 My 29 '87
Jovanovich charges Maxwell is 'unfit' [takeover controversy; with interview] M. Reuter. *Publ Wkly* 231:13-14 Je 5 '87
Jovanovich sees nothing friendly in Maxwell's bid. P. Engardio. il por *Bus Week* p47 Je 1 '87
Maxwell may back Gallo. B. J. Culliton. *Science* 238:1643 D 18 '87
Maxwell sues to block HBJ's $3 billion plan. *Publ Wkly* 231:23 Je 12 '87
Power of the press. E. A. Finn, Jr. il por *Forbes* 139:91 Ja 26 '87
Maxwell, Robert B.
The "graying" of America [address, May 15, 1987] *Vital Speeches Day* 53:710-12 S 15 '87
Maxwell, Ted A.
Exploring deserts. il *Earth Sci* 39:12-14 Wint '86
Maxwell, William
about
Trying to profit from child's play. J. Alexander. il por *Money* 16:162-4 F '87
Maxwell House Division *See* General Foods Corp. Maxwell House Division
Maxxam Group Inc.
A takeover artist who's turning redwoods into quick cash [C. E. Hurwitz's takeover of Pacific Lumber through Maxxam Group] J. R. Norman. il por *Bus Week* p64-5 F 2 '87
Maxym, Lucy
about
When only the best will do. R. Hotch. il por *Nations Bus* 75:78+ My '87
May, Charles *See* May, Karl Friedrich, 1842-1912
May, Clifford, 1908-
about
Architectural digest visits: Robert Wagner. J. Allen. il pors *Archit Dig* 44:124-31+ My '87
May, Elaine
about
Ishtar [film] Reviews
America 156:466+ Je 6 '87. R. A. Blake
Glamour il 85:101 Jl '87. J. G. Boyum
Macleans il 100:54 My 25 '87. L. O'Toole
N Y il 20:105+ My 25 '87. D. Denby
Natl Rev 39:52 Jl 3 '87. J. Simon
New Repub 196:26 Je 8 '87. S. Kauffmann
New Yorker 63:102+ Je 1 '87. P. Kael
Newsweek il por 109:76-8 My 18 '87. D. Ansen
People Wkly 27:8 Je 1 '87. P. Travers
Time il 129:85 My 18 '87. R. Schickel
Vogue il 177:306-7 My '87. T. Young
The road to 'Ishtar'. D. Blum. il pors *N Y* 20:34-43 Mr 16 '87
May, John Lawrence, 1922-, and others
What we have heard and what we will say. *America* 157:102-4 Ag 29-S 5 '87
May, John R.
Tell us your story and we will know who you are. *Am Craft* 47:22+ Je/Jl '87
May, Karl Friedrich, 1842-1912
about
Tales of the Grand Teutons: Karl May among the Indians. F. Morton. por *N Y Times Book Rev* 92:15-16 Ja 4 '87
May, Leland C.
Collecting patented medicine bottles. il *Antiques Collect Hobbies* 91:22-4 Ja '87
May, Peter
about
Who's getting the deal in the Triangle shuffle? C. Power. il por *Bus Week* p78 N 23 '87
May, Philip A.
Suicide among American Indian youth: a look at the issues. bibl f il *Child Today* 16:22-5 Jl/Ag '87
May, Willard
about
Fear and salvation. R. Koselka. por *Forbes* 139:38-9 Je 1 '87
May
The May almanac. il *Atlantic* 259:16 My '87
May Department Stores Co.
David Farrell [acquisition of Associated Dry Goods] M. D. Oneal. il por *Bus Week* Sp Issue:236 Ap 17 '87

May Department Stores Co.—cont.
Powerhouse potential [May Department Stores buys Associated Dry Goods] T. Jaffe. il *Forbes* 139:110 Ja 26 '87
May-Pressley, DeLores
about
Essence woman. J. C. McAdams. il por *Essence* 18:38 Je '87
Mayakovsky, Vladimir, 1894-1930
The Sandinistas' favorite poet. I. Karetnikova. il *Natl Rev* 39:40-2 My 8 '87
Mayan Dude Ranch (Bandera, Tex.) *See* Ranches—Texas
Mayapples
Sex choice and reproductive costs in Jack-in-the-pulpit. D. Policansky. bibl f il *BioScience* 37:476-81 Jl/Ag '87
Mayas

Agriculture
Pollen probe of early Maya farming [work of David J. Rue] *Sci News* 131:218 Ap 4 '87
Unraveling another Mayan mystery. A. Chen. il map *Discover* 8:40-1+ Je '87

Antiquities
See also
Chichén Itzá (Mexico)
Copán (Ancient city)
El Mirador site (Guatemala)
New findings on ancient Maya [satellite images] map *USA Today (Periodical)* 115:11-12 Je '87
Satellites help in study of ancient civilization. *Astronomy* 15:64 Ag '87

Art
Exhibitions
Cenote of sacrifice. V. G. Stoddart. il *Américas* 39:60-2 My/Je '87
Food of the gods [Blood of kings exhibit at Kimbell Art Museum]; tr. by Eliot Weinberger. O. Paz. il *N Y Rev Books* 34:3-7 F 26 '87

History
Why were the Aztecs and Mayas stuck in the Stone Age? Obsidian, a kind of volcanic glass, may be the answer. T. Stocker. *Earth Sci* 40:32 Summ '87

Medicine
'Let the days come in'. J. F. Garcia Ruiz. il *Courier* 40:7 Ag '87

Writing
Column [World Symposium on Maya Epigraphy in Guatemala City] W. E. Garrett. *Natl Geogr* 171:561 My '87
Reading Mayan images. L. Schele. il map *Américas* 39:38-43 Mr/Ap '87
Maychick, Diana
Mel Gibson unbuttoned. por *Mademoiselle* 93:232-4 Mr '87
Mayco Petroleum, Inc.
Staying up when your industry's down [A. L. Holland] D. Holder. il pors *Work Woman* 12:45-6 My '87
Mayeda, Mikko
about
The triumph of Mikko Mayeda. V. Scott. il por *Good Housekeep* 204:40 Mr '87
Mayer, Francois J. P.
about
The young turks making over L.F. Rothschild. C. Farrell. il pors *Bus Week* p58-9 Ag 31 '87
Mayer, Martin, 1928-
The Altmeyer story. il pors *Opera News* 51:8-10 F 28 '87
How capitalism survived the twentieth century. il *Am Herit* 38:46-51 N '87
Make me a star [cover story] il pors *Opera News* 52:10-12+ Jl '87
A random walk through Wall Street. il por *U S News World Rep* 103:64-5 N 16 '87
Seeking the light [cover story] il pors *Opera News* 52:12-15 D 5 '87
Strong medicine for the markets. il *U S News World Rep* 103:34 N 2 '87
Mayer, Robert E.
Paterson PCS 2500 universal pro enlarger. il *Petersens Photogr Mag* 16:60-1+ Jl '87
Mayer (Oscar) & Co. *See* Oscar Mayer & Co.
Mayersohn, Norman
Cycles. See issues of Popular Mechanics beginning January 1986
Mayes, Dennis
"Any time I can be of service". il *Read Dig* 130:9-10 F '87

Mayes, Rueben
about
The saint from Shiloh. J. Lieber. il pors *Sports Illus* 67:50-2+ Ag 17 '87
Mayfair, Billy
about
Mayfairest of them all. J. Diaz. il por *Sports Illus* 67:75 S 7 '87
Mayflower Madam [television program] See Television program reviews—Single works
Maynard, Joyce, 1953-
Books. See issues of Mademoiselle beginning January 1985
Visit with my grandmother [excerpt from Domestic affairs] il pors *Ladies Home J* 104:42+ Ap '87
Maynes, Charles William
America's chance. *Foreign Policy* 68:88-99 Fall '87
Mayo, John S.
New developments in computer and communications technologies [address, March 31, 1987] *Vital Speeches Day* 53:499-503 Je 1 '87
Mayo Clinic (Rochester, Minn.)
The world's greatest hospital. B. Keating. il *50 Plus* 27:60-2+ Ja '87
Mayonnaise
Pleasant occasions [75th birthday of Hellmann's] N. Hazelton. *Natl Rev* 39:60+ D 4 '87
Sweet and tart fruit aïoli. il *Sunset* 178:212 Ap '87
Mayor, Federico
about
A scientist back at the helm of Unesco? D. Dickson. por *Science* 238:473-4 O 23 '87
Mayor Zaragoza, Federico *See* Mayor, Federico
Mayors
See also
Black mayors
The best of city hall. il *U S News World Rep* 103:54-5 D 21 '87

Conferences
Prichard, Ala.'s Smith is black mayors' leader [J. H. Smith] por *Jet* 72:24 My 18 '87
Mayotte Island
Sovereignty of Comoros over island of Mayotte reaffirmed by Assembly. *UN Chron* 24:82 F '87
Mays, Benjamin Elijah, 1895-1984
about
New HU Divinity School named for Benjamin E. Mays gets $750,000 Lilly Award. *Jet* 72:30 My 18 '87
Mays, John Bentley
Stylistic ensembles [cover story] il por *Am Craft* 47:42-9 O/N '87
Mays, Lyle
about
Lyle Mays: catching a (sound) wave [interview; cover story] G. Santoro. il pors *Down Beat* 54:16-19 Jl '87
Mays, Michael
about
Willie Mays' cancer-ill son faces charges of guns, pot possession. il pors *Jet* 72:18 Ag 3 '87
Mays (Benjamin E.) Academy of Scholars See Benjamin E. Mays Academy of Scholars
Mayson, Frank
about
Should a Mormon-owned corporation be able to fire a Mormon who does not tithe? R. F. Drinan. il *America* 156:375-6 My 9 '87
Supreme Court hears challenge to church hiring policies. E. J. Larson. *Christ Today* 31:49-50 My 15 '87
Maytag Co.
Maytag's new girth will test its marketing muscle [Magic Chef acquisition] K. Deveny. il *Bus Week* p68+ F 16 '87
Mazankowski, Don
about
The Minister of Everything. P. Gessell. il por *Macleans* 100:12 S 14 '87
Mazda (Automobile) *See* Automobiles, Foreign; Sports cars
Mazel, Charles
Technology and the marine archaeologist. il *Courier* 40:15-21 N '87
Mazer, Roslyn A.
Take a kid to the ball game. por *Newsweek* 109:8 Ap 6 '87
Mazes *See* Labyrinths
Mazie, David M.
(jt. auth) See Rowan, Carl Thomas, 1925-, and Mazie, David M.
Mazlish, Elaine
(jt. auth) See Faber, Adele, and Mazlish, Elaine

Mazoué, Jo Ann
I saved my family from asbestos contamination. il por *Good Housekeep* 204:108 Ap '87
Mazur, Jay
Industrial homework and sweatshops [address, July 20, 1987] *Vital Speeches Day* 53:701-2 S 1 '87
The return of the sweat shop. il *USA Today (Periodical)* 115:31-3 Mr '87
Should the "Minimum Wage Restoration Act of 1987" be approved? [excerpts from testimony, July 23, 1987] *Congr Dig* 66:216+ Ag/S '87
MBA/Strategies (Firm)
A little friendly advice—at $100 an hour. por *Bus Week* p46 Mr 9 '87
MBAs (Masters of Business Administration) *See* Business schools and colleges—Graduates
M'Baye, Malick
(jt. auth) *See* Ndoye, Thianar, and M'Baye, Malick
MBB *See* Messerschmitt-Bölkow-Blohm GmbH
Mbeki, Govan
about
ANC leader Mbeki freed after 23 years in jail. il *Jet* 73:28 N 23 '87
'The government smashes our hope'. il por *Newsweek* 110:49 D 21 '87
Out of jail and on his feet. R. Nordland. il por *Newsweek* 110:81 N 16 '87
The return of a rebel. il por *U S News World Rep* 103:16-17 N 16 '87
Why free Mbeki? S. Mufson. *Nation* 245:670-1 D 5 '87
MBFR (Mutual and Balanced Force Reductions Talks) *See* Disarmament—Conferences
MCA Inc.
Entertaining offers. A. D. Frank. il *Forbes* 140:33-4 N 2 '87
A Hollywood thriller: MCA vs. the sharks. J. Egan. il por *U S News World Rep* 103:44-5 S 7 '87
It's King Kong vs. the 'ravenous rat' [MCA and Disney compete for theme park market in Europe] K. Kelly. il *Bus Week* p54 O 5 '87
Theme parks: this slugfest is no fantasy [Disney vs. MCA] R. Grover. il *Bus Week* p38 Mr 23 '87
MCA Records, Inc.
2120 S. Michigan Ave. [MCA rereleases Chess archives] J. Brinsfield. *Down Beat* 54:30 Mr '87
The pulse of Impulse [digitally remastered discs from Impulse catalog] J. Balleras. *Down Beat* 54:32+ Ja '87
Second Impulse [second batch of Impulse jazz reissues] K. Whitehead. il *Down Beat* 54:38+ S '87
McAdam, Dale
Terms of complaint. *Change* 19:7 Mr/Ap '87
McAdam, Denise
about
Thanks to Denise McAdam, Fergie always turns up tressed for success. il por *People Wkly* 28:30-1 Jl 20 '87
McAdams, A. James (Arthur James)
A new deal for Eastern Europe. *Nation* 244:799-800+ Je 13 '87
McAdams, Arthur James *See* McAdams, A. James (Arthur James)
McAdoo, Bob, 1951-
about
McAdoo a driving force in Italy. por *Jet* 73:50 N 2 '87
McAdoo does it right for Italian league hoop team. por *Jet* 72:50 Je 1 '87
McAleer, Neil, 1942-
Archaeology from above. il map *Space World* X-2-278:21-5 F '87
The light stuff: laser propulsion. il *Space World* X-7-283:9-11 Jl '87
The sixth mission: a space station diary. il *Space World* X-5-281:12-19 My '87
The space age turns 30. il *Space World* X-10-286:7-13 O '87
McAllister, Bruce
Kingdom come [fiction] il *Omni* 9:60-2+ F '87
McArdle, Andrea
about
Jumpin' Jehoshaphat! It's little Annie, Andrea McArdle, who's now pumping life into Starlight Express. D. Hutchings. il pors *People Wkly* 27:67-8 Ap 27 '87
McArdle, Frank B.
Congress and the work place: tax reform and employee benefits [address, December 3, 1986] *Vital Speeches Day* 53:215-19 Ja 15 '87

McArthur, Edwin, 1907-1987
about
Obituary
Opera News il por 51:13 Je '87. S. Flatow
McArtor, T. Allan
about
McArtor cites quality control in call for inspection program. E. H. Phillips. *Aviat Week Space Technol* 127:41 O 5 '87
McArtor orders industry-wide assessment of pilot training. *Aviat Week Space Technol* 127:20-1 Ag 24 '87
McArtor presses for safety gains, airport construction in 1988 plan. P. Proctor. *Aviat Week Space Technol* 127:36 S 21 '87
The new FAA chief flies into a storm of flak. S. Payne. por *Bus Week* p33 Ag 24 '87
Nominee for FAA administrator cites safety, improved ATC as priorities. P. Proctor. *Aviat Week Space Technol* 127:32 Jl 13 '87
McAuliffe, Christa
about
The death and life of Christa McAuliffe [excerpt from I touch the future] R. T. Hohler. il pors *Good Housekeep* 204:90-3+ Ja '87
"I touch the future . . . " [condensation] R. T. Hohler. il pors *Read Dig* 130:78-85 Je '87
Remembering Christa [special section] il pors *Ladies Home J* 104:76+ F '87
McAuliffe, Kathleen
Genes that predict disease. il *Read Dig* 131:17-18+ S '87
McBain, Laurie
Some problems for the historical novelist. *Writer* 100:24-7 Ag '87
McBarton, Bob
A caveat for candidates. por *Newsweek* 110:14 O 19 '87
McBride, Bunny
Game watching in Tanzania. il *Travel Holiday* 168:22+ Jl '87
Outward bound for chimps. il map *Int Wildl* 17:18-21 S/O '87
McBride, James
Tillich in an Alice-in-Wonderland world. *Christ Century* 104:519-20 Je 3-10 '87
McBride, Jim
about
The Big Easy [film] Reviews
Glamour il 85:227 O '87. J. G. Boyum
Macleans 100:49 Ag 24 '87. L. O'Toole
N Y il 20:110+ Ag 24 '87. D. Denby
New Repub 197:27 S 28 '87. S. Kauffmann
New Yorker 63:100 S 7 '87. P. Kael
People Wkly il 28:8 Ag 31 '87. P. Travers
Time il 130:65 Ag 24 '87. R. Schickel
McBride, Margaret
about
Madame ambassador. L. Fleischer. *Publ Wkly* 232:153 S 18 '87
McBride, Patricia
about
McBride gets to the pointe. O. Stuart. por *Harpers Bazaar* 120:139+ Ag '87
McBride, Stewart
Racing's record-breaker. il pors *N Y Times Mag* p42+ N 8 '87
McBrien, Richard P.
Free speech in the Catholic Church [address, December 19, 1986] *Vital Speeches Day* 53:237-40 F 1 '87
Homosexuality & the priesthood. *Commonweal* 114:380-3 Je 19 '87
Homosexuality & the priesthood [discussion of June 19, 1987 article] *Commonweal* 114:493-7 S 11 '87
about
Of many things. G. W. Hunt. *America* 156:inside cover Mr 28 '87
McBroom, Patricia
You won't get ahead without a mentor (and other executive phony tales). il *Mademoiselle* 93:238-9+ Ap '87
McCabe, Edward A.
Eight thousand miles of bad road. il pors map *Esquire* 108:96-104 Jl '87
McCabe, J. Terrence, and Ellis, J. E.
Beating the odds in arid Africa. il map *Nat Hist* 96:32-41 Ja '87
McCabe, Joe
Members only: what every guy wants a girl to know. *Mademoiselle* 93:278-9+ Mr '87
McCabe, Stephen
(jt. auth) *See* Edwords, Frederick, and McCabe, Stephen

McCaffrey, Kathleen
 Breaking the silence. il *Commonweal* 114:418-20 Jl 17
  '87
McCaig, Donald
 The legendary Dodge Power Wagon. il *Ctry J* 14:28-33
  My '87
McCain, John S., 1936-
 Should Congress move to invoke the War Powers Resolu-
  tion? [excerpts from debate, October 9, 1987] *Congr
  Dig* 66:299+ D '87
McCall, Bruce
 World Expo Larry 'n' Dot '87: an appraisal. il *New
  Yorker* 63:32-3 F 23 '87
McCall, Nathan
 Atlanta: the city of the next generation. il *Black Enterp*
  17:56-8 My '87
 How Herman Russell built his business . . . brick by
  brick. il pors *Black Enterp* 17:176-80+ Je '87
 Making fast money in high finance. il *Black Enterp*
  17:52-6 F '87
 Universal Life's policy for growth. il por *Black Enterp*
  17:232-4+ Je '87
McCall, Robert B.
 About fathers. See issues of Parents beginning July 1985
McCall Pattern Co.
 Black investor realizes mammoth 90-to-1 return [R. F.
  Lewis] por *Jet* 72:6 Jl 27 '87
McCalla, Gary E.
 Life at Southern living. See issues of Southern Living
McCall's (Periodical)
 From our editor. E. Sloan. See issues of McCall's begin-
  ning March 1986
 Reader of the Year [S. Eberhardt] il pors *McCalls*
  115:41-6+ O '87
McCallum, Jack, 1949-
 Atop the Pacific Rim. il *Sports Illus* 67:22-3 D 14
  '87
 Back to haunt the Sixers. il pors *Sports Illus* 66:28-9
  Mr 16 '87
 The battle of the band-aids. il *Sports Illus* 67:32-4+
  D 21 '87
 Big birds on the wing. il *Sports Illus* 66:44-6+ Ap 20
  '87
 Building a basis for dreams. il pors *Sports Illus* 67:22-3
  D 21 '87
 Crunch time [cover story] il *Sports Illus* 66:18-23 Je
  15 '87
 Doc across America. il *Sports Illus* 66:74-5 My 4 '87
 Don't play it again: the NFL should do away with
  the instant replay. por *Sports Illus* 67 Sp Issue:130
  S 9 '87
 Getting fooled by drugs: the perils of taking NBA cocaine
  users at their word. il por *Sports Illus* 66:70 Ja 26
  '87
 Give the NBA a break. por *Sports Illus* 67:116 N 9
  '87
 Green and mean. il *Sports Illus* 66:22-7 My 25 '87
 Hey, Tom can smile! il pors *Sports Illus* 67:64+ N
  23 '87
 In your face, comrades! il *Sports Illus* 67:50-2+ N 2
  '87
 It's a brave new World. il por *Sports Illus* 67:78 D
  14 '87
 Jock lit. il *Sports Illus* 67:80-4+ S 21 '87
 The joy of getting even. il por *Sports Illus* 66:28-30
  My 4 '87
 The king at his new court. il pors *Sports Illus* 67:36-9+
  N 16 '87
 Laying down the L.A. law. il *Sports Illus* 66:20-3 F
  23 '87
 Like father, like sons. il por *Sports Illus* 67:32-3 Jl
  6 '87
 More than meets the eye. il por *Sports Illus* 66:162+
  F 9 '87
 The mystique goes on [cover story] il *Sports Illus* 66:30-2+
  Je 8 '87
 The NBA's unsung heroes. il *Sports Illus* 66:42-4+ Mr
  9 '87
 No apple for the Orangemen. il *Sports Illus* 66:18-19
  Mr 30 '87
 Not first class, coach: Rick Pitino deserted Providence,
  and so his players suffer. por *Sports Illus* 67:86 Ag
  3 '87
 Opening tips. il *Sports Illus* 67:70-3 N 9 '87
 Playing it tough in the East. il *Sports Illus* 66:34-6+
  Je 1 '87
 Pop in his bat, or in his corner? il pors *Sports Illus*
  66:24-5 Mr 23 '87
 Scouting reports. il *Sports Illus* 67:74-8+ N 9 '87
 Slap crackles and pops. il por *Sports Illus* 67:66 N
  16 '87

 There's just no doubting Thomas [cover story] il pors
  Sports Illus 66:30-2+ My 18 '87
 They can't get off the ground. il *Sports Illus* 66:54+
  Ja 19 '87
 They're front and Central. il *Sports Illus* 66:14-17 Mr
  2 '87
 The three-point uproar. il *Sports Illus* 66:40-3 Ja 5 '87
 Tom McMillen (D., Md.). il pors *Sports Illus* 66:70-4
  F 23 '87
 Twenty-seven's a crowd: the last thing the NBA needed
  was four new franchises. por *Sports Illus* 66:92 My
  25 '87
 Wake me when it's over. por *Sports Illus* 67:112 D
  14 '87
 What's going on here? por *Sports Illus* 67:74 S 28 '87
 Your ball, L.A. [cover story] il *Sports Illus* 66:14-21
  Je 22 '87
McCallum, Mike, 1957?-
   about
 Loud left from a quiet champ. P. Putnam. il pors *Sports
  Illus* 67:34-5 Jl 27 '87
McCallum, Napoleon
   about
 Navy tackles McCallum, and checks Robinson. pors
  Jet 72:50 My 11 '87
McCammon, J. Andrew
 Computer-aided molecular design. bibl f il *Science*
  238:486-91 O 23 '87
McCann, Peggy
   about
 To be whole again: mastectomy treated Peggy McCann's
  cancer, but breast reconstruction made her well. D.
  E. Haupt. il pors *Life* 10:78-83+ My '87
McCardell, Claire, 1905-1958
   about
 Designing women. D. Drier. il pors *Art Am* 75:21-3
  My '87
McCarran-Walter Act
 May the U.S. ban "undesirable" foreigners? [case of
  E. Mandel] S. Flack. *Sch Update* 120:35-6 O 2 '87
 U.S. visa policy: the machinery of exclusion [Act of
  1952; cover story; with editorial comment] J. Kalven.
  bibl f il *Bull At Sci* 43:2, 21-30 My '87
McCarroll, Anne
 Raising chair awareness. il *Saturday Evening Post* 259:22
  S '87
McCarroll, Tolbert
 Where does God live? il *Parents* 62:102-4+ D '87
McCarron, Chris
   about
 The hands have it: jockey Chris McCarron and Alysheba
  grab for racing's Triple Crown. il pors *People Wkly*
  27:48-50 Je 8 '87
McCarter, Brooke
   about
 The Lost Boys: behind the scenes [interview] il pors
  Teen 31:49+ Jl '87
McCarther twins *See* Siamese twins
McCarthy, Abigail
 Of several minds. See alternate issues of Commonweal
McCarthy, Colman
 Big man on campus. *Nation* 244:252-4 F 28 '87
McCarthy, Eugene J., 1916-
 Capital takes advantage. il *Commonweal* 114:37-8 Ja
  30 '87
 Fawn Hall among the Antinomians [poem] *New Repub*
  197:14 S 14-21 '87
   about
 Of many things. G. W. Hunt. *America* 156:inside cover
  My 2 '87
McCarthy, Laura Flynn
 The addictive personality: are you a creature of habits?
  il *Mademoiselle* 93:184 S '87
 Do you have diet know-how? il *Mademoiselle* 93:136+
  Ap '87
 How to buy a used car. il *Seventeen* 46:90 My '87
 How to outsmart a headache. il *Mademoiselle* 93:116+
  Mr '87
 My best—and worst—date ever. il *Seventeen* 46:192+
  Mr '87
 Test your clutter quotient. il *Seventeen* 46:50+ F '87
McCarthy, Mary, 1912-
   about
 Our woman of letters. M. Kakutani. il pors *N Y Times
  Mag* p60-1+ Mr 29 '87
McCarthy, Paul
 Sterilization and its discontents. il *Psychol Today* 21:10+
  O '87
 Yawning to breathe free? il *Psychol Today* 21:9-10 F
  '87

McCarthy, Rebecca
  Trouble in the underworld. il *Ctry J* 14:18-21 S '87
McCarthy, Sheila
          about
  Mermaids' star Sheila McCarthy, who's heard the critics
    singing. il por *People Wkly* 28:89 N 9 '87
McCarthy, Crisanti & Maffei, Inc.
  Junkyard analyst [P. Maffei] J. Willoughby. il por *Forbes*
    140:230+ N 2 '87
McCarthyism *See* Anti-Communist movements—History
McCartney, Paul
          about
  Goals of 'Sgt. Pepper' yet to materialize: McCartney.
    por *Jet* 72:59 Je 22 '87
  Paul McCartney [interview] A. DeCurtis. por *Roll Stone*
    p39-40+ N 5-D 10 '87
McCarty, Kim
          about
  View from Malibu: Michael and Kim McCarty in Califor-
    nia. B. D. Colen. il pors *Archit Dig* 44:96-101+ Jl
    '87
McCarty, Michael
          about
  View from Malibu: Michael and Kim McCarty in Califor-
    nia. B. D. Colen. il pors *Archit Dig* 44:96-101+ Jl
    '87
McCarty, Willy
          about
  Exercise for life: new expert thinking [interview] il *Vogue*
    177:346-7+ D '87
McCarver, Tim
  Catchers and pitchers [excerpt from Oh, baby, I love
    it!] il *Sport Mag* 78:56 Jl '87
McCauley, George
  Faith in Jesus. *America* 156:282 Ap 4 '87
  Faith, institution and community. *America* 156:259+ Mr
    28 '87
  Goodbye to some of that. il *America* 157:328-30 N
    7 '87
  New Testament perspectives on faith (I). il *America*
    156:200 Mr 7 '87
  New Testament perspectives on faith (II). *America*
    156:217 Mr 14 '87
  New Testament perspectives on faith (III). *America*
    156:236 Mr 21 '87
  Old Testament forms of faith. *America* 156:177 F 28
    '87
McCausland, Peter
          about
  Life is a gas. R. Simon. il por *Forbes* 140:114+ D
    14 '87
McCaw Cellular Communications Inc.
  Hot number. E. B. Gibbs. il *Channels* 7:69 S '87
MccGwire, Michael K., 1924-
  The changing role of the Soviet Navy. il *Bull At Sci*
    43:34-9 S '87
  Why the Soviets want arms control. il *Technol Rev*
    90:36-45 F/Mr '87
McClain, John
          about
  John McClain creates solid gold money-makers. A. Ed-
    mond, Jr. il por *Black Enterp* 18:54-7+ N '87
McClain, Thomas
          about
  Welcome aboard. The champagne is on ice. S. Toy.
    il por *Bus Week* p61-2 Ja 19 '87
McClain, William H., and others
  Model substrates for an RNA enzyme. bibl f il *Science*
    238:527-30 O 23 '87
McClain Airlines Inc.
  Welcome aboard. The champagne is on ice. S. Toy.
    il por *Bus Week* p61-2 Ja 19 '87
McClanahan, Rue
          about
  Rue on the road [cover story] il pors *50 Plus* 27:38-49
    S '87
  The world according to Blanche [interview] J. Porcino.
    il por *50 Plus* 27:31 S '87
McClane, A. J. (Albert Jules), 1922-
  Claws for celebration. il *Esquire* 108:21-2 Ag '87
  A new angle on trout. il *Esquire* 107:36 My '87
  The nine lives of the catfish. il *Esquire* 107:25-6 F
    '87
McClane, Albert Jules *See* McClane, A. J. (Albert Jules),
    1922-
McClaney, Eula
          about
  From Alabama fields to Holmby Hills. P. F. Stewart.
    il por *Ladies Home J* 104:154 O '87

McCleary, Kathleen
  Take care of your working back. il *Work Woman* 12:154+
    Ap '87
McClellan, Gary
  New life for old car radios (I). il *Radio-Electron* 58:42-4
    My '87
  New life for old car radios (II). il *Radio-Electron* 58:50-2
    Je '87
McClellan, J. Mac
  Technicalities. See alternate issues of Flying
McClellan, Mary C.
  (jt. auth) See Barber, Larry W., and McClellan, Mary
    C.
McClelland, Jack
          about
  A bookman bids farewell. P. Young. il por *Macleans*
    100:50 Mr 2 '87
  McClelland leaves publishing; sells Seal interest to Key
    Porter. B. Slopen. por *Publ Wkly* 231:35 Mr 6 '87
McClelland, Kacy R.
          about
  A friend on their side. E. J. Kahn. *New Yorker* 62:72-7
    Ja 19 '87
McClelland & Stewart
  A bookman bids farewell [J. McClelland retires] P. Young.
    il por *Macleans* 100:50 Mr 2 '87
  McClelland leaves publishing; sells Seal interest to Key
    Porter. B. Slopen. por *Publ Wkly* 231:35 Mr 6 '87
McClendon, Lowery
  Woman of the leaves [poem] *Essence* 18:122 D
    '87
McClester, Cedric
  The view from 40. por *Essence* 18:12 D '87
McClintock, Jack
  Real trouble ahead. il *N Y Times Mag* p40 Ag 9 '87
  Remote sensing: adding to our knowledge of oceans—and
    earth. il *Sea Front* 33:105-13 Mr/Ap '87
McClintock, Jessica
          about
  Meet designer Jessica McClintock. K. Evans. il pors
    Seventeen 46:206-9+ Ap '87
McClinton, Katharine Morrison
  Children's tea sets. il *Antiques Collect Hobbies* 92:18-21
    Jl '87
  Collectible kitchenware. il *Antiques Collect Hobbies*
    92:13-16 My '87
  Stevengraph bookmarkers. il *Antiques Collect Hobbies*
    91:51-4 Ja '87
McClinton, O. B., 1942-1987
          about
  Obituary
    Jet por 73:13 O 19 '87
McClory, Robert
  Sanctuary: should parishes break the law for a stranger?
    il *U S Cathol* 52:32-8 My '87
McCloskey, Frank, 1939-
  Should Congress adopt the House-passed "Gephardt
    Amendment"? [excerpts from debate, April 29, 1987]
    Congr Dig 66:186+ Je/Jl '87
McCloskey, Robert, 1914-
          about
  Boston makes way for ducklings: the Mallard family
    in bronze. A. Meeker. il *Publ Wkly* 232:27 O 30
    '87
McCloskey, William
  Why men fish. il *Int Wildl* 17:34-40 Mr/Ap '87
McCloud, Mac
  Deliberately decorative: the ceramics of Ralph Bacerra.
    il por *Am Craft* 47:50-5 Je/Jl '87
McCluggage, Denise
  [Column on automobiles] See occasional issues of
    Glamour beginning February 1983
  When you're driving alone. il *Essence* 18:112 S '87
McCluggage, Kerry
          about
  Universal changing the rules. J. Von Herrmann. por
    Channels 7:12 My '87
McClure, Bruce
  Watching earth move with the shadow clock. il *Astronomy*
    15:32-5 Ag '87
McClure, Jessica
          about
  Baby Jessica. il por *People Wkly* 28:34-5 D 28 '87-Ja
    4 '88
  A brave little girl. G. Hackett. il por *Newsweek* 110:41
    O 26 '87
  The epic rescue of Jessica McClure [cover story] L.
    Hart and A. Maier. il pors *People Wkly* 28:42-7 N
    2 '87
  Good news for Baby Jessica. il *Newsweek* 110:8 N 2
    '87

McClure, Jessica—about—*cont.*
One went right. W. Shapiro. il pors *Time* 130:30-1 O 26 '87
Saving the babies. il por *Macleans* 100:49 O 26 '87
McClure [drama] See Scott, Munroe
McColl, Patricia
Bohan: the power behind Dior. il pors *Harpers Bazaar* 120:162+ S '87
McCollister, John
George Burns: an American treasure. il pors *Saturday Evening Post* 259:58-9 My/Je '87
The violinist from left field. il pors *Saturday Evening Post* 259:30+ D '87
McConaghy, Tom
Internships in Alberta. *Phi Delta Kappan* 68:794-5 Je '87
Legislation threatens B.C. Teachers' Federation. *Phi Delta Kappan* 69:310-11 D '87
Teachers as researchers: learning through teaching. il *Phi Delta Kappan* 68:630-1 Ap '87
McConkey, Phil, 1957-
about
McConkey: an unlikely hero. E. M. Swift. il *Sports Illus* 66:22-3 F 2 '87
McConnell, David
Clouds of the twilight. il *Astronomy* 15:42-7 Jl '87
McConnell, J. R.
about
J. R. McConnell: the ballad of a Texas tornado. T. Vogel. il por *Bus Week* p80+ N 9 '87
McConnell, Jean
Come soar with me [story] il *Good Housekeep* 204:110+ Ap '87
McConnell, John M.
Brief encounter. il *America* 157:101 Ag 29-S 5 '87
McConnell, Kevin
American historical flasks: glassware symbolic of a growing nation. il *Antiques Collect Hobbies* 92:40-2 O '87
Ceramic inkwells: pottery gems from the past. bibl il *Antiques Collect Hobbies* 92:28-31 S '87
Collecting redware: America's folk art pottery. bibl il *Antiques Collect Hobbies* 92:24-7 Mr '87
McConnell, Malcolm
about
Lost in space. G. Easterbrook. *Wash Mon* 19:48-54 Ap '87
McConnell, Michael
Europe's sanctuary movement: grappling with governments. il *Christ Century* 104:1001-3 N 11 '87
McConnell, Mitch
Should the proposed Product Liability Reform Act be approved? [excerpts from debate, September 22, 1986] *Congr Dig* 66:22+ Ja '87
McConnell, Scott
Campus controversy. *New Repub* 196:13-14 My 25 '87
Resurrecting the new left. *Commentary* 84:31-8 O '87
McConnell, Shay
Top-notch foot care. il *Harpers Bazaar* 120:80+ Mr '87
Will your face-lift be a letdown? *Harpers Bazaar* 120:97+ Ag '87
McCord, Gary
about
The course jester of CBS. W. Taaffe. il por *Sports Illus* 66:93 Je 8 '87
McCorkle, Susannah
about
Susannah McCorkle. C. Albertson. il por *Stereo Rev* 52:180 D '87
McCormack, Mark H.
about
Mark McCormack does everything but play the game. D. Cook and others. il por *Bus Week* p52-3 Ag 31 '87
McCormick, Brian
The shame of wanting. il *Atlantic* 259:36-7 F '87
McCormick, Frank
(jt. auth) See Trahey, Meg, and McCormick, Frank
McCormick, John, 1918-
Francis Fergusson, 1904-1986. *Am Sch* 56:557-64 Aut '87
McCormick, Kathleen
AIDS instruction: a troubling test for educators. *Educ Dig* 53:56-9 S '87
The school executive shortage: how serious is it? *Educ Dig* 53:2-5 D '87
McCormick, Richard A., 1922-
The Vatican document on bioethics: some unsolicited suggestions. il *America* 156:24-8+ Ja 17 '87
The Vatican document on bioethics: two responses. *America* 156:247-8 Mr 28 '87

(jt. auth) See Paris, John J., and McCormick, Richard A., 1922-
McCormick, Robert, and Meiners, Roger
Bust the college sports cartel. il pors *Fortune* 116:235-6 O 12 '87
McCormick, Virginia
When teaching excellence does not pay off. *Educ Dig* 52:14-15 F '87
McCormick & Co. Inc.
A close call. J. Novack. il *Forbes* 139:38 Ja 26 '87
McCormick County (S.C.)
Politics and government
First black sheriff is elected in McCormick, S.C. [G. Reid] por *Jet* 71:17 F 2 '87
Give us just one honest man . . . please [race for sheriff] il *Newsweek* 109:31 F 9 '87
McCosh, Dan
Automotive newsfront. See issues of Popular Science beginning January 1986
Honda four-wheel steering. il *Pop Sci* 230:18 F '87
McCoy, Elin
Child labor. il *Parents* 62:94-9 Ag '87
McCoy, Frank
What to do with your severance package. il *Black Enterp* 17:63-4 Mr '87
McCoy, Jean L.
An angel from Tennessee. il pors *McCalls* 114:132-4 Je '87
McCoy, John A.
The Catholic Church in Bolivia. *America* 157:263-5 O 24 '87
McCoy, Karrie
about
The sound of a miracle. T. Rademacher. il pors *Seventeen* 46:96-8 My '87
McCoy, Kathleen
Arctic dreams. il pors *Women's Sports Fitness* 9:22-7+ F '87
McCoy, Kathleen, 1945-
Overweight or underconfident? Coming to terms with your body. *Seventeen* 46:32+ F '87
Sex and your body. See issues of Seventeen beginning June 1983
McCoy, Kathy See McCoy, Kathleen, 1945-
McCoy, Sharon
A water workout that works! il *Teen* 31:90-1 Je '87
McCoy, William
about
The real McCoy. J. F. Mariani. il *Mot Boat Sail* 160:30 O '87
McCracken, Gary F., and Gustin, Mary K.
Batmom's daily nightmare. il map *Nat Hist* 96:66-73 O '87
McCracken, James, 1926-1988
about
Singing day to day. D. McGovern. pors *Opera News* 52:38+ O '87
McCracken, John, 1934-
about
John McCracken at P.S. 1. S. Westfall. *Art Am* 75:214 Ap '87
McCrackin, Maurice F.
about
The restoration of Maurice McCrackin. D. Peerman. il *Christ Century* 104:998-1000 N 11 '87
McCreary, David
John Bennett on Oxford '37. il por *Christ Century* 104:942-4 O 28 '87
McCree, Wade H., 1920-1987
about
Obituary
Jet por 72:55 S 14 '87
McCrory, Patti
Create armour from junkyard scrap. il *Theatre Crafts* 21:66 F '87
McCulley, Mary
about
Pro challenge. il por *Pop Photogr* 94:58 Ag '87
McCullough, R. Michael
about
Is Booz Allen having a mid-life crisis? L. Baum. il por *Bus Week* p76+ Mr 9 '87
McCune, Kate
The Jeffery Amherst Bookshop: cultivating a narrow specialty. il pors *Publ Wkly* 232:29-31 Jl 3 '87
McCutcheon, Shaw
Armorica the beautiful: France's land by the sea. il map *Travel Holiday* 168:66-71+ Jl '87
Beached in Belau: the South Pacific's water playground. il map *Travel Holiday* 168:60-5 D '87

McDaniel, Thomas R.
Using positive reinforcement. *Educ Dig* 53:36-9 O '87
McDavid, David
about
Science at McDonald Observatory. R. Reeves. il pors *Astronomy* 15:6-17 Jl '87
McDermott, Barry
Switching signals. il *Life* 10:43+ N '87
McDermott, Irene S.
Mother & child. See issues of Good Housekeeping beginning January 1986
McDermott, James E.
All about spread spectrum communications. il *Radio-Electron* 58:55-8 Ap '87
McDermott, John W.
Defining the role of religion in the American classroom. *Educ Dig* 52:14-17 Ap '87
McDermott International, Inc.
Oil service service. T. Jaffe. *Forbes* 139:154 F 9 '87
McDonald, Ann Gilbert
Samuel Weller: illustrious citizen of Zanesville. il *Antiques Collect Hobbies* 92:32-5 Ap '87
McDonald, Dick
Marketing [address, April 3, 1987] *Vital Speeches Day* 53:566-72 Jl 1 '87
McDonald, Donald
Can the press tell the truth? il por *Cent Mag* 20:19-32 S/O '87
about
Donald McDonald—a career of commitment. P. McDonald. *Cent Mag* 20:18 S/O '87
McDonald, Erroll
about
A talk with Erroll McDonald, editor of the 1986 Nobel laureate for literature. G. Blooston. por *Publ Wkly* 231:86+ Mr 6 '87
McDonald, Frank B.
Space research: at a crossroads. bibl f *Science* 235:751-4 F 13 '87
McDonald, Gregory A., and others
Cloned gene of rickettsia rickettsii surface antigen: candidate vaccine for Rocky Mountain spotted fever. bibl f il *Science* 235:83-5 Ja 2 '87
McDonald, H. Gregory
(jt. auth) See Shaw, Christopher A., and McDonald, H. Gregory
McDonald, Joe
One picture . . . il *Audubon* 89:80-1 Ja '87
McDonald, Kitt
about
Eartha Kitt's daughter weds attorney in N.Y. il pors *Jet* 72:60-1 Jl 6 '87
McDonald, Marci
Undermining the Sandinistas. il *World Press Rev* 34:21-3 Ap '87
Would you believe . . . Iranian moderates? [cover story] *Wash Mon* 19:39-45+ Mr '87
McDonald, Tim
about
A little UHF group tries a great big gamble. C. S. Eklund. il por *Bus Week* p84+ F 2 '87
McDonald, Walter
Cattle in rain [poem] *Ctry J* 14:54 Ja '87
Moses, at Jordan [poem] *America* 156:158 F 21 '87
Night missions [poem] *America* 156:176 F 28 '87
The Southern Pacific [poem] *America* 156:481 Je 13 '87
McDonald Observatory (Austin, Tex.) See Astronomical observatories
McDonald's Corp.
60 billion burgers—and counting. P. O. D'Aulaire and E. D'Aulaire. il *Read Dig* 131:39-40+ D '87
Big Mac strikes back. S. Koepp. il *Time* 129:58-60 Ap 13 '87
A McDonald's coins big McMoney [A. Lencioni's restaurants in Chicago] J. Alexander. il *Money* 16:37+ D '87
McQueen of the Golden Arches [black franchisee L. Heard] L. Gite. il pors *Black Enterp* 18:64-6+ S '87
McDonell, Keri
about
Great Model Search '87 [special section] il pors *Teen* 31:82-91 O '87
McDonnell, Donald P., and others
Molecular cloning of complementary DNA encoding the avian receptor for vitamin D. bibl f il *Science* 235:1214-17 Mr 6 '87

McDonnell, Jim
about
The husband who vanished. J. P. Blank. il pors *Read Dig* 130:131-5 Ja '87
McDonnell, John F.
about
The odd couple at McDonnell Douglas. C. Leinster. il pors *Fortune* 115:120-1+ Je 22 '87
McDonnell, Sanford N.
First word. por *Omni* 9:4 Jl '87
about
The odd couple at McDonnell Douglas. C. Leinster. il pors *Fortune* 115:120-1+ Je 22 '87
McDonnell Douglas Corp.
Air-India considers MD-11 for key role in fleet rejuvenation. *Aviat Week Space Technol* 126:30 My 25 '87
Airframe makers near key technology decisions. R. G. O'Lone. il *Aviat Week Space Technol* 126:183-5+ Mr 9 '87
Bids in a jumbo gamble [MD-11 vs. A-340] J. Barber. il *Macleans* 100:46-7 Ja 19 '87
Boeing, McDonnell Douglas programs reflect need for collaborative efforts. R. G. O'Lone. il *Aviat Week Space Technol* 126:301-2+ Je 15 '87
British Aerospace, McDonnell Douglas will propose new Harrier version [AV-8B/GR. 5 Advanced Harrier] *Aviat Week Space Technol* 126:24 Je 22 '87
Chinese join wing, fuselage of second coproduced MD-82. W. B. Scott. *Aviat Week Space Technol* 127:38-9 Ag 17 '87
Commercial Delta 2 to be priced lower than international competitors. T. M. Foley. *Aviat Week Space Technol* 126:23-4 F 2 '87
Douglas advances MD-91X target launch date by half-year. *Aviat Week Space Technol* 126:33 My 25 '87
Douglas Aircraft realigns program office structure. *Aviat Week Space Technol* 126:34 Ja 19 '87
Douglas approaches airlines with stretched MD-11 concept. il *Aviat Week Space Technol* 127:41 O 19 '87
Douglas begins building long-lead MD-11 components. il *Aviat Week Space Technol* 126:50+ Ap 6 '87
Douglas plans UHB-powered MD-91X as successor to turbofan transports. M. A. Dornheim. il *Aviat Week Space Technol* 126:90-3 Ap 13 '87
Douglas stresses reliability early in C-17 development. B. A. Smith. il *Aviat Week Space Technol* 127:61-2 Jl 20 '87
Expanded Exim credit could aid Douglas aircraft negotiations. *Aviat Week Space Technol* 126:31 My 11 '87
FAA officials visit MD-82 facilities in China [inspect controls and procedures for coproduction of MD-82 transports in Shanghai] *Aviat Week Space Technol* 126:42 Ap 6 '87
First Chinese-assembled MD-82 nears completion in SAIC facilities. il *Aviat Week Space Technol* 126:34-5 Je 1 '87
International carriers weigh A340, MD-11 acquisition options. J. M. Lenorovitz. *Aviat Week Space Technol* 126:53+ Ap 6 '87
McDonnell displays engineering mockup of SDI integrated space experiment. il *Aviat Week Space Technol* 127:26-7 Ag 17 '87
McDonnell Douglas/European talks include larger version of MD-11. B. A. Smith. *Aviat Week Space Technol* 126:42 Ap 13 '87
McDonnell Douglas Astronautics receives nine $50,000 deposits for commercial satellite launches [Delta 2s] *Aviat Week Space Technol* 126:29 Ap 13 '87
McDonnell Douglas discussing MD-11 with potential customers. B. A. Smith. il *Aviat Week Space Technol* 126:40+ Ja 12 '87
McDonnell Douglas establishes New Aircraft Products Division. J. D. Morrocco. *Aviat Week Space Technol* 127:84 O 26 '87
McDonnell Douglas focusing resources on MD-90, MD-11 transport programs. B. A. Smith. il *Aviat Week Space Technol* 127:59+ N 9 '87
McDonnell Douglas grabs a piece of China's sky. D. J. Yang. il *Bus Week* p35 Ag 17 '87
McDonnell Douglas offers F/A-18 for French Navy's carrier air fleet. J. D. Morrocco. *Aviat Week Space Technol* 127:33-5 S 7 '87
McDonnell Douglas receives firm commercial Delta launch orders [Hughes Aircraft to purchase for launch of British Satellite Broadcasting spacecraft] *Aviat Week Space Technol* 127:24 Jl 20 '87
McDonnell Douglas reports reduced earnings for first quarter 1987. *Aviat Week Space Technol* 126:139 My 11 '87

McDonnell Douglas Corp.—*cont.*

McDonnell Douglas resumes flight tests with GE UDF engine [unducted fan engine] *Aviat Week Space Technol* 127:35 N 2 '87

McDonnell Douglas signing partners in MD-11 development program. *Aviat Week Space Technol* 126:34-5 Ja 26 '87

McDonnell Douglas studies larger payload assist modules. *Aviat Week Space Technol* 127:136 Ag 10 '87

McDonnell Douglas team to test neutral-particle beam accelerator in orbit. *Aviat Week Space Technol* 126:27 Je 8 '87

McDonnell Douglas team will plan assembly of key elements in space [space station] il *Aviat Week Space Technol* 127:22-3 D 7 '87

McDonnell Douglas to launch Airbus A330 competitor. *Aviat Week Space Technol* 126:40 Je 22 '87

McDonnell Douglas UHB demonstrator flies with GE unducted fan engine [ultrahigh bypass ratio engine] M. A. Dornheim. il *Aviat Week Space Technol* 126:32-4 My 25 '87

McDonnell Douglas will develop expanded aerial refueling system for USAF KC-10s. il *Aviat Week Space Technol* 126:72 Je 22 '87

McDonnell executives question target date of SuperFan engine. R. G. O'Lone. *Aviat Week Space Technol* 126:30-1 F 16 '87

McDonnell plans rapid buildup of Delta launcher fleet. B. A. Smith. il *Aviat Week Space Technol* 126:114-15 F 16 '87

MD-11, A340 competition gains momentum at Thai International. R. G. O'Lone. *Aviat Week Space Technol* 126:30-1 Mr 16 '87

MD-11 continues to add orders despite A340 SuperFan sales effort. B. A. Smith. *Aviat Week Space Technol* 126:32-3 Mr 16 '87

MD-80 delivery delays force some airlines to curb expansion. B. A. Smith. il *Aviat Week Space Technol* 127:34-6 Jl 6 '87

MD-82 coproduction could aid in forming U.S.-China bilateral. B. A. Smith. il *Aviat Week Space Technol* 126:43+ Ap 6 '87

The odd couple at McDonnell Douglas [S. McDonnell and J. F. McDonnell] C. Leinster. il pors *Fortune* 115:120-1+ Je 22 '87

Orders spur McDonnell to launch MD-11 program. *Aviat Week Space Technol* 126:35 Ja 5 '87

T-45A trainer will be built, tested at Palmdale. *Aviat Week Space Technol* 127:136 O 12 '87

TWA discussing aircraft order with McDonnell Douglas, Boeing. C. Preble. *Aviat Week Space Technol* 126:38-9 Mr 30 '87

UHB demonstrator aircraft continues unducted fan tests [GE UDF engine] il *Aviat Week Space Technol* 127:81 O 26 '87

USAF awards McDonnell Douglas contract to build, operate MLVs [medium launch vehicles] B. A. Smith. *Aviat Week Space Technol* 126:20-1 Ja 26 '87

Widebody wars: Airbus decides 'to go for the kill' [fierce battle with McDonnell Douglas] F. J. Comes. il *Bus Week* p80-1 Jl 6 '87

The widebody wars are about to flare up again [MD-11s] J. E. Ellis. il *Bus Week* p41-2 Ja 12 '87

McDonnell Douglas Corp. Information Systems Group

Can McDonnell Douglas make its computers fly? S. Toy. il por *Bus Week* p121-2 My 4 '87

McDonnell Douglas Helicopter Company

Bell/McDonnell team reviews design of Army LHX entry. *Aviat Week Space Technol* 126:85-6 Ja 19 '87

McDonnell Douglas Helicopter may select development partner for new light model by fall. *Aviat Week Space Technol* 126:71 Je 15 '87

McDonnell Douglas studies updated maritime AH-64A Apache derivative. il *Aviat Week Space Technol* 126:26-7 Ap 6 '87

McDonnell Douglas to propose Apache target handoff system. *Aviat Week Space Technol* 127:22 O 19 '87

McDonnell to include no-tail rotor concept in future designs [Notar] *Aviat Week Space Technol* 127:90 Jl 6 '87

McDonough, Jimmy

Great balls of fire. il por *Film Comment* 23:38-40+ Mr/Ap '87

McDonough, John

Anatomy of the game [photographs] il *Sports Illus* 67 Sp Issue:34-43 N 18 '87

Dream fight [photographs] il pors *Sport Mag* 78:56-63 D '87

A week of Sundays [photographs] il *Sport Mag* 78:36-45 F '87

McDonough, Tom

That great blank page, the screen. il *N Y Times Book Rev* 92:1+ N 15 '87

McDonough, Will

about

A breath of fresh air. W. Taaffe. il por *Sports Illus* 67:97 N 23 '87

McDougall, Ian

The electronic pencil; one small-firm approach. il *Archit Rec* 175:45+ Je '87

McDougall, Mary

Style of a lifetime. il *House Gard* 159:178-83+ Mr '87

McDowell, Bart

New Mexico: between frontier and future. il map *Natl Geogr* 172:602-33 N '87

McDowell, Edwin

'Exodus' in samizdat: still popular and still subversive. il *N Y Times Book Rev* 92:13 Ap 26 '87

McDowell, Jane

"My son, my daughter". il por *Ladies Home J* 104:18+ F '87

McDowell, Robert, 1953-

How good is John Ashbery? *Am Sch* 56:275-8+ Spr '87

McDowell-Head, Leila

On surrogate motherhood. por *Essence* 18:136 Jl '87

McElligott, Tom

about

Admen for heaven. D. Neff. il pors *Christ Today* 31:12-13 S 18 '87

McElroy, Charles

Casa Romero closes: where do they go from here? il map *Focus* 37:28-9 Spr '87

McElroy, Colleen J.

about

Word star. M. Southgate. por *Essence* 18:26 D '87

McElroy, Martin C. P.

The architect as facility manager—fiction and fact. il *Archit Rec* 175:42-3 O '87

McElwee, Ross

about

Sherman's March [film] Reviews
  Mademoiselle 93:168 Ja '87. R. Rosenbaum

McEnroe, John

Mac says: overcome the mental challenge. il por *World Tennis* 35:58 Jl '87

about

Advantage, Mr. McEnroe? [cover story] M. Lupica. il pors *Esquire* 108:84-8+ Jl '87

Before the parade passes by. N. Amdur. il pors *World Tennis* 34:14-16 Ja '87

Mac gets a new Mr. Fix-it. R. Sullivan. il pors *Sports Illus* 67:26-7 Ag 17 '87

McEnroe's on a roll. K. Cunningham. il por *World Tennis* 35:12+ Jl '87

Tennis champ McEnroe thanks Leonard for hope. pors *Jet* 72:47 My 18 '87

That period of adjustment. P. Gonzalez. il por *World Tennis* 35:80 Ag '87

Yankee flameout in Hartford. F. Lidz. il pors *Sports Illus* 67:20-1 Ag 3 '87

McEntire, Reba

about

Reba McEntire: country singer of the year. J. R. Adams. il pors *McCalls* 114:51-2 Ja '87

McEntyre, John E.

James Luguri's haiku. *Christ Century* 104:486-8 My 20-27 '87

McErlean, Michael

about

Judgment of liability. R. Corelli. il por *Macleans* 100:52 O 12 '87

McEwan, Ian

The child in time [story] il *Esquire* 108:69-72 Ag '87

about

PW interviews. A. Smith. il por *Publ Wkly* 232:68-9 S 11 '87

McEwen, John

Report from London. il *Art Am* 75:30-7+ Jl '87

Report from London. il *Art Am* 75:29-33+ Ja '87

McEwen, Kally

By the time I get to Davenport. il *U S Cathol* 52:34-9 F '87

McFadden, Geoff

Not-so-naked ancestors. il *Sea Front* 33:46-51 Ja/F '87

McFadden, Kenny

about

Cleveland's big cheese. C. Pierce. por *Sports Illus* 66:56-7 Mr 2 '87

McFadden, Maureen
How to sell the job you have to the person you want. il *Work Woman* 12:86-7+ Je '87
McFadden, Mouse *See* McFadden, Kenny
McFarlane, Jonda
The meaning of marriage. por *Newsweek* 110:8 Ag 17 '87
McFarlane, Robert C.
about
The good soldier. J. V. Lamar, Jr. il pors map *Time* 129:30-1+ My 25 '87
Iranscam's near tragedy. G. J. Church. il por *Time* 129:25 F 23 '87
'It was my idea'. L. Martz. il pors *Newsweek* 109:16-19 My 25 '87
McFarlane: a question of candor. T. E. Johnson. il por *Newsweek* 109:40 My 18 '87
McFarlane's folly. D. Schorr. *New Leader* 70:3-4 F 9-23 '87
Out of the basement. M. Kondracke. *New Repub* 196:10+ Ja 5-12 '87
The price of not 'breaking faith'. M. McDonald. il por *Macleans* 100:16-17 My 25 '87
Three Thanksgivings: the saga of Robert McFarlane. T. B. Feldman. il pors *McCalls* 115:22+ N '87
Under pressure, a Marine loses control. B. Barol. il pors *Newsweek* 109:22-4 F 23 '87
A Washington corner trip to the edge and back. S. Powell. il por *U S News World Rep* 102:11 F 23 '87
Week 2: more troubling questions. B. Duffy. il por *U S News World Rep* 102:24-5 My 25 '87
McFarlin, Whitney
about
The perils of being too successful. E. Paris. il *Forbes* 139:88+ F 9 '87
McFee, Michael
Snow goat [poem] *New Yorker* 62:69 Ja 19 '87
McFerrin, Bobby
about
Bobby McFerrin sings 'Cosby show' theme song. por *Jet* 73:53 O 26 '87
Every song is a cliff-hanger for improviser Bobby McFerrin, a one-man, no-instrument band. D. Grogan. il pors *People Wkly* 28:109-10 S 21 '87
Showstopper Bobby McFerrin. M. Johnson. por *Essence* 17:24 Ap '87
The wizard of ahs. L. Gourse. il pors *Horizon* 30:34-7 Jl/Ag '87
McGee, Celia
Reads: picking through the paperbacks. il *N Y* 20:140+ Je 29-Jl 6 '87
McGee, Susan Morris
The watercolor page. il por *Am Artist* 51:60 Je '87
McGee, Vonetta
about
Jimmie Walker, Vonetta McGee star in TV's 'Bustin loose' [cover story] il pors *Jet* 73:58-60 N 2 '87
McGhee, Howard, 1918-1987
about
Obituary
Jet por 72:55 Ag 10 '87
McGill, David
about
A meeting of the twain. J. Biggar. bibl (p65) il *Psychol Today* 21:46-50+ N '87
McGill University. Motor Sport Research Group
Fit to win. T. West. il *Road Track* 38:126-8+ Je '87
McGilligan, Pat
Point man [interview with O. Stone] il pors *Film Comment* 23:11-14+ Ja/F '87
Tender comrades. il *Film Comment* 23:38-9+ N/D '87
McGillis, Kelly
about
Chameleon. S. Peters and M. Daugherty. il pors *Life* 10:145-6+ N '87
McGinnis, Alan Loy
Are you neglecting your marriage? *Redbook* 168:86-7+ Ja '87
McGinniss, Joe
about
Suit against 'Fatal vision' author is settled out of court. C. Reid. il *Publ Wkly* 232:12 D 11 '87
McGinty, Brian
Clement C. Moore: "A visit from St. Nicholas". por *Am Hist Illus* 22:28-9 D '87
Isaac Jefferson: the slave who remembered. il por *Am Hist Illus* 21:32-3 F '87
Joyce Kilmer: soldier and poet. por *Am Hist Illus* 22:46-7 My '87

Monument to a discoverer? il *Am Hist Illus* 22:38-41 O '87
Paul Morphy: the pride and sorrow of chess. por *Am Hist Illus* 22:50-1 Mr '87
Shays' Rebellion: a black cloud that rose in the East. il *Am Hist Illus* 21:10-13+ Ja '87
We the people [cover story; special issue; with editorial comment by Ed Holm] il *Am Hist Illus* 22:4, 10-48+ Summ '87
McGlashan, Sandy, and Clausen, John
Is it time for an ad agency? il *Nations Bus* 75:74+ O '87
McGleno, Phil *See* O'Grady, Mac
McGoldrick, Fred
Problems of assurance of nuclear supplies [address, May 27, 1987] *Dep State Bull* 87:48-52 S '87
McGonagill, Grady
Board/staff partnership: the key to the effectiveness of state and local boards. bibl f *Phi Delta Kappan* 69:65-8 S '87
McGough, Michael
Area Man. *New Repub* 197:17 S 14-21 '87
McGourty, Brian M.
Manufacturing today [address, June 24, 1987] *Vital Speeches Day* 53:752-5 O 1 '87
McGourty, Frederick
Garden American. por *Rodale's Org Gard* 34:111-12 D '87
McGovern, Dennis
Singing day to day. pors *Opera News* 52:38+ O '87 (jt. auth) See Winer, Deborah Grace, and McGovern, Dennis
McGovern, George S. (George Stanley), 1922-
about
George McGovern [interview] W. Greider. il por *Roll Stone* p103-4+ N 5-D 10 '87
McGowan, Alan
Sakharov: the folly of SDI [interview] *Harpers* 275:20 O '87
McGowan, Elsie
about
White woman jailed for hitting black principal who paddled her son. il por *Jet* 73:6-7 N 30 '87
McGowan, Jo
The poor break through. il *Commonweal* 114:383-6 Je 19 '87
McGowan, William
A sense of belonging. il *N Y Times Mag* p46-8 Ag 23 '87
McGowan, William G.
about
The CEO who got a new heart. W. J. Cook. il pors *U S News World Rep* 103:60-2+ O 19 '87
Parting MCI's veil of secrecy. J. J. Keller. *Bus Week* p54 My 18 '87
McGowin, Ed, 1938-
about
Ed McGowin at Gracie Mansion. E. Heartney. il *Art Am* 75:141-2 Mr '87
McGrady, Patrick M.
about
The lone ranger of cancer care. E. Kiester. il pors *50 Plus* 27:88-94 Ap '87
McGrath, Camilla
about
Entertaining. W. P. Rayner and C. Rayner. il pors *Vogue* 177:120+ Jl '87
McGrath, Kathryn
about
The SEC's Kathryn McGrath keeps mutual funds in line. L. N. Vreeland. il por *Money* 16:160 Jl '87
McGrath, Mary R.
A reading program that works as a community effort. il *Phi Delta Kappan* 68:475-6 F '87
McGrath, Tom
Bring back the sin of selfishness [with readers' comments] *U S Cathol* 52:14-19 O '87
McGraw-Hill, Inc.
McGraw-Hill gets serious about audio. il *Publ Wkly* 232:36-7 Jl 17 '87
McGraw-Hill purchases TDM. *Publ Wkly* 232:416 Ag 7 '87
McGraw-Hill to sell South Africa branch. *Publ Wkly* 231:10 Mr 13 '87
When freedom to read suffers [implications of decision to terminate South African operations] I. L. Horowitz. por *Publ Wkly* 232:38 Jl 17 '87
McGriff, Jimmy
about
Hank Crawford/Jimmy McGriff. M. Bourne. il pors *Down Beat* 54:14 S '87

McGuane, Thomas
Midstream. il *Harpers* 274:60-4 Ap '87
McGuigan, Barry
about
A real nobody did it better. R. Wiley. il pors *Sports Illus* 66:32-4+ Ja 12 '87
McGuigan, Cathleen
Forms of fantasy. il pors *N Y Times Mag* p62-4+ D 6 '87
McGuire, John
about
The gift of sight [with editorial comment by Bard Lindeman] P. Spencer. il pors *50 Plus* 27:4, 24-7+ Je '87
McGuire, John
KYTV. il *Channels* 7:34-5+ O '87
McGuire, Rick
Good knees: how to take care of your most precious joint. il *Women's Sports Fitness* 9:46-9 D '87
McGuire, Wayne
I didn't kill Dian. She was my friend; ed. by Beverly Trainer and Gina Maranto. il pors maps *Discover* 8:28-32+ F '87
about
Rwandan justice: a show of pomp and circumstantial evidence. B. A. Borst. il *Discover* 8:45 F '87
McGwire, Mark
about
Fence buster Mark McGwire is Oakland's Babe by the Bay. C. Neuhaus. il por *People Wkly* 28:49 Ag 31 '87
Mark McGwire. H. Hersch. il pors *Sports Illus* 67:42+ Jl 13 '87
McGwire on fire. P. Axthelm. il por *Newsweek* 110:49 Jl 13 '87
The stuff of baseball legend. C. Stier. il *Macleans* 100:36 Ag 24 '87
McHenry, Susan
Producer Diane Silver and the making of "Native son". por *Ms* 15:15-17 Mr '87
Spelman College gets its first "sister president". il por *Ms* 16:58-61+ O '87
MCI Communications Corp.
AT&T is eating 'em alive. J. J. Keller. il *Bus Week* p28-9 F 16 '87
Can MCI go the distance? J. Mendes. *Fortune* 116:106-7 Jl 20 '87
The CEO who got a new heart [restored health of W. McGowan] W. J. Cook. il pors *U S News World Rep* 103:60-2+ O 19 '87
MCI's fight for a future in the world it helped create. F. Seghers and J. J. Keller. il *Bus Week* p114-15 My 25 '87
Parting MCI's veil of secrecy [secrecy surrounding president W. G. McGowan's heart transplant surgery] J. J. Keller. *Bus Week* p54 My 18 '87
McIlhenny, Henry Plumer, 1910-1986
about
Last of a breed. D. Solomon. il *Harpers Bazaar* 121:88+ D '87
Philadelphia's pride. C. Vogel. il *N Y Times Mag* p70-2 My 10 '87
McIlhenny (Henry P.) Collection *See* Art—Collectors and collecting
McIlvanney, Hugh
The illusion of victory: another view of the Leonard-Hagler decision. il por *Sports Illus* 66:120 Ap 20 '87
McInerney, Jay
Reunion [story] il *Esquire* 107:178-80+ Mr '87
Smoke [story] il *Atlantic* 259:68-72+ Mr '87
Story of my life [story] il *Esquire* 108:106-8+ Ag '87
McIntosh, Winston Hubert *See* Tosh, Peter, 1944-1987
McIntyre, Annie
Enter, speaker right. il *Publ Wkly* 232:39-41 D 11 '87
McIntyre, Loren
The High Andes: South America's islands in the sky. il maps *Natl Geogr* 171:422-59 Ap '87
McIntyre, Robert S.
Loopholes at large. *New Repub* 196:12+ Je 15 '87
Rich man's populist. *New Repub* 196:16-17 Mr 23 '87
Tax the Forbes 400! *New Repub* 197:15-17 Ag 31 '87
VAT is a bad idea. il *Atlantic* 259:26-8+ Ja '87
McJimsey, George T.
about
Wild about Harry. J. K. Galbraith. il por *Wash Mon* 19:44-5 Je '87
McKay, Linda Back
Oil spill [poem] *America* 157:134 S 12-19 '87

McKee, Chris
(jt. auth) See Mori, Jim, and McKee, Chris
McKee, Clarence
about
Clarence McKee takes helm of $365 million TV station. por *Jet* 72:36-7 Ag 24 '87
McKee, Gillett Co. buy $365 mil. Fla. TV station. por *Jet* 72:6 Mr 30 '87
McKee, Russell
Tales of two rails. il *Audubon* 89:79+ S '87
McKeegan, Kevin D.
Oxygen isotopes in refractory stratospheric dust particles: proof of extraterrestrial origin. bibl f il *Science* 237:1468-71 S 18 '87
McKenna, David L.
Financing the Great Commission. il por *Christ Today* 31:26-31 My 15 '87
McKenna, Frank
about
All the earmarks of a Liberal sweep. K. Harley. il por *Macleans* 100:26-7 O 12 '87
Clean sweep [cover story; special section; with editorial comment by Kevin Doyle] il pors *Macleans* 100:2, 14-16+ O 26 '87
An unaffected kid on the block. M. Janigan. por *Macleans* 100:12 D 7 '87
McKenzie, Alecia
Jamaicans fuel a skyrocketing market. il por map *Black Enterp* 18:93-4+ D '87
McKenzie, Heather
about
BMX racer: beating the boys at their own game. K. Dickerson. il *Teen* 31:67 S '87
McKenzie, Richard B.
The bright side of economic failure. *Society* 24:39-42 S/O '87
Jobilism, or, Is the world really flat? il *Forbes* 140:68-70 Jl 13 '87
McKeon, Nancy, and Pollan, Corky
Best bets. See issues of New York
McKeown, Bill
Boating. See issues of Outdoor Life beginning May 1983
McKesson Corp.
Adviser beware: cooked books may burn you, too [investment bankers face fraud charges in CPC International's suit against McKesson and Morgan Stanley over sale of C. F. Mueller] L. J. Tell. il *Bus Week* p58+ O 26 '87
Billion-dollar brainstorm [service merchandising] G. Bronson. il *Forbes* 140:98 O 19 '87
McKiernan, Janet
about
Janet McKiernan at Semaphore. E. Heartney. il *Art Am* 75:129-30 Jl '87
McKinley, William, 1843-1901
Statues, portraits, etc.
President and Mrs. McKinley portraits. M. Wollett and B. Wollett. il por *Antiques Collect Hobbies* 91:37 F '87
McKinna, J. S.
Divers' dilemma. il *Oceans* 20:10 N/D '87
McKinney, Billy
about
Bulls 1st black executive: 'I've got a lot to learn'. por *Jet* 72:46 Je 29 '87
McKinney, Rhoda E.
High schools that work. il *Ebony* 43:34+ N '87
How to get a piece of the $21 billion scholarship pie. bibl il *Ebony* 43:124+ D '87
Introducing: Pulitzer Prize-winning poet Rita Dove. il pors *Ebony* 42:44+ O '87
McKinney, Stewart B., 1931-1987
about
AIDS makes another chilling advance, claiming the life of a congressman. il por *People Wkly* 27:53 My 25 '87
AIDS strikes down a congressman. por *Newsweek* 109:47 My 18 '87
McKinney (Tex.)
Climate
Inside a Texas tornado [reprint from June 1951 issue] R. S. Hall. *Weatherwise* 40:72-5 Ap '87
McKinnon, Carmen
about
Detroit girl stays in school; wins trip to Japan. *Jet* 72:12 S 7 '87
McKinsey & Company
News by the numbers [analysis of NBC News] E. Diamond. il *N Y* 20:20-1 My 25 '87

McKinsey & Company—*cont.*
"We don't learn from our clients, we learn from each other" [cover story] J. Merwin. il *Forbes* 140:122-8 O 19 '87

McLain, Denny, 1944-
about
Starting over. W. Nack. il pors *Sports Illus* 67:92-6+ D 14 '87

McLain, Gary
The downfall of a champion; ed. by Jeffrey Marx. il pors *Sports Illus* 66:42-6+ Mr 16 '87

McLaren, Norman, 1914-1987
about
Obituary
Macleans il por 100:50 F 9 '87. P. Young

McLaughlin, Ann Dore
about
Reagan picks a 'good soldier'. S. B. Garland and H. Bradford. *Bus Week* p71 N 16 '87

McLaughlin, Clara
about
Texas TV pioneer: Clara McLaughlin is first black woman to own stations. M. Marshall. il pors *Ebony* 42:78+ Mr '87

McLaughlin, David
about
"Civility" for Dartmouth. por *Time* 129:85 Ap 27 '87

McLaughlin, Ed
about
Pinker than the pinks? por *Forbes* 140:146-7 D 28 '87

McLaughlin, John
From Washington straight. See issues of National Review
about
Masters of babble. L. Wainwright. il *Life* 10:26 D '87

McLaughlin, John
about
Adventures in Fusionland. H. Bordowitz. il por *High Fidel* 37:87-8+ Ja '87

McLaughlin, John
Interesting the media in serious arts education. *Des Arts Educ* 88:6-9 Jl/Ag '87

McLaughlin, John, 1898-1976
about
John McLaughlin. N. Grimes. *Art News* 86:148+ My '87
John McLaughlin at Andre Emmerich. J. Weinberg. *Art Am* 75:182 O '87

McLaughlin, Milbrey Wallin, 1941-
(jt. auth) See Heath, Shirley Brice, and McLaughlin, Milbrey Wallin, 1941-

McLaughlin, Milbrey Wallin, 1941-, and Shields, Patrick M.
Involving low-income parents in the schools: a role for policy? bibl f il *Phi Delta Kappan* 69:156-60 O '87

McLaughlin, Thomas
about
"I was an incredibly wild child". B. Leonard. il por *Forbes* 140:56-7 Ag 24 '87

The McLaughlin Group [television program] See Television program reviews—Single works

McLaurin, Melton Alonza
The day I learned I was a racist. il por *Wash Mon* 19:32-6 N '87

McLean, Malcolm
about
Malcom McLean's pirate ships. A. D. Frank. il por *Forbes* 139:32-3 Mr 23 '87

McLean, Malcolm Dallas
about
Finding a lost colony. L. Thomas. il por *South Living* 22:136 S '87

McLean, Ross
about
Obituary
Macleans 100:50 Je 15 '87. P. Young

McLean Industries Inc.
Malcom McLean's pirate ships. A. D. Frank. il por *Forbes* 139:32-3 Mr 23 '87
Will USL join Davy Jones? S. Payne. *Bus Week* p30-1 Mr 30 '87

McLellan, Iain
TV's shortcomings in Africa. *World Press Rev* 34:60-1 Ja '87

McLemore, Lamonte
about
Lamonte McLemore's best. il por *Ebony* 42:124+ Mr '87

McLeod, Catherine Styles- *See* Styles-McLeod, Catherine

McLeod, Kenneth J., and others
Frequency dependence of electric field modulation of fibroblast protein synthesis. bibl f il *Science* 236:1465-9 Je 12 '87

McLin, Clarence Josef, 1921-
about
Ohio's most powerful black lawmaker reveals fight to conquer cancer. il por *Jet* 73:29 S 28 '87

McMahan, David
about
The Revenger offers drivers a shot at life in the blast lane. il por *People Wkly* 28:179 D 14 '87

McMahon, Don, d. 1987
about
Obituary
Sports Illus il por 67:12 Ag 3 '87

McMahon, Ed
about
On board with Ed McMahon. S. Duke. il por *Mot Boat Sail* 160:54-5+ Jl '87

McMahon, Hugh
about
Come Halloween, pumpkin carver Hugh McMahon has no trouble scaring up famous faces. V. R. Peterson. il por *People Wkly* 28:143-4 N 2 '87

McMahon, Jim
Reading is fun-damental. il por *Sport Mag* 78:22-3 Ja '87
about
Beers with [interview] C. Pesmen. il por *Sport Mag* 78:23-5 Jl '87
Chicago's weighty issue [cover story] R. Telander. il pors *Sports Illus* 67:28-32+ Ag 24 '87
Miracles of the Midway. P. Zimmerman. il *Sports Illus* 67:28-30+ N 16 '87
Sic transit McMahon: the cheering has stopped for the NFL's bad boy—now he's rich, famous and hurt. J. Friedman. il pors *People Wkly* 27:46-8 Ja 19 '87

McMahon, Lynn
(jt. auth) See Kabat, Donald, and McMahon, Lynn

McMahon, Lynne
Going back [poem] *Nation* 244:695 My 23 '87
Unbuilding [poem] il *Atlantic* 260:43 Ag '87

McMahon, Thomas A., 1943-
about
A Harvard prof tells runners: on your Marx; get set; Groucho! il *People Wkly* 28:85 S 21 '87
PW interviews. R. Herbert. por *Publ Wkly* 231:52-3 Ja 23 '87

McMains, Kate
I was a teen-age cosmonaut. il *Space World* X-2-278:32-3+ F '87

McManis, Sam
The Reds' menace. il por *Sport Mag* 78:22-4 Mr '87

McManus, Doyle
Dateline Washington: Gipperdämmerung. *Foreign Policy* 66:156-72 Spr '87

McManus, Jason
about
A new chieftain for Time Inc. J. Alter. il por *Newsweek* 109:63 Ap 27 '87
Their Time. E. Diamond. il pors *N Y* 20:29-31 O 12 '87

McManus, Michael J.
Another kind of censorship. por *Publ Wkly* 231:70 Ja 23 '87

McManus, Patrick F.
The last laugh. See issues of Outdoor Life

McMartin family
about
Can the 'abused' kids be believed? T. Gest. il *U S News World Rep* 103:10 Jl 27 '87

McMenamin, Mark A. S.
The emergence of animals. bibl (p128) il map *Sci Am* 256:94-102 Ap '87

McMillan, Ian
Tall in the saddle [poem] *Harpers* 275:27 S '87

McMillan, James F., 1948-
The Third Republic. il *Hist Today* 37:50-2 Je '87

McMillan, Terry
Mama [fiction] il *Essence* 17:72-4+ Ap '87

McMillan, Tom
about
Business 101. S. B. Weiner. il por *Forbes* 140:52 Ag 24 '87

McMillen, Tom, 1952-
about
Tom McMillen (D., Md.). J. McCallum. il pors *Sports Illus* 66:70-4 F 23 '87

McMillian, John G.
about
Full speed ahead. B. Waitzkin. il por *Mot Boat Sail* 159:54-7+ My '87
McMinn, Douglas W.
Competitiveness in America: is protectionism the answer? [address, May 27, 1987] *Dep State Bull* 87:56-9 Ag '87
Global economic powers with global responsibilities [address, August 3, 1987] *Dep State Bull* 87:24-6 O '87
U.S. foreign agricultural policy and the sugar program [address, February 24, 1987] *Dep State Bull* 87:40-3 My '87
McMullen-Pastrick, Miriam, and Weimer, Maryellen Gleason
Student exams: accentuating the positive. *Educ Dig* 52:14-17 My '87
McMurtry, Larry
Bibliography
The bard of Wichita Falls. R. M. Adams. il *N Y Rev Books* 34:39-41 Ag 13 '87
McNabb, Polly
'A walk a day keeps my back pain away'. il *Prevention* 39:45-6+ Ag '87
McNair, Barbara
about
Singer Barbara McNair files for bankruptcy. il por *Jet* 72:22 S 14 '87
McNair, Cheryl
about
Astronaut McNair's widow settles with rocket maker. *Jet* 72:18 My 25 '87
Cheryl McNair: surviving the shuttle disaster. il pors *Ebony* 42:162+ My '87
McNair, Harold M.
High-performance liquid chromatography, gas chromatography, and supercritical fluid chromatography. *Science* 235 pt2:G43 F 27 '87
McNair, Ronald E.
about
Astronaut McNair's widow settles with rocket maker. *Jet* 72:18 My 25 '87
Cheryl McNair: surviving the shuttle disaster. il pors *Ebony* 42:162+ My '87
Jackson, Miss., theater named for Ronald McNair. il *Jet* 71:37 F 2 '87
Ronald McNair's family copes with memories of Challenger tragedy. il *Jet* 71:53 F 9 '87
McNally, Terrence, 1939-
about
Frankie and Johnny in the Clair de Lune [drama] Reviews
Commonweal 114:749 D 18 '87. G. Weales
N Y 20:124+ N 9 '87. J. Simon
Nation 245:695 D 5 '87. T. M. Disch
New Yorker 63:129-30 N 9 '87. E. Oliver
McNamara, Mary
South Africa's medical front. il *Ms* 16:76 D '87
Southern African women caught in the middle. il *Ms* 15:23 Mr '87
McNamara, Robert F.
More thoughts about the declining number of vocations [discussion of December 13, 1986 article, A jubilarian reflects on the declining number of priests] *America* 156:142-4 F 14 '87
McNamara, Robert J.
An inside story. il *Conservationist* 41:27-9 Ja/F '87
McNamara, Robert S., 1916-
Blundering into disaster [address, February 17, 1987] *Vital Speeches Day* 53:390-4 Ap 15 '87
McNeil, Lori
about
Black tennis stars winning big bucks but snubbed for commercials. pors *Jet* 72:48 Jl 20 '87
Lori McNeil accepts an apparel endorsement deal. por *Jet* 73:48 N 2 '87
Lori McNeil challenges tennis elite at US Open. il por *Jet* 73:51 S 28 '87
Winning is only half the battle. M. Witherell. il pors *World Tennis* 34:38-41+ My '87
McNeil, Paul L.
(jt. auth) See Swanson, Joel A., and McNeil, Paul L.
McNeil, Wally
about
No bad hops with Wally. F. Lidz. il pors *Sports Illus* 67:54+ Jl 6 '87
McNeill, John J.
Homosexuality: challenging the church to grow. il *Christ Century* 104:242-6 Mr 11 '87
McNeill on the church and gays [discussion of March 11, 1987 article, Homosexuality: challenging the church to grow] *Christ Century* 104:443-4+ My 6 '87

McNeill, William Hardy, 1917-
about
Unlike AIDS, says a historian, ancient plagues swept the world scythelike and suddenly [interview] G. Breu. il por *People Wkly* 28:123-4+ O 12 '87
McNerney, John E.
The agony of de-feet. il *World Tennis* 34:8-9 F '87
Prevention's the best medicine. il *World Tennis* 35:16-17 Jl '87
Shoe guide (I). il *World Tennis* 34:53-4+ Ap '87
Shoe guide (II). il *World Tennis* 35:55-8+ Ag '87
Shoe guide (III). il *World Tennis* 35:51-3 O '87
McNichol, Tom
False profits. *New Repub* 196:11-12 Ap 13 '87
Moonie journalism. *Wash Mon* 19:23-8 O '87
McNickle, Larry, and Deacon, Beverly
Old buildings come alive. il *Aging* no356:6-12 '87
McNulty, Faith
Children's books for Christmas. *New Yorker* 63:132+ N 30 '87
McNulty, James
Where to get good investment advice. il *Work Woman* 12:122-4 My '87
McNulty, Robert J.
about
Robert McNulty: back on discounting's fast track. K. Kelly. il por *Bus Week* p91 N 9 '87
McPartland, Brendan
about
When to upgrade your electrical service [interview] il *Home Mech* 83:18-19+ S '87
McPhee, John A.
Atchafalaya. *New Yorker* 63:39-44+ F 23 '87
McPherson, Don
about
Syracuse QB Don McPherson gives his team a season with a sugary ending. J. Friedman. il pors *People Wkly* 28:73-4 D 21 '87
A touch of class. C. Kirkpatrick. il pors *Sports Illus* 67:40-2+ D 14 '87
McPherson, M. Peter
FY 1988 request for foreign assistance programs [statement, March 17, 1987] *Dep State Bull* 87:61-6 Je '87
U.S. development strategy for Sub-Saharan Africa [statement, February 26, 1987] *Dep State Bull* 87:56-8 My '87
U.S. initiative for Southern Africa [address, February 5, 1987] *Dep State Bull* 87:54-5 My '87
McPherson, Mary Patterson, and Korshin, Paul
Taking on Secretary Bennett. pors *U S News World Rep* 102:6 Je 29 '87
McPherson, Sandra
Note to Sappho [poem] *New Repub* 196:39 F 2 '87
McPherson, William
about
PW interviews. S. Staggs. por *Publ Wkly* 231:58-9 My 22 '87
McQueen, John
about
John McQueen/Bellas artes. E. Lebow. il *Am Craft* 47:88-9 O/N '87
McQuilkin, Rennie, 1936-
The Rev. Robert Walker skates [poem] il *Atlantic* 259:60-1 F '87
McRae, Dianne, and Smith, Melba
First aid for pets. il *FDA Consum* 21:24-7 Je '87
McRae, Hal
about
K.C.'s Hal McRae makes mid-season career move. por *Jet* 72:48 Ag 10 '87
McRae, Lee
about
Number one at the gun. H. Hersch. il pors *Sports Illus* 66:64+ My 18 '87
McRae, Michael
Meet 'Grandmother Nature'. il pors *50 Plus* 27:25-8 Jl '87
McRobbie, Joan
The unsung heroines of Vietnam. il pors *McCalls* 114:159 My '87
McTaggart, David Fraser, 1932-
about
The zeal of disapproval. M. H. Brown. il por *Oceans* 20:36-41 My/Je '87
McTaggart, Douglas
about
The tangle of disability claims. D. Francis. il *Macleans* 100:11 D 14 '87

McTiernan, John
> *about*
> Predator [film] Reviews
> *People Wkly* il 27:10 Je 29 '87. R. Novak

McTigue, Gerard
> An American in Romania. il *Travel Holiday* 167:60-3+
> Ap '87
> Mohonk Mountain House. il *Travel Holiday* 168:12-13
> D '87
> Smooth sailing in Stockholm. il *Travel Holiday* 168:18
> D '87

McVey, Charles J., II
> *about*
> Tracking a technobandit. D. Pauly. il por *Newsweek*
> 110:66 D 7 '87

McVie, Christine
> *about*
> Talking about each other: the women of Fleetwood Mac.
> C. Krupp. por *Glamour* 85:302 S '87

McWalter, Keith G.
> Couch dancing. il *N Y Times Mag* p138 D 6 '87

McWey, Michael
> Cruise control [story] il *Seventeen* 46:212-13+ Ap
> '87

McWherter, Ned
> *about*
> Tennessee's new governor finds good fortune in a cookie.
> il por *People Wkly* 27:75 F 2 '87

McWilliam, Martha
> One man's romance with fiber created the Textile
> Museum. il por *Smithsonian* 17:108-10+ Mr '87

McWilliams, James C.
> (jt. auth) See Holland, William R., and McWilliams,
> James C.

McWilliams, Michael
> Second to none. il *Roll Stone* p49+ Ap 23 '87

McWilliams, Patricia G.
> April, come she will: celebrate spring with the first
> fresh foods of the season. il *Ctry J* 14:75-8 Ap '87
> Asparagus. il *Ctry J* 14:47-50 My '87
> Companion planting. il *Ctry J* 14:42-5 Je '87
> The life of spice. il *Ctry J* 14:47-9+ Ag '87
> (jt. auth) See Gibson, Carol, and McWilliams, Patricia
> G.

MDC, Inc.
> Preparing disenchanted students to succeed in society.
> R. C. Smith. il *USA Today (Periodical)* 116:87-9 N
> '87

Me and my girl [musical] See Musicals, revues,
> etc.—Reviews—Single works

Mead, Margaret, 1901-1978
> *about*
> Ghosts to believe in: recalling Bateson and Mead. M.
> C. Bateson. *N Y Times Book Rev* 92:49 N 15 '87
> Letters [discussion of November 1986 article, Untrashing
> Margaret Mead] *Sci Am* 256:6 F '87

Meadow gardening
> A bit of wilderness in your own backyard [wildflowers]
> L. C. Martin. il por *Natl Wildl* 25:22-8 Ap/My '87
> The flowering hayfield. M. Rothschild. il por *Archit*
> *Dig* 44:24+ Ja '87

Meadowlands Pace See Harness racing
Meadowlands Sports Complex
> My blue heaven [celebration of Giants' Super Bowl
> victory] il *N Y* 20:34-5 F 9 '87

Meals
> *See also*
> Breakfasts
> Brunches
> Buffet meals
> Cooking
> Diet
> Dinners and dining
> Entertaining
> Luncheons
> Lunches
> Menus
> Outdoor meals
> Snacks
> Suppers
> Table setting
> Thanksgiving dinners
> Wedding meals
> 15-minute gourmet. J. T. Hazard. il *Ladies Home J*
> 104:122-3+ O '87
> 30-minute menu. See issues of Good Housekeeping
> After-work cooking. B. Greenwood. il *Better Homes Gard*
> 65:104-10+ F '87
> Diana's hillock. N. Hazelton. *Natl Rev* 39:53-4+ Jl 3
> '87
> Easy as 1-2-3. See issues of Ladies' Home Journal

Food for (uninterrupted) thought. E. Toretto. il *Work*
> *Woman* 12:86 Ag '87
> Four 30 minute menus. A. Bailey. il *Parents* 62:169-70+
> Ag '87
> Gourmet on the run. See issues of Glamour
> Make it snappy! [nutritious quick meals] il *Seventeen*
> 46:132-3 F '87
> Tray meals. il *Gourmet* 47:130-8+ O '87
> Wonderful one-dish family dinners [microwaving] il
> *Redbook* 169:85+ O '87

Meals on Wheels program See Aged—Nutrition
Means, Catherine S.
> The watercolor page. il por *Am Artist* 51:52-5 Mr '87

Means, Gordon P.
> The politics of ethnicity in Malaysia. bibl f *Curr Hist*
> 86:168-71+ Ap '87

Meares, John L.
> *about*
> Black members who gave white minister money to build
> church change minds and sue. D. M. Cheers. il pors
> *Jet* 72:24-7 Ag 10 '87

Mearns' quail shooting See Quail shooting
Measell, James S.
> The Findlay Flint Glass Company. il *Antiques Collect*
> *Hobbies* 91:18-19 Ja '87

Measles
> A new rash of measles. A. C. Heller. *Redbook* 169:30
> Jl '87
> Spot check on measles. *Sci News* 131:377 Je 13 '87
> **Vaccines and vaccination**
> The spotted story about measles after childhood. I. A.
> Oppenheim. il *Curr Health 2* 13:16-17 Ap '87

Measurement
> *See also*
> Astronomical measurements
> Blood pressure—Measurement
> Calibration
> Earth sciences—Measurement
> Lasers—Measurement use
> Time measurement
> Measurement scales on the continuum. R. D. Luce and
> L. Narens. bibl f il *Science* 236:1527-32 Je 19 '87

Measurement-driven instruction
> The merits of measurement-driven instruction [with reply
> by G. W. Bracey] W. J. Popham. bibl f il *Phi Delta*
> *Kappan* 68:679-89 My '87

Measuring equipment
> *See also*
> Gages
> Micrometers

Meat
> *See also*
> Beef
> Buffalo meat
> Cooking—Meat
> Ham
> Spam
> Meat and nutrition . . . here's a scorecard. il *Sunset*
> 179:186 N '87
> **Grading**
> Packers don't want to pay for fat [hot fat trimming
> of cattle carcasses] B. Eftink. il *Success Farm* 85:60-1
> Ag '87
> **Packaging**
> Buyers say Excel is OK [vacuum-packed beef] il *Success*
> *Farm* 85:48 O '87
> **Prices**
> There's the beef. S. W. Angrist. il *Forbes* 139:264 My
> 18 '87

Meat contamination
> *See also*
> Poultry contamination
> Drugged livestock [beef cattle from Gordon Riley's farm]
> il *FDA Consum* 21:30-1 Jl/Ag '87
> Lapp life after Chernobyl. S. Stephens. il map *Nat Hist*
> 96:32-41 D '87
> The legacy of Chernobyl: disaster for the Lapps [reindeer
> meat contamination] R. Knight. il map *U S News*
> *World Rep* 102:36 Mr 23 '87

Meat industry
> *See also*
> B3R Country Meat, Inc.
> Buffalo industry
> Cattle industry
> Excel Beef Corporation
> Geo. A. Hormel & Co.
> Hebrew National Kosher Foods, Inc.
> IBP, Inc.
> Monfort of Colorado, Inc.
> Oscar Mayer & Co.

Meat industry—*cont.*

Acquisitions and mergers
Cattle feeding and packing too concentrated. *Success Farm* 85 no4:B24 F '87
Some worry, others applaud packer mergers. *Success Farm* 85:66A S '87

Advertising
Are beef ads making fun of our target audience? B. Eftink. il *Success Farm* 85 no6:B1 Mr '87
Beef checkoff funds are working. *Success Farm* 85:66A S '87
Call me anything, just call me [pork] G. Johnston. *Success Farm* 85 no3:H1 F '87
Canadians happy to support U.S. beef checkoff. *Success Farm* 85 no4:B17 F '87
How now to sell a cow? E. Zuckerman. il *N Y Times Mag* p68-70+ N 29 '87
Meat meet draws urban runners [10 km fitness run in Illinois] il *Success Farm* 85 no4:B24 F '87
Oscar Mayer Wienermobile. J. R. Nerad. il *Mot Trend* 39:108-13 D '87

Ethical aspects
A meat-packing magnate gets boxed in [Swift's E. L. Cox] J. Weber, Jr. il por *Bus Week* p50+ Je 22 '87

Export-import trade
Canadians fear study will lead to import duties [beef] *Success Farm* 85 no2:B8 Ja '87
Exports equal all of the beef in Colorado. *Success Farm* 85:42B Je '87
Hamburgers are killing trees [boycott of fast-food outlets until they stop using Central American beef] il *Newsweek* 110:74 S 14 '87
One costly hamburger [importation of Central American beef contributes to tropical deforestation; views of Christopher Uhl] *Ctry J* 14:12-13 Ag '87
Why we'll sell more beef to Japan in coming years. G. Johnston. il *Success Farm* 85:68 Ag '87

Finance
Packers don't want to pay for fat [hot fat trimming of cattle carcasses] B. Eftink. il *Success Farm* 85:60-1 Ag '87

Marketing
See also
   Beeler's Meat Market and Bakery
Baby beef could be the answer. *Success Farm* 85 no6:B1 Mr '87
The granddaddy of branded beef [Certified Angus Beef] B. Eftink. *Success Farm* 85:32 S '87
'It's our beef from ranch to retail'. B. Eftink. il *Success Farm* 85 no4:B10 F '87
Some good news, and some bad. G. Johnston. il *Success Farm* 85:5 Ag '87

Canada
Canadians happy to support U.S. beef checkoff. *Success Farm* 85 no4:B17 F '87

Meat industry workers
See also
   United Food and Commercial Workers International Union
Meat loaf, pies, etc. *See* Cooking—Meat
Meat tenderizers
Not an ant-idote [effectiveness in treating fire ant stings] *Sci News* 131:374 Je 13 '87
Meatballs *See* Cooking—Meat
Meatless meals *See* Vegetarianism
Mecca (Saudi Arabia)

Riots
A chain of violence. il *Macleans* 100:17 Ag 10 '87
Confronting the 'monster' [Saudi Arabia clashes with Iran] T. Clifton. il *Newsweek* 110:36 S 7 '87
Death by misunderstanding. G. Shamis. il *U S News World Rep* 103:23 Ag 17 '87
Pressing the Saudis. *New Repub* 197:9 Ag 24 '87
Swept up in the tides of the Gulf. H. Anderson. il *Newsweek* 110:40-2 Ag 10 '87
Mech, L. David
At home with the Arctic wolf. il map *Natl Geogr* 171:562-93 My '87
Mecham, Evan
about
Arizona airhead. P. Goudinoff and S. Tobias. *New Repub* 197:15-16 O 26 '87
Arizona gov. stirs rift by denying racial slur. *Jet* 72:29 Ap 13 '87
Arizona gov. vows to repeal King holiday. *Jet* 71:37 Ja 19 '87
Arizona gov's stance on King holiday may cost state $18 million loss. *Jet* 72:36 Je 22 '87
Arizona loses NBNA confab. A. Edmond, Jr. il *Black Enterp* 17:62 Je '87

Arizona observes King holiday despite repeal of state bill by governor. *Jet* 71:12 F 2 '87
Arizona's outspoken new governor, Evan Mecham, seems to enjoy diving straight into political hot water. D. Chu. il por *People Wkly* 28:39-40 Ag 24 '87
At odds in Arizona. S. L. Hawkins. il por *U S News World Rep* 102:26 Mr 23 '87
Critics: Mecham's offer to honor Martin Luther King is unacceptable. *Jet* 72:12 Jl 6 '87
Evan Mecham, please go home. J. D. Hull. il por *Time* 130:61 N 9 '87
Governor's stance on King holiday stirs controversy in Arizona: tempers flare. W. Wofford, Jr. il por *Jet* 73:24-6 N 2 '87
Group wants recall of Arizona Gov. Mecham; NBA cancels meeting. *Jet* 72:14 Jl 27 '87
A land rush—or the bum's rush? D. Gates. il por *Newsweek* 110:10 O 12 '87
No rebates. por *Time* 129:42 Mr 9 '87
Shooting from the lip. C. O'Connor. il por *Newsweek* 109:31 F 9 '87
Up in arms in Arizona. A. Weisman. il por *N Y Times Mag* p50-1+ N 1 '87
When Evan Mecham talks, Arizona shudders. R. Grover. il por *Bus Week* p110+ S 28 '87

Caricatures and cartoons
'Doonesbury' in Arizona. il *Newsweek* 110:41 S 14 '87
Mecham, Robert P., and others
Smooth muscle-mediated connective tissue remodeling in pulmonary hypertension. bibl f il *Science* 237:423-6 Jl 24 '87
Mechanical animals *See* Animals, Mechanical
Mechanical banks *See* Banks, Coin
Mechanical models

Exhibitions
After five centuries, a devoted modeler gives shape to genius [R. Guatelli's models made from Leonardo's sketches] J. P. Wiley, Jr. bibl (p145) il por *Smithsonian* 18:90-5 Ag '87
Mechanics
See also
   Horsepower (Mechanics)
   Many-body problem
   Micromechanics
   Perpetual motion
   Statistical mechanics
   Strains and stresses
   Torque
   Vibration
Mechanics, Celestial
See also
   Orbits
   Solar system—Motion in space
The librations of the moon. A. MacRobert. il *Sky Telesc* 74:60-2 Jl '87
Newton vindicated—Einstein, too! il *Sky Telesc* 73:484-5 My '87
Viewing libration with the naked eye. J. Meketa. il *Sky Telesc* 74:63 Jl '87
Mechanics, Household *See* Houses—Maintenance and repair
Mechanics (Persons)
See also
   Airplane mechanics (Persons)
   Automobile mechanics (Persons)
Mechanics & Farmers Bank
Mechanics & Farmers: branch banking at its best. C. Mitchell. il *Black Enterp* 17:196-8+ Je '87
Mechanics Hall (Worcester, Mass.)
Mechanics Hall is the showpiece of a city where the arts thrive. M. Wade. il *Horizon* 30:17-19 My '87
Mechanics' liens
Here's one way to deal with clients' unpaid bills [architects' rights provided in mechanics' lien statutes] S. A. Glazer. *Archit Rec* 175:39 Mr '87
Mecir, Miloslav
about
Big Cat on the prowl. J. Diaz. il por *Sports Illus* 66:91-2 Ap 20 '87
Change of pace [cover story] S. Flink. il pors *World Tennis* 34:28-31 My '87
Mecking, J. Garvin
about
A practiced eye: J. Garvin Mecking in Greenwich Village. S. M. L. Aronson. il *Archit Dig* 44:156-63+ Ap '87
Mecklenburger, James A.
History of 20th-century American education [poem] il *Phi Delta Kappan* 68:396 Ja '87
Medal of Arts, National *See* National Medal of Arts
Medal of Freedom
Trained as animal doctor, Medal of Freedom winner Patterson founded UNCF. il por *Jet* 72:22 Jl 27 '87

Medal of Freedom—*cont.*
UNCF founder Patterson to get presidential honor [F. D. Patterson to receive Medal of Freedom] por *Jet* 72:24 My 11 '87
Medal of Science, National *See* National Medal of Science
Medal of Technology, National *See* National Medal of Technology
Medallion Books
Los Angeles financial firm is acquiring assets of Medallion Books. *Publ Wkly* 232:18 Ag 14 '87
Medallions *See* Medals
Medals

Collectors and collecting
McKinley to Reagan: collecting U.S. presidents [inaugural medals] A. Schwartz. il *Antiques Collect Hobbies* 92:79-80 S '87
Women's Pavilion Centennial medallion [Philadelphia Centennial Exposition] M. Wollett and B. Wollett. il *Antiques Collect Hobbies* 91:26 Ja '87
Medavoy, Mike

about
Rise and shine [interview] A. Thompson. il por *Film Comment* 23:54-6+ My/Je '87
Meddin, Barbara J., and Rosen, Anita L.
Child abuse and neglect: prevention and reporting. *Educ Dig* 52:52-5 Ja '87
Medex Inc.
Aching back? Arthur Jones says he has the answer. M. Frons. il por *Bus Week* p59+ D 14 '87
Medflies *See* Fruit flies
Medi-Rx America, Inc.
What's not in the prospectus [management linked to drug diversion business] G. Morgenson. il *Forbes* 140:61-2 Jl 27 '87
Media *See* Mass media
Media cabinets *See* Cabinets (Furniture)
Media industry *See* Mass media industry
MediaNews Group Inc.
Beneath the mogul, paradox [acquisitions of W. D. Singleton] N. J. Perry. il por *Fortune* 116:191-2 O 12 '87
Dean Singleton: the making of a media baron. T. Mason and others. il por *Bus Week* p29 S 28 '87
Extra: Texan builds newspaper empire [W. D. Singleton] J. Schwartz. il por *Newsweek* 110:48 S 28 '87
Forget about art and cars [acquisitions of W. D. Singleton] L. Zuckerman. il por *Time* 130:55 S 28 '87
Is Dean Singleton a media king in the making? Check his papers. V. Balfour. il pors *People Wkly* 28:47-8 O 5 '87
Mediation *See* Arbitration and award
Mediation, Commercial *See* Arbitration, Commercial
Mediation, Environmental *See* Environmental mediation
Mediation, Sports *See* Arbitration, Sports
Medicaid
Caught in the VA-Medicaid trap [veterans needing nursing home care] S. Nohlgren. *50 Plus* 27:23 O '87
Medicare and Medicaid programs. *Congr Dig* 66:100-1+ Ap '87
A welfare mother's battle to clean up the Medicaid mess [class action suit in California] S. B. Garland. il *Bus Week* p42 D 21 '87
Medical botany *See* Botany, Medical
Medical care

See also
Aged—Medical care
Airplanes in medical care
Ambulance service
Blacks—Medical care
Children—Medical care
Chiropractic
Diagnosis
First aid in illness and injury
Group medical practice
Health facilities
Helicopters in medical care
Home care services
Hospitals
Iatrogenic diseases
Infants—Medical care
Malpractice
Medical ethics
Missions, Medical
Nurses and nursing
Physicians
Physicians and patients
Poor—Medical care
Public schools—Medical care
Quacks and quackery
Rich—Medical care
Sex discrimination in medicine

Telephone in medical care
Trauma care units
Medical care revolution. il *USA Today (Periodical)* 115:1-2 F '87
"A pothole system" [report by the Department of Health and Human Services] *Sci Am* 256:71 Mr '87
Quick tips to unkink sore spots [self care; excerpts from Listen to your body] E. Michaud and L. Anastas. il *Prevention* 39:96 O '87
The revolution in medicine. G. Easterbrook. il *Newsweek* 109:40-4+ Ja 26 '87

Costs

See also
AIDS (Disease)—Costs
Alzheimer's disease—Costs
Hospital care—Costs
Nursing homes—Costs
Psychotherapy—Costs
7 ways to cut your medical costs. L. Lamberg. *Better Homes Gard* 65:70+ Mr '87
Alcoholism and the medical cost crunch. C. Holden. il *Science* 235:1132-3 Mr 6 '87
A blow for the doctors [British Columbia policy limits number of physicians allowed to practice in move to cut billings] J. O'Hara. il *Macleans* 100:16 Ja 19 '87
Buying health care in the new era of medicine [address, April 28, 1987] E. W. Spencer. *Vital Speeches Day* 53:713-16 S 15 '87
Comparing medical care expenditures of two diverse U.S. data sources [Consumer Expenditure Survey and data from Health Care Financing Administration] E. R. Branch. bibl f il *Mon Labor Rev* 110:15-18 Mr '87
Counting the cost [ratio of different grades of health personnel best for spending limited budgets] B. Abel-Smith. il *World Health* p18-19 Ap '87
The crisis in health benefits. S. B. Garland. il *Bus Week* p36 Je 15 '87
Doctors and markets. *New Repub* 196:4+ Ja 19 '87
Doctors find a prescription for profits. B. Robinson. il *Black Enterp* 17:70-2+ Mr '87
Examining the limits of life [views of D. Callahan] B. Angelo. il por *Time* 130:76-7 N 2 '87
Health care in America [address, December 4-5, 1986] F. E. Samuel, Jr. *Vital Speeches Day* 53:335-7 Mr 15 '87
How not to control medical costs [gatekeeping] C. M. Lindsay. il por *Fortune* 116:105-6 Jl 6 '87
In a doctor's wallet [fee for service vs. HMO payment system] R. A. Berenson. *New Repub* 196:11-13 My 18 '87
Is there a doctor in the house? H. Banks. *Forbes* 139:27 Ap 6 '87
It's fever time for doctors. C. P. Work. il *U S News World Rep* 102:44-6 Ja 26 '87
Letters [discussion of August 15-22, 1987 article, Limiting health care for the old] D. Callahan. *Nation* 245:362+ O 10 '87
Limiting health care for the old [cover story] D. Callahan. *Nation* 245:109+ Ag 15-22 '87
Medical care and pauperization. G. P. Brockway. *New Leader* 70:11-12 D 28 '87
Medical "miracles" cost more than money. A. E. Miller, Jr. *Read Dig* 131:101-4 D '87
Medical technology [address, October 14, 1987] R. A. Schoellhorn. *Vital Speeches Day* 54:122-5 D 1 '87
The medicine vendors. E. Kiester. il *50 Plus* 27:36-40+ Ja '87
No more shooting for the moon [impact on technology] R. Greene. il *Forbes* 140:221-2 D 14 '87
On penalty of penury. *Progressive* 51:10 Ap '87
Reducing health-care costs. *Futurist* 21:54 S/O '87
The rising cost of health care: what it means to the nation, the elderly, and you [cover story; special issue] il *Sch Update* 119:2-12+ Ap 20 '87
Sick retirees could kill your company. J. Nielsen. il *Fortune* 115:98-9 Mr 2 '87
The silent killer [accounting treatment of employee health benefits] L. Jereski. il *Forbes* 139:112 F 23 '87
Some docs charge you 200% more. *Money* 16:13 Mr '87
Strong medicine for health bills [companies bargaining for better deals] S. Gannes. il *Fortune* 115:70-2+ Ap 13 '87
The Ten Commandments of health care. R. D. Lamm. il por *Humanist* 47:16-20+ My/Je '87
What price life? R. Greene. il *Forbes* 140:42+ S 7 '87
Anecdotes, facetiae, satire, etc.
The humiliating cost of health [American medical system] A. Fotheringham. il *Macleans* 100:60 My 11 '87

Medical care—*cont.*

Evaluation

Saving money and improving health by evaluating medical technology. V. Miké. il *Technol Rev* 90:22+ Ap '87

Federal aid

See Medical care, State

Africa

See also

Confederation of African Medical Associations and Societies

A third world perspective. O. O. Akinkugbe. il *World Health* p24-5 Ap '87

Alabama

Granny midwives: portrait of a timeless profession. E. I. M. Holland. il pors *Ms* 15:48-51+ Je '87

Algeria

More prevention, less treatment. O. Zemor. il *World Health* p11 Ap '87

California

See also

San Francisco (Calif.)—Medical care

A welfare mother's battle to clean up the Medicaid mess. S. B. Garland. il *Bus Week* p42 D 21 '87

Canada

Canada: too many and too few. *World Health* p13 Ap '87

Caribbean region

Eye services in the Caribbean. A. M. S. Connell. il *World Health* p27-8 My '87

China

Reaching the grass-roots. Deng Yuzhen. il *World Health* p20-1 Je '87

Colombia

An overdose of physicians. A. Mejia. il *World Health* p26-9 Ap '87

Developing countries

Save sight [cover story; special issue] il *World Health* p3-15+ My '87

Florida

In Florida, everybody loses [medical malpractice insurance] R. Goudreau. *50 Plus* 27:18 S '87

Georgia

See also

Brunswick (Ga.)—Medical care

All the hours of the night: the recollections of a country midwife [P. Burton] M. F. Greene. il pors *Ctry J* 14:58-63 N '87

India

Cataract in India. G. Venkataswamy. il *World Health* p25-6 My '87

Iowa

Rural elderly need new heart attack rescue rules [defibrillation equipment] *Success Farm* 85:54 O '87

Latin America

Health services for all. J. Osuna. il *World Health* p23-5 O '87

Malawi

Ophthalmic medical assistants. M. C. Chirambo. il *World Health* p9-11 My '87

Mexico

Health manpower out of balance. G. Soberón Acevedo. il *World Health* p16-17 Ap '87

Mexico faces the challenge. J. Frenk. il *World Health* p20-3 Ap '87

Psst, you wanna plastic surgeon? [Americans seeking health care services] J. Borrell. il *Time* 129:60 Je 15 '87

Oklahoma

See also

Jenks (Okla.)—Medical care

South Africa

South Africa's medical front [Alexandra Health Center and University Clinic aids black patients] M. McNamara. il *Ms* 16:76 D '87

Soviet Union

Doctor with a mission [G. Batist presses Soviet authorities to release refusenik patients with cancer] L. Van Dusen. il por *Macleans* 100:49-50 My 18 '87

United States

See Medical care

Medical care, Rural

New rural health care programs help fill need. C. Tevis. il *Success Farm* 85 no6:18L-18M Mr '87

Medical care, State

See also

Medicaid

Medicare

Health care bites the bullet [health care competes with military budget] H. H. Hiatt. *Bull At Sci* 43:7-8 Je '87

Medical care industry

See also

Baxter Travenol Laboratories Inc.

Biotherapeutics Inc.

Caremark, Inc.

Clinical Homecare Corporation

Healthsouth (Firm)

Hospital management industry

Kaiser-Permanente Medical Care Program

New England Critical Care

TME, Inc.

The bottom line is society loses [privatization] M. Abramovitz. il *Nation* 245:410-12 O 17 '87

Doctors as entrepreneurs: drawing the bottom line [views of Alexander Capron] il *USA Today (Periodical)* 115:16 F '87

Health. M. Fritz. il *Forbes* 139:140+ Ja 12 '87

Prognosis: empty beds and falling profits. J. O. Hamilton. il *Bus Week* p102 Ja 12 '87

Acquisitions and mergers

A booster shot for Baxter Labs [acquisition of Caremark Inc.] K. Deveny. il *Bus Week* p63 My 25 '87

Securities

See also

Fidelity Select-Health Care Fund

What the doctor ordered: medical mutual funds. T. Segal. il *Bus Week* p96 Ag 3 '87

Canada

Profits in health care. T. Tedesco. il *Macleans* 100:26-7 Je 8 '87

Medical centers *See* Health facilities; Hospitals

Medical colleges

See also

Black medical colleges

Charles R. Drew Postgraduate Medical School

Cornell University. Medical College

Meharry Medical College

Yale University. School of Medicine

Curing—plus caring. il *U S News World Rep* 103:78-9 N 2 '87

Enrollment

Med schools learn humility [fewer applications] J. N. Baker. il *Newsweek* 109:61-2 Je 29 '87

Caribbean region

The outcasts from the Caribbean [offshore medical school graduates] J. Langone. il *Discover* 8:68-70+ Je '87

Grenada

See also

St. George's University School of Medicine

Pakistan

See also

Aga Khan University Hospital and Medical College

Medical education

See also

Black medical students

Interns (Medicine)

Medical colleges

Medical teachers

Nurses and nursing—Study and teaching

First do no harm [education of a neurosurgeon; condensation] J. K. Rainer. il *Read Dig* 131:282-9+ N '87

Great expectations [health manpower out of balance; cover story; special issue] il *World Health* p3-29 Ap '87

The new doctors [learning compassion] A. B. Eagan. il *Health* 19:25-9+ Ap '87

A note to health-care policy makers [low morale] W. V. Healey. *America* 156:435-6 My 30 '87

Aids and devices

Anecdotes, facetiae, satire, etc.

What happened when I gave a proctoscopy to Eugene Wilson [DxTer interactive system] J. Gorman. il *Discover* 8:20+ Je '87

Medical electronics

See also

Biosensors

Biotelemetry

Computers—Medical use

Defibrillators

Magnetic resonance imaging—Medical use

Monitoring (Medical care)

Radiography, Medical

Chip nerves [reconnecting nerve fibers; work of Morton Grosser and Joseph M. Rosen] J. I. Mattill. il *Technol Rev* 90:15 O '87

Good connections? It's in the chips [reconnecting nerve fibers; work of Joseph M. Rosen and Morton Grosser] D. D. Edwards. il *Sci News* 131:86 F 7 '87

Medical technology in the 21st century. R. Fish. il *Radio-Electron* 58:112-14 My '87

Medical electronics—*cont.*
Repair shop [reconnecting nerve fibers] O. Davies. il
  Omni 10:140 N '87
Medical electronics industry
  See also
  Acuson Corporation
Medical equipment
  See also
  Electrotherapy—Equipment
  Hemodialysis equipment
  Image processing—Medical use
  Intravenous therapy—Equipment
  Medical electronics
  Oxygen equipment
  Polymers in medicine
  Sphygmomanometers
  Syringes
Be your own doctor, up to a point [use of at-home
  medical tests] *U S News World Rep* 103:69 N 23
  '87
A consumer's guide to over-the-counter tests. E.
  Greenspan. il *Ms* 15:60+ Je '87
Docs-in-a-box [home medical tests] C. Schaeffer. il
  Changing Times 41:137-40 N '87
Don't forget first-aid kit [vacation supplies; views of
  Patty Gerou] il *USA Today (Periodical)* 116:15 Ag
  '87
Tracking your health [home medical tests] *Vogue* 177:260
  Jl '87
What to pack in your medicine chest. C. Schaeffer.
  Changing Times 41:18+ Ag '87
          Safety devices and measures
A 'complaint department' for medical devices [Food
  and Drug Administration's Device Experience Network]
  R. C. Thompson. il *FDA Consum* 21:10-13 Mr '87
Looking for trouble in medical devices [FDA's Mechanics
  and Materials Laboratory] D. W. Stearman. il *FDA
  Consum* 21:18-23 S '87
Medical equipment industry
  See also
  Becton, Dickinson & Co.
  Biomet, Inc.
  Cordis Corporation
  Customedix Corporation
  Everest & Jennings International
  Foster Medical Corp.
  Intermedics Inc.
  Medex Inc.
  Q-Med, Inc.
  Shiley, Inc.
  Women in the medical equipment industry
          Suits and claims
$4.5 mil. lawsuit won in Mississippi medical case [suit
  against Pharmaseal Laboratories by family of T. Wells]
  Jet 72:14 Jl 20 '87
Medical ethics
  See also
  Baby Doe rules
  Cancer research—Ethical aspects
  Euthanasia
  Fertilization in vitro—Ethical aspects
  Gene therapy—Ethical aspects
  Genetic research—Ethical aspects
  Heart research—Ethical aspects
  Informed consent (Medical law)
  Medical research—Ethical aspects
  Medical research—Experimentation on man
  Pharmaceutical research—Ethical aspects
  Pharmaceutical research—Experimentation on man
  Psychiatric ethics
  Psychiatric research—Ethical aspects
  Right to die
  Transplantation of organs, tissues, etc.—Ethical
    aspects
Courage, Doc [C. E. Koop reprimands health professionals
  who refuse to treat AIDS patients] por *Time* 130:57
  S 21 '87
Doctors as entrepreneurs: drawing the bottom line [views
  of Alexander Capron] il *USA Today (Periodical)* 115:16
  F '87
Doctors grapple with ethics. M. Clark. il *Newsweek*
  110:62-3 D 28 '87
Fateful decisions on treating AIDS. E. Bowen. il *Time*
  129:62 F 2 '87
Health, ethics and human values [conference in Athens,
  Greece] Z. Bankowski and F. Gutteridge. il *World
  Health* p9-11 Je '87
Last rights [redefining death; cover story] K. Stein. il
  Omni 9:58-60+ S '87
Life & death, heart & mind [excerpt from Mortal choices]
  R. Macklin. *Vogue* 177:348-9+ Ap '87

Life and death [discussion of September 1987 article,
  Last rights] K. Stein. *Omni* 10:18 D '87
Life and death decisions: do you trust yourself to play
  God? [cover story; interview with E. Pellegrino] por
  U S Cathol 52:6-13 O '87
Medicine: the tough new questions [interview with R.
  Macklin] il por *Vogue* 177:350-1+ Ap '87
The Vatican document on bioethics: some unsolicited
  suggestions. R. A. McCormick. il *America* 156:24-8+
  Ja 17 '87
          Anecdotes, facetiae, satire, etc.
Last word. J. Fodor. il *Omni* 10:182 O '87
          Bibliography
'A man is ethical only when life, as such, is sacred
  to him'. L. S. Cahill. *America* 157:250+ O 17 '87
Medical examinations *See* Physical examinations
Medical facilities *See* Health facilities
Medical fakers *See* Quacks and quackery
Medical fees *See* Medical care—Costs
Medical genetics *See* Heredity of disease
Medical geography
The geography of influenza. G. F. Pyle and K. D.
  Patterson. il maps *Focus* 37:16-23 Fall '87
Medical history *See* Medicine—History
Medical hypnosis *See* Hypnotism—Therapeutic use
Medical identification
Have your kids been tagged? [Wager Lifesaver] il *Read
  Dig* 131:11-12 N '87
The symbol that speaks for you. il *Curr Health 2* 14:28-9
  D '87
Medical insurance *See* Insurance, Health
Medical jargon *See* Medicine—Terminology
Medical jurisprudence
  See also
  Forensic psychiatry
  Insanity—Jurisprudence
  Malpractice
DNA prints [analysis of nuclear DNA patterns in criminal
  investigations] *Time* 129:66 Ja 26 '87
Leaving Holmes in the dust [DNA fingerprints] S. Begley.
  il *Newsweek* 110:81 O 26 '87
Ultra-sensitive blood test is a new anti-crime weapon
  [isoelectric focusing] R. Layne. *Pop Sci* 230:104 Ap
  '87
Medical kits *See* Medical equipment
Medical laboratories
Can you really trust a lab test? The scary truth. M.
  Lawrence. il *Glamour* 85:74+ N '87
Medical laboratory workers *See* Health workers
Medical laws and regulations *See* Medical policy
Medical libraries
  See also
  National Library of Medicine (U.S.)
Medical literature
          Authorship
Turning my words against me [accusations of plagiarism]
  P. Klass. *N Y Times Book Rev* 92:1+ Ap 5 '87
Medical missions *See* Missions, Medical
Medical museums
  See also
  Deutsches Hygiene-Museum (Dresden, Germany)
Medical news
Breakthroughs. See issues of Health (New York, N.Y.)
Family doctor. A. E. Nourse. See issues of Good
  Housekeeping
Feel & look your best! C. Schrader. il *Harpers Bazaar*
  120:130-1+ Ja '87
Health. M. Weber. See issues of Vogue
Health front. See issues of Prevention (Emmaus, Pa.)
Healthsmart. C. Schrader. *Harpers Bazaar* 120:68+ Ag
  '87
Medical-care news. See issues of Prevention (Emmaus,
  Pa.) beginning May 1985
Medical mailbox. C. SerVaas. See issues of The Saturday
  Evening Post
Medical news. il *Parents* 62:26 F '87
Medical report. See issues of Glamour
Medinews. B. Weinhouse. See issues of Ladies' Home
  Journal
News. F. Davis. See issues of Mademoiselle
News from the world of medicine. See issues of Reader's
  Digest
A question of health. See issues of Consumer Reports
Read between the lines of a health study. *Glamour*
  85:97 S '87
Stethoscope. See issues of Current Health 2
Vital signs. See issues of McCall's beginning October
  1983

Medical newsletters *See* Newsletters
Medical physics
Forensic physics of vehicle accidents [cover story] A. C. Damask. bibl f il *Phys Today* 40:36-44 Mr '87
Medical physics. il *Phys Today* 40:S42-S45 Ja '87
Medical policy
See also
Informed consent (Medical law)
Medical care, State
United States. Dept. of Health and Human Services
United States. Surgeon-General's Office
The bottom line is society loses [privatization] M. Abramovitz. il *Nation* 245:410-12 O 17 '87
Health policy and chronic illness. A. L. Strauss. *Society* 25:33-9 N/D '87
How high a priority will society accord to health care? [address, December 5, 1986] T. M. Cooper. *Vital Speeches Day* 53:242-5 F 1 '87
Memo to the president: U.S. health policy. L. Kravitz. il *Sch Update* 119:17-18 Ap 20 '87
The revolution in medicine. G. Easterbrook. il *Newsweek* 109:40-4+ Ja 26 '87
The Ten Commandments of health care. R. D. Lamm. il por *Humanist* 47:16-20+ My/Je '87

International aspects
Health, ethics and human values [conference in Athens, Greece] Z. Bankowski and F. Gutteridge. il *World Health* p9-11 Je '87

Bavaria (Germany)
Bavaria requires AIDS testing. D. Dickson. *Science* 236:1057 My 29 '87

British Columbia
A blow for the doctors [policy limits number of physicians allowed to practice in move to cut billings] J. O'Hara. il *Macleans* 100:16 Ja 19 '87

Connecticut
Medicare and seniors [address, February 2, 1987] T. Norbek. *Vital Speeches Day* 53:414-16 Ap 15 '87
Medical radiography *See* Radiography, Medical
Medical research
See also
Cancer research
Heart research
Howard Hughes Medical Institute
National Institute of Arthritis, Musculoskeletal, and Skin Diseases (U.S.)
National Institutes of Health (U.S.)
Pharmaceutical research
Psychiatric research
Vollum Institute for Advanced Biomedical Research
Read between the lines of a health study. *Glamour* 85:97 S '87
Science discovers women. R. Wolkomir and J. Wolkomir. *Omni* 10:37 O '87

Ethical aspects
Dashed hopes and debate over 'cures'. J. Barber. il *Macleans* 100:72-3 F 2 '87
NIH moves to debar cholesterol researcher [case of C. J. Glueck] C. Holden. por *Science* 237:718-19 Ag 14 '87

Experimentation on man
See also
Self experimentation in medicine
America's human guinea pigs. R. C. Cowen. il *Technol Rev* 90:20-1 F/Mr '87
The death doctors [Nazi doctors] N. Ascherson. il *N Y Rev Books* 34:29-34 My 28 '87
(Lab) works in progress. A. Hornaday. il *Omni* 9 Omni Exper:11-13 Ap '87

Federal aid
See also
National Institutes of Health (U.S.)—Appropriations and expenditures

Developing countries
See also
Independent International Commission on Health Research for Development

France
See also
Institut Pasteur (Paris, France)

Great Britain
See also
Common Cold Unit (Great Britain)
British government rekindles debate on embryo research. D. Dickson. *Science* 238:1348 D 4 '87

Soviet Union
Surveillance and research [smallpox eradication research] S. Marennikova. il *World Health* p22-3 Ag/S '87

Medical schools *See* Medical colleges
Medical science *See* Medicine
Medical self care *See* Medical care
Medical service *See* Medical care
Medical societies
See also
American College of Surgeons
American Medical Association
Canadian Medical Association
Confederation of African Medical Associations and Societies
Institute of Medicine (U.S.)
National Medical Association
Medical students
See also
Black medical students
Women medical students
Medical symbolism *See* Symbolism in medicine
Medical teachers
A note to health-care policy makers [low morale] W. V. Healey. *America* 156:435-6 My 30 '87
Medical technology
Medical miracles [special section] D. Nimmons. il *Ladies Home J* 104:125-8+ F '87
Medical technology [address, October 14, 1987] R. A. Schoellhorn. *Vital Speeches Day* 54:122-5 D 1 '87
Medical technology and the poor. V. W. Sidel. il *Technol Rev* 90:24-5 My/Je '87
Medical technology in the 21st century. R. Fish. il *Radio-Electron* 58:112-14 My '87
No more shooting for the moon [impact of medical costs] R. Greene. il *Forbes* 140:221-2 D 14 '87
Saving money and improving health by evaluating medical technology. V. Miké. il *Technol Rev* 90:22+ Ap '87
Tomorrow's medicine. Y. Villedieu. il *Courier* 40:28-33 Ag '87
What price life? R. Greene. il *Forbes* 140:42+ S 7 '87
Wildcatters in the laboratory [medical technology ventures in Houston] T. Mack. il *Forbes* 140:258+ N 16 '87

Conferences
A consensus view. S. Perry. il *World Health* p12-13 Je '87

Securities
See also
Medical Technology Fund
Venture capital is changing course. il *Bus Week* p71 Ag 31 '87
Medical Technology Fund
Medical assistance. R. Phalon. il *Forbes* 139:114 Ap 20 '87
Medical television programs *See* Television broadcasting—Medical programs
Medical terminology *See* Medicine—Terminology
Medical thermography *See* Thermography—Medical use
Medical ultrasonics *See* Ultrasonic waves—Medical use
Medical waste disposal
The garbage health scare. M. Clark. il *Newsweek* 110:56 Jl 20 '87
Medical workers *See* Health workers
Medicare
See also
Medicaid
National Committee to Preserve Social Security and Medicare
Are the elderly overinsured? [medigap insurance] A. R. Dennon. il *Consum Res Mag* 70:16-19 Mr '87
Beyond Medicare [catastrophic illness] il *Newsweek* 109:3 Ja 5 '87
Catastrophic coverage. R. Coorsh. *Consum Res Mag* 70:4 D '87
Catastrophic health care may be flat on its back. S. B. Garland. *Bus Week* p45 Jl 13 '87
Catastrophic health insurance. *Congr Dig* 66:97-128 Ap '87
Catastrophic-illness insurance: not if, but when. M. A. Pollock and R. Fly. il *Bus Week* p46-7 Ja 12 '87
Catastrophic insurance for all. J. Hook. il *Wash Mon* 19:37-40 F '87
The company that has HMOs sick with worry [International Medical Centers Inc.] G. DeGeorge. il *Bus Week* p52 My 11 '87
Congress wakes up to Medicare reform [catastrophic care] C. Murphy. il *50 Plus* 27:26-9 Ap '87
Deathbed politics: Medicare and the baby boom generation. P. Longman. *New Repub* 196:18-20 Mr 30 '87
Doctors and markets. *New Repub* 196:4+ Ja 19 '87
Dr. Bowen's catastrophic insurance is bad medicine. il *Consum Res Mag* 70:30-3 Je '87
A grim outlook for hospitals [government might limit Medicare capital cost payouts] G. Weiss. il *Bus Week* p126+ My 11 '87

Medicare—*cont.*

The health gift repossessed. R. J. Margolis. il *New Leader* 70:13-14 Ap 6 '87

Health insurance: Democrats borrow a line from Reagan [treating Medicare benefits as taxable income] S. B. Garland. il *Bus Week* p43 My 4 '87

How Medicare puts the elderly on hold. R. J. Margolis. *New Leader* 70:12-13 Jl 1-15 '87

Letters [discussion of August 15-22, 1987 article, Limiting health care for the old] D. Callahan. *Nation* 245:362+ O 10 '87

Limiting health care for the old [cover story] D. Callahan. *Nation* 245:109+ Ag 15-22 '87

Medicare and Medicaid programs. *Congr Dig* 66:100-1+ Ap '87

Medicare and seniors [address, February 2, 1987] T. Norbek. *Vital Speeches Day* 53:414-16 Ap 15 '87

"Medicare must be rewritten, now!" [views of R. N. Butler] E. Kiester. il por *50 Plus* 27:30-2+ Ja '87

Medicare street smarts. E. Kiester. il *50 Plus* 27:30-1+ Ap '87

Next, the McDRG [diagnostic related groups] J. Feinglass. il *Progressive* 51:28 Ja '87

No socialized medicine now [catastrophic illness legislation] J. McLaughlin. *Natl Rev* 39:24 S 11 '87

Peace of mind [catastrophic illness] *America* 156:185 Mr 7 '87

Profiting from the medigap [TV ads for health insurance] G. P. Brockway. *New Leader* 70:11-12 Ap 20 '87

An Rx for catastrophe [O. R. Bowen's proposal for catastrophic illness insurance] O. Friedrich. il por *Time* 129:38-9 Ja 5 '87

Should it cover millionaires? F. Greve. *50 Plus* 27:20+ My '87

Transplant by the numbers [heart transplants and Medicare] R. Rosenblatt. *50 Plus* 27:19 O '87

What you need to know to protect your life's savings. P. Martin. bibl il *50 Plus* 27:32-40+ O '87

Canada

A blow for the doctors [British Columbia policy limits number of physicians allowed to practice in move to cut billings] J. O'Hara. il *Macleans* 100:16 Ja 19 '87

Medici, Lorenz de'

about

A cooking school in Chianti. Z. E. Zakroff. il pors *Gourmet* 47:70-5+ My '87

Medicinal plants *See* Botany, Medical

Medicine

See also
Acupuncture
Adhesives—Medical use
American Medical Association
Anesthesia and anesthetics
Balloons—Medical use
Carbon fibers—Medical use
Computers—Medical use
Dentistry
Diseases
Group medical practice
Holistic medicine
Homeopathy
Humor in medicine
Image processing—Medical use
Indians of North America—Medicine
Information storage and retrieval systems—Medical use
Lasers—Medical use
Leeches—Medical use
Mayas—Medicine
Medical research
Nuclear medicine
Paleopathology
Polymers in medicine
Quacks and quackery
Sex discrimination in medicine
Space medicine
Surgery
Tropical medicine
Ultrasonic waves—Medical use
Veterinary medicine

The revolution in medicine. G. Easterbrook. il *Newsweek* 109:40-4+ Ja 26 '87

Emblems and symbols
See Symbolism in medicine

Equipment
See Medical equipment

History

A brief history of American medicine. J. Ross. il *Sch Update* 119:10-12 Ap 20 '87

Information services

When your child is seriously ill: lifelines for parents. S. Lowe. il *McCalls* 114:40-1 Je '87

Where to get help if you hurt. il *U S News World Rep* 102:57 Je 29 '87

Where to go for help [information on preventive medicine] il *U S News World Rep* 103:62-3 Ag 17 '87

International aspects

See also
Council for International Organizations of Medical Sciences

Medicine and health [cover story; special issue] il *Courier* 40:3-34 Ag '87

Laws and regulations
See Medical policy

Periodicals

See also
New England journal of medicine

Practice
See Physicians

Scholarships and fellowships

See also
National Medical Fellowships

Study and teaching
See Medical education

Terminology

Healing words from the worlds of medicine and public health care. P. M. Jones. *Sch Update* 119:26 Ap 20 '87

Medical terms in plain English. P. Gadsby. il *Good Housekeep* 205:253 O '87

Operating on the English language. *Newsweek* 109:44 Ja 26 '87

Africa

See also
Confederation of African Medical Associations and Societies

Canada

See also
Canadian Medical Association

Germany

The death doctors [Nazi doctors] N. Ascherson. il *N Y Rev Books* 34:29-34 My 28 '87

United States
See Medicine

Medicine, Chinese

Acupuncture and me [knee injury treated with herbal tea and acupuncture] S. R. Brady. il por *Good Housekeep* 205:58+ Ag '87

Chinese folk remedy may promote cancer [plants containing phorbal esters linked to nasopharyngeal cancer; research by L. David Tomei and others] R. Weiss. *Sci News* 132:148 S 5 '87

Plant therapy in the fight against cancer. Xing Sishao. il *Courier* 40:20 Ag '87

A side order of sea slugs [herbal cookery at Emperor Herbal Restaurant, San Francisco] L. Shapiro. il *Newsweek* 110:77 S 14 '87

Medicine, Military

See also
Civilian Health and Medical Program of the Uniformed Services
World War, 1914-1918—Medical and sanitary affairs

Medicine, Preventive

See also
Vaccines and vaccination

Fending off the leading killers [cover story; special section] J. Carey and J. Silberner. il *U S News World Rep* 103:56-8+ Ag 17 '87

Personal autonomy and public health: an ethical imperative for preventing disease. R. C. Greene. il por *Humanist* 47:6-9 Jl/Ag '87

Prevention should be for everyone [proposed President's Prevention Council] il *Prevention* 39:27-31 F '87

Medicine, Psychosomatic

See also
Faith cure
Hospital patients—Psychology
Psychoneuroimmunology

Are your thoughts killing you? D. Chopra. il *Nations Bus* 75:87 O '87

Blaming the victim. E. Switzer. *Vogue* 177:782-3+ S '87

Can you psych yourself into good health? [excerpt from The healing brain] R. E. Ornstein and D. S. Sobel. il *Glamour* 85:280-1+ Ag '87

Can you think yourself healthy? J. M. Toal. il *Mademoiselle* 93:164+ S '87

Dr. Bernie Siegel's prescription for cancer victims (and a best-seller): 'Patient, heal thyself'. K. Gross. il pors *People Wkly* 28:61+ S 21 '87

Medicine, Psychosomatic—*cont.*
Generic disposition for disease? *Sci News* 132:46 Jl 18
'87
Help for the worried well. C. Turkington. il *Psychol
Today* 21:44-8 Ag '87
Mind games taken to heart [post-operative cardiac patients
at Children's Hospital in San Diego] N. Benford and
D. Gage. il *Health* 19:25 N '87
The mind over the body [behavioral medicine] D.
Goleman. il *N Y Times Mag* p36+ S 27 '87
Psychosomatic illness: is it all in your head? R. D.
France. por *McCalls* 114:81 Ap '87
Stop blaming yourself [linking explanatory style with
learned helplessness, depression, and illness; research
by M. E. P. Seligman] R. J. Trotter. bibl (p64) il
pors *Psychol Today* 21:30-2+ F '87
Think yourself healthy. R. Manuel. il *Harpers Bazaar*
120:118+ F '87
Three medical miracles: the medicine was love; ed. by
Susan Schneider. B. S. Siegel. *Redbook* 170:84-5+ D
'87
Winter in Antarctica: health despite discomfort [positive
stress; study by Lawrence A. Palinkas] E. Smith. il
Psychol Today 21:60-1 Mr '87
Medicine and art
See also
Anatomy, Artistic
Medicine and religion
Embarrassed physicians. R. Clapp. il *Christ Today*
31:16-17 N 20 '87
Life and death decisions: do you trust yourself to play
God? [cover story; interview with E. Pellegrino] por
U S Cathol 52:6-13 O '87
To your health. M. A. Noll. il *Christ Today* 31:14-15
Je 12 '87
The Vatican document on bioethics: some unsolicited
suggestions. R. A. McCormick. il *America* 156:24-8+
Ja 17 '87
Medicine and state *See* Medical policy
Medicine bottles *See* Bottles
Medicine cabinet supplies *See* Medical equipment
Medicine men
See also
Shamans and shamanism
Dr. Plotkin's jungle pharmacy: an ethnobotanist goes
native for science [work among the Tirió tribe in
Suriname] A. Fadiman. il pors *Life* 10:15-17 Je '87
Medicines *See* Drugs
Medicines, Nonprescription
See also
Cold (Disease) remedies
Cough medicines
Eye drops, washes, etc.
Home remedies
Mouthwashes
Over-the-counter drugs: handle with care! D. Hymes.
il *Curr Health 2* 13:14-15 Ja '87
A special system for OTC drugs [FDA review] *FDA
Consum* 21:12 D '87/Ja '88
Medieval civilization *See* Civilization, Medieval
Medieval music *See* Music, Medieval
Medigap insurance *See* Insurance, Health
Medina, Mario
about
The 'red' bishop of Benjamín Aceval. T. H. Stahel.
America 156:453-4 Je 6 '87
Meditation
Centering prayer. M. B. Pennington. *America* 156:169-71
F 28 '87
Give Randy Adamadama 40 minutes—he'll have you
seeing the light [owner of Synchro-Energizer salon in
California] il por *People Wkly* 28:134-5 D 14 '87
Mellow out: meditate. C. Elflein. il *Seventeen* 46:143
S '87
Mind over muscle [use of meditation techniques to boost
athlete performance] L. Brummell and B. Weisbrot.
il *Women's Sports Fitness* 9:60 My '87
Stress relief: the 15-minute breather. P. Kripke. il *Work
Woman* 12:148 Ap '87
Mediterranean fruit flies *See* Fruit flies
Mediterranean region
See also
Bronze Age—Mediterranean region
Eating—Mediterranean region
Malta
Antiquities
The Mediterranean, an underwater museum. A. J. Parker.
il *Courier* 40:8-10 N '87
Mediterranean Sea
See also
Marine pollution—Mediterranean Sea

Medium format cameras *See* Cameras
Medjugorje (Yugoslavia)
Religious institutions and affairs
Medjugorje's miracles: faith and profit [appearances of
the Virgin Mary] D. R. Janz. il *Christ Century* 104:724-5
Ag 26-S 2 '87
Visitations of the Virgin. K. L. Woodward. il *Newsweek*
110:54-5 Jl 20 '87
Medley, Donald M. (Donald Matthias), and Coker, Homer
How valid are principals' judgments of teacher effective-
ness? bibl f il *Phi Delta Kappan* 69:138-40 O '87
MEDLINE (Data base) *See* Information storage and
retrieval systems—Medical use
Mednick, Murray
about
The coyote cycle [drama] Reviews
People Wkly il 28:83-4 Ag 24 '87. D. Grogan
Medoff, Mark Howard
In praise of teachers. pors *Read Dig* 130:69-73 F '87
Medulla, Adrenal *See* Adrenal glands
Medvescek, Chris
8 silly little games (and why they're so important). il
Parents 62:92-4+ Je '87
Mee, Charles L.
The non-signers. pors *Am Herit* 38:78-9 S/O '87
Meeh, Gregory
about
Still life in motion. C. Bush. il *Theatre Crafts* 21:32-3+
F '87
Meehan, Denise Duffy
Handmade in Massachusetts: Pioneer Valley crafts. il
Travel Holiday 167:44-7 Ja '87
Meehan, Mary
Wombs shouldn't be for rent [with readers' comments]
U S Cathol 52:16-21 S '87
Meeker, Amy
Boston makes way for ducklings: the Mallard family
in bronze. il *Publ Wkly* 232:27 O 30 '87
Marketing on two fronts. *Publ Wkly* 232:44-7 N 27
'87
Meeker, Darcy
Clean greens. il *Health* 19:43-4+ Ag '87
Meekins, Dorothy
Please disturb [poem] *Essence* 17:108 F '87
Meer, Jeff
(jt. auth) See Horn, Jack C., and Meer, Jeff
Meerkats
Photographs and photography
Together we stand . . . [cover story] A. Degré. il *Nat
Hist* 96:34-9 Je '87
Meerson, Felix Z.
Survival: human adaptation to extreme conditions. il
Courier 40:4-7 Je '87
Meese, Edwin, III
The law of the Constitution. il *Natl Rev* 39:30-3 Jl
17 '87
UN narcotics conference meets in Vienna [statement,
June 17, 1987] *Dep State Bull* 87:77-9 S '87
about
Another blow for Ed Meese. T. Jacoby. il por *Newsweek*
110:24-5 N 30 '87
A Bronx scandal tars Meese. C. O'Connor. il por
Newsweek 109:20 My 25 '87
Civil rights setbacks. F. D. Brown. *Essence* 18:30 Jl
'87
The Constitution and the Court: could Meese be right?
S. Levinson. *Current* 292:32-5 My '87
Edwin Meese and the Wedtech web. D. Baer. il por
U S News World Rep 102:14 My 18 '87
Edwin Meese's power trip—the downhill slope. D. Baer.
il por *U S News World Rep* 103:14 Jl 13 '87
Edwin Meese's quiet year turns unquiet. D. Baer and
P. Cary. il por *U S News World Rep* 102:14-15 My
25 '87
The growing difficulties of Ed Meese. T. Jacoby. il por
Newsweek 110:24 Jl 13 '87
An introduction to the attorney general. D. Oliver. *Natl
Rev* 39:18 Jl 17 '87
Investigating the investigator. R. Parry. il por *Newsweek*
110:16-17 Ag 3 '87
"It's very difficult to accept". J. V. Lamar, Jr. il pors
Time 130:11 Ag 10 '87
John Conyers asks that Edwin Meese resign. *Jet* 72:29
Ag 31 '87
Meese and AIDS. *Nation* 244:837-8 Je 20 '87
The Meese factor: packing the lower courts. I. Silver.
Commonweal 114:102 F 27 '87
The Meese lie. S. Gillers. *Nation* 244:205 F 21 '87
The Meese mess gets muddier. P. Dwyer. por *Bus Week*
p68 D 28 '87-Ja 4 '88

Meese, Edwin, III—about—*cont.*
'Meese messes' galore. D. Baer. por *U S News World Rep* 103:18 N 30 '87
Meese's legal troubles have him hog-tied at Justice. P. Dwyer. por *Bus Week* p39 Je 29 '87
Meese's troubles go way beyond Wedtech. P. Dwyer and H. Collingwood. il por *Bus Week* p26-7 Jl 27 '87
New doubts about Meese and the contra inquiry. L. Martz. il por *Newsweek* 109:29-30 Ap 20 '87
The new questions about Ed Meese's finances. P. Dwyer. il por *Bus Week* p46-7 My 11 '87
Of principles and politics [interview] il *U S News World Rep* 103:20 O 19 '87
Pulling the plug on antitrust law. J. S. Cohen and J. W. Cuneo. il *Nation* 245:296-7 S 26 '87
Resign, Ed Meese. il *New Repub* 197:7-9 N 9 '87
The resilient loyalist. E. Shannon. il por *Time* 130:15 Ag 3 '87
The trial and errors of Edwin Meese. D. Baer. il pors *U S News World Rep* 103:16-18 Ag 3 '87
Viva Miranda. J. Toobin. *New Repub* 196:11-12 F 16 '87
Why Meese spoke. D. Lindorff. *Nation* 244:349 Mr 21 '87
With a friend like this . . . E. Magnuson. por *Time* 130:20 N 16 '87
Anecdotes, facetiae, satire, etc.
Last word. T. Runté. il *Omni* 9:126 F '87
Meese Commission on Pornography *See* United States. Attorney General's Commission on Pornography
Meese Partners
The Meese mess gets muddier. P. Dwyer. por *Bus Week* p68 D 28 '87-Ja 4 '88
Meese's troubles go way beyond Wedtech. P. Dwyer and H. Collingwood. il por *Bus Week* p26-7 Jl 27 '87
Meetings
See also
Conventions
Corporations—Meetings
Mefistofele [opera] *See* Boito, Arrigo, 1842-1918
Megalithic monuments
See also
America's Stonehenge (North Salem, N.H.)
Stonehenge (England)
Megavitamins *See* Vitamins
Meggyesy, Dave
about
Still on the outside. D. Remnick. il pors *Sports Illus* 67:44-7+ O 5 '87
Meharry Medical College
Jackson State, Meharry get $100,000 each from grads. *Jet* 72:25 Je 22 '87
Mehera, S. K.
India and Pakistan: brothers and enemies. map *World Press Rev* 34:32-4 S '87
Meherani, Candyce
Choosing wines. il *Ms* 15:12+ Ja '87
Mehl, Duane
The downward trajectory of John Updike. *Natl Rev* 39:53-4+ F 13 '87
Mehlman, Peter
Cracking the manspeak code. *Mademoiselle* 93:138-9+ Ja '87
Fête accompli. il *Harpers Bazaar* 121:68+ D '87
In search of the rare redhead. *Harpers Bazaar* 120:111+ Jl '87
Male guilt. il *Glamour* 85:332 Ap '87
Men, myths & movies. il *Harpers Bazaar* 120:380+ S '87
Mehrten, Greg
about
It's a man's world [drama] Reviews
Nation 244:862 Je 20 '87. T. M. Disch
New Yorker 63:69-70 Je 8 '87. M. Kramer
Mehta, A. S. (Ajai Singh)
about
The heart of the Mehta. R. Koenig. il *N Y* 20:23 Mr 2 '87
Sonny Mehta named president of Knopf. M. Reuter. por *Publ Wkly* 231:289 Ja 30 '87
Mehta, Ajai Singh *See* Mehta, A. S. (Ajai Singh)
Mehta, Ved, 1934-
Among the seven pillars of wisdom. *New Yorker* 63:34-6+ Ag 24 '87
At the gates of California. *New Yorker* 63:82-97 My 11 '87
Letter from New Delhi. il *New Yorker* 62:52+ Ja 19 '87

Mehta, Zubin
about
Seeking the light [cover story] M. Mayer. il pors *Opera News* 52:12-15 D 5 '87
Meier, Daniel
One man's kids. il *N Y Times Mag* p56 N 1 '87
Meier, Deborah
Central Park East: an alternative story. il *Phi Delta Kappan* 68:753-7 Je '87
Meier, Eduard
about
UFO update. B. Lawren. il *Omni* 9:95 Jl '87
Meier, Joan
Battered justice. *Wash Mon* 19:37-45 My '87
Meier, Richard, 1934-
about
Architecture: Richard Meier [cover story] R. Hughes. il *Archit Dig* 44:152-9+ O '87
Classic modern. C. Vogel. il *N Y Times Mag* p60-4 F 1 '87
Eminent domain. M. Filler. il *House Gard* 159:162-9+ Ap '87
Richard Meier, abroad and at home. T. Metz. il *Archit Rec* 175:51 Jl '87
Meigs, James B.
Band on the run. il *Roll Stone* p86-9+ S 24 '87
Home video. See issues of Popular Mechanics beginning January 1986
Meindl, James D.
Chips for advanced computing. il *Sci Am* 257:78-84+ O '87
Meine, Curt
How Leopold learned to think like a mountain. *Wilderness* 51:57-8+ Wint '87
Meiners, Roger
(jt. auth) See McCormick, Robert, and Meiners, Roger
Meinke, Peter
Writing short stories. *Writer* 100:12-14 Ja '87
Meisler, Laurie
Managing your money pro. il *Work Woman* 12:36+ F '87
Meisner, Edward H.
about
Meet the men who invented vibrating bedroom slippers. P. Finch. il pors *Bus Week* p91 N 9 '87
Meissen porcelain *See* Pottery, German
Mejia, Alfonso
An overdose of physicians. il *World Health* p26-9 Ap '87
Melamid, Aleksandr, 1945-
about
Nobody's fools. R. B. Woodward. il pors *Art News* 86:172-8 N '87
Melancholia *See* Depression, Mental
Melançon, André
about
Bach and broccoli [film] Reviews
Macleans il 100:58 Mr 16 '87. B. D. Johnson
Macleans il 100:57 Mr 16 '87. B. D. Johnson
Melanesia
See also
Fiji
Melanin
Parkinson's protection? [chloroquine offers partial protection from MPTP-induced symptoms; research by Robert J. D'Amato and others] B. Bower. *Sci News* 131:359 Je 6 '87
Melanomas *See* Skin—Cancer
Melatonin
Antidepressant and circadian phase-shifting effects of light. A. J. Lewy and others. bibl f il *Science* 235:352-4 Ja 16 '87
Winter depression: day for night [correction of melatonin production timing; research by Alfred J. Lewy and others] J. Meer. il *Psychol Today* 21:12 Je '87
Melbin, Murray
Night, the final frontier [excerpt from Night as frontier] *Harpers* 274:30+ Mr '87
about
Into the night. G. Williams. il *Omni* 9:36-8+ Jl '87
Melbourne (Australia)
Music
See also
Opera—Australia
Mell, Michael
Retrofitting the sixties: upgrading your lighting booth. il *Theatre Crafts* 21:32+ D '87
Mellencamp, John Cougar
about
Hero of the heartland. J. Jerome. il pors *Life* 10:102-4 O '87

Mellencamp, John Cougar—about—*cont.*
Mellencamp's melancholy 'Jubilee'. A. DeCurtis. il *Roll Stone* p105-7 O 8 '87
Rebel with a cause. T. White. il pors *N Y Times Mag* p40-1+ S 27 '87

Mellini, Peter, and Matthews, Roy T.
John Bull's family arises. bibl il *Hist Today* 37:17-23 My '87

Mellish, Xander
No foreigners needed here. *Progressive* 51:14-15 My '87

Mello, Thiago de
A land of contrasts. il map *Courier* 39:4-10 D '86

Mellon, Marc Richard
about
Pygmalion. *New Yorker* 63:33-5 O 19 '87

Mellon Bank NA
Mellon Bank looks for a repairman [resignation of J. D. Barnes] M. Rothman. il por *Bus Week* p97 Ap 27 '87
Mellon muscle [family fires chairman J. D. Barnes] *Time* 129:54 Ap 27 '87
Mellon's turnaround man is racing the clock [F. V. Cahouet] M. Schroeder. il por *Bus Week* p146 S 14 '87
A muddled future for Mellon Bank. R. E. Norton. il *Fortune* 115:68-70+ Mr 30 '87
Once-mighty Mellon is busy 'plugging holes'. M. Rothman. il por *Bus Week* p68 F 2 '87

Mellor, John Williams, 1928-, and Gavian, Sarah
Famine: causes, prevention, and relief. bibl f il *Science* 235:539-45 Ja 30 '87

Mellow, James R.
Antiques: birdcages. il *Archit Dig* 44:116-21 Ag '87
Art: schoolgirl paintings: nineteenth-century works by American amateur artists. il *Archit Dig* 44:140-5+ D '87

Melman, Rich
about
A Beverly Hills diner-saur named Ed Debevic's takes customers back to the Stone Age of rock 'n' roll. M. Neill. il por *People Wkly* 28:180-1 N 30 '87

Melo Neto, João Cabral de, 1920-
The voice of the canefield [poem]; tr. by Richard Zenith. *Atlantic* 259:52 F '87

Melody
Linear development. E. Kloss. il *Down Beat* 11:54-5 N '87

Melody farm [drama] See Mitchell, Ken

Melone, Joseph J.
The competitiveness challenge [address, August 21, 1987] *Vital Speeches Day* 54:100-4 D 1 '87

Melons
See also
Cooking—Fruit
Is it ripe? [winter melons; cover story] S. Milius. il *Rodale's Org Gard* 34:44+ S '87
Playing for keeps [casabas; cover story] J. H. Sanchez. il *Rodale's Org Gard* 34:38-42 S '87

Melosh, H. J.
(jt. auth) See Vickery, Ann M., and Melosh, H. J.

Melotti, Fausto, 1901-1986
about
Fausto Melotti: San Nicola dei Greci, Madonna delle Virtù. J. Turner. il *Art News* 86:174 D '87

Melridge, Inc.
Hotter than a pistil [G. R. Heublein] M. Gill. il por *Esquire* 107:72 My '87
Planting the seeds of a blossoming business. M. J. Parks. il por *Bus Week* p82 Je 1 '87

Melrose (Natchez, Miss.: Historic house) See Natchez (Miss.)—Historic houses, sites, etc.

Melrose (New York, N.Y.: Restaurant) See New York (N.Y.)—Restaurants, nightclubs, bars, etc.

Melting
Central heating [estimating temperature of the earth's core from the melting point of iron at immense pressure] *Sci Am* 256:25-6 Je '87
How hot is the heart of the earth? [research by Quentin Williams and others] S. Weisburd. *Sci News* 131:245 Ap 18 '87
The melting curve of iron to 250 gigapascals: a constraint on the temperature at earth's center. Q. Williams and others. bibl f il *Science* 236:181-2 Ap 10 '87

Melton, Charles, d. 1987
about
Crusader Charles Melton gets last wish; new vote system for Westchester, Pa. il por *Jet* 73:6-7 S 28 '87

Melton, J. Gordon
(jt. auth) See Lewis, James R., and Melton, J. Gordon

Melton, Mel
about
Instead of just squeaking by, retiree Mel Melton snaps at the chance to easily trap the common mouse. il por *People Wkly* 27:114 F 2 '87

Meltsner, Michael
Cool with Coolidge. *Nation* 245:365 O 10 '87

Melville Corporation
Melville's new crew aims to get back to speed. F. McCoy. il por *Bus Week* p94 Jl 13 '87

Melzack, Ronald
about
Pain's gatekeeper. C. Warga. bibl (p67) il pors *Psychol Today* 21:50-6 Ag '87

Membrane transport systems See Biological transport

Membranes (Biology)
See also
Amnion
Blood-brain barrier
Epithelium
Assembly of clathrin-coated pits onto purified plasma membranes. M. S. Moore and others. bibl f il *Science* 236:558-63 My 1 '87
Bacteriophage M13 procoat protein inserts into the plasma membrane as a loop structure. A. Kuhn. bibl f il *Science* 238:1413-15 D 4 '87
Bespoke bactericide [for gram-negative bacteria; work of Stephen M. Hammond] J. Benditt. *Sci Am* 257:32+ S '87
Family study of platelet membrane fluidity in Alzheimer's disease. G. S. Zubenko and others. bibl f il *Science* 238:539-42 O 23 '87
How animal cells move. M. S. Bretscher. bibl (p158) il *Sci Am* 257:72-6+ D '87
Inherited membranes predict Alzheimer's? [fluidity of platelet membranes] *Sci News* 132:301 N 7 '87
Leader peptidase of Escherichia coli: critical role of a small domain in membrane assembly. R. E. Dalbey and W. T. Wickner. bibl f il *Science* 235:783-7 F 13 '87
Lipid takes a stand against alcohol [phosphatidylinositol; research by Theodore F. Taraschi and others] D. D. Edwards. *Sci News* 131:38-9 Ja 17 '87
Photodynamic action [photosensitization] D. P. Valenzeno and J. P. Pooler. bibl f il *BioScience* 37:270-6 Ap '87
Second wind for second-messenger research: how do G proteins and external signals influence intracellular activity? C. Vaughan. il *BioScience* 37:642-6 O '87
Signal for attachment of a phospholipid membrane anchor in decay accelerating factor. I. W. Caras and others. bibl f il *Science* 238:1280-3 N 27 '87
Structure, function, and assembly of membrane proteins. E. Racker. bibl f *Science* 235:959-61 F 27 '87

Mementos See Souvenirs (Keepsakes)
Memorabilia See Souvenirs (Keepsakes)
Memorandums
Memo of the month. See issues of The Washington Monthly

Memorial Sloan-Kettering Cancer Center
Dr. Marks' crusade: shaking up Sloan-Kettering for a new assault on cancer [cover story] P. M. Boffey. il pors *N Y Times Mag* p26-31+ Ap 26 '87

Memorials
See also
Stone Mountain Memorial (Ga.)
War memorials
Anecdotes, facetiae, satire, etc.
Uncivil liberties. C. Trillin. *Nation* 244:566 My 2 '87

Memories See Memory

Memory
See also
Amnesia
Attention
Past
Recognition (Psychology)
Advice from a sentimentalist: don't worry if he forgets your "shared memories". B.-J. Raphael. *Glamour* 85:243 O '87
Amnesia in litteris. P. Süskind. il *Harpers* 274:71-3 Mr '87
The anatomy of memory. M. Mishkin and T. Appenzeller. bibl (p136) il *Sci Am* 256:80-9 Je '87
Answering autobiographical questions: the impact of memory and inference on surveys. N. M. Bradburn and others. bibl f il *Science* 236:157-61 Ap 10 '87
Beside the still waters. H. L. Bahr. il *South Living* 22:140 My '87
Biochemistry of information storage in the nervous system. I. B. Black and others. bibl f il *Science* 236:1263-8 Je 5 '87

Memory—*cont.*

Brain boost? [lecithin] K. Freifeld. il *Health* 19:9-10 S '87

Bringing back fading memories [work of Anders Björklund and others with nerve growth factor] D. D. Edwards. *Sci News* 132:149-50 S 5 '87

The cerebellum and memory storage [discussion of August 29, 1986 article, The neurobiology of learning and memory] R. F. Thompson. *Science* 238:1728-30 D 18 '87

Childhood memories we can't erase. R. Westen. il *Glamour* 85:168+ O '87

Do 15 million cat neurons mediate the memory of a circle and a star? [discussion of September 12, 1986 article, Double-labeled metabolic maps of memory] E. R. John and others. *Science* 238:1586-8 D 11 '87

Eat to remember [role of the vagus nerve; research by James F. Flood and others] S. Weisburd. *Sci News* 131:327 My 23 '87

Feeding pigeons serial chunks [work of Herbert S. Terrace] *Sci News* 131:40 Ja 17 '87

Golden scrapbooks of the mind [family memories] B. Bartocci. il *Read Dig* 131:137-40 D '87

Knowing without knowing [tip-of-the-tonque effect; study by Gregory Jones and Sally Langford] J. Rubin. *Psychol Today* 21:16 D '87

Making the memory fit the man. L. Wainwright. il *Life* 10:13 S '87

Memory: age or practice? [prose recall; study by Hilary Horn Ratner] E. Stark. *Psychol Today* 21:24 O '87

Memory boost from spaced-out learning [long-term retention of foreign languages; study by Harry P. Bahrick and Elizabeth Phelps] B. Bower. *Sci News* 131:244 Ap 18 '87

Memory: learning how it works [cover story] G. Johnson. il por *N Y Times Mag* p16-21+ Ag 9 '87

Mind over matter: memory. S. Perry. il *Curr Health 2* 13:22-3 My '87

Modulation of memory processing by cholecystokinin: dependence on the vagus nerve. J. F. Flood and others. bibl f il *Science* 236:832-4 My 15 '87

Neural Darwinism: an exchange [discussion of October 9, 1986 article, Neural Darwinism: a new approach to memory and perception] I. Rosenfield. *N Y Rev Books* 34:44-5 Mr 12 '87

New routes to early memories [split brain research] D. Kucharski and W. G. Hall. bibl f il *Science* 238:786-8 N 6 '87

Old memories [work of Elisabeth Koss and others] *Sci Am* 256:26+ Je '87

Remembering how it was [using childhood memories in writing for children] L. Lowry. il *Writer* 100:16-19 Jl '87

Se habla español [language proficiency of former students of Spanish; study by Harry Bahrick] J. Meer. *Psychol Today* 21:12 My '87

Smell and tell [odor and memory; studies by Trygg Engen] H. Hall. *Psychol Today* 21:11 Ag '87

The subjects came in for a cold [effects of common cold on coordination and memory; study by Andrew P. Smith] V. Bozzi and G. Lowe. il *Psychol Today* 21:14 D '87

Unlocking the managerial memory. W. Kiechel, III. il *Fortune* 116:183-4 D 21 '87

Variety, the spice of memory [improving memory in Alzheimers patients; study by Curt Sandman] C. Simon. il *Psychol Today* 21:20 N '87

Weakened, memories, but sound minds [views of Elizabeth Zelinski] *USA Today (Periodical)* 116:5-6 Ag '87

When words elude you [tip-of-the-tongue state] *Better Homes Gard* 65:101 O '87

The workings of working memory. M. M. Waldrop. il *Science* 237:1564-7 S 25 '87

Anecdotes, facetiae, satire, etc.

Running on his rims [R. Reagan's memory] M. Ivins. il *Progressive* 51:17 My '87

Memory cards

Credit cards: the U.S. is taking its time getting 'smart'. T. Peterson and P. Heywood. il *Bus Week* p88-9 F 9 '87

Data card [Hi-Lite optical card] W. J. Hawkins. il *Pop Sci* 231:20 Jl '87

Hurry up and wait for optical-memory cards [LaserCards] J. W. Wilson. il por *Bus Week* p89+ F 9 '87

Raising the intelligence of credit cards. S. N. Wellborn. il *U S News World Rep* 102:50-1 F 2 '87

They bombed in Columbia [MasterCard's test marketing of the smart card] L. J. Moore. il *U S News World Rep* 102:50-1 F 2 '87

Memory devices (Computers) *See* Computers—Memory systems

Memos *See* Memorandums

Memotec Data Inc.

A buyer for Teleglobe. *Macleans* 100:38 F 23 '87

A giant charts its future [Bell Canada Enterprises buys stake in Memotec Data] B. Wallace. il *Macleans* 100:26-7 My 25 '87

The Memotec affair [insider trading scandal] B. Wallace. il *Macleans* 100:38 O 5 '87

Memotec's tangled roots [takeover of Teleglobe Canada] T. Fennell. il *Macleans* 100:42+ Mr 23 '87

Memphis (Tenn.)

Education

Needy kids, perpetual aid [A. Fogelman subsidizes college tuition for Memphis students] por *Time* 130:70 N 30 '87

Historic houses, sites, etc.

See also
Graceland

Hotels, motels, etc.

Lucky ducks! [trained ducks at Peabody Hotel] il *Natl Geogr World* 140:3-5 Ap '87

Housing

Downtown Memphis: they're moving in [converted buildings] L. Joyner. il *South Living* 22:96-8 N '87

Music

The King is dead, but his rich legacy still grows [E. Presley and rebirth of music] J. P. Shapiro. il *U S News World Rep* 103:56 Ag 24 '87

Religious institutions and affairs

Memphis churches back Rep. Ford with $100,000. il por *Jet* 72:7 Je 15 '87

Streets

See also
Beale Street (Memphis, Tenn.)

Men

See also
Beauty, Personal—Men
Christmas gifts for men
Cooking by men
Fathers
Heroes and heroines
Husbands
Men's liberation movement
Patriarchy
Sex differences
Single men
Young men

The 10 most handsome men on TV [results of survey] il *Good Housekeep* 204:124-5 F '87

The 15 dumbest men in America. G. Jacobs and G. Steinem. il *Ms* 16:118 Jl/Ag '87

About men. See issues of The New York Times Magazine

Heroic proportions [most admired men and women polls; study by Tom W. Smith] A. H. Rosenfeld. il *Psychol Today* 21:15 Jl '87

Look who won our most admired women and men polls. il *Good Housekeep* 204:48 Ja '87

Anecdotes, facetiae, satire, etc.

20 things a 30-year-old regular guy should know. B. Barol. il *Newsweek* 109:82 Je 22 '87

Is he husband material or a boyfriend kind of guy? K. Heller. il *Mademoiselle* 93:162-3+ O '87

Attitudes

His. B. Weber. See issues of Mademoiselle beginning October 1986

Hot commodities: will the man shortage spoil men? R. Wetzsteon. *Mademoiselle* 93:184-5+ F '87

How men really feel about condoms. P. Richmond. il *Glamour* 85:304-5+ N '87

Jake: a man's opinion. See issues of Glamour

Say, brother. See issues of Essence beginning May 1983

The women we love: a definitive selection [symposium] il *Esquire* 107:154-68 Je '87

Clothing and dress

See Clothing and dress—Men

Hairstyling

See Hairstyling

Health and hygiene

See also
Beauty, Personal—Men

Health smart. D. Longstreet. il *Harpers Bazaar* 120:44+ My '87

Help him lose extra pounds . . . while you get in shape, too. il *Glamour* 85:206+ Ja '87

His four biggest health fears. S. Friedlander. il *Health* 19:34-6 N '87

The save-his-life weight loss diet [excerpt from The underburner's diet] B. Edelstein. il *Ladies Home J* 104:62+ F '87

Men—*cont.*

Height

See Stature

Language

Man talk. B. Lustig. il *Glamour* 85:252 F '87

Anecdotes, facetiae, satire, etc.

Cracking the manspeak code. P. Mehlman. *Mademoiselle* 93:138-9+ Ja '87

Psychology

See also

Beauty, Personal—Psychological aspects

Masculinity (Psychology)

Are you turning men off? [special section] il *Harpers Bazaar* 120:300+ S '87

Confessions of a leg man. J. P. Davis. il *Glamour* 85:142-3 Jl '87

The dark playground [male response to rape] D. Voll. il *N Y Times Mag* p86 O 4 '87

Do men always fall for beauties? B. Weber. *Mademoiselle* 93:178 Ap '87

He's feeling sick? Take two aspirin and watch out. B.-J. Raphael. *Glamour* 85:30 Jl '87

How do men feel about their bodies? P. Richmond. il *Glamour* 85:312-13+ Ap '87

Male guilt [men perceived as criminals by women] P. Mehlman. il *Glamour* 85:332 Ap '87

Men in the eighties: multiplying roles: the next stage. D. Hellerstein. il *Ms* 16:48-50 O '87

The passions of men, 1987 [cover story; special issues; with editorial comment by Lee Eisenberg] il *Esquire* 107:29, 63+ Je '87

Say, brother [lack of communication between black men] C. Marberry. por *Essence* 18:9 My '87

Say, brother [rape of friend] M. W. Griffith. por *Essence* 18:10 S '87

Today's troubled men. H. J. Freudenberger. bibl (p63) il *Psychol Today* 21:46-7 D '87

Understanding the reasons behind men's new sexual fears. S. S. Cohen. il *Glamour* 85:206-7+ Je '87

What men really want from women in bed. J. P. Davis. il *Glamour* 85:178-9+ Ja '87

When women fight for equality, says Warren Farrell, fairness to men may be one of the casualties [interview] L. Powell. il pors *People Wkly* 27:49-50+ Je 15 '87

Why men cheat. R. Masello. il *Glamour* 85:146-7+ Jl '87

Why men confuse the women they love [condensed from Sexual static] M. H. Shaevitz. il *Read Dig* 131:65-6+ N '87

Why men divorce. L. L. Davitz. *McCalls* 145:26+ Mr '87

Why smart men still want dumb women. R. Grant. il *Ladies Home J* 104:78+ S '87

Sexual behavior

See Sexual behavior

Men, Women and God: Christians for Biblical Equality (Organization)

Christian feminists form new organization. *Christ Today* 31:44 O 16 '87

Men . . . [film] *See* Motion picture reviews—Single works

Men and women *See* Women and men

Men in literature *See* Characters in literature

Men teachers *See* Teachers

Ménage à Trois (New York, N.Y.: Restaurant) *See* New York (N.Y.)—Restaurants, nightclubs, bars, etc.

Menaker, Daniel

The spoils of success. il *N Y Times Mag* p24-5+ Ag 9 '87

Menand, Louis

Talk talk. *New Repub* 196:28-33 F 16 '87

Mencken, H. L. (Henry Louis), 1880-1956

about

At home with H. L. Mencken. il por *South Living* 22:30 S '87

Mencken and the great American boob. A. Kazin. il *N Y Rev Books* 34:8-11 F 26 '87

Rodgers and Haardt. L. Fleischer. il *Publ Wkly* 231:77 Ja 16 '87

Unpublished work by H. L. Mencken coming from Roberts Rinehart. B. Levine. *Publ Wkly* 232:62 O 9 '87

Mencken, Henry Louis *See* Mencken, H. L. (Henry Louis), 1880-1956

Mencken, Sara Haardt, 1898-1935

about

Rodgers and Haardt. L. Fleischer. il *Publ Wkly* 231:77 Ja 16 '87

Mencken (H. L.) House (Baltimore, Md.) *See* Baltimore (Md.)—Historic houses, sites, etc.

Mendel, Perry, 1922-

about

Kinder-Care may stick to its sitting. D. Foust. il por *Bus Week* p36 Jl 13 '87

Mendel, Richard A.

The first Chrysler bail-out: the M-1 tank. il *Wash Mon* 19:17-23 F '87

Mendenhall, Dan

about

Hurt books, remainders or what? A. Symons and S. Bolle. il *Publ Wkly* 232:31+ N 20 '87

Mendenhall Enterprises

Hurt books, remainders or what? A. Symons and S. Bolle. il *Publ Wkly* 232:31+ N 20 '87

Mendillo, M., and others

Spacelab-2 plasma depletion experiments for ionospheric and radio astronomical studies. bibl f il *Science* 238:1260-4 N 27 '87

Mendocino (Calif.)

Restaurants, nightclubs, bars, etc.

California idyll [Café Beaujolais] N. Hazelton. *Natl Rev* 39:67-9 S 11 '87

Mendocino County (Calif.)

Description and travel

The September-glorious Mendocino-Sonoma coast. il map *Sunset* 179:60-5 S '87

Mendoza, Terri

The A's and C's of vitamins. il *Curr Health 2* 14:18-21 D '87

Food equivalents: an easy equation. il *Curr Health 2* 13:22-5 Ap '87

Wanted: someone to watch my weight while I get on with the rest of my life. il *Curr Health 2* 13:25-7 F '87

Mendoza, Tony

about

A family framed. T. Young. il *Vogue* 177:98 My '87

Meneely, Philip M.

(jt. auth) *See* Sedensky, Margaret M., and Meneely, Philip M.

Meneses, Antonio

about

Unstrung when they first met, Cecile Licad and Antonio Meneses now harmonize onstage and off. H. Shapiro. il pors *People Wkly* 27:105-6 Ap 27 '87

Mengo virus *See* Viruses

Menil Collection (Houston, Tex.) *See* De Menil Collection (Houston, Tex.)

Meningitis

"We thought our faith could save our son" [death of M. Swan from meningitis after Christian Scientist parents withhold medical treatment] K. Delaney. il pors *Redbook* 168:104-6 Ja '87

Vaccines and vaccination

Meningitis vaccine stirs controversy. R. Weiss. *Sci News* 132:260 O 24 '87

Mennonites

See also

Amish

Can the Mennonites survive success? P. W. Cohen. il *N Y Times Mag* p114-16+ N 8 '87

Menopause

Blue moods. L. Claverie. il *Health* 19:47-51 S '87

An energy boost for menopause [testosterone treatment; research by Barbara Sherwin] il *Prevention* 39:6 N '87

Estrogens exonerated in breast cancer. *Sci News* 131:57 Ja 24 '87

Female trouble [menopause-heart disease link] *Sci Am* 257:24+ Jl '87

Hot flash! [use of clonidine transdermal patches to counter menopausal flashes] P. McCarthy. *Health* 19:29 N '87

Managing menopause. P. M. Sarrel and L. J. Sarrel. il *Work Woman* 12:150+ O '87

Menopause: a complete medical report. P. Phillips. il *McCalls* 115:89-95 N '87

More about estrogen skin patches. C. SerVaas. il *Saturday Evening Post* 259:52-4+ Ja/F '87

Pregnancy, PMS and menopause: no need to cramp your style. A. Krueger. *Work Woman* 12:158+ Ap '87

Menotti, Gian Carlo, 1911-

about

Amelia goes to the ball [opera] Reviews

N Y 20:64+ My 11 '87. P. G. Davis

Goya [opera] Reviews

New Repub 196:27-9 Ja 26 '87. E. Rothstein

Opera News il 51:38 Mr 14 '87. D. P. Stearns

Tamu-tamu [opera] Reviews

N Y il 20:64+ My 11 '87. P. G. Davis

Menoyo, Eloy Gutiérrez *See* Gutiérrez Menoyo, Eloy
Men's clothes *See* Clothing and dress—Men
Men's clothing stores *See* Clothing stores
Men's clubs *See* Clubs
Men's friendships *See* Friendship
Men's hairstyling *See* Hairstyling
Men's jewelry *See* Jewelry
Men's liberation movement
What men really want. M. Gallagher. *Natl Rev* 39:39-40
My 22 '87
Men's shirts *See* Shirts
Men's shoes *See* Footwear
Men's sweaters *See* Sweaters
Menstrual cycle *See* Menstruation
Menstruation
See also
Menopause
Menstruation: that time of the month. *Teen* 31:80-1
Mr '87
Perspiration: a chemical communicator? [research by
Winnifred B. Cutler and George Preti] P. McCarthy.
Psychol Today 21:16 Jl '87
Disorders
See also
Premenstrual syndrome
How exercise can K-O your period. S. Festa. il
Mademoiselle 93:120 Ag '87
It's not how far you go [low calorie intake may contribute
to amenorrhea in athletes] J. Venturino. il *Women's
Sports Fitness* 9:20 S '87
No periods? New clues. E. T. Becker. *Women's Sports
Fitness* 9:57 F '87
The unpredictable period. D. Pine. *Redbook* 168:28 F
'87
A young runner faces osteoporosis [amenorrhea] E. Car-
son. il *Women's Sports Fitness* 9:58-9 Ja '87
Therapy
Cramps. K. McCoy. *Seventeen* 46:38+ Je '87
That time of month: when menstrual cramps hit, will
exercise help? S. Festa. il *Women's Sports Fitness*
9:29-31 Ag '87
Mental depression *See* Depression, Mental
Mental development of children *See* Children—Growth
and development
Mental development of infants *See* Infants—Growth and
development
Mental healing
See also
Faith cure
Mental health
See also
Boredom
Maturity
Mental illness
Mind and body
National Institute of Mental Health (U.S.)
Psychiatry
Psychology
Psychotherapy
Relaxation
Mind health. C. Tavris. See issues of Vogue
Research
See Psychiatric research
Mental health centers
An open door [Pesach Tikvah, mental health center
serving the Orthodox community in Williamsburg,
Brooklyn] J. Meer. *Psychol Today* 21:17 Ap '87
Who cares for the mentally ill? M. Hope and J. Young.
il *Nation* 245:782-4 D 26 '87-Ja 2 '88
Mental health insurance *See* Insurance, Mental health
Mental health laws
See also
Insanity—Jurisprudence
Mentally ill—Civil rights
Mental hospitals *See* Hospitals, Psychiatric
Mental illness
See also
Art and mental illness
Autism
Depression, Mental
Insanity
Mentally ill
Paranoia
Schizophrenia
Elizabeth Hartman. M. Ryan. il pors *People Wkly*
28:135-7+ S 7 '87
The politics of psychiatry. R. E. Vatz and L. S. Weinberg.
il *USA Today (Periodical)* 116:71-3 Jl '87
Psychological disorders: turbulence of the mind. S. R.
Arbetter. il *Curr Health 2* 14:10-12 N '87

Diagnosis
The parable of the cheek-turners and the cheek-smiters
[feminist opposition to proposed revision of the
Diagnostic and statistical manual of mental disorders]
S. Boxer. il *Discover* 8:80-3 Ag '87
The politics of masochism [feminists challenge proposed
revisions to Diagnostic and statistical manual of mental
disorders] D. Franklin. il *Psychol Today* 21:52-7 Ja
'87
Research
See Psychiatric research
Therapy
See also
Psychopharmacology
Psychotherapy
Mental illness in literature
"Canst thou not minister to a mind diseas'd?". C. C.
Park. *Am Sch* 56:219-34 Spr '87
Mental illness in motion pictures
Through a lens, darkly. M. Fleming and R. Manvell.
il *Psychol Today* 21:26-30+ Jl '87
Mental maps *See* Geographical perception
Mental prayer *See* Meditation
Mentally handicapped
See also
Fragile X syndrome
Hi Hopes (Musical group)
Savant syndrome
Everybody smiles at Santa. R. Riddell. il *Ladies Home
J* 104:134+ D '87
Retarded couple face the new year with a baby boy
[R. and D. Thornton] pors *Jet* 71:8 Ja 12 '87
Care and treatment
"It was too good to be true" [false data used by mental
retardation researcher S. Breuning] D. Brand. il por
Time 129:59 Je 1 '87
NIMH finds a case of "serious misconduct" [case of
S. E. Breuning] C. Holden. *Science* 235:1566-7 Mr
27 '87
Prosecution urged in fraud case [case of S. E. Breuning]
C. Norman. *Science* 236:1057 My 29 '87
Education
See also
Hope University
Employment
See also
Rainbow Acres (Organization)
Family relationships
My Aunt Rosie. J. Kelman. il por *Good Housekeep*
204:120 Ap '87
Institutional care
All in the family [severely retarded Bowes-Lyon sisters,
relatives of the royal family, secretly institutionalized
in Great Britain] il *Time* 129:45 Ap 20 '87
A royal family secret [confinement of Queen Mother's
nieces to a mental institution] il *Macleans* 100:24
Ap 20 '87
The royal family's gothic shocker [Queen Mother's nieces
locked in mental hospital] N. Cooper. il *Newsweek*
109:49 Ap 20 '87
The state vs. the retarded. A. Press. il *Newsweek* 110:57
Jl 20 '87
Mentally handicapped children
See also
Autism
Down syndrome
Parents of the mentally handicapped
Slow learning children
"My son was hit by lightning" [struggle with resulting
brain damage]; ed. by Lorene Hanley Duquin. S.
Schunk. il por *Redbook* 169:17+ Ag '87
Education
The "perfect" student: being alert to autism. M. A.
Coppola. *Educ Dig* 52:33-5 My '87
Mentally ill
See also
Children of the mentally ill
Drugs and the mentally ill
Insane, Criminal and dangerous
Parents of the mentally ill
Care and treatment
See also
Hospitals, Psychiatric
Crazy in the streets [deinstitutionalized mentally ill] P.
S. Appelbaum. *Commentary* 83:34-9 My '87
Crazy in the streets: the policy of deinstitutionalization.
P. S. Appelbaum. *Current* 296:4-10 O '87
The homeless: a mental-health debate. H. Hall. il *Psychol
Today* 21:65 F '87

Mentally ill—Care and treatment—*cont.*
Profiles [L. and K. Looper run the Chateau, a board-and-care home for schizophrenics in San Francisco] B. Barich. il *New Yorker* 63:51-2+ O 12 '87
Psychiatric 'stretch' in the hospital [research by George Fulop and others] *Sci News* 132:94 Ag 8 '87
Street people [discussion of May 1987 article, Crazy in the streets] P. S. Appelbaum. *Commentary* 84:14-16+ S '87
Who cares for the mentally ill? M. Hope and J. Young. il *Nation* 245:782-4 D 26 '87-Ja 2 '88

Civil rights
At issue: freedom for the irrational [institutionalizing the homeless mentally ill] R. Stengel. il *Time* 130:88 S 14 '87
Down and out—but determined [J. Brown, homeless woman deemed mentally ill by New York City] M. Hornblower. il *Time* 130:29 N 23 '87
Forcing the mentally ill to get help [rounding up the homeless] D. Gelman. il *Newsweek* 110:47-8 N 9 '87
The mayor is right [New York City program to hospitalize mentally ill homeless people] *America* 157:396 N 28 '87
Saying 'no' to psychiatry [patient rights activist G. Ebert vs. Willard Psychiatric Center, Ithaca, N.Y.] M. Schultz. il por *Progressive* 51:17 F '87

Imprisonment
Criminal treatment: the jails become holding tanks for the mentally ill. J. Wax. il *Progressive* 51:26-7 O '87

Mentally ill children
See also
    Autism
    Parents of the mentally ill

Care and treatment
Alaska native youth: a new approach to serving emotionally disturbed children and youth. J. VanDenBerg and B. A. Minton. il *Child Today* 16:15-18 S/O '87
Children's mental health. il *Futurist* 21:50-1 Jl/Ag '87
Helping our children [mentally disturbed Alaskan Eskimo youth] S. Polk. il *Child Today* 16:19-20 S/O '87
Meeting the mental health needs of severely emotionally disturbed minority children and adolescents: a national perspective. J. Katz-Leavy and others. il *Child Today* 16:10-14 S/O '87

Mentally retarded *See* Mentally handicapped
Mentally retarded children *See* Mentally handicapped children
Menthol
Strong medicine [FDA investigates high concentrations of menthol in cough syrup] *FDA Consum* 21:38-9 Je '87
Mentor, Johane, d. 1987
about
Ex-boyfriend beheads teen girl with samurai sword in New York. por *Jet* 72:17 Je 8 '87
Mentors in business
Let a mentor lead you—but beware the pitfalls. J. A. Byrne. il *Bus Week* p95 Ap 20 '87
Mentors in education *See* Educational counseling
Mentors in education (Peers) *See* Peer counseling
Menuhin, Yehudi, 1916-
about
Music: the universal language [interview] A. P. Sanoff. por *U S News World Rep* 102:68 Ap 13 '87
Menus
See also
    Breakfasts
    Brunches
    Buffet meals
    Dinners and dining
    Luncheons
    Lunches
    Meals
Gourmet's menus. See issues of Gourmet
[Month] menus. See issues of Sunset (Central edition)
Menus (Computer programming)
A hard disk menu shell [PreCursor] R. Lockwood. il *Pers Comput* 11:242 Je '87
Pull-down menus in C. J. L. Pinson. il *Byte* 12:108-10+ My '87
Menyuk, Norman
(jt. auth) See Killinger, D. K. (Dennis K.), 1945-, and Menyuk, Norman
Menzel, Jiri
about
My sweet little village [film] Reviews
    Commonweal 114:82 F 13 '87. T. O'Brien
Mercado, Sergio Ramírez *See* Ramírez Mercado, Sergio, 1942-

Mercaldo, Steve
Taking care of your car. See issues of Popular Science
Mercantile system
Playing by different rules [Japan] J. M. Fallows. il *Atlantic* 260:22+ S '87
Merce Cunningham Dance Company
Jigs, japes and Joyce [Roaratorio, an Irish circus on Finnegans wake] J. Johnston. il *Art Am* 75:102-5 Ja '87
The lonely crowd [performance of Fabrications] T. Tobias. il *N Y* 20:73-4 Mr 23 '87
Reviews:
    Performances of Roaratorio at the Brooklyn Academy of Music. E. Zimmer. *Dance Mag* 61:80-1 F '87
    Visible spirit: the Cunningham continuum [performances at City Center, New York City] N. V. Dalva. il por *Dance Mag* 61:46-8 Ag '87
Merced River (Calif.)
Rafting, hiking, fishing in and around Yosemite's river . . . the Merced. il map *Sunset* 178:14-16 My '87
Mercedes-Benz (Automobile) *See* Automobiles, Foreign
Mercenaries (Soldiers) *See* Mercenary troops
Mercenary troops
See also
    United Nations. Ad Hoc Committee on the Drafting of an International Convention against the Recruitment, Use, Financing and Training of Mercenaries
Assembly appeals for intensified activities to combat racism, condemns increased use of mercenaries. *UN Chron* 24:126 F '87
Covert loophole [executive order authorizes privatization of covert operations] I. F. Stone. *Nation* 245:184-5 S 5 '87
Mercenary with a cause [J. Terrell turns from contra mercenary to contra whistleblower] B. Connie and D. Bernstein. *Progressive* 51:13 Ag '87
Mercer, Marilyn
The complete book of colds and flu. il *Good Housekeep* 205:62+ N '87
What parents are doing right. il *Good Housekeep* 205:75+ S '87
Mercer, Robert E.
Terrorists in three-piece suits [address, March 3, 1987] *Vital Speeches Day* 53:421-3 My 1 '87
about
Back to basics. S. N. Chakravarty. il por *Forbes* 140:40-1 S 21 '87
Robert Mercer. Z. Schiller. il por *Bus Week* Sp Issue:266 Ap 17 '87
Mercer University
Going topless and other sins. B. Kantrowitz and A. Murr. il *Newsweek* 110:79-80 O 26 '87
Merchandise *See* Commercial products
Merchandise, Quality of *See* Quality of products
Merchandise, Secondhand *See* Secondhand trade
Merchandising
See also
    CCI/ICE (Firm)
    Display of merchandise
    Rebates
    Samples (Merchandising)
Billion-dollar brainstorm [service merchandising by McKesson Corp.] G. Bronson. il *Forbes* 140:98 O 19 '87
The risky world of licensing [children's books written around TV and film characters] E. Klavan. il *Publ Wkly* 231:97-100 F 27 '87
Merchant, Ismail
about
India's Merchant with a view. M. P. Trehan. por *World Press Rev* 34:60 My '87
Partners and friends for 26 years, James Ivory and Ismail Merchant film a hotly debated gay love story. J. Stark. il pors *People Wkly* 28:119-22 O 26 '87
Producer with a view. R. Morais. il por *Forbes* 139:68+ Mr 23 '87
The Raj duet. D. Smith. il pors *N Y* 20:58-60+ O 5 '87
View from Prospero's Island. G. Clarke. il pors *Time* 129:70 Ja 12 '87
Merchant banking *See* Investment banking
Merchant Ivory Productions
India's Merchant with a view. M. P. Trehan. por *World Press Rev* 34:60 My '87
Producer with a view. R. Morais. il por *Forbes* 139:68+ Mr 23 '87
The Raj duet. D. Smith. il pors *N Y* 20:58-60+ O 5 '87
View from Prospero's Island [work of I. Merchant and J. Ivory] G. Clarke. il pors *Time* 129:70 Ja 12 '87

Merchant marine
See also
Shipping
United States. Merchant Marine Academy
The Soviet maritime threat [address, March 17, 1987]
F. Drozak. *Vital Speeches Day* 53:534-7 Je 15 '87
Will Congress rescue the listing merchant marine? S.
Payne. il *Bus Week* p39 Mr 2 '87
Soviet Union
The Soviet maritime threat [address, March 17, 1987]
F. Drozak. *Vital Speeches Day* 53:534-7 Je 15 '87
United States
See Merchant marine
Merchant Marine Academy *See* United States. Merchant
Marine Academy
Merck & Co., Inc.
An act of vision for the third world [donation of ivermec-
tin to treat river blindness] S. Budiansky. il *U S
News World Rep* 103:14 N 2 '87
The devil we know [Mevacor vs. niacin for reducing
cholesterol] S. N. Chakravarty. il *Forbes* 140:203-4
N 2 '87
Merck donates drug for river blindness [ivermectin] J.
Walsh. *Science* 238:610 O 30 '87
Merck has made biotech work. S. Gannes. il *Fortune*
115:58-60+ Ja 19 '87
The miracle company [cover story] J. A. Byrne. il pors
Bus Week p84-8+ O 19 '87
Miracle worker [donation of ivermectin to cure river
blindness in the third world] il *Time* 130:78 N 2
'87
Mercouri, Melina
The time has come for American travelers to return
to Europe. il *USA Today (Periodical)* 115:70-3 My
'87
Mercury
Metalloregulator DNA-binding protein encoded by the
*mer*R gene: isolation and characterization. T. O'Hal-
loran and C. Walsh. bibl f il *Science* 235:211-14 Ja
9 '87
Mercury (Planet)
Transits
Photographs and photography
The November 13th transit of Mercury. il *Sky Telesc*
73:223 F '87
Mercury House Publishing
Mercury House: moving away from fiction. L. See. *Publ
Wkly* 231:24 Mr 27 '87
Mercury in the body
See also
Mercury poisoning
How safe are your dental fillings? [mercury amalgam
fillings] il *Glamour* 85:330+ My '87
Mercury poisoning
Playing with poison [Pymm Thermometer plant, Brook-
lyn, N.Y.] K. Dobie and A. Goodman. il *Progressive*
51:19-23 F '87
Mercury space vehicles *See* Space vehicles
Mercury telescope mirrors, Liquid *See* Telescopes—Mirrors
Mercy killing *See* Euthanasia
Meredith, David
Imperial images: the Empire Marketing Board, 1926-32.
bibl f il *Hist Today* 37:30-6 Ja '87
Meredith, Scott
Making book on Oliver North. *Harpers* 274:54-5 Mr
'87
Meredith, William, 1919-
Partial accounts [poem] *New Yorker* 62:34 F 16
'87
What I remember the writers telling me when I was
young [poem] *Atlantic* 259:67 My '87
Mereson, Amy
Surgery women should think about twice. *McCalls*
114:139-40 Jl '87
(jt. auth) See Rothman, Tony, and Mereson, Amy
Meret, Inc.
Off with their heads. S. B. Weiner. il *Forbes* 139:34-5
F 9 '87
Mericle, William C.
Last word. il *Omni* 9:118 Mr '87
Meridian circle telescopes *See* Telescopes
Mérimée, Prosper, 1803-1870
about
Storyteller. B. L. Scherer. il por *Opera News* 51:32+
Mr 14 '87
Merims, Belden Randolph
Best Birmingham barbecue sauce. il *Ctry J* 14:22-3 S
'87
Meringue
Cooking with Jacques Pépin [orange vacherin Jeannette]
J. Pépin. il *Gourmet* 48:169-71+ Je '87

Merisotis, Jamie P.
Income contingent loans. il *Change* 19:10-11 Mr/Ap
'87
Merit certificates *See* Certificates of merit
Merkin, Geraldine
Readin', ritin' and real estate. por *U S News World
Rep* 103:9 N 2 '87
Merkling, Frank
Escape from the shadow. il *Opera News* 51:30-1+ Mr
28 '87
Merle Norman Cosmetics, Inc.
Career makeover: from typist to training specialist without
a college degree [J. Dowd] il *Glamour* 85:144+ My
'87
Merlino, Kate
Potomac: food and fantasy in Washington, D.C. il *USA
Today (Periodical)* 116:38-43 S '87
Mermelstein, Aaron
Comedy clubs. il *Travel Holiday* 167:56-8 Mr '87
Merrell, Purless
about
Miami judge nixes will awarding $1.5 mil. real estate
to black gardener. *Jet* 72:24 Jl 13 '87
Merrell Dow Pharmaceutical Inc.
Deformed D.C. boy gets $95 million award in product
liability suit [award to S. Ealy in Bendectin case]
por *Jet* 72:26 Ag 3 '87
Merriam, Eve, 1916-
Going seventy [poem] il *Ms* 16:98 D '87
Merrick, Joseph Carey, 1862 or 3-1890
about
As of '87, he's Proteus Man. *Sci News* 132:55 Jl 25
'87
Merrill, Charles, 1920-
about
Giving it away. B. Leonard. il por *Forbes* 140 Sp
Issue:380+ O 26 '87
Merrill Lynch & Co., Inc.
The big loss at Merrill Lynch: why it was blindsided
[mortgage bond debacle] E. Spragins. il *Bus Week*
p112-13 My 18 '87
Bond bombshell [Merrill Lynch bond trader H. Rubin's
mortgage securities loss] il *Time* 129:53 My 11 '87
The British connection [insider trading scandals] A. Miller.
il por *Newsweek* 109:39 Mr 23 '87
Can Merrill catch up? R. Behar. il *Forbes* 139:39-40
Je 1 '87
A fan of smokestack America [interview with C. Clough]
A. E. Serwer. il por *Fortune* 116:192 O 26 '87
Hidden gems in a high market [interview with P. Hoff-
mann] A. E. Serwer. il por *Fortune* 115:126 My 25
'87
The insider scandal travels abroad [charges against N.
Vaskevitch and D. Sofer] S. Koepp. il por *Time* 129:51
Mr 23 '87
Merrill Lynch, discount king? [Blueprint program] G.
Weiss. *Bus Week* p72 Mr 30 '87
Merrill Lynch takes a bath [mortgage securities trading
loss] D. Pauly. il *Newsweek* 109:53 My 11 '87
Merrill's loss: why the numbers keep changing [trading
fiasco in mortgage-backed securities] E. Spragins. il
Bus Week p72 Ag 3 '87
This bull likes two brokerages [views of Mason S. Sexton]
G. G. Marcial. *Bus Week* p148 Mr 23 '87
Merrill Lynch Capital Markets
Bullish on takeovers. J. Crudele. il *N Y* 20:14 My 25
'87
Can Merrill catch up? R. Behar. il *Forbes* 139:39-40
Je 1 '87
Cash, flash, and dash: can this be Merrill? E. Spragins.
il *Bus Week* p124+ My 11 '87
Will GAF cash in its Borg-Warner chips—or up the
ante? [leveraged buyout led by Merrill Lynch] J. E.
Ellis. *Bus Week* p34-5 Ap 27 '87
Merritt, J. I.
Schools for fly-fishers. il *Money* 16:67-8+ Jl '87
Merritt, Jay
Heck on wheels. *Esquire* 107:30+ Mr '87
Merritt, Nancy L.
Bank of America's blueprint for a policy on AIDS.
por *Bus Week* p127 Mr 23 '87
The merry widow [ballet] See Ballet reviews—Single works
Merschel, Sylvia E.
(ed) See Perry, Donald R. As cities crumble, plants
may be at the root of it
(ed) See Perry, Donald R. Plants that eat cities
Merser, Cheryl
about
Is writing a career for 'Grown-ups'? B. Levine. por
Publ Wkly 232:23 S 4 '87

Mertz, Barbara, 1927-
about
PW interviews. D. Brainard. il por *Publ Wkly* 232:39-40 O 23 '87
Mertz, Edward H.
about
The Buick stops here. R. Ceppos. por *Car Driv* 33:46 S '87
Merwin, Clarence Edgar
about
How to lose the coke war. D. Kline. il *Atlantic* 259:22-7 My '87
Merwin, W. S. (William Stanley), 1927-
Airport [poem] *New Yorker* 63:46 O 19 '87
Chord [poem] *Atlantic* 260:41 Jl '87
Kanaloa [poem] *New Yorker* 63:32 Ap 13 '87
Paper [poem] *Nation* 244:152 F 7 '87
Place [poem] *Nation* 244:230 F 21 '87
Refugee [poem] *Nation* 244:152 F 7 '87
The rose beetle [poem] *New Yorker* 63:32 Je 1 '87
Thanks [poem] *Nation* 244:334 Mr 14 '87
Utterance [poem] *Nation* 244:152 F 7 '87
Merwin, William Stanley See Merwin, W. S. (William Stanley), 1927-
Meryman, Richard, 1926-
MacGyver's Richard Dean Anderson: TV's gentle daredevil. il por *McCalls* 114:35-6+ F '87
Wyeth's world: how a woman named Helga came to haunt the art of America's foremost realist. il pors *Life* 10:72-6+ Je '87
Merz, Gerhard, 1947-
about
Gerhard Merz at Barbara Gladstone. S. Ellis. *Art Am* 75:155-6 D '87
Mesa Limited Partnership
The best Pickens play may be in his own backyard. G. G. Marcial. por *Bus Week* p100 S 7 '87
Blitz on Boeing [targeted for takeover by T. B. Pickens] por *Time* 130:35 Ag 10 '87
Boone buys a bunch of Boeing. il por *Newsweek* 110:50 Ag 10 '87
A gold miner helps Pickens chip away at Newmont [R. M. Friedland cut into Ivanhoe Partners deal] S. D. Atchison. il por *Bus Week* p36 Ag 31 '87
Is Boone bluffing? [buying into Boeing] K. M. Hafner. il por *Bus Week* p22-3 Ag 10 '87
Mesa purchase of Boeing stock highlights industry pressures. R. G. O'Lone. *Aviat Week Space Technol* 127:24-5 Ag 3 '87
One swallow could make Pickens' summer [pursuit of Newmont Mining] J. E. Davis. il por *Bus Week* p37 S 14 '87
Pickens picks: a Boone for investors? [aerospace stocks] J. P. Newport, Jr. il *Fortune* 116:126+ S 14 '87
Ripe enough for Pickens [T. B. Pickens stalks Singer] R. Mitchell. il *Bus Week* p23 Ag 24 '87
Mesa Petroleum Co.
Boone speaks [excerpt from Boone] T. B. Pickens, Jr. il pors *Fortune* 115:42-5+ F 16 '87
Mesa Verde National Park (Colo.)
Helicopters at Mesa Verde cause run-in with Utes. il *Natl Parks* 61:8 N/D '87
MESBIC (Minority enterprise small business investment companies) See Small business investment companies
Mesches, Arnold, 1923-
about
Arnold Mesches at Jack Shainman. S. Westfall. *Art Am* 75:221-2 Ap '87
Mesclun See Greens, Edible
Meske, Eunice Boardman
Learning to learn—music. *Des Arts Educ* 89:45-8 S/O '87
The (musical) arts and teacher education. bibl f *Des Arts Educ* 88:15-18 Ja/F '87
Mesle, Bob
A friend's love: why process theology matters. *Christ Century* 104:622-5 Jl 15-22 '87
Meslin, Jane
Part-time mom. *Good Housekeep* 205:136+ S '87
Mesolithic period See Stone Age
Mesons See Particles (Nuclear physics)
Mesopotamia
See also
Babylon (Ancient city)
Has the Garden of Eden been located at last? [views of J. Zarins] D. J. Hamblin. bibl (p184) il map *Smithsonian* 18:127-35 My '87

Mesquite (Tex.)
Public health
'I want him crucified' [pediatrician R. J. Huse loses his practice after testing positive for AIDS] G. Hackett. il por *Newsweek* 110:36 O 5 '87
Messages in bottles See Drift bottles
Messarovitch, Yves
All eyes on the U.S. *World Press Rev* 34:25-6 N '87
The perils of trading money for money. *World Press Rev* 34:46-7 Jl '87
Messel, Thomas
about
Regency redux. C. Aslet. il por *House Gard* 159:106+ N '87
Messel (Germany) See Grube Messel (Germany)
Messenger RNA See RNA
Messengers
See also
Bicycle messengers
Messerer, Sulamith
about
The indomitable Sulamith Messerer: the eyes have it. J. K. Nelson. il pors *Dance Mag* 61:70-3 Mr '87
Messerschmitt-Bölkow-Blohm GmbH
Conflicting requirements stymie German/French PAH-2 project. *Aviat Week Space Technol* 126:80-1 Ja 19 '87
Fokker, MBB agree to study future cooperation. *Aviat Week Space Technol* 127:30 O 19 '87
France, Germany agree on common specifications for combat helicopter [PAH-2 program] il *Aviat Week Space Technol* 126:61-2 Ap 6 '87
MBB focuses on airframes, rotors for the PAH-2, NH-90. il *Aviat Week Space Technol* 126:111-12 Ja 19 '87
MBB seeks members for consortium to develop medium-size transport. il *Aviat Week Space Technol* 126:53-4 Mr 16 '87
MBB to test composite helicopter airframe. K. F. Mordoff. il *Aviat Week Space Technol* 127:87 Ag 3 '87
Messianic Judaism See Judaism
Messier, Charles, 1730-1817
about
Nature. *New Yorker* 62:26 F 2 '87
Messina, P. C. (Paul C.), 1943-
(jt. auth) See Fox, Geoffrey C., and Messina, P. C. (Paul C.), 1943-
Messina, Paul C. See Messina, P. C. (Paul C.), 1943-
Messiness
Beat the messy room rap [teen bedrooms] S. Harris. il *Teen* 31:26+ N '87
The good, the bad, and the messy. N. Stedman. il *Health* 19:70-2+ My '87
In a mess. J. Fowles. il por *Archit Dig* 44:24+ Je '87
Learning to live with a sloppy kid. C. Berman. il *Parents* 62:128-30+ N '87
An officer's mess. S. Bing. il *Esquire* 107:44 Ja '87
Why I clutter. H. H. Broun. il por *50 Plus* 27:88 Ja '87
Messmer, William B.
If Labour wins. *Foreign Policy* 67:137-53 Summ '87
Metabolism
See also
Bioenergetics
Brain—Metabolism
Carbohydrate metabolism
Fungi—Metabolism
Heart—Metabolism
Insects—Metabolism
Counting calories: your metabolism may be slower than you think. B. Kevles. *Women's Sports Fitness* 9:16 Je '87
Metabolic catch-22 of exercise regimens. G. Kolata. il *Science* 236:146-7 Ap 10 '87
Metabolism studies predict obesity [Pima Indians; research by Clifton Bogardus and others] D. D. Edwards. *Sci News* 132:309 N 14 '87
Running the numbers [figuring calories burned while running] M. Brzycki. il *Women's Sports Fitness* 9:20 S '87
Disorders
See also
Anorexia nervosa
Cystic fibrosis
Diabetes
Gaucher's disease
Gout
Hypercholesteremia
Lactose intolerance
Lesch-Nyhan syndrome

Metal beds *See* Beds
Metal castings
    See also
      Steel castings
Metal ceilings *See* Ceilings
Metal construction
  Heavy metal [three buildings in Canada designed by IKOY Partnership] P. M. Sachner. il *Archit Rec* 175:126-35 My '87
Metal furniture *See* Furniture, Metal
Metal industry
    See also
      AMAX Inc.
      ASARCO Inc.
      Collective bargaining—Metal industry
      Steel industry
Metal mining industry *See* Mining industry
Metal oxide semiconductors
  Solid pictures, or gathering MOS. D. Ranada. il *High Fidel* 37:16 O '87
Metal poisoning
    See also
      Lead poisoning
Metal sculpture
    See also
      Bronzes
Metal work
    See also
      Brass work
      Solder and soldering
Metal workers
    See also
      Trade unions—Metal workers
Metalloorganic compounds *See* Organometallic compounds
Metallothionein
  Regulation in vitro of metallothionein gene binding factors. C. Seguin and D. H. Hamer. bibl f il *Science* 235:1383-7 Mr 13 '87
Metallurgy
    See also
      Uranium metallurgy
  The art and science of microstructural control. F. Spaepen. bibl f il *Science* 235:1010-14 F 27 '87
Metals
    See also
      Metallurgy
      Mines and mineral resources
      Plants—Metal content
      Rare earth metals
      Transition metals
      See also names of metals
  Glasnost comes to Soviet physics [misdirection of high-pressure physics research] A. L. Robinson. il *Science* 236:671-2 My 8 '87
  Looking into metal specimens [Mossbauer imaging; work of Stephen J. Norton] *Sci News* 132:361 D 5 '87
      Corrosion
    See Corrosion and anticorrosives
Metals, Effect of temperature on
  Frozen tools [use of deep-cryogenic processing; cover story] V. E. Gilmore. il *Pop Sci* 230:64-7+ Je '87
Metals in the body
    See also
      Aluminum in the body
      Iron in the body
      Trace elements
      Zinc in the body
Metaphor
  The action of metaphor. L. Michaels. *Harpers* 274:30+ Ja '87
  The earth makes its move [metaphor for orgasm] W. Safire. il *N Y Times Mag* p12+ Je 14 '87
Metaphysics
    See also
      Absolute
      Soul
  Metaphysical hints and tips: how to find health in the strangest places. R. Rodale. il *Prevention* 39:23-5 D '87
  Papal metaphysics. I. F. Stone. *Nation* 245:292-3 S 26 '87
Metastasis
  β1-6 branching of Asn-linked oligosaccharides is directly associated with metastasis. J. W. Dennis and others. bibl f il *Science* 236:582-5 My 1 '87
  Nicotine: addictive and spreads cancer? [research by Gesina L. Longenecker and others] D. D. Edwards. *Sci News* 131:213 Ap 4 '87
  Transformation by oncogenes encoding protein kinases induces the metastatic phenotype. S. E. Egan and others. bibl f il *Science* 238:202-5 O 9 '87

  YIGSR, a synthetic laminin pentapeptide, inhibits experimental metastasis formation. Y. Iwamoto and others. bibl f il *Science* 238:1132-4 N 20 '87
Metaxas, Eric
  That post-modernism! il *Atlantic* 259:36-7 Ja '87
Metcalf, Harold J.
  (jt. auth) *See* Phillips, William D., 1948-, and Metcalf, Harold J.
Meteor burst communication
  Agriculture Dept. terminals demonstrate reliability of meteor-burst communications. map *Aviat Week Space Technol* 126:81 Ja 26 '87
  GTE transmits messages by bouncing voice signals off meteor trails. J. C. Lowndes. il *Aviat Week Space Technol* 126:80-1 Ja 26 '87
Meteor showers *See* Meteors
Meteorites
    See also
      Tektites
  Amino acids from space [Murchison meteorite] *Astronomy* 15:95-6 D '87
  Diamonds from outer space [research by Roy Lewis] il *USA Today (Periodical)* 115:4-5 Je '87
  Escape from Mars [SNC meteorites; work of John D. O'Keefe and Thomas J. Ahrens] il *Sky Telesc* 73:155 F '87
  Getting Mars' rocks off [SNC meteorites; research by A. M. Vickery and H. J. Melosh] il *Discover* 8:12-13 D '87
  Interstellar ooze? [study of Murchison meteorite; work of Samuel Epstein and others] il *Sky Telesc* 74:233-4 S '87
  Interstellar polycyclic aromatic hydrocarbons and carbon in interplanetary dust particles and meteorites. L. J. Allamandola and others. bibl f il *Science* 237:56-9 Jl 3 '87
  The large crater origin of SNC meteorites. A. M. Vickery and H. J. Melosh. bibl f il *Science* 237:738-43 Ag 14 '87
  Life from outer space, or Panspermia redux [views of John Cronin] il *Discover* 8:10 Jl '87
  Martian meteorites are arriving. R. A. Kerr. *Science* 237:721-3 Ag 14 '87
  Meteorites make a planet [Basaltic Achondrite Planetoid; work of Jeremy Delaney] E. R. C. Capulong. *Pop Sci* 231:33 O '87
  Signs of Nemesis: meteors, magnetism. D. E. Thomsen. *Sci News* 131:100 F 14 '87
  Star dust in the sky with diamonds [research by Edward Anders and others] I. Peterson. *Sci News* 131:166 Mr 14 '87
  Stardust on earth [interstellar diamonds] J. K. Beatty. il *Sky Telesc* 73:610 Je '87
Meteoroids *See* Meteors
Meteorological equipment
    See also
      Barometers
      Bolometers and bolometry
  How to be your own weatherman. il *Sunset* 179:237-8 N '87
Meteorological models
  Capturing El Niño in models. R. A. Kerr. *Science* 238:1507-8 D 11 '87
  Climate modeling [cover story] S. H. Schneider. il *Sci Am* 256:72-8+ My '87
  Cloudy crystal balls [computer models used by climatologists] D. Bjerklie. il *Time* 130:64 O 19 '87
  Milankovitch climate cycles through the ages. R. A. Kerr. il *Science* 235:973-4 F 27 '87
  Scientific basis of modern weather prediction. J. J. Tribbia and R. A. Anthes. bibl f il map *Science* 237:493-9 Jl 31 '87
  Weather regimes: the challenge in extended-range forecasting. B. Reinhold. bibl f il maps *Science* 235:437-41 Ja 23 '87
Meteorological optics
    See also
      Haze
      Noctilucent clouds
Meteorological photography
  1986 Photo Contest winners [Weatherwise Contest; cover story] il *Weatherwise* 40:189-96 Jl/Ag '87
Meteorological research *See* Meteorology
Meteorologists
    See also
      Burgess, Don
  The few, the proud, the meteorologists. M. Reed. *Weatherwise* 40:155 Je '87
Meteorology
    See also
      Airplanes in meteorology

Meteorology—See also—*cont.*
　Artificial satellites—Meteorological use
　Atmosphere
　Auroras
　Blocking (Meteorology)
　Climate
　Clouds
　Computers—Meteorological use
　Condensation (Meteorology)
　Cyclones
　Dew
　Floods
　Fronts (Meteorology)
　Hurricanes
　Information storage and retrieval systems—
　　Meteorological use
　Jet stream
　Lasers—Meteorological use
　Lightning
　Meteorologists
　Motion pictures—Meteorological films
　Radar meteorology
　Rain and rainfall
　Snow
　Storms
　Sun and meteorology
　Thunderstorms
　Tornadoes
　United States. National Weather Service
　Videotapes—Meteorological use
　Weather
　Weather forecasting
　Windchill index
　Winds
　World Meteorological Organization
Immiscible investigators: oceanographers, meteorologists, and fishery scientists. W. S. Wooster. *BioScience* 37:728-30 N '87

Charts, diagrams, etc.
The world's cheapest weather recording instruments [weather chart developed for use by students] D. Barstow. il *Weatherwise* 40:146-8 Je '87
Study and teaching
The world's cheapest weather recording instruments [weather chart developed for use by students] D. Barstow. il *Weatherwise* 40:146-8 Je '87
Aids and devices
Audio visuals about the weather. E. Brotak. il *Weatherwise* 40:107 Ap '87
Audio visuals about the weather. E. Brotak. *Weatherwise* 40:218 Jl/Ag '87
Audio visuals about the weather. E. Brotak. *Weatherwise* 40:159 Je '87
Audio visuals about the weather. E. Brotak. *Weatherwise* 40:271-2 O '87
Balloons launch National Science & Technology Week. *Earth Sci* 40:6 Summ '87
Up, up, and away: students will launch thousands of helium-filled balloons in nationwide experiment [cover story] A. H. Livermore. il map *Earth Sci* 40:12-13 Spr '87
Meteorology, Agricultural *See* Plants, Effect of climate on
Meteorology, Aviation
　See also
　Computers—Meteorological use
　Information storage and retrieval systems—
　　Meteorological use
　Radar meteorology
　United States. Federal Aviation Administration—
　　Flight service stations
　Wind shear
Hoodwinked over Oklahoma [flying in the clouds] M. Coan. il *Flying* 114:104-5 Ap '87
Improved weather alerts offset by poor delivery to cockpit. J. Ott. *Aviat Week Space Technol* 127:33-4 O 5 '87
Out of control. J. M. McClellan. il *Flying* 114:48-50+ Jl '87
Storm window [Stormscope] R. L. Collins. il *Flying* 114:76-8+ N '87
Tailwinds, thunderstorms and turbulence: the weather story of the Voyager flight [cover story] P. Mueller and L. Burch. il map *Weatherwise* 40:240-7 O '87
Meteorology, Maritime
　See also
　Ocean-atmosphere interaction
　Waterspouts
Watching the weather. S. Stapleton. il *Mot Boat Sail* 159:24 Ja '87

Meteorology, Military
History
　See also
　World War, 1939-1945—Meteorological aspects
Meteors
Calculating the distance to the sun by observing the trail of a meteor. J. Walker. il *Sci Am* 256:122-6 Mr '87
Close to home. D. H. Levy. *Space World* X-12-288:36 D '87
The flight of a meteor [computer program] R. W. Snnott and J. A. Kennewell. il *Sky Telesc* 73:83-4 Ja '87
Geologic events. See issues of Earth Science
In Canada: strong acceleration . . . and mysterious objects. J. Silberner. *Sci News* 131:233 Ap 11 '87
The quadrantids: bright prospects for 1987. P. M. Bagnall. il *Astronomy* 15:39-42 Ja '87
The Ursid meteor stream. P. Roggemans and others. il *Sky Telesc* 74:678-9 D '87
Meteors in art
A mysterious woodcut [1833 Leonid shower] D. W. Hughes. il *Sky Telesc* 74:252 S '87
Meter (Standard of length) *See* Metric system
Meters
　See also
　Electric meters
　Micrometers
　Moisture meters
　Odometers
Methane
　See also
　Bacteria, Methanogenic
Are landfills a major threat to climate? [source of atmospheric methane; study by Paul J. Crutzen and H. G. Bingemer] J. Raloff. *Sci News* 131:150 Mr 7 '87
Cloud conundrums [possible methane plumes in Soviet Arctic; cover story] S. Weisburd. il map *Sci News* 131:204-6 Mr 28 '87
"Don't blame me". G. Reiger. *Field Stream* 92:14+ Ag '87
Drilling into a deep controversy [deep-earth-gas theory of Thomas Gold] R. Monastersky. *Sci News* 131:380-1 Je 13 '87
Sounding the inner earth for gas and oil [deep-earth-gas theory of Thomas Gold] *Environment* 29:22-3 Jl/Ag '87
The termite connection [atmospheric methane; work of P. Zimmerman] D. M. Schwartz. il por *Int Wildl* 17:38-42 Jl/Ag '87
Uranus' methane cloud [work of Gunnar F. Lindal and others] il *Sky Telesc* 73:273 Mr '87
Methanogenic bacteria *See* Bacteria, Methanogenic
Metheny, Mike
　about
Mike Metheny. F. Bouchard. il por *Down Beat* 54:15 Ap '87
Methionine
Kitty odor product seized [Scent-free product mislabeled as drug] D. Farley. il *FDA Consum* 21:37-8 Je '87
Methodist Church
Fiji
Methodists involved in Fiji coup. D. C. White. *Christ Century* 104:548-9 Je 17-24 '87
South Africa
Peter Storey: hope for South Africa. W. H. Willimon. *Christ Century* 104:1109-11 D 9 '87
United States
　See also
　African Methodist Episcopal Church
　United Methodist Church
Methodist Hospital (Houston, Tex.) *See* Houston (Tex.)—Hospitals
Methody, Hieromonk
　about
An Orthodox monk and a Lutheran pastor witness the survival of faith in an atheistic state. M. Brower. il pors *People Wkly* 27:110-13 Ap 6 '87
Methvin, Eugene H.
The case of common sense vs. Miranda. il *Read Dig* 131:96-100 Ag '87
Gorbachev's dilemma. *Natl Rev* 39:42+ D 4 '87
A Texas tornado hits the Senate. il por *Read Dig* 130:17-18+ Ap '87
A union in bondage to the mob. *Read Dig* 131:171-5 N '87
Methyl isocyanate
　See also
　Bhopal poisonous gas disaster, India, 1984

Methyl-phenyl-tetrahydropyridine *See* MPTP (Drug)

Methyl sulfide

Climate control [influence of plankton on cloud formation; work of Robert J. Charlson and James E. Lovelock] *Sci Am* 257:24 Jl '87

Methylation

CH₃ips off the old genetic block [DNA methylation] D. D. Edwards. *Sci News* 132:36 Jl 18 '87

Fungi: California's answer to selenium? [Kesterson National Wildlife Refuge] *Sci News* 132:8 Jl 4 '87

The inheritance of epigenetic defects. R. Holliday. bibl f il *Science* 238:163-70 O 9 '87

Methylation gives mom/dad distinction [DNA methylation] *BioScience* 37:651 O '87

A portable signal causing faithful DNA methylation de novo in Neurospora crassa. E. U. Selker and others. bibl f il *Science* 238:48-53 O 2 '87

Methylene chloride

Covert chemical. K. Freifeld. il *Health* 19:75 Ja '87

Métraux, Guy

The ranz des vaches. il *Courier* 40:32-3 F '87

Metric system

What ever happened to metric? Despite some changes, the U.S. hardly gave an inch. M. D. Lemonick. il *Time* 130:80-1 Jl 6 '87

Metro-Goldwyn-Mayer, Inc.

MGM vet Lucille Ryman Carroll recalls the reel adventures of Liz, Rock, Marilyn and Nancy [interview] R. Natale. il por *People Wkly* 28:135-7+ N 2 '87

Metro Mobile CTS Inc.

Wrong numbers? G. Morgenson. il *Forbes* 139:50-1 My 18 '87

Metrodome (Minneapolis, Minn.) *See* Hubert H. Humphrey Metrodome (Minneapolis, Minn.)

Metrology *See* Measurement

Metronomes

How to build a $13 darkroom metronome. T. F. Fuller. il *Petersens Photogr Mag* 16:82-3 My '87

Metropolitan areas

See also
　　City planning
　　Suburbs

The best places to live in America. R. Eisenberg and D. W. Englander. il map *Money* 16:34-42+ Ag '87

Where to live—and prosper [1990s] G. Breckenfeld. il map *Fortune* 115:52-4+ F 2 '87

Metropolitan Life Insurance Co.

Picking up the pieces [purchase offer for Principal Group's assets] J. Howse. il *Macleans* 100:26-7 Ag 31 '87

Metropolitan Museum of Art (New York, N.Y.)

Japanesque silver by Tiffany and Company in the Metropolitan Museum of Art. F. G. Safford and R. W. Caccavale. bibl f il *Antiques* 132:808-19 O '87

Morris to Memphis: modern design at the Metropolitan Museum of Art. R. C. Miller. il *Antiques* 131:278-81 Ja '87

Six decades in exile [Statue of a Young Woman, originally called forgery, reclassified as genuine] il *U S News World Rep* 103:53 Ag 10 '87

Star tours [celebrity taped tours] il *Art News* 86:11 D '87

Metropolitan Museum of Art (New York, N.Y.). American Wing

The Gothic revival library at the Metropolitan Museum of Art. A. Peck. il *Antiques* 131:824-7 Ap '87

Of time and place [Gothic revival library] C. Vogel. il *N Y Times Mag* p50-1 F 15 '87

Metropolitan Museum of Art (New York, N.Y.). Costume Institute

"Dance" at Met Museum is lavish but laconic. B. Laine. il *Dance Mag* 61:14-15 Ap '87

Unmaking history at the Costume Institute [Debora Silverman's book Selling culture] R. Storr. bibl f il *Art Am* 75:15-17+ F '87

Metropolitan Museum of Art (New York, N.Y.). Dept. of Paintings Conservation

Profiles [chairman J. M. Brealey] C. Tomkins. por *New Yorker* 63:44-6+ Mr 16 '87

Metropolitan Museum of Art (New York, N.Y.). Lila Acheson Wallace Wing

Amazing space. B. Rose. il *Vogue* 177:394-401+ F '87

Another temple for modernism. R. Hughes. il *Time* 129:78-9 F 2 '87

The art world. C. Tomkins. *New Yorker* 63:114-17 F 23 '87

Contemporary craft at the Met. J. Tognini. il *Am Craft* 47:50-5 Ap/My '87

Gamble at the Met. J. Perl. il *Vogue* 177:40 Ja '87

Met opens Wallace Wing. il *Art Am* 75:168 Mr '87

The modern Met. R. Atkins. il *Horizon* 30:33-6 Mr '87

Modern remastered [design section] M. Filler. il *House Gard* 159:136-43+ Ja '87

Money changes everything. K. Larson. il *N Y* 20:88+ F 16 '87

New York's Metropolitan enters the 20th century with a bang. H. Dudar. bibl (p183) il *Smithsonian* 18:46-54+ My '87

One woman's gift to the 20th century. P. B. Osborne. il por *Read Dig* 131:274-81 N '87

Rediscovering an early modern vision [S. Thayer's Dial Collection] J. Richardson. il por *House Gard* 159:158-63+ F '87

Thoroughly modern Met. S. Hochfield. il *Art News* 86:112-17 F '87

Winging into modernism. il *Harpers Bazaar* 120:142+ F '87

Metropolitan Museum of Art (New York, N.Y.). Sackler Galleries for Asian Art

Empire of the sun [Arts of Japan galleries] J. Spayde. il *Art News* 86:155 D '87

A visual wisdom [new portion of Sackler Galleries devoted to Japanese art] M. Filler. il *House Gard* 159:174-7+ Je '87

Zen and the art of museum installation. K. Larson. il *N Y* 20:58-9 Ag 31 '87

Metropolitan Opera (New York, N.Y.)

Age of gold [opening week of 1987 season] P. G. Davis. il *N Y* 20:80+ O 12 '87

Arias alfresco [summer performances] D. G. Winer and D. McGovern. il *Opera News* 51:24+ Je '87

Battered 'Bat' [Die Fledermaus] P. G. Davis. il *N Y* 20:43-4 Ja 5 '87

Chinese junk [F. Zeffirelli's production of Turandot] P. G. Davis. il *N Y* 20:62+ Mr 30 '87

Fledermaus without fizz. M. Walsh. il *Time* 129:71 Ja 5 '87

Franco Zeffirelli in Chinatown [production of Turandot] M. Walsh. il *Time* 129:92 Mr 23 '87

Jimmy's Met [J. Levine] P. G. Davis. il por *N Y* 20:52-4+ Ap 20 '87

Light show [G. Wechsler and staff, lighting technicians] C. Mobley. il pors *Opera News* 51:14-16+ Mr 14 '87

Mais non [production of Manon] P. G. Davis. il *N Y* 20:60+ F 23 '87

The Met goes for the gold [production of Il Trovatore] L. Shapiro. il *Newsweek* 110:86 N 23 '87

Musical events:

Manon and Carmen. A. Porter. *New Yorker* 63:104-5 Mr 2 '87

Das Rheingold. A. Porter. *New Yorker* 63:136+ O 26 '87

Il Trovatore. A. Porter. *New Yorker* 63:129-30 N 30 '87

Turandot. A. Porter. *New Yorker* 63:104+ Mr 30 '87

New York. J. W. Freeman; G. Schmidgall. il *Opera News* 51:36-8 Mr 28 '87

New York City. J. W. Freeman. il *Opera News* 51:51-2 Je '87

New York City. G. Schmidgall. il *Opera News* 51:34 Ja 31 '87

New York City. J. W. Freeman; G. Schmidgall. il *Opera News* 52:40-1 Jl '87

Ongoing Dialogues [performance of Dialogues of the Carmelites] P. G. Davis. il *N Y* 20:82+ Ap 6 '87

Ringing in the new [production of Das Rheingold] P. G. Davis. il *N Y* 20:112-13 O 26 '87

Sound sense [performance of Carmen] P. G. Davis. il *N Y* 20:104-6 Mr 2 '87

Staged by Scotto [Madama Butterfly at the Metropolitan Opera; with editorial comment by Jane L. Poole] C. Battaglia. il pors *Opera News* 51:4, 10-13 Ja 17 '87

Texaco-Metropolitan Opera radio network: 1987-88 season. *Opera News* 52:22 D 5 '87

Viewpoint [new managerial structure evolving under Bruce Crawford] J. W. Freeman. *Opera News* 52:4 S '87

Viewpoint [plans for 1987-88 season] G. Fitzgerald. *Opera News* 51:4 Ap 11 '87

Voices of spring [performance of Samson et Dalila] P. G. Davis. il *N Y* 20:97-8 Ap 13 '87

Wild goose chase [performance of Il Trovatore] P. G. Davis. il *N Y* 20:83-5 N 30 '87

Metropolitan Opera Archives

Treasures and trifles. D. J. Soria. il *Opera News* 52:24-6+ S '87

Metropolitan Opera Guild

MOG annual report. A. E. Peters. *Opera News* 52:4 O '87

With enormous pleasure . . . [annual luncheon] il *Opera News* 51:48-9 Je '87

Metropolitan Opera House (New York, N.Y.)
The Met's Jane Hermann: offstage assoluta. J. Gruen. il por *Dance Mag* 61:48-51 Jl '87
Mettam, Roger
Conflict in continuity in 17th-century France. bibl il *Hist Today* 37:30-5 F '87
Metter, Bertram Milton, 1927-
about
Turnover, not turnaround, at J. Walter Thompson. C. Dugas. *Bus Week* p49-50 My 11 '87
Mettler, Ruben Frederick, 1924-
about
Can they keep it up? J. Flint. il por *Forbes* 139:46+ F 9 '87
Metts, Wally, Jr.
Home-grown kids need a full-time mom. il por *Christ Today* 31:12 Mr 6 '87
Metz, E. Michael
about
A bear in '87, but a bull in '88. G. G. Marcial. il por *Bus Week* p135 D 28 '87-Ja 4 '88
Metz, Holly
Grass-roots art seeks a haven. il por *Progressive* 51:14 O '87
Metz, Tracy
Design awards/competitions: competition for a new city hall in The Hague, Holland. il *Archit Rec* 175:54-5 Ap '87
Metzenbaum, Howard M.
Should the proposed Product Liability Reform Act be approved? [excerpts from address, September 22, 1986] *Congr Dig* 66:23+ Ja '87
Metzger, Juan E.
about
Mr. Yogurt takes a chance on tofu. F. McCoy. il por *Bus Week* p115 Jl 20 '87
Metzner, Raven
Son of sixties parents. il *Seventeen* 46:14+ F '87
Mevacor *See* Lovastatin
Mexican Americans
Here to stay at last in Arizona [Javier and Juana Quintero] E. Schurenberg. il *Money* 16:86-90 Ag '87
In Texas, a grim new Appalachia [Rio Grande Valley] F. Gibney. il *Newsweek* 109:27-8 Je 8 '87
Education
When good intentions aren't enough [culture conflict between student and teacher] S. S. Wineburg. il *Phi Delta Kappan* 68:544-5 Mr '87
Political activities
See also
Southwest Voter Registration Education Project
San Antonio: putting family first [Mayor H. Cisneros declines race for governor; chooses to care for new son ailing from birth defects] D. Pedersen. il por *Newsweek* 110:8 S 14 '87
Psychiatric care
In search of self [E. Cacho, psychotherapist to Mexican American women] M. Rochlin. il pors *Ms* 16:58-60 N '87
Mexican Americans in motion pictures
'La bamba' is no bomb. J. Podhoretz. il *U S News World Rep* 103:48-9 Ag 10 '87
Mexican architecture *See* Architecture, Mexican
Mexican art *See* Art, Mexican
Mexican cooking *See* Cooking, Mexican
Mexican diet *See* Diet
Mexican folk art *See* Folk art
Mexican freetail bats *See* Bats
Mexican Grand Prix *See* Automobile racing—Mexico
Mexican house decoration *See* House decoration, Mexican
Mexican restaurants *See* Restaurants
Mexican sunflowers
You'll look up to tithonia. C. B. Hipps. il *Flower Gard* 31:69+ Ap/My '87
Mexican Workers Confederation
Death watch in Mexico [F. Velázquez] T. Rosenberg. il *Nation* 244:500-2+ Ap 18 '87
Mexicanos *See* Mexican Americans
Mexicans
United States
See also
Mexican Americans
A boxcar horror in Sierra Blanca [death of illegal Mexican aliens] il *U S News World Rep* 103:15 Jl 13 '87
The boxcar that became a coffin [Mexican aliens suffocate in Texas] E. Magnuson. il *Time* 130:21 Jl 13 '87
Can the trek to El Norte be curbed? [enforcing new immigration law; special section] il *U S News World Rep* 102:22-6 Ja 19 '87

Confusion on both sides of the border [amnesty and illegal aliens] A. Bernstein and others. il *Bus Week* p68-9 Jl 20 '87
Death ride to the American Dream [Mexican aliens suffocate in boxcar] F. Bruning. por *Macleans* 100:7 Ag 3 '87
New law won't stop illegals' influx [immigration reform law; views of David Heer] *USA Today (Periodical)* 115:7 Ap '87
Peonage in the pines [migrant Mexican forest workers] J. Juffer. il *Progressive* 51:24-7 N '87
Sad return of the prodigal sons [Mexicans returning to Huandacareo as result of new immigration law] J. Moody. il *Time* 129:52 My 18 '87
The social process of international migration. D. S. Massey and F. García-España. bibl f il *Science* 237:733-8 Ag 14 '87
Tragedy in Texas [Mexican aliens suffocate in boxcar] A. Bilski. il *Macleans* 100:19 Jl 13 '87
Mexico
See also
Acapulco (Mexico)
Agricultural administration—Mexico
Americans—Mexico
Atotonilco (Mexico)
Automobile racing—Mexico
Baja California (Mexico: Peninsula)
Barranca de Cobre (Mexico)
Birds—Mexico
Bullfights—Mexico
Children—Mexico
Cholula (Mexico)
Country estates—Mexico
Cultural property—Protection—Mexico
Dance festivals—Mexico
Drug abuse—Mexico
Earthquakes—Mexico
Eating—Mexico
Education and state—Mexico
El Chichón (Mexico)
Finance—Mexico
Forests and forestry—Mexico
Guadalupe Island (Mexico)
Gulf of California (Mexico)
Health education—Mexico
Hotels, motels, etc.—Mexico
Huandacareo (Mexico)
Hunting—Mexico
Immigration and emigration—Mexico
Investments, American—Mexico
Investments, Japanese—Mexico
Jazz music—Mexico
Labor supply—Mexico
Loans, Bank—Mexico
Medical care—Mexico
Mexicans
Mexico City (Mexico)
Money—Mexico
Morelia (Mexico)
Motion pictures—Mexico
Narcotics trade—Mexico
Neo-Nazis—Mexico
New River (Mexico and Calif.)
Orphans and orphanages—Mexico
Paleontology—Mexico
Puebla (Mexico)
Railroads—Mexico
Real estate investment—Mexico
Regionalism—Mexico
Relief work—Mexico
Resorts—Mexico
San Miguel de Allende (Mexico)
Sonora (Mexico: State)
Sonoran Desert
Strikes—Automobile industry workers—Mexico
Student protests, demonstrations, etc.—Mexico
Tijuana (Mexico)
Trade unions—Mexico
United Nations—Mexico
Veracruz (Mexico: State)
Water pollution—Mexico
Wildlife conservation—Mexico
Wildlife sanctuaries—Mexico
Women—Mexico
Wrestling, Professional—Mexico
Xilitla (Mexico)
Yucatan (Mexico: State)
Zihuatanejo (Mexico)
Antiquities
See also
Cities and towns, Ruined, extinct, etc.—Mexico

Mexico—*cont.*

Bibliography
Book reviews. *Curr Hist* 86:125+ Mr '87

Description and travel
All across Mexico [special section] il map *Saturday Evening Post* 259:68-70+ O '87

Hammock land [smaller resorts and beach towns along Pacific coast] il map *Sunset* 178:46-51 Ja '87

A Mexican state of mind. D. G. Salter and R. J. Christmas. il *Essence* 18:20+ My '87

Mexico. P. Plawin. il *Changing Times* 41:95-8+ N '87

Economic conditions
A swelling tide of troubles. J. Moody. il *Time* 129:60 F 23 '87

Economic policy
For De la Madrid, it's almost like being reelected [hand picked heir C. Salinas de Gortari] S. Baker. il por *Bus Week* p78-9 O 19 '87

Mexico's development crisis. J. H. Street. bibl f *Curr Hist* 86:101-4+ Mr '87

Mexico's precarious balancing act. S. Baker and E. Weiner. il por *Bus Week* p54-5 S 14 '87

Mexico's slow recovery. T. Fennell. il *Macleans* 100:38+ O 12 '87

Nothing left to steal. G. B. Lake. *Natl Rev* 39:40-1 Jl 3 '87

Why De la Madrid's successor won't be another De la Madrid. S. Baker. por *Bus Week* p65 My 11 '87

Foreign relations
Latin America
Mexico and Latin America: the limits of cooperation. C. Rico. bibl f *Curr Hist* 86:121-4+ Mr '87

United States
See United States—Foreign relations—Mexico

History
The road to Veracruz. M. Richie. il *Américas* 39:22-5+ Mr/Ap '87

Spanish colony, 1540-1810
Splendors of the Golden Age: three centuries of Spanish colonial art [cover story; catalog of exhibit at EPCOT] il *Horizon* 30:41-56 Jl/Ag '87

Industries
See also
> Automobile factories—Mexico
> Candy industry—Mexico
> Shellfish fisheries—Mexico
> Volkswagen de Mexico SA de CV

Labor policy
The dilemma of Mexican labor. J. Bortz. *Curr Hist* 86:105-8+ Mr '87

Politics and government
See also
> Institutional Revolutionary Party (Mexico)
> Political candidates—Mexico
> Politics, Corruption in—Mexico

The CIA sizes up the Mexican domino. *Harpers* 274:21 My '87

The machine and the tiger. M. Kondracke. *New Repub* 196:16-21 F 23 '87

Mexico [special issue] bibl f map (inside back cover) *Curr Hist* 86:95-137 Mr '87

Mexico: the presidential problem. A. Aguilar Zinser. bibl f *Foreign Policy* 69:40-60 Wint '87/'88

A swelling tide of troubles. J. Moody. il *Time* 129:60 F 23 '87

United States relations with Mexico [address, April 23, 1987] S. W. Sanders. *Vital Speeches Day* 53:525-8 Je 15 '87

Statistics
Basic data on Mexico. il *Curr Hist* 86:126 Mr '87

Mexico City (Mexico)

Air pollution
Stepping up the war on smog. S. Baker. *Bus Week* p60 F 23 '87

Architecture
International style: Oriental touch for Mexico City [interior design by Jay Spectre] P. Warner. il *Archit Dig* 44:84-91 Jl '87

Art
Restoring Mexican murals. *Américas* 39:56 Mr/Ap '87

Description
Mexico City. J. Hooper. il *Esquire* 107 Summ Traveler:T8+ Ap '87

Mexico City Olympics, 1968 *See* Olympic Games—1968—Summer Olympics

Mexico Stock Exchange *See* Stock exchanges—Mexico exchange

Meyer, Edgar
about
Edgar Meyer. K. Whitehead. il por *Down Beat* 11:14 N '87

Meyer, Galen H.
Easter on Hill 17. il por *Christ Today* 31:18-22 Ap 17 '87

Meyer, Marsha
The right and wrong ways to buy gold. il *Money* 16:47-8+ Ag '87

Why stockbrokers sleep at night. il *Money* 16:105-8+ Jl '87

Meyer, Peter
Getting to the top: the conquest of the great peaks. il *Courier* 40:24-8 F '87

Meyer Stone Books
To further 'A global theology'. W. Griffin. *Publ Wkly* 231:24+ Ap 17 '87

Meyers, Eugene
Shuttle external tanks offer U.S. a shortcut to large space stations. por *Aviat Week Space Technol* 127:60-1+ Jl 27 '87

Meyers, Jeffrey
about
A rejoinder from Dmitri Nabokov. D. Nabokov. *Natl Rev* 39:42-3 Ja 30 '87

Meyers, Joan Rohr
Poems [poem] *Commonweal* 114:87 F 13 '87

Meyers, John A.
A letter from the publisher. See issues of Time through February 2, 1987

Meyerson, Harold
Bork and Bird. *New Repub* 197:21+ S 14-21 '87

Meyerson, Morton H.
about
Git along, little thrifts. T. Mason. il por *Bus Week* p33 O 26 '87

MFN (Most-favored-nation) tariff policy *See* Tariff—United States

MGM *See* Metro-Goldwyn-Mayer, Inc.

MGM Grand Air Inc.
The little luxury airline that might. E. Paris. il *Forbes* 140:170-1 O 19 '87

MGM Grand Air begins all-first-class transcontinental service with 727-100s. B. A. Smith. il *Aviat Week Space Technol* 127:41 S 21 '87

Welcome aboard. The champagne is on ice. S. Toy. il por *Bus Week* p61-2 Ja 19 '87

MGM/UA Communications Co.
Can Kerkorian breathe new life into the old lion? R. Grover. il *Bus Week* p33 N 23 '87

Doing the Hollywood shuffle [K. Kerkorian] M. Beauchamp. il por *Forbes* 140:35-6 O 19 '87

MHC *See* Major histocompatibility complex

MHD *See* Magnetohydrodynamics

Miami (Fla.)

Airports
"We enterprised it" [Miami International's manager R. Judy] J. Parr. il por *Forbes* 140:298+ N 16 '87

Architecture
Conference report: the AIA takes a new look at 'America's Sunporch' [conference sponsored by design committee that investigated The fantasy architecture of Miami] P. M. Sachner. il *Archit Rec* 175:39 Ja '87

Crime
Can Miami save itself? [cover story] R. Sherrill. il *N Y Times Mag* p18-24+ Jl 19 '87

Don Aronow's murder leaves Miami wondering: were 'Cigarettes' hazardous to his health? J. Hammer. il por *People Wkly* 27:75-6+ Mr 30 '87

Ex-champ Pryor shot, held in Miami for rape [A. Pryor] por *Jet* 71:50 Mr 23 '87

The hitchhiker [disappearance of A. Billig: excerpt from The corpse had a familiar face] E. Buchanan. il por *Glamour* 85:140+ O '87

Judge drops case against mom who fed sons on train [case of T. Jinks] *Jet* 72:24 S 14 '87

Miami mom jailed for feeding 'hungry' sons [T. Jinks arrested for disobeying 'no eating' sign on Metrorail] il por *Jet* 72:55 S 7 '87

Pryor preps for battle on rape charge in Miami [A. Pryor] por *Jet* 72:51 Mr 30 '87

Criminal justice, Administration of
Miami preacher convicted for selling heroin [case of C. Scott] *Jet* 72:10 Je 15 '87

Pryor gets no record in Miami kidnapping case [rape charges dropped against A. Pryor] *Jet* 72:52 S 14 '87

Description
Miami. J. Didion. il *N Y Rev Books* 34:43-8 My 28 '87

Galleries and museums
See also
> Gold Coast Railroad Museum

Miami (Fla.)—*cont.*

Health facilities
See also
University of Miami. Comprehensive Pain Center
Historic houses, sites, etc.
See also
Vizcaya Museum and Gardens
Newspapers
See also
Miami herald
Miami news
Police
Miami Vice: sorting good guys from bad guys [police involved in drug dealing] M. A. Moore. il *U S News World Rep* 102:28 F 2 '87
On the beat with two Miami cops. M. A. Esquivel. il *Sch Update* 120:6 D 4 '87
Politics and government
NBL's Teele launches bid to become Miami's mayor. por *Jet* 72:28 Ag 10 '87
Revenge in a hot place [views of J. Didion] J. Rothchild. *Wash Mon* 19:45-6+ D '87
Washington in Miami. J. Didion. il *N Y Rev Books* 34:22+ Jl 16 '87
Population
Are contras living it up in Miami? R. Parry. il *Newsweek* 109:25 My 4 '87
Miami [Cubans] J. Didion. il *N Y Rev Books* 34:43-8 My 28 '87
Miami: exiles. J. Didion. il *N Y Rev Books* 34:35-9 Je 25 '87
Miami: 'la lucha'. J. Didion. il *N Y Rev Books* 34:15-18 Je 11 '87
Revenge in a hot place [views of J. Didion] J. Rothchild. *Wash Mon* 19:45-6+ D '87
The second Havana. D. Rieff. il *New Yorker* 63:65-9+ My 18 '87
Race relations
Casket on steps evokes apology from judge who denounced King's memory [Judge J. Turner's remarks] *Jet* 71:4 F 16 '87
Social conditions
Can Miami save itself? [cover story] R. Sherrill. il *N Y Times Mag* p18-24+ Jl 19 '87
Stores
Minority businesses open at new mall in Miami. *Jet* 72:23 My 4 '87
Transit systems
Judge drops case against mom who fed sons on train [case of T. Jinks] *Jet* 72:24 S 14 '87
Miami mom jailed for feeding 'hungry' sons [T. Jinks arrested for disobeying 'no eating' sign on Metrorail] il por *Jet* 72:55 S 7 '87
Transportation
How to get to both Miami boat shows. map *Mot Boat Sail* 159:84-5 F '87
Miami (Fla.) in literature
1987: Miami's year in the literary limelight. R. Kaye. il pors *Publ Wkly* 232:46-7 N 13 '87
The mirage of Miami. N. Lemann. *New Repub* 197:37-42 N 23 '87
Urban razzle, fatal glamour. R. Z. Sheppard. il *Time* 130:65-6 S 28 '87
Miami Beach (Fla.)
Hotels, motels, etc.
A bargain: 130 rooms, ocean vu, wet bar. il *Newsweek* 109:30 F 23 '87
Miami Book Fair International *See* Book fairs
Miami City Ballet
Reviews:
Performance of 1953 version of Valse fantaisie. L. Horn. *Dance Mag* 61:176-7 Je '87
Miami Film Festival *See* Motion picture festivals—Florida
Miami herald
Stakeouts and shouted questions [stakeout of Gary Hart's townhouse] R. Zoglin. il *Time* 129:28-9 My 18 '87
Miami International Airport *See* Miami (Fla.)—Airports
Miami International Boat Show *See* Boats and boating—Exhibitions
Miami news
Hounded by woes, Miamians beg for more of Ryan the Advice Dog. il por *People Wkly* 28:113 O 19 '87
Miami Sound Machine (Musical group)
Miami Sound Machine: nothing gets in their way. il *Teen* 31:45 Ja '87
Miami Vice [television program] *See* Television program reviews—Single works
MIAs (Vietnamese War) *See* Vietnamese War, 1957-1975—Missing in action

MIAs (World War II) *See* World War, 1939-1945—Missing in action
Mice
See also
Milk, Mouse
Building a better mouse [model of Down's syndrome] J. A. Miller. il *BioScience* 37:103-6 F '87
The mice shall stay [house mice] J. Page. il *Ctry J* 14:6+ D '87
Control
See also
Mousetraps
Embryology
See Embryology—Rodents
Eye
See Eye—Rodents
Hearing
See Hearing—Rodents
Mutation
See Mutation—Rodents
Michael, Prince of Greece, 1939-
House of cards: Niki de Saint Phalle's Tuscan fantasy [cover story] il por *Archit Dig* 44:124-31 S '87
Michael, Clifford
about
An untimely departure. J. O'Hara. *Macleans* 100:20 N 30 '87
Michael, George
about
Traditional values? M. E. Marty. *Christ Century* 104:775 S 9-16 '87
Michael Clark and Company
Reviews:
Performance of No fire escape in hell at the Brooklyn Academy of Music. O. Stuart. *Dance Mag* 61:81-2 Mr '87
Michaels, Jack D.
The importance and impact of standards [address, December 17, 1986] *Vital Speeches Day* 53:441-4 My 1 '87
Michaels, Leonard
The action of metaphor. *Harpers* 274:30+ Ja '87
Jealousy [story] *Harpers* 274:36-7 Mr '87
Literary talk. *Harpers* 275:30+ D '87
Michaels, Patrick J., and Hayden, Bruce P.
Modeling the climate dynamics of tree death. bibl il maps *BioScience* 37:603-10 S '87
Michael's Waterside Inn (Santa Barbara, Calif.: Restaurant) *See* Santa Barbara (Calif.)—Restaurants, nightclubs, bars, etc.
Michalske, Terry A., and Bunker, Bruce C.
The fracturing of glass. il *Sci Am* 257:122-9 D '87
Michalski, Franek
WiPing Poland into shape. il *Nation* 244:680-2 My 23 '87
Michanie, Silvia, and Bryan, Frank L.
Spin-off from space travel. il *World Health* p26-7 Ag/S '87
Michaud, Ellen, and Anastas, Lila
Quick health tips for women only [excerpt from Listen to your body] *Prevention* 39:89 D '87
Quick tips for cold comfort [excerpt from Listen to your body] *Prevention* 39:66 N '87
Quick tips to unkink sore spots [excerpts from Listen to your body] il *Prevention* 39:96 O '87
Michaud, Stephen G., 1948-
Identifying Argentina's 'disappeared'. il *N Y Times Mag* p18-21+ D 27 '87
Michel, F. Curtis, and others
When will a pulsar in supernova 1987A be seen? bibl f il *Science* 238:938-40 N 13 '87
Michel, Thomas
Mount Hiei day of prayer for peace. il *America* 157:475-7 D 19 '87
Michelangelo Buonarroti, 1475-1564
about
Art historian James Beck urges the Vatican to clean up its act, not Michelangelo's frescoes [interview] H. Shapiro. il por *People Wkly* 27:69+ Mr 30 '87
Controversy over the Sistine ceiling. J. Dillenberger. *Christ Century* 104:708-9 Ag 26-S 2 '87
Crown moves up Sistine Chapel video. il *Publ Wkly* 231:32 Mr 27 '87
Dispelling clouds. J. Gardner. *Commonweal* 114:599-601 O 23 '87
He didn't paint by the numbers, but he's getting digitized now [restoration of Sistine Chapel frescoes] il *Discover* 8:8 My '87
A long-lost little brother? [discovery of model for sculpture David] il *U S News World Rep* 102:12 Mr 16 '87
Michelangelo rediscovered [cover story] M. K. Talley, Jr. il *Art News* 86:159-70 Summ '87

Michelangelo Buonarroti, 1475-1564—about—*cont.*

A model for David? J. Tully. il *Art News* 86:53-4 Summ '87

Out of grime, a domain of light. R. Hughes. il *Time* 129:86-7 Ap 27 '87

Recovering Michelangelo's true colors. J. Arias. *World Press Rev* 34:60 Ap '87

Storm over the Sistine ceiling. J. Pope-Hennessy. il *N Y Rev Books* 34:16+ O 8 '87

Michelin Canada Ltd.

A setback for labor [workers in Nova Scotia vote against joining the Canadian Auto Workers union] D. Jones. il *Macleans* 100:14 Ja 26 '87

Michelin et Cie

Michelin is burning rubber. F. J. Comes and Z. Schiller. il *Bus Week* p60 O 12 '87

Michelmore, Peter

Alone in the shark-filled sea. il *Read Dig* 131:116-21 O '87

"Bail out, Tommy! Eject!". il *Read Dig* 130:106-11 F '87

Emergency aid that works—enhanced. il *Read Dig* 131:165-8 N '87

Nightmare in the hayfield. il *Read Dig* 130:64-9 Je '87

Michels, Robert, 1936-

about

Textbook credits bruise psychiatrists' egos. E. Marshall. por *Science* 235:835-6 F 20 '87

Textbook dispute [discussion of February 20, 1987 article, Textbook credits bruise psychiatrists' egos] E. Marshall. *Science* 236:655-7 My 8 '87

Michelson, Albert Abraham, 1852-1931

about

Centennial of the Michelson-Morley experiment [cover story; special issue] bibl f il pors *Phys Today* 40:23-30+ My '87

Michelson, Peter F., and others

Resonant-mass detectors of gravitational radiation [cover story] bibl f il *Science* 237:150-7 Jl 10 '87

Michener, Charles

Britain's brat of letters. por *Esquire* 107:108-11 Ja '87

Madrid. il *Esquire* 107 Summ Traveler:T10 Ap '87

Michener, James A. (James Albert), 1907-

Legacy [fiction] il *Ladies Home J* 104:104+ S '87

Together for life [fiction] il *Read Dig* 131:106-9 S '87

about

What makes love last. S. Arnout. il pors *McCalls* 114:166+ F '87

Michener, Mari

about

What makes love last. S. Arnout. il pors *McCalls* 114:166+ F '87

Michiels, Frank, and others

Derivation of clones close to *met* by preparative field inversion gel electrophoresis. bibl f il *Science* 236:1305-8 Je 5 '87

Michigan

See also

Birds—Michigan

Criminal justice, Administration of—Michigan

Isle Royale National Park (Mich.)

Macomb County (Mich.)

Wayne County (Mich.)

Legislature

Black woman speaker pro tempore of Michigan House [T. P. Hunter] por *Jet* 71:22 Ja 12 '87

Politics and government

See also

Michigan—Legislature

Kemp's surprising victory [Kemp-Robertson alliance wins delegate contest in Michigan] L. Schiffren. *Natl Rev* 39:37+ Ap 10 '87

Religious institutions and affairs

Dispensing forgiveness and justice in equal measure, Father Mike Callahan is a man of the cloth and the law. S. K. Reed. il pors *People Wkly* 28:143-4+ D 7 '87

Michigan, Lake *See* Lake Michigan

Michigan Avenue (Chicago, Ill.)

The Magnificent Mile. T. Bross. il *Travel Holiday* 167:10+ Je '87

Michigan Education Trust

Michigan gov. enacts guaranteed tuition law. *Jet* 71:23 Ja 26 '87

Michigan Opera Theatre

Detroit. N. Malitz. *Opera News* 51:38 Mr 28 '87

Michigan State Bar Association *See* State Bar of Michigan

Michigan State University. Institute for Research on Teaching

Teacher collaboration: new partnerships to attack old problems [classroom teachers and university professors] A. C. Porter. bibl f il *Phi Delta Kappan* 69:147-52 O '87

Michnik, Adam

Gorbachev: the great counter-reformer; tr. by Pat Hunt and Jonathan Kozol. *Harpers* 275:19-20 N '87

about

Poland's plucky activist. M. T. Kaufman. il por *N Y Times Mag* p38+ Ap 26 '87

Mick, Larry

about

A wrenching separation ends an Iowa couple's hope of adopting the five Cooper kids. G. Pick. il *People Wkly* 27:40-3 F 2 '87

Micklus, Sam

about

Mental agility, not plodding scholarship, gets the gold in the 'Odyssey of the Mind'. T. Kahn. il por *People Wkly* 28:75+ Jl 6 '87

Micro-Books, Inc.

New reading system promises to increase data retention [Kwikscan New Testament] J. P. Frank. il *Publ Wkly* 232:64-5 O 16 '87

Microbial degradation *See* Biodegradation

Microbial genetics

See also

Gene transfer

Altered bacteria released [frost preventing bacteria] *Sci News* 131:277 My 2 '87

Assessing the risks of microbial release. J. L. Marx. bibl il *Science* 237:1413-17 S 18 '87

BioTechnica tests EPA review process [field test of Rhizobium bacteria] M. Crawford. *Science* 235:840 F 20 '87

Bozeman chain saw massacre [G. A. Strobel's Dutch elm disease experiment] W. E. Brock. il pors *Discover* 8:78-82+ N '87

California field test goes forward [Frostban bacteria] M. Crawford. il *Science* 236:511 My 1 '87

Engineered bacteria released [preventing frost damage] L. Tangley. *BioScience* 37:461 Jl/Ag '87

The importance of being blue [South Carolina experiment attempts to track genetically altered Pseudomonas in soil] M. D. Lemonick. il *Time* 130:82-3 N 9 '87

Metalloregulator DNA-binding protein encoded by the *mer*R gene: isolation and characterization. T. O'Halloran and C. Walsh. bibl f il *Science* 235:211-14 Ja 9 '87

Montana State's troublesome elms [G. Strobel illegally injects diseased trees with genetically altered bacteria] M. D. Lemonick. il por *Time* 130:67 S 14 '87

MSU faults Strobel for Dutch elm test. L. Roberts. *Science* 237:1286 S 11 '87

New questions in Strobel case [field test of Dutch elm disease] L. Roberts. *Science* 237:1097-8 S 4 '87

One potato patch that is making genetic history [test of genetically engineered Ice-minus bacteria at Tulelake, Calif.] S. S. Hall. il *Smithsonian* 18:125-6+ Ag '87

Researcher flouts gene-splicing rules [G. Strobel's Dutch elm disease experiment] M. Crawford. *Science* 237:838-9 Ag 21 '87

Tubers, berries and bugs [bacteria designed to inhibit frost formation sprayed on plants] P. Elmer-Dewitt. il *Time* 129:63 My 11 '87

Microbiology

See also

Bacteriology

Biodegradation

Industrial microbiology

Intestines—Microbiology

Water—Microbiology

Microburst wind shear *See* Wind shear

Microchemistry

Very, very, very small scale [devices developed by N. J. Dovichi; cover story] J. Raloff. il *Sci News* 132:74-5 Ag 1 '87

Microcircuits *See* Integrated circuits

Microcomputer industry *See* Computer industry

Microcomputers *See* Computers

Microelectronics

See also

Integrated circuits

National Nanofabrication Facility

How are Japanese unions responding to microelectronics-based automation? W. E. Klay. bibl f *Mon Labor Rev* 110:39-40 Mr '87

Microelectronics and Computer Technology Corporation
Three members will leave research group. *Aviat Week Space Technol* 126:135 F 9 '87
Uneasy alliance. il *Time* 129:51 Ja 19 '87
Microelectronics industry *See* Electronic industries
Microfiche
Acid test [Nineteenth century short title catalog on microfiche] il *Hist Today* 37:61-2 Ag '87
MicroGeneSys Inc.
AIDS vaccine: a sliver of hope? R. Rhein, Jr. *Bus Week* p30-1 Ag 31 '87
Micromechanics
A small world grows tinier. W. D. Marbach. il *Newsweek* 110:65 N 30 '87
Micrometers
A wire micrometer for photographs. L. Balbi. il *Sky Telesc* 74:310-11+ S '87
Anecdotes, facetiae, satire, etc.
First, find your spider [renovating old brass filar micrometer] S. D. Ringwood. il *Astronomy* 15:28+ Ja '87
Micron Technology, Inc.
Hard times may be over for the high techs. G. G. Marcial. il *Bus Week* p120 My 18 '87
Micronav Ltd.
A future in smart boxes. il por *Macleans* 100:40 Ap 20 '87
Micronesia
See also
Pacific Islands (Trust territory)
Foreign relations
United States
See United States—Foreign relations—Micronesia
Micronesia (Federated States)
Politics and government
Compact of free association with Pacific Islands [text of executive order, October 16, 1986] R. Reagan. *Dep State Bull* 86:74-5 D '86
Micronutrients *See* Trace elements
Microorganisms
See also
Archaebacteria
Bacteria
Growth regulators—Microorganisms
Staphylococci
Viruses
Microorganisms, Fossil *See* Micropaleontology
Microorganisms, Pathogenic
See also
Mycoplasmas
Protozoa, Pathogenic
Spiroplasmas
Micropaleontology
Bacterial bedfellows [symbiotic theory of evolution] D. Sagan and L. Margulis. il *Nat Hist* 96:26+ Mr '87
Early Archean (3.3-billion to 3.5-billion-year-old) microfossils from Warrawoona Group, Australia. J. W. Schopf and B. M. Packer. bibl f il map *Science* 237:70-3 Jl 3 '87
Microbial trace-fossil formation, biogenous, and abiotic weathering in the Antarctic cold desert. E. I. Friedmann and R. Weed. bibl f il *Science* 236:703-5 My 8 '87
Who spread syphilis? [Indiana bear fossil found to have had disease] *Newsweek* 110:73 S 21 '87
Microphones
Diversity microphone transmission. H. Friedman. il *Radio-Electron* 58:26-7+ Ag '87
Microphone techniques and sound quality. M. Riggs. il *High Fidel* 37:24 Ja '87
Missing link: a practical guide to wireless mics. F. Ginsburg. il *Theatre Crafts* 21:49-52 Ap '87
MicroPro International Corporation
The rebirth of a classic [WordStar] C. Spencer. il *Pers Comput* 11:62-5+ F '87
Microprocessors
286/386 protected-mode programming [IBM PC] J. Barnum. il *Byte* 12 no12 Sp Issue:125-9 '87
The 386 and DOS 5.0: hard questions and not-so-easy answers [Compaq Deskpro 386; cover story] S. R. Reed and P. Honan. il *Pers Comput* 11:62-5+ Mr '87
68000 update. il *Radio-Electron* 58 ComputerDigest:63 Ag '87
80286 accelerators. R. G. A. Cote. il *Byte* 12:161-6 N '87
The 80286 problem. il *Byte* 12:88-9 My '87
80386 accelerator boards [American Computer and Peripheral's 386 Turbo and Intel's Inboard 386] D. E. Crabb. il *Byte* 12:213-16 Ag '87
Accelerator boards [BIX product focus] C. Franklin, Jr. *Byte* 12:169-70+ N '87

Accelerator boards for the Macintosh SE [Prodigy SE and HyperCharger 020] L. H. Loeb. il *Byte* 12:177-80 N '87
Atari 520ST projects: an interface board for the Atari ST cartridge port. T. G. Hunkler. il *Byte* 12:161-2+ Je '87
Build the MC 68000. T. Schrader and others. il *Radio-Electron* 58 ComputerDigest:101-4 Mr '87
Build the PT-68K (I). P. Stark. il *Radio-Electron* 58 ComputerDigest:90-5 O '87
The Cheetah Adapter/386 [translator card] J. Shiell. il *Byte* 12:135-7 Ap '87
A closer look [relative speeds of 80386- and 68020-based machines] R. Grehan. il *Byte* 12:110-11 S '87
Computer chip supplies personal computers with greater speed and power. S. Bentley. *Black Enterp* 17:34 Jl '87
Exploring the 386 offerings. M. Liskin. il *Pers Comput* 11:45-6+ F '87
The Fairchild Clipper. M. Ackerman and G. Baum. il *Byte* 12:161-2+ Ap '87
Hauppauge 386 Motherboard. R. Malloy. *Byte* 12:102 N '87
High-tech horsepower [Intel 80386 and Motorola 68020 microprocessors] il *Byte* 12:101-2+ Jl '87
Intel and Sequent kiss and make up [80386 microprocessors] J. W. Wilson. il *Bus Week* p120 My 25 '87
A look inside the 6502. L. Solomon. il *Radio-Electron* 58 ComputerDigest:141-3 My '87
The MC 68000. T. Schrader and others. il *Radio-Electron* 58 ComputerDigest:138-40 My '87
New life for 80286 computers [Inboard 386/AT] P. Honan. il *Pers Comput* 11:196 S '87
PCs that can roar almost as loud as the giants. G. Lewis. il *Bus Week* p118 N 30 '87
Simulating a microprocessor [Prolog program] A. Lane. il *Byte* 12:161+ Ag '87
Stack machines and compiler design: the Novix CPU's FORTH instruction set and the design of a C compiler. D. L. Miller. bibl il *Byte* 12:177-8+ Ap '87
Three accelerator boards for the Macintosh Plus. C. Crawford. il *Byte* 12:161-2+ D '87
Two brief conversations with Ben Rosen. P. Lemmons. *Byte* 12:6 Ja '87
VIPC 386: top-flight price and performance. A. C. Hixson. il *Pers Comput* 11:187-8 S '87
Microscopes and microscopy
See also
Electron microscopes and microscopy
Microchemistry
Photomicrography
X ray microscopes and microscopy
In the light spot [optical trapping and manipulation of viruses and bacteria; work of Arthur Ashkin and Joseph M. Dziedzic] *Sci Am* 256:32 Je '87
Microscopy and optical equipment. *Science* 235 pt2:G135+ F 27 '87
Optical trapping and manipulation of viruses and bacteria. A. Ashkin and J. M. Dziedzic. bibl f il *Science* 235:1517-20 Mr 20 '87
Today's microscopy [cover story] E. S. Boatman and others. bibl f il *BioScience* 37:384-94 Je '87
The use of a charge-coupled device for quantitative optical microscopy of biological structures. Y. Hiraoka and others. bibl f il *Science* 238:36-41 O 2 '87
Microscopic Septet
The Microscopic Septet. A. Kahn. il *Down Beat* 54:43-5 My '87
Microsoft Corporation
Bill Gates on: a platform for the next 10 years [cover story; interview] S. R. Reed. il pors *Pers Comput* 11:74-5+ My '87
The billion-dollar whiz kid [W. Gates gets IBM to endorse Microsoft operating system; cover story] R. Brandt. il pors *Bus Week* p68-72+ Ap 13 '87
Both sides may win this war [spreadsheet market] A. Field. il *Bus Week* p104-5 O 19 '87
A CD-ROM with a view [Microsoft Bookshelf] il *Pers Comput* 11:27 My '87
A computer jock's $550-million jackpot [W. H. Gates] B. Uttal. il por *Fortune* 115:84-5 Ja 5 '87
Self-made billionaire [W. H. Gates] il por *U S News World Rep* 103:48-9 Jl 6 '87
Microsoft Word (Word processor program) *See* Word processors and processing—Programming
Microsurgery
Surgery without sutures [use of adhesives] S. Weisburd. il *Sci News* 131:234-5 Ap 11 '87
Microtomography
Superscope [work of Brian P. Flannery and others] il *Sci Am* 257:29-30 Jl '87

Microtomography—*cont.*

Three-dimensional X-ray microtomography. B. P. Flannery and others. bibl f il *Science* 237:1439-44 S 18 '87

X-ray microscopy in 3-D [cover story] D. E. Thomsen. il *Sci News* 131:300-1 My 9 '87

Microtubules

See also

Tubulin

Aluminum: a high price for a surrogate? [research by Timothy L. MacDonald and others] D. D. Edwards. il *Sci News* 131:245 Ap 18 '87

F-actin and microtubule suspensions as indeterminate fluids. R. E. Buxbaum and others. bibl f il *Science* 235:1511-14 Mr 20 '87

The microtubule as an intracellular engine. R. D. Allen. il *Sci Am* 256:42-9 F '87

Microtubule gelation-contraction: essential components and relation to slow axonal transport. R. C. Weisenberg and others. bibl f il *Science* 238:1119-22 N 20 '87

Preferred microtubules for vesicle transport in lobster axons. R. H. Miller and others. bibl f il *Science* 235:220-2 Ja 9 '87

Promotion of tubulin assembly by aluminum ion in vitro. T. L. MacDonald and others. bibl f il *Science* 236:183-6 Ap 10 '87

Microwave aircraft

Can a plane fly forever? M. Rogers. il *Newsweek* 110:42+ S 28 '87

Companies testing Long-EZ derivative for unmanned aerial vehicle market [California Microwave CM-44 designed by Burt Rutan] W. B. Scott. il *Aviat Week Space Technol* 126:128+ Ap 27 '87

A ride on Voyager's tail [drone aircraft designed for California Microwave Inc. by Burt Rutan] G. G. Marcial. *Bus Week* p117 Ja 12 '87

Soaring into history. M. Gray. il *Macleans* 100:45 O 19 '87

Microwave communication systems

See also

Multichannel multipoint distribution service

Microwave cooking

See also

Golden Valley Microwave Foods Inc.

Cool it for summer. J. R. Nyenhuis. il *Saturday Evening Post* 259:18+ Jl/Ag '87

Dessert is easy with fruit sauces. il *South Living* 22:110 Ag '87

Easy meals in minutes. L. Hoppe. il *Better Homes Gard* 65:176 N '87

Fast fish. C. Kummer. il *Atlantic* 260:96-9 D '87

Favorite recipes—only faster. il *South Living* 22:166 F '87

Fish in a flash. il *South Living* 22:206 Ap '87

The flavors of China. J. R. Nyenhuis. il *Saturday Evening Post* 259:16+ Mr '87

Food in Vogue. B. Kafka. il *Vogue* 177:488+ S '87

Healthy microwaving. J. B. Hurley. See issues of Prevention (Emmaus, Pa.) beginning January 1987

Helpful hints and a few good tips. il *South Living* 22:192+ Mr '87

Hey, Ma, what's in the microwave? M. J. Pitzer. il *Bus Week* p68+ N 30 '87

Holiday baking in minutes. il *South Living* 22:216 N '87

How to bake a cake in a microwave oven [cake mix] il *Consum Rep* 52:330-1 Je '87

Junior chefs on their own with a microwave. il *Sunset* 179:116-17 Jl '87

Mechanical love. E. Crow. il *Parents* 62:6 Je '87

Micro-way cooking. See issues of McCall's beginning March 1986

Microwave! [special section] T. P. Wolf. il *Better Homes Gard* 65:140-6+ Ap '87

The microwave cookbook. See issues of Good Housekeeping beginning November 1985

Microwave cooking for kids. D. W. Hansen. il *Ladies Home J* 104:66+ S '87

Microwave cooking tips. J. A. Kenneally. See issues of Good Housekeeping beginning October 1985

Microwave custard in just 5 minutes. il *Sunset* 178:172-3 Mr '87

Microwave desserts. il *Better Homes Gard* 65:111-12 Je '87

Microwave food: a hot investment idea? T. Segal. *Bus Week* p104 Mr 30 '87

Microwave for your health. il *Glamour* 85:320-3 Mr '87

Microwave magic 1987 [special section] il *Good Housekeep* 205:113-14+ N '87

Microwave main dishes. il *Better Homes Gard* 65:153-4 S '87

Microwave mastery:

Candy. il *Gourmet* 47:92-3+ D '87

Seafood. il *Gourmet* 47:62-3+ Jl '87

Winter vegetables. il *Gourmet* 47:64+ F '87

Microwave one-dish meals. B. Greenwood. il *Better Homes Gard* 65:86-7 Ag '87

Microwave your fish and game. P. J. Del Giudice. il *Outdoor Life* 179:72-4+ Je '87

Microwaving goes big time [B. Kafka's Microwave gourmet] L. Shapiro. il por *Newsweek* 110:79 O 12 '87

Microwaving it! J. Nash. il *Essence* 17:88 Mr '87

New foods for your microwave. C. Sugarman. il *Consum Res Mag* 70:24-5 Mr '87

New ways with microwaves [special section] il *Redbook* 169:85+ O '87

The old new wave. B. Kafka. il *N Y Times Mag* p41-2 Ag 2 '87

Promote even cooking with foil. il *South Living* 22:130+ D '87

Quick and easy cakes. il *South Living* 22:200 My '87

Quick cooking for summer. il *South Living* 22:140-2 Je '87

Quick-cooking garden fare. il *South Living* 22:141-2 Jl '87

Soup and sandwich—a natural combo. il *South Living* 22:106+ Ja '87

Sprightly spring salads. J. R. Nyenhuis. il *Saturday Evening Post* 259:17-19 Ap '87

Summer microwaving. J. B. Hurley. il *Prevention* 39:50-2+ Ag '87

Tapas: delicious little dishes of Spain. J. R. Nyenhuis. il *Saturday Evening Post* 259:18+ Ja/F '87

Timesaving entrées. il *South Living* 22:206 O '87

Tips from top cooks. M. Siegel. il *Good Housekeep* 205:179-80+ N '87

Try your hand at adapting recipes. il *South Living* 22:172-3 S '87

The working kids' cookbook. R. Coyle. il *Work Woman* 12:168+ S '87

Anecdotes, facetiae, satire, etc.

Getting zapped by technology. L. Stone. por *U S News World Rep* 103:7 S 7 '87

Microwave cookware

Microwave gifts & gadgets. il *Redbook* 170:140+ D '87

What's new in microwave cookware. il *Good Housekeep* 205:120+ N '87

Microwave integrated circuits

ITT invests $20 million to obtain gallium-arsenide MMIC benefits. il *Aviat Week Space Technol* 126:111-13 F 16 '87

Microwave landing systems

FAA initiates two-phase effort to speed acceptance of MLS. K. J. Stein. *Aviat Week Space Technol* 126:36+ Mr 23 '87

FAA plans MLS installation at major New York airports. K. J. Stein. *Aviat Week Space Technol* 127:65+ Jl 27 '87

Microwave landing system effort gaining momentum. K. J. Stein. il *Aviat Week Space Technol* 127:120+ N 9 '87

Microwave ovens

Compact microwave ovens. il *Consum Rep* 52:16-20 D '87

Microwave ovens: watt differences. *Better Homes Gard* 65:140 Je '87

The new wave in microwaves. il *U S News World Rep* 102:64-5 Mr 30 '87

Safety rules for a microwave oven. il *Glamour* 85:57 D '87

The secret of a microwave oven's rapid cooking action is disclosed. J. Walker. il *Sci Am* 256:134-8 F '87

What's new in microwave ovens. il *Good Housekeep* 205:124+ N '87

Mid-Atlantic Booksellers Association

A smaller turnout for MABA-NYRA meeting. D. Maryles. *Publ Wkly* 232:60 N 27 '87

Midas (Greek mythology)

The Midas touch. G. Reiger and M. Nichols. *Field Stream* 91:14+ Ja '87

Middle age

49 turning 50 [celebrities; quiz] M. Opsata. il *50 Plus* 27:26-8 Ja '87

Brides at last: women over 40 who beat the odds [cover story] B. Lovenheim. il *N Y* 20:20-8 Ag 3 '87

Fit at forty: the new "middle age". A. Gottlieb. *Vogue* 177:270 O '87

Is there sexy after 40? E. Jong. *Vogue* 177:304-5 My '87

Middle age—*cont.*

Middle-aged America [baby boomers] R. J. Samuelson. il *Newsweek* 110:45 Jl 27 '87

'Middle aged' spread tied to lack of exercise. *Jet* 73:28 S 28 '87

Over-40 & young! [special section] il *Harpers Bazaar* 120:124-37+ Ag '87

Psychology

Brokenhearted me. E. Pell. il *Ms* 15:80 Je '87

Captain Midlife faces Christmas. R. Rosenblatt. il *Time* 130:96 D 14 '87

Conquest of Aconcagua [Andes peak] W. Broyles. il pors *Read Dig* 131:144-50 N '87

Lucky, plucky Becky Sinkler. D. Hurford. il por *50 Plus* 27:50+ Ag '87

Midlife music [40 yr. old can't keep up with contemporary rock] M. Goldensohn. il *N Y Times Mag* p48 Je 21 '87

Pushing the mid-life envelope [climbing Aconcagua in the Andes] W. Broyles. il pors *Esquire* 107:72-4+ Je '87

Sex improves with age [views of Herant Katchadourian] il *USA Today (Periodical)* 116:11 S '87

So long, great expectations. H. H. Broun. il *50 Plus* 27:76 Jl '87

So you're 40, baby boomer [advice of Morris Spier] il *USA Today (Periodical)* 116:8-9 N '87

Thirty-fourth winter. C. F. Wall. il *South Living* 22:80 Ja '87

The view from 40. C. McClester. por *Essence* 18:12 D '87

What mid-life crisis? K. Marquardt. il *Health* 19:16 D '87

Women and the new midlife crisis. R. Grant. il *Ladies Home J* 104:87-9+ Ag '87

Middle age market

Those big-spending middle-aged baby boomers. G. Koretz. il *Bus Week* p20 O 19 '87

Middle age pregnancy *See* Pregnancy

Middle Ages

See also
Chivalry
Civilization, Medieval
Crusades
Feudalism

The Swahili corridor. M. Horton. il maps *Sci Am* 257:86-8+ S '87

Bibliography

Paperback history [twelfth and thirteenth centuries] H. Lawrence. *Hist Today* 37:57 Mr '87

Middle classes

The black middle class: moving up at last? *Current* 293:9-15 Je '87

Chicken Little is wrong again [address, August 17, 1987] P. Laxalt. *Vital Speeches Day* 53:741-2 O 1 '87

Ebony examines new black middle class. il *Jet* 72:40 Ag 17 '87

The high-living middle class. J. Fierman. il *Fortune* 115:27 Ap 13 '87

Home is where the hurt is [upper middle class battered wives] A. Toufexis. il *Time* 130:68 D 21 '87

Middle-class child abuse worsening [study by Dean Knudsen] il *USA Today (Periodical)* 115:6-7 My '87

Moving up at last? [black middle class; Harper's forum] il *Harpers* 274:35-9+ F '87

The new black middle class [cover story; special issue] il *Ebony* 42:22+ Ag '87

The new vise on the middle class [housing crunch] R. Eisenberg. il *Money* 16:48-9 S '87

The patrimony society [cover story] R. Kuttner. *New Repub* 196:18-21 My 11 '87

Too much ain't enough. J. Flint. il *Forbes* 140:92-4+ Jl 13 '87

Anecdotes, facetiae, satire, etc.

A comedic look at the black middle class [views of D. Gregory and R. Foxx] W. Leavy. il pors *Ebony* 42:68+ Ag '87

Iran

'Revolutionizing' a middle-class society. M. Field. il *World Press Rev* 34:19-20 My '87

Japan

Is Japan as rich as you think? B. Powell. il *Newsweek* 109:48-50 Je 8 '87

Middle East

See also
Birth control—Middle East
Economic assistance, American—Middle East
Iran
Iraq
Israel
Jerusalem
Jordan
Lebanon
Narcotics laws and regulations—Middle East
Oman
Petroleum pipelines—Middle East
Syria
Terrorism—Middle East
Trade unions—Middle East
Turkey
United Nations—Middle East
United Nations Relief and Works Agency for Palestine Refugees in the Near East

Regional report: the Middle East. S. Pope. See issues of World Press Review beginning June 1986

Antiquities

Arches and vaults in the ancient Near East [cover story] G. W. Van Beek. il map *Sci Am* 257:96-103 Jl '87

Bibliography

Book reviews. *Curr Hist* 86:81+ F '87

Commerce

See also
Iranian-Iraqi War, 1980- —Economic aspects

United States
See United States—Commerce—Middle East

Defenses

See also
United Nations—Armed Forces—Forces in the Middle East

The nuclear arsenal in the Middle East. F. Barnaby. il map *Technol Rev* 90:27-34 My/Je '87

Foreign relations

Jordan
See Jordan—Foreign relations—Middle East

Soviet Union
See Soviet Union—Foreign relations—Middle East

Syria
See Syria—Foreign relations—Middle East

United States
See United States—Foreign relations—Middle East

Politics and government

See also
Israel-Arab Wars, 1967-
Jewish-Arab relations

Islam: seeking the future in the past [Shiite fundamentalists] P. R. Range. il map *U S News World Rep* 103:33-5 Jl 6 '87

The Middle East, 1987 [special issue] bibl f map (inside back cover) *Curr Hist* 86:49-91 F '87

Middle East developments [statement, April 21, 1987] R. W. Murphy. *Dep State Bull* 87:70-2 Je '87

The Middle East in the year 2000 [address, April 24, 1987] A. Ghandour. *Vital Speeches Day* 53:450-5 My 15 '87

Religious institutions and affairs

See also
Muslims—Middle East

Middle Eastern art *See* Art, Middle Eastern

Middle Eastern furniture *See* Furniture, Middle Eastern

Middle Europe *See* Central Europe

Middle school students *See* High school students

Middle schools

Curriculum

See also
Decision making—Study and teaching

Middle South Utilities, Inc.

Still surviving—maybe. M. Fritz. il *Forbes* 139:8 Je 29 '87

Middle Western States

See also
Agriculture—Middle Western States
Earthquakes—Middle Western States

Description and travel

See also
Motorcycling—Middle Western States

Politics and government

Japan is winning friends in the Rust Belt [midwesterners becoming less protectionist as a result of Japanese auto plant locations] W. J. Holstein. il *Bus Week* p54 O 19 '87

Middleton, Lillian

Training respite workers for Alzheimer's families. il *Aging* no356:24-6 '87

Midgetman (Missile) *See* Guided missiles

Midgets *See* Dwarfs and dwarfism

MIDI (Musical instrument digital interface)

Programming

Master Tracks Pro MIDI sequencer. D. Swearingen. *Byte* 12:212+ N '87

Midland Bank plc
And now, the Saatchi & Saatchi bank? [attempt to merge with Midland Bank] M. Maremont. il *Bus Week* p92 S 28 '87
Midland College (Tex.)
Teachers can be ousted for swearing at students [case of professor J. D. Martin] *Jet* 71:23 F 23 '87
Midler, Bette
about
Adventures in Tinseltown. T. Janowitz. il por *N Y Times Mag* p32-3+ Mr 22 '87
The best Bette yet. J. Goodman. il pors *Ladies Home J* 104:30+ Je '87
Bette steals Hollywood. R. Corliss. il pors *Time* 129:64-7+ Mr 2 '87
Anecdotes, facetiae, satire, etc.
A day in the life of a screen goddess. G. Gorman. il pors *Life* 10:122-5+ Ap '87
Midlothian (Tex.)
Crime
The new kid [undercover narcotics cop G. Raffield murdered at Midlothian High School] por *Time* 130:61 N 9 '87
Midori, 1971-
about
The soul of a prodigy. M. J. Walters. il por *Read Dig* 130:84-8 Mr '87
A midsummer nights dream [drama] See Shakespeare, William, 1564-1616
Midway Airlines, Inc.
Heeding a gospel of measured growth. J. E. Ellis. il por *Bus Week* p62 S 21 '87
Midway's option on MD-91/92X represents gamble on fuel prices. J. Ott. il *Aviat Week Space Technol* 127:43+ Jl 6 '87
A profitable survivor. S. B. Weiner. *Forbes* 139:106 Mr 9 '87
Midway Airport See Chicago (Ill.)—Airports
Midway Islands
See also
Birds—Midway Islands
Midwest See Middle Western States
Midwest Stock Exchange See Stock exchanges—Midwest exchange
Midwestern Council of Sports Car Clubs
The Empty Bleacher League revisited. P. Egan. il *Road Track* 38:168-70+ Ap '87
Midwives
All the hours of the night: the recollections of a country midwife [P. Burton] M. F. Greene. il pors *Ctry J* 14:58-63 N '87
Granny midwives: portrait of a timeless profession [Alabama] E. I. M. Holland. il pors *Ms* 15:48-51+ Je '87
The insurance crisis [dwindling numbers of lay midwives] L. Holmes. *Ms* 15:74 Je '87
Modern midwifery: new childbirth options. S. Fibich and T. Yulsman. *McCalls* 114:92-3 S '87
Mieher, Stuart
Spike Lee's gotta have it. il pors *N Y Times Mag* p26-9+ Ag 9 '87
Miesfeld, Roger, and others
Glucocorticoid receptor mutants that define a small region sufficient for enhancer activation. bibl f il *Science* 236:423-7 Ap 24 '87
MiG airplanes See Airplanes, Military
Migraine See Headache
Migrant children See Children of migrant laborers
Migrant labor
See also
Children of migrant laborers
United Farm Workers of America
Walsers
Peonage in the pines [migrant Mexican forest workers] J. Juffer. il *Progressive* 51:24-7 N '87
Rotten shame [immigration reform creates shortage of migrant farm workers] S. Koepp. il *Time* 129:49 Je 22 '87
Wooing the migrant farmer [growers' campaign to explain Immigration Reform and Control Act] J. B. Copeland. il *Newsweek* 109:47 Je 29 '87
Migration
See also
Birds—Migration
Butterflies—Migration
Cranes (Birds)—Migration
Egrets—Migration
Eskimos—Migration
Man—Migrations
Polar bears—Migration
Shore birds—Migration

Turtles—Migration
Water birds—Migration
Wildebeest—Migration
Migration, Internal
See also
Blacks—Migration
Cities and towns—Growth
Labor mobility
Land settlement
Rural hot spots . . . rural cold spots. B. Trebilcock. il *Ctry J* 14:32-5+ Je '87
Migratory workers See Migrant labor
Mihajlov, Mihajlo
Absolutes and my grandfather's Aunt Sarah [discussion of September 7, 1987 article, A talk with Leszek Kolakowski] *New Leader* 70:19-20 D 14 '87
A talk with Leszek Kolakowski [cover story; interview] *New Leader* 70:10-12 S 7 '87
Mijalkov, Nikita See Mikhalkov, Nikita
The Mikado [operetta] See Sullivan, Sir Arthur, 1842-1900
Miké, Valerie, 1934-
Saving money and improving health by evaluating medical technology. il *Technol Rev* 90:22+ Ap '87
Mikhailov, Fyodor
about
The instructors and principal at a Leningrad school challenge rigidities in Soviet education. J. W. Seymore. il por *People Wkly* 27:104-7 Ap 6 '87
Mikhailov, Georgi
about
Gulag eyewitness: daring photographs by a Soviet prisoner. il pors *Life* 10:73-5 S '87
Mikhalkov, Nikita
about
The Brothers M-K. K. Jaehne. il por *Film Comment* 23:66-8 S/O '87
Dark eyes [film] Reviews
Commonweal 114:601-2 O 23 '87. T. O'Brien
Macleans il 100:71 N 16 '87. L. O'Toole
N Y il 20:116 O 5 '87. D. Denby
Natl Rev 39:56-9 N 6 '87. J. Simon
New Repub 197:32-3 O 12 '87. S. Kauffmann
New Yorker 63:93-4 O 5 '87. P. Kael
Newsweek il 110:84 O 5 '87. D. Ansen
People Wkly 28:14 N 2 '87. P. Travers
Vogue il 177:442-3+ O '87. A. Harvey
Miklowitz, Gloria
Why deny the children? por *Publ Wkly* 232:66 O 9 '87
Mikowski family
about
One big happy family. M. Miller. il *People Wkly* 27:22-9 Ja 12 '87
Mikulski, Barbara A.
about
Barbara Mikulski. L. Edmunds. por *Ms* 15:63+ Ja '87
Md. Sen. blasts negative reports on black family. *Jet* 72:8 Mr 30 '87
Our two women in the Senate: influential and respected. M. Engel. por *Glamour* 85:50+ My '87
Milam, Kathryn
Albuquerque: casting a spell. il *Horizon* 30:33-8+ O '87
Monterey County: a cultural mission. il *Horizon* 30:64-70+ Jl/Ag '87
Santa Fe/Taos: southwestern gems. il *Horizon* 30:53-6 O '87
Tucson: a cultural oasis. il *Horizon* 30:49-54+ My '87
Milan (Ind.)
Sports
Hoosiermania [Milan High School's basketball championship in 1954] H. Nuwer. il *Saturday Evening Post* 259:52-3+ Mr '87
Milan, Indiana still weeps for joy over its 1954 championship team that inspired Hoosiers. L. Aitken. il *People Wkly* 27:34-5 Mr 30 '87
Milan (Italy)
Art
Luminous visions, dark moods. H. Martin. il *Art News* 86:35+ F '87
Crime
Letter from Europe [A. Verdiglione's psychoanalysis scam] J. Kramer. *New Yorker* 63:88+ Je 8 '87
Description
Italy's chic showcase. T. Skall. il map *Travel Holiday* 168:50-7 S '87
Stores
Milan bazaar. G. Whitmore. il *Harpers Bazaar* 120:54+ Jl '87
Shopping in Milan. A. M. Zwack. il *Gourmet* 47:86-91+ N '87

Milan (Italy) fashion shows *See* Fashion shows
Milan Furniture Fair *See* Furniture, Italian—Exhibitions
Milankovitch cycles *See* Meteorological models
Milanov, Zinka, 1906-
					about
Brava Zinka! B. Burroughs. il pors *Opera News* 52:18+ D 19 '87
Milbank, Tweed, Hadley & McCloy
A gale of fresh air at Milbank Tweed [new partners T. Puccio and A. Young] L. J. Tell. il pors *Bus Week* p102-4 Jl 20 '87
Milbrandt, Jeffrey
A nerve growth factor-induced gene encodes a possible transcriptional regulatory factor. bibl f il *Science* 238:797-9 N 6 '87
Mildew
Doing battle with mildew. *Better Homes Gard* 65:39 Ag '87
Mile running *See* Track and field athletics
Mileage indicators *See* Odometers
Milek, Gary, 1941-
					about
Gary Milek. E. Feit. il *Am Artist* 51:64-9+ O '87
Milenkovic, Stefan, 1977-
					about
Stefan Milenkovic, who plays like a kid when he isn't playing a violin. M. Runnion. il pors *People Wkly* 28:93-4 S 7 '87
Miles, Sarah
					about
Sarah Miles stars in an incredible story of scandal and love—and no, it's not her new film, Hope and glory, it's her life. J. Stark. il pors *People Wkly* 28:73-4+ N 23 '87
Miles Homes (Firm)
A buyer-manufacturer partnership. R. Barnhart. il *Home Mech* 83:26-7 My '87
Miles Laboratories, Inc.
Block, Block, fizz, fizz [Alka-Seltzer and H&R Block join advertising forces] S. D. Atchison. il *Bus Week* p36 Mr 30 '87
Milford Plaza Hotel (New York, N.Y.) *See* New York (N.Y.)—Hotels, motels, etc.
Milhollin, Gary
Heavy water cheaters. bibl f *Foreign Policy* 69:100-19 Wint '87/'88
Militarism
Return of the big stick. T. C. Muck. il *Christ Today* 31:18-19 S 4 '87
Military administration
Into the vacuum stepped Ollie North [U.S. needs a bureaucracy on the European model to counteract reliance on the military] J. Keegan. por *U S News World Rep* 103:14 Ag 31 '87
Military Airlift Command (U.S.) *See* United States. Air Force. Military Airlift Command
Military airplanes *See* Airplanes, Military
Military and day care *See* Day care and the military
Military and television *See* Television in military art and science
Military and the environment
					See also
		Air bases—Environmental aspects
		Military training camps—Environmental aspects
Decontaminating federal facilities: the case of the Rocky Mountain Arsenal [with editorial comment by Wallace N. Quintrell] K. B. Wiley and S. L. Rhodes. bibl f il maps *Environment* 29:2-3, 16-20+ Ap '87
Linking environment and security. N. Myers. il *Bull At Sci* 43:46-7 Je '87
Military art and science
					See also
		Computers—Military use
		Electronics—Military use
		Mines, Military
		Optoelectronics—Military use
		Superconductors and superconductivity—Military use
		Television in military art and science
		War
		War games
		World War, 1939-1945—Strategy
					Collectibles
					See also
		Military miniatures—Collectors and collecting
					Terminology
Strategic words: a short dictionary of defense. J. Ferber. *Sch Update* 119:25 F 23 '87
Military assistance, American
					See also
		United States. Army. Special Operations Division

Calling a halt to covert actions. R. Goetz. *Christ Century* 104:349-50 Ap 15 '87
The case against covert action [cover story] M. H. Halperin. *Nation* 244:345+ Mr 21 '87
Covert action and open society. G. F. Treverton. bibl f *Foreign Aff* 65:995-1014 Summ '87
Covert loophole [executive order authorizes privatization of covert operations] I. F. Stone. *Nation* 245:184-5 S 5 '87
Covert operations: play by the rules. M. Kramer. il *U S News World Rep* 103:15-16 Jl 20 '87
A cult of 'covert ops'. T. Jacoby. il *Newsweek* 110:22+ Jl 20 '87
Global intervention and a new imperial presidency. T. G. Carpenter. il *USA Today (Periodical)* 115:10-18 Mr '87
Hidden commitments. T. L. Deibel. *Foreign Policy* 67:46-63 Summ '87
Military aid bid represents 15% rise over fiscal 1987. *Aviat Week Space Technol* 126:19 Ja 12 '87
Proposed Saudi sale spurs review of arms export controls. M. Mecham. *Aviat Week Space Technol* 126:69+ Mr 30 '87
Protecting America's interests: defense and foreign aid [special issue] il maps *Sch Update* 119:6-16+ F 23 '87
The Reagan revival of arms deals. W. D. Hartung. bibl f il *Bull At Sci* 43:20-5 Jl/Ag '87
Reagan's vow: never again [covert operations procedure] il por *U S News World Rep* 103:11 Ag 17 '87
Rules governing covert operations [ACLU report Covert operations and the democratic process: the implications of the Iran-contra affair] *Cent Mag* 20:57-8 N/D '87
Saving covert action from Ollie North. *New Repub* 197:5-7 Ag 3 '87
The tangled web [deceit as component of covert actions] *Nation* 245:39-40 Jl 18-25 '87
U.S. weapon export sales face waning demand, rising competition. P. Mann. il *Aviat Week Space Technol* 126:134-5 F 9 '87
					Afghanistan
The alchemy of turning guns into luxury villas [diversion of U.S. aid] E. Girardet. il *U S News World Rep* 103:36 N 30 '87
The great game. S. R. Weisman. *New Repub* 197:20-3 Ag 10-17 '87
How did Iran get Stinger missiles? [missiles sent by U.S. to Afghan resistance] il *Newsweek* 110:42-3 O 26 '87
Insurgencies: two of a kind [U.S.-backed rebels in Afghanistan] R. Watson. il *Newsweek* 109:32-3 Mr 23 '87
Lost in Afghanistan [C.I.A.-run aid program] D. Corn and J. Morley. *Nation* 245:43 Jl 18-25 '87
The sting [Reagan administration could spoil peace process by stepping up arms to Afghan guerrillas] A. Rashid. *Nation* 244:241-2 F 28 '87
U.S. credits Afghan resistance with thwarting Soviet air power. M. Mecham. *Aviat Week Space Technol* 127:26-7 Jl 13 '87
					Angola
The right's last, best hope [J. Savimbi's UNITA] M. Maren. il *Nation* 245:744-6 D 19 '87
Yet another Saudi connection [businessman S. Bamieh claims U.S. supplied covert aid to UNITA rebels] E. Magnuson. il *Time* 129:16 Je 29 '87
					Caribbean region
Pentagon banking on Castro phobia. W. M. Arkin. *Bull At Sci* 43:4-5 My '87
					Central America
					See also
		National Bipartisan Commission on Central America (U.S.)
Ambiguous war: the United States and low-intensity conflict. M. Miller. il *Technol Rev* 90:60-7 Ag/S '87
Body on the line [B. Willson run over by train while protesting against U.S. arms shipments to Central America] B. Kessler. *Nation* 245:329 O 3 '87
The future belongs to the free [address, February 14, 1987] L. A. Tambs. *Vital Speeches Day* 53:379-81 Ap 1 '87
Give 'em hell. A. Tonelson. *New Repub* 197:20-1+ O 5 '87
In search of change. R. Rivard. il *Newsweek* 109:40+ Ap 27 '87
Litmus test [1988 presidential campaign issue] *Nation* 244:528-9 Ap 25 '87
Stealing a march [Mobilization for Justice and Peace] M. Kondracke. *New Repub* 196:10+ My 4 '87

Military assistance, American—Nicaragua—*cont.*

Could it be? [Nicaraguan ceasefire peace initiative] W. F. Buckley. *Natl Rev* 39:72-3 S 11 '87

Covert action and national policy: beyond North and Poindexter. R. J. Bresler. il *USA Today (Periodical)* 115:6-7 Mr '87

Crunch time for the contras. R. Watson. il map *Newsweek* 109:24-6 Ja 19 '87

Development of U.S.-Nicaragua policy [statements, February 5, 1987] E. Abrams; P. C. Habib. *Dep State Bull* 87:75-82 My '87

A do-or-die offensive [trip with the contras] R. Nordland. il *Newsweek* 109:47 My 11 '87

Encore! [call for additional hearings on contra aid] *Commonweal* 114:435-7 Ag 14 '87

The end of the affair? [Central American peace plans and contra aid] J. Chace. bibl f il *N Y Rev Books* 34:24-6+ O 8 '87

The execution of Ben Linder. A. Cockburn. *Nation* 245:402-3 O 17 '87

Eyeing a dialogue [D. Ortega Saavedra agrees to peace talks with contras; with interview] J. Smolowe. il por *Time* 130:34-6 N 16 '87

Facing down Congress. D. Schorr. *New Leader* 70:3 D 28 '87

Fallout from a defector [revelations from Nicaraguan defector R. Miranda] H. Anderson. il por *Newsweek* 110:26 D 28 '87

Fighting the Sandinistas with dollars. M. D. Wilde. *Christ Century* 104:957-8 N 4 '87

Foggy Bottom agit prop [pro-contra propaganda] *Harpers* 275:22 D '87

Four men in North's safe: the uses of intellectuals [Elie Wiesel, Joachim Maitre, Max Singer and Michael Ledeen] A. Cockburn. *Nation* 244:350-1+ Mr 21 '87

A fragile peace plan [indirect talks with the contras] A. Bilski. il *Macleans* 100:24 N 16 '87

Give 'em hell. A. Tonelson. *New Repub* 197:20-1+ O 5 '87

Gorbachev's offer forces tough choices on contra aid. B. Javetski and L. Boyd. il *Bus Week* p93 D 28 '87-Ja 4 '88

The hearings, and after. *Natl Rev* 39:17-18 Ag 14 '87

A hero's mission [O. L. North] M. Kempton. il *N Y Rev Books* 34:13 Ag 13 '87

High stakes in Nicaragua. D. Reed. il *Read Dig* 131:72-7 S '87

Honduran sting [aid to contras funneled through Ilopango air base in El Salvador] *Time* 129:29 Ap 6 '87

The hunger artists [fast by veterans protesting U.S. policy] W. F. Schulz, Jr. il *Progressive* 51:14-15 Je '87

If it's Tuesday, this must be Managua [work of S. Rushdie and P. Davis] C. Lane. *Wash Mon* 19:48-51 Je '87

An Indian view of the contras. B. S. Gupta. il *World Press Rev* 34:15-16 S '87

Into the jungle. M. Kondracke. *New Repub* 196:14-17 Ap 6 '87

Is it the contras' last stand? A. Landaburu. *World Press Rev* 34:41 Mr '87

Is there a contra drug connection? [cocaine smuggling for guns] R. Nordland. il *Newsweek* 109:26 Ja 26 '87

It ain't over till it's over [renewed campaign for funds] M. Duffy. il *Time* 130:19 Jl 27 '87

The Jim Wright shuffle [Central American peace plan] J. Morley. *Nation* 245:185+ S 5 '87

Keeping Faith [role of F. R. Whittlesey and other U.S. diplomats in Switzerland in promoting the contra cause] M. Schapiro and E. Burnand. *Nation* 244:42 Ja 17 '87

Labor & Nicaragua [urging condemnation of aid to the contras] *Nation* 245:472-3 O 31 '87

The last hurrahs [Reagan administration moves on contra aid, arms control and R. Bork nomination] *Nation* 245:291-2 S 26 '87

The last puppet show? *Nation* 244:237 F 28 '87

LeMoyne's progress [J. LeMoyne's Nicaraguan coverage in New York times] A. Cockburn. *Nation* 244:423 Ap 4 '87

Letter from Washington. Cato. *Natl Rev* 39:13 Ag 28 '87

Letter from Washington [effect of Central American peace initiative on contra aid] Cato. *Natl Rev* 39:15 S 11 '87

Lies about Nicaragua. W. S. Smith. *Foreign Policy* 67:87-103 Summ '87

Lifeline for a rebellion [contras establish vital supply links] R. Chavira. il *Time* 129:40 Ap 27 '87

Memo to: Gary Hart from: National review [foreign policy campaign issue] *Natl Rev* 39:17-18 Mr 27 '87

A memo to Reagan [alleged harassment of contra critic J. Terrell by O. North and staff] il pors *Newsweek* 110:7 S 21 '87

Mercenary with a cause [J. Terrell turns from contra mercenary to contra whistleblower] B. Connie and D. Bernstein. *Progressive* 51:13 Ag '87

Miami: exiles. J. Didion. il *N Y Rev Books* 34:35-9 Je 25 '87

Minority report. C. Hitchens. *Nation* 244:244 F 28 '87

Minority report [evidence of C.I.A.-contra-narcotics connection] C. Hitchens. *Nation* 244:531 Ap 25 '87

Miranda's tempest [Nicaraguan defector R. Miranda used to manipulate U.S. press] A. Cockburn. *Nation* 245:780-1 D 26 '87-Ja 2 '88

Money, drugs and the contras [cover story] J. Kwitny. il *Nation* 245:145+ Ag 29 '87

Mrs. Kirkpatrick visits Managua. W. F. Buckley. *Natl Rev* 39:67 N 20 '87

The new contras? R. Nordland. il map *Newsweek* 109:32-6+ Je 1 '87

Nicaragua. M. S. Forbes, Jr. il *Forbes* 139 Ann Directory:45 Ap 27 '87

Nicaragua [statement, November 3, 1986] H. S. Okun. *Dep State Bull* 87:82-4 Ja '87

Nicaragua cliffhanger. R. S. Leiken. *New Repub* 197:17-21 D 14 '87

Nicaragua: the moral and strategic stakes [address, February 12, 1987] G. P. Shultz. *Dep State Bull* 87:14-18 Mr '87

Nicaragua: the undeclared war hits home [special section] il *World Press Rev* 34:21-5 Ap '87

The Nobel difference [O. Arias wins Peace Prize for his Central American plan] H. Anderson. il por *Newsweek* 110:44+ O 26 '87

Notes and comment [U.S. reaction to peace plan] *New Yorker* 63:35-6 O 12 '87

Notes and comment [who are the contras?] *New Yorker* 63:19-20 Je 29 '87

Odds against the contras. J. McLaughlin. *Natl Rev* 39:24 Mr 27 '87

Of drugs, money and contras [discussion of August 29, 1987 article, Money, drugs and the contras] J. Kwitny. *Nation* 245:254+ S 19 '87

Oh, brother—not again! [blunders by the Ortegas lend support to contra aid] J. Smolowe. il pors *Time* 130:33 D 28 '87

Ollie's gang [lack of reporting on O. North's secret teams in Nicaragua] A. Cockburn. *Nation* 245:115 Ag 15-22 '87

On reconsidering contra funding. *America* 156:22 Ja 17 '87

One last chance for the contras. T. Jenkins. il *Nation* 244:638-40 My 16 '87

Ortega gunplay [blunders may lead to new aid for contras] il por *U S News World Rep* 103:13 D 28 '87-Ja 4 '88

Pack it in [resignation of A. Cruz] C. Lane. il *New Repub* 196:17-19 Ap 6 '87

The peace (death) movement. *Natl Rev* 39:16-17 F 27 '87

Peace scare. *New Repub* 197:4+ S 28 '87

Peaced off [Reagan-Wright plan upstaged by Central American peace proposal] F. Barnes. *New Repub* 197:10-11 Ag 31 '87

The phony peace [Reagan peace plan for Central America] *Nation* 245:147-8 Ag 29 '87

A plea to 'give peace a chance' [aid to contras undercut by peace plan] M. McDonald. il *Macleans* 100:32 O 5 '87

Positive containment in Nicaragua. V. P. Vaky. *Foreign Policy* 68:42-58 Fall '87

The president's passion. M. B. Zuckerman. il *U S News World Rep* 102:66 F 23 '87

'Pricing the contras' [Central American peace initiative's effect on contra aid] H. Anderson. il *Newsweek* 110:24-5 Ag 24 '87

Promoting freedom and democracy in Central America [address, May 3, 1987] R. Reagan. *Dep State Bull* 87:1-4 Jl '87

Pseudo-talks in Nicaragua. *Natl Rev* 39:16-17 D 4 '87

Putting the arm on rich, right-wing widows [C. Channell's fund raising activities for the contras] G. Hackett. il por *Newsweek* 109:30 Ap 20 '87

Reagan and Hegel. A. Cockburn. *Nation* 244:709 My 30 '87

Reagan isn't calling the shots in Central America anymore. B. Javetski and others. il *Bus Week* p65 O 12 '87

Reagan's secret wars and missed opportunities [revelations from B. Woodward's Veil] J. M. Wall. *Christ Century* 104:907-8 O 21 '87

Military assistance, American—Nicaragua—*cont.*

Reinventing the contras [U.S. switches allegiance from A. Calero to A. Cruz] R. Watson. il pors *Newsweek* 109:32-4 Mr 2 '87

A reluctant contra's struggle for survival [N. Rivas] J. McPhaul. por *Sch Update* 119:16 Mr 9 '87

Retreating from a retreat. M. S. Forbes, Jr. il *Forbes* 140:25 O 5 '87

Rival plans, rival goals [Central American peace plans] B. Crozier. *Natl Rev* 39:30 S 25 '87

Robelo calls it quits [last major moderate leader of contras] por *Newsweek* 109:7 Ap 20 '87

The secret team behind contragate. P. D. Scott. il *Nation* 244:97+ Ja 31 '87

The secret warriors tell their story [American pilots making airdrops over Nicaragua] E. Calonius. il *Newsweek* 109:26-8 F 9 '87

Security Council considers Nicaraguan complaint against United States, takes no action. il *UN Chron* 23:79-82 N '86

Security Council considers Nicaraguan complaint of 'serious incidents' in Central America. il *UN Chron* 24:64 F '87

Security Council does not adopt text calling for compliance with International Court ruling regarding Nicaraguan case. il *UN Chron* 24:62-3 F '87

Security Council does not adopt text calling for full compliance with International Court ruling in case of 'military and paramilitary activities in and against Nicaragua'. il *UN Chron* 23:83-8 N '86

The selling of the F.D.N. [CIA-backed contra propaganda operations] P. Kornbluh. il *Nation* 244:40-4 Ja 17 '87

Sending signals on the contras. *America* 156:185-6 Mr 7 '87

Sergio Ramirez: the view from Managua [interview] C. Dreifus. il por *Progressive* 51:19-20 S '87

Should the contras get more U.S. aid? [interviews with W. Walker and C. Dodd] S. Manning. pors *Sch Update* 119:10 Mr 9 '87

Should the U.S. support the contras? C. Krauthammer. il *Time* 129:81-2 Mr 2 '87

'Sleazy' is the word for it [Senate votes against immediate cut-off of aid to Nicaraguan resistance] *America* 156:266 Ap 4 '87

So long, contras? *Natl Rev* 39:17 S 11 '87

A 'successful' failure. I. Austen. por *Macleans* 100:20 Ag 17 '87

Torpedoing the peace process? [Reagan's support for the contras] H. Anderson. il *Newsweek* 110:49 O 19 '87

U.S. policies in Central America: choices on Nicaragua. R. W. Fontaine. *Current* 291:34-40 Mr/Ap '87

Uncivil targets. *Commonweal* 114:195-8 Ap 10 '87

United States policy in Central America. E. Kenworthy. bibl f *Curr Hist* 86:401-4+ D '87

Upping the ante at home [views of House Speaker J. Wright] G. Borger. il por *U S News World Rep* 103:25 Ag 17 '87

Video vérité: Jackson Browne makes his point about U.S. policy in Central America. A. DeCurtis. il por *Roll Stone* p12 Ja 29 '87

A visit to Salvador. M. Kondracke. *New Repub* 197:10-12 Ag 10-17 '87

The war for Nicaragua [special section; with editorial comment by Kevin Doyle] il map *Macleans* 100:2, 16-20+ F 23 '87

War of words [Reagan's commitment to the contras blocks peace plan] P. R. Range. il *U S News World Rep* 103:10 O 19 '87

War on the installment plan [contras] J. V. Lamar, Jr. il *Time* 129:24 F 23 '87

Washington in Miami. J. Didion. il *N Y Rev Books* 34:22+ Jl 16 '87

What North might have wrought [cover story] P. Kornbluh. il *Nation* 244:871+ Je 27 '87

Why Iranscam won't keep Congress from aiding the contras. D. Harbrecht and S. J. Dryden. *Bus Week* p57 Je 22 '87

With aid, contras talk a better war. L. Balmaseda. il *U S News World Rep* 102:32-3 Ja 26 '87

Pakistan

Administration expected to back lease of E-2Cs to Pakistan. M. Mecham. *Aviat Week Space Technol* 126:27-8 My 4 '87

An aid package for Pakistan stirs up India's Yankee-bashers. V. Tenorio. il *Bus Week* p54 Je 15 '87

Aid to Pakistan: megatons of trouble for the U.S.? B. Javetski. il *Bus Week* p57 Ap 6 '87

A bad case of nuclear friction [Pakistan rejects U.S. attempt to link inspection of nuclear facilities to aid package] M. S. Serrill. il *Time* 130:40 Ag 17 '87

Flying into a tight corner [U.S. promise to supply AWACs to Pakistan] E. W. Desmond. il *Time* 129:41 Je 22 '87

Glenn asks Reagan to halt Pakistan aid pending review of nuclear programs. M. Crawford. por *Science* 235:1321 Mr 13 '87

House to consider $670-million aid package for Pakistan. *Aviat Week Space Technol* 126:22 Mr 16 '87

How lies proliferate [Pakistan's nuclear capabilities] *Nation* 244:381 Mr 28 '87

Pakistani smuggling riles Congress [nuclear smuggling] L. S. Spector. il *Bull At Sci* 43:3-4 O '87

A rock and a hard place [Pakistan caught trying to illegally import maraging steel intended for bomb program] R. Nordland. il *Newsweek* 110:30+ Jl 27 '87

Wanted: the bomb [possible cutoff of military aid after Pakistan's attempt buy steel alloy for nuclear weapons] il *U S News World Rep* 103:8 Jl 27 '87

Philippines

The Army can't back up Aquino's tough talk. R. Gourlay. *Bus Week* p57 Ap 6 '87

Defense vs. Cory [views of George Talbot on fighting Communist insurgents] L. Howard. il *Newsweek* 109:5 My 4 '87

Turkey

Turkey offered U.S. military equipment. *Aviat Week Space Technol* 126:28 Mr 23 '87

Military assistance, Cuban

Africa

Cuba in Africa. P. S. Falk. map *Foreign Aff* 65:1077-96 Summ '87

Angola

Cuba in Africa. P. S. Falk. map *Foreign Aff* 65:1077-96 Summ '87

Cuba's strange mission in Angola. J. Brooke. il *N Y Times Mag* p24+ F 1 '87

Ideological contradictions in U.S. policy toward Angola. R. A. Fangmeier. il *Christ Century* 104:1061-3 N 25 '87

Caribbean region

Pentagon banking on Castro phobia. W. M. Arkin. *Bull At Sci* 43:4-5 My '87

Military assistance, French

Chad

Chad: Kaddafi on the run. F. Coleman. il map *Newsweek* 109:28 Ja 19 '87

Standoff in the Sahara. B. Levin. il map *Macleans* 100:26-7 S 21 '87

War by proxy in the dunes [French air attack on Libyan forces in Chad] W. E. Smith. il *Time* 129:37 Ja 19 '87

Military assistance, Israeli

Byzantine bedfellows. Y. Karny. *New Repub* 196:23-5 F 2 '87

Military assistance, Russian

Step by step [address, May 2, 1987] J. A. Courter. *Vital Speeches Day* 53:581-5 Jl 15 '87

Where is linkage? W. F. Buckley. *Natl Rev* 39:59 Ag 28 '87

Iraq

See also
Iranian-Iraqi War, 1980- —Russian participation

Nicaragua

Gorbachev's offer forces tough choices on contra aid. B. Javetski and L. Boyd. il *Bus Week* p93 D 28 '87-Ja 4 '88

Soviet helicopters perform medical, reconnaissance missions in Nicaragua. il *Aviat Week Space Technol* 127:16-17 Ag 31 '87

Military assistance, Saudi Arabian

Angola

Yet another Saudi connection [businessman S. Bamieh claims U.S. supplied covert aid to UNITA rebels] E. Magnuson. il *Time* 129:16 Je 29 '87

Military astronautics *See* Space flight—Military use

Military aviation *See* Aviation, Military

Military bands *See* Bands (Music)

Military bases

See also
Air bases
Guided missile bases
Navy yards and naval stations

The bigger the bases, the bigger the trouble [Clark and Subic Bay in the Philippines] J. M. Fallows. il *U S News World Rep* 103:32 N 23 '87

Greece's balancing act [U.S. bases and nuclear weapons] W. M. Arkin. *Bull At Sci* 43:11-12 Mr '87

Military bases—*cont.*
Papandreou's 'whipping boy' [U.S. bases in Greece] N. Cooper. il por *Newsweek* 110:35 Jl 27 '87
Testing an ally's resolve [future of American bases in the Philippines] W. L. Chaze. il por map *U S News World Rep* 103:73-5 S 28 '87
When the stepping stones of world power are rocky bases. J. Wallace. il *U S News World Rep* 103:30-1 N 23 '87

Day care
See Day care and the military

Security measures
Security shock at dawn in Lahr [saboteurs attack Canadian base in West Germany] M. Nichols. il *Macleans* 100:10-11 Jl 20 '87
Tracking an inside job [explosion at Canadian base in West Germany] P. Lewis. *Macleans* 100:19 Ag 3 '87

Military bases, Russian
See also
Navy yards and naval stations, Russian
Soviet strategic laser sites imaged by French Spot satellite. C. Covault. il *Aviat Week Space Technol* 127:26-7 O 26 '87
Soviets extend air, sea power with buildup at Cam Ranh Bay. B. M. Greeley, Jr. il *Aviat Week Space Technol* 126:76-7 Mr 2 '87

Military budget *See* United States. Dept. of Defense—Appropriations and expenditures
Military budgets, International *See* Armed Forces—Appropriations and expenditures
Military chaplains *See* Chaplains, Military
Military chartering of airplanes *See* Airlines—Military use
Military-civil relations *See* Civil supremacy over the military
Military communications *See* Communications, Military
Military communications satellites *See* Communications satellites—Military use
Military contracts *See* Contracts, Government
Military draft *See* Military service, Compulsory

Military education
See also
Citadel (Military academy)
Military training camps
United States. Coast Guard—Education
United States. Merchant Marine Academy
United States Air Force Academy
United States Military Academy

Military electronics *See* Electronics—Military use; Superconductors and superconductivity—Military use

Military engineering
See also
Fortification

Military ethics

Study and teaching
Military duty and moral scruple [Naval War College] E. Hillman. il *America* 157:185+ O 3 '87
Military expenditures *See* United States. Dept. of Defense—Appropriations and expenditures
Military expenditures, International *See* Armed Forces—Appropriations and expenditures
Military exports *See* Munitions—Export-import trade

Military history
See also
United States—History, Military

Military-industrial complex
See also
National Committee for Employer Support of the Guard and Reserve (U.S.)
Administration opposes House bill on offsets. P. Mann. *Aviat Week Space Technol* 127:26-7 Jl 6 '87
Aerospace/defense executives must put their own shops in order [discussion of November 23, 1987 article, The aerospace leadership void] P. Mann. por *Aviat Week Space Technol* 127:61-3 D 21 '87
The aerospace leadership void [address, November 13, 1987] P. Mann. *Aviat Week Space Technol* 127:15 N 23 '87
Business versus Star Wars. A. M. Cunningham. il *Technol Rev* 90:17 My/Je '87
Defense Dept. analyzes problems in strengthening industrial base. P. Mann. *Aviat Week Space Technol* 127:21-2 Jl 13 '87
Defense industry and government: partners or antagonists? D. Fuqua. por *Aviat Week Space Technol* 127:133+ S 7 '87
Defense spending's role in the economy. M. Christopher. map *Sch Update* 119:17 F 23 '87
Harris chief warns of economic chaos if manufacturing continues overseas move [views of J. A. Boyd] E. H. Kolcum. *Aviat Week Space Technol* 127:89 S 14 '87

A hidden cost of military research: less national security. D. S. Greenberg. il *Discover* 8:94+ Ja '87
Ike's nightmare is upon us [views of K. Glennan] H. Sidey. il por *Time* 130:24 S 14 '87
It's time for economic conversion. J. Ritter-Murray. *Humanist* 47:30+ S/O '87
Militarism in America. *Cent Mag* 20:62-3 Mr/Ap '87
Panel finds defense policies erode U.S. technology base [Senate Armed Services Committee report] M. Mecham. *Aviat Week Space Technol* 126:21-2 My 18 '87
The political economy of military waste. J. B. Anderson and D. R. Lee. il *USA Today (Periodical)* 115:30-3 My '87
Priorities in a military culture. B. Smith. il *Bull At Sci* 43:9-10 Je '87
Soviets interested in study on economic conversion. M. Crawford. *Science* 235:1133 Mr 6 '87
The war business. J. R. Saul. il *World Press Rev* 34:19-21 Je '87

Military intelligence
See also
United States. Army. Special Operations Division
The secret Army. G. J. Church. il *Time* 130:12-14 Ag 31 '87

Military law
See also
Courts martial and courts of inquiry

Military maneuvers
Airex 87 tests French Air Force in chemical, EW environments. J. M. Lenorovitz. *Aviat Week Space Technol* 126:70-1 Mr 16 '87
Back to the front [Certain Strike maneuvers in West Germany] A. T. Hadley. *New Repub* 197:16-18 N 16 '87
F-15s complete intercepts, operations over North Pole [Alaskan Air Command's Cobbler Freeze '87] il *Aviat Week Space Technol* 126:76-7 My 25 '87
Flying units ready for Green Flag exercise [electronic combat training exercise] *Aviat Week Space Technol* 126:113 F 9 '87

Inspection
NATO's war-game guests [Soviet bloc military observers] K. Scanlon. il *Macleans* 100:20-1 S 28 '87
U.S. inspects Soviet military exercise [State Dept. statement and report, September 22, 1987] *Dep State Bull* 87:44-6 N '87
Military men *See* Servicemen
Military mines *See* Mines, Military
Military miniatures

Collectors and collecting
An investment worth a salute. R. Brady. il *Nations Bus* 75:84 D '87

Exhibitions
See also
Toys and Soldiers Museum (Vicksburg, Miss.)
Military motorcycles *See* Motorcycles, Military

Military museums
See also
Titan II Missile Museum (Ariz.)
Military officers *See* United States—Armed Forces—Officers
Military pay *See* United States. Army—Pay, allowances, etc.
Military pilots *See* Air pilots

Military policy
See also
Denmark—Military policy
Soviet Union—Military policy
United States—Military policy
Military psychology *See* Psychology, Military
Military radar *See* Radar—Military use

Military reconnaissance
See also
Aerial reconnaissance

Military research
See also
George C. Marshall Institute
Technology transfer
United States. Defense Advanced Research Projects Agency
United States. Defense Science Board
1988 defense bill emphasizes new science initiatives. *Aviat Week Space Technol* 127:25-6 N 23 '87
Academy helps Army be all that it can be [report on human performance enhancement] C. Holden. *Science* 238:1501-2 D 11 '87
Air Force altering budget priorities for Project Forecast 2. J. D. Morrocco. il *Aviat Week Space Technol* 126:22-3 Ap 13 '87

Military research—*cont.*

Air Force defines milestones for Project Forecast 2 initiatives. J. D. Morrocco. *Aviat Week Space Technol* 126:139+ My 11 '87

Berkeley changes tack on reactor [decision to shut down reactor used for military-related research] J. Walsh. *Science* 235:273 Ja 16 '87

Black holes in the budget [line item requests for Air Force research and development programs that are classified] D. C. Morrison. il *Harpers* 274:50-1 Ja '87

Computer combat [technological revolution in conventional warfare; cover story] E. A. Cohen. *New Repub* 196:15-17 Ap 20 '87

Defense Dept. analyzes problems in strengthening industrial base. P. Mann. *Aviat Week Space Technol* 127:21-2 Jl 13 '87

Geographical limit on research funds in bill seen as swipe at peer review [University Research Initiative program] J. Walsh. *Science* 238:1506 D 11 '87

Gramm-Rudman threatens to disrupt defense contracts, research programs. P. Mann. *Aviat Week Space Technol* 127:22-4 N 9 '87

A hidden cost of military research: less national security. D. S. Greenberg. il *Discover* 8:94+ Ja '87

Panel finds defense policies erode U.S. technology base [Senate Armed Services Committee report] M. Mecham. *Aviat Week Space Technol* 126:21-2 My 18 '87

A physicist objects [C. Schwartz stops teaching classes in higher physics at Berkeley] J. J. Neuburger. il por *Progressive* 51:12-13 Jl '87

R&D enriched by 1988 budget but science policy impoverished. I. Goodwin. il *Phys Today* 40:59-65 My '87

Report finds R&D budget growth could limit readiness funds. *Aviat Week Space Technol* 127:111 Jl 13 '87

Research reactor closed at Berkeley for mixed reasons. W. Sweet. *Phys Today* 40:56 Je '87

Thinking strategically [competitive strategies doctrine] P. Mann. *Aviat Week Space Technol* 127:13 Jl 6 '87

U.S. formulates strategic doctrine for high technology [competitive strategies doctrine] P. Mann. il map *Aviat Week Space Technol* 126:110-11+ Je 15 '87

Use of Berkeley reactor questioned on military-related research [views of Charles Schwartz] J. Walsh. *Science* 235:23 Ja 2 '87

International aspects

France, USAF discuss joint efforts on Project Forecast 2 technologies. *Aviat Week Space Technol* 126:78-9 Je 1 '87

SDIO selects five U.S./allied teams for phase 2 missile defense studies. *Aviat Week Space Technol* 127:28 Ag 3 '87

Senate study acclaims U.S./NATO weapons R&D. *Aviat Week Space Technol* 126:316 Je 15 '87

Germany (West)

Star Wars controversy in West Germany. T. Risse-Kappen. *Bull At Sci* 43:50-2 Jl/Ag '87

Great Britain

British researchers seek SDI funds. D. Dickson. il *Science* 235:736-7 F 13 '87

Cuts promised in U.K. military R&D. D. Dickson. *Science* 236:772 My 15 '87

Israel

Navy evaluates Israeli R&D programs for use on U.S. weapon systems. M. Mecham. *Aviat Week Space Technol* 126:20-1 Je 1 '87

Japan

Japan, U.S. agree on SDI participation. *Aviat Week Space Technol* 127:23 Jl 27 '87

Western Europe

Defense research: promises, promises. D. Dickson. il *Science* 237:1109-10 S 4 '87

Murdering SDI [suspicious murders and suicides of Europeans connected with SDI] J. S. Denton and P. Schweizer. *Natl Rev* 39:37-9 Jl 31 '87

Military satellites *See* Artificial satellites—Military use
Military science *See* Military art and science
Military secrets, Classified *See* Classified information
Military service, Compulsory

See also

Conscientious objectors

Involuntary servitude. E. Knoll. *Progressive* 51:4 Ja '87

Mercenary morality [argument against the draft] D. Bandow. *New Repub* 197:20-2 O 19 '87

Draft resisters

Costs of a flimsy card. M. Wehle. il *Progressive* 51:50 Ap '87

How to beat the draft in Teheran? Flee to Turkey. J. P. Shapiro. il map *U S News World Rep* 102:30 F 23 '87

Moral and religious aspects

No benefit of appeal: registration & basic rights. P. J. Riga. *Commonweal* 114:582-4 O 23 '87

Recruiters for peace [counter-recruiters] O. Davidson. *Nation* 244:175-7 F 14 '87

Iran

How to beat the draft in Teheran? Flee to Turkey. J. P. Shapiro. il map *U S News World Rep* 102:30 F 23 '87

Yugoslavia

Yugoslav youth stir it up [case of I. Cecko] S. Drakulich. il *Nation* 244:601-3 My 9 '87

Military telegraph

History

The telegraph and WWI. R. D. Fitch. il *Radio-Electron* 58:88-91 F '87

Military training

See also

Military maneuvers

United States. Navy. Reserve Officers' Training Corps

Military training camps

The combat Kawis [Marine motorcycle training at Camp Pendleton, Calif.] P. Lyons. il *Cycle* 38:63-6 Je '87

Environmental aspects

The Corps (Marine) and the only natural river [Camp Pendleton and proposed Santa Margarita dams in Calif.] J. Sunila. il map *Audubon* 89:114-16+ S '87

Old adversaries guard the woods [protest against proposed Minnesota National Guard training facility] M. Helmberger. il *Sierra* 72:81-2 Mr/Ap '87

Military trials *See* Courts martial and courts of inquiry
Military uniforms

See also

United States. Air Force—Uniforms

Future battlefield fashion will be a knockout. il *Pop Mech* 164:119 F '87

Milk

See also

Cream

Whey

The dawn of supermilks. A. Stern. il *Work Woman* 12:43+ Jl '87

How does a cow give soy milk? J. Silberner. il *U S News World Rep* 103:61 Ag 3 '87

Milk's great white way. B. Prescott. il *Health* 19:71-3 S '87

Contamination

See Milk contamination

Prices

Milking the consumer. M. S. Evans. *Consum Res Mag* 70:3 F '87

Taste of victory [Farmland Dairies wins fight on New York City milk prices] M. Fritz. il por *Forbes* 139:234 My 18 '87

Production

1987 dairy market trends still show mixed signals. J. R. Borcherding. *Success Farm* 85:D1 My '87

A debate over more milk [bovine somatotropin] M. Salter. *Macleans* 100:80 F 2 '87

Growth hormone work gets a health checkup [bovine somatotropin] J. R. Borcherding. *Success Farm* 85:30 S '87

Hold milk output in line to avoid 1988 support cut. J. R. Borcherding. *Success Farm* 85:D1 Je '87

Monthly shots of BST boost milk output 22%; Milk drinkers appear ready to accept BST use [bovine somatotropin] *Success Farm* 85:68 O '87

New flurry of growth hormone developments [bovine growth hormone] *Success Farm* 85 no5:D6 Mr '87

Product report: Megalac [protected fat for cows] J. R. Borcherding and D. Wanner. il *Success Farm* 85:54 N '87

Milk, Acidophilus

See also

Yogurt

Milk, Carbonated

Bessie goes bubbly. J. Zimmer. il *Health* 19:11 F '87

Milk, Human

See also

Breast feeding

Is mother's milk safe? Dioxin climbs to the top of the food chain. K. Hart. il *Progressive* 51:32-4 Mr '87

Milk, Mouse

Biotech's bid to build a better mouse [transferring human genes into mice to make human proteins] R. Rhein, Jr. il *Bus Week* p102 N 9 '87

Manipulating milk in mammals [betalactoglobulin gene in mice; research by J. Paul Simons and others] R. Weiss. *Sci News* 132:84 Ag 8 '87

Milk contamination
From tainted feed to mothers' milk [heptachlor contamination] D. Farley. il *FDA Consum* 21:38-40 Mr '87
Is mother's milk safe? Dioxin climbs to the top of the food chain. K. Hart. il *Progressive* 51:32-4 Mr '87
West Germany pours hot milk [disposition of milk contaminated by Chernobyl] D. Egger. il *Nation* 244:392-4+ Mr 28 '87

Milk crates
Theft
If you're missing milk crates, Mike Massey will crack the case. il por *People Wkly* 28:114 S 21 '87

Milk drinks *See* Beverages
Milk industry
Marketing
The dawn of supermilks. A. Stern. il *Work Woman* 12:43+ Jl '87

Milk production *See* Milk—Production
The milk train doesn't stop here anymore [drama] *See* Williams, Tennessee, 1911-1983

Milken, Michael R.
about
The case against Drexel: will the government come up short? C. Welles. il por *Bus Week* p56-60 Ag 10 '87
A chat with Michael Milken. A. Sloan. il por *Forbes* 140:248+ Jl 13 '87
Drexel's clients are rallying 'round Milken. C. Welles. il *Bus Week* p74 Ap 20 '87
A 'junk' king takes on the third world. B. Powell and C. Friday. il por *Newsweek* 110:56 S 21 '87
Mystery man of mergers. A. E. Serwer. il por *Fortune* 115:50 Ja 5 '87
Now Drexel Burnham is fighting on two fronts. C. Welles. il por *Bus Week* p90-3+ F 16 '87
A record turnout for Drexel's junk-bond bash. A. Bianco. il por *Bus Week* p80 Ap 13 '87
Why Mike Milken is suddenly taking himself public. C. Welles. il pors *Bus Week* p27-8 S 7 '87

Milkowski, Bill
Jeff Berlin: beyond the bas(s)ics. il pors *Down Beat* 54:22-4 Ap '87
John Scofield: all shades of blue. il pors *Down Beat* 54:16-18+ Ja '87
Marcus Miller: Miles' man in the studio. il pors *Down Beat* 54:20-2 F '87
Michael Brecker on Impulse [interview] il pors *Down Beat* 54:16-19 Je '87
Mike Stern's new lease on life. il pors *Down Beat* 54:28-30 Ag '87
Terje Rypdal: sculptor in sound. il por *Down Beat* 54:20-2 O '87

Milkshakes
Skinny-shake maker. il *McCalls* 114:118-19 Jl '87
Milkweed
Underachiever of the plant world. D. M. Schwartz. il *Audubon* 89:46-61 S '87
Vein-cutting behavior: insect counterploy to the latex defense of plants. D. E. Dussourd and T. Eisner. bibl f il *Science* 237:898-901 Ag 21 '87

Milky Way
The large-scale streaming of galaxies. A. Dressler. bibl (p120) il *Sci Am* 257:46-54 S '87
Looking for a few good stars [cover story] K. Croswell. il *Space World* X-7-283:12-15 Jl '87
Milky Way meanderings. G. Lovi. il *Sky Telesc* 74:167-8 Ag '87
The Milky Way's fountain [work of Christopher Martin and Stuart Bowyer] *Sky Telesc* 73:485 My '87
News from the center of our galaxy [lunar occultation] D. E. Thomsen. *Sci News* 131:24 Ja 10 '87
Star motions may alter view of galaxy [Lick Northern Proper Motion program] D. E. Thomsen. *Sci News* 132:69 Ag 1 '87

Photographs and photography
Exploring the summer Milky Way. R. Reeves. il *Astronomy* 15:99-102 S '87
Images. il *Sky Telesc* 74:16-17 Jl '87
Project Milky Way. S. J. O'Meara. il *Sky Telesc* 73:656-7 Je '87

Mill, John Stuart, 1806-1873
about
The Columbus argument. D. C. Stove. *Commentary* 84:57-8 D '87

Millar, Debbie Crandall- *See* Crandall-Millar, Debbie
Millar, M. Stuart
about
Calling all pilots. W. J. Cook. il por *U S News World Rep* 103:53+ D 7 '87

Piper's new tune. R. L. Collins. il *Flying* 114:58-64+ N '87

Millar, Sue
about
The past mastered. T. Aldous. *Hist Today* 37:4-5 My '87

Millard, William
about
A billionaire no longer. K. K. Wiegner and J. Littman. il por *Forbes* 140:37-8 O 19 '87
ComputerLand celebrates a sea change. K. M. Hafner. *Bus Week* p70 Je 15 '87

Millay, Norma, d. 1986
about
Obituary
Ms il por 15:82 F '87. N. Milford

Mille Fleurs (Rancho Santa Fe, Calif.: Restaurant) *See* Rancho Santa Fe (Calif.)—Restaurants, nightclubs, bars, etc.
Mille Miglia (Race) *See* Automobile racing—Italy
Millen, Steve
about
Millen around . . . and about. J. Dinkel. il por *Road Track* 38:33-4 Ap '87
Toyota's off-road racer . . . tanks but no tanks. J. Dinkel. il *Road Track* 38:33-6 My '87

Millennium
Our future hope: eschatology and its role in the church [special section] il *Christ Today* 31:1I-14I F 6 '87

Miller, A. E., Jr.
Medical "miracles" cost more than money. *Read Dig* 131:101-4 D '87

Miller, Alan
about
This family has seltzer in its blood. T. Carson. il pors *Bus Week* p92 Jl 6 '87

Miller, Alice
about
Alice Miller: the cost of parental tyranny. L. Van Gelder. il por *Ms* 16:82+ O '87
Interview. D. Connors. por *Omni* 9:72-4+ Mr '87

Miller, Andy
about
Kickoff of a craze: aerobics get competitive with beach-front bouts. M. A. Fischer. il pors *Life* 10:53-4+ Ag '87

Miller, Arthur, 1915-
A new candor at Issyk-Kul. por *Newsweek* 109:8 Ja 19 '87
O.K., but who was I? [excerpt from Timebends] il pors *Life* 10:72-88 N '87
about
All my sons [drama] Reviews
America 156:507-8 Je 20-27 '87. G. G. Seibert
N Y 20:122+ My 4 '87. J. Simon
Nation 244:695 My 23 '87. M. Hodgson
New Leader il 70:20-1 Ap 20 '87. L. Sauvage
New Yorker 63:127 My 4 '87. E. Oliver
Time il 129:107 My 4 '87. W. A. Henry
Danger: memory! [drama] Reviews
Commonweal 114:184-5 Mr 27 '87. G. Weales
N Y il 20:127-8 F 23 '87. J. Simon
New Leader 70:17 F 9-23 '87. L. Sauvage
New Repub 196:26 Mr 9 '87. R. Brustein
New Yorker 63:105 F 23 '87. E. Oliver
Time il 129:88 Mr 9 '87. W. A. Henry
PW interviews. W. Smith. por *Publ Wkly* 232:51-2 N 6 '87

Miller, Bryan
Chewing on words. il *N Y Times Mag* p10+ Jl 19 '87
about
In a gastronomic grudge match, a seasoned contender from Italy taunts the Times's top taster. A. Richman. il por *People Wkly* 28:7-8 D 7 '87

Miller, Charles D., 1928-
about
A sticky business. M. Beauchamp. il por *Forbes* 139:61 Ja 26 '87

Miller, Chris
about
A sleeper awakens. G. Norman. il pors *Sport Mag* 78:67+ My '87

Miller, Don Ethan, 1947-
Brick breaker. il *Atlantic* 259:79-81 Ap '87
Miller, Earl
about
Preachin' at the Guthrie Theater. P. Alsdurf. il por *Christ Today* 31:58-60 Jl 10 '87

Miller, Edwin
Spotlight. See issues of Seventeen

Miller, Frank R.

about

Watch out, here come more cheap imports. A. B. Block. il por *Forbes* 139:150 Mr 9 '87

Miller, George, 1945-

about

The witches of Eastwick [film] Reviews
   Christ Century 104:600 Jl 1-8 '87. J. M. Wall
   Commonweal 114:421-2 Jl 17 '87. T. O'Brien
   Macleans 100:48 Je 22 '87. L. O'Toole
   Mademoiselle il 93:84+ O '87. R. Rosenbaum
   N Y il 20:71 Je 22 '87. D. Denby
   Natl Rev 39:52-3 Jl 31 '87. J. Simon
   New Repub 197:26 Jl 13-20 '87. S. Kauffmann
   New Yorker 63:72 Je 29 '87. P. Kael
   Newsweek il 109:71 Je 15 '87. D. Ansen
   People Wkly il 27:12 Je 22 '87. P. Travers
   Time il 129:76 Je 22 '87. R. Corliss

Miller, George Armitage, 1920-, and Gildea, Patricia M.
How children learn words. il *Sci Am* 257:94-9 S '87

Miller, George H., and others
Facing nuclear reality. bibl f *Science* 238:455+ O 23 '87

Miller, George Oxford, 1943-
Training your eye [excerpt from Texas photo safaris] il *Natl Parks* 61:10-11 S/O '87

Miller, Helen L.
Elementary school dilemma: cheating or helping? *Educ Dig* 52:40-1 Ap '87

Miller, Henry I.
The case for qualifying "case by case". *Science* 236:133 Ap 10 '87

Miller, Inette
Diary of a divorce. il por *Ladies Home J* 104:67-70+ Ja '87

Miller, J. David (Joseph David), 1964-
The 1987 first round preview. *Sport Mag* 78:70-1 My '87
Lightning strikes back. il por *Sport Mag* 78:34-7+ Ja '87
Man down on the field. il *Sport Mag* 78:102 Ag '87
The new specialists. il *Sport Mag* 78:45-6 O '87

Miller, J. David (Joseph David), 1964-, and Whitford, David
Trouble in Tennessee. il *Sport Mag* 78:6, 68-73+ N '87

Miller, J. Houston
(jt. auth) See Smyth, Kermit C., and Miller, J. Houston

Miller, James C., III

about

'Jim, no tax increase' [interview] por *U S News World Rep* 102:47 Ja 12 '87
The OMB is digging in its heels on the budget. H. Gleckman. por *Bus Week* p41 F 9 '87

Miller, Janice

about

Legacy of a mother's murder. P. Maas. il pors *N Y Times Mag* p40-4+ Ap 12 '87
Winning back a child. P. Maas. il por *N Y Times Mag* p42+ Je 7 '87

Miller, Jason

about

That championship season long past, author-actor Jason Miller tests the new weather in Scranton. K. Hubbard. il pors *People Wkly* 28:58-60+ N 23 '87

Miller, Jo Ann, and Weissman, Susan
Helping your child learn [excerpt from The parents' guide to daycare] *Work Woman* 12:146+ Mr '87

Miller, Joel S., and Dixon, David A.
Dianion stabilization by $(M(C_5(CH_3)_5)_2)^+$: theoretical evidence for a localized ring in $(DDQ)^{2-}$. bibl f il *Science* 235:871-3 F 20 '87

Miller, John W.
Ice magic. il *Read Dig* 130:43-6 F '87

Miller, Jon

about

'Still very sweet indeed'. W. Taaffe. il pors *Sports Illus* 67:80 Jl 6 '87

Miller, Joni
Cruel shoes. il *Ms* 16:54 S '87
Glorious gluttony. il *Ms* 16:36 N '87
Halloween redux. il *Ms* 16:24 O '87
Scout's honor: the new uniform is blue. il *Ms* 15:58-9 Mr '87
Yoo hoo, Santa! il *Ms* 16:28 D '87

Miller, Joni K.
Pit power. il *Omni* 9:22 S '87

Miller, Joseph David See Miller, J. David (Joseph David), 1964-

Miller, Judea B.
Reviving Judaica—without Jews—in Poland. il *Christ Century* 104:916-17 O 21 '87

Miller, Judith
The Istanbul synagogue massacre: an investigation. il *N Y Times Mag* p14-20+ Ja 4 '87

Miller, Judith, and Miller, Mark
Earthquake threat to the Mississippi Valley. il *USA Today (Periodical)* 116:66-9 S '87

Miller, Ken
What's so special about Bryan Adams? por *Seventeen* 46:51+ Ag '87

Miller, Kenneth M.
Spying on the stars. il *Esquire* 108:15+ Jl '87
The two-wheeled time machine. il *Esquire* 107:17-18 Ja '87
What's your major? il *Roll Stone* p104-6+ Mr 26 '87

Miller, Laurence
REM sleep: pilot light of the mind? il *Psychol Today* 21:8+ S '87
This brain's for hire. *Omni* 9:14 Mr '87

Miller, Lee

about

What's foul is fair game. B. Anderson. il por *Sports Illus* 67:98 Jl 6 '87

Miller, Louis H., and others
Stable integration and expression of a bacterial gene in the mosquito Anopheles gambiae. bibl f il *Science* 237:779-81 Ag 14 '87

Miller, Marc
Ambiguous war: the United States and low-intensity conflict. il *Technol Rev* 90:60-7 Ag/S '87

Miller, Marcus

about

Marcus Miller: Miles' man in the studio. B. Milkowski. il pors *Down Beat* 54:20-2 F '87

Miller, Mark
(jt. auth) See Miller, Judith, and Miller, Mark

Miller, Marvin

about

Divided they fell. D. Whitford. il por *Sport Mag* 78:84-5 Jl '87

Miller, Marvin M.
Stemming the spread of nuclear weapons. il *Technol Rev* 90:68-75 Ag/S '87

Miller, Mary Susan
1987 Teacher of the Year. il por *Good Housekeep* 204:144+ My '87

Miller, Matthew

about

Grandson power. R. King, Jr. il por *Forbes* 140 Sp Issue:376+ O 26 '87

Miller, Neal

about

Putting his money where the trends are [interview] A. E. Serwer. il por *Fortune* 115:174 Je 22 '87

Miller, Peter

about

Peter Miller Books: where design professionals go to shop. K. Harmon. il pors *Publ Wkly* 231:56-8 F 20 '87

Miller, Peter, 1934-
Golden Girl. il pors *Skiing* 40:44+ N '87
Tornado! il map *Natl Geogr* 171:690-715 Je '87
The ups and downs of clambering on the roof of Europe. bibl (p154) il *Smithsonian* 18:92-8+ Je '87

Miller, R. Craig
Morris to Memphis: modern design at the Metropolitan Museum of Art. il *Antiques* 131:278-81 Ja '87

about

Contemporary craft at the Met. J. Tognini. il *Am Craft* 47:50-5 Ap/My '87

Miller, Randy

about

Fizz-biz whiz Randy Miller leaps into high-rise hype. il *People Wkly* 27:74 Mr 2 '87
This family has seltzer in its blood. T. Carson. il pors *Bus Week* p92 Jl 6 '87

Miller, Raymond Francis, 1941-

about

After the feast. J. Willoughby. por *Forbes* 140:38+ O 5 '87

Miller, Richard J.
Multiple calcium channels and neuronal function. bibl f il *Science* 235:46-52 Ja 2 '87

Miller, Robert H., and others
Preferred microtubules for vesicle transport in lobster axons. bibl f il *Science* 235:220-2 Ja 9 '87

Miller, Robert L.
A letter from the publisher. See issues of Time beginning February 9, 1987

Miller, Robert L.—*cont.*
The new American downtown: Tyson's Corner as a case study. il *Archit Rec* 175:79+ S '87

Miller, Roger H.
Proteolytic self-cleavage of hepatitis B virus core protein may generate serum e antigen. bibl f il *Science* 236:722-5 My 8 '87

Miller, Roger W.
Athletes and steroids: playing a deadly game. il *FDA Consum* 21:16-21 N '87
Can herbs really heal? il *FDA Consum* 21:32-4 Je '87
The digestive discomfort of gas. il *FDA Consum* 21:32-4 Ap '87

Miller, Ron, 1947-
Astronauts by gaslight [cover story] il *Space World* X-9-285:26-9 S '87

Miller, Ron, 1947-, and Durant, Frederick C., 1916-
Lunar fantasies. il *Omni* 9:50-5 F '87

Miller, Ross M., Jr.
about
Miller named 1st black pres. of the American College of Surgeons S. Calif. chapter. por *Jet* 72:26 Ap 27 '87

Miller, Sara
A Christmas tradition that grows and grows. il *Good Housekeep* 205:206 D '87

Miller, Shoshana
about
Israel's new conversion crisis. R. N. Ostling. il por *Time* 129:75 Ja 19 '87

Miller, Stephen
Black enterprise guide to home entertainment [special section] il *Black Enterp* 18:81-8 S '87

Miller, Steven
Men and child care: the plot thickens. il por *Ms* 16:54-6 O '87

Miller, Ted
The value of a life. *Cent Mag* 20:62-3 Jl/Ag '87

Miller, William Lee
Sola gratia in Lake Wobegon [cover story] il por *Christ Century* 104:526-8 Je 3-10 '87

Miller (Herman) Inc. *See* Herman Miller, Inc.
Miller & Schroeder's Municipal Investors Trust of America
Municipal garbage. G. Morgenson. il *Forbes* 139:42-3 Mr 9 '87

Miller Brewing Company
Miller Brewing Co. honors publisher John H. Johnson. il pors *Jet* 71:5 F 16 '87
Miller jumps into a cooler cooler market. M. D. Oneal. il *Bus Week* p36+ O 26 '87

Miller family
about
Everybody in this picture is named Miller or Yoder except for one poor guy [postmaster T. Hagedorn's problem with family names in town of Kalona, Iowa] D. Van Biema. il por *People Wkly* 27:46-8 Mr 30 '87

Milles, Carl, 1875-1955
about
Green men. J. Herzfeld. il *Art News* 86:13-14 N '87

Millet, Richard
The Honduran dilemma. bibl f *Curr Hist* 86:409-12+ D '87

Millet
A grain revolution: the impact of imported rice on millet-based African civilizations. T. Ndoye and M. M'Baye. il *Courier* 40:8-9 My '87

Millhouses, Converted *See* Houses, Remodeled
Millican, Ron
about
The right mix. G. Wen. il por *N Y* 20:42 S 21 '87

Millicent Rogers Museum (Taos, N.M.)
Tiffany's of the Southwest. M. Wade. il *Horizon* 30:45 O '87

Milligan, Susan
Eyes on the lies. il *Wash Mon* 19:39-42 Je '87

Milliken, Robert
Australia's nuclear graveyard. il map *Bull At Sci* 43:38-44 Ap '87

Millinery *See* Hats
Millington-Drake, Teddy
about
Painting Petworth. M. Egremont. il *House Gard* 159:116+ N '87

Millionaires
Football's millionaires [black players] il *Ebony* 43:132+ N '87
The forgotten four hundred: Chicago's first millionaires. B. A. Weisberger. il *Am Herit* 38:34-45 N '87
What it takes to be rich in America [cover story; special section] il *Fortune* 115:22-9+ Ap 13 '87

Millisecond pulsars *See* Pulsars
Millman, Lawrence
America's Stonehenge. il *Travel Holiday* 168:28-9 Jl '87

Mills, Alan
about
Chief arbiter [interview] N. Amdur. il por *World Tennis* 35:50+ Jl '87

Mills, Erie
about
Ego intact. G. Heymont. il pors *Opera News* 52:38+ D 5 '87

Mills, Jack
about
Jack be nimble: a day in the life of an agent. D. S. Looney. il por *Sports Illus* 67:100-1 O 19 '87

Mills, Joey
From bland to all-day beautiful in 16 minutes [excerpt from New classic beauty] il *Good Housekeep* 205:150-1+ N '87

Mills, Joshua
Hockey's big brother act. il *N Y Times Mag* p64-5+ Mr 29 '87

Mills, Judy, and Delehanty, Hugh
Highway to glory. il *Women's Sports Fitness* 9:48-53 N '87

Mills, Lia
Best friends and other strangers [story] il *Teen* 31:64+ S '87

Mills, Phoebe
about
Game and gutsy, three tiny teens limber up for the '88 Olympics. A. Chambers. il pors *People Wkly* 28:130-2 N 2 '87

Mills, Steve
about
A Beverly Hills bar has water, water from everywhere, and that's all there is to drink. il *People Wkly* 27:109-10 F 9 '87

Mills, Terry
about
The waiting game is over. H. Hersch. il pors *Sports Illus* 67 Sp Issue:67 N 18 '87

Mills
See also
Paper mills

Mills, Remodeled
Moulin refuge [B. Fouret's remodeled mill outside Paris] C. de Liagre. il por *House Gard* 159:138-47+ Ap '87

Mills (R. M.) Bookstores (Nashville, Tenn.) *See* Booksellers and bookselling—Tennessee
Mills College
Degrees of art. il *Horizon* 30:37 Ja/F '87

Mills College. Jane Baerwald Aron Art Center *See* Jane Baerwald Aron Art Center
Mills family
about
High-flying household [sports-oriented Mills clan of Northfield, Ill.] H. Hersch. il *Sports Illus* 66:44-6+ Je 22 '87

Milne, Brian
Warming to an Arctic spring [photographs] il *Int Wildl* 17:30-4 My/Je '87

Milne, James Lees- *See* Lees-Milne, James
Milner, Eddie
about
Milner quietly beat drugs, but he's talking about it. *Jet* 72:46 S 7 '87

Milner, Thirman L.
about
New England's 1st black mayor to step down at end of his third term. por *Jet* 72:29 Ag 10 '87

Milner, Virginia
about
Rancho La Vista: western themes in California's Ojai Valley. M. Webb. il pors *Archit Dig* 44:112-19 D '87

Milosz, Czeslaw
All Hallows' Eve [poem; tr. by the author and Leonard Nathan. *New Yorker* 63:42 N 2 '87
Mary Magdalene and I [poem] *New Yorker* 63:40 F 23 '87
about
Separate nations: poetry and the people [excerpt from Conversations with Czeslaw Milosz]; tr. by Richard Lourie. A. Fiut. il *N Y Times Book Rev* 92:3+ O 11 '87

Milpitas (Calif.)
Crime
Bitter memories of murder [movie River's edge recalls murder and coverup by teens] P. Abramson. il *Newsweek* 109:25 Je 22 '87

Milpitas (Calif.)—*cont.*
Education
Man poses as 14-year-old for chance at education [R. Turner] il por *Jet* 72:8 Je 1 '87
Milton, Karla Garrett
about
Dayton Newspapers Inc. names asst. business mgr. por *Jet* 73:25 O 5 '87
Milton (Vt.)
Social work
Developing partnerships between families and service providers in rural Vermont [work of the Milton Family Community Center] L. Horel. il *Child Today* 16:17-19 Ja/F '87
Milwaukee (Wis.)
Criminal justice, Administration of
Ex-cop Lawrencia Bembenek claims she was wrongly convicted of murder in the case of the unsmoking gun. J. S. Kunen. il pors *People Wkly* 28:116-18+ D 7 '87
Description
Talkin' M'Waukee. J. S. Lewis. il *Travel Holiday* 168:25-7 D '87
Galleries and museums
See also
Milwaukee Public Museum
Music
See also
Opera—Wisconsin
Newspapers
See also
Milwaukee community journal
Politics and government
History in Sherman Park (I) [views of ordinary citizens during the 1984 presidential campaign] J. Schell. *New Yorker* 62:35-6+ Ja 5 '87
History in Sherman Park (II) [views of ordinary citizens during the 1984 presidential campaign] J. Schell. *New Yorker* 62:57-8+ Ja 12 '87
Milwaukee community journal
Black press organization names 1st woman president [P. O. Thomas] por *Jet* 72:31 Jl 27 '87
Milwaukee Public Museum
Geology in Milwaukee [dinosaur dioramas] P. M. Sheehan. il *Earth Sci* 39:18-19 Wint '86
Mimara, Ante Topić, 1898-1987
about
Real and fake in the 'Zagreb Louvre'. A. Decker. il pors *Art News* 86:151-8 Summ '87
Mimas (Satellite) *See* Saturn (Planet)—Satellites
Mime
See also
Marcel Marceau World Centre for Mime
British television's Catholic pioneer [mime H. Pepler] M. E. Evans. il *America* 157:501-3 D 26 '87
Speaking out from behind the mask of mime [interview with M. Marceau] R. Z. Chesnoff. il pors *U S News World Rep* 102:62-3 F 23 '87
Mimicry (Biology)
Chemical mimicry: bolas spiders emit components of moth prey species sex pheromones. M. K. Stowe and others. bibl f il *Science* 236:964-7 My 22 '87
Deceit and corruption in the blueberry patch [flower mimicry by mummy berry fungus (Monilinia)] S. W. T. Batra. il *Nat Hist* 96:56-9 Ag '87
On display: the stars of the stripes [fruit fly mimicry of jumping spider territorial display; research by Erick Greene and others] il *Discover* 8:9-10 My '87
A sheep in wolf's clothing: tephritid flies mimic spider predators. M. H. Mather and B. D. Roitberg. bibl f il *Science* 236:308-10 Ap 17 '87
Snow place to hide [Arctic animals] il *Natl Geogr World* 148:24-5+ D '87
Spider's perfume fatal for moths [research by Mark K. Stowe and others] S. Weisburd. il *Sci News* 131:340 My 30 '87
A tephritid fly mimics the territorial displays of its jumping spider predators. E. Greene and others. bibl f il *Science* 236:310-12 Ap 17 '87
Why the spider did not eat the fly [jumping spider mimicry among fruit flies] S. Weisburd. il *Sci News* 131:261 Ap 25 '87
Mimicry (Botany)
Mimicry in plants. S. C. H. Barrett. bibl (p120) il *Sci Am* 257:76-83 S '87
Mims, Forrest M.
Surface-mount technology [special section] il *Radio-Electron* 58:57-79+ N '87

Mims, Madeline Manning- *See* Manning-Mims, Madeline
Minard, Sally
about
The power of positive stress. K. Brady. il pors *Work Woman* 12:74-7 Jl '87
Minassian, Daniel H.
Profiles: Count and Countess Lennart Bernadotte. il pors *Archit Dig* 44:174-9+ D '87
Profiles: Thor Heyerdahl. il pors *Archit Dig* 44:102-9 F '87
Mind
See also
Brain
Intelligence
Memory
Wisdom
The Omni wholemind. il *Omni* 10:125-32 O '87
The origin of the modern human mind [special section] R. Lewin. il *Science* 236:668-70 My 8 '87
Your mindless brain [views of M. L. Minsky] P. Hoffman. il *Discover* 8:84-5+ S '87
Mind and body
See also
Biofeedback training
Consciousness
Holistic medicine
Hypnotism
Medicine, Psychosomatic
Parapsychology
Psychoneuroimmunology
Sleep
New mind/body basics [special section] il *Vogue* 177:354-73+ Ap '87
Mind control *See* Brainwashing
Minden, Larry
Feathers. il *Sierra* 72:90-1 Mr/Ap '87
Mine accidents and explosions
19 hours in "Devil's Icebox" [rescue of D. Easter, pinned by boulder in Missouri mine] S. Kelly. il *Read Dig* 131:60-6 Ag '87
Mine pumps
Cornish pumps kept California gold mines dry, but forced miners to take a strange and dangerous route to work. M. Hill. *Earth Sci* 40:38 Summ '87
Mineral licks *See* Salt licks
Mineral resources *See* Mines and mineral resources
Mineralocorticoid receptors *See* Hormone receptors
Mineralogy *See* Minerals
Minerals
See also
Marine mineral resources
Meteorites
Mines and mineral resources
Soils—Mineral content
Geologist's hammer is joined by spectrometers [work of Gregg Vane] R. A. Kerr. *Science* 236:1625 Je 26 '87
Minerals & Resources Corporation
What color is your mail? [Salomon Brothers pays greenmail to Minerals & Resources Corp.] A. Sloan. il *Forbes* 140:36-7 O 19 '87
Minerals in the body
See also
Cadmium in the body
Calcium in the body
Chromium in the body
Copper in the body
Iron in the body
Magnesium in the body
Trace elements
Vitamins
Mineral mania: sorting facts from myths. L. Hoppe. il *Better Homes Gard* 65:45+ Je '87
Vitamin and mineral supplements: do you need them? il *Glamour* 85:238 Je '87
Miners
See also
Strikes—Miners
United Mine Workers of America
Mines, Military
See also
Mines, Submarine
UH-60A tested with Volcano multiple delivery mine system. il *Aviat Week Space Technol* 126:73 Mr 2 '87
Mines, Submarine
See also
Minesweepers
An attack in the Gulf [U.S. Navy attack on Iranian ship laying mines] M. Nichols. il map *Macleans* 100:26-8 O 5 '87

Mines, Submarine—*cont.*

Can't anybody here play this game? [U.S. unpreparedness in Persian Gulf] M. Kramer. il *U S News World Rep* 103:11 Ag 10 '87

Caught in the act [U.S. captures Iranians laying mines in the Persian Gulf] E. Magnuson. il map *Time* 130:20-3 O 5 '87

Combined U.S. forces defeat Iranian mine-laying mission. B. M. Greeley, Jr. il map *Aviat Week Space Technol* 127:32-3 S 28 '87

Convoy to a minefield [mine blast hits Kuwaiti tanker under American escort] B. Levin. il *Macleans* 100:20-1 Ag 3 '87

Dealing with primitive—but deadly—mines [Persian Gulf] il *Newsweek* 110:16-17 Ag 31 '87

The Gulf: an important success [trapping Iran in minelaying operations] *Natl Rev* 39:20 O 23 '87

Here a mine, there a mine [Persian Gulf] J. Greenwald. il *Time* 130:24-7 Ag 24 '87

Into rough water [U.S./Kuwaiti tankers encounter mines in the Persian Gulf] W. Isaacson. il *Time* 130:8-10 Ag 10 '87

Iran: 'producing mines like seeds'. il *U S News World Rep* 103:28 Ag 31 '87

The mines of August [Persian Gulf] R. Watson. il map *Newsweek* 110:22-4 Ag 24 '87

The mining episode . . . and more to come? [U.S.-flagged tanker Bridgeton hits mine in Persian Gulf] il maps *U S News World Rep* 103:26-7 Ag 3 '87

Running the gauntlet [U.S.-flagged Kuwaiti tanker hits Iranian mine in the Persian Gulf] W. E. Smith. il map *Time* 130:24-7 Ag 3 '87

A sting in the Gulf [mine blast hits Kuwaiti tanker under American escort] H. Anderson. il map *Newsweek* 110:24-6 Ag 3 '87

Time bombs in the ocean [mines in the Persian Gulf] A. Bilski. il *Macleans* 100:24 Ag 24 '87

Time for sweeping gestures [mines in the Persian Gulf] M. S. Serrill. *Time* 130:26 Ag 31 '87

A U.S. ambush in the Gulf [trapping Iran in the act of laying mines] R. Watson. il map *Newsweek* 110:24-7 O 5 '87

Waiting for Iran [U.S. capture of Iranian mine laying vessels; with editorial comment by Mortimer B. Zuckerman] W. L. Chaze. il map *U S News World Rep* 103:22-4, 88 O 5 '87

Mines and mineral resources

See also

Coal mines and mining
Copper mines and mining
Emerald mines and mining
Gold mines and mining
Marine mineral resources
Mining industry
Ocean mining
Ore deposits
Platinum mines and mining
Prospecting
Strip mining
United States. Bureau of Mines
Uranium mines and mining
Zinc mines and mining

Maine

Maine's tourmaline gems. il *Earth Sci* 40:14-16 Wint '87

Montana

Deep breath down under [sick people seeking radon cure in old mines] M. Dobbin. il *U S News World Rep* 102:40 Ap 27 '87

United States

See Mines and mineral resources

Minesweepers

Missing mine sweepers. H. Evans. il *U S News World Rep* 103:68 Ag 24 '87

Navy deploys helicopters to counter Gulf mine threat [Sikorsky RH-53D Sea Stallion] M. Mecham. *Aviat Week Space Technol* 127:25-6 Ag 3 '87

Oops, we forgot minesweepers [Persian Gulf] F. Willey. il *Newsweek* 110:40-1 Ag 10 '87

The weapons that wait. il *Time* 130:10 Ag 10 '87

Where are U.S. minesweepers? Out of service and out-of-date, says arms expert William Lind [interview] M. Wilhelm. il por *People Wkly* 28:30-1 Ag 24 '87

Mineta, Norman Y.

The wounds of war; ed. by Susan Schindehette. il pors *People Wkly* 28:173-4+ D 14 '87

Minetree, Harry

Fast company: rich & racy. il pors *Harpers Bazaar* 120:22-5+ My '87

High art in the Low Countries. il *Harpers Bazaar* 120:78+ Ag '87

Red, white & American. il *Harpers Bazaar* 120:108+ O '87

Ming dynasty, 1368-1644 *See* China—History—Ming dynasty, 1368-1644

Mingei (Japanese folk art) *See* Folk art

Mingo, Frank L., Sr.

about

Obituary
Jet 72:17 Je 1 '87

Mingo-Jones Advertising Inc.

Mingo-Jones affiliate makes historic merger. il *Jet* 71:33 F 9 '87

Miniature castles *See* Castle models

Miniature gardens and gardening

The wonders of gardening . . . in a saucer [kindergarten project] il *Sunset* 179:90-1 O '87

Miniature golf

Mini golf [theme party given by K. Brown and L. Crafts] *New Yorker* 63:31-2 O 26 '87

Miniature golf in your backyard. L. M. Dalsgaard. il *Home Mech* 83:52-4+ Je '87

We couldn't stop playing to save our soles. C. Bond. il *Smithsonian* 18:120-5 Je '87

Photographs and photography

Fanciful fairways. J. Margolies. il *Americana* 15:80-1 My/Je '87

Miniature horses *See* Horses, Miniature

Miniature objects

See also

Architectural models
Automobile models
Cameras, Miniature
Circus, Miniature
Furniture, Miniature
House models
Military miniatures
Models of cities, towns, etc.
Needlework, Miniature
Rugs and carpets, Miniature
Ship and boat models
Tea services, Miniature
Toys, Miniature

Miniatures. A. Bahar. See issues of Antiques & Collecting Hobbies beginning March 1985

Miniatures. A. Bahar. See issues of Hobbies through February 1985

Collectors and collecting

Ingenuity and genius: the Rogers Collection. A. Bahar. il *Antiques Collect Hobbies* 92:43-6 Jl '87

Miniature painting

Art: tiny paintings. R. Rosenblum. il *Archit Dig* 44:222-7 N '87

Britain's Charles shows his colors [Prince Charles' work] L. S. Healy. il por *Life* 10:82-3 Ag '87

Miniature roses *See* Roses

Minicucci, Robert A.

about

Hardball on Wall Street [cover story] J. Sterngold. il pors *N Y Times Mag* p22-7+ Ag 16 '87

Minimal music *See* Music, Experimental

Minimum competency tests *See* Educational tests and measurements

Minimum competency tests for teachers *See* Teachers—Examinations

Minimum disclosure proofs *See* Zero knowledge proofs

Minimum security prisons *See* Prisons

Minimum wage

Dispelling the myths about a higher minimum wage. A. Bernstein. il *Bus Week* p146 O 19 '87

Don't raise the minimum wage. J. Campbell. il por *Fortune* 116:103-4 Ag 31 '87

It's time to raise the minimum wage. S. L. Gottovi. por *Seventeen* 46:126 Ag '87

Job loss from wage hike. il *Nations Bus* 75:103 S '87

Minimum employment. *Natl Rev* 39:18-19 My 22 '87

The minimum wage: its relation to incomes and poverty. R. E. Smith and B. Vavrichek. bibl f il *Mon Labor Rev* 110:24-30 Ag '87

Minimum wage myths. il *Nations Bus* 75:35-8 Je '87

Perils of a new minimum wage. R. W. Haseltine. il *USA Today (Periodical)* 116:21 Jl '87

Raising the $3.35 minimum. J. V. Lamar, Jr. il *Time* 129:19 Ja 26 '87

Raising the minimum wage. *Congr Dig* 66:193-224 Ag/S '87

The real costs of a higher minimum wage. J. Berger. il *Bus Week* p64-5 Jl 27 '87

A wage debate with no real winners. il *Nations Bus* 75:64 Ap '87

Wage showdown. il *Newsweek* 109:7 Mr 9 '87

Minimum wage—*cont.*
Workers at the minimum wage or less: who they are and the jobs they hold. E. F. Mellor. bibl f il *Mon Labor Rev* 110:34-8 Jl '87
Mining *See* Mines and mineral resources
Mining, Petroleum *See* Petroleum engineering
Mining accidents *See* Mine accidents and explosions
Mining equipment industry
Management
The mining machinery industry: labor productivity trends, 1972-84. B. A. O'Neil. bibl f il *Mon Labor Rev* 110:31-6 Je '87
Mining industry
> *See also*
> AMAX Inc.
> ASARCO Inc.
> Hughes Mining Company
> Newmont Mining Corp.
> Yuba Natural Resources, Inc.
Acquisitions and mergers
A gold miner helps Pickens chip away at Newmont [R. M. Friedland cut into Ivanhoe Partners deal] S. D. Atchison. il por *Bus Week* p36 Ag 31 '87
One swallow could make Pickens' summer [pursuit of Newmont Mining] J. E. Davis. il por *Bus Week* p37 S 14 '87
Canada
Defence of a gold mine [run on Dome Mines] D. Jenish. il *Macleans* 100:32-3 Ag 17 '87
Placer Dome: will it pan out? E. B. Terry. *Bus Week* p42+ S 7 '87
Finance
Metals [nonferrous mining industry] J. Merwin. il *Forbes* 139:162-3 Ja 12 '87
International aspects
> *See also*
> Minerals & Resources Corporation
Canada
> *See also*
> Echo Bay Mines Ltd.
> Galactic Resources Ltd.
> Placer Dome Inc.
> Teck Corp.
New life stirs for natural resource companies. E. B. Terry. il *Bus Week* p47 Mr 2 '87
South Africa
> *See also*
> Anglo American Corp. of South Africa, Ltd.
Mining leases
> *See also*
> Oil and gas leases
Royalties
> *See also*
> United States. Office of Royalty Management
Miniseries (Television) *See* Television broadcasting—Miniseries
Miniskirts *See* Skirts (Clothing)
Ministers (Clergy) *See* Black clergy; Clergy
Ministorage *See* Self storage warehouses
Ministry *See* Church work
Ministry of International Trade and Industry (Japan) *See* Japan. Ministry of International Trade and Industry
Minitel (Videotex system) *See* Information storage and retrieval systems—France
Minivans *See* Vans
Miniwarehouses *See* Self storage warehouses
Mink coats, wraps, etc. *See* Fur coats, wraps, etc.
Minker, Ralph L.
Mandatory retirement: its time has passed. *Christ Century* 104:463-4 My 13 '87
Minkow, Barry
> *about*
Wall-to-wall trouble for the carpet-cleaning king. K. Kelly. il por *Bus Week* p83 Jl 13 '87
A whiz kid goes wrong. J. B. Copeland. il por *Newsweek* 110:40 Jl 20 '87
ZZZZ Best may be ZZZZ worst. P. Elmer-Dewitt. por *Time* 130:56 Jl 20 '87
Minneapolis (Minn.)
Bookstores
See Booksellers and bookselling—Minnesota
Economic conditions
The could-do city could do it again. F. S. Worthy. il *Fortune* 115:82-4+ Ja 19 '87
Restaurants, nightclubs, bars, etc.
Where to eat in . . . Minneapolis. C. Beason. il *Work Woman* 12:102 My '87

Minnelli, Liza
> *about*
Bouncing back from drugs and booze, lissome Liza Minnelli takes a stand at Carnegie Hall. il pors *People Wkly* 27:36-7 Je 15 '87
If she can make it there. il por *Newsweek* 109:75 Je 15 '87
Liza battles back. E. Sherman. il pors *Ladies Home J* 104:50+ Jl '87
Minnesota
> *See also*
> Agriculture—Minnesota
> Architecture, Domestic—Minnesota
> Booksellers and bookselling—Minnesota
> Child welfare—Minnesota
> Criminal justice, Administration of—Minnesota
> Education—Minnesota
> Environmental movement—Minnesota
> Fishing—Minnesota
> Hennepin County (Minn.)
> Law—Minnesota
> Organic gardens and gardening—Minnesota
> Superior National Forest (Minn.)
> Wildlife—Minnesota
Minnesota. National Guard
Old adversaries guard the woods [protest against proposed Minnesota National Guard training facility] M. Helmberger. il *Sierra* 72:81-2 Mr/Ap '87
Minnesota Dance Theatre
Reviews:
> Fall season in St. Paul. J. Timmis. *Dance Mag* 61:34+ Mr '87
Minnesota Institute for Theoretical Physics *See* Institute for Theoretical Physics (Minn.)
Minnesota Mining & Mfg. Co.
Earnings gains from a new-products blitz. il *Money* 16:8 S '87
NASA agreement with 3M sets precedent for large commercial space commitments [shuttle research] T. M. Foley. *Aviat Week Space Technol* 126:102-3 Ja 12 '87
Shuttle mission 26 will extend 3M materials experimentation. *Aviat Week Space Technol* 127:110+ O 12 '87
Minnesota Multiphasic Personality Inventory
Nuclear psych-out [workers at Davis Besse nuclear plant fired as security risks after failing psychological test] P. Kruger. il *Progressive* 51:24-5 Je '87
Minnesota Opera
St. Paul. M. Anthony. *Opera News* 51:38-9 Mr 28 '87
Minnesota Public Radio
MPR ends exclusive arrangement with Newman. *Publ Wkly* 231:70-1 Ap 10 '87
Minnows
> *See also*
> Shiners (Fish)
Minolta Camera Co. Ltd.
Canon finally challenges Minolta's mighty Maxxum [EOS autofocus SLRs] O. Port. il *Bus Week* p89-90 Mr 2 '87
Minor, Wendell
> *about*
Wendell Minor. M. S. Doherty. il por *Am Artist* 51:42-7 Ja '87
Minor league baseball *See* Baseball, Professional
Minor league baseball stadiums *See* Stadiums
Minor planets *See* Asteroids
Minorities
> *See also*
> Discrimination
Let's get rid of 'minority'. Y. T. De Mola. *America* 157:284-5 O 31 '87
U.S. could become a nation of minorities. *Futurist* 21:57 Mr/Ap '87
Civil rights
The new McCarthyism. G. F. Kreyche. il *USA Today (Periodical)* 116:98 S '87
Education
> *See also*
> Bilingual education
> Institute for Independent Education
> Minorities—Vocational-technical education
> National Urban Fellows
> Public schools—Desegregation
6,000 hours [Special Public School 31 in the South Bronx] *New Yorker* 62:25-7 F 16 '87
American High: at Seward Park, the melting pot still bubbles [New York City high school] K. D. Fishman. il *N Y* 20:78-80+ Mr 2 '87
The case of Our Lady of Sorrows [Catholic school on the Lower East Side of New York City] D. E. DeCosse. *Commonweal* 114:210-15 Ap 10 '87

Minorities—Education—*cont.*

Demographic changes: what meaning for arts education? [effect of growing minorities] D. Funes. *Des Arts Educ* 89:29-33 N/D '87

A dream come true [followup on students of P.S. 121 in East Harlem helped by E. M. Lang] M. deC. Hinds. il por *N Y Times Mag* p32-6 Ap 26 '87

Group pushes MBAs for minorities with forum tour [Graduate Management Admission Council] *Jet* 72:24 Ag 31 '87

Improving urban schools. E. L. Boyer. *Educ Dig* 53:6-9 S '87

Minorities do better at Catholic schools: study. *Jet* 72:24 Je 22 '87

Minorities get $25 million boost from Columbia gift [gift by J. W. Kluge] *Jet* 72:32 My 18 '87

Minorities in Catholic schools: why do they read better? V. Lee. *Educ Dig* 52:20-3 F '87

N.J. officials pushing for more minority college grads. *Jet* 72:25 Ag 31 '87

Needy kids, perpetual aid [A. Fogelman subsidizes college tuition for Memphis students] por *Time* 130:70 N 30 '87

Storm warnings [report of the National Commission on the Role and Future of State Colleges and Universities] *Cent Mag* 20:58 Ja/F '87

Employment

See also

United States. Equal Employment Opportunity Commission

Fate of labor force depends on minorities' skills: Brock. *Jet* 72:38 My 4 '87

Minority firms likely to hire more minorities. *Jet* 73:25 O 5 '87

Health and hygiene

Meeting the mental health needs of severely emotionally disturbed minority children and adolescents: a national perspective. J. Katz-Leavy and others. il *Child Today* 16:10-14 S/O '87

Political activities

What went wrong with the Voting Rights Act [views of A. M. Thernstrom] P. H. Schuck. *Wash Mon* 19:51-5 N '87

Vocational-technical education

Why few ghetto factories are making it. A. Beam. il *Bus Week* p86+ F 16 '87

Great Britain

"Our time has come" [minority candidates for Parliament] L. Garrison. il *Time* 129:36 Je 1 '87

Soviet Union

Can Moscow control restive minorities? S. Powell. il map *U S News World Rep* 102:40-2 F 2 '87

Gorbachev facing faith & nationality. E. von Kuehnelt-Leddihn. *Natl Rev* 39:48 Mr 27 '87

The nationality question. R. G. Suny. il *Nation* 244:808-10 Je 13 '87

United States

See Minorities

Minorities and the environment

Saving the world. P. A. A. Berle. *Audubon* 89:6 N '87

Minorities and the press

Only news that's nice to print [suppression of racial identification in criminal cases] G. Bain. il *Macleans* 100:47 Ja 26 '87

Minorities in science

Spotlight brighter on minorities in science. J. Walsh. il *Science* 238:265-6 O 16 '87

Minorities in the mass media industry

Affirmative action, FCC-style [preference policies for minorities and women in broadcasting] N. Gunther. *Channels* 7:12 My '87

F.C.C. launches inquiry into policies preferential to minorities and women. *Jet* 71:16 Ja 12 '87

Minority brokers

Federal aid

Reverse discrimination on the Street [Dept. of Agriculture decision to distribute Rural Housing Senior Mortgage passthroughs by minority firms] D. Seligman. il *Fortune* 116:142 O 26 '87

Minority Business Development Agency (U.S.) *See* United States. Minority Business Development Agency

Minority Business Enterprise Legal Defense and Education Fund Inc.

Mitchell rigs 'hot line' for black firm contracts. *Jet* 73:38 O 12 '87

Minority business enterprises

See also

Black business enterprises

Filipino American business enterprises

Minority Business Enterprise Legal Defense and Education Fund Inc.

Minority businesses open at new mall in Miami. *Jet* 72:23 My 4 '87

Minority firms likely to hire more minorities. *Jet* 73:25 O 5 '87

Federal aid

See also

United States. Minority Business Development Agency

$4 billion worth of temptation [corruption of set-aside programs for minority firms as evidenced in Wedtech scandal] W. Shapiro. il *Time* 129:20 Je 15 '87

The 8(a) follies [minority set-asides] il *Fortune* 115:17-18 F 2 '87

"Give me back my reputation!" [ex-Labor Secretary R. Donovan] G. J. Church. il por *Time* 129:31 Je 8 '87

'A political snake pit' comes under the spotlight [Wedtech scandal] P. Cary. il *U S News World Rep* 102:22-4 Je 15 '87

Reagan lauds civil rights era at White House meet for minority businesses. *Jet* 72:12 Ag 3 '87

Location

Top 10 states with Asian, Indian and Hispanic businesses. R. Thompson. il *Nations Bus* 75:10 F '87

Minority college graduates

Graduating minority students: lessons from ten success stories. R. C. Richardson and others. il *Change* 19:20-7 My/Je '87

Minority contractors

See also

Black contractors

Minority Enterprise Development Week

Reagan announces salute for minority businesses. *Jet* 72:36 S 7 '87

Minority enterprise small business investment companies *See* Small business investment companies

Minors, Employment of *See* Children—Employment

Minors (Law) *See* Children—Law; Parent and child (Law)

Minotaur Designs (Firm)

It is easy to get bushed when you're threading a maze. R. Wolkomir. il *Smithsonian* 18:108-12+ D '87

Minoxidil

Anti-baldness drug linked with sexual staying power. *Jet* 71:38 F 23 '87

Baldness drug gets a boost. il *Prevention* 39:14 S '87

Hair-raising news. il *Time* 129:62 Mr 30 '87

A hairy problem [minoxidil as hair restorative not yet proven] il *FDA Consum* 21:37-8 Ap '87

Putting the brakes on the baldness-cure bandwagon [Minox-a-gro] il *FDA Consum* 21:34-5 S '87

Minsky, Marvin Lee, 1927-

about

Your mindless brain. P. Hoffman. il *Discover* 8:84-5+ S '87

Minsky, Terri

The death of dress for success. il *Mademoiselle* 93:308-9+ S '87

Prisoners of psychotherapy [cover story] il *N Y* 20:34-40 Ag 31 '87

Who'll win with the tax law. il *Esquire* 107:44 F '87

Who's that girl? por *Roll Stone* p40-2+ My 21 '87

Yuppievision. il *Roll Stone* p41-2 D 3 '87

Minstar Inc.

Irv Jacobs is calling 'time out'. P. Houston. il *Bus Week* p46 Je 1 '87

Mint (Herb)

See also

Cooking—Herbs and spices

Peppermint

Minton, Barbara A.

(jt. auth) See VanDenBerg, John, and Minton, Barbara A.

Minton, Eric

Beatrix Potter country. il *Travel Holiday* 168:28-30 D '87

Minuteman (Missile) basing system *See* Guided missile bases

Miocene period *See* Paleontology—Miocene

Mir (Space station) *See* Space stations, Russian

Mira (Star) *See* Stars, Variable

Mirabel International Airport *See* Montreal (Québec)—Airports

Miracles

See also

Faith cure

Jesus Christ—Apparitions and miracles

Fuller Seminary releases study on the miraculous. il *Christ Today* 31:44-5 F 6 '87

Miracles—*cont.*

The scientist who makes icons weep [S. Carlson] il por *Newsweek* 110:79 O 26 '87

Mirage (Firm)

On Pollack's plate. P. S. Nathan. *Publ Wkly* 231:248 My 15 '87

Mirage airplanes *See* Airplanes, Military

Miralda, Antoni, 1942-

about

Mixed marriage. C. Peck. il *Art News* 86:15-16 Mr '87

Miramichi River region (N.B.)

Death on the Miramichi [heat wave endangers salmon] K. Harley. il *Macleans* 100:41 Ag 3 '87

Miranda, Roger

about

A defector's damaging tale. N. Cooper. il por *Newsweek* 110:49 D 21 '87

Fallout from a defector. H. Anderson. il por *Newsweek* 110:26 D 28 '87

'Little worm' or big fish? N. Cooper. por *Newsweek* 110:80 N 16 '87

Miranda's tempest. A. Cockburn. *Nation* 245:780-1 D 26 '87-Ja 2 '88

Tales of a Sandinista defector. J. Smolowe. il por *Time* 130:47 D 21 '87

Miranda (Satellite) *See* Uranus (Planet)—Satellites

Miranda decision *See* United States. Supreme Court—Decisions

Mirhoseini, Mahmood

about

Leapin' lizards! This doc zaps hearts. J. Langone. il por *Discover* 8:56-8+ Ag '87

Mirkin, Barry Alan

Early retirement as a labor force policy: an international overview. bibl f il *Mon Labor Rev* 110:19-33 Mr '87

Miró, Joan, 1893-1983

about

Art. A. C. Danto. *Nation* 244:863-6 Je 20 '87

Hemingway's Miró. S. Staggs. il *Art News* 86:12 D '87

Joan Miró. M. Feist. il *Art News* 86:179 O '87

The Krazy Kat of painters. J. Kroll. il *Newsweek* 109:70-1 My 25 '87

Miró: conjurer of earthy magic. B. Adams. il *Harpers Bazaar* 120:184-5+ My '87

Mirror Fusion Test Facility *See* Nuclear reactors

Mirror lenses *See* Lenses, Photographic

Mirror reactors *See* Nuclear reactors

Mirrors

See also

Automobiles—Mirrors

Lasers—Mirrors

Telescopes—Mirrors

Dew drops on a bathroom mirror. C. F. Bohren. il *Weatherwise* 40:102-6 Ap '87

Unique cheval mirror. W. Waltner and E. Waltner. il *Workbench* 43:18+ Ja/F '87

Photographs and photography

Into the looking glass [work of J. Hernandez-Claire] S. Piperato. il *Pop Photogr* 94:46-9 Mr '87

Mirsky, Jonathan

Broken China. *Foreign Policy* 66:57-76 Spr '87

Miscarriage

Childbearing: the dangers of high tech [AT&T policy regarding pregnant semiconductor workers] il *U S News World Rep* 102:12 Ja 26 '87

Clean-room controversy [study by Digital Equipment Corp. on toxic hazards that affect a worker's ability to have children] R. Wilson. il *Technol Rev* 90:10+ Ag/S '87

Danger in the clean room [semiconductor workers have increased risk of miscarriage at AT&T] il *Time* 129:48 Ja 26 '87

Moms-to-be banned from 'chip room' [AT&T policy] *Sci News* 131:73 Ja 31 '87

Psychological aspects

After miscarriage: healing the hurt. K. W. Wiley. il *Health* 19:80-5 My '87

It might have been: mourning the unborn. D. Cole. *Psychol Today* 21:64-5 Jl '87

Miscarriage: the baby who wasn't. P.-L. Moffitt. bibl il *Parents* 62:132-4+ Ap '87

Mourning a miscarriage. J. Rose. por *Newsweek* 110:7 Ag 3 '87

Religious aspects

A pastoral and theological response to losses in pregnancy. J. S. Peterman. *Christ Century* 104:750-3 S 9-16 '87

Miscarriage of justice *See* Justice, Miscarriage of

Miscegenation *See* Interracial marriage

Misconduct in office

See also

Politics, Corruption in

Miss Feasance of 1987. W. Safire. *N Y Times Mag* p6+ Mr 15 '87

Les misérables [musical] *See* Musicals, revues, etc.—Reviews—Single works

Misfeasance in office *See* Misconduct in office

Mishima, Osamu, and others

High-temperature cubic boron nitride P-N junction diode made at high pressure. bibl f il *Science* 238:181-3 O 9 '87

Mishkin, Mortimer, and Appenzeller, Tim

The anatomy of memory. bibl (p136) il *Sci Am* 256:80-9 Je '87

Mishra, Hemanta Raj, and Dinerstein, Eric

New ZIP codes for resident rhinos in Nepal. il *Smithsonian* 18:66-73 S '87

MISL (Major Indoor Soccer League) *See* Soccer, Professional

Misogyny

Blueprints for survival and change [views of S. Forward] A. Steacy. por *Macleans* 100:42 Je 22 '87

Counselor to the women men hate, Susan Forward is still looking for love. K. McMurran. il pors *People Wkly* 27:71-2+ Ap 27 '87

Smart women—and men—read this one [views of S. Forward] L. Shapiro. il por *Newsweek* 109:65 Je 1 '87

Misogyny in music

How rock gives love a bad name [hostility towards women in lyrics] J. Pareles. il *Mademoiselle* 93:92+ My '87

Misogyny and racism top the charts [views of Alix Dobkin] il *USA Today (Periodical)* 116:14-15 Ag '87

Misrepresentation *See* Fraud

Miss America Pageant

First black Miss Mississippi to compete for Miss America [T. Seawright] por *Jet* 72:14-15 Ag 3 '87

Simone Stephens is 1st black 'Miss California'. il por *Jet* 72:53 Jl 6 '87

Miss Mary [film] *See* Motion picture reviews—Single works

Miss Rheingold (Beauty contest)

Miss Rheingold. J. Della Femina. il *N Y* 20:74-5 D 21-28 '87

Miss Teenage America Pageant

Miss Teenage America 1988 [finalists] il *Teen* 31:90-1 D '87

Miss Teenage America '87. il *Teen* 31:60-7 F '87

On a winning streak [K. Johansen] il pors *Teen* 31:100-1 Ag '87

Sporting a winning look [winner K. Johansen] il pors *Teen* 31:68-9 F '87

Teen to teen. K. Johansen. See issues of 'Teen beginning March 1987 through December 1987

Miss USA Pageant

Beyond the valley of the beautiful dolls [R. Guy and R. Holt, beauty pageant experts] D. Heyn. il *Mademoiselle* 93:182+ N '87

Black first runner-up in 1987 Miss USA Pageant [C. Cabrera] il pors *Jet* 71:36 Mr 9 '87

The crowning touch of Richard Guy and Rex Holt shapes Texas teens into lovelies who just can't lose. L. Aitken. il pors *People Wkly* 27:53-4 My 4 '87

Missile bases *See* Guided missile bases

Missiles, Guided *See* Guided missiles

Missing and found art *See* Art—Missing and found works

Missing children

Lost innocents: the myth of missing children. P. Schneider. il *Harpers* 274:47-53 F '87

A new way to find missing children [drawings that simulate the way children would look today] J. Hope. il *Good Housekeep* 204:50+ Mr '87

Argentina

Finding the children [identifying missing children through genetic testing] B. Beckwith. il *Ms* 16:88 S '87

Fingerprints on file: the search for missing children. J. B. Elshtain. il *Commonweal* 114:229-30 Ap 24 '87

Canada

Terror in the forest [failure to find missing boy, A. Warburton, spurs efforts to teach wilderness survival] il *Macleans* 100:45 Ap 20 '87

Missing in action

See also

Vietnamese War, 1957-1975—Missing in action

World War, 1939-1945—Missing in action

Missing money *See* Lost money
Missing persons
> *See also*
> Fugitives from justice

The hacker who vanished [B. Landreth] G. Hackett. il por *Newsweek* 109:22 Ja 19 '87
The hitchhiker [disappearance of A. Billig: excerpt from The corpse had a familiar face] E. Buchanan. il por *Glamour* 85:140+ O '87
The husband who vanished [J. McDonnell] J. P. Blank. il pors *Read Dig* 130:131-5 Ja '87
The mission [film] *See* Motion picture reviews—Single works
Missionaries
> *See also*
> Black missionaries
> Missions
> Women missionaries

Protestantism's foreign legion. R. N. Ostling. il *Time* 129:62 F 16 '87
Protection
Missions held hostage. S. Mumper. il *Christ Today* 31:37+ S 18 '87
U.S. policy, not militia gunfire, drives missionary teacher Nancie Wingo out of Lebanon. M. Avrech. il pors *People Wkly* 27:32-4+ Mr 16 '87
Supply and demand
Does attrition threaten the future of missions? S. Mumper. *Christ Today* 31:53-5 N 6 '87
Missionaries of Charity
Mother Teresa's work of grace. C. Tower. il pors *Read Dig* 131:163-75+ D '87
Missionary conferences *See* Religious conferences
Missions
> *See also*
> Black missionaries
> Inter-Varsity Christian Fellowship
> Missionaries
> Salesians—Missions
> Women missionaries
> World Vision (Organization)
Conferences
See Religious conferences
Africa
Christian missions and the Western guilt complex [cover story] L. O. Sanneh. il *Christ Century* 104:330-4 Ap 8 '87
Brazil
The gospel and the gold rush [Tucano Indians caught between Salesian missionaries and gold mining interests] R. N. Ostling. il *Time* 129:64 Je 1 '87
California
See California—Missions
Developing countries
Christian missions and the Western guilt complex [cover story] L. O. Sanneh. il *Christ Century* 104:330-4 Ap 8 '87
Kenya
The plot that never was [questionable memo implicates American missionaries in plot to overthrow Kenyan government] M. Hornblower. il por *Time* 130:37 N 30 '87
Korea (South)
Nevius: starting on the right foot. S. H. Moffett. il *Christ Today* 31:34 N 20 '87
Lebanon
U.S. policy, not militia gunfire, drives missionary teacher Nancie Wingo out of Lebanon. M. Avrech. il pors *People Wkly* 27:32-4+ Mr 16 '87
Mozambique
Missionaries gain their freedom. il *Christ Today* 31:35 S 18 '87
Murder in Mozambique [attack on United Methodist mission station] *Christ Century* 104:850 O 7 '87
Nigeria
Learning from missionaries. P. Schineller. *America* 156:249-51 Mr 28 '87
Paraguay
Paraguay's mission towns. B. Wrenn. il *Travel Holiday* 168:8+ O '87
United States
Sun dances, corn pollen, & the cross [Native American Catholics] C. Vecsey. il *Commonweal* 114:345-51 Je 5 '87
Zimbabwe
Commune murders. *Christ Century* 104:1171 D 23-30 '87
Massacre in Matabeleland. *Macleans* 100:24 D 7 '87
A massacre's message: get out or die. il *Newsweek* 110:52 D 7 '87

Missions, Medical
Ethiopia
An angel from Tennessee [G. Williams brings medical aid to Ethiopia and 14 yr. old Tefera to the U.S. for heart surgery] J. L. McCoy. il pors *McCalls* 114:132-4 Je '87
Tanzania
A mission of service to leprosy sufferers [R. Lamburn's work in Tanzania] F. Nowikowski. *Christ Century* 104:782-3 S 23 '87
Mississippi
> *See also*
> Architecture, Domestic—Mississippi
> Bars and barrooms—Mississippi
> Bolivar County (Miss.)
> Child welfare—Mississippi
> Criminal justice, Administration of—Mississippi
> Environmental movement—Mississippi
> Marriage law—Mississippi
> Marshall County (Miss.)
> Wetlands—Mississippi
> Wildlife sanctuaries—Mississippi
> Yazoo River (Miss.)
Politics and government
> *See also*
> Politics, Corruption in—Mississippi

A man of the people [black congressman M. Espy] W. Rabb. il por *Black Enterp* 17:19 F '87
Mississippi rises again [Gov. R. Mabus] D. Winbush. il por *Time* 130:32 N 16 '87
Mississippi Queen (Steamboat)
Big wheel, big river. C. Males. il map *Travel Holiday* 168:50-5 Jl '87
Steamboat on the upper Mississippi. C. Davidson. il *Am Herit* 38:24+ Ap '87
Mississippi River
Big wheel, big river [Mississippi Queen excursion] C. Males. il map *Travel Holiday* 168:50-5 Jl '87
Steamboat on the upper Mississippi [Mississippi Queen] C. Davidson. il *Am Herit* 38:24+ Ap '87
Regulation
Atchafalaya [Army Corps of Engineers' Old River Control operation] J. A. McPhee. *New Yorker* 63:39-44+ F 23 '87
Mississippi River Valley
> *See also*
> Earthquakes—Mississippi River Valley
Exploring expeditions
1687 [murder of R. C. LaSalle] il *Am Herit* 38:108 F/Mr '87
Missouri
> *See also*
> Abortion clinics—Missouri
> Agriculture—Missouri
> Black River (Ark. and Mo.)
> Criminal justice, Administration of—Missouri
> Crowley's Ridge (Ark. and Mo.)
> Hunting—Missouri
> Ozark Mountains region
> Trails—Missouri
> Vegetable gardens and gardening—Missouri
> Wetlands—Missouri
Politics and government
A hero pilot's new flight plan [J. Testrake may run for state legislature] D. Gates. il por *Newsweek* 110:6 N 23 '87
Religious institutions and affairs
America's most generous diocese [Springfield-Cape Girardeau] M. F. Dorion. il *Fortune* 116:40 D 21 '87
Missouri River Trail *See* Trails—Missouri
Mistakes *See* Errors
Mistletoe
The mistletoe mystique. G. H. Harrison. il *Natl Wildl* 26:40-1 D '87/Ja '88
MIT *See* Massachusetts Institute of Technology
Mita, Katsushige
> *about*

The mountain priest. F. H. Katayama. il por *Fortune* 116:42 Ag 3 '87
Mitcham, Carl
Schools for whistle blowers. bibl il *Commonweal* 114:201-5 Ap 10 '87
Mitcham, Marylee
Contemplation exploded in my heart. il *Commonweal* 114:474-6 S 11 '87
Mitchell, Arthur
> *about*

D.T.H. *New Yorker* 63:35-6 D 28 '87

Mitchell, Barbara J.
When the wheels began to turn. il *Women's Sports Fitness* 9:14 Mr '87
Mitchell, Brett Webb- *See* Webb-Mitchell, Brett
Mitchell, Bruce M., and Williams, William G.
Education of the gifted and talented in the world community. *Phi Delta Kappan* 68:531-4 Mr '87
Mitchell, Charlene, 1950-, and Burdick, Thomas, 1950-
A teenager's tragedy: birth and death in a Florida town. il por *Ms* 16:60-3 D '87
Mitchell, Clarence, III
about
Mitchell sons indicted in a federal bribery case. *Jet* 72:14 Ap 20 '87
Mitchell, Constance
Hot careers in banking. il *Black Enterp* 17:62-4+ F '87
Mechanics & Farmers: branch banking at its best. il *Black Enterp* 17:196-8+ Je '87
Mitchell, D. L., and others
Evidence for chain molecules enriched in carbon, hydrogen, and oxygen in Comet Halley. bibl f il *Science* 237:626-8 Ag 7 '87
Mitchell, David T. *See* Mitchell, Tom
Mitchell, Elvis
What's wrong with this picture? il *Roll Stone* p31-2 D 3 '87
Mitchell, George J.
Clean Air: Congress must get tough. il por *Natl Parks* 61:12-13 Jl/Ag '87
Mitchell, Greg, 1947-
Baseball at ground zero. il *Progressive* 51:20-1 Ag '87
Mitchell, Henry, 1923-
Rare species. il por *House Gard* 159:56+ O '87
Summer bounty. il *House Gard* 159:46+ Ag '87
Mitchell, Jack
Age bias: the uphill battle. *50 Plus* 27:32+ Mr '87
Mitchell, Jan
about
Jan Mitchell—the varied tastes of a New York connoisseur. C. Ratcliff. il por *Archit Dig* 44:298+ N '87
Mitchell, Joseph, 1908-
about
Joseph Mitchell's secret. B. Ivry. il por *N Y* 20:20 F 9 '87
Mitchell, Joseph N., 1922-
about
A drum, a drum, Renouf doth come. H. Rudnitsky. il *Forbes* 139:146+ My 18 '87
Mitchell, Joyce Slayton, 1933-
The back-to-work handbook [excerpt from Making more money] il *50 Plus* 27:36+ Jl '87
Mitchell, Ken
about
Melody farm [drama] Reviews
Macleans 100:55 F 23 '87. R. Marken
Mitchell, Leona
about
Dramatic leanings. G. Schmidgall. por *Opera News* 51:21-2 Ja 31 '87
Mitchell, Michael
about
Mitchell sons indicted in a federal bribery case. *Jet* 72:14 Ap 20 '87
Mitchell, Norman *See* Lobsenz, Norman M., 1919-
Mitchell, Parren J.
about
Mitchell rigs 'hot line' for black firm contracts. *Jet* 73:38 O 12 '87
Mitchell, Peter Todd
Gourmet holidays: Barcelona. il *Gourmet* 48:48-53+ Je '87
Gourmet holidays: La Rioja. il map *Gourmet* 47:74-9+ N '87
Gourmet holidays: the coast of Languedoc. il map *Gourmet* 47:60-5+ O '87
Mitchell, Peter W.
How to buy a tuner. il *Stereo Rev* 52:93-7 N '87
The perfect match. il *High Fidel* 37:44-6 F '87
Mitchell, Susan, 1944-
Women in profile: bas-relief, left section missing [poem] *New Yorker* 63:38 Ap 20 '87
Mitchell, Tom
about
How Tom Mitchell lays out the competition. B. O'Reilly. il pors *Fortune* 115:90-3+ Mr 30 '87
Mitchell, W. O. (William Ormond), 1914-
about
Royalty is royalty [drama] Reviews
Macleans 100:70 O 19 '87. J. Bemrose

Mitchell, William F.
about
Destination: lunar industrial base. W. H. Ganoe. il *Space World* X-9-285:39 S '87
Mitchell, William Ormond *See* Mitchell, W. O. (William Ormond), 1914-
Mitchell & Ness Sporting Goods
Baseball flannels are hot [reproductions of classic jerseys] D. Butwin. il por *Sports Illus* 67:105 Jl 6 '87
Mitchell-Smith, Ilan
about
Ilan Mitchell-Smith. por *Teen* 31:44 Ja '87
Miter boxes, gages, etc.
Help for making miters [mitermate] il *Workbench* 43:91 Mr/Ap '87
Making a miterbox. R. Capotosto. il *Pop Mech* 164:33 Jl '87
Miter saws *See* Saws and sawing
Mites
Control
Induced resistance and interspecific competition between spider mites and a vascular wilt fungus [verticillium wilt] R. Karban and others. bibl f il *Science* 235:678-80 F 6 '87
Minimize your mite problem [spider mites] M. D. Eskilson. il *Rodale's Org Gard* 34:77-80+ Je '87
Mite and fungus: foe and friend? [spider mites and verticillium wilt; research by Richard Karban and others] D. D. Edwards. *Sci News* 131:101 F 14 '87
Mitford, Jessica, 1917-
Grace Darling—the lighthouse heroine. il por *Archit Dig* 44:30+ S '87
Mitgang, Herbert
Policing America's writers. *New Yorker* 63:47-8+ O 5 '87
about
Two writers probe FBI surveillance of American authors. W. Goldstein. *Publ Wkly* 232:38 O 30 '87
Mithers, Carol Lynn
Considering the way most of us learned about sex, it's a wonder we can do it, do it well or have any interest in doing it at all. il *Glamour* 85:44+ Mr '87
"My husband is so bossy". il *Ladies Home J* 104:14+ Mr '87
Sexual ethics. See issues of Glamour beginning April 1987
MITI *See* Japan. Ministry of International Trade and Industry
Mitigation, Environmental *See* Environmental mitigation
Mitnick, Barbara J.
J.L.G. Ferris. il por *Am Hist Illus* 21:14-21 F '87
Mitochondria
Bacterial bedfellows [symbiotic theory of evolution] D. Sagan and L. Margulis. il *Nat Hist* 96:26+ Mr '87
Mitochondrial DNA *See* DNA
Mitochondrial RNA *See* RNA
Mitogens
Activation of the HIV-1 LTR by T cell mitogens and the trans-activator protein of HTLV-I. M. Siekevitz and others. bibl f il *Science* 238:1575-8 D 11 '87
Mitogens and oncogenes can block the induction of specific voltage-gated ion channels. J. M. Caffrey and others. bibl f il *Science* 236:570-3 My 1 '87
Mitomycin
Isolation and structure of a covalent cross-link adduct between mitomycin C and DNA. M. Tomasz and others. bibl f il *Science* 235:1204-8 Mr 6 '87
Mitral valve prolapse *See* Heart—Diseases
Mitsubishi (Automobile) *See* Automobiles, Foreign; Sports cars
Mitsubishi Heavy Industries, Ltd.
The romantic of heavy industry [Y. Iida] F. H. Katayama. il por *Fortune* 116:54 Ag 3 '87
Swords to plowshares . . . and back to swords. A. Tanzer. il *Forbes* 139:32-3 Ja 26 '87
Mitsubishi Motors Corp.
Castle under siege. A. Tanzer. il *Forbes* 139:104-5 F 9 '87
Mitsui & Co., Ltd
End-run strategy. il *U S News World Rep* 103:42-3 Ag 24 '87
Mitteldorf, Arthur J., and Weis, Judith S.
No safe harbor for marine life. il *Sierra* 72:27+ S/O '87
Mitteleuropa *See* Central Europe
Mittelstaedt, Martin
The gentrification of Harlem. *World Press Rev* 34:44 Ap '87

Mittens *See* Gloves
Mittermeier, Russell
Rescuing Brazil's muriqui: monkey in peril. il map *Natl Geogr* 171:386-95 Mr '87
Mitterrand, François, 1916-
about
The future of cohabitation in France. J. Valls-Russell. il *New Leader* 70:3-4 Mr 9 '87
Giving French lessons in *le scandale*. R. Z. Chesnoff. il pors *U S News World Rep* 103:56 N 16 '87
The perils of power sharing [with interview] W. R. Doerner. il pors *Time* 129:43-4 Ap 6 '87
The president of France speaks out [interview] M. S. Forbes. il pors *Forbes* 140:22-3+ D 28 '87
Visit to Canada, 1987
The French president's triumphal tour. M. Rose. il por *Macleans* 100:14-15 Je 8 '87
Mix, Miguel Rojas- *See* Rojas-Mix, Miguel
Mix, Ron
So little gain for the pain. il *Sports Illus* 67:54-6+ O 19 '87
Mixed drinks *See* Cocktails
Mixed marriage *See* Interfaith marriage
Mixes, Beverage *See* Beverage mixes
Mixes, Food *See* Food mixes
Miyamoto, Michael M., and others
Phylogenetic relations of humans and African apes from DNA sequences in the ψη-globin region. bibl f il *Science* 238:369-73 O 16 '87
Miyazawa, Kiichi, 1919-
about
Japan's problems with exports [interview] B. Blohm. *World Press Rev* 34:51 Ja '87
Mize, Larry
about
Mr. Chip. D. Granger. il por *Sport Mag* 78:10 D '87
My, oh Mize. S. Ballard. il pors *Sports Illus* 66:36-43 Ap 20 '87
Mizejewski, Linda
The erotic stripped bare. il *Harpers* 274:57-62 Mr '87
MLA *See* Modern Language Association of America
MMDS *See* Multichannel multipoint distribution service
MMPI *See* Minnesota Multiphasic Personality Inventory
MMT (Multiple mirror telescopes) *See* Telescopes—Mirrors
Mob (Criminals) *See* Mafia; Organized crime
Moberg, Peggy Dye
Working for a living. *Essence* 17:100+ Mr '87
Mobil Corporation
Give it to the stockholders? [Mobil may spinoff Montgomery Ward] C. Siler. il *Forbes* 140:55-6 S 7 '87
Mobil may be the slickest oil play. G. G. Marcial. *Bus Week* p61 Jl 27 '87
Oil king from Queens [A. Murray] D. Kirkpatrick. il por *Fortune* 116:30 Ag 3 '87
Triple reverse [appeals court reverses decision in W. Tavoulareas' libel suit against the Washington post] por *Time* 129:70 Mr 23 '87
Mobile (Ala.)
Architecture
A House for Spring Hill. L. Hallam. il *South Living* 22:150-2+ Mr '87
Cemeteries
The gift of Magnolia Cemetery. C. Powell. il *South Living* 22:155 Ap '87
Race relations
Black lawyer forces KKK to pay $7 million for lynching black, 19 [M. Figures work on the M. Donald case] T. S. Moore. il pors *Jet* 71:6-8 Mr 9 '87
Going after the Klan [verdict in case brought by lynching victim M. Donald's family] A. Press. il *Newsweek* 109:29 F 23 '87
Mother of slain black son takes possession of KKK building won in lawsuit [mother of M. Donald] il por *Jet* 72:8 Je 8 '87
Seeking justice for her lynched son, an Alabama mother ruins the Klan that killed him [B. M. Donald] J. S. Kunen. il pors *People Wkly* 27:55-6+ Je 8 '87
The woman who beat the Klan [B. M. Donald fights for justice for her lynched son] J. Kornbluth. il pors *N Y Times Mag* p26-32+ N 1 '87
Mobile health facilities
Help needed [Mammobile] C. SerVaas. il *Saturday Evening Post* 259:98+ Mr '87
Prostate manograms on the MaleMobile. C. SerVaas. il *Saturday Evening Post* 259:106+ Ja/F '87
What the AIDS MOBILE has taught us [free tests offered] C. SerVaas. il *Saturday Evening Post* 259:54-5+ O '87
Mobile home parks
Some like it hot! [retirees in Hemet, Calif.] S. Angel. il *50 Plus* 27:54-8 Je '87

Mobile satellite system *See* Communications satellites—Radiotelephone use
Mobile senior centers
Nassau County puts services on the road [Seniormobile] il *Aging* no355:32-3 '87
Mobile telephones *See* Cellular radio; Radiotelephone
Mobilehome parks *See* Mobile home parks
Mobility, Residential *See* Migration, Internal
Mobley, Cole
Light show. il pors *Opera News* 51:14-16+ Mr 14 '87
What it's all about. il *Opera News* 52:32-5 Jl '87
Mobley, Hank, 1930-1986
about
Down Mobley's way. L. Kart. il por *Down Beat* 54:61 F '87
Mobutu Sese Seko, 1930-
Visit of Zaire's president [remarks, December 9, 1986] il por *Dep State Bull* 87:15 Ap '87
Visit to the United States, 1986
Visit of Zaire's president [remarks, December 9, 1986] R. Reagan; Mobutu Sese Seko. il por *Dep State Bull* 87:15 Ap '87
MOCA *See* Museum of Contemporary Art (Los Angeles, Calif.)
Mocatta Group
Keith Smith, gold's raging bull. R. A. Melcher. il por *Bus Week* p70-1 Je 22 '87
Moccasin flower *See* Lady's slipper
Mock jury
Focus groups for lawyers. G. Bronson. il *Forbes* 140:148 S 21 '87
Mockingbirds
Sexual behavior
See Sexual behavior—Birds
Mod Squad (Firm)
The high Chaparral. R. L. Collins. il *Flying* 114:40-5 Je '87
Model cars *See* Automobile models
Model houses
Building on innovations [Concept IV House] M. Morris. il *Home Mech* 83:12-14 Ja '87
A House for Spring Hill [deep South architecture] L. Hallam. il *South Living* 22:150-2+ Mr '87
Idea house '87 [joint Home mechanix/American Wood Council venture] H. Wicks. il *Home Mech* 83:40-3+ F '87
Modeling
See also
Dough craft
Soap sculpture
Modeling agencies
See also
Dimensions (Firm)
PaVage Fitness Images (Firm)
Models
See also
Airplane models
Astronomical models
Automobile models
Biological models
Circus, Miniature
Dioramas
Ecological models
House models
Mechanical models
Meteorological models
Miniature objects
Molecular models
Paleontological models and exhibits
Pistol models
Railroad models
Ship and boat models
Space vehicle models
Theater models
Models (Display figures)
See also
Dress forms
Models (Persons)
See also
Alt, Carol
Ayler, Ethel
Blair, Billie
Hanson, Marla
Hardison, Bethann
Johnson, Beverly
Mounia
Nicholson, Ivy
Nygren, Carrie
O'Neill, Gail
Petty, Ramona
Phillips, Laura

Models (Persons)—See also—*cont.*
  Phillips, Linda Morand
  Porizkova, Paulina
  Richardson, Ashley
  Sadiya
  Schnarre, Monika
  Smith, Mandy
  Stephanie, Princess of Monaco
  Towles, Dorothea
  Turlington, Christy
  Tyler, Kathie
  Valentine, Laura
Beauty and the beat [rock stars who marry models]
  J. Pareles. il *Mademoiselle* 93:60+ Je '87
Beauty exposé: Teen models tell all. il *Teen* 31:70-2
  Mr '87
Beauty sells. G. Bernstein. il *Petersens Photogr Mag*
  15:12 Mr '87
From 'Teen to the screen [models become actresses]
  il *Teen* 31:50 Ap '87
Linda Gray interview [discussion of photography
  modeling; cover story] D. Brooks. il pors *Petersens
  Photogr Mag* 16:49-50+ N '87
On top! [black fashion models; special section; with
  editorial comment by Susan L. Taylor] il *Essence*
  17:37-45+ Ja '87
The super models [cover story; special section] il pors
  Macleans 100:36-42+ Ap 13 '87
When a beauty needs a boost . . . 28 tips from four
  top models. il *Mademoiselle* 93:18 D '87
Whose breasts are they, anyway? [models and breast
  implants] J. Kaufman. il *Mademoiselle* 93:70 Ag '87
Competitions
Fall's winning looks [McCall's competition winners] il
  McCalls 114:27-33 S '87
Great Model Search 1987: meet the finalists. il *Teen*
  31:30-1 Jl '87
Great Model Search '87 [special section] il pors *Teen*
  31:82-91 O '87
Seventeen's 1987 Cover Model Contest finalists. il
  Seventeen 46:66+ O '87
Models of cities, towns, etc.
Exhibitions
New York City gets small [model on exhibit at the
  Queens Museum] B. Barol. il *Newsweek* 109:54 Je
  29 '87
Modems
A fast CRC [XMODEM cyclic redundancy check al-
  gorithm] J. LeVan. bibl il *Byte* 12:339-41 N '87
Modem in the side pocket [Pocket Modem MM-1200]
  J. Bell. il *Pers Comput* 11:198 My '87
Modem madness: telecommunications at a crossroads.
  S. Shulman. il *Technol Rev* 90:8 Jl '87
Modems operandi. R. Lockwood. il *Pers Comput* 11:25
  Jl '87
Okidata moves into modems [Okitel 2400B] R. Lock-
  wood. *Pers Comput* 11:278 D '87
Smartmodems get smarter [V-series Smartmodems] R.
  Lockwood. il *Pers Comput* 11:258+ N '87
The smooth Zoom/Modem. J. Bell. il *Pers Comput* 11:154
  Mr '87
Traveling modems [Pocket Modem and Worldport 1200]
  P. White. il *Byte* 12:180-3 N '87
Working together via modem. R. Lockwood. *Pers Comput*
  11:42 D '87
Speed
High-speed internal modems. S. Satchell. bibl il *Byte*
  12:209-15 My '87
High-speed modems. R. Lockwood. il *Pers Comput*
  11:233+ D '87
Modern architecture *See* Architecture, Modern
Modern art *See* Art, Modern
Modern civilization *See* Civilization
Modern dance *See* Dance
Modern furniture *See* Furniture
Modern Language Association of America
  MIA at the MLA. J. Atlas. *New Repub* 196:12-13 Ja
  26 '87
Modernism (Aesthetics)
The idea of tradition in American art criticism [R.
  Cortissoz and C. Greenberg] H. Kramer. *Am Sch*
  56:319-27 Summ '87
Modernism (Art) *See* Art, Modern
Modernism (Literature)
The muse, postmodern and homeless. C. Ozick. il *N
  Y Times Book Rev* 92:9 Ja 18 '87
Modernization *See* Social change
Modes, Musical *See* Musical intervals and scales
Modesty
Lessons in modesty [for children] L. G. Katz. il *Parents*
  62:198 Ap '87

Modified airplanes *See* Airplanes, Remodeled
Modula-2 (Computer language)
Crafting reusable software in Modula-2. H. Oktaba and
  R. Berber. bibl *Byte* 12:123-4+ S '87
Three Modula-2 programming systems. P. A. Sand. il
  Byte 12:333-6 Ja '87
Modular construction
  See also
  Cardinal Industries
  Houses, Prefabricated
  Prisons, Prefabricated
Modulation (Electronics)
  See also
  Pulse code modulation
  Radio frequency modulation
Modulators
  See also
  Modems
Moenjodaro site (Pakistan) *See* Mohenjo-Daro site
  (Pakistan)
Moerschel, James H.
  Autumn leaves. il *Conservationist* 42:32-5 S/O '87
Moët Hennessy
  Moet and Vuitton: the dernier cri in chic [merger] F.
  J. Comes. *Bus Week* p49 Je 15 '87
Moffatt, BettyClare
                          about
  The need to self-publish AIDS books. L. See. *Publ Wkly*
  232:56 Ag 28 '87
Moffett, Luisa
  Béjart's bye-bye to Brussels. por *Dance Mag* 61:62 S
  '87
  Kylián changes keys. il por *Dance Mag* 61:46-50 My
  '87
Moffitt, John, 1908-1987
  The pattern [poem] *America* 156:323 Ap 18 '87
                          about
  Obituary
  America 157:52 Ag 1-8 '87
Moffitt, Perry-Lynn
  Miscarriage: the baby who wasn't. bibl il *Parents*
  62:132-4+ Ap '87
Moffitt, Phillip
  Esquire magazine. *Writer* 100:28 F '87
Mofungo (Musical group)
  Mofungo. J. Macnie. il *Down Beat* 54:14 Ag '87
Mogador (Morocco) *See* Essaouira (Morocco)
Mogil, H. Michael
  Geology from 37,000 feet. il *Earth Sci* 40:20-2 Wint
  '87
Mogul Empire
  The East India Company and the Emperor Aurangzeb.
  B. Lenman. bibl il map *Hist Today* 37:23-9 F '87
Mohaber, Nick
  Exemplary antique and decorative Persian rugs [cover
  story] il *Antiques Collect Hobbies* 92:28-31 Ap '87
Mohammed Ag Albakaye *See* Albakaye, Mohammed Ag
Mohammed Zahir Shah, King of Afghanistan, 1914-
                          about
  The once and future king? F. Willey. por *Newsweek*
  109:39 Je 1 '87
Mohammedanism *See* Islam
Mohan, C. Raja
  The media's new spies in the sky. il *World Press Rev*
  34:55-6 Je '87
Mohenjo-Daro site (Pakistan)
  Fighting the flood at Mohenjodaro. A. Bingham. il *Hist
  Today* 37:4-5 Mr '87
Mohlenbrock, Robert H., 1931-
  Alum Cove, Arkansas. il map *Nat Hist* 96:60-2 Ap
  '87
  Blackie's Hollow, Virginia. il map *Nat Hist* 96:70-2 Jl
  '87
  Crowley's Ridge, Arkansas. il map *Nat Hist* 96:84-6
  N '87
  Devils Hopyard, New Hampshire. il map *Nat Hist*
  96:38-40+ O '87
  Dolly Sods, West Virginia. il maps *Nat Hist* 96:76-9
  Ja '87
  El Yunque Rain Forest, Puerto Rico. il map *Nat Hist*
  96:76-9 F '87
  Elfin Forest, Puerto Rico. il map *Nat Hist* 96:20-2 D
  '87
  Garden of the Gods, Illinois. il map *Nat Hist* 96:66-8
  Je '87
  Grand Mesa, Colorado. il map *Nat Hist* 96:14-16 My
  '87
  Little Wambaw Swamp, South Carolina. il map *Nat
  Hist* 96:68-70 Ag '87
  Mount Graham, Arizona. il map *Nat Hist* 96:88-90 Mr
  '87

Mohlenbrock, Robert H., 1931-—*cont.*
Sycamore Canyon, Arizona. il map *Nat Hist* 96:16-18 S '87
Mohler, Chaco
Cat tracks. il *Skiing* 39:52-9 F '87
Up, up, and away! il *Skiing* 39:70-3 F '87
Mohler, Mary
News for parents. See occasional issues of Ladies' Home Journal beginning September 1984 through August 1987
Parents' journal. See issues of Ladies' Home Journal beginning September 1987
Moholy, Noel Francis
about
So you want to be a saint. L. Gomez and W. Wynn. il pors *Life* 10:68-9+ S '87
Mohonk Mountain House
Mohonk Mountain House. G. McTigue. il *Travel Holiday* 168:12-13 D '87
Mohs, Mayo
Where has all the fragrance gone? il *Discover* 8:90-1+ Je '87
Moi, Daniel Arap
Visit of Kenyan president [remarks, March 12, 1987] il por *Dep State Bull* 87:28 Je '87
about
Kenya: the dissolution of democracy. M. Maren. bibl f *Curr Hist* 86:209-12+ My '87
Moi? Yes, Moi. *World Press Rev* 34:41 My '87
Visit to the United States, 1987
Visit of Kenyan president [remarks, March 12, 1987] R. Reagan; D. A. Moi. il por *Dep State Bull* 87:28 Je '87
Moisture
Trouble in the underworld [excess moisture can cause rot] R. McCarthy. il *Ctry J* 14:18-21 S '87
Moisture meters
A new relative humidity sensor [work of Peter H. Huang] *Sci News* 132:236 O 10 '87
Moisturizers *See* Cosmetics
Mojave Airport *See* Airports—California
Moktarian, Mark
The 10 most asked tax reform questions. il *Nations Bus* 75:28-9+ Ag '87
Molasses
Molasses day. R. Mashburn. il *Ctry J* 14:57-61 O '87
Mold toxins *See* Toxins and antitoxins
Moldea, Dan E., 1950-
about
Penguin rushes paperback of book on Reagan. *Publ Wkly* 231:74 Ap 10 '87
Moldex/Metric, Inc.
His cups runneth over [president M. Magidson] M. Beauchamp. il por *Forbes* 139:105 Ap 20 '87
Moldings (Architecture)
Get dramatic detail with molded millwork system. S. Ross. il *Fam Handyman* 37:28-9 Ap '87
Molds (Botany)
See also
Mildew
Slime molds
What's the diagnosis? [sooty mold] W. S. Moore. il *Flower Gard* 31:26 O/N '87
Mole National Park (Ghana) *See* National parks and reserves—Ghana
Molecular beams
Molecular beam studies of elementary chemical processes [adaptation of Nobel Prize address, December 8, 1986] Y. T. Lee. bibl f il *Science* 236:793-8 My 15 '87
Molecular biology
See also
Computers—Biological use
European Molecular Biology Laboratory
Africa: cradle of modern humans. R. Lewin. *Science* 237:1292-5 S 11 '87
Biochemistry of information storage in the nervous system. I. B. Black and others. bibl f il *Science* 236:1263-8 Je 5 '87
The molecular biology of aging. J. P. Cohn. il *BioScience* 37:99-102 F '87
Molecular clouds *See* Matter, Interstellar
Molecular data storage *See* Optical storage devices
Molecular dynamics
Crystallographic R factor refinement by molecular dynamics. A. T. Brünger and others. bibl f il *Science* 235:458-60 Ja 23 '87
Molecular dynamics of a cytochrome c-cytochrome b₅ electron transfer complex. J. J. Wendoloski and others. bibl f il *Science* 238:794-7 N 6 '87
Molecular dynamics simulations of proteins. M. Karplus. bibl f il *Phys Today* 40:68-72 O '87

Multiple conformational states of proteins: a molecular dynamics analysis of myoglobin. R. Elber and M. Karplus. bibl f il *Science* 235:318-21 Ja 16 '87
Molecular genetics
The ancestry of the giant panda [cover story] S. J. O'Brien. il map *Sci Am* 257:102-7 N '87
Everyone's genealogical mother [study of mtDNA indicates "Eve" lived in sub-Saharan Africa; research by Allan Wilson and others] M. D. Lemonick. il *Time* 129:66 Ja 26 '87
Molecular genetics: applications to the clinical neurosciences [linkage analysis with restriction fragment length polymorphisms] J. B. Martin. bibl f il *Science* 238:765-72 N 6 '87
The molecular genetics of cancer. J. M. Bishop. bibl f il *Science* 235:305-11 Ja 16 '87
Molecular mechanisms of photosynthesis [study of rhodo-pseudomonas; cover story] D. C. Youvan and B. L. Marrs. bibl (p136) il *Sci Am* 256:42-8 Je '87
My close cousin the chimpanzee. R. Lewin. il *Science* 238:273-5 O 16 '87
Phylogenetic relations of humans and African apes from DNA sequences in the ψη-globin region. M. M. Miyamoto and others. bibl f il *Science* 238:369-73 O 16 '87
Regulation of inducible and tissue-specific gene expression. T. Maniatis and others. bibl f il *Science* 236:1237-45 Je 5 '87
Tics in the tocks of molecular clocks. I. Amato. il *Sci News* 131:74-5 Ja 31 '87
The unmasking of mitochondrial Eve. R. Lewin. il *Science* 238:24-6 O 2 '87
Molecular models
Computer-aided molecular design. J. A. McCammon. bibl f il *Science* 238:486-91 O 23 '87
Model studies in molecular recognition [cover story] J. Rebek, Jr. il *Science* 235:1478-84 Mr 20 '87
Molecular rotation
See also
Isomers and isomerism
Rotation and solvation of ammonium ion. C. L. Perrin and R. K. Gipe. bibl f il *Science* 238:1393-4 D 4 '87
Molecular spin
Going for a molecular spin [electron stimulated desorption ion angular distribution method of probing structure and bonding at surfaces] S. Weisburd. il *Sci News* 132:199 S 26 '87
Molecular synthesis *See* Synthesis
Molecules
See also
Polymers and polymerization
A periodic table for molecules [work of Ray Hefferlin] D. E. Thomsen. *Sci News* 131:87 F 7 '87
Models
See Molecular models
Molecules, Interstellar *See* Matter, Interstellar
Moles (Animals)
Control
Anecdotes, facetiae, satire, etc.
A farewell to arms. R. B. Elsberry. il *N Y Times Mag* p54 S 27 '87
Moles (Dermatology)
Birthmarks and moles: what they are, what you can do about them. L. Rosch. *Glamour* 85:30 N '87
Molesting, Child *See* Child molesting
Molex Incorporated
Molex: far-flung but close-knit. K. Dreyfack. il *Bus Week* p62-3 Ap 13 '87
Molière, 1622-1673
about
Tartuffe [drama] Reviews
Nation 244:586 My 2 '87. T. M. Disch
Molina, Mario J., and others
Antarctic stratospheric chemistry of chlorine nitrate, hydrogen chloride, and ice: release of active chlorine. bibl f il *Science* 238:1253-7 N 27 '87
Molinari, Guy V.
How safe is the air traffic control system? [cover story] il *USA Today (Periodical)* 116:12-14 N '87
Molitor, Paul
about
The hit parade. il *Sports Illus* 67:13 Ag 31 '87
More than halfway there. M. Bishop. il pors *Sports Illus* 67:26-7 Ag 24 '87
Mollison, Bill
about
Farming with a future: the passing of the plow [interview] P. Stone. bibl il pors *Mother Earth News* 104:110-14+ Mr/Ap '87

Mollusks
See also
  Clams
  Growth—Mollusks
  Mussels
  Nautilus
  Nervous system—Mollusks
  Octopuses
  Sea slugs
  Shells (Conchology)
  Slugs
  Snails
  Squid
  Thyca
Food and feeding
Herbivory in rocks and the weathering of a desert [impact of lichen feeding by snails] M. Shachak and others. bibl f il *Science* 236:1098-9 My 29 '87
Snails dine at desert dust depot [research by Clive G. Jones and others] K. Hartley. il *Sci News* 131:373 Je 13 '87
Muscle
See Muscle
Mollusks, Fossil
Heritability at the species level: analysis of geographic ranges of Cretaceous mollusks. D. Jablonski. bibl f il *Science* 238:360-3 O 16 '87
Molnar, Peter Hale, and others
Geologic evolution of northern Tibet: results of an expedition to Ulugh Muztagh. bibl f il maps *Science* 235:299-305 Ja 16 '87
Molnar, Thomas
Camouflaged power. *Natl Rev* 39:39+ My 8 '87
Exporting the drug war. *Natl Rev* 39:38 My 22 '87
Moloise, Benjamin
about
Execution of ANC member deplored and condemned. por *UN Chron* 22:14 N/D '85
Molokai (Hawaii)
Description and travel
Sheer beauty. R. W. Bone. il *Travel Holiday* 167:13-17 Mr '87
Molony, Brian
about
Taxing a gambler's loss. D. Jenish. il por *Macleans* 100:34+ D 14 '87
Moltmann, Jürgen
about
Christianity today talks to Jürgen Moltmann [interview] A. J. Conyers. por *Christ Today* 31:67 Mr 20 '87
Molton, Warren Lane
He descended into Hell [poem] *Christ Century* 104:351 Ap 15 '87
Maundy Thursday [poem] *Christ Century* 104:264 Mr 18-25 '87
Waking in winter [poem] *Christ Century* 104:236 Mr 11 '87
Molybdenum
Edge surfaces in lithographically textured molybdenum disulfide. C. B. Roxlo and others. bibl f il *Science* 235:1629-31 Mr 27 '87
Molyneux, Juan Pablo
about
A civilized intuition. D. Harris. il por *Archit Dig* 44:148-55 N '87
MOMA See Museum of Modern Art (New York, N.Y.)
Momatiuk, Yva, and Eastcott, John
Slovakia's spirit of survival. il map *Natl Geogr* 171:120-46 Ja '87
Momix (Dance company)
World of wonders [performances at the 92nd Street Y, New York City] T. Tobias. il *N Y* 20:70 Ja 26 '87
Mon Petit (Cordele, Ga.: Restaurant) See Cordele (Ga.)—Restaurants, nightclubs, bars, etc.
Mona Island (Puerto Rico)
See also
  Wildlife conservation—Mona Island (Puerto Rico)
Monacella, Suzana
about
Blame it on Rio. il pors *Vogue* 177:252 D '87
Monaco
See also
  Automobile racing—Monaco
Description and travel
Letter from Monaco. W. Murray. *New Yorker* 63:96-108 O 5 '87
Royal family
See also
  Grace, Princess of Monaco, 1929-1982

Pierre, Prince of Monaco, 1987-
Stephanie, Princess of Monaco
Taking Grace's place [cover story] M. Green. il *People Wkly* 28:84-9 S 28 '87
Monaco Grand Prix See Automobile racing—Monaco
Monaghan, Robert
Building fun telescopes for less than $10. il *Astronomy* 15:46-9 My '87
Monaghan, Thomas
about
Dawn and Tom. *New Yorker* 63:37-8 N 23 '87
Monahan, Terry
Get turned on. *Women's Sports Fitness* 9:28-9 O '87
The training effect: enough is just right. il *Work Woman* 12:117-18+ Je '87
Monarch butterflies See Butterflies
Monarch Capital Corp.
Monarch buys its own insurance policy [acquisition of BankAmerica's investment management subsidiaries] K. H. Hammonds. il *Bus Week* p93+ S 7 '87
Monasteries
Canada
Lives of heart and soul [Benedictine Priory in Montreal] G. Ferzoco. il *Macleans* 100:42 S 14 '87
The monks of St. Peters [Benedictine abbey in Muenster, Sask.] il *Macleans* 100:6+ Je 29 '87
Finland
Finland's New Valamo: orthodoxy meets culture. A. Ugolnik. il *Christ Century* 104:1176-8 D 23-30 '87
France
See also
  Communauté de Taizé
Italy
See also
  Monte Cassino (Monastery: Cassino, Italy)
Yugoslavia
Yugoslavia's monastery route. C.-L. Parison. il *World Press Rev* 34:62 S '87
Monasticism
See also
  Benedictines
  Communauté de Taizé
Moncton (N.B.)
Education
One teacher's prejudice [J. Israeli urges New Brunswick to take action against anti-Semitic school teacher M. Ross] K. Harley. il pors *Macleans* 100:17 Ap 27 '87
Mondadori Viaggi SpA
1986 earnings show Mondadori and Hachette top their home markets. H. R. Lottman. *Publ Wkly* 232:312 Ag 7 '87
Mondale, Eleanor
about
Smart on-the-go getters. il pors *Harpers Bazaar* 120:290-7 Mr '87
Mondale, Walter F., 1928-
about
'Vindicated'—not gloating. D. Gates. il por *Newsweek* 110:6 N 23 '87
Mondavi, Robert
about
The Mondavi method. N. Hazelton. *Natl Rev* 39:60+ N 6 '87
Mondavi (Robert) Winery See Robert Mondavi Winery
Monday
Monday-morning jump starts: how to hit the ground running. S. Mernit. il *Work Woman* 12:59 F '87
Anecdotes, facetiae, satire, etc.
Christmas does not fall on Monday this year—hallelujah! K. Fury. il *Work Woman* 12:136 D '87
Monday sportsnite [television program] See Television program reviews—Single works
Mondeschein, Brian
To vault over the moon [story] il *Women's Sports Fitness* 9:48-50+ Ap '87
Monetary policy (U.S.) See Federal Reserve System (U.S.)
Money
See also
  Bank notes
  Capital
  Coins
  Credit
  Deflation (Finance)
  Finance
  Gold as money
  Inflation (Finance)
  Interest (Economics)
  Laundering of money
  Liquidity (Economics)
  Lost money
  Paper money

Money—See also—*cont.*
    Silver as money
    Tokens
    United States. Dept. of the Treasury
    Wealth

'Another 15 to 20 percent' drop [dollar's future; interview with M. S. Feldstein] por *U S News World Rep* 102:43 Mr 9 '87

Betting against the greenback. E. A. Finn, Jr. il *Forbes* 140:33-4 D 14 '87

Betting on the buck. M. Schiffres. il *Changing Times* 41:48-50 S '87

Beware the deadly endive [decline of dollar and trade deficits] L. H. Lapham. *Harpers* 274:8-10 Ap '87

The buck stops where? *New Repub* 196:6-8 F 16 '87

Budget gridlock. B. Powell. il *Newsweek* 110:53+ N 16 '87

Calm before a storm? [markets battered by weakening dollar] W. Glasgall. il *Bus Week* p30-2 D 14 '87

Currencies in free fall [plunging dollar] A. Walmsley. il *Macleans* 100:46-7 Ap 27 '87

Dangerous drift. M. S. Forbes, Jr. il *Forbes* 139:25 My 4 '87

Debt and the dollar: the markets are making all the rules [meetings of the World Bank and International Monetary Fund] W. Glasgall and M. McNamee. il *Bus Week* p57 O 12 '87

A declining dollar is just one piece in the puzzle. A. M. Solomon. il *Bus Week* p20 Ap 13 '87

The declining dollar: not a simple cure. C. P. Alexander. il *Time* 130:57 N 16 '87

Did Baker call the right play? [dollar bashing] B. Powell. il por *Newsweek* 109:22 My 4 '87

The dollar. M. S. Forbes, Jr. il *Forbes* 140:25 N 30 '87

The dollar and the deficits: what to do [cover story; special section] il *Fortune* 116:36-40+ D 7 '87

Dollar in distress. M. McNamee. il *Bus Week* p60-1 N 16 '87

The dollar: No, garçon, I ordered a Big Mac, not a cognac [tables] il *Money* 16:40 Ap '87

The dollar: should we worry? *Natl Rev* 39:20 F 27 '87

Dollar wars: waiting for the Germans. D. Pauly. il *Newsweek* 109:53 F 9 '87

Double-talk on the dollar [plunging dollar] R. Thomas. il *Newsweek* 109:45 F 2 '87

The falling dollar has thrown the trade deficit a curve. J. Berger. il *Bus Week* p68 My 11 '87

The falling dollar is improving the trade picture. W. B. Franklin and J. C. Cooper. il *Bus Week* p39-40 Je 1 '87

Finance ministers meet on exchange rates [statement, February 22, 1987] *Dep State Bull* 87:31-2 Ap '87

A game of chicken [drop in value of dollar fails to help trade deficit] G. Russell. il *Time* 129:44-6 Ja 26 '87

The gnomes behind the dollar's fall. P. Sherrid. il *U S News World Rep* 102:43-4 F 16 '87

The greenback may get black and blue again. W. Glasgall. il *Bus Week* p122-3 Jl 20 '87

The high-stakes showdown on the dollar. K. R. Sheets. il *U S News World Rep* 102:16-17 F 2 '87

How far the dollar goes in far-flung places. D. H. Dunn. il *Bus Week* p149 O 19 '87

Imposing order on a global economy [Group of 7 meeting in Washington] il *Macleans* 100:30 Ap 20 '87

In search of leadership. I. Austen. il *Macleans* 100:22-3 N 16 '87

In this corner, Uncle Sam [lower dollar helps American industry] D. Pauly. il *Newsweek* 110:61-2 D 7 '87

Interest rates have nowhere to go but up [dollar decline] S. Bartlett. il *Bus Week* p142-3 S 14 '87

Is the dollar doomed? [economic conference in Venice] A. Smith. il *Esquire* 107:51-2 Ja '87

Is the dollar too high—or too low? S. Nasar. il *Fortune* 115:85-6 My 11 '87

Is Uncle Sam putting up the price of oil? [views of Federal Reserve economist Bharat Trehan] R. McGough. il *Forbes* 139:144 F 23 '87

Looking the other way [falling dollar] S. Koepp. il *Time* 130:54-6 N 16 '87

The market wants the dollar to fall. Let it happen. A. S. Blinder. por *Bus Week* p18 O 19 '87

Money & banking. See issues of Business Week

New lows ahead for the incredible diving dollar. B. Riemer and W. Glasgall. il *Bus Week* p30 Ja 19 '87

The Paris pact may not buoy the dollar for long [February 1987 meeting] B. Riemer and others. il *Bus Week* p40-1 Mr 9 '87

People are talking about money [special section] il *Vogue* 177:204-9+ Ja '87

Playing for a fall [investment outlook in light of falling dollar] E. A. Finn, Jr. il *Forbes* 139:98-101 F 23 '87

Rise and fall of the dollar. R. Thompson. il *Nations Bus* 75:9-10 F '87

The risks of a free-fall [plunging dollar] B. Riemer and W. Glasgall. il *Bus Week* p28-9 F 2 '87

A roll of the dice on the dollar [with interview with S. Pardee] J. Egan. il *U S News World Rep* 103:60-1 N 16 '87

See the world—and pinch pfennigs [effect of weak dollar on American G.I.s stationed in Germany] J. D. Reed. il *Time* 130:24 D 28 '87

Sound as a dollar [Reaganism] *Nation* 244:99-100 Ja 31 '87

Spurious worries and real cares. H. Banks. *Forbes* 139:27 Ap 20 '87

Supporting the dollar [Group of Five meeting in Paris] A. Finlayson. *Macleans* 100:38 Mr 9 '87

A surprising rally cheers the dollar's boosters. W. Glasgall. il *Bus Week* p36 Je 8 '87

Taking the sting out of the plunging dollar [European companies exporting from U.S. subsidiaries] B. Riemer and F. J. Comes. il *Bus Week* p72-3 D 7 '87

Taming the wild buck [Group of Five intervention] M. R. Meyer. il *Newsweek* 109:53 Mr 2 '87

Testing time for Jim Baker [dollar and trade deficit policies] E. Mervosh. il por *U S News World Rep* 102:43-4 Ja 19 '87

There's no panacea for six years of bad policy. R. Kuttner. il *Bus Week* p28 My 11 '87

They won't feel like partying at the IMF meetings [pressure to halt dollar's slide] M. McNamee. il *Bus Week* p36 S 28 '87

Too many hopes are riding on a falling dollar. J. Berger. il *Bus Week* p92 D 7 '87

The trade gap is still hammering the dollar. W. B. Franklin and J. C. Cooper. *Bus Week* p25-6 O 26 '87

Twin deficits and the G-7 [Paris accord] il *Natl Rev* 39:19-20 Ap 24 '87

Uncle Sam's supermoney. R. J. Samuelson. il *Newsweek* 109:50 Mr 9 '87

We better keep them happy [Japanese investment in the U.S.; interview with R. D. Hormats] A. D. Frank. il por *Forbes* 140:37-8 N 30 '87

Weak dollar begets weak stocks and bonds [stemming the dollar's fall] M. S. Forbes, Jr. il *Forbes* 140:25 S 21 '87

A weaker dollar may blunt Asia's trade claws . . . and send more U.S. goods to the Pacific. G. Koretz. il *Bus Week* p22 Mr 16 '87

Weaving a dollar crisis out of whole cloth [weak dollar] P. C. Roberts. il *Bus Week* p31 F 23 '87

Where the dollar is headed—with luck [down] V. Brownstein. il *Fortune* 115:39-40 F 16 '87

Where will the buck stop? B. Powell. il *Newsweek* 109:37 Ja 26 '87

Why Americans aren't likely to start buying American [import prices] L. Therrien. il *Bus Week* p34 N 23 '87

Why the dollar could head south again . . . and send the economy into recession next year [U.S. as debtor nation] G. Koretz. il *Bus Week* p20 Jl 13 '87

Why the dollar will fall. L. C. Thurow. il *Technol Rev* 90:24-5 N/D '87

International aspects
    See also
    Capital movements
    Foreign exchange
    Gold as money
    International Monetary Fund
    Paris Club

Crisis and reform [address, November 13, 1986] C. F. Bergsten. *Vital Speeches Day* 53:281-8 F 15 '87

The global funny money game. H. M. Wachtel. il *Nation* 245:784-6+ D 26 '87-Ja 2 '88

One way to win high marks from future historians [new international monetary system] M. S. Forbes, Jr. il *Forbes* 139:25 Ap 6 '87

Psychological aspects
Am I a loser if I don't earn big bucks? B. Patrick. il *Glamour* 85:222 D '87

Elementary 'psychological accounting' [study by Helene J. Krouse] *Sci News* 131:89 F 7 '87

Money and freedom [retirement at age 24] M. Glickman. il *N Y Times Mag* p62 Ap 26 '87

Notes and comment. *New Yorker* 63:21-2 Je 15 '87

Psyching it out. S. Drucker. *Vogue* 177:208-9+ Ja '87

Money—Psychological aspects—*cont.*

Say, brother [change in economic status affects relationships with women] R. Clements. por *Essence* 18:6 O '87

A theory of the panic. R. Rosenblatt. il *Time* 130:112 N 9 '87

The trouble with money [coming between friends] M. Jacobson. il *Esquire* 107:49-50 Ap '87

What's your attitude toward money? L. Stains. il *Prevention* 39:74-6 F '87

When everyone has more money than you [teenagers] L. Dormen. il *Seventeen* 46:29-30+ D '87

Why Jerry Moore left River Oaks [Houston millionaire craves social esteem] E. F. Cone. il pors *Forbes* 140 Sp Issue:102+ O 26 '87

Why women are afraid of money [excerpt from Unbalanced accounts] A. R. Lieberman and V. Lindner. il *Glamour* 85:318-19+ Ap '87

Social aspects

Money and the moral vacuum. B. Amiel. il *Macleans* 100:9 N 9 '87

The money society [cover story] M. Magnet. il *Fortune* 116:26-31 Jl 6 '87

Australia

Head Down Under for double-digit bond yields. T. Segal. *Bus Week* p126 S 21 '87

Canada

Currencies in free fall [plunging dollar] A. Walmsley. il *Macleans* 100:46-7 Ap 27 '87

World money wars. D. Jenish. il *Macleans* 100:60-1 F 2 '87

Cuba

Cuba chases the dollar [austerity measures] F. D. Colburn. il *New Leader* 70:13-14 Mr 9 '87

Germany (West)

The Bundesbank's hardliner has a change of heart [H. Schlesinger willing to cut interest rates] B. Riemer. il por *Bus Week* p32 D 14 '87

The mark puts a stranglehold on exporters. F. A. Miller. il *Bus Week* p60 F 23 '87

Unexpected ally for the dollar? [labor leader E. Breit] L. Minard. por *Forbes* 139:158+ Mr 23 '87

With national elections out of the way. M. S. Forbes, Jr. il *Forbes* 139:25 F 9 '87

Great Britain

See also

Bank of England

A jolly good show for the economy [devalued pound] R. A. Melcher. il *Bus Week* p47 F 16 '87

New glitter for sterling. G. Slutsker. il *Forbes* 139:37 Je 1 '87

Japan

The ballad of Ron and Yasu [effects of high yen; cover story] M. Sayle. *New Repub* 196:18-21 Je 15 '87

Bridgestone may try an end run around the yen [construction of U.S. plant to make car tires] Z. Schiller and J. B. Treece. il *Bus Week* p31 F 2 '87

Damn the dollar, full speed ahead. M. Tharp. il *U S News World Rep* 103:50-1 D 14 '87

Do you have the yen to travel? H. Katayama. il *Forbes* 139:222+ My 18 '87

Harnessing the 'yen monster'. M. R. Meyer. il *Newsweek* 110:60 S 21 '87

A hot American car may hit Japan: the Honda [strong yen could prompt Japanese carmakers to reexport from the U.S.] W. J. Hampton and others. il *Bus Week* p50 Ja 26 '87

Japan can't make a quick yen in the U.S. any more [consumer electronics] K. Dreyfack. il *Bus Week* p120-1 F 23 '87

The rampaging yen is leaving a trail of misery. J. B. Treece. il *Bus Week* p46-7 F 16 '87

The swollen yen is weighing heavily on Japan. M. Berger. il *Bus Week* p34 My 4 '87

Waiting for the yen to stop pummeling profits. L. Armstrong. il *Bus Week* p58-9 Je 1 '87

Mexico

A haymaker for Mexico [peso devaluation] J. Contreras. il *Newsweek* 110:53 N 30 '87

Peso panic. il *Time* 130:66 N 30 '87

Why De La Madrid is letting the peso fend for itself. J. Anderson and S. Baker. il *Bus Week* p73 D 7 '87

Switzerland

Check your options [Swiss francs] S. W. Angrist. il *Forbes* 139:125 Ap 20 '87

Taiwan

Liquidity trap. A. Tanzer. il *Forbes* 139:37-8 Ap 6 '87

Taiwan's wealth crisis. M. Shao. il *Bus Week* p46-7 Ap 13 '87

Why Taiwan's doors should swing wide open. M. Shao. il *Bus Week* p41 Ag 3 '87

United States

See Money

Money (Periodical)

Money anniversary issue. il *Money* Sp Issue:8-9+ Fall '87

Money brokers

"We're the lifeblood" [regulators turn to money brokers for help with weak thrifts] M. Schifrin. il *Forbes* 140:43-4 Jl 27 '87

Money cards *See* Debit cards

Money lending *See* Loans, Personal

Money management *See* Budget, Household; Finance, Personal; Financial services; Investment advisers

Money management accounts *See* Cash management accounts

Money market accounts (Banking) *See* Bank accounts—Interest (Economics)

Money market funds *See* Investment trusts

Money markets

See also

Foreign exchange

A bad case of nerves [April's market jolts] S. Bartlett. il *Bus Week* p30-2 Ap 27 '87

A case of the jitters [financial markets] L. Martz. il *Newsweek* 109:18-22+ My 4 '87

Coping with the markets [April jitters] B. Powell. il *Newsweek* 109:54 Ap 27 '87

Financial markets [address, June 9, 1987] A. M. Solomon. *Vital Speeches Day* 53:725-9 S 15 '87

Jitters! [cover story; special section] il *Bus Week* p40-5 My 11 '87

New capitals for raising capital? [interview with J. Hennessy] R. Morais. por *Forbes* 139:64 Mr 9 '87

A new kind of free speech. W. B. Wriston. il por *Forbes* 140:264 D 14 '87

Our changing capital markets [address, April 30, 1987] D. B. Marron. *Vital Speeches Day* 53:586-8 Jl 15 '87

The perils of trading money for money. Y. Messarovitch. *World Press Rev* 34:46-7 Jl '87

Risky moments in the money markets. M. W. Karmin. il *U S News World Rep* 102:44-5 Mr 2 '87

A storm in the markets. il *Macleans* 100:28-9 Ap 13 '87

Sunrise, sunset. *Nation* 244:455-6 Ap 11 '87

Money raising campaigns *See* Fund raising

Money rates *See* Interest (Economics)

Money supply

See also

Federal Reserve System (U.S.)

Is the Fed behind the stock boom? D. Pauly. il *Newsweek* 109:36-7 Ja 26 '87

Is the Fed playing it too close to the vest? G. Koretz. il *Bus Week* p24 D 14 '87

Tight money and loose fiscal policy. A. S. Blinder. bibl *Society* 24:80-3 Jl/Ag '87

Why the Fed may zero in on the money targets. J. Berger. il *Bus Week* p73+ Jl 13 '87

Money traders *See* Foreign exchange brokers

Monfort, Kenneth

about

Beefed-up profits. M. Fritz. il por *Forbes* 139:159 My 4 '87

Monfort of Colorado, Inc.

Beefed-up profits. M. Fritz. il por *Forbes* 139:159 My 4 '87

How ConAgra grew big—and now, beefy [acquisition of Monfort] M. Ivey. il por *Bus Week* p87-8 My 18 '87

Mongiardino, Renzo

about

Orientalist opulence in Belgravia: the London residence of Princess Firyal of Jordan. G. Y. Dryansky. il *Archit Dig* 44:216-20 My '87

Mongolia

See also

Paleontology—Mongolia

United States—Diplomatic and consular service—Mongolia

Cultural relations

United States

See United States—Cultural relations—Mongolia

Mongolism *See* Down syndrome

Monhegan Island (Me.)

Monhegan: an artist's island. E. Agar. il map *Am Artist* 51:46-51+ My '87

Monheit, Jonathan

about

The one and only. por *Time* 129:68 My 18 '87

Monilia rot *See* Brown rot

Monitor (Ironclad)
Probing the Monitor with a deep drone. M. D. Lemonick. il map *Time* 129:77 Je 22 '87

Monitor roofs *See* Roofs and roofing

Monitoring
See also
Employees—Monitoring
Women prisoners—Monitoring

Monitoring (Medical care)
Labor-saving device [Term Guard, a device that can detect premature labor] D. Tonnessen. il *Health* 19:23 Je '87
Premature labor takes a holiday thanks to a new pregnancy monitor [Term Guard home monitoring device] *Prevention* 39:79-80 N '87

Monitors, Video *See* Video monitors

Moniz, David
The Pope came to South Carolina: unfortunately, so did the Yankee press. il por *Wash Mon* 19:28-9 D '87

Monjo, John C.
The Cambodian issue [statement, March 11, 1987] *Dep State Bull* 87:29-30 My '87

Monk, Dennis C.
The "flaw" in the ointment: who will teach the understanding of music? bibl f *Des Arts Educ* 89:2-7 N/D '87

Monk, Thelonious, 1917-1982
about
Down by the Riverside: truth and ugly beauty. P. Kostakis. *Down Beat* 54:32+ Je '87
Thelonious Monk's great nephews start new quartet. *Jet* 72:38 Je 15 '87

Monk Family (Musical group)
Thelonious Monk's great nephews start new quartet. *Jet* 72:38 Je 15 '87

Monkees (Musical group)
Monkees: here they come . . . again. K. Silverman. il *Teen* 31:42-3 Ja '87

Monkeyface prickleback fishing *See* Prickleback fishing

Monkeys
See also
Baboons
Earth station, can you read me? [monkey onboard Soviet space vehicle frees arm from restraints] il *Time* 130:36 O 19 '87
Japan's monkey treasures [macaques; cover story] il map *Natl Geogr World* 147:4-9 N '87
Monkey business in orbit [rhesus monkey launched by Soviets] M. Gray. il *Macleans* 100:54 O 19 '87
Rescuing Brazil's muriqui: monkey in peril. R. Mittermeier. il map *Natl Geogr* 171:386-95 Mr '87
Eye
See Eye—Animals
Food and feeding
These are real swinging primates [muriqui monkeys] S. Brownlee. il map *Discover* 8:66-8+ Ap '87
Sexual behavior
See Sexual behavior—Animals

Monkeys, Fossil
An ancient relative for the owl monkey [skull found in Colombia] B. Bower. il *Sci News* 131:263 Ap 25 '87

Monmaney, Terence
Are we led by the nose? il *Discover* 8:48-54+ S '87
Key notes on the mind. il *Omni* 9:44-6+ Ja '87

Monmouth, James Scott, Duke of, 1649-1685
about
A morbid curiosity. J. Prendergast. il *Hist Today* 37:62 My '87

Monnet, Jean, 1888-1979
about
Wanted: leaders with vision. J. M. Wall. *Christ Century* 104:779 S 23 '87

Monnet, Philippe
about
On board with Philippe Monnet. M. Pennybaker. il por *Mot Boat Sail* 160:54-5+ N '87

Monninger, Joseph
My mother's Easter hat. il *Glamour* 85:108+ Ap '87

Mono Lake (Calif.)
Trouble ahead for exotic Mono Lake. M. Sun. il *Science* 237:716-17 Ag 14 '87

Monoamine oxidase *See* Oxidases

Monoclonal antibodies
Abzymes [catalytic antibodies] *Sci Am* 256:84-5 F '87
Antibodies, monoclonal antibodies, immunologics, and antigens. *Science* 235 pt2:G26-G29 F 27 '87
Coming: Star Wars medicine. G. Bylinsky. il *Fortune* 115:153-4+ Ap 27 '87

Immunochemical proof that a novel rearranging gene encodes the T cell receptor δ subunit. H. Band and others. bibl f il *Science* 238:682-4 O 30 '87
In treatment, Centocor is breaking new ground. C. S. Eklund. il por *Bus Week* p91 Je 1 '87
Islet allograft survival after a single course of treatment of recipient with antibody to L3T4. J. A. Shizuru and others. bibl il *Science* 237:278-80 Jl 17 '87
A mab to a unique cerebellar neuron generated by immunosuppression and rapid immunization. S. Hockfield. bibl f il *Science* 237:67-70 Jl 3 '87
Monoclonal antibodies as phylogenetic labels [discussion of July 3, 1987 article, A mab to a unique cerebellar neuron generated by immunosuppression and rapid immunization] S. Hockfield. *Science* 238:1730-1 D 18 '87
Mutations in diphtheria toxin separate binding from entry and amplify immunotoxin selectivity. L. Greenfield and others. bibl f il *Science* 238:536-9 O 23 '87
Recombinant interferon enhances monoclonal antibody-targeting of carcinoma lesions in vivo. J. W. Greiner and others. bibl f il *Science* 235:895-8 F 20 '87
Seeking antibodies against chickenpox. *USA Today (Periodical)* 115:9-10 F '87
A stereospecific cyclization catalyzed by an antibody. A. D. Napper and others. bibl f il *Science* 237:1041-3 Ag 28 '87

Monogamy
The four-year itch: do divorce patterns reflect our evolutionary heritage? H. E. Fisher. il *Nat Hist* 96:22+ O '87

Monogamy in animals *See* Sexual behavior—Animals

Monograms
Monograms at work: a do or a don't? J. Mattera. il *Glamour* 85:164 O '87

Monongahela National Forest (W. Va.)
Dolly Sods, West Virginia. R. H. Mohlenbrock. il maps *Nat Hist* 96:76-9 Ja '87
Some plain dealing pays off [management plan] D. G. Hanson. il *Sierra* 72:20-2 Ja/F '87

Mononucleosis
The Epstein-Barr virus: beyond mono. I. A. Oppenheim. il *Curr Health 2* 13:18-19 Ja '87

Monopod camera supports *See* Camera supports

Monotony *See* Boredom

Monoun, Lake (Cameroon) *See* Lake Monoun (Cameroon)

Monroe, James, 1758-1831
Homes
James Monroe's Highland home. il *South Living* 22:22 My '87
Statues, portraits, etc.
Monroe portrait unveiled [remarks, April 28, 1987] G. P. Shultz. il por *Dep State Bull* 87:81 Jl '87

Monroe, Marilyn, 1926-1962
about
Marilyn Monroe [excerpt from Marilyn] G. Steinem. il pors *Redbook* 168:102-3+ Ja '87
Marilyn: the legend lives on. S. Marchant. il pors *Ladies Home J* 104:92+ Ag '87
Some like it hot. B. Greene. il pors *Esquire* 108:59-60+ O '87
There's a little bit of Marilyn in all of us. il pors *Ladies Home J* 104:93-5 Ag '87
Unforgettable faces [makeup and hairstyles that reinterpret legendary looks] il pors *Seventeen* 46:120-5 F '87
Anecdotes, facetiae, satire, etc.
Who does know Marilyn? R. Schoenstein. por *Publ Wkly* 231:82 Ja 9 '87
Photographs and photography
I remember Norma Jean [excerpt from Marilyn Monroe] E. Arnold. il pors *People Wkly* 28:72-4+ Ag 10 '87

Monroe (Mich.)
Education
Helping kids: the ripple effect [elderly volunteers] il *Aging* no355:28 '87

Monroe Doctrine
The spirit behind the Monroe Doctrine [address, April 28, 1987] E. Abrams. *Dep State Bull* 87:80-3 Jl '87

Monsanto Company
The chemistry that may put Monsanto in play. G. G. Marcial. il *Bus Week* p165 O 12 '87
In Illinois: the longest jury trial drones on [Kemner et al. v. Monsanto] L. Griggs. il *Time* 129:1 Mr 23 '87
Most improved. il *Forbes* 139:93 Ja 12 '87
Never to be accused of rushing to judgment, a jury goes home after a trying 44 months [dioxin-spill suit] M. Green. il *People Wkly* 28:48-50 N 9 '87
Weed killer [Roundup] A. L. Kimery. il *Progressive* 51:20-1 Jl '87

Monsma, Stephen V., 1936-
Should the poor earn their keep? il por *Christ Today* 31:28-31 Je 12 '87
Monsod, Solita Collas
Debt to democracy. *New Repub* 197:16-18 D 7 '87
about
Who's afraid of Solita Monsod? U.S. bankers, that's who. D. J. Yang. il por *Bus Week* p54 Ja 26 '87
Monster in the closet [film] *See* Motion picture reviews—Single works
The Monster Squad [film] *See* Motion picture reviews—Single works
Monsters
See also
    Loch Ness monster
    Sea monsters
Mont Blanc (France and Italy)
The ups and downs of clambering on the roof of Europe. P. Miller. bibl (p154) il *Smithsonian* 18:92-8+ Je '87
Mont Pelerin Society conferences *See* Economic conferences
Montage
See also
    Photomontage
Montagnards (Vietnamese people)
Warm welcomes for forgotten allies [Montagnard refugees resettled in North Carolina] J. Bennett. il *Macleans* 100:5+ Mr 23 '87
Montague, Joel B., Jr.
Security risk. il *Progressive* 51:34 S '87
Montaigne (Natchez, Miss.: Historic house) *See* Natchez (Miss.)—Historic houses, sites, etc.
Montalcini, Rita Levi- *See* Levi-Montalcini, Rita, 1909-
Montale, Eugenio, 1896-1981
Little testament [poem]; tr. by Jonathan Galassi. *N Y Rev Books* 34:7 N 19 '87
Wind and flags [poem]; tr. by Jonathan Galassi. *N Y Rev Books* 34:4 Jl 16 '87
Montana, Jennifer
about
Couples. M. Orth. il pors *Vogue* 177:392 F '87
Montana, Joe
about
Couples. M. Orth. il pors *Vogue* 177:392 F '87
Fast comeback for a quarterback with a bad back. il *Discover* 8:14 Ja '87
Montana
See also
    Architecture, Domestic—Montana
    Crime and criminals—Montana
    Earthquakes—Montana
    Fishing—Montana
    Glacier National Park (Mont.)
    Hunting—Montana
    Lewis and Clark National Forest (Mont.)
    Mines and mineral resources—Montana
    Paleontology—Montana
    Ranches—Montana
    Resorts—Montana
    Smith River (Mont.)
    Waterton-Glacier International Peace Park (Alta. and Mont.)
    Wilderness areas—Montana
    Wildlife management—Montana
    Wildlife sanctuaries—Montana
Climate
The summer Montana burned [1984] R. Heim, Jr. il map *Weatherwise* 40:184-7 Jl/Ag '87
Description and travel
Scars and legends of Montana's 1959 earthquake. il *Sunset* 179:44-5 Ag '87
Forest fires
See Forest fires
Social life and customs
Redneck secrets [excerpt from Owning it all] W. Kittredge. *Harpers* 275:34-8 O '87
Montana State University (Bozeman)
Bozeman chain saw massacre [G. A. Strobel's Dutch elm disease experiment] W. E. Brock. il pors *Discover* 8:78-82+ N '87
MSU faults Strobel for Dutch elm test. L. Roberts. *Science* 237:1286 S 11 '87
Montand, Yves
about
Montand [interview] H. Jacobson. por *Film Comment* 23:28-32 S/O '87
Monte (Elisa) Dance Company *See* Elisa Monte Dance Company
Monte Carlo method
Electron tunneling paths in proteins. A. Kuki and P. G. Wolynes. bibl f il *Science* 236:1647-52 Je 26 '87

Monte Carlo morons [computer program] A. Blackadar. *Weatherwise* 40:338-41 D '87
Stars and spikes [finding stellar diffraction patterns for different telescope types; computer program] R. W. Sinnott. il *Sky Telesc* 74:294-6 S '87
Monte Cassino (Monastery: Cassino, Italy)
Monte Cassino: a story of death and resurrection. O. Friedrich. bibl (p163) il map *Smithsonian* 18:128-32+ Ap '87
Monteleon, Francine
about
Career makeover: high school teacher to high-tech sales. il por *Glamour* 85:156 Mr '87
Monterey Bay (Calif.)
Kayak tours of Monterey Bay. il *Sunset* 179:31 S '87
Monterey Bay Aquarium
Star trek in Monterey. il *Sunset* 178:44 F '87
Monterey County (Calif.)
Arts
Monterey County [special section] il *Horizon* 30:57-70+ Jl/Ag '87
Description and travel
Monterey County [special section] il *Horizon* 30:57-70+ Jl/Ag '87
Wine industry
See Wine industry
Monterey Film Festival *See* Motion picture festivals—California
Monterey Historic Automobile Races *See* Automobile racing
Monterey Peninsula (Calif.)
Description and travel
Nature's mellow canvas. B. St. Pierre. il map *50 Plus* 27:62-6+ O '87
Monterey Peninsula Museum of Art
The Monterey Peninsula Museum of Art: a legacy in the county. M. Wade. il *Horizon* 30:57-8 Jl/Ag '87
Monterey Pop Festival *See* Music festivals—California
Montesinos, Jorge Nieto
Embattled in Peru. *World Press Rev* 34:39 My '87
Montessori method of education
What's the Montessori method? F. Roberts. *Parents* 62:53-5 S '87
Monteverdi, Claudio, 1567-1643
about
Monteverdi's modernity. W. H. Youngren. il *Atlantic* 259:82-5 Ap '87
Montgomery, Beauregard Houston- *See* Houston-Montgomery, Beauregard
Montgomery, David
A Dickens Christmas. il *Good Housekeep* 205:160-5 D '87
Montgomery, Geoffrey
Worm watching: the case of the suicidal sex cell. il por *Discover* 8:44-6+ O '87
Montgomery, James F.
about
How playing it safe worked for Great Western. T. Carson. il por *Bus Week* p70 S 7 '87
Montgomery, John C., and Macdonald, John A.
Sensory tuning of lateral line receptors in Antarctic fish to the movements of planktonic prey. bibl f il *Science* 235:195-6 Ja 9 '87
Montgomery, L. M. (Lucy Maud), 1874-1942
about
An author's painful secrets. A. Shortell. por *Macleans* 100:50 D 7 '87
Montgomery, Lee
about
Hunks & heartthrobs. pors *Teen* 31:54 Mr '87
Montgomery, Lucy Maud *See* Montgomery, L. M. (Lucy Maud), 1874-1942
Montgomery, Nancy S.
Song in a weary throat. *Christ Century* 104:828+ S 30 '87
Montgomery, Parker G.
about
A fire sale at Cooper? J. O. Hamilton. il por *Bus Week* p37 N 23 '87
Inside Parker Montgomery's tangle of troubled companies. J. O. Hamilton and J. H. Dobrzynski. il por *Bus Week* p110-11 F 23 '87
Montgomery, Sy
Planning parenthood: can you time the birth of your child? il *Work Woman* 12:139-40+ O '87
The truth about the common cold (and similar ills). il *Work Woman* 12:142+ Ap '87
Montgomery (Ala.)
Photographs and photography
Epochs of Montgomery. il *Am Herit* 38:106-7 S/O '87

Montgomery (Ala.)—*cont.*

Theater

See also

Alabama Shakespeare Festival

Montgomery bus boycott, 1955 *See* Civil rights demonstrations—History

Montgomery-Massingberd, Hugh

Forever Ashley. il *House Gard* 159:158-65+ S '87

Montgomery Ward & Co., Inc.

Give it to the stockholders? [Mobil may spinoff Montgomery Ward] C. Siler. il *Forbes* 140:55-6 S 7 '87

A month of Sundays [drama] *See* Larbey, Bob

Monthly labor review

Klein Award. *Mon Labor Rev* 110:2 Mr '87

Monthly Review Press

Left, but not left out. J. Mutter. il *Publ Wkly* 232:18-19 Jl 17 '87

Months

See also

April

August

December

February

January

July

March

May

November

October

September

Monticello (Va.: Estate)

Gardens

In Mr. Jefferson's garden. P. L. Hudson. il por *Americana* 14:50-5 Ja/F '87

Thomas Jefferson, gardener. N. Bubel. il *Ctry J* 14:11-13 Ap '87

Montoya, Richard T.

The foreign aid cancer [address, May 28, 1987] *Vital Speeches Day* 53:616-18 Ag 1 '87

Montreal (Québec)

Airports

A murder mystery [murder of M. Taddeo, subject of Mirabel Airport land sales investigation] L. Van Dusen. por *Macleans* 100:19-20 D 21 '87

Buildings

Montreal's hot property market [office space broker S. Leopold] P. C. Newman. il por *Macleans* 100:34 S 7 '87

Crime

Crackdown on the Montreal connection [drug trafficking] D. Burke. il *Macleans* 100:45 Ap 6 '87

Criminal justice, Administration of

'We just want the truth' [child witnesses and sex abuse cases] L. Van Dusen. il *Macleans* 100:56+ N 2 '87

Description

Montreal. J. Hooper. il *Esquire* 107 Summ Traveler:T5-T6 Ap '87

Montreal. B. Keating. il *50 Plus* 27:42-6 Ap '87

Finance

See also

Montreal (Québec)—Taxation

Newspapers

Montreal's widening newspaper wars [P. Péladeau seeks to introduce English language daily] A. Wilson-Smith. il por *Macleans* 100:46 Mr 9 '87

Office buildings

See Montreal (Québec)—Buildings

Police

Charges of racism [black youth A. Griffin killed by Montreal police] L. Van Dusen. il *Macleans* 100:14+ N 30 '87

Politics and government

Montreal's controversial reformers [J. Doré administration] A. Wilson-Smith. il por *Macleans* 100:36 F 9 '87

Race relations

Charges of racism [black youth A. Griffin killed by Montreal police] L. Van Dusen. il *Macleans* 100:14+ N 30 '87

Religious institutions and affairs

Lives of heart and soul [Benedictine Priory] G. Ferzoco. il *Macleans* 100:42 S 14 '87

Streets

Commemorated by controversy [boulevard renamed after R. Lévesque] B. Wallace. *Macleans* 100:19 N 30 '87

Taxation

New shocks at tax time [property tax] B. Wallace. il *Macleans* 100:56 Mr 30 '87

Montreal (Québec) in television

High drama in the world of film [dispute between Telefilm Canada and R. Lantos over adult soap series Mont Royal] B. Amiel. il *Macleans* 100:7 S 14 '87

Montréal Danse

Reviews:

Performances at the National Arts Centre in Ottawa. L. Howe-Beck. *Dance Mag* 61:81-2 S '87

Montreal Film Festival *See* Motion picture festivals—Quebec (Province)

Montreal Protocol to the Vienna Convention for the Protection of the Ozone Layer *See* Vienna Convention for the Protection of the Ozone Layer (1985). Montreal Protocol (1987)

Montreal Stock Exchange *See* Stock exchanges—Montreal exchange

Montrose Capital Corporation

How to win friends and enrich people [C. Hamner] S. B. Weiner. il por *Forbes* 140:196+ D 14 '87

Montt, José Efraín Ríos *See* Ríos Montt, José Efraín

Montville, Leigh

Everything under the sun. il *Sports Illus* 67:66-8+ S 7 '87

To Boston with love. il *Sports Illus* 66:94-8+ Ap 20 '87

Where fouls are fair. il *Sports Illus* 67:66-9 N 9 '87

You're an old smoothie. il pors *Sports Illus* 66:38-40+ Mr 30 '87

Monuments

See also

Amsterdam (Netherlands)—Monuments, statues, etc.

Memorials

San Antonio (Tex.)—Monuments, statues, etc.

War memorials

Germany (West)

See also

Hamburg (Germany)—Monuments, statues, etc.

MONY *See* Mutual Life Insurance Co. of New York

Mood, John

Star hopping to a quasar. il *Astronomy* 15:49-52 Ap '87

Moodie, Alexander Forbes

about

Cowley and Moodie honored for work in crystallography. por *Phys Today* 40:105 D '87

Moods

Go away! (A guy in a bad mood means it). W. D. Leight. *Mademoiselle* 93:116 D '87

How to live with a moody man. L. Lague. il *Glamour* 85:74+ Jl '87

Laughter: a creative muse? [mood and creativity; research by Alice M. Isen] C. Russo. *Psychol Today* 21:21 S '87

Moody, Jim

(jt. auth) See Downey, Thomas J., and others

Moody, Shearn, Jr.

about

In Galveston, Moody's blues. G. Hackett. il por *Newsweek* 109:33 F 2 '87

Moody (Ala.)

Race relations

White woman jailed for hitting black principal who paddled her son. il por *Jet* 73:6-7 N 30 '87

Moody Foundation

In Galveston, Moody's blues [investigation of fraud] G. Hackett. il por *Newsweek* 109:33 F 2 '87

Moon

See also

Eclipses, Lunar

Lunar geology

Space flight to the moon

Tides

A daytime occultation of Spica. A. MacRobert. il *Sky Telesc* 74:174 Ag '87

A grand Pleiades occultation. D. W. Dunham. il *Sky Telesc* 74:284-7 S '87

Lunar occultation highlights for 1987. D. W. Dunham. il map *Sky Telesc* 73:68-9 Ja '87

The March 5th Pleiades occultation. D. W. Dunham. il *Sky Telesc* 73:296-7 Mr '87

The moon covers Spica. il *Sky Telesc* 73:183 F '87

The moon's highs and lows. T. D. Nicholson. il *Nat Hist* 96:68-9 Jl '87

News from the center of our galaxy [lunar occultation] D. E. Thomsen. *Sci News* 131:24 Ja 10 '87

The sun, moon, and planets this month. D. Byrd. See issues of Sky and Telescope beginning August 1985

Evolution

Birth of the moon [giant impact theory] A. Fisher. il *Pop Sci* 230:60-4+ Ja '87

Moon—*cont.*

Exploration

See also

Lunar bases

Magnetic properties

The moon's ancient magnetism [cover story] S. K. Runcorn. bibl (p158) il *Sci Am* 257:60-8 D '87

Orbit

The high-low moon for 1987. G. Lovi. il *Sky Telesc* 73:57-8 Ja '87

The librations of the moon. A. MacRobert. il *Sky Telesc* 74:60-2 Jl '87

Viewing libration with the naked eye. J. Meketa. il *Sky Telesc* 74:63 Jl '87

Origin

See Moon—Evolution

Phases

Eastward slow, the sea slugs [research by A. O. Dennis Willows and Kenneth J. Lohmann] D. D. Edwards. *Sci News* 131:54 Ja 24 '87

How dark was the night of the Boston Tea Party? S. W. Schultz. il *Astronomy* 15:24 Ag '87

Lunar-modulated geomagnetic orientation by a marine mollusk. K. J. Lohmann and A. O. D. Willows. bibl f il *Science* 235:331-4 Ja 16 '87

Photographs and photography

Crescent earth. il *Natl Geogr World* 145:33 S '87

Earth and moon together. H. Brandli. il *Astronomy* 15:20-2 O '87

The moon on a silver plate [experimenting with daguerreotype process] J. K. Herman and M. S. Barger. il *Astronomy* 15:98-103 O '87

Surface

The "great black lake" of Plato. A. MacRobert. il *Sky Telesc* 74:396-7 O '87

Invitation to Imbrium. G. Lovi. il *Sky Telesc* 74:55-6 Jl '87

The lunar straight wall [Rupes Recta] S. J. O'Meara. il *Sky Telesc* 73:639-42 Je '87

Sculpting the moon. M. T. Kitt. il *Astronomy* 15:82-7 F '87

Moon bases *See* Lunar bases

Moon Pies (Cookies) *See* Cookies

Moon vehicles *See* Lunar vehicles

Moonchildren [drama] *See* Weller, Michael

Mooney, Harold A., and Drake, J. A.

The ecology of biological invasions. bibl f il maps *Environment* 29:10-15+ Je '87

Mooney, Harold A., and others

Exchange of materials between terrestrial ecosystems and the atmosphere. bibl f il *Science* 238:926-32 N 13 '87

Plant physiological ecology today. bibl f *BioScience* 37:18-20 Ja '87

Mooney, Michael J.

Forest in the dunes. il map *Sea Front* 33:120-7 Mr/Ap '87

Mooney Aircraft Corporation

European air forces interested in Socata/Mooney TBM 700 [single-engine business turboprop as transport aircraft for military officials] *Aviat Week Space Technol* 127:147 O 12 '87

Moonlighting *See* Supplementary employment

Moonlighting [television program] *See* Television program reviews—Single works

Moonstruck [film] *See* Motion picture reviews—Single works

Moore, Allen J.

Teen-age sexuality and public morality. il *Christ Century* 104:747-50 S 9-16 '87

Moore, Arch A., Jr.

about

Economic paralysis could stop Arch Moore cold. M. Rothman. il por *Bus Week* p86+ N 30 '87

Moore, Arnold R.

about

Obituary

Phys Today por 40:114 N '87. J. Dressner

Moore, Arthur Cotton

about

Cooking with history [with editorial comment by Mildred F. Schmertz] D. Dietsch. il *Archit Rec* 175:9, 84-93 Ja '87

Moore, Brian, 1921-

Sea-struck living. il por *House Gard* 159:78+ S '87

Moore, Carolyn E.

(jt. auth) *See* Cooley, Denton A., 1920-, and Moore, Carolyn E.

Moore, Charles Willard

about

The architecture of Charles Moore: 1949-1986. J. H. Kay. *Nation* 244:27-8 Ja 10 '87

Charles Moore at Williams. V. J. Scully. il por *Archit Dig* 44:66+ D '87

Good neighbors. K. Norment and C. Giuliano. il *Art News* 86:51-2 Ja '87

Moore, Clement Clarke, 1779-1863

about

Clement C. Moore: "A visit from St. Nicholas". B. McGinty. por *Am Hist Illus* 22:28-9 D '87

Moore, Cynthia B.

A reflection [poem] *Essence* 17:123 F '87

Moore, Demi

about

Gambling that their love is here to stay, Bruce Willis and Demi Moore hit Vegas to get seriously married. il pors *People Wkly* 28:71 D 7 '87

Now playing. pors *Teen* 31:52 Mr '87

Moore, Gaylen

(ed) *See* Sarnoff, Dorothy. Never be nervous again

Moore, George S. (George Stevens), 1905-

about

Bank to the future. E. A. Finn, Jr. il por *Forbes* 140:450+ Jl 13 '87

Moore, Henry, 1898-1986

about

Henry Moore. G. Henry. il *Art News* 86:171 O '87

Obituary

Art News il por 86:37 F '87. W. S. Lieberman

Moore, Howard W.

about

The longest war. R. F. Sayre. *Nation* 244:133 F 7 '87

Moore, James V.

about

Black man's teeth a deadly weapon, jury rules. il por *Jet* 72:24 Jl 13 '87

Moore, Jerry J.

about

Why Jerry Moore left River Oaks. E. F. Cone. il pors *Forbes* 140 Sp Issue:102+ O 26 '87

Moore, Jonathan

FY 1988 assistance requests for migration and refugees [statement, March 26, 1987] *Dep State Bull* 87:83-4 Je '87

Perspectives on U.S. refugee programs [address, June 11, 1987; statement June 30, 1987] *Dep State Bull* 87:54-8 S '87

Proposed refugee admissions for FY 1988 [statement, September 23, 1987] il *Dep State Bull* 87:47-52 N '87

Refugees and foreign policy: immediate needs and durable solutions [address, April 6, 1987] *Dep State Bull* 87:70-4 Jl '87

U.S. refugee policy and programs for FY 1987 [statements, September 16 and 26, 1986] il *Dep State Bull* 86:78-81 D '86

about

U.S. Coordinator for Refugee Affairs, Director, Bureau for Refugee Programs. por *Dep State Bull* 87:71 Jl '87

Moore, Kathleen

about

Trials by Fire. M. Hunt. il pors *Dance Mag* 61:42-5 My '87

Moore, Kenny, 1943-

A bad deal for track: it's time for the top runners to start racing one another. il por *Sports Illus* 67:70 Jl 20 '87

Bravos for a Roman candle. il por *Sports Illus* 67:18-21 S 7 '87

Bursting from the shadows. il pors *Sports Illus* 67:94-8+ N 30 '87

Dash and crash on an Indy track. il *Sports Illus* 66:22-4+ Mr 16 '87

Double dip for Daly City. il pors *Sports Illus* 67:106-10+ O 26 '87

Giants on the earth. il pors *Sports Illus* 66:48-50+ Je 29 '87

Indy lights up. il *Sports Illus* 67:18-21 Ag 24 '87

A life on the run. il pors *Sports Illus* 66:76-80+ My 18 '87

On top of the worlds [cover story] il pors *Sports Illus* 67:18-23 S 14 '87

Preparing a big move. il pors *Sports Illus* 67:36-8+ S 7 '87

Reaching out to the kids. il pors *Sports Illus* 67:18-19 D 21 '87

The road to Rome. il *Sports Illus* 67:20-1 Jl 6 '87

Rude hello for an old foe. il pors *Sports Illus* 66:16-17 Ja 26 '87

Sweden's new royal highness. il por *Sports Illus* 67:26-7 Jl 13 '87

Moore, Kenny, 1943-—*cont.*
Ties that bind. il pors *Sports Illus* 66:76-80+ Ap 27 '87
Moore, Laverne Galeener- *See* Galeener-Moore, Laverne, 1930-
Moore, Lorrie
about
Post-counterculture tristesse. C. Iannone. *Commentary* 83:57-61 F '87
Moore, M. Thomas, 1934-
about
Dilution control. P. Fuhrman. il *Forbes* 140:174 O 5 '87
Moore, Marianne, 1887-1972
about
Moore in Maine [Marianne Moore Centennial Conference at the University of Maine] *New Yorker* 63:20-1 Jl 20 '87
Moore, Mary Shannon, and others
Assembly of clathrin-coated pits onto purified plasma membranes. bibl f il *Science* 236:558-63 My 1 '87
Moore, Melba
about
Melba Moore returns to TV as 'Falcon Crest' star. *Jet* 71:28 Ja 26 '87
Moore, Michael
In Flint, tough times last. il *Nation* 244:753-6 Je 6 '87
Moore, Miles David
Villanelle: traffic in Washington [poem] *Natl Rev* 39:30 Ag 28 '87
Moore, Myles E.
Don't promote "one of the boys". por *Nations Bus* 75:4 Mr '87
Moore, Phil, d. 1987
about
Obituary
Jet il por 72:17 Je 1 '87
Moore, Sally
Ben Franklin's Philadelphia. il *Saturday Evening Post* 259:82-4 Jl/Ag '87
Moore, Shelley
An audible impact. il por *Essence* 18:118 O '87
Moore, Susan J.
Meeting Mossie [story] il *Teen* 31:62+ Mr '87
Moore, Tracey
about
Essence woman. M. Scott. il por *Essence* 18:30 Jl '87
Moore, Wayne S.
What's the diagnosis? See issues of Flower and Garden beginning February/March 1984
Moore, William
about
Pittsburgh's black police chief quits over authority. *Jet* 72:8 Je 1 '87
Moorestown (N.J.)
Education
The 'Kids for Peace' reach out [Friends School exchange program with East Germany] D. Dahlke. il *World Press Rev* 34:45 Ap '87
Mooring of boats *See* Anchorage
Moorman, Margaret
In a timeless world [cover story] il pors *Art News* 86:90-8 My '87
Moose
Giants of the wilderness: Alaskan moose [Denali National Park] V. Van Ballenberghe. il map *Natl Geogr* 172:260-80 Ag '87
Of moose and men. D. D. Jackson. il *Audubon* 89:94-101 Jl '87
Moose hunting
Anecdotes, facetiae, satire, etc.
The skunked hunt. J. B. Middleton. il *Outdoor Life* 180:86-7+ N '87
Mopane worms *See* Caterpillars
Mopeds
Kamasura contretemps [mail order motorcycles turn out to be mopeds] T. Carrithers. il *Cycle* 38:93-6 Ag '87
YSRage [YSR50] P. Schilling. il *Cycle* 38:7 Ag '87
Testing
Down the rabbit hole [Yamaha YSR50] il *Cycle* 38:26-30 O '87
Full-honk Yamaha YSR [stock exhaust replaced with Toomey Tunes Racing Pipe Kit] K. Vreeke. il *Cycle* 38:48-51 D '87
Galloping Suzuki GSX-R50. K. Vreeke. il *Cycle* 38:48-51 D '87
Moral codes *See* Ethics
Moral conditions
See also subhead Moral conditions under names of countries, states, cities, etc.

What's shocking? T. Young. il *Vogue* 177:758-61 S '87
Moral development
The crayon man [R. Coles] P. Yancey. il pors *Christ Today* 31:14-20 F 6 '87
Does Dr. Ruth talk to your kids more than you do? [interview with R. Coles] por *U S Cathol* 52:22-9 Ag '87
A question of morality [testing L. Kohlberg's theory of moral development] J. R. Snarey. il *Psychol Today* 21:6+ Je '87
Moral education
Bill Bennett's dilemma. D. Wagner. il *Natl Rev* 39:28-31+ Je 19 '87
Calling for a commission on values in public education [T. Hall] *Christ Today* 31:43-4 S 18 '87
Character education and clinical intervention: a paradigm shift for U.S. schools. P. London. bibl f il *Phi Delta Kappan* 68:667-73 My '87
Education and values [address, October 12, 1987] T. Ehrlich. *Vital Speeches Day* 54:106-9 D 1 '87
Education of the heart [college] J. T. Laney. il *Christ Today* 31:21 F 6 '87
Escape into esthetics. J. J. Pelikan. *Cent Mag* 20:57-8 Ja/F '87
Higher education [address, September 8, 1987] J. A. Howard. *Vital Speeches Day* 54:13-17 O 15 '87
How faith helps parents raise good kids. J. Breig. il *U S Cathol* 52:26-31 Mr '87
The humanist family and moral education. D. Carroll. por *Humanist* 47:35-6 Mr/Ap '87
In teens we trust. M. Mantle. il *U S Cathol* 52:29-31 My '87
A matter of mission: the dilemma of teaching in expensive places. B. DeMott. *Change* 19:62 My/Je '87
Morality and education [address, January 27, 1987] S. J. Trachtenberg. *Vital Speeches Day* 53:333-5 Mr 15 '87
Nothing less will do. G. L. Bauer. por *Saturday Evening Post* 259:14+ N '87
Sex, psychology and censorship: preserving the freedoms of the mind. P. Scales. il por *Humanist* 47:18-22+ S/O '87
Superkids and superparents. H. Smith. il *Christ Today* 31:14-15 S 18 '87
Teaching morality in the classroom. G. L. Bauer. *Educ Dig* 52:2-5 Mr '87
True stories [use of real events to teach values] F. K. Lord. il *Parents* 62:81-2+ Ag '87
Understanding right and wrong [two year olds] B. Weissbourd. il *Parents* 62:197 D '87
Using a hidden curriculum for moral education [democratic processes can teach values] C. Power and L. Kohlberg. *Educ Dig* 52:10-13 My '87
The value of 'values education' [California] P. Dworkin. il *U S News World Rep* 102:61 F 23 '87
Values education demands fortitude. *America* 156:474-5 Je 13 '87
What we must teach our children about character. W. J. Bennett. il *Read Dig* 130:100-2 My '87
A word about character. A. C. Lewis. *Phi Delta Kappan* 68:724-5 Je '87
Anecdotes, facetiae, satire, etc.
Of Ivy and success. R. Baker. il *N Y Times Mag* p20 Ag 30 '87
Moral Majority
See also
Liberty Federation
Falwell puts politics behind him—for the most part. *Christ Today* 31:53-4 D 11 '87
For Falwell: new job, new questions [questionable use of funds donated for Sudanese famine relief] S. Emerson and G. Witkin. il por *U S News World Rep* 102:60-1 Ap 6 '87
Goodbye to all that [J. Falwell steps down] M. Miller. por *Newsweek* 110:10 N 16 '87
A Jerry-built coalition regroups [resignation of J. Falwell] R. N. Ostling. il por *Time* 130:68-9 N 16 '87
Moral philosophy *See* Ethics
Moral theology *See* Christian ethics
Morale
See also
Employee morale
Optimism
Morale, National
"Citty upon a hill". T. R. Davis and S. M. Lynn-Jones. bibl f *Foreign Policy* 66:20-38 Spr '87
Cultural failure: the American preoccupation. W. F. Gavin. *Current* 293:16-19 Je '87
Feeling good about America [American children; survey] il *USA Today (Periodical)* 116:4-5 Ag '87

Morale, National—*cont.*
Is America going to the dogs? J. McLaughlin. *Natl Rev* 39:22 Jl 31 '87
Notes and comment [mood of happy feelings has run its course] *New Yorker* 62:25 F 2 '87
Presidents: men of the hour don't stand the test of time ["national mood" candidates; study by David G. Winter] J. Fischman. *Psychol Today* 21:13 My '87
'We should have listened to Jimmy Carter'. C. Bremner. *World Press Rev* 34:64 My '87
Canada
Nothing to fear but the fearful [free trade accord with the U.S.] D. Francis. il *Macleans* 100:13 O 19 '87
The Peter Mansbridge syndrome [talented Canadians opting to leave Canada] C. Gordon. il *Macleans* 100:52 N 30 '87
A turning away from politics [Maclean's/Decima poll; special section; with editorial comment by Kevin Doyle] il *Macleans* 100:2, 24-8+ Ja 5 '87
Germany (West)
Hitler's shadow. P. Schneider. il *Harpers* 275:49-54 S '87
West Germany's old demons. D. C. Marsh. il *World Press Rev* 34:22-4 S '87
Japan
Japan just can't believe it's a superstar. B. Buell. il *Bus Week* p64 Jl 13 '87
Philippines
A damaged culture. J. M. Fallows. il *Atlantic* 260:49-54+ N '87
United States
See Morale, National
Morales, Andrés
(tr) *See* Rivarola Matto, Juan Bautista. Soul brother
Morales, Armando, 1927-
about
Armando Morales. M. McCombie. il *Art News* 86:29 F '87
Morales, Arqueles
Vice president and author. il por *World Press Rev* 34:58 N '87
Morales, Edwin
about
Against all odds. R. Arias. il pors *People Wkly* 28:32-42+ O 26 '87
Morales, Ernesto Barreto- *See* Barreto-Morales, Ernesto
Morales, Pablo
about
Graduating with honors. C. Neff. il pors *Sports Illus* 66:52+ Ap 13 '87
Morality *See* Ethics
Morality and religion *See* Christian ethics
Morals *See* Ethics
Morals and politics *See* Political ethics
Morals and war *See* War and morals
Moran, Gabriel
Dominion over the earth [cover story] bibl il *Commonweal* 114:697-701 D 4 '87
Moran, Malcolm
Will instant replay trip the ref? il *N Y Times Mag* p24-30+ Ja 25 '87
Moran, Mount (Wyo.) climbs *See* Mountaineering
Moravia, Alberto, 1907-
The terrorist aesthetic; tr. by John Satriano. *Harpers* 274:37-9+ Je '87
Morden, Reid
about
Ottawa's unlikely spymaster. il por *Macleans* 100:13 S 28 '87
More than the news [television program] *See* Television program reviews—Single works
Morehouse College
Dr. Gloster weeps as he awards Wonder last degree as president of Morehouse. il pors *Jet* 72:24 Je 8 '87
Dr. Leroy Keith elected new Morehouse president. por *Jet* 72:7 My 11 '87
Nobel winner will accept a Morehouse degree only [African writer W. Soyinka] il por *Jet* 72:28 Ap 27 '87
Spike Lee filming banned at alma mater in Atlanta. *Jet* 72:55 My 11 '87
Morehouse School of Medicine
Winfield joins Morehouse School of Medicine board. por *Jet* 72:26 Je 1 '87
Moreira, Airto
about
Flora Purim/Airto Moreira. M. Bourne. il pors *Down Beat* 54:15 Ja '87

Morel, Benoit
ATBM—a solution in search of a problem. bibl f *Bull At Sci* 43:39-41 My '87
Morel cooking *See* Cooking—Mushrooms
Morelia (Mexico)
Description
Morelia: Mexico's candy capital. R. Bulter. il *Américas* 39:56-7 My/Je '87
Morell, Virginia
Announcing the birth of a heresy [cover story] il *Discover* 8:26-8+ Mr '87
Moreno, Eliseo, d. 1987
about
An everyday death. I. Austen. il por *Macleans* 100:16+ Mr 16 '87
Moreno, Elsa M., and others
Children of Latin America and the Caribbean. il *World Health* p14-15+ O '87
Moreschi, Daniel G.
about
Houston facility wages a war against AIDS. E. Fudge. *Christ Today* 31:52+ Mr 6 '87
Morgan, Brian L. G.
Kitchen alert: the right way to store and prepare food. il *Ladies Home J* 104:50+ Ap '87
Morgan, C. Allan
Green mansion. il *Nat Hist* 96:108-9 N '87
Morgan, Charles D., Jr.
about
Cutting out the guesswork. M. Barrier. il *Nations Bus* 75:77-8 Jl '87
Morgan, Edmund S.
Popular fiction. il *New Repub* 196:25-32+ Je 29 '87
Morgan, Ernest
The long-term effects of death education and counseling. *Humanist* 47:27-8+ Mr/Ap '87
Morgan, Frank
about
A newfound jazz master. D. Gates. il por *Newsweek* 109:69 Ap 6 '87
West Coast ghost. F. Davis. il *Atlantic* 260:97-9 O '87
Morgan, Gwen G.
For-profit vs. not-for-profit. il *Parents* 62:108-9 Ap '87
Morgan, H. Wayne (Howard Wayne)
An epitaph for Mr. Lincoln. il por *Am Herit* 38:58-63 F/Mr '87
Morgan, Howard Wayne *See* Morgan, H. Wayne (Howard Wayne)
Morgan, J. P. (John Pierpont), 1867-1943
about
European decorative arts. S. B. Sherrill. il *Antiques* 131:48+ Ja '87
J. P. Morgan and Kaiser Wilhelm II. E. Sorel and N. C. Sorel. il *Atlantic* 259:67 Mr '87
J.P. Morgan: the agglomerator. J. Merwin. il por *Forbes* 140:275+ Jl 13 '87
Tycoon taste. J. Strouse. il por *House Gard* 159:94+ My '87
Morgan, Jacqui, 1939-
The watercolor page. il por *Am Artist* 51:38-41+ Ja '87
Morgan, James I., and others
Mapping patterns of c-*fos* expression in the central nervous system after seizure. bibl f il *Science* 237:192-7 Jl 10 '87
Morgan, Jeffrey R., and others
Expression of an exogenous growth hormone gene by transplantable human epidermal cells. bibl f il *Science* 237:1476-9 S 18 '87
Morgan, Joe
about
Morgan says he'd manage only with the right team. por *Jet* 72:46 Jl 27 '87
Morgan, John Pierpont *See* Morgan, J. P. (John Pierpont), 1867-1943
Morgan, Julia
about
California Xanadu. A. Cockburn. il pors *House Gard* 159:222-30+ O '87
Morgan, Len
Vectors. *See* issues of Flying
Morgan, Michael
about
Morgan replaces ill Chicago Symphony conductor Solti. por *Jet* 72:38 Je 15 '87
Morgan, Robert P., 1934-
(jt. auth) *See* Barber, Elinor G., and Morgan, Robert P., 1934-
Morgan, Robin
Dry your smile [fiction] il *Ms* 16:54-7 N '87

Morgan, Sherard Y., d. 1987
about
Obituary
Jet 73:28 D 14 '87
Morgan, Stanley
about
Steamin' Stanley. A. Murphy. il pors *Sports Illus* 67 Sp Issue:86-8+ S 9 '87
Morgan, Ted, 1932-
The Barbie file [cover story] il pors *N Y Times Mag* p18-24+ My 10 '87
Voices from the Barbie trial [cover story] il pors *N Y Times Mag* p20-5+ Ag 2 '87
Morgan, Thomas Bruce, 1926-
What does a sixty-year-old man see when he looks in the mirror? il *Esquire* 107:161-4+ My '87
Morgan (J.E.) Knitting Mills, Inc. See J.E. Morgan Knitting Mills, Inc.
Morgan (J. P.) & Co. Incorporated See J. P. Morgan & Co. Incorporated
Morgan Stanley and Company
Adviser beware: cooked books may burn you, too [investment bankers face fraud charges in CPC International's suit against McKesson and Morgan Stanley over sale of C. F. Mueller] L. J. Tell. il *Bus Week* p58+ O 26 '87
Grabbing a fair share [doing business in Japan] il *U S News World Rep* 103:40-1 Ag 24 '87
The Street is fretting over 'Street sweeps' [P. Bilzerian loses Pay 'N Pak when Morgan Stanley cancels trade] A. Bianco. il por *Bus Week* p71-2 Ag 3 '87
Morgenstern, Steve
Business simulations. il *Work Woman* 12:54+ My '87
Morgenthau, Hans Joachim, 1904-
about
Words and deeds in foreign policy. K. W. Thompson. *Society* 24:24-8 My/Je '87
Morgret, Jessie
about
From the jaws of death. H. Hurt. il *Read Dig* 130:116-20 Ap '87
Morgret, Michael
about
From the jaws of death. H. Hurt. il *Read Dig* 130:116-20 Ap '87
Mori, Hanae
about
Paris, Tokyo, New York: Hanae Mori's style goes everywhere—and so does her chef. W. P. Rayner and C. Rayner. il por *Vogue* 177:300 O '87
Mori, Hiroshi, and others
Ubiquitin is a component of paired helical filaments in Alzheimer's disease. bibl f il *Science* 235:1641-4 Mr 27 '87
Mori, Jim, and McKee, Chris
Outward-dipping ring-fault structure at Rabaul caldera as shown by earthquake locations. bibl f il map *Science* 235:193-5 Ja 9 '87
Moriarty-Schieven, G. H.
(jt. auth) See Huang, Y.-L., and Moriarty-Schieven, G. H.
Morice, Laura
Endometriosis: the new young women's infertility disease. il *Mademoiselle* 93:94 D '87
Should you trust the touch of a chiropractor? il *Mademoiselle* 93:82 Je '87
Morisot, Berthe, 1841-1895
about
Berthe Morisot's experimental techniques and impressionist style. W. P. Scott. il *Am Artist* 51:42-7 D '87
Fragments of reverie. M. Stevens. il *Newsweek* 110:80 S 28 '87
Revising the history of impressionism. il *Publ Wkly* 232:29-30 S 11 '87
A woman of substance. K. Larson. il *N Y* 20:130+ S 28 '87
Morita, Akio
about
Sony's challenge [cover story] L. Armstrong. il pors *Bus Week* p64-9 Je 1 '87
Morita, Pat
Photographs and photography
The background of a shot. G. Bernstein. il pors *Petersens Photogr Mag* 16:20 Jl '87
Morita & Company
The saga of Sony all started with sake. A. Borrus. il *Bus Week* p66 Je 1 '87
Morley, Jefferson
The ballad of Fawn and Arturo [cover story] il *Nation* 245:397+ O 17 '87

Darkness on the edge of the shining city. il *New Repub* 196:20-3 Mr 23 '87
Ollie's blueprint. *New Repub* 196:16-18 My 25 '87
The paradox of North's popularity. il *Nation* 245:122-5 Ag 15-22 '87
Story of a consummate bureaucrat [cover story] *Nation* 245:737+ D 19 '87
(jt. auth) See Corn, David, and Morley, Jefferson
Morley, Jefferson, and Rosenberg, Tina
The real heroes of contra-gate. il pors *Roll Stone* p48-50+ S 10 '87
La Mormaire (France: Garden) See Gardens and gardening—France
Mormons and Mormonism
A Latter-Day forger [Mormon M. Hofmann pleads guilty to murder] A. Wilentz. il por *Time* 129:32 F 2 '87
A motion picture Bible according to Mormonism [edited version of the New Media Bible] R. Frame. il *Christ Today* 31:44+ S 18 '87
Salt Lake City diarist. H. Fairlie. *New Repub* 196:42 Mr 2 '87
Temple on a hill [Manti, Utah] il *Americana* 15:51-3 S/O '87

Employees
Should a Mormon-owned corporation be able to fire a Mormon who does not tithe? [Supreme Court considers discrimination case of F. Mayson] R. F. Drinan. il *America* 156:375-6 My 9 '87
Supreme Court hears challenge to church hiring policies [discrimination case filed by F. Mayson against the Mormon church] E. J. Larson. *Christ Today* 31:49-50 My 15 '87

Great Britain
The first Mormon mission to Britain. A. M. Smith. bibl il *Hist Today* 37:24-31 Jl '87
The morning after [film] See Motion picture reviews—Single works
Morning news (Dallas, Tex.) See Dallas morning news
The morning program [television program] See Television program reviews—Single works
Morning rooms See Dining alcoves, etc.
Moroccan cooking See Cooking, Moroccan
Morocco
See also
Airports—Morocco
Essaouira (Morocco)
Marrakesh (Morocco)
Tangier (Morocco)
United Nations—Morocco
United States—Diplomatic and consular service—Morocco

Description and travel
See also
Automobile touring—Morocco

Foreign relations
United States
See United States—Foreign relations—Morocco

Territorial expansion
See also
Western Sahara conflict, 1975-
Moroles, Jesus Bautista, 1950-
about
Jesús Bautista Moroles. M. McCombie. il *Art News* 86:57-8 Ja '87
Morphogenesis
See also
Differentiation (Biology)
Form-fitting genes [identification of morphogen; research by Christina Thaller and Gregor Eichele] *Discover* 8:8+ S '87
Shape-inducing chemical identified [retinoic acid; research by Christina Thaller and Gregor Eichele] R. Weiss. il *Sci News* 131:406 Je 27 '87
Morphology
See also
Body size
Homology (Biology)
Morphogenesis
Morphy, Paul, 1837-1884
about
Paul Morphy: the pride and sorrow of chess. B. McGinty. por *Am Hist Illus* 22:50-1 Mr '87
Morra, Marion, and Potts, Eve
Breast cancer. *Good Housekeep* 204:153-6 My '87
Morricone, Ennio
about
The lyrical assassin at 5 a.m. J. Cocks. il por *Time* 129:83 Mr 16 '87

Morris, Adrian G., Jr.
about
The charge: AIDS assault. A. Press. il por *Newsweek* 109:24 Je 22 '87
Morris, Charles S.
The eye's view of Comet Halley. il *Astronomy* 15:90-6 Ja '87
Morris, Cynthia
Ageproofing our skin: the latest achievements. il *Essence* 18:72-3+ Ag '87
Beauty, health and fitness! il *Essence* 18:64-5 Je '87
Morris, Daniel
Can parents of toddlers find time to pamper their faith? il *U S Cathol* 52:21-8 My '87
Covetousness: the one who dies with the most toys wins. il *U S Cathol* 52:13-14 Ag '87
Morris, Desmond
The secret lives of dogs and cats [condensed from Dogwatching and Catwatching] il *Read Dig* 131:47-8+ D '87
Morris, Edmund
about
Upstairs at the White House [interview] il por *U S News World Rep* 103:51 Ag 3 '87
Morris, Glenn
(jt. auth) See Belwood, Jacqueline J., and Morris, Glenn
Morris, Gouverneur, 1752-1816
about
American efforts to free Madame de Lafayette. A. L. Levin. il *Am Hist Illus* 22:22-3 O '87
Morris, H. H.
Vanity of vanities. *Christ Century* 104:932 O 28 '87
Morris, James, 1926-
See also
Morris, Jan, 1926-
Morris, James R.
Those burgeoning worker benefits. il *Nations Bus* 75:53-4 F '87
Morris, Jan, 1926-
Future shock in Hong Kong. il *N Y Times Mag* p48-51+ O 25 '87
The pink oasis. il *Vogue* 177:228+ D '87
Splendor in the dust. il *Vogue* 177:348+ Mr '87
Morris, Jill
Your dreams: what you can learn from them! il *Good Housekeep* 204:12+ Ap '87
Morris, Jim
about
The tiny troops of Vicksburg. il por *South Living* 22:17-18 Ag '87
Morris, John N.
On the list [poem] *New Yorker* 63:49 D 7 '87
Morris, Keith
about
Obituary
Sports Illus il por 66:4 Ap 13 '87. D. J. Barr
Morris, Leon, 1914-
More than a symbol. il por *Christ Today* 31:23-5 Ap 17 '87
Morris, Leona
about
It's take two for former teacher Leona Morris as she starts another career on Baltimore TV. il por *People Wkly* 27:84 Ap 27 '87
Morris, Mark
about
Dancevision. J. Gruen. por *Dance Mag* 61:74-5 F '87
Morris to replace Bejart in Brussels. L. Moffett. por *Dance Mag* 61:14 D '87
Mythologies [dance] Reviews
New Yorker 63:83-4 Je 8 '87. A. Croce
Stabat mater [dance] Reviews
Dance Mag 61:35-6 Ap '87. J. R. Acocella
Morris, Max
about
In the beginning was the word. W. G. Flanagan. il por *Forbes* 139:100-1 Ap 20 '87
New reading system promises to increase data retention. J. P. Frank. il *Publ Wkly* 232:64-5 O 16 '87
Morris, Patricia H.
Nasturtium notes. il *Rodale's Org Gard* 34:80 My '87
Morris, Richard B.
A few parchment pages two hundred years later. bibl il *Am Herit* 38:46-51 My/Je '87
Morris, Richard Brandon, 1904-
Empty pockets. il *Life* 10:24 Fall '87
Morris, Robert Lee, 1948-
about
Jewelry designer Robert Lee Morris sinks his claws into heavy metal. B. Johnson. il por *People Wkly* 27:121-2+ My 11 '87

Morris, Roger
Architecture: Antoine Predock. il por *Archit Dig* 44:90-7+ Ag '87
Morris, Scot
Games. See issues of Omni (New York, N.Y.)
Morris, Steveland *See* Wonder, Stevie
Morris (Mark) Dance Group *See* Mark Morris Dance Group
Morris Brown College
Morris Brown College has more than proud tradition. il *Jet* 72:14 Ap 27 '87
Morrison, Ann M., and others
Executive women: substance plus style. il *Psychol Today* 21:18-21+ Ag '87
Women with promise: who succeeds, who fails? [excerpt from Breaking the glass ceiling] il *Work Woman* 12:79-82+ Je '87
Morrison, Bruce
about
Tearaway [film] Reviews
Macleans 100:54 S 14 '87. P. Hluchy
Morrison, Charles C.
Save the queen! il *Conservationist* 42:6-11 Jl/Ag '87
Morrison, Charles E. *See* Morrison, Chuck
Morrison, Chuck
about
These guys don't blink. A. Edmond, Jr. il pors *Black Enterp* 17:310-12+ Je '87
Morrison, David, 1940-
Is the U.S. abandoning the solar system? il *Sky Telesc* 73:580 Je '87
U.S. must renew commitment to planetary exploration. por *Aviat Week Space Technol* 127:143 Ag 10 '87
Morrison, David C.
Black holes in the budget. il *Harpers* 274:50-1 Ja '87
Morrison, Dwight
Nine-station intercom. il *Radio-Electron* 58:57-60 Ja '87
Morrison, Jim, 1943-1971
about
New Jim Morrison writings discovered. M. Goldberg. *Roll Stone* p11+ Ja 29 '87
Morrison, Mark
Michael J. Fox unwinds. il pors *Roll Stone* p30-2+ Mr 12 '87
Morrison, Martha
My 17 years as a drug addict; ed. by Dick Harris. il por *Read Dig* 130:123-6 My '87
Morrison, Philip
Books. See issues of Scientific American
about
Morrison is first recipient of AIP's Gemant Award. por *Phys Today* 40:58 Je '87
Morrison, Richard S., and others
Trophic stimulation of cultured neurons from neonatal rat brain by epidermal growth factor. bibl f il *Science* 238:72-5 O 2 '87
Morrison, Toni, 1931-
Life in his language. il por *N Y Times Book Rev* 92:27 D 20 '87
about
'Five years of terror' [interview] M. Horn. por *U S News World Rep* 103:75 O 19 '87
The ghosts of 'sixty million and more'. W. Clemons. il *Newsweek* 110:75 S 28 '87
PW interviews. A. Smith. por *Publ Wkly* 232:50-1 Ag 21 '87
Telling how it was. G. C. Ward. il *Am Herit* 38:14+ D '87
Toni Morrison now [interview] E. B. Washington. il por *Essence* 18:58-9+ O '87
Toni Morrison's career. C. Iannone. *Commentary* 84:59-63 D '87
Morrisroe, Patricia
Bess and the mess: Myerson's slide into scandal [cover story] il pors *N Y* 20:30-44 Mr 30 '87
Mega-Mort: superagent Janklow's blockbuster life. il pors *N Y* 20:34-40+ F 2 '87
Report from the front. il *N Y* 20:58-70 N 30 '87
'Too much money, too much time': the life and death of Sandy Marsh [cover story] il pors *N Y* 20:42-51 S 14 '87
Morrissey, John F.
Shark research at sea. bibl il map *Sea Front* 33:244-55 Jl/Ag '87
Morrocco, Anthony
about
Mane man Anthony Morrocco works on moon time to deliver the kindest cut of all. il por *People Wkly* 28:113 Jl 13 '87

Morrow, Richard Martin
about
One cautious gambler. C. Knowlton. por *Fortune* 116:51
Ag 3 '87
Morrow, W. Scot
Should public schools teach creation science? por *Christ
Today* 31:50 S 18 '87
Morrow, Walter E., Jr.
SDI research is critical. il *Technol Rev* 90:24-5+ Jl '87
Morrow (William) & Co., Inc. *See* William Morrow &
Co., Inc.
Morse, Barry
about
Profiles in greasepaint. P. Hluchy. por *Macleans* 100:56
O 26 '87
Morse, Bradford, 1921-
about
UNDP chief Bradford Morse to retire. il por *UN Chron*
23:62 Ja '86
Morse, Kingsley G.
about
Airline president predicts demise of independent U.S.
commuters. il *Aviat Week Space Technol* 126:53 Je
29 '87
Morse, Margaret
Penthouse poise. il *House Gard* 159:126-33 Ja '87
Russian folk in Taos. il *House Gard* 159:198-203 Ap
'87
Morse, Roger A.
Bee fever. bibl il *Conservationist* 41:33-5 My/Je '87
Morse, Ronald A.
Japan's drive to pre-eminence. *Foreign Policy* 69:3-21
Wint '87/'88
The United States-Japan economic Olympics [address,
December 11-12, 1986] *Vital Speeches Day* 53:409-11
Ap 15 '87
Morse, Steve
about
Steve Morse: guitar power. R. Tolleson. il pors *Down
Beat* 54:16-18+ Ap '87
Steve Morse's The whistle—a guitar transcription. J.
Dennison. il *Down Beat* 54:59 Ap '87
Mort, Jo-Ann
The vanishing labor beat. il *Nation* 245:588-90 N 21
'87
Mortality
See also
AIDS (Disease)—Mortality
Black women—Mortality
Cancer—Mortality
Cerebrovascular disease—Mortality
Children—Mortality
Death
Dolphins—Mortality
Executives—Mortality
Heart—Diseases—Mortality
Indochinese—United States—Mortality
Infant mortality
Veterans—Mortality
Youth—Mortality
The century's top five. il *U S News World Rep* 103:62
Ag 17 '87
"Drivin' my life away" [epidemiology of fatal motor
vehicle crashes] maps *Sci Am* 257:28+ Ag '87
Great quake body count [1906 quake in San Francisco]
J. Silberner. *Sci News* 131:255 Ap 18 '87
Tobacco's toll [leading cause of preventable deaths]
Newsweek 110:62 N 9 '87
Mortensen, Lance
about
For sale: the rich look. J. Adler. il *Newsweek* 109:80
Je 22 '87
Mortgage banks
See also
Citicorp Mortgage, Inc.
ComFed Savings Bank
Accounting
Mystery profits [accrual accounting] L. Jereski. il *Forbes*
139:54 Ap 20 '87
Acquisitions and mergers
At 69, J.B. Fuqua still keeps 'em guessing [selling Georgia
Federal Bank] S. Ticer. il por *Bus Week* p82 N 23
'87
Mortgage bonds and notes
Bear Stearns: hitting its stride while others trip [com-
puterized mortgage securities trading] D. Zigas. il por
Bus Week p59-60 Ag 31 '87
The big loss at Merrill Lynch: why it was blindsided
[mortgage bond debacle] E. Spragins. il *Bus Week*
p112-13 My 18 '87

Bond bombshell [Merrill Lynch bond trader H. Rubin's
mortgage securities loss] il *Time* 129:53 My 11 '87
Burned by Fannie, Ginnie, or Freddie? Try a CMO
[collateralized mortgage obligations] D. Zigas. il *Bus
Week* p112 Je 15 '87
Buy mortgages [Ginnie Mae pools] B. Weberman. il
Forbes 139:193 Je 1 '87
Eat your heart out, Ginnie Mae [collateralized mortgage
obligations] D. Zigas. il *Changing Times* 41:31-4 Jl
'87
Fed up with GNMAs? Check out CMOs [collateralized
mortgage obligations] *Money* 16:14 S '87
The fickle ways of Ginnie Mae. J. Blyskal. il *50 Plus*
27:78-83 F '87
Ginnie Mae's woes. P. Brandon. il *Changing Times*
41:12+ N '87
Government minus [misrepresentation of government
bond fund yields] B. Weberman. il *Forbes* 139:117
Ap 20 '87
High-yield alternative to Ginnie Maes [collateralized
mortgage obligations] *Changing Times* 41:11 Ja '87
How Wall Street is driving the mortgage market. C.
Farrell. il *Bus Week* p108-9 My 4 '87
Merrill Lynch takes a bath [mortgage securities trading
loss] D. Pauly. il *Newsweek* 109:53 My 11 '87
Merrill's loss: why the numbers keep changing [trading
fiasco in mortgage-backed securities] E. Spragins. il
Bus Week p72 Ag 3 '87
Move over, corporate bonds. D. Zigas. il *Bus Week*
p118 Je 8 '87
Move over Ginnie Mae, here comes Farmer Mac. T.
Smart. *Bus Week* p72 Ag 24 '87
Profits from mortgages [Canada] A. Walmsley. il *Macleans*
100:26 Ja 12 '87
Reverse discrimination on the Street [Dept. of Agriculture
decision to distribute Rural Housing Senior Mortgage
passthroughs by minority firms] D. Seligman. il *Fortune*
116:142 O 26 '87
Wall Street reaches for the skyscraper market [commercial
mortgage securities] E. Spragins. il *Bus Week* p88-9
Je 15 '87
Mortgage brokers
Ethical aspects
The big loss at Merrill Lynch: why it was blindsided
[mortgage bond debacle] E. Spragins. il *Bus Week*
p112-13 My 18 '87
Bond bombshell [Merrill Lynch bond trader H. Rubin's
mortgage securities loss] il *Time* 129:53 My 11 '87
Home loan horrors. D. M. Topolnicki. il *Money* 16:69-70+
Ag '87
Merrill Lynch takes a bath [mortgage securities trading
loss] D. Pauly. il *Newsweek* 109:53 My 11 '87
Merrill's loss: why the numbers keep changing [trading
fiasco in mortgage-backed securities] E. Spragins. il
Bus Week p72 Ag 3 '87
Mortgage companies *See* Mortgage banks
Mortgage insurance *See* Insurance, Mortgage
Mortgages
See also
Discrimination in mortgages
Federal National Mortgage Association
Foreclosure
Home equity conversion
Information storage and retrieval systems—Real
estate use
Insurance, Mortgage
United States. Federal Home Loan Bank Board
Accelerated payments cut years off mortgage. H. Porter.
il *Fam Handyman* 37:16 My/Je '87
Adjustable mortgages: they're not created equal. A. Z.
Cuneo. il *Bus Week* p150 F 23 '87
Attack of sticker shock [interest rates jump] *Time* 129:58
Ap 27 '87
Computerized mortgage shopping: a lack of interest.
P. E. Godwin. il *Changing Times* 41:20 Je '87
Deciphering mortgages. T. Tilling. *Parents* 62:48+ Ag
'87
Fast-track loans. H. J. Lehman. il *Changing Times* 41:14
Ja '87
Government still backs energy-saving improvements
[Energy Efficient Mortgage] H. Porter. *Fam Handyman*
37:22 F '87
Here's the point of it all. M. Schiffres. *U S News World
Rep* 102:49 Ap 13 '87
Home loan horrors. D. M. Topolnicki. il *Money* 16:69-70+
Ag '87
Home loan strategies: what to do about rising rates.
M. Daly. il *Better Homes Gard* 65:52 Ag '87
Homing in on a home loan. J. Bodnar. *Changing Times*
41:8 Ag '87

Mortgages—*cont.*

How to hedge against rising mortgage rates. J. N. Frank. *Bus Week* p142 My 4 '87

How to win the struggle to fit a mortgage lender's mold [self-employed] H. Porter. il *Fam Handyman* 37:9+ D '87

Ill-informed buyer gets duped [unexpected second mortgage from signing document for home improvement loan] H. Porter. *Fam Handyman* 37:14+ Jl/Ag '87

Interest rates may nail housing. W. B. Franklin and J. C. Cooper. il *Bus Week* p27-8 My 4 '87

Keeping loan commitments locked up. *Consum Rep* 52:407 Jl '87

A look at adjustable rate mortgages. il *Consum Res Mag* 70:27-31 Jl '87

Making the best deal in today's mortgage market. D. Lamaute. il *Black Enterp* 17:23-4 My '87

Money-saving mortgage math [figuring accuracy of ARM payment adjustments] il *Changing Times* 41:79-80+ N '87

Mortgage-hunting? ARMs have some new twists. D. Zigas. *Bus Week* p118 Jl 13 '87

Mortgage rates: catch the best deal. M. Schiffres. il *Changing Times* 41:76-80 S '87

Mortgages: buy that house now—or pay more later. il *Money* 16:24 N '87

Mortgages: fixed rates go below 9% for the first time since '78. il *Money* 16:40 Ja '87

Mortgages: how to look smart by missing the points. il *Money* 16:30 O '87

Mortgages: how to put the ARM on your banker. il *Money* 16:28 D '87

Mortgages: lenders pull a fast one by slowing down. il *Money* 16:32 Jl '87

Mortgages: now at least you will know how high is up. il *Money* 16:28 S '87

Mortgages: now there are quick fixes on adjustable loans. il *Money* 16:26 Ag '87

Mortgages: rates are even low enough to revive Detroit. il *Money* 16:36 Ap '87

Mortgages: rates aren't likely to spurt till spring. il *Money* 16:44 F '87

Mortgages: rates may be about as low as they will go. il *Money* 16:36 Mr '87

Mortgages: rush is on to close deals before rates hit 11%. il *Money* 16:41 Je '87

Mortgages: sooner or later, what goes down must come up. il *Money* 16:26 My '87

Mortgages that go bump in the night [adjustable rate mortgages] A. McGrath. il *U S News World Rep* 103:54 Jl 13 '87

Moving in without moving down [trailing spouse mortgages] P. E. Godwin. il *Changing Times* 41:20 Jl '87

News on the home front. J. A. Conway. il *Forbes* 139:8 Je 1 '87

Return of the low rates [Canada] D. Jenish. il *Macleans* 100:27 F 9 '87

A second mortgage that turned into a first-class nightmare [Richard D. Price family] D. Cook. il *Bus Week* p68 F 9 '87

Second thoughts on second mortgages. B. Weberman. il *Forbes* 140:42 O 5 '87

Shopping the mortgage supermarket. H. Wheelwright. il *Money* 16:78 Je '87

Sorry, sir, that was this morning's rate. S. Bartlett. il *Bus Week* p109 My 4 '87

Test-drive a convertible mortgage. *Money* 16:13 S '87

Thinking of your house as a cash cow. C. P. Work. il *U S News World Rep* 102:56-7 Je 8 '87

Winning the ARM's race. J. B. Quinn. il *Newsweek* 109:43 Ja 19 '87

Prepayment

Unmortgaging the future. L. Scheer. il *Forbes* 140:218+ N 30 '87

Refinancing

Taxation

See Mortgages—Taxation

Taxation

Just one more form . . . [home mortgage interest deduction] M. Kaus. il *Newsweek* 110:21 Ag 24 '87

New tax law. M. C. Thomsett. il *Home Mech* 83:16 N '87

New tax laws save mortgage interest deduction. H. Porter. *Fam Handyman* 37:12 Ja '87

Pitfalls of refinancing. G. W. Padwe. il *Nations Bus* 75:44 Je '87

Refinancing: when to play your points. P. Philipps. il *Bus Week* p182 Jl 20 '87

Refinancing your home. G. W. Padwe. *Nations Bus* 75:66-7 Ja '87

Rules change for the income tax game. H. Porter. il *Fam Handyman* 37:20 Ap '87

What the new tax law means to homeowners. M. Daly. il *Better Homes Gard* 65:27+ F '87

Morticians *See* Undertakers and undertaking

Mortimer, Edward

The quest for a leader. *World Press Rev* 34:12 D '87

Mortise and tenon joints *See* Joints (Carpentry)

Morton, Alexandra

Into the world of orcas. il *Int Wildl* 17:12-17 S/O '87

Morton, Frederic

The boys of winter. il *N Y Times Mag* p54 Mr 1 '87

Tales of the Grand Teutons: Karl May among the Indians. por *N Y Times Book Rev* 92:15-16 Ja 4 '87

about

PW interviews. S. S. Steinberg. por *Publ Wkly* 231:69-70 Je 12 '87

Morton, James Parks

about

Architecture. C. Wiseman. il *N Y* 20:122-3 S 21 '87

Dogs in the manger. D. K. Mano. *Natl Rev* 39:65-6 Ja 30 '87

Morton, Nelle, 1905-1987

about

Obituary

Christ Century 104:711-12 Ag 26-S 2 '87. B. Thompson

Morton, Robin, 1953-1986

about

Obituary

Int Wildl il por 17:17 S/O '87. A. Morton

Morton-Norwich Products Inc.

See also

Morton Thiokol, Inc.

Morton Thiokol, Inc.

Can Thiokol rise from Challenger's ashes? J. Mendes. *Fortune* 115:152+ Je 8 '87

Congress, booster manufacturers criticize joint redesign program [design for shuttle booster] C. Covault. il *Aviat Week Space Technol* 126:116-17 F 9 '87

FBI investigating fraud charges against Morton Thiokol in manufacture of shuttle solid rocket motors. *Aviat Week Space Technol* 126:41-2 Ap 27 '87

Life beyond Challenger. C. Siler. por *Forbes* 140:44 S 21 '87

Morton Thiokol hot-fires redesigned space shuttle solid rocket motor joint. il *Aviat Week Space Technol* 127:23 Ag 10 '87

Morton Thiokol will forfeit $10 million in lieu of contract penalty. *Aviat Week Space Technol* 126:28 Mr 2 '87

Rocket scientists [stock price] T. Jaffe. il *Forbes* 140:180 Jl 27 '87

Thiokol begins full-diameter tests of redesigned SRB field joint [shuttle solid rocket booster] M. A. Dornheim. il *Aviat Week Space Technol* 126:119+ F 9 '87

Thiokol evaluates first full-scale test of redesigned shuttle booster. il *Aviat Week Space Technol* 127:26-7 S 7 '87

Thiokol test fires shuttle motor, reinstates old O-ring material. M. A. Dornheim. il *Aviat Week Space Technol* 126:26 Je 1 '87

MOS *See* Metal oxide semiconductors

Mosaic Systems, Inc.

Mosaic Systems develops circuit board with electrically programmable network [wafer scale integration technique] il *Aviat Week Space Technol* 126:81 Ap 6 '87

Mosaic viruses *See* Viruses, Plant

Mosaics

Exhibitions

Carthage [D. Soren and Carthaginian exhibit at American Museum of Natural History] *New Yorker* 63:36-7 D 14 '87

A fanciful way with ferocity [Carthage: a mosaic of ancient Tunisia] M. Stevens. il *Newsweek* 110:95-6 D 7 '87

The treasures of ancient Tunisia [Carthage: a mosaic of ancient Tunisia] R. Bacher. il *Nat Hist* 96:68+ D '87

Mosaics (Biology)

A chimeric, ligan-binding v-erbB/EGF receptor retains transforming potential. H. Riedel and others. bibl f il *Science* 236:197-200 Ap 10 '87

Heritable somatic excision of a Drosophila transposon. G. J. Bryan and others. bibl f il *Science* 235:1636-8 Mr 27 '87

Tolerance induced by thymic epithelial grafts in birds. H. Ohki and others. bibl f il *Science* 237:1032-5 Ag 28 '87

Mosasaurs *See* Reptiles, Fossil
Moscardini, Thomas
about
Art cop. H. Polskin. il por *N Y* 20:28+ O 26 '87
Moscow (Soviet Union)
Description
Asymmetry [meeting of the International Physicians for the Prevention of Nuclear War in Moscow] J. Hersey. *New Yorker* 63:36-40+ S 7 '87
From Russia with *glasnost*. K. Rodeghier. il *Travel Holiday* 168:60-6 Ag '87
Moscow revisited. J. Woll. il *New Leader* 70:7-9 F 9-23 '87
Galleries and museums
See also
Pushkin Museum of Fine Arts (Moscow, Soviet Union)
Hospitals
Automation and microsurgery [Moscow Scientific Research Institute of Eye Microsurgery] S. Fedorov. il *Courier* 40:33-4 Ag '87
Newspapers
See also
Moscow news
Protests, demonstrations, etc.
Testing the limits of *glasnost* [Crimean Tatars demonstrate in Red Square] S. Thomas. il *Time* 130:22 Ag 10 '87
Restaurants, nightclubs, bars, etc.
Capitalism on Kropotkinskaya Street [Café 36] J. O. Jackson. il *Time* 130:39 Jl 27 '87
Stores
See also
GUM (Moscow, Soviet Union)
Theater
Director without a country [Soviet exile Y. Lyubimov of Taganka Theater] R. B. Cullen. il por *Newsweek* 109:60 Ja 19 '87
Moscow Ballet
Dancing:
Baltimore performances. A. Croce. *New Yorker* 63:115-17 O 12 '87
Solo flights [performances at the War Memorial Auditorium, Trenton, N.J.] T. Tobias. il *N Y* 20:84-5 D 14 '87
Moscow Book Fair *See* Book fairs
Moscow M. V. Lomonosov State University
Satellites for the classroom [joint U.S.-U.S.S.R. course on the nuclear arms race] S. Begley. il *Newsweek* 110:103 N 16 '87
Moscow news
'Glasnost' in print. L. Branson. il *World Press Rev* 34:34-5 Ag '87
Mosedale, Laura
Breaking up with my out-laws. il *Glamour* 85:324 N '87
How to wear a miniskirt. il pors *Glamour* 85:192-3+ D '87
Women right now. See issues of Glamour
Moser, Diane, 1944-
(jt. auth) See Spangenburg, Ray, 1939-, and Moser, Diane, 1944-
Moser, Heinz E., and Dervan, Peter B.
Sequence-specific cleavage of double helical DNA by triple helix formation. bibl f il *Science* 238:645-50 O 30 '87
Moser, Penny Ward
Maybe it was something you ate (I). il *Saturday Evening Post* 259:62-3+ Ap '87
Maybe it was something you ate (II). il *Saturday Evening Post* 259:46-9 My/Je '87
Watch out for food poisoning! il *Read Dig* 131:113-17 S '87
Moser, Winfried L.
Mozambicans in diaspora. *America* 156:440-1+ My 30 '87
Moses, Edwin
about
Ed Moses looks forward to new streak after loss. il pors *Jet* 72:51 Je 22 '87
Moses wins, Nehemiah falls at track meet in England. *Jet* 72:46 Ag 17 '87
The reign ended in Spain. P. Butcher. il pors *Sports Illus* 66:34-5 Je 15 '87
Moses, Gilbert
about
A conversation with . . . D. Armstrong. il por *Essence* 17:26 Ja '87
Moses, Phyllis B.
Strange bedfellows. il *BioScience* 37:6-10 Ja '87

Moses, Robert, 1888-1981
about
Oral history: remembering Robert Moses. M. F. Schmertz. *Archit Rec* 175:9 Jl '87
Moses, Sam
Dale turns 'em pale. il pors *Sports Illus* 67:32-5 S 7 '87
Fit, fast and feisty. il pors *Sports Illus* 67:50+ Jl 20 '87
Gallant victory for an odd bird. il pors *Sports Illus* 66:36-9 Ja 5 '87
Going flat out on the briny. il *Sports Illus* 67:28-9 N 23 '87
Good to the last drop. il *Sports Illus* 66:32-3 F 23 '87
Have helmet, will travel. il por *Sports Illus* 66:30-3 Je 1 '87
Indy air show. il *Sports Illus* 66:22-7 My 18 '87
They burned up the track. il *Sports Illus* 66:72-3 F 9 '87
Very much an Indy-vidual. il pors *Sports Illus* 66:46-8+ My 25 '87
Moses, Sherry
about
Burning alive! S. Kelly. il *Read Dig* 131:95-9 S '87
Mosher, Steven
A mother's ordeal. il *Read Dig* 130:49-55 F '87
Mosier, John
Film. See issues of Américas
Moskin, J. Robert
World beat. See issues of World Press Review through April 1987
Moslems *See* Muslims
Mosley, James L.
about
Teen sues for being denied love role opposite white. *Jet* 72:22 Mr 30 '87
The Mosquito Coast [film] *See* Motion picture reviews—Single works
Mosquito repellents *See* Insect baits and repellents
Mosquitoes
Color-conscious mosquitoes [homochromy; work of Mark Q. Benedict and Jack A. Seawright] il *Sci Am* 257:24+ Ag '87
Mosquitoes may be beneficial [views of Charles L. Hogue] il *USA Today (Periodical)* 116:14 Ag '87
Stable integration and expression of a bacterial gene in the mosquito Anopheles gambiae. L. H. Miller and others. bibl f il *Science* 237:779-81 Ag 14 '87
Control
See also
Malaria—Prevention and control
Mosquitoes as carriers of infection
See also
Malaria
Rift Valley fever
Aedes albopictus in North America: probable introduction in used tires from northern Asia. W. A. Hawley and others. bibl f il *Science* 236:1114-16 My 29 '87
AIDS and insects. W. Booth. il *Science* 237:355-6 Jl 24 '87
A G1 glycoprotein epitope of La Crosse virus: a determinant of infection of Aedes triseriatus. D. R. Sundin and others. bibl f il *Science* 235:591-3 Ja 30 '87
Hold that tiger: a very tiresome pursuit [probable introduction of Asian tiger mosquitoes in used tires from northern Asia; research by Paul Reiter] il map *Discover* 8:8-9 Ag '87
The mosquito AIDS scare. M. Clark. il *Newsweek* 110:47 Jl 13 '87
Slapping down the mosquito [AIDS carrier scare] il *Time* 130:56 Jl 13 '87
Mosquitofish
Now here's a case of you eat what you are [work of Gary Meffe and Martha Crump] il *Discover* 8:10 Je '87
Moss, Ambler H., Jr.
The Panama Canal Treaties: looking back—and ahead. *Américas* 39:53-4 My/Je '87
Moss, Eric Owen
about
Eric Owen Moss: watching his garden grow. K. D. Stein. il *Archit Rec* 175:51 Je '87
Moss, Howard, 1922-1987
Naming a painting [poem] *New Repub* 196:32 My 4 '87
about
Obituary
New Yorker 63:128 O 5 '87

Moss, Jackie
  Contagious skin diseases: things that go itch in the night. il *Curr Health 2* 14:22-3 S '87
  What every teen should know about cancer. il *Curr Health 2* 14:27-9 O '87
Moss, Stanley
  Allegory of evil in Italy [poem] *Nation* 244:696 My 23 '87
  The bathers [poem] *New Yorker* 63:38 Je 1 '87
  Hannibal crossing the Alps [poem] *New Repub* 197:38 N 30 '87
  New York song [poem] *Nation* 245:60 Jl 18-25 '87
  Song of imperfection [poem] *Nation* 244:696 My 23 '87
Moss, Vicki A., and Webster, Judith A.
  Avoiding knee injuries. il *Nations Bus* 75:43-4 Je '87
Moss *See* Mosses
Moss, Spanish *See* Spanish moss
Mossad (Israel) *See* Israel. Mossad
Mössbauer effect
  Looking into metal specimens [Mossbauer imaging; work of Stephen J. Norton] *Sci News* 132:361 D 5 '87
Mosses
  Devils Hopyard, New Hampshire. R. H. Mohlenbrock. il map *Nat Hist* 96:38-40+ O '87
  Gathering moss [J. Biesenkamp's garden in Cherry Hill, N.J.] K. Whiteside. il *House Gard* 159:144-9+ My '87
Mosset, Olivier
about
  Olivier Mosset at John Gibson. J. Rian. il *Art Am* 75:177 S '87
Most-favored-nation tariff policy *See* Tariff—United States
Mostafa, Yaser S. Abu- *See* Abu-Mostafa, Yaser S.
Mostel, Josh
  In your face, mate. il *Esquire* 108:42 N '87
about
  More than Zero. P. Blauner. il por *N Y* 20:22 F 2 '87
Mostly Mozart Festival *See* Music festivals—New York (State)
Mota, Atico Vilas-Boas da
  Black theatre, black consciousness. *Courier* 39:18 D '86
Motavalli, Jim
  A dissident turned back. il por *Progressive* 51:14-15 F '87
Motels *See* Hotels, motels, etc.
Motets
See also
  Compact discs—Motets
Moth orchids *See* Orchids
Mother Earth news
  High tech in the country? [use of personal computers] B. Woods. *Mother Earth News* 105:10 My/Je '87
Mother Goose
Bibliography
  Don't cook Mother Goose. M. C. Livingston. *N Y Times Book Rev* 92:20 Jl 26 '87
Mother-in-law's tongue (Plant) *See* Snake plant
Mother love *See* Love, Maternal
Mother Teresa [film] *See* Motion picture reviews—Single works
Mother Teresa's Mission of Charity *See* Missionaries of Charity
Motherhood *See* Mothers
Mothers
See also
  Childbirth
  Divorced mothers
  Homemakers
  Love, Maternal
  Maternal deprivation
  Mother's Day
  Parent education
  Pregnancy
  Single mothers
  Stepparents and stepchildren
  Surrogate mothers
  Career change [choosing motherhood] E. W. Fielding. il por *Christ Today* 31:26-8 D 11 '87
  Could you be a better mother? [excerpt from The woman who works: the parent who cares] S. Sanger and J. Kelly. *Redbook* 169:94-5+ Je '87
  The go-between. P. Theroux. il *Parents* 62:80+ N '87
  Mother as joymonger. P. Theroux. il *Parents* 62:55-7 D '87
  Mother love. A. Banks. il *Parents* 62:114-15 Ag '87
  Mother told jokes [condensed from An American childhood] A. Dillard. il *Read Dig* 131:122-5 O '87
  Mothering. See issues of Essence

The mothers' page. See issues of McCall's beginning January 1984
  My mother, in memory. R. Ford. il *Harpers* 275:44-57 Ag '87
  My mother's Easter hat. J. Monninger. il *Glamour* 85:108+ Ap '87
  One day a year we give mom flowers; the other 364 we give her grief. Why? il *Glamour* 85:106 My '87
  The private lives of star moms [excerpt from Starring mothers] J. Barber. il pors *McCalls* 114:57+ My '87
  Special mother-daughter issue [cover story] il *Teen* 31:10+ D '87
  Support thy wife [good husbands help make good mothers] R. B. McCall. il *Parents* 62:168 Jl '87
  Till birth do us part [women's friendships vs. motherhood] K. E. Livingston. il *Parents* 62:87-91 Mr '87
  Where are the cheerleaders for a mother's daily marathon? C. Gould. il *Glamour* 85:178 N '87
  A young mother's story. See issues of Redbook
Anecdotes, facetiae, satire, etc.
  My hotel weekend. E. Berg. il *Parents* 62:48+ F '87
  Night & day. E. Berg. il *Parents* 62:100-1 Ag '87
  Stomach flu & toddlers, too. M. Stevenson. il *Parents* 62:92-4 F '87
Attitudes
  Happy Mother's Day [interview with L. Genevie and E. Margolies] B. Johnson. il pors *People Wkly* 27:57-8+ My 11 '87
  How women feel about "helpful" husbands & how children affect a marriage [excerpts from The motherhood report] L. E. Genevie and E. Margolies. *Good Housekeep* 204:188-9+ My '87
  The motherhood report [excerpts] L. E. Genevie and E. Margolies. il *Good Housekeep* 204:73-6 Ap '87
  Mothers talk about mothering [excerpt from Mother: a collective portrait] M. M. Kalergis. il *Ladies Home J* 104:43-4+ My '87
  'What I wish I'd known': the surprising reality of motherhood. B. M. Campbell. il *Essence* 18:116 O '87
Awards
See also
  Outstanding Mothers Award
Employment
See also
  Children of working parents
  Maternity leaves
  Are kids a handicap? K. Levine. il *Parents* 62:71+ O '87
  Breast-feeding and work. K. Levine. il *Parents* 62:64+ D '87
  Can't is a coward too lazy to try [address, July 14, 1987] P. A. Weir. *Vital Speeches Day* 54:26-9 O 15 '87
  Caring about child care [cover story; with list of resources] K. Rubin. bibl il *Ms* 15:31-6+, 60+ Mr '87
  Child care issues [report of Population Reference Bureau, Inc.] *Child Today* 16:3-4 My/Je '87
  Dear Betty Harragan. B. L. Harragan. *Work Woman* 12:28+ Mr '87
  Different kinds of mothering [homemakers vs. working moms] L. Harris. il *Parents* 62:59-60+ Jl '87
  Families that work [two career black couples] P. V. Pressley. il *Essence* 17:75-7+ Mr '87
  Good news for working moms. M. Mohler. il *Ladies Home J* 104:80 Mr '87
  The guilt that drives working mothers crazy. B. J. Berg. il *Ms* 15:56-9+ My '87
  How to be a better (working) mother [excerpt from The modern mother] S. Sanger and J. Kelly. *Redbook* 168:94-5+ Mr '87
  Is "homework" the answer? J. Walsh. il *Ms* 16:124-5+ Jl/Ag '87
  The managerial mother [special section] il *Work Woman* 12:117-18+ D '87
  Managing maternity. D. L. Gittens. il *Essence* 18:106+ Je '87
  Part-time mom. J. Meslin. *Good Housekeep* 205:136+ S '87
  A story about professionalism, attachment and women's hearts. S. Weller. *Glamour* 85:134+ Mr '87
  The toughest choice [career vs. staying home] M. D. Leonard. il por *Ladies Home J* 104:22+ O '87
  "What's a smart woman like you doing at home?" [search for child care; excerpt] L. Burton. il *Read Dig* 131:29-30+ O '87
  Women: where we are today [special section] il *Ladies Home J* 104:93-5+ Mr '87
  Women who have it all. S. Nelton and K. Berney. il *Nations Bus* 75:18-20+ My '87

Mothers—Employment—*cont.*
The working nursing mother [excerpt from The complete book of breastfeeding] M. S. Eiger and S. W. Olds. *Work Woman* 12:186+ My '87

Mothers, Handicapped
A lesson of love [paraplegic wife and mother] K. Burns. il por *Ladies Home J* 104:20+ D '87

Mothers, Unmarried *See* Single mothers

Mothers Against Drunk Driving
MADD's winning posters. il *Seventeen* 46:216 Ag '87

Mothers and children *See* Parent-child relationship

Mothers and children in literature *See* Parent-child relationship in literature

Mothers Are Women (Organization)
The mother lobby. J. Bayly. il *Ms* 16:75 D '87

Mother's Day
Celebrities salute their mothers on 'Mother's Day'. il *Jet* 72:58 My 11 '87
Granting a mother's wish [A. Jarvis, initiator of holiday] il por *South Living* 22:46 My '87

Mother's Day cards *See* Greeting cards

Mother's Day gifts *See* Gifts

Mother's helpers *See* Household employees

Mothers-in-law
How to make peace (not war) with a difficult mother-in-law. L. Felder. il *Redbook* 168:104-5+ Ap '87

Mothers' milk *See* Milk, Human

Moths
See also
Caterpillars
Gypsy moths
Chemical mimicry: bolas spiders emit components of moth prey species sex pheromones. M. K. Stowe and others. bibl f il *Science* 236:964-7 My 22 '87
Pheromone components and active spaces: what do moths smell and where do they smell it? C. E. Linn, Jr. and others. bibl f il *Science* 237:650-2 Ag 7 '87
Smart bird gets the moth! [jays learn to find camouflaged moths] il *Natl Geogr World* 143:30-1 Jl '87
Spider's perfume fatal for moths [research by Mark K. Stowe and others] S. Weisburd. il *Sci News* 131:340 My 30 '87
Thermoregulation in winter moths. B. Heinrich. bibl (p128) il *Sci Am* 256:104-11 Mr '87

Sexual behavior
See Sexual behavior—Insects

Motion
See also
Perpetual motion
Precession
Stars—Motion
Vibration

Motion, Human *See* Biomechanics

Motion of the solar system in space *See* Solar system—Motion in space

Motion perception
Focus! [development of eye-tracking skills in athletes] S. Schneider. il *Women's Sports Fitness* 9:18 Je '87
Open your eyes to vision training [improving athletes' vision; views of Harvey Ratner] L. N. DeLuca. il *World Tennis* 35:16-17 Ag '87
Parallel and serial processes in motion detection. M. Dick and others. bibl f il *Science* 237:400-2 Jl 24 '87
Synapses that compute motion [study of ganglion cells] T. Poggio and C. Koch. il *Sci Am* 256:46-52 My '87

Motion picture actors and actresses
See also
Academy Awards
American Cinema Awards
Children as actors and actresses
Youth as actors and actresses
See also names of motion picture actors and actresses
100 years of Hollywood [special section] il *People Wkly* 27:25-31+ F 9 '87
Amour fools [directors directing their wives] A. White. il *Film Comment* 23:26-31 Ja/F '87
Canada's rising 'Brat Pack'. B. D. Johnson. il *Macleans* 100:52-3 D 7 '87
Crossing over in Hollywood [TV stars in movies] M. Reese. il *Newsweek* 109:76-7+ My 11 '87
Hot in Hollywood [actresses] C. Kramer. il *McCalls* 114:42-3+ S '87
How the stars make love on-screen [chemistry between couples] M. Musto. il *Mademoiselle* 93:68 My '87
The lady moguls. A. Thompson. il *Ms* 16:18+ N '87
Men, myths & movies. P. Mehlman. il *Harpers Bazaar* 120:380+ S '87

MGM vet Lucille Ryman Carroll recalls the reel adventures of Liz, Rock, Marilyn and Nancy [interview] R. Natale. il por *People Wkly* 28:135-7+ N 2 '87
New faces of 1986. L. O'Toole. il *Film Comment* 23:56-7 Ja/F '87
People [actors who have overcome typecasting as bad guys] G. D. Garcia. il *Time* 129:66-7 Mr 30 '87
Personal style: the new moods of beauty. L. Hirschberg. il *Harpers Bazaar* 120:147+ F '87
Show biz's boring beauties. M. Musto. il *Mademoiselle* 93:140 S '87

Anecdotes, facetiae, satire, etc.
Hollywood in the fifties. G. Keillor. *New Yorker* 63:40-1 N 16 '87

Health and hygiene
Movie muscle [exercise regimens] il *Life* 10:64-6 F '87

Photographs and photography
100 years of Hollywood [cover story: special section; with editorial comment by Franklin Cameron] il *Petersens Photogr Mag* 16:4, 16-21 S '87
I am a camera. N. Almendros. il *Film Comment* 23:18-21 Jl/Ag '87
The movies [cover story; special issue; with editorial comment by Judith Daniels] il *Life* 10:4, 12-20+ Ap '87

Political activities
Pols of India [actor-politicians M. G. Ramachandran and N. T. Ramo Rao] C. Das Gupta and J. Hoberman. il pors *Film Comment* 23:20-4 My/Je '87

Motion picture adaptations
Don't put your drama onscreen [84 Charing Cross Road, Duet for one and Beyond therapy] R. Corliss. il *Time* 129:74+ Mr 2 '87
Mailer's minuet [film adaptation of Tough guys don't dance] K. Jaehne. il pors *Film Comment* 23:11-17 Jl/Ag '87
No sequels [J. Rossner won't sell movie rights to her novel August unless she can hold rights to possible sequel movies] P. S. Nathan. *Publ Wkly* 232:27 Jl 31 '87
A papal writ with mass appeal [filming of John Paul II's play The jeweller's shop] P. Young. il *Macleans* 100:50 Ag 31 '87
Partners and friends for 26 years, James Ivory and Ismail Merchant film a hotly debated gay love story [adaptation of E. M. Forster's Maurice] J. Stark. il pors *People Wkly* 28:119-22 O 26 '87
Producer Diane Silver and the making of "Native son". S. McHenry. por *Ms* 15:15-17 Mr '87
Rights. P. S. Nathan. *See issues of Publishers Weekly*
Tough guys make movie [making of Tough guys don't dance] D. Smith. il pors *N Y* 20:32-5+ Ja 12 '87
What it takes to make a good book a good movie [with interview with J. Ivory] A. P. Sanoff. il *U S News World Rep* 103:66-8 D 21 '87
The year in rights. P. S. Nathan. *Publ Wkly* 231:42 Ja 9 '87

Motion Picture Association of America
Hollywood goes to war [Canada's plan to give Canadians larger share of movie distribution business] I. Austen. il *Macleans* 100:53-4 Je 22 '87

Motion picture audiences
Hollywood's change of art [test audiences vote for different endings] P. H. Broeske. il *Roll Stone* p24+ F 12 '87
Silent community in the afternoon. G. G. Seibert. *America* 157:274+ O 24 '87

Anecdotes, facetiae, satire, etc.
Cinéma vérité. M. Richler. il *N Y Times Mag* p16 Mr 8 '87

Motion picture authorship
Blacks find jobs scarce for writers in Hollywood. *Jet* 71:25 Mr 23 '87
Facing a flop [failed motion picture] J. Boorstin. il *N Y Times Mag* p102 O 11 '87
Frontiersman [interview with R. Wurlitzer] M. Golden. il por *Film Comment* 23:40-4 Jl/Ag '87
Gin-soaked boy [cover story; interview with C. Bukowski] C. Hodenfield. il pors *Film Comment* 23:53-4+ Jl/Ag '87
Hanif Kureishi. M. Glicksman. por *Roll Stone* p33-4 N 19 '87
The hope of Hollywood? [young screenwriters] J. Roberts. il *N Y* 20:22 Jl 27 '87
I. A. L. Diamond. I. A. L. Diamond. il por *People Wkly* 27:66+ F 9 '87
Lethal weapon gives writer Shane Black a shot at fame. il por *People Wkly* 27:121 Je 15 '87
Limbo land [development of new films] B. Walker. il *Film Comment* 23:34-8+ Ja/F '87

Motion picture authorship—*cont.*
Ordeal by Disney [writing the script for The magnificent rebel in 1958 post-blacklist period] J. Scott. il pors *Film Comment* 23:52-4+ N/D '87
Some down and dirty zingers [L. Dixon, screenwriter of Outrageous fortune] D. Ansen. il *Newsweek* 109:76 Ja 26 '87

Motion picture cameras
See also
Film-to-video transfer system

Motion picture cartoons *See* Motion pictures—Animated films

Motion picture credits
Where credit is due: the heads and tails of title design. J. Calhoun. il *Theatre Crafts* 21:79-82 Ag/S '87

Motion picture critics and criticism
See also
Ebert, Roger
Motion picture reviews
Siskel, Gene
Television broadcasting—Motion picture criticism programs

Motion picture directors
See also
Allen, Woody
Beineix, Jean-Jacques
Brooks, Mel
Coen, Joel
De Palma, Brian
Demme, Jonathan
Directors Guild of America
Ecaré, Désiré
Frank, Melvin, 1913-
Frears, Stephen, 1931-
Gordon, Stuart
Huston, John, 1906-1987
Ivory, James
Jabor, Arnaldo
Konchalovsky, Andrei
Kubrick, Stanley
Leonard, Terry J.
Levinson, Barry
Lynch, David
Mikhalkov, Nikita
Panfilov, Gleb
Pinsent, Gordon, 1930-
Polanski, Roman
Ray, Satyajit
Reiner, Rob
Sayles, John, 1950-
Schroeder, Barbet
Sevela, Efraim
Stoller, Bryan Michael
Stone, Oliver
Strikes—Motion picture directors
Walker, Giles
Amour fools [directors directing their wives] A. White. il *Film Comment* 23:26-31 Ja/F '87
New faces of 1986. L. O'Toole. il *Film Comment* 23:56-7 Ja/F '87
Taking direct action. D. Hershkovits. pors *Harpers Bazaar* 121:144-5 N '87

Attitudes
A night at the movies [seven directors describe movies they'd like to do in 2001; cover story] M. Long. il *Omni* 9:44-6+ Je '87

Motion picture editing *See* Motion pictures—Editing
Motion picture festivals
The 16th New Directors/New Films Series. A. White; M. Pally. il *Film Comment* 23:64-71 My/Je '87

California
A red-carpet festival [Monterey Film Festival] B. Golightly. il *Horizon* 30:59 Jl/Ag '87

Colombia
Nieto's show [Cartagena Film Festival] E. Stein. il *Film Comment* 23:4+ Ja/F '87

Colorado
Rocky Mountain 'hi' [Telluride Film Festival] M. Sragow. *Film Comment* 23:6+ N/D '87

Florida
Miami nice [Miami Film Festival] E. Stein. *Film Comment* 23:6+ Jl/Ag '87

France
See also
Cannes Film Festival

Germany (West)
Berlin Film Festival: art as political bridge. J. M. Wall. *Christ Century* 104:235-6 Mr 11 '87
Berlin Film Festival: mirrors and windows. J. M. Wall. *Christ Century* 104:259-60 Mr 18-25 '87

Movies [Berlin Film Festival] D. Denby. *N Y* 20:84-5 Mr 23 '87
Wall-eyed [Berlin Film Festival] H. Kennedy. il *Film Comment* 23:2+ My/Je '87

Hawaii
Hawaii International Film Festival. il *Travel Holiday* 168:39 Ag '87

Illinois
MUMM V.S.O.P. Cognac presents black filmfest [Chicago] il *Jet* 72:60-3 Je 29 '87

Italy
A tent in Venice. H. Kennedy. *Film Comment* 23:70+ N/D '87

New York (State)
25th New York Film Festival. S. Harvey; E. Stein; H. Jacobson. il *Film Comment* 23:60-9 N/D '87
Margaret Mead Film Festival. A. White. *Nation* 245:353-4 O 3 '87
A queer kind of film [Lesbian and Gay Experimental Film Festival in New York City] J. Stuart. *Film Comment* 23:4+ N/D '87
Raisins [use of popular commercial to celebrate Festival of Claymation at the Metro Cinema in Manhattan] *New Yorker* 63:29 My 4 '87
Silver streak: the N.Y. Film Festival at 25 [special section] il *Film Comment* 23:35-6+ S/O '87
Anecdotes, facetiae, satire, etc.
25th New York, New York, Film Festival. M. Groening. il *Film Comment* 23:56-7 S/O '87

Ontario
Cinematic riches of the Pacific Rim [program being shown at the Toronto Festival of Festivals] B. D. Johnson. il *Macleans* 100:57-8 S 21 '87
A festival's voyage among the stars [Toronto's annual Festival of Festivals] N. Jennings. il *Macleans* 100:46+ S 28 '87
Oriental insurgents [Eastern Horizons retrospective at the Festival of Festivals in Toronto] P. Aufderheide. *Film Comment* 23:73-6 N/D '87
A zoo for films [Festival of Festivals in Toronto] D. Chute. il *Film Comment* 23:71-3 N/D '87

Québec (Province)
Cinema's critical mass [Montreal Film Festival] G. Peary. il *Macleans* 100:62 S 7 '87
'Moments' in movies: Montreal's World Film Festival. J. M. Wall. il *Christ Century* 104:787-90 S 23 '87

Scotland
Edinburgh at 40. H. Kennedy. il *Film Comment* 23:7-8 Ja/F '87
It's the dinosaur show [Edinburgh Film Festival] H. Kennedy. *Film Comment* 23:7+ N/D '87

Soviet Union
Glasnost on the screen [Moscow Film Festival] C. Redden. *Macleans* 100:46 Jl 20 '87
Overheard in Moscow . . . [Moscow Film Festival] P. Aufderheide. *Film Comment* 23:6 S/O '87

Utah
Downhill at Park City [U.S. Film Festival] J. Powers. il *Film Comment* 23:4+ Mr/Ap '87
The United States Film Festival. T. Rafferty. *Nation* 244:338-40 Mr 14 '87

Motion picture industry
See also
Alive Films (Firm)
Cannon Group Inc.
Carolco Service, Inc.
Cinecom Entertainment Group
Columbia Pictures Entertainment Inc.
Columbia Pictures Industries, Inc.
De Laurentiis Entertainment Group
DEG Film Studio
Fox Inc.
Hal Roach Studios Inc.
Hemdale Film Corporation
Hollywood Way (Firm)
MCA Inc.
Merchant Ivory Productions
MGM/UA Communications Co.
Mirage (Firm)
Motion Picture Association of America
Motion picture production and direction
Motion picture theaters
Motown Productions
New World Pictures Ltd.
Orion Pictures Corporation
Ormond Organization
Paramount Pictures Corp.
Pytka Productions
Republic Pictures Corporation
Robert Halmi, Inc.
Showscan Film Corporation

Motion picture industry—See also—*cont.*
　Todd-AO Corp.
　Tri-Star Pictures Inc.
　Troma, Inc.
　Twentieth Century-Fox Film Corp.
　United Artists Corp.
　Universal Pictures
　Walt Disney Company
　Warner Bros. Inc.
　Weintraub Entertainment Group Inc.
　Women in the motion picture industry
Dark visions on the silver screen. M. Horn. il por
　U S News World Rep 102:75 Mr 30 '87
Hollywood goes independent. D. Ansen. il *Newsweek*
　109:64-6 Ap 6 '87
The Hollywood of the East [Florida] A. Miller. il
　Newsweek 110:63 O 19 '87
In development [special section] il *Film Comment*
　23:33-8+ Ja/F '87

Acquisitions and mergers
At Columbia, things might go better with Tri-Star [Coca-
　Cola merging two studios] R. Grover. il por *Bus
　Week* p74-5 N 30 '87

Advertising
Mini masterpieces: teasers, trailers and spots before your
　eyes. P. Wadsley. il *Theatre Crafts* 21:69-72 Ja '87

Anecdotes, facetiae, satire, etc.
A salute to Klassik Klassix year-and-a-half anniversary:
　eighteen months of quality entertainment. M. Wilkins
　and J. Barth. il *Film Comment* 23:63-7 Ja/F '87

Communist activities
Memories of HUAC. P. Bosworth. *Nation* 245:436-7
　O 24 '87
Notes on the . . . blacklist [Hollywood blacklisting period;
　special section] il *Film Comment* 23:37-9+ N/D '87

Conferences
Cinema summit [Soviet filmmakers meet American coun-
　terparts in Hollywood] B. Strauss. il *Film Comment*
　23:37-8 My/Je '87
Gorbashow and the flicks [Moscow conference entitled
　War and peace on the world screen since 1945] P.
　Kenez. il *New Leader* 70:10-12 Ap 6 '87
Soviets' cinema vérité [Los Angeles conference between
　American and Soviet filmmakers] S. L. Hawkins. il
　U S News World Rep 102:26 Ap 6 '87

Employees
　See also
　International Alliance of Theatrical Stage Employees
　　and Moving Picture Machine Operators of the
　　U.S. and Canada
　Trade unions—Motion picture industry employees
Starstruck. J. Ash. il *Life* 10:107-8+ Ap '87

Health and hygiene
A promise of renewal [recovering alcoholic] D. B. Smith.
　il *N Y Times Mag* p52 F 15 '87

Finance
　See also
　Film Finances, Ltd.
The 12th annual grosses gloss. A. Thompson. il *Film
　Comment* 23:62-4+ Mr/Ap '87
The Hollywood superstar no one's ever heard of [W.
　F. Thompson of Boston Ventures Management] G.
　Geipel. il por *Bus Week* p98-9 Ja 26 '87
Hollywood's ticket to a hot summer. J. Egan. il *U
　S News World Rep* 103:47 Jl 13 '87
Hollywood's video boom is stuck on pause. R. Grover.
　il *Bus Week* p56 Je 29 '87
Lights! Camera! Cut the budget! [independent filmmakers]
　S. Koepp. il *Time* 129:57 Mr 30 '87
Make money, not war. A. Gibney and A. Thompson.
　il *Film Comment* 23:17-18+ N/D '87
Summertime, and the movies are sequels. R. Grover.
　il *Bus Week* p49 My 11 '87
Too many goodies under Hollywood's tree [Christmas
　releases] R. Grover. il *Bus Week* p39 D 21 '87
What's the point? [dispute over distribution of profits
　from Platoon] il *Fortune* 116:9 N 23 '87

History
100 years of Hollywood [cover story; special section;
　with editorial comment by Franklin Cameron] il
　Petersens Photogr Mag 16:4, 16-21 S '87
100 years of Hollywood [special section] il *People Wkly*
　27:25-31+ F 9 '87
Hollywood hits 100 [cover story; special section; with
　editorial comment by Kevin Doyle] il *Macleans* 100:2,
　32-9 Je 8 '87
Hollywood turns 100: Tinseltown glitters again. P. L.
　Brosnan. il *Travel Holiday* 168:42-7 Ag '87
Hooray for Hollywood. G. Hackett. il *Newsweek* 109:24-5
　F 16 '87

The movies [cover story; special issue; with editorial
　comment by Judith Daniels] il *Life* 10:4, 12-20+ Ap
　'87
The stars shine at the shrine as Hollywood wishes itself
　a happy 100th birthday. il *People Wkly* 27:40-1 My
　11 '87
Tales of imperial Hollywood [views of O. Friedrich]
　J. Skow. il *Time* 129:74 Ja 5 '87

International aspects
Moviemaking around the world [special section] il *Life*
　10:26-8+ Ap '87

Laws and regulations
　See Motion picture laws and regulations

Securities
Ought you to be in pictures? *Money* 16:13 Mr '87
Suddenly Wall Street stops going to the movies. R.
　Grover. il *Bus Week* p112 Je 1 '87
Wall Street's movie critics. il *Fortune* 115:9 Je 22 '87

Canada
　See also
　Film Arts Ltd.
　Genie Awards
　Telefilm Canada
Canada's talent bank [Canadians in Hollywood] P.
　Hluchy. il *Macleans* 100:38-9 Je 8 '87
Hollywood goes to war [Canada's plan to give Canadians
　larger share of movie distribution business] I. Austen.
　il *Macleans* 100:53-4 Je 22 '87
Movie magic for the child in everyone [R. Demers]
　B. D. Johnson. il por *Macleans* 100:57 Mr 16 '87

Germany (West)
Germany's 'international' producer [B. Eichinger] A.
　Fisher. *World Press Rev* 34:58 Ap '87

Great Britain
The Brit pack [producers E. Fellner, R. Randall-Cutler
　and T. Bevan] R. Nicolson. il pors *Vogue* 177:80
　D '87
'Picture shows': the early British film industry in Wal-
　thamstow. M. O'Brien and J. Holland. bibl il *Hist
　Today* 37:9-15 F '87
Whither Britain? H. Kennedy. il *Film Comment* 23:50-1
　Ja/F '87

India
Hollywood East. P. Gupte. il *Forbes* 140:90 D 28 '87

Soviet Union
After seven years Gleb Panfilov's film, Tema, sees daylight
　at last and wrests an award from Platoon. S. K.
　Reed. il pors *People Wkly* 27:57-8 Ap 6 '87
Glasnost [special section] il *Film Comment* 23:33-8+
　My/Je '87
Gorbashow and the flicks [Moscow conference entitled
　War and peace on the world screen since 1945] P.
　Kenez. il *New Leader* 70:10-12 Ap 6 '87
Soviets' cinema vérité [Los Angeles conference between
　American and Soviet filmmakers] S. L. Hawkins. il
　U S News World Rep 102:26 Ap 6 '87

United States
　See Motion picture industry
Motion picture insurance *See* Insurance, Motion picture
Motion picture laws and regulations

Canada
Beat the devil [R. Reagan's visit to Canada] A. Cockburn.
　Nation 244:494-5 Ap 18 '87
Hollywood goes to war [Canada's plan to give Canadians
　larger share of movie distribution business] I. Austen.
　il *Macleans* 100:53-4 Je 22 '87
Motion picture locations *See* Motion pictures—Setting and
　scenery
Motion picture makeup *See* Makeup, Theatrical
Motion picture music *See* Motion pictures—Music
Motion picture novels *See* Motion pictures and literature
Motion picture photography
　See also
　Motion pictures—Special effects
Connie's comeback [C. Hall] L. Klady. il por *Film
　Comment* 23:6-8 Mr/Ap '87
I am a camera. N. Almendros. il *Film Comment* 23:18-21
　Jl/Ag '87
Motion picture premieres
Who's that girl [glimpses of Madonna at New York
　premiere] *New Yorker* 63:23-4 Ag 24 '87
Motion picture producers
　See also
　Bevan, Tim
　Bruckheimer, Jerry
　Coen, Ethan
　De Laurentiis, Dino
　Demers, Rock
　Eichinger, Bernd, 1953-
　Fellner, Eric
　Kopelson, Arnold

Motion picture producers—See also—_cont._
  Merchant, Ismail
  Randall-Cutler, Roger
  Simpson, Don, 1945-
  Tisch, Steve
Motion picture production and direction
  See also
  Motion picture credits
  Motion picture directors
  Motion pictures—Setting and scenery
Cane and Able [filming of The whales of August] J. Ney. il por _Film Comment_ 23:2+ Ja/F '87
Contra-courant [A. Cox's film Walker] G. Fuller. il _Film Comment_ 23:50-1 Jl/Ag '87
Grand old Lillian Gish makes a big splash in The whales of August [battle of wills with actress B. Davis] B. Darrach. il pors _People Wkly_ 28:70-2+ D 14 '87
'Hamburger Hill' star says filming was hell [C. B. Vance] il pors _Jet_ 72:56 S 21 '87
Help us cast "The Ollie North story". C. Krupp and J. Powell. il por _Glamour_ 85:310 S '87
How the war was won [retired Marine D. Dye, technical adviser for Platoon] D. Goodgame. il por _Time_ 129:58 Ja 26 '87
In development [special section] il _Film Comment_ 23:33-8+ Ja/F '87
In the trenches of Wall Street. G. D. Garcia. il _Time_ 130:76-7 Jl 20 '87
John Huston raises The dead. M. Walsh. il pors _Time_ 129:92-3 Mr 16 '87
John Sayles's labor of love [Matewan] S. G. Freedman. il pors _Roll Stone_ p27-8 O 8 '87
Kurys makes her bed [making of A man in love] M. Pally. il por _Film Comment_ 23:84-6 S/O '87
Lovers leap: behind the scenes with Baryshnikov [making of Dancers] H. Brubach. il pors _Vogue_ 177:220-3+ Jl '87
Mailer's minuet [film adaptation of Tough guys don't dance] K. Jaehne. il pors _Film Comment_ 23:11-17 Jl/Ag '87
Making a legend [filming Bethune: the making of a hero in China; cover story; special section; with editorial comment by Kevin Doyle] il pors _Macleans_ 100:2, 26-34 Ag 10 '87
Making Malcolm [work of Australians N. Tass and D. Parker] W. Harris. il pors _Theatre Crafts_ 21:73-4 F '87
'The making of "The African Queen"'. K. Hepburn. il por _Newsweek_ 110:53-5 Ag 31 '87
The making of The African Queen. K. Hepburn. il pors _Ladies Home J_ 104:77-80+ N '87
Midnacht at the oasis [making of P. Adlon's Brenda's palace, a comedy fable] B. Walker. il por _Film Comment_ 23:4+ Jl/Ag '87
Mini masterpieces: teasers, trailers and spots before your eyes. P. Wadsley. il _Theatre Crafts_ 21:69-72 Ja '87
Moviemaking around the world [special section] il _Life_ 10:26-8+ Ap '87
Nicaragua: radical flick [A. Cox shoots movie based on exploits of American adventurer William Walker] R. Nordland. il por _Newsweek_ 109:44 Ap 20 '87
Our gangsters [The Untouchables] J. Salamon. il _Vogue_ 177:58+ Je '87
A papal writ with mass appeal [filming of John Paul II's play The jeweller's shop] P. Young. il _Macleans_ 100:50 Ag 31 '87
Point man [interview with O. Stone] P. McGilligan. il pors _Film Comment_ 23:11-14+ Ja/F '87
Post-mod squad [making of M. Lambert's Siesta] G. Smith. il por _Film Comment_ 23:24-9 N/D '87
Praising 'Arizona' [work of J. and E. Coen] J. Barth. il por _Film Comment_ 23:18-20+ Mr/Ap '87
Rebel rouser [making of A. Cox's Walker] F. Schruers. il por _Roll Stone_ p29+ S 10 '87
The road to 'Ishtar'. D. Blum. il pors _N Y_ 20:34-43 Mr 16 '87
Sayles talk. R. Seidenberg. il por _Horizon_ 30:12-14 S '87
Susan Seidelman directs post-feminist fun [Making Mr. Right] C. Krupp. il pors _Glamour_ 85:224 My '87
Tough guys make movie [making of Tough guys don't dance] D. Smith. il pors _N Y_ 20:32-5+ Ja 12 '87
Trading places [J. Jett and M. J. Fox in Light of day] S. Pond. il _Roll Stone_ p25-6 Ja 15 '87
The Untouchables [film version of TV program] F. Schruers. il _Roll Stone_ p47-8+ Mr 26 '87
Warped in America: the dark vision of moviemakers Joel and Ethan Coen. E. Pooley. il pors _N Y_ 20:44-8 Mr 23 '87

Accidents
Twilight Zone: the verdict. _Time_ 129:69 Je 8 '87

The 'Twilight Zone' verdict: not guilty. por _Newsweek_ 109:83 Je 8 '87
Motion picture reviews
100 years of screen. il _People Wkly_ 27:8 F 9 '87
Brian De Palma's guilty pleasures. B. De Palma. il por _Film Comment_ 23:52-3 My/Je '87
Cue: a complete entertainment guide for the week. See issues of New York
The current cinema. P. Kael. See issues of The New Yorker
Film. M. H. Seitz. See issues of The Progressive
Film. J. Simon. See occasional issues of National Review
Film clips. il _Teen_ 31:54 F '87
Film review. H. M. Geduld. See issues of The Humanist
Films. See issues of Maclean's
Films. K. R. Hey. See alternate issues of USA Today (Periodical) through March 1987
Goings on about town. See issues of The New Yorker
Good films in small packages [1987 releases] K. Dieckmann. il _Roll Stone_ p153+ D 17-31 '87
Hot tickets, cold turkeys [summer releases] D. Edelstein. il _Roll Stone_ p27+ Je 18 '87
Movies. J. G. Boyum. See issues of Glamour
Movies. D. Denby. See issues of New York
Movies [fall releases] R. Gilbert. il _N Y_ 20:56-9 S 21 '87
Movies. R. Rosenbaum. See issues of Mademoiselle
Movies to see. See issues of Jet beginning February 10, 1986
Old movies through new eyes: sexual politics at your video store. G. Steinem. il _Ms_ 16:46 Jl/Ag '87
People are talking about . . . movies. M. Haskell. See issues of Vogue
People picks & pans. See issues of People Weekly
The reel world. K. R. Hey. See alternate issues of USA Today (Periodical) beginning May 1987
Screen [fall previews] il _People Wkly_ 28:73-5 Ag 31 '87
Screen. T. O'Brien. See occasional issues of Commonweal beginning February 10, 1984
Screen '87. il _People Wkly_ 27:52-4+ Ja 5 '87
Spotlight. E. Miller. See issues of Seventeen
Stanley Kauffmann on films. S. Kauffmann. See issues of The New Republic
Starpower summer nights. il _Harpers Bazaar_ 120:110-13 Je '87
Summer fare. D. Scheuer. il _Sch Update_ 119:16 My 18 '87
Summertime, and the movies are sequels. R. Grover. il _Bus Week_ p49 My 11 '87
'Teen goes to the movies. il _Teen_ 31:64-5 Je '87
Single works
84 Charing Cross Road
    Christ Today 31:61 Jl 10 '87. S. Ulstein
    Glamour 85:244 Ap '87. J. G. Boyum
    _Ms_ il 15:35 Ap '87. L. Stone
    _N Y_ il 20:100+ Mr 2 '87. D. Denby
    New Repub 196:24 F 23 '87. S. Kauffmann
    Newsweek 109:72 F 16 '87. D. Ansen
    People Wkly 27:12+ Mr 30 '87. T. Cunneff
    Time il 129:74+ Mr 2 '87. R. Corliss
Adventures in babysitting
    Newsweek 110:60 Jl 13 '87. D. Ansen
    People Wkly 28:10 Jl 20 '87. S. Haller
The African Queen
    Ladies Home J il pors 104:77-80+ N '87. K. Hepburn
    Newsweek il 110:53-5 Ag 31 '87. K. Hepburn
Amazing Grace and Chuck
    Newsweek il 109:74 My 4 '87. J. Kroll
    People Wkly il 27:10 Je 8 '87. R. Novak
Amazon women on the moon
    Time il 130:69 S 28 '87. R. Corliss
Angel heart
    Glamour 85:217-18 My '87. J. G. Boyum
    Jet il 71:16 Mr 2 '87
    Jet 71:59 Mr 9 '87
    Jet il 71:60-1 Mr 16 '87
    Jet il 71:60-1 Mr 23 '87. C. Waldron
    Macleans 100:58 Mr 16 '87. L. O'Toole
    Mademoiselle il 93:46+ Je '87. R. Rosenbaum
    New Leader il 70:20 Mr 23 '87. J. Gardner
    New Yorker 63:85-6 Ap 6 '87. P. Kael
    Newsweek il 109:72 Mr 16 '87. D. Ansen
    People Wkly il 27:10 Mr 16 '87. P. Travers
    Time il 129:86 Mr 9 '87. R. Corliss
    Vogue il 177:72 My '87. M. Haskell
Anna
    _N Y_ 20:116 N 9 '87. D. Denby
    Vogue il 177:82 O '87. M. Haskell
The aristocats
    People Wkly il 27:8 My 4 '87. P. Travers

Motion picture reviews—Single works—*cont.*
Assassination
    People Wkly 27:16 F 2 '87. I. Hellman
The assault
    Macleans 100:58 My 4 '87. L. O'Toole
    N Y 20:77 F 16 '87. D. Denby
    Time il 129:80 Ap 6 '87. R. Schickel
Athens, Ga.
    Roll Stone p27 Ap 23 '87. A. DeCurtis
Baby boom
    Commonweal 114:602 O 23 '87. T. O'Brien
    Glamour il 85:160 D '87. J. G. Boyum
    Glamour il 85:256+ N '87. C. Krupp
    Macleans il 100:63 O 26 '87. L. O'Toole
    N Y 20:91-2 O 12 '87. D. Denby
    New Repub 197:24-5 N 9 '87. S. Kauffmann
    New Yorker 63:109-10 O 19 '87. P. Kael
    Newsweek il 110:84 O 12 '87. D. Ansen
    People Wkly il 28:16 O 19 '87. R. Novak
    Time 130:85 O 12 '87
Bach and broccoli
    Macleans il 100:58 Mr 16 '87. B. D. Johnson
    Macleans il 100:57 Mr 16 '87. B. D. Johnson
Back to the beach
    Macleans 100:51 Ag 17 '87. L. O'Toole
La bamba
    Glamour 85:200 Ag '87
    Macleans il 100:47 Jl 27 '87. N. Jennings
    New Yorker 63:71-2 Ag 10 '87. P. Kael
    Newsweek il 110:66-7 Ag 17 '87. J. Foote
    Roll Stone il p13 Ag 13 '87. A. DeCurtis
    Time il 130:62 Ag 17 '87. R. Corliss
    U S News World Rep il 103:48-9 Ag 10 '87. J. Podhoretz
Barfly
    Film Comment il 23:53-4+ Jl/Ag '87. C. Hodenfield
    Macleans il 100:66 N 30 '87. L. O'Toole
    Mademoiselle il 93:108+ N '87. R. Rosenbaum
    N Y il 20:114-15 O 26 '87. D. Denby
    Natl Rev 39:57-8+ D 4 '87. J. Simon
    New Yorker 63:137-40 N 2 '87. P. Kael
    Newsweek il 110:86 O 26 '87. D. Ansen
    People Wkly il 28:14 N 2 '87. P. Travers
The bedroom window
    Glamour 85:225-6 Mr '87. J. G. Boyum
    Macleans 100:56 Ja 19 '87. L. O'Toole
    N Y 20:57 F 2 '87. D. Denby
    New Yorker 62:94-5 F 9 '87. P. Kael
    People Wkly il 27:14 Ja 26 '87. P. Travers
    Time il 129:76+ F 16 '87. R. Corliss
The believers
    Newsweek 109:66 Je 29 '87. D. Ansen
    People Wkly il 27:12 Je 22 '87. P. Travers
    Time il 129:76 Je 22 '87. R. Schickel
    Vogue il 177:36 Jl '87. M. Haskell
The bell jar
    Nation 244:132-3 F 7 '87
    Newsweek 109:58 F 9 '87
    Newsweek il 109:63 F 2 '87. A. Press
    Publ Wkly 231:290 Ja 30 '87. M. Yen
    Time il 129:60-1 F 9 '87. R. Lacayo
Benji the hunted
    People Wkly il 27:10 Je 29 '87. P. Travers
Best seller
    Macleans 100:58 O 5 '87. L. O'Toole
    Newsweek 110:84 O 5 '87. D. Ansen
    Time 130:85 O 12 '87
Betty Blue
    Film Comment il 23:21-4 Ja/F '87. M. Pally
    New Leader 70:22 Ja 12-26 '87. J. Gardner
    Time il 129:72-3 Ja 19 '87. R. Schickel
Beverly Hills cop II
    Jet il 72:56-8 Je 15 '87
    Macleans il 100:55 Je 1 '87. L. O'Toole
    N Y il 20:95 Je 1 '87. D. Denby
    N Y 20:71-3 Je 22 '87. D. Denby
    New Repub 196:25 Je 29 '87. S. Kauffmann
    Newsweek il 109:69 Je 1 '87. D. Ansen
    People Wkly il 27:10 My 25 '87. P. Travers
    Roll Stone il p27-9 Jl 2 '87. D. Handelman
    Time il 129:73 Je 1 '87. R. Schickel
Beyond therapy
    Commonweal 114:183-4 Mr 27 '87. T. O'Brien
    Macleans il 100:57 Mr 9 '87. L. O'Toole
    New Repub 196:25 Mr 23 '87. S. Kauffmann
    Time il 129:74+ Mr 2 '87. R. Corliss
The Big Easy
    Glamour il 85:227 O '87. J. G. Boyum
    Macleans 100:49 Ag 24 '87. L. O'Toole
    N Y il 20:110+ Ag 24 '87. D. Denby
    New Repub 197:27 S 28 '87. S. Kauffmann

    New Yorker 63:100 S 7 '87. P. Kael
    People Wkly il 28:8 Ag 31 '87. P. Travers
    Time il 130:65 Ag 24 '87. R. Schickel
Billy Galvin
    People Wkly 27:10 Mr 16 '87. I. Hellman
Black widow
    Macleans 100:52 F 16 '87. L. O'Toole
    N Y il 20:72 F 16 '87. D. Denby
    New Repub 196:24-5 Mr 2 '87. S. Kauffmann
    New Yorker 63:111-12 F 23 '87. P. Kael
    Newsweek il 109:72 F 16 '87. D. Ansen
    People Wkly il 27:6 Mr 2 '87. P. Travers
    Roll Stone il p19+ Mr 12 '87. A. DeCurtis
    Time il 129:76 F 16 '87. R. Corliss
Blind date
    Macleans il 100:54 Ap 6 '87. L. O'Toole
    New Leader 70:23 Ap 6 '87. J. Gardner
    New Repub 196:27 Ap 27 '87. S. Kauffmann
    Newsweek il 109:77-8 Ap 13 '87. J. Kroll
    People Wkly il 27:12 Ap 13 '87. P. Travers
    Time il 129:76 Ap 20 '87. R. Schickel
Blue snake
    Dance Mag 61:74 Ja '87. J. Gruen
Blue velvet
    Christ Century 104:7-9 Ja 7-14 '87. J. M. Wall
    Progressive 51:36 Ja '87. P. Aufderheide
Born in East L.A.
    People Wkly il por 28:14 S 14 '87. T. Cunneff
Brenda's palace, a comedy fable
    Film Comment il 23:4+ Jl/Ag '87. B. Walker
Brighton Beach memoirs
    Glamour il 85:131 Ja '87. J. G. Boyum
    Macleans il 100:20 Ja 5 '87. L. O'Toole
    N Y il 20:77-8 Ja 19 '87. D. Denby
    New Repub 196:26-7 Ja 26 '87. S. Kauffmann
    New Yorker 62:74-5 Ja 26 '87. P. Kael
Broadcast news
    Newsweek il 110:50 D 28 '87. C. Gould
    Newsweek il por 110:44-9 D 28 '87. D. Ansen
    People Wkly il 28:10 D 21 '87. P. Travers
    Time il por 130:82-3 D 14 '87. R. Corliss
Broken mirrors
    New Repub 196:26-7 Mr 16 '87. S. Kauffmann
Burglar
    Jet il 72:56-7 Ap 20 '87
    Macleans 100:55 Ap 6 '87. L. O'Toole
    People Wkly il 27:12 Ap 13 '87. R. Novak
    Time il 129:78 Ap 13 '87. R. Schickel
Business as usual
    Christ Century 104:739-40 S 9-16 '87. J. M. Wall
Candy mountain
    Film Comment il 23:32-9 Jl/Ag '87. M. Glicksman
Can't buy me love
    People Wkly il 28:14 S 7 '87. T. Cunneff
Captain EO
    USA Today (Periodical) 115:33 Ja '87. J. Saltzman
Caravaggio
    Art Am il 75:21-3 Ja '87. L. Tillman
Castaway
    Time 130:69 S 28 '87. R. Schickel
Chief Zabú
    Life il 10:44-5+ Ap '87. D. C. Craig
Children of a lesser god
    USA Today (Periodical) il 115:96-7 Ja '87. K. R. Hey
Chuck Berry Hail! Hail! Rock 'n' roll
    N Y 20:102-3 O 19 '87. D. Denby
Cinderella
    Art Am il 75:31-3 Ap '87. V. Dika
The color of money
    Film Comment il 23:72+ My/Je '87. J. McDonough
The color purple
    Harpers 274:29 Ja '87
    N Y Rev Books 34:17-20 Ja 29 '87. D. Pinckney
Come and see
    N Y 20:64 F 23 '87. D. Denby
Creepshow 2
    People Wkly il 27:10 My 25 '87. R. Novak
Crimes of the heart
    Christ Century 104:60 Ja 21 '87. J. M. Wall
    Commonweal 114:55 Ja 30 '87. T. O'Brien
    Glamour il 85:134 Ja '87. C. Krupp
    Glamour 85:176 F '87. J. G. Boyum
    Ms il 15:12+ F '87. M. Rochlin
    Natl Rev 39:56 F 13 '87. J. Simon
    New Repub 196:26-7 F 2 '87. S. Kauffmann
    USA Today (Periodical) il 115:95 Mr '87. K. R. Hey
    Vogue il 177:82+ F '87. M. Haskell
Critical condition
    Jet il 71:58-9 F 9 '87

Motion picture reviews—Single works—Critical condi-
tion—*cont.*
   Macleans 100:54 Ja 26 '87. M. Jackson
   People Wkly il 27:16 F 2 '87. T. Cunneff
Cross my heart
   Glamour il 85:250 N '87. J. Powell
   Macleans il 100:66-7 N 30 '87. L. O'Toole
   People Wkly il 28:12 D 7 '87. T. Cunneff
Cry freedom
   America 157:482+ D 19 '87. R. A. Blake
   Commonweal 114:655 N 20 '87. T. O'Brien
   Ebony il pors 43:60-2+ D '87. C. Tyson
   Film Comment il 23:11-12+ N/D '87. A. White
   Glamour 85:159-60 D '87. J. G. Boyum
   Horizon il 30:37-8 N '87. G. Stern
   Macleans il 100:59 N 23 '87. L. O'Toole
   Mademoiselle il 93:108 N '87. L. Morice
   N Y il 20:54-5 S 21 '87. D. Denby
   N Y il 20:113-15 N 16 '87. D. Denby
   New Repub 197:42 D 21 '87. M. Peretz
   New Repub 197:26 D 7 '87. S. Kauffmann
   New Yorker 63:101-4 N 30 '87. P. Kael
   Newsweek il 110:79+ N 9 '87. J. Kroll
   People Wkly il 28:18 N 30 '87. P. Travers
   People Wkly il 28:64+ N 23 '87. W. Plummer
   Roll Stone il p31-2 D 3 '87. E. Mitchell
   Time il 130:91 N 9 '87. R. Corliss
   Vogue il 177:82 N '87. M. Haskell
Dancers
   Dance Mag il 61:36-43 O '87. J. Gruen
   Film Comment il 23:81 S/O '87. M. Pally
   New Repub 197:25-6 N 9 '87. S. Kauffmann
   Newsweek il 110:86 O 26 '87. D. Ansen
   Sch Update il 120:36-7 O 16 '87. D. Scheuer
   Vogue il 177:220-3+ Jl '87. H. Brubach
Dark eyes
   Commonweal 114:601-2 O 23 '87. T. O'Brien
   Macleans il 100:71 N 16 '87. L. O'Toole
   N Y il 20:116 O 5 '87. D. Denby
   Natl Rev 39:56-9 N 6 '87. J. Simon
   New Repub 197:32-3 O 12 '87. S. Kauffmann
   New Yorker 63:93-4 O 5 '87. P. Kael
   Newsweek il 110:84 O 5 '87. D. Ansen
   People Wkly 28:14 N 2 '87. P. Travers
   Vogue il 177:442-3+ O '87. A. Harvey
Date with an angel
   Teen il 31:63 N '87
The dead
   Commonweal 114:748-9 D 18 '87. T. O'Brien
   Macleans 100:66 D 14 '87. L. O'Toole
   New Repub 197:26-8 D 21 '87. S. Kauffmann
   New Yorker 63:144+ D 14 '87. P. Kael
   Newsweek il 110:68 D 21 '87. D. Ansen
   Time il 129:92-3 Mr 16 '87. M. Walsh
Dead of winter
   Macleans 100:52 F 23 '87. L. O'Toole
   New Repub 196:24-5 Mr 9 '87. S. Kauffmann
   Newsweek il 109:79 F 23 '87. D. Ansen
   People Wkly 27:6 Mr 2 '87. T. Cunneff
   Time il 129:76+ F 16 '87. R. Corliss
Deadline
   New Repub 197:26 S 28 '87. S. Kauffmann
Death before dishonor
   New Leader 70:22-3 Mr 9 '87. J. Gardner
The decline of the American empire
   Natl Rev 39:61-3 Ja 30 '87. J. Simon
   Time il 129:70+ Ja 19 '87. R. Schickel
Defense of the realm
   New Yorker 63:99-100 Mr 9 '87. P. Kael
   Newsweek il 109:61 Ja 19 '87. D. Ansen
Devil in the flesh
   Commonweal 114:387 Je 19 '87. T. O'Brien
   N Y 20:69 Je 8 '87. D. Denby
   Natl Rev 39:52-3 Jl 3 '87. J. Simon
   New Repub 196:24-5 Je 15 '87. S. Kauffmann
Dirty dancing
   Dance Mag il 61:64 O '87. D. Towers
   Glamour 85:297-8 S '87. J. G. Boyum
   Macleans 100:50 Ag 24 '87. L. O'Toole
   N Y il 20:60-1 S 7 '87. D. Denby
   New Yorker il 63:79-80 Ag 24 '87. P. Kael
   Newsweek il 110:63 D 21 '87. C. Leerhsen
   People Wkly il 28:8 Ag 31 '87. T. Cunneff
   Time il 130:77 S 14 '87. R. Schickel
   Vogue il 177:64 Ag '87. M. Haskell
Dragnet
   Life il 10:26-8+ Ap '87. M. Dougherty
   Macleans il 100:46 Jl 13 '87. L. O'Toole
   Newsweek il 110:60 Jl 13 '87. D. Ansen
   People Wkly il 28:10 Jl 20 '87. R. Novak
   Time il 130:68 Jl 13 '87. R. Schickel

Duet for one
   Commonweal 114:83 F 13 '87. T. O'Brien
   Macleans il 100:46 Mr 2 '87. L. O'Toole
   People Wkly il 27:16 F 2 '87. P. Travers
   Time il 129:74+ Mr 2 '87. R. Corliss
The duxorcist
   Newsweek il 110:83 N 30 '87. B. Barol
Eat the peach
   Macleans 100:46 Ag 31 '87. N. Jennings
   New Yorker 63:64-5 Jl 27 '87. P. Kael
Empire of the sun
   Macleans il 100:65 D 14 '87. L. O'Toole
   N Y il 20:86-7 D 14 '87. D. Denby
   New Yorker 63:93-5 D 28 '87. P. Kael
   Newsweek il 110:82-3 D 14 '87. D. Ansen
   Time il 130:79 D 7 '87. R. Corliss
Extreme prejudice
   Macleans il 100:58 My 4 '87. L. O'Toole
   N Y 20:70+ My 11 '87. D. Denby
   Newsweek il 109:75 My 4 '87. D. Ansen
   People Wkly il 27:10 My 11 '87. R. Novak
   Time il 129:97 My 4 '87. R. Schickel
Faces of women
   New Repub 196:24-5 F 16 '87. S. Kauffmann
Family viewing
   Macleans il 100:64 D 7 '87. B. D. Johnson
Fatal attraction
   Commonweal 114:565-6 O 9 '87. T. O'Brien
   Macleans 100:58 S 21 '87. L. O'Toole
   Macleans il 100:7 N 23 '87. F. Bruning
   Ms il 16:78-9 D '87. L. Stone
   N Y 20:116+ O 5 '87. D. Denby
   Natl Rev 39:56-7 D 4 '87. J. Simon
   New Repub 197:27 O 19 '87. S. Kauffmann
   New Yorker 63:106-7+ O 19 '87. P. Kael
   Newsweek il 110:76 S 28 '87. D. Ansen
   Newsweek il 110:76-7 O 12 '87. C. McGuigan
   People Wkly il 28:10 O 5 '87. P. Travers
   Roll Stone il p34 N 19 '87. L. Hirschberg
   Time il 130:69 S 28 '87. R. Schickel
   Time il 130:72-6+ N 16 '87. R. Corliss
Fatal beauty
   Jet il 73:58-60 N 16 '87
   Jet il 73:63 O 5 '87
Filming Othello
   New Repub 196:24-5 F 23 '87. S. Kauffmann
Forever Lulu
   Commonweal 114:319-20 My 22 '87. T. O'Brien
   People Wkly il 27:8 My 4 '87. R. Novak
The fourth protocol
   Macleans il 100:54 S 14 '87. G. Peary
   New Repub 197:26 S 28 '87. S. Kauffmann
   Newsweek il 110:82 S 14 '87. D. Ansen
   People Wkly il 28:14 S 7 '87. R. Novak
The fringe dwellers
   Ms 15:20-1 Mr '87. L. Stone
From the hip
   Macleans 100:52 F 23 '87. L. O'Toole
   N Y 20:72+ F 16 '87. D. Denby
   People Wkly il 27:12 Mr 9 '87. S. Haller
Full metal jacket
   America 157:66 Ag 1-8 '87. R. A. Blake
   Commonweal 114:457-8 Ag 14 '87. T. O'Brien
   Film Comment il 23:11-14 S/O '87. R. Lacayo
   Macleans il por 100:55 Jl 6 '87. L. O'Toole
   N Y il 20:54-5 Jl 13 '87. D. Denby
   Nation 245:98-9 Ag 1-8 '87. T. Rafferty
   Natl Rev 39:52-3 Ag 14 '87. J. Simon
   New Repub 197:28-9 Jl 27 '87. S. Kauffmann
   New Yorker 63:75-6 Jl 13 '87. P. Kael
   Newsweek il 109:64-5 Je 29 '87. J. Kroll
   People Wkly il 28:10 Jl 13 '87. R. Novak
   Time il 129:66 Je 29 '87. R. Corliss
Gaby—a true story
   Macleans 100:67 N 30 '87. L. O'Toole
Gardens of stone
   America 156:506+ Je 20-27 '87. R. A. Blake
   Commonweal 114:320 My 22 '87. T. O'Brien
   Macleans il 100:57 My 11 '87. L. O'Toole
   N Y 20:93 My 18 '87. D. Denby
   New Repub 196:24-5 My 25 '87. S. Kauffmann
   New Yorker 63:84-6 My 18 '87. P. Kael
   Newsweek il 109:79 My 11 '87. D. Ansen
   People Wkly il 27:10 My 11 '87. P. Travers
   Time 129:74 Je 15 '87
   Vogue il 177:90 Mr '87. T. Young
The gate
   People Wkly il 27:10 Je 8 '87. T. Cunneff
Girls apart
   Nation 245:463-4 O 24 '87. M. Gevisser

Motion picture reviews—Single works—*cont.*
The glass menagerie
  Glamour il 85:159 D '87. J. G. Boyum
  Macleans il 100:42 S 28 '87. J. Bemrose
  New Repub 197:25 N 23 '87. S. Kauffmann
  People Wkly il 28:14 N 23 '87. S. Haller
  Sch Update il 120:12-13 N 20 '87. D. Scheuer
The golden child
  N Y 20:46 Ja 5 '87. D. Denby
  People Wkly il 27:10 Ja 12 '87. T. Cunneff
The good father
  N Y il 20:63-4 F 23 '87. D. Denby
  Natl Rev 39:54 My 8 '87. J. Simon
  New Repub 196:28-9 F 9 '87. S. Kauffmann
  New Yorker 63:83-4 Ap 6 '87. P. Kael
  Newsweek 109:78 Mr 2 '87. D. Ansen
Good morning, Babylon
  N Y 20:64-5 Jl 27 '87. D. Denby
  New Repub 197:26-7 Ag 24 '87. S. Kauffmann
  New Yorker 63:70-1 Ag 10 '87. P. Kael
  Newsweek 110:68 Ag 3 '87. D. Ansen
Good morning, Vietnam
  Time il 130:74 D 28 '87. R. Schickel
The good wife
  Macleans 100:46 Mr 2 '87. L. O'Toole
  New Repub 196:27-8 Mr 16 '87. S. Kauffmann
Gothic
  America 156:445 My 30 '87. R. A. Blake
  Newsweek il 109:79 Ap 27 '87. J. Kroll
  People Wkly 27:14 Ap 20 '87. P. Travers
  Time 129:76 Ap 20 '87. R. Corliss
Hail Mary
  Phi Delta Kappan il 68:401-2 Ja '87. T. J. Flygare
Half Moon Street
  Mademoiselle il 93:66+ Ja '87. R. Rosenbaum
Hamburger Hill
  Jet il 72:56 S 21 '87
  Macleans 100:54 S 14 '87. L. O'Toole
  N Y il 20:108-9+ S 14 '87. D. Denby
  New Repub 197:32-3 S 14-21 '87. S. Kauffmann
  New Yorker 63:97-8 S 7 '87. P. Kael
  Newsweek il 110:83 S 14 '87. J. Kroll
  People Wkly il 28:14 S 14 '87. R. Novak
Hannah and her sisters
  Commonweal 114:294-6 My 8 '87. M. Burkhart
The Hanoi Hilton
  Macleans 100:57 My 11 '87. L. O'Toole
  N Y il 20:90-1 Ap 13 '87. D. Denby
  New Repub 196:26-7 Ap 27 '87. S. Kauffmann
  People Wkly il 27:14 Ap 20 '87. R. Novak
  Time il 129:78 Ap 13 '87. R. Schickel
A hard day's night
  High Fidel il 37:79-80 Je '87. D. Browne
Harry and the Hendersons
  Glamour 85:101+ Jl '87. J. G. Boyum
  Macleans 100:51 Je 15 '87. L. O'Toole
  Mademoiselle il 93:146+ S '87. R. Rosenbaum
  Newsweek il 109:78 Je 8 '87. D. Ansen
  People Wkly il 28:10 Jl 6 '87. T. Cunneff
  Time 129:74 Je 15 '87
Heartbreak Ridge
  N Y il 20:45 Ja 5 '87. D. Denby
  New Repub 196:24-5 Ja 5-12 '87. S. Kauffmann
  People Wkly il por 27:10 Ja 5 '87. R. Novak
Hearts of fire
  Vogue il 177:54 Jl '87. R. O'Connor
Heat
  People Wkly 27:12 Mr 30 '87. R. Novak
Heaven
  Christ Century 104:600 Jl 1-8 '87. D. Peerman
  Film Comment il 23:32-7 Mr/Ap '87. M. Glickman
  Newsweek il por 109:79 Ap 27 '87. D. Ansen
  People Wkly 27:10 My 11 '87. P. Travers
  Roll Stone il p23-4+ My 7 '87. D. Edelstein
  Time 129:79 Ap 27 '87. R. Corliss
Hello again
  Newsweek il 110:108-9 N 16 '87. D. Ansen
Help!
  High Fidel il 37:79-80 Je '87. D. Browne
  Stereo Rev il 52:205 N '87. L. Meredith
High season
  Vogue por 177:146+ S '87. R. Koenig
Hollywood shuffle
  Ebony il 42:54D+ Jl '87. M. Marshall
  Essence il 18:28 My '87. H. Als
  Film Comment il 23:11-14 Mr/Ap '87. A. White
  Jet il 72:58-60 Je 1 '87. C. Waldron
  Macleans 100:55 Je 1 '87. L. O'Toole
  Mademoiselle il 93:46-7+ Jl '87. R. Rosenbaum
  N Y il 20:90-1 Ap 6 '87. D. Denby
  New Repub 196:26 My 4 '87. S. Kauffmann

Time il 129:79 Ap 27 '87. R. Corliss
The home and the world
  N Y Rev Books il 34:12+ N 19 '87. I. Buruma
Hoosiers
  Commonweal 114:215-16 Ap 10 '87. T. O'Brien
  Macleans il 100:46 Mr 2 '87. L. O'Toole
  New Repub 196:26-7 Ap 6 '87. S. Kauffmann
  Newsweek il 109:73 F 9 '87. D. Ansen
  People Wkly il 27:12 F 23 '87. S. Haller
  People Wkly il 27:34-5 Mr 30 '87. L. Aitken
  Saturday Evening Post il 259:52-3+ Mr '87. H. Nuwer
  Time il 129:74 F 9 '87. R. Schickel
Hope and glory
  Commonweal 114:704-6 D 4 '87. T. O'Brien
  Glamour il 85:249 N '87. J. G. Boyum
  Macleans 100:52 N 2 '87. L. O'Toole
  N Y 20:115-16 O 26 '87. D. Denby
  New Repub 197:28-9 N 2 '87. S. Kauffmann
  New Yorker 63:91-2 O 5 '87. P. Kael
  Newsweek il 110:84 O 19 '87. D. Ansen
  People Wkly il 28:14 N 2 '87. P. Travers
  Time il 130:76 O 19 '87. R. Corliss
Hot pursuit
  People Wkly 27:10 Je 8 '87. T. Cunneff
The hour of the star
  Américas 39:62-3 My/Je '87. J. Mosier
  New Yorker 63:110-11 F 23 '87. P. Kael
  Vogue il 177:32+ Ja '87. M. Haskell
House of games
  Commonweal 114:703-4 D 4 '87. T. O'Brien
  Glamour 85:227 O '87. J. G. Boyum
  Macleans 100:63 O 26 '87. L. O'Toole
  N Y il 20:101-2 O 19 '87. D. Denby
  New Repub 197:22-3 N 16 '87. S. Kauffmann
  Newsweek il 110:85 O 19 '87. J. Kroll
  People Wkly il 28:14 N 16 '87. P. Travers
  Time il 130:76 O 19 '87. R. Schickel
  Vogue il 177:140+ S '87. M. Haskell
Housekeeping
  Macleans 100:67 D 14 '87. L. O'Toole
  New Yorker 63:147-9 D 14 '87. P. Kael
  Newsweek 110:89 D 7 '87. J. Kroll
  Time il 130:101 N 23 '87. R. Schickel
  Vogue il 177:72 D '87. M. Haskell
I lived, but . . .
  New Repub 196:24-6 Ap 13 '87. S. Kauffmann
In the mood
  Newsweek il 110:77 S 28 '87. M. Reese
  People Wkly il 28:12 O 12 '87. T. Cunneff
In the shadow of the wind
  Macleans il 100:54 Ja 26 '87. M. Abley
Innerspace
  Macleans 100:46 Jl 13 '87. L. O'Toole
  N Y 20:51 Jl 20 '87. D. Denby
  New Yorker 63:65 Jl 27 '87. P. Kael
  Newsweek il 110:60 Jl 13 '87. D. Ansen
  People Wkly il 28:10 Jl 20 '87. S. Haller
  Time il 130:68-9 Jl 13 '87. R. Corliss
Ironweed
  Horizon il 30:35-6 D '87. J. Parini
  Newsweek il 110:68 D 21 '87. D. Ansen
  Time il 130:74 D 21 '87. R. Corliss
Ishtar
  America 156:466+ Je 6 '87. R. A. Blake
  Bus Week il p75 N 30 '87. R. Grover
  Glamour il 85:101 Jl '87. J. G. Boyum
  Life il 10:62-5+ My '87. S. Allison
  Macleans il 100:54 My 25 '87. L. O'Toole
  N Y il 20:105+ My 25 '87. D. Denby
  N Y il 20:34-43 Mr 16 '87. D. Blum
  Natl Rev 39:52 Jl 3 '87. J. Simon
  New Repub 196:26 Je 8 '87. S. Kauffmann
  New Yorker 63:102+ Je 1 '87. P. Kael
  Newsweek il por 109:76-8 My 18 '87. D. Ansen
  People Wkly 27:8 Je 1 '87. P. Travers
  Time il 129:85 My 18 '87. R. Schickel
  Vogue il 177:306-7 My '87. T. Young
I've heard the mermaids singing
  Commonweal 114:498 S 11 '87. T. O'Brien
  Macleans il 100:48 S 28 '87. L. O'Toole
  Natl Rev 39:60-1 O 23 '87. J. Simon
  Time il 130:77 S 14 '87. R. Corliss
Jaws the revenge
  Macleans 100:49 Ag 3 '87. L. O'Toole
  People Wkly il 28:12 Ag 3 '87. T. Cunneff
Jean de Florette
  Commonweal 114:420-1 Jl 17 '87. T. O'Brien
  Glamour 85:102 Jl '87. J. G. Boyum
  N Y il 20:50-1 Jl 20 '87. D. Denby
  New Repub 197:26-7 Jl 6 '87. S. Kauffmann
  New Yorker 63:76-7 Jl 13 '87. P. Kael

Motion picture reviews—Single works—Jean de Florette
—cont.

   Newsweek il 110:61 Jl 13 '87. J. Kroll
   Time il 130:75 Jl 20 '87. R. Schickel
The jeweller's shop
   Macleans il 100:50 Ag 31 '87. P. Young
John and the missus
   Macleans il 100:78 F 2 '87. L. O'Toole
Kangaroo
   Commonweal 114:182-3 Mr 27 '87. T. O'Brien
   Macleans 100:69 Mr 23 '87. J. Bemrose
   Ms il 15:35-6 Ap '87. L. Stone
   New Repub 196:24-5 Mr 30 '87. S. Kauffmann
   People Wkly 27:12 Ap 13 '87. I. Hellman
Keeping track
   Macleans il 100:55 Ap 6 '87. B. D. Johnson
The kid brother
   Macleans il 100:60 O 19 '87. C. Bell
King Kong lives
   People Wkly 27:14 Ja 26 '87. R. Novak
Lady and the Tramp
   People Wkly il 27:10 Ja 12 '87. R. Novak
The last emperor
   Commonweal 114:747-8 D 18 '87. T. O'Brien
   Film Comment il 23:31-2+ N/D '87. T. Rayns
   Life il 10:36-40 Ap '87. D. Leigh-Kile
   Macleans il 100:66 D 14 '87. L. O'Toole
   N Y il 20:76-8 N 30 '87. D. Denby
   Natl Rev 39:54-7 D 18 '87. J. Simon
   New Repub 197:22-3 D 14 '87. S. Kauffmann
   New Yorker 63:98-101 N 30 '87. P. Kael
   Newsweek 1 110:81-2 N 23 '87. D. Ansen
   People Wkly il 28:12 D 7 '87. P. Travers
   Time il 130:100 N 23 '87. R. Schickel
The last straw
   Macleans il 100:60 O 19 '87. B. D. Johnson
Law of desire
   New Yorker 63:80-1 Ap 20 '87. P. Kael
   People Wkly 28:12 Ag 3 '87. P. Travers
Leonard part 6
   Jet il 73:54-7 D 21 '87
Less than zero
   N Y il 20:104-5 N 23 '87. D. Denby
   Newsweek il 110:108 N 16 '87. D. Ansen
   People Wkly 28:14 D 14 '87. S. Haller
   Vogue il 177:76 N '87. B. Roe
Lethal weapon
   Jet il 72:58-60 Ap 6 '87. C. Waldron
   New Repub 196:24 Ap 13 '87. S. Kauffmann
   Newsweek il 109:72 Mr 16 '87. D. Ansen
   People Wkly il 27:8 Mr 23 '87. T. Cunneff
   Time il 129:86 Mr 23 '87. R. Schickel
Life classes
   Macleans 100:64 D 7 '87. S. Pedersen
Light of day
   Christ Today il 31:66 My 15 '87. S. Ulstein
   Macleans il 100:46 F 9 '87. B. D. Johnson
   N Y 20:102-3 Mr 2 '87. D. Denby
   Newsweek il 109:73 F 9 '87. D. Ansen
   People Wkly il 27:12 F 23 '87. P. Travers
   Roll Stone il por p25-6 Ja 15 '87. S. Pond
   Time il 129:74 F 9 '87. R. Corliss
Lily Tomlin: the film behind the show
   New Repub 196:24-5 Mr 23 '87. S. Kauffmann
Little shop of horrors
   Commonweal 114:55-6 Ja 30 '87. T. O'Brien
   Glamour il 85:175 F '87. J. G. Boyum
   Macleans il 100:18-19 Ja 5 '87. L. O'Toole
   N Y il 20:51 Ja 12 '87. D. Denby
   New Repub 196:26 Ja 26 '87. S. Kauffmann
   New Yorker 62:92+ Ja 12 '87. P. Kael
   Newsweek il 109:56 Ja 5 '87. D. Ansen
   People Wkly 27:10 Ja 12 '87. P. Travers
   USA Today (Periodical) il 115:96-7 Mr '87. K. R.
     Hey
The living daylights
   Humanist il 47:43 N/D '87. H. M. Geduld
   Macleans il 100:49 Ag 3 '87. L. O'Toole
   N Y il 20:54 Ag 10 '87. D. Denby
   Newsweek il 110:56-7 Jl 27 '87. C. McGuigan
   People Wkly 28:8 Ag 31 '87. R. Novak
   Roll Stone il p37-9 Jl 16-30 '87. G. Hirshey
   Time il 130:55 Ag 10 '87. R. Corliss
The lonely passion of Judith Hearne
   New Yorker 63:92-3 D 28 '87. P. Kael
Long live the lady!
   New Repub 197:24 N 9 '87. S. Kauffmann
The Lost Boys
   Glamour il 85:199 Ag '87. J. G. Boyum
   Macleans 100:49 Ag 3 '87. P. Young
   Newsweek il 110:67 Ag 3 '87. D. Ansen

   People Wkly 28:10 Ag 17 '87. J. Calio
   Teen il 31:49+ Jl '87
Love me now or never
   Américas 39:59 Mr/Ap '87. J. Mosier
Made in heaven
   New Yorker 63:145 N 16 '87. P. Kael
   Newsweek 110:108 N 16 '87. D. Ansen
   People Wkly 28:18 N 30 '87. P. Travers
The magnificent rebel
   Film Comment il 23:52-4+ N/D '87. J. Scott
Maid to order
   Glamour 85:199-200 Ag '87. J. G. Boyum
   People Wkly il 28:12 Ag 3 '87. R. Novak
   Sch Update il 120:48 S 18 '87. D. Scheuer
Making Mr. Right
   Glamour il 85:154 Je '87. J. G. Boyum
   Glamour il 85:224 My '87. C. Krupp
   Macleans 100:49 Ap 13 '87
   Ms 15:22 My '87. S. Dworkin
   N Y il 20:46-9 Mr 30 '87. A. Virshup
   N Y il 20:125-6 Ap 27 '87. D. Denby
   New Repub 196:26-7 My 4 '87. S. Kauffmann
   Newsweek il 109:77-8 Ap 13 '87. J. Kroll
   People Wkly il 27:8 Ap 27 '87. R. Novak
   Time il 129:78 Ap 13 '87. R. Schickel
Malandro's opera
   Américas 39:60-1 S/O '87. J. Mosier
Malcolm
   Theatre Crafts il 21:73-4 F '87. W. Harris
Malone
   People Wkly il 27:10 My 18 '87. R. Novak
Man facing southeast
   Américas 39:60-1 N/D '87. J. Mosier
   Commonweal 114:243-4 Ap 24 '87. T. O'Brien
   Macleans il 100:49 Ap 13 '87
   New Repub 196:26 Ap 6 '87. S. Kauffmann
A man in love
   Film Comment il 23:84-6 S/O '87. M. Pally
   Macleans 100:50 Ag 24 '87. L. O'Toole
   N Y 20:54-5 Ag 10 '87. D. Denby
Manhunter
   Christ Century 104:46-7 Ja 21 '87. M. Horst
Mannequin
   Macleans 100:57 Mr 9 '87. P. Young
Manon of the spring
   N Y 20:115 N 16 '87. D. Denby
   Natl Rev 39:57 D 18 '87. J. Simon
   New Repub il 197:24-5 N 23 '87. S. Kauffmann
   Newsweek il 110:77 N 9 '87. D. Ansen
Marlene
   Macleans il 100:48 Ja 12 '87. L. O'Toole
   People Wkly 27:12 Ja 5 '87. P. Travers
   USA Today (Periodical) il 115:96 Mr '87. K. R.
     Hey
Matewan
   Commonweal il 114:626-7 N 6 '87. T. O'Brien
   Glamour 85:298 S '87. J. G. Boyum
   Horizon il por 30:12-14 S '87. R. Seidenberg
   Macleans 100:56 O 12 '87. L. O'Toole
   Nation 245:427-8 O 17 '87. M. Margaronis
   New Repub 197:24-5 S 7 '87. S. Kauffmann
   Newsweek il 110:82 S 14 '87. D. Ansen
   People Wkly il 28:12 S 21 '87. R. Novak
   Roll Stone il p27-8 O 8 '87. S. G. Freedman
   Theatre Crafts il 21:45-8 Ap '87. R. Seidenberg
   Time il 130:77 S 14 '87. R. Corliss
Maurice
   Macleans 100:59 S 21 '87. L. O'Toole
   N Y il 20:136+ S 28 '87. D. Denby
   Nation 245:498-500 O 31 '87. V. Russo
   Natl Rev 39:59-60 N 6 '87. J. Simon
   New Repub 197:28 O 5 '87. S. Kauffmann
   New Yorker 63:103+ S 21 '87. P. Kael
   Newsweek il 110:76 S 21 '87. D. Ansen
   People Wkly il 28:14-15 S 28 '87. P. Travers
   Vogue il 177:62+ My '87. V. Radin
Men . . .
   New Leader 70:21-2 Ja 12-26 '87. J. Gardner
Miss Mary
   Commonweal 114:16 Ja 16 '87. T. O'Brien
   Glamour 85:175+ F '87. J. G. Boyum
   Ms 15:14 F '87. L. Stone
   Time il 129:70 Ja 19 '87. R. Corliss
The mission
   USA Today (Periodical) il 115:94-5 Ja '87. K. R.
     Hey
Monster in the closet
   People Wkly il 27:8 Je 1 '87. R. Novak
The Monster Squad
   People Wkly 28:14 S 7 '87. T. Cunneff

Motion picture reviews—Single works—*cont.*
Moonstruck
   Macleans 100:65 D 14 '87. L. O'Toole
   Newsweek 110:69 D 21 '87. D. Ansen
The morning after
   Commonweal 114:55 Ja 30 '87. T. O'Brien
   Macleans 100:19-20 Ja 5 '87. L. O'Toole
   Mademoiselle il 93:102+ Mr '87. R. Rosenbaum
   N Y 20:45-6 Ja 5 '87. D. Denby
   Natl Rev 39:56-7 F 13 '87. J. Simon
   New Repub 196:24 Ja 5-12 '87. S. Kauffmann
   People Wkly il 27:12 Ja 5 '87. S. Haller
The Mosquito Coast
   Glamour il 85:132 Ja '87. J. G. Boyum
   Theatre Crafts il 21:71-2 F '87. S. Gowin
   USA Today (Periodical) il 115:95-6 Mr '87. K. R.
     Hey
Mother Teresa
   Christ Century 104:260-1 Mr 18-25 '87. J. D. Lynch
   Commonweal 114:82-3 F 13 '87. T. O'Brien
The Mozart brothers
   Opera News il 52:55 D 5 '87. A. Rich
My demon lover
   People Wkly il 27:10 My 18 '87. T. Cunneff
My life as a dog
   Commonweal 114:420 Jl 17 '87. T. O'Brien
   Macleans 100:51 Je 15 '87. L. O'Toole
   N Y il 20:70 My 11 '87. D. Denby
   Natl Rev 39:56 Je 19 '87. J. Simon
   New Repub 196:24 My 25 '87. S. Kauffmann
   People Wkly 28:6 Ag 24 '87. S. Haller
   Vogue il 177:32 Je '87. M. Haskell
My sweet little village
   Commonweal 114:82 F 13 '87. T. O'Brien
Nadine
   Commonweal 114:499 S 11 '87. T. O'Brien
   Macleans 100:51 Ag 17 '87. L. O'Toole
   New Yorker 63:81-2 Ag 24 '87. P. Kael
   Newsweek 110:58 Ag 10 '87. J. Kroll
   People Wkly il 28:8 Ag 10 '87. P. Travers
   Time il 130:62 Ag 17 '87. R. Corliss
   Vogue il 177:132+ S '87. M. Haskell
The name of the rose
   Humanist il 47:39-40 Mr/Ap '87. H. M. Geduld
   USA Today (Periodical) il 115:95-6 Ja '87. K. R.
     Hey
Napoleon
   Stereo Rev il 52:111 Mr '87. S. Simels
Native son
   Essence il 17:40-2+ Ap '87. B. Allen
   Macleans 100:18 Ja 5 '87. L. O'Toole
   Ms il 15:15-17 Mr '87. S. McHenry
   People Wkly il 27:8 Ja 19 '87. S. Haller
A nightmare on Elm Street, part 3: Dream warriors
   New Leader 70:19-20 Mr 23 '87. J. Gardner
No man's land
   People Wkly il 28:14 N 16 '87. R. Novak
No mercy
   N Y 20:45 Ja 5 '87. D. Denby
   People Wkly il 27:10 Ja 5 '87. P. Travers
No way out
   Glamour il 85:297 S '87. J. G. Boyum
   Macleans il 100:46 Ag 31 '87. B. D. Johnson
   N Y il 20:62-3 Ag 17 '87. D. Denby
   Natl Rev 39:59-61 S 25 '87. J. Simon
   New Yorker 63:98-100 S 7 '87. P. Kael
   People Wkly il 28:6 Ag 24 '87. S. Haller
   Time il 130:62 Ag 17 '87. R. Schickel
Nuts
   America il 157:506 D 26 '87. R. A. Blake
   Macleans il 100:66 N 30 '87. L. O'Toole
   New Repub 197:23-4 D 14 '87. S. Kauffmann
   Newsweek il 110:83 N 23 '87. D. Ansen
   People Wkly il 28:14 N 23 '87. P. Travers
   Time il 130:104 N 30 '87. R. Corliss
On the waterfront
   N Y Times Book Rev il 92:1+ Ap 26 '87. B. Schulberg
The only son
   New Repub 196:24-6 Ap 13 '87. S. Kauffmann
Orphans
   Glamour il 85:228 O '87. J. G. Boyum
   Natl Rev 39:61-2 O 23 '87. J. Simon
   New Repub 197:26-7 O 19 '87. S. Kauffmann
   Newsweek 110:76 S 28 '87. D. Ansen
   People Wkly il 28:10 O 5 '87. P. Travers
   Time 130:85 O 12 '87
   Vogue il 177:462+ S '87. D. Mason
Outrageous fortune
   Commonweal 114:182 Mr 27 '87. T. O'Brien
   Macleans 100:47 F 9 '87. L. O'Toole
   N Y 20:96 F 9 '87. D. Denby

   New Leader 70:23 Ap 6 '87. J. Gardner
   New Repub 196:24 Mr 2 '87. S. Kauffmann
   New Yorker 63:112-13 F 23 '87. P. Kael
   Newsweek il 109:76 Ja 26 '87. D. Ansen
   People Wkly 27:10 F 16 '87. P. Travers
   Time il 129:73 F 2 '87. R. Corliss
Over the top
   Macleans il 100:52 F 23 '87. L. O'Toole
   Newsweek il 109:79 F 23 '87. D. Ansen
   People Wkly il 27:6 Mr 2 '87. T. Cunneff
Peggy Sue got married
   Christ Century 104:61 Ja 21 '87. J. M. Wall
   Humanist il 47:44-5 Ja/F '87. H. M. Geduld
   Progressive 51:36 Ja '87. P. Aufderheide
   USA Today (Periodical) il 115:97 Ja '87. K. R.
     Hey
Personal services
   Macleans 100:56 O 12 '87. L. O'Toole
   Ms 15:21-2 My '87. A. B. Snitow
   N Y 20:95-6 Je 1 '87. D. Denby
   New Repub 196:27 My 4 '87. S. Kauffmann
   New Yorker 63:84 My 18 '87. P. Kael
   People Wkly 28:12 Jl 27 '87. T. Cunneff
The pick-up artist
   N Y 20:93 O 12 '87. D. Denby
   New Yorker 63:92-3 O 5 '87. P. Kael
   Newsweek 110:77 S 28 '87. D. Ansen
   People Wkly 28:12 O 12 '87. T. Cunneff
   Time il 130:69 S 28 '87. R. Corliss
Pink Floyd the wall
   Phi Delta Kappan il 69:237-8 N '87. T. J. Flygare
Place of weeping
   Commonweal 114:16-17 Ja 16 '87. T. O'Brien
Planes, trains and automobiles
   Macleans 100:67 D 14 '87. L. O'Toole
   N Y il 20:152 D 7 '87. D. Denby
   People Wkly il 28:14 D 14 '87. P. Travers
   Time il 130:104 N 30 '87. R. Schickel
Platoon
   Am Herit il 38:12+ Jl/Ag '87. G. C. Ward
   America 156:159+ F 21 '87. R. A. Blake
   Channels il 7:59 O '87. J. Vitale
   Christ Century 104:60-1 Ja 21 '87. J. M. Wall
   Commonweal 114:17-18 Ja 16 '87. T. O'Brien
   Film Comment il 23:11-14+ Ja/F '87. P. McGilligan
   Forbes il 140:33 Ag 10 '87. W. Harris
   Forbes il 139:170 Ap 6 '87. A. B. Block
   Fortune il 116:9 N 23 '87
   Humanist il 47:41 My/Je '87. H. M. Geduld
   Macleans il 100:61-2 Mr 30 '87. G. Peary
   Macleans il 100:7 Mr 16 '87. F. Bruning
   Mademoiselle il 93:96+ Ap '87. R. Rosenbaum
   N Y 20:78+ Ja 19 '87. D. Denby
   Nation 244:54-6 Ja 17 '87. T. Rafferty
   Natl Rev 39:54-7 Mr 13 '87. J. Simon
   New Leader 70:22-3 Mr 9 '87. J. Gardner
   New Repub 196:24-5 Ja 19 '87. S. Kauffmann
   New Repub 196:4+ Mr 9 '87
   New Yorker 62:94-6 Ja 12 '87. P. Kael
   Newsweek il 109:57 Ja 5 '87. D. Ansen
   Newsweek il 110:56 N 23 '87
   People Wkly il 27:82-3+ Mr 2 '87. A. Richman
   People Wkly il 27:8 Ja 19 '87. R. Novak
   People Wkly il 27:48-50+ Mr 9 '87
   People Wkly il 27:101-2+ Ap 20 '87. W. Terry
   Roll Stone il p23-4+ Ja 29 '87. F. Schruers
   Time il 129:54-61 Ja 26 '87. R. Corliss
   U S News World Rep 102:78 Mr 2 '87. H. Evans
   USA Today (Periodical) il 115:94-5 Mr '87. K. R.
     Hey
Police
   Time 129:72 Ja 19 '87. R. Corliss
Police Academy 4
   People Wkly il 27:14 Ap 20 '87. R. Novak
The pornographers
   New Repub 196:25-6 Je 15 '87. S. Kauffmann
A prayer for the dying
   Macleans 100:59 S 21 '87. L. O'Toole
   New Repub 197:26-7 S 28 '87. S. Kauffmann
   People Wkly 28:10 O 5 '87. R. Novak
Predator
   People Wkly il 27:10 Je 29 '87. R. Novak
Prick up your ears
   Macleans il 100:48 My 18 '87. L. O'Toole
   N Y il 20:76+ Ap 20 '87. D. Denby
   N Y Rev Books il 34:3-4 S 24 '87. G. Annan
   Nation 244:618-19 My 9 '87. T. Rafferty
   Natl Rev 39:52-4 My 22 '87. J. Simon
   New Repub 196:28-9 Ap 20 '87. S. Kauffmann
   New Yorker 63:128+ My 4 '87. P. Kael
   Newsweek il 109:89 Ap 20 '87. D. Ansen

Motion picture reviews—Single works—Prick up your ears—*cont.*

People Wkly 27:8 My 4 '87. P. Travers
Time il 129:76 Ap 20 '87. R. Corliss
Vogue il 177:70 Ap '87. M. Haskell

The princess bride
Film Comment il 23:58+ S/O '87. H. Jacobson
Glamour il 85:250 N '87. J. G. Boyum
Macleans il 100:58 O 5 '87. L. O'Toole
New Yorker 63:110-12 O 19 '87. P. Kael
Newsweek il 110:85 O 5 '87. D. Ansen
People Wkly 28:14 S 28 '87. P. Travers
Sch Update il 120:40 O 2 '87. D. Scheuer
Time il 130:74 S 21 '87. R. Corliss

Project X
Glamour il 85:153 Je '87. J. G. Boyum
Macleans il 100:62 Ap 27 '87. L. O'Toole
Newsweek il 109:75 My 4 '87. D. Ansen
People Wkly 27:12 Je 15 '87. S. Haller
Time il 129:97 My 4 '87. R. Corliss

Radio days
America 156:237+ Mr 21 '87. R. A. Blake
Commonweal il 114:111-12 F 27 '87. T. O'Brien
Film Comment il 23:11-14 Mr/Ap '87. A. White
Glamour il 85:225 Mr '87. J. G. Boyum
Macleans il 100:47 F 9 '87. L. O'Toole
Mademoiselle il 93:76+ My '87. R. Rosenbaum
Ms 15:17+ Mr '87. L. Stone
N Y il 20:95-6 F 9 '87. D. Denby
Nation 244:229-31 F 21 '87. T. Rafferty
Natl Rev 39:57-9 Mr 27 '87. J. Simon
New Leader il 70:19-20 F 9-23 '87. J. Gardner
New Repub 196:24 Mr 9 '87. S. Kauffmann
New Yorker 63:96+ Mr 9 '87. P. Kael
Newsweek il 109:71 F 2 '87. D. Ansen
People Wkly il 27:10 F 16 '87. P. Travers
Time il 129:73 F 2 '87. R. Schickel
Vogue il 177:90+ Mr '87. M. Haskell

Raising Arizona
Christ Century 104:598 Jl 1-8 '87. J. H. Mahan
Commonweal il 114:242-3 Ap 24 '87. T. O'Brien
Film Comment il 23:19-20+ Mr/Ap '87. J. Barth
Glamour il 85:243 Ap '87. J. G. Boyum
Macleans il 100:69 Mr 23 '87. L. O'Toole
N Y il 20:44-8 Mr 23 '87. E. Pooley
N Y il 20:60+ Mr 16 '87. D. Denby
Natl Rev 39:52-4 My 8 '87. J. Simon
New Leader 70:22-3 Ap 6 '87. J. Gardner
New Repub 196:24 Ap 13 '87. S. Kauffmann
New Yorker 63:81-2 Ap 20 '87. P. Kael
People Wkly il 27:8 Mr 23 '87. P. Travers
Time il 129:86 Mr 23 '87. R. Corliss
USA Today (Periodical) 116:43 Jl '87. K. R. Hey
Vogue il 177:62 Ap '87. M. Haskell

Rate it X
Christ Today il pors 31:64 Mr 6 '87. S. Ulstein

Red kiss
Ms 15:16 F '87. L. Stone

Rendez-vous
Nation 244:154-6 F 7 '87. T. Rafferty

Repentance
Christ Century 104:676-7 Ag 12-19 '87. J. Forest
Newsweek il 109:20-1 Ja 5 '87
Time il 130:54 D 14 '87. T. A. Sancton

Rita, Sue and Bob too
New Repub 197:24-5 Ag 10-17 '87. S. Kauffmann
Newsweek 110:67 Ag 3 '87. D. Ansen

River's edge
Film Comment il 23:70-1 Jl/Ag '87. G. Smith
Glamour 85:153-4 Je '87. J. G. Boyum
Macleans il 100:48 Je '87. L. O'Toole
Mademoiselle il 93:80 My '87. R. Rosenbaum
Ms il 16:26 S '87. J. Barthel
N Y il 20:90+ My 18 '87. D. Denby
Nation 245:386-7 O 10 '87. F. P. Smoler
Natl Rev 39:55-6 Je 19 '87. J. Simon
New Repub 196:26-7 Je 8 '87. S. Kauffmann
New Yorker 63:78-9 Je 15 '87. P. Kael
Newsweek il 109:69 Je 1 '87. D. Ansen
Newsweek il 109:25 Je 22 '87. P. Abramson
People Wkly il 27:8 Je 1 '87. P. Travers
Roll Stone il p43-4 Ap 23 '87. D. Edelstein
Time il 129:73 Je 1 '87. R. Schickel

Robinson's garden
Film Comment il 23:6+ My/Je '87. A. Vogel

RoboCop
Macleans 100:47 Jl 27 '87. L. O'Toole
N Y il 20:58+ Jl 27 '87. D. Denby
New Yorker 63:72-3 Ag 10 '87. P. Kael
Newsweek il 110:58-9 Jl 20 '87. D. Ansen
People Wkly il 28:12 Jl 27 '87. S. Haller

Time il 130:75 Jl 27 '87. R. Corliss

Rosa Luxemburg
Ms 15:22-3 My '87. L. Stone
N Y 20:96-7 Je 1 '87. D. Denby
Nation 244:546-9 Ap 25 '87. D. Egger
New Repub 196:24-5 My 18 '87. S. Kauffmann

Round midnight
Down Beat il 54:22-3 Ja '87. H. Mandel

Roxanne
America 157:66+ Ag 1-8 '87. R. A. Blake
Commonweal 114:387-8 Je 19 '87. T. O'Brien
Macleans il 100:48 Je 29 '87. L. O'Toole
N Y il 20:87+ Je 15 '87. D. Denby
Natl Rev 39:51-2 Jl 31 '87. J. Simon
New Repub 196:24-5 Je 29 '87. S. Kauffmann
New Yorker 63:77-8 Je 15 '87. P. Kael
Newsweek il 109:73 Je 22 '87. D. Ansen
People Wkly il 28:10 Jl 6 '87. P. Travers
Time il 129:74 Je 15 '87. R. Corliss

The running man
People Wkly il 28:18 N 30 '87. R. Novak

Russkies
Mot Boat Sail il 159:60-1 Ap '87. J. Clemans
Sch Update il 120:TE8 O 16 '87. C. McHugh

Sammy and Rosie get laid
Macleans 100:71 N 16 '87. P. Hluchy
N Y il 20:114+ N 9 '87. D. Denby
Nation 245:606-8 N 21 '87. T. Rafferty
New Repub 197:24-6 N 30 '87. S. Kauffmann
New Yorker 63:140-2+ N 16 '87. P. Kael
Newsweek 110:77 N 9 '87. D. Ansen
Time il 130:91 N 9 '87. R. Corliss
Vogue il 177:74 D '87. M. Haskell

Scene of the crime
Macleans il 100:53 Ap 20 '87
N Y il 20:56-7 F 2 '87. D. Denby
Nation 244:154-6 F 7 '87. T. Rafferty

The secret of my success
Commonweal 114:318-19 My 22 '87. T. O'Brien
Macleans il 100:53-4 Ap 20 '87
N Y 20:126+ Ap 27 '87. D. Denby
New Repub 196:24 My 11 '87. S. Kauffmann
New Yorker 63:130+ My 4 '87. P. Kael
People Wkly il 27:8 Ap 27 '87. S. Haller
Time il 129:97 My 4 '87. R. Corliss
USA Today (Periodical) 116:43 Jl '87. K. R. Hey

September
Macleans 100:61 D 21 '87. B. D. Johnson
People Wkly il 28:10 D 21 '87. R. Novak
Time il 130:74 D 21 '87. R. Schickel

Sherman's March
Mademoiselle 93:168 Ja '87. R. Rosenbaum

She's gotta have it
Ebony il 42:42+ Ja '87

The Sicilian
People Wkly 28:14 N 16 '87. R. Novak

Siesta
Film Comment il 23:24-9 N/D '87. G. Smith

Sign o' the times
Roll Stone il p16 D 3 '87. A. DeCurtis

Slam dance
Vogue il 177:154 S '87. M. Haskell

Snow White and the seven dwarfs
Am Hist Illus il 22:30-9 D '87. E. Oxford
Life il 10:52-4+ Ap '87. M. Dougherty
Read Dig il 131:114-19 D '87. J. Culhane

Some kind of wonderful
Newsweek 109:72 Mr 16 '87. D. Ansen
People Wkly il 27:12 Mr 9 '87. P. Travers
Time il 129:86 Mr 9 '87. R. Schickel

Someone to watch over me
Macleans 100:63 O 26 '87. L. O'Toole
N Y 20:95 N 2 '87. D. Denby
Nation 245:461-2 O 24 '87. T. Rafferty
New Yorker 63:140 N 2 '87. P. Kael
People Wkly il 28:16 O 19 '87. P. Travers
Time il 130:84 O 12 '87. R. Corliss

Something wild
Glamour 85:131 Ja '87. J. G. Boyum

Spaceballs
Macleans il 100:46 Jl 13 '87. L. O'Toole
New Repub 197:26-7 Ag 3 '87. S. Kauffmann
Newsweek il 109:66 Je 29 '87. D. Ansen
People Wkly il 28:10 Jl 13 '87. P. Travers
Time il 130:68 Jl 13 '87. R. Schickel

The spider game
Américas 39:58 Jl/Ag '87. J. Mosier

Sport aviation
Flying il 114:88 Ja '87. J. M. McClellan

Square dance
Glamour 85:226 Mr '87. J. G. Boyum

Motion picture reviews—Single works—Square dance—
cont.

   Ms 15:36 Ap '87. S. Dworkin
   Sch Update il 119:32-3 Mr 23 '87. D. Scheuer
The squeeze
   Macleans il 100:46 Jl 20 '87. L. O'Toole
   People Wkly il 28:12 Jl 27 '87. R. Novak
Stacking
   Macleans 100:59 N 23 '87. B. D. Johnson
Stakeout
   Macleans il 100:51 Ag 17 '87. L. O'Toole
   New Yorker il 63:80-1 Ag 24 '87. P. Kael
   Newsweek il 110:56-7 Ag 10 '87. D. Ansen
   People Wkly il 28:10 Ag 17 '87. R. Novak
   Time il 130:62 Ag 17 '87. R. Schickel
The stepfather
   N Y 20:107 My 25 '87. D. Denby
   Nation 244:740-2 My 30 '87. T. Rafferty
   New Yorker 62:92-3 F 9 '87. P. Kael
   Newsweek 109:79 F 23 '87. D. Ansen
   People Wkly 27:10 My 18 '87. P. Travers
   Time 129:74 Je 15 '87
   Vogue il 177:34 Je '87. M. Haskell
Stranded
   Theatre Crafts il 21:83-6 N '87. R. Seidenberg
The street of crocodiles
   Film Comment il 23:8 My/Je '87. A. Vogel
Street smart
   Glamour il 85:243-4 Ap '87. J. G. Boyum
   Macleans il 100:54 Ap 20 '87
   N Y il 20:89-90 Mr 30 '87. D. Denby
   New Yorker 63:82-3 Ap 20 '87. P. Kael
   People Wkly il 27:12 Mr 30 '87. P. Travers
   Vogue il 177:62 Ap '87. M. Haskell
Street trash
   Theatre Crafts il 21:20 N '87. J. Calhoun
Summer heat
   People Wkly il 27:12 Je 15 '87. R. Novak
Summer night
   New Repub 197:27-8 Jl 6 '87. S. Kauffmann
Summer school
   Macleans il 100:47 Jl 27 '87. P. Young
   People Wkly 28:8 Ag 10 '87. T. Cunneff
Superman IV
   People Wkly il 28:8 Ag 10 '87. R. Novak
Surrender
   People Wkly il 28:14 N 9 '87. R. Novak
Suspect
   Macleans 100:71 N 16 '87. L. O'Toole
   N Y il 20:94-5 N 2 '87. D. Denby
   New Yorker 63:145-6 N 16 '87. P. Kael
   Newsweek il 110:86 O 26 '87. D. Ansen
   People Wkly il 28:14 N 9 '87. R. Novak
Swimming to Cambodia
   Glamour 85:218 My '87. J. G. Boyum
   Macleans 100:62 Ap 27 '87. L. O'Toole
   Mademoiselle il 93:46-7+ Jl '87. R. Rosenbaum
   N Y il 20:82+ Mr 23 '87. D. Denby
   N Y Times Mag il p40+ Mr 8 '87. M. Simpson
   Nation 244:518-20 Ap 18 '87. T. Rafferty
   New Repub 196:24 Mr 23 '87. S. Kauffmann
   New Yorker 63:84-5 Ap 6 '87. P. Kael
   Time 129:79 Ap 27 '87. R. Schickel
Tampopo
   Macleans 100:46 Ag 31 '87. C. Bell
   New Repub 196:26 Je 1 '87. S. Kauffmann
   New Yorker 63:101-2 Je 1 '87. P. Kael
   Newsweek 109:71 Je 15 '87. D. Ansen
   Time il 130:65 Ag 3 '87. R. Schickel
Tearaway
   Macleans 100:54 S 14 '87. P. Hluchy
Tema
   People Wkly il 27:57-8 Ap 6 '87. S. K. Reed
Theme
   New Repub 197:24-5 O 26 '87. S. Kauffmann
Thérèse
   America 156:55-6 Ja 24 '87. R. A. Blake
   America 156:137-8+ F 14 '87. J. W. Donohue
   Christ Century 104:260-1 Mr 18-25 '87. J. D. Lynch
   Macleans il 100:54 Ap 6 '87. L. O'Toole
   N Y 20:51-2 Ja 12 '87. D. Denby
   New Yorker 62:73-4 Ja 26 '87. P. Kael
   Newsweek il 109:61 Ja 19 '87. D. Ansen
   Time il 129:75 Ja 5 '87. R. Corliss
Three amigos
   N Y 20:46 Ja 5 '87. D. Denby
   People Wkly il 27:10+ Ja 5 '87. P. Travers
Three for the road
   People Wkly 27:10 My 25 '87. T. Cunneff
Three men and a baby
   Good Housekeep il 205:106+ N '87

Newsweek il 110:73 N 30 '87. D. Ansen
   People Wkly il 28:14 D 14 '87. T. Cunneff
   Redbook il 170:44+ N '87. K. Henderson
Throw momma from the train
   Macleans il 100:61 D 21 '87. L. O'Toole
   Newsweek il 110:69 D 21 '87. D. Ansen
A time to die
   Américas 39:60-1 Ja/F '87. J. Mosier
Tin men
   Commonweal 114:215 Ap 10 '87. T. O'Brien
   Glamour il 85:217 My '87. J. G. Boyum
   Macleans il 100:57 Mr 9 '87. L. O'Toole
   N Y il 20:106-7 Mr 9 '87. D. Denby
   Nation 244:445-6 Ap 4 '87. T. Rafferty
   Natl Rev 39:52-3 Ap 10 '87. J. Simon
   New Repub 196:25-6 Mr 30 '87. S. Kauffmann
   New Yorker 63:82-3 Ap 6 '87. P. Kael
   Newsweek il 109:78 Mr 2 '87. D. Ansen
   People Wkly il 27:10 Mr 16 '87. R. Novak
   Time il 129:80 Ap 6 '87. R. Corliss
   Vogue 177:82 My '87. M. Haskell
Too outrageous!
   Macleans 100:58 O 5 '87. L. O'Toole
Touch and go
   New Yorker 62:93-4 F 9 '87. P. Kael
Tough guys don't dance
   Commonweal 114:566 O 9 '87. T. O'Brien
   Film Comment il 23:11-17 Jl/Ag '87. K. Jaehne
   Glamour 85:249-50 N '87. J. G. Boyum
   Mademoiselle il 93:108+ N '87. R. Rosenbaum
   N Y 20:138+ S 28 '87. D. Denby
   N Y il 20:32-5+ Ja 12 '87. D. Smith
   New Repub 197:28-9 O 5 '87. S. Kauffmann
   New Yorker 63:105-6 S 21 '87. P. Kael
   Newsweek il 110:76 S 21 '87. D. Ansen
   People Wkly il 28:12 O 12 '87. P. Travers
True stories
   New Repub 196:26+ Mr 23 '87. C. Coulson
   Progressive il 51:36-7 Ja '87. P. Aufderheide
The Untouchables
   America 157:66 Ag 1-8 '87. R. A. Blake
   Christ Century 104:598 Jl 1-8 '87. J. M. Wall
   Commonweal 114:354-6 Je 5 '87. T. O'Brien
   Humanist il 47:43 S/O '87. H. M. Geduld
   Macleans il 100:51 Je 15 '87. L. O'Toole
   N Y il 20:68-9 Je 8 '87. D. Denby
   Nation 244:900-2 Je 27 '87. T. Rafferty
   New Repub 196:26-7 Je 22 '87. S. Kauffmann
   New Yorker 63:70-2 Je 29 '87. P. Kael
   Newsweek il 109:78 Je 8 '87. D. Ansen
   Newsweek il 109:62-6+ Je 22 '87. T. Mathews
   People Wkly il 27:12 Je 15 '87. R. Novak
   Roll Stone il p47-8+ Mr 26 '87. F. Schruers
   Time il 129:78-9 Je 22 '87. R. Corliss
   Time il 129:83 Je 8 '87. R. Schickel
   Vogue il 177:58+ Je '87. J. Salamon
La vie est à nous
   New Repub 196:26-7 Je 1 '87. S. Kauffmann
Waiting for the moon
   Christ Today il 31:61 Jl 10 '87. S. Ulstein
   Macleans 100:48 My 18 '87. L. O'Toole
   Nation 244:773-4 Je 6 '87. R. Drexler
   New Repub 196:25-6 Mr 2 '87. S. Kauffmann
Walker
   Film Comment il 23:50-1 Jl/Ag '87. G. Fuller
   Macleans il 100:67 D 14 '87. L. O'Toole
   New Repub 197:26-7 D 28 '87. S. Kauffmann
   Newsweek il 110:88+ D 7 '87. D. Ansen
   Roll Stone il p29+ S 10 '87. F. Schruers
   Time il 130:79 D 7 '87. R. Schickel
Wall Street
   Bus Week il p38-9 D 21 '87. C. Welles
   Macleans il 100:46 D 28 '87. P. C. Newman
   Macleans il 100:61 D 21 '87. L. O'Toole
   N Y 20:87-8 D 14 '87. D. Denby
   Newsweek il 110:78-9 D 14 '87. C. McGuigan
   Newsweek il 110:80 D 14 '87. S. Rattner
   Time il 130:76-7 Jl 20 '87. G. D. Garcia
   Time il 130:82-3 D 14 '87. R. Corliss
   Time il 130:53 N 2 '87
   Vogue il 177:166+ D '87. M. Orth
The Wannsee Conference
   Commonweal 114:749 D 18 '87. T. O'Brien
   Macleans 100:67 N 30 '87. L. O'Toole
   N Y 20:152+ D 7 '87. D. Denby
   Nation 245:767-8 D 19 '87. M. Pally
   New Repub 197:26-7 D 7 '87. S. Kauffmann
Wanted dead or alive
   People Wkly 27:12 Mr 9 '87. J. Calio
Weeds
   Macleans il 100:52 N 2 '87. L. O'Toole

Motion picture reviews—Single works—Weeds—*cont.*
New Yorker 63:136-7 N 2 '87. P. Kael
Newsweek 110:109 N 16 '87. D. Ansen
People Wkly il 28:14 O 26 '87. R. Novak
The whales of August
America 157:384 N 21 '87. R. A. Blake
Film Comment il 23:2+ Ja/F '87. J. Ney
New Repub 197:28 N 2 '87. S. Kauffmann
People Wkly il 28:70-2+ D 14 '87. B. Darrach
People Wkly il 28:14 O 26 '87. P. Travers
Sch Update il 120:35 O 16 '87. D. Scheuer
The whistle blower
Macleans il 100:49 Ag 24 '87. L. O'Toole
Natl Rev 39:65-6 S 11 '87. J. Simon
New Repub 197:24 Ag 10-17 '87. S. Kauffmann
People Wkly 28:12 S 21 '87. T. Cunneff
Who's that girl
Macleans il 100:50 Ag 24 '87. N. Jennings
New Repub 197:25 S 7 '87. S. Kauffmann
People Wkly il 28:6 Ag 24 '87. R. Novak
Roll Stone il p23 S 24 '87. J. Rosenbluth
The wild one
Cycle il 38:55 Ag '87. J. Dorrance
Wisdom
People Wkly il 27:14 Ja 26 '87. T. Cunneff
Wish you were here
Commonweal 114:498-9 S 11 '87. T. O'Brien
Macleans il 100:56 O 12 '87. L. O'Toole
N Y il 20:54 Ag 3 '87. D. Denby
Nation 245:246-8 S 12 '87. T. Rafferty
Natl Rev 39:66-7 S 11 '87. J. Simon
New Repub 197:27 Ag 3 '87. S. Kauffmann
New Yorker 63:63-4 Jl 27 '87. P. Kael
Newsweek il 110:67 Ag 3 '87. D. Ansen
People Wkly il 28:10 Ag 17 '87. S. Haller
Vogue 177:64 Ag '87. M. Haskell
The witches of Eastwick
Christ Century 104:600 Jl 1-8 '87. J. M. Wall
Commonweal 114:421-2 Jl 17 '87. T. O'Brien
Macleans 100:48 Je 22 '87. L. O'Toole
Mademoiselle il 93:84+ O '87. R. Rosenbaum
N Y il 20:71 Je 22 '87. D. Denby
Natl Rev 39:52-3 Jl 31 '87. J. Simon
New Repub 197:26 Jl 13-20 '87. S. Kauffmann
New Yorker 63:72 Je 29 '87. P. Kael
Newsweek il 109:71 Je 15 '87. D. Ansen
People Wkly il 27:12 Je 22 '87. P. Travers
Time il 129:76 Je 22 '87. R. Corliss
Withnail and I
Macleans 100:55 Jl 6 '87. L. O'Toole
New Repub 197:26-7 Jl 13-20 '87. S. Kauffmann
Vogue il 177:40 Jl '87. M. Haskell
Wolf at the door
America 157:162 S 26 '87. R. A. Blake
New Repub 197:26 Ag 24 '87. S. Kauffmann
Working girls
Macleans 100:55 Je 1 '87. L. O'Toole
Ms il 15:20-1 My '87. A. B. Snitow
Nation 244:482-4 Ap 11 '87. M. Pally
New Repub 196:26 Mr 16 '87. S. Kauffmann
Time il 129:79 Ap 27 '87. R. Schickel
Vogue il por 177:218-19+ Jl '87. M. Kramer
Un zoo, la nuit
Macleans il 100:50 S 28 '87. B. D. Johnson
Motion picture scripts
'Sammy & Rosie' [excerpts from screenplay] H. Kureishi.
il *Film Comment* 23:70-4+ S/O '87
Motion picture sets *See* Motion pictures—Setting and scenery
Motion picture studios
A down-home movie mogul [North Carolina studio owned by E. Owensby] J. B. Copeland. il por *Newsweek* 109:41 Ja 12 '87
Motion picture theaters
See also
Bronx (New York, N.Y.)—Motion picture theaters
Cinema 'N' Drafthouse International Inc.
Cineplex Odeon Corporation
General Cinema Corporation
National Amusements, Inc.
New York (N.Y.)—Motion picture theaters
United Artists Communications, Inc.
The last picture shows [revival houses are dying out] B. Barol. il *Newsweek* 109:76-7 Je 8 '87
Motion picture trailers *See* Motion picture industry—Advertising
Motion picture workers *See* Motion picture industry—Employees
Motion pictures
See also
Computers—Motion picture use

Copyright—Motion pictures
Film-to-video transfer system
Television broadcasting—Motion pictures
Videotapes—Motion pictures
Violence in motion pictures
The movies [cover story; special issue; with editorial comment by Judith Daniels] il *Life* 10:4, 12-20+ Ap '87
Siskel on Ebert—Ebert on Siskel [interview] *Omni* 9:52+ Je '87
Advertising
See Motion picture industry—Advertising
Animated films
See also
Clay animation
Computer animation
Daffy Duck (Fictional character)
Donald Duck (Fictional character)
Walt Disney Company
Will Vinton Productions Inc.
Disney's enduring masterpiece [Snow White and the seven dwarfs; cover story] E. Oxford. il por *Am Hist Illus* 22:30-9 D '87
His X-rated Fritz (and L.A.) behind him, cartoonist Ralph Bakshi tries to make the grade as a painter. R. Arias. il pors *People Wkly* 28:91-2+ D 7 '87
The lost Snow White: working sketches reveal how Disney's fairy tale came true. M. Dougherty. il *Life* 10:52-4+ Ap '87
Twin cinema [work of T. and S. Quay] T. Rafferty. il *Atlantic* 259:74-6 Je '87
Unforgettable Snow White. J. Culhane. il *Read Dig* 131:114-19 D '87
Audiences
See Motion picture audiences
Awards
See also
Academy Awards
American Cinema Awards
Genie Awards
Golden Globe Awards
Spike Lee wins honor for 'She's gotta have it' [New Generation Award] por *Jet* 71:26 Ja 19 '87
Anecdotes, facetiae, satire, etc.
1986 & all that. S. Harvey and R. Corliss. il *Film Comment* 23:58-9 Ja/F '87
Best films
Best of '86. il *Time* 129:75 Ja 5 '87
Movies [1987] D. Denby. il *N Y* 20:110+ D 21-28 '87
Our holiday lists. *Nation* 245:793-804 D 26 '87-Ja 2 '88
Ten-bests [1986 lists] *Film Comment* 23:58-9 Ja/F '87
Top motion pictures of 1986. J. M. Wall and G. E. Forshey. il *Christ Century* 104:194+ F 25 '87
Bibliography
Books. See issues of Film Comment
Censorship
After seven years Gleb Panfilov's film, Tema, sees daylight at last and wrests an award from Platoon. S. K. Reed. il pors *People Wkly* 27:57-8 Ap 6 '87
Federal judge orders showing of controversial film [attempt to censor Hail Mary in Lincoln, Neb.] T. J. Flygare. il *Phi Delta Kappan* 68:401-2 Ja '87
Glasnost [Soviet Union; special section] il *Film Comment* 23:33-8+ My/Je '87
Gorbashow and the flicks [Moscow conference entitled War and peace on the world screen since 1945] P. Kenez. il *New Leader* 70:10-12 Ap 6 '87
Movies and censorship: who will protect freedom? J. M. Wall. il *Christ Century* 104:277-8 Mr 18-25 '87
Soviets' cinema vérité [Los Angeles conference between American and Soviet filmmakers] S. L. Hawkins. il *U S News World Rep* 102:26 Ap 6 '87
Children's films
Movie magic for the child in everyone [R. Demers] B. D. Johnson. il por *Macleans* 100:57 Mr 16 '87
Classification
See Motion pictures—Ratings
Coloring
Black and white and green. J. Vitale. *Channels* 7:17 Ja '87
Casablanca in color? I'm shocked, shocked! C. Krauthammer. il *Time* 129:82 Ja 12 '87
Color-by-numbers. S. Parker. il *Pop Mech* 164:98-101 Ap '87
Colorizing black-and-white films is a crime against art! R. Ascher. por *Seventeen* 46:78-9 N '87
Emotion pictures. D. Blum. *New Repub* 196:13-15 F 9 '87
A film of a different color [colorization process] K. Sheldon. il *Byte* 12:164-5 Mr '87

Motion pictures—Coloring—*cont.*

Tampering with tradition [special section] *Society* 24:4-23 My/Je '87

True colors. W. Allen. il *N Y Rev Books* 34:38 Ag 13 '87

Using the ImageWise video digitizer (II). S. Ciarcia. il *Byte* 12:117-21 Ag '87

Anecdotes, facetiae, satire, etc.

Pensées: on the 'colorization' of classics [Picasso's Guernica] il *Film Comment* 23:76-7 Ja/F '87

Comedy films

Funny man Frank [work of M. Frank] J. Benair. il por *Film Comment* 23:58-61 Mr/Ap '87

Costs

See Motion picture industry—Finance

Costume

See Costume, Theatrical

Crime films

The ghost of Alfred Hitchcock [thrillers The bedroom window, Dead of winter and Black widow] R. Corliss. il *Time* 129:76+ F 16 '87

Sin, psychopathology and Father Brown [comparison with M. Mann's Manhunter] M. Horst. *Christ Century* 104:46-7 Ja 21 '87

Cult films

Getting down and dirty [Dirty dancing] C. Leerhsen. il *Newsweek* 110:63 D 21 '87

Dance films

See also

Dance Films Association

Dancefilms. See occasional issues of Dance Magazine

Editing

See also

Film Arts Ltd.

Motion pictures—Sound editing

Hollywood's change of art [test audiences vote for different endings] P. H. Broeske. il *Roll Stone* p24+ F 12 '87

Educational films

See Motion pictures in education

Experimental films

Exile on Main Street [special section] il *Film Comment* 23:31-46+ Jl/Ag '87

History

The last picture shows [revival houses are dying out] B. Barol. il *Newsweek* 109:76-7 Je 8 '87

Exhibitions

Hollywood: legend and reality. M. Webb. il *USA Today (Periodical)* 116:44-59 Jl '87

Horror films

Blood, sweat, & fears: why are horror movies such a slashing success? J. Farber. il *Seventeen* 46:108-9+ Jl '87

Killer bimbos & galactic gigolos star in video's grade Z future [low budget exploitation movies] D. Hutchings and D. Lindeman. il *People Wkly* 28:159-60+ S 7 '87

We killed 'em in Chicago [work of S. Gordon] M. Brody. il por *Film Comment* 23:68-70+ Ja/F '87

Insurance

See Insurance, Motion picture

Laws and regulations

See Motion picture laws and regulations

Meteorological films

Audio visuals about the weather. E. Brotak. il *Weatherwise* 40:107 Ap '87

Audio visuals about the weather. E. Brotak. *Weatherwise* 40:218 Jl/Ag '87

Audio visuals about the weather. E. Brotak. *Weatherwise* 40:159 Je '87

Moral and religious aspects

See also

Good and evil in motion pictures

Motion pictures—Censorship

Motion pictures—Religious films

Pornography

Sex in motion pictures

Violence in motion pictures

Beauty in a world of schlock [W. Allen's Hannah and her sisters] M. Burkhart. il *Commonweal* 114:294-6 My 8 '87

Federal judge orders showing of controversial film [attempt to censor Hail Mary in Lincoln, Neb.] T. J. Flygare. il *Phi Delta Kappan* 68:401-2 Ja '87

Kentucky teacher hits The wall with Pink Floyd [J. Fowler fights dismissal for showing R-rated movie] T. J. Flygare. il *Phi Delta Kappan* 69:237-8 N '87

'Moments' in movies: Montreal's World Film Festival. J. M. Wall. il *Christ Century* 104:787-90 S 23 '87

Moral shadow-boxing. K. R. Hey. il *USA Today (Periodical)* 116:55 S '87

Only a glimpse of grace [Light of day] S. Ulstein. il *Christ Today* 31:66 My 15 '87

Private lives [Waiting for the moon and 84 Charing Cross Road] S. Ulstein. il *Christ Today* 31:60-1 Jl 10 '87

Top motion pictures of 1986. J. M. Wall and G. E. Forshey. il *Christ Century* 104:194+ F 25 '87

Music

See also

Compact discs—Motion picture music

Phonograph records—Motion picture music

The lyrical assassin at 5 a.m. [movie theme composer E. Morricone] J. Cocks. il por *Time* 129:83 Mr 16 '87

Music at the movies: turn it down! J. Pareles. il *Mademoiselle* 93:96+ O '87

Round midnight. H. Mandel. il *Down Beat* 54:22-3 Ja '87

The sound of silents [C. Davis' scores for silent films] D. Shaw. il por *N Y* 20:22 Mr 2 '87

Sounds of silents. M. Walsh. il *Film Comment* 23:66-9 Jl/Ag '87

Musical films

Celebration! [Broadway and Hollywood stills celebrating dance] W. Como. il *Dance Mag* 61:34-7 Ag '87

Plots, themes, etc.

See also

Abortion in motion pictures

Adultery in motion pictures

Alienation (Social psychology) in motion pictures

Apartheid in motion pictures

Art in motion pictures

Bible in motion pictures

Blacks in motion pictures

Boats in motion pictures

Business in motion pictures

China in motion pictures

Dance in motion pictures

Family in motion pictures

Feminism in motion pictures

Good and evil in motion pictures

Handicapped in motion pictures

Hawaii in motion pictures

Hispanic Americans in motion pictures

History in motion pictures

Holocaust, Jewish (1939-1945), in motion pictures

Homosexuality in motion pictures

Infants in motion pictures

Investment banking in motion pictures

Italian Americans in motion pictures

Jews in motion pictures

Love in motion pictures

Mental illness in motion pictures

Motorcycle gangs in motion pictures

National parks and reserves in motion pictures

Nelson (B.C.) in motion pictures

New York (N.Y.) in motion pictures

Nicaragua in motion pictures

Nostalgia in motion pictures

Prostitution in motion pictures

Psychiatry in motion pictures

Robots in motion pictures

Self in motion pictures

Sharks in motion pictures

Soviet Union in motion pictures

Space flight in motion pictures

Sports in motion pictures

Titanic (Steamship) in motion pictures

Tucson (Ariz.) in motion pictures

Violence in motion pictures

Voodooism in motion pictures

Women executives in motion pictures

Women in motion pictures

Wrestling in motion pictures

A night at the movies [seven directors describe movies they'd like to do in 2001; cover story] M. Long. il *Omni* 9:44-6+ Je '87

Political films

Hollywood takes a gamble on movies with a message. A. P. Sanoff. il *U S News World Rep* 103:76-7 N 16 '87

Hollywood's new vision. B. D. Johnson. il *Macleans* 100:58-9 My 11 '87

Propaganda films

Keeping the word [Supreme Court rules that 3 Canadian films are propaganda] *Time* 129:49 My 11 '87

Psychological aspects

Beyond dreams: the mysterious power of movies. L. Wainwright. il *Life* 10:22 Ap '87

Motion pictures—Psychological aspects—*cont.*
Blood, sweat, & fears: why are horror movies such a slashing success? J. Farber. il *Seventeen* 46:108-9+ Jl '87

Ratings
'Angel' heart is rated X; likely to be edited for R. *Jet* 71:59 Mr 9 '87
Film group to reconsider Bonet's 'Angel heart' film. il por *Jet* 71:16 Mr 2 '87
Movies. See issues of Consumer Reports
Should sex rate an "X"? R. Rosenbaum. il *Mademoiselle* 93:46+ Je '87
What the critics say about movies. See issues of Consumers' Research Magazine
Why Lisa Bonet of 'Cosby' fame made X-rated film. il pors *Jet* 71:60-1 Mr 16 '87

Religious films
See also
Bible in motion pictures
Christian film and video: hard questions and entertaining answers. il *Christ Today* 31:57+ S 18 '87
Heaven [special section] il *Film Comment* 23:31-40+ Mr/Ap '87

Science fiction films
See also
Star trek
As time warps by [tenth anniversary celebration of Star wars] M. Mancini. il *Film Comment* 23:2+ S/O '87
Lights! Camera! NASA! L. Suid. il *Space World* X-6-282:16-20 Je '87
Physics, Hollywood style [J. Weyland, physicist who critiques science fiction films] B. Lawren. *Omni* 9:35 Je '87

Special effects
See Motion pictures—Special effects
Setting and scenery
See also
Hollywood on Location (Firm)
At the movies [special section; with editorial comment by Scott Shane] il *Travel Holiday* 168:8+ Ag '87
Konchalovsky: the force of nature. R. Gentry. il por *Theatre Crafts* 21:63-6 Mr '87
Matewan: Nora Chavooshian creates major miners. R. Seidenberg. il *Theatre Crafts* 21:45-8 Ap '87
A nose for the tragic heart of comedy [filming of Roxanne in Nelson, B.C.] P. Young. il *Macleans* 100:48 Je 29 '87
On location [national parks] J. Carman. il *Natl Parks* 61:30-6 N/D '87
Trash splats the streets [J. Muro's Street trash] J. Calhoun. il *Theatre Crafts* 21:20 N '87
You must remember this [movies shot on location in New York] H. Karren. il *N Y* 20:60-3 My 4 '87

Silent films
The sound of silents [C. Davis' scores] D. Shaw. il por *N Y* 20:22 Mr 2 '87
Sounds of silents. M. Walsh. il *Film Comment* 23:66-9 Jl/Ag '87

Songs
See Motion pictures—Music
Sound editing
Sound by Splet [Mosquito Coast] S. Gowin. il *Theatre Crafts* 21:71-2 F '87

Spanish language films
Hispanic Hollywood. J. Foote. il *Newsweek* 110:66-7 Ag 17 '87
Miami nice [Miami Film Festival] E. Stein. *Film Comment* 23:6+ Jl/Ag '87

Special effects
Reel illusions [science fiction effects created by Industrial Light and Magic studio] T. G. Smith. il *Omni* 9:70-9 Je '87
Simple special effects illustrate the art of converting algorithms into programs. A. K. Dewdney. il *Sci Am* 257:142-6 D '87
Stranded: Michele Burke's friendly foreigners [science fiction film makeup] R. Seidenberg. il por *Theatre Crafts* 21:83-6 N '87

Spy films
Double trouble. R. Rosenbaum. il *Mademoiselle* 93:64+ D '87

Titling
Where credit is due: the heads and tails of title design. J. Calhoun. il *Theatre Crafts* 21:79-82 Ag/S '87

War films
See also
Vietnamese War, 1957-1975, in motion pictures
Westerns
Cowboy. J. P. Sisk. *Am Sch* 56:400-6 Summ '87
Old Tucson [movie location] C. Buhl. il *Travel Holiday* 168:10+ Ag '87

Western movie stars: yesterday's heroes. M. A. DeMarco. il *Antiques Collect Hobbies* 92:50-4 O '87
Wide screen films
EAA thrill theater [wide-screen film Sport aviation] J. M. McClellan. *Flying* 114:88 Ja '87
Brazil
'Cinema novo'. P. A. Paranaguá. il *Courier* 39:33-6 D '86
Canada
See also
Genie Awards
National Film Board of Canada
Canadian gems at a glittery festival [Cannes] B. D. Johnson. il *Macleans* 100:53-4 My 25 '87
East Asia
Cinematic riches of the Pacific Rim [program being shown at the Toronto Festival of Festivals] B. D. Johnson. il *Macleans* 100:57-8 S 21 '87
Oriental insurgents [Eastern Horizons retrospective at the Festival of Festivals in Toronto] P. Aufderheide. *Film Comment* 23:73-6 N/D '87
France
Beineix blue. M. Pally. il pors *Film Comment* 23:21-4 Ja/F '87
Paris journal [cinema and after-cinema supping] C. P. Reynolds. il *Gourmet* 47:24+ Ja '87
Great Britain
Disasterpiece theater. R. Schickel. il *Time* 130:68 S 7 '87
Gritty Brit [S. Frears] H. Kennedy. il por *Film Comment* 23:15-17 Mr/Ap '87
A young filmmaker with a sense of purpose [L. Barrett's Business as usual] J. M. Wall. *Christ Century* 104:739-40 S 9-16 '87
India
The last Bengali renaissance man [filmmaker S. Ray] I. Buruma. bibl f il *N Y Rev Books* 34:12+ N 19 '87
Italy
Rosi and the Italian film crisis. P. Lennon. por *World Press Rev* 34:56 Jl '87
Latin America
Film. J. Mosier. See issues of Américas
Mexico
Slugfests del sur [Mexican wrestling films] A. Coe. il *Film Comment* 23:27-8+ Jl/Ag '87
Soviet Union
The Brothers M-K [N. Mikhalkov and A. Konchalovsky] K. Jaehne. il por *Film Comment* 23:66-8 S/O '87
Glasnost [special section] il *Film Comment* 23:33-8+ My/Je '87
Motion pictures and children
See also
Motion pictures—Children's films
Motion pictures and literature
See also
Motion picture adaptations
That great blank page, the screen [questioning the concept of cinematic fiction] T. McDonough. il *N Y Times Book Rev* 92:1+ N 15 '87
'Waterfront'—'more than a 90-minute movie'. B. Schulberg. il *N Y Times Book Rev* 92:1+ Ap 26 '87
Motion pictures and television
See also
Television broadcasting—Motion picture criticism programs
Crossing over in Hollywood [TV stars in movies] M. Reese. il *Newsweek* 109:76-7+ My 11 '87
Motion pictures and theater
See also
Motion picture adaptations
Motion pictures in education
Rae Dawn Chong draws heat with an education film on sex and AIDS. il *People Wkly* 27:112 Ap 13 '87
Motion pictures in industry
The Bingo Long traveling all-star industrialists [business training films] D. M. Kimmel. il por *Film Comment* 23:41-3 Ja/F '87
Motion sickness
Queasy rider [airsickness] D. Pine. il *Health* 19:73-4 Ja '87
Seasick? Here's why, and what to do [views of Charles M. Oman] *Technol Rev* 90:79 Jl '87
Motion sickness in space *See* Weightlessness
Motivation (Education)
The key to improving schools: an interview with William Glasser. P. B. Gough. il *Phi Delta Kappan* 68:656-62 My '87
Motivation (Psychology)
See also
Goals (Psychology)

Motivation (Psychology)—See also—*cont.*
Risk taking (Psychology)
The fizzle phenomenon [exercise plans] J. L. Lippert. il *Health* 19:55-7+ F '87
Handling the overachiever. K. Samon. il *Work Woman* 12:24+ Mr '87
How to motivate people [employees] T. L. Quick. il *Work Woman* 12:15+ S '87
Mental games: ten strategies for staying motivated [excerpt from The total runner] J. Lynch. il *Women's Sports Fitness* 9:26-8 Mr '87
Merchants of inspiration [motivational speakers] J. Main. il *Fortune* 116:69-71+ Jl 6 '87
Motivating the teams on your staff. G. Bakoulis. *Work Woman* 12:23+ D '87
Motivating without money: a strokes and perks primer. S. Mernit. il *Work Woman* 12:75 D '87
Wisdom from the well. R. T. Harwood. il *Mother Earth News* 108:8+ N/D '87
You can make exercise fun. J. L. Lippert. il *Read Dig* 131:108-10 Ag '87

Motley, Michael T.
What I meant to say. bibl (p64) il *Psychol Today* 21:24-8 F '87

Mötley Crüe (Musical group)
Money for nothing and the chicks for free: on the road with Mötley Crüe [cover story] D. Handelman. il *Roll Stone* p34-6+ Ag 13 '87

Motocross racing (Bicycle) *See* Bicycle racing

Motor ability
See also
Ataxia
Agility: learn to respond quickly to the ball [tennis] J. L. Groppel. il *World Tennis* 35:36 Ag '87
The subjects came in for a cold [effects of common cold on coordination and memory; study by Andrew P. Smith] V. Bozzi and G. Lowe. il *Psychol Today* 21:14 D '87

Motor boat engines
Gas engines '88—what's new? What's right for you? T. Banse. il *Mot Boat Sail* 160:86-7 N '87
The jetdrive option. T. Banse. il *Mot Boat Sail* 159:71-2 My '87
Jets are bustin' out all over. E. Dennis. *Mot Boat Sail* 160:51+ Jl '87
Power play [outboards] J. Wooldridge. il *Pop Mech* 164:100-3 Mr '87
Stealth outboard [military amphibious reconnaissance system outboard motors] B. McKeown. il *Pop Sci* 230:75 Je '87
Lubrication and lubricants
See Motor boats—Lubrication and lubricants
Maintenance and repair
How to care for your beast [outboards] T. Banse. *Mot Boat Sail* 159:69+ Je '87
Testing
Get set for jets. B. McKeown. il *Outdoor Life* 179:38+ Je '87
Hang on to your transom [new outboard motors] T. Banse. il *Mot Boat Sail* 159:64-9+ Je '87
Jets! [jet-drive outboards] B. McKeown. il *Pop Sci* 230:54-5 My '87
Merc's new 9.9 [fishing motor] B. Stearns. *Field Stream* 92:119 My '87
New outboards for 1987. B. Stearns. il *Field Stream* 91:51-2+ Mr '87

Motor boat racing
Don Johnson tames the Mississippi [winner of New Orleans to St. Louis race; cover story] P. Whittell. il pors *Mot Boat Sail* 160:34-7+ N '87
Going flat out on the briny [Key West's World Offshore Championships] S. Moses. il *Sports Illus* 67:28-9 N 23 '87
Magnum opus redux [Miami-Nassau-Miami race] C. Davis. il *Mot Boat Sail* 160:34-7+ O '87
Popeye's punch [A. Copeland wins offshore championship at Key West] C. Davis. il *Mot Boat Sail* 159:46-9+ Ja '87
Accidents and injuries
Death of a champion [powerboat racer M. Lavin] P. A. Janssen. il *Mot Boat Sail* 159:11 Ja '87
Ethical aspects
Offshore racing's image problems [drug scandals] D. Wallace and C. Davis. il *Mot Boat Sail* 160:42-5+ D '87
Social aspects
Like father, like son [racing families] C. Davis. il *Mot Boat Sail* 160:34-7+ Ag '87

Motor boating and sailing (Periodical)
At the helm. P. A. Janssen. See issues of Motor Boating & Sailing

Motor boats
See also
Fishing boats
Fountain Powerboats Industries
Hydrofoils
Getting wet. T. H. Cole. il *Pop Mech* 164:94-5 Mr '87
High performance: the hottest boats, owners, gear [cover story; special section; with editorial comment by Peter A. Janssen] il *Mot Boat Sail* 160:11, 32-47+ Jl '87
New dazzle from Donzi [Ragazza line] J. Skorupa. il *Pop Mech* 164:33 Ag '87
Powering up for '88. B. McKeown. il *Outdoor Life* 180:56+ O '87
Trends '88: powerboats. D. Fales. il *Mot Boat Sail* 160:42-7 S '87
Trends '88: sportboats. D. Wallace. il *Mot Boat Sail* 160:48-51 S '87
Equipment
Signal rod shows outdrive position. J. Shreve. il *Pop Sci* 230:126 F '87
Leasing and renting
Directories
Worldwide power & sail charter directory. il *Mot Boat Sail* 160:69-80 Ag '87
Lubrication and lubricants
Oil injection and premix [automatic oiling systems for outboard motors] T. Banse. *Mot Boat Sail* 159:68+ Je '87
Materials
The unsinkable allure of 'antique' boats [wooden boats] il *Bus Week* p108-9 Je 29 '87
Purchasing
The baby boomers take to the waves [powerboat industry] R. McGough. il *Forbes* 139:72-3 Ap 20 '87
Breaking away [entry-level high performance boats] C. Davis. *Mot Boat Sail* 160:116-17 Jl '87
Steering gear
See Boats and boating—Steering gear
Testing
The longest ride [trip from Miami to Maine in 38-foot Tempest speedboat] P. A. Janssen. il *Mot Boat Sail* 160:38-41 S '87
Mark Twain MTC 195 [long term test] T. H. Cole. il *Pop Mech* 164:142+ Mr '87
Muscle boats. F. Sargeant. il *Pop Mech* 164:102-5+ Jl '87
Ski boat shootout. F. Sargeant. il *Pop Mech* 164:86-9+ N '87
Sonic RS 33. C. Davis. il *Mot Boat Sail* 160:44-5 Jl '87
Stacked decks. F. Sargeant. il *Pop Mech* 164:82-5+ Je '87
Wellcraft 38 Scarab KV. P. Whittell. il *Mot Boat Sail* 160:42-3 Jl '87

Motor clubs *See* Automobile clubs
Motor cortex *See* Brain
Motor fuels
See also
Gasoline
Motor homes *See* Campers, Truck
Motor oils, Airplane *See* Airplanes, Jet—Lubrication and lubricants
Motor oils, Automotive *See* Automobiles—Lubrication and lubricants
Motor scooters
End of the road [Vespa ceases production] il *Newsweek* 110:10 D 7 '87
To scoot. L. C. Pogrebin. il por *Ms* 16:18+ O '87
Motor Sport Research Group *See* McGill University. Motor Sport Research Group
Motor Trend Awards
1987 Car of the Year [Ford Thunderbird Turbo Coupe] il *Mot Trend* 39:27-32+ F '87
Motor Trend's 1987 Import Car of the Year [Acura Legend Coupe] J. R. Nerad. il *Mot Trend* 39:35-9+ Ap '87
Preview: 1987 Car of the Year. G. Brown. il *Mot Trend* 39:55-7 Ja '87
Preview: 1987 Import Car of the Year. B. Nagy. il *Mot Trend* 39:102-5 Mr '87
Motor Vehicle Administration (Md.) *See* Maryland. Motor Vehicle Administration
Motor vehicle driving
Trip the two-track [off-road driving] T. Opre. il *Outdoor Life* 179:52+ My '87
Motor vehicle industries *See* Automobile industry; Automotive industries; Truck industry
Motor vehicle racing
See also
Automobile racing

Motor vehicle racing—See also—*cont.*
> Drag racing
> Motor vehicle rallies
> Motorcycle racing
> Mud racing
> Truck racing

Off-road odyssey. L. C. Crane. il *Road Track* 38:118+ Ag '87

Toyota's off-road racer . . . tanks but no tanks [S. Millen in off-road race at Anaheim Stadium] J. Dinkel. il *Road Track* 38:33-6 My '87

Motor vehicle rallies
Manhattan or bust [R. Harding and K. Hill drive Model T in Great American Race] J. Paris. il pors *Read Dig* 131:5-6+ Jl '87

Motor vehicles
> See also
> All terrain vehicles
> Automobiles
> Four wheel drive vehicles
> Jeep automobiles
> Mopeds
> Motor scooters
> Motorcycles
> Recreational vehicles
> Snowmobiles and snowmobiling
> Station wagons
> Trucks
> Vans

Vehicles. B. Kilpatrick. See issues of Field & Stream
Traction
Bog-cogs slog on. D. Scott. il *Pop Sci* 230:14 F '87

Motor vehicles, Military
> See also
> Autonomous land vehicles
> Motorcycles, Military

Motor vehicles, Three wheel
Three-wheelers likely to be history in a few years. *Success Farm* 85:18BD Ap '87

Motor yachts See Yachts and yachting
Motorbikes See Mopeds; Motorcycles
Motorboats See Motor boats
Motorcycle accidents See Traffic accidents
Motorcycle brakes See Brakes, Motorcycle
Motorcycle engineering
Bibliography
Tech maven's library. K. Cameron. il *Cycle* 38:86-8 F '87

Motorcycle engines
Ducatis on the dyno [desmo twin engines] K. Vreeke. il *Cycle* 38:31-2 My '87
Engine performance: beyond the dyno. K. Cameron. il *Cycle* 38:63-7 S '87
Engine performance: the dyno room. K. Cameron. il *Cycle* 38:72-5+ Ag '87
Extending the limit. K. Cameron. il *Cycle* 38:23 Mr '87
Working under pressure [power loss represented by pressure on the undersides of descending pistons] K. Cameron. il *Cycle* 38:15 Je '87
YB4 and 5: the Yamaha connection [Yamaha engines used by Bimota] B. De Prato. il *Cycle* 38:87-8 Jl '87
Design
Ducati 850 tech tour. K. Cameron. il *Cycle* 38:27-31+ S '87
Duck of the decade [Ducati's four-valve Desmo] B. De Prato. il *Cycle* 38:77-9 Ja '87
Exotic excess. J. Karr. il *Mot Trend* 39:96-9 F '87
Norton Rotary Rocket. M. Oxley. il *Cycle* 38:64-9 D '87
Project Hurricane: CBR chassis tune-up. K. Vreeke. il *Cycle* 38:50-3 N '87
Project Hurricane: off to war on Honda's CBR600 [modified for box-stock racing] K. Vreeke. il *Cycle* 38:58-61+ O '87
Energy usage
Energy alert: where the power goes. K. Cameron. il *Cycle* 38:74 Ag '87
Exhaust
> See also
> Motorcycles—Pollution control devices
Full-honk Yamaha YSR [stock exhaust replaced with Toomey Tunes Racing Pipe Kit] K. Vreeke. il *Cycle* 38:48-51 D '87
Fuel feeding
FI primer [fuel injection] M. Lindemann. il *Cycle* 38:61-4 N '87
Maintenance and repair
The inside mirror [Extrude Hone process used to polish wall surfaces] P. Schilling. il *Cycle* 38:109-12 My '87

Pass it on [mechanical skills] A. Girdler. il *Road Track* 38:20 Ja '87
Temperature
Engines: how hot? [motorcycle engines measured with Probeye infrared system] P. Gordon. il *Cycle* 38:33-8 S '87
Valves
Desmodromics then & now. K. Vreeke. il *Cycle* 38:36-9 My '87
Motorcycle gangs
> See also
> Hell's Angels
Motorcycle gangs in motion pictures
The wild one. J. Dorrance. il *Cycle* 38:55 Ag '87
Motorcycle helmets See Helmets
Motorcycle industry
> See also
> Harley-Davidson Motor Co., Inc.
Indian: on the road again [J. Junker's restoration and parts supply company] E. Borin. il pors *Cycle* 38:68-72+ S '87
Advertising
Dogs and Tigers [Triumph Engineering brochure, 1949] P. Schilling. il *Cycle* 38:8 Ap '87
Export-import trade
> See Motorcycles—Export-import trade
Public relations
Virus. P. Schilling. il *Cycle* 38:7-8 D '87
Great Britain
Back from the dead? J. Greening. il *Cycle* 38:20 My '87
British survivors in America [American motorcyclists views on British bikes] C. Wimpey. il *Cycle* 38:78-82 My '87
Italy
> See also
> Bimota (Firm)
Japan
> See also
> Honda Motor Co., Ltd
> Suzuki Motor Company Ltd.
> Yamaha Motor Co. Ltd.
Goners and foundlings [Japanese bikes dropped by manufacturers for 1987] il *Cycle* 38:94-6+ Mr '87
Why Milwaukee won't die [Japanese motorcycles imitate Harleys] il *Cycle* 38:35-7+ Je '87
Motorcycle insurance See Insurance, Motorcycle
Motorcycle jackets See Jackets
Motorcycle journalism See Journalism, Automotive
Motorcycle junkyards
Rebuilt and running, but not by the book [repairing Honda CBR600 Hurricane] M. Lindemann. il *Cycle* 38:54-6+ N '87
Motorcycle ownership
Initiations. K. Cameron. il *Cycle* 38:14 D '87
Ruminations on a New Year's Day. P. Schilling. il *Cycle* 38:7 Ja '87
Anecdotes, facetiae, satire, etc.
No! [letting someone else ride my motorcycle] P. Schilling. il *Cycle* 38:8 F '87
Motorcycle parts
> See also
> Motorcycle junkyards
Motorcycle racers (Persons) See Motorcyclists
Motorcycle racing
> See also
> Drag racing
> Motorcycle rallies
Box-stock balance sheet [Suzuki GSX-R and Honda Interceptor series for club road racers] P. Van Zuyle. il *Cycle* 38:30-2 Mr '87
Come, Daytona [winter preparations] K. Cameron. il *Cycle* 38:17 Ap '87
Daytona showcase. K. Cameron. il *Cycle* 38:74-81+ Je '87
Full circle. B. Ross. il *Cycle* 38:12 D '87
Laguna Seca '87. K. Cameron. il *Cycle* 38:74-84 O '87
Mike Baldwin. K. Cameron. il pors *Cycle* 38:76-80+ Mr '87
Pipeline. J. Greening. See issues of Cycle
Racetrack flashback [vintage racing] N. Mayersohn. il *Pop Mech* 164:20 Ag '87
Two American heroes [videotapes by E. Knievel and Freddie Spencer] C. Hodenfield. il *Cycle* 38:14 F '87
Economic aspects
Nothing is forever [Honda Britain Racing disbands] J. Greening. il *Cycle* 38:21 Mr '87
History
American racer [S. Wright's book] P. Schilling. il *Cycle* 38:9 My '87

Motorcycle racing—History—cont.

J.N. Roberts: "what's a mother to do?". T. O'Connor. il pors Cycle 38:54-7+ Jl '87

John Surtees [seven-time world motorcycling champion and winner of the 1964 World Grand Prix Championship] C. Fox. il pors Cycle 38:68-71+ My '87

Photographs and photography

Ascot then and now [southern California dirt-tracking, 1968 and 1987] il Cycle 38:47-9+ Jl '87

King on a coconut [Laguna Seca] il Cycle 38:14-15 O '87

Baja California (Mexico: Peninsula)

A splash of La Carrera #5. C. Hodenfield. il Cycle 38:31-5+ D '87

Belgium

Down and out at Spa [track conditions force cancellation of Belgian Grand Prix] J. Greening. il Cycle 38:12 O '87

Great Britain

Bantam racing. J. Greening. il Cycle 38:12+ Jl '87

Nothing is forever [Honda Britain Racing disbands] J. Greening. il Cycle 38:21 Mr '87

Silverstone says no [Grand Prix races at Donington Park] J. Greening. il Cycle 38:104 Je '87

Transatlantic '87. J. Greening. il Cycle 38:77 S '87

Italy

Minor league, major hopes [European Championship] J. Greening. il Cycle 38:9 Ja '87

Western Europe

1986 GP season [Powersports Video Grand Prix tapes] C. Hodenfield. il Cycle 38:17+ Ag '87

Motorcycle rallies

Demo [demonstration rides at Americade Rockies touring rally] R. J. Roach. il Cycle 38:45 D '87

History

Forty hours in Hollister [legendary riots during 1947 motorcycle rally] J. Dorrance. il Cycle 38:50-4+ Ag '87

Motorcycle riding See Motorcycling

Motorcycle speed records

The day they broke 200 [NSU streamliner at Bonneville in 1956] P. Lyons. il Cycle 38:42-8 Ap '87

Faster, faster, faster [records since 1908] P. Lyons. il Cycle 38:55 Ap '87

Motorcycle tires See Tires, Motorcycle

Motorcycles

See also
  Mopeds
  Motor scooters
  Motorcycling

Cycles. N. Mayersohn. See issues of Popular Mechanics beginning January 1986

Goners and foundlings [Japanese bikes dropped by manufacturers for 1987] il Cycle 38:94-6+ Mr '87

Accidents

See Traffic accidents

Advertising

See Motorcycle industry—Advertising

Aerodynamics

Aero age. K. Cooper. il Cycle 38:38-41+ Ap '87

Brakes

See Brakes, Motorcycle

Cleaning

S100 cleaner. il Cycle 38:71 Ja '87

Collectors and collecting

Motor mouth [collection owned by J. Leno] C. Hodenfield. il pors Cycle 38:80-4 F '87

Where a grand buys a great time. W. C. Banks. il Money 16:65 Jl '87

Design

1988 Honda VFR750R. il Cycle 38:32-3 O '87

Bullet bikes. S. F. Brown. il Pop Sci 231:75+ O '87

Harmony in design [Honda CBR600] K. Cameron. il Cycle 38:63-6+ O '87

Honda: high-performance Hurricanes [1987 models] il Cycle 38:42-3 Ja '87

Honda's transatlantic Transalp. il Cycle 38:45 Ja '87

The Italian connection: Cagiva/Ducati/Husqvarna. il Cycle 38:29-31 F '87

Kawasaki: turning twenty [1987 models] il Cycle 38:48-9+ Ja '87

Suzuki: Reno dealing [1987 models] il Cycle 38:46-7 Ja '87

Why Milwaukee won't die [Japanese motorcycles imitate Harleys] il Cycle 38:35-7+ Je '87

Equipment

Lockhart Kwik Lift [stand] il Cycle 38:40+ S '87

Lockhart Swing-Arm Stand. il Cycle 38:110 Je '87

Storz Superbike Bar Mounts. il Cycle 38:106 Mr '87

Exhibitions

Official recognition [Motorcycling in American history, 1900-1940 at the Smithsonian] K. Cameron. il Cycle 38:82-3+ Ap '87

Export-import trade

Harley-Davidson: ready to ride on its own [asking to end import restraints against Japan] Newsweek 109:50 Mr 30 '87

Fairings

Targa Formula Cowling [add-on lower fairing and replacement front fender] il Cycle 38:42 Jl '87

Fenders

Targa Formula Cowling [add-on lower fairing and replacement front fender] il Cycle 38:42 Jl '87

Fuel systems

See Motorcycle engines—Fuel feeding

Gas mileage

See Motorcycle engines—Energy usage

Gearing

Where's the redline? il Cycle 38:47 Je '87

History

The gentleman's express. P. Schilling. il Cycle 38:61-4 My '87

Insurance

See Insurance, Motorcycle

Laws and regulations

The Danforth bill [Motorcycle Safety Bill of 1987; with editorial comment by Phil Schilling] P. Gordon. il Cycle 38:7, 66-9+ N '87

A straw in the wind. P. Schilling. il Cycle 38:7 O '87

Maintenance and repair

Rebuilt and running, but not by the book [repairing Honda CBR600 Hurricane] M. Lindemann. il Cycle 38:54-6+ N '87

TDC. K. Cameron. See issues of Cycle

Totalled or not: no easy answer [totalling vs. repairing Honda 600 Hurricane] T. Carrithers. il Cycle 38:47-9 N '87

Noise

For your ears only. A. Girdler. il Road Track 38:18 My '87

Ownership

See Motorcycle ownership

Photographs and photography

Beyond the off-ramp [motorcycles in Los Angeles] J. Terranova. il Cycle 38:72-4 Mr '87

Big Apple bikes [New York City] J. Terranova. il Cycle 38:75-9 N '87

Pollution control devices

Jealousy [differences between California motorcycles and those sold in other states] P. Schilling. il Cycle 38:9 Jl '87

Prices

Three-grand conspiracy [motorcycles under $3000] il Cycle 38:57-63 F '87

Restoration

See Motorcycles, Restored

Safety devices and measures

The Danforth bill [Motorcycle Safety Bill of 1987; with editorial comment by Phil Schilling] P. Gordon. il Cycle 38:7, 66-9+ N '87

A straw in the wind. P. Schilling. il Cycle 38:7 O '87

Virus. P. Schilling. il Cycle 38:7-8 D '87

Speed

Top-speed streak-off: Ninja vs. Hurricane [Honda CBR1000 and Kawasaki Ninja 1000] il Cycle 38:26-8+ Ap '87

Springs and suspension

Beyond telescopic forks. K. Cameron. il Cycle 38:58-67 Ja '87

GCB fork. K. Cameron. il Cycle 38:84 O '87

Testing

The 600s: Hurricane vs. Ninja [Honda CBR600 vs. Kawasaki ZX600R] il Cycle 38:34-9 Ag '87

1000 Hurricane [Honda] J. Karr. il Mot Trend 39:75-6 Ap '87

America's choice [Honda CBR600, Suzuki LS650, Yamaha YX600 Radian, Kawasaki EX500 and Harley-Davidson XLH883; cover story] il Cycle 38:12-15+ N '87

Beat the press: Kawasaki KLR650. T. Carrithers. il Cycle 38:60-3+ Ap '87

The best of East & West [Honda CBR600F Hurricane & Ducati 750 Paso; cover story] il Cycle 38:26-32+ My '87

A better Bimota: db1 SR. B. De Prato. il Cycle 38:84-5+ Jl '87

Better yet: Harley's FXRS-Sp Low Rider Sport Edition. il Cycle 38:8-9 O '87

BMW K100LT. il Cycle 38:32-8 Jl '87

BMW K100LT. J. Karr. il Mot Trend 39:99+ Ag '87

Motorcycles—Testing—*cont.*

BMW K100RS. il *Cycle* 38:22-5+ N '87

Cagiva/Ducati 650 Indiana. il *Cycle* 38:62-5+ Mr '87

Demo [demonstration rides at Americade Rockies touring rally] R. J. Roach. il *Cycle* 38:45 D '87

Euro enduro twins: Cagiva Elefant 750 & BMW R100GS. B. De Prato. il *Cycle* 38:52-4+ D '87

Famous last words [concluding paragraphs of motorcycle road tests] C. Hodenfield. il *Cycle* 38:41-3 S '87

Ferrari Mondial & Ducati Paso [cover story] R. Grable. il *Mot Trend* 39:50-6+ N '87

FZRs at Paul Ricard [Yamaha FZR750 and FZR1000] D. Coe. il *Cycle* 38:25-7 Mr '87

Harley-Davidson 883 Sportster [cover story] il *Cycle* 38:20-5 O '87

Harley-Davidson FLHS Electra Glide Sport. il *Cycle* 38:36-9+ Mr '87

Harley-Davidson FLST Heritage Softail. il *Cycle* 38:46-7 Mr '87

Harley-Davidson FXRS low rider. il *Cycle* 38:34-9+ O '87

Harley-Davidson XL 1100 Sportster. il *Cycle* 38:97-8+ My '87

Harley-Davidson XL 883 Hugger. il *Cycle* 38:89-90 My '87

Honda CBR1000F Hurricane [cover story] il *Cycle* 38:22-8+ Ap '87

Honda VF700C Magna. il *Cycle* 38:18-24 F '87

Honda VFR700F Interceptor. il *Cycle* 38:48-51+ Mr '87

Honda VT1100C Shadow. il *Cycle* 38:44-8+ Je '87

Honda VT700C Shadow. il *Cycle* 38:84+ My '87

Jealousy [differences between California motorcycles and those sold in other states] P. Schilling. il *Cycle* 38:9 Jl '87

Kawasaki EL 250 Eliminator. il *Cycle* 38:44-9 O '87

Kawasaki EX250-F2 Ninja. il *Cycle* 38:24-9 D '87

Kawasaki EX500. il *Cycle* 38:50-1+ Ja '87

Kawasaki GPX750R Ninja. il *Cycle* 38:20-5+ Ja '87

Kawasaki VN1500 Vulcan. il *Cycle* 38:24-9+ Je '87

Kawasaki ZG1000 Concours. il *Cycle* 38:36-7 Jl '87

Kawasaki ZG1200 Voyager XII. il *Cycle* 38:80-1 S '87

Kawasaki ZX600 Ninja [cover story] il *Cycle* 38:22-7+ Ag '87

The loyal opposition [Honda CBR1000 Hurricane, Kawasaki ZX1000R Ninja and Suzuki GSX-R1100] il *Cycle* 38:24-6 Jl '87

Middleweights on the mountain [Honda CBR600F Hurricane, Yamaha FZ600, Kawasaki EX500 and ZX600R Ninja] il *Cycle* 38:48-9+ My '87

Near-crimes of passion [1987 Ducati F1B 750 Desmo and 1974 Ducati 750SS] il *Cycle* 38:48-55+ F '87

Off to the future: Ducati's fuel-injected 850. B. De Prato. il *Cycle* 38:57-9 N '87

Six-wheeling the Alps [BMW K75 and BMW325i in the Tyrolean Alps] T. West. il *Road Track* 38:132-4+ F '87

Sold! From crate to customer: the Hurricane papers [manufacturer-supplied Honda vs. Honda purchased from dealer] il *Cycle* 38:43-6 Ag '87

Starship: Ducati 850 Superbike [cover story] D. Coe. il *Cycle* 38:18-25+ S '87

Suzuki GSX-R 1100. R. Grable. il *Mot Trend* 39:98-9 F '87

Suzuki GSX-R1100. il *Cycle* 38:40-5 N '87

Suzuki GV1400 LXE Cavalcade. il *Cycle* 38:38-9+ D '87

Suzuki VS1400GL Intruder. il *Cycle* 38:72-5+ Ap '87

Suzuki VS700 Intruder: direct hit. il *Cycle* 38:75 Ap '87

Three-grand conspiracy [motorcycles under $3000] il *Cycle* 38:57-63 F '87

Yamaha '88 [cover story] il *Cycle* 38:15-22 D '87

Yamaha FZ700. il *Cycle* 38:19-20 Je '87

Yamaha FZR. N. Mayersohn. il *Pop Mech* 164:48-9 N '87

Yamaha FZR1000 [cover story] il *Cycle* 38:20-8+ Jl '87

Yamaha SRX250. il *Cycle* 38:56-60 Ag '87

Yamaha XV1100 Virago. il *Cycle* 38:46-50 S '87

Yamaha XV535 Virago. il *Cycle* 38:36-9+ F '87

Yamaha YX600. il *Cycle* 38:78-9 S '87

Tires

See Tires, Motorcycle

Vibration

Bad vibes. K. Cameron. il *Cycle* 38:10 F '87

Wheels

Toomey static wheel balancing stand. il *Cycle* 38:18 Ja '87

Motorcycles, Antique

American original [Cyclone] M. Jordan. il *Cycle* 38:52-7 O '87

Photographs and photography

Art in decay. J. Owens. il *Cycle* 38:96-9 Je '87

Motorcycles, Experimental

Futurebike [FalcoRustyco show bike] K. Radley. il *Pop Sci* 230:82-3 F '87

Motorcycles, Military

The combat Kawis [Marine motorcycle training at Camp Pendleton, Calif.] P. Lyons. il *Cycle* 38:63-6 Je '87

Motorcycles, Racing

Daytona showcase. K. Cameron. il *Cycle* 38:74-81+ Je '87

Pipeline. J. Greening. See issues of Cycle

Chassis

Project Hurricane: CBR chassis tune-up. K. Vreeke. il *Cycle* 38:50-3 N '87

Design

Lucky thirteens. K. Cameron. il *Cycle* 38:17 Jl '87

Photographs and photography

On the salt [at Bonneville] Freud. il *Cycle* 38:50-3 Ap '87

Testing

Norton Rotary Rocket. M. Oxley. il *Cycle* 38:64-9 D '87

Oval-piston endurance racer: Honda's NR750. K. Cameron. il *Cycle* 38:62-3+ Ag '87

Yamaha FZR750RT [cover story] il *Cycle* 38:66-70+ Jl '87

Yoshimura GSX-R Superbike: track testing Daytona's pole sitter. K. Vreeke. il *Cycle* 38:89+ Je '87

YZR500: acronym for speed [E. Lawson's Yamaha GP bike] D. Coe. il pors *Cycle* 38:62-4+ Jl '87

Motorcycles, Remodeled

Testing

The road not taken [Ducati owned by B. De Prato] M. Lindemann. il *Cycle* 38:86-7 S '87

Motorcycles, Restored

Indian: on the road again [J. Junker's restoration and parts supply company] E. Borin. il pors *Cycle* 38:68-72+ S '87

Motorcycles, Used

Ruminations on a New Year's Day. P. Schilling. il *Cycle* 38:7 Ja '87

Motorcycles in education

Professor Honda [high school teacher uses his motorcycle to relate to students] M. Miller. il *Cycle* 38:20 N '87

Motorcycling

See also

Motorcycle racing

Heck on wheels. J. Merritt. *Esquire* 107:30+ Mr '87

Anecdotes, facetiae, satire, etc.

Famous last words. P. Schilling. il *Cycle* 38:11 Mr '87

History

Official recognition [Motorcycling in American history, 1900-1940 at the Smithsonian] K. Cameron. il *Cycle* 38:82-3+ Ap '87

International aspects

The art of motorcycle touring. M. S. Forbes. il pors *Pop Mech* 164:90-4+ Je '87

Storm hazards

Waterskiing [riding in the rain] K. Cameron. il *Cycle* 38:17 S '87

Stunt cycling

Daredevil: the man who fell to earth [D. Wade] C. Hodenfield. il pors *Cycle* 38:29-34 N '87

Two American heroes [videotapes by E. Knievel and Freddie Spencer] C. Hodenfield. il *Cycle* 38:14 F '87

Winter cycling

Come, Daytona [winter preparations] K. Cameron. il *Cycle* 38:17 Ap '87

California

Beat the press: Kawasaki KLR650. T. Carrithers. il *Cycle* 38:60-3+ Ap '87

Germany (West)

Ich bin ein ballooner [M. Forbes' motorcycle and hot air balloon trip] B. Conrad, III. il map *Forbes* 140:116-20+ Ag 24 '87

Japan

The quest [motorcycle licensing exams] R. Goldstein. il *Cycle* 38:132-3+ Ap '87

Middle Western States

Backroads [autumn ride from Murray, Ky. to Columbus, Ohio] H. R. Nett. il *Cycle* 38:35-7 N '87

Motorcycling clothes *See* Clothing and dress—Sports clothes

Motorcycling gloves *See* Gloves

Motorcyclists

See also

Baldwin, Mike

Lawson, Eddie

Manning, Dennis

Roberts, J. N. (James Nelson)

Motorcyclists—See also—*cont.*
   Surtees, John
   Diseases of enthusiasm. K. Cameron. il *Cycle* 38:8 O '87
   A view from the grid [1987's outstanding racers] il *Cycle* 38:80-3 O '87

   Attitudes
   British survivors in America [American motorcyclists views on British bikes] C. Wimpey. il *Cycle* 38:78-82 My '87

   Health and hygiene
   Racer Rx. K. Cameron. il *Cycle* 38:8 N '87

   Licenses
   The quest [motorcycle licensing exams in Japan] R. Goldstein. il *Cycle* 38:132-3+ Ap '87

   Psychology
   A sense of drama [motorcyclist and young son] T. Simmons. il *N Y Times Mag* p130 S 13 '87
Motoren-und-Turbinen-Union *See* MTU Motoren-und-Turbinen-Union
Motorhomes *See* Campers, Truck
Motorists *See* Automobile drivers
Motors, Electric *See* Electric motors
Motovun Group
   The floating book fair [annual meeting] H. R. Lottman. il *Publ Wkly* 232:28-30 Ag 14 '87
Motown Productions
   Judge OKs Mary Wilson's use of the name 'Supremes'. por *Jet* 71:56 Ja 26 '87
   Motown names new execs, starts $38 mil. promo plan. il *Jet* 72:61 S 14 '87
   Motown returns to classic LPs to old music format. *Jet* 72:58 Ap 27 '87
   Motown sings new tune. M. Bernstein. il *Black Enterp* 18:22 N '87
   Motown's other mogul [S. De Passe] J. Hopewell. il por *Channels* 7:38-9 S '87
   Smokey Robinson [interview] M. Goldberg. il por *Roll Stone* p61-2 N 5-D 10 '87
Motsenbocker, Judson M.
   about
   What you should know about replacing windows [interview] L. Stains. il por *Home Mech* 83:28+ Mr '87
Mott, Michael
   Air and water [poem] *America* 157:398 N 28 '87
   Gifts [poem] *America* 157:481 D 19 '87
Mott, William Penn, Jr.
   The national park system: looking back and moving ahead. il *USA Today (Periodical)* 115:18-28 My '87
   about
   Disputed territory. R. Cahn and P. Cahn. il *Natl Parks* 61:28-33 My/Je '87
   Takeover at the Park Service. R. Cahn. *Natl Parks* 61:53 Mr/Ap '87
Mottoes
   The man who put God's trust in your pocket! [motto on paper money suggested by M. H. Rothert] E. Rochette. il *Antiques Collect Hobbies* 92:80-1 Jl '87
Moty, Eleanor
   about
   Eleanor Moty [cover story] S. Foley. il por *Am Craft* 47:34-9+ Je/Jl '87
Motyl, Alexander J.
   Meanwhile, back in the Kazakh SSR . . . *New Leader* 70:9 F 9-23 '87
Moufarrege, Nicolas A., 1947-1985
   about
   A postmodern dandy. J. Perl. il *Vogue* 177:86 D '87
Moulden, Julia
   Porn: new battle, old war. il *Ms* 16:92 N '87
Moult, John
   (jt. auth) See Herzberg, Osnat, and Moult, John
Mounia
   about
   Mounia! P. A. Taylor. il por *Essence* 17:62-3 Ja '87
Mount, Charles Merrill
   about
   The tale of a frog prince. M. Stevens. il por *Newsweek* 110:22 Ag 31 '87
   Walking papers. D. Seideman. il pors *Time* 130:16 Ag 31 '87
Mount Airy (Md.)
   Radon pollution
   How one family solved a deadly dilemma. M. Lipske. il *Natl Wildl* 25:38 Ap/My '87
Mount Cuba (Wilmington, Del.: Historic house) *See* Wilmington (Del.)—Historic houses, sites, etc.
Mount Desert Island (Me.)
   See also
   Historic houses, sites, etc.—Mount Desert Island (Me.)

Mount Elbrus (Soviet Union) climbs *See* Mountaineering
Mount Etna (Sicily)
   Volcanic winter [study of volcanic aerosols] il *Sci Am* 256:83-4 F '87
Mount Everest (China and Nepal)
   After all is said and done, will Everest still be number one? [Navstar satellite altitude measurement; work of George Wallerstein] J. Krakauer. bibl (p231) il map *Smithsonian* 18:176-8+ O '87
   Can you top this? [abstract quality of mountain's height] M. W. Browne. il *N Y Times Mag* p50 Je 14 '87
   Everest toppled [Navstar satellite altitude measurement; work of George Wallerstein] il *Sky Telesc* 74:121 Ag '87
   King of the mountains [Navstar satellite measurements prove Everest is higher than K2] il *Time* 130:75 N 2 '87
   Mallory's camera [search conducted by T. Holzel] J. Taylor. il por *Omni* 9:90 F '87
   Pique over peaks: K2 versus Everest [use of Navstar satellite to determine height] J. Kluger. il *Discover* 8:16 O '87
   Race to the top of the world: who will be the first American woman to reach the summit of Mount Everest? E. Kaufmann. il *Women's Sports Fitness* 9:22-6 O '87
Mount Fuji (Japan)
   Ah, Fuji! C. N. Barnard. il *Int Wildl* 17:24-7 S/O '87
Mount Graham (Ariz.)
   Mount Graham, Arizona. R. H. Mohlenbrock. il map *Nat Hist* 96:88-90 Mr '87
Mount Holyoke College. Art Museum
   American art in the Mount Holyoke College Art Museum. P. J. Staiti and W. M. Watson. il *Antiques* 132:1122-31 N '87
Mount McKinley National Park (Alaska) *See* Denali National Park and Preserve (Alaska)
Mount Moran (Wyo.) climbs *See* Mountaineering
Mount Pelée (Martinique)
   Saint-Pierre Bay: Mont Pelée's underwater graveyard [reminders of 1902 eruption] J. C. Fine. il *Sea Front* 33:288-95 Jl/Ag '87
Mount Pleasant (Iowa)
   Crime
   Murder as usual. N. Pearson. il *Progressive* 51:50 F '87
Mount Pleasant (Mich.)
   Hospitals
   Getting set for a sibling [program at Central Michigan Hospital] J. Smith. il *Good Housekeep* 205:132 S '87
Mount Rainier National Park (Wash.)
   Mount Rainier [excerpt] R. Snow. il *Natl Parks* 61:46-7 N/D '87
   Shake hands with a glacier. il maps *Sunset* 179:44-8 Jl '87
Mount Saint Helens (Wash.)
   New life under the volcano. P. A. Witteman. il *Time* 129:63 Je 15 '87
   Raising the stakes at Mount St. Helens. R. A. Kerr. il *Science* 236:254-5 Ap 17 '87
   Replanting Mt. St. Helens. S. Kaveski. il *Technol Rev* 90:14-15 Ag/S '87
Mount Saint Helens National Volcanic Monument (Wash.)
   Hiking to Spirit Lake . . . or up to the rim of Mount St. Helens. il *Sunset* 179:62 Jl '87
Mount Shasta region (Calif.)
   Description and travel
   User-friendly Shasta [cover story] il maps *Sunset* 179:50-5 Ag '87
Mount Snow (Vt.: Resort) *See* Resorts—Vermont
Mount Wilson Observatory (Calif.) *See* Astronomical observatories
Mountain bicycle racing *See* Bicycle racing
Mountain bicycles *See* Bicycles
Mountain climbing *See* Mountaineering
Mountain curs
   The mountain cur. L. Mueller. il *Outdoor Life* 179:50+ Je '87
Mountain cycling *See* Cycling
Mountain ecology
   'Green death' in the Alps. E. Brunner. *World Press Rev* 34:53 D '87
   In harmony with nature [Alps] L. Lienert. il map *Courier* 40:4-8 F '87
   Mountain challenge. il *Courier* 40:27-9 O '87
   When men and mountains meet [Alps] J. Schaller. il map *Courier* 40:9-10 F '87
Mountain flying *See* Aviation—Mountain flying
Mountain gardens and gardening *See* High-altitude gardens and gardening

Mountain goats *See* Rocky Mountain goats
Mountain lions *See* Pumas
Mountain lodges *See* Lodges
Mountain men (Trappers) *See* Trappers
Mountain of the Mists Expedition *See* Scientific expeditions
Mountain plants *See* Alpine flora
Mountain sculpture
    See also
      Stone Mountain Memorial (Ga.)
Mountain sheep
      Diseases and pests
Ancient ram's death foreshadows disaster [decimation of Oregon bighorn herd] il *Audubon* 89:18 N '87
Mountain sickness
Feeling dizzy [advice for mountain climbers] D. Murphy. *Women's Sports Fitness* 9:87 Mr '87
It goes to your head. S. Festa. il *Women's Sports Fitness* 9:10 O '87
Mountain View (Calif.)
      Restaurants, nightclubs, bars, etc.
Spécialités de la maison:
    Chez TJ. C. Bates. il *Gourmet* 47:22+ Ja '87
Mountaineering
    See also
    Mount Everest (China and Nepal)
    Mountain sickness
    Snow and ice climbing
Arlene Blum: from molecules to mountains. M. Nelson. il pors *Ms* 16:106+ S '87
At the summit meeting [Soviet-American climb of Mount Elbrus] G. Warner. il map *Sierra* 72:57-60 Jl/Ag '87
Away from it all on a granite wall [rock climbing] M. Wellemeyer. il *Fortune* 115:119-20 Ap 13 '87
Conquest of Aconcagua [Andes peak] W. Broyles. il pors *Read Dig* 131:144-50 N '87
Exploring Patagonia's ranges [Andes] P. Smith. il map *Américas* 39:8-15 Jl/Ag '87
Getting to the top: the conquest of the great peaks [Alps] P. Meyer. il *Courier* 40:24-8 F '87
The Gunks [Will Colgan discusses climbing New York's Shawangunk cliffs] *New Yorker* 63:32-4 My 18 '87
Out on a ledge [women rock climbers] N. Wartik. il *Ms* 15:34 My '87
Pushing the mid-life envelope [climbing Aconcagua in the Andes] W. Broyles. il pors *Esquire* 107:72-4+ Je '87
Rock out: learn to scale new heights. B. Harrington. il *Women's Sports Fitness* 9:94-5 S '87
Take a hike! [women hikers in the Himalayas] D. Ravitch. il *Vogue* 177:248-9+ Je '87
The ups and downs of clambering on the roof of Europe [Mont Blanc] P. Miller. bibl (p154) il *Smithsonian* 18:92-8+ Je '87
      Accidents
Hazards involved [1986 Mt. Moran climb] E. J. Kahn. *New Yorker* 63:64-70 Ag 17 '87
In memory of David Koop [excerpt from Sometimes mountains move] C. E. Koop and E. Koop. il pors *Saturday Evening Post* 259:62-3+ N '87
      Bibliography
Climb and tell: or, It's a long way from Annapurna. C. S. Wren. il *N Y Times Book Rev* 92:7 F 15 '87
      Equipment
On the rocks. J. Roskelly. il *Pop Mech* 164:79-81+ Mr '87
      Psychological aspects
Facing fear on the mountain. D. Skafte. il *Women's Sports Fitness* 9:78 Ap '87
MountainNET (Firm)
Government agencies promote business, industry access to Ada. B. D. Nordwall. il *Aviat Week Space Technol* 127:91+ N 16 '87
Mountains
    See also
    Adirondack Mountains (N.Y.)
    Alps
    Andes
    Davis Mountains (Tex.)
    Grand Mesa (Colo.)
    Jemez Mountains (N.M.)
    Jura Mountains (France and Switzerland)
    K2 Mountain (Pakistan)
    Karakoram Range
    Mont Blanc (France and Italy)
    Mount Graham (Ariz.)
    Rocky Mountains
    Seamounts
    Volcanoes
    Watersheds
    Yucca Mountain (Nev.)

      Photographs and photography
Either/or on the old Silk Road. G. A. Rowell. il *Petersens Photogr Mag* 16:20-1 Ag '87
Mountains and Plains Booksellers Association
Colorado booksellers challenge obscenity law. *Publ Wkly* 231:87 F 27 '87
Mountains in art
    See also
    Sierra Nevada Mountains (Calif. and Nev.) in art
Mounted animals *See* Hunting trophies
Mounting (Taxidermy) *See* Taxidermy
Mountings, Telescope *See* Telescopes—Mounting
Mounts (Decorative arts)
Antiques: ormolu: opulent adornment for fine French furniture. M. M. Thomas. il *Archit Dig* 44:84-9+ F '87
      Exhibitions
Mounted oriental porcelain [cover story] F. J. B. Watson. il *Antiques* 131:812-23 Ap '87
Moure, Joseph
      about
Joseph Moure's California impressionist paintings. I. Borger. il por *Archit Dig* 44:86+ Mr '87
Mourning *See* Grief
Mourning dove shooting
In search of the perfect dove hunt [Kansas] M. Pearce. il *Outdoor Life* 180:66-7+ Ag '87
Mouse *See* Mice
Mouse (Computers) *See* Computers—Input-output equipment
Mousetraps
A better mousetrap. G. Levoy. il *N Y Times Mag* p58 Ag 23 '87
Instead of just squeaking by, retiree Mel Melton snaps at the chance to easily trap the common mouse. il por *People Wkly* 27:114 F 2 '87
Mouth
    See also
    Gums
    Teeth
      Care and hygiene
    See also
    Mouthwashes
      Diseases
    See also
    Leukoplakia, Oral
      Wounds and injuries
    See also
    Teeth—Wounds and injuries
Mouthwashes
Glorious gargle [chlorhexidine gluconate] D. Groves. *Health* 19:22-3 F '87
Super solutions for tooth decay. D. Born. il *Saturday Evening Post* 259:16+ Ja/F '87
Moutoussamy-Ashe, Jeanne, 1951-
      about
Arthur Ashe and wife Jeanne Moutoussamy-Ashe are parents of baby girl. il pors *Jet* 71:22 F 9 '87
Movalli, Charles
A conversation with Maurice Kennedy. il *Am Artist* 51:74-9+ N '87
A conversation with Robert Duffy. il *Am Artist* 51:54-9+ N '87
In praise of painterly painters. il *Am Artist* 51:36-41+ My '87
Movement, Creative *See* Dance
Movement, Psychology of
    See also
    Communication, Nonverbal
    Motion perception
    Motor ability
Movement disorders
    See also
    Ataxia
    Paralysis
    Tic
Movement of animals *See* Animal locomotion
Movement of cells *See* Cells—Motility
Movements of man *See* Biomechanics
Movie musicals *See* Motion pictures—Musical films
Movie theaters *See* Motion picture theaters
Movies *See* Motion pictures
Moving
    See also
    Executives—Relocation
    Migration, Internal
    Moving and storage companies
    Packing of household furnishings
That moving experience. J. Anthony. *Changing Times* 41:18-19 S '87

Moving—*cont.*
Psychological aspects
All over the map. A. Perrill. il *Seventeen* 46:176-7 S '87
Helping children adjust to moving. F. A. Smardo. bibl f il *Child Today* 16:10-13 My/Je '87
Rites of passage. D. D. Sleeper. il *Ctry J* 14:16+ O '87
Moving and storage companies
Making the right move. il *Consum Res Mag* 70:32-4 Ja '87
Moving companies. il *Consum Rep* 52:298-300 D '87
Japan
See also
Art Moving Center (Firm)
Moving of structures, etc.
Move it or lose it [Cape Hatteras Light] O. H. Pilkey, Jr. il *Oceans* 20:23+ Mr/Ap '87
Photographs and photography
Household effects. S. Piperato. il por *Pop Photogr* 94:96-7 N '87
Moving pictures *See* Motion pictures
Mowat, Farley
about
PW interviews. B. Slopen. por *Publ Wkly* 232:79-80 O 2 '87
Mowing machines
See also
Lawn mowers
Rotary discs send conditioner market spinning. B. Eftink. il *Success Farm* 85:36B-37B Je '87
Mowry, Kimberly L., and Steitz, Joan A.
Identification of the human U7 snRNP as one of several factors involved in the 3' end maturation of histone premessenger RNA's. bibl f il *Science* 238:1682-7 D 18 '87
Moy, Tzu
about
All-American-Girl talk. il por *Teen* 31:77 O '87
Moyer, Albert E., 1945-
Michelson in 1887. bibl f il *Phys Today* 40:50-6 My '87
Moyer, Robin
about
Robin Moyer's Bayan ko! honors the Philippine revolt. H. Chapnick. il por *Pop Photogr* 94:16 Mr '87
Moyers, Bill
about
Bill Moyers on our U.S. Constitution [interview] L. Kravitz. por *Sch Update* 119:29 My 18 '87
Listening to both sides of the 'divided kingdom'. J. M. Wall. *Christ Century* 104:1166-7 D 23-30 '87
Moyers and Mudd: seers or soreheads? W. A. Henry. il por *Channels* 7:57 Ap '87
Our 200-year fight for freedom [interview] L. Kravitz. por *Sch Update* 120:6 S 4 '87
Moyers: in search of the Constitution [television program] See Television program reviews—Single works
Moyers: report from Philadelphia [television program] See Television program reviews—Single works
Moynahan, Brian
Marseilles: a city at sea. il *World Press Rev* 34:56 Ap '87
Moynihan, Daniel P. (Daniel Patrick), 1927-
How the Soviets are bugging America. il map *Pop Mech* 164:102-5 Ap '87
Lessons of the Iran-contra affair. por *Read Dig* 130:74-5 Je '87
The Tecumseh Club. il *N Y* 20:96 D 21-28 '87
about
His way. J. Klein. il pors *N Y* 20:34+ O 26 '87
The presence of malice. G. F. Will. il *Newsweek* 110:106 D 7 '87
Sounder of alarms. por *Time* 129:21 F 16 '87
Tough, tightfisted and traditional. W. Shapiro. il por *Time* 130:19 Ag 3 '87
A welfare reform mirage. M. Kaus. il por *Newsweek* 110:21 Ag 3 '87
Moynihan, Maura
Food wars: diet and irradiation. *Vogue* 177:405+ O '87
Out of India: karma & Christ. il *Commonweal* 114:446-52 Ag 14 '87
Sam Nunn: "After two hours of walking NYC's streets, three people had asked me to run! Three!". il por *Vogue* 177:248+ O '87
Moynihan, Rodrigo, 1910-
about
Rodrigo Moynihan at Robert Miller. G. Henry. *Art Am* 75:216 Ap '87

Mozambican refugees *See* Refugees, Mozambican
Mozambique
See also
Massacres—Mozambique
Relief work—Mozambique
United Nations—Mozambique
Foreign relations
South Africa
See South Africa—Foreign relations—Mozambique
Southern Africa
Mozambique and the regional conflict in Southern Africa. A. F. Isaacman. bibl f *Curr Hist* 86:213-16+ My '87
United States
See United States—Foreign relations—Mozambique
Industries
See also
Nut industry—Mozambique
Politics and government
Hunger and armed conflict threaten Mozambique. R. Frame. il *Christ Today* 31:60-1 O 2 '87
Massacre deep in the African bush. W. E. Smith. il map *Time* 130:28-9 Ag 3 '87
More than $200 million pledged for humanitarian assistance to Mozambique. il *UN Chron* 24:29 My '87
Mozambicans in diaspora. W. L. Moser. *America* 156:440-1+ My 30 '87
Mozambique and the regional conflict in Southern Africa. A. F. Isaacman. bibl f *Curr Hist* 86:213-16+ My '87
The Renamo menace: hunger and carnage in Mozambique [cover story; with editorial comment] A. R. Norton. il *New Leader* 70:2, 5-8 N 16 '87
Religious institutions and affairs
See also
Missions—Mozambique
Mozambique National Resistance Movement
Massacre deep in the African bush. W. E. Smith. il map *Time* 130:28-9 Ag 3 '87
Massacre in Mozambique. S. Reiss. *Newsweek* 110:28 Ag 3 '87
Mozambique: a rebel reign of terror. R. Wilkinson. il *Newsweek* 110:29 Ag 24 '87
Mozambique massacre. B. Shelby. *World Press Rev* 34:43 S '87
Notes and comment [American policy regarding Renamo] *New Yorker* 63:35-6 N 16 '87
The Renamo menace: hunger and carnage in Mozambique [cover story; with editorial comment] A. R. Norton. il *New Leader* 70:2, 5-8 N 16 '87
Mozart, Johann Chrysostom Wolfgang Amadeus *See* Mozart, Wolfgang Amadeus, 1756-1791
Mozart, Wolfgang Amadeus, 1756-1791
about
La clemenza di Tito [opera] Reviews
Opera News il 51:22-4+ F 14 '87
Don Giovanni [opera] Reviews
N Y il 20:48-9 Ag 3 '87. P. G. Davis
Nation 245:208-9 S 5 '87. M. Hodgson
Nation 245:319-20 S 26 '87. E. W. Said
New Yorker il 63:66-9 Ag 10 '87. A. Porter
Opera News 52:52-3 N '87. C. J. Luten
Die Entführung aus dem Serail [opera] Reviews
Opera News il 52:32-4, 36 D 5 '87
La finta giardiniera [opera] Reviews
New Yorker 63:110-11 S 14 '87. A. Porter
In defense of embellishment. K. Stern. il *Opera News* 51:18-21 F 14 '87
The marriage of Figaro [opera] Reviews
Opera News il 51:24-8+ Ja 31 '87
Mozart: the basic repertoire on compact disc. R. Freed. il *Stereo Rev* 52:78-9 Jl '87
L'oca del Cairo [opera] Reviews
N Y 20:83 N 30 '87. P. G. Davis
New Yorker 63:130-1 N 30 '87. A. Porter
Il re pastore [opera] Reviews
New Yorker 63:111-12 S 14 '87. A. Porter
Die Zauberflöte [opera] Reviews
N Y il 20:56 Ag 31 '87. P. G. Davis
New Yorker 63:112+ S 14 '87. A. Porter
Opera News il 52:42 O '87
The Mozart brothers [film] See Motion picture reviews—Single works
Mozart violin concerto [ballet] See Ballet reviews—Single works
Mozzarelli, Andrea, and others
Delay time of hemoglobin S polymerization prevents most cells from sickling in vivo. bibl f il *Science* 237:500-6 Jl 31 '87
MPAA *See* Motion Picture Association of America
MPD (Myofacial pain dysfunction) syndrome *See* TMJ syndrome

MPR *See* Minnesota Public Radio
MPTP (Drug)
Parkinson's protection? [chloroquine offers partial protection from MPTP-induced symptoms; research by Robert J. D'Amato and others] B. Bower. *Sci News* 131:359 Je 6 '87
Mr. B's (New Orleans, La.: Restaurant) *See* New Orleans (La.)—Restaurants, nightclubs, bars, etc.
Mr. T
about
For Bruce Willis and Mr. T, the good-neighbor policy has just been canceled. N. Geeslin. il pors *People Wkly* 27:34-5 Je 15 '87
Mr. T chops down trees on his property; angers his neighbors in suburb. por *Jet* 72:57 Je 8 '87
Mr. T files counter harassment suit against New York photographer. *Jet* 72:60 Ag 24 '87
Mr. T suffers backlash after tree-cutting spree. il por *Jet* 72:54 Je 15 '87
Suburb plans to legally axe Mr. T.'s tree-chopping. por *Jet* 72:33 Je 22 '87
Mraz, Barb
about
A garden gone wild. J. Burnett. il por *Rodale's Org Gard* 34:84-6 N '87
MRI *See* Magnetic resonance imaging
Mrs. Fields Cookies
Just once I wanted to hear that maybe I was different, individual, that I had something of my own to offer [excerpt from One smart cookie] D. Fields. il pors *Glamour* 85:122+ S '87
Mrs. Sam Houston House (Independence, Tex.) *See* Independence (Tex.)—Historic houses, sites, etc.
Ms. (Periodical)
Inside Ms. S. B. Levine. See issues of Ms. beginning September 1987 through December 1987
Let the celebration begin . . . [15th anniversary issue; cover story] S. B. Levine. il *Ms* 16:1+ Jl/Ag '87
Women of the Year: the 1986 awards [special section] il *Ms* 15:39-41+ Ja '87
MSD (Marine sanitation devices) *See* Boats and boating—Toilet facilities
Mswati III, King of Swaziland
about
In the kingdom of "Fire Eyes". W. E. Smith. il *Time* 130:34 S 7 '87
Mtingwa, Sekazi K.
about
Black scientist is named Soviet exchange scholar. por *Jet* 73:36 O 12 '87
MTU Motoren-und-Turbinen-Union
MTU plans key shrouded propfan tests for 1988. K. F. Mordoff. *Aviat Week Space Technol* 127:88-9 Jl 6 '87
Mtume, A. Kamili
about
On the rise! L. Barrett. pors *Essence* 18:42 My '87
MTV Networks Inc.
MTV faces a mid-life crisis. R. Zoglin. il *Time* 129:67 Je 29 '87
MTV's great leap backward. F. Dannen. il *Channels* 7:45-7 Jl/Ag '87
MTV Video Music Awards
MTV draws a crowd. S. Rogers. il *Roll Stone* p9 O 22 '87
Mubarak, Hosni
about
Egypt: repression and liberalization. H. Ansari. *Curr Hist* 86:77-80+ F '87
Egypt: the Islamic issue. M. Sid-Ahmed. *Foreign Policy* 69:22-39 Wint '87/'88
Mubarak maneuver. S. Reed. *Nation* 244:421 Ap 4 '87
Mucha, Janusz
Polish humanist in a Communist world: Stanislaw Ossowski. *Society* 24:70-7 My/Je '87
Muchmore, Elaine A., and Varki, Ajit P.
Selective inactivation of influenza C esterase: a probe for detecting 9-O-acetylated sialic acids. bibl f il *Science* 236:1293-5 Je 5 '87
Muckraking
Mellowing of a muckraker [J. Anderson; cover story] D. Corn. il *Nation* 245:541+ N 14 '87
Mucus
Isolation of an olfactory cDNA: similarity to retinol-binding protein suggests a role in olfaction. K.-H. Lee and others. bibl f il *Science* 235:1053-6 F 27 '87
Mud
See also
Automobile driving—Mud hazards

Mud racing
Just mucking around [Swamp Buggy Races in Naples, Florida] B. W. Yates. il *Car Driv* 32:191-7 My '87
Muda Hassanal Bolkiah *See* Hassanal Bolkiah, Sultan of Brunei, 1946-
Mudd, E. J.
Stop that music! [story] il *Redbook* 169:46+ My '87
Mudd, Roger Harrison
about
Moyers and Mudd: seers or soreheads? W. A. Henry. il por *Channels* 7:57 Ap '87
Mueller, John E.
The Astaire illusion. *Dance Mag* 61:34 N '87
Mueller, Larry
Hunting dogs. See issues of Outdoor Life
Mueller, Peter, and Burch, Larry
Tailwinds, thunderstorms and turbulence: the weather story of the Voyager flight [cover story] il map *Weatherwise* 40:240-7 O '87
Mueller, R. J.
(jt. auth) See Johnston, M. J. S., and Mueller, R. J.
Mueller, Van D.
Choice: the parents' perspective. *Phi Delta Kappan* 68:761-2 Je '87
Mueller (C. F.) & Co. *See* C. F. Mueller & Co.
Mueller-Dombois, Dieter, 1925-
Natural dieback in forests. bibl il *BioScience* 37:575-83 S '87
Muesli
Muesli. il *Gourmet* 47:84-5+ O '87
Muffins
Fast breads and muffins. il *Better Homes Gard* 65:163-4 My '87
Hot buns. B. Kanner. il *N Y* 20:16+ Mr 30 '87
Muffins. M. Cunningham. il *Gourmet* 47:74-5+ S '87
MUFON *See* Mutual UFO Network
Mufson, Steven
Anglo-American faces life. *New Repub* 197:26+ S 14-21 '87
The fall of the Front. *New Repub* 196:17-19 Mr 23 '87
Uncle Joe. *New Repub* 197:20-3 S 28 '87
Why free Mbeki? *Nation* 245:670-1 D 5 '87
Mugabe, Robert Gabriel, 1924-
Struggle for Southern Africa. *Foreign Aff* 66:311-27 Wint '87/'88
Muggeridge, Anne Roche, 1936-
Reclaiming the Catholic heritage. *Commentary* 84:39-44 S '87
Mugging (Crime) *See* Assault and battery
Mugs
Arsonist immortalized on transfer-printed mug [1829 York Minster fire] S. Bagdade and A. Bagdade. il *Antiques Collect Hobbies* 92:46 Mr '87
Muhammad ibn 'Abd Allāh ibn Baṭūṭah *See* Ibn Battuta, 1304-1377
Muirfield (Scotland: Golf course) *See* Golf courses—Scotland
Mujica Gallo, Miguel
about
All that glitters [cover story] P. E. Rogers. il *Américas* 39:8-13 Mr/Ap '87
Mukhamedov, Irek
about
The Bolshoi's big news: Irek Mukhamedov, superstar. M. E. Willis. il pors *Dance Mag* 61:58-63 Ap '87
Mukherjee, Bharati
(jt. auth) See Blaise, Clark, and Mukherjee, Bharati
Mulberries
Mulberries . . . keep birds at bay. M. Leister. il *Rodale's Org Gard* 34:40 Mr '87
Mulching
Deep mulch. P. Dennis, Jr. bibl il *Mother Earth News* 105:89-90+ My/Je '87
Deep mulch on the High Plains [Podoll family garden] J. Ruttle. il *Rodale's Org Gard* 34:42-4+ Mr '87
Mulch? Tomatoes prefer red. *Sci News* 132:73 Ag 1 '87
The new high-tech mulches that keep weeds down. il *Sunset* 178:270 My '87
Muldavin, Phyllis Smirle
about
Ann Page and Phyllis Muldavin at the Woman's Building. M. Laurence. *Art Am* 75:141-2 Ja '87
Mule deer hunting *See* Deer hunting
Mulholland, William D.
The safety of the world's funds [address, September 10, 1987] *Vital Speeches Day* 54:86-8 N 15 '87

Mullane, Robert E., 1932-
about
Zero-sum game. R. Phalon. il pors *Forbes* 139:110-12 Mr 23 '87
Mullen, Daniel P.
Forecasting for the frigid desert of Antarctica [cover story] il map *Weatherwise* 40:304-11 D '87
Müller, K. Alex, 1927-
about
The 1987 Nobel Prize for Physics. M. M. Waldrop. il pors *Science* 238:481-2 O 23 '87
Bednorz and Müller win Nobel Prize for new superconducting materials. A. Khurana. il pors *Phys Today* 40:17-19 D '87
Nobel prizes: physics. J. Horgan. *Sci Am* 257:46 D '87
Müller, K. Alex, 1927-, and Bednorz, J. Georg
The discovery of a class of high-temperature superconductors. bibl f il *Science* 237:1133-9 S 4 '87
Muller, Karen, 1948-
(jt. auth) See Edelman, Hendrik, 1937-, and Muller, Karen, 1948-
Muller, Marcia
Plotting the realistic detective novel. *Writer* 100:12-15+ Je '87
Müller, Mario
Song without words. il *Courier* 40:31 F '87
Muller, Steven
The university presidency today. *Science* 237:705 Ag 14 '87
Mullet fishing
Net gain [use of cast nets for mullet] G. Norman. il *Oceans* 20:56 N/D '87
Mullets
Beautiful leapers. G. Norman. il *South Living* 22:104 Je '87
Mullican, Matt, 1951-
about
Matt Mullican. J. Kutner. il *Art News* 86:29+ Ap '87
Mulligan, Joseph E.
Religion and the Nicaraguan constitution. il *Christ Century* 104:398-9 Ap 29 '87
Mulligan, Tim, 1938-
Joining the inn crowd. il *50 Plus* 27:44-8 Ag '87
Mullins, Carolyn J.
How to tell good software by its cover. *Work Woman* 12:44+ D '87
Mullins, Hattie-Jo P.
The rocky courtship of teens and birth control. il *Ms* 15:25 Mr '87
Women and the law: will real life catch up to TV? il *Ms* 15:64-5 Je '87
Mullis, Ina V. S.
(jt. auth) See Applebee, Arthur N., and others
Mulloy, Gardnar, 1913-
about
Advantage: Gardnar Mulloy. L. Lindeman. il pors *50 Plus* 27:68-70+ Ja '87
Mulroney, Brian
Behind closed doors. il *Macleans* 100:15-16 Je 15 '87
about
Fraternity at the top. il pors *Macleans* 100:12-13 Ap 20 '87
Going public on trade. M. Janigan. il por *Macleans* 100:16+ Mr 23 '87
A hint of election fever. M. Janigan. il pors *Macleans* 100:12-13 N 30 '87
How the free-trade talks are clobbering Canada's Tories. E. B. Terry. il *Bus Week* p61 Mr 9 '87
How to track a plummeting star. P. Stoler. il por *Time* 129:32 Mr 2 '87
It is déjà vu all over again. S. MacLeod. por *Macleans* 100:84 F 2 '87
Judgment in hard-cover. P. Gessell. il *Macleans* 100:17 N 2 '87
Low marks for the government. P. Gessell. il pors *Macleans* 100:32-5 Ja 5 '87
Mulroney on his record [interview] il pors *Macleans* 100:14-17 D 21 '87
Mulroney's magic moment. P. Gessell. *Macleans* 100:17 Je 15 '87
Mulroney's new offensive. M. Janigan. il por *Macleans* 100:6-8 F 23 '87
Mulroney's red-hot summer. P. Gessell. il por *Macleans* 100:8 Jl 13 '87
A political minefield [special section; with editorial comment by Kevin Doyle] il pors *Macleans* 100:2, 8-9+ F 2 '87
Reagan and Mulroney: the bloom is off the shamrock. M. Whitaker. il por *Newsweek* 109:34-5 Ap 6 '87

The tastes of the Mulroney family. M. Janigan. il por *Macleans* 100:13 Ap 27 '87
An unflattering portrait of Mulroney. M. Rose. il por *Macleans* 100:17 S 28 '87
Why Brian Mulroney is up against a trade wall. E. B. Terry and others. il *Bus Week* p44-5 Je 15 '87
Anecdotes, facetiae, satire, etc.
May your best friend fail, too. A. Fotheringham. il *Macleans* 100:60 Mr 9 '87
Press relations
Prejudice in Ottawa's attack pack. G. Bain. il *Macleans* 100:56 Mr 23 '87
Staff
At the eye of a blistering storm [J. A. Doucet and B. Roy] M. Rose. il pors *Macleans* 100:9 F 23 '87
A man with a mandate [chief of staff D. Burney] H. Mackenzie. il pors *Macleans* 100:10-11 My 25 '87
Mulroney's new team. H. Mackenzie. il *Macleans* 100:21 Mr 23 '87
Speaking with fewer tongues. S. MacLeod. por *Macleans* 100:52 Ag 24 '87
A Tory veteran bows out. H. Mackenzie and M. Janigan. il pors *Macleans* 100:11 Mr 2 '87
Visit to Africa, 1987
Africa's warm welcome. M. Rose. il pors *Macleans* 100:8-9 F 9 '87
Getting away from it all. M. Rose. il *Macleans* 100:23 F 2 '87
Mulroney, Mila
about
The tastes of the Mulroney family. M. Janigan. il por *Macleans* 100:13 Ap 27 '87
Multichannel multipoint distribution service
Maneuvering for growth. N. Gunther. *Channels* 7 Sp Issue:91 D '87
Multicultural education *See* Intercultural education
Multidimensional scaling
Rating the IBM compatibles. R. G. Brookshire. bibl il *Byte* 12 no12 Sp Issue:193-6+ '87
Multilevel marketing
Dreams and downlines. D. Owen. il *Atlantic* 260:84-90 O '87
The mess called multilevel marketing. R. Eisenberg. il *Money* 16:136-8+ Je '87
MultiMate (Word processor program) *See* Word processors and processing—Programming
Multimedia, Inc.
Multimedia's maverick [R. E. Hamby] J. Baker. por *Channels* 7:55 Je '87
Multimeters
Beckman Industrial DM 800 DMM. il *Radio-Electron* 58:71 Ja '87
Fluke LCA-10 line current test adapter [multimeter accessory] il *Radio-Electron* 58:28+ Mr '87
Leader LCD-100 portable DMM/storage oscilloscope. il *Radio-Electron* 58:21+ Je '87
Using a multimeter. G. Branson. il *Fam Handyman* 37:79 My/Je '87
Using a multimeter. E. Morrissey. il *Workbench* 43:36+ S/O '87
Multinational corporations *See* Corporations, International
Multiple birth *See* Birth, Multiple
Multiple/choice crimes [dance] *See* Dance reviews—Single works
Multiple jobholding *See* Supplementary employment
Multiple mirror telescopes *See* Telescopes—Mirrors
Multiple Opportunities Portfolio
In this new fund, anything goes. C. J. Loomis. *Fortune* 115:294+ Ap 27 '87
Multiple personality
The many faces of Audrey Anne Wilder. J. Fincher. il *Read Dig* 130:36-8+ Ap '87
Multiple sclerosis
After years of lying, actress Madlyn Rhue reveals the truth about her multiple sclerosis [interview] L. Armstrong. il pors *People Wkly* 28:105+ N 16 '87
Award of honor [courage of P. Gust] R. V. Araskog. il *N Y Times Mag* p54 S 6 '87
The Baby M case: pregnancy and M.S. il *Discover* 8:13 Je '87
Chemical factors may alter disease course. D. M. Barnes. il *Science* 237:1569 S 25 '87
Multiple sclerosis: a riddle wrapped in a mystery. P. C. Shaw. il *USA Today (Periodical)* 116:87-91 Jl '87
Searching for the key to the mystery of multiple sclerosis. il *Curr Health 2* 13:14-15 F '87
Still stalking MS. D. D. Edwards. il *Sci News* 132:234-5 O 10 '87
The triumph of Mikko Mayeda [multiple sclerosis victim becomes a competitive equestrian] V. Scott. il por *Good Housekeep* 204:40 Mr '87

Multiple sclerosis—*cont.*
Varying influences on cell-cell interactions. D. M. Barnes. *Science* 237:1568-9 S 25 '87

Therapy
Drug shows potential as MS treatment [Cop 1] *Sci News* 132:120 Ag 22 '87
New hope for MS victims [Cop 1] L. Drew. il *Newsweek* 110:46 Ag 24 '87

Multiprocessors
See also
Parallel processing (Computers)
The Definicon DSI-780: a 68020-based XT/AT coprocessor for scientific and engineering applications. D. Thomas. il *Byte* 12:209-10+ O '87
Fast math [Motorola's 68882 math coprocessor] T. Thompson. il *Byte* 12:120-1 D '87
Graphics co-processors. J. Bernard. il *Radio-Electron* 58 ComputerDigest:82-5 S '87
Inside the 82786 graphics chip. B. Nicholls. il *Byte* 12:135-41 Ag '87
PC-Elevator 386 [80386 add-in board] F. Langa. il *Byte* 12:98 D '87
The state of numerics [floating-point coprocessors] S. S. Fried. il *Byte* 12 no12 Sp Issue:115-18+ '87
Turbo-Amiga: a peripheral for the Amiga 1000 that's actually another computer. W. Block. il *Byte* 12:235-8 Je '87
Turbocharge your PC. J. Holtzman. il *Radio-Electron* 58 ComputerDigest:95-100+ N '87

Multiprogramming (Computers)
Breaking the bottleneck. J. Jainschigg. il *Work Woman* 12:64 Ap '87

Multitech Industrial Corp.
Stan Shih wants 'made in Taiwan' to mean first-rate. M. Shao. il por *Bus Week* p109+ Je 8 '87

Multiuser systems (Computers) *See* Computers—Multiuser systems

MultiVision Products, Inc.
The Rabbit punch [R. Wright charges Rabbit Systems and MarketCorp Venture Associates with misappropriation of trade secrets] K. Healy. il por *Forbes* 140:175-6 S 21 '87

Multnomah Press
The Multnomah formula. R. P. Nelson. il *Publ Wkly* 231:41-2 Mr 6 '87

Mumford, George S.
The legacy of E. E. Barnard. il por *Sky Telesc* 74:30-4 Jl '87

Mumford, J. L., and others
Lung cancer and indoor air pollution in Xuan Wei, China. bibl f il map *Science* 235:217-20 Ja 9 '87

Mumford, Lewis, 1895-
about
The sky line. B. Gill. *New Yorker* 63:106-9 F 23 '87

Mummies
Mummy dearest [studying Egyptian mummies with CT scan] S. Allison. il *Life* 10:106-9 O '87

Mummy berry fungus
Deceit and corruption in the blueberry patch [flower mimicry by mummy berry fungus (Monilinia)] S. W. T. Batra. il *Nat Hist* 96:56-9 Ag '87

Mundigo, Axel
What people believe. il *World Health* p8-9 N '87

Mung beans *See* Beans

Mungin, Horace
A fatherless father. por *Essence* 18:10 N '87

Munich (Germany)
Industries
See also
Publishers and publishing—Germany (West)

Municipal advertising
See also
West Chester (Pa.)—Advertising

Municipal bond funds *See* Investment trusts

Municipal bonds
See also
Bonds, Housing authority
Bonds, Industrial development
Stripped municipal bonds
Bargains in muni bonds. B. Weberman. il *Forbes* 140:311 N 16 '87
Battered bonds? Try swapping them. D. Zigas. *Bus Week* p182 O 12 '87
Buying those magnificent muni bonds. L. Marsa. *Black Enterp* 17:320 Je '87
Can Salomon grow by shrinking? [shutting down municipal bond unit and laying off staff] A. Bianco. il *Bus Week* p30-1 O 26 '87
Carpetbaggers [Georgia objects to tax reform restrictions on tax-exempt status] *Time* 130:63 S 14 '87

How 'tax-free' are these bonds? [munis underwritten by Matthews & Wright] D. Zigas. *Bus Week* p122 Ag 17 '87
Making the most of the bond debacle. D. Zigas. il *Bus Week* p202-3 N 2 '87
Muni market mayhem. il *Fortune* 116:8 N 9 '87
The municipal-bond alternative. *Consum Rep* 52:12 Ja '87
Municipal bonds: a surviving tax shelter. il *Consum Rep* 52:572 S '87
Municipal bonds: the next big scandal? [collapsible escrow bonds] J. Bodnar. *Changing Times* 41:8 O '87
Required reading [muni prospectus] B. Weberman. il *Forbes* 139:183 Ap 6 '87
Seizing the golden moment in tax-free bonds. D. Harris. il *Money* 16:106-8+ Ja '87
Smoke signals [brokers promote American Indian tax free municipals] M. Schifrin. il *Forbes* 139:42+ Je 15 '87
A strong rebound for municipals. J. Rachlin. il *U S News World Rep* 102:46-7 Je 29 '87
Tax reform puts the squeeze on muni bonds. D. Zigas. il *Bus Week* p76-7 Ag 17 '87
Taxable munis: worth a look. M. Brill. il *Changing Times* 41:84-8 Ap '87
Van Peebles makes most of stock market crash. il por *Jet* 73:6 N 9 '87
Wall Street's puny 'muni' markets. D. P. Wiener. il *U S News World Rep* 103:43 O 26 '87
Why muni bond funds got massacred. D. Zigas. il *Bus Week* p108 Je 1 '87
The wonder woman of muni bonds [C. A. Fitts of Dillon, Read] A. Bianco. il por *Bus Week* p112-13 F 23 '87

Default
Clear as MUD [defaults of municipal utility district bonds in Texas] W. P. Barrett. il *Forbes* 139:96-8 Je 15 '87
Listen up. B. Weberman. il *Forbes* 139:117 Je 29 '87
Municipal garbage [Miller & Schroeder's Municipal Investors Trust of America] G. Morgenson. il *Forbes* 139:42-3 Mr 9 '87

Insurance
Belt and suspenders. B. Weberman. il *Forbes* 139 Ann Directory:333 Ap 27 '87
The risky business of insuring muni debt. C. Farrell. il *Bus Week* p96-7 Ap 27 '87

Rating
The best and nearly best. B. Weberman. il *Forbes* 140:465 Jl 13 '87

Redemption
Moral obligation [refinanced munis] B. Weberman. il *Forbes* 139:161 F 23 '87

Refunding
A safe harbor in a choppy bond market [pre-refunded bonds] J. Mendes. il *Fortune* 116:102-3 Jl 6 '87

Municipal budget *See* Municipal finance

Municipal employees
See also
Albuquerque (N.M.)—Employees
Detroit (Mich.)—Employees
Long Branch (N.J.)—Employees
Women municipal employees

Salaries, allowances, etc.
State and local government pay increases outpace five-year rise in private industry. R. Schumann. il *Mon Labor Rev* 110:18-20 F '87

Municipal finance
See also
Local taxation
Municipal bonds
States and cities won't be building up the economy. G. Koretz. il *Bus Week* p24 Ag 17 '87

Municipal garages *See* Garages, Municipal

Municipal government
See also
Mayors
Municipal home rule
Municipal incorporation
Municipal services

Municipal home rule
Fauntroy renews bid to gain statehood for D.C. *Jet* 71:5 Mr 23 '87
Walter Fauntroy closer to gaining statehood for D.C. *Jet* 72:4 Je 22 '87
Whistle stop campaigning for D.C. statehood drive. il *Jet* 72:6 Ag 3 '87

Municipal improvement
See also
Business districts
City planning

Municipal improvement—See also—*cont.*
    Jacksonville (Fla.)—Municipal improvement
    Public works
    Royston (Ga.)—Municipal improvement
    Waterfronts

Municipal incorporation
  The city that isn't [vote to dissolve government in Crystal Beach, Tex.] il *Time* 129:33 Ap 27 '87

Municipal liability *See* Government liability

Municipal officers
    See also
    Mayors
    Women municipal officers

Municipal ordinances
    See also
    Baltimore (Md.)—Ordinances
    Bedford (Tex.)—Ordinances
    New York (N.Y.)—Ordinances
    Thousand Oaks (Calif.)—Ordinances

Municipal services
  Lotus Land isn't what it used to be [California's declining services] S. L. Hawkins. il *U S News World Rep* 103:23-4 O 19 '87
  Privatizing city services [address, February 24, 1987] R. W. Poole. *Vital Speeches Day* 53:588-90 Jl 15 '87

Municipal taxation *See* Local taxation
Municipal transit *See* Local transit
Municipal utilities *See* Public utilities

Munitions
    See also
    Boeing Co.
    Firearms industry
    Military-industrial complex
    Nuclear weapons
    Projectiles
    Weapons
  Industry observer. See issues of Aviation Week & Space Technology
  Pentagon Council to review new munitions master plan. J. D. Morrocco. *Aviat Week Space Technol* 127:23-4 Jl 13 '87
  Scientists find corporate support building for deployment of SDI. J. D. Morrocco. il *Aviat Week Space Technol* 126:81 Ap 27 '87

Automation
  USAF initiatives promote automation of weapon subcontractors' shops. E. H. Phillips. *Aviat Week Space Technol* 127:89 D 7 '87

Export-import trade
    See also
    Iran-contra affair
  Administration opposes House bill on offsets. P. Mann. *Aviat Week Space Technol* 127:26-7 Jl 6 '87
  Administration to cite Saudi involvement in Gulf as justification for arms sale. M. Mecham. *Aviat Week Space Technol* 127:31 Ag 24 '87
  The Canadian connection [South Africa using Canadian-designed weaponry in Angola] A. Bilski. il map *Macleans* 100:36 O 19 '87
  Caught in the cross-fire [Canadian defense industry threatened by U.S. protectionism] M. Drohan. il *Macleans* 100:15 Mr 9 '87
  Congress warns administration not to attempt Saudi arms sale. M. Mecham. *Aviat Week Space Technol* 127:28-9 O 5 '87
  The deadly world of the arms trade. M. Christopher. il *Sch Update* 119:13 My 4 '87
  Europe's arms pipeline to Iran. K. R. Timmerman. *Nation* 245:47-8+ Jl 18-25 '87
  Everybody's doing it [European arms sales to Iran] G. Russell. il *Time* 129:31 Mr 16 '87
  How U.S. arms dealers are making a killing. A. R. Dowd. il *Fortune* 115:58-61+ F 16 '87
  Industry presses congressional review of marketing cost ban. M. Mecham. *Aviat Week Space Technol* 127:77 N 2 '87
  Nations vie for arms markets. W. D. Hartung. bibl f il *Bull At Sci* 43:27-35 D '87
  Peking guns for hard cash. F. Willey. il *Newsweek* 109:36 Mr 23 '87
  Pentagon reviews trade pacts to standardize joint projects. J. D. Morrocco. il *Aviat Week Space Technol* 127:45+ O 19 '87
  Pretoria connection [Israeli arms sales to South Africa] H. Goodman. *New Repub* 196:20-1 Ap 20 '87
  A profitable irony of the war [Western Europe as supplier of arms to Iran] R. J. Gwyn. il *World Press Rev* 34:19-20 O '87
  Profiteering on the Iran-Iraq War. M. Brzoska. bibl f il *Bull At Sci* 43:42-5 Je '87

  Proposed Saudi sale spurs review of arms export controls. M. Mecham. *Aviat Week Space Technol* 126:69+ Mr 30 '87
  The Reagan revival of arms deals. W. D. Hartung. bibl f il *Bull At Sci* 43:20-5 Jl/Ag '87
  Rhetoric and reality in the Iranian arms trade. P. Gupte. il por *Forbes* 140:32-5 O 19 '87
  Russia: arms merchant to the world. P. Gupte. il *Forbes* 140:168+ N 2 '87
  The shame of the game [European arms sales to Iran] E. Clift. il *Newsweek* 110:44 S 21 '87
  Soviet weapons exports increase battlefield threat worldwide. il *Aviat Week Space Technol* 126:49 Ja 19 '87
  State Dept. faulted for poor control of munitions exports [Office of Munitions Control] *Aviat Week Space Technol* 127:30 S 21 '87
  Strict implementation of 1977 arms embargo against South Africa asked by Council. *UN Chron* 24:46 F '87
  U.S. weapon export sales face waning demand, rising competition. P. Mann. il *Aviat Week Space Technol* 126:134-5 F 9 '87
  Value of third-world arms pacts is lowest in eight years. P. Mann. il *Aviat Week Space Technol* 126:323-4 Je 15 '87
  The war business. J. R. Saul. il *World Press Rev* 34:19-21 Je '87
  Who arms Iran? Almost everyone. W. L. Chaze. il *U S News World Rep* 103:26-8 Ag 31 '87
  The world's greatest middleman [S. Eisenberg] H. Kestin. il pors *Forbes* 140 Sp Issue:98+ O 26 '87
  Your Constitution: can the president ban private arms sales? D. Pawelek. *Sch Update* 119:20 Mr 9 '87

Finance
  Aerospace and defense. H. Banks. il *Forbes* 139:64-5 Ja 12 '87
  Defense faces a slowdown—sort of. S. Toy. il *Bus Week* p69-70 Ja 12 '87
  The incredible shrinking business. il *Fortune* 115:68 F 16 '87

International aspects
  Defense Dept. will ask allies to fund cooperative projects. *Aviat Week Space Technol* 126:26 F 2 '87
  NATO arms cooperation enters critical period. M. Feazel. il *Aviat Week Space Technol* 126:77+ Mr 9 '87
  NATO to weigh long-term arms planning. *Aviat Week Space Technol* 126:18 Je 1 '87
  Navy evaluates Israeli R&D programs for use on U.S. weapon systems. M. Mecham. *Aviat Week Space Technol* 126:20-1 Je 1 '87
  Pentagon forms unit to coordinate arms projects with allies [Defense Cooperation Working Group] *Aviat Week Space Technol* 126:21 Ja 26 '87
  U.S. will propose structure to revive arms cooperation. *Aviat Week Space Technol* 126:82 Mr 30 '87

Quality control
  Defense Dept. acknowledges weak quality control. *Aviat Week Space Technol* 126:23 Ja 19 '87

Securities
  Investing in the dark [investors in black programs] M. Beauchamp. il *Forbes* 140:131+ S 21 '87
  Market focus. J. R. Stodden. See issues of Aviation Week & Space Technology beginning December 1, 1986

Canada
  Caught in the cross-fire [Canadian defense industry threatened by U.S. protectionism] M. Drohan. il *Macleans* 100:15 Mr 9 '87

China
  Peking guns for hard cash. F. Willey. il *Newsweek* 109:36 Mr 23 '87

Developing countries
  Nations vie for arms markets. W. D. Hartung. bibl f il *Bull At Sci* 43:27-35 D '87
  Value of third-world arms pacts is lowest in eight years. P. Mann. il *Aviat Week Space Technol* 126:323-4 Je 15 '87

France
    See also
    Matra SA
  France weighing value of political autonomy against trend toward defense cooperation. *Aviat Week Space Technol* 127:129+ O 12 '87

Great Britain
  British list top defense contractors. il *Aviat Week Space Technol* 127:69 Ag 17 '87

Iran
  A profitable irony of the war [Western Europe as supplier of arms to Iran] R. J. Gwyn. il *World Press Rev* 34:19-20 O '87

Munitions—Iran—cont.

The shame of the game [European arms sales to Iran]
E. Clift. il *Newsweek* 110:44 S 21 '87

Who arms Iran? Almost everyone. W. L. Chaze. il *U S News World Rep* 103:26-8 Ag 31 '87

Italy

See also
Valsella Meccanotecnica (Firm)

Japan

Japan, the armsmaker. P. Genet. *World Press Rev* 34:52-3 O '87

Sweden

See also
Bofors Nobel AB

Western Europe

IEPG seeks broader European arms market [Independent European Program Group] *Aviat Week Space Technol* 127:30 Jl 20 '87

NATO group recommends forming common European arms market. M. Feazel. *Aviat Week Space Technol* 126:18-19 F 23 '87

Munitions Control Office (U.S.) *See* United States. Office of Munitions Control

Munitions industries *See* Munitions

Munitions trade *See* Munitions—Export-import trade

Munk, Peter
about
Munk's glittering gamble. D. Jenish. il por *Macleans* 100:22-3 Ja 12 '87

Munn, Geoffrey C.
The jewelry of René Lalique. il *Antiques* 131:1288-91 Je '87

Muñoz, Alejandra
about
A split decision. il *Time* 129:66 Mr 9 '87

Muñoz, Annette Lopez- *See* Lopez-Muñoz, Annette

Munro, Alice
Oh, what avails [story] *New Yorker* 63:42-52+ N 16 '87

Munro, J. Richard
Whose business is defense? [address, January 16, 1987] *Vital Speeches Day* 53:360-2 Ap 1 '87
about
Time's Nick & Dick show [cover story] B. Nussbaum. il pors *Bus Week* p54-7+ Ag 3 '87

Münster (Germany)
Monuments, statues, etc.
Essen: Scenes; Münster: Sculptural projects. M. Hübl. il *Art News* 86:200 O '87
Sighted in Münster [Skulptur projekte exhibition] E. Heartney. il *Art Am* 75:140-3+ S '87

Münter, Gabriele, 1877-1962
about
Murnau and Kochel: where the Blue Rider was born. J. Dornberg. il pors *Art News* 86:77-8+ D '87

Muons *See* Particles (Nuclear physics)

Mura, David
Grandfather and grandmother in love [poem] *Nation* 244:545 Ap 25 '87

Mural painting and decoration
See also
Cave drawings and paintings
Frescoes
Photographic murals
Art underground [mural art in the subways of Brussels] B. Grauman. il *Art News* 86:69-70 My '87
Painting in medieval England: the wall-to-wall message. P. Tudor-Craig. bibl il *Hist Today* 37:39-45 N '87
Pattern & decoration in the public eye [J. Kozloff's large tile and mosaic murals in public spaces] S. Webster. il *Art Am* 75:118-25 F '87
Politics outlives art [controversy surrounding murals by A. Mason and M. Spafford for the state capitol in Olympia, Wash.] L. Smallwood. il *Art News* 86:28 D '87

Conservation and restoration
A master painter and his aging collective bring life and color back to the Catherine Palace [Y. Kazakov] S. K. Reed. il pors *People Wkly* 27:92-4+ Ap 6 '87
Restoring Mexican murals. *Américas* 39:56 Mr/Ap '87
Restoring The Last Supper. il *Travel Holiday* 168:54 S '87
Up against the walls [New York City murals] K. Larson. il *N Y* 20:46-51 F 2 '87

Murarka, Dev
A new revolution in consciousness. il *Nation* 245:486-8+ O 31 '87
Recovering the buried Stalin years [cover story] il *Nation* 245:433+ O 24 '87

Muravchik, Joshua
Maximum feasible containment. *New Repub* 196:23-5 Je 1 '87
What is to be done? *New Repub* 197:16-17 N 30 '87

Muravchik, Joshua, and others
Sandinista anti-Semitism [discussion of September 1986 article, Sandinista anti-Semitism and its apologists] *Commentary* 83:2+ Ja '87

Murch, Walter Tandy, 1907-1967
about
Walter Murch at the Whitney Museum at Philip Morris and Sid Deutsch. P. Smith. *Art Am* 75:145-6 F '87

Murchison meteorite *See* Meteorites

Murder
See also
Assassination
Capital punishment
Euthanasia
Howard Beach case
Lynching
Parents of murdered children
Popieluszko, Jerzy—Murder case
Small, Stephen, d. 1987—Kidnapping
Steinberg, Elizabeth, d. 1987—Child abuse case
Trials (Murder)
Alabama man cleared of murder 15 years later [case of B. J. Leaster] il por *Jet* 71:26 Ja 19 '87
Atlanta probes murder mystery of black wife of white millionaire [murder of L. M. Sullivan] D. M. Cheers. il pors *Jet* 72:24-7 My 25 '87
Auguries of innocence [K. Buckner posthumously cleared of murdering his family in Elkland, Mo.] L. Zuckerman. il por *Time* 130:21 O 19 '87
Bitter memories of murder [movie River's edge recalls murder and coverup by Milpitas, Calif. teens] P. Abramson. il *Newsweek* 109:25 Je 22 '87
Black Nashville youth killed by whites over $2 vase at flea market [K. Majors] *Jet* 72:36 Je 15 '87
Black women report of sex, torture, murder at hands of white Philadelphia 'bishop' [G. Heidnik case] il por *Jet* 72:6-7 Ap 13 '87
Blood and money: the unsolved murder of a Long Island woman leads to a novel suit against her husband [case of M. S. Schwartz] M. Ryan. il pors *N Y* 20:38-44 Je 8 '87
A bloody rage in rural England [M. Ryan's shooting spree in Hungerford] il *U S News World Rep* 103:11 Ag 31 '87
Breaking the crack murders [solving the murder of a crack dealer in Brooklyn] R. Rosenbaum. il *N Y Times Mag* p44-6+ N 15 '87
Brutal treatment, vicious deeds [C. Pierson and other abused children who murder their parents] J. D. Hull. il por *Time* 130:68 O 19 '87
Carnage at a shopping mall [W. Cruse's killing spree in Palm Bay, Fla.] *Macleans* 100:24 My 4 '87
The case against Brian Spencer [accused of M. Dalfo's murder in Palm Beach Gardens, Fla.] P. Dexter. il *Sports Illus* 66:98-102+ My 11 '87
Casting a net at Green River [serial murderer manhunt in Washington State] C. Garcia. il *Time* 130:61 Jl 27 '87
The child custody murder [battle for P. A. Taylor] P. Maas. il pors *Good Housekeep* 205:154-5+ O '87
Claude Dallas update. R. P. Stuart. por *Outdoor Life* 179:49 Mr '87
The con man [FBI informer M. Raymond] M. A. Farber. il por *N Y Times Mag* p34+ Je 21 '87
Could they get away with murder? [E. Woodward and A. Woodward] B. Darrach. il pors *People Wkly* 27:52-4+ F 16 '87
Countdown to the electric chair [18-year-old killer P. Cooper] F. Bruning. por *Macleans* 100:13 O 26 '87
Crack murder: a detective story [solving the murder of a crack dealer in Brooklyn] R. Rosenbaum. il pors *N Y Times Mag* p24-30+ F 15 '87
D.C. police seek black van linked to murdered women [Suitland, Md. murders] *Jet* 71:17 F 2 '87
David Burke's deadly revenge [fired USAir employee causes PSA jet to crash] E. Magnuson. il por *Time* 130:30 D 21 '87
Deaf-mute must stay in mental hospital for 1971 slaying in Chicago [case of D. Lang] *Jet* 72:17 Je 8 '87
A death at work can put the boss in jail [homicide conviction against Sabine Consolidated Inc.] J. Tasini. *Bus Week* p37-8 Mr 2 '87
Dial om for murder [involvement of guru Bhaktipada in murder of S. Bryant] J. Hubner and L. Gruson. il pors *Roll Stone* p53-4+ Ap 9 '87

Murder—*cont.*

Don Aronow's murder leaves Miami wondering: were 'Cigarettes' hazardous to his health? J. Hammer. il por *People Wkly* 27:75-6+ Mr 30 '87

Epidemic of murder [Vancouver, B.C. murders thought to be linked to Washington State serial murderer] J. O'Hara. *Macleans* 100:12 Jl 20 '87

Etta Smith's inspiration cost her four days in jail [vision of victim's body in Pacoima section of Los Angeles] J. Kelley. il por *People Wkly* 27:33 My 25 '87

Ex-boyfriend beheads teen girl with samurai sword in New York [E. Rodrique kills J. Mentor] por *Jet* 72:17 Je 8 '87

Exercising her right to madness, accused killer Gena Spero poses a legal problem without a solution [pleading insanity] J. S. Kunen. il pors *People Wkly* 28:115-16+ O 5 '87

Exploring an injustice [inquiry into Sydney, N.S. conviction of D. Marshall] M. Gee. *Macleans* 100:29 O 19 '87

Family business: murder would settle it, and Debra Banister knew who to ask [hit man J. W. Hearn] J. Wadler. il pors *People Wkly* 28:57-8+ Jl 6 '87

The Fat Man: the life and high times of Irwin Schiff [cover story] M. Daly. il pors *N Y* 20:46-61 O 19 '87

Fears of a serial killer [Edmonton, Alta.] *Macleans* 100:14 Ap 13 '87

Find 7 bodies in Philly, jail tenant [case of H. Graham] *Jet* 72:18 Ag 31 '87

Georgia sisters indicted for their mother's murder [R. Golden and M. Collier] *Jet* 73:47 N 2 '87

Gunman seen as key to crash of PSA flight that killed 43 [D. A. Burke] M. A. Dornheim. il *Aviat Week Space Technol* 127:31 D 14 '87

A hand from the grave [E. LeBaron and the polygamy murders case] P. Abramson. il pors *Newsweek* 110:45 D 21 '87

Hidden histories on death row [neurological disorders and homicidal behavior; study of death row juveniles by Dorothy Otnow Lewis] *Sci News* 132:287 O 31 '87

Hold Georgia physician in death of white patient [V. D. Mallory held in murder of S. Fields] *Jet* 72:4 My 11 '87

House of horrors [murderer G. Heidnik in Philadelphia] por *Time* 129:34 Ap 6 '87

Houston man waits in dark, kills assailant [B. Gibson slays man who had robbed him of his social security money] *Jet* 72:12 Ag 24 '87

Husband tosses wife 18 stories in heated dispute [J. Burgos] *Jet* 73:32 O 26 '87

I didn't kill Dian. She was my friend [murder of gorilla protector D. Fossey]; ed. by Beverly Trainer and Gina Maranto. W. McGuire. il pors maps *Discover* 8:28-32+ F '87

In Detroit, kids kill kids [searching students for weapons used in school-related attacks] E. Salholz. il *Newsweek* 109:74 My 11 '87

In Idaho: a killer becomes a mythic hero [C. Dallas] M. Riley. il por *Time* 129:10-11 Ja 26 '87

In Manson's eyes [interview with C. Manson] R. Healy. il pors *Life* 10:54-6 Mr '87

In the shadows a killer waited [M. Chapman's murder of J. Lennon] J. R. Gaines. il por *People Wkly* 27:50-2+ Mr 2 '87

Indiana killer, Italian martyr [Italians show support for juvenile killer P. Cooper] G. Hackett. il por *Newsweek* 110:37 S 21 '87

A killer still on the loose [Green River serial murderer] M. Ryan. il *People Wkly* 28:24-9 Ag 24 '87

The killer takes his fall [M. Chapman, murderer of J. Lennon] J. R. Gaines. il por *People Wkly* 27:60-2+ Mr 9 '87

The lady killer: should Jean Harris go free? B. G. Harrison. *Mademoiselle* 93:164 Ag '87

A Latter-Day forger [Mormon M. Hofmann pleads guilty to murder] A. Wilentz. il por *Time* 129:32 F 2 '87

Legacy of a mother's murder [custody battle for P. A. Taylor] P. Maas. il pors *N Y Times Mag* p40-4+ Ap 12 '87

Lethal doses [orderly D. Harvey accused of 34 murders at various hospitals in Cincinnati] por *Time* 130:17 Ag 24 '87

Life with father was nasty, brutish and scary, so Johnny Junatanov tried to have him murdered—repeatedly. A. Richman. il pors *People Wkly* 27:83+ Ja 19 '87

Little Boy Blue of Chester, Nebraska [child found dead by roadside] H. Hurt. *Read Dig* 131:73-8 D '87

A little house of horrors [murderer G. Heidnik in Philadelphia] T. E. Johnson. il por *Newsweek* 109:29 Ap 6 '87

Long Island's 'angel of death' [male nurse R. Angelo charged with murder of patients at Good Samaritan Hospital in West Islip, N.Y.] D. Gates. il por *Newsweek* 110:35 N 30 '87

Machine gunman, high on crack, pumps 26 fatal bullets into boy, 3 [murder of L. Horris in Brooklyn] por *Jet* 73:36 D 7 '87

A made-for-television movie brings biathlete Kari Swenson face-to-face with her past. M. Neill. il pors *People Wkly* 27:76-8+ Mr 16 '87

The man who shot Lennon [M. Chapman] J. R. Gaines. il pors *People Wkly* 27:58-60+ F 23 '87

The market-day massacre [Hungerford, England] B. Levin. il *Macleans* 100:20 Ag 31 '87

Mass murder in the clouds [D. A. Burke and crash of PSA Flight 1771] M. Satchell. il por *U S News World Rep* 103:14-15 D 21 '87

Master of cant and recant [serial murderer H. L. Lucas] R. Lacayo. por *Time* 129:66 Ja 12 '87

More intrigue involved in Peter Tosh's murder. por *Jet* 73:32 O 26 '87

Murder as usual [Mt. Pleasant, Iowa] N. Pearson. il *Progressive* 51:50 F '87

Murder hits home [murder of school principal W. H. Donahue of Highland Park, N.J.] S. G. Freedman. il *N Y Times Mag* p20+ My 31 '87

Murder in mind [neurological disorders and homicidal behavior; study of death row juveniles by Dorothy Otnow Lewis] J. Meer. *Psychol Today* 21:62 Mr '87

Murder in mind [views of homicide authority D. Archer] J. Wilkes. il pors *Psychol Today* 21:26-8+ Je '87

A murder mystery [murder of M. Taddeo, subject of Mirabel Airport land sales investigation] L. Van Dusen. por *Macleans* 100:19-20 D 21 '87

The new kid [undercover narcotics cop G. Raffield murdered at Midlothian High School in Texas] por *Time* 130:61 N 9 '87

The nightmare of his mother's murder is echoed in James Ellroy's grisly new novel, The black dahlia. S. Dougherty. il pors *People Wkly* 28:122-4 D 14 '87

Pennsylvania gothic [death of K. Umstadter in alcohol-related traffic accident results in her brother's murdering of driver in Honesdale] G. Hackett. il por *Newsweek* 110:27 Ag 17 '87

Philadelphia's house of horrors [arrest of G. Heidnik] il *U S News World Rep* 102:11 Ap 6 '87

Primed to kill, an angry young man shoots his dead sister's boyfriend, leaving two families in ruins [T. Umstadter kills G. Evans] J. Hammer. il *People Wkly* 28:159-60+ N 16 '87

Reggae great Peter Tosh murdered. M. Goldberg. por *Roll Stone* p24+ O 22 '87

Reggae star Peter Tosh fatally shot in Jamaica. por *Jet* 73:62 S 28 '87

Search for a serial killer [Ontario] R. Corelli. il *Macleans* 100:54 O 5 '87

Settling a score [murders aboard PSA airliner linked to USAir ex-employee D. Burke] G. Hackett. il por *Newsweek* 110:43 D 21 '87

A shocking arrest breaks the case of a Missouri farm family's murder—and rescues a boy's reputation [J. Schnick charged; K. Buckner cleared] M. Green. il pors *People Wkly* 28:101-2+ O 26 '87

Strange and contradictory testimony [testimony of R. N. Ebsary at inquiry into Sydney, N.S. murder conviction of D. Marshall] M. Gee. il pors *Macleans* 100:23 S 21 '87

The tale of a remarkably loyal husband [S. Creviston linked to attempted murder of J. Creviston] *Newsweek* 110:45 D 21 '87

A tale of two Minnesota mothers: one seeks the truth behind their son's death, the other stands accused [investigation into death of Dennis Jurgens] D. Chu. il pors *People Wkly* 27:28-31 Mr 2 '87

A teenager's tragedy: birth and death in a Florida town [M. Clark charged with murder of her newborn child in Golden Gate] C. Mitchell and T. Burdick. il por *Ms* 16:60-3 D '87

They shoot only in America, don't they? [M. Ryan's killing spree in Hungerford, England] por *Newsweek* 110:34 Ag 31 '87

The three lives of . . . Marie Hilley [excerpt from Poisoned blood] P. E. Ginsburg. il pors *Good Housekeep* 205:148-9+ N '87

Three police killed in shootout near Detroit. il *Jet* 72:8 Jl 27 '87

Murder—*cont.*

A torch held on high [legacy of murdered priest R. Grande in El Salvador] J. R. Brockman. *America* 156:214-16+ Mr 14 '87

Two Georgia sisters held for their mother's murder [M. Collier and R. Golden held in murder of Frances Golden] il pors *Jet* 72:32 Ag 17 '87

Unmasking a murderous mother, crime writer Ann Rule closes the book on another psychopath [case of D. Downs] M. Brower. il pors *People Wkly* 28:125 S 14 '87

Urban murders: on the rise [cocaine-related killings] T. E. Johnson. il *Newsweek* 109:30 F 9 '87

A vision of murder [S. Linscott tried for murder on basis of dream] M. Green. il pors *People Wkly* 27:30-2 My 25 '87

Wednesday, bloody Wednesday [gunman M. Ryan in Hungerford, England] C. Ogden. il *Time* 130:27 Ag 31 '87

Why are there Angels in the Dells? [Guardian Angels in Wisconsin] il *Newsweek* 110:21 Ag 24 '87

Why our children are killing one another. A. Poinsett. il *Ebony* 43:88+ D '87

Winning back a child [custody battle for P. A. Taylor concludes] P. Maas. il por *N Y Times Mag* p42+ Je 7 '87

Women right to kill men who brutalize them: group [Committee on Domestic Violence and Incarcerated Women] *Jet* 72:28 Jl 13 '87

Murder board (Term)

Murder board at the skunk works. W. Safire. il *N Y Times Mag* p18+ O 11 '87

Murder in the cathedral [opera] See Pizzetti, Ildebrando, 1880-1968

Murder mystery plays See Detective and mystery plays

Murder mystery stories See Detective and mystery stories

Murderers See Murder

Murdoch, Anna
about
The woman who stands up to him. T. Moore. il por *Fortune* 116:94 Jl 6 '87

Murdoch, Rupert
about
Citizen Murdoch makes his mark in books and television. D. Pauly. il por *Newsweek* 109:47+ Ap 13 '87

Citizen Murdoch presses for more. T. Moore. il pors *Fortune* 116:90-6 Jl 6 '87

A media magnate on a buying spree. M. Janigan. il por *Macleans* 100:40 Ja 12 '87

Murdoch increases stake in Pearson conglomerate to 14.7%. V. Menkes. *Publ Wkly* 232:28 O 9 '87

Murdoch to sell half of Harper & Row to Collins, to become co-chairman. J. Mutter and V. Menkes. *Publ Wkly* 232:70 S 18 '87

Pearson in a pickle. S. Miller. *Bus Week* p60 O 12 '87

Rupert Murdoch. R. Grover. il por *Bus Week* Sp Issue:246 Ap 17 '87

Rupert Murdoch, can we talk? R. Grover. il por *Bus Week* p50 Je 1 '87

Rupert Murdoch to acquire Harper & Row for $65 a share. M. Reuter. il por *Publ Wkly* 231:16-17 Ap 10 '87

Tally-ho, Rupert [interview] M. Brown and R. Buck. il pors *Channels* 7:70-1 Ja '87

"We'll get back to you on that". R. Behar. il *Forbes* 139:42+ Ap 6 '87

Murdock, David H.
about
Bellagio House: the David Murdock estate in Bel-Air. M. M. Thomas. il por *Archit Dig* 44:52-61 F '87

David Murdock is picking plums. T. Carson. il por *Bus Week* p43 O 12 '87

"I just make ideas happen". J. Heins. il por *Forbes* 140 Sp Issue:32-5 O 26 '87

Murdock, Gabriele, 1941?-1985
about
Bellagio House: the David Murdock estate in Bel-Air. M. M. Thomas. il por *Archit Dig* 44:52-61 F '87

Murie, Olaus Johan, 1889-1963
about
The natural magic of Olaus Murie. J. Glover and R. Glover. il pors *Sierra* 72:69-73 S/O '87

Muriqui monkey sexual behavior See Sexual behavior—Animals

Muriqui monkeys See Monkeys

Murkowski, Frank H.
Should Congress move to invoke the War Powers Resolution? [excerpts from debate, October 9, 1987] *Congr Dig* 66:300+ D '87

Murnau (Germany)
Historic houses, sites, etc.
Murnau and Kochel: where the Blue Rider was born. J. Dornberg. il pors *Art News* 86:77-8+ D '87

Muro, Jim
about
Street trash [film] Reviews
Theatre Crafts il 21:20 N '87. J. Calhoun

Murph the Surf See Murphy, Jack

Murphy, Ann Pleshette
When I was grieving. il *Glamour* 85:302 My '87

Murphy, Austin
Another case of the South Bends. il *Sports Illus* 66:32-4 Mr 9 '87

The Battle of Quebec. il *Sports Illus* 66:20-5 My 4 '87

The Bear bit the Badger. il *Sports Illus* 67:24-5 S 14 '87

A bloody mess. il *Sports Illus* 66:24-6+ Mr 30 '87

Break up the Colts! [cover story] il *Sports Illus* 67:18-23 N 9 '87

A burden gallantly borne. il pors *Sports Illus* 67:26-7 D 21 '87

Capital punishment. il *Sports Illus* 66:26-8+ Ap 27 '87

Doing time in the pen. il *Sports Illus* 67:88-91 Jl 6 '87

Edgy from lack of Coffey. il *Sports Illus* 67:26-7 N 16 '87

Edmonton's Rx for D. il pors *Sports Illus* 66:42-4 My 25 '87

Grand grapple in the Midwest. il *Sports Illus* 66:20-1 Mr 2 '87

Having a Devil of a time. il *Sports Illus* 67:20-1 N 23 '87

Hot shots on ice [cover story] il por *Sports Illus* 66:26-9 Je 1 '87

It's still a gusher. il *Sports Illus* 67:102-4+ O 12 '87

Make way for Hartford. il *Sports Illus* 66:69-70 Mr 23 '87

New model in Motown. il pors *Sports Illus* 66:30-2 Mr 16 '87

A new set of Twins. il *Sports Illus* 67:36-8+ Jl 27 '87

One for the books. il *Sports Illus* 67 Sp Issue:96-9 N 18 '87

Party time in Edmonton. il *Sports Illus* 66:22-5 Je 8 '87

Playing for lunch money. il *Sports Illus* 67:50-2+ D 21 '87

Playing two for the show. il *Sports Illus* 67:74+ S 21 '87

Running for redemption. il pors *Sports Illus* 67:103-4 O 26 '87

A series with punch. il *Sports Illus* 66:82+ Ap 20 '87

The shooter and the stopper. il *Sports Illus* 66:42-3 My 18 '87

Steamin' Stanley. il pors *Sports Illus* 67 Sp Issue:86-8+ S 9 '87

Those low-flying Flyers. il *Sports Illus* 67:44-6+ D 7 '87

about
From the publisher. D. J. Barr. il por *Sports Illus* 66:4 My 4 '87

Murphy, Brendan
A nation of readers. il *Atlantic* 260:21-5 Ag '87

Murphy, Brian Alfred
about
Building his own bridges. J. Giovannini. il *House Gard* 159:112-21+ Mr '87

Murphy, Cait
The game's still afoot. il *Atlantic* 259:58-62+ Mr '87

Murphy, Caryle
Congress wakes up to Medicare reform. il *50 Plus* 27:26-9 Ap '87

Murphy, Cullen
A blaze of glory. il *Atlantic* 259:16+ Ap '87
Deliverance. il *Atlantic* 260:22+ N '87
Going to the cats. il *Atlantic* 260:14+ Ag '87
Life in the slow lane. il *Read Dig* 130:47-8 Ap '87
The longest day. il *Atlantic* 259:14+ Je '87
The speech. il *Atlantic* 260:20 D '87

Murphy, Dale
about
A man who can't say no. P. Gammons. il pors *Sports Illus* 67:16-17 D 21 '87

Murphy, Denis
Peace in the Philippines. *America* 156:406-8 My 16 '87

Murphy, Eddie
about
Eddie Murphy hit with paternity suit in L.A. por *Jet* 72:56 My 25 '87

Murphy, Eddie—about—cont.

Eddie Murphy scores again with 'Beverly Hills cop II' [cover story] il pors *Jet* 72:56-8 Je 15 '87

Eddie Murphy's dad and black promoter now book comedian's concert tour. il pors *Jet* 73:28-30 O 19 '87

Free Eddie Murphy. D. Handelman. il por *Roll Stone* p27-9 Jl 2 '87

Jury selection under way in Eddie Murphy dispute. *Jet* 71:16 Mr 23 '87

Murphy settles battle with ex-manager out of court. il por *Jet* 72:54 Ap 6 '87

Murphy to do 'Fences' as part of new Paramount contract worth millions. il por *Jet* 72:56 S 14 '87

Murphy's law. E. Sherman. por *Ladies Home J* 104:84 My '87

Yo, Broder! Eddie Murphy has to pay the King's ransom. K. Gross. il pors *People Wkly* 27:103-4+ Ap 13 '87

Murphy, Erin

Alaskan adventure. map *Seventeen* 46:90+ D '87

Murphy, Jack

about

Murph the Surf rides again. J. Lombardi. il por *Esquire* 108:114-16+ N '87

Murphy, Jill, 1949-

Five minutes' peace [story] il *Parents* 62:147-8+ O '87

Murphy, Kevin J.

Do you spend too much time in meetings? [excerpt from Effective listening] *Work Woman* 12:30 D '87

Murphy, Kevin P.

Where do article ideas come from? *Writer* 100:28-9 Ag '87

Murphy, Richard W.

Assistant Secretary Murphy's interview on "Meet the press" [transcript of program, August 23, 1987] *Dep State Bull* 87:44-8 O '87

FY 1988 assistance requests for the Middle East and South Asia [statement, March 23, 1987] *Dep State Bull* 87:59-64 My '87

Middle East activities [statement, July 28, 1987] *Dep State Bull* 87:45-8 S '87

Middle East developments [statement, April 21, 1987] *Dep State Bull* 87:70-2 Je '87

Pakistan and the nuclear issue [statement, July 22, 1987] *Dep State Bull* 87:53-4 O '87

The Persian Gulf: stakes and risks [statement, May 29, 1987] *Dep State Bull* 87:64-7 Jl '87

Supporting U.S. interests in the Middle East [statement, October 8, 1986] *Dep State Bull* 86:70-2 D '86

Murphy, Thomas S.

about

An exception to Murphy's Law? S. N. Chakravarty. il por *Forbes* 140:36-8 Ag 10 '87

Not ready for prime time? G. Fabrikant. il pors *N Y Times Mag* p30+ Ap 12 '87

Murphy, Timothy F.

Winning against whining. il *Parents* 62:110-12 Ag '87

Murphy, Walter F., 1929-

The Constitution and the 14th Amendment [with discussion] il por *Cent Mag* 20:9-30 Jl/Ag '87

Murray, Alan S., 1954-

about

Inside tax reform. P. Glastris. *Wash Mon* 19:52-6 Je '87

Murray, Allen Edward

about

Oil king from Queens. D. Kirkpatrick. il por *Fortune* 116:30 Ag 3 '87

Murray, Andrew W., and Szostak, Jack W.

Artificial chromosomes. bibl (p150) il *Sci Am* 257:62-6+ N '87

Murray, Charles A.

about

Will reform work? Two experts debate [interview] M. Christopher. pors *Sch Update* 119:20 Mr 23 '87

Murray, David, 1955-

about

David Murray [with discography] G. Santoro. *Nation* 244:554-6 Ap 25 '87

David Murray Orchestra & Strings. F. Bouchard. il por *Down Beat* 54:52-3 F '87

Murray, Donald Morison, 1924-

When I retire . . . *Writer* 100:5-6 F '87

Murray, Elizabeth

about

Abstraction and Popeye's biceps. R. Hughes. il por *Time* 130:65 Jl 13 '87

Elizabeth Murray. J. Kutner. il *Art News* 86:45-6 My '87

Elizabeth Murray at Paula Cooper. S. Tillim. il *Art Am* 75:177 O '87

Elizabeth Murray: the shape of things to come. B. Rose. il por *Vogue* 177:224-5+ Jl '87

Murray, Jean Ritter- *See* Ritter-Murray, Jean

Murray, Jonn

about

The Christmas Island Phosphate Company. A. L. Rice. bibl il por map *Sea Front* 33:444-53 N/D '87

Murray, Les A., 1938-

Max Fabre's yachts [poem] *N Y Rev Books* 34:25 D 3 '87

The Megaethon: 1850, 1906-1929 [poem] il *Atlantic* 260:74-5 S '87

Mercurial September [poem] *N Y Rev Books* 34:25 D 3 '87

Murray, Linda

Sexual destinies. il *Omni* 9:100-2+ Ap '87

Murray, Mary

VB 8B or not VB 8B? il *Space World* X-3-279:27-9 Mr '87

Murray, Pauli, 1910-1985

about

Song in a weary throat. N. S. Montgomery. *Christ Century* 104:828+ S 30 '87

Murray, Thomas H.

The growing danger from gene-spliced hormones. il *Discover* 8:88+ F '87

Murray, William, 1926-

Letter from Monaco. *New Yorker* 63:96-108 O 5 '87

Letter from Sperlonga. *New Yorker* 63:94-103 Mr 30 '87

Letter from the Ticino. *New Yorker* 63:61+ Je 1 '87

Murray Hill (New York, N.Y.)

Murray Hill: mansions with pedigrees from the Age of Innocence. C. Jakobson. il map *N Y* 20:42-4 My 4 '87

Murray Louis Dance Company

News watch [performance of Black and white at the Joyce Theater, New York City] T. Tobias. il *N Y* 20:80-1 Ap 6 '87

Reviews:

Performances at the Joyce Theater, New York City. K. Onoda. il *Dance Mag* 61:18-19 N '87

Murray Ohio Mfg. Co.

Lots of eggs, several baskets. K. Hannon. il *Forbes* 139:75 Ap 20 '87

Murres

Murre mysteries. F. Graham. il map *Audubon* 89:16+ Ja '87

Seabird citadels of the Arctic [thick-billed murres] A. J. Gaston. il *Nat Hist* 96:54-9 Ap '87

Murrow, Edward R.

about

Seeing Murrow now. G. C. Ward. il *Am Herit* 38:16+ F/Mr '87

Murrow, Liza K.

Summer camp and compost. il *Ctry J* 14:61-8 Ja '87

Muscarinic receptors *See* Chemoreceptors

Muscat wines *See* Wine

Muschamp, Herbert

The L.A. Museum of Contemporary Art: what's in a name? il *Archit Rec* 175:83+ My '87

The temple of marketing. il *New Repub* 197:25-8 O 26 '87

Muschg, Adolf, 1934-

Staying alive by learning to write. il *N Y Times Book Rev* 92:1+ F 1 '87

Muscle

See also

Heart—Muscle

Ligaments

Tendons

Basic muscle moves. J. Mandelbaum-Schmid. il *Vogue* 177:370-1+ Ap '87

Corkscrew-like shortening in single smooth muscle cells. D. M. Warshaw and others. bibl f il *Science* 236:1457-9 Je 12 '87

Fat & muscle. R. B. Pearce. il *Women's Sports Fitness* 9:36-9 Jl '87

How food/fitness breakthroughs can take you from mush to muscle. il *Glamour* 85:312-15 My '87

Mitogens and oncogenes can block the induction of specific voltage-gated ion channels. J. M. Caffrey and others. bibl f il *Science* 236:570-3 My 1 '87

Muscle balance [women athletes] S. Zakin. il *Women's Sports Fitness* 9:38-41 My '87

Skin reborn from muscle [research by Ioannis Yannas] S. Weisburd. *Sci News* 132:164 S 12 '87

Muscle—*cont.*
Smooth-muscle cells: twist and clout [research by David M. Warshaw and others] S. Weisburd. il *Sci News* 131:389 Je 20 '87
Stand tall against osteoporosis [link with back muscles] il *Prevention* 39:6 Je '87

Diseases
See also
Muscular dystrophy

Proteins
See also
Actin
Myoglobin
Vinculin

Transplantation
Skeletal muscle as the potential power source for a cardiovascular pump: assessment in vivo. M. A. Acker and others. bibl f il *Science* 236:324-7 Ap 17 '87

Wounds and injuries
Electricity may have the potential to heal injured back muscles. *Prevention* 39:63 O '87
Super-C for hunters and dogs [preventing muscle soreness] L. Mueller. il *Outdoor Life* 180:76+ S '87

Muscle contraction
See also
Heart—Muscle—Contraction
Corkscrew-like shortening in single smooth muscle cells. D. M. Warshaw and others. bibl f il *Science* 236:1457-9 Je 12 '87
It is diprotonated inorganic phosphate that depresses force in skinned skeletal muscle fibers. T. M. Nosek and others. bibl f il *Science* 236:191-3 Ap 10 '87
Laser-stimulated luminescence used to measure X-ray diffraction of a contracting striated muscle. Y. Amemiya and others. bibl f il *Science* 237:164-8 Jl 10 '87
Myosin rod phosphorylation and the catch state of molluscan muscles. L. Castellani and C. Cohen. bibl f il *Science* 235:334-7 Ja 16 '87
Peptide turn-on for the ACh receptor gene [research by Jean-Pierre Changeux and others] D. M. Barnes. *Science* 238:1652-3 D 18 '87
Regional changes in calcium underlying contraction of single smooth muscle cells. D. A. Williams and others. bibl f il *Science* 235:1644-8 Mr 27 '87
Smooth-muscle cells: twist and clout [research by David M. Warshaw and others] S. Weisburd. il *Sci News* 131:389 Je 20 '87

Muscle powered aircraft *See* Human powered aircraft

Muscle strength
See also
Body building
Are your muscles old before their time? [excerpt from Dr. Nagler's Body maintenance and repair book] W. Nagler. il *Women's Sports Fitness* 9:68 Ap '87
How fit—muscles. il *Good Housekeep* 204:92 My '87
The mysterious world of strength. T. Osborne. il *Curr Health 2* 13:20-1 Ja '87
Pink and blue: the power of suggestion [influence of color on strength; research by Jeffrey M. Smith] P. McCarthy. *Psychol Today* 21:24-5 Jl '87

Muscle stretch *See* Stretch (Physiology); Stretching exercises

Muscular dystrophy
Muscular dystrophy: defective inhibitor? *Sci News* 131:41 Ja 17 '87
Sammy Davis and Jerry Lewis star on telethon to fight muscular dystrophy [cover story] il pors *Jet* 72:60-1 S 7 '87

Diagnosis
A new probe for the diagnosis of myotonic muscular dystrophy. R. J. Bartlett and others. bibl f il *Science* 235:1648-50 Mr 27 '87

Genetic aspects
Conservation of the Duchenne muscular dystrophy gene in mice and humans. E. P. Hoffman and others. bibl f il *Science* 238:347-50 O 16 '87
Molecular analysis of a constitutional X-autosome translocation in a female with muscular dystrophy. S. E. Bodrug and others. bibl f il *Science* 237:1620-4 S 25 '87
Progress toward eliminating a killer [Duchenne muscular dystrophy] R. Corelli. il *Macleans* 100:49 Ag 10 '87

Therapy
Steroid helpful in muscular dystrophy [prednisone] *Sci News* 132:120 Ag 22 '87
War on muscular dystrophy achieves a first [use of prednisone] J. Silberner. il *U S News World Rep* 103:12 Ag 17 '87

Muscular power *See* Muscle strength
Muse-Cordero-Chen & Baca Advertising
Mingo-Jones affiliate makes historic merger. il *Jet* 71:33 F 9 '87

Musée des Arts Décoratifs (Paris, France)
Art deco rooms at the Musée des Arts Décoratifs. O. Bernier. il *Antiques* 132:776-81 O '87
Musée d'Orsay (Paris, France)
Amazing space. B. Rose. il *Vogue* 177:394-401+ F '87
The Aulenti uproar. C. Vogel. il por *N Y Times Mag* p26-32+ N 22 '87
The avant-garde and the academy: an exchange [discussion of February 26, 1987 article, The judgment of Paris] C. Rosen and H. Zerner. *N Y Rev Books* 34:48-9 Jl 16 '87
A critic's complaints. B. Bernard. *World Press Rev* 34:62 F '87
From Paris, with love, a new palace for art now shines on the Seine. B. Conrad, III. il *Smithsonian* 17:82-8+ Mr '87
The judgment of Paris. C. Rosen and H. Zerner. il *N Y Rev Books* 34:21-5 F 26 '87
Missed connections [G. Aulenti's design] C. K. Gandee. il por *Archit Rec* 175:128-39 Mr '87
The Musée d'Orsay: a new and different 19th century. M. Gibson. il *Art News* 86:142-6 Ap '87
Musée extraordinaire. P. L. Buckley. il *Horizon* 30:11-13 Mr '87
The new temples of art. P. Young. il *Macleans* 100:82-3 F 2 '87
Paris journal. C. P. Reynolds. il *Gourmet* 47:28+ Ap '87
A train station becomes a major museum. il *World Press Rev* 34:61-2 F '87
Whose century was it, anyway? J. Perl. *New Repub* 197:30-3 N 2 '87
Musée du Louvre
Balladur's last stand. B. Grauman. il *Art News* 86:39 D '87
Tour of Louvre from Stewart Tabori & Chang. il *Publ Wkly* 231:250 My 15 '87
Musée Napoléonien (Fontainebleau, France)
Musée Napoléon Premier, Fontainebleau. P. Mansel. il *Hist Today* 37:62-3 S '87
Musée van Buuren (Brussels, Belgium)
Artful traveler. B. Grauman. il *Art News* 86:75-6 S '87
Museo Oro del Peru
All that glitters [cover story] P. E. Rogers. il *Américas* 39:8-13 Mr/Ap '87
Musetto, Vincent
Tots nix blazing coeds!; ed. by David Van Biema. il por *People Wkly* 27:65+ Je 1 '87
Museum conservation methods
Behind the scenes at the Smithsonian. D. Young. il *South Living* 22:173-4+ N '87
Museum directors
See also
Guillaud, Jacqueline
Guillaud, Maurice
Klindt, Steven
Krens, Thomas
Lawton, Thomas, 1931-
Smith, Paul J.
The great director chase [art museums] il *U S News World Rep* 102:72 Ap 27 '87

Attitudes
Representing realist artists [views of gallery directors] P. Van Gelder. il *Am Artist* 51:64-9+ My '87
Museum exhibits
See also
Paleontological models and exhibits
Museum für Deutsche Geschichte (Berlin, Germany: East)
Reichstag Museum and Museum of German History. I. R. Mitchell. il *Hist Today* 37:61 Ag '87
Museum of American Folk Art
Amish quilts in the Museum of American Folk Art. E. V. Warren. bibl f il *Antiques* 132:514-23 S '87
Museum of Appalachia
John Rice Irwin's gift of the past. D. Young. il pors *South Living* 22:92+ D '87
Museum of Archaeology (Durham, England)
Durham's hidden gems. D. Byrne. il *Hist Today* 37:5-6 Jl '87
Museum of Arts and Sciences (Daytona Beach, Fla.)
Daytona's quieter side. il *South Living* 22:21 S '87
Museum of Broadcasting (New York, N.Y.)
New York's library of TV and radio. il *Sunset* 179:60 O '87
Museum of Contemporary Art (Antwerp, Belgium)
Starting from scratch. B. Grauman. il *Art News* 86:50 N '87
Museum of Contemporary Art (Los Angeles, Calif.)
The buildings in close-up. S. Stephens. il *Art Am* 75:152-5 My '87

Museum of Contemporary Art (Los Angeles, Calif.)— *cont.*
From oil to oils [chairman W. F. Kieschnick] G. Buchalter. il por *Forbes* 139:283 Ja 12 '87
Getting on the map. R. Hughes. il *Time* 129:78-81 Ja 12 '87
L.A. elevation [designed by A. Isozaki] M. Filler. il *House Gard* 159:86-9+ Ja '87
The L.A. Museum of Contemporary Art: what's in a name? H. Muschamp. il *Archit Rec* 175:83+ My '87
Los Angeles: two for the show. P. Plagens. il *Art Am* 75:146-52+ My '87
MOCA and more: the future of California Plaza at Bunker Hill. M. F. Schmertz. il *Archit Rec* 175:82 My '87
MOCA-Panza dispute settled [dispute over possible sale of Panza Collection] R. W. Walker. *Art News* 86:21-2 Mr '87
The new temples of art. P. Young. il *Macleans* 100:82-3 F 2 '87
Why collectors buy contemporary art [interview with E. Broad] M. S. Doherty. por *Am Artist* 51:10-11 Ap '87
Museum of Fine Arts (Houston, Tex.). Lillie and Hugh Roy Cullen Sculpture Garden
Mixing art and nature in Houston. il *South Living* 22:48+ My '87
Museum of Flight (Seattle, Wash.)
Seattle's grand aircraft showcase [Great Gallery] il *Sunset* 179:11 Ag '87
Museum of German History (Berlin, Germany: East) *See* Museum für Deutsche Geschichte (Berlin, Germany: East)
Museum of Holography (New York, N.Y.)
Holography [demonstration by A. M. Nicholson] *New Yorker* 63:20-2 Ag 24 '87
Museum of Islamic Art (Marrakesh, Morocco)
Gardens: Majorelle remembered: Yves Saint Laurent and Pierre Bergé in Marrakesh. C. Aillaud. il pors *Archit Dig* 44:160-5 O '87
Museum of Medical Quackery (Saint Louis, Mo.)
Patently absurd. N. Guccione. il *Omni* 10:100-5+ N '87
Museum of Modern Art (New York, N.Y.)
Oedipal complex. K. Larson. il *N Y* 20:65-6 Ja 26 '87
Museum of Modern Art (San Francisco, Calif.) *See* San Francisco Museum of Modern Art
Museum of Natural History (New York, N.Y.) *See* American Museum of Natural History
Museum of Natural History (Portales, N.M.)
A natural view of art. J. P. Forsthoffer. il *Horizon* 30:27 O '87
Museum of New Mexico
The Museum of New Mexico is a cultural digest of the state. S. Osborne. il *Horizon* 30:41-3 O '87
Museum of Photographic Arts (San Diego, Calif.). Bookstore
Focus on photography books [work of manager D. Kinney] B. Teague. il por *Publ Wkly* 232:50-2 Jl 31 '87
Museum of the Borough of Brooklyn
Out of the commonplace [display system of mutable floating walls] M. Gaskie. il *Archit Rec* 175:162-5 mid-S '87
Museum of the Gold of Peru *See* Museo Oro del Peru
Museum stores
Making prehistory [dinosaur models at Reproductions Shop of American Museum of Natural History] C. Rubin. il *Vogue* 177:58 Jl '87
Museum buys in D.C. D. P. Marshall. *Travel Holiday* 167:66-8 Ja '87
Museum Support Center *See* Smithsonian Institution. Museum Support Center
Museum van Hedendaagse Kunst Antwerpen *See* Museum of Contemporary Art (Antwerp, Belgium)
Museum villages *See* Villages, Restored
Museum workers, Handicapped
Blind tour guide describes exhibits at famous museum [J. Luckett of the DuSable Museum] il pors *Jet* 72:24-5+ Ag 17 '87
Museums
See also
Agricultural museums
Art galleries and museums
Children's museums
Halls of fame
Historic houses, sites, etc.
Science museums
See also names of museums; also subhead Galleries and museums under names of cities
Museum news. See issues of Antiques & Collecting Hobbies beginning March 1985

Museum news. See issues of Hobbies through February 1985
Museum trivia [quiz] il *Americana* 15:13 S/O '87
Museums for every brow. T. Segal. il *Bus Week* p124 Ap 6 '87
Architecture
See also
Art galleries and museums—Architecture
Building beyond limitations [Canadian Museum of Civilization architect D. Cardinal] il por *Macleans* 100:18-19 D 28 '87
A go-ahead for "bad manners" [controversy over J. I. Freed's design for the U.S. Holocaust Memorial Museum] K. Andersen. il por *Time* 129:65 Je 29 '87
Underneath a garden [Smithsonian Institution's Center for African, Near Eastern and Asian Culture; cover story] M. F. Schmertz. il *Archit Rec* 175:112-21 S '87
Fires and fire prevention
Around the Mall and beyond [Smithsonian fire of 1865] E. Park. il *Smithsonian* 18:22+ D '87
Management
See also
Museum directors
Arizona
See also
Titan II Missile Museum (Ariz.)
California
See also
Ardenwood Historic Farm
San Francisco (Calif.)—Galleries and museums
Santa Monica (Calif.)—Galleries and museums
Venice (Calif.)—Galleries and museums
Ecuador
See also
Chordeleg (Ecuador)—Galleries and museums
France
See also
Musée Napoléonien (Fontainebleau, France)
Paris (France)—Galleries and museums
Georgia
See also
Antique Auto and Music Museum (Stone Mountain, Ga.)
Savannah Science Museum, Inc.
Germany (West)
See also
Frankfurt am Main (Germany)—Galleries and museums
Great Britain
See also
London (England)—Galleries and museums
Sigmund Freud Museum (London, England)
Massachusetts
See also
Historic Deerfield, Inc.
Springfield (Mass.)—Galleries and museums
Michigan
See also
Henry Ford Museum and Greenfield Village
Mississippi
See also
Jackson (Miss.)—Galleries and museums
Eiw Mexico
See also
Museum of Natural History (Portales, N.M.)
North America
Focal points: observatories, planetariums, and museums for astronomy enthusiasts to visit throughout the United States and Canada. il *Astronomy* 15:42-53 Je '87
Planetariums and museums. *Sky Telesc* 74 Sky Telesc Handb:2-8 S '87
Ontario
See also
Royal Ontario Museum
Toronto (Ont.)—Galleries and museums
Toronto's group of five: museums as varied as Canada. H. Loverseed. il *Travel Holiday* 168:44-50 O '87
Sweden
See also
Stockholm (Sweden)—Galleries and museums
Tennessee
See also
Museum of Appalachia
Texas
See also
Vida's Vintage Vehicles Antique Car Museum
Yugoslavia
See also
Zagreb (Yugoslavia)—Galleries and museums

Museums and blacks
Four blacks on Smithsonian Cultural Education Board. *Jet* 71:22 F 2 '87
Museums and children
See also
Children's museums
Museums and single people
Singles mingle [Singles Sunday at the Baltimore Museum of Art] M. Giuliano. il *Art News* 86:21 My '87
Museums and the blind
Blind tour guide describes exhibits at famous museum [J. Luckett of the DuSable Museum] il pors *Jet* 72:24-5+ Ag 17 '87
Museveni, Yoweri
about
Starting over. R. D. Kaplan. il *Atlantic* 259:18-21+ Ap '87
Mushakoji, Kinhide
How unique is UNU? il por *UN Chron* 23:114-15 N '86
Mushroom soups *See* Soups
Mushrooms
See also
Cooking—Mushrooms
Truffles
Celebrating the wild mushroom [excerpt] S. A. Friedman. bibl il *Mother Earth News* 104:76-83 Mr/Ap '87
Find 'pearls' with oyster mushrooms; Shiitake mushrooms spawn profits for dairy farmer. P. Smith. il *Success Farm* 85:48 N '87
Mushrooms in the mountains [shiitake mushroom grower P. Goland] J. O'Brien. il pors *Ctry J* 14:28-32 S '87
Musial, Stan, 1920-
about
A baseball for dad. P. Thomson. il *Read Dig* 130:13-14+ Mr '87
Music
See also
Accordion music
Animals and music
Bands (Music)
Black music
Blues music
Booksellers and bookselling—Music
Calypso music
Chamber music
Composition (Music)
Computers—Musical use
Concerts
Conductors (Music)
Copyright—Music
Country music
Embellishment (Music)
Fanfares
Fashion and music
Gospel music
Improvisation (Music)
Jazz music
Melody
Metronomes
Motion pictures—Music
New Age music
Opera
Orchestras
Parody (Music)
Phonograph records
Piano music
Radio broadcasting—Music
Religious music
Rock music
Singing
Television broadcasting—Music
Edward Rothstein on music. E. Rothstein. See occasional issues of The New Republic beginning August 27, 1984
Medley. K. Richardson. See issues of High Fidelity (New York, N.Y.) beginning November 1986
Record makers. C. Barter and S. Simels. See issues of Stereo Review beginning March 1984
Speaking my piece. L. G. Boundas. See issues of Stereo Review beginning May 1987
Speaking my piece. W. Livingstone. See issues of Stereo Review through April 1987
Acoustics and physics
Acoustics of ancient Chinese bells. S. Shen. il map *Sci Am* 256:104-10 Ap '87
Fiddling with the future [work of C. M. Hutchins] T. Rothman and A. Mereson. il pors *Discover* 8:58-64+ S '87

Key notes on the mind [neuropsychology of music] T. Monmaney. il *Omni* 9:44-6+ Ja '87
Appreciation
A new and awful silence. B. Holland. il *Harpers* 275:70-1 Jl '87
Competitions
See also
Albert Schweitzer Music Award
Singing—Competitions
Seventeen Magazine & General Motors National Concerto Competition. E. Miller. il *Seventeen* 46:42+ Je '87
Composition
See Composition (Music)
History
Changing your tune [standards of pitch] S. Zucker. il *Opera News* 51:32-4+ Ja 3 '87
Memories of his master's voice [interview with R. K. Anderson] E. E. Swenson. il por *High Fidel* 37:56-9 My '87
Stereo review's calender of classical composers. W. Livingstone. il *Stereo Rev* 52:105-9 N '87
Who shot the piano player? [amateurism] E. Rothstein. *New Repub* 196:26+ Mr 30 '87
Modes
See Musical intervals and scales
Performance
See also
Improvisation (Music)
Periodicals
See also
Musical America (Periodical)
Stereo review (Periodical)
Psychological aspects
See also
Music therapy
Key notes on the mind [neuropsychology of music] T. Monmaney. il *Omni* 9:44-6+ Ja '87
Makin' music: exercise for the spirit. M. Golin. il *Prevention* 39:55-8 O '87
Music (any ol' kind) hath charm . . . [effect on students] G. W. Bracey. il *Phi Delta Kappan* 68:399-400 Ja '87
The sound of purple [colors associated with music; study by Robert A. Cutietta and Kelly J. Haggerty] A. H. Rosenfeld. *Psychol Today* 21:18-19 D '87
Recording and reproducing
See Sound—Recording and reproducing
Scores
See also
Sheet music
Social aspects
Who shot the piano player? [amateurism] E. Rothstein. *New Repub* 196:26+ Mr 30 '87
Study and teaching
See also
Cello—Study and teaching
Guitar—Study and teaching
Music teachers
Opera—Study and teaching
Violin—Study and teaching
A case history of one foundation's philanthropy [Ford Foundation's Contemporary Music Project] R. J. Werner. *Des Arts Educ* 88:19-22 Mr/Ap '87
The gap between music research and music teaching. J. A. Taylor. *Des Arts Educ* 88:27-30 My/Je '87
Higher education and teacher preparation in music. B. R. Lundquist. bibl f *Des Arts Educ* 88:6-11 Ja/F '87
Learning to learn—music. E. B. Meske. *Des Arts Educ* 89:45-8 S/O '87
The (musical) arts and teacher education. E. B. Meske. bibl f *Des Arts Educ* 88:15-18 Ja/F '87
The sound of music [St. Augustine parochial school, South Bronx] E. Hopkins. il *N Y* 20:54-7 N 23 '87
Themes, motives, etc.
See also
Child abuse in music
Death in music
Ice cream, ices, etc. in music
Misogyny in music
Theory
See also
Atonality
Melody
Musical intervals and scales
Therapeutic use
See Music therapy
Caribbean region
Sounds of the Caribbean. D. Palmer. il *Black Enterp* 17:42-4 My '87

Music—*cont.*

Finland

Northern lights. T. W. Libbey, Jr. il *High Fidel* 37:71 N '87

Great Britain

Music notes. S. Billen. il *Horizon* 30:32-4 N '87

Illinois

See also

Chicago (Ill.)—Music

Louisiana

See also

New Orleans (La.)—Music

New York (State)

See also

New York (N.Y.)—Music

Pennsylvania

See also

Philadelphia (Pa.)—Music

Tennessee

See also

Memphis (Tenn.)—Music

Texas

See also

Austin (Tex.)—Music

Music, African

See also

Juju music

Phonograph records—African music

Rendezvous in Mali [songs of the griots] J. Fox. il *House Gard* 159:94+ S '87

Music, American

See also

Compact discs—American music

Jazz music

Big-Mac attack [American music featured at Japanese festivals] T. W. Libbey, Jr. il *High Fidel* 37:58 O '87

Dictionaries

American soundings [New Grove dictionary of American music] W. H. Youngren. il *Atlantic* 259:83-5 Mr '87

The New Grove dictionary of American music. J. Idema. *Smithsonian* 18:158-9 Ap '87

Viewpoint [New Grove dictionary of American music] J. W. Freeman. *Opera News* 51:4 F 28 '87

Music, Baroque

The musical offering. A. Basso. il *Courier* 40:11-13 S '87

Music, Black *See* Black music

Music, Brazilian

Music, the pulse of a people. T. de Souza. il *Courier* 39:29-32 D '86

Music, Cajun *See* Cajun music

Music, Caribbean

Sounds of the Caribbean. D. Palmer. il *Black Enterp* 17:42-4 My '87

Music, Chamber *See* Chamber music

Music, Church *See* Religious music

Music, Electronic

See also

Compact discs—Electronic music

Computers—Musical use

Musical instruments, Electronic

Videotapes—Electronic music

Larry Fast. J. Diliberto. il por *Down Beat* 54:50+ S '87

Music's electronic future. T. Charbeneau. il por *Futurist* 21:35-7 S/O '87

Steve Roach. J. Diliberto. il por *Down Beat* 54:46-8 Mr '87

Steve Winwood's solo on Empty pages—an electric piano transcription. J. T. Cohen. il *Down Beat* 54:60-1 Ag '87

Wendy Carlos: A.D. (after digital). J. Diliberto. il pors *Down Beat* 54:20-2+ Mr '87

Music, English

See also

Compact discs—English music

Music, Experimental

See also

Compact discs—Experimental music

Phonograph records—Experimental music

La Monte Young's minimalist marathon [The well-tuned piano] A. Rich. *Newsweek* 110:58 Jl 27 '87

The minimalist with the mostest [J. Adams] K. R. Schwarz. il pors *High Fidel* 37:57-9 Ag '87

Music, French

Musical events:

Performances of 17th century music. A. Porter. il *New Yorker* 63:155-6 D 7 '87

Music, Jamaican

See also

Reggae music

Music, Japanese

See also

Kodo (Musical group)

Music, Latin American

See also

Phonograph records—Latin American music

Eddie Palmieri/Hilton Ruiz/Papo Lucca [Salsa meets Jazz series] L. Birnbaum. il *Down Beat* 54:52-3 Ag '87

Music. See issues of *Américas* beginning May/June 1984

The Palladium [dance hall in New York City] J. Torres. il *N Y* 20:99 D 21-28 '87

The spicy bite of Latin music. F. Hernandez. il *Essence* 17:30 Ap '87

Music, Medieval

Musical events:

Medieval English music performed by Sequentia. A. Porter. *New Yorker* 63:90-1 Mr 9 '87

Music, Modern

See also

Phonograph records—Modern music

Music, South African

See also

Ladysmith Black Mambazo (Musical group)

Phonograph records—South African music

Music, Spanish

See also

Compact discs—Spanish music

Phonograph records—Spanish music

Music, Swiss

See also

Folk songs, Swiss

Music, Zydeco *See* Zydeco music

Music and animals *See* Animals and music

Music and children

See also

Children's songs

Phonograph records—Children's music

Conning kids. W. Livingstone. il *Stereo Rev* 52:8 F '87

Have baton, will travel [conductor R. Worby's concerts for children] S. Mieses. il por *N Y* 20:25 F 16 '87

There goes my song again. L. Wainwright. il *Life* 10:18 Mr '87

Music and fashion *See* Fashion and music

Music and literature

A movie star goes to Watts to make sure the Bard gets a good rap [work of J. Agutter] K. Hubbard. il pors *People Wkly* 27:83-4 Je 29 '87

Music and motion pictures *See* Motion pictures—Music

Music and science

Play the right bases, and you'll hear Bach [music derived from DNA bases; work of S. Ohno] il *Discover* 8:10+ Mr '87

Music and state

Grenada

Grenada fights the calypso menace. *Newsweek* 110:38 Jl 27 '87

Soviet Union

Aquarium's leader rises to the surface [B. Grebenschikov] N. Traver. il por *People Wkly* 27:51 Ap 6 '87

Rock in Russia. M. R. Benson. il *Roll Stone* p15-16+ Mr 26 '87

Rock 'n' roll in Red. C. Redden. il *Macleans* 100:8+ S 7 '87

Stas Namin and Ludmila Senchina reign over the pop scene while rock's underground rumbles. S. K. Reed. il pors *People Wkly* 27:46-8+ Ap 6 '87

Music and the blind

After years of hard traveling, mountain maestro Doc Watson looks to find some easy pickin' at last. R. Wolmuth. il pors *People Wkly* 28:57-8+ Ag 10 '87

Blind boy, 3, learns to play 50 songs on piano [J. Gardner] D. M. Cheers. il pors *Jet* 72:22-3 My 25 '87

Blind piano player, 3, visits Stevie Wonder [J. Gardner] il pors *Jet* 72:18 Je 22 '87

Blind piano prodigy, age 4, gets free facial surgery [J. Gardner] il por *Jet* 72:24 S 14 '87

Blind since birth and barely 4, Jermaine Gardner happily hits all the right keys—and heartstrings. K. Hubbard. il pors *People Wkly* 27:53+ Je 22 '87

Music and the handicapped

See also

Guitarists, Handicapped

Hi Hopes (Musical group)

Pianists, Handicapped

Music and the press *See* Music news
Music and women
Music. E. W. Said. *Nation* 244:158-60 F 7 '87
Music boxes
  See also
  Rita Ford, Inc.
Music conductors *See* Conductors (Music)
Music contests *See* Music—Competitions
Music Corporation of America *See* MCA Inc.
Music critics and criticism
  See also
  Hanslick, Eduard, 1825-1904
  Hume, Paul
  Jacobson, Robert
  Opera reviews
  Operetta reviews
  Oratorio reviews
  Rosenthal, Harold D., 1917-1987
Cleveland rock critic Jane Scott may be pushing 70, but she's still got the beat. K. Myers. il pors *People Wkly* 27:91-2 Je 8 '87
Rock's most influential album? [reaction to Sgt. Pepper] M. Goldberg. *Roll Stone* p57+ Je 18 '87
Viewpoint [F. Zeffirelli upset with criticism of Metropolitan Opera production of Turandot] J. W. Freeman. *Opera News* 51:4 Je '87
Where are we, and where do we go from here? R. Freeman. *Des Arts Educ* 88:29-32 Jl/Ag '87
  Caricatures and cartoons
How to be a feisty rock critic. K. Richardson. il *High Fidel* 37:69 Ja '87
Music directors *See* Conductors (Music)
Music education *See* Music—Study and teaching
Music festivals
Calendar. See issues of Opera News
Summer fests. E. Copage. il *Essence* 18:40 Je '87
  Austria
Mozart, Moses and money [Salzburg Festival] M. Walsh. il *Time* 130:58 Ag 31 '87
Salzburg [Salzburg Easter Festival] J. H. Sutcliffe. il *Opera News* 52:56 O '87
  Belgium
Flamenco puro [guitar festival] D. Gordon. il *Down Beat* 54:12 Jl '87
  British Columbia
Vancouver [La Scala's visit for Expo '86 World Festival] F. B. St. Clair. *Opera News* 51:37-8 Ja 3 '87
  California
Jazz and turtles just outside Sequoia [Jazzaffair] il *Sunset* 178:56-7 Ap '87
Monterey Pop: the dawning of an age [1967] M. Goldberg. il *Roll Stone* p116+ Je 4 '87
  Colorado
Aspen. G. Giffin. *Opera News* 52:50-2 D 5 '87
Dick Gibson Jazz Party. L. Feather. il *Down Beat* 54:50-1 Ja '87
Dick Gibson Jazz Party. L. Feather. il *Down Beat* 54:56+ D '87
  Connecticut
Old pros, kids featured at debut Yale Jazzfest. A. Light. il *Down Beat* 54:13 S '87
  Europe
An operaphiles' Baedeker 1987. il *Opera News* 51:36-8+ My '87
  France
Nice Festival [Grande Parade du Jazz] J. McDonough. il *Down Beat* 11:51-2 N '87
Verona/Ravenna/Vienne festivals [jazz festivals] D. Keller. il *Down Beat* 11:52-3 N '87
  Germany (East)
Dresden [opera] J. H. Sutcliffe. *Opera News* 52:38-9 D 19 '87
  Germany (West)
Berlin Jazztage. H. Mandel. il *Down Beat* 54:53 F '87
  Great Britain
Glyndebourne/Brighton. N. Goodwin. il *Opera News* 52:43 D 5 '87
Musical events:
  London Proms. A. Porter. *New Yorker* 62:70+ Ja 5 '87
Wexford [opera productions] E. Forbes. il *Opera News* 51:36 F 28 '87
  Illinois
Blues fest draws 550,000 [Chicago Blues Festival] M. McCormick. il *Roll Stone* p18+ Ag 13 '87
Chicago Blues Festival. G. Easterling. il *Down Beat* 54:56-7 S '87
Chicago Jazz Festival. D. Helland. il *Down Beat* 54:56 D '87
Musicfest U.S.A./Chicago! B. Beuttler. il *Down Beat* 54:26-31 Jl '87

  Italy
Florence [opera at the Maggio Musicale] M. A. Zaccaria. *Opera News* 52:41+ D 19 '87
In quest of Rossini [annual festival held in Pesaro] C. Battaglia. il *Opera News* 52:30-1+ Ag '87
Musical events:
  Performance of La donna del lago at the Rossini Opera Festival. A. Porter. *New Yorker* 62:81-2 Ja 26 '87
  Rossini Opera Festival. A. Porter. *New Yorker* 63:110+ O 5 '87
The two faces of Umbria [Umbria Jazz Festival] A. Lange. il *Down Beat* 54:12+ O '87
Verona/Ravenna/Vienne festivals [jazz festivals] D. Keller. il *Down Beat* 11:52-3 N '87
Whitney Houston a hit at Italian music show [San Remo Festival] *Jet* 71:63 F 23 '87
  Jamaica
Reggae: death, life [Sunsplash] L. Jaffee. il *High Fidel* 37:63 D '87
Round-the-clock reggae [Sunsplash Festival] M. Point. *Down Beat* 54:12 D '87
  Japan
Big-Mac attack [American music featured at Japanese festivals] T. W. Libbey, Jr. il *High Fidel* 37:58 O '87
  Kentucky
The Big Singing [annual gathering in Benton, Ky. to sing from the Southern harmony songbook] W. White. il *New Yorker* 62:78-84+ Ja 19 '87
  Louisiana
Fun on the bayou [New Orleans Jazz and Heritage Festival] D. Fricke. il *Roll Stone* p15-16 Je 18 '87
  Martinique
Martinique guitar fest [Seventh International Guitar Festival] D. Gordon. il *Down Beat* 54:12 Mr '87
  Maryland
Musical events:
  Israel in Egypt at Maryland Handel Festival. A. Porter. *New Yorker* 63:137-9 N 23 '87
  Maryland Handel Festival performance of Saul. A. Porter. *New Yorker* 63:72-3 Mr 16 '87
  Massachusetts
Musical events:
  Performance of works by G. Perle and W. Lutoslawski at Tanglewood. A. Porter. *New Yorker* 63:68-9 Ag 31 '87
  Netherlands
Northsea Festival. M. Bourne. il *Down Beat* 11:50-1 N '87
  New Jersey
  See also
  Hollybush Festival
  New York (State)
JVC Jazz Festival. M. Bourne and H. Mandel. il *Down Beat* 54:50-3 O '87
JVC Jazz Festival New York. G. Santoro. *Nation* 245:100-4 Ag 1-8 '87
Musical events:
  Mostly Mozart Festival. A. Porter. *New Yorker* 63:110-12 S 14 '87
  Plus and minus at Mostly Mozart. P. G. Davis. il *N Y* 20:56 Jl 27 '87
  Ontario
MusicFest Canada '87. B. Beuttler. il *Down Beat* 54:11 Ag '87
  Pennsylvania
Elvis meets the Bacchae [American Music Theater Festival] M. Walsh. il *Time* 130:126+ O 26 '87
Fatal flaw [American Music Theater Festival] P. G. Davis. il *N Y* 20:110-11 O 19 '87
Philadelphia on pitch [American Music Theater Festival] G. Weales. *Commonweal* 114:623+ N 6 '87
  Rhode Island
Seaside festival [Newport Music Festival] P. G. Davis. il *N Y* 20:56-7 Ag 10 '87
  Saint Thomas (Virgin Islands of the U.S.)
On the beach [Virgin Island Jazz Festival] B. Beuttler. *Down Beat* 11:6 N '87
  Soviet Union
Glasnost rock: American and Russian musicians rock & roll for disarmament at Moscow festival. M. R. Benson. il *Roll Stone* p15-16+ Ag 27 '87
  Switzerland
  Anecdotes, facetiae, satire, etc.
The festival that never was [Matterhorn Music Festival] T. W. Libbey, Jr. il *High Fidel* 37:69 Ja '87
  Texas
Hot debut for Austin music conference [South By Southwest Regional Music and Media Conference] B. Beuttler. il *Down Beat* 54:12 Je '87

Musical events:
Vivaldi's Giustino presented as part of Italy in Houston festival. A. Porter. *New Yorker* 63:141-5 N 2 '87

Trinidad and Tobago
Pan-demonium [National Steelband Music Festival] H. Mandel. *Down Beat* 54:13 Ja '87

Virginia
Fiddling [Old Fiddlers' Convention in Galax, Va.] W. White. *New Yorker* 63:74+ Jl 20 '87

Washington (D.C.)
D.C. festival in April to salute Duke Ellington. por *Jet* 71:16 Mr 23 '87

West Virginia
Mountain music lives at Vandalia. C. Griffith. il *South Living* 22:10-11 My '87

Western States
Western mountains and bluegrass music . . . they go together like banjo and fiddle. il *Sunset* 178:10-12 Je '87

Music for children *See* Music and children
Music in advertising
See also
Advertising jingles
Radio Kings (Firm)
Beatles buy-out [Beatles song Revolution used in Nike TV ad] J. Wiener. *New Repub* 196:13-14 My 11 '87
Beatles sue over Nike commercial. A. DeCurtis. *Roll Stone* p15 S 10 '87
Look what they've done to my song [rock music in TV commercials] J. Pareles. il *Mademoiselle* 93:102+ Ag '87
Running on recall [Beatles' song Revolution used in Nike commercial] A. White. il *Film Comment* 23:72+ Jl/Ag '87
Twin ads: a case of mistaken identity [Michelob and ABC Sports run commercials using song Everybody have fun tonight by Wang Chung] *Newsweek* 110:37 Ag 24 '87
Wanna buy a Revolution? [Beatles song in Nike commercial] J. Cocks. il *Time* 129:78 My 18 '87

Music industry
See also
Computers—Music industry use
Four Seasons Partnership
National Association of School Music Dealers
Radio Kings (Firm)

Music news
Where are we, and where do we go from here? R. Freeman. *Des Arts Educ* 88:29-32 Jl/Ag '87

Music research *See* Musicology
Music schools
See also
Indiana University, Bloomington. School of Music
Manhattan School of Music
University of Idaho. Lionel Hampton School of Music

Canada
See also
Royal Conservatory of Music (Toronto, Ont.)

Music societies
See also
American Society of Composers, Authors and Publishers
Rossini Foundation

Music teachers
See also
Singing teachers

Education
The "flaw" in the ointment: who will teach the understanding of music? D. C. Monk. bibl f *Des Arts Educ* 89:2-7 N/D '87
Reform in music teacher education: what to do until we reach utopia. P. R. Lehman. bibl f *Des Arts Educ* 89:2-11 S/O '87
The role of music research in teacher training programs [music education research] J. N. Anderson. bibl f *Des Arts Educ* 88:42-4 My/Je '87

Music therapy
Mind-bending music. M. Scofield and M. Teich. il *Health* 19:69-70+ F '87
Music as medicine. il *Parents* 62:14 Jl '87
Music as medicine [use in pain treatment] J. R. Goldberg. *McCalls* 114:105 Ja '87
Music hath charms to soothe a throbbing head [migraine treatment; research by Janet Lapp] P. Chance. il *Psychol Today* 21:14 F '87

Music writing *See* Composition (Music); Rock music—Writing

Musical accompaniment
See also
Tape recordings—Musical accompaniment
How to become a house musician [J. Spencer and K. Sill] M. Stryker. pors *Down Beat* 54:54+ F '87
Sharing the music [interview with opera voice coach and accompanist J. Wustman] J. W. Freeman. il pors *Opera News* 52:16-18+ Jl '87

Musical America (Periodical)
Welcome back, Musical America. W. Tynan. il *High Fidel* 37:8 Ja '87

Musical comedies, revues, etc. *See* Musicals, revues, etc.
The musical comedy murders of 1940 [drama] *See* Bishop, John, 1929-
Musical composition *See* Composition (Music)
Musical films *See* Motion pictures—Musical films
Musical instrument digital interface *See* MIDI (Musical instrument digital interface)
Musical instruments
See also
Keyboard instruments
See also names of musical instruments
Pro shop. See issues of Down Beat

Musical instruments, Electronic
See also
Drum
Keyboard instruments
MIDI (Musical instrument digital interface)
The computer as a musical instrument. M. V. Mathews and J. R. Pierce. il *Sci Am* 256:126-33 F '87
Music is alive with the sound of high tech. T. Thompson. il *Bus Week* p114-16 O 26 '87
The new music biz. S. Gordon. il *Technol Rev* 90:10-11 Ja '87
Not for listeners only (I). C. J. Esse. il *High Fidel* 37:14+ O '87

Study and teaching
Aids and devices
The secrets of analog and digital synthesis [videotape] J. Balleras. *Down Beat* 54:53 My '87

Musical instruments, Mechanical
Exhibitions
What I did on my summer vacation [Lightner Museum] B. Ault. il *Antiques Collect Hobbies* 92:62-4 O '87

Musical instruments industry
See also
National Association of Music Merchants

Musical intervals and scales
The well-tempered ear. R. Hodges. il *Stereo Rev* 52:128 S '87

Musical pitch
Changing your tune [standards of pitch] S. Zucker. il *Opera News* 51:32-4+ Ja 3 '87

Musical prodigies *See* Children as musicians
Musicals, revues, etc.
See also
College and school drama
Compact discs—Musicals, revues, etc.
Frohman Academy for Musical Theatre Education
Phonograph records—Musicals, revues, etc.
Broadway and beyond. K. Grubb. See issues of Dance Magazine
Razzle-dazzle on Broadway [British musicals] M. Horn. il *U S News World Rep* 102:72-3 Mr 16 '87
Risky business [black musicals created from operettas] S. Flatow. il *Opera News* 51:18-20+ My '87

Choreography
See Choreography
Conducting
See Conducting (Music)
Photographs and photography
Celebration! [Broadway and Hollywood stills celebrating dance] W. Como. il *Dance Mag* 61:34-7 Ag '87
Production and direction
Bringing a Smile to Broadway. A. M. Hale. il *Theatre Crafts* 21:18-23+ Ja '87
Fantastick voyage [bringing The fantasticks to China] B. R. Marriott. il *Horizon* 30:64-5 O '87
Goodspeed Opera House. M. Loeffler and M. Sommers. il *Theatre Crafts* 21:32-7+ N '87
I've got the horse right here: producer Rocco Landesman's big Broadway gamble [Into the woods] E. Pooley. il pors *N Y* 20:74-6+ S 28 '87
Les miz. D. Kaufman. il *Horizon* 30:37-9 Mr '87
A show of all shows [Les misérables; cover story] J. Kroll. il *Newsweek* 109:62-6+ Mr 30 '87
The stage manager: Off-Broadway or on, the buck stops here [A. Hall, stage manager of Smile] R. Conniff. il pors *Smithsonian* 17:92-4+ F '87

Musicals, revues, etc.—*cont.*

Reviews
Single works

Anything goes
 N Y 20:111 N 2 '87. J. Simon
 Nation 245:570-2 N 14 '87. T. M. Disch
 New Leader 70:22 N 16 '87. L. Sauvage
 New Repub 197:28-9 D 21 '87. R. Brustein
 New Yorker 63:146 N 2 '87. E. Oliver
 Time il 130:95 N 2 '87. W. A. Henry
Barbara Cook: a concert for the theatre
 N Y 20:139-40 Ap 27 '87. J. Simon
 New Yorker 63:127 My 4 '87. E. Oliver
Barnum
 Theatre Crafts il 21:30-2+ Ja '87. M. LaRue
Birds of paradise
 New Yorker 63:131-2 N 9 '87. M. Kramer
Black Sea follies
 N Y il 20:49-50 Ja 12 '87. J. Simon
Cabaret
 Dance Mag il 61:66-7 O '87. K. Grubb
 Harpers Bazaar il 120:134-5 Je '87
 N Y il 20:112 N 2 '87. J. Simon
 Nation 245:571-2 N 14 '87. T. M. Disch
 New Leader 70:19 D 28 '87. L. Sauvage
 New Yorker 63:148-9 N 2 '87. M. Kramer
 Time 130:95 N 2 '87. W. A. Henry
 Vogue il 177:128 O '87. R. Alleman
La cage aux folles
 Dance Mag il 61:70-1 D '87. K. Grubb
Chess
 Newsweek il 109:64-5 Mr 30 '87. J. Kroll
Company
 New Yorker 63:148 N 16 '87. M. Kramer
Don't get God started
 Nation 245:694-5 D 5 '87. T. M. Disch
Dreamgirls
 America 157:88+ Ag 15-22 '87. G. G. Seibert
 Jet il 72:59 Jl 20 '87. S. P. Flanagan
 N Y il 20:62-3 Jl 13 '87. J. Simon
 Nation 245:174-5 Ag 29 '87. T. M. Disch
The fantasticks
 Horizon il 30:64-5 O '87. B. R. Marriott
Funny feet
 Nation 244:775 Je 6 '87. T. M. Disch
The gospel at Colonus
 Christ Today il 31:58-60 Jl 10 '87. P. Alsdurf
Have I got a girl for you!
 Dance Mag 61:89 Ja '87. K. Grubb
Into the light
 America 156:283 Ap 4 '87. G. G. Seibert
Into the woods
 America 157:458 D 12 '87. G. G. Seibert
 N Y il 20:74-6+ S 28 '87. E. Pooley
 N Y il 20:50-1 S 21 '87. R. D. Story
 N Y il 20:109-10 N 16 '87. J. Simon
 Nation 245:726-7 D 12 '87. T. M. Disch
 New Leader 70:18-19 D 28 '87. L. Sauvage
 New Repub 197:29-30 D 21 '87. R. Brustein
 New Yorker 63:147-8 N 16 '87. M. Kramer
 Newsweek il 110:106-7 N 16 '87. J. Kroll
 Time il 130:96-7 N 16 '87. W. A. Henry
The knife
 Harpers Bazaar il 120:206-7+ Ap '87. D. Shewey
 N Y 20:89-90 Mr 23 '87. J. Simon
 Nation 244:480 Ap 11 '87. T. M. Disch
 New Yorker 63:77 Mr 23 '87. E. Oliver
Lady, be good!
 Nation 245:173-4 Ag 29 '87. T. M. Disch
Late nite comic
 New Yorker 63:130+ O 26 '87. M. Kramer
Magdalena
 New Yorker 63:163-4 D 7 '87. A. Porter
Mama I want to sing
 Jet 72:53 Jl 13 '87
Me and my girl
 Saturday Evening Post il 259:22+ O '87. J. McCollister
Les misérables
 America 156:427+ My 23 '87. G. G. Seibert
 Commonweal 114:245-7 Ap 24 '87. G. Weales
 Horizon il 30:37-9 Mr '87. D. Kaufman
 N Y il 20:88-9 Mr 23 '87. J. Simon
 N Y Rev Books il 34:14-16 My 7 '87. L. Sante
 New Leader 70:17-18 Mr 23 '87. L. Sauvage
 New Yorker 63:77 Mr 23 '87. E. Oliver
 Newsweek il 109:62-6+ Mr 30 '87. J. Kroll
 Newsweek il 109:44 Mr 23 '87. J. Kroll
 Opera News 52:41 Jl '87. S. Flatow
 Time il 129:90-1 Mr 23 '87. W. A. Henry
 U S News World Rep il 102:72-3 Mr 16 '87. M. Horn

 Vogue il 177:92 F '87. B. Nightingale
No way to treat a lady
 N Y 20:68+ Je 22 '87. J. Simon
 New Yorker 63:69 Je 22 '87. E. Oliver
Nunsense
 America 156:283-4 Ap 4 '87. G. G. Seibert
Oil City Symphony
 Time il 130:67 D 21 '87. M. Walsh
Oklahoma!
 Americana il 15:15 My/Je '87. V. Nash
On the Twentieth Century
 Time 129:11-13 Ap 20 '87. R. Coniff
The Phantom of the Opera
 Newsweek il 109:64 Mr 30 '87. J. Kroll
Roza
 N Y il 20:98 O 12 '87. J. Simon
 Nation 245:460-1 O 24 '87. T. M. Disch
 New Leader il 70:21 N 16 '87. L. Sauvage
 New Yorker 63:118+ O 12 '87. M. Kramer
Sarafina!
 N Y il 20:124 N 9 '87. J. Simon
 Nation 245:694 D 5 '87. T. M. Disch
 New Yorker 63:130 N 9 '87. E. Oliver
 Newsweek il 110:82 N 9 '87. J. Kroll
Satchmo: America's musical legend
 Jet il 72:18 Ag 24 '87
Smile
 Smithsonian il 17:92-4+ F '87. R. Conniff
 Theatre Crafts il 21:18-23+ Ja '87. A. M. Hale
Songs on a shipwrecked sofa
 New Yorker 63:72-3 Je 15 '87. M. Kramer
South Pacific
 N Y 20:92+ Mr 23 '87. P. G. Davis
Staggerlee
 N Y 20:97 Mr 30 '87. J. Simon
 New Yorker 63:93 Mr 30 '87. E. Oliver
 Roll Stone il p18 My 21 '87. M. Coleman
Standup Shakespeare
 New Yorker 63:75 Ap 20 '87. E. Oliver
Stardust
 N Y il 20:111 Mr 2 '87. J. Simon
 New Leader 70:21 Mr 9 '87. L. Sauvage
 New Yorker 63:76 Mr 2 '87. E. Oliver
Starlight Express
 America 156:427 My 23 '87. G. G. Seibert
 Dance Mag il 61:86-7 Ap '87. K. Grubb
 N Y il 20:96-7 Mr 30 '87. J. Simon
 N Y il 20:66-8 Mr 9 '87
 Nation 244:516 Ap 18 '87. T. M. Disch
 New Leader 70:21 Ap 6 '87. L. Sauvage
 New Yorker 63:93 Mr 30 '87. E. Oliver
 Pop Mech il 164:85 D '87. J. Skorupa
 Theatre Crafts il 21:8 Mr '87. D. F. Sisk
 Time il 129:83 Mr 30 '87. W. A. Henry
 U S News World Rep il 102:72-3 Mr 16 '87. M. Horn
Stepping out
 Dance Mag il 61:87 Ap '87. K. Grubb
Sunday in the park with George
 Theatre Crafts il 21:48-55+ N '87. J. Calhoun
Tango apasionado
 N Y 20:115-16 N 23 '87. J. Simon
 New Yorker 63:103-4 D 21 '87. A. Croce
Teddy & Alice
 America il 157:430 D 5 '87. G. G. Seibert
 N Y il 20:115 N 23 '87. J. Simon
 New Yorker 63:153 N 23 '87. E. Oliver
Three postcards
 N Y il 20:108+ My 25 '87. J. Simon
 New Yorker 63:87 My 25 '87. E. Oliver
 Time 129:71 My 25 '87. W. A. Henry
Time
 Newsweek il 109:65 Mr 30 '87. J. Kroll
Too many girls
 Nation 244:480-1 Ap 11 '87. T. M. Disch

Scores
Reclaiming a vital heritage [scores to Broadway musicals found in warehouse in Secaucus, N.J.] R. Corliss. il *Time* 129:82 Mr 23 '87

Special effects
See Theater—Special effects

Stage setting and scenery
Barnum. M. LaRue. il *Theatre Crafts* 21:30-2+ Ja '87
Broadway steels for Starlight. D. F. Sisk. il *Theatre Crafts* 21:8 Mr '87
Don't be a sucker—rig for safety [mounting a production of Barnum] R. Libbon. il *Theatre Crafts* 21:32-3+ Ja '87

Musicals, revues, etc.—Stage setting and scenery—*cont.*
More Majestic than ever [Frederick Olsson oversees modifications in Broadway's Majestic Theater to accommodate The Phantom of the Opera] B. Weber. il *N Y Times Mag* p62 S 6 '87
Roller derby: 'Starlight Express' arrives on wheels of steel. il *N Y* 20:66-8 Mr 9 '87
Sunday in the park with George [design ideas for university and regional companies] J. Calhoun. il *Theatre Crafts* 21:48-55+ N '87

Writing
Andrew Lloyd Webber: superstar [cover story] J. Rockwell. il pors *N Y Times Mag* p28-31+ D 20 '87
Lost Beatles script to emerge [musical based on unfinished screenplay by J. Orton to be composed by T. Rundgren] M. Jenkins. *Roll Stone* p14 Mr 12 '87
Master of the musical [S. Sondheim] W. A. Henry. il por *Time* 130:80-2 D 7 '87
The multimillion-dollar music man [A. Lloyd Webber] P. Young. il por *Macleans* 100:53-4 Je 8 '87

Musicfest U.S.A. Awards
Musicfest U.S.A./Chicago! B. Beuttler. il *Down Beat* 54:26-31 Jl '87
Musicfest U.S.A. expands; existing fests affiliate. B. Beuttler. il *Down Beat* 11:12 N '87

Musicians
　　See also
　　　Artistic Ambassador Program (U.S.)
　　　Black musicians
　　　Children as musicians
　　　Composers
　　　Conductors (Music)
　　　Drugs and musicians
　　　Fiddlers
　　　Jazz musicians
　　　Rock musicians
　　　Street music and musicians
Musician cars. P. Egan. il *Road Track* 38:18 F '87
Record makers. C. Barter and S. Simels. See issues of Stereo Review beginning March 1984

Agencies and agents
See Theatrical agencies and agents

Religious life
The "good life" wasn't good enough [C. Parkening] T. Mattingly. il por *Christ Today* 31:64+ My 15 '87

Musicians, Amateur
Who shot the piano player? E. Rothstein. *New Repub* 196:26+ Mr 30 '87

Musick, Greg
(jt. auth) See Hogge, Allison, and Musick, Greg

Musicology
The gap between music research and music teaching. J. A. Taylor. *Des Arts Educ* 88:27-30 My/Je '87
Research in music: science or art? C. K. Madsen. bibl *Des Arts Educ* 88:10-14 My/Je '87

Musk thistle weevils *See* Weevils
Musk thistles *See* Thistles

Muskellunge fishing
A doctor's prize catch [comparison of the retrieval of a catheter lodged in a lung with muskie fishing] P. Skalka. il *Read Dig* 130:128-32 Mr '87
River of giant muskies [Saint Lawrence] K. Schultz. il *Field Stream* 92:117-18 S '87

Muskie, Edmund S.
The chains of liberty [address, September 17, 1987] *Vital Speeches Day* 54:4-7 O 15 '87
　　about
The story that still nags at me [excerpt from Behind the front page] D. S. Broder. il *Wash Mon* 19:29-32+ F '87

Muskie fishing *See* Muskellunge fishing
Muslim architecture *See* Architecture, Islamic
Muslims
　　See also
　　　Islam

Afghanistan
The alchemy of turning guns into luxury villas [diversion of U.S. aid] E. Girardet. il *U S News World Rep* 103:36 N 30 '87
The catastrophe [visiting places related to the Afghan resistance] D. M. Lessing. *New Yorker* 63:74-90+ Mr 16 '87
The great game. S. R. Weisman. *New Repub* 197:20-3 Ag 10-17 '87
How did Iran get Stinger missiles? [missiles sent by U.S. to Afghan resistance] il *Newsweek* 110:42-3 O 26 '87
Inside an unlovely war. W. Burger. il *Newsweek* 110:46-8 O 12 '87

Insurgencies: two of a kind [U.S.-backed rebels in Afghanistan] R. Watson. il *Newsweek* 109:32-3 Mr 23 '87
J-school for Afghan rebels [Boston University project in Pakistan] E. Salholz. il *Newsweek* 109:75-6 Mr 30 '87
On the receiving end. B. Crozier. *Natl Rev* 39:26+ Jl 17 '87
The Soviet Union and Afghanistan in 1987. L. Dupree. bibl f *Curr Hist* 86:333-5 O '87
The sting [Reagan administration could spoil peace process by stepping up arms to Afghan guerrillas] A. Rashid. *Nation* 244:241-2 F 28 '87
U.S. credits Afghan resistance with thwarting Soviet air power. M. Mecham. *Aviat Week Space Technol* 127:26-7 Jl 13 '87

Egypt
Egypt: the Islamic issue. M. Sid-Ahmed. *Foreign Policy* 69:22-39 Wint '87/'88
A flood of radicalism in the land of the Nile [Shiite fundamentalists] J. L. Galloway. il *U S News World Rep* 103:35-6 Jl 6 '87

Iran
　　See also
　　Iranian seizure of United States embassy, 1979-1981
Spreading the faith. B. Levin. il *Macleans* 100:14-17 Jl 27 '87

Iraq
The view from the Mustansiriyah. M. Viorst. map *New Yorker* 63:92+ O 12 '87

Lebanon
　　See also
　　Lebanon hostage cases, 1984-
The battle for Beirut: a close shave [Syria's war on beards] C. Dickey and S. Issa. il *Newsweek* 109:47 Mr 16 '87
Council members ask urgent measures for UNIFIL security [Shiites clash with French troops] *UN Chron* 23:58 N '86
Security Council condemns attacks against UNIFIL as 'criminal', calls for end to 'any military presence' unacceptable to Lebanon [Shiites clash with French troops] il *UN Chron* 23:59-62 N '86

Middle East
　　See also
　　Beirut airplane hijacking, 1985
Confronting the 'monster' [Saudi Arabia clashes with Iran] T. Clifton. il *Newsweek* 110:36 S 7 '87
Islam: seeking the future in the past [Shiite fundamentalists] P. R. Range. il map *U S News World Rep* 103:33-5 Jl 6 '87
Militant Islam: defying Israel's control [violence in the West Bank and Gaza] J. Barnes. il *U S News World Rep* 103:39 O 26 '87
Militant Islam gains ground. R. Wright. il *Nation* 244:675-7 My 23 '87
Moslem radicals: idealism and intolerance [views of Richard Dekmejian] il *USA Today (Periodical)* 115:14 Ap '87
The unending feud: Shi'tes vs. Sunnis. il *Time* 130:26 Ag 17 '87
A who's who [Shiite terrorist organizations] S. Emerson and C. Fenyvesi. il *U S News World Rep* 102:26-7 F 9 '87

Nigeria
Did Muslims plan religious violence? *Christ Today* 31:43 Jl 10 '87

Pakistan
"Friend by day, enemy by night" [blood feuds in village of Thull] R. L. Keiser. il *Nat Hist* 96:8+ N '87

Soviet Union
Taking a firm stand against faith [growing population] R. N. Ostling. il *Time* 129:60 Ja 12 '87
Winning the war for Afghanistan. A. Bennigsen. *Natl Rev* 39:36-8 My 8 '87

Tunisia
Punishing the pious [sentencing of fundamentalists for plotting to overthrow H. Bourguiba] M. S. Serrill. il por *Time* 130:42 O 12 '87
'The worst has been avoided'. S. Seibert. il por *Newsweek* 110:52 O 12 '87

Muslims, Black *See* Black Muslims
Muslims and Christians *See* Christianity and other religions
Musorgsky, Modest Petrovich *See* Mussorgsky, Modest Petrovich, 1839-1881
Mussau Islands (Papua New Guinea) *See* Saint Matthias Islands (Papua New Guinea)

Mussel culture See Shellfish culture
Mussels
Hard times on mussel beach [oystercatcher competition for food on the Exe estuary, England] J. Goss-Custard. il *Nat Hist* 96:64-71 Mr '87
Musseling in on novel cryoprotectants [research by Stephen Loomis and others] S. Weisburd. *Sci News* 132:9 Jl 4 '87
Mussels munch methane [research by James Childress] il *Technol Rev* 90:18 F/Mr '87
Musser, Cynthia Erfurt
about
Cutouts of fashion. J. Ware. il por *Americana* 15:41-5 Jl/Ag '87
Musser, R. D.
about
100 years later, the Grand Hotel still boasts the biggest front porch in America. K. Gross. il por *People Wkly* 28:80-1 Ag 3 '87
Mussorgsky, Modest Petrovich, 1839-1881
about
Boris Godunov [opera] Reviews
New Yorker 63:83-5 Ap 13 '87. A. Porter
Opera News il 51:20, 22-4 Mr 14 '87
Must-carry rules (Cable television) See Television laws and regulations
Mustangs See Horses, Wild
Mustard, Prepared
Marvelous mustards. B. R. Rogers. il *Ctry J* 14:28-31 Mr '87
Mustique (Saint Vincent and the Grenadines)
See also
Country estates—Mustique (Saint Vincent and the Grenadines)
Musto, Michael, 1955-
Are these stars sick of being stars? il *Mademoiselle* 93:90 Ap '87
Cool in the shades. il *Harpers Bazaar* 120:32+ Ap '87
The importance of being hippest: a 60-second history of trends. *Mademoiselle* 93:147+ D '87
Late-night glitz. il *Harpers Bazaar* 120:72+ Ja '87
Mustoe, Thomas A., and others
Accelerated healing of incisional wounds in rats induced by transforming growth factor-β. bibl f il *Science* 237:1333-6 S 11 '87
Mutagenic substances
See also
Cancer—Causes
Mutation
See also
Chromosome abnormalities
Dysgenesis
Transposons
The approaching era of the tumor suppressor genes. G. Klein. bibl f *Science* 238:1539-45 D 11 '87
Better animal models for genetic defects [technique developed by Mario R. Capecchi and Kirk R. Thomas] S. Eisenberg. *Sci News* 132:327 N 21 '87
A cytoplasmic protein stimulates normal N-*ras* p21 GTPase, but does not affect oncogenic mutants. M. Trahey and F. McCormick. bibl f il *Science* 238:542-5 O 23 '87
Evidence for increased somatic cell mutations at the glycophorin A locus in atomic bomb survivors. R. G. Langlois and others. bibl f il *Science* 236:445-8 Ap 24 '87
Gene defect located for Gaucher's disease [research by Shoji Tsuji and others] B. Bower. *Sci News* 131:167-8 Mr 14 '87
Gene for von Recklinghausen neurofibromatosis is in the pericentromeric region of chromosome 17. D. Barker and others. bibl f il *Science* 236:1100-2 My 29 '87
Gene search narrows [neurofibromatosis] R. Weiss. *Sci News* 131:359 Je 6 '87
Identification and localization of mutations at the Lesch-Nyhan locus by ribonuclease A cleavage. R. A. Gibbs and C. T. Caskey. bibl f il *Science* 236:303-5 Ap 17 '87
Mutants of bovine pancreatic trypsin inhibitor lacking cysteines 14 and 38 can fold properly. C. B. Marks and others. bibl f il *Science* 235:1370-3 Mr 13 '87
Mutations in the first exon are associated with altered transcription of c-*myc* in Burkitt lymphoma [chromosomal translocations] E. Cesarman and others. bibl f il *Science* 238:1272-5 N 27 '87
New understanding of Gaucher's disease [research by Edward Ginns and others] G. Kolata. *Science* 235:1328 Mr 13 '87
Tinkering with enzymes: what are we learning? J. R. Knowles. bibl f il *Science* 236:1252-8 Je 5 '87

Bacteria
Mutations in diphtheria toxin separate binding from entry and amplify immunotoxin selectivity. L. Greenfield and others. bibl f il *Science* 238:536-9 O 23 '87
Fungi
Yeast KEX2 protease has the properties of a human proalbumin converting enzyme. I. C. Bathurst and others. bibl f il *Science* 235:348-50 Ja 16 '87
Nematodes
Genetic analysis of halothane sensitivity in Caenorhabditis elegans. M. M. Sedensky and P. M. Meneely. bibl f il *Science* 236:952-4 My 22 '87
Rodents
Evolutionary and somatic selection of the antibody repertoire in the mouse. K. Rajewsky and others. bibl f il *Science* 238:1088-94 N 20 '87
Glucocorticoid receptor mutants that define a small region sufficient for enhancer activation. R. Miesfeld and others. bibl f il *Science* 236:423-7 Ap 24 '87
The molecular basis of the sparse fur mouse mutation [ornithine transcarbamylase] G. Veres and others. bibl f il *Science* 237:415-17 Jl 24 '87
Viruses
Clustering of genes dispensable for growth in culture in the S component of the HSV-1 genome. R. Longnecker and B. Roizman. bibl f il *Science* 236:573-6 My 1 '87
HTLV *x* gene mutants exhibit novel transcriptional regulatory phenotypes. W. Wachsman and others. bibl f il *Science* 235:674-7 F 6 '87
Rapid identification of nonessential genes of herpes simplex virus type 1 by Tn5 mutagenesis. P. C. Weber and others. bibl f il *Science* 236:576-9 My 1 '87
Mutchnick, Brenda
about
L.A.'s eclectic entertainment executive. J. Giambanco. il pors *Work Woman* 12:128+ Ap '87
Muti, Riccardo
about
Muti of Milan [interview] N. Lebrecht. il por *Opera News* 51:18-19+ Ja 17 '87
Mutiny
See also
Bounty Mutiny, 1789
Muttontown (N.Y.)
Historic houses, sites, etc.
William Adams Delano and the Muttontown enclave. M. A. Hewitt. bibl f il *Antiques* 132:316-27 Ag '87
Mutual and Balanced Force Reductions Talks See Disarmament—Conferences
Mutual Broadcasting System, Inc.
The Pattiz treatment. C. Capuzzi. il *Channels* 7:31 Ap '87
Mutual fund forecaster (Newsletter) See Investment newsletters
Mutual fund managers See Investment advisers
Mutual funds See Investment trusts
Mutual Life Insurance Co. of New York
Stodgy no more. J. A. Conway. il por *Forbes* 139:8 My 4 '87
Mutual of New York-MONY See Mutual Life Insurance Co. of New York
Mutual Publishing Company
Regional reissues are new directions in San Francisco and Honolulu. L. See. *Publ Wkly* 231:34 Ap 24 '87
Mutual Shares Corp.
Distressed merchandise [Cambrian & General Securities] R. Phalon. por *Forbes* 139:180 Ap 6 '87
Falling off a limb at Harcourt [Salomon and Mutual Shares lost on convertible bond gamble] D. Zigas. por *Bus Week* p32 Jl 6 '87
Mutual UFO Network
Closer encounters [annual convention] E. Dolnick. *New Repub* 197:15-16 Ag 10-17 '87
Mutualism (Biology) See Symbiosis
Muwakkil, Salim
Jackson's challenge [cover story] il *Progressive* 51:16-19 Jl '87
Muybridge, Eadweard, 1830-1904
about
A portrait of change [excerpt from Eadweard Muybridge in Guatemala, 1875] E. B. Burns. il *Américas* 39:26-33 Jl/Ag '87
Muziektheater (Amsterdam, Netherlands) See Opera houses
Mvelase
about
Out of South Africa. J. Levine. il pors *N Y Times Mag* p81+ S 20 '87
MVP Athletic Network See Information storage and retrieval systems—Educational use

Mwiria, Kilemi
(jt. auth) See Shiman, David A., and Mwiria, Kilemi
MX (Missile) See Guided missiles
MX (Missile) basing system See Guided missile bases
My darling Judith [drama] See Foster, Norm, 1949-
My demon lover [film] See Motion picture reviews—Single works
My Gene [drama] See Gelb, Barbara
My life as a dog [film] See Motion picture reviews—Single works
My sweet little village [film] See Motion picture reviews—Single works
Myatt, Art
Health care economics and AIDS. il por *Humanist* 47:18-20+ Jl/Ag '87
Mycobacterial diseases
See also
Leprosy
Tuberculosis
Mycoplasmas
Cloning and detection of DNA from a nonculturable plant pathogenic mycoplasma-like organism. B. C. Kirkpatrick and others. bibl f il *Science* 238:197-200 O 9 '87
Transposition of gram-positive transposon Tn916 in Acholeplasma laidlawii and Mycoplasma pulmonis. K. Dybvig and G. H. Cassell. bibl f il *Science* 235:1392-4 Mr 13 '87
Mycorrhiza
Fossil mycorrhizae: a case for symbiosis. S. P. Stubblefield and others. bibl f il *Science* 237:59-60 Jl 3 '87
Pulling each other through bad times [fossil mycorrhiza; research by Sara P. Stubblefield and others] *Sci News* 132:47 Jl 18 '87
Mydans, Seth
The embattled Mrs. Aquino. il pors *N Y Times Mag* p42-3+ N 15 '87
The Marcoses' moonlight sonata. il pors *N Y Times Mag* p34-6+ Ap 19 '87
Myelin disease See Demyelination
Myelitis
The million-dollar baby nobody wants [P. Carnes, suffering from diffuse myelitis, lives in Texas hospital] C. C. Frink. il pors *Ladies Home J* 104:48+ D '87
Myers, Alan
(tr) See Brodsky, Joseph, 1940-. The bust of Tiberius
Myers, Arthur, 1917-
That's the spirit. il *Travel Holiday* 168:114 O '87
Myers, Debbie
about
How they do it. J. Traub. pors *Channels* 7:39 My '87
Myers, Dennis, and Ewing, Darrell
Tar Heel Tinseltown: De Laurentiis does it in North Carolina. il *Theatre Crafts* 21:53-4 Ap '87
Myers, Gary
This gun for hire. il por *Sport Mag* 78:26 Ja '87
Myers, George Hewitt, 1865-1957
about
One man's romance with fiber created the Textile Museum. M. McWilliam. il por *Smithsonian* 17:108-10+ Mr '87
Myers, Jane
The active gourmet. il pors *Women's Sports Fitness* 9:37-9 N '87
Myers, Joan Rohr
Preliminaries [poem] *Christ Century* 104:303 Ap 1 '87
Towards morning [poem] *Commonweal* 114:618 N 6 '87
Myers, M. Ruth
A touch of magic [fiction] il por *Good Housekeep* 205:153-6+ Ag '87
Myers, Miles
When research does not help teachers. *Educ Dig* 52:14-17 Ja '87
Myers, Norman
Kuna Indians: building a bright future. il map *Int Wildl* 17:18-24 Jl/Ag '87
Linking environment and security. il *Bull At Sci* 43:46-7 Je '87
Myers, Ramon H.
The Republic of Korea [address, September 22, 1987] *Vital Speeches Day* 54:72-6 N 15 '87
Myers, Woodrow A.
about
Indiana's health chief got sick of life in the fat lane, and he's never svelte better. M. Neill. il pors *People Wkly* 28:185-6 N 16 '87
Reagan names black MD to AIDS Commission. il por *Jet* 72:6 Ag 10 '87

Myers-Briggs Type Indicator
Personality tests are back. T. Moore. il *Fortune* 115:74-6+ Mr 30 '87
Myerson, Bess
about
Bess and the mess: Myerson's slide into scandal [cover story] P. Morrisroe. il pors *N Y* 20:30-44 Mr 30 '87
Bess Myerson's got a secret. D. Collins. il por *U S News World Rep* 102:14 Ja 26 '87
Between friends. J. Hull. il por *Time* 129:22 Ja 26 '87
'Dallas' on the Hudson. il pors *Newsweek* 110:10 O 26 '87
Downfall of an American idol [cover story] M. Green. il pors *People Wkly* 27:44-6+ Je 29 '87
Knowing the right people. A. Logan. *New Yorker* 63:121-4+ O 26 '87
Mylan Laboratories Inc.
Mylan Laboratories has a new formula for profits. il *Money* 16:8 N '87
Mylander, Maureen
Gut reactions! il *Ladies Home J* 104:80+ Ag '87
Myler, Cammy
about
Woman to watch: Cammy Myler. A. Osius. il por *Women's Sports Fitness* 9:70 D '87
Mylrea, Mindy
about
Kickoff of a craze: aerobics get competitive with beachfront bouts. M. A. Fischer. il pors *Life* 10:53-4+ Ag '87
Mylroie, Laurie
(jt. auth) See Pipes, Daniel, 1949-, and Mylroie, Laurie
Mynors, Arthur Clynton Baskerville, d. 1879
about
The good, the true, the beautiful. J. Hart. *Natl Rev* 39:46 Mr 27 '87
Myocardial ischemia See Heart—Diseases
Myocardium See Heart—Muscle
Myofacial pain dysfunction syndrome See TMJ syndrome
Myoglobin
Multiple conformational states of proteins: a molecular dynamics analysis of myoglobin. R. Elber and M. Karplus. bibl f il *Science* 235:318-21 Ja 16 '87
Spectra and spectroscopy
Linkage of functional and structural heterogeneity in proteins: dynamic hole burning in carboxymyoglobin. B. F. Campbell and others. bibl f il *Science* 238:373-6 O 16 '87
Myohemerythrin See Hemerythrin
Myopia
'Boring' reading and nearsightedness [work of Josh Wallman and others] D. D. Edwards. *Sci News* 132:23 Jl 11 '87
Eyeing myopia [how reading could lead to nearsightedness; research by Josh Wallman] E. Collins. *Sci Am* 257:36 O '87
Local retinal regions control local eye growth and myopia [impoverished stimulus situation of reading; cover story] J. Wallman and others. bibl f il *Science* 237:73-7 Jl 3 '87
Therapy
What behavioral optometrists see [cover story] J. Pace. *Consum Res Mag* 70:11-15 Ap '87
Myopia surgery See Cornea—Surgery
Myosin
Antisense RNA inactivation of myosin heavy chain gene expression in Dictyostelium discoideum [cover story] D. A. Knecht and W. F. Loomis. bibl f il *Science* 236:1081-6 My 29 '87
Cracking the mold [gene targeting and anti-sense techniques used in Dictyostelium myosin research] *Sci Am* 257:26 Ag '87
Disruption of the Dictyostelium myosin heavy chain gene by homologous recombination. A. De Lozanne and J. A. Spudich. bibl f il *Science* 236:1086-91 My 29 '87
What myosin might do. F. Solomon. bibl f *Science* 236:1043-4 My 29 '87
Myosin phosphorylation See Phosphorylation
Myrdal, Gunnar, 1898-1987
about
Obituary
Jet 72:17 Je 1 '87
Natl Rev 39:20 Je 19 '87
Myrdal, Jan
Thoughts from the roof of the world [excerpt from Silk Road] il *Courier* 40:37-8 Ap '87

Myrica faya *See* Candleberry myrtle

Myristic acid

Acylation of proteins with myristic acid occurs cotranslationally. C. Wilcox and others. bibl f il *Science* 238:1275-8 N 27 '87

Mysids

The spangled reef. il *Sea Front* 33:183-5 My/Je '87

The mystery of Al Capone's vaults [television program] See Television program reviews—Single works

Mystery plays (Modern) *See* Detective and mystery plays

Mystery stories *See* Detective and mystery stories

Mystic Seaport Museum

Mystic: a whale of a time. M. Andersson. il *Saturday Evening Post* 259:90 Jl/Ag '87

Mysticism

See also

Yoga

Hinduism

See also

Krishna consciousness movement

Judaism

A fateful intellectual friendship [G. Scholem and W. Benjamin] E. Rothstein. *Commentary* 84:41-9 D '87

Mythologies [dance] See Dance reviews—Single works

Mythology

See also

Geographical myths

Women in mythology

The Iran arms scandal, says a historian, shows how the power of myth can cloud a president's mind [interview with R. Slotkin] D. Van Biema. il pors *People Wkly* 27:97-8+ Ja 19 '87

Bibliography

Saviors, myths, & sacred heroes. M. Gerhart. il *Commonweal* 114:250-1 Ap 24 '87

Mythology, Aboriginal *See* Australian aborigines—Religion and mythology

Mythology, Greek

See also

Amazons

Midas (Greek mythology)

Odysseus (Greek mythology)

Mythology, Indian (American) *See* Indians of North America—Religion and mythology

Myths *See* Mythology

MyWord! (Word processor program) *See* Word processors and processing—Programming

Myxicola infundibulum *See* Annelids

N

N-ROSS (Navy Remote Ocean Sensing System) satellite *See* Artificial satellites—Oceanographic use

N. W. Ayer & Son, Inc.

An ad agency's war with the Army. P. Dwyer. *Bus Week* p102+ Ap 13 '87

N.W. Ayer bags itself a whopper [Burger King account] M. N. Vamos. il *Bus Week* p42 O 12 '87

NAAB *See* National Architectural Accrediting Board (U.S.)

NAACP *See* National Association for the Advancement of Colored People

NABET *See* National Association of Broadcast Employees and Technicians

Nabisco Brands, Inc.

Soggy cookie monster. J. A. Trachtenberg. il *Forbes* 140:156+ O 19 '87

Nabokov, Dmitri

A rejoinder from Dmitri Nabokov. *Natl Rev* 39:42-3 Ja 30 '87

Nabokov, Vladimir Vladimirovich, 1899-1977

about

A rejoinder from Dmitri Nabokov. D. Nabokov. *Natl Rev* 39:42-3 Ja 30 '87

Nabucco [opera] See Verdi, Giuseppe, 1813-1901

Nacco Industries

Most improved. il *Forbes* 139:97 Ja 12 '87

Nacelles (Airplanes) *See* Airplanes, Jet—Nacelles

Nack, William

Busting out for a cool million. il *Sports Illus* 66:26-8+ Je 15 '87

Classic fit for an old Shoe. il *Sports Illus* 67:36-8+ N 30 '87

Comeback for the ages. il pors *Sports Illus* 66:18-25 Ap 13 '87

Doing battle with the Demon. il por *Sports Illus* 66:42-4+ My 4 '87

A dud in the mud. il *Sports Illus* 67:14-15 Ag 31 '87

'Everything I did worked'. il pors *Sports Illus* 66:50-2+ Ap 20 '87

Fighting is in his blood. il pors *Sports Illus* 67:58-61+ N 16 '87

The good Doctor has a bad scrape. il pors *Sports Illus* 66:28-30+ Ja 5 '87

'I have got to do right'. il pors *Sports Illus* 66:60-4+ Ja 19 '87

In the groove at long last. il *Sports Illus* 67:50-3 O 19 '87

'Let the world know I'm O.K.'. il pors *Sports Illus* 67:34-7 S 28 '87

Old foes, new race. il *Sports Illus* 66:44-6+ Je 8 '87

Prediction. il pors *Sports Illus* 66:70-2+ Mr 30 '87

Say good night, Gerry. il pors *Sports Illus* 66:22-3 Je 22 '87

Slip-slidin' away to '88. il por *Sports Illus* 66:64-5 Mr 9 '87

The son shines bright. il *Sports Illus* 66:26-31 My 11 '87

Starting over. il pors *Sports Illus* 67:92-6+ D 14 '87

Two down, now the Crown. il *Sports Illus* 66:30-2+ My 25 '87

Very tough night at the office. il pors *Sports Illus* 67:64+ O 26 '87

What goes up comes down. il pors *Sports Illus* 67:68+ D 14 '87

NACS *See* National Association of College Stores (U.S.)

Nadelman, Cynthia

Gabo's progeny. il por *Art News* 86:123-7 D '87

Rewriting sculpture. il por *Art News* 86:120-7 My '87

Nader, Alceu

Bolivia beats 5-digit inflation. il *World Press Rev* 34:44-5 S '87

Nader, Laura

Cultural control [with discussion] il por *Cent Mag* 20:50-9 Mr/Ap '87

Nader, Ralph

about

It's still full speed ahead for Ralph Nader. I. Wolfman. il por *50 Plus* 27:24-7 N '87

Ralph Nader [interview] W. Greider. il por *Roll Stone* p115-16+ N 5-D 10 '87

Nadin, Peter

about

Peter Nadin. J. Sturman. il *Art News* 86:181 O '87

Nadine [film] See Motion picture reviews—Single works

Nadis, Steven J.

Asleep in the cosmos. il *Omni* 9:26+ Je '87

Cosmic mergers. il *Omni* 9:24+ Ag '87

Sky graffiti. il *Omni* 10:24+ O '87

NAE *See* National Association of Evangelicals

NAEP *See* National Assessment of Educational Progress

Naft, Mabel Wood, d. 1987

about

Obituary

Natl Rev 39:18-19 Jl 31 '87. P. L. Buckley

Nagan, Peter

about

Those who can, do. D. Machan. il por *Forbes* 140:113-14 D 14 '87

Nagasaki (Japan)

Bombardment, 1945

Atomic bomb doses reassessed. L. Roberts. il *Science* 238:1649-51 D 18 '87

Nagel, E. Victoria

Who is William Wharton? il *Horizon* 30:33-5 My '87

Nagel, Ed

about

Building blocks or stumbling blocks? S. Flink. il *World Tennis* 35:16-17 O '87

Nagel, Paul C.

Adamses at home [cover story] il por *Americana* 15:28-32 S/O '87

Naggar, Patrick

about

Rooms for art. J. Plumb. il por *House Gard* 159:142-51+ O '87

Nagle, Darragh E., and others

Pion physics at the meson factories. bibl f il *Phys Today* 40:56-64 Ap '87

Nagler, Willibald

Are your muscles old before their time? [excerpt from Dr. Nagler's Body maintenance and repair book] il *Women's Sports Fitness* 9:68 Ap '87

Nagy, Peter

about

Peter Nagy. M. Poirier. il *Art News* 86:179+ O '87

NAIA *See* National Association of Intercollegiate Athletics

Naify, Marshall
about
What a performance. A. B. Block. il *Forbes* 139:136 Ap 6 '87

Naify, Robert A.
about
What a performance. A. B. Block. il *Forbes* 139:136 Ap 6 '87

Nail biting
How to nip the nail-biting habit. *Teen* 31:130 S '87

Nail polish
Nail polish know-how. il *Ladies Home J* 104:34 N '87

Nail salons *See* Beauty shops

Nailing *See* Nails

Nails
See also
Tremont Nail Company
Driving small nails and brads. H. Wicks. il *Home Mech* 83:10 O '87
Nail selection chart. il *Workbench* 43:80 My/Je '87
Nails. J. Truini. il *Pop Mech* 164:65-7 Ja '87
Plastic nails. P. McCafferty. il *Pop Sci* 230:66-7 Ap '87
Popped drywall nails. B. Duggan. il *Home Mech* 83:30 F '87
Pound for pound, aluminum nails measure up. L. Swercinski. il *Workbench* 43:12 Mr/Ap '87

Nails (Anatomy)
See also
Manicuring
Nail biting
The newest beauty asset: hands & nails. il *Glamour* 85:364-9 S '87
Remedies for your biggest nail problems. il *Glamour* 85:20 Ja '87

Naimoli, Vincent Joseph, 1937-
about
What keeps Anchor Glass steady: buying shaky rivals. G. DeGeorge. il por *Bus Week* p72-3 Jl 27 '87

Naipaul, V. S. (Vidiadhar Surajprasad), 1932-
The ceremony of farewell [fiction] il *N Y Rev Books* 34:9-10 F 12 '87
On being a writer. il *N Y Rev Books* 34:7 Ap 23 '87
about
An elusive master [interview] A. Robinson. por *World Press Rev* 34:32-3 O '87

Naipaul, Vidiadhar Surajprasad *See* Naipaul, V. S. (Vidiadhar Surajprasad), 1932-

Nairn, Allan
The Bush connection [cover story] il *Progressive* 51:19-23 My '87
The contras' little list. il *Progressive* 51:24-6 Mr '87
The White House tapes, again. il *Progressive* 51:20-3 Ap '87

Nairobi (Kenya)
Child welfare
The street boys of Nairobi. I. Ndirangu. *World Press Rev* 34:57 S '87

Naisbitt, John, and Aburdene, Patricia
When companies are great places to work [condensed from Re-inventing the corporation] il *Read Dig* 130:141-4 Ja '87

Naismith Memorial Basketball Hall of Fame
Walt Frazier feels great becoming an NBA legend. por *Jet* 71:49 Mr 2 '87

Naison, Mark, 1946-
A failed game plan. il *Commonweal* 114:199-200 Ap 10 '87

Naivete *See* Innocence (Psychology)

Najibullah, Mohammed
about
Najibullah—Moscow's new man in Kabul. por *Dep State Bull* 87:14 F '87
'People need peace, not Stingers' [interview] D. Foote. por *Newsweek* 110:48 O 12 '87

Nakamura, Yusuke, and others
Variable number of tandem repeat (VNTR) markers for human gene mapping. bibl f il *Science* 235:1616-22 Mr 27 '87

Nakash family
about
Does Guess have a friend in the IRS? R. Behar. il map *Forbes* 140:146-50+ N 16 '87
The IRS mess. R. Behar. il *Forbes* 140:8 N 30 '87

Nakasone, Yasuhiro
Visit of Japanese Prime Minister Nakasone [remarks and text of joint statement, April 30-May 1, 1987] il por *Dep State Bull* 87:37-41 Jl '87

about
A back-room man steps forward. H. G. Chua-Eoan. il por *Time* 130:65 N 2 '87
The ballad of Ron and Yasu [cover story] M. Sayle. *New Repub* 196:18-21 Je 15 '87
Japan. *Bus Week* p53 Mr 2 '87
Nakasone: from prime minister to 'shadow shogun'? B. Buell. il *Bus Week* p83 O 19 '87
Political poker game, Japanese style. M. Lord. il por *U S News World Rep* 103:32 Jl 20 '87
A whiff of blood in the water. B. Hillenbrand. il *Time* 129:35 Mr 23 '87
Yasu, the chips are down. H. G. Chua-Eoan. il por *Time* 129:38 Ap 27 '87
Anecdotes, facetiae, satire, etc.
Trading letters [imaginary correspondence between R. Reagan and Y. Nakasone] R. Baker. il *N Y Times Mag* p14 My 10 '87
Visit to the United States, 1987
America vs. Japan: a no-win game [special section] il por *Bus Week* p30-4 My 4 '87
A meeting for the books. il por *Fortune* 115:8 My 25 '87
Playing it cool. J. Greenwald. il por *Time* 129:32-3 My 11 '87
The U.S. and Japan: trying to head off a slump. B. Powell. il por *Newsweek* 109:50+ My 11 '87
Visit of Japanese Prime Minister Nakasone [remarks and text of joint statement, April 30-May 1, 1987] R. Reagan; Y. Nakasone; G. P. Shultz. il por *Dep State Bull* 87:37-41 Jl '87
A war between friends [protectionist frenzy unleashed during visit] M. McDonald. il por *Macleans* 100:32-3 My 11 '87

Nakedness *See* Nudity

Nally, Kenneth
about
Clergy malpractice. *Christ Century* 104:850 O 7 '87

Naltrexone
Are autistic children high on themselves? [Barbara Herman's work with opioid-blocking drug naltrexone] *Discover* 8:6-7 F '87
Autism: a chemical excess? [naltrexone used to treat children with abnormal opioid levels; research by Barbara Herman] S. Vandershaf. *Psychol Today* 21:15-16 Mr '87
A drug that lets the real world in [work of Barbara Herman and Kathryn Hammock] K. McAuliffe. il *U S News World Rep* 102:66 F 2 '87
Healthy addiction [use of opioid receptor blocking agent in treating autistic children; research by Barbara H. Herman] J. R. Goldberg. il *Health* 19:18 Ag '87

The name of the rose [film] *See* Motion picture reviews—Single works

Names
See also
Astronomy—Nomenclature
Corporations—Names
Wine—Names
Anecdotes, facetiae, satire, etc.
A rose by any other name. R. H. Bell. *Commonweal* 114:470-1 S 11 '87

Names, Geographical
English village names. B. Bryson. il *Travel Holiday* 168:94 S '87

Names, Personal
See also
Football players—Names
Nicknames
Presidential candidates—Names
Pseudonyms
Don't call me Fred. F. Eberstadt. il *Vogue* 177:267 Ap '87
Anecdotes, facetiae, satire, etc.
First-name fixation. R. Baker. il *N Y Times Mag* p14 Je 7 '87
What's in a name, Moonbeam? P. F. McManus. il *Outdoor Life* 179:130+ Ap '87
Pronunciation
Call him Vincent [van Gogh] J. Herzfeld. por *Art News* 86:15 Summ '87

Namibia
See also
United Nations—Namibia
United Nations Council for Namibia
Politics and government
See also
International Conference for the Immediate Independence of Namibia

Namibia—Politics and government—*cont.*

Assembly urges Security Council to impose mandatory oil embargo against South Africa: thirteen texts adopted on apartheid, Namibia issues. il *UN Chron* 24:40-4 F '87

Council commemorates Week of Solidarity with Namibians, SWAPO [U.N. Council for Namibia] il *UN Chron* 22:16 N/D '85

Council for Namibia calls for decisive action for territory's independence. il *UN Chron* 24:26 Ag '87

Council for Namibia president asks body to work for earliest independence for territory. *UN Chron* 23:32 N '86

General Assembly demands action for immediate implementation of Namibian independence plan, comprehensive sanctions and South African withdrawal from the territory. il *UN Chron* 23:37-46 N '86

An independent Namibia? It's still a pipe dream. G. Yalowitz. il *U S News World Rep* 103:76 S 28 '87

Namibia! Namibia! E. von Kuehnelt-Leddihn. *Natl Rev* 39:26 My 22 '87

Solemn meetings mark twentieth anniversary of start of Namibian liberation struggle. *UN Chron* 23:36 N '86

Text calling for comprehensive mandatory sanctions against South Africa vetoed after discussion in eight meetings. il *UN Chron* 24:22-5 Ag '87

The United Nations plan for Namibian independence. *UN Chron* 23:33 N '86

Social conditions

See also
Women—Namibia

Namin, Stas
about

Stas Namin and Ludmila Senchina reign over the pop scene while rock's underground rumbles. S. K. Reed. il pors *People Wkly* 27:46-8+ Ap 6 '87

NAMM *See* National Association of Music Merchants

Namphy, Henri, 1932-
about

Haiti robbed of hope [cover story] C. Cleaver. il *New Leader* 70:8-10 D 28 '87

Living with a nightmare. J. Smolowe. il *Time* 130:48+ D 21 '87

Visit to the United States, 1986

Visit of Haiti President Namphy [White House statement, November 21, 1986] il por *Dep State Bull* 87:78 F '87

Nancy Atkins, Inc.

Socks with soul: Nancy Atkins, Inc. [N. A. Keresty] J. Ciabattari. il por *Work Woman* 12:136-7 N '87

Nannies *See* Nursemaids

Nanotechnology

Great things from tiny beginnings. S. Budiansky. il *U S News World Rep* 103:54 Ag 31 '87

Nanotechnology [Space Development Conference] J. Rhea. il *Space World* X-6-282:8-9 Je '87

Nantucket (Mass.)
See also
Historic houses, sites, etc.—Nantucket (Mass.)

Art

Decorative arts in New England [The decorative arts and crafts of Nantucket] S. B. Sherrill. il *Antiques* 132:64+ Jl '87

Description and travel

Gourmet holidays: Christmas in Nantucket. T. Weeks. il map *Gourmet* 47:66-71+ D '87

Nantucket: the faraway land [cover story] D. Strickland. il map *Oceans* 20:14-23 My/Je '87

Napa Valley (Calif.)

Architecture

See Architecture—California

Art

See Art—California

Wine industry

See Wine industry

Napier, Augustus Y.

Couples on the couch. *Vogue* 177:386+ F '87

Napoleon I, Emperor of the French, 1769-1821
about

Napoleonic New York. A. Keefe. *Travel Holiday* 167:32-4 Je '87

Napoleon's grand designs. O. Bernier. il *House Gard* 159:146-51+ D '87

Napoleon [film] *See* Motion picture reviews—Single works

Napoleon and Josephine: a love story [television program] *See* Television program reviews—Single works

Napoleonic Wars
See also
Waterloo, Battle of, 1815

Napoli [ballet] *See* Ballet reviews—Single works

Napper, Andrew D., and others

A stereospecific cyclization catalyzed by an antibody. bibl f il *Science* 237:1041-3 Ag 28 '87

Napping (Sleep) *See* Sleep

Napsu, Izat
about

A pileup of scandals in Israel. N. Cooper. il por *Newsweek* 109:42 Je 8 '87

A scandal in the ranks. E. Silver. *Macleans* 100:28+ My 4 '87

Security on trial. B. Levin. il por *Macleans* 100:22 Je 8 '87

Thrice rebuked. il por *Time* 129:40 Je 8 '87

Narayanamurti, Venkatesh

Artificially structured thin-film materials and interfaces. bibl f il *Science* 235:1023-8 F 27 '87

Narcissism

The death of social conscience. B. G. Harrison. *Mademoiselle* 93:124 D '87

Narcissus, absorb thyself. W. Safire. *N Y Times Mag* p14 Mr 1 '87

Narcissus

How to make cut daffodils last longer. il *Sunset* 178:194 Mr '87

Paperwhites' sweet perfume. il *South Living* 22:60 O '87

Some bulbs are almost foolproof. il *Sunset* 179:220-1 O '87

Anecdotes, facetiae, satire, etc.

The sneaky woman's garden [daffodils] K. Fury. il *50 Plus* 27:90 Je '87

Narcotic addicts *See* Drug abuse

Narcotic antagonists
See also
Naltrexone

Narcotics
See also
Endorphins
Heroin

Narcotics laws and regulations
See also
Airplanes in narcotics regulation
Boats in narcotics regulation
Marijuana—Laws and regulations
United States. Congress. House. Select Committee on Narcotics Abuse and Control
United States. Drug Enforcement Administration

The biggest drug bust. J. A. Conway. il *Forbes* 139:8 Je 1 '87

Black mayors rap funding for U.S. war on drugs. *Jet* 73:6 N 16 '87

Calif. 'Big Spin' winner pleads guilty to theft [cocaine charge against T. Garrett dismissed] *Jet* 71:36 Ja 12 '87

Citizen Ueberroth [interview] R. B. Cramer. il pors *Esquire* 107:69-72+ F '87

Cleaver is arrested in L.A. on cocaine charges. por *Jet* 73:38 O 26 '87

Dark clouds over Sun country [drug bust implicating present and former members of the Phoenix Suns basketball team] A. Keteyian. il *Sports Illus* 66:24-5 Ap 27 '87

The drug war bogs down. J. V. Lamar, Jr. il *Time* 130:28 N 23 '87

Drug withdrawal [cut in funds in 1988 budget] il *Time* 129:22 Ja 19 '87

Eldridge Cleaver fights charge; holds fund-raiser. por *Jet* 73:26 N 16 '87

Ex-Hawks star John Drew sentenced in drug case [selling cocaine] *Jet* 71:49 F 2 '87

Fighting drugs. M. S. Kreiter. il *Curr Health 2* 13:12-15 Ap '87

From hot tips to hard drugs—another Wall Street bust [brokers as cocaine dealers] K. R. Sheets. il *U S News World Rep* 102:55 Ap 27 '87

Georgia woman tied to Julian Bond in drug probe gets 22-year sentence [C. Butler] por *Jet* 72:52 S 21 '87

Getting high on it [legalization] R. O'Connor. *Vogue* 177:209+ Ja '87

Miami preacher convicted for selling heroin [case of C. Scott] *Jet* 72:10 Je 15 '87

Odom gets early release from Calif. drug sentence. *Jet* 71:50 Ja 12 '87

Parsing a sentence [N. Mailer accuses federal authorities of attempting to implicate him in drug smuggling case] por *Time* 130:61 Jl 27 '87

Quickly. Death is going on [treating terminal cancer with heroin] W. F. Buckley. *Natl Rev* 39:63 N 6 '87

Narcotics laws and regulations—*cont.*

Quiz sports stars after probe produces pictures [connections to heroin kingpin J. Jackson] il *Jet* 72:46 Je 1 '87

Reducing the demand for drugs [excerpts from report of the President's Commission on Organized Crime] *Congr Dig* 66:134-5 My '87

Reefer madness [Reagan antidrug campaign] A. Hoffman. *Nation* 245:580-1 N 21 '87

The rise and fall of Glenn Loury [drug possession charges] il por *Newsweek* 110:53 D 14 '87

Seattle's Gene Anderson throws the book at white-collar coke users who once knew no fear. M. Green. il por *People Wkly* 27:111-12 F 2 '87

Self-loathing on the Street [cocaine on Wall Street] il *Newsweek* 109:53 Ap 27 '87

A shaky Operation Alliance. E. Magnuson. il *Time* 129:31 F 23 '87

Should drug use be legalized? G. S. Becker. il *Bus Week* p22 Ag 17 '87

Sniffing out a line of coke brokers [drug dealing on Wall Street] S. Koepp. il *Time* 129:54 Ap 27 '87

The Southwest drug connection. S. Strasser. il map *Newsweek* 110:29-30+ N 23 '87

'They used to call me McEnroe' [satellite circuit tennis player, D. Herman, imprisoned for drug dealing] P. M. Coan. il *World Tennis* 34:20-1 My '87

We can conquer cocaine. T. Armbrister. il *Read Dig* 130:63-8 F '87

What's behind 'Jar Wars'. H. Levine and C. Reinarman. il *Nation* 244:388-90 Mr 28 '87

Conferences

See also

International Conference on Drug Abuse and Illicit Trafficking

International aspects

See also

International Narcotics Control Board

United Nations. Commission on Narcotic Drugs

United Nations. Division of Narcotic Drugs

FY 1988 assistance requests for narcotics control [statement, April 22, 1987] A. B. Wrobleski. *Dep State Bull* 87:73-6 Je '87

International Narcotics Control Strategy Report released. *Dep State Bull* 87:52-3 Ap '87

A long campaign. J. R. Thomas. *Cent Mag* 20:55 Ja/F '87

Narcotics: a global threat [address, May 4, 1987] G. P. Shultz. *Dep State Bull* 87:45-6 Ag '87

Bolivia

Exporting the drug war [U.S. efforts against cocaine trade] T. Molnar. *Natl Rev* 39:38 My 22 '87

How to lose the coke war [U.S.-Bolivian campaign] D. Kline. il *Atlantic* 259:22-7 My '87

Canada

Cashing in on ill-gotten gains [seizing proceeds derived from drug trafficking] D. Francis. il *Macleans* 100:13 N 2 '87

Crackdown on the Montreal connection. D. Burke. il *Macleans* 100:45 Ap 6 '87

Escape from a Dutch jail [Peruvian E. Barreto-Morales wanted by Canada for cocaine trafficking] D. Burke. por *Macleans* 100:44 Je 15 '87

New campaigns in the war on drugs. M. McIver. il *Macleans* 100:44 Je 8 '87

Colombia

Breaking a drug lord [cocaine dealer C. E. Lehder Rivas] K. Scanlon. por *Macleans* 100:45 F 23 '87

Caught: cocaine's 'Mr. Big' [C. Lehder Rivas] M. Satchell. il por *U S News World Rep* 102:12 F 16 '87

Cocaine billionaires: the men who hold Colombia hostage. A. Riding. il map *N Y Times Mag* p26-32+ Mr 8 '87

Colombia to drug lords: enough is enough [cocaine] C. A. Robbins. il *U S News World Rep* 102:12 Ja 19 '87

Crackdown on the drug lords [cocaine] A. Guillermoprieto. *Newsweek* 109:33 Ja 19 '87

Crazy Charlie [arrest of C. Lehder Rivas] *Nation* 244:203-5 F 21 '87

The fall of a cocaine kingpin [capture of Colombian C. Lehder Rivas] J. Smolowe. il por *Time* 129:37 F 16 '87

How the drug czar got away [Drug Enforcement Administration botches case against Colombian J. L. Ochoa Vasquez] M. A. Lee. il *Nation* 245:189-92 S 5 '87

Snaring the king of coke [capture of C. Lehder Rivas] R. Nordland. il por *Newsweek* 109:16-18 F 16 '87

Italy

Life in a Roman limbo [Canadians M. and L. Lévesque held on charges of heroin trafficking] A. Wilson-Smith. il pors *Macleans* 100:15-16 Ja 26 '87

Triumph for two sisters [M. and L. Lévesque cleared of heroin smuggling charges in Rome] J. Barber. il pors *Macleans* 100:44 F 23 '87

Latin America

Dealing against illegal drugs. A. Quiroga G. *Américas* 39:55 My/Je '87

Malaysia

Deadly traffic. M. Schwarz. il *N Y Times Mag* p54+ Mr 22 '87

Middle East

Mideast drug busting. T. Land. *New Leader* 70:4 O 19 '87

Panama

Dirty dollars [new law aimed at drug traffickers] J. Moody. il por *Time* 129:44-5 Ja 19 '87

Peru

Busted [false arrest of Americans for cocaine possession] J. Jameson. *New Repub* 196:9-10 My 25 '87

Soviet Union

The raiders of 'Tashkent Vice'. il *U S News World Rep* 103:13 Ag 31 '87

United States

See Narcotics laws and regulations

Narcotics smuggling *See* Narcotics trade

Narcotics trade

See also

Airplanes in narcotics regulation

Airplanes in narcotics trade

Boats in narcotics regulation

Boats in narcotics trade

Narcotics laws and regulations

United Nations. Commission on Narcotic Drugs

United Nations. Division of Narcotic Drugs

Drug smuggling increases. il *Futurist* 21:56 S/O '87

'Fat Cat' and the crack wars: brash young dealers muscle the drug establishment [Queens, N.Y.] P. Blauner. il por *N Y* 20:46-54 S 7 '87

Miami Vice: sorting good guys from bad guys [police involved in drug dealing] M. A. Moore. il *U S News World Rep* 102:28 F 2 '87

Pizza penance [New York City jury convicts Mafia members of smuggling drugs] il *Time* 129:34 Mr 16 '87

International aspects

Narcotics: terror's new ally [cover story; special section] M. Satchell. il map *U S News World Rep* 102:30-7 My 4 '87

The return of the French connection [cover story] A. Press. il *Newsweek* 109:56-63 Ap 13 '87

Bolivia

The sacred and the corrupt [cocaine] *World Press Rev* 34:44 S '87

Colombia

Cocaine billionaires: the men who hold Colombia hostage. A. Riding. il map *N Y Times Mag* p26-32+ Mr 8 '87

How to make $7 billion in 7 years [Medellín Cartel] D. Henry. il *Forbes* 140:154 O 5 '87

France

The return of the French connection [cover story] A. Press. il *Newsweek* 109:56-63 Ap 13 '87

Mexico

The Southwest drug connection. S. Strasser. il map *Newsweek* 110:29-30+ N 23 '87

Nicaragua

Contra-gate: a black issue. R. Knight. por *Essence* 18:144 Je '87

Drugs and contras. *Nation* 244:786-7 Je 13 '87

How the drug czar got away [Drug Enforcement Administration botches case against Colombian J. L. Ochoa Vasquez] M. A. Lee. il *Nation* 245:189-92 S 5 '87

Is there a contra drug connection? [cocaine smuggling for guns] R. Nordland. il *Newsweek* 109:26 Ja 26 '87

Minority report [evidence of C.I.A.-contra-narcotics connection] C. Hitchens. *Nation* 244:531 Ap 25 '87

The misadventures of El Patrón [involvement of contra supporter J. Hull] J. V. Lamar, Jr. il por *Time* 130:31-2 N 16 '87

Money, drugs and the contras [cover story] J. Kwitny. il *Nation* 245:145+ Ag 29 '87

Of drugs, money and contras [discussion of August 29, 1987 article, Money, drugs and the contras] J. Kwitny. *Nation* 245:254+ S 19 '87

Narcotics trade—*cont.*

Southeast Asia
New kingpins of heroin [Chinese traffickers] M. Gray. il *Macleans* 100:55+ S 7 '87
Reign of an opium warlord [Khun Sa] M. Satchell. il por *U S News World Rep* 102:33 My 4 '87

Soviet Union
What is the Kremlin's role? [involvement in narco-terrorism] M. Satchell. il *U S News World Rep* 102:34 My 4 '87

United States
See Narcotics trade

Nardone, Angelo
about
Grass-roots art seeks a haven. H. Metz. il por *Progressive* 51:14 O '87

Narens, Louis
(jt. auth) See Luce, R. Duncan (Robert Duncan), and Narens, Louis

Narration (Rhetoric)
See also
Fiction—Narration

NASA *See* United States. National Aeronautics and Space Administration

NASA Alumni League
NASA Alumni League news. See issues of Space World beginning June 1987

Nasal sprays
By a nose [addiction] K. Freifeld. il *Health* 19:10 Ag '87
Hot new cold treatment [Viralizer] D. Pine. il *Health* 19:21 Ap '87
Medicating through the nose. S. Weisburd. *Sci News* 132:190 S 19 '87

NASCAR *See* National Association for Stock Car Auto Racing
NASD *See* National Association of Securities Dealers
Nash, J. Daniel
Florida: working with the phosphate factor. bibl f il map *Environment* 29:13+ Mr '87

Nash, Jonell
Fix food fast. See issues of Essence
Recipes. See issues of Essence

Nash, Knowlton
about
The face of the news. J. Bennett. il por *Macleans* 100:10+ D 21 '87
The National's new man. P. Young. il pors *Macleans* 100:58 N 23 '87

Nash, Victor
Americana in miniature. il *Americana* 15:21 N/D '87

Nasher, Patsy
about
The collectors: a passion for sculpture: Patsy and Raymond D. Nasher's Dallas residence and gardens. J. Chatfield-Taylor. il *Archit Dig* 44:112-21 O '87
Just getting started. K. Gregor. il pors *Art News* 86:59-60+ N '87

Nasher, Raymond
about
Buy what you love—but make sure it's first-rate. J. H. Dobrzynski. il por *Bus Week* p185 D 28 '87-Ja 4 '88
The collectors: a passion for sculpture: Patsy and Raymond D. Nasher's Dallas residence and gardens. J. Chatfield-Taylor. il *Archit Dig* 44:112-21 O '87
Just getting started. K. Gregor. il pors *Art News* 86:59-60+ N '87

Nashua Corporation
Why Nashua looks even richer now [acquisition of Lin Data] G. G. Marcial. *Bus Week* p126 Jl 20 '87

Nashville (Tenn.)
Bookstores
See Booksellers and bookselling—Tennessee
Crime
Black Nashville youth killed by whites over $2 vase at flea market [K. Majors] *Jet* 72:36 Je 15 '87
Hotels, motels, etc.
Tempering a landscape [hvac system of Cascades atrium, Opryland Hotel] D. Rastorfer. il *Archit Rec* 175:154-7 My '87
Politics and government
The battle of Nashville [mayoral race between B. Boner and P. Bredesen] T. E. Johnson. il por *Newsweek* 110:38 S 21 '87
Race relations
Whites protect black youth; four arrested [case of John Kelly] *Jet* 72:8 Ag 10 '87

Nasmyth, Kim, and Shore, David
Transcriptional regulation in the yeast life cycle. bibl f il *Science* 237:1162-70 S 4 '87

Nasopharynx
Cancer
Causes
Chinese folk remedy may promote cancer [plants containing phorbal esters linked to nasopharyngeal cancer; research by L. David Tomei and others] R. Weiss. *Sci News* 132:148 S 5 '87

NASP *See* National Association of Securities Professionals
Nasr Automotive Manufacturing Company
GM's grand design in Egypt may be a mirage. B. Slavin. il *Bus Week* p46 Mr 30 '87

Nasrallah, Emily
about
Voice of a war-torn land. J. Bennett. il por *Macleans* 100:7 Je 1 '87

Nassau (Bahamas)
Hotels, motels, etc.
Success in the sun [N. Symonette, black woman owner of Casuarinas Hotel] J. C. McAdams and J. Simmons. il pors *Essence* 17:101-2+ Ap '87

Nassau County (N.Y.)
Social work
Nassau County puts services on the road [Seniormobile] il *Aging* no355:32-3 '87

Nasser, Gamal Abdel, 1918-1970
about
The cost of self-deception. il por *U S News World Rep* 102:36 Je 8 '87

Nasturtiums
Nasturtium notes. P. H. Morris. il *Rodale's Org Gard* 34:80 My '87

Naszinski, Lara
about
Taking it easy. il pors *Vogue* 177:308-13 D '87

Natchez (Miss.)
Historic houses, sites, etc.
Living with antiques:
 Melrose in Natchez, Mississippi. W. N. Banks. bibl f il *Antiques* 131:650-7 Mr '87
Montaigne's invitation to the past: a historic residence in Natchez, Mississippi. R. Ford. il por *Archit Dig* 44:114-17+ Jl '87
The Old South comes alive in Natchez. B. Keating. il *50 Plus* 27:61-6 Mr '87
Plan a pilgrimage to Natchez. il *South Living* 22:47 O '87

History
Photographs and photography
Steamboats on the Mississippi [late 19th century photographer H. C. Norman] J. W. Gandy and T. H. Gandy. il *Am Hist Illus* 22:36-49 Mr '87

Nathan, Bethel
about
Getting the black vote. M. Eaton. il por *Black Enterp* 17:20 F '87

Nathan, Joan
Deep in the heart of Texas. il *Mother Earth News* 106:54-9 Jl/Ag '87
Fresh from the sea. il *N Y Times Mag* p67-8 Mr 22 '87
A Passover seder. il *N Y Times Mag* p63-4 Ap 5 '87

Nathan, Joe, 1948-
Results and future prospects of state efforts to increase choice among schools. bibl f il *Phi Delta Kappan* 68:746-52 Je '87

Nathan, Leonard, 1924-
(tr) See Miłosz, Czesław. All Hallows' Eve

Nathan, Otto, 1893-1987
about
Obituary
 Nation 244:169 F 14 '87. L. B. Boudin

Nathan, Paul S.
Rights. See issues of Publishers Weekly

Nathan, Richard P.
Will the underclass always be with us? il *Society* 24:57-62 Mr/Ap '87

Nathan Group
Getting the black vote. M. Eaton. il por *Black Enterp* 17:20 F '87

Nathanson, J. A. (James A.), 1947-
(jt. auth) See Steardo, Luca, and Nathanson, J. A. (James A.), 1947-

Nathanson, James A. *See* Nathanson, J. A. (James A.), 1947-

Nathanson, Jo
Virginia Madsen. il pors *Harpers Bazaar* 120:74, 344-7 S '87

Nation (Periodical)
Anti-Semitism, left & right [discussion of November 1986 article, The hate that dare not speak its name] N. Podhoretz. *Commentary* 83:2+ Mr '87

Nation (Periodical)—*cont.*
Covering alternative writing [S. Klawan's column] J. Barbato. *Publ Wkly* 232:56 N 27 '87
National Academy of Engineering
Academies select panel to judge ideal SSC site. I. Goodwin. *Phys Today* 40 pt1:52 Ag '87
Engineering Academy honors two, elects new members. il *Phys Today* 40:109-11 My '87
NAE elects new members. *Science* 235:1569 Mr 27 '87
National Academy of Recording Arts and Sciences (U.S.)
Drummer Stix Hooper heads the L.A. chapter of NARAS. por *Jet* 72:57 S 21 '87
National Academy of Sciences (U.S.)
Academies select panel to judge ideal SSC site. I. Goodwin. *Phys Today* 40 pt1:52 Ag '87
Academy rejects Huntington nomination. E. Marshall. por *Science* 236:661-2 My 8 '87
Blood lust in academia [S. P. Huntington denied membership] F. Zakaria. *New Repub* 197:16-18 Jl 27 '87
Cornell unit surveys some US Academy members on SDI. W. Sweet. *Phys Today* 40:72-3 Ja '87
NAS elects new members. *Science* 236:662 My 8 '87
The posse stops a "softie" [denial of entry to S. P. Huntington] E. Bowen. il *Time* 129:76-7 My 11 '87
Reelected to lead Academy, Press talks about science issues [interview] I. Goodwin. por *Phys Today* 40:47-52 Ap '87
Scholars bite Mad Dog [S. P. Huntington denied membership] *Nation* 244:595 My 9 '87
Soft sciences are often harder than hard sciences [opposition of S. Lang to S. P. Huntington's membership] J. M. Diamond. il *Discover* 8:34-5+ Ag '87
National Academy of Sciences (U.S.). Institute of Medicine *See* Institute of Medicine (U.S.)
National Academy of Sciences (U.S.). National Academy of Engineering *See* National Academy of Engineering
National Aeronautics and Space Administration (U.S.) *See* United States. National Aeronautics and Space Administration
National Aeronautics and Space Administration Alumni League *See* NASA Alumni League
National Agriculture Day
Joint venture. C. Tevis. il *Success Farm* 85 no6:18AW Mr '87
National Air Traffic Controllers Association
Air-traffic controllers: getting organized again? S. B. Garland. il *Bus Week* p52 My 18 '87
Full circle. A. A. Lappen. il *Forbes* 140:12 Jl 13 '87
Six years after PATCO's crash, fired air controller John Thornton helps a new union get off the ground. D. Chu. il por *People Wkly* 28:38-9 S 14 '87
Talking union. J. Merwin. il *Forbes* 139:35-6 Ap 6 '87
National Amusements, Inc.
Now Redstone is a media giant [S. Redstone wins Viacom] D. Lieberman and L. Therrien. il por *Bus Week* p42 Mr 16 '87
National Arboretum (U.S.)
Washington after the cherry blossoms fall. C. H. Crowley. il *Saturday Evening Post* 259:84-6+ Ap '87
National Architectural Accrediting Board (U.S.)
Accreditation criteria revive some standards, tighten others. J. M. Maudlin-Jeronimo and P. Hoffmann. *Archit Rec* 175:33 Ja '87
National Archives and Records Administration (U.S.) *See* United States. National Archives and Records Administration
National Assessment of Educational Progress
Improving literacy level is crucial: NAEP. *Phi Delta Kappan* 68:711+ My '87
Johnny can't write, either. il *Consum Res Mag* 70:18-21+ Ag '87
The national assessments in reading: are we misreading the findings? J. B. Carroll. bibl f il *Phi Delta Kappan* 68:424-30 F '87
National writing assessments: trends across 10 years [excerpt from Writing] A. N. Applebee and others. *Educ Dig* 52:24-6 F '87
Students lack skills in writing and critical thinking: NAEP. *Phi Delta Kappan* 68:484-5 F '87
Testing the winds. A. C. Lewis. *Phi Delta Kappan* 68:652-3 My '87
National Association for Home Care
The growing Halamandaris empire. R. Rosenblatt. il pors *50 Plus* 27:14-17 Jl '87
National Association for Stock Car Auto Racing
Close company [Winston Cup series] A. Girdler. il *Road Track* 39:120-2+ D '87
NASCAR '87: Winston Cup preview. B. Nagy. il *Mot Trend* 39:111-12+ My '87

National Association for the Advancement of Colored People
Atlanta NAACP is fuming over white talk show host's calling Lewis 'Buckwheat' [E. Tyll's remarks concerning Congressman J. Lewis] il pors *Jet* 72:22 Ag 10 '87
Atlanta NAACP targets Turner's Hawks, Braves. *Jet* 73:48 D 14 '87
Detroit NAACP raises record $720,000 at Freedom banquet. il *Jet* 72:23 My 18 '87
Frank Sinatra to receive NAACP achievement honor. *Jet* 71:16 Mr 23 '87
Homestead NAACP chided on fingerprint support. il *Jet* 73:7 S 28 '87
L.A. branch of NAACP gives Sinatra achievement award. il por *Jet* 72:56 Je 1 '87
L.A. NAACP wants judge fired for 'nigger' slur [removal of D. Calabro] *Jet* 72:12 S 14 '87
NAACP blasts record biz. A. DeCurtis. *Roll Stone* p15+ My 21 '87
NAACP hits Tulsa with voting rights suit. *Jet* 72:29 Ag 10 '87
NAACP, NEA opposing Reagan's pick for Court [R. Bork nomination] il *Jet* 72:8 Jl 20 '87
Percy Sutton lauded; past year's battles celebrated at NAACP confab in N.Y. il por *Jet* 72:4-5 Jl 27 '87
National Association of Air Traffic Specialists
Air traffic controllers sue to block FAA drug testing. C. Preble. *Aviat Week Space Technol* 126:32-3 Mr 2 '87
National Association of Arab Americans
Arabs anonymous [sponsorship of essay contest on America's Middle East policy] J. L. Pasley. *New Repub* 197:17-18 Ag 10-17 '87
National Association of Area Agencies on Aging
Agencies on Aging can serve developmentally disabled older adults. T. Rose. il *Aging* no356:32-3 '87
The one agency you can't do without. M. Opsata. *50 Plus* 27:20+ Mr '87
National Association of Black Journalists
Publisher John H. Johnson accepts lifetime achievement award from black journalists. il por *Jet* 72:16 S 14 '87
National Association of Boards of Pharmacy
Henry Cade named new Pharmacy Board prexy. por *Jet* 72:14 Jl 13 '87
National Association of Broadcast Employees and Technicians
Sammy Davis refuses to cross line of pickets. *Jet* 72:10 Ag 31 '87
Union shopping. A. B. Block. il *Forbes* 139:106+ Je 15 '87
National Association of Broadcasters
The NAB's low power signal. M. Frankel. il *Channels* 7:36-42 Mr '87
Public service and the bottom line [antidrug public service announcements] J. L. Swerdlow. il *Channels* 7:66 Ja '87
National Association of College Stores (U.S.)
College stores CAMEX show draws record turnout in Anaheim. L. See. il *Publ Wkly* 231:44-5 Je 5 '87
National Association of Evangelicals
Expanding the peace movement. R. J. Neuhaus. *Natl Rev* 39:46 F 27 '87
Gospel or government? H. Smith. il *Christ Today* 31:38-9 Ap 3 '87
Weaving a seamless garment out of peace, freedom, and security [guidelines on war and peace] R. Frame. il *Christ Today* 31:42-4 My 15 '87
National Association of Intercollegiate Athletics
Central State University returns sports to NAIA. *Jet* 72:48 Jl 27 '87
National Association of Manufacturers of the United States of America
Computer congressmen [video game, Congressional Insight] T. Noah. *New Repub* 196:10-12 Ap 6 '87
National Association of Music Merchants
Obsolescence battled at NAMM Convention. D. Andrews. il *Down Beat* 54:12 S '87
Refinement, innovation displayed at NAMM. B. O'Donnell. il *Down Beat* 54:12 Ap '87
National Association of Radiation Survivors
Putting vets in the shredder [suit against the Veterans Administration] M. Perry. il *Nation* 245:554-6 N 14 '87
National Association of Real Estate Brokers
Nation's black real estate brokers hold 40th confab. il *Jet* 72:8 S 21 '87
National Association of School Music Dealers
NASMD at 25. B. O'Donnell. *Down Beat* 54:6+ My '87

National Association of Securities Dealers
Excessive markups? D. Henry. il *Forbes* 139:98 Ja 26 '87
Hardiman could be just what the NASD needs. V. Cahan. *Bus Week* p32 Jl 6 '87

National Association of Securities Professionals
NASP: blacks should buy part of American economy. il *Jet* 72:33 S 21 '87

National Association of Television Program Executives
Sizing up a down market. il *Channels* 7:58-9 Ap '87
Who's hot at NATPE [special section; with editorial comment by Les Brown] il *Channels* 7:4, 45-51+ F '87

National Audubon Society
Audubon ecology camp [Hog Island, Me.] P. Salmansohn. il *Ctry J* 14:60-2 Je '87
How fare the Audubon birds a century later? [wading birds] F. Graham. il *Audubon* 89:14-16+ Mr '87

National Automobile, Aerospace and Agricultural Implement Workers Union of Canada
From working stiff to political hero [R. White] E. B. Terry. il por *Bus Week* p60-1 Mr 30 '87
A pension breakthrough [Chrysler Canada agrees to index pensions against inflation] D. Jenish. il *Macleans* 100:32-3 S 28 '87
A setback for labor [Michelin workers in Nova Scotia vote against joining the Canadian Auto Workers union] D. Jones. il *Macleans* 100:14 Ja 26 '87
Unions fighting unions [R. Cashin switches Newfoundland fishermen's union affiliation from United Food and Commercial Workers to Canadian Auto Workers] D. Jenish. il *Macleans* 100:41-2 Ap 27 '87
White knight on a crusade [R. H. White] M. McIver. il por *Macleans* 100:34 Jl 13 '87

National Ballet of Canada
The art of dirty dancing [G. Tetley's La ronde] P. Hluchy. il *Macleans* 100:65 N 30 '87
Bold steps in London [performance of Alice] M. Crabb. il *Macleans* 100:44 Jl 13 '87
Reviews:
    Performances of Alice and other works at the Metropolitan Opera House, New York City. C. Hardy. *Dance Mag* 61:36-8 F '87
The widow's a peak [production of The merry widow; cover story] M. Crabb. il *Dance Mag* 61:62-7 Mr '87

National Bank of Catalina
His customers bank on service [president A. T. Gibson] H. Morris. il por *Nations Bus* 75:69 Ja '87

National Baptist Convention of the United States of America
See Baptists—United States

National Bar Association
NBA pres. urges High Court to uphold affirm. action [views of T. J. Broome] por *Jet* 71:26 Ja 12 '87
Walter Sutton Jr. named head of Bar Association. *Jet* 72:55 S 7 '87

National Baseball Hall of Fame and Museum
Billy Williams joins his friends in baseball hall. il pors *Jet* 71:46-7 F 2 '87
Billy Williams' speech fans Hall of Fame fires. il por *Jet* 72:51+ Ag 10 '87
An error for baseball: why aren't Leo Durocher and Roger Maris in the Hall? S. Wulf. il por *Sports Illus* 67:92 Ag 10 '87
Getting to first base [All-American Girls Professional Baseball League to be commemorated in exhibit] J. Rodewald. il *Women's Sports Fitness* 9:48-9 O '87
Negro League star gets Hall of Fame surprise [R. Dandridge] il por *Jet* 71:46 Mr 23 '87
Up at the Hall. R. Angell. il *New Yorker* 63:35-8+ Ag 31 '87

National Basketball Association
Group wants recall of Arizona Gov. Mecham; NBA cancels meeting. *Jet* 72:14 Jl 27 '87
NBA leading pro sports in hiring of minorities. *Jet* 73:46 N 9 '87
NBA players sue league over draft, salary cap. *Jet* 73:49 O 19 '87
Twenty-seven's a crowd: the last thing the NBA needed was four new franchises. J. McCallum. por *Sports Illus* 66:92 My 25 '87

National Basketball Players Association
'Save up,' says Magic, as NBA strike looms. *Jet* 73:48 N 2 '87

National Bible Week
Celebrity ads promote National Bible Week. *Jet* 73:32 N 16 '87

National Bipartisan Commission on Central America (U.S.)
A plan for fully funding NBCCA recommendations. il *Dep State Bull* 87:59-86 Ap '87

National Black Catholic Congress
Director sought for Black Catholic Congress, Inc. *Jet* 71:24 Ja 19 '87
The National Black Catholic Congress [cover story] E. K. Braxton. *America* 157:29-34 Jl 18-25 '87

National Black Caucus of State Legislators
Blacks get group of state legislators to dump Bork. *Jet* 72:29 S 21 '87

National Black Nurses Association
Arizona loses NBNA confab. A. Edmond, Jr. il *Black Enterp* 17:62 Je '87

National Black United Fund
Black NY group seeks Harry Edwards' ouster [Black United Fund of New York] il por *Jet* 72:46 S 14 '87

National Book Awards
FS & G garners three fiction nominees for National Book Award. *Publ Wkly* 232:14 O 30 '87
National Book Awards announces new board, grants, traveling show. *Publ Wkly* 232:14 Jl 3 '87
Surprise winner, and political tone, mark National Book Awards. J. F. Baker. il *Publ Wkly* 232:15 N 20 '87
What are book awards for? J. F. Baker. *Publ Wkly* 232:9 D 18 '87

National Book Critics Circle Awards
Humanism is saluted at NBCC Award ceremonies. J. F. Baker. il *Publ Wkly* 231:22 F 13 '87
Knopf collects seven of 25 NBCC awards nominees. *Publ Wkly* 232:16 D 18 '87

National Broadcasting Co., Inc.
Black viewers turn to NBC. il *Channels* 7:64 N '87
Bob Wright's surprising script for NBC: grow, grow, grow. J. R. Norman. il por *Bus Week* p70+ Mr 9 '87
GE's hard driver at NBC [R. C. Wright] A. L. Taylor, III. il pors *Fortune* 115:97-8+ Mr 16 '87
Is NBC getting hooked up to cable? [deal with Disney Channel and Turner Broadcasting] D. Lieberman. il por *Bus Week* p73 D 28 '87-Ja 4 '88
The man who turns on America [B. Tartikoff] L. Hirschberg. il pors *Roll Stone* p59-60+ O 22 '87
Mr. Wright? [new president R. C. Wright] E. Diamond. il por *N Y* 20:11-13 Ja 19 '87
NBC's catalytic anchor [interview with T. Brokaw] pors *Channels* 7:62-3 My '87
News by the numbers [McKinsey & Co.'s analysis of NBC News] E. Diamond. il *N Y* 20:20-1 My 25 '87
The perils of a programmer [B. Tartikoff] W. A. Henry. il *Channels* 7:56 N '87
The quest for cable-resilience. B. Tartikoff. il *Channels* 7:71 O '87
Suing the bosses who bounced her, a bitter Valerie Harper fights to save her reputation. D. Hutchings. il pors *People Wkly* 28:46-8 O 19 '87
Will checkerboarding survive? [stations' campaign to promote fall lineup of checkerboard sitcoms] P. Ellis-Simons. *Channels* 7:10 Je '87

National Brotherhood of Skiers
National Brotherhood of Skiers. J. C. Baker. il *Black Enterp* 17:146 F '87
Ski tripping. K. Burns. il *Essence* 18:21+ D '87

National Business Aircraft Association
Business and pleasure mix. D. Eskow. il *Pop Mech* 164:30 Ja '87
Crossroads [interview with J. Howe] E. Weiner. il pors *Flying* 114:82-4+ N '87
NBAA Show [special section] il *Aviat Week Space Technol* 127:18-21 O 5 '87

National Business League
NBL, Black Caucus at odds over status of the MBDA. *Jet* 72:30 My 4 '87

National Cancer Institute (U.S.)
Biologics gain influence in expanding NCI program. D. M. Barnes. il *Science* 237:848-50 Ag 21 '87
Recollections on the war on cancer. B. J. Culliton. il *Science* 237:843 Ag 21 '87

National Capital Trolley Museum
D.C.'s trolleys still run. il *South Living* 22:28 Ja '87

National Car Rental System, Inc.
First, kick the tires. S. B. Weiner. il por *Forbes* 140:50+ O 5 '87

National Catholic Educational Association
'The gift of teaching'. *America* 156:334 Ap 25 '87

National cemeteries
    See also
    Arlington National Cemetery (Va.)

National Center for Space Studies (France) *See* Centre National d'Études Spatiales (France)

National Coalition Against the Misuse of Pesticides
Pesticide SOS. S. Milius. il *Rodale's Org Gard* 34:74-9 O '87

National Coalition of Black Voter Participation
Gracia Hillman pilots voter group for political victories across nation. S. Booker. il por *Jet* 71:12-13 Ja 26 '87

National Collegiate Athletic Association
Another NCAA fumble [judge rules against drug testing policy] B. Newman. il por *Sports Illus* 67:100 D 7 '87
Big-time college athletics: academic eligibility rules are elitist. G. R. Roberts. il *USA Today (Periodical)* 116:68-70 Jl '87
Big-time college athletics: commercialization and corruption. T. A. Luken. il *USA Today (Periodical)* 116:64-7 Jl '87
Bust the college sports cartel. R. McCormick and R. Meiners. il pors *Fortune* 116:235-6 O 12 '87
Cheap labor on campus. D. Glasner. por *Newsweek* 110:12 N 9 '87
"Death" to S.M.U. football. *Time* 129:72 Mr 9 '87
Howard U. battles NCAA over grid playoff snub. *Jet* 73:50 D 14 '87
Mr. Clean comes to the NCAA [R. D. Schultz] M. Ivey. il por *Bus Week* p51+ S 7 '87
The NCAA: a cartel in sheepskin clothing. G. S. Becker. il *Bus Week* p24 S 14 '87
NCAA panel to address minorities in management. *Jet* 73:50 O 12 '87
Shame on you, SMU [football program suspended] R. Sullivan and C. Neff. il *Sports Illus* 66:18-21+ Mr 9 '87
SMU [football program suspended] S. Bayless. il *Sport Mag* 78:98 D '87
SMU football is called for illegal motion. il *Newsweek* 109:55 Mr 9 '87

National Commission on Libraries and Information Science (U.S.)
See also
White House Conference on Library and Information Services

National Commission on Space (U.S.)
America in space: where next? [cover story] L. David. il *Sky Telesc* 74:23-9 Jl '87
First word. H. Downs. il *Omni* 9:6 Mr '87

National Committee for Employer Support of the Guard and Reserve (U.S.)
Pentagon gives lifts to bosses. O. Davidson. *Progressive* 51:14 Jl '87

National Committee for Prevention of Child Abuse
Ombudsman of child abuse [Dr. F. C. Green] il pors *Ebony* 42:82+ F '87

National Committee for the Berne Convention
New coalition of 47 joins battle over Berne. H. Fields. *Publ Wkly* 232:10 S 25 '87

National Committee to Preserve Social Security and Medicare
Geezer sleaze. C. Coulson. *New Repub* 196:21-3 Ap 20 '87
Roosevelt Committee draws heavy fire. R. Rosenblatt. il por *50 Plus* 27:14-16+ My '87

National committees (Political)
See also
Democratic National Committee
Republican National Committee

National Concrete Masonry Association
Changing the shape of things to come. D. Rastorfer. il *Archit Rec* 175:20-1 D '87

National Conference of Catholic Bishops *See* Catholic Church. National Conference of Catholic Bishops

National Conference of State Legislatures
Blacks get group of state legislators to dump Bork. *Jet* 72:29 S 21 '87

National conventions, Democratic
All booked up [Atlanta facilities] il *Newsweek* 109:7 Mr 2 '87
Big chips to play at convention time [J. Jackson] H. Rainie. *U S News World Rep* 103:41 N 16 '87
The Democrats' script for 1988 [model for acceptance speech] R. Shrum. *Harpers* 275:14+ S '87
Their own worst enemies? G. Borger. il *U S News World Rep* 103:23 Ag 24 '87

National conventions (Political)
Black mayors of Atlanta, New Orleans will host 1988 political conventions. il pors *Jet* 71:5 Mr 2 '87
Let us entertain you [competition among cities to host 1988 presidential conventions] A. Stanley. il *Time* 129:23 Ja 12 '87

National Corporate Fund for Dance
Corporate fund fuels dance; choreographer awards announced. il *Dance Mag* 61:12-13 Ag '87

National Council of Architectural Registration Boards
Architectural education: on NCARB's horizon—a computer-adaptive exam. W. T. Carry. il *Archit Rec* 175:59 N '87

National Council of Black Engineers and Scientists
Engineers' conference. S. Herbert. il *Black Enterp* 17:17 Mr '87

National Council of Churches
Pentecostals and NCC begin dialogue. K. Houghland. *Christ Century* 104:87-9 Ja 28 '87

National Council of Churches. Church World Service
'Integration' sparks NCC showdown. J. M. Wall. *Christ Century* 104:955-6 N 4 '87
NCC officials put dispute on hold. J. C. Lyles. *Christ Century* 104:1021-2 N 18 '87

National Council of Jewish Women
Getting the homebound out of the house [recreation program at senior center in Brooklyn, N.Y.] il *Aging* no355:22 '87

National Council of Negro Women
Family reunions helping blacks face unsure future. il *Jet* 73:20+ O 5 '87
A show of strength: celebrating the black family with 'reunions'. B. Kantrowitz. il *Newsweek* 110:73 Ag 17 '87

National Council of the Churches of Christ in the United States of America *See* National Council of Churches

National Council on Education for the Ceramic Arts (U.S.)
Clay for art's sake [annual conference] B. Sanders. il *Am Craft* 47:12-13+ Ag/S '87

National Council on Independent Living
Fighting for their rights. M. Marshall. il *Ebony* 42:68-70+ O '87

National Dairy Board
Dairy board moves through 1987 with strong plans. *Success Farm* 85:D3 My '87

National Dance Week
National Dance Week is April 26-May 2 [activities in Rochester, N.Y.] H. M. Simpson. il *Dance Mag* 61:14-15 Ap '87

National debt *See* Debts, Public

National Democratic Institute for International Affairs
While Haiti burns. M. Massing. *New Repub* 197:14-16 N 16 '87

National Dental Association
Nat. Dental Assn. staff to ask members to take precautions for AIDS. *Jet* 72:6 Ag 10 '87

National Distillers & Chemical Corp.
Why National Distillers went on the wagon. C. Power. il por *Bus Week* p78+ S 14 '87

National Earthquake Information Center
If your problem is earthshaking, call Waverly Person. A. Collier. il pors *Ebony* 42:134+ S '87

National Education Association of the United States
NAACP, NEA opposing Reagan's pick for Court [R. Bork nomination] il *Jet* 72:8 Jl 20 '87

National Endowment for Democracy
The quiet Americans. *Nation* 244:273 Mr 7 '87

National Endowment for the Arts
The new NEA Arts-in-Education program. *Des Arts Educ* 88:25-33 N/D '86
. . . Uncle Sam's way [opera funding] P. J. Smith. il *Opera News* 51:10-12 Ja 31 '87

National enquirer
Frisco judge dismisses Thomas libel lawsuit [suit by P. M. Thomas] por *Jet* 72:32 Je 8 '87

National Equipment Servicing Dealers Association
Buying and servicing outdoor power equipment [interview with N. Beck] M. Ferrara. il por *Home Mech* 83:24-5 Ja '87

National Federation for Decency
Attack on pornography misses the mark [calling on Holiday Inn to remove "pornographic movies" from its motels] J. M. Wall. *Christ Century* 104:811-12 S 30 '87

National Federation of Business and Professional Women's Clubs
Broadcasting exec gets apology from organization following racial insult [X. Clayton snubbed by Rome, Ga. affiliate] il por *Jet* 72:32 My 18 '87

National Film Board of Canada
A nation's home movies [video program] B. D. Johnson. il *Macleans* 100:46 Jl 27 '87

National Football League
Meeting of minds in Maui [annual meeting] P. Zimmerman. il *Sports Illus* 66:51-2 Mr 30 '87
NFL appoints black to monitor minority hiring [D. Cornwell] *Jet* 73:46 O 12 '87

National Football League—*cont.*
NFL owners may have fumbled away their victory. A. Bernstein. il *Bus Week* p162 N 2 '87
NFL training camp aids black college coaches. *Jet* 72:50 S 21 '87
The NFL's big game [television rights] il *Fortune* 115:14 Mr 2 '87
The not-so-super state of pro football [interview with P. Rozelle] il por *U S News World Rep* 102:68 Ja 26 '87

National Football League Players Association
The guard who would be quarterback [executive director G. Upshaw] F. Deford. il pors *Sports Illus* 67:64-9+ S 14 '87
The life of a $725,000 scab [M. Gastineau] B. Saporito. il por *Fortune* 116:91-2+ O 26 '87
NFL Players' dinner fetes Mom of Year [J. Browner] il pors *Jet* 72:52-3 Ap 20 '87
Still on the outside [western director D. Meggyesy] D. Remnick. il pors *Sports Illus* 67:44-7+ O 5 '87
Upshaw claims racism influences NFL strike. por *Jet* 73:49 O 19 '87

National forests
   See also
   United States. Forest Service
Congress should investigate Forest Service violations [with editorial comment by George T. Frampton] il *Wilderness* 50:2-3 Summ '87
Firewood gathering hits a snag [endangering bird habitats] M. Kantor. il *Sierra* 72:24+ Mr/Ap '87
The lopsided ledger [management of the national forests] L. Williamson. il *Outdoor Life* 179:18+ Ja '87

Roads
The Forest Service's road to nowhere [timber contracts and roadbuilding projects threaten Tongass National Forest] K. E. Franklin. il *Progressive* 51:12 Je '87

Alaska
   See also
   Tongass National Forest (Alaska)

Arizona
   See also
   Coronado National Forest (Ariz. and N.M.)

Arkansas
   See also
   Ozark National Forest (Ark.)
   Saint Francis National Forest (Ark.)

California
   See also
   Tahoe National Forest (Calif.)

Idaho
Idaho batholith. B. G. Norton. il map *Wilderness* 50:30-1 Spr '87

Illinois
   See also
   Shawnee National Forest (Ill.)

Maine
   See also
   White Mountain National Forest (N.H. and Me.)

Minnesota
   See also
   Superior National Forest (Minn.)

Montana
   See also
   Lewis and Clark National Forest (Mont.)

New Hampshire
   See also
   White Mountain National Forest (N.H. and Me.)

New Mexico
   See also
   Coronado National Forest (Ariz. and N.M.)

Pacific Northwest
Old-growth forests. B. G. Norton. il map *Wilderness* 50:25-6 Spr '87

Puerto Rico
   See also
   Caribbean National Forest (Puerto Rico)

South Carolina
   See also
   Francis Marion National Forest (S.C.)

Virginia
   See also
   George Washington National Forest (Va. and W. Va.)

West Virginia
   See also
   George Washington National Forest (Va. and W. Va.)
   Monongahela National Forest (W. Va.)

Western States
The degradation factor [timber management and watershed protection in western national forests] M. Anderson and C. Gehrke. il *Wilderness* 51:38-40 Fall '87
Threatening the Yellowstone Complex. *Wilderness* 50:3 Spr '87
The Yellowstone Complex. B. G. Norton. il map *Wilderness* 50:26-30 Spr '87

National Forum of State Leaders
State leaders join to form a national group. il *Jet* 72:6 Ap 6 '87

National Gallery (Great Britain)
The Sainsbury Wing: an extension to the National Gallery in London. K. D. Stein. il *Archit Rec* 175:65 My '87

National Gallery of Art (U.S.)
The installation of American furniture from the Kaufman Collection at the National Gallery of Art. W. A. Cooper. bibl f il *Antiques* 131:1096-1105 My '87
The National Gallery model: a miniature with a purpose. A. Bahar. il *Antiques Collect Hobbies* 92:55-7 My '87

National Geodetic Survey (U.S.)
The regridding of North America. *Sea Front* 33:461 N/D '87

National Geographic Kids Network
The grade-schoolers unraveling acid rain's mysteries. M. Bluestone. *Bus Week* p116 O 19 '87

National Geographic Society (U.S.)
Abrams celebrates National Geographic 1988 centennial. il *Publ Wkly* 231:51 My 29 '87
Happy 100, National Geographic. D. Thompson. il *Time* 130:69-70 D 28 '87
"A society for the increase and diffusion of geographical knowledge" [excerpt from The National Geographic Society; with editorial comment by Ed Holm] C. D. B. Bryan. il *Am Hist Illus* 22:4, 16-27 D '87

National geographic world (Periodical)
Winners named in World T-shirt contest. il *Natl Geogr World* 138:22-9 F '87

National Governors' Association
National Governors' Association report on education reform. L. Alexander. *Educ Dig* 52:2-5 Ap '87
National Guard (Minn.) *See* Minnesota. National Guard
National Guard (Tenn.) *See* Tennessee. National Guard
National health insurance *See* Insurance, Health
National Healthcare, Inc.
Single minded [fleet of Cessna 210s] R. L. Collins. il *Flying* 114:34-8 Je '87
National Heart, Lung, and Blood Institute (U.S.)
Heart Institute is major player in clinical trials. G. Kolata. il *Science* 237:851-3 Ag 21 '87
National High School Football Recruiting Service
Mad Max, video recruiter. D. Whitford. il por *Sport Mag* 78:19 Ag '87
National Highway Traffic Safety Administration (U.S.)
See United States. National Highway Traffic Safety Administration
National Hockey League
John Ziegler's spectacular save: the NHL. B. Welling. il por *Bus Week* p110 My 18 '87
National Housing Partnership
The NHP starts playing for profit. J. Novack. il *Forbes* 139:52 F 9 '87
National Hurricane Center
The human dimension in hurricane forecasting. M. Clary. il *Weatherwise* 40:197-9 Jl/Ag '87
National Industries, Inc.
The heroine of homegrown manufacturing [J.-C. Mason] S. Wilkinson. il pors *Work Woman* 12:108-9+ N '87
National Institute for Architectural Education
The apprentice system: should it make a comeback? [views of J. F. Hartray] M. F. Schmertz. *Archit Rec* 175:9 N '87
National Institute of Arthritis, Musculoskeletal, and Skin Diseases (U.S.)
Arthritis Institute tackles sports. W. Booth. il *Science* 237:846-7 Ag 21 '87
National Institute of Arts and Letters *See* American Academy and Institute of Arts and Letters
National Institute of Mental Health (U.S.)
"It was too good to be true" [false data used by mental retardation researcher S. Breuning] D. Brand. il por *Time* 129:59 Je 1 '87
NIMH finds a case of "serious misconduct" [case of S. E. Breuning] C. Holden. *Science* 235:1566-7 Mr 27 '87
Prosecution urged in fraud case [case of S. E. Breuning] C. Norman. *Science* 236:1057 My 29 '87
A top priority at NIMH [schizophrenia research] C. Holden. *Science* 235:431 Ja 23 '87

National Institutes of Health (U.S.)
A consensus view. S. Perry. il *World Health* p12-13 Je '87
Gallo gets itchy feet, looks to academe. W. Booth. *Science* 238:1223 N 27 '87
Maxwell may back Gallo [proposed laboratory funding] B. J. Culliton. *Science* 238:1643 D 18 '87
National Institutes of Health: the centennial year [special section; with editorial comment by Daniel E. Koshland, Jr.] *Science* 237:821, 841-53+ Ag 21 '87
NIH celebrates 100 [special section] D. M. Barnes. il *Science* 238:892-4 N 13 '87
NIH finally resolves 7-year dispute [case of J. S. Borer] C. Holden. *Science* 238:151 O 9 '87
PHS revitalization plan stirs up NIH [views of C. E. Koop] G. Kolata. il por *Science* 236:1055-6 My 29 '87

Appropriations and expenditures
A battle over NIH funds. B. J. Culliton. il *Science* 235:1129-30 Mr 6 '87
The NIH legislators. W. Booth. il *Science* 237:844-5 Ag 21 '87
NIH to restore slashed grants. B. J. Culliton. *Science* 235:1321 Mr 13 '87
NIH urged to forge new ties to Congress. B. J. Culliton. il *Science* 237:841-2 Ag 21 '87
OMB stalks the "burgeoning growth of biomedicine". E. Marshall. *Science* 237:847-8 Ag 21 '87

National Intercollegiate Flying Association
High school. R. L. Collins. il *Flying* 114:17-18 Ag '87

National interest *See* Nationalism

National Intergroup Inc.
The best-laid plans of Howard Love . . . G. L. Miles. il por *Bus Week* p74 Ag 10 '87
Bonuses for steelworkers? S. W. Angrist. il por *Forbes* 139 Ann Directory:126 Ap 27 '87

National Jewelers Exchange
Not strictly all business [retired wedding ring salesman B. Schifrin] *New Yorker* 63:27-9 My 25 '87

National Labor Relations Board (U.S.) *See* United States. National Labor Relations Board

National Lead Company *See* NL Industries, Inc.

National liberation movements
Debate over the U.S. role in foreign wars. J. Martin. il *Sch Update* 119:11-12 My 4 '87
Guerrilla warfare: morality and the Reagan Doctrine. C. Krauthammer. *Current* 290:32-40 F '87
The two faces of the Reagan administration's foreign policy approach [Reagan Doctrine] C. W. Kegley and E. R. Wittkopf. il *USA Today (Periodical)* 115:10-15 Ja '87

National Library of Medicine (U.S.)
When your doctor needs to know—fast [MEDLINE] M. E. DeBakey. il *Read Dig* 131:110-13 Jl '87

National Magazine Awards (U.S.)
Bulletin wins top award. *Bull At Sci* 43:2 Je '87

National Marine Fisheries Service (U.S.) *See* United States. National Marine Fisheries Service

National Maritime Museum (U.S.)
Chantey sing in San Francisco. il *Sunset* 178:34 F '87

National Medal of Arts
Fitzgerald, Bearden get president's Medal of Arts. il por *Jet* 72:52 Jl 6 '87

National Medal of Science
Abelson receives National Medal of Science. J. L. Teramani. il por *Science* 237:661 Ag 7 '87
Science medals presented at White House. il *Science* 236:1621 Je 26 '87

National Medal of Technology
Science medals presented at White House. il *Science* 236:1621 Je 26 '87

National Mediation Board (U.S.) *See* United States. National Mediation Board

National Medical Association
Black doctors elect Joyner head of NMA. por *Jet* 72:25 Ag 24 '87
Black M.D.'s convene in Atlanta on hypertension. il *Jet* 72:16 Ap 13 '87

National Medical Fellowships
$4 mil. loan set to aid minority medical students. il *Jet* 73:12 N 16 '87

National monuments
See also
Death Valley National Monument (Calif. and Nev.)
El Malpais National Monument (N.M.)
Mount Saint Helens National Volcanic Monument (Wash.)
Petroglyphs National Monument (N.M.)
America's little-known parklands. il *Better Homes Gard* 65:169-71 My '87

National morale *See* Morale, National

National mottoes *See* Mottoes

National Museum of African Art (U.S.)
Cavern fever. B. Forgey. il *Art News* 86:27 D '87
Discover an African oasis . . . in Washington, D.C. A. Reid-Dove. il *Black Enterp* 18:99-100+ D '87
New treasures on the Mall. H. Dudar. il *Smithsonian* 18:44-63 S '87
Peering into a people's soul. M. Horn. il *U S News World Rep* 103:67-8 O 5 '87
Smithsonian opens new museum complex on National Mall. il *Am Craft* 47:12 O/N '87
Sylvia Williams: equal time. A. Thorson. il por *Art News* 86:91-2 O '87

National Museum of American Art (U.S.)
Museum accessions [folk art collection of Herbert Waide Hemphill Jr.] E. H. Gustafson. il *Antiques* 132:438-9+ S '87

National Museum of American Art (U.S.). Renwick Gallery *See* Renwick Gallery

National Museum of American History (U.S.)
Accepted notions of the family and its function have changed profoundly; how do we exhibit this in a museum? R. M. Adams. il *Smithsonian* 18:10 Je '87
Congress buys Ellington collection for Smithsonian. il por *Jet* 71:27 Mr 9 '87
Keeper of the Attic [director R. G. Kennedy] M. Durham. il pors *Americana* 15:43-8 N/D '87
New exhibit at Smithsonian [Engines of change: the American Industrial revolution, 1790-1860] il *Am Hist Illus* 21:8-9 Ja '87
Two recent events raise the question of how Smithsonian museums should deal with artifacts of our own time. R. M. Adams. il *Smithsonian* 17:12 Mr '87

National Museum of Dance (U.S.)
Founders of American dance to be honored July 11 at Saratoga's National Museum. R. Philp. il *Dance Mag* 61:8-9 Jl '87

National Museum of Man (Canada)
See also
Canadian Museum of Civilization

National Museum of Modern Art (Kyoto, Japan)
Eastern diplomacy [F. Maki's design; cover story] D. Dietsch. il *Archit Rec* 175:116-27 O '87

National Museum of Modern Art (Seoul, Korea)
Bastion of culture. D. Dietsch. il *Archit Rec* 175:138-47 N '87

National Museum of Natural History (U.S.)
Around the Mall and beyond [new director R. S. Hoffmann] E. Park. il por *Smithsonian* 18:18+ Jl '87
Around the Mall and beyond [photographer K. B. Sandved] E. Park. il por *Smithsonian* 18:24+ S '87
Roxie Laybourne: feather detective. R. Wolkomir. il pors *Natl Wildl* 26:20-5 D '87/Ja '88

National Museum of Women in the Arts (U.S.)
American women artists, 1830-1930. M. Moorman. il *Art News* 86:57-8 Summ '87
Exhibits. il *Am Artist* 51:104 Ap '87
How to start a museum. R. Hughes. il *Time* 130:48-50 Ag 10 '87
Is a woman's place in a woman's museum? B. E. Quick. il *U S News World Rep* 102:70 Ap 20 '87
A museum of one's own. C. McGuigan. il *Newsweek* 109:76+ Ap 13 '87
A new museum for women artists. S. B. Sherrill. il *Antiques* 131:716+ Ap '87
A new showcase for women artists. M. McDonald. il *Macleans* 100:53-4 My 18 '87
To bravos and boos, a daring Wilhelmina Holladay brings women a museum they can call their own. H. Shapiro. il por *People Wkly* 27:113-15 Ap 27 '87
A woman's place. A. Schwartz. il *Americana* 15:30-2+ Mr/Ap '87
Women artists: pro and con. B. Rose. il *Vogue* 177:150+ Ap '87
The women's museum—a house is not a home? [founder W. C. Holladay] il *Ms* 16:24 S '87

National Nanofabrication Facility
Dancing on the head of a pin. G. Bronson. il *Forbes* 139:152-3 Ap 6 '87

National Negro Golf Association
National golf group sets minority college tourney. *Jet* 72:50 Ap 27 '87

National Newspaper Publishers Association
Black press organization names 1st woman president [P. O. Thomas] por *Jet* 72:31 Jl 27 '87
Black publishers pull out of Arizona confab [protest against repeal of Martin Luther King Day] *Jet* 71:8 F 9 '87

National Oceanic and Atmospheric Administration (U.S.)
See United States. National Oceanic and Atmospheric Administration
National Oceans Policy Commission (U.S.)
House approvals. *Sea Front* 33:381 S/O '87
Oceans policy legislation. *Oceans* 20:4 My/Je '87
National Organization for Women
A new battlefield for NOW's fearless leader [efforts of E. Smeal] por *Newsweek* 110:30-1 Jl 20 '87
Not NOW [renewed campaign for the ERA] J. J. Mansbridge. *Nation* 244:5 Ja 10 '87
NOW now. *Natl Rev* 39:19-20 Ag 14 '87
NOW redux. A. Kopkind. *Nation* 245:76-7 Ag 1-8 '87
Septuagenarian Molly Yard may not be unsinkable, but she's just the thing for NOW. K. McMurran. il pors *People Wkly* 28:38-9 O 12 '87
When picketing pays [Adopt-a-Picket program run by NOW to raise money for abortions in Concord, Calif.] D. G. Albrecht. il *Ms* 16:91 N '87
National Organization of Black Law Enforcement Executives
Houston police chief receives NOBLE award [L. P. Brown] *Jet* 72:40 Ag 3 '87
National Organization on the Status of Minorities in Sports
Group to monitor black progress in white colleges. *Jet* 72:27 Je 1 '87
National park personnel *See* National parks and reserves—Employees
National Park Service (U.S.) *See* United States. National Park Service
National Park Trust
Missing pieces. F. H. Kennedy. il *Natl Parks* 61:30-3 S/O '87
National Parks and Conservation Association
Commentary. See issues of National Parks
National Parks and Conservation Association annual report: 1986. *Natl Parks* 61:24A-24H Jl/Ag '87
NPCA report. See issues of National Parks
Prescribed burning: NPCA's position. R. D. Butcher. *Natl Parks* 61:27 Ja/F '87
National parks and reserves
See also
Marine parks and reserves
National Park Trust
United States. National Park Service
United States. Park Police
Wild and scenic rivers
Ah, wilderness! D. Gergen. il *U S News World Rep* 103:68 Ag 31 '87
Clean Air should start in the parks. P. C. Pritchard. *Natl Parks* 61:5 Jl/Ag '87
Congress examines aircraft noise issue [national parks] *Aviat Week Space Technol* 126:112 My 18 '87
Gallery. See issues of National Parks beginning March/April 1987
How to save our national parks [cover story] A. Chase. il *Atlantic* 260:35-44 Jl '87
It's festival time! L. Tuttle. il *Natl Parks* 61:14-15+ Jl/Ag '87
The latest word. See issues of National Parks
The national park system: looking back and moving ahead. W. P. Mott, Jr. il *USA Today (Periodical)* 115:18-28 My '87
The national view [problems of the parks system; interview with D. Hodel] R. A. Taylor. por *U S News World Rep* 103:51 Ag 31 '87
NPCA report reveals state of acid rain in parks. il *Natl Parks* 61:38 S/O '87
Parks and the Constitution: celebrating on common soil [cover story; special section; with editorial comment by Paul C. Pritchard] il *Natl Parks* 61:5, 12-29+ Mr/Ap '87
Scenic sites under siege [air pollution in national parks] C. Peterson. il *Natl Wildl* 25:44-5 Je/Jl '87
Ski the backcountry. K. Sferra. il *Natl Parks* 61:12-13+ Ja/F '87
Smokey would never believe this [views of D. Hummel] A. Chase. *Wash Mon* 19:45-6+ N '87
Taking a count of threats [natural resource inventories and monitoring] R. Cahn. il *Natl Parks* 61:33-4 Jl/Ag '87
'Tis the season [Christmas events] L. Tuttle. il *Natl Parks* 61:38-9 N/D '87
Travelers' respite [park hostels] T. Stroll. il *Natl Parks* 61:14-15 My/Je '87
Trivia trek. T. Kilpatrick. il *Natl Parks* 61:22-3+ Jl/Ag '87
Violating history [American archeological sites] J. Robbins. il *Natl Parks* 61:26-31 Jl/Ag '87
Wins outweigh losses in 99th Congress. *Natl Parks* 61:39-40 Ja/F '87

Crowd control
The four-percent solution [increase in national park visitors] P. C. Pritchard. *Natl Parks* 61:5 N/D '87
Employees
Awards
Phillip Evans named Interpreter of Year. il por *Natl Parks* 61:41 Ja/F '87
Fees
Investing in parks. D. Durenberger. il *Natl Parks* 61:10-11 Ja/F '87
New funds and new programs for our national parks. il *Sunset* 179:164 Ag '87
Park entrance fees raised for this year at least. *Natl Parks* 61:40 Mr/Ap '87
This land is your land? il *Money* 16:16 Ag '87
Alaska
See also
Denali National Park and Preserve (Alaska)
Alberta
See also
Jasper National Park (Alta.)
Arizona
See also
Grand Canyon National Park (Ariz.)
British Columbia
See also
South Moresby National Park (B.C.)
California
See also
Death Valley National Monument (Calif. and Nev.)
Golden Gate National Recreation Area (Calif.)
Point Reyes National Seashore (Calif.)
Sequoia and King's Canyon National Park (Calif.)
Yosemite National Park (Calif.)
Haute skiing [ski touring the Sierra High Route in comparison to Europe's Haute Route] D. Robinson. il *Natl Parks* 61:14-19 Ja/F '87
Colorado
See also
Mesa Verde National Park (Colo.)
Costa Rica
Coast of riches. P. Cahn and R. Cahn. il map *Natl Parks* 61:18-20 S/O '87
Growing a forest from scratch [Guanacaste National Park re-created tropical dry forest; work of Daniel H. Janzen] E. C. Wolf. il por *Futurist* 21:41-2 Jl/Ag '87
France
See also
Cévennes Biosphere Reserve and National Park (France)
Gambia
Outward bound for chimps [reintroduction to the wild at Abuko Nature Reserve, Gambia] B. McBride. il map *Int Wildl* 17:18-21 S/O '87
Ghana
Return to Ghana [Mole National Park] B. Jamieson. il *Int Wildl* 17:38-41 N/D '87
Hawaii
See also
Haleakala National Park (Hawaii)
India
A contemptuous tiger's loss of innocence [man-eating tiger in Corbett National Park] G. C. Ward. il *Audubon* 89:50-1 Jl '87
Photographs and photography
Some birds of Corbett Park. il *Audubon* 89:56-7 Jl '87
Japan
Jets to invade a national park [Fuji-Hakone-Izu National Park] J. Hamilton. il *Sierra* 72:132-3 Ja/F '87
Landscape of the mind. B. Culhane and L. Tuttle. il map *Natl Parks* 61:24-5 S/O '87
Kentucky
See also
Big South Fork National River and Recreation Area (Tenn. and Ky.)
Kenya
Elephants in musth, lust [Amboseli National Park] J. H. Poole. il *Nat Hist* 96:46-55 N '87
Madagascar
Saving paradise [Beza-Mahafaly reserve] R. G. Brock. il *Technol Rev* 90:13-15 My/Je '87
Maryland
See also
Assateague Island National Seashore (Md. and Va.)
Michigan
See also
Isle Royale National Park (Mich.)
Montana
See also
Glacier National Park (Mont.)

National parks and reserves—*cont.*
Nepal
How to drive an elephant. C. R. Capos. il *Ms* 16:108 S '87

New ZIP codes for resident rhinos in Nepal [restocking Bardia Wildlife Reserve with rhinos captured from Royal Chitawan National Park] H. R. Mishra and E. Dinerstein. il *Smithsonian* 18:66-73 S '87
Nevada
See also
Death Valley National Monument (Calif. and Nev.)
Great Basin National Park (Nev.)
New Mexico
See also
Chaco Culture National Historical Park (N.M.)
El Malpais National Monument (N.M.)
Petroglyphs National Monument (N.M.)
New York (State)
See also
Fire Island National Seashore (N.Y.)
Saratoga National Historical Park (N.Y.)
North Carolina
See also
Cape Hatteras National Seashore (N.C.)
Great Smoky Mountains National Park (N.C. and Tenn.)
Northwest Territories
See also
Ellesmere Island National Park (N.W.T.)
Pennsylvania
See also
Gettysburg National Military Park (Pa.)
Independence National Historical Park (Pa.)
Valley Forge National Historical Park (Pa.)
Saint Lucia
See also
Pigeon Island National Historic Park (Saint Lucia)
South Dakota
See also
Wind Cave National Park (S.D.)
Tanzania
Game watching in Tanzania [Lake Manyara National Park] B. McBride. il *Travel Holiday* 168:22+ Jl '87
Tennessee
See also
Big South Fork National River and Recreation Area (Tenn. and Ky.)
Great Smoky Mountains National Park (N.C. and Tenn.)
Texas
See also
Big Thicket National Preserve (Tex.)
San Antonio Missions National Historical Park (Tex.)
United States
See National parks and reserves
Utah
See also
Bryce Canyon National Park (Utah)
Virginia
See also
Appomattox Court House National Historical Park (Va.)
Assateague Island National Seashore (Md. and Va.)
Shenandoah National Park (Va.)
Wolf Trap Farm Park for the Performing Arts
Washington (State)
See also
Mount Rainier National Park (Wash.)
Olympic National Park (Wash.)
Western States
See also
Yellowstone National Park
Nature classes and seminars in the national parks. il map *Sunset* 178:50+ Ap '87
New funds and new programs for our national parks. il *Sunset* 179:164 Ag '87
Wyoming
See also
Grand Teton National Park (Wyo.)
Zimbabwe
Where elephants die [Hwange National Park] G. Haynes. il *Nat Hist* 96:28-33 Je '87

National parks and reserves in motion pictures
On location. J. Carman. il *Natl Parks* 61:30-6 N/D '87

National Portrait Gallery (Great Britain)
A morbid curiosity [deathbed portrait of man wrongly assumed to be the Duke of Monmouth] J. Prendergast. il *Hist Today* 37:62 My '87

National Prayer Breakfast *See* Prayer breakfasts
National Public Radio (U.S.)
Adam Clayton Powell III is National Public Radio V.P. il por *Jet* 73:22 O 26 '87
To be or not to be commercial?—That is the question. R. L. Fischer. *USA Today (Periodical)* 116:89-91 S '87

National Railroad Passenger Corp.
In New Mexico: visions along the Amtrak line [Apparitions and Amtrak performed in Canyoncito] L. Schulman. il *Time* 129:10 Mr 2 '87
Waiting for the right phone call [W. S. Norman] D. Machan. il por *Forbes* 140:110-11 Ag 10 '87

National Rainbow Coalition
Jackson's challenge [J. L. Jackson; cover story] S. Muwakkil. il *Progressive* 51:16-19 Jl '87
The 'new voters' find their voice [cover story] A. Kopkind. il *Nation* 245:505+ N 7 '87

National Real Estate Stock Fund
A fund manager who separates REITs from wrongs [M. Cohen] G. Anrig, Jr. il por *Money* 16:232 Ap '87

National Reconciliation Commission (Nicaragua)
Evangelical leader named to national peace commission [G. Parajon] S. Wykstra. il por *Christ Today* 31:52 O 2 '87

National Religious Broadcasters. Ethics and Financial Integrity Commission
Policing its ranks. R. Frame. il *Christ Today* 31:44+ O 16 '87

National Research Council (U.S.)
Committee calls for SRB alternatives [shuttle solid rocket booster] *Aviat Week Space Technol* 126:24-5 Je 29 '87
Panel backs space station design, but warns of flaws in program. T. M. Foley. *Aviat Week Space Technol* 127:28-9 S 21 '87

National Research Council (U.S.). Committee on the Status of Black Americans
American dilemmas and black responses [special section] bibl *Society* 24:3-38 Ja/F '87

National Resource Center for Children in Poverty
Services to poor families. *Child Today* 16:2 S/O '87

National Resource Center on Family Based Services
Progress towards change: the National Resource Center on Family Based Services. J. R. Hutchinson. *Child Today* 15:6-7 N/D '86

National Rifle Association of America
Battle over the plastic gun. G. Hackett. il *Newsweek* 109:31 Je 1 '87
Dissidents, old allies shake NRA. T. Gest. il *U S News World Rep* 102:44 Ap 27 '87
Mrs. Brady's letter. D. E. Petzal. *Field Stream* 91:31 Ap '87
The NRA is right [need to ban handguns] J. Sugarmann. il *Wash Mon* 19:11-15 Je '87

National Science Foundation (U.S.)
Document links NSF official to biotech firm [case of D. T. Kingsbury] M. Crawford. *Science* 238:742 N 6 '87
Evolution and growth at NSF. P. H. Abelson. *Science* 236:893 My 22 '87
NSF official's finances probed by Justice [case of D. T. Kingsbury] M. Crawford. por *Science* 238:478 O 23 '87
Sally Ride to leave NASA orbit; exodus at NSF. I. Goodwin. *Phys Today* 40:45 Jl '87
SURA gets new president from DOE: NSF loses two computer chiefs. I. Goodwin. *Phys Today* 40:60-1 D '87

Appropriations and expenditures
Committee cuts NSF, NASA funds. M. Crawford. *Science* 236:1517 Je 19 '87
Congress considers upgrading labs. J. Walsh. il *Science* 237:351-2 Jl 24 '87
Duke's heart center in bureaucratic jam. M. Basgall. *Science* 238:882-3 N 13 '87
GAO finds fault with NSF award [earthquake engineering research center] J. Walsh. il *Science* 237:241-2 Jl 17 '87
Gossip and peer review at NSF [case of J. Kalb] E. Marshall. *Science* 238:1502 D 11 '87
NASA, NSF await the ax. M. Crawford. *Science* 237:717 Ag 14 '87
NSF centers: yes, but . . . C. Norman. *Science* 237:21 Jl 3 '87
NSF goes to Congress with plans for growth. J. Walsh. *Science* 235:1458 Mr 20 '87
NSF lends a hand with DOD award [Sematech project] J. Walsh. il *Science* 238:748 N 6 '87

National Science Foundation (U.S.)—Appropriations and expenditures—*cont.*
NSF puts big stake on research centers. J. Walsh. il *Science* 236:18-19 Ap 3 '87
NSF supercomputer centers plan for next leap into research. I. Goodwin. il map *Phys Today* 40:61-4 O '87
NSF to formulate 5-year plan, budget. J. Walsh. *Science* 235:967 F 27 '87
NSF undergrad programs upset scientists. I. Goodwin. il *Phys Today* 40:66-7 F '87
NSF's budget and economic competitiveness. E. Bloch. *Science* 235:621 F 6 '87
Peer review—'oops—merit review in for some changes at NSF. J. Walsh. *Science* 235:153 Ja 9 '87
Security Council blocks NSF grant to IIASA. C. Norman. il *Science* 236:514-15 My 1 '87
Upgrading basic science education. *Sci News* 131:106 F 14 '87

National Science Week
Balloons launch National Science & Technology Week. *Earth Sci* 40:6 Summ '87
Up, up, and away: students will launch thousands of helium-filled balloons in nationwide experiment to learn about wind and weather [cover story] A. H. Livermore. il map *Earth Sci* 40:12-13 Spr '87

National Scientific Balloon Facility
NASA's giant research balloons are out of sight. J. R. Chiles. bibl (p132) il *Smithsonian* 17:82-8+ Ja '87

National Sea Products Ltd.
Newfound riches for National Sea. P. C. Newman. il por *Macleans* 100:39 Ja 19 '87

National security *See* Internal security; United States—Defenses

National Security Archive
Must reading [chronology of Iran-contra scandal published by S. Armstrong] il por *Time* 129:29 Je 1 '87

National Security Council (U.S.) *See* United States. National Security Council

National Semiconductor Corp.
Why National came to the Fairchild fire sale. J. B. Levine and O. Port. il *Bus Week* p38-9 S 14 '87

National Senior Citizens Law Center (U.S.)
Legal eagles. F. Greve. *50 Plus* 27:16+ D '87

National service
Enlisting with Uncle Sam. J. V. Lamar, Jr. il *Time* 129:30 F 23 '87
Involuntary servitude. E. Knoll. *Progressive* 51:4 Ja '87
Sparking life into our youth. A. Bacard. il *Humanist* 47:46 Jl/Ag '87

National Service Industries, Inc.
Lights on [stock price] T. Jaffe. il *Forbes* 140:310 S 7 '87

National Severe Storms Forecast Center (U.S.) *See* United States. National Severe Storms Forecast Center

National socialism
See also
Holocaust, Jewish (1939-1945)
Anti-'fascism'. E. von Kuehnelt-Leddihn. *Natl Rev* 39:50 Ja 30 '87
Dutch tribute to gay pride [Amsterdam monument to homosexuals killed during Nazi regime] K. Golden. *Ms* 15:32 Je '87
Europe faces its Nazi past. S. Sullivan. il pors *Newsweek* 109:34-6 Ap 20 '87
Ferdinand Toennies: dark times for a liberal intellectual. J. Samples. bibl *Society* 24:65-8 S/O '87
Hitler's shadow. P. Schneider. il *Harpers* 275:49-54 S '87
Invasion of the German left [American misperception of Nazism] E. von Kuehnelt-Leddihn. *Natl Rev* 39:28 S 11 '87
Jottings from the Third Reich [publication of J. Goebbels diaries] J. Smolowe. il por *Time* 130:44 S 14 '87

National socialism and art
Austria reviews claims on looted art [artworks confiscated under the Nazi regime] A. Decker. *Art News* 86:37-8 F '87
A slow process [claims proceedings for Austrian-held artworks confiscated under the Nazi regime] A. Decker. il *Art News* 86:71-2 O '87

National songs
See also
Star spangled banner (Song)

National Space Center (Great Britain)
British refusal to boost space funding threatens European Space Agency unity. *Aviat Week Space Technol* 127:26-7 O 19 '87
British space chief quits in protest [R. Gibson] D. Dickson. *Science* 237:719 Ag 14 '87

The model of a modern director general: a conversation with Roy Gibson. T. Furniss. il por *Space World* X-5-281:26-7 My '87
U.K. space chief resigns over funding; ESA reevaluates impact on polar platform. J. M. Lenorovitz. il *Aviat Week Space Technol* 127:26-7 Ag 10 '87

National Space Institute (U.S.)
See also
National Space Society (U.S.)

National Space Society (U.S.)
See also
Spacecause
Spacepac
Inside NSS. E. S. Wynn. See issues of Space World beginning June 1987
The making of Mir Watch. E. S. Wynn. il *Space World* X-10-286:31-2 O '87
Society pages. See issues of Space World beginning January 1986 through May 1987
Space advocate. See issues of Space World beginning June 1987
Space politics forum. G. P. Wilson. See issues of Space World beginning December 1987
Who are we? G. Woodcock. por *Space World* X-6-282:36 Je '87

National Space Technology Laboratories (U.S.)
The National Space Technology Laboratories. H. A. Butowsky. il *Space World* X-9-285:34-5 S '87

National Steel Corp. *See* National Intergroup Inc.

National Stolen Art File (U.S.) *See* United States. Federal Bureau of Investigation. National Stolen Art File

National Symphony Orchestra
To Slava with love [M. Rostropovich] T. W. Libbey, Jr. il *High Fidel* 37:54 Jl '87

National Tap Dance Company of Canada
New works celebrate a tap troupe's tenth anniversary. P. Citron. il *Dance Mag* 61:10 F '87

National Teacher of the Year award *See* Teachers—Awards

National Technical Information Service (U.S.) *See* United States. National Technical Information Service

National Teen Challenge (Organization)
Teen Challenge: conquering drugs and AIDS [Teen Challenge groups voluntarily take AIDS tests] D. Manuel. il *Saturday Evening Post* 259:52-5+ D '87

National Test Pilot School
Demand for flight test training prompts NTPS to expand facilities. W. B. Scott. il *Aviat Week Space Technol* 126:62-4 My 4 '87

National Theater Workshop of the Handicapped
May we come in? R. Curry. il *America* 156:442-4 My 30 '87

National Tourism Week
Why a National Tourism Week. S. Shane. *Travel Holiday* 167:6 My '87

National Transportation Safety Board (U.S.) *See* United States. National Transportation Safety Board

National Trust (Great Britain)
Rare species [G. S. Thomas, overseer of the gardens] H. Mitchell. il por *House Gard* 159:56+ O '87

National Union for the Total Independence of Angola
Can this man save Africa? [UNITA's J. Savimbi] D. Reed. il por *Read Dig* 130:221-2+ My '87
A remote-control war. A. Bilski. il map *Macleans* 100:33 O 12 '87
The right's last, best hope. M. Maren. il *Nation* 245:744-6 D 19 '87
Yet another Saudi connection [businessman S. Bamieh claims U.S. supplied covert aid to UNITA rebels] E. Magnuson. il *Time* 129:16 Je 29 '87

National Union of Mineworkers (South Africa)
Black labor power. *Nation* 245:183-4 S 5 '87
Digging out to avoid a cave-in [strike settled] B. W. Nelan. il *Time* 130:32 S 7 '87
S. African mines hit hard with 'big' strike. il *Jet* 72:4 Ag 24 '87
South Africa: a clash of wills. S. Reiss. il *Newsweek* 110:28-9 Ag 24 '87
South Africa: lessons of a bitter strike. S. Reiss. il *Newsweek* 110:35 S 7 '87
South African miners test political clout. M. August. il *Black Enterp* 18:19-20 N '87
South Africa's whites face a new reality [striking black miners] J. Jones. il *U S News World Rep* 103:29 Ag 24 '87
A strike at a nation's heart. il *Macleans* 100:23 Ag 24 '87
Striking figure [leader C. Ramaphosa] J. Greenwald. il por *Time* 130:42+ S 14 '87
This miners' strike may hit political pay dirt. A. Fine. il *Bus Week* p35 Ag 24 '87

National Union of Mineworkers (South Africa)—*cont.*
Trouble from belowground [miners' strike] W. E. Smith. il *Time* 130:33 Ag 24 '87
National University of Chile *See* Universidad de Chile
National Urban Fellows
Urban Fellows Group awards grants to workers in rural and public administration. *Jet* 71:9 Ja 26 '87
National Weather Service (U.S.) *See* United States. National Weather Service
National Westminster Bank plc
How NatWest plans to stretch its string of successes. R. A. Melcher. il por *Bus Week* p46 Jl 6 '87
National Wildflower Research Center
In from the fields, wildflowers find a new welcome among gardeners. B. Gilbert. bibl (p162) il por *Smithsonian* 18:36-45 Ap '87
National wildlife (Periodical)
25 years of National wildlife [with editorial comment by Jay D. Hair] J. Strohm. il *Natl Wildl* 25:30, 58-9 O/N '87
National Wildlife Federation
NWF takes up call for natural resources protection [superfund] J. D. Hair. *Environment* 29:9-10 My '87
Report on the 51st NWF annual meeting. il *Natl Wildl* 25:25-7 Je/Jl '87
Report to members on NWF activities in 1986. J. D. Hair. il *Natl Wildl* 25:29-32 Ap/My '87
Wildlife digest. See issues of International Wildlife
National Wildlife Refuge System *See* Wildlife sanctuaries
National Women in Sports Day
February 4: National Women in Sports Day. il *Women's Sports Fitness* 9:74 F '87
What a day it was! L. Fink. il *Women's Sports Fitness* 9:75-6 My '87
National Women's Political Caucus
Belafonte, Lynch cited by women's political caucus. *Jet* 73:28 N 2 '87
National Wrestling Hall of Fame
ASU grappling mentor named to Wrestling Hall [B. Douglas] por *Jet* 73:46 O 26 '87
National Year of the Americas (1987)
Celebrating the Americas in 1987. *Américas* 39:51-3 Ja/F '87
Nationalism
See also
China—Nationalism
Ethnocentrism
Great Britain—Nationalism
Japan—Nationalism
National liberation movements
Nicaragua—Nationalism
Patriotism
Québec (Province)—Nationalism
Regionalism
Soviet Union—Nationalism
Spain—Nationalism
United States—Nationalism
Yugoslavia—Nationalism
Nationalism revisited [special section] il map *U S News World Rep* 103:42-50 D 28 '87-Ja 4 '88
On nationalism. W. Pfaff. *New Yorker* 63:44+ My 25 '87
Nationality (Citizenship) *See* Citizenship
Nationalization of industry *See* Government ownership
Nations
How the other haves live [world's richest countries] R. H. Bork, Jr. il *U S News World Rep* 102:47 Je 22 '87
The world in focus. il *Sch Update* 120:13-18 O 2 '87
Nation's business (Periodical)
American enterprise: then, now and tomorrow: 75th anniversary issue [cover story; special issue] il *Nations Bus* 75:10-12+ S '87
Change and continuity [H. Fish resigns as publisher] *Nation* 245:73 Ag 1-8 '87
From the editor. R. T. Gray. *Nations Bus* 75:8 Ja '87
Native peoples
See also
Ethnology
Native son [film] See Motion picture reviews—Single works
Nativity groups *See* Christmas cribs
Nativity of Christ *See* Jesus Christ—Nativity
NATO *See* North Atlantic Treaty Organization
Natori, Josie
about
The luminary of luxury lingerie. W. Konrad. il pors *Work Woman* 12:54-7 N '87
Natori Company
The luminary of luxury lingerie [J. Natori] W. Konrad. il pors *Work Woman* 12:54-7 N '87

Natow, Annette B.
(jt. auth) See Heslin, Jo-Ann, and Natow, Annette B.
Natriuretic factor, Atrial *See* Atrial natriuretic factor
Natural areas
See also
Wilderness areas
California
Where the Cosumnes still runs wild [Cosumnes River Preserve] il *Sunset* 179:38 O '87
Maryland
Soldiers Delight. S. Newcomb. il map *Earth Sci* 40:24-5 Summ '87
Soviet Union
Nature reserves of the USSR. J. F. King. il map *Sierra* 72:38-45 My/Je '87
Natural childbirth *See* Childbirth
Natural cosmetics *See* Cosmetics
Natural food *See* Food, Organic
Natural food cooking *See* Cooking—Organic food
Natural gas
See also
Gas industry
Gas supply
Methane
Guess which fuel is looking hot. P. Nulty. il map *Fortune* 115:94-6+ Je 8 '87
Leases
See Oil and gas leases
Pipelines
See Gas pipelines
Prices
Heating up the gas wars [Manitoba purchases supply network belonging to Inter-City Gas Corp.] D. Smith. il *Macleans* 100:37 Je 22 '87
How to make everyone unhappy [gas pipeline take-or-pay contracts] L. M. Keefe. il *Forbes* 140:40-1 Ag 10 '87
Rates
See Gas utilities—Rates; Natural gas—Prices
Natural gas industry *See* Gas industry
Natural history
Australia
Exhibitions
Liverpool 'Down Under' [Australia 1788—a mine of botanical novelty at Liverpool Museum] S. J. Evans. il *Hist Today* 37:4-5 O '87
Madagascar
Madagascar: a world apart. A. Jolly. il maps *Natl Geogr* 171:148-83 F '87
New York (State)
A man ahead of his time [60 years of records kept by D. Smiley] M. Winerip. il por *Natl Wildl* 25:10 F/Mr '87
Trinidad and Tobago
The lavish tropics in tandem. A. R. Williams. il *Américas* 39:14-21 Mr/Ap '87
Venezuela
Expedition to a 'lost' world [Cerro de la Neblina] A. Conover. il map *Int Wildl* 17:38-42 My/Je '87
Natural history literature *See* Nature literature
Natural history museums
See also
American Museum of Natural History
California Academy of Sciences. Natural History Museum
Museum of Natural History (Portales, N.M.)
National Museum of Natural History (U.S.)
Roger Tory Peterson Institute of Natural History
Natural killer cells *See* Lymphocytes
Natural language processing
Natural language [cover story; special section] il *Byte* 12:223-8+ D '87
Natural resources
See also
Conservation of resources
Forests and forestry
Marine resources
Mines and mineral resources
Peat
Power resources
United Nations. Committee on Natural Resources
Water
Water resources development
International aspects
The 1987 State of the world describes a planet crossing thresholds. A global science effort will look for some answers. J. P. Wiley, Jr. il *Smithsonian* 18:28+ Ap '87
Thresholds of change. L. R. Brown and S. Postel. il pors *Futurist* 21:9-14 S/O '87

Natural resources—*cont.*
Antarctic regions
Antarctica. P. J. Vesilind. il map *Natl Geogr* 171:556-60 Ap '87
Resources of Antarctica. il *Oceans* 20:69 S/O '87
Brazil
The wealth of a nation. il *Courier* 39:43-5 D '86
Natural Resources Committee (United Nations) *See* United Nations. Committee on Natural Resources
Natural Resources Defense Council
Gaining ground zero [joint Soviet-American seismic detection of underground explosions] L. Y. Lin. il *Sierra* 72:33-6 Ja/F '87
The grounds for a test ban treaty [joint Soviet-American seismic detection of underground explosions] G. Garelik. il maps *Discover* 8:50-2+ Je '87
Natural science *See* Natural history
Natural selection
See also
Competition (Biology)
Variation (Biology)
Asymmetries in mating preferences between species: female swordtails prefer heterospecific males. M. J. Ryan and W. E. Wagner, Jr. bibl f il *Science* 236:595-7 My 1 '87
Natural selection: bird seeds of change [research by Peter R. Grant and H. Lisle Gibbs] R. Monastersky. il *Sci News* 131:373-4 Je 13 '87
Runaway sexual selection [diversity of male genitalia] W. G. Eberhard. *Nat Hist* 96:4+ D '87
Naturalists
See also
Burroughs, John, 1837-1921
Leopold, Aldo, 1886-1948
Murie, Olaus Johan, 1889-1963
Thoreau, Henry David, 1817-1862
Nature
See also
Man—Influence of environment
Man—Influence on nature
Natural history
Outdoor life
Reading nature [excerpt from The lost notebooks of Loren Eiseley] L. C. Eiseley. *Harpers* 275:27 S '87
Silent bones and fallen kingdoms [excerpts from The lost notebooks of Loren Eiseley] L. C. Eiseley. *Nat Hist* 96:20+ Je '87
Bibliography
Books. J. Taylor. See issues of The Conservationist
Reviews. See issues of Natural History
Religious interpretations
The God who can't be tamed. P. Yancey. il *Christ Today* 31:72 S 18 '87
Nature (Aesthetics)
See also
Landscape
Let nature help you decorate. C. Engle. il *South Living* 22:170 Mr '87
Nature and art *See* Nature (Aesthetics)
Nature and man *See* Man—Influence of environment; Man—Influence on nature
Nature and nurture *See* Heredity and environment
Nature centers
See also
Terwilliger Nature Education Center
Wildlife watching at three Bay Area nature centers. il *Sunset* 178:48 Mr '87
Trinidad and Tobago
Asa Wright and her tropical forest ark. F. Graham. il maps *Audubon* 89:82-95 My '87
Nature Company
Marketing nature tie-ins at Nature Company [books] A. Symons. il *Publ Wkly* 231:36-8 My 1 '87
Nature Conservancy (U.S.)
Casting about in Montana [float fishing trips for trout] V. Klinkenborg. il *Esquire* 107:31+ My '87
Conservation's best-kept secret. J. Murphy. il *Time* 129:54 F 9 '87
Nature conservation
See also
Estuarine area conservation
Forest conservation
Shore protection
Wildlife conservation
Biodiversity and the public lands [cover story; special section; with editorial comment by T. H. Watkins] il maps *Wilderness* 50:10-38+ Spr '87
Profiles [M. Rothschild] K. Fraser. il *New Yorker* 63:45-8+ O 19 '87

Reflections from a dragonfly's wing [excerpt from Life in the balance] D. R. Wallace. *Wilderness* 51:51-2+ Fall '87
Species richness: a geographic approach to protecting future biological diversity [cover story] J. M. Scott and others. bibl f il map *BioScience* 37:782-8 D '87
The storehouse of the possible. P. Caws. *Wilderness* 51:64 Fall '87
A universal gift [reprint from December 1974 issue] T. Trueblood. il *Field Stream* 92:50-1 D '87
Nature in art
See also
Animals in art
Flowers in art
Gardens and gardening in art
Leaves in art
Plants in art
Using rice paper to transfer color. B. Senter. il *Am Artist* 51:60-3 My '87
Watching the artist watch nature [J. Arnosky's Drawing from nature TV series] K. O. Fakih. il por *Publ Wkly* 231:43-4 My 29 '87
Nature in literature
See also
Animals in literature
Nature literature
See also
Nature—Bibliography
A guide to the field guides. *Nat Hist* 96:62+ My '87
Nature photography
See also
Flowers—Photographs and photography
Marine photography
Photography—Landscapes
Wildlife—Photographs and photography
Around the Mall and beyond [National Museum of Natural History photographer K. B. Sandved] E. Park. il por *Smithsonian* 18:24+ S '87
The dreamer's eye. il *Conservationist* 41:30-7 Ja/F '87
Mountain light. G. A. Rowell. See issues of Petersen's Photographic Magazine beginning June 1987 through August 1987
The natural moment. See issues of Natural History beginning November 1983
Natural resources [equipment for nature photography] E. Stecker. il *Pop Photogr* 94:62-5 Ag '87
Natural splendors: Sierra's annual Photo Contest winners [cover story] il *Sierra* 72:49-57 S/O '87
Nature. J. Shaw. See issues of Popular Photography beginning June 1987
Photo contest winners. il *Natl Wildl* 26:50-9 D '87/Ja '88
Training your eye [excerpt from Texas photo safaris] G. O. Miller. il *Natl Parks* 61:10-11 S/O '87
Exhibitions
Through the eye of the beholder [exhibition of E. Porter's work at the Amon Carter Museum] M. Harwood. il *Nat Hist* 96:24-9 D '87
Nature protection *See* Nature conservation
Nature sanctuaries *See* Wildlife sanctuaries
Nature study
See also
Bird study
Environmental education
Nature centers
Nature photography
Roger Tory Peterson Institute of Natural History
Terwilliger Nature Education Center
The importance of "tweety birds". S. Cook. il *Natl Wildl* 25:46-7 O/N '87
Nature classes and seminars in the national parks [Western States] il map *Sunset* 178:50+ Ap '87
Nature trails *See* Trails
Naughton, Tom
Exercise ailments: when your used parts break down. il *Curr Health 2* 14:26-7 S '87
Naughty Marietta [operetta] *See* Herbert, Victor
Nausea
See also
Motion sickness
Nauset Beach (Cape Cod, Mass.) *See* Beaches—Cape Cod (Mass.)
Nautical archeology *See* Archeology, Submarine
Nautical charts
1988 buyer's guide: Lorans, radars, sat navs, plotters. G. West. il *Mot Boat Sail* 160:67+ D '87
Notices to boatmen. E. S. Maloney. See issues of Motor Boating & Sailing

Nautical terms *See* Seamen—Language

Nautilus
Chambered nautilus redux. J. Page. *Oceans* 20:9 Jl/Ag '87

Growth
See Growth—Mollusks

Navaho blankets, rugs, etc. *See* Indian blankets, rugs, etc. (American)

Navaho Indians
Chairman of the tribe [P. MacDonald] J. Cook. il por *Forbes* 139:238+ My 18 '87
Indian land, white greed [Navajo-Hopi relocation issue] T. Johnson. il *Nation* 245:15-18 Jl 4-11 '87
The land of the Navajo and the Hopi [cover story] il maps *Sunset* 178:96-109 My '87
The Navajo Nation [address, January 13, 1987] P. Macdonald. *Vital Speeches Day* 53:342-4 Mr 15 '87
On the land for good [Navajo missionary A. Garber] R. Wilkins. il pors *Christ Today* 31:12-13 Je 12 '87
Suddenly Peter MacDonald is business' best friend. S. D. Atchison. il por *Bus Week* p64 Ag 10 '87

Navaho weaving *See* Weaving

Navaids *See* Air navigation—Aids and devices

Naval Air Reserve *See* United States. Naval Air Reserve

Naval Air Systems Command (U.S.) *See* United States. Naval Air Systems Command

Naval Air Test Center (U.S.)
Increasingly complex systems will double testing workload [electronic warfare testing] il *Aviat Week Space Technol* 126:69-71 F 9 '87

Naval airplanes *See* Airplanes, Military

Naval architecture
See also
Boatbuilding
Yachts and yachting—Design

Naval bases *See* Navy yards and naval stations

Naval battles
See also
World War, 1939-1945—Naval operations

Naval history
See also
Greece—History, Naval
Pirates
Rome—History, Naval
Spain—History, Naval

Naval museums
See also
Constitution (Frigate)
Mystic Seaport Museum
National Maritime Museum (U.S.)

Naval Security and Investigative Command (U.S.) *See* United States. Naval Security and Investigative Command

Naval stations *See* Navy yards and naval stations

Naval War College (U.S.)
Military duty and moral scruple [study of ethics] E. Hillman. il *America* 157:185+ O 3 '87

Naval warfare
See also
Submarine warfare
In harm's way [Navy's strategy for global conventional war; cover story] J. Beatty. il map *Atlantic* 259:37-46+ My '87
Naval strategy: America rules the waves? D. Charles. *Science* 236:24 Ap 3 '87
Seapower [address, October 28, 1987] J. H. Webb. *Vital Speeches Day* 54:98-100 D 1 '87
Superpower arms race at sea [cover story; special section] bibl f il *Bull At Sci* 43:13-28+ S '87

Navasky, Victor S.
Ronald Reagan and the Supremes. il *Esquire* 107:77-80+ Ap '87

Navel *See* Umbilical cord

Navellier, Louis G.
about
How to find top small stocks before the big guys do. L. Laurence. il por *Money* 16:216 Mr '87

Naversen, Ronald
Mold models out of Flexwax. il *Theatre Crafts* 21:104-5 O '87

Navies
See also
Argentina—Navy
Canada. Royal Canadian Navy
France—Navy
Italy—Navy
Soviet Union—Navy
United States. Navy
Venezuela—Navy

Navigation
See also
Air navigation
Lighthouses
Lightships
Sailing
Seamanship
Boat handling. H. Halsted. See issues of Motor Boating & Sailing
Easy navigation. S. Netherby. il *Field Stream* 91:102+ Ap '87

Aids and devices
See also
Artificial satellites—Navigational use
Computers—Navigational use
Depth indicators
Fog signals
Loran
Nautical charts
Radar in navigation

Navigation satellites *See* Artificial satellites—Navigational use

Navistar International Corporation
Can the man who saved Navistar run it, too? [J. C. Cotting] K. Deveny. il por *Bus Week* p88 Mr 9 '87

Navratilova, Martina, 1956-
Dynamic duos. il *World Tennis* 34:40-1 Mr '87
Emotional rescue. il *World Tennis* 35:86 S '87
The players. il por *World Tennis* 35:39 Jl '87
Tips for the club player. il *World Tennis* 34:33 Ap '87
Winning dishes. il *World Tennis* 34:56-7 My '87
about
Ex-tennis star Gibson sees herself in Martina. il pors *Jet* 72:49 Mr 30 '87
Flo Hyman Sports Award brings Martina to tears. *Jet* 71:5 F 23 '87
Look who's on top again. F. Deford. il por *Sports Illus* 67:40-3 S 21 '87
Out of this world. S. Flink. il por *World Tennis* 34:28-31 F '87
Score one more for Steffi. F. Deford. il pors *Sports Illus* 66:38-42 Je 15 '87
Slims Championship: Martina marches on. C. Shmerler. il por *World Tennis* 34:57+ F '87
Smash acts on centre court. C. Kirkpatrick. il pors *Sports Illus* 67:28-30+ Jl 13 '87
Yes you can [cover story] S. Flink. il pors *World Tennis* 35:22-4 N '87
Anecdotes, facetiae, satire, etc.
Exclusive! Martina's dog tells all. H. Delehanty. il por *Women's Sports Fitness* 9:62 Ja '87
Golden girls. M. Lupica. il *World Tennis* 35:40-2+ S '87

Navstar satellites *See* Artificial satellites—Navigational use

Navy planes *See* Airplanes, Military

Navy Remote Ocean Sensing System (Satellite) *See* Artificial satellites—Oceanographic use

Navy yards and naval stations
Soviet break-ins? [Spetsnaz unit suspected in U.S. naval base espionage] L. Howard. il *Newsweek* 110:6 N 9 '87

Navy yards and naval stations, Russian
French Spot satellite shows Soviet Northern Fleet facilities. il *Aviat Week Space Technol* 126:44-5 Mr 2 '87
Spot photographs secret base for USSR nuclear submarines [Barents Sea] C. Covault. il *Aviat Week Space Technol* 127:18-19 Jl 20 '87

Nayak, Ranganath P.
(jt. auth) See Ketteringham, John M., and Nayak, Ranganath P.

Naylor, Jack
about
One shutterbug wears more than meets the eye [cover story] D. Stewart. il pors *Smithsonian* 18:108-12+ O '87

Naylor, R. T., 1945-
about
American bank loans line the pockets of the third world's elite. S. C. Gwynne. *Wash Mon* 19:51-2 O '87

Naylor, Thomas H., 1936-
The ban that boomeranged. *Nation* 245:755-6 D 19 '87
about
Dirty money and the debt crisis. P. C. Newman. il por *Macleans* 100:39 Mr 9 '87

Naylor Museum of Photography
One shutterbug wears more than meets the eye [J. Naylor's Collection; cover story] D. Stewart. il pors *Smithsonian* 18:108-12+ O '87

Nazi art *See* National socialism and art
Nazi war criminals *See* World War, 1939-1945—War criminals
Nazis *See* National socialism
Nazis (Neo-Nazis) *See* Neo-Nazis
Nazor, Maria
about
Maria Nazor: mapping the mindscape. S. R. Goldberg. il por *Art News* 86:97-8 Ap '87
NBA *See* National Basketball Association
NBAA *See* National Business Aircraft Association
NBC *See* National Broadcasting Co., Inc.
NBC Radio Network
Jumping Jack strikes again [J. Welch sells NBC Radio Network] P. Elmer-Dewitt. il *Time* 130:44 Ag 3 '87
NBUF *See* National Black United Fund
NCAA *See* National Collegiate Athletic Association
NCARB *See* National Council of Architectural Registration Boards
NCBA *See* Northern California Booksellers Association
NCC *See* National Council of Churches
NCEA *See* National Catholic Educational Association
NCECA *See* National Council on Education for the Ceramic Arts (U.S.)
NCI *See* National Cancer Institute (U.S.)
N'Diaye, Babacar, 1937-
about
Out of Africa. E. A. Finn, Jr. il por *Forbes* 140:246 D 14 '87
Ndirangu, Irungu
The street boys of Nairobi. *World Press Rev* 34:57 S '87
N'Dour, Youssou
about
Youssou N'Dour. L. Birnbaum. il por *Down Beat* 54:14 My '87
Ndoye, Thianar, and M'Baye, Malick
A grain revolution: the impact of imported rice on millet-based African civilizations. il *Courier* 40:8-9 My '87
NEA *See* National Education Association of the United States
Neal, Edward C.
about
Neal stays as lone black SBA policymaker in D.C. *Jet* 72:12 Ag 24 '87
Near-death experiences
Is there life after life? A scholar goes out on a limb [views of C. G. Zaleski on near-death experience] J. Cott. il *Vogue* 177:312+ My '87
Near East *See* Middle East
Nearsightedness *See* Myopia
Nearsightedness surgery *See* Cornea—Surgery
Neary, Patricia
about
La Scala's Patricia Neary: this lady is a champ. G. Parks. il pors *Dance Mag* 61:64-5 Ja '87
Neas, Richard Lowell
about
Fabulous fakery. E. Greene. il *House Gard* 159:134-43 S '87
Neatness
See also
Messiness
The good, the bad, and the messy. N. Stedman. il *Health* 19:70-2+ My '87
Neave, Charles
Drawn to politics. il *Esquire* 107:29-30 Mr '87
Neblina Expedition *See* Scientific expeditions
Nebraska
See also
Agriculture—Nebraska
Irrigation—Nebraska
Nebraskans
Midwestern state [Nebraskans living on East Coast] *New Yorker* 63:22-3 Je 8 '87
Nebulae
Bubbles from a dying star [OH 231.8+4.2; work by Bo Reipurth] il *Astronomy* 15:77 Je '87
Ceres sails by the Lagoon. il *Sky Telesc* 73:639 Je '87
Deep-sky wonders [Lagoon nebula] W. S. Houston. il *Sky Telesc* 74:106-7 Jl '87
Deep-sky wonders [Rosette nebula] W. S. Houston. il *Sky Telesc* 73:227-9 F '87
Deuterium, dust, and infant stars [study of Kleinmann-Low nebula; work of Malcolm Walmsley and others] *Sky Telesc* 74:236 S '87
Discovering M31's spiral shape. G. H. de Vaucouleurs. il por *Sky Telesc* 74:595-8 D '87
Fossil stellar shell stumps astronomers [R Coronae Borealis] il *Astronomy* 15:76-7 Mr '87

In the shadow of the Horsehead [cover story] D. Malin. il *Sky Telesc* 74:253-7 S '87
R Cor Bor's cold nebula. il *Sky Telesc* 73:369-70 Ap '87
The secret world of dark nebulae. D. Higgins and D. J. Eicher. il *Astronomy* 15:46-51 S '87
The shaping of planetary nebulae. B. Balick. il *Sky Telesc* 73:125-7+ F '87
The splendor of Eta Carinae. D. Malin. il *Sky Telesc* 73:14-18 Ja '87
Star-forming globule [Bok globule; research by D. J. King] il *Sky Telesc* 74:461-2 N '87
Photographs and photography
Hidden images: dissecting bright nebulae. R. Reeves. il *Astronomy* 15:72-5 Mr '87
Tips for shooting clusters and nebulae. M. F. Willson. il *Astronomy* 15:56-9 Ag '87
Spectra and spectroscopy
Frosty the . . . nebula? [IRAS 09371 + 1212; work of Thierry Forveille and others] il *Sky Telesc* 74:346 O '87
NEC Corp.
Japanese data center in Australia [NEC Halley's Comet Observation Center] S. J. O'Meara. il *Sky Telesc* 73:201-3 F '87
Necciai, Ron
about
Kid K. P. Jordan. il pors *Sports Illus* 66:82-6+ Je 1 '87
Neck pain
Get rid of that pain in your neck [cyclists' problems] C. R. Wolpert. il *Women's Sports Fitness* 9:56 Ja '87
Necklaces
Fantasy in blue [platinum, diamond and sapphire necklace from Hammerman Bros.] B. Weber. il por *N Y Times Mag* p102 O 25 '87
Neckties
Strong ties [woven neckties] R. La Ferla. il *N Y Times Mag* p50 Ag 30 '87
The tie that binds. G. Martin. il por *Esquire* 107:F65 Mr '87
Ties that bind [tight neckwear affects perceptual skills; report by Leonora M. Langan and Susan M. Watkins] B. L. Benderly. il *Psychol Today* 21:16 O '87
Necrologies *See* Obituaries
Needlepoint embroidery *See* Embroidery
Needles (Syringes) *See* Syringes
Needlework
See also
Appliqué work
Crocheting
Embroidery
Knitting
Quilts and quilting
Samplers
Conservation and restoration
See also
Atelier Brocard
Patterns
Try Transgraph-X for photo needleart [instant needlework chart] K. Geller-Shinn. il *Petersens Photogr Mag* 16:50-1 Ag '87
Needlework, Miniature
Golden hands: an overview of needlework in miniature. A. Bahar. il *Antiques Collect Hobbies* 92:42-5 D '87
Neel, Alexandra David- *See* David-Neel, Alexandra, 1868-1969
Neeley, Dennis J.
about
Designing where less is best. E. King. il por *Pers Comput* 11:161+ O '87
Neeley/Lofrano Inc.
Designing where less is best. E. King. il por *Pers Comput* 11:161+ O '87
Neely, Mark E., Jr.
(jt. auth) See Holzer, Harold, and Neely, Mark E., Jr.
Neely, Mark E., Jr., and others
Lost cause art. il *Americana* 15:59-62 Jl/Ag '87
Neely, Richard, 1941-
The politicalization of America's courts [address, October 16, 1987] *Vital Speeches Day* 54:147-50 D 15 '87
Neff, Craig
Agents of turmoil. il pors *Sports Illus* 67:34-40+ Ag 3 '87
Bosworth faces the music. il pors *Sports Illus* 66:20-2+ Ja 5 '87
The CAPE of good hopes. il *Sports Illus* 67:84+ O 26 '87
A clean sweep: how to deal with the agents. il *Sports Illus* 67:102+ O 19 '87

Neff, Craig—*cont.*
A double with trouble. il por *Sports Illus* 66:69 My 25 '87
Flash out of the blocks. il *Sports Illus* 66:56-7 F 23 '87
Graduating with honors. il pors *Sports Illus* 66:52+ Ap 13 '87
The hottest American import in Japan. il pors *Sports Illus* 66:72-6+ Mr 23 '87
Money talked, nobody walked. il *Sports Illus* 66:34-5 Ap 27 '87
A Murderers' Row of one. il pors *Sports Illus* 67:24-5 Jl 27 '87
New look in the long run. il pors *Sports Illus* 67:24-5 N 9 '87
Den of vipers: a sports scourge: bad agents. il *Sports Illus* 67:76-8+ O 19 '87
On to the White House. il por *Sports Illus* 67:102 N 16 '87
Pluck of the Irish. il pors *Sports Illus* 66:158+ F 9 '87
A reborn Russian, a new Nadia. il *Sports Illus* 67:74+ N 2 '87
Rolling a six the hard way. il por *Sports Illus* 67:42-3 D 7 '87
A sea dog primes his guns. il pors *Sports Illus* 66:56-62 Ja 5 '87
That wheeling feeling. il por *Sports Illus* 66:96 My 4 '87
Time to rise and shine. il *Sports Illus* 67:30-2+ N 23 '87
Triumph for Pigg power. il *Sports Illus* 67:62-3 O 5 '87
Upset time. il *Sports Illus* 67:15-17 Ag 31 '87
'What times, Silvia!'. il *Sports Illus* 67:22-3+ Ag 24 '87
(jt. auth) See Sullivan, Robert, and Neff, Craig
Neff, John B.
about
An encouraging word from Windsor's John Neff [interview] L. N. Vreeland. il por *Money* 16:130 D '87
The manager his peers admire most. L. N. Vreeland. il por *Money* Sp Issue:66-7 Fall '87
Neffson, Robert
Using photographs to interpret the modern world. il *Am Artist* 51:72-5 D '87
Negative advertising *See* Advertising
Negative ions *See* Ions
Negatives (Photography) *See* Photography—Negatives
Negev (Israel)
Israel's miracle food from the desert. J. D. Auerbach. il *Saturday Evening Post* 259:48-9+ S '87
Negligence
See also
Liability (Law)
Malpractice
Torts
Wrongful life
Negotiable instruments
See also
Certificates of deposit
Negotiation
Focus: great negotiations [special section] il *Seventeen* 46:150-1 Mr '87
The manly art of win-win negotiating. M. Willens. il *Money* 16:199-202 F '87
Negotiation, International *See* Diplomacy
Negri, Maxine
Ambitions and strategies of the religious right. *Humanist* 47:29-32 My/Je '87
Pope John Paul II and freedom. por *Humanist* 47:23-5+ S/O '87
Negritude
Negritude: an old term promotes a new movement. *Jet* 72:30 Mr 30 '87
Negro baseball leagues *See* Baseball, Professional—History
Negro Ensemble Company
20 years of theatrical excellence. R. Howell. il pors *Ebony* 42:92+ Mr '87
Negroes *See* Blacks
Negroponte, John
The environmental agenda and foreign policy [address, April 16, 1987] *Dep State Bull* 87:52-4 Jl '87
International prospects for civil nuclear power in the post-Chernobyl era [address, November 5, 1986] *Dep State Bull* 87:75-8 Ja '87
Nonproliferation and the peaceful uses of nuclear energy [address, May 20, 1987] *Dep State Bull* 87:67-70 Jl '87
Protecting the ozone layer. *Dep State Bull* 87:58-60 Je '87

Science and technology cooperation with Latin America [statement, July 30, 1987] *Dep State Bull* 87:50-2 O '87
Science and technology exchanges with the Soviet Union [statement, June 25, 1987] *Dep State Bull* 87:58-61 S '87
The success of the Antarctic Treaty [address, March 27, 1987] *Dep State Bull* 87:29-30 Je '87
U.S. role in wildlife conservation [remarks, May 18, 1987] *Dep State Bull* 87:34-5 S '87
Negroponte, Nicholas P.
about
Inventing the future. E. Dolnick. il por *N Y Times Mag* p30-3+ Ag 23 '87
Negros Island (Philippines)
Resistance on the right. M. Liu. il *Newsweek* 110:44 Ag 10 '87
The thin edge (II) [C. Aquino and problems of government] R. Shaplen. *New Yorker* 63:63-74+ S 28 '87
Nehamas, Alexander, 1946-
Truth and consequences. *New Repub* 197:31-6 O 5 '87
Nehemiah, Renaldo, 1959-
about
Moses wins, Nehemiah falls at track meet in England. *Jet* 72:46 Ag 17 '87
Nehemiah hopes surgery will improve his comeback. *Jet* 71:50 Mr 9 '87
Nehemiah ready for U.S. debut against Olympians. por *Jet* 71:49 Ja 19 '87
Rude hello for an old foe. K. Moore. il pors *Sports Illus* 66:16-17 Ja 26 '87
Neher, Bonnie O'Neal
Herb vinegars. il *Ctry J* 14:26-9 Jl '87
Neher, Ross, 1949-
about
Ross Neher at Beitzel. A. Slaton. *Art Am* 75:131 Jl '87
Neier, Aryeh, 1937-
The contra contradiction. il *N Y Rev Books* 34:5-6 Ap 9 '87
Neifert, Marianne R.
Dr. Mom's page. See issues of McCall's beginning May 1986
Neighborhood organization *See* Community organization
Neighborhoods
See also
Gentrification
NIMBY syndrome
A neighborhood. G. Pollock. il *N Y Times Mag* p104 N 8 '87
Neighbors
The front porch connection. J. Culhane. il *Read Dig* 130:106-9 Je '87
Living in peace with neighbors. E. E. Goode. il *U S News World Rep* 103:66 Ag 17 '87
Anecdotes, facetiae, satire, etc.
The best me possible. M. Kriegman. *New Yorker* 63:36-7 O 19 '87
Neil, Barbara
In the shadow of Clarendon House. il por *House Gard* 159:230-8 N '87
Neil Young and Crazy Horse (Musical group)
Neil Young and Crazy Horse: U.S. tour, September-October 1978. D. Fricke. il pors *Roll Stone* p99-100 Je 4 '87
Neill, Robert H.
about
A farmer turns to writing. B. Summer. *Publ Wkly* 232:38 D 18 '87
Neilson, Sandy
about
Woman to watch: Sandy Neilson. il pors *Women's Sports Fitness* 9:54 Jl '87
Neiman Marcus
The new show at Neiman-Marcus [General Cinema takeover] J. P. Newport, Jr. il por *Fortune* 115:103-4+ Ap 27 '87
Neisseria
Antibiotic-resistant VD on increase. *Sci News* 131:200 Mr 28 '87
Belligerent bug makes Korean debut [spectinomycin-resistant Neisseria gonorrhoeae; research by John W. Boslego and others] *Sci News* 132:94 Ag 8 '87
A new venereal threat [penicillin-resistant gonorrhea] N. Underwood. il *Macleans* 100:51 S 21 '87
Neizvestnyi, Ernst, 1926-
about
The New Statue of Liberty. *New Yorker* 63:21-2 Jl 13 '87

Nekoloff, Joe
about
A stroke victim's road to recovery. B. Perris. il por
Sch Update 119:5 Ap 20 '87
Nelkin, Dorothy
The culture of science journalism. bibl *Society* 24:17-25
S/O '87
Show and sell. *Society* 24:16-18 My/Je '87
Nell's (New York, N.Y.: Nightclub) *See* New York (N.Y.)—
Restaurants, nightclubs, bars, etc.
Nelson, Bill
about
Rep. Nelson criticizes administration space station fund-
ing estimate. T. M. Foley. *Aviat Week Space Technol*
126:27-8 Ap 13 '87
Nelson, C. Hans, and Johnson, Kirk R.
Whales and walruses as tillers of the sea floor. il maps
Sci Am 256:112-17 F '87
Nelson, Daniel
Unions' struggle to survive goes beyond modern tech-
nology. bibl f il *Mon Labor Rev* 110:41-5 Ag '87
Nelson, David
about
Hunter and Nelson named to DOE posts. I. Goodwin.
Phys Today 40 pt1:53 Ag '87
Nelson, David D., Jr., and others
Does ammonia hydrogen bond? bibl f il *Science*
238:1670-4 D 18 '87
Nelson, Gaylord
First word. por *Omni* 10:8 N '87
Nelson, Ingrid
The many lives of Kay Fanning. il por *50 Plus* 27:78+
Ja '87
More on the Adirondack Park [discussion of September
1986 article, Green hills, blue lakes, and red tape]
il *Ctry J* 14:4+ F '87
Nelson, James Bruce
Reuniting sexuality and spirituality. il *Christ Century*
104:187-90 F 25 '87
Nelson, Jill
The demise of a marriage. *Essence* 18:63+ N '87
Nelson, Julie K.
The indomitable Sulamith Messerer: the eyes have it.
il pors *Dance Mag* 61:70-3 Mr '87
Nelson, Kristin
about
Life after Ozzie & Harriet [cover story] B. Darrach.
il pors *People Wkly* 28:40-5 S 7 '87
Nelson, Larry
about
Cool customer in a hot PGA. J. Diaz. il pors *Sports
Illus* 67:28-30+ Ag 17 '87
Nelson, Lisa
about
Reviews:
S. Paxton and L. Nelson at The Kitchen, New
York City. S. Sommer. pors *Dance Mag* 61:22
S '87
Nelson, Lorna L.
about
Prince's sis says he stole lyrics from her. *Jet* 72:62
S 7 '87
Nelson, Mariah Burton
Tall. il *Ms* 15:60+ Ap '87
Nelson, Mark
Sleep on it. il *Nations Bus* 75:72+ D '87
Nelson, Martha
From the editor. See issues of Women's Sports & Fitness
beginning July 1985
Nelson, Mary Carroll
Catherine Burchfield Parker. il por *Am Artist* 51:58-61+
D '87
Twenty-six artists describe a crystallizing experience. il
Am Artist 51:74-6+ F '87
Nelson, Meredith
Arlene Blum: from molecules to mountains. il pors *Ms*
16:106+ S '87
Nelson, Niall C. W.
(jt. auth) See Johnson, Susan Moore, and Nelson, Niall
C. W.
Nelson, Olof
about
The value of a dam. J. Merwin. il por *Forbes* 139:160
Mr 23 '87
Nelson, Peter
Present & accounted for. *Harpers Bazaar* 121:127+ D
'87
Sylvia Smith-Smith and . . . the cigar-smoking ghost
[story] il *Seventeen* 46:120-1+ Je '87
Sylvia Smith-Smith and . . . the cigar-smoking ghost
[story] *Seventeen* 46:122-3+ Jl '87

Sylvia Smith-Smith's mixed-up masquerade [story] il
Seventeen 46:150-1+ O '87
Why gentlemen still prefer blondes. il *Harpers Bazaar*
120:174-5+ Ap '87
Nelson, Prince Rogers *See* Prince
Nelson, Richard K.
Shooting a buck. *Harpers* 274:29-30 Ja '87
Nelson, Roy Paul
The Multnomah formula. il *Publ Wkly* 231:41-2 Mr
6 '87
Nelson, Sam
about
Life after Ozzie & Harriet [cover story] B. Darrach.
il pors *People Wkly* 28:40-5 S 7 '87
Nelson, Sara
Finding your heart . . . away from home. il *Seventeen*
46:152-3+ My '87
Gossip: why we love it. il *Seventeen* 46:140-1 O '87
Sex, AIDS and pillow talk. il *Glamour* 85:350-1+ S
'87
Ten-boy summer. il *Glamour* 85:44+ Jl '87
When your mom is fat. il *Seventeen* 46:164-5+ N '87
(ed) See Belanger, Diana. 3 children who needed a medical
miracle
Nelson, Sara, and Simels, Steve
The long and bumpy road from lovers to just friends.
il *Glamour* 85:194-5+ Je '87
Nelson, Theodor H.
On the road to Xanadu. *Pers Comput* 11:170 D '87
about
The big link. S. Ditlea. il *Omni* 9:16+ S '87
Nelson, Willie
about
Farm Aid's founder Willie Nelson [cover story] P. Carr.
il pors *Mother Earth News* 105:42-5 My/Je '87
The stars who make Christmas special. L. Feldman.
il pors *McCalls* 115:90+ D '87
Willie Nelson's harvest of hope. E. Hawkes. il pors
Ladies Home J 104:88+ S '87
Nelson (B.C.) in motion pictures
A nose for the tragic heart of comedy [filming of Roxanne]
P. Young. il *Macleans* 100:48 Je 29 '87
Nelson (Thomas) Inc. *See* Thomas Nelson, Inc.
Nelson-Herber, Joan
(jt. auth) See Herber, Harold L., and Nelson-Herber,
Joan
Nelson Ledges (Race) *See* Automobile racing
Nematodes
See also
Embryology—Nematodes
Mutation—Nematodes
Bugs bite the dust on bitter pill [use of parasitic nematodes
as biological controls] *Sci News* 132:377 D 12 '87
Nemerov, Howard
The shadow side [poem] *America* 157:41 Jl 18-25
'87
Nemesis (Star) *See* Stars
Nenaschev, Mikhail
about
'They must not print books that nobody buys' [interview]
por *Publ Wkly* 232:30-1 O 16 '87
Nenzel, Andrea
about
The long trip home. G. Palumbo. *Commonweal* 114:377
Je 19 '87
Neo-expressionism (Art)
The four brushmen of the apocalypse. L. Hirschberg.
il pors *Esquire* 107:76-84+ Mr '87
Neo-geo (Art)
Neo-geo: art's computer hum. M. Stevens. il *Newsweek*
110:119 N 16 '87
Neo-Nazis
Facing up to the farm crisis [Interreligious Conference
on Rural Life; cover story] V. Rebeck. *Christ Century*
104:381-3 Ap 22 '87
Foiling a revolt [white supremacists indicted for sedition]
il *Time* 129:24 My 4 '87
Greg Withrow's neo-Nazi past returns to inflict the
ultimate scourge: crucifixion. M. Green. il pors *People
Wkly* 28:41-2+ S 21 '87
Hi-tech racism. S. Miller. *Black Enterp* 18:22 O '87
San Jose blacks angered over white racist group's threat
to black woman. *Jet* 72:4 Ag 31 '87
Skinheads on the rampage [youths in California] G.
Hackett. il *Newsweek* 110:22 S 7 '87
Photographs and photography
White patriots. J. Friar. il *Society* 25:87-93 N/D '87
Mexico
Neo-Nazi U [Autonomous University of Guadalajara
is stronghold of secret society Los Tecos] C. Pyes.
il *New Repub* 196:17-18+ Ja 19 '87

Neoclassicism

Classicism and the American Revolution. S. Andrews. bibl f il *Hist Today* 37:37-42 Ja '87

Neoclassicism (Architecture)

Neoclassic beauty [Villa Melzi] A. Lambton. il *House Gard* 159:190-9+ S '87

Exhibitions

British architecture [Robert Adam and Kedleston Hall at the Cooper-Hewitt] S. B. Sherrill. il *Antiques* 131:1170+ Je '87

Neoclassicism (Art)

Editorial [Victorian classicism] W. Garrett. il *Antiques* 131:223 Ja '87

Neocortex *See* Brain

Neoliberalism *See* Liberalism

Neolithic period *See* Stone Age

Neologisms *See* Words, New

Neon light in art *See* Light in art

Neon signs

Neon. il *Natl Geogr World* 140:36-9 Ap '87

Neonatology *See* Infants, Newborn—Hospital care

Nepal

See also

Education—Nepal
Environment—Nepal
Forests and forestry—Nepal
Hiking—Nepal
Kathmandu (Nepal)
Mount Everest (China and Nepal)
National parks and reserves—Nepal
Phalabang (Nepal)
Wildlife—Nepal
Wildlife sanctuaries—Nepal

Kingdom of Nepal. map *Dep State Bull* 87:68-72 S '87

Foreign relations

United States

See United States—Foreign relations—Nepal

Nepeta *See* Catmint

Nepomuceno, Eric

Brazil and its neighbours. il *Courier* 39:11-15 D '86

Nepotism

Dear Betty Harragan [anti-nepotism policy instituted after corporate merger] B. L. Harragan. il *Work Woman* 12:38+ D '87

China

Princes of privilege. J. Greenwald. il *Time* 130:41 S 28 '87

Neptune (Planet)

Photographs and photography

New views of Neptune [work of Heidi Hammel and Marc Buie] il *Sky Telesc* 74:235 S '87

Neptune Theatre

Getting back on the theatrical track [artistic director R. Ouzounian] il por *Macleans* 100:47-8 Ap 20 '87

Neptune's Car (Clipper ship)

"Captain" Mary Patten [1854-55 voyage from New York to San Francisco via Cape Horn] P. L. Brosnan. il por *Oceans* 20:36-9 S/O '87

The nerd [drama] *See* Shue, Larry

Nerenberg, Michael, and others

The *tat* gene of human T-lymphotropic virus type 1 induces mesenchymal tumors in transgenic mice. bibl f il *Science* 237:1324-9 S 11 '87

Neruda, Pablo, 1904-1973

Birds of a poet's native land [poem]; tr. by Jack Schmitt. il *Int Wildl* 17:16-17 My/Je '87

Nerval, Gérard de, 1808-1855

about

Folies de grandeur. R. M. Adams. il map *House Gard* 159:48+ Ja '87

Nerve cell adhesion *See* Adhesion

Nerve cell regeneration *See* Regeneration (Biology)

Nerve cells

See also

Electrophysiology
Synapses

Brainy ties that bind [astrocytes; research by Robert C. Janzer and Martin C. Raff] D. D. Edwards. il *Sci News* 131:68 Ja 31 '87

Cellular mechanisms of epilepsy: a status report. M. A. Dichter and G. F. Ayala. bibl f il *Science* 237:157-64 Jl 10 '87

Conduction velocity variations minimize conduction time differences among retinal ganglion cell axons. L. R. Stanford. bibl f il *Science* 238:358-60 O 16 '87

Delayed transneuronal death of substantia nigra neurons prevented by γ-aminobutyric acid agonist. M. Saji and D. J. Reis. bibl f il *Science* 235:66-9 Ja 2 '87

Depolarization without calcium can release γ-aminobutyric acid from a retinal neuron. E. A. Schwartz. bibl f il *Science* 238:350-5 O 16 '87

Does the release of potassium from astrocyte endfeet regulate cerebral blood flow? O. B. Paulson and E. A. Newman. bibl f il *Science* 237:896-8 Ag 21 '87

The dynamics of free calcium in dendritic spines in response to repetitive synaptic input. E. Gamble and C. Koch. bibl f il *Science* 236:1311-15 Je 5 '87

External calcium ions are required for potassium channel gating in squid neurons. C. M. Armstrong and J. Lopez-Barneo. bibl f il *Science* 236:712-14 My 8 '87

Fans of the worms [Myxicola worms raised for axon research by David Dean] P. A. Erickson. il *Oceans* 20:62-3 S/O '87

Mapping patterns of c-*fos* expression in the central nervous system after seizure. J. I. Morgan and others. bibl f il *Science* 237:192-7 Jl 10 '87

Multiple calcium channels and neuronal function. R. J. Miller. bibl f il *Science* 235:46-52 Ja 2 '87

Nerve terminal remodeling visualized in living mice by repeated examination of the same neuron. D. Purves and others. bibl f il *Science* 238:1122-6 N 20 '87

Neuronal pp60^{c-src} contains a six-amino acid insertion relative to its non-neuronal counterpart. R. Martinez and others. bibl f il *Science* 237:411-15 Jl 24 '87

New clue [effect of quinolinic acid on brain cells in Huntington's disease; work of Dennis Choi and others] *USA Today (Periodical)* 115:9 F '87

Newly identified 'glutamate interneurons' and their role in locomotion in the lamprey spinal cord. J. T. Buchanan and S. Grillner. bibl f il *Science* 236:312-14 Ap 17 '87

Preferred microtubules for vesicle transport in lobster axons. R. H. Miller and others. bibl f il *Science* 235:220-2 Ja 9 '87

Protobrain [embryonic cat brain cells; work of Jerald J. M. Chun and others] *Sci Am* 256:68+ My '87

RNA complementary to a herpesvirus α gene mRNA is prominent in latently infected neurons. J. G. Stevens and others. bibl f il *Science* 235:1056-9 F 27 '87

Slow transport of tubulin in the neurites of differentiated PC 12 cells. C. H. Keith. bibl f il *Science* 235:337-9 Ja 16 '87

Synapses that compute motion [study of ganglion cells] T. Poggio and C. Koch. il *Sci Am* 256:46-52 My '87

Transient morphological features of identified ganglion cells in living fetal and neonatal retina. A. S. Ramoa and others. bibl f il *Science* 237:522-5 Jl 31 '87

Culture

Concanavalin A alters synaptic specificity between cultured Aplysia neurons. S. S. Lin and I. B. Levitan. bibl f il *Science* 237:648-50 Ag 7 '87

Development of two types of calcium channels in cultured mammalian hippocampal neurons. Y. Yaari and others. bibl f il *Science* 235:680-2 F 6 '87

Forskolin and phorbol esters reduce the same potassium conductance of mouse neurons in culture. D. S. Grega and others. bibl f il *Science* 235:345-8 Ja 16 '87

Networking [culturing neurons on arrays of microelectrodes] il *Sci Am* 256:62 Ja '87

Growth

Astrocytes block axonal regeneration in mammals by activating the physiological stop pathway. F. J. Liuzzi and R. J. Lasek. bibl f il *Science* 237:642-5 Ag 7 '87

Cloning of complementary DNA for GAP-43, a neuronal growth-related protein. L. R. Karns and others. bibl f il *Science* 236:597-600 My 1 '87

Trophic stimulation of cultured neurons from neonatal rat brain by epidermal growth factor. R. S. Morrison and others. bibl f il *Science* 238:72-5 O 2 '87

Nerve conduction *See* Electrophysiology

Nerve endings

Nerve terminal remodeling visualized in living mice by repeated examination of the same neuron. D. Purves and others. bibl f il *Science* 238:1122-6 N 20 '87

Nerve gases *See* Chemical and biological weapons

Nerve growth factor

Bringing back fading memories [work of Anders Björklund and others] D. D. Edwards. *Sci News* 132:149-50 S 5 '87

The heart & mind of a genius [R. Levi-Montalcini] F. Randall. il por *Vogue* 177:480-1+ Mr '87

The nerve growth factor 35 years later [address, December 8, 1986] R. Levi-Montalcini. bibl f il *Science* 237:1154-62 S 4 '87

A nerve growth factor-induced gene encodes a possible transcriptional regulatory factor. J. Milbrandt. bibl f il *Science* 238:797-9 N 6 '87

Nerve growth factor—*cont.*

Nerve growth factor treatment after brain injury prevents neuronal death. L. F. Kromer. bibl f il *Science* 235:214-16 Ja 9 '87

Nerve regeneration *See* Regeneration (Biology)

Nerve tissue

Transplantation

Nerve transplant: proceed with caution. D. D. Edwards. *Sci News* 131:135 F 28 '87

Retina transplant restores rat reflex [pupillary reflex; work of Henry Klassen and Raymond D. Lund] R. Weiss. il *Sci News* 132:245 O 17 '87

Nerve transmitter substances *See* Neurotransmitters

Nerves

See also
Nervous system
Sciatic nerve
Synapses
Vagus nerve

Nervous system

See also
Biological control systems
Brain
Electrophysiology
Nerve tissue
Neural tube
Neurobiology
Reflexes
Sensory receptors
Shock
Spinal cord
Synapses

Identification of a novel thyroid hormone receptor expressed in the mammalian central nervous system. C. C. Thompson and others. bibl f il *Science* 237:1610-14 S 25 '87

Annelids

Fans of the worms [Myxicola worms raised for axon research by David Dean] P. A. Erickson. il *Oceans* 20:62-3 S/O '87

Crustaceans

Full-wave rectification from a mixed electrical-chemical synapse [lobsters] K. Graubard and D. K. Hartline. bibl f il *Science* 237:535-7 Jl 31 '87

Preferred microtubules for vesicle transport in lobster axons. R. H. Miller and others. bibl f il *Science* 235:220-2 Ja 9 '87

Diseases

See also
AIDS (Disease)
Amyotrophic lateral sclerosis
Brain—Diseases
Demyelination
Huntington's disease
Lesch-Nyhan syndrome
Multiple sclerosis
Tourette syndrome

Leukemia virus linked to nerve disease [HTLV-I] J. L. Marx. bibl il *Science* 236:1059-61 My 29 '87

Fish

Sensory tuning of lateral line receptors in Antarctic fish to the movements of planktonic prey [teleosts] J. C. Montgomery and J. A. Macdonald. bibl f il *Science* 235:195-6 Ja 9 '87

Growth

See Developmental neurology

Invertebrates

Neuronal circuits and evolution [discussion of August 22, 1986 article, Neuronal circuits: an evolutionary perspective] J. P. C. Dumont and R. M. Robertson. *Science* 236:1681-2 Je 26 '87

Mollusks

Concanavalin A alters synaptic specificity between cultured Aplysia neurons. S. S. Lin and I. B. Levitan. bibl f il *Science* 237:648-50 Ag 7 '87

Dissecting learning in Aplysia [research by Thomas J. Carew and others] S. Weisburd. *Sci News* 132:286 O 31 '87

Long-term sensitization in Aplysia: biophysical correlates in tail sensory neurons. K. P. Scholz and J. H. Byrne. bibl f il *Science* 235:685-7 F 6 '87

New bearers of nerve tidings? [effect of eicosanoids on Aplysia neurons; research by Daniele Piomelli and others] D. D. Edwards. *Sci News* 132:5 Jl 4 '87

Surgery

See also
Spinal cord—Surgery

Wounds and injuries

See also
Carpal tunnel syndrome

Nervous tension *See* Stress

Nervousness

See also
Stage fright

Here comes that sinking feeling! [conquering nervousness during a tennis match] J. E. Loehr. il *World Tennis* 34:16-17 Mr '87

Never be nervous again [condensation]; ed. by Gaylen Moore. D. Sarnoff. *Read Dig* 131:27-8+ D '87

Nnnerves: how to overcome them. A. Bell. il *Teen* 31:84+ My '87

Nesbit, W. Ben

Establishing a local education foundation. *Educ Dig* 52:21-3 My '87

Nesbitt, Scott

Snow removal equipment. il *Flower Gard* 32:74-5 D '87/Ja '88

Nesbitt Thomson Deacon Inc.

Frantic week for a broker [D. Doritty's activities during stock market crash] A. Shortell. il por *Macleans* 100:31-2 N 2 '87

Nesmith, N. Graham

Say, brother. por *Essence* 17:8 Ja '87

Ness, Eliot, 1903-1957

about

The first Untouchable of them all. L. Shapiro. il por *Newsweek* 109:68 Je 22 '87

The last Untouchable; ed. by Civia Tamarkin. A. Wolff. il pors *People Wkly* 28:53-4+ Jl 13 '87

The real Eliot Ness. S. Nickel. il pors *Am Hist Illus* 22:42-52 O '87

Nessel, Denise

Reading comprehension: asking the right questions. bibl il *Phi Delta Kappan* 68:442-5 F '87

Nesting habits of birds *See* Birds—Habits and behavior

Nestle SA

Stirring the coffee pot [H. Maucher] S. Tully. il por *Fortune* 116:44 Ag 3 '87

Nests

See also
Birds—Nests
Dinosaurs—Nests

Nesvisky, Matt

So who's confused? *World Press Rev* 34:16 F '87

Netherby, Steve

Camping. See issues of Field & Stream

Netherlands

See also
Amsterdam (Netherlands)
Art and state—Netherlands
Astronomical observatories—Netherlands
British—Netherlands
Dance concerts—Netherlands
Dance festivals—Netherlands
Eating—Netherlands
Hague (Netherlands)
Housing projects—Netherlands
Jews—Netherlands
Music festivals—Netherlands
Opera—Netherlands
Physics—Netherlands
Prisons—Netherlands
Technical assistance, Dutch

Air Force

Three European Air Forces step up training at Goose Bay. *Aviat Week Space Technol* 127:86 O 5 '87

Commerce

United States

See United States—Commerce—Netherlands

Defenses

See also
Netherlands—Air Force

Description and travel

Dutch treat. H. Koenig. il map *Travel Holiday* 168:48-53+ Ag '87

History

See also
World War, 1939-1945—Campaigns and battles—Netherlands

Wars of Independence, 1556-1648

A patriot for whom? Stanley, York and Elizabeth's Catholics [1587 defection of key officers in the Netherlands] S. Adams. bibl il *Hist Today* 37:46-50 Jl '87

Industries

See also
Elsevier (Firm)
Fokker BV
Kluwer NV
Philips Industries, NV
Publishers and publishing—Acquisitions and mergers—Netherlands

Netherlands—Industries—See also—cont.
Royal Dutch/Shell Group
Unilever NV
Kings and rulers
See also
Beatrix, Queen of the Netherlands, 1938-
Social history
Holland's feast of life [eating habits in the 17th and 18th centuries; excerpt from The embarrassment of riches] S. Schama. il *House Gard* 159:68+ Je '87
Social policy
Tolerance finally finds its limits. F. Painton. il *Time* 130:28-9 Ag 31 '87
Netherlands Antilles
See also
Aruba
Saba (Netherlands Antilles)
Saint Eustatius (Netherlands Antilles)
The sun isn't setting on this tax haven. G. DeGeorge. il *Bus Week* p57-8 Ag 31 '87
Treaties
United States
See United States—Treaties—Netherlands Antilles
Netherlands Dance Theater
Kylián changes keys. L. Moffett. il por *Dance Mag* 61:46-50 My '87
Letdown at Lincoln Center. L. A. Jacobs. *New Leader* 70:21-2 Jl 13-27 '87
Love finds a way [performances in New York City] T. Tobias. il *N Y* 20:56-7 Jl 13 '87
Reviews:
Performances at Circustheater in the Netherlands. H. Klooss. *Dance Mag* 61:70-2 Jl '87
Performances at the Metropolitan Opera House, New York City. J. R. Acocella. *Dance Mag* 61:19+ N '87
Netherlands-United States air agreements See Aviation—International aspects
Neto, João Cabral de Melo See Melo Neto, João Cabral de, 1920-
Nets, Fishing See Fishing nets
Nett, H. R.
Backroads. il *Cycle* 38:35-7 N '87
Network Productions Inc.
Pay TV's descrambling wars. C. Gerber. *Channels* 7:11 Je '87
Networking
Don't know anyone in the room? How to take charge. il *Glamour* 85:108 F '87
A nation of networkers. P. Baida. il *Am Herit* 38:20+ Ap '87
A network model. J. Lipnack and J. Stamps. il pors *Futurist* 21:23-5 Jl/Ag '87
Network to network [black professionals] D. Wickham. il *Black Enterp* 17:123-4+ F '87
Networking: better than creating new centers? [European research] D. Dickson. *Science* 237:1106-7 S 4 '87
Networking news. See issues of Black Enterprise beginning November 1987
Networking update [Black Enterprise Professional Exchange] il *Black Enterp* 18:25 Ag '87
Networking update [Black Enterprise Professional Exchange] C. Bullock. il *Black Enterp* 18:26 S '87
Office pals: it pays to stay in touch. J. A. Byrne. il *Bus Week* p126 Ap 6 '87
On the network. L. Whitten. *Essence* 18:114 Jl '87
Power networking Black enterprise style. S. R. King. il *Black Enterp* 18:70-3 N '87
Networks, Computer See Computer networks
Neuberger & Berman Money Market Plus
A hybrid money fund with pop. il *Money* 16:39 Jl '87
Neuburger, Jerrold J.
A physicist objects. il por *Progressive* 51:12-13 Jl '87
Neugarten, Bernice L., and Neugarten, Dail A.
The changing meanings of age. bibl (p94) il *Psychol Today* 21:29-30+ My '87
Neugarten, Dail A.
(jt. auth) See Neugarten, Bernice L., and Neugarten, Dail A.
Neugebauer, Marcia
Comet rendezvous—the next step. il *Sky Telesc* 73:266+ Mr '87
Neuharth, Allen
about
Allen H. Neuharth. P. Jordan. il pors *People Wkly* 28:65+ S 28 '87
Gatsby with a typewriter. D. Hutchins. il por *Fortune* 115:92 Ja 5 '87
Good news is no news. D. Remnick. il pors *Esquire* 108:156-8+ O '87

The growing gets tougher. S. N. Chakravarty. il pors *Forbes* 139:68+ Je 15 '87
Invasion of the Gannettoids. P. Weiss. il *New Repub* 196:18-20+ F 2 '87
The king of the road. J. Alter. il por *Newsweek* 109:66-7 My 4 '87
Never forget the egomania. R. J. Samuelson. il *Newsweek* 110:65 S 21 '87
Neuhaus, Cable
(ed) See Lindsay, Bertha. The Shakers face their last amen
Neuhaus, Max
about
Max Neuhaus: aural spaces. C. Ratcliff. il *Art Am* 75:154-63 O '87
Neuhaus, Richard John
Pilgrim. See occasional issues of National Review beginning September 12, 1986
Prophets with tenure. *Commentary* 84:49-52 Jl '87
Neuma Inc.
One woman's smart formula: don't only tend to your knitting [founder N. Agins] J. Alexander. il por *Money* 16:41-2+ N '87
Neuman, Frances
about
And they called it puppy love. D. Hurley. *50 Plus* 27:18+ F '87
Neuman, Jeffrey
about
'A season on the brink' is the season's surprise #1 bestseller. D. Masello. il pors *Publ Wkly* 231:28-30 Mr 27 '87
Neural network computers
Back-propagation. W. P. Jones and J. Hoskins. bibl il *Byte* 12:155-6+ O '87
Collective computation in neuronlike circuits. D. W. Tank and J. J. Hopfield. il *Sci Am* 257:104-8+ D '87
Computing with neural networks [discussion of August 8, 1986 article, Computing with neural circuits: a model] J. J. Hopfield and D. W. Tank. bibl f il *Science* 235:1226-9 Mr 6 '87
Constructing an associative memory. B. Kosko. bibl il *Byte* 12:137-8+ S '87
Creating an "electronic nose" [electronically reproduced fragment of the olfactory cortex; work of Gary Lynch and others] il *USA Today (Periodical)* 115:13 Je '87
Designing computers that think the way we do. W. F. Allman. il *Technol Rev* 90:58-65 My/Je '87
Exploiting highly concurrent computers for physics. K. C. Bowler and others. bibl f il *Phys Today* 40:40-8 O '87
Growing 'brains' in a computer. I. Amato. il *Sci News* 131:60-1 Ja 24 '87
Mimicking the human mind. M. Rogers. il *Newsweek* 110:52-3 Jl 20 '87
Modeling the brain. M. Zeidenberg. bibl il *Byte* 12:237-8+ D '87
Neural computing not just for the very rich. *Byte* 12:38+ S '87
Neural nets catch the ABCs of DNA [research by Alan Lapedes and others] S. Weisburd. *Sci News* 132:76 Ag 1 '87
Neural-network heuristics. G. Josin. bibl il *Byte* 12:183-4+ O '87
Neural networks: from heyday to nayday and back. R. Spangenburg and D. Moser. *Space World* X-9-285:18 S '87
Optical neural computers. Y. S. Abu-Mostafa and D. Psaltis. bibl (p128) il *Sci Am* 256:88-95 Mr '87
Seeing the need for 'ART' [adaptive resonance theory represents another step in neural networks; work of Gail A. Carpenter] K. Hartley. il *Sci News* 132:14 Jl 4 '87
They're here: computers that 'think'. O. Port. *Bus Week* p94+ Ja 26 '87
Three neural-network programs; Turn your AT into a neurocomputer. *Byte* 12:45-6 O '87
Neural receptors See Sensory receptors
Neural tube
Diseases
See also
Spina bifida
Diagnosis
Screening for neural tube defects. P. A. Hillard. il *Parents* 62:194+ S '87
Neuraminidase
Similarity of cruzin, an inhibitor of Trypanosoma cruzi neuraminidase, to high-density lipoprotein. R. P. Prioli and others. bibl f il *Science* 238:1417-19 D 4 '87

Neurites *See* Nerve cells
Neurobiology
  See also
  Neural network computers
Broad attack launched on the nervous system [special section] D. M. Barnes. il *Science* 238:1651-3 D 18 '87
The cerebellum and memory storage [discussion of August 29, 1986 article, The neurobiology of learning and memory] R. F. Thompson. *Science* 238:1728-30 D 18 '87
Memory: learning how it works [cover story] G. Johnson. il por *N Y Times Mag* p16-21+ Ag 9 '87
Neural models yield data on learning [special section] D. M. Barnes. *Science* 236:1628-9 Je 26 '87
Neurochemistry
  See also
  Brain—Analysis and chemistry
  Neurotransmitters
Biochemistry of information storage in the nervous system. I. B. Black and others. bibl f il *Science* 236:1263-8 Je 5 '87
Neurofibromatosis
As of '87, he's Proteus Man [cause of the Elephant Man's deformities] *Sci News* 132:55 Jl 25 '87
Common pathogenetic mechanism for three tumor types in bilateral acoustic neurofibromatosis. B. R. Seizinger and others. bibl f il *Science* 236:317-19 Ap 17 '87
Gene for von Recklinghausen neurofibromatosis is in the pericentromeric region of chromosome 17. D. Barker and others. bibl f il *Science* 236:1100-2 My 29 '87
Gene search narrows. R. Weiss. *Sci News* 131:359 Je 6 '87
A transgenic mouse model for human neurofibromatosis. S. H. Hinrichs and others. bibl f il *Science* 237:1340-3 S 11 '87
Neuroimmunology
  See also
  Psychoneuroimmunology
Neuroimmunology sits on broad research base [special section] D. M. Barnes. il *Science* 237:1568-9 S 25 '87
Neuroleptics *See* Psychopharmacology
Neuroleukin
'Competition' cause of AIDS dementia? [work of Mark E. Gurney and others] D. D. Edwards. *Sci News* 132:150-1 S 5 '87
Functional interaction and partial homology between human immunodeficiency virus and neuroleukin [cause of AIDS dementia] M. R. Lee and others. bibl f il *Science* 237:1047-51 Ag 28 '87
Neurolinguistics
The language of the brain [cover story] B. Bower. il *Sci News* 132:40-1 Jl 18 '87
Old familiar voices [familiar-voice recognition] D. Van Lancker. il *Psychol Today* 21:12-13 N '87
The right turn of phrase [processing of familiar language in the brain's right hemisphere] D. Kempler and D. Van Lancker. il *Psychol Today* 21:20+ Ap '87
Neurology
  See also
  Developmental neurology
  Neuroimmunology
Oliver Sacks: "I began to think that wellness might be a disease, that one might suffer from chronic health in California". H. Brubach. il pors *Vogue* 177:230+ N '87
  Anecdotes, facetiae, satire, etc.
More clinical tales. R. Liebmann-Smith. *New Yorker* 63:30-1 My 4 '87
Neuromuscular junctions *See* Junctions (Physiology)
Neuron degeneration *See* Cell death
Neurons *See* Nerve cells
Neuropeptides *See* Peptides
Neurophysiology *See* Nervous system
Neuropsychology
Braitenberg memoirs: vehicles for probing behavior roam a dark plain marked by lights. A. K. Dewdney. il *Sci Am* 256:16-18+ Mr '87
Neurogenetic adaptive mechanisms in alcoholism. C. R. Cloninger. bibl f il *Science* 236:410-16 Ap 24 '87
This brain's for hire. L. Miller. *Omni* 9:14 Mr '87
Neurosecretion
  See also
  Pituitary hormone releasing factors
Neuroses
  See also
  Depression, Mental
  Phobias

Neurospora
A portable signal causing faithful DNA methylation de novo in Neurospora crassa. E. U. Selker and others. bibl f il *Science* 238:48-53 O 2 '87
Neurosurgery *See* Brain—Surgery
Neurotoxins *See* Toxins and antitoxins
Neurotransmitter receptors *See* Chemoreceptors
Neurotransmitters
  See also
  Aminobutyric acid
  Cholecystokinin
  Dopamine
  Serotonin
  Substance P
Brain food: eat smart to stay sharp. S. C. Finn. il *50 Plus* 27:65+ Je '87
New bearers of nerve tidings? [effect of eicosanoids on Aplysia neurons; research by Daniele Piomelli and others] D. D. Edwards. *Sci News* 132:5 Jl 4 '87
Polyphosphoinositide research updated. J. L. Marx. il *Science* 235:974-6 F 27 '87
Quantal release of transmitter is not associated with channel opening on the neuronal membrane [neuromuscular junction] S. H. Young and I. Chow. bibl f il *Science* 238:1712-13 D 18 '87
Neusner, Jacob, 1932-
Ethnic studies: the coming crisis: the case of "Jewish studies". il *Change* 19:8-10 Jl/Ag '87
Neutrality
  See also
  Treaties of guaranty
Neutrinos
Bang: the supernova of 1987. D. Helfand. bibl il *Phys Today* 40 pt1:24-32 Ag '87
The first news from the supernova was the last to be read [1987A] S. Vogel. il *Discover* 8:58-9 Jl '87
From neutrinos to quasiparticles. L. P. Kadanoff. por *Phys Today* 40 pt1:7+ Ag '87
A hint of gamma rays; Blank about Mont Blanc [supernova 1987A] D. E. Thomsen. *Sci News* 132:286 O 31 '87
Limits on sensitivity of large silicon bolometers for solar neutrino detection. C. J. Martoff. bibl f il *Science* 237:507-9 Jl 31 '87
Neutrino astronomy born in a supernova [1987A] D. E. Thomsen. *Sci News* 131:180 Mr 21 '87
Neutrino mass: a positive view [work of Hong-Yee Chiu and others] D. E. Thomsen. *Sci News* 131:246 Ap 18 '87
Neutrino mass: a tritium disagreement. D. E. Thomsen. *Sci News* 131:342 My 30 '87
Neutrino physics after the supernova [explosion of 1987A] D. E. Thomsen. *Sci News* 131:231 Ap 11 '87
Neutrinos from hell [detected from supernova 1987A] R. A. Schorn. il *Sky Telesc* 73:477-9 My '87
Observational neutrino astrophysics [Japanese research] M.-T. Koshiba. bibl il map *Phys Today* 40:38-42 D '87
Regenerating neutrinos. D. E. Thomsen. *Sci News* 131:303 My 9 '87
Scientists, 'boxed in', scramble after supernova, find neutrinos [1987A] D. E. Thomsen. *Sci News* 131:165 Mr 14 '87
A simple model for neutrino cooling of the Large Magellanic Cloud supernova. D. N. Spergel and others. bibl f il *Science* 237:1471-3 S 18 '87
Solar neutrinos: experimental approaches. G. Friedlander and J. Weneser. bibl f il *Science* 235:760-5 F 13 '87
Solar neutrinos: questions and hypotheses. J. Weneser and G. Friedlander. bibl f il *Science* 235:755-9 F 13 '87
A star's subatomic message [neutrinos spit out by supernova 1987A] S. Budiansky. il *U S News World Rep* 102:75 Mr 23 '87
Supernova 1987A: notes from all over [special section] M. M. Waldrop. il *Science* 236:522-3 My 1 '87
The supernova 1987A shows a mind of its own—and a burst of neutrinos. M. M. Waldrop. il *Science* 235:1322-3 Mr 13 '87
Supernova neutrinos [1987A] il *Sci Am* 256:18+ Je '87
Supernova neutrinos at IMB [explosion of 1987A] M. M. Waldrop. *Science* 235:1461 Mr 20 '87
Vanishing solar neutrinos. A. Franco and D. H. Smith. il *Sky Telesc* 73:149 F '87
Were the supernova's neutrinos pulsed? [1987A; work of Martin Harwit and others] D. E. Thomsen. *Sci News* 132:117 Ag 22 '87
Neutron stars
The birth of neutron stars and black holes [cover story] A. Burrows. bibl f il *Phys Today* 40:28-37 S '87

Neutron stars—*cont.*

New-wave pulsars. N. E. White. il *Sky Telesc* 73:22-4 Ja '87

Two gamma-ray sources and ancient guest stars. Z.-R. Wang. bibl f il *Science* 235:1485-6 Mr 20 '87

Neutrons

Diffraction

See also
Crystallography

Scattering

See Scattering (Physics)

Neutrophils *See* Leukocytes

Nevada

See also
Booksellers and bookselling—Nevada
Death Valley National Monument (Calif. and Nev.)
Elko County (Nev.)
Great Basin National Park (Nev.)
Radioactive waste disposal—Nevada
Sierra Nevada Mountains (Calif. and Nev.)
Wilderness areas—Nevada
Wildlife sanctuaries—Nevada
Yucca Mountain (Nev.)

Industries

See also
Gold mines and mining—Nevada

Nevada Dance Theatre

Vassili Sulich's desert song. M. Veljkovic. il pors *Dance Mag* 61:66-9 Ja '87

Nevado del Ruiz (Colombia)

Assembly urges international support to alleviate effects of Colombian volcanic eruption. il *UN Chron* 23:21-2 Ja '86

Neve Shalom (Israel)

Middle East oasis of hope. L. Press. *Macleans* 100:8 F 16 '87

Water from the rock [Jewish-Arab cooperation at the School for Peace] *Commonweal* 114:198 Ap 10 '87

Neves, Kenneth W.

(jt. auth) See Erisman, Albert M., and Neves, Kenneth W.

Neveux, Michael, and Hause, Irene

Graduated backgrounds. il *Petersens Photogr Mag* 15:60-1 Ap '87

Nevi, Charles

In defense of tracking. *Educ Dig* 53:50-2 S '87

Nevil, Robbie

about

In/sight. E. Miller. il por *Seventeen* 46:85 O '87

Robbie Nevil: from sidelines to center stage. M. L. Baer. por *Teen* 31:75 Ag '87

Nevill, Guy

about

Of horse and hound. C. Gibbs. il por *House Gard* 159:76+ N '87

Neville Brothers (Musical group)

Funky but chic. R. Tannenbaum. il *Roll Stone* p23-4+ Jl 2 '87

Nevin, John J.

about

John Nevin rescued Firestone—his way. Z. Schiller. il por *Bus Week* p96+ My 11 '87

Nevins, Carol

about

Obituary

Space World por X-8-284 Space Advocate:1 Ag '87. S. Nevins

Nevis (Saint Kitts-Nevis)

See also
Charlestown (Saint Kitts-Nevis)

New Age literature

See also
Booksellers and bookselling—New Age materials
Publishers and publishing—New Age literature

Entities in print. B. Alexander. il *Christ Today* 31:26 S 18 '87

Ex libris [typical titles] M. E. Marty. *Christ Century* 104:1047 N 18 '87

An old New Age in publishing. M. E. Marty. *Christ Century* 104:1019 N 18 '87

Writing for Celestial Arts. P. Reed and D. Hinds. *Writer* 100:26-7 Ja '87

Authorship

Inner visions. A. Symons. il *Publ Wkly* 232:75-7 S 25 '87

New Age movement

See also
Channelers
Harmonic Convergence
Tape recordings—New Age movement
Videotapes—New Age movement

Aura watching. D. K. Mano. *Natl Rev* 39:66-7 O 23 '87

Channelers. K. Lowry. il por *Omni* 10:46-8+ O '87

Good vibrations: the new peace offensive. D. Brooks. il *Natl Rev* 39:36-9 N 6 '87

Metaphysical healing [interview with P. A. Valentine] K. J. Halliburton. il por *Essence* 18:20 S '87

Mystics on Main Street. A. Levine. il *U S News World Rep* 102:67-9 F 9 '87

New Age harmonies [cover story] O. Friedrich. il *Time* 130:62-6+ D 7 '87

Pet rocks [crystals] *Harpers* 274:20 Ja '87

Rock power for health and wealth [new uses for crystals] M. Smilgis. il *Time* 129:66 Ja 19 '87

The rocks with good vibrations [crystals] il *Newsweek* 110:78 O 12 '87

Soul of a New Age. C. Lasch. il *Omni* 10:78-80+ O '87

Supreme quartz [crystals] J. Page. il *Omni* 10:94-6+ O '87

Theology from the Twilight Zone. B. Alexander. il por *Christ Today* 31:22-6 S 18 '87

Under fire [cover story] il *Christ Today* 31:17-21 S 18 '87

Where not to find new ideas [American universities] K. Sale. *Nation* 244:320-3 Mr 14 '87

You don't need a crystal ball to see that New Age rocks are clearly on a roll. L. Aitken. il *People Wkly* 27:67+ Je 15 '87

Bibliography

New Age titles. il *Publ Wkly* 232:37-8+ S 25 '87; Addendum. 232:28 D 18 '87

New Age movement and business

Corporate mind control. A. Miller. il *Newsweek* 109:38-9 My 4 '87

Mainstream metaphysics. J. A. Trachtenberg and E. Giltenan. il *Forbes* 139:156-8 Je 1 '87

Trying to bend managers' minds [human potential gurus] J. Main. il *Fortune* 116:95-6+ N 23 '87

New Age music

See also
Phonograph records—New Age music
Radio broadcasting—New Age music

Christian music enters the New Age. S. Rabey. il *Christ Today* 31:52-3 F 6 '87

Music to buy books by. J. Zinsser. il *Publ Wkly* 231:40+ Ap 17 '87

New Aladdin (Periodical)

Magazine on floppy disk. il *Futurist* 21:48 Jl/Ag '87

New American Bible *See* Bible—Versions

New American Library, Inc.

Archbishop to appeal ruling on NAL novel [privacy suit brought by P. Marcinkus] C. Reid. *Publ Wkly* 232:20 D 25 '87

New Avanti Motor Corp.

From the '60s with care [views of president M. Kelly] J. A. Seamonds. il *U S News World Rep* 102:50 Je 1 '87

New Brunswick

See also
Fishing—New Brunswick
Miramichi River region (N.B.)
Moncton (N.B.)
New Kincardineshire (N.B.)
Saint Andrews (N.B.)

Description and travel

Crow's nest. G. L. Voss. il *Sea Front* 33:402-3 N/D '87

Languages

Angry words in the East [decision to appoint a francophone postmaster ignites protest] M. Gee. *Macleans* 100:13 Ag 31 '87

Politics and government

All the earmarks of a Liberal sweep. K. Harley. il por *Macleans* 100:26-7 O 12 '87

Clean sweep [Liberal election victory; cover story; special section; with editorial comment by Kevin Doyle] il pors *Macleans* 100:2, 14-16+ O 26 '87

Hatfield's toughest fight [campaign for a fifth term] K. Harley. il por *Macleans* 100:13 S 14 '87

An unaffected kid on the block [F. McKenna] M. Janigan. por *Macleans* 100:12 D 7 '87

A very political mistress [career of R. Hatfield] A. Fotheringham. il *Macleans* 100:64 N 2 '87

New Caledonia

See also
United Nations—New Caledonia

Politics and government

Assembly decides New Caledonia is non-self-governing territory. *UN Chron* 24:131 F '87

New cities and towns
See also
   Heathrow (Fla.)
   Las Colinas (Tex.)
   Victory City
New Deal, 1933-1939
Wild about Harry [H. Hopkins] J. K. Galbraith. il por *Wash Mon* 19:44-5 Je '87
    Photographs and photography
Images from the New Deal [Official images: New Deal photography] K. M. Burke. il *Smithsonian* 18:151 Jl '87
New Delhi (India)
    Stores
Delhi's cuisine and craftsmen. L. Nicholson. il *Gourmet* 47:66-71+ S '87
New Democratic Party (Canada)
Canada looks leftward. *Natl Rev* 39:20-1 D 4 '87
Canada's sober socialists. H. M. Waller. il *New Leader* 70:10-11 O 5 '87
Changing of the guard [R. Romanow chosen leader of Saskatchewan New Democrats] D. Eisler. il por *Macleans* 100:10+ N 23 '87
The end of an accord [Liberals and New Democrats in Ontario] S. Aikenhead. il *Macleans* 100:14 Jl 6 '87
From working stiff to political hero [R. White] E. B. Terry. il por *Bus Week* p60-1 Mr 30 '87
Hard questions for the NDP. M. Rose. il *Macleans* 100:20+ Mr 16 '87
A heady new scent of coalition [views of A. Reid] P. C. Newman. il por *Macleans* 100:35 S 28 '87
The message in the NDP's book [economic policies] D. Francis. il *Macleans* 100:7 Ag 24 '87
A moderate takes over [M. Harcourt acclaimed leader of British Columbia's New Democratic Party] J. O'Hara. *Macleans* 100:16 Ap 27 '87
The NDP's Quebec gamble. B. Wallace. il *Macleans* 100:20-1 D 14 '87
New views on defense. G. Dyer; R. J. Jackson. *World Press Rev* 34:45 N '87
On the march [cover story; special section; with editorial comment by Kevin Doyle] il *Macleans* 100:2, 8-16 Ag 3 '87
    Anecdotes, facetiae, satire, etc.
Alerting America to 'Red Ed'. A. Fotheringham. il *Macleans* 100:52 Ag 10 '87
When summer blues turn pink [commonly held views surrounding an NDP federal government] C. Gordon. por *Macleans* 100:35 Ag 10 '87
New Edition (Musical group)
Zoro makes his mark [interview] por *Teen* 31:57 My '87
New England
See also
   Airports—New England
   Architecture—New England
   Architecture, Domestic—New England
   Art galleries and museums—New England
   Banks and banking—New England
   Dance—New England
   Historic houses, sites, etc.—New England
   Hotels, motels, etc.—New England
   Wildlife—New England
    Description and travel
Great escapes: New England [special section] T. Bross. il *Travel Holiday* 167:67-8+ My '87
    History
See also
   Puritans and puritanism
Letters home: old and New England in the seventeenth century. D. Cressy. bibl il map *Hist Today* 37:37-41 O '87
    Religious institutions and affairs
See also
   Puritans and puritanism
New England Apple Products Company Inc.
Veryfine: oh, what a difference packaging makes. K. H. Hammonds. il por *Bus Week* p71 Ag 31 '87
New England Aquarium
Born free—home free [pilot whales] M. Starr. il *Newsweek* 110:56 Jl 13 '87
Whales' new lease on life [pilot whales] M. B. Simpson. il *Oceans* 20:57-8 S/O '87
New England Booksellers Association
NEBA marks first decade. S. Bolle and D. E. Roback. il *Publ Wkly* 232:43-6 O 30 '87
New England Critical Care
The boss said no. B. Leonard. il por *Forbes* 139:94+ F 9 '87

New England in literature
Invoking America: a Gitche Gumee memoir [adaptation of address] H. Yglesias. il *N Y Times Book Rev* 92:1+ Jl 5 '87
New England journal of medicine
Hippocratic humor [letters to the New England journal of medicine] J. Schuster. il *Technol Rev* 90:14 O '87
New Englanders
See also
   Vermonters
New English Song and Daunce Companie
The zest of the past. C. Mahoney. il *Americana* 15:40-4 My/Je '87
New Hampshire
See also
   Agriculture—New Hampshire
   Architecture, Domestic—New Hampshire
   Banks and banking—New Hampshire
   Rural planning—New Hampshire
    Antiquities
See also
   America's Stonehenge (North Salem, N.H.)
    Description and travel
Old roses and birdsong [summer] D. Hall. il *Harpers* 275:35-41 Ag '87
    Politics and government
See also
   Presidential primaries—New Hampshire
    Race relations
Aide to Kemp dismissed for making racial slurs [state senator J. Chandler] *Jet* 73:37 S 28 '87
New Haven (Conn.)
    Music
See also
   Opera—Connecticut
New Horizons Mutual Fund *See* T. Rowe Price New Horizons Mutual Fund Inc.
New issues (Stock) *See* Stocks—Marketing
New Jersey
See also
   Architecture, Domestic—New Jersey
   Camps—New Jersey
   Colleges and universities—New Jersey
   Criminal justice, Administration of—New Jersey
   Educational laws and regulations—New Jersey
   Environmental policy—New Jersey
   Forests and forestry—New Jersey
   Gardens and gardening—New Jersey
   Hudson River Valley (N.Y. and N.J.)
   Literary festivals—New Jersey
   Port Authority of New York and New Jersey
   Prisons—New Jersey
   Probate law and practice—New Jersey
   Radioactive pollution—New Jersey
   Radon pollution—New Jersey
   Reading Prong
   Shore protection—New Jersey
New Jersey gets a bit of respect. D. Collins. il *U S News World Rep* 102:24 My 11 '87
    Anecdotes, facetiae, satire, etc.
Give my regards to Jersey. A. B. Hanauer. por *Seventeen* 46:80-1 My '87
    Industries
See also
   Tourist trade—New Jersey
New Jersey. Casino Control Commission
Donald Trump gets a $200 million Christmas gift [contract to manage Resorts International Atlantic City casino approved] L. J. Tell and S. Benway. il por *Bus Week* p76 D 28 '87-Ja 4 '88
New Jersey. Meadowlands Sports Complex *See* Meadowlands Sports Complex
New Jersey Symphony Orchestra
Between a rock (New York) and another hard place (Philadelphia), Hugh Wolff conducts a revival. V. Burns. il por *People Wkly* 28:87-8 Ag 31 '87
New Kincardineshire (N.B.)
    History
'A family affair': colonising New Kincardineshire. M. Harper. bibl il map *Hist Today* 37:42-8 O '87
New Korea Democratic Party (Korea: South)
2 Kims + 3 Lees = trouble. R. Watson. il *Newsweek* 109:40 Ap 20 '87
New Man *See* Masculinity (Psychology)
New Media Bible *See* Bible in motion pictures
New Mexico
See also
   Art—New Mexico
   Booksellers and bookselling—New Mexico
   Chaco Culture National Historical Park (N.M.)
   Churches (Buildings)—New Mexico

New Mexico—See also—*cont.*
Colorado Plateau
Conservation of resources—New Mexico
Education—New Mexico
El Malpais National Monument (N.M.)
Gardens and gardening—New Mexico
Geology—New Mexico
Geothermal resources—New Mexico
Homesteads—New Mexico
Jemez Mountains (N.M.)
Petroglyphs National Monument (N.M.)
Pueblo Indians
Radioactive pollution—New Mexico
Radioactive waste disposal—New Mexico
Santo Domingo Pueblo (N.M.)
Wildlife sanctuaries—New Mexico

Antiquities

See also
Chaco Culture National Historical Park (N.M.)

Description and travel

New Mexico: between frontier and future. B. McDowell. il map *Natl Geogr* 172:602-33 N '87

History
Bibliography

Natives and others. R. M. Adams. il *N Y Rev Books* 34:32-6 Mr 26 '87
On the trail of Santa Fe. R. M. Adams. il *N Y Rev Books* 34:28-31 Mr 12 '87

New Mexico Repertory Theatre
A theater company leads a double life and becomes a cultural resource in the process. J. P. Forsthoffer. il *Horizon* 30:25-6 O '87

New Mexico Symphony Orchestra
Enticing with quality. G. Chow. il *Horizon* 30:29 O '87

New moon stories [dance] See Dance reviews—Single works

The new Newlywed game [television program] See Television program reviews—Single works

New Oregon Trail (Or.)
Blazing a New Oregon Trail [cover story] W. L. Sullivan. il map *Sierra* 72:54-60 My/Je '87

New Orleans (La.)

Architecture

Filled with art and style [renovated cottage] L. Hallam. il *South Living* 22:84-5 Je '87

Cemeteries

Touring the cemeteries of New Orleans. il *South Living* 22:32+ N '87

Historic houses, sites, etc.

Take a tour of historic New Orleans [Gallier, Beauregard-Keyes, and Hermann-Grima Houses] C. Maddox. il *South Living* 22:36+ S '87

Music

New Orleans now. B. Sandmel. il *Down Beat* 54:60-1 Ja '87

Politics and government

Hard times in the Big Easy. N. Lemann. il *Atlantic* 260:16-18+ Ag '87

Race relations

Wall stirs rift between New Orleans and suburb; mayor orders it torn down. il *Jet* 71:25 Mr 16 '87

Restaurants, nightclubs, bars, etc.

Bayou boast [recipes from Flagon's Wine Bar & Bistro] M. Fox. il *Health* 19:65-6+ S '87
City dining: New Orleans [Mr. B's, Upperline, Gautreau's] G. Trotta. il *Gourmet* 47:48+ My '87
A well-traveled bistro brings an Eiffel-utin air to New Orleans [Restaurant de la Tour Eiffel moved from Paris] J. Greene. il pors *People Wkly* 28:83-4 O 26 '87

Stores

The joy of shopping Royal Street. il *South Living* 22:31+ Mr '87

Taxicabs

New Orleans cabbies were making the Big Easy queasy, so the city has sent them to charm school [Jazzy Cabby course] J. Greene. il *People Wkly* 28:115-16 O 19 '87

Waterfront

Get away to the lakefront. il *South Living* 22:36 D '87
A new riverfront for New Orleans. il map *South Living* 22:8-10 Ja '87

New Orleans Jazz and Heritage Festival *See* Music festivals—Louisiana

New People's Army (Philippines)
The careful Communists. W. Steif. il *Progressive* 51:24-7 F '87
Ceasefire with the Communists. T. Lansner. *World Press Rev* 34:25 Ja '87

The day of the sparrow [U.S. airmen murdered near Clark Air Base] H. Anderson. il *Newsweek* 110:54 N 9 '87
Defense vs. Cory [views of George Talbot on fighting Communist insurgents] L. Howard. il *Newsweek* 109:5 My 4 '87
A military renaissance [Philippine Army's success in Cagayan] R. Laver. il *Macleans* 100:6+ Ja 26 '87
Peace in the Philippines. D. Murphy. *America* 156:406-8 My 16 '87
Philippines: danger signs. H. Anderson. il por *Newsweek* 109:36-8 My 11 '87
Rebels left and right. H. G. Chua-Eoan. il *Time* 130:38 O 5 '87
Rebirth of a rebel army. W. A. Taylor. il *U S News World Rep* 103:75 S 28 '87
Sharpening the swords of war. W. Stewart. il *Time* 129:46 Mr 30 '87
They saw the future and it didn't work [city of Davao] R. Vokey. *Newsweek* 109:38-9 F 16 '87
Tough words from the top [C. Aquino changes policy in dealing with rebels] W. Svoboda. il por *Time* 129:41 Ap 6 '87
A truce gives way to gunplay. S. Allis. il *Time* 129:57 F 23 '87
Vigilantes for Aquino. F. Willey. il por *Newsweek* 109:34+ Mr 30 '87
Who's winning the cease-fire? H. Anderson. il *Newsweek* 109:34 Ja 26 '87

New Port Richey (Fla.)

Gardens and gardening

A Florida success story [work of J. Fritch] M. Kane. il por *Rodale's Org Gard* 34:60-4 D '87

New products See Products, New

New Ralston House (Philadelphia, Pa.: Nursing home) See Nursing homes

New Regal Theater (Chicago, Ill.)
Chicago's New Regal Theater debuts with weeklong gala. il *Jet* 72:56-8 S 7 '87

New republic (Periodical)
Minority report. C. Hitchens. *Nation* 244:39 Ja 17 '87

New River (Mexico and Calif.)
Dead cats, toxins and typhoid. M. Riley. il *Time* 129:68-9 Ap 20 '87

New River (N.C.-W. Va.)
Dubious mining operations continue at New River. *Natl Parks* 61:40 S/O '87
New River suffering from benign neglect. il *Natl Parks* 61:41 Mr/Ap '87
State wants to spray pesticide on New River [use of Bti to exterminate breeding grounds of the black fly] *Natl Parks* 61:43 Mr/Ap '87

New Society Publishers
Left, but not left out. J. Mutter. il *Publ Wkly* 232:18-19 Jl 17 '87

New stars *See* Stars, New

New Start Health Center (Saint Petersburg, Fla.) *See* Saint Petersburg (Fla.)—Health facilities

New statesman (Periodical)
New statesman downed by law [government harassment] C. Hitchens. il *Nation* 244:217-19 F 21 '87

New stock issues *See* Stocks—Marketing

New Testament *See* Bible. N.T.

New United Motor Mfg., Inc.
The NUMMI experience [joint venture between Toyota and General Motors] M. Keller. il *Mot Trend* 39:126-7 Mr '87

New Valamo (Finland: Monastery) *See* Monasteries—Finland

New words *See* Words, New

New world (Periodical)
Where glasnost has its limits [trying to get published in Novy mir]; tr. by John Glad and Marie Arana-Ward. V. Voĭnovich and S. Zalygin. por *N Y Times Mag* p30-1 Jl 19 '87

New World man *See* Paleo-Indians

New World Pictures Ltd.
Another toymaker may be in play [New World Pictures to go after Mattel] G. G. Marcial. *Bus Week* p108 S 21 '87
Can Monopoly find happiness in Spiderman's arms? [Kenner Parker Toys weighs bid from New World Pictures] K. H. Hammonds. il *Bus Week* p34 Ag 3 '87
Getting rich on TV's new austerity. R. Grover. il *Bus Week* p109-10+ Ap 6 '87
High drama from the folks who brought you Godzilla '85 [New World's play for Kenner] R. Grover. il pors *Bus Week* p30 S 7 '87
Tough New World. G. Critser. il *Channels* 7:20-6 Mr '87

New World Video (Firm)
Marvel, New World plan book-video line. il *Publ Wkly* 232:138 S 18 '87
New Year
Happy New Year! [special section] il *Seventeen* 46:64-5 D '87
New Year's brunches *See* Brunches
New Year's Eve dinners *See* Dinners and dining
New Year's parties *See* Entertaining
New York (N.Y.)
See also
Bronx (New York, N.Y.)
Brooklyn (New York, N.Y.)
New Yorkers
Queens (New York, N.Y.)
Best bets. N. McKeon and C. Pollan. See issues of New York
Fast track. See issues of New York beginning February 13, 1984

Airports
Cocaine arrests prompt efforts to investigate airline employee records [smuggling rings uncovered at Kennedy Airport] *Aviat Week Space Technol* 126:36 Mr 16 '87
FAA plans MLS installation at major New York airports [microwave landing systems] K. J. Stein. *Aviat Week Space Technol* 127:65+ Jl 27 '87
How the Mafia loots JFK Airport. R. Rowan. il *Fortune* 115:54-7+ Je 22 '87
New radar sectors improve metropolitan area traffic flow [New York Terminal Radar Control] *Aviat Week Space Technol* 127:119 Jl 6 '87
Pan Am adds flights at Kennedy using separate access system. *Aviat Week Space Technol* 127:119 N 9 '87
Positive control: two TCAs, and the controllers in the ATC shuffle. P. Scott. il *Flying* 114:30-2 D '87

Architecture
See also
New York (N.Y.)—Buildings
New York (N.Y.)—Historic houses, sites, etc.
Chronicles of a [New York] brownstone (I). G. Talese. il por *Archit Dig* 44:44+ N '87
Chronicles of a New York brownstone (II). G. Talese. il por *Archit Dig* 44:28+ D '87
Cityscape. C. Wiseman. See occasional issues of New York
Experiencing places (I) [space and environment in architecture] T. Hiss. *New Yorker* 63:45-9+ Je 22 '87
Experiencing places (II) [space and environment in architecture] T. Hiss. *New Yorker* 63:73-80+ Je 29 '87
New York City gets small [model on exhibit at the Queens Museum] B. Barol. il *Newsweek* 109:54 Je 29 '87
The sky line. B. Gill. See occasional issues of The New Yorker beginning February 23, 1987

Art
See also
New York (N.Y.)—Monuments, statues, etc.
New York (N.Y.). Art Commission
Art [1987] K. Larson. il *N Y* 20:122-3 D 21-28 '87
Art. A. C. Danto. See issues of The Nation beginning October 20, 1984
Art. K. Larson. See issues of New York
The Cedars [Cedar Street Tavern] J. Oppenheimer. il *N Y* 20:82-3 D 21-28 '87
Color-blind art history [exhibition entitled Masters and pupils: the education of the black artist in New York, 1900-1980] S. Staggs. *Art News* 86:15+ Ap '87
The fun's over: the East Village scene gets burned by success. A. Virshup. il *N Y* 20:48-50+ Je 22 '87
The hot new cool art: simulationism. E. Heartney. il *Art News* 86:130-7 Ja '87
Portraits of the artists [R. Grooms's parodic drawings of New York School artist-heroes] H. Cotter. il *Art Am* 75:154-7 N '87
Up against the walls [murals] K. Larson. il *N Y* 20:46-51 F 2 '87

Arts
See also
92nd Street Y (New York, N.Y.)
New York (N.Y.). Dept. of Cultural Affairs
The arts [1987; special section] il *N Y* 20:105-8+ D 21-28 '87
Cue: a complete entertainment guide for the week. See issues of New York
Fall preview [special issue] il *N Y* 20:49-66+ S 21 '87
Goings on about town. See issues of The New Yorker
Ruth recommends. R. Gilbert. See issues of New York beginning February 13, 1984

Banks
See also
Bank of New York
Bowery Savings Bank
Central National Bank of New York
Chase Manhattan Bank, N. A.
Citibank N.A.
Freedom National Bank of New York
Irving Trust Co.
Birds
See Birds—New York (State)
Blacks
See also
Harlem (New York, N.Y.)
New York: the good, the bad and the ugly. R. Howell. il *Black Enterp* 17:294-6+ Je '87
Bookstores
See Booksellers and bookselling—New York (State)
Buildings
480 Lex. P. Bosworth. por *N Y* 20:100 D 21-28 '87
Black Monday's silver lining [effect on Cityspire and other new construction] C. Wiseman. il *N Y* 20:136+ D 7 '87
The buildings New Yorkers love to hate [cover story] R. D. Story. il *N Y* 20:30-5 Je 15 '87
Outflanked, outmaneuvered [Integrated Resources vs. Cohen Brothers Realty over 666 5th Ave.] H. Rudnitsky. il *Forbes* 140:343-4 Jl 13 '87
Perfect pitch [St. Thomas Choir School] P. M. Sachner. il *Archit Rec* 175:116-19 N '87
Tarted up [Park Avenue Tower and 53rd at Third] C. Wiseman. il *N Y* 20:72+ Ap 20 '87
When buildings needn't be preserved. S. C. Florman. il *Technol Rev* 90:19+ Ap '87
Charities
See also
Associated Black Charities
Essence woman [L. Turner's Men Who Cook benefit] M. Southgate. il por *Essence* 17:28 Ap '87
Child welfare
See also
Covenant House (New York, N.Y.)
Where Christmas never comes [children in shelters and hotels for the homeless] M. Small. il *People Wkly* 28:50-60 D 14 '87
Children
City child [cover story; special issue] il *N Y* 20:33-46+ N 23 '87
Trying to raise children in the city. M. Stone. il *N Y* 20:26-33 F 2 '87
Churches (Buildings)
See also
Cathedral of St. John the Divine (New York, N.Y.)
City planning
See also
Columbus Center (New York, N.Y.)
Television City (New York, N.Y.)
Oral history: remembering Robert Moses. M. F. Schmertz. *Archit Rec* 175:9 Jl '87
Climate
The blizzard of '88. P. E. Hughes. il *Weatherwise* 40:312-14+ D '87
The great blizzard of '88. L. Ponte. il *Read Dig* 131:11-12+ D '87
Notes and comment [snowstorms] *New Yorker* 63:23-4 Mr 2 '87
Notes and comment [remembering the snowstorm of 1947] *New Yorker* 63:34-5 D 28 '87
Clubs
See also
Tecumseh Club
Crime
See also
Bronx (New York, N.Y.)—Crime
Brooklyn (New York, N.Y.)—Crime
Goetz, Bernhard—Subway shooting case
New York (N.Y.)—Police
New York (N.Y.)—Prisons and reformatories
Queens (New York, N.Y.)—Crime
Steinberg, Elizabeth, d. 1987—Child abuse case
The Fat Man: the life and high times of Irwin Schiff [cover story] M. Daly. il pors *N Y* 20:46-61 O 19 '87
Fishy business [Fulton Fish Market and the Mafia] A. A. Lappen. il *Forbes* 140:8 N 16 '87
Frenchy and the Persians [N. Sakhai and H. Mahboubian mastermind theft of Near Eastern antiquities for insurance recovery] C. Trillin. *New Yorker* 63:44+ Je 29 '87

New York (N.Y.)—Crime—*cont.*

Incident in the park [mugging and theft of bicycle in Central Park] D. Galef. il *N Y Times Mag* p56 F 8 '87

The lords of Hell's Kitchen [Westies] J. Traub. il pors *N Y Times Mag* p38+ Ap 5 '87

Marla Hanson: "All of a sudden I'm on the 'in' list for parties. I sit next to Bianca Jagger at dinner". R. O'Connor. por *Vogue* 177:438+ S '87

Model Marla Hanson, showing the face of courage to a jury, helps convict the thug who maimed her. J. Wadler. il pors *People Wkly* 27:38-40+ Ja 5 '87

New kingpins of heroin [Chinese traffickers] M. Gray. il *Macleans* 100:55+ S 7 '87

Notes and comment [buying a burglar alarm after moving out of Mafia-protected neighborhood] *New Yorker* 63:21-2 Ag 31 '87

The worms in the Big Apple [Mafia] J. Cook. il *Forbes* 140:102-6 S 21 '87

Criminal justice, Administration of

See also

Goetz, Bernhard—Subway shooting case

Dance

After postmodernism: waiting for the end of the world. E. Zimmer. il *Dance Mag* 61:64-9 F '87

Broadway and beyond. K. Grubb. See issues of Dance Magazine

Dance [1987 performances] T. Tobias. il *N Y* 20:124-5 D 21-28 '87

Dance [fall preview] R. Gilbert. il *N Y* 20:100+ S 21 '87

Dance. T. Tobias. See issues of New York

New works from Jacob's Pillow land in lower Manhattan's Triplex theater. il *Dance Mag* 61:15 Ja '87

Reviews:

Joyce Sampler at the Joyce Theater. S. Sommer. *Dance Mag* 61:82+ S '87

Sex & dance at P.S. 122 and Bessie Schönberg Theater, New York City. E. Zimmer. il *Dance Mag* 61:22+ Mr '87

Shall we dance? [dance element of the Gershwin gala at the Brooklyn Academy of Music] T. Tobias. il *N Y* 20:92-3 Mr 30 '87

Dance halls

See also

Roseland Dance City (New York, N.Y.)

The Palladium [Latin American dance hall] J. Torres. il *N Y* 20:99 D 21-28 '87

Description

The day New York became harmless. A. Broyard. il *N Y Times Book Rev* 92:11 O 4 '87

Holiday time in New York. il *Glamour* 85:174-6+ D '87

In New York City: an incantation. G. Jaynes. il *Time* 129:13-14 Ja 12 '87

Inside New York [cover story; special issue] il *Archit Dig* 44:44+ N '87

My New York, my New York. R. Brookhiser. *Natl Rev* 39:37-9 F 13 '87

Notes and comment [colors of the city] *New Yorker* 63:31 Ap 6 '87

Reading the noises. *New Yorker* 62:26-7 Ja 19 '87

The ultimate insider's guide to New York [cover story; special issue] il maps *N Y* 20:26+ My 4 '87

A walker in the city—again. A. Kazin. il *N Y* 20:32-5 Ja 19 '87

Anecdotes, facetiae, satire, etc.

Miami to New York: drop dead. D. Barry. *Harpers* 275:36+ D '87

Docks, wharves, etc.

Pier 40: a remembrance [closing of parking garage built on unsound pier] *New Yorker* 63:31-2 S 14 '87

Photographs and photography

The art of decay [R. Colbert's photographs] M. Wade. il *Horizon* 30:39-40 D '87

Economic conditions

What things cost [cover story] il *N Y* 20:32-40 S 7 '87

The worms in the Big Apple [Mafia] J. Cook. il *Forbes* 140:102-6 S 21 '87

Education

See also

Bronx (New York, N.Y.)—Education

The admissions-go-round: private school fever. B. Kanner. il *N Y* 20:40-6 N 23 '87

Adult education: classes of '87. L. Dyett. il *N Y* 20:38-42+ Ag 17 '87

American High: at Seward Park, the melting pot still bubbles. K. D. Fishman. il *N Y* 20:78-80+ Mr 2 '87

Balloons [Greenwich Village School participates in the Triangle Coalition National Balloon Launch] *New Yorker* 63:26-8 Ap 20 '87

Better than rubies [High School for the Humanities] J. W. Donohue. il *America* 157:319-26 N 7 '87

The case of Our Lady of Sorrows [Catholic school on the Lower East Side] D. E. DeCosse. *Commonweal* 114:210-15 Ap 10 '87

Central Park East: an alternative story. D. Meier. il *Phi Delta Kappan* 68:753-7 Je '87

A dream come true [followup on students of P.S. 121 in East Harlem helped by E. M. Lang] M. deC. Hinds. il por *N Y Times Mag* p32-6 Ap 26 '87

Experiment at P.S. 192: Babar and Horton teach reading. M. Reuter. il *Publ Wkly* 231:88-9 F 27 '87

Fish trip [Corlears School makes field trip to De Martino's Fish Market] *New Yorker* 62:25 Ja 12 '87

Retooling teachers: the New York experience [replenishing supply of science and math teachers] B. S. Cooper. il *Phi Delta Kappan* 68:606-9 Ap '87

Sex education: a matter of body & soul [New York City program vs. Catholic Church] K. S. Smith. il *Commonweal* 114:206-10 Ap 10 '87

Teaching s-e-x in school: the facts of life in Mrs. Roseman's class. D. Prince. il por *N Y* 20:56-8+ Ap 6 '87

Three views from the trenches: teaching high school religion in the city. D. H. Powell. *America* 157:212-16 O 10 '87

Festivals

See also

Brooklyn (New York, N.Y.)—Festivals

Queens (New York, N.Y.)—Festivals

Harlem hospitality [focus of month long celebration] P. A. Taylor. il *Essence* 18:18+ O '87

Finance

See also

New York (N.Y.)—Taxation

Firefighters

Out of the fire and into the frying pan [J. Sineno's The firefighters cookbook] il *Newsweek* 109:58 Mr 9 '87

Galleries and museums

See also

American Craft Museum (New York, N.Y.)

American Museum of Natural History

Artweave Textile Gallery

Barry Friedman Ltd.

Cooper-Hewitt Museum

Fraunces Tavern Museum

Kentshire Galleries Ltd.

L'Art et L'Automobile Gallery

Leo Castelli Gallery

Lucien Goldschmidt Inc.

Metropolitan Museum of Art (New York, N.Y.)

Museum of American Folk Art

Museum of Broadcasting (New York, N.Y.)

Museum of Holography (New York, N.Y.)

Museum of Modern Art (New York, N.Y.)

New York Historical Society

Paula Cooper Gallery

Richard York Gallery

Sidney Janis Gallery

Solomon R. Guggenheim Museum

Whitney Museum of American Art

Art [fall preview] K. Larson and E. Newhall. il *N Y* 20:66+ S 21 '87

Offbeat offerings. B. Kandel. il *Travel Holiday* 167:6-7+ Ja '87

The post-Beaubourg generation [shows featuring new French work] A. Rochette. il *Art Am* 75:41-7+ Je '87

SoHo: downtown boomtown. P. Gardner. il *Art News* 86:128-33 Mr '87

Gardens and gardening

See also

Brooklyn (New York, N.Y.)—Gardens and gardening

Operation GreenThumb (New York, N.Y.)

Harbor

Like his father before him, a brave tugboat skipper battles wind and sea to bring great ships to port [P. Mahoney] D. Grogan. il pors *People Wkly* 28:88-9+ O 12 '87

Losing jobs by trying to save them. J. Cook. il *Forbes* 139:56+ Je 1 '87

Health facilities

See also

Brooklyn (New York, N.Y.)—Health facilities

New York (N.Y.)—*cont.*

Highways

See Express highways—New York (State)

Historic houses, sites, etc.

See also

New York (N.Y.). Landmarks Preservation Commission

Staten Island (New York, N.Y.)—Historic houses, sites, etc.

The fat man's garden and other landmarks [literary landmarks] R. Starr. il *N Y Times Book Rev* 92:34+ N 22 '87

In the presence of the past. B. Gill. il por *Archit Dig* 44:98+ N '87

Murray Hill: mansions with pedigrees from the Age of Innocence. C. Jakobson. il map *N Y* 20:42-4 My 4 '87

On Ladies' Mile. il map *Americana* 14:36-40 Ja/F '87

When buildings needn't be preserved. S. C. Florman. il *Technol Rev* 90:19+ Ap '87

History

New York 1865 [W. M. Tweed] G. Dallas. bibl il *Hist Today* 37:17-22 D '87

Hospitals

See also

Bellevue Hospital

Columbia Presbyterian Medical Center (New York, N.Y.)

Memorial Sloan-Kettering Cancer Center

New York Hospital-Cornell Medical Center

St. Luke's-Roosevelt Hospital Center (New York, N.Y.)

Hospital gets facelift [North General Hospital, Harlem] M. Scott. *Black Enterp* 18:20 N '87

Hospital hype: competition for patients spurs a marketing blitz. B. Holcomb. il *N Y* 20:30-5 Ag 3 '87

Kevin Porter's house calls [lawyer for hospitals] O. Jaffe. il por *N Y* 20:20 Jl 20 '87

Hotels, motels, etc.

The Algonquin faces life. M. Stone. il *N Y* 20:52-4+ N 2 '87

The Blue Room [Milford Plaza Hotel] *New Yorker* 63:31-3 S 21 '87

The Box Tree Hotel: Augustin Paege's opulent setting in Turtle Bay. G. Greene. il por *Archit Dig* 44:170-7 N '87

The Marriott Marquis: Renaissance on Broadway. il *USA Today (Periodical)* 115:34-44 Mr '87

Want a room with a view? This hotel has one of hell [paintings on walls of Carlton Arms Hotel] M. Small. il por *People Wkly* 28:175-7 N 16 '87

Housing

See also

Brooklyn (New York, N.Y.)—Housing

The $37,000 slum [system for housing its homeless] C. Coulson. *New Repub* 196:15-16 Ja 19 '87

The gentrification of Harlem. M. Mittelstaedt. *World Press Rev* 34:44 Ap '87

Homeless in New York. D. K. Mano. *Natl Rev* 39:64-5+ O 9 '87

How to find an apartment (seriously) [cover story] J. Goldman. il *N Y* 20:30-8 Je 22 '87

Little house on the prairie ["cabin" built by homeless family] P. Weber. il *N Y* 20:40 D 14 '87

Lords, serfs, psychics, apples [tour of Rutherford Place, newly remodeled into rental units] *New Yorker* 63:23-5 Mr 30 '87

Manhattan's Martinique [hotel for homeless families] R. Hirschfield. *Commonweal* 114:71-2 F 13 '87

The Martinique Hotel: housing the homeless. R. Hirschfield. *America* 156:90-1 F 7 '87

The right mix [R. Millican's mixed-use building provides housing for the elderly] G. Wen. il por *N Y* 20:42 S 21 '87

Scenes from the squatting life [New York City owned buildings inhabited by squatters] P. Weber. il *Natl Rev* 39:28-32 F 27 '87

Sweet 'n' low [revision of zoning law] C. Wiseman. il *N Y* 20:62-3 Ag 31 '87

There goes the neighborhood: gangs of yuppies move onto the turf of New York's Hells Angels [East Village] J. S. Kunen. il *People Wkly* 28:119-20+ S 7 '87

Where Christmas never comes [children in shelters and hotels for the homeless] M. Small. il *People Wkly* 28:50-60 D 14 '87

With our own hands [excerpt from Everything to gain] J. Carter and R. Carter. il pors *McCalls* 114:44+ Jl '87

Industries

See also

Clothing industry

How to start your own business (I) [cover story] S. M. Pollan and M. Levine. il *N Y* 20:28-37 Je 8 '87

How to start your own business (II). S. M. Pollan and M. Levine. il *N Y* 20:44-8+ Je 15 '87

Intellectual life

The New York (Jewish) intellectuals. R. R. Wisse. *Commentary* 84:28-38 N '87

Bibliography

The New York intellectuals & the socialist legacy. J. Hart. *Natl Rev* 39:58+ S 11 '87

Law

See New York (N.Y.)—Ordinances

Markets

See also

Fulton Fish Market

Market watch [Greenmarket system] L. Sombke. il *N Y* 20:23 Jl 27 '87

Monuments, statues, etc.

See also

Statue of Liberty (New York, N.Y.)

A loss for Serra [R. Serra loses court fight to save Tilted arc from being removed from Federal Plaza] G. Danto. il *Art News* 86:61 O '87

Mother Goose and Henry Moore. J. Herzfeld. il *Art News* 86:61+ O '87

On the waterfront [N. Smyth's installation on the esplanade at Battery Park City] N. Princenthal. il *Art Am* 75:210-11+ Ap '87

Serra goes to court [R. Serra's battle with the General Services Administration over Tilted arc] A. Decker. *Art News* 86:29 Ap '87

Tilted arc goes to court [R. Serra files suit against General Services Administration] *Art Am* 75:168 F '87

Motion picture theaters

See also

Bronx (New York, N.Y.)—Motion picture theaters

Notes and comment [Regency Theatre to close as a revival house] *New Yorker* 63:23 S 7 '87

Museums

See New York (N.Y.)—Galleries and museums

Music

See also

Amato Opera Theatre

Bel Canto Opera (Company)

Carnegie Hall (New York, N.Y.)

Concert Opera of Manhattan

Metropolitan Opera (New York, N.Y.)

New York City Opera Company

New York Music Awards

New York Philharmonic-Symphony Orchestra

Opera—New York (State)

Opera at the Academy

Opera Ensemble of New York

Opera Orchestra of New York

Riverside Symphony

Vineyard Opera (New York, N.Y.)

Jazz. W. Balliett. See occasional issues of The New Yorker

Music [1987] P. G. Davis. il *N Y* 20:114+ D 21-28 '87

Music. P. G. Davis. See issues of New York

Music [fall preview] F. Fletcher. il *N Y* 20:88+ S 21 '87

Musical events. A. Porter. See issues of The New Yorker

Nightclub nightmares: a musician's view [jazz scene] J. Forrester. *Down Beat* 54:52-3 My '87

Nightlife [fall preview] K. Pryor. il *N Y* 20:126+ S 21 '87

Sounds of the city. E. Pooley. il *N Y* 20:70-6+ My 4 '87

Music festivals

See Music festivals—New York (State)

Newspapers

See also

Daily news (New York, N.Y.)

El diario-La prensa (New York, N.Y.)

New York observer (Newspaper)

New York post

New York times

An upstart from the 'burbs: Newsday's inroads in New York City. D. Lieberman. il *Bus Week* p89+ My 11 '87

History

Nellie Bly. C. Bergman and M. Nussbaum. il pors *Am Hist Illus* 22:22-6+ Mr '87

New York (N.Y.)—*cont.*

Office buildings
See New York (N.Y.)—Buildings

Ordinances
Bernstein for the defenseless [lawyer enforces animal protection laws] K. Pritzker. il por *McCalls* 114:62 Jl '87

Parades
Black serves as marshall of N.Y. Labor Day Parade [P. J. Ottley] *Jet* 72:55 S 21 '87
Notes and comment [Gay/Lesbian Pride Parade] *New Yorker* 63:17-18 Jl 13 '87
Stars & Stripes [parade for D. Conner and victorious crew] *New Yorker* 63:26-7 F 23 '87

Parks and playgrounds
See also
Central Park (New York, N.Y.)
Riverside Park (New York, N.Y.)

Photographs and photography
Big Apple bikes [motorcycles] J. Terranova. il *Cycle* 38:75-9 N '87
Getting close to Gotham. M. Heiferman and C. Kismaric. il *Art News* 86:106-11 S '87
Time and Detroit . . . and New York . . . and Santa Barbara [then and now photographs] il *Am Herit* 38:100-5 Ap '87
Vintage New York PolaGraphs [color prints made from high-contrast B&W slides] D. Cook. il *Petersens Photogr Mag* 16:28-30 S '87

Police
Art cop [Detective T. Moscardini tracks art theft] H. Polskin. il por *N Y* 20:28+ O 26 '87
Best intentions: Edmund Perry's path from Harlem to Exeter to death on a street in Morningside Heights [excerpt] R. S. Anson. il pors map *N Y* 20:30-45 My 11 '87
Black and white cops duel in lovers' quarrel; he is critical and she is dead [J. Hill shoots John Kopek] *Jet* 73:8 N 2 '87
Black N.Y. police officer turns down a promotion; says he's no 'quota cop' [S. Brown] *Jet* 71:25 Mr 23 '87
Cops fear AIDS after bites from alleged prostitutes. il *Jet* 72:8 Je 29 '87
Fighting the school for scoundrels [Transit Police Pickpocket Squad] T. Cochran. il *N Y* 20:25 My 25 '87
The Police Shack [old hangout for police reporters] N. Pileggi. il por *N Y* 20:95 D 21-28 '87
'Sorry' for comment to white woman: Ward [Police Commissioner B. Ward] por *Jet* 72:28 Ag 24 '87

Politics and government
See also
Brooklyn (New York, N.Y.)—Politics and government
New York (N.Y.)—Ordinances
Tammany Hall
Around City Hall. A. Logan. See occasional issues of The New Yorker
Bess and the mess: Myerson's slide into scandal [cover story] P. Morrisroe. il pors *N Y* 20:30-44 Mr 30 '87
Bess Myerson's got a secret [possible involvement in political scandal] D. Collins. il por *U S News World Rep* 102:14 Ja 26 '87
Between friends [B. Myerson's possible involvement in political scandal] J. Hull. il por *Time* 129:22 Ja 26 '87
The Big Apple is beset by rotten apples. C. O'Connor. il *Newsweek* 109:30 Mr 30 '87
'Dallas' on the Hudson [B. Myerson scandal] il pors *Newsweek* 110:10 O 26 '87
Downfall of an American idol [B. Myerson; cover story] M. Green. il pors *People Wkly* 27:44-6+ Je 29 '87
Koch agonistes [corruption scandal] J. Klein. il pors *N Y* 20:28-32 Jl 13 '87
The Koch-Newfield letters [discussion of April 4, 1987 article, Mayor Daley is alive and well in N.Y.C.] J. Newfield. *Nation* 245:2+ Jl 4-11 '87
Mayor Daley is alive and well in N.Y.C. [city corruption; cover story] J. Newfield. il *Nation* 244:417+ Ap 4 '87
Putting a shine on the Big Apple [blacks] R. Howell. *Black Enterp* 17:308 Je '87
The streets were paved with gold diggers [corruption scandals; cover story] P. Weber. il *Natl Rev* 39:24-7 Je 5 '87
Troubled times for Hizzoner [Mayor E. Koch] B. Angelo. il por *Time* 130:21-2+ N 30 '87
The unplugged city: the story of New York cable is a model municipal mess. P. Blauner. il map *N Y* 20:36-42 Jl 20 '87

Wisenheimer's disease [E. Koch] J. Klein. il por *N Y* 20:26+ Ag 24 '87

Anecdotes, facetiae, satire, etc.
The New York idea [Inner Circle show presented by press] A. Logan. *New Yorker* 63:84-6+ Mr 23 '87

Poor
See also
New York (N.Y.)—Public welfare
Down and out in the 'Path Hotel' [homeless living in a tunnel] D. Whitman. il *U S News World Rep* 102:69-71 Mr 23 '87
Down and out—but determined [J. Brown, homeless woman deemed mentally ill] M. Hornblower. il *Time* 130:29 N 23 '87
Homeless in New York. D. K. Mano. *Natl Rev* 39:64-5+ O 9 '87
Inhuman rights [U.S. forces U.N. to omit footage of homeless from documentary] *Nation* 244:36-7 Ja 17 '87
The mayor is right [program to hospitalize mentally ill homeless people] *America* 157:396 N 28 '87
Notes and comment [volunteer shelter for the homeless at Ansche Chesed Synagogue] *New Yorker* 63:27-8 S 14 '87

Population
Foreign intrigue [ethnic neighborhoods] B. Costikyan. il *N Y* 20:46-52 My 4 '87
If I can make it there, I'll make it anywhere [Cambodians] B. Doyle. il *U S Cathol* 52:26-33 D '87

Prisons and reformatories
NY prison ship boasts only convicts at sea. il *Jet* 73:36 S 28 '87

Public health
Eyes on the lies [black leaders team up with tobacco industry in fight against smoking ban as a civil rights issue] S. Milligan. il *Wash Mon* 19:39-42 Je '87
A necessary offense [various New York groups objecting to advertising of condoms to prevent AIDS] H. Evans. il *U S News World Rep* 102:80 My 25 '87
An unflinching AIDS campaign [condom ads] T. E. Johnson. il *Newsweek* 109:24 My 25 '87

Public utilities
It takes a 'sixth sense' to operate underneath the streets of New York. D. D. Jackson. il *Smithsonian* 18:38-47 Ag '87

Public welfare
The $37,000 slum [system for housing its homeless] C. Coulson. *New Repub* 196:15-16 Ja 19 '87

Race relations
The fire this time: two tough lawyers spur a new black activism [A. H. Maddox and C. V. Mason] P. Blauner. il pors *N Y* 20:42-7 Ap 27 '87

Recreation
Summer pleasures [cover story; special issue] il *N Y* 20:21-36+ Je 29-Jl 6 '87
Up, up, and away [weekend outdoor adventure vacations close to New York City] J. Seabury. il *N Y* 20:36-42 Ag 3 '87

Religious institutions and affairs
Brief encounter [discussing the plight of Harlem with white man on Manhattan's East Side] J. M. McConnell. il *America* 157:101 Ag 29-S 5 '87
Denominational moves raise questions [relocating church offices has implications for ecumenism] C. Iosso. *Christ Century* 104:484-6 My 20-27 '87
Dignity groups barred [conflict between Roman Catholic homosexuals and the Archdiocese of New York] *Christ Century* 104:376-7 Ap 22 '87
Profiles (I) [Cardinal J. J. O'Connor] N. Hentoff. por *New Yorker* 63:59-76 Mr 23 '87
Profiles (II) [Cardinal J. J. O'Connor] N. Hentoff. il *New Yorker* 63:37-8+ Mr 30 '87
Sex education: a matter of body & soul [New York City program vs. Catholic Church] K. S. Smith. il *Commonweal* 114:206-10 Ap 10 '87

Restaurants, nightclubs, bars, etc.
See also
Brooklyn (New York, N.Y.)—Restaurants, nightclubs, bars, etc.
Sarabeth's Kitchen
"21" and still counting . . . M. Sheraton. il *Time* 129:66 Je 1 '87
"21" plus [Manhattan restaurant redecorated by C. Pfister] M. Filler. il *House Gard* 159:24+ S '87
Adding up the new '21'. G. Greene. il *N Y* 20:40-7 Je 1 '87
Afternoon tea in New York. A. R. Gochman. il *Gourmet* 47:92-7+ N '87
Art wanes in clubland. G. Danto. il *Art News* 86:16 O '87

New York (N.Y.)—Restaurants, nightclubs, bars, etc.—
cont.

Ask Gael: where our critic tells her friends to eat. G.
Greene. il *N Y* 20:20-6+ Ja 5 '87

The Automat. N. Simon. il *N Y* 20:66-7 D 21-28 '87

Birdland. N. Hentoff. il *N Y* 20:92 D 21-28 '87

Bistro's best [wines] F. J. Prial. il *N Y Times Mag*
p48 My 10 '87

Bistro's new simplicity [Chez Louis in New York City]
C. Claiborne and P. Franey. il *N Y Times Mag* p51-2
My 10 '87

Borscht belt [St. Petersbourg, Odessa and Kavkazian]
G. Greene. il *N Y* 20:116-18 O 19 '87

Branching out [Albero d'Oro and Cafe at Arizona 206]
G. Greene. il *N Y* 20:130+ Ap 27 '87

Brunch. J. Freiman. il *N Y* 20:66-8+ Je 29-Jl 6 '87

Cafe au Go Go. P. Herbst. il *N Y* 20:81 D 21-28
'87

California dreaming [Melrose and China Grill] G. Greene.
il *N Y* 20:102-4 N 16 '87

Canta e pasta [annual concert sponsored by the Frisari
family at the Veronica Ristorante Italiano] *New Yorker*
63:27-9 Mr 23 '87

The Cedars. J. Oppenheimer. il *N Y* 20:82-3 D 21-28
'87

Coastal discoveries [Coastal] G. Greene. il *N Y* 20:70-1
Je 8 '87

A couple of swells [Provence and Barocco] G. Greene.
il *N Y* 20:60+ Ja 26 '87

Cue: a complete entertainment guide for the week. See
issues of New York

Discos in the '80s: stayin' alive. D. L. Lewis. il *N
Y* 20:24 Je 8 '87

Dreams of Victory [Sweet Victory Café] J. Freiman.
il *N Y* 20:80 Je 8 '87

East is West [Bo Ky and Dagon Burmese Restaurant]
J. Freiman. il *N Y* 20:85 Ap 20 '87

Eddie Condon's. V. Ziegel. il por *N Y* 20:70-1 D 21-28
'87

Family-style: the Lattanzis have built a restaurant dynasty
on anti-chic. S. Squire. il *N Y* 20:90-2+ Ag 24 '87

Food in Vogue [Bice and Sofi] B. Kafka. il *Vogue* 177:280+
N '87

Food in Vogue [Le Cirque] B. Kafka. il *Vogue* 177:216+
D '87

For adults only [designer A. Tihany] D. Shaw. il por
N Y 20:42 D 7 '87

The Forbes "choice" restaurants of 1987. M. S. Forbes.
il *Forbes* 140:18 D 28 '87

Foreign intrigue [ethnic neighborhoods] B. Costikyan.
il *N Y* 20:46-52 My 4 '87

Four for the money [Safari Grill, Bud's, Cinco de Mayo
and Border Cafe] G. Greene. il *N Y* 20:102+ Mr
9 '87

The fourth season at The Four Seasons. N. Hazelton.
Natl Rev 39:51-2 D 31 '87

The French evolution [Le Cirque, Le Régence, Le Chantilly and Le Festival] G. Greene. il *N Y* 20:50-5 Mr
23 '87

Goings on about town. See issues of The New Yorker

Great new places to have a party (I). B. Costikyan.
il *N Y* 20:52-66+ F 16 '87

Great new places to have a party (II). B. Costikyan.
il *N Y* 20:40-57 F 23 '87

High Thai [Bangkok House and Thai Taste] J. Freiman.
il *N Y* 20:76 Mr 16 '87

Home on two ranges [David K's and Zarela] G. Greene.
il *N Y* 20:90+ N 30 '87

Hot restaurants—how they get that way . . . B. Kafka.
il *Vogue* 177:338+ Mr '87

Hot tickets: caviar, vodka, then off to Broadway . .
. [Petrossian] W. P. Rayner and C. Rayner. il *Vogue*
177:210 Ag '87

If you want to lounge on a love seat in New York's
hippest club, you'll have to get Nell Campbell's okay.
M. Small. il por *People Wkly* 27:117-19 F 2 '87

In a gastronomic grudge match, a seasoned contender
from Italy taunts the Times's top taster [feud between
B. Miller and H. Cipriani over reviews of restaurants
named Bellini and Harry Cipriani] A. Richman. il
por *People Wkly* 28:67-8 D 7 '87

In the fourth dimension [4D] il *Horizon* 30:33-4 S '87

In the nabes [Extra! Extra!, Cameos, Vico and Manhattan
Island] G. Greene. il *N Y* 20:62-5 S 14 '87

Indulgences [Casual Quilted Giraffe and Ménage à Trois]
B. Kafka. il *Vogue* 177:272+ F '87

Italics [signs outside restaurants along Madison Avenue]
New Yorker 63:30-1 Ap 27 '87

Late-night glitz. M. Musto. il *Harpers Bazaar* 120:72+
Ja '87

The Les Paul fan club [Monday night shows at Fat
Tuesday's] M. Walker. il por *N Y* 20:28 S 7 '87

Let's eat out. See issues of Gourmet

A lifetime in the Vanguard [M. Gordon] J. Levenson.
il por *Down Beat* 54:65 S '87

Making old '21' young. J. Homans. il *N Y Times Mag*
p42-3+ F 15 '87

The miracle cure for holiday indulgence . . . the new
Q.V., a worthy splurge. B. Kafka. il *Vogue* 177:112+
Ja '87

New spice [Thai House Cafe and Curry in a Hurry]
J. Freiman. il *N Y* 20:62 S 7 '87

Night club [the Tunnel] *New Yorker* 63:26-7 Mr 23
'87

Nightclub nightmares: a musician's view [jazz scene]
J. Forrester. *Down Beat* 54:52-3 My '87

Nostalgia food: the diner updated and fond memories
of forties and fifties fare. A. Batterberry. il por *House
Gard* 159:54+ Mr '87

On the Springsteen scene: one Boss Club. E. Byron.
il por *Mademoiselle* 93:52 Je '87

Once it was Jack and Charlie's and now it's Ken and
Anne's, but is it still the 21 Club? A. Richman. il
pors *People Wkly* 27:49-50 My 25 '87

Out of India [Gaylord and Everest] J. Freiman. il *N
Y* 20:68 F 2 '87

Out of the cellar [A. Stillman of Smith & Wollensky
buys M. Tucci's wine cellar from Oscar's Delmonico's
restaurant] F. J. Prial. il por *N Y Times Mag* p56
N 29 '87

Le Pavillon. G. Greene. il *N Y* 20:86 D 21-28 '87

Pretty in pink [Bellini by Cipriani] S. Drucker. il *Vogue*
177:120 Ag '87

Restaurants [fall preview] B. Costikyan. il *N Y* 20:150-1+
S 21 '87

Restaurants—go, consider, stop. M. S. Forbes. il *Forbes*
139:18-19 F 9 '87

Restaurants—go, consider, stop. M. S. Forbes. *Forbes*
140:18-19 O 5 '87

Restaurants—go, consider, stop. M. S. Forbes. *Forbes*
140:22 Jl 27 '87

Restaurants—go, consider, stop. M. S. Forbes. *Forbes*
139:18 My 4 '87

The road back to El Morocco: Usha Singh and the
$2-million gamble. W. Norwich. il por *N Y* 20:48-51
Ap 27 '87

Salsa and samovars [Blue Moon Mexican Cafe and White
Night Cafe] J. Freiman. il *N Y* 20:105 D 14 '87

Sam Lopata, the clown prince of restaurant designers,
lets nothing interfere with atmosphere. E. Levin. il
pors *People Wkly* 28:103-4+ N 23 '87

Scenes: the big idea this summer is escape. D. Shaw.
il *N Y* 20:42-6 Je 29-Jl 6 '87

Schrafft's. J. Baumgold. il *N Y* 20:72-3 D 21-28 '87

Seems like old times [Frank's Trattoria] J. Freiman.
il *N Y* 20:113 N 2 '87

Sofi's choice. G. Greene. il *N Y* 20:80-1 My 11 '87

Sounds of the city. E. Pooley. il *N Y* 20:70-6+ My
4 '87

Spécialités de la maison:
Argenteuil, Primola, Bridge Cafe. A. Birsh. il *Gourmet*
47:28+ O '87
Aurora, Bukhara, Zinno. A. Birsh. il *Gourmet* 47:34+
Mr '87
Le Bernardin, La Bohême, Taormina. A. Birsh.
Gourmet 47:30+ Ja '87
Brive, Nishi NoHo, Chapiteau. A. Birsh. il *Gourmet*
48:20+ Je '87
Le Chantilly, Arizona 206, "before the theater". A.
Birsh. il *Gourmet* 47:24+ Ap '87
Le Cirque, Tommy Tang's, Hard Rock Cafe. A.
Birsh. il *Gourmet* 47:26+ D '87
The Coach House, Andrée's Restaurant, "Thanks-
giving Day". A. Birsh. il *Gourmet* 47:44+ N '87
Le Cygne, Sparks Steak House, The Nice Restaurant.
A. Birsh. il *Gourmet* 47:34+ S '87
Gotham Bar and Grill, Prunelle, Kom Tang. A.
Birsh. il *Gourmet* 47:26+ F '87
Lafayette, Cent' Anni, Claire. A. Birsh. il *Gourmet*
47:34+ My '87
Lattanzi, Brighton Grill & Oyster Bar. A. Birsh.
il *Gourmet* 47:28+ Ag '87
Ménage à Trois, Dawat, Onini. A. Birsh. il *Gourmet*
47:38+ Jl '87
Stars come in at night [light projection system at Saint
nightclub] il *Pop Mech* 164:125 Mr '87

The Stork Club. C. Amory. il *N Y* 20:78-9 D 21-28
'87

Such good fronds [Le Palmier and Bellini by Cipriani]
G. Greene. il *N Y* 20:52-3 Ag 10 '87

New York (N.Y.)—Restaurants, nightclubs, bars, etc.—*cont.*
This year's remodels. J. Freiman. il *N Y* 20:15 Ja 12 '87
The trouble with Harry's: behind the coup at Cipriani. J. Taylor. il por *N Y* 20:62-7 O 19 '87
Turkey on a roll [Anatolia] G. Greene. il *N Y* 20:76-7 Je 22 '87
Uptown gets smart [El Morocco] T. Connors. il *Vogue* 177:52 Je '87
Vaulting ambition [Bouley] G. Greene. il *N Y* 20:75-6 O 5 '87
West Side, East Side [Positively 104th Street Cafe and Little Mushroom Cafe] J. Freiman. il *N Y* 20:54 Jl 20 '87
Where have you gone, Woody Allen? [celebrities have forsaken Elaine's and are now dining at Elio's, Primola, Orso, and Columbus] D. Blum. il *N Y* 20:48-53 O 12 '87
Where the foodies go. J. Freiman. il *N Y* 20:86-9 My 4 '87
Wining and dining out. A. Bespaloff. il *N Y* 20:105-8 N 16 '87
The young man and the sea [G. Le Coze and Le Bernardin] M. Cantwell. il por *Vogue* 177:236-7+ Jl '87

Savings and loan associations
See also
Carver Federal Savings Bank

Schools
See New York (N.Y.)—Education

Social conditions
One block: a tale of two cities on West 80th Street. D. Blum. il *N Y* 20:24-32 F 9 '87

Social history
See also
Brooklyn (New York, N.Y.)—Social history
You must remember this: the New York we've lost [cover story; special issue] il *N Y* 20:47-8+ D 21-28 '87

Social life and customs
The aristobrats: they're young, they're rich, they're oh-so-shallow (could you be one of them?). D. Handelman. il *Mademoiselle* 93:230-1+ Ap '87
Club Lit: reading groups of the rich and famous. E. Hopkins. il *N Y* 20:32-5 Jl 20 '87
Couch potatoes: the new nightlife [stay-at-home New Yorkers] D. Blum. il *N Y* 20:24-30 Jl 20 '87
Dancing on the lip of the volcano: Christian Lacroix's crash chic [cover story] J. Baumgold. il pors *N Y* 20:36-49 N 30 '87
Late-night glitz. M. Musto. il *Harpers Bazaar* 120:72+ Ja '87
Life in the slow lane. R. Lynes. il *Archit Dig* 44:65+ N '87
Love: the fervid quest for the 'L' word. E. Hopkins. il *N Y* 20:32-6+ Je 29-Jl 6 '87
Manners for the eighties: how to master the daily dance of life in New York [cover story] G. Mahon. il *N Y* 20:46-54 D 14 '87
Mr. Peepers goes the way of all flesh [benefit dinner hosted by G. Steinberg] il *N Y* 20:29-30 Ap 13 '87
Mr. Peepers's nights: the Versailles squeak [receptions prior to the Winter Antiques Show] il *N Y* 20:21-2 Ja 26 '87
On the streets of New York. A. Fotheringham. il *Macleans* 100:72 O 19 '87
Rio on a plate [M. O'Donoghue's Bal Existential] *New Yorker* 63:25-6 Je 15 '87
Typical [Schwartzman and Xu families dine out] *New Yorker* 63:24-5 Je 15 '87
Where have you gone, Woody Allen? [celebrities have forsaken Elaine's and are now dining at Elio's, Primola, Orso, and Columbus] D. Blum. il *N Y* 20:48-53 O 12 '87

Stations
See also
Pennsylvania Station (New York, N.Y.)
Eager beaver [restoration and improvement of Astor Place Station] G. Anderson. il *Archit Rec* 175:80-3 Ja '87
Gold rush to hell [A. Jaar's installation of photographs of Brazilian gold rush in subway station] S. Staggs. il *Art News* 86:9 F '87

Stores
See also
Angus Wilkie Antiques (Firm)
B. Altman & Co.
Clodagh, Ross & Williams Inc.
F. A. O. Schwarz
Fairway Fruits & Vegetables (New York, N.Y.)

Hyde Park Antiques Ltd.
Lord & Taylor
Maxilla & Mandible (Firm)
National Jewelers Exchange
Place des Antiquaires (New York, N.Y.)
Portantina Ltd.
R. H. Macy & Co., Inc.
Rita Ford, Inc.
Tiffany & Co.
Turning Heads (Firm)
Bake sale [auction of the equipment from out-of-business Lichtman's bakery] *New Yorker* 63:23-4 Jl 20 '87
The Christmas table. *New Yorker* 63:84+ D 21 '87
Designer cheek. J. Dolce. il *Harpers Bazaar* 120:210+ Mr '87
Fish trip [Corlears School makes field trip to De Martino's Fish Market] *New Yorker* 62:25 Ja 12 '87
Fish window [F. Lara's window displays at the Citarella Fish Company] *New Yorker* 63:23-5 Jl 6 '87
Folding [art of folding sweaters at a Benetton store] *New Yorker* 63:30-1 My 25 '87
Here's a bit of Europe in old New York [Madison Avenue] T. Segal. il *Bus Week* p119 F 16 '87
Into the valley of death? [Abraham & Straus opens in Herald Square] J. Flint. il *Forbes* 140:160 O 19 '87
Mr. Smith comes to New York [fashion designer P. Smith's store] B. Boehlert. il por *N Y* 20:28 Ap 20 '87
Nails [nail salons] *New Yorker* 63:23-4 S 7 '87
New York area lighting rental houses. D. F. Sisk. *Theatre Crafts* 21:14+ Ja '87
The New York Flower Show and Uncle Sam Umbrella Shop. H. Bridges. il *Gourmet* 47:42+ Mr '87
On and off the avenue [Christmas gifts for children] *New Yorker* 63:118+ D 7 '87
On and off the avenue [Christmas gifts for men] *New Yorker* 63:106-18 D 14 '87
On and off the avenue [Christmas gifts for women] *New Yorker* 63:114-32 N 16 '87
On and off the avenue [gifts for the house] *New Yorker* 63:105-18 N 23 '87
Sales & bargains. L. Fleischer. See issues of New York
Shopping [fall preview] L. Dyett. il *N Y* 20:140-9 S 21 '87

Street trades
See Street trades

Street traffic
Wild in the streets [woman bicycle messenger M. Sprizzo] D. Frost. il pors *Women's Sports Fitness* 9:33-6 My '87

Streets
See also
Fifth Avenue (New York, N.Y.)
Madison Avenue (New York, N.Y.)
Freedom [Freedom Place, where student drivers can practice] *New Yorker* 63:22-3 Ag 24 '87
One block: a tale of two cities on West 80th Street. D. Blum. il *N Y* 20:24-32 F 9 '87

Subways
See also
Goetz, Bernhard—Subway shooting case
Fighting the school for scoundrels [Transit Police Pickpocket Squad] T. Cochran. il *N Y* 20:25 My 25 '87
Mr. Personality [P. Schimmel, clarinet player] *New Yorker* 63:25-7 Ap 13 '87
Notes and comment [observations made while riding the subway during the holidays] *New Yorker* 62:19-23 Ja 5 '87

Transit police
See New York (N.Y.)—Police

Taxation
My troubles with the taxman [New York City Unincorporated Business Tax] A. P. Tobias. il *N Y Times Mag* p40+ Ja 18 '87

Terminals
See New York (N.Y.)—Stations

Theater
See also
AMAS Repertory Theatre, Inc.
Apollo Theatre (New York, N.Y.)
Harlem Opera House (New York, N.Y.)
Jujamcyn Theaters
Majestic Theater (New York, N.Y.)
Martin Beck Theatre (New York, N.Y.)
Promethean Theatre Company
Bright lights, Big Apple. L. Black. il *Macleans* 100:69-70 D 7 '87
Broadway and beyond. K. Grubb. See issues of Dance Magazine

New York (N.Y.)—Theater—*cont.*

Guerrillas [street theater advertising a real estate broker] *New Yorker* 63:31-2 N 30 '87

The late arrivals lighting up broadway. D. H. Dunn. il *Bus Week* p93 Ap 20 '87

Leaving his imprint on Broadway [L. Richards] S. G. Freedman. il pors *N Y Times Mag* p38+ N 22 '87

Musical 'Mama' eviction cleared by N.Y. judge. *Jet* 72:53 Jl 13 '87

Off Broadway [early days] J. Tallmer. il *N Y* 20:73 D 21-28 '87

Razzle-dazzle on Broadway [British musicals] M. Horn. il *U S News World Rep* 102:72-3 Mr 16 '87

Robert Brustein on theater. R. Brustein. See occasional issues of The New Republic

Snarls, continued [British conquest of Broadway] R. Brustein. *New Repub* 196:27-8+ My 4 '87

Take the freeway to Broadway [imports from California] R. Alleman. il *Vogue* 177:128 O '87

Theater. See occasional issues of The Nation

Theater [1987] J. Simon. il *N Y* 20:105-6 D 21-28 '87

Theater [fall season] M. Morgan. il *N Y* 20:52-3 S 21 '87

Theater. J. Simon. See issues of New York

The theatre. M. Kramer. See issues of The New Yorker beginning June 8, 1987

The theatre. E. Oliver. See issues of The New Yorker beginning February 16, 1987

Transit police

See New York (N.Y.)—Police

Transit systems

See also

New York (N.Y.)—Subways

Port Authority of New York and New Jersey

Floating the Hudson: Big Apple commuters get mellow [ferries] G. Langer. il *Sierra* 72:12 N/D '87

New York Boat Show directions. map *Mot Boat Sail* 159:58-9 Ja '87

Tunnels and tunneling

It takes a 'sixth sense' to operate underneath the streets of New York. D. D. Jackson. il *Smithsonian* 18:38-47 Ag '87

Zoning

Sweet 'n' low [revision of law on housing] C. Wiseman. il *N Y* 20:62-3 Ag 31 '87

Battery Park City

See Battery Park City (New York, N.Y.)

Greenwich Village

See Greenwich Village (New York, N.Y.)

Harlem

See Harlem (New York, N.Y.)

Herald Square

See Herald Square (New York, N.Y.)

Lower East Side

See Lower East Side (New York, N.Y.)

Murray Hill

See Murray Hill (New York, N.Y.)

SoHo

See SoHo (New York, N.Y.)

Television City

See Television City (New York, N.Y.)

Times Square

See Times Square (New York, N.Y.)

Tribeca

See Tribeca (New York, N.Y.)

Upper West Side

See Upper West Side (New York, N.Y.)

Wall Street

See Wall Street (New York, N.Y.)

New York (N.Y.). Art Commission

Mother Goose and Henry Moore. J. Herzfeld. il *Art News* 86:61+ O '87

New York (N.Y.). Cathedral of St. John the Divine *See* Cathedral of St. John the Divine (New York, N.Y.)

New York (N.Y.). City University *See* City University of New York

New York (N.Y.). Dept. of Cultural Affairs

Mary Campbell is cultural affairs chief of New York. il por *Jet* 72:23 Ag 17 '87

NY gets new cultural head [M. S. Campbell] B. Blondin. *Black Enterp* 18:24 N '87

New York (N.Y.). Dept. of General Services. Operation GreenThumb *See* Operation GreenThumb (New York, N.Y.)

New York (N.Y.). Dept. of the Aging

Easing the burden on Alzheimer's families. L. B. Cheek. il *Aging* no355:16-19 '87

Old friends [Meals on Wheels program] G. Greene. il *N Y* 20:10-11 Ja 12 '87

New York (N.Y.). Landmarks Preservation Commission

Landmarks crossroads. C. Wiseman. il *N Y* 20:98-100 Je 1 '87

New York (N.Y.). Metropolitan Opera *See* Metropolitan Opera (New York, N.Y.)

New York (N.Y.). Post Office

Why your mail is so slow [cover story] J. Blyskal and M. Hodge. il *N Y* 20:42-52+ N 9 '87

New York (N.Y.). Statue of Liberty *See* Statue of Liberty (New York, N.Y.)

New York (N.Y.). World Trade Center *See* World Trade Center (New York, N.Y.)

New York (N.Y.) fashion shows *See* Fashion shows

New York (N.Y.) in art

Richard Pantell. F. Johnson. il *Am Artist* 51:64-7+ F '87

New York (N.Y.) in literature

The fat man's garden and other landmarks [literary landmarks] R. Starr. il *N Y Times Book Rev* 92:34+ N 22 '87

Tom Wolfe's walk on the wild side [The bonfire of the vanities; interview] A. P. Sanoff. il pors *U S News World Rep* 103:57-8 N 23 '87

New York (N.Y.) in motion pictures

You must remember this [movies shot on location] H. Karren. il *N Y* 20:60-3 My 4 '87

New York (State)

See also

Adirondack Mountains (N.Y.)

Architecture, Domestic—New York (State)

Ballet—New York (State)

Birds—New York (State)

Booksellers and bookselling—New York (State)

Camps—New York (State)

Carlton Hill Multiple Use Area (N.Y.)

Catskill Mountains region (N.Y.)

Cemeteries—New York (State)

Chautauqua County (N.Y.)

Country estates—New York (State)

Criminal justice, Administration of—New York (State)

Dance festivals—New York (State)

Drama festivals—New York (State)

Dutchess County (N.Y.)

Express highways—New York (State)

Finger Lakes region (N.Y.)

Fire Island National Seashore (N.Y.)

Fishing—New York (State)

Forests and forestry—New York (State)

Gardens and gardening—New York (State)

Historic houses, sites, etc.—New York (State)

Hospices—New York (State)

Hospitals—New York (State)

Hospitals, Psychiatric—New York (State)

Hudson River (N.Y. and N.J.)

Hudson River Valley (N.Y. and N.J.)

Hunting—New York (State)

Income tax—New York (State)

Insurance law—New York (State)

Kaaterskill Falls (N.Y.)

Labor laws and regulations—New York (State)

Lake Awosting (N.Y.)

Lake George (N.Y.)

Lakes—New York (State)

Law—New York (State)

Long Island (N.Y.)

Motion picture festivals—New York (State)

Music festivals—New York (State)

Nassau County (N.Y.)

Niagara Falls (N.Y. and Ont.)

Oil pollution—New York (State)

Opera—New York (State)

Paleontology—New York (State)

Pollution—New York (State)

Prisons—New York (State)

Reading Prong

Saint Lawrence River

Saratoga National Historical Park (N.Y.)

Water pollution—New York (State)

Westchester County (N.Y.)

Wildflowers—New York (State)

Wildlife—New York (State)

Wildlife conservation—New York (State)

Youth—New York (State)

Antiquities

Digging into history [amateur archeologists excavate Saratoga battlefield] J. E. Stevens. il *Americana* 14:41-4 Ja/F '87

New York (State)—*cont.*
Climate
Lake acidification [effect of Big Blow of November 25, 1950 on Adirondack lakes; with reply by A. H. Johnson, D. F. Charles, and S. B. Andersen] J. E. Dobson and others. bibl f il *Environment* 29:2-5 Je '87
Fisheries
See Fisheries
Parks and reserves
See also
Artpark (Lewiston, N.Y.)
The Adirondack Park—a 2020 vision. R. Beamish. il map *Conservationist* 42:22-5 Jl/Ag '87
A beleaguered beauty faces the future [Adirondack State Park] G. Witkin. il map *U S News World Rep* 103:50-1 Ag 31 '87
More on the Adirondack Park [discussion of September 1986 article, Green hills, blue lakes, and red tape] I. Nelson. il *Ctry J* 14:4+ F '87
Politics and government
Cuomo and those rumors: getting to the bottom of all the 'Mob' talk [cover story] N. Pileggi. il pors *N Y* 20:44-8+ N 2 '87
The Fish family feud. M. Kaus. il pors *Newsweek* 110:18 Ag 24 '87
His way [challenging Sen. D. P. Moynihan] J. Klein. il pors *N Y* 20:34+ O 26 '87
Sanitary affairs
Five pounds a day. B. Hogan and M. Kadlecek. il *Conservationist* 41:18-25 My/Je '87
New York (State). Air National Guard
Weekend warriors [C-5 Galaxies] P. Scott. il *Flying* 114:60-4 Je '87
New York (State). Dept. of Environmental Conservation
Consumers protected from unclean shellfish. B. Hogan. il *Conservationist* 42:19 S/O '87
The continuing success of Return a Gift to Wildlife [tax checkoff] S. Keeler. il *Conservationist* 41:2-5 Mr/Ap '87
DEC welcomes new commissioner [T. C. Jorling] por *Conservationist* 42:49 S/O '87
DEC's 1987 migratory waterfowl print and stamp. il *Conservationist* 42:54 Jl/Ag '87
In search of wintering bats. A. Hicks. *Conservationist* 41:14-17+ Ja/F '87
Landowners and sportsmen united [cooperative program allowing public to hunt or fish on private lands] J. Major. il *Conservationist* 41:42-5 Ja/F '87
Managing New York's marine fishery. G. C. Colvin. il *Conservationist* 42:10-17 S/O '87
Toxics in a great river—putting the pieces together [pollution flowing from Niagara River into Lake Ontario] M. Kadlecek. il *Conservationist* 42:34-9 N/D '87
New York (State). Power Authority *See* Power Authority of the State of New York
New York (State) in art
Harry Orlyk [cover story] M. Mathews-Berenson. il *Am Artist* 51:38-41+ Jl '87
New York Academy of Art
'This incredible machine' [cadaver studied in anatomy class] R. Bass. il *Art News* 86:182 Mr '87
New York Academy of Sciences
New York Academy presents awards. *BioScience* 37:300 Ap '87
New York Air
People Express, New York Air merging under Continental umbrella. C. Preble. *Aviat Week Space Technol* 126:32-3 Ja 19 '87
New York Aquarium
Alysoun Seacat is number one in Nuka's heart—by a whisker. B. Rowes. il por *People Wkly* 28:110-11 Ag 10 '87
Aquarium news [tour led by G. Ruggieri] *New Yorker* 62:22-4 Ja 26 '87
New York Baroque Dance Company
Bringing back baroque [performance of Les fêtes d'Hébé] P. J. Rosenwald. il *Horizon* 30:42 Mr '87
Dance [Terpsicore at Marymount Manhattan Theatre] M. Aloff. *Nation* 244:624-6 My 9 '87
Reviews:
Performances of Les fêtes d'Hébé and Ariodante at Hunter College, New York City. L. Garafola. il *Dance Mag* 61:20+ F '87
New York Book Fair *See* Book fairs
New York City Ballet
Blossom time in New York [production of Variations pour une porte et un soupir] L. A. Jacobs. il *New Leader* 70:22-3 Jl 1-15 '87
The company wunderkind [R. Marsden] B. Ivry. por *N Y* 20:24 My 25 '87

A dancer's nightmare [S. Lavery] L. Leivick. il pors *N Y Times Mag* p66+ N 8 '87
Dancing:
P. Martins' Green, Purple, and Ecstatic orange and comparison with the American Ballet Theatre. A. Croce. *New Yorker* 63:75-6 Jl 6 '87
P. Martins' Les gentilhommes. A. Croce. *New Yorker* 63:82-3 Je 8 '87
Swan Lake and La sonnambula. A. Croce. *New Yorker* 63:71-4 Je 22 '87
Dressing up [performances of La sonnambula and Bournonville divertissements] T. Tobias. il *N Y* 20:64-5 Je 22 '87
Happy families [revival of Le tombeau de Couperin] T. Tobias. il *N Y* 20:100-1 My 18 '87
A kid lands every child's dream job: fighting mice in The Nutcracker [M. Parvin] il pors *People Wkly* 28:119-21 D 21 '87
Martins talks back: Peter's perspectives [cover story] J. Gruen. il pors *Dance Mag* 61:38-42 N '87
New faces at the New York City Ballet: future indicative. O. Stuart. il *Dance Mag* 61:70-3 Ja '87
NYCB unveils new plans. il *Dance Mag* 61:6 Ag '87
One for my master [performance of Les gentilhommes] T. Tobias. il *N Y* 20:64+ Je 1 '87
Peter Martins' little nothings. M. Duffy. il por *Time* 129:77 F 2 '87
Post-Balanchine breakthroughs [ballerinas M. Calegari and K. Nichols] E. Kendall. pors *Vogue* 177:48 Je '87
Reviews:
1987 spring season at the New York State Theater. O. Stuart. il *Dance Mag* 61:18-19+ O '87
Choreography project with dancers from the New York City Ballet at Jacob's Pillow. L. Garafola. *Dance Mag* 61:74-5 D '87
Winter season at City Center. M. Aloff. *Dance Mag* 61:184-9 Je '87
Second comings [performance of Variations pour une porte et un soupir] T. Tobias. il *N Y* 20:60-1+ F 9 '87
Solo flights [D. Kistler's performance in La sonnambula] T. Tobias. il *N Y* 20:84-5 D 14 '87
Taking stock [P. Martins' Les petits riens and Ecstatic orange] T. Tobias. il *N Y* 20:58 F 2 '87
New York City Marathon *See* Marathon running
New York City Opera Company
An angel's way . . . [L. E. Rigler, major benefactor] L. Kandell. il por *Opera News* 51:8-10 Ja 31 '87
Architectural digest visits: Beverly Sills. J. Gruen. il pors *Archit Dig* 44:184-9 N '87
The executive superstar of the opera [B. Sills] K. Brady. il pors *Work Woman* 12:62-3+ Je '87
A flat 'Flute'. P. G. Davis. il *N Y* 20:56 Ag 31 '87
Musical events:
Where the Wild Things are and L'oca del Cairo. A. Porter. *New Yorker* 63:130-1 N 30 '87
Die Zauberflöte. A. Porter. *New Yorker* 63:112+ S 14 '87
New York City. T. Eckert, Jr. *Opera News* 51:36-8 Ja 17 '87
New York City. T. Eckert, Jr. il *Opera News* 52:51-2 N '87
The shadow glows [production of The desert song] P. G. Davis. il *N Y* 20:104 S 14 '87
Small world [revival of South Pacific] P. G. Davis. il *N Y* 20:92+ Mr 23 '87
Vitamins of happiness [new music director] S. Comissiona. il *Opera News* 52:26-7 Jl '87
Wild goose chase [performances of L'oca del Cairo and Where the Wild Things are] P. G. Davis. il *N Y* 20:83-5 N 30 '87
X (The life and times of Malcolm X). H. Mandel. *Down Beat* 54:50 Ja '87
New York daily news *See* Daily news (New York, N.Y.)
New York Film Festival *See* Motion picture festivals—New York (State)
New York Flower Show *See* Flower exhibits
New York Historical Society
Bicentennial of the Constitution—New York City [Government by choice: inventing the United States Constitution] S. B. Sherrill. il *Antiques* 132:410+ S '87

New York Hospital-Cornell Medical Center
A hospital stands accused [mystery surrounding A. Warhol's death] C. Wallis. il por *Time* 129:64 Ap 27 '87
New York Hospital on the spot: three baffling deaths jolt a proud institution. M. Stone. il pors *N Y* 20:40-7 Je 22 '87

New York International Ballet Competition *See* Ballet—Competitions

New York Mercantile Exchange
A hot commodity [W. Bradt of the New York Merc pushes for mergers] S. W. Angrist. il por *Forbes* 139:256 Je 15 '87
The hot new low-stakes play in oil [crude options] T. Thompson. il *Bus Week* p80 Ja 26 '87
Not so crude options [oil options] S. W. Angrist. il *Forbes* 139:176 Mr 9 '87

New York Music Awards
The sound of success [founders M. Lash and R. Woliver] S. Mieses. il por *N Y* 20:22 Ap 6 '87

New York National Boat Show *See* Boats and boating—Exhibitions

New York newsday (Newspaper)
An upstart from the 'burbs: Newsday's inroads in New York City. D. Lieberman. il *Bus Week* p89+ My 11 '87

New York observer (Newspaper)
Now, the New York 'observer' [publisher A. L. Carter] E. Diamond. il por *N Y* 20:21-3 Jl 13 '87

New York Philharmonic-Symphony Orchestra
Applause! Applause! [conductor E.-P. Salonen] P. G. Davis. il por *N Y* 20:53-4 Ja 12 '87
Dexter Gordon/New York Philharmonic. M. Bourne. *Down Beat* 54:56 S '87
Doctor in the house [concerts conducted by G. Sinopoli] P. G. Davis. il por *N Y* 20:63 Je 8 '87
Enthusiastic response [C. Davis conducts The damnation of Faust] P. G. Davis. il por *N Y* 20:114-15 O 5 '87
Ongoing Dialogues [M. Rostropovich conducts B. Britten's War requiem] P. G. Davis. il *N Y* 20:82+ Ap 6 '87

New York post
Tots nix blazing coeds! [writing headlines]; ed. by David Van Biema. V. Musetto. il por *People Wkly* 27:65+ Je 1 '87

New York Power Authority *See* Power Authority of the State of New York

New York Public Library. Dance Collection
Dance Collection names archive for Robbins, launches campaign. por *Dance Mag* 61:7 Ag '87
Oswald retires. D. Cox. il por *Dance Mag* 61:4 N '87

New York Public Library. Schomburg Center for Research in Black Culture *See* Schomburg Center for Research in Black Culture

New York Regional Booksellers Association
A smaller turnout for MABA-NYRA meeting. D. Maryles. *Publ Wkly* 232:60 N 27 '87

New York review of books
Cover-up at 'The New York review' [criticism of R. Leiken's reports from Nicaragua by Tony Jenkins] A. Cockburn. *Nation* 245:9 Jl 4-11 '87
Shamed [R. Leiken's reporting on Nicaragua criticized by Tony Jenkins] A. Cockburn. *Nation* 245:79 Ag 1-8 '87

New York Rights & Permissions Group
New York Permissions Group holds two-day meeting in Ottawa. M. E. Phelps. *Publ Wkly* 232:12-13 Jl 17 '87

New York State Museum
The Ice Age returns [exhibit] il *Conservationist* 41:48-9 My/Je '87

New York State Ranger School (Wanakena, N.Y.)
Wanakena—the New York State Ranger School. K. Smith and J. E. Coufal. il *Conservationist* 42:42-5 S/O '87

New York Stock Exchange *See* Stock exchanges—New York exchange

New York Telephone Co.
How one guy beat the system [small claims suit brought by Bhaichand Patel] *Consum Rep* 52:74 F '87

New York Theatre Ballet
Reviews:
Performances at the Riverside Dance Festival. C. Hardy. *Dance Mag* 61:78-9 D '87
Second sight [performances at the Roundabout Theater] T. Tobias. por *N Y* 20:111-12 My 25 '87

New York times
Abe speaks his mind [A. M. Rosenthal's column] J. Alter. il por *Newsweek* 109:54 Mr 9 '87
All the corrections that are fit to print. J. Alter. *Newsweek* 110:52-3 Jl 27 '87
The best journalist of his time [retirement of J. Reston] T. Griffith. il por *Time* 130:60 Ag 31 '87
From Nixon to Lincoln [W. Safire] L. Weymouth. il pors *N Y* 20:42-7 Ag 31 '87
Full disclosure, semi-outrage [survey of presidential candidates] L. Zuckerman. il *Time* 129:67 Je 22 '87
James Reston steps down. *Natl Rev* 39:20 Ag 28 '87

A legend in his Times [retirement of J. Reston] por *Time* 130:55 Ag 17 '87
LeMoyne's progress [J. LeMoyne's Nicaraguan coverage] A. Cockburn. *Nation* 244:423 Ap 4 '87
The other day (as culled from the New York "Times" of August 9th). R. Harris. *New Yorker* 63:90-2+ S 21 '87
Pundit to pasture [J. Reston gives up his column] A. Cockburn. *Nation* 245:114 Ag 15-22 '87
Sections [S. Bronsky sells discarded sections of the Sunday New York times on Manhattan sidewalk] *New Yorker* 62:24 Ja 26 '87
Some hits, some runs, one error [editor M. Frankel] L. Zuckerman. il por *Time* 130:59 Jl 27 '87
The Times of Frankel [cover story] E. Diamond. il pors *N Y* 20:26-34 Ag 10 '87

New York times book review
A look at the issues in Blatty's appeal to the Supreme Court [best seller list dispute with N.Y. times] C. E. Rinzler. *Publ Wkly* 232:16-17 Ag 28 '87

New York Times Company
What's free, full of ads, and read all over? [antitrust suit against New York Times Co. by direct mailer Advo-System] C. Welles. il *Bus Week* p122+ N 2 '87

New York University
Tsk, tsk, Larry Tisch [investment portfolio performance] il por *Fortune* 116:118 O 26 '87

New York wines *See* Wine

New York Woodwind Quintet
Musical events:
Merkin Hall recital. A. Porter. *New Yorker* 63:124+ O 12 '87

New York Youth Symphony Orchestra *See* Youth Symphony Orchestra of New York

New York Zoological Park *See* Bronx Zoo

New Yorker (Madrid, Spain: Restaurant) *See* Madrid (Spain)—Restaurants, nightclubs, bars, etc.

New Yorker (Periodical)
After Shawn [editor R. Gottlieb] E. Diamond. il por *N Y* 20:14+ Je 8 '87
Barking up the family tree [The art of the New Yorker—a 60 year retrospective] T. Young. il *Vogue* 177:96 Ag '87
E. J. Kahn book about 'New Yorker' to be published by Stephen Greene. *Publ Wkly* 232:76 O 2 '87
The fate of the earth [R. Gottlieb chosen to succeed W. Shawn] E. Diamond. il por *N Y* 20:12-13 Ja 26 '87
Fear and loathing at the New Yorker [R. Gottlieb to succeed W. Shawn as editor] M. Salter. il por *Macleans* 100:46 Ja 26 '87
Gottlieb to leave Knopf for New Yorker. por *Publ Wkly* 231:20 Ja 23 '87
Joseph Mitchell's secret. B. Ivry. il por *N Y* 20:20 F 9 '87
Masson loses libel suit against 'New Yorker,' Malcolm and Knopf. M. Colin. *Publ Wkly* 232:11 S 4 '87
The New Yorker lists at this season some books by its contributors published during the year. *New Yorker* 63:100-1 D 21 '87
Shawn with the wind [R. Gottlieb succeeding W. Shawn as editor] A. Gingold. il *New Repub* 196:10-12 F 9 '87
The sky line [revival of column] B. Gill. *New Yorker* 63:106-9 F 23 '87
The squawk of the town [R. Gottlieb picked as new editor] J. Alter. il pors *Newsweek* 109:83 Ja 26 '87
Still here at the New Yorker. B. Gill. il *N Y Times Book Rev* 92:1+ O 4 '87
The talk of the town [R. Gottlieb to succeed W. Shawn as editor] J. Kelly. il pors *Time* 129:69 Ja 26 '87

New Yorkers
The buildings New Yorkers love to hate [cover story] R. D. Story. il *N Y* 20:30-5 Je 15 '87
Notes and comment [observations made while riding the subway during the holidays] *New Yorker* 62:19-23 Ja 5 '87
Places in the heart: where real New Yorkers find the real New York. M. Morgan. il *N Y* 20:26+ My 4 '87
You must remember this: the New York we've lost [cover story; special issue] il *N Y* 20:47-8+ D 21-28 '87

New Zealand
See also
Agriculture—New Zealand
Anti-nuclear movement—New Zealand
Architecture, Domestic—New Zealand
Birds—New Zealand
Fishing—New Zealand

New Zealand—See also—*cont.*
Hotels, motels, etc.—New Zealand
Investments, New Zealand
Skis and skiing—New Zealand
United Nations—New Zealand
Defenses
See also
Airplanes, Military—New Zealand
Description and travel
Britain in the South Pacific. C. Hitchens. il *Harpers Bazaar* 120:264+ S '87
Kiwi gothic: Grant Wood farmstays in New Zealand [farmers who invite travelers into their homes] D. P. Marshall. il map *Travel Holiday* 168:42-7 N '87
New Zealand: the last utopia? R. P. Jordan. il map *Natl Geogr* 171:654-81 My '87
Nine lives in New Zealand. D. A. Rose. il *Esquire* 108:29-30 Ag '87
Sheep Down Under. *New Yorker* 63:27-9 My 4 '87
Thumbs up for Down Under. P. Plawin. il *Changing Times* 41:138-42+ Ja '87
Foreign relations
New Zealand and an interdependent world [address, March 13, 1987] P. M. Cleveland. map *Dep State Bull* 87:80-3 Je '87
United States
See United States—Foreign relations—New Zealand
Industries
See also
Fruit industry—New Zealand
Wine industry—New Zealand
Politics and government
Beyond California. R. Sandall. *Commentary* 83:56-60 Je '87
Newark (N.J.)
Airports
Newark Airport to expand passenger capacity. il *Aviat Week Space Technol* 126:48 Mr 30 '87
Operational problems at Newark hub reducing Continental traffic. M. Feazel. il *Aviat Week Space Technol* 126:44-5 Mr 30 '87
Blacks
Down and out and no place to go [Wolf family] T. McCarroll. il *Time* 130:20-1 Ag 24 '87
Photographs and photography
Ordinary miseries. H. M. Stummer. il *Society* 24:83-7 Mr/Ap '87
Monuments, statues, etc.
Grass-roots art seeks a haven [K. Tawana's ark] H. Metz. il por *Progressive* 51:14 O '87
Pollution
Chemical cleanup [EPA cleanup at closed facilities of Arkansas Chemical Co.] B. Weber. il *N Y Times Mag* p42 D 27 '87
Stores
See also
Giordano's Bakery
Newark [dance] See Dance reviews—Single works
Newark International Airport *See* Newark (N.J.)—Airports
Newbert, Chris
Chasing rainbows in the sea. il por *Natl Wildl* 25:52-9 F/Mr '87
Une liaison dangereuse. il *Nat Hist* 96:88-9 S '87
Newborn animals *See* Animals, Infancy of
Newborn infants *See* Infants, Newborn
Newbound, Christopher
Tennis or what [story] il *Seventeen* 46:164-5+ My '87
Newburn, Ray L.
about
Inside the IHW: the professionals [interview] J. K. Beatty. pors *Sky Telesc* 73:256-7 Mr '87
Newburyport (Mass.)
Hospitals
Hospital offers senior suppers [Anna Jaques Hospital] il *Aging* no356:29 '87
Newby, Eric
Travel. il *N Y Times Book Rev* 92:48-9 My 31 '87
Newcastle Upon Tyne (England)
Youth
Photographs and photography
Skinheads of Newcastle. C. Killip. il *Society* 24:84-6 Jl/Ag '87
Newcomb, Sally
Soldiers Delight. il map *Earth Sci* 40:24-5 Summ '87
Newcombe, Jack
Taking to the road. il *Americana* 15:26-31 N/D '87

Newell, Mike
about
Amazing Grace and Chuck [film] Reviews
Newsweek il 109:74 My 4 '87. J. Kroll
People Wkly il 27:10 Je 8 '87. R. Novak
The good father [film] Reviews
N Y il 20:63-4 F 23 '87. D. Denby
Natl Rev 39:54 My 8 '87. J. Simon
New Repub 196:28-9 F 9 '87. S. Kauffmann
New Yorker 63:83-4 Ap 6 '87. P. Kael
Newsweek 109:78 Mr 2 '87. D. Ansen
Newell, Roger D.
about
It's all relative. J. Heins. il por *Forbes* 140:54-5 Jl 27 '87
Newell Associates
It's all relative [using relative yield as forecasting tool; views of R. Newell] J. Heins. il por *Forbes* 140:54-5 Jl 27 '87
Newell Co.
Still expanding [acquisition of Anchor Hocking] A. A. Lappen. il *Forbes* 140:8 O 19 '87
Newfield, Jack
The Koch-Newfield letters [discussion of April 4, 1987 article, Mayor Daley is alive and well in N.Y.C.] *Nation* 245:2+ Jl 4-11 '87
Mayor Daley is alive and well in N.Y.C. [cover story] il *Nation* 244:417+ Ap 4 '87
Newfoundland
History
Echoes and voices summoned from a half-hour in hell [Royal Newfoundland Regiment casualties at the Battle of the Somme] J. D. Atwater. bibl (p271) il map *Smithsonian* 18:196-200+ N '87
Politics and government
Bringing down the House [political humor used by MP G. Baker] M. Drohan. por *Macleans* 100:8+ N 30 '87
Support for a legend [plan for financial bailout of former premier J. R. Smallwood] *Macleans* 100:25 F 2 '87
Newfoundland Energy Ltd.
A new life for Come By Chance [reopening of oil refinery] D. Jenish. il *Macleans* 100:32-3 S 7 '87
Newhouse, Donald
about
The biggest private fortune. C. J. Loomis. il pors *Fortune* 116:60-4+ Ag 17 '87
Newhouse, Samuel I., Jr.
about
The biggest private fortune. C. J. Loomis. il pors *Fortune* 116:60-4+ Ag 17 '87
Newhouse Broadcasting Corporation
The biggest private fortune [S. I. and D. Newhouse] C. J. Loomis. il pors *Fortune* 116:60-4+ Ag 17 '87
Newkirk, Lucille
about
Miami judge nixes will awarding $1.5 mil. real estate to black gardener. *Jet* 72:24 Jl 13 '87
Newlin, Jeanne T.
A Charleston, South Carolina, playbill of 1794. il *Antiques* 131:432-3 F '87
Newman, Arnold, 1918-
about
Newman's people. S. Weiley. il por *Art News* 86:128-34 D '87
Newman, Barbara
Nora Kaye on Nora Kaye: character and caring [interview] il pors *Dance Mag* 61:54-9 S '87
Newman, Bruce
All that he can be. il pors *Sports Illus* 66:30-1 Ja 19 '87
Another NCAA fumble. il por *Sports Illus* 67:100 D 7 '87
Bob's job is his calling. il pors *Sports Illus* 67:86-7 Jl 6 '87
The Broncos busted 'em. il *Sports Illus* 66:29-31 Ja 12 '87
A championship season. il *Sports Illus* 66:81-2 My 4 '87
Game for a good meal? il *Sports Illus* 66:93 Mr 9 '87
A heady start. il *Sports Illus* 66:18-23 Ap 27 '87
How Indiana got Smart. il pors *Sports Illus* 67 Sp Issue:14-16 N 18 '87
A King eyes a court comeback. il por *Sports Illus* 66:32-3 Mr 30 '87
Let's get physical. il *Sports Illus* 67:46-54+ N 9 '87
Now you see him. il pors *Sports Illus* 67:67-8+ N 30 '87
The road to nowhere. il *Sports Illus* 66:56-60 Mr 23 '87

Newman, Bruce—*cont.*
Three strikes and he's . . . back. il pors *Sports Illus* 66:18-19 Mr 2 '87
A true Jet fighter. il pors *Sports Illus* 67:108-12 O 12 '87
(jt. auth) See Hersch, Hank, and Newman, Bruce
Newman, Bruce
about
An antiques dealer's secret sources: Bruce Newman in Paris and England. J. Kornbluth. il pors *Archit Dig* 44 Archit Dig Travels:20-31+ O '87
Newman, Charles Hamilton, 1938-
What's left out of literature. il *N Y Times Book Rev* 92:1+ Jl 12 '87
Newman, Eric A.
(jt. auth) See Paulson, Olaf B., and Newman, Eric A.
Newman, James L.
The hybrids. *Focus* 36:36 Wint '86
Newman, Joseph Westley
about
Is Newman's car for real? il *Pop Mech* 164:82 Jl '87
A man who defies the laws. D. Noland. por *Discover* 8:46-8+ My '87
Newman, Judith B.
Poetic license. il por *Horizon* 30:39-40 N '87
Newman, Marion E.
about
Doll house furnishings to be auctioned August 14 and 15. *Antiques Collect Hobbies* 92:36 Ag '87
Newman, Michelle Spletzer- *See* Spletzer-Newman, Michelle
Newman, Paul, 1925-
about
The glass menagerie [film] Reviews
Glamour il 85:159 D '87. J. G. Boyum
Macleans il 100:42 S 28 '87. J. Bemrose
New Repub 197:25 N 23 '87. S. Kauffmann
People Wkly il 28:14 N 23 '87. S. Haller
Sch Update il 120:12-13 N 20 '87. D. Scheuer
Paul Newman and Tom Cruise spend a so-so day at the races, but fans lap it up anyway. il pors *People Wkly* 28:36-7 Jl 13 '87
Paul Newman, no longer a loser, finally hustles up that Oscar for The color of money. il pors *People Wkly* 27:122-3 Ap 13 '87
When Jim Fitzgerald was killed, racing lost its grand old man, and Paul Newman lost a friend. il pors *People Wkly* 28:122-3 N 23 '87
Newman, Peter C., 1929-
Business watch. See issues of Maclean's
Caesars of the wilderness [excerpt] il map *Macleans* 100:42-6+ O 12 '87
Canada's fur-trading empire. il map *Natl Geogr* 172:192-229 Ag '87
Newman, Rosalind
about
Roz Newman forms a multi-national alliance. E. Zimmer. il por *Dance Mag* 61:4 F '87
Newman, Stephen A.
Will power. il *N Y* 20:75+ Mr 23 '87
Newman, Steve
about
World-girdler Steve Newman sets a record by walking in a very, very big circle. R. Wolmuth. il pors *People Wkly* 27:38-40 Mr 30 '87
Newman, Warren Bennett
Arts education, the board of education, and you. *Des Arts Educ* 89:34-7 N/D '87
Newman (Rosalind) and Dancers *See* Rosalind Newman and Dancers
Newman Communications
MPR ends exclusive arrangement with Newman. *Publ Wkly* 231:70-1 Ap 10 '87
Newmarket Press
Making that first million [work of E. Margolis] R. A. Carter. il pors *Publ Wkly* 231:18-20 Mr 27 '87
Newmont Mining Corp.
A gold miner helps Pickens chip away at Newmont [R. M. Friedland cut into Ivanhoe Partners deal] S. D. Atchison. il por *Bus Week* p36 Ag 31 '87
One swallow could make Pickens' summer. J. E. Davis. il por *Bus Week* p37 S 14 '87
Newport, Curt
about
ISO: Liberty Bell. T. Reichhardt. il por *Space World* X-1-277:25-8 Ja '87
Newport (R.I.)
Historic houses, sites, etc.
The golden age of Newport [Wetmore family, owners of Château-sur-Mer] A. Pryce-Jones. il *House Gard* 159:190-7+ Je '87

Newport Beach (Calif.)
Restaurants, nightclubs, bars, etc.
Spécialités de la maison:
Pavilion. C. Bates. il *Gourmet* 47:20+ S '87
Newport Harbor Art Museum (Balboa, Calif.)
Art on the go. T. Bailey. il *Horizon* 30:51-2 Ja/F '87
Newport Music Festival *See* Music festivals—Rhode Island
News
See also
Art news
Cable television—News
Communications satellites—Journalistic use
Current events
Economic news
Educational news
Environmental news
Foreign news
Government and the press
Journalism
Medical news
Music news
Newsletters
Radio broadcasting—News
Religious news
Science news
Television broadcasting—News
The other day (as culled from the New York "Times" of August 9th). R. Harris. *New Yorker* 63:90-2+ S 21 '87
Anecdotes, facetiae, satire, etc.
Les neues. H. Flesch. *Nation* 245:174 Ag 29 '87
Of many things [Man suffocated by potatoes, William Marsano's collection of wacky news items] G. W. Hunt. *America* 157:178 O 3 '87
Serving up a new slice of news [food as news] C. Gordon. il *Macleans* 100:10 D 28 '87
News 12 Long Island (Television channel)
Cable grows its first regional all-news channel on Long Island. R. Buck. il *Channels* 7:13 S '87
News agencies
See also
Associated Press
Reuters Holdings plc
Soviet Union
See also
TASS (Soviet Union)
News broadcasts *See* Radio broadcasting—News; Television broadcasting—News
News commentators *See* Radio broadcasting—News
News Corporation Ltd.
Citizen Murdoch presses for more. T. Moore. il pors *Fortune* 116:90-6 Jl 6 '87
A media magnate on a buying spree [R. Murdoch] M. Janigan. il por *Macleans* 100:40 Ag 12 '87
Murdoch increases stake in Pearson conglomerate to 14.7%. V. Menkes. *Publ Wkly* 232:28 O 9 '87
Pearson in a pickle [R. Murdoch's stake in publishing operations of Pearson plc] S. Miller. *Bus Week* p60 O 12 '87
Thomas and 13 others leave Harper & Row [reorganization in wake of takeover] M. Reuter. il *Publ Wkly* 231:21-2 My 29 '87
News media *See* Mass media
News media ethics *See* Journalistic ethics
News photographs *See* Current events—Photographs and photography
News photography *See* Photography, Journalistic
News releases *See* Press releases
Newscasters *See* Radio broadcasting—News; Television broadcasting—News
Newscasts *See* Radio broadcasting—News; Television broadcasting—News
Newsgathering satellites *See* Communications satellites—Journalistic use
Newsletter Services, Inc.
Those who can, do. D. Machan. il por *Forbes* 140:113-14 D 14 '87
Newsletters
See also
House organs
Investment newsletters
Wine newsletters
Rating the health advisers. J. Carey. il *U S News World Rep* 103:54-5 S 7 '87
Newson, Roger
The ALPEX experiment. il *Courier* 40:34-6 F '87
Newspaper advertising *See* Advertising, Newspaper
Newspaper court reporting
Jury selection series cited by Marshall wins an award [Dallas morning news series on jury discrimination] *Jet* 72:23 Jl 20 '87

Newspaper errors *See* Errors, Literary
Newspaper ethics *See* Journalistic ethics
Newspaper fillers
An ode to newspaper fillers, those rich tidbits of the mind. P. Dickson. il *Smithsonian* 18:280 N '87
Newspaper publishers and publishing
> *See also*
> American Newspaper Publishers Association
> Blacks in newspaper publishing
> Computers—Newspaper publishing use
> Courier-Journal & Louisville Times Co.
> Dayton Newspapers, Inc.
> Freedom Newspapers, Inc.
> Gannett Co., Inc.
> Hearst Corporation
> Ingersoll Publications Company
> Knight-Ridder Inc.
> MediaNews Group Inc.
> National Newspaper Publishers Association
> New York Times Company
> Newhouse Broadcasting Corporation
> Women in newspaper publishing

Acquisitions and mergers
Beneath the mogul, paradox [acquisitions of W. D. Singleton] N. J. Perry. il por *Fortune* 116:191-2 O 12 '87
Dean Singleton: the making of a media baron. T. Mason and others. il por *Bus Week* p29 S 28 '87
Extra: Texan builds newspaper empire [W. D. Singleton] J. Schwartz. il por *Newsweek* 110:48 S 28 '87
Forget about art and cars [acquisitions of W. D. Singleton] L. Zuckerman. il por *Time* 130:55 S 28 '87
Is Dean Singleton a media king in the making? Check his papers. V. Balfour. il pors *People Wkly* 28:47-8 O 5 '87
A quixotic father's acquisitive son [R. Ingersoll II] P. Berman. il por *Forbes* 140:8 O 5 '87

International aspects
Black and white and read all over [Canada's C. Black] T. Fennell. il por *Macleans* 100:32-3 Je 15 '87
Partners for the Post [Financial post venture by Toronto Sun Publishing to include London's Financial times] P. Best. por *Macleans* 100:40 O 19 '87

Canada
Front-page challenge [Sherbrooke daily, The record, sold to Quebecor Inc.] B. Wallace. *Macleans* 100:49 O 26 '87
A new voice for business [Toronto Sun Publishing buys the Financial post] P. Best. il *Macleans* 100:37-8 O 12 '87

Antitrust cases
What's free, full of ads, and read all over? [antitrust suit against New York Times Co. by direct mailer Advo-System] C. Welles. il *Bus Week* p122+ N 2 '87

Finance
> *See also*
> Advertising, Newspaper

International aspects
The global newspaper game. R. Z. Chesnoff. il *U S News World Rep* 102:53 My 25 '87

Securities
All the newspaper stocks that are fit to buy? G. G. Marcial. il *Bus Week* p122 D 14 '87

Canada
> *See also*
> Hollinger, Inc.
> Toronto Sun Publishing Corp.
A challenge to big-city dailies. G. Bain. il *Macleans* 100:44 Je 22 '87

China
> *See also*
> World economic herald

Great Britain
Fleet Street's shake-out. R. Laver. il *Macleans* 100:38-40 O 19 '87
Power of the press [R. Maxwell] E. A. Finn, Jr. il por *Forbes* 139:91 Ja 26 '87
"The whole thing is breaking up" [Fleet Street] R. Morais. il *Forbes* 139:148+ My 18 '87
Newspaper reading

Anecdotes, facetiae, satire, etc.
With tabloids, 'Zip! You're in another world!'. R. Wolkomir. il *Smithsonian* 18:240 O '87
Newspapers
> *See also*
> Advertising, Newspaper
> Black press
> Freedom of the press
> Journalism
> Journalistic ethics

> Newsletters
> Palestinian Arab press
> Photography, Journalistic
> USA today (Newspaper)

Advice columns
Dear Ann Landers: anything you can do, I can do better, write 22 dazzled but eager column hopefuls. L. Aitken. il por *People Wkly* 27:42-4+ Ap 20 '87
Defeating 12,000, odd couple Diane Crowley and Jeff Zaslow win Ann Landers' old job. M. Vespa. il pors *People Wkly* 27:49-50 Je 22 '87
Hounded by woes, Miamians beg for more of Ryan the Advice Dog. il por *People Wkly* 28:113 O 19 '87
Looking for Miss Lonelyhearts [Chicago sun-times holds contest to replace Ann Landers who moved to the Chicago tribune] M. Bosc. il por *U S News World Rep* 102:13 Mr 23 '87
Mr. and Ms. Lonelyhearts [J. Zaslow and D. Crowley replace A. Landers at the Chicago sun-times] M. Bosc. il pors *U S News World Rep* 102:12 Je 15 '87

Book reviews
> *See* Book reviews and reviewing

Color printing
Extra! Extra! Red all about it! [influence of color use in newspapers; study by Robert Bohle and Mario R. Garcia] J. Goetz. il *Psychol Today* 21:24 Jl '87

Columns
> *See* Newspapers—Advice columns; Newspapers—Sections, columns, etc.

Headlines
Tots nix blazing coeds! [writing headlines for the New York post]; ed. by David Van Biema. V. Musetto. il por *People Wkly* 27:65+ Je 1 '87
What really mattered [10 most important headlines of the twentieth century] O. Friedrich. il *Time* 130:94 O 12 '87

History
It was a big day for 'Big Jule'—and me [birthdate newspapers] J. Kastner. il *Smithsonian* 18:154 Jl '87

International aspects
> *See also*
> International herald tribune

Letters to the editor
> *Anecdotes, facetiae, satire, etc.*
Vox populi. See issues of World Press Review

Magazine sections
An inviting market for free lancers . . . Sunday magazines [directory] *Writer* 100:25-9 Ap '87

Political news
> *See* Newspapers and politics

Sections, columns, etc.
> *See also*
> Book reviews and reviewing
> Newspapers—Advice columns
> Newspapers—Magazine sections
Abe speaks his mind [A. M. Rosenthal's column] J. Alter. il por *Newsweek* 109:54 Mr 9 '87
He's the wisest of wise guys [C. Adams, author of syndicated column The straight dope] E. Dolnick. il por *Discover* 8:82-4+ Ja '87
Is a yawn really contagious? [syndicated science column, The straight dope, by C. Adams] E. Dolnick. il *Read Dig* 131:99-102 Jl '87
Short-notice wisdom [new columnist A. M. Rosenthal] T. Griffith. il por *Time* 129:62 F 9 '87

Sports news
> *See* Sports journalism

California
> *See also*
> San Francisco chronicle

Canada
> *See also*
> Financial post (Canada)

Florida
> *See also*
> Miami herald
> Miami news

Great Britain
> *See also*
> Financial times
> Independent (Newspaper: Great Britain)
> Star (London, England: Newspaper)
Donkey business and asinine journalism [British mass circulation dailies' coverage of false Spanish donkey abuse story fed them by an animal rights group] J. Valls-Russell. il *New Leader* 70:5-7 Ap 6 '87
Spanish grill [British newspapers' anti-Hispanic bias] R. Alan. *New Leader* 70:9 O 5 '87

Newspapers—*cont.*

Illinois

See also
Chicago sun-times (Newspaper)

Louisiana

See also
Baton Rouge advocate

Nebraska

See also
Omaha world-herald

New Hampshire

See also
Manchester union leader (Newspaper)

New York (State)

See also
Daily news (New York, N.Y.)
El diario-La prensa (New York, N.Y.)
New York (N.Y.)—Newspapers
New York newsday (Newspaper)
New York observer (Newspaper)
New York post
New York times

Newfoundland

See also
Sunday express (Saint John's, Nfld.: Newspaper)

Nicaragua

See also
La prensa (Nicaragua)

Ohio

See also
Cleveland plain dealer (Newspaper)

Pennsylvania

See also
Philadelphia inquirer (Newspaper)
Reporting on radon: the role of local newspapers. S.
M. Friedman and others. *Environment* 29:4-5+ Mr
'87

Québec (Province)

See also
Montreal (Québec)—Newspapers
Record (Newspaper: Sherbrooke, Québec)

South Africa

See also
Star (Johannesburg, South Africa: Newspaper)

Soviet Union

See also
Moscow news

Texas

See also
Dallas morning news

Wisconsin

See also
Milwaukee community journal

Newspapers, Electronic *See* Information storage and retrieval
systems

Newspapers, Student *See* College and school journalism

Newspapers and politics
Area Man [rivalry between national and local newspapers
as demonstrated by R. Bork nomination coverage]
M. McGough. *New Repub* 197:17 S 14-21 '87
From Nixon to Lincoln [W. Safire] L. Weymouth. il
pors *N Y* 20:42-7 Ag 31 '87
Mellowing of a muckraker [J. Anderson; cover story]
D. Corn. il *Nation* 245:541+ N 14 '87
Readers take on one-paper town [Omaha world-herald
monitoring group] B. E. Johansen. il *Progressive* 51:16
Ap '87

International aspects
The bums on the front page. A. Fotheringham. il *Macleans*
100:64 O 12 '87

Newsweek (Periodical)
Now 'Impactweek'. E. Diamond. il *N Y* 20:20+ My
11 '87

Newton, Donna

about
Buddies. J. Stern and M. Stern. *New Yorker* 63:78+
S 21 '87

Newton, Helmut

about
Mr. Peepers's nights: dangerous liaisons. il por *N Y*
20:23-4 Ap 6 '87

Newton, Huey

about
Huey Newton sentenced for firearm possession. il por
Jet 72:38 Ap 13 '87
Huey Newton spared additional prison time. por *Jet*
72:29 Ag 17 '87

Newton, Sir Isaac, 1642-1727

about
Celebrating Newton [cover story] S. Weisburd. il por
Sci News 132:11-13 Jl 4 '87

Isaac Newton goofed, and it took student Robert Garisto
to get to the core of the matter. R. Wolmuth. il
por *People Wkly* 27:43 Je 29 '87
Museums mark tercentenary of Newton's Principia. R.
Hart. *Phys Today* 40:78 D '87
New superhero at Sigma Xi. il por *Time* 129:77 Je
22 '87
Newton's Principia: a retrospective. G. E. Christianson.
il por *Sky Telesc* 74:18-20 Jl '87

Nexrad *See* Radar meteorology

Next Inc.
Next from Steve Jobs. il por *U S News World Rep*
102:49 Ja 26 '87
Perot and Jobs: who's Next? M. Rogers. il pors *Newsweek*
109:48 F 9 '87
Ross Perot turns into an angel for Steve Jobs. K. M.
Hafner. il pors *Bus Week* p32 F 9 '87
Steven Jobs. K. M. Hafner. il por *Bus Week* Sp Issue:245
Ap 17 '87

Next Wave Festival
BAM goes boom [cover story] A. Virshup. il *N Y* 20:38-47
O 12 '87
In its fifth year, BAM's Next Wave Festival becomes
an institution. N. FitzGerald. *Dance Mag* 61:100 O
'87

Ney, Joanna
Cane and Able. il por *Film Comment* 23:2+ Ja/F '87

Ney, Tom
Steak dinners from the sea. il *Prevention* 39:62+ S '87

NFL *See* National Football League

NFL Players Association *See* National Football League
Players Association

NGA *See* National Governors' Association

Ngema, Mbongeni

about
Asinamali! [drama] Reviews
Nation 244:695-6 My 23 '87. M. Hodgson

**NGOs (Non-governmental organizations) of the United
Nations** *See* United Nations—Non-governmental
organizations

Nguyen, Cat

about
This is against my rights! Three who felt wronged—and
determined to battle for redress. G. Jaynes. il pors
Time 130:40-2 Jl 6 '87

Nguyen, Dustin

about
Class acts: guys who make the grade. M. L. Baer. il
pors *Teen* 31:59-60 N '87

Nguyên, Van Khoa
Domination and deprivation. il *Courier* 40:24-6 Ja '87

Nguyen, Van Linh, 1913-

about
An interview with Viet Nam's Nguyen Van Linh. D.
Brelis. il por *Time* 130:40 S 21 '87

NHL *See* National Hockey League

NHTSA *See* United States. National Highway Traffic Safety
Administration

Niacin
The devil we know [Mevacor vs. niacin for reducing
cholesterol] S. N. Chakravarty. il *Forbes* 140:203-4
N 2 '87
Niacin for the heart. G. Maleskey. *Prevention* 39:28-31
Jl '87

Niacinamide *See* Nicotinamide

Niagara (Ship)
USS Niagara restoration. il *Am Hist Illus* 22:8 D '87

Niagara Falls (N.Y.)

Pollution

See also
Love Canal case

Niagara Falls (N.Y. and Ont.)
Niagara rapids rescue [1918 breeches buoy rescue] *Sea
Front* 33:145-6 Mr/Ap '87

Niagara River (N.Y. and Ont.)
Toxics in a great river—putting the pieces together
[pollution flowing from Niagara River into Lake On-
tario] M. Kadlecek. il *Conservationist* 42:34-9 N/D
'87

Nicaragua

See also
Americans—Nicaragua
Anti-Semitism—Nicaragua
Censorship—Nicaragua
Civil rights—Nicaragua
College education and state—Nicaragua
Economic assistance, American—Nicaragua
Economic assistance, Canadian—Nicaragua
Economic assistance, European—Nicaragua
Espionage, American—Nicaragua
Government and the press—Nicaragua

Army
Bracing for the contras [Sandinista Army] C. A. Robbins. il *U S News World Rep* 102:30-1 Mr 9 '87

Commerce
Latin America
Nicaragua [oil shipments] *Bus Week* p49 Jl 6 '87
Soviet Union
See Soviet Union—Commerce—Nicaragua

Economic policy
Managua's wounded economy. R. Nordland. il *Newsweek* 109:35 Je 22 '87
The Nicaraguan economic system. B. M. Carl. map *America* 156:155-8 F 21 '87
War is crippling Nicaragua's economy. R. Graham. *World Press Rev* 34:50 Jl '87

Foreign opinion
European
Why Europeans support the Sandinistas. M. Falcoff. *Commentary* 84:61-5 Ag '87

Foreign relations
Central America
The Central American crisis and the Contadora process. P. M. Alvergue. *USA Today (Periodical)* 115:29-30 Ja '87
Costa Rica
See Costa Rica—Foreign relations—Nicaragua
Honduras
See Honduras—Foreign relations—Nicaragua
United States
See United States—Foreign relations—Nicaragua

History
One hundred years of turpitude [cover story] A. Cruz, Jr. il *New Repub* 197:26-8+ N 16 '87
The Sandinista heritage. C. Foster. il *Hist Today* 37:5-8 Ap '87
Two democrats betrayed [J. Marti and P. J. Chamorro] pors *Dep State Bull* 87:66 Mr '87

Industries
See also
Publishers and publishing—Nicaragua
Tourist trade—Nicaragua

Nationalism
Sandinismo: the nationalist faith of Nicaragua. C. C. O'Brien. *Cent Mag* 20:31-4 Jl/Ag '87

Politics and government
See also
National Reconciliation Commission (Nicaragua)
Nicaragua. Constitution
Press and politics—Nicaragua
After the contra war: time for peacemaking. M. D. Wilde. *Christ Century* 104:45 Ja 21 '87
The agony in Nicaragua. J. C. Erlick. il *U S News World Rep* 103:31 Jl 20 '87
Another grenade goes off under Reagan's contra strategy. B. Javetski and others. il *Bus Week* p53 Mr 2 '87
Another useful tool [discussion of April 18, 1987 article, Democrats and the Arias plan] L. Annunziata. *Nation* 244:565 My 2 '87
Apocalypse soon [effect of Central American peace plan on contra aid] J. Smolowe. il *Time* 130:34-6 S 21 '87
The battle of the isthmus [Reagan administration opposition to Central American peace plan] il *Progressive* 51:8-9 O '87
Beat the devil [pro contra reporting by W. Branigin of the Washington post] A. Cockburn. *Nation* 244:790-1 Je 13 '87
Beat the devil [reporting on death of B. E. Linder] A. Cockburn. *Nation* 244:636-7 My 16 '87
Bracing for the contras [Sandinista Army] C. A. Robbins. il *U S News World Rep* 102:30-1 Mr 9 '87
A bumpy road to democracy. H. Anderson. il *Newsweek* 110:38-9 O 5 '87
Can the contras go on? [cover story] J. LeMoyne. il map *N Y Times Mag* p32-5+ O 4 '87
Can the contras win? M. Singer. *Natl Rev* 39:30-4 F 13 '87

Can the Sandinistas still be stopped? G. Russell. *Commentary* 84:26-34 Jl '87
Captain Ahab vs. Moby Dick [Reagan roadblocks to Central American peace plan] G. J. Church. il *Time* 130:28 O 19 '87
The case for the contras. M. Kramer. il *U S News World Rep* 102:39-40 Je 1 '87
Caught in the cross fire [death of American engineer B. Linder] il *Newsweek* 109:47 My 11 '87
Central America: what are the alternatives? [address, April 21, 1987] E. Abrams. *Dep State Bull* 87:83-7 Jl '87
Central America: why peace talks aren't just talk. B. Javetski. il *Bus Week* p41 Ag 24 '87
Central America: will it be peace now? C. A. Robbins. il *U S News World Rep* 103:39-40 O 5 '87
Central American peace plan [address, August 22, 1987] R. Reagan. *Dep State Bull* 87:8 N '87
A Central American Yalta? [peace agreement] M. Kramer. il *U S News World Rep* 103:13 Ag 24 '87
The choice in Central America [peace plans] S. K. Purcell. bibl f map *Foreign Aff* 66:109-28 Fall '87
Congress shows its impatience [House votes for moratorium on aid to contras] R. Stengel. il *Time* 129:16+ Mr 23 '87
The contra contradiction. A. Neier. il *N Y Rev Books* 34:5-6 Ap 9 '87
A contra defection [resignation of A. Cruz] M. Satchell. il por *U S News World Rep* 102:18-19 Mr 23 '87
Contras: ending the pipe dreams. M. Kramer. il *U S News World Rep* 103:9 Ag 3 '87
Contras fear they're losing the peace. M. Speck. il *U S News World Rep* 103:36 S 21 '87
The contras in a squeeze. C. Lane. il *Newsweek* 110:55 N 9 '87
The contras' little list [American mercenary J. Adams discloses assassination plots against Nicaraguan leaders by the contras] A. Nairn. il *Progressive* 51:24-6 Mr '87
Contras to Ortega: your move. N. Cooper. il *Newsweek* 110:30 S 7 '87
Coping with the contras. J. Smolowe. il *Time* 129:38-9 Mr 30 '87
Costa Rican initiative [Arias plan; statement, March 6, 1987] E. Abrams. *Dep State Bull* 87:90-1 My '87
Could it be? [Nicaraguan ceasefire peace initiative] W. F. Buckley. *Natl Rev* 39:72-3 S 11 '87
Cover-up at 'The New York review' [criticism of R. Leiken's reports from Nicaragua by Tony Jenkins] A. Cockburn. *Nation* 245:9 Jl 4-11 '87
A crash course in democracy? [Sandinistas sign Guatemala accords] C. A. Robbins. il *U S News World Rep* 103:35 S 21 '87
Crunch time for the contras. R. Watson. il map *Newsweek* 109:24-6 Ja 19 '87
Cursed are the peacemakers. M. S. Serrill. il *Time* 130:30-1 Ag 24 '87
Deadline [Central American peace plan] *Time* 130:68 N 2 '87
Debating the peace plan [D. Ortega's visit to Washington] I. Austen. il por *Macleans* 100:18 N 23 '87
A defector's damaging tale [Nicaraguan defector R. Miranda's revelations] N. Cooper. il por *Newsweek* 110:49 D 21 '87
Democrats and the Arias plan [cover story] L. Annunziata. il *Nation* 244:489+ Ap 18 '87
A do-or-die offensive [trip with the contras] R. Nordland. il *Newsweek* 109:47 My 11 '87
An elusive cease-fire [Central American peace plan] C. A. Robbins. il *U S News World Rep* 103:49-50 N 16 '87
Embattled Nicaragua. F. D. Colburn. bibl f *Curr Hist* 86:405-8+ D '87
The end of the affair? [Central American peace plans and contra aid] J. Chace. bibl f il *N Y Rev Books* 34:24-6+ O 8 '87
The execution of Ben Linder. A. Cockburn. *Nation* 245:402-3 O 17 '87
Eyeing a dialogue [D. Ortega Saavedra agrees to peace talks with contras; with interview] J. Smolowe. il por *Time* 130:34-6 N 16 '87
Fallout from a defector [revelations from Nicaraguan defector R. Miranda] H. Anderson. il por *Newsweek* 110:26 D 28 '87
Feet people [fleeing refugees] R. Radosh. *New Repub* 196:15-17 Mr 9 '87
A fragile peace plan [indirect talks with the contras] A. Bilski. il *Macleans* 100:24 N 16 '87
The glimmer [Central American peace initiative] J. Klein. il *N Y* 20:16+ S 14 '87

Nicaragua—Politics and government—*cont.*

Golden opportunity for Don Oscar [O. Arias Sanchez awarded Nobel Peace Prize] J. Smolowe. il por *Time* 130:44+ O 26 '87

The growing enemies of a Managua cease-fire [Sandinista's amnesty program] C. A. Robbins. il *U S News World Rep* 103:37-8 O 26 '87

High stakes in Nicaragua. D. Reed. il *Read Dig* 131:72-7 S '87

The hole in the summit agenda. M. Kramer. il *U S News World Rep* 103:40 D 21 '87

How credible is the proposal on Nicaragua? [U.S. proposal] J. M. Wall. *Christ Century* 104:675-6 Ag 12-19 '87

How democratic is the Sandinista government? [debate at the Carter Presidential Center of Emory University] B. Spring. il *Christ Today* 31:48+ Ja 16 '87

If it's Tuesday, this must be Managua [work of S. Rushdie and P. Davis] C. Lane. *Wash Mon* 19:48-51 Je '87

Into the jungle. M. Kondracke. *New Repub* 196:14-17 Ap 6 '87

Is it the contras' last stand? A. Landaburu. *World Press Rev* 34:41 Mr '87

The Jim Wright shuffle [Central American peace plan] J. Morley. *Nation* 245:185+ S 5 '87

LeMoyne's progress [J. LeMoyne's Nicaraguan coverage in New York times] A. Cockburn. *Nation* 244:423 Ap 4 '87

Letter from Managua. R. O'Connor. il *Vogue* 177:176+ Ag '87

Lifeline for a rebellion [contras establish vital supply links] R. Chavira. il *Time* 129:40 Ap 27 '87

Little steps. *Natl Rev* 39:20-1 O 23 '87

Managua is waiting [excerpt from Where is Nicaragua?] P. Davis. il *Esquire* 107:171-4+ Mr '87

Mrs. Kirkpatrick visits Managua. W. F. Buckley. *Natl Rev* 39:67 N 20 '87

The new contras? R. Nordland. il map *Newsweek* 109:32-6+ Je 1 '87

New steps to Central American peace. M. Nichols. il *Macleans* 100:18-19 Ag 17 '87

Nicaragua. E. Bibb. il *Sch Update* 119:11-12 Mr 9 '87

Nicaragua [statement, November 3, 1986] H. S. Okun. *Dep State Bull* 87:82-4 Ja '87

Nicaragua: appearance v. reality. *Dep State Bull* 87:78 Mr '87

Nicaragua: at war with itself. J. Borrell. il *Time* 130:41-2 N 16 '87

Nicaragua cliffhanger. R. S. Leiken. *New Repub* 197:17-21 D 14 '87

Nicaragua revisited. R. Radosh. *New Repub* 197:20-2 Ag 3 '87

Nicaragua: the undeclared war hits home [special section] il *World Press Rev* 34:21-5 Ap '87

The Nicaraguan Catholic Church vs. the Sandinista Front. J. E. Cassidy. il *USA Today (Periodical)* 115:31-2 Ja '87

The Nobel difference [O. Arias wins Peace Prize for his Central American plan] H. Anderson. il por *Newsweek* 110:44+ O 26 '87

Not just one peace plan for Nicaragua, but two: Reagan and Central Americans unveil proposals. E. Magnuson. il *Time* 130:14-15 Ag 17 '87

Notes and comment [death of B. E. Linder and letter from friend Mira Brown] *New Yorker* 63:21-2 Je 8 '87

Notes and comment [U.S. reaction to peace plan] *New Yorker* 63:35-6 O 12 '87

Notes and comment [who are the contras?] *New Yorker* 63:19-20 Je 29 '87

Oh, brother—not again! [blunders by the Ortegas lend support to contra aid] J. Smolowe. il pors *Time* 130:33 D 28 '87

On the battle fronts [Central America and the Persian Gulf] D. Schorr. *New Leader* 70:6 O 19 '87

One hundred years of turpitude [cover story] A. Cruz, Jr. il *New Repub* 197:26-8+ N 16 '87

One last chance for the contras. T. Jenkins. il *Nation* 244:638-40 My 16 '87

Ortega gets the Wright stuff [Nicaraguan leader meets with congressman] C. A. Robbins. il por *U S News World Rep* 103:35 N 23 '87

Ortega gunplay [blunders may lead to new aid for contras] il por *U S News World Rep* 103:13 D 28 '87-Ja 4 '88

Ortega's dilemma. *Nation* 245:579-80 N 21 '87

Oscar's Nobel [Arias peace plan] M. Kondracke. *New Repub* 197:14-16 N 9 '87

Pack it in [resignation of A. Cruz] C. Lane. il *New Repub* 196:17-19 Ap 6 '87

Peace and the Central American drama. *America* 157:395-6 N 28 '87

Peace, democracy, and security in Central America [statement, September 10, 1987] G. P. Shultz. *Dep State Bull* 87:13-16 N '87

Peace plan problems [Arias plan] L. S. Robinson. *Commonweal* 114:580-2 O 23 '87

Peace scare. *New Repub* 197:4+ S 28 '87

Peaced off [Reagan-Wright plan upstaged by Central American peace proposal] F. Barnes. *New Repub* 197:10-11 Ag 31 '87

The phony peace [Reagan peace plan for Central America] *Nation* 245:147-8 Ag 29 '87

A plea to 'give peace a chance' [aid to contras undercut by peace plan] M. McDonald. il *Macleans* 100:32 O 5 '87

Positive containment in Nicaragua. V. P. Vaky. *Foreign Policy* 68:42-58 Fall '87

Potholes on the road to peace [U.S. delays Central American summit meeting; with interview with O. Arias Sánchez] J. Smolowe. il por *Time* 129:34+ Je 29 '87

The price of peace [Central American peace plan] M. Kempton. *N Y Rev Books* 34:46 S 24 '87

'Pricing the contras' [Central American peace initiative's effect on contra aid] H. Anderson. il *Newsweek* 110:24-5 Ag 24 '87

Pseudo-talks in Nicaragua. *Natl Rev* 39:16-17 D 4 '87

Puzzling out a peace plan. H. Rainie. il *U S News World Rep* 103:19 S 7 '87

Reagan peace plan: a win if it fails? J. Wallace. il *U S News World Rep* 103:24-5 Ag 17 '87

Reagan's dirty trick. W. Greider. il *Roll Stone* p31-2+ Ja 29 '87

Reinventing the contras [U.S. switches allegiance from A. Calero to A. Cruz] R. Watson. il pors *Newsweek* 109:32-4 My 2 '87

A reluctant contra's struggle for survival [N. Rivas] J. McPhaul. por *Sch Update* 119:16 Mr 9 '87

Rival plans, rival goals [Central American peace plans] B. Crozier. *Natl Rev* 39:30 S 25 '87

Robelo calls it quits [last major moderate leader of contras] por *Newsweek* 109:7 Ap 20 '87

The rule of reason [Central American peace plan] *Commonweal* 114:549 O 9 '87

The sad saga of a Sandalista [American volunteer worker B. Linder killed by contras] J. Smolowe. il por *Time* 129:34 My 11 '87

Security Council considers Nicaraguan complaint of 'serious incidents' in Central America. il *UN Chron* 24:64 F '87

Sergio Ramirez: the view from Managua [interview] C. Dreifus. il por *Progressive* 51:19-20 S '87

Shamed [R. Leiken's reporting criticized by Tony Jenkins] A. Cockburn. *Nation* 245:1-8 Jl '87

Should the Sandinistas be trusted? [peace plans] H. Anderson. il *Newsweek* 110:28+ Ag 31 '87

Should the U.S. support the contras? C. Krauthammer. il *Time* 129:81-2 Mr 2 '87

Sightseeing in Sandinistaland. P. J. O'Rourke. il *Roll Stone* p37-8 D 3 '87

Slipping and sliding around peace. J. Smolowe. il *Time* 130:28+ S 7 '87

Speaking his peace [O. Arias Sanchez addresses Congress] J. Smolowe. il por *Time* 130:34-5 O 5 '87

Still gunning for peace. J. Smolowe. il *Time* 130:72 N 9 '87

A tale of two cities. J. P. Fitzpatrick. *America* 157:4-5 Jl 4-11 '87

Tales of a Sandinista defector [Sandinista defector R. Miranda] J. Smolowe. il por *Time* 130:47 D 21 '87

Tangled Nicaragua: an exchange [discussion of December 5, 1985 article, The Nicaraguan tangle] R. S. Leiken. il *N Y Rev Books* 34:59-61 Ag 13 '87

Torpedoing the peace process? [Reagan's support for the contras] H. Anderson. il *Newsweek* 110:49 O 19 '87

A tug of war over peace [D. Ortega meets with Congressman J. Wright] H. Anderson. il pors *Newsweek* 110:34-6 N 23 '87

A twisting road to peace. C. Wood. il *Macleans* 100:19 Ag 31 '87

The war for Nicaragua [special section; with editorial comment by Kevin Doyle] il map *Macleans* 100:2, 16-20+ F 23 '87

War of words [Reagan's commitment to the contras blocks peace plan] P. R. Range. il *U S News World Rep* 103:10 O 19 '87

War on the installment plan [contras] J. V. Lamar, Jr. il *Time* 129:24 F 23 '87

Nicaragua—Politics and government—_cont._

The war that no one can cover [reporting on the contras] J. Borrell. il _Time_ 129:60 F 16 '87

Who wants peace? [Arias plan; cover story] M. Kondracke. _New Repub_ 197:16-19 S 28 '87

Whose peace plan is it anyway? J. Smolowe. por _Time_ 130:34 S 28 '87

Will Ortega play for peace—or play for time? [Central American peace agreement] J. L. Galloway. il por _U S News World Rep_ 103:30-1 Ag 24 '87

Will peace break out? [initiatives by R. Reagan and Central American governments] H. Anderson. il _Newsweek_ 110:16-18 Ag 17 '87

Will the Arias peace plan work? _World Press Rev_ 34:22-3 O '87

With aid, contras talk a better war. L. Balmaseda. il _U S News World Rep_ 102:32-3 Ja 26 '87

Wright is wrong [J. Wright meets with D. Ortega in Washington] _New Repub_ 197:7-8+ D 7 '87

The Wright stuff [congressman meets with Nicaraguan leader D. Ortega] J. Smolowe. il pors _Time_ 130:32-3 N 23 '87

A young Sandinista's effort to serve her nation [M. Arguello] J. Lantigua. il por _Sch Update_ 119:17 Mr 9 '87

Religious institutions and affairs
See also
　Catholic Church—Nicaragua
　Church and social problems—Nicaragua
　Church and state—Nicaragua

Nicaragua. Constitution

Religion and the Nicaraguan constitution. J. E. Mulligan. il _Christ Century_ 104:398-9 Ap 29 '87

Nicaragua and Europe
See also
　Nicaragua—Foreign opinion—European

Nicaragua and the United States

Notes and comment [Ann Arbor, Mich. donates garbage truck to sister city Juigalpa, Nicaragua] _New Yorker_ 63:15-16 Ag 17 '87

The other aid network [humanitarian aid from U.S.] R. Nordland. il _Newsweek_ 110:37 Jl 27 '87

Twisted sisters. J. L. Pasley. _New Repub_ 196:14+ Je 22 '87

Nicaragua in focus (Periodical)

The right books. C. Williamson. _Natl Rev_ 39:50 My 22 '87

Nicaragua in motion pictures

Contra-courant [A. Cox's film Walker] G. Fuller. il _Film Comment_ 23:50-1 Jl/Ag '87

Nicaragua: radical flick [A. Cox shoots movie based on exploits of American adventurer William Walker] R. Nordland. il por _Newsweek_ 109:44 Ap 20 '87

Rebel rouser [making of A. Cox's Walker] F. Schruers. il por _Roll Stone_ p29+ S 10 '87

Nicaraguan defectors _See_ Defectors, Political

Nicaraguan Humanitarian Assistance Office (U.S.)

Down the drain. P. Kornbluh. _Nation_ 245:452 O 24 '87

Nicaraguan refugees _See_ Refugees, Nicaraguan

Nicaraguans

United States

Are contras living it up in Miami? R. Parry. il _Newsweek_ 109:25 My 4 '87

The ballad of Fawn and Arturo [F. Hall and A. Cruz Jr.; cover story] J. Morley. il _Nation_ 245:397+ O 17 '87

'Little worm' or big fish? [Sandinista R. Miranda defects to the U.S.] N. Cooper. por _Newsweek_ 110:80 N 16 '87

Nice Restaurant (New York, N.Y.) _See_ New York (N.Y.)—Restaurants, nightclubs, bars, etc.

Niceness

Niceness (seasonally adjusted) is all. R. Alan. _New Leader_ 70:8-9 Ap 6 '87

Nicgorski, Darlene
about

Sister Darlene Nicgorski. R. Brown. il por _Ms_ 15:54+ Ja '87

Nichihara Observatory _See_ Astronomical observatories—Japan

Nicholas, Nicholas J., Jr.
about

Nick Nicholas. D. Lieberman. por _Bus Week_ Sp Issue:238 Ap 17 '87

Their Time. E. Diamond. il pors _N Y_ 20:29-31 O 12 '87

Time's Nick & Dick show [cover story] B. Nussbaum. il pors _Bus Week_ p54-7+ Ag 3 '87

Nicholls, Gerald P., and Deieso, Donald A.

New Jersey: involving the commercial sector. bibl f il map _Environment_ 29:12+ Mr '87

Nichols, Annabel

A tale of two brownstones: the New York residence of Annabel and Mike Nichols. il _Archit Dig_ 44:96-101+ F '87

Nichols, Bill
about

Nighttime smallmouths. M. Hicks. il por _Outdoor Life_ 180:78-9+ Jl '87

Nichols, Dan
about

A made-for-television movie brings biathlete Kari Swenson face-to-face with her past. M. Neill. il pors _People Wkly_ 27:76-8+ Mr 16 '87

Nichols, Don
about

A made-for-television movie brings biathlete Kari Swenson face-to-face with her past. M. Neill. il pors _People Wkly_ 27:76-8+ Mr 16 '87

Nichols, Frederick D.

Rooms architecturally redesigned by John Blatteau and Walter M. Macomber. il _Antiques_ 132:144-5 Jl '87

Nichols, John Treadwell, 1940-
Bibliography

Down the beanstalk. F. Pfeil. _Nation_ 244:857-60 Je 20 '87

Nichols, Kyra
about

Post-Balanchine breakthroughs. E. Kendall. pors _Vogue_ 177:48 Je '87

Nichols, Lisa
about

Designer Lisa Nichols can't make a stitch but she's a great knit-picker. K. Johnson. il por _People Wkly_ 27:98-9 F 16 '87

Nichols, Lorenzo
about

'Fat Cat' and the crack wars: brash young dealers muscle the drug establishment. P. Blauner. il por _N Y_ 20:46-54 S 7 '87

Nichols, Mike
about

A tale of two brownstones: the New York residence of Annabel and Mike Nichols. A. Nichols. il _Archit Dig_ 44:96-101+ F '87

Nichols, Robert G.

Satellites on a string. il _Sky Telesc_ 73:383-5 Ap '87

Nichols, Ron
about

Commerce Dept. black cites job bias and is demoted. por _Jet_ 73:17 N 30 '87

Nicholson, Ana Maria
about

Holography. _New Yorker_ 63:20-2 Ag 24 '87

Nicholson, Ivy
about

Ex-fashion model Ivy Nicholson hits the skids. il pors _People Wkly_ 27:37 F 16 '87

Nicholson, Jack
about

Jack Nicholson [interview] L. Hirschberg. il por _Roll Stone_ p236-9 N 5-D 10 '87

Nicholson, Louise

Delhi's cuisine and craftsmen. il _Gourmet_ 47:66-71+ S '87

Nicholson, Susan Brown

Collecting Christmas paper memorabilia [cover story] il _Antiques Collect Hobbies_ 92:52-3+ D '87

Nicholson, Thomas D.

Celestial events. See issues of Natural History

Nick Bollettieri Tennis Academy (Bradenton, Fla.)

Camp diary: blistered are the weak. L. Bragga. il _World Tennis_ 34:38-9 Ja '87

Sports schools go high tech. M. Wellemeyer. il _Fortune_ 115:119-20 F 16 '87

Nick Lyons Books

Angling for sales at Nick Lyons Books. M. Reuter. il _Publ Wkly_ 231:20-1 Ja 16 '87

Nickel, Steven

The real Eliot Ness. il pors _Am Hist Illus_ 22:42-52 O '87

Nickel

Sound waves for activating nickel [research by Kenneth S. Suslick and Dominick J. Casadonte] I. Peterson. _Sci News_ 131:388 Je 20 '87

Nickel-hydrogen storage batteries _See_ Storage batteries

Nickelodeon (Firm)

Selling the children. C. Capuzzi. il _Channels_ 7:60-1 Je '87

Nicklaus, Jack
about
One more time, Jack. J. G. Hubbell. il pors *Read Dig* 130:121-6 Ap '87
Nicklaus (Jack) Academy of Golf (Orlando, Fla.) *See* Jack Nicklaus Academy of Golf (Orlando, Fla.)
Nicknames
What's in a nickname? [college and professional sports teams] J. Leo. il *Time* 129:82 Ja 19 '87
Nicks, Stevie
about
Talking about each other: the women of Fleetwood Mac. C. Krupp. por *Glamour* 85:302 S '87
Nicogossian, Arnauld E.
about
The human factor: a conversation with Dr. Arnauld Nicogossian. T. Reichhardt and J. Rhea. il por *Space World* X-3-279:8-13 Mr '87
Nicol, Charles, 1940-
The hard-boiled go to brunch. il *Harpers* 275:61-5 O '87
Nicol, Stephen
Krill: food of the future? il *Sea Front* 33:12-17 Ja/F '87
Nicole, Roger
Universalism: will everyone be saved? il por *Christ Today* 31:32-9 Mr 20 '87
Nicoll, Peggy
Hypnosis power: tranceforming. il *Harpers Bazaar* 120:184+ Mr '87
Nicotinamide
Niacin: sweet hope for slowing diabetes [niacinamide] *Prevention* 39:52-3 O '87
Nicotine
Nicotine: addictive and spreads cancer? [research by Gesina L. Longenecker and others] D. D. Edwards. *Sci News* 131:213 Ap 4 '87
Nicotine chewing gum *See* Chewing gum
Nidal, Abu *See* Abu Nidal
Niebuhr, Reinhold, 1892-1971
about
Letters to Reinhold: Easter memories. U. M. Niebuhr. il *Christ Century* 104:357-8 Ap 15 '87
Letters to Reinhold: eating dill pickles in paradise. U. M. Niebuhr. *Christ Century* 104:663-4 Jl 29-Ag 5 '87
Prudence, humility and the Niebuhrian ethic. J. M. Wall. *Christ Century* 104:875-6 O 14 '87
Niebuhr, Ursula M.
Letters to Reinhold: Easter memories. il *Christ Century* 104:357-8 Ap 15 '87
Letters to Reinhold: eating dill pickles in paradise. *Christ Century* 104:663-4 Jl 29-Ag 5 '87
Niedner, Malcolm B., Jr., and Liller, William, 1927-
The IHW island network. il *Sky Telesc* 73:258-63 Mr '87
Niedzialek, Terry
about
New York artist Terry Niedzialek specializes in turban blight. il por *People Wkly* 27:47 Ja 12 '87
Niefer, Werner
about
"We are still saying hello to each other". P. Berman. il *Forbes* 139:94+ My 18 '87
Niekro, Phil
about
A season to remember. H. Quinn. il por *Macleans* 100:37 Ag 24 '87
Nielsen, Brigitte
about
Brigitte Nielsen. por *People Wkly* 28:68-9 D 28 '87-Ja 4 '88
Sly says bye, bye, Brigitte, and so a rocky marriage ends with a split decision. A. Richman. il pors *People Wkly* 28:38-9 Jl 27 '87
The Stallones: sex on the Sly? [cover story] J. Ash and others. pors *People Wkly* 28:48-9 Ag 10 '87
Nielsen, Erik, 1924-
about
'Yukon Erik' steps down. C. Barrett. il por *Macleans* 100:26 F 2 '87
Nielsen, John
Last chance for the condor. il *Sports Illus* 66:62+ Mr 23 '87
Nielsen (A. C.) Co. *See* A. C. Nielsen Co.
Nieves, Juan
about
Juan Nieves and the Brewers: miracles on tap in Milwaukee. S. K. Reed. il pors *People Wkly* 27:49-50 My 11 '87

Niger
See also
Deserts—Niger
Nigeria
See also
Nigerians
Public health—Nigeria
Riots—Nigeria
Politics and government
Nigeria between dictatorship and democracy. L. Diamond. bibl f *Curr Hist* 86:201-4+ My '87
Religious institutions and affairs
See also
Catholic Church—Nigeria
Missions—Nigeria
Muslims—Nigeria
Nigerians
United States
A bruiser from Azusa [football player C. Okoye] J. Lieber. il pors *Sports Illus* 66:42-4+ Ap 27 '87
Night
Into the night [views of M. Melbin] G. Williams. il *Omni* 9:36-8+ Jl '87
Night, the final frontier [excerpt from Night as frontier] M. Melbin. *Harpers* 274:30+ Mr '87
Night walking. J. Harrison. il *Roll Stone* p91+ Mr 26 '87
Night fishing *See* Fishing
Night flying *See* Aviation—Night flying
Night photography *See* Photography, Night
Night sky *See* Sky
Night vision devices
Expanded night-fighting capability shapes Army flight training needs [helicopters] il *Aviat Week Space Technol* 126:115+ Ja 19 '87
Martin develops simplified Flir for night-vision attack capability. *Aviat Week Space Technol* 127:101 S 21 '87
Nightclubs
See also
Comedy nightclubs
Discotheques
Tracks International Inc.
Everything old becomes new again [classy clubs] J. Conant. il *Newsweek* 109:67-8 My 11 '87
Hip hangouts for the jazz lover on the road. R. Hoffman. il *Bus Week* p118 Je 1 '87
Turn up the juice! [teenage nights at adult hot spots] il *Seventeen* 46:138 N '87
Nightgowns, pajamas, etc. *See* Sleepwear
Nightingale-Conant Corp.
'Instant' audios due from S & S, Nightingale-Conant. *Publ Wkly* 232:47-8 O 30 '87
S & S adds Nightingale-Conant audio line. *Publ Wkly* 231:57 My 22 '87
Nightline [television program] *See* Television program reviews—Single works
A nightmare on Elm Street, part 3: Dream warriors [film] *See* Motion picture reviews—Single works
Nightmares
All about nightmares. B. Davidson. il *Seventeen* 46:40 Ja '87
The fragile, creative side of nightmares [research by Ernest Hartmann and others] B. Bower. *Sci News* 131:37 Ja 17 '87
The Jung and the restless [college students' nightmares about exams] H. Ward. il *N Y* 20:23 Je 8 '87
Major league nightmares [baseball players] H. Hewes. il *Sport Mag* 78:79-81 Ag '87
Night of the living dread [views of Ernest Hartmann] L. Sage. il *Health* 19:20 Ag '87
Night visitors. A. S. Brodoff. *Vogue* 177:446 F '87
When bad dreams happen to good people. D. Carlson. *McCalls* 114:98 My '87
Nightshade (Plant)
See also
Jerusalem cherry
Long-blooming, flexible, easygoing . . . the solanum clan. il *Sunset* 178:178 Mr '87
Nigro, Peter D.
Reflections of an individual investor. il *USA Today (Periodical)* 116:27-8 N '87
NIH *See* National Institutes of Health (U.S.)
Nihon Keizai Shimbun, Inc.
Watch out Reuters, you, too, Dow Jones. M. Beauchamp. il *Forbes* 139:116+ My 4 '87
Nijinska, Bronislava, 1891-1972
about
Shakespeare's sister. H. Brubach. il *Atlantic* 259:86-8 F '87

Nijinsky, Waslaw, 1890-1950
about
Le sacre du printemps [ballet] Reviews
Dance Mag il 61:44-8 N '87. J. R. Acocella
Dance Mag il 61:49-51 N '87. R. Philp
N Y il 20:100 N 16 '87. T. Tobias
New Leader il por 70:22-3 N 30 '87. L. A. Jacobs
New Yorker il 63:140-2+ N 23 '87. A. Croce
Newsweek il 110:109 N 16 '87. L. Shapiro
Theatre Crafts il 21:15 D '87. B. Howard
Time il 130:97 N 16 '87. M. Duffy
Vogue il 177:114 N '87. L. Friedman
Nike Inc.
Beatles buy-out [Beatles song Revolution used in Nike
TV ad] J. Wiener. *New Repub* 196:13-14 My 11 '87
Beatles sue over Nike commercial. A. DeCurtis. *Roll
Stone* p15 S 10 '87
Looking for that strong finish. J. Heins. il por *Forbes*
139:74-5 My 4 '87
Nike hits its stride [stock price] A. E. Serwer. *Fortune*
116:98-9 Ag 31 '87
No pain, no gain. J. Sherman. il *Work Woman* 12:92
My '87
Running on recall [Beatles' song Revolution used in
Nike commercial] A. White. il *Film Comment* 23:72+
Jl/Ag '87
Wanna buy a Revolution? [Beatles song in Nike commer-
cial] J. Cocks. il *Time* 129:78 My 18 '87
Nikitin, Afanasii, d. 1472
Reflections on solitude. il *Courier* 40:15 Ap '87
Nikitine, Serge, 1904-1986
about
Obituary
Phys Today 40:126+ F '87. H. Haken
Nikkei Group *See* Nihon Keizai Shimbun, Inc.
Nikko Securities Co. Ltd.
Better late than never [New York subsidiary's government
bond chief R. Strausberg] B. Weberman. il por *Forbes*
139:282-3 Ja 12 '87
Niklas, Karl J.
Aerodynamics of wind pollination. bibl (p116) il *Sci
Am* 257:90-5 Jl '87
Nikolais, Alwin
about
Reviews:
Performances at the Joyce Theater, New York City.
R. A. Thom. *Dance Mag* 61:68-9+ Jl '87
Nikolais Dance Theatre
Reviews:
Performances at the Joyce Theater, New York City.
R. A. Thom. *Dance Mag* 61:68-9+ Jl '87
Nilson, Lisbet
Chicago's art explosion. il *Art News* 86:110-19 My '87
Nilsson, Birgit
about
Our favorite force of nature. G. Schmidgall. il pors
Opera News 52:20-2+ Jl '87
Nilsson, Sten, and Duinker, Peter
The extent of forest decline in Europe. bibl f il maps
Environment 29:4-9+ N '87
NIMBY syndrome
The NIMBY syndrome [not in my backyard rationale
in objecting to placement of public facilities]
Commonweal 114:310 My 22 '87
The NIMBY syndrome: is it inevitable? J. H. Gervers.
bibl f il *Environment* 29:18-20+ O '87
Nimmons, David
Medical miracles [special section] il *Ladies Home J*
104:125-8+ F '87
Nimmons, Willie Cam
about
First she did good, then she did well. R. Chepesiuk.
il por *Nations Bus* 75:66 N '87
Nimoy, Leonard
about
Three men and a baby [film] Reviews
Good Housekeep il 205:106+ N '87
Newsweek il 110:73 N 30 '87. D. Ansen
People Wkly il 28:14 D 14 '87. T. Cunneff
Nims, John Frederick, 1913-
Trick or treat [poem] *Atlantic* 260:92 N '87
Nina Wiener and Dancers
Hold me tight [performance of Fierce attachments at
the Brooklyn Academy of Music] T. Tobias. il *N
Y* 20:81-2 N 30 '87
Nindooinbah House (Queensland, Australia) *See* Historic
houses, sites, etc.—Queensland (Australia)
Nine (The number)
Nine: a nifty number, nein? S. Morris. il *Omni* 10:178-9
O '87

Nine Winds (Firm)
A fresh breeze. B. Shoemaker. *Down Beat* 11:34 N
'87
Nineteen hundred and eighty-eight
From Super Bowl to Super Tuesdays. D. Kalb and
I. Pazner. il *U S News World Rep* 103:5 D 28 '87-Ja
4 '88
A gaggle of New Year's guesses [celebrities' forecasts]
S. F. Golden and others. il *U S News World Rep*
103:116 D 28 '87-Ja 4 '88
Outlook '88 and beyond. il *Futurist* 21:53-60 N/D '87
Predictions '88. il *Health* 19:29 D '87
That was the year that will be [sports in 1988] M.
Lupica. il *Esquire* 108:81-2 D '87
Nineteen hundred and eighty-seven
The arts [special section] il *N Y* 20:105-8+ D 21-28
'87
The best and the worst of 1987. P. C. Newman. il
Macleans 100:32 D 21 '87
Health's 1987 annual report [special section] G. Bakoulis.
il *Health* 19:25-9+ D '87
The Honor Roll [cover story; special section; with editorial
comment by Kevin Doyle] il *Macleans* 100:2, 11-35
D 28 '87
Images of '87 [special section; with editorial comment
by Carl Mollins] il *Macleans* 100:34-48 D 21 '87
Music yearbook 1987 [cover story; special issue] il *Roll
Stone* p6-10+ D 17-31 '87
The national interest: winners and sinners. J. Klein.
il *N Y* 20:20+ D 21-28 '87
Of many things [Catholic news events] G. W. Hunt.
America 157:490 D 26 '87
Oliver North and the music of the night: reflections
on a year out of tune. L. Eisenberg. il *Esquire* 108:141+
D '87
Opinions: from Lacroix to La bamba: '87's high points
and low lives. il *Vogue* 177:314-17 D '87
Picks & pans. il *People Wkly* 28:12-14+ D 28 '87-Ja
4 '88
Science news of the year. il *Sci News* 132:400-6 D
19-26 '87
The televangelist fiasco: top '87 religion story. *Christ
Century* 104:1163-5 D 23-30 '87
The top 10 stories of 1987; Looking to 1988 and beyond.
R. Frame. il *Christ Today* 31:34-6+ D 11 '87
What's new for American families in '87 [special section]
K. Stechert. il *Better Homes Gard* 65:15+ Ja '87
Win a few, lose a few [review of events in women's
sports] il *Women's Sports Fitness* 9:74 D '87
Winners and sinners: media. E. Diamond. il *N Y* 20:34+
D 21-28 '87
Winners and sinners: the bottom line. J. Crudele. il
N Y 20:26+ D 21-28 '87
　　　　Anecdotes, facetiae, satire, etc.
Here today, gone today. R. Baker. il *N Y Times Mag*
p8 D 27 '87
Winners and sinners: on Madison Avenue. B. Kanner.
il *N Y* 20:30-2 D 21-28 '87
　　　　Photographs and photography
The best photos of 1987. il *Jet* 73:33+ D 28 '87-Ja
4 '88
Images 1987. il *Time* 130:36-44+ D 28 '87
Nineteen hundred and eighty-six
After 1986, nowhere to go but up [science and technology]
World Press Rev 34:56 F '87
America and the world 1986. bibl f *Foreign Aff* 65
Sp Issue:423-696 ['87]
The best outstanding achievements of 1986. il *Bus Week*
p123-31 Ja 12 '87
Cory Aquino: religious newsmaker no. 1. D. Peerman.
Christ Century 104:3-4 Ja 7-14 '87
A disturbing year past [religious news] M. E. Marty.
Christ Century 104:39 Ja 7-14 '87
The highs, the lows: lasting memories of 1986 [events
concerning women] K. Burkett and M. McNamara.
il *Ms* 15:19-21+ Ja '87
Nadirism [ten most depressing events of 1986] D. Selig-
man. il *Fortune* 115:119-20 Ja 19 '87
Physics news in 1986 [special section] P. F. Schewe.
il *Phys Today* 40:S1-S70 Ja '87
Three balls, two strikes. G. F. Will. il *Newsweek* 109:64
Ja 5 '87
The top 10 news stories of 1986. B. Shelby. il *World
Press Rev* 34:8+ F '87
The top ten stories of 1986 [religious news] R. Frame.
il *Christ Today* 31:38-9+ Ja 16 '87
The weather of 1986 [cover story; special issue] il
Weatherwise 40:8-44 F '87
　　　　Anecdotes, facetiae, satire, etc.
Dubious achievements of 1986! il *Esquire* 107:55-8+ Ja
'87

Nineteen hundred and eighty-six—Anecdotes, facetiae, satire, etc.—*cont.*

The year that was [1986] M. Ivins. il *Progressive* 51:18 F '87

Photographs and photography

The year in pictures '86 [special issue; with editorial comment by Judith Daniels] il *Life* 10:5, 8-19+ Ja '87

Nineteen hundred and fifties

The '50s have gotten a bum rap [interview with W. L. O'Neill] A. P. Sanoff. il por *U S News World Rep* 102:74 Mr 23 '87

Back to the 'fifties [fashion] K. Beckett. *Vogue* 177:168+ F '87

Fab '50s [special section] il *Harpers Bazaar* 120:254-63 Mr '87

Fab '50s: the now look. R. Horn. il *Harpers Bazaar* 120:274-7+ Mr '87

Joe College: memories of a fifties education [cover story] P. Roth. il *Atlantic* 260:41-8+ D '87

Look back with glamour. il *Vogue* 177:388+ Mr '87

Mom was mad for 'em (you will be too!). J. Romberger. il *Teen* 31:22+ D '87

Trivial pursuits: investing for fun in the toys and kitsch of the fabulous '50s. H. Wheelwright. il *Money* 16:65-6+ D '87

Anecdotes, facetiae, satire, etc.

Fast forward to the past. P. Frost. *New Yorker* 63:26-7 Jl 6 '87

Nineteen hundred and fifty-one

Down in the wiregrass [memories of Ozark, Ala. youth] L. Wells. il *South Living* 22:108 Jl '87

Nineteen hundred and forty-five

Was 1945 a break in history? M. S. Sherry. bibl f il *Bull At Sci* 43:12-15 Jl/Ag '87

Nineteen hundred and forty-seven

1947, a year to remember [first issue of Road & track] L. Keeton. il *Road Track* 38:120+ Je '87

Nineteen hundred and nineties

The 1990s [special section] il *Fortune* 115:22-4+ F 2 '87

Nineteen hundred and sixties

See also

Student movement—History

Dreams of the sixties. A. Brinkley. bibl f il *N Y Rev Books* 34:10+ O 22 '87

Mom was mad for 'em (you will be too!). J. Romberger. il *Teen* 31:22+ D '87

Resurrecting the new left. S. McConnell. *Commentary* 84:31-8 O '87

Twentieth anniversary [Rolling stone; cover story; special issue] il *Roll Stone* p7+ N 5-D 10 '87

Anecdotes, facetiae, satire, etc.

Blowing up the 60's. B. Stein. il *N Y Times Mag* p14 F 22 '87

Fast forward to the past. P. Frost. *New Yorker* 63:26-7 Jl 6 '87

Harry, Krishna, and me. P. J. O'Rourke. *New Repub* 197:16-18 N 2 '87

Let the sixties die. P. J. O'Rourke. il *Roll Stone* p114-16 S 24 '87

Photographs and photography

An easy rider's lens [photos by D. Hooper] D. Davis. il *Newsweek* 109:83 Je 8 '87

Nineteen hundred and sixty-four

1964 [excerpt from Be true to your school] B. Greene. il por *Esquire* 107:86-90+ F '87

Nineteen hundred and sixty-seven

20 years ago. M. LaRue. il *Theatre Crafts* 21:10-11+ My '87

Flower power revisited [cover story] R. Wolmuth. il *People Wkly* 27:92-7+ Je 22 '87

Nineteen hundred and thirty-seven

The year of living nervously [marking the fiftieth anniversary of a great many things] B. Barol. il *Newsweek* 109:84-5 Je 8 '87

Nineteen hundred and twelve

A glimpse of 1912. H. Altman. il *Nations Bus* 75:20-1 S '87

Nineteen hundred and two

1902 [American art] R. Lynes. il *Art News* 86:154-6 N '87

Nineties (Decade) *See* Nineteen hundred and nineties

Nintendo Co. Ltd.

Here come the Super Mario Bros. N. Gross. il *Bus Week* p138 N 9 '87

Nios, Lake (Cameroon) *See* Lake Nyos (Cameroon)

Nipon, Albert

about

After 20 months behind bars, a chastened Albert Nipon is trying to sew up the dress market again. B. Johnson. il pors *People Wkly* 28:91-2 Ag 31 '87

Pearl picks up the pieces. M. Rowland. il pors *Work Woman* 12:114-17 My '87

Nipon, Pearl

about

Pearl picks up the pieces. M. Rowland. il pors *Work Woman* 12:114-17 My '87

Nipon (Albert), Inc. *See* Albert Nipon, Inc.

Nipp, Susan Hagen

about

Take a gander at Mother Goose's newest champions, Pam Beall and Susan Nipp of Wee Sing. A. Chambers. il pors *People Wkly* 28:66+ S 14 '87

Nippon Electric Co., Ltd. *See* NEC Corp.

Nippon Gakki Co. Ltd.

Create or die. A. Tanzer. il *Forbes* 139:52+ Ap 6 '87

Nippon Life Insurance Co.

It won't stop with the Shearson deal [buys stake in Shearson Lehman Brothers] W. Glasgall and T. Aritake. il *Bus Week* p36 Ap 6 '87

No place like home. J. Heins. il *Forbes* 140:104 N 16 '87

Nippon Telegraph & Telephone Corporation

A 16-megabit memory chip from Japan [dynamic random access memory] A. L. Robinson. il *Science* 235:1324-5 Mr 13 '87

Data General gets the call. L. Helm and N. Gross. il *Bus Week* p96 O 19 '87

The submicron era may belong to the Japanese [dynamic random access memory chips] O. Port. il *Bus Week* p98 Mr 16 '87

Nippon Telegraph & Telephone Public Corporation

See also

Nippon Telegraph & Telephone Corporation

Nipson, Herb

about

Backstage. pors *Ebony* 42:29 O '87

Nisbet, Robert A.

America as utopia: the city upon a hill. *Current* 293:4-8 Je '87

Nisbett, Richard E., and others

Teaching reasoning. bibl f il *Science* 238:625-31 O 30 '87

Nishioka, Charles K.

about

Slow and steady wins the race. R. Thompson. il pors *Nations Bus* 75:63-4 Ag '87

Nishioka (Charles K.) & Son *See* Charles K. Nishioka & Son

Nisho NoHo (New York, N.Y.: Restaurant) *See* New York (N.Y.)—Restaurants, nightclubs, bars, etc.

Nissan (Automobile) *See* Automobiles, Foreign; Sports cars

Nissan Design International

Miscellaneous ramblings [designer G. Hirshberg, formerly know as singer Jerry Paul] J. Dinkel. il *Road Track* 38:33-4 Ja '87

Nissan Motor Co. Ltd.

Creating a new culture [Y. Kume] F. H. Katayama. il por *Fortune* 116:48 Ag 3 '87

Jackson buys California automobile dealership [R. Jackson] por *Jet* 73:48 N 9 '87

Life at Nissan: paradise lost? [UAW's new drive to unionize Smyrna, Tenn. plant] B. Turque and J. B. Copeland. il *Newsweek* 110:50 Ag 10 '87

Nissan, Tennessee [poor treatment of workers at Smyrna plant; cover story] J. Junkerman. il *Progressive* 51:16-18+ Je '87

Reggie purchases stake in Nissan dealership [R. Jackson] *Jet* 73:50 O 26 '87

Shoot-out in Los Angeles: how Chiat/Day captured Nissan. J. Flynn and R. Grover. il *Bus Week* p70-1 Ag 17 '87

Nitinol

New uses for nitinol, the miracle metal. S. Morris. il *Omni* 9:123-4 F '87

Nitrides

See also

Boron nitrides

Nitrites

A safer strip [bacon curer Cure-trol avoids use of sodium nitrite] P. McCarthy. il *Health* 19:11 F '87

Nitrogen

See also

Feeds—Nitrogen content

Plants—Nitrogen content

Water—Nitrogen content

Nitrogen—*cont.*

Quantitative three-dimensional optical tomographic imaging of supersonic flows. G. W. Faris and R. L. Byer. bibl f il *Science* 238:1700-2 D 18 '87

Nitrogen cycle (Biogeochemistry)

Nitrogen: regional contributions to the global cycle. G. P. Robertson. bibl il *Environment* 28:16-20+ D '86

Nitrogen dioxide pollution of the air *See* Air pollution

Nitrogen fertilizers *See* Fertilizers and manures

Nitrogen oxide pollution of the air *See* Air pollution

Nitrogenous bases

Play the right bases, and you'll hear Bach [music derived from DNA bases; work of S. Ohno] il *Discover* 8:10+ Mr '87

Nitrosamines

Needed: a cure for curing snuff [research by William J. Chamberlain and others] S. Weisburd. *Sci News* 132:169 S 12 '87

Nitze, Paul H.

Developments in NST issues after Reykjavik [statement, December 4, 1986] *Dep State Bull* 87:33-6 Mr '87

Interpreting the ABM Treaty [address, April 1, 1987] *Dep State Bull* 87:31-3 Je '87

The nuclear and space negotiations: translating promise to progress [address, January 14, 1987] *Dep State Bull* 87:29-33 Mr '87

Permitted and prohibited activities under the ABM Treaty [address, October 31, 1986] *Dep State Bull* 87:39-40 Ja '87

about

Arms and the man. S. Talbott. por *Time* 130:76-8 D 21 '87

Niven, Fernanda

Late summer spice. il por *House Gard* 159:200-2 S '87

about

Down the garden path. C. Vogel. il *N Y Times Mag* p68-71 Je 28 '87

Nivens, Beatryce

Work it out! See occasional issues of Essence

Nix, Robert N. C., d. 1987

about

Obituary

Jet por 72:6 Jl 13 '87

Nixon, E. D.

about

Obituary

Jet il por 71:7 Mr 16 '87

Nixon, Jimmy

about

Keeping flamingos under his wing. B. Krist. il por *Int Wildl* 17:46-51 Ja/F '87

Nixon, Joan Lowery, 1927-

Creating suspense in the young mystery. *Writer* 100:19-21+ O '87

Nixon, Julie *See* Eisenhower, Julie Nixon, 1947-

Nixon, Patricia

about

"I think your mommy's had a stroke" [excerpt from Pat Nixon: the untold story] J. N. Eisenhower. il por *Saturday Evening Post* 259:60-1+ Ap '87

Nixon, Richard M. (Richard Milhous), 1913-

Richard Nixon on world leadership's indispensable ingredient. il por *Life* 10:30-1 O '87

about

Advice from the third man. S. Talbott. il pors *Time* 130:18 N 30 '87

Benefits of an INF agreement. G. P. Shultz. *Dep State Bull* 87:17-18 Jl '87

'The best and worst of presidents' [interview with S. E. Ambrose] A. P. Sanoff. il pors *U S News World Rep* 102:67-8 My 4 '87

Déjà vu all over again. *Nation* 245:665 D 5 '87

An interview with Richard Nixon. J. F. Stacks and S. Talbott. il por *Time* 129:23 My 4 '87

Making up the truth. G. C. Ward. il *Am Herit* 38:18+ S/O '87

Protocol and peace. W. F. Buckley. *Natl Rev* 39:54 Je 5 '87

A reply to Nixon and Kissinger. G. P. Shultz. il por *Time* 129:40 My 18 '87

Requiem for a deposed leader [conference at Hofstra University] J. Adler. il pors *Newsweek* 110:60-1 N 30 '87

Archives

History deleted [Justice Dept.'s attempt to win R. M. Nixon the right to keep secret thousands of historically significant documents] *Nation* 244:669-70 My 23 '87

Homes

A small town fights for native son Nixon [Yorba Linda, Calif.] S. Angel. il *50 Plus* 27:14+ Ja '87

Press relations

How I made the enemies list. H. Sidey. il por *Time* 129:26 Je 8 '87

Sports

Nixon: the fairway tapes [excerpt from Slammin' Sam] S. Snead. *Harpers* 274:28 Ja '87

Nixon, Richard M. (Richard Milhous), 1913-, and Kissinger, Henry, 1923-

A real peace. *Natl Rev* 39:32-4 My 22 '87

Nixon, Rob

Optimistic tragedies. *Nation* 245:453-4 O 24 '87

Nixon in China [opera] *See* Adams, John

NKDP *See* New Korea Democratic Party (Korea: South)

NL Industries, Inc.

Harold Simmons is set to roll another seven [proposal to merge into Valhi] G. G. Marcial. il por *Bus Week* p106 O 5 '87

NLM *See* National Library of Medicine (U.S.)

NLRB *See* United States. National Labor Relations Board

NMF *See* National Medical Fellowships

NMR (Nuclear magnetic resonance) *See* Magnetic resonance imaging

NNPA *See* National Newspaper Publishers Association

No exit [drama] *See* Sartre, Jean Paul, 1905-1980

No fire escape in hell [dance] *See* Dance reviews—Single works

No man's land [film] *See* Motion picture reviews—Single works

No mercy [film] *See* Motion picture reviews—Single works

No smoking laws and regulations *See* Smoking—Laws and regulations

No-tillage agriculture *See* Tillage

No way out [film] *See* Motion picture reviews—Single works

No way to treat a lady [musical] *See* Musicals, revues, etc.—Reviews—Single works

NOAA *See* United States. National Oceanic and Atmospheric Administration

Noah, Barbara

about

Barbara Noah. L. Smallwood. *Art News* 86:57 My '87

Noah, Timothy

Computer congressmen. *New Repub* 196:10-12 Ap 6 '87

War Powers inaction. *New Repub* 197:11-12 Jl 6 '87

Noah, Yannick

about

Yannick Noah to divorce, resumes tennis career. il por *Jet* 73:48 O 26 '87

Noah's ark toys *See* Toys

Nobel Foundation

Fattening up the Nobel Prize [going public] J. Kapstein. *Bus Week* p48 O 26 '87

Nobel prizes

The 1987 Nobel Prize for Physics [awarded to J. G. Bednorz and K. A. Muller] M. M. Waldrop. il pors *Science* 238:481-2 O 23 '87

Antibody research garners Nobel Prize [work of S. Tonagawa] J. L. Marx. il por *Science* 238:484-5 O 23 '87

Bednorz and Müller win Nobel Prize for new superconducting materials. A. Khurana. il pors *Phys Today* 40:17-19 D '87

Blessed are the peacemakers [O. Arias wins Nobel Peace Prize for Central American plan] *America* 157:283-4 O 31 '87

Brodsky's Nobel: what the applause was about [Literature Prize winner] S. Heaney. por *N Y Times Book Rev* 92:1+ N 8 '87

Chemistry in the image of biology [molecular recognition research] R. Lewin. il pors *Science* 238:611-12 O 30 '87

Fattening up the Nobel Prize [Nobel Foundation going public] J. Kapstein. *Bus Week* p48 O 26 '87

Feats of inspiration and originality [winners in the fields of physics, chemistry, and medicine] M. D. Lemonick. il *Time* 130:134 O 26 '87

Golden opportunity for Don Oscar [O. Arias Sanchez awarded Peace Prize] J. Smolowe. il por *Time* 130:44+ O 26 '87

Hard chargers find the keys to glory [S. Tonegawa and other science winners] S. Budiansky. il por *U S News World Rep* 103:12-13 O 26 '87

The heart & mind of a genius [R. Levi-Montalcini] F. Randall. il por *Vogue* 177:480-1+ Mr '87

Herschbach, Lee and Polanyi receive 1986 Chemistry Nobel. P. H. Andersen. il pors *Phys Today* 40:17-20 Mr '87

Light, darkness and bridges in Norway [E. Wiesel's acceptance of Peace Prize] R. M. Brown. *Christ Century* 104:5-6 Ja 7-14 '87

Nobel prizes—*cont.*

Lyrics of loss, theories of gain [awarded to J. Brodsky for literature and R. Solow for economics] P. Gray; P. Elmer-DeWitt. il pors *Time* 130:80 N 2 '87

Medicine, chemistry, physics Nobels announced [S. Tonegawa and others] S. Eisenberg. il por *Sci News* 132:244 O 17 '87

The Nobel difference [O. Arias wins Peace Prize for his Central American plan] H. Anderson. il por *Newsweek* 110:44+ O 26 '87

Nobel dynamite [J. Brodsky wins Literature Prize] *Natl Rev* 39:21 N 20 '87

The Nobel Prize deferred again [R. P. Warren] P. H. Samway. *America* 157:359+ N 14 '87

Nobel Prize for theory of economic growth [theories of R. M. Solow] E. Marshall. il por *Science* 238:754-5 N 6 '87

Nobel prizes. *Sci Am* 257:45-6+ D '87

Nobel winner Oscar Arias makes Costa Rica the mouse that roars for peace in Central America. M. Brower. il pors *People Wkly* 28:57-8+ N 9 '87

Of many things [Peace Prize winner M. Corrigan] G. W. Hunt. *America* 157:370 N 21 '87

Oscar's Nobel [Arias peace plan] M. Kondracke. *New Repub* 197:14-16 N 9 '87

Outstanding Nobel achievements. M. McIver. il *Macleans* 100:48 O 26 '87

Physics Nobel Prize. P. F. Schewe. bibl f *Phys Today* 40:S70 Ja '87

Physics Nobel Prize awarded for microscopies old and new. B. M. Schwarzschild. il pors *Phys Today* 40:17-21 Ja '87

Poetry's laureate in exile [J. Brodsky wins Literature Prize] J. Kroll. il por *Newsweek* 110:66 N 2 '87

What's in a middle name? Ask Donald Cram, carpet cleaner, and Donald Cram, Nobel laureate. il pors *People Wkly* 28:61 N 2 '87

Wole Soyinka: Nobel laureate. P. Garland. il pors *Ebony* 42:141-2+ Ap '87

Anecdotes, facetiae, satire, etc.

Nobel undertakings. E. Larson. *Omni* 9 Omni Exper:10 Ap '87

History

Bumps and falls on the road to Stockholm. D. Dickson. il *Science* 238:263-4 O 16 '87

Nobility

See also

Titles of honor and nobility

France

Conflict in continuity in 17th-century France. R. Mettam. bibl il *Hist Today* 37:30-5 F '87

Germany (West)

Need a little blueblood to go? Does Germany's Wolfgang Schrell have a princess for you! M. Neill. il pors *People Wkly* 28:159-60 D 7 '87

Great Britain

London journal [R. A. Smith, auctioneer of English titles] J. Bainbridge. il *Gourmet* 47:28+ My '87

Poor little rich girls [19th century American heiresses who married British nobility] C. M. Wallace. il *Forbes* 140 Sp Issue:62+ O 26 '87

Richard Wortley, a Yankee from Maine, joins Britain's ruling class as the new Earl of Wharncliffe. W. Plummer. il por *People Wkly* 27:94-5 Je 29 '87

Noble, Betsy

about

Win, place and sew. D. Marth. il por *Nations Bus* 75:65 F '87

Noble, David F.

about

Professor sues MIT over tenure. D. L. Goodman. *Progressive* 51:13 Je '87

Noble, Holcomb B.

A joyful noise. il *N Y Times Mag* p31 D 27 '87

Noble, Mark

about

Engineering his way to success. L. Gite. il por *Black Enterp* 17:92-3 F '87

Nocera, Joseph

Amy's day. *New Repub* 196:11-13 My 11 '87

Iacocc-heads. *New Repub* 196:32-6 Mr 2 '87

My life as a Texan. *New Repub* 196:19-23 Ap 13 '87

Les noces [ballet] See Ballet reviews—Single works

Nochlin, Linda

Art: a sense of fashion: paintings that capture the elements of style. il *Archit Dig* 44:110-15+ F '87

Noctilucent clouds

Clouds of the twilight. D. McConnell. il *Astronomy* 15:42-7 Jl '87

More on noctilucent clouds. il *Sky Telesc* 74:7 Jl '87

Noe, Alfonso

Maximum beauty. *50 Plus* 27:49 S '87

Noe, Booker

about

Whiskey Land, USA, Booker Noe, Prop. J. E. Bradley. il pors *Esquire* 108:204-8+ S '87

Noel, Claude

about

What's ahead for the church in Haiti? [interview] il por *Christ Today* 31:60-1 N 20 '87

Noel, Patrick

about

Breaking ground. L. Brown. il por *Black Enterp* 18:76-8+ O '87

Noga, Edward J.

Propagation in cell culture of the dinoflagellate Amyloodinium, an ectoparasite of marine fishes. bibl f il *Science* 236:1302-4 Je 5 '87

Noglows, Paul

How they got that story. il *Channels* 7:29-30+ N '87

Nogrady, John

Patterned play: a lost art. il *World Tennis* 35:76 S '87

Noguchi, Isamu, 1904-

One carves the whole of the hole. il por *Art News* 86:15 O '87

about

Metaphors for the world. R. Tracy. il por *Archit Dig* 44:72+ O '87

Noguchi (Isamu) Garden Museum See Isamu Noguchi Garden Museum

Noise

See also

Airplanes—Noise

Airplanes, Military—Noise

Airports—Noise

Audio systems—Noise

Automobiles—Noise

Fishing—Noise

Helicopters—Noise

Hunting—Noise

Motorcycles—Noise

Radio receivers—Noise

Silence

Tape recorders and recording—Noise

Tinnitus

Videotape recorders and recording—Noise

Physiological effects

Developmental stability of the tonotopic organization of the chick's basilar papilla. G. A. Manley and others. bibl f il *Science* 237:655-6 Ag 7 '87

How noise can harm your hearing. H. Twidale. il *Good Housekeep* 204:215 Je '87

Noise control

See also

Airports—Noise

Soundproofing

Noise zapper [selective sound wave cancellation] J. Free. il *Pop Sci* 230:76-7+ Ja '87

Noise reduction systems See Tape recorders and recording—Noise

Nokes, Matt

about

Matt Nokes. A. Murphy. il pors *Sports Illus* 67:53 Jl 13 '87

Nolan, David

Airline safety: a shocking truth. il *Read Dig* 130:125-30 Ja '87

Nolan, William F., 1928-

Horror fiction: exploring the dark side. *Writer* 100:20-3 D '87

Noland, David

A man who defies the laws. por *Discover* 8:46-8+ My '87

Nolen, William A., 1928-1986

Bellevue: no one was ever turned away. il *Am Herit* 38:36-43 F/Mr '87

about

Obituary

50 Plus por 27:4 Mr '87. B. Lindeman

Noles, Janice

[Month] in the South. See issues of Southern Living beginning February 1987

Noll, Mark A., 1946-

Reasons and arguments in the Constitution. il *Christ Century* 104:499-500+ My 20-27 '87

Should Christians join the celebration? il por *Christ Today* 31:18-23 Jl 10 '87

Nolley, Betty

Last gas for 22,000 miles. il *Space World* X-2-278:26-8 F '87

Nolting, Mark
about
African safari guide from new Florida publisher. por *Publ Wkly* 231:60 Je 12 '87
Nomads
See also
Bedouins
Tuaregs
Beating the odds in arid Africa [Turkana of Kenya] J. T. McCabe and J. E. Ellis. il map *Nat Hist* 96:32-41 Ja '87
Tibetan nomads: 'high' living . . . combined with low blood pressure [Phala nomads] *Sci News* 131:312 My 16 '87
Nominations for office
See also
Presidents—Nomination
Nomura Securities Co. Ltd.
'Making money, winning fame' [chairman Y. Tabuchi] *U S News World Rep* 102:63-4 My 11 '87
More than a yen [buys interest in Eastdil Realty] J. Willoughby. il por *Forbes* 139:122 F 9 '87
Nomura: land of the rising young. B. Buell. il por *Bus Week* p51-2 N 30 '87
Non-Governmental Organizations Committee (United Nations) *See* United Nations. Committee on Non-Governmental Organizations
Non-governmental organizations of the United Nations *See* United Nations—Non-governmental organizations
Non sedative antihistamines *See* Antihistamines
Non-wage payments *See* Fringe benefits
Nonalcoholic wine *See* Wine, Nonalcoholic
Nonaligned nations conferences *See* International conferences
Nondasuta, Amorn, and Piyarath, Prapont
Basic minimum needs. il *World Health* p14-15 Je '87
Nonenzymatic browning *See* Browning
Nonferrous metal mining industry *See* Mining industry
Nonfiction *See* Literature
Nonkin, Lesley Jane, 1957-
Catch-28. il *Work Woman* 12:118-20+ My '87
Women and cars. See issues of Vogue beginning January 1986
Nonprescription drugs *See* Medicines, Nonprescription
Nonprofit hospitals *See* Hospitals
Nonprofit institutions
See also
Charities
There's big money in the 'nonprofits'. E. Calonius. il *Newsweek* 109:38 Ja 5 '87
Employees
Characteristics of workers in nonprofit organizations. D. Johnston and G. Rudney. bibl f il *Mon Labor Rev* 110:28-33 Jl '87
Salaries, pensions, etc.
How to negotiate nonprofit salaries. L. Angell. *Work Woman* 12:27-8 D '87
Taxation
Profits? Who, me? L. Saunders. il *Forbes* 139:106+ Mr 23 '87
What's a nonprofit business, anyway? il *Fortune* 116:12+ Ag 3 '87
Nonproliferation policy *See* Disarmament
Nonsense literature
Let's talk nonsense. A. Burgess. il *N Y Times Book Rev* 92:1+ Ag 9 '87
Nonverbal communication *See* Communication, Nonverbal
Nonviolence
See also
Hunger strikes
Martin Luther King, Jr. Center for Nonviolent Social Change
Martin Luther King, Jr. Nonviolent Peace Prize
Palestine Center for Non-Violent Resistance
The nonviolent alternative [interview with L. E. Norman] D. McDonald. por *Cent Mag* 20:20-5 Ja/F '87
Notes and comment [N. O'Brien's views on revolutionary nonviolence in the Philippines] *New Yorker* 62:23-5 Ja 19 '87
Noonday Press
Wasserman named publisher of Noonday Press, Hill and Wang. por *Publ Wkly* 232:12 S 11 '87
Noor al-Hussein *See* Nur el Hussein, Queen, consort of Hussein, King of Jordan
Noorda, Raymond J.
The shifting meaning of connectivity. por *Pers Comput* 11:248 O '87

NORAD *See* North American Aerospace Defense Command
NORAID
An Ulster blast heard in Boston [Enniskillen bombing] M. Satchell. il *U S News World Rep* 103:14 N 23 '87
Norbek, Tim
Medicare and seniors [address, February 2, 1987] *Vital Speeches Day* 53:414-16 Ap 15 '87
Norberg, John
AIDS is a human disease. il pors *Saturday Evening Post* 259:52-3 O '87
Norberg-Hodge, Helena
about
Tibetan society bridges the future. T. L. Barnett. il por *Progressive* 51:15 Ap '87
Norberg-Schulz, Christian
The art of persuasion. il *Courier* 40:42-5 S '87
Norcross (Ga.)
Police
NFL Falcons' star sues Ga. police for $400,000 [W. Andrews] *Jet* 72:50 Jl 27 '87
Nordic machines *See* Exercising equipment
Nordic ski racing *See* Ski racing
Nordio, Umberto
Of cookies, convoys and Cassandra [address, January 10, 1987] *Vital Speeches Day* 53:439-41 My 1 '87
Nordquist, Doug
about
A man of bars and measures. R. Wiley. il pors *Sports Illus* 66:50+ Je 15 '87
Nordstrom, Inc.
Nordstrom's high style. P. Abramson. il *Newsweek* 109:43 Ja 5 '87
Why rivals are quaking as Nordstrom heads east. J. O. Hamilton. il *Bus Week* p99-100 Je 15 '87
Norfleet, Janet
about
Chicago woman tabbed for top Post Office job. por *Jet* 72:18 Ap 6 '87
Janet Norfleet: in charge of the world's largest post office. F. White, III. il pors *Ebony* 42:80+ Jl '87
Norfolk (Va.)
Education
Aid for unwed teens [job training program subsidized by Systems Management American Corp.] S. S. Harrison. *Black Enterp* 17:17 Mr '87
A call for Comer [J. P. Comer hired as consultant] S. S. Harrison. por *Black Enterp* 17:20 Ap '87
Festivals
Norfolk salutes spring [International Azalea Festival] C. Griffith. il *South Living* 22:12-13+ Ap '87
Galleries and museums
See also
Chrysler Museum
Waterfront
John Sears has brought Norfolk change. D. Young. il por *South Living* 22:160+ Ap '87
Norfolk Southern Corporation
Piedmont is in play—and Norfolk Southern is flying. C. S. Eklund and S. Ticer. il *Bus Week* p37 F 9 '87
Norfork Lake (Ark.)
Relaxing on Norfork Lake. il *South Living* 22:35 Ag '87
Noriega, Manuel Antonio
about
Backing away from a Latin dictator. T. Gup. il por *Time* 130:21 S 7 '87
The battle for 50th Street. N. Cooper. il por *Newsweek* 110:42-3 Ag 10 '87
A colonel takes on the general. M. S. Serrill. il por *Time* 129:40 Je 22 '87
Cracking down on Panama's general. C. A. Robbins. il por *U S News World Rep* 103:30 Ag 10 '87
Defying the strong man. B. Levin. il por *Macleans* 100:18 Ag 10 '87
Dirty dollars. J. Moody. il por *Time* 129:44-5 Ja 19 '87
Dishonor thy general. H. Anderson. il por *Newsweek* 109:37 Je 22 '87
Down and dirty. *Time* 130:42 Ag 17 '87
The general went to work. J. Smolowe. il por *Time* 130:21 Ag 10 '87
The general who won't go [interview] J. Smolowe. il por *Time* 130:36-8 Jl 20 '87
No, no Noriega. M. Kondracke. *New Repub* 197:4 O 5 '87
Panama: disaster or democracy. R. Arias Calderón. bibl f *Foreign Aff* 66:328-47 Wint '87/'88
Panama fallen among thieves. G. Sánchez Borbón. il *Harpers* 275:57-67 D '87

Noriega, Manuel Antonio—about—*cont.*
Panama's struggle for democracy. S. C. Ropp. bibl f *Curr Hist* 86:421-4+ D '87
The rumbles grow in the isthmus. M. Satchell. il por *U S News World Rep* 102:18 Je 22 '87
Sending Reagan a message. F. Willey. il por *Newsweek* 110:30 Jl 13 '87
Turmoil in Panama has its strongman tottering. S. Baker. il *Bus Week* p42 Ag 3 '87
Twilight for a dictator? J. L. Galloway. il por map *U S News World Rep* 103:29-31 Jl 20 '87
U.S. and Panama—push comes to shove. J. L. Galloway. il por *U S News World Rep* 103:17 Jl 13 '87
Will this man control the Panama Canal? D. Reed. por *Read Dig* 130:136-40 Ja '87
Norma (Constellation) *See* Constellations
Norman, Carlos
(jt. auth) *See* Reuben, William A., and Norman, Carlos
Norman, Edward
Stewart Headlam and the Christian Socialists. bibl il por *Hist Today* 37:27-32 Ap '87
Norman, Geoffrey
The art of trout fishing. il *Natl Wildl* 25:52-9 Ap/My '87
Beautiful leapers. il *South Living* 22:104 Je '87
A Cowboy's long way home. il pors *Sport Mag* 78:79-80+ D '87
Net gain. il *Oceans* 20:56 N/D '87
Resurrection at Notre Dame. il por *Sport Mag* 78:26-8+ O '87
A sleeper awakens. il pors *Sport Mag* 78:67+ My '87
Take a dive. il *50 Plus* 27:32-6 S '87
Norman, Greg, 1955-
about
Beers with [interview] D. Granger. il por *Sport Mag* 78:23-4 S '87
Bowed but not broken. R. Reilly. il pors *Sports Illus* 66:32-4+ Je 22 '87
My, oh Mize. S. Ballard. il pors *Sports Illus* 66:36-43 Ap 20 '87
PGA Shark alert: Greg Norman is still hungry—and circling. J. Friedman. il pors *People Wkly* 27:149-50+ Ap 13 '87
Norman, Henry C.
about
Steamboats on the Mississippi. J. W. Gandy and T. H. Gandy. il *Am Hist Illus* 22:36-49 Mr '87
Norman, Liane Ellison
about
The nonviolent alternative [interview] D. McDonald. por *Cent Mag* 20:20-5 Ja/F '87
Norman, Marsha
TV families. il *Ms* 16:38+ Jl/Ag '87
about
Tarot cards catch the eye of a master writer [interview] A. P. Sanoff. por *U S News World Rep* 102:78 Je 8 '87
Norman, Michael
The road to self-reliance. il *N Y Times Mag* p82 D 13 '87
Norman, Ron
Techniques of landscape painting. il *Am Artist* 51:54-7 Ag '87
Norman, Royal, Jr., and Balling, Robert C., Jr.
Live at five! il pors *Weatherwise* 40:36-7 F '87
Norman, William Stanley, 1938-
about
Waiting for the right phone call. D. Machan. il por *Forbes* 140:110-11 Ag 10 '87
Norman, Zack
about
Cut-rate moguls. D. C. Craig. il pors *Life* 10:44-5+ Ap '87
Norman (Merle) Cosmetics, Inc. *See* Merle Norman Cosmetics, Inc.
Norman Rockwell's Breaking home ties [television program] *See* Television program reviews—Single works
Normandy Invasion, 1944 *See* D-Day Invasion, 1944
Norodom Sihanouk, Prince, 1922-
about
Sihanouk's 'open door'. F. Willey. il por *Newsweek* 110:56 D 14 '87
Norris, Bill
Getting the massage. il *World Tennis* 34:6-7 Ja '87
Head-to-toe treatments. il *World Tennis* 35:14-15 Je '87
Norris, Leslie, 1921-
Two poems [poem] *New Yorker* 63:34 Jl 27 '87

Norris, Merry
about
Lessons of a judicious couple who won big collecting art. M. Willens. il pors *Money* 16:152 Ja '87
Norris, Robert C.
about
The quiet cowboy who helped lasso the deal. P. Finch. por *Bus Week* p67 D 28 '87-Ja 4 '88
Norris, Walter
about
Jazz. W. Balliett. il *New Yorker* 62:88-91 Ja 12 '87
Norris, William Albert, 1927-
about
Lessons of a judicious couple who won big collecting art. M. Willens. il pors *Money* 16:152 Ja '87
Norris, William C.
Balancing US-Japan technology flow [discussion of February 1987 article, Equalizing US-Japan technology flow] *Phys Today* 40 pt1:11+ Ag '87
Equalizing US-Japan technology flow. *Phys Today* 40:168 F '87
North, Betsy
about
The colonel and his wife: 'my best friend'. por *Newsweek* 110:20 Jl 20 '87
A man of many faces [cover story] D. Friend. il pors *Life* 10:12-17 Ag '87
The women in North's life. W. Lowther. il pors *Macleans* 100:19 Jl 20 '87
North, Carol S.
Her own mental illness behind her, a young doctor reaches out to the victims of schizophrenia; ed. by Giovanna Breu. il por *People Wkly* 28:127-8+ N 9 '87
North, Jay
about
West Coast petal pushers Jay and Pamela North foster a flowering culinary fad. N. Geeslin. il pors *People Wkly* 28:95+ Ag 17 '87
North, Oliver L., Jr.
about
Albert, Fawn and Ollie. W. Goodman. il *New Leader* 70:5-7 Jl 13-27 '87
Beat the devil. A. Cockburn. *Nation* 245:78 Ag 1-8 '87
Begging his pardon. J. V. Lamar, Jr. il *Time* 130:16-17 Ag 3 '87
The "Belly Button" file. M. McDonald. il pors *Macleans* 100:26 Je 15 '87
A big bonus for "Belly Button". J. V. Lamar, Jr. il pors *Time* 129:18-19 Je 15 '87
Black judge dismisses two suits in Iran arms case. por *Jet* 72:4 Mr 30 '87
Breaking a confidence. L. Zuckerman. il *Time* 130:61 Ag 3 '87
Can North be believed? E. Magnuson. il por *Time* 130:12 Jl 6 '87
Charge of the lightweight brigade. F. FitzGerald. il map *Roll Stone* p46-8+ O 22 '87
Charging up Capitol Hill [cover story; special section] il pors *Time* 130:12-18+ Jl 20 '87
Coming attractions. il pors *Time* 130:18 Ag 17 '87
Communist view: Ollie is Rambo. T. Kolesnichenko. *World Press Rev* 34:13-14 S '87
The contra con. J. S. DeMott. por *Time* 129:16+ My 11 '87
Democracy and Colonel North. L. Wieseltier. *New Repub* 196:22-5 Ja 26 '87
Everybody came but 'Larry'. M. Grevatt. il *Nation* 245:228-9 S 12 '87
Faith in a true believer. A. Stanley. por *Time* 129:23 F 16 '87
The fall of a hero. M. McDonald. *Macleans* 100:20-1 Je 1 '87
Fawn Hall, Ollie's ally and shredder, wows the Hill. M. Green. il por *People Wkly* 27:32-3 Je 22 '87
Fifth Amendment patriots. *New Repub* 196:4 Ja 5-12 '87
Four men in North's safe: the uses of intellectuals. A. Cockburn. *Nation* 244:350-1+ Mr 21 '87
Full medal jackoff: what ever happened with Oliver North? R. Corliss. *Film Comment* 23:16 S/O '87
Hanging Ollie out to dry. T. Morganthau. il por *Newsweek* 109:16-17 Ja 19 '87
Help us cast "The Ollie North story". C. Krupp and J. Powell. il por *Glamour* 85:310 S '87
Hero or outlaw? [cover story; special section; with editorial comment by Kevin Doyle] il pors *Macleans* 100:2, 14-21 Jl 20 '87
A hero's mission. M. Kempton. il *N Y Rev Books* 34:13 Ag 13 '87

North, Oliver L., Jr.—about—*cont.*

How a Macy's engineer and his pals became rogue American agents. N. M. Renfrew and P. Blauner. il pors *N Y* 20:102-4+ D 7 '87

Inside dopes. J. L. Pasley. *New Repub* 196:14-16 F 23 '87

Inside Ollie's mind. E. Alterman. il *New Repub* 196:12-15 F 16 '87

Into the vacuum stepped Ollie North. J. Keegan. por *U S News World Rep* 103:14 Ag 31 '87

Iranscam: the real meaning of Oliver North. il pors *Ms* 15:24-7 My '87

Keeping up his guard. F. Trippett. il por *Time* 129:14+ Je 29 '87

Landscape with trolls. L. H. Lapham. *Harpers* 275:6-8 S '87

Letter from Washington. E. Drew. *New Yorker* 63:71-89 Ag 31 '87

Like a John Wayne movie. M. W. Davies. *World Press Rev* 34:16 S '87

A lone ranger or just a good soldier? R. Stengel. por *Time* 129:35 Ja 5 '87

Making book on Oliver North. S. Meredith. *Harpers* 274:54-5 Mr '87

The making of a folk hero. C. W. Colson. il *Christ Today* 31:80 S 4 '87

A man of many faces [cover story] D. Friend. il pors *Life* 10:12-17 Ag '87

The man who did too much. D. Chu. il pors *People Wkly* 28:30-5 Jl 13 '87

A memo to Reagan. il pors *Newsweek* 110:7 S 21 '87

Nancy: no pardons. L. Howard. por *Newsweek* 110:7 N 30 '87

Next step for North? W. F. Buckley. *Natl Rev* 39:55 Ag 14 '87

No pardon. *New Repub* 197:7-9 D 28 '87

North displays talent for television politics. J. M. Wall. il *Christ Century* 104:611-12 Jl 15-22 '87

North falls for a hostage scam. G. J. Church. il pors *Time* 129:25 Je 8 '87

North: felon or fall guy? T. Morganthau. il pors *Newsweek* 109:28+ Je 15 '87

North, Goetz, and the American audience. J. Saltzman. *USA Today (Periodical)* 116:55 N '87

North's other secret [hospitalization for emotional problems] por *Time* 129:45 Ja 5 '87

Not with a bang [cover story; special section] il pors *Newsweek* 110:14-21 Jl 13 '87

Notes and comment. *New Yorker* 63:19-20 Jl 20 '87

Of many things. G. W. Hunt. *America* 157:50 Ag 1-8 '87

The old boys' role in the Iran-contra affair. P. Cary. il pors *U S News World Rep* 103:16-17 Ag 10 '87

Oliver North. il por *People Wkly* 28:38-9 D 28 '87-Ja 4 '88

Oliver North and his merry band. R. Sandza and D. Newell. il *Newsweek* 109:18-19 My 25 '87

Oliver North's blank check. R. Stengel. il por *Time* 129:38-9 Mr 9 '87

Oliver North's strange recruits. P. Maas. il *N Y Times Mag* p20-2+ Ja 18 '87

Oliver's twist [cover story; special section] B. Duffy. il pors *U S News World Rep* 103:18-22+ Jl 20 '87

Oliver's twists. N. Atkins. il *Roll Stone* p65-6+ Jl 16-30 '87

Ollie and Old Gimlet Eye. G. C. Ward. il *Am Herit* 38:14+ N '87

Ollie? Golly! T. Lencz. *Natl Rev* 39:40 Ag 14 '87

Ollie North and the trajectory of fame. C. Krauthammer. il *Time* 130:76 Jl 27 '87

Ollie North, the movie. D. Denby. il *New Repub* 197:7-9 Ag 3 '87

Ollie North's private network. S. Emerson and R. A. Manning. il *U S News World Rep* 102:16-17 Mr 9 '87

Ollie North's secret network. T. Morganthau. il pors *Newsweek* 109:32-7 Mr 9 '87

Ollie-oop! B. Darrach. il pors *People Wkly* 28:32-7 Jl 27 '87

Ollie takes the Hill [cover story; special section] il pors *Newsweek* 110:12-22+ Jl 20 '87

Ollie's blueprint. J. Morley. *New Repub* 196:16-18 My 25 '87

Ollie's gang. A. Cockburn. *Nation* 245:115 Ag 15-22 '87

Ollie's shadow operators. N. Cooper. il por *Newsweek* 109:24-6 Mr 2 '87

Ollie's turn [cover story; special section] il pors *Time* 130:22-6+ Jl 13 '87

Out of the shadows [cover story] B. Duffy. il pors *U S News World Rep* 103:20-7 Jl 13 '87

The paradox of North's popularity. J. Morley. il *Nation* 245:122-5 Ag 15-22 '87

Pardon? F. Barnes. *New Repub* 196:13-15 Ja 5-12 '87

Pardon my Spanish. R. Paulson. *New Repub* 197:4+ Ag 10-17 '87

Pressing North. J. Garvey. *Commonweal* 114:437-8 Ag 14 '87

Questions for the colonel. il por *U S News World Rep* 103:26-7 Jl 13 '87

Saving covert action from Ollie North. *New Repub* 197:5-7 Ag 3 '87

See no evil, hear no evil, speak no evil. M. Kramer. il *U S News World Rep* 103:12 Jl 27 '87

Soldier of misfortune. il por *U S News World Rep* 102:19 Mr 9 '87

Stokes lectures Col. North, nation on law and America. il pors *Jet* 72:28-9 Ag 3 '87

Stones unturned. *Nation* 245:75-6 Ag 1-8 '87

The stuff of patriotism. H. Evans. il *U S News World Rep* 103:66 Ag 10 '87

Television's blinding power [cover story] M. McLoughlin. il pors *U S News World Rep* 103:18-21 Jl 27 '87

Timing tiff. *Time* 129:26 Mr 23 '87

Tracking Oliver North. L. Gomez and P. Meyer. il pors *Life* 10:30-4+ My '87

Two leaks, but by whom? il por *Newsweek* 110:16 Jl 27 '87

The untouchables. J. Klein. il por *N Y* 20:12-13 Jl 27 '87

Walsh vs. Congress. T. Morganthau. il pors *Newsweek* 109:24+ Mr 23 '87

Wayward ship. il *Time* 129:17 Mr 2 '87

Week 3: a Marine's problems multiply. M. Healy and K. T. Walsh. il *U S News World Rep* 102:19 Je 1 '87

Week 5: the strangest tales yet. M. Healy. il por *U S News World Rep* 102:20-1 Je 15 '87

What North might have wrought [cover story] P. Kornbluh. il *Nation* 244:871+ Je 27 '87

What Ollie North told me before he took the Fifth. N. C. Livingstone. *Natl Rev* 39:37-8+ Ja 30 '87

What will Ollie say—and when? D. Baer and M. Healy. il por *U S News World Rep* 102:23-4 Je 29 '87

What will they say—and when? M. Healy. il pors *U S News World Rep* 102:20 Mr 23 '87

When sources get immunity. J. Alter. il *Newsweek* 109:54 Ja 19 '87

Who will believe Oliver North? M. Healy. il por *U S News World Rep* 103:12-13 Jl 6 '87

Zeal without understanding: reflections on Rambo and Oliver North. R. Jewett. il *Christ Century* 104:753-6 S 9-16 '87

Anecdotes, facetiae, satire, etc.

Baloney hero. P. J. O'Rourke. il *Roll Stone* p34-5 S 10 '87

Maggie in Ollieland. M. Gallagher. il *Natl Rev* 39:42+ N 6 '87

Poll. V. Geng. *New Yorker* 63:21 Ag 3 '87

True North. T. Southern. *Nation* 245:41-2 Jl 18-25 '87

Collectibles

And coming soon: Ollie-pops candy. il *Newsweek* 110:60 Jl 27 '87

Olliemania coast to coast. I. Austen. il *Macleans* 100:16-17 Jl 20 '87

North, Pamela

about

West Coast petal pushers Jay and Pamela North foster a flowering culinary fad. N. Geeslin. il pors *People Wkly* 28:95+ Ag 17 '87

North Adams (Mass.)

Galleries and museums

See also

Massachusetts Museum of Contemporary Art and Architecture

North Aegean Petroleum Company

Storm clouds over the Aegean [Greece-Turkey dispute] J. Bierman. il map *Macleans* 100:26-7 Ap 6 '87

North Africa

See also

Libya

Sahara

Tunisia

United Nations—North Africa

History

See also

Barbary States

North African cooking *See* Cooking, North African

North America

See also

Astronomical observatories—North America

Botany—North America

North American Aerospace Defense Command
NORAD, Space Command request system for surveillance of Soviet weapons. C. Covault. *Aviat Week Space Technol* 126:73+ Ap 6 '87

North American Aerospace Defense Command. Space Defense Operations Center
New Space Operations Center will improve threat assessment. C. Covault. il *Aviat Week Space Technol* 126:50+ My 25 '87

North American Blue-Bird Society
A bird in the helping hand [work of L. Zeleny] D. Young. il por *South Living* 22:136+ My '87

North American Essay Contest *See* Essays—Competitions

North American Philips Corp.
How far can Philips elbow its way into the U.S.? J. Kapstein and F. McCoy. il *Bus Week* p46-7 Mr 2 '87

North Atlantic Treaty Organization
After arms control: what does NATO do now? D. Griffiths. il *Bus Week* p124-5 O 19 '87
Allies approach agreement on joint ATM programs [antitactical missile] J. D. Morrocco. *Aviat Week Space Technol* 126:18-20 Je 29 '87
Allies weigh new deployments to offset proposed INF cuts. J. D. Morrocco. *Aviat Week Space Technol* 126:18-19 My 18 '87
Arms talks [cover story; special section] il *World Press Rev* 34:9-15 Je '87
Atlanticism without NATO. C. Layne. bibl f *Foreign Policy* 67:22-45 Summ '87
Battle of the bean counters [effect of zero option proposal on NATO and Warsaw Pact forces] C. Redman. il map *Time* 129:33-4 Je 15 '87
Big idea, little future: Europe eyes own defenses. H. Trewhitt. il *U S News World Rep* 103:36 Jl 20 '87
Bombs away [INF deal] *New Repub* 197:7-8 O 12 '87
Can Europe stand on its own feet? J. Barry and R. Watson. il map *Newsweek* 110:31-2+ D 7 '87
Can NATO survive an arms deal? [views of B. W. Rogers] J. Keegan. il *U S News World Rep* 103:30 Jl 27 '87
Cautious optimism on high-tech weapons for NATO forces [report by the Office of Technology Assessment] D. Charles. *Science* 236:1622 Je 26 '87
The complexities of nuclear diplomacy [INF proposals] R. J. Bresler. il *USA Today (Periodical)* 116:7 Jl '87
Conventional defense must be strengthened. L. Aspin. *Aviat Week Space Technol* 127:15 N 2 '87
Conventional forces in Europe [special section] bibl f il *Bull At Sci* 43:9-20 D '87
Dealing at last [M. Gorbachev's offer to cut back Euromissiles; cover story; special section] il pors map *Newsweek* 109:20-8+ Ap 27 '87
Defense Dept. will ask allies to fund cooperative projects. *Aviat Week Space Technol* 126:26 F 2 '87
Euromissile pact may affect NATO's conventional/high-technology balance. J. D. Morrocco. il map *Aviat Week Space Technol* 126:122+ Je 15 '87
Europe's decoupling anxiety [disarmament proposals frighten Western European leaders] N. Gelb. il *New Leader* 70:7-8 Ap 20 '87
Europe's security dilemmas. C. Bertram. *Foreign Aff* 65:942-57 Summ '87
Exploiting the Soviet "threat" to Europe [European Defense Initiative] M. A. Evangelista. bibl f *Bull At Sci* 43:14-16+ Ja/F '87
Former NATO chief calls for force improvements to offset INF cuts [Bernard W. Rogers] *Aviat Week Space Technol* 127:24 D 14 '87
France weighing value of political autonomy against trend toward defense cooperation. *Aviat Week Space Technol* 127:129+ O 12 '87

Future missile cuts would force NATO to improve conventional arms planning. *Aviat Week Space Technol* 126:212-14 Je 15 '87
Generals can be right [B. Rogers on proposed INF Treaty] W. F. Buckley. *Natl Rev* 39:56 Jl 31 '87
A Gorbachev arms offer even Europe may not refuse. B. Javetski and P. Galuszka. il por *Bus Week* p53 Ap 27 '87
Gorbachev is making nice—and that makes NATO nervous. J. Templeman. il *Bus Week* p37 D 21 '87
Happy birthday, flexible response [nuclear stragegy] W. M. Arkin. *Bull At Sci* 43:5-6 D '87
Ike was right [reducing deployment of our troops in Europe] J. Chace. il *Atlantic* 260:39-41 Ag '87
Improving the balance of conventional forces in Europe [address, March 27, 1987] J. H. Hawes. *Dep State Bull* 87:18-21 Jl '87
Inauguration of NATO E-3A force boosts Norway's mountain defenses [airborne warning and control system] *Aviat Week Space Technol* 126:88 My 25 '87
Italian RPV wins $16-million bid for NATO missile range service [Mirach 100/Mizar remotely piloted vehicle] J. M. Lenorovitz. il *Aviat Week Space Technol* 126:52-3 F 23 '87
Kissinger: a new era for NATO. H. Kissinger. il *Newsweek* 110:57-8+ O 12 '87
Kissinger and INF. il *Natl Rev* 39:17 N 6 '87
A Labour Britain, NATO and the bomb. D. Healey. *Foreign Aff* 65:716-29 Spr '87
Make 'em pay [getting America's allies to shoulder more of the burden for their own defense] M. Kondracke. *New Repub* 197:15-17 O 12 '87
Meeting of NATO's Special Consultative Group [statement, December 10, 1986] A. Holmes. *Dep State Bull* 87:46 Mr '87
Memo to the Senate [views of B. Rogers on INF deal] *Natl Rev* 39:15 Jl 17 '87
The message from Madrid [U.S. asked to remove F-16s from Torrejón Air Base, Spain] H. Anderson. il *Newsweek* 110:83 N 16 '87
Military security in Europe. J. Dean. *Foreign Aff* 66:22-40 Fall '87
Missile pact edges closer. C. Norman. il *Science* 236:378-9 Ap 24 '87
NATO allies narrow gap in defense spending as U.S. outlays decline. *Aviat Week Space Technol* 126:20-1 My 18 '87
NATO armaments programs hinge on technology transfer benefits. M. A. Dornheim. il *Aviat Week Space Technol* 126:220-2+ Je 15 '87
NATO arms cooperation enters critical period. M. Feazel. il *Aviat Week Space Technol* 126:77+ Mr 9 '87
NATO defense ministers affirm need for conventional weapon upgrades. K. F. Mordoff. *Aviat Week Space Technol* 127:28-9 D 7 '87
NATO defense ministers back INF agreement. B. A. Smith. *Aviat Week Space Technol* 127:26-7 N 9 '87
NATO Defense Planning Committee meets in Brussels [text of communique, December 4-5, 1986] *Dep State Bull* 87:57-9 F '87
NATO defense planning committee meets in Brussels [text of final communique, May 27, 1987] *Dep State Bull* 87:63-4 Ag '87
NATO emphasizes joint efforts to meet Soviet EW threat. *Aviat Week Space Technol* 126:83+ F 9 '87
NATO group recommends forming common European arms market. M. Feazel. *Aviat Week Space Technol* 126:18-19 F 23 '87
NATO, industry groups study use of RPVs for small ships. *Aviat Week Space Technol* 127:95+ S 14 '87
NATO looks for arms control loopholes [prospect of an INF accord] D. Charles. il *Bull At Sci* 43:7-12 S '87
NATO NH-90 helicopter program enters one-year definition phase. K. F. Mordoff. il *Aviat Week Space Technol* 127:28 Jl 20 '87
NATO Nuclear Planning Group meets in Norway [text of final communique, May 15, 1987] *Dep State Bull* 87:57 Jl '87
NATO Nuclear Planning Group meets in the U.K. [text of communique, October 22, 1986] *Dep State Bull* 86:65-6 D '86
NATO orders two military satellites from British firms [versions of the Skynet 4 series] *Aviat Week Space Technol* 126:27 Ja 26 '87
NATO planning group to discuss post-INF tactical nuclear strategy. J. D. Morrocco. *Aviat Week Space Technol* 127:125+ O 12 '87
NATO ponders its nuclear options. C. Norman. il *Science* 238:1498-500 D 11 '87

North Atlantic Treaty Organization—*cont.*

NATO pushes the 'eject' button on U.S. contractors [replacement program for F-16 fighters] J. Kapstein. *Bus Week* p50 F 2 '87

NATO suffers separation anxieties. R. Knight. il *U S News World Rep* 103:38-40 D 7 '87

NATO: the best investment in peace [excerpts from address, May 23, 1987] G. Bush. *Dep State Bull* 87:27-8 Ag '87

NATO to weigh long-term arms planning. *Aviat Week Space Technol* 126:18 Je 1 '87

NATO's fallback: can 'battlefield' nukes hold the line? N. Cooper. il *Newsweek* 109:28-9 My 4 '87

NATO's middle course. D. P. Calleo. bibl f *Foreign Policy* 69:135-47 Wint '87/'88

NATO's security dilemma. J. M. O. Sharp. il *Bull At Sci* 43:42-4 Mr '87

NATO's shake-up: exit a European favorite [General B. Rogers] por *Newsweek* 109:44 Mr 9 '87

The need for nuclear arms [interview with B. W. Rogers] R. Knight. por *U S News World Rep* 102:22-3 Je 22 '87

Negotiations on Intermediate-range Nuclear Forces. il *Dep State Bull* 87:24-7 S '87

Nervous about nuclear security [NATO allies object to possible removal of INF missiles] C. Redman. il *Time* 129:37 My 11 '87

North Atlantic Council meets in Brussels [texts of final communique, declaration on conventional arms control, and press conference, December 12, 1986] *Dep State Bull* 87:42-6 Mr '87

North Atlantic Council meets in Iceland [texts of final communique and news conference, June 12, 1987] G. P. Shultz. *Dep State Bull* 87:59-63 Ag '87

Now at center stage, NATO's leading lady [M. Thatcher] S. Jenkins. il por *U S News World Rep* 102:33 Ap 6 '87

Now, super-zero? [M. Gorbachev's proposal to NATO] G. J. Church. il pors *Time* 129:20-3 Ap 27 '87

Nunn calls for conventional upgrades to balance possible nuclear cuts. K. F. Mordoff. *Aviat Week Space Technol* 126:30-1 Ap 20 '87

Nunn's view: a chance to 'educate' Europe [deficiency in conventional weapons] T. Jacoby. il por *Newsweek* 109:30 My 4 '87

One way to arms-control unity: twist allied arms. P. Hassner. il *U S News World Rep* 102:24-5 Je 22 '87

OTA faults allies' deep strike ability. B. M. Greeley, Jr. map *Aviat Week Space Technol* 126:18-19 Je 29 '87

Pentagon forms unit to coordinate arms projects with allies [Defense Cooperation Working Group] *Aviat Week Space Technol* 126:21 Ja 26 '87

Pentagon reviews trade pacts to standardize joint projects. J. D. Morrocco. il *Aviat Week Space Technol* 127:45+ O 19 '87

Pentagon will develop defense against Soviet tactical missiles [antitactical ballistic missile defense] J. D. Morrocco. *Aviat Week Space Technol* 126:22 Ja 19 '87

Rejecting the suicide pact [opposition to proposed INF agreement] *Natl Rev* 39:12-13 Je 5 '87

Removing Gorbachev's edge. M. Svec. il *Foreign Policy* 69:148-65 Wint '87/'88

Retreating from Norway [Canada abandons commitment to help defend Norway in wartime] H. Mackenzie. *Macleans* 100:14-15 F 23 '87

Secretary's trip to Helsinki, Moscow, and Brussels. G. P. Shultz. il por *Dep State Bull* 87:12-24 Je '87

Senate study acclaims U.S./NATO weapons R&D. *Aviat Week Space Technol* 126:316 Je 15 '87

The singular threat to the Atlantic Alliance [excerpts from address, May 28, 1987] H. Kissinger. *Natl Rev* 39:18-19 Jl 3 '87

A tactical defense initiative for Western Europe? I. H. Daalder. bibl f il *Bull At Sci* 43:34-9 My '87

U.S. will propose structure to revive arms cooperation. *Aviat Week Space Technol* 126:82 Mr 30 '87

The uneasy nuclear balance [Soviet offers to reduce the number of nuclear missiles deployed in Europe] D. E. Fink. *Aviat Week Space Technol* 126:25 Ap 27 '87

Unsung force in science exchanges. C. Norman. *Science* 237:1113 S 4 '87

USAF pursues standardized allied reconnaissance data. *Aviat Week Space Technol* 127:25 S 21 '87

The wary warlords [views of Joint Chiefs on Euromissile treaty] D. Gates. il *Newsweek* 109:5 My 11 '87

Washington could get burned by putting the heat on Madrid. J. Patterson and others. il *Bus Week* p58 N 23 '87

Western Europe's dilemma: is a strong defense possible without nuclear arms? H. Cleveland. il *USA Today (Periodical)* 116:52-4 S '87

When the stepping stones of world power are rocky bases [Spain-U.S. dispute over Torrejón Air Base] J. Wallace. il *U S News World Rep* 103:30-1 N 23 '87

Why arms talks unnerve NATO. J. Keegan. il *U S News World Rep* 102:28-30 Ap 20 '87

Why Gorbachev's arms offer gives NATO the jitters. D. Griffiths. il *Bus Week* p49 Mr 30 '87

Yalta II [implications of Soviet Union's zero option INF proposal] J. Morley. *New Repub* 196:14-15 Mr 30 '87

Military maneuvers
See Military maneuvers

North Carolina

See also
Bird sanctuaries—North Carolina
Cape Hatteras National Seashore (N.C.)
Forests and forestry—North Carolina
Franklin County (N.C.)
Gardens and gardening—North Carolina
Great Smoky Mountains National Park (N.C. and Tenn.)
Historic houses, sites, etc.—North Carolina
Hotels, motels, etc.—North Carolina
New River (N.C.-W. Va.)
Oil pollution—North Carolina
Outer Banks (N.C.)
Resorts—North Carolina
Skis and skiing—North Carolina

Fisheries
See Fisheries

Industries
See also
Furniture industry

Population
Warm welcomes for forgotten allies [Montagnard refugees resettled] J. Bennett. il *Macleans* 100:5+ Mr 23 '87

Race relations
The day I learned I was a racist. M. A. McLaurin. il por *Wash Mon* 19:32-6 N '87

National center helps victims of racist acts rampant across nation [Center for Democratic Renewal] *Jet* 71:18 F 23 '87

North Carolina Dance Theater

Reviews:
Performances at the Joyce Theater, New York City. L. Garafola. *Dance Mag* 61:25-7 Jl '87

Wanted: a choreographer [performances at the Joyce Theater] T. Tobias. il *N Y* 20:47-8 Ja 5 '87

North Carolina Memorial Hospital. Preconception Clinic

A new program offers important advice to couples just thinking of having a baby [advice of W. A. Bowes] G. Williams. *McCalls* 115:62-3 O '87

North Carolina Museum of Art

Art has a place in the South. il *South Living* 22:62-7 F '87

North Carolina School of Science and Mathematics

The North Carolina School of Science and Mathematics. C. R. Eilber. *Phi Delta Kappan* 68:773-7 Je '87

North Dakota

See also
Agriculture—North Dakota
Environmental movement—North Dakota
Vegetable gardens and gardening—North Dakota

Description and travel
North Dakota: tough times on the prairie. B. Hodgson. il map *Natl Geogr* 171:320-47 Mr '87

Industries
The challenge of the future [address, September 22, 1987] A. Harrigan. *Vital Speeches Day* 54:109-11 D 1 '87

North Detroit General Hospital *See* Detroit (Mich.)—Hospitals

North General Hospital (New York, N.Y.) *See* New York (N.Y.)—Hospitals

North Haledon (N.J.)

Police
Barbara Schein finally gets a shot at walking the beat. A. Abrahams. il pors *People Wkly* 27:139-40 My 4 '87

North Korea *See* Korea (North)

North Plainfield (N.J.)

Gardens and gardening
Cultivating community spirit [R. Seymour] P. H. Johnson. por *Rodale's Org Gard* 34:103-4 D '87

North Pole
    See also
    Arctic exploration
North Saint Vrain Creek (Colo.)
    A city says no to canyon dams. T. Turner. il *Sierra* 72:133-5 Ja/F '87
North Sea
    See also
    Petroleum—North Sea region
North West Company
    Caesars of the wilderness [excerpt] P. C. Newman. il map *Macleans* 100:42-6+ O 12 '87
Northampton (Mass.)
          Galleries and museums
    See also
    Smith College. Museum of Art
Northcott, Kaye
    Tex mess. il *Progressive* 51:36-9 Ap '87
Northeast Investors Growth Fund
    This preppy's buttoned-down fund is beating the S&P 500 [W. A. Oates] D. M. Topolnicki. il por *Money* 16:214 Je '87
Northeastern States
    See also
    New England
Northern California Booksellers Association
    Carrying the torch for children's books in California [advertising efforts] L. See. il *Publ Wkly* 231:104 F 27 '87
    Crown to countersue NCBA and individual booksellers [antitrust suit] M. Reuter. *Publ Wkly* 231:19 F 13 '87
    Giving no ground, Avon and NCBA settle suit. M. Colin. *Publ Wkly* 232:9 N 13 '87
    Judge dismisses suits between NCBA, chains. M. Colin. *Publ Wkly* 232:13 O 23 '87
    Judge freezes NCBA-chain lawsuit until September. M. Colin. *Publ Wkly* 231:15 My 1 '87
    NCBA moves trade show to Oakland site. L. See. il *Publ Wkly* 232:58-9 N 27 '87
    NCBA sues three chains for 'inducing' unfair discounts. M. Reuter. *Publ Wkly* 231:16 F 6 '87
Northern Ireland
    See also
    Belfast (Northern Ireland)
    Discrimination in employment—Northern Ireland
    Investments, American—Northern Ireland
    Organized crime—Northern Ireland
    Terrorism—Northern Ireland
    Traffic accidents—Northern Ireland
          Defenses
    See also
    Fortification—Northern Ireland
          Industries
    See also
    Short Brothers Ltd.
          Politics and government
    See also
    Irish unification question
    Belfast: the allure of the 'troubles' [excerpt from Living with war] S. Belfrage. *Harpers* 275:27+ O '87
    The empire's last nervous twitch [Anglo-Irish cooperation] C. C. Mann. *Commonweal* 114:562-5 O 9 '87
    In Belfast, war is a way of life [excerpt from Living with war] S. Belfrage. il *Nation* 245:156-8 Ag 29 '87
          Religious institutions and affairs
    See also
    Catholics—Northern Ireland
    Corrymeela Community (Northern Ireland)
Northern Ireland and the United States
    See also
    NORAID
Northern States Power Co. (Minn.)
    Profit without pollution. S. B. Weiner. il *Forbes* 139:46 My 18 '87
Northern Telecom Ltd.
    How Northern Telecom is riding out the storm. J. J. Keller. il por *Bus Week* p84-5 Ja 26 '87
    Productivity in a customer vein [address, February 23, 1987] R. A. Ferchat. *Vital Speeches Day* 53:602-5 Jl 15 '87
    A revolution in chip power. il *Macleans* 100:42 Ap 20 '87
Northrop, David K.
          about
    In search of historic observatories. S. J. O'Meara. il *Sky Telesc* 73:315-16 Mr '87
Northrop Corp.
    Air Force defends MX management as Northrop is charged with fraud. M. Mecham. *Aviat Week Space Technol* 127:16-18 Ag 31 '87

Air Force refers Northrop investigation to U.S. Attorney; Late IMUs delay scheduled MX deployment [inertial measurement units] B. A. Smith. *Aviat Week Space Technol* 126:72 Je 15 '87
Crew systems lab offers rapid feedback on cockpit concepts. il *Aviat Week Space Technol* 127:98-9+ N 23 '87
Guidance unit shortage keeps 8 MXs off alert. M. Mecham. *Aviat Week Space Technol* 127:22-3 Jl 6 '87
Multipilot air-to-air combat evaluated in Northrop simulator. M. A. Dornheim. il *Aviat Week Space Technol* 127:64-5+ N 30 '87
Northrop boosts IMU deliveries, expects to meet schedule in March [inertial measurement units for MX intercontinental ballistic missile] B. A. Smith. il *Aviat Week Space Technol* 127:31-2 S 7 '87
Northrop developing tactical infrared focal plane array. il *Aviat Week Space Technol* 127:82-3 N 2 '87
Northrop leads U.S. production of airborne jamming equipment. il *Aviat Week Space Technol* 126:83+ F 16 '87
Northrop mid-range RPV contender stresses operational flexibility [NV-144R remotely piloted vehicle] B. A. Smith. il *Aviat Week Space Technol* 126:326-7 Je 15 '87
Northrop upgrades simulator center to bolster ATF program effort [advanced tactical fighter] M. A. Dornheim. il *Aviat Week Space Technol* 127:95-8 N 23 '87
Rockwell sneaks up on the Stealth bomber [challenging Northrop] D. Griffiths. il *Bus Week* p96 Je 29 '87
Science board seeks new MX test procedures, affirms IMU reliability. M. Mecham. *Aviat Week Space Technol* 127:32-3 N 2 '87
USAF probes Northrop's MX program purchases. *Aviat Week Space Technol* 126:27 Je 1 '87
USAF withholds MX progress payments from Northrop. *Aviat Week Space Technol* 126:23 Ap 13 '87
The wages of Stealth [Stealth bomber] *Commonweal* 114:644 N 20 '87
Northsea Jazz Festival *See* Music festivals—Netherlands
Northwest Aerospace Training Corporation
    Training firm, university plan ab initio program. il *Aviat Week Space Technol* 127:96-7 O 5 '87
Northwest Airlines, Inc.
    Most improved. il *Forbes* 139:67 Ja 12 '87
    Northwest configures 747-400 as model for rest of aircraft. il *Aviat Week Space Technol* 127:64+ Jl 6 '87
    Northwest suit charges nine with organizing job slowdown. *Aviat Week Space Technol* 127:34 S 21 '87
    Northwest's A330/A340 choice fuels aircraft subsidy debate. J. Ott. il *Aviat Week Space Technol* 126:38-9 Ap 13 '87
    Northwest's aircraft orders, options designed to meet 1990s traffic boom. J. Ott. il *Aviat Week Space Technol* 127:59+ Jl 6 '87
    NWA funds training center for zero-time pilot candidates. il *Aviat Week Space Technol* 127:69+ Jl 6 '87
    Steve Rothmeier's Northwest looks great—on paper. P. Houston. il por *Bus Week* p58-9 S 28 '87
Northwest Coast Indians *See* Indians of North America
Northwest Harris County Municipal Utility District No. 19 (Tex.)
    Clear as MUD [defaults] W. P. Barrett. il *Forbes* 139:96-8 Je 15 '87
Northwest Industries, Inc.
    See also
    Farley/Northwest Industries, Inc.
Northwest ordinance (1787)
    1787. K. Ide. *Am Herit* 38:107 Jl/Ag '87
    Neutrality and religious freedom. M. E. Marty. *Christ Century* 104:580-1 Jl 1-8 '87
Northwest Passage
    See also
    Franklin Expedition (1845)
    An epic Arctic journey [expedition retracing Inuit migration and demonstrating Canadian Arctic sovereignty; special section; with editorial comment by Kevin Doyle] il map *Macleans* 100:2, 20-8+ My 11 '87
    Larsen of the Northwest Passage [1940's voyage to bolster Canadian claims to sovereignty] J. Roe. il pors map *Oceans* 20:48-53+ N/D '87
    Standing up to the United States [Canadian sovereignty in the Arctic] S. Shallhorn. *Bull At Sci* 43:16-17 O '87
    Threats to the North [U.S. threat to Canadian sovereignty in the Arctic and dispute over Arctic National Wildlife Refuge] M. Janigan. il map *Macleans* 100:10-11 Ja 26 '87

Northwest Passage—*cont.*
Uncle Sam's sovereignty promise [agreement on sovereignty in the Canadian Arctic between Ottawa and Washington] P. C. Newman. il *Macleans* 100:33 Mr 30 '87

Northwest Power Company
A nonrenewable river [proposed hydroelectric dams on the South Yuba] D. Carter. il *Sierra* 72:66-7 My/Je '87

Northwest Territories
See also
Ellesmere Island National Park (N.W.T.)
Fishing—Northwest Territories
Wildlife—Northwest Territories
Industries
See also
Gold mines and mining—Northwest Territories
Politics and government
A new leader for the North [D. Patterson] B. Jones. *Macleans* 100:12 N 23 '87

Northwest Territory (U.S.) *See* Old Northwest

Northwestern States
See also
Pacific Northwest

Norton, Arthur J.
Families and children in the year 2000. il *Child Today* 16:6-9 Jl/Ag '87

Norton, Augustus Richard
The Renamo menace: hunger and carnage in Mozambique [cover story; with editorial comment] il *New Leader* 70:2, 5-8 N 16 '87

Norton, B. W. L.
about
Three for the road [film] Reviews
People Wkly 27:10 My 25 '87. T. Cunneff

Norton, Bryan G.
The spiral of life. il maps *Wilderness* 50:16-38 Spr '87

Norton, Ken, Jr.
about
Like father, like son. R. Wiley. il pors *Sports Illus* 67:74-6+ O 12 '87

Norton, Ken, 1945-
about
Like father, like son. R. Wiley. il pors *Sports Illus* 67:74-6+ O 12 '87

Norton-Welsh, Christopher
Lyric taste. por *Opera News* 52:42+ D 5 '87

Norville, Deborah
about
NBC's crack (of dawn) news anchor, Deborah Norville, shoots for a spot as the next morning star. J. Hall. il pors *People Wkly* 28:79-80 Jl 27 '87

Norwalk (Wis.)
Crime
The tale of a remarkably loyal husband [S. Creviston linked to attempted murder of J. Creviston] *Newsweek* 110:45 D 21 '87

Norway
See also
Hydroelectric plants—Norway
Oslo (Norway)
Securities—Norway
Wave power—Norway
Air Force
Norway's job market drains officer cadre. *Aviat Week Space Technol* 126:88 My 25 '87
Norwegian Air Force to weigh replacing F-16 fighter force. D. A. Brown. *Aviat Week Space Technol* 126:81+ My 25 '87
Commerce
Soviet Union
See Soviet Union—Commerce—Norway
Defenses
See also
Airplanes, Military—Norway
Canada—Armed Forces—Forces in Norway
Guided missiles, Norwegian
Norway—Air Force
Inauguration of NATO E-3A force boosts Norway's mountain defenses [airborne warning and control system] *Aviat Week Space Technol* 126:88 My 25 '87
Description and travel
Oslo: a taste of things to come. B. Walker. il map *Travel Holiday* 167:62-7+ Je '87
Foreign relations
United States
See United States—Foreign relations—Norway
Industries
See also
Bik Bok Gruppen
Fish culture—Norway

Kongsberg Vaapenfabrikk AS
VIP Scandinavia
Politics and government
On top of the world [G. Brundtland, Norwegian prime minister] F. Hauptfuhrer. il pors *People Wkly* 27:34-9 Ap 20 '87

Norwegian cooking *See* Cooking, Norwegian

Norwegian Sea
Greenland Sea Project uses tomography. *Sea Front* 33:143 Mr/Ap '87
Greenland Sea research [seawater circulation] il *Oceans* 20:4 Ja/F '87

Norwest Corporation
The brave new world of swaps [dealings in Brazil] P. Sherrid. il *U S News World Rep* 103:41 Ag 31 '87

Norwich, William
The road back to El Morocco: Usha Singh and the $2-million gamble. il por *N Y* 20:48-51 Ap 27 '87

Norwood, Christopher
Is preventing AIDS the responsibility of women? The media seem to think so [excerpt from Advice for life] il *Glamour* 85:18 Jl '87
P.I.D.: the "pay later" threat to your sexual health. *Mademoiselle* 93:122 Mr '87

Norwood, Janet L.
The future of employment [address, October 18, 1986] *Current* 292:18-23 My '87
Quality [excerpts from address, March 30, 1987] *Mon Labor Rev* 110:2 Ap '87

Norwood, Lori
about
Did she or didn't she? S. Francis. il *Women's Sports Fitness* 9:22 Ap '87

Norwood, Robin
about
Loving too much. C. Leerhsen. il por *Newsweek* 109:52-3 Mr 9 '87
Pocket to start hardcover line ahead of schedule. W. Goldstein. il por *Publ Wkly* 232:74 O 2 '87

Nose
See also
Nasopharynx
Smell
Surgery, Plastic
See Surgery, Plastic

Nosebleed
Nosebleeds: first-aid advice. S. R. Boone. *McCalls* 115:89 O '87

Noseguards (Football players) *See* Football players

Nosek, Thomas M., and others
It is diprotonated inorganic phosphate that depresses force in skinned skeletal muscle fibers. bibl f il *Science* 236:191-3 Ap 10 '87

Nossal, G. J. V. (Gustav Joseph Victor), 1931-
(jt. auth) See Ada, Gordon L., and Nossal, G. J. V. (Gustav Joseph Victor), 1931-

Nossal, Gustav Joseph Victor *See* Nossal, G. J. V. (Gustav Joseph Victor), 1931-

Nossal, Kim Richard
(jt. auth) See Bromke, Adam, and Nossal, Kim Richard

Nossiter, Bernard D.
Reagan's road to stabilization. il *Nation* 244:12+ Ja 10 '87

Nostalgia
See also
Homesickness
Collectible adolescence [nostalgia for 1950s youth] A. M. Dershowitz. il *N Y Times Mag* p46 My 31 '87
The deep currents of nostalgia [Buenos Aires residents] M. Kogan. il *Américas* 39:26-31 Mr/Ap '87
Editorial ["the good old days"] D. Barnes. *Field Stream* 92:8 Je '87
Good enough [nostalgia for fishing with grandfather] G. Hill. il *Field Stream* 92:20 Je '87
The way we weren't. M. Jacobson. il *Esquire* 108:65+ O '87
When the town pizza parlor shut down. D. Geigis. il *Glamour* 85:278+ S '87

Nostalgia in motion pictures
Nostalgia and dis-history. K. R. Hey. *USA Today (Periodical)* 116:93 N '87

Not in my backyard syndrome *See* NIMBY syndrome
Notables *See* Black celebrities; Celebrities
Notaries
Ethical aspects
Robber stamps. W. P. Barrett. il *Forbes* 140:144+ S 21 '87

Nourse, Alan E.
Family doctor. See issues of Good Housekeeping

Nouvelle cuisine *See* Cooking, French
Nova Health Services
　Abort/adopt. *Time* 130:60 N 2 '87
Nova Pharmaceutical Corp.
　Pain relief may make Nova feel good again. G. G.
　　Marcial. il *Bus Week* p114 Je 1 '87
Nova Scotia
　　See also
　　Charlesville (N.S.)
　　Drama festivals—Nova Scotia
　　Family courts—Nova Scotia
　　Fishing—Nova Scotia
　　Halifax (N.S.)
　　Oak Island (N.S.)
　　Paleontology—Nova Scotia
　　Port Medway (N.S.)
　　Sydney (N.S.)
　　　　Anecdotes, facetiae, satire, etc.
　Gentility with tennis and gin. A. Fotheringham. il
　　Macleans 100:52 Ag 3 '87
　　　　Description and travel
　Crow's nest. G. L. Voss. il *Sea Front* 33:402-3 N/D
　　'87
　　　　Industries
　　See also
　　Shellfish fisheries—Canada
　　　　Politics and government
　　See also
　　Politics, Corruption in—Nova Scotia
　The return of Billy Joe MacLean. C. Wood. il por
　　Macleans 100:14 Mr 9 '87
Nova Scotia Savings & Loan Company
　Victory to the outsiders [takeover defense ruled illegal
　　in court] C. Wood. il *Macleans* 100:28 F 16 '87
Novack, Phyllis Stein- *See* Stein-Novack, Phyllis
Novak, Lorie
　　　　about
　Projecting the past: Lorie Novak portrays memory by
　　projecting slides from her past in empty rooms. S.
　　Piperato. il *Pop Photogr* 94:48-53 Je '87
Novak, Michael
　Buying & selling babies. il *Commonweal* 114:406-7 Jl
　　17 '87
　The new science. *Natl Rev* 39:36-7+ Jl 17 '87
　　　　about
　Christianity today talks to Michael Novak. D. Neff.
　　por *Christ Today* 31:54-5 Jl 10 '87
　Reclaiming the Catholic heritage. A. R. Muggeridge.
　　Commentary 84:39-44 S '87
Novak, Robert D.
　The politics of the crash. il *Natl Rev* 39:49-50+ N 20
　　'87
　(jt. auth) See Evans, Rowland, and Novak, Robert D.
Novas *See* Stars, New
NovAtel Communications Ltd.
　The cellular-phone star that's burning dimmer. E. B.
　　Terry. il por *Bus Week* p100+ D 7 '87
Novelists, American
　　See also
　　Auel, Jean M.
　　Austin, Doris Jean
　　Barth, John
　　Bell, Madison Smartt
　　Bellow, Saul
　　Boyle, T. Coraghessan
　　Bukowski, Charles
　　Chabon, Michael
　　Clancy, Tom, 1947-
　　Coonts, Stephen, 1946-
　　Crews, Harry, 1935-
　　Dillard, Annie
　　Doig, Ivan
　　Eisenstadt, Jill
　　Ellis, Bret Easton
　　Ellroy, James
　　Fante, John, 1909-1983
　　Faulkner, William, 1897-1962
　　Fitzgerald, F. Scott (Francis Scott), 1896-1940
　　Forward, Robert L.
　　Gaddis, William, 1922-
　　Gibbons, Kaye, 1960-
　　Gordon, Mary, 1949-
　　Greeley, Andrew M., 1928-
　　Green, Judith H.
　　Grimes, Martha
　　Haley, Alex
　　Hearon, Shelby, 1931-
　　Heller, Joseph
　　Hemingway, Ernest, 1899-1961
　　Howells, William Dean, 1837-1920
　　Hoyt, Richard, 1941-

　　Humphreys, Josephine
　　Ignatius, David, 1950-
　　Isaacs, Susan, 1943-
　　James, Henry, 1843-1916
　　Janowitz, Tama
　　Kleypas, Lisa
　　Koen, Karleen
　　Koontz, Dean, 1945-
　　L'Amour, Louis, 1908-
　　Lawrence, Rae
　　Leonard, Elmore, 1925-
　　Lewis, Sinclair, 1885-1951
　　Marquand, John P. (John Phillips), 1893-1960
　　McCarthy, Mary, 1912-
　　McMahon, Thomas A., 1943-
　　McMurtry, Larry
　　McPherson, William
　　Michener, James A. (James Albert), 1907-
　　Morrison, Toni, 1931-
　　O'Marie, Carol Anne
　　Parker, Robert B., 1932-
　　Percy, Walker
　　Piercy, Marge
　　Powell, Dawn
　　Price, Reynolds, 1933-
　　Raskin, Barbara
　　Roth, Henry, 1906-
　　Roth, Philip
　　Saint, H. F. (Harry F.)
　　Salinger, J. D. (Jerome David), 1919-
　　Simpson, Mona
　　Stegner, Wallace Earle, 1909-
　　Steinbeck, John, 1902-1968
　　Thomas, Elizabeth Marshall, 1931-
　　Thomas, Ross, 1926-
　　Tunis, John R., 1889-1975
　　Twain, Mark, 1835-1910
　　Updike, John
　　Vachss, Andrew H.
　　Walker, Alice, 1944-
　　Wharton, Edith, 1862-1937
　　Wharton, William
　　Willeford, Charles Ray, 1919-1988
　　Wolfe, Thomas, 1900-1938
　Beyond the first novel. J. Dolce. il *Harpers Bazaar*
　　120:108+ Ag '87
　The selling of the young. J. Giles. *Natl Rev* 39:64-5
　　N 20 '87
Novelists, Canadian
　　See also
　　Atwood, Margaret, 1939-
　　Davies, Robertson, 1913-
　　MacLennan, Hugh
　　Montgomery, L. M. (Lucy Maud), 1874-1942
Novelists, Chilean
　　See also
　　Donoso, José
Novelists, Chinese American
　　See also
　　Lee, C. Y., 1917-
Novelists, English
　　See also
　　Amis, Martin
　　Austen, Jane, 1775-1817
　　Beauman, Sally
　　Drabble, Margaret, 1939-
　　Forsyth, Frederick, 1938-
　　Howatch, Susan
　　Lawrence, D. H. (David Herbert), 1885-1930
　　McEwan, Ian
　　Rendell, Ruth, 1930-
　　Rutherfurd, Edward
　The comic bad men of English letters. M. Bradbury.
　　il *N Y Times Book Rev* 92:15 Mr 22 '87
Novelists, French
　　See also
　　Balzac, Honoré de, 1799-1850
　　Céline, Louis-Ferdinand, 1894-1961
　　Hugo, Victor, 1802-1885
Novelists, German
　　See also
　　Mann, Thomas, 1875-1955
　　May, Karl Friedrich, 1842-1912
Novelists, Irish
　　See also
　　Joyce, James, 1882-1941
Novelists, Italian
　　See also
　　Calvino, Italo
　　Ortese, Anna Maria
　　Sciascia, Leonardo

Novelists, Italian—See also—*cont.*
  Silone, Ignazio, 1900-1978
Novelists, Lebanese
    See also
  Nasrallah, Emily
Novelists, Peruvian
    See also
  Arguedas, José María
  Vargas Llosa, Mario, 1936-
Novelists, Russian
    See also
  Aksenov, Vasiliĭ Pavlovich, 1932-
  Dostoyevsky, Fyodor, 1821-1881
  Rasputin, Valentin Grigor'evich
  Russian fiction
  Rybakov, Anatoliĭ Naumovich
  Semenov, IŪlian Semenovich, 1931-
  Solzhenitsyn, Aleksandr, 1918-
Novelists, South African
    See also
  Gordimer, Nadine, 1923-
Novelizations of motion pictures *See* Motion pictures and
  literature
Novell Inc.
  It's high noon for the little guys. J. W. Wilson. il *Bus
  Week* p111 Ap 27 '87
Novello, John
  Practice disciplines. il *Down Beat* 54:53-4 Mr '87
Novels *See* Fiction
Novels, Computer *See* Computer novels
Novels, Graphic *See* Graphic novels
Novelties
    See also
  Russ Berrie & Co., Inc.
  Sanrio Co., Ltd.
  Spirit Novelties (Firm)
November
  The November almanac. il *Atlantic* 260:20 N '87
  The November transition. D. M. Ludlum. *Ctry J* 14:72
  D '87
Novick, Robert E.
  Shelter and health. il *World Health* p6-9 Jl '87
NOW *See* National Organization for Women
Nowick, Walter
    about
  Barnyard diplomacy. M. Baldwin. il *Opera News* 52:38-9
  Jl '87
  From a Maine barn to a Soviet stage, Walter Nowick's
  opera company raises the Iron Curtain to promote
  harmony. L. Aitken. il por *People Wkly* 27:93-4 Ja
  12 '87
Nowicki, Edward J.
  The TV teacher trivia test. il *Phi Delta Kappan* 69:69-70
  S '87
Nowikowski, Frank
  A mission of service to leprosy sufferers. *Christ Century*
  104:782-3 S 23 '87
Noxell Corporation
  Making millions on women over 30. F. Rice. il *Fortune*
  115:75+ My 25 '87
Noyes, Dorothy
  Your house may be hazardous to your health. il *Parents*
  62:180-2+ N '87
Noyes, Kirk
  Surplus schools can serve the community. il *Aging*
  no356:13-16 '87
Nozko, Henry W., Sr.
    about
  Life after death. B. Leonard. il por *Forbes* 139:132-3
  My 4 '87
Nozzles
    See also
  Pitot tubes
  Remotely piloted vehicle engines—Nozzles
  New calibrator tunes sprayer in 10 minutes. il *Success
  Farm* 85 no5:26F Mr '87
  Next revolution in spraying? [air-assisted nozzles] D.
  Mowitz. il *Success Farm* 85 no2:26 Ja '87
  Will CDAs spin or spin out? [controlled droplet ap-
  plication] D. Mowitz. il *Success Farm* 85 no1:26AN
  Ja '87
NPA (Firm)
  Two regional commuters expand market base beyond
  traditional areas. *Aviat Week Space Technol* 127:52
  S 28 '87
NPCA *See* National Parks and Conservation Association
NPR *See* National Public Radio (U.S.)
NRA *See* National Rifle Association of America
NRC *See* National Research Council (U.S.) U.S. Nuclear
  Regulatory Commission

Nriagu, Jerome O., and others
  Biogenic sulfur and the acidity of rainfall in remote
  areas of Canada. bibl f il *Science* 237:1189-92 S 4
  '87
NSAF *See* United States. Federal Bureau of Investigation.
  National Stolen Art File
NSC *See* United States. National Security Council
NTIS *See* United States. National Technical Information
  Service
NTSB *See* United States. National Transportation Safety
  Board
Nucci, Leo
    about
  Sound and fury. L. Valdes. il por *Vogue* 177:174 S
  '87
Nuclear aircraft carriers
          Costs
  House, Senate panels support Navy plan to replace
  carriers. B. M. Greeley, Jr. il *Aviat Week Space Technol*
  126:127+ My 11 '87
Nuclear bombs *See* Atomic bombs
Nuclear chemistry
  Chemical chaos in a runaway reactor [data from Three
  Mile Island] J. I. Mattill. il *Technol Rev* 90:18 My/Je
  '87
Nuclear energy
    See also
  Anti-nuclear movement
  Nuclear fission
  Nuclear fusion
  Nuclear reactors
  How do we produce electricity from nuclear power?
  USA Today (Periodical) 116:51 N '87
          Awards
    See also
  Enrico Fermi Award
          Conferences
    See also
  United Nations Conference for the Promotion of
  International Co-operation in the Peaceful Uses
  of Nuclear Energy
          Economic aspects
    See also
  Nuclear industry
          Environmental aspects
  The future of nuclear power: seeking new energy sources.
  C. Flavin. *Current* 298:24-9 D '87
  Nuclear power's burdened future. C. Flavin. bibl f il
  Bull At Sci 43:26-31 Jl/Ag '87
  Revising the nuclear dream. C. Flavin. il *USA Today
  (Periodical)* 116:60-2 Jl '87
          Insurance
  See Insurance, Nuclear hazards
          International aspects
    See also
  International Atomic Energy Agency
  United Nations Conference for the Promotion of
  International Co-operation in the Peaceful Uses
  of Nuclear Energy
  The future of nuclear power: seeking new energy sources.
  C. Flavin. *Current* 298:24-9 D '87
  International prospects for civil nuclear power in the
  post-Chernobyl era [address, November 5, 1986] J.
  Negroponte. *Dep State Bull* 87:75-8 Ja '87
  Nuclear cooperation with EURATOM [letter to Congress,
  February 28, 1986] R. Reagan. *Dep State Bull* 87:77
  Je '87
  Nuclear power's burdened future. C. Flavin. bibl f il
  Bull At Sci 43:26-31 Jl/Ag '87
  Revising the nuclear dream. C. Flavin. il *USA Today
  (Periodical)* 116:60-2 Jl '87
          Laws and regulations
    See also
  Nuclear industry—Suits and claims
  Radioactive waste disposal—Laws and regulations
  U.S. Nuclear Regulatory Commission
          Physiological effects
  See Radiation—Physiological effects
          Central Europe
  Nuclear power's Faustian bargain. E. V. Kohák. *Harpers*
  274:15-16+ My '87
          Western Europe
    See also
  Euratom
Nuclear excited states *See* Energy levels (Quantum
  mechanics)
Nuclear explosions *See* Nuclear weapons—Testing
Nuclear exports *See* Nuclear industry—Export-import trade
Nuclear facilities
    See also
  Hanford Reservation (Wash.)

Nuclear facilities—See also—*cont.*
   Nuclear power plants
   Nuclear research laboratories
   Nuclear weapons—Manufacture
   Radioactive waste disposal
         Decommissioning
Hot waste goes down the tubes [nuclear reprocessing plant in West Valley, N.Y.] S. N. Wellborn. il *U S News World Rep* 102:76 My 25 '87
      Protests, demonstrations, etc.
   See Anti-nuclear movement
Nuclear fallout *See* Radioactive pollution
Nuclear fission
Reminiscences of the early days of fission. H. H. Barschall. bibl f il *Phys Today* 40:27-32 Je '87
Nuclear-free zones
County blocks bomb exercise [Clatsop County, Or., self-declared nuclear free zone, subjected to mock nuclear attack by Federal Emergency Management Agency] D. Friedrich. *Progressive* 51:16 My '87
         Oceania
Connecting the dots on the map. G. Alcalay. il *Nation* 245:84-7 Ag 1-8 '87
A nuclear free Pacific: enlisting U.S. support [South Pacific Nuclear Free Zone Treaty] R. A. Evans. *Christ Century* 104:373-4 Ap 22 '87
Red herring in the Pacific. W. M. Arkin. *Bull At Sci* 43:6-7 Ap '87
South Pacific Nuclear Free Zone [statement, December 15, 1986] J. S. Roy. *Dep State Bull* 87:52-4 S '87
Nuclear freeze *See* Disarmament
Nuclear fuel reprocessing *See* Reactor fuel reprocessing
Nuclear fuels
   See also
   Reactor fuel reprocessing
   Uranium
         Disposal
   See Radioactive waste disposal
Nuclear fusion
   See also
   Magnetic fusion
   Tokamaks
Cold fusion [work of Steven E. Jones] A. Fisher. il *Pop Sci* 230:54-5+ Ap '87
Cold nuclear fusion. J. Rafelski and S. E. Jones. bibl (p116) il *Sci Am* 257:84-9 Jl '87
The fusion quest. D. Eskow. il *Pop Mech* 164:52+ Je '87
Getting nuked [aneutronic energy; work of B. Maglich] P. Patton. il por *Omni* 9:82-4+ F '87
Keep cool with cold nuclear fusion [work of Steven E. Jones] D. E. Thomsen. *Sci News* 131:133 F 28 '87
Plasma and fusion physics. *Phys Today* 40:S59-S63 Ja '87
The road to magnetic fusion? [international cooperation] D. E. Thomsen. *Sci News* 132:294 N 7 '87
Seeking aneutronic nuclear fusion. D. E. Thomsen. *Sci News* 132:181 S 19 '87
Nuclear fusion reactors *See* Nuclear reactors
Nuclear industry
   See also
   Computers—Nuclear industry use
   Nuclear Support Services, Inc.
   Nuclear weapons—Manufacture
   Reactor fuel reprocessing
   Washington Public Power Supply System
Celebrating 30 years of nuclear energy. H. B. Finger. il *USA Today (Periodical)* 116:52-4 N '87
Nuclear reactions [discussion of December 1986 article, First word] H. B. Finger. *Omni* 9:15 Ap '87
Safe nuclear power [cover story] L. M. Lidsky. *New Repub* 197:20-3 D 28 '87
      Export-import trade
DOD sees risks in plutonium trade. D. Charles. il *Science* 238:886 N 13 '87
Heavy water cheaters. G. Milhollin. bibl f *Foreign Policy* 69:100-19 Wint '87/'88
Nonproliferation and the peaceful uses of nuclear energy [address, May 20, 1987] J. Negroponte. *Dep State Bull* 87:67-70 Jl '87
The nuclear arsenal in the Middle East. F. Barnaby. il map *Technol Rev* 90:27-34 My/Je '87
The nuclear caper [arrest of Arshad Pervez in Philadelphia on charges of trying to illegally export materials for Pakistan's weapons program] I. Austen. il *Macleans* 100:19 Jl 27 '87
Nuclear proliferation: who's next? L. S. Spector. bibl f il *Bull At Sci* 43:17-20 My '87
The Pakistan syndrome [halting nuclear proliferation] *New Repub* 197:7-8+ S 28 '87

Pakistani smuggling riles Congress. L. S. Spector. il *Bull At Sci* 43:3-4 O '87
Problems of assurance of nuclear supplies [address, May 27, 1987] F. McGoldrick. *Dep State Bull* 87:48-52 S '87
A rock and a hard place [Pakistan caught trying to illegally import maraging steel intended for bomb program] R. Nordland. il *Newsweek* 110:30+ Jl 27 '87
Stemming the spread of nuclear weapons. M. M. Miller. il *Technol Rev* 90:68-75 Ag/S '87
Wanted: the bomb [possible cutoff of U.S. military aid after Pakistan's attempt buy steel alloy for nuclear weapons] il *U S News World Rep* 103:8 Jl 27 '87
        Management
America's big risk. W. D. Marbach. il map *Newsweek* 109:58+ Ap 27 '87
      Suits and claims
A $78 million check from GE [settlement of suit over failed Zimmer nuclear plant] Z. Schiller. *Bus Week* p64 D 7 '87
Price tag for Price-Anderson Act. K. Hartley. *Sci News* 132:70 Ag 1 '87
A push for 'quick justice' has GE squirming [summary trial in suit over Zimmer nuclear plant] Z. Schiller. *Bus Week* p31-2 S 21 '87
         Canada
   See also
   Atomic Energy of Canada Ltd.
        United States
   See Nuclear industry
Nuclear insurance *See* Insurance, Nuclear hazards
Nuclear magnetic resonance *See* Magnetic resonance imaging
Nuclear medicine
   See also
   Magnetic resonance imaging—Medical use
Nuclear healing [work of Dr. R. Holmes] J. Gruber. il por *Black Enterp* 18:24 O '87
The talking tumor's guide to surgery? D. D. Edwards. *Sci News* 131:232 Ap 11 '87
Using medical radiation from the inside out. J. Thompson. il *FDA Consum* 21:10-13 Jl/Ag '87
Nuclear nonproliferation policy *See* Disarmament
Nuclear physics
   See also
   Accelerators (Electrons, etc.)
   Cluster theory (Nuclear physics)
   Collisions (Nuclear physics)
   Cosmic rays
   Energy levels (Quantum mechanics)
   European Organization for Nuclear Research
   Mössbauer effect
   Particles (Nuclear physics)
   Quantum chromodynamics
   Scattering (Physics)
Electron and atomic physics. *Phys Today* 40:S23-S26 Ja '87
Nuclear physics. *Phys Today* 40:S46-S47 Ja '87
         History
Reminiscences of the early days of fission. H. H. Barschall. bibl f il *Phys Today* 40:27-32 Je '87
Nuclear policy *See* Nuclear energy
Nuclear pollution *See* Radioactive pollution
Nuclear power *See* Nuclear energy
Nuclear power plants
   See also
   Nuclear reactors
   Tokamaks
The woman who tackled Black Fox [C. Dickerson's fight against Black Fox plant in Oklahoma] N. H. Perreault. il por *Progressive* 51:12 D '87
      Accidents and explosions
   See also
   Chernobyl nuclear disaster, 1986
Can Chernobyl happen here? [comparison to Three Mile Island]; ed. by Mary Hopkins. M. Copulos. il *Consum Res Mag* 70:35-7 Ja '87
Chemical chaos in a runaway reactor [data from Three Mile Island] J. I. Mattill. il *Technol Rev* 90:18 My/Je '87
The human factor. *Progressive* 51:8-9 Ag '87
Nuclear power after Chernobyl [comparison to Three Mile Island] J. F. Ahearne. bibl f il *Science* 236:673-9 My 8 '87
Postmortem on Three Mile Island. W. Booth. il *Science* 238:1342-5 D 4 '87
Superphénix springs a leak. D. Dickson. *Science* 236:248 Ap 17 '87
World enough & time. *Commonweal* 114:227-8 Ap 24 '87

Nuclear power plants—*cont.*

Automation
Troubleshooting with robots. *USA Today (Periodical)* 115:14 Je '87

Decommissioning
Death of a nuclear plant [Shippingport] S. Minerbrook. il *U S News World Rep* 103:57-8 N 2 '87

Decommissioning nuclear power plants. C. Pollock. il *USA Today (Periodical)* 115:50-3 Mr '87

Headed for the last shutdown [Rancho Seco nuclear power plant] H. Rubin. il *Sierra* 72:74-5 S/O '87

Is Maine Yankee headed for the dump? [proposal to ban production of nuclear waste] J. Kriesberg. *Progressive* 51:12-13 N '87

Nuclear-power industry gets a wake-up call [NRC shuts down Peach Bottom plant in Pa.] R. A. Taylor. il *U S News World Rep* 102:14 Ap 13 '87

Design
Under pressure: U.S. plants with pressure-suppression containments. R. Poole. maps *Sierra* 72:21 Mr/Ap '87

Economic aspects
A $78 million check from GE [settlement of suit over failed Zimmer nuclear plant] Z. Schiller. *Bus Week* p64 D 7 '87

Humble pie [Central Maine Power's nuclear problems] J. Cook. il por *Forbes* 139:50-1 Ap 20 '87

The jury's still out on 'WHOOPS'—way out [Washington Public Power Supply System] H. Gleckman. il *Bus Week* p168 N 2 '87

A nuclear cloud hangs over GE's reputation [flawed plant designs and responsibility for cost overruns] D. Cook. il *Bus Week* p32 Je 15 '87

A push for 'quick justice' has GE squirming [summary trial in suit over Zimmer nuclear plant] Z. Schiller. *Bus Week* p31-2 S 21 '87

The safe Whoopses [projects 1, 2 and 3] B. Weberman. il *Forbes* 139:297 Ja 12 '87

A utility runs out of juice [Public Service Co. of New Hampshire's Seabrook plant] K. H. Hammonds. il *Bus Week* p26 Ag 24 '87

"We are in a heap of trouble" [Seabrook] J. Attinger. il *Time* 130:114 O 26 '87

Who says utilities can't be raider bait? [M. J. Whitman's play for Public Service of N.H. includes debt by Seabrook nuclear plant] C. Brown. il por *Bus Week* p112 N 23 '87

WHOOPS haunts the Street [SEC investigation] C. Farrell. *Bus Week* p122 Mr 16 '87

Wonders never cease [comeback in bonds of Washington Public Power Supply System] B. Weberman. il *Forbes* 140:213 O 19 '87

Employees
See Nuclear power workers

Protests, demonstrations, etc.
See Anti-nuclear movement

Safety devices and measures
See also
Institute of Nuclear Power Operations (U.S.)

After Chernobyl: where do we go from here? C. Reed. il *USA Today (Periodical)* 116:48-51 N '87

America's big risk. W. D. Marbach. il map *Newsweek* 109:58+ Ap 27 '87

Controversy over nuclear evacuation planning. J. Raloff. *Sci News* 131:100 F 14 '87

Foreseeing failure [computers that predict problems may make nuclear plants safer] *Futurist* 21:42 Ja/F '87

Holes in the U.S. nuclear safety net. D. Utroska. bibl f il *Bull At Sci* 43:36-40 Jl/Ag '87

IAEA conventions on nuclear safety provide for co-operation in wake of nuclear accident. il *UN Chron* 23:74 N '86

Legality of new NRC rule is challenged [licensing of nuclear power plants] R. Weiss. *Sci News* 132:309 N 14 '87

Moscow "radicals" stop a nuclear plant [Zimmer Ohio Nuclear Power Station] J. Lawless. il por *Sierra* 72:125-30 Ja/F '87

Nonproliferation and the peaceful uses of nuclear energy [address, May 20, 1987] J. Negroponte. *Dep State Bull* 87:67-70 Jl '87

NRC to vote on new evacuation rule. R. Weiss. *Sci News* 132:279 O 31 '87

A nuclear cloud hangs over GE's reputation [flawed plant designs and responsibility for cost overruns] D. Cook. il *Bus Week* p32 Je 15 '87

Nuclear power plants under fire. *Environment* 29:21 Ap '87

The safety goals of the U.S. Nuclear Regulatory Commission. D. Okrent. bibl f il *Science* 236:296-300 Ap 17 '87

Summer of our discontent. H. Wasserman. *Nation* 245:233-4 S 12 '87

Three conventions on nuclear safety now in force. *UN Chron* 24:52 My '87

U.S., Soviets renew an exchange [nuclear safety] E. Marshall. *Science* 235:1568 Mr 27 '87

Security measures
Nuclear psych-out [workers at Davis Besse nuclear plant fired as security risks after failing psychological test] P. Kruger. il *Progressive* 51:24-5 Je '87

Canada
Nuclear deal-making. M. Drohan. il *Macleans* 100:28+ N 23 '87

Nuclear slowdown. C. Wood. il *Macleans* 100:24 Ag 10 '87

France
Slowdown for French fast breeders? D. Dickson. *Science* 238:472 O 23 '87

Superphénix springs a leak. D. Dickson. *Science* 236:248 Ap 17 '87

Great Britain
Britain chooses U.S.-designed reactor [pressurized water reactor] D. Dickson. *Science* 235:629 F 6 '87

Iran
A nuclear Gulf. S. Pope. il *World Press Rev* 34:38 S '87

Iraq
IAEA asked to consider measures to ensure Israel does not attack 'peaceful nuclear facilities' [General Assembly resolution prompted by Israel's attack on the Tammuz nuclear reactor] *UN Chron* 23:11 Ja '86

A nuclear Gulf. S. Pope. il *World Press Rev* 34:38 S '87

Ukraine
See also
Chernobyl nuclear disaster, 1986

Nuclear power workers
See also
Nuclear Support Services, Inc.

Health and hygiene
Human instability and nuclear weapons. H. L. Abrams. bibl f il *Bull At Sci* 43:34-9 Ja/F '87

Psychology
Nuclear psych-out [workers at Davis Besse nuclear plant fired as security risks after failing psychological test] P. Kruger. il *Progressive* 51:24-5 Je '87

Nuclear powered artificial satellites *See* Artificial satellites—Power supply

Nuclear powered space vehicles *See* Space vehicles—Power supply

Nuclear reactions
Small systems: when does thermodynamics apply? H. Feshbach. il *Phys Today* 40:9+ N '87

Solar neutrinos: questions and hypotheses. J. Weneser and G. Friedlander. bibl f il *Science* 235:755-9 F 13 '87

Vanishing solar neutrinos. A. Franco and D. H. Smith. il *Sky Telesc* 73:149 F '87

Nuclear reactors
See also
Nuclear power plants
Reactor fuel reprocessing
Tokamaks

Berkeley changes tack on reactor [decision to shut down reactor used for military-related research] J. Walsh. *Science* 235:273 Ja 16 '87

Britain chooses U.S.-designed reactor [pressurized water reactor] D. Dickson. *Science* 235:629 F 6 '87

Fusion's $372-million mothball [Mirror Fusion Test Facility] W. Booth. il *Science* 238:152-5 O 9 '87

JET: uncertainty follows success [Joint European Torus] C. Norman. il *Science* 237:1112 S 4 '87

Plutonium by the ton. E. Marshall. il *Science* 236:515-16 My 1 '87

Research reactor closed at Berkeley for mixed reasons. W. Sweet. *Phys Today* 40:56 Je '87

Slowdown for French fast breeders? D. Dickson. *Science* 238:472 O 23 '87

Use of Berkeley reactor questioned on military-related research [views of Charles Schwartz] J. Walsh. *Science* 235:23 Ja 2 '87

Accidents and explosions
See also
Chernobyl nuclear disaster, 1986

Manufacture
See Nuclear industry

Safety devices and measures
DOE shuts N-reactor for safety repairs but fears persist [Hanford] I. Goodwin. il *Phys Today* 40:63-4 F '87

End game for the N reactor? [Hanford reactor] E. Marshall. il *Science* 235:17-18 Ja 2 '87

Nuclear reactors—Safety devices and measures—*cont.*
How safe Savannah River reactors? E. Marshall. *Science* 235:1563-4 Mr 27 '87
Nuclear reactor safety assailed in report [GAO report] R. Weiss. *Sci News* 132:213 O 3 '87
Plutonium blues in Hanford [reactor temporarily closed] O. Friedrich. il *Time* 129:22 Ja 12 '87
Safe nuclear power [cover story] L. M. Lidsky. *New Repub* 197:20-3 D 28 '87
Safety of DOE reactors questioned [National Research Council report] E. Marshall. *Science* 238:741 N 6 '87
Uncle Sam's risky bomb plants. S. Budiansky. il map *U S News World Rep* 102:75-6 My 25 '87

Nuclear Regulatory Commission (U.S.) *See* U.S. Nuclear Regulatory Commission

Nuclear research
See also
Hanford Reservation (Wash.)
NRC's research program comes under fire [National Academy of Sciences report] J. Raloff. *Sci News* 131:38 Ja 17 '87

International aspects
No nation can be an island in science. R. C. Cowen. il *Technol Rev* 90:20+ My/Je '87
The road to magnetic fusion? D. E. Thomsen. *Sci News* 132:294 N 7 '87
U.S.S.R. eyes role in U.S. Compact Tokamak Ignition experiment. M. Crawford. il *Science* 238:1035 N 20 '87
US and EC conclude fusion agreement [magnetic fusion] W. Sweet. *Phys Today* 40:56-7 Je '87
What course for U.S. fusion energy R&D? [magnetic fusion] M. Crawford. *Science* 237:966-7 Ag 28 '87

Germany (West)
Jülich lab sets new priorities, opens neutron guide hall. W. Sweet. il *Phys Today* 40:61 Jl '87

Japan
Reflections of a Japanese physicist. M. Kimura. il pors *Bull At Sci* 43:7-10 N '87
Tristan e^+ e^- collider in Japan yields 50 GeV center of mass. G. B. Lubkin. il *Phys Today* 40:21-3 Ja '87

Soviet Union
Early years of Soviet nuclear physics. P. Josephson. bibl f il *Bull At Sci* 43:36-9 D '87
The making of the Soviet bomb [excerpt from How it began]; tr. by John Crowfoot. V. S. Yemelyanov. *Bull At Sci* 43:39-41 D '87
Soviet physicists map collider strategy. M. Crawford. il *Science* 238:1036-7 N 20 '87
Soviets plan huge linear collider. M. Crawford. *Science* 238:16-17 O 2 '87
UNK: the accelerator that couldn't shoot straight. R. P. Crease and C. C. Mann. il *Omni* 9:63-6+ Je '87

Western Europe
See also
Euratom
European Organization for Nuclear Research
JET: uncertainty follows success [Joint European Torus] C. Norman. il *Science* 237:1112 S 4 '87

Nuclear research laboratories
See also
Argonne National Laboratory
Brookhaven National Laboratory
Los Alamos Scientific Laboratory
Jülich lab sets new priorities, opens neutron guide hall [West Germany] W. Sweet. il *Phys Today* 40:61 Jl '87

Nuclear spin
Collisions between spinning protons. A. D. Krisch. bibl (p116) il *Sci Am* 257:42-50 Ag '87
Novel magnetic properties of solid helium-3. M. C. Cross and D. D. Osheroff. bibl f il *Phys Today* 40:34-41 F '87

Nuclear submarines
The race for sneaky subs: run silent, run deadly [cover story] T. Dworetzky. il map *Discover* 8:44-52 D '87
Run silent, run deadly [cover story] S. R. Southard. il *Pop Mech* 164:86-9+ Ap '87

Accidents and explosions
Naval reactors: the silent proliferation. D. E. Kaplan. il *Technol Rev* 90:10-11 Ap '87

Nuclear submarines, Canadian
The battle of the subs [nuclear subs contract] M. Clark. il *Macleans* 100:16 D 7 '87
Canada sees nuclear subs as key to Arctic defenses. il *Aviat Week Space Technol* 127:85+ S 21 '87
Canadian agency rejects nuclear subs, favors surface vessels and patrol aircraft. P. Mann. *Aviat Week Space Technol* 126:77-8 Je 1 '87

The case for the new policy. J. J. Sokolsky. il *Bull At Sci* 43:13-16 O '87
Cool criticism from Washington [Canadian plan to purchase fleet of nuclear-powered submarines] I. Austen. il *Macleans* 100:17 My 18 '87
Standing up to the United States [Canadian sovereignty in the Arctic] S. Shallhorn. *Bull At Sci* 43:16-17 O '87

Nuclear submarines, Russian
Deep secrets [Soviets guard sunken nuclear submarine] T. Gup. *Time* 130:28 O 5 '87
Spot photographs secret base for USSR nuclear submarines [Barents Sea] C. Covault. il *Aviat Week Space Technol* 127:18-19 Jl 20 '87

Nuclear Support Services, Inc.
The road to recovery? A. A. Lappen. il *Forbes* 140:8 S 7 '87

Nuclear test ban *See* Nuclear weapons—Testing—Suspension

Nuclear warfare
See also
Anti-nuclear movement
Children and nuclear warfare
Nuclear winter
Space warfare
"After MAD": a computer game of nuclear strategy that ends in a Prisoner's Dilemma. A. K. Dewdney. il *Sci Am* 257:174-7 O '87
Armageddon revisited. E. Marshall. *Science* 236:1421-2 Je 12 '87
The dangers of quick launch. R. N. Lebow. bibl f il *Bull At Sci* 43:36-9 N '87
Exploiting the Soviet "threat" to Europe [European Defense Initiative] M. A. Evangelista. bibl f *Bull At Sci* 43:14-16+ Ja/F '87
Happy birthday, flexible response [NATO nuclear strategy] W. M. Arkin. *Bull At Sci* 43:5-6 D '87
Hardguy software [Balance of Power strategic computer game designed by C. Crawford] J. Ledbetter. *Nation* 244:150-3 F 7 '87
Korean tripwire [possibility of nuclear war erupting in Korea] P. Hayes and others. *Nation* 245:256-7 S 19 '87
Learning to live with the bomb. D. O. Relin. il *Sch Update* 120:31 N 20 '87
A neglected lesson of the Chernobyl disaster [relationship to effects of a nuclear war] R. E. Powaski. *America* 156:167-8 F 28 '87
A new deterrent ["successful" nuclear first strikes] I. F. Stone. *Nation* 244:598-9 My 9 '87
Notes and comment. *New Yorker* 63:27-8 Mr 16 '87
Nuclear crash [computer simulation of the post-attack economy] C. Norman. *Science* 236:1517 Je 19 '87
Nuke City: wake up, America, to another sunny doomsday in Washington, District of Catastrophe. M. Amis. il *Esquire* 108:97-100+ O '87
Off with their heads: how Zbigniew Brzezinski hawked the doctrine of nuclear decapitation. M. Kaku and D. Axelrod. il *Progressive* 51:29-31 Ja '87
U.S. nuclear strategy: theory vs. practice. D. A. Rosenberg. bibl f *Bull At Sci* 43:20-6 Mr '87

Anecdotes, facetiae, satire, etc.
Last word [postnuclear scenarios] T. Runté. il *Omni* 9:114 Ag '87

Defenses
See also
Civil defense
Guided missiles—Defenses

Economic aspects
Return to the dark ages? The high price of nuclear war. il *Technol Rev* 90:80 O '87

Environmental aspects
Nuclear war as an environmental issue. J. Salzman. *Environment* 29:4-5+ Ja/F '87

Bibliography
Books. J. Dowling. *Phys Today* 40:97-8 N '87

Ethical aspects
Philosophers discover the bomb. M. E. Levin. *Natl Rev* 39:34+ D 4 '87
Waking up. A. Su. il por *Humanist* 47:20-1+ Mr/Ap '87

Prevention
See also
Disarmament
International Physicians for the Prevention of Nuclear War
Blundering into disaster [address, February 17, 1987] R. S. McNamara. *Vital Speeches Day* 53:390-4 Ap 15 '87
Crises and nuclear control. C. Norman. *Science* 235:1135 Mr 6 '87

Nuclear warfare—Prevention—cont.

How many fingers on the button? [views of D. Aaron in novel State scarlet] B. Van Voorst. il por *Time* 129:32 Ap 20 '87

Independent initiatives: an alternative peace process. M. Sommer and G. Feller. *Current* 292:36-9 My '87

Needed: a tactical defense initiative. J. Rhea. il *Space World* X-11-287:4 N '87

Soviet foreign minister visits Washington [agreement on establishing Nuclear Risk Reduction Centers] R. Reagan; E. Shevardnadze; G. P. Shultz. il *Dep State Bull* 87:34-40 N '87

Soviets will pay U.S. for risk center equipment. P. Mann. *Aviat Week Space Technol* 127:31 S 21 '87

Talk with a stranger. R. Redfield. *Cent Mag* 20:51-7 My/Je '87

U.S.-Soviet move toward risk reduction. J. Borawski. bibl f *Bull At Sci* 43:16-18 Jl/Ag '87

U.S., Soviet Union to establish Nuclear Risk Reduction Centers [White House statement, May 5, 1987] *Dep State Bull* 87:21-2 Jl '87

Psychological aspects

Nuclear language and how we learned to pat the bomb [cover story] C. Cohn. bibl f il *Bull At Sci* 43:17-24 Je '87

Patting the missile: making nuclear war less threatening. il *Discover* 8:6 Ag '87

Saving for what future? [perception of nuclear threat and savings habits; study by Joel Slemrod] J. A. Natale. *Psychol Today* 21:16 Ag '87

Sex, power, and nuclear language [discussion of June 1987 article, Nuclear language and how we learned to pat the bomb] C. Cohn. *Bull At Sci* 43:58-61 S '87

Public opinion

A growing fear of total war [Maclean's/Decima poll] B. Levin. il *Macleans* 100:50+ Ja 5 '87

Nuclear warfare and children *See* Children and nuclear warfare

Nuclear warfare and religion

A classic case of consequentialism [criticism of Cardinal Ratzinger's views on the morality of deterrence] E. W. Doherty. *Commonweal* 114:10-11 Ja 16 '87

An editorial dissent [discussion of May 8, 1987 article, Is deterrence moral?] P. Jordan. *Commonweal* 114:309-10 My 22 '87

Expanding the peace movement [National Association of Evangelicals] R. J. Neuhaus. *Natl Rev* 39:46 F 27 '87

Is deterrence moral? [Catholic view] *Commonweal* 114:259-61 My 8 '87

Is nuclear deterrence immoral? [Catholic bishops' stand] R. E. Powaski. *America* 156:401-5 My 16 '87

Is nuclear deterrence moral? [Catholic views] J. M. Cameron. bibl f il *N Y Rev Books* 34:38-43 N 5 '87

Sidestepping The challenge of peace [Catholic bishops' pastoral on nuclear deterrence] M. Gallagher. il *Commonweal* 114:9-13 Ja 16 '87

Weaving a seamless garment out of peace, freedom, and security [National Association of Evangelicals guidelines on war and peace] R. Frame. il *Christ Today* 31:42-4 My 15 '87

Nuclear warfare in literature

Yooks, zooks and the bomb [children's literature] R. Sutton. *N Y Times Book Rev* 92:22 F 22 '87

Nuclear waste disposal *See* Radioactive waste disposal

Nuclear weapons

See also
    Anti-nuclear movement
    Atomic bombs
    Guided missiles
    Nuclear-free zones
    Strategic Defense Initiative

Aid to Pakistan: megatons of trouble for the U.S.? B. Javetski. il *Bus Week* p57 Ap 6 '87

The arms race is a universal issue. P. Ochieng. il *World Press Rev* 34:36-7 Ja '87

A bad case of nuclear friction [Pakistan rejects U.S. attempt to link inspection of nuclear facilities to aid package] M. S. Serrill. il *Time* 130:40 Ag 17 '87

British, French, and Chinese nuclear weapons. il *Bull At Sci* 43:52 D '87

A case of treason [trial of M. Vanunu in Israel] A. Bilski. il por *Macleans* 100:25 S 14 '87

Controlling deadly weapons [special section] *Society* 24:38-79 Jl/Ag '87

Defense Dept. plans to study earth-penetrating nuclear weapons. J. D. Morrocco. *Aviat Week Space Technol* 126:28-9 Je 8 '87

A European deterrent? B. Crozier. *Natl Rev* 39:24 Jl 31 '87

Explosive power of the U.S. nuclear weapons stockpile. il *Bull At Sci* 43:64 Jl/Ag '87

The game of perceptions in arms racing [with discussion] S. Kull. por *Cent Mag* 20:43-57 S/O '87

Glenn asks Reagan to halt Pakistan aid pending review of nuclear programs. M. Crawford. por *Science* 235:1321 Mr 13 '87

Greece's balancing act [U.S. bases and nuclear weapons] W. M. Arkin. *Bull At Sci* 43:11-12 Mr '87

How lies proliferate [Pakistan's nuclear capabilities] *Nation* 244:381 Mr 28 '87

In the shadow of the 'Islamic bomb' [Pakistan's nuclear capability] A. Bilski. il *Macleans* 100:24+ Mr 23 '87

India, Pakistan racing to be last. R. V. R. Chandrasekhar Rao. il *Bull At Sci* 43:32-4 N '87

Israel's nuclear ambiguity. A. Cohen and B. Frankel. bibl f il *Bull At Sci* 43:15-19 Mr '87

Israel's nuclear ambiguity. A. Cohen and B. Frankel. *Current* 294:34-8 Jl/Ag '87

Knocking at the nuclear door [Pakistan; with interview with M. Zia-ul-Haq] W. R. Doerner. il por *Time* 129:42-3 Mr 30 '87

Minority report [case of M. Vanunu] C. Hitchens. *Nation* 244:387 Mr 28 '87

NATO Nuclear Planning Group meets in Norway [text of final communique, May 15, 1987] *Dep State Bull* 87:57 Jl '87

NATO Nuclear Planning Group meets in the U.K. [text of communique, October 22, 1986] *Dep State Bull* 86:65-6 D '86

NATO planning group to discuss post-INF tactical nuclear strategy. J. D. Morrocco. *Aviat Week Space Technol* 127:125+ O 12 '87

NATO ponders its nuclear options. C. Norman. il *Science* 238:1498-500 D 11 '87

NATO's fallback: can 'battlefield' nukes hold the line? N. Cooper. il *Newsweek* 109:28-9 My 4 '87

The nuclear arsenal in the Middle East. F. Barnaby. il map *Technol Rev* 90:27-34 My/Je '87

The nuclear caper [arrest of Arshad Pervez in Philadelphia on charges of trying to illegally export materials for Pakistan's weapons program] I. Austen. il *Macleans* 100:19 Jl 27 '87

The nuclear club grows, but new members are shy [with interview with J. Nye] R. A. Manning. il *U S News World Rep* 102:34-5 Mr 23 '87

Nuclear proliferation: who's next? L. S. Spector. bibl f il *Bull At Sci* 43:17-20 My '87

Nuclear weapons, arms control, and the future of deterrence [address, November 17, 1986] G. P. Shultz. *Dep State Bull* 87:31-5 Ja '87

Nuke City: wake up, America, to another sunny doomsday in Washington, District of Catastrophe. M. Amis. il *Esquire* 108:97-100+ O '87

Pakistan and the nuclear issue [statement, July 22, 1987] R. W. Murphy. *Dep State Bull* 87:53-4 O '87

A Pakistan bombshell [evidence it has nuclear arms] R. Nordland. il *Newsweek* 109:45 Mr 16 '87

The Pakistan syndrome [halting nuclear proliferation] *New Repub* 197:7-8+ S 28 '87

Pakistan thought to possess atomic bomb. M. Crawford. il *Science* 235:1131 Mr 6 '87

Pakistani smuggling riles Congress. L. S. Spector. il *Bull At Sci* 43:3-4 O '87

Plutonium by the ton. E. Marshall. il *Science* 236:515-16 My 1 '87

A right to disobedience? [trial of M. Vanunu in Israel] S. Seibert. il por *Newsweek* 110:41 S 7 '87

A rock and a hard place [Pakistan caught trying to illegally import maraging steel intended for bomb program] R. Nordland. il *Newsweek* 110:30+ Jl 27 '87

Seven nations curb nuclear weapon launch system exports [Missile Technology Control Regime] D. M. North. *Aviat Week Space Technol* 126:28-9 Ap 20 '87

Stemming the spread of nuclear weapons. M. M. Miller. il *Technol Rev* 90:68-75 Ag/S '87

Superpower arms race at sea [cover story; special section] bibl f il *Bull At Sci* 43:13-28+ S '87

Third-generation nuclear weapons. T. B. Taylor. bibl (p128) il *Sci Am* 256:30-9 Ap '87

A third generation of nukes. M. D. Lemonick. il *Time* 129:36 My 25 '87

U.S. and Soviet nuclear weapons under development. *Bull At Sci* 43:56 O '87

U.S. nuclear weapons stockpile (June 1987). il *Bull At Sci* 43:56 Je '87

Nuclear weapons—*cont.*

Wanted: the bomb [possible cutoff of U.S. military aid after Pakistan's attempt buy steel alloy for nuclear weapons] il *U S News World Rep* 103:8 Jl 27 '87

"We don't have the bomb" [interview with R. Gandhi] P. Gupte. il pors *Forbes* 139:156+ My 18 '87

Weapons that must never be used. E. Weiner. il *Sch Update* 119:21 F 23 '87

Western Europe's dilemma: is a strong defense possible without nuclear arms? H. Cleveland. il *USA Today (Periodical)* 116:52-4 S '87

Who has nuclear weapons? D. Plater. il *Sch Update* 120:30 N 20 '87

A world without nuclear weapons [address, November 13, 1986] K. L. Adelman. *Dep State Bull* 87:35-8 Ja '87

A world without nuclear weapons? [special section] il *N Y Times Mag* p45-9+ Ap 5 '87

Disarmament
See Disarmament

Manufacture
See also
Pantex

Atomic gaffe [House Subcommittee on Oversight and Investigations' study of security at nuclear weapons manufacturing plants] *Nation* 244:349 Mr 21 '87

Energy Department blurs line between civilian, military reactors [plan to convert Unit One of the Washington Public Power Supply System to weapons purposes] M. M. Hoenig. bibl f *Bull At Sci* 43:25-7 Je '87

Heavy water cheaters. G. Milhollin. bibl f *Foreign Policy* 69:100-19 Wint '87/'88

Human instability and nuclear weapons. H. L. Abrams. bibl f il *Bull At Sci* 43:34-9 Ja/F '87

Pakistan's bomb-making capacity [gas centrifuge enrichment plant at Kahuta] D. Albright. bibl f il *Bull At Sci* 43:30-3 Je '87

Uncle Sam's risky bomb plants. S. Budiansky. il map *U S News World Rep* 102:75-6 My 25 '87

Why is D.O.E. for food irradiation? [justifying the extraction of plutonium from commercial nuclear wastes for use in nuclear weapons] K. Terry. il *Nation* 244:142+ F 7 '87

Moral and religious aspects

The churches and the peace movement in France. M. B. Davis. il *Christ Century* 104:826-8 S 30 '87

Living in sin with nuclear arms [views of M. Gallagher on Catholic bishops' peace pastoral] J. M. Wall. *Christ Century* 104:155-6 F 18 '87

Ministering to the collective soul amid the arms race. J. Smith. il *Christ Century* 104:17-20 Ja 7-14 '87

Moral rhetoric, moral confusion in the Star Wars debate. E. T. Linenthal. il *Christ Century* 104:1058-61 N 25 '87

One night in the Beatty lockup [anti-nuclear protest] L. R. Peattie. il *Commonweal* 114:140-3 Mr 13 '87

Our backs against the bomb, our eyes on the stars. R. L. Schweickart. il *Discover* 8:62+ Jl '87

The present and the apocalypse [Pantex factory] C. Widmann. *World Press Rev* 34:51 Mr '87

'The things that make for peace' [United Methodist pastoral In defense of creation] W. H. Willimon. *Christ Century* 104:453-4 My 6 '87

Willimon hollering at bishops? [discussion of May 6, 1987 article, The things that make for peace] W. H. Willimon. *Christ Century* 104:632-4 Jl 15-22 '87

Photographs and photography

The bomb we never see [work of R. Del Tredici] J. Schell. il *Progressive* 51:25-8 D '87

Physiological effects
See Radiation—Physiological effects

Protests, demonstrations, etc.
See Anti-nuclear movement

Security measures

Atomic gaffe [House Subcommittee on Oversight and Investigations' study of security at nuclear weapons manufacturing plants] *Nation* 244:349 Mr 21 '87

Human instability and nuclear weapons. H. L. Abrams. bibl f il *Bull At Sci* 43:34-9 Ja/F '87

Study and teaching

Politics and "peace education." A. Ryerson. *Read Dig* 130:133-8 Je '87

International aspects

Satellites for the classroom [joint U.S.-U.S.S.R. course on the nuclear arms race] S. Begley. il *Newsweek* 110:103 N 16 '87

Terminology

Nuclear language and how we learned to pat the bomb [cover story] C. Cohn. bibl f il *Bull At Sci* 43:17-24 Je '87

Patting the missile: making nuclear war less threatening. il *Discover* 8:6 Ag '87

Sex, power, and nuclear language [discussion of June 1987 article, Nuclear language and how we learned to pat the bomb] C. Cohn. *Bull At Sci* 43:58-61 S '87

Talking nukespeak. D. O. Relin. il *Sch Update* 120:33 N 20 '87

Testing

See also
National Association of Radiation Survivors

Australia's nuclear graveyard [British nuclear tests in the outback during the 1950s and 1960s] R. Milliken. il map *Bull At Sci* 43:38-44 Ap '87

Bombs without test blasts? [Pakistan] D. Albright. bibl f *Bull At Sci* 43:32 Je '87

Bottling the bomb [reusable underground test chambers] *Sci Am* 256:68-9 Ja '87

Nuclear tests defended [views of George Miller] C. Norman. *Science* 235:963-4 F 27 '87

An opening closed [Haysbrook underground bomb test, February 1986] *Nation* 244:131-2 F 7 '87

A simulated goddess [Aurora nuclear blast simulator] D. Eskow. il *Pop Mech* 164:21 My '87

Testers and protesters [Nevada test site] M. Riley. il *Time* 129:28 F 16 '87

"What has happened is incredible" [increased cancer incidence in Utah near site of 1950's atomic bomb tests]; ed. by Dena Kleiman. C. Peterson. il por *Redbook* 168:44+ Ja '87

The yields of Soviet strategic weapons. L. R. Sykes and D. M. Davis. bibl (p128) il map *Sci Am* 256:29-37 Ja '87

Detection

Gaining ground zero [joint Soviet-American seismic detection of underground explosions] L. Y. Lin. il *Sierra* 72:33-6 Ja/F '87

The grounds for a test ban treaty [joint Soviet-American seismic detection of underground explosions] G. Garelik. il maps *Discover* 8:50-2+ Je '87

Mexico Declaration on nuclear testing contains verification proposals. *UN Chron* 23:71 N '86

Monitoring the sounds of silence [seismic monitoring] R. Monastersky. *Sci News* 131:345 My 30 '87

Nuclear test ban verification agreements yield new seismic data. W. Sweet. il *Phys Today* 40:83-5 N '87

Nuclear test watchers feel political heat [joint Soviet-American seismic monitoring] E. Marshall. map *Science* 237:594-6 Ag 7 '87

The Soviet mantle and nuclear test monitoring. R. A. Kerr. *Science* 236:1426 Je 12 '87

A Soviet official on verification. R. Timerbaev. *Bull At Sci* 43:8-10 Ja/F '87

Soviets to allow monitoring in USSR. R. Monastersky. *Sci News* 132:6 Jl 4 '87

Test ban compliance: is seismology enough? [U.S. prefers Continuous Reflectometry for Radius versus Time Experiments] D. C. Morrison. il *Science* 236:383-6 Ap 24 '87

U.S.-Soviet seismic monitoring advances. R. A. Kerr. *Science* 235:434-5 Ja 23 '87

Verification: will it work? [cover story] D. Aaron. il *N Y Times Mag* p36-40+ O 11 '87

Yields of US and Soviet nuclear tests [seismic detection verification of Threshold Test Ban Treaty compliance; cover story] J. F. Evernden and G. E. Marsh. bibl il *Phys Today* 40 pt1:36-44 Ag '87

Suspension

Before we cheer [comparison between impending INF Treaty and the nuclear test ban treaty of 1963] S. H. Day, Jr. *Progressive* 51:14-15 N '87

The Hazebrook folly. H. Evans. il *U S News World Rep* 102:70 F 2 '87

Make the partial test ban comprehensive. G. T. Seaborg and B. S. Loeb. *Bull At Sci* 43:3 My '87

"New thinking" in the Kremlin. F. Griffiths. bibl f *Bull At Sci* 43:20-4 Ap '87

A nuclear test ban. P. Doty. bibl f *Foreign Aff* 65:750-69 Spr '87

Nuclear testing: illusion and reality. W. Epstein. *Bull At Sci* 43:8 Ap '87

Policy forum [views of six experts] *Science* 238:455-64 O 23 '87

The quest for a comprehensive test ban treaty. R. E. Powaski. il *America* 157:61-5 Ag 1-8 '87

Senate consideration of unratified treaties to limit nuclear testing [Threshold Test Ban Treaty and the Peaceful Nuclear Explosions Treaty] *Dep State Bull* 87:48-52 Je '87

Would a test ban strengthen SDI? S. Fetter. il *Bull At Sci* 43:40-1 N '87

Nuclear weapons—Testing—Suspension—_cont._

Yields of US and Soviet nuclear tests [seismic detection verification of Threshold Test Ban Treaty compliance; cover story] J. F. Evernden and G. E. Marsh. bibl il _Phys Today_ 40 pt1:36-44 Ag '87

Nuclear weapons and disarmament _See_ Disarmament

Nuclear Weapons Freeze Campaign
> _See also_
> SANE/FREEZE (Organization)

Nuclear winter

Climate modeling [cover story] S. H. Schneider. il _Sci Am_ 256:72-8+ My '87

The infrared herring of nuclear summer [views of Fred Singer] _Discover_ 8:8-9 My '87

The little chill. E. Marshall. _New Repub_ 196:4+ F 16 '87

Nuclear winter debate heats up [study by the National Center for Atmospheric Research] E. Marshall. il _Science_ 235:271-3 Ja 16 '87

Severe global-scale effects of nuclear war reaffirmed. _Environment_ 29:4-5+ My '87

Updating the "nuclear winter" debate [SCOPE-ENUWAR Bangkok workshop] M. A. Harwell and C. C. Harwell. _Bull At Sci_ 43:42-4 O '87

Nuclear winter and religion

Nuclear winter and the call for disarmament. A. Geyer. il _Christ Century_ 104:677-8 Ag 12-19 '87

Nucleases
> _See also_
> Deoxyribonuclease
> Ribonucleases

Chemical conversion of a DNA-binding protein into a site-specific nuclease. C.-H. B. Chen and D. S. Sigman. bibl f il _Science_ 237:1197-1201 S 4 '87

Nucleic acids
> _See also_
> DNA
> Nitrogenous bases
> Nucleotides
> RNA

Nucleoproteins
> _See also_
> Interferon
> Ribosomes

Nucleosides
> _See also_
> Adenosine

Nucleosynthesis

The cosmic synthesis of lithium, beryllium and boron. V. E. Viola and G. J. Mathews. il _Sci Am_ 256:38-45 My '87

Nucleotide sequences _See_ Genetic code

Nucleotides
> _See also_
> Adenosine monophosphate
> Adenosine triphosphate
> Guanosine monophosphate
> Guanosine triphosphate

The immunoglobulin octanucleotide: independent activity and selective interaction with enhancers. T. G. Parslow and others. bibl f il _Science_ 235:1498-1501 Mr 20 '87

A system for rapid DNA sequencing with fluorescent chain-terminating dideoxynucleotides. J. M. Prober and others. bibl f il _Science_ 238:336-41 O 16 '87

Nucleus (Cells) _See_ Cell nuclei

Nude in art

Matisse's Two negresses [sculpture] J. Hobhouse. il por _Art News_ 86:91-2 D '87

Nude photography _See_ Photography of the nude

Nudibranchs _See_ Sea slugs

Nudity

On the beach: plovers vs. nudists [Rhode Island] il _Newsweek_ 110:63 Ag 3 '87

Wanted: a nude _glasnost_ [women's magazines in the Soviet Union] S. Drakulich. il _Nation_ 244:846-8 Je 20 '87

Nudity in advertising

Leer campaign [ads for Lear's magazine] N. J. Perry. il _Fortune_ 116:159 N 9 '87

Sex and salesmanship [nudity in ads for Lear's magazine] A. Steacy. il _Macleans_ 100:64 O 5 '87

Nuechterlein, James

A farewell to civil rights. _Commentary_ 84:25-36 Ag '87

The feminization of the American left. _Commentary_ 84:43-8 N '87

Nuestra Señora de Atocha (Ship)

Despite centuries underwater, seeds from a sunken galleon prove life begins at 365 [research by C. Malcom] il por _People Wkly_ 28:59 Ag 3 '87

A fabulous lady from Spain [cover story] R. A. Green. il por _Antiques Collect Hobbies_ 92:30-4 My '87

Number concept

Asian languages aid mathematics skills [research by Irene T. Miura] B. Bower. _Sci News_ 132:183 S 19 '87

Number systems _See_ Numeration

Number theory
> _See also_
> Fermat's theorem

Numbers
> _See also_
> Nine (The number)
> Pi
> Thirteen (The number)

The "coincidence" of the large numbers isn't coincidental. T. Rothman. il _Discover_ 8:93 My '87

Points of reference [how impersonal numbers take on a life of their own in crises] E. Levin. il _People Wkly_ 28:40-1 N 2 '87

Terminology

Head over googol [terminology of large numbers] A. W. Powers. il _N Y Times Mag_ p10+ Ag 9 '87

Numbers, Complex

Complex math in Pascal. D. Gedeon. il _Byte_ 12:121-2+ Jl '87

Numbers, Prime

Once more through the Sieve [Sieve of Eratosthenes prime number generator] S. Ciarcia. il _Byte_ 12:36+ D '87

Numbers, Random
> _See also_
> Random number generators

Craps, the Monkey Test, and other ways of proving that a series of numbers isn't random [work of George Marsaglia] il _Discover_ 8:78-9 Ja '87

Numeration
> _See also_
> Counting
> Ternary system

History

Lumps of clay that gave birth to numbers [Sumerian tablets; work of Denise Schmandt-Besserat] il _Discover_ 8:7-8 Mr '87

Numerical ability _See_ Mathematical ability

Numerology _See_ Symbolism of numbers

Numismatics
> _See also_
> American Numismatic Association
> Coins as an investment
> Dollar sign
> Seals (Numismatics)

Numismatics. E. Rochette. See issues of Antiques & Collecting Hobbies beginning March 1985

Numismatics. E. Rochette. See issues of Hobbies through February 1985

Nunery, Leroy D.
> _about_

Leroy Nunery: working for a bigger crop of minority MBAs. M. Mallory. por _Bus Week_ p76 O 26 '87

Nunes, Shirley

The boy who wouldn't say his name [story] il _Ladies Home J_ 104:56+ Jl '87

Nunn, Kem

Chairman of the board: Tom Curren. il pors _Roll Stone_ p81-4 Jl 16-30 '87

Nunn, Sam

Should the Levin-Nunn Amendment be approved? [excerpts from address, May 13, 1987] _Congr Dig_ 66:264+ N '87
> _about_

Arms Control Agency challenges Nunn's contention on legality of testing kinetic systems. _Aviat Week Space Technol_ 126:29 Mr 23 '87

Big Foot South sits it out. D. Baer. il por _U S News World Rep_ 103:12 S 7 '87

Hard choice for the Hamlet of the South. D. Baer. il por _U S News World Rep_ 103:22-3 Ag 24 '87

Leading roles: the stature of Schroeder & Nunn. J. B. Hehir. _Commonweal_ 114:645-6 N 20 '87

A lot of Nunnsense. W. Greider. il _Roll Stone_ p57+ Mr 26 '87

Memo to Sam: it's going to be tough. H. Fineman. por _Newsweek_ 110:19 Ag 31 '87

Nunn affirms 1972 ABM pact, finding kinetic tests illegal. P. Mann. _Aviat Week Space Technol_ 126:21-3 Mr 16 '87

Nunn calls for conventional upgrades to balance possible nuclear cuts. K. F. Mordoff. _Aviat Week Space Technol_ 126:30-1 Ap 20 '87

Nunn, Sam—about—*cont.*

Nunn threatens INF pact with link to ABM Treaty. P. Mann. *Aviat Week Space Technol* 126:30 My 11 '87

Nunn too soon for president? [interview] il *U S News World Rep* 102:20 Ja 19 '87

Nunn's countdown. por *Newsweek* 109:7 F 23 '87

Nunn's view: a chance to 'educate' Europe. T. Jacoby. il por *Newsweek* 109:30 My 4 '87

'Renegotiate the ABM Treaty' [interview] por *U S News World Rep* 103:30-1 D 14 '87

Rising star Sam Nunn ponders a presidential bid. D. Harbrecht. il por *Bus Week* p43 Ja 12 '87

Sam Nunn: "After two hours of walking NYC's streets, three people had asked me to run! Three!". M. Moynihan. il por *Vogue* 177:248+ O '87

Sam Nunn is sticking to his guns. D. Griffiths. il por *Bus Week* p52-3 Ag 24 '87

Sam Nunn's rising star. P. Gailey. il pors *N Y Times Mag* p24-9+ Ja 4 '87

The songs of the South. W. Shapiro. il por *Time* 130:17 Ag 31 '87

Southern scramble. J. B. Copeland. por *Newsweek* 110:5 S 7 '87

When Nunn speaks . . . C. Norman. il por *Science* 235:1457 Mr 20 '87

Anecdotes, facetiae, satire, etc.

President Nunn's team. G. F. Will. il *Newsweek* 110:74 Ag 3 '87

Nunneries *See* Convents

Nuns

American nuns: are they still a class act? [interview with M. L. Tobin] por *U S Cathol* 52:27-34 Ja '87

Nuns as authors

Mysteries from a novelist nun [C. A. O'Marie] J. Horowitz. il por *N Y Times Mag* p34-5 Ag 30 '87

Nuns as physicians

The healing of soul and body [work of Sister Anne Brooks] L. Lindeman. il pors *50 Plus* 27:20-3+ D '87

Sister Anne Brooks, doctor and nun, practices without preaching to the poor. B. Shaw. il pors *People Wkly* 27:82-3+ Mr 23 '87

Nunsense [musical]   See   Musicals,   revues, etc.—Reviews—Single works

Nur el Hussein, Queen, consort of Hussein, King of Jordan

about

Architectural digest visits: King Hussein and Queen Noor of Jordan. G. Y. Dryansky. il pors *Archit Dig* 44:68-77+ Ja '87

Nureyev, Rudolf, 1938-

about

Cinderella [ballet] Reviews

Art Am il 75:43-5 S '87. J. R. Acocella

Dance Mag il 61:58-63 F '87. M. E. Willis

Dance Mag il 61:32 S '87. W. Como

Dance Mag 61:76-7 D '87. A. Smith

N Y 20:57-8 Jl 13 '87. T. Tobias

New Leader 70:21-2 Jl 13-27 '87. L. A. Jacobs

Nursemaids

Baba says ta ta to Wills and Harry—the question is, did Charles and Di get the nanny's goat? [B. Barnes dismissed] B. Johnson. il pors *People Wkly* 27:44+ F 2 '87

A no-nonsense nanny strolls into Charles and Di's nursery [R. Wallace] il pors *People Wkly* 27:45 Mr 30 '87

Princess Di's nanny remembers . . . the custody battle for Diana. M. Clarke. il pors *Redbook* 169:88-9+ Ag '87

A story about professionalism, attachment and women's hearts. S. Weller. *Glamour* 85:134+ Mr '87

Where to turn when you need a nanny. E. Ehrlich. il *Bus Week* p133 D 21 '87

Nurseries (Horticulture)

See also

Garden centers (Retail trade)

Mail order business

See Mail order business

Nursery rhymes

See also

Mother Goose

Nursery schools

See also

Day care

Smart, magical, funny 3-year-olds [work of V. G. Paley at the University of Chicago Laboratory Nursery School] P. La Farge. il pors *Parents* 62:160-4+ N '87

Why we skipped nursery school. L. Kotrosits. il *Parents* 62:68+ S '87

Nurses and nursing

See also

National Black Nurses Association

Computers for nurses. J. I. Mattill. il *Technol Rev* 90:8+ Ap '87

Critical care nurses. S. Wilding. il *Good Housekeep* 204:136+ My '87

"Don't let my baby die!" [preeclampsia; excerpt from Intensive care] E. Heron. il por *Redbook* 168:122-4+ Ap '87

Emergency room nurse [excerpt from Intensive care] E. Heron. il *Glamour* 85:330-1+ Ap '87

A nurse. D. K. Mano. *Natl Rev* 39:59-60 Mr 27 '87

Attitudes

AIDS: treating it, fearing it [survey of nurses] *Sci News* 131:89 F 7 '87

Crime

Long Island's 'angel of death' [male nurse R. Angelo charged with murder of patients at Good Samaritan Hospital in West Islip, N.Y.] D. Gates. il por *Newsweek* 110:35 N 30 '87

Religious life

Contemplation exploded in my heart. M. Mitcham. il *Commonweal* 114:474-6 S 11 '87

Salaries, pensions, etc.

Occupational pay structure in nursing and personal care facilities. il *Mon Labor Rev* 110:41-2 Jl '87

The road to greater job satisfaction—and more money. G. Bakoulis. *Work Woman* 12:80 Ag '87

Study and teaching

Nursing careers: new and improved. G. Hechinger. il *Glamour* 85:364 Ap '87

Spotlight on schools. *Teen* 31:110 O '87

Fiji

Training rural-based nurses. V. G. Hawley. il *World Health* p12-15 My '87

Supply and demand

Nurses: few and fatigued. M. Clark. il *Newsweek* 109:59+ Je 29 '87

Too few nurses? G. Biscoe. il *World Health* p14-15 Ap '87

Nursing (Infant feeding) *See* Breast feeding

Nursing (Suckling) *See* Suckling

Nursing home patients

The last stop [letter] M. M. Rice. *Harpers* 274:4-7 My '87

Son, behold your mother. T. Unsworth. *U S Cathol* 52:28-30 Jl '87

Whose best interest? [use of restraints in nursing homes] B. Lindeman. il *50 Plus* 27:4 D '87

Nutrition

A home for malnutrition [study by Gayle D. Pinchcofsky-Devin] *Prevention* 39:68 N '87

Recreation

Mystery rides for nursing home residents [Woodview Health Care facility in Fort Wayne, Ind.] M. Hammer. il *Aging* no356:30-1 '87

Visitors

See Nursing homes—Visitors

Nursing homes

See also

Insurance, Nursing home care

The fast-care industry. R. J. Margolis. il *New Leader* 70:13-14 Ja 12-26 '87

The nursing home dilemma. T. Stafford. il *Christ Today* 31:22 N 6 '87

What you need to know [choosing a nursing home] il *U S News World Rep* 103:58+ Jl 20 '87

Where time stands still [New Ralston House, Philadelphia] J. Buckley. il *U S News World Rep* 103:50-7 Jl 20 '87

Costs

Caught in the VA-Medicaid trap [veterans needing nursing home care] S. Nohlgren. *50 Plus* 27:23 O '87

Medical care and pauperization. G. P. Brockway. *New Leader* 70:11-12 D 28 '87

Ethical aspects

A concerned Christian goes the Second Mile [J. A. Peterson's effort to refund investors bilked in bankrupt nursing home fraud] *Christ Today* 31:47-8 F 6 '87

Visitors

While demons howl, folks in a Florida nursing home scare kids every witch way but loose [Green Briar Nursing Home in Kendall] il *People Wkly* 28:98 N 2 '87

Canada

Profits in health care. T. Tedesco. il *Macleans* 100:26-7 Je 8 '87

Nuseibeh, Sari
about
The strange bedfellows. M. J. Kubic. il por *Newsweek* 110:42 O 5 '87
Nussbaum, Hedda, 1942-
about
A tragic life and death. M. Gray. il pors *Macleans* 100:50 N 23 '87
A wicked rage claims a child. K. Gross. il pors *People Wkly* 28:44-9 N 23 '87
Nussbaum, Martha Craven, 1947-
Undemocratic vistas. bibl f il *N Y Rev Books* 34:20-6 N 5 '87
Nussbaum, Muriel
(jt. auth) See Bergman, Carol, and Nussbaum, Muriel
Nussenzweig, Michel C., and others
Allelic exclusion in transgenic mice that express the membrane form of immunoglobulin μ. bibl f il *Science* 236:816-19 My 15 '87
Nüsslein-Volhard, Christiane, and others
Determination of anteroposterior polarity in Drosophila. bibl f il *Science* 238:1675-81 D 18 '87
Nut industry
Mozambique
Meanwhile, back in Mozambique [cashews] il *Forbes* 140:110 N 16 '87
Nut trees
See also
Filbert trees
The Nutcracker [ballet] See Ballet reviews—Single works
Nutcracker: money, madness, murder [television program]
See Television program reviews—Single works
Nutley (N.J.)
Monuments, statues, etc.
Grass-roots art seeks a haven [A. Nardone's Roman ruins] H. Metz. il por *Progressive* 51:14 O '87
Nutmeg
Nutmeg. E. Schneider. il *Gourmet* 47:86-7+ D '87
NutraSweet *See* Sugar substitutes
NutriClean Inc.
Pesticide protection [California markets test produce] J. Adler. il *Newsweek* 110:69+ N 9 '87
Nutrient capsules
Hiking light: meal in a capsule [Sustain SP] J. Venturino. il *Women's Sports Fitness* 9:59 My '87
Nutrient labeling of food *See* Food—Labeling
Nutrition
See also
Aged—Nutrition
Aging—Nutritional aspects
Aluminum in the body
Alzheimer's disease—Nutritional aspects
Arteriosclerosis—Nutritional aspects
Arthritis—Nutritional aspects
Athletes—Nutrition
Baseball players—Nutrition
Breakfasts
Calcium in the body
Cancer—Nutritional aspects
Carbohydrates
Children—Nutrition
Chromium in the body
Copper in the body
Dancers—Nutrition
Diabetes—Nutritional aspects
Diet
Dietary supplements
Dietitians
Digestion
Fiber in diet
Firefighters—Nutrition
Gallstones—Nutritional aspects
Gingivitis—Nutritional aspects
Headache—Nutritional aspects
Heart—Diseases—Nutritional aspects
Human Nutrition Research Center (U.S.)
Hyperactivity—Nutritional aspects
Hypertension—Nutritional aspects
Infants—Nutrition
Iodine in the body
Iron in the body
Juvenile delinquents and delinquency—Nutrition
Magnesium in the body
Malnutrition
Minerals in the body
Nursing home patients—Nutrition
Nutrient capsules
Plants—Nutrition
Pregnancy—Nutritional aspects
Premenstrual syndrome—Nutritional aspects
Proteins

Regional ileitis—Nutritional aspects
Skiers—Nutrition
Snacks
Stress—Nutritional aspects
Tennis players—Nutrition
Trace elements
Tube feeding
Vitamins
Women—Nutrition
Women athletes—Nutrition
Xerophthalmia—Nutritional aspects
Youth—Nutrition
Zinc in the body
101 great nutrition ideas for busy people; ed. by Maria Mihalik. il *Prevention* 39:34-6+ Ap '87
1987 smart eater's guide. il *Seventeen* 46:118-19 Ja '87
Brain food: eat smart to stay sharp. S. C. Finn. il *50 Plus* 27:65+ Je '87
The clip-out catalog of super foods. J. Carper. il *Redbook* 168:127-30 Ap '87
Companion planting, companion eating [benefits of eating diverse foods] A. Hirsch. il *Rodale's Org Gard* 34:92-3 Ja '87
Diet and health. See issues of Better Homes and Gardens beginning March 1985
Dining out with a healthy appetite. il *FDA Consum* 21:18-23 Mr '87
Do you have shopping savvy? il *Seventeen* 46:214-15 Ap '87
Eat more, weigh less, feel great [condensed from Jane Brody's Good food book] J. E. Brody. *Read Dig* 131:159-62 N '87
Eating healthfully: for appearance' sake [study by Diane Hayes and Catherine E. Ross] S. Walton. *Psychol Today* 21:18 D '87
Fan fare [healthy food selections at the National Tennis Center during the U.S. Open] L. C. Garrett. il *World Tennis* 35:45-6 S '87
Fit, fast food. il *Good Housekeep* 204:120+ My '87
Food foolers and other little-known facts about food. B. Hayton. il *Curr Health 2* 13:24-7 Ja '87
Food for thought. B. T. Hunter. See issues of Consumers' Research Magazine
Get shrewd about food: five nutrition updates. L. Bellini-Gergley. il *Mademoiselle* 93:114 Ag '87
The good nutrition almanac. K. Stechert and others. il *Better Homes Gard* 65:36+ Mr '87
The great energy game. il *Seventeen* 46:260-1 Mr '87
How to eat for more energy. N. Stedman. il *Read Dig* 130:112-15 F '87
How to get more health from your food. J. B. Hurley. il *Prevention* 39:57-8+ D '87
Make it snappy! [nutritious quick meals] il *Seventeen* 46:132-3 F '87
Mood foods to raise your energy or lower your stress [excerpt from Managing your mind and mood through food]; ed. by Margaret Danbrot. J. J. Wurtman. il *Redbook* 168:106-9+ F '87
Nutrient interactions: the inner-digestive struggle. il *Curr Health 2* 13:11-13 My '87
Nutrition/fitness. D. W. Hatfield. See issues of McCall's beginning March 1986
Nutrition all-stars. P. Cobe. il *Ladies Home J* 104:142-5+ O '87
Nutrition digest. See issues of Prevention (Emmaus, Pa.) beginning February 1986 through February 1988
Nutrition in your life. H. Fisher. See issues of Prevention (Emmaus, Pa.) beginning January 1987
Nutrition information: how to tell fact from fiction. *Glamour* 85:352 Ap '87
Old-fashioned food, first-class nutrition [symposium] il *Good Housekeep* 205:114+ O '87
Q & A food. See issues of Rodale's Organic Gardening through February 1987
The regenerating power of nutrition. R. Rodale. il *Prevention* 39:17-18+ Ja '87
A sizzling food fight [high cholesterol products push nutrition in ads] A. Miller. il *Newsweek* 109:56 Ap 20 '87
What's news: nutrition, diet, fitness. See occasional issues of Good Housekeeping beginning May 1985
What's your nutrition IQ? il *Seventeen* 46:190 Mr '87
Wild livin'. J. R. Goldberg. il *Health* 19:51-2 Ap '87
Study and teaching
See Nutrition education
China
China's health food tradition. L. Ruifen. il *Courier* 40:24-7 My '87
Nutrition education
The advice diet counselors fork out. S. Neale. il *Changing Times* 41:67-8+ Je '87

Nutrition education—*cont.*

How zucchini won 5th-grade hearts [Arizona gardening program; cover story] D. Cavaliere. il *Child Today* 16:18-21 My/Je '87

Nutrition know-how. J. Schmid. il *Vogue* 177:359+ Ag '87

Nutritional illiterates [views of Karen Konzelmann] il *Futurist* 21:52 My/Je '87

Special "cooking friends" add spice to Head Start nutrition programs [American Home Economics Association's Volunteer Nutrition Consultant Project] S. A. Koblinsky and M. G. Phillips. il *Child Today* 16:26-9 Jl/Ag '87

The "weight shrinks" dig in [nutrition counseling] P. Blake. il *Time* 129:64 Ja 12 '87

Nutrition policy

Hunger in the U.S. J. L. Brown. il *Sci Am* 256:36-41 F '87

Letters [discussion of February 1987 article, Hunger in the U.S.] J. L. Brown. *Sci Am* 256:6+ Je '87

Meeting America's 1990 nutrition goals: we'll need a strong finish [Public Health Service objectives] M. Stephenson. il *FDA Consum* 21:15-17 S '87

Will RDAs keep you healthy? [recommended daily allowances] J. Schein. il *Consum Res Mag* 70:15-19 Jl '87

United States

See Nutrition policy

Nutrition problems

See also

Deficiency diseases

Nutritionists

See also

Finn, Susan Calvert

The advice diet counselors fork out. S. Neale. il *Changing Times* 41:67-8+ Je '87

First aid for bad eaters. H. Marsh. il *Mademoiselle* 93:98 D '87

Nutritionists: how to get advice you can trust. L. Hoppe. il *Better Homes Gard* 65:109 Ap '87

The "weight shrinks" dig in [nutrition counseling] P. Blake. il *Time* 129:64 Ja 12 '87

Nuts

See also

Cashew nuts

Cooking—Nuts

Peanuts

Nuts (Machinery) *See* Bolts and nuts

Nuts [film] *See* Motion picture reviews—Single works

Nutting, Wallace H.

about

General Nutting and the invaders. W. M. Arkin. *Bull At Sci* 43:6-7 Ja/F '87

Nuwer, Hank

Hoosiermania. il *Saturday Evening Post* 259:52-3+ Mr '87

NV Homes L. P.

Pyrrhic possibilities [NV Homes' acquisition of Ryan Homes] K. Hannon. il por *Forbes* 139:94 Je 15 '87

NVF Company

Every man for himself [V. Posner buys controlling block of APL Corp. from NVF Co.] A. Sloan. il por *Forbes* 139:37-8 Je 29 '87

NYCB *See* New York City Ballet

Nye, Hethea

about

For ever England. E. Greene. il por *House Gard* 159:198-203 My '87

Nye, Joseph S., Jr.

about

When is the threshold crossed? [interview] por *U S News World Rep* 102:35 Mr 23 '87

Nye, Peter *See* White, Wallace, 1930-

Nyenhuis, Jacquelyn R.

Berries: the just dessert. il *Saturday Evening Post* 259:22+ My/Je '87

Cool it for summer. il *Saturday Evening Post* 259:18+ Jl/Ag '87

A fashionable Sunday brunch. il *Saturday Evening Post* 259:20-1 O '87

The flavors of China. il *Saturday Evening Post* 259:16+ Mr '87

Prime time for pumpkin. il *Saturday Evening Post* 259:90-3 N '87

Sprightly spring salads. il *Saturday Evening Post* 259:17-19 Ap '87

Tapas: delicious little dishes of Spain. il *Saturday Evening Post* 259:18+ Ja/F '87

Taste tempters from the garden. il *Saturday Evening Post* 259:18+ S '87

Warm greetings for the holidays. il *Saturday Evening Post* 259:76-8 D '87

Nygren, Carrie

about

Carrie Nygren is a model import—ain't she Swede? por *People Wkly* 27:98 F 9 '87

Nyland, Larry

Win/win bargaining pays off. *Educ Dig* 53:28-9 S '87

Nylon

1937 [inventor W. H. Carothers] por *Am Herit* 38:108-9 F/Mr '87

Nynex Corporation

How NYNEX' Bud Staley is dialing for dollars. J. J. Keller. il por *Bus Week* p84-6 Jl 6 '87

Nyos, Lake (Cameroon) *See* Lake Nyos (Cameroon)

O

O stars

Lambda Orionis' molecular ring [work of Ronald J. Maddalena and Mark Morris] il *Sky Telesc* 74:455 N '87

Science at McDonald Observatory. R. Reeves. il pors *Astronomy* 15:6-17 Jl '87

The spectacular O stars. J. B. Kaler. il *Sky Telesc* 74:464-9 N '87

Oak

Praise for the mighty oaks. S. Bender. il *South Living* 22:76-81 O '87

Oak Island (N.S.)

The mystery of Oak Island [pirate's treasure] R. Surette. il *Macleans* 100:42 Ag 10 '87

Oak Park (Ill.)

Criminal justice, Administration of

Court orders new trial for Steven Linscott. il por *Christ Today* 31:68+ S 4 '87

A vision of murder [S. Linscott tried for murder on basis of dream] M. Green. il pors *People Wkly* 27:30-2 My 25 '87

Oak Ridge Boys (Musical group)

Oak Ridge Boys help out USDA [Take Pride in America campaign] P. Smith. il *Success Farm* 85:24 N '87

Oakey, Philip

about

No matter the question, music's the answer. Ask the Human League's Philip Oakey. E. Miller. il por *Seventeen* 46:66-7 My '87

Oakland (Calif.)

Architecture

Oakland's past, present, and visions of the future come together in its architecture. N. Steidtmann. il *Horizon* 30:33-5 Ja/F '87

Arts

Oakland: Alameda County [special section] N. Steidtmann. il *Horizon* 30:33-46+ Ja/F '87

Blacks

Keeper of the faith [community activist D. Woods-Jones] M. Marshall. il pors *Ebony* 42:92+ Ag '87

Description

Oakland: Alameda County [special section] N. Steidtmann. il *Horizon* 30:33-46+ Ja/F '87

Galleries and museums

See also

Oakland Museum

Theater

Grand palaces. il *Horizon* 30:36 Ja/F '87

Oakland Ballet

Ballet on the East Bay. il *Horizon* 30:38-9 Ja/F '87

Reviews:

Season in the Bay Area. J. Ross. il *Dance Mag* 61:26-7 My '87

Shakespeare's sister [exhibition Bronislava Nijinska: a dancer's legacy and revivals of Les biches and Les noces] H. Brubach. il *Atlantic* 259:86-8 F '87

Oakland Museum

Collecting California. il *Horizon* 30:40-1 Ja/F '87

Oakley, Robert B.

International terrorism. *Foreign Aff* 65 Sp Issue:611-29 ['87]

Oarsmanship *See* Rowing

OAS *See* Organization of American States

Oates, Joyce Carol, 1938-

The abduction [story] il *Seventeen* 46:176-7+ N '87

The double-edged knife [story] il *Redbook* 169:50+ My '87

Kid Dynamite. il pors *Life* 10:64-6+ Mr '87

Oates, Joyce Carol, 1938——cont.
Killer instinct [excerpt from On boxing] il *Sport Mag* 78:57 Jl '87
Shopping [story] il *Ms* 15:50-3+ Mr '87
Snapshot album [poem] *Nation* 244:231 F 21 '87
Success and the pseudonymous writer: turning over a new self. il *N Y Times Book Rev* 92:12+ D 6 '87
The world's worst critics. il *N Y Times Book Rev* 92:1+ Ja 18 '87

Oates, William A.
about
This preppy's buttoned-down fund is beating the S&P 500. D. M. Topolnicki. il por *Money* 16:214 Je '87

Oatmeal
Marketing
Food fight! [General Mills to challenge Quaker Oats with Total Oatmeal] S. B. Weiner. il *Forbes* 140:86+ Jl 27 '87

Oats
See also
Cooking—Grain

OAU *See* Organization of African Unity

Oaxaca (Mexico)
Dance festivals
See Dance festivals—Mexico

Obando y Bravo, Miguel, Cardinal
about
Covert aid and the Church. R. Parry and T. Jacoby. il por *Newsweek* 109:27-8 Je 15 '87

Obedience
Lenten meditation:
A question of faith. J. F. Scholer. *Christ Century* 104:237-8 Mr 11 '87
The tyranny of subjectivism [address, September 18, 1987] G. Leonard. *Vital Speeches Day* 54:50-7 N 1 '87

Obee, Bruce
Seal-salmon controversy escalates in B.C. il *Oceans* 20:8-9 S/O '87

Oberg, Alcestis R., 1949-
Interview [J. Fletcher] il por *Omni* 10:120-2+ D '87
Lives of the cell. il *Omni* 9:20+ Ag '87
New exits. il *Omni* 9:28 My '87

Oberlin College
Black admissions director hired at Oberlin College [J. L. Washington] *Jet* 73:22 S 28 '87

Obern, Sara
about
Easing the city squeeze. K. Martin. il pors *Rodale's Org Gard* 34:78+ Ap '87

Obesity
See also
Weight reducing preparations
After 27 years in his bedroom, 1,200-lb. Walter Hudson decides to take a load off [D. Gregory to help with diet] W. Plummer. il pors *People Wkly* 28:60-1 O 26 '87
Baby fat [study by Douglas S. Lewis and others] J. Silberner. *Sci News* 131:73 Ja 31 '87
Battling the bulge at an early age. J. Carey. il *U S News World Rep* 102:66-7 Mr 2 '87
Being a heavy in a skinny world [teenagers] B. Laskoski. il *Seventeen* 46:336-7+ Ag '87
A British town's cemeteries begin charging extra for oversize clients, and the plot thickens. il *People Wkly* 27:129 My 18 '87
A chemical thermostat for fat? [adipsin] D. D. Edwards. *Sci News* 132:70-1 Ag 1 '87
Danger! Marriage can make you fat [excerpt from Weight, sex and marriage] R. B. Stuart and B. Jacobson. il *Redbook* 169:92-3+ Ag '87
Diabetics should lose weight, avoid diet fads. G. Kolata. *Science* 235:163-4 Ja 9 '87
Extra pounds can weigh down your career. L. Baum. il *Bus Week* p96 Ag 3 '87
Fat, shmat, so long as you feel OK [study by Diane Hayes and Catherine E. Ross] A. H. Rosenfeld. il *Psychol Today* 21:18 Jl '87
Gregory comes to rescue of 1,000-pound Walter Hudson. il pors *Jet* 73:17-18 N 9 '87
Inability to get up, go to mother's funeral, gives 700-pounder will to diet [W. Hudson] R. L. Haywood. il pors *Jet* 73:54-6 O 5 '87
Poussaint: money, play keeps black kids slimmer than fat white kids. *Jet* 72:36 Jl 13 '87
Severely impaired adipsin expression in genetic and acquired obesity. J. S. Flier and others. bibl f il *Science* 237:405-8 Jl 24 '87
Stomach 'bubble': diet device not without risks. E. Zamula. il *FDA Consum* 21:28-31 Ap '87

Think you're too fat? [with introd. by Melody Trask] N. Roberts. pors *McCalls* 114:34, 38-9 S '87
The waist span/life span link. il *Prevention* 39:12+ O '87
When your mom is fat. S. Nelson. il *Seventeen* 46:164-5+ N '87
Genetic aspects
Family fat; ed. by Bill Lawren. A. J. Stunkard. il *Health* 19:8 F '87
Metabolism studies predict obesity [Pima Indians; research by Clifton Bogardus and others] D. D. Edwards. *Sci News* 132:309 N 14 '87
Your body blueprint—born to be fat? M. Katahn. il *Mademoiselle* 93:337+ S '87

Obey, Ebenezer, 1942-
about
Talking drums and juju joy. S. Bergman. il pors *Christ Today* 31:10-11 Ag 7 '87

Obituaries
Bidding goodbye to a few late greats. il *Life* 10:117-18+ Ja '87
The deaths [1987] il *Macleans* 100:48 D 21 '87
Images: farewells. il *Time* 130:58-9 D 28 '87
Obituaries. il *People Wkly* 28:124-6+ D 28 '87-Ja 4 '88
Obituaries [art world] il *Art Am* 75:55 Ag '87
Remembering other Christian leaders. il *Christ Today* 31:40+ D 11 '87
Tributes [1987] il *Roll Stone* p61-2+ D 17-31 '87

Objects, Miniature *See* Miniature objects

Oboe music
See also
Compact discs—Oboe music

O'Boyle, Laurie M.
Houseplants. il *Mother Earth News* 108:56-9 N/D '87

O'Brien, Beth
(tr) *See* Fuchs, Rudi. Spotlight

O'Brien, Conor Cruise, 1917-
Coping with terrorism. il por *Cent Mag* 20:45-9 Mr/Ap '87
Sandinismo: the nationalist faith of Nicaragua. *Cent Mag* 20:31-4 Jl/Ag '87

O'Brien, David J.
The American laity: memory, meaning and mission [adaptation of address, September 1986] *America* 156:189-93 Mr 7 '87

O'Brien, Dennis
One, holy, Catholic and somewhat infallible. *America* 156:276-8 Ap 4 '87
Synchronicity and the liberal arts. *Des Arts Educ* 88:42-5 Jl/Ag '87

O'Brien, Edna
Epitaph [story] *New Yorker* 63:34-41 Ap 27 '87
A little holiday [story] *New Yorker* 63:26-8 Jl 27 '87

O'Brien, Geoffrey
Thoreau's book of life. il *N Y Rev Books* 33:46-51 Ja 15 '87

O'Brien, Jim
about
The last Super Bowl hero. D. Whitford. il pors *Sport Mag* 78:26-7 F '87

O'Brien, John
Mushrooms in the mountains. il pors *Ctry J* 14:28-32 S '87

O'Brien, Joseph
about
A city sanctuary. K. Wilson. il por *Rodale's Org Gard* 34:18+ My '87

O'Brien, Margaret, and Holland, Julia
'Picture shows': the early British film industry in Walthamstow. bibl il *Hist Today* 37:9-15 F '87

O'Brien, Mark, 1950-
Desk-top investing aids. il *Nations Bus* 75:45-6 Mr '87
The slump that wasn't. il *Nations Bus* 75:29-30 S '87

O'Brien, Michael
about
A fair share; ed. by Micki Siegel. R. Maloney. il por *Good Housekeep* 205:54+ N '87

O'Brien, Niall
about
Notes and comment. *New Yorker* 62:23-5 Ja 19 '87

O'Brien, Stephen J.
The ancestry of the giant panda. il map *Sci Am* 257:102-7 N '87

O'Brien, Tim
How to tell a true war story [story] il *Esquire* 108:208-10+ O '87

O'Brien, Tom
Screen. *See* occasional issues of Commonweal beginning February 10, 1984

Obscene language See Words, Obscene

Obscenity (Law)
> See also
> Trials (Obscenity)
> United States. Attorney General's Commission on
> Pornography

Author and publisher groups make filings in two Supreme Court cases [challenge to a Virginia law on how certain books may be displayed] H. Fields. *Publ Wkly* 232:12 S 4 '87

Blue boys of the airwaves [FCC broadens definition of indecency] R. H. Bork, Jr. il *U S News World Rep* 102:16-17 Ap 27 '87

Colorado booksellers challenge obscenity law. *Publ Wkly* 231:87 F 27 '87

Debunking the 'reasonable man' rule [Supreme Court ruling] C. Rembar. por *Publ Wkly* 231:16 Je 26 '87

The F.C.C. cleans up the airways. R. Corn. il *Nation* 245:679-81 D 5 '87

A far-reaching drive against obscenity. *Christ Today* 31:44+ N 6 '87

FCC doublespeak [indecency standard] L. P. Sheinfeld. il *Film Comment* 23:87-90 S/O '87

The First Amendment and obscenity [address, November 13, 1986] B. C. Hafen. *Vital Speeches Day* 53:210-12 Ja 15 '87

High Court asked to rule on RICO bookstore case [adult bookstore in Indiana] *Publ Wkly* 232:10 N 13 '87

High Court to review Va. minors access law. M. Yen. *Publ Wkly* 231:30 Mr 6 '87

An indecent proposal [FCC's new definition of indecency] J. Saltzman. il *USA Today (Periodical)* 116:95 Jl '87

Midnight blue [FCC guidelines on "indecent" programming] *Time* 130:61 D 7 '87

Obscenity test challenged in U.S. Supreme Court [intent of Miller test questioned in Pope v. Illinois] H. Fields. *Publ Wkly* 231:10 Mr 13 '87

Pornography and its discontents [special section] bibl *Society* 24:6-32 Jl/Ag '87

Radio daze [FCC issues warnings to radio stations for broadcasting obscene material] R. Stengel. il por *Time* 129:32 Ap 27 '87

Reach out and touch someone [limiting access of children to dial-a-porn] R. Lacayo. il *Time* 130:58 D 21 '87

Reagan proposes RICO law based on Meese porno recommendations. H. Fields. *Publ Wkly* 232:13 D 4 '87

Suing Ma Bell over dirty language [parents sue over child's access to dial-a-porn] *Newsweek* 110:47 D 7 '87

Supreme Court fine-tunes third part of 'Miller' test [Pope v. Illinois] *Publ Wkly* 231:20 My 22 '87

Supreme Court justices quiz both sides in Virginia minors access law. H. Fields. *Publ Wkly* 232:16 N 20 '87

Trying to close some obscenity law loopholes. J. H. DeDakis. *Christ Today* 31:57 D 11 '87

Unpublished work by H. L. Mencken coming from Roberts Rinehart [1926 Hatrack obscenity case] B. Levine. *Publ Wkly* 232:62 O 9 '87

Bibliography
Recommended reading. *Nation* 244:724 My 30 '87

Canada
Canada tries a second time to tighten laws against pornography. B. Slopen. *Publ Wkly* 232:15 Jl 3 '87

New pornography wars. M. Clark. il *Macleans* 100:44 My 18 '87

Porn: new battle, old war. J. Moulden. il *Ms* 16:92 N '87

Toronto book shop wins suit against customs over 'Joy of gay sex' [Glad Day Bookshop wins obscenity suit] B. Slopen. *Publ Wkly* 231:20 Ap 17 '87

Western Europe
Less sex please—we're European. R. Laver. il *Macleans* 100:50 O 12 '87

Observation (Psychology)
The writer's eye. R. Silvis. *Writer* 100:7-8 O '87

Observation decks
Baltimore from the top [Top of the World observation deck] il *South Living* 22:33 Je '87

Observation towers
Trying to unload a 90-foot-high home is one very tall order [D. Cappelletti trying to sell Massachusetts observation tower] il por *People Wkly* 28:57 N 23 '87

Observations, Astronomical See Astronomy—Observations

Observatories
> See also
> Astronomical observatories

Observer (London, England)
'U.S. motivation is benign, but often misguided' [interview with D. Trelford] J. R. Moskin. por *World Press Rev* 34:27-8 N '87

Obsession (Psychology) See Obsessive-compulsive behavior

Obsessive-compulsive behavior
Attack of the obsessive managers. W. Kiechel, III. il *Fortune* 115:127-8 F 16 '87

The dark side of love [cover story] J. S. Kunen. il *People Wkly* 28:88-90+ O 26 '87

Doctor reveals sexual addiction a growing problem [M. Lee] T. S. Moore. il pors *Jet* 72:24-5 Mr 30 '87

High anxiety. W. Gallagher. il *Roll Stone* p34-5+ Mr 12 '87

Images of obsession [positron emission tomography; cover story] B. Bower. il *Sci News* 131:236-7 Ap 11 '87

It's compulsory. M. O'Brian. il *Health* 19:19 O '87

Obsidian
Why were the Aztecs and Mayas stuck in the Stone Age? Obsidian, a kind of volcanic glass, may be the answer. T. Stocker. *Earth Sci* 40:32 Summ '87

Obstetrical nurses See Nurses and nursing

Obstetrics
> See also
> Abortion
> Cesarean section
> Midwives

The malpractice mess: why you should worry. A. B. Lieberman. il *Parents* 62:106-10+ Mr '87

Policing pregnancy [views on forced obstetrical procedures] *Sci Am* 257:26+ Ag '87

A special ob-gyn section. il *McCalls* 114:85-8+ S '87

When doctors refuse to treat lawyers [obstetricians vs. women lawyers in Brunswick, Ga.] P. Cooke. il *Read Dig* 131:100-4 O '87

When the obstetrician says "no" [malpractice suits forcing physicians to drop practices] R. Sandroff. il *Health* 19:52-4+ N '87

L'oca del Cairo [opera] See Mozart, Wolfgang Amadeus, 1756-1791

O'Callahan, Jay
> about
> Told from the heart. P. Mandell. il por *Americana* 15:38-40+ Jl/Ag '87

Ocasio, Ossie
> about
> Holyfield stops Ocasio, setting up Qawi rematch. *Jet* 72:46 S 7 '87

Occident and Orient See East and West

Occidental Petroleum Corp.
A geriatric who won't slow down [A. Hammer] B. O'Reilly. il por *Fortune* 116:58 Ag 3 '87

Occult sciences
> See also
> Astrology
> Demonology
> Magic
> Parapsychology
> Spiritualism

Great Britain
Signs & wonders & the English Civil War. C. Durston. bibl il *Hist Today* 37:22-8 O '87

Occult sciences and Christianity See Christianity and occult sciences

Occultations
April's occultation of Venus. D. Di Cicco. il *Sky Telesc* 74:214-16 Ag '87

A beautiful occultation of Venus. S. J. O'Meara. il *Sky Telesc* 73:412 Ap '87

A daytime occultation of Spica. A. MacRobert. il *Sky Telesc* 74:174 Ag '87

A grand Pleiades occultation. D. W. Dunham. il *Sky Telesc* 74:284-7 S '87

Lunar occultation highlights for 1987. D. W. Dunham. il map *Sky Telesc* 73:68-9 Ja '87

The March 5th Pleiades occultation. D. W. Dunham. il *Sky Telesc* 73:296-7 Mr '87

The moon covers Spica. il *Sky Telesc* 73:183 F '87

News from the center of our galaxy [lunar occultation] D. E. Thomsen. *Sci News* 131:24 Ja 10 '87

Planetary occultations of stars in 1987. D. W. Dunham. il map *Sky Telesc* 73:70-1 Ja '87

Pluto and Charon: the dance goes on. J. K. Beatty. il *Sky Telesc* 74:248-51 S '87

Occupational aptitude tests See Aptitude tests
Occupational education See Vocational-technical education
Occupational guidance See Vocational guidance
Occupational health and safety
> See also
> AIDS (Disease) and employment
> Black government employees—Health and hygiene

Occupational health and safety—See also—*cont.*
    Drugs and employment
    Farm labor—Health and hygiene
    Farmers—Health and hygiene
    Government employees—Health and hygiene
    Health workers—Health and hygiene
    Industrial accidents
    Industry—Physical fitness programs
    Insurance, Workers' compensation
    Nuclear power plants—Safety devices and measures
    Nuclear power workers—Health and hygiene
    Postal employees—Health and hygiene
    Smoking and employment
    United States. Occupational Safety and Health Administration
    Women electronics workers—Health and hygiene
Asleep at the switch: the human machine. il *Newsweek* 109:62 Ap 27 '87
Bad backs: pains in the wallet. R. J. Chapel. il *Nations Bus* 75:43-4 Ja '87
Deaths in industry, 1985: BLS survey findings. D. M. Cotter and J. Macon. il *Mon Labor Rev* 110:45-7 Ap '87
Disability days. *Mon Labor Rev* 110:2 Ja '87
Employee health can spell profits [views of John Harper] *USA Today (Periodical)* 115:2-3 Ap '87
Health hazard from copier exhaust [air pollution from wet process copiers; research by Yoshio Tsuchiya] S. Weisburd. *Sci News* 132:166 S 12 '87
Healthsmart. C. Schrader. *Harpers Bazaar* 121:94+ N '87
Is your office toxic? H. Manley. il *Good Housekeep* 205:268 S '87
Is your work harmful to your unborn baby? C. Loomis. il *Parents* 62:13 Jl '87
Job security: a healthy bonus [survey by Karl W. Kuhnert] M. Schanback. il *Psychol Today* 21:16 My '87
Kids' leukemia from parents' exposures? J. Raloff. *Sci News* 132:38-9 Jl 18 '87
Managing VDT safety and comfort. H. McCandless. *Work Woman* 12:20+ Jl '87
Office workers suffer more than physical laborers [study by Rene Caillet] *USA Today (Periodical)* 115:11-12 F '87
Skin in the workplace [special section] il *Vogue* 177:156-61+ Ja '87
Top priority: job health. il *Harpers Bazaar* 120:156+ Mr '87
VDT comfort. M. S. Dolan. *Consum Res Mag* 70:2 Ag '87
Workplace safety [National Research Council study] *Mon Labor Rev* 110:2 N '87

International aspects
It could be your office that is 'sick' [sick building syndrome] E. Verdecchia. *World Press Rev* 34:50 My '87

Laws and regulations
    See also
    California. Division of Occupational Health and Safety
A death at work can put the boss in jail [homicide conviction against Sabine Consolidated Inc.] J. Tasini. *Bus Week* p37-8 Mr 2 '87
An excuse for workplace hazard [fetal protection policies discriminate against women] C. Marshall. il *Nation* 244:532-4 Ap 25 '87
Playing with poison [mercury poisoning at Pymm Thermometer, Brooklyn, N.Y.] K. Dobie and A. Goodman. il *Progressive* 51:19-23 F '87

Canada
A struggle for safe workplaces. J. Bennett and N. Underwood. il *Macleans* 100:32-3 Jl 13 '87

Occupational mobility
    See also
    Labor turnover
8 steps to your own career makeover. M. M. Kennedy. il *Glamour* 85:168+ S '87
All the right moves . . . work/love [career changes by women] il *Vogue* 177:300-4+ Ag '87
Career makeover: high school teacher to high-tech sales [F. Monteleon, computer components distributer] il por *Glamour* 85:156 Mr '87
Dream jobs: the big switch. P. Bernstein. *Harpers Bazaar* 120:299+ Mr '87
Lessons from late bloomers. F. Rice. il *Fortune* 116:87-91 Ag 31 '87
Second careers. S. Blotnick. il *Forbes* 139:150-1 F 9 '87

Occupational retraining *See* Retraining, Occupational
Occupational safety *See* Occupational health and safety
Occupational Safety and Health Administration (U.S.) *See* United States. Occupational Safety and Health Administration
Occupational stress *See* Job stress
Occupational therapy
Study and teaching
New curriculum in gerontology for occupational therapists. L. J. Davis. il *Aging* no356:34 '87
Occupational training *See* Vocational-technical education
Occupations
    See also
    Aged—Occupations
    Black women—Occupations
    Blacks—Occupations
    Job descriptions
    Job evaluation
    Women—Occupations
Best jobs, bright futures: your brilliant career [cover story] J. Bodnar. il *Changing Times* 41:26-31+ N '87
An evaluation of state projections of industry, occupational employment. H. A. Goldstein and A. M. Cruze. bibl f il *Mon Labor Rev* 110:29-38 O '87
A look at occupational employment trends to the year 2000. G. T. Silvestri and J. M. Lukasiewicz. il *Mon Labor Rev* 110:46-63 S '87
Today's kids with yesterday's goals. il *Parents* 62:15 Ap '87

Ocean, Billy
    about
The man behind the voice. M. Marshall. il pors *Ebony* 42:96+ Ja '87

Ocean
    See also
    Atlantic Ocean
    Drift bottles
    Icebergs
    Indian Ocean
    Marine biology
    Marine fauna
    Meteorology, Maritime
    Pacific Ocean
    Red Sea
    Sea level changes
    Sea water
    Territorial waters
    Tide power
    Waste disposal in the ocean
    Wave power
    Waves
Economic aspects
    See Marine mineral resources; Marine resources
Laws and regulations
    See Maritime law
Ocean and civilization
The sea within us. D. Behrman. il *Courier* 40:23-6 Je '87
Ocean-atmosphere interaction
    See also
    El Niño (Ocean current)
    Southern Oscillation
The biggest chill. W. S. Broecker. il maps *Nat Hist* 96:74-80+ O '87
Climate and chlorophyll a: long-term trends in the central North Pacific Ocean. E. L. Venrick and others. bibl f il maps *Science* 238:70-2 O 2 '87
Climate control [influence of plankton on cloud formation; work of Robert J. Charlson and James E. Lovelock] *Sci Am* 257:24 Jl '87
Of whales and weather [biotelemetry tracking of whales in deep water; work of Bruce Mate] S. Strauss. il *Technol Rev* 90:11 Jl '87
On the trail of ocean bubbles [work of S. A. Thorpe and A. J. Hall] R. Monastersky. *Sci News* 132:21 Jl 11 '87
The plankton-climate connection [cover story] R. Monastersky. il *Sci News* 132:362-5 D 5 '87
Sea surface temperature, surface wind divergence, and convection over tropical oceans. N. E. Graham and T. P. Barnett. bibl f il *Science* 238:657-9 O 30 '87
Variations on a Pacific theme [wind patterns] *Sci News* 131:377 Je 13 '87
Wind-driven ocean currents and Ekman transport. J. F. Price and others. bibl f il *Science* 238:1534-8 D 11 '87

Ocean birds *See* Sea birds
Ocean bottles *See* Drift bottles
Ocean bottom
    See also
    Marine mineral resources

Ocean bottom—See also—cont.
　　Marine sediments
　　Ocean Drilling Program
　　Seamounts
　　Submarine geology
ArgoRise: outline of an oceanographic expedition [East Pacific Rise] C. L. Van Dover. il *Sea Front* 33:186-94 My/Je '87
Big splash from an ancient fall [Montagnais crater off Nova Scotia coast] R. Monastersky. *Sci News* 131:404 Je 27 '87
Deep-sea hydrocarbon seep communities: evidence for energy and nutritional carbon sources. J. M. Brooks and others. bibl f il *Science* 238:1138-42 N 20 '87
Ocean hot springs similar around globe. R. A. Kerr. il *Science* 235:435 Ja 23 '87
There's a hole in the bottom of the sea [impact crater off Nova Scotia coast; research by Lubomir Jansa and Georgia Pe-Piper] map *Discover* 8:20 S '87
Underwater canyons [Atlantic trip in submarine Alvin] R. Gannon. il *Pop Sci* 231:60-4+ Jl '87
Whales and walruses as tillers of the sea floor [side-scan sonar studies of the Bering Sea] C. H. Nelson and K. R. Johnson. il maps *Sci Am* 256:112-17 F '87
　　　　　　　　Maps
East Coast EEZ mapping [Exclusive Economic Zone] *Oceans* 20:4-5 My/Je '87
Mapping the nation's underseas wealth [Exclusive Economic Zone] R. C. Cowen. il *Technol Rev* 90:23 N/D '87
Sea-bottom road maps. il *Sea Front* 33:381-3 S/O '87
Ocean circulation
　　　See also
　　Ocean currents
Computer modeling in physical oceanography from the global circulation to turbulence. W. R. Holland and J. C. McWilliams. bibl f il *Phys Today* 40:51-7 O '87
Greenland Sea Project uses tomography. *Sea Front* 33:143 Mr/Ap '87
Greenland Sea research. il *Oceans* 20:4 Ja/F '87
Mesoscale oceanographic processes beneath the ice of Fram Strait. T. O. Manley and others. bibl f il maps *Science* 236:432-4 Ap 24 '87
Ocean-climate interaction See Ocean-atmosphere interaction
Ocean currents
　　　See also
　　Eddies
　　El Niño (Ocean current)
Turbidity current activity in a British Columbia fjord. D. B. Prior and others. bibl f il map *Science* 237:1330-3 S 11 '87
Wind-driven ocean currents and Ekman transport. J. F. Price and others. bibl f il *Science* 238:1534-8 D 11 '87
Ocean Drilling & Exploration Co.
A double play for contrarians. C. Farrell. *Bus Week* p69 F 2 '87
How two offshore drillers kept their heads above water. T. Vogel. il *Bus Week* p87-8 Ag 3 '87
Ocean Drilling Program
Delving deep into the Indian past [hot spots] R. Monastersky. map *Sci News* 132:56 Jl 25 '87
Drill ship probes Indian Ocean mysteries. K. Riedel. il *Oceans* 20:6-7 S/O '87
Drilling discoveries in the Pacific. S. Weisburd. *Sci News* 131:102-3 F 14 '87
Leg 113: drilling into Antarctica's past. S. Weisburd. map *Sci News* 131:278-9 My 2 '87
National security and the environment. W. C. Clark. bibl *Environment* 29:inside cover+ Je '87
NSC and Ocean Drilling [Soviet participation] J. A. Knauss. *Environment* 29:2-3 Jl/Ag '87
Ocean drilling details steps to an icy world [Antarctica] R. A. Kerr. il map *Science* 236:912-13 My 22 '87
Soviet-ODP partnership on or off? S. Weisburd. *Sci News* 131:280 My 2 '87
Soviets disinvited to join Drilling Program [objections by the Dept. of Defense] C. Norman. il *Science* 236:659-60 My 8 '87
Ocean farming See Aquaculture
Ocean festivals See Festivals
Ocean fishing See Salt water fishing
Ocean floor See Ocean bottom
Ocean in art
　　　See also
　　Marine painting
Ocean life See Marine biology
Ocean liners
　　　See also
　　Art on ocean liners

　　Queen Elizabeth 2 (Ship)
　　Republic (Steamship)
　　Royal Princess (Ship)
　　Titanic (Steamship)
Five new ways to sail the seven seas [miniliners] D. Butwin. il *Esquire* 107:20+ Ja '87
Ocean mining
　　　See also
　　Exclusive Economic Zone
　　United Nations. Preparatory Commission for the International Sea-Bed Authority and the International Tribunal for the Law of the Sea
Pulling the plug on ocean minerals. R. Monastersky. *Sci News* 132:86 Ag 8 '87
Seabed materials. J. M. Broadus. bibl f il map *Science* 235:853-60 F 20 '87
Ocean pollution See Marine pollution
Ocean Reef (Key Largo, Fla.: Resort) See Resorts—Florida Keys (Fla.)
Ocean resources See Marine resources
Ocean temperature
Finding the comfort zone [how water temperature affects saltwater fishing] B. Stearns. il *Field Stream* 92:91+ Je '87
Of whales and weather [biotelemetry tracking of whales in deep water; work of Bruce Mate] S. Strauss. il *Technol Rev* 90:11 Jl '87
Sea surface temperature, surface wind divergence, and convection over tropical oceans. N. E. Graham and T. P. Barnett. bibl f il *Science* 238:657-9 O 30 '87
Ocean thermal power plants
Power from the sea. T. R. Penney and D. Bharathan. bibl (p128) il map *Sci Am* 256:86-92 Ja '87
　　　　　　　　Indonesia
Tapping ocean thermal power. E. R. C. Capulong. il *Pop Sci* 231:97 N '87
Ocean travel
　　　See also
　　Cruising
　　Ocean liners
　　Voyages
　　Voyages around the world
　　　　　　Anecdotes, facetiae, satire, etc.
How to travel in peace [excerpt from Chips off the old Benchley] R. Benchley. il *50 Plus* 27:59-61 Je '87
Ocean wave power See Wave power
Ocean waves See Waves
Oceania
　　　See also
　　Nuclear-free zones—Oceania
　　　　　　Foreign relations
　　　　　　　Libya
　　See Libya—Foreign relations—Oceania
　　　　　　Politics and government
Connecting the dots on the map. G. Alcalay. il *Nation* 245:84-7 Ag 1-8 '87
Oceanic Society
Log of the Oceanic Society. See issues of Oceans
Oceanographic research See Oceanography
Oceanographic submersibles
ArgoRise: outline of an oceanographic expedition [East Pacific Rise] C. L. Van Dover. il *Sea Front* 33:186-94 My/Je '87
Birth of an island [Alvin explores Loihi] J. C. Borg. il map *Oceans* 20:26-33 Jl/Ag '87
A man with Titanic vision [R. D. Ballard] F. Golden. il pors *Discover* 8:50-3+ Ja '87
Probing the Monitor with a deep drone. M. D. Lemonick. il map *Time* 129:77 Je 22 '87
Roving the deep [M. Hawkes' adventures in piloting Deep Rover] il por map *Natl Geogr World* 144:6-11 Ag '87
Submarine crew finds volcano, minerals and exotic animals [Alvin explores Loihi] il *Earth Sci* 40:7 Fall '87
Underwater canyons [Atlantic trip in submarine Alvin] R. Gannon. il *Pop Sci* 231:60-4+ Jl '87
A yellow submarine pops up from Down Under [C'Cat] C. Debes. il *Bus Week* p104 S 28 '87
Oceanography
　　　See also
　　Artificial satellites—Oceanographic use
　　Computers—Oceanographic use
　　International Oceanographic Foundation
　　Marine resources
　　National Oceans Policy Commission (U.S.)
　　Ocean-atmosphere interaction
　　Ocean bottom
　　Ocean circulation
　　Ocean Drilling Program

Oceanography—See also—*cont.*
  Oceanic Society
  Oceanographic submersibles
  Sea water
  Tides
  Tomography—Oceanographic use
Crow's nest. G. L. Voss. See issues of Sea Frontiers beginning November/December 1986
Immiscible investigators: oceanographers, meteorologists, and fishery scientists. W. S. Wooster. *BioScience* 37:728-30 N '87
A man with Titanic vision [R. D. Ballard] F. Golden. il pors *Discover* 8:50-3+ Ja '87
Sea secrets [questions and answers] F. Schaefer. See issues of Sea Frontiers beginning January/February 1986
The sea within us. D. Behrman. il *Courier* 40:23-6 Je '87

Bibliography
Reviews. See issues of Oceans
Science of the sea in books. See issues of Sea Frontiers

Soviet Union
NSC and Ocean Drilling [Soviet participation] J. A. Knauss. *Environment* 29:2-3 Jl/Ag '87
Soviet-ODP partnership on or off? [Ocean Drilling Program] S. Weisburd. *Sci News* 131:280 My 2 '87
Soviets disinvited to join Drilling Program [objections by the Dept. of Defense] C. Norman. il *Science* 236:659-60 My 8 '87

Ochieng, Philip
The arms race is a universal issue. il *World Press Rev* 34:36-7 Ja '87

Ochoa Vasquez, Jorge Luis
about
How the drug czar got away. M. A. Lee. il *Nation* 245:189-92 S 5 '87

Ocko, Stephanie
The business of selling adventure. il *Technol Rev* 90:64-9+ F/Mr '87

OCO *See* Olympiques Calgary Olympics (Organization)

O'Collins, Gerald
The appearances of the risen Jesus [cover story] il *America* 156:317-20 Ap 18 '87
Interpreting Christmas. il *America* 157:470-1 D 19 '87

O'Connell, Daniel
The short end of the stick. il *World Tennis* 35:80+ O '87

O'Connell, Mary
Is feminism God's gift to the Catholic Church? il *U S Cathol* 52:12-19 Je '87
The least you can do is vote [with readers' comments] *U S Cathol* 52:14-20 My '87
Past imperfect: is it time to let your parents off the hook? [cover story] il *U S Cathol* 52:6-13 Ja '87

O'Connell-Cahill, Michael
The church needs married priests [with readers' comments] *U S Cathol* 52:14-19 D '87
Drug abuse: who says it can't happen to your kid? il *U S Cathol* 52:20-5 O '87

O'Connor, Flannery
about
'The meaning is in you': Flannery O'Connor in her letters. J. P. Baumgaertner. *Christ Century* 104:1172-6 D 23-30 '87

O'Connor, Harvey, 1897-1987
about
Obituary
  Nation 245:257 S 19 '87. E. Tiger

O'Connor, James V.
Geoquiz. See issues of Earth Science beginning Summer 1985

O'Connor, John Joseph, Cardinal, 1920-
The Pope's call to holiness. il pors *Saturday Evening Post* 259:56-9 D '87
about
But does God get 15%? L. Fleischer. *Publ Wkly* 232:48 S 4 '87
The Cardinal & Israel. *Commonweal* 114:36-7 Ja 30 '87
The Cardinal goes calling. *New Repub* 196:9 Ja 19 '87
Diplomatic impasse. *Christ Century* 104:48 Ja 21 '87
George Will overboard. W. F. Buckley. *Natl Rev* 39:62-3 F 27 '87
A holy row from a visit to a holy city. W. L. Chaze. il por *U S News World Rep* 102:14 Ja 12 '87
Jerusalem and the pluck of the Irish. *America* 156:41-2 Ja 24 '87
Minority report. C. Hitchens. *Nation* 244:170 F 14 '87
O'Connor's critics misconstrue terms. J. M. Wall. *Christ Century* 104:75-6 Ja 28 '87
Office politics. *New Repub* 196:9 Ja 26 '87

On challenging a few clichés. *America* 156:62-3 Ja 31 '87
Profiles (I). N. Hentoff. por *New Yorker* 63:59-76 Mr 23 '87
Profiles (II). N. Hentoff. il *New Yorker* 63:37-8+ Mr 30 '87

O'Connor, Karen
The best gift we can give. il *Read Dig* 130:61-2+ My '87

O'Connor, Mary Flannery *See* O'Connor, Flannery

O'Connor, Rory
Getting high on it. *Vogue* 177:209+ Ja '87
Letter from Managua. il *Vogue* 177:176+ Ag '87

O'Connor, Thomas
J.N. Roberts: "what's a mother to do?". il pors *Cycle* 38:54-7+ Jl '87

OCR (Optical character recognition) devices *See* Optical scanners

Octagonal houses *See* Houses, Octagonal

Octane rating *See* Gasoline—Octane rating

October
The October almanac. il *Atlantic* 260:16 O '87
October farewell. C. T. Dennis. il *Conservationist* 42:56 S/O '87

Octopus Publishing Group plc
Macmillan buys out Octopus to be sole owner of Pan for $36.5 million. V. Menkes. *Publ Wkly* 232:15 O 2 '87
Octopus to acquire ABP's trade publishing lines. V. Menkes. *Publ Wkly* 232:12 D 18 '87
Reed acquires Octopus, leads British publishing. V. Menkes. il *Publ Wkly* 232:11 Jl 17 '87

Octopuses
See also
  Cooking—Shellfish
Around the Mall and beyond [work of C. Roper with squid and blue-ringed octopus] E. Park. *Smithsonian* 18:28+ My '87

Oda, Minoru
What do we learn from space? Space science in Japan. bibl il *Phys Today* 40:26-33 D '87

Oda, Minoru, and Tanaka, Yasuo
Japan's blossoming space science. il map *Sky Telesc* 73:7-11 Ja '87

Odean, Kathleen
At an all-girls school you're taught to believe in yourself. il *Glamour* 85:112 Ag '87

O'Dell, C. R.
The physics of aerobatic flight [cover story] il *Phys Today* 40:24-30 N '87

O'Dell, Tony
about
Class acts: guys who make the grade. M. L. Baer. il pors *Teen* 31:59-60 N '87

Oden, Thomas C.
about
Napping through the revolution. D. F. Kinlaw. il *Christ Today* 31:9 Ag 7 '87

Odenwald, Sten
To the Big Bang and beyond. il *Astronomy* 15:90-5 My '87

Odessa (Brooklyn, N.Y.: Nightclub) *See* Brooklyn (New York, N.Y.)—Restaurants, nightclubs, bars, etc.

Odets, Clifford, 1906-1963
about
Waiting for Lefty [drama] Reviews
  America 157:430 D 5 '87. G. G. Seibert

Odhiambo, Thomas
about
Top African leaders Diouf, Odhiambo hailed for fight against hunger. il pors *Jet* 73:6 O 5 '87

Odiorne, George S.
Bait and switch, corporate-style [excerpt from The human side of management] *Work Woman* 12:50+ My '87
How am I doing? [excerpt from The human side of management] il *Work Woman* 12:32+ Je '87
Nine rules for hiring [excerpt from The human side of management] *Work Woman* 12:40+ N '87
Where do the best goals come from? [excerpt from The human side of management] il *Work Woman* 12:32+ D '87

O'Doherty, Brian *See* Ireland, Patrick

Odom, John
about
Odom gets early release from Calif. drug sentence. *Jet* 71:50 Ja 12 '87

Odometers
A free ride at Chrysler. G. Carroll and J. B. Copeland. il *Newsweek* 110:37 Jl 6 '87
Iacocca: 'Did we screw up? You bet'. *Newsweek* 110:42 Jl 13 '87

Odometers—*cont.*
　Odometer fraud: it's worse than you think. D. B. Zukowski. il *Changing Times* 41:55-6+ S '87
　Would you buy a used Chrysler from this man? [disconnected odometers] C. P. Work. *U S News World Rep* 103:44 Jl 6 '87

Odon (Ind.)
Protests, demonstrations, etc.
　Street sign [B. Breeden arrested for stealing street sign named to honor J. Poindexter] *Progressive* 51:4 Ag '87

Odone family
about
　They won't let their son die. J. Adler. il *Newsweek* 110:98-100 N 16 '87

O'Donnell, Bob
　NASMD at 25. *Down Beat* 54:6+ My '87

O'Donnell, Donat *See* O'Brien, Conor Cruise, 1917-

O'Donnell, James
　To the graduates of 1987: on losing one's self in finance [adaptation of address] *America* 156:415-16 My 23 '87

O'Donnell, Joseph
about
　Blood on the carpet: the coup that failed at J. Walter Thompson. B. Kanner. il pors *N Y* 20:36-40 F 16 '87
　Et tu, Brutus? This time Caesar won. C. J. Loomis. il pors *Fortune* 115:54-6 Mr 2 '87
　Even golden boys can tarnish. B. Rudolph. il por *Time* 129:51 F 9 '87
　The incredible shrinking William Esty. A. Dunkin. por *Bus Week* p54 My 18 '87

O'Donnell, Kendra Stearns
about
　A woman at old Exeter. F. Schumer. il pors *N Y Times Mag* p98-101 O 11 '87

O'Donoghue, Michael
about
　Rio on a plate. *New Yorker* 63:25-6 Je 15 '87

Odors
See also
　Aroma therapy
　Perfumes
　Pheromones
　Aromatic machines [automotive odors] K. Cameron. il *Cycle* 38:15 Ag '87
　Thelma Williams' daredevil nose probes the pungent secrets of America's toes [testing for Hill Top Research] R. Arias. il por *People Wkly* 28:164-5 S 7 '87
　The underrated power of scent [body odor] H. S. Kaplan. il por *Redbook* 169:38+ My '87
Control
　Deer hunting's big stink [controlling body odor to get closer] J. Weiss. il *Outdoor Life* 180:56-7+ Ag '87

O'Dowd, George *See* Boy George

Odysseus (Greek mythology)
　Odyssey: dig on Ithaca seeks the dwelling of Homer's famed wanderer [work of Sarantis Symeonoglou] J. Horgan. il *Sci Am* 257:18+ N '87

Odyssey of the Mind
　Mental agility, not plodding scholarship, gets the gold in the 'Odyssey of the Mind'. T. Kahn. il por *People Wkly* 28:75+ Jl 6 '87

OECD *See* Organisation for Economic Co-operation and Development

Oecophylla smaragdina *See* Ants

OED (Oxford English dictionary) *See* English language—Dictionaries

Oerlikon Aerospace Inc.
　Fever in a climate of scandal. G. Bain. il *Macleans* 100:49 F 23 '87
　A new senator's troubled debut [J. Bazin's involvement in land speculation controversy in Canada] M. Gee. il por *Macleans* 100:14 F 16 '87
　The police and the MP [A. Bissonnette charged in Oerlikon land sale scandal] M. Rose. *Macleans* 100:9 Ag 31 '87
　A political minefield [resignation of Canadian transport minister A. Bissonnette over land sale; special section; with editorial comment by Kevin Doyle] il pors *Macleans* 100:2, 8-9+ F 2 '87
　The Tories strike back [resignation of A. Bissonnette over land sale in Quebec] M. Gee. il por *Macleans* 100:10-11 F 9 '87

Oest family
about
　In New Mexico: a family lives in its own world. J. Ackermann-Blount. il *Time* 130:12-13 O 5 '87

Off Broadway theater *See* New York (N.Y.)—Theater
Off-road driving *See* Motor vehicle driving
Off-road racing *See* Motor vehicle racing
Off-road vehicles *See* All terrain vehicles
Offenbach, Jacques, 1819-1880
about
　Orphée aux enfers [operetta] Reviews
　　Opera News 51:38 Mr 28 '87. N. Malitz
　The tales of Hoffmann [opera] Reviews
　　Macleans il 100:70 N 9 '87. S. Pedersen

Offerings of stock, Public *See* Stocks—Marketing
Office buildings
See also
　Canton (Mass.)—Buildings
　Charlotte (N.C.)—Buildings
　London (England)—Buildings
　New York (N.Y.)—Buildings
　Is your office toxic? H. Manley. il *Good Housekeep* 205:268 S '87
　It could be your office that is 'sick' [sick building syndrome] E. Verdecchia. *World Press Rev* 34:50 My '87
Architecture
　Five by KPF [Kohn Pedersen Fox] G. Anderson. il *Archit Rec* 175:126-35 F '87
Environmental engineering
　See Environmental engineering (Buildings)

Office decoration
See also
　G N Associates
　Big fish, nice pond [broker E. DeVries' office] F. Greenberg. il por *Work Woman* 12:54-5 Jl '87
　Book-smart style [office of S. Petersen, president of Ballantine Books] P. Kripke. il por *Work Woman* 12:118-19 N '87
　Flexibility for interiors. R. Crawmer. *Nations Bus* 75:44 Mr '87
　In her own image [office of R. Gomez, literary agent for Triad Artists] F. Greenberg. il por *Work Woman* 12:76-7 D '87
　Life and work at the same address [C. Koblenzer] F. Greenberg. il por *Work Woman* 12:92-3 Ap '87
　The new look: offices with zing. R. Farmanfarmaian. il *Work Woman* 12:54-5 O '87
　Taking creative control [B. August's office] P. Kripke. il por *Work Woman* 12:50-1 Ag '87
　Total communication [C. Cloutier's styling agency office] F. Greenberg. il por *Work Woman* 12:102-3 My '87
　Très chair [Juan Montoya's New York City office] M. Bethany. il *N Y* 20:58-60 My 11 '87

Office equipment
See also
　Computers—Business use
　The complete home office. R. R. Roha. il *Changing Times* 41:105-6+ D '87
　How to get colleagues to keep hands off. il *Glamour* 85:86 Ja '87
　Old office, new office [special section] il *Work Woman* 12:49+ Ap '87
　Old office, new office: reaching decisions that get results [special section] il *Work Woman* 12:47+ O '87
　Product reports 1988. il *Archit Rec* 175:24-7+ D '87
　The well-equipped home office. C. Begole. il *Better Homes Gard* 65:37-9 Ap '87
Exhibitions
　Techniques for getting the tools you need. H. McCandless. il *Work Woman* 12:64+ O '87

Office equipment industry
See also
　Bell & Howell Co.
　International Business Machines Corp.
　Kroy Inc.
　Minnesota Mining & Mfg. Co.
　Nashua Corporation
　Xerox Corp.
Finance
　Industrial and office services. A. Snitzer. il *Forbes* 139:148+ Ja 12 '87
Marketing
See also
　Staples, Inc.
Italy
See also
　Ing. C. Olivetti & Co., SpA
Japan
See also
　Canon Inc.

Office etiquette *See* Business etiquette
Office furniture
　Product reports 1988. il *Archit Rec* 175:166-72+ D '87

Office furniture—*cont.*
Toward a personal workplace. C. Alexander and others. il *Archit Rec* 175:130-41 mid-S '87

Office furniture industry
See also
Herman Miller, Inc.
Shelby Williams Industries, Inc.
SunarHauserman (Firm)

Office management
See also
Information managers
Office paperwork
Computerizing with confidence (III). K. Berney. il *Nations Bus* 75:33-5 Ja '87
The menace of high-tech employment [office of the future] J. H. Foegen. il por *Futurist* 21:38-40 S/O '87
Office automation: making it pay off [special section] C. L. Harris. il *Bus Week* p134-8+ O 12 '87
Rethinking how we work: the office of the future. S. E. Bleecker. il por *Futurist* 21:15-21 Jl/Ag '87
Technology in action [special section] il *Work Woman* 12:67+ N '87

Office of Emergency Operations in Africa *See* United Nations. Office of Emergency Operations in Africa
Office of Legislative Operations (House) *See* United States. Congress. House. Office of Legislative Operations
Office of Policy Development (U.S.) *See* United States. Office of Policy Development
Office of the United Nations Disaster Relief Co-ordinator
More than $200 million pledged for humanitarian assistance to Mozambique. il *UN Chron* 24:29 My '87
Office of Vocational and Adult Education (U.S.) *See* United States. Office of Vocational and Adult Education
Office paperwork
Ten ways to cut paperwork and do your job better [excerpt from Cutting paperwork in the corporate culture] D. D. Booher. *Work Woman* 12:136-7 S '87
Office parties
Quick but classy office parties. L. Wittels. il *Work Woman* 12:76 D '87
Walking the fine line at holiday office parties [employer liability for alcohol-related damages] L. J. Moore. il *U S News World Rep* 103:75 D 21 '87
Office politics *See* Psychology, Industrial
Office romances *See* Sex in business
Office supplies *See* Office equipment
Office workers
See also
Secretaries

Health and hygiene
See Occupational health and safety
Psychology
See Psychology, Industrial
Officer, Carl
about
E. St. Louis mayor wins 3rd term, but spectre of dead man may mar victory. il por *Jet* 72:38 Ag 24 '87
East St. Louis mayor in dispute over election. *Jet* 72:29 Ap 13 '87
Officers, Military *See* United States—Armed Forces—Officers
Offices
See also
Architects' offices
Home offices
Lawyers' offices
Physicians' offices

Automation
See also
Digital Equipment Corp.
Electronic data processing departments
Harris Corp.
Ing. C. Olivetti & Co., SpA
International Business Machines Corp.
Minnesota Mining & Mfg. Co.
Northern Telecom Ltd.
Voice mail systems
Wang Laboratories Inc.
Xerox Corp.
Computerizing with confidence (III). K. Berney. il *Nations Bus* 75:33-5 Ja '87
Computerizing with confidence (V). K. Berney. il *Nations Bus* 75:23-4 Mr '87
The menace of high-tech employment [office of the future] J. H. Foegen. il por *Futurist* 21:38-40 S/O '87
Office automation: making it pay off [special section] C. L. Harris. il *Bus Week* p134-8+ O 12 '87
Old office, new office [special section] il *Work Woman* 12:49+ Ap '87
Old office, new office: reaching decisions that get results [special section] il *Work Woman* 12:47+ O '87

Rethinking how we work: the office of the future. S. E. Bleecker. il por *Futurist* 21:15-21 Jl/Ag '87
Technology in action [special section] il *Work Woman* 12:67+ N '87
When to give your technology a boost. H. McCandless. *Work Woman* 12:25+ S '87
OfficeWriter (Word processor program) *See* Word processors and processing—Programming
Official misconduct *See* Misconduct in office
Official residences

Canada
The tastes of the Mulroney family [use of Conservative Party donations to renovate official residences] M. Janigan. il por *Macleans* 100:13 Ap 27 '87
Official secrets
See also
Classified information
Executive privilege (Government information)
Government and the press
Pentagon Papers
Calling a halt to covert actions. R. Goetz. *Christ Century* 104:349-50 Ap 15 '87
Can an open society protect its secrets? D. Baer. il *U S News World Rep* 102:26-8 Je 1 '87
The CIA-Harvard controversy over secrecy. T. A. Idinopulos. il *USA Today (Periodical)* 115:38-40 My '87
Covert action and open society. G. F. Treverton. bibl f *Foreign Aff* 65:995-1014 Summ '87
Getting high on secrecy. M. Greenfield. il *Newsweek* 109:82 F 23 '87
Secret government. E. Knoll. *Progressive* 51:4 S '87
When secrecy meets democracy. C. Krauthammer. il *Read Dig* 130:116-18 F '87
Why the First Amendment is not incompatible with national security interests [address, January 14, 1987] M. L. Feldman. *Vital Speeches Day* 53:394-8 Ap 15 '87
Why the secrets slip out [cover story] M. Satchell. il *U S News World Rep* 102:20-2 Je 1 '87

Great Britain
Imperial reach. D. Campbell. *Nation* 245:669-70 D 5 '87
Offshore boundaries *See* Territorial waters
Offshore drilling rig workers *See* Petroleum workers
Offshore oil well rigs *See* Oil well drilling rigs
Offshore petroleum workers *See* Petroleum workers
Offshore powerboat racing *See* Motor boat racing
Ogallala Aquifer
The Great American aquifer. C. E. Little. il *Wilderness* 51:43-7 Fall '87
O'Gara, Geoff
Saga of a High country newsman. por *Sierra* 72:72-7 Mr/Ap '87
Ogarkov, Nikolai
about
The Ogarkov factor. B. Crozier. *Natl Rev* 39:22 Je 5 '87
Ogburn, Charlton, 1911-
about
Some ado about who was, or was not, Shakespeare. J. D. Reed. bibl (p187) il pors *Smithsonian* 18:155-8+ S '87
Ogden, Ellen E.
Cut-your-own bouquets. il *Rodale's Org Gard* 34:81-2+ Ja '87
Ogden, Shepherd
Onions. il *Ctry J* 14:66-70 Ap '87
Ogilvie, Bruce
about
Interview. P. Weintraub and M. Teich. por *Omni* 9:80-2+ S '87
Ogilvy, David, 1911-
Memos from an advertising man [condensed from The unpublished David Ogilvy; ed. by Joel Raphaelson. il por *Read Dig* 131:69-72 Ag '87
Ogilvy & Mather
Memos from an advertising man [condensed from The unpublished David Ogilvy]; ed. by Joel Raphaelson. D. Ogilvy. il por *Read Dig* 131:69-72 Ag '87
Ogimi, Kaoru
about
Tompkins's big chance. J. Lowenstein. il *Oceans* 20:72 S/O '87
O'Grady, Mac
about
Mac is back and right on track. J. Diaz. il por *Sports Illus* 66:50-1 Ja 19 '87

Ohain, Hans von
about
The inventions that change our lives often meet with indifference, even active resistance—as did the jet engine. R. M. Adams. *Smithsonian* 18:12 Jl '87
They created the Jet Age. N. Vietmeyer. il *Read Dig* 130:162-6 My '87

O'Halloran, Thomas, and Walsh, Christopher
Metalloregulator DNA-binding protein encoded by the *mer*R gene: isolation and characterization. bibl f il *Science* 235:211-14 Ja 9 '87

Ohanian, Susan
Japanese education in America? *Educ Dig* 53:10-14 S '87
Notes on Japan from an American schoolteacher. il *Phi Delta Kappan* 68:360-7 Ja '87
The paper chase. il *Phi Delta Kappan* 69:153-5 O '87
Ruffles and flourishes. il *Atlantic* 260:20+ S '87

O'Hanlon, Redmond
Ways to go. *Harpers* 274:23 Je '87

O'Hare, Joseph A.
Reflections on the Pope's visit [cover story] il *America* 157:375-8 N 21 '87

O'Hare International Airport *See* Chicago (Ill.)—Airports

Ohio
See also
Booksellers and bookselling—Ohio
Cross Creek (Ohio)
Fishing—Ohio
Taxation—Ohio
Unemployment—Ohio
Description and travel
Ohio. M. Elder. il map *Gourmet* 47:80-5+ N '87
Industries
National economic competitiveness [Thomas Edison Program; address, February 6, 1987] C. M. Coburn. *Vital Speeches Day* 53:478-80 My 15 '87
Legislature
Ohio's most powerful black lawmaker reveals fight to conquer cancer [C. J. McLin] il por *Jet* 73:29 S 28 '87
Politics and government
See also
Ohio—Legislature

Ohio Art Company
Etch a future [Etch A Sketch] G. Slutsker. il por *Forbes* 139:72 Mr 23 '87
Lego wars: a Christmas tale [Ohio Art's Zaks vs. Lego construction toys] il *Newsweek* 110:40-1 D 28 '87

Ohio Mattress Company
Mattress wars [Ohio Mattress acquires Sealy] J. Andresky. il por *Forbes* 139:41 Je 15 '87

Ohio River
Riding the river with a Kentucky Belle. J. T. Black. il *South Living* 22:22+ Je '87
Will the river stay 'way from their door? [1937 Ohio River flood and current prevention efforts] J. G. Mitchell. il *Audubon* 89:28-32+ My '87

Ohio State University
Teaching [address, October 31, 1986] K. Brooks. *Vital Speeches Day* 53:434-9 My 1 '87

Ohio University
This course is a joke [M. Helitzer's comedy course] N. Karlen. il por *Roll Stone* p106+ S 24 '87

Ohki, Hiroko, and others
Tolerance induced by thymic epithelial grafts in birds. bibl f il *Science* 237:1032-5 Ag 28 '87

Ohmae, Kenichi
A storm gathers in Japan [address, June 15, 1987] *Vital Speeches Day* 53:729-30 S 15 '87

Ohmmeters
See also
Voltohmmeters

Ohno, Susumu
about
Play the right bases, and you'll hear Bach. il *Discover* 8:10+ Mr '87

Ohr, George E., 1857-1918
about
The mad potter of Biloxi. K. Kertess. il por *House Gard* 159:104+ Je '87

Oil *See* Petroleum
Oil and gas leases
The Alaska lands debate, part two [opening Arctic National Wildlife Refuge to oil and gas exploration] J. D. Hair. il *Int Wildl* 17:26 Ja/F '87
All caribou are not the same [petroleum development threatens Arctic National Wildlife Refuge] L. Minard. il maps *Forbes* 139:43-5 Mr 9 '87
Arctic National Wildlife Refuge: oil field or wilderness? A. L. Spitler. *BioScience* 37:714 N '87

Arctic schemes [proposed oil exploration in the Arctic National Wildlife Refuge] M. K. Udall. *Wilderness* 50:60 Spr '87
A compromise the caribou will like [oil exploration in Arctic National Wildlife Refuge] il *Fortune* 115:9 My 25 '87
Cumulative impacts of oil fields on northern Alaskan landscapes [Arctic National Wildlife Refuge] D. A. Walker and others. bibl f il map *Science* 238:757-61 N 6 '87
Edge of the Arctic [Arctic National Wildlife Refuge; cover story] D. Frazier. il *Natl Parks* 61:18-23 N/D '87
Fighting a new threat to the North [proposed oil development in the Arctic National Wildlife Refuge] I. Austen. il map *Macleans* 100:12 My 4 '87
First word [proposed oil exploration of the Arctic National Wildlife Refuge] G. Nelson. por *Omni* 10:8 N '87
Forest Service steps on Blackfeet [Blackfeet Indians vs. Lewis and Clark National Forest Plan] J. Bruggers. il *Progressive* 51:14 Ap '87
Fuel for an Arctic controversy [opening Arctic National Wildlife Refuge to oil and gas exploration] L. Williamson. il *Outdoor Life* 179:42+ Mr '87
High stakes in a land of plenty [Arctic National Wildlife Refuge; cover story; with editorial comment by Jay D. Hair] T. A. Lewis. il map *Natl Wildl* 25:4-11, 28 Je/Jl '87
Into the second century [Arctic National Wildlife Refuge in Alaska] P. A. A. Berle. *Audubon* 89:4 Mr '87
NPCA opposes damage to Arctic Wildlife Refuge [proposed oil and gas exploration] il *Natl Parks* 61:36 My/Je '87
Polar opposites [oil development versus wilderness in the Arctic National Wildlife Refuge] J. R. Udall. il map *Sierra* 72:40-8 S/O '87
Preserving Alaska's wildlife [Arctic National Wildlife Refuge] L. Williamson. il *Outdoor Life* 180:40+ O '87
Staking out the last frontier [Arctic National Wildlife Refuge] M. K. Udall. il por *Natl Parks* 61:16-17 N/D '87
Wilderness and worship—or wells? [Lewis and Clark National Forest Plan vs. Blackfeet Indians] M. Kantor. il *Sierra* 72:67-8 My/Je '87
Royalties
See also
United States. Office of Royalty Management

Oil Can Henrys (Firm) *See* American Lubrication Company
Oil City Symphony [musical] *See* Musicals, revues, etc.—Reviews—Single works
Oil companies *See* Petroleum industry
Oil crisis *See* Petroleum supply
Oil drilling funds *See* Petroleum investment trusts
Oil exploration *See* Petroleum—Prospecting
Oil field investment trusts *See* Petroleum investment trusts
Oil filters
See also
Automobile engines—Filters
Oil furnaces *See* Furnaces
Oil imports and exports *See* Petroleum industry—Export-import trade
Oil leases *See* Oil and gas leases
Oil options *See* Commodity options
Oil pollution
Laws and regulations
Costly cleanups at the gas pump [EPA storage tank rules] T. Smart. *Bus Week* p28-9 Ap 20 '87
Oil spill bill. *Oceans* 20:69-70 My/Je '87
Proposed EPA rules on petroleum storage may boost fuel costs [underground fuel tanks] *Aviat Week Space Technol* 127:33 Jl 6 '87
New York (State)
A focus on oil and hazardous materials spills. L. Smith. il *Conservationist* 41:46-9 Ja/F '87
North Carolina
The onshore transport of an oil spill by internal waves. A. L. Shanks. bibl f il map *Science* 235:1198-200 Mr 6 '87
Oil refineries *See* Petroleum refineries
Oil shale industry
See also
Tosco Corp.
Return to oil shale. A. Fisher. il *Pop Sci* 231:10+ S '87
Environmental aspects
Shale shock on the western slope. S. M. Voynick. il *Sierra* 72:29-31 My/Je '87

Oil spills *See* Oil pollution
Oil supply *See* Petroleum supply
Oil tankers *See* Tankers
Oil tanks
Costly cleanups at the gas pump [EPA storage tank rules] T. Smart. *Bus Week* p28-9 Ap 20 '87
Proposed EPA rules on petroleum storage may boost fuel costs [underground fuel tanks] *Aviat Week Space Technol* 127:33 Jl 6 '87
Oil well drilling
Environmental aspects
See Petroleum industry—Environmental aspects
Equipment
See also
Oil well drilling rigs
Oil well drilling, Submarine
Environmental aspects
See Petroleum industry—Environmental aspects
Rigs
See Oil well drilling rigs
Oil well drilling rig workers *See* Petroleum workers
Oil well drilling rights *See* Oil and gas leases
Oil well drilling rigs
Mussel colonies thrive on oil platform legs. J. Stuller. il *Oceans* 20:6-7+ Ja/F '87
Oil rigs and sea life: a shotgun marriage that works. P. K. Driessen. il *Sea Front* 33:362-72 S/O '87
Recycling oil rigs. *Oceans* 20:69 Jl/Ag '87
A state's scheme to rig the reefs [Louisiana Rigs-to-Reefs project] C. R. Cotton. il *Sierra* 72:19 Jl/Ag '87
Safety devices and measures
Oil rigs near Vandenberg concern USAF. *Aviat Week Space Technol* 126:110 My 11 '87
Wrecking
Divers' dilemma [offshore rig removal vs. endangered marine species] J. S. McKinna. il *Oceans* 20:10 N/D '87
Oils and fats
See also
Lubrication and lubricants
Soybean oil
Oils and fats, Edible
See also
Evening primrose oil
Feeds—Fat content
Fish oil
Food—Fat content
Rapeseed oil
Dietary fats: a primer. H. Fisher. il *Prevention* 39:98-100+ Mr '87
Oingo Boingo (Musical group)
Oingo Boingo's Danny Elfman. il pors *Seventeen* 46:158+ Ag '87
Ojora, Adekunle
about
Central State University lands Nigerian business exec. at commencement. il por *Jet* 72:25 Jl 27 '87
O'Kanes (Musical group)
The glimmer twins of Nashville. D. Gates. il *Newsweek* 109:80-1 My 18 '87
OKC Limited Partnership
Shootout at the OKC Corral. E. F. Cone. por *Forbes* 140:86+ D 14 '87
O'Keefe, Anne Marie
The case against drug testing. *Psychol Today* 21:34-5+ Je '87
O'Keefe, John Cavanaugh- *See* Cavanaugh-O'Keefe, John
O'Keefe, M. Timothy
Fort Wilderness: Disney World's "Hinterland". il *Saturday Evening Post* 259:92-4+ Ja/F '87
Try the Bermuda angle. il *Saturday Evening Post* 259:82-4 Ap '87
O'Keefe, Michael
A new look at college costs [cover story; with editorial comment by Theodore J. Marchese] il *Change* 19:4, 11-27+ N/D '87
O'Keefe, Patrick J.
(jt. auth) See Prott, Lyndel V., and O'Keefe, Patrick J.
O'Keeffe, Georgia, 1887-1986
about
The $70 million battle over Georgia O'Keeffe's will. S. D. Atchison. il pors *Bus Week* p44 Ja 26 '87
And what about those red hills she painted? J. Herzfeld. il *Art News* 86:198 Ap '87
The battle over Georgia O'Keeffe's multimillion-dollar legacy. A. Decker. il pors *Art News* 86:120-7 Ap '87
Beyond flower power. H. Drohojowska. il por *Harpers Bazaar* 121:224-5+ N '87
A dignified settlement. A. Decker. *Art News* 86:57+ O '87

Georgia O'Keeffe. J. A. Lewis. bibl (p270) il pors *Smithsonian* 18:154-69 N '87
The great big little paintings of Georgia O'Keeffe. B. Rose. il por *House Gard* 159:160-1+ D '87
'Let them all be damned—I'll do as I please' [cover story] E. Abrahams. *Am Herit* 38:44-57 S/O '87
The letters of Georgia O'Keeffe. S. Greenough. bibl f il por *Antiques* 132:1110-17 N '87
A peculiar road to sainthood. J. Hobhouse. il pors *Newsweek* 110:74-6+ N 9 '87
A remarkable book from the 'greatest painter of flowers'. W. Goldstein. il *Publ Wkly* 232:27+ S 11 '87
The self, the style, the art of Georgia O'Keeffe. B. Rose. il por *Vogue* 177:430-3+ O '87
The unknown O'Keeffe. il por *Ms* 16:16+ N '87
The world according to O'Keeffe. M. Wade. il *Horizon* 30:21-4 O '87
O'Keeffe family
about
The $70 million battle over Georgia O'Keeffe's will. S. D. Atchison. il pors *Bus Week* p44 Ja 26 '87
The battle over Georgia O'Keeffe's multimillion-dollar legacy. A. Decker. il pors *Art News* 86:120-7 Ap '87
Okefenokee Swamp (Ga. and Fla.)
See also
Fishing—Okefenokee Swamp (Ga. and Fla.)
Gator riding in the Okefenokee [tour] W. Schemmel. il *Travel Holiday* 168:90+ N '87
Okey, Roberta
Trekking in nature's terrarium. il map *Américas* 39:8-13 S/O '87
Okinawa, Battle of, 1945
The bloodiest battle of all. W. Manchester. il *N Y Times Mag* p42+ Je 14 '87
Oklahoma
See also
Fortification—Oklahoma
Osage Hills (Okla.)
Radioactive pollution—Oklahoma
Wildlife sanctuaries—Oklahoma
Oklahoma! [musical] *See* Musicals, revues, etc.—Reviews—Single works
Oklahoma City Zoo. Aquaticus
Marine life in Oklahoma? il *South Living* 22:28 O '87
O'Koon, Marcy
Take our Constitution quiz. *Good Housekeep* 205:267 S '87
Okoye, Christian
about
A bruiser from Azusa. J. Lieber. il pors *Sports Illus* 66:42-4+ Ap 27 '87
We kid you not—Kansas City rookie Christian Okoye is powered by goodness and goat meat. J. Friedman. il pors *People Wkly* 28:91-2 N 30 '87
Okra
See also
Cooking—Vegetables
The long and short of okra. L. B. Trigg. il *South Living* 22:74-5 My '87
Stretch your harvest. D. J. Young. il *Flower Gard* 31:71 Je/Jl '87
A taste for okra [cover story] M. Kane. il *Rodale's Org Gard* 34:33+ Jl '87
Okrent, Daniel
Saint Francis of Hoboken. il pors *Esquire* 108:211-16 D '87
Okrent, David
The safety goals of the U.S. Nuclear Regulatory Commission. bibl f il *Science* 236:296-300 Ap 17 '87
OK's Company
With hydraulic skillets and enormous toasters, OK's caterers feed the fight against forest fires. M. Grant. il *People Wkly* 28:47-8 S 21 '87
Oksenberg, Michel, 1938-
China's confident nationalism. bibl f *Foreign Aff* 65 Sp Issue:501-23 ['87]
Okun, Alexander
about
Emotional spaces. M. Sommers. il por *Theatre Crafts* 21:44-7+ N '87
Okun, Herbert S.
Libyan occupation of northern Chad [statement, November 18, 1986] *Dep State Bull* 87:87 Ja '87
Nicaragua [statement, November 3, 1986] *Dep State Bull* 87:82-4 Ja '87
Situation in Afghanistan [statement, November 4, 1986] *Dep State Bull* 87:84-6 Ja '87
Olaguer, Eduardo B.
about
Visa denied. W. Steif. il *Progressive* 51:27 F '87

Olajide, Michael

about

Dressed to kill. P. Blauner. il pors *N Y* 20:50-4 Mr 9 '87

Fateful date against Tate. P. Putnam. pors *Sports Illus* 67:48-9 O 19 '87

Olbers' paradox

Goodbye Olbers' paradox! [work of Paul S. Wesson and others] il *Sky Telesc* 74:458 N '87

Light from the depths of time. R. Kippenhahn. il *Sky Telesc* 73:140-2 F '87

Olbrich, Josef Maria, 1867-1908

about

Historic architecture: Joseph Maria Olbrich: a jugendstil design at the Mathildenhöhe artists' colony. J. Rykwert. il por *Archit Dig* 44:180-5+ Ap '87

Olcott-Reid, Brenda

More on plums and Crandall currant ancestry [discussion of January 1987 article, A wealth of plums (I)] *Rodale's Org Gard* 34:8 Ap '87

A wealth of plums (I). il *Rodale's Org Gard* 34:26-32 Ja '87

A wealth of plums (II). il *Rodale's Org Gard* 34:88-92 F '87

Old age

See also

Aged
Ageism
Aging
Centenarians
Longevity
Retirement
Senility

Psychological aspects

See Aged—Psychology

Old age assistance

See also

National Association of Area Agencies on Aging
Townsend pension plan
United States. Administration on Aging

Life planning for old age, focus of AoA projects. J. H. Wehling. *Aging* no356:37-8 '87

Out front. See issue of 50 Plus beginning September 1986

Resources for Hispanic and other minorities. il *Aging* no355:23 '87

State and community news. See issues of Aging

The Ten Commandments of an aging society [address, November 6, 1987] R. D. Lamm. *Vital Speeches Day* 54:133-9 D 15 '87

The use of community services. D. Fowles. il *Aging* no355:36-inside back cover '87

Canada

The growing claims of the aged. D. Cohen. por *Macleans* 100:7 Mr 2 '87

Old age centers *See* Senior centers

Old age homes

See also

Life care communities
Nursing homes

Old age market *See* Aged market

Old business [drama] *See* Cacaci, Joe

Old Court House Museum-Eva Whitaker Davis Memorial

Once a prison, always a courthouse. il *South Living* 22:25 Je '87

Old Fiddlers' Convention (Galax, Va.) *See* Music festivals—Virginia

Old Ironsides *See* Constitution (Frigate)

Old masters drawings *See* Drawing

Old Northwest

Northwest Territory expedition rolling again [reenactment] il *Am Hist Illus* 22:4 N '87

Old Pueblo Museum (Tucson, Ariz.)

An unusual location brings visitors in droves to the Old Pueblo Museum. B. Golightly. il *Horizon* 30:41-2 My '87

Old Salem, Inc.

What did women do? [Domestic Skills Program; with editorial comment by Sandra Wilmot] R. Mashburn. il *Americana* 15:4, 49-52 Mr/Ap '87

Old Slave Mart Museum

Charleston's African connection. il *South Living* 22:24 F '87

Old Spice perfumes for men *See* Perfumes for men

Old Sturbridge Village

Once upon a time in America. D. Lyon. il *Travel Holiday* 168:60-4 O '87

Stepping back in time. B. Golightly. il *Horizon* 30:20-1 My '87

Old Testament *See* Bible. O.T.

Old-time music festivals *See* Music festivals

Old-timers games *See* Baseball, Professional—Old-timers games

Old Westbury Gardens

Old Westbury Gardens, Old Westbury, New York. W. H. Adams. bibl f il *Antiques* 132:304-15 Ag '87

Olden, Tim

"Two saves, partial panel". il *Flying* 114:110-11 Ag '87

Oldenburg, Claes, 1929-

about

An outsize Oldenburg cuts a wide swath at the Guggenheim. il por *People Wkly* 27:102-3 Ja 26 '87

Oldenburg, Kirsten U., and Hirschhorn, Joel S.

Waste reduction: a new strategy to avoid pollution. bibl f il *Environment* 29:16-20+ Mr '87

Oldfield, Bruce

about

Bruce Oldfield makes clothes fit for a (future) queen. B. Johnson. il pors *People Wkly* 27:137-8+ Ap 13 '87

Oldfield, Margery L., and Alcorn, Janis B.

Conservation of traditional agroecosystems. bibl f il *BioScience* 37:199-208 Mr '87

Oldham, Joe

Editor's notes. See issues of Popular Mechanics beginning August 1985

Oldham, Robert K.

Patients as research partners [address, August 14, 1987] *Vital Speeches Day* 53:763-6 O 1 '87

Oldman River Dam (Alta.) *See* Dams—Canada

Olds, Sally Wendkos

America's grandmother fixation. il *Ms* 15:104 Ja '87

(jt. auth) See Eiger, Marvin S., and Olds, Sally Wendkos

Olds, Sharon

The Empire State Building as the moon [poem] *New Yorker* 62:91 F 16 '87

Mrs. Krikorian [poem] *Nation* 245:727 D 12 '87

Olduvai Gorge (Tanzania) fossils *See* Paleontology—Tanzania

Olefins

Synthesis

Putting a spin into chemistry [propellahexaene; work of Leo A. Paquette and Liladhar Waykole] I. Peterson. il *Sci News* 131:357 Je 6 '87

Olestra *See* Sucrose polyesters

Olfactory bulb *See* Brain

Olfactory sense *See* Smell

Oligosaccharides

β1-6 branching of Asn-linked oligosaccharides is directly associated with metastasis. J. W. Dennis and others. bibl f il *Science* 236:582-5 My 1 '87

Olin, Dirk

The right not to know. *New Repub* 197:18-19 Ag 10-17 '87

Olitski, Jules, 1922-

about

Jules Olitski at Knoedler. S. Tillim. *Art Am* 75:215-16 Ap '87

Olivarez, Jose

Jupiter's best show in twelve years [cover story] il *Astronomy* 15:64-70 N '87

Olive baboons *See* Baboons

Olive Branch Awards *See* Journalism—Awards

Olive industry

See also

Lindsay Olive Growers

Olive pit recycling *See* Recycling (Waste, etc.)

Olive trees

The tree of life. J. D. Scott. il *Read Dig* 131:43-4+ N '87

Oliveira, Paulo de *See* Colina, Paulo

Oliver, Anthony

about

A new way to cash in on 'dirty phone calls'. il *Newsweek* 110:55 N 30 '87

Oliver, Augustus K.

about

The trio that humbled Allegis. S. P. Sherman. il pors *Fortune* 116:52-4+ Jl 20 '87

Oliver, Charles

about

Down the primrose path. K. Wilson. il pors *Rodale's Org Gard* 34:32+ Ap '87

Oliver, Daniel

An introduction to the attorney general. *Natl Rev* 39:18 Jl 17 '87

about

Thunder from the right at the Federal Trade Commission. P. Dwyer. il por *Bus Week* p139-40 Ja 12 '87

Oliver, Donna
about
1987 Teacher of the Year. M. S. Miller. il por *Good Housekeep* 204:144+ My '87
Introducing: "Teacher of the Year" Donna Oliver. il pors *Ebony* 43:148+ N '87
Oliver, Edith
The theatre. See issues of The New Yorker beginning February 16, 1987
Oliver, Jay
about
Local TV fights back in Palm Beach. M. Clary. il map *Channels* 7:21-2 Ap '87
Oliver, Mario
about
Hey, Prince Rainier, guess who's coming to the palace! Stephanie's latest beau, what's-his-name. il pors *People Wkly* 27:90-2 Mr 23 '87
Oliver, Martha
about
Down the primrose path. K. Wilson. il pors *Rodale's Org Gard* 34:32+ Ap '87
Oliver, Mary, 1935-
Moccasin flowers [poem] *Atlantic* 259:64 Je '87
Oliver, Peter
A buyer's guide to ski racks. il *Skiing* 40:220+ D '87
Jackson for tourists. il *Skiing* 40:198-202+ S '87
Rec racing revs up. il *Skiing* 39:102+ Ja '87
The ultimate ski adventure. il *Skiing* 40:114 O '87
Oliver, Stephen, 1950-
about
Beauty and the beast [opera] Reviews
New Yorker 63:59-60 Jl 6 '87. A. Porter
Olivetti (Ing. C.) & Co., SpA *See* Ing. C. Olivetti & Co., SpA
Olivines
See also
Forsterite
Ollard, Richard
Clarendon and the Great Rebellion. bibl il por *Hist Today* 37:47-52 S '87
Olmi, Ermanno, 1931-
about
Long live the lady! [film] Reviews
New Repub 197:24 N 9 '87. S. Kauffmann
Olmstead, Marty
7,300 days . . . and counting. il *Sierra* 72:96-8+ N/D '87
Olmstead, Fred
An uncompromising position. il *World Tennis* 34:14-15 F '87
Olmsted, Frederick Law, 1822-1903
about
Olmsted Heritage Landscapes Act. J. H. Kay. *Nation* 244:552-4 Ap 25 '87
Olmsted, Ruth M.
I teach for love—I'm too smart to be in it for the money. il *Glamour* 85:50 S '87
Olney, David
about
The eye of David Olney. A. Nash. il por *Stereo Rev* 52:106 Ap '87
Olsen, Barbara
about
Inspired by quilts and samplers. S. Ferraro. il por *Americana* 15:53-7 Mr/Ap '87
Olsen, Paul E., and others
New early Jurassic tetrapod assemblages constrain Triassic-Jurassic tetrapod extinction event. bibl f il map *Science* 237:1025-9 Ag 28 '87
Olsen, Robert E.
(jt. auth) See Whelan, Elizabeth M., and Olsen, Robert E.
Olsen, William
Breughel's peasants and the month of August [poem] *New Repub* 197:41 Ag 10-17 '87
Olson, James E., 1925-1988
about
Broad shoulders to bear the burden. P. Petre. il por *Fortune* 116:31+ Ag 3 '87
Olson, Lynn
An overview of the Holmes Group. *Phi Delta Kappan* 68:619-21 Ap '87
Olson, Mark
Annual report illustration. il *Petersens Photogr Mag* 16:70-1 S '87
Olsson, Lennart
Report on reports: Continuing the commitment: agricultural development in the Sahel. il *Environment* 29:25-7 Mr '87

Olsson's Books · Records (Firm)
Books as partners in success at Olssons'. H. Fields. il *Publ Wkly* 231:151-3 My 15 '87
Olympia (Wash.)
Art
Politics outlives art [controversy surrounding murals by A. Mason and M. Spafford for the state capitol in Olympia] L. Smallwood. il *Art News* 86:28 D '87
Olympia & York Developments Ltd.
Bloody Monday was a blessing in disguise for the Reichmanns. E. B. Terry. il *Bus Week* p56 D 21 '87
Capital developments. D. Jenish. il *Macleans* 100:28-9 Ag 24 '87
The expansive Reichmanns. D. Jenish. il *Macleans* 100:36 D 7 '87
The Reichmann touch: facing the toughest test yet. E. B. Terry. il *Bus Week* p96-7+ Mr 23 '87
Santa Fe's pursuers may have to settle for pieces. S. Toy. il *Bus Week* p74 D 28 '87-Ja 4 '88
Olympic Arts Festival (1988: Calgary, Alta.)
Culture and conflict. P. Young. il *Macleans* 100:52+ N 9 '87
Olympic athletes *See* Athletes
Olympic athletes, Women *See* Women athletes
Olympic Committee (U.S.) *See* United States Olympic Committee
Olympic Country Club (Calif.: Golf course) *See* Golf courses
Olympic Games
See also
International Olympic Committee
United States Olympic Committee
Bobsleigh, luge and speed skating [U.S. competitors] W. Bingham. il *Sports Illus* 67:51+ D 14 '87
Goodbye, olive wreaths; hello, riches and reality. W. O. Johnson. il *Sports Illus* 66:168+ F 9 '87
The race for gold [skiing champions] W. Bingham. il *Sports Illus* 67:41+ N 23 '87
1936
Winter Olympics
1936: Garmisch-Partenkirchen [ski racing] N. Howe. il *Skiing* 40:56+ S '87
1956
Winter Olympics
1956: Cortina D'Ampezzo [ski racing] N. Howe. il *Skiing* 40:24+ O '87
1960
Winter Olympics
The miracle upsets [U.S. hockey team] W. Bingham. il *Sports Illus* 67:47+ S 21 '87
1968
Summer Olympics
Giants on the earth [B. Beamon's long jump record and L. Evans' 400 meters record still stand] K. Moore. il pors *Sports Illus* 66:48-50+ Je 29 '87
Winter Olympics
1968: Grenoble [ski racing] N. Howe. il *Skiing* 40:24-5+ N '87
1972
Winter Olympics
1972: Sapporo [ski racing] N. Howe. il *Skiing* 40:42+ D '87
1980
Winter Olympics
The miracle upsets [U.S. hockey team] W. Bingham. il *Sports Illus* 67:47+ S 21 '87
1984
Summer Olympics
Black woman named prexy of Olympic surplus fund. por *Jet* 72:48 Jl 27 '87
1988
The reach for athletic gold [American contenders] il *U S News World Rep* 103:70-3 D 28 '87-Ja 4 '88
Summer Olympics
Cable domes [arenas in Seoul] J. Free. il *Pop Sci* 231:88-9 N '87
Carl Lewis predicts calm for 1988 Seoul Olympics. por *Jet* 72:51 Mr 30 '87
A golden opportunity for tennis. N. Amdur. il *World Tennis* 35:4 Jl '87
Gumbel to become NBC's Seoul man for Olympics. por *Jet* 72:46 Jl 20 '87
High-stakes games: are the Olympics at risk? N. Cooper. il *Newsweek* 109:32-3 Je 29 '87
North Korea: games across the border. *Newsweek* 109:45 F 23 '87
Olympic tennis: a bad idea. B. Colson. por *Sports Illus* 66:96 Je 29 '87
South Korea: anticipating visitors. O. Barrot. il *World Press Rev* 34:62 Jl '87

Olympic Games—1988—Summer Olympics—*cont.*
A strange and resolute calm [South Korea's political climate] W. O. Johnson. il *Sports Illus* 66:38-40+ Je 8 '87
The Summer Games. J. Orsini. il *Travel Holiday* 168:9-11 D '87
Surprising Seoul. P. Plawin. il *Changing Times* 41:62-6+ O '87
A symbol of pride and concern [political situation in South Korea] J. D. Reed. il *Time* 129:28-9 Je 29 '87
A vote for South Korea: it's too soon to push the panic button over the Seoul Olympics. W. O. Johnson. por *Sports Illus* 67:94 Jl 13 '87
    Summer Olympics—Boycott
Gold-medal diplomacy [North Korean demand to cohost Olympics] B. Wallace. il *Macleans* 100:21 Ag 17 '87
Pyongyang's Olympic game [North Korea's desire to cohost the Olympics] F. Willey. il *Newsweek* 110:43 O 5 '87
    Summer Olympics—Economic aspects
An all-star entrepreneur [Drew Pearson Enterprises wins Olympic contract] L. Gite. il por *Black Enterp* 17:22 F '87
    Winter Olympics
    See also
    Olympiques Calgary Olympics (Organization)
Calgary's five-ring Stampede [indoor Olympic rodeo] J. Howse. il *Macleans* 100:26 Jl 20 '87
Canada's long glide to gold [national cross-country ski team; with editorial comment by Kevin Doyle] D. Keefler. il *Macleans* 100:2, 46-7 My 25 '87
Competing for tickets. R. Savage. il *Travel Holiday* 168:22-3 Ag '87
Countdown to Calgary [special section] il *Macleans* 100:42-7 O 5 '87
Countdown to the cowtown hoedown. E. M. Swift. il map *Sports Illus* 66:72-8+ Mr 9 '87
From Olympia to the Calgary Games [carrying Olympic flame] R. Surette. il *Macleans* 100:54-5 N 30 '87
High hopes on the slopes [America's female ski racers] W. Roessing. il *Saturday Evening Post* 259:64-5+ D '87
In the tracks of the Olympians. il map *Sunset* 179:50+ D '87
Injunction withdrawn [dispute over Maclean's plans for special edition on Calgary Olympics] il *Macleans* 100:51 N 23 '87
Olym-tix: meanwhile, up in Calgary . . . S. Krasnow. il *Sport Mag* 78:85-6 O '87
An Olympian journey [right to carry the Olympic torch] J. Howse. il *Macleans* 100:47 My 25 '87
An Olympian struggle [Maclean's and Olympic organizers heading for confrontation in the courts over a special issue of the magazine] *Macleans* 100:59 N 9 '87
Olympic countdown. J. Howse. il *Macleans* 100:46-7+ F 16 '87
Olympic countdown (I). il *Women's Sports Fitness* 9:67-8 N '87
Olympic countdown (II). il *Women's Sports Fitness* 9:70-2 D '87
Preparing for snowless slopes [Mount Allan as site for downhill and slalom races] D. Keefler. il *Macleans* 100:42 Mr 2 '87
The price of glory [cover story; special section; with editorial comment by Kevin Doyle] il *Macleans* 100:40-6 D 14 '87
Readying an Olympic mountain [Mt. Allan in western Alberta] *Skiing* 39:50 F '87
Trying to prevent a free ride [growth in contestants] J. Howse. il *Macleans* 100:46 Je 22 '87
The Winter Olympics [special section] il *Macleans* 100:58-61 D 7 '87
The Winter Olympics [special section] il *Macleans* 100:50-2+ N 9 '87
    Winter Olympics—Economic aspects
Accounting for the Games. H. Quinn. il *Macleans* 100:43 D 14 '87
Ceasing and desisting [trademark protection effort in Canada] H. Quinn. il *Macleans* 100:61 D 7 '87
Going for gold with Olympic pins [collectible lapel pins] J. Howse. il *Macleans* 100:56 N 9 '87
The gold rush [Calgary Olympics; cover story; special section; with editorial comment by Kevin Doyle] il *Macleans* 100:2, 28-39 Mr 23 '87
OCO's symbolic victory [Olympic lapel pin distributor B. Hipson taken to court over trademark rights in Calgary] H. Quinn. il por *Macleans* 100:40 Je 8 '87
The selling of the Olympics [official sponsor deals for Calgary Games] R. Manning. il *Newsweek* 110:40-1 D 28 '87

    Winter Olympics—Security measures
Securing the Games. J. Howse. il *Macleans* 100:38-9 Jl 27 '87
    1994
    Winter Olympics
Anchorage's King snub may imperil Olympic bid. *Jet* 73:48 O 26 '87
    Anecdotes, facetiae, satire, etc.
To open the Olympics—lift this tab. M. Lopez. il *Women's Sports Fitness* 9:68 Jl '87
Olympic National Park (Wash.)
A mountainous appetite [mountain goats in Olympic National Park] J. Burger. il *Natl Parks* 61:28-31 Ja/F '87
Olympic National Park [excerpt from Olympic] H. C. Warren. il *Natl Parks* 61:46-7 My/Je '87
Olympic torch
An Olympian journey [right to carry the Calgary Olympics torch] J. Howse. il *Macleans* 100:47 My 25 '87
Olympics, Junior *See* Junior Olympics
Olympics, Senior *See* Senior Olympics
Olympics, Special *See* Special Olympics
Olympics of the Mind *See* Odyssey of the Mind
Olympiques Calgary Olympics (Organization)
An Olympian booster [chief executive officer F. King] J. Howse. il por *Macleans* 100:33 Mr 23 '87
Omaha (Neb.)
    Newspapers
    See also
    Omaha world-herald
    Theater
    See also
    Omaha Community Playhouse
Omaha Community Playhouse
Omaha Community Playhouse. M. LaRue. il *Theatre Crafts* 21:44-5+ D '87
Omaha world-herald
Readers take on one-paper town [monitoring group] B. E. Johansen. il *Progressive* 51:16 Ap '87
O'Mahony, T. P.
After the Irish elections. *America* 156:267-8 Ap 4 '87
O'Malley, Anne
Agent Gail Hochman's role in the ascent of 'Presumed innocent'. il por *Publ Wkly* 231:35-6 Ap 3 '87
Taking the pulse of crime. por *Publ Wkly* 231:71-2 F 6 '87
O'Malley, Christopher
Home office. See issues of Personal Computing beginning July 1987
O'Malley, William J.
P.T. Barnum and the catechetical quest. il *America* 157:206-10 O 10 '87
The priests of Dachau. il *America* 157:351-3 N 14 '87
Oman
    Politics and government
One dagger not aimed at America [rule of Sultan Qabus] J. Barnes. il por map *U S News World Rep* 102:52 Ap 27 '87
Omang, Joanne
In the tropics, still rolling back the rain forest primeval. bibl (p182) il *Smithsonian* 17:56-60+ Mr '87
Omar, Gomaa, and others
Fission-track dating of Haughton Astrobleme and included biota, Devon Island, Canada. bibl f il map *Science* 237:1603-5 S 25 '87
O'Marie, Carol Anne
    about
Mysteries from a novelist nun. J. Horowitz. il por *N Y Times Mag* p34-5 Ag 30 '87
Omark, Johanna
Trimming the fat. il *Women's Sports Fitness* 9:14+ S '87
Omary, M. Bishr, and Kagnoff, Martin F.
Identification of nuclear receptors for VIP on a human colonic adenocarcinoma cell line. bibl f il *Science* 238:1578-81 D 11 '87
OMB *See* United States. Office of Management and Budget
Ombudsman
    See also
    Hospital patient representatives
O'Meara, Stephen James
Amateur astronomers. See issues of Sky and Telescope
Omega (Automobile) *See* Automobiles, Foreign
Omega-3 fatty acids *See* Acids, Fatty
Omelets
Mother, may I? [brie-berry omelet] il *Seventeen* 46:95 My '87
Omelet of the year? il *Sunset* 179:66-7 Ag '87
The original tortilla [in Spain it's an egg-potato omelet] il *Sunset* 178:196-7 Ap '87

Omicron Ceti (Star) *See* Stars, Variable
Omm Sety, 1904-1981
about
Walk like an Egyptian [excerpt from The search for Omm Sety] J. Cott. il *Omni* 9:66-8+ Jl '87
Omni (Periodical)
Omni [manuscript submission policy] P. G. Adcroft. *Writer* 100:22 My '87
Omniflight Helicopter Services, Inc.
Agency suspends Omniflight scheduled services in New York [FAA] *Aviat Week Space Technol* 126:37 Je 8 '87
Omnivex, Inc.
A brand-new way to organize fine art. A. Oshins. il por *Work Woman* 12:66+ My '87
Clever, and it's art [Omnivex Network] il *Pers Comput* 11:257 Jl '87
Omolade, Barbara
Best girlfriends. il *Ms* 16:138-40 Jl/Ag '87
On line data bases *See* Information storage and retrieval systems
On line searching
Finders keepers [Dragnet text-retrieval program] A. C. Hixson. il *Pers Comput* 11:184+ Ap '87
Finding it fast: new software features that search your system [utilities] C. Bermant. il *Pers Comput* 11:125-7+ N '87
Gofer finds what you've lost [RAM-resident utility] C. Bermant. il *Pers Comput* 11:294 D '87
The output side of data bases. C. O'Malley. *Pers Comput* 11:89+ Jl '87
Search and destroy [book index program] D. Pountain. il *Byte* 12:257-60 Ag '87
A search strategy for commonsense logic programming. P. V. Haley. *Byte* 12:173-5 O '87
Solving the riddle of on-line searches. T. Badgett. il *Pers Comput* 11:157-9+ D '87
Super searcher [Fast Data Finder designed by Kwang-I Yu] J. Schefter. il *Pop Sci* 231:60-1 D '87
On-the-job training *See* Employees—Training
On the Twentieth Century [musical] *See* Musicals, revues, etc.—Reviews—Single works
On the verge [drama] *See* Overmyer, Eric
On the waterfront [film] *See* Motion picture reviews—Single works
Onassis, Jacqueline Kennedy
about
Dressing for Camelot [excerpt from In my own fashion; cover story] O. Cassini. il pors *People Wkly* 28:66-8+ Ag 24 '87
For a woman of independent means, an uncluttered, fulfilling life. V. Balfour. il pors *People Wkly* 28:76-8 Ag 24 '87
Onchocerciasis
Victory in sight against 'river blindness' [West Africa] D. D. Silva. il *UN Chron* 24:75-6 My '87
Therapy
An act of vision for the third world [Merck & Co.'s donation of ivermectin to treat river blindness] S. Budiansky. il *U S News World Rep* 103:14 N 2 '87
End of river blindness in sight? [Ivermectin] *Sci News* 132:287 O 31 '87
Merck donates drug for river blindness [ivermectin] J. Walsh. *Science* 238:610 O 30 '87
Miracle worker [Merck & Co.'s donation of ivermectin to cure river blindness in the third world] il *Time* 130:78 N 2 '87
Oncogenes *See* Cancer—Genetic aspects
Oncogenic viruses
See also
HIV viruses
HTLV viruses
Human papilloma virus
Leukemia viruses
Papilloma viruses
Efficient packaging of readthrough RNA in ALV: implications for oncogene transduction [avian leukosis virus] S. A. Herman and J. M. Coffin. bibl f il *Science* 236:845-8 My 15 '87
Human proto-oncogene c-*jun* encodes a DNA binding protein with structural and functional properties of transcription factor AP-1. D. Bohmann and others. bibl f il *Science* 238:1386-92 D 4 '87
Oncogenes and transcriptional control. H. E. Varmus. bibl f *Science* 238:1337-9 D 4 '87
Post-transcriptional control of class I MHC mRNA expression in adenovirus 12-transformed cells. R. T. M. J. Vaessen and others. bibl f il *Science* 235:1486-8 Mr 20 '87

Transformation of rat fibroblasts by FSV rapidly increases glucose transporter gene transcription [Fujinami sarcoma virus] M. J. Birnbaum and others. bibl f il *Science* 235:1495-8 Mr 20 '87
One Lap of America (Rally) *See* Automobile rallies
One life to live [television program] *See* Television program reviews—Single works
One Night Stand (Firm)
Party time? Rent-a-dress. J. Conant. il *Newsweek* 110:104 D 7 '87
Serving Cinderellas on both sides of the ocean, Joanna Doniger rents out gowns fit for a princess. L. Lague. il pors *People Wkly* 28:51-2 D 21 '87
One Price Clothing Stores
A clothing store where one price fits all. il *Newsweek* 110:64 O 19 '87
O'Neal, Alexander
about
Alexander O'Neal's time has come. R. Hoerburger. por *Roll Stone* p22 O 22 '87
O'Neal, Tatum
about
Advantage, Mr. McEnroe? [cover story] M. Lupica. il pors *Esquire* 108:84-8+ Jl '87
O'Neil, Charles Roderick
about
One plus one plus one equals zero. D. Machan. il por *Forbes* 139:58+ Ap 20 '87
O'Neil, Edward H.
The public conversation. *Cent Mag* 20:60-1 Jl/Ag '87
O'Neil, Elaine
(jt. auth) See Horenstein, Henry, and O'Neil, Elaine
O'Neil, Isabel, 1908-1981
about
Isabel O'Neil and the Art of the Painted Finish. S. Wilding. il *Gourmet* 47:76-9+ My '87
O'Neil, Karyn T., and others
Fluorescence properties of calmodulin-binding peptides reflect alpha-helical periodicity. bibl f il *Science* 236:1454-6 Je 12 '87
O'Neil, William J.
about
Look who's nipping at the Wall Street journal. S. Toy. il por *Bus Week* p121-2+ D 21 '87
O'Neil (Isabel) Foundation for the Art of the Painted Finish *See* Isabel O'Neil Foundation for the Art of the Painted Finish
O'Neil (William) & Co., Inc. *See* William O'Neil & Co., Inc.
O'Neill, Gail
about
Making of a star. B. Brandon. por *Essence* 17:45+ Ja '87
O'Neill, Malcolm
about
O'Neill leaves SDI after Senate dust-up. I. Goodwin. *Phys Today* 40:57 S '87
O'Neill, Michael J., 1922-
Lets hear it for losers! por *Newsweek* 110:9 N 2 '87
O'Neill, Terry
'The best show in town': a big birthday album from Paramount. il *Life* 10:130-4+ Ap '87
about
Faye & Terry have Dunaway with living together. il pors *People Wkly* 27:47 Mr 9 '87
O'Neill, Thomas P. *See* O'Neill, Tip
O'Neill, Tip
about
In Tip-top shape. il por *Time* 129:18 Ja 26 '87
Tip: the birth of a pitchman. il por *Newsweek* 110:19 Ag 31 '87
Washington confidential: an interview with Tip O'Neill. C. Hunter-Gault. por *Vogue* 177:756-7+ S '87
O'Neill, William L.
about
The '50s have gotten a bum rap [interview] A. P. Sanoff. il por *U S News World Rep* 102:74 Mr 23 '87
Onex Capital Corporation
Building a first for Canada. D. Jenish. il por *Macleans* 100:22+ Jl 27 '87
Can-do Canadian [G. Schwartz] L. Jereski. il por *Forbes* 140:124 S 7 '87
Oney, Steve
Portman's complaint. il por *Esquire* 107:182-9 Je '87
Ongpin, Jaime Velayo, 1938-1987
about
Foreign money runs scared. L. Reaves. *Bus Week* p54 O 5 '87
Onini (New York, N.Y.: Restaurant) *See* New York (N.Y.)—Restaurants, nightclubs, bars, etc.

O'Nions, R. Keith
(jt. auth) See Oxburgh, E. R., and O'Nions, R. Keith
Onions
See also
Cooking—Vegetables
Onions. S. Ogden. il *Ctry J* 14:66-70 Ap '87
Onions from seed. D. Skilton. il *Rodale's Org Gard* 34:60-1 Ja '87
Will the real Vidalia please stand up? G. Abraham and K. Abraham. il *Flower Gard* 31:64+ F/Mr '87
Only child
Bringing up baby, one by one [single child policy in China] H. G. Chua-Eoan. il *Time* 130:38 D 7 '87
China's only child. E. Hall. bibl (p68) il *Psychol Today* 21:44-7 Jl '87
The only child. L. G. Katz. il *Parents* 62:199 D '87
The only son [film] See Motion picture reviews—Single works
Only you [drama] See Mason, Timothy
Ono, Yōko
about
Yoko Ono [interview] D. Fricke. por *Roll Stone* p53-4 N 5-D 10 '87
Yoko Ono attends Soviet peace parley. A. DeCurtis. il pors *Roll Stone* p14 Ap 9 '87
Ono, Yoshitaka, and others
Expression and properties of two types of protein kinase C: alternative splicing from a single gene. bibl f il *Science* 236:1116-20 My 29 '87
Onorio, John
about
A well-traveled bistro brings an Eiffel-utin air to New Orleans. J. Greene. il pors *People Wkly* 28:83-4 O 26 '87
Ontario
See also
Abortion clinics—Ontario
Booksellers and bookselling—Ontario
Brampton (Ont.)
Criminal justice, Administration of—Ontario
Dance festivals—Ontario
Drama festivals—Ontario
Education—Ontario
Educational laws and regulations—Ontario
Finance—Ontario
Hamilton (Ont.)
Insurance law—Ontario
Kingston (Ont.)
Labor laws and regulations—Ontario
Liquor laws and regulations—Ontario
Motion picture festivals—Ontario
Museums—Ontario
Music festivals—Ontario
Niagara Falls (N.Y. and Ont.)
Ottawa (Ont.)
Saint Thomas (Ont.)
Toronto (Ont.)
Wilderness areas—Ontario
Economic policy
Capitalizing on the good times. P. Best. il *Macleans* 100:20-1 S 21 '87
Learning to compete [address, April 23, 1987] D. R. Peterson. *Vital Speeches Day* 53:528-31 Je 15 '87
Industries
Tremors in the heartland. D. Jenish. il *Macleans* 100:28-9 Mr 30 '87
Languages
Backlash over language. S. Aikenhead. il *Macleans* 100:12-13 Ag 17 '87
Politics and government
The big red wave [Liberal election victory; cover story; special section; with editorial comment by Kevin Doyle] il pors *Macleans* 100:12-14+ S 21 '87
An election budget. S. Aikenhead. il *Macleans* 100:11 Je 1 '87
The end of an accord [Liberals and New Democrats] S. Aikenhead. il *Macleans* 100:14 Jl 6 '87
Ontario's election fever. S. Aikenhead. il *Macleans* 100:24 Ap 6 '87
Ontario's power struggle [D. Peterson calls for an election] S. Aikenhead. il por *Macleans* 100:14-15 Ag 10 '87
Ready for combat [Premier D. Peterson] S. Aikenhead. il por *Macleans* 100:9 Jl 20 '87
A tide of change sweeps Ontario [D. Peterson government] S. Aikenhead. il *Macleans* 100:12-13 Ja 12 '87
Turning up the heat [L. Grossman's campaign] S. Aikenhead. il por *Macleans* 100:8-9 Ag 31 '87
Ontario Securities Commission
Crackdown on Bay Street [insider trading probe] T. Tedesco. il *Macleans* 100:22-3 Jl 13 '87

Explosive questions about trading. A. Walmsley. il *Macleans* 100:33 Jl 20 '87
Policing the stock market. A. Shortell. il *Macleans* 100:32-3 Ag 3 '87
Oocytes See Ova
Op amps See Amplifiers
OPEC See Organization of Petroleum Exporting Countries
Opel, John R.
Technology and the wealth of nations. *Society* 24:51-4 S/O '87
Opel (Adam) AG See Adam Opel AG
Opel (Automobile) See Automobiles, Foreign
Open adoption See Adoption and adopted children
Open air museums
See also
Agricultural museums
Villages, Restored
Open-air opera See Opera, Open-air
Open education See Education, Experimental
Open-pit mining See Strip mining
Open-reel tape recorders See Tape recorders and recording
Opera
See also
Phonograph records—Opera
Radio broadcasting—Opera
Television broadcasting—Opera
Videotapes—Opera
Calendar. See issues of Opera News
The Opera news 1987-88 American opera forecast. il *Opera News* 52:33-6+ S '87
The Opera news 1987 American summer opera forecast. il *Opera News* 51:28-9+ Je '87
Operascope. See issues of Opera News beginning July 1986
A painful process [state of U.S. opera; cover story] G. Heymont. il *Opera News* 52:12-15 N '87
Playing it safe [U.S. opera survey 1986-87] M. F. Rich. il *Opera News* 52:20+ N '87
Viewpoint. See issues of Opera News
Appreciation
Do we need opera? G. Gale. *World Press Rev* 34:60 S '87
Archives
See also
Metropolitan Opera Archives
Choreography
See Choreography
Conducting
See Conducting (Music)
Economic aspects
An angel's way . . . [L. E. Rigler, major benefactor of the New York City Opera] L. Kandell. il por *Opera News* 51:8-10 Ja 31 '87
Funding opera: an endearing attitude [work of G. P. Getty] S. Von Buchau. il por *Opera News* 51:14+ Je '87
Viewpoint. J. L. Poole. *Opera News* 51:4 Ja 31 '87
Viewpoint [corporate sponsorship] J. L. Poole. *Opera News* 52:6 D 5 '87
Federal aid
. . . Uncle Sam's way [funding by the National Endowment for the Arts] P. J. Smith. il *Opera News* 51:10-12 Ja 31 '87
History
Full cycle [staging of the Ring since Wagner's day] D. Harris. il *Opera News* 51:12-14+ F 28 '87
In defense of embellishment [ornamenting Mozart's vocal music] K. Stern. il *Opera News* 51:18-21 F 14 '87
Production and direction
Dancing with Carmen [L. Wertmuller's and T. Brown's collaboration on experimental production of Carmen in Naples] K. Kertess. il pors *Art Am* 75:180-5+ Ap '87
In it together [thirteen companies co-producing Porgy and Bess] G. Heymont. il *Opera News* 51:10-13 Mr 28 '87
Pure and simple [director G. Järvefelt] G. Loney. por *Opera News* 51:18-20+ Je '87
Reviving the dinosaur [work of Y. Lyubimov] G. Loney. il por *Opera News* 52:34-6 N '87
Staged by Scotto [Madama Butterfly at the Metropolitan Opera; with editorial comment by Jane L. Poole] C. Battaglia. il pors *Opera News* 51:4, 10-13 Ja 17 '87
Three cheers for the partisans [radical restagings of classic operas in Europe] M. Walsh. il *Time* 129:81-2 F 23 '87
Stage lighting
Light show [G. Wechsler and staff, lighting technicians at the Metropolitan Opera] C. Mobley. il pors *Opera News* 51:14-16+ Mr 14 '87

Opera—*cont.*

Stage setting and scenery

A fairy-tale Wagner in L.A. [D. Hockney's sets for Tristan] J. Huck. il por *Newsweek* 110:73 D 21 '87

Full cycle [staging of the Ring since Wagner's day] D. Harris. il *Opera News* 51:12-14+ F 28 '87

Opera on a grand scale [A. Lobel's set for Nixon in China] B. Weber. il por *N Y Times Mag* p126 O 11 '87

"Pigeons on the grass"—at last [1986 production of Four saints in three acts by the Opera Ensemble of New York] R. Smith. il *Theatre Crafts* 21:14 My '87

Study and teaching

See also
Indiana University, Bloomington. School of Music
Academic questions [opera training] B. L. Scherer. il *Opera News* 52:16-18+ N '87

Themes

See also
Femmes fatales in opera
Flowers in opera
Grail in opera
An artist's salvation [Richard Wagner's recurrent myth of love as expressed in Tannhäuser] J. Potter and S. Potter. il *Opera News* 51:30-3+ Ja 17 '87

Titling

Viewpoint [use of surtitles by major companies] J. L. Poole. *Opera News* 51:4 F 14 '87

Argentina

Eighty years of elegance and excellence [Colón Theater in Buenos Aires] A. R. Williams. il *Américas* 39:14-19 S/O '87

Arizona

See also
Arizona Opera Company

Australia

Melbourne/Brisbane. J. Cargher. *Opera News* 52:69-70 N '87

Austria

Vienna. C. Norton-Welsh. *Opera News* 52:46-7 D 5 '87

History

A critic's nightmare [E. Hanslick's criticism of Vienna premiere of La bohème in 1897] S. W. Shrader. por *Opera News* 51:20-1 Ja 3 '87

Belgium

Brussels [National Opera of Belgium] D. P. Stearns. *Opera News* 52:46 Jl '87

California

See also
Los Angeles Music Center Opera
San Francisco Opera

Colorado

See also
Opera Colorado

Connecticut

See also
Underground Opera (Opera company)
Tilling 'The tender land' [production at the Long Wharf Theatre, New Haven] P. G. Davis. il *N Y* 20:96 My 18 '87

Egypt

Glitz on the Nile [production of Aida at the Temple of Luxor] il *Time* 129:87 My 18 '87

Florida

See also
Sarasota Opera Association

France

History

Breaking the rules [co-librettist recalls difficult beginnings of Bizet's Carmen in the 1870s]; tr. by Clarence H. Russell. L. Halévy. il *Opera News* 51:36-7+ Mr 14 '87

Germany

Birthdays in Berlin (I). J. H. Sutcliffe. il *Opera News* 51:32-5 F 14 '87

Birthdays in Berlin (II). J. H. Sutcliffe. il *Opera News* 51:32-5+ Mr 28 '87

Germany (East)

East Germany. J. H. Sutcliffe. *Opera News* 52:56-7 O '87

Germany (West)

Bonn. E. Forbes. *Opera News* 52:60+ S '87
Bremen. J. H. Sutcliffe. *Opera News* 52:62+ S '87
Cologne. E. Forbes. *Opera News* 51:37 F 28 '87
Düsseldorf/Duisburg. E. Forbes. *Opera News* 51:39-40 Ja 31 '87
Frankfurt. E. Forbes. *Opera News* 51:38 F 28 '87
Hamburg [Staatsoper] J. H. Sutcliffe. *Opera News* 52:44 Jl '87

Stuttgart. H. Koegler. *Opera News* 51:40 Ja 17 '87
Stuttgart. H. Koegler. *Opera News* 52:62 N '87
Stuttgart. H. Koegler. *Opera News* 51:46-7 Ap 11 '87
West Berlin. J. H. Sutcliffe. *Opera News* 52:57-9 O '87

Great Britain

See also
English National Opera
Glyndebourne Festival Opera Company
Opera North
Royal Opera House (London, England)
London. N. Goodwin. *Opera News* 52:40-1 Ag '87
London. N. Goodwin. *Opera News* 52:60 S '87
London. N. Goodwin. il *Opera News* 51:56+ Je '87
London. N. Goodwin. *Opera News* 52:43-4 D 5 '87
London. N. Goodwin. il *Opera News* 52:59-61 N '87
London [Opera Factory/London Sinfonietta productions] N. Goodwin. il *Opera News* 51:39 Ja 3 '87

Hawaii

See also
Hawaii Opera Theatre

Illinois

See also
Chicago Opera Theater
Lyric Opera of Chicago
Viewpoint [Chicago's opera heritage] R. Holman. *Opera News* 51:4 My '87

Indiana

See also
Indiana University Opera Theatre

Italy

Dancing with Carmen [L. Wertmuller's and T. Brown's collaboration on experimental production of Carmen in Naples] K. Kertess. il pors *Art Am* 75:180-5+ Ap '87

Florence. M. A. Zaccaria. *Opera News* 51:44-6 Ap 11 '87

Genoa. S. Modi. *Opera News* 52:44 Ag '87
Musical events:
Nabucco performed at La Scala. A. Porter. *New Yorker* 62:76+ Ja 26 '87
Performance of J.-B. Lully's Atys by Les Arts Florissants. A. Porter. *New Yorker* 62:79-81 Ja 26 '87
Muti of Milan [interview with new artistic director of La Scala] N. Lebrecht. il por *Opera News* 51:18-19+ Ja 17 '87
Rome [Teatro dell'Opera] M. A. Zaccaria. *Opera News* 51:40 Mr 28 '87
Turin [Teatro Regio] S. Modi. il *Opera News* 51:40+ Mr 28 '87
Vancouver [La Scala's visit for Expo '86 World Festival] F. B. St. Clair. *Opera News* 51:37-8 Ja 3 '87
Verona. C. Battaglia. il *Opera News* 51:38-9 Ja 17 '87

History

Twin glories (I) [singers M. Battistini and F. De Lucia] W. Crutchfield. il pors *Opera News* 52:10-13 D 19 '87

Japan

Tokyo. J. Roussos. *Opera News* 52:47 D 5 '87

Kentucky

See also
Kentucky Opera

Maine

See also
Surry Opera Company

Massachusetts

See also
Opera Company of Boston

Michigan

See also
Michigan Opera Theatre

Minnesota

See also
Minnesota Opera

Mississippi

See also
Opera/South (Opera company)

Missouri

See also
Opera Theatre of Saint Louis

Netherlands

Amsterdam. B. Wechsler. *Opera News* 51:36-7 F 28 '87

New Jersey

See also
Hollybush Festival

New Mexico

See also
Albuquerque Civic Light Opera Association
Opera SouthWest
Santa Fe Opera

Opera—*cont.*
New York (State)
See also
Amato Opera Theatre
Artpark (Lewiston, N.Y.)
Bel Canto Opera (Company)
Center for Contemporary Opera
Chautauqua Opera
Concert Opera of Manhattan
Eastman Opera Theatre
Glimmerglass Opera Theater
Juilliard American Opera Center
Manhattan School of Music
Metropolitan Opera (New York, N.Y.)
New York City Opera Company
Opera at the Academy
Opera Ensemble of New York
Opera Orchestra of New York
PepsiCo Summerfare
Syracuse Opera Company
Vineyard Opera (New York, N.Y.)
New York City. S. Casale; G. Loney; B. L. Scherer. *Opera News* 52:54+ S '87
Ontario
See also
Canadian Opera Company
Opera Atelier (Ont.)
Pennsylvania
See also
Opera Company of Philadelphia
San Francisco Bay region (Calif.)
Barbary Coast bonanza. S. Von Buchau. il *Opera News* 52:18+ S '87
Scotland
See also
Scottish Opera
Sicily
Palermo. M. A. Zaccaria. il *Opera News* 52:41+ Ag '87
Spain
Return to Barcelona [Gran Teatre del Liceu] J. Tassel. il *Opera News* 52:41-2 S '87
Spell it M-A-D-R-I-D [Teatro Lírico Nacional La Zarzuela] F. Kinkaid. il *Opera News* 51:50-1 My '87
Switzerland
Geneva. E. Forbes. *Opera News* 52:54-6 O '87
Texas
See also
Dallas Opera
Houston Grand Opera Association
United States
See Opera
See also
Washington Opera
Washington (D.C.)
See also
Washington Opera
Washington (State)
See also
Seattle Opera
Western Europe
Three cheers for the partisans [radical restagings of classic operas] M. Walsh. il *Time* 129:81-2 F 23 '87
Wisconsin
Milwaukee. J. Koopman; L. Singer. *Opera News* 52:58-9 S '87
Opera, American
See also
Fry, William Henry, 1813-1864
Opera, English
See also
Britten, Benjamin, 1913-1976
Opera, French
See also
Massenet, Jules, 1842-1912
Fournet—à la française [conductor to bow at the Met] A. Ulrich. il por *Opera News* 51:38-9+ Ap 11 '87
Opera, German
See also
Wagner, Richard, 1813-1883
Zimmermann, Bernd Alois, 1918-1970
Opera, Italian
See also
Alfano, Franco, 1876-1954
Puccini, Giacomo, 1858-1924
Opera, Open-air
Arias alfresco [Metropolitan Opera's summer performances] D. G. Winer and D. McGovern. il *Opera News* 51:24+ Je '87
Opera America (Organization)
In it together [thirteen companies co-producing Porgy and Bess] G. Heymont. il *Opera News* 51:10-13 Mr 28 '87

Viewpoint [annual convention] J. L. Poole. *Opera News* 51:4 Mr 14 '87
Opera at the Academy
Musical events:
Performance of Cavalli's La Calisto. A. Porter. *New Yorker* 63:140-1 O 26 '87
Opera Atelier (Ont.)
Going for baroque. P. Young. il *Macleans* 100:70 N 16 '87
Opera broadcasts *See* Radio broadcasting—Opera; Television broadcasting—Opera
Opera Colorado
Denver. G. Giffin. *Opera News* 52:50-1 O '87
Opera Company of Boston
Musical events:
Madama Butterfly. A. Porter. *New Yorker* 63:82-3 Ap 13 '87
Opera Company of Philadelphia
Musical events:
Boris Godunov. A. Porter. *New Yorker* 63:83-5 Ap 13 '87
Death in Venice. A. Porter. *New Yorker* 63:61-2 Ag 3 '87
Philadelphia. R. Baxter. *Opera News* 51:41-2 Ap 11 '87
Reviews:
Performance of Death in Venice. L. M. Brooks. il *Dance Mag* 61:25+ Mr '87
Opera critics and criticism *See* Music critics and criticism
Opera direction *See* Opera—Production and direction
Opera directors
See also
Holby, Grethe Barrett
Järvefelt, Göran
Ross, Glynn
Opera Ensemble of New York
"Pigeons on the grass"—at last [1986 production of Four saints in three acts] R. Smith. il *Theatre Crafts* 21:14 My '87
Opera festivals *See* Music festivals
Opera guilds
See also
Metropolitan Opera Guild
Opera houses
Can do [Wortham Theater Center, home of the Houston Grand Opera; special section] G. Schmidgall. il *Opera News* 52:12-16+ O '87
Eighty years of elegance and excellence [Colón Theater in Buenos Aires] A. R. Williams. il *Américas* 39:14-19 S/O '87
Musical events:
Alice Busch Opera Theatre, new opera house in Cooperstown, N.Y. A. Porter. *New Yorker* 63:72-4 Jl 13 '87
Het Muziektheater in Holland. J. Dolan. il *Theatre Crafts* 21:16-17 O '87
Opera North
Leeds. N. Goodwin. il *Opera News* 51:39 Ja 31 '87
Opera Orchestra of New York
Most happy cello [performance of concluding segments of the Ring operas at Carnegie Hall] P. G. Davis. il por *N Y* 20:108-9 Mr 9 '87
Musical events:
1987 season. A. Porter. *New Yorker* 63:92-3 My 25 '87
Natural wonder [concert performance of Rusalka] P. G. Davis. il *N Y* 20:114-15 My 25 '87
Opera reviews
Single works
See name of composer for full entry
The accomplish'd maid. Piccinni, Niccolò, 1728-1800
Agnes von Hohenstaufen. Spontini, Gaspato, 1774-1851
Aida. Verdi, Giuseppe, 1813-1901
Alceste. Gluck, Christoph Willibald, Ritter von, 1714-1787
Alcina. Handel, George Frideric, 1685-1759
Amelia goes to the ball. Menotti, Gian Carlo, 1911-
Atys. Lully, Jean Baptiste, 1632-1687
Un ballo in maschera. Verdi, Giuseppe, 1813-1901
The barber of Seville. Rossini, Gioacchino, 1792-1868
Beauty and the beast. Oliver, Stephen, 1950-
La bohème. Puccini, Giacomo, 1858-1924
Boris Godunov. Mussorgsky, Modest Petrovich, 1839-1881
La buona figliuola. Piccinni, Niccolò, 1728-1800
La Calisto. Cavalli, Pier Francesco, 1602-1676
Carmen. Bizet, Georges, 1838-1875
La Cenerentola. Rossini, Gioacchino, 1792-1868
Chérubin. Massenet, Jules, 1842-1912
Christopher Sly. Argento, Dominick
La clemenza di Tito. Mozart, Wolfgang Amadeus, 1756-1791

Opera reviews—Single works—*cont.*

Czar Saltan. Rimsky-Korsakov, Nikolay, 1844-1908
Death in Venice. Britten, Benjamin, 1913-1976
Dialogues of the Carmelites. Poulenc, Francis, 1899-1963
Don Giovanni. Mozart, Wolfgang Amadeus, 1756-1791
La donna del lago. Rossini, Gioacchino, 1792-1868
I due litiganti. Sarti, Giuseppe, 1729-1802
Die Entführung aus dem Serail. Mozart, Wolfgang Amadeus, 1756-1791
Ermione. Rossini, Gioacchino, 1792-1868
Les fêtes d'Hébé. Rameau, Jean Philippe
La finta giardiniera. Mozart, Wolfgang Amadeus, 1756-1791
Four saints in three acts. Thomson, Virgil, 1896-
Giasone. Cavalli, Pier Francesco, 1602-1676
Giustino. Vivaldi, Antonio, 1678-1741
The golden cockerel. Rimsky-Korsakov, Nikolay, 1844-1908
Goya. Menotti, Gian Carlo, 1911-
Leonora. Fry, William Henry, 1813-1864
The love of three oranges. Prokofiev, Sergey, 1891-1953
Lulu. Berg, Alban, 1885-1935
Madama Butterfly. Puccini, Giacomo, 1858-1924
Manon. Massenet, Jules, 1842-1912
Manon Lescaut. Puccini, Giacomo, 1858-1924
The marriage of Figaro. Mozart, Wolfgang Amadeus, 1756-1791
Mefistofele. Boito, Arrigo, 1842-1918
Murder in the cathedral. Pizzetti, Ildebrando, 1880-1968
Nabucco. Verdi, Giuseppe, 1813-1901
Nixon in China. Adams, John
L'oca del Cairo. Mozart, Wolfgang Amadeus, 1756-1791
Parsifal. Wagner, Richard, 1813-1883
Porgy and Bess. Gershwin, George, 1898-1937
The postman always rings twice. Paulus, Stephen
Il re pastore. Mozart, Wolfgang Amadeus, 1756-1791
Das Rheingold. Wagner, Richard, 1813-1883
Rigoletto. Verdi, Giuseppe, 1813-1901
Le rivali concordi. Steffani, Agostino
Der Rosenkavalier. Strauss, Richard, 1864-1949
Rusalka. Dvořák, Antonín, 1841-1904
Salvator Rosa. Gomes, Antonio Carlos, 1836-1896
Samson et Dalila. Saint-Saëns, Camille, 1835-1921
Das Schloss. Laporte, André, 1931-
Die Soldaten. Zimmermann, Bernd Alois, 1918-1970
The tales of Hoffmann. Offenbach, Jacques, 1819-1880
Tamu-tamu. Menotti, Gian Carlo, 1911-
Tannhäuser. Wagner, Richard, 1813-1883
The tender land. Copland, Aaron, 1900-
Tolomeo. Handel, George Frideric, 1685-1759
Tomorrow and tomorrow. Sullivan, Timothy
Tosca. Puccini, Giacomo, 1858-1924
La traviata. Verdi, Giuseppe, 1813-1901
Tristan und Isolde. Wagner, Richard, 1813-1883
Il Trovatore. Verdi, Giuseppe, 1813-1901
Turandot. Puccini, Giacomo, 1858-1924
Il viaggio a Reims. Rossini, Gioacchino, 1792-1868
La virtù de' strali d'Amore. Cavalli, Pier Francesco, 1602-1676
Die Walküre. Wagner, Richard, 1813-1883
Where the Wild Things are. Knussen, Oliver, 1952-
Wozzeck. Gurlitt, Manfred, 1890-1973
X. Davis, Anthony
Die Zauberflöte. Mozart, Wolfgang Amadeus, 1756-1791

Opera singers

See also

Alexander, Roberta
Altmeyer, Jeannine, 1948-
Battistini, Mattia, 1856-1928
Bori, Lucrezia, 1887-1960
Budai, Livia
Callas, Maria, 1923-1977
Cuénod, Hugues, 1902-
Daniels, Barbara
De Lucia, Fernando, 1860-1925
Domingo, Placido
Dunn, Susan
Esswood, Paul
Fischer-Dieskau, Dietrich, 1925-
Freni, Mirella
Hynninen, Jorma
Lorengar, Pilar, 1928-
Lott, Felicity, 1948-
Marton, Eva
McCracken, James, 1926-1988
Milanov, Zinka, 1906-
Mills, Erie
Mitchell, Leona
Nilsson, Birgit
Nucci, Leo
Pavarotti, Luciano

Price, Margaret, 1941-
Ramey, Samuel
Randova, Eva
Rossi-Lemeni, Nicola Makedon, 1920-
Sayão, Bidú, 1902-
Scotto, Renata, 1934-
Sénéchal, Michel, 1927-
Shirai, Mitsuko
Simpson, Joy
Singher, Martial
Söderström, Elisabeth, 1927-
Stevens, Risë, 1913-
Sutherland, Joan, 1926-
Winbergh, Gösta, 1943-
Zeani, Virginia, 1928-

Keep your eye on . . . sixteen young American singers on the rise. il *Opera News* 52:36-7 Jl '87
No mere curiosity [resurging art of the countertenor] A. Kozinn. il por *Opera News* 52:26+ Ag '87
Operascope. See issues of Opera News beginning July 1986

Voice training

See Singing—Study and teaching

Opera/South (Opera company)

Jackson State Univ. names white to run Opera/South [B. J. Schooley] *Jet* 72:25 Ag 31 '87

Opera SouthWest

The total package. N. D'Ambrosio. il *Horizon* 30:30 O '87

Opera Theatre of Saint Louis

Musical events:

Beauty and the beast, Alcina, Carmen, La Cenerentola. A. Porter. *New Yorker* 63:59-61 Jl 6 '87
St. Louis. J. Wierzbicki. il *Opera News* 52:50-1 S '87

Operating systems (Computers) *See* Computers—Operating systems

Operation Get Down Food Co-op

Feeding the masses. L. Gite. il *Black Enterp* 17:16 Mr '87

Operation GreenThumb (New York, N.Y.)

Operation GreenThumb [Brooklyn gardens] P. H. Johnson. il *Rodale's Org Gard* 34:20-2 N '87

Operation PUSH *See* People United to Serve Humanity (Organization)

Operation Raleigh

Grace under pressure. A. Finlayson. il *Macleans* 100:6 Je 1 '87

Operational amplifiers *See* Amplifiers

Operations, Surgical *See* Surgery

Operetta

See also

Compact discs—Operetta
Phonograph records—Operetta

Risky business [black musicals created from operettas] S. Flatow. il *Opera News* 51:18-20+ My '87

Operetta reviews

Single works

See name of composer for full entry

The desert song. Romberg, Sigmund, 1887-1951
Die Fledermaus. Strauss, Johann, 1825-1899
HMS Pinafore. Sullivan, Sir Arthur, 1842-1900
The Mikado. Sullivan, Sir Arthur, 1842-1900
Naughty Marietta. Herbert, Victor
Orphée aux enfers. Offenbach, Jacques, 1819-1880
The sorcerer. Sullivan, Sir Arthur, 1842-1900

Ophthalmic assistants

Ophthalmic medical assistants [Malawi] M. C. Chirambo. il *World Health* p9-11 My '87

Ophuls, Marcel, 1927-

Barbie on trial. *Nation* 244:634-5 My 16 '87
Klaus Barbie's circus of evil. il *Nation* 244:884-7 Je 27 '87

about

Shame and punishment. J. J. Buck. il pors *Vogue* 177:392-3+ N '87

Opinion, Public *See* Public opinion

Opinion research *See* Public opinion polls

Oplatka, Avraham

(jt. auth) See Yuli, Itzhak, and Oplatka, Avraham

Opossum shrimp *See* Mysids

Opossums

Photographs and photography

Pint-size possum [pygmy] il *Natl Geogr World* 142:30-1 Je '87

Oppenheim, Bruce

about

Cybill marries her other Bruce. L. Armstrong and others. il pors *People Wkly* 27:98-9+ Mr 16 '87

Oppenheim, Irwin A.

The Epstein-Barr virus: beyond mono. il *Curr Health* 2 13:18-19 Ja '87

Oppenheim, Irwin A.—*cont.*
The spotted story about measles after childhood. il *Curr Health 2* 13:16-17 Ap '87

Oppenheim, Janet, 1948-
Physics and psychics [discussion of May 1986 article, Physics and psychic research in Victorian and Edwardian England] *Phys Today* 40:144-5 My '87

Oppenheim, Joanne
The best new toys for brighter kids. il *Redbook* 170:30+ D '87

Oppenheimer, Harry Frederick, 1908-
about
Apartheid: 'a slippery slope' [interview] S. Reiss. il *Newsweek* 110:53 S 14 '87

Oppenheimer, Helga
about
An aesthetic concern: the Los Angeles apartment of Walter and Helga Oppenheimer. I. Borger. il *Archit Dig* 44:180-5 D '87

Oppenheimer, Joel, 1930-
The Cedars. il *N Y* 20:82-3 D 21-28 '87

Oppenheimer & Co., Inc.
A bear in '87, but a bull in '88 [E. M. Metz] G. G. Marcial. il por *Bus Week* p135 D 28 '87-Ja 4 '88

Oppens, Ursula
about
Musical events. A. Porter. *New Yorker* 63:105-6 Mr 2 '87

Opre, Tom
Sport vehicles. See issues of Outdoor Life

Opryland Hotel (Nashville, Tenn.) *See* Nashville (Tenn.)—Hotels, motels, etc.

Opsata, Margaret
49 turning 50. il *50 Plus* 27:26-8 Ja '87

Optic tectum *See* Brain

Optical character recognition devices *See* Optical scanners

Optical circuits, Integrated *See* Fiber optics

Optical data processing
The Cauzin Softstrip system. J. Holtzman. il *Radio-Electron* 58 ComputerDigest:93-5+ Ap '87
Computing on a beam of light [work of Joseph Goodman and others] *USA Today (Periodical)* 115:13-14 Je '87
Optical materials. A. M. Glass. bibl f il *Science* 235:1003-9 F 27 '87

Optical discs *See* Optical storage devices

Optical equipment
See also
Amplifiers—Optical equipment
Binoculars
Compact disc players—Optical equipment
Eyeglasses
Guided missiles—Optical equipment
Lenses
Night vision devices
Remotely piloted vehicles—Optical equipment
Telescopes
Microscopy and optical equipment. *Science* 235 pt2:G135+ F 27 '87

Optical fibers *See* Fiber optics

Optical illusions
Alice in Wonderland: the Oregon challenge [investigation of the Oregon Vortex] S. Morris. il *Omni* 10:176-7 D '87
Concerning disappearances, including the Cheshire Cat's odd vanishing act. J. Walker. il *Sci Am* 256:122-6 My '87

Optical industry
See also
Bausch & Lomb Inc.
CooperVision, Inc.
Marketing
Safer contacts may ease the strain on lensmakers. S. Siwolop. il *Bus Week* p121 Ja 12 '87

Optical interferometers *See* Interferometers and interferometry

Optical memory cards *See* Memory cards

Optical pattern recognition
See also
Optical scanners
Optical neural computers. Y. S. Abu-Mostafa and D. Psaltis. bibl (p128) il *Sci Am* 256:88-95 Mr '87

Optical radar
Laser remote sensing of the atmosphere [lidar systems] D. K. Killinger and N. Menyuk. bibl f il *Science* 235:37-45 Ja 2 '87

Optical scanners
Machines that read. T. A. Heppenheimer. il *Pop Sci* 230:82-5+ Mr '87
Reading pictures into your computer [Princeton Graphic Systems LS-300] R. Lockwood. il *Pers Comput* 11:240 Je '87

Saba Handscan. J. McCormick. il *Byte* 12:165-7 D '87
Scanning images into your computer [Microtek MS-300A] J. Bell. il *Pers Comput* 11:158 Mr '87
Text scanners for the IBM PC: five OCR machines form CompuScan, Dest, Canon, IOC, and EIT. J. McCormick. il *Byte* 12:233-6+ Ap '87

Optical Society of America
Kogelnik is elected 1987 vice president of OSA. por *Phys Today* 40:73-4 Ja '87
OSA expands programs for teachers. *Phys Today* 40:101 F '87
OSA honored eleven in 1986. il *Phys Today* 40 pt1:82-4 Ag '87

Optical storage devices
See also
CD-ROM (Compact disc-Read only memory)
Drexler Technology Corp.
Videodiscs
Erasable optical discs. N. Metzger and N. J. Freundlich. il *Pop Sci* 230:56-9+ My '87
The ISI WC 525 optical disk drive. R. Malloy. il *Byte* 12:231-3 Jl '87
Kodak introduces high-capacity, high-speed optical-disc system. il *Radio-Electron* 58:6 Je '87
Langley develops optical technique for storing satellite data [Earth Radiation Budget Experiment satellites] *Aviat Week Space Technol* 127:145 Ag 10 '87
Molecular memory. N. J. Freundlich. il *Pop Sci* 230:62-3+ Je '87
Muddy waters in laser land: new formats take the plunge. R. L. Miller. il *Channels* 7 Sp Issue:129 D '87
An optical memory that can be wiped clean. E. T. Smith. il *Bus Week* p56+ Je 15 '87
Optical storage growing up, facing the magnetic challenge. *Byte* 12:37-8 O '87
Storage by light. S. R. Reed. *Pers Comput* 11:123 Jl '87

Optical switching
Computing with light beams [work of Desmond Smith and others] S. Budiansky. *U S News World Rep* 102:68 F 2 '87
Light switch [work of André Mysyrowicz and others] *Sci Am* 256:74-5 Mr '87

Optics
See also
Diffraction
Fiber optics
Light
Optical Society of America
Optoelectronics
Perspective
Reflection (Optics)
Resolution (Optics)
Spectrum analysis
Squeezed light
Optics. il *Phys Today* 40:S47-S51 Ja '87

Optics, Physiological
See also
Optical illusions
Vision

Optimal foraging theory
Large herbivore foraging and ecological hierarchies. R. L. Senft and others. bibl il *BioScience* 37:789-95+ D '87

Optimism
See also
Pessimism
Are you an optimist or a pessimist? [quiz] K. Stechert. il *Glamour* 85:148+ S '87
The birth of an optimist. M. Jacobson. il *Esquire* 108:35-6 Jl '87
The greatest gift you can give your children for Christmas [positive thinking]; ed. by William T. Buckley. N. V. Peale. il *Good Housekeep* 205:116+ D '87
How optimistic are American women? [results of poll] il *Ms* 16:172-4+ Jl/Ag '87
Pollyanna, ex-bubblehead [character created by E. H. Porter] J. Griswold. *N Y Times Book Rev* 92:51 O 25 '87
Put a smile on your face. S. Perry. il *Curr Health 2* 14:14-15 O '87
Think yourself healthy. R. Manuel. il *Harpers Bazaar* 120:118+ F '87
You are what you think [positive thinking] C. Safran. il *Read Dig* 131:44-6 Ag '87
Anecdotes, facetiae, satire, etc.
Why pessimism is better than optimism (on a global scale). J. Gorman. il *Discover* 8:14+ Ag '87

Optimization, Mathematical See Mathematical optimization
Options, Automobile See Automobiles—Equipment
Options, Boat See Boats and boating—Equipment
Options (Contracts)
    See also
    Commodity options
    Foreign exchange options
    Interest rate options
    Put and call transactions
    Stock index options
    Stock purchase options
Optoelectronics
    See also
    Digitizers (Computers)
                    Conferences
CLEO and IQEC in Baltimore [Conference on Lasers
    and Electro-optics and the International Quantum
    Electronics Conference] M. Marynowski. il *Phys Today*
    40:62-3 Mr '87
                    Military use
USAF pursues standardized allied reconnaissance data.
    Aviat Week Space Technol 127:25 S 21 '87
Optoelectronics industry
                    Israel
    See also
    Electro-optics Industries, Ltd.
Opus (Fictional character)
Opus goes home: Bloom County's penguin returns to
    his roots in Antarctica. B. Breathed. il *Life* 10:42-7+
    My '87
Opus Dei (Society)
The autonomous kingdoms of Opus Dei. J. Creighton.
    il por *Humanist* 47:9-13+ Mr/Ap '87
Oral communication
    See also
    Listening
    Public speaking
The elusive language of pleasure and pain. R. Selzer.
    il *N Y Times Book Rev* 92:38-9 Ap 5 '87
Oral contraceptives See Contraceptives
Oral history
Bournonville lives in oral memoirs [work of T. Tobias]
    por *Dance Mag* 61:108-9 Mr '87
A gift to the future [family oral histories] R. Long.
    il *High Fidel* 37:21 D '87
Prepare an oral history. B. M. Stave. il *Americana* 15:14+
    N/D '87
Oral leukoplakia See Leukoplakia, Oral
Orange, Cynthia
A creative approach to learning. por *Progressive* 51:12
    N '87
Orange County (Calif.)
Orange County, California. il map *Time* 129:16 Je 15
    '87
                    Arts
Orange County [special section] il *Horizon* 30:49-62+
    Ja/F '87
                    Crime
Côte de Fraud [boiler room scam operators] M.
    Beauchamp. il *Forbes* 140:32-3 N 2 '87
Dial-a-dupe on Con Man's Coast [boiler room phone
    scams] P. Cary. il *U S News World Rep* 103:62-3
    D 21 '87
                    Description and travel
Orange County [special section] il *Horizon* 30:49-62+
    Ja/F '87
                    Public health
AIDS tests for teachers [teacher V. Chalk fights to regain
    position in Orange County, Calif.] J. N. Baker. por
    Newsweek 110:81 O 19 '87
Orange County Performing Arts Center
The new Orange County Performing Arts Center sym-
    bolizes the county's coming of age. T. Bailey. il *Horizon*
    30:49-50 Ja/F '87
Orange County opens center for the arts [suitability
    for dance] O. Maynard. il *Dance Mag* 61:7 Ap '87
Orange industry See Citrus fruit industry
Orange juice
    See also
    TreeSweet Products Co.
Orange juice. il *Consum Rep* 52:377-80 D '87
Orange juice. il *Consum Rep* 52:76-80 F '87
                    Export-import trade
    See also
    Citrosuco Paulista (Firm)
                    Labeling
The state of the Sunshine Tree. il *Consum Rep* 52:77
    F '87
                    Marketing
A juice maker squeezes itself dry [TreeSweet] J. E. Davis.
    il por *Bus Week* p42 Ag 10 '87

What's for breakfast? Juice wars. Z. Schiller. il *Bus
    Week* p110+ O 5 '87
Oranges
About oranges. A. Burgess. il *Gourmet* 47:60+ N '87
Orangutans
Interview [B. Galdikas] D. Lessem. por *Omni* 9:76-8+
    Jl '87
Oratorio
    See also
    Phonograph records—Oratorio
Oratorio reviews
                    Single works
    See name of composer for full entry
Acis and Galatea. Handel, George Frideric, 1685-1759
Athalia. Handel, George Frideric, 1685-1759
Esther. Handel, George Frideric, 1685-1759
Israel in Egypt. Handel, George Frideric, 1685-1759
Joshua. Handel, George Frideric, 1685-1759
Saul. Handel, George Frideric, 1685-1759
Oratory See Rhetoric
Orbison, Roy, 1936-
                    about
An all-star band rocks with Roy Orbison at the Coconut
    Grove. S. Rogers. il por *Roll Stone* p9 N 19 '87
The Boss is just one of the guys as an all-star band
    salutes rock 'n' roll great Roy Orbison. il por *People
    Wkly* 28:44-5 O 19 '87
Orbita Aerospace Systems (Firm)
Brazil forms high-technology venture to develop advanced
    weapon systems. *Aviat Week Space Technol* 127:52-3
    Ag 17 '87
Orbital Engine Company
Can the two-stroke make it this time? D. Scott. il *Pop
    Sci* 230:74-6 F '87
Two strokes revisited [Orbital Combustion Process] P.
    L. Albrecht. il *Road Track* 38:64+ Ap '87
Orbital platforms See Space stations
Orbital rendezvous (Space flight)
CNES discusses Hermes-Mir compatibility with Soviets.
    Aviat Week Space Technol 126:25 My 11 '87
Mir mockup reveals docking hub for vehicle expansion.
    il *Aviat Week Space Technol* 127:38-9 Jl 27 '87
Soviet long-duration crew activates Mir space station.
    C. Covault. il *Aviat Week Space Technol* 126:19-20
    F 16 '87
Soviets conduct space tanker flight tests [docking
    maneuvers with Mir] *Aviat Week Space Technol* 127:25
    N 16 '87
Soviets prepare to place cosmonaut crew on Mir for
    long-duration station flight. il *Aviat Week Space Technol*
    126:28-9 Ja 26 '87
Orbital Sciences Corporation
Commercial space firms propose booster, free-flier [Mars
    Observer] il *Aviat Week Space Technol* 126:76 Ap
    6 '87
Company offers to buy NASA a rocket [Titan 3] M.
    M. Waldrop. *Science* 235:1568 Mr 27 '87
Orbital Sciences, Space Agency disagree on cost of using
    transfer orbit stage as upper stage for the Mars Observer.
    Aviat Week Space Technol 126:27 My 11 '87
OSC offers to finance Titan 34D for Mars Observer.
    Aviat Week Space Technol 126:24-5 Mr 23 '87
Orbits
    See also
    Artificial satellites—Orbits
    Asteroids—Orbits
    Comets—Orbits
    Earth—Orbit
    Mechanics, Celestial
    Moon—Orbit
    Planets—Orbits
    Stars—Orbits
More on Kepler's equation. W. Landgraf. il *Sky Telesc*
    73:535-6 My '87
Orcas See Killer whales
Orchard Books
Orchard Books: '80 years of experience' behind a brand-
    new list. *Publ Wkly* 231:26 Ap 24 '87
Orchestra directors See Conductors (Music)
Orchestra New England
Musical events:
    Concert performance of H. Villa-Lobos' Magdalena
        at Alice Tully Hall. A. Porter. *New Yorker* 63:163-4
        D 7 '87
Orchestra of Santa Fe
Point, counterpoint. J. P. Forsthoffer. il *Horizon* 30:44
    O '87
Orchestra of the Eighteenth Century
The real thing [New York City performances] P. G.
    Davis. il *N Y* 20:146+ D 7 '87

Orchestral music
See also
Compact discs—Orchestral music
Phonograph records—Orchestral music
Tape recordings—Orchestral music
Orchestras
See also
Amor Artis Chorale and Orchestra
Bands (Music)
Boston Early Music Festival Orchestra
Boston Symphony Orchestra
Brooklyn Philharmonic Symphony Orchestra
Conductors (Music)
Detroit Symphony Orchestra
Eastman Philharmonia
Fairfax Symphony Orchestra
Handel & Haydn Society
Houston Symphony Orchestra
Indianapolis Symphony Orchestra
Jacksonville Symphony Orchestra
Lester Lanin Orchestras
National Symphony Orchestra
New Jersey Symphony Orchestra
New Mexico Symphony Orchestra
New York Philharmonic-Symphony Orchestra
Opera Orchestra of New York
Orchestra New England
Orchestra of Santa Fe
Orchestra of the Eighteenth Century
Riverside Symphony
Royal Philharmonic Orchestra
Santa Fe Symphony
Senior Citizens' Orchestra of Miami Beach
Springfield Symphony Orchestra (Mass.)
Tucson Symphony Orchestra
Vienna Philharmonic
Youth Symphony Orchestra of New York
The glorious symphony. A. Rich. il *Newsweek* 109:54-6
Ja 5 '87
Orchid amaryllis *See* Jacobean lilies
Orchids
See also
Lady's slipper
Cattleya orchids as a gift? Yes, even without a greenhouse.
il *Sunset* 179:188 D '87
Orchid mania. T. Ferraro. il *Flower Gard* 31:30-2+ O/N
'87
Orchids indoors? [moth orchids and lady's slippers] il
Sunset 178:182 F '87
Order of Our Lady of Mount Carmel *See* Carmelites
Order of Saint Benedict *See* Benedictines
Ordinaires (Musical group)
The Ordinaires. B. Milkowski. il *Down Beat* 54:14-15
My '87
Ordinance of 1787 *See* Northwest ordinance (1787)
Ordination of homosexuals
Anglicans compromise on gay clergy. T. Beeson. *Christ
Century* 104:1080-1 D 2 '87
A Methodist on trial [trial of lesbian clergywoman R.
Denman in Dover, N.H.] M. Starr. il por *Newsweek*
110:62 S 7 '87
Ordination of women
Anglicans move toward women's ordination. K. Slack.
il *Christ Century* 104:374-5 Ap 22 '87
Episcopal 'gentlemen's club' now open? J. C. Lyles. *Christ
Century* 104:909-10 O 21 '87
Hour of decision for women priests [Church of England]
M. P. Harris. il *Time* 129:43 Mr 2 '87
Sailing to the edge of the world [role of women in
the Church of England] S. Fletcher. il *Hist Today*
37:10-11 S '87
Ordnance
See also
Ballistics
Ordovician period *See* Paleontology—Ordovician
Ordway, Frederick Ira, 1927-
Last of the rocket team: a conversation with Georg
von Tiesenhausen. il por *Space World* X-6-282:29-32
Je '87
Report from the IAF. *Space World* X-12-288 Space
Advocate:2 D '87
Ore deposits
Present at the birth of an ore deposit [Salton Sea area]
R. A. Kerr. il *Science* 238:890-1 N 13 '87
Oregon
See also
Booksellers and bookselling—Oregon
Civil defense—Oregon
Clatsop County (Or.)
Columbia River
Gardens and gardening—Oregon

Geology—Oregon
Hunting—Oregon
New Oregon Trail (Or.)
Rogue River (Or.)
Wilderness areas—Oregon
Wildlife—Oregon
Wildlife sanctuaries—Oregon
Description and travel
A coast of many moods. A. Furst. il map *50 Plus*
27:78-82 O '87
Lakes, lava, llamas [central Oregon] il maps *Sunset*
179:64-9 Jl '87
**Oregon Health Sciences University. Vollum Institute for
Advanced Biomedical Research** *See* Vollum Institute
for Advanced Biomedical Research
O'Reilly, Bill
You can go home—sort of. por *Newsweek* 110:14-15
D 7 '87
O'Reilly, Jane
A global click! il *Ms* 16:60-1+ Jl/Ag '87
(jt. auth) See Ehrenreich, Barbara, and O'Reilly, Jane
Oreskes, Michael
(jt. auth) See Purnick, Joyce, and Oreskes, Michael
Oresman, Janice C.
Steven Barbash. il por *Am Artist* 51:26 F '87
Orford String Quartet
An up-tempo quartet. J. Pearce. il *Macleans* 100:42
Jl 13 '87
Organ, Claude, Jr.
about
Claude Organ Jr.: super surgeon. il pors *Ebony* 42:88+
Ja '87
Organ donation *See* Donation of organs, tissues, etc.
Organ industry
See also
Fritts-Richards Organ Builders (Firm)
Organ music
See also
Compact discs—Organ music
Organ preservation *See* Preservation of organs, tissues,
etc.
Organ transplantation *See* Transplantation of organs, tissues,
etc.
Organic cosmetics *See* Cosmetics
Organic farming
See also
Community-Supported Agriculture (Organization)
International Federation of Organic Agriculture
Movements
Beyond the farming crisis. D. Ehrenfeld. il *Technol Rev*
90:46-56 Jl '87
The time is ripe for organic agriculture. L. Shapiro.
Newsweek 110:88 O 5 '87
Economic aspects
Can sustainable agriculture be profitable? P. Madden.
bibl f il *Environment* 29:18-20+ My '87
Iowa
Two Iowa farmers sow the seeds of change [D. and
S. Thompson] C. Isenhart. il pors *Sierra* 72:79-82
N/D '87
Sweden
Life after Chernobyl. J. Forssell and E. Forssell. il pors
Mother Earth News 105:94-8+ My/Je '87
Washington (State)
Keeping topsoil down on the farm [study of effect of
farming techniques on soil; work of John P. Reganold]
I. Peterson. *Sci News* 132:357-8 D 5 '87
Organic food *See* Food, Organic
Organic food cooking *See* Cooking—Organic food
Organic gardening (Periodical)
Inside. S. O. Daniels. See issues of Rodale's Organic
Gardening beginning August 1985 through January
1987
Organic gardens and gardening
See also
Compost
Mulching
Vegetable gardens and gardening
Calendar. See issues of Rodale's Organic Gardening
through July 1987
Concentrate your garden's greening power. R. Rodale.
il *Rodale's Org Gard* 34:16-18 Ap '87
Garden gate. S. O. Daniels. See issues of Rodale's Organic
Gardening beginning February 1987
Healing garden. W. Gottlieb. See issues of Rodale's
Organic Gardening beginning August 1987
The healing garden [regeneration gardening] R. Rodale.
il *Rodale's Org Gard* 34:24-6 F '87
New ground. See issues of Rodale's Organic Gardening
beginning January 1987

Organic gardens and gardening—*cont.*

Q & A. See issues of Rodale's Organic Gardening beginning April 1987

Q & A gardening. See issues of Rodale's Organic Gardening through March 1987

What my first garden taught me. il *Rodale's Org Gard* 34:54-6+ F '87

Competitions

The winners: 1986 Organic Gardener of the Year contest. il *Rodale's Org Gard* 34:34-6 F '87

Periodicals

See also

Organic gardening (Periodical)

California

Growin' in the wind. M. V. Look. il *Rodale's Org Gard* 34:64-5 Ap '87

Minnesota

Black earth bounty [Gardener of the Year J. Smith] P. H. Johnson. il por *Rodale's Org Gard* 34:38-40+ F '87

Pennsylvania

Down the primrose path [gardeners C. and M. Oliver] K. Wilson. il pors *Rodale's Org Gard* 34:32+ Ap '87

Organic insect control *See* Insect control

Organic matter in soils *See* Humus

Organic metals *See* Organometallic compounds

Organic spraying and dusting *See* Spraying and dusting

Organisation for Economic Co-operation and Development

OECD Council meets in Paris [text of final communique] *Dep State Bull* 87:43-5 Jl '87

OECD meeting calls for job growth, flexibility, and readjustment. M. Brodsky. il *Mon Labor Rev* 110:53-4 Je '87

OECD to set rules for international science. D. Dickson. il *Science* 238:743 N 6 '87

Organization

Could you be better organized? [quiz] K. Abel. *Redbook* 169:27-8 My '87

Getting organized for 1987. K. V. Brailsford. il *Black Enterp* 17:54-6 Ja '87

How to work without a secretary. E. W. Allison and M. A. Allison. *Work Woman* 12:22 Ag '87

An officer's mess. S. Bing. il *Esquire* 107:44 Ja '87

What-to-do checklist before the baby arrives [excerpt from Organize yourself!]; ed. by Kate Kelly. R. Eisenberg. il *Glamour* 85:160+ F '87

Where to find more time for yourself [excerpt from Organize yourself!]; ed. by Kate Kelly. R. Eisenberg. il *Redbook* 168:74-5+ Ja '87

Organization for Economic Cooperation and Development *See* Organisation for Economic Co-operation and Development

Organization of African Unity

OAU leader meets with black politicos in D.C. to cement U.S. African ties [I. Oumarou] il por *Jet* 72:14 Je 1 '87

Organization of American States

Collective security and the inter-American system. D. S. Painter. il *Dep State Bull* 87:56-8 Ap '87

Dealing against illegal drugs. A. Quiroga G. *Américas* 39:55 My/Je '87

Learning democracy's ways [Model OAS General Assembly] C. Whelan. il *Américas* 39:50-2 S/O '87

Promoting inter-American cooperation [address, November 11, 1986] G. P. Shultz. *Dep State Bull* 87:27-30 Ja '87

San Martín and the OAS. C. Godoy-García. il *Américas* 39:55-6 Jl/Ag '87

Organization of Petroleum Exporting Countries

The cold wave that sent warm shivers to Riyadh. K. R. Sheets. *U S News World Rep* 102:41 Ja 26 '87

Iranamok and OPEC. P. J. Sloyan. *New Repub* 197:19-21 N 9 '87

Is OPEC bluffing again? T. Thompson. *Bus Week* p92 Mr 9 '87

It's comeback time for $1-a-gallon gasoline and OPEC. K. R. Sheets. *U S News World Rep* 102:36 Je 29 '87

New clout for the oil cartel. il *Fortune* 115:8 F 16 '87

A new member? Moscow plays oil politics with OPEC. il *Newsweek* 109:4 Mr 30 '87

OPEC makes $18 oil stick—for now. W. C. Symonds. il *Bus Week* p32-3 F 16 '87

'There's too much damn oil around'. T. Smart. *Bus Week* p24-5 S 7 '87

The U.S. is better braced for another oil shock . . . while OPEC seems less likely to maintain high prices. G. Koretz. il *Bus Week* p14 Ag 24 '87

Why oil prices could rise again. D. Blake. *World Press Rev* 34:48+ Jl '87

Conferences

Can OPEC keep its foot off the gas in Vienna? W. C. Symonds. il *Bus Week* p32 Je 29 '87

Crude calculations [price drop] il *U S News World Rep* 103:14 D 28 '87-Ja 4 '88

OPEC is staring at $15 oil—once more [Vienna meeting] W. C. Symonds. il *Bus Week* p33 D 14 '87

OPEC smartens up. W. C. Symonds. *Bus Week* p34-5 Jl 13 '87

OPEC's troubled future. T. Tedesco. il *Macleans* 100:37-8 D 14 '87

Organizational behavior

"Achieve or leave" [United Technologies] H. Banks. por *Forbes* 140:344-5 Jl 13 '87

Big firm, small firm: which is better for you? M. M. Kennedy. il *Glamour* 85:140 My '87

Bureaucracy as life [W. H. Whyte's Organization man] R. J. Samuelson. il *Newsweek* 109:43 Ja 12 '87

Computer headaches. J. Schwartz. il *Newsweek* 110:34-5 Jl 6 '87

Corporate countercultures. *Society* 24:2-3 My/Je '87

Corporate mind control [New Age gurus] A. Miller. il *Newsweek* 109:38-9 My 4 '87

Creativity and enterprise [address, June 1, 1987] A. W. Elliott. *Vital Speeches Day* 53:637-40 Ag 1 '87

Culture shock at Xerox. J. A. Byrne. il por *Bus Week* p106+ Je 22 '87

Imposing a corporate culture. P. C. Reynolds. il *Psychol Today* 21:32-4+ Mr '87

The perils of persistence [Profiles of Organizational Influence Strategies test results] S. Schmidt and D. Kipnis. bibl (p65) il *Psychol Today* 21:32+ N '87

The role of the manager: the use of power. F. Bartolomé and A. Laurent. *Current* 291:12-16 Mr/Ap '87

Trying to bend managers' minds [human potential gurus] J. Main. il *Fortune* 116:95-6+ N 23 '87

Why so many mergers fail [clash of corporate cultures] M. Lefkoe. il por *Fortune* 116:113-14 Jl 20 '87

Organizational change

How the best get better [R. H. Waterman's The renewal factor; cover story] J. A. Byrne. il por *Bus Week* p98-9 S 14 '87

An inside view of change in schools. E. E. Eubanks and R. Parish. il *Phi Delta Kappan* 68:610-15 Ap '87

Making changes: how to budge the office mule. M. J. Parson. il *Work Woman* 12:139-41 S '87

The protean corporation [cover story] S. Lee and C. Brown. il *Forbes* 140:76-9 Ag 24 '87

The renewal factor [excerpt] R. H. Waterman, Jr. il *Bus Week* p100-1+ S 14 '87

When change is in the wind . . . heads up! J. Ciabattari. il *Work Woman* 12:63-6+ F '87

When companies are great places to work [condensed from Re-inventing the corporation] J. Naisbitt and P. Aburdene. il *Read Dig* 130:141-4 Ja '87

Organizational development *See* Organizational change

Organized crime

See also

Mafia

Capone to Kefauver: organised crime in America. M. Woodiwiss. bibl il *Hist Today* 37:8-15 Je '87

Rooting out organized crime [address, November 17, 1986] W. H. Webster. *Vital Speeches Day* 53:262-5 F 15 '87

Hong Kong

The criminal element. A. Finlayson. *Macleans* 100:27 Ag 17 '87

Northern Ireland

A different kind of terror. M. S. Serrill. *Time* 130:45 O 12 '87

Organized labor *See* Trade unions

Organometallic compounds

Dianion stabilization by $(M(C_5(CH_3)_5)_2)^+$: theoretical evidence for a localized ring in $(DDQ)^{2-}$. J. S. Miller and D. A. Dixon. bibl f il *Science* 235:871-3 F 20 '87

Orgasm

Ardent adaptationism [discussion of February 1987 article, Freudian slip] S. J. Gould. il *Nat Hist* 96:4+ Ap '87

Are you lying in bed? [faking an orgasm] H. S. Kaplan. por *Redbook* 169:14 Je '87

The earth makes its move [metaphor for orgasm] W. Safire. il *N Y Times Mag* p12+ Je 14 '87

Freudian slip [female orgasm] S. J. Gould. *Nat Hist* 96:14+ F '87

The politics of orgasm, continued. C. Tavris. *Vogue* 177:100 S '87

Orians, Gordon H.
Expanding adaptive management principles [discussion of November 1986 article, The place of science in environmental problem solving] *Environment* 29:3-4 Ja/F '87

Orient and Occident *See* East and West

Oriental Americans *See* Asian Americans

Oriental art *See* Art, Oriental

Oriental house decoration *See* House decoration, Oriental

Oriental languages
Asian languages aid mathematics skills [research by Irene T. Miura] B. Bower. *Sci News* 132:183 S 19 '87

Oriental pottery *See* Pottery, Oriental

Oriental rugs and carpets *See* Rugs and carpets, Oriental

Oriental vegetables *See* Vegetables

Orientation
> *See also*
> Chemotaxis
> Echolocation (Physiology)
> Geographical perception

Eastward slow, the sea slugs [research by A. O. Dennis Willows and Kenneth J. Lohmann] D. D. Edwards. *Sci News* 131:54 Ja 24 '87

Easy navigation. S. Netherby. il *Field Stream* 91:102+ Ap '87

Fungi feel their way to feast [bean rust fungi; research by Harvey C. Hoch and others] S. Weisburd. il *Sci News* 131:214 Ap 4 '87

Lost! (but not for long) [survival instruction course at Big Thicket National Preserve] M. W. Perin. il *Parents* 62:92-4+ Jl '87

Lunar-modulated geomagnetic orientation by a marine mollusk. K. J. Lohmann and A. O. D. Willows. bibl f il *Science* 235:331-4 Ja 16 '87

Signaling for growth orientation and cell differentiation by surface topography in Uromyces. H. C. Hoch and others. bibl f il *Science* 235:1659-62 Mr 27 '87

What to do when you're lost. il *Natl Wildl* 25:23 F/Mr '87

Origen
> *about*

Origen. C. E. White. il *Christ Today* 31:36 Mr 20 '87

Origin of languages *See* Language and languages—Origin

Origin of life *See* Life (Biology)—Origin

Origin of man *See* Man, Prehistoric

Origin of species *See* Evolution; Species

Original New York Seltzer (Firm)
Fizz-biz whiz Randy Miller leaps into high-rise hype. il *People Wkly* 27:74 Mr 2 '87

This family has seltzer in its blood. T. Carson. il pors *Bus Week* p92 Jl 6 '87

Original Sonora Cafe (Los Angeles, Calif.) *See* Los Angeles (Calif.)—Restaurants, nightclubs, bars, etc.

Origny, Henri d', vicomte
> *about*

Habitation Pécoul: Vicomte and Vicomtesse d'Origny on Martinique. L. Dennis. il *Archit Dig* 44:192-7+ O '87

Origny, Sybil d', vicomtesse
> *about*

Habitation Pécoul: Vicomte and Vicomtesse d'Origny on Martinique. L. Dennis. il *Archit Dig* 44:192-7+ O '87

Orinoco River (Venezuela)
The earthly paradise [Orinoco River as Eden; excerpt from The four voyages of Christopher Columbus] C. Columbus. il *Courier* 40:8-9 Ap '87

A major food web component in the Orinoco River channel: evidence from planktivorous electric fishes. J. G. Lundberg and others. bibl f il *Science* 237:81-3 Jl 3 '87

Orioli, Esther M., and Jaffe, Dennis T.
StressMap [excerpt] il *Ms* 15:38-9+ My '87

Orion airplanes *See* Airplanes, Military

Orion Pictures Corporation
The little studio that could. J. Kornbluth. il *N Y* 20:48-52+ Ap 6 '87

Orion can't wait to hear 'The envelope, please'. R. Grover. il *Bus Week* p98 Mr 30 '87

Rise and shine [interview with M. Medavoy] A. Thompson. il por *Film Comment* 23:54-6+ My/Je '87

Orlando, Tom, 1931-
> *about*

Tom Orlando. E. Agar. il por *Am Artist* 51:40-3+ S '87

Orlando (Fla.)
> **Airports**

KLM gains Orlando gateway over U.S. carriers' protests. *Aviat Week Space Technol* 127:44 Ag 3 '87

U.S. airlines oppose KLM service to Orlando. *Aviat Week Space Technol* 126:42 My 11 '87

> **Industries**

Down on the levy [ad tax dampens Orlando TV market boom] M. Clary. il *Channels* 7:53-5 N '87

Orlando Helicopter Airways
Orlando helicopter will modify H-19/S-55s into 'Hind look-alikes'. il *Aviat Week Space Technol* 127:53 Ag 10 '87

Orlaskey, Chris
> *about*

"I deserve a change". S. Schneider. il pors *Redbook* 168:82-5 Ja '87

Orlean, Susan
California girls. il *Roll Stone* p62-4+ Mr 26 '87

Making a splash with Traci Wolfe. il pors *Seventeen* 46:112-13+ F '87

Tanorexia: when girls just gotta have sun. il *Mademoiselle* 93:166-7+ Je '87

Working girl by day/party animal by night. il *Mademoiselle* 93:132-3+ F '87

Orlofsky, Patsy
> *about*

Textile tending. E. Greene. il por *House Gard* 159:87-8+ Mr '87

Orlov, Yuri
My life in exile; tr. by Catherine A. Fitzpatrick. il pors *N Y Times Mag* p26-8+ Mr 15 '87

Orlyk, Harry
> *about*

Harry Orlyk [cover story] M. Mathews-Berenson. il *Am Artist* 51:38-41+ Jl '87

Orme, Nicholas
The Reformation & the red light. il *Hist Today* 37:36-41 Mr '87

Orme, William A., Jr.
Mexico. *Nation* 244:468-9 Ap 11 '87

Ormolu
Antiques: ormolu: opulent adornment for fine French furniture. M. M. Thomas. il *Archit Dig* 44:84-9+ F '87

Ormond, June
> *about*

Great balls of fire. J. McDonough. il por *Film Comment* 23:38-40+ Mr/Ap '87

Ormond Organization
Great balls of fire. J. McDonough. il por *Film Comment* 23:38-40+ Mr/Ap '87

Ormrod, Peter
> *about*

Eat the peach [film] Reviews
Macleans 100:46 Ag 31 '87. N. Jennings
New Yorker 63:64-5 Jl 27 '87. P. Kael

Ornament *See* Decoration and ornament

Ornamental cooking *See* Cooking, Ornamental

Ornamental glass *See* Glassware

Ornaments, Christmas tree *See* Christmas decorations

Ornish, Dean
> *about*

Can heart diseases be reversed? D. Grady. il pors *Discover* 8:54-6+ Mr '87

Ornithine transcarbamylase *See* Transferases

Ornithology *See* Bird study

Ornitz, David M., and others
Pancreatic neoplasia induced by SV40 T-antigen expression in acinar cells of transgenic mice. bibl f il *Science* 238:188-93 O 9 '87

Ornitz, Samuel, 1890-1957
> *about*

Naming names [excerpt from Worms in a wine cup] J. Bright. il por *Film Comment* 23:48-51 N/D '87

Ornstein, Norman J.
How to win in '88: meld the unmeldable. il *U S News World Rep* 103:31-2+ O 12 '87

Ornstein, Robert Evans, and Sobel, David S. (David Stuart)
Can you psych yourself into good health? [excerpt from The healing brain] il *Glamour* 85:280-1+ Ag '87

The healing brain. bibl (p59) il *Psychol Today* 21:48-52 Mr '87

Orogrande (N.M.)
> **Economic conditions**

Star Wars in Orogrande [laser testing site] F. Gibney. il map *Newsweek* 110:42 O 19 '87

Oron, Yoram, and others
Decreased TRH receptor mRNA activity precedes homologous downregulation: assay in oocytes. bibl f il *Science* 238:1406-8 D 4 '87

O'Rourke, P. J.
Baloney hero. il *Roll Stone* p34-5 S 10 '87

Captains and kangaroos. il *Roll Stone* p60-2+ Ap 9 '87

Confessions of a non-cook. il *Read Dig* 130:67-9 Mr '87

O'Rourke, P. J.—*cont.*
Good sports. il *House Gard* 159:108+ O '87
Harry, Krishna, and me. *New Repub* 197:16-18 N 2 '87
Holiday in hell. il *Roll Stone* p45-6+ F 26 '87
Let the sixties die. il *Roll Stone* p114-16 S 24 '87
Sightseeing in Sandinistaland. il *Roll Stone* p37-8 D 3 '87
Your basic bachelor [excerpt from The bachelor home companion] il *Mademoiselle* 93:156-7+ Je '87

Orphan drugs
Genentech's custody case over an orphan drug [gene-spliced human growth hormone] J. O. Hamilton. il *Bus Week* p39 Mr 23 '87
Who wants an "orphan drug"? S. Forbes. *McCalls* 115:99-100 N '87

Orphans [film] See Motion picture reviews—Single works
Orphans and orphanages
　　See also
　　Adoption and adopted children
And they called it puppy love [35-year reunion of former orphans results in marriage of Robert Young and Frances Neuman] D. Hurley. *50 Plus* 27:18+ F '87
　　　　Japan
"The children I could never forget" [C. Smith adopts a child from a Japanese orphanage]; ed. by Maria Karagianis. C. Smith. il pors *Redbook* 170:30+ N '87
　　　　Kenya
'They're all my children' [Olympic gold medalist K. Keino gives home to orphans] F. Lidz. il pors *Sports Illus* 67:24-5 D 21 '87
　　　　Mexico
A ring and a prayer [Mexican priest S. Gutierrez wrestles to earn money for orphanage] R. Reilly. il pors *Sports Illus* 67:88-92+ D 21 '87

Orphée aux enfers [operetta] See Offenbach, Jacques, 1819-1880
Orser, Brian
　　　　about
A championship in pure gold. il por *Macleans* 100:20-1 D 28 '87
Sweet victory. D. Jenish. il por *Macleans* 100:31 Mr 23 '87
Orso (New York, N.Y.: Restaurant) *See* New York (N.Y.)—Restaurants, nightclubs, bars, etc.
Ortega, Magno
　　　　about
High Court splits on search of public employee's office. T. J. Flygare. *Phi Delta Kappan* 68:792-4 Je '87
Ortega, Novar
　　　　about
PCs convert convicts. il por *Pers Comput* 11:397 N '87
Ortega Saavedra, Daniel
　　　　about
Eyeing a dialogue [with interview] J. Smolowe. il por *Time* 130:34-6 N 16 '87
Oh, brother—not again! J. Smolowe. il pors *Time* 130:33 D 28 '87
Ortega gunplay. il por *U S News World Rep* 103:13 D 28 '87-Ja 4 '88
Ortega's version [interview] M. McDonald. il por *Macleans* 100:20 F 23 '87
　　Visit to the United States, 1987
Debating the peace plan. I. Austen. il por *Macleans* 100:18 N 23 '87
Nicaragua cliffhanger. R. S. Leiken. *New Repub* 197:17-21 D 14 '87
Ortega gets the Wright stuff [Nicaraguan leader meets with congressman] C. A. Robbins. il por *U S News World Rep* 103:35 N 23 '87
A tug of war over peace [meeting with Congressman J. Wright] H. Anderson. il pors *Newsweek* 110:34-6 N 23 '87
Wright is wrong. *New Repub* 197:7-8+ D 7 '87
The Wright stuff [congressman meets with Nicaraguan leader] J. Smolowe. il pors *Time* 130:32-3 N 23 '87
Ortese, Anna Maria
　　　　about
Day of 'The iguana'. L. Fleischer. *Publ Wkly* 231:34 My 8 '87
Orth, Maureen
All the candidates' wives. il *Vogue* 177:394-5+ N '87
Is there a wrong way to make babies? il *Glamour* 85:272-3+ O '87
Ortho Books
Ortho plans fall introduction for how-to video series. il *Publ Wkly* 231:69-70 Ap 10 '87
Ortho Pharmaceutical Corporation
Understanding women [excerpt from recruiting memo] *Harpers* 274:23-4 Ap '87

Ortho Research Center
On the Pacific Rim. G. Anderson. il *Archit Rec* 175:100-3 Jl '87
Orthodontics
Bye-bye braces [Occlus-o-Guide, developed by Earl Berger-sen] J. R. Goldberg. il *Health* 19:18 Ap '87
Dental esthetics: a bridge too far? [study by Naham C. Cons and others] E. Bird. il *Psychol Today* 21:16 S '87
Embraceable you. il *Seventeen* 46:144-5 O '87
It's never too late to untangle your teeth. D. Zigas. il *Bus Week* p94-5 Ag 3 '87
Set in stone [sapphire braces] E.-L. Greene. *Health* 19:26 O '87
Straight talk about braces. C. Schaeffer. il *Changing Times* 41:55-6+ Jl '87
Straightening out your smile [braces for adults] C. Schaeffer. il *Changing Times* 41:73-7 F '87
Orthodox Eastern Church
Evangelical denomination gains official acceptance into the Orthodox Church [Evangelical Orthodox Church will join the Antiochian Orthodox Church] B. Nassif. il *Christ Today* 31:40 F 6 '87
A new vision for Eastern Orthodoxy? [cover story] Y. Eldar and T. A. Idinopulos. il *Christ Century* 104:995-8 N 11 '87
　　　　Finland
Finland's New Valamo: orthodoxy meets culture. A. Ugolnik. il *Christ Century* 104:1176-8 D 23-30 '87
　　　　Turkey
Mission to Moscow [Dimitrios I of Constantinople makes pilgrimage to daughter church of Russia] il por *Time* 130:66 S 14 '87
　　　　United States
A black prince of the church [Greek Orthodox Bishop A. Draconakis seduces D. Gallas] G. Clifford. il pors *People Wkly* 28:30-5 S 28 '87
In an Eastern Orthodox Chicago church, a weeping Madonna and Child bring throngs to pray and hope for miracles [first sighted by Father P. Koufos at St. Nicholas Church] C. Tamarkin. il *People Wkly* 27:44-5 Ja 19 '87
Orthodox Eastern Church, Russian
Mission to Moscow [Dimitrios I of Constantinople makes pilgrimage to daughter church of Russia] il por *Time* 130:66 S 14 '87
Orthodox Judaism See Judaism
Orthodoxy
Napping through the revolution [postmodern orthodoxy] D. F. Kinlaw. il *Christ Today* 31:9 Ag 7 '87
Orthography See Spelling
Orthopedic equipment
Foot support [Dr. SportStep custom orthotics] *Field Stream* 91:31 Ja '87
Orthotics See Orthopedic equipment
Ortiz, Elisabeth Lambert
Mexican vegetables and salads. il *Gourmet* 47:80-1+ My '87
Ortman, Ross
Digital speedometer for your car. il *Radio-Electron* 58:47-51+ Jl '87
Digital tachometer for your car [cover story] il *Radio-Electron* 58:45-9 Je '87
Versatile digital timer. il *Radio-Electron* 58:45-7 Ag '87
Ortoli, François-Xavier
　　　　about
A diplomat turned businessman. S. Tully. il por *Fortune* 116:66 Ag 3 '87
Orton, Joe
　　　　about
Lost Beatles script to emerge. M. Jenkins. *Roll Stone* p14 Mr 12 '87
Love and death. D. Kaufman. il pors *Horizon* 30:38-40 My '87
Sex, violence, & gratuitous social comment. F. Simon. por *Vogue* 177:70+ Ap '87
　　　　Bibliography
Changeling. G. Annan. il *N Y Rev Books* 34:3-4 S 24 '87
Orzac, Edward S.
Travel health. See alternate issues of Travel Holiday
Orzoff, Sylvia
　　　　about
Talk about gelt trips! With only a tin cup, Sylvia Orzoff, 77, has begged $2 million for charity. il por *People Wkly* 27:91 Je 1 '87
Osage Hills (Okla.)
A budding prairie preserve. J. Hamilton. il *Sierra* 72:83-4 Jl/Ag '87

Osaka (Japan)

Airports

Japanese building international offshore airport to serve Osaka; Kansai developers survey experts. D. A. Brown. il map *Aviat Week Space Technol* 127:38+ Jl 13 '87

City planning

Big plans for Japan's second city. P. Pons. il *World Press Rev* 34:55 Jl '87

Description

Osaka: a lesson in Japanese character. A. M. Stinchecum. il *Travel Holiday* 167:64-8 Ap '87

Osborn, Patricia

Let's not teach bad writing: five commonly taught fallacies. *Educ Dig* 52:42 Ap '87

Osborne, Adam

The changing corporate market. por *Pers Comput* 11:256 O '87

Osborne, Philip B.

One woman's gift to the 20th century. il por *Read Dig* 131:274-81 N '87

Osborne, Richard De Jongh, 1934-

about

Lean, mean and prosperous. J. Cook. il por *Forbes* 140:48-9 D 28 '87

Osborne, S.

The Museum of New Mexico is a cultural digest of the state. il *Horizon* 30:41-3 O '87

Osborne, Terry

All-star fitness [cover story] bibl il *Curr Health 2* 14:3-8 S '87

The case of the missing creative fitness games. il *Curr Health 2* 13:26-7 My '87

Exercise and fluid replacement: your body's balancing act. il *Curr Health 2* 14:16-17 N '87

Fancy footwork: exercise shoes in the '80s. il *Curr Health 2* 13:19-21 Ap '87

The mysterious world of strength. il *Curr Health 2* 13:20-1 Ja '87

Shooting baskets & flying without wings. il *Curr Health 2* 14:22-3 D '87

The taming of stress. il *Curr Health 2* 14:22-3 O '87

When athletes and machines meet. il *Curr Health 2* 13:16-17 F '87

Oscar Mayer & Co.

Oscar Mayer Wienermobile. J. R. Nerad. il *Mot Trend* 39:108-13 D '87

Oscars (Prizes) *See* Academy Awards

Oscillations

See also

Stars—Oscillations

Sun—Oscillations

In tune with nature [computer program for studying characteristics of vertically oscillating column of air] A. Blackadar. il *Weatherwise* 40:95-8 Ap '87

Oscillators

How to design oscillator circuits (VII). J. J. Carr. il *Radio-Electron* 58:65-6+ Ja '87

Oscillators, Crystal

A simple CMOS oscillator. R. Grossblatt. il *Radio-Electron* 58:96 F '87

Oscilloscopes

He's walking tall where IBM wouldn't tread [S. Faris' Josephson junction oscilloscope] O. Port. il por *Bus Week* p124 My 4 '87

How to analyze waveforms. G. D. Carey. il *Radio-Electron* 58:59-60+ D '87

Leader LCD-100 portable DMM/storage oscilloscope. il *Radio-Electron* 58:21+ Je '87

Poor man's storage scope. D. Bernard. il *Radio-Electron* 58:113-14 N '87

Using the new generation oscilloscopes. C. Diller. il *Radio-Electron* 58:55-7 F '87

Osei, Kwame

about

Osei 1st black to head UCC conference in D.C. *Jet* 72:38 Jl 27 '87

OSHA *See* United States. Occupational Safety and Health Administration

O'Shaughnessy, Hugh

Brazil throws down the gauntlet. il *World Press Rev* 34:46-7 Ap '87

O'Shea, Catherine Lower

Someone to share the hurt. il por *Read Dig* 131:67-71 S '87

Osheroff, Douglas D.

(jt. auth) See Cross, Michael C., and Osheroff, Douglas D.

Oshins, Alice

A brand-new way to organize fine art. il por *Work Woman* 12:66+ My '87

Oshkosh B'Gosh, Inc.

B'Gosh, it's OshKosh. G. Perlick. il *Work Woman* 12:39+ Ag '87

Oshkosh Fly-In *See* Aviation—Exhibitions

Oshman, M. Kenneth

about

Little Orphan Ampex looks for Daddy Warbucks. J. B. Levine. *Bus Week* p39-40 Ap 13 '87

Oshman's Sporting Goods, Inc.

Endangered species? [Abercrombie & Fitch] E. Paris. il por *Forbes* 139:136-7 Mr 9 '87

O'Sickey, Joseph B.

about

Joseph B. O'Sickey. S. Kirby. il pors *Am Artist* 51:60-5+ Ja '87

Oslo (Norway)

Description

Oslo: a taste of things to come. B. Walker. il map *Travel Holiday* 167:62-7+ Je '87

Restaurants, nightclubs, bars, etc.

Food fit for a Viking. M. Polvay. il *Travel Holiday* 167:67 Je '87

Osmium

Isotopes

Cosmic clock dates the universe [rhenium-osmium isotopes] R. Layne. *Pop Sci* 230:53 Mr '87

Osmond, C. B., and others

Stress physiology and the distribution of plants. bibl f il *BioScience* 37:38-48 Ja '87

Osmond, Marie, 1959-

about

Marie Osmond: starting over. C. Kramer. il pors *McCalls* 114:14-16 Ap '87

Osmond, Olive Marie *See* Osmond, Marie, 1959-

Osmoregulation

Absence of significant cellular dilution during ADH-stimulated water reabsorption. K. Strange and K. R. Spring. bibl f il *Science* 235:1068-70 F 27 '87

The strange case of the freshwater marine fishes. D. Perrine. il *Sea Front* 33:114-19 Mr/Ap '87

Osmosis

See also

Biological transport

Osmoregulation

Ospreys

Flocking together: it may help ospreys to fish more efficiently [research by Erick Greene] J. Horgan. il *Sci Am* 257:40 D '87

Ossofsky, Jack

Should the financing of U.S. catastrophic health care emphasize private insurance methods? [excerpts from testimony, January 28, 1987] *Congr Dig* 66:117+ Ap '87

Ossowski, Stanislaw

about

Polish humanist in a Communist world: Stanislaw Ossowski. J. Mucha. *Society* 24:70-7 My/Je '87

Osten, Suzanne

about

The Mozart brothers [film] Reviews

Opera News il 52:55 D 5 '87. A. Rich

Osteomyelitis

Therapy

Firing squad [antibiotic pump implant developed by Clayton R. Perry] W. Barnhill. *Health* 19:24 Jl '87

Osteoporosis

All in the name of science, Houston's Richard Fitzpatrick goes flat out for NASA—in bed [researching connection between weightlessness and bone loss] B. Stewart. il pors *People Wkly* 28:59-60 D 21 '87

The calcium controversy: an expert warns that supplements are not the cure-all for dowager's hump [interview with B. L. Riggs] G. Breu. il pors *People Wkly* 27:69-70+ Ap 13 '87

The calcium craze. B. T. Hunter. il por *Consum Res Mag* 70:8-9 Ja '87

Calcium for steroid users. il *Prevention* 39:8+ Ja '87

Fluoride: not just for teeth. E. T. Becker. il *Women's Sports Fitness* 9:14 Jl '87

Going crazy over calcium. A. Toufexis. il *Time* 129:88-9 F 23 '87

Good for the old bones [post-menopausal women] K. S. Zimmeth. il *Health* 19:16 F '87

A little estrogen, fewer broken hips. il *Newsweek* 110:99 N 16 '87

Losing it. R. Lewis. il *Health* 19:54-6+ Ap '87

New bone-loss risk factors in young women [research by Pamela Jensen] S. Weisburd. *Sci News* 132:347 N 28 '87

Osteoporosis—*cont.*

New leads in osteoporosis [estrogen receptors in osteoblasts; research by B. Lawrence Riggs and others] D. M. Barnes. *Science* 236:915 My 22 '87

No calcium fix. *Sci Am* 256:72 Ap '87

Osteoporosis: a bone disease you can do something about. *Teen* 31:86 Jl '87

Osteoporosis: most answers yet to come. J. Silberner. *Sci News* 131:116 F 21 '87

The osteoporosis protection plan from the National Institutes of Health. il *Prevention* 39:34+ Ag '87

Osteoporosis reexamined: complexity of bone biology is a challenge. B. J. Culliton. *Science* 235:833-4 F 20 '87

Stand tall against osteoporosis [link with back muscles] il *Prevention* 39:6 Je '87

Swim for strong bones. L. Fink. il *Women's Sports Fitness* 9:19 Ag '87

Well-rounded exercise may build more bone [work of Jon E. Block] il *Prevention* 39:12 Ag '87

A young runner faces osteoporosis. E. Carson. il *Women's Sports Fitness* 9:58-9 Ja '87

Diagnosis

Detecting osteoporosis early [use of dual photon absorptiometry] il *USA Today (Periodical)* 115:15 F '87

It came from outer space [osteo-analyzer developed by John M. Vogel] G. Ertel. *Health* 19:23 F '87

Scanning your bones: can these tests do any good? [computerized tomography or dual photon absorptiometry] S. Festa. il *Women's Sports Fitness* 9:18 Jl '87

Osterlund, Peter
The Democrats' zero options. *Natl Rev* 39:36+ Je 19 '87

Ostlere, Hilary
Tampa Bay Performing Arts Center: the miracle works. il *Dance Mag* 61:68 N '87

Oston, Ann
Dinks: a practical partnership. *Harpers Bazaar* 120:139+ Jl '87

Ostracods
Marine firefleas. il *Sea Front* 33:386 S/O '87

Sexual behavior

See Sexual behavior—Crustaceans

Ostreicher, David, and Klein, Diane
Maximize your immune system. *McCalls* 115:79-80 O '87

Ostriches

Photographs and photography

How to stay a shade cooler [ostriches protect their young] il *Natl Geogr World* 139:10-11 Mr '87

Ostriker, Alicia
Move [poem] *New Yorker* 63:38 Ap 13 '87

Ostro, Marc J.
Liposomes. il *Sci Am* 256:102-4+ Ja '87

Ostrom, Cheryll K.
Do you feel like his mother or his wife? il *Ladies Home J* 104:100+ N '87

O'Sullivan, Maureen

about

Mama Mia! "My daughter has a gift with children" [interview] K. Henderson. il pors *Redbook* 169:50+ S '87

O'Sullivan, Richard
Red badge revivalists. il *Hist Today* 37:6-8 D '87

Osuna, Jorge
Eighty-five years of dedication. il *World Health* p2-4 O '87

Health services for all. il *World Health* p23-5 O '87

Oswald, Genevieve

about

Oswald retires. D. Cox. il por *Dance Mag* 61:4 N '87

Oswald, Rudolph A.
The tragic impact of joblessness. il *USA Today (Periodical)* 115:28-30 Mr '87

Oswego (N.Y.)

History

Hope and despair through refugees' eyes [Bitter hope: from Holocaust to haven; exhibit at the New York State Museum] il *USA Today (Periodical)* 115:50-9 Ja '87

OTC insight (Newsletter) *See* Investment newsletters

OTC trading *See* Over-the-counter securities markets

OTEC (Ocean thermal energy conversion) *See* Ocean thermal power plants

Othello [drama] *See* Shakespeare, William, 1564-1616

Otis, Elisha Graves, 1811-1861

about

A mechanic gave the world a lift. S. C. Drain. il *Am Hist Illus* 22:42-6+ N '87

Otis Elevator Co., Ltd.
A mechanic gave the world a lift [E. Otis] S. C. Drain. il *Am Hist Illus* 22:42-6+ N '87

Otitis externa (Ear infection) *See* Ear—Diseases
Otitis media (Ear infection) *See* Ear—Diseases

O'Toole, Joanne
(jt. auth) See O'Toole, Thomas, and O'Toole, Joanne

O'Toole, Lawrence
New faces of 1986. il *Film Comment* 23:56-7 Ja/F '87

O'Toole, Peter

about

Though he is plagued by a custody fight over his son, Peter O'Toole is triumph in Pygmalion. A. Chambers. il pors *People Wkly* 27:96-8 Je 29 '87

O'Toole, Thomas, and O'Toole, Joanne
Hypothermia: a springtime hazard. il *Saturday Evening Post* 259:60-2 My/Je '87

Ottawa (Ont.)

Galleries and museums

See also

Canadian Museum of Civilization

Hospitals

Doctor under examination [psychiatrist S. Smith of Royal Ottawa Hospital accused of misappropriating funds] A. Finlayson. *Macleans* 100:5 Ja 12 '87

Otterness, Tom, 1952-

about

Tom Otterness at Brooke Alexander and MOMA "Projects". E. Heartney. il *Art Am* 75:175-6 N '87

Otters
Otter comeback [river otters] il map *Natl Geogr World* 139:19-23 Mr '87

Outermost otters [Shetland] H. Kruuk. il *Nat Hist* 96:34-41 Jl '87

Photographs and photography

Otter delight. T. Walker. il *Nat Hist* 96:80-1 My '87

Otterstetter, Horst, and Flores, Alberto
Water, source of life. il *World Health* p11-13 O '87

Ottley, Peter J.

about

Black serves as marshall of N.Y. Labor Day Parade. *Jet* 72:55 S 21 '87

Ottman, Klaus
Berlin: a place for painting. il *Harpers Bazaar* 120:136-7+ Je '87

Ouabain
Ouabain resistance conferred by expression of the cDNA for a murine Na^+,K^+-ATPase α subunit. R. B. Kent and others. bibl f il *Science* 237:901-3 Ag 21 '87

Ouano, E. A. R.
"His slum, not mine". il *World Health* p10-11 Jl '87

Oumarou, Ide

about

OAU leader meets with black politicos in D.C. to cement U.S. African ties. il por *Jet* 72:14 Je 1 '87

Our Sunday visitor (Periodical)
Of many things [75th anniversary] G. W. Hunt. *America* 156:inside cover My 16 '87

Out of court settlements *See* Arbitration and award

Out on a limb [television program] See Television program reviews—Single works

Outboard motors *See* Motor boat engines
Outdoor cooking *See* Cooking, Outdoor
Outdoor education

See also

Environmental education
Outward Bound Inc.
Reevis Mountain School of Self-Reliance
Wilderness survival

Outdoor furniture *See* Furniture, Outdoor
Outdoor kitchens *See* Kitchens, Outdoor
Outdoor life

See also

Backpacks and backpacking
Camping
Country life
Fishing
Hiking
Hunting
Mountaineering
Nature
Picnics
Snow and ice climbing
United States. President's Commission on Americans Outdoors
Walking
Wilderness survival
Winter sports

Hill country. G. Hill. See issues of Field & Stream
Into the outdoors. M. Ingebretsen. il *Better Homes Gard* 65:195-6 O '87

Outdoor life—*cont.*
Outdoors. T. H. Cole. See issues of Popular Mechanics beginning August 1985 through June 1987
Outdoors. J. Skorupa. See issues of Popular Mechanics beginning July 1987
Outdoors South [month] See issues of Southern Living
Up, up, and away [weekend outdoor adventure vacations close to New York City] J. Seabury. il *N Y* 20:36-42 Ag 3 '87
What's new: a fresh air guide to the summer of '87. il *Life* 10:58 Jl '87

Anecdotes, facetiae, satire, etc.
Inward bound. D. Seligman. il *Fortune* 115:107-8 Mr 16 '87

Periodicals
See also
Sports afield (Periodical)
Sports, recreation, conservation, and outdoors magazines. *Writer* 100:33-42 Ja '87
Outdoor lighting *See* Lighting, Outdoor
Outdoor living areas *See* Decks, patios, terraces, etc.
Outdoor meals
See also
Barbecue cooking
Picnics
This is a fish fry? il *Sunset* 179:78-9, 164 S '87
Outdoor opera *See* Opera, Open-air
Outdoor rooms *See* Decks, patios, terraces, etc.
Outdoor sculpture *See* Sculpture
Outdoor survival *See* Wilderness survival
Outer Banks (N.C.)
Description and travel
Awash in change. C. E. Cobb. il maps *Natl Geogr* 172:484-513 O '87
Outer Banks [problems brought by real estate development] A. Bailey. *New Yorker* 63:94-104+ My 25 '87
Outer space in art *See* Space flight in art
Outfield (Musical group)
Musical chairs with the Outfield. E. Miller. il *Seventeen* 46:63-4+ Ja '87
Outlets, Electric *See* Electric wire and wiring
Outlines (Authorship)
Outlining with InLine. S. Quigley. il *Pers Comput* 11:210 My '87
Outplacement consultant services
Finding work for Wall Street's exiles. *Fortune* 116:8 D 7 '87
How to hire the best outplacement firm. J. Sherman. *Work Woman* 12:18+ Ja '87
Pink-slip time. D. Machan. il *Forbes* 139:118+ F 9 '87
Japan
Saying sayonara in a way that saves face. A. Borrus. il *Bus Week* p54 Ap 6 '87
Output of workers *See* Productivity, Industrial
Outrageous fortune [film] *See* Motion picture reviews—Single works
Outstanding Mothers Award
Moms. *New Yorker* 63:32-3 My 11 '87
Outward Bound Inc.
True grit [program for sedentary women over 30] I. Borger. il *Vogue* 177:356-7+ Ag '87
Ouzounian, Richard
about
Barometer rising [drama] Reviews
Macleans il 100:57 N 23 '87. S. Pedersen
Getting back on the theatrical track. il por *Macleans* 100:47-8 Ap 20 '87
Ova
Decreased TRH receptor mRNA activity precedes homologous downregulation: assay in oocytes. Y. Oron and others. bibl f il *Science* 238:1406-8 D 4 '87
Electrical responses of eggs to acrosomal protein similar to those induced by sperm. M. Gould and J. L. Stephano. bibl f il *Science* 235:1654-6 Mr 27 '87
Expression of functional cell-cell channels from cloned rat liver gap junction complementary DNA. G. Dahl and others. bibl f il *Science* 236:1290-3 Je 5 '87
Rapid stimulation of diacylglycerol production in Xenopus oocytes by microinjection of H-*ras* p21. J. C. Lacal and others. bibl f il *Science* 238:533-6 O 23 '87
ras p21 as a potential mediator of insulin action in Xenopus oocytes. L. J. Korn and others. bibl f il *Science* 236:840-3 My 15 '87
Rat brain N-methyl-D-aspartate receptors expressed in Xenopus oocytes. T. A. Verdoorn and others. bibl f il *Science* 238:1114-16 N 20 '87
Xenopus oocytes injected with rat uterine RNA express very slowly activating potassium currents. M. B. Boyle and others. bibl f il *Science* 235:1221-4 Mr 6 '87

Transplantation
And baby makes four: for the first time a surrogate bears a child genetically not her own. B. Johnson. il por *People Wkly* 27:95-6+ My 4 '87
Building a winning horse with biotech [embryo transfer used on Grand Prix jumpers] S. Budiansky. il *U S News World Rep* 103:63 N 2 '87
High-tech horses. J. Horgan. il *Sci Am* 257:29-31 S '87
The miracle baby [frozen embryo in vitro fertilization] B. Weinhouse and F. Feldinger. il *Ladies Home J* 104:104+ Ap '87
Ovarian cysts *See* Cysts
Ovaries
Cancer
Pill/cancer: another look [protection from ovarian cancer] *Sci News* 131:180 Mr 21 '87
Therapy
Drug 'nukes' ovarian cancer [estrogen linked with radioactive bromine] J. Raloff. *Sci News* 131:389 Je 20 '87
Ove Arup Partnership
Ove Arup & Partners: the engineer as designer. D. Dietsch. il *Archit Rec* 175:122-33 S '87
Oven cleaners *See* Cleaning compositions
Ovens
See also
Microwave ovens
Stoves
Over-the-counter drugs *See* Medicines, Nonprescription
Over-the-counter securities markets
See also
National Association of Securities Dealers
Penny stocks
The battle of the exchanges. J. A. Conway. il *Forbes* 139:8 My 4 '87
A big new plus for small stocks. P. Nulty. il *Fortune* 116:173-4 D 21 '87
Excessive markups? D. Henry. il *Forbes* 139:98 Ja 26 '87
How the spike in interest rates snagged First Boston [Treasury bond options] D. Zigas. *Bus Week* p30-1 Je 29 '87
How to find top small stocks before the big guys do [OTC insight, newsletter edited by L. G. Navallier] L. Laurence. il por *Money* 16:216 Mr '87
Look over-the-counter for the fast action. G. G. Marcial. il *Bus Week* p60-1 Jl 6 '87
The OTC: a few stars stand out against the dark sky. il *Money* 16:50 F '87
Small stocks to sock away [interview with C. Royce] M. McFadden. il por *Fortune* 115:133 Mr 2 '87
Sound picks in small stocks [interview with T. Cashman] A. E. Serwer. il por *Fortune* 115:164 My 11 '87
Where Kidder's brokers bet [secondary stocks] G. G. Marcial. *Bus Week* p78 Ag 3 '87
Japan
Avon calling—at the Tokyo Exchange [selling 40% of Japanese subsidiary to the Japanese] T. Holden. il *Bus Week* p116 D 14 '87
Over the top [film] *See* Motion picture reviews—Single works
Overbrook Herb Farm (Lansdale, Pa.)
Marketing miniatures [baby vegetables for upscale restaurants] K. Pechter. il por *Rodale's Org Gard* 34:72-6 D '87
Overeating *See* Bulimia
Overhead projection
Slideless slide show for groups [Datashow System electronic transparency system for displaying computer images through an overhead projector] S. Makrias. il *Pers Comput* 11:162 Mr '87
Overhome (N.C.: Historic site) *See* Historic houses, sites, etc.—North Carolina
Overmyer, Eric
about
On the verge [drama] Reviews
N Y il 20:56 Mr 16 '87. J. Simon
New Yorker 63:93 Mr 30 '87. E. Oliver
Overnight delivery service *See* Air freight service
Overnite Transportation Co.
From two used trucks to a $1.2-billion deal [Overnite Transportation's H. Cochrane sells out to Union Pacific Corp.] A. B. Rea. il por *Fortune* 115:67 Ja 5 '87
Overpopulation *See* Population
Overseas Adventure Travel (Firm)
The company's bigger, but is it better? W. Lowe. il pors *Work Woman* 12:45-8 Je '87
Overseas Development Network
Grass roots partnerships for development. C. Wise. *Américas* 39:52-3 S/O '87

Overseas employees *See* Americans—Foreign countries—Employment

Overseas forces, American *See* United States—Armed Forces—Forces in foreign countries

Oversight and Investigations Subcommittee (House Committee on Energy and Commerce) *See* United States. Congress. House. Committee on Energy and Commerce. Subcommittee on Oversight and Investigations

Overtime
Is it smart to work late? L. Lebowitz. il *Work Woman* 12:117 N '87
What price peace? [upcoming decision on whether lump-sum payments should be computed as overtime] D. Fanning. il *Forbes* 140:56 D 28 '87

Overwater flying *See* Aviation—Overwater flying

Overweight *See* Obesity

Ovshinsky, Stanford R.
about
An investment that turned into a nightmare. E. T. Smith. il por *Bus Week* p102+ N 30 '87
The promised land may be near for 'Ovonics'. E. T. Smith. il por *Bus Week* p58 Je 15 '87

Ovum *See* Ova

Owen, David, 1938-
about
A bad stumble for a man in a hurry. por *Newsweek* 110:32 Ag 17 '87
Two Davids and Goliath. R. Watson. il pors *Newsweek* 109:26-7 My 25 '87

Owen, David, 1955-
Dreams and downlines. il *Atlantic* 260:84-90 O '87
Help for the TV-shy. il *Atlantic* 260:18 S '87
Octane and knock. il *Atlantic* 260:53-60 Ag '87
The walls around us. il *Atlantic* 259:71-9 My '87
Work marriage. il *Atlantic* 259:22 F '87

Owen, Edward Roger John *See* Owen, Roger

Owen, Ken
In South Africa, white makes right. il *World Press Rev* 34:43 Jl '87

Owen, Leslie E.
The changing foreign rights market. il *Publ Wkly* 231:28-30+ Mr 20 '87
Children's science fiction and fantasy grows up. il *Publ Wkly* 232:32+ O 30 '87

Owen, Robert W.
The all new, improved contras! *Harpers* 275:22-3 Ag '87
A 'contra' democracy? *Harpers* 275:19-20 O '87
about
Down a sinkhole. M. Kempton. *N Y Rev Books* 34:53-4 Je 25 '87

Owen, Roger
On becoming a Jew. *Commentary* 84:55-62 N '87

Owens, C. E. (Clinton E.)
about
A juice maker squeezes itself dry. J. E. Davis. il por *Bus Week* p42 Ag 10 '87

Owens, Carlton
about
He knows how to take a shot. R. Demak. il por *Sports Illus* 67 Sp Issue:89 N 18 '87

Owens, Clinton E. *See* Owens, C. E. (Clinton E.)

Owens, Ethel
about
U.S. Rep. Major Owens fights ex-wife on charges of race bias, back alimony. il pors *Jet* 73:16-17 N 2 '87

Owens, John
Art in decay [photographs] il *Cycle* 38:96-9 Je '87

Owens, Joyce
about
University 'madam' gets $1000 fine, probation. il por *Jet* 73:22 N 16 '87

Owens, Major
about
Owens fouls with Edwards; now pitches to Ueberroth. por *Jet* 73:49 N 2 '87
U.S. Rep. Major Owens fights ex-wife on charges of race bias, back alimony. il pors *Jet* 73:16-17 N 2 '87

Owens-Corning Fiberglas Corp.
What a raider hath wrought. J. Willoughby. il *Forbes* 139:56-7 Mr 23 '87

Owensby, Earl
about
A down-home movie mogul. J. B. Copeland. il por *Newsweek* 109:41 Ja 12 '87

Owings, Thomas
Frost bitten. il *Flying* 114:110 Mr '87

Owls
End of the old-growth canopy [destruction of Pacific Northwest forests endangers spotted owls] L. Tuttle. il *Natl Parks* 61:16-21 My/Je '87
The neighborly great gray owl [cover story] E. L. Bull and M. G. Henjum. il *Nat Hist* 96:32-41 S '87
Preserving old-growth forests [spotted owl controversy] D. B. Edelson. bibl f il *Environment* 29:3-5 O '87
A tale of two kitties [great horned owl] D. Petersen. il map *Mother Earth News* 106:102+ Jl/Ag '87
Threat to the spotted owl [destruction of Pacific Northwest forests] L. Burnham. il *Sci Am* 257:34+ O '87

Photographs and photography
Food for the brood. A. Wolfe. il *Nat Hist* 96:92-3 F '87
From beyond the horizon [snowy owls] D. Harding. il *Conservationist* 41:20-1 Mr/Ap '87
Looking ahead [burrowing owls] J. L. Ferrara. il *Natl Wildl* 25:10-11 O/N '87

Owls in art
The spotted owl: a diptych. R. Bateman. il *Audubon* 89:74-5 Mr '87

Oxalis
The good oxalis. il *Sunset* 179:214 O '87

Oxburgh, E. R., and O'Nions, R. Keith
Helium loss, tectonics, and the terrestrial heat budget. bibl f il map *Science* 237:1583-8 S 25 '87

Oxenberg, Catherine
about
New star style! il pors *Harpers Bazaar* 121:178-97 N '87

Oxenbury, Helen, 1938-
about
PW interviews. M. Field. il pors *Publ Wkly* 232:168-9 Jl 24 '87

Oxford, Edward
Disney's enduring masterpiece [cover story] il por *Am Hist Illus* 22:30-9 D '87

Oxford, Edward De Vere, Earl of, 1550-1604
about
A fair shake for Oxford. J. Sobran. *Natl Rev* 39:54-6 N 6 '87
Some ado about who was, or was not, Shakespeare. J. D. Reed. bibl (p187) il pors *Smithsonian* 18:155-8+ S '87

Oxford (England)
Galleries and museums
See also
Pitt Rivers Museum (Oxford, England)

Oxford (Miss.)
Education
Teen sues for being denied love role opposite white [J. L. Mosley's suit over role in school musical] *Jet* 72:22 Mr 30 '87
Historic houses, sites, etc.
Looking for Mr. Faulkner. W. Cobb. il *South Living* 22:128 Mr '87
Rowan Oak—Faulkner's Mississippi refuge. il *South Living* 22:19 Ag '87

Oxford Conference on Church, Community, and State (1937) *See* World Conference on Church, Community, and State (1937)

Oxford English dictionary *See* English language—Dictionaries

Oxford University *See* University of Oxford

Oxford University Press
Oxford to publish 19th century black women writers series. B. Levine. il *Publ Wkly* 231:48-9 Je 5 '87

Oxidases
Mapping human brain monoamine oxidase A and B with [11]-labeled suicide inactivators and PET. J. S. Fowler and others. bibl f il *Science* 235:481-5 Ja 23 '87

Inactivation
Drug trial for Parkinson's [Deprenyl/tocopherol] R. Lewin. *Science* 236:1420 Je 12 '87
Parkinson's treatment to be tested [Deprenyl/tocopherol; research by Ira Shoulson] *Prevention* 39:78 N '87

Oxidation
Disulfate ion as an intermediate to sulfuric acid in acid rain formation. S. G. Chang and others. bibl f il *Science* 237:756-8 Ag 14 '87

Oxidation, Physiological
See also
Bacteria, Sulfur oxidizing
Cytochromes
Bypass heart damage with vitamin E [free radical formation; research by Nicholas Cavarocchi] *Prevention* 39:11 O '87

Oxidation, Physiological—*cont.*
Chemical energy fuels ecosystems [gutless clam able to oxidize and get energy directly from sulfides] il *Sea Front* 33:62-4 Ja/F '87
Macrophage cytotoxicity: role for L-arginine deiminase and imino nitrogen oxidation to nitrite. J. B. Hibbs, Jr. and others. bibl f il *Science* 235:473-6 Ja 23 '87
Oxygen free radicals linked to many diseases. J. L. Marx. *Science* 235:529-31 Ja 30 '87
Radical therapy: drugs may combat brain damage by toxic oxygen free radicals. K. Wright. *Sci Am* 257:34 S '87
Why does gold help arthritics? [research by Elias J. Corey and others] *Sci News* 131:264 Ap 25 '87

Oxides
See also
Ceramic oxides
Deuterium oxide
High-resolution electron microscopy and scanning tunneling microscopy of native oxides on silicon. A. H. Carim and others. bibl f il *Science* 237:630-3 Ag 7 '87
Painting with superconductors [use of oxide compounds to make SQUIDs] il *Sci News* 131:293 My 9 '87

Oxley, Mat
Norton Rotary Rocket. il *Cycle* 38:64-9 D '87

Oxmoor House Inc.
The return of 'Jericho,' a southern classic. B. Summer. *Publ Wkly* 232:66 O 16 '87

Oxygen
See also
Ozone
Amber yields samples of ancient air [work of Robert A. Berner and Gary P. Landis] R. Monastersky. *Sci News* 132:293 N 7 '87
Ancient air analyzed in dinosaur-age amber [research by Robert Berner and Gary Landis] R. A. Kerr. *Science* 238:890 N 13 '87
Putting on ancient airs [ancient atmosphere trapped in amber found to contain 50% more oxygen] il *Time* 130:82 N 9 '87

Isotopes
Oxygen isotope effect in high-temperature oxide superconductors. H.-C. Zur Loye and others. bibl f il *Science* 238:1558-60 D 11 '87
Oxygen isotopes in refractory stratospheric dust particles: proof of extraterrestrial origin. K. D. McKeegan. bibl f il *Science* 237:1468-71 S 18 '87

Oxygen detectors
Performance sentinels [oxygen sensors in automobiles] K. Zino. il *Pop Sci* 230:25-6+ My '87

Oxygen equipment
If you're 20 fathoms down and out of oxygen, the answer is Larry Williamson's Spare Air. il por *People Wkly* 27:65 My 18 '87

Oxygen in sea water *See* Sea water
Oxygen therapy
See also
Hyperbaric oxygenation

Oyster Bay (N.Y.)
Historic houses, sites, etc.
See also
Sagamore Hill National Historic Site (N.Y.)

Oyster bisque *See* Bisques (Cooking)
Oyster catchers (Birds) *See* Oystercatchers (Birds)
Oyster fisheries *See* Shellfish fisheries
Oyster mushrooms *See* Mushrooms
Oyster stew *See* Stew
Oystercatchers (Birds)
Hard times on mussel beach [oystercatcher competition for food on the Exe estuary, England] J. Goss-Custard. il *Nat Hist* 96:64-71 Mr '87

Oysters (Santa Barbara, Calif.: Restaurant) *See* Santa Barbara (Calif.)—Restaurants, nightclubs, bars, etc.

Oysters as food
See also
Cooking—Shellfish
Westcott Bay Sea Farms
A new oyster for all seasons [triploids edible year-round; research by Standish Allen and Sandra Downing] R. M. Strickland and L. Bevan. *Oceans* 20:7-8 S/O '87

Oz, Frank
about
Little shop of horrors [film] Reviews
Commonweal 114:55-6 Ja 30 '87. T. O'Brien
Glamour il 85:175 F '87. J. G. Boyum
Macleans il 100:18-19 Ja 5 '87. L. O'Toole
N Y il 20:51 Ja 12 '87. D. Denby
New Repub 196:26 Ja 26 '87. S. Kauffmann
New Yorker 62:92+ Ja 12 '87. P. Kael
Newsweek il 109:56 Ja 5 '87. D. Ansen

People Wkly 27:10 Ja 12 '87. P. Travers
USA Today (Periodical) il 115:96-7 Mr '87. K. R. Hey

Ozal, Turgut
about
Ankara's search for identity [with interview] J. P. Shapiro. il pors *U S News World Rep* 102:35-6 F 16 '87

Ozark (Ala.)
Down in the wiregrass [memories of youth] L. Wells. il *South Living* 22:108 Jl '87

Ozark cooking *See* Cooking, American
Ozark Mountains region
See also
Fishing—Ozark Mountains region
The American scene. E. Jones. il *Gourmet* 47:62+ F '87

Ozark National Forest (Ark.)
Alum Cove, Arkansas [French's shooting stars] R. H. Mohlenbrock. il map *Nat Hist* 96:60-2 Ap '87

Ozawa, Seiji
about
What makes Seiji run? M. Walsh. il por *Time* 129:80 Mr 30 '87

Ozick, Cynthia
Good novelists, bad citizens. il *N Y Times Book Rev* 92:13 F 15 '87
The library of nonexistent classics. il *N Y Times Book Rev* 92:12 Ap 12 '87
The muse, postmodern and homeless. il *N Y Times Book Rev* 92:9 Ja 18 '87
Science and letters: God's work—and ours. il *N Y Times Book Rev* 92:3+ S 27 '87
Where orphans can still become heiresses. il *N Y Times Book Rev* 92:13 Mr 8 '87
about
Defenders of the faith. R. Alter. *Commentary* 84:52-5 Jl '87
PW interviews. P. Kaganoff. por *Publ Wkly* 231:33-4 Mr 27 '87

Ozone
See also
Plants, Effect of ozone on
Vienna Convention for the Protection of the Ozone Layer (1985)
Another antismog device? [controlling ozone by trapping vapors from gasoline refueling] il *U S News World Rep* 103:8 Ag 3 '87
Antarctic ozone reaches lowest levels. R. Monastersky. *Sci News* 132:230 O 10 '87
Antarctic ozone: the plot thickens. R. Monastersky. *Sci News* 131:326 My 23 '87
Antarctic stratospheric chemistry of chlorine nitrate, hydrogen chloride, and ice: release of active chlorine. M. J. Molina and others. bibl f il *Science* 238:1253-7 N 27 '87
Assessing the threat to the ozone [cover story] S. F. Singer and C. Crandall. il *Consum Res Mag* 70:11-14 Jl '87
Can we close the ozone hole? F. S. Rowland. il *Technol Rev* 90:50-8 Ag/S '87
Changes in stratospheric ozone. R. J. Cicerone. bibl f il *Science* 237:35-42 Jl 3 '87
Chlorofluorocarbons and the incredible shrinking ozone. J. P. Cohn. il *FDA Consum* 21:32-5 D '87/Ja '88
Chlorofluorocarbons and the ozone layer. J. P. Cohn. *BioScience* 37:647-50 O '87
Culprits of the stratosphere [study by Crofton Farmer on the Antarctic ozone hole] M. D. Lemonick. il *Time* 130:57 S 21 '87
The endangered ozone layer [cover story; with editorial comment by Gilbert F. White] G. Brasseur. bibl il *Environment* 29:inside cover, 6-11+ Ja/F '87
Energetic electrons: an ozone killer? *Sci News* 131:377 Je 13 '87
EPA attacks vapor villain [reducing ozone pollution by trapping gasoline vapors emitted during refueling] *Mot Trend* 39:44 N '87
EPA to cut U.S. CFC production to protect ozone in stratosphere. M. Crawford. il *Science* 238:1505 D 11 '87
Flying into an ozone hole [Airborne Antarctic Ozone Experiment] *Sci News* 132:95 Ag 8 '87
Forecast for disaster. R. H. Boyle. il *Sports Illus* 67:78-84+ N 16 '87
Halocarbons linked to ozone hole [research by Philip Solomon and others] R. A. Kerr. il *Science* 236:1182-3 Je 5 '87
Has stratospheric ozone started to disappear? R. A. Kerr. il *Science* 237:131-2 Jl 10 '87
The heat is on [cover story] M. D. Lemonick. il *Time* 130:58-63+ O 19 '87

Ozone—*cont.*

High noon for smog control. D. S. Strait and R. E. Ayres. bibl f *Environment* 29:43-5 S '87

How to protect the ozone layer. D. Starr. il *Natl Wildl* 26:26-8 D '87/Ja '88

Layers of complexity in ozone hole. J. Silberner. *Sci News* 131:164 Mr 14 '87

A lethal filibuster [dangers of chlorofluorocarbons] H. Evans. il *U S News World Rep* 102:72 Je 22 '87

Life, the great chemistry experiment [State of the earth 1987] S. Postel. il *Nat Hist* 96:41-8 Ap '87

Made in the shade? No way [Antarctic ozone hole] G. Taubes. il *Discover* 8:62-71 Ag '87

Missing the deadline on ozone. M. D. Uehling. il *Natl Wildl* 25:34-7 O/N '87

The Missouri standard [U.S. failure to curb acid rain and chlorofluorocarbons] H. Evans. il *U S News World Rep* 103:90 O 12 '87

More clues to the mysterious ozone hole. R. Monastersky. *Sci News* 132:182 S 19 '87

The new soldier in the clean-air war: you. S. N. Wellborn. il *U S News World Rep* 103:50-1 Ag 10 '87

New threats to the sky [depletion in Antarctic ozone layer] A. Steacy. il *Macleans* 100:44-5 S 14 '87

Ozone [theories of depletion causes] *Sci Am* 256:67-8 Ja '87

Ozone and acid rain. P. H. Abelson. *Science* 238:141 O 9 '87

The ozone hole [Antarctic] *Sci Am* 257:19-20 Ag '87

Ozone hole updates. *Sci News* 132:302 N 7 '87

Ozone watch [Antarctic ozone hole] T. Beardsley. *Sci Am* 257:18 N '87

Policies on global warming and ozone depletion. B. Green. *Environment* 29:5+ Ap '87

Reaction of chlorine nitrate with hydrogen chloride and water at Antarctic stratospheric temperatures. M. A. Tolbert and others. bibl f il *Science* 238:1258-60 N 27 '87

Smog-ozone policy shift. J. Raloff. *Sci News* 131:244 Ap 18 '87

U.S., Soviets to study Antarctic ozone. R. Monastersky. *Sci News* 131:408 Je 27 '87

Volcanic residue cited as possible source of misleading ozone data [Antarctic ozone hole] R. G. O'Lone. *Aviat Week Space Technol* 126:91-2 Ja 12 '87

Watch this space [Antarctic ozone hole] E. R. Shell. il *Omni* 9:36-8+ Ag '87

Weather versus chemicals [controversy over chlorofluorocarbons and Antarctic ozone hole] E. R. Shell. il *Atlantic* 259:27-31 My '87

Winds, pollutants drive ozone hole. R. A. Kerr. il map *Science* 238:156-8 O 9 '87

Physiological effects

Circadian variation in ozone tolerance [research by Leendert van Bree and others] J. Raloff. *Sci News* 131:169 Mr 14 '87

New clues to smog's effects on lungs. J. Raloff. *Sci News* 132:86 Ag 8 '87

Ozu, Yasujiro, 1903-1963

about

The only son [film] Reviews

New Repub 196:24-6 Ap 13 '87. S. Kauffmann

P

P-3C (Airplane) *See* Airplanes, Military

PAAF *See* Professional Actors Association of Florida

PACCAR Inc.

Shift gears on a steep hill. J. Heins. il *Forbes* 139:40+ F 9 '87

Pace, Jana

Radial keratotomy: a cure for myopia? il *Consum Res Mag* 70:27-31 O '87

What behavioral optometrists see [cover story] *Consum Res Mag* 70:11-15 Ap '87

(jt. auth) See Lehrman, Karen, and Pace, Jana

Pace cars *See* Automobiles, Racing

Pacelli, Eugenio *See* Pius XII, Pope, 1876-1958

Pacemaker, Artificial (Heart)

Defects

Why Cordis' heart wasn't in pacemakers. P. Engardio. il *Bus Week* p80 Mr 16 '87

Pacemaker systems *See* Biological rhythms

Pacheco, Maria Luisa

about

The abstract landscapes of Pacheco. A. Sanjurjo de Casciero. il por *Américas* 39:14-17+ Ja/F '87

Pacher, Sara

Cream of the country. See issues of The Mother Earth News beginning September/October 1986

Pachur, H.-J., and Kröpelin, S.

Wadi Howar: paleoclimatic evidence from an extinct river system in the southeastern Sahara. bibl f il map *Science* 237:298-300 Jl 17 '87

Pacific Asset Holdings, Inc.

The Drexel connection [potential partners in Western Union takeover offer scared off by Pacific Asset's dealings with Drexel] J. Crudele. *N Y* 20:24 Ap 20 '87

Pacific Bell

Are you ready for Pacific Bell's 'wonder phone'? [Project Victoria] il *U S News World Rep* 102:61 Mr 30 '87

Pacific coast

See also

Cruising—Pacific coast

Pacific Coast Stock Exchange *See* Stock exchanges—Pacific Coast exchange

Pacific Horizon Aggressive Growth Mutual Fund

Picking small high-tech winners [views of W. H. Duncan] G. G. Marcial. *Bus Week* p72 Ap 6 '87

Pacific Islands (Trust territory)

See also

Environmental policy—Pacific Islands (Trust territory)

Marshall Islands

Micronesia (Federated States)

Palau

United Nations—Pacific Islands (Trust territory)

United States reports agreement on compacts. *UN Chron* 24:132 F '87

Pacific Lumber Co.

Razing the giant redwoods. P. Abramson. il por *Newsweek* 110:38 Jl 6 '87

A takeover artist who's turning redwoods into quick cash [C. E. Hurwitz's takeover of Pacific Lumber through Maxxam Group] J. R. Norman. il por *Bus Week* p64-5 F 2 '87

Pacific Northwest

See also

Beaches—Pacific Northwest

Columbia River Gorge (Or. and Wash.)

Earthquakes—Pacific Northwest

Fishing—Pacific Northwest

Forests and forestry—Pacific Northwest

Hunting—Pacific Northwest

National forests—Pacific Northwest

Radioactive pollution—Pacific Northwest

Resorts—Pacific Northwest

Wilderness areas—Pacific Northwest

Antiquities

Echoes of a shaman's song: artifacts and ethics in the Northwest [Native Americans] J. Magnuson. il *Christ Century* 104:406-8 Ap 29 '87

Description and travel

Northwest exploring by seaplane . . . cities, waterways, wild high country. il *Sunset* 178:66 Je '87

Pacific Northwest Ballet

Reviews:

Performances at Kennedy Center, Washington, D.C. G. Jackson. *Dance Mag* 61:22+ D '87

Pacific Ocean

See also

El Niño (Ocean current)

Petroleum—Pacific Ocean

Acantharian fluxes and strontium to chlorinity ratios in the North Pacific Ocean. R. E. Bernstein and others. bibl f il *Science* 237:1490-4 S 18 '87

Climate and chlorophyll a: long-term trends in the central North Pacific Ocean. E. L. Venrick and others. bibl f il maps *Science* 238:70-2 O 2 '87

Drilling discoveries in the Pacific. S. Weisburd. *Sci News* 131:102-3 F 14 '87

Large warm spot in the Pacific [megaplume discovered by Edward T. Baker] *Sci News* 132:238 O 10 '87

Variations on a Pacific theme [wind patterns] *Sci News* 131:377 Je 13 '87

Pacific region

See also

Aviation—Pacific region

Economic assistance, American—Pacific region

Financial institutions—Pacific region

Investments, American—Pacific region

Oceania

Resorts—Pacific region

Space research—Pacific region

Regional report: Asia/Pacific. A. Giarelli. See issues of World Press Review beginning October 1986

Pacific region—*cont.*

Commerce

Japan and the Pacific Rim: economic challenge to America [cover story; special issue] il *Sch Update* 119:2-24 Ap 6 '87

United States

See United States—Commerce—Pacific region

Defenses

See also

ANZUS Council

Soviet Union—Armed Forces—Forces in the Pacific

The strategic importance of the emerging Pacific [address, September 29, 1986] G. J. Sigur. *Dep State Bull* 86:75-8 D '86

Description and travel

Daybreak on the Pacific. G. Hesse. il *Travel Holiday* 167:91-2+ Ap '87

Economic conditions

See also

United Nations. Economic and Social Commission for Asia and the Pacific

The Pacific Basin's challenge to America: myth and reality. C. Johnson. il *USA Today (Periodical)* 115:20-4 Mr '87

Economic relations

United States

See United States—Economic relations—Pacific region

Foreign relations

The great Pacific game [Peking, Washington and Moscow jockey for power] H. Trewhitt. il *U S News World Rep* 102:30-1 Mr 2 '87

Australia

See Australia—Foreign relations—Pacific region

United States

See United States—Foreign relations—Pacific region

Industries

See also

Aerospace industries—Pacific region

Investment trusts—Pacific region

Shellfish fisheries—Pacific region

Pacific region communications satellites *See* Communications satellites, Pacific region

Pacific Southwest Airlines

Teamsters' vote clears path for USAir's acquisition of PSA. C. Preble. il *Aviat Week Space Technol* 126:41 My 25 '87

Pacific States

See also

Transportation—Pacific States

Pacific Trust Territory *See* Pacific Islands (Trust territory)

Pacific voyages *See* Voyages

Pacifism

See also

Conscientious objectors

Nonviolence

More tears of God. M. E. Marty. *Christ Century* 104:639 Jl 15-22 '87

Once a G-man, now a pacifist [J. C. Ryan] T. E. Johnson. il por *Newsweek* 110:24 N 23 '87

The price of pacifism [discussion of October 22, 1986 article, A practical Christian pacifism] D. A. Hoekema. *Christ Century* 104:20-2 Ja 7-14 '87

Recruiters for peace [counter-recruiters] O. Davidson. *Nation* 244:175-7 F 14 '87

The restoration of Maurice McCrackin [Presbyterian activist minister] D. Peerman. il *Christ Century* 104:998-1000 N 11 '87

Pacifists *See* Pacifism

Pack of lies [television program] *See* Television program reviews—Single works

Pack transportation

See also

Backpacks and backpacking

High on llamas: you do the walking, they'll do the work. E. McGrath. il *Women's Sports Fitness* 9:20-3 Ag '87

Pack trips *See* Horseback trips

Package delivery services *See* Parcel post

Package tours *See* Travel

Packaged mixes *See* Food mixes

Packages, Wrapping of *See* Wrapping of packages

Packaging

See also

Cereal foods—Packaging

Container industry

Cosmetics—Packaging

Drugs—Packaging

Hair care products—Packaging

Meat—Packaging

Packaging Corp. of America

Shorewood Packaging Corporation

Packaging for the older consumer [address, March 6, 1987] M. Bender. *Vital Speeches Day* 53:490-2 Je 1 '87

Packaging Corp. of America

Ilene Gordon: hey, what's she doing here? [vice president in charge of corporate development] M. Mallory. il por *Bus Week* p76 O 26 '87

Packard, David

about

A quartet of high-tech pioneers. B. O'Reilly. il pors *Fortune* 116:148-9 O 12 '87

Packard, George R.

The coming U.S.-Japan crisis. bibl f *Foreign Aff* 66:348-67 Wint '87/'88

Packard Commission *See* United States. President's Commission on Defense Management

Packer, Alex J., 1951-

A view from the back seat. *U S News World Rep* 102:59 My 25 '87

Packer, Billy

about

Racist, sexist comment by CBS sports anchors riles nation's women's groups. il por *Jet* 72:54 S 14 '87

Packer, Bonnie M.

(jt. auth) See Schopf, J. William, 1941-, and Packer, Bonnie M.

Packer, David

about

Conscience over duty. C. Barrett. *Macleans* 100:24 S 21 '87

Packet switching (Data transmission)

Networks for advanced computing. R. E. Kahn. bibl (p184) il *Sci Am* 257:136-43 O '87

Packing of household furnishings

It's your move. S. L. White. il *Home Mech* 83:72+ My '87

Packing of luggage

Packing light. N. Strung. il *Field Stream* 91:72+ Mr '87

Ten trusty tips for packing light. A. Keefe. il *50 Plus* 27:78+ Mr '87

Packs

See also

Backpacks and backpacking

Packwood, Robert

Should Congress approve the Fairness Doctrine? [excerpts from remarks, April 21, 1987] *Congr Dig* 66:237+ O '87

about

Washington's odd couple shakes up taxes. A. R. Dowd. il pors *Fortune* 115:40-1 Ja 5 '87

PACs *See* Political action committees

Pad sanders *See* Sanding and sanding equipment

Paddling *See* Canoes and canoeing

Paddling (Punishment) *See* Corporal punishment

Paddock, Barbara

about

Barbara Paddock: keeping Manny Hanny ahead of the game. P. Finch. il por *Bus Week* p91 N 9 '87

Padilla Bay (Wash.)

Fecund mysteries. P. Johnson. il *Wilderness* 50:37-44+ Summ '87

Pado, Tom

about

A yellow submarine pops up from Down Under. C. Debes. il *Bus Week* p104 S 28 '87

Padoch, Christine

Risky business. il *Nat Hist* 96:56-65 O '87

Padunov, Vladimir

(jt. auth) See Condee, Nancy P., and Padunov, Vladimir

Padus, Emrika

Eat out and lose weight! il *Prevention* 39:68-74 Ag '87

Padwe, Gerald W.

For your tax file. See issues of Nation's Business beginning July 1983

Paege, Augustin

about

The Box Tree Hotel: Augustin Paege's opulent setting in Turtle Bay. G. Greene. il por *Archit Dig* 44:170-7 N '87

Pagan (Ancient city)

Temples

Journey to Pagan. A. Harvey. il *House Gard* 159:72+ Mr '87

Paganism

Pagans, Christians, Jews. C. Raphael. *Commentary* 84:39-44 O '87

Paganism—*cont.*

History

Constantine's pagan triumph [R. Lane Fox's Pagans and Christians] P. Pettingell. *New Leader* 70:15-16 Ap 6 '87

Page, Alan C., 1945-
about
Mandatory drug testing may spark racism: Page. por *Jet* 72:46 Ag 31 '87

Page, Ann Takayoshi
about
Ann Page and Phyllis Muldavin at the Woman's Building. M. Laurence. *Art Am* 75:141-2 Ja '87

Page, Clarence
Spoils and spoilers. *New Repub* 196:13-15 Mr 2 '87

Page, Diana
Cutting the debt, saving the forest. *Environment* 29:4-5+ S '87

Page, Geraldine, 1924-1987
about
Obituary
People Wkly il por 27:71 Je 29 '87. P. Travers

Page, Jake
Jake's turn. See issues of Oceans beginning July/August 1987
The mice shall stay. il *Ctry J* 14:6+ D '87
"Mother-in-chief" with a mission. il por *McCalls* 114:138 S '87
Shore hits. *Oceans* 20:57 Mr/Ap '87
The Suffolk punch [cover story] il *Mother Earth News* 106:72-9 Jl/Ag '87
Supreme quartz. il *Omni* 10:94-6+ O '87

Page, John C.
One man's fertilizer [cover story] il *Ctry J* 14:33-7 Ap '87

Page, Louise
about
Real estate [drama] Reviews
New Yorker 63:119 D 14 '87. E. Oliver

Page, Russell
about
Reshaping a corner of Connecticut. K. Whiteside. il *House Gard* 159:152-5+ Jl '87

Page Avjet Corporation
Page Avjet, Kollsman completing design for Boeing 727 flight deck conversion. E. H. Kolcum. *Aviat Week Space Technol* 127:52+ S 28 '87

Pageants
See also
Christmas pageants

PageMaker (Desktop publishing program) *See* Desktop publishing—Programming

Paget, Dennis, and Majzlin, Leonard
How to tell when it's time to visit your mother [excerpt from How to visit your mother] il *Work Woman* 12:76-7 Ja '87

Paging devices
Beepers for roadrunners. A. Oshins. il *Work Woman* 12:90 N '87
Don't ask for whom the beeper beeps, it beeps for thee [hospital interns] P. Klass. il *Discover* 8:16-18 Je '87
The latest show-offs in electronic gadgetry. S. Woolley. il *Bus Week* p204 N 2 '87

Pagodas
Journey to Pagan. A. Harvey. il *House Gard* 159:72+ Mr '87

Paha, Michael
about
Michael Paha at Perimeter. S. Taylor. il *Art Am* 75:186-7 N '87

Paher, Stanley W.
Scotty's Castle [excerpt] il *Natl Parks* 61:46-7 S/O '87

Paige, Connie
Watch on the right. por *Ms* 15:24-8 F '87

Paik, Nam June
about
Nam June Paik at Holly Solomon. W. Robinson. il *Art Am* 75:157 Je '87

Pain
See also
Analgesia and analgesics
Backache
Headache
Neck pain
Pelvic pain
Sadomasochism
Suffering
TMJ syndrome
University of Miami. Comprehensive Pain Center

Do dentists know when it hurts? [facial expressions of juvenile patients; study by Ann Rowland] G. Lowe. *Psychol Today* 21:12 Ag '87
How to help your doctor diagnose your pain. P. Gadsby. il *Good Housekeep* 205:182-3 Ag '87
Office workers suffer more than physical laborers [study by Rene Caillet] *USA Today (Periodical)* 115:11-12 F '87
Pain centers. S. Levin. *McCalls* 115:80-1 O '87
The pain-pleasure connection. P. L. DeVito. il *USA Today (Periodical)* 115:47-9 Ja '87
Pain's gatekeeper [researcher R. Melzack] C. Warga. bibl (p67) il pors *Psychol Today* 21:50-6 Ag '87
Stress can be painful [research by Thomas F. Lundeen] *Prevention* 39:13 Je '87
Taking the pain out of pain [cover story; special section] il *U S News World Rep* 102:50-7 Je 29 '87

Paine, John Knowles, 1839-1906
about
An American original. R. Freed. il *Stereo Rev* 52:109 Je '87

Paine, Thomas, 1737-1809
about
The forgotten Founding Father: the impact of Thomas Paine [address, January 29, 1987] D. Braff. il pors *Humanist* 47:21-3+ My/Je '87
Sir Richard Attenborough on Thomas Paine. R. Attenborough. *Humanist* 47:22 My/Je '87

Paine, Thomas O.
Who will lead the world's next age of discovery? por *Aviat Week Space Technol* 127:43+ S 21 '87

Paine Webber Group Inc. *See* PaineWebber Group Inc.

PaineWebber Group Inc.
PaineWebber gets a little insurance from Japan [18% stake bought by Yasuda Mutual Life Insurance] C. Farrell. il *Bus Week* p118 D 14 '87
This bull likes two brokerages [views of Mason S. Sexton] G. G. Marcial. *Bus Week* p148 Mr 23 '87

Paint
See also
Lead based paint
Drip-free, semisolid paint [Sears Ready-To-Roll paint] R. Capotosto. il *Pop Mech* 164:36 F '87
Exterior paint and stain. K. Childers. il *Fam Handyman* 37:76-7 Mr '87
Exterior paint: cosmetic or preservative? J. Vara. il *Ctry J* 14:20+ O '87
Exterior paint: problems and cures. il *Consum Res Mag* 70:29-33 Ag '87
House paints & stains. il *Consum Rep* 52:365-74 Je '87
House paints and stains. il *Consum Rep* 52:207-20 D '87
What you really need to know about house paint and painting. il *Sunset* 179:80-6 S '87

Paint, Protective
No safe harbor for marine life [TBT based paint and the marine environment] A. J. Mitteldorf and J. S. Weis. il *Sierra* 72:27+ S/O '87
Painting with pesticides: the controversial organotin paints. S. Scott. il *Sea Front* 33:414-21 N/D '87

Paint and varnish removers
Powered paint removers. J. R. Provey. il *Home Mech* 83:32-5+ Jl '87
Step-by-step to perfect painted woodwork. il *Fam Handyman* 37:60+ My/Je '87

Paint industry
See also
PPG Industries, Inc.
Standard Brands Paint Company

Paint removers *See* Paint and varnish removers

Paint rollers
EZ Roller: not so easy to paint with. il *Consum Rep* 52:74 F '87
Painting with power [cover story] J. R. Provey. il *Home Mech* 83:36-9 Jl '87

Paint spraying and sprayers
See also
Airbrush art
Fingertip painting and finishing [can sprayers] A. Rooze. il *Fam Handyman* 37:8+ Ap '87
Painting with power [cover story] J. R. Provey. il *Home Mech* 83:36-9 Jl '87

Paint strippers *See* Paint and varnish removers

Painted furniture *See* Furniture, Painted

Painter, David S.
Collective security and the inter-American system. il *Dep State Bull* 87:56-8 Ap '87

Painter, Pamela
Kate and Allie and Kate [story] il *Redbook* 168:54+ Mr '87

Painting
See also
Cubism
Floor painting and decoration
Frescoes
Human figure in art
Impressionism (Art)
Landscape painting
Marine painting
Miniature painting
Mural painting and decoration
Portrait painting
Still life painting
Tempera painting
Textile painting
Watercolor painting
Appreciation
See Art—Appreciation
Collectors and collecting
See Art—Collectors and collecting
Conservation and restoration
See also
Metropolitan Museum of Art (New York, N.Y.).
Dept. of Paintings Conservation
Digital image processing in art conservation [secrets of
the Mona Lisa] J. F. Asmus. bibl il *Byte* 12:151-60+
Mr '87
True colors of a classic canvas [work of David Bull
in restoring The feast of the gods by Bellini] il *N
Y Times Mag* p54 Jl 26 '87
Unmasking a 'Mona Lisa' coverup [work of John F.
Asmus] I. Peterson. *Sci News* 131:152 Mr 7 '87
Expertising
See Art—Expertising
Prices
See Art—Prices
Purchasing
See Art trade
Reproductions
See Art—Reproductions
Study and teaching
Instant art [M. Katz's speed-painting course] *New Yorker*
63:23-4 Je 29 '87
Technique
See also
Airbrush art
Eleven artists paint the same location [paintings of the
Alamo on exhibit at the San Antonio Museum of
Art] M. S. Doherty. il *Am Artist* 51:30-41 F '87
In praise of painterly painters. C. Movalli. il *Am Artist*
51:36-41+ My '87
Painting skin the color of life. F. Alexander. il *Am
Artist* 51:66-70 Mr '87
Technical page [technique of C. Demuth] J. R. Doyle.
il *Am Artist* 51:32+ S '87
Techniques of landscape painting. R. Norman. il *Am
Artist* 51:54-7 Ag '87
Using rice paper to transfer color. B. Senter. il *Am
Artist* 51:60-3 My '87
Painting, Abstract See Art, Abstract
Painting, American
See also
Anderson, Doug, 1954?-
Anderson, Walter Inglis, 1903-1965
Asher, Elise
Banks, Allan R., 1948-
Bartlett, Jennifer, 1941-
Bearden, Romare, 1914-1988
Bell, Leland, 1922-
Blakelock, Ralph Albert, 1847-1919
Bleckner, Ross, 1949-
Boston school of painting
Brown, Roger, 1941-
Burgess, Roy
Canright, Sarah, 1941-
Cantrell, Jim, 1935-
Chandler, Michael
Chase, William Merritt, 1849-1916
Coffey, Susanna
Coheleach, Guy
Cole, Thomas, 1801-1848
Cropsey, Jasper Francis, 1823-1900
Dallmann, Daniel
Davis, Joe, 1957?-
Davis, Michael, 1956-
Deas, Charles, 1818-1867
Demuth, Charles, 1883-1935
Diebenkorn, Richard, 1922-
Duffy, Robert
Eddy, Don, 1944-
Estes, Merion

Faulkner, Frank
Ferris, Jean Léon Gérôme, 1863-1930
Fischl, Eric
Frey, Jane
Garet, Jedd
Gechtoff, Sonia, 1926-
Gemberling, Stephen
Gentling, Scott
Gentling, Stuart
Goodman, Sidney, 1936-
Graham, John D., 1886-1961
Grosser, Maurice, 1903-1986
Gruenebaum, Thomas
Haas, Richard
Haberle, John, 1856-1933
Halley, Peter, 1953-
Harrington, James
Hathaway, Rufus, 1770-1822
Held, Al, 1928-
Hoover, Ron
Hudson River School
Hughes, Allen
Hughes, Holly, 1951-
Innerst, Mark, 1958?-
Jaecks, Joel
Jenks, David
Jenney, Neil, 1945-
Jessup, Robert
Johns, Jasper
Johnson, Joshua, 1765-1830
Katz, Alex, 1927-
Katz, Morris, 1932-
Kennedy, Maurice
Klein, Pat
Kligman, Ruth
Knippers, Edward
Komoski, Bill, 1954-
Krasner, Lee, 1908-1984
La Farge, John, 1835-1910
Lawrence, Jacob
Layton, Elizabeth
Lee-Smith, Hughie
Lemieux, Suzanne
Lichtenstein, Roy, 1923-
Loe, Kathleen, 1953-
Lynch, Tom, 1950-
Mangold, Robert, 1937-
Marden, Brice, 1938-
Martin, Agnes, 1912-
McCracken, John, 1934-
McGowin, Ed, 1938-
McKiernan, Janet
McLaughlin, John, 1898-1976
Mesches, Arnold, 1923-
Milek, Gary, 1941-
Minor, Wendell
Murray, Elizabeth
Neas, Richard Lowell
Neher, Ross, 1949-
O'Keeffe, Georgia, 1887-1986
Olitski, Jules, 1922-
Orlando, Tom, 1931-
Orlyk, Harry
O'Sickey, Joseph B.
Pantell, Richard, 1951-
Park, David, 1911-1960
Parker, Catherine Burchfield
Payne, David Mode, 1907-1985
Peacock, Cliffton
Phillips, Ammi
Polk, Kay
Porter, Katherine, 1941-
Portraits, American
Pousette-Dart, Richard, 1916-
Preston, Astrid
Quin, Langdon
Rauschenberg, Robert, 1925-
Reed, David Frederick, 1946-
Robinson, Theodore, 1852-1896
Rockburne, Dorothea, 1934-
Rook, Edward Francis, 1870-1960
Rosenquist, James, 1933-
Rothenberg, Susan
Salle, David
Sargent, John Singer, 1856-1925
Schickel, William
Schley, Reeve
Schnabel, Julian
Shannon, Joseph, 1933-
Shapinsky, Harold
Sheeler, Charles, 1883-1965

Painting, American—See also—*cont.*
    Shuptrine, Hubert
    Skaggs, Robert
    Slavick, Susanne
    Small, Deborah
    Smith, Lee N., 1951-
    Smith, Leon Polk, 1906-
    Snyder, Joan, 1940-
    Sorman, Steven, 1948-
    Sprick, Daniel
    Steir, Pat, 1940-
    Stella, Frank
    Stella, Joseph, 1877-1946
    Stuart, Michelle
    Sullivan, Bill, 1942-
    Sultan, Donald K., 1951-
    Taaffe, Philip, 1955-
    Tanning, Dorothea, 1913-
    Tarbell, Edmund Charles, 1862-1938
    Terpning, Howard, 1927-
    Theobald, Gillian
    Trefny, Frank, 1948-
    Trumbull, John, 1756-1843
    Ushenko, Audrey Andreyevna, 1945-
    Van Horn, Dana
    Walker, Chuck, 1952-
    Warhol, Andy, 1928?-1987
    Weisberg, Ruth
    Welliver, Neil
    Weymouth, George A.
    Wharton, William
    Whitaker, Eileen Monaghan, 1911-
    Wiley, William
    Williams, Neil, 1934-1988
    Williamson, Philemona
    Wilson, Donald Roller, 1940?-
    Wilson, Helen Miranda
    Wofford, Dan
    Wolff, Anita
    Wonner, Paul, 1920-
    Wood, Grant, 1892-1942
    Wyeth, Andrew, 1917-
    Wyeth, Jamie, 1946-
    Wyeth, N. C. (Newell Convers), 1882-1945
    Young, Michael, 1952-
    Youngerman, Jack, 1926-
American painting [cover story; special issue] il *Antiques* 132:1082-1139 N '87
Art: schoolgirl paintings: nineteenth-century works by American amateur artists. J. R. Mellow. il *Archit Dig* 44:140-5+ D '87
The California school of watercolor. J. Lovoos. il por *Am Artist* 51:62-9+ Ap '87
A family vision: the Wyeth legacy. il *Read Dig* 131:25-31 S '87
The national image: American paintings in the State Department. J. Wilmerding. il *Antiques* 132:146-59 Jl '87
Our third annual winter art show. il *Am Herit* 38:72-81 D '87
Sublime views [market for romantic landscapes] F. Donegan. il *Americana* 15:62-4 N/D '87
Talking abstract (I) [cover story; interviews with eight American painters] L. Wei. il *Art Am* 75:80-97 Jl '87
Talking abstract (II) [cover story; interviews with nine American painters] L. Wei. il *Art Am* 75:112-29+ D '87

Exhibitions
See also
    Corcoran Gallery of Art. Biennial Exhibition of Contemporary American Painting
    R.H. Love Galleries, Inc.
    Richard York Gallery
    Whitney Museum of American Art
American art in the Mount Holyoke College Art Museum. P. J. Staiti and W. M. Watson. il *Antiques* 132:1122-31 N '87
American painting [In nature's ways: American landscape painting of the late 19th century] S. B. Sherrill. il *Antiques* 131:360+ F '87
Artsmart [American traditions in watercolor from Worcester Art Museum] il *Harpers Bazaar* 120:190 Mr '87
"Empowered painting" at the Santa Fe Museum of Fine Arts. D. Bell. *Art Am* 75:143+ Ja '87
The heart of the seasons [American impressionist paintings from the Terra Museum; cover story] E. Hardwick. il *House Gard* 159:122-31+ My '87
"Liars" at State of Illinois Art Gallery. S. Taylor. il *Art Am* 75:187+ S '87

"Modern times" at Hirschl & Adler. J. Weinberg. *Art Am* 75:144-5 F '87
New museum of American art [inaugural exhibit entitled A proud heritage: two centuries of American art at Terra Museum] S. B. Sherrill. il *Antiques* 131:926+ My '87
A sense of light and air in landscapes [exhibition of 19th century American landscape paintings] B. Weber. bibl f il *Am Artist* 51:40-7+ Ap '87
Technique in American watercolors from the Worcester Art Museum, Worcester, Massachusetts. S. E. Strickler and J. C. Walsh. bibl f il *Antiques* 131:412-25 F '87
The watercolors from Worcester [American traditions in watercolor] K. M. Burke. il *Smithsonian* 18:192 S '87
Painting, Argentine
    See also
    Fontana, Lucio, 1899-1968
Painting, Australian
    See also
    Tillers, Imants, 1950-
The vivid imagery of Australia's artists. P. Fuller. il *Archit Dig* 44:204+ S '87
Painting, Austrian
    See also
    Kokoschka, Oskar, 1886-1980
Painting, Baroque
The Italian baroque paintings of Morton and Mary Jane Harris. C. Ratcliff. il por *Archit Dig* 44:50+ My '87
Painting, Belgian
    See also
    Alechinsky, Pierre, 1927-
    Verheylewegen, Jamy
Painting, Bolivian
    See also
    Pacheco, Maria Luisa
Painting, Canadian
    See also
    Eckart, Christian
    Goodwin, Betty
    Wieland, Joyce, 1931-
Painting, Christian *See* Christian art and symbolism
Painting, Decorative *See* Decoration and ornament
Painting, Dutch
    See also
    Appel, Karel, 1921-
    Gogh, Vincent van, 1853-1890
    Houckgeest, Gerard, ca. 1600-1661
    Rembrandt Harmenszoon van Rijn, 1606-1669
The pleasure of the image [paintings of church interiors] S. Sontag. il *Art Am* 75:122-31 N '87
Painting, English
    See also
    Bacon, Francis, 1909-
    Coe, Sue, 1951-
    Freud, Lucian
    Hayman, Francis, 1708-1776
    Hodgkin, Howard, 1932-
    Leighton, Sir Frederic, 1830-1896
    Millington-Drake, Teddy
    Nadin, Peter
    Portraits, English
    Turner, J. M. W. (Joseph Mallord William), 1775-1851
Painting in medieval England: the wall-to-wall message. P. Tudor-Craig. bibl il *Hist Today* 37:39-45 N '87
Exhibitions
    See also
    Tate Gallery. Clore Wing
British marine painting [Masters of the sea: British marine watercolors, 1650-1930 at the Yale Center for British Art] S. B. Sherrill. il *Antiques* 131:1182 Je '87
Painting, European
Art: European watercolors: luminous washes by nineteenth-century painters. C. Finch. il *Archit Dig* 44:140-5 S '87
Painting, Flemish
    See also
    Brueghel, Pieter, the Elder, 1522?-1569
Painting, French
    See also
    Alberola, Jean-Michel, 1953-
    Balthus, 1908-
    Ecole de Rouen
    Fauvism
    Favier, Philippe
    Majorelle, Jacques
    Matisse, Henri
    Morisot, Berthe, 1841-1895
    Mosset, Olivier

Painting, French—See also—*cont.*
Poussin, Nicolas, 1594?-1665
Rohan-Chabot, Joy de
Exhibitions
See also
Galerie Schmit
Painting, German
See also
Bach, Elvira
Beckmann, Max, 1884-1950
Blaue Reiter (Group)
Ernst, Max, 1891-1976
Haacke, Hans
Kiefer, Anselm, 1945-
Klee, Paul, 1879-1940
Marc, Franz, 1880-1916
Münter, Gabriele, 1877-1962
Umberg, Günter
Painting, Haitian
Hunting art in Haiti. J. B. Harris. il *Black Enterp* 17:36
My '87
Painting, Industrial and practical
See also
Automobiles—Painting
Bridges—Painting
Gilding
House painting
Paint
Paint spraying and sprayers
Answering your questions about fall repainting jobs.
A. W. Lees. *Pop Sci* 231:121 O '87
Scene painting. R. Long. il *Theatre Crafts* 21:44-6+ O
'87
Equipment
See also
Paint rollers
Painting basics: the right tools. C. Self and B. Gould.
il *Workbench* 43:106-9 Mr/Ap '87
Tool charts. G. Branson. il *Fam Handyman* 37:32 Mr
'87
Painting, Israeli
See also
Arikha, Avigdor, 1929-
Painting, Italian
See also
Arcimboldo, Giuseppe, ca. 1527-1593
Clemente, Francesco
Cremonini, Leonardo, 1925-
Gallo, Giuseppe, 1954-
Leonardo, da Vinci, 1452-1519
Macchiaioli
Michelangelo Buonarroti, 1475-1564
Nazor, Maria
Raphael, 1483-1520
Denis Mahon and his 'old friends' [collector of 17th-
century paintings] I. Shenker. il por *Art News* 86:121-7
Mr '87
The Italian baroque paintings of Morton and Mary Jane
Harris. C. Ratcliff. il por *Archit Dig* 44:50+ My '87
The rediscovery of the Bolognese school. D. S. Pepper.
il *Antiques* 131:846-7 Ap '87
Exhibitions
The Age of Correggio and the Carracci [exhibition at
the Metropolitan Museum of Art] A. C. Danto. *Nation*
244:586-90 My 2 '87
Faith in the flesh [The Age of Correggio and the Carracci]
D. Rosand. il *New Repub* 196:29-33 F 9 '87
Mannerism at its best [The Age of Correggio and the
Carracci] J. Gardner. il *Commonweal* 114:244-5 Ap
24 '87
Sometimes a great notion [The Age of Correggio and
the Carracci: Emilian painting of the sixteenth and
seventeenth centuries at the Metropolitan Museum]
K. Larson. il *N Y* 20:100+ Ap 13 '87
Unexpected pleasures [The Age of Correggio and the
Carracci] M. Stevens. il *Newsweek* 109:64-6 Ja 12
'87
Anecdotes, facetiae, satire, etc.
Vickie Lou's letters from Long Island [The Age of
Correggio and the Carracci] il *Am Artist* 51:18+ Ap
'87
Painting, Japanese
See also
Kimura, Chūta, 1917-
Painting, Manuscript *See* Illumination of books and
manuscripts
Painting, Mexican
See also
Lepe, Manuel
Tamayo, Rufino, 1899-

Painting, Modern *See* Art, Modern
Painting, Nicaraguan
See also
Morales, Armando, 1927-
Painting, Panamanian
See also
Arias, Susana
Painting, Polish
See also
Klement, Vera, 1929-
Painting, Russian
See also
Chagall, Marc, 1887-1985
Kandinsky, Wassily, 1866-1944
Komar, Vitali, 1943-
Melamid, Aleksandr, 1945-
Exhibitions
Russian painting at the dawn of modernism [exhibit
entitled Russia, the land, the people: Russian painting
1850-1910] A. Hilton. il *Art News* 86:110-15 Mr '87
Painting, Spanish
See also
Barceló, Miquel, 1957-
Miró, Joan, 1893-1983
Perejaume, 1957-
Picasso, Pablo, 1881-1973
Sicilia, José Maria, 1954-
Zurbarán, Francisco de, 1598-1664
Exhibitions
Spanish masterworks from the Meadows Museum: Wil-
denstein. R. Bass. il *Art News* 86:158 D '87
Painting, Swedish
See also
Larsson, Carl Olof, 1853-1919
Painting, Swiss
See also
Hodler, Ferdinand, 1853-1918
Painting, Uruguayan
See also
Torres-García, Joaquín, 1874-1949
Painting, Venezuelan
See also
Borges, Jacobo, 1932-
Painting, Victorian
Attic attitudes: Leighton and aesthetic philosophy. S.
Jones. bibl il *Hist Today* 37:31-7 Je '87
Painting on glass *See* Glass painting and staining
Painting on textiles *See* Textile painting
Paints *See* Paint
Paisley, David
about
Prescription for profits. G. Bronson. il por *Forbes* 140:65-6
O 19 '87
Paisley shawls *See* Shawls
Pajamas *See* Sleepwear
Pake, George Edward, 1924-
Physics, Japan and US competitiveness. por *Phys Today*
40:9+ D '87
Pakenham, Elizabeth Harman Pakenham, Baroness *See*
Longford, Elizabeth Harman Pakenham, Countess of,
1906-
Pakistan
See also
Airplanes, Military—Pakistan
Baltistan (Pakistan)
Immigration and emigration—Pakistan
Journalism—Study and teaching—Pakistan
K2 Mountain (Pakistan)
Karachi (Pakistan)
Marriage customs and rites—Pakistan
Military assistance, American—Pakistan
Muslims—Pakistan
Peshawar (Pakistan)
Public health—Pakistan
Relief work—Pakistan
Thull (Pakistan)
United Nations—Pakistan
Antiquities
See also
Mohenjo-Daro site (Pakistan)
Commerce
United States
See United States—Commerce—Pakistan
Defenses
Aid to Pakistan: megatons of trouble for the U.S.? B.
Javetski. il *Bus Week* p57 Ap 6 '87
A bad case of nuclear friction [Pakistan rejects U.S.
attempt to link inspection of nuclear facilities to aid
package] M. S. Serrill. il *Time* 130:40 Ag 17 '87
Bombs without test blasts? D. Albright. bibl f *Bull At
Sci* 43:32 Je '87

Pakistan—*Defenses*—*cont.*

Glenn asks Reagan to halt Pakistan aid pending review of nuclear programs. M. Crawford. por *Science* 235:1321 Mr 13 '87

How lies proliferate [nuclear capabilities] *Nation* 244:381 Mr 28 '87

In the shadow of the 'Islamic bomb' [nuclear capability] A. Bilski. il *Macleans* 100:24+ Mr 23 '87

India, Pakistan racing to be last [nuclear weapons] R. V. R. Chandrasekhar Rao. il *Bull At Sci* 43:32-4 N '87

Knocking at the nuclear door [with interview with M. Zia-ul-Haq] W. R. Doerner. il por *Time* 129:42-3 Mr 30 '87

The nuclear caper [arrest of Arshad Pervez in Philadelphia on charges of trying to illegally export materials for Pakistan's weapons program] I. Austen. il *Macleans* 100:19 Jl 27 '87

Pakistan and the nuclear issue [statement, July 22, 1987] R. W. Murphy. *Dep State Bull* 87:53-4 O '87

A Pakistan bombshell [evidence it has nuclear arms] R. Nordland. il *Newsweek* 109:45 Mr 16 '87

Pakistan thought to possess atomic bomb. M. Crawford. il *Science* 235:1131 Mr 6 '87

Pakistani smuggling riles Congress [nuclear smuggling] L. S. Spector. il *Bull At Sci* 43:3-4 O '87

Pakistan's bomb-making capacity [gas centrifuge enrichment plant at Kahuta] D. Albright. bibl f il *Bull At Sci* 43:30-3 Je '87

A rock and a hard place [Pakistan caught trying to illegally import maraging steel intended for bomb program] R. Nordland. il *Newsweek* 110:30+ Jl 27 '87

Wanted: the bomb [possible cutoff of U.S. military aid after Pakistan's attempt buy steel alloy for nuclear weapons] il *U S News World Rep* 103:8 Jl 27 '87

Foreign relations
Afghanistan
See Afghanistan—Foreign relations—Pakistan
India
See India—Foreign relations—Pakistan
Soviet Union
See Soviet Union—Foreign relations—Pakistan
United States
See United States—Foreign relations—Pakistan

Politics and government
The perils of Pakistan. M. Ispahani. *New Repub* 196:19-21+ Mr 16 '87
See also
Church and social problems—Pakistan

Pakula, Alan J., 1928-
about
Orphans [film] Reviews
Glamour il 85:228 O '87. J. G. Boyum
Natl Rev 39:61-2 O 23 '87. J. Simon
New Repub 197:26-7 O 19 '87. S. Kauffmann
Newsweek 110:76 S 28 '87. D. Ansen
People Wkly il 28:10 O 5 '87. P. Travers
Time 130:85 O 12 '87
Vogue il 177:462+ S '87. D. Mason

PAL *See* Programmable array logic

Palace Cafe (Santa Barbara, Calif.) *See* Santa Barbara (Calif.)—Restaurants, nightclubs, bars, etc.

Palaces
See also
Castles
Czechoslovakia
Open house in Prague [Petschek Palace functions as U.S. embassy] W. W. Luers. il pors *House Gard* 159:150-5+ My '87
Great Britain
See also
Hampton Court Palace (London, England)
Haiti
Haiti's majestic monuments [Citadelle Laferriére and Sans Souci Palace] R. Bishop. il *Américas* 39:2-7+ Ja/F '87
'We will confound the calumniators of our race . . .' [Citadelle and Sans Souci Palace of H. Christophe] F. Maclean. il por map *Smithsonian* 18:160-6+ O '87
India
Princely palaces. V. Fass. il *Horizon* 30:24-5 Mr '87
Italy
A charmed life [Palazzo Frescobaldi in Florence] G. Y. Dryansky. il *Vogue* 177:446-53+ O '87
Traces of the future's past: Nicola Trussardi's palazzo in Bergamo. G. Y. Dryansky. il por *Archit Dig* 44:152-9 My '87

Soviet Union
Homes of the czars [Leningrad] F. Maclean. il *House Gard* 159:56+ Ap '87
A master painter and his aging collective bring life and color back to the Catherine Palace [Y. Kazakov] S. K. Reed. il pors *People Wkly* 27:92-4+ Ap 6 '87
A Russian Versailles [Paul's summer palace at Pavlosk and Catherine's palace at Pushkin] A. Cooper. *Travel Holiday* 167:8 F '87
Where the czars shined [Grand Palace Petrodvorets] J. Gillette. il *Travel Holiday* 167:6+ F '87
Spain
See also
Escorial (San Lorenzo, Spain)
Generalife (Granada, Spain)
Syria
Syria's disappearing palace. T. Mirabelli. il *Hist Today* 37:4-5 Ag '87

Palacio de Generalife (Granada, Spain) *See* Generalife (Granada, Spain)

Palacio Nacional de Montjuich (Barcelona, Spain)
The Aulenti uproar. C. Vogel. il por *N Y Times Mag* p26-32+ N 22 '87

Palacios, Alvar González- *See* González-Palacios, Alvar

Palade, Laurentiu
Hunter-gatherers of the tropical forest. il maps *Courier* 40:20-2 Je '87

Palau
See also
United Nations—Palau
Description and travel
Beached in Belau: the South Pacific's water playground. S. McCutcheon. il map *Travel Holiday* 168:60-5 D '87
Photographs and photography
Coral gardens: a textured treasure. D. Faulkner. il *Int Wildl* 17:46-51 N/D '87
Politics and government
Compact of free association with Pacific Islands [text of executive order, October 16, 1986] R. Reagan. *Dep State Bull* 86:74-5 D '86
Trusteeship Council recommends early completion of process of approval of compact for Palau. il *UN Chron* 24:37-9 Ag '87
Trusteeship Council sends mission to Palau. *UN Chron* 24:132 F '87
Visiting mission reports on plebiscite in Palau. il *UN Chron* 24:41-2 My '87
Visiting mission to Palau observes plebiscite. *UN Chron* 24:55 N '87

Palen, Kathy
Family leave: a needed guarantee. *Christ Century* 104:372-3 Ap 22 '87

Paleo-Americans *See* Paleo-Indians

Paleo-Indians
The American blitzkrieg: a mammoth undertaking [Clovis hunters] J. M. Diamond. il *Discover* 8:82-4+ Je '87
Blood test [clues to New World migration from genetic analysis] S. L. Zegura. il *Nat Hist* 96:8+ Jl '87
By the banks of the Chinchihuapi [Monte Vercle site, Chile] T. D. Dillehay. il map *Nat Hist* 96:8+ Ap '87
Cliff notes [rock-shelter paintings at Pedra Furada site and vicinity, Brazil] N. Guidon. il map *Nat Hist* 96:6+ Ag '87
Clovisia the Beautiful! P. S. Martin. *Nat Hist* 96:10+ O '87
Death by natural causes [Pleistocene extinctions of animals may have been caused by human hunters] D. K. Grayson. il *Nat Hist* 96:8+ My '87
Did early North Americans mount a mammoth 'blitzkrieg'? il *Earth Sci* 40:6-7 Wint '87
Earlier appearance of humans in New World [work of Barbara Purdy] il *USA Today (Periodical)* 115:12 Je '87
Extinctions on ice [North American land mammals and Clovis hunters; theories of Paul S. Martin and others; cover story] B. Bower. il *Sci News* 132:284-5 O 31 '87
The first Americans are getting younger. R. Lewin. il map *Science* 238:1230-2 N 27 '87
Flakes, breaks and the first Americans [controversy over date of human migration to North America] B. Bower. il *Sci News* 131:172-3 Mr 14 '87
The Ginsberg experiment [Clovis and pre-Clovis artifacts] D. J. Stanford. il *Nat Hist* 96:10+ S '87
How did the giants die? [North American land mammals and Clovis hunters; theory of P. S. Martin] T. A. Lewis. il por *Int Wildl* 17:4-11 S/O '87
New dates from old bones [Old Crow site in Yukon Territory] W. N. Irving. map *Nat Hist* 96:8+ F '87

Paleo-Indians—cont.

Points of order: excavations in Venezuela and Colombia put the Ice Age hunters of North America in a new perspective. A. L. Bryan. maps *Nat Hist* 96:6+ Je '87

Prehistoric adventurers explored Kentucky cave passages 3,000 years before modern cavers came along [excerpt from The Longest cave] R. Brucker and R. A. Watson. *Earth Sci* 40:23 Fall '87

Telltale teeth. C. G. Turner, II. maps *Nat Hist* 96:6+ Ja '87

Voices from the past [clues to New World migrations from study of Indian languages] M. Ruhlen. map *Nat Hist* 96:6+ Mr '87

Paleoanthropology *See* Man, Prehistoric

Paleobiology
    See also
    Paleoecology

Paleobotany
    See also
    Pollen, Fossil

Triassic

Fossil mycorrhizae: a case for symbiosis. S. P. Stubblefield and others. bibl f il *Science* 237:59-60 Jl 3 '87

Pollen and spores date origin of rift basins from Texas to Nova Scotia as early late Triassic. A. Traverse. bibl f il map *Science* 236:1469-72 Je 12 '87

Pulling each other through bad times [fossil mycorrhiza; research by Sara P. Stubblefield and others] *Sci News* 132:47 Jl 18 '87

Antarctic regions

Fossil mycorrhizae: a case for symbiosis. S. P. Stubblefield and others. bibl f il *Science* 237:59-60 Jl 3 '87

Pulling each other through bad times [fossil mycorrhiza; research by Sara P. Stubblefield and others] *Sci News* 132:47 Jl 18 '87

Paleoclimatology
    See also
    Glacial epochs

The biggest chill. W. S. Broecker. il maps *Nat Hist* 96:74-80+ O '87

Leg 113: drilling into Antarctica's past. S. Weisburd. map *Sci News* 131:278-9 My 2 '87

Ocean drilling details steps to an icy world [Antarctica] R. A. Kerr. il map *Science* 236:912-13 My 22 '87

Precise timing of the last interglacial period from mass spectrometric determination of thorium-230 in corals. R. L. Edwards and others. bibl f il *Science* 236:1547-53 Je 19 '87

Volcanic history in the Aleutian arc [research by Thomas P. Miller and Robert L. Smith] R. Monastersky. il *Sci News* 131:357 Je 6 '87

Windfalls of dust [determining ancient wind patterns from core samples of ocean sediments] D. K. Rea. il map *Nat Hist* 96:28+ F '87

Cretaceous

Amber yields samples of ancient air [work of Robert A. Berner and Gary P. Landis] R. Monastersky. *Sci News* 132:293 N 7 '87

Ancient air analyzed in dinosaur-age amber [research by Robert Berner and Gary Landis] R. A. Kerr. *Science* 238:890 N 13 '87

Putting on ancient airs [ancient atmosphere trapped in amber found to contain 50% more oxygen] il *Time* 130:82 N 9 '87

Precambrian

Solar records set in stone [Australian study] il *Sky Telesc* 73:153-4 F '87

Quaternary

Vapor lock [air bubbles in Antarctic ice record carbon dioxide and climate] T. Beardsley. *Sci Am* 257:32 D '87

Wadi Howar: paleoclimatic evidence from an extinct river system in the southeastern Sahara. H.-J. Pachur and S. Kröpelin. bibl f il map *Science* 237:298-300 Jl 17 '87

Paleoecology

In search of ancient shores [Catskill clastic wedge; work of Patricia Bonamo and others] P. Barnes-Svarney. il *Earth Sci* 40:22-3 Spr '87

Paleogeography
    See also
    Continental drift

Paleologos, Nicholas

Pacific overtures. il *Phi Delta Kappan* 68:368 Ja '87

Paleontological models and exhibits

Before the dinosaurs [reconstruction of Placerias skeleton; work of R. A. Long] B. Weber. il pors *N Y Times Mag* p66 Ag 23 '87

Building beasts. J. T. Hannibal. il *Earth Sci* 39:20-1 Wint '86

Eastern homes for western dinosaurs. il *Sunset* 178:61-2 Je '87

Geology in Milwaukee [dinosaur dioramas at the Milwaukee Public Museum] P. M. Sheehan. il *Earth Sci* 39:18-19 Wint '86

Making prehistory [dinosaur models at Reproductions Shop of American Museum of Natural History] C. Rubin. il *Vogue* 177:58 Jl '87

Paleontologists
Anecdotes, facetiae, satire, etc.

Fossil news. J. Stevenson. il *New Yorker* 63:36-7 My 11 '87

Paleontology
    See also
    Animals, Extinct
    Anteaters, Fossil
    Apes, Fossil
    Bears, Fossil
    Birds, Fossil
    Computers—Paleontological use
    Corals, Fossil
    Dinosaurs
    Echinoderms, Fossil
    Eggs, Fossil
    Fish, Extinct
    Fish, Fossil
    Frogs, Fossil
    Fungi, Fossil
    Horses, Fossil
    Invertebrates, Fossil
    Mammals, Fossil
    Man, Prehistoric
    Marine fauna, Fossil
    Mass extinction of species
    Micropaleontology
    Mollusks, Fossil
    Monkeys, Fossil
    Paleoecology
    Paleontological models and exhibits
    Paleopathology
    Reefs, Fossil
    Reptiles, Fossil
    Rhinoceros, Fossil
    Sea birds, Fossil
    Sirenia, Fossil
    State fossils
    Teeth, Fossil
    Tomography—Paleontological use
    Trace fossils
    Turtles, Fossil
    Tusks, Fossil
    Whales, Fossil

Archean

Early Archean (3.3-billion to 3.5-billion-year-old) microfossils from Warrawoona Group, Australia. J. W. Schopf and B. M. Packer. bibl f il map *Science* 237:70-3 Jl 3 '87

Cambrian

The emergence of animals. M. A. S. McMenamin. bibl (p128) il map *Sci Am* 256:94-102 Ap '87

Cretaceous

Avascular necrosis: occurrence in diving Cretaceous mosasaurs. B. Rothschild and L. D. Martin. bibl f il *Science* 236:75-7 Ap 3 '87

Badlands fossils [Kansas] R. Buchanan. il *Earth Sci* 40:13-15 Fall '87

Dinosaurs: decline or fall? *Sci Am* 256:62-3 Ja '87

Dinosaurs on the North Slope, Alaska: high latitude, latest Cretaceous environments. E. M. Brouwers and others. bibl f il map *Science* 237:1608-10 S 25 '87

Heritability at the species level: analysis of geographic ranges of Cretaceous mollusks. D. Jablonski. bibl f il *Science* 238:360-3 O 16 '87

K-T mass extinctions: abrupt or what? [work of William J. Zinsmeister] R. Monastersky. *Sci News* 132:277 O 31 '87

Mass extinctions caused by large bolide impacts [adaptation of address, December 11, 1986; cover story] L. W. Alvarez. bibl f il *Phys Today* 40:24-33 Jl '87

Where have all the dinos gone? [work of L. Alvarez] il *U S News World Rep* 103:67 Jl 6 '87

Devonian

In search of ancient shores [Catskill clastic wedge; work of Patricia Bonamo and others] P. Barnes-Svarney. il *Earth Sci* 40:22-3 Spr '87

Eocene

Climbing adaptations in the early Eocene mammal Chriacus and the origin of Artiodactyla. K. D. Rose. bibl f il *Science* 236:314-16 Ap 17 '87

Paleontology—Eocene—*cont.*

An upper Eocene frog from the Dominican Republic and its implication for Caribbean biogeography. G. O. Poinar and D. C. Cannatella. bibl f il *Science* 237:1215-16 S 4 '87

Whale of a discovery [Seymour Island] *Sea Front* 33:303 Jl/Ag '87

Jurassic

Modern turtle origins: the oldest known cryptodire [northeastern Arizona discovery] E. S. Gaffney and others. bibl f il *Science* 237:289-91 Jl 17 '87

Methodology

Statistical traps lurk in the fossil record [views of Carl Koch] R. Lewin. il *Science* 236:521-2 My 1 '87

Miocene

Empire of the apes [Lake Turkana fossils; work of Richard Leakey] S. J. Gould. il *Nat Hist* 96:20+ My '87

Ordovician

Dry run [trace fossils evidence for late Ordovician land animals in Pennsylvania; work of Gregory J. Retallack and Carolyn R. Feakes] *Sci Am* 256:64-5 My '87

Facing up to a backwards fossil [work of David K. Elliott] *Sci News* 132:47 Jl 18 '87

A reassessment of Astraspis desiderata, the oldest North American vertebrate. D. K. Elliott. bibl f il *Science* 237:190-2 Jl 10 '87

Trace fossil evidence for late Ordovician animals on land [Pennsylvania] G. J. Retallack and C. R. Feakes. bibl f il *Science* 235:61-3 Ja 2 '87

Paleozoic

Environmental trends in extinction during the Paleozoic. J. J. Sepkoski, Jr. bibl f il *Science* 235:64-6 Ja 2 '87

Pleistocene

Calcium-41 concentration in terrestrial materials: prospects for dating of Pleistocene samples. W. Henning and others. bibl f il *Science* 236:725-7 My 8 '87

Clovisia the Beautiful! P. S. Martin. *Nat Hist* 96:10+ O '87

Death by natural causes [Pleistocene extinctions of animals may have been caused by human hunters] D. K. Grayson. il *Nat Hist* 96:8+ My '87

Extinctions on ice [North American land mammals and Clovis hunters; theories of Paul S. Martin and others; cover story] B. Bower. il *Sci News* 132:284-5 O 31 '87

First record of giant anteater (Xenarthra, Myrmecophagidae) in North America. C. A. Shaw and H. G. McDonald. bibl f il map *Science* 236:186-8 Ap 10 '87

Have land bridge, will travel [research by H. Gregory McDonald and others] *Sci News* 131:296 My 9 '87

How did the giants die? [North American land mammals and Clovis hunters; theory of P. S. Martin] T. A. Lewis. il por *Int Wildl* 17:4-11 S/O '87

Precambrian

The emergence of animals. M. A. S. McMenamin. bibl (p128) il map *Sci Am* 256:94-102 Ap '87

Has the biosphere done a flip-flop? [changes from the Archean; views of James C. G. Walker] S. Eisenberg. *Sci News* 132:278 O 31 '87

Triassic

Abrupt extinctions at end of Triassic [research by Paul E. Olsen and others] R. Monastersky. map *Sci News* 132:149 S 5 '87

New early Jurassic tetrapod assemblages constrain Triassic-Jurassic tetrapod extinction event [Nova Scotia discovery] P. E. Olsen and others. bibl f il map *Science* 237:1025-9 Ag 28 '87

Africa

Africa: cradle of modern humans. R. Lewin. *Science* 237:1292-5 S 11 '87

Bushes all the way down: we are all products of a recent African twig [mitochondrial DNA] S. J. Gould. *Nat Hist* 96:12+ Je '87

Discoveries in Africa are clues to early humans. il *Earth Sci* 40:8-9 Spr '87

Alaska

Dinosaurs on the North Slope, Alaska: high latitude, latest Cretaceous environments. E. M. Brouwers and others. bibl f il map *Science* 237:1608-10 S 25 '87

Make no bones about it, dinosaur theory challenged [Alaskan Hadrosaur remains found by Elisabeth Brouwers and William Clemens] il *Earth Sci* 40:6 Wint '87

Alberta

Digging for dinosaurs [Dinosaur Project findings] J. Howse. il *Macleans* 100:62 N 30 '87

Dinosaur country. il maps *Sunset* 178:82-91 Je '87

Drop that bone! [deposits of dinosaur bones] P. Johnston. il *Hist Today* 37:4-6 D '87

Arctic regions

Fission-track dating of Haughton Astrobleme and included biota, Devon Island, Canada. G. Omar and others. bibl f il map *Science* 237:1603-5 S 25 '87

Arizona

Age and diet of fossil California condors in Grand Canyon, Arizona. S. D. Emslie. bibl f il *Science* 237:768-70 Ag 14 '87

Modern turtle origins: the oldest known cryptodire. E. S. Gaffney and others. bibl f il *Science* 237:289-91 Jl 17 '87

Australia

Early Archean (3.3-billion to 3.5-billion-year-old) microfossils from Warrawoona Group, Australia. J. W. Schopf and B. M. Packer. bibl f il map *Science* 237:70-3 Jl 3 '87

China

Digging for dinosaurs [Dinosaur Project findings] J. Howse. il *Macleans* 100:62 N 30 '87

Dinosaurs: decline or fall? *Sci Am* 256:62-3 Ja '87

Colombia

An ancient relative for the owl monkey. B. Bower. il *Sci News* 131:263 Ap 25 '87

Colorado

Dinosaur eggs unscrambled [discovered in Wells Gulch] il *Time* 130:56 Ag 3 '87

Facing up to a backwards fossil [work of David K. Elliott] *Sci News* 132:47 Jl 18 '87

The Ginsberg experiment [Clovis and pre-Clovis artifacts] D. J. Stanford. il *Nat Hist* 96:10+ S '87

A reassessment of Astraspis desiderata, the oldest North American vertebrate. D. K. Elliott. bibl f il *Science* 237:190-2 Jl 10 '87

They dig dinos. il map *Natl Geogr World* 146:6-9 O '87

Dominican Republic

An upper Eocene frog from the Dominican Republic and its implication for Caribbean biogeography. G. O. Poinar and D. C. Cannatella. bibl f il *Science* 237:1215-16 S 4 '87

Germany (West)

Dumping on science [plan to use fossil rich Grube Messel as a garbage dump] P. Shipman. il map *Discover* 8:60-6 D '87

Great Britain

Mammoth find fuels extinction debate. B. Bower. *Sci News* 132:372 D 12 '87

Italy

Rising above a prehistoric handicap [adolescent male dwarf skeleton from southern Italy; research by David W. Frayer and others] *Sci News* 132:334 N 21 '87

Kansas

Badlands fossils. R. Buchanan. il *Earth Sci* 40:13-15 Fall '87

Kenya

Empire of the apes [Lake Turkana fossils; work of Richard Leakey] S. J. Gould. il *Nat Hist* 96:20+ My '87

Family feud: enter the 'black skull' [Alan Walker's controversial discovery] B. Bower. il *Sci News* 131:58-9 Ja 24 '87

The prehumans: our family tree [skull related to Australopithecus boisei discovered] P. Shipman. *Current* 290:4-8 F '87

Stone Age site gets pushed back in time [potassium-argon dating of Olorgesailie site; work of Bethany A. Bye and others] B. Bower. *Sci News* 132:199 S 26 '87

Uncovering life by an ancient lake [Olorgesailie lake basin] B. Bower. *Sci News* 131:264 Ap 25 '87

Mexico

First record of giant anteater (Xenarthra, Myrmecophagidae) in North America. C. A. Shaw and H. G. McDonald. bibl f il map *Science* 236:186-8 Ap 10 '87

Have land bridge, will travel [research by H. Gregory McDonald and others] *Sci News* 131:296 My 9 '87

Mongolia

A daring gamble in the Gobi Desert took the jackpot [R. C. Andrews' search for dinosaur fossils] D. J. Preston. il pors *Smithsonian* 18:94-8+ D '87

Montana

Dinosaurs: decline or fall? *Sci Am* 256:62-3 Ja '87

New York (State)

Fossils extend condor's range, pose questions [discovery of three fossil California condor bones] il *Audubon* 89:14 Jl '87

In search of ancient shores [Catskill clastic wedge; work of Patricia Bonamo and others] P. Barnes-Svarney. il *Earth Sci* 40:22-3 Spr '87

Nature [views of David Steadman] *New Yorker* 62:25-6 F 2 '87

Paleontology—*cont.*

North America
The rise and fall of the American rhino. D. R. Prothero. il *Nat Hist* 96:26-33 Ag '87

Nova Scotia
Abrupt extinctions at end of Triassic [research by Paul E. Olsen and others] R. Monastersky. map *Sci News* 132:149 S 5 '87

New early Jurassic tetrapod assemblages constrain Triassic-Jurassic tetrapod extinction event. P. E. Olsen and others. bibl f il map *Science* 237:1025-9 Ag 28 '87

Pennsylvania
Dry run [trace fossils evidence for late Ordovician land animals] *Sci Am* 256:64-5 My '87

Landing the earliest plants and animals. *Sci News* 131:41 Ja 17 '87

Trace fossil evidence for late Ordovician animals on land. G. J. Retallack and C. R. Feakes. bibl f il *Science* 235:61-3 Ja 2 '87

Poland
Prehistoric tusk: early boomerang? [mammoth tusk found in Polish cave; research by Pawel Valde-Nowak and others] B. Bower. *Sci News* 132:215 O 3 '87

Seymour Island (Antarctic regions)
K-T mass extinctions: abrupt or what? [work of William J. Zinsmeister] R. Monastersky. *Sci News* 132:277 O 31 '87

Whale of a discovery. *Sea Front* 33:303 Jl/Ag '87

South Carolina
Fossil skeleton sets seabird size record [pseudodontorn bound in South Carolina; work of Storrs L. Olson] B. Bower. *Sci News* 132:310 N 14 '87

Sudan
Wadi Howar: paleoclimatic evidence from an extinct river system in the southeastern Sahara. H.-J. Pachur and S. Kröpelin. bibl f il map *Science* 237:298-300 Jl 17 '87

Tanzania
The 2-million-year-old meat and marrow diet resurfaces [research by Henry T. Bunn and Ellen M. Kroll] B. Bower. *Sci News* 131:7 Ja 3 '87

The earliest "humans" were more like apes [Homo habilis found in Olduvai Gorge] R. Lewin. il *Science* 236:1061-3 My 29 '87

Early human skeleton apes its ancestors [Homo habilis found in Olduvai Gorge by Donald Johanson] B. Bower. il *Sci News* 131:340 My 30 '87

Family ties [Homo habilis skeleton unearthed in Olduvai Gorge] il *Sci Am* 257:16+ Jl '87

Lucy gets a younger sister [Homo habilis skeleton unearthed in Olduvai Gorge by Donald Johanson] A. Toufexis. il *Time* 129:63 Je 1 '87

New light on when man came down from the trees [Homo habilis skeleton discovered by Donald Johanson in Olduvai Gorge] S. Budiansky. il *U S News World Rep* 102:10-11 Je 1 '87

Woman of the year, 1.8 million B.C. [fossils from Olduvai Gorge] il *Newsweek* 109:59 Je 1 '87

Texas
Fossils of ancient bird unearthed in west Texas [Protoavis discovered by Sankar Chatterjee] il *Earth Sci* 40:7 Spr '87

Western States
Dinosaur country. il maps *Sunset* 178:82-91 Je '87

Wyoming
Climbing adaptations in the early Eocene mammal Chriacus and the origin of Artiodactyla. K. D. Rose. bibl f il *Science* 236:314-16 Ap 17 '87

Yugoslavia
Sizing up Neanderthals [work of Rachel Caspari at Krapina site] B. Bower. *Sci News* 131:255 Ap 18 '87

Paleopathology
Bad news bear [prehistoric syphilis] il *Discover* 8:8 D '87

Prehistoric syphilis [found in bear bones] *Sci News* 132:205 S 26 '87

Rising above a prehistoric handicap [adolescent male dwarf skeleton from southern Italy; research by David W. Frayer and others] *Sci News* 132:334 N 21 '87

Why these bones were so weary. S. Budiansky. il *U S News World Rep* 103:68-9 O 19 '87

Paleotemperature *See* Paleoclimatology
Paleozoic period *See* Paleontology—Paleozoic
Palermo (Italy)

Music
See also
Opera—Sicily

Palestine
See also
Art—Palestine

History
See also
Philistines
Zionism

Among the anti-Semites: memoirs of a British Zionist. H. Fairlie. *New Repub* 196:24 Je 8 '87

Palestine Center for Non-Violent Resistance
Seeking justice through nonviolent resistance. W. G. Pippert. *Christ Today* 31:53-4 Mr 20 '87

Palestine Information Office
Minority report [closure of U.S. office] C. Hitchens. *Nation* 245:366 O 10 '87

U.S. orders closure of Palestine Information Office [State Dept. statement, September 15, 1987] *Dep State Bull* 87:43 N '87

Palestine Liberation Organization
Arab vs. Arab over Palestine. D. Pipes. *Commentary* 84:17-25 Jl '87

Arafat makes another comeback [Lebanon] S. Reed. il *Nation* 244:137-41 F 7 '87

Arafat: still first among equals. F. Willey. il por *Newsweek* 109:42 Ap 27 '87

Arafat's answer [meeting in Algiers] *New Repub* 196:9 My 4 '87

Arafat's back, reshaping outlook for Mideast talks. W. L. Chaze. il por *U S News World Rep* 102:40 My 4 '87

Beirut spring [presence of Syrian troops and expected clash with PLO] *New Repub* 196:7-8 Ap 6 '87

Conference call [meeting of the Palestine National Council in Algiers] *Nation* 244:670-1 My 23 '87

Death from the skies [guerrilla attacks Israeli soldiers from hang glider] il *Time* 130:36 D 7 '87

Hussein's game [willingness to enter peace negotiations with Israel independent of the P.L.O.] S. Reed. *Nation* 244:839-40 Je 20 '87

An interview with Yasser Arafat (I). S. MacLeod. bibl f il *N Y Rev Books* 34:36-40 Je 11 '87

An interview with [Yasser] Arafat (II). S. MacLeod. bibl f il pors *N Y Rev Books* 34:41-5 Je 25 '87

Israel and the Palestinian question: 1987. K. J. Kelly. *America* 156:424-6 My 23 '87

An Israeli and an Arab tour for peace [views of M. Peled] J. M. Wall. *Christ Century* 104:427-8 My 6 '87

Minority report [State Dept. orders closing of Washington information office] C. Hitchens. *Nation* 245:366 O 10 '87

On the brink of cannibalism [food shortage at Beirut refugee camps] il *Time* 129:55 F 23 '87

Security Council 'vigorously' condemns Israeli 'aggression' against Tunisian territory. il *UN Chron* 22:3-6 N/D '85

A show of PLO unity. J. Bierman. il por *Macleans* 100:27 My 4 '87

Show of unity [meeting of the Palestine National Council] il por *Time* 129:40 My 4 '87

The siege of the camps [Palestinians in Lebanon]. N. Cooper. il *Newsweek* 109:34 F 23 '87

U.S. orders closure of Palestine Information Office [State Dept. statement, September 15, 1987] *Dep State Bull* 87:43 N '87

A voice of hope and moderation [interview with Hassan bin Talal] H. Mackenzie. il por *Macleans* 100:21 Je 22 '87

When Israelis and Palestinians meet [meeting in Rumania, November 1986] Y. Lotan. *Nation* 244:141-2 F 7 '87

Palestinian Arab press
Israel's censored Palestinians. J. Greenberg. *World Press Rev* 34:56 My '87

Palestinian Arab students
A new-breed Palestinian. A. Deming. il *Newsweek* 109:38 Ap 6 '87

Palestinian Arabs
See also
International Day of Solidarity with the Palestinian People
Jewish-Arab relations
Palestine Center for Non-Violent Resistance
United Nations. Committee on the Exercise of the Inalienable Rights of the Palestinian People
United Nations Relief and Works Agency for Palestine Refugees in the Near East
Beirut camps: is the carnival of carnage over? P. R. Range. il *U S News World Rep* 102:14 Ap 20 '87

Palestinian Arabs—*cont.*

Days of rage in the territories [Israeli troops crack down on Arab rioters] M. S. Serrill. il *Time* 130:32 D 28 '87

Edward Said: an exile's exile [interview] M. Stevenson. il *Progressive* 51:30-4 F '87

Interpreting Palestine. E. W. Said. *Harpers* 274:19-22 Mr '87

Invisible Palestinians: ideology and reality in Israel. R. R. Ruether. il *Christ Century* 104:587-91 Jl 1-8 '87

A land that history forgot [Gaza] J. McGeary. il *Time* 130:40 N 30 '87

Myths about Palestinians. K. Christison. bibl f *Foreign Policy* 66:109-27 Spr '87

On the brink of cannibalism [food shortage at Beirut refugee camps] il *Time* 129:55 F 23 '87

The siege of the camps [Palestinians trapped in embattled refugee camps in Lebanon] N. Cooper. il *Newsweek* 109:34 F 23 '87

Trouble in the Holy Land [violence in the West Bank and Gaza] E. Silver. il *Macleans* 100:40-1 D 28 '87

Violence in Gaza. A. Kenan. *Nation* 245:777-8 D 26 '87-Ja 2 '88

'We hate the occupation' [insurrection in the Gaza Strip] R. Watson. il *Newsweek* 110:25 D 28 '87

Education

The Palestinian campus [Birzeit University] L. Wolfe. il *N Y Times Mag* p67-8+ Ap 19 '87

Employment

Force for change in the West Bank [Palestinian labor movement] J. R. Hiltermann. il *Nation* 245:338-40 O 3 '87

Palestinian question *See* Israel-Arab Wars, 1967- : Jewish-Arab relations; United Nations—Middle East

Palevsky, Max, 1924-

about

California crafted. il *House Gard* 159:182-9 Ap '87

Paley, Maggie

Squash: the court of appeal. il *Harpers Bazaar* 120:130+ O '87

Paley, Vivian Gussin, 1929-

about

Smart, magical, funny 3-year-olds. P. La Farge. il pors *Parents* 62:160-4+ N '87

Paley, William S., 1901-

about

The last tycoon. J. Cooney and G. Winslow. il pors *Channels* 7:34-5 F '87

A legendary chairman. P. Baida. il *Am Herit* 38:16+ Jl/Ag '87

Nice cop, tough cop. E. Diamond. pors *N Y* 20:14+ F 9 '87

O.K., Larry and Bill, take your places. It's showtime. D. Lieberman and M. N. Vamos. il por *Bus Week* p36-7 Ja 26 '87

Palimony

5 of 6 charges dismissed against 'Miami Vice' star [P. M. Thomas] *Jet* 72:28 Je 22 '87

Eric Dickerson must pay pregnant ex-girlfriend. pors *Jet* 72:25 S 7 '87

White ex-girlfriend hits Dickerson with paternity and palimony lawsuits [E. Dickerson] pors *Jet* 72:52 Ag 3 '87

Palinkas, Almuth

Comment. il *Am Craft* 47:20+ D '87/Ja '88

Palio di Siena (Italy)

Photographs and photography

Passion in the piazza [with report by Sam Toperoff] L. Stewart. il *Sports Illus* 67:42-9 Jl 20 '87

Palladin, Jean-Louis

about

Fresh from the sea. J. Nathan. il *N Y Times Mag* p67-8 Mr 22 '87

Palladium (New York, N.Y.: Dance hall) *See* New York (N.Y.)—Dance halls

Pallas (Asteroid) *See* Asteroids

Pallottine Institute for Lay Leadership and Apostolate Research

Strong support for dialogue [conference entitled Faith and culture: historic moment for American Catholic laity?] *America* 156:186-7 Mr 7 '87

Pally, Marcia

The 16th New Directors/New Films Series. il *Film Comment* 23:65-9 My/Je '87

Beineix blue. il pors *Film Comment* 23:21-4 Ja/F '87

'Farbrengen' my baby back home. il por *Film Comment* 23:75-7 My/Je '87

'Giselle' goes to Hollywood. il por *Film Comment* 23:80+ S/O '87

Kurys makes her bed. il por *Film Comment* 23:84-6 S/O '87

Palm Bay (Fla.)

Crime

Carnage at a shopping mall [W. Cruse's killing spree] *Macleans* 100:24 My 4 '87

Palm Beach (Fla.)

Sports

Palm Beach game plan. A. Ash. il *Harpers Bazaar* 120:122-33+ Je '87

Palm Beach Gardens (Fla.)

Crime

The case against Brian Spencer [accused of M. Dalfo's murder] P. Dexter. il *Sports Illus* 66:98-102+ My 11 '87

Palm Dairies Ltd.

Unicorp fuels a fight [sale of Palm Dairies blocked by Competition Act tribunal] T. Fennell. il *Macleans* 100:14-15 Ja 5 '87

Palm Springs (Calif.)

Water supply

Drink and be merry. E. Paris. il *Forbes* 140:42+ Ag 10 '87

Palm trees *See* Palms

Palme, Olof, 1927-1986

about

Rhetoric and reality in the Iranian arms trade. P. Gupte. il por *Forbes* 140:32-5 O 19 '87

Assassination

The Palme obsession. R. Reeves. il pors *N Y Times Mag* p20-4+ Mr 1 '87

Palmer, Arnold, 1929-

about

Seven ahead, nine to go, and then . . . R. Reilly. il *Sports Illus* 66:62-6+ Je 15 '87

Palmer, Charles

about

Big man in the kitchen. L. Wells. il pors *N Y Times Mag* p40-1+ D 13 '87

Catch as chef can. M. Burros. il por *N Y Times Mag* p75-6 Je 14 '87

Palmer, Don

Sounds of the Caribbean. il *Black Enterp* 17:42-4 My '87

Palmer, Mark J.

Guarding Neptune's sacred grounds. il *Sierra* 72:20+ N/D '87

Palmer, Parker J.

Community, conflict, and ways of knowing [address, March 1987] il *Change* 19:20-5 S/O '87

Palmer, Paul

about

Great-grandma dies after getting good draft news. por *Jet* 72:46 My 18 '87

Palmer, Robert

In the lair of the lusca. il *Nat Hist* 96:42-7 Ja '87

Palmer, Ronald DeWayne

about

The untold story of black ambassador who weds Asian princess. S. Booker. il pors *Jet* 73:12+ O 12 '87

Palmer, Thelma

Maple tree [poem] *Rodale's Org Gard* 34:102 D '87

Palmer, Tim

The Kings up close: focus on a threatened river. *Sierra* 72:43 Ja/F '87

Le Palmier (New York, N.Y.: Restaurant) *See* New York (N.Y.)—Restaurants, nightclubs, bars, etc.

Palmieri, Eddie

about

Eddie Palmieri/Hilton Ruiz/Papo Lucca. L. Birnbaum. il *Down Beat* 54:52-3 Ag '87

Palmieri, Victor H.

about

Only 'high-profile' disasters need apply. il por *Bus Week* p112 S 21 '87

Palms

Diseases and pests

The curse of cadang-cadang [Philippine coconut palm disease] K. Maramorosch. il *Nat Hist* 96:20-2 Jl '87

Palo Alto (Calif.)

Fear and loathing in Palo Alto [lawsuit over cable TV franchises] L. Ballard. *Channels* 7:15 Jl/Ag '87

Paltrow, Bruce

about

Bruce Paltrow. L. Margulies. il por *Channels* 7:26-7+ O '87

Palumbo, Gene

The long trip home. *Commonweal* 114:377 Je 19 '87

Ruben Zamora: politics & belief [interview] il *Commonweal* 114:733-5 D 18 '87

PAM (Payload assist modules) *See* Space vehicles—Propulsion systems

Pamphlets
  Booklets worth writing for [title varies] See issues of Good Housekeeping
  Clothesline literature [folhetos of Brazil] C. Pisa. il *Courier* 39:26-8 D '86
  Freebies and cheapies. *Teen* 31:14+ Ja '87
  Kitchen remodeling how-to-do-it information. D. Chermak. *Fam Handyman* 37:88 Mr '87
  'Teen classifieds. *Teen* 31:38+ Jl '87
  Worth getting. See issues of Changing Times
Pamplin, Robert B., 1911-
about
  Bob Pamplin's second career. G. Eisler. il por *Forbes* 139:182 My 18 '87
Pamplin (R. B.) Corporation See R. B. Pamplin Corporation
Pamplona (Spain)
Social life and customs
  Pamplona in July [excerpt from Dateline Toronto] E. Hemingway. il *50 Plus* 27:50-4 Jl '87
Pamyat (Organization)
  Glasnost's ghosts. W. Laqueur. *New Repub* 197:13-14 Ag 3 '87
  Under *glasnost*, a dark fringe. D. Stanglin. il *U S News World Rep* 102:30 Je 29 '87
Pan Am See Pan American World Airways, Inc.
Pan American Day and Week
  Pan American Day and Week, 1987 [proclamation, April 9, 1987] R. Reagan. *Dep State Bull* 87:86 Jl '87
Pan American Exposition (1901: Buffalo, N.Y.)
Collectibles
  Pan American Exposition wine. M. Wollett and B. Wollett. il *Antiques Collect Hobbies* 92:43 O '87
Pan American Games
  Amateur sports capital prepares for Pan Am Games [Indianapolis] il *Black Enterp* 17:80 Jl '87
  Fast breaks [preview of women's events] M. Kort. il *Women's Sports Fitness* 9:47-8+ Ag '87
  The games countries play [political aspects] il *Newsweek* 110:24-5 Ag 24 '87
  Heavy harps and Pan Am heroes. T. Callahan. il *Time* 130:44-5 Ag 24 '87
  "High" hurdle [Sports Medicine Drug Identification Laboratory] R. Callahan. il *Saturday Evening Post* 259:32-3 Jl/Ag '87
  Joyner-Kersee's record leads U.S. Pan Am team. il por *Jet* 72:50+ Ag 31 '87
  Pan Am Games [special section] il *Sports Illus* 67:18-25 Ag 24 '87
  Pan Am: let the games begin. P. Gambaccini. il *Sport Mag* 78:15 Ag '87
  Pans for the Pan Ams [television coverage] W. Taaffe. il *Sports Illus* 67:87 Ag 24 '87
  Politics snarl the Pan Am Games. D. Carpenter. *Progressive* 51:12 Ag '87
  Racist, sexist comment by CBS sports anchors riles nation's women's groups [comments by B. Packer about J. Gillom] il por *Jet* 72:54 S 14 '87
  Swifter, higher, stronger around the hemisphere. R. Ruck. il *Américas* 39:2-7 Jl/Ag '87
  A U.S.-Cuba showdown. H. Quinn. *Macleans* 100:38 Ag 24 '87
  Upset time. C. Neff. il *Sports Illus* 67:15-17 Ag 31 '87
History
  The Pan American Games: stepping stone to the Olympics. W. Bingham. il *Sports Illus* 67:39+ Jl 27 '87
Pan American Health Organization
  The Americas [cover story; special issue] il *World Health* p2-29 O '87
Pan American World Airways, Inc.
  AMR, Pan Am end pact on Sabre system use [computer reservations system] C. A. Shifrin. *Aviat Week Space Technol* 127:33-4 Ag 24 '87
  Desperately seeking survival. B. Rudolph. il *Time* 129:60 Mr 9 '87
  Exchange of stock signals Pan Am, Braniff merger. *Aviat Week Space Technol* 127:36 D 14 '87
  A high roller moves in on Pan Am [bid by K. Kerkorian] R. Grover. il por *Bus Week* p30-3 N 23 '87
  Pan Am adds flights at Kennedy using separate access system. *Aviat Week Space Technol* 127:119 N 9 '87
  Pan Am, American continue negotiations [joint frequent-flier program] *Aviat Week Space Technol* 127:54 Ag 3 '87
  Pan Am plan to restore profits depends on capacity, labor gains. J. Ott. il *Aviat Week Space Technol* 127:33-4 N 23 '87
  Pan Am seeks labor concessions following $469-million 1986 loss. *Aviat Week Space Technol* 126:34 Mr 30 '87

Pan Am seeks partner/buyer following $400-million loss. J. Ott. *Aviat Week Space Technol* 126:30-1 Mr 2 '87
Pan Am Shuttle aims for half share of Northeast market. *Aviat Week Space Technol* 126:56 Mr 16 '87
Pan Am union coalition attempts buyout. *Aviat Week Space Technol* 127:32 Jl 27 '87
Pan American council examines takeover, restructure plan [K. Kerkorian plan] J. Ott. *Aviat Week Space Technol* 127:34 O 19 '87
Reports of Pan Am's sale may not be greatly exaggerated. C. Hawkins. il *Bus Week* p33 F 2 '87
Sure, Pan Am could be sold—but not 'as is'. G. G. Marcial. il *Bus Week* p108 S 21 '87
This shareholder uprising may give Pan Am a tailwind. G. G. Marcial. por *Bus Week* p130 My 25 '87
Will it be Kerkorian to the rescue at Pan Am? C. Hawkins and R. Grover. il *Bus Week* p57-8 O 19 '87
Yes, Pan Am stock is up. No, the airline isn't healthy. C. Hawkins. il *Bus Week* p37-8 Jl 13 '87
Pan Americanism
See also
  Alliance for Progress
  Monroe Doctrine
  National Year of the Americas (1987)
  Organization of American States
  United States—Foreign relations—Latin America
Pan Books Ltd.
  Macmillan buys out Octopus to be sole owner of Pan for $36.5 million. V. Menkes. *Publ Wkly* 232:15 O 2 '87
Panagakos, Steven
about
  Looking for that significant udder? Try calling the Panagakos family and their new agency, Adopt-A-Cow. il por *People Wkly* 28:89 Jl 20 '87
Panagrellus redivivus embryos See Embryology—Nematodes
Panama
See also
  Americans—Panama
  Economic assistance, Japanese—Panama
  Narcotics laws and regulations—Panama
  Panama (Panama)
  Panama Canal
  Panama Canal Zone
  Rain forests—Panama
  Riots—Panama
  Strikes—Panama
  United States—Diplomatic and consular service—Panama
Economic conditions
  The color of money. C. Lane. il *Newsweek* 110:27 Ag 24 '87
Foreign relations
  "Everyone wants us". A. D. Frank. il *Forbes* 139:37-8 F 23 '87
United States
  See United States—Foreign relations—Panama
Politics and government
See also
  Politics, Corruption in—Panama
  The battle for 50th Street [opposition to M. A. Noriega] N. Cooper. il por *Newsweek* 110:42-3 Ag 10 '87
  Cracking down on Panama's general [M. A. Noriega] C. A. Robbins. il por *U S News World Rep* 103:30 Ag 10 '87
  Defying the strong man [anti-Noriega sentiment] B. Levin. il por *Macleans* 100:18 Ag 10 '87
  Down and dirty [M. A. Noriega's tactics] *Time* 130:42 Ag 17 '87
  The general went to work [opposition to M. A. Noriega] J. Smolowe. il por *Time* 130:21 Ag 10 '87
  The general who won't go [M. A. Noriega; with interview] J. Smolowe. il por *Time* 130:36-8 Jl 20 '87
  Latin America and the Caribbean: the paths to democracy [address, June 30, 1987] E. Abrams. *Dep State Bull* 87:81-5 S '87
  Panama. D. Sussman. *Sch Update* 119:15 Mr 9 '87
  Panama banal: the revolution turns into an all-too-civil war. P. J. O'Rourke. il *Roll Stone* p50-2+ O 8 '87
  Panama: disaster or democracy. R. Arias Calderón. bibl f *Foreign Aff* 66:328-47 Wint '87/'88
  Panama's struggle for democracy. S. C. Ropp. bibl f *Curr Hist* 86:421-4+ D '87
  Sending Reagan a message. F. Willey. il por *Newsweek* 110:30 Jl 13 '87
  Turmoil in Panama has its strongman tottering [M. A. Noriega] S. Baker. il *Bus Week* p42 Ag 3 '87

Panama—Politics and government—*cont.*
Twilight for a dictator? [M. A. Noriega] J. L. Galloway. il por map *U S News World Rep* 103:29-31 Jl 20 '87
U.S. and Panama—push comes to shove. J. L. Galloway. il por *U S News World Rep* 103:17 Jl 13 '87

Panama (Panama)
Buses
See Panama (Panama)—Transit systems
Riots
A colonel takes on the general [charges against M. A. Noriega] M. S. Serrill. il por *Time* 129:40 Je 22 '87
Dishonor thy general [accusations against M. A. Noriega] H. Anderson. il por *Newsweek* 109:37 Je 22 '87
The rumbles grow in the isthmus [charges against M. A. Noriega] M. Satchell. il por *U S News World Rep* 102:18 Je 22 '87
Transit systems
Panama's moving murals [decorated buses] M. L. Wilkinson. il *Américas* 39:44-7 Mr/Ap '87

Panama Canal
Trouble ahead for the Canal? [deforestation may cause water shortage] J. Borrell. il *Time* 129:63 Mr 2 '87
Turmoil in Panama has its strongman tottering [M. A. Noriega] S. Baker. il *Bus Week* p42 Ag 3 '87
History
Across the isthmus. O. Jaén Suárez. il *Américas* 39:28-35 My/Je '87

Panama Canal Treaties (1977)
The Panama Canal Treaties: looking back—and ahead. A. H. Moss, Jr. *Américas* 39:53-4 My/Je '87
The Panama Canal Treaties: negotiating a new order. C. A. López Guevara. *Américas* 39:52-3 My/Je '87

Panama Canal Zone
In the Zone: the end of an American enclave. J. Borrell. il *Time* 130:8-9 Jl 20 '87

Panama City (Panama) *See* Panama (Panama)

Panavia Aircraft GmbH
Eurofighter, Panavia explore restructuring of EFA program [European fighter aircraft] il *Aviat Week Space Technol* 126:65 Je 29 '87

Pancake eating competitions *See* Eating—Competitions

Pancakes, waffles, etc.
See also
Crêpes
Feast before fast. J. Pruess. il *N Y Times Mag* p57-8 Mr 1 '87
The perfect pancake. K. Haedrich. il *Ctry J* 14:18-21 Ja '87
Potato cakes. D. L. Parker. il *Gourmet* 47:82-3+ O '87

Pancreas
Cancer
Genetic aspects
Pancreatic neoplasia induced by SV40 T-antigen expression in acinar cells of transgenic mice. D. M. Ornitz and others. bibl f il *Science* 238:188-93 O 9 '87
Diseases
See also
Diabetes
Transplantation
Islet allograft survival after a single course of treatment of recipient with antibody to L3T4. J. A. Shizuru and others. bibl il *Science* 237:278-80 Jl 17 '87
Sweet success in freezing islets. S. Weisburd. *Sci News* 132:47 Jl 18 '87

Pandas
The ancestry of the giant panda [molecular analysis; cover story] S. J. O'Brien. il map *Sci Am* 257:102-7 N '87
New plan drafted to save the panda. J. Raloff. *Sci News* 131:168 Mr 14 '87
Panda outposts [Wolong Natural Reserve] G. E. Machlis and K. Johnson. il map *Natl Parks* 61:14-16 S/O '87
Pandas [J. A. Cohen's work in securing loan of pandas from Beijing for the Bronx Zoo] *New Yorker* 63:23-4 Ap 13 '87
Take a ganda at this panda, the queen of China's bear market and now the zoo's who of N.Y.C. il *People Wkly* 27:79 My 18 '87
The whole world goes pandas [Chinese pandas at the Bronx Zoo] G. Clarke. il *Time* 129:79 My 11 '87

Panel saws *See* Saws and sawing

Paneling
How to install solid wood paneling. P. Barrett. il *Pop Mech* 164:123-6 Ja '87
Paneling in unexpected places. A. W. Lees. il *Pop Sci* 230:72-4 Ap '87
Paneling: new looks for old walls. V. Hahn. il *Parents* 62:180-2+ Ap '87

Redwood renovation. J. Truini. il *Pop Mech* 164:112-14+ Ap '87
Texture, pattern, and color with solid wood paneling. il *Sunset* 178:124-5 Mr '87

Panelized houses *See* Houses, Prefabricated

Panfilov, Gleb
about
After seven years Gleb Panfilov's film, Tema, sees daylight at last and wrests an award from Platoon. S. K. Reed. il pors *People Wkly* 27:57-8 Ap 6 '87
Theme [film] Reviews
New Repub 197:24-5 O 26 '87. S. Kauffmann

Panfish fishing
Double duty [fly tackle for trout works for panfish] C. Hauptman. il *Field Stream* 92:48-9+ Ag '87

Pang, Eul-Soo, and Jarnagin, Laura
Brazil's Cruzado Plan. bibl f *Curr Hist* 86:13-16+ Ja '87

Panhandle Eastern Corporation
Most improved. il *Forbes* 139:165 Ja 12 '87
The performance took a beating, the paychecks didn't [R. D. Hunsucker] J. E. Davis and K. Deveny. il pors *Bus Week* p54 My 4 '87

Panhandling *See* Begging and beggars

Panic disorder *See* Anxiety

Panic of 1837 *See* Business depression, 1837

Panic of 1893 *See* Business depression, 1893

Panics (Finance) *See* Business depression

Pankey, Eric
Into happiness [poem] *New Repub* 196:41 F 16 '87

Pankratz, David B.
Toward an integrated study of cultural and educational policy. bibl f *Des Arts Educ* 89:12-21 N/D '87

Panmure Gordon & Company
Panmure Gordon & Co. [interview with M. Henderson] il por *Fortune* 116 Sp Issue:182-3 Fall '87

Pannenberg, Wolfhart, 1928-
about
Pannenberg on Marxism: insights and generalizations. S. Grenz. *Christ Century* 104:824-6 S 30 '87

Panoramic photography *See* Photography, Panoramic

Pantell, Richard, 1951-
about
Richard Pantell. F. Johnson. il *Am Artist* 51:64-7+ F '87

Pantex
The present and the apocalypse. C. Widmann. *World Press Rev* 34:51 Mr '87

Pantheon Books, Inc.
Random buys Schocken for unit of Pantheon. *Publ Wkly* 232:101 Jl 24 '87

Panthers
See also
Pumas

Panthers, Florida *See* Pumas

Pantomime
See also
Mime

Pants
Smart on-the-go getters [J. Bruno and E. Mondale] il pors *Harpers Bazaar* 120:290-7 Mr '87

Pantyhose *See* Hosiery

Panza di Biumo, Giuseppe
about
MOCA-Panza dispute settled. R. W. Walker. *Art News* 86:21-2 Mr '87
Williams College coup. C. Giuliano. *Art News* 86:58+ Summ '87

Pao, Y. K.
about
A free market? J. Willoughby. il por *Forbes* 139:158 Mr 23 '87

Pap test
Pap comes home. C. P. Weinstock. *Health* 19:21 Mr '87
Pap smears: a closer look. R. Lewis. il *Health* 19:69-70+ Ap '87
Pap smears: what every woman must know. B. Weinhouse. *Ladies Home J* 104:104+ O '87
A sexually transmitted cancer virus [views of D. Norman Dahm on papilloma viruses] C. SerVaas. il *Saturday Evening Post* 259:104-5 My/Je '87

Papa Manteo's Life-Sized Marionettes *See* Puppets and puppet plays

Papacy
Of many things [Patrick Granfield's The limits of the papacy] G. W. Hunt. *America* 157:234 O 17 '87

Papain
Not an ant-idote [effectiveness of meat tenderizer in treating fire ant stings] *Sci News* 131:374 Je 13 '87

Papandreou, Andreas George
about
Papandreou's 'whipping boy'. N. Cooper. il por *Newsweek* 110:35 Jl 27 '87
While Andreas Papandreou, Greece's prime minister, dallies with a dame, all *hellas* is breaking loose. il pors *People Wkly* 28:62 O 26 '87

Papandreou, Margaret
about
Margarita Papandreou [interview] C. Dreifus. il *Progressive* 51:21-4 D '87

Papanek, John
Athletes or role models? Demanding higher standards from players is unrealistic. por *Sports Illus* 66:84 Je 15 '87
A lot of hurt: inaction got Kareem creamed. il pors *Sports Illus* 67:89-92+ O 19 '87
A series for the ages. il *Sports Illus* 66:76+ My 4 '87

Papayas
See also
Papain

Papazian, Diane M., and others
Cloning of genomic and complementary DNA from Shaker, a putative potassium channel gene from Drosophila. bibl f il *Science* 237:749-53 Ag 14 '87

Paper
See also
Photographic paper
Preservation
For the record [National Archives documents] *Sci Am* 256:59-60 Ja '87
Preserving the past. il *Futurist* 21:40-1 Ja/F '87
Prices
Paper buying strategies. J. P. Frank. *Publ Wkly* 232:42-3 N 20 '87
Paper prices climb in Asia. S. A. Taylor. *Publ Wkly* 232:47 S 4 '87
Standards
Book publishers are attracting a wide range of new paper grades. *Publ Wkly* 231:258 My 15 '87
Lighter-weight paper for mass market 'Whirlwind' saves Avon some heavy cost. J. P. Frank. il *Publ Wkly* 232:59-63 O 16 '87
Warren introduces glare-free and lightweight gloss grades to book publishers. il *Publ Wkly* 231:254+ My 15 '87

Paper airplanes *See* Airplane models
Paper dolls
Collectors and collecting
Cutouts of fashion [collection of C. Musser] J. Ware. il por *Americana* 15:41-5 Jl/Ag '87

Paper industry
See also
American Paper Institute
Fort Howard Paper Co.
Georgia-Pacific Corp.
International Paper Co.
James River Corp. of Virginia
Paper mills
S. D. Warren Co.
Stone Container Corp.
Wood pulp industry
Book publishers are attracting a wide range of new paper grades. *Publ Wkly* 231:258 My 15 '87
Paper buying strategies. J. P. Frank. *Publ Wkly* 232:42-3 N 20 '87
Acquisitions and mergers
International aspects
An Irishman feasts on American trees [M. Smurfit] K. Labich. il por *Fortune* 116:62-4+ Jl 20 '87
Export-import trade
Paper prices climb in Asia. S. A. Taylor. *Publ Wkly* 232:47 S 4 '87
Finance
Paper. K. K. Wiegner. il *Forbes* 139:204-5 Ja 12 '87
Reams of profits for the paper business. J. B. Levine. il *Bus Week* p87 Ja 12 '87
East Asia
Paper prices climb in Asia. S. A. Taylor. *Publ Wkly* 232:47 S 4 '87
Ireland
See also
Jefferson Smurfit Group Ltd.

Paper industry workers
See also
Strikes—Paper industry workers

Paper mills
Environmental aspects
Alarm over paper goods [dioxin contamination] M. Gray. *Macleans* 100:57-8 O 26 '87

Scientist Vladimir Fialkov focuses on the future of a unique natural wonder: crystalline Lake Baikal. S. K. Reed. il pors *People Wkly* 27:121+ Ap 6 '87
Showdown over pollution [Kimberly-Clark paper mill on Lake Superior ordered to install pollution controls] S. Aikenhead. il *Macleans* 100:81 F 2 '87
Warning: the Friday night fish fry may be hazardous to your health [pollution of Wisconsin's Fox River and Green Bay by waste from the Fort Howard Paper Co.] M. Hudson. il maps *Audubon* 89:24-6+ Jl '87

Paper money
See also
Bank notes
Confederate money
The man who put God's trust in your pocket! [motto on paper money suggested by M. H. Rothert] E. Rochette. il *Antiques Collect Hobbies* 92:80-1 Jl '87
Papal visit recalls America's "Catholic note"! [1869 dollar] E. Rochette. il *Antiques Collect Hobbies* 92:76-7 S '87
Yesterday's lemon is today's watermelon! [Panic of 1893 and issuance of watermelon notes] E. Rochette. il *Antiques Collect Hobbies* 92:71-2 Ap '87

Paper money in art
The Monet of money paints himself into a corner [J. S. G. Boggs to be prosecuted in England for his reproductions of legal tender] il por *People Wkly* 27:77 Mr 2 '87
Exhibitions
Making money [The fine art of making money] R. Green. il *Art News* 86:174 F '87

Paper products
See also
Paper towels
Contamination
Alarm over paper goods [dioxin contamination] M. Gray. *Macleans* 100:57-8 O 26 '87

Paper towels
Paper towels. il *Consum Rep* 52:581-3 S '87
Paper towels. il *Consum Rep* 52:48-50 D '87

Paper work (Art)
See also
Decoupage
Papier-mâché
Paper and plants, simple and cheerful [Christmas decorations] il *Sunset* 179:64-7 D '87

Paperback book covers *See* Book covers
Paperback books
See also
Publishers and publishing—Paperback books
Soft covers for children. S. Wilkinson. *N Y Times Book Rev* 92:47 My 3 '87
Bibliography
See also
Best sellers
Forecasts. See issues of Publishers Weekly
Great summer paperbacks. L. Mathews. il *Glamour* 85:104+ Jl '87
Paperbacks: new and noteworthy. See issues of The New York Times Book Review
Reads: picking through the paperbacks. C. McGee. il *N Y* 20:140+ Je 29-Jl 6 '87
Trade paperbacks. *Publ Wkly* 232:353-83 Ag 7 '87
Collectors and collecting
See Books—Collectors and collecting
Marketing
Bantam mixed-media promotions feature audio, paperbacks. il *Publ Wkly* 231:31-2 Mr 27 '87

Paperhanging *See* Wallpaper and wallpapering
Papert, Seymour
about
Computers in the classroom. A. Bass. il por *Technol Rev* 90:52-62+ Ap '87
Now even Lego is going high-tech. P. Angiolillo and M. Bluestone. il *Bus Week* p40 Ag 17 '87

Paperweights
See also
Lampwork (Paperweights)
Collectors and collecting
Columbian Exposition paperweight. M. Wollett and B. Wollett. il *Antiques Collect Hobbies* 92:21 D '87
Columbus paperweight. M. Wollett and B. Wollett. il *Antiques Collect Hobbies* 92:29 My '87

Paperwork (Art) *See* Paper work (Art)
Papier-mâché
Collectors and collecting
Antiques: papier-mâché. A. Berman. il *Archit Dig* 44:108-13+ Jl '87

Papilloma viruses
See also
Human papilloma virus

Papilloma viruses—*cont.*
A promoter with an internal regulatory domain is part of the origin of replication in BPV-1 [bovine papilloma virus] A. Stenlund and others. bibl f il *Science* 236:1666-71 Je 26 '87

Papillote cooking
Seafood en papillote [salmon and halibut steak] il *Good Housekeep* 204:42 Mr '87

Papp, Tony
about
Another Papp sparkles. S. Mieses. il por *N Y* 20:14 Ja 5 '87

Papua New Guinea
See also
Earthquakes—Papua New Guinea
Eating—Papua New Guinea
Saint Matthias Islands (Papua New Guinea)

Parachutes
Developmental Sciences tests parafoil recovery on Skyeye RPV. il *Aviat Week Space Technol* 126:92 Je 1 '87
Probe of Harrier crash focuses on emergency parachute system. D. A. Brown. il *Aviat Week Space Technol* 127:30-1 N 2 '87
This parachute keeps the whole plane aloft. P. Houston. il *Bus Week* p86 N 2 '87

Parachuting
My first jump [skydiving at age 70] D. Fitzpatrick. il *Read Dig* 130:29-30+ Mr '87
Accidents and injuries
A miraculous sky rescue [G. Robertson rescues fellow skydiver] il por *Time* 129:26 My 4 '87
Rescue in midair! [G. Robertson saves free-falling parachutist D. Williams] P. O. D'Aulaire and E. D'Aulaire. il *Read Dig* 131:100-5 N '87

Parade balloons *See* Balloons

Parade floats
Mechanics go bowling [electronic Bubble Trouble float in the 1986 Tournament of Roses parade] il *Pop Mech* 164:43 Ja '87
Parading the Constitution ["We the People 200" parade in Philadelphia] B. Weber. il *N Y Times Mag* p162 S 13 '87

Parades
Equipment
See also
Glendale Industries
California
See also
Pasadena (Calif.)—Parades
New York (State)
See also
New York (N.Y.)—Parades
Pennsylvania
See also
Philadelphia (Pa.)—Parades

Paradox
See also
Olbers' paradox

Paradyne Corp.
Picking up the pieces at Paradyne. G. DeGeorge. il por *Bus Week* p102 Ap 6 '87

Parafoils *See* Parachutes

Paraguay
See also
Asunción (Paraguay)
Description and travel
Paraguay's mission towns. B. Wrenn. il *Travel Holiday* 168:8+ O '87
Politics and government
See also
Politics, Corruption in—Paraguay
Paraguay's Stroessner: losing control? J. H. Williams. bibl f *Curr Hist* 86:25-8+ Ja '87
Trying to ignore the winds of change [special section] il *World Press Rev* 34:26-8 D '87
Religious institutions and affairs
See also
Church and civil rights—Paraguay
Missions—Paraguay

Parajon, Gustavo
about
Evangelical leader named to national peace commission. S. Wykstra. il por *Christ Today* 31:52 O 2 '87

Parallax
Star tracks [Solar Neighborhood Astrometric Parallax Survey] D. E. Thomsen. il *Sci News* 131:140-2 F 28 '87

Parallel processing (Computers)
See also
Multiprocessors

Advanced computer architectures. G. C. Fox and P. C. Messina. bibl (p183) il *Sci Am* 257:66-74 O '87
Computing cornucopia [massively parallel machines] T. Beardsley. *Sci Am* 257:22 D '87
Concurrency. M. Stern. il *Radio-Electron* 58 ComputerDigest:112-14 F '87
Concurrent PC DOS. W. Rash, Jr. *Byte* 12:226-8 Mr '87
Concurrent programming in Turbo Pascal. M. S. Krishnamoorthy and S. Agnarsson. il *Byte* 12:127-30+ Ap '87
The Connection Machine. D. Hillis. il *Sci Am* 256:108-15 Je '87
Exploiting highly concurrent computers for physics. K. C. Bowler and others. bibl f il *Phys Today* 40:40-8 O '87
Intel and Sequent kiss and make up [80386 microprocessors] J. W. Wilson. il *Bus Week* p120 My 25 '87
Modeling the brain. M. Zeidenberg. bibl il *Byte* 12:237-8+ D '87
Parallel paths [massively parallel processor] I. Peterson. il *Sci News* 131:28-30 Ja 10 '87
Programming for advanced computing. D. Gelernter. bibl (p183) il *Sci Am* 257:90-6+ O '87
The search for a thinking computer. N. Doi and others. il *Courier* 40:16-19 Jl '87

Paralysis
See also
Cerebral palsy
Parkinson's disease
Therapy
Pressure to find a cure. J. Barber. il por *Macleans* 100:38-9 Mr 30 '87

Paralytics
Against all odds: Suzy Gilstrap. M. Altman. il por *Seventeen* 46:214 Ag '87
At home with Tira [J. Wolff, mother of quadriplegic daughter] M. Weissman. il por *Ms* 16:36+ S '87
The end of an odyssey [wheelchair athlete R. Hansen] M. Gray. il por *Macleans* 100:46+ Je 1 '87
First Andres Vasquez learned about pain, suffering and patience; then he became a doctor. J. Calio. il pors *People Wkly* 28:73-4 Ag 17 '87
A hero comes home [wheelchair athlete R. Hansen; cover story; special section] il pors map *Macleans* 100:34-40+ Mr 30 '87
A lesson of love [paraplegic wife and mother] K. Burns. il por *Ladies Home J* 104:20+ D '87
Monkeys with helping hands [capuchin monkeys aid quadriplegics: work of M. J. Willard] J. T. MacFadyen. il por *Read Dig* 131:38-43 Ag '87
Paralyzed after a near-fatal accident, director Jack Hofsiss stages a dramatic comeback; ed. by Bonnie Johnson. J. Hofsiss. il pors *People Wkly* 28:131-2+ S 14 '87
Paraplegic Rick Hansen proves a wheelchair is no handicap with a 25,000-mile marathon. W. Plummer. il pors *People Wkly* 27:36-8+ Ap 27 '87

Paramount Pictures Corp.
'The best show in town': a big birthday album from Paramount. T. O'Neill. il *Life* 10:130-4+ Ap '87
Murphy to do 'Fences' as part of new Paramount contract worth millions. il por *Jet* 72:56 S 14 '87
Paramount's hot streak is untouchable—for now. R. Grover. il por *Bus Week* p153 S 14 '87
The studio with the Midas touch. M. Reese. il *Newsweek* 110:62-3 D 14 '87
You don't know them—but they know moviegoers [D. Simpson and J. Bruckheimer] R. Grover. il pors *Bus Week* p166+ My 25 '87

Paramount Pictures Corp. Television Group
Family ties: the day-care center a TV show built [G. D. Goldberg and Paramount studio's day care center] N. Gittelson. il *McCalls* 114:61-4 Ag '87

Paranaguá, Paulo Antonio
'Cinema novo'. il *Courier* 39:33-6 D '86

Paranoia
Paranoia for fun and profit [on the job paranoia] S. Bing. il *Esquire* 107:40 F '87

Parapsychology
See also
Channelers
Extrasensory perception
Psychics
Spiritualism
Antimatter. See issues of Omni (New York, N.Y.)
Censoring the paranormal. J. Clark. *Omni* 9:33 F '87
Great Britain
Physics and psychics [discussion of May 1986 article, Physics and psychic research in Victorian and Edwardian England] J. Oppenheim. *Phys Today* 40:144-5 My '87

Parapsychology and archeology
Walk like an Egyptian [excerpt from The search for Omm Sety] J. Cott. il *Omni* 9:66-8+ Jl '87
Parapsychology and criminal investigation
Clairvoyant crime busters [work of J. Catchings] R. Wolkomir and J. Wolkomir. il por *McCalls* 115:162-4+ O '87
Courtroom psychics. H. E. Goldfluss. *Omni* 9:12 Jl '87
Parapsychology and disarmament
A Twilight Zone defense? [U. Geller's influence on U.S.-Soviet negotiations] D. Gates. il por *Newsweek* 109:5 My 11 '87
Pararajasegaram, R.
Partners in eye health. il *World Health* p6-8 My '87
Parasite-host relationships *See* Host-parasite relationships
Parasites
    See also
    Fleas
    Host-parasite relationships
    Lice
    Plasmodium (Parasite)
    Protozoa, Pathogenic
    Ticks
    Trematodes
    Trypanosomes
    Wasps
Parasitic diseases
    See also
    Babesiosis
    Giardiasis
    Onchocerciasis
    Q fever
    Schistosomiasis
    Toxoplasmosis
        Vaccines and vaccination
Parasite vaccine hunt follows new roads. D. D. Edwards. *Sci News* 131:181 Mr 21 '87
Parasitic plants
    See also
    Air plants
    Mistletoe
    Witchweed
Parathyroid hormone
New tumor factor may disrupt calcium levels [development of hypercalcemia in cancer patients] D. M. Barnes. bibl il *Science* 237:363-4 Jl 24 '87
A parathyroid hormone-related protein implicated in malignant hypercalcemia: cloning and expression. L. J. Suva and others. bibl f il *Science* 237:893-6 Ag 21 '87
Parathyroid hormone-related protein of malignancy: active synthetic fragments. B. E. Kemp and others. bibl f il *Science* 238:1568-70 D 11 '87
Similarity of synthetic peptide from human tumor to parathyroid hormone in vivo and in vitro. N. Horiuchi and others. bibl f il *Science* 238:1566-8 D 11 '87
Parcel post
    See also
    Air freight service
There's still time to get it there [Christmas gifts] D. Moreau. il *Changing Times* 41:113-14 D '87
What's the best way to send presents? [eight package delivery services] il *Consum Rep* 52:662-6 N '87
Parcells, Bill
        about
A Giants man, all the way. J. Kaplan. il pors *N Y Times Mag* p28-30+ S 6 '87
Sports. E. Pooley. il por *N Y* 20:136-7 S 21 '87
Parchment paper in cooking *See* Papillote cooking
Pardee, Scott
        about
'We're giving assets away' [interview] por *U S News World Rep* 103:60-1 N 16 '87
Pardes, Herbert, 1934-
First word. il *Omni* 9:6 Ja '87
Pardo, Arvid
        about
Hope amid hopelessness: a conversation about arms control with Arvid Pardo. M. Davidson. il por *USA Today (Periodical)* 115:26-8 Ja '87
Pardo de Carugati, Dirma
Leaving yesterday behind. il *World Press Rev* 34:28 D '87
Pardon, Leonard
        about
Going with the grain of tradition. S. Wood. il por *Home Mech* 83:62-3 Mr '87
Pardon
    See also
    Amnesty
    Forgiveness

Begging his pardon [possible presidential pardon for J. M. Poindexter and O. L. North] J. V. Lamar, Jr. il *Time* 130:16-17 Ag 3 '87
Nancy: no pardons [opposition to pardoning O. North and J. Poindexter over Iranscam] L. Howard. por *Newsweek* 110:7 N 30 '87
No pardon [presidential pardon for O. North and J. Poindexter] *New Repub* 197:7-9 D 28 '87
Pardon? [discussion of presidential pardon for J. Poindexter and O. North] F. Barnes. *New Repub* 196:13-15 Ja 5-12 '87
Pardon my Spanish [presidential pardon for J. Poindexter and O. North] R. Paulson. *New Repub* 197:4+ Ag 10-17 '87
Rangel urges Congress to clear record of Garvey. *Jet* 72:22 Ap 20 '87
Paree, Paul
The beauty of humble things. il *Petersens Photogr Mag* 16:58-9 My '87
Pareles, Jon
Music. See issues of Mademoiselle
Parent, Gail
        about
Panic attack? No. Sex with a new man can be funny if Gail Parent writes the script. J. Powell. il por *Glamour* 85:250 N '87
Parent and child (Law)
    See also
    Adoption and adopted children
    Baby Doe rules
    Custody of children
    Paternity
    Support (Domestic relations)
Abortion law complications [parental notification argument before the Supreme Court] *Christ Today* 31:47+ D 11 '87
Can states restrict a minor's access to abortion? [upcoming Supreme Court decision] *Christ Today* 31:44+ Ap 3 '87
Fighting to see the grandkids they love. F. Greve. *50 Plus* 27:18-20 Ap '87
"Nana, I can't visit you". B. Lindeman. il *50 Plus* 27:4 Jl '87
Parents also have rights [teenage pregnancy] R. Gunnerson. por *Newsweek* 109:10-11 Mr 2 '87
Teenagers and abortion [parental consent] B. Kantrowitz. *Newsweek* 110:81 O 12 '87
This is what you thought: 59% disapprove of gay couples adopting children [results of survey] *Glamour* 85:63 Ja '87
When the children visit the weekend parent. J. K. Rosemond. il *Better Homes Gard* 65:56 My '87
Parent-child relationship
    See also
    Adoption and adopted children
    Aged—Family relationships
    Cancer patients—Family relationships
    Child abuse
    Children—Management and training
    Children of alcoholics
    Children of artists
    Children of celebrities
    Children of divorced parents
    Children of drug addicts
    Children of executives
    Children of hippies
    Children of Holocaust survivors
    Children of homosexuals
    Children of prisoners
    Children of prostitutes
    Children of rock musicians
    Children of separated parents
    Children of servicemen
    Children of the deaf
    Children of the mentally ill
    Children of the rich
    Children of working parents
    Homeless children
    Love, Maternal
    Maternal deprivation
    Paternal deprivation
    Sick—Family relationships
    Stepparents and stepchildren
    Youth—Management and training
10 tips on talking with your child. M. B. Brinley. il *McCalls* 114:53 Ag '87
The aged mother. R. Rosenblatt. il *Time* 129:78 Je 1 '87
All in the family [views of E. Maccoby] E. Hall. il pors *Psychol Today* 21:54-8+ N '87

Parent-child relationship—*cont.*

Are you picking up your parents' bad habits? [teenagers] D. Gage and M. Hibsch. il *Seventeen* 46:132+ Mr '87

Attention, shoppers! [shopping with mom] R. Ascher. il *Seventeen* 46:235 Ag '87

Baby love [parent-child relationship's role in development of adult beliefs about romance; studies by Phillip Shaver and Cindy Hazan] M. Roberts. *Psychol Today* 21:22 Mr '87

A baseball for dad [ball autographed by S. Musial] P. Thomson. il *Read Dig* 130:13-14+ Mr '87

Being there. P. Theroux. il *Parents* 62:56+ O '87

Blame the kid, not the parent [problem children; study by Kathleen E. Anderson] V. Bozzi. il *Psychol Today* 21:16 Mr '87

Bonding: eight years later. D. F. Bjorklund and B. Bjorklund. il *Parents* 62:160 F '87

Bound to bicker [adolescents] L. D. Steinberg. il *Psychol Today* 21:36-9 S '87

Children affect parents' mental health [study by Debra Umberson] il *USA Today (Periodical)* 116:9 S '87

Choosing between your lover and your family. C. L. Mithers. *Glamour* 85:334 Ap '87

Daughter/mother. A. Sheedy. il pors *Ms* 16:158-9 Jl/Ag '87

A daughter's father. R. Sandza. il *N Y Times Mag* p59 F 1 '87

Dear Dad [letters from celebrities to their fathers; excerpts] L. N. Cox. *Ladies Home J* 104:53 Je '87

Depressed moms: mixed messages for kids [research by Zvia Breznitz and Tracy Sherman] E. Grant. *Psychol Today* 21:14 O '87

"Don't forget to eat!" [parents and adult children] E. Handman. *Read Dig* 131:23-4 Jl '87

Equal is less [problem of favoritism; with editorial comment by Elizabeth Crow] A. Faber and E. Mazlish. il *Parents* 62:10, 96-100 Ap '87

Father bonding. R. B. McCall. il *Parents* 62:133 Ja '87

Father of the bride [D. Fox's relationship with his daughter] J. Adler. il pors *Esquire* 107:170-2+ Je '87

Fathers and sons [excerpt from Father to the man] C. Hallowell. il *Glamour* 85:68+ Je '87

A father's pictures [family history through photographs] D. Pitchford. il *N Y Times Mag* p44 Jl 12 '87

Fierce attachments [memoir of mother-daughter relationship; excerpts] V. Gornick. il por *Ms* 15:52-4+ Je '87

Gentle into that good night [son learns to accept father's impending death] W. Wangerin. il por *Christ Today* 31:23-5 N 6 '87

The gold watch [son's separation from parents] G. Jellinek. il *N Y Times Mag* p42 Je 28 '87

Good grades for day-care [day-care and infant-mother bond; studies by Margaret Burchinal] R. J. Moss. il *Psychol Today* 21:20 F '87

The good mother [mothers and daughters; interview with O. Silverstein] *Vogue* 177:84+ Je '87

A grandmother too soon! [mothers of pregnant teenagers] C. Berman. il *McCalls* 114:84-6 My '87

"Hey, Dad, thanks for coming". E. Goodman. il *Read Dig* 130:151-2 Ap '87

Home sex ed: values 1, facts 0 [results of survey] V. Bozzi. *Psychol Today* 21:14 My '87

How to handle a parent's visit [excerpt from Do your parents drive you crazy?] J. Dight. il *Glamour* 85:153-4 N '87

How to help when your child feels bad. N. Samalin and M. M. Jablow. il *Parents* 62:73-8 F '87

How to talk to your parents. J. A. Baggett. il *Sch Update* 119:21 Mr 23 '87

I moved back into my parents' house. il *Good Housekeep* 205:24+ Ag '87

"I'm sorry!" [parents' apologies] J. Vedral. il *Parents* 62:91-4 Ap '87

In teens we trust. M. Mantle. il *U S Cathol* 52:29-31 My '87

Kyoiku mama: secret of Japan's schools. C. Simons. il *Read Dig* 131:117-20 Jl '87

A magic I almost missed [sharing a joyful moment with a child] A. Lindstrom. il *Read Dig* 130:71-2 Ap '87

Maternal scents [mothers most likely to recognize newborns by smell] E. Comte. *Health* 19:26 N '87

Michael Landon: "My mother tried to stab me" [interview] T. Reinhold. il pors *Redbook* 169:59-60+ S '87

Mom, I want to have the baby. M. C. Funk. il por *Ladies Home J* 104:22+ N '87

Mother/daughter. L. Ellerbee and V. Veselka. pors *Ms* 16:126-8+ Jl/Ag '87

Mother of a pearl [6-year-old tennis player A. Stevenson] S. Stevenson. il pors *World Tennis* 34:38-41+ Ap '87

Motherly love works a miracle [P. Anthony is surrogate for her daughter; cover story] E. Levin. il pors *People Wkly* 28:38-43 O 19 '87

A Mother's Day challenge [discussion of sex with teenage daughter] M. Cartledge-Hayes. il *Ms* 15:80 My '87

My family, my team [serving as parent-tennis coach to five children] W. A. Washington. il *World Tennis* 35:18+ O '87

My father, Mr. Lincoln and me. E. Ziegler. il *Read Dig* 130:35-40 F '87

My father's song [condensed from God's best for you] M. M. Helleberg. il *Read Dig* 131:53-6 S '87

My mother's cookbook [discovery of cookbook prompts memories of recently deceased mother] S. Flynn. il por *McCalls* 114:47+ My '87

My mother's mystery. J. Gage. il pors *N Y Times Mag* p36-7+ My 17 '87

My parents were risking their future. il *Good Housekeep* 205:22+ O '87

"My son, my daughter" [sex change surgery] J. McDowell. il por *Ladies Home J* 104:18+ F '87

My son the man [teenager] M. K. Blakely. por *Ms* 15:28-9 Mr '87

My teenage daughter was pregnant. il *Good Housekeep* 204:24+ Mr '87

Offspring stay at home with mom, dad longer. *Jet* 72:32 S 21 '87

One from the heart [pro golfer P. Stewart and father] R. Reilly. il pors *Sports Illus* 66:44-6+ My 18 '87

Past imperfect: is it time to let your parents off the hook? [cover story] M. O'Connell. il *U S Cathol* 52:6-13 Ja '87

The play's the thing [importance of parental interaction with infants; research by T. Field] R. J. Trotter. bibl (p63) il pors *Psychol Today* 21:26-34 Ja '87

The railing on the stairs [son makes repair for handicapped father] E. Ziegler. il *Read Dig* 131:97-9 N '87

Rejected fathers. R. B. McCall. il *Parents* 62:221 Mr '87

Sending a daughter to college. J. Fonda. il pors *Ladies Home J* 104:22+ Ja '87

A sense of drama [motorcyclist and young son] T. Simmons. il *N Y Times Mag* p130 S 13 '87

Show me the way to go home [young adults living with their parents] A. Toufexis. il *Time* 129:106 My 4 '87

Small moments [mother captures fleeting magic of childhood] E. Berg. il *Parents* 62:108-10+ D '87

Sons & daughters. R. B. McCall. il *Parents* 62:240 My '87

Special mother-daughter issue [cover story] il *Teen* 31:10+ D '87

Speech for a high school graduate [father's advice to daughter] R. Rosenblatt. il *Time* 129:72 Je 29 '87

"Stuck on you!" [effects of maternal-infant attachment] N. S. Schwartzberg. il *Parents* 62:100-2+ O '87

Sugar babies and clucking mommies [newborns; research by Elliott Blass] il *Discover* 8:10 N '87

Tactics for living with your teen. K. Henderson. il *McCalls* 115:63-5 N '87

"There's got to be a better way" [conflict resolution] J. Marks. il *Parents* 62:106-8+ S '87

They get by with a lot of help from their kyoiku mamas [Japanese students; cover story] C. Simons. bibl (p182) il *Smithsonian* 17:44-53 Mr '87

Things his mother taught him [impact on relationships with other women] R. Wetzsteon. *Mademoiselle* 93:110+ S '87

To Meg, on becoming thirteen. P. Sherlock. il *Read Dig* 131:189-90 D '87

Travels with my father: what we learned from working together. R. J. Christmas. il por *Ms* 15:66+ Mr '87

What babies know, and noises parents make [newborns; research by Elliott Blass] G. Kolata. *Science* 237:726 Ag 14 '87

What do you do with a baby? L. Albert. il *Parents* 62:156-7 N '87

What fathers really think [excerpt from Fathers] il *Parents* 62:82-5 Je '87

When a brother or sister is ill [parents' treatment of healthy children] C. Wallinga and others. *Psychol Today* 21:42-3 Ag '87

When my wife's mother died, the loss tore us apart. N. Dillon. *Glamour* 85:234+ Mr '87

When you and your parents disagree: should you rebel, conform or compromise? S. Helgesen. *Glamour* 85:118-19 Ja '87

Parent-child relationship—*cont.*

When your mom is fat. S. Nelson. il *Seventeen* 46:164-5+ N '87

When you're really hassled [mothers of toddlers] J. T. Gibson. il *Parents* 62:148 Jl '87

Where did I go wrong? R. B. McCall. il *Parents* 62:246 S '87

Why mothers get a hard time. J. Marzollo. il *Parents* 62:103-5+ N '87

Why you can't talk to your parents anymore. W. Lamb. il *Seventeen* 46:114-15 F '87

William Bloomer's footprints. V. G. Beers. il *Christ Today* 31:11 Je 12 '87

"You make me so mad!"; ed. by Martha Moraghan Jablow. N. Samalin. il *Parents* 62:53-7 Ja '87

"You were great, Dad" [son admires father's basketball skills] B. Cohen. il *Read Dig* 131:124-6 D '87

Your parents' house—or his? [excerpt from Do your parents drive you crazy?] J. Dight. il *Ladies Home J* 104:70+ D '87

Anecdotes, facetiae, satire, etc.

The high cost of raising a daughter. E. Bombeck. por *Teen* 31:64 D '87

How to tell when it's time to visit your mother [excerpt from How to visit your mother] D. Paget and L. Majzlin. il *Work Woman* 12:76-7 Ja '87

Mommie barest [mother-son relationship tested by search for sexy swimsuit] R. Rothenstein. il *50 Plus* 27:84+ Je '87

Mr. Cool meets the king [father and teenage son go king salmon fishing] A. Liere. il *Field Stream* 92:47-8+ My '87

Visit from mom. D. Stillman. il *Mademoiselle* 93:202-3+ O '87

Parent-child relationship in literature

The world and our mothers. V. Gornick. il *N Y Times Book Rev* 92:1+ N 22 '87

Parent education

    See also

      Parents as Teachers (Program)

      Tape recordings—Parent education

Education eases parenting [study by University of California Cooperative Extension and Dept. of Agriculture] il *Child Today* 16:5 Mr/Ap '87

In San Francisco, teacher Robert Valverde fights teen pregnancy with flour power. D. Gorgan. il por *People Wkly* 27:34-5 Ap 27 '87

Mama, talk to your baby [Rene Van de Carr's Prenatal University] il *Newsweek* 110:75 N 2 '87

Parent-teacher cooperation *See* School and the home

Parental behavior in animals

Fatherhood in frogdom [coqui forest frogs of Puerto Rico] D. S. Townsend. il *Nat Hist* 96:28-35 My '87

The multiple benefits of babysitting duties. R. Lewin. il *Science* 236:775-6 My 15 '87

Seals under the sun [Galapagos fur seals] F. Trillmich. il *Nat Hist* 96:42-9 O '87

Parental behavior in birds

Grouse and spouse [willow ptarmigan] K. Martin. il *Nat Hist* 96:62-9 F '87

How to stay a shade cooler [ostriches protect their young] il *Natl Geogr World* 139:10-11 Mr '87

Parental deprivation

    See also

      Maternal deprivation

      Paternal deprivation

Parental leaves

Family leave: a needed guarantee. K. Palen. *Christ Century* 104:372-3 Ap 22 '87

A one-size-fits-all leave policy? [proposed Family and Medical Leave Act] L. Dehmlow. por *U S News World Rep* 103:11 D 7 '87

Parental leave: a policy for the future. A. Finkelstein. il *Parents* 62:240+ S '87

Parental leave is snowballing. S. B. Garland. *Bus Week* p32 Ag 31 '87

Should business be forced to help bring up baby? [battle over 'mandated benefits'] M. E. Recio. il *Bus Week* p39-40 Ap 6 '87

Parents

    See also

      Children

      Family

      Fathers

      Mothers

      Parent education

      Parental leaves

      School and the home

      School management and organization—Parent participation

      Single parent families

      Stepparents and stepchildren

Baby makes three. E. Fishel. il *Parents* 62:73-6+ S '87

Children affect parents' mental health [study by Debra Umberson] il *USA Today (Periodical)* 116:9 S '87

Choosing parenthood: help for couples who can't decide [excerpt from The pre-pregnancy planner] J. Wilson. il *Glamour* 85:128 Ja '87

"How I'd like mom & dad to change". G. N. Edelman. il *Parents* 62:122-6 N '87

A report card for parents. S. F. Enos. il *Ladies Home J* 104:87-9+ Je '87

Should you sell your empty nest? L. Stains. il *Prevention* 39:62-4 My '87

What parents are doing right. M. Mercer. il *Good Housekeep* 205:75+ S '87

When baby makes three. D. Hales. il *McCalls* 115:54+ N '87

Anecdotes, facetiae, satire, etc.

'The cat would never admit her mistakes' [empty nest syndrome] D. D. Jackson. il *Smithsonian* 17:140 Ja '87

How to talk to new parents. D. Barry. il *Glamour* 85:30+ My '87

Attitudes

Childhood: then vs. now [results of survey] I. Groller. il *Parents* 62:30 Ap '87

Disorderly conduct [results of survey] I. Groller. il *Parents* 62:33 Ag '87

Fatherese & motherese. P. Perry. il *Parents* 62:100-4 Mr '87

What is a successful parent? [results of survey] O. S. Nordberg. il *Parents* 62:12 Mr '87

Who's minding the kids? [results of survey] il *Parents* 62:106-10+ Ap '87

Political activities

Getting involved. E. Berg. il *Parents* 62:100-2 My '87

Religious life

Can parents of toddlers find time to pamper their faith? D. Morris. il *U S Cathol* 52:21-8 My '87

How faith helps parents raise good kids. J. Breig. il *U S Cathol* 52:26-31 Mr '87

Kids deserve better than perfect parents. J. G. Hermes. *U S Cathol* 52:38-40 Mr '87

Superkids and superparents. H. Smith. il *Christ Today* 31:14-15 S 18 '87

Parents (Periodical)

Happy birthday, Parents magazine. C. Loomis. il *Parents* 62:17 Mr '87

Inside Parents. E. Crow. See issues of Parents

Parents' and teachers' associations

Sprucing up the classroom. F. Roberts. il *Parents* 62:58 Ap '87

Parents as Teachers (Program)

Teaching parents to be better parents. N. Eberle. il *McCalls* 114:49+ Je '87

Parents' grief *See* Grief

Parents' Music Resource Center

Tipper de doo dah [T. Gore] H. Hertzberg. *New Repub* 197:22-3 D 7 '87

Tipper Gore: the PMRC swings back into action. R. Love. por *Seventeen* 46:56 Jl '87

Parents of actors and actresses

Enter worried [parents footing the bills of child's acting career] D. Machan. il *Forbes* 139:246+ Je 15 '87

Parents of homosexuals

The AIDS epidemic hits home [results of survey] B. E. Robinson and others. bibl (p65) il *Psychol Today* 21:48-52 Ap '87

Parents of murdered children

Avenging a murder [D. Thompson seeks justice for murdered son in Alabama] D. O. Relin. il por *Sch Update* 120:7 D 4 '87

Parents of the handicapped

At home with Tira [J. Wolff, mother of quadriplegic daughter] M. Weissman. il por *Ms* 16:36+ S '87

A burden gallantly borne [hockey player B. Bourne's son born with spina bifida] A. Murphy. il pors *Sports Illus* 67:26-7 D 21 '87

"Sergeant Mom" [Army sergeant has child with spina bifida] B. A. Kidwell. il por *Ladies Home J* 104:16+ Ja '87

Zachary [son born with spina bifida] N. Lund. il por *Parents* 62:117-18+ Ag '87

Parents of the mentally handicapped

The fine art of child appreciation. M. Mantle. *U S Cathol* 52:30-1 S '87

Parents of the mentally ill

Madness in the family. N. Harlow. il *Redbook* 169:130-1+ My '87

The sound and fury of mania. S. Garson. por *Newsweek* 109:10 Ap 13 '87

Parents' quarrels *See* Quarrels

Parès, Yvette
about
Easing leprosy's pain. M. Rose. il por *Macleans* 100:6+ Mr 30 '87

Parfit, Michael
Blackout! What happens in a power failure. il *Read Dig* 130:197-8+ Je '87
Coping with blackout: what happens when the lights go out? bibl (p143) M. *Smithsonian* 17:38-49 F '87
Retracing Lindy's victorious trip across the country. bibl (p231) il pors map *Smithsonian* 18:200-2+ O '87
They learn to work calmly while instinct warns they're about to die. il *Smithsonian* 18:98-102+ My '87

Parian ware
Collectors and collecting
Worcester Parian and Parian ivory porcelain of the 19th century [cover story] M. L. Loch. il *Antiques Collect Hobbies* 92:33-9 O '87

Parikh, Vandana S., and others
The mitochondrial genotype can influence nuclear gene expression in yeast. bibl f il *Science* 235:576-80 Ja 30 '87

Parini, Jay
History [poem] *Am Sch* 56:414 Summ '87
The literary impulse. il *Horizon* 30:27-8 N '87
Man of Ironweed. il por *Horizon* 30:35-6 D '87
Robert Penn Warren. por *Horizon* 30:36-7 Je '87
Writers reading. il *Horizon* 30:63 O '87
Writing and the devout life. *Christ Century* 104:815-16 S 30 '87

Paris, Bubba
about
49ers' Paris grapples with a weighty problem. *Jet* 72:50 S 7 '87

Paris, Jay
Manhattan or bust. il pors *Read Dig* 131:5-6+ Jl '87
When the dinosaur hit Lodi, Ohio. il *Read Dig* 130:145-8 Ap '87

Paris, John J., and McCormick, Richard A., 1922-
The Catholic tradition on the use of nutrition and fluids. *America* 156:356-61 My 2 '87
Letters in reaction [discussion of May 2, 1987 article, The Catholic tradition on the use of nutrition and fluids] *America* 156:449-52 My 30 '87

Paris, Michael
The American film industry & Vietnam [cover story] bibl il *Hist Today* 37:19-26 Ap '87

Paris (France)
Art
Aesthetics in fashion. C. Worthington. il *Harpers Bazaar* 120:88+ Ag '87
Cooper-Hewitt Museum [Art nouveau Bing: Paris style 1900 exhibition; cover story] il *Antiques Collect Hobbies* 92:49+ Jl '87
The other fin de siècle [The Dreyfus affair and Art nouveau Bing] K. Silver. bibl f il *Art Am* 75:104-11+ D '87
Arts
Letter from Paris. J. J. Buck. il *Vogue* 177:138+ Ap '87
The new créateurs. C. Worthington. il *Harpers Bazaar* 120:246+ S '87
Paris where it sizzles [the Bastille] E. White. il *Vogue* 177:134+ Jl '87
Banks
Now, the Bourse is in the game for real [le Big Bang] J. Rossant. il *Bus Week* p88 Jl 20 '87
Blacks
Americans in Paris. S. S. Oliver. il *Essence* 18:97-9 O '87
Why Paris? [blacks; cover story] B. Chase-Riboud. il *Essence* 18:65-6 O '87
Cemeteries
Paris journal [Père-Lachaise: an historic resting place] C. P. Reynolds. il *Gourmet* 47:28+ Jl '87
City planning
The next time you see Paris. J. Valls-Russell. il *New Leader* 70:7-8 Jl 1-15 '87
Clubs
See also
Saint James's Club (Paris, France)
Dance halls
Dance-floor democracy [1846; excerpt from Travels] D. F. Sarmiento. il *Courier* 40:30 Ap '87
Description
Imagine Paris. J. Berger. il *Harpers* 274:72-4 Ja '87
Paris hot spots. H. Cole and C. Mongo. il *Essence* 18:102+ O '87

Paris journal. C. P. Reynolds. See occasional issues of *Gourmet*
Paris where it sizzles [the Bastille] E. White. il *Vogue* 177:134+ Jl '87
The whole slice of Paris life. A. Fotheringham. il *Macleans* 100:56 Ap 6 '87
Galleries and museums
See also
Centre National d'Art et de Culture Georges Pompidou
La Cité des Sciences et de l'Industrie (Paris, France)
Galerie Schmit
Musée des Arts Décoratifs (Paris, France)
Musée d'Orsay (Paris, France)
Musée du Louvre
Even more great museums for Paris. il *Sunset* 179:44+ O '87
Gardens and gardening
See also
Jardin des Plantes (Paris, France)
History
Siege, 1870-1871
On war letters: pigeons, planes, and philatelists. H. Herst, Jr. il *Antiques Collect Hobbies* 92:82+ N '87
Housing
Buying a second house in Paris [experience of B. and C. Haber] C. Styles-McLeod. il pors *Archit Dig* 44 Archit Dig Travels:10+ O '87
Industries
See also
Publishers and publishing—France
Intellectual life
Bibliography
Pilgrims in Paris. J. E. Seigel. *New Repub* 197:30-4 S 28 '87
Monuments, statues, etc.
See also
Eiffel Tower (Paris, France)
Museums
See Paris (France)—Galleries and museums
Restaurants, nightclubs, bars, etc.
Bistro's best [wines] F. J. Prial. il *N Y Times Mag* p48 My 10 '87
Fantasy after dark. L. Chaplin. il *Harpers Bazaar* 120:214+ F '87
The gastronomic world of Balzac. N. Barry. il *Gourmet* 47:48-53+ S '87
Paris journal [cinema and after-cinema supping] C. P. Reynolds. il *Gourmet* 47:24+ Ja '87
Savory merriment [New Year's Eve at Taillevent] S. M. Dinhofer. il *Harpers Bazaar* 121:82+ D '87
Social history
The gastronomic world of Balzac. N. Barry. il *Gourmet* 47:48-53+ S '87
Paris in the thirties: some letters home. V. Lawford. il por *Archit Dig* 44:210+ Mr '87
Social life and customs
Christmas chic: Gallic galas. J. B. Rafferty. il *Harpers Bazaar* 121:80+ D '87
Fantasy after dark. L. Chaplin. il *Harpers Bazaar* 120:214+ F '87
Mr. Peepers in Paris: le hot center. il *N Y* 20:26-8 N 2 '87
Paris in the pink. C. Worthington. il *Harpers Bazaar* 120:40+ Je '87
The rules of the game [entertaining in France] J. Kramer. il *House Gard* 159:86+ O '87
Le snob appeal. C. Worthington. il *Harpers Bazaar* 120:172+ O '87
Stores
See also
Atelier Brocard
An antiques dealer's secret sources: Bruce Newman in Paris and England. J. Kornbluth. il pors *Archit Dig* 44 Archit Dig Travels:20-31+ O '87
Let them eat pastry [Paris patisserie Xavier Gourmet] K. Hom. il *N Y Times Mag* p55-6 D 20 '87
Paris bazaar. C. Worthington. il *Harpers Bazaar* 120:54+ Jl '87
Paris' haute chocolaterie. N. Barry. il *Gourmet* 47:58-63+ Mr '87
Theater
Letter from Europe [lives of singer L. Mariano and a Portuguese fan] J. Kramer. il *New Yorker* 63:66-70+ Ag 24 '87
Paris (France). Eiffel Tower *See* Eiffel Tower (Paris, France)
Paris (France). La Villette *See* La Villette (Paris, France)
Paris (France) fashion shows *See* Fashion shows
Paris (France) in art
Tom Lynch: Paris sketchbook [watercolors] V. R. Rivers. il por *Am Artist* 51:S7-S10 N '87

Paris Auto Show *See* Automobiles—Exhibitions
Paris Club
  In debt? Ring up the Louvre [work in rescheduling third world debt] F. Ungeheuer. il *Time* 130:50 Jl 13 '87
Paris fashion *See* Fashion
Paris International Air Show *See* Aviation—Exhibitions
Paris Opera Ballet
  Cinderella in America. J. R. Acocella. il *Art Am* 75:43-5 S '87
  Editor's log [performances of Cinderella in New York City] W. Como. il *Dance Mag* 61:32 S '87
  Letdown at Lincoln Center. L. A. Jacobs. *New Leader* 70:21-2 Jl 13-27 '87
  Love finds a way [performances of Cinderella in New York City] T. Tobias. il *N Y* 20:56-7 Jl 13 '87
  A night at the Opéra: Cinderella in Tinseltown. M. E. Willis. il *Dance Mag* 61:58-63 F '87
  Paris Opéra Ballet at the Met: compagnie de cristal. M. Hunt. il *Dance Mag* 61:50-5 Ja '87
  Reviews:
    Performances in Paris. B. Merrill. *Dance Mag* 61:67-9 D '87
    Performances of Cinderella at the Metropolitan Opera House, New York City. A. Smith. *Dance Mag* 61:76-8 D '87
Paris to Dakar automobile rally *See* Automobile rallies—International aspects
Parish, Ralph
  (jt. auth) See Eubanks, Eugene E., and Parish, Ralph
Parish, Robert, 1953-
    about
  Burglary adds to losses for Boston star Parish. por *Jet* 72:46 Jl 6 '87
Parish, Sister
    about
  Back country Greenwich. S. M. L. Aronson. il *House Gard* 159:132-9+ Ag '87
Parishes
  Does the RENEW program renew? [Catholic evangelism] J. R. Kelly. *America* 156:197-9 Mr 7 '87
  Growing together in spirituality: pastor and parish have a check-up. A. C. Krass. il *Christ Century* 104:311-14 Ap 1 '87
  Parish finances: are Catholics reluctant to pay their own way? [with editorial comment by Robert E. Burns] T. Unsworth. il *U S Cathol* 52:2, 32-8 S '87
  Parishes for Anglican usage. J. H. Fichter. *America* 157:354-7 N 14 '87
  The Pope's foot soldiers [B. Frawley and R. Dlugos, parish priests; cover story] J. Buckley. il pors *U S News World Rep* 103:60-4+ S 21 '87
  A second collection on Catholic giving [discussion of September 1987 article, Parish finances] T. Unsworth. *U S Cathol* 52:46-7 D '87
Parisi, Bruno
  The great transalpine routes. il *Courier* 40:11-13 F '87
Parison, Christian-Luc
  Yugoslavia's monastery route. il *World Press Rev* 34:62 S '87
Parizeau, Jacques, 1930-
    about
  The PQ in turmoil. B. Wallace. il pors *Macleans* 100:8-10 N 23 '87
Park, Clara Claiborne
  "Canst thou not minister to a mind diseas'd?". *Am Sch* 56:219-34 Spr '87
Park, Darragh
    about
  Darragh Park at Tibor de Nagy. J. Ashbery. il *Art Am* 75:186 My '87
Park, David, 1911-1960
    about
  David Park: facing Eden. B. Berkson. bibl f il *Art Am* 75:164-71+ O '87
Park, Edwards
  Around the Mall and beyond. See issues of Smithsonian
  Could Canada have ever been our Fourteenth Colony? [cover story] bibl (p204) il map *Smithsonian* 18:40-9 D '87
Park, Mungo, 1771-1806
  Long nose, white skin and 'honey mouth' [excerpt from Travels into the interior of Africa] por *Courier* 40:18+ Ap '87
Park employees
    See also
  National parks and reserves—Employees

Park Police (U.S.) *See* United States. Park Police
Park rangers
  The last working horses [use by U.S. Park Police and park rangers] C. Carnie. il *Natl Parks* 61:30-5 Mr/Ap '87
  Patrolling the park beat [National Park Service rangers] L. Peach. il *Natl Parks* 61:24-9 N/D '87
  Risky business [national park rangers] J. Heinrichs. il *Natl Wildl* 25:12-15 Je/Jl '87
Parkdale Mills, Inc.
  The fast track isn't always the best track. P. Berman. il por *Forbes* 140:60+ N 2 '87
Parkening, Christopher, 1947-
    about
  The "good life" wasn't good enough. T. Mattingly. il por *Christ Today* 31:64+ My 15 '87
Parker, Alan, 1944-
    about
  Angel heart [film] Reviews
    Glamour 85:217-18 My '87. J. G. Boyum
    Jet il 71:60-1 Mr 23 '87. C. Waldron
    Jet il 71:60-1 Mr 16 '87
    Macleans 100:58 Mr 16 '87. L. O'Toole
    Mademoiselle il 93:46+ Je '87. R. Rosenbaum
    New Leader il 70:20 Mr 23 '87. J. Gardner
    New Yorker 63:85-6 Ap 6 '87. P. Kael
    Newsweek il 109:72 Mr 16 '87. D. Ansen
    People Wkly il 27:10 Mr 16 '87. P. Travers
    Time il 129:86 Mr 9 '87. R. Corliss
    Vogue il 177:72 My '87. M. Haskell
Parker, Anthony J.
  The Mediterranean, an underwater museum. il *Courier* 40:8-10 N '87
Parker, Barrington D.
    about
  Black judge dismisses two suits in Iran arms case. por *Jet* 72:4 Mr 30 '87
Parker, Catherine Burchfield
    about
  Catherine Burchfield Parker. M. C. Nelson. il por *Am Artist* 51:58-61+ D '87
Parker, Charlie, 1920-1955
    about
  Celebrating Bird. M. Bourne. il por *Down Beat* 54:63 Ap '87
Parker, Dave, 1951-
    about
  The anatomy of an at-bat. D. Granger. il pors *Sport Mag* 78:26-9 Jl '87
Parker, David
    about
  Making Malcolm. W. Harris. il pors *Theatre Crafts* 21:73-4 F '87
Parker, Dorian Leigh
  An excursion from Milan: Bergamo. il *Gourmet* 47:60-5+ S '87
  Potato cakes. il *Gourmet* 47:82-3+ O '87
Parker, Dorothy, 1893-1967
    about
  Three neighbors. T. Capote. il pors *Esquire* 108:223-4 D '87
Parker, Eugene Newman, 1927-
  Why do stars emit X rays? bibl f il *Phys Today* 40:36-42 Jl '87
Parker, Evan
    about
  Evan Parker: the breath and breadth of the saxophone. P. Keegan. il pors *Down Beat* 54:26-8 Ap '87
Parker, Frank J., 1940-
  South Africa hemorrhages. *America* 156:10-12 Ja 3-10 '87
Parker, Karl E.
  Spirit of the northern waters. il *Conservationist* 42:16-21 Jl/Ag '87
Parker, Kathleen
    about
  From nurse to medical-supply executive. J. Giambanco. il pors *Work Woman* 12:77-8+ Ag '87
Parker, Robert
    about
  Parker's mood. J. Sohmer. *Down Beat* 54:47-8+ D '87
Parker, Robert B., 1932-
    about
  Robert Parker: "We weren't blessed with an ideal close relationship. We earned it". S. Wright. por *Vogue* 177:176+ D '87
Parker, Robert M., Jr.
    about
  The man with a paragon palate. J. Elson. il por *Time* 130:89 D 14 '87

Parker, Robert M., Jr.—about—cont.
The merciless man of wine. J. Adler. il por *Newsweek*
110:77 D 14 '87
Parker, Tom, 1950-
Every day in America . . . [condensed from In one
day] il *Read Dig* 131:85 S '87
Parking (Securities)
Ivan Boesky's secret 'parking lots'. C. Welles. il por
Bus Week p130 Je 22 '87
Jefferies's fall worries more than insiders. il por *Fortune*
115:8 Ap 13 '87
Nabbing the stealth broker [B. Jefferies charged] B. Powell
and C. Friday. il por *Newsweek* 109:48 Mr 30 '87
Serving his clients all too well [criminal charges against
B. Jefferies] S. Koepp. il por *Time* 129:52 Mr 30
'87
When Boyd Jefferies talks, all of Wall Street will be
listening. C. Farrell and others. il por *Bus Week* p37
Ap 6 '87
Parking garages *See* Garages, Municipal
Parkinson's disease
Causes
Environmental roots to Parkinsonism [research by Donald
B. Calne and others] *Sci News* 132:120 Ag 22 '87
More clues to the cause of Parkinson's disease [study
by Donald Calne and others] R. Lewin. *Science* 237:978
Ag 28 '87
Therapy
Adrenal medulla grafts enhance recovery of striatal
dopaminergic fibers. M. C. Bohn and others. bibl
f il *Science* 237:913-16 Ag 21 '87
Ali denies seeking cure for Parkinson's disease. por *Jet*
72:53 Jl 27 '87
Ali shows he's sharp enough to say 'no' to brain surgery.
il pors *Jet* 72:47 Ag 3 '87
The amazing new brain surgery for Parkinson's disease.
E. Kiester. il *50 Plus* 27:24-6+ O '87
Back to normal [cells from adrenal glands transplanted
into brain] C. Wallis. il *Time* 129:57 Ap 13 '87
Brain grafts benefit Parkinson's patients [work of Ignacio
Madrazo and others] R. Lewin. *Science* 236:149 Ap
10 '87
Breakthrough for Parkinson's disease? [cells from adrenal
glands transplanted into brain] B. Wallace. il *Macleans*
100:46-7 My 18 '87
Cell grafts proceed, value uncertain [fetal brain cell
transplants] R. Weiss. *Sci News* 132:341 N 28 '87
Dramatic results with brain grafts. R. Lewin. il *Science*
237:245-7 Jl 17 '87
Drug trial for Parkinson's [Deprenyl/tocopherol] R. Lewin.
Science 236:1420 Je 12 '87
The edge of knife [adrenal glands grafted to brain] J.
Carpi. *Health* 19:25 Jl '87
Hole in the head [uncertainties surrounding adrenal cell
transplants into the brain as cure for Parkinson's]
R. Bazell. *New Repub* 197:13-14 Ag 10-17 '87
Human fetal-cell transplants planned. R. Weiss. *Sci News*
132:22 Jl 11 '87
New Parkinson's surgery [adrenal glands transplanted
into brain] *Sci News* 131:244 Ap 18 '87
Parkinson's: is this the cure? [adrenal cell transplants
into the brain] K. McAuliffe. il *U S News World
Rep* 102:12-13 Ap 13 '87
Parkinson's protection? [chloroquine offers partial protec-
tion from MPTP-induced symptoms; research by Robert
J. D'Amato and others] B. Bower. *Sci News* 131:359
Je 6 '87
Parkinson's treatment to be tested [Deprenyl/tocopherol;
research by Ira Shoulson] *Prevention* 39:78 N '87
Progress in Parkinsonism [transferring adrenal gland cells
into the brain] *Time* 129:59 Ap 20 '87
Therapy by transplant [adrenal cells transplanted into
brains of Parkinson's victims; work of Ignacio Madrazo
and others] *Sci Am* 256:29-30 Je '87
Transplants in the brain [adrenal grafts] S. Begley. il
Newsweek 109:64 Ap 13 '87
Parkmerced (San Francisco, Calif.) *See* San Francisco (Calif.)
Parks, Gary
Deanmusicdance. il por *Dance Mag* 61:54-5 Ap '87
Keeping dance forever. il por *Dance Mag* 61:46-8 D
'87
La Scala's Patricia Neary: this lady is a champ. il pors
Dance Mag 61:64-5 Ja '87
Parks, Henry G., 1916-
about
Parks, Smale feted at annual UNCF gala held in New
York City. il pors *Jet* 72:12-13 Ap 6 '87
Parks, Rosa, 1913-
about
A visit from Rosa Parks: power of the ordinary. D.
C. Skinner. *Christ Century* 104:300-1 Ap 1 '87

Parks, William S.
A president in trouble—so what's new? por *U S News
World Rep* 102:8 Ja 26 '87
Parks
See also
Amusement parks
Greenbelts
National parks and reserves
Playgrounds
Sculpture gardens and parks
Parkway Grill (Pasadena, Calif.) *See* Pasadena (Calif.)—
Restaurants, nightclubs, bars, etc.
Parliaments
See also
South Africa. Parliament
Parlors *See* Living rooms
Parma (Italy)
Industries
See also
Cheese industry—Italy
Parmesan cheese industry *See* Cheese industry—Italy
Parmiggiani, Claudio
about
Claudio Parmiggiani at Albert Totah. P. Smith. il *Art
Am* 75:135-6 Mr '87
Parmigiano cheese industry *See* Cheese industry—Italy
Parnas, David
Why I quit. *Cent Mag* 20:56-7 Ja/F '87
Parnassus (Instrumental ensemble)
Musical events:
American premiere of J. Harvey's Bhakti. A. Porter.
New Yorker 63:121 D 14 '87
Parnell, Dale
High school-community college cooperation creates a
degree. *Educ Dig* 52:40-1 Mr '87
Parochial schools *See* Church schools
Parochial schools, Catholic *See* Catholic schools
Parodies
Puns and parodies pay off. S. Glasser. *Writer* 100:19-20+
Je '87
Parody (Music)
Oh my aching ear! The (bang!) music of Spike (splat!)
Jones is revived by a new (tweet!) band of merry
makers. M. Shaughnessy. il pors *People Wkly* 27:77+
My 4 '87
Parole
Not in my town [problems of paroled rapist L. Singleton]
il por *Time* 129:31 Je 1 '87
The 'Onion Field' parole: Rose Bird's parting shot [case
of G. Powell] por *Newsweek* 109:26 Ja 12 '87
Parquet flooring *See* Flooring
Parr, Mike
about
Mike Parr at Ruth Siegel. E. Heartney. il *Art Am* 75:132-3
Ja '87
Parricide *See* Murder
Parrill, Gene
Cars in scale. See occasional issues of Road & Track
Parriott, Sara
If you're free Friday night, read this. il *Mademoiselle*
93:232-3+ My '87
Parris, Guichard
about
Recovering black history [cover story] J. W. Donohue.
America 157:35-7 Jl 18-25 '87
Parris, Mark R.
The U.S.-Soviet bilateral relationship [address, February
25, 1987] *Dep State Bull* 87:45-8 My '87
Parrots
Seized parrots could restore a lost species [thick-billed
parrot] il *Audubon* 89:22 Jl '87
Parrott, Bruce, 1945-
The Soviet debate on missile defense. bibl f il *Bull
At Sci* 43:9-12 Ap '87
Parrott, Robert E.
One day in August. *Christ Century* 104:679-80 Ag 12-19
'87
Parry, Charles William
about
Alcoa: recycling itself to become a pioneer in new
materials. G. L. Miles and M. Rothman. il por *Bus
Week* p56-8 F 9 '87
Parry, Robert
about
The real heroes of contra-gate. J. Morley and T. Rosen-
berg. il pors *Roll Stone* p48-50+ S 10 '87
Parsifal [opera] *See* Wagner, Richard, 1813-1883
Parslow, Tristram G., and others
The immunoglobulin octanucleotide: independent activity
and selective interaction with enhancers. bibl f il *Science*
235:1498-1501 Mr 20 '87

Parson, Mary Jean
Creating solutions, not showdowns. il *Work Woman* 12:127-9 My '87
Making changes: how to budge the office mule. il *Work Woman* 12:139-41 S '87

Parsons, David
about
David Parsons takes off. L. Friedman. il por *Vogue* 177:46 Je '87
On edge [cover story] M. Hunt. il pors *Dance Mag* 61:43-7 S '87
Reviews:
    Performances at Bessie Schönberg Theater, New York City. S. Sommer. *Dance Mag* 61:77-8 D '87
Taking stock. T. Tobias. il *N Y* 20:58-9 F 2 '87

Parsons, Edward L.
(jt. auth) See Botwin, Carol, and Parsons, Edward L.

Parsons, Paul F.
The fourth "R" [cover story] il por *Christ Today* 31:21-7 S 4 '87

Parsons (David) Company *See* David Parsons Company

Part time employment
See also
    College teachers, Part time
    Supplementary employment
More benefits in store for part-timers. J. Bodnar. *Changing Times* 41:11 N '87
Why you should hire peak-time employees. L. Washer. *Work Woman* 12:21+ F '87

Japan
Wanted: part-time mourners, too. M. Lord. il *U S News World Rep* 103:46 N 23 '87

Partello-Hollingsworth, Helen
about
Lessons in simplicity. C. D. B. Bryan. il por *Archit Dig* 44:92+ O '87
Rejuvenating a Connecticut parsonage: a designer's Litchfield County colonial. R. Conniff. il *Archit Dig* 44:108-17+ Je '87

Parthenogenesis
Courtship in unisexual lizards: a model for brain evolution. D. Crews. bibl (p158) il *Sci Am* 257:116-21 D '87
Does pseudosex enhance virgin birth? [desert grassland whiptail lizard; research by David Crews] il *Discover* 8:5-6 Ap '87
Leaping lizards and male impersonators: are there hidden messages? [research by David Crews and others] D. D. Edwards. il *Sci News* 131:348-9 My 30 '87
Mammals need moms and dads. J. A. Miller. il *BioScience* 37:379-82 Je '87

Parthenon (Athens, Greece)
The Parthenon at dusk [excerpt from The journey to the East; tr. by Ivan Zaknic and Nicola Pertuiset. Le Corbusier. *Harpers* 275:27-8+ Jl '87

Parti québécois
Mourning a patriot son [R. Lévesque; special section] il *Macleans* 100:10-12+ N 16 '87
The PQ in turmoil [resignation of P. M. Johnson] B. Wallace. il pors *Macleans* 100:8-10 N 23 '87

Parti Rhinoceros
A tongue in a bearded cheek. S. MacLeod. por *Macleans* 100:11 S 21 '87

Participation, Political *See* Political participation

Participative management
See also
    Employee ownership
    Team work in industry
Blue collars in the boardroom: putting business first. J. Hoerr. il *Bus Week* p126+ D 14 '87
Mega mergers [address, September 7, 1987] R. H. Guest. *Vital Speeches Day* 54:20-2 O 15 '87
U.A.W. backs the wrong team. E. Mann. il *Nation* 244:171-2+ F 14 '87

Particle accelerators *See* Accelerators (Electrons, etc.)

Particle beam weapons
The APS Council and the DEW study [letters] *Phys Today* 40:9+ O '87
APS releases report on directed-energy weapons [special section] bibl f il *Phys Today* 40:S1-S16 My '87
SDI attempts to zap APS directed-energy weapons report. I. Goodwin. il *Phys Today* 40:43-6 Je '87
Space-based neutral particle beam weapon [SDI program] il *Aviat Week Space Technol* 127:68-9 N 23 '87
Strategic defense and directed-energy weapons. C. K. N. Patel and N. Bloembergen. il map *Sci Am* 257:39-45 S '87

Testing
Army expedites demonstration program for neutral particle beam technology; McDonnell displays engineering mockup of SDI integrated space experiment. P. J. Klass. il *Aviat Week Space Technol* 127:26-7 Ag 17 '87
Los Alamos begins work on NPB test accelerator [Neutral Particle Beam Ground Test Accelerator] T. M. Foley. il *Aviat Week Space Technol* 127:93-4+ O 19 '87
McDonnell Douglas team to test neutral-particle beam accelerator in orbit. *Aviat Week Space Technol* 126:27 Je 8 '87

Particle beams
See also
    Atomic beams
    Electron beams

Particles
See also
    Colloids
Forest fires, barnacles and trickling oil [interacting particle systems; cover story] I. Peterson. il *Sci News* 132:220-3 O 3 '87
Ultrafine particles [Japanese research] C. Hayashi. bibl il *Phys Today* 40:44-51 D '87

Particles (Nuclear physics)
See also
    Antiprotons
    Cosmic rays
    Cosmic strings
    Electrons
    Neutrinos
    Positronium
    Protons
    Scattering (Physics)
    Superstring theories (Physics)
    Tunneling (Physics)
Elementary particle physics. *Phys Today* 40:S27-S33 Ja '87
Holes and loose ends in particle physics [adaptation of address, July 1986] S. Weinberg. por *Phys Today* 40:7+ Ja '87
Is anything left out there? G. Taubes. il *Discover* 8:42-6+ Ap '87
Marvelous mystery cosmic radiation [muons; work of Marvin Marshak] D. E. Thomsen. *Sci News* 131:228-9 Ap 11 '87
Neutral B mesons show surprisingly large flavor mixing [observed at the DORIS electron-positron storage ring] B. M. Schwarzschild. bibl il *Phys Today* 40 pt1:17-20 Ag '87
On the trail of elemental matter. D. E. Thomsen. il *Sci News* 131:202-3 Mr 28 '87
Particle physics and inflationary cosmology. A. Linde. bibl f il *Phys Today* 40:61-8 S '87
Particle physics for everybody [cover story] P. C. W. Davies. il *Sky Telesc* 74:582-7+ D '87
Pion physics at the meson factories. D. E. Nagle and others. bibl f il *Phys Today* 40:56-64 Ap '87
Quarks realistic and naive [discussion of January 1987 article, Asymptotic freedom] D. J. Gross. bibl *Phys Today* 40:112+ D '87
Rattling WIMPs. D. E. Thomsen. *Sci News* 131:303 My 9 '87
Strange stars don't glitch [quarks] *Sky Telesc* 74:580 D '87
Through a peephole tantalizingly [hadrons produced along single muon at DESY-PETRA laboratory] *Sci News* 132:219 O 3 '87
Ugly ducklings redux [cygnets from Cygnus X-3] D. E. Thomsen. *Sci News* 131:8 Ja 3 '87
Wimps [search for axions by W. Wuensch and others at Brookhaven National Laboratory] *New Yorker* 63:18-19 Jl 13 '87

Accelerators
See Accelerators (Electrons, etc.)

Parties *See* Balls (Parties); Entertaining
Parties, Birthday *See* Birthday parties
Parties, Christmas *See* Christmas entertaining
Parties, Office *See* Office parties
Parties, Political *See* Political parties

Partisan review
Minority report. C. Hitchens. *Nation* 244:39 Ja 17 '87
The New York intellectuals & the socialist legacy. J. Hart. *Natl Rev* 39:58+ S 11 '87

Partitions
See also
    Room dividers
For places where you want a wall but you don't. il *Sunset* 178:70-1 Ja '87
Room partition gives them efficient work space, family dining. il *Sunset* 178:110-11 Mr '87

Partnership
See also
Joint ventures
Limited partnership
Master limited partnership
My partner, my spouse. D. Machan. il *Forbes* 140:240+ D 14 '87
Starting a business: two heads are better than one. J. E. Cohn. il *Changing Times* 41:78-80+ F '87
Two for the money. S. Blotnick. il *Forbes* 139:166 F 23 '87
Wall Street's growing money pot [investment partnerships] H. Banks. il *Forbes* 140:110+ S 21 '87
Taxation
Congress, spare us this reform. G. W. Padwe. il *Nations Bus* 75:58 Ag '87
Preserving fiscal years. il *Nations Bus* 75:10 O '87
Parton, Dolly
about
A different Dolly. M.-A. Bendel. il por *Ladies Home J* 104:118+ N '87
Dolly. D. E. Haupt. il pors *Life* 10:58-62 Mr '87
Dolly Parton. G. Steinem. il *Ms* 15:66+ Ja '87
Dolly Parton on turning 40, and turning her life around [cover story; interview] A. W. Petrucelli. il pors *Redbook* 169:16+ Jl '87
Dolly Parton: "We had nothing but love" [cover story] A. W. Petrucelli. por *Redbook* 170:64 D '87
Here she comes, again. C. Leerhsen. il por *Newsweek* 110:73-4 N 23 '87
Partridge shooting
"A tough, strange bird" [Hungarian partridge] T. Davis. il *Field Stream* 92:52-3+ S '87
Parturition See Childbirth
Party dinners See Dinners and dining
Party guests See Guests
Party lines, Telephone See Telephone
Parviainen, Pekka
about
Sky photography near the Arctic circle. D. Di Cicco. il *Sky Telesc* 73:343-5 Mr '87
Parvin, Landon
about
George Bush polishes up his comedy routines. *Newsweek* 109:27 Ja 5 '87
Parvin, Margaret
about
A kid lands every child's dream job: fighting mice in The Nutcracker. il pors *People Wkly* 28:119-21 D 21 '87
Pasadena (Calif.)
Parades
Doo Dah, Doo Dah [Doo Dah Parade] I. Silden. il *Travel Holiday* 168:66 D '87
Doo Dah Parade. *New Yorker* 63:31-3 D 21 '87
Mechanics go bowling [electronic Bubble Trouble float in the 1986 Tournament of Roses parade] il *Pop Mech* 164:43 Ja '87
Restaurants, nightclubs, bars, etc.
Spécialités de la maison:
Parkway Grill. il *Gourmet* 48:32+ Je '87
Pasadena (Calif.). Rose Bowl (Stadium) See Rose Bowl (Pasadena, Calif.: Stadium)
Pasarell, Charles
about
A new racquet. E. Paris. il por *Forbes* 139:144-5 F 23 '87
Pascal, Blaise, 1623-1662
about
"I sez to myself, sez I". D. F. Kinlaw. il *Christ Today* 31:11 Ap 17 '87
Pascal (Computer language)
Building a random-number generator. B. A. Wichmann and D. Hill. il *Byte* 12:127-8 Mr '87
Complex math in Pascal. D. Gedeon. il *Byte* 12:121-2+ Jl '87
Concurrent programming in Turbo Pascal. M. S. Krishnamoorthy and S. Agnarsson. il *Byte* 12:127-30+ Ap '87
Dynamic memory allocation. A. Fernandes. il *Byte* 12:169-73 Ja '87
Mapping the world in Pascal. R. Miller and F. Reddy. il maps *Byte* 12:329-32+ D '87
Marshal Pascal and Pascal-2. M. Bridger. il *Byte* 12:185-6+ D '87
Processor wars. B. F. Webster. il *Byte* 12:297-8+ Je '87
Turbo Pascal 4.0. G. A. Stewart. *Byte* 12:97 N '87
Turbo Pascal debuggers. il *Radio-Electron* 58 ComputerDigest:88-90 D '87

Turbo Pascal toolboxes. N. C. Shammas. *Byte* 12:244+ Ap '87
Paschal, John H., and Schwahn, Linda
Intensive crisis counseling in Florida. il *Child Today* 15:12-16 N/D '86
Pasco (Wash.)
Education
Win/win bargaining pays off. L. Nyland. *Educ Dig* 53:28-9 S '87
Pasley, Jeffrey L.
The aides virus. *New Repub* 197:22+ O 19 '87
Green thumbs: the PIK and Roll and other scams from the farm belt. il *Wash Mon* 19:11-14+ S '87
Not-so-good books. *New Repub* 196:20-2 Ap 27 '87
PASNY See Power Authority of the State of New York
Pasquariello, Ronald D.
The skewing of America: disparities in wealth and income. il *Christ Century* 104:164-6 F 18 '87
(jt. auth) See Rybeck, Walter, and Pasquariello, Ronald D.
Pass, Joe
about
Blindfold test. L. Feather. il por *Down Beat* 54:41 O '87
Pass the blutwurst, bitte (The Egon Schiele story) [drama] See Kelly, John
Pass-throughs (Architecture)
Bigger pass-through links rooms. il *South Living* 22:156 Mr '87
Kitchen divider is a pass-through. il *Sunset* 178:118 Mr '87
Pass-through has prebuilt units above and below. il *Sunset* 179:142-3 O '87
Passamaquoddy Indians
A new band of Tribal tycoons [Tribal Assets handling investment of land claim settlements] F. Ungeheuer. il *Time* 129:56+ Mr 16 '87
Passenger entertainment (Airlines) See Airlines—Passenger entertainment
Passenger fares, Airline See Airlines—Fares
Passenger service on airlines See Airlines—Passenger service
Passengers, Airline See Air travel
Passiflora See Passionflowers
Passion flowers See Passionflowers
Passion music
See also
Phonograph records—Passion music
Passion of Christ See Jesus Christ—Passion
Passionflowers
War & passion. P. Fogden. il *Int Wildl* 17:12-17 Ja/F '87
Passive exercise equipment See Exercising equipment
Passive income generators See Limited partnership
Passive safety restraints See Automobiles—Safety devices and measures
Passive seat belt systems See Automobiles—Safety belts
Passive smoking See Smoking
Passover
Bibliography
All about Passover. il *Parents* 62:20 Ap '87
Passover cooking See Cooking, Jewish
Passports
Easy visas [visa service companies] A. S. Blask. *Travel Holiday* 168:41+ Jl '87
May the U.S. ban "undesirable" foreigners? [case of E. Mandel] S. Flack. *Sch Update* 120:35-6 O 2 '87
Stricter visa rules could keep new acts out of U.S. [foreign rock bands] M. Goldberg. *Roll Stone* p25+ F 26 '87
U.S. passports invalid for travel to Lebanon [statement, January 28, 1987] *Dep State Bull* 87:51 Mr '87
U.S. visa policy: the machinery of exclusion [McCarran-Walter Act of 1952; cover story; with editorial comment] J. Kalven. bibl f il *Bull At Sci* 43:2, 21-30 My '87
Vis-à-visas: how to cut the red tape [visa services] G. Eichler. il *Esquire* 108:72 N '87
Visa denied [U.S. denies visa to anti-Marcos activist E. B. Olaguer of the Philippines] W. Steif. il *Progressive* 51:27 F '87
France
Vexing visa. D. H. Dunn. il *Bus Week* p117 Je 1 '87
Western Europe
No foreigners needed here. X. Mellish. *Progressive* 51:14-15 My '87
Past
See also
Nostalgia
How we shred the past. M. Greenfield. il *Newsweek* 110:98 O 5 '87

Past—*cont.*
Remembering [the past as a fundamental problem for the Soviet Union] W. Pfaff. *New Yorker* 63:140-6+ D 7 '87
Pasta
See also
C. F. Mueller & Co.
Pasta! il *Seventeen* 46:116 My '87
Contamination
Mourners felled by pasta poisoning [salmonellosis] il *FDA Consum* 21:41-2 Mr '87
Pasta cooking *See* Cooking—Pasta
Pasta industry
Italy
See also
Barilla Group
Pasta sauces *See* Sauces
Pasta soups *See* Soups
Pastan, Linda, 1932-
Turnabout [poem] *New Repub* 196:46 Je 8 '87
Pastel drawing
Anita Wolff's portraits and landscapes in pastel. M. S. Schulzke. il por *Am Artist* 51:60-3+ S '87
Discovering my potential with pastel. B. Scott. il por *Am Artist* 51:56-7+ Jl '87
Kay Polk: combining pastels and watercolors to paint portraits. B. D. Stroud. il *Am Artist* 51:60-3 O '87
Suzanne Lemieux. B. S. Goldman. il por *Am Artist* 51:64-9+ N '87
Exhibitions
The late watercolor/pastels of Maurice Prendergast [exhibition at the Coe Kerr Gallery in New York City; cover story] C. Langdale. bibl f il *Antiques* 132:1084-95 N '87
Pasteur Institute (Paris, France) *See* Institut Pasteur (Paris, France)
Pastin, Mark, 1944-
Losing the future to the past. il por *Nations Bus* 75:4 F '87
Pastoral counseling
Growing together in spirituality: pastor and parish have a check-up. A. C. Krass. il *Christ Century* 104:311-14 Ap 1 '87
Seizing the moment for teaching pastoral care. I. Dixon. *Christ Century* 104:103-4 F 4-11 '87
Pastoral peoples *See* Nomads
Pastorius, Jaco
about
Obituary
Down Beat il por 54:11-12 D '87. B. Beuttler
Roll Stone por p29-30 N 19 '87. S. Benarde
Pastrick, Miriam McMullen- *See* McMullen-Pastrick, Miriam
Pastry
See also
Pie
Tarts
Beautiful pastries—without the trouble [use of commercially prepared doughs] S. Payne. il *South Living* 22:224+ N '87
Brunch bundle: it's gift-wrapped eggs, sausage [filawrapped torta] il *Sunset* 179:74-5 D '87
Fast puff pastry. C. Kummer. il *Atlantic* 259:81-3 Ja '87
French fast food: cream puff creations. A. Bailey. il *Parents* 62:127-8+ F '87
Fresh peach galette. il *Good Housekeep* 205:28 Ag '87
Fruit & cream puffs. il *Good Housekeep* 205:30 O '87
Have fun with phyllo appetizers. il *South Living* 22:207 Mr '87
Hot & hearty savory dinner pies. H. Garrison. il *Parents* 62:166-8+ O '87
Hot apple kisses. J. B. Hurley. il *Rodale's Org Gard* 34:50-1 O '87
Let them eat pastry [Paris patisserie Xavier Gourmet] K. Hom. il *N Y Times Mag* p55-6 D 20 '87
Savory turnovers. K. Haedrich. il *Ctry J* 14:29-32 Ja '87
Pastry cutters
Picture-perfect pies—the easy way. M. Langan. il *McCalls* 114:92+ Ja '87
Pastry shops *See* Bakers and bakeries
Pastures
See also
Grazing
Livestock ranges
Patagonia (Argentina and Chile)
Description and travel
Exploring Patagonia's ranges. P. Smith. il map *Américas* 39:8-15 Jl/Ag '87

Patano, Patricia
about
Making a healthy business out of fitness. M. Kort. il pors *Ms* 15:14+ Ap '87
Patch, Margaret Merwin, 1894-1987
about
Obituary
Am Craft il por 47:68+ Je/Jl '87. J. S. Plaut
Patching materials
See also
Spackling compounds
Four easy patches [wallboard] S. Clarke. il *Pop Sci* 231:136 N '87
Patel, Ambalal Somabhai
Class, caste and power. il *Courier* 40:26-7 Ja '87
Patel, C. Kumar N., and Bloembergen, Nicolaas, 1920-
Strategic defense and directed-energy weapons. il map *Sci Am* 257:39-45 S '87
Patent and Trademark Office *See* United States. Patent and Trademark Office
Patent infringement
Invasion of the patent pirates [foreign companies] C. Sims. il *Read Dig* 131:33-6 O '87
Loophole closing time. G. Bronson. il *Forbes* 139:144-5 My 4 '87
Patent pirates may soon be walking the plank [infringement by foreign companies] R. Rhein, Jr. il *Bus Week* p62-3 Je 15 '87
Protecting against patent piracy. D. DeConcini. il *USA Today (Periodical)* 116:25-6 N '87
When the going gets tough, the tough go to court [chipmakers wage intellectual property battles] K. K. Wiegner. il *Forbes* 140:36-7 D 28 '87
Patent lawyers *See* Lawyers
Patents
See also
Blood—Testing—Patents
Drugs—Patents
Genetic research—Patents
Lasers—Patents
TPA (Drug)—Patents
Apply for a patent. D. J. Sweeney. bibl il *Radio-Electron* 58:48-52+ Ja '87
Laws and regulations
See also
Patents and government-developed inventions
United States. Patent and Trademark Office
Licensing
See also
Refac Technology Development Corp.
Patents and government-developed inventions
Technology for sale. *Sci Am* 256:62 My '87
Paternal deprivation
Absentee fathers [Japan] P. Hartcher. il *World Press Rev* 34:59 O '87
The legacy of father-loss: "men that I love will leave me". E. Wakerman. *Glamour* 85:132+ My '87
Paternity
Are you lonesome tonight? [E. Presley's unknown daughter; excerpt] L. De Barbin and D. Matera. il pors *Redbook* 169:106-8+ Jl '87
Daughters of the King? [E. Presley's alleged daughters] D. Chu. il pors *People Wkly* 27:28-31 Je 22 '87
Eddie Murphy hit with paternity suit in L.A. por *Jet* 72:56 My 25 '87
Eric Dickerson must pay pregnant ex-girlfriend. pors *Jet* 72:25 S 7 '87
LBJ's 'mistress' signs with Contemporary [M. Brown] il por *Publ Wkly* 232:42-3 O 16 '87
Man sues for paternity of child that was born to his ex-girlfriend now wed [G. E. Cline] por *Jet* 71:15 Ja 26 '87
Was LBJ's final secret a son? [M. Brown claims she was president's mistress] M. Brower. il pors *People Wkly* 28:30-5 Ag 3 '87
White ex-girlfriend hits Dickerson with paternity and palimony lawsuits [E. Dickerson] pors *Jet* 72:52 Ag 3 '87
Anecdotes, facetiae, satire, etc.
Thanks to a Detroit dee jay, even death hasn't stopped Elvis from turning out more Presleys [fake "daughter of Elvis Presley" certificates issued to raise funds for hospital; work of D. Purtan] il por *People Wkly* 28:45 Jl 27 '87
Paternity leaves
Time off for new fathers. A. Levine. il *U S News World Rep* 102:69 Ap 13 '87
Paterson, Katherine
People I have known. *Writer* 100:22-4 Ap '87

Pathology
See also
Paleopathology
Paths *See* Walks (Paths)
Patient representatives *See* Hospital patient representatives
Patient restraint *See* Restraint of patients
Patients *See* Hospital patients
Patients and dentists *See* Dentists and patients
Patients and gynecologists *See* Gynecologists and patients
Patients and physicians *See* Physicians and patients
Patients and psychiatrists *See* Psychiatrists and patients
Patients and psychotherapists *See* Psychotherapists and patients
Patients' rights *See* Cancer patients—Civil rights
Patinkin, Mandy, 1953?-
about
The song of Mandy Patinkin. D. Blum. il pors *N Y* 20:52-61 S 14 '87
Patinkin, Mark
African Noel [excerpt from An African journey] il *Omni* 10:26+ D '87
Patios *See* Decks, patios, terraces, etc.
Patlak, Margie
Children's all-too-common ear infections. il *FDA Consum* 21:28-31 D '87/Ja '88
Patnaude, Dale
about
From campus to business. J. Schwartz. il por *Pers Comput* 11:189+ O '87
Paton Walsh, Jill, 1937-
A sense of audience. *Writer* 100:19-21 F '87
Patou (Jean) (Firm) *See* Jean Patou (Firm)
Patout's (Los Angeles, Calif.: Restaurant) *See* Los Angeles (Calif.)—Restaurants, nightclubs, bars, etc.
Patowmack Canal (Va.)
George Washington's Patowmack Canal. W. E. Garrett. il maps *Natl Geogr* 171:716-53 Je '87
Patowmack Canal connection. B. Culhane. il *Natl Parks* 61:16-17 Mr/Ap '87
Patriarchy
The chalice and the blade: an interview with Riane Eisler. F. P. Hosken. *Humanist* 47:26-30+ Jl/Ag '87
Patricide *See* Murder
Patrick, Brennan
Am I a loser if I don't earn big bucks? il *Glamour* 85:222 D '87
Patrick, Dennis Roy
about
The FCC's new chief will keep dialing deregulation. F. Seghers. il por *Bus Week* p156 Mr 23 '87
Kid gloves, same punch. F. Seghers. *Bus Week* p37 F 2 '87
Patrick, Jane Gassner
Your sex switch: why do you turn off when you want to turn on? *Redbook* 168:94-5+ Ap '87
Patrick, John, 1931-
Paperback history. *Hist Today* 37:59 N '87
Patrick, Margaret
about
For two New Jersey grannies misfortune sets the stage for a musical collaboration. il pors *People Wkly* 28:121 D 14 '87
Patrick County (Va.)
Economic conditions
A rural not-so-hot spot. B. Trebilcock. *Ctry J* 14:35 Je '87
Patriot missiles *See* Guided missiles
Patriotism
"Citty upon a hill". T. R. Davis and S. M. Lynn-Jones. bibl f *Foreign Policy* 66:20-38 Spr '87
Culture shock on the prairie. M. S. Van Leeuwen. il *Christ Today* 31:9 N 20 '87
Operation scare-the-pants-off-'em [Tennessee National Guard stages mock invasions of high schools to promote patriotism] *Harpers* 274:22-3 Ap '87
The religious character of American patriotism. F. Edwords. il por *Humanist* 47:20-4+ N/D '87
The stuff of patriotism [O. L. North and what makes a patriot] H. Evans. il *U S News World Rep* 103:66 Ag 10 '87
The unilateral disarmament of the American spirit [address, October 10, 1986] P. C. Roberts. *Vital Speeches Day* 53:212-15 Ja 15 '87
Anecdotes, facetiae, satire, etc.
Patriotic lying. R. Baker. il *N Y Times Mag* p14 Ag 9 '87

Patrol airplanes *See* Airplanes in patrol work
Patrol airplanes, Military *See* Airplanes, Military
Patrol airships *See* Airships in patrol work
Patrol boats
Propellers
Power prop [new Coast Guard design] D. H. Van Liew. il *Pop Sci* 231:80-1+ O '87
Patrouille de France (Flight squadron)
Alpha Jet soup. M. Phelps. il *Flying* 114:100 Mr '87
Pattee, Nanette
about
You don't need a great body at L.A.'s cushiest health club, but a big name and fat wallet help. S. K. Reed. il pors *People Wkly* 28:113-14 N 30 '87
Patten, Harry
about
Ex-hick sells sticks, is market pick. N. J. Perry. il por *Fortune* 115:52 Ja 5 '87
Patten, Joshua A., 1826 or 7-1857
about
"Captain" Mary Patten. P. L. Brosnan. il por *Oceans* 20:36-9 S/O '87
Patten, Mary Anne Brown, 1837-1861
about
"Captain" Mary Patten. P. L. Brosnan. il por *Oceans* 20:36-9 S/O '87
Patten Corporation
Ex-hick sells sticks, is market pick [H. Patten] N. J. Perry. il por *Fortune* 115:52 Ja 5 '87
Old game, new twist [bookkeeping] G. Morgenson. il *Forbes* 139:44-5+ Ja 12 '87
Pattern generators *See* Signal generators
Pattern perception
See also
Optical pattern recognition
Sound pattern recognition
Pattern recognition systems
Seeing the need for 'ART' [adaptive resonance theory represents another step in neural networks; work of Gail A. Carpenter] K. Hartley. il *Sci News* 132:14 Jl 4 '87
Patterns (Sewing)
See also
McCall Pattern Co.
Patterson, David
The causes of Down syndrome. il *Sci Am* 257:52-7+ Ag '87
Patterson, Dennis
about
A new leader for the North. B. Jones. *Macleans* 100:12 N 23 '87
Patterson, Donald W.
The watercolor page. il por *Am Artist* 51:48-51+ D '87
Patterson, Evelyn
about
Dressing in the rich tradition. W. Konrad. il pors *Work Woman* 12:83-4+ Jl '87
Patterson, Floyd
about
Floyd Patterson: still making a mark in the ring. il pors *Ebony* 42:46+ Mr '87
Manager, trainer, father, Patterson guides his son. il pors *Jet* 71:52 Mr 2 '87
Patterson, Frederick D.
about
Trained as animal doctor, Medal of Freedom winner Patterson founded UNCF. il por *Jet* 72:22 Jl 27 '87
UNCF founder Patterson to get presidential honor. por *Jet* 72:24 My 11 '87
Patterson, Freeman, 1937-
Re:vision. See alternate issues of Petersen's Photographic Magazine beginning March 1987
about
Better photography. B. Hurter. il por *Petersens Photogr Mag* 15:6 Mr '87
Patterson, K. David (Karl David), 1941-
(jt. auth) See Pyle, Gerald F., and Patterson, K. David (Karl David), 1941-
Patterson, Karl David *See* Patterson, K. David (Karl David), 1941-
Patterson, Nicholas J.
There are no sacred trusts when you're broke [address, March 26, 1987] *Vital Speeches Day* 53:484-7 Je 1 '87
Patterson, Richard S.
(jt. auth) See Koehler, Philip G., and Patterson, Richard S.
Pattison, Bill
about
Delta's spreading welcome mat. P. C. Newman. il por *Macleans* 100:35 Ag 3 '87

Pattison, Robert
Connect the dots. il *Nation* 244:295-8 Mr 7 '87
Pattiz, Norm
about
The Norman conquest. C. Capuzzi. il pors *Channels* 7:28-31+ Ap '87
Patton, Curtis
Health care and black communities. *Cent Mag* 20:61-2 Jl/Ag '87
Patton, Phil
The essential mallmanac. *Seventeen* 46:323-4+ Ag '87
Getting nuked. il *Omni* 9:82-4+ F '87
Made on the place. il *Esquire* 108:41-2 O '87
The shape of Ford's success [cover story] il pors *N Y Times Mag* p18-22+ My 24 '87
Paugh, Tom
Sports afield. il *Writer* 100:26 S '87
Paul, the Apostle, Saint
about
A new paradigm for Paul. D. J. Harrington. il *America* 157:290-3 O 31 '87
Paul, Alexandra
about
In Dragnet, Alexandra Paul proves that even a squeaky-clean virgin can get her man, Friday. M. Dougherty. il por *People Wkly* 28:58-9 Jl 27 '87
Sexy looks: celebrity secrets. il pors *Harpers Bazaar* 120:146-57 My '87
Paul, Annette av
about
Working with music, muscle and motion. P. Hluchy. pors *Macleans* 100:54 Mr 9 '87
Paul, Anthony
Can Aquino break the grip of crony corruption? il pors *Read Dig* 131:83-7 Jl '87
Paul, Aranjaniyil K., and others
Coexistence of guanylate cyclase and atrial natriuretic factor receptor in a 180-kD protein. bibl f il *Science* 235:1224-6 Mr 6 '87
Paul, Jerry *See* Hirshberg, Gerald
Paul, Les, 1915-
about
The Les Paul fan club. M. Walker. il por *N Y* 20:28 S 7 '87
Paul, William E.
(jt. auth) *See* Snapper, Clifford M., and Paul, William E.
Paul, Epistles of *See* Bible. N.T. Epistles of Paul
Paul Bunyan (Legendary character)
Paul Bunyan dons a giant T-shirt—are tall tails next? [Autotype U.S.A. dresses statue in Bemidji, Minn.] il *People Wkly* 28:97 Ag 3 '87
Paul Taylor Dance Company
The big Sleep [performance of Syzygy at City Center, New York City] T. Tobias. il *N Y* 20:76-7 My 11 '87
Happy families [performance of Kith and kin at City Center, New York City] T. Tobias. il *N Y* 20:100-1 My 18 '87
On edge [dancer D. Parsons; cover story] M. Hunt. il pors *Dance Mag* 61:43-7 S '87
Paul Taylor, pace maker: those who can, do [performances at City Center, New York City] E. Zimmer. il *Dance Mag* 61:36-40 S '87
Taylor and York to show a decade's collaboration. S. Reiter. por *Dance Mag* 61:6 Ap '87
Taylor-made design. S. Flatow. il *Theatre Crafts* 21:24-5+ Ja '87
Paula Cooper Gallery
Contemporary energies at the Paula Cooper Gallery. A. Haden-Guest. il por *Archit Dig* 44:78+ Ap '87
Pauley, Jane
about
Jane Pauley's charmed life. J. Stone. il por *McCalls* 114:152+ Ap '87
Pauley Petroleum Inc.
Robert Anderson is shaking up the oil patch again [merging Hondo into Pauley] J. Flynn. il por *Bus Week* p39 Ag 17 '87
Pauli, U., and others
Protein-DNA interactions in vivo upstream of a cell cycle-regulated human H4 histone gene. bibl f il *Science* 236:1308-11 Je 5 '87
Paulist Productions
Of many things [TV movie We are the children] J. W. Donohue. *America* 156:inside cover Mr 14 '87
Paulsen, Don
about
"We will never, ever give up!" [with editorial comment by Elizabeth Sloan] B. Raymond. il pors *McCalls* 145:10, 66+ Mr '87

Paulsen, Eileen
about
"We will never, ever give up!" [with editorial comment by Elizabeth Sloan] B. Raymond. il pors *McCalls* 145:10, 66+ Mr '87
Paulson, Alan
about
On the road. S. Staggs. il por *Art News* 86:15-16 O '87
Paulson, Allen E.
about
Why Gulfstream's rivals are gazing up in envy. S. Ticer. il por *Bus Week* p66+ F 16 '87
Paulson, Olaf B., and Newman, Eric A.
Does the release of potassium from astrocyte endfeet regulate cerebral blood flow? bibl f il *Science* 237:896-8 Ag 21 '87
Paulucci, Jeno F.
about
Jeno Paulucci's dream: bring fiber optics home. S. Ticer. il por *Bus Week* p34-5 S 21 '87
Paulus, Stephen
about
The postman always rings twice [opera] Reviews *Opera News* 51:38-9 Mr 28 '87. M. Anthony
PaVage Fitness Images (Firm)
Making a healthy business out of fitness. M. Kort. il pors *Ms* 15:14+ Ap '87
PaVage Fitness Innovations (Firm)
Making a healthy business out of fitness. M. Kort. il pors *Ms* 15:14+ Ap '87
Pavarotti, Luciano
about
Dead from Lincoln Center. S. Lipman. *Commentary* 83:59-63 My '87
Music. P. G. Davis. *N Y* 20:72 Ja 26 '87
The Sutherland/Pavarotti anniversary gala. il pors *Opera News* 51:40-1 F 28 '87
Pave Paws *See* Radar defense networks
Pavements
See also
Potholes (Pavements)
Roads
Paving can be easy [dry-laid method] il *South Living* 22:102-3+ Mr '87
Pavia, Phillip, 1912-
about
Phillip Pavia at Edward Thorp. N. Princenthal. il *Art Am* 75:149 Je '87
Pavilion (Newport Beach, Calif.: Restaurant) *See* Newport Beach (Calif.)—Restaurants, nightclubs, bars, etc.
Pavilions
Classical allusions: a hillside pavilion in Greece [designed by Hugh Newell Jacobsen] C. Aillaud. il *Archit Dig* 44:72-7 Jl '87
Life at Heron Bay: Palladian pavilion on the island of Barbados [cover story] M. Tree. il *Archit Dig* 44:54-9+ Ag '87
Pavilions, Garden *See* Garden houses, shelters, etc.
Le Pavillon (New York, N.Y.: Restaurant) *See* New York (N.Y.)—Restaurants, nightclubs, bars, etc.
Pavo (Constellation) *See* Constellations
Pawnbroking
See also
Cash America Investments (Firm)
Paxson, Lowell
about
The rise and rise of HSN. M. Gill. il pors *Esquire* 107:70 Ap '87
Paxton, Steve
about
Reviews:
S. Paxton and L. Nelson at The Kitchen, New York City. S. Sommer. pors *Dance Mag* 61:22 S '87
Pay differentials *See* Wage differentials
Pay-for-knowledge plans *See* Skill-based pay
Pay-in-kind securities
Never-never money. B. Weberman. il *Forbes* 139:265 Je 15 '87
PIK 'em with care. A. Sloan. il *Forbes* 140:32-3 D 14 '87
Pay N Pak Stores, Inc.
The Street is fretting over 'Street sweeps' [P. Bilzerian loses Pay 'N Pak when Morgan Stanley cancels trade] A. Bianco. il por *Bus Week* p71-2 Ag 3 '87
Pay N Save Inc.
No customers, no profits. D. Henry. il *Forbes* 139:52+ F 23 '87

Pay-per-view cable television *See* Cable television
Pay raises *See* Wages and salaries
Pay television, Cable *See* Cable television
Payload assist modules *See* Space vehicles—Propulsion systems
Payment in kind program *See* Agricultural administration
Payments, Balance of *See* Balance of payments
Payne, Cynthia
> *about*

Sex and 'Madam Cyn'. N. Underwood. *Macleans* 100:48 F 23 '87
Payne, David Mode, 1907-1985
> *about*

Portraits in style: David Mode Payne's paintings of interiors. M. M. Thomas. il *Archit Dig* 44:196-201 Ap '87
Payne, Freda
> *about*

Freda Payne sings backup on new 'Band of gold'. il por *Jet* 71:54 Ja 26 '87
Payne, Janice
My experience with the peer mentor program. *Child Today* 16:20 Jl/Ag '87
Payne, Rolce Redard
Banking land. il *House Gard* 159:56+ S '87
Payroll withholding taxes *See* Withholding tax
Pays, Amanda
> *about*

Amanda's style pays off. B. Goodwin. pors *Harpers Bazaar* 120:222-3 O '87
A high-tech heroine heats up the screen. J. Conant. por *Newsweek* 109:62 Ap 20 '87
Max Headroom's steel-souled co-star, Amanda Pays, takes off her hat to nobody but herself. M. Ginsberg and F. Sanello. il pors *People Wkly* 28:129-30 O 19 '87
Payson, Charles Shipman, 1898-1985
> *about*

The outsider. L. Gubernick. il pors *Forbes* 140 Sp Issue:38+ O 26 '87
Payson, Virginia
> *about*

The outsider. L. Gubernick. il pors *Forbes* 140 Sp Issue:38+ O 26 '87
Payton, Robert L.
Tainted money: the ethics and rhetoric of divestment. il *Change* 19:55-60 My/Je '87
Payton, Walter, 1954-
> *about*

Ditka praises Payton as best running back. il pors *Jet* 73:48 D 28 '87-Ja 4 '88
Payton pursues pioneer plan to become NFL owner. il por *Jet* 72:52 Je 1 '87
Payton says he may be first owner/coach/player. por *Jet* 72:48 Je 29 '87
Payton signs contract for likely final year. *Jet* 72:47 Ag 17 '87
Payton's agent could pose a problem with NFL plans. *Jet* 72:50 Jl 13 '87
Paz, Octavio, 1914-
The barricades and beyond. *New Repub* 197:26-30 N 9 '87
Edith Piaf among the pygmies; tr. by Helen R. Lane. il *N Y Times Book Rev* 92:1+ S 6 '87
Food of the gods; tr. by Eliot Weinberger. il *N Y Rev Books* 34:3-7 F 26 '87
Pazienza, Vinny
> *about*

Local boy makes good. P. Putnam. il pors *Sports Illus* 66:59 Je 15 '87
The Paz that refreshes. D. S. Looney. il pors *Sports Illus* 66:62+ Je 1 '87
PBS *See* Public Broadcasting Service
PBX (Private branch exchanges) *See* Telephone exchanges
PC Network (Firm)
PC Network [letter] *Pers Comput* 11:15-16+ S '87
PC-Write (Word processor program) *See* Word processors and processing—Programming
PCBs *See* Polychlorinated biphenyls
PCS, Inc.
Arizona high. S. N. Chakravarty. il por *Forbes* 140:178+ N 2 '87
PC's Ltd.
> *See also*
> Dell Computer Corporation
Pea coats *See* Coats
Peabody, Elizabeth Palmer, 1804-1894
> *about*

Three sisters who showed the way. M. Marshall. il pors *Am Herit* 38:58-63+ S/O '87
Peabody, Sophia *See* Hawthorne, Sophia Amelia Peabody, 1811-1871

Peabody (Memphis, Tenn.: Hotel) *See* Memphis (Tenn.)—Hotels, motels, etc.
Peabody Awards
'Cosby show' captures coveted Peabody honor. *Jet* 72:32 Je 1 '87
A quantity of quality. L. Brown. il *Channels* 7:20 Je '87
Peabody family
> *about*

Three sisters who showed the way. M. Marshall. il pors *Am Herit* 38:58-63+ S/O '87
Peace
> *See also*
> International Year of Peace, 1986
> Pacifism
> Religion and peace
> United Nations
> Women and peace
> World Peace Run, 1987

Causes of war and causes of peace [address, February 12, 1987] F. A. Rodgers. *Vital Speeches Day* 53:375-9 Ap 1 '87
U.S. presidents on war and peace. O. Berger. il *Saturday Evening Post* 259:36+ Ja/F '87
Peace and literature
Fighting words: the myth of the 'hereditary enemy'. J. Blot. il *Courier* 40:25-8 Jl '87
Peace conferences
> *See also*
> Religion and peace—Conferences
Peace Corps (U.S.)
How the Peace Corps exports friendship [Dominican Republic] H. Browne. il *Sch Update* 119:27 F 23 '87
Peace [Family Night celebration for relatives of volunteers] *New Yorker* 63:29-30 My 25 '87
Peace Corps follies [Belize] S. Donziger. il *Progressive* 51:28-31 Mr '87
Peace movement
> *See also*
> Anti-nuclear movement
> Great Peace March, 1986

The ballot trap. R. Jahnkow. il *Progressive* 51:14-15 Ag '87
Be your own peacemaker [views of A. Ayvazian and M. T. Klare] S. H. Day, Jr. il *Progressive* 51:17-18 Ap '87
Body on the line [B. Willson run over by train while protesting against U.S. arms shipments to Central America] B. Kessler. *Nation* 245:329 O 3 '87
Making a career of it [unemployed steel worker becomes professional peace worker] L. Evans. il *Progressive* 51:34 D '87

> **Northern Ireland**
> *See also*
> Community of Peace People of Northern Ireland
> **Poland**
> *See also*
> Freedom and Peace (Organization)

Peace of Mind (Organization)
Single and free—of AIDS. T. Gallant-Stokes. por *Black Enterp* 18:24 Ag '87
Peace studies
> *See also*
> United States Institute of Peace

Education for peace [address, October 9, 1987] J. L. Carro. *Vital Speeches Day* 54:157-60 D 15 '87
The 'Kids for Peace' reach out [Moorestown, N.J. Friends School exchange program with East Germany] D. Dahlke. il *World Press Rev* 34:45 Ap '87
Politics and "peace education". A. Ryerson. *Read Dig* 130:133-8 Je '87
Peacekeeper (Missile) *See* Guided missiles
Peach, Lucinda
Patrolling the park beat. il *Natl Parks* 61:24-9 N/D '87
Peach Bottom nuclear power plant (Delta, Pa.) *See* Nuclear power plants
Peach desserts *See* Desserts
Peach pie *See* Pie
Peacock, Cliffton
> *about*

Cliffton Peacock. D. Bonetti. il *Art News* 86:34 Mr '87
Peale, Norman Vincent
The greatest gift you can give your children for Christmas; ed. by William T. Buckley. il *Good Housekeep* 205:116+ D '87
Why I believe there is life after death. il *Read Dig* 130:139-40 My '87

Peale, Norman Vincent—*cont.*
about
Peale launches audio publisher for positive-thinking authors. T. Spain. il *Publ Wkly* 232:39-40 N 20 '87
Peanut butter
See also
Cooking—Peanut butter
Peanut butter. il *Consum Rep* 52:475-8 Ag '87
Peanut butter. il *Consum Rep* 52:356-9 D '87
Advertising
Peanut butter: a dip for the health-conscious [Procter & Gamble's campaign for Jif] il *Newsweek* 110:42 Jl 20 '87
Peanuts
See also
Cooking—Nuts
Grow your own peanuts! N. Bubel. il *Rodale's Org Gard* 34:24-8 Je '87
Peanuts (Comic strip) *See* Comic books, strips, etc.
Pear desserts *See* Desserts
Pearce, Carol Ann
The fast-food diet. il *Harpers Bazaar* 120:84+ Mr '87
Sweet tooth diet: the latest scoop. il *Harpers Bazaar* 120:62+ Jl '87
Thin thighs in 3 weeks. il *Harpers Bazaar* 120:116-17+ Ja '87
Pearce, Fred
With IT in the scientific jet set. *World Press Rev* 34:55 Ja '87
Pearce, Richard
about
No mercy [film] Reviews
N Y 20:45 Ja 5 '87. D. Denby
People Wkly il 27:10 Ja 5 '87. P. Travers
Pearce, Richard B.
Fat & muscle. il *Women's Sports Fitness* 9:36-9 Jl '87
Pearce, Simon
about
An everyday luxury. N. F. Weber. il *House Gard* 159:76+ F '87
Pearcy, Robert W., and others
Carbon gain by plants in natural environments. bibl f il *BioScience* 37:21-9 Ja '87
Pearl, Minnie, 1912-
about
Minnie Pearl. L. Rozen. il pors *People Wkly* 28:65-6+ O 26 '87
Pearsall, Paul
8 wrong ideas about sex: his and yours [excerpt from Super marital sex] il *Glamour* 85:216+ N '87
Love busters [excerpt from Super marital sex] *Ladies Home J* 104:96+ O '87
Pearson, Carol Lynn
about
Carol Lynn Pearson pens a moving memoir on her gay husband's death from AIDS. K. McMurran. il pors *People Wkly* 27:91+ F 2 '87
Pearson, Charlene
about
Gooden's ex-fiancée nabbed en route to reconciliation. il por *Jet* 71:12 F 16 '87
Pearson, David E. (David Eric), 1953-
Questions that won't go away [excerpt from KAL 007: the cover-up; cover story] *Nation* 245:181+ S 5 '87
Pearson, Drew
about
An all-star entrepreneur. L. Gite. il por *Black Enterp* 17:22 F '87
Pearson, Gerald
about
Carol Lynn Pearson pens a moving memoir on her gay husband's death from AIDS. K. McMurran. il pors *People Wkly* 27:91+ F 2 '87
Pearson, Natalie
Murder as usual. il *Progressive* 51:50 F '87
Pearson, Peter
about
High drama in the world of film. B. Amiel. il *Macleans* 100:7 S 14 '87
Pearson, Richard L.
Laser listener [cover story] il *Radio-Electron* 58:39-44 O '87
Laser listener legalities [discussion of October 1987 article, Laser listener] il *Radio-Electron* 58:8-9 N '87
Pearson (Drew) Enterprises *See* Drew Pearson Enterprises
Pearson plc
Murdoch increases stake in Pearson conglomerate to 14.7%. V. Menkes. *Publ Wkly* 232:28 O 9 '87
Pearson, in a pickle [R. Murdoch's stake in publishing operations] S. Miller. *Bus Week* p60 O 12 '87

Peary, Robert Edwin, 1856-1920
about
The Eskimo offspring of Matthew Henson. S. A. Counter. il pors *Ebony* 42:50+ Ja '87
Explorers' Eskimo offspring visit America. il *Ebony* 42:84+ S '87
No slouches at breaking the ice, polar explorers Peary and Henson each left behind a son in the Arctic. C. Neuhaus. il pors *People Wkly* 27:41-2 Je 1 '87
Peary Expeditions (1886-1909)
The Eskimo offspring of Matthew Henson. S. A. Counter. il pors *Ebony* 42:50+ Ja '87
Eskimo son of explorer Matthew Henson dies in Greenland of cancer. pors *Jet* 72:12 Jl 27 '87
Explorers' Eskimo offspring visit America [children of M. Henson and R. Peary] il *Ebony* 42:84+ S '87
Matthew Henson will be reburied in Arlington. por *Jet* 73:26 N 23 '87
Matthew Henson's Eskimo son comes to U.S. for a reunion with relatives. il pors *Jet* 72:6 Je 15 '87
No slouches at breaking the ice, polar explorers Peary and Henson each left behind a son in the Arctic. C. Neuhaus. il pors *People Wkly* 27:41-2 Je 1 '87
Peas
See also
Winged peas
Peas and potatoes. P. H. Dunphy. il *Ctry J* 14:53-9 Ap '87
Purple's the new color for edible-pod peas. il *Sunset* 179:240 N '87
Peasant Restaurants (Firm)
Career makeover: from bank officer to restaurant V.P. [B. Van] il por *Glamour* 85:170 Ap '87
Peat, F. David, 1938-
(jt. auth) See Briggs, John, and Peat, F. David, 1938-
Peat
Mysteries of the bog. L. E. Levathes. il *Natl Geogr* 171:396-420 Mr '87
Peattie, Lisa Redfield
One night in the Beatty lockup. il *Commonweal* 114:140-3 Mr 13 '87
Pecans
See also
Cooking—Nuts
Pechman, Joseph A., 1918-
Taxes abroad: pressures for tax reform. il *Current* 295:30-8 S '87
Pechter, Kerry
Marketing miniatures. il por *Rodale's Org Gard* 34:72-6 D '87
Peck, Amelia
The Gothic revival library at the Metropolitan Museum of Art. il *Antiques* 131:824-7 Ap '87
Peck, Gregory, 1916-
about
Gregory Peck. B. Darrach. il pors *People Wkly* 27:78-82 Je 15 '87
Peck, Jim
Noam Chomsky: an American dissident [interview; excerpt from The Chomsky reader] il *Progressive* 51:22-5 Jl '87
Peck, Keenen
Just shut up and shop. il *Progressive* 51:4, 23-5 O '87
On the way to the forum. il *Progressive* 51:28-9 F '87
Peck, M. Scott (Morgan Scott)
about
The best kind of advertising. J. A. Trachtenberg. il por *Forbes* 139:91-2 Ap 20 '87
Self-help guru M. Scott Peck seeks the road to peace—for the world and himself. M. Brower. il pors *People Wkly* 28:125-8+ O 26 '87
Peck, Morgan Scott *See* Peck, M. Scott (Morgan Scott)
Peck, Robert A.
Resolving the Sri Lankan conflict [statement, March 12, 1987] *Dep State Bull* 87:68-71 My '87
Peck, Robert McCracken, 1952-
Terry Shortt: a life's journey into nature. il por *Int Wildl* 17:4-11 Jl/Ag '87
Peckinpaugh, Janet
about
Connecticut's on-air authority. J. Giambanco. il pors *Work Woman* 12:91-2+ Ja '87
Pécoul (Martinique: Plantation) *See* Plantations—Martinique
Pecqueur, Michel
about
Turning Elf into a giant. S. Tully. il por *Fortune* 116:52 Ag 3 '87
Pectins
Grapefruit pectin reduces cholesterol [research by James Cerda] *Sci News* 132:63 Jl 25 '87

Pectins—*cont.*
Low-sugar jams. A. Hirsch. il *Rodale's Org Gard* 34:46+ Je '87
Pectin promises [lowers cholesterol] D. Welch. il *Health* 19:13 D '87
Pectin—the super fiber. G. Maleskey. il *Prevention* 39:60-4 Mr '87
Why carrots may reduce cholesterol. *Sci News* 131:409 Je 27 '87
Pedagogy *See* College teaching; Teaching
Pedal powered aircraft *See* Human powered aircraft
Pedal powered vehicles *See* Human powered vehicles
Pedder, Alan
about
Synthesizing success. C. Brown. il por *Forbes* 139:179 Je 1 '87
Peddlers and peddling
See also
Street trades
Pedersen, Charles J., 1904-
about
Chemistry in the image of biology. R. Lewin. il pors *Science* 238:611-12 O 30 '87
Pedersen, Niels C., and others
Isolation of a T-lymphotropic virus from domestic cats with an immunodeficiency-like syndrome. bibl f il *Science* 235:790-3 F 13 '87
Pedersen, Robert C., and Brownie, Alexander C.
Steroidogenesis-activator polypeptide isolated from a rat Leydig cell tumor. bibl f il *Science* 236:188-90 Ap 10 '87
Pedersen, William
about
William Pedersen: the postmodernist. B. Dumaine. il por *Fortune* 115:160-1 Je 22 '87
Pedersen-Lane, Joan, and Belfort, Marlene
Variable occurrence of the *nrd*B intron in the T-even phages suggests intron mobility. bibl f il *Science* 237:182-4 Jl 10 '87
Pederson Custom Golf Clubs Inc.
The swing's the thing. G. Waggoner. il *Esquire* 107:25-6 My '87
Pedestrians
Doin' the pedestrian two-step. D. C. Ross. il *Mot Trend* 39:116 S '87
Pediatricians
Baby doctors: choice & prime. P. Theroux. il *Parents* 62:78+ Ap '87
Choosing your child's pediatrician. S. S. Stautberg. *Work Woman* 12:94+ Jl '87
Health and hygiene
'I want him crucified' [pediatrician R. J. Huse loses his practice after testing positive for AIDS] G. Hackett. il por *Newsweek* 110:36 O 5 '87
Pedicure *See* Foot—Care and hygiene
Pedodontics
Dental care for children: an expert's advice. H. Simmons, Jr. *McCalls* 114:114+ F '87
The new dental care for children. il *Good Housekeep* 205:94 S '87
Open wide! D. Edmondson. il *Parents* 62:112-16+ Mr '87
Pedra Furada site (Brazil) *See* Brazil—Antiquities
Pee (Term)
Somewhat vulgar. W. Safire. *N Y Times Mag* p8+ Ja 4 '87
Pee-wee's playhouse [television program] See Television program reviews—Single works
Peer counseling
Keeping youth in school: a public-private collaboration [peer mentor program for high school students sponsored by Catholic University and Marriott; with reports by J. Payne and J. Smith] S. Lee and others. il *Child Today* 16:15-21 Jl/Ag '87
Peer groups
Are your kid's friends bad influences? B. Spock. por *Redbook* 169:22 Je '87
Peer influence. D. Elkind. il *Parents* 62:206 Ap '87
Positive peer pressure. J. P. Comer. il *Parents* 62:205 D '87
Peer review
Geographical limit on research funds in bill seen as swipe at peer review [University Research Initiative program] J. Walsh. *Science* 238:1506 D 11 '87
Gossip and peer review at NSF [case of J. Kalb] E. Marshall. *Science* 238:1502 D 11 '87
Peer review—'oops—merit review in for some changes at NSF. J. Walsh. *Science* 235:153 Ja 9 '87
Anecdotes, facetiae, satire, etc.
Scaling the ivory tower [publishing mediocre articles] H. J. Bullford. il *Change* 19:56-7 S/O '87

Peer tutoring *See* Tutors and tutoring
Peerman, Dean
Twenty-two years in Castro's prisons. il por *Christ Century* 104:1029-33 N 18 '87
Peet, R. K., and Christensen, Norman L.
Competition and tree death. bibl il *BioScience* 37:586-95 S '87
Peete, Calvin
about
Golf carts 'killing' caddies and blacks on PGA tour. por *Jet* 71:46 Ja 26 '87
The greener grass of Calvin Peete. T. Huth. il pors *Esquire* 107:108-12+ F '87
Peete drops by course in time for $105G prize. por *Jet* 72:50 Ap 13 '87
PGAer Calvin Peete hosts Fla. benefit golf tourney. por *Jet* 71:49 F 23 '87
Peeves
Pet peeves: when they drive you wild! W. J. Rohr. il *Teen* 31:100-2 Je '87
Pegase (Clos) Winery *See* Clos Pegase Winery
Peggy Sue got married [film] *See* Motion picture reviews—Single works
Pegram Medal *See* Physics—Awards
Peguis Indians *See* Indians of North America—Canada
Peirce, James
Is the administration approach to federal employee drug testing sound? [excerpts from testimony, March 18, 1986] *Congr Dig* 66:155+ My '87
Pekinel, Güher
about
When Güher and Süher Pekinel take the stage, classical piano buffs savor a twin Turkish delight. D. Grogan. il pors *People Wkly* 27:48+ Mr 16 '87
Pekinel, Süher
about
When Güher and Süher Pekinel take the stage, classical piano buffs savor a twin Turkish delight. D. Grogan. il pors *People Wkly* 27:48+ Mr 16 '87
Peking (China) *See* Beijing (China)
Pekkanen, John, 1939-
AIDS: the plague that knows no boundaries [with editorial comment] *Read Dig* 130:9-11, 49-58 Je '87
Doctors who use drugs. il *Good Housekeep* 205:198-9+ S '87
Péladeau, Pierre
about
Montreal's widening newspaper wars. A. Wilson-Smith. il por *Macleans* 100:46 Mr 9 '87
Peled, Abraham
The next computer revolution. bibl (p183) il *Sci Am* 257:56-64 O '87
Peled, Matti
about
An Israeli and an Arab tour for peace. J. M. Wall. *Christ Century* 104:427-8 My 6 '87
Pelée, Mount (Martinique) *See* Mount Pelée (Martinique)
Pelican Publishing Company Inc.
'Best editorial cartoons' series: a southern perennial. B. Summer. *Publ Wkly* 232:42 S 4 '87
Pelicans
Pelicans vs. pesticides. il *Nat Hist* 96:6 S '87
Treatment
This doctor is for the birds [H. Albers; cover story] E. Boddie. il pors *50 Plus* 27:20-4 Jl '87
Pelicci, Pier Giuseppe, and others
Molecular diversity of the human T-gamma constant region genes. bibl f il *Science* 237:1051-5 Ag 28 '87
Pelikan, Jaroslav Jan, 1923-
Escape into esthetics. *Cent Mag* 20:57-8 Ja/F '87
Speak of the devil. *Commentary* 83:63-6 Ap '87
Pell, Claiborne
about
Coming soon: the odd couple. T. Noah and E. Clift. il pors *Newsweek* 109:28 F 2 '87
Pell, Eve
Brokenhearted me. il *Ms* 15:80 Je '87
Quit telling women to slow down. il *Women's Sports Fitness* 9:68 Je '87
Pellauer, Mary
Pornography: an agenda for the churches [cover story] il *Christ Century* 104:651-5 Jl 29-Ag 5 '87
Pellegrino, Edmund D.
about
Life and death decisions: do you trust yourself to play God? [cover story; interview] por *U S Cathol* 52:6-13 O '87
Pellegrino, Renaud
about
Charm: in the bag . . . il por *Vogue* 177:346 O '87

Pellizzari, Valerio
The 'apex of civilization'. il *World Press Rev* 34:54 D '87
Peloponnesian War, 431-404 B.C. *See* Greece—History—Peloponnesian War, 431-404 B.C.
Pelton, Ronald William
about
Secrets storm. *Nation* 244:4-5 Ja 10 '87
Pelts *See* Hides and skins
Peltz, Nelson
about
Who's getting the deal in the Triangle shuffle? C. Power. il por *Bus Week* p78 N 23 '87
Pelvic examinations *See* Gynecologic examinations
Pelvic inflammatory disease
P.I.D.: the "pay later" threat to your sexual health. C. Norwood. *Mademoiselle* 93:122 Mr '87
Pelvic inflammatory disease. P. A. Hillard. il *Parents* 62:188+ D '87
Pelvic pain
The posture of pelvic pain. *Prevention* 39:10+ D '87
Pelzel, Thomas
Art: paintings from the Arts and crafts period. il *Archit Dig* 44:78-83+ Jl '87
Pemberton, Hilda R.
about
Prince George's County, Md. Council gets woman leader. *Jet* 71:22 Ja 12 '87
PEN
Mr. Peepers: PEN goes the way of all flesh [benefit dinner hosted by G. Steinberg] il *N Y* 20:29-30 Ap 13 '87
My dinner with Imelda. R. Howard. *Harpers* 275:29-30+ O '87
Pen and ink drawing *See* Pen drawing
Pen drawing
Pen & ink: John Anderson. M. S. Doherty. il *Am Artist* 51:64-7 Ag '87
Pen names *See* Pseudonyms
Pen pals
The best of pen pals. M. Dorris. il *Seventeen* 46:272 Ag '87
Find a letter-perfect friend. il *Teen* 31:82 S '87
Friendship: it's in the mail [picking pen pals by numerology] il *Teen* 31:56 F '87
Pen pals: from quills to keyboards [Keylink computer network] *Newsweek* 110:60 D 21 '87
Peña, Federico
The challenge of immigration. il *USA Today (Periodical)* 115:60-2 Ja '87
about
A dogfight in Denver. M. Ivey. il por *Bus Week* p38 Ap 27 '87
Penal institutions *See* Prisons
Penance
Penance in crisis. J. J. Gallen and J. J. Lopresti. *America* 157:217-22 O 10 '87
Reconciliation rooms: I'd rather be kept in the dark. M. Scheiber. *U S Cathol* 52:30-2 Ap '87
Pencil drawing
Drawn to the past [M. Leonard's pencil portraits of contemporary people in the style of famous artists] L. Kirstein. il por *House Gard* 159:168-71+ N '87
Further techniques for using colored pencils [cover story] B. Borgeson. il por *Am Artist* 51:52-7 Ap '87
Sigmund Abeles: the Max drawings [drawings of premature son] T. Bolt. il *Am Artist* 51:50-5 O '87
Talk about lines! A guy paid $26,400 for this drawing—and then they demolished it [auction of conceptual art by S. LeWitt] M. Small. il por *People Wkly* 27:43-4 My 25 '87
William A. Berry [colored pencil still lifes] B. S. Goldman. il por *Am Artist* 51:68-73+ F '87
Pencils
A gripping invention [Stetro pencil grippers invented by C. Rusk] D. Marth. il por *Nations Bus* 75:82 My '87
Penck, A. R., 1939-
about
A.R. Penck at Jule Kewenig and Ropac. C. Vielhaber. il *Art Am* 75:167 D '87
Penderecki, Krzysztof
about
Penderecki and Shostakovich: death affirms life. L. Mendes. *Christ Century* 104:287-8 Mr 18-25 '87
Pendergrass, Teddy
about
Pendergrass marries in ceremony at his home. il por *Jet* 72:64 Jl 6 '87
Teddy Pendergrass starts new life with new wife [cover story] il pors *Jet* 72:26-7 Jl 20 '87

Peng, Chen *See* Peng Zhen, 1899-
Peng Zhen, 1899-
about
China's new Year of the Mule. F. Willey. il por *Newsweek* 109:43 F 9 '87
Penguin Books Inc.
Marie Winn and Penguin designate November 'No TV Month' [forthcoming publication of Unplugging the plug-in drug] *Publ Wkly* 231:49-50 Je 5 '87
Penguin rushes paperback of book on Reagan [D. E. Moldea's Dark victory] *Publ Wkly* 231:74 Ap 10 '87
Penguins
No room for a hermit [yellow-eyed penguin] A. Vernon. il *Int Wildl* 17:22-4 N/D '87
Sexual behavior
See Sexual behavior—Birds
Penguins in advertising
Foot and Falconetti are TV's most popular penguin pitchmen, and it serves them right. il por *People Wkly* 28:50 Ag 24 '87
Penis
Members only: what every guy wants a girl to know. J. McCabe. *Mademoiselle* 93:278-9+ Mr '87
Penitence *See* Repentance
Penitentiaries *See* Prisons
Penmanship
Study and teaching
Aids and devices
A gripping invention [Stetro pencil grippers invented by C. Rusk] D. Marth. il por *Nations Bus* 75:82 My '87
Penn, Arthur, 1922-
about
Dead of winter [film] Reviews
Macleans 100:52 F 23 '87. L. O'Toole
New Repub 196:24-5 Mr 9 '87. S. Kauffmann
Newsweek il 109:79 F 23 '87. D. Ansen
People Wkly 27:6 Mr 2 '87. T. Cunneff
Time il 129:76+ F 16 '87. R. Corliss
Penn, Sagon
about
Black who killed white cop, wounded others; acquitted. *Jet* 73:47 N 2 '87
Penn, Sean
about
As Hollywood's fastest fists fly again, a prosecutor plans to give Sean Pennance. E. Levin. il pors *People Wkly* 27:38-9 My 18 '87
Everyone said it wouldn't last . . . [cover story] J. Kaufman. il pors *People Wkly* 28:138-9+ D 14 '87
First he lost his temper, now he's lost his freedom: Sean Penn is going to jail. il por *People Wkly* 28:38 Jl 6 '87
Penn & Teller
about
The theatre. M. Kramer. *New Yorker* 63:106-7 D 21 '87
Penn Central Corp.
This Penn Central spinoff may soar [Sprague Technologies] G. G. Marcial. *Bus Week* p61 Ag 31 '87
With Lindner in charge, Penn Central is on the prowl. R. Mitchell. il *Bus Week* p80-1 Ap 20 '87
Pennacchia, Michael
Pedaling Vermont. il map *Travel Holiday* 167:62-6+ My '87
Villa Vera. il *Travel Holiday* 168:8+ N '87
Pennant-Rea, Rupert
about
Mrs. Thatcher's election prospects [interview] A. Balk. il por *World Press Rev* 34:30-3 Ja '87
Pennathur, Sudha Messerly
about
Shamianas, anyone? P. Gupte. il pors *Forbes* 140:190+ O 5 '87
Pennell, H. Barrett, Jr.
The quality of mercy [story] il *Saturday Evening Post* 259:64-5 O '87
Penney, Alexandra
I'll never forgive you! il *Ladies Home J* 104:42+ Mr '87
Penney, Terry R., and Bharathan, Desikan
Power from the sea. bibl (p128) il map *Sci Am* 256:86-92 Ja '87
Penney (J. C.) Company, Inc. *See* J. C. Penney Company, Inc.
Pennica, Diane, and others
Identification of human uromodulin as the Tamm-Horsfall urinary glycoprotein. bibl f il *Science* 236:83-8 Ap 3 '87

Pennies *See* Coins
Penniman, Richard *See* Little Richard
Pennington, M. Basil
　　Centering prayer. *America* 156:169-71 F 28 '87
Pennison, Marleen
　　　　　　　about
　　Marleen Pennison: if a dance has a script, is it a play?
　　il *Dance Mag* 61:7 D '87
Pennsylvania
　　　　See also
　　Architecture, Domestic—Pennsylvania
　　Brandywine Valley (Pa. and Del.)
　　Bucks County (Pa.)
　　Express highways—Pennsylvania
　　Flower gardens and gardening—Pennsylvania
　　Gardens and gardening—Pennsylvania
　　Gettysburg National Military Park (Pa.)
　　Hunting—Pennsylvania
　　Independence National Historical Park (Pa.)
　　Liquor laws and regulations—Pennsylvania
　　Music festivals—Pennsylvania
　　Newspapers—Pennsylvania
　　Organic gardens and gardening—Pennsylvania
　　Paleontology—Pennsylvania
　　Police—Pennsylvania
　　Radon pollution—Pennsylvania
　　Reading Prong
　　Valley Forge National Historical Park (Pa.)
　　Wildlife management—Pennsylvania
　　　　　　　Climate
　　Day of the killer tornadoes [condensed from Tornado
　　watch #211] J. G. Fuller. il map *Read Dig* 130:152-61+
　　My '87
　　　　Description and travel
　　　　See also
　　Automobile touring—Pennsylvania
Pennsylvania Avenue (Washington, D.C.)
　　Pennsylvania Ave: making an American place. P. Morris.
　　il map *South Living* 22:66-71 S '87
Pennsylvania Ballet
　　Reviews
　　　　Performance of Winter dreams at the Philadelphia
　　　　Academy of Music. C. Hardy. *Dance Mag* 61:28-9
　　　　N '87
Pennsylvania Dutch *See* Pennsylvania Germans
Pennsylvania Dutch cooking *See* Cooking, American
Pennsylvania Engineering Corporation
　　Victor Posner is on the ropes—and slipping. G. DeGeorge
　　and P. Engardio. il por *Bus Week* p36 N 23 '87
　　Victor, victorious [V. Posner tries to strong-arm employees
　　into lending money to the firm] G. Morgenson. il
　　por *Forbes* 140:108 Ag 24 '87
Pennsylvania furniture *See* Furniture, American
Pennsylvania Germans
　　At the Kutztown Fair [with editorial comment by Sandra
　　Wilmot] C. Berglie and A. M. Geffen. il map *Americana*
　　15:2, 33-7 Jl/Ag '87
Pennsylvania Mutual Fund
　　Small stocks to sock away [interview] M. McFadden.
　　il por *Fortune* 115:133 Mr 2 '87
Pennsylvania quilts *See* Quilts and quilting
Pennsylvania Station (New York, N.Y.)
　　Penn Station. C. Wiseman. il *N Y* 20:84-5 D 21-28
　　'87
Penny stocks
　　Blinder, Robinson—blind 'em and rob 'em. M. Schifrin.
　　il *Forbes* 139:33-8 Ap 20 '87
　　Meet the prince of penny stocks: Meyer Blinder. D.
　　R. Katz. il por *Fortune* 115:108-10+ Ja 19 '87
　　Penny stocks: do they make cents? M. Hodge. il *50
　　Plus* 27:66-8 Ag '87
　　Poison wine in new bottles [Stuart-James Co. Inc.] D.
　　Henry. il *Forbes* 140:32-4 O 5 '87
Penny Whistle Toys (Firm)
　　This Brokaw is cashing in on classy toys [M. Brokaw]
　　M. Frons. il por *Bus Week* p107 My 11 '87
Pennypacker, Carl
　　Searching for supernovae: the discovery in M-99. il
　　Astronomy 15:74-9 Ag '87
Pennzoil Company
　　Bankruptcy court for Texaco: the lesser evil—barely.
　　T. Thompson and others. il *Bus Week* p102-3+ Ap
　　27 '87
　　Behind the scenes at Texaco's settlement. J. R. Norman
　　and T. Vogel. il *Bus Week* p66-8 D 28 '87-Ja 4
　　'88
　　Bonds: the safest play on Texaco. G. G. Marcial. *Bus
　　Week* p124 Je 8 '87
　　A break in the action [Texaco files for Chapter 11]
　　J. Castro. il *Time* 129:52-3 Ap 27 '87

Carl Icahn deals himself in [controls 12% of Texaco]
　　J. R. Norman. il por *Bus Week* p38 D 14 '87
Chapter 11 for Texaco. D. Pauly. il *Newsweek* 109:52
　　Ap 20 '87
David Boies: the ace litigator playing Texaco's hand.
　　L. J. Tell. il por *Bus Week* p79 Ap 20 '87
Et tu, Pennzoil? [Texaco-Pennzoil case] *New Repub* 196:4+
　　My 4 '87
The gambler who refused $2 billion [Pennzoil's J. H.
　　Liedtke's fight with Texaco; cover story] S. P. Sherman.
　　il pors *Fortune* 115:50-4+ My 11 '87
Gushing money [Texas court rules in favor of Pennzoil
　　in takeover dispute with Texaco] *Newsweek* 109:56
　　F 23 '87
Knocked down in round 2 [Texas court upholds judgment
　　against Texaco] il *Time* 129:67 F 23 '87
Let 'Icahn do your work for you' [buying TWA stock
　　to get in on Texaco-Pennzoil deal] G. G. Marcial.
　　Bus Week p106 D 21 '87
Meet Larry Tribe, Pennzoil's hole card [bested Texaco
　　in Supreme Court] L. Helm and P. Dwyer. il por
　　Bus Week p78-9 Ap 20 '87
On tap: a $3 billion solution? [settlement in Pennzoil
　　vs. Texaco] K. R. Sheets and W. J. Cook. *U S News
　　World Rep* 103:16 D 21 '87
The shootout at Texaco corral [petition for Chapter
　　11] J. Egan. il *U S News World Rep* 102:62+ Ap
　　27 '87
A small price to pay [settlement of Texaco-Pennzoil
　　case] G. Bock. il *Time* 130:63 D 28 '87
Texaco starts a new life [bankruptcy] J. B. Copeland.
　　il *Newsweek* 109:50 Ap 27 '87
Texaco takes a knockdown punch [Supreme Court sends
　　Pennzoil case back to Texas] T. Thompson. il *Bus
　　Week* p27 Ap 20 '87
Texaco vs. Pennzoil: next stop, Washington [Texas
　　Supreme Court refuses to review judgment won by
　　Pennzoil] T. Vogel. il *Bus Week* p68 N 16 '87
Texaco's $3 billion deal with Pennzoil. *Newsweek* 110:52
　　D 21 '87
Texaco's big gamble [bankruptcy gambit] T. Tedesco.
　　il *Macleans* 100:42 Ap 27 '87
Texaco's last stand [negotiations over Pennzoil settlement]
　　T. Tedesco. il *Macleans* 100:43 D 28 '87
Texaco's last stand in Texas [judgment won by Pennzoil]
　　J. E. Davis and T. Vogel. il *Bus Week* p36 Mr 2
　　'87
Texaco's star falls. J. Castro. il *Time* 129:50-2 Ap 20
　　'87
Triumph of the sore-back lawyer [J. Jamail's skills in
　　Texaco-Pennzoil battle] T. Mack. il por *Forbes* 139:33-4
　　My 4 '87
Penobscot Bay (Me.)
　　　　　　Fisheries
　　　　See Fisheries
Penobscot Indians
　　A new band of Tribal tycoons [Tribal Assets handling
　　investment of land claim settlements] F. Ungeheuer.
　　il *Time* 129:56+ Mr 16 '87
Penpad *See* Computers—Input-output equipment
Penrice, Daniel
　　Great ad copy in American poetry: an anthology. il
　　Atlantic 260:40-1 O '87
Pens
　　　　　　Manufacture
　　　　See also
　　A. T. Cross Co.
Pensacola (Fla.)
　　　　　　Description
　　On the sugar sands of Florida's panhandle [cover story]
　　D. Young. il map *South Living* 22:54-61 Jl '87
Penser, Erik
　　　　　　　about
　　A financial gambler tries to trump the Wallenbergs again.
　　J. Kapstein. *Bus Week* p50+ Ja 19 '87
Pension Benefit Guaranty Corporation
　　The feds are facing the easy part of the pension-fund
　　problem. V. Cahan. il *Bus Week* p48 F 23 '87
　　How safe is your pension? J. B. Quinn. il *Newsweek*
　　110:47 Ag 3 '87
　　Who's going to pay steel's pensions? G. L. Miles. il
　　Bus Week p115+ N 2 '87
Pension funds and funding *See* Pensions
Pensions
　　　　See also
　　Civil service pensions
　　Individual retirement accounts
　　Keogh plans
　　Portfolio insurance (Securities)
　　Simplified employee pensions
　　Social security

Pensions—See also—*cont.*
Townsend pension plan
Trade unions—Benefit funds
Agonizing reappraisals [pension fund real estate holdings]
H. Rudnitsky. *Forbes* 140:40 S 7 '87
Do pensions and stocks mix? il *U S News World Rep*
103:43 N 9 '87
How safe is your pension? J. B. Quinn. il *Newsweek*
110:47 Ag 3 '87
Pension help: it's on the way. M. Engel. *Glamour* 85:276+
F '87
Trends in retirement eligibility and pension benefits,
1974-83. D. Bell and W. Marclay. bibl f il *Mon Labor
Rev* 110:18-25 Ap '87
When George Russell talks, pension funds listen. H.
Gleckman. il por *Bus Week* p134-5 N 30 '87
Accounting
Pension funds are fat—so why the long faces? C. Farrell.
il *Bus Week* p102-3 O 26 '87
Some choice! L. Jereski. il *Forbes* 139:58 My 4 '87
Laws and regulations
See also
Pension Benefit Guaranty Corporation
Courts v. EEOC on over-65 pension rights. A. J. Shein-
man. *50 Plus* 27:19-20 Je 4 '87
The feds are facing the easy part of the pension-fund
problem. V. Cahan. il *Bus Week* p48 F 23 '87
The good news about pensions. M. Rowland. il *Work
Woman* 12:32 F '87
National project to help seniors with pension problems.
T. Chaw. *Aging* no356:32 '87
Trying to shore up the private pension system. R.
Rosenblatt and C. McLaughlin. il *50 Plus* 27:10+ Ag
'87
Taxation
How the new tax law could trim your pension. I. Pave.
il *Bus Week* p130-1 D 14 '87
Make your payout pay off. M. C. Paulson. il *Changing
Times* 41:51-5 Ap '87
New rules for borrowing against retirement plans. il
Changing Times 41:9 Mr '87
Pension rollover timing. G. W. Padwe. il *Nations Bus*
75:75 N '87
Rolling with new rollover rules [rolling over pension
money into an IRA] A. Rock. *Money* 16:74-5 Mr
'87
Taxes for young retirees. L. Saunders. il *Forbes* 139
Ann Directory:71+ Ap 27 '87
Why early retirement may not work for you. P. Philipps.
il *Bus Week* p166 My 11 '87
Termination
Is your pension safe from your company? M. Hodge.
il *50 Plus* 27:50-1 My '87
Great Britain
See also
British Rail Pension Fund
Penske, Roger
about
Hard driver. N. J. Perry. il por *Fortune* 116:195 N
23 '87
Roger Penske: running on 16 cylinders. P. Finch. il
por *Bus Week* p71+ Je 1 '87
Penske Corporation
Hard driver. N. J. Perry. il por *Fortune* 116:195 N
23 '87
Roger Penske: running on 16 cylinders. P. Finch. il
por *Bus Week* p71+ Je 1 '87
Penstemons
Pine-leaf penstemon. L. Goldstein. il *Flower Gard* 31:36-7
Ap/My '87
Penta Systems International, Inc.
Penta files breach of contract suit against Harper &
Row. *Publ Wkly* 232:25 Jl 17 '87
Pentacle (DanceWorks, Inc.)
Dance organizations: Pentacle offers the luxury of time
to create. il *Dance Mag* 61:18 Jl '87
Pentagon *See* United States. Dept. of Defense
Pentagon Papers
Daniel Ellsberg [interview] D. Sheff. il por *Roll Stone*
p221-2+ N 5-D 10 '87
Pentane Partners
Why is Tesoro so popular? T. Vogel. il *Bus Week* p40
D 21 '87
Pentateuch *See* Bible. O.T. Pentateuch
Pentathlon
Did she or didn't she? [L. Norwood banned after positive
drug test] S. Francis. il *Women's Sports Fitness* 9:22
Ap '87
Penteado, Sebastião Ferraz de Camargo *See* Camargo Pen-
teado, Sebastião Ferraz de

Pentecost
Cardinal Suenens calls for a new Pentecost [interview]
J. Catoir. *America* 156:457-9 Je 6 '87
Receive the Spirit. M. K. Hellwig. *America* 156:inside
back cover My 30 '87
Pentecostal churches
See also
Assemblies of God
Pentecostals and NCC begin dialogue. K. Houghland.
Christ Century 104:87-9 Ja 28 '87
Guatemala
Ríos Montt: from president to full-time church elder
[Verbo Church] K. Piecuch. il por *Christ Today* 31:46-7
F 20 '87
Korea (South)
Presbyterian, Pentecostal—or both? W. W. Menzies. il
Christ Today 31:41 N 20 '87
Pentecostal movement *See* Pentecostalism
Pentecostalism
America's Pentecostals [cover story; special section] il
Christ Today 31:16-30 O 16 '87
The Holy Spirit and world evangelization [North
American Congress on the Holy Spirit and World
Evangelization] J. Duin. il *Christ Today* 31:44-5 S
4 '87
A language spoken only by believers [Brown family,
Charlotte, N.C. charismatics] P. R. Range. il *U S
News World Rep* 102:66 Ap 6 '87
Spiritual lifts. T. C. Muck. il *Christ Today* 31:14-15
O 16 '87
Pentecostalism (Catholic)
Who are the Catholic charismatics? il *Christ Today* 31:47+
S 4 '87
Penthouses *See* Apartments
Pentos plc
Pentos to expand Dillons. C. T. Anthony. il *Publ Wkly*
232:28-9 N 27 '87
Pentstemons *See* Penstemons
Pentzell, Raymond J.
Cracked theatrical mirrors. *Society* 24:78-82 Ja/F '87
Penumbra (Term)
The penumbra of desuetude. W. Safire. il *N Y Times
Mag* p16+ O 4 '87
Penwest, Ltd.
There's a lot of interest brewing in this maltmaker.
G. G. Marcial. il *Bus Week* p126 Jl 20 '87
Peonies
Tree peonies. A. J. De Blasi. il *Flower Gard* 31:70-1+
Ap/My '87
People, Single *See* Single people
People Express Inc.
People Express, New York Air merging under Continental
umbrella. C. Preble. *Aviat Week Space Technol* 126:32-3
Ja 19 '87
People for the American Way
People for the American Way [interview with A. T.
Podesta] R. Love. il por *Seventeen* 46:237 Ag '87
Winning one from the Gipper [campaign against R.
H. Bork] A. R. Dowd. il pors *Fortune* 116:125+ N
9 '87
People in Faith United Housing Corporation
Housing and hope for census tract 5130. M. Goodell.
Christ Century 104:213-15 Mr 4 '87
People meters (TV audience research)
Attack of the people meters. E. Diamond. il *N Y* 20:38-41
Ag 24 '87
The networks' big headache. D. Lieberman. il *Bus Week*
p26-8 Jl 6 '87
No go. TV networks nix new high-tech rating system.
K. R. Sheets. *U S News World Rep* 103:39 Jl 20
'87
People meters [symposium sponsored by the International
Radio and Television Society] *New Yorker* 63:24-5
Mr 2 '87
People meters arrive. A. A. Lappen. il *Forbes* 140:8
S 21 '87
People meters' upside. S. Behrens. il *Channels* 7:19 My
'87
People meters vs. the gold standard. S. Behrens. il
Channels 7:72 S '87
Perfecting the body count. R. Barbieri. il *Channels* 7:15
Je '87
Ratings brawl [CBS and ABC allow contracts with Nielsen
to expire] *Time* 130:57 Jl 20 '87
A ratings revolution? H. F. Waters. il *Newsweek* 110:76
S 14 '87
Who's gypping whom in TV ads? B. Dumaine. il *Fortune*
116:78-9 Jl 6 '87

People Organized & Working for Economic Rebirth (Firm)
See POWER (Firm)

People United to Serve Humanity (Organization)
The disorganization man [J. L. Jackson] J. Weisberg. il por *Newsweek* 110:19 Ag 17 '87
Miss. tot needs transplant; parents seek financial help at PUSH in Chicago [case of Tabari Davis] *Jet* 72:4 Ag 10 '87
Operation PUSH continues boycott of Revlon products. *Jet* 71:17 Ja 12 '87
Operation PUSH debts cleared through gifts. il *Jet* 73:16 O 26 '87

People's Choice Awards
Bill Cosby wins three People's Choice Awards. il por *Jet* 72:55 Mr 30 '87

The people's court [television program] See Television program reviews—Single works

Pepi, John W.
The summer simmer index. il *Weatherwise* 40:143-5 Je '87

Pépin, Jacques
Cooking with Jacques Pépin. See issues of Gourmet beginning January 1985

Pepin, Yvonne
Sea kayaking: a water-lover's workout. il *Women's Sports Fitness* 9:60-1 Je '87

Pepler, Hilary D. C.
about
British television's Catholic pioneer. M. E. Evans. il *America* 157:501-3 D 26 '87

Peploe, Clare
about
High season [film] Reviews
Vogue por 177:146+ S '87. R. Koenig

Pepper, Beverly, 1924-
about
Hot Pepper. K. Larson. il por *N Y* 20:46-8+ Je 8 '87
A monumental vision. B. Rose. il pors *Vogue* 177:484-7+ Mr '87
Woman of steel. D. Solomon. il por *Art News* 86:112-17 D '87

Pepper, Claude
Should the financing of U.S. catastrophic health care emphasize private insurance methods? [excerpts from remarks, January 21, 1987] *Congr Dig* 66:105+ Ap '87
about
Lobbies rock the retirement boat. C. Murphy. il *50 Plus* 27:13-14 Ja '87

Pepper, Curtis Bill
Still Mastroianni [cover story] il pors *N Y Times Mag* p46-51+ S 20 '87

Pepper, D. Stephen
The rediscovery of the Bolognese school. il *Antiques* 131:846-7 Ap '87

Pepper, Jon
How to get more done in the 8-hour day. il *Work Woman* 12:47+ O '87

Peppermint
Relief is just a mint away [peppermint oil for excess stomach gas; work of Thomas L. Kun] il *Prevention* 39:14 My '87

Peppers
See also
Cooking—Vegetables
Are yellow peppers sweeter? K. Martin. il *Rodale's Org Gard* 34:51-2+ Mr '87
Hot ideas for sweet peppers [cover story; with editorial comment by Stevie Daniels] J. Ruttle. il *Rodale's Org Gard* 34:4, 34+ Je '87
Hot peppers. N. Bubel. il *Ctry J* 14:66-9 Jl '87

Peppiatt, Michael
Architectural digest visits: Sophia Loren. il pors *Archit Dig* 44:116-23 Mr '87
An art of constant renewal. il por *Archit Dig* 44:40+ Ag '87
Drawing on an old passion. il *Archit Dig* 44:40+ Ja '87
Perpetuating the Bauhaus ideal. il por *Archit Dig* 44:48+ Ag '87
A place for roses: the inimitable world of Ned and Marlo Phillips. il por *Archit Dig* 44:206-11 N '87

Peppler, Kathy Zar
Save our seeds. il *Rodale's Org Gard* 34:38-41 D '87

Pepsi-Cola Company See Pepsico, Inc.

Pepsico, Inc.
Michael Jackson to get about $10M for Pepsi ads. *Jet* 71:22 F 9 '87
The mouse that roared at Pepsi [Double-Cola in India] S. Tefft. il *Bus Week* p42 S 7 '87

Pepsi and Coca-Cola: the all-American worldwide war. S. Caminiti. il *Fortune* 116:56 O 26 '87
Pepsi's bubble. T. Jaffe. il *Forbes* 139:178 Mr 9 '87
Wayne Calloway's nonstop cash machine. S. N. Chakravarty. il por *Forbes* 140:35-7 S 7 '87

PepsiCo Summerfare
Don Juan in hell [P. Sellars' production of opera Don Giovanni] P. G. Davis. il *N Y* 20:48-9 Ag 3 '87
Music [production of Don Giovanni] E. W. Said. *Nation* 245:318-20 S 26 '87
Musical events:
　Mozart's opera, Don Giovanni. A. Porter. il *New Yorker* 63:66-9 Ag 10 '87
PepsiCo Summerfare [P. Sellars' production of Don Giovanni and Y. Lyubimov's production of A feast in the plague-time] M. Hodgson. *Nation* 245:208-10 S 5 '87
Purchase, N.Y. [Peter Sellars' production of Mozart's opera Don Giovanni] C. J. Luten. *Opera News* 52:52-3 N '87

Peptic ulcers
Bugged by an ulcer? You could have a bug [work of Barry Marshall] il *Discover* 8:10 My '87
Therapy
A bug, not what's bugging you, may cause ulcers [development of bacteria fighting drugs] Z. Schiller and S. Siwolop. il *Bus Week* p90 Ag 3 '87
Ulcers: on the brink of a cure [work of Barry Marshall and others] D. Foley. *Prevention* 39:49-52 My '87

Peptidases
See also
Thermolysin
Leader peptidase of Escherichia coli: critical role of a small domain in membrane assembly. R. E. Dalbey and W. T. Wickner. bibl f il *Science* 235:783-7 F 13 '87

Peptide T
Clinical trials planned for new AIDS drug. G. Kolata. il *Science* 235:1138-9 Mr 6 '87
Debate over potential AIDS drug. D. M. Barnes. il *Science* 237:128-30 Jl 10 '87
Peptide T: future AIDS treatment? D. D. Edwards. *Sci News* 131:376 Je 13 '87
Questions raised about peptide T's action [proposed AIDS therapy] J. L. Marx. *Science* 236:1523 Je 19 '87

Peptides
See also
Amino acid sequence
Atrial natriuretic factor
Cholecystokinin
Endorphins
Somatomedins
Substance P
Vasoactive intestinal polypeptide
Bug brains [pesticides based on insect neuropeptides] B. Lawren. il *Omni* 9:18 Ap '87
The case of the frog that healed leads Dr. Michael Zasloff to a medical leap ahead. M. Brower. il por *People Wkly* 28:34-5 Ag 17 '87
Characterization by tandem mass spectrometry of structural modifications in proteins. K. Biemann and H. A. Scoble. bibl f il *Science* 237:992-8 Ag 28 '87
D-alanine in the frog skin peptide dermorphin is derived from L-alanine in the precursor. K. Richter and others. bibl f il *Science* 238:200-2 O 9 '87
Fluorescence properties of calmodulin-binding peptides reflect alpha-helical periodicity. K. T. O'Neil and others. bibl f il *Science* 236:1454-6 Je 12 '87
Frogs get the jump on microbes [research by Michael Zasloff] S. Weisburd. *Sci News* 132:85 Ag 8 '87
Frog's gift to man [Michael Zasloff discovers natural antibiotic in frog skin] il *U S News World Rep* 103:6 Ag 10 '87
Immunological self, nonself discrimination. J.-G. Guillet and others. bibl f il *Science* 235:865-70 F 20 '87
New perspectives in cell adhesion: RGD and integrins. E. Ruoslahti and M. D. Pierschbacher. bibl f il *Science* 238:491-7 O 23 '87
A new prosomatostatin-derived peptide reveals a pattern for prohormone cleavage at monobasic sites. R. Benoit and others. bibl f il *Science* 238:1126-9 N 20 '87
Parathyroid hormone-related protein of malignancy: active synthetic fragments. B. E. Kemp and others. bibl f il *Science* 238:1568-70 D 11 '87
Peptide turn-on for the ACh receptor gene [research by Jean-Pierre Changeux and others] D. M. Barnes. *Science* 238:1652-3 D 18 '87
Polypeptide sequences essential for RNA recognition by an enzyme. L. Regan and others. bibl f il *Science* 235:1651-3 Mr 27 '87

Peptides—*cont.*

The relation between major histocompatibility complex (MHC) restriction and the capacity of Ia to bind immunogenic peptides. S. Buus and others. bibl f il *Science* 235:1353-8 Mr 13 '87

Ribbiting evidence [anti-infection peptides in skin of African clawed frog; work of Michael Zasloff] il *Time* 130:31 Ag 10 '87

A sea urchin gene encodes a polypeptide homologous to epidermal growth factor. D. A. Hursh and others. bibl f il *Science* 237:1487-90 S 18 '87

Similarity of synthetic peptide from human tumor to parathyroid hormone in vivo and in vitro. N. Horiuchi and others. bibl f il *Science* 238:1566-8 D 11 '87

Skin of frog . . . [natural antibiotic found by Michael Zasloff] T. Beardsley. il *Sci Am* 257:36+ O '87

Steroidogenesis-activator polypeptide isolated from a rat Leydig cell tumor. R. C. Pedersen and A. C. Brownie. bibl f il *Science* 236:188-90 Ap 10 '87

Synthesis

Synthesis of a sequence-specific DNA-cleaving peptide. J. P. Sluka and others. bibl f il *Science* 238:1129-32 N 20 '87

Synthesis of a site-specific DNA-binding peptide. M. F. Bruist and others. bibl f il *Science* 235:777-80 F 13 '87

Peralta, Ernest G., and others

Primary structure and biochemical properties of an M_2 muscarinic receptor. bibl f il *Science* 236:600-5 My 1 '87

Peras, Steve

about

To be franc, currency trader Steve Peras has a yen to make sure the buck doesn't stop here. E. Levin. il por *People Wkly* 27:95-6 F 16 '87

Perception

See also

Body image
Cognition
Consciousness
Extrasensory perception
Geographical perception
Human information processing
Motion perception
Self perception
Sensory stimulation
Space perception
Speech perception
Subliminal projection
Synesthesia
Time perception
Visual perception

Neural Darwinism: an exchange [discussion of October 9, 1986 article, Neural Darwinism: a new approach to memory and perception] I. Rosenfield. *N Y Rev Books* 34:44-5 Mr 12 '87

Perception of risk. P. Slovic. bibl f il *Science* 236:280-5 Ap 17 '87

Percussion instruments

See also

Drum
Steel bands (Music)

From a new Sunset book, musical instruments to make ahead for Christmas [rhythm instruments] il *Sunset* 179:132+ O '87

Percy, Roger

about

Beyond the people meter. M. Fritz. il por *Forbes* 140:248 D 14 '87

Percy, Walker, 1916-

about

'The last southern gentleman'. J. Reed. il pors *U S News World Rep* 102:75-6 Mr 16 '87

Moralist of the South. M. Jones. il por *N Y Times Mag* p42+ Mr 22 '87

Percy's syndrome [discussion of October 7, 1987 article, The Thanatos syndrome] J. L. Womack. *Christ Century* 104:1003-4 N 11 '87

The Thanatos syndrome: exciting, horrifying, disappointing. R. C. Wood. il por *Christ Century* 104:857-8 O 7 '87

Percy (R.D.) & Company *See* R.D. Percy & Company

Perdition [drama] *See* Allen, Jim

Perdue, Frank

about

C.E.O., TV. T. Whiteside. *New Yorker* 63:39-40+ Jl 6 '87

Perdue Farms Inc.

C.E.O., TV [F. Perdue's television commercials] T. Whiteside. *New Yorker* 63:39-40+ Jl 6 '87

They're fencing beak to beak [ready-to-eat chicken products] M. Sheraton. il *Time* 130:76 S 28 '87

Père-Lachaise Cemetery (Paris, France) *See* Paris (France)—Cemeteries

Perejaume, 1957-

about

Five from Spain. J. Gambrell. il pors *Art Am* 75:160-71 S '87

Perelman, Ronald Owen, 1943-

about

Back to business. J. Cook. il por *Forbes* 140:40-1 O 5 '87

Big investors on Wall Street. pors *Fortune* 116:8 O 26 '87

Has Perelman taken a shine to Sterling Drug? G. G. Marcial. il por *Bus Week* p101 Jl 13 '87

How Ron Perelman scared Gillette into shape. K. H. Hammonds. il *Bus Week* p40-1 O 12 '87

The raider who runs Revlon. A. Ramirez. il pors *Fortune* 116:56-8+ S 14 '87

Revlon's striving makeover man. A. Ramirez. il por *Fortune* 115:54-5 Ja 5 '87

Salomon and Revlon: what really happened. A. Bianco. il pors *Bus Week* p156+ O 12 '87

A tale of our times. A. Sloan and L. Jereski. il *Forbes* 139:180 My 18 '87

A white knight saves Salomon. B. Powell. il por *Newsweek* 110:66 O 12 '87

White-knight time on Wall Street. J. Egan. il pors *U S News World Rep* 103:60 O 12 '87

Perelman, S. J. (Sidney Joseph), 1904-1979

about

Knowing S. J. Perelman. P. Crowther. il *N Y Rev Books* 34:14-19 Jl 16 '87

Sid, you made the prose too thin. J. Epstein. *Commentary* 84:53-60 S '87

Perelman, Sidney Joseph *See* Perelman, S. J. (Sidney Joseph), 1904-1979

Perennials (Plants)

See also

Dahlias
Peonies

Are perennials for you? E. Sheldon. il *Flower Gard* 31:16-17+ Ap/My '87

Bellflowers, cranesbills and lilies [excerpt from The perennial garden] J. Cox and M. Cox. il *Rodale's Org Gard* 34:46-8+ F '87

Downsizing [miniature bedding plants and bulbs] il *Sunset* 179:256-7 N '87

Hardy ageratums, chrysanthemums and petunias [excerpt from The perennial garden] J. Cox and M. Cox. il *Rodale's Org Gard* 34:48 S '87

Perennial beauty. E. Henke. il *Saturday Evening Post* 259:94-5 My/Je '87

Spread the roots to get more blooms. il *South Living* 22:94-5 Ap '87

These perennials color the fall [cover story] L. C. Askey. il *South Living* 22:74-7 S '87

Peres, Shimon, 1923-

Visit of Israeli Prime Minister Peres [remarks, September 15, 1986] *Dep State Bull* 86:73 D '86

about

Destined for a dogfight. W. E. Smith. il pors *Time* 129:39 My 11 '87

Face-off in Israel [cover story] E. Salpeter. il *New Leader* 70:5-6 Ap 20 '87

A government at war over peace. B. Levin. il pors *Macleans* 100:18 My 25 '87

Israel: at war with itself. M. J. Kubic. il pors *Newsweek* 109:30 My 25 '87

Israel: the Peres era and its legacy. S. W. Lewis. *Foreign Aff* 65 Sp Issue:582-610 ['87]

Israel's year of transition. B. Reich. bibl f *Curr Hist* 86:69-72+ F '87

Letter from Israel. A. Elon. *New Yorker* 63:33-8+ Jl 27 '87

The Mideast: crying wolf? N. Cooper. il por *Newsweek* 109:54-5 My 18 '87

Peace nix. M. Kondracke. il *New Repub* 196:20-2 Je 8 '87

Peace-talks plan: push comes to shove in Israel. il *U S News World Rep* 102:16 My 25 '87

Peres' big mistake. A. Whitley. *World Press Rev* 34:15 Jl '87

The Peres peace plan: battling extremism. J. M. Wall. *Christ Century* 104:931-2 O 28 '87

Shut up and deal. *New Repub* 197:7-9 O 26 '87

So much for national unity. il por *Time* 129:50 My 25 '87

Peres, Shimon, 1923——*cont.*
Visit to the United States, 1986
Visit of Israeli Prime Minister Peres [remarks, September 15, 1986] S. Peres; R. Reagan. *Dep State Bull* 86:73 D '86
Peress, Gilles
about
Eyes behind the camera, then and now [interview] M. Horn. il *U S News World Rep* 103:88-9 N 9 '87
Pérez, Alan García *See* García Pérez, Alan
Pérez, Carlos Andrés
about
Trust me. L. Gubernick. il por *Forbes* 139:152 Mr 9 '87
Perez, Mike
about
San Jose's Sweet P. J. Diaz. il pors *Sports Illus* 67:96-7 Ag 31 '87
Pérez de Cuellar, Javier
The 38th floor. See issues of UN Chronicle
Decent shelter for all . . . *UN Chron* 24:inside cover Ag '87
Secretary-General urges fullest use of young peoples' wealth of knowledge [excerpt from address] *UN Chron* 23:37 Ja '86
about
Secretary-General appointed to a second five-year term. il por *UN Chron* 24:4-5 F '87
Secretary-General discusses 'outline plan' during trip to Teheran, Baghdad. il pors *UN Chron* 24:16-18 N '87
Secretary-General reaffirms support for Contadora efforts after four-day peace mission to region. il pors *UN Chron* 24:7-10 My '87
Perez-Stable, Marifeli
Castro takes the economy in hand. il *Nation* 245:298-300 S 26 '87
Perfection (Philosophy)
See also
Utopias
Perfection (Psychology)
Are you too tough on yourself? When to lighten up, when to tighten up. J. Stone. *Glamour* 85:88 D '87
Is perfectionism killing your kid? M. Conroy. il *Better Homes Gard* 65:76+ N '87
Perfectionism: a serious impediment to creativity. J. Croghan. *Am Artist* 51:14+ Je '87
Too hard on yourself? [excerpt from Perfectionism] M. Adderholdt-Elliott. *Teen* 31:40+ S '87
Performance appraisal *See* Employees—Rating; Women executives—Rating
Performance art
See also
Bogosian, Eric
Higby, Sha Sha
Jonas, Joan
Kelley, Michael, 1954?-
Sound in art
Survival Research Laboratories (Group)
Thomas, Philippe
After postmodernism: waiting for the end of the world. E. Zimmer. il *Dance Mag* 61:64-9 F '87
In New Mexico: visions along the Amtrak line [Apparitions and Amtrak performed in Canyoncito] L. Schulman. il *Time* 129:10 Mr 2 '87
Movin' uptown [A. Magnuson] A. Virshup. il pors *N Y* 20:46-9 Mr 30 '87
New-Age visions: Zangezi goes west. P. Clothier. il *Art Am* 75:25+ My '87
News watch [performance of Black and white at the Joyce Theater, New York City] T. Tobias. il *N Y* 20:80-1 Ap 6 '87
Performance standards
Bait and switch, corporate-style [excerpt from The human side of management] G. S. Odiorne. *Work Woman* 12:50+ My '87
How picking favorites can improve performance [excerpt from Managing people at work desk guide] T. L. Quick. *Work Woman* 12:21 Ja '87
Performers *See* Actors and actresses; Entertainers
Performing arts
See also
Ballet
Computers—Performing arts use
Dance
Entertainment industry
Motion pictures
Music
Next Wave Festival
Opera
Theater
Theatrical agencies and agents

Vaudeville
Cross country. See issues of Horizon (Tuscaloosa, Ala.)
Glitz! D. Harris. il *Vogue* 177:318-19+ D '87
Awards
See also
Kennedy Center Honors
Performing Arts Journal Publications
PAJ branches out dramatically into fiction. B. Levine. il *Publ Wkly* 232:28-9 N 20 '87
Perfume industry
See also
Alfin Fragrances, Inc.
Ethical aspects
'Obsession' by any other name sells sweetly. A. Dunkin. il *Bus Week* p97 Je 1 '87
Marketing
For Avon, Rodeo Drive is no easy street. W. Konrad. il *Bus Week* p78 D 28 '87-Ja 4 '88
Liz Taylor leaps into a vial business with Passion. R. Wolmuth. il pors *People Wkly* 28:38-9 O 5 '87
A new smell for success [launching of Tiffany and Colors de Benetton] L. Wells. il *N Y Times Mag* p62 Jl 12 '87
What's in a smell? T. Kalich. il *Atlantic* 260:34+ O '87
France
See also
Jean Patou (Firm)
The essence of Grasse. T. Skari. il *Life* 10:66-8 N '87
Perfume patches
From making hearts to winning them [Thermedics drug delivery skin patches redesigned to release fragrances] C. Brown. il *Bus Week* p153+ N 16 '87
Perfumes
All he could taste was the smell of her . . . il *Mademoiselle* 93:152-5 Je '87
Day-to-night fragrance. il *Harpers Bazaar* 120:32 Mr '87
Day-to-night scents. il *Essence* 18:44 D '87
Designer scents. C. Morris. il *Essence* 18:52 S '87
Eau know! B. L. Ascher. il *Seventeen* 46:114 S '87
Fragrance: the news! il *Essence* 17:38 F '87
Good scents: a fragrance buyer's guide. il *Mademoiselle* 93:56 Ap '87
Light scents with strong appeal. il *Glamour* 85:386-7 S '87
Perfume primer. il *Teen* 31:84-7 N '87
Perfumed girls . . . how scents keep a man spellbound. D. Seeley. il *Mademoiselle* 93:150-1+ Je '87
The power of fragrance. il *Essence* 18:64-9 My '87
Scent: fragrant escapes. il *Harpers Bazaar* 120:14 Jl '87
Scents of encounter [special section] il *Vogue* 177:322-9+ My '87
Spring in the air. J. L. Lippert. il *Health* 19:38-40 Ap '87
Stoppers. S. Lord. il *Vogue* 177:408-15+ N '87
Top-secret scents. il *Glamour* 85:218-19 D '87
What's that wonderful scent you're wearing? il *Redbook* 168:8 Ap '87
Perfumes for animals
At last there's something more for the pooch who has everything (including odor)—doggie perfume [work of L. Gilford] il por *People Wkly* 28:117 S 21 '87
Perfumes for men
Eau no, eau yes. M. Johnson. il *Esquire* 107:F20+ Mr '87
Give your nose a break. *Esquire* 108:233 S '87
Scent's the thing. R. La Ferla. il *N Y Times Mag* p68 Ap 26 '87
The sweet smell of success [Old Spice] J. A. Trachtenberg. il *Forbes* 140:92-3 Ag 10 '87
Pergolas
New pergola keeps you dry, house to garage. il *Sunset* 178:78 Ja '87
Planter fences and pergolas. A. W. Lees. il *Pop Sci* 231:72-4 Ag '87
This pergola welcomes spring. il *South Living* 22:120-1 Mr '87
Pergonal
Clarifying cause of multiple pregnancy [work of Oscar A. Kletzky] il *USA Today (Periodical)* 115:10 F '87
Pericles Prince of Tyre by William Shakespeare [drama] See Dubois, René-Daniel
Peridance
Reviews:
Performances at the Joyce Theater, New York City. C. Hardy. *Dance Mag* 61:110-11 My '87
Perin, Monica Wilch
Lost! (but not for long). il *Parents* 62:92-4+ Jl '87

Period rooms, Gothic revival *See* House decoration, Gothic revival

Periodic law

A periodic table for molecules [work of Ray Hefferlin] D. E. Thomsen. *Sci News* 131:87 F 7 '87

Periodical advertising *See* Advertising, Magazine

Periodical articles

See also

Journalism, Religious

As they said in the Writer in 1887 . . . [reprint of April 1887 article] C. M. Hammond. *Writer* 100:1 S '87

Beating the rejection blues. J. Harayda. *Writer* 100:21-3 S '87

Brainstorming alone. J. S. Boyanton. *Writer* 100:29-30 Ag '87

Erasing the blue-pencil blues. D. Petersen. *Writer* 100:14-16 F '87

Fictive techniques for nonfiction writing. K. Sale. *Writer* 100:16-18 Ap '87

Finding a subject for short nonfiction. G. A. Reims. *Writer* 100:25-6 F '87

Getting into travel writing. J. Steinberg. *Writer* 100:14-15+ My '87

Give them what they want. R. A. Caras. *Writer* 100:7-8 Je '87

How to write good article leads. M. Cook. *Writer* 100:16-18 Je '87

Inspiring story ideas: a baker's dozen. C. Kyle and L. A. Walker. *Writer* 100:5-6 N '87

Juvenile articles that sell. M. Johnston. *Writer* 100:28-9 S '87

Making it as a free-lance writer-photographer. R. Tolley. il *Petersens Photogr Mag* 15:51-3 Ja '87

Market newsletter. See issues of The Writer

Personally yours [personal experience articles] S. Lueth. *Writer* 100:25-7 O '87

Special to the Writer. See issues of The Writer beginning February 1987

Ten ways to make your articles sparkle. L. Felder. *Writer* 100:14-16 D '87

This month's special market 'sts. See issues of The Writer

Using your vacation for article ideas. J. Watlington. *Writer* 100:19-21 Ag '87

Where do article ideas come from? K. P. Murphy. *Writer* 100:28-9 Ag '87

Where to sell manuscripts. See issues of The Writer

Anecdotes, facetiae, satire, etc.

From a free-lancer's notebook. P. Frost. *New Yorker* 62:29-30 Ja 19 '87

Periodical covers

Exhibitions

Covering Time's Men of the Year [exhibit at the National Portrait Gallery] C. Bond. il *Smithsonian* 17:188 Mr '87

Periodical design

Now 'Impactweek' [Newsweek] E. Diamond. il *N Y* 20:20+ My 11 '87

Periodical reading

Anecdotes, facetiae, satire, etc.

A magazine junkie. J. Atlas. il *N Y Times Mag* p22 N 1 '87

Periodicals

See also

Children's periodicals

House organs

Interactive computer periodicals

Journalism

Libraries—Periodical collections

See also names of periodicals; *also* subhead Periodicals under various subjects

The small time [small presses] S. Klawans. *Nation* 244:263-4+ F 28 '87

Illustration

See Illustration

Letters to the editor

For art's sake [letters to the Progressive commenting on illustrations] E. Knoll. *Progressive* 51:4 N '87

Hippocratic humor [letters to the New England journal of medicine] J. Schuster. il *Technol Rev* 90:14 O '87

Horsewhipped [letters to Progressive] E. Knoll. *Progressive* 51:4 Ap '87

How it all comes right [fan letter to Road & track addressed to the wrong editor] A. Girdler. il *Road Track* 39:24 N '87

The postman rings—frequently [letters to Space world] J. Rhea. il *Space World* X-12-288:4 D '87

The readers speak: 1986's mail [Time magazine] il *Time* 129:16 F 16 '87

Prices

Journal price increases [discussion of May 22, 1987 article, Libraries stunned by journal price increases] C. Holden. *Science* 238:597-8 O 30 '87

Libraries stunned by journal price increases. C. Holden. *Science* 236:908-9 My 22 '87

Subscriptions

Bits and bytes [new computer subscription fulfillment system for Sky and telescope] il *Sky Telesc* 73:427 Ap '87

From the publisher [major magazine subscription promotional offers] D. K. Graham. *Antiques Collect Hobbies* 92:6+ O '87

Canada

See also

Idler (Periodical)

Maclean's (Periodical)

Saturday night (Periodical)

China

See also

Humanities: theory and criticism (Periodical)

Great Britain

See also

Builder (Periodical)

Economist (Periodical)

Spectator (Periodical)

Literary London. G. Smith. *New Leader* 70:20-1 My 4-18 '87

Poland

See also

Res publica (Periodical)

Soviet Union

See also

Glasnost (Periodical)

Soviet photo (Periodical)

Taiwan

See also

Journalist (Taiwan: Periodical)

Periodicals, Publishing of *See* Publishers and publishing—Periodicals

Periodicals for men

See also

Esquire (Periodical)

Gentlemen's quarterly

Hustler (Periodical)

Periodicals for women

See also

Feminism—Periodicals

Good housekeeping (Periodical)

Lear's (Periodical)

Ms. (Periodical)

Savvy (Periodical)

Woman's day (Periodical)

Wanted: a nude *glasnost* [women's magazines in the Soviet Union] S. Drakulich. il *Nation* 244:846-8 Je 20 '87

What women want to read. J. Conant. il *Newsweek* 109:61 F 23 '87

Why seven magazines pretend you don't exist [women's magazines] D. Heyn. il *50 Plus* 27:38-41 Mr '87

Periodicity *See* Biological rhythms

Periodontal disease *See* Gums—Diseases

Peripheral equipment (Computers) *See* Computers—Equipment

Perjury

See also

Deaver, Michael K.—Conflict of interests case

Perkins, Charles M.

Where Moscow embassy went awry. por *U S News World Rep* 102:8 My 18 '87

Perkins, Edward J.

about

New man in the townships. B. W. Nelan. il por *Time* 129:58 F 23 '87

Perkins makes 1st public protest against S. Africa. por *Jet* 72:24 My 11 '87

Quiet sting. W. R. Doerner. il por *Time* 130:50 D 21 '87

S. Africa banquet fails to invite speaker—Perkins. *Jet* 72:18 Ap 20 '87

Perkins, Helen

about

Black woman wins mayor's race in Hollandale, Miss. *Jet* 72:8 My 4 '87

Perkins, Lori

The truth about agents. il *Publ Wkly* 231:58 Mr 6 '87

Perkins, Pheme

Biblical traditions and women's experience. il *America* 157:294-6 O 31 '87

Perkovich, George
Bear in a briarpatch: prospects for a Soviet pullout. il *Commonweal* 114:725-6 D 18 '87
Moscow turns east. il *Atlantic* 260:30+ D '87
Perl, Jed, 1951-
Artburn. il *Vogue* 177:308-11+ My '87
Perlberg, Deborah
Talking good art talk. *Art News* 86:81 O '87
Perle, George, 1915-
about
Musical events:
Performance of works by G. Perle and W. Lutoslawski at Tanglewood. A. Porter. *New Yorker* 63:68-9 Ag 31 '87
Perle, Richard N.
[Column] See issues of U.S. News & World Report beginning May 25, 1987
about
Farewell, Dark Prince. il por *Time* 129:14 Mr 23 '87
The Iran/arms control connection. M. Krepon. il *Bull At Sci* 43:9-10 Mr '87
The 'Prince of Darkness' calls it quits. T. Jacoby. il por *Newsweek* 109:27 Mr 23 '87
Reagan admin. spawns two books: memoir and novel. *Publ Wkly* 232:81 Ag 14 '87
Richard Perle did his best. *Natl Rev* 39:21 Ap 10 '87
Perlman, Eric
New life for waterproof/breathables. *Skiing* 39:101 Spr '87
A short guide to long johns. il *Skiing* 39:87-9 F '87
Perlman, Itzhak, 1945-
"To help the handicapped, talk to them". il por *Glamour* 85:64 Mr '87
Perlman, Rhea
about
Danny De Vito & Rhea Perlman. W. Urbanska. il pors *McCalls* 145:36+ Mr '87
Perlmutter, Cathy
The news & the bad news. il *Prevention* 39:69-72+ N '87
Perlmutter, Nate
about
Obituary
Natl Rev 39:21 Ag 14 '87. W. F. Buckley
Perm State Ballet School *See* Dance schools—Soviet Union
Permaculture *See* Agricultural ecology
Permafrost *See* Frozen ground
Permanent Court of International Justice
See also
International Court of Justice
Permanent waves *See* Hairstyling
Permutations
Now there is Rubik's Magic, a new puzzle that provides a study in permutation operators. J. Walker. il *Sci Am* 257:170-3 O '87
Pernfors, Mikael
about
Hot dawg. C. Shmerler. il por *World Tennis* 35:56-8+ Je '87
Perón, Juan Domingo, 1895-1974
Tomb
Holding (Peron's) hands in Argentina. A. M. Shapiro. il *New Leader* 70:5-7 Ag 10-24 '87
Perosa, Sergio
The heirs of Calvino and the Eco effect. il *N Y Times Book Rev* 92:1+ Ag 16 '87
Perot, H. Ross, 1930-
Business leaders [address, December 8, 1986] *Vital Speeches Day* 53:337-42 Mr 15 '87
about
The $750 million muzzle. D. Sherman. il *Car Driv* 32:7 Mr '87
A billionaire for the common man. B. O'Reilly. il por *Fortune* 115:47 Ja 5 '87
Detroit. P. Lienert. il pors *Road Track* 38:110 Mr '87
How G.M. bought itself a lemon. M. M. Thomas. il *Nation* 244:108-9 Ja 31 '87
North falls for a hostage scam. G. J. Church. il pors *Time* 129:25 Je 8 '87
Perot and Jobs: who's Next? M. Rogers. il pors *Newsweek* 109:48 F 9 '87
Perot's private probes. G. J. Church. il por *Time* 129:18 My 4 '87
A quartet of high-tech pioneers. B. O'Reilly. il pors *Fortune* 116:148-9 O 12 '87
Ross Perot turns into an angel for Steve Jobs. K. M. Hafner. il pors *Bus Week* p32 F 9 '87
True-life adventures of H. Ross Perot. D. Remnick. por *Read Dig* 131:165-6+ S '87
You don't lose 'em all. C. Siler. il por *Forbes* 140:34 Ag 10 '87

Perovskite
Earth's most abundant mineral [research by Elise Knittle and Raymond Jeanloz] S. Weisburd. *Sci News* 131:103 F 14 '87
Superconductivity at 40 K in the oxygen-defect perovskites $La_{2-x}Sr_xCuO_{4-y}$. J. M. Tarascon and others. bibl f il *Science* 235:1373-6 Mr 13 '87
Synthesis and equation of state of $(Mg,Fe)SiO_3$ perovskite to over 100 gigapascals. E. Knittle and R. Jeanloz. bibl f il *Science* 235:668-70 F 6 '87
Perpetual motion
A man who defies the laws [J. W. Newman's electric motor] D. Noland. por *Discover* 8:46-8+ My '87
Perpich, Joseph G.
about
Perpich to head new Hughes program. B. J. Culliton. por *Science* 236:141 Ap 10 '87
Perreault, Nancy Hanback
The woman who tackled Black Fox. il por *Progressive* 51:12 D '87
Perrelli, Gianni, and Regazzoni, Enrico
Red Square chic. il *World Press Rev* 34:19-20 Ap '87
Perret, Gene
Having fun writing humor. *Writer* 100:13-15 Mr '87
Perrier, Source SA *See* Source Perrier SA
Perrill, Amy
All over the map. il *Seventeen* 46:176-7 S '87
Perrin, Charles L., and Gipe, Robert K.
Rotation and solvation of ammonium ion. bibl f il *Science* 238:1393-4 D 4 '87
Perrine, Doug
The strange case of the freshwater marine fishes. il *Sea Front* 33:114-19 Mr/Ap '87
Perrone, Arthur
about
Sell now. J. Heins. il por *Forbes* 139 Ann Directory:124+ Ap 27 '87
Perry, Charles R.
about
"Publish and be damned" [interview] J. Novack. por *Forbes* 140:380+ Jl 13 '87
Perry, Donald R.
As cities crumble, plants may be at the root of it; ed. by Sylvia E. Merschel. il *Smithsonian* 17:72-9 Ja '87
Plants that eat cities; ed. by Sylvia E. Merschel. il *Read Dig* 131:126-8 O '87
Perry, Edmund
about
Best intentions: Edmund Perry's path from Harlem to Exeter to death on a street in Morningside Heights [excerpt] R. S. Anson. il pors map *N Y* 20:30-45 My 11 '87
A black American youth torn between cultures [cover story] R. J. Rousseve. il por *Humanist* 47:5-8 Mr/Ap '87
Perry, Frank
about
Hello again [film] Reviews
Newsweek il 110:108-9 N 16 '87. D. Ansen
Perry, Jack, 1930-
Looking for the great bookstore. por *Publ Wkly* 232:58 D 25 '87
Perry, Jason
Clean heating with wood stoves. il *Consum Res Mag* 70:10-13 D '87
Perry, Mark
Conditions less than honorable. il *Progressive* 51:24-7 My '87
The I.S.A. behind the N.S.C. il *Nation* 244:33+ Ja 17 '87
Putting vets in the shredder. il *Nation* 245:554-6 N 14 '87
Perry, Nancy J.
Fortune people. See issues of Fortune beginning August 17, 1987
Perry, Patricia, 1949-
Fatherese & motherese. il *Parents* 62:100-4 Mr '87
Perry, Seymour
A consensus view. il *World Health* p12-13 Je '87
Perry, Susan
Dreams: a journey into the mind. il *Curr Health 2* 13:11-13 Ja '87
Mind over matter: memory. il *Curr Health 2* 13:22-3 My '87
Put a smile on your face. il *Curr Health 2* 14:14-15 O '87
Staying out of crime's way. il *Curr Health 2* 14:20-1 O '87

Perry, William
about
'Fridge' Perry is tops, say U.S. teens. *Jet* 71:32 Ja 19 '87
Fridge says keep wife out of weight saga. il por *Jet* 72:51 S 21 '87
NFL's lone black kicker recalls a bigger 'Fridge'. pors *Jet* 71:51 Ja 12 '87
Perry, William James, 1927-
about
The powers that shouldn't be: five Washington insiders the next Democratic president shouldn't hire [cover story] P. Glastris. pors *Wash Mon* 19:39-46+ O '87
Perseus (Constellation) *See* Constellations
Perseverance
Helping children persevere. J. Segal and Z. Segal. il *Parents* 62:162 Je '87
Persian Gulf
Has the Garden of Eden been located at last? [views of J. Zarins] D. J. Hamblin. bibl (p184) il map *Smithsonian* 18:127-35 My '87
Persian Gulf region
See also
Cities and towns—Persian Gulf region
Crime and criminals—Persian Gulf region
Commerce
See also
Iranian-Iraqi War, 1980- —Economic aspects
Ship attacks boom: so do the profits. J. Barnes. il *U S News World Rep* 103:38 S 14 '87
Japan
See Japan—Commerce—Persian Gulf region
United States
See United States—Commerce—Persian Gulf region
Western Europe
See Western Europe—Commerce—Persian Gulf region
Defenses
See also
Great Britain. Royal Navy—Forces in the Persian Gulf region
Italy—Navy—Forces in the Persian Gulf region
United States—Armed Forces—Forces in the Persian Gulf region
United States. Navy—Forces in the Persian Gulf region
Foreign relations
Soviet Union
See Soviet Union—Foreign relations—Persian Gulf region
United States
See United States—Foreign relations—Persian Gulf region
Persian rugs *See* Rugs and carpets, Oriental
Persians *See* Iranians
Persimmon trees
Oriental persimmons. T. E. Eltzroth. il *Flower Gard* 31:52-3 O/N '87
Persimmons
See also
Cooking—Fruit
Just when should you pick persimmons? il *Sunset* 179:255 N '87
Persky, Lester
about
The Farrah Fawcett/Barbara Hutton connection [interview] M. J. Bandler. il pors *McCalls* 115:186-8 N '87
Person, Chuck
about
A very special Person. D. S. Looney. il por *Sports Illus* 66:88-9 Ja 12 '87
Person, Ethel Spector
about
Grown-up love [interview] D. Mason. *Vogue* 177:58 O '87
Person, Waverly
about
If your problem is earthshaking, call Waverly Person. A. Collier. il pors *Ebony* 42:134+ S '87
Personal bankruptcy *See* Bankruptcy
Personal beauty *See* Beauty, Personal
Personal care appliances
See also
Hair dryers
Here's to your health! il *Essence* 18:92 Je '87
Personal care products
See also
Bath products
Cosmetics

Feminine hygiene products
Hair care products
Personal care products industry
See also
Alberto-Culver Co.
American Health and Beauty Aids Institute
Colgate-Palmolive Co. (Delaware)
Combe Inc.
Cosmetics industry
Gillette Co.
Hair care products industry
Hill Top Research, Inc.
Lee Pharmaceuticals
Procter & Gamble Co.
S. C. Johnson & Son, Inc.
Shaklee Corp.
Acquisitions and mergers
How Ron Perelman scared Gillette into shape. K. H. Hammonds. il *Bus Week* p40-1 O 12 '87
An unlikely savior for Gillette? [W. E. Buffett] G. G. Marcial. *Bus Week* p188 N 16 '87
Finance
Consumer products. R. Koselka. il *Forbes* 139:114-15 Ja 12 '87
Personal computer industry *See* Computer industry
Personal Computer Network (Firm) *See* PC Network (Firm)
Personal computer software industry *See* Computer service industries
Personal computers *See* Computers
Personal computing (Periodical)
Readers pick best of bunch [Personal computing survey] P. Honan. il *Pers Comput* 11:41-2 F '87
Some things old—and new. F. Abatemarco. il *Pers Comput* 11:5 S '87
Personal criticism *See* Criticism, Personal
Personal data banks *See* Information storage and retrieval systems
Personal finance *See* Finance, Personal
Personal financial planning *See* Investment advisers
Personal flotation devices *See* Life preservers
Personal liberty *See* Liberty
Personal loans *See* Loans, Personal
Personal names *See* Names, Personal
Personal portfolio manager (Newsletter) *See* Investment newsletters
Personal property *See* Property
Personal rights *See* Civil rights
Personal secrets
See also
Self disclosure
3 secrets about men that women won't keep. il *Jet* 73:34 N 16 '87
Do you betray a lover when you discuss your relationship with a friend? C. L. Mithers. *Glamour* 85:392 S '87
Spare me: secrets you shouldn't spill. B. Weber. *Mademoiselle* 93:200 Mr '87
Your deep, dark secrets revealed. il *Teen* 31:34+ Je '87
Personal services [film] *See* Motion picture reviews—Single works
Personal shoppers
Do your clothes need help? A. Sands. il *Redbook* 168:106-9 Ap '87
Personal shoppers: their services will save you time, maybe money, and let you enjoy shopping again. il *Glamour* 85:40 Ap '87
Personal space
See also
Crowding stress
Help, at a distance [effect of distance and personal space on helping behavior] P. Glick. *Psychol Today* 21:66-7 F '87
Personal style *See* Fashion
Personal trainers *See* Exercise teachers
Personality
See also
Body image
Character
Identity (Psychology)
Individuality
Innocence (Psychology)
Introversion and extroversion
Leadership
Minnesota Multiphasic Personality Inventory
Moods
Self
Typology (Psychology)
The character of cancer [work of Pirkko L. Graves and others] B. Bower. *Sci News* 131:120-1 F 21 '87
The character of personality. C. Wood. il *Psychol Today* 21:8+ Mr '87

Personality—*cont.*
The diet that nurtures your nature. S. Waldman. il *Mademoiselle* 93:167-9+ F '87
Generic disposition for disease? *Sci News* 132:46 Jl 18 '87
What mid-life crisis? K. Marquardt. il *Health* 19:16 D '87
What traits bring success? il *Glamour* 85:150 N '87
Your child's temperament: easy, difficult, or slow-to-warm-up? N. Rubin. il *Parents* 62:94-6+ S '87

Disorders

See also
Multiple personality
Narcissism
Schizophrenia
Crossing the border [medications and borderline personalities] M. Mintzer. il *Health* 19:16 D '87

Genetic aspects
The genetics of personality. C. Holden. il *Science* 237:598-601 Ag 7 '87
How genes shape personality [cover story; special section] S. N. Wellborn. il *U S News World Rep* 102:58-62+ Ap 13 '87
Sins and twins. R. Bazell. *New Repub* 197:17-18 D 21 '87
To the manner born [study of twins] W. Gallagher. il *Roll Stone* p56+ N 19 '87

Personality tests *See* Psychological tests

Personals
'A chorus of groans,' notes Sherlock Holmes. J. Harkison. il *Smithsonian* 18:196 S '87
Getting personal. D. K. Mano. *Natl Rev* 39:52-3 D 31 '87
I know you're out there. *Harpers* 274:17-18 F '87

Anecdotes, facetiae, satire, etc.
Dream lovers (on reading the personals). K. Fury. il *Work Woman* 12:192 My '87

Personics Corporation
Labels split on in-store taping. N. Arnett and A. DeCurtis. *Roll Stone* p14+ Jl 2 '87
Taping at retail. C. J. Esse. il *High Fidel* 37:14 S '87

Personnel management

See also
Absenteeism
AIDS (Disease) and employment
Alcohol and employment
Communication in management
Drugs and employment
Employee counseling
Employees—Dismissal
Employees—Rating
Employees—Recruiting
Employees—Training
Employment tests
Factory management
Incentives in industry
Job evaluation
Job satisfaction
Labor discipline
Labor turnover
Layoffs
Nepotism
Personnel records
Profit sharing
Promotions
Psychology, Industrial
Smoking and employment
Coping with pain-in-the-neck employes [interview with C. Sherman] il por *U S News World Rep* 103:74 D 14 '87
Delegating your way to job survival. L. Baum. il *Bus Week* p206 N 2 '87
Don't call me honey [managing a secretary] S. Bing. il *Esquire* 108:49 Jl '87
Employee development: is your company just paying lip service. W. Konrad. il *Work Woman* 12:23+ Je '87
Giving—and getting—feedback [excerpt from The art of managing people] P. L. Hunsaker and A. J. Alessandra. il *Work Woman* 12:30+ Ap '87
Goodbye, corporate staff. T. Moore. il *Fortune* 116:65+ D 21 '87
Handling the overachiever. K. Samon. il *Work Woman* 12:24+ Mr '87
How to groom a great successor. K. Berman. *Work Woman* 12:28 My '87
How to manage people whose jobs are different from yours. W. Konrad. il *Work Woman* 12:32+ My '87
How to manage the staff procrastinator. C. Golden. *Work Woman* 12:31 N '87
Making changes: how to budge the office mule. M. J. Parson. il *Work Woman* 12:139-41 S '87

Managing sideways. R. E. Lefton. il *Work Woman* 12:34+ O '87
Managing the excusaholic employee [excerpt from Managing people at work desk guide] T. L. Quick. *Work Woman* 12:15 Ag '87
Maternity leaves: how managers should handle them. H. McCrum. *Work Woman* 12:18 Ja '87
Moving a key subordinate out of a rut [excerpt from Managing people at work desk guide] T. L. Quick. *Work Woman* 12:33 N '87
The new careerists [views of C. Brooklyn Derr] il *Futurist* 21:23-4 Mr/Ap '87
The right way to welcome a new employee. M. Rathie. *Work Woman* 12:23 D '87
Seven delegating mistakes—and how to avoid them. J. Iaconetti. *Work Woman* 12:24+ Jl '87
Tips for the hands-off CEO. B. Powell. il *Newsweek* 109:52 Mr 16 '87
What every manager should know about discrimination. J. Sherman. *Work Woman* 12:31+ N '87

Personnel records
Keep an up-to-date file on yourself [excerpt from Managing people at work desk guide] T. L. Quick. *Work Woman* 12:23 D '87

Perspective
Creating the illusion of three dimensions in two-dimensional space [photography] F. Patterson. il *Petersens Photogr Mag* 16:56-7 N '87
Perspective based on math alone isn't the whole picture. N. Rothschild. il *Pop Photogr* 94:18 Je '87
Three-dimensional perspective plotting. T. Daulton. il *Byte* 12:307-8+ D '87

Perspiration
Perspiration: track down no-sweat solutions. L. Kelly. il *Teen* 31:32+ My '87
Sweat: how sweet it is! K. Cunningham and P. Stites. il *World Tennis* 34:60+ My '87
Sweating it out. L. J. Nonkin. *Vogue* 177:266 Jl '87

Persuasion (Psychology)
How persuasive are you? Ways to make others believe in your ideas. B. L. Stern. *Vogue* 177:264 Jl '87
The perils of persistence [Profiles of Organizational Influence Strategies test results] S. Schmidt and D. Kipnis. bibl (p65) il *Psychol Today* 21:32+ N '87

Pertschuk, Michael, 1933-
about
What every lobbyist should know. J. L. Swerdlow. il por *Channels* 7:76 F '87

Pertuiset, Nicola
(tr) *See* Le Corbusier, 1887-1965. The Parthenon at dusk

Peru

See also
Americans—Peru
Andes
Festivals—Peru
Financial institutions—Laws and regulations—Peru
Government ownership—Peru
Iquitos (Peru)
Narcotics laws and regulations—Peru
Wildlife conservation—Peru
Wildlife sanctuaries—Peru

Antiquities
See also
Machu Picchu (Peru)

Economic conditions
See also
Underground economy—Peru

Economic policy
Debt, democracy and terrorism in Peru. D. P. Werlich. bibl f *Curr Hist* 86:29-32+ Ja '87

Industries
See also
Wool industry—Peru

Native peoples
See Indians of South America—Peru

Politics and government
Debt, democracy and terrorism in Peru. D. P. Werlich. bibl f *Curr Hist* 86:29-32+ Ja '87
Embattled in Peru. J. N. Montesinos. *World Press Rev* 34:39 My '87
Shining Path burns with a hotter flame. B. Durr. il *U S News World Rep* 102:35 My 25 '87

Religious institutions and affairs
See also
Church and social problems—Peru

Peru in literature
José María Arguedas: godfather of liberationism. S. B. Wall-Smith. *Christ Century* 104:1034-9 N 18 '87

Peruvian cooking *See* Cooking, Peruvian
Peruvian folk art *See* Folk art
Pesaro (Italy)

Music festivals
See Music festivals—Italy

Pesavento, Peter
Sputnik's heirs: what the Soviets are doing in space [cover story] il *Technol Rev* 90:26-35 O '87
Tsander's dream. il por *Space World* X-5-281:28-31 My '87

Peschke, Virginia M., and others
Discovery of transposable element activity among progeny of tissue culture-derived maize plants. bibl f il *Science* 238:804-7 N 6 '87

Peshawar (Pakistan)

Description
The catastrophe [visiting places related to the Afghan resistance] D. M. Lessing. *New Yorker* 63:74-90+ Mr 16 '87

Peskin, Marietta Esposito
Kindergarten all day? *Educ Dig* 52:17-19 Mr '87

Pessac (France)

Housing
Le Corbusier's Pessac: an experiment in urbanism continues. T. Matthews. il *Archit Rec* 175:87+ N '87

Pessimism
Are you an optimist or a pessimist? [quiz] K. Stechert. il *Glamour* 85:148+ S '87
The power of negative thinking [research by Julie K. Norem and Nancy Cantor] C. Wade. il *Psychol Today* 21:18 My '87

Anecdotes, facetiae, satire, etc.
Why pessimism is better than optimism (on a global scale). J. Gorman. il *Discover* 8:14+ Ag '87

Pest control
See also
  Garden symphylans—Control
  Insect control
  Mites—Control
  Moles (Animals)—Control
  Pesticides
  Slugs—Control
  Squirrels—Control
  Traps
A close watch on U.S. borders to keep the world's bugs out. E. Larson. bibl (p154) *Smithsonian* 18:106-8+ Je '87; il
Fiddling around with nature means better pest control. *Success Farm* 85:18R My '87
Learning how to control pests. il *World Health* p22 Jl '87
Pets and the garden [readers' tips] S. Milius. il *Rodale's Org Gard* 34:30-1 Je '87
What to do when man's best friend is your garden's worst enemy? il *Sunset* 178:106-9 Ap '87

Pest control services
See also
  Bugs Burger Bug Killer Inc.
When to call the exterminator [interview with A. M. Katz] P. Easton. il por *Home Mech* 83:14-15 Ap '87

Environmental aspects
Safety first [crusade of pest control operator S. Tvedten] P. H. Johnson. il por *Rodale's Org Gard* 34:82-4+ D '87

Pesticide pollution *See* Pesticides—Environmental aspects
Pesticide residues in food *See* Food contamination
Pesticide residues in milk *See* Milk contamination
Pesticide resistance
Report on reports: Pesticide resistance: strategies and tactics for management [report of National Research Council conference, 1984] S. H. Dreistadt and D. L. Dahlsten. bibl f *Environment* 29:25-7 Ap '87
Pesticide spraying equipment *See* Spraying equipment
Pesticides
See also
  Chlordane
  Heptachlor
  Herbicides
  National Coalition Against the Misuse of Pesticides
Bug brains [pesticides based on insect neuropeptides] B. Lawren. il *Omni* 9:18 Ap '87

Environmental aspects
See also
  Pest control services—Environmental aspects
  Pesticides and wildlife
Pesticidal rains. *Sci News* 131:360 Je 6 '87
Reducing pesticide use. *Futurist* 21:52-3 Jl/Ag '87

Export-import trade
Disaster for sale [pesticides exported from the United States] P. A. A. Berle. *Audubon* 89:6 My '87

Handling
No-hands handling of corn insecticides [hopper system] J. Walter. il *Success Farm* 85 no1:26H Ja '87

Injurious effects
Bug-spray alert [potentially poisonous inert substances] W. Kistner and A. Porterfield. il *Technol Rev* 90:10+ My/Je '87
The dangers of lawn care. J. Burnett. il *Rodale's Org Gard* 34:24-32 N '87
Disaster for sale [pesticides exported from the United States] P. A. A. Berle. *Audubon* 89:6 My '87
Farmworkers out on the line again [proposed UFW grape boycott] A. Stine. il *Sierra* 72:14+ Jl/Ag '87
Green dreams [potential problems from lawn chemicals] J. R. Provey. il *Home Mech* 83:4 Mr '87
Hazards of the game [golf courses] J. Edmondson. il *Audubon* 89:24-8+ N '87
In the journals [link between household pesticides and childhood leukemia] *Child Today* 16:3 S/O '87
No time for termites [EPA forces end to production of Termide] *Time* 130:46 Ag 24 '87
One washing won't remove pesticides from clothing. *Success Farm* 85:D My '87
Pesticide health risks [farmers] B. Freese and D. Mowitz. il *Success Farm* 85 no3:18AB F '87
Pesticides: a growing concern. B. T. Hunter. *Consum Res Mag* 70:27-8 Ag '87
Safety first [crusade of pest control operator S. Tvedten] P. H. Johnson. il por *Rodale's Org Gard* 34:82-4+ D '87

Labeling
Bug spray-drug spray mix-up [pesticide mislabeled as an aerosol drug] *FDA Consum* 21:40 Mr '87

Laws and regulations
Chemical warfare. T. Beardsley. *Sci Am* 257:18+ S '87
Crates of fresh poison [EDB levels in mangoes imported from Haiti] R. Caplan. *Harpers* 275:58-9 O '87
EPA's predicament over regulating pesticides. M. Sun. il *Science* 238:20-1 O 2 '87
Regulating pesticides in food [National Academy of Sciences report] L. Tangley. il *BioScience* 37:452-6 Jl/Ag '87
Regulating pesticides: the "Delaney paradox". C. Norman. il *Science* 236:1054-5 My 29 '87

Safety devices and measures
Personal protection from pesticides. C. Tevis. il *Success Farm* 85 no1:26D-26E Ja '87

Testing
How safe is your food? [cancer threat from pesticides] K. McAuliffe. il *U S News World Rep* 103:70-2 N 16 '87
Pesticide protection [California markets test produce] J. Adler. il *Newsweek* 110:69+ N 9 '87

Pesticides and wildlife
Courage of Rachel Carson [excerpt from Two Park Street] P. Brooks. il por *Audubon* 89:12+ Ja '87
Pelicans vs. pesticides. il *Nat Hist* 96:6 S '87
Wildlife [Environmental Quality Index] il *Natl Wildl* 25:34 F/Mr '87

Pests

Control
See Pest control

PET (Positron emission tomography) *See* Tomography
Pet allergy
Living with pet allergies. H. E. Whiteley. il *Saturday Evening Post* 259:26+ O '87
Pet food
See also
  Cats—Food and feeding
  Dogs—Food and feeding
  Lick Your Chops (Firm)
Pet food moves upscale—and profits fatten. L. Therrien. il *Bus Week* p80+ Je 15 '87
Special diets for special pets. H. E. Whiteley. il *Saturday Evening Post* 259:20-1 My/Je '87
Pet Incorporated
Take the high ground. J. Flint. il *Forbes* 139:228+ Je 15 '87
Pet industries

Advertising
Upscale dogs: clipping coupons for chow. il *Newsweek* 109:62 My 18 '87

Export-import trade
Morris the Cat is learning Japanese [U.S. cat food exports] B. Buell. il *Bus Week* p82 Je 15 '87

Finance
Pet food moves upscale—and profits fatten. L. Therrien. il *Bus Week* p80+ Je 15 '87

Japan
Morris the Cat is learning Japanese [U.S. cat food exports] B. Buell. il *Bus Week* p82 Je 15 '87

Pet shows
See also
Dog shows

Pet stores
For sale: the Gloved One's cast-off main squeeze [Sherman Oaks, Calif. pet store owner L. de Borondy attempts to sell singer M. Jackson's former pet python] il por *People Wkly* 27:88 My 25 '87

Pet therapy See Pets—Therapeutic use

Peter, the Apostle, Saint
about
St. Peter and Lord Acton? . . . and suffering. G. G. Seibert. *America* 157:95 Ag 15-22 '87

Peter Kiewit Sons, Inc.
Dow Jones average? What's that? J. R. Hayes. il *Forbes* 140:151-2 D 14 '87

Peter Miller Architecture and Design Books (Seattle, Wash.: Bookstore) See Booksellers and bookselling—Washington (State)

Peter Pan [drama] See Barrie, J. M. (James Matthew), 1860-1937

Peter Rabbit (Fictional character)
So, what did happen to Peter Rabbit's dad? [new, sanitized version] il *Newsweek* 110:36 S 28 '87

Peterborough (N.H.)
Population
Rural hot spots . . . rural cold spots. B. Trebilcock. il *Ctry J* 14:32-5+ Je '87

Peterman, Janet S.
A pastoral and theological response to losses in pregnancy. *Christ Century* 104:750-3 S 9-16 '87

Peterman, Randall M., and Bradford, Michael J.
Wind speed and mortality rate of a marine fish, the northern anchovy (Engraulis mordax). bibl f il *Science* 235:354-6 Ja 16 '87

Peters, Alton E.
MOG annual report. *Opera News* 52:4 O '87

Peters, Ann
The government as a matchmaker. il *World Press Rev* 34:58 F '87

Peters, Anne
Legends [poem] *America* 156:459 Je 6 '87

Peters, Bernadette
about
Theater. R. D. Story. il por *N Y* 20:50-1 S 21 '87

Peters, Brock
about
Brock Peters. il pors *Ebony* 43:92+ N '87

Peters, Charles, 1926-
The Kennedy hustle. il *Wash Mon* 19:47-9 My '87
Tilting at windmills. See issues of The Washington Monthly

Peters, Georges
Overdose. il *Courier* 40:21-4 Ag '87

Peters, Stephen, and others
Zinc selectively blocks the action of N-methyl-D-aspartate on cortical neurons. bibl f il *Science* 236:589-93 My 1 '87

Peters, Thomas J.
Robert Reich takes on Rambo. *Wash Mon* 19:51-6 Mr '87
There are no excellent companies. il por *Fortune* 115:341+ Ap 27 '87
To: Corporate managers. Re: Bureaucracy. Don't send memos! il *Wash Mon* 19:12-14+ N '87

Petersburg (Va.)
Crime
Convicted Va. minister quits council, churches [case of C. Johnson] por *Jet* 72:6 Ag 24 '87
Minister/councilman's rape conviction still stuns his church, city [Rev. C. Johnson] D. M. Cheers. il por *Jet* 72:16-17 Jl 13 '87
Minister/lawmaker may get 161 years in prison for rape, sexual battery [case of C. Johnson] il por *Jet* 72:4-6 Je 29 '87
Petersburg, Va. pastor charged with alleged sexual abuse of 6 girls [case of C. L. Johnson] *Jet* 72:10 Je 15 '87
Va. minister convicted of sex crimes gets 120 years [case of C. L. Johnson] por *Jet* 73:51 O 5 '87

Petersen, Anne C.
Those gangly years [cover story] il *Psychol Today* 21:28-34 S '87

Petersen, Chris W.
(jt. auth) See Fischer, Eric A., and Petersen, Chris W.

Petersen, David
Erasing the blue-pencil blues. *Writer* 100:14-16 F '87

Petersen, Donald E.
The automotive world of the 21st century. il *Radio-Electron* 58:91-5 My '87

about
1987 Man of the Year. il por *Mot Trend* 39:43 F '87
Can Ford stay on top? [cover story] J. B. Treece. il pors *Bus Week* p78-82+ S 28 '87
Miscellaneous ramblings. J. Dinkel. il *Road Track* 39:37-9 O '87
The poor boy who outearned GM. A. L. Taylor, III. il por *Fortune* 116:28-9 Ag 3 '87
The U.S.: team at the top of no. 2. il pors *Fortune* 116:82 N 9 '87

Petersen, Erik Brinch
(jt. auth) See Price, T. Douglas (Theron Douglas), and Petersen, Erik Brinch

Petersen, Norman
about
Gaijin makes good. M. Beauchamp. il por *Forbes* 140:124 S 7 '87

Petersen, Pat
about
Pat Petersen: happy landings! K. Silverman. por *Teen* 31:49 F '87

Petersen, Susan J.
about
Book-smart style. P. Kripke. il por *Work Woman* 12:118-19 N '87

Petersen's photographic magazine
Better photography [new column, Re: vision by F. Patterson] B. Hurter. il por *Petersens Photogr Mag* 15:6 Mr '87
More results of the "opinion poll". J. Augustine. il *Petersens Photogr Mag* 16:6 My '87
Photographic debuts a new design. J. Augustine. il *Petersens Photogr Mag* 16:6 N '87
Photographic's Outstanding Achievement Award debuts. J. Augustine. il *Petersens Photogr Mag* 16:6 D '87
Quick & easy studio portraiture [photographing Petersen's editors] A. Stone. il *Petersens Photogr Mag* 15:50-3 Mr '87
Results of the opinion poll. J. Augustine. il *Petersens Photogr Mag* 15:6 Ap '87
Team depth [new columnist G. A. Rowell] B. Hurter. por *Petersens Photogr Mag* 16:10 Je '87
To video or not to video . . . [results of reader survey] J. Augustine. il *Petersens Photogr Mag* 15:4 Ja '87

Peterson, Ann
Home on the range. il *Seventeen* 46:268+ Ag '87

Peterson, Cass
Scenic sites under siege. il *Natl Wildl* 25:44-5 Je/Jl '87

Peterson, Claudia
"What has happened is incredible"; ed. by Dena Kleiman. il por *Redbook* 168:44+ Ja '87

Peterson, Clinton
about
What's up, docs? Supercarrot is on the way. il pors *People Wkly* 27:40 Mr 16 '87

Peterson, David Robert
Learning to compete [address, April 23, 1987] *Vital Speeches Day* 53:528-31 Je 15 '87
Neo-protectionism [address, November 6, 1986] *Vital Speeches Day* 53:230-1 F 1 '87
about
The big red wave [cover story; special section; with editorial comment by Kevin Doyle] il pors *Macleans* 100:12-14+ S 21 '87
Ontario's power struggle. S. Aikenhead. il por *Macleans* 100:14-15 Ag 10 '87
Ready for combat. S. Aikenhead. il por *Macleans* 100:9 Jl 20 '87
A tide of change sweeps Ontario. S. Aikenhead. il *Macleans* 100:12-13 Ja 12 '87

Peterson, Eugene H., 1932-
Christmas shame [cover story] il por *Christ Today* 31:17-19 D 11 '87
about
Eugene Peterson: a monk out of habit [interview] R. Clapp. il pors *Christ Today* 31:24-8 Ap 3 '87

Peterson, Ivars
Hvac systems: in pursuit of comfort. *Archit Rec* 175:150-3 My '87
The Statue of Liberty project: lessons learned from a Lady. *Current* 292:4-8 My '87

Peterson, J. Allan
about
A concerned Christian goes the Second Mile. *Christ Today* 31:47-8 F 6 '87

Peterson, John I.
Laboratory experimentation with a personal computer. *Science* 235 pt2:G162 F 27 '87

Peterson, Michael R., 1943-1987
about
As Father Michael Peterson lay dying of AIDS, his Catholic Church showed it cared deeply for one of its own. D. Chu. il por *People Wkly* 27:131-2 My 11 '87
Peterson, Norma
Mind over disease: Warning! Daily hassles are hazardous. il *Read Dig* 130:76-8 Ap '87
Peterson, Norman L., 1935-1986
about
Obituary
Phys Today 40:113 My '87. J. N. Mundy
Peterson, Peter G.
After an economic heart attack. il *Newsweek* 110:50+ N 2 '87
Gorbachev's bottom line. bibl f il *N Y Rev Books* 34:29-33 Je 25 '87
The morning after [cover story] il *Atlantic* 260:43-50+ O '87
about
Meet Pete Peterson, the new merchant banker on the block. S. Bartlett. il por *Bus Week* p108-9 N 23 '87
Peterson, Roger Tory, 1908-
'The most vivid expression of life'. il por *Life* 10:56 Jl '87
Peterson, Tom
Child survival: an achievable goal in hunger relief [cover story] il *Christ Century* 104:594-5 Jl 1-8 '87
Peterson, Wallace C.
Prescription for a slump. *New Leader* 70:14 N 30 '87
Peterson (Roger Tory) Institute of Natural History See Roger Tory Peterson Institute of Natural History
Petit, Philippe, 1949-
about
Profiles. G. Kinkhead. *New Yorker* 63:35-8+ Je 15 '87
Petit, Roland
about
The Blue Angel [ballet] Reviews
Dance Mag il 61:20-1+ Ag '87. M. E. Willis
Les petits riens [ballet] See Ballet reviews—Single works
Petosa, Rick
Self-management skills and student health practices. *Educ Dig* 52:56-9 Ja '87
PETRA electron-positron colliding-beam accelerator See Accelerators (Electrons, etc.)
Petraglia, Felice, and others
Localization, secretion, and action of inhibin in human placenta. bibl f il *Science* 237:187-9 Jl 10 '87
Petri dishes
Photographs and photography
Work dramatization. T. Strand. il *Petersens Photogr Mag* 16:66-7 Je '87
Petrich, Perla
Of maize and meat: culinary traditions and cultural identity in Mexico and Argentina. il *Courier* 40:10-13 My '87
Petrie, Daniel
about
Square dance [film] Reviews
Glamour 85:226 Mr '87. J. G. Boyum
Ms 15:36 Ap '87. S. Dworkin
Petrie, Milton, 1902?-
about
Grandson power. R. King, Jr. il por *Forbes* 140 Sp Issue:376+ O 26 '87
Petrie, Paul
The composition [poem] *Christ Century* 104:1076 D 2 '87
Stamp store [poem] *America* 156:380 My 9 '87
Petrie Stores Corp.
Grandson power [heir apparent M. Miller] R. King, Jr. il por *Forbes* 140 Sp Issue:376+ O 26 '87
Petrobras See Petroleo Brasileiro SA
Petrochemical industry
See also
Cain Chemical Inc.
Ethyl Corp.
Acquisitions and mergers
Leaning against the wind [deals by G. Cain] J. Willoughby. il por *Forbes* 140:208+ Jl 13 '87
Petroglyphs
See also
Cave drawings and paintings
Petroglyphs National Monument (N.M.)
The push for a petroglyph park. F. Urquhart. il *Sierra* 72:82-3 Mr/Ap '87
Petroleo Brasileiro SA
The Iacocca of Brazil [O. Silva] J. Barham. il por *Fortune* 116:60+ Ag 3 '87

Petroleum
An invariance in the isoheptanes of petroleum. F. D. Mango. bibl f il *Science* 237:514-17 Jl 31 '87
Conferences
See also
Organization of Petroleum Exporting Countries—Conferences
Export-import trade
See Petroleum industry—Export-import trade
Geology
Drilling into a deep controversy [deep-earth-gas theory of Thomas Gold] R. Monastersky. *Sci News* 131:380-1 Je 13 '87
Sounding the inner earth for gas and oil [deep-earth-gas theory of Thomas Gold] *Environment* 29:22-3 Jl/Ag '87
International aspects
See also
Organization of Petroleum Exporting Countries
Petroleum industry—Export-import trade
Pipelines
See Petroleum pipelines
Prices
See also
Gasoline—Prices
Bailing out oil. *Progressive* 51:11-12 My '87
The big dip is history. S. Koepp. il *Time* 130:40-1 Ag 3 '87
Can OPEC keep its foot off the gas in Vienna? W. C. Symonds. il *Bus Week* p32 Je 29 '87
Chalk one up for the permanent government [oil overcharge cases] R. Jaroslovsky. *Wash Mon* 19:33-7 O '87
The cold wave that sent warm shivers to Riyadh. K. R. Sheets. *U S News World Rep* 102:41 Ja 26 '87
Crude calculations [price drop] il *U S News World Rep* 103:14 D 28 '87-Ja 4 '88
Fuel refund of $80 waiting for users who file forms. *Success Farm* 85:66C S '87
Gas lines again? *Natl Rev* 39:20-1 Ap 10 '87
Get ready for the coming oil crisis. J. P. Newport, Jr. il *Fortune* 115:46-52+ Mr 16 '87
The great oil giveaway [address, September 4, 1987] R. G. Wallace. *Vital Speeches Day* 54:17-20 O 15 '87
The hot new low-stakes play in oil [crude options] T. Thompson. il *Bus Week* p80 Ja 26 '87
Impending energy crisis? [discussion of March 20, 1987 article, Impending United States energy crisis] R. L. Hirsch. *Science* 236:763-5 My 15 '87
Impending United States energy crisis. R. L. Hirsch. bibl f il *Science* 235:1467-73 Mr 20 '87
Import price declines in 1986 reflected reduced oil prices. E. Gibbons and G. F. Halpin. bibl f il *Mon Labor Rev* 110:3-17 Ap '87
Iranamok and OPEC. P. J. Sloyan. *New Repub* 197:19-21 N 9 '87
Is OPEC bluffing again? T. Thompson. *Bus Week* p92 Mr 9 '87
Is Uncle Sam putting up the price of oil? [views of Federal Reserve economist Bharat Trehan] R. McGough. il *Forbes* 139:144 F 23 '87
Low-cost oil is fueling energy worries [report by the Department of Energy] *Sci News* 131:201 Mr 28 '87
New clout for the oil cartel. il *Fortune* 115:8 F 16 '87
New directions for oil policy. R. W. Fri. bibl f il *Environment* 29:16-20+ Je '87
The new energy challenge [address, February 3, 1987] G. M. Keller. *Vital Speeches Day* 53:314-17 Mr 1 '87
The next oil crisis [cover story] M. Lynch. il *Technol Rev* 90:38-45+ N/D '87
Not so crude options [oil options] S. W. Angrist. il *Forbes* 139:176 Mr 9 '87
Oil, the Gulf and the Iranians. D. Hiro. *Nation* 245:261-3 S 19 '87
Oil together now. F. Barnes. *New Repub* 196:12-13 F 9 '87
Oilmen have a new way to cope with falling prices [energy asset insurance guarantees a price floor] T. Thompson. il *Bus Week* p74 Ag 3 '87
OPEC is staring at $15 oil—once more [Vienna meeting] W. C. Symonds. il *Bus Week* p33 D 14 '87
OPEC makes $18 oil stick—for now. W. C. Symonds. il *Bus Week* p32-3 F 16 '87
OPEC smartens up. W. C. Symonds. *Bus Week* p34-5 Jl 13 '87
OPEC's troubled future. T. Tedesco. il *Macleans* 100:37-8 D 14 '87

Petroleum—Prices—cont.

Supersap [U.S. effort to protect access to Persian Gulf oil results in price rise] New Repub 197:4 Ag 31 '87

'There's too much damn oil around'. T. Smart. Bus Week p24-5 S 7 '87

The third oil crisis. J. Cook. il map Forbes 140:37+ D 14 '87

The U.S. is better braced for another oil shock . . . while OPEC seems less likely to maintain high prices. G. Koretz. il Bus Week p14 Ag 24 '87

Undertow from the Gulf [Persian Gulf tensions] W. Glasgall. il Bus Week p32-4 Ag 17 '87

Why oil prices could rise again. D. Blake. World Press Rev 34:48+ Jl '87

Production methods
See Petroleum engineering

Prospecting
See also
Airplanes in the petroleum industry
Pennzoil Company
Shell Oil Company

Is there oil in Iowa? [prospecting in Halbur] C. O'Connor. il Newsweek 109:26 Je 22 '87

The new breed of wildcatters. P. Nulty. il Fortune 116:110-12+ S 28 '87

Oil's gutsy new mavericks. F. Gibney and P. Wang. il Newsweek 110:42 Ag 31 '87

Recovery methods
See Petroleum engineering

Refining
From crud to crude [emulsion technology] J. Keebler. il Pop Sci 230:79 My '87

Storage
See also
Oil tanks

Transportation
See also
Petroleum pipelines
Tankers

Aegean Sea
Storm clouds over the Aegean [Greece-Turkey dispute] J. Bierman. il map Macleans 100:26-7 Ap 6 '87

Alaska
The Alaska lands debate, part two [endangering Arctic National Wildlife Refuge] J. D. Hair. il Int Wildl 17:26 Ja/F '87

All caribou are not the same [petroleum development threatens Arctic National Wildlife Refuge] L. Minard. il maps Forbes 139:43-5 Mr 9 '87

Arctic National Wildlife Refuge: oil field or wilderness? A. L. Spitler. BioScience 37:714 N '87

Arctic schemes [proposed oil exploration in the Arctic National Wildlife Refuge] M. K. Udall. Wilderness 50:60 Spr '87

A compromise the caribou will like [oil exploration in Arctic National Wildlife Refuge] il Fortune 115:9 My 25 '87

Cumulative impacts of oil fields on northern Alaskan landscapes [Arctic National Wildlife Refuge] D. A. Walker and others. bibl f il map Science 238:757-61 N 6 '87

Edge of the Arctic [Arctic National Wildlife Refuge; cover story] D. Frazier. il Natl Parks 61:18-23 N/D '87

Fighting a new threat to the North [proposed oil development in the Arctic National Wildlife Refuge] I. Austen. il map Macleans 100:12 My 4 '87

First word [proposed oil exploration of the Arctic National Wildlife Refuge] G. Nelson. por Omni 10:8 N '87

Fuel for an Arctic controversy [opening Arctic National Wildlife Refuge to oil and gas exploration] L. Williamson. il Outdoor Life 179:42+ Mr '87

High stakes in a land of plenty [Arctic National Wildlife Refuge; cover story; with editorial comment by Jay D. Hair] T. A. Lewis. il map Natl Wildl 25:4-11, 28 Je/Jl '87

Into the second century [Arctic National Wildlife Refuge] P. A. A. Berle. Audubon 89:4 Mr '87

NPCA opposes damage to Arctic Wildlife Refuge [proposed oil and gas exploration] il Natl Parks 61:36 My/Je '87

Polar opposites [oil development versus wilderness in the Arctic National Wildlife Refuge] J. R. Udall. il map Sierra 72:40-8 S/O '87

Preserving Alaska's wildlife [Arctic National Wildlife Refuge] L. Williamson. il Outdoor Life 180:40+ O '87

Staking out the last frontier [Arctic National Wildlife Refuge] M. K. Udall. il por Natl Parks 61:16-17 N/D '87

Arctic regions
See also
Petroleum—Alaska

Gulf of Mexico
It's white-knuckle time for the Hunts [bankruptcy court to decide fate of Placid Oil Gulf drilling project] T. Mason. il Bus Week p29 Mr 30 '87

North Sea region
Offshore outpost [life and work in the North Sea oil fields] C. Swann. il Oceans 20:42-7 N/D '87

A squall over oil whips up the North Sea [British independents scurrying for white knights] S. Miller. il Bus Week p89-90 D 28 '87-Ja 4 '88

Pacific Ocean
Oil and fishing industries negotiate: mediation and scientific issues [conflicts arising off California coast] G. W. Cormick and A. Knaster. bibl il Environment 28:6-15+ D '86

United States
See Petroleum

Petroleum engineering
See also
Computers—Petroleum engineering use

Molasses and microbes mix to sustain oil flow in Oklahoma. Earth Sci 40:7-8 Summ '87

Petroleum research centers. P. H. Abelson. Science 237:117 Jl 10 '87

Roughnecks [use of bacteria in petroleum production] Sci Am 256:60+ My '87

Petroleum equipment industry
See also
Baker International Corp.
Hughes Tool Company
Kendavis Industries International Inc.
L. B. Foster Co.
NL Industries, Inc.
Ocean Drilling & Exploration Co.
Petroleum Equipment Tools Co.
Rowan Companies, Inc.
Schlumberger Ltd.

Oil. T. Mack. il Forbes 139:198-200 Ja 12 '87

Acquisitions and mergers
Why the Baker-Hughes merger almost didn't happen. C. S. Eklund and T. Vogel. il pors Bus Week p110-11 My 11 '87

Export-import trade
Easing the high-tech sales ban: U.S. firms can now sell oil equipment to Moscow. J. B. Copeland. il Newsweek 109:38 Ja 26 '87

Our grip slips. T. Mack. il Forbes 139:45-6 Mr 9 '87

Finance
Oil drillers bounce back—to their lenders' doors. T. Vogel. il Bus Week p96 S 7 '87

Petroleum Equipment Tools Co.
Thanks, Dad. B. Leonard. il por Forbes 140:53-4+ Ag 10 '87

Petroleum geology *See* Petroleum—Geology

Petroleum income funds *See* Petroleum investment trusts

Petroleum industry
See also
Airplanes in the petroleum industry
Amerada Hess Corp.
Amoco Corporation
Atlantic Richfield Co.
Blocker Energy Corp.
Chevron Corporation
Exxon Corporation
Getty Petroleum Corp.
Hondo Oil & Gas Company
Mesa Limited Partnership
Mesa Petroleum Co.
Mobil Corporation
Occidental Petroleum Corp.
Oil shale industry
Pauley Petroleum Inc.
Pennzoil Company
Petrochemical industry
Petroleum refineries
Petroleum workers
Phillips Petroleum Company
Placid Oil Company
Shell Oil Company
Standard Oil Company
Tesoro Petroleum Corp.
Texaco Inc.
Tosco Corp.
Wagner & Brown
Wolverine Exploration Company
Women in the petroleum industry

Is there oil in Iowa? [prospecting in Halbur] C. O'Connor. il Newsweek 109:26 Je 22 '87

Petroleum industry—*cont.*

Acquisitions and mergers

Behind the scenes at Texaco's settlement [Pennzoil agreement] J. R. Norman and T. Vogel. il *Bus Week* p66-8 D 28 '87-Ja 4 '88

Carl Icahn deals himself in [controls 12% of Texaco] J. R. Norman. il por *Bus Week* p38 D 14 '87

Creating value [R. Rainwater's petroleum plays] J. Merwin. il *Forbes* 139 Ann Directory:57 Ap 27 '87

Gushing money [Texas court rules in favor of Pennzoil in takeover dispute with Texaco] *Newsweek* 109:56 F 23 '87

Icahn thickens the Texaco plot. *Newsweek* 110:66 D 7 '87

Knocked down in round 2 [Texas court upholds judgment against Texaco] il *Time* 129:67 F 23 '87

Let 'Icahn do your work for you' [buying TWA stock to get in on Texaco-Pennzoil deal] G. G. Marcial. *Bus Week* p106 D 21 '87

On tap: a $3 billion solution? [settlement in Pennzoil vs. Texaco] K. R. Sheets and W. J. Cook. *U S News World Rep* 103:16 D 21 '87

Robert Anderson is shaking up the oil patch again [merging Hondo into Pauley] J. Flynn. il por *Bus Week* p39 Ag 17 '87

A small price to pay [settlement of Texaco-Pennzoil case] G. Bock. il *Time* 130:63 D 28 '87

Texaco takes a knockdown punch [Supreme Court sends Pennzoil case back to Texas] T. Thompson. il *Bus Week* p27 Ap 20 '87

Texaco vs. Pennzoil: next stop, Washington [Texas Supreme Court refuses to review judgment won by Pennzoil] T. Vogel. il *Bus Week* p68 N 16 '87

Texaco's $3 billion deal with Pennzoil. *Newsweek* 110:52 D 21 '87

Texaco's last stand [negotiations over Pennzoil settlement] T. Tedesco. il *Macleans* 100:43 D 28 '87

Texaco's last stand in Texas [judgment won by Pennzoil] J. E. Davis and T. Vogel. il *Bus Week* p36 Mr 2 '87

Triumph of the sore-back lawyer [J. Jamail's skills in Texaco-Pennzoil battle] T. Mack. il por *Forbes* 139:33-4 My 4 '87

Why is Tesoro so popular? T. Vogel. il *Bus Week* p40 D 21 '87

International aspects

Is Holmes a Court trying to lasso Texaco? T. Thompson. il por *Bus Week* p59 Jl 27 '87

Jaws: the Australian [accumulation of Texaco stock by R. Holmes à Court] J. Castro. il por *Time* 130:53 Jl 27 '87

An oil-patch marriage [British Gas buys major stake in Bow Valley Industries] J. Howse. il *Macleans* 100:33 Ag 17 '87

Putting out the welcome mat [takeover of Husky Oil by Li Ka-shing] D. Francis. por *Macleans* 100:9 My 18 '87

Stalker of wounded game [R. Holmes à Court's interest in Texaco stock] T. Jaffe. il por *Forbes* 139:38+ Je 15 '87

Stalking Texaco [stock purchase by R. Holmes à Court] *Time* 129:52 Je 1 '87

Why BP is going all out for all of Standard Oil. S. Miller. il *Bus Week* p50 Ap 13 '87

Will Aussie raider deliver coup de grace to crippled Texaco? [plans of R. Holmes à Court] K. R. Sheets. *U S News World Rep* 102:43 Je 1 '87

Will he, or won't he? Australia keeps Texaco on edge [R. Holmes à Court plans to boost holdings] K. R. Sheets. *U S News World Rep* 103:37 Jl 27 '87

Canada

Amoco becomes bolder [bid for Dome] C. Siler. il *Forbes* 140:88 N 2 '87

A bidding war shapes up for debt-ridden Dome [bid by TransCanada PipeLines] E. B. Terry. il *Bus Week* p50 Ap 27 '87

Dome's day of reckoning [creditors disappointed with Amoco Canada bid] T. Tedesco. il *Macleans* 100:29 My 25 '87

Dome's deepening saga [proposed sale of Dome to Amoco Canada Petroleum Co. Ltd.] D. Jenish. il *Macleans* 100:26 Jl 6 '87

Dome's last deal [bid by Amoco Canada; cover story; special section; with editorial comment by Kevin Doyle] il *Macleans* 100:2, 34-42 My 4 '87

Dome's light at the end of the tunnel [Amoco raises its takeover offer] D. Jenish. il *Macleans* 100:50 N 30 '87

Dome's lingering drama [agreement with Amoco Canada Petroleum] T. Tedesco. il *Macleans* 100:40 My 18 '87

Dome's trans-Canadian vision [bid by TransCanada PipeLines] T. Fennell. il *Macleans* 100:45 Ap 27 '87

The Reichmann touch: facing the toughest test yet. E. B. Terry. il *Bus Week* p96-7+ Mr 23 '87

A special interest in Dome [J. P. Gallagher wants Dome to stay in Canadian hands] P. C. Newman. il por *Macleans* 100:48 Ap 27 '87

A threat to the public interest [loss to Canada of Dome to Amoco] P. C. Newman. il *Macleans* 100:31 Jl 6 '87

Great Britain

A squall over oil whips up the North Sea [British independents scurrying for white knights] S. Miller. il *Bus Week* p89-90 D 28 '87-Ja 4 '88

Antitrust cases

Chalk one up for the permanent government [oil overcharge cases] R. Jaroslovsky. *Wash Mon* 19:33-7 O '87

Fuel refund of $80 waiting for users who file forms. *Success Farm* 85:66C S '87

Environmental aspects

Cumulative impacts of oil fields on northern Alaskan landscapes [Arctic National Wildlife Refuge] D. A. Walker and others. bibl f il map *Science* 238:757-61 N 6 '87

Oil and fishing industries negotiate: mediation and scientific issues [conflicts arising off California coast] G. W. Cormick and A. Knaster. bibl il *Environment* 28:6-15+ D '86

Ethical aspects

Making crime pay [gasoline bootlegging] J. Cook. il *Forbes* 140:56+ Jl 27 '87

Export-import trade

See also
    Organization of Petroleum Exporting Countries
    United Nations. Intergovernmental Group to Monitor the Supply and Shipping of Oil and Petroleum Products to South Africa

Enjoy now, pay later [rising oil imports and falling domestic production] B. Rudolph. il *Time* 129:54-5 Mr 16 '87

Foreign oil: the scourge of the '70s may be a blessing now. B. Starr and T. Smart. il *Bus Week* p40 Mr 23 '87

Nicaragua. *Bus Week* p49 Jl 6 '87

Tax relief sought for oil industry. M. Crawford. *Science* 235:1568-9 Mr 27 '87

Trends in oil imports. D. H. Hickcox. *Focus* 37:33 Spr '87

Finance

See also
    Petroleum investment trusts

An economic uptick in the oil patch [Texas] S. A. Peterson. il *U S News World Rep* 103:23 Ag 3 '87

It won't get any easier for U.S. oil companies. T. Thompson. il *Bus Week* p84 Ja 12 '87

My life as a Texan [oil bust] J. Nocera. *New Repub* 196:19-23 Ap 13 '87

Oil. T. Mack. il *Forbes* 139:198-200 Ja 12 '87

There's still money to be made in oil—but not as much [wildcatter C. W. Williams] P. Nulty. il por *Fortune* 115:53 Mr 16 '87

Management

Billions don't buy happiness [billionaires] A. Ramirez. il *Fortune* 116:153-4 O 12 '87

The new breed of wildcatters. P. Nulty. il *Fortune* 116:110-12+ S 28 '87

Oil's gutsy new mavericks. F. Gibney and P. Wang. il *Newsweek* 110:42 Ag 31 '87

Who's afraid of the new Kurt Wulff? J. R. Norman. il por *Bus Week* p74 Je 15 '87

Press relations

Triple reverse [appeals court reverses decision in W. Tavoulareas' libel suit against the Washington post] por *Time* 129:70 Mr 23 '87

Public relations

Give the people light [address, June 9, 1987] M. T. Halbouty. *Vital Speeches Day* 53:653-5 Ag 15 '87

Securities

See also
    Petroleum investment trusts

Arresting new warrants [British Petroleum] S. Miller. il *Bus Week* p126 My 25 '87

Bonds: the safest play on Texaco. G. G. Marcial. *Bus Week* p124 Je 8 '87

Creating value [R. Rainwater's petroleum plays] J. Merwin. il *Forbes* 139 Ann Directory:57 Ap 27 '87

A good time to buy oil stocks? E. C. Baig. il *Fortune* 115:109-10 Mr 16 '87

Oil: getting a bet down. J. B. Quinn. il *Newsweek* 109:52 F 2 '87

Petroleum industry—Securities—*cont.*

The oil stocks' siren song. S. Weiss. il *Bus Week* p126 My 25 '87

Sheik, rattle and roll. M. Sivy. il *Money* 16:49 Ja '87

Texaco stocks and bonds: they may still be no bargain. G. Weiss. il *Bus Week* p106 Ap 27 '87

Who's afraid of the new Kurt Wulff? J. R. Norman. il por *Bus Week* p74 Je 15 '87

Taxation

Irving's taxing battle [Revenue Canada vs. Irving Oil over Bermudan tax shelter] C. Wood. il por *Macleans* 100:34 Ag 3 '87

An oil tax makes sense. R. J. Samuelson. il *Newsweek* 109:48 Ap 6 '87

The petroleum industry at its crossroads [address, February 19, 1987] M. T. Halbouty. *Vital Speeches Day* 53:381-4 Ap 1 '87

Tax relief sought for oil industry. M. Crawford. *Science* 235:1568-9 Mr 27 '87

Brazil

See also
Petroleo Brasileiro SA

Canada

See also
Amoco Canada Petroleum Company Ltd.
Bow Valley Industries Ltd.
Dome Petroleum Ltd.
Gulf Canada Limited
Husky Oil Ltd.
Irving Oil Company
Newfoundland Energy Ltd.

Ottawa aids the oilmen [western Canada] T. Tedesco. *Macleans* 100:31 Ap 6 '87

France

See also
Elf Aquitaine
TOTAL-Compagnie Française des Pétroles

Great Britain

See also
British Petroleum Co. plc
Britoil plc

Italy

See also
Ente Nazionale Idrocarburi

Kuwait

See also
Kuwait Petroleum Corporation

Netherlands

See also
Royal Dutch/Shell Group

Soviet Union

A new member? Moscow plays oil politics with OPEC. il *Newsweek* 109:4 Mr 30 '87

United States

See Petroleum industry

Venezuela

Venezuelan oil firms maintain fleets to service remote sites. il *Aviat Week Space Technol* 127:55+ Ag 31 '87

Petroleum investment trusts

See also
OKC Limited Partnership

Oil: getting a bet down. J. B. Quinn. il *Newsweek* 109:52 F 2 '87

Petroleum laws and regulations

See also
Oil and gas leases
Petroleum—Prices

Petroleum options *See* Commodity options

Petroleum pipelines

Middle East

Who needs the Gulf, anyway? M. Gart. map *Time* 130:27 Ag 24 '87

Petroleum pollution *See* Oil pollution

Petroleum refineries

Shutdowns

A new life for Come By Chance [reopening of oil refinery in Newfoundland] D. Jenish. il *Macleans* 100:32-3 S 7 '87

Petroleum refining *See* Petroleum—Refining

Petroleum supply

Another oil crisis? *Futurist* 21:57 S/O '87

The avoidable oil crisis. A. B. Lovins and L. H. Lovins. il *Atlantic* 260:22+ D '87

Back to the energy crisis. M. Crawford. bibl il *Science* 235:626-7 F 6 '87

Bailing out oil. *Progressive* 51:11-12 My '87

Can the U.S. oil and gas resource base support sustained production? W. L. Fisher. bibl f il *Science* 236:1631-6 Je 26 '87

Energy security [message to Congress, May 6, 1987] R. Reagan. *Dep State Bull* 87:51-2 Jl '87

Enjoy now, pay later [rising oil imports and falling domestic production] B. Rudolph. il *Time* 129:54-5 Mr 16 '87

Food or fuel: the ultimate choice? J. Chapline. il *Ctry J* 14:11 Mr '87

Foreign oil: the scourge of the '70s may be a blessing now. B. Starr and T. Smart. il *Bus Week* p40 Mr 23 '87

Gas lines again? *Natl Rev* 39:20-1 Ap 10 '87

Get ready for the coming oil crisis. J. P. Newport, Jr. il *Fortune* 115:46-52+ Mr 16 '87

Give the people light [address, June 9, 1987] M. T. Halbouty. *Vital Speeches Day* 53:653-5 Ag 15 '87

The great oil giveaway [address, September 4, 1987] R. G. Wallace. *Vital Speeches Day* 54:17-20 O 15 '87

Impending energy crisis? [discussion of March 20, 1987 article, Impending United States energy crisis] R. L. Hirsch. *Science* 236:763-5 My 15 '87

Impending United States energy crisis. R. L. Hirsch. bibl f il *Science* 235:1467-73 Mr 20 '87

Is OPEC bluffing again? T. Thompson. *Bus Week* p92 Mr 9 '87

Low-cost oil is fueling energy worries [report by the Department of Energy] *Sci News* 131:201 Mr 28 '87

New directions for oil policy. R. W. Fri. bibl f il *Environment* 29:16-20+ Je '87

The new energy challenge [address, February 3, 1987] G. M. Keller. *Vital Speeches Day* 53:314-17 Mr 1 '87

The next oil crisis. *Commonweal* 114:132-3 Mr 13 '87

The next oil crisis [cover story] M. Lynch. il *Technol Rev* 90:38-45+ N/D '87

Oil and gas discovery rates [discussion of June 26, 1987 article, Can the U.S. oil and gas resource base support sustained production?] W. L. Fisher. *Science* 238:878-9 N 13 '87

Oil slick. *New Repub* 196:7-9 Ap 13 '87

OPEC smartens up. W. C. Symonds. *Bus Week* p34-5 Jl 13 '87

Report on reports: Energy security: a report to the president of the United States. J. Darmstadter. bibl f il *Environment* 29:25-7 Jl/Ag '87

'There's too much damn oil around'. T. Smart. *Bus Week* p24-5 S 7 '87

The third oil crisis. J. Cook. il map *Forbes* 140:37+ D 14 '87

Trends in oil imports. D. H. Hickcox. *Focus* 37:33 Spr '87

Troubled waters [European and Japanese dependence on oil from the Persian Gulf] il *Time* 129:22 Je 1 '87

The U.S. is better braced for another oil shock . . . while OPEC seems less likely to maintain high prices. G. Koretz. il *Bus Week* p14 Ag 24 '87

When the Gulf coughs, the oil market shivers. W. J. Cook. il map *U S News World Rep* 103:20-1 Ag 17 '87

Why Europe and Japan won't help [keeping Persian Gulf lanes open] F. Willey. il *Newsweek* 109:35 Je 8 '87

Petroleum workers

Offshore outpost [life and work in the North Sea oil fields] C. Swann. il *Oceans* 20:42-7 N/D '87

Petronio, Stephen

about

Tousling with choreography. L. Friedman. il por *Vogue* 177:98 F '87

Petrossian (New York, N.Y.: Restaurant) *See* New York (N.Y.)—Restaurants, nightclubs, bars, etc.

Petryanov-Sokolov, Igor

An open book. il *Courier* 40:28-9 Ja '87

Pets

See also
Birds
Cats
Celebrities—Pets
Dogs
Pet stores
Rabbits
Swine
Travel with pets

Animal love. J. Glass. See alternate issues of Glamour beginning July 1987

Common pet myths: sorting fact from fiction. C. Lamb. il *Better Homes Gard* 65:182+ O '87

Do house pets belong in research labs? M. Engel. il *Glamour* 85:252 S '87

Pets—*cont.*

Pet concerns. See issues of The Mother Earth News beginning September/October 1986

Pet news. See occasional issues of Ladies' Home Journal

Pet set. S. L. Gerstenfeld. See occasional issues of Parents

Pets. See occasional issues of Better Homes and Gardens

Pets and the garden [readers' tips] S. Milius. il *Rodale's Org Gard* 34:30-1 Je '87

Pets for those with exotic tastes—and deep pockets. T. Segal. il *Bus Week* p148-9 F 23 '87

Test your pet IQ. F. S. Goulart. il *Saturday Evening Post* 259:32+ Ja/F '87

Therapy [sessions for pet owners run by S. P. Cohen at Animal Medical Center in Manhattan] *New Yorker* 63:30-1 O 26 '87

Vets on pets. H. E. Whiteley. See issues of The Saturday Evening Post beginning January/February 1984

Accidents and hazards

Is your home safe for pets? H. E. Whiteley. il *Saturday Evening Post* 259:22+ N '87

Care

See also

First aid for animals

Kennels

Animal birthdays. R. Kidd. il *Mother Earth News* 104:36-9 Mr/Ap '87

Animal emergencies. R. Kidd. il *Mother Earth News* 103:26 Ja/F '87

Can you afford to keep that pet? P. J. Adams. il *Essence* 18:95-6 Je '87

How to help your pet to a longer life. A. R. Marder. *Prevention* 39:71+ D '87

How to take a (guilt free) vacation. J. Glass. il *Glamour* 85:94 Jl '87

Pet survival tips: critical steps for families and pets [escaping a fire] V. Webster. *Better Homes Gard* 65:83 Ap '87

Your healthy pet. A. R. Marder. See issues of Prevention (Emmaus, Pa.) beginning July 1987

Your healthy pet. R. H. Pitcairn. See issues of Prevention (Emmaus, Pa.) through June 1987

Diseases and pests

Licking summer ills. H. E. Whiteley. il *Saturday Evening Post* 259:22-3+ Jl/Ag '87

Equipment

See also

Christmas gifts for pets

First aid

See First aid for animals

Food and feeding

See Pet food

Housing

See also

Kennels

Laws and regulations

See Domestic animals—Laws and regulations

Therapeutic use

Can Fido save this marriage? il *Prevention* 39:6 F '87

Feathered friends are good for us. il *Prevention* 39:12 Mr '87

Furry and feathery therapists. A. Toufexis. il *Time* 129:74 Mr 30 '87

Patients' best friend [pet room at the Swedish American Hospital in Rockford, Ill.] il *Prevention* 39:8 Ap '87

Take two pets and call me in the morning. B. J. Culliton. il *Science* 237:1560-1 S 25 '87

Treatment

See Animals—Treatment

Pets and children *See* Children and animals

Pets as carriers of infection *See* Animals as carriers of infection

Pets as gifts

Holiday pets. S. Gerstenfeld. il *Parents* 62:346 N '87

Pets in videotapes

Anecdotes, facetiae, satire, etc.

Cassette-deck kids and pets [Video Dog and Video Cat] A. Steacy. il *Macleans* 100:52-3 D 14 '87

Petschek Palace (Prague, Czechoslovakia) *See* Palaces—Czechoslovakia

PetSong (Firm)

To animals, Dennis Knick is Johann Sebastian Bark, maybe even Moo-zart. J. Kaufman. il pors *People Wkly* 28:153-4 N 2 '87

Pettaway, Clarence

about

Calls from Cosby give sick teen will to live. *Jet* 71:24 F 23 '87

Pettingell, Phoebe

Writers & writing. See occasional issues of The New Leader

Petty, Ramona

about

Body by design. M. Kort. il pors *Women's Sports Fitness* 9:34-8 S '87

Who is Ramona, anyway? M. Nelson. il por *Women's Sports Fitness* 9:8 Ap '87

Petty, Tom

about

Tom Petty's new LP: back to basics. A. DeCurtis. il por *Roll Stone* p10 My 7 '87

Petty (Tom) and the Heartbreakers (Musical group) *See* Tom Petty and the Heartbreakers (Musical group)

Petworth (Sussex, England: Historic house) *See* Historic houses, sites, etc.—Great Britain

Petzal, David E.

Endangered tradition. See issues of Field & Stream beginning March 1985

Peugeot (Automobile) *See* Automobiles, Foreign

Peugeot SA

Europe: a battling bureaucrat. S. Tully. il por *Fortune* 116:86 N 9 '87

France's no-frills manager [J. Calvet] S. Tully. il por *Fortune* 116:58 Ag 3 '87

Let them drive Peugeots. R. Morais. il por *Forbes* 139:153-4 My 18 '87

Pewter

Collectors and collecting

Do you know this . . . about silver and pewter? C. Thompson. il por *Antiques Collect Hobbies* 92:19-21 O '87

Peyron, Bruno

about

Sibling rivalry. P. Whittell. il pors *Mot Boat Sail* 159:58-61+ Je '87

Peyron, Loick

about

Sibling rivalry. P. Whittell. il pors *Mot Boat Sail* 159:58-61+ Je '87

Peyser, Joan

about

A frank biography finds that Leonard Bernstein's passions, like his talents, are boundless [interview] E. Levin. il pors *People Wkly* 27:48-50 My 4 '87

Portrait of the artist, with smudges. M. Walsh. il por *Time* 129:87 My 18 '87

PW interviews. J. F. Baker. por *Publ Wkly* 231:63-4 Je 5 '87

Pfaff, William

On nationalism. *New Yorker* 63:44+ My 25 '87

Perils of policy: the Marshall Plan only worked once. *Harpers* 274:70-2 My '87

Remembering. *New Yorker* 63:140-6+ D 7 '87

Pfahl, Magnus

(jt. auth) See Benbrook, Doris, and Pfahl, Magnus

Pfeffer, Barbara

about

The indomitable human spirit. P. Gardner. il por *Art News* 86:13 Mr '87

Pfeiffer, Carolyn

about

The moviemaker. A. P. Sanoff. il por *U S News World Rep* 102:61 Ja 26 '87

Pfeiffer, Jack

about

New look at an old failure. J. Peterzell. il por *Time* 129:29 Je 1 '87

Pfeiffer, John E., 1915-

Six months and half a million dollars, all for 15 seconds. il *Smithsonian* 18:134-8+ O '87

Pfeiffer, Michelle

about

Michelle Pfeiffer. J. Nathanson. pors *Harpers Bazaar* 120:280, 364-5 S '87

Pfeiffer, Reiner

about

A deadly game of dirty tricks. S. Seibert. il *Newsweek* 110:49 O 26 '87

Pfeil, Fred

Down the beanstalk. *Nation* 244:857-60 Je 20 '87

Pfister, Charles, 1940-

about

"21" plus. M. Filler. il *House Gard* 159:24+ S '87

Pfizer Inc.

Where research rules. G. Slutsker. il *Forbes* 139:128-9 F 23 '87

PGA Tour Inc.

Spreading the wealth [commissioner D. Beman] R. Behar. il pors *Forbes* 140:74-7+ Ag 10 '87

PGL Young Adventure (Organization)
River adventure [canoeing and kayaking on the Wye River, England] il map *Natl Geogr World* 142:24-9 Je '87
pH *See* Hydrogen ion concentration
Ph.D. degrees *See* Degrees, Academic
pH of soil *See* Soil acidity
Phaedra [ballet] See Ballet reviews—Single works
Phages *See* Bacteriophages
Phagocytes and phagocytosis
　　See also
　　Macrophages
Phagocytosis of Candida albicans enhances malignant behavior of murine tumor cells. I. Ginsburg and others. bibl f il *Science* 238:1573-5 D 11 '87
Phalabang (Nepal)
A question of balance. D. Zurick. il *Sierra* 72:46-50 Jl/Ag '87
Phalaenopsis *See* Orchids
The Phantom of the Opera [musical] See Musicals, revues, etc.—Reviews—Single works
Pharmaceutical industry *See* Drug industry
Pharmaceutical research
　　See also
　　United States. Food and Drug Administration
Battling illness with body proteins. M. Murray. il *Sci News* 131:42-5 Ja 17 '87
Body doubles [engineering of healing proteins] J. Kluger. il *Omni* 9:48-50+ Ag '87
From test tube to patient: new drug development in the United States [cover story; special section] il *FDA Consum* 21:4-15 N '87
Giving free rein to Merck's best and brightest. il *Bus Week* p90 O 19 '87
New drugs with that enzymatic touch. D. D. Edwards. *Sci News* 131:407-8 Je 27 '87
Search for a drug to fight AIDS. T. Jackson. il *World Press Rev* 34:52-3 Mr '87
Where research rules [Pfizer] G. Slutsker. il *Forbes* 139:128-9 F 23 '87
Who has the next wonder drug? il *Fortune* 116:8 S 28 '87
Ethical aspects
Researcher disqualified [case of J. Weiss] *FDA Consum* 21:30 Jl/Ag '87
Experimentation on man
AIDS: the search for a vaccine [D. Zagury serves as his own guinea pig] M. Clark. il por *Newsweek* 109:79 Mr 30 '87
AIDS vaccine? Now, tests on humans. J. Silberner. il *U S News World Rep* 103:10 Ag 31 '87
AIDS vaccine trial OKed. D. M. Barnes. *Science* 237:973 Ag 28 '87
AIDS vaccines: the problems of human testing. S. Weisburd. *Sci News* 131:329-32 My 23 '87
Heaven sent? [priests test vaccine for pregnant women that could prevent cytomegalovirus] D. Tonnessen. il *Health* 19:18 D '87
Human test of AIDS vaccine approved. D. D. Edwards. *Sci News* 132:116 Ag 22 '87
Playing roulette with experimental drugs. S. Budiansky. il *U S News World Rep* 103:58-9 Jl 13 '87
Taking his own medicine [D. Zagury innoculates himself] E. Magnuson. il por *Time* 129:25 Mr 30 '87
Testing in 'real people'. K. Flieger. il *FDA Consum* 21:10-12+ N '87
A tough old soldier joins the fight against AIDS [J. Salk] S. Siwolop and R. Rhein, Jr. il por *Bus Week* p69-70 Jl 27 '87
"You first" [human tests of VaxSyn] *Time* 130:56 Ag 31 '87
International aspects
Indo-U.S. vaccine pact disputed. J. Walsh. *Science* 238:19 O 2 '87
India
Indo-U.S. vaccine pact disputed. J. Walsh. *Science* 238:19 O 2 '87
Pharmaceutical services *See* Hospitals—Pharmaceutical services; Physicians—Pharmaceutical services
Pharmaceutical services insurance *See* Insurance, Pharmaceutical services
Pharmacists
　　See also
　　Black pharmacists
　　National Association of Boards of Pharmacy
New trends in over-the-counter care. B. S. Rabin. il *50 Plus* 27:20+ Ja '87
Professional ethics
"Operation Rx" sting [D. Hall helps break pharmacists' prescription drug scam in Los Angeles] J. Fincher. il *Read Dig* 131:36-41 S '87

Pharmacology
　　See also
　　Drug receptors
　　Drug resistance
　　Psychopharmacology
Research
See Pharmaceutical research
Pharmacy colleges
　　See also
　　University of Georgia. School of Pharmacy
Pharmaseal Laboratories
$4.5 mil. lawsuit won in Mississippi medical case [suit against Pharmaseal Laboratories by family of T. Wells] *Jet* 72:14 Jl 20 '87
Pharynx
　　See also
　　Nasopharynx
Surgery
Surgery that could put snoring to rest. D. B. Moskowitz. il *Bus Week* p154 Je 8 '87
Phase transitions
Alpha-decay-induced fracturing in zircon: the transition from the crystalline to the metamict state [cover story] B. C. Chakoumakos and others. bibl f il *Science* 236:1556-9 Je 19 '87
Electrons and ions at the helium surface. A. J. Dahm and W. F. Vinen. bibl f il *Phys Today* 40:43-50 F '87
Freezing. A. D. J. Haymet. bibl f il *Science* 236:1076-80 My 29 '87
Mechanism of the body-centered cubic-hexagonal close-packed phase transition in iron. W. A. Bassett and E. Huang. bibl f il *Science* 238:780-3 N 6 '87
Observation of phase transitions in spreading activation networks. J. Shrager and others. bibl f il *Science* 236:1092-4 My 29 '87
Reappearing phases. J. S. Walker and C. A. Vause. bibl (p128) il *Sci Am* 256:98-105 My '87
Phases of the moon *See* Moon—Phases
Pheasant shooting
Grandpa and the kid. D. Sisson. il *Field Stream* 92:41+ D '87
Pheasants in frigid weather. J. Bashline. il *Field Stream* 92:66+ N '87
Phool a pheasant. D. Zutz. il *Outdoor Life* 180:92-3+ N '87
Roosters within reach [cock pheasants] J. Murray. il *Outdoor Life* 180:78-9+ O '87
Pheasants
　　See also
　　Cooking—Game
Phelan, Jacquie
　　about
High on the mountain. S. Rubin. il pors *Women's Sports Fitness* 9:29-32 My '87
Phelan, John J., Jr.
　　about
The Big Board's crusade against program trading. J. M. Laderman and B. Nussbaum. il por *Bus Week* p134-6+ Mr 23 '87
Phelan, P. Larry, and Baker, Thomas C.
Evolution of male pheromones in moths: reproductive isolation through sexual selection? bibl f il *Science* 235:205-7 Ja 9 '87
Phelps, Barton
　　about
Configuration for a canyon. T. S. Hines. il *Archit Dig* 44:166-9+ S '87
Phelps, D. Gray
Getting honest. il *N Y Times Mag* p53 Mr 15 '87
Phelps, Mark
On the record. See issues of Flying
Phelps Dodge Corporation
Back from the brink. A. A. Lappen. il *Forbes* 140:8 S 21 '87
Most improved. il *Forbes* 139:162 Ja 12 '87
Phenobarbital
Cytochrome P-450-catalyzed formation of Δ^4-VPA, a toxic metabolite of valproic acid. A. E. Rettie and others. bibl f il *Science* 235:890-3 F 20 '87
Phenology
　　See also
　　Plants, Effect of climate on
Phenols
　　See also
　　Dinitrophenol
　　Hydroquinones
Phenylalanine
Hyperactivity: no go for amino acid [research by Alan J. Zametkin and others] *Sci News* 131:376 Je 13 '87
Sweet talk [aspartame] *Sci Am* 257:16 Jl '87

Pheromones

The chemistry between people. T. Monmaney. il *Newsweek* 109:54-5 Ja 12 '87

Perspiration: a chemical communicator? [menstrual cycles; research by Winnifred B. Cutler and George Preti] P. McCarthy. *Psychol Today* 21:16 Jl '87

Animals

A sense of scents. K. Ambrus. il *Conservationist* 42:42-7 Jl/Ag '87

Insects

Bugs vs. bugs [work of Jeffrey Aldrich] *USA Today (Periodical)* 115:8 Je '87

Chemical mimicry: bolas spiders emit components of moth prey species sex pheromones. M. K. Stowe and others. bibl f il *Science* 236:964-7 My 22 '87

Chemistry of pheromone and hormone metabolism in insects. G. D. Prestwich. bibl f il *Science* 237:999-1006 Ag 28 '87

Evolution of male pheromones in moths: reproductive isolation through sexual selection? P. L. Phelan and T. C. Baker. bibl f il *Science* 235:205-7 Ja 9 '87

Insects that mark host plants. B. D. Roitberg and R. J. Prokopy. il *BioScience* 37:400-6 Je '87

Pheromone components and active spaces: what do moths smell and where do they smell it? C. E. Linn, Jr. and others. bibl f il *Science* 237:650-2 Ag 7 '87

A sense of scents. K. Ambrus. il *Conservationist* 42:42-7 Jl/Ag '87

Spider's perfume fatal for moths [research by Mark K. Stowe and others] S. Weisburd. il *Sci News* 131:340 My 30 '87

PHH Group Inc.

Growth by takeover. J. A. Conway. il *Forbes* 139:8 F 23 '87

Phi Delta Kappan (Periodical)

The editor's page. R. W. Cole, Jr. See issues of Phi Delta Kappan through January 1988

Philadelphia (Pa.)

See also

Walk of Fame (Philadelphia, Pa.)

Tales of sister cities [Philadelphia, Pa. and Douala, Cameroon] L. Hazelton. *Black Enterp* 17:16 Mr '87

Anniversaries, etc.

A bicentennial botch-up. P. McKillop and J. Schwartz. il *Newsweek* 109:62 My 18 '87

Congress goes home again [ceremonies marking 200th anniversary] F. Trippett. il *Time* 130:26 Jl 27 '87

Philadelphia, 1987 [celebration marking the bicentennial of the U.S. Constitution] il *Am Hist Illus* 22:26-33 My '87

The Philadelphia story [commemorating 200th birthday of U.S. Constitution] G. Bain. il *Travel Holiday* 167:44-8 Ap '87

Philadelphia: the city that gave us a nation. A. Green. il *Natl Parks* 61:24-9 Mr/Ap '87

Tale of two cities: did party poopers prevail? [plans for celebration of the Constitution's bicentennial] W. L. Chaze. il *U S News World Rep* 102:26 My 4 '87

Unexpected Philadelphia. J. Lukacs. il *Am Herit* 38:72-6+ My/Je '87

Art

American decorative arts [Federal Philadelphia, 1785-1825] S. B. Sherrill. il *Antiques* 132:42+ Jl '87

Athens on these shores [Federal Philadelphia, 1785-1825] S. Weaver. il *Americana* 15:22-5 Jl/Ag '87

Banks

See also

Fidelity Bank, N.A.

Provident National Bank

Blacks

Philadelphia: a big city with small-town appeal. L. Hazelton. il *Black Enterp* 17:71-2+ My '87

Philadelphia In the black [directory of black-owned business] W. J. Dawkins. il pors *Black Enterp* 17:66 Je '87

Child welfare

SCAN: providing preventive services in an urban setting [Supportive Child Adult Network] T. Tatara and others. il *Child Today* 15:17-22 N/D '86

Climate

Constitution-making weather: Philadelphia, 1787. D. M. Ludlum. *Ctry J* 14:70 Jl '87

Courts

Philadelphia takes a fall [suspension of 15 judges] E. Bowen. il *Time* 129:72 F 23 '87

Crime

Black women report of sex, torture, murder at hands of white Philadelphia 'bishop' [G. Heidnik case] il por *Jet* 72:6-7 Ap 13 '87

A boy and his dog in hell [illegal dog fighting with pit bull terriers] M. Sager. il *Roll Stone* p36-7+ Jl 2 '87

Find 7 bodies in Philly, jail tenant [case of H. Graham] *Jet* 72:18 Ag 31 '87

House of horrors [murderer G. Heidnik] por *Time* 129:34 Ap 6 '87

A little house of horrors [murderer G. Heidnik] T. E. Johnson. il por *Newsweek* 109:29 Ap 6 '87

Philadelphia's house of horrors [arrest of G. Heidnik] il *U S News World Rep* 102:11 Ap 6 '87

Description

. . . culturally sophisticated. J. Powell. il *Travel Holiday* 167:48-53 Ap '87

Even W.C. Fields might like Philadelphia now. C. S. Eklund. il *Bus Week* p178-9 Jl 20 '87

Economic history

Editorial. W. Garrett. il *Antiques* 131:1043 My '87

Galleries and museums

See also

Philadelphia Museum of Art

Historic houses, sites, etc.

See also

Independence National Historical Park (Pa.)

Ben Franklin's Philadelphia. S. Moore. il *Saturday Evening Post* 259:82-4 Jl/Ag '87

A house tour of colonial Philadelphia. il *Redbook* 169:105-11 Ag '87

Philadelphia, 1987 [celebration marking the bicentennial of the U.S. Constitution] il *Am Hist Illus* 22:26-33 My '87

The Philadelphia story [commemorating 200th birthday of U.S. Constitution] G. Bain. il *Travel Holiday* 167:44-8 Ap '87

Unexpected Philadelphia. J. Lukacs. il *Am Herit* 38:72-6+ My/Je '87

History

Birthplace of the new republic. D. G. Kinney. il *Life* 10:44-8 Fall '87

Philadelphia, 1787. H. Holzer. il *Am Hist Illus* 22:20-5 My '87

Hospitals

See also

University of Pennsylvania. Hospital

Industries

See also

Furniture industry

Philadelphia In the black [directory of black-owned business] W. J. Dawkins. il pors *Black Enterp* 17:66 Je '87

Monuments, statues, etc.

Pygmalion [M. R. Mellon's statue of singer K. Smith to stand at entrance to the Spectrum in Philadelphia] *New Yorker* 63:33-5 O 19 '87

Music

See also

Opera Company of Philadelphia

Philly Jazz goes national on NPR [Jazz impressions from Philadelphia] R. Woessner. *Down Beat* 54:60 S '87

Tribute to John Coltrane [Trane Stop Resource Institute] R. Woessner. *Down Beat* 54:47 My '87

Newspapers

See also

Philadelphia inquirer (Newspaper)

Parades

Dr. J goes out on top, but raps parade violence [J. Erving] il por *Jet* 72:48 My 11 '87

Parading the Constitution ["We the People 200" parade] B. Weber. il *N Y Times Mag* p162 S 13 '87

When springtime comes to Philadelphia, even the robins sing Louie Louie [parade to celebrate song] il *People Wkly* 27:34-5 My 25 '87

Politics and government

A fracas in Philadelphia [mayoral election between W. Goode and F. Rizzo] il pors *U S News World Rep* 103:20 N 16 '87

Philadelphia's bare-knuckled political brawl [mayoral race between F. Rizzo and W. Goode] T. E. Johnson. il pors *Newsweek* 110:59 N 2 '87

Wilson Goode, Frank Rizzo stump for mayor's seat in Philadelphia election. *Jet* 72:12 Je 8 '87

Poor

An evening with Trevor's dad [work with the homeless by T. and F. Ferrell] E. S. Vaughn. il pors *Christ Today* 31:12-13 F 20 '87

Slow descent into hell [homeless] J. D. Hull. il *Time* 129:26-7+ F 2 '87

Prisons and reformatories

A new-generation jail [Philadelphia Industrial Correctional Center] il *Archit Rec* 175:82-7 Ap '87

Philadelphia (Pa.)—*cont.*

Protests, demonstrations, etc.

'Reagan people only' [protestors banned from ceremonies commemorating bicenntenial of Constitution] K. Kilimnik. *Progressive* 51:11 S '87

Restaurants, nightclubs, bars, etc.

Filling up in Philadelphia. M. Sheraton. il *Time* 130:65 Jl 6 '87

Fourth stars [Fountain Restaurant] M. Fox. il *Health* 19:55-6+ Je '87

Savings and loan associations

See also

Firstrust Savings Bank

Social work

See also

Coalition of Advocates for the Rights of the Infirm Elderly

Philadelphia Flower Show *See* Flower exhibits

Philadelphia Industrial Correctional Center *See* Philadelphia (Pa.)—Prisons and reformatories

Philadelphia inquirer (Newspaper)

Philadelphia stories [3 Pulitzers awarded] R. Zoglin. il *Time* 129:62 Ap 27 '87

'Philadephia inquirer' changes format, editor of book coverage. *Publ Wkly* 232:13 D 18 '87

Philadelphia Museum of Art

Last of a breed [collection of H. P. McIlhenny] D. Solomon. il *Harpers Bazaar* 121:88+ D '87

Museum accessions [restoration of R. Adam's drawing room from the Lansdowne House] E. H. Gustafson. il *Antiques* 131:1228-9 Je '87

Philadelphia Society

What hope for the courts? L. Bridges. *Natl Rev* 39:36-7+ Ag 28 '87

Philadelphia Zoological Garden

Animal house [World of Primates] K. D. Stein. il *Archit Rec* 175:120-5 F '87

Philanthropic foundations *See* Foundations, Charitable and educational

Philanthropy *See* Charities; Giving

Philately and philatelists *See* Postage stamps—Collectors and collecting

Philharmonic Symphony Orchestra of New York *See* New York Philharmonic-Symphony Orchestra

Philip II, King of Spain, 1527-1598

about

Philip II's grand design for the glory of God and empire. R. Wernick. bibl (p205) il pors *Smithsonian* 18:152-6+ D '87

Philip, Prince, consort of Elizabeth II, Queen of Great Britain, 1921-

about

The Queen and Prince Philip toast a 40-year Windsor knot. il pors *People Wkly* 28:54 N 23 '87

Philip, Prince of Hesse

about

A royal family heritage [cover story] A. González-Palacios. il *House Gard* 159:162-72+ Jl '87

Philip, Cynthia Owen

Robert Fulton. bibl f il por *Antiques* 132:1132-9 N '87

Philip Morris, Inc.

The call for Philip Morris gets louder. G. G. Marcial. il *Bus Week* p78 Ag 17 '87

Cigarettes anyone? Tennis and smoking [Virginia Slims tournaments] R. Doar. *Wash Mon* 19:40 Je '87

Here's one tough cowboy [Marlboro Man] J. A. Trachtenberg. il *Forbes* 139:108-10 F 9 '87

His own best customer [H. Maxwell] A. Farnham. il por *Fortune* 116:44-5 Ag 3 '87

Profit growth is still smoking at Philip Morris. il *Money* 16:8 Ag '87

Will Philip Morris nibble at Hershey? G. G. Marcial. *Bus Week* p106 O 5 '87

Philipp, Peter

Which road to peace? *World Press Rev* 34:12-13 Jl '87

Philipp Brothers, Inc.

A giant trader under fire. D. Pauly and B. Powell. il *Newsweek* 109:36-40 Ja 19 '87

Philippines

See also

AIDS (Disease)—Philippines

Americans—Philippines

Anti-Communist movements—Philippines

Arabs—Philippines

Astronomy—Philippines

Botany—Philippines

Cagayan (Philippines: Province)

Civil rights—Philippines

Dams—Philippines

Davao City (Philippines)

Eating—Philippines

Economic assistance, American—Philippines

Environmental movement—Philippines

Filipinos

Immigration and emigration—Philippines

Industry and state—Philippines

Investments, Foreign—Philippines

Land reform—Philippines

Literature and state—Philippines

Loans, Bank—Philippines

Manila (Philippines)

Military assistance, American—Philippines

Morale, National—Philippines

Negros Island (Philippines)

Riots—Philippines

Roads—Philippines

Terrorism—Philippines

Armed Forces

Leandro Alejandro: victim of militarism. D. Friesen. *Christ Century* 104:877-8 O 14 '87

Philippines: danger signs. H. Anderson. il por *Newsweek* 109:36-8 My 11 '87

Army

The Army can't back up Aquino's tough talk. R. Gourlay. *Bus Week* p57 Ap 6 '87

A military renaissance [success against New People's Army in Cagayan] R. Laver. il *Macleans* 100:6+ Ja 26 '87

Commerce

United States

See United States—Commerce—Philippines

Defenses

See also

United States—Armed Forces—Forces in the Philippines

United States. Air Force—Forces in the Philippines

Discovery and exploration

Mass to the sound of gunfire [Easter Mass in the Philippines; excerpt from Magellan's voyage around the world] A. Pigafetta. il *Courier* 40:11 Ap '87

Economic conditions

A damaged culture. J. M. Fallows. il *Atlantic* 260:49-54+ N '87

New optimism in the Philippines. *World Press Rev* 34:47-8 Jl '87

A new road in the Philippines spurs development [project supported by World Bank loan] L. V. Coronel. il *UN Chron* 24:66-7 Ag '87

Economic policy

Aquino needs a new miracle. L. Kraar. il por *Fortune* 116:90-2+ S 14 '87

Debt to democracy. S. C. Monsod. *New Repub* 197:16-18 D 7 '87

Foreign money runs scared. L. Reaves. *Bus Week* p54 O 5 '87

The Philippine economy rises from its sickbed. M. Shao. il *Bus Week* p46 Je 29 '87

Slowly turning the corner. W. Stewart. il *Time* 129:59 Ap 27 '87

Who's afraid of Solita Monsod? U.S. bankers, that's who [Economic Planning Minister] D. J. Yang. il por *Bus Week* p54 Ja 26 '87

Foreign relations

United States

See United States—Foreign relations—Philippines

Industries

See also

Fisheries—Philippines

San Miguel Corp.

Native peoples

One for the spirits [defeat of Chico River Dam project by tribal peoples] C. Fay. il *Sierra* 72:22-4 Mr/Ap '87

Photographs and photography

Robin Moyer's Bayan ko! honors the Philippine revolt. H. Chapnick. il por *Pop Photogr* 94:16 Mr '87

Politics and government

See also

Communist Party (Philippines)

Elections—Philippines

Philippines. Cabinet

Philippines. Congress

Philippines. Constitution

Political campaigns—Philippines

Politics, Corruption in—Philippines

'After Aquino'. A. Doronila. *World Press Rev* 34:41 D '87

Aquino: an end to innocence. N. Cooper. il *Newsweek* 109:37 F 2 '87

Philippines—Politics and government—*cont.*

Aquino in the corner. H. Anderson. il por *Newsweek* 110:46+ S 14 '87

Aquino under fire. T. Jacoby. il *Newsweek* 110:40 O 5 '87

Aquino wins a victory—but can she govern? H. Anderson. il por *Newsweek* 109:38-9 F 16 '87

Aquino's close call [coup attempt] B. Levin. il *Macleans* 100:26-7 S 7 '87

Aquino's first year. P. Tarr. il *Nation* 244:353-7 Mr 21 '87

Aquino's Philippines: the center holds. S. Burton. *Foreign Aff* 65 Sp Issue:524-37 ['87]

'Bloody Thursday'. L. Neumann. il *Macleans* 100:55 F 2 '87

A brave woman's fight to heal a troubled U.S. ally [C. Aquino] J. Martin. il pors *Sch Update* 119:14-15 Ap 6 '87

Bungled coup, foiled return. J. Smolowe. il *Time* 129:34-5 F 9 '87

Can Aquino take charge? [coup attempt] H. Anderson. il por *Newsweek* 109:40-1 F 9 '87

The center holds in the Philippines. *America* 156:145 F 21 '87

Chiller in Manila [coup attempt] *Nation* 245:219-20 S 12 '87

Cory [C. Aquino, Time's Woman of the Year; special section] il pors *Time* 129:18-27+ Ja 5 '87

Cory Aquino and the psychology of bubbles. M. Singer. il *Natl Rev* 39:34-8 Ag 14 '87

Cory Aquino: religious newsmaker no. 1. D. Peerman. *Christ Century* 104:3-4 Ja 7-14 '87

Cory hallelujah. *New Repub* 196:7-9 Mr 2 '87

The Cory myth. A. Cockburn. *Nation* 245:258-9 S 19 '87

The coup that failed. H. G. Chua-Eoan and E. W. Desmond. il por *Time* 130:24-7 S 7 '87

Death in Manila [demonstrators shot by riot policemen] E. W. Desmond. il por *Time* 129:34-6 F 2 '87

Democracy in the Philippines [statement, September 10, 1987] D. F. Lambertson. *Dep State Bull* 87:27-9 N '87

Divine guidance? Aquino may need it. J. M. Fallows. il por *U S News World Rep* 102:41-2 Mr 16 '87

Divisions in the ranks [coup attempt] A. Bilski. il *Macleans* 100:22 F 9 '87

Embattled Aquino gets a new mandate. B. D. Williams and D. Cunningham. *Christ Century* 104:157-8 F 18 '87

The embattled Mrs. Aquino. S. Mydans. il pors *N Y Times Mag* p42-3+ N 15 '87

Exiled Marcos: 'We shall return' [interview] R. Z. Chesnoff. il por *U S News World Rep* 103:33 Ag 3 '87

First Family in exile [F. and I. Marcos] P. S. Greenberg. il pors *Macleans* 100:23-5 Ap 27 '87

The foiling of Ferdinand [Marcos' plot to overthrow Aquino] H. Anderson. il por *Newsweek* 110:35 Jl 20 '87

For Aquino, another thriller in Manila [attempted coup] W. L. Chaze. il por *U S News World Rep* 103:10-11 S 7 '87

For Aquino, crisis is a way of life. W. A. Taylor. il *U S News World Rep* 102:42 F 9 '87

The ground is crumbling under Aquino. W. A. Taylor. il por *U S News World Rep* 103:51 N 2 '87

Has Aquino used up last of miracles? [attempted coup] W. A. Taylor. il por *U S News World Rep* 103:49 S 14 '87

How Aquino can recoup [cover story] R. J. Kessler. il *New Leader* 70:3-5 O 5 '87

"I know you still love me". J. D. Reed. il *Time* 129:44 Ja 19 '87

Inside the rebel camp [views of G. Honasan] M. Liu. il pors *Newsweek* 110:40-2 S 21 '87

Last call for Cory? *Commonweal* 114:643-4 N 20 '87

The last days of Aquino? H. Anderson. il *Newsweek* 110:50 O 12 '87

Letter from Manila. R. E. Huke. *Focus* 37:33 Summ '87

Making the Constitution work [cover story] R. J. Kessler. por *New Leader* 70:8-10 Mr 9 '87

Manila fudge [views of W. Chapman and R. Bonner] J. M. Fallows. *Wash Mon* 19:53-6 S '87

Manila's threatening new storm. L. Neumann. il por *Macleans* 100:21 S 14 '87

Marcos at bay. F. Barnes. *New Repub* 196:9-11 Mr 2 '87

The Marcos plot. A. Giarelli. il *World Press Rev* 34:40 S '87

The Marcoses' moonlight sonata. S. Mydans. il pors *N Y Times Mag* p34-6+ Ap 19 '87

Mean momma [C. Aquino] H. G. Chua-Eoan. il por *Time* 130:68 N 2 '87

Mutiny in Manila. H. Anderson. il pors map *Newsweek* 110:26-9 S 7 '87

New troubles for Aquino. W. A. Taylor. il por *U S News World Rep* 102:33-4 F 2 '87

Notes and comment [N. O'Brien's views on revolutionary nonviolence] *New Yorker* 62:23-5 Ja 19 '87

Peace in the Philippines. D. Murphy. *America* 156:406-8 My 16 '87

The Philippine revolution: a year later. F. F. Claver. *America* 156:232-5 Mr 21 '87

The Philippines: a land in shadow [visit in preparation for 1988 solar eclipse expedition] S. J. O'Meara. il *Sky Telesc* 73:432-3 Ap '87

The Philippines: Aquino's first year. D. A. Rosenberg. bibl f *Curr Hist* 86:160-3+ Ap '87

Philippines: danger signs. H. Anderson. il por *Newsweek* 109:36-8 My 11 '87

Please speak into the microphone [F. Marcos' plans for insurrection] S. Tifft. il por *Time* 130:50 Jl 20 '87

Praying for time [C. Aquino's presidency] H. G. Chua-Eoan. il por *Time* 130:36-7 N 23 '87

Putting Corypower to the test. J. Clad. il *World Press Rev* 34:24-6 Ja '87

Rebels left and right. H. G. Chua-Eoan. il *Time* 130:38 O 5 '87

Rebirth of a rebel army [New People's Army] W. A. Taylor. il *U S News World Rep* 103:75 S 28 '87

Rise of the vigilantes [anti-Communist groups] M. S. Serrill. il *Time* 129:40 My 11 '87

Robin Moyer's Bayan ko! honors the Philippine revolt [photographic book project] H. Chapnick. il por *Pop Photogr* 94:16 Mr '87

Roundup of an elusive renegade [capture of rebel leader G. Honasan] H. G. Chua-Eoan. il *Time* 130:48 D 21 '87

Save Cory. *New Repub* 197:7-9 N 2 '87

Seizing a most wanted man [capture of G. Honasan] M. Liu. il por *Newsweek* 110:48 D 21 '87

Sharpening the swords of war. W. Stewart. il *Time* 129:46 Mr 30 '87

The slum behind the Sheraton. J. DeParle. il *Wash Mon* 19:32-44 D '87

Snapping at the revolution [massacre in Manila and aborted military coup] *New Repub* 196:5-6 F 16 '87

The thin edge (I) [C. Aquino and problems of government] R. Shaplen. *New Yorker* 63:43-6+ S 21 '87

The thin edge (II) [C. Aquino and problems of government] R. Shaplen. *New Yorker* 63:63-74+ S 28 '87

Things fall apart. H. G. Chua-Eoan. il por *Time* 130:32-3 S 28 '87

Tough words from the top [C. Aquino changes policy in dealing with rebels] W. Svoboda. il por *Time* 129:41 Ap 6 '87

A truce gives way to gunplay. S. Allis. il *Time* 129:57 F 23 '87

Under Secretary Armacost's interview on "Meet the press" [transcript of program, August 30, 1987] *Dep State Bull* 87:32-4 O '87

Vigilantes for Aquino. F. Willey. il por *Newsweek* 109:34+ Mr 30 '87

Vigilantes resurgent [right wing Alsa Masa movement] D. Friesen. il *Progressive* 51:21-3 N '87

Visa denied [U.S. denies visa to anti-Marcos activist E. B. Olaguer] W. Steif. il *Progressive* 51:27 F '87

A war of vigilantes [anti-Communist paramilitary groups] B. Levin. il *Macleans* 100:26 Mr 30 '87

When the cheering stopped [aftermath of coup attempt] H. G. Chua-Eoan. il por *Time* 130:40-1 S 14 '87

Who's winning the cease-fire? H. Anderson. il *Newsweek* 109:34 Ja 26 '87

Will a sudden show of spine save Cory Aquino? W. L. Chaze. il por *U S News World Rep* 103:12 S 21 '87

Will Aquino finally trade velvet glove for iron fist? M. Shao and L. Reaves. il *Bus Week* p51 S 14 '87

Religious institutions and affairs

See also

Catholic Church—Philippines

Church and social problems—Philippines

Evangelical churches—Philippines

Philippines. Cabinet

Aquino's muddle in Manila. R. Vokey. il por *Newsweek* 110:35 S 28 '87

The Joker was not laughing [C. Aquino forces Cabinet to resign] H. G. Chua-Eoan. il por *Time* 130:37 S 21 '87

Philippines. Congress
Aquino hands over power and problems. W. A. Taylor. il por *U S News World Rep* 103:31-2 Ag 3 '87
Philippines. Constitution
Aquino wins a victory—but can she govern? H. Anderson. il por *Newsweek* 109:38-9 F 16 '87
Aquino's mandate won't make the tightrope any less shaky. D. J. Yang. il *Bus Week* p51 F 16 '87
Aquino's troubled win [approval of new constitution] L. Neumann. il por *Macleans* 100:24 F 16 '87
"I know you still love me" [upcoming vote] J. D. Reed. il *Time* 129:44 Ja 19 '87
Making the Constitution work [cover story] R. J. Kessler. por *New Leader* 70:8-10 Mr 9 '87
The sweet, sweet taste of victory. W. R. Doerner. il por *Time* 129:36 F 16 '87
Philips Industries, NV
A competitor who smells gunpowder [C. van der Klugt] S. Tully. il por *Fortune* 116:43-4 Ag 3 '87
How far can Philips elbow its way into the U.S.? J. Kapstein and F. McCoy. il *Bus Week* p46-7 Mr 2 '87
Philips Industries Inc.
This wheelmaker is on a roll. G. G. Marcial. *Bus Week* p94 Mr 9 '87
Philipson, Lori
Shades of summer. il *Seventeen* 46:92 Ag '87
Philistines
A lost people. M. Dismore. map *Opera News* 51:32-3+ Ap 11 '87
Philistines [drama] See Gorky, Maksim, 1868-1936
Phillips, Ammi
about
Ammi Phillips portraits rediscovered. M. C. Black. bibl f il *Antiques* 132:558-9 S '87
Phillips, Arlene
about
Aboard the Starlight Express: choreographing human trains. K. Grubb. il *Dance Mag* 61:86-7 Ap '87
Phillips, Bob
Mario Lemieux: Pittsburgh's premier Penguin. il por *Sch Update* 119:20-1 F 9 '87
Phillips, Channing E., 1928-1987
about
Obituary
Jet il por 73:12 N 30 '87
Phillips, Chynna
about
Star mothers & daughters. pors *Harpers Bazaar* 120:130+ Ag '87
Phillips, Euan Hywel
about
Phillips named AAUP director. por *Publ Wkly* 232:32 O 9 '87
Phillips, Fred M., 1954-
(jt. auth) See Elmore, David, and Phillips, Fred M., 1954-
Phillips, Geoffrey
After the hippies and the yuppies . . . *World Press Rev* 34:34 Je '87
Phillips, Harry R.
Wildflowers for a sunny border. il *Rodale's Org Gard* 34:72-7+ My '87
Phillips, J. D.
about
Black Methodist minister heads white Texas church. por *Jet* 72:22 Jl 13 '87
Phillips, John
about
At 72, John Phillips looks at today's "super press". H. Chapnick. il por *Pop Photogr* 94:37 N '87
Phillips, Kristie
about
Game and gutsy, three tiny teens limber up for the '88 Olympics. A. Chambers. il pors *People Wkly* 28:130-2 N 2 '87
Mary Lou II. B. Phillips. il por *Sch Update* 119:12 Mr 23 '87
Phillips, Laura
about
A model family. il pors *Teen* 31:10 D '87
Phillips, Linda Morand
about
A model family. il pors *Teen* 31:10 D '87
Phillips, Lou Diamond
about
A bright new Diamond brings a fading legend to life in La bamba. J. Stark. il pors *People Wkly* 28:58+ Ag 17 '87

Phillips, Mackenzie
about
Mackenzie Phillips comes clean. D. Maychick. il por *Mademoiselle* 93:54 Ja '87
Phillips, Margaret G.
(jt. auth) See Koblinsky, Sally A., and Phillips, Margaret G.
Phillips, Margaret G., and Stubbs, Phyllis E.
Head Start combats baby bottle tooth decay. il *Child Today* 16:25-8 S/O '87
Phillips, Marlo
about
A place for roses: the inimitable world of Ned and Marlo Phillips. M. Peppiatt. il por *Archit Dig* 44:206-11 N '87
Phillips, Melba, 1907-
Arthur Gordon Webster, founder of the APS. il pors *Phys Today* 40:48-52 Je '87
Phillips, Michelle
about
Michelle Phillips—"I'm a proud Mama". V. J. Radovsky. il pors *Redbook* 169:12+ Ag '87
Star mothers & daughters. pors *Harpers Bazaar* 120:130+ Ag '87
Phillips, Norma
Recognition and preparedness will protect you from poison ivy. il *Flower Gard* 31:20+ Je/Jl '87
Phillips, Pat
Menopause: a complete medical report. il *McCalls* 115:89-95 N '87
Phillips, Thomas L., 1924-
about
Flying on a wing and a half. R. Simon. il por *Forbes* 140:350+ Jl 13 '87
Phillips, Valerie
This summer, see Wimbledon . . . live. il *Sport Mag* 78:93-4 Mr '87
Phillips, William D., 1948-, and Metcalf, Harold J.
Cooling and trapping atoms. bibl (p128) il *Sci Am* 256:50-6 Mr '87
Phillips Academy (Andover, Mass.) See Private schools
Phillips Exeter Academy See Private schools
Phillips Petroleum Company
Air-minded enterprise. J. M. McClellan. il *Flying* 114:90+ S '87
Philmont (N.Y.)
Politics and government
Everybody came but 'Larry' [Oliver North Day] M. Grevatt. il *Nation* 245:228-9 S 12 '87
Anecdotes, facetiae, satire, etc.
Maggie in Ollieland [O. North Day in Philmont] M. Gallagher. il *Natl Rev* 39:42+ N 6 '87
Philology
Portrait of Justus Lipsius. A. Grafton. *Am Sch* 56:382-90 Summ '87
Philosophical anthropology
Talk with a stranger. R. Redfield. *Cent Mag* 20:51-7 My/Je '87
Philosophical Library Inc.
Philosophical Library redux. R. Larkin. il por *Publ Wkly* 232:26-8 Ag 21 '87
Philosophy
See also
Absolute
Art—Philosophy
Atheism
Biology—Philosophy
Christianity—Philosophy
Civilization
College education—Philosophy
Consciousness
Education—Philosophy
Evolution
Hedonism
Humanism
Idealism
Irrationalism (Philosophy)
Language and languages—Philosophy
Materialism
Mathematics—Philosophy
Metaphysics
Mind and body
Mysticism
Pessimism
Pragmatism
Psychology
Reality
Science—Philosophy
Self (Philosophy)
Soul
Terrorism—Philosophy

Philosophy—See also—*cont.*
    Truth
Anecdotes, facetiae, satire, etc.
Let's be philosophical. R. Baker. il *N Y Times Mag* p16 Ja 25 '87
Paths of enlightenment. J. Kulpa. il *Field Stream* 92:39-40 Jl '87

Philosophy, American
    See also
    Adler, Mortimer Jerome, 1902-

Philosophy, English
    See also
    Burke, Edmund, 1729?-1797
    Spencer, Herbert, 1820-1903

Philosophy, French
    See also
    Sartre, Jean Paul, 1905-1980

Philosophy, Hindu
    See also
    Yoga

Philosophy and religion
    See also
    Christianity—Philosophy
Absolutes and my grandfather's Aunt Sarah [discussion of September 7, 1987 article, A talk with Leszek Kolakowski] M. Mihajlov. *New Leader* 70:19-20 D 14 '87
A talk with Leszek Kolakowski [cover story; interview] M. Mihajlov. *New Leader* 70:10-12 S 7 '87
Two decades of ultimate dialogue [conference in Toronto on ultimate reality and meaning; work of T. Horvath] D. J. Leigh. *America* 157:504-5 D 26 '87

Philp, Richard
Ailey launches a Katherine Dunham renaissance: Miss D's day. il pors *Dance Mag* 61:50-5 D '87
In touch with tradition [cover story] il *Dance Mag* 61:HC4-HC5 D '87
Sacre: the Joffrey connection. il *Dance Mag* 61:49-51 N '87
Summerspace at Watch Hill. il *Dance Mag* 61:46-9 O '87
A wishbook of danceworks we'd like to see again: revivals. il *Dance Mag* 61:136-49 Je '87

Phipps, Susie
    about
Louisiana woman losing her bid to be categorized white. por *Jet* 71:36 Ja 12 '87

Phipps family
Photographs and photography
Rich kids. B. Klaw. il *Am Herit* 38:102-11 N '87

PHLCorp Inc.
A fight over Baldwin's ghost [Leucadia goes after PHLCorp] C. S. Eklund. il *Bus Week* p72 Mr 30 '87

Phobias
    See also
    Aquaphobia
    Fear of flying
    Fear of snakes
    School phobia
    Thirteen (The number)
Famous people tell what they fear most. il *Jet* 72:54+ Je 8 '87
Food phobias. C. Tevis. il *Success Farm* 85 no2:18H-18I Ja '87
Nothing to fear but ear itself [malfunctions of ear as cause of phobic behavior] L. S. Dumas. il *Health* 19:19 Je '87
Tips on conquering paralyzing anxiety: fearing the worst [panic attacks and social phobias] J. H. Tanne and E. Rapp. il *N Y* 20:44-9 F 9 '87

Phobos (Satellite) *See* Mars (Planet)—Satellites

Phoenix, River
    about
River Phoenix. E. Miller. il pors *Seventeen* 46:163-4+ Mr '87
River Phoenix: on the rise. il pors *Teen* 31:51 Mr '87

Phoenix (Ariz.)
Climate
Live at five! [television coverage of November 18, 1986 Arizona tornado] R. Norman, Jr. and R. C. Balling, Jr. il pors *Weatherwise* 40:36-7 F '87

Phoenix family
    about
One big hippy family. S. Peters. il *Life* 10:46-8+ Ag '87

Phoenix Mutual Life Insurance Co.
A successful balancing act [interview with P. Bannan] A. E. Serwer. il por *Fortune* 116:180 D 7 '87

Phoenix Technologies Ltd.
IBM's 'clone killers' don't scare Phoenix Technologies. L. Helm. il *Bus Week* p113 D 21 '87

Phonics method *See* Reading—Study and teaching

Phonograph
History
The Bell-Tainter Graphophone. B. Ault. il *Antiques Collect Hobbies* 92:72-4 Jl '87
A few observations on the art of playing old records. B. Ault. il *Antiques Collect Hobbies* 91:48-50 F '87
Pickup
Moving-magnet vs. moving-coil cartridges. J. D. Hirsch. il *Stereo Rev* 52:30+ Ja '87
Ortofon X3-MC phono cartridge. il *High Fidel* 37:40-1 Ja '87
Ortofon X3-MC phono cartridge. J. D. Hirsch. il *Stereo Rev* 52:45-6 Mr '87
Turntables & cartridges. E. B. Meyer. *High Fidel* 37:46-7 S '87
Record changers
See Phonograph—Turntables
Turntables
Choosing a turntable. M. Smolen. il *Stereo Rev* 52:88-92+ Ja '87
Linn Axis turntable. il *High Fidel* 37:30+ Mr '87
Linn Axis turntable. J. D. Hirsch. il *Stereo Rev* 52:35-6 Ja '87
Thorens TD 520 turntable. J. D. Hirsch. il *Stereo Rev* 52:31-2 Ag '87
Turntable Rx. R. Hodges. il *Stereo Rev* 52:67-9 Ag '87
Turntables. il *Stereo Rev* 52:115-20 F '87
Turntables & cartridges. E. B. Meyer. *High Fidel* 37:46-7 S '87

Phonograph record covers
The Sarge at 20 [photographing cover of Sgt. Pepper album twenty years ago] il *People Wkly* 27:159-61 Je 8 '87

Phonograph record industry
    See also
    A&M Records (Firm)
    Alligator Records (Firm)
    Atlantic Records (Firm)
    Blacks in the phonograph record industry
    Capitol Industries-EMI, Inc.
    CBS Inc. Records Division
    Folkways Records
    Gold Castle Records
    Island Records
    Keynote Records (Firm)
    MCA Records, Inc.
    Motown Productions
    National Academy of Recording Arts and Sciences (U.S.)
    Nine Winds (Firm)
    Phonograph records—Recording
    RCA Corp.
    Riverside Records (Firm)
    Virgin Records America
    Warner Bros. Inc.
Local heroes [record company interest in T. Conwell and band named Jane's Addiction] D. Handelman. il pors *Roll Stone* p68-70+ O 22 '87
Looking for the Jolly Roger [record industry vs. digital audio tape recorders] M. Riggs. *High Fidel* 37:4 My '87
Record executives are on pins and needles [digital tape scare] B. Buell and others. il *Bus Week* p112 F 16 '87
Record industry battles digital tape. A. DeCurtis. *Roll Stone* p13+ Ap 9 '87
The sound of money [battle over digital audio tape] J. B. Copeland. il *Newsweek* 110:72-3 O 5 '87
Things are looking up [classical music outlook] T. W. Libbey, Jr. il *High Fidel* 37:63 D '87
What is DAT, and why are the record companies trying to keep it away from you? P. Wilkinson. il *Roll Stone* p69-70+ S 10 '87
Who DAT? M. Costello. *Omni* 10:43 D '87
Acquisitions and mergers
Capitol shake-up: EMI America merges with Manhattan. M. Goldberg. *Roll Stone* p18+ Ag 13 '87
International aspects
Born in the U.S.A., sold to Japan [Sony acquires CBS Records] S. Koepp. il *Time* 130:66 N 30 '87
CBS Records: if you can't beat 'em, sell [sold to Sony Corp.] il *Newsweek* 110:53 N 30 '87
A solid gold record deal [Sony acquires CBS Records] D. Lieberman and W. J. Holstein. il *Bus Week* p36 N 30 '87

Phonograph record industry—*cont.*

Employees

Getting a good rep [student field representatives] M. Kaplan. il *Roll Stone* p115-16+ Mr 26 '87

Ethical aspects

L.A. probe focusing on record returns. B. Haring. *Roll Stone* p11+ Ja 29 '87

Export-import trade

Imports under fire. M. Goldberg. *Roll Stone* p14+ Jl 2 '87

Finance

And the beat goes on. A. D. Frank. il *Forbes* 139:40-2+ My 18 '87

Cassette singles emerge as 45s fade. M. Walker. *Roll Stone* p29+ Mr 26 '87

Execs assess a year of mixed messages. D. Fricke. *Roll Stone* p11+ Mr 12 '87

The LP's wobbly future. P. Wang. il *Newsweek* 109:52 F 9 '87

History

Nipper and his friends [phonograph label trademarks; cover story] J. L. Poole. il *Opera News* 52:8-12 Ag '87

Marketing

See Phonograph records—Marketing

Canada

See also

Juno Awards

Daniel Lanois [interview] J. Henke. por *Roll Stone* p93-4+ D 17-31 '87

The sound alternative [Canadian children's albums] P. Young. *Macleans* 100:53 D 14 '87

Hungary

See also

Hungaroton (Firm)

Japan

A cruel cut for Sergeant Pepper [losing copyright] N. Gross. il *Bus Week* p62 Je 22 '87

Scandinavia

Home-grown labels from Scandinavia. B. Wechsler. il *High Fidel* 37:76-7 Ja '87

Phonograph record stores

See also

Tower Records (Firm)

Labels split on in-store taping. N. Arnett and A. DeCurtis. *Roll Stone* p14+ Jl 2 '87

Taping at retail [Personics System] C. J. Esse. il *High Fidel* 37:14 S '87

Phonograph records

See also

Compact discs

Best of '86. il *Time* 129:71 Ja 5 '87

Classical music. See issues of Stereo Review

Classical reviews. See issues of High Fidelity (New York, N.Y.)

For the record. See occasional issues of Maclean's

Gimme a break [recent releases by underappreciated artists] P. G. Davis. il *N Y* 20:54+ Ja 19 '87

Hit Liszt. P. G. Davis. il *N Y* 20:68+ Mr 16 '87

New discs offer sound trips. J. Cocks and M. Walsh. il *Time* 129:78 Mr 2 '87

People picks & pans. See issues of People Weekly

Recorded music in review. W. F. Grueninger. See issues of Consumers' Research Magazine

Records. J. W. Freeman. See issues of Opera News

The shape of things to come [preview 1988] il *High Fidel* 37:61-71 S '87

Sound adventures [new fall releases] P. G. Davis. il *N Y* 20:78-80 D 14 '87

Sound on disc. R. De Toledano. See occasional issues of National Review

Spotlight. E. Miller. See issues of Seventeen

African music

Foday Musa Suso: Mansa bendung; Malamini Jobarteh/Dembo Konte: Jaliya; Jali Nyama Suso; Master drummers of Dagbon. L. Birnbaum. il *Down Beat* 54:36-8 Ap '87

Nelson Mandela [release by Youssou N'Dour] J. Guterman. il *Roll Stone* p103-4 My 21 '87

Archives

See also

ARChive of Contemporary Music

Arias

What are the French doing in Frisco? [recording Handel's Arias for Senesino] P. Moor. il *High Fidel* 37:62 Ap '87

Avant-garde music

See Phonograph records—Experimental music

Awards

See also

American Music Awards

Grammy Awards

Juno Awards

20th annual International Record Critics Awards. T. W. Libbey, Jr. il *High Fidel* 37:72+ N '87

Stereo Review's Record of the Year Awards for 1986. C. Barter. il *Stereo Rev* 52:59-62 F '87

Ballet music

Charles Dutoit: a surpassing "Firebird". R. Freed. il por *Stereo Rev* 52:72+ Mr '87

Falla's "El amor brujo". W. Livingstone. il *Stereo Rev* 52:105 My '87

Black music

30 greatest hits; Aretha [Aretha Franklin's new releases] R. Hoerburger. il *Roll Stone* p48-9 Ja 29 '87

The Badder they come [M. Jackson's album Bad] J. Cocks. il pors *Time* 130:85 S 14 '87

Call me: Al Green. il *Roll Stone* p143 Ag 27 '87

Greatest hits: Sly and the Family Stone. il *Roll Stone* p146 Ag 27 '87

History of Otis Redding: Otis Redding. il *Roll Stone* p167 Ag 27 '87

Hot together [Pointer Sisters' new release] R. Hoerburger. il *Roll Stone* p90+ F 12 '87

I never loved a man the way I love you: Aretha Franklin. il *Roll Stone* p162 Ag 27 '87

Innervisions: Stevie Wonder. il *Roll Stone* p101 Ag 27 '87

Introducing: 'Producers of the Year' Jimmy (Jam) Harris and Terry Lewis. pors *Ebony* 42:126 Jl '87

Jackson's "Bad": good music for every taste. P. Garland. il *Stereo Rev* 52:135-6 D '87

Jam and Lewis take control. M. Goldberg. il pors *Roll Stone* p30+ Ap 23 '87

Jet's top 20 albums; Singles. See issues of Jet

Jody Watley. V. Aletti. il *Roll Stone* p99+ My 21 '87

John McClain creates solid gold money-makers [A&M Records] A. Edmond, Jr. il por *Black Enterp* 18:54-7+ N '87

Lady Soul: Aretha Franklin. il *Roll Stone* p111+ Ag 27 '87

Michael grows up [release of Bad] D. Sigerson. il por *Roll Stone* p87-8 O 22 '87

Michael Jackson: Bad. N. Jennings. *Macleans* 100:58 S 14 '87

Michael Jackson: Bad; Prince: Sign o' the times. D. Wolff. *Nation* 245:728-9 D 12 '87

The new soul men [Luther Vandross' Give me the reason, Gregory Abbott's Shake you down and Freddie Jackson's Just like the first time] V. Aletti. il *Roll Stone* p43-4 Mr 12 '87

Off the wall: Michael Jackson. il *Roll Stone* p130+ Ag 27 '87

One heartbeat [release of Smokey Robinson] D. Wild. il *Roll Stone* p148 Ap 23 '87

RCA Victor blues & rhythm revue. L. Birnbaum. il *Down Beat* 54:40-2 D '87

Soul queen Aretha Franklin [release of Aretha] J. A. Baggett. por *Sch Update* 119:32 F 23 '87

Soul survivors [J. Brown's Gravity and A. Franklin's Aretha] T. Young. por *Vogue* 177:36+ Ja '87

Stand! Sly and the Family Stone. il *Roll Stone* p155 Ag 27 '87

Superior pop music from Al Jarreau [L is for lover] P. Garland. il *Stereo Rev* 52:170+ F '87

Taj Mahal goes his own way [release of Taj] P. Garland. il *Stereo Rev* 52:71-2 Mr '87

Talking book: Stevie Wonder. il *Roll Stone* p129 Ag 27 '87

There's a riot goin' on: Sly and the Family Stone. il *Roll Stone* p93-4 Ag 27 '87

Thriller: Michael Jackson. il *Roll Stone* p154 Ag 27 '87

Tina Turner: Break every rule. A. Nash. il *Stereo Rev* 52:130 Ja '87

Tina Turner: Break every rule. R. Wynn. *High Fidel* 37:75 Mr '87

What's going on: Marvin Gaye. il *Roll Stone* p69 Ag 27 '87

Whitney plays it safe [release of Whitney] V. Aletti. il por *Roll Stone* p49-51 Ag 13 '87

Blues music

See also

Alligator Records (Firm)

2120 S. Michigan Ave. [MCA rereleases Chess archives] J. Brinsfield. *Down Beat* 54:30 Mr '87

Atlantic blues. D. Fricke. il *Roll Stone* p87-8+ F 12 '87

Big mamas who made the most of the blues [reissued blues recordings compiled by Rosetta Reitz] C. Brown. il *Essence* 18:28 Jl '87

Phonograph records—Blues music—*cont.*
The blues, volume 1 [Chess archives] K. Loder. il *Roll Stone* p55 F 26 '87
Count Basie: Mostly blues . . . and some others. J. McDonough. il *Down Beat* 54:32 Ag '87
The new bluebloods. L. Birnbaum. il *Down Beat* 54:38 Jl '87
New blues. L. Birnbaum. *Down Beat* 11:39-42 N '87
New blues. J. Roberts and B. Sandmel. *Down Beat* 54:34-7 My '87
Reissue blues. G. Santoro. *Down Beat* 54:32 Ap '87
Robert Cray's new blues power [release of Strong persuader] J. Pareles. il por *Roll Stone* p45-6 Ja 29 '87

Canadian music
See also
Juno Awards

Cantatas
Davies, Peter Maxwell: Into the labyrinth; Sinfonietta accademica [Scottish Chamber Orchestra] J. Wierzbicki. *High Fidel* 37:83-4 Ja '87

Chamber music
Davies, Peter Maxwell: Into the labyrinth; Sinfonietta accademica [Scottish Chamber Orchestra] J. Wierzbicki. *High Fidel* 37:83-4 Ja '87

Children's music
Children's music parents love [Kevin Roth's Unbearable bears] il *Parents* 62:20 Ap '87
Conning kids. W. Livingstone. il *Stereo Rev* 52:8 F '87
Recordings kids will love! [picks of Linda Dimitroff] S. Berkman. il *Good Housekeep* 205:143 S '87
The sound alternative [Canadian children's albums] P. Young. *Macleans* 100:53 D 14 '87

Christmas music
Music for Christmas. C. Barter. *Stereo Rev* 52:182 D '87
Rock elves from Sting to Springsteen give the Special Olympics a very Special Christmas. M. Green. il por *People Wkly* 28:157-9 N 2 '87
Sing we now of Christmas. K. Ames. il *Newsweek* 110:52 D 28 '87
Sounds of Christmas past. B. Ault. il *Antiques Collect Hobbies* 92:58-60 D '87
Switched-on Santa Claus. N. Jennings. il *Macleans* 100:62 D 14 '87

Clarinet music
Smooth new sounds from Woody Herman's heirs. R. Hoffman. il *Bus Week* p158 N 30 '87

Collectors and collecting
A groovy way to make a buck. J. Rachlin. il *U S News World Rep* 102:59-60 My 18 '87
Music memorabilia. B. Ault. See issues of Antiques & Collecting Hobbies beginning May 1986
Music memorabilia. S. M. Stroff. See issues of Antiques & Collecting Hobbies beginning February 1986

Comedy records
Homer and Jethro. S. M. Stroff. il *Antiques Collect Hobbies* 92:50-2 Ag '87
Komedy kuts. A. Sarko. il *Seventeen* 46:113 N '87

Concertos
See also
Phonograph records—Piano music
Phonograph records—Violin music

Country music
Dolly Parton, Linda Ronstadt, Emmylou Harris: Trio. A. Nash. il *Stereo Rev* 52:90+ Jl '87
Dwight Yoakam [release of Hillbilly deluxe] A. Nash. por *Stereo Rev* 52:87 Jl '87
Early tracks [release by Steve Earle] C. Willman. il *Roll Stone* p151-2 Ap 23 '87
Exit 0: Steve Earle and the Dukes. D. Browne. il *Roll Stone* p133-4 Jl 16-30 '87
The eye of David Olney [release of Eye of the storm] A. Nash. il por *Stereo Rev* 52:106 Ap '87
Heart land and Ain't no binds [releases by the Judds and the Whites] A. DeCurtis. il *Roll Stone* p74 Ap 9 '87
Homer and Jethro. S. M. Stroff. il *Antiques Collect Hobbies* 92:50-2 Ag '87
Judds: Heart land. A. Nash. il *Stereo Rev* 52:120 Je '87
The Judds: Heart land; John Anderson: Countrified. R. Wynn. *High Fidel* 37:79 Ag '87
Lyle Lovett. A. Nash. por *Stereo Rev* 52:128 Ja '87
Music [Heart land by The Judds and Trio] D. Wolff. *Nation* 245:137-9 Ag 15-22 '87
The O'Kanes. A. Nash. il *Stereo Rev* 52:194 F '87
Randy Travis [release of Always & forever] A. Nash. por *Stereo Rev* 52:95 S '87

Rosanne Cash gets back to basics [release of King's Record Shop] A. Nash. il por *Stereo Rev* 52:147+ N '87
Trio [Dolly Parton, Linda Ronstadt, Emmylou Harris] D. Gates. il *Roll Stone* p54 My 7 '87

Dance music
See also
Phonograph records—Ballet music

Experimental music
David Sylvian: Gone to earth. J. Diliberto. il *Down Beat* 54:37 S '87
A John Adams sampler. R. Freed. por *Stereo Rev* 52:190 N '87
John Zorn: Big gundown. B. Milkowski. il *Down Beat* 54:26 Mr '87
John Zorn: Cobra. B. Shoemaker. il *Down Beat* 54:32+ S '87
Minimal extensions. J. Diliberto. *Down Beat* 54:32 Mr '87
The well-tuned piano [L. Young's composition] B. Wentz. *Down Beat* 54:34 Ag '87

Folk music
See also
Folkways Records
Gold Castle Records
Nick Drake: Fruit tree. D. Browne. *High Fidel* 37:78-9 Jl '87
Vega's good 'Standing' [release of Solitude standing] D. Browne. il por *Roll Stone* p81-3 Je 18 '87
Vega's "Solitude standing". M. Peel. por *Stereo Rev* 52:73 Ag '87
The Washington Squares. D. Handelman. il *Roll Stone* p135 Je 4 '87

Gospel music
Aretha Franklin records gospel album in her late father's church in Detroit [cover story] C. Waldron. il pors *Jet* 73:56-9 D 7 '87
Aretha sings up a soulful storm at gospel recording. *Jet* 72:60 Ag 17 '87
God's great gift, Aretha [One Lord, one faith, one baptism] B. Allen. il por *Ms* 16:77-8 D '87
Mamas and papas [R. H. Harris and The Soul Stirrers on Father and sons and M. Williams on I've come so far] M. Jefferson. il pors *Vogue* 177:100 O '87

Guitar music
Bireli Lagrene. B. Milkowski. *Down Beat* 54:34 Jl '87
Henry Kaiser: Devil in the drain. P. Kostakis. il *Down Beat* 54:30-1 O '87
Liona Boyd [release of Persona] A. Nash. por *Stereo Rev* 52:82 Mr '87
Six-string sizzle [jazz] B. Milkowski. *Down Beat* 54:28-9 Mr '87
Stanley Jordan: Standards: volume 1. F.-J. Hadley. il *Down Beat* 54:26-7 Mr '87

History
A visit with Ernest L. Stevens. P. Malvern and M. Malvern. il por *Antiques Collect Hobbies* 92:48-9+ Ag '87

Jazz music
See also
Keynote Records (Firm)
Phonograph records—Blues music
Atlantic at 40 [N. Ertegun] G. Santoro. por *Down Beat* 54:63 Ag '87
Now's the time [renaissance] M. Bourne. il *Down Beat* 54:6+ Ja '87

Reviews
America's real music. R. De Toledano. *Natl Rev* 39:57-8 Mr 13 '87
Back to the future. K. Whitehead. *Down Beat* 54:36 F '87
Blindfold test. See issues of Down Beat
Columbia jazz masterpieces [series] F. Davis. il *Roll Stone* p54+ My 7 '87
Great & imperishable. R. De Toledano. *Natl Rev* 39:56-7 Je 19 '87
Jazz: from LP to CD. R. De Toledano. *Natl Rev* 39:61-2 S 25 '87
Jazz glasnost. B. Shoemaker. il *Down Beat* 54:28-9 O '87
Jazz with new muscle. B. Testa. *Macleans* 100:48 Jl 20 '87
OJC Ltd. [Original Jazz Classics line] K. Whitehead. *Down Beat* 54:38-40 Ja '87
The pulse of Impulse [digitally remastered discs from Impulse catalog] J. Balleras. *Down Beat* 54:32+ Ja '87
Record reviews. See issues of Down Beat
Second Impulse [second batch of Impulse reissues from MCA] K. Whitehead. il *Down Beat* 54:38+ S '87

Phonograph records—Jazz music—Reviews—*cont.*

Suddenly, it's swing time all over again. R. Hoffman. il *Bus Week* p120 F 16 '87

Updating the mainstream [acoustic mainstream jazz] O. Cardle. *Down Beat* 54:30 Ja '87

Waxing on. See issues of Down Beat

What is this thing called bop? F.-J. Hadley. il *Down Beat* 54:30 S '87

Yessir, that's Count Basie. C. Albertson. por *Stereo Rev* 52:180 N '87

Reviews—Single works

Allen, Geri: In the middle
 Nation 245:426 O 17 '87. G. Santoro

Alvin, Phil: Un "sung stories"
 High Fidel il 37:78 Mr '87. D. Browne

Art Farmer/Benny Golson Jazztet: Back to the city
 Down Beat il 54:35-7 F '87. K. Whitehead

Atlantic jazz
 Roll Stone il p87-8+ F 12 '87. D. Fricke

Basie, Count: Mostly blues . . . and some others
 Down Beat il 54:32 Ag '87. J. McDonough

Berne, Tim: Fulton Street maul
 Down Beat il 54:39 Jl '87. J. Diliberto

Big band jazz
 New Yorker 62:70-2 Ja 26 '87. W. Balliett

Blades, Rubén: Agua de luna
 Roll Stone il p134 Mr 26 '87. L. Fissinger

Bley, Paul: Fragments
 Down Beat il 54:35-6 Ap '87. P. Kostakis

Bley, Paul: Hot
 Down Beat il 54:35-6 Ap '87. P. Kostakis

Brackeen, Joanne: Fi-Fi goes to heaven
 Down Beat il 54:27 O '87. E. Guregian

Brecker, Michael: Michael Brecker
 Down Beat il 54:39-40 S '87. O. Cordle

Bruford, Bill: Earthworks
 Down Beat il 54:27 My '87. B. Milkowski

Bruford, Bill: Master strokes
 Down Beat il 54:27 My '87. B. Milkowski

Carlton, Larry: Discovery
 Down Beat il 11:36-7 N '87. F.-J. Hadley

Carlton, Larry: Last nite
 Down Beat 11:36-7 N '87. F.-J. Hadley

Coleman, Ornette: In all languages
 Down Beat il 54:27 O '87. B. Shoemaker

The complete Keynote Collection
 Down Beat 54:28 Ja '87. J. McDonough
 High Fidel il 37:74+ Mr '87. S. Futterman
 New Yorker 62:78-80 F 9 '87. W. Balliett
 Stereo Rev il 52:126-7 Je '87. C. Albertson

Corea, Chick: Light years
 Down Beat 54:34 Ag '87. J. Balleras

Corea, Chick: Trio music/Live in Europe
 Down Beat il 54:32+ Ag '87. J. Balleras

Daniels, Eddie: To Bird with love
 Down Beat il 54:28 S '87. O. Cordle

David Baker's 21st Century Bebop Band: Struttin'
 Down Beat il 54:27-8 My '87. O. Cordle

David Murray Octet: New life
 Down Beat il 54:29-30 S '87. J. Roberts

Davis, Miles: Bitches brew
 Roll Stone il p151 Ag 27 '87

Davis, Miles: Tutu
 Down Beat il 54:27 Ja '87. B. Milkowski

De Franco, Buddy: Complete Verve recordings of the Buddy De Franco Quartet/Quintet with Sonny Clark
 Down Beat il 54:32+ Mr '87. J. Sohmer

Dolphy, Eric: Other aspects
 Down Beat 54:34 Jl '87. E. Guregian

Dolphy, Eric: Vintage Dolphy
 Down Beat il 54:34-5 Jl '87. E. Guregian

Ellington, Duke: Blanton-Webster Band
 Stereo Rev il 52:90+ Mr '87. C. Albertson

Farmer, Art: Something to live for: the music of Billy Strayhorn
 Down Beat il 54:31 D '87. E. Guregian

Garbarek, Jan: To all those born with wings
 Down Beat il 54:32 S '87. J. Diliberto

Getz, Stan: Voyage
 Down Beat 54:31-2 Ja '87. B. Shoemaker

Gordon, Dexter: Other side of Round midnight
 Down Beat il 54:31+ Ap '87. R. Welburn

Gordon, Dexter: Round midnight
 Down Beat 54:31+ Ap '87. R. Welburn

Grappelli, Stephane: Live in San Francisco
 Down Beat il 54:38 F '87. J. Roberts

Grappelli, Stephane: Plays Jerome Kern
 Down Beat il 54:36+ D '87. F. Bouchard

Grappelli, Stephane: Together at last
 Down Beat il 54:36+ D '87. F. Bouchard

Haden, Charlie: Quartet west
 Down Beat il 54:34 O '87. K. Whitehead

Harris, Craig/Tailgaters Tales: Shelter
 Down Beat il 11:31+ N '87. K. Whitehead

Helias, Mark: Split image
 Down Beat il 54:35-6 Jl '87. B. Shoemaker

Hill, Andrew: Shades
 Down Beat il 54:39-40 D '87. K. Whitehead

Hodes, Art: Complete Art Hodes Blue Note sessions
 Down Beat il 54:40-1 Je '87. J. Sohmer

Jack DeJohnette's Special Edition: Irresistible forces
 Down Beat il 54:35-6 Ag '87. J. Roberts

Jarreau, Al: L is for lover
 Stereo Rev il 52:170+ F '87. P. Garland

Johnson, Henry: You're the one
 Down Beat 54:40 Ap '87. P. Welding

Jones, Elvin/Tyner, McCoy: Reunited
 Down Beat il 54:38 Jl '87. F.-J. Hadley

Jordan, Stanley: Standards: volume 1
 Down Beat il 54:26-7 Mr '87. F.-J. Hadley

Konitz, Lee: Ideal scene
 Down Beat il 54:34-5 D '87. J. Roberts

Kuhn, Steve: Life's magic
 Down Beat il 11:37-8 N '87. J. Balleras

Kuhn, Steve: Mostly ballads
 Down Beat il 11:37-8 N '87. J. Balleras

Lagrene, Bireli: Bireli Lagrene
 Down Beat 54:34 Jl '87. B. Milkowski

Lagrene, Bireli: Stuttgart aria
 Down Beat il 54:34 Jl '87. B. Milkowski

Lake, Oliver: Gallery
 Down Beat il 54:44-5 Je '87. F.-J. Hadley

Lester Bowie's Brass Fantasy: Twilight dreams
 Macleans 100:60 N 30 '87. B. Testa

Lounge Lizards: Big heart
 Down Beat il 54:32-3 Ja '87. B. Milkowski

Marsalis, Branford: Royal Garden blues
 Down Beat il 54:33-5 F '87. J. Roberts

Marsalis, Wynton: Marsalis standard time vol. 1
 Macleans 100:60 N 30 '87. B. Testa

McPartland, Marian: Music of Billy Strayhorn
 Down Beat 54:31 D '87. E. Guregian

McPhee, Joe: Po music—a future retrospective
 Down Beat il 54:28-9 My '87. K. Whitehead

Mingus, Charles: Mingus at Antibes
 Down Beat il 54:30-1 Je '87. L. Birnbaum

Mingus, Charles: New Tijuana moods
 Down Beat il 54:30-1 Je '87. L. Birnbaum

Modern Jazz Quartet with the New York Chamber Symphony: Three windows
 Roll Stone p131 S 24 '87. F. Davis

Monk, Thelonious: Complete Riverside recordings
 Down Beat 54:32+ Je '87. P. Kostakis

Moody, James: Something special
 Down Beat il 54:36-7 Je '87. O. Cordle

Morgan, Frank: Lament
 Down Beat il 54:27+ Ja '87. O. Cordle

Moses, Bob: Story of Moses
 Down Beat il 54:38-9 Ag '87. K. Whitehead

Newman, David: Heads up
 Down Beat il 54:37-8 Ag '87. R. Welburn

Newton, James: Romance and revolution
 Down Beat il 54:30 Je '87. K. Whitehead

Newton, James: Water mystery
 Down Beat il 54:36 Ja '87. E. Guregian

Pat Metheny Group: Still life (talking)
 Down Beat il 54:31-2 D '87. F.-J. Hadley

Pickett, Lenny: Lenny Pickett with the Borneo Horns
 Down Beat il 54:43-4 D '87. J. Roberts

Pine, Courtney: Journey to the urge within
 Stereo Rev il 52:94 Jl '87. C. Albertson

Professor Longhair: Houseparty New Orleans style: the lost sessions, 1971-1972
 Down Beat il 54:38 Ag '87. J. Roberts

Pullen, Don/Adams, George: Song everlasting
 Down Beat il 54:32+ D '87. K. Whitehead

Riverside history of classic jazz
 Stereo Rev il 52:200 F '87. C. Albertson

Roach, Max: Bright moments
 Down Beat il 54:40-1 S '87. J. Diliberto

Rollins, Sonny: Quartets, featuring Jim Hall
 Down Beat il 54:38-9 Je '87. R. Welburn
 Stereo Rev il 52:92+ Mr '87. C. Albertson

Ronald Shannon Jackson & The Decoding Society with Twins Seven Seven: Live at the Caravan of Dreams
 Down Beat il 54:45 Je '87. J. Brinsfield

Round midnight
 Stereo Rev 52:138 Ja '87. C. Albertson

Sanborn, David: A change of heart
 Down Beat il 54:29+ My '87. F.-J. Hadley

Phonograph records—Jazz music—Reviews—Single works —*cont.*

Saxophone Choir: Saxophone shop
  Down Beat il 54:35+ S '87. R. Welburn
Scofield, John: Blue matter
  Down Beat il 54:30 Je '87. J. Roberts
Shearing, George: Lullaby of Birdland
  Down Beat 54:36-8 Ja '87. P. Welding
Shorter, Wayne: Phantom navigator
  Down Beat il 54:36 Je '87. J. Roberts
Sonny Clark Memorial Quartet: Voodoo
  Down Beat il 54:39 Je '87. K. Whitehead
Sphere: On tour
  Down Beat il 54:31-2 Ja '87. B. Shoemaker
Tatum, Art: 20th century piano genius
  Down Beat il 54:36-8 Ja '87. P. Welding
Taylor, Cecil: Eighth
  Down Beat il 54:27 My '87. B. Shoemaker
Taylor, Cecil: For Olim
  Down Beat il 11:30 N '87. K. Whitehead
Tonight Show Band: World premier performance
  Down Beat il 54:32-3 F '87. J. McDonough
Turre, Steve: Viewpoint
  Down Beat 11:31+ N '87. K. Whitehead
Tyler, Alvin "Red": Graciously
  Down Beat il 11:38 N '87. K. Whitehead
Vital Information: Global beat
  Down Beat il 54:28 My '87. B. Milkowski
Weiss, Michael: Presenting Michael Weiss
  Stereo Rev il 52:90+ O '87. C. Albertson
Williams, Tony: Civilization
  Down Beat il 54:33-4 Jl '87. O. Cordle
Winter, Stefan F.: Little trumpet
  Down Beat 54:35-6 Jl '87. B. Shoemaker
World Saxophone Quartet: World Saxophone Quartet live at Brooklyn Academy of Music
  Roll Stone il p56 F 26 '87. F. Davis
World Saxophone Quartet: World Saxophone Quartet plays Duke Ellington
  Roll Stone il p56 F 26 '87. F. Davis
Yellowjackets: Four corners
  Down Beat il 11:30 N '87. R. Tolleson
Zappa, Frank: Jazz from hell
  Down Beat 54:40-1 Ap '87. B. Milkowski
  Roll Stone il p48 Mr 12 '87. D. Fricke

Latin American music

Agua de luna [release by Ruben Blades] L. Fissinger. il *Roll Stone* p134 Mr 26 '87

Marketing

See also
Phonograph record stores

Bruce live set slips. M. Goldberg. *Roll Stone* p9 My 7 '87
Charts. See issues of Rolling Stone
Demise of the 45 [new cassette singles] P. Newcomb. il *Forbes* 139:91 Je 29 '87
Execs assess a year of mixed messages. D. Fricke. *Roll Stone* p11+ Mr 12 '87
Getting a good rep [student field representatives] M. Kaplan. il *Roll Stone* p115-16+ Mr 26 '87
The top 100 albums of 1987. *Roll Stone* p192 D 17-31 '87

Modern music

Carter, Elliott: Triple duo; In sleep, in thunder. K. R. Schwarz. il *High Fidel* 37:61-2 F '87
Denisov, Edison Vasilyevich: La vie en rouge; "Colin and Chloé," from L'écume des jours. P. Moor. *High Fidel* 37:65 Ap '87

Motion picture music

La bamba [soundtrack] A. DeCurtis. il *Roll Stone* p110 O 8 '87
Dexter Gordon: Round midnight; The other side of Round midnight. R. Welburn. il *Down Beat* 54:31+ Ap '87
Ritchie Valens lives! [La bamba] S. Simels. il *Stereo Rev* 52:172 N '87
Round midnight. C. Albertson. *Stereo Rev* 52:138 Ja '87
Symphonic splendor and the silver screen [scores by Erich Korngold, Miklos Rozsa and Franz Waxman] B. Zakariasen. il *High Fidel* 37:60-1 F '87
Talking Heads: True stories. G. Santoro. il *Down Beat* 54:38-9 F '87
"True stories": Talking Heads at their best. M. Peel. il *Stereo Rev* 52:108 Ja '87
The Untouchables. S. Simels. il *Stereo Rev* 52:106 S '87
Who's that girl [soundtrack] V. Aletti. il *Roll Stone* p112 O 8 '87

Musicals, revues, etc.

Barbara Cook reheats Carousel. R. J. Lehmann. *Vogue* 177:54 Jl '87

Crossover schemes [celebrity casts] P. G. Davis. il *N Y* 20:104+ N 2 '87

New Age music

New wave forms. J. Diliberto. *Down Beat* 54:34 F '87

Opera

See also
Phonograph records—Arias

Great expectations. *Opera News* 52:24-5 Ag '87
An open ear [how to listen to historic records] W. Crutchfield. il *Opera News* 52:18-20+ Ag '87
Valhalla on Thirty-fourth Street [joint Metropolitan Opera-Deutsche Grammaphon recording of Ring cycle] W. Livingstone. il *Opera News* 52:14-16 Ag '87

Reviews

Baton twirlers [releases by various conductors] P. G. Davis. il *N Y* 20:127-8 S 28 '87

Reviews—Single works

Berlioz, Hector: Roméo et Juliette
  Opera News 51:42-3 Ja 3 '87. J. W. Freeman
Dargomizhsky, Alexander: Stone guest
  Opera News il 51:51 Mr 14 '87. J. W. Freeman
Dvořák, Antonín: Rusalka
  Opera News il 51:58 My '87. J. W. Freeman
Giordano, Umberto: Fedora
  Opera News il 52:48 Jl '87. J. W. Freeman
Gounod, Charles: Faust
  Opera News il 52:66 S '87. J. W. Freeman
Handel, George Frideric: Imeneo
  Opera News il 52:49 Jl '87. J. W. Freeman
Lully, Jean Baptiste: Atys
  Stereo Rev il 52:85 Ag '87. C. Barter
Meyerbeer, Giacomo: Le pardon de Ploërmel
  High Fidel 37:63-4 F '87. R. Levine
Mozart, Wolfgang Amadeus: Così fan tutte
  Stereo Rev il 52:92 O '87. R. Ackart
Mozart, Wolfgang Amadeus: Don Giovanni
  High Fidel il 37:53 F '87. T. W. Libbey, Jr.
  Opera News il 51:42 Ja 31 '87. J. W. Freeman
Mozart, Wolfgang Amadeus: Die Entführung aus dem Serail
  Opera News il 52:64 O '87. J. W. Freeman
Mozart, Wolfgang Amadeus: Marriage of Figaro
  Opera News il 51:14-16 Ja 31 '87. N. Malitz
  Opera News il 52:42 D 19 '87. J. W. Freeman
  Stereo Rev il 52:106 Ja '87. R. Ackart
Offenbach, Jacques: Tales of Hoffmann
  Opera News il 52:72 N '87. J. W. Freeman
Pasatieri, Thomas: Three sisters
  Opera News il 51:59 My '87. J. W. Freeman
Puccini, Giacomo: Tosca
  Opera News il 51:44-5 Ja 17 '87. J. W. Freeman
  Opera News il 51:42 Ja 3 '87. J. W. Freeman
  Stereo Rev il 52:104-5 Mr '87. R. Ackart
Strauss, Richard: Ariadne auf Naxos
  Opera News il 52:72 N '87. J. W. Freeman
  Stereo Rev il 52:152+ D '87. R. Ackart
Verdi, Giuseppe: La forza del destino
  Opera News il 52:65 O '87. J. W. Freeman
  Stereo Rev il 52:111 S '87. R. Ackart
  Stereo Rev il 52:77-8 My '87. R. Ackart
Verdi, Giuseppe: I Lombardi
  Opera News il 51:42 Ja 3 '87. J. W. Freeman
Verdi, Giuseppe: Otello
  Stereo Rev 52:182+ F '87. R. Ackart
Vivaldi, Antonio: L'incoronazione di Dario
  Stereo Rev 52:98 Ap '87. S. Lincoln
Wagner, Richard: Tannhäuser
  Opera News il 51:44 Ja 17 '87. J. W. Freeman

Operetta

Very model records of the major Gilbert & Sullivan. P. Kresh. il pors *High Fidel* 37:56-8 Je '87

Oratorio

A child of our time [André Previn recording of Michael Tippett work] R. Freed. il *Stereo Rev* 52:97 Jl '87
Handel, George Frideric: Athalia. S. Lincoln. *Stereo Rev* 52:112+ Je '87

Orchestral music

See also
Phonograph records—Symphonic poems

Abbado's appealing Ravel package [Boléro; Rapsodie espagnole; Ma Mère l'Oye; Pavane pour une infante défunte] D. Hall. il *Stereo Rev* 52:172 F '87
Loeffler, Charles Martin: La mort de Tintagiles; Five Irish fantasies. H. Halbreich. il *High Fidel* 37:65+ Mr '87
Musical chairs [star conductors] T. W. Libbey, Jr. il *High Fidel* 37:55-7 Jl '87
Record royalty [Royal Philharmonic Orchestra] T. W. Libbey, Jr. il *High Fidel* 37:56 Ap '87

Phonograph records—*cont.*

Passion music
Gardiner's magnificent Bach Passion [St. John Passion] S. Lincoln. por *Stereo Rev* 52:81 Jl '87

Piano music
András Schiff's fresh-sounding Tchaikovsky [Piano concerto no. 1] R. Freed. *Stereo Rev* 52:71 Mr '87

Art Tatum: 20th century piano genius. P. Welding. il *Down Beat* 54:36-8 Ja '87

"The birth of Rhapsody in blue" [recreation of Paul Whiteman's historic Aeolian Hall concert of 1924] E. Salzman. il *Stereo Rev* 52:110 Ap '87

Brahms, with warmth, wit, and fantasy [Richard Goode's Brahms collection on Nonesuch] R. Freed. il *Stereo Rev* 52:152+ N '87

Cecil Taylor: For Olim. K. Whitehead. il *Down Beat* 11:30 N '87

Cziffra's incomparable Liszt. R. Freed. il por *Stereo Rev* 52:105 Ja '87

Edelmann: Irresistible Chopin. R. Freed. por *Stereo Rev* 52:76 Ag '87

Edward Rothstein on music. *New Repub* 197:26-8 Ag 10-17 '87

Horszowski: honest, vital authority. R. Freed. il por *Stereo Rev* 52:88+ S '87

Liszt and Prokofiev [concertos performed by Janis Vakarelis] R. Freed. il por *Stereo Rev* 52:127 O '87

Miraculous Beethoven from Arrau and Davis [Fourth Concerto] D. Hall. il *Stereo Rev* 52:136+ D '87

Music for three pianos [recordings by A. Toradze, B. Douglas and R. Shirk] R. Freed. pors *Stereo Rev* 52:132 O '87

Peter Serkin: happy discoveries [music by Stravinsky, Stefan Wolpe and Peter Lieberson] R. Freed. il *Stereo Rev* 52:170 F '87

Rogé's Poulenc. R. Freed. il por *Stereo Rev* 52:141 D '87

Schubert, Franz: Sonata for piano, in B flat, Allegretto in C minor; Impromptu in A flat [Richard Goode performance] T. Hathaway. il *High Fidel* 37:86+ Ja '87

Serkin's Reger [Variations and fugue on a theme by J. S. Bach and Haydn's Piano sonata in C major] R. Freed. por *Stereo Rev* 52:141 Ja '87

Vlad tidings from Milan [V. Horowitz recording sessions of Mozart's Piano concerto in A] E. Greenfield. il pors *High Fidel* 37:58-9 S '87

The well-tuned piano [L. Young's composition] B. Wentz. *Down Beat* 54:34 Ag '87

Popular music
See also
    Phonograph records—Black music
    Phonograph records—Blues music
    Phonograph records—Country music
    Phonograph records—Jazz music
    Phonograph records—Motion picture music
    Phonograph records—Musicals, revues, etc.
    Phonograph records—Rock music

Popular music. See issues of Stereo Review

Reviews
America's real music. R. De Toledano. *Natl Rev* 39:57-8 Mr 13 '87

Backbeat. See issues of High Fidelity (New York, N.Y.)
Disc and tape reviews. See issues of Stereo Review
Editor on the loose! K. Richardson. il *High Fidel* 37:75+ S '87

In short order. See issues of High Fidelity (New York, N.Y.)

Mini-a-tour. il *High Fidel* 37:70-2+ My '87
Music. T. Bentkowski. See occasional issues of New York

Records. See issues of Rolling Stone
They sing for their supper. J. McDonough. *Down Beat* 54:34-8 O '87

Reviews—Single works
Grappelli, Stephane: Plays Jerome Kern
    Down Beat il 54:36+ D '87. F. Bouchard
Houston, Whitney: Whitney
    Roll Stone il p49-51 Ag 13 '87. V. Aletti
Jackson, Joe: Will power
    Stereo Rev il 52:106 O '87. M. Peel
Manhattan Transfer: Live
    Down Beat il 54:27+ O '87. O. Cordle
McCorkle, Susannah: Dream
    Stereo Rev il 52:180 D '87. C. Albertson
Ronstadt, Linda: For sentimental reasons
    Down Beat 54:37-8 F '87. J. McDonough
    Stereo Rev il 52:85 Ap '87. M. Peel
Simon, Carly: Coming around again
    Roll Stone il p85 Je 18 '87. R. Hoerburger

Streisand, Barbra: One voice
    Stereo Rev il 52:98 S '87. R. Hemming
Wainwright, Loudon, III: More love songs
    Roll Stone il p152-3 Ap 23 '87. D. Browne
Warnes, Jennifer: Famous blue raincoat
    Stereo Rev il 52:78+ My '87. A. Nash

Rap music
In the case of the bum rap song, Richard Golub courts justice for his fellow lawyers. L. Wohlfert. il por *People Wkly* 27:71+ F 2 '87

Recording
The beat goes off: how technology has gummed up rock's grooves. M. Hunter. il *Harpers* 274:53-7 My '87

A church marriage [recording of The marriage of Figaro conducted by N. Marriner] N. Malitz. il por *Opera News* 51:14-16 Ja 31 '87

An interview with Bob Ludwig. M. Dery. il por *Stereo Rev* 52:113-15 N '87

Live vs. studio. L. Berman. il *High Fidel* 37:55 My '87

Memories of his master's voice [interview with R. K. Anderson] E. E. Swenson. il por *High Fidel* 37:56-9 My '87

Red Seal revival. T. W. Libbey, Jr. il *High Fidel* 37:54 Je '87

Stevie Wonder, Nile Rodgers produce disc from 2 coasts. il pors *Jet* 71:56 Mr 23 '87

Valhalla on Thirty-fourth Street [joint Metropolitan Opera-Deutsche Grammaphon recording of Ring cycle] W. Livingstone. il *Opera News* 52:14-16 Ag '87

Vlad tidings from Milan [V. Horowitz recording sessions of Mozart's Piano concerto in A] E. Greenfield. il pors *High Fidel* 37:58-9 S '87

Will there be recordings? [new Carnegie Hall] T. W. Libbey, Jr. *High Fidel* 37:59 Ap '87

Reggae music
The harder they come. il *Roll Stone* p124 Ag 27 '87

Reissues
East St. Louis Toodle-oo [pop reissues on compact disc] J. Miller. il *Newsweek* 109:57-8 Ja 19 '87

Old wine in new bottles no. 2: vintage music on compact discs. S. M. Stroff. il *Antiques Collect Hobbies* 92:66-7+ N '87

Old wine in new bottles: vintage music on compact discs. S. M. Stroff. il *Antiques Collect Hobbies* 92:48-51 My '87

Reissues of the year [rock reissues of 1987] *Roll Stone* p191 D 17-31 '87

Through the hourglass. R. D. Darrell. il *High Fidel* 37:54-6+ F '87

Religious music
See also
    Phonograph records—Passion music

Rock music
The beat goes off: how technology has gummed up rock's grooves. M. Hunter. il *Harpers* 274:53-7 My '87

Local heroes [record company interest in T. Conwell and band named Jane's Addiction] D. Handelman. il pors *Roll Stone* p68-70+ O 22 '87

Reviews
An autumn harvest. il *Time* 130:92 O 12 '87
Ladies pay their dues. T. Young. il *Vogue* 177:54 Je '87
Music. T. Bentkowski. See occasional issues of New York
Music. J. Pareles. See issues of Mademoiselle
Records. See issues of Rolling Stone
Reissue blues. G. Santoro. *Down Beat* 54:32 Ap '87
So long on Lonely Street [releases commemorating 10th anniversary of E. Presley's death] J. Cocks. il pors *Time* 130:78 Jl 20 '87
The top 100: the best albums of the last twenty years [cover story; special issue] il *Roll Stone* p45-52+ Ag 27 '87
The year in records [1987] D. Fricke. il *Roll Stone* p171-2+ D 17-31 '87

Reviews—Single works
10,000 Maniacs: In my tribe
    Roll Stone il p93 O 22 '87. J. D. Considine
Abbott, Gregory: Shake you down
    Roll Stone il p43-4 Mr 12 '87. V. Aletti
Adams, Bryan: Into the fire
    Roll Stone il p93-4 My 21 '87. S. Hochman
    Stereo Rev 52:79-80 Ag '87. M. Peel
Alvin, Dave: Romeo's escape
    Down Beat il 54:31 D '87. G. Santoro
Baker, Ginger: Horses and trees
    Down Beat il 54:31+ Je '87. R. Tolleson

Phonograph records—Rock music—Reviews—Single works
—*cont.*
   La bamba
    Roll Stone il p110 O 8 '87. A. DeCurtis
    Stereo Rev il 52:172 N '87. S. Simels
  Band: Band
    Roll Stone il p78 Ag 27 '87
  Band: Music from Big Pink
    Roll Stone il p104 Ag 27 '87
  Barton, Lou Ann: Forbidden tones
    Roll Stone il p46 Mr 12 '87. K. Loder
  Beastie Boys: Licensed to ill
    Roll Stone il p53 F 26 '87. M. Coleman
  Beat Rodeo: Home in the heart of the Beat
    Stereo Rev il 52:125 Ja '87. M. Peel
  Beatles: Abbey Road
    Roll Stone il p76 Ag 27 '87
  Beatles: Beatles [White album]
    Roll Stone il p66 Ag 27 '87
  Beatles: Sgt. Pepper's Lonely Hearts Club Band
    Roll Stone il p51-2+ Je 18 '87. K. Loder
    Roll Stone il p46-7 Ag 27 '87
    Roll Stone p57+ Je 18 '87. M. Goldberg
  Big Audio Dynamite: No. 10, Upping St.
    Roll Stone il p48 Mr 12 '87. J. Guterman
  Big Brother and the Holding Company: Cheap thrills
    Roll Stone il p115 Ag 27 '87
  Bob Dylan and the Band: Basement tapes
    Roll Stone il p74 Ag 27 '87
  BoDeans: Outside looking in
    Roll Stone il p116-17 N 19 '87. D. Browne
  Bowie, David: ChangesOneBowie
    Roll Stone il p168 Ag 27 '87
  Bowie, David: Never let me down
    High Fidel 37:74-5 Ag '87. R. C. Walls
    Roll Stone il p129-30 Je 4 '87. S. Pond
  Bowie, David: Rise and fall of Ziggy Stardust and the
    Spiders from Mars
    Roll Stone il p61 Ag 27 '87
  Boy George: Sold
    Roll Stone il p52-3 Ag 13 '87. R. Tannenbaum
  Bragg, Billy: Talking with the taxman about poetry
    Roll Stone il p135 Mr 26 '87. D. Handelman
  Breakfast Club: Breakfast Club
    Stereo Rev il 52:90 Jl '87. M. Peel
  Burnett, T-Bone: T Bone Burnett
    Roll Stone il p92-3 F 12 '87. A. DeCurtis
  Byrds: Sweetheart of the rodeo
    Roll Stone il p151 Ag 27 '87
  Camper Van Beethoven: Camper Van Beethoven
    Roll Stone il p136+ Mr 26 '87. E. Wurtzel
  Captain Beefheart and his Magic Band: Trout mask
    replica
    Roll Stone il p95+ Ag 27 '87
  Cars: Door to door
    Roll Stone il p107+ O 8 '87. D. Browne
  Celibate Rifles: Mina mina mina
    Roll Stone p94 F 12 '87. D. Fricke
  Celibate Rifles: Turgid miasma of existence
    Roll Stone il p94 F 12 '87. D. Fricke
  Chilton, Alex: High priest
    Roll Stone il p85 D 3 '87. M. Azerrad
  Clapton, Eric: August
    Down Beat il 54:30+ Mr '87. G. Santoro
    Roll Stone il p90 F 12 '87. A. DeCurtis
    Stereo Rev il 52:77 Mr '87. M. Peel
  Clash: Clash
    Roll Stone il p89 Ag 27 '87
  Clash: London calling
    Roll Stone il p74-5 Ag 27 '87
  Colourfield: Deception
    Roll Stone il p101 My 21 '87. S. Hochman
  Communards: Communards
    Stereo Rev 52:187-8 F '87. M. Peel
  Concrete Blonde: Concrete Blonde
    Roll Stone il p151 Ap 23 '87. L. Fissinger
  Costello, Elvis: My aim is true
    Roll Stone il p93 Ag 27 '87
  Costello, Elvis: This year's model
    Roll Stone il p72 Ag 27 '87
  Creedence Clearwater Revival: Green River
    Roll Stone il p107 Ag 27 '87
  Creedence Clearwater Revival: Willy and the poor boys
    Roll Stone il p101 Ag 27 '87
  Crenshaw, Marshall: Mary Jean & 9 others
    Down Beat il 54:30+ S '87. G. Santoro
    Roll Stone il p51 Ag 13 '87. A. DeCurtis
  Crosby, Stills and Nash: Crosby, Stills and Nash
    Roll Stone il p140+ Ag 27 '87
  Crowded House: Crowded House
    Roll Stone il p54 F 26 '87. C. Willman
    Stereo Rev il 52:81-2 Jl '87. M. Peel

Cruzados: After dark
    Stereo Rev il 52:152 N '87. M. Peel
Cure: Kiss me, kiss me, kiss me
    Stereo Rev il 52:97 O '87. M. Peel
dB's: Sound of music
    Roll Stone il p130 S 24 '87. D. Browne
    Stereo Rev il 52:89 O '87. S. Simels
Deep Purple: House of blue light
    Roll Stone il p56 F 26 '87. D. Fricke
Def Leppard: Hysteria
    Roll Stone il p16 S 10 '87. R. Tannenbaum
    Roll Stone il p127-8 S 24 '87. K. Loder
Derek and the Dominos: Layla
    Roll Stone il p82 Ag 27 '87
Dixon, Don: Most of the girls like to dance but only
    some of the boys like to
    Roll Stone il p46 Mr 12 '87. R. Tannenbaum
Dixon, Don: Romeo at Juilliard
    Roll Stone il p86-7 D 3 '87. D. Browne
Doors: Doors
    Roll Stone il p84 Ag 27 '87
Dr. John: Gris-gris
    Down Beat il 54:32 Ag '87. L. Birnbaum
Dr. John: Gumbo
    Down Beat il 54:27 Ja '87. J. Roberts
Dukes of Stratosphear: Psonic psunspot
    Stereo Rev il 52:138+ D '87. S. Simels
Duran Duran: Notorious
    Roll Stone il p46+ Ja 29 '87. M. Coleman
Dylan, Bob: Blood on the tracks
    Roll Stone il p72 Ag 27 '87
Dylan, Bob: John Wesley Harding
    Roll Stone il p130 Ag 27 '87
Earle, Steve: Early tracks
    Roll Stone il p151-2 Ap 23 '87. C. Willman
Echo and the Bunnymen: Echo & the Bunnymen
    Roll Stone il p90 O 22 '87. J. D. Considine
Edmunds, Dave: I hear you rockin'
    Stereo Rev il 52:101 Ap '87. S. Simels
Elvis Costello and the Attractions: Blood & chocolate
    High Fidel 37:70-1 F '87. D. Browne
Elvis Costello and the Attractions: Get happy!!
    Roll Stone il p129 Ag 27 '87
Ely, Joe: Lord of the highway
    Down Beat il 54:42-3 D '87. G. Santoro
Europe: Final countdown
    Roll Stone il p52+ My 7 '87. J. D. Considine
Fabulous Thunderbirds: Hot number
    Down Beat il 54:30 O '87. G. Santoro
    Roll Stone il p53-4 Ag 13 '87. J. Guterman
Fatal Flowers: Younger days
    Roll Stone il p133+ S 24 '87. D. Fricke
Fire Town: In the heart of the heart country
    Stereo Rev il 52:74 Mr '87. S. Simels
Fleetwood Mac: Rumours
    Roll Stone il p140 Ag 27 '87
Fleetwood Mac: Tango in the night
    Roll Stone il p51-2 My 7 '87. J. Pareles
    Stereo Rev il 52:84 Jl '87. S. Simels
Fogerty, John: Eye of the zombie
    Down Beat il 54:30-1 Ja '87. G. Santoro
    High Fidel il 37:89 Ja '87. K. Richardson
    Stereo Rev 52:126 Ja '87. S. Simels
Frankie Goes to Hollywood: Liverpool
    Stereo Rev il 52:85 My '87. M. Peel
Franklin, Aretha: 30 greatest hits
    Roll Stone il p48-9 Ja 29 '87. R. Hoerburger
Franklin, Aretha: Aretha
    Roll Stone il p48-9 Ja 29 '87. R. Hoerburger
    Sch Update il 119:32 F 23 '87. J. A. Baggett
    Vogue il 177:36+ Ja '87. T. Young
Franklin, Aretha: I never loved a man the way I love
    you
    Roll Stone il p162 Ag 27 '87
Franklin, Aretha: Lady Soul
    Roll Stone il p111+ Ag 27 '87
French/Frith/Kaiser/Thompson: Live, love, larf & loaf
    Down Beat 54:32 O '87. P. Kostakis
Gaye, Marvin: What's going on
    Roll Stone il p69 Ag 27 '87
General Public: Hand to mouth
    Stereo Rev il 52:187 F '87. M. Peel
Golden Palominos: Blast of silence
    Down Beat il 54:38 Ap '87. B. Milkowski
    Roll Stone il p133-4 Mr 26 '87. A. DeCurtis
Graham Parker and the Rumour: Howlin wind
    Roll Stone il p118 Ag 27 '87
Graham Parker and the Rumour: Squeezing out sparks
    Roll Stone il p108 Ag 27 '87
Gramm, Lou: Ready or not
    Roll Stone il p148+ Ap 23 '87. A. DeCurtis

Phonograph records—Rock music—Reviews—Single works —*cont.*

Grateful Dead: In the dark
    High Fidel 37:94 D '87. A. Nash
    Roll Stone il p51-2 Ag 13 '87. D. Browne
Green, Al: Call me
    Roll Stone il p143 Ag 27 '87
Harrison, George: Cloud nine
    Roll Stone il p80 D 3 '87. D. Wild
Harry, Debbie: Rockbird
    Roll Stone il p46 Ja 29 '87. A. DeCurtis
Hooters: One way home
    Roll Stone il p81-2 S 10 '87. D. Fricke
Hüsker Dü: Warehouse: songs and stories
    Roll Stone il p131-3 Mr 26 '87. D. Fricke
Iggy and the Stooges: Raw power
    Roll Stone il p157 Ag 27 '87
Isaak, Chris: Chris Isaak
    Roll Stone il p52 My 7 '87. D. Wild
Jackson, Freddie: Just like the first time
    Roll Stone il p43-4 Mr 12 '87. V. Aletti
Jackson, Michael: Bad
    Macleans 100:58 S 14 '87. N. Jennings
    Roll Stone il p87-8 O 22 '87. D. Sigerson
    Stereo Rev il 52:135-6 D '87. P. Garland
    Time il 130:85 S 14 '87. J. Cocks
Jackson, Michael: Off the wall
    Roll Stone il p130+ Ag 27 '87
Jackson, Michael: Thriller
    Roll Stone il p154 Ag 27 '87
Jagger, Mick: Primitive cool
    Roll Stone il p113+ N 19 '87. M. Gilmore
Jefferson Airplane: 2400 Fulton Street—an anthology
    Roll Stone il p98-9 My 21 '87. D. Fricke
    Stereo Rev il 52:120 Je '87. S. Simels
Jefferson Airplane: Surrealistic pillow
    Roll Stone il p107-8 Ag 27 '87
Jellybean: Just visiting this planet
    Roll Stone il p118 N 19 '87. V. Aletti
Jimi Hendrix Experience: Are you experienced?
    Roll Stone il p55 Ag 27 '87
Jimi Hendrix Experience: Electric Ladyland
    Roll Stone il p125+ Ag 27 '87
Kaiser, Henry: Crazy-backwards alphabet
    Down Beat 54:31-2 O '87. P. Kostakis
Kid Creole and the Coconuts: I, too, have seen the woods
    Nation 245:426-7 O 17 '87. G. Santoro
Kinks: Think visual
    Roll Stone il p54 Ja 15 '87. D. Wild
Led Zeppelin: Led Zeppelin II
    Roll Stone il p152 Ag 27 '87
Led Zeppelin: Led Zeppelin IV
    Roll Stone il p110-11 Ag 27 '87
Lennon, John: Imagine
    Roll Stone il p125 Ag 27 '87
Lennon, John: Menlove Ave.
    Roll Stone il p52+ Ja 15 '87. D. Fricke
Lennon, John: Plastic Ono Band
    Roll Stone il p52 Ag 27 '87
Little Steven: Freedom—no compromise
    Roll Stone il p52+ Jl 2 '87. A. DeCurtis
Lone Justice: Shelter
    Roll Stone il p93 F 12 '87. J. Guterman
Los Lobos: By the light of the moon
    Down Beat il 54:31 Ap '87. G. Santoro
    Roll Stone il p51+ F 26 '87. A. DeCurtis
    Stereo Rev il 52:86+ Ap '87. S. Simels
Love and Rockets: Express
    Roll Stone il p44+ Mr 12 '87. M. Coleman
Madonna: Who's that girl
    Roll Stone il p112 O 8 '87. V. Aletti
Mahal, Taj: Taj
    Stereo Rev il 52:71-2 Mr '87. P. Garland
McCartney, Paul: Press to play
    High Fidel il 37:89 Ja '87. K. Richardson
Mellencamp, John Cougar: Lonesome jubilee
    High Fidel 37:93-4 D '87. D. Browne
    Roll Stone il p105-7 O 8 '87. A. DeCurtis
Mitchell, Joni: Blue
    Roll Stone il p108 Ag 27 '87
Modern Lovers: Modern Lovers
    Roll Stone il p116 Ag 27 '87
Morrison, Van: Astral weeks
    Roll Stone il p63 Ag 27 '87
Morrison, Van: Moondance
    Roll Stone il p122+ Ag 27 '87
Mothers of Invention: We're only in it for the money
    Roll Stone il p144-6 Ag 27 '87
Murphy, Elliott: Milwaukee
    Roll Stone il p138 Mr 26 '87. D. Wild

Neil Young and Crazy Horse: Life
    Roll Stone il p129 S 24 '87. S. Hochman
Neil Young and Crazy Horse: Rust never sleeps
    Roll Stone il p129 Ag 27 '87
Neville Brothers: Treacherous: a history of the Neville Brothers 1955-85
    Down Beat il 54:40-2 Jl '87. F.-J. Hadley
Neville Brothers: Uptown
    Down Beat il 54:40-2 Jl '87. F.-J. Hadley
New York Dolls: New York Dolls
    Roll Stone il p118+ Ag 27 '87
Newman, Randy: 12 songs
    Roll Stone il p114-15 Ag 27 '87
Newman, Randy: Sail away
    Roll Stone il p157-8 Ag 27 '87
Nixon, Mojo, and Roper, Skid: Bo-day-shus!!!
    Roll Stone il p111 O 8 '87. K. Loder
Nuggets: Original artyfacts from the first psychedelic era, 1965-1968
    Roll Stone il p158+ Ag 27 '87
Osbourne, Ozzy, and Rhoads, Randy: Tribute
    Roll Stone il p52 Jl 2 '87. M. Coleman
Paul Kelly and the Messengers: Gossip
    Roll Stone il p118 N 19 '87. D. Fricke
Pfeifer, Bob: After words
    Roll Stone il p54 Ag 13 '87. D. Fricke
Pink Floyd: A momentary lapse of reason
    Stereo Rev il 52:159 D '87. M. Peel
Pink Floyd: Dark side of the moon
    Roll Stone il p97+ Ag 27 '87
Pink Floyd: Piper at the gates of dawn
    Roll Stone il p146 Ag 27 '87
Pointer Sisters: Hot together
    Roll Stone il p90+ F 12 '87. R. Hoerburger
Presley, Elvis: Complete Sun sessions
    Roll Stone il p79+ S 10 '87. S. Pond
Presley, Elvis: From Elvis in Memphis
    Roll Stone il p144 Ag 27 '87
Presley, Elvis: Memphis record
    Roll Stone il p79+ S 10 '87. S. Pond
Presley, Elvis: Number one hits
    Roll Stone il p79+ S 10 '87. S. Pond
Presley, Elvis: Top ten hits
    Roll Stone il p79+ S 10 '87. S. Pond
Pretenders: Get close
    Roll Stone il p52 Ja 15 '87. R. Tannenbaum
Pretenders: Pretenders
    Roll Stone il p104-5 Ag 27 '87
Prince: Dirty mind
    Roll Stone il p78 Ag 27 '87
Prince: Purple rain
    Roll Stone il p102 Ag 27 '87
Prince: Sign o' the times
    Down Beat il 54:33 Jl '87. G. Santoro
    Nation 245:728-9 D 12 '87. D. Wolff
    Newsweek il 109:72-3 My 4 '87. B. Barol
    Roll Stone il p145-6 Ap 23 '87. K. Loder
R.E.M.: Document
    Roll Stone il p18 Ag 27 '87. A. DeCurtis
    Roll Stone il p88+ O 22 '87. D. Fricke
R.E.M.: Murmur
    Roll Stone il p122 Ag 27 '87
Ramones: Ramones
    Roll Stone il p135 Ag 27 '87
RCA Victor blues & rhythm revue
    Down Beat il 54:40-2 D '87. L. Birnbaum
Redding, Otis: History of Otis Redding
    Roll Stone il p167 Ag 27 '87
Replacements: Pleased to meet me
    Roll Stone il p51-2 Jl 2 '87. D. Fricke
Robertson, Robbie: Robbie Robertson
    Roll Stone il p113-15 N 19 '87. S. Pond
Robinson, Smokey: One heartbeat
    Roll Stone il p148 Ap 23 '87. D. Wild
Robyn Hitchcock and the Egyptians: Element of light
    High Fidel il 37:70 F '87. A. Nash
Rolling Stones: Beggars banquet
    Roll Stone il p75 Ag 27 '87
Rolling Stones: Between the buttons
    Roll Stone il p135+ Ag 27 '87
Rolling Stones: Exile on Main Street
    Roll Stone il p50-1 Ag 27 '87
Rolling Stones: Let it bleed
    Roll Stone il p76-8 Ag 27 '87
Rolling Stones: Sticky fingers
    Roll Stone il p94 Ag 27 '87
Roxy Music: Siren
    Roll Stone il p152 Ag 27 '87
Ruffner, Mason: Gypsy blood
    Roll Stone il p132-3 Jl 16-30 '87. D. Fricke

Phonograph records—Rock music—Reviews—Single works —*cont.*

Rundgren, Todd: Something/anything?
 Roll Stone il p140 Ag 27 '87

Saints: All fools day
 Roll Stone il p83-4 Je 18 '87. D. Fricke

Screaming Blue Messiahs: Bikini red
 Roll Stone il p80 D 3 '87. D. Browne

Sex Pistols: Never mind the Bollocks here's the Sex Pistols
 Roll Stone il p48-9 Ag 27 '87

Silencers: Letter from St. Paul
 Stereo Rev il 52:157 N '87. M. Peel

Simon and Garfunkel: Bridge over troubled water
 Roll Stone il p165 Ag 27 '87

Simon, Paul: Graceland
 Roll Stone il p121 Ag 27 '87

Simply Red: Men and women
 Roll Stone il p72 Ap 9 '87. M. Coleman
 Stereo Rev il 52:117 Je '87. M. Peel

Sly and the Family Stone: Greatest hits
 Roll Stone il p146 Ag 27 '87

Sly and the Family Stone: Stand!
 Roll Stone il p155 Ag 27 '87

Sly and the Family Stone: There's a riot goin' on
 Roll Stone il p93-4 Ag 27 '87

Smith, Patti: Horses
 Roll Stone il p75-6 Ag 27 '87

Smiths: Louder than bombs
 Roll Stone il p95+ My 21 '87. J. Farber

Smiths: Strangeways, here we come
 Roll Stone il p84-5 D 3 '87. D. Browne

Southside Johnny and the Asbury Jukes: Hearts of stone
 Roll Stone il p162 Ag 27 '87

Springsteen, Bruce: Born in the U.S.A.
 Roll Stone il p89+ Ag 27 '87

Springsteen, Bruce: Born to run
 Roll Stone il p64 Ag 27 '87

Springsteen, Bruce: Bruce Springsteen & the E Street Band live/1975-85
 Down Beat il 54:32 F '87. G. Santoro
 High Fidel il 37:74-5 Mr '87. W. King
 Roll Stone il p50-2 Ja 15 '87. D. Fricke
 Stereo Rev il 52:169 F '87. S. Simels

Springsteen, Bruce: Darkness on the edge of town
 Roll Stone il p102 Ag 27 '87

Springsteen, Bruce: River
 Roll Stone il p127 Ag 27 '87

Springsteen, Bruce: Tunnel of love
 Macleans il 100:54 O 12 '87. N. Jennings
 Roll Stone il p77-9 D 3 '87. S. Pond
 Time il 130:92 O 12 '87. J. Cocks

Springsteen, Bruce: Wild, the innocent and the E Street shuffle
 Roll Stone il p115-16 Ag 27 '87

Squeeze: Babylon and on
 Roll Stone il p117 N 19 '87. D. Wild

Steely Dan: Katy lied
 Roll Stone il p170 Ag 27 '87

Stewart, Rod: Every picture tells a story
 Roll Stone il p97 Ag 27 '87

Sting: . . . Nothing like the sun
 Roll Stone il p79-80 D 3 '87. A. DeCurtis

Summers, Andy: XYZ
 Down Beat il 54:38-9 D '87. B. Milkowski

T. Rex: Electric warrior
 Roll Stone il p173 Ag 27 '87

Talking Heads: Fear of music
 Roll Stone il p167 Ag 27 '87

Talking Heads: More songs about buildings and food
 Roll Stone il p121-2 Ag 27 '87

Talking Heads: Remain in light
 Roll Stone il p116 Ag 27 '87

Talking Heads: Talking Heads: 77
 Roll Stone il p148 Ag 27 '87

Talking Heads: True stories
 Down Beat il 54:38-9 F '87. G. Santoro
 New Repub 196:26+ Mr 23 '87. C. Coulson
 Stereo Rev il 52:108 Ja '87. M. Peel

Television: Marquee moon
 Roll Stone il p102 Ag 27 '87

They Might Be Giants: They Might Be Giants
 High Fidel 37:75 Ag '87. L. Berman

Thompson, Richard: Daring adventures
 Down Beat il 54:34+ Mr '87. F.-J. Hadley
 High Fidel 37:75+ Mr '87. D. Browne

Thompson, Richard/Thompson, Linda: I want to see the bright lights tonight
 Roll Stone il p155 Ag 27 '87

Thompson, Richard/Thompson, Linda: Shoot out the lights
 Roll Stone il p82+ Ag 27 '87

Timbuk 3: Greetings from Timbuk 3
 Stereo Rev il 52:106 Ja '87. S. Simels

Tom Petty and the Heartbreakers: Let me up (I've had enough)
 Roll Stone il p131 Je 4 '87. A. DeCurtis
 Stereo Rev il 52:79 Ag '87. S. Simels

Townshend, Pete: Another scoop
 Roll Stone il p146+ Ap 23 '87. D. Fricke

Turner, Tina: Break every rule
 High Fidel 37:75 Mr '87. R. Wynn
 Stereo Rev il 52:130 Ja '87. A. Nash

U2: Joshua tree
 Down Beat il 54:36 Ag '87. G. Santoro
 High Fidel 37:75 Jl '87. D. Browne
 Roll Stone il p71-2 Ap 9 '87. S. Pond
 Stereo Rev il 52:102+ Je '87. M. Peel

Van Zandt, Steve: Freedom—no compromise
 Roll Stone il p19 My 21 '87. A. DeCurtis

Vandross, Luther: Give me the reason
 Roll Stone il p43-4 Mr 12 '87. V. Aletti

Velvet Underground: Loaded
 Roll Stone il p94-5 Ag 27 '87

Velvet Underground: Velvet Underground
 Roll Stone il p168+ Ag 27 '87

Velvet Underground: Velvet Underground and Nico
 Roll Stone il p80 Ag 27 '87

A very Special Christmas
 People Wkly il 28:157-9 N 2 '87. M. Green

Waits, Tom: Franks wild years
 Roll Stone il p110-11 O 8 '87. S. Hochman
 Stereo Rev il 52:88 S '87. M. Peel

Waters, Roger: Radio K.A.O.S.
 Roll Stone il p134 Jl 16-30 '87. J. D. Considine

Watley, Jody: Jody Watley
 Roll Stone il p99+ My 21 '87. V. Aletti

White Animals: In the last days
 Stereo Rev il 52:87 S '87. S. Simels

Whitesnake: Whitesnake
 Roll Stone il p83 Je 18 '87. J. D. Considine

Who: Meaty beaty big and bouncy
 Roll Stone il p170 Ag 27 '87

Who: Who's next
 Roll Stone il p80+ Ag 27 '87

Williams Bros: Two stories
 Roll Stone il p86 Je 18 '87. D. Browne

Willis, Bruce: Return of Bruno
 Roll Stone il p72+ Ap 9 '87. J. Guterman

Wolf, Peter: Come as you are
 Roll Stone il p94-5 My 21 '87. A. DeCurtis
 Stereo Rev il 52:101 Je '87. S. Simels

Wonder, Stevie: Innervisions
 Roll Stone il p101 Ag 27 '87

Wonder, Stevie: Talking book
 Roll Stone il p129 Ag 27 '87

XTC: Skylarking
 Roll Stone il p134-5 Mr 26 '87. R. Tannenbaum
 Stereo Rev il 52:77 My '87. S. Simels

Young, Neil: After the Gold Rush
 Roll Stone il p138-9 Ag 27 '87

Young, Neil: Tonight's the night
 Roll Stone il p84+ Ag 27 '87

Zevon, Warren: Sentimental hygiene
 Roll Stone il p131-2 Jl 16-30 '87. D. Handelman
 Roll Stone il p19 Je 18 '87. A. DeCurtis
 Stereo Rev il 52:74+ Ag '87. S. Simels

Rock opera

Bob Moses: Story of Moses. K. Whitehead. il *Down Beat* 54:38-9 Ag '87

Saxophone music

Reeds & deeds [jazz quartets] B. Shoemaker. il *Down Beat* 54:42 Ap '87

Saxophone Choir: Saxophone shop. R. Welburn. il *Down Beat* 54:35+ S '87

World Saxophone Quartet plays Duke Ellington; World Saxophone Quartet live at Brooklyn Academy of Music. F. Davis. il *Roll Stone* p56 F 26 '87

A year in the life of a sopranoist [D. Liebman discography] F. Bouchard. *Down Beat* 54:36 Jl '87

Sonatas

See also
Phonograph records—Piano music

Songs

See also
Phonograph records—Arias

The enchanting Kathleen Battle [release of Salzburg recital] R. Freed. il *Stereo Rev* 52:88 Ap '87

Weill, Kurt: Songs [Teresa Stratas] P. Bloom. *High Fidel* 37:67 Je '87

Phonograph records—cont.

Soul music

See Phonograph records—Black music

South African music

Hugh Masekela [release of Tomorrow] P. Garland. il por *Stereo Rev* 52:116 O '87

Spanish music

Falla's "El amor brujo". W. Livingstone. il *Stereo Rev* 52:105 My '87

Symphonic poems

Loeffler, Charles Martin: La mort de Tintagiles; Five Irish fantasies. H. Halbreich. il *High Fidel* 37:65+ Mr '87

Symphonies

As American as Pittsburgh [Pittsburgh Symphony Orchestra's recording of William Schuman's Symphony no. 7 and Leonardo Balada's Steel Symphony] E. Salzman. il por *Stereo Rev* 52:118 S '87

Bychkov's stirring Shostakovich [recording of Symphony no. 5, in D major] R. Freed. por *Stereo Rev* 52:87-8 S '87

Giulini's elegant Bruckner [Symphony no. 7] D. Hall. il por *Stereo Rev* 52:150+ N '87

Haydn, Beethoven & old instruments [recordings by L'Estro Armonico conducted by Derek Solomons] R. De Toledano. *Natl Rev* 39:53-4 Ap 10 '87

Haydn, Joseph: Symphonies: nos. 60, 63, 66, 67, 68 and 69. K. R. Schwarz. *High Fidel* 37:65-6 My '87

Hogwood's Beethoven [recording of Symphony no 3] R. Freed. por *Stereo Rev* 52:99 Mr '87

The symphonic Furtwängler. W. H. Youngren. il *Atlantic* 259:77-80 Ja '87

Tennstedt's poetic Mahler [Eighth symphony] D. Hall. il por *Stereo Rev* 52:89-90 O '87

Television music

Jarreau wins new fans with 'Moonlighting' tune. por *Jet* 73:18 N 16 '87

Television's greatest hits, volume II. S. Simels. *Stereo Rev* 52:132 Ja '87

Tone poems

See Phonograph records—Symphonic poems

Trumpet music

Band-shell bop: putting the corn in cornet [W. Marsalis' Carnaval] D. Gates. *Newsweek* 109:69 Ap 6 '87

Unauthorized recording

Looking for the Jolly Roger [record industry vs. digital audio tape recorders] M. Riggs. *High Fidel* 37:4 My '87

Record executives are on pins and needles [digital tape scare] B. Buell and others. il *Bus Week* p112 F 16 '87

Record industry battles digital tape. A. DeCurtis. *Roll Stone* p13+ Ap 9 '87

What is DAT, and why are the record companies trying to keep it away from you? P. Wilkinson. il *Roll Stone* p69-70+ S 10 '87

Violin music

Lively Mozart concertos from Lin and Leppard. R. Freed. il *Stereo Rev* 52:135 D '87

Vocal music

See also

Phonograph records—Arias

Phonograph records—Cantatas

Phonograph records—Opera

Phonograph records—Passion music

Phonograph records—Songs

Best of the year: the editors of Opera news choose outstanding vocal recordings of 1987. il *Opera News* 52:44 D 19 '87

Denisov, Edison Vasilyevich: La vie en rouge; "Colin and Chloé," from L'écume des jours. P. Moor. *High Fidel* 37:65 Ap '87

Zydeco music

On a night like this [release by Buckwheat Zydeco] D. Browne. il *Roll Stone* p90 O 22 '87

Phonograph records as gifts

Hi-fi holiday gifts [with editorial comment by Louise Boundas] il *Stereo Rev* 52:8, 79-83 D '87

Our holiday lists. *Nation* 245:793-804 D 26 '87-Ja 2 '88

Phonons

Phonon density of states and specific heat of forsterite, Mg_2SiO_4. K. R. Rao and others. bibl f il *Science* 236:64-5 Ap 3 '87

Shaking up quasicrystals [work of Hartmut Zabel and others] I. Peterson. *Sci News* 131:152 Mr 7 '87

Phorbol esters

Chinese folk remedy may promote cancer [plants containing phorbol esters linked to nasopharyngeal cancer; research by L. David Tomei and others] R. Weiss. *Sci News* 132:148 S 5 '87

Forskolin and phorbol esters reduce the same potassium conductance of mouse neurons in culture. D. S. Grega and others. bibl f il *Science* 235:345-8 Ja 16 '87

Phosphatases

See also

Adenosine triphosphatase

Chemoattractant-regulated mobilization of a novel intracellular compartment in human neutrophils. N. Borregaard and others. bibl f il *Science* 237:1204-6 S 4 '87

Phosphate industry

Christmas Island (Indian Ocean)

History

The Christmas Island Phosphate Company. A. L. Rice. bibl il por map *Sea Front* 33:444-53 N/D '87

Phosphates

See also

Adenosine triphosphate

Guanosine diphosphate

Guanosine triphosphate

Phosphorylation

Florida: working with the phosphate factor. J. D. Nash. bibl f il map *Environment* 29:13+ Mr '87

Focusing on brain-tumor phosphates [use of nuclear magnetic resonance spectroscopy; work of Klaus Roth and others] S. Weisburd. il *Sci News* 132:375 D 12 '87

Why nature chose phosphates. F. H. Westheimer. bibl f il *Science* 235:1173-8 Mr 6 '87

Physiological effects

It is diprotonated inorganic phosphate that depresses force in skinned skeletal muscle fibers. T. M. Nosek and others. bibl f il *Science* 236:191-3 Ap 10 '87

Phosphatides

See also

Lecithin

Phosphatidylinositol

Phosphoinositides

Insulin rapidly increases diacylglycerol by activating de novo phosphatidic acid synthesis. R. V. Farese and others. bibl f il *Science* 236:586-9 My 1 '87

Polyphosphoinositide research updated. J. L. Marx. il *Science* 235:974-6 F 27 '87

Signal for attachment of a phospholipid membrane anchor in decay accelerating factor. I. W. Caras and others. bibl f il *Science* 238:1280-3 N 27 '87

Phosphatidylinositol

A glycan-phosphatidylinositol-specific phospholipase D in human serum. M. A. Davitz and others. bibl f il *Science* 238:81-4 O 2 '87

Lipid takes a stand against alcohol [research by Theodore F. Taraschi and others] D. D. Edwards. *Sci News* 131:38-9 Ja 17 '87

Phosphoinositides

An M2 muscarinic receptor subtype coupled to both adenylyl cyclase and phosphoinositide turnover. A. Ashkenazi and others. bibl f il *Science* 238:672-5 O 30 '87

Phospholipases *See* Lipases

Phospholipid vesicles *See* Liposomes

Phospholipids *See* Phosphatides

Phosphorescence

See also

Bioluminescence

On the prevalence of room-temperature protein phosphorescence. J. M. Vanderkooi and others. bibl f il *Science* 236:568-9 My 1 '87

Phosphorus

See also

Soils—Phosphorus content

Phosphorus in antique iron music wire. M. Goodway. bibl f il *Science* 236:927-32 My 22 '87

The well-tempered clavier [use of phosphorus alloy in harpsichord strings; research by Martha Goodway] il *Sci Am* 257:20+ Ag '87

Phosphorylases

Structure of the nucleotide activation switch in glycogen phosphorylase a. S. Sprang and others. bibl f il *Science* 237:1012-19 Ag 28 '87

Phosphorylation

Myosin rod phosphorylation and the catch state of molluscan muscles. L. Castellani and C. Cohen. bibl f il *Science* 235:334-7 Ja 16 '87

Protein kinase C contains a pseudosubstrate prototope in its regulatory domain. C. House and B. E. Kemp. bibl f il *Science* 238:1726-8 D 18 '87

Photinia

Diseases and pests

Check for leaf spot [disease that attacks photinias] il *South Living* 22:100 Ap '87

Photo Marketing Association Show *See* Photography—Exhibitions

Photo-realism
Joel Jaecks. J. H. Glassie. il por *Am Artist* 51:34-9 S '87
Using photographs to interpret the modern world. R. Neffson. il *Am Artist* 51:72-5 D '87

Photo stylists
Ellen Silverstein, photo stylist. J. Dolce. il por *Seventeen* 46:232 Ag '87

Photobiology *See* Light—Physiological effects

Photochemistry
See also
Photosynthesis

Photocopier art *See* Photocopying—Art use

Photocopying
Art use
Acetate meets copy machine for cards, decorations. il *Sunset* 179:110-11 D '87
Educational use
Danish agent fights to disburse copying fees to foreign authors [payment for school photocopying] H. R. Lottman. *Publ Wkly* 232:14 Ag 14 '87

Photocopying equipment
See also
Canon Inc.
KCR Technology, Inc.
Minnesota Mining & Mfg. Co.
Nashua Corporation
Xerox Corp.
Copier craze [pocket copies] J. Jainschigg. il *Work Woman* 12:69 Ap '87
Health hazard from copier exhaust [air pollution from wet process copiers; research by Yoshio Tsuchiya] S. Weisburd. *Sci News* 132:166 S 12 '87
Print it or copy it on this double-duty printer [Xerox 4045 CP laser printer/photocopier] D. B. Trivette. il *Pop Sci* 230:42 Ja '87
Xerox's laser with copier option. P. Honan. il *Pers Comput* 11:154 Ja '87

Photocopying law *See* Copyright

Photoelectric cells
See also
Solar cells

Photoelectrochemical cells *See* Solar cells

Photoelectronics
In the blink of a laser. S. Budiansky. il *U S News World Rep* 102:68 F 2 '87

Photoemission spectroscopy *See* Spectrum analysis

Photograph albums
Family photo albums [excerpt from The Russian album] M. Ignatieff. *Harpers* 274:27-8 Je '87
Postal photography [mailable photo greetings] L. Nielsen. il *Petersens Photogr Mag* 15:70-1 Ap '87

Photographers
See also
Authors as photographers
Celebrities as photographers
Photography as a profession
Meet the masters. F. Cameron. See alternate issues of Petersen's Photographic Magazine beginning March 1985
Profiles. H. Chapnick. See issues of Popular Photography beginning February 1987
Legal status, laws, etc.
Are you a photographer or a hired gun? J. W. Brewer. il *Petersens Photogr Mag* 16:64-7 O '87

Photographers, American
See also
Abell, Sam
Adams, Ansel, 1902-1984
Avedon, Richard
Banks, Steve
Bergman, Alan
Bloom, Barbara
Carey, Ellen
Colbert, Richard
DeMello, Dennis
Dexter, King
Elmi, Ross
Feininger, Andreas, 1906-
Fowler, Brad
Frank, Robert, 1924-
Gagliani, Oliver
Gibson, Ralph
Gilpin, Laura
Going, Michael
Haller, Grant
Handler, Lowell
Heinecken, Robert, 1931-
Heisler, Gregory

Heyman, Abigail
Hofer, Evelyn
Hurrell, George
Iooss, Walter, Jr.
Klein, William, 1928-
Kral, Jon
Kruger, Barbara
Loengard, John
Maisel, Jay, 1931-
Mapplethorpe, Robert
Mark, Mary Ellen, 1940-
McCulley, Mary
Newman, Arnold, 1918-
Noah, Barbara
Novak, Lorie
Phillips, John
Porter, Eliot, 1901-
Rau, William, 1855-1920
Rothschild, Norman
Rowell, Galen A.
Saunders, Richard
Schulke, Flip
Sherman, Cindy
Sklute, Ken
Skoglund, Sandy, 1946-
Sleet, Moneta
Starn Twins
Stern, Bert
Sternfeld, Joel, 1944-
Stoller, Ezra, 1916?-
Sturtevant, Roger
Thorp, Gregory
Thorson, Bruce
Trindl, Gene
Turner, Pete, 1934-
Weber, Bruce
Wegman, William
Weston, Edward, 1886-1958
Witkin, Joel-Peter, 1939-

Photographers, Austrian
See also
Rainer, Arnulf, 1929-

Photographers, Brazilian
See also
Salgado, Sebastiao

Photographers, Dutch
See also
Dibbets, Jan, 1941-

Photographers, English
See also
O'Neill, Terry

Photographers, French
See also
Cartier-Bresson, Henri, 1908-
Peress, Gilles
Rousse, Georges

Photographers, German
See also
Hoefer, Hans
Lehmann, Hans G.
Wolf, Reinhart, 1930-
Remnants of authenticity [International Center of Photography show of contemporary photographers] M. E. Haus. il *Art News* 86:186 O '87

Photographers, Handicapped
The courage to adapt [work of A. Shahrouzi] P. Skinner. il por *Petersens Photogr Mag* 15:36-7+ Ap '87
Two pros overcome handicaps for successful careers [L. Handler and B. Thorson] H. Chapnick. il pors *Pop Photogr* 94:20 F '87

Photographers, Hungarian
See also
Capa, Robert, 1913-1954
Kertész, André

Photographers, Indian (East Indian)
See also
Bedi, Rajesh

Photographers, Latin American
Hispanic photography: new traditions [New traditions: thirteen Hispanic photographers] V. G. Stoddart. il *Américas* 39:54-6 Mr/Ap '87

Photographers, Lithuanian
"The republic of photographers" exhibits a special vitality. A. Goldsmith. il *Pop Photogr* 94:18 Ap '87

Photographers, Mexican
See also
Alvarez Bravo, Manuel, 1902-
Hernandez-Claire, José

Photographers, Russian
The state of photography behind the Iron Curtain [Soviet photo's 60th anniversary exhibition] A. Goldsmith. il por *Pop Photogr* 94:15 F '87
Photographers' markets *See* Photographs—Marketing
Photographic batteries *See* Electric batteries
Photographic calendars *See* Calendars
Photographic chemistry
   See also
   Photography—Developing and developers
   Photography—Processing
$18 darkroom chemical balance [scale] T. F. Fuller. il *Petersens Photogr Mag* 16:66-7 Ag '87
Photographic Christmas cards *See* Christmas cards
Photographic copying *See* Photography—Copying
Photographic enlargers *See* Photography—Enlargers and enlarging
Photographic equipment *See* Photography—Equipment
Photographic exhibitions *See* Photography—Exhibitions
Photographic films *See* Photography—Films
Photographic filters *See* Light filters
Photographic greeting cards *See* Greeting cards
Photographic industry
   See also
   Bell & Howell Co.
   Eastman Kodak Co.
   GAF Corp.
   Photographic laboratories
   Polaroid Corp.
   Tekno, Inc.
                     Employees
Beyond Blow-up: career opportunities in the photo industry. G. Schaub. il *Pop Photogr* 94:36+ Ag '87
                  Ethical aspects
Is KIS beating a retreat from the U.S.? C. Gaffney. il *Bus Week* p58 Mr 16 '87
                      France
   See also
   Key Independent System
                      Japan
   See also
   Canon Inc.
   Fuji Photo Film Co., Ltd.
   Minolta Camera Co. Ltd.
Japan news. See issues of Petersen's Photographic Magazine beginning June 1985 through August 1987
Photographic laboratories
   See also
   Key Independent System
Film-processing labs. il *Consum Rep* 52:316-18 D '87
Independent Kodachrome labs. B. Hurter. il *Petersens Photogr Mag* 16:94 N '87
Out of the shadows [black-and-white photofinishing] R. Hart. il *Pop Photogr* 94:62-7 S '87
Three film processing options that may be better, faster, more convenient for you. C. Begole. il *Glamour* 85:302+ Ag '87
Who makes the best color prints? il *Consum Rep* 52:643-6 O '87
Photographic laboratory workers
                     Training
Staples Institute: a launching pad for photo lab technicians. G. Schaub. il *Pop Photogr* 94:46 N '87
Photographic lenses *See* Lenses, Photographic
Photographic literature
   See also
   Photography—Bibliography
   Publishers and publishing—Photographic literature
Photographic murals
Doc [102 foot Duratrans mural of baseball player D. Gooden that hangs in Penn Station] *New Yorker* 63:29-30+ Mr 23 '87
Photographic optics
   See also
   Lenses, Photographic
   Perspective
Photographic paper
Color crossover [combination of Konica SR-V 3200 color print film and panchromatic paper] R. Hart. il *Pop Photogr* 94:94-5 N '87
Exhibition papers: the color of black and white. C. W. Kennedy. il *Pop Photogr* 94:22-3 Ap '87
Plastic's fantastic: RC paper internegatives. R. Hart. il *Pop Photogr* 94:44+ D '87
Shades of color [black-and-white prints from color negatives with panchromatic papers] R. Hart. il *Pop Photogr* 94:88-93 N '87

Photographic postcards *See* Postcards
Photographic posters *See* Posters
Photographic processing *See* Photography—Processing
Photographic silk screen printing *See* Silk screen printing
Photographic slides *See* Slides (Photography)
Photographic supplies *See* Photography—Equipment
Photographs
   See also
   Daguerreotypes
   Slides (Photography)
      See also subhead Photographs and photography under various subjects
The snapshot at 100: a tradition of spontaneous imagery. A. Goldsmith. il *Pop Photogr* 94:62+ D '87
                     Cleaning
Clean up your photos. M. Crook and W. Crook. bibl il *Petersens Photogr Mag* 15:47-8 Mr '87
              Collectors and collecting
   See Photography—Collectors and collecting
                    Cropping
   See Photographs—Trimming, mounting, etc.
                   Exhibitions
   See Photography—Exhibitions
                     Framing
   See Photographs—Trimming, mounting, etc.
                    Marketing
Contemporary greeting cards: more than hearts and flowers [selling photographs to greeting card companies] G. Schaub. il *Pop Photogr* 94:21 Mr '87
Culling the shots: how to edit your marketable photographs. G. Schaub. il *Pop Photogr* 94:30 Ap '87
Making it as a free-lance writer-photographer. R. Tolley. il *Petersens Photogr Mag* 15:51-3 Ja '87
                     Prices
Photo market upswing. A. Decker. il *Art News* 86:18 F '87
                   Reproducing
   See Photography—Copying
                     Theft
Free lance photog who worked for Jet has her life's work stolen [E. Tomlin] *Jet* 72:22 S 14 '87
              Trimming, mounting, etc.
Free-standing photo collages. K. Geller-Shinn. il *Petersens Photogr Mag* 16:14 O '87
Who says you should never crop your prints or slides? N. Rothschild. il *Pop Photogr* 94:24 Jl '87
Photographs on cloth
Transfer your photos for summer fun [use of Transfer Magic] K. Geller-Shinn. il *Petersens Photogr Mag* 16:14 Jl '87
Try Transgraph-X for photo needleart [instant needlework chart] K. Geller-Shinn. il *Petersens Photogr Mag* 16:50-1 Ag '87
Photography
   See also
   Art and photography
   Astronomical photography
   Candid photography
   Computers—Photographic use
   Daguerreotypes
   Erotic photography
   Information storage and retrieval systems—Photographic use
   Macrophotography
   Marine photography
   Motion picture photography
   Nature photography
   Photographs
   Photomicrography
   Photomontage
   Radiography
   Reflections (Photography)
   Set photography
   Slides (Photography)
   Television photography
   Texture (Photography)
   Travel photography
   Ultraviolet photography
Falling in love with photography: our readers tell all. A. Goldsmith. il *Pop Photogr* 94:22 N '87
Focus [special section] il *Pop Mech* 164:79-82+ Ja '87
Keppler's SLR world. H. Keppler. See issues of Popular Photography beginning September 1987
Love at first sight isn't always the case in photography. A. Goldsmith. il *Pop Photogr* 94:22 Je '87
Meet the masters [color photography of P. Turner; cover story] F. Cameron. il por *Petersens Photogr Mag* 16:20-5 My '87
Offbeat. N. Rothschild. See issues of Popular Photography through September 1987

Photography—*cont.*

One to one [questions and answers] B. Hurter. See issues of Petersen's Photographic Magazine

Photography. S. A. Booth. See issues of Popular Mechanics beginning January 1986

Pro tips. B. Hagin. See issues of Popular Photography beginning November 1987

Reflections. J. Loengard. See issues of Popular Photography beginning September 1987

Re:vision. F. Patterson. See alternate issues of Petersen's Photographic Magazine beginning March 1987

Snapshots. S. Piperato. See issues of Popular Photography beginning November 1986

Take better pictures. C. Begole. See issues of Glamour

Tools & techniques. C. W. Kennedy. See issues of Popular Photography

Viewfinder. See issues of Petersen's Photographic Magazine beginning April 1987

Viewfinder. R. Ermshar. See issues of Petersen's Photographic Magazine beginning June 1986 through March 1987

Why shoot black & white? B. Schwalberg. il *Pop Photogr* 94:30-5 F '87

Bibliography

Books in brief. See issues of Popular Photography

New books about photography. F. Cameron. *Petersens Photogr Mag* 16:42-4 Je '87

Cold weather conditions

Gearing up for ski photography. L. Calvacca. il *Pop Photogr* 94:67 Ja '87

Collectors and collecting

See also

Cameras—Collectors and collecting

A collectible comes of age. D. Moreau. il *Changing Times* 41:67-71 S '87

"Hard" photographs from the 19th century. J. Leckel and C. Robbins. il *Antiques Collect Hobbies* 92:72-5 My '87

Photographic masterpieces from a midwestern bank [collection of the Exchange National Bank of Chicago] H. Kahn. il *USA Today (Periodical)* 115:42-53 My '87

Professional page. D. Grant. *Am Artist* 51:14+ O '87

Competitions

See also

Scholastic Awards

1986 Photo Contest winners [Weatherwise Contest; cover story] il *Weatherwise* 40:189-96 Jl/Ag '87

Américas Photo '88 Contest rules. *Américas* 39:55 S/O '87

Having a wonderful time! [contest winners] il *Ladies Home J* 104:62+ Jl '87

Instant success . . . ! [C. Gandolfo's photograph of Cinnamon the wet cat; cover story] J. Gray. il *Petersens Photogr Mag* 15:28-9+ Mr '87

International photo competition: Health for all, all for health. il *World Health* p31 My '87

Monthly contest winners. See issues of Petersen's Photographic Magazine beginning June 1985

Natural splendors: Sierra's annual Photo Contest winners [cover story] il *Sierra* 72:49-57 S/O '87

Photo '87 winners [Americas Photo Contest] C. Healy. il *Américas* 39:20-7 My/Je '87

Photo contest winners. il *Natl Wildl* 26:50-9 D '87/Ja '88

Photographic's Outstanding Achievement Award debuts. J. Augustine. il *Petersens Photogr Mag* 16:6 D '87

A portfolio of photography contest winners [sea-related and underwater] il *Sea Front* 33:273-9 Jl/Ag '87

Portrait of a golden day [amateur contest sponsored by Popular photography in coordination with the Day in the life of America book project] il *Pop Photogr* 94:36-51 Ja '87

The winners [Life's Contest for Young Photographers] il *Life* 10:51-6+ N '87

Composition

See Composition (Photography)

Contrast

See Photography—Light and lighting

Copying

See also

Slides (Photography)—Copying

Not so hot way to make copies. H. Keppler. il *Pop Photogr* 94:94+ O '87

Developing and developers

See also

Photography—Negatives

A developing crisis: T-Max processing options. D. Brooks. il *Petersens Photogr Mag* 16:44-6+ D '87

Electronic equipment

See also

Camera shutters—Control

Photography—Flash equipment

Enlargers and enlarging

Looking sharp in the dark [enlarger problems] R. Hart. il *Pop Photogr* 94:52-7 F '87

Paterson PCS 2500 universal pro enlarger. R. E. Mayer. il *Petersens Photogr Mag* 16:60-1+ Jl '87

Zone VI Cold Light [enlarger light system] D. Brooks. il *Petersens Photogr Mag* 15:33-5 Mr '87

Equipment

See also

Astronomical photography—Equipment

Camera bags, cases, etc.

Camera supports

Camera tripods

Cameras

Lenses, Photographic

Light filters

Photography—Flash equipment

Photography—Processing—Equipment

21 for the road. E. Stecker. il *Pop Photogr* 94:68-71 Ap '87

Brand X accessory won't operate with camera Y? It ain't necessarily so [autowinders] H. Keppler. il *Pop Photogr* 94:76+ S '87

Christmas gift guide. il *Pop Photogr* 94:22+ D '87

Gear on the go: indispensable items for the traveler. C. Purcell and A. Purcell. il *Pop Photogr* 94:24+ O '87

Gyrostabilizers: steady as she goes. R. Attaway. il *Pop Photogr* 94:77 Jl '87

Just out. B. Hagin. See issues of Popular Photography beginning February 1987

Just out. G. Schaub. See issues of Popular Photography beginning March 1986 through January 1987

Modifying a conventional lens [soft-focus attachments] E. Stecker. il *Pop Photogr* 94:44-5 Mr '87

Natural resources [equipment for nature photography] E. Stecker. il *Pop Photogr* 94:62-5 Ag '87

A portable copy stand. T. F. Fuller. il *Petersens Photogr Mag* 16:72-3 S '87

Practical little photo gifts. K. Geller-Shinn. il *Petersens Photogr Mag* 16:16 D '87

Proof sheet. See issues of Petersen's Photographic Magazine beginning November 1985

Set shots [accessories for still lifes] E. Stecker. il *Pop Photogr* 94:36-9 F '87

Shoptalk. N. Goldberg. See issues of Popular Photography through November 1987

Tools & techniques. C. W. Kennedy. See issues of Popular Photography

Tools of the trade. K. Geller-Shinn. See issues of Petersen's Photographic Magazine

What's new in photography. A. Fisher. See alternate issues of Popular Science beginning January 1986

Exhibitions

See Photography—Exhibitions

Maintenance and repair

See also

Camera repairmen

Dry goods: protective gear can keep your equipment safe from the perils of water and sand. E. Stecker. il *Pop Photogr* 94:78-81 Jl '87

Testing

First look. See issues of Popular Photography

Exhibitions

The artistry of Moneta Sleet Jr. il por *Ebony* 42:66-8+ Ja '87

Come on, baby, do the locomotion [work of W. Klein] R. Lacayo. il *Time* 129:78 Mr 9 '87

Gear of the year [PMA Show; special section] il *Pop Photogr* 94:63-73 My '87

Hispanic photography: new traditions [New traditions: thirteen Hispanic photographers] V. G. Stoddart. il *Américas* 39:54-6 Mr/Ap '87

Lovelorn tracts, minced wilderness [work of J. Sternfeld] R. Lacayo. il *Time* 129:84 Ap 20 '87

Photographic masterpieces from a midwestern bank [collection of the Exchange National Bank of Chicago] H. Kahn. il *USA Today (Periodical)* 115:42-53 My '87

Photography [New York City; fall preview] D. Shaw. il *N Y* 20:82+ S 21 '87

Sharper images [Photo Marketing Association Show] S. A. Booth. il *Pop Mech* 164:28+ N '87

Shows we've seen. See issues of Popular Photography through January 1987

Photography—cont.

Exposure

16 F-number formulas. J. Drafahl and S. Drafahl. il *Petersens Photogr Mag* 15:61-2 F '87

Automatic rescue [overriding your autoexposure SLR] B. Hagin. il *Pop Photogr* 94:56-61 Ap '87

Decent exposure: your lightmeter, slide film, and the "sunny f/16" rule. J. Shaw. il *Pop Photogr* 94:30-1 Ag '87

Film exposure and the custom lab: some options. il *Pop Photogr* 94:67 S '87

Hidden images: dissecting bright nebulae. R. Reeves. il *Astronomy* 15:72-5 Mr '87

Motion light traces [time exposure] R. Barnes and T. M. Smith. il *Petersens Photogr Mag* 15:36-7 Mr '87

The perfect film speed: a simple way to do what the zone system does. S. Griswold, Jr. il *Petersens Photogr Mag* 16:54-6 My '87

Slow motion [long exposures let you transform moving subjects into beautiful blurs] E. Stecker. il *Pop Photogr* 94:80-1 N '87

Zone system (I). L. Radeka. il *Petersens Photogr Mag* 16:34-6 Jl '87

Zone system (II). L. Radeka. il *Petersens Photogr Mag* 16:27-9 Ag '87

Films

Adventures in gas hypering. B. Iburg. il *Sky Telesc* 73:110-12 Ja '87

Balancing act [use of tungsten balanced slide film for difficult lighting situations] G. Schaub. il *Pop Photogr* 94:30-7 Mr '87

The color controversy [print vs. slide film] B. Schwalberg and G. Schaub. il *Pop Photogr* 94:45-51 Jl '87

Color crossover [combination of Konica SR-V 3200 color print film and panchromatic paper] R. Hart. il *Pop Photogr* 94:94-5 N '87

Everything you need to know about choosing the right film. C. Begole. il *Glamour* 85:284 Ap '87

Less is more. T. Arruza. il *Pop Photogr* 94:38-43 Ap '87

Negative vision: staying on the reverse side of Vericolor slide film. C. Braendle. il *Petersens Photogr Mag* 16:20-2 O '87

Print film vs slides: which, when? H. Keppler. il *Pop Photogr* 94:84+ O '87

Skyshooting with the fastest color film [Konica SR-V3200] D. Di Cicco. il *Sky Telesc* 74:558-61 N '87

Travel-protect your film [getting film through airport security] W. Hampton. il *Petersens Photogr Mag* 16:24+ O '87

Traveling with color. G. Schaub and B. Schwalberg. il *Pop Photogr* 94:50-3 Ag '87

Vintage New York PolaGraphs [color prints made from high-contrast B&W slides] D. Cook. il *Petersens Photogr Mag* 16:28-30 S '87

Testing

Breaking the speed limit [Konica SR-V 3200] B. Schwalberg. il *Pop Photogr* 94:44-9 S '87

Color slide sampler. G. Schaub. il *Pop Photogr* 94:46-53 My '87

A developing crisis: T-Max processing options. D. Brooks. il *Petersens Photogr Mag* 16:44-6+ D '87

Efke 4x5 sheet film. D. Brooks. il *Petersens Photogr Mag* 16:64-5 Je '87

Fuji joins the 400 club [Neopan 400] B. Schwalberg. il *Pop Photogr* 94:60-5 Je '87

Fuji Neopan 400 professional [black and white film] D. Brooks. il *Petersens Photogr Mag* 16:88-9 N '87

Gang of four [Ektachrome, Agfachrome, Fujichrome and Scotch Color Slide ISO 100 films] G. Schaub. il *Pop Photogr* 94:46-51 O '87

Instant 35 [Polaroid slide films] G. Schaub. il *Pop Photogr* 94:82-4+ N '87

Kodacolor VR-G 100/120: an autoexposure film for 120 shooters. J. Drafahl and S. Drafahl. il *Petersens Photogr Mag* 16:32-3 N '87

Kodak T-Max 4x5 professional film. D. Brooks. il *Petersens Photogr Mag* 16:52-4 S '87

Kodak Vericolor HC professional film. D. Brooks. il *Petersens Photogr Mag* 16:42-3 Ag '87

Konica SR-V3200 [color negative film] B. Hurter. il *Petersens Photogr Mag* 16:80-1 O '87

Medium-format Kodachrome 64 120. D. Brooks. il *Petersens Photogr Mag* 16:64-5 My '87

Polaroid films: High-Contrast Polachrome & PolaBlue in action! J. Drafahl and S. Drafahl. il *Petersens Photogr Mag* 16:24-5 Jl '87

Second coming [Kodacolor VR-G 400 color print film] B. Schwalberg. il *Pop Photogr* 94:92-3 D '87

SR-V 3200: the superfilm from Konica. R. Berry. il *Astronomy* 15:78-83 N '87

Super HR films! [Fujicolor Super HR 200 & 1600] J. Drafahl and S. Drafahl. il *Petersens Photogr Mag* 15:52-3 F '87

Flash equipment

Fine-tuning your electronic flash. il *Pop Photogr* 94:44-5 Ag '87

How to make your own bicycle wheel flash sequencer. il *Petersens Photogr Mag* 16:20 N '87

Testing

Canon Macro Ring Lite ML-2. D. Brooks. il *Petersens Photogr Mag* 15:46-7 Ap '87

Courtenay Computaflash 1000 C. D. Brooks. il *Petersens Photogr Mag* 16:68-9 Ag '87

Nikon autofocus closeup system [SB-21 flash and 55mm macro lens] J. Drafahl and S. Drafahl. il *Petersens Photogr Mag* 16:68-70 Je '87

Norman Superlite 800. G. Lewis. il *Petersens Photogr Mag* 16:48-9 Ag '87

Profoto studio flash. D. Brooks. il *Petersens Photogr Mag* 16:48-9 S '87

PSI Prolites: self-contained studio flash at an affordable price. D. O'Neill. il *Petersens Photogr Mag* 15:74+ Ap '87

Quantum Turbo battery [power pack for electronic flash] G. Lewis. il *Petersens Photogr Mag* 16:32+ D '87

Speedotron Brown Line [flash power generators] D. Brooks. il *Petersens Photogr Mag* 16:70-1 N '87

Starblitz flash. A. Stone. il *Petersens Photogr Mag* 15:64-7 F '87

White Lightning Ultra [studio flash units] D. Brooks. il *Petersens Photogr Mag* 16:78-9+ D '87

Focusing

Autofocus: how to get around problems. H. Keppler. il *Pop Photogr* 94:102+ D '87

Black-dot diffusion helps capture a subject's character [work of G. Heisler] B. Hagin. il por *Pop Photogr* 94:68 D '87

Illusion of sharpness: the way to razor-sharp black-and-white images. S. Griswold, Jr. il *Petersens Photogr Mag* 16:40-2 D '87

Sharpness and long lenses: tips for movers and shakers. C. W. Kennedy. il *Pop Photogr* 94:68-9 Ag '87

Through a lens, softly. il *Pop Photogr* 94:38-45 Mr '87

Grain

Grain and the color negative. il *Pop Photogr* 94:93 N '87

History

See also
Daguerreotypes

Special 50th-anniversary issue. il *Pop Photogr* 94:10+ Ja '87

Time exposure. E. S. Lothrop. See occasional issues of Popular Photography

Interiors

Projecting the past: Lorie Novak portrays memory by projecting slides from her past in empty rooms. S. Piperato. il *Pop Photogr* 94:48-53 Je '87

Landscapes

Golden light. J. Zuckerman. il *Petersens Photogr Mag* 16:52-5 O '87

Light and lighting

See also
Photography—Exposure
Photography—Flash equipment
Photography, Flashlight

Automatic rescue [overriding your autoexposure SLR] B. Hagin. il *Pop Photogr* 94:56-61 Ap '87

Balancing act [use of tungsten balanced slide film for difficult lighting situations] G. Schaub. il *Pop Photogr* 94:30-7 Mr '87

Beauty lighting [cover story] G. Bernstein. il *Petersens Photogr Mag* 16:30-1 Je '87

Boxers, Leicas, and available light. B. Witkowski. il *Petersens Photogr Mag* 16:50-3 D '87

Collins on basics. D. Collins. See occasional issues of Petersen's Photographic Magazine beginning July 1983 through April 1987

Exterior architecture: a study in natural light. L. Bullis. il *Petersens Photogr Mag* 16:32-3 My '87

Golden light. J. Zuckerman. il *Petersens Photogr Mag* 16:52-5 O '87

High contrast. H. Horenstein and E. O'Neil. il *Pop Photogr* 94:56-61 Jl '87

How to carry bright overcast with you. H. Keppler. il *Pop Photogr* 94:108+ N '87

Matthews Survival Kit. D. Brooks. il *Petersens Photogr Mag* 15:62-3 Mr '87

Mola: a new name in beautiful light [reflector] D. Brooks. il *Petersens Photogr Mag* 16:16 Je '87

Painting with light. M. J. Hanzek and C. L. Waddell. il *Petersens Photogr Mag* 16:72-3 D '87

Photography—Light and lighting—*cont.*

Patience makes perfect: waiting for better light. J. Shaw. il *Pop Photogr* 94:32-3 Je '87

Small product lighting: floating a subject on a white background. A. Stone. il *Petersens Photogr Mag* 16:36-7 S '87

Smith-Victor Vari-Flector. D. Brooks. il *Petersens Photogr Mag* 15:60-1 Ja '87

Subjective light: feeling begins where seeing ends. A. Goldsmith. il *Pop Photogr* 94:22 S '87

Thank you for your support: Cora's low-light photo tips. C. W. Kennedy. il *Pop Photogr* 94:24-5 My '87

Traveling light: Jay Maisel's portable Mylar reflector. B. Hagin. il por *Pop Photogr* 94:56-7 N '87

Universal soft-light modifiers. J. A. Dickerson. il *Petersens Photogr Mag* 16:62-6 S '87

Zone VI Cold Light [enlarger light system] D. Brooks. il *Petersens Photogr Mag* 15:33-5 Mr '87

Masking

Miraculous MinitMask. D. Brooks. il *Petersens Photogr Mag* 16:34+ O '87

Negatives

Plastic's fantastic: RC paper internegatives. R. Hart. il *Pop Photogr* 94:44+ D '87

Periodicals

See also

Petersen's photographic magazine

Popular photography (Periodical)

Soviet photo (Periodical)

Perspective

See Perspective

Philosophy

The eternal question: which comes first, technique or art? N. Rothschild. il *Pop Photogr* 94:14 Mr '87

Portraits

See also

Artists, American—Photographs and photography

Black women—Photographs and photography

Celebrities—Photographs and photography

Motion picture actors and actresses—Photographs and photography

Women—Photographs and photography

Arnulf Rainer: self-exposures. D. B. Kuspit. bibl f il pors *Art Am* 75:170-9 Ap '87

Avoiding the weakest link syndrome [post-production finishing phase] G. Bernstein. il *Petersens Photogr Mag* 15:14-15 F '87

Black-dot diffusion helps capture a subject's character [work of G. Heisler] B. Hagin. il por *Pop Photogr* 94:68 D '87

Capturing a subject in action makes a powerful portrait. J. Loengard. il *Pop Photogr* 94:18 O '87

Characters: sparking the joy and finding the eccentricity. A. Bergman. il *Petersens Photogr Mag* 15:44-6 Ja '87

Claudio Edinger: portraiture is a way to understand mankind. S. Piperato. il por *Pop Photogr* 94:40 D '87

Collins on basics. D. Collins. See occasional issues of Petersen's Photographic Magazine beginning July 1983 through April 1987

Coupling. D. Egan. il *Society* 24:78-81 My/Je '87

Environmental portrait. E. A. Johnson. il *Petersens Photogr Mag* 16:62-3 Jl '87

Graphic self-promotion. B. A. DeBrask. il *Petersens Photogr Mag* 15:42-3 F '87

The group is a balanced equation [photographing the cast of Bustin' loose] G. Bernstein. il *Petersens Photogr Mag* 16:10 S '87

How to look perfect in a picture. il *Mademoiselle* 93:64 S '87

If you don't like most pictures of yourself, take time to set things straight—get out your camera and do a self-portrait. C. Begole. il *Glamour* 85:256 Mr '87

In the Hurrell style. M. Raboy. il *Petersens Photogr Mag* 16:20-1 S '87

Into the looking glass [work of J. Hernandez-Claire] S. Piperato. il *Pop Photogr* 94:46-9 Mr '87

Newman's people [work of A. Newman] S. Weiley. il por *Art News* 86:128-34 D '87

Opaque disclosures. M. Kozloff. il *Art Am* 75:144-53+ O '87

Portraiture: when subtlety is the key. G. Bernstein. il *Petersens Photogr Mag* 15:26 Ap '87

The power of profile. T. Gray. il *Petersens Photogr Mag* 16:36-7 Je '87

Quick & easy studio portraiture [photographing Petersen's editors] A. Stone. il *Petersens Photogr Mag* 15:50-3 Mr '87

Printing processes

See Photography—Processing

Processing

See also

Photographic laboratories

Photography—Developing and developers

Slides (Photography)—Processing

Color crossover [combination of Konica SR-V 3200 color print film and panchromatic paper] R. Hart. il *Pop Photogr* 94:94-5 N '87

A flash in the dark [print flashing] J. Dow. il *Pop Photogr* 94:50-5 N '87

A flash of color [print flashing] J. Dow. il *Pop Photogr* 94:94-7 D '87

Going beyond Polaroid: the artful manipulations of Michael Going. F. Cameron. il por *Petersens Photogr Mag* 15:22-4 F '87

Goof-proof your black-and-white film processing (I). C. W. Kennedy. il *Pop Photogr* 94:42+ O '87

Goof-proof your black-and-white film processing (II). C. W. Kennedy. il *Pop Photogr* 94:104 N '87

Personal posterization. R. Zen. il *Petersens Photogr Mag* 16:64-6 D '87

Photodrawings [solarization] R. T. Stephens. il *Petersens Photogr Mag* 15:38-40 Ja '87

Plastic's fantastic: RC paper internegatives. R. Hart. il *Pop Photogr* 94:44+ D '87

Push processing primer. G. Schaub. il *Pop Photogr* 94:66-71 O '87

Shades of color [black-and-white prints from color negatives with panchromatic papers] R. Hart. il *Pop Photogr* 94:88-93 N '87

Soup's on: how black-and-white film is processed. il *Pop Photogr* 94:66 S '87

Spacious sky: double printing makes it always glorious. R. T. Stephens. il *Petersens Photogr Mag* 16:44-6 N '87

Equipment

See also

Photography—Enlargers and enlarging

Slides (Photography)—Processing—Equipment

$18 darkroom chemical balance [scale] T. F. Fuller. il *Petersens Photogr Mag* 16:66-7 Ag '87

Darkroom [PMA Show] R. Hart. il *Pop Photogr* 94:72-3 My '87

Great FX: easy with texture screens. K. Geller-Shinn. il *Petersens Photogr Mag* 16:14 Je '87

How to build a $13 darkroom metronome. T. F. Fuller. il *Petersens Photogr Mag* 16:82-3 My '87

Process your own color film: Beseler's liquid color film & slide processing kits. D. O'Neill. il *Petersens Photogr Mag* 15:56-7 Ja '87

Scientific use

See also

Photomicrography

Self portraits

See Photography—Portraits

Setting and scenery

The background of a shot [photographing J. Leno and P. Morita] G. Bernstein. il pors *Petersens Photogr Mag* 16:20 Jl '87

Graduated backgrounds. M. Neveux and I. Hause. il *Petersens Photogr Mag* 15:60-1 Ap '87

The long and short of it: background and focal length. J. Shaw. il *Pop Photogr* 94:36-7 Jl '87

Still life

The beauty of humble things. P. Paree. il *Petersens Photogr Mag* 16:58-9 My '87

Evoking an era. B. Gammon. il *Petersens Photogr Mag* 15:42-3 Ja '87

Set shots [accessories for still lifes] E. Stecker. il *Pop Photogr* 94:36-9 F '87

Studios and darkrooms

Equipment

See Photography—Processing—Equipment

Leasing and renting

See also

Tekno, Inc.

Study and teaching

Comp book. See issues of Petersen's Photographic Magazine

Fall workshops. L. Nielsen. *Petersens Photogr Mag* 16:55-7+ S '87

Getting the most from a photography workshop. G. Schaub. il *Pop Photogr* 94:101 D '87

Spring workshops. L. Nielsen. *Petersens Photogr Mag* 15:60-1+ Mr '87

Summer workshops. L. Nielsen. *Petersens Photogr Mag* 16:53-8 Je '87

Photography—Study and teaching—*cont.*
Symbol, a single flower: an exercise in point of view by students of photography at Art Center College of Design. B. Hurter. il *Petersens Photogr Mag* 16:36-8 Ag '87
Training your eye [excerpt from Texas photo safaris] G. O. Miller. il *Natl Parks* 61:10-11 S/O '87
Winter workshops. M. Kiwak. il *Petersens Photogr Mag* 16:47-8 D '87
Workshops. C. Rosenthal. See issues of Popular Photography beginning June 1986

             Aids and devices
Instructional video. L. Nielsen. il *Petersens Photogr Mag* 16:57-9 Ag '87

             Terminology
A short course in making sense of photo jargon. N. Goldberg. il *Pop Photogr* 94:70 Ag '87

Photography, Aerial
   See also
     Aerial reconnaissance
     Artificial satellites—Military use
Camera in flight. M. Stensvold. il *Petersens Photogr Mag* 16:26-8+ N '87
Geology from 37,000 feet. H. M. Mogil. il *Earth Sci* 40:20-2 Wint '87

Photography, Architectural
   See also
     Photography—Interiors
Architecture challenges the traveling photographer. C. Purcell. il *Pop Photogr* 94:18 Mr '87
Color forms [work of R. Elmi] B. Hagin. il *Pop Photogr* 94:46-9 F '87
Exterior architecture: a study in natural light. L. Bullis. il *Petersens Photogr Mag* 16:32-3 My '87
Ezra Stoller: the architectural landscape. il *Art News* 86:160-6 N '87
Painting with light. M. J. Hanzek and C. L. Waddell. il *Petersens Photogr Mag* 16:72-3 D '87

             Exhibitions
In Oakland, the architectural photography of Roger Sturtevant. il por *Sunset* 178:34 Ja '87

Photography, Artistic
   See also
     Photography of the nude
Color forms [work of R. Elmi] B. Hagin. il *Pop Photogr* 94:46-9 F '87
Going beyond Polaroid: the artful manipulations of Michael Going. F. Cameron. il por *Petersens Photogr Mag* 15:22-4 F '87
Photodrawings [solarization] R. T. Stephens. il *Petersens Photogr Mag* 15:38-40 Ja '87
Social science fiction [cover story; interview with R. Prince] J. Rian. il *Art Am* 75:86-95 Mr '87
Spring dreams: in pursuit of the idealized image. C. Kunin. il *Petersens Photogr Mag* 16:40-2 My '87

             Exhibitions
Alvin Langdon Coburn [retrospective exhibition at the International Center of Photography] J. Sturman. il *Art News* 86:154+ My '87
Ansel Adams: one with beauty [exhibit at M. H. de Young Memorial Museum] C. D. Long. il *USA Today (Periodical)* 116:56-65 S '87
Art [work of C. Sherman at the Whitney] A. C. Danto. *Nation* 245:134-7 Ag 15-22 '87
Barbara Bloom at Nature Morte. J. Rian. il *Art Am* 75:127-8 Jl '87
Barbara Kasten. E. Heartney. il *Art News* 86:140+ S '87
Candide camera [work of H. Cartier-Bresson] J. Perl. il *Vogue* 177:98 N '87
Cartier-Bresson [Museum of Modern Art exhibitions] J. Loengard. il pors *Life* 10:124-5+ D '87
Cindy Sherman [exhibits at Metro Pictures and the Whitney] M. E. Haus. il *Art News* 86:167-8 O '87
Cindy Sherman at Metro Pictures and the Whitney Museum. S. Tillim. il *Art Am* 75:162-3 D '87
Drunk on a world served straight [work of H. Cartier-Bresson] R. Lacayo. il *Time* 130:88 O 12 '87
Edward Weston [traveling exhibit entitled Supreme instants: the photography of Edward Weston] G. Morris. il *Art News* 86:37 Ap '87
Ellen Carey at ICP and Simon Cerigo. S. Westfall. il *Art Am* 75:181 N '87
Georges Rousse at Farideh Cadot. E. Heartney. *Art Am* 75:130 Ja '87
Henri Cartier-Bresson. R. B. Woodward. il *Art News* 86:200+ N '87
Henri Cartier-Bresson [exhibit at the Museum of Modern Art] A. C. Danto. *Nation* 245:346-8 O 3 '87
Jan Groover: melancholy modernist. M. Kozloff. il *Art Am* 75:144-7 Je '87

A master with a double image [H. Cartier-Bresson] D. Davis. il *Newsweek* 110:78 S 21 '87
Photo forecast [Future of photography at the Corcoran] M. Power. il *Art Am* 75:47+ D '87
Photography [A. Kertesz] V. Goldberg. il *N Y* 20:80-1 S 21 '87
Photography becomes art [Photography and art: interactions since 1946] R. Atkins. il *Horizon* 30:38-40 Je '87
Portraits by the artist as a young man [H. Cartier-Bresson] G. James. il *Macleans* 100:62+ N 9 '87
Remnants of authenticity [International Center of Photography show of contemporary German photographers] M. E. Haus. il *Art News* 86:186 O '87
Supreme instants: photography of Edward Weston. T. Pitts and N. Solomon. il por *USA Today (Periodical)* 116:56-65 N '87
Who's that girl? [work of C. Sherman at the Whitney] K. Larson. il por *N Y* 20:52-3 Ag 3 '87

Photography, Close-up
   See also
     Macrophotography
Close encounters: magnifying images with a teleconverter. N. Rothschild. il *Pop Photogr* 94:16 Ap '87
You don't have to be that close to shoot closeups. J. Shaw. il *Pop Photogr* 94:56 D '87

Photography, Cold weather *See* Photography—Cold weather conditions

Photography, Commercial
   See also
     Photography, Fashion
     Photography, Journalistic
     Photography as a profession
Pro talk. G. Bernstein. See issues of Petersen's Photographic Magazine

Photography, Composite *See* Photomontage

Photography, Documentary
             Exhibitions
Outside report: Robert Frank [traveling retrospective entitled Robert Frank from New York to Nova Scotia] R. Silberman. il *Art Am* 75:130-9 F '87
             History
Street photography with almost-instant cameras. E. S. Lothrop. il *Pop Photogr* 94:58 D '87

Photography, Fashion
Bathing beauties on the beach & in the studio [cover story] J. Britt. il *Petersens Photogr Mag* 16:16-19+ Jl '87
Beauty and the bubbly [photographing J. Harry for Black elegance layout] G. Bernstein. il por *Petersens Photogr Mag* 16:24 N '87
Beauty sells. G. Bernstein. il *Petersens Photogr Mag* 15:12 Mr '87
Fashion plus personality [photographing J. Harry for Black elegance layout] G. Bernstein. il pors *Petersens Photogr Mag* 16:18 My '87
Flash with daylight [shooting a fashion layout for Black elegance magazine] G. Bernstein. il *Petersens Photogr Mag* 16:28 O '87
Picture perfectionist: my life as a photographer. F. Scavullo. il por *Saturday Evening Post* 259:50-3+ My/Je '87

Photography, Flashlight
"Doc" Edgerton: the man who made time stand still. E. Zwingle. il pors *Natl Geogr* 172:464-83 O '87
Flash with daylight [shooting a fashion layout for Black elegance magazine] G. Bernstein. il *Petersens Photogr Mag* 16:28 O '87
Painting with flash. D. Ferguson. il *Petersens Photogr Mag* 16:72-3 My '87
Rainbow strobo: a tribute to Ben Rose. D. Brooks. il *Petersens Photogr Mag* 16:16-20+ N '87
Second sun [use of electronic fill flash outdoors] G. Schaub. il *Pop Photogr* 94:42-4+ Ag '87
             Equipment
   See Photography—Flash equipment

Photography, High speed
   See also
     Photography of moving objects
"Doc" Edgerton: the man who made time stand still. E. Zwingle. il pors *Natl Geogr* 172:464-83 O '87
Split seconds [excerpt from Split second] S. Dalton. il *Read Dig* 131:155-61 Ag '87

Photography, Humorous
Onomatopoeias: the wily photo pun strikes again! H. Werran. il *Petersens Photogr Mag* 16:40-2 N '87
Playful plagiarism: imitating art with Alan Bergman. B. Hurter. il por *Petersens Photogr Mag* 15:44-9 F '87

Photography, Industrial *See* Photography in industry

Photography, Journalistic

And let us not forget [with introd. by Nadine Gordimer] il *Esquire* 108:229-35 D '87

At 72, John Phillips looks at today's "super press". H. Chapnick. il por *Pop Photogr* 94:37 N '87

Eyes behind the camera, then and now [interviews with H. Cartier-Bresson and G. Peress] M. Horn. il *U S News World Rep* 103:88-9 N 9 '87

Flip Schulke's philosophy forms his photographic style. H. Chapnick. il por *Pop Photogr* 94:28 Je '87

Getting the scoop on careers in photojournalism [fourth grade project at John S. Clarke Elementary Center, Pottsville, Pa.] G. Schaub. il *Pop Photogr* 94:26 Je '87

Hal Buell leads the Associated Press into the future. H. Chapnick. il por *Pop Photogr* 94:40 Jl '87

Making it as a free-lance writer-photographer. R. Tolley. il *Petersens Photogr Mag* 15:51-3 Ja '87

Talking pictures [excerpts from Pictures under discussion] J. Loengard. il *Life* 10:71-2+ My '87

The unflinching eye [M. E. Mark; cover story] V. Goldberg. il pors *N Y Times Mag* p12-18+ Jl 12 '87

The winners [Life's Contest for Young Photographers] il *Life* 10:51-6+ N '87

Exhibitions

The Cultural Center [Robert Capa: a retrospective, 1932-1954] il por *Antiques Collect Hobbies* 92:54-5 S '87

Photojournalism's colorful era [exhibition at the International Center of Photography] il *N Y Times Mag* p32-7 Mr 1 '87

History

American photojournalism: highlights of an evolution. H. Chapnick. il *Pop Photogr* 94:76-7 Ja '87

Photography, Medical
See also
Radiography, Medical

Photography, Meteorological *See* Meteorological photography

Photography, Military
See also
Aerial reconnaissance
Artificial satellites—Military use

Photography, Night

Night photography and in-camera special effects. M. Stensvold. il *Petersens Photogr Mag* 16:41+ Jl '87

Photography, Panoramic

360° panorama assemblages [interview with B. Fowler] F. Cameron. il *Petersens Photogr Mag* 15:22-5 Mr '87

Photography, Pinhole

Barbara Ess: the mind's eye. M. E. Haus. il *Art News* 86:119-20+ N '87

A gamma-ray pinhole camera. W. J. Wild. il *Sky Telesc* 74:126-7 Ag '87

Photography, Submarine

Adirondacks underwater [photographing acid-killed lakes] A. LaBastille. il por *Conservationist* 42:12-15 Jl/Ag '87

Chasing rainbows in the sea. C. Newbert. il por *Natl Wildl* 25:52-9 F/Mr '87

A portfolio of photography contest winners. il *Sea Front* 33:273-9 Jl/Ag '87

Photography, Surrealistic *See* Surrealism

Photography, Trick

Airbrushing your photos. M. Bright and D. Bright. il *Petersens Photogr Mag* 15:38-41 Ap '87

Grouper steals the show! A special-effects system incorporates 16 images on just one slide! J. Drafahl and S. Drafahl. il *Petersens Photogr Mag* 15:42-4 Mr '87

Night photography and in-camera special effects. M. Stensvold. il *Petersens Photogr Mag* 16:41+ Jl '87

Rainbow strobo: a tribute to Ben Rose. D. Brooks. il *Petersens Photogr Mag* 16:16-20+ N '87

Photography and art *See* Art and photography

Photography as a profession

Beyond Blow-up: career opportunities in the photo industry. G. Schaub. il *Pop Photogr* 94:36+ Ag '87

Markets & careers. H. Chapnick. See issues of Popular Photography through January 1987

Markets & careers. G. Schaub. See issues of Popular Photography beginning February 1987

Photography galleries and museums
California
See also
California Museum of Photography
Museum of Photographic Arts (San Diego, Calif.)
San Francisco (Calif.)—Galleries and museums
Massachusetts
See also
Naylor Museum of Photography

New York (State)
See also
International Museum of Photography at George Eastman House

Photography in archeology
See also
Antiquities—Photographs and photography

Photography in industry

Annual report illustration. M. Olson. il *Petersens Photogr Mag* 16:70-1 S '87

Work dramatization. T. Strand. il *Petersens Photogr Mag* 16:66-7 Je '87

Photography models *See* Models (Persons)

Photography of moving objects
See also
Fireworks—Photographs and photography

Motion light traces [time exposure] R. Barnes and T. M. Smith. il *Petersens Photogr Mag* 15:36-7 Mr '87

Pan & zoom. P. Utz. il *Pop Photogr* 94:68-9 Ja '87

Slow motion [long exposures let you transform moving subjects into beautiful blurs] E. Stecker. il *Pop Photogr* 94:80-1 N '87

Photography of the nude

Some of her parts. A. MacWeeney. il *Esquire* 107:200-3 Je '87

Why would a woman peel off her clothes and pose nude for Playboy? Three women tell their stories. S. Helgesen. il *Glamour* 85:218-19+ Je '87

Photography trade *See* Photographs—Marketing

Photojournalism *See* Photography, Journalistic

Photolithography
See also
Electron beam lithography

Photomacrography *See* Macrophotography

Photometers and photometry

SMT project: light meter [surface mount technology] F. M. Mims. il *Radio-Electron* 58:75-6+ N '87

Photometry, Astronomical

The wandering stars of Allegheny [addition of Multichannel Astrometric Photometer to 30-inch Thaw refractor; cover story] R. W. Sinnott. il *Sky Telesc* 74:360-3 O '87

Photomicrography

Botanical close encounters. G. W. Verderber. il *Conservationist* 42:40-3 N/D '87

Little drop of horrors [life in a drop of pond water; work of A. Rakosy] H. Wouk. il *Omni* 10:84-9 N '87

Photomontage

360° panorama assemblages [interview with B. Fowler] F. Cameron. il *Petersens Photogr Mag* 15:22-5 Mr '87

Drawing with a camera [work of D. Hockney] S. Piperato. il por *Pop Photogr* 94:50-5 S '87

Free-standing photo collages. K. Geller-Shinn. il *Petersens Photogr Mag* 16:14 O '87

Photometrics. M. Fay. bibl il *Petersens Photogr Mag* 16:26+ Je '87

Photomurals *See* Photographic murals

Photons
See also
Exciton theory

The impossible dream [excited rubidium atom in resonant cavity; work of Gerhard Rempe and others] *Sci Am* 256:25 Je '87

Photoperiodism

Lens crystallins may be moonlighting [determination of nucleotide sequence for mole rat crystallin gene; work of Wiljan Hendriks and others] *Sci News* 132:104 Ag 15 '87

Photopheresis

Exposing cancer to a 'light' therapy [cutaneous T-cell lymphoma] J. Silberner. *Sci News* 131:101 F 14 '87

Let there be light [photopheresis to treat cutaneous T-cell lymphoma] R. Boling. *Health* 19:24 Je '87

New clues to the immune system [photopheresis treatment of lymphatic cancer and immunologic function of skin] S. Squire. il por *N Y Times Mag* p32-3+ F 1 '87

Photopolarimeters *See* Polariscopes

Photoreceptor cells *See* Rods and cones

Photoreceptors

Developmental control gene sequenced [fruit flies; work of Gerald Rubin and others] J. L. Marx. *Science* 236:26-7 Ap 3 '87

Sevenless, a cell-specific homeotic gene of Drosophila, encodes a putative transmembrane receptor with a tyrosine kinase domain. E. Hafen and others. bibl f il *Science* 236:55-63 Ap 3 '87

Photosensitization *See* Light—Physiological effects
Photosynthesis
See also
Chloroplasts
Carbon gain by plants in natural environments. R. W. Pearcy and others. bibl f il *BioScience* 37:21-9 Ja '87
Diel periodicity of photosynthesis in polar phytoplankton: influence on primary production. R. B. Rivkin and M. Putt. bibl f il *Science* 238:1285-8 N 27 '87
Keys to help unlock photosynthesis. J. Raloff. *Sci News* 131:168 Mr 14 '87
Molecular mechanisms of photosynthesis [study of rhodo-pseudomonas; cover story] D. C. Youvan and B. L. Marrs. bibl (p136) il *Sci Am* 256:42-8 Je '87
New light on seaweeds [role of light harvesting pigments in depth zonation of seaweeds; cover story] M. B. Saffo. bibl il *BioScience* 37:654-64 O '87
Solar-powered animals [aeolid nudibranchs growing zoox-anthellae inside their bodies; cover story] W. B. Rudman. il *Nat Hist* 96:50-3 O '87
Phototherapy
See also
Photopheresis
Seasonal affective disorder—Therapy
Photovoltaics *See* Solar cells
Phrasebooks
Useful Zulu phrases [managing servants in South Africa] L. Freed. il *Harpers* 274:26-8 My '87
Phrases *See* English language—Terms and phrases
Phycoerythrins
New light on seaweeds [role of light harvesting pigments in depth zonation of seaweeds; cover story] M. B. Saffo. bibl il *BioScience* 37:654-64 O '87
Phyfe, Duncan, 1768-1854
about
American furniture. S. B. Sherrill. il *Antiques* 131:1176+ Je '87
A Duncan Phyfe bill and the furniture it documents. J. V. Sloane. bibl f il *Antiques* 131:1106-13 My '87
Phyllo pastry *See* Pastry
Phylogeny
See also
Cladistic analysis
Homology (Biology)
The ancestry of the giant panda [molecular analysis; cover story] S. J. O'Brien. il map *Sci Am* 257:102-7 N '87
Freud's phylogenetic fantasy. S. J. Gould. *Nat Hist* 96:10+ D '87
Hominid evolution: a tale of two trees. B. Bower. il *Sci News* 132:7 Jl 4 '87
My close cousin the chimpanzee. R. Lewin. il *Science* 238:273-5 O 16 '87
Phylogenetic relations of humans and African apes from DNA sequences in the ψη-globin region. M. M. Miyamoto and others. bibl f il *Science* 238:369-73 O 16 '87
Phymatids *See* Ambush bugs
Physical astronomy *See* Astrophysics
Physical constants
See also
Hubble constant
Borehole measurement of the Newtonian gravitational constant. A. T. Hsui. bibl f il map *Science* 237:881-3 Ag 21 '87
Changing constants: measuring progress. I. Peterson. il *Sci News* 131:104 F 14 '87
The fundamental physical constants. E. R. Cohen and B. N. Taylor. bibl il *Phys Today* 40 pt2:BG11-BG15 Ag '87
Values of fundamental constants adjusted. A. L. Robinson. *Science* 235:633-4 F 6 '87
Physical education and training
See also
Cincinnati Academy of Physical Education
Making a difference [work of J. Pyfer with children with motor problems] D. Young. il pors *South Living* 22:98+ Je '87
Physical equipment
Fourth annual Physics today buyers' guide [with editorial comment by Robert N. Ubell] il *Phys Today* 40 pt2:BG3+ Ag '87
New products. See issues of Physics Today
Nuclear instruments. *Science* 235 pt2:G159-G161 F 27 '87
Physical examinations
See also
Gynecologic examinations
Bogus health tests. P. L. Spencer. *Consum Res Mag* 70:2 Mr '87

Physical exercise *See* Exercise
Physical fitness
See also
Aged—Care and hygiene
Black entertainers—Health and hygiene
Celebrities—Health and hygiene
Children—Care and hygiene
Endurance
Exercise
Health clubs
Hunters—Health and hygiene
Industry—Physical fitness programs
Muscle strength
PaVage Fitness Innovations (Firm)
Physical education and training
U.S. Fitness Academy
Vitality
Young women—Health and hygiene
Youth—Health and hygiene
1987 winter body shop [special section] il *Health* 19:25-7+ Ja '87
The American way of fitness [special issue; with editorial comment by Judith Daniels] il *Life* 10:4, 22-31+ F '87
Body basics. See issues of 'Teen beginning November 1987
Body be beautiful (I) [special section] il *Good Housekeep* 204:79+ My '87
Body be beautiful (II) [special section] il *Good Housekeep* 205:79-80+ O '87
Can you be fit without being healthy? D. Pine. il *Women's Sports Fitness* 9:34-7 Je '87
Fitness now. See issues of Vogue
He made the climb to fitness [S. Silva going for vertical mile record] il por *Sports Illus* 67:20 O 5 '87
Nutrition/fitness. D. W. Hatfield. See issues of McCall's beginning March 1986
The price you'll pay to sweat [special section] il *Changing Times* 41:38-44+ Ag '87
The rebuilding of Remar Sutton. A. Toufexis. pors *Time* 129:72 Ap 6 '87
Shape-up. L. Gordon. See issues of Glamour
Sports clinic. See issues of Esquire
Super-fit climber Steve Silva is a new man since first he chose to aim for the stairs [attempt to set vertical mile record] il pors *People Wkly* 28:147-8 N 2 '87
Ultimate fitness [cover story; special section] il *Esquire* 107:113-16+ My '87
What's news: nutrition, diet, fitness. See occasional issues of Good Housekeeping beginning May 1985
Yeah, but can he keep it off? [R. Sutton] B. Barol. pors *Newsweek* 109:70 Ap 27 '87
Your healthy body now: what hurts, what helps, what works. il *Glamour* 85:180-1 Ja '87
Bibliography
A roundup of fitness guides. S. Kiesling. il *50 Plus* 27:66-7 Ja '87
Testing
A-plus in fitness [Fitnessgram developed by the Institute for Aerobics Research] D. Zevin. il *Health* 19:18 Ap '87
Are your muscles old before their time? [excerpt from Dr. Nagler's Body maintenance and repair book] W. Nagler. il *Women's Sports Fitness* 9:68 Ap '87
The body test [women] L. Villarosa. il *Mademoiselle* 93:100 Je '87
Do-it-yourself test for cardiovascular fitness. B. Weinhouse. il *Ladies Home J* 104:58 Je '87
How fit—heart. K. McCleary. il *Good Housekeep* 204:90 My '87
How fit—muscles. il *Good Housekeep* 204:92 My '87
Rate your shape [women] J. Jones. il *Redbook* 168:88-93 F '87
Test yourself [women] K. Delhagen. il *Women's Sports Fitness* 9:32-6+ Ja '87
What kind of shape are you in? [quiz] il *Teen* 31:30 S '87
Physical fitness cruises *See* Cruising
Physical geography
See also
Climate
Islands
Volcanoes
Physical restraint of patients *See* Restraint of patients
Physical therapy
See also
Healthsouth (Firm)
Massage

Physically handicapped *See* Handicapped

Physicians

> *See also*
>
> AIDS (Disease) and physicians
> American Medical Association
> Black physicians
> Drugs and physicians
> Group medical practice
> International Physicians for the Prevention of Nuclear War
> Interns (Medicine)
> Medical care
> Medicine
> Pediatricians
> Surgeons
> Women physicians
> > *See also* names of physicians

The guinea pig closest at hand [researchers experiment on themselves] il *U S News World Rep* 103:58-9 Jl 13 '87

House calls 2000 [family doctors] M. J. Slocum. *Omni* 9:27 Jl '87

It's fever time for doctors. C. P. Work. il *U S News World Rep* 102:44-6 Ja 26 '87

Anecdotes, facetiae, satire, etc.

Confessions of an M.D. O. London. il *Saturday Evening Post* 259:46-9+ O '87

Attitudes

Ageism is bad medicine. B. Lindeman. il *50 Plus* 27:4 Ja '87

Fees

See Medical care—Costs

Licenses

A fair share [N.Y. divorce ruling holds M. O'Brien's medical license to be form of property]; ed. by Micki Siegel. R. Maloney. il por *Good Housekeep* 205:54+ N '87

Quackus tyrannus. R. Greene. il *Forbes* 140:67 O 5 '87

Malpractice

See Malpractice

Pharmaceutical services

Doctor drugs. J. W. Merline. il *Consum Res Mag* 70:38 Jl '87

Drug money [Direct Pharmaceutical Corp.] J. Wynn. il por *Forbes* 139:254 Je 15 '87

Now, one-stop medicine? J. Schwartz. il *Newsweek* 109:32-3 My 25 '87

One-stop medicine. T. Beardsley. *Sci Am* 257:34 N '87

Professional ethics

See Medical ethics

Psychology

Cutting too close to the bone [physicians' reactions to patients who mirror their own lives] P. Klass. il *Discover* 8:26+ S '87

A degree of detachment [physician and cancer patient] B. Shragg. il *N Y Times Mag* p48 Jl 26 '87

Supply and demand

Great expectations [health manpower out of balance; cover story; special issue] il *World Health* p3-29 Ap '87

Med schools learn humility [fewer applications] J. N. Baker. il *Newsweek* 109:61-2 Je 29 '87

The outcasts from the Caribbean [offshore medical school graduates] J. Langone. il *Discover* 8:68-70+ Je '87

Physicians, Handicapped

First Andres Vasquez learned about pain, suffering and patience; then he became a doctor. J. Calio. il pors *People Wkly* 28:73-4 Ag 17 '87

Physicians and patients

> *See also*
>
> Gynecologists and patients
> Physical examinations

Be the kind of patient a doctor loves to help. *Glamour* 85:46 Ja '87

The crisis of overtreatment: doctors protect themselves; so should you. *Glamour* 85:92 Mr '87

Cutting too close to the bone [physicians' reactions to patients who mirror their own lives] P. Klass. il *Discover* 8:26+ S '87

A degree of detachment [physician and cancer patient] B. Shragg. il *N Y Times Mag* p48 Jl 26 '87

Doctor search. M. S. Dolan. *Consum Res Mag* 70:2 S '87

"Don't worry!" [daughter's bout with bronchiectasis] A. R. Roiphe. il por *McCalls* 114:58-60 Ja '87

How to pick a good family doctor. P. Krantz. il *Better Homes Gard* 65:80 N '87

Knowing when to call the doctor [sizing up symptoms; study by George D. Bishop] A. H. Rosenfeld. il *Psychol Today* 21:12 O '87

My father is my patient. Z. Rosen. il *Newsweek* 109:10-11 Mr 30 '87

The new doctors [learning compassion] A. B. Eagan. il *Health* 19:25-9+ Ap '87

No patience for elder patients [ageism among physicians; study by Michele G. Greene] M. Schanback. il *Psychol Today* 21:22 F '87

Patient knows best [predicting heart attack recovery; study by Dan Bar-On] M. Roberts. *Psychol Today* 21:10 Je '87

Patients. M. L. Magie. *Commentary* 83:48-52 F '87

Questions about your medicine? Go ahead—ask. F. E. Young. il *FDA Consum* 21:2-3 O '87

When the doctor-patient relationship breaks down. P. Klass. il *Discover* 8:16+ Mr '87

Anecdotes, facetiae, satire, etc.

Just be patient. A. W. Hoppe. il *Read Dig* 130:139-40 Je '87

Physicians as artists

Art for the outdoorsman [work of A. Hughes] H. Middleton. il por *South Living* 22:100+ Je '87

Physicians' liability insurance *See* Insurance, Malpractice liability

Physicians' offices

Life and work at the same address [C. Koblenzer] F. Greenberg. il por *Work Woman* 12:92-3 Ap '87

Office tests for doctors. R. Simon. il *Forbes* 139 Ann Directory:90+ Ap 27 '87

Physicists

> *See also*
>
> Einstein, Albert, 1879-1955
> Forrester, A. Theodore
> Forward, Robert L.
> Hawking, S. W. (Stephen W.)
> Moore, Arnold R.
> Newton, Sir Isaac, 1642-1727
> Szilard, Leo
> Weyland, Jack
> Witten, E.
> Wuensch, Walter
> Zumino, Bruno

The life it brings (I). J. Bernstein. *New Yorker* 62:35-8+ Ja 26 '87

The life it brings (II). J. Bernstein. *New Yorker* 62:39-42+ F 2 '87

Nyaah-nyaah [solid state physicists vs. particle physicists] C. C. Mann. *Omni* 9:27 S '87

The physics community. See issues of Physics Today

We hear that. See issues of Physics Today

Political activities

See Scientists—Political activities

Professional ethics

APS Council adopts statement on integrity in physics. *Phys Today* 40:81 Je '87

Supply and demand

Advice on applying for a postdoc. P. W. Anderson. por *Phys Today* 40:7+ S '87

Enrollments and degrees survey is available. il *Phys Today* 40:86 N '87

Survey of physics bachelors finds that more plan to teach. *Phys Today* 40:76 S '87

Physics

> *See also*
>
> Acoustical Society of America
> American Institute of Physics
> American Physical Society
> American Vacuum Society
> Astrophysics
> Computers—Physics use
> Dynamics
> Electricity
> Entropy
> Field theory (Physics)
> Fifth force (Physics)
> Fluid dynamics
> Fluids
> Gases
> Geophysics
> Gravity and gravitation
> Lasers—Physics use
> Light
> Magnetism
> Mass (Physics)
> Mathematical physics
> Matter
> Medical physics
> Nuclear physics
> Quantum theory
> Relativity (Physics)
> Sixth force (Physics)
> Sound

Physics—See also—*cont.*

Space stations—Physics use
Statistical mechanics
Symmetry (Physics)
Thermodynamics
Tomography—Physics use
Vibration
Viscosity

Physics, Hollywood style [J. Weyland, physicist who critiques science fiction films] B. Lawren. *Omni* 9:35 Je '87

Awards

See also

Ernest Orlando Lawrence Memorial Awards
Ewald Prize
Gemant Award
International Physics Olympiad
Wolf prizes

Acoustical Society of America 1986 awards. il *Phys Today* 40:99-101 Ap '87

Bruno Zumino and Bryce Dewitt receive Dirac medals. pors *Phys Today* 40:111 N '87

Four Canadian physicists honored in 1986-87. *Phys Today* 40:96 S '87

Franklin Institute honors eight physicists. il *Phys Today* 40:101-2+ Ap '87

Franklin Institute honors seven physicists with 1987 awards. il *Phys Today* 40:139-40 O '87

Gürsey receives Wigner Medal for symmetry work. por *Phys Today* 40:89 Ja '87

Hwa is the recipient of the 1986 Apker Award. il por *Phys Today* 40:95 Ja '87

ICTP honors four with Dirac Medals. il *Phys Today* 40:107-8 My '87

NSF honors Rabi and Witten, names Young Investigators [Vannevar Bush and Alan T. Waterman Awards] il *Phys Today* 40:95-6 S '87

OSA honored eleven in 1986. il *Phys Today* 40 pt1:82-4 Ag '87

Pegram and Beams awards presented. il *Phys Today* 40:108-9 My '87

Spinrad receives Heineman Prize for Astrophysics. por *Phys Today* 40:123 F '87

Templetons honored for work in crystallography. il pors *Phys Today* 40:83 Jl '87

Three receive APS plasma physics awards. il *Phys Today* 40:85-6 Mr '87

Wong and Yeh win 1987 Apker Award for achievements as undergraduates. *Phys Today* 40:103 D '87

Bibliography

Books. See issues of Physics Today

Conferences

See also

American Physical Society—Meetings
Calendar. See alternate issues of Physics Today

Equipment

See Physical equipment

Experiments

The amateur scientist. J. Walker. See issues of Scientific American

Federal aid

ERAB sets priorities for Energy Department's physics research. M. Crawford. *Science* 235:1317 Mr 13 '87

History

Centennial of the Michelson-Morley experiment [cover story; special issue] bibl f il pors *Phys Today* 40:23-30+ My '87

Museums mark tercentenary of Newton's Principia. R. Hart. *Phys Today* 40:78 D '87

Newton's Principia: a retrospective. G. E. Christianson. il por *Sky Telesc* 74:18-20 Jl '87

Physics centennial [1887 Michelson-Morley experiment] T. H. Cole. il *Pop Mech* 164:56 Jl '87

International aspects

See also

American Physical Society. International Physics Group
International Union of Pure and Applied Physics

Council adopts statement on US-Soviet scientific cooperation [American Physical Society] *Phys Today* 40:121 F '87

Periodicals

See also

Computers in physics (Periodical)

Philosophy

On complexity. L. P. Kadanoff. il por *Phys Today* 40:7+ Mr '87

Research

See also

Franklin Institute (Philadelphia, Pa.)
Institute for Theoretical Physics (Minn.)

Physics news in 1986 [special section] P. F. Schewe. il *Phys Today* 40:S1-S70 Ja '87

Search & discovery. See issues of Physics Today

Ethical aspects

How to win a Nobel Prize [G. Taubes' book criticizing methods of C. Rubbia] M. D. Lemonick. il por *Time* 129:55 F 9 '87

Federal aid

See Physics—Federal aid

Study and teaching

Education projects look at introductory courses. W. Sweet. il *Phys Today* 40:107-8+ O '87

Enrollments and degrees survey is available. il *Phys Today* 40:86 N '87

High-school students make $YBa_2Cu_3O_{7-x}$ [Gilroy, Calif. class produces superconducting material] W. Sweet. il *Phys Today* 40:111-12 O '87

New approaches to introductory physics. D. F. Holcomb and others. *Phys Today* 40:87 My '87

A physicist objects [C. Schwartz stops teaching classes in higher physics at Berkeley] J. J. Neuburger. il por *Progressive* 51:12-13 Jl '87

Physics education. *Phys Today* 40:S56-S58 Ja '87

The PSSC course in retrospect [discussion of September 1986 article, Setting new directions in physics teaching: PSSC thirty years later] A. P. French. *Phys Today* 40:11+ Ap '87

Summer intern program places students in industry. il *Phys Today* 40:93 S '87

Watkins starts work as AIP senior education fellow. por *Phys Today* 40:85 N '87

Textbooks

Books [college texts] A. P. French. bibl *Phys Today* 40:98+ N '87

Canada

See also

Canadian Institute for Theoretical Astrophysics

Germany

Einstein and Germany [discussion of February 1986 article] F. R. Stern. *Phys Today* 40:15+ Jl '87

Great Britain

Physics and psychics [discussion of May 1986 article, Physics and psychic research in Victorian and Edwardian England] J. Oppenheim. *Phys Today* 40:144-5 My '87

Japan

Physics in Japan [cover story; special issue] il *Phys Today* 40:25-33+ D '87

Physics, Japan and US competitiveness. G. E. Pake. por *Phys Today* 40:9+ D '87

Netherlands

Life in the Kamerlingh Onnes lab. L. I. Dana. *Phys Today* 40:42 Ap '87

Soviet Union

Glasnost comes to Soviet physics [misdirection of high-pressure physics research] A. L. Robinson. il *Science* 236:671-2 My 8 '87

Western Europe

See also

European Organization for Nuclear Research

Physics and state *See* Science and state

Physics students

See also

International Physics Olympiad

Physics teachers

See also

American Association of Physics Teachers

Physiognomy

See also

Facial expression

Physiological oxidation *See* Oxidation, Physiological

Physiology

See also

Absorption (Physiology)
Body, Human
Digestion
Electrophysiology
Flexibility (Physiology)
Growth
Obesity
Respiration
Senses and sensation
Stretch (Physiology)
Temperature, Animal and human
Weight (Physiology)
Women—Anatomy and physiology
See also subheads Physiological aspects; Physiological effects under various subjects

Physiology—*cont.*

Study and teaching
Aids and devices
Acid-base balance: an educational computer game. J. Boyle and G. Robinson. il *BioScience* 37:511-13 Jl/Ag '87

Physiology, Comparative
See also
Body size
Phytopathogenic fungi *See* Fungi, Pathogenic
Phytoplankton *See* Plankton
Pi
Pi wars: dueling supercomputers [work of Peter and Jonathan Borwein] I. Peterson. *Sci News* 131:118 F 21 '87
Piaggio (Rinaldo) (Firm) *See* Rinaldo Piaggio (Firm)
Pialat, Maurice
about
Police [film] Reviews
Time 129:72 Ja 19 '87. R. Corliss
Pianists
See also
Ashkenazy, Vladimir
Brendel, Alfred
Buechner, David
Butler, Henry
Cerovsek, Katja
Ciccolini, Aldo
Cliburn, Van, 1934-
Davidovich, Bella
Edelmann, Sergei
Feinstein, Michael
Feltsman, Vladimir
Gavrilov, Andrei
Gould, Glenn, 1932-1982
Hinderas, Natalie, 1927-1987
Horowitz, Vladimir, 1904-
Horszowski, Mieczyslaw
Istomin, Eugene, 1925-
Jarvis, John
Kocsis, Zoltán, 1952-
Liberace, 1919-1987
Licad, Cecile
Loh, Sandra Tsing
Norris, Walter
Oppens, Ursula
Pekinel, Güher
Pekinel, Süher
Pollini, Maurizio
Powell, Mel, 1923-
Rogé, Pascal, 1951-
Rosser, Eric
Ruiz, Hilton
Schnabel, Artur, 1882-1951
Serkin, Peter
Shearing, George
Solzhenitsyn, Ignat
Toradze, Alexander
Uchida, Mitsuko
Vakarelis, Janis
Watts, André, 1946-
Weiss, Michael
Weston, Randy
Pianists, Handicapped
Blind boy, 3, learns to play 50 songs on piano [J. Gardner] D. M. Cheers. il pors *Jet* 72:22-3 My 25 '87
Blind piano player, 3, visits Stevie Wonder [J. Gardner] il pors *Jet* 72:18 Je 22 '87
Blind piano prodigy, age 4, gets free facial surgery [J. Gardner] il por *Jet* 72:24 S 14 '87
Blind since birth and barely 4, Jermaine Gardner happily hits all the right keys—and heartstrings. K. Hubbard. il pors *People Wkly* 27:53+ Je 22 '87
For two New Jersey grannies misfortune sets the stage for a musical collaboration [stroke victims M. Patrick and R. Eisenberg] il pors *People Wkly* 28:121 D 14 '87
Piano
See also
Harpsichord
In tune with the right piano [excerpt from The piano book; cover story] L. Fine. il *Consum Res Mag* 70:11-15 S '87

Maintenance and repair
Piano man [restorer H. A. Buchman] I. Ross. il por *N Y* 20:24 Jl 13 '87

Piano industry
History
When the music in our parlors brought death to darkest Africa [19th century use of ivory for piano keys] R. Conniff. il *Audubon* 89:76-93 Jl '87
Piano music
See also
Compact discs—Piano music
Phonograph records—Piano music
Tape recordings—Piano music
Videotapes—Piano music
La Monte Young's minimalist marathon [The well-tuned piano] A. Rich. *Newsweek* 110:58 Jl 27 '87
Steve Winwood's solo on Empty pages—an electric piano transcription. J. T. Cohen. il *Down Beat* 54:60-1 Ag '87
Piatigorsky, Joram
(jt. auth) See Wistow, Graeme, and Piatigorsky, Joram
Pica (Pathology)
Anecdotes, facetiae, satire, etc.
My geophagy problem—and yours. R. Blount. il *Atlantic* 260:46-7 N '87
Picante sauce *See* Sauces
Picasso, Jacqueline
about
Jacqueline Picasso and me: the widow-of-the-great-man syndrome. J. T. Steichen. il por *Ms* 15:76 Mr '87
Picasso, Pablo, 1881-1973
about
For an impatient sitter, Picasso à la mode. il *Art News* 86:198 Ja '87
'My angel . . . I love you in every color'. K. Ames. il por *Newsweek* 110:86 S 28 '87
Picasso gets a hit. J. Yood. il *Art News* 86:16 N '87
Picasso's apocalyptic whorehouse. J. Richardson. bibl f il *N Y Rev Books* 34:40-7 Ap 23 '87
Picasso's motif. J. Gardner. *Commentary* 83:56-9 My '87
Picasso's secret love. J. Richardson. il pors *House Gard* 159:174-83+ O '87
Picasso's time of decisive encounters; tr. by Tom Repensek. P. Daix. il *Art News* 86:136-41 Ap '87
Picasso, Paloma
about
Women facing women. il pors *Vogue* 177:54 Ag '87
Picchi, Mario
Don Quixote's Spain. il *World Press Rev* 34:61 N '87
Piccinni, Niccolò, 1728-1800
about
The accomplish'd maid [opera] Reviews
N Y 20:113 O 26 '87. P. G. Davis
La buona figliuola [opera] Reviews
New Yorker 63:146+ N 9 '87. A. Porter
Pich, Tom
Blue grit [with photographs] il *Oceans* 20:28-35 S/O '87
Pick, Richard A.
about
Cleaning up his act may help Dick Pick clean up. J. Flynn. il por *Bus Week* p76 S 28 '87
Pick Systems Inc.
Cleaning up his act may help Dick Pick clean up. J. Flynn. il por *Bus Week* p76 S 28 '87
The pick-up artist [film] See Motion picture reviews—Single works
Pick Up Company *See* David Gordon/Pick Up Company
Pickavance, William W.
about
This Bud's for Bear. P. Lyons. il pors *Car Driv* 32:158 Ap '87
Pickens, T. Boone, III *See* Pickens, Tom
Pickens, T. Boone, Jr.
Boone speaks [excerpt from Boone] il pors *Fortune* 115:42-5+ F 16 '87
about
The best Pickens play may be in his own backyard. G. G. Marcial. por *Bus Week* p100 S 7 '87
Blitz on Boeing. por *Time* 130:35 Ag 10 '87
Boone buys a bunch of Boeing. il por *Newsweek* 110:50 Ag 10 '87
A gold miner helps Pickens chip away at Newmont. S. D. Atchison. il por *Bus Week* p36 Ag 31 '87
Is Boone bluffing? K. M. Hafner. il por *Bus Week* p22-3 Ag 10 '87
Mesa purchase of Boeing stock highlights industry pressures. R. G. O'Lone. *Aviat Week Space Technol* 127:24-5 Ag 3 '87
One swallow could make Pickens' summer. J. E. Davis. il por *Bus Week* p37 S 14 '87
Pickens picks: a Boone for investors? J. P. Newport, Jr. il *Fortune* 116:126+ S 14 '87

Pickens, T. Boone, Jr.—about—*cont.*
Ripe enough for Pickens. R. Mitchell. il *Bus Week* p23 Ag 24 '87
Pickens, Tom
about
Leave it to T. Boone's son to sniff out a bargain. W. Glasgall. il por *Bus Week* p113-14 Mr 16 '87
Pickerel fishing
Pickerel on purpose. C. Hauptman. il *Field Stream* 91:74-5+ Ap '87
Picketing
A novel union role: picketing for the boss [Ohio supermarkets enlist workers in push against nonunion rivals] S. Phillips. il *Bus Week* p80 D 28 '87-Ja 4 '88
Sammy Davis refuses to cross line of pickets [National Assn. of Broadcast Employees and Technicians] *Jet* 72:10 Ag 31 '87
When picketing pays [Adopt-a-Picket program run by NOW to raise money for abortions in Concord, Calif.] D. G. Albrecht. il *Ms* 16:91 N '87
Pickett, Wilson, 1941-
about
Singer Wilson Pickett convicted of gun charge. il por *Jet* 72:56 Jl 20 '87
Pickford, Kaylan
Keep it simple [cover story; excerpt from Always beautiful] il por *50 Plus* 27:26-30 Ag '87
Picking of apples *See* Apples—Picking
Pickle, J. J. *See* Pickle, Jake
Pickle, Jake
about
Taking yet another look at television evangelism. il por *Christ Today* 31:48-9+ S 18 '87
Pickles and relishes
A chutney sampler. T. Dudley. il *Ctry J* 14:58-60 Jl '87
Condiments from the garden. R. Haskell. il *Flower Gard* 31:10-11 Ag/S '87
From our kitchen to yours. K. Adams. *South Living* 22:140 Jl '87
In a pickle. T. Dudley. il *Ctry J* 14:36-9 S '87
It's time for pickling [Jerusalem artichoke pickles] W. E. Wooldridge. il *Flower Gard* 31:50 O/N '87
Last-minute condiments & relishes. A. Bailey. il *Parents* 62:246+ N '87
Patient or quick, ways to make perfect pickles. il *Sunset* 179:80-5 Jl '87
Pickles the quick way. D. G. Lowery. il *South Living* 22:62-3 Jl '87
Pickles with pizzazz! il *Mother Earth News* 106:80-2+ Jl/Ag '87
Quick relishes and pickles. il *Gourmet* 47:162 Ag '87
A relish you'll rave about [zucchini relish] il *South Living* 22:171 S '87
Sauces and relishes for meat. il *Better Homes Gard* 65:175-6 O '87
Pickover, Clifford A.
about
Picture this [cover story] I. Peterson. il *Sci News* 131:392-5 Je 20 '87
Portraits of equations [cover story] I. Peterson. il *Sci News* 132:184-6 S 19 '87
Pickpockets *See* Stealing
Pickup campers *See* Campers, Truck
Pickup trucks *See* Trucks
Pickvance, Ronald
Van Gogh in Saint-Remy and Auvers. il por *USA Today (Periodical)* 115:74-83 Ja '87
Picnic tables *See* Tables
Picnics
Food to go: picnicking with pizzazz. C. Lyons. il *Ebony* 42:94-6+ S '87
Four thermos feasts. C. Wapner. il *Good Housekeep* 205:94+ O '87
Have an Italian-style picnic. J. B. Hurley. il *Prevention* 39:60+ Jl '87
Movable feasts. il *Gourmet* 47:66-8+ Jl '87
North, south, west, east, try these for your tailgate feast! *50 Plus* 27:71-2 S '87
A picnic among the violets. il *Gourmet* 47:86-8 My '87
Plan a four-star picnic [recipes from New York City chefs] C. Rossant. il *McCalls* 114:103 Jl '87
Polo picnic. L. Wells. il *N Y Times Mag* p51-2 My 31 '87
Scrumptious picnic fare. il *South Living* 22:190+ My '87
A summer feast. K. Haedrich. il *Ctry J* 14:40-3+ S '87
Summer foods to go! L. Hoppe. il *Better Homes Gard* 65:88-92+ Ag '87

Sunday in the park. il *Seventeen* 46:349-50 Ag '87
A tailgate picnic. il *Gourmet* 47:88-90+ O '87
Tailgating: nobody does it better than seniors! L. Wheeler. il *50 Plus* 27:68-70 S '87
Picoult, Jodi
Keeping count [story] il *Seventeen* 46:126-7+ F '87
Road stop [story] il *Seventeen* 46:330-1+ Ag '87
Picozzi, James
about
Trial by fire. T. Senger. il *Roll Stone* p111-12+ S 24 '87
Pictor (Constellation) *See* Constellations
Picture books
See also
Pop-up books
Publishers and publishing—Picture books
Bibliography
Art. J. Russell. il *N Y Times Book Rev* 92:11+ D 6 '87
Illustrated books for Christmas. il *Hist Today* 37:52-3 D '87
Illustrated books for Christmas: give the big picture. il *N Y Times Book Rev* 92:26-9 D 13 '87
New books about photography. F. Cameron. *Petersens Photogr Mag* 16:42-4 Je '87
Photography. A. Grundberg. il *N Y Times Book Rev* 92:20-1 D 6 '87
Picture this! The most beautiful books of the year. E. P. Williams. il *Vogue* 177:186+ D '87
Pretty pages [art books for Christmas] K. Larson. il *N Y* 20:89-90 D 14 '87
Picture books for children
See also
Pop-up books
Awards
The year's best illustrated books [N Y times book review choices] il *N Y Times Book Rev* 92:34-5 N 8 '87
Bibliography
The 10 best new picturebooks. W. Lamb. il *Redbook* 170:24+ D '87
Picture enlargers, Television *See* Television projection
Picture frames and framing
Frame pictures with granite? [spatter-finished mat board] D. Hastings. il *South Living* 22:84 Ag '87
The parameters of framing. M. Hampton. il *House Gard* 159:48+ Ap '87
Picture postcards *See* Postcards
Picture processing *See* Image processing
Picture writing
See also
Mayas—Writing
Picturephones
Reinventing the picture-transmitting phone [Luma telephone] *Futurist* 21:47 Ja/F '87
Video phones. D. Lampe. *Pop Sci* 231:56 O '87
Pictures
See also
Illustration
Photographs
Framing
See Picture frames and framing
Hanging
Pictures locator. K. Oberrecht. il *Pop Mech* 164:150 O '87
Trimming, mounting, etc.
Making your own mat-cutting clamp and guide. G. R. Cohen. il *Am Artist* 51:84+ N '87
Pie
American pie. L. Land. il *N Y Times Mag* p33-4 Jl 5 '87
Cobblers. K. Haedrich. il *Ctry J* 14:14-16+ Je '87
Fabulous fall pies. il *Ladies Home J* 104:136-7+ N '87
The gasparilla cookbook [sweet potato pie] il *Good Housekeep* 204:180 Mr '87
Glorious pies. L. Hoppe. il *Better Homes Gard* 65:152-3+ N '87
Knee-deep in blackberries. E. Sahatjian. il *Esquire* 108:20 Jl '87
Lower the fat . . . in pie crusts. M. Gorman. il *Rodale's Org Gard* 34:65-7 D '87
Picture-perfect pastry. J. Herwig. il *Better Homes Gard* 65:158 N '87
Picture-perfect pies—the easy way [apple pie] M. Langan. il *McCalls* 114:92+ Ja '87
Piecrusts you don't have to roll. il *Good Housekeep* 205:256 N '87
Pies and tarts from the garden [made with fruits] R. Haskell. il *Flower Gard* 31:16+ Je/Jl '87
Pleasingly plum [David Liederman's fresh-plum pie] B. Costikyan. il *N Y* 20:77 O 12 '87

Pie—cont.
Recipe of the week [easy peach pie] il *Jet* 72:33 Je 29 '87
Sweet sugar-crust pies. il *Redbook* 170:96-9+ N '87
Traditional fall pies. S. Dosier. il *South Living* 22:160-2 O '87
Pie crust *See* Pie
Piece of work (Term)
Piece of work. W. Safire. il *N Y Times Mag* p14+ O 18 '87
Piedmont (Calif.)
Historic houses, sites, etc.
Before remodeling, they dug back into the house's roots [Craftsman era house in Piedmont, Calif.] il *Sunset* 179:118+ O '87
Piedmont Aviation, Inc.
How USAir cut Icahn out [plan to buy Piedmont] S. Payne. il por *Bus Week* p35 Mr 23 '87
Law judge rejects USAir/Piedmont merger on regional antitrust grounds. M. Mecham. *Aviat Week Space Technol* 127:41+ S 28 '87
Piedmont delays acquisition decision, invites new bids. il *Aviat Week Space Technol* 126:34 F 23 '87
Piedmont is in play—and Norfolk Southern is flying. C. S. Eklund and S. Ticer. il *Bus Week* p37 F 9 '87
Piedmont to spend $4 million for T/CAS fleet installation [traffic alert/collision avoidance system] *Aviat Week Space Technol* 127:37 N 23 '87
Piedmont will start frequent service to Florida, Bahamas. *Aviat Week Space Technol* 126:37 Ja 26 '87
Transportation Dept. approves proposed USAir/Piedmont merger. J. Ott. *Aviat Week Space Technol* 127:44 N 9 '87
USAir, Piedmont ask administration to overturn decision against merger. *Aviat Week Space Technol* 127:44 O 12 '87
USAir-Piedmont merger pending government, shareholder approval. C. Preble. map *Aviat Week Space Technol* 126:34-6 Mr 16 '87
What's standing between USAir and Piedmont. S. Payne. il *Bus Week* p40 O 5 '87
Piedra, Alberto Martinez
about
The U.S. view from Guatemala City [interview] J. A. Briggs and J. W. Michaels. il por *Forbes* 139:174+ My 18 '87
Pielmeier, John
about
Sleight of hand [drama] Reviews
N Y il 20:25 My 11 '87. L. Schulte
New Yorker 63:88 My 18 '87. E. Oliver
Pienza (Italy)
Description
Pienza: the reward of patience [built by Pope Pius II] M. Kempton. il *House Gard* 159:74+ D '87
Pieper, Josef, 1904-
about
Josef Pieper and the pursuit of virtue. D. Heim. *Christ Century* 104:1076-7 D 2 '87
Pierce, Barbara Hanson
(ed) *See* Rex, Betty. The tears—and rage—of a foster mother
Pierce, Barry A. Costa- *See* Costa-Pierce, Barry A.
Pierce, Charles
Comin' back at San Jac. il *Sports Illus* 67 Sp Issue:18-19 N 18 '87
Pierce, Jim
Environmental Task Force. *Environment* 28:3-4 D '86
Pierce, John
about
John Pierce proved that the writing on the wall was a relic. il por *People Wkly* 27:51 F 16 '87
Pierce, John Robinson, 1910-
(jt. auth) *See* Mathews, Max V., and Pierce, John Robinson, 1910-
Pierce, Nona Prettyman
Creative patio crafting. il *Flower Gard* 31:16+ Ag/S '87
Pierce, Samuel R., Jr.
about
HUD grants $4.3 billion to black business under Pierce. il por *Jet* 72:12 Ap 20 '87
Pierce takes U.S. group on tour of Soviet Union. por *Jet* 73:4 O 26 '87
Piercy, Marge
Of arms and the woman. *Harpers* 274:30+ Je '87
about
A woman writer treads on male turf [interview] A. P. Sanoff. por *U S News World Rep* 102:74 My 18 '87

Pierotti, Ray
about
The real birdman of Alcatraz. K. Schafer. il pors *Natl Wildl* 25:18-21 Ag/S '87
Pierre, Prince of Monaco, 1987-
about
Say hello to Prince Pierre, the littlest Monegasque. il pors *People Wkly* 28:38 S 21 '87
Pierre Balmain (Firm)
A fashionable Canadian connection. B. Janssen. il por *Macleans* 100:37 N 16 '87
Pierrepont, Nancy
about
The quality of comfort. S. M. Alsop. il por *Archit Dig* 44:250+ Je '87
Pierschbacher, Michael D.
(jt. auth) *See* Ruoslahti, Erkki, and Pierschbacher, Michael D.
Pierson, Cheryl
about
Brutal treatment, vicious deeds. J. D. Hull. il por *Time* 130:68 O 19 '87
Pierson, Julie
Stand up for yourself. il *Read Dig* 130:103-5 F '87
Pies *See* Pie
Pietig, Jeanne
Strengths and weaknesses of the Holmes Group report. *Educ Dig* 52:32-5 Mr '87
Piezoelectric equipment
See also
Oscillators, Crystal
Piezoelectric plastic film. J. Iovine. il *Radio-Electron* 58:57-8+ Mr '87
Pifer, Alan
Universities and apartheid. *Cent Mag* 20:61-2 Mr/Ap '87
Pig racing *See* Swine racing
Pigafetta, Antonio, 1491?-1534?
Mass to the sound of gunfire [excerpt from Magellan's voyage around the world] il *Courier* 40:11 Ap '87
Pigeon Island National Historic Park (Saint Lucia)
Pigeon Island. S. Alcorn. il *Travel Holiday* 167:14+ Je '87
Pigeon postal service
France
On war letters: pigeons, planes, and philatelists. H. Herst, Jr. il *Antiques Collect Hobbies* 92:82+ N '87
Pigeon racing
The astonishing flight of pigeon 309. W. Ecenbarger. il *Read Dig* 130:94-8 Mr '87
Pigeon shooting
See also
Mourning dove shooting
Treasure of Tamaulipas [whitewing doves] W. L. Bourne. il *Field Stream* 92:58-9+ S '87
Pigeons
See also
Pigeon postal service
Pigeon racing
Feeding pigeons serial chunks [work of Herbert S. Terrace] *Sci News* 131:40 Ja 17 '87
". . . it would be a pity to kill the birds" [attempt to train carrier pigeons to fly messages over a hundred miles, 1896-1900] *Forbes* 140:18+ S 21 '87
Keeping a key pigeon in the Keys [work of T. Bancroft with white-crowned pigeons] G. Laycock. il por *Audubon* 89:76-80 Mr '87
Pigford, Aretha Butler
Teacher evaluation: more than a game that principals play. il *Phi Delta Kappan* 69:141-2 O '87
Pigg, Mike
about
Triumph for Pigg power. C. Neff. il *Sports Illus* 67:62-3 O 5 '87
Piggott, Lester, 1935-
about
Riding for a fall. il por *Sports Illus* 67:24 N 2 '87
Piggy banks *See* Banks, Coin
Piggyback transportation
Train, ahoy! [American President Companies] J. Cook. il por *Forbes* 139:60+ My 18 '87
Pigmentation (Biology) *See* Color of man
Pigments (Biology)
See also
Bilirubin
Carotene
Cytochromes
Hemerythrin
Melanin
Phycoerythrins
Porphyrins

Pigments (Biology)—*cont.*
How purple was my valley [bacteriorhodopsin; work of Andrew Goldsworthy] il *Discover* 8:14+ N '87
Pigs *See* Swine
PIK (Payment in kind) program *See* Agricultural administration
Pikas
Snack-packing pika. il map *Natl Geogr World* 145:14-16 S '87
Pike
See also
Cooking—Fish
Pike fishing
Bassic strategy for pike. T. Mandile. il *Outdoor Life* 179:62-3+ Je '87
Pikes Peak Auto Hill Climb *See* Automobile racing
Pilaf *See* Cooking—Rice
Pilarczyk, Daniel E.
Taking it on the chin—for life: reflections on a Vatican instruction. *America* 156:295-6 Ap 11 '87
about
On challenging opponents. *America* 156:434 My 30 '87
Pilates system *See* Biomechanics—Therapeutic use
Pileggi, Nicholas
Cuomo and those rumors: getting to the bottom of all the 'Mob' talk [cover story] il pors *N Y* 20:44-8+ N 2 '87
Daylighting: going undercover with Gillian Farrell and the new private eyes. il pors *N Y* 20:44-8 Ap 20 '87
The Police Shack. il por *N Y* 20:95 D 21-28 '87
Pilgrims and pilgrimages
Return of the Pleiades [festival of Qoyllur Rit'i in Peru] R. Randall. il *Nat Hist* 96:42-53 Je '87
Pilkey, Orrin H., Jr.
Move it or lose it. il *Oceans* 20:23+ Mr/Ap '87
about
The gospel according to Pilkey. K. Ringle. pors *Oceans* 20:18-22 Mr/Ap '87
Pill (Birth control) *See* Contraceptives
Pill bugs *See* Pillbugs
Pilla, Anthony M.
How to implement 'Economic justice for all'. il *America* 156:76-8+ Ja 31 '87
Pillage
The amphora war [looting of ancient shipwrecks] il *Courier* 40:25 N '87
Violating history [American archeological sites] J. Robbins. il *Natl Parks* 61:26-31 Jl/Ag '87
PILLAR *See* Pallottine Institute for Lay Leadership and Apostolate Research
Pillar of fire [ballet] *See* Ballet reviews—Single works
Pillbugs
Control
Sowbugs, pillbugs. W. S. Moore. il *Flower Gard* 31:33 F/Mr '87
Pillows
Leaf-print pillows. il *South Living* 22:174 Ap '87
Pills
Make sure bedtime pills go down. *Prevention* 39:10 Jl '87
Pillsbury Baptist Bible College
Minn. Bible College jock says he was expelled for dating white girl there [case of C. Addison] il por *Jet* 72:14 My 11 '87
Probe interracial dating policy at Bible College. *Jet* 71:21 F 23 '87
Pillsbury Co.
Can Burger King's man spice up Pillsbury's eateries? [J. J. Campbell] M. J. Pitzer. il por *Bus Week* p50-1 My 18 '87
A CEO bake-off at Pillsbury [former CEO W. Spoor called back] B. Dumaine. il pors *Fortune* 116:109+ N 23 '87
Pilobolus Dance Theatre
Close encounters [performance of Land's edge at the Joyce Theater, New York City] T. Tobias. il *N Y* 20:84-5 F 16 '87
Creatures in motion: the shapes of Pilobolus [performances at Joyce Theater, New York City] D. McDonagh. *Commonweal* 114:293-4 My 8 '87
'Phototropic' and fun too. G. G. Seibert. *America* 156:239 Mr 21 '87
Reviews:
Performances at the Joyce Theater, New York City. K. Onoda. il *Dance Mag* 61:23-4+ S '87
Pilon, Roger
The systematic repression of Soviet Jews [address, September 28, 1986] *Dep State Bull* 86:67-70 D '86

Pilot, Automatic (Airplanes) *See* Automatic pilot (Airplanes)
Pilot ejection seats, capsules, etc. *See* Airplanes, Military—Escape devices
Pilot training *See* Aviation—Study and teaching
Pilot whales *See* Whales
Piloting of airplanes *See* Airplanes—Piloting; Airplanes, Light—Piloting; Airplanes, Military transport—Piloting; Seaplanes—Piloting
Piloting of airships *See* Airships—Piloting
Pilots, Aviation *See* Air pilots
Pilots, Helicopter *See* Helicopter pilots
Pima Indians
Metabolism studies predict obesity [research by Clifton Bogardus and others] D. D. Edwards. *Sci News* 132:309 N 14 '87
Pimentel, David, 1925-
Down on the farm: genetic engineering meets ecology. il *Technol Rev* 90:24-30 Ja '87
Report on reports: Partners against hunger. bibl f *Environment* 29:25-7 S '87
Pimentel, David, 1925-, and others
World agriculture and soil erosion. bibl f il *BioScience* 37:277-83 Ap '87
Pincherle, Alberto *See* Moravia, Alberto, 1907-
Pinckney, Callan
about
Callan Pinckney: the thighs have it. P. Brandt. il *Ms* 16:20+ N '87
Pinckney, Darryl
Black victims, black villains. bibl f il *N Y Rev Books* 34:17-20 Ja 29 '87
Pincus, Jonathan
Indonesia votes. *Nation* 244:493 Ap 18 '87
Pincus, Walter
about
The power and the story [interview] L. Hirschberg. por *Roll Stone* p45-6+ My 21 '87
Pindling, Sir Lynden Oscar
about
Pindling reelected as Bahamian prime minister. il por *Jet* 72:8 Jl 6 '87
Pine, Courtney
about
Courtney Pine. C. Albertson. il por *Stereo Rev* 52:94 Jl '87
Pine, Devera
Can you be fit without being healthy? il *Women's Sports Fitness* 9:34-7 Je '87
The unpredictable period. *Redbook* 168:28 F '87
(jt. auth) *See* Griffith, Linda Lewis, 1953-, and Pine, Devera
Pine, Katie
about
In motion. il pors *Seventeen* 46:48 D '87
Pine
Diseases and pests
See also
Beetles
Pine-leaf penstemon *See* Penstemons
Pine Manor College. Annenberg Library and Communications Center (Mass.) *See* Annenberg Library and Communications Center (Mass.)
Pines, Deborah
Kids' time. il *McCalls* 114:73 Ap '87
Piney Flats (Tenn.)
Historic houses, sites, etc.
It's 1791 at Rocky Mount. il *South Living* 22:40 S '87
Pinheiro Machado, Anesia
about
The doyenne of Brazilian skies. A. Fernández. il por *Américas* 39:54-5 Ja/F '87
Pinhole photography *See* Photography, Pinhole
Pininfarina, Sergio
about
Pininfarina heads for the U.S. in a Caddy. W. C. Symonds. il por *Bus Week* p58-9 F 9 '87
Pininfarina SpA *See* Industrie Pininfarina SpA
Pink, William T., and Liebert, Robert E.
Reforming reading instruction. *Educ Dig* 52:24-7 Mr '87
Pink Floyd (Musical group)
Pink Floyd hits the road [concert at the Forum in Montreal] D. Fricke. il *Roll Stone* p17 O 22 '87
Pink Floyd plays the name game. D. Wild. *Roll Stone* p13 Ja 15 '87
Pink Floyd: the inside story [cover story] D. Fricke. il *Roll Stone* p44-6+ N 19 '87
Pink Floyd: the Wall tour, February-August 1980. D. Fricke. il *Roll Stone* p105-6 Je 4 '87

Pink Floyd the wall [film] See Motion picture reviews—Single works
Pink sheet securities See Under-the-counter securities
Pinkham, Mary Ellen
25 tips for good health and great looks [condensed from How to become a healthier, prettier you] il *Read Dig* 130:112-14 Ja '87
Pinks (Plants)
Think pinks. J. Larmoth. il *House Gard* 159:44+ D '87
Pinkston, Jim
(jt. auth) See Brown, Peter H., and Pinkston, Jim
Pinnacle West Capital Corporation
Overload? J. Heins. il por *Forbes* 140:124+ D 14 '87
Pinnipedia
See also
Seals (Animals)
Walruses
Seals and their kin [cover story] R. L. Gentry. il supp (folded map) *Natl Geogr* 171:474-501 Ap '87
Pinnock, Clark H., 1937-
Fire, then nothing. por *Christ Today* 31:40-2 Mr 20 '87
Piño Díaz, Rafael del
about
A flight to freedom. *Macleans* 100:24 Je 8 '87
Hero to go. *Time* 129:26 Je 8 '87
Just how big a fish is the man from Havana? C. A. Robbins. por *U S News World Rep* 102:12 Je 8 '87
Their man from Havana: true confessions? *Newsweek* 109:42 Je 8 '87
Pinochet Ugarte, Augusto
about
Derailing Pinochet. J. Dinges and S. Landau. il *Nation* 244:280-2 Mr 7 '87
Getting away with murder. H. Evans. il *U S News World Rep* 102:80 Mr 23 '87
In Chile, all sides angle for a nod from the Pope. M. Santini. il por *U S News World Rep* 102:38 Ap 6 '87
Life goes on under Pinochet's yoke. S. J. Ungar. il *U S News World Rep* 103:40 N 30 '87
Pinochet's grip on Chile. P. Constable. bibl f *Curr Hist* 86:17-20+ Ja '87
Pinochet's way. C. G. Brown. il por *N Y Rev Books* 34:47-9 Je 25 '87
A tight grip on the reins. C. Lane. il por *Newsweek* 110:29 Jl 6 '87
Under the dictator; tr. by Robert Cox. J. Timerman. *New Yorker* 63:47-50+ N 2 '87
Bibliography
Going to extremes [cover story] M. Falcoff. il *New Repub* 197:26-33 S 7 '87
Pinola, Joseph J., 1925-
about
The man who would be boss at BankAmerica. R. E. Norton. il pors *Fortune* 115:88-90+ F 16 '87
Suddenly, First Interstate looks a whole lot slimmer. T. Carson. il por *Bus Week* p126 N 9 '87
Who needs BankAmerica? Not Joe Pinola. T. Carson. il por *Bus Week* p46 F 23 '87
Pins
See also
Brooches
Hatpins
Lapel pins
Pinsent, Gordon, 1930-
about
John and the missus [film] Reviews
Macleans il 100:78 F 2 '87. L. O'Toole
The restless dreamer from the Rock. B. D. Johnson. il por *Macleans* 100:76-8 F 2 '87
Pinsker, Jeff
about
Prankster Jeff Pinsker profits profoundly from improbable practical jokes. S. Dougherty. il por *People Wkly* 27:58-9 Je 15 '87
Pinsky, Robert
The Hearts [poem] *New Repub* 196:40 F 23 '87
The Lenore Marshall Prize. *Nation* 245:496-8 O 31 '87
about
Responsibilities of the poet. *Harpers* 275:31-2+ Ag '87
You are what you read. D. Lehman. il pors *Newsweek* 109:67 Ja 12 '87
Pintauro, Joseph
about
Wild blue [drama] Reviews
Nation 245:459 O 24 '87. T. M. Disch

Pinto Coelho, Duarte
about
Spain's doyen of interiors. N. Shrady. il por *Archit Dig* 44:246+ Ap '87
Pinzon, Leopoldo
about
The spider game [film] Reviews
Américas 39:58 Jl/Ag '87. J. Mosier
Pion, P. D., and others
Myocardial failure in cats associated with low plasma taurine: a reversible cardiomyopathy [cover story] bibl f il *Science* 237:764-8 Ag 14 '87
Pioneer flights See Space flight—Pioneer flights
Pioneer life See Frontier and pioneer life
Pions See Particles (Nuclear physics)
Piotrowski, John L.
In defense of Strategic Defense [address, August 16, 1987] *Vital Speeches Day* 53:742-5 O 1 '87
Pipeline companies
See also
Coastal Corporation
Enron Corp.
Panhandle Eastern Corporation
Tenneco Inc.
Texas Eastern Corp.
Transco Energy Co.
Finance
How to make everyone unhappy [gas pipeline take-or-pay contracts] L. M. Keefe. il *Forbes* 140:40-1 Ag 10 '87
Laws and regulations
Can Transco wriggle out of the 'take-or-pay' mess? J. E. Davis. il por *Bus Week* p66-7 S 28 '87
How to make everyone unhappy [gas pipeline take-or-pay contracts] L. M. Keefe. il *Forbes* 140:40-1 Ag 10 '87
Canada
See also
Inter-City Gas Corp.
Manitoba Consumers Gas Corporation
TransCanada PipeLines Limited
Pipelines
See also
Gas pipelines
Petroleum pipelines
Water pipes
Piper, John
Just say no to condom ads. il por *Christ Today* 31:16 S 4 '87
Piper, Kathy
Plant hellebores to herald springtime. il *Flower Gard* 32:58-61 D '87/Ja '88
Sweet alyssum gives the finishing touch. il *Flower Gard* 31:41 F/Mr '87
Piper Aircraft Corp.
Bear country [fly-in celebrating 50th anniversary of the Piper Cub] R. Munson. il *Flying* 114:64-9 O '87
Calling all pilots [new generation of small private planes] W. J. Cook. il por *U S News World Rep* 103:53+ D 7 '87
FAA uncovers additional PA-28s with cracked wing spars. *Aviat Week Space Technol* 127:53 Ag 10 '87
Malibu U. [Malibu training center in Vero Beach, Fla.] E. Weiner. il *Flying* 114:82-5+ Jl '87
Piper then and now [J-3 Cub and Malibu] F. Mackerodt. il *Pop Mech* 164:12+ Ag '87
Piper to expand its product line, seeks partners for joint programs. il *Aviat Week Space Technol* 127:86-7 S 28 '87
Piper's new tune. R. L. Collins. il *Flying* 114:58-64+ N '87
Piperato, Susan
Snapshots. See issues of Popular Photography beginning November 1986
Pipes, Daniel, 1949-
Arab vs. Arab over Palestine. *Commentary* 84:17-25 Jl '87
Pipes, Daniel, 1949-, and Mylroie, Laurie
Back Iraq. *New Repub* 196:14-15 Ap 27 '87
Pipes, R. Byron
(jt. auth) See Kerr, Arnold D., and Pipes, R. Byron
Pipes, Richard
The 'glasnost' test. *New Repub* 196:16-17 F 2 '87
Pipes
See also
Sewer pipes
Water pipes
Pipes, Plastic
See also
Water pipes, Plastic
Pipes, Tobacco See Tobacco pipes
Pipho, Chris
Stateline. See issues of Phi Delta Kappan

Pipp, Wally
about
Just a Pipp of a legend. B. Anderson. il pors *Sports Illus* 66:78-82+ Je 29 '87

Pippen, Scott
about
Bulls' top pick Pippen inks unique 6-year deal. *Jet* 73:50 N 2 '87
Now you see him. B. Newman. il pors *Sports Illus* 67:67-8+ N 30 '87

Piquet, Nelson
about
Black flag, black mood for Prost. I. Ireland. il pors *Road Track* 38:128-30 Ja '87
Now Nelson, now Nigel. I. Ireland. il *Road Track* 39:134-8+ D '87
Williams again. I. Ireland. il *Road Track* 39:152-4+ N '87

Piracy *See* Pirates

Piranesi, Giambattista, 1720-1778
about
Next time, ask. R. W. Walker. *Art News* 86:25-6 O '87

Pirani, Mario
The epoch of dislocation. il *World Press Rev* 34:18 D '87

Pirates
The truth about pirates [knowledge gained from salvage of the Whidah] B. Lawren. il *Omni* 9:30+ Je '87

Pirating of books *See* Copyright infringement
Pirating of cable television broadcasts *See* Cable television—Unauthorized use
Pirating of compact discs *See* Compact discs—Unauthorized recording
Pirating of computer software *See* Computer programming—Unauthorized use
Pirating of phonograph records *See* Phonograph records—Unauthorized recording
Pirating of radio broadcasts *See* Radio broadcasting—Unauthorized use
Pirating of tape recordings *See* Tape recordings—Unauthorized recording

Pirelli Société Générale
Old and new [Pirelli race cars] D. Sherman. il *Car Driv* 33:9 N '87

Piret's (Los Angeles, Calif.: Restaurant) *See* Los Angeles (Calif.)—Restaurants, nightclubs, bars, etc.

Pirie, Madsen
The principles and practice of privatization [address, March 30, 1987] *Vital Speeches Day* 53:655-8 Ag 15 '87

Pisa, Clelia
Clothesline literature. il *Courier* 39:26-8 D '86

Pistachios
See also
Cooking—Nuts

Pistol models
A phone shaped like a Colt .45 has its critics up in arms. il por *People Wkly* 27:38 F 16 '87

Pistols
Battle over the plastic gun. G. Hackett. il *Newsweek* 109:31 Je 1 '87
The gun as whipping boy [plastic pistol legislation] D. E. Petzal. *Field Stream* 92:26 Je '87
Praise Madison and pass the ammunition [limited edition pistol to commemorate the 200th anniversary of the U.S. Constitution] il *Harpers* 275:21+ N '87

Pistorio, Pasquale
about
An Italian chipmaker shows the way. W. C. Symonds. il por *Bus Week* p134+ My 25 '87

Pistorius, Alan
The big sleep. il *Ctry J* 14:45-9 Ja '87

Pit bull terriers
Are pit bulls a menace? N. Keilin. il *Ladies Home J* 104:122 N '87
A boy and his dog in hell [illegal dog fighting with pit bull terriers in Philadelphia] M. Sager. il *Roll Stone* p36-7+ Jl 2 '87
An instinct for the kill. M. Green. il *People Wkly* 28:28-31 Jl 6 '87
L.A. animal control officer attacked by pit bull dog [Florence Crowell] il *Jet* 72:28 Jl 13 '87
Life is the pits for pit bulls. M. Bosc. il *U S News World Rep* 103:12 Ag 17 '87
The most dangerous dog in America. M. Satchell. il *U S News World Rep* 102:24 Ap 20 '87
The pit bull: friend and killer [cover story] E. M. Swift. il *Sports Illus* 67:72-8+ Jl 27 '87
"Time bombs on legs" [attacks on humans] D. Brand. il *Time* 130:60 Jl 27 '87

Pitcairn, Richard H.
Your healthy pet. See issues of Prevention (Emmaus, Pa.) through June 1987

Pitcairn Island
Pitcairn lives. W. F. Buckley. *Natl Rev* 39:63 D 18 '87

Pitch, Musical *See* Musical pitch

Pitchers (Pottery, glass, etc.)
Ceramic teapots, pitchers recalled [Dutch pottery] il *FDA Consum* 21:6 S '87

Collectors and collecting
Jan Emens' "penny jug". S. Bagdade and A. Bagdade. il *Antiques Collect Hobbies* 92:43 Ag '87
A Wood Family Toby jug. S. Bagdade and A. Bagdade. il *Antiques Collect Hobbies* 92:37 Je '87

Pitchford, Dean
A father's pictures. il *N Y Times Mag* p44 Jl 12 '87

Pitching (Baseball)
The anatomy of an at-bat [Houston pitcher M. Scott vs. Cincinnati batter D. Granger; cover story] D. Granger. il pors *Sport Mag* 78:26-9 Jl '87
The arms talks. R. Angell. *New Yorker* 63:103-12+ My 4 '87
Baseball is for robots [study of pitching motion as applied to robotics] E. R. C. Capulong. *Pop Sci* 231:39 Ag '87
Doing time in the pen [Oakland A's relievers] A. Murphy. il *Sports Illus* 67:88-91 Jl 6 '87
Knuckleballs [study by Joel W. Hollenberg] il *Sci Am* 257:22 Jl '87
The pitch that ate baseball [splitfingered fastball] D. Levine. il *Sport Mag* 78:45+ My '87
What's wrong with pitching? P. Gammons. il *Sports Illus* 67:58-60 Ag 17 '87

Anecdotes, facetiae, satire, etc.
Post-season knucklers [influence in non-baseball areas] J. Stevenson. il *New Yorker* 63:33 O 26 '87

Records
See Baseball records

Pitember, Sunita
about
Entertaining. W. P. Rayner and C. Rayner. il por *Vogue* 177:128 Je '87

Pitino, Rick
about
Not first class, coach: Rick Pitino deserted Providence, and so his players suffer. J. McCallum. por *Sports Illus* 67:86 Ag 3 '87

Pitney, John J., Jr.
Neo-Gephardt. *New Repub* 197:13-14 D 14 '87

Pitot tubes
Bugged pitot [airplane] J. Holloway. il *Flying* 114:104 D '87

Pitshanger Manor (Ealing, London, England) *See* Ealing (London, England)—Historic houses, sites, etc.

Pitt, William, 1759-1806
about
Whose crazy idea was this? L. Saunders. il por *Forbes* 140:290 Jl 13 '87

Pitt Rivers Museum (Oxford, England)
Pitt Rivers Museum at Oxford offers a cultural cornucopia. J. Reader. il *Smithsonian* 18:108-14+ Jl '87

Pittman, Bob
about
Quantum leaps. J. A. Trachtenberg. il por *Forbes* 139:178-9 Je 1 '87

Pittock, A. Barrie, 1938-
Report on reports: the carbon dioxide debate: reports from SCOPE and DOE. bibl *Environment* 29:25-30 Ja/F '87

Pitts, Cornelius
about
How the homeless bought a Rolls for Cornelius Pitts. M. Szegedy-Maszak. il por *Wash Mon* 19:11-15 Jl/Ag '87

Pitts, Milt
about
Tips from a tonsorial tout. H. Sidey. il por *Time* 129:25 F 16 '87

Pitts, Terence, and Solomon, Nancy
Supreme instants: photography of Edward Weston. il por *USA Today (Periodical)* 116:56-65 N '87

Pittsburgh (Pa.)

Crime
Pittsburgh's Nate Smith shot in hip near diner. por *Jet* 72:10 Ag 31 '87

Hospitals
Senior Center becomes medical satellite to hospital in Pittsburgh [Vintage Senior Adult Center and West Penn Hospital] il *Aging* no355:29-30 '87

Pittsburgh (Pa.)—*cont.*

Housing

Slum community saves itself [efforts of single mothers to insure survival of low cost housing] R. Kahn. *Ms* 15:32 Je '87

Police

Pittsburgh's black police chief quits over authority [W. Moore] *Jet* 72:8 Je 1 '87

Politics and government

Pittsburgh voters approve new system; ups chances for black candidates. *Jet* 72:12 Je 8 '87

Population

The nationality rooms [Cathedral of Learning on the campus of the University of Pittsburgh] M. A. Zimmermann. il *Focus* 36:34-5 Wint '86

Religious institutions and affairs

Happy hour at Mr. C's [Episcopal pastor S. Boehmig brings his band into Pittsburgh clubs] R. Frame. il por *Christ Today* 31:12-13 O 16 '87

Theater

See also

Pittsburgh Public Theater

Water supply

Hunting for Legionnaire's bacteria. S. Weisburd. *Sci News* 132:169 S 12 '87

Pittsburgh Ballet Theatre

The Gatsby gamble [A. Prokovsky adapts F. S. Fitzgerald's Gatsby] S. Flatow. il *Horizon* 30:60-2 O '87

Pittsburgh Public Theater

Born in the USA. J. Dolan. il *Theatre Crafts* 21:32-7+ Ag/S '87

Pittsfield (Mass.)

Galleries and museums

See also

Berkshire Museum (Pittsfield, Mass.)

Pituitary hormone releasing factors

See also

Factrel

Gonadotropin releasing hormone

Thyrotropin releasing factor

Corticotropin-releasing factor-producing neurons in the rat activated by interleukin-1. F. Berkenbosch and others. bibl f il *Science* 238:524-6 O 23 '87

Interleukin-1 stimulates the secretion of hypothalamic corticotropin-releasing factor. R. M. Sapolsky and others. bibl f il *Science* 238:522-4 O 23 '87

Pituitary hormones

See also

Gonadotropins

Melatonin

Vasopressin

Expression of an exogenous growth hormone gene by transplantable human epidermal cells. J. R. Morgan and others. bibl f il *Science* 237:1476-9 S 18 '87

Implantation of genetically engineered fibroblasts into mice: implications for gene therapy. R. F. Selden and others. bibl f il *Science* 236:714-18 My 8 '87

Release of multiple hormones by a direct action of interleukin-1 on pituitary cells. E. W. Bernton and others. bibl f il *Science* 238:519-21 O 23 '87

Pituitary hormones, Synthetic

A debate over more milk [bovine somatotropin] M. Salter. *Macleans* 100:80 F 2 '87

The facts behind those amazing growth hormones [porcine growth hormone] *Success Farm* 85:H6-H7 Ap '87

Genentech sues FDA on growth hormone. M. Crawford. il *Science* 235:1454-5 Mr 20 '87

Genentech's custody case over an orphan drug [gene-spliced human growth hormone] J. O. Hamilton. il *Bus Week* p39 Mr 23 '87

The growing danger from gene-spliced hormones. T. H. Murray. il *Discover* 8:88+ F '87

Growth hormone work gets a health checkup [bovine somatotropin] J. R. Borcherding. *Success Farm* 85:30 S '87

Help for slow-growing children. M. Vogel. il *FDA Consum* 21:14-17 Mr '87

High-speed pork [use of porcine somatotropin and beta adrenergic agonists] K. Coble. il *Success Farm* 85:42 N '87

Introducing the skinny pig [porcine somatotropin] R. Rhein, Jr. il *Bus Week* p37 Mr 23 '87

Monthly shots of BST boost milk output 22%; Milk drinkers appear ready to accept BST use [bovine somatotropin] *Success Farm* 85:68 O '87

New flurry of growth hormone developments [bovine growth hormone] *Success Farm* 85 no5:D6 Mr '87

Piturro, Marlene

The high price of low pay. il por *Work Woman* 12:157-8 Mr '87

Pity *See* Sympathy

Pius II, Pope, 1405-1464

about

Pienza: the reward of patience. M. Kempton. il *House Gard* 159:74+ D '87

Pius XII, Pope, 1876-1958

about

Shameful silence. *Natl Rev* 39:17 F 13 '87

The 'silence' of Pius XII: again. J. Gallagher. il *America* 156:279-81 Ap 4 '87

Pivar, Stuart

about

The collectors: a rare aesthetic: Stuart Pivar's cornucopia of art in Manhattan. S. M. L. Aronson. il *Archit Dig* 44:124-31+ Mr '87

Pivot, Bernard

about

Au flair. J. Bernstein. *Am Sch* 56:167-70+ Spr '87

The Carson of the literary set. L. Zuckerman. il por *Time* 130:64 Jl 13 '87

A nation of readers. B. Murphy. il *Atlantic* 260:21-5 Ag '87

Pixar (Firm)

Hip graphics. B. Weber. il *N Y Times Mag* p110 D 13 '87

Piyarath, Prapont

(jt. auth) *See* Nondasuta, Amorn, and Piyarath, Prapont

Pizza

Fast pizza variations. il *Glamour* 85:320 O '87

It was inevitable, pizza on the barbecue [cover story] il *Sunset* 179:70-1 Jl '87

Not the same old pizza. S. Payne. il *South Living* 22:162+ S '87

Pizza! T. P. Wolf. il *Better Homes Gard* 65:132-3 O '87

Pizza: have it your way. il *Seventeen* 46:225-6 Ap '87

Advertising

Pizza wars. B. Kanner. il *N Y* 20:20+ S 21 '87

Pizza restaurants

See also

Shakey's Incorporated

When the town pizza parlor shut down. D. Geigis. il *Glamour* 85:278+ S '87

Pizzetti, Ildebrando, 1880-1968

about

Murder in the cathedral [opera] Reviews

N Y 20:111 N 23 '87. P. G. Davis

Place des Antiquaires (New York, N.Y.)

Judith's place [J. Applegate] M. Bethany. il por *N Y* 20:30 N 30 '87

Place in fiction *See* Fiction—Setting

Place names *See* Names, Geographical

Place of weeping [film] *See* Motion picture reviews—Single works

A place with the pigs [drama] *See* Fugard, Athol

Placemats *See* Table mats, tiles, etc.

Placenta

See also

Maternal-fetal exchange

Localization, secretion, and action of inhibin in human placenta. F. Petraglia and others. bibl f il *Science* 237:187-9 Jl 10 '87

Placer Dome Inc.

Defence of a gold mine. D. Jenish. il *Macleans* 100:32-3 Ag 17 '87

Placer Dome: will it pan out? E. B. Terry. *Bus Week* p42+ S 7 '87

Placerias *See* Reptiles, Fossil

Places of retirement *See* Retirement, Places of

Placid Oil Company

It's white-knuckle time for the Hunts [bankruptcy court to decide fate of Placid Oil Gulf drilling project] T. Mason. il *Bus Week* p29 Mr 30 '87

Plagens, Peter, 1941-

Los Angeles: two for the show. il *Art Am* 75:146-52+ My '87

Plagiarism

And then there were six [J. Biden withdraws from race] G. J. Church. il por *Time* 130:24-5 O 5 '87

Biden's belly flop. M. Kaus. il pors *Newsweek* 110:23-4 S 28 '87

Biden's familiar quotations. W. Shapiro. il por *Time* 130:17 S 28 '87

Biden's truth. *Nation* 245:328-9 O 3 '87

A candidate's character in question [J. Biden's plagiarism] M. McDonald. il por *Macleans* 100:24+ S 28 '87

A case of plagiarized passion? [charges against J. R. Biden] *Newsweek* 110:35 S 21 '87

No heavy lifting. W. Safire. il *N Y Times Mag* p12+ S 27 '87

Plagiarism—*cont.*

Of many things [J. Biden] G. W. Hunt. *America* 157:202 O 10 '87

On trial: character [charges against J. Biden] G. Borger. il pors *U S News World Rep* 103:26-7 S 28 '87

Peccadillos and presidents [J. R. Biden] A. Fotheringham. il *Macleans* 100:68 S 28 '87

The reduction of Joe Biden. J. Klein. por *N Y* 20:26+ O 5 '87

Researcher accused of plagiarism resigns [case of R. J. Shamberger] C. Holden. *Science* 237:1098 S 4 '87

Swaggart column nixed [Baton Rouge advocate charges plagiarism] *Christ Century* 104:552 Je 17-24 '87

Turning my words against me. P. Klass. *N Y Times Book Rev* 92:1+ Ap 5 '87

Anecdotes, facetiae, satire, etc.

Talking head [J. R. Biden] A. Z. Posner. *New Repub* 197:8+ O 12 '87

Plaid

Paris—mad for plaid! il *Harpers Bazaar* 120:372-7 S '87

With a plaid hand. il *Vogue* 177:154 Jl '87

Plains (Ga.)

Historic houses, sites, etc.

See also

Jimmy Carter National Historic Site

Water pollution

The problem is not peanuts in Plains [groundwater quality] il *Success Farm* 85:13 S '87

Planers *See* Planes and planing

Planes and planing

Portable surface planer [Ryobi AP-10] R. Capotosto. il *Pop Mech* 164:48 Je '87

A portable tabletop planer [Ryobi AP-10 planer] S. H. Ostrow. il *Workbench* 43:119 Mr/Ap '87

Power plane handles tough stuff. R. Capotosto. il *Pop Mech* 164:40 N '87

Square edges, clean surfaces the easy way [power planers] A. Rooze. il *Fam Handyman* 37:14+ D '87

Planes, trains and automobiles [film] *See* Motion picture reviews—Single works

Planetariums

See also

Adler Planetarium

Russel Davis Planetarium

Equipment

The soccer-ball sky [how a planetarium projector works] G. Lovi. il *Sky Telesc* 74:279-80 S '87

France

New Paris planetarium and Omnimax theater [Space Voyager] il *Sky Telesc* 73:152 F '87

North America

Focal points: observatories, planetariums, and museums for astronomy enthusiasts to visit throughout the United States and Canada. il *Astronomy* 15:42-53 Je '87

Planetariums and museums. *Sky Telesc* 74 Sky Telesc Handb:2-8 S '87

Planetary nebulae *See* Nebulae

Planetary systems *See* Solar system

Planetesimal hypothesis

Birth of the moon [giant impact theory] A. Fisher. il *Pop Sci* 230:60-4+ Ja '87

Protoplanetary disks are common. D. E. Thomsen. *Sci News* 132:24 Jl 11 '87

Planets

See also

Earth

Jupiter (Planet)

Life on other planets

Mars (Planet)

Mechanics, Celestial

Mercury (Planet)

Neptune (Planet)

Occultations

Planetesimal hypothesis

Pluto (Planet)

Saturn (Planet)

Solar system

Uranus (Planet)

Venus (Planet)

A 1987 planet preview. il *Sky Telesc* 73:66-7 Ja '87

Alien worlds: the search heats up [cover story; with editorial comment by Paul Hoffman] R. Wolkomir. il *Discover* 8:4, 66-8+ O '87

The art of planetary observing (I). D. C. Parker and T. A. Dobbins. il *Sky Telesc* 74:370-2 O '87

The art of planetary observing (II). D. C. Parker and T. A. Dobbins. il *Sky Telesc* 74:603-7 D '87

The backyard astronomer. See issues of Astronomy

A 'brown dwarf' in the heavens [discovery by Benjamin Zuckerman and Eric Becklin] il *U S News World Rep* 103:15 N 23 '87

Extrasolar planets, maybe—but brown dwarfs, no. M. M. Waldrop. il *Science* 236:1623-4 Je 26 '87

Finding the planets [computer program] A. Blackadar. il *Weatherwise* 40:45-9 F '87

Hunting Planet X: a nothing that counts. J. Eberhart. *Sci News* 132:21 Jl 11 '87

Meteorites make a planet [Basaltic Achondrite Planetoid; work of Jeremy Delaney] E. R. C. Capulong. *Pop Sci* 231:33 O '87

Pioneer data support theory of tenth planet. *Aviat Week Space Technol* 127:32 Jl 6 '87

Planet stalkers [Canadian research] J. Hecht. il *Omni* 10:34 N '87

The planets of summer. J. Kanipe. il *Astronomy* 15:58-63 F '87

'Possible' and 'probable' alien planets [research by Bruce Campbell and others] D. E. Thomsen. *Sci News* 131:405 Je 27 '87

Possible planetary systems discovered [Canadian research] R. Talcott. il *Astronomy* 15:18-19 S '87

The search for Planet X. W. D. Marbach. il *Newsweek* 110:55 Jl 13 '87

The strange case of the disappearing star—or was that a planet? [VB 8B] il *Discover* 8:9-10 Ja '87

The sun, moon, and planets this month. D. Byrd. See issues of Sky and Telescope beginning August 1985

Telltale wobbles [Canadian astronomers discover planet orbiting around star Epsilon Eridani] il *Time* 129:53 Je 29 '87

Alignment

See Conjunctions (Astronomy)

Conferences

Halley in Heidelberg, planets in Paris. R. Berry. il *Astronomy* 15:24+ Mr '87

Letter from the Space Center [Lunar and Planetary Science Conference] H. S. F. Cooper. *New Yorker* 63:71-81 Je 8 '87

Conjunctions

See Conjunctions (Astronomy)

Exploration

See also

Space flight to Jupiter

Space flight to Mars

Space flight to Saturn

Space flight to Venus

Is the U.S. abandoning the solar system? [Solar System Exploration Committee report] D. Morrison. il *Sky Telesc* 73:580 Je '87

Scientists urge immediate change in planetary exploration policies [report of the Solar System Exploration Committee] T. M. Foley. *Aviat Week Space Technol* 126:68 Je 15 '87

U.S. must renew commitment to planetary exploration. D. Morrison. por *Aviat Week Space Technol* 127:143 Ag 10 '87

Measurements

See Astronomical measurements

Orbits

Do orbits change in 100 million years? [Project Longstop] R. W. Sinnott. il *Sky Telesc* 74:182-3 Ag '87

Uranus is perturbed: usual suspect rounded up [Planet X; research by John Anderson] il *Discover* 8:16+ S '87

Were Titius and Bode right? il *Sky Telesc* 73:371 Ap '87

Ring system

See Ring systems (Astronomy)

Planets, Minor *See* Asteroids

Planispheres

Star finding with a planisphere. A. MacRobert. il *Sky Telesc* 73:143-5 F '87

Plank, Karl A.

Broken continuities: Night and White crucifixion [cover story] il por *Christ Century* 104:963-6 N 4 '87

Plankton

See also

Water bloom

Acantharian fluxes and strontium to chlorinity ratios in the North Pacific Ocean. R. E. Bernstein and others. bibl f il *Science* 237:1490-4 S 18 '87

Bacteria: link or sink? [discussion of May 16, 1986 article, Bacterioplankton: a sink for carbon in a coastal marine plankton community] H. W. Ducklow and others. *Science* 235:88-9 Ja 2 '87

Can microscale chemical patches persist in the sea? Microelectrode study of marine snow fecal pellets. A. L. Alldredge and Y. Cohen. bib f il *Science* 235:689-91 F 6 '87

Plankton—*cont.*

Climate control [influence of plankton on cloud formation; work of Robert J. Charlson and James E. Lovelock] *Sci Am* 257:24 Jl '87

Diel periodicity of photosynthesis in polar phytoplankton: influence on primary production. R. B. Rivkin and M. Putt. bibl f il *Science* 238:1285-8 N 27 '87

A major food web component in the Orinoco River channel: evidence from planktivorous electric fishes. J. G. Lundberg and others. bibl f il *Science* 237:81-3 Jl 3 '87

The plankton-climate connection [cover story] R. Monastersky. il *Sci News* 132:362-5 D 5 '87

Solar-powered animals [aeolid nudibranchs growing zooxanthellae inside their bodies; cover story] W. B. Rudman. il *Nat Hist* 96:50-3 O '87

Stimulation of heterotrophic microplankton production by resuspended marine sediments. S. C. Wainright. bibl f il *Science* 238:1710-12 D 18 '87

Planned Parenthood Federation of America
    See also
    Family Planning International Assistance
Faye Wattleton. C. Green. *Black Enterp* 17:42+ Ap '87

Planning, Agricultural *See* Farm management
Planning, Business *See* Business planning
Planning, City *See* City planning
Planning, Economic *See* Economic policy
Planning, Land *See* Land utilization
Planning, Product *See* Product planning
Planning, Regional *See* Regional planning
Plans (Architecture) *See* Architecture, Domestic—Designs and plans
Plant analysis *See* Plants—Analysis and chemistry
Plant Biological Institute (Canada)
Cloning new foods. il *Macleans* 100:43 Ap 20 '87
Plant boxes *See* Flower boxes, planters, etc.
Plant cells and tissues
    See also
    Chloroplasts
    Chromosomes (Botany)
    Plants—Analysis and chemistry
    Protoplasts

Culture
    See also
    Clones (Botany)

Photographs and photography
Botanical close encounters. G. W. Verderber. il *Conservationist* 42:40-3 N/D '87

Plant chemistry *See* Plants—Analysis and chemistry
Plant competition
Competition and tree death. R. K. Peet and N. L. Christensen. bibl il *BioScience* 37:586-95 S '87
Plant conservation
    See also
    Forest conservation
Plant defenses *See* Defense mechanisms (Botany)
Plant eating animals *See* Herbivores
Plant ecology *See* Botany—Ecology
Plant foods *See* Plants—Nutrition
Plant genetics
    See also
    Chromosomes (Botany)
    Clones (Botany)
    Germplasm resources—Plants
    Plant Biological Institute (Canada)

Agricultural biotechnology: strategies for competitiveness [report by the National Research Council] L. Tangley. *BioScience* 37:463 Jl/Ag '87

Biotechnology, agriculture and development [cover story; special issue; with editorial comment by Edouard Glissant] il *Courier* 40:3-34 Mr '87

Can a banana splice save the banana split? [breeding against black sigatoka disease; work of Phillip Rowe] il *Discover* 8:7-8 Ag '87

Coming from RJR: high-tech vegetables [joint venture with Biotechnica International] il *Bus Week* p44 O 5 '87

Discovery of transposable element activity among progeny of tissue culture-derived maize plants. V. M. Peschke and others. bibl f il *Science* 238:804-7 N 6 '87

Does more food mean less famine? A. Smith. il *Esquire* 108:55-6 Jl '87

Down on the farm: genetic engineering meets ecology. D. Pimentel. il *Technol Rev* 90:24-30 Ja '87

Duplication of CaMV 35S promoter sequences creates a strong enhancer for plant genes [cauliflower mosaic virus] R. Kay and others. bibl f il *Science* 236:1299-302 Je 5 '87

Electrophoretic evidence for genetic diploidy in the bracken fern (Pteridium aquilinum). P. G. Wolf and others. bibl f il *Science* 236:947-9 My 22 '87

Fiddling around with nature means better pest control. *Success Farm* 85:18R My '87

Gene transfer in cereals. E. C. Cocking and M. R. Davey. bibl f *Science* 236:1259-62 Je 5 '87

Gene transfer in corn. D. D. Edwards. *Sci News* 131:37 Ja 17 '87

Gene transfer in crop improvement. R. M. Goodman and others. bibl f il *Science* 236:48-54 Ap 3 '87

Glowing tobacco [gene tagging with luciferase] A. Fisher. il *Pop Sci* 230:8 Ap '87

Here come the bionic piglets. G. Bylinsky. il *Fortune* 116:74-6+ O 26 '87

Ingrained genes. *Sci Am* 256:68 Mr '87

Lab-built plants, animals mean change. G. Vincent. il *Success Farm* 85:B-C My '87

Lighting up [gene tagging with luciferase] il *Sci Am* 256:60-2 Ja '87

The maize transposable element Ds is spliced from RNA. S. R. Wessler and others. bibl f il *Science* 237:916-18 Ag 21 '87

Progress toward engineering monocots. L. Tangley. *BioScience* 37:462 Jl/Ag '87

Rice plants regenerated from protoplasts. J. L. Marx. il *Science* 235:31-2 Ja 2 '87

Shotgun approach to genetic engineering [work of Theodore M. Klein and others] J. Raloff. *Sci News* 131:310 My 16 '87

Shotgun marriage [use of microprojectiles for delivering nucleic acids into living plant cells; work of Theodore M. Klein and others] il *Sci Am* 257:23-4 Jl '87

Strange bedfellows. P. B. Moses. il *BioScience* 37:6-10 Ja '87

Transgenic plants as tools to study the molecular organization of plant genes. J. St. Schell. bibl f *Science* 237:1176-83 S 4 '87

Transposon tagging and molecular analysis of the maize regulatory locus opaque-2. R. J. Schmidt and others. bibl f il *Science* 238:960-3 N 13 '87

Virginia Walbot. B. Lawren. *Omni* 9:40+ S '87
Plant holders *See* Flower boxes, planters, etc.
Plant hormones *See* Hormones, Plant
Plant introduction
Biological invasion by Myrica faya alters ecosystem development in Hawaii. P. M. Vitousek and others. bibl f il *Science* 238:802-4 N 6 '87

Ecological invasions offer opportunities [Hawaii as a research area] R. Lewin. il *Science* 238:752-3 N 6 '87

The ecology of biological invasions. H. A. Mooney and J. A. Drake. bibl f il maps *Environment* 29:10-15+ Je '87
Plant lice
One giant leap for aphid-kind [escape-response behavior of parasitized aphids; research by Murdoch K. McAllister and Bernard D. Roitberg] *Sci News* 132:158 S 5 '87
Plant mail order business *See* Mail order business
Plant nutrition *See* Plants—Nutrition
Plant physiology *See* Botany—Physiology
Plant propagation
    See also
    Clones (Botany)
    Grafting
    Seedlings
    Seeds

How to multiply Matilija poppies . . . challenging to very difficult. il *Sunset* 178:202-3 Je '87

How to propagate baby's-tears. E. Waltner. il *Flower Gard* 31:60 Ap/My '87

Layering: a sure way to increase your shrubs and vines. P. Byers. il *Flower Gard* 31:93-4 Ap/My '87
Plant research *See* Agricultural research; Botanical research
Plant roots *See* Roots
Plant sales *See* Sales
Plant shelves and racks *See* Shelves and racks
Plant stands, flower stands, etc.
Sleek 'n' sturdy grow-light stand. B. A. Lewis. il *Better Homes Gard* 65:178+ O '87
Plant supports
    See also
    Trellises
Plant therapy *See* Gardens and gardening—Therapeutic use
Plant tissues *See* Plant cells and tissues
Plant toxins *See* Toxins and antitoxins
Plant viruses *See* Viruses, Plant
Plantations

Brazil
Two giant U.S. business efforts that failed in Brazil [H. Ford's Fordlandia and D. Ludwig's Jari Project] M. S. Forbes. il *Forbes* 140:18-19 O 19 '87

Plantations—*cont.*

Louisiana

The last of the belles. L. Bailey. il *Vogue* 177:536+ S '87

Martinique

Habitation Pécoul: Vicomte and Vicomtesse d'Origny on Martinique. L. Dennis. il *Archit Dig* 44:192-7+ O '87

Virginia

See also

Stratford Hall Plantation, Robert E. Lee Memorial Association (Stratford, Va.)

Along the river flows a golden past [James River] K. Lingo. il map *South Living* 22:58-63 Ag '87

Planters (Farm machines)

Equipment

Anhydrous on drill, but seed feels no pain [no-till wheat] M. Holmberg. il *Success Farm* 85 no1:30 Ja '87

Planting-time conveniences. D. Mowitz. il *Success Farm* 85:18AB Ap '87

Ridge planting on a roll. D. Mowitz and C. Finck. il *Success Farm* 85 no6:10-13 Mr '87

Planters (Flower boxes) *See* Flower boxes, planters, etc.

Planting *See* Flower gardens and gardening; Gardens and gardening; Landscape gardening; Seeding; Vegetable gardens and gardening

Planting machinery *See* Planters (Farm machines)

Planting of trees *See* Tree planting

Plants

See also

Alpine flora

Biennials (Plants)

Biomass energy

Botany

Bulbs

Climbing plants

Color of plants

Desert flora

Electrophysiology of plants

Flowers

Forage plants

Forcing (Plants)

Ground cover plants

Growth regulators—Plants

Herbs

Leaves

Perennials (Plants)

Pollen

Roots

Seeds

Shrubs

Succulent plants

Urban flora

Weeds

[Month] in your garden. See issues of Sunset (Central edition)

All-America Selections

AARS names three 1988 winners [roses] il *Flower Gard* 31:8 O/N '87

AAS winners for 1988. L. C. Askey. il *South Living* 22:50 D '87

All-America Selections '88. il *Flower Gard* 32:14-16+ D '87/Ja '88

Analysis and chemistry

They read the leaves to target fertilizer [DRIS analysis] M. Holmberg. il *Success Farm* 85 no3:18AH F '87

Breeding

See also

Germplasm resources—Plants

Plant genetics

Introducing zunkins [zucchini-pumpkin hybrids] W. Bilozir. il por *Rodale's Org Gard* 34:88-9 O '87

Ted Torrey interview. J. Lowe. il por *Flower Gard* 32:48+ D '87/Ja '88

Carbon content

Carbon gain by plants in natural environments. R. W. Pearcy and others. bibl f il *BioScience* 37:21-9 Ja '87

Plant responses to multiple environmental factors. F. S. Chapin and others. bibl f il *BioScience* 37:49-57 Ja '87

Classification

See Botany—Classification

Defense mechanisms

See Defense mechanisms (Botany)

Disease and pest resistance

A deer-proof garden. P. Holm. il *Rodale's Org Gard* 34:31-3 D '87

The deer still visit, but they ignore most of the plants [deer-resistant plants] il *Sunset* 179:224-5 O '87

Diseases and pests

See also

Brown rot

Cutworms

Earwigs

Fungi, Pathogenic

Insects

Leaf spot

Plant lice

Viruses, Plant

Wilt diseases

The role of drought in outbreaks of plant-eating insects. W. J. Mattson and R. A. Haack. bibl f il *BioScience* 37:110-18 F '87

What's the diagnosis? W. S. Moore. See issues of Flower and Garden beginning February/March 1984

Evolution

Gender modification in North American ginsengs. M. A. Schlessman. bibl f il *BioScience* 37:469-75 Jl/Ag '87

Not-so-naked ancestors [electron microscope study of naked algae] G. McFadden. il *Sea Front* 33:46-51 Ja/F '87

Fertilization

See Fertilization of plants

Genetics

See Plant genetics

Irritability and movements

See also

Geotropism

Metal content

Prospecting with plants. F. R. Siegel. il *Earth Sci* 40:18-19 Fall '87

Nitrogen content

Plant responses to multiple environmental factors. F. S. Chapin and others. bibl f il *BioScience* 37:49-57 Ja '87

Nutrition

Apogeotropic roots in an Amazon rain forest. R. L. Sanford. bibl f il *Science* 235:1062-4 F 27 '87

When growing down isn't good enough [apogeotropic roots; study by Robert L. Sanford, Jr.] *Sci News* 131:188 Mr 21 '87

Physiology

See Botany—Physiology

Protection

See also

Mulching

Agricultural fleece: boon to gardeners. J. Ball. il *Home Mech* 83:58+ Ap '87

Altered bacteria released [frost preventing bacteria] *Sci News* 131:277 My 2 '87

California field test goes forward [Frostban bacteria] M. Crawford. il *Science* 236:511 My 1 '87

Engineered bacteria released [preventing frost damage] L. Tangley. *BioScience* 37:461 Jl/Ag '87

Extend the growing season [use of row covers] L. C. Askey. il *South Living* 22:62 N '87

Garden netting to foil berry-eating birds. il *Sunset* 178:208 Je '87

Headstart garden [use of black plastic mulch and floating row covers] J. Cook. il *Ctry J* 14:34-5 My '87

Miracle blankets for vegetables? [floating row covers] il *Sunset* 178:86-8+ F '87

One potato patch that is making genetic history [test of genetically engineered Ice-minus bacteria at Tulelake, Calif.] S. S. Hall. il *Smithsonian* 18:125-6+ Ag '87

Pest protection by the yard [soft row covers] M. Kane. il *Rodale's Org Gard* 34:24-6+ Mr '87

Sow lettuce now [use of floating row covers] K. Martin. il *Rodale's Org Gard* 34:53-4+ S '87

Tubers, berries and bugs [bacteria designed to inhibit frost formation sprayed on plants] P. Elmer-Dewitt. il *Time* 129:63 My 11 '87

Weatherproofing the garden. S. Sides and F. Sides. il *Mother Earth News* 104:87-91 Mr/Ap '87

Reproduction

See also

Plants, Sex in

Allocating resources to reproduction and defense. F. A. Bazzaz and others. bibl f il *BioScience* 37:58-67 Ja '87

Resistance to disease and pests

See Plants—Disease and pest resistance

Soilless culture

See Hydroponics

Temperature

See also

Plants, Effect of temperature on

Plants—Temperature—*cont.*
Salicylic acid: a natural inducer of heat production in Arum lilies. I. Raskin and others. bibl f il *Science* 237:1601-2 S 25 '87
Training
A blooming azalea column . . . train your own. il *Sunset* 178:273 My '87
High standards [training house plants] J. Rapp. il *Redbook* 169:126-9+ My '87
Training a vine to perform in tight space. il *Sunset* 178:244-5 My '87
Water requirements
Just in case it's another dry winter. il *Sunset* 179:210 O '87
Plant water balance. E.-D. Schulze and others. bibl f il *BioScience* 37:30-7 Ja '87
Plants 'tell' when thirsty [work of Mike Dixon] G. L. Vincent. il *Success Farm* 85 no3:20 F '87
Plants, Artificial
See also
Flowers, Artificial
Plants, Edible
See also
Cattails
Flowers as food
Greens, Edible
Vegetables
The American scene [Ozark forager B. J. Tatum] E. Jones. il *Gourmet* 47:62+ F '87
For forager Justin Rashid, the woods are lovely, dark and deep—and filled with things that he can eat. M. Neill. il pors *People Wkly* 28:125-7 O 19 '87
A garden gone wild [Vermont forager B. Mraz] J. Burnett. il por *Rodale's Org Gard* 34:84-6 N '87
Plants, Effect of air pollution on
Acid showers and damage to plants [crops] *Sci News* 132:158 S 5 '87
Plants, Effect of climate on
The role of drought in outbreaks of plant-eating insects. W. J. Mattson and R. A. Haack. bibl f il *BioScience* 37:110-18 F '87
Plants, Effect of ethylene on
Plant hormone: key to ozone toxicity? [research by Horst Mehlhorn and Alan R. Wellburn] J. Raloff. *Sci News* 131:357-8 Je 6 '87
Plants, Effect of gravity on *See* Geotropism
Plants, Effect of light on
See also
Photoperiodism
Plants, Effect of ozone on
Changing perspectives on air-pollution stress. F. H. Bormann and G. E. Likens. *BioScience* 37:370 Je '87
Ozone's major effects on trees may be hidden [work of Deane Wang and others] *Environment* 28:21 D '86
Plant hormone: key to ozone toxicity? [research by Horst Mehlhorn and Alan R. Wellburn] J. Raloff. *Sci News* 131:357-8 Je 6 '87
Plants, Effect of stress on
Stress physiology and the distribution of plants. C. B. Osmond and others. bibl f il *BioScience* 37:38-48 Ja '87
Plants, Effect of temperature on
Better beans [protection from stressful temperature swings] D. Bilderback. il *Rodale's Org Gard* 34:25-9 Ag '87
Don't leave houseplants in the cold. il *South Living* 22:55 F '87
Plants, Effect of wind on
Growin' in the wind. M. V. Look. il *Rodale's Org Gard* 34:64-5 Ap '87
Plants, Extinct
See also
Mass extinction of species
Plants, Food *See* Plants, Edible
Plants, Fossil *See* Paleobotany
Plants, Fragrant
Where has all the fragrance gone? [roses] M. Mohs. il *Discover* 8:90-1+ Je '87
Plants, Geographical distribution of *See* Geographical distribution of animals and plants
Plants, Hanging *See* Hanging plants
Plants, Industrial *See* Factories
Plants, Medicinal *See* Botany, Medical
Plants, Ornamental
See also
Aspidistra
Caladiums
Espaliers
Hanging plants
House plants

Plants, Potted
See also
Flower boxes, planters, etc.
House plants
Plants, Sex in
See also
Plants—Reproduction
Gender modification in North American ginsengs. M. A. Schlessman. bibl f il *BioScience* 37:469-75 Jl/Ag '87
Sex choice and reproductive costs in Jack-in-the-pulpit. D. Policansky. bibl f il *BioScience* 37:476-81 Jl/Ag '87
Plants, Size of
Sex choice and reproductive costs in Jack-in-the-pulpit. D. Policansky. bibl f il *BioScience* 37:476-81 Jl/Ag '87
Plants and civilization
See also
Ethnobotany
As cities crumble, plants may be at the root of it; ed. by Sylvia E. Merschel. D. R. Perry. il *Smithsonian* 17:72-9 Ja '87
Plants that eat cities; ed. by Sylvia E. Merschel. D. R. Perry. il *Read Dig* 131:126-8 O '87
Plants as energy sources *See* Biomass energy
Plants as gifts
Cattleya orchids as a gift? Yes, even without a greenhouse. il *Sunset* 179:188 D '87
The season's best gift plants. D. A. Jimerson. il *Better Homes Gard* 65:142-3 N '87
Plants in art
See also
Leaves in art
The Hans Sloane plate [botanicals] S. Bagdade and A. Bagdade. il *Antiques Collect Hobbies* 92:76 My '87
Plants in house decoration
Living flowers for your table [cover story] D. Hastings. il *South Living* 22:116-17 Mr '87
Reinaldo and Carolina Herrera in Manhattan [brownstone decorated by Robert Metzger] C. T. Buckley. il pors *Archit Dig* 44:128-35+ Ap '87
Plaque, Dental *See* Dental plaque
Plaques and plaquettes
Butterfly wall plaques. F. D. Thompson. il *Workbench* 43:48 Mr/Ap '87
Plaskett, Thomas G., 1943-
about
Plaskett replaced as Continental chief; Lorenzo takes over. *Aviat Week Space Technol* 127:32 Jl 27 '87
Taking over the controls. pors *Time* 130:43 Ag 3 '87
Plasma (Ionized gases)
See also
Solar wind
Tokamaks
Big-Bang bashers. J. Horgan. il *Sci Am* 257:22+ S '87
Electrons and ions at the helium surface. A. J. Dahm and W. F. Vinen. bibl f il *Phys Today* 40:43-50 F '87
Gas jet seen projecting from Seyfert Galaxy [Markarian 315; work of John W. MacKenty] *Astronomy* 15:84-5 Ja '87
A Herbig-Haro object unmasked [cosmic jets of HH34] *Sky Telesc* 73:30-1 Ja '87
Lab for the universe [International Solar-Terrestrial Physics Program] T. Kiely. il *Technol Rev* 90:8+ N/D '87
M-87: describing the indescribable [cover story] J. Kanipe. il *Astronomy* 15:6-13 My '87
Matter flow from a Seyfert nucleus [work of Jean W. Goad and John S. Gallagher] *Sci News* 132:254 O 17 '87
The Milky Way's fountain [work of Christopher Martin and Stuart Bowyer] *Sky Telesc* 73:485 My '87
Plasma and fusion physics. *Phys Today* 40:S59-S63 Ja '87
Surfing on a plasma wave [plasma wake-field acceleration] il *Sci Am* 256:66-7 Ap '87
Three receive APS plasma physics awards. il *Phys Today* 40:85-6 Mr '87
Plasma confinement
See also
Magnetic fusion
Tokamaks
Plasma display systems
The lava light returns [Eye of the Storm light show] S. A. Booth. il *Pop Mech* 164:14 S '87
Plasma membranes *See* Membranes (Biology)
Plasma propulsion of space vehicles *See* Space vehicles—Propulsion systems

Plasma waves
See also
Alfvén waves
Plasmacytomas See Blood cells—Cancer
Plasmapheresis
See also
Photopheresis
Plasmids
See also
Transposons
Linear plasmids of the bacterium Borrelia burgdorferi have covalently closed ends. A. G. Barbour and C. F. Garon. bibl f il *Science* 237:409-11 Jl 24 '87
New questions in Strobel case [field test of Dutch elm disease] L. Roberts. *Science* 237:1097-8 S 4 '87
Redesigning metabolic routes: manipulation of TOL plasmid pathway for catabolism of alkylbenzoates. J. L. Ramos and others. bibl f il *Science* 235:593-6 Ja 30 '87
Site-specific nick in the T-DNA border sequence as a result of Agrobacterium vir gene expression. K. Wang and others. bibl f il *Science* 235:587-91 Ja 30 '87
Transgenic plants as tools to study the molecular organization of plant genes. J. St. Schell. bibl f *Science* 237:1176-83 S 4 '87
Plasminogen
See also
TPA (Drug)
Gene makeup a surprise [apolipoprotein(a) and plasminogen] D. M. Barnes. *Science* 238:1513 D 11 '87
Plasmodium (Parasite)
An antidrug malaria pump? [resistance to chloroquine] *Sci News* 132:359 D 5 '87
Efflux of chloroquine from Plasmodium falciparum: mechanism of chloroquine resistance. D. J. Krogstad and others. bibl f il *Science* 238:1283-5 N 27 '87
Genetic analysis of the human malaria parasite Plasmodium falciparum. D. Walliker and others. bibl f il *Science* 236:1661-6 Je 26 '87
Reversal of chloroquine resistance in Plasmodium falciparum by verapamil. S. K. Martin and others. bibl f il *Science* 235:899-901 F 20 '87
Structurally distinct, stage-specific ribosomes occur in Plasmodium. J. H. Gunderson and others. bibl f il *Science* 238:933-7 N 13 '87
Plasmodium (Parasite) infection See Malaria
Plaster and plastering
See also
Spackling compounds
Stucco
Pigments of imagination [work of Art In Construction studio] K. D. Stein. il *Archit Rec* 175:18-19 D '87
Plaster repair. M. Morris. il *Home Mech* 83:26+ S '87
A plasterlike finish for basement walls. R. Barnhart. il *Home Mech* 83:132+ O '87
Repair plaster cracks/holes. G. Branson. il *Fam Handyman* 37:52 F '87
Plaster board See Wallboard
Plaster casts (Sculpture)
Ghosts of sculpture past. R. Lynes. il *Archit Dig* 44:26+ Ag '87
Plastic coins See Coins
Plastic flooring See Flooring, Plastic
Plastic food wraps See Food wraps
Plastic houses
Foam-block house. V. E. Gilmore. il *Pop Sci* 231:52-4+ D '87
Homes of foam [cover story] V. E. Gilmore. il *Pop Sci* 230:78-81+ Mr '87
Plastic nails See Nails
Plastic pistols See Pistols
Plastic surgery See Surgery, Plastic
Plastic tubes See Tubes, Plastic
Plastic water pipes See Water pipes, Plastic
Plastic worms See Fishing lures, flies, etc.
Plasticity (Physiology) See Adaptation (Biology)
Plastics
See also
Laminated plastics
Polyacetylene
Styrene
Thermoplastics
New uses for plastics. G. Bronson. il *Forbes* 139:216-17 My 18 '87
Deterioration
Bagging it [starch-based plastics] *Sci Am* 257:22 Ag '87
Degradable polymers? J. Parr. il *Forbes* 140:206+ O 5 '87
Wash-away plastics [developed by Belland AG] S. Ashley. il *Pop Sci* 230:45+ Je '87

Plastics in automobiles See Automobiles, Foreign—Materials
Plastics in medicine See Polymers in medicine
Plastics industry
See also
Envirodyne Industries, Inc.
Switzerland
See also
Belland AG
Plastics pollution of the sea See Marine pollution
Plastics work
Clearly beautiful [acrylic plastic projects] L. M. Dalsgaard. il *Home Mech* 83:76-9 Ap '87
Protect your collectibles [acrylic display case] E. Waltner and W. Waltner. il *Workbench* 43:78-80 S/O '87
Plate
See also
Pewter
Silverware
Plate tectonics See Geology
Platelet aggregation See Blood cell aggregation
Platelet-derived growth factor See Growth regulators
Platelets (Blood) See Blood cells
Platforms, Plant See Plant stands, flower stands, etc.
Plath, Sylvia
about
Any resemblance . . . *Nation* 244:132-3 F 7 '87
Closing accounts on Plath's 'Bell jar'. *Newsweek* 109:58 F 9 '87
From book to film: a novel case of libel. A. Press. il por *Newsweek* 109:63 F 2 '87
Libel in fiction to be tested in Bell jar suit. M. Yen. *Publ Wkly* 231:290 Ja 30 '87
Of whom the Bell told. R. Lacayo. il por *Time* 129:60-1 F 9 '87
Parties settle Bell suit out of court. *Publ Wkly* 231:19 F 13 '87
Salinger and 'The bell jar': what do they mean to publishers? C. E. Rinzler. il *Publ Wkly* 231:20-2 Ap 24 '87
Platinum
Prices
More precious than gold. S. W. Angrist. il *Forbes* 139:191 Ap 6 '87
Platinum as an investment
Platinum's new luster. B. Kallen. il *Forbes* 139:85 Ja 26 '87
Platinum mines and mining
See also
Hughes Mining Company
North America
The platinum rush of 1987 is on. S. D. Atchison. il *Bus Week* p67 S 7 '87
Platoon [film] See Motion picture reviews—Single works
Platt, Harty
Fitness times two. *Harpers Bazaar* 120:132+ Ja '87
Sport specs: play it safe! il *Harpers Bazaar* 120:44+ Ap '87
Water play: sports afloat. il *Harpers Bazaar* 120:137+ My '87
Platt, John Rader, 1918-
The future of AIDS. il por *Futurist* 21:10-17 N/D '87
Platt, John W. S.
Oregon Eden. il *House Gard* 159:142-9+ F '87
Platt, Rutherford H.
Coastal wetland management: the advance designation approach. bibl f il maps *Environment* 29:16-20+ N '87
Plaut, W. Gunther, 1912-
about
'A hysterical overreaction' [interview] M. Gee. il por *Macleans* 100:12 Ag 24 '87
Play
See also
Games
Playgrounds
Toys
8 silly little games (and why they're so important) [playing with baby] C. Medvescek. il *Parents* 62:92-4+ Je '87
Games babies play [research by Hildy S. Ross and Susan P. Lollis] J. Fischman. il *Psychol Today* 21:14 O '87
Games parents play [interacting with infants] il *Psychol Today* 21:31 Ja '87
The importance of play [cover story] B. Bettelheim. il *Atlantic* 259:35-46 Mr '87
Peer play [two year olds] B. Weissbourd. il *Parents* 62:208 O '87
A place to play. B. Weissbourd. il *Parents* 62:202 My '87
Play's the thing [results of poll] I. Groller. il *Parents* 62:27 Jl '87

Play—*cont.*
Your toddler's social life. J. T. Gibson. il *Parents* 62:190 Ag '87
Play behavior (Animals) *See* Animals—Habits and behavior
Play groups
The care-giver [Parkbench playgroup at the 92nd St. Y, New York City] E. Hopkins. il *N Y* 20:26 Je 15 '87
Teaching "entry" behavior to elementary schoolers. G. L. Macklem. *Educ Dig* 53:40-3 N '87
Play houses *See* Playhouses
Play production and direction *See* Theater—Production and direction
Playbills
A Charleston, South Carolina, playbill of 1794. J. T. Newlin. il *Antiques* 131:432-3 F '87
Playboy (Periodical)
Why would a woman peel off her clothes and pose nude for Playboy? Three women tell their stories. S. Helgesen. il *Glamour* 85:218-19+ Je '87
Playboy Enterprises, Inc.
A move to uncover Playboy's hidden assets. G. G. Marcial. il *Bus Week* p148 Mr 23 '87
Player, Corrie Lynne
"Joy comes from sharing". il *McCalls* 115:133-5 D '87
Player, Gary
about
Another era, same Player. J. Diaz. il por *Sports Illus* 67:18-19 Jl 20 '87
Player, William
about
Downfall of a schemer. P. Best. il por *Macleans* 100:32 Jl 20 '87
Playfair, John
about
Tinkering with tax reform. P. C. Newman. il por *Macleans* 100:42 Je 29 '87
Playgrounds
Outdoor play . . . one Head Start program's approach [Adams County, Colo.; cover story] F. Wardle. il *Child Today* 16:16-19 Mr/Ap '87
Playgrounds, Home
Equipment
Parents guide to backyard play sets. il *Good Housekeep* 205:130 S '87
Personal playgrounds. A. Rooze. il *Fam Handyman* 37:40+ Mr '87
Play structure grows and changes as the children do. il *Sunset* 178:142+ Ap '87
Wisteria and children are both welcome. il *Sunset* 179:128 O '87
Playgroups *See* Play groups
Playhouses
See also
Tree houses
Best outdoor projects [Victorian playhouse] il *Fam Handyman* 37:38-9 My/Je '87
Fold-up playhouse made from two sheets of plywood. il *Sunset* 178:108 F '87
Pegboard, shoelaces, and square knots . . . these play shelters couldn't be simpler. il *Sunset* 179:76-8 D '87
Personal playgrounds. R. Bischof. il *Fam Handyman* 37:40 Mr '87
Playmates *See* Friendship
Playrooms *See* Children's rooms
Plays *See* Drama
Plays, Filmed *See* Motion picture adaptations
Playwriting *See* Drama—Technique
Plaza Guadalupe (San Antonio, Tex.) *See* San Antonio (Tex.)—Plazas
Plaza Lasso, Galo, 1906-1987
about
Obituary
Américas por 39:51 Mr/Ap '87. R. C. Schroeder
Plazas
See also
Barcelona (Spain)—Plazas
Los Angeles (Calif.)—Plazas
San Antonio (Tex.)—Plazas
Plea bargaining *See* Pleas (Legal procedure)
Pleas (Legal procedure)
A new legal defense: Ollie made me do it. T. Jacoby. il *Newsweek* 110:24-5 N 30 '87
"Plea bargaining should be abolished" [condensed from Escape of the guilty] R. A. Fine. il *Read Dig* 131:233-4+ N '87
Pleas of insanity (Legal procedure) *See* Insanity—Jurisprudence

Pleasant, Barbara
Biennial flowers for easy care. il *Rodale's Org Gard* 34:54-6+ Je '87
Looking at the lupines. il *Rodale's Org Gard* 34:74-9 Ja '87
Stalking the perfect ear [cover story] il *Rodale's Org Gard* 34:28-30 My '87
Please Touch (Castro Valley, Calif.: Store) *See* Castro Valley (Calif.)—Stores
Pleasure
See also
Comfort
Happiness
Hedonism
The pain-pleasure connection. P. L. DeVito. il *USA Today (Periodical)* 115:47-9 Ja '87
Popularity contest [results of poll on sources of pleasure or satisfaction] J. Queenan. *New Repub* 196:14-15 Mr 23 '87
Pleck, Joseph H.
about
Real man redux. M. S. Kimmel. bibl (p68) il pors *Psychol Today* 21:48-52 Jl '87
Pledging Conference for Development Activities (United Nations) *See* United Nations Pledging Conference for Development Activities
Pleiades
A grand Pleiades occultation. D. W. Dunham. il *Sky Telesc* 74:284-7 S '87
The March 5th Pleiades occultation. D. W. Dunham. il *Sky Telesc* 73:296-7 Mr '87
Skylore. R. Burnham. il *Astronomy* 15:61 N '87
Pleistocene period *See* Paleontology—Pleistocene
Plenum Publishing Corp.
Can this canary swallow a cat? [Plenum wants Arthur D. Little] K. H. Hammonds. *Bus Week* p30-1 Jl 27 '87
Fish or cut bait. F. Meeks. il por *Forbes* 139:57+ Je 15 '87
Plessey Co. plc
Plessey's new face in the U.S. [Stromberg-Carlson purchase in 1982] J. J. Keller. il *Bus Week* p32 Ap 20 '87
Pliers
Pliers & wrenches. H. Wicks. il *Home Mech* 83:20 Jl '87
Selecting pliers for home tasks. H. Wicks. il *Home Mech* 83:36 F '87
Plimpton, George
Literary lair: Freddy and George Plimpton in Sagaponack. il por *Archit Dig* 44:126-31 Je '87
Plisetskaya, Maya
about
Technique: Plisetskaya teaches. M. Horosko. il pors *Dance Mag* 61:54-6 O '87
PLO *See* Palestine Liberation Organization
Ploscowe, Stephen A., and Goldstein, Marvin M.
Trouble on the firing line. il *Nations Bus* 75:36-7 Mr '87
Plotkin, Mark
about
Dr. Plotkin's jungle pharmacy: an ethnobotanist goes native for science. A. Fadiman. il pors *Life* 10:15-17 Je '87
Plots (Drama, novel, etc.)
See also
Television broadcasting—Plots, themes, etc.
Plotting the realistic detective novel. M. Muller. *Writer* 100:12-15+ Je '87
Using imagination in plotting. J. Aiken. *Writer* 100:7-10+ D '87
Plous, S.
Ban missile flight testing. *Nation* 244:219-20 F 21 '87
Plovers
On the beach: plovers vs. nudists [Rhode Island] il *Newsweek* 110:63 Ag 3 '87
Photographs and photography
Back off, springbok! [pesky plover] il *Natl Geogr World* 146:10-11 O '87
Plowing *See* Tillage
Ploy (Term)
State of ploy. W. Safire. il *N Y Times Mag* p16 Ag 30 '87
PLR (Power line radiation) *See* Electromagnetic waves
Plugs (Fishing lures) *See* Fishing lures, flies, etc.
Plum Creek Timber Company, Inc.
Public dismay over private cuts [clearcutting by Plum Creek Timber Company on private land in the Pacific Northwest] J. Sher. il *Sierra* 72:83-4 Mr/Ap '87

Plum jam *See* Jelly, jam, etc.
Plum pie *See* Pie
Plum trees
More on plums and Crandall currant ancestry [discussion of January 1987 article, A wealth of plums (I)] B. Olcott-Reid. *Rodale's Org Gard* 34:8 Ap '87
Treat yourself to homegrown plums. il *South Living* 22:90 Ap '87
A wealth of plums (I). B. Olcott-Reid. il *Rodale's Org Gard* 34:26-32 Ja '87
A wealth of plums (II). B. Olcott-Reid. il *Rodale's Org Gard* 34:88-92 F '87
Plumage, Color of *See* Color of birds
Plumb, Barbara
Living. See issues of Vogue
Plumb, John
Rooms for art. il por *House Gard* 159:142-51+ O '87
A short history of furniture. il *House Gard* 159:120+ Ap '87
Vintage memories. il por *House Gard* 159:30+ Ag '87
Plumbing
See also
    Boats and boating—Water supply
    Sinks
    Toilets
    Water pipes
    Water pipes, Plastic
Maintenance and repair
5 foolproof fixes [common bathroom repairs] M. Henkenius. il *Pop Mech* 164:132-4+ Ap '87
Clearing clogged drains. M. Henkenius. il *Home Mech* 83:20 D '87
How to fix a pop-up drain. M. Thompson. il *Fam Handyman* 37:78 Mr '87
How to repair a bathtub drain. M. Henkenius. il *Pop Mech* 164:138 Jl '87
Keep your plumbing humming [bathroom fixtures] A. Rooze. il *Fam Handyman* 37:48+ O '87
Stopping water hammer. G. Branson. il *Fam Handyman* 37:88-9 My/Je '87
Plumbing industry
See also
    Waxman Industries, Inc.
Plumly, Stanley
Hedgerows [poem] il *Atlantic* 259:46-7 Je '87
The Wyoming poetry tour [poem] *New Yorker* 63:38 N 30 '87
Plummer, Bill
about
Bass fishing the old way. J. Gibbs. il por *Outdoor Life* 180:74-5+ O '87
Plums
See also
    Prunes
Plundering *See* Pillage
Pluralism (Social sciences)
See also
    Ethnicity
Plus System, Inc.
Plastic profits [D. D. Browning] A. Snitzer. il por *Forbes* 140:116 Ag 10 '87
Pluto (Planet)
See also
    Space flight to Pluto
Getting small [measurement of Pluto and its satellite] *Sci Am* 256:68 Ap '87
Pluto: limits on its atmosphere, ice on its moon. J. Eberhart. il *Sci News* 132:207 S 26 '87
Pluto the planetoid. D. Garr. il *Omni* 9:25 Jl '87
Pluto's identity crisis. il *Discover* 8:18 D '87
Satellites
How to view this summer's Pluto-Charon transits. D. J. Eicher. il *Astronomy* 15:97-101 My '87
Improved orbital and physical parameters for the Pluto-Charon system. D. J. Tholen and others. bibl f il *Science* 237:512-14 Jl 31 '87
IRAS serendipitous survey observations of Pluto and Charon. M. V. Sykes and others. bibl f il *Science* 237:1336-40 S 11 '87
Mysterious Pluto may shrink no longer [Pluto-Charon mutual events; research by David Tholen and others] R. A. Kerr. il *Science* 235:30 Ja 2 '87
Pluto and Charon: the dance goes on. J. K. Beatty. il *Sky Telesc* 74:248-51 S '87
Spectrophotometry of Pluto-Charon mutual events: individual spectra of Pluto and Charon. S. R. Sawyer and others. bibl f il *Science* 238:1560-3 D 11 '87
The surface composition of Charon: tentative identification of water ice. R. L. Marcialis and others. bibl f il *Science* 237:1349-51 S 11 '87

Watching Pluto blink [Pluto-Charon mutual events] il *Sky Telesc* 73:413 Ap '87
Spectra and spectroscopy
Spectrophotometry of Pluto-Charon mutual events: individual spectra of Pluto and Charon. S. R. Sawyer and others. bibl f il *Science* 238:1560-3 D 11 '87
Transits
How to view this summer's Pluto-Charon transits. D. J. Eicher. il *Astronomy* 15:97-101 My '87
Pluto and Charon: the dance goes on. J. K. Beatty. il *Sky Telesc* 74:248-51 S '87
Watching Pluto blink [Pluto-Charon mutual events] il *Sky Telesc* 73:413 Ap '87
Plutonium reactors *See* Nuclear reactors
Plutonium recycling *See* Reactor fuel reprocessing
Plyometrics
Look before you leap. M. Brzycki. il *Women's Sports Fitness* 9:86 Mr '87
Plywood
Understanding plywood. J. Vara. il *Ctry J* 14:18-19 F '87
Plywood construction
Wood-epoxy construction makes a featherweight camper cap. P. Butler and M. Butler. il *Pop Sci* 231:86-8 O '87
PMS *See* Premenstrual syndrome
Pneumatic equipment
See also
    Airplanes—Pneumatic equipment
Blown-on weed control. D. Mowitz. il *Success Farm* 85 no5:26J Mr '87
Pneumatics enjoy whirlwind success [farm applicators] D. Mowitz. il *Success Farm* 85 no4:22-5 F '87
Pneumonia
See also
    Q fever
Double (whammy) pneumonia [combined viral-bacterial pneumonia] D. D. Edwards. *Sci News* 131:101 F 14 '87
Pneumonia: lungs under bacterial siege. il *Curr Health* 2 14:26-7 D '87
Still a killer: pneumonia targets the ill, the elderly. C. Lecos. il *FDA Consum* 21:8-13 Je '87
Therapy
Extending AIDS patients' lives [two-drug combination used to attack Pneumocystis carinii pneumonia] M. Clark. il *Newsweek* 110:85 N 2 '87
Fighting a killer virus [Pneumocystis carinii pneumonia] N. Underwood. il *Macleans* 100:68 N 9 '87
Poaching
Egg thieves of Playa Grande [leatherback turtle eggs] R. Hamm. il map *Sea Front* 33:27-33 Ja/F '87
I didn't kill Dian. She was my friend [murder of gorilla protector D. Fossey]; ed. by Beverly Trainer and Gina Maranto. W. McGuire. il pors maps *Discover* 8:28-32+ F '87
Putting the sting on poachers [undercover agent K. Corey conducts sting operation on fish poachers in California] M. Tennesen. il *Natl Wildl* 25:26-8 O/N '87
The rhino wars [battling black rhino poachers in Zimbabwe] M. Vollers. il *Sports Illus* 66:60-8+ Mr 2 '87
The rhino's fatal flaw [horn trade in Africa and Asia] P. Jackson. il maps *Int Wildl* 17:4-11 Ja/F '87
A small misunderstanding [interest in salmon spawning on Scotland's Endrick River] R. Holland. il *Audubon* 89:62-3 S '87
A war to save the black rhino [battle against poachers in Zimbabwe] M. Vollers. il *Time* 130:62-3 S 7 '87
When the music in our parlors brought death to darkest Africa [19th century use of ivory for piano keys] R. Conniff. il *Audubon* 89:76-93 Jl '87
Pochivalov, Leonid
The Soviets abroad. il *World Press Rev* 34:30-1 D '87
Pochoir *See* Stencil work
Pocket Books
Pocket to start hardcover line ahead of schedule [R. Norwood's Letters from women who love too much] W. Goldstein. il por *Publ Wkly* 232:74 O 2 '87
Realizing the potential at Pocket Books [work of I. Applebaum] J. Davis. il pors *Publ Wkly* 231:45-8 Ja 23 '87
Updated Bobbsey Twins series follows Nancy Drew, Hardy Boys. il *Publ Wkly* 232:32 Ag 28 '87
Pocket television receivers *See* Television receivers
Pocketbooks *See* Handbags
Poddubny, Walt
about
He's not a Stooge on the ice. F. Lidz. il pors *Sports Illus* 67:68-71 N 16 '87

Podesta, Anthony T.
A word from the right on rights. il por *Progressive* 51:13-14 Jl '87

about

People for the American Way [interview] R. Love. il por *Seventeen* 46:237 Ag '87

Podgursky, Michael, and Swaim, Paul
Health insurance loss: the case of the displaced worker. bibl f il *Mon Labor Rev* 110:30-3 Ap '87

Podhoretz, John
An open letter to Allan Bloom. *Natl Rev* 39:34-7 O 9 '87

Podhoretz, Norman
Anti-Semitism, left & right [discussion of November 1986 article, The hate that dare not speak its name] *Commentary* 83:2+ Mr '87

Podiatry
Top-notch foot care. S. McConnell. il *Harpers Bazaar* 120:80+ Mr '87

Podlisny, Marcia Berman, and others
Gene dosage of the amyloid β precursor protein in Alzheimer's disease. bibl f il *Science* 238:669-71 O 30 '87

Poe, Edgar Allan, 1809-1849

about

Beyond the pale with Edgar Allan Poe. M. Robinson. il *N Y Times Book Rev* 92:11 F 8 '87

Poems

Single works

See also

Christmas poems—Single works

See name of author for full entry

Above the world. Levine, Philip, 1928-
Acts. Cairns, Scott
Acts. Cochran, Leonard
Acuity. Alexander, Pamela, 1948-
After reading the Detroit news. Thorndike, Nick
After the death of a neighbor's child. Rosenberg, Liz
After the fact. Libbey, Elizabeth
The ages of rock. Holloway, Glenna
Air and water. Mott, Michael
Airport. Merwin, W. S. (William Stanley), 1927-
All Hallows' Eve. Miłosz, Czesław
Allegory of evil in Italy. Moss, Stanley
Alzheimer's. Williams, C. K. (Charles Kenneth), 1936-
Amanda's garden. Schoyen, Warner O.
America. Irwin, Mark
An American naturalist writes to a Londoner, 1758. Galvin, Brendan
Amortization. Westerfield, Nancy G.
And be merry. Kumbalek, Tom
Anniversary. Davidson, Mark
Another song. Cairns, Scott
April galleons. Ashbery, John
Aquarium. Willard, Nancy
The art of fiction. Santos, Sherod, 1948-
Art songs. Ashbery, John
As if in prayer. Roe, Margie McCreless
Ashes, ashes. Wangerin, Walter
At Hemingway's house. Stanton, Maura
At the jazz concert. Sadoff, Ira
August mirage. Liu, Stephen Shu-Ning
August poem. Absher, Tom
Aunt Sadie's visit. Dugger, Edward Anthony
Automatic natural. Gilyard, Keith
Azania. Reynolds, A. H.
The bad physician. Gregerson, Linda
Baize doors. Raine, Craig
The bathers. Moss, Stanley
Beautiful loser. Galassi, Jonathan
The Belfast tune. Brodsky, Joseph, 1940-
Bells above Bretaye. Kirchwey, Karl
Between 6:37 p.m. and 9:04 p.m. Brodkey, Harold
Beverly Hills bride. Stefan, Jon
Birds of a poet's native land. Neruda, Pablo, 1904-1973
A birthday tribute III. Green, Jaki Shelton, 1953-
The black lace fan my mother gave me. Boland, Eavan
Blizzard. Christopher, Nicholas
A bouquet for Battista. Giordan, Alma Roberts
Breakdown. Wallace, Ronald, 1945-
Breughel's peasants and the month of August. Olsen, William
The Brooklyn Museum of Art. Collins, Billy
The bust of Tiberius. Brodsky, Joseph, 1940-
Buying and selling. Levine, Philip, 1928-
By the sound. Hollander, John
Caryatid. Ryan, Kay
Casting back. Weiner, Joshua
Castrati in Caesar's court. Reiss, James
Catching the light. Lohmann, Jeanne
Cattle in rain. McDonald, Walter

Chapel. Fasel, Ida
Chichikov's driver. Lyons, Richard
Child on the marsh. Hudgins, Andrew
The children of paradise. Santos, Sherod, 1948-
Child's moon. Zeidner, Lisa
Chimes. Jensen, Laura, 1948-
Chord. Merwin, W. S. (William Stanley), 1927-
Circadian rhythms. Digges, Deborah
Circe revisited. Christopher, Nicholas
Clearing. Goodenough, J. B.
The clock turns backwards. Simmons, Judy
Collecting future lives. Dunn, Stephen, 1939-
Cologne. Fasel, Ida
Comin strong. Madhubuti, Haki R.
Companionship. Dunn, Stephen, 1939-
The composition. Petrie, Paul
Cool lightning over Tucson. Elman, Richard M.
The corners of my mind remember. Curtis, Jeannette
Correct blinking. Hollander, Jean
Cosmetics. Hammond, Mary Stewart
Counterclockwise. Espaillat, Rhina P.
Coyote. Bennett, Paul
Crab house. Smith, Dave, 1942-
Crabbing for blue-claws. Ulmer, James
Crossroads Inn. Ryan, Michael
Custer dreams 'The tonight show'. Pomerance, Bernard
Daniel da Volterra, "the breeches-maker," on Michelangelo's last judgment. Kamenetz, Rodger, 1950-
Desperate character. Christopher, Nicholas
The difficulty of moonlight in the 6th arrondissement. Wong, May
Drab shutters. Ashbery, John
The dream of birds. Ludvigson, Susan
Dreams: a Darwinian view. Disch, Thomas M.
Dropping acid at Aunt Bea's. Wormser, Baron
Drought: sure signs in Merkle, Texas. Fink, Robert A.
The duration. Flahive, Peg
Each is one. Charles, Pepsi
Eclogue V: summer. Brodsky, Joseph, 1940-
Ecstasy. Reynolds, A. H.
Electronically yours. Jonas, Gerald
Elegy. Balk, Christianne
Elemental colloquy. Hollander, John
Elves. Lowry, Betty
The Empire State Building as the moon. Olds, Sharon
The empress of the laundromat. Cooperman, Robert
Erebus. Bierds, Linda
Esau's birthright. Hamilton, Carol
Escuintla. Gray, Jeffrey
Eva I. Green, Jaki Shelton, 1953-
Evening star. Hirsch, Edward
Fall's end. Ammons, A. R., 1926-
The famous scene. Strand, Mark, 1934-
Fantasiestücke 3. Ann Landers comes to me for advice. Schwartz, Hillel, 1948-
A farmstead with a hayrick and weirs beside a stream. Carper, Thomas
Fawn Hall among the Antinomians. McCarthy, Eugene J., 1916-
Feedback. Collier, Michael
Fettuccine. Alladice, Darryl
Fine lines. Rotter, Pat
First frost. Applin, Stephen
Fisherman's wife. Der Hovanessian, Diana
For once. Stern, Gerald
For Stuart Porter, who asked for a poem that would not depress him further. Skinner, Jeffrey
(For William Cook, drowned in Maine, and for Roy Huss, lost in Indonesia). Ponsot, Marie
For you, my children. Whitford, Genevieve Smith
Forsaken sea. Sundiata, Sekou
Four poems. Berry, Wendell, 1934-
Four poems. Cassian, Nina
Friends in high places. Shea, John
Frog. Voigt, Ellen Bryant, 1943-
From a journal of the Year of the Ox. Wright, Charles, 1935-
From a photograph. Stap, Don
From 'Le ricordanze' ('Memories'). Leopardi, Giacomo, 1798-1837
Frost. Ashbery, John
Gentlemen at the barber shop. Barnes, S. Brandi
Ginestra. Baumel, Judith
Give me a nickname, prison. Ratushinskaya, Irina
Glass. Karp, Vickie
Going back. Austin, Penelope
Going back. McMahon, Lynne
Going seventy. Merriam, Eve, 1916-
Goodbye, Göteborg. Updike, John
Grandfather and grandmother in love. Mura, David
Grandmother's rug. Hammond, Mary Stewart

Poems—Single works—*cont.*
Grandmother's spit. Hudgins, Andrew
Grappling in the central blue. Kumin, Maxine, 1925-
Grete Samsa's letter to H. Strand, Mark, 1934-
Growth. Coulthard, Leslie Jean
Gulls on dumps. Di Piero, W. S.
Halfway-to-two. Cannon, Maureen
Halley's comet. Foerster, Richard
Hannibal crossing the Alps. Moss, Stanley
Hard rain. Williams, Steve
Harvard 8/9/85. Keller, Bernard J.
He descended into Hell. Molton, Warren Lane
Heart art. Ghigna, Charles
The Hearts. Pinsky, Robert
Heat. Ullman, Leslie
Hedgerows. Plumly, Stanley
Herd of buffalo crossing the Missouri River on ice.
 Matthews, William, 1942-
Here. Hickoff, Stephen
Hidebound. Ude, Chema
Hills. House, Amelia Blossom
History. Parini, Jay
History of 20th-century American education.
 Mecklenburger, James A.
The holly tree. Smith, Charlie, 1947-
Holy Name School, 1951. Carson, Mike
Homage to O'Keeffe. Hirsch, Edward
Homer's 'Iliad,' updated. Logue, Christopher, 1926-
Hope. Hall-Evans, Jo Ann
Horse-chestnut trees and roses. Schuyler, James
The horses' water. Barnes, Kate
The hunt. Siegel, Robert
Hunting. Mattern, Evelyn
I think of flags. Cannon, Maureen
In a remote Korean village. Chang, Soo Ko
In extremadura. Irion, Mary Jean
In memoriam. Brodsky, Joseph, 1940-
In memoriam: Robert Fitzgerald. Heaney, Seamus
In praise of darkness. Cairns, Scott
In praise of the potato. Williams, David
In the country of dreamers. Rosenberg, Liz
In the hardware store. Hickoff, Stephen
In the museum. Loots, Barbara
In the shadow of the pine. Bennett, Paul
In this photograph. Espaillat, Rhina P.
Indistinguishable from the darkness. Smith, Charlie, 1947-
Infertility. Hirsch, Edward
Inside. Banks, C. Tillery
Into happiness. Pankey, Eric
Isaac. Hamilton, Carol
Jacksonville/Charleston. Engles, Eric C.
Jaws 4. Woddis, Roger
A jazz festival. Barnes, S. Brandi
The jellyfish. Kinsolving, Susan
John Muir remembers Eliza Hendricks. Balk, Christianne
Joy ride. Finkel, Donald
Just a few laughs, some fun nothing serious. Karriem,
 Jaleelah
The Kama Sutra according to Fiat. St. John, David,
 1949-
Kanaloa. Merwin, W. S. (William Stanley), 1927-
Karma causes condensation. Fatisha
Kelomyakki. Brodsky, Joseph, 1940-
The kite. Turco, Lewis, 1934-
Krazy Kat's confession. Christopher, Nicholas
Late love, a comic opera. Coulette, Henri
Late marsh. Dings, Fred
The least of things. Smith, Arthur
Leaving forever. Smith, Ron
The legacy. Drury, Michael
Legends. Peters, Anne
Letter from a friend on her anniversary. Coles, Katharine
Likewise. Hiestand, Emily
Lines for a dead sister, reawakening. Rubin, Larry
Lines for a simple computer to sort out. Hollander,
 John
Little elegy with books and beasts. Willard, Nancy
The little professor. Cummins, James
Little testament. Montale, Eugenio, 1896-1981
Lollypop kiss. King, Dorothy E.
Lost love. Allen, Dick, 1939-
Lotto. Bloomfield, Maureen
Lovesick. Rosenberg, Liz
Luminism. Strand, Mark, 1934-
Magnolia season. Eimers, Nancy
Man feeding pigeons. Clampitt, Amy
Mandarin oranges. Pollitt, Katha
Mandelstam. Donaldson, Jeffery
The maple keys. Skinner, Jeffrey
Maple tree. Palmer, Thelma
March. Shepherd, J. Barrie

Marcus Aurelius. Aleshire, Joan
Mary Magdalene and I. Miłosz, Czesław
Mass for the imprisoned. Herbert, Zbigniew
Maundy Thursday. Molton, Warren Lane
Maundy Thursday: Thomas's testimony. Shepherd, J.
 Barrie
Max Fabre's yachts. Murray, Les A., 1938-
Max Planck and the squirrel. Atlee, Champ
Meadowlark country. Clampitt, Amy
The Megaethon: 1850, 1906-1929. Murray, Les A., 1938-
Memorial days. Fandel, John
Mercurial September. Murray, Les A., 1938-
Midsummer. Santos, Sherod, 1948-
The mind-body problem. Richardson, James, 1950-
Miranda in Reno. Christopher, Nicholas
Moccasin flowers. Oliver, Mary, 1935-
Modernism. Austin, Penelope
A mood of quiet beauty. Ashbery, John
Moon waters back home. Ude, Chema
Moses, at Jordan. McDonald, Walter
Mourning song. Barnes, S. Brandi
Move. Ostriker, Alicia
Mozartian. Gregor, Arthur, 1923-
Mr. Wakeville on Interstate 90. Hall, Donald, 1928-
Mrs. Krikorian. Olds, Sharon
Mrs. Overholt's garden. Quinn, John Robert
Museum of Holography. Kirchwey, Karl
The music of lost hours. Harney, John
My brothers. Madhubuti, Haki R.
My favorite farewell. Stern, Gerald
Naming a painting. Moss, Howard, 1922-1987
Napping in trees. Boruch, Marianne
Native Americans. Porter, Anne
Les natures profondement bonnes sont toujours indecises.
 Ryan, Kay
Never once. Lynskey, Edward
Never to get it really right. Ashbery, John
New Year's Day. Smith, Dave, 1942-
New York song. Moss, Stanley
Night casting: Epiphany in Galilee. Harmless, William
Night missions. McDonald, Walter
Nightmare on Elm Street. Disch, Thomas M.
Nightscape with doves. Watterson, William Collins
Noche triste. Wright, Tennant C.
North & south. Davie, Donald
Not this year. Ponsot, Marie
Note to Sappho. McPherson, Sandra
November garden with moon. Boruch, Marianne
Nuclear medicine. Johnston, Stella
O boy. Irion, Mary Jean
Octavian in Alexandria. Johnson, W. R. (Walter Ralph),
 1933-
October 29, 1855: variation on Thoreau's journal entry.
 Larson, Rustin
October tune. Brodsky, Joseph, 1940-
Oil spill. McKay, Linda Back
On the list. Morris, John N.
On the river. Levine, Philip, 1928-
On wings made of gauze. Finney, Nikky
Once removed. Stern, Cathy
One of the citizens. Jones, Rodney, 1950-
An open letter. Heaney, Seamus
Ordeal by devotion. Root, William Pitt, 1941-
Our lives are here and now. Halbo, Sverre
Owls. Seid, Christopher
Pale ambience: browsing a bookstore in Appalachia.
 DeFoe, Mark
The palm at the end of the mind. Ryan, Kay
Paper. Merwin, W. S. (William Stanley), 1927-
Partial accounts. Meredith, William, 1919-
A past-due notice. Macdonald, Cynthia
The patience of white birches. Galvin, Brendan
The pattern. Moffitt, John, 1908-1987
Pennsylvania: small scale strip mining. Hurdelsh, Mark
Perennial peeves. Marsh, Corinna
Philosophy I. Porter, Caryl
Pinned. Kleinzahler, August
Place. Merwin, W. S. (William Stanley), 1927-
Planting by the stars. Makofske, Mary
Play it again, Sam. Coffer, Helene Lewis
Playing pizzicato. James, Joyce
Please disturb. Meekins, Dorothy
Poems. Meyers, Joan Rohr
Political song. Logan, William, 1950-
Polonaise: a variation. Brodsky, Joseph, 1940-
The pool of tears. Prospere, Susan
The poor in the bus depot. Ivo, Lêdo
Popcorn man. Tully, John
The potato picker. Willard, Nancy
Prayer to cottonmouth blocking the road to the pond.
 Skinner, Jeffrey

Poems—Single works—*cont.*

Prayer to sparrow in two seasons. Skinner, Jeffrey
Preliminaries. Myers, Joan Rohr
Presbyopia. Getty, Sarah
Prophecy. Hall, Donald, 1928-
Proserpine, packing. Ponsot, Marie
Rain. Schuyler, James
Raising animals: Esther and Eve. James, Joyce
Rapture: a dream of dying. Baysa, Fred O.
Receive this white garment. Yvonne
A reflection. Moore, Cynthia B.
Refugee. Merwin, W. S. (William Stanley), 1927-
Rembrandt prepares for a walk along the Amstel River. Carper, Thomas
Reminder. Ponsot, Marie
Returning native. Updike, John
The Rev. Robert Walker skates. McQuilkin, Rennie, 1936-
The right way to escape from a sinking ship. Spence, Michael, 1952-
Ripening. Crooker, Barbara
The road. Simon, Francesca
The road to Damascus. Adkins, Vincent
Robert Bly quelling riots in Miami. Bosch, Daniel
Robert's friends. Urdang, Constance
Rock Creek Cemetery: Washington, D.C. Kane, Paul
The rose beetle. Merwin, W. S. (William Stanley), 1927-
Rt. 91, Vermont. Evarts, Prescott
Ruth's love letters, 1918-1919. Porter, Pamela Rice
Safisha. Madhubuti, Haki R.
Saints are not born to it. Squire-Buresh, Anne
The saints' wives. Socolow, Elizabeth Anne
Salt bread. Hamilton, Carol
A seashell from the Seychelles. Wickers, Brian
Seasonal blooms. Bariteau, Corinne Adria
September. Cassian, Nina
The shadow side. Nemerov, Howard
Shaking the tree. Lohmann, Jeanne
She reminds. Reddy, T. J.
Showered! Britt, Angela M.
Sighs and inhibitions. Ashbery, John
A sister on the tracks. Hall, Donald, 1928-
Sixty-third summer. Cannon, Maureen
A sketch from the campaign in the north. Seshadri, Vijay
'Slave, come to my service!'. Brodsky, Joseph, 1940-
Smoke. Westerfield, Nancy G.
Snapshot album. Oates, Joyce Carol, 1938-
Snow goat. McFee, Michael
Snow White and Rose Red. Greger, Debora, 1949-
So. Banks, C. Tillery
Song of imperfection. Moss, Stanley
Song of salt and pepper. Storace, Patricia
Sonnet to Orpheus. Drury, John
Southern hospitality. Storace, Patricia
The Southern Pacific. McDonald, Walter
Spring and. Libbey, Elizabeth
Spring sewing. Grossman, Florence
Spring-shock. Dickey, James
The stairs. Barnes, Kate
Stamp store. Petrie, Paul
The star story. Ebalo, Dan
The steeple. Dickson, John
Stepping in the same river. Chamberlain, Karen
Still life. Grossman, Florence
Stocking trout. Lewandowski, Stephen
Stopping Schubert. Stern, Gerald
Straight at the blue. Siegel, Robert
Strawberrying. Swenson, May, 1919-
Strike. Bierds, Linda
The summer before the moon. Stewart, Susan
Summer elegy. Walcott, Derek
Summer elegy II. Walcott, Derek
Summerizing. Ghigna, Charles
Summer's children. Shelton, Richard, 1933-
Sunday. Kratt, Mary
Sunday in the old republic. Walcott, Derek
Sundays. Walcott, Derek
Supermarket and then some. Comas, Beatrice H.
Swimming party on the Hayfork River. Maino, Jeannette
Switzerland. Updike, John
Sycamores. Digges, Deborah
Sync. Swafford-Choyce, Alice
Tall in the saddle. McMillan, Ian
Telling mother. Klander, Sharon
Thanks. Merwin, W. S. (William Stanley), 1927-
These are for your consideration. Hiestand, Emily
This is where I draw the line. Finkel, Donald
This last piece of paper. Sharp, Saundra
Three poems. Mandel'stam, Osip Yemilyevich, 1891-1938
Tics. Janowitz, Phyllis

To Charlotte Brontë. Aleshire, Joan
To S. K. Glosser, John L.
A toast for a composer's widow in Tashkent. Talbott, Strobe
Togetherness—suburban style. Goldsmith, Del
Tomatoes of the Lord. Thorndike, Nick
Tonight you dine on the water. Shomer, Enid
Towards morning. Myers, Joan Rohr
Traffic watch. Rutsala, Vern
Transactions. Ryan, Martin
The trembling. Grego, Daniel
A trenta-sei for John Ciardi. Stone, John, 1936-
Trick or treat. Nims, John Frederick, 1913-
Turnabout. Pastan, Linda, 1932-
Two poems. Asekoff, L. S.
Two poems. Levi, Primo, 1919-1987
Two poems. Norris, Leslie, 1921-
Two poems from prison. Ratushinskaya, Irina
Unbuilding. McMahon, Lynne
Underdeveloped criminals. Ude, Chema
United States. Booth, Philip E.
Until the next time. Heyen, William, 1940-
Untitled. Viveros, Joy
Untitled. Woodson, Jacqueline
Utterance. Merwin, W. S. (William Stanley), 1927-
Velocity of money. Ginsberg, Allen, 1926-
A verse from 'Fuku'. Yevtushenko, Yevgeny Aleksandrovich, 1933-
The very first dream of morning. Siegel, Robert
Villanelle: traffic in Washington. Moore, Miles David
Visiting Emily Dickinson. Wright, Charles, 1935-
The voice of the canefield. Melo Neto, João Cabral de, 1920-
Waiting. Wayne, Jane O.
Waiting for Jay. Cannon, Maureen
Waiting for the train. Liu, Stephen Shu-Ning
Waking in winter. Molton, Warren Lane
We got stuff. Barnes, S. Brandi
Weather radio. Grossman, Florence
What about rainbows? Rotter, Pat
What guys hate! Blount, Roy
What I remember the writers telling me when I was young. Meredith, William, 1919-
What the end is for. Graham, Jorie, 1951-
What time does a Chinaman go to the dentist? Ivry, Benjamin
What we hear toward morning. Garrison, Deborah Gottlieb
The whelk. Santos, Sherod, 1948-
When it stopped singing. Hunter, Donnell
Widow. Harrell, Lorraine
Wildlife. Zarin, Cynthia
Wind and flags. Montale, Eugenio, 1896-1981
Window. Hamilton, Carol
Winter aconite. Quinn, John Robert
Winter wail. Cannon, Maureen
A woman fully grown. Reynolds, A. H.
Woman of the leaves. McClendon, Lowery
Women are the superstars. Akili, John-Michael
Women in profile: bas-relief, left section missing. Mitchell, Susan, 1944-
A word about the artist. Holloway, Glenna
The word "love". Blumenthal, Michael
The wrong way home. Green, Vincent S.
The Wyoming poetry tour. Plumly, Stanley
Yes. Kiley, John

Poetics *See* Poetry

Poetry

See also

Art and poetry
Brazilian poetry
Children's poetry
Christmas poems
Cowboy poetry
Erotic poetry
Feminist poetry
Limericks
Sufi poetry

Light verse: dead but remarkably robust. B. Leithauser. il *N Y Times Book Rev* 92:1+ Je 7 '87
Writers & writing. P. Pettingell. See occasional issues of The New Leader

Authorship

Making a name in poetry, or, How did Emily Dickinson do it? X. J. Kennedy. *Writer* 100:18-21+ N '87
The poet's pursuit: capturing dreams [interview with A. Ginsberg] A. P. Sanoff. il por *U S News World Rep* 102:74 F 16 '87
Questions and answers on writing poetry. U. Fanthorpe. *Writer* 100:22-3 Ag '87

Poetry—Authorship—*cont.*
Separate nations: poetry and the people [excerpt from Conversations with Czeslaw Milosz]; tr. by Richard Lourie. A. Fiut. il *N Y Times Book Rev* 92:3+ O 11 '87

Awards
The Lenore Marshall Prize [awarded to D. Hall] R. Pinsky. *Nation* 245:496-8 O 31 '87

Bibliography
The Romantics return. P. Pettingell. *New Leader* 70:14-16 Je 29 '87

Book reviews
See Book reviews and reviewing

Competitions
Prizewinning poets—1987 [winners of Discovery—The Nation, '87] G. Schulman. *Nation* 244:544-5 Ap 25 '87

Moral and religious aspects
Writing and the devout life. J. Parini. *Christ Century* 104:815-16 S 30 '87

Periodicals
This month's special market list. *Writer* 100:29-43 Mr '87

Technique
Form and experimentation in poetry. L. Rosenberg. *Writer* 100:17-18 F '87
The poet's workshop. F. Trefethen. See alternate issues of The Writer through May 1987

Themes
See also
Fathers in poetry
Humanism in poetry
Romanticism in poetry
Poetry and art *See* Art and poetry
Poetry and society *See* Literature and society
Poetry and state *See* Literature and state
Poetry festivals *See* Literary festivals
Poets
See also
Children as poets
Poets, American
See also
Ashbery, John
Brooks, Gwendolyn
Dickey, James
Dickinson, Emily, 1830-1886
Dove, Rita
Gallagher, Tess
Ginsberg, Allen, 1926-
Hall, Donald, 1928-
Jacobsen, Josephine
Kelly, Brigit Pegeen, 1951-
Kilmer, Joyce, 1886-1918
Moore, Clement Clarke, 1779-1863
Moore, Marianne, 1887-1972
Plath, Sylvia
Stevens, Wallace, 1879-1955
Taylor, Henry, 1942-
Warren, Robert Penn, 1905-
Whitman, Walt, 1819-1892
Wilbur, Richard, 1921-
Wright, James Arlington, 1927-1980
Poets, Argentine
See also
Borges, Jorge Luis, 1899-1986
Poets, Austrian
See also
Hofmannsthal, Hugo von, 1874-1929
Poets, English
See also
Cowper, William, 1731-1800
Shakespeare, William, 1564-1616
Tennyson, Alfred Tennyson, Baron, 1809-1892
Poets, French
See also
Hugo, Victor, 1802-1885
Poets, Italian
See also
Leopardi, Giacomo, 1798-1837
Poets, Nicaraguan
See also
Cuadra, Pablo Antonio, 1912-
Darío, Rubén, 1867-1916
Poets, Polish
See also
Miłosz, Czesław
Poets, Russian
See also
Mayakovsky, Vladimir, 1894-1930
Ratushinskaya, Irina
TSvetaeva, Marina Ivanovna, 1892-1941

Voznesenskiĭ, Andreĭ, 1933-
Yevtushenko, Yevgeny Aleksandrovich, 1933-
Poets, Uruguayan
See also
Agustini, Delmira, 1886-1914
Poets, Welsh
See also
Thomas, Dylan, 1914-1953
Poets & Writers, Inc.
Poets & Writers expands its reach. J. Barbato. *Publ Wkly* 232:56 N 27 '87
Poets and publishers *See* Authors and publishers
Poets laureate, American
Richard Wilbur. D. Van Biema. il pors *People Wkly* 28:91-2+ O 5 '87
Robert Penn Warren. J. Parini. por *Horizon* 30:36-7 Je '87
Poggio, Tomaso, and Koch, Christof
Synapses that compute motion. il *Sci Am* 256:46-52 My '87
Pogrebin, Letty Cottin
Going public as a Jew. *Ms* 16:76-7+ Jl/Ag '87
To scoot. il por *Ms* 16:18+ O '87
What men can teach women—and women teach men—about friendship. il *Glamour* 85:278-9+ Mr '87
Pohl, Frederik, 1919-
Adeste fideles [fiction] il *Omni* 10:68-70+ D '87
Pohl, Herbert Ackland, 1916-1986
about
Obituary
Phys Today 40:90-1 Ja '87. P. A. Westhaus
Pohlad, Carl R., 1915-
about
The Twins have clinched stardom for Carl Pohlad. P. Houston. il por *Bus Week* p79-80 O 26 '87
Poinar, George O., and Cannatella, David C.
An upper Eocene frog from the Dominican Republic and its implication for Caribbean biogeography. bibl f il *Science* 237:1215-16 S 4 '87
Poincaré conjecture
What happens when hubris meets nemesis. G. Taubes. il *Discover* 8:66-70+ Jl '87
Poindexter, John M.
about
Awaiting the admiral. M. Healy and K. T. Walsh. il por *U S News World Rep* 103:26-7 Jl 13 '87
Begging his pardon. J. V. Lamar, Jr. il *Time* 130:16-17 Ag 3 '87
'The buck stops here'. M. McDonald. il por *Macleans* 100:12-13 Jl 27 '87
Calm in the eye of the storm. il por *Time* 129:29 Ap 6 '87
For Reagan, a bit of relief [special section] il por *U S News World Rep* 103:14-21 Jl 27 '87
Letter from Washington. E. Drew. *New Yorker* 63:71-89 Ag 31 '87
Making waves: Poindexter sails into scientific databases. I. Goodwin. por *Phys Today* 40:51-2 Ja '87
Nancy: no pardons. L. Howard. por *Newsweek* 110:7 N 30 '87
Next, the most important witness? G. J. Church. il pors *Time* 130:28-9 Jl 20 '87
The next witness. G. Hackett. il por *Newsweek* 110:27-8 Jl 20 '87
No pardon. *New Repub* 197:7-9 D 28 '87
Pardon? F. Barnes. *New Repub* 196:13-15 Ja 5-12 '87
Pardon my Spanish. R. Paulson. *New Repub* 197:4+ Ag 10-17 '87
Passing the buck [special section] il pors *Time* 130:8-14+ Jl 27 '87
See no evil, hear no evil, speak no evil. M. Kramer. il *U S News World Rep* 103:12 Jl 27 '87
Street sign. *Progressive* 51:4 Ag '87
Taking blame [special section] il por *Newsweek* 110:14-19 Jl 27 '87
Timing tiff. *Time* 129:26 Mr 23 '87
The untouchables. J. Klein. il por *N Y* 20:12-13 Jl 27 '87
Walsh vs. Congress. T. Morganthau. il pors *Newsweek* 109:24+ Mr 23 '87
What will they say—and when? M. Healy. il pors *U S News World Rep* 102:20 Mr 23 '87
Anecdotes, facetiae, satire, etc.
Poindexter file. R. R. Lingeman. *Nation* 244:68-9 Ja 24 '87
Poinsett, Alex
August Wilson: hottest new playwright. il pors *Ebony* 43:68+ N '87
Why our children are killing one another. il *Ebony* 43:88+ D '87

Point of view (Fiction) *See* Fiction—Narration
Point Reyes National Seashore (Calif.)
Balancing act at Point Reyes [seals and sharks; cover story] K. Evans. il *Natl Parks* 61:16-21 Jl/Ag '87
Point Reyes views and other diversions from Mount Vision. il *Sunset* 179:66-8 N '87
Pointers (Dogs)
Life with Trixie. B. Stein. il *N Y Times Mag* p48 Ap 19 '87
Poirier, Anne

about

Readymade ruins. A. Thorson. il *Art News* 86:32-3 F '87
Poirier, Patrick

about

Readymade ruins. A. Thorson. il *Art News* 86:32-3 F '87
Poirier, Richard
Human, all too inhuman. *New Repub* 196:29-32+ F 2 '87
Where is Emerson now that we need him? or, Why literature can't save us [excerpt from The renewal of literature] il *N Y Times Book Rev* 92:3+ F 8 '87
Poison control centers
Poison control centers—timing is everything. il *Curr Health 2* 13:28-9 F '87
Poison ivy
Heidi had an itch to be festival queen [Poison Oak Festival, Forestville, Calif.] il *Audubon* 89:20 N '87
Life's an itch. D. Mermon. il *Outdoor Life* 180:76-7+ O '87
Poison ivy primer. C. Le Master. il *Seventeen* 46:102 Je '87
Recognition and preparedness will protect you from poison ivy. N. Phillips. il *Flower Gard* 31:20+ Je/Jl '87

Control

Get rid of poison ivy. il *South Living* 22:48 Jl '87
Poison oak *See* Poison ivy
Poisoning *See* Poisons and poisoning
Poisonous fish
See also
Scorpionfish
Poisonous gases
See also
Bhopal poisonous gas disaster, India, 1984
Carbon monoxide
Hydrogen sulfide
The 1986 Lake Nyos gas disaster in Cameroon, West Africa [cover story] G. W. Kling and others. bibl f il maps *Science* 236:169-75 Ap 10 '87
Cameroon clouds: soda source? R. Monastersky. il *Sci News* 131:388 Je 20 '87
Cameroon lake: new clues, new clouds? [Lake Nyos] S. Weisburd. *Sci News* 131:36-7 Ja 17 '87
A dead chief's revenge? [Lake Nyos gas burst] H. Sigurdsson. il maps *Nat Hist* 96:44-9 Ag '87
Lake Nyos reported red and rumbling. S. Weisburd. *Sci News* 131:134 F 28 '87
Lake Nyos was rigged for disaster. R. A. Kerr. il *Science* 235:528-9 Ja 30 '87
Plumbing the depths of a lethal lake [Nyos in Cameroon; work of George Kling] il map *Discover* 8:12 My '87
Prehistoric Cameroon-style lake events [ancient Arizona crater lake; research by James D. White and Richard Fisher] R. Monastersky. *Sci News* 132:335 N 21 '87
Seasonal mixing and catastrophic degassing in tropical lakes, Cameroon, West Africa. G. W. Kling. bibl f il *Science* 237:1022-4 Ag 28 '87
Silent death from Cameroon's killer lake [Lake Nyos] C. Stager. il map *Natl Geogr* 172:404-20 S '87
Poisonous plants
See also
Poison ivy
Poisons and poisoning
See also
Cadmium poisoning
Carbon monoxide
Food poisoning
Lead poisoning
Mercury poisoning
Scombroid poisoning
Selenium
Snake venom
Toxins and antitoxins
Boric-acid poisoning. il *Parents* 62:20 D '87
Don't get poisoned this summer. il *USA Today (Periodical)* 116:8 Jl '87
Embedded sentinels of toxicity [cover story] J. Raloff. il *Sci News* 131:123-5 F 21 '87

Poisons in your home: a disposal dilemma. A. Schwartz. il *Audubon* 89:12-16 My '87
Protecting tots from drug poisonings. B. Rados. il *FDA Consum* 21:24-5 Mr '87
Poisons and poisoning, Industrial
See also
Bhopal poisonous gas disaster, India, 1984
Mercury poisoning
Trade waste
Poissy (France)

Historic houses, sites, etc.

Le Corbusier's true colors [Villa Savoye] M. Filler. il por *House Gard* 159:174-81+ My '87
Poitier, Sidney

about

Sidney Poitier, 60, begins his 42nd film. por *Jet* 71:56 Mr 23 '87
PoKempner, Marc
Playing the blues, Chicago-style [photographs] il *N Y Times Mag* p80-1 Ja 18 '87
Poker (Game)
Trading tips from a poker player turned options pro [J. Keller] il por *Money* 16:242 N '87

Anecdotes, facetiae, satire, etc.

The poker game: what is it about cards that turns sensitive New Men into Neanderthals? N. Karlen. il *Glamour* 85:68+ S '87
Pol Pot

about

Cambodia [discussion of April 1987 article, Pol Pot in retrospect] A. Puddington. *Commentary* 84:14-15 Ag '87
Pol Pot in retrospect. A. Puddington. *Commentary* 83:49-54 Ap '87
Polakov, Alexander
Terry-fied on the beach. il *Harpers Bazaar* 120:20+ Jl '87
Poland
See also
Anti-Semitism—Poland
Concentration camps—Poland
Jews—Poland
Kraków (Poland)
Paleontology—Poland
Underground literature—Poland
Warsaw (Poland)
Warships—Poland

Commerce
United States
See United States—Commerce—Poland

Economic policy

Poles at the polls [referendum on proposed austerity plan] *New Repub* 197:4 D 21 '87
Thanks for asking, but no [referendum for economic reform] W. R. Doerner. il *Time* 130:43 D 14 '87
There are no garage sales here. J. Cook. il *Forbes* 139:72-3+ F 23 '87

Foreign relations
Canada
See Canada—Foreign relations—Poland
Germany (West)
See Germany (West)—Foreign relations—Poland
Soviet Union
See Soviet Union—Foreign relations—Poland
United States
See United States—Foreign relations—Poland

History
20th century

Poland's 20th-century struggles [television series The struggles for Poland; cover story] N. Ascherson. il *Hist Today* 37:44-9 Je '87

Intellectual life

Another country. A. Applebaum. *New Repub* 197:12-13 Ag 24 '87

Politics and government
See also
Referendum—Poland
A bitter anniversary [fifth anniversary of the declaration of martial law] *America* 156:1 Ja 3-10 '87
From a U.S. mole: inside story of what might have been [views of R. Kuklinski] R. Z. Chesnoff and D. Stanglin. il por *U S News World Rep* 102:32-3 Ap 20 '87
Gorbachev may be setting the stage for more unrest in Poland. W. Echikson. il *Bus Week* p53 Ja 19 '87
Jaruzelski walks a fine line. A. Bromke. *World Press Rev* 34:37 Je '87
Lunch with Lech. N. Bethell. *New Repub* 197:13-14 N 2 '87

Poland—Politics and government—*cont.*
A new deal in Poland? A. Brumberg. bibl f il *N Y Rev Books* 33:32-6 Ja 15 '87
Poland [statements, December 12, 1986 and February 19, 1987] R. Reagan. *Dep State Bull* 87:33-4 Ap '87
Poland's plucky activist [A. Michnik] M. T. Kaufman. il por *N Y Times Mag* p38+ Ap 26 '87
The Polish road to the abyss. A. R. Rachwald. bibl f *Curr Hist* 86:369-72+ N '87
Searching for signs of spring [J. Clark's visit] H. Mackenzie. il *Macleans* 100:20-1 My 18 '87
Solidarity forsaken. *New Repub* 196:7-9 Ja 5-12 '87
Top down or bottom up? D. Singer. il *Nation* 244:756-8 Je 6 '87

Religious institutions and affairs
See also
Catholic Church—Poland
Convents—Poland
John Paul II, Pope, 1920——Visit to Poland, 1987
Poland and Hungary *See* Hungary and Poland
Polanski, Roman
about
The rise & fall of Roman Polanski. T. Lindberg. *Commentary* 83:61-5 Ja '87
Polansky, Frank
Collecting early electro-medical apparatuses. il *Antiques Collect Hobbies* 92:61-2+ D '87
Polansky, Norman Alburt, 1918-
Cynical notes on change. *Society* 24:40-4 Mr/Ap '87
Polanyi, John C., 1929-
Some concepts in reaction dynamics [adaptation of Nobel Prize address, December 8, 1986] bibl f il *Science* 236:680-90 My 8 '87
about
Herschbach, Lee and Polanyi receive 1986 Chemistry Nobel. P. H. Andersen. il pors *Phys Today* 40:17-20 Mr '87
Polar bears
Boy, 11, begged 'help' before bears ate him [polar bear attack on Juan Perez at Prospect Park Zoo] il *Jet* 72:16 Je 8 '87
Migration
Camping out in polar bear country [Churchill, Man.] D. Matthews. il map *50 Plus* 27:44-8+ F '87
Polar exploration
See also
Antarctic exploration
Arctic exploration
Polar flights *See* Aviation—Polar flights
Polar regions
See also
Antarctic regions
Arctic regions
Ice—Polar regions
Polar research
See also
Antarctic research
Polar ring galaxies *See* Galaxies
Polar wander
Magnetic field reversals, polar wander, and core-mantle coupling. V. Courtillot and J. Besse. bibl f il maps *Science* 237:1140-7 S 4 '87
Tracking the wandering poles of ancient earth. R. A. Kerr. bibl il *Science* 236:147-8 Ap 10 '87
Polarimeters *See* Polariscopes
Polariscopes
White light sunspot observations from the solar optical universal polarimeter on Spacelab-2. R. A. Shine and others. bibl f il *Science* 238:1264-7 N 27 '87
Polarity (Biology)
Determination of anteroposterior polarity in Drosophila. C. Nüsslein-Volhard and others. bibl f il *Science* 238:1675-81 D 18 '87
Polarization (Light)
See also
Polariscopes
Radio lobes revealed [galaxy 3C33; work of Klaus Meisenheimer and Hermann-Josef Röser] il *Sky Telesc* 73:25 Ja '87
Polarizing filters *See* Light filters
Polaroid cameras *See* Cameras, Instant print
Polaroid Corp.
Golden legend: a toast to Polaroid's 50th anniversary. N. Goldberg. il pors *Pop Photogr* 94:48+ N '87
How Polaroid flashed back. B. Dumaine. il *Fortune* 115:72-3+ F 16 '87
The Polaroid promise [Spectra instant camera] J. A. Conway. il *Forbes* 139:8 F 9 '87
Polaroid's Spectra may be losing its flash. K. H. Hammonds. il *Bus Week* p31-2 Je 29 '87

The vindication of Edwin Land. S. N. Chakravarty. il por *Forbes* 139:83-4 My 4 '87
Zooming in on Polaroid [views of Stuart A. Shikiar] G. G. Marcial. *Bus Week* p108 O 26 '87
Polaroid film *See* Photography—Films
Pole sitting
Tell some folks to sit on it, and they might do just that—for 104 hours [Netherlands contest] il *People Wkly* 28:83 Ag 17 '87
Polenz, Robert *See* Tomato Bob
Poles, Fishing *See* Fishing tackle
Poles, Ski *See* Skis and skiing—Equipment
Poles, Wood *See* Wood poles
Polgar family
about
Nurtured to be geniuses, Hungary's Polgar sisters put winning moves on chess masters. il *People Wkly* 27:65 My 4 '87
Policansky, David
Evolution, sex, and sex allocation. bibl f *BioScience* 37:466-8 Jl/Ag '87
Sex choice and reproductive costs in Jack-in-the-pulpit. bibl f il *BioScience* 37:476-81 Jl/Ag '87
Policastro, Michael
Why can't men dress themselves? il *50 Plus* 27:56+ S '87
Police
See also
Arrest
Black police
Computers—Police use
Policewomen
United States. Park Police
Three [relations between police partners of opposite sexes] *New Yorker* 63:38-9 O 12 '87
War stories [encounters with traffic police over 55mph speed limit] P. Bedard. il *Car Driv* 33:164 Jl '87
Anecdotes, facetiae, satire, etc.
Ten best cop stories. D. Coulter. il *Car Driv* 32:85-7 Ja '87
Education
Cops and college. G. W. Lynch. *America* 156:274-5 Ap 4 '87
Psychological aspects
See Police psychology
Retirement
A cop prepares to slip his leash [Richard Will considers early retirement] M. Willens. il *Money* 16:128-33 Je '87
Salaries, pensions, etc.
A cop prepares to slip his leash [Richard Will considers early retirement] M. Willens. il *Money* 16:128-33 Je '87
Alabama
Blacks, state police in Alabama reach agreement in $2.5 million suit. *Jet* 72:8 S 7 '87
Court upholds racial quota [blacks in the Alabama state trooper force; Supreme Court decision] D. Camper. il *Black Enterp* 17:15 My '87
A one-white, one-black quota for promotions [Supreme Court decision in state trooper case] T. Gest. il *U S News World Rep* 102:8 Mr 9 '87
A racial quota for Alabama [state trooper hirings; Supreme Court decision] A. Press. il *Newsweek* 109:55 Mr 9 '87
Replying in the affirmative [Supreme Court approves promotion quotas for black state troopers] R. Lacayo. il *Time* 129:66 Mr 9 '87
Supreme Court approves quotas for promotions [state troopers case] *Jet* 71:8 Mr 16 '87
Supreme Court upholds promotion quotas [state troopers case] *Mon Labor Rev* 110:41 My '87
Brazil
Scenes from Brazilian Vice. C. Wood. il *Macleans* 100:24-5 Ja 19 '87
California
See also
Los Angeles (Calif.)—Police
San Diego (Calif.)—Police
Canada
See also
Royal Canadian Mounted Police
Florida
See also
Manatee County (Fla.)—Police
Miami (Fla.)—Police
Tampa (Fla.)—Police
Georgia
See also
Brooks County (Ga.)—Police
Norcross (Ga.)—Police

Police—cont.

Great Britain
History
Keeping the peace? Policing strikes 1906-26. B. Weinberger. bibl il *Hist Today* 37:29-35 D '87
Illinois
See also
Chicago (Ill.)—Police
Des Plaines (Ill.)—Police
Indiana
See also
Indianapolis (Ind.)—Police
Italy
Going undercover for art's sake. R. Suro. il *N Y Times Mag* p42-3+ D 13 '87
Kentucky
See also
Louisville (Ky.)—Police
Maryland
Baltimore police chief is new top cop for Maryland [B. Robinson] *Jet* 71:4 Mr 9 '87
Massachusetts
See also
Boston (Mass.)—Police
Michigan
See also
Detroit (Mich.)—Police
Inkster (Mich.)—Police
Mississippi
See also
Greenville (Miss.)—Police
New Jersey
See also
North Haledon (N.J.)—Police
New York (State)
See also
Brooklyn (New York, N.Y.)—Police
New York (N.Y.)—Police
North Carolina
See also
Chadbourn (N.C.)—Police
Greensboro (N.C.)—Police
Ohio
See also
Cleveland (Ohio)—Police
Ontario
See also
Toronto (Ont.)—Police
Pennsylvania
See also
Pittsburgh (Pa.)—Police
Black wins case against Pennsylvania state police; will receive $485,000 [case of black policeman R. Clanagan] *Jet* 72:38 My 11 '87
Pennsylvania gets first black state police major [R. M. Sharpe] por *Jet* 71:32 Mr 23 '87
Sharpe is 1st black tabbed to head Pa. state police. por *Jet* 72:8 Ag 31 '87
Sharpe is first black Pa. state police chief. por *Jet* 73:47 N 2 '87
Québec (Province)
See also
Montreal (Québec)—Police
Showdown in Quebec [police raids on the Confederation of National Trade Unions] M. Rose. il *Macleans* 100:12 Je 29 '87
South Carolina
See also
Aiken (S.C.)—Police
Texas
See also
Houston (Tex.)—Police
Washington (State)
See also
Seattle (Wash.)—Police

Police, Mounted
See also
Police horses
Royal Canadian Mounted Police
United States. Park Police

Police (Musical group)
The Police: U.S. tour, October-November 1978. D. Fricke. il *Roll Stone* p103+ Je 4 '87

Police [film] See Motion picture reviews—Single works
Police Academy 4 [film] See Motion picture reviews—Single works

Police auctions *See* Auctions
Police bicycles *See* Bicycles—Police use
Police brutality *See* Police cruelty
Police chiefs
See also
Black police chiefs
Police communication systems
See also
Computers—Police use
Police corruption
Miami Vice: sorting good guys from bad guys [police involved in drug dealing] M. A. Moore. il *U S News World Rep* 102:28 F 2 '87
Police cruelty
Choke-hold death of black sparks violence in Tampa. *Jet* 71:15 Mr 9 '87
Detroit man gets $1 million in police brutality case [R. Steward] *Jet* 72:29 My 4 '87
Fla. race issue clouds Dwight Gooden arrest. il pors *Jet* 71:46-7 Ja 12 '87
James Brown says he was mistreated by police, after alleged accident. por *Jet* 73:54 N 30 '87
Racial mishap sparks buy boycott in Isola, Miss. [treatment of B. Greenwood by police sparks boycott] *Jet* 73:32 N 2 '87
White cop cleared in choke hold death of black man [D. D'Agresta of Tampa police] *Jet* 72:33 Ap 27 '87
Police ethics
See also
Police corruption
An Illinois policeman puts his job on the line by rushing to the aid of his family [C. Launius] il por *People Wkly* 28:59 O 19 '87
Police horses
The last working horses [use by U.S. Park Police and park rangers] C. Carnie. il *Natl Parks* 61:30-5 Mr/Ap '87
Police interrogation *See* Police questioning
Police psychology
Psychologist with a badge [T. H. Blau of Manatee County, Fla.] R. J. Trotter. il pors *Psychol Today* 21:26+ N '87
Police questioning
The case of common sense vs. Miranda. E. H. Methvin. il *Read Dig* 131:96-100 Ag '87
Crime and the Constitution [Miranda Rule] D. O. Relin and C. Lawrence. il *Sch Update* 120:10-11 D 4 '87
The Meese lie [effort to overturn Miranda decision] S. Gillers. *Nation* 244:205 F 21 '87
Viva Miranda [Justice Dept. offensive against Miranda decision] J. Toobin. *New Repub* 196:11-12 F 16 '87
Police radar *See* Radar in traffic control
Police shootings
Best intentions: Edmund Perry's path from Harlem to Exeter to death on a street in Morningside Heights [excerpt] R. S. Anson. il pors map *N Y* 20:30-45 My 11 '87
Charges of racism [black youth A. Griffin killed by Montreal police] L. Van Dusen. il *Macleans* 100:14+ N 30 '87
Shot by a cop [J. Yates of Cleveland] D. O. Relin. il por *Sch Update* 120:7 D 4 '87
Police television shows *See* Television broadcasting—Crime programs
Policewomen
Barbara Schein finally gets a shot at walking the beat. A. Abrahams. il pors *People Wkly* 27:139-40 My 4 '87
Jury awards $900,000 to black female officer in Detroit police case [case of C. Preston] *Jet* 72:33 Ap 27 '87
Policies, Insurance *See* Insurance
Policy analysis *See* Policy sciences
Policy Analysis for California Education
Bridging the gap between policy and research [interview with M. W. Kirst] D. B. Strother. il por *Phi Delta Kappan* 69:161-4 O '87
Data: a by-product of reform. C. Pipho. il *Phi Delta Kappan* 69:102-3 O '87
Policy loans *See* Insurance, Life—Policy loans
Policy Management Systems Corp.
One insider bet his boat on this stock. G. G. Marcial. *Bus Week* p100 S 7 '87
Policy sciences
See also
International Center for Development Policy
United States. Office of Policy Development
Urban Institute
Future histories: a new approach to scenarios [SIGMA computer simulation] W. L. Renfro. il por *Futurist* 21:38-41 Mr/Ap '87

Policy sciences—*cont.*
The politics of blame: public policy and avoidance behavior. R. K. Weaver. *Current* 296:11-15 O '87
Polikoff, Barbara Garland
The write stuff. il *Parents* 62:140-4 O '87
Poling, Harold A.
Can we make U.S. industry competitive again? il *USA Today (Periodical)* 116:22-4 N '87
about
The U.S.: team at the top of no. 2. il pors *Fortune* 116:82 N 9 '87
Poliomyelitis virus
The structure of poliovirus. J. M. Hogle and others. bibl (p128) il *Sci Am* 256:42-9 Mr '87
Poliovirus *See* Poliomyelitis virus
Polishes *See* Polishing materials
Polishing materials
Face lift for furniture [Formby's Furniture Face Lift] N. Negovetich. il *Pop Sci* 230:121 Je '87
Polisi, Salvatore Daniel
about
The sins of the father: a mobster's past shadows his sons' football stardom. N. Taylor. il *N Y* 20:42-4+ Ja 26 '87
Polit, Denise F.
Routes to self-sufficiency: teenage mothers and employment. bibl f il *Child Today* 16:6-11 Ja/F '87
Politeness *See* Courtesy
Political action committees
See also
Effective Government Committee
Impac '88
JustLife (Organization)
Spacepac
As the new right stumbles, its PACs pick up speed. R. Fly. il *Bus Week* p72-3 Mr 2 '87
Nice PAC you've got here . . . a pity if anything should happen to it: how politicians shake down the special interests. A. Dockser. *Wash Mon* 18:21-2+ Ja '87
Rating the com-PACs [broadcasting] R. Buck. *Channels* 7:42 Mr '87

Laws and regulations
Inside Gephardt's PACscam [cover story] D. Corn. il *Nation* 244:559+ My 2 '87
Is Congress ready to bite the hands that feed it? D. Harbrecht and R. Fly. il *Bus Week* p102-3 Je 1 '87
Limiting political action committees. *Congr Dig* 66:33-62 F '87
Senate's big PAC attack. A. Holzinger. il *Nations Bus* 75:10 Ap '87
UnPAC. *Nation* 244:456-7 Ap 11 '87
Political advertising *See* Advertising, Political
Political and Security Committee (United Nations) *See* United Nations. Political and Security Committee
Political asylum *See* Asylum, Right of
Political attitudes
See also
Aged—Political activities
Anti-nuclear movement
Baby boom generation—Political activities
Blacks—Political activities
Business—Political aspects
Cardinals—Political activities
College students—Political activities
College teachers—Political activities
Cuban Americans—Political activities
Farmers—Political activities
High school students—Political activities
Iran-contra affair—Public opinion
Jews—Political activities
Jews—United States—Political activities
Mexican Americans—Political activities
Nuclear warfare—Public opinion
Parents—Political activities
Reagan-Gorbachev summit conference, 1987—Public opinion
Rock musicians—Political activities
Scientists—Political activities
Women—Political activities
Yuppies—Political activities
After the fall [Time poll on Democratic presidential candidates] il *Time* 129:26 My 18 '87
America's state of mind [foreign affairs] J. E. Rielly. il *Foreign Policy* 66:39-56 Spr '87
At the turn of the year, an upbeat America. il *U S News World Rep* 103:28-9 D 28 '87-Ja 4 '88
Business week/Harris poll. See issues of Business Week
Do conservatives discriminate against blacks? *Society* 25:4+ N/D '87
The GOP: it's up for grabs. T. Morganthau. il *Newsweek* 110:30-1 O 19 '87

A growing sense of disillusion [Iowa voters' views on G. Hart case] A. Plattner. il *U S News World Rep* 102:22-3 My 18 '87
Gung ho in the Gulf [support for U.S. presence in the Persian Gulf; Time poll] il *Time* 130:26 Ag 31 '87
The Hart poll [Gallup/Nation poll shows that G. Hart would be frontrunner if he were to reenter race] V. S. Navasky. *Nation* 245:112-13 Ag 15-22 '87
Has Reagan changed? [public's perception has changed] J. Alter. il por *Newsweek* 110:20 N 23 '87
History in Sherman Park (I) [views of ordinary citizens in Milwaukee during the 1984 presidential campaign] J. Schell. *New Yorker* 62:35-6+ Ja 5 '87
History in Sherman Park (II) [views of ordinary citizens in Milwaukee during the 1984 presidential campaign] J. Schell. *New Yorker* 62:57-8+ Ja 12 '87
How to win in '88: meld the unmeldable. N. J. Ornstein. il *U S News World Rep* 103:31-2+ O 12 '87
Interpreting public opinion: five common fallacies. J. Doble. *Current* 294:20-5 Jl/Ag '87
Jackson a top contender for U.S. president: poll [J. Jackson] il por *Jet* 72:4-5 Ap 6 '87
Jesse Jackson and the polls. W. F. Buckley. *Natl Rev* 39:62 Je 19 '87
Jesse Jackson leads poll since Gary Hart withdrew. por *Jet* 72:4 Je 22 '87
A Newsweek poll: Bork, the Court and the issues. il *Newsweek* 110:26 S 14 '87
Notes and comment [change in the political climate] *New Yorker* 63:25 F 23 '87
Notes and comment [President Reagan's loss of power to define the political agenda] *New Yorker* 62:25 F 16 '87
Notes and comment [public mood dictating policy] *New Yorker* 62:23 Ja 19 '87
Others as we see them. il *Society* 24:2 My/Je '87
The paradox of North's popularity [O. L. North] J. Morley. il *Nation* 245:122-5 Ag 15-22 '87
Polls, pollution, and politics revisited: public opinion on the environment in the Reagan era [cover story; with editorial comment by Gilbert F. White] R. E. Dunlap. bibl f il *Environment* 29:6-11+ Jl/Ag '87
Public backs Marshall in his views on Constitution [Supreme Court Justice T. Marshall] por *Jet* 72:32 Je 1 '87
Public opinion on the environment [discussion of July/August 1987 article, Polls, pollution and politics revisited] R. E. Dunlap. il *Environment* 29:2-3 N '87
The public's agenda [results of Time poll] il *Time* 129:37 Mr 30 '87
Sex and the presidency [Life polls America] M. Dubrow and others. il *Life* 10:70-2+ Ag '87
Southern attitudes and world affairs [Main Street America and the third world] J. H. Wolfe. *USA Today (Periodical)* 115:9 Ja '87
Unhappy Democrats, a loyal G.O.P. [Time poll on presidential contenders] L. I. Barrett. il *Time* 130:22+ S 14 '87

Canada
The decline of Lean and Mean [disenchantment with economic conservatism] C. Gordon. il *Macleans* 100:9 Ap 6 '87
A growing fear of total war [Maclean's/Decima poll] B. Levin. il *Macleans* 100:50+ Ja 5 '87
A heady new scent of coalition [views of A. Reid] P. C. Newman. il por *Macleans* 100:35 S 28 '87
It is déjà vu all over again [Tories out of favor] S. MacLeod. por *Macleans* 100:84 F 2 '87
Low marks for the government [Maclean's/Decima poll] P. Gessell. il pors *Macleans* 100:32-5 Ja 5 '87
A move toward self-reliance [Maclean's/Decima poll on the economy] P. Best. il *Macleans* 100:46+ Ja 5 '87
Tempering the old idealism [Maclean's/Decima poll] C. Wood. il *Macleans* 100:36-7 Ja 5 '87
Voice of the people [Maclean's poll on the constitutional accord] A. Phillips. il *Macleans* 100:12-14 Je 15 '87
Anecdotes, facetiae, satire, etc.
When summer blues turn pink [commonly held views surrounding an NDP federal government] C. Gordon. por *Macleans* 100:35 Ag 10 '87
Germany (West)
The view from West Germany [views on arms control] O. Weber. il *Sch Update* 120:18 N 20 '87
Israel
History and the body politic in Israel. D. Ashkenazy. il *Christ Century* 104:822-3 S 30 '87
Soviet Union
Soviet specimens. W. Goodman. il *New Leader* 70:7-8 N 2 '87

Political attitudes—Soviet Union—*cont.*
The view from Moscow [views on arms control] N. Marcus. il *Sch Update* 120:19 N 20 '87
United States
See Political attitudes
Political bosses *See* Boss rule (Politics)
Political campaign consultants *See* Campaign management
Political campaigns
  See also
  Advertising, Political
  Campaign funds
  Campaign issues
  Campaign management
  Campaign workers
  Political candidates
  Political ethics
  Presidential campaigns
  Television and politics
  Television broadcasting—Election results
    See also subhead Politics and government under names of states and cities
Political notes [Senate races] J. McLaughlin. *Natl Rev* 39:20 Je 5 '87
Canada
  See also subhead Politics and government under names of provinces and cities
Testing party power [byelections] M. Janigan. il *Macleans* 100:9-10 Jl 13 '87
Egypt
Mubarak maneuver. S. Reed. *Nation* 244:421 Ap 4 '87
France
Giving French lessons in *le scandale* [F. Mitterrand and J. Chirac] R. Z. Chesnoff. il pors *U S News World Rep* 103:56 N 16 '87
Germany (West)
Campaigning with a free conscience [H. Kohl] R. Laver. il por *Macleans* 100:22-3 Ja 26 '87
Candidate for a confident time [H. Kohl] M. S. Serrill. il por *Time* 129:32 Ja 26 '87
Kohl by default. N. Birnbaum. *Nation* 244:69 Ja 24 '87
'The shadows of the Reich' [H. Kohl's campaign remark concerning East German concentration camps] N. Cooper. il por *Newsweek* 109:32 Ja 19 '87
The strange appeal of Helmut Kohl. J. E. Pluenneke and F. A. Miller. il por *Bus Week* p48-9 Ja 26 '87
West Germany chooses a chancellor. F. O. Bonkovsky. il *Commonweal* 114:14-16 Ja 16 '87
Great Britain
The battle for Britain. R. Laver. il *Macleans* 100:22-5 Je 15 '87
Britain's cheesy campaign [cover story] F. Barnes. il *New Repub* 196:22-5 Je 22 '87
Campaigning for a record [M. Thatcher calls election] P. C. Winslow. il por *Macleans* 100:20+ My 25 '87
Headed for the finish line. C. Ogden. il por *Time* 129:39 Je 15 '87
In the telly's eye: an American-style British campaign. R. Knight. il pors *U S News World Rep* 102:10-11 Je 15 '87
Maggie's revolution on the line. A. Lejeune. *Natl Rev* 39:32+ Je 19 '87
Minority report. C. Hitchens. *Nation* 244:752 Je 6 '87
Off and running. F. Painton. il por *Time* 129:34-6 Je 1 '87
On and on. *New Repub* 196:4+ Je 15 '87
On the stump with the Iron Lady [M. Thatcher] B. Amiel. il *Macleans* 100:9 Je 22 '87
Politics American style. G. C. Lubenow. il *Newsweek* 109:41 Je 8 '87
Thatcher pushes ahead [cover story; special section] il *World Press Rev* 34:11-16 My '87
Thatcher's capitalist revolution [cover story] H. Raines. il pors *N Y Times Mag* p16-19+ My 31 '87
Thatcher's revolution: act III. R. A. Melcher. il por *Bus Week* p72-4 My 25 '87
Two Davids and Goliath [D. Owen and D. Steel challenge M. Thatcher] R. Watson. il pors *Newsweek* 109:26-7 My 25 '87
What Maggie has wrought. R. I. Kirkland, Jr. il pors *Fortune* 115:91-2 Je 8 '87
Haiti
Can Haiti conjure up a miracle? C. A. Robbins. il *U S News World Rep* 103:30-2 N 30 '87
Moment of decision arrives in Haiti. W. T. Boots. *Christ Century* 104:1077-8 D 2 '87
Taking a stab at democracy. N. Cooper. il *Newsweek* 110:42 N 30 '87
While Haiti burns. M. Massing. *New Repub* 197:14-16 N 16 '87

Indonesia
Indonesia votes. J. Pincus. *Nation* 244:493 Ap 18 '87
Indonesia's economic downswing and political reforms. G. B. Hainsworth. bibl f *Curr Hist* 86:172-5+ Ap '87
Italy
Back in the game [Communist Party] G. Conti. *Nation* 244:706-7 My 30 '87
Italy gets set to vote on its future. W. C. Symonds and K. Wolman. il *Bus Week* p52-3 Je 8 '87
Korea (South)
Heading down the homestretch. J. Greenwald. il *Time* 130:46+ D 14 '87
Korea: a three-way tossup. F. Willey. il *Newsweek* 110:59 D 7 '87
Korea's election gamble. H. Anderson. il *Newsweek* 110:47-8 D 21 '87
Korea's elections: high stakes for the economy. L. Armstrong and L. Nakarmi. il *Bus Week* p50-2 D 14 '87
Potholes on the highway to democracy. J. Wallace. il *U S News World Rep* 103:34-5 N 30 '87
Reform movement endangered in Korea. L.-M. Delloff. *Christ Century* 104:990 N 11 '87
Philippines
Big Red machine. W. Chapman. *New Repub* 196:19-20 Ap 6 '87
Rallying the body politic [cover story] D. Kirk. il *New Leader* 70:5-7 Mr 9 '87
South Africa
Bashing heads before balloting. W. E. Smith. il *Time* 129:38 My 11 '87
A bloody campaign trail. A. Bilski. il *Macleans* 100:26-7 My 4 '87
Botha defies the tides, gets tougher. J. Jones. il por *U S News World Rep* 102:32-3 F 16 '87
Dealing from strength [call for a general election] S. Reiss. il *Newsweek* 109:32 Ja 12 '87
Pretoria's 'New Nats'. S. Reiss. il *Newsweek* 109:44 Mr 9 '87
Running against America. B. W. Nelan. il *Time* 129:40 F 16 '87
South Africa. S. Mufson. *Bus Week* p65 My 11 '87
South Africa: subtle stakes. J. Jones. il *U S News World Rep* 102:29-30 My 11 '87
South Africa's fault lines. S. Reiss. il *Newsweek* 109:42 My 11 '87
A vote under siege. A. Bilski. il *Macleans* 100:34 My 11 '87
Voting in South Africa. D. L. Lewis. il *Nation* 244:534+ Ap 25 '87
Political candidates
  See also
  Black political candidates
  Political campaigns
  Presidential candidates
  Television broadcasting—Election results
  Women political candidates
Ethics
  See Political ethics
Expenditures
  See Campaign funds
Religious life
Evangelical politicians defeat themselves. B. Hallman. il por *Christ Today* 31:12 N 6 '87
France
Fanning French fears [presidential candidate J.-M. Le Pen] R. Bernstein. il por *N Y Times Mag* p50+ O 4 '87
New fire on the far right [J.-M. Le Pen emerges as a serious force in presidential politics] W. R. Doerner. il por *Time* 129:40 Je 8 '87
Great Britain
"Our time has come" [minority candidates for Parliament] L. Garrison. il *Time* 129:36 Je 1 '87
Japan
Nakasone: from prime minister to 'shadow shogun'? B. Buell. il *Bus Week* p83 O 19 '87
Political poker game, Japanese style [Y. Nakasone and possible successors] M. Lord. il por *U S News World Rep* 103:32 Jl 20 '87
The political rivals jockeying for Japan's top job. B. Buell. il *Bus Week* p36-7 Ap 20 '87
Tee time for the threesome [Liberal Democratic Party presidency candidates] B. Hillenbrand. il *Time* 130:38 O 19 '87
Korea (South)
Kim out, Kim out, whoever you are. H. G. Chua-Eoan. il pors *Time* 130:36 O 12 '87
Kim vs. Kim. il por *Time* 130:74 N 9 '87

Political candidates—Korea (South)—*cont.*
Korean politics: Kim for a day [presidential candidate Kim Jong Pil] B. Martin. il por *Newsweek* 110:51 O 12 '87

Mexico

Continuity for Mexico [C. Salinas de Gortari] A. Landaburu. por *World Press Rev* 34:25 D '87

The fickle finger of a president [M. de la Madrid to pick successor] J. Contreras. il *Newsweek* 109:35 Ja 12 '87

For De la Madrid, it's almost like being reelected [hand picked heir C. Salinas de Gortari] S. Baker. il por *Bus Week* p78-9 O 19 '87

Let us now await the hidden one [possible PRI presidential candidates] J. Smolowe. il *Time* 129:34 Mr 23 '87

Mexico chooses a new president [C. Salinas de Gortari] por *Newsweek* 110:52 O 12 '87

Mexico: the presidential problem. A. Aguilar Zinser. bibl f *Foreign Policy* 69:40-60 Wint '87/'88

Mexico's precarious balancing act. S. Baker and E. Weiner. il por *Bus Week* p54-5 S 14 '87

Mexico's race is on. P. Chapman. *World Press Rev* 34:45 Ja '87

A political split in Mexico [dissension in PRI over president's selection of candidate] J. Contreras. il *Newsweek* 110:32 Jl 6 '87

A professor's pupil makes good [P.R.I. candidate C. Salinas de Gortari] J. Smolowe. por *Time* 130:37 O 19 '87

Why De la Madrid's successor won't be another De la Madrid. S. Baker. por *Bus Week* p65 My 11 '87

Political cartoon publishing *See* Publishers and publishing—Cartoons
Political cartoons *See* Caricatures and cartoons
Political clubs and associations
See also
Philadelphia Society
Tecumseh Club

Canada
See also
Reform Association of Canada

Soviet Union
See also
Pamyat (Organization)
Rebirth of political activity. J. Steele. *World Press Rev* 34:38-9 N '87

Political consultants
See also
Campaign management
Nathan Group
Sawyer-Miller Group
Debate distress? Call the spin doctors. E. Clift. il *Newsweek* 110:51 D 14 '87

Political contributions *See* Campaign funds
Political conventions
See also
National conventions, Democratic
National conventions (Political)
Political corruption *See* Politics, Corruption in
Political crimes and offenses
See also
Assassination
Impeachments
Sedition
Terrorism
Treason

Political defectors *See* Defectors, Political
Political diaries *See* Diaries
Political ethics
See also
Conflict of interests (Public office)
Debategate case
Government, Resistance to
Politics, Corruption in
Again: character tests [problems of J. Jackson and P. Robertson] il por *U S News World Rep* 103:8 O 19 '87

The bums on the front page. A. Fotheringham. il *Macleans* 100:64 O 12 '87

A case of rank vs. privilege [Senator A. Specter's attempt to get Navy to reimburse Dravo Corp. for plant construction cost overruns] T. Gup. il *Time* 130:29 S 14 '87

Cassette principles. D. E. Koshland, Jr. *Science* 238:445 O 23 '87

Did Gorbachev smoke pot? M. Greenfield. il *Newsweek* 110:94 N 30 '87

Edwin Meese's power trip—the downhill slope. D. Baer. il por *U S News World Rep* 103:14 Jl 13 '87

Fraternalist manifesto [excerpt from address, November 1986] C. Lasch. *Harpers* 274:17-20 Ap '87

The growing difficulties of Ed Meese. T. Jacoby. il por *Newsweek* 110:24 Jl 13 '87

The high price of indictment [problems of public officials] T. Gest and D. Baer. il *U S News World Rep* 102:23-4 Je 8 '87

'I am for morality' [interview with R. Reagan] por *U S News World Rep* 102:25 My 25 '87

John Conyers asks that Edwin Meese resign. *Jet* 72:29 Ag 31 '87

Letter from Washington [House Democrats] Cato. *Natl Rev* 39:14 Ag 14 '87

Making the world safe for difference. R. J. Neuhaus. *Natl Rev* 39:24 N 20 '87

'Meese messes' galore. D. Baer. por *U S News World Rep* 103:18 N 30 '87

Moral judgment and political action [address, October 26, 1987] P. L. Berger. *Vital Speeches Day* 54:115-22 D 1 '87

Morality among the supply-siders [Reagan administration members with ethical or legal charges against them] R. Stengel. il *Time* 129:18-20 My 25 '87

Planning a secret-poll scam [tactics by R. Gephardt's Iowa organization] M. Duffy. il por *Time* 130:27 N 23 '87

Political hardball: the new fall classic [dirty tricks in the presidential campaign] G. Borger. il *U S News World Rep* 103:28-9 S 28 '87

Politicians and professors: a double standard. S. M. Walt. il *Bull At Sci* 43:3-4 Jl/Ag '87

The public image of public figures. D. Schorr. il *New Leader* 70:3-4 N 16 '87

The real sins of politicians. A. Fotheringham. il *Macleans* 100:68 D 14 '87

Republican dirty tricks [anti-Kemp mailing traced to G. Bush operatives] F. Barnes. *New Repub* 197:18+ Jl 27 '87

Sounds of the Righteous Brothers [1988 presidential candidates] L. I. Barrett. il *Time* 129:21 My 25 '87

'A stone in one's shoe': running with integrity. J. M. Wall. *Christ Century* 104:843 O 7 '87

Why it hurts: the murky worlds of Hart and Secord raise painful questions about what America expects of its leaders and institutions. R. Stengel. il *Time* 129:14-15 My 18 '87

Why not the truth? M. Kramer. il *U S News World Rep* 102:22 My 25 '87

With a friend like this . . . [controversies surrounding E. Meese] E. Magnuson. por *Time* 130:20 N 16 '87

Anecdotes, facetiae, satire, etc.
The character issue. *New Repub* 197:6+ O 26 '87

Political films *See* Motion pictures—Political films
Political forecasting
Needed: a new political agenda for the 1990s. W. J. Cohen. por *U S News World Rep* 102:7 Mr 16 '87

Politics after Reagan. R. J. Bresler. il *USA Today (Periodical)* 116:7 S '87

A return to the center. R. J. Bresler. il *USA Today (Periodical)* 116:7 N '87

The U.S.S.R. in the 1990's [address, April 17, 1987] R. F. Staar. *Vital Speeches Day* 53:487-90 Je 1 '87

Why the Reagan era won't end in 1989. R. Fly and others. il por *Bus Week* p33 Jl 13 '87

Political humor *See* Politics—Anecdotes, facetiae, satire, etc.
Political indoctrination *See* Indoctrination
Political interest groups *See* Special interest groups
Political journalism *See* Press and politics
Political leaders *See* Politicians
Political machine *See* Boss rule (Politics)
Political participation
See also
Lobbyists and lobbying
Voting
The ballot trap. R. Jahnkow. il *Progressive* 51:14-15 Ag '87

Political parties
See also
Communist Party (U.S.)
Democratic Party (U.S.)
Green Party (U.S.)
National conventions (Political)
Republican Party (U.S.)
The political impasse. T. B. Edsall. il *N Y Rev Books* 34:8-10+ Mr 26 '87

Canada
See also
Christian Heritage Party (Canada)
Conservative Party (Canada)
Liberal Party (Canada)
New Democratic Party (Canada)
Parti québécois

Political parties—Canada—See also—*cont.*
   Parti Rhinoceros
   Reform Party of Canada
   Social Credit Party (B.C.)

China
   See also
   Communist Party (China)

Czechoslovakia
   See also
   Communist Party (Czechoslovakia)

Germany (West)
   See also
   Social Democratic Party (Germany: West)

Great Britain
   See also
   Conservative Party (Great Britain)
   Labour Party (Great Britain)
   Liberal Party (Great Britain)
   Social Democratic Party (Great Britain)

Hungary
   See also
   Communist Party (Hungary)

Iceland
Iceland's feminists: power at the top of the world [Kven-nalistinn Party] J. Edgar. il *Ms* 16:30+ D '87

Italy
   See also
   Communist Party (Italy)
   Radical Party (Italy)

Japan
   See also
   Liberal-Democratic Party (Japan)

Mexico
   See also
   Institutional Revolutionary Party (Mexico)

Philippines
   See also
   Communist Party (Philippines)

South Africa
   See also
   Communist Party (South Africa)

Soviet Union
   See also
   Communist Party (Soviet Union)

Vietnam
   See also
   Communist Party (Vietnam)

Western Europe
   See also
   Green Party (Western Europe)

Political patronage
   See also
   Nepotism

Political philosophy
   See also
   Communism
   Conservatism
   Democracy
   Liberalism
   Political ethics
   Radicalism
   Right and left (Political science)
   Socialism
The cult of Leo Strauss. J. Weisberg. il por *Newsweek* 110:61 Ag 3 '87
How history's great minds inspired the framers. P. M. Jones. il *Sch Update* 120:22-3 S 4 '87
Is a science of politics possible?: The view from Mannheim. D. Kettler and others. *Society* 24:76-82 Mr/Ap '87
Legality, legitimacy, and Carl Schmitt. P. Gottfried. *Natl Rev* 39:52-4 Ag 28 '87
Watch out for herdthink. M. Greenfield. il *Newsweek* 110:68 Jl 13 '87

Political prisoners
   See also
   Amnesty International
   Concentration camps

Brazil
A bizarre escape from Brazil [American mercenary T. Carmody] por *Newsweek* 109:35 Ja 5 '87
A miracle, a universe (I) [involvement of Presbyterian minister J. Wright and Cardinal Arns in project to document torture by Brazilian military governments, 1964-1979] L. Weschler. *New Yorker* 63:69-84+ My 25 '87
A miracle, a universe (II) [involvement of Presbyterian minister J. Wright and Cardinal Arns in project to document torture by Brazilian military governments, 1964-1979] L. Weschler. *New Yorker* 63:72-80+ Je 1 '87

China
Life and death in Shanghai [excerpts; cover story] N. Cheng. il por *Time* 129:42-8+ Je 8 '87
Surviving the hurricane [Nien Cheng] J. Shapiro. il *N Y Rev Books* 34:5-6+ Jl 16 '87
The threat of the gulag. M. Achiron. il *Newsweek* 109:33 Ja 19 '87

Cuba
Against all hope: the prison memoirs of Armando Valladares [condensation] A. Valladares. il *Read Dig* 131:172-6+ Jl '87
In Castro's gulag [E. Gutiérrez Menoyo] G. Volsky. il pors *N Y Times Mag* p80-2+ O 18 '87
Twenty-two years in Castro's prisons [A. Valladares] D. Peerman. il por *Christ Century* 104:1029-33 N 18 '87

Czechoslovakia
Human rights and all that jazz [crackdown on Jazz Section members] *Newsweek* 109:36 Mr 23 '87
Jazz leaders face trial in Czechoslovakia. J. A. Glusman. *Roll Stone* p16 Ap 9 '87
Notes and comment [arrests of members of the Jazz Section of the Union of Musicians] *New Yorker* 63:25-6 Mr 23 '87
Prague & the perils of jazz [persecution of Czechoslovak Union of Musicians' Jazz Section] K. Roth. il *Commonweal* 114:351-4 Je 5 '87

Guatemala
Four candles in the wind [disappearance of four Catholic activists] G. L. Bowen. il *Commonweal* 114:726-7 D 18 '87

Iran
A champagne homecoming [release of Canadian P. Engs] S. Aikenhead. *Macleans* 100:13 F 23 '87
An execution in Tehran [execution of M. Hashemi] K. Scanlon and C. Jerome. il por *Macleans* 100:32 O 12 '87
The mullahs reconsider [release of Canadian P. Engs] A. Bilski. il por *Macleans* 100:19 F 16 '87

Israel
A pileup of scandals in Israel [government reports on the Pollard case and role of Shin Bet in I. Napsu's imprisonment] N. Cooper. il por *Newsweek* 109:42 Je 8 '87
A scandal in the ranks [I. Napsu's claims against Shin Bet arrouses Circassian community] E. Silver. *Macleans* 100:28+ My 4 '87
Security on trial [J. Pollard and I. Napsu cases] B. Levin. il por *Macleans* 100:22 Je 8 '87
Thrice rebuked [cases of J. Pollard and I. Napsu] il por *Time* 129:40 Je 8 '87

Korea (South)
Amnesty for the opposition. il *Macleans* 100:24 Jl 20 '87

Portugal
Letter from Europe [O. Carvalho, leader of 1974 revolution, convicted of terrorism] J. Kramer. *New Yorker* 63:105-20 N 30 '87

South Africa
   See also
   Day of Solidarity with South African Political Prisoners
ANC leader Mbeki freed after 23 years in jail. il *Jet* 73:28 N 23 '87
Apartheid chic [Cry freedom and Mandela] A. White. il *Film Comment* 23:11-12+ N/D '87
Apartheid persecution [clergy opposed to the government's policies] *Christ Century* 104:49-50 Ja 21 '87
Black and white [Cry freedom] M. Peretz. *New Repub* 197:42 D 21 '87
A black Gandhi [Cry freedom depicts life of S. Biko] G. Stern. il *Horizon* 30:37-8 N '87
Cosby heads 'Unlock Apartheid Jails' drive; hits reporter's insult. il por *Jet* 73:56 O 19 '87
Crockett heads drive for a day honoring Mandela. pors *Jet* 73:4 N 9 '87
Cry freedom [story of S. Biko] C. Tyson. il pors *Ebony* 43:60-2+ D '87
Donald and Wendy Woods talk about the real-life drama behind Cry freedom [interview] C. Krupp. il pors *Glamour* 85:166+ D '87
'The government smashes our hope' [restrictions placed on G. Mbeki] il por *Newsweek* 110:49 D 21 '87
Gray calls on Reagan to help S. African detainees. por *Jet* 72:12 Ag 31 '87
Mandela: 25 years later, still a force in South Africa. *Jet* 72:6 Ag 24 '87
Movies [D. Washington portrays S. Biko in Cry freedom] D. Denby. il por *N Y* 20:54-5 S 21 '87

Political prisoners—South Africa—_cont._

Newsman Donald Woods still seeks justice for Stephen Biko in the film Cry freedom. W. Plummer. il pors *People Wkly* 28:64+ N 23 '87

Out of jail and on his feet [release of African National Congress leader G. Mbeki] R. Nordland. il por *Newsweek* 110:81 N 16 '87

The return of a rebel [release of G. Mbeki] il por *U S News World Rep* 103:16-17 N 16 '87

Richard Attenborough's 'Biko'. L. Shaw. il *World Press Rev* 34:60 Je '87

Robert Brown oversees the enrollment of Mandela's daughter at Boston Univ. il por *Jet* 72:28 Je 8 '87

South Africa's war on children. R. A. Falk. il *Nation* 245:516-17 N 7 '87

Special Committee against Apartheid calls for release of political prisoners. il *UN Chron* 23:47 N '86

Stop the torture! [South African youth] B. F. Chavis. por *Essence* 18:146 O '87

Two voices that will not be stilled [N. and W. Mandela] B. W. Nelan. il pors *Time* 129:37 Ja 5 '87

What's wrong with this picture? [Cry freedom] E. Mitchell. il *Roll Stone* p31-2 D 3 '87

Why free Mbeki? S. Mufson. *Nation* 245:670-1 D 5 '87

Soviet Union

A day in the depths of the gulag [I. Begun describes prison regimen] J. O. Jackson. il por *Time* 129:52 Mr 9 '87

Emigrés express caution on Soviet human rights. C. Holden. il *Science* 235:738-40 F 13 '87

Five poems that spelled danger [I. Ratushinskaya] B. Wolfer. il *Commonweal* 114:107-11 F 27 '87

Freedom for a refusenik [interview with I. Begun] il por *Macleans* 100:6+ Ap 27 '87

Gulag eyewitness: daring photographs by a Soviet prisoner. il pors *Life* 10:73-5 S '87

A hard bargain [freeing of A. Sakharov and E. Bonner; special section] il pors *Newsweek* 109:12-23 Ja 5 '87

Houses of the dead [relevance of F. Dostoyevsky's Notes from the House of the Dead to G. Herling's A world apart] F. Eberstadt. *Commentary* 83:43-7 F '87

An interview with Irina Ratushinskaya. E. Kuryluk. il por *N Y Rev Books* 34:16-20 My 7 '87

Koryagin skeptical on *glasnost*. C. Holden. il por *Science* 238:476 O 23 '87

A meeting with Sakharov [interview] H. Feshbach. il pors *Phys Today* 40:7+ Ap '87

More glazed than *glasnost*. I. F. Stone. *Nation* 244:240-1 F 28 '87

Moscow's mixed signals. B. Levin. il *Macleans* 100:29 F 23 '87

My life in exile; tr. by Catherine A. Fitzpatrick. Y. Orlov. il pors *N Y Times Mag* p26-8+ Mr 15 '87

On accepting a prize. A. D. Sakharov. il *N Y Rev Books* 34:49 Ag 13 '87

Orlov provides perspectives on Gorbachev's reforms [interview] W. Sweet. por *Phys Today* 40:79-82 My '87

Picking up where he left off [A. Sakharov freed] J. Smolowe. il pors *Time* 129:53-4 Ja 5 '87

Raising the stakes in Soviet reform [with interview with A. Sakharov] S. Powell. il por *U S News World Rep* 102:30-1 Ja 12 '87

Russia's "gift" to the West [interview with I. Ratushinskaya] il por *Christ Today* 31:41 Je 12 '87

Sakharov and Gorky [release] M. A. Evangelista. *Bull At Sci* 43:21 Ap '87

Sakharov's list. B. Keller. il por *N Y Times Mag* p34-7+ F 15 '87

Sounds of freedom. W. E. Smith. il *Time* 129:52-3 F 23 '87

Soviet believers: still paying a high cost for commitment. K. A. Lawton. il *Christ Today* 31:40-2 Je 12 '87

Soviet psychiatrist describes abuse [views of A. Koryagin] J. Greenberg and B. Bower. *Sci News* 131:328 My 23 '87

A test case [A. Koryagin] D. Satter. il por *N Y Rev Books* 34:3-4 F 12 '87

Ukraine

The KGB admits a mistake [dismissal of senior officer over arrest of Ukrainian journalist] il *Newsweek* 109:32 Ja 19 '87

The KGB gets spanked [officer dismissed over arrest of Ukrainian journalist] il *Time* 129:43 Ja 19 '87

Political protests, demonstrations, etc. *See* Protests, demonstrations, etc.

Political psychology

    See also

    Propaganda

    Voting—Psychological aspects

Avoiding the hard part. M. Greenfield. il *Newsweek* 110:76 S 7 '87

The politics of blame: public policy and avoidance behavior. R. K. Weaver. *Current* 296:11-15 O '87

A republic of souls: puritanism and the American presidency. R. Sennett. il *Harpers* 275:41-6 Jl '87

Political publicity *See* Advertising, Political

Political refugees *See* Refugees

Political reporting *See* Press and politics

Political rhetoric *See* Rhetoric

Political satire *See* Politics—Anecdotes, facetiae, satire, etc.

Political scandals *See* Politics, Corruption in

Political science

    See also

    Authority

    Citizenship

    Communism

    Democracy

    Diplomacy

    Fascism

    Geopolitics

    Law

    Liberalism

    Liberty

    Nations

    Policy sciences

    Populism

    Radicalism

    Revolutions

    Right and left (Political science)

    Separation of powers

    Socialism

    State (Political science)

    Totalitarianism

    Utopias

Textbooks

What do U.S. government and civics textbooks teach? [excerpt from We the people] J. D. Carroll and others. *Educ Dig* 53:36-8 S '87

Political terminology *See* Politics—Terminology

Politicians

    See also

    Boss rule (Politics)

    Drugs and politicians

    Public officers

    Statesmen

Ethics

    See Political ethics

Sexual behavior

Again, sex and politics [disclosures concerning R. Celeste, B. Frank and J. Jackson] C. O'Connor. il por *Newsweek* 109:33 Je 15 '87

Are the sex lives of all politicians now fair game? [cases of G. Hart and R. Celeste] A. P. Sanoff. il por *U S News World Rep* 102:12 Je 15 '87

Only the chaste may apply. A. Fotheringham. il *Macleans* 100:56 Je 29 '87

Sexual hysteria [press coverage] E. Diamond. il *N Y* 20:14-16 Je 22 '87

Should the press play vice cop? [cover story] N. Von Hoffman. *Nation* 244:835+ Je 20 '87

Politicians' wives

    See also

    Congressmen's wives

    Presidential candidates—Wives

More than just a mama bear. M. Greenfield. il *Newsweek* 109:88 Mr 23 '87

Politics

    See also

    Art and politics

    Cable television and politics

    Comic books, strips, etc.—Political aspects

    Computers—Political use

    Conservatism

    Economics and politics

    Elections

    Geopolitics

    Information storage and retrieval systems—Political use

    Law and politics

    Liberalism

    Newspapers and politics

    Political science

    Public relations and politics

    Television and politics

    Voting

    World politics

    See also subhead Politics and government under names of continents, countries, states, cities

Politics—*cont.*

Anecdotes, facetiae, satire, etc.

Bringing down the House [political humor used by Newfoundland MP G. Baker] M. Drohan. por *Macleans* 100:8+ N 30 '87

Not going gentle into that good night, caustic comic Mort Sahl gears up for a Broadway comeback. K. Gross. il pors *People Wkly* 28:134-6 O 12 '87

Bibliography

Political booknotes. See issues of The Washington Monthly

The Washington monthly 17th annual Book Award [special section] *Wash Mon* 19:38-54 Ap '87

Terminology

A dictionary of world affairs words. J. Ferber. il *Sch Update* 120:36 O 2 '87

Let us distance ourselves. W. Safire. il *N Y Times Mag* p9-10 Ja 11 '87

Negative phenomena come to Nexis [current terms used by Tass] D. Seligman. il *Fortune* 115:166 Je 22 '87

One thing is certain [Nexis data base searches] *New Repub* 196:4+ F 2 '87

Workaday words from the halls of the Capitol. J. Ferber. *Sch Update* 119:22 Ja 12 '87

Anecdotes, facetiae, satire, etc.

Uncivil liberties. C. Trillin. il *Nation* 245:222 S 12 '87

Politics, Corruption in

See also
Boss rule (Politics)
Campaign funds
Conflict of interests (Public office)
Muckraking
Watergate case

$4 billion worth of temptation [corruption of set-aside programs for minority firms as evidenced in Wedtech scandal] W. Shapiro. il *Time* 129:20 Je 15 '87

Corruption's 'good old days' are back [bribery cases soar] il *U S News World Rep* 103:10 Ag 24 '87

Did the good guys go too far? [crackdown on political corruption hamstrung by Supreme Court ruling on mail fraud] P. Dwyer. il *Bus Week* p29 Ag 31 '87

Mitchell sons indicted in a federal bribery case [Wedtech case] *Jet* 72:14 Ap 20 '87

Morality among the supply-siders [Reagan administration members with ethical or legal charges against them] R. Stengel. il *Time* 129:18-20 My 25 '87

Nice PAC you've got here . . . a pity if anything should happen to it: how politicians shake down the special interests. A. Dockser. *Wash Mon* 18:21-2+ Ja '87

'A political snake pit' comes under the spotlight [Wedtech scandal] P. Cary. il *U S News World Rep* 102:22-4 Je 15 '87

Scandal sheet. E. Alterman. *New Repub* 196:17-18+ Ap 20 '87

A tale of urban greed [Wedtech scandal] R. Stengel. il *Time* 129:30+ Ap 20 '87

Wedtech—and the web it wove. *U S News World Rep* 102:12 F 16 '87

History

The presidential follies. I. F. Fredman. il *Am Herit* 38:38-43 S/O '87

British Columbia

An untimely departure [conflict of interest charges force resignation of Highways Minister C. Michael] J. O'Hara. *Macleans* 100:20 N 30 '87

Canada

Conflicts and credibility gaps [media coverage of case against S. Stevens] G. Bain. il *Macleans* 100:52 D 21 '87

Government under siege [accusations of Tory corruption] M. Janigan and A. Wilson-Smith. il *Macleans* 100:10-12 F 16 '87

Harsh lessons from an inquiry [S. Stevens affair and the press] G. Bain. il *Macleans* 100:44 Ag 24 '87

How to track a plummeting star [scandals surrounding B. Mulroney] P. Stoler. il por *Time* 129:32 Mr 2 '87

Mulroney's new offensive. M. Janigan. il por *Macleans* 100:6-8 F 23 '87

Wrapping up an inquiry [conflict of interest charges against former cabinet minister S. Stevens] S. Aikenhead. il *Macleans* 100:13 Mr 2 '87

'Wrong by any measure' [report on S. Stevens' conflict of interest investigation issued] M. Rose. il por *Macleans* 100:12-14 D 14 '87

Anecdotes, facetiae, satire, etc.

May your best friend fail, too. A. Fotheringham. il *Macleans* 100:60 Mr 9 '87

China

Princes of privilege [nepotism] J. Greenwald. il *Time* 130:41 S 28 '87

France

See also
Greenpeace bombing incident, 1985

Georgia

See also
Fulton County (Ga.)—Politics and government

Germany (West)

See also
Schleswig-Holstein (Germany)—Politics and government

Haiti

Judge: $115,000 Duvalier aide's condo in Miami belongs to Haiti Republic. *Jet* 71:6 Mr 2 '87

India

Millions for expansion but not one cent for tribute [Tata Group's refusal to pay bribes] S. N. Chakravarty. il por *Forbes* 140:46+ O 5 '87

Politics and the university [examination fixing scandal] P. G. Altbach. il *Change* 19:56-9 Jl/Ag '87

Shades of a cover-up [Fairfax scandal] il por *Macleans* 100:22-3 Ap 20 '87

Singh a song of discord [R. Gandhi forces out V. P. Singh] F. Willey. il por *Newsweek* 110:28 Ag 3 '87

Italy

'Irangate' unfolds in Italy [arms smuggling charges against F. Borletti] W. C. Symonds. *Bus Week* p46 S 21 '87

Louisiana

The trials and jubilations of Governor Edwin Edwards. N. Lemann. il por *Esquire* 107:79-82+ My '87

Mexico

Nothing left to steal. G. B. Lake. *Natl Rev* 39:40-1 Jl 3 '87

Mississippi

Stinging the good ole boys. C. O'Connor. il *Newsweek* 110:21 Ag 10 '87

New Jersey

See also
Jersey City (N.J.)—Politics and government

New York (State)

See also
New York (N.Y.)—Politics and government
Queens (New York, N.Y.)—Politics and government
Tammany Hall

Nova Scotia

The return of Billy Joe MacLean. C. Wood. il por *Macleans* 100:14 Mr 9 '87

Panama

Backing away from a Latin dictator [M. A. Noriega] T. Gup. il por *Time* 130:21 S 7 '87

A colonel takes on the general [charges against M. A. Noriega] M. S. Serrill. il por *Time* 129:40 Je 22 '87

Dirty dollars [new law aimed at drug traffickers] J. Moody. il por *Time* 129:44-5 Ja 19 '87

Dishonor thy general [accusations against M. A. Noriega] H. Anderson. il por *Newsweek* 109:37 Je 22 '87

Panama fallen among thieves. G. Sánchez Borbón. il *Harpers* 275:57-67 D '87

The rumbles grow in the isthmus [charges against M. A. Noriega] M. Satchell. il por *U S News World Rep* 102:18 Je 22 '87

Will this man control the Panama Canal? [M. A. Noriega] D. Reed. por *Read Dig* 130:136-40 Ja '87

Paraguay

Smuggler's paradise. T. Rosenberg. *New Repub* 196:14-16 Je 8 '87

Philippines

Can Aquino break the grip of crony corruption? A. Paul. il pors *Read Dig* 131:83-7 Jl '87

Cory Aquino and the psychology of bubbles [legislative election of May 11, 1987] M. Singer. il *Natl Rev* 39:34-8 Ag 14 '87

Hot on the trail of the Marcos billions. M. Shao. il pors *Bus Week* p52-3 Ag 17 '87

The quest for Marcos's gold. N. Cooper. il por *Newsweek* 110:33 Ag 3 '87

Unclean elections. M. Singer. *New Repub* 197:9-10 Ag 3 '87

Where do you hide $10 billion? Aquino wants to know [F. Marcos' fortune] L. Kraar. por *Fortune* 116:97 S 14 '87

Québec (Province)

Fever in a climate of scandal [reporting on the Oerlikon affair] G. Bain. il *Macleans* 100:49 F 23 '87

A new senator's troubled debut [J. Bazin's involvement in Oerlikon land speculation controversy] M. Gee. il por *Macleans* 100:14 F 16 '87

Politics, Corruption in—Québec (Province)—*cont.*

The police and the MP [A. Bissonnette charged in Oerlikon land sale scandal in Canada] M. Rose. *Macleans* 100:9 Ag 31 '87

A political minefield [resignation of Canadian transport minister A. Bissonnette over land sale to Oerlikon Aerospace; special section; with editorial comment by Kevin Doyle] il pors *Macleans* 100:2, 8-9+ F 2 '87

Questions about a firing [criminal allegations against R. La Salle aide F. Majeau] D. Burke. por *Macleans* 100:11-12 Ja 19 '87

The Tories strike back [resignation of A. Bissonnette over land sale to Oerlikon Aerospace] M. Gee. il por *Macleans* 100:10-11 F 9 '87

A Tory veteran bows out [R. LaSalle] H. Mackenzie and M. Janigan. il pors *Macleans* 100:11 Mr 2 '87

Uproar over a firing [criminal allegations against R. LaSalle aide F. Majeau] A. Wilson-Smith. por *Macleans* 100:16 Ja 26 '87

South Carolina

See also

McCormick County (S.C.)—Politics and government

Soviet Union

Sending a message loud and clear: no more graft. P. Galuszka. il *Bus Week* p44-5 Jl 6 '87

Tennessee

Gag order lifted in Harold Ford fraud case. por *Jet* 73:39 O 26 '87

Memphis churches back Rep. Ford with $100,000. il por *Jet* 72:7 Je 15 '87

Rep. Ford indicted and says he will fight charges. por *Jet* 72:4 My 11 '87

Western Europe

Iranscam couldn't happen there. J. Bonfante. il *Time* 129:36 Ja 26 '87

Yugoslavia

All the party chief's men [Agrokomerc scandal] K. W. Banta. il *Time* 130:40 S 28 '87

Corruption and scandal [F. Abdic scandal's effect on Yugoslavia's economic system] T. Fennell. il por *Macleans* 100:38 S 21 '87

Politics and art *See* Art and politics
Politics and blacks *See* Blacks—Political activities
Politics and business *See* Business—Political aspects
Politics and economics *See* Economics and politics
Politics and education

See also

College students—Political activities

College teachers—Political activities

Politicians and professors: a double standard. S. M. Walt. il *Bull At Sci* 43:3-4 Jl/Ag '87

Politics and industry *See* Industry and state
Politics and law *See* Law and politics
Politics and literature

See also

Literature and state

Be reasonable—unless you're a writer. W. Kennedy. il *N Y Times Book Rev* 92:3 Ja 25 '87

Politics and newspapers *See* Newspapers and politics
Politics and public relations *See* Public relations and politics
Politics and religion *See* Religion and politics
Politics and science *See* Science and state
Politics and the press *See* Press and politics
Politics in art

Diversionary (syn)tactics [work of B. Kruger] C. Squiers. il por *Art News* 86:76-85 F '87

Prints, politics & people: The English satirical print, 1600-1832 [Chadwyck-Healey's seven volume collection of satirical prints] I. Roots. il *Hist Today* 37:47-53 Mr '87

Sue Coe's inferno [cover story] S. Gill. il pors *Art News* 86:110-15 O '87

Exhibitions

Urban disturbances [work of K. Wodiczko] E. Lajer-Burcharth. bibl f il *Art Am* 75:146-53+ N '87

Politics in literature

See also

Publishers and publishing—Political literature

Anecdotes, facetiae, satire, etc.

Snap books [books by big-name authors about their brief experiences in foreign countries] M. Massing. *New Repub* 196:21+ My 4 '87

Polizzi, Catherine

A part of him revealed [story] il por *McCalls* 145:150-2 Mr '87

Polk, Kay

about

Kay Polk: combining pastels and watercolors to paint portraits. B. D. Stroud. il *Am Artist* 51:60-3 O '87

Polk, Milbry C.

Organize a family reunion. il *Americana* 15:14-16 Jl/Ag '87

Polk, Sophie

Helping our children. il *Child Today* 16:19-20 S/O '87

Polk Audio, Inc.

Polk Audio sounds like a winner. J. M. Laderman. *Bus Week* p82 Ja 26 '87

Polke, Sigmar

about

Modern times. J. Perl. il *Vogue* 177:90+ Ag '87

Polkow, Dennis

Andrew Lloyd Webber: from Superstar to Requiem [cover story; interview] il por *Christ Century* 104:272-6 Mr 18-25 '87

Poll tax

Great Britain

England's last poll tax [1641] C. Russell. il *Hist Today* 37:9-11 O '87

Thatcher on dangerous ground. N. Gelb. il *New Leader* 70:5-6 N 2 '87

Pollack, J. D.

My sister is in love . . . again. il *Seventeen* 46:196+ Mr '87

Pollack, Sheldon D.

Unraveling the Constitution. bibl *Society* 24:56-9 Ja/F '87

Unraveling the Constitution: a rule of law. *Current* 297:18-21 N '87

Pollack, Sydney, 1934-

about

On Pollack's plate. P. S. Nathan. *Publ Wkly* 231:248 My 15 '87

Pollak, Patricia Baron

Housing options for seniors today. il *Aging* no356:2-5 '87

Pollak, Richard

Witnessing for peace. *Nation* 244:567-8 My 2 '87

Pollan, Corky

Christmas gifts [cover story] il *N Y* 20:57-77+ D 7 '87

(jt. auth) See McKeon, Nancy, and Pollan, Corky

Pollan, Michael

Cultivating virtue. il *Harpers* 274:66-9 My '87

Cultivating virtue. por *Rodale's Org Gard* 34:95-6 O '87

Pollan, Stephen M., and Levine, Mark

How to start your own business (I) [cover story] il *N Y* 20:28-37 Je 8 '87

How to start your own business (II). il *N Y* 20:44-8+ Je 15 '87

Pollard, C. William, 1938-

about

ServiceMaster: looking for new worlds to clean. M. D. Oneal. il pors *Bus Week* p60-1 Ja 19 '87

Pollard, Jonathan

about

Brothers with blood in their eyes. W. E. Smith. il *Time* 129:40 Mr 30 '87

I spy, you spy. W. Blitzer. *New Repub* 196:15-16 Ap 13 '87

Israel and Pollard. *World Press Rev* 34:36-7 My '87

Israelamok. *New Repub* 196:9 Mr 30 '87

Jay Pollard's peculiar tale. M. Satchell. il pors *U S News World Rep* 102:23-5 Je 1 '87

Life for an Israeli spy. H. Anderson. il por *Newsweek* 109:26+ Mr 16 '87

Official rogues. G. Carver. *New Repub* 196:12-15 Ap 13 '87

One step ahead, two backward. J. Branegan. il por *Time* 129:53 Ap 13 '87

A pileup of scandals in Israel. N. Cooper. il por *Newsweek* 109:42 Je 8 '87

The Pollard case. *Nation* 244:457 Ap 11 '87

Security on trial. B. Levin. il por *Macleans* 100:22 Je 8 '87

The spy who came between friends. M. Satchell. il por *U S News World Rep* 102:32-3 Mr 30 '87

Spying between friends. W. E. Smith. il por *Time* 129:44+ Mr 16 '87

Spying between friends: Pollard case simmers on. S. Powell. il por *U S News World Rep* 102:12 Mr 16 '87

Strains in the family. M. Whitaker. il por *Newsweek* 109:32-4 Mr 30 '87

Thrice rebuked. il por *Time* 129:40 Je 8 '87

Triple trouble in Israel [with editorial comment] E. Salpeter. il *New Leader* 70:2, 5-7 Mr 23 '87

Uproar over a spy. W. E. Smith. il *Time* 129:30-2 Mr 23 '87

Pollen
Tracking a trail of pollen [work of Vaughn M. Bryant] D. Lampe. il *Pop Sci* 231:38 N '87
Pollen, Fossil
Pollen and spores date origin of rift basins from Texas to Nova Scotia as early late Triassic. A. Traverse. bibl f il map *Science* 236:1469-72 Je 12 '87
Pollen probe of early Maya farming [work of David J. Rue] *Sci News* 131:218 Ap 4 '87
Pollick, Michael
Preparing for the worst. il *Nations Bus* 75:28+ O '87
Pollin, Robert
(jt. auth) See Cockburn, Alexander, and Pollin, Robert
Pollination *See* Fertilization of plants
Pollini, Maurizio
about
The Pollini sound. K. Botsford. il pors *N Y Times Mag* p30-1+ Mr 1 '87
Pollitt, Katha
Letters [discussion of May 23, 1987 article, The strange case of Baby M] *Nation* 245:38+ Jl 18-25 '87
Mandarin oranges [poem] *New Yorker* 63:36 F 23 '87
The mind of an anti-abortionist. il *Nation* 244:65+ Ja 24 '87
Sonata for two pianos [story] il *Ms* 15:64-6+ My '87
The strange case of Baby M [cover story] *Nation* 244:667+ My 23 '87
Pollock, Cynthia
Decommissioning nuclear power plants. il *USA Today (Periodical)* 115:50-3 Mr '87
Pollock, George
A neighborhood. il *N Y Times Mag* p104 N 8 '87
Pollock, Randle
Build an image for your firm. *Archit Rec* 175:44-5 O '87
Polls, College basketball *See* Basketball, College—Polls
Polls, College football *See* Football, College—Polls
Pollution
See also
Acid dew
Acid rain
Air pollution
Chemical plants—Environmental aspects
Electric plants—Environmental aspects
Insurance, Pollution liability
Marine pollution
Medical waste disposal
Oil pollution
Pesticides—Environmental aspects
Radioactive pollution
Radon pollution
Resorts—Environmental aspects
Smelters—Environmental aspects
Soil pollution
Space pollution
Trade waste—Disposal
Uranium industry—Environmental aspects
Water pollution
The environment. B. Commoner. *New Yorker* 63:46-7+ Je 15 '87
Control
See also
Environmental movement
Industry and the environment
Pollution control industries
United States. Environmental Protection Agency
International aspects
Transboundary pollution and environmental health [Canadian perspective; cover story] E. Somers. il *Environment* 29:6-9+ Je '87
Canada
Transboundary pollution and environmental health [Canadian perspective; cover story] E. Somers. il *Environment* 29:6-9+ Je '87
Denmark
The hazards of leadshot in soil. *Sci News* 131:233 Ap 11 '87
New Jersey
See also
Newark (N.J.)—Pollution
New York (State)
See also
Love Canal case
A focus on oil and hazardous materials spills. L. Smith. il *Conservationist* 41:46-9 Ja/F '87

United States
See Pollution
Pollution, Outdoor light *See* Lighting, Outdoor
Pollution control devices (Automobiles) *See* Automobiles—Pollution control devices
Pollution control devices (Diesel engines) *See* Diesel engines, Automotive—Pollution control devices
Pollution control industries
See also
American Toxxic Control (Firm)
Cleaning up after industry's slobs. E. Pomice. il *Forbes* 139:90 Ap 20 '87
Securities
Cleaning up. B. Leonard. il *Forbes* 139:52-3 Je 1 '87
Pollution liability insurance *See* Insurance, Pollution liability
Pollution policy *See* Environmental policy
Pollyanna (Fictional character)
Pollyanna, ex-bubblehead [character created by E. H. Porter] J. Griswold. *N Y Times Book Rev* 92:51 O 25 '87
Polo
Don't set the table, Mabel, we're going into extra chukkers! K. J. Gross and J. Mather. il *Esquire* 108:192-7 S '87
Polo picnic. L. Wells. il *N Y Times Mag* p51-2 My 31 '87
Canada
A game for all classes. B. Wallace. il *Macleans* 100:6+ O 12 '87
Polo Grounds (New York, N.Y.)
The Polo Grounds. J. Klein. il *N Y* 20:80-1 D 21-28 '87
Polo/Ralph Lauren, Inc.
Ralph Lauren's achievement. H. Brubach. il *Atlantic* 260:70-3 Ag '87
Polskin, Howard
Art cop. il por *N Y* 20:28+ O 26 '87
Polvay, Marina
Food fit for a Viking. il *Travel Holiday* 167:67 Je '87
What's cooking in Europe: schools with flavor. il *Travel Holiday* 167:56-60 F '87
Polyacetylene
Currents in plastics [doping polyacetylene; work of Herbert Naarmann and N. Theophilou] J. Horgan. *Sci Am* 257:26-7 S '87
Polyandry
Tibet
When brothers share a wife. M. C. Goldstein. il *Nat Hist* 96:38-49 Mr '87
Polychlorinated biphenyls
Blue flame, black gunk [PCB-laced oil buried along Texas Eastern's pipelines] J. Egginton. il map *Audubon* 89:106-12 S '87
Citizens douse a hazardous burn [plan to incinerate PCBs at University of North Dakota's Energy Research Center] J. Hamilton. il *Sierra* 72:88-9 N/D '87
Cleanup target: 10,000 miles of toxic soup [PCBs dumped along Texas Eastern pipeline] map *U S News World Rep* 103:16 N 23 '87
Detoxifying PCBs [cover story] J. Raloff. il *Sci News* 132:154-5+ S 5 '87
Discovering microbes with a taste for PCBs. L. Roberts. il *Science* 237:975-7 Ag 28 '87
Mopping up the PCB mess [problem at Texas Eastern] J. Castro. il *Time* 130:50 N 23 '87
PCB-polluted fishes cause seal decline [Waddenzee, Netherlands] *Sea Front* 33:305-6 Jl/Ag '87
Polychlorinated biphenyl dechlorination in aquatic sediments [river sediments] J. F. Brown and others. bibl f il *Science* 236:709-12 My 8 '87
Sunken PCBs taint the Housatonic. J. Fahys. il *Sierra* 72:85 Jl/Ag '87
Polychlorinated dibenzodioxin *See* Dioxin
Polyesters, Sucrose *See* Sucrose polyesters
Polygamy
A hand from the grave [E. LeBaron and the polygamy murders case] P. Abramson. il pors *Newsweek* 110:45 D 21 '87
Polygonatum *See* Solomon's seal (Plant)
Polymer soil conditioners *See* Soil conditioners
Polymers and polymerization
See also
Plastics
Polyacetylene
Polysilanes
Styrene
Actin polymerization and ATP hydrolysis. E. D. Korn and others. bibl f il *Science* 238:638-44 O 30 '87
An amylose antiparallel double helix at atomic resolution. W. Hinrichs and others. bibl f il *Science* 238:205-8 O 9 '87

Polymers and polymerization—*cont.*
Delay time of hemoglobin S polymerization prevents most cells from sickling in vivo. A. Mozzarelli and others. bibl f il *Science* 237:500-6 Jl 31 '87
Evidence for chain molecules enriched in carbon, hydrogen, and oxygen in Comet Halley [Giotto data] D. L. Mitchell and others. bibl f il *Science* 237:626-8 Ag 7 '87
First polymer in space identified in Comet Halley [Giotto data] W. F. Huebner. bibl f il *Science* 237:628-30 Ag 7 '87
Gas-phase polymerization: ultraslow chemistry. H. Reiss. bibl f il *Science* 238:1368-73 D 4 '87
Hierarchical structure in polymeric materials. E. Baer and others. bibl f il *Science* 235:1015-22 F 27 '87
Imitating iron's magnetism [cover story] I. Peterson. il *Sci News* 131:252-3 Ap 18 '87
New uses for plastics. G. Bronson. il *Forbes* 139:216-17 My 18 '87
Polymer physics. *Phys Today* 40:S64-S66 Ja '87
Polymers in medicine
Eyes prefer plasma-coated contacts [work of Hirotsugu Yasuda] J. Raloff. *Sci News* 131:251 Ap 18 '87
Loosening bacteria's hold on implants [preventing staphylococci from adhering to polymers; research by Bernd Jansen] S. Weisburd. *Sci News* 132:190 S 19 '87
Making drugs stick to your stomach [work of David Harris] J. Raloff. *Sci News* 131:251 Ap 18 '87
Skin reborn from muscle [research by Ioannis Yannas] S. Weisburd. *Sci News* 132:164 S 12 '87
Polymorphism (Biology)
Clonal analysis of human colorectal tumors [use of restriction fragment length polymorphisms] E. R. Fearon and others. bibl f il *Science* 238:193-7 O 9 '87
Genetic promise [restriction fragment length polymorphism mapping] *Sci Am* 257:30-1 Ag '87
Molecular genetics: applications to the clinical neurosciences [linkage analysis with restriction fragment length polymorphisms] J. B. Martin. bibl f il *Science* 238:765-72 N 6 '87
Variable number of tandem repeat (VNTR) markers for human gene mapping. Y. Nakamura and others. bibl f il *Science* 235:1616-22 Mr 27 '87
The world's most polymorphic species. W. R. Catton. bibl f il *BioScience* 37:413-19 Je '87
Polynesia
See also
French Polynesia
Hawaii
Marquesas Islands
Pitcairn Island
Tonga
Polynomials
Polynomial curve fitter [Basic program] W. G. Hood. il *Byte* 12:155-6+ Je '87
Polyoxymethylene
Halley's whiskers: first space polymer detected [work of Walter F. Huebner] J. Eberhart. il *Sci News* 132:100 Ag 15 '87
Polymer found in Comet Halley. il *Astronomy* 15:94 D '87
Polypeptides *See* Peptides
Polyps (Tumors) *See* Tumors (Benign)
Polysaccharides
See also
Amyloses
Cellulose
Dextrans
Polysilanes
Polysilane potential [work of John M. Zeigler and Larry A. Harrah] *Sci Am* 257:22 Ag '87
Polystyrene *See* Styrene
Polyvinylidene fluoride
Piezoelectric plastic film. J. Iovine. il *Radio-Electron* 58:57-8+ Mr '87
Pomerance, Bernard
Custer dreams 'The tonight show' [poem] *Harpers* 274:31-2 Ap '87
Pomeranz, Virginia E.
about
Obituary
Parents il 62:8 F '87. E. Crow
Pomona College
Among the seven pillars of wisdom [blind East Indian student] V. Mehta. *New Yorker* 63:34-6+ Ag 24 '87
Pompeii (Ancient city)
Pompeii: a new eruption [proposed highway] B. Hewitt. il *Newsweek* 109:46 F 23 '87

Small eruption at Pompeii [plan to build a highway] *World Press Rev* 34:59 Mr '87
Pompidou Centre *See* Centre National d'Art et de Culture Georges Pompidou
Pond, Steve
Big time. il pors *Roll Stone* p36-8+ Ja 29 '87
R.E.M. [cover story] il *Roll Stone* p46-8+ D 3 '87
Pond ecology
Little drop of horrors [life in a drop of pond water; work of A. Rakosy] H. Wouk. il *Omni* 10:84-9 N '87
Science in a tub. J. Carey. il *Natl Wildl* 25:32-5 Je/Jl '87
Ponds
See also
Walden Pond (Mass.)
Beaver-pond trout. P. Barrett. il *Field Stream* 92:121-2+ S '87
Getting your feet wet [ponds in landscaping] G. Norman. il *Esquire* 107:28 My '87
New life for old ponds. T. Matson. il *Ctry J* 14:48-53 Jl '87
Ponds. J. D. Randolph. il *Ctry J* 14:8-9 Ag '87
Science in a tub. J. Carey. il *Natl Wildl* 25:32-5 Je/Jl '87
Small-water bass. K. Schultz. il *Field Stream* 92:48+ Jl '87
Pons, Philippe
Big plans for Japan's second city. il *World Press Rev* 34:55 Jl '87
Pons, T. P., and others
Physiological evidence for serial processing in somatosensory cortex. bibl f il *Science* 237:417-20 Jl 24 '87
Ponsford, Alan
Grenada revisited: better than ever. il *World Press Rev* 34:63 F '87
Ponsot, Marie
(For William Cook, drowned in Maine, and for Roy Huss, lost in Indonesia) [poem] *Commonweal* 114:289 My 8 '87
Not this year [poem] *Commonweal* 114:421 Jl 17 '87
Proserpine, packing [poem] *Commonweal* 114:13 Ja 16 '87
Reminder [poem] *Commonweal* 114:84 F 13 '87
Ponte, Lowell
The bugs that bug us: what you should know about colds. il *Read Dig* 131:85-9 O '87
Dawn of the new Stone Age. il *Read Dig* 131:128-33 Jl '87
The great blizzard of '88. il *Read Dig* 131:11-12+ D '87
Jumping genes—nature's secret agents. *Read Dig* 130:132-6 Ap '87
SOS—save our seeds! il *Read Dig* 130:118-22 Je '87
Pontifical Commission for Social Communication *See* Catholic Church. Pontifical Commission for Social Communication
Pool (Game) *See* Billiards
Pool houses
Alpine undercurrents: the subterranean poolhouse of a mountain chalet [decorated by Tessa Kennedy] E. Lambert. il *Archit Dig* 44:96-9 Ja '87
Living poolside. il *South Living* 22:82-3 Je '87
This pavilion and deck give space for poolside entertaining. il *Sunset* 179:106-7 Jl '87
Poole, Joyce H.
Elephants in musth, lust. il *Nat Hist* 96:46-55 N '87
Poole, Robert W., 1944-
Freeway privatization [address, April 10, 1987] *Vital Speeches Day* 53:553-6 Jl 1 '87
Privatizing city services [address, February 24, 1987] *Vital Speeches Day* 53:588-90 Jl 15 '87
Pooler, John P.
(jt. auth) See Valenzeno, Dennis Paul, and Pooler, John P.
Pooley, Don
about
Grooving on a Sunday afternoon. J. Diaz. il pors *Sports Illus* 66:73-4 Je 8 '87
Pooley, Eric
Dave's kids: the twisted minds behind the Letterman show. il por *N Y* 20:36-45 Ja 19 '87
Hey, man, it's Holly Hunter! il pors *N Y* 20:70-4 D 14 '87
I've got the horse right here: producer Rocco Landesman's big Broadway gamble. il pors *N Y* 20:74-6+ S 28 '87

Pooley, Eric—*cont.*
The last angry man: lawyer Andrew Vachss takes to novels to fight child abuse. il por *N Y* 20:42-4+ My 25 '87
Sounds of the city. il *N Y* 20:70-6+ My 4 '87
True blue: from Giants to supermen. il *N Y* 20:26-34 Ja 26 '87
Village voice. il pors *N Y* 20:52-5 Ap 27 '87
Warped in America: the dark vision of moviemakers Joel and Ethan Coen. il pors *N Y* 20:44-8 Mr 23 '87

Pools, Garden *See* Garden pools
Pools, Home *See* Swimming pools, Home
Pools, Swimming *See* Swimming pools
Poor
    See also
    Hunger
    Public welfare
America's underclass: what can be done? M. Magnet. *Current* 295:17-24 S '87
America's underclass: what to do? M. Magnet. il *Fortune* 115:130-4+ My 11 '87
Breaking out of the ghetto: the origins of the underclass. N. Lemann. *Current* 289:4-15 Ja '87
Consumer spending: how many are poor? *Society* 24:2 Jl/Ag '87
Inequality in America: where do we stand? G. T. Burtless. il *Current* 297:4-10 N '87
Life at the edge (I). il *Consum Rep* 52:375-8 Je '87
Life at the edge (II). il *Consum Rep* 52:436-9 Jl '87
Life at the edge (III). il *Consum Rep* 52:504-7 Ag '87
Malthus then and now. J. L. Hess. il *Nation* 244:496-500 Ap 18 '87
New efforts to help America's poor [special issue] il maps *Sch Update* 119:3-10+ Mr 23 '87
Progress and poverty. R. J. Samuelson. por *Newsweek* 110:41 Ag 24 '87
Rescuing the urban poor. T. H. Kean. il *USA Today (Periodical)* 116:72-5 N '87
Will the underclass always be with us? R. P. Nathan. il *Society* 24:57-62 Mr/Ap '87
    Housing
    See also
    Habitat for Humanity Inc.
    Housing vouchers
    International Year of Shelter for the Homeless, 1987
    People in Faith United Housing Corporation
    Slums
The coming of the 'couch people'. D. Whitman. il *U S News World Rep* 103:19-21 Ag 3 '87
Down and out in L.A. [not-quite-homeless forced to live in garages, automobiles, etc.] F. Trippett. il *Time* 129:23 Je 22 '87
Hitch 22 [tax credits intended to draw investment into housing for the poor] J. Novack. il *Forbes* 139:54 F 9 '87
Pro bono architecture in Appalachia and elsewhere [L. J. Currie and his staff provide free architectural services to the poor] M. F. Schmertz. *Archit Rec* 175:9 Mr '87
Shelter skelter [Federal housing programs] *New Repub* 196:7-8 My 11 '87
Want a tax shelter—and a good conscience? [tax credits for investing in housing for the poor] C. Yang. *Bus Week* p130 O 5 '87
    International aspects
Poverty and progress [special section] bibl f il *Courier* 40:20-7 Ja '87
    Medical care
    See also
    Medicaid
Catastrophic costs and the poor [views of Leon Wyszewianski] *USA Today (Periodical)* 115:3 Ap '87
The healing of soul and body [work of Sister Anne Brooks] L. Lindeman. il pors *50 Plus* 27:20-3+ D '87
Medical technology and the poor. V. W. Sidel. il *Technol Rev* 90:24-5 My/Je '87
No money, no vacancy! [patient dumping] L. David and I. David. *Health* 19:64 Ag '87
Sister Anne Brooks, doctor and nun, practices without preaching to the poor. B. Shaw. il pors *People Wkly* 27:82-3+ Mr 23 '87
Women's health insurance: old problems, new programs [services for low income women] D. Lipson. *Ms* 15:24 Mr '87
Your money or your life. P. Downs. il *Progressive* 51:24-8 Ja '87
    California
    See also
    Los Angeles (Calif.)—Poor

    Georgia
    See also
    Atlanta (Ga.)—Poor
    Illinois
    See also
    Chicago (Ill.)—Poor
    India
Class, caste and power. A. S. Patel. il *Courier* 40:26-7 Ja '87
The poor break through. J. McGowan. il *Commonweal* 114:383-6 Je 19 '87
    Massachusetts
    See also
    Boston (Mass.)—Poor
    Mississippi
    See also
    Tutwiler (Miss.)—Poor
    Missouri
    See also
    Kansas City (Mo.)—Poor
    Nevada
    See also
    Las Vegas (Nev.)—Poor
    New Jersey
    See also
    Atlantic City (N.J.)—Poor
    New York (State)
    See also
    New York (N.Y.)—Poor
    Pakistan
    See also
    Karachi (Pakistan)—Poor
    Pennsylvania
    See also
    Philadelphia (Pa.)—Poor
    Philippines
    See also
    Manila (Philippines)—Poor
    Texas
In Texas, a grim new Appalachia [Mexicans of the Rio Grande Valley] F. Gibney. il *Newsweek* 109:27-8 Je 8 '87
    United States
    See Poor
    Washington (D.C.)
    See Washington (D.C.)—Poor
    Western Europe
The 'new poor'. G. Sarpellon. il *Courier* 40:22-4 Ja '87

Poor and the church *See* Church and social problems
Poor children *See* Socially handicapped children
Poor in the Bible
A humble and holy people. M. K. Hellwig. *America* 156:inside back cover Ja 24 '87
Poor little rich girl: the Barbara Hutton story [television program] See Television program reviews—Single works
Poor relief *See* Public welfare
Poore, Patricia
    about
Finding materials for a restoration [interview] S. Romeo. il por *Home Mech* 83:22+ Je '87
Pop art
Saturday disasters: trace and reference in early Warhol [cover story] T. E. Crow. bibl f il por *Art Am* 75:128-36 My '87
Social science fiction [cover story; interview with R. Prince] J. Rian. il *Art Am* 75:86-95 Mr '87
    Exhibitions
The art behind the dots [work of R. Lichtenstein] D. Solomon. il por *N Y Times Mag* p42-6+ Mr 8 '87
The luck of the draw [The drawings of Roy Lichtenstein at the Museum of Modern Art] K. Larson. il *N Y* 20:98-9 My 18 '87
Roy Lichtenstein: master of the Benday dot [The drawings of Roy Lichtenstein at the Museum of Modern Art] E. Heartney. il *Art News* 86:210 Summ '87
Pop music *See* Popular music
Pop-up books
    See also
    Carvajal SA
    Exhibitions
Books that won't sit still [exhibit at the Cooper-Hewitt] D. M. Bolz. il *Smithsonian* 18:208 D '87
Popcorn, Faith
    about
Putting Faith in trends. A. Miller. il pors *Newsweek* 109:46-7 Je 15 '87
Popcorn
    See also
    Golden Valley Microwave Foods Inc.

Popcorn—*cont.*
Even more irresistible popcorn? Grow your own. il *Sunset* 178:114-15, 246 My '87
Meet the presidents: Orville Redenbacher. C. P. Andersen. il por *Good Housekeep* 204:164+ My '87
Pop goes the corn! [microwaved] J. B. Hurley. il *Prevention* 39:72 O '87
Popcorn that steals the show. T. Segal. il *Bus Week* p126 Ap 6 '87

Popcorn diet *See* Diet

Pope, Brenda
about
Wringing profits out of towels. M. S. Goodman and D. Harris. il por *Money* 16:164-6 F '87

Pope, Carl
Undamming Hetch Hetchy. il *Sierra* 72:34-8 N/D '87

Pope, Peter
about
Violence on the Island. M. Gee. por *Macleans* 100:12 Ja 19 '87

Pope, Sterett
Regional report: the Middle East. See issues of World Press Review beginning June 1986

Pope-Hennessy, John
Storm over the Sistine ceiling. il *N Y Rev Books* 34:16+ O 8 '87

Popejoy, William J.
about
Going once, going twice . . . T. Carson. il por *Bus Week* p102 O 5 '87
Psst! Wanna buy the big daddy of thrifts? T. Carson. *Bus Week* p36 Mr 30 '87

Popeo, Dan
about
Capital punishment: just or cruel? [interview] A. Kenney. pors *Sch Update* 119:13 F 9 '87

Popes
See also
John Paul II, Pope, 1920-
Papacy
Pius II, Pope, 1405-1464

Popham, W. James
The merits of measurement-driven instruction [with reply by G. W. Bracey] bibl f il *Phi Delta Kappan* 68:679-89 My '87

Popham, W. James, and Kirby, W. N.
Recertification tests for teachers: a defensible safeguard for society. il *Phi Delta Kappan* 69:45-9 S '87

Popieluszko, Jerzy
Murder case
Of many things. J. W. Donohue. *America* 157:26 Jl 18-25 '87

Poplar
See also
Aspen

Poplar Hall (Kent County, Del.: Historic house) *See* Kent County (Del.)—Historic houses, sites, etc.

Popoff, Peter
about
Fleecing the flock. J. Tierney. il pors *Discover* 8:50-4+ N '87

Popov, Boris
about
This parachute keeps the whole plane aloft. P. Houston. il *Bus Week* p86 N 2 '87

Popovers *See* Bread

Poppa, Ryal R.
about
Surviving the cure. J. Parr. il por *Forbes* 140:52-3 Jl 27 '87

Poppies, Matilija *See* Matilija poppies

Poppleton, Lou Anne, and Cornman, Reba
A bridge between hospital and home. il *Aging* no355:12-13 [14-15] '87

Poppy, John
Gut strength. il *Esquire* 108:71+ S '87
The keys to mastery. il *Esquire* 107:119-22+ My '87
The running debate. il *Esquire* 107:49-50 Mr '87
The sleepless sportsman. il *Esquire* 108:71-2 O '87
Slim pickings. il *Esquire* 108:59-60 N '87
The tao of walking. il *Esquire* 107:31-2 F '87
Turbocharge on wheels. il *Esquire* 107:57-8 Ap '87
Windjamming. il *Esquire* 108:39+ Jl '87

Popular culture
See also
Canada—Popular culture
China—Popular culture
Ethiopia—Popular culture
Great Britain—Popular culture
London (England)—Popular culture
Los Angeles (Calif.)—Popular culture

Punk culture
United States—Popular culture
The best of everything else. il *U S News World Rep* 103:56-7 D 21 '87
Opinions: from Lacroix to La bamba: '87's high points and low lives. il *Vogue* 177:314-17 D '87
What's shocking? T. Young. il *Vogue* 177:758-61 S '87

Popular mechanics (Periodical)
Staff cars. W. Hoyt. il *Pop Mech* 164:41 My '87

Popular music
See also
Blues music
Christian contemporary music
Compact discs—Popular music
Country music
Gospel music
Phonograph records—Popular music
Radio broadcasting—Popular music
Rock music
Videotapes—Popular music
Backbeat. See issues of High Fidelity (New York, N.Y.)
Heart strings: in praise of the melancholy ballad. il *Esquire* 107:114-15 Je '87
Record makers. C. Barter and S. Simels. See issues of Stereo Review beginning March 1984
International aspects
Music for export: pop! T. W. Libbey, Jr. il *High Fidel* 37:56 Mr '87
Brazil
Music, the pulse of a people. T. de Souza. il *Courier* 39:29-32 D '86
South Africa
'Graceland' in Africa [controversy surrounding P. Simon's album] N. Cooper. il por *Newsweek* 109:45 F 23 '87
Julian Bond hired to promote Paul Simon tour [Graceland U.S. tour] il *Jet* 72:55 Je 1 '87
Paul Simon goes on tour with black South Africans. *Jet* 71:17 Mr 2 '87
Paul Simon's amazing Graceland tour [cover story] D. Fricke. il pors *Roll Stone* p42-4+ Jl 2 '87
Singer Paul Simon strikes sour chord with students at Howard U. over album [Graceland] *Jet* 71:59 F 2 '87
Tapping pop music's African roots [P. Simon's Graceland album and tour] N. Jennings. il por *Macleans* 100:52-3 My 4 '87
UN forgives Paul Simon for 'Graceland' album. *Jet* 71:30 F 23 '87
UN group attacks Paul Simon: says 'Graceland' broke cultural boycott of South Africa. R. Tannenbaum. *Roll Stone* p11+ F 12 '87

Popular photography (Periodical)
Special 50th-anniversary issue. il *Pop Photogr* 94:10+ Ja '87

Popular reality (Periodical)
The small time. S. Klawans. *Nation* 244:407-9 Mr 28 '87

Popularity
Are you too concerned with being liked? [teenagers] W. J. Rohr. *Teen* 31:22+ My '87
How to be liked. G. Maleskey. il *Prevention* 39:84-8 Je '87

Population
See also
Birth control
Birth rate
United Nations. Population Commission
United Nations Fund for Population Activities
See also subhead Population under names of continents, countries, states, cities, etc.
"Don't blame me". G. Reiger. *Field Stream* 92:14+ Ag '87
Expert group meets on 1990 World Population and Housing Census Programme. *UN Chron* 23:85 Ja '86
Five billion and counting. P. A. A. Berle. *Audubon* 89:6 Jl '87
Population update. See issues of The Humanist beginning July/August 1986
The threat of population growth. il *World Press Rev* 34:58-9 Ag '87
Toward a world demographic balance. S. J. Burki. *World Press Rev* 34:59 Ja '87
Triumph or threat? [baby in Yugoslavia proclaimed five billionth person on the planet] il *UN Chron* 24:40-1 N '87

Population biology
See also
Animal populations
Fish populations

Population biology—*cont.*

How many creatures? [discussion of October 1986 article, Cultural carrying capacity: a biological approach to human problems] G. J. Hardin. *BioScience* 37:246-7 Ap '87

Population biology, conservation biology, and the future of humanity [address, August 10, 1987] P. R. Ehrlich. *BioScience* 37:757-63 N '87

Population Commission (United Nations) *See* United Nations. Population Commission

Population control *See* Birth control

Population forecasting

The arrival of the 5-billionth human. R. E. Hamil. il por *Futurist* 21:36-7 Jl/Ag '87

Battling over birth policy [views of B. J. Wattenberg] E. Bowen. il *Time* 130:58 Ag 24 '87

The birth dearth. T. Kaye. *New Repub* 196:20-3 Ja 19 '87

The birth dearth: dangers ahead? [excerpts; cover story] B. J. Wattenberg. il por *U S News World Rep* 102:56-62+ Je 22 '87

The birth dearth debate [criticism of B. J. Wattenberg's arguments] A. Levine. il *U S News World Rep* 102:64-5 Je 22 '87

Depleting asset? [views of Ben Wattenberg] M. S. Forbes, Jr. il *Forbes* 140:41 Jl 13 '87

U.S. could become a nation of minorities. *Futurist* 21:57 Mr/Ap '87

Population genetics

Blood test [clues to New World migration from genetic analysis] S. L. Zegura. il *Nat Hist* 96:8+ Jl '87

Gene flow and the geographic structure of natural populations. M. Slatkin. bibl f il *Science* 236:787-92 My 15 '87

Telltale teeth [prehistoric Indians] C. G. Turner, II. maps *Nat Hist* 96:6+ Ja '87

Animals

Bottlenecked cheetahs [research by Stephen O'Brien and others] R. Lewin. il *Science* 235:1327 Mr 13 '87

Two bottlenecks for cheetahs? *Sci News* 131:88 F 7 '87

Birds

DNA fingerprinting of birds. *Sci News* 131:344 My 30 '87

Insects

The surprising genetics of bottlenecked flies [research by Edwin Bryant and others] R. Lewin. *Science* 235:1325-7 Mr 13 '87

Population policy

See also

Birth control

Immigration and emigration

Human population [address, June 22, 1987] M. R. Cutler. *Vital Speeches Day* 53:691-6 S 1 '87

The ultimate wildlife threat [human population expansion] L. Williamson. il *Outdoor Life* 180:28+ D '87

Populations, Animal *See* Animal populations

Populations, Fish *See* Fish populations

Populism

Beyond tax populism. R. Darman. *Society* 24:35-8 S/O '87

Is Reagan conservative? C. Krauthammer. *New Repub* 197:12-14 Jl 27 '87

Populism and tax reform. R. Darman. il *USA Today (Periodical)* 116:29-31 S '87

Porcelli, Mary J.

Treating tension headaches. il *Essence* 18:12+ My '87

Porches

All-American add-on. M. Morris. il *Home Mech* 83:34-6+ Je '87

All-seasons sun porch. A. W. Lees. il *Pop Sci* 230:88-90 Ja '87

The best of both indoor and outdoor worlds: a multiuse screened porch. il *Sunset* 179:108-9 Jl '87

The front porch connection. J. Culhane. il *Read Dig* 130:106-9 Je '87

Porchless. M. E. Marty. *Christ Century* 104:735 Ag 26-S 2 '87

The South has always loved porches. L. Joyner. il *South Living* 22:130-4 Ap '87

Spruce up your porch! S. Wood and E. Young. il *McCalls* 114:142-4+ Je '87

Summertime getaway [gazebo-style porch] P. Rusten. il *Fam Handyman* 37:67-70+ Ap '87

Maintenance and repair

How to repair a porch. P. Barrett. il *Pop Mech* 164:193-7 My '87

Porcine growth hormone, Synthetic *See* Pituitary hormones, Synthetic

Porcupines

C. subspinosus, I presume? [thin-spined porcupine rediscovered in Brazil] il *Sci News* 131:88 F 7 '87

Photographs and photography

Stick 'em up! il *Natl Geogr World* 142:9 Je '87

Porgy and Bess [opera] See Gershwin, George, 1898-1937

Porizkova, Paulina

about

All about Paulina. M. Haskell. il por *Vogue* 177:82 O '87

New star style! il pors *Harpers Bazaar* 121:178-97 N '87

The perils of being Paulina. G. Sikes. il pors *Mademoiselle* 93:78 O '87

Sexy looks: celebrity secrets. il pors *Harpers Bazaar* 120:146-57 My '87

Pork

See also

Cooking—Meat

Ham

Advertising

See Meat industry—Advertising

Pork barrel legislation

Adapting to pork-barrel science. J. Walsh. il *Science* 238:1639-40 D 18 '87

Funding facilities: who's getting what [research universities and the pork barrel issue] I. Peterson. *Sci News* 131:246 Ap 18 '87

A halt to earmarking [vote of the Association of American Universities] *Sci News* 131:341 My 30 '87

Horse-trading on Capitol Hill [trade bill subjected to pork barrel politics] T. Noah. il *Newsweek* 110:71 O 12 '87

Pork barrel science: no end in sight. C. Norman. *Science* 236:16-17 Ap 3 '87

Pork barrel unbound? [funds for the Center for Molecular Medicine and Immunology in N.J.] J. Walsh. *Science* 237:352 Jl 24 '87

The pornographers [film] See Motion picture reviews—Single works

Pornography

See also

Obscenity (Law)

Parents' Music Resource Center

Telephone pornography

United States. Attorney General's Commission on Pornography

Attack on pornography misses the mark [National Federation for Decency calls on Holiday Inn to remove "pornographic movies" from its motels] J. M. Wall. *Christ Century* 104:811-12 S 30 '87

Bedroom eyes: erotic movies come home. E. Abeel. il *Mademoiselle* 93:194-5+ O '87

Child-abuse charges rock UNICEF. *Newsweek* 110:33 Jl 6 '87

A far-reaching drive against obscenity. *Christ Today* 31:44+ N 6 '87

Porn and the novelist: freedom to read [symposium] *Current* 290:27-31 F '87

Pornography: an agenda for the churches [cover story] M. Pellauer. il *Christ Century* 104:651-5 Jl 29-Ag 5 '87

Pornography and its discontents [special section] bibl *Society* 24:6-32 Jl/Ag '87

Pornography on the march. B. Wein. il *Read Dig* 131:153-8 N '87

The real sex ed battle. K. S. Kantzer. il *Christ Today* 31:16-17 Ap 17 '87

Romantic porn in the boudoir [influence of women filmmakers] J. Leo. il *Time* 129:63+ Mr 30 '87

Turned on? Turn it off: switching channels may be one cure for the contagion of porn. R. Corliss. il *Time* 130:72-3 Jl 6 '87

Whip me, beat me and while you're at it cancel my N.O.W. membership: feminists war against each other over pornography. A. Levine and K. Currie. *Wash Mon* 19:17-21 Je '87

Canada

New pornography wars. M. Clark. il *Macleans* 100:44 My 18 '87

Denmark

Deception and propaganda. B. Kutchinsky. *Society* 24:21-4 Jl/Ag '87

Porphyrins

Embedded sentinels of toxicity [cover story] J. Raloff. il *Sci News* 131:123-5 F 21 '87

Porpoises *See* Dolphins

Porrata, Magdalena

Heads, you lose—tails, I win. por *U S News World Rep* 102:11 Ap 27 '87

Porsche (Automobile) *See* Sports cars
Porsche AG
Body by Cessna, power by Porsche. R. L. Collins. il
Flying 114:38-44+ N '87
Flying Porsche [light aircraft engine] B. Kocivar. il *Pop
Sci* 230:39 My '87
Porsche develops torque-shaft system for light aircraft.
Aviat Week Space Technol 126:97 Je 29 '87
The racer's edge. J. A. Conway. *Forbes* 139:8 Mr 9
'87
Port Authority of New York and New Jersey
Newark Airport to expand passenger capacity. il *Aviat
Week Space Technol* 126:48 Mr 30 '87
Port Blair (India)
              Hotels, motels, etc.
Climate as context [Bay Island Hotel] M. F. Schmertz.
il *Archit Rec* 175:114-19 Ag '87
Port Medway (N.S.)
              Description
Coastal retreat. A. Trillin. il *Seventeen* 46:250+ Ag '87
Port wine *See* Wine
Portable astronomical observatories *See* Astronomical obser-
vatories
Portable computers *See* Computers
Portable computers and air travel *See* Computers and air
travel
Portable heaters *See* Heaters
Portable radio-cassette players *See* Radio receivers—Tape
recorder combination
Portable radio receivers *See* Radio receivers
Portals *See* Doorways
Portantina Ltd.
Past perfect: Bernard and Barbara Bergreen on Fifth
Avenue. J. Allen. il por *Archit Dig* 44:190-9 N '87
Portaro, Sam A.
On the stewardship of property. *Christ Century* 104:846-7
O 7 '87
Porter, Andrew, 1928-
Musical events. See issues of The New Yorker
Porter, Andrew C.
Teacher collaboration: new partnerships to attack old
problems. bibl f il *Phi Delta Kappan* 69:147-52 O
'87
Porter, Anne
La bella notizia [poem] *Commonweal* 114:732 D
18 '87
Native Americans [poem] *Commonweal* 114:386 Je
19 '87
Porter, Caryl
Philosophy I [poem] *Christ Century* 104:644 Jl 29-Ag
5 '87
Porter, Cole, 1891-1964
              about
Anything goes [musical] Reviews
N Y 20:111 N 2 '87. J. Simon
Nation 245:570-2 N 14 '87. T. M. Disch
New Leader 70:22 N 16 '87. L. Sauvage
New Yorker 63:146 N 2 '87. E. Oliver
Time il 130:95 N 2 '87. W. A. Henry
Porter, Eleanor H., 1868-1920
              about
Pollyanna, ex-bubblehead. J. Griswold. *N Y Times Book
Rev* 92:51 O 25 '87
Porter, Eliot, 1901-
              about
Through the eye of the beholder. M. Harwood. il *Nat
Hist* 96:24-9 D '87
Porter, Hal
Home finances. See issues of The Family Handyman
beginning September 1986
Porter, Katherine, 1941-
              about
Guerrilla tactics. K. Larson. il *N Y* 20:54 F 2 '87
Katherine Porter at Sidney Janis. R. G. Edelman. il
Art Am 75:135 Mr '87
Porter, Kay, and Foster, Judy
Who will stop the pain. il *World Tennis* 35:28-30 Jl
'87
Porter, Kevin
              about
Kevin Porter's house calls. O. Jaffe. il por *N Y* 20:20
Jl 20 '87
Porter, Michael E., 1947-
              about
The case of Michael Porter, superstar. por *Fortune* 116:44
N 9 '87
Porter, Mike
Needed: more steering of the feet and legs; ed. by Doug
Smith. il por *Skiing* 40:48 O '87

Porter, Pamela Rice
Ruth's love letters, 1918-1919 [poem] *Commonweal*
114:529 S 25 '87
Porter, Pat, 1960?-
              about
Rolling a six the hard way. C. Neff. il por *Sports Illus*
67:42-3 D 7 '87
Porter, Patricia
(jt. auth) See Leatherman, Glenda, and Porter, Patricia
Porter, Rosalie Pedalino
Should Congress enact the Quayle amendments to the
Bilingual Education Act? [excerpts from statement,
June 5, 1986] *Congr Dig* 66:86+ Mr '87
Porter, Tom, and Dombek, George
Architectural education: drawing the line—graphics should
clearly communicate design. pors *Archit Rec* 175:45
My '87
Porterfield, Andrew, and Weir, David, 1947-
The export of U.S. toxic wastes [cover story] il *Nation*
245:325+ O 3 '87
Porter's Camera Store, Inc.
Porter's: the photo fabric store. K. Geller-Shinn. il
Petersens Photogr Mag 16:10 N '87
Portfolio insurance (Securities)
Bear-market protection? [funds offering portfolio
insurance] J. B. Quinn. il *Newsweek* 109:43 My 25
'87
Money managers after the crash. J. P. Newport, Jr.
il *Fortune* 116:71-2 D 7 '87
Risk business [mutual funds using portfolio insurance]
Money 16:31+ Je '87
Thanks, professor. D. N. Dreman. il *Forbes* 140:314-15
N 16 '87
What happened and what's next [post crash reforms]
A. L. Taylor, III. il *Fortune* 116:76-9+ N 23 '87
Portfolio managers *See* Investment advisers
Portfolios, Investment *See* Investments
Porticoes
Portico helps define entry. il *South Living* 22:155 S
'87
Portland (Or.)
              Architecture
See also
Portland (Or.)—Buildings
              Bookstores
See Booksellers and bookselling—Oregon
              Buildings
All in the family [RiverPlace Athletic Club] D. Dietsch.
il *Archit Rec* 175:100-5 Ag '87
Minds over matter [Vollum Institute for Advanced
Biomedical Research] D. Brenner. il *Archit Rec*
175:102-11 S '87
              Criminal justice, Administration of
Scarlet lettering [child molester required to post warning
signs] *Time* 130:60 S 7 '87
              Galleries and museums
See also
Contemporary Crafts Association (Portland, Or.)
              Gardens and gardening
Gardening for self-respect [D. Barker's Home Gardening
Project] P. H. Johnson. il por *Rodale's Org Gard*
34:59-62 Jl '87
Portland General Electric Co.
Systems matchmaking [Information Center for Client
Computing] R. Dalton. il *Pers Comput* 11:75-6+ N
'87
Portman, John Calvin
              about
Architecture: John C. Portman, Jr. [cover story] P.
Goldberger. il por *Archit Dig* 44:98-111 D '87
Portman's complaint. S. Oney. il por *Esquire* 107:182-9
Je '87
Portnoy, Mindy Avra
Ima on the bima [story] il *Ms* 15:57-8 Je '87
Portrait drawing
Anita Wolff's portraits and landscapes in pastel. M.
S. Schulzke. il por *Am Artist* 51:60-3+ S '87
Drawn to the past [M. Leonard's pencil portraits of
contemporary people in the style of famous artists]
L. Kirstein. il por *House Gard* 159:168-71+ N '87
Elizabeth Layton: portrait of the artist as an old woman.
A. Fadiman. il pors *Life* 10:21-2 Mr '87
Portrait painting
Allan R. Banks [cover story] M. E. Stegmaier. il por
Am Artist 51:42-7+ Ag '87
Daniel Dallmann. T. Bolt. il *Am Artist* 51:56-61 Mr
'87
Kay Polk: combining pastels and watercolors to paint
portraits. B. D. Stroud. il *Am Artist* 51:60-3 O '87
Painting skin the color of life. F. Alexander. il *Am
Artist* 51:66-70 Mr '87

Portrait painting—*cont.*
A reasonable definition of love [work of L. Freud] W. Feaver. il *Archit Dig* 44:34+ Jl '87
You oughta be in paintings. L. S. Brady. il *Esquire* 108:54 O '87

Portrait prints
Exhibitions
Lost cause art [prints the North published for the South; Confederate image exhibit] M. E. Neely, Jr. and others. il *Americana* 15:59-62 Jl/Ag '87

Portraits
See also
Photography—Portraits
Anecdotes, facetiae, satire, etc.
The self once seen: reflective images in time. J. Stevenson. il *New Yorker* 63:26-7 Ag 31 '87

Portraits, American
Ammi Phillips portraits rediscovered. M. C. Black. bibl f il *Antiques* 132:558-9 S '87
Rufus Hathaway, artist and physician. L. Valentine and N. F. Little. bibl f il *Antiques* 131:628-41 Mr '87
Exhibitions
American portraits [National Portrait Gallery exhibition entitled Portraits from the American Academy and Institute of Arts and Letters] S. B. Sherrill. il *Antiques* 131:1186 Je '87
China's odd couple [exhibit cancelled after Chinese refuse to include portraits of Douglas MacArthur and Golda Meir] il *U S News World Rep* 103:10 Jl 27 '87
Joshua Johnson. C. J. Weekley. bibl f il *Antiques* 132:524-37 S '87
Politically incorrect [Beijing exhibit of portraits canceled after Chinese insisted that paintings of Golda Meir and General Douglas MacArthur be removed] D. Lanchner. il *Art News* 86:71 O '87
Portraits in colonial America [exhibition at National Portrait Gallery] S. B. Sherrill. il *Antiques* 132:626+ O '87

Portraits, English
A morbid curiosity [deathbed portrait of man wrongly assumed to be the Duke of Monmouth] J. Prendergast. il *Hist Today* 37:62 My '87
Portraits in reflection [dance] *See* Dance reviews—Single works

Ports
See also
Boston (Mass.)—Harbor
Hamilton (Ont.)—Harbor
New York (N.Y.)—Harbor
Saint-Pierre (Martinique)—Harbor
East Coast redux. E. A. Finn, Jr. il *Forbes* 139:162 My 18 '87

Portsmouth (Va.)
Politics and government
Portsmouth, Va., mayor is cited in hate mail scandal [J. G. Holley] *Jet* 72:4 Ag 3 '87
Race relations
Portsmouth, Va., mayor is cited in hate mail scandal [J. G. Holley] *Jet* 72:4 Ag 3 '87

Portugal
See also
Automobile racing—Portugal
Country estates—Portugal
Education—Portugal
Historic houses, sites, etc.—Portugal
Hotels, motels, etc.—Portugal
Immigration and emigration—Portugal
Lisbon (Portugal)
Political prisoners—Portugal
Portuguese
Terrorism—Portugal
Women—Portugal
Colonies
See also
Macao
Cultural relations
Brazil
See Brazil—Cultural relations—Portugal
Description and travel
Portugal if you can. D. Machan. il *Forbes* 140:104-5 Ag 10 '87
Economic policy
Portugal turns right. il por *Fortune* 116:8 Ag 31 '87
A small victory [A. Cavaco Silva's election] E. von Kuehnelt-Leddihn. *Natl Rev* 39:46 N 6 '87

Foreign relations
China
See China—Foreign relations—Portugal
History
Revolution, 1974
Letter from Europe [O. Carvalho, leader of 1974 revolution, convicted of terrorism] J. Kramer. *New Yorker* 63:105-20 N 30 '87
Politics and government
See also
Elections—Portugal

Portuguese
France
Letter from Europe [lives of singer L. Mariano and a Portuguese fan] J. Kramer. il *New Yorker* 63:66-70+ Ag 24 '87

Portuguese architecture *See* Architecture, Portuguese
Portuguese Grand Prix *See* Automobile racing—Portugal
Portuguese house decoration *See* House decoration, Portuguese

Posen, Barry R.
U.S. maritime strategy: a dangerous game. bibl f map *Bull At Sci* 43:24-8 S '87

Poses, Jonathan W.
Our blues. il *High Fidel* 37:84-5 D '87

Positions, Applications for *See* Job applications
Positions, Sleep *See* Sleep positions

Positive Communications Inc.
Peale launches audio publisher for positive-thinking authors. T. Spain. il *Publ Wkly* 232:39-40 N 20 '87

Positive ions *See* Ions
Positive thinking *See* Optimism
Positively 104th Street Cafe (New York, N.Y.) *See* New York (N.Y.)—Restaurants, nightclubs, bars, etc.
Positron emission tomography *See* Tomography

Positronium
Experiment challenges theory in positronium measurements [research by Chris Westbrook and others] B. G. Levi. bibl f il *Phys Today* 40:22-4 S '87

Posner, Richard A., 1939-
What am I? A potted plant? *New Repub* 197:23-5 S 28 '87

Posner, Victor
about
Every man for himself. A. Sloan. il por *Forbes* 139:37-8 Je 29 '87
A shark gets bitten. J. A. Conway. il *Forbes* 139:8 My 18 '87
Three sparkling turnarounds: can this really be Victor Posner? P. Engardio. il por *Bus Week* p56-7 Jl 27 '87
Victor Posner is on the ropes—and slipping. G. DeGeorge and P. Engardio. il por *Bus Week* p36 N 23 '87
Victor reverts to type. J. A. Conway. por *Forbes* 139:8 Mr 9 '87
Victor, victorious. G. Morgenson. il por *Forbes* 140:108 Ag 24 '87
Why Posner backed out of a bailout for Sharon Steel. P. Engardio. il por *Bus Week* p40 My 4 '87

Possessions *See* Property
Possessiveness (Psychology)
The girl who showed too much [attractive woman shopping with possessive boyfriend] L. Darling. *Mademoiselle* 93:102 Je '87

Possums *See* Opossums
Post, Elizabeth L.
Etiquette for every day. See issues of Good Housekeeping
Post, Robert
about
Cash-machine magician. *Time* 129:61 Je 1 '87
Post (New York, N.Y.) *See* New York post
Post cards *See* Postcards
Post Group
F/X on $5 a day. A. Meisler. il *Channels* 7:10 F '87
Post-impressionism (Art)
See also
Ecole de Rouen
Post Office (Chicago, Ill.) *See* Chicago (Ill.). Post Office
Post Office (New York, N.Y.) *See* New York (N.Y.). Post Office

Post office buildings
The postman cometh with a lot of new construction. P. Hoffmann. il *Archit Rec* 175:35 S '87
Postage stamp dealers
See also
International Stamp Exchange Corporation
International aspects
Around the world with stamps. H. Herst, Jr. il *Antiques Collect Hobbies* 91:83-4 F '87

Postage stamps
See also
Covers (Philately)
Americana in miniature [quiz] V. Nash. il *Americana* 15:21 N/D '87
The Christmas Island Phosphate Company. A. L. Rice. bibl il por map *Sea Front* 33:444-53 N/D '87
Postage-size propaganda [Iranian stamps] il *N Y Times Mag* p38-41 F 15 '87
Truth and reason upside down [CIA employees accused of selling rare postage stamps that were government property] J. V. Lamar, Jr. il *Time* 130:32 S 14 '87
Wildlife on stamps. P. Schullery. il *Ctry J* 14:11-12 N '87

Collectors and collecting
Philately. H. Herst, Jr. See issues of Antiques & Collecting Hobbies beginning March 1985
Philately. H. Herst, Jr. See issues of Hobbies through February 1985
A wide world of sports, in stamps. B. Loeffelbein. il *Sport Mag* 78:99 Ag '87

Rates
See Postal rates

Postage stamps as an investment
Beware the stamp man [M. Rousso of International Stamp Exchange] J. Clements. il por *Forbes* 139:232+ My 18 '87
No higher yields exist [Salomon Brothers' survey on coins and stamps] *Changing Times* 41:126 N '87
Stamp investing. J. W. Merline. il *Consum Res Mag* 70:38 N '87

Postal covers *See* Covers (Philately)

Postal employees
See also
Black postal employees
Collective bargaining—Postal service
Strikes—Postal employees
Women postal employees
Everybody in this picture is named Miller or Yoder except for one poor guy [postmaster T. Hagedorn's problem with family names in town of Kalona, Iowa] D. Van Biema. il por *People Wkly* 27:46-8 Mr 30 '87

Health and hygiene
Walking up your HDL [study of mailmen by Timothy Cook] il *Prevention* 39:6 My '87

Postal Inspection Service (U.S.) *See* United States Postal Service. Postal Inspection Service

Postal rates
House unit would stop subsidizing postal 'library rate'. H. Fields. *Publ Wkly* 231:32 Je 19 '87
'Library rate' appears safe, with possible increase next year. H. Fields. *Publ Wkly* 232:13 D 11 '87
The twenty-five cent stamp: why it's here and why it shouldn't be. M. Szegedy-Maszak. il *Wash Mon* 19:39-42 N '87
USPS seeks 16% rate increase. H. Fields. *Publ Wkly* 231:14 Je 5 '87

Postal service
See also
Air freight service
Collective labor agreements—Postal service
Parcel post
Pigeon postal service
United States Postal Service
By land? By air? By sea? W. A. Kleinschrod. il *Work Woman* 12:82+ N '87

Employees
See Postal employees

History
Around the world with stamps. H. Herst, Jr. il *Antiques Collect Hobbies* 92:73-4 Ap '87

International aspects
See also
Universal Postal Union
Moving the mail in other countries. M. Gee. il *Macleans* 100:17-18 O 12 '87

Amazon River Valley
The swimming postman [letters delivered in Amazon region by Indian swimmers in 1802] A. Humboldt, Freiherr von. il *Courier* 40:14 Ap '87

Canada
See also
Canada Post Corporation
Threats to smalltown post offices. C. Barrett. il *Macleans* 100:18 O 12 '87

Postal Service (U.S.) *See* United States Postal Service
Postal workers *See* Postal employees

Postcards
Postal photography [mailable photo greetings] L. Nielsen. il *Petersens Photogr Mag* 15:70-1 Ap '87

Collectors and collecting
The picture postcard. S. S. Carver. See issues of Hobbies through February 1985
Picture postcards. S. S. Carver. See issues of Antiques & Collecting Hobbies beginning March 1985

History
The greatest moments in a girl's life [postcards by H. Fisher] C. E. Rinzler. il *Am Herit* 38:34-5 F/Mr '87

Postel, Sandra
Life, the great chemistry experiment. il *Nat Hist* 96:41-8 Ap '87
(jt. auth) See Brown, Lester Russell, 1934-, and Postel, Sandra

Posterization *See* Photography—Processing

Posters
See also
Playbills
Around the Mall and beyond [selling posters of Smithsonian illustrations] E. Park. il *Smithsonian* 18:30+ N '87
Art rock [excerpt from The art of rock] P. Grushkin. il *Roll Stone* p71-5 S 24 '87
Artists sue over posters: San Francisco battle focuses on rights to psychedelic artwork from the sixties. M. Goldberg. *Roll Stone* p29 Ap 23 '87
Expanding your market with multiples [posters, prints, and reproductions based on paintings] M. S. Doherty. il *Am Artist* 51:52-9 My '87
The first sign of a Wimsey [work of P. Davis] B. Weber. il por *N Y Times Mag* p62 Ag 30 '87
Handsome, helpful posters to send for. L. J. Brown. il *Good Housekeep* 204:205 F '87
Poster artist Robbie Conal paints satiric dislikenesses of the great, the wrinkled and the powerful. il por *People Wkly* 28:138 N 23 '87
Poster girls [ads celebrating benefits of women's participation in sports] *Women's Sports Fitness* 9:62 Ag '87
Shooting a self-promotional poster. S. Farhad. il *Petersens Photogr Mag* 16:38-9 N '87
Some vintage advertising [use of Bartles and Jaymes takeoffs to promote Iowa State football program] il *Sports Illus* 67:18 O 12 '87

Collectors and collecting
Collectors' finds in Paris: discoveries in painting, wallpaper and posters [papier peint wallpapers and art deco advertising posters] J. A. Cuadrado. il *Archit Dig* 44:210+ D '87

Competitions
MADD's winning posters. il *Seventeen* 46:216 Ag '87

Exhibitions
Take the SVA train [School of Visual Arts posters exhibited at the Cooper-Hewitt Museum] J. W. Graham. il *Horizon* 30:73 Jl/Ag '87

Posting of land *See* Trespass

Postman, Andrew
Celebrity autobiographies on audio. il *Publ Wkly* 231:56-7 My 29 '87
Commercial fiction on tape. il *Publ Wkly* 232:27-30+ S 4 '87
Horror fiction on audio. bibl il *Publ Wkly* 232:33-6+ Jl 3 '87
In their own voices. il *Publ Wkly* 232:33-7+ N 6 '87

The postman always rings twice [opera] See Paulus, Stephen

Postmodern architecture *See* Architecture, Modern

Postmodernism
Napping through the revolution [postmodern orthodoxy] D. F. Kinlaw. il *Christ Today* 31:9 Ag 7 '87

Postmodernism (Literature)
The muse, postmodern and homeless. C. Ozick. il *N Y Times Book Rev* 92:9 Ja 18 '87

Anecdotes, facetiae, satire, etc.
That post-modernism! E. Metaxas. il *Atlantic* 259:36-7 Ja '87

Postnatal exercises *See* Pregnancy exercises

Postpartum depression
Blue moods. L. Claverie. il *Health* 19:47-51 S '87
New-baby blues [role of stress in maternal postpartum depression; research by Carolyn E. Cutrona and Beth R. Troutman] S. Vandershaf. il *Psychol Today* 21:18 Ap '87
Ready for the blues [diagnostic quiz developed by Norman Ames Posner] M. Mintzer. il *Health* 19:14 Ap '87

Postpartum exercises *See* Pregnancy exercises
Postpartum hemorrhage *See* Hemorrhage

PostScript (Computer language)
IBM adopts PostScript. *Pers Comput* 11:27-8 My '87
PostScript possibilities. P. Saffo. il *Pers Comput* 11:57-8+ S '87
Programming in PostScript. D. G. Pelli. bibl il *Byte* 12:185-8+ My '87

Postsecondary education *See* Adult education

Posture

    See also

    Sleep positions

How to survive sitting. J. Mandelbaum-Schmid. il *Vogue* 177:446-8+ Mr '87

The posture of pelvic pain. *Prevention* 39:10+ D '87

Posture: the lowdown on straightening up. L. Rosch. il *Glamour* 85:306 Ag '87

Posture: the straight story. il *Teen* 31:94+ S '87

Stand up for yourself. J. Pierson. il *Read Dig* 130:103-5 F '87

Pot, Pol *See* Pol Pot

Pot *See* Marijuana

Pot roasting *See* Cooking—Meat

Potash Corporation of Saskatchewan

Canadian-United States trade [address, September 14, 1987] G. Devine. *Vital Speeches Day* 54:76-9 N 15 '87

Devine's control zone [Saskatchewan enacts potash protectionist measures to counteract U.S. duties] D. Eisler. il *Macleans* 100:14-15 S 14 '87

Fertilizer trade wars [Saskatchewan potash in the U.S.] T. Tedesco. il *Macleans* 100:35 Mr 9 '87

Firing up a new potash war [U.S. duty on Saskatchewan potash] D. Eisler. il *Macleans* 100:32-3 S 7 '87

Potash industry

    Export-import trade

Canadian-United States trade [address, September 14, 1987] G. Devine. *Vital Speeches Day* 54:76-9 N 15 '87

Devine's control zone [Saskatchewan enacts potash protectionist measures to counteract U.S. duties] D. Eisler. il *Macleans* 100:14-15 S 14 '87

Fertilizer trade wars [Saskatchewan potash in the U.S.] T. Tedesco. il *Macleans* 100:35 Mr 9 '87

Firing up a new potash war [U.S. duty on Saskatchewan potash] D. Eisler. il *Macleans* 100:32-3 S 7 '87

    Canada

    See also

    Potash Corporation of Saskatchewan

Potassium-argon dating *See* Radioactive dating

Potassium in the body

The α subunit of the GTP binding protein G_k opens atrial potassium channels. J. Codina and others. bibl f il *Science* 236:442-5 Ap 24 '87

Block a stroke with better nutrition. M. Mihalik. il *Prevention* 39:24-8 Ag '87

Cyclic AMP-modulated potassium channels in murine B cells and their precursors. D. Choquet and others. bibl f il *Science* 235:1211-14 Mr 6 '87

Does the release of potassium from astrocyte endfeet regulate cerebral blood flow? O. B. Paulson and E. A. Newman. bibl f il *Science* 237:896-8 Ag 21 '87

Forskolin and phorbol esters reduce the same potassium conductance of mouse neurons in culture. D. S. Grega and others. bibl f il *Science* 235:345-8 Ja 16 '87

Potassium power. G. A. Levey. il *Health* 19:13 Je '87

The protective potato. W. Gottlieb. il *Rodale's Org Gard* 34:16+ O '87

Xenopus oocytes injected with rat uterine RNA express very slowly activating potassium currents. M. B. Boyle and others. bibl f il *Science* 235:1221-4 Mr 6 '87

Potassium transport *See* Biological transport

Potato beans *See* Groundnuts

Potato bread *See* Bread

Potato chips

One potato, two potato . . . M. Sheraton. il *Time* 129:77 Mr 30 '87

Ron Zappe's Cajun potato chips are really hot in Louisiana, and he'd like to run them bayou too. il por *People Wkly* 27:81 Ja 19 '87

That greasy kid stuff. R. Sokolov. *Nat Hist* 96:78-81 Ap '87

When the chips are down, make chips! [Hoot N Annie Potato Chips] W. Mueller. il *Success Farm* 85:18G My '87

Potato pancakes *See* Pancakes, waffles, etc.

Potato salads *See* Salads

Potatoes

    See also

    Cooking—Potatoes

About potatoes. il *Mother Earth News* 103:30-2+ Ja/F '87

Peas and potatoes. P. H. Dunphy. il *Ctry J* 14:53-9 Ap '87

The protective potato. W. Gottlieb. il *Rodale's Org Gard* 34:16+ O '87

Reflections on the potato. N. M. Joaquin. il *Courier* 40:14-15 My '87

    Contamination

Potato eaters [glycoalkaloid dangers] E. Collins. *Sci Am* 257:31 S '87

Warning: peel potatoes before cooking [glycoalkaloid dangers] *Sci News* 132:8 Jl 4 '87

    Disease and pest resistance

Helping spuds defend themselves. *Sci News* 132:8 Jl 4 '87

Potato eaters. E. Collins. *Sci Am* 257:31 S '87

Potatoes, Frozen

'Lite' fries aren't quite as light as you might like [Ore-Ida Lites] il *Consum Rep* 52:655 N '87

Potentiometers

An electronic potentiometer. R. F. Scott. il *Radio-Electron* 58:42-3 D '87

Potholes (Pavements)

A civil engineer declares holey war on the city's mean streets [CU-31 pothole lining devised by J. Ahmad] il por *People Wkly* 27:63 Ja 12 '87

Potok, Chaim, 1929-

Neighbors. *Seventeen* 46:128 D '87

Potomac (Washington, D.C.: Restaurant) *See* Washington (D.C.)—Restaurants, nightclubs, bars, etc.

Potomac River

    See also

    Patowmack Canal (Va.)

Pots and pans *See* Kitchen utensils and appliances

Potter, Beatrix, 1866-1943

    about

Beatrix Potter country. E. Minton. il *Travel Holiday* 168:28-30 D '87

Brightening up Beatrix. K. O. Fakih. il pors *Publ Wkly* 232:25-6 S 25 '87

So, what did happen to Peter Rabbit's dad? il *Newsweek* 110:36 S 28 '87

Updated Beatrix Potter brews a storm in Britain. J. Taylor. il *Publ Wkly* 232:26 O 30 '87

Potter, John, and Potter, Suzanne

An artist's salvation. il *Opera News* 51:30-3+ Ja 17 '87

Potter, Michael, and others

Avian v-*myc* replaces chromosomal translocation in murine plasmacytomagenesis. bibl f il *Science* 235:787-9 F 13 '87

Potter, Suzanne

(jt. auth) *See* Potter, John, and Potter, Suzanne

Potteries

    See also

    MacKenzie-Childs Ltd.

    History

    See also

    Weller Pottery Company

    Great Britain

    See also

    Wedgwood plc

Potters

    See also

    Bacerra, Ralph, 1938-

    Brown, Charles Moses, 1904-1987

    Ohr, George E., 1857-1918

    Saxe, Adrian

    Zeisel, Eva, 1906-

Pottery

    See also

    Ceramic sculpture

    Figurines

    Lusterware

    Majolica

    Parian ware

    Pitchers (Pottery, glass, etc.)

    Terracotta

Baby's first china. J. Williams and J. Severson. il *Better Homes Gard* 65:80-1 F '87

Pretty poison: lead and ceramic ware. C. Lecos. il *FDA Consum* 21:6-9 Jl/Ag '87

Putting the lid on dangerous dinnerware [lead-glazed pottery] E. E. Goode. il *U S News World Rep* 103:56 Ag 10 '87

Still some serious questions about lead in pottery. il *Sunset* 179:168 Jl '87

    Collectors and collecting

Classics in china. S. Bagdade and A. Bagdade. *See* issues of *Antiques & Collecting Hobbies* beginning March 1985

Classics in china. S. Bagdade and A. Bagdade. *See* issues of *Hobbies* beginning May 1984 through February 1985

    Decoration

The architecture of Charles Bulfinch on historical blue Staffordshire (II). H. Goldberg. bibl f il *Antiques* 131:434-43 F '87

Pottery—Decoration—_cont._

Collecting pot lids: Staffordshire Pratt ware painted by Jesse Austin. M. Ginaven. il *Antiques Collect Hobbies* 92:22-4 D '87

Deliberately decorative: the ceramics of Ralph Bacerra. M. McCloud. il por *Am Craft* 47:50-5 Je/Jl '87

Study and teaching

See also

National Council on Education for the Ceramic Arts (U.S.)

Themes

A Don Quixote discovery [ninth plate in Don Quixote series of transfer-printed earthenware attributed to Staffordshire potters James and Ralph Clews] E. H. Gustafson. il *Antiques* 132:740+ O '87

Pottery, American

The mad potter of Biloxi [G. E. Ohr] K. Kertess. il por *House Gard* 159:104+ Je '87

Collectors and collecting

Collecting redware: America's folk art pottery. K. McConnell. bibl il *Antiques Collect Hobbies* 92:24-7 Mr '87

Exhibitions

American ceramics now: the 27th Ceramic National. E. Lebow. il *Am Craft* 47:26-33+ Ag/S '87

In defense of Ceramic National [discussion of August/September 1987 article, American ceramics now: the 27th Ceramic National] E. Lebow. *Am Craft* 47:24 O/N '87

Stylistic ensembles [work of A. Saxe exhibited at the University of Missouri-Kansas City Gallery of Art; cover story] J. B. Mays. il por *Am Craft* 47:42-9 O/N '87

Pottery, Chinese

See also

China trade porcelain

Ixing. A. Derham. il *House Gard* 159:36-41+ F '87

Pottery, Dutch

Ceramic teapots, pitchers recalled. il *FDA Consum* 21:6 S '87

Pottery, English

See also

Parian ware

The architecture of Charles Bulfinch on historical blue Staffordshire (II). H. Goldberg. bibl f il *Antiques* 131:434-43 F '87

British election ceramics. J. Priestley. bibl f il *Antiques* 131:1304-13 Je '87

Collectors and collecting

The Adam and Eve blue dash charger. S. Bagdade and A. Bagdade. il *Antiques Collect Hobbies* 91:75 Ja '87

Chelsea porcelain: 1745-69. S. Jones. il *Antiques Collect Hobbies* 92:18-22 Je '87

Collecting pot lids: Staffordshire Pratt ware painted by Jesse Austin. M. Ginaven. il *Antiques Collect Hobbies* 92:22-4 D '87

A Don Quixote discovery [ninth plate in Don Quixote series of transfer-printed earthenware attributed to Staffordshire potters James and Ralph Clews] E. H. Gustafson. il *Antiques* 132:740+ O '87

The Hans Sloane plate [botanicals] S. Bagdade and A. Bagdade. il *Antiques Collect Hobbies* 92:76 My '87

The Staffordshire tithe pig group [figural grouping] S. Bagdade and A. Bagdade. il *Antiques Collect Hobbies* 92:27 Ap '87

A Wood Family Toby jug. S. Bagdade and A. Bagdade. il *Antiques Collect Hobbies* 92:37 Je '87

Pottery, European

Collectors and collecting

A deco discovery [collection of H. P. Rothberg] A. Duncan. il *House Gard* 159:156-9+ My '87

Pottery, French

Collectors and collecting

Paris cache pot decorated to fool the eye. S. Bagdade and A. Bagdade. il *Antiques Collect Hobbies* 92:39 Jl '87

Pottery, German

Collectors and collecting

Art nouveau Meissen emerges from long neglect. S. Jones. il *Antiques Collect Hobbies* 91:11-14 F '87

Pottery, Irish

See also

Belleek ware

Pottery, Italian

See also

Majolica

Pottery, Korean

Exhibitions

Brooklyn Museum [seventeenth-century iron-painted Korean dragon jar] il *Antiques Collect Hobbies* 92:58-9 My '87

Pottery, Oriental

A touch of the Orient [porcelain bowls] il *South Living* 22:94-5 N '87

Exhibitions

Mounted oriental porcelain [cover story] F. J. B. Watson. il *Antiques* 131:812-23 Ap '87

The Oriental porcelains at Burghley House, Lincolnshire, England [Cecil family collection] G. Lang. il *Antiques* 131:236-47 Ja '87

Potts, Annie

about

Those remarkable Designing women. H. Yorkshire. il pors *McCalls* 115:78-9+ N '87

Potts, Eve

(jt. auth) See Morra, Marion, and Potts, Eve

Potts, Keith

about

Official position. E. Weiner. *Flying* 114:38 D '87

Potts, Yank

Should you pull the plug on utility stocks? il *50 Plus* 27:76-9+ S '87

Pottsville (Pa.)

Education

Getting the scoop on careers in photojournalism [fourth grade project at John S. Clarke Elementary Center] G. Schaub. il *Pop Photogr* 94:26 Je '87

Pouchepadass, Emmanuel

Twenty years of cultural co-operation. il *Courier* 40:9 Ja '87

Pouches, Food See Food pouches

Poulenc, Francis, 1899-1963

about

Dialogues of the Carmelites [opera] Reviews

N Y il 20:82 Ap 6 '87. P. G. Davis

Opera News il 51:26-9 Mr 28 '87. S. Flatow

Opera News il por 51:30-1+ Mr 28 '87. F. Merkling

Opera News il 51:12-13 My '87

Poulin, Jeanne

Publishing in French Canada. il *Publ Wkly* 232:36+ Jl 31 '87

Quebec's French connection. il *Publ Wkly* 232:24 N 13 '87

Poulin, John E.

Personal competence and government control. *Society* 24:45-8 Mr/Ap '87

Poulos, Constantine, d. 1986

about

Secret history. A. Cockburn. *Nation* 244:70-1 Ja 24 '87

Poultry

See also

Bursa Fabricii

Cooking—Poultry

Ducks

Eggs

Feathered friends [raising bantams] D. Barker. il por *Mother Earth News* 103:29 Ja/F '87

Poultry contamination

Another flap over contaminated chicken. il *Newsweek* 109:24 My 25 '87

Avoiding sick chicks [Chik Chek test for salmonella bacteria] M. Kemp. il *Discover* 8:20 O '87

Foul chickens. B. Costikyan. il *N Y* 20:44-8 Ag 10 '87

NAS reports on pathogens in poultry . . . and pesticides in food. *Sci News* 131:361 Je 6 '87

Poultry industry

See also

Gold Kist Inc.

Holly Farms Poultry Industries

Perdue Farms Inc.

Advertising

C.E.O., TV [F. Perdue's television commercials] T. Whiteside. *New Yorker* 63:39-40+ Jl 6 '87

Management

Two decades of productivity growth in poultry dressing and processing. Z. Z. Ahmed and M. S. Sieling. bibl f il *Mon Labor Rev* 110:34-9 Ap '87

Marketing

Poultry gobbles more meat market [turkeys] *Success Farm* 85 no5:26 Mr '87

They're fencing beak to beak [ready-to-eat chicken products by Perdue and Holly Farms] M. Sheraton. il *Time* 130:76 S 28 '87

Will the turkey fly this time? R. Simon. il *Forbes* 139:210+ My 18 '87

Poultry industry workers

Two decades of productivity growth in poultry dressing and processing. Z. Z. Ahmed and M. S. Sieling. bibl f il *Mon Labor Rev* 110:34-9 Ap '87

Pound cake *See* Cake
Pountain, Dick
  Byte U.K. See issues of Byte through April 1987
  Focus on algorithms. See issues of Byte beginning June 1987
Pournelle, Jerry, 1933-
  Computing at Chaos Manor. See issues of Byte beginning June 1984
Pousette-Dart, Richard, 1916-
        about
  Pousette-Dart's windows into the unknowing. J. Higgins. il por *Art News* 86:108-16 Ja '87
Poussaint, Alvin F.
  The price of success. il por *Ebony* 42:76+ Ag '87
Poussin, Nicolas, 1594?-1665
        about
  Warrant for Lee's arrest dropped. R. W. Walker. *Art News* 86:30 Summ '87
Poverty *See* Poor
Povod, Reinaldo
        about
  La puta vida trilogy [drama] Reviews
    New Yorker 63:165 D 7 '87. E. Oliver
Powaski, Ronald E.
  Is nuclear deterrence immoral? *America* 156:401-5 My 16 '87
  A neglected lesson of the Chernobyl disaster. *America* 156:167-8 F 28 '87
  The proposed Euromissile agreement: an important step toward nuclear sanity. *America* 157:183-4+ O 3 '87
  The quest for a comprehensive test ban treaty. il *America* 157:61-5 Ag 1-8 '87
Powder (Face, toilet, etc.)
  The power of powder. il *Mademoiselle* 93:28 F '87
Powe, Marc
        about
  An American spy in Kuwait. S. Emerson. *U S News World Rep* 102:18-19 Ap 13 '87
Powel, Nick
  Courts of appeal. See issues of World Tennis
Powell, Adam Clayton, III
        about
  Adam Clayton Powell III is National Public Radio V.P. il por *Jet* 73:22 O 26 '87
Powell, Bess
  (tr) See Aksenov, Vasiliĭ Pavlovich, 1932-. Beatniks and Bolsheviks
Powell, Bill
  Your next boss may be Japanese. il *Read Dig* 130:141-4 Je '87
Powell, Clark
  The gift of Magnolia Cemetery. il *South Living* 22:155 Ap '87
Powell, Clifton
  Say, brother. por *Essence* 18:10 Ag '87
Powell, Colin L.
        about
  Army Gen. Colin Powell is picked for NSC's no. 2 spot. il por *Jet* 71:24 Ja 12 '87
  Gen. Colin Powell cites black military legacy at D.C. Veterans Day affair. il por *Jet* 73:18 N 30 '87
  Gen. Colin Powell steps in as National Security chief. il por *Jet* 73:10 N 23 '87
  The general takes command. J. V. Lamar, Jr. il por *Time* 130:22 N 16 '87
  'The ultimate no. 2' for NSC. T. M. DeFrank. il por *Newsweek* 110:63 N 16 '87
Powell, David H.
  Three views from the trenches: teaching high school religion in the city. *America* 15˜:212-16 O 10 '87
Powell, Dawn
        about
  Dawn Powell, the American writer. G. Vidal. il *N Y Rev Books* 34:52-60 N 5 '87
Powell, Geoffrey
  John Buchan's Richard Hannay. bibl il pors map *Hist Today* 37:32-9 Ag '87
Powell, Gregory
        about
  The 'Onion Field' parole: Rose Bird's parting shot. por *Newsweek* 109:26 Ja 12 '87
Powell, Gregory
  Say, brother. por *Essence* 17:10 Mr '87
Powell, Jim
  . . . culturally sophisticated. il *Travel Holiday* 167:48-53 Ap '87
  New adventure & romance in East Asia [special section] il map *Travel Holiday* 167:61-2+ F '87
Powell, Jody
  Pushiness we can respect. *Wash Mon* 19:55-6 F '87

Powell, Lewis F., Jr.
        about
  The ball's in Reagan's court. T. Gest. il por *U S News World Rep* 103:20-1 Jl 6 '87
  The Court's pivot man. G. J. Church. il por *Time* 130:10-11 Jl 6 '87
  Lewis F. Powell, Jr.: his warning brought a new era of business activism. il por *Nations Bus* 75:66 Ag '87
  Will the Court turn right? A. Press. il por *Newsweek* 110:16-18 Jl 6 '87
Powell, Mel, 1923-
        about
  Profiles. W. Balliett. por *New Yorker* 63:37-43 My 25 '87
Powell, Padgett
  Learning to hit back. *Harpers* 275:23+ Ag '87
  Voice from the grave [story] il *Esquire* 107:100-3 Ja '87
Powell, Lake (Utah and Ariz.) *See* Lake Powell (Utah and Ariz.)
Powell Observatory (Louisburg, Kan.) *See* Astronomical observatories
Powell's Books (Portland, Or.: Bookstores) *See* Booksellers and bookselling—Oregon
Power, Clark, and Kohlberg, Lawrence, 1927-1987
  Using a hidden curriculum for moral education. *Educ Dig* 52:10-13 My '87
Power, J. David, III
        about
  Does GM rate shelf space? M. Beauchamp. il por *Forbes* 139:144 F 23 '87
Power, J. F., and Follett, R. F. (Ronald F.), 1939-
  Monoculture. il *Sci Am* 256:78-86 Mr '87
Power, Mark, 1937-
  Photo forecast. il *Art Am* 75:47+ D '87
Power (Congressional) *See* United States. Congress—Powers and duties
POWER (Firm)
  Islam's new entrepreneur. S. Monroe and J. Schwartz. il por *Newsweek* 110:38-9 Jl 13 '87
Power (Judicial) *See* Judicial power
Power (Mechanics)
        See also
  Horsepower (Mechanics)
Power (Social sciences)
        See also
  Authority
  Elite (Social sciences)
  The boss [cover story; special section] il *Forbes* 139:145-7+ Je 15 '87
  Camouflaged power. T. Molnar. *Natl Rev* 39:39+ My 8 '87
  The finer points of power building [excerpt from Company manners] L. Wyse. il *Work Woman* 12:78-80+ Ja '87
  If you're so powerful, how come you're fetching coffee? [quiz] A. Gates. *Mademoiselle* 93:256-7+ N '87
  The making of a top manager. B. Insel. il *Work Woman* 12:105-8+ My '87
  Power. D. Wickham. bibl il *Black Enterp* 17:52-4+ Ap '87
  The power of politics and the politics of power. S. M. Buchanan. por *Cent Mag* 20:4-8 Jl/Ag '87
  The role of the manager: the use of power. F. Bartolomé and A. Laurent. *Current* 291:12-16 Mr/Ap '87
  A true test of power [quiz] P. Jordan. *Black Enterp* 17:59 Ap '87
  A view from the top [black women executives; cover story] il *Black Enterp* 17:40-2+ Ap '87
  Waiting is a power game [cover story] R. Levine. il *Psychol Today* 21:24-6+ Ap '87
        Anecdotes, facetiae, satire, etc.
  Turning on the power. R. Baker. il *N Y Times Mag* p12 Ja 18 '87
Power amplifiers *See* Amplifiers
Power Authority of the State of New York
  Power to the people. J. Cook. il por *Forbes* 140:110+ O 19 '87
  The utility industry [address, March 9-11, 1987] R. M. Flynn. *Vital Speeches Day* 53:463-5 My 15 '87
Power boats *See* Motor boats
Power Corporation of Canada
  Power's new Siberian connection. P. C. Newman. il por *Macleans* 100:44 Je 1 '87

Power failures *See* Electric power failures
Power lawn mowers *See* Lawn mowers
Power line radiation *See* Electromagnetic waves
Power lines *See* Electric lines
Power of attorney

Canada

A bleak tale of riches to rags [case of W. Richardson] D. Francis. il *Macleans* 100:7 Ag 10 '87
Power plants
  See also
  Electric plants
  Hydroelectric plants
  Nuclear power plants
  Ocean thermal power plants
Power plants, Solar *See* Solar energy
Power policy *See* Energy policy
Power production, Electric *See* Electric power production
Power resources
  See also
  Biomass energy
  Coal
  Coal supply
  Electronic equipment—Energy usage
  Energy industries
  Energy policy
  Geothermal resources
  Hydroelectric power
  Natural gas
  Nuclear energy
  Ocean thermal power plants
  Peat
  Petroleum
  Solar energy
  Tide power
  Wave power

Conservation

See Energy conservation

Economic aspects

See also
Petroleum—Prices
Sharp drop in energy prices holds inflation in check during 1986. C. Howell and others. il *Mon Labor Rev* 110:3-9 My '87

International aspects

See also
International Energy Agency

Laws and regulations

See Energy policy

Research

See also
University of North Dakota. Energy Research Center

Developing countries

Bioenergy can meet global needs [report from World Resources Institute] *Futurist* 21:44 Ja/F '87
Power resources industry *See* Energy industries
Power resources policy *See* Energy policy
Power saws *See* Saws and sawing
Power supply *See* Power resources
Power Test Corp.
  See also
  Getty Petroleum Corp.
Power tools *See* Tools
Power transistors *See* Transistors
Power washers *See* Pressure washers
Powerboat racing *See* Motor boat racing
Powers, Alan W.
Head over googol. il *N Y Times Mag* p10+ Ag 9 '87
Powers, Arthur
The great Brazilian land grab. *Commonweal* 114:288-90 My 8 '87
Land and violence in Brazil. *America* 156:324-6 Ap 18 '87
Powers, Brian M., 1949-
  about
Jardine's giant step from Hong Kong to Wall Street. D. J. Yang and others. il por *Bus Week* p39-40 O 12 '87
Powers, Connie
  about
Since he got Connie Powers' number, long-distance operator Scott Luczak is hearing a steady aisle tone. il pors *People Wkly* 27:57 Mr 30 '87
Powers, Harry L.
(jt. auth) See Stevenson, Robert G., and Powers, Harry L.
Powers, John
Downhill at Park City. il *Film Comment* 23:4+ Mr/Ap '87
Powers, Marla N.
The Americanization of Indian girls. il *Society* 24:83-6 Ja/F '87

Powers, Richard Gid, 1944-
  about
The Sunday school fascist. T. Branch. *Wash Mon* 19:46-8 Ap '87
Powers, Robert M., 1942-
Fast Forward: a conversation with Robert L. Forward. il por *Space World* X-1-277:30-6 Ja '87
Powers, Separation of *See* Separation of powers
Powledge, Fred
Fighting back. *Nation* 244:120-2 Ja 31 '87
The poisoned well. il *Wilderness* 51:40-3 Fall '87
Pownall, David, 1938-
  about
Pride & prejudice [drama] Reviews
  Macleans il 100:55 Ja 12 '87. M. Schoenberg
Pox viruses
Candidate AIDS vaccine [recombinant vaccinia virus; work of Daniel Zagury] D. M. Barnes. *Science* 235:1575 Mr 27 '87
PPG Industries, Inc.
Setting up shop in China: three paths to success. D. J. Yang. il *Bus Week* p74 O 19 '87
Vincent Sarni is shattering the old PPG. M. Schroeder. il por *Bus Week* p74-5 Ag 17 '87
PR *See* Public relations
Practical arts *See* Home economics
Practical jokes
  See also
  Amazing Events, Inc.
  Joke's on You!, Inc.
At witty Caltech, pranks aren't purely a laughing matter. J. Ellis. il *Smithsonian* 18:100-2+ S '87
Practice jury *See* Mock jury
Pragmatism
F.C.S. Schiller: an appreciation. D. Lawson. *Humanist* 47:35 S/O '87
Prague (Czechoslovakia)

Galleries and museums

See also
Smetana Museum (Prague, Czechoslovakia)

Palaces

See Palaces—Czechoslovakia
Prague Quadrennial *See* Theater—Exhibitions
Prahus (Boats) *See* Praus (Boats)
Prairie dogs
A prairie dog companion [work of J. Hoogland in Wind Cave National Park, S.D.] J. Grossmann. il pors *Audubon* 89:52-4+ Mr '87
Prairie ecology
Tale of the tallgrass. E. Docekal. il map *Sierra* 72:76-9 My/Je '87
A prairie home companion [radio program] See Radio program reviews—Single works
Prairie schooner trips *See* Wagon trains
Prairie View A & M University
Prairie View gets $109,500 in funds. *Jet* 73:22 O 19 '87
Prairie View A & M University. Benjamin Banneker Honors College
Benjamin Banneker Honors College at Prairie View A&M offers wide range of studies. *Jet* 72:16 Ap 27 '87
Prairies

Kansas

See also
Tallgrass Prairie National Preserve (Kan. and Okla.)

Oklahoma

See also
Tallgrass Prairie National Preserve (Kan. and Okla.)
Praise
In praise of praise. P. Theroux. il *Parents* 62:60+ Ag '87
Take out some marriage insurance. H. N. Ferguson. il *Read Dig* 130:213-14+ My '87
What writers live on. K. Reed. por *Publ Wkly* 232:55 Ag 28 '87
Pralines
Pralines. A. Matthews. il *Americana* 15:42-4+ Mr/Ap '87
Pranks *See* Practical jokes
Prater, Yvonne, 1932-
Snowshoeing: making tracks. il por *Women's Sports Fitness* 9:78-9 D '87
Pratt & Whitney Aircraft Group
Allison, Pratt & Whitney team for propfan engine market. il *Aviat Week Space Technol* 126:32-3 Mr 2 '87
Component deliveries delay PW-Allison propfan first flight. S. W. Kandebo. *Aviat Week Space Technol* 127:28-9 N 30 '87
Lavi cancellation sets back Pratt's PW1120 engine program. *Aviat Week Space Technol* 127:24-5 S 7 '87

Pratt & Whitney Aircraft Group—*cont.*
One thing after another. H. Banks. *Forbes* 140:184 N 16 '87
P&W, Williams joint venture for helicopter engine work. il *Aviat Week Space Technol* 127:33 N 2 '87
Pratt & Whitney captures lead in USAF fighter engine competition. *Aviat Week Space Technol* 126:30 F 9 '87
Pratt & Whitney expands role in V2500 compressor work; Rolls-Royce retains lead in IAE V2500 cold-section development. *Aviat Week Space Technol* 126:32-3 Mr 16 '87
Pratt & Whitney expects to regain market share with PW2000, PW4000. S. W. Kandebo. il *Aviat Week Space Technol* 127:70-1 Ag 31 '87
Pratt & Whitney plans expanded operations to pursue growth in overhaul, repair work. *Aviat Week Space Technol* 127:66 Jl 20 '87
Pratt & Whitney reorganizes its large engine business. S. W. Kandebo. *Aviat Week Space Technol* 127:33 O 12 '87
Pratt & Whitney's stall is turning into a tailspin. R. Mitchell. il *Bus Week* p37 D 14 '87
Pratt, Allison team for P-3 follow-on engine candidate. *Aviat Week Space Technol* 127:32 D 21 '87
Pratt testing increased-thrust F100 engine. il *Aviat Week Space Technol* 126:55 F 23 '87
Pratt's cautious research reflects uncertain UHB market [ultrahigh bypass engine] il *Aviat Week Space Technol* 126:70+ Ap 13 '87
Why Pratt & Whitney is sputtering [investment in International Aero Engines] R. W. King and F. J. Comes. il *Bus Week* p24 Ap 20 '87

Praus (Boats)
Plying the Java Sea [traditional wooden prahu; cover story] S. P. Breslow. il map *Oceans* 20:20-7 S/O '87

Pray, Roger T.
How did our prisons get that way? bibl il *Am Herit* 38:92-6+ Jl/Ag '87

Prayer
   See also
   Meditation
   Prayers
Centering prayer. M. B. Pennington. *America* 156:169-71 F 28 '87
For God's sake, pray for favors. K. Hughes. *U S Cathol* 52:35-6 Ja '87
How prayer can strengthen your love for God [cover story; interview with W. J. Burghardt] por *U S Cathol* 52:6-13 D '87:
Lenten meditation:
   Petitionary prayer reconsidered. C. E. Simcox. *Christ Century* 104:212-13 Mr 4 '87
A lot of tired prayer warriors [South Korea] H. Smith and K. Myung-Hyuk. il *Christ Today* 31:37 N 20 '87
On providence and prayer. J. A. Keller. *Christ Century* 104:967-9 N 4 '87
The power of prayer. R. Coles. il *50 Plus* 27:44-6 D '87
Prayer & the pursuit of public virtue. F. J. Macchiarola. *Commonweal* 114:440-2 Ag 14 '87
Prowlers, prayers and a dream. M. A. King. *Christ Century* 104:959-60 N 4 '87
Real Christians pray every day [with readers' comments] M. Finley. *U S Cathol* 52:14-19 F '87
The role of prayer in gaining the release of hostages. K. A. Lawton. il *Christ Today* 31:34-6 S 18 '87
U.S. judge rules prayer before a game is illegal [high school football] *Jet* 71:6 Mr 2 '87
Why to, how to, when to. H. Fehren. *U S Cathol* 52:38-40 N '87
Writing and the devout life. J. Parini. *Christ Century* 104:815-16 S 30 '87

Prayer books
   See also
   Catholic Church—Prayer books and devotions

Prayer breakfasts
Washington's movers and shakers gather for prayer [National Prayer Breakfast] E. E. Plowman. il *Christ Today* 31:65 Mr 20 '87

Prayer Canada (Organization)
An unholy prayer fight [meetings in British Columbia legislature provoke protests] il *Macleans* 100:12 Ap 13 '87

A prayer for the dying [film] See Motion picture reviews—Single works

Prayer in the schools *See* Public schools and religion

Prayers
   See also
   Lord's prayer

Prayers of confession: let's get unspecific. B. Barr. *Christ Century* 104:844 O 7 '87
Pre-Columbian art *See* Art, Pre-Columbian
Pre-Paid Legal Services, Inc.
Ready, fire, aim. R. Thompson. il por *Nations Bus* 75:77-8 N '87
Preaching
   See also
   Sermons
Warning: God's been known to speak through a jackass [excerpt from Preaching] W. J. Burghardt. il *U S Cathol* 52:13-15 S '87
Preakness (Race) *See* Horse racing
Preamplifiers *See* Amplifiers
Precambrian period *See* Geology, Stratigraphic—Precambrian; Paleoclimatology—Precambrian; Paleontology—Precambrian
Precession
Misreading the stars. N. Henbest. il *World Press Rev* 34:55 S '87
Prechter, Robert Rougelot
   about
Ace analyst Robert Prechter says when skirts rise, so does the stock market—no bull. L. Aitken. il pors *People Wkly* 27:42-4 My 11 '87
The champion market forecaster. M. A. Elliott. il por *Fortune* 115:75 Ja 5 '87
Chartists. J. K. Glassman. *New Repub* 196:8-10 Ap 6 '87
The guru who saw a 2000 Dow. A. Miller. il por *Newsweek* 109:40+ Ja 19 '87
The stock market catches a big wave. il por *Discover* 8:12 Mr '87
Precious metals
   See also
   Gold
   Platinum
Precious metals as an investment
   See also
   A-Mark Precious Metals Inc.
Avoiding the gold rush stampede [metals funds] *Money* 16:27+ Je '87
Gold is back. J. Kosnett. il *Changing Times* 41:95-6+ S '87
The new risk in precious metals. R. Eisenberg. il *Money* 16:113+ D '87
Protecting your portfolio with a gold lining. G. Weiss. il *Bus Week* p76 Jl 6 '87
When the going gets tough, the tough get hedging. T. Segal. il *Bus Week* p180-2 D 28 '87-Ja 4 '88
Precious stones
   See also
   Crown jewels
   Diamonds
   Garnets
   Rubies
   Sapphires
   Tourmalines
Precipitation (Meteorology)
   See also
   Rain and rainfall
   Snow
How often does it rain where you live? N. J. Doesken and W. P. Eckrich. il maps *Weatherwise* 40:200-3 Jl/Ag '87
Precipitation fluctuations over Northern Hemisphere land areas since the mid-19th century. R. S. Bradley and others. bibl f il maps *Science* 237:171-5 Jl 10 '87
Precision *See* Accuracy
Precognition *See* Extrasensory perception
Preconception Clinic *See* North Carolina Memorial Hospital. Preconception Clinic
Predation (Biology)
Chemical mimicry: bolas spiders emit components of moth prey species sex pheromones. M. K. Stowe and others. bibl f il *Science* 236:964-7 My 22 '87
Complex dynamics link islands' predators [research by Thomas Schoener and David Spiller] R. Lewin. *Science* 236:917 My 22 '87
Diadema antillarum was not a keystone predator in cryptic reef environments. J. B. C. Jackson and K. W. Kaufmann. bibl f il *Science* 235:687-9 F 6 '87
Effect of lizards on spider populations: manipulative reconstruction of a natural experiment. T. W. Schoener and D. A. Spiller. bibl f il *Science* 236:949-52 My 22 '87
Sensory tuning of lateral line receptors in Antarctic fish to the movements of planktonic prey [teleosts] J. C. Montgomery and J. A. Macdonald. bibl f il *Science* 235:195-6 Ja 9 '87

Predation (Biology)—*cont.*

Spider's perfume fatal for moths [research by Mark K. Stowe and others] S. Weisburd. il *Sci News* 131:340 My 30 '87

Predator [film] *See* Motion picture reviews—Single works

Predatory insects *See* Insects, Predatory

Prediction *See* Forecasting

Prednisone

Steroid helpful in muscular dystrophy. *Sci News* 132:120 Ag 22 '87

War on muscular dystrophy achieves a first. J. Silberner. il *U S News World Rep* 103:12 Ag 17 '87

Predock, Antoine

about

Architecture: Antoine Predock. R. Morris. il por *Archit Dig* 44:90-7+ Ag '87

Preeclampsia *See* Pregnancy—Complications

Prefabrication

See also

Furniture, Prefabricated

Houses, Prefabricated

Prisons, Prefabricated

Preferred stocks

See also

Pay-in-kind securities

Bad calls [use of preferred stock in bond refundings] B. Weberman. il *Forbes* 140:129 Ag 24 '87

Pregnancy

See also

Abortion

Alternative pregnancy centers

Amniotic liquid

Artificial insemination, Human

Childbirth

Conception

Fetus

Maternity leaves

North Carolina Memorial Hospital. Preconception Clinic

Obstetrics

Prenatal influences

Teenage pregnancy

As they grow/pregnancy and birth. P. A. Hillard. *See* issues of Parents

How we can save our babies [prenatal care] L. David and I. David. il *Health* 19:29-31+ Ag '87

Managing your pregnancy. G. Bakoulis. *Work Woman* 12:122 D '87

Nairobi Safe Motherhood Conference reviews concerns, activities to help pregnant women and mothers. il *UN Chron* 24:63-4 My '87

New perspective on pregnancy after 35. D. Calkins. *McCalls* 114:107 Ja '87

Pregnancy, PMS and menopause: no need to cramp your style. A. Krueger. *Work Woman* 12:158+ Ap '87

The pregnancy test—how to get positive results [effect of unplanned pregnancy on relationship to the baby's father] C. Rickey. *Mademoiselle* 93:100 F '87

What pregnant women need from friends. il *Glamour* 85:60 F '87

Your baby, your way [excerpt] S. Kitzinger. il *Glamour* 85:50+ Ag '87

Your pregnancy. L. MacCallum. *See* issues of Glamour

Complications

See also

Fetus, Effect of hormones on the

Miscarriage

Umbilical cord—Prolapse

The Baby M case: pregnancy and M.S. il *Discover* 8:13 Je '87

A child for Christmas [cardiac N. Claar risks pregnancy] W. Barnhill. il pors *Good Housekeep* 205:66+ D '87

Childbearing and age. M. Konner. il *N Y Times Mag* p22-3 D 27 '87

Dental alert: how pregnancy affects your teeth and gums. D. Burden. *Work Woman* 12:140 O '87

"Don't let my baby die!" [preeclampsia; excerpt from Intensive care] E. Heron. il por *Redbook* 168:122-4+ Ap '87

Eat right, stay off your feet—or go to jail [proposed measures protecting fetal rights at the expense of the mother] M. Takas. *Vogue* 177:148 My '87

Ectopic pregnancies: are they on the rise? J. Randal. il *Glamour* 85:254+ Ap '87

An excuse for workplace hazard [fetal protection policies discriminate against women] C. Marshall. il *Nation* 244:532-4 Ap 25 '87

Fertility and family [ectopic pregnancies after infertility problems] K. Bouton. *Ms* 15:92 Ap '87

Is your work harmful to your unborn baby? C. Loomis. il *Parents* 62:13 Jl '87

A matter of neglect [fetal rights vs. maternal rights] J. Bermel. il *Parents* 62:335-6+ N '87

The ordeal of Pamela Rae Stewart [charged with irresponsible prenatal care] A. Bonavoglia. il pors *Ms* 16:92-5+ Jl/Ag '87

Policing pregnancy [views on forced obstetrical procedures] *Sci Am* 257:26+ Ag '87

Poverty makes pregnancy dangerous to black women. *Jet* 71:29 F 2 '87

Pregnancy hypertension marker found. *Sci News* 131:344 My 30 '87

Viral exposure boosts schizophrenia risk [research by Sarnoff A. Mednick and others] B. Bower. *Sci News* 132:180 S 19 '87

When pregnancy can be life-threatening [ectopic pregnancy] D. Klein. il *McCalls* 115:100+ N '87

The wisest decision I ever made [postponing chemotherapy to complete pregnancy]; ed. by Jack Hope. E. Eaton. il pors *Good Housekeep* 205:48+ Jl '87

Immunological aspects

Autoimmunity may cause infertility [research by Norbert Gleicher and others] R. Weiss. *Sci News* 132:52-3 Jl 25 '87

Nutritional aspects

Calcium may take the pressure off pregnancy. *Prevention* 39:10 F '87

Does fetal zinc affect later immunity? [research by Pamela Fraker and others] J. Raloff. *Sci News* 131:375 Je 13 '87

Eating for two. G. Williams and L. Williams. il *Health* 19:47-9+ F '87

Psychological aspects

Don't panic, you're pregnant [work of David T. George and others] *Sci News* 132:120 Ag 22 '87

The expectant father. J. L. Shapiro. bibl (p63) il *Psychol Today* 21:36-9+ Ja '87

What pregnant dreams mean. M. Vogel. il *Parents* 62:120-2+ My '87

Signs and diagnosis

Home pregnancy tests: a user's guide. S. Rose. *Work Woman* 12:143 O '87

Pregnancy exercises

After the baby: shedding 25 inches and 25 pounds [M. Spletzer-Newman] *See* issues of Glamour beginning June 1987 through December 1987

Coming back after pregnancy. S. Festa. il *Women's Sports Fitness* 9:32 Ap '87

A new mother's fitness plan [K. Shaefer] C. Straley. il pors *Parents* 62:134-5+ Mr '87

One-minute overall stretch. L. MacCallum. il *Glamour* 85:244 Mr '87

Vive la différence! M. Carpenter. il *Women's Sports Fitness* 9:88 Mr '87

Pregnancy kits *See* Pregnancy—Signs and diagnosis

Pregnancy tests *See* Pregnancy—Signs and diagnosis

Pregnant schoolgirls *See* Teenage pregnancy

Prego (Irvine, Calif.: Restaurant) *See* Irvine (Calif.)— Restaurants, nightclubs, bars, etc.

Prehistoric agriculture *See* Agriculture, Prehistoric

Prehistoric astronomy *See* Astronomy, Ancient

Prehistoric man *See* Man, Prehistoric

Prejudice

See also

Anti-Catholicism

Anti-Semitism

Ethnocentrism

Race discrimination

Big and little bigots. E. Crow. il *Parents* 62:6 Jl '87

Le nouveau canard [accusations of bigotry used as ad hominem argument by liberals] J. Sobran. *Natl Rev* 39:44-5+ F 13 '87

Prejudice. P. A. Feuerstein. il *Curr Health 2* 13:28-9 Ap '87

The ugly faces of prejudice [against the handicapped] B. Davidson. il *McCalls* 114:62-3 S '87

Prelee, Michael

Life is sunnier for this now-fit Florida man; ed. by Maria Mihalik. il *Prevention* 39:98-100+ S '87

Prelutsky, Jack

Read-aloud rhymes for the very young [excerpt] il *Parents* 62:141-2+ S '87

Premadasa, Ranasinghe

about

Investing in human beings [interview] il por *World Health* p2-5 Jl '87

Premark International Inc.

How Premark is shrinking to the occasion. J. E. Ellis. il *Bus Week* p75 Mr 9 '87

Premature infants See Infants, Premature
Premature labor See Childbirth
Premenstrual syndrome
Blue moods. L. Claverie. il *Health* 19:47-51 S '87
The lowdown on PMS. D. Hales. *Seventeen* 46:116-17
  Ja '87
Winter doldrums. il *Ms* 16:53 D '87
Nutritional aspects
Eat to beat PMS. G. Burtis. il *Mademoiselle* 93:180
  My '87
PMS eased by vitamin E [study by Robert London]
  il *Prevention* 39:14+ D '87
Therapy
Can exercise cure PMS? D. Fortino. il *Women's Sports
  Fitness* 9:44-7 N '87
A cure for PMS? [thyroid hormones] *Women's Sports
  Fitness* 9:60 My '87
Pregnancy, PMS and menopause: no need to cramp
  your style. A. Krueger. *Work Woman* 12:158+ Ap
  '87
Premieres, Motion picture See Motion picture premieres
Premiums
See also
  Coupons
Toasters are not the only bank gifts. S. Woolley. il
  Bus Week p152 Mr 16 '87
Collectors and collecting
Childhood memories are preserved in radio premiums.
  S. Bagdade and A. Bagdade. il *Antiques Collect Hobbies*
  92:76-9 Mr '87
Premiums, Insurance See Insurance—Rates and tables
Prenatal care See Pregnancy
Prenatal diagnosis See Fetus—Diseases—Diagnosis
Prenatal influences
Class before birth [fetal learning] M. Roberts. il *Psychol
  Today* 21:41 My '87
Lead in utero: low-level danger [effect on mental develop-
  ment in first two years of life; research by David
  Bellinger and others] B. Bower. *Sci News* 131:277
  My 2 '87
Leaden development [lead in the womb and mental
  development; study by David Bellinger] J. Rubin. il
  Psychol Today 21:13 S '87
Mama, talk to your baby [Rene Van de Carr's Prenatal
  University] il *Newsweek* 110:75 N 2 '87
Prendergast, Maurice Brazil, 1859-1924
about
The late watercolor/pastels of Maurice Prendergast [cover
  story] C. Langdale. bibl f il *Antiques* 132:1084-95 N
  '87
La prensa (New York, N.Y.) See El diario-La prensa (New
  York, N.Y.)
La prensa (Nicaragua)
A bumpy road to democracy [reopening] H. Anderson.
  il *Newsweek* 110:38-9 O 5 '87
How "La prensa" was silenced; tr. by Steven Blakemore.
  J. Chamorro. *Commentary* 83:39-44 Ja '87
Minority report. C. Hitchens. *Nation* 244:458 Ap 11
  '87
"Our people cannot be silenced"; tr. by Steven Blakemore.
  J. Chamorro. *Read Dig* 130:169-70+ My '87
Playing to the crowd [discussion of April 11, 1987 article,
  Minority report] C. Hitchens. *Nation* 244:564-5 My
  2 '87
Prentice-Hall, Inc. Business and Professional Division
Direct-mail audio line due from Prentice Hall. il *Publ
  Wkly* 232:70 O 9 '87
Prenuptial contracts See Marriage contracts
Prep schools See Private schools
Prepaid legal services
See also
  Pre-Paid Legal Services, Inc.
Charge-a-lawyer is here. R. R. Roha. il *Changing Times*
  41:112+ Mr '87
Prepaid legal services: they offer advice without criminally
  high prices. J. Reid. il *Money* 16:43+ Ap '87
Those dial-a-lawyer plans. A. E. LaForge. *Good Housekeep*
  205:186 Ag '87
Preparation of manuscripts See Authorship—Copy prepara-
  tion
Preparatory schools See Private schools
Preparedness, Military See United States—Military policy
Prepayment of mortgages See Mortgages—Prepayment
Prepositions See English language—Prepositions
Presbyterian Church
United States
Choosing sites [selection of headquarters by Presbyterian
  Church (U.S.A.)] *Christ Century* 104:104 F 4-11 '87
Coming to terms with Judaism [Presbyterian Church
  U.S.A.] R. N. Ostling. il *Time* 129:57 Je 29 '87

Free office space [Louisville, Ky. bids for Presbyterian
  Church (U.S.A.) headquarters] *Christ Century* 104:401
  Ap 29 '87
Hick rejected [bid to be accepted as a Presbyterian
  minister] *Christ Century* 104:304-5 Ap 1 '87
Major Maryland Presbyterian Church switches its affilia-
  tion [Fourth Presbyterian Church to join Evangelical
  Presbyterian Church] *Christ Today* 31:59 Ja 16 '87
The Presbyterian moment. D. Ritchie. il *Natl Rev* 39:30-1
  Jl 31 '87
Presbyterians: politics and responsibility. G. Telford.
  Christ Century 104:614-16 Jl 15-22 '87
The restoration of Maurice McCrackin [Presbyterian
  activist minister] D. Peerman. il *Christ Century*
  104:998-1000 N 11 '87
Presbyterian Church (U.S.A.) See Presbyterian Church—
  United States
Preschool education See Education, Preschool
Prescott, Bonnie
I was a junk food addict. il *Health* 19:12+ S '87
Prescott, Eileen
What it takes to be an entrepreneur. *Work Woman*
  12:34 Ag '87
Prescott, James W.
AIDS, sexual oppression, and violence: a call for preven-
  tion. il por *Humanist* 47:15-17+ Jl/Ag '87
Prescott, Katherine
about
Katherine Prescott: a chat with a candy maker. il por
  McCalls 114:110-11 Ag '87
Prescott, Peter S.
about
S & S buys bio of Knopf by Peter Prescott. *Publ Wkly*
  231:87 F 27 '87
Prescott, Ted
about
Crucifying machine. D. Neff. il *Christ Today* 31:58 N
  6 '87
Prescribed burning See Forest fires—Controlled fires
Prescription drug insurance See Insurance, Pharmaceutical
  services
Prescription drugs See Drugs
Presenile dementia See Alzheimer's disease
Presentations (Business) See Business presentations
Presents See Gifts
Preservation of architecture See Architecture—Conservation
  and restoration
Preservation of books See Books—Conservation and restora-
  tion
Preservation of food See Food preservation and preservatives
Preservation of historic sites See Historic houses, sites,
  etc.
Preservation of organs, tissues, etc.
Beyond the cutting edge of cold [vitrification of organs;
  cover story] S. Weisburd. il *Sci News* 132:138-41 Ag
  29 '87
Fluid flushed with promise [Belzer's solution] S. Weisburd.
  Sci News 132:5 Jl 4 '87
Sweet success in freezing islets. S. Weisburd. *Sci News*
  132:47 Jl 18 '87
Preservation of paper See Paper—Preservation
Preservation of wood See Wood—Preservation and preserva-
  tives
Preserves, Shooting See Shooting preserves
Preserving See Canning and preserving
Presidential advisers
See also
  Council of Economic Advisers (U.S.)
The powers that shouldn't be: five Washington insiders
  the next Democratic president shouldn't hire [cover
  story] P. Glastris. pors *Wash Mon* 19:39-46+ O '87
Presidential airplanes See Airplanes, Government
Presidential automobiles See Automobiles, Government
Presidential campaigns
See also
  Advertising, Political
  Campaign issues
  Campaign management
  Campaign workers
  Caucuses
  National conventions, Democratic
  National conventions (Political)
  Presidential candidates
  Presidential debates
  Presidential primaries
  Television and politics
The press, the process, and Gary Hart [address, May
  29, 1987] O. C. Henkel. *Vital Speeches Day* 53:697-700
  S 1 '87

Presidential candidates—1988—cont.

The lightweight philosopher [views of G. F. Will] S. Blumenthal. *Wash Mon* 19:53-7 O '87

A little spice for the tapioca [noncandidates G. Hart, M. Cuomo, and J. Jackson] G. Witkin. il pors *U S News World Rep* 103:14 S 21 '87

Look who wants to be president [Fruit of the Loom executive W. Farley] B. Saporito. il pors *Fortune* 116:141+ N 23 '87

The man Gorbachev didn't circle [M. Cuomo] M. Kramer. por *U S News World Rep* 103:20 D 14 '87

Manufacturing the next president [Harper's forum simulating process of 1988 Democratic nomination] il *Harpers* 275:43-54 D '87

Mario Cuomo's coy politics. *Newsweek* 109:28 Je 1 '87

Mario's moves. por *Time* 129:26 F 23 '87

Memo to Sam: it's going to be tough. H. Fineman. por *Newsweek* 110:19 Ag 31 '87

The New York idea [M. Cuomo declines to seek Democratic nomination] A. Logan. *New Yorker* 63:84-6+ Mr 23 '87

Now, please welcome The Platitudes [Democratic candidates] M. Kramer. il *U S News World Rep* 103:18 O 5 '87

Now the Democrats have a pack of front-runners. R. Fly and D. Harbrecht. por *Bus Week* p61 My 18 '87

Nunn too soon for president? [interview] il *U S News World Rep* 102:20 Ja 19 '87

On deck [Democratic lineup] *Natl Rev* 39:13-14 Je 5 '87

One remove from the real. A. McCarthy. *Commonweal* 114:343-4 Je 5 '87

Outside, looking in. *Natl Rev* 39:16-17 Ap 24 '87

Overdue Bill [B. Bradley] J. Klein. il por *N Y* 20:22-3 N 23 '87

Pat Schroeder's ambition to be First Lady in the Oval Office nears the moment of truth. M. Green. il pors *People Wkly* 28:48-50 S 7 '87

Picking among the leftovers [Democrats] il *World Press Rev* 34:34 Jl '87

Playing politics by the numbers [Democratic candidates figuring how to win baby boomers' votes] G. Borger and D. Baer. il *U S News World Rep* 102:28-9 Je 22 '87

Playing politics on Wall Street. J. Crudele. il *N Y* 20:16+ Ag 10 '87

President Bradley? J. McLaughlin. *Natl Rev* 39:26 F 13 '87

A president for space. J. Muncy. *Space World* X-7-283 Space Advocate:4-5 Jl '87

A presidential straw poll [National Association of Evangelicals convention] *Christ Today* 31:39 Ap 3 '87

The Republicans in '88. W. Schneider. il *Atlantic* 260:58-62+ Jl '87

Rethinking the fair game rules [press coverage] L. I. Barrett. il *Time* 130:76+ N 30 '87

Rising star Sam Nunn ponders a presidential bid. D. Harbrecht. il por *Bus Week* p43 Ja 12 '87

"Run, Pat, run!" [P. Schroeder] A. Stanley. il *Time* 130:20 Ag 3 '87

Rushing to an early kickoff. L. I. Barrett. il *Time* 129:18-20 Ja 19 '87

Sam Nunn: "After two hours of walking NYC's streets, three people had asked me to run! Three!". M. Moynihan. il por *Vogue* 177:248+ O '87

Sam Nunn's rising star. P. Gailey. il pors *N Y Times Mag* p24-9+ Ja 4 '87

Savior on the right? [P. Buchanan] M. G. Warner. il por *Newsweek* 109:18 Ja 19 '87

The search for personal flaws [press treatment] J. Alter. il *Newsweek* 110:79 O 19 '87

See how they run [Democrats] *New Repub* 196:7-9 My 4 '87

Seeking oomph on the stump. L. I. Barrett. il *Time* 130:15 Ag 10 '87

'Seven dwarfs' asleeping. A. Brummer. il *World Press Rev* 34:64 O '87

Shallow sounds of campaign '88. M. Kramer. il *U S News World Rep* 103:24-6+ D 28 '87-Ja 4 '88

Shrinking violets [urging B. Bradley and M. Cuomo to enter race] *New Repub* 196:4+ Je 22 '87

So now who's likely to be the Democratic nominee? M. S. Forbes. *Forbes* 139:19 Je 1 '87

So what do you want to be when you grow up? President! il *Life* 10:102-4+ D '87

So why is the A Team sitting on the bench? [Democrat's leading vote getters choose not to run] E. Clift. il *Newsweek* 109:33-4 Ap 27 '87

The songs of the South [Democrat S. Nunn] W. Shapiro. il por *Time* 130:17 Ag 31 '87

Southern scramble [effect of S. Nunn's withdrawal on Democratic contenders] J. B. Copeland. por *Newsweek* 110:5 S 7 '87

The sprint to the finish. G. F. Will. il *Newsweek* 110:90 S 28 '87

'A stone in one's shoe': running with integrity. J. M. Wall. *Christ Century* 104:843 O 7 '87

Suffering toward the White House. R. Harris. *New Yorker* 63:65-6+ Ag 3 '87

The summer line [Republicans] F. Barnes. *New Repub* 197:14-16 Jl 6 '87

Taking shots at the 'Sphinx of Albany' [M. Cuomo] H. Fineman. il por *Newsweek* 109:25-6 Ja 26 '87

Testing ideas on education. G. J. Church. il *Time* 130:32 S 21 '87

Those fractious Republicans. H. Smith. il *N Y Times Mag* p30+ O 25 '87

Tips from a tonsorial tout [barber M. Pitts' analysis of candidates' hairstyles] H. Sidey. il por *Time* 129:25 F 16 '87

Trouble for the early birds. H. Fineman. il *Newsweek* 110:22 N 23 '87

Trump for president? G. Hackett. il por *Newsweek* 110:41 S 14 '87

The "turn-to" scenarios [H. Baker and M. Cuomo] L. I. Barrett. il pors *Time* 129:26 Ap 13 '87

TV's David Frost quizzes the men who would be president. J. Hall. il pors *People Wkly* 28:78-80 D 7 '87

Unhappy Democrats, a loyal G.O.P. [Time poll] L. I. Barrett. il *Time* 130:22+ S 14 '87

The unreal campaign. W. Shapiro. il *Time* 130:18-21 S 14 '87

A visitation of phantoms [G. Hart's televised apology and M. Cuomo's noncandidacy] M. Kaus. il pors *Newsweek* 110:32-3 S 21 '87

Wanted: leaders with vision. J. M. Wall. *Christ Century* 104:779 S 23 '87

Watch Baker [H. H. Baker] J. McLaughlin. *Natl Rev* 39:24 Ap 10 '87

We hardly knew ye [M. Cuomo declines to seek nomination] *Nation* 244:275-6 Mr 7 '87

What the darkest horses hope to gain by running [Democrats] R. Fly. *Bus Week* p55 Je 1 '87

Where are the wingers? [Republican candidates] L. I. Barrett. il *Time* 130:34+ O 26 '87

Where's the beef? [Republicans; cover story] M. Kondracke. *New Repub* 197:16-18+ Jl 6 '87

While others are running, Mario Cuomo's stature is growing. M. S. Forbes. *Forbes* 140:17-18 O 5 '87

Whistling Dixie [A. Gore and B. Clinton] pors *Time* 129:32 Ap 6 '87

Whom are the conservatives backing? W. F. Buckley. *Natl Rev* 39:56-7 My 22 '87

Who's going to be the next president? M. S. Forbes. *Forbes* 140:17 N 2 '87

Why Bradley isn't running. R. Rothenberg. il pors *N Y Times Mag* p28-31+ Ag 2 '87

Why the Democrats lose elections [cover story] G. F. Will. il *Natl Rev* 39:28-9+ D 18 '87

The year of the refuseniks. L. I. Barrett. il *Time* 130:14 S 7 '87

Anecdotes, facetiae, satire, etc.

I dream of Jeanie [J. Kirkpatrick] G. F. Will. il *Newsweek* 109:82 F 2 '87

Notes and comment [M. Gorbachev as presidential candidate] *New Yorker* 63:33-4 D 28 '87

On to the White House [how sports will elect B. Bradley president] C. Neff. il por *Sports Illus* 67:102 N 16 '87

Outdated candidates. R. Baker. il *N Y Times Mag* p14 F 8 '87

Reasons to believe. R. Baker. il *N Y Times Mag* p40 D 6 '87

Running on empty. A. A. Rooney. il *N Y Times Mag* p26 N 8 '87

This is one candidate who's not afraid to admit he's a dog [Punch Burger is registered with the Federal Election Commission] il *People Wkly* 28:45 Jl 13 '87

Uncivil liberties. C. Trillin. il *Nation* 245:438 O 24 '87

Addresses, messages, etc.
Anecdotes, facetiae, satire, etc.

The speech. C. Murphy. il *Atlantic* 260:20 D '87

Advertising
See Advertising, Political

Anecdotes, facetiae, satire, etc.

Notes and comment. *New Yorker* 63:27 S 28 '87

Potomac fever. L. H. Lapham. *Harpers* 275:12-13 N '87

Presidential candidates—Anecdotes, facetiae, satire, etc. —*cont.*

Presidential illusions. R. Baker. *N Y Times Mag* p12 Jl 5 '87

Economic conditions

And now, 'log cabin chic'. H. Fineman. il *Newsweek* 110:27 N 30 '87

Ethics

See Political ethics

Expenditures

See Campaign funds

Families

See Dick run, see Jane run. M. Kaus. il *Newsweek* 109:21-2 My 25 '87

Names

Anecdotes, facetiae, satire, etc.

Name that carcass. R. Baker. il *N Y Times Mag* p20 N 29 '87

Psychology

The character debate: how much is too much? K. A. Lawton. il *Christ Today* 31:49-50+ D 11 '87

Character issue. W. Safire. il *N Y Times Mag* p18+ N 22 '87

The character issue: enough already. W. Shapiro. il *Time* 130:93-4 D 7 '87

Hail to the (macho) chief [desired presidential traits; study by D. Anthony Butterfield and Gary N. Powell] A. Kohn. il *Psychol Today* 21:21 D '87

Kennedy going on Nixon [G. Hart] L. Morrow. il *Time* 129:90 My 18 '87

Presidents: men of the hour don't stand the test of time ["national mood" candidates; study by David G. Winter] J. Fischman. *Psychol Today* 21:13 My '87

The public and the private Gary Hart. J. M. Wall. *Christ Century* 104:483-4 My 20-27 '87

Reading

Summer reading for candidates [recommendations by D. Boorstin] H. Sidey. bibl il por *Time* 130:21 Ag 3 '87

Religion

Presidential candidates: preachers and pragmatists. J. M. Wall. *Christ Century* 104:1051-2 N 25 '87

Religion in politics: a little goes a long way. J. M. Wall. *Christ Century* 104:1107-8 D 9 '87

Sexual behavior

After sticking with a troubled marriage, Lee Hart watches a dream die. M. Green. il pors *People Wkly* 27:38-40 My 25 '87

After the fall: how Hart's workers picked up the pieces. L. Glynn and J. Mathewson. il por *Glamour* 85:362-3+ S '87

Boston diarist [press treatment of G. Hart] H. Hertzberg. *New Repub* 196:42 Je 15 '87

Chronicle of a ruinous affair [G. Hart and D. Rice; views of L. Armandt; cover story] M. Green. il pors *People Wkly* 27:104-8 Je 15 '87

Donna Rice tells her story; ed. by James Grant. D. Rice. il *Life* 10:82-6+ Jl '87

Donna Rice: 'the woman in question' [G. Hart case] A. Richman. il pors *People Wkly* 27:32-7 My 18 '87

Fall from grace [G. Hart's withdrawal; cover story; special section] il pors *Time* 129:16-20+ My 18 '87

Femme is fatal [G. Hart scandal] B. Ehrenreich and J. O'Reilly. *New Repub* 196:15-16 Je 1 '87

The Gary Hart affair: the media's role. J. B. Judis. *Current* 297:28-32 N '87

Gary-kari—& after [G. Hart case] *Commonweal* 114:307-9 My 22 '87

Gotta have Hart [Moscow's reaction to G. Hart's sudden fall from electoral grace] J. E. Oberg. *Natl Rev* 39:40 Jl 17 '87

The Hart poll [Gallup/Nation poll shows that G. Hart would be frontrunner if he were to reenter race] V. S. Navasky. *Nation* 245:112-13 Ag 15-22 '87

Hart's problem & ours [press treatment of scandal] W. F. Buckley. *Natl Rev* 39:55 Je 5 '87

Infidelity [G. Hart] *Nation* 244:633-4 My 16 '87

Jack Kennedy's private side [previously unreleased campaign notes] *Newsweek* 109:22 Je 8 '87

Keeping the press at bay [G. Hart] L. Zuckerman. il *Time* 130:18 D 28 '87

The loss of Hart. *New Repub* 196:9-11 Je 1 '87

The mourning after [G. Hart] F. Trippett. il *Time* 129:34 My 25 '87

New morality, new journalism [coverage of G. Hart scandal] *Natl Rev* 39:15 Je 5 '87

New photos behind the fall [G. Hart scandal] il pors *Newsweek* 109:22 Je 8 '87

Notes and comment [G. Hart case] *New Yorker* 63:27 My 25 '87

Now after Hart, the questions [cover story; special section] il pors *U S News World Rep* 102:18-25 My 18 '87

On the zipper beat [press coverage of G. Hart scandal] *New Repub* 196:4+ My 25 '87

Preaching & practice [case of G. Hart] D. R. Carlin, Jr. *Commonweal* 114:342-3 Je 5 '87

The press, the process, and Gary Hart [address, May 29, 1987] O. C. Henkel. *Vital Speeches Day* 53:697-700 S 1 '87

Private lives and public people [repercussions from the G. Hart sex scandal] M. McDonald. il por *Macleans* 100:28-9 S 21 '87

Private lives, public values [G. Hart case] M. Greenfield. il *Newsweek* 109:92 My 18 '87

Private sex and public exposure [G. Hart case] G. Bain. il *Macleans* 100:48 My 25 '87

The public and the private Gary Hart. J. M. Wall. *Christ Century* 104:483-4 My 20-27 '87

Sex and the presidency. J. Alter. il *Newsweek* 109:26 My 4 '87

Sex and the presidency [Life polls America] M. Dubrow and others. il *Life* 10:70-2+ Ag '87

Sex, privacy and journalism [G. Hart case] T. Griffith. il por *Time* 129:90 Je 8 '87

Should the press play vice cop? [cover story] N. Von Hoffman. *Nation* 244:835+ Je 20 '87

Sluicegate [press treatment of G. Hart scandal] H. Hertzberg. *New Repub* 196:11-12 Je 1 '87

The sting of scandal [G. Hart case and ramifications for Canada; cover story; special section; with editorial comment by Kevin Doyle] il pors *Macleans* 100:2, 24-8+ My 18 '87

The sudden fall of Gary Hart [cover story; special section] il pors *Newsweek* 109:22-8+ My 18 '87

This is what you thought: 63% say candidate's sex life is irrelevant [results of survey] *Glamour* 85:129 N '87

A visitation of phantoms [G. Hart's televised apology] M. Kaus. il pors *Newsweek* 110:32-3 S 21 '87

X-rated politicians: going public with private lies [G. Hart] B. G. Harrison. *Mademoiselle* 93:234 S '87

Anecdotes, facetiae, satire, etc.

A truly Hart-stopping chickadee. A. Fotheringham. il *Macleans* 100:56 My 18 '87

Speechwriters and speechwriting

The Democrats' script for 1988 [model for acceptance speech at Democratic convention] R. Shrum. *Harpers* 275:14+ S '87

Notes on a brief campaign [G. Hart's speechwriter] P. Tauber. il *N Y Times Mag* p48-50+ My 31 '87

Wives

All the candidates' wives. M. Orth. il *Vogue* 177:394-5+ N '87

First Ladies in waiting. J. Conant and E. Clift. il *Newsweek* 110:20+ Ag 17 '87

The other hot race for the White House. H. Rainie. il *U S News World Rep* 103:34-6 S 28 '87

Presidential Commission on AIDS (U.S.) *See* United States. Presidential Commission on AIDS

Presidential debates

See also

Debategate case

Are we having any fun yet? G. F. Will. il *Newsweek* 110:88 N 9 '87

Debate distress? Call the spin doctors. E. Clift. il *Newsweek* 110:51 D 14 '87

Debate strategies. L. Howard. il *Newsweek* 110:6 N 2 '87

Democratic second string [Firing line debate] M. McDonald. il *Macleans* 100:12-14 Jl 13 '87

G.O.P. follies. H. Hertzberg. *New Repub* 197:15-17 N 23 '87

The great debate spate. W. Shapiro. il *Time* 130:15 S 7 '87

Heigh-ho, heigh-ho [Firing line debate] *Natl Rev* 39:16 Jl 31 '87

'I am not a dwarf' [Firing line debate] J. Klein. il *N Y* 20:12-13 Jl 20 '87

Jesse Jackson stands tall in first Democrats debate [Firing line debate] D. M. Cheers. il pors *Jet* 72:4+ Jl 20 '87

Of dwarfs and Giants [Democratic candidates] D. Seligman. il *Fortune* 116:220 O 12 '87

On the Firing line, mostly blanks. W. Shapiro. il *Time* 130:16 Jl 13 '87

Parade of the seven pygmies [Firing line appearance] M. Kramer. il *U S News World Rep* 103:18 Jl 13 '87

Presidential debates—*cont.*

Saying bye-bye to the wimp factor [G. Bush's performance in Republican debate] M. Kramer. il por *U S News World Rep* 103:46 N 9 '87

Six in Houston [Republican candidates] *Natl Rev* 39:18 D 4 '87

Throwing the 'long bomb' [debate between P. Du Pont and B. Babbitt] M. Kaus. pors *Newsweek* 109:20 Je 8 '87

Tuesday night Patball. H. Hertzberg. *New Repub* 197:9-10 D 21 '87

TV's week: of gab and *glasnost*. R. Zoglin. il por *Time* 130:67-8 D 14 '87

The unbeaten Bush. A. Brummer. il *World Press Rev* 34:64 D '87

The vox pop hit parade. H. Fineman. il *Newsweek* 110:17 Ag 10 '87

When worlds collide. J. Klein. il por *N Y* 20:35-6+ D 14 '87

Yapping from the right [Republican debate] W. Shapiro. il *Time* 130:31 N 9 '87

Presidential elections *See* Presidents—Election
Presidential entertaining *See* Government entertaining
Presidential helicopters *See* Helicopters, Government
Presidential Medal of Freedom *See* Medal of Freedom
Presidential power *See* Presidents—Powers and duties
Presidential press corps *See* Presidents—Press relations
Reagan, Ronald, 1911—Press relations

Presidential primaries

The favorite-son myth. J. McLaughlin. *Natl Rev* 39:24 Jl 3 '87

New Hampshire

Aide to Kemp dismissed for making racial slurs [state senator J. Chandler] *Jet* 73:37 S 28 '87

Southern States

The South will rise again. M. Cleland. por *U S News World Rep* 102:5 Ja 19 '87

Super Tuesday: a day of reckoning for Democrats? G. Borger. il *U S News World Rep* 102:21 Ap 20 '87

Super Tuesday, super mistake [March 8, 1988] J. McLaughlin. *Natl Rev* 39:24 Ap 24 '87

Presidential Young Investigators Awards

NSF honors Rabi and Witten, names Young Investigators. il *Phys Today* 40:95-6 S '87

Presidents

See also

Carter, Jimmy, 1924-
Eisenhower, Dwight D. (Dwight David), 1890-1969
Ford, Gerald R., 1913-
Grant, Ulysses S. (Ulysses Simpson), 1822-1885
Hoover, Herbert, 1874-1964
Jefferson, Thomas, 1743-1826
Johnson, Lyndon B. (Lyndon Baines), 1908-1973
Kennedy, John F. (John Fitzgerald), 1917-1963
Lincoln, Abraham, 1809-1865
Madison, James, 1751-1836
Monroe, James, 1758-1831
Nixon, Richard M. (Richard Milhous), 1913-
Reagan, Ronald, 1911-
Roosevelt, Franklin D. (Franklin Delano), 1882-1945

Fade to black [provisional nature of American presidency] L. H. Lapham. *Harpers* 274:8+ My '87

Four presidents challenge America [special section] il *Life* 10:24-31 O '87

Grading the presidents [civil rights records; views of T. Marshall] por *Newsweek* 110:33 S 21 '87

A president in trouble—so what's new? W. S. Parks. por *U S News World Rep* 102:8 Ja 26 '87

The presidential follies. I. F. Fredman. il *Am Herit* 38:38-43 S/O '87

Presidents, imperial and otherwise. G. C. Ward. il *Am Herit* 38:18+ My/Je '87

President's weather. D. M. Ludlum. *Ctry J* 14:76-7 Mr '87

Thurgood Marshall ranks Reagan last among U.S. presidents he observed. il por *Jet* 73:12-13 S 28 '87

U.S. presidents on war and peace. O. Berger. il *Saturday Evening Post* 259:36+ Ja/F '87

Advisers

See Presidential advisers

Age

See also

Reagan, Ronald, 1911—Age

Archives

See also

Nixon, Richard M. (Richard Milhous), 1913—Archives

Reagan, Ronald, 1911—Archives

Bibliography

Summer reading for candidates [recommendations by D. Boorstin] H. Sidey. bibl il por *Time* 130:21 Ag 3 '87

Collectibles

McKinley to Reagan: collecting U.S. presidents [inaugural medals] A. Schwartz. il *Antiques Collect Hobbies* 92:79-80 S '87

Correspondence

See also

Truman, Harry S., 1884-1972—Correspondence

Discipline

No confidence [call for no confidence in presidency mechanism in wake of Iran arms scandal] M. Kaus. *New Repub* 196:15-16 Mr 23 '87

Election

See also

Presidential campaigns
Presidential candidates
Voting

Presidential elections and democratic persuasions [special section] bibl *Society* 24:29-62 My/Je '87

The right not to know [universal poll-closing time bill] D. Olin. *New Repub* 197:18-19 Ag 10-17 '87

Why the Democrats lose elections [cover story] G. F. Will. il *Natl Rev* 39:28-9+ D 18 '87

Health

See also

Reagan, Ronald, 1911—Health

Homes

See also

Adams, John, 1735-1826—Homes
Carter, Jimmy, 1924—Homes
Lincoln, Abraham, 1809-1865—Homes
Monroe, James, 1758-1831—Homes
Nixon, Richard M. (Richard Milhous), 1913—Homes
Reagan, Ronald, 1911—Homes
Roosevelt, Franklin D. (Franklin Delano), 1882-1945—Homes
Roosevelt, Theodore, 1858-1919—Homes
Washington, George, 1732-1799—Homes

Inaugurations

McKinley to Reagan: collecting U.S. presidents [inaugural medals] A. Schwartz. il *Antiques Collect Hobbies* 92:79-80 S '87

Nomination

Farewell to reform—almost. A. Ranney. bibl *Society* 24:29-38 My/Je '87

Manufacturing the next president [Harper's forum simulating process of 1988 Democratic nomination] il *Harpers* 275:43-54 D '87

Powers and duties

See also

Pardon
Veto
War and emergency powers
War Powers Resolution

The chains of liberty [address, September 17, 1987] E. S. Muskie. *Vital Speeches Day* 54:4-7 O 15 '87

Disease of distrust [presidential and congressional duties in foreign policy] D. Gergen. il *U S News World Rep* 103:64 Jl 27 '87

Does the U.S. president have the right to cancel a treaty? [mutual defense treaty with Taiwan] T. Fung. il *Sch Update* 120:40 S 18 '87

Foreign affairs and the Constitution. L. Henkin. bibl f *Foreign Aff* 66:284-310 Wint '87/'88

Fragmentation of powers: have the arguments preserved liberty or brought government to a stalemate? H. Sidey. il *Time* 130:36-7 Jl 6 '87

Global intervention and a new imperial presidency. T. G. Carpenter. il *USA Today (Periodical)* 115:10-18 Mr '87

The imperial temptation: Reagan's presidency succumbs. A. M. Schlesinger. *New Repub* 196:17 Mr 16 '87

Letter from Washington [Iran-contra affair] E. Drew. *New Yorker* 63:75-6+ Je 22 '87

Notes and comment [question of presidential responsibility for actions of staff] *New Yorker* 63:21 Jl 27 '87

The paranoid presidency. C. Lasch. *Cent Mag* 20:42-8 Jl/Ag '87

Personal politics. J. C. Alexander. *New Repub* 196:12-13 Ap 6 '87

The president and the Secretary of State. T. C. Sorensen. *Foreign Aff* 66:231-48 Wint '87/'88

Shrinking the Oval Office [state of the presidency] M. Elfin. il *U S News World Rep* 103:26-9 D 7 '87

Who's in charge here? [Congress's role in foreign policy] T. Jacoby. il *Newsweek* 110:18 Jl 27 '87

Presidents—Powers and duties—cont.
Your Constitution: can the president ban private arms sales? D. Pawelek. *Sch Update* 119:20 Mr 9 '87
Press conferences
See also
Lincoln, Abraham, 1809-1865—Press conferences
Reagan, Ronald, 1911—Press conferences
Press relations
See also
Nixon, Richard M. (Richard Milhous), 1913—Press relations
Reagan, Ronald, 1911—Press relations
Of many things [S. Donaldson] G. W. Hunt. *America* 156:inside cover My 9 '87
Pushiness we can respect [S. Donaldson] J. Powell. *Wash Mon* 19:55-6 F '87
Privileges and immunities
See also
Executive privilege (Government information)
Protection
See also
Reagan, Ronald, 1911—Protection
Public relations
See also
Reagan, Ronald, 1911—Public relations
The paranoid presidency. C. Lasch. *Cent Mag* 20:42-8 Jl/Ag '87
A republic of souls: puritanism and the American presidency. R. Sennett. il *Harpers* 275:41-6 Jl '87
Sending messages, getting replies. K. L. Schlozman and S. Verba. *Society* 24:48-55 My/Je '87
Relations with Congress
See also
Reagan, Ronald, 1911—Relations with Congress
Religion
See also
Jefferson, Thomas, 1743-1826—Religion
Madison, James, 1751-1836—Religion
Reagan, Ronald, 1911—Religion
Sexual behavior
Sex and the presidency. J. Alter. il *Newsweek* 109:26 My 4 '87
Sex and the presidency [Life polls America] M. Dubrow and others. il *Life* 10:70-2+ Ag '87
Upstairs at the White House. H. Sidey. il por *Time* 129:20 My 18 '87
Speechwriters and speechwriting
See also
Reagan, Ronald, 1911—Speechwriters and speechwriting
Sports
See also
Nixon, Richard M. (Richard Milhous), 1913—Sports
Staff
See also
Reagan, Ronald, 1911—Staff
Firing is hard to do [reluctance of presidents to fire officials and staff members] il *Time* 129:15 Mr 2 '87
President Nunn's team. G. F. Will. il *Newsweek* 110:74 Ag 3 '87
Tales from the top: inside the White House with eight former presidential aides [excerpt from Chief of staff; cover story] il *Wash Mon* 19:23-7+ Ap '87
Victims of good fortune. M. Greenfield. il *Newsweek* 110:68 D 28 '87
State of the Union messages
See also
Reagan, Ronald, 1911—State of the Union messages
Statues, portraits, etc.
See also
Monroe, James, 1758-1831—Statues, portraits, etc.
Washington, George, 1732-1799—Statues, portraits, etc.
Term
Eight (years) is enough. G. F. Will. il *Newsweek* 110:92 N 23 '87
Transportation
See also
Airplanes, Government
Automobiles, Government
Helicopters, Government
Wives
First Helpmate. A. McCarthy. il *Commonweal* 114:230-1 Ap 24 '87
First Lady or second fiddle [symposium] il *Ladies Home J* 104:66+ Ag '87
Reflections on life in a fishbowl. M. Dobbin. il *U S News World Rep* 103:37-8 S 28 '87

Too old, too bold, too pushy, too plastic—First Ladies hear it all, but never 'she's perfect!' [interview with B. B. Caroli] M. Wilhelm. il por *People Wkly* 27:93-4+ My 18 '87
When the First Lady speaks her mind. R. Bourne. il *Am Herit* 38:108-9 S/O '87
Anecdotes, facetiae, satire, etc.
The New First Lady. R. Cohen. *New Yorker* 63:36-7 My 18 '87
United States
See Presidents
Presidents, College *See* College presidents
President's Commission on Americans Outdoors (U.S.) *See* United States. President's Commission on Americans Outdoors
President's Commission on Defense Management *See* United States. President's Commission on Defense Management
President's Foreign Intelligence Advisory Board (U.S.) *See* United States. President's Foreign Intelligence Advisory Board
Presley, Deborah
about
Daughters of the King? D. Chu. il pors *People Wkly* 27:28-31 Je 22 '87
Presley, Desirée
about
Are you lonesome tonight? [excerpt] L. De Barbin and D. Matera. il pors *Redbook* 169:106-8+ Jl '87
Daughters of the King? D. Chu. il pors *People Wkly* 27:28-31 Je 22 '87
Presley, Elvis, 1935-1977
about
Amazing Graceland. V. Balfour. il pors *Life* 10:44-6+ S '87
Are you lonesome tonight? [excerpt] L. De Barbin and D. Matera. il pors *Redbook* 169:106-8+ Jl '87
Critics dispute Elvis as king of rock 'n' roll. il por *Jet* 72:53 Ag 31 '87
Daughters of the King? D. Chu. il pors *People Wkly* 27:28-31 Je 22 '87
Elvis is back, again. S. Pond. il pors *Roll Stone* p79+ S 10 '87
Elvis Presley: 'Elvis' NBC TV, December 3rd, 1968. D. Fricke. il pors *Roll Stone* p53+ Je 4 '87
Forever Elvis [cover story] J. Miller. il pors *Newsweek* 110:48-54+ Ag 3 '87
Greetings from Graceland. B. Greene. il por *Esquire* 108:53-4+ D '87
Honoring a pop legend. N. Jennings. il por *Macleans* 100:50 Ag 17 '87
A hot property. L. Fleischer. *Publ Wkly* 231:69 Mr 13 '87
The King is dead, but his rich legacy still grows. J. P. Shapiro. il *U S News World Rep* 103:56 Ag 24 '87
The King of Rock keeps on rollin' [cover story] R. Wolmuth. il pors *People Wkly* 28:84-6+ Ag 17 '87
So long on Lonely Street. J. Cocks. il pors *Time* 130:78 Jl 20 '87
Two Presley books commemorate his musical immortality. il pors *Publ Wkly* 231:49 Je 5 '87
Anecdotes, facetiae, satire, etc.
From 100 Elvis stories. L. Walker. *New Yorker* 63:38-9 N 2 '87
Thanks to a Detroit dee jay, even death hasn't stopped Elvis from turning out more Presleys [fake "daughter of Elvis Presley" certificates issued to raise funds for hospital; work of D. Purtan] il por *People Wkly* 28:45 Jl 27 '87
Collectibles
Elvis' great career move. P. Tai. il pors *Money* 16:30-1 Ag '87
Photographs and photography
Elvis world [excerpts] J. Stern and M. Stern. il *Ladies Home J* 104:53-6 Ag '87
The King is gone but not forgotten. K. Loder. il pors *Roll Stone* p29-33 Ag 13 '87
Presley, Priscilla Beaulieu
about
Her life since Elvis: Priscilla Presley. B. Davidson. il pors *McCalls* 145:12-14+ Mr '87
Priscilla Presley just gets more gorgeous [interview] E. Byron. il pors *Redbook* 168:8+ Ja '87
Presley pieces [dance] See Dance reviews—Single works
Press, Frank
about
Reelected to lead Academy, Press talks about science issues [interview] I. Goodwin. por *Phys Today* 40:47-52 Ap '87

Press

   See also

   Aged and the press
   AIDS (Disease) and the press
   Baseball players—Press relations
   Black press
   Blacks and the press
   Communications satellites—Journalistic use
   Confidential communications—Press
   Drugs and the press
   Foreign news
   Freedom of the press
   Government and the press
   Homeless and the press
   Journalistic ethics
   Minorities and the press
   Newspapers
   Palestinian Arab press
   Presidents—Press relations
   Reagan, Ronald, 1911——Press relations
   Terrorism and the press
Media. E. Diamond. See issues of New York beginning January 28, 1985
Newswatch. T. Griffith. See issues of Time

Press and art *See* Art news
Press and blacks *See* Blacks and the press
Press and business *See* Business and the press
Press and crime *See* Crime and the press
Press and disarmament
Arms control. il *World Press Rev* 34:7 S '87
Arms control. il *World Press Rev* 34:8 O '87
Protocol and peace [J. Reston's comments on proposed INF Treaty] W. F. Buckley. *Natl Rev* 39:54 Je 5 '87
USA today wins peace award [Olive Branch Award] *USA Today (Periodical)* 116:4 Ag '87
Views on arms. il *World Press Rev* 34:12-13 Je '87
Press and economics *See* Economic news
Press and education *See* Educational news
Press and feminism
Media savvy. G. Blair and C. C. Mann. *Ms* 16:40+ Jl/Ag '87
Press and government *See* Government and the press
Press and minorities *See* Minorities and the press
Press and music *See* Music news
Press and politics
   See also
   Newspapers and politics
   Presidents—Press relations
   Reagan, Ronald, 1911——Press relations
Again, sex and politics [disclosures concerning R. Celeste, B. Frank and J. Jackson] C. O'Connor. il por *Newsweek* 109:33 Je 15 '87
Are the sex lives of all politicians now fair game? [cases of G. Hart and R. Celeste] A. P. Sanoff. il por *U S News World Rep* 102:12 Je 15 '87
Beat the devil. A. Cockburn. See issues of The Nation
Betrayal. H. S. Scott. *New Repub* 197:12-13 D 14 '87
Boston diarist [press treatment of G. Hart] H. Hertzberg. *New Repub* 196:42 Je 15 '87
Can the media be reformed? S. Garment. *Commentary* 84:37-43 Ag '87
Can the press tell the truth? D. McDonald. il por *Cent Mag* 20:19-32 S/O '87
Character cops on patrol [G. Hart case] J. Alter. il *Newsweek* 109:26-7 My 18 '87
Cuomo and those rumors: getting to the bottom of all the 'Mob' talk [cover story] N. Pileggi. il pors *N Y* 20:44-8+ N 2 '87
The fall of Joe Biden. J. Alter and H. Fineman. il por *Newsweek* 110:28 O 5 '87
Femme is fatal [G. Hart scandal] B. Ehrenreich and J. O'Reilly. *New Repub* 196:15-16 Je 1 '87
Fighting for their right to the party [Democratic candidates in Iowa] W. Greider. il *Roll Stone* p93-4+ N 19 '87
Fresh-baked political wisdom [Presidential Campaign Hotline compendium of political news and analysis] M. Kaus. il *Newsweek* 110:83 N 2 '87
Full disclosure, semi-outrage [New York times survey of presidential candidates] L. Zuckerman. il *Time* 129:67 Je 22 '87
The Gary Hart affair: the media's role. J. B. Judis. *Current* 297:28-32 N '87
Gary Hart and the press: can the media be reformed? S. Garment. *Current* 298:11-17 D '87
George Will among the polysyllables. W. A. Henry. il por *Esquire* 107:87-92 Ja '87
Gotcha! The media's frenzied patrol of the candidates [presidential candidates] E. Diamond. il *N Y* 20:50-3 O 26 '87

Hart's problem & ours [press treatment of scandal] W. F. Buckley. *Natl Rev* 39:55 Je 5 '87
The hunt for the killer anecdote. H. Rainie. il *U S News World Rep* 103:27-8 N 23 '87
Invisible man [reluctance of press to acknowledge J. Jackson as front-runner] A. Cockburn. *Nation* 244:708-9 My 30 '87
Journalistic ethics [discussion of August 1987 article, Can the media be reformed?] S. Garment. *Commentary* 84:2+ D '87
Keeping the press at bay [G. Hart] L. Zuckerman. il *Time* 130:18 D 28 '87
Look out for the ideolog! [media's use of ideologue to characterize personages struggling for influence in the Reagan White House] D. Seligman. il *Fortune* 116:169-70 D 21 '87
The necrophiles [liberal journalists uncovering "truths" about liberalism's past] J. L. Hess. *Nation* 244:37-8 Ja 17 '87
New morality, new journalism [coverage of G. Hart scandal] *Natl Rev* 39:15 Je 5 '87
On the zipper beat [press coverage of G. Hart scandal] *New Repub* 196:4+ My 25 '87
One thing is certain [Nexis data base searches] *New Repub* 196:4+ F 2 '87
The petty inquisitors. M. Charen. il *Natl Rev* 39:36+ D 18 '87
The press and the public discourse [cover story; with discussion] J. W. Carey. il por *Cent Mag* 20:4-32 Mr/Ap '87
The press, the process, and Gary Hart [address, May 29, 1987] O. C. Henkel. *Vital Speeches Day* 53:697-700 S 1 '87
Private lives and public people [repercussions from the G. Hart sex scandal] M. McDonald. il por *Macleans* 100:28-9 S 21 '87
Private lives, public figures [G. Hart case] G. Borger. il *U S News World Rep* 102:20-1+ My 18 '87
Private lives, public values [G. Hart case] M. Greenfield. il *Newsweek* 109:92 My 18 '87
Private sex and public exposure [G. Hart case] G. Bain. il *Macleans* 100:48 My 25 '87
Rethinking the fair game rules [press coverage of presidential candidates] L. I. Barrett. il *Time* 130:76+ N 30 '87
The search for personal flaws [press treatment of presidential candidates] J. Alter. il *Newsweek* 110:79 O 19 '87
Sex, privacy and journalism [G. Hart case] T. Griffith. il por *Time* 129:90 Je 8 '87
Sexual hysteria [press coverage of politicians' sex lives] E. Diamond. il *N Y* 20:14-16 Je 22 '87
Should the press play vice cop? [cover story] N. Von Hoffman. *Nation* 244:835+ Je 20 '87
Sluicegate [press treatment of G. Hart scandal] H. Hertzberg. *New Repub* 196:11-12 Je 1 '87
Stakeouts and shouted questions [Miami herald's stakeout of Gary Hart's townhouse] R. Zoglin. il *Time* 129:28-9 My 18 '87
The sting of scandal [G. Hart case and ramifications for Canada; cover story; special section; with editorial comment by Kevin Doyle] il pors *Macleans* 100:2, 24-8+ My 18 '87
The story that still nags at me [press coverage of E. Muskie's emotional reaction to W. Loeb's attacks in invisible man union leader, 1972; excerpt from Behind the front page] D. S. Broder. il *Wash Mon* 19:29-32+ F '87
That's entertainment: public scrutiny & the press. J. Garvey. il *Commonweal* 114:378-9 Je 19 '87
Voyeurism in politics. J. Boyle. por *Newsweek* 109:8 My 25 '87
World beat. J. R. Moskin. See issues of World Press Review through April 1987
The world looks at. See issues of World Press Review

Anecdotes, facetiae, satire, etc.
The character issue. *New Repub* 197:6+ O 26 '87
The New York idea [Inner Circle show presented by New York City press] A. Logan. *New Yorker* 63:84-6+ Mr 23 '87
Running on empty. A. A. Rooney. il *N Y Times Mag* p26 N 8 '87

Angola
Birth of a Soviet satellite. B. Amiel. il *Macleans* 100:9 Ag 17 '87

Canada
Paying homage to a best friend [G. Jonas] B. Amiel. il *Macleans* 100:9 My 25 '87
The press and a new puritanism. G. Bain. il *Macleans* 100:48 N 23 '87

Press and politics—Canada—*cont.*

The sting of scandal [G. Hart case and ramifications for Canada; cover story; special section; with editorial comment by Kevin Doyle] il pors *Macleans* 100:2, 24-8+ My 18 '87

An unflattering portrait of Mulroney [M. Gratton's So what are the boys saying?] M. Rose. il por *Macleans* 100:17 S 28 '87

Chile

The tricoteuse of counterrevolution [S. Christian's reporting] A. Cockburn. *Nation* 245:44-5 Jl 18-25 '87

Great Britain

On the stump with the Iron Lady [M. Thatcher] B. Amiel. il *Macleans* 100:9 Je 22 '87

Israel

The focus on Israel. T. L. Friedman. il *N Y Times Mag* p14-19+ F 1 '87

Israel enjoys silent airwaves. M. R. Halton. il *Christ Century* 104:1111-12 D 9 '87

Twenty years on. A. Cockburn. *Nation* 245:45 Jl 18-25 '87

Nicaragua

Beat the devil [pro contra reporting by W. Branigin of the Washington post] A. Cockburn. *Nation* 244:790-1 Je 13 '87

Beat the devil [reporting on death of B. E. Linder] A. Cockburn. *Nation* 244:636-7 My 16 '87

Cover-up at 'The New York review' [criticism of R. Leiken's reports from Nicaragua by Tony Jenkins] A. Cockburn. *Nation* 245:9 Jl 4-11 '87

LeMoyne's progress [J. LeMoyne's Nicaraguan coverage in New York times] A. Cockburn. *Nation* 244:423 Ap 4 '87

Miranda's tempest [Nicaraguan defector R. Miranda used to manipulate U.S. press] A. Cockburn. *Nation* 245:780-1 D 26 '87-Ja 2 '88

Reagan and Hegel. A. Cockburn. *Nation* 244:709 My 30 '87

Shamed [R. Leiken's reporting criticized by Tony Jenkins] A. Cockburn. *Nation* 245:79 Ag 1-8 '87

The war that no one can cover [reporting on the contras] J. Borrell. il *Time* 129:60 F 16 '87

United States

See Press and politics

Press and terrorism *See* Terrorism and the press

Press and the aged *See* Aged and the press

Press and the church *See* Church and the press

Press and the environment *See* Environmental news

Press and the homeless *See* Homeless and the press

Press law

See also

Confidential communications—Press

Libel and slander

Press photography *See* Photography, Journalistic

Press releases

See also

Government and the press

Fit to print [getting press releases published] G. P. Tyson and others. *Des Arts Educ* 88:13-16 Jl/Ag '87

The press release [theater events] C. Boneau. il *Theatre Crafts* 21:92+ N '87

Presser, Jackie

about

Letter from Washington. Cato. *Natl Rev* 39:13 Jl 31 '87

Presses

See also

Printing presses

Pressler, Larry

Libya [statement, November 19, 1986] *Dep State Bull* 87:87-90 Ja '87

Should Congress approve the Fairness Doctrine? [excerpts from remarks, April 21, 1987] *Congr Dig* 66:246+ O '87

Pressley, DeLores May- *See* May-Pressley, DeLores

Pressley, Patsy V.

Families that work. il *Essence* 17:75-7+ Mr '87

Pressman, Carol

about

Natural instincts. I. C. Selinger. il por *Work Woman* 12:54-5 Mr '87

Pressman, Edward

about

The Hollywood Way. S. Flack. por *Forbes* 139:174+ Je 1 '87

Pressure

See also

High pressure (Science)

Pressure, Atmospheric *See* Atmospheric pressure

Pressure (Psychology) *See* Stress

Pressure canning *See* Canning and preserving

Pressure groups *See* Special interest groups

Pressure suits

See also

Spacesuits

Pressure washers

Do power washers really work? M. Thompson. il *Fam Handyman* 37:81-2 Jl/Ag '87

Pressurized water reactors *See* Nuclear reactors

Preston, Astrid

about

Astrid Preston. M. Schipper. il *Art News* 86:50 My '87

Astrid Preston at Patty Aande. R. L. Pincus. il *Art Am* 75:191 O '87

Preston, Cheryl

about

Jury awards $900,000 to black female officer in Detroit police case. *Jet* 72:33 Ap 27 '87

Preston, Don

about

Don Preston: synthesizer from Apocalypse now to Zappa. J. Woodard. il por *Down Beat* 54:25-7 Ag '87

Preston, Douglas J.

A daring gamble in the Gobi Desert took the jackpot. il pors *Smithsonian* 18:94-8+ D '87

Preston, Frances W.

about

In the music biz, a star behind the scenes. D. L. Dennis. il por *Fortune* 115:77-8 Ja 5 '87

Preston, Richard

Dark time. *New Yorker* 63:64+ O 26 '87

Prestwich, Glenn D.

Chemistry of pheromone and hormone metabolism in insects. bibl f il *Science* 237:999-1006 Ag 28 '87

Pretenders (Musical group)

The Chrissie Hynde story: sex & drugs & rock 'n' roll & politics & motherhood & vegetables. R. Wolmuth. il pors *People Wkly* 27:68+ Mr 23 '87

The Pretenders [performance in New Orleans] S. Bloom. il *Roll Stone* p34 Mr 26 '87

Pretrial detention *See* Preventive detention

Pretrial publicity *See* Crime and the press

Prevention of accidents *See* Accidents—Prevention

Prevention of crime *See* Crime prevention

Prevention of cruelty to animals *See* Animals—Treatment

Prevention of suicide *See* Suicide—Prevention

Preventive detention

First jail, then a trial [Supreme Court upholds preventive detention] il *Newsweek* 109:19 Je 8 '87

First the sentence, then the trial [Supreme Court ruling] R. Lacayo. il *Time* 129:69 Je 8 '87

High Court backs jailing without bail; Justice Thurgood Marshall dissents. por *Jet* 72:4 Je 15 '87

No bail for the baddest [Supreme Court ruling] T. Gest. il *U S News World Rep* 102:12 Je 8 '87

Preventive medicine *See* Medicine, Preventive

Previn, André, 1929-

about

André Previn: recipient of the 1987 Mabel Mercer Award. H. Kupferberg. il pors *Stereo Rev* 52:63-7 F '87

Previte, Bobby

about

Bobby Previte. B. Milkowski. il por *Down Beat* 54:54-5 D '87

Prewitt, C. T., and others

New opportunities in synchrotron X-ray crystallography. bibl f il *Science* 238:312-19 O 16 '87

Prial, Frank J.

Wine. See occasional issues of The New York Times Magazine

Price, Bonni

17 boffo things to do on prom night (instead of going to prom). il *Seventeen* 46:172-3 My '87

Price, H. H.

Country medicine. il *Gourmet* 47:58+ O '87

Price, J. William

The marsh that Arcata built. il *Sierra* 72:51-3 My/Je '87

Price, James F., and others

Wind-driven ocean currents and Ekman transport. bibl f il *Science* 238:1534-8 D 11 '87

Price, Jay

Beers with [interview with J. Kelly and B. Esiason] il pors *Sport Mag* 78:23-5 O '87

Beers with . . . [interview with M. Tyson] il por *Sport Mag* 78:25-6 My '87

Price, Jennifer
Dryland farmers say no to water. il *Progressive* 51:11 Jl '87

Price, Laurence
about
Family fun. J. Flint. il *Forbes* 140:246 D 14 '87

Price, Margaret, 1941-
about
Margaret Price sings Liszt gems. R. Freed. il por *Stereo Rev* 52:82 Jl '87
Natural instincts. P. G. Davis. il por *N Y* 20:111-12 N 16 '87

Price, Martin
about
A seed of prayer. M. Kane. il pors *Rodale's Org Gard* 34:80-2+ Mr '87

Price, Michael F.
about
Distressed merchandise. R. Phalon. por *Forbes* 139:180 Ap 6 '87
Falling off a limb at Harcourt. D. Zigas. por *Bus Week* p32 Jl 6 '87

Price, Reynolds, 1933-
about
A writer at his best. M. Ruhlman. il por *N Y Times Mag* p60-1+ S 20 '87

Price, Robert, 1932-
about
Running to stay in place. T. Pouschine. il por *Forbes* 139:133+ My 4 '87

Price, Robert E.
about
These penny-pinchers deliver a big bang for their bucks. C. S. Eklund and J. Flynn. pors *Bus Week* p52 My 4 '87

Price, Robert M.
about
How Bob Price is reprogramming Control Data. P. Houston. il pors *Bus Week* p102+ F 16 '87

Price, Sol, 1932-
about
Family fun. J. Flint. il por *Forbes* 140:246 D 14 '87

Price, T. Douglas (Theron Douglas), and Petersen, Erik Brinch
A Mesolithic camp in Denmark. il maps *Sci Am* 256:112-19+ Mr '87

Price, Theron Douglas *See* Price, T. Douglas (Theron Douglas)

Price, Walter
Irreplaceable. il pors *Opera News* 51:8-12 Mr 14 '87

Price Club *See* Price Co.

Price Co.
Family fun [L. Price sues father S. Price] J. Flint. il por *Forbes* 140:246 D 14 '87
These penny-pinchers deliver a big bang for their bucks [R. E. Price] C. S. Eklund and J. Flynn. pors *Bus Week* p52 My 4 '87

Price Communications Corp.
Running to stay in place. T. Pouschine. il por *Forbes* 139:133+ My 4 '87

Price cutting
See also
Discount houses (Retail trade)

Price-earnings ratios *See* Stocks—Price-earnings ratios

Price index futures
A glimpse today of tomorrow [Commodity Research Bureau's futures price index] S. W. Angrist. il *Forbes* 139:109 Ja 26 '87
A hedge against inflation [Consumer Price Index futures] J. Egan. *U S News World Rep* 102:56 F 2 '87

Price indexes
Baker's plan: no glitter [gold based price index] M. McNamee. por *Bus Week* p56 O 19 '87
The changes behind the CPI's new look [Consumer Price Index] G. Koretz. il *Bus Week* p24 Mr 2 '87
Comparison of the revised and the old CPI. M. L. Schmidt. il *Mon Labor Rev* 110:3-6 N '87
Consumer spending: how many are poor? [Consumer Price Index] *Society* 24:2 Jl/Ag '87
The CPI's new look [Consumer Price Index] il *Fortune* 115:9 Mr 16 '87
Golden promise [J. A. Baker's proposed commodity price index tied to gold] il *Natl Rev* 39:17-18 N 6 '87
Import price declines in 1986 reflected reduced oil prices. E. Gibbons and G. F. Halpin. bibl f il *Mon Labor Rev* 110:3-17 Ap '87
Investors should rejoice [J. A. Baker's proposed gold based price index] M. S. Forbes, Jr. il por *Forbes* 140 Sp Issue:29 O 26 '87

Jim Baker shakes up a little gold dust [proposed commodity price index tied to gold] *Newsweek* 110:66 O 12 '87
New basket of goods and services being priced in revised CPI. C. Mason and C. Butler. bibl f il *Mon Labor Rev* 110:3-22 Ja '87
New weight structure being used in Producer Price Index. A. Clem and W. Thomas. il *Mon Labor Rev* 110:12-21 Ag '87
Price data. See issues of Monthly Labor Review
Right price [Consumer Price Index] J. W. Merline. *Consum Res Mag* 70:38 My '87
Sharp drop in energy prices holds inflation in check during 1986. C. Howell and others. il *Mon Labor Rev* 110:3-9 My '87
This economic barometer has a broken spring [commodity price indexes] K. Pennar. il *Bus Week* p71 D 28 '87-Ja 4 '88
Why consumers still see inflation as a threat [Irwin L. Keller's nuisance index tracks small ticket items] G. Koretz. *Bus Week* p24 Mr 23 '87

Price maintenance by industry
See also
Freight rates
Petroleum—Prices

Price policies
'The best price in town'? What to do if it isn't. D. H. Dunn. il *Bus Week* p118 S 28 '87
Brockway's paradox [theories of J. M. Buchanan] G. P. Brockway. il *New Leader* 69:10-11 D 29 '86
Who's gored by gouging? H. Altman. il *Nations Bus* 75:6 Je '87
Why business is at a loss in a free market. R. Kuttner. *Bus Week* p18 S 28 '87

Price regulation by government
See also
Natural gas—Prices
Petroleum—Prices
Wage-price policy

Price-sales ratios *See* Stocks—Price-sales ratios

Price supports, Agricultural *See* Agricultural administration

Price-wage policy *See* Wage-price policy

Prices
See also
Cost and standard of living
Deflation (Finance)
Inflation (Finance)
Supply and demand
Wage-price policy
See also subhead Prices under various subjects
All that glitters . . . [commodities prices] G. Slutsker. il *Forbes* 139:33-4 Je 15 '87
Are exporters settling for a fast buck? W. B. Franklin and J. C. Cooper. il *Bus Week* p30 Ag 17 '87
The crosswinds buffeting commodity prices. G. Koretz. il *Bus Week* p28 Ja 26 '87
Debating the impact of higher materials costs [commodity prices] G. Koretz. il *Bus Week* p26 Je 8 '87
Dumping? Or just defending markets? [prices of imported goods] G. Slutsker. il *Forbes* 139:166+ My 18 '87
Guess who's stuck with the check [U.S. trade deficit results in higher prices for imported goods] B. Bauer. il *U S News World Rep* 102:52-3 F 2 '87
Imports cost more—and they'll keep going up. W. B. Franklin and J. C. Cooper. il *Bus Week* p43-4 My 18 '87
An inflationary sign does a disappearing act [commodity prices have leveled off] G. Koretz. il *Bus Week* p22 S 28 '87
Price rises do not an inflation cycle make [views of Joseph G. Carson and Jeffrey R. Leeds] G. Koretz. il *Bus Week* p30 My 11 '87
Raw materials haven't been bloodied much [no sign of recession yet in commodity prices] G. Koretz. il *Bus Week* p24 N 30 '87
Why Americans aren't likely to start buying American [import prices] L. Therrien. il *Bus Week* p34 N 23 '87

United States
See Prices

Pricing *See* Price policies

Prick up your ears [film] *See* Motion picture reviews—Single works

Pricketts Fort State Park (W. Va.) *See* Fortification—West Virginia

Prickleback fishing
Poke-poling for the homely but delicious monkeyface prickleback. il *Sunset* 179:56 S '87

Prickly pears

Walk on the dry side [coastal areas of New York and southern New England] J. E. Connolly. il *Conservationist* 42:26-7 Jl/Ag '87

Pride

Pride: a legend in your own mind. J. Shea. il *U S Cathol* 52:7-8 Ag '87

Pride & prejudice [drama] *See* Pownall, David, 1938-

Pride of Baltimore (Schooner)

Board finding on Pride of Baltimore. *Oceans* 20:58 My/Je '87

Pride of Baltimore [discussion of May/June 1987 article, Board finding on Pride of Baltimore] il *Oceans* 20:65 Jl/Ag '87

A question of stability. J. Lowenstein. il *Oceans* 20:72 Jl/Ag '87

Priesthood *See* Priests

Priestley, John

British election ceramics. bibl f il *Antiques* 131:1304-13 Je '87

Priests

See also

Black priests
Cardinals
Celibacy
Marriage of priests

The Pope's foot soldiers [B. Frawley and R. Dlugos, parish priests; cover story] J. Buckley. il pors *U S News World Rep* 103:60-4+ S 21 '87

Should a priest serve on a jury? V. A. Lapomarda. il *America* 156:495-6 Je 20-27 '87

Attitudes

Of many things [CBS-New York times poll] G. W. Hunt. *America* 157:146 S 26 '87

Health and hygiene

See also

AIDS (Disease) and priests

Heaven sent? [priests test vaccine for pregnant women that could prevent cytomegalovirus] D. Tonnessen. il *Health* 19:18 D '87

Political activities

The priest who fights the regime [J.-B. Aristide of Haiti; cover story] A. Wilentz. *Nation* 245:217+ S 12 '87

Sexual behavior

Homosexuality & the priesthood. R. P. McBrien. *Commonweal* 114:380-3 Je 19 '87

Homosexuality & the priesthood [discussion of June 19, 1987 article] R. P. McBrien. *Commonweal* 114:493-7 S 11 '87

Wanting a woman's hand to hold. J. Seligmann. il *Newsweek* 109:60 F 23 '87

Sports

A ring and a prayer [Mexican priest S. Gutierrez wrestles to earn money for orphanage] R. Reilly. il pors *Sports Illus* 67:88-92+ D 21 '87

Supply and demand

Lay ministers won't put priests out of business. W. F. Sullivan. *U S Cathol* 52:22-3 N '87

More thoughts about the declining number of vocations [discussion of December 13, 1986 article, A jubilarian reflects on the declining number of priests] R. F. McNamara. *America* 156:142-4 F 14 '87

Priests as lawyers

Dispensing forgiveness and justice in equal measure, Father Mike Callahan is a man of the cloth and the law. S. K. Reed. il pors *People Wkly* 28:143-4+ D 7 '87

Primack, Phil

Flight of the butterflies. il *Travel Holiday* 168:96 N '87

Primaries, Presidential *See* Presidential primaries

Primary education *See* Education, Elementary

Primary productivity (Biology) *See* Productivity, Biological

Primates

See also

Baboons
Chimpanzees
Gorillas
Man
Monkeys
Orangutans

Do animals read minds, tell lies? [deceptive behavior] R. Lewin. il *Science* 238:1350-1 D 4 '87

My close cousin the chimpanzee. R. Lewin. il *Science* 238:273-5 O 16 '87

Phylogenetic relations of humans and African apes from DNA sequences in the ψη-globin region. M. M. Miyamoto and others. bibl f il *Science* 238:369-73 O 16 '87

Prime Cable Corporation

Keeping the bankers at bay. D. Holder. il por *Channels* 7:55-6 My '87

Prime ministers

Sexual behavior

While Andreas Papandreou, Greece's prime minister, dallies with a dame, all *hellas* is breaking loose [affair with D. Liani] il pors *People Wkly* 28:62 O 26 '87

Prime numbers *See* Numbers, Prime

Prime rate *See* Interest (Economics)

Primerica Corp.

For Smith Barney, the go-go years have just begun. R. Mitchell. il por *Bus Week* p39-40 Je 8 '87

Jerry Tsai listens to his mother. C. Leinster. il por *Fortune* 116:82-4+ Ag 17 '87

Primetime (Firm)

Is this article worth $19,260? J. Alter. il por *Newsweek* 109:77 Ap 20 '87

Primitive and early church *See* Church history—Primitive and early church

Primitives (Puppets)

Post-Muppet Primitives. B. Weber. il por *N Y Times Mag* p78 Ag 16 '87

Primitivism in art

America's "primitive" dolls. M. Jailer. il *Antiques Collect Hobbies* 92:33-5 Ag '87

A naïf vision of paradise [paintings of M. Lepe] M. Kroll. il por *Américas* 39:20-4 S/O '87

Picasso's time of decisive encounters; tr. by Tom Repensek. P. Daix. il *Art News* 86:136-41 Ap '87

Primm, Beny

about

Fresh troops for president's AIDS panel. W. Booth. pors *Science* 238:1034 N 20 '87

Mandatory tests for AIDS? [interview] pors *U S News World Rep* 102:62 Mr 9 '87

Primola (New York, N.Y.: Restaurant) *See* New York (N.Y.)—Restaurants, nightclubs, bars, etc.

Primrose oil, Evening *See* Evening primrose oil

Prince

about

His Royal Badness, Inc. B. Barol. il por *Newsweek* 109:72-3 My 4 '87

Michael Jackson: Bad; Prince: Sign o' the times. D. Wolff. *Nation* 245:728-9 D 12 '87

Prince in Europe: a preview of his new show. K. Loder. il pors *Roll Stone* p11-12+ Jl 2 '87

Prince: U.S. tour, November 1982-March 1983. D. Fricke. il pors *Roll Stone* p113-14 Je 4 '87

Prince working on new full-length concert film. por *Jet* 72:53 Ag 31 '87

Prince's baffling brilliance. K. Loder. il *Roll Stone* p145-6 Ap 23 '87

Prince's intriguing women [cover story] L. Norment. il pors *Ebony* 43:162-3+ N '87

Prince's 'Sign o' times' highlights his European tour [cover story] il pors *Jet* 73:56-8 N 30 '87

Prince's sis says he stole lyrics from her. *Jet* 72:62 S 7 '87

Sign o' the times [film] Reviews

Roll Stone il p16 D 3 '87. A. DeCurtis

Prince, Dinah

Marriage in the '80s. il *N Y* 20:30-8 Je 1 '87

Street inspirations. il pors *N Y* 20:32-7 Ag 17 '87

Teaching s-e-x in school: the facts of life in Mrs. Roseman's class. il por *N Y* 20:56-8+ Ap 6 '87

Prince, Larry L.

about

Grease monkey's dream. K. Hannon. il por *Forbes* 140:193 N 30 '87

Prince, Richard, 1949-

about

Social science fiction [cover story; interview] J. Rian. il *Art Am* 75:86-95 Mr '87

Prince Edward Island

See also

Charlottetown (P.E.I.)
Drama festivals—Prince Edward Island
Indian River (P.E.I.)
Public health—Prince Edward Island

Bridges

See Bridges—Canada

Politics and government

Plans for an Island link. C. Barrett. il *Macleans* 100:18 N 30 '87

Violence on the Island [P. Pope resigns from legislature after admitting to beating a woman] M. Gee. por *Macleans* 100:12 Ja 19 '87

Prince Georges County (Md.)
County contracts
Black computer firm wins $15 million contract in Md. [Maxima] *Jet* 72:8 Jl 13 '87
Politics and government
Prince George's County, Md. Council gets woman leader [H. R. Pemberton] *Jet* 71:22 Ja 12 '87
Prince Leopold Island (N.W.T.)
See also
Birds—Prince Leopold Island (N.W.T.)
Princenthal, Nancy
Fragments and frames. il *Art Am* 75:144-5 My '87
On the waterfront. il *Art Am* 75:210-11+ Ap '87
The self in parts. il *Art Am* 75:170-1+ N '87
Social seating [cover story] bibl f il *Art Am* 75:130-7 Je '87
The princess bride [film] See Motion picture reviews—Single works
Princeton, Battle of, 1777
Trenton and Princeton. R. F. Snow. il *Am Herit* 38:26+ D '87
Princeton (N.J.)
Politics and government
Tough hide/soft heart? [Mayor B. Sigmund] L. Davis. *Vogue* 177:392 S '87
Savings and loan associations
See also
College Savings Bank
Princeton Air Link
Islander hopping. P. Scott. il *Flying* 114:46-8+ My '87
Princeton Review, Ltd.
"This isn't school". B. Kallen. il por *Forbes* 140:246+ N 16 '87
Princeton University
The graduate [B. Shields' transcript] il por *Life* 10:24-5 Ag '87
Great university presidents have to be miracle men [W. Bowen] M. S. Forbes. por *Forbes* 139:26 My 18 '87
A new kind of Tiger [new president H. Shapiro] por *Time* 129:77 My 11 '87
Quadrangle keep [Feinberg Hall] il *Archit Rec* 175:100-5 Mr '87
Those growls at Brooke's commencement weren't coming from the Princeton Tiger. il pors *People Wkly* 27:34-5 Je 22 '87
Princeton University. Dept. of History
The hot History Department. M. Silk. il pors *N Y Times Mag* p42-3+ Ap 19 '87
Principal, Victoria
Victoria's diet Principals [excerpt from The diet Principal] il pors *Redbook* 168:8+ F '87
Principal Group Ltd.
Accounting in the West [outraged investors demand inquiry] D. Jenish. il *Macleans* 100:20-1 Jl 27 '87
Giving business a bad name [D. Cormie] P. C. Newman. il por *Macleans* 100:35 Ag 17 '87
Picking up the pieces [Metropolitan Life's purchase offer for Principal Group's assets] J. Howse. il *Macleans* 100:26-7 Ag 31 '87
Principal's stunning loss. D. Jenish. il *Macleans* 100:30-1 Ag 24 '87
Threats of another failure. D. Jenish. il *Macleans* 100:23 Jl 13 '87
Principals, School See School superintendents and principals
Principles
Anecdotes, facetiae, satire, etc.
Beyond principles. R. Baker. il *N Y Times Mag* p16 Ag 2 '87
Prinn, Ronald G., and others
Atmospheric trends in methylchloroform and the global average for the hydroxyl radical. bibl f il *Science* 238:945-50 N 13 '87
Printed circuits
PC service. See issues of Radio-Electronics beginning July 1985
Design
Computer-aided routing of printed circuit boards [Lee's Algorithm] S. E. Belter. bibl il *Byte* 12:199-200+ Je '87
Designing PC boards on your computer (I). R. Grossblatt. il *Radio-Electron* 58 ComputerDigest:97-9 Je '87
Designing PC boards on your computer (II). R. Grossblatt. il *Radio-Electron* 58 ComputerDigest:69-71+ Ag '87
Printers (Computers) See Computers—Print-out equipment
Printing
See also
Computers—Printing use
Photography—Processing
Silk screen printing
Type and typefounding

The future of the printed word [symposium] il *USA Today (Periodical)* 115:88-90 Mr '87
History
See also
American Printing History Association
Printing industry
See also
Bitstream Inc.
Chas. P. Young Co.
Dickinson Press Inc.
George Banta Company, Inc.
R. R. Donnelley & Sons Co.
Semline, Inc.
Service Resources Corp.
Sorg Incorporated
W. A. Krueger Co.
Short runs—an update. *Publ Wkly* 231:60-1 Je 5 '87
Acquisitions and mergers
Pat Rooney's back—and he hasn't changed a bit [financial printing] A. Bianco. il por *Bus Week* p110-11 My 4 '87
Chain and franchise operations
Printing franchises: quick, growing. R. Hotch and D. Shipley. il *Nations Bus* 75:28-30 Jl '87
International aspects
Banta to print 85 titles for Brazil's Distribuidora. J. P. Frank. *Publ Wkly* 231:24 Ja 23 '87
Book manufacturing in Spain [assessment of potential for American publishers] R. Ross. il *Publ Wkly* 232:47-8+ D 4 '87
Spanish printers cast glances at U.S. market. R. Ross. il *Publ Wkly* 232:44+ N 20 '87
East Asia
Farewell to pirate printing in Asia? S. A. Taylor. il *Publ Wkly* 231:23-4 Ap 24 '87
Singapore
See also
Koon Wah Printing, Pte., Ltd.
Spain
Book manufacturing in Spain. R. Ross. il *Publ Wkly* 232:47-8+ D 4 '87
Spanish printers cast glances at U.S. market. R. Ross. il *Publ Wkly* 232:44+ N 20 '87
Printing ink
Soybean ink could print more profits for farmers. *Success Farm* 85:62P O '87
Printing machinery
Color separations: a new level of quality. J. P. Frank. il *Publ Wkly* 232:145-50 S 18 '87
Printing machinery and supplies industry
See also
Autotype U.S.A. (Firm)
Printing paper (Photography) *See* Photographic paper
Printing presses
Short runs—an update. *Publ Wkly* 231:60-1 Je 5 '87
Prints
See also
Portrait prints
Wood engraving
Botanical illustration. S. J. Zietz. il *Antiques* 131:600-13 Mr '87
Expanding your market with multiples [posters, prints, and reproductions based on paintings] M. S. Doherty. il *Am Artist* 51:52-9 My '87
New editions. il *Art News* 86:131-6 O '87
Prints, politics & people: The English satirical print, 1600-1832 [Chadwyck-Healey's seven volume collection of satirical prints] I. Roots. il *Hist Today* 37:47-53 Mr '87
Views of Edo: high and low [Hiroshige] K. Varnedoe. il *Art Am* 75:98-105 Jl '87
Collectors and collecting
Art for the pensioners' sake [prices of Japanese print collection of British Rail Pension Fund] L. Scheer. il *Forbes* 140:117-18 D 28 '87
Art: woodland prints. H. H. Broun. il *Archit Dig* 44:178-83 Je '87
Drawn to the masters—David Tunick. J. Kornbluth. il por *Archit Dig* 44:74+ My '87
The eighteenth-century French print. M. Forrest. il *Antiques Collect Hobbies* 92:58-60 Je '87
The pochoir prints of Charles Rahn Fry. J. Gruen. il por *Archit Dig* 44:94+ Ap '87
To win big on a print, bet on the artist. R. W. King. il *Bus Week* p178-9 My 25 '87
Exhibitions
Prints in the Golden Anniversary National Art Exhibition. il *Am Artist* 51:66-9 Je '87

Prints—cont.

Prices

See Art—Prices

Technique

See also
Lithography
Silk screen printing

Prinz, Bernhard
Causes of forest damage in Europe. bibl f il map *Environment* 29:10-15+ N '87

Prinzmetal, Jan
about
A tough assignment—working out inside. M. Kort. il por *Ms* 16:32 O '87

Prioli, R. P., and others
Similarity of cruzin, an inhibitor of Trypanosoma cruzi neuraminidase, to high-density lipoprotein. bibl f il *Science* 238:1417-19 D 4 '87

Prior, David B., and others
Turbidity current activity in a British Columbia fjord. bibl f il map *Science* 237:1330-3 S 11 '87

Prior, William E.
about
Almost Japanese. M. Kuntz. il por *Forbes* 139:179 Je 1 '87

Prison construction
Turning penance to profit [P. Eaton instructs other Delaware Correctional Center inmates] R. Arias. il por *People Wkly* 27:30-3 Mr 30 '87

Prison escapes *See* Escapes

Prison industries *See* Convict labor

Prison labor *See* Convict labor

Prison management industry
Jails could be Texas' next ten-gallon business. T. Vogel. il *Bus Week* p33 Ap 20 '87
'A person, not a number'. A. Press. il *Newsweek* 109:63 Je 29 '87

Prison mirror (Newspaper)
The best prison paper in the U.S.—bar none—turns 100. J. Kaufman. il por *People Wkly* 28:66+ O 5 '87
'Mirror' marks 100th year of reflecting prison life. *Jet* 72:40 S 7 '87

Prison mother, prison daughter [television program] See Television program reviews—Single works

Prison psychology
Building better jails [direct supervision facilities] R. Wener and others. bibl (p56) il *Psychol Today* 21:40-4+ Je '87
Growing old behind bars [aged prisoners] S. Chaneles. bibl (p62) il *Psychol Today* 21:46-51 O '87
In Massachusetts: theater therapy [Geese Company includes prisoners in performances] D. Brand. il *Time* 130:12+ N 9 '87

Prison publications
See also
Prison mirror (Newspaper)

Prison reform
Lock 'em up: America's all-purpose cure for crime [cover story] L. Rocawich. il *Progressive* 51:16-19 Ag '87

Prison riots
Come home to roost [Cuban prison riots] *Nation* 245:701 D 12 '87
A Cuban explosion [Marielitos seize two U.S. prisons] A. Press. il *Newsweek* 110:38-40 D 7 '87
The flames of fear [Marielitos riot in two U.S. prisons] B. Duffy. il *U S News World Rep* 103:20-2 D 7 '87
Lessons of the Cuban prison crisis: what the Marielitos won. G. Hackett. il *Newsweek* 110:53 D 14 '87
Miami's bishop Agustin Roman defuses a human time bomb to end the Cuban prison riots peacefully [Marielito uprising] R. Arias. il pors *People Wkly* 28:104-6 D 21 '87
Promises, promises [Marielitos and prison riots] E. Magnuson. il *Time* 130:36 D 14 '87
Revolt of the Cubans [Marielitos riot in two U.S. prisions] A. Bilski. il *Macleans* 100:24 D 7 '87
'This is a moment of peace' [Miami bishop A. Román helps end Cuban prisoner takeovers] *America* 157:468-9 D 19 '87
"We are the abandoned ones" [Cuban Marielitos riot in two U.S. prisons] J. V. Lamar, Jr. il *Time* 130:23-4 D 7 '87

Prison ships
NY prison ship boasts only convicts at sea. il *Jet* 73:36 S 28 '87

Prison theater
See also
Geese Company

Prisoners
See also
Black prisoners
Children of prisoners
Convict labor
Escapes
Ex-convicts
Mentally ill—Imprisonment
Parole
Political prisoners
Prisons
Refugee children—Imprisonment
Women prisoners
Growing old behind bars [aged prisoners] S. Chaneles. bibl (p62) il *Psychol Today* 21:46-51 O '87

Attitudes
A verdict by their peers [views of prison inmates on B. Goetz verdict] R. Blecker. il *Nation* 245:334-6 O 3 '87

Employment
See Convict labor

Health and hygiene
'AIDS: a bad way to die'. A. Press. il *Newsweek* 109:30 Mr 23 '87
AIDS behind bars—a prisoner's concern. H. Rowe. il *U S News World Rep* 102:7 F 2 '87

Political activities
Extremist groups seek recruits in prisons. I. Suall. il *USA Today (Periodical)* 116:22-8 S '87

Psychology
See Prison psychology

Recreation
Laurel and Hardy in the big house [Somers Prison chapter of Sons of the Desert folds in Connecticut] D. M. Kimmel. il pors *Film Comment* 23:2+ Jl/Ag '87

Rehabilitation
Foster grandparents go inside prison walls. E. Sklar and C. M. Carlson. il *Aging* no356:20-3 '87
Teaching convicts real street smarts. T. Gest. il *U S News World Rep* 102:72 My 18 '87

Religious life
See also
Church work with prisoners
Va. fed. judge says 'Rasta' cons must eat prison food. *Jet* 72:12 Ag 3 '87

Sexual behavior
Married N.Y. inmates get condoms to battle AIDS. *Jet* 71:38 Ja 26 '87

Sports
'They used to call me McEnroe' [satellite circuit tennis player, D. Herman, imprisoned for drug dealing] P. M. Coan. il *World Tennis* 34:20-1 My '87

Suicide
See Suicide

Treatment
See also
Torture
America's troubled prisons [special issue] il *Sch Update* 119:4-17 F 9 '87
Rough justice in Australia? [jail deaths of aborigines] S. Seibert. il *Newsweek* 110:34 Ag 31 '87
The toughest prison in America [Marion Federal Penitentiary] M. Satchell. il *U S News World Rep* 103:23-4 Jl 27 '87

Prisoners as air pilots
Teach a jailbird to fly [Big Spring Federal Prison Camp, Tex.] G. Haddaway. *Flying* 114:102 Ag '87

Prisoners as cowboys
These cowboys are convicts [taming wild mustangs at Colorado State Penitentiary] J. Willwerth. il *Time* 130:20 Ag 31 '87

Prisoners of war
See also
Vietnamese War, 1957-1975—Prisoners and prisons
World War, 1939-1945—Prisoners and prisons

Prisons
See also
Art in prisons
Black prisoners
Computers—Prison use
Mentally ill—Imprisonment
Parole
Preventive detention
Prison reform
Prison riots
Prisoners
Women prisoners
America's troubled prisons [special issue] il *Sch Update* 119:4-17 F 9 '87
Clubs fed: a guide [minimum security federal prisons] *Harpers* 274:24+ Ap '87

Prisons—*cont.*

Lock 'em up: America's all-purpose cure for crime [cover story] L. Rocawich. il *Progressive* 51:16-19 Ag '87

More rooms for the big house [alternative prison spaces used to deal with overcrowding] R. Woodbury. il *Time* 130:25 Ag 10 '87

Architecture

Building better jails [direct supervision facilities] R. Wener and others. bibl (p56) il *Psychol Today* 21:40-4+ Je '87

Crime and punishment [with introd. by Karen D. Stein] il *Archit Rec* 175:81-97 Ap '87

Collectibles

Museum [J. Baranyi's collection of New Jersey prison artifacts] *New Yorker* 63:34-6 N 23 '87

History

A 196-year push to make prisons work. K. Bair. il *Sch Update* 119:16-17 F 9 '87

How did our prisons get that way? R. T. Pray. bibl il *Am Herit* 38:92-6+ Jl/Ag '87

Officials and employees

When women do men's work [guarding both male and female prisoners in Canada] B. Amiel. il *Macleans* 100:9 O 12 '87

Race relations

Charges prisons ruled by 'institutional racism' [views of B. Ward] por *Jet* 73:22 N 16 '87

Australia

Rough justice in Australia? [jail deaths of aborigines] S. Seibert. il *Newsweek* 110:34 Ag 31 '87

California

Prison versus probation [report of Joan Petersilia and Susan Turner] *Society* 24:3 My/Je '87

A tough assignment—working out inside [J. Prinzmetal runs exercise program at California Institution for Women] M. Kort. il por *Ms* 16:32 O '87

Canada

When women do men's work [guarding both male and female prisoners] B. Amiel. il *Macleans* 100:9 O 12 '87

Colorado

These cowboys are convicts [taming wild mustangs at Colorado State Penitentiary] J. Willwerth. il *Time* 130:20 Ag 31 '87

Connecticut

See also
Somers (Conn.)—Prisons and reformatories

Delaware

Turning penance to profit [P. Eaton instructs other Delaware Correctional Center inmates in prison construction] R. Arias. il por *People Wkly* 27:30-3 Mr 30 '87

Georgia

See also
Atlanta (Ga.)—Prisons and reformatories
Jackson (Ga.)—Prisons and reformatories

Illinois

See also
Flora (Ill.)—Prisons and reformatories
Marion (Ill.)—Prisons and reformatories

Kentucky

See also
Lexington (Ky.)—Prisons and reformatories

Louisiana

Prison life: one convict's story [Louisiana State Penitentiary] T. R. Mason. il por *Sch Update* 119:6-7 F 9 '87

Massachusetts

In Massachusetts: theater therapy [Geese Company includes prisoners in performances] D. Brand. il *Time* 130:12+ N 9 '87

Michigan

See also
Detroit (Mich.)—Prisons and reformatories
Macomb County (Mich.)—Prisons and reformatories

Netherlands

Escape from a Dutch jail [Peruvian E. Barreto-Morales wanted by Canada for cocaine trafficking] D. Burke. por *Macleans* 100:44 Je 15 '87

Nevada

See also
Las Vegas (Nev.)—Prisons and reformatories

New Jersey

Museum [J. Baranyi's collection of prison artifacts] *New Yorker* 63:34-6 N 23 '87

New York (State)

See also
Binghamton (N.Y.)—Prisons and reformatories
New York (N.Y.)—Prisons and reformatories

Married N.Y. inmates get condoms to battle AIDS. *Jet* 71:38 Ja 26 '87

Prison parenting: a challenge for children's advocates [male prisoners] V. Bauhofer. il *Child Today* 16:15-16 Ja/F '87

Ontario

See also
Kingston (Ont.)—Prisons and reformatories

Pennsylvania

See also
Philadelphia (Pa.)—Prisons and reformatories

Soviet Union

See also
Concentration camps—Soviet Union

Texas

The eyes of Justice are on Texas [Judge W. Justice finds system sorely deficient] il por *Newsweek* 109:55 Ja 19 '87

Jails could be Texas' next ten-gallon business. T. Vogel. il *Bus Week* p33 Ap 20 '87

Teach a jailbird to fly [Big Spring Federal Prison Camp] G. Haddaway. *Flying* 114:102 My '87

United States

See Prisons

Virginia

Va. fed. judge says 'Rasta' cons must eat prison food. *Jet* 72:12 Ag 3 '87

Washington (State)

PCs convert convicts [computer education program at Washington State Reformatory] il por *Pers Comput* 11:397 N '87

Wyoming

Prison house [Wyoming Women's Center in Lusk] il *Archit Rec* 175:94-7 Ap '87

Prisons, Prefabricated

Prefab pokeys: when prison space is tight. D. Foust. il por *Bus Week* p86 N 2 '87

Pritchard, Ambrose Evans- *See* Evans-Pritchard, Ambrose

Pritchard, Paul C.

Americans outdoors. il *Natl Parks* 61:12-13 My/Je '87

Pritikin Longevity Centers

Live-in Pritikin. M. S. Balter. *Health* 19:68 Je '87

The Pritikin "promise". H. Brubach. il *Vogue* 177:422-3+ F '87

Pritikin Program diet *See* Diet

Pritzker, Jay A.

about
Glitzy resorts and suburban hotels: Hyatt breaks new ground. J. E. Ellis. il por *Bus Week* p100-1 My 4 '87

Pritzker, Karen

Bernstein for the defenseless. il por *McCalls* 114:62 Jl '87

Pritzker Architecture Prize

An elegant sweep toward heaven [awarded to K. Tange] K. Andersen. il por *Time* 129:81 Mr 30 '87

Privacy

"I want to be alone" [with editorial comment by Elizabeth Crow] J. G. Fitzpatrick. il *Parents* 62:8, 77-80 My '87

The rewards, and risks, of snooping. B.-J. Raphael. *Glamour* 85:48 Ap '87

When you want to be alone. C. L. Mithers. *Glamour* 85:232 Je '87

Would you spy on your man? Meet 8 women who did. J. Ralston. il *Glamour* 85:266+ S '87

Privacy, Right of

See also
Confidential communications
Trade secrets
Wiretapping

Archbishop to appeal ruling on NAL novel [privacy suit brought by P. Marcinkus] C. Reid. *Publ Wkly* 232:20 D 25 '87

'Big Brother' in the office. *Newsweek* 110:78 O 5 '87

'Big Brother Inc.' may be closer than you thought. A. Field. il *Bus Week* p84-6 F 9 '87

Big Brother is counting your keystrokes [report by the Office of Technology Assessment] W. Booth. *Science* 238:17 O 2 '87

Can a system keep a secret? [privacy issue raised by Iran arms-contra aid case] P. Elmer-Dewitt. il *Time* 129:68-9 Ap 6 '87

Congress heads for an ugly battle over AIDS. D. Harbrecht. il *Bus Week* p53 O 12 '87

Don't tread on my data: protecting individual privacy in the information age. P. Elmer-Dewitt. il *Time* 130:84 Jl 6 '87

Electronic taskmasters [computer monitoring of employees] T. Beardsley. *Sci Am* 257:32+ D '87

How not to control the AIDS epidemic [adaptation of address, June 1987] M. Krim. il por *Humanist* 47:14-15+ N/D '87

Privacy, Right of—*cont.*
Privacy and the undressed. M. Greenfield. il *Newsweek* 110:100 O 19 '87
Telecommunications and computers: whither privacy policy? J. E. Katz. *Society* 25:81-6 N/D '87
Private branch exchanges (Telephone) *See* Telephone exchanges
Private brands
What's in a name? Store brands offer the best value for your money. il *Glamour* 85:84 Je '87
Private clubs *See* Clubs
Private corporations *See* Closely held corporations
Private enterprise *See* Free enterprise
Private eye [television program] See Television program reviews—Single works
Private flying
See also
Airplanes—Private ownership
Airlines vs. private pilots. il *U S News World Rep* 103:56 D 7 '87
Birthday blues. R. L. Collins. il *Flying* 114:17-18 Jl '87
Grounded grassroots [proposed Mode C rule] M. Phelps. il *Flying* 114:40 D '87
Tailored training. R. L. Collins. *Flying* 114:27 D '87
Private institutions, Nonprofit *See* Nonprofit institutions
Private libraries *See* Libraries, Private
Private placements (Securities)
Every risk has its price [private placements by Prudential] R. Greene. il *Forbes* 140:156+ N 16 '87
Private presses
See also
Janus Press
Private prison industry *See* Prison management industry
Private property *See* Property
Private school teachers *See* Teachers
Private schools
See also
Church schools
Andover's mission to Moscow [exchange of high school students] J. N. Baker. il *Newsweek* 110:102-3 N 16 '87
At an all-girls school you're taught to believe in yourself. K. Odean. il *Glamour* 85:112 Ag '87
Beyond designer prep schools. B. Leonard. il *Forbes* 140:220+ N 30 '87
— A continuing conundrum? [research on effectiveness of public vs. private schools] G. W. Bracey. il *Phi Delta Kappan* 69:74-5 S '87
Escape to freedom [independent schools; address, March 6, 1987] J. D. Ratteray. *Vital Speeches Day* 53:497-8 Je 1 '87
Miles from nowhere [Virginia's Oak Hill Academy] H. Hersch. il *Sports Illus* 66:78-82+ F 16 '87
The road to self-reliance [lesson of boarding school] M. Norman. il *N Y Times Mag* p82 D 13 '87
A woman at old Exeter [principal K. S. O'Donnell] F. Schumer. il pors *N Y Times Mag* p98-101 O 11 '87

Admission
The admissions-go-round: private school fever [New York City] B. Kanner. il *N Y* 20:40-6 N 23 '87

Federal aid
The French experience with public aid to private schools. F. C. Fowler. bibl f *Phi Delta Kappan* 68:356-9 Ja '87

France
The French experience with public aid to private schools. F. C. Fowler. bibl f *Phi Delta Kappan* 68:356-9 Ja '87

Switzerland
The scions of sovereigns and stars form a ring around Le Rosey, the world's poshest prep school. S. Dougherty. il *People Wkly* 28:82-4 Ag 3 '87
Privatization
The bottom line is society loses. M. Abramovitz. il *Nation* 245:410-12 O 17 '87
Corporate control [privatization of air traffic control system] R. L. Collins. *Flying* 114:28-9 O '87
An economic bill of rights. il *Nations Bus* 75:54 Ag '87
Freeway privatization [address, April 10, 1987] R. W. Poole. *Vital Speeches Day* 53:553-6 Jl 1 '87
Going once, going twice—going nowhere fast [loan sales by federal government] R. Brady. il *Bus Week* p35 Jl 13 '87
Housing solutions sought as federal subsidy agreements run out [projects that owners will have option of taking onto open market] J. Trewhitt. il *Archit Rec* 175:35 O '87

The making of a privatization boondoggle. *Newsweek* 110:57 S 21 '87
A new squeeze on housing: publicly assisted projects are imperiled. S. Dentzer. il *Newsweek* 110:48-9 Ag 10 '87
A painless way to slash the deficit [shifting public services to the private sector] R. Fitzgerald. *Read Dig* 130:79-82 Mr '87
Patients as research partners [privatization of cancer research; address, August 14, 1987] R. K. Oldham. *Vital Speeches Day* 53:763-6 O 1 '87
President acts on privatization. il *Nations Bus* 75:12 O '87
Privatization: boon for smalls. *Nations Bus* 75:15-16 Ag '87
Privatizing city services [address, February 24, 1987] R. W. Poole. *Vital Speeches Day* 53:588-90 Jl 15 '87
Privatizing tech info [National Technical Information Service] R. Chalk. il *Technol Rev* 90:8+ F/Mr '87
Selling Uncle Sam's assets: why Reagan has a real shot now. P. Magnusson. il por *Bus Week* p41 S 28 '87
Uncle Sam's loan sale: low prices, no guarantees. H. Gleckman. *Bus Week* p41-2 Ja 26 '87
Up from public housing [tenant management] M. Wooster and J. Fund. il *Read Dig* 131:139-43 Jl '87
The view from the White House. R. Reagan. pors *Forbes* 140:35-6 S 21 '87
What do we mean by "privatization"? T. Kolderie. *Society* 24:46-51 S/O '87
Why privatization is stalled. *Fortune* 115:98 My 25 '87
Will NTIS go private? M. Crawford. *Science* 236:140 Ap 10 '87

International aspects
Global privatization. *Futurist* 21:39-41 N/D '87
Going private: France . . . Britain . . . Soviet Union. *World Press Rev* 34:51 F '87
'Privatization' becomes a global byword. G. de Jonquieres. *World Press Rev* 34:50 F '87

British Columbia
Revolution on the right. J. Pifer. il por *Macleans* 100:28 Ag 31 '87
Vander Zalm's bold plans. J. O'Hara. il por *Macleans* 100:14-16 N 2 '87
A West Coast sell-off. J. O'Hara. il *Macleans* 100:17 D 7 '87

France
Can France's great sell-off sell Chirac as president? J. Rossant. il *Bus Week* p76 My 25 '87
Chirac's chance to remake France may be slipping away. F. J. Comes and J. Rossant. por *Bus Week* p44-5 Mr 30 '87
'Chirac's Yalta': the selling of French TV. J. Rossant. il *Bus Week* p48 F 16 '87
A choice menu from Jacques Chirac. M. McFadden. il *Fortune* 115:18-19 Ja 5 '87
Giving French business a new message: sink or swim [A. Madelin] S. Tully. il por *Fortune* 115:39-40 Ja 5 '87
People's sellout. D. Singer. *Nation* 245:545 N 14 '87

Great Britain
First you slim your fat cats. S. Jenkins. il *U S News World Rep* 103:62 N 9 '87
People's sellout. D. Singer. *Nation* 245:545 N 14 '87
The principles and practice of privatization [address, March 30, 1987] M. Pirie. *Vital Speeches Day* 53:655-8 Ag 15 '87
Privatization sparks scramble for competitive edge in England [airline industry] il *Aviat Week Space Technol* 127:128+ N 9 '87
A spanner in the works [privatization of Rolls-Royce endangered by V2500 setbacks] H. Banks. il *Forbes* 139:36-7 Je 1 '87

Anecdotes, facetiae, satire, etc.
Talk about a buyout! [leveraged buyout for all of Britain] B. Stein. il *N Y Times Mag* p50+ Mr 1 '87

Israel
Israel thinks it's time to get out of business. N. Sandler. il *Bus Week* p36 Ag 24 '87

Italy
Mussolini's corporate legacy. P. C. Newman. il por *Macleans* 100:31 N 23 '87

United States
See Privatization

Western Europe
Europe goes wild over privatization. S. Tully. il *Fortune* 115:68-70 Mr 2 '87
Governments must strive to make private enterprise work in space. R. Gibson. por *Aviat Week Space Technol* 127:91-2 N 2 '87

Privatization—Western Europe—*cont.*
Slump at the sales window [effect of stock market crash] C. Redman. il *Time* 130:47 N 9 '87

Privé, Gilbert G., and others
Helix geometry, hydration, and G·A mismatch in a B-DNA decamer. bibl f il *Science* 238:498-504 O 23 '87

Privileged communications *See* Confidential communications
Privileges and immunities
Timing tiff [Senate Select Committee and L. Walsh clash over granting immunity to J. Poindexter and O. North] *Time* 129:26 Mr 23 '87
Walsh vs. Congress [granting immunity in Iran arms case] T. Morganthau. il pors *Newsweek* 109:24+ Mr 23 '87
What will they say—and when? [tussle over who gets immunity in the Iran-contra affair] M. Healy. il pors *U S News World Rep* 102:20 Mr 23 '87

Privy Council (Great Britain) *See* Great Britain. Privy Council
Prix de Lausanne *See* Ballet—Competitions
Prize contests
Alan Klimpke's career as a singer is running hot and cold [winner of Coast-to-Coast Shower Sing-Off] il por *People Wkly* 28:79 N 30 '87
How Beatrice lost at its own game [football prize contest] L. Baum. il *Bus Week* p66 Mr 2 '87
Madison Ave.'s amateur hour [marketing contests] A. Miller. il *Newsweek* 110:56 N 23 '87
No consolation from this prize [Sweepstakes Clearing House using credit vouchers as prizes] il *Consum Rep* 52:270 My '87

Anecdotes, facetiae, satire, etc.
Uncivil liberties. C. Trillin. il *Nation* 244:459 Ap 11 '87

Prize fighting *See* Boxing
Pro Football Hall of Fame
Proud NFL Hall of Famers bring black total to 26. il *Jet* 71:51 F 16 '87
Pro life movement
See also
Black Americans for Life
Feminists for Life of America
JustLife (Organization)
AIDS and the death penalty as consistency tests for the prolife movement. J. R. Kelly. *America* 157:151-5 S 26 '87
Attracting clients and controversy [centers that counsel women against abortion] P. P. Wong. il *Christ Today* 31:32-3 S 18 '87
Domestic terrorism: on the front line at an abortion clinic [work of clinic director J. Widdicombe in St. Louis] M. Kort. il por *Ms* 15:48-51+ My '87
How to keep the pro-life movement small. J. Thomas-Bailey. *Commonweal* 114:308-9 My 22 '87
The mind of an anti-abortionist. K. Pollitt. il *Nation* 244:65+ Ja 24 '87
Prolife and prochoice activists renew the battle. B. Spring. il *Christ Today* 31:48-50 F 20 '87
Real prolifers defend women, too [with readers' comments] J. Ball. *U S Cathol* 52:16-21 Ag '87
When picketing pays [Adopt-a-Picket program run by NOW to raise money for abortions in Concord, Calif.] D. G. Albrecht. il *Ms* 16:91 N '87

Proaño, Leonidas
about
Sowing justice in Ecuador. P. R. Greene. *Christ Century* 104:910-12 O 21 '87

Probabilities
See also
Risk
Stochastic processes
Forest fires, barnacles and trickling oil [interacting particle systems; cover story] I. Peterson. il *Sci News* 132:220-3 O 3 '87
Our wild, weird world of coincidence. R. Blodgett. il *Read Dig* 131:125-8 S '87
The shapes of random walks. J. Rudnick and G. Gaspari. bibl f il *Science* 237:384-9 Jl 24 '87

Probate law and practice
See also
Wills
New Jersey
First black named deputy surrogate in New Jersey [H. Davis] *Jet* 72:8 Ag 31 '87

Probation
Prison versus probation [report of Joan Petersilia and Susan Turner] *Society* 24:3 My/Je '87

Prober, James M., and others
A system for rapid DNA sequencing with fluorescent chain-terminating dideoxynucleotides. bibl f il *Science* 238:336-41 O 16 '87

Probes, Testing *See* Testing equipment
Probiotics, Veterinary *See* Veterinary drugs
Problem children
See also
Bullying
Hyperactivity
Juvenile delinquents and delinquency
Blame the kid, not the parent [study by Kathleen E. Anderson] V. Bozzi. il *Psychol Today* 21:16 Mr '87
Coping with a difficult child [one year olds] J. T. Gibson. il *Parents* 62:258 N '87
See me, help me [bizarre behavior as communication] E. G. Carr and V. M. Durand. bibl (p65) il *Psychol Today* 21:62-4 N '87

Education
After-school discussion helps problem students [program at Central High School in Indianapolis] W. Bourke and R. D. Furniss. il *Phi Delta Kappan* 69:241-2 N '87
Behavior pills [disciplining unruly kids with Ritalin] E. Salholz. il *Newsweek* 109:76 Ap 20 '87
Beyond designer prep schools. B. Leonard. il *Forbes* 140:220+ N 30 '87
Parental separation and school problems. F. Roberts. *Parents* 62:53 D '87

Problem solving
See also
Crisis management (Psychology)
Creating solutions, not showdowns. M. J. Parson. il *Work Woman* 12:127-9 My '87
Get unstuck: look at an old problem in a new way. il *Glamour* 85:34 Jl '87
Problems not worth solving. S. Blotnick. il *Forbes* 139:197 Je 1 '87
Take a break and incubate. M. Golin. *Prevention* 39:75-7 S '87
"There's got to be a better way" [conflict resolution] J. Marks. il *Parents* 62:106-8+ S '87

Probst, Gerald Graham, 1923-
Applying tomorrow's technology today [address, September 9, 1986] *Vital Speeches Day* 53:166-8 Ja 1 '87

Procare Industries Ltd.
Gender kits—caveat emptor [FDA censures Gender Choice kit manufacturer] il *U S News World Rep* 102:12 F 9 '87

Procedure (Law) *See* Legal procedure
Process theology
A friend's love: why process theology matters. B. Mesle. *Christ Century* 104:622-5 Jl 15-22 '87

Processing, Signal *See* Signal processing
Processors, Food (Appliances) *See* Food processors (Appliances)
Prochazka, Michal, and others
Three recessive loci required for insulin-dependent diabetes in nonobese diabetic mice. bibl f il *Science* 237:286-9 Jl 17 '87

Procrastination
Help for procrastinators. E. E. Goode. il *U S News World Rep* 103:106 N 9 '87
How to beat procrastination [views of Steven Booth] il *USA Today (Periodical)* 116:10 Ag '87
How to manage the staff procrastinator. C. Golden. *Work Woman* 12:31 N '87
Now is the time to stop procrastinating. il *Glamour* 85:95 S '87
The power of positive procrastination. G. M. Galles. *Read Dig* 131:9-10 Ag '87
Thirteen ways to procrastinate efficiently and gain control of your time. C. R. Hobbs. *Work Woman* 12:96-7 O '87

Procter & Gamble Co.
Dieters delight—P&G asks O.K. for no-cal fat additive [olestra] K. R. Sheets. *U S News World Rep* 102:47 My 18 '87
Fast food freaks, this will do your heart good [fat substitute olestra] T. Dworetzky. il *Discover* 8:12 Ag '87
Fat without calories [synthetic fat substitute olestra] A. Steacy. il *Macleans* 100:49-50 Je 8 '87
Luv that market [J. G. Smale] B. Saporito. il por *Fortune* 116:56 Ag 3 '87
Peanut butter: a dip for the health-conscious [campaign for Jif] il *Newsweek* 110:42 Jl 20 '87
Procter & Gamble goes on a health kick. Z. Schiller. il *Bus Week* p90-2 Je 29 '87
Will fake fat yield plump profits? [fat substitute olestra] G. M. Bock. il *Time* 129:57 My 25 '87

Procurement, Military *See* United States. Air Force—Procurement; United States. Army—Procurement; United States. Dept. of Defense—Procurement; United States. Navy—Procurement

Prodi, Romano

about

Europe's quiet revolution [interview] S. Solomon. il por *Forbes* 140:52+ D 14 '87

Lessons from a master. R. I. Kirkland, Jr. il por *Fortune* 116:34-5 Ag 3 '87

Mussolini's corporate legacy. P. C. Newman. il por *Macleans* 100:31 N 23 '87

The turnaround sparking a new Italian renaissance. W. C. Symonds. il por *Bus Week* p60-1 Mr 2 '87

Prodigies, Musical *See* Children as musicians

Produce, Farm *See* Farm produce

Produce trade

See also

Cashew nuts—Export-import trade

Frieda's Finest/Produce Specialties, Inc.

Grain trade

Maggio Inc.

Rice—Export-import trade

Soybean industry—Export-import trade

Wheat trade

America's agricultural future. O. L. Freeman. il por *Futurist* 21:15-17 S/O '87

Better veggies ahead. L. Shapiro. il *Newsweek* 110:87-8 O 5 '87

Can we put U.S. agriculture on the road to recovery? D. Amstutz. il *USA Today (Periodical)* 116:18-20 N '87

International agricultural trade reform [statement, July 6, 1987] R. Reagan. *Dep State Bull* 87:33 S '87

Line on U.S. exports: fast starters stumble. T. White. il *Success Farm* 85 no2:5 Ja '87

Pleading for the farmers [western Canadian leaders call for increased federal aid and end to global subsidies] J. Howse. *Macleans* 100:15 Je 8 '87

Subsidies, science more powerful than demand [views of Dennis Avery] *Success Farm* 85 no1:27 Ja '87

Tomato Bob. *New Yorker* 63:36-8 O 12 '87

Trade frictions and farm subsidies. H. Banks. *Forbes* 139:27 Ja 26 '87

Trade wars: Reagan plays with fire [U.S. duties imposed on European agricultural products] *Natl Rev* 39:21-2 Ja 30 '87

Transatlantic showdown [U.S.-European Community agricultural trade war] P. Lewis. il *Macleans* 100:30 Ja 19 '87

The war over subsidies [Canada's campaign to end international agricultural support payments] M. Janigan. il *Macleans* 100:14 Je 1 '87

A worldwide glut of food. M. Drohan. il *Macleans* 100:37-8 N 9 '87

Producer Price Index *See* Price indexes

Producers, Television *See* Television producers

Product coding *See* Bar coding

Product development *See* Product planning

Product liability *See* Liability (Law)

Product planning

Riding a product to the top [computer industry] R. A. Shaffer. il *Pers Comput* 11:39 Ja '87

Speeding new ideas to market. B. Uttal. il *Fortune* 115:62-4+ Mr 2 '87

Production, Agricultural

See also

Crop yields

World Food Council

Food security: a technological alternative: biotechnology can convert biomass into a stable food supply. M. H. Rogoff and S. L. Rawlins. bibl il *BioScience* 37:800-7 D '87

How U.S. farmers rate in world competition. D. Ohrtman. il *Success Farm* 85:10-13 Ap '87

Use it or lose it. C. Siler. il *Forbes* 140:80+ D 14 '87

Production, Industrial *See* Productivity, Industrial

Production, Theatrical *See* Theater—Production and direction

Production control

See also

Quality control

Productivity, Biological

Diel periodicity of photosynthesis in polar phytoplankton: influence on primary production. R. B. Rivkin and M. Putt. bibl f il *Science* 238:1285-8 N 27 '87

Energy for life among the waves [research by Egbert G. Leigh, Jr. and others] I. Peterson. *Sci News* 131:183 Mr 21 '87

Food production in low-nutrient seas. W. H. Adey. bibl f il *BioScience* 37:340-8 My '87

Life thrives under breaking ocean waves [research by Egbert Leigh and others] R. Lewin. il *Science* 235:1465-6 Mr 20 '87

Oxygen supersaturation in the ocean: biological versus physical contributions. H. Craig and T. Hayward. bibl f il *Science* 235:199-202 Ja 9 '87

Terrestrial metabolism and atmospheric CO_2 concentrations. R. A. Houghton. bibl il *BioScience* 37:672-8 O '87

Productivity, Industrial

See also

Gross national product

Supply and demand

Can America compete? [growth crisis; cover story; special section] il *Bus Week* p44-9+ Ap 20 '87

Casting light on the mystery of low productivity . . . G. Koretz. il *Bus Week* p32 Je 1 '87

The defense buildup, 1977-85: effects on production and employment. D. K. Henry and R. P. Oliver. bibl f il *Mon Labor Rev* 110:3-11 Ag '87

GM's not-so-radical proposal [productivity of each plant to determine wage increases and job security] *Fortune* 116:10 S 14 '87

Industry output and employment through the end of the century. V. A. Personick. bibl f il *Mon Labor Rev* 110:30-45 S '87

Industry productivity. il *Mon Labor Rev* 110:2 O '87

Is America over-managed? [dismal white collar productivity] il *World Press Rev* 34:55 F '87

The job engine is going great guns . . . but it's one reason the productivity motor is backfiring. G. Koretz. il *Bus Week* p20 Mr 30 '87

Just-in-time people. S. Blotnick. il *Forbes* 140:109-10+ Jl 13 '87

A lament: all work and less pay [rise in productivity as wages are cut] S. Koepp. il *Time* 130:48 Jl 13 '87

Lee Iacocca's production whiz [R. E. Dauch] A. L. Taylor, III. il pors *Fortune* 115:36-8+ Je 22 '87

The mining machinery industry: labor productivity trends, 1972-84. B. A. O'Neil. bibl f il *Mon Labor Rev* 110:31-6 Je '87

Multifactor productivity in U.S. manufacturing, 1949-83. W. Gullickson and M. J. Harper. bibl f il *Mon Labor Rev* 110:18-28 O '87

Performance of multifactor productivity in the steel and motor vehicles industries. M. K. Sherwood. bibl f il *Mon Labor Rev* 110:22-31 Ag '87

Productivity data. See issues of Monthly Labor Review

Productivity gains continued in many industries during 1985. A. S. Herman. il *Mon Labor Rev* 110:48-52 Ap '87

Productivity in a customer vein [address, February 23, 1987] R. A. Ferchat. *Vital Speeches Day* 53:602-5 Jl 15 '87

Productivity is the best affirmative action plan [women's economic position] G. S. Becker. il *Bus Week* p18 Ap 27 '87

Productivity perks up. S. Nasar. il *Fortune* 116:62 S 28 '87

Productivity puzzle. S. Nasar. il *Fortune* 115:44 Je 8 '87

Productivity trends in the furniture and home furnishings stores industry. A. S. Herman and J. E. Henneberger. bibl f il *Mon Labor Rev* 110:24-9 My '87

Pumping up productivity. il *Fortune* 116:9 D 7 '87

R&D and productivity: measurement issues and econometric results. Z. Griliches. bibl f il *Science* 237:31-5 Jl 3 '87

Retail liquor stores experience flat trend in productivity. J. D. York. bibl f il *Mon Labor Rev* 110:25-9 F '87

Service with a smile [productivity in the service sectors] S. Lee and C. Brown. *Forbes* 140:79 Ag 24 '87

Two decades of productivity growth in poultry dressing and processing. Z. Z. Ahmed and M. S. Sieling. bibl f il *Mon Labor Rev* 110:34-9 Ag '87

Using body rhythms to boost productivity. L. Washer. *Work Woman* 12:19-20 Ag '87

A weakness in process technology. L. C. Thurow. bibl f *Science* 238:1659-63 D 18 '87

Productivity, Labor *See* Productivity, Industrial

Products, Animal *See* Animal products

Products, Commercial *See* Commercial products

Products, New

See also

Product planning

Products, New—*cont.*

Betting on a better mousetrap [influence of new products on company stocks] J. Crudele. il *N Y* 20:16+ S 28 '87

Buy better. See issues of Home Mechanix beginning January 1985

Home & shop improvements. M. Thompson. See issues of The Family Handyman beginning September 1986

Home mechanix picks: 14 great home products. il *Home Mech* 83:10+ Ag '87

Innovations. See issues of Essence beginning August 1987

Just out. See issues of Better Homes and Gardens

Mishaps that mothered invention. B. Gatty. il *Nations Bus* 75:58-9 F '87

Mom's marketplace. See issues of The Mother Earth News through September/October 1987

New/home. See issues of Popular Mechanics beginning February 1987

New products. il *Bus Week* p124-5 Ja 12 '87

New tech. C. Begole. See occasional issues of Glamour

Product reports 1988 [cover story; special issue; with editorial comment by Mildred F. Schmertz] il *Archit Rec* 175:23-7+ D '87

Products. il *Workbench* 43:38-9 Jl/Ag '87

Products of the year. H. J. Steinbreder. il *Fortune* 116:120-5 D 7 '87

Speeding new ideas to market. B. Uttal. il *Fortune* 115:62-4+ Mr 2 '87

Star tech. See issues of Omni (New York, N.Y.) beginning October 1986

What's new. See issues of Popular Science through December 1986

What's new! A. Elkins. See issues of Good Housekeeping

What's new: products/technology. D. Stover. See issues of Popular Science beginning January 1987

Products, Quality of *See* Quality of products

Profanity *See* Words, Obscene

Professional Actors Association of Florida

PAAF. *New Yorker* 63:31-2 My 18 '87

Professional associations *See* Trade and professional associations

Professional ethics

See also

Automobile mechanics (Persons)—Professional ethics

Automobile sales personnel—Professional ethics

Business ethics

College teachers—Professional ethics

Engineers—Professional ethics

Journalistic ethics

Legal ethics

Medical ethics

Pharmacists—Professional ethics

Physicists—Professional ethics

Teachers—Professional ethics

Wedtech: where fingers are pointing now [accountants, lawyers, and bankers] P. Dwyer. il *Bus Week* p34+ O 5 '87

Professional Secretaries International

Black woman new prexy for Ill. secretary group [E. B. G. Hickman] por *Jet* 72:30 Je 15 '87

Professional sports *See* Sports

Professionals

See also

Black professionals

Yuppies

Geologists and lawyers needn't apply [question of teacher certification for professionals] L. Solórzano. il *U S News World Rep* 103:58 Jl 27 '87

Professionals and their computers [Apple's Macintosh] J. Sculley. por *Pers Comput* 11:236 O '87

Professionals and their setups [personal computer use] C. Spezzano. il *Pers Comput* 11:127-9+ S '87

Religious life

Professionals must adjust their fees [Christian professionals] J. Hilt. il *Christ Today* 31:30 F 6 '87

Salaries, fees, etc.

Professionals must adjust their fees [Christian professionals] J. Hilt. il *Christ Today* 31:30 F 6 '87

Professions

See also

Black women—Occupations

Blacks—Occupations

Occupations

Women—Occupations

Professors *See* College teachers

Profit

See also

Capitalism

Corporations—Finance

A dirty word [profit in the Soviet Union] D. Seligman. il *Fortune* 116:203 Ag 3 '87

Morality and capitalism: is there virtue in profit? *Current* 292:11-17 My '87

Profit forecasting *See* Business forecasting

Profit sharing

An anesthetist seeks to invest her profit sharing [Louise Weizer] D. Harris. il *Money* 16:185-6 S '87

Taxation

Make your payout pay off. M. C. Paulson. il *Changing Times* 41:51-5 Ap '87

Profiteering

See also

Black markets

Program trading (Securities)

Are computers to blame? [stock market crash] *Time* 130:32 N 2 '87

Ban program trading. *New Repub* 197:9 N 30 '87

The Big Board's crusade against program trading [New York Stock Exchange] J. M. Laderman and B. Nussbaum. il por *Bus Week* p134-6+ Mr 23 '87

Casino Royale [January 23, 1986] J. J. Cramer. *New Repub* 196:10-11 F 16 '87

Chicago's traders are trying to be their own best watchdogs. J. N. Frank. il *Bus Week* p38 Mr 2 '87

The Merc starts to clean up its pit [Chicago Mercantile Exchange] J. N. Frank. il *Bus Week* p114+ Mr 16 '87

A new invisible hand. D. Pauly. il *Newsweek* 110:21 N 2 '87

The not so awful truth. S. W. Angrist. il *Forbes* 139:180-1 Mr 23 '87

Program previews. J. Crudele. *N Y* 20:16+ N 16 '87

Program trading has lost its punch. J. N. Frank and J. M. Laderman. il *Bus Week* p58 Jl 27 '87

The SEC report: program trading gets off easy. J. N. Frank and S. Zucker. il *Bus Week* p38 Ap 6 '87

Thanks, professor. D. N. Dreman. il *Forbes* 140:314-15 N 16 '87

This triple witching hour could last all day [June 19, 1987] J. N. Frank. il *Bus Week* p126+ Je 22 '87

Two key questions: was program trading to blame . . . and did the specialists do their jobs? il *Bus Week* p51 N 2 '87

A way to stop a stock-market 'meltdown'? [SEC chairman D. Ruder's proposals for curbing program trading] por *Newsweek* 110:60 O 19 '87

What's making the market swing so wildly [program traders using the Major Market Index] J. M. Laderman and J. N. Frank. il *Bus Week* p72-3 F 9 '87

Why stocks are such swingers; Foretelling with futures. J. Rachlin. il *U S News World Rep* 102:50-1 F 9 '87

Programmable array logic

Programmable hardware [special section] bibl il *Byte* 12:194-5+ Ja '87

TI/P-CAD PAL starter kit. il *Radio-Electron* 58:32-4 Mr '87

Programme on Man and the Biosphere *See* Man and the Biosphere Programme

Programming (Cable television) *See* Cable television—Programming

Programming (Computers) *See* Computer programming

Programming (Linear) *See* Linear programming

Programming (Television) *See* Television broadcasting—Programming

Progress

See also

Social change

Technological innovations

Does improved technology mean progress? L. Marx. il *Technol Rev* 90:32-41+ Ja '87

Herbert Spencer and 'inevitable' progress. R. M. Young. bibl il por *Hist Today* 37:18-22 Ag '87

Anecdotes, facetiae, satire, etc.

The problem with progress. K. Fury. il *Work Woman* 12:104 Ag '87

Progressive (Periodical)

Memo. E. Knoll. See issues of The Progressive

Progressive Conservative Party (Canada) *See* Conservative Party (Canada)

Prohibition

Fish dry and vote wet! C. Ford. il *50 Plus* 27:62-4 Je '87

The last Untouchable; ed. by Civia Tamarkin. A. Wolff. il pors *People Wkly* 28:53-4+ Jl 13 '87

The real Eliot Ness. S. Nickel. il pors *Am Hist Illus* 22:42-52 O '87

The real McCoy [W. McCoy, rum runner] J. F. Mariani. il *Mot Boat Sail* 160:30 O '87

Prohibition—*cont.*

United States

See Prohibition

Project 714 (Organization)

Positive peer pressure: a new weapon against drugs. C. Lutes. il *Christ Today* 31:40-1+ F 20 '87

Project ELF *See* Radio, Military

Project Head Start (U.S.)

Head Start combats baby bottle tooth decay [American Indians] M. G. Phillips and P. E. Stubbs. il *Child Today* 16:25-8 S/O '87

Outdoor play . . . one Head Start program's approach [Adams County, Colo.; cover story] F. Wardle. il *Child Today* 16:16-19 Mr/Ap '87

Special "cooking friends" add spice to Head Start nutrition programs [American Home Economics Association's Volunteer Nutrition Consultant Project] S. A. Koblinsky and M. G. Phillips. il *Child Today* 16:26-9 Jl/Ag '87

Project Liberty *See* Proyecto Libertad

Project management *See* Business management

Project management software *See* Computers—Business use—Programming

Project Mercury space vehicles *See* Space vehicles

Project on Military Procurement

Dina Rasor: patriot with a purpose. A. Steinbach. il pors *McCalls* 114:52 F '87

Project STAR

Secret weapon: astronomy. P. M. Sadler. il *Sky Telesc* 74:452 N '87

Project X [film] See Motion picture reviews—Single works

Projectiles

See also

Ballistics

Bullets

Rockets

USAF Center develops lightweight projectiles for SDI applications [Lightweight Exoatmospheric Projectile program] T. M. Foley. il *Aviat Week Space Technol* 127:46-7 N 2 '87

Projection, Overhead *See* Overhead projection

Projection, Spherical *See* Spherical projection

Projection angiography *See* Radiography, Medical

Projection of slides *See* Slides (Photography)—Projection

Projection television *See* Television projection

Projectors

See also

Television projection

Dukane Pro-100 slide projector. J. Drafahl and S. Drafahl. il *Petersens Photogr Mag* 16:82-3 O '87

The soccer-ball sky [how a planetarium projector works] G. Lovi. il *Sky Telesc* 74:279-80 S '87

History

Exhibitions

Optical amusements before movies and TV [exhibit at Museum of Our National Heritage] M. Jailer. il *Antiques Collect Hobbies* 92:46-9 Je '87

Projects (Teaching)

See also

Astronomy—Study and teaching—Projects

Science—Study and teaching—Projects

Collecting for fun, education, and the Arizona Kidney Foundation [Glendale American School in Arizona] E. Walker. *Phi Delta Kappan* 68:402-3 Ja '87

Prokofiev, Sergey, 1891-1953

about

The love of three oranges [opera] Reviews

New Yorker 63:63-5 Ag 24 '87. A. Porter

Prokopy, Ronald J.

(jt. auth) See Roitberg, Bernard D., and Prokopy, Ronald J.

Prokovsky, André

about

The Gatsby gamble. S. Flatow. il *Horizon* 30:60-2 O '87

Prolapse of the umbilical cord *See* Umbilical cord—Prolapse

Prolog (Computer language)

ALS Prolog. A. Lane. il *Byte* 12:269-72 S '87

DOS in English [Turbo Prolog program] A. Lane. *Byte* 12:261-2+ D '87

Intelligent databases. C. D. S. Moss. il *Byte* 12:97-8+ Ja '87

Mathematical reasoning: a Prolog program uses heuristic methods to solve equations. L. Sterling. il *Byte* 12:177-80 O '87

Prolog [cover story; special section] bibl il *Byte* 12:145-50+ Ag '87

Promethean Theatre Company

A heroic theater for the rational mind. R. A. Cooper. *Humanist* 47:33-4 Jl/Ag '87

Prometheus Books

Prometheus unbound [publisher P. W. Kurtz] M. Berkley. il por *Publ Wkly* 231:32-4 Ja 16 '87

Promoters and promoting

See also

Abercrombie, Josephine

Arum, Bob, 1931-

International Creative Management (Firm)

Theatrical agencies and agents

Promotion (School)

See also

Grade repetition (Education)

Promotion check-offs (Meat industry) See Meat industry—Advertising

Promotions

See also

Black executives—Promotion

Executives—Promotion

Women executives—Promotion

2 smart women, one top job: who got the VP promotion? M. Gordon. il *Mademoiselle* 93:144-5+ Je '87

Big bucks, baby—get wise to the ways to rise. A. Gates. *Mademoiselle* 93:154-5 F '87

Don't promote "one of the boys". M. E. Moore. por *Nations Bus* 75:4 Mr '87

What to do when an employee turns down a promotion [excerpt from Managing people at work desk guide] T. L. Quick. *Work Woman* 12:18 Jl '87

You promoted a weak person? Here's how to set things right. H. C. Rogers. *Work Woman* 12:15 Ag '87

Proms (Dances)

A night to remember. il *Teen* 31:8+ Ap '87

Prom pizazz! il *Teen* 31:57-8+ Ap '87

Anecdotes, facetiae, satire, etc.

17 boffo things to do on prom night (instead of going to prom). B. Price. il *Seventeen* 46:172-3 My '87

Proms (London, England: Festival) *See* Music festivals—Great Britain

Pronghorn hunting

Approach to antelope. B. Journey. il *Outdoor Life* 180:92-3+ S '87

Blood brothers [pronghorn hunting in Montana] K. McCafferty. il *Field Stream* 92:44-5 D '87

Myths of the plains runner. J. Barsness. il *Field Stream* 92:62-3+ Jl '87

Pronghorns

A prairie goat companion. D. Petersen. il map *Mother Earth News* 108:70-1+ N/D '87

Pronunciation

See also

Accents

English language—Pronunciation

Names, Personal—Pronunciation

Proof (Law) *See* Evidence (Law)

Proof theory

See also

Zero knowledge proofs

Rectangles within rectangles [proof of tiling theorem] *Sci News* 132:187 S 19 '87

What happens when hubris meets nemesis [obsession with proving Poincaré conjecture] G. Taubes. il *Discover* 8:66-70+ Jl '87

Proofreading

The importance of copy editing [boosting pay and prestige] L. Stearns. il *Publ Wkly* 232:48 Jl 10 '87

On the road to mediocrity [decline of copy editing] T. Rogers. il *Publ Wkly* 232:42 D 4 '87

Propaganda

See also

Foreign propagandists

Indoctrination

Motion pictures—Propaganda films

United States. Information Agency

World War, 1914-1918—Propaganda

Casey's domestic 'covert op' [CIA domestic propaganda campaign designed to rally support for Nicaraguan contras] T. Jacoby. il *Newsweek* 110:36 O 12 '87

Faking the red menace [Reagan administration's invention of a Soviet threat to Iran] *Nation* 244:65 Ja 24 '87

Foggy Bottom agit prop [pro-contra propaganda] *Harpers* 275:22 D '87

The selling of the F.D.N. [CIA-backed contra propaganda operations] P. Kornbluh. il *Nation* 244:40-4 Ja 17 '87

Anecdotes, facetiae, satire, etc.

Poindexter file [disinformation supplied to Iran and Iraq concerning Soviet threat] R. R. Lingeman. *Nation* 244:68-9 Ja 24 '87

Propaganda, American *See* Propaganda
Propaganda, Iranian
Postage-size propaganda [Iranian stamps] il *N Y Times Mag* p38-41 F 15 '87
Propaganda, Russian
See also
Radio Moscow
Glasnost [address, March 11, 1987] V. Bukovsky. *Vital Speeches Day* 53:596-600 Jl 15 '87
Glasnost [address, March 13, 1987] C. Z. Wick. *Vital Speeches Day* 53:418-20 My 1 '87
Red star blazes on [M. Gorbachev's tactics] B. Crozier. *Natl Rev* 39:26 Ag 14 '87
The threat from a failed system [address, June 8, 1987] M. Tugwell. *Vital Speeches Day* 53:645-7 Ag 15 '87
What the Soviets think about American liberals. D. D'Souza. *Natl Rev* 39:39-41+ Ja 30 '87
Propellanes
Synthesis
Putting a spin into chemistry [propellahexaene; work of Leo A. Paquette and Liladhar Waykole] I. Peterson. il *Sci News* 131:357 Je 6 '87
Propellers
See also
Airplanes—Propellers
Airplanes, Jet—Propellers
Airplanes, Light—Propellers
Boats and boating—Propellers
Patrol boats—Propellers
Property
See also
Airspace (Law)
Confiscations
Estates, Decedents'
Intellectual property
Joint ownership
Land tenure
Real property
Trespass
Wills
The case for a cheap dog [folly of putting your trust in things] C. Gordon. por *Macleans* 100:39 Je 15 '87
Test your clutter quotient [what your possessions reveal about you; quiz] L. F. McCarthy. il *Seventeen* 46:50+ F '87
Taxation
See also
Real property—Taxation
Property, Unclaimed *See* Estates, Unclaimed
Property appraisal *See* Real property—Valuation
Property insurance *See* Insurance, Property and casualty
Property rights *See* Land tenure
Property surveys *See* Surveying
Propfan propellers *See* Airplanes, Jet—Propellers
Prophecies
See also
Apocalyptic literature
Astrology
Forecasting
Prophets
Prophets
The Bible's "fusty old men". P. Yancey. il *Christ Today* 31:17-21 O 2 '87
Liberalism & the Hebrew prophets. J. S. Auerbach. *Commentary* 84:58-60 Ag '87
Proportional representation
Let's get representative [proposed constitutional amendment calling for national proportional representation] H. Hertzberg. *New Repub* 196:15-18 Je 29 '87
Proposals of marriage *See* Marriage proposals
Propranolol
And our next speaker is . . . drugged [treating stage fright] C. Schaeffer. il *Changing Times* 41:18 Ag '87
Proprietary hospitals *See* Hospital management industry
Proprietary rights *See* Intellectual property
Proprietary schools
Proprietary schools. W. W. Wilms. il *Change* 19:10-22 Ja/F '87
Prosciutto
See also
Cooking—Meat
Prose, Francine, 1947-
Tangerine dreams [story] il *Redbook* 170:52+ D '87
Women and children first [story] *New Yorker* 62:32-7 Ja 19 '87
(tr) See Fink, Ida. A scrap of time

Prosecutors, Public *See* Public prosecutors
Prospect Park Zoo (New York, N.Y.)
Boy, 11, begged 'help' before bears ate him [polar bear attack on Juan Perez] il *Jet* 72:16 Je 8 '87
Prospecting
See also
Petroleum—Prospecting
Prospecting with plants. F. R. Siegel. il *Earth Sci* 40:18-19 Fall '87
Prospectuses *See* Securities—Prospectuses
Prospere, Susan
The pool of tears [poem] *New Yorker* 63:36 Je 22 '87
Prosperity
Testing the theory of less government, more prosperity. G. Koretz. il *Bus Week* p22+ F 2 '87
Prost, Alain
about
The 1986 Grand Prix season. J. Thompson. il *Road Track* 38:148-50+ Mr '87
Alain Prost: world champion. P. Windsor. il pors *Car Driv* 32:111-16+ F '87
The champ, like a champ. I. Ireland. il *Road Track* 38:140-2+ Jl '87
Nigel's championship hopes go flat. I. Ireland. il *Road Track* 38:126-8+ F '87
Prost claims the magic 27 [Belgian Grand Prix] I. Ireland. il *Road Track* 39:128-30+ S '87
Racing's record-breaker. S. McBride. il pors *N Y Times Mag* p42+ N 8 '87
Street smart in Motown. R. F. Jones. il pors *Sports Illus* 66:68-9 Je 29 '87
Prostacyclin *See* Prostaglandins
Prostaglandins
Pregnancy hypertension marker found. *Sci News* 131:344 My 30 '87
Smoking, the pill, and coronary disease [lowered prostacyclin levels; studies by Jerry L. Nadler] il *USA Today (Periodical)* 115:4 F '87
Prostate gland
Cancer
My father's best gift [living will] N. P. Randall. il *Read Dig* 130:11-16 Ja '87
Prostate cancer consensus hampered by lack of data. G. Kolata. *Science* 236:1626-7 Je 26 '87
Diagnosis
For president or plain citizen, prostate problems come with age, says surgeon Haakon Ragde [interview] R. Sackett. il por *People Wkly* 27:72+ Ja 12 '87
Prostate manograms on the MaleMobile. C. SerVaas. il *Saturday Evening Post* 259:106+ Ja/F '87
Therapy
Ohio's most powerful black lawmaker reveals fight to conquer cancer [C. J. McLin] il por *Jet* 73:29 S 28 '87
Diseases
For men only: coping with a bad prostate. I. Pave. *Bus Week* p89 F 2 '87
This gland is your gland. K. B. Taylor. il *50 Plus* 27:64-7 S '87
Surgery
Prostate surgery and time for a cancer checkup [R. Reagan] M. Clark. *Newsweek* 109:20 Ja 12 '87
Prosthesis
See also
Arm, Artificial
Heart, Artificial
Hip joint, Artificial
Joints, Artificial
Ligaments, Artificial
Biomaterial-centered infection: microbial adhesion versus tissue integration. A. G. Gristina. bibl f il *Science* 237:1588-95 S 25 '87
Bionic breakthroughs. D. Todd. il *Macleans* 100:34-5 N 23 '87
Loosening bacteria's hold on implants [preventing staphylococci from adhering to polymers; research by Bernd Jansen] S. Weisburd. *Sci News* 132:190 S 19 '87
Prostitution
See also
Children of prostitutes
A commercial overture [sexual solicitation] B. Staples. il *N Y Times Mag* p106 S 20 '87
Cops fear AIDS after bites from alleged prostitutes [New York City] il *Jet* 72:8 Je 29 '87
Teen sex for sale: who pays the price? M. Barbera-Hogan. il *Teen* 31:20+ Ja '87
University 'madam' gets $1000 fine, probation [J. Owens' business at De Paul] il por *Jet* 73:22 N 16 '87

Prostitution—*cont.*

The wages of sin [S. Barrows permitted to keep profits from sale of book; Son of Sam laws not applicable] *Time* 129:77 Mr 23 '87

International aspects

Fear of AIDS chills sex industry [Nevada and Japan] W. L. Chaze. il *U S News World Rep* 102:25 F 16 '87

Canada

Epidemic of murder [Vancouver, B.C. murders thought to be linked to Washington State serial murderer] J. O'Hara. *Macleans* 100:12 Jl 20 '87

Europe

History

The Reformation & the red light [medieval attitudes toward prostitution] N. Orme. il *Hist Today* 37:36-41 Mr '87

Great Britain

Author's life imitates his art [libel suit won by J. Archer] A. Deming. il por *Newsweek* 110:62 Ag 3 '87

Sex and 'Madam Cyn' [cleared of managing prostitutes] N. Underwood. *Macleans* 100:48 F 23 '87

Spare pennies [J. Archer wins libel suit against the Star] W. R. Doerner. il por *Time* 130:31-2 Ag 3 '87

India

Bombay's 'red-light' children. B. Sadasivam. *World Press Rev* 34:54 Jl '87

Prostitution in motion pictures

Hooker. K. Jaehne. il *Film Comment* 23:25-32 My/Je '87

Undressed for success. M. Kramer. il *Vogue* 177:218-19+ Jl '87

Proteas

Can you really grow proteas in northern California? il *Sunset* 179:234-5 N '87

Proteases

See also

Renin

Adipsin: a circulating serine protease homolog secreted by adipose tissue and sciatic nerve. K. S. Cook and others. bibl f il *Science* 237:402-5 Jl 24 '87

The catalytic role of the active site aspartic acid in serine proteases. C. S. Craik and others. bibl f il *Science* 237:909-13 Ag 21 '87

A chemical thermostat for fat? [adipsin] D. D. Edwards. *Sci News* 132:70-1 Ag 1 '87

A new wave of enzymes for cleaving prohormones. J. L. Marx. il *Science* 235:285-6 Ja 16 '87

Proteolytic self-cleavage of hepatitis B virus core protein may generate serum e antigen. R. H. Miller. bibl f il *Science* 236:722-5 My 8 '87

Severely impaired adipsin expression in genetic and acquired obesity. J. S. Flier and others. bibl f il *Science* 237:405-8 Jl 24 '87

The three-dimensional structure of Asn^{102} mutant of trypsin: role of Asp^{102} in serine protease catalysis. S. Sprang and others. bibl f il *Science* 237:905-9 Ag 21 '87

X-ray holograms at improved resolution: a study of zymogen granules. M. Howells and others. bibl f il *Science* 238:514-17 O 23 '87

Yeast KEX2 protease has the properties of a human proalbumin converting enzyme. I. C. Bathurst and others. bibl f il *Science* 235:348-50 Ja 16 '87

Inactivation

Coming—dietary aids to prevent cancer? [protease inhibitors; research by Ann Kennedy and others] J. Raloff. *Sci News* 131:206 Mr 28 '87

Muscular dystrophy: defective inhibitor? *Sci News* 131:41 Ja 17 '87

Protection (Trade) *See* Free trade and protection

Protection against burglary *See* Burglary protection

Protection from lightning *See* Lightning protection

Protection of cultural property *See* Cultural property—Protection

Protection of missionaries *See* Missionaries—Protection

Protection of plants *See* Plants—Protection

Protective clothing *See* Clothing, Protective

Protective gloves *See* Gloves

Protective masks *See* Dust masks

Protective mechanisms (Biology) *See* Defense mechanisms (Biology)

Protective mimicry *See* Mimicry (Biology)

Protein kinase *See* Kinases

Protein receptors

Blocking of HIV-1 infectivity by a soluble, secreted form of the CD4 antigen. D. H. Smith and others. bibl f il *Science* 238:1704-7 D 18 '87

Brain barrier tissues: end organs for atriopeptins. L. Steardo and J. A. Nathanson. bibl f il *Science* 235:470-3 Ja 23 '87

Heart peptide goes to the head [research by James A. Nathanson and Luca Steardo] D. D. Edwards. *Sci News* 131:68 Ja 31 '87

Identification of nuclear receptors for VIP on a human colonic adenocarcinoma cell line. M. B. Omary and M. F. Kagnoff. bibl f il *Science* 238:1578-81 D 11 '87

The IL-2 receptor β chain (p70): role in mediating signals for LAK, NK, and proliferative activities. J. P. Siegel and others. bibl f il *Science* 238:75-8 O 2 '87

New perspectives in cell adhesion: RGD and integrins. E. Ruoslahti and M. D. Pierschbacher. bibl f il *Science* 238:491-7 O 23 '87

A novel putative tyrosine kinase receptor encoded by the *eph* gene. H. Hirai and others. bibl f il *Science* 238:1717-20 D 18 '87

Physiological role of silent receptors of atrial natriuretic factor. T. Maack and others. bibl f il *Science* 238:675-8 O 30 '87

Protein-binding sites in Ig gene enhancers determine transcriptional activity and inducibility. M. Lenardo and others. bibl f il *Science* 236:1573-7 Je 19 '87

Restoration of LDL receptor activity in mutant cells by intercellular junctional communication. L. Hobbie and others. bibl f il *Science* 235:69-73 Ja 2 '87

Therapy by mimicry [thyromimetic SK&F L-94901 reduces blood cholesterol without increasing heart rate] *Sci Am* 256:88 F '87

Proteins

See also

Actin
Albumins
Amino acid sequence
Amino acids
Amyloid
Bacterial proteins
Clathrin
Collagen
Crystallins
Cytochromes
Ferritin
Fetoprotein
G proteins
Glycoproteins
Histones
Insulin
Interferon
Interleukin
Laminin
Lipoproteins
Metallothionein
Myoglobin
Myosin
Nerve growth factor
Peptides
Transducin
Transferrin
Tryptophan
Tubulin
Ubiquitin
Urine—Proteins
Vinculin
Visual purple

Activation of adenovirus promoters by the adenovirus E1A protein in cell-free extracts. R. Spangler and others. bibl f il *Science* 237:1044-6 Ag 28 '87

Acylation of proteins with myristic acid occurs cotranslationally. C. Wilcox and others. bibl f il *Science* 238:1275-8 N 27 '87

Alzheimer's protein is also in infant brains [research by Peter Davies and others] D. M. Barnes. *Science* 238:1652 D 18 '87

Cloning of complementary DNA for GAP-43, a neuronal growth-related protein. L. R. Karns and others. bibl f il *Science* 236:597-600 My 1 '87

The CML-specific P210 *bcr/abl* protein, unlike v-*abl*, does not transform NIH/3T3 fibroblasts. G. Q. Daley and others. bibl f il *Science* 237:532-5 Jl 31 '87

Control protein for AIDS virus identified [research by Gary Nabel and David Baltimore] J. L. Marx. il *Science* 236:393 Ap 24 '87

Electron tunneling paths in proteins. A. Kuki and P. G. Wolynes. bibl f il *Science* 236:1647-52 Je 26 '87

Epitope mapping by chemical modification of free and antibody-bound protein antigen. A. Burnens and others. bibl f il *Science* 235:780-3 F 13 '87

Mapping patterns of c-*fos* expression in the central nervous system after seizure. J. I. Morgan and others. bibl f il *Science* 237:192-7 Jl 10 '87

The ones that get away [low protein diet in Papua New Guinea] J. Durnin. il *Courier* 40:17 My '87

Proteins—*cont.*

Protein defect in diabetes? D. D. Edwards. *Sci News* 131:327 My 23 '87

ras p21 as a potential mediator of insulin action in Xenopus oocytes. L. J. Korn and others. bibl f il *Science* 236:840-3 My 15 '87

The regulation of natural anticoagulant pathways [protein C] C. T. Esmon. bibl f il *Science* 235:1348-52 Mr 13 '87

Signal for attachment of a phospholipid membrane anchor in decay accelerating factor. I. W. Caras and others. bibl f il *Science* 238:1280-3 N 27 '87

Stop-transfer regions do not halt translocation of proteins into chloroplasts. T. H. Lubben and others. bibl f il *Science* 238:1112-14 N 20 '87

Structure, function, and assembly of membrane proteins. E. Racker. bibl f *Science* 235:959-61 F 27 '87

Your diet: high-protein promises. J. S. Stern. *Vogue* 177:358 D '87

Analysis

A complete mapping of the proteins in the small ribosomal subunit of Escherichia coli [neutron scattering data] M. S. Capel and others. bibl f il *Science* 238:1403-6 D 4 '87

Crystallographic R factor refinement by molecular dynamics. A. T. Brünger and others. bibl f il *Science* 235:458-60 Ja 23 '87

Global flexibility in a sensory receptor: a site-directed cross-linking approach. J. J. Falke and D. E. Koshland, Jr. bibl f il *Science* 237:1596-600 S 25 '87

Molecular dynamics simulations of proteins. M. Karplus. bibl f il *Phys Today* 40:68-72 O '87

Mutants of bovine pancreatic trypsin inhibitor lacking cysteines 14 and 38 can fold properly. C. B. Marks and others. bibl f il *Science* 235:1370-3 Mr 13 '87

Organic origami: scientists study the art of protein folding [cover story] R. Weiss. il *Sci News* 132:344-6 N 28 '87

Purification and properties of Drosophila heat shock activator protein. C. Wu and others. bibl f il *Science* 238:1247-53 N 27 '87

The role of protein structure in chromatographic behavior. F. E. Regnier. bibl f *Science* 238:319-23 O 16 '87

Solution of a protein crystal structure with a model obtained from NMR interproton distance restraints. A. T. Brünger and others. bibl f il *Science* 235:1049-53 F 27 '87

Structurally divergent human T cell receptor γ proteins encoded by distinct Cγ genes. M. S. Krangel and others. bibl f il *Science* 237:64-7 Ja 3 '87

X-ray snapshots of proteins in motion. I. Peterson. *Sci News* 132:182 S 19 '87

Spectra and spectroscopy

On the prevalence of room-temperature protein phosphorescence. J. M. Vanderkooi and others. bibl f il *Science* 236:568-9 My 1 '87

Synthesis

Battling illness with body proteins. M. Murray. il *Sci News* 131:42-5 Ja 17 '87

Body doubles [engineering of healing proteins] J. Kluger. il *Omni* 9:48-50+ Ag '87

Designer proteins: the next boom in biotech. M. Bluestone. il *Bus Week* p94+ Ap 13 '87

Frequency dependence of electric field modulation of fibroblast protein synthesis. K. J. McLeod and others. bibl f il *Science* 236:1465-9 Je 12 '87

Proteolytic enzymes *See* Proteases

Protestant churches

See also

Catholic Church—Relations—Protestant churches
Lutheran Church
National Council of Churches

Clergy

See Clergy

Education

See also

Theological seminaries

China

The church the Gang of Four built [cover story] S. Mumper. il *Christ Today* 31:17-21 My 15 '87

The Protestant church in the People's Republic of China. D. S. Browning. *Christ Century* 104:218-21 Mr 4 '87

Korea (South)

Will success spoil the South Korean church? il *Christ Today* 31:29-44 N 20 '87

United States

See also

Assemblies of God
Christian Church (Disciples of Christ)
Episcopal Church—United States
Lutheran Church—United States

Presbyterian Church—United States
Reformed Church in America
Unitarian Universalist Association
United Church of Christ
United Methodist Church

Denominational moves raise questions [relocating church offices out of New York City has implications for ecumenism] C. Iosso. *Christ Century* 104:484-6 My 20-27 '87

Religion's social ladders [decline of liberal Protestant churches] R. J. Neuhaus. *Natl Rev* 39:52 O 23 '87

Protestant theology *See* Theology

Protestantism

See also

Evangelicalism
Fundamentalism
Protestant churches

The liberal ethic and the spirit of Protestantism [cover story; with discussion] R. W. Fox. il por *Cent Mag* 20:4-14 S/O '87

Liberation theology is remarkably Protestant. C. R. Padilla. il por *Christ Today* 31:12 My 15 '87

Protestants and Jews *See* Christianity and other religions

Protests, demonstrations, etc.

See also

Animal experimentation—Protests, demonstrations, etc.
Anti-nuclear movement
Hunger strikes
Student protests, demonstrations, etc.

Connecticut

See also

Groton (Conn.)—Protests, demonstrations, etc.

Indiana

See also

Odon (Ind.)—Protests, demonstrations, etc.

Massachusetts

See also

Boston (Mass.)—Protests, demonstrations, etc.

Missouri

See also

Saint Louis (Mo.)—Protests, demonstrations, etc.

Soviet Union

See also

Moscow (Soviet Union)—Protests, demonstrations, etc.

Taiwan

Quiet victories in Taipei [opposition to martial law] E. W. Desmond. il *Time* 129:43 Je 1 '87

Washington (D.C.)

See Washington (D.C.)—Protests, demonstrations, etc.

Proteus syndrome

As of '87, he's Proteus Man [cause of the Elephant Man's deformities] *Sci News* 132:55 Jl 25 '87

Prothero, Donald R.

The rise and fall of the American rhino. il *Nat Hist* 96:26-33 Ag '87

Prothero, R. Mansell (Ralph Mansell)

Mankind and the mosquito. il *World Health* p18-19 Je '87

Prothero, Ralph Mansell *See* Prothero, R. Mansell (Ralph Mansell)

Protoavis *See* Birds, Fossil

Proton (Launch vehicle) *See* Space vehicles—Propulsion systems

Protons

See also

Antiprotons

Collisions between spinning protons. A. D. Krisch. bibl (p116) il *Sci Am* 257:42-50 Ag '87

Protoplasts

Progress toward engineering monocots. L. Tangley. *BioScience* 37:462 Jl/Ag '87

Rice plants regenerated from protoplasts. J. L. Marx. il *Science* 235:31-2 Ja 2 '87

Protozoa

See also

Dinoflagellates

Protozoa, Pathogenic

See also

Plasmodium (Parasite)
Trypanosomes

Encystation and expression of cyst antigens by Giardia lamblia in vitro. F. D. Gillin and others. bibl f il *Science* 235:1040-3 F 27 '87

A parasite with the guts of a burglar [Leishmania; research by David M. Mosser and Paul J. Edelson] K. Hartley. *Sci News* 131:359 Je 6 '87

Protozoa, Pathogenic—*cont.*
Resistance and sensitivity
An antidrug malaria pump? [resistance to chloroquine] *Sci News* 132:359 D 5 '87
Efflux of chloroquine from Plasmodium falciparum: mechanism of chloroquine resistance. D. J. Krogstad and others. bibl f il *Science* 238:1283-5 N 27 '87
Reversal of chloroquine resistance in Plasmodium falciparum by verapamil. S. K. Martin and others. bibl f il *Science* 235:899-901 F 20 '87
Prott, Lyndel V., and O'Keefe, Patrick J.
Law and the underwater heritage. *Courier* 40:24 N '87
Provençal cooking *See* Cooking, French
Provence (France)
The new Provence allure. S. M. Dinhofer. il *Harpers Bazaar* 120:86+ My '87
Provence (New York, N.Y.: Restaurant) *See* New York (N.Y.)—Restaurants, nightclubs, bars, etc.
Provey, Joseph R.
Editor's notes. See issues of Home Mechanix beginning January 1985
Providence of God *See* God—Providence
Provident National Bank
Riding the rate curve. B. Weberman. il *Forbes* 140 Sp Issue:395 O 26 '87
Provincialism *See* Regionalism
Proving grounds
See also
United States. Air Force. Eastern Test Range
White Sands Missile Range (N.M.)
Environmental aspects
Trouble in Hell Canyon [Indians oppose Honeywell's proposed munitions testing site in South Dakota] T. E. Johnson. il *Newsweek* 110:30 S 28 '87
Provost, Gary, 1944-
Worcester County: arts in Heritage Country. il *Horizon* 30:24-30+ My '87
Prowse, Michael
Lessons and questions. *World Press Rev* 34:12 Ag '87
Proxies
Dilution control [stockholders vs. management over share value at Cleveland-Cliffs Inc.] P. Fuhrman. il *Forbes* 140:174 O 5 '87
The net drops on Crazy Eddie [E. Zinn's proxy] T. Vogel. il *Bus Week* p62 N 2 '87
Shareholders aren't just rolling over anymore. C. Power. il *Bus Week* p32-3 Ap 27 '87
Who's afraid of the new Kurt Wulff? J. R. Norman. il por *Bus Week* p74 Je 15 '87
Proxmire, William
Should Congress approve the Fairness Doctrine? [excerpts from statement, March 18, 1987] *Congr Dig* 66:235+ O '87
about
. . . and Proxmire takes aim at takeover abuses. V. Cahan. *Bus Week* p35 Ap 20 '87
Suddenly, Proxmire the gadfly looks more like a godsend. V. Cahan. *Bus Week* p47 S 14 '87
Proyecto Libertad
Reprieves from the war zone. J. Juffer. il *Progressive* 51:11 D '87
Prudden, Bonnie, 1914-
Mother & daughter workout [excerpt from How to keep your child fit from birth to six] il pors *Good Housekeep* 205:138 S '87
Prudent speculator (Newsletter) *See* Investment newsletters
Prudential Insurance Co. of America
Every risk has its price [private placements] R. Greene. il *Forbes* 140:156+ N 16 '87
Prudhomme, Paul
The recipe that launched a thousand boats. il por *Oceans* 20:12 My/Je '87
Pruess, Joanna
At last, tomato time. il *N Y Times Mag* p37-8 Ag 9 '87
A chili winter. il *N Y Times Mag* p57-8 Ja 18 '87
Decadent desserts. il *N Y Times Mag* p63-4 My 3 '87
Feast before fast. il *N Y Times Mag* p57-8 Mr 1 '87
French with an English accent. il *N Y Times Mag* p50-2 F 22 '87
Not the same old rice. il *N Y Times Mag* p49-50 S 6 '87
Winter vegetables. il *N Y Times Mag* p73-4 N 29 '87
Pruitt, Dean G.
Solutions, not winners. bibl (p63) il *Psychol Today* 21:58-62 D '87
Pruitt, Derek
about
Derek's herd. R. Gavin. il por *Ctry J* 14:21-5 Jl '87

Prunelle (New York, N.Y.: Restaurant) *See* New York (N.Y.)—Restaurants, nightclubs, bars, etc.
Prunes
See also
Cooking—Fruit
The power of prunes. il *Parents* 62:20 Jl '87
Pruning
Giving a hedge new life. il *South Living* 22:106 Mr '87
Kiwi control. il *Sunset* 178:112-13 Ja '87
Limbing up trees. il *South Living* 22:91 Mr '87
Pruning flowering shrubs . . . what, when, where, how. il *Flower Gard* 31:44+ F/Mr '87
Pruning fruit trees [excerpt from Pruning simplified] L. Hill. il *Mother Earth News* 103:51-5 Ja/F '87
Think before you prune. L. C. Askey. il *South Living* 22:47 Ja '87
Time to prune roses [excerpt from Basic gardening] M. MacCaskey. il *Flower Gard* 31:72-3 F/Mr '87
Training new apple trees. J. Ruttle. il *Rodale's Org Gard* 34:48-9 D '87
Pryce-Jones, Alan, 1908-
The golden age of Newport. il *House Gard* 159:190-7+ Je '87
Pryce-Jones, David
Foul play. *New Repub* 196:15-17 Mr 2 '87
Pryor, Aaron
about
Ex-champ Pryor shot, held in Miami for rape. por *Jet* 71:50 Mr 23 '87
The Hawk tries his wings on return to boxing ring. por *Jet* 72:46 Ag 10 '87
The Hawk's toughest fight. P. Axthelm. il por *Newsweek* 110:56 Ag 3 '87
Pryor gets no record in Miami kidnapping case. *Jet* 72:52 S 14 '87
Pryor preps for battle on rape charge in Miami. por *Jet* 72:51 Mr 30 '87
Pryor's comeback KO'd, now faces court fight. il por *Jet* 72:49 Ag 31 '87
Sunset in Sunrise for the Hawk. P. Putnam. il por *Sports Illus* 67:16 Ag 17 '87
Pryor, Richard
about
Fifth wife pregnant again, Pryor re-files for divorce. *Jet* 72:56 Ap 6 '87
Pryor, ex-wife have second child; feud over Xmas visit. il por *Jet* 73:22 D 21 '87
Richard Pryor: "I wanted to do 'Critical condition' . . . I needed to make people laugh". il pors *Jet* 71:58-9 F 9 '87
Richard Pryor talks about what caused his fifth marriage to fail. il por *Jet* 72:16-17 Ap 20 '87
Richard Pryor's estranged wife tells why their marriage failed. A. Collier. il pors *Jet* 72:54-6 My 4 '87
Richard Pryor's fifth marriage on the rocks; divorce petition filed. il por *Jet* 71:12 Mr 23 '87
Psaltis, Demetri
(jt. auth) See Abu-Mostafa, Yaser S., and Psaltis, Demetri
Pseudomonas
The importance of being blue [South Carolina experiment attempts to track genetically altered Pseudomonas in soil] M. D. Lemonick. il *Time* 130:82-3 N 9 '87
Redesigning metabolic routes: manipulation of TOL plasmid pathway for catabolism of alkylbenzoates. J. L. Ramos and others. bibl f il *Science* 235:593-6 Ja 30 '87
Pseudonyms
Success and the pseudonymous writer: turning over a new self. J. C. Oates. il *N Y Times Book Rev* 92:12+ D 6 '87
Pseudorabies in swine *See* Swine—Diseases and pests
Pseudoscience *See* Occult sciences
Psi phenomena *See* Parapsychology
Psoralens
Structure of a psoralen cross-linked DNA in solution by nuclear magnetic resonance. M. T. Tomic and others. bibl f il *Science* 238:1722-5 D 18 '87
Psoriasis
Therapy
Vitamin D for psoriasis? *Prevention* 39:14 S '87
PSR prophet (Newsletter) *See* Investment newsletters
Psychedelic Furs (Musical group)
Let's dance! Top tunemakers. il por *Teen* 31:55 Jl '87
Psychedelic posters *See* Posters
Psychiatric diagnosis *See* Mental illness—Diagnosis
Psychiatric ethics
See also
Psychiatric research—Ethical aspects

Psychiatric ethics—*cont.*
Doctor under examination [psychiatrist S. Smith of Royal Ottawa Hospital accused of misappropriating funds] A. Finlayson. *Macleans* 100:5 Ja 12 '87
Psychiatric hospitals *See* Hospitals, Psychiatric
Psychiatric insurance *See* Insurance, Mental health
Psychiatric research
>*See also*
>National Institute of Mental Health (U.S.)
>>**Ethical aspects**
"It was too good to be true" [false data used by mental retardation researcher S. Breuning] D. Brand. il por *Time* 129:59 Je 1 '87
NIMH finds a case of "serious misconduct" [case of S. E. Breuning] C. Holden. *Science* 235:1566-7 Mr 27 '87
Prosecution urged in fraud case [case of S. E. Breuning] C. Norman. *Science* 236:1057 My 29 '87
Psychiatrist gets reality therapy [case of Dr. D. O. Sherwin] *FDA Consum* 21:44 F '87
Stanford psychiatrist resigns under a cloud [P. A. Berger] C. Holden. por *Science* 237:479-80 Jl 31 '87
>>**Experimentation on man**
America's human guinea pigs. R. C. Cowen. il *Technol Rev* 90:20-1 F/Mr '87
Nominating a hero for 1987 [J. Rauh's suit against CIA mind control experiments performed on Canadians] A. Fotheringham. il *Macleans* 100:64 Ja 19 '87
Psychiatrists
>*See also*
>Black psychiatrists
Yale takes action against psychiatrists for financial improprieties. C. Holden. *Science* 238:745 N 6 '87
Psychiatrists and patients
Harvard researcher's study of sex between doctors and patients helps stir strong debate. *Jet* 73:24+ D 21 '87
Psychiatry
>*See also*
>American Psychiatric Association
>Forensic psychiatry
>Mexican Americans—Psychiatric care
>Psychiatrists and patients
>Psychoanalysis
>Psychotherapists—Psychiatric care
>Psychotherapy
>Women—Psychiatric care
>>**Experimentation on man**
>*See* Psychiatric research—Experimentation on man
>>**Textbooks**
Textbook credits bruise psychiatrists' egos [R. Michels vs. J. O. Cavenar] E. Marshall. por *Science* 235:835-6 F 20 '87
Textbook dispute [discussion of February 20, 1987 article, Textbook credits bruise psychiatrists' egos] E. Marshall. *Science* 236:655-7 My 8 '87
>>**China**
Analyzing China. G. Wahl. *World Press Rev* 34:55 N '87
>>**Soviet Union**
Koryagin skeptical on *glasnost*. C. Holden. il por *Science* 238:476 O 23 '87
Soviet psychiatrist describes abuse [views of A. Koryagin] J. Greenberg and B. Bower. *Sci News* 131:328 My 23 '87
A test case [political prisoner A. Koryagin] D. Satter. il por *N Y Rev Books* 34:3-4 F 12 '87
Psychiatry and society
The politics of psychiatry. R. E. Vatz and L. S. Weinberg. il *USA Today (Periodical)* 116:71-3 Jl '87
Psychiatry in motion pictures
Reel psychiatry. B. Bower. il *Sci News* 132:188-9 S 19 '87
Psychiatry in television
Reality shows: the syndicated couch. J. Vitale. il *Channels* 7:56-7 Jl/Ag '87
Psychic phenomena *See* Parapsychology
Psychical research *See* Parapsychology
Psychics
>*See also*
>Cosmic Contact Psychic Services
>Geller, Uri, 1946-
Are you a little bit psychic? [excerpt from Intangible evidence] B. Gittelson and L. Torbet. *Redbook* 169:76+ O '87
Psychics at work. J. M. Leder. il *McCalls* 115:159-62 O '87
Psychics: should one be in your future? il *Glamour* 85:85 Mr '87
Psychics and criminal investigation *See* Parapsychology and criminal investigation

Psycho beach party [drama] *See* Busch, Charles
Psychoacoustics
Can you believe your ears? L. Klein. il *Radio-Electron* 58:40-1+ D '87
Psychoacoustics and stereo imagery. L. Klein. il *Radio-Electron* 58:80-1 Mr '87
Why a blackboard screech drives us crazy [research by Lynn Halpern] *Prevention* 39:14 Je '87
Why stereo doesn't work. L. Klein. il *Radio-Electron* 58:68+ Ap '87
Psychoactive drugs *See* Psychopharmacology
Psychoanalysis
>*See also*
>Dreams
Letter from Europe [A. Verdiglione's psychoanalysis scam in Milan] J. Kramer. *New Yorker* 63:88+ Je 8 '87
My six years on the couch [excerpt from Returning] D. Wakefield. il *N Y Times Mag* p32-3+ D 20 '87
Psychoanalysis and art
Paintings, manifest and latent content. J. Croghan. il *Am Artist* 51:14+ Ap '87
Psychoanalysis and history *See* History—Psychological aspects
Psychoanalysis and literature
Psychotales. il *Omni* 10:92-4+ D '87
Psychoanalysts
>*See also*
>Freud, Sigmund, 1856-1939
>Miller, Alice
Psychohistory *See* History—Psychological aspects
Psycholinguistics
Dr. Jekyll, Señor Hyde [personality and coordinate bilinguals; study by Philip V. Hull] C. Simon. il *Psychol Today* 21:16 D '87
What I meant to say [verbal slips] M. T. Motley. bibl (p64) il *Psychol Today* 21:24-8 F '87
Psychological equipment
Give Randy Adamadama 40 minutes—he'll have you seeing the light [owner of Synchro-Energizer salon in California] il por *People Wkly* 28:134-5 D 14 '87
Psychological measurement *See* Psychometrics
Psychological research
>*See also*
>Wellesley College. Stone Center for Developmental Services and Studies
Academy helps Army be all that it can be [report on human performance enhancement] C. Holden. *Science* 238:1501-2 D 11 '87
The case of the falling nightwatchmen: in behavorial biology, not all facts are created equal. R. M. Sapolsky. il *Discover* 8:42-5 Jl '87
Psychology and the Constitution [impact on Supreme Court decisions] A. J. Tomkins. bibl (p58) *Psychol Today* 21:48-50 S '87
>>**Ethical aspects**
Secret of a success [Forbes business psychologist S. Blotnick exposed as a fraud] por *Time* 130:61 Ag 3 '87
>>**Experimentation on man**
(Lab) works in progress. A. Hornaday. il *Omni* 9 Omni Exper:11-13 Ap '87
Psychological tests
>*See also*
>Aptitude tests
>Intelligence tests
>Lie detectors and detection
>Minnesota Multiphasic Personality Inventory
>Myers-Briggs Type Indicator
>Rorschach test
The Farley test for risk takers. il *U S News World Rep* 102:64-5 Ja 26 '87
Love your job! [determining your work personality] K. Koontz. il *Health* 19:29-33 Je '87
Psychological types *See* Typology (Psychology)
Psychological warfare
>*See also*
>Terrorism
Psychologists
>*See also*
>Blau, Theodore H.
>Ogilvie, Bruce
>Rogers, Carl R. (Carl Ransom), 1902-1987
>Seligman, Martin E. P.
Psychology
>*See also*
>Behavior (Psychology)
>Behavior modification
>Child psychology
>Cognition
>Computers—Psychological use
>Consciousness

Psychology—See also—*cont.*
Control (Psychology)
Counseling
Criminal psychology
Ethnopsychology
Helplessness (Psychology)
Infant psychology
Mental illness
Observation (Psychology)
Parapsychology
Police psychology
Political psychology
Prison psychology
Psychiatry
Psychoanalysis
Psychotherapy
Social psychology
Soul
    See also subheads Psychological aspects; Psychology under various subjects
Toward a universal law of generalization for psychological science. R. N. Shepard. bibl f il *Science* 237:1317-23 S 11 '87

Anecdotes, facetiae, satire, etc.
Notes from the overblown. B. Zilbergeld. il *Psychol Today* 21:10-12 My '87

Experimentation on man
    See Psychological research—Experimentation on man

Measurement
    See Psychometrics

Periodicals
    See also
Psychology today (Periodical)

Research
    See Psychological research

Psychology, Comparative
    See also
Instinct
Born to be shy? [studies of infants and monkeys by Jerome Kagan and Stephen Suomi] J. Asher. bibl (p65) il *Psychol Today* 21:56-9+ Ap '87
Boys will be boys, girls will be . . . [spotted hyenas may help answer questions about gender and aggression in humans] J. L. Hopson. bibl (p67) il *Psychol Today* 21:60-6 Ag '87
What happens when the boss is a baboon [study by Anthony Coelho] il *Discover* 8:12-13 Je '87

Psychology, Educational
    See also
Black college teachers—Psychology
Incentives in education
Learning, Psychology of
Students—Psychology
Teachers—Psychology

Psychology, Industrial
    See also
Black executives—Psychology
Business etiquette
Employee counseling
Employee morale
Executives—Psychology
Job satisfaction
Job stress
Motivation (Psychology)
Women executives—Psychology
Workaholics
The actualized worker [cover story] M. Sinetar. il por *Futurist* 21:21-2+ Mr/Ap '87
Are you in or out with the boss? J. Sherman. *Work Woman* 12:20+ Ap '87
The art of constructive criticism. E. Davidowitz. il *Work Woman* 12:101 My '87
Assertiveness breeds contempt [male vs. female evaluations of assertive female managers; study by David L. Mathison] V. Bozzi. *Psychol Today* 21:15 S '87
Corporate compassion: striking the balance between personal pain and company policy. P. R. Satran. il *Work Woman* 12:105 Mr '87
Creating solutions, not showdowns. M. J. Parson. il *Work Woman* 12:127-9 My '87
Dealing with difficult bosses. P. Plawin. il *Changing Times* 41:92 Je '87
Dealing with the problem boss. S. Nelton. *Nations Bus* 75:61-2 F '87
Dear Betty Harragan [learning to "play the game"] B. L. Harragan. il *Work Woman* 12:30+ Ja '87
Do you work for a jerk? P. King. il *Ladies Home J* 104:52+ My '87
Feeling bored and restless? How to stay fresh on the job. M. M. Kennedy. il *Glamour* 85:216-18+ F '87

The finer points of power building [excerpt from Company manners] L. Wyse. il *Work Woman* 12:78-80+ Ja '87
Food for thought [drop in concentration after meals; research by Andrew Smith and Christopher Miles] G. Lowe. *Psychol Today* 21:14 F '87
Getting along with your boss [condensed from How to manage your boss] G. Berkley. il *Read Dig* 131:13-16 Jl '87
Have a good cry—but not at the office. B. Brophy. il *U S News World Rep* 102:63 Mr 16 '87
How picking favorites can improve performance [excerpt from Managing people at work desk guide] T. L. Quick. *Work Woman* 12:21 Ja '87
How to be a graceful winner [excerpt from Managing people at work desk guide] T. L. Quick. *Work Woman* 12:20 Ap '87
How to be smarter than the boss and keep your job. L. Baum. il *Bus Week* p112 Je 29 '87
How to cope with a problem boss: 4 key strategies. A. Thompson. *McCalls* 145:34 Mr '87
How to deal with an unbearable boss [interview with M. Grothe] il por *U S News World Rep* 102:56 Ja 19 '87
How to deal with bizarre employee behavior. M. Brooks. *Work Woman* 12:15+ Ag '87
How to get along with a difficult co-worker. R. V. Weinstein. il *McCalls* 114:129 S '87
How to keep that new-job 'honeymoon' alive. H. McCandless. *Work Woman* 12:17 Jl '87
How to learn from your mistakes [excerpt from Managing people at work desk guide] T. L. Quick. *Work Woman* 12:27 My '87
How to make the grapevine work for you [excerpt from Managing people at work desk guide] T. L. Quick. *Work Woman* 12:23 S '87
How to tell off your boss—and get away with it. B. Brophy. il *U S News World Rep* 102:48-9 My 4 '87
If your boss is in trouble, what do you do? M. M. Kennedy. il *Glamour* 85:104 F '87
If you're so powerful, how come you're fetching coffee? [quiz] A. Gates. *Mademoiselle* 93:256-7+ N '87
Is your job right for you? [quiz] R. Hillhouse and S. La Rosa. il *McCalls* 114:73-4 Jl '87
Love your job! [determining your work personality] K. Koontz. il *Health* 19:29-33 Je '87
Monday-morning jump starts: how to hit the ground running. S. Mernit. il *Work Woman* 12:59 F '87
My co-worker didn't do any work. il *Good Housekeep* 204:40+ Ap '87
Office gossip: is your name on more lips than Chap Stick? J. Stone. *Glamour* 85:21 Ap '87
Office politics: when to push for your point of view—and when not to. *Glamour* 85:172 S '87
Paranoia for fun and profit. S. Bing. il *Esquire* 107:40 F '87
The perils of persistence [Profiles of Organizational Influence Strategies test results] S. Schmidt and D. Kipnis. bibl (p65) il *Psychol Today* 21:32+ N '87
Problem bosses: they come in all sizes, shapes and styles—and everybody thinks that he's got one [interview with P. Wylie and M. Grothe] T. Cunneff. il pors *People Wkly* 27:95-6+ Je 8 '87
Problems not worth solving. S. Blotnick. il *Forbes* 139:197 Je 1 '87
Revenge is sweet, but . . . S. Blotnick. il *Forbes* 139 Ann Directory:338 Ap 27 '87
Standard issue [employees in uniform] M. R. Solomon. bibl (p63) il *Psychol Today* 21:30-1 D '87
Stuck in a rut? 6 ways to dig out. M. M. Kennedy. il *Glamour* 85:62 Jl '87
Surviving office politics. il *McCalls* 114:97 My '87
What to do if your boss is a bully. M. M. Kennedy. il *Glamour* 85:150 Mr '87
What to do when you don't like your boss [excerpt from Managing people at work desk guide] T. L. Quick. *Work Woman* 12:27 O '87
Where do the best goals come from? [excerpt from The human side of management] G. S. Odiorne. il *Work Woman* 12:32+ D '87
Whiz kids: why they need special attention. *Work Woman* 12:18-19 Ag '87
Who thrives in which job? R. Sandroff. il *Work Woman* 12:126-8+ N '87
Why smart people fail [interview with C. Hyatt] il por *U S News World Rep* 102:55 Ap 6 '87
With friends like these [office politics] S. Bing. il *Esquire* 107:63 Mr '87

Anecdotes, facetiae, satire, etc.
Work marriage [relationship between people of the opposite sex who work at the same place] D. Owen. il *Atlantic* 259:22 F '87

Psychology, Military
Iranscam: the real meaning of Oliver North. il pors *Ms* 15:24-7 My '87

Psychology, Pathological
See also
Autism
Depression, Mental
Mental illness
Narcissism
Paranoia
Personality—Disorders

Psychology, Physiological
See also
Body image
Brain—Localization of functions
Conditioned responses
Eating—Psychological aspects
Emotions
Facial expression
Laterality
Left- and right-handedness
Medicine, Psychosomatic
Memory
Mind and body
Neuropsychology
Optical illusions
Pain
Reaction time
Reflexes
Reinforcement (Psychology)
Senses and sensation
Sleep
Space perception
Time perception

Psychology, Religious
Christianity & mental health [cover story; with reply by P. R. Breggin] W. W. Watters. il *Humanist* 47:5-13+ N/D '87
Finding a place for emotions in Christian theology. G. S. Clapper. il *Christ Century* 104:409-11 Ap 29 '87
Self-help guru M. Scott Peck seeks the road to peace—for the world and himself. M. Brower. il pors *People Wkly* 28:125-8+ O 26 '87

Psychology and weather *See* Weather—Mental and physiological effects

Psychology today (Periodical)
Just spell our name right [20th anniversary] J. Fischman. il *Psychol Today* 21:22-3 My '87

Psychometrics
See also
Multidimensional scaling
Reading the buyer's mind [use of psychometric surveys in automobile marketing] *U S News World Rep* 102:59 Mr 16 '87

Psychoneuroimmunology
Complex characters handle stress better [study by Patricia W. Linville] D. Schechter. *Psychol Today* 21:26 O '87
Getting tough: can people learn to have disease-resistant personalities? [hardiness training; work of Salvatore Maddi] J. Fischman. bibl (p63) il *Psychol Today* 21:26-8 D '87
The healing brain. R. E. Ornstein and D. S. Sobel. bibl (p59) il *Psychol Today* 21:48-52 Mr '87
Laugh and be well? P. Long. bibl (p62) il *Psychol Today* 21:28-9 O '87
Lone dangers. R. E. Borgman. il *Omni* 9:24 My '87
Mind over disease: Warning! Daily hassles are hazardous. N. Peterson. il *Read Dig* 130:76-8 Ap '87
Mind over disease: your attitude can make you well. D. Robinson. il *Read Dig* 130:73-6 Ap '87
A new prescription: mind over malady. R. Wechsler. il *Discover* 8:50-3+ F '87
The pain of loneliness. M. W. Lear. il *N Y Times Mag* p47-8 D 20 '87
Stress & disease. B. G. Barley. *Ladies Home J* 104:38+ My '87
Taking care of immunity [lowered immune function in families caring for Alzheimer's patients; research by Janice K. Kiecolt-Glaser and others] B. Bower. *Sci News* 132:168 S 12 '87
Worried sick: hassles and herpes [research by Susan Kennedy and others] R. Weiss. *Sci News* 132:360 D 5 '87
Your new path to a stronger immune system. R. Rodale. il *Prevention* 39:20-1+ S '87

Psychopharmacology
See also
Antidepressants
Tranquilizing drugs

Crossing the border [medications and borderline personalities] M. Mintzer. il *Health* 19:16 D '87
D_1 dopamine receptor activation required for postsynaptic expression of D_2 agonist effects. J. R. Walters and others. bibl f il *Science* 236:719-22 My 8 '87
The doors of perception. G. Bronson. il *Forbes* 140:222+ D 14 '87
Drugs on the mind [psychological side effects of pharmaceutical drugs] *Sci Am* 256:70-1 Ja '87
"It was too good to be true" [false data used by mental retardation researcher S. Breuning] D. Brand. il por *Time* 129:59 Je 1 '87
Low-dose caveat for schizophrenia [research by Stephen R. Marder and others] B. Bower. *Sci News* 131:374 Je 13 '87
Neurogenetic adaptive mechanisms in alcoholism. C. R. Cloninger. bibl f il *Science* 236:410-16 Ap 24 '87
NIMH finds a case of "serious misconduct" [case of S. E. Breuning] C. Holden. *Science* 235:1566-7 Mr 27 '87
Prosecution urged in fraud case [case of S. E. Breuning] C. Norman. *Science* 236:1057 My 29 '87
Psychiatric side-effects of interleukin-2 [research by Kirk D. Denicoff and others] R. Weiss. *Sci News* 132:196 S 26 '87
Psychiatrist gets reality therapy [case of Dr. D. O. Sherwin] *FDA Consum* 21:44 F '87
Treating the mind, risking the body [drugs linked to hip fractures; study by Wayne A. Ray and others] *Sci News* 131:122 F 21 '87

Psychoses
See also
Depression, Mental
Paranoia
Schizophrenia

Psychosomatic medicine *See* Medicine, Psychosomatic

Psychotherapists
Growing pains for the shrinks. D. Gelman. il *Newsweek* 110:70-2 D 14 '87

Psychiatric care
When therapists need help [study by John C. Norcross] P. Chance. il *Psychol Today* 21:17 S '87

Psychotherapists and patients
For a little peace of mind [finding the right therapist] E. E. Goode. il *U S News World Rep* 103:98-9+ S 28 '87
Prisoners of psychotherapy [cover story] T. Minsky. il *N Y* 20:34-40 Ag 31 '87
Therapists: a cultural bias? [study by Steven Lopez and Priscilla Hernandez] P. Chance. *Psychol Today* 21:16-17 S '87

Anecdotes, facetiae, satire, etc.
'Therapist dyed, sessions canceled'. R. E. Lovett. il *Smithsonian* 18:152 Ag '87

Psychotherapy
See also
Biofeedback training
Child psychotherapy
Cognitive therapy
Computers—Psychotherapeutic use
Dance therapy
Family psychotherapy
Hypnotism—Therapeutic use
Psychopharmacology
Puppets and puppet plays—Therapeutic use
Self help groups
Shock therapy
Story telling—Therapeutic use
Beyond the purchase of friendship. W. Schofield. *Society* 24:69-75 Mr/Ap '87
Can you—should you—play therapist to your lover? C. L. Mithers. *Glamour* 85:224 D '87
Make believers [therapeutic use of enhanced states; work of M. M. Watkins] R. Katz. il *Omni* 10:126-8+ N '87
Navigating the therapy maze. M. M. Hunt. il *N Y Times Mag* p28-31+ Ag 30 '87
Self-help: a bargain? [views of Gerald M. Rosen] P. Chance. *Psychol Today* 21:17 Ag '87
Short-term therapies. M. A. Kellogg. il *Harpers Bazaar* 120:78+ F '87
Their own worst enemy [rational-emotive therapy; views of A. Ellis] C. Wood. il *Psychol Today* 21:18 F '87
Therapy [sessions for pet owners run by S. P. Cohen at Animal Medical Center in Manhattan] *New Yorker* 63:30-1 O 26 '87
Time travel [imagining one's future as a therapeutic tool; work of J. Hart] B. Lawren. il *Omni* 10:20+ N '87
When you need psychotherapy. R. Hyatt. il *USA Today (Periodical)* 116:84-6 N '87

Psychotherapy—cont.

Costs

That minor problem of paying for therapy. il *U S News World Rep* 103:101 S 28 '87

History

Therapies: a brief history. il *N Y Times Mag* p49 Ag 30 '87

Psychotropic drugs *See* Psychopharmacology

Psyllids

The bird that farms the dell [relationship between bell miners, psyllids, and eucalyptus dieback] R. H. Loyn. il *Nat Hist* 96:54-60 Je '87

PTA *See* Parents' and teachers' associations

Ptarmigans

Grouse and spouse [willow ptarmigan] K. Martin. il *Nat Hist* 96:62-9 F '87

Pterosaurs

Prehistoric pelves: bones of contention [work of David Unwin] il *Discover* 8:6-7 Jl '87

Pterosaurs waddled when they walked? [theory of David M. Unwin] *Sci News* 131:344 My 30 '87

PTL Network

Ankerberg discusses the part he played [uncovering the J. Bakker sex scandal] il por *Christ Today* 31:52 Je 12 '87

As the spiritual soap opera plays on, an expert assesses how Jim Bakker's fall could change television preaching [interview with J. K. Hadden] J. S. Podesta. il pors *People Wkly* 27:44-6 Ap 13 '87

At the helm of PTL [J. Falwell] C. Neuhaus. il pors *People Wkly* 27:30-3 Je 15 '87

Auctioning an empire. M. Green. il pors *People Wkly* 27:40-3 Je 8 '87

Bakker quits [J. Bakker] *Christ Century* 104:328 Ap 8 '87

The Bakker tragedy [danger of mixing television and ministry] T. C. Muck. il por *Christ Today* 31:14-15 My 15 '87

The Bakkers vs. the hired gun [conflict of interest charges brought against lawyer N. R. Grutman] G. Carroll. il por *Newsweek* 110:61-2 S 7 '87

Baring body and soul [J. Hahn, J. Bakker and PTL scandal; cover story] il pors *People Wkly* 28:32-7 O 5 '87

Beyond Bakker. W. F. Buckley. *Natl Rev* 39:59 Jl 3 '87

Breaking faith, two TV idols fall [J. and T. Bakker] J. Wadler. il pors *People Wkly* 27:80-2+ My 18 '87

Can Jim and Tammy make a comeback? G. Witkin. il por *U S News World Rep* 103:21 O 19 '87

A crackdown at PTL. il por *Christ Today* 31:51+ Je 12 '87

Divided Pentecostals: Bakker vs. Swaggart. E. L. Blumhofer. *Christ Century* 104:430-1 My 6 '87

Dropping the reins at PTL [J. Falwell] il por *Christ Today* 31:40 N 6 '87

The fall of the House of Bakker. J. M. Wall. *Christ Century* 104:323-4 Ap 8 '87

False profits [televangelists] T. McNichol. *New Repub* 196:11-12 Ap 13 '87

Falwell and the PTL: 'send money'. D. Gates. il por *Newsweek* 109:6 My 25 '87

Falwell says media ministers need more accountability. por *Christ Today* 31:42 Jl 10 '87

Falwell throws in the towel [resignation] R. N. Ostling. il por *Time* 130:74 O 19 '87

Folding the PTL tent? L. Howard. il *Newsweek* 110:7 S 28 '87

Fresh out of miracles [J. Bakker loses TV ministry] R. Watson. il por *Newsweek* 109:70-2 My 11 '87

God and money [PTL scandal; cover story; special section] il pors *Time* 130:48-55 Ag 3 '87

God and money [TV evangelists; cover story; special section] il pors *Newsweek* 109:16-23 Ap 6 '87

The gospel according to the free market [shakeout among TV evangelists] T. Mason and S. Ticer. il por *Bus Week* p43-4 Ap 6 '87

Gospelgate II: target Falwell. L. Martz. il pors *Newsweek* 109:56-7+ Je 1 '87

Hahn bares her soul, etc. G. Hackett. il pors *Newsweek* 110:43 O 12 '87

Heaven can wait [J. and T. Bakker; cover story; special section] il pors *Newsweek* 109:58-62+ Je 8 '87

Heaven in 15 minutes or less [J. Bakker sex scandal] A. Fotheringham. il *Macleans* 100:56 Ap 20 '87

Hellfire, brimstone—and a TV scandal [J. Bakker sex scandal] B. Levin. il pors *Macleans* 100:42-3 Ap 6 '87

How much money did Jim and Tammy need? il por *Newsweek* 110:60-1 Ag 3 '87

Jerry Falwell's anti-AIDS dollar drive. M. Doan. il por *U S News World Rep* 102:12-13 My 4 '87

Jim and Tammy rise again. J. Adler. il por *Newsweek* 110:77 O 19 '87

The Jim Bakker affair. il pors *Christ Today* 31:36-7 Ap 17 '87

Jim Bakker made me do it. P. Yancey. il *Christ Today* 31:64 O 16 '87

Jim Bakker's lost America. A. Kopkind. il pors *Esquire* 108:174-8+ D '87

New Bakker charge [sexual misconduct charges by J. Hahn] K. L. Woodward. il por *Newsweek* 109:6 Ap 13 '87

Of God and greed [J. Bakker-J. Falwell feud] R. N. Ostling. il pors *Time* 129:70-2+ Je 8 '87

On having fun with fundamentalists [J. Bakker sex scandal] W. F. Buckley. *Natl Rev* 39:60 My 8 '87

Ousting two from the clergy [J. Bakker and R. Dortch fired from the Assemblies of God] R. N. Ostling. il por *Time* 129:65 My 18 '87

An "outrageous" ministry [J. Bakker scandal] D. Brand. il por *Time* 129:82 My 4 '87

Paying the wages of sin [J. Bakker] G. Hackett. il por *Newsweek* 109:28 Mr 30 '87

Pearlygate satires are weak on substance [press coverage of J. Bakker scandal] L. I. Sweet. *Christ Century* 104:644-5 Jl 29-Ag 5 '87

Preacher-bashing and the public life [J. Bakker scandal and media overkill] J. M. Wall. *Christ Century* 104:347-8 Ap 15 '87

PTL: a battle of words in the holy war [J. Bakker hires lawyer M. Belli] il pors *Newsweek* 110:25 Jl 6 '87

A really bad day at Fort Mill [J. Bakker forced to resign from PTL in wake of sex scandal] R. N. Ostling. il por *Time* 129:70 Mr 30 '87

Religious distraction. K. Burris. *Commonweal* 114:310-11 My 22 '87

Spring cleaning at Jim Bakker's PTL. J. L. Sheler and J. Thornton. il *U S News World Rep* 102:8-9 My 11 '87

Stones fly in the TV temple [J. Bakker-J. Falwell feud] G. Witkin. il pors *U S News World Rep* 102:10-11 Je 8 '87

Taking command at Fort Mill [J. Bakker loses TV ministry] R. N. Ostling. il pors *Time* 129:60 My 11 '87

The televangelist fiasco: top '87 religion story. *Christ Century* 104:1163-5 D 23-30 '87

Thou shalt not smirk [J. Bakker sex scandal] *Natl Rev* 39:17 Ap 24 '87

A troubled homecoming [files for bankruptcy] L. Martz. il pors *Newsweek* 109:21+ Je 22 '87

TV's endless holy wars [Bakkers' attempt to regain ministry] M. Gray. *Macleans* 100:45 Jl 6 '87

TV's raging holy wars [J. Bakker scandal] L. Black. il por *Macleans* 100:54 My 11 '87

TV's unholy row [sex scandal involving J. Bakker; cover story] R. N. Ostling. il pors *Time* 129:60-4+ Ap 6 '87

Untold story of black founder of Pentecostal church body rocked by sex scandal of whites [W. J. Seymour of the Assemblies of God and reaction to J. Bakker scandal] S. Booker. il pors *Jet* 72:12-14+ My 18 '87

The value of preacher-bashing [discussion of April 15, 1987 article, Preacher-bashing and the public life] J. M. Wall. *Christ Century* 104:532-4 Je 3-10 '87

War of the evangelists: unfunny reflections [J. Bakker and J. Swaggart] T. H. Stahel. *America* 156:293 Ap 11 '87

What profits a preacher? [televangelists] K. L. Woodward. il *Newsweek* 109:68 My 4 '87

Anecdotes, facetiae, satire, etc.

Hostile takeovers. M. E. Marty. *Christ Century* 104:343 Ap 8 '87

Pu Yi, 1906-1967

about

Billions of emperors. B. Bertolucci. il por *Film Comment* 23:34 N/D '87

Puberty

Girl to woman: a growing-up guide. A. Bell. il *Teen* 31:50+ N '87

My son the man [teenager] M. K. Blakely. por *Ms* 15:28-9 Mr '87

Public accounting *See* Government accounting

Public administration

See also
Bureaucracy
Crisis management in government
Military administration

Public art
1986 in review: public art. il *Art Am* 75:50-1 Ag '87
Get rid of that eyesore! T. Morganthau. il *Newsweek* 110:23+ Ag 17 '87
Gold rush to hell [A. Jaar's installation of photographs of Brazilian gold rush in New York subway station] S. Staggs. il *Art News* 86:9 F '87
Liability insurance for artists. D. Grant. *Am Artist* 51:66-7 Jl '87
On public art and the public interest. A. C. Danto. *Art News* 86:208 O '87
Pattern & decoration in the public eye [J. Kozloff's large tile and mosaic murals] S. Webster. il *Art Am* 75:118-25 F '87
The perils of public sculpture [West Germany] D. Galloway. il *Art Am* 75:37-9+ D '87
Public support for artists through percent for art. J. Jevnikar. il *Am Artist* 51:12+ Mr '87

Anecdotes, facetiae, satire, etc.
Szyrk v. Village of Tatamount et al. W. Gaddis. *New Yorker* 63:44-50 O 12 '87

Exhibitions
Site reading: British art in public spaces [TSWA 3D show] R. Cork. il *Art Am* 75:144-51 S '87
Urban disturbances [work of K. Wodiczko] E. Lajer-Burcharth. bibl f il *Art Am* 75:146-53+ N '87

Public Broadcasting Service
And now, for something completely cheap [programming] J. Hitt. il *Harpers* 275:58-9 N '87
Opportunities abound on PBS and cable [miniseries and movies based on novels] L. See. *Publ Wkly* 231:30 Ap 3 '87
PBS and nonfiction. *Publ Wkly* 231:56-7 Je 12 '87
What's up this fall on PBS. W. A. Henry. il *Channels* 7:66 S '87

Public buildings
See also
Chicago (Ill.)—Public buildings
Courthouses
Library architecture
Post office buildings
Public art
School buildings
Visitor centers

Public comfort stations
Toilet training for adults: learn what you can catch in public bathrooms. A. Cassidy. il *Redbook* 169:118-19+ O '87

Public debt *See* Debts, Public
Public documents *See* Government publications
Public employees *See* Government employees
Public figures *See* Celebrities
Public finance *See* Finance
Public gardens *See* Gardens and gardening
Public health
See also
Children—Mortality
Environmental health
Epidemics
Epidemiology
Food inspection
Health facilities
Housing and health
Infant mortality
Mass media and public health
Medical care
Medical policy
Medicine, Preventive
Mortality
Occupational health and safety
Public comfort stations
United States. Public Health Service
Venereal diseases
Health hoax and a health scare [address, September 22, 1987] E. M. Whelan. il *Vital Speeches Day* 54:57-61 N 1 '87
How healthy is your town? (I) [community regeneration] R. Rodale. il *Rodale's Org Gard* 34:19-20 O '87; Same. *Prevention* 39:18-20+ O '87
How healthy is your town? (II) [community regeneration] R. Rodale. il *Rodale's Org Gard* 34:18-19 N '87
The public health payoffs of FDA research. F. E. Young. il *FDA Consum* 21:4-5 D '87/Ja '88
The truth about Americans' health [cover story] E. M. Whelan. il *USA Today (Periodical)* 115:54-8 My '87

Conferences
See also
World Health Assembly

Finance
Paying for HFA [Health for all by the year 2000] il *World Health* p27 Mr '87

International aspects
See also
Council for International Organizations of Medical Sciences
World Health Organization
Ottawa charter for health promotion [charter for action to achieve Health for all by the year 2000 and beyond] il *World Health* p16-17 My '87

Photographs and photography
International photo competition: Health for all, all for health. il *World Health* p31 My '87

Africa
Human T-lymphotropic virus type 4 and the human immunodeficiency virus in West Africa. P. J. Kanki and others. bibl f il *Science* 236:827-31 My 15 '87
Malaria: fighting the African scourge. L. Tangley. il *BioScience* 37:94-8 F '87

California
See also
California. Division of Occupational Health and Safety
Los Angeles (Calif.)—Public health
Orange County (Calif.)—Public health
San Francisco (Calif.)—Public health

Canada
See also
Canada. Health Protection Branch

Caribbean region
Islands in the sun [immunization program] H. C. Smith. il *World Health* p21-2 Ja/F '87

Central America
Health as a bridge for peace. M. L. Schneider. il *World Health* p4-6 O '87

Colorado
The AIDS tracers [contact tracing program] R. Healy. il *Life* 10:52-5 O '87

Developing countries
See also
Independent International Commission on Health Research for Development
Cigarettes smoked outstrip population growth. il *World Health* p30 Mr '87
Does wealth equal health? D.-C. Lambert. il *Courier* 40:8-12 Ag '87
Nairobi Safe Motherhood Conference reviews concerns, activities to help pregnant women and mothers. il *UN Chron* 24:63-4 My '87
Ottawa charter for health promotion [charter for action to achieve Health for all by the year 2000 and beyond] il *World Health* p16-17 My '87
Preventing child mortality [Child survival: risks and the road to health report] il *Futurist* 21:41 N/D '87

Finland
Viral exposure boosts schizophrenia risk [research by Sarnoff A. Mednick and others] B. Bower. *Sci News* 132:180 S 19 '87

France
Vive la difference! M. Carpenter. il *Women's Sports Fitness* 9:88 Mr '87

Guam
The bad seed [connection between neurotoxins in food and brain disease; research by Peter S. Spencer and others] K. Wright. *Sci Am* 257:44 O '87
Environmental hypothesis for brain diseases strengthened by new data [plant toxins] R. Lewin. il *Science* 237:483-4 Jl 31 '87
Guam amyotrophic lateral sclerosis-Parkinsonism-dementia linked to a plant excitant neurotoxin [cover story] P. S. Spencer and others. bibl f il map *Science* 237:517-22 Jl 31 '87
Plant at the root of neural disorders [research by Peter S. Spencer and others] *Sci News* 132:94 Ag 8 '87

Illinois
See also
Chicago (Ill.)—Public health

India
Mankind and the mosquito [National Malaria Eradication Programme] R. M. Prothero. il *World Health* p18-19 Je '87

Kenya
Detection of Rift Valley fever viral activity in Kenya by satellite remote sensing imagery [vegetation measurement linked to flood conditions that produce mosquitoes] K. J. Linthicum and others. bibl f il maps *Science* 235:1656-9 Mr 27 '87
Rift Valley fever: long-distance diagnosis [vegetation measurement linked to floods and mosquitoes; study by Kenneth J. Linthicum and others] J. Silberner. *Sci News* 131:199 Mr 28 '87

Public health—*cont.*

Latin America

See also
Pan American Health Organization
The Americas [cover story; special issue] il *World Health*
p2-29 O '87

Massachusetts

See also
Cambridge (Mass.)—Public health
Framingham (Mass.)—Public health

New York (State)

See also
Love Canal case
New York (N.Y.)—Public health

Nigeria

Compare two nations' care: the Soviet Union and Nigeria.
P. M. Jones. il *Sch Update* 119:24-5 Ap 20 '87

Pakistan

Motivating parents [immunization program] M. I. Burney
and F. A. Lari. il *World Health* p19-20 Ja/F '87

Prince Edward Island

A grim milestone on P.E.I [first recorded death from
AIDS] B. MacAndrew. *Macleans* 100:52 O 5 '87

Soviet Union

Compare two nations' care: the Soviet Union and Nigeria.
P. M. Jones. il *Sch Update* 119:24-5 Ap 20 '87
The sickening Soviet reality. G. F. Will. il *Newsweek*
109:68 Ja 19 '87

Spain

Spain's deadly elixir [toxic industrial rapeseed oil
poisoning case] il *Macleans* 100:35 Ap 13 '87

Tanzania

Schisto comes to town. R. K. Sarda. il *World Health*
p27-9 Je '87

Texas

See also
Mesquite (Tex.)—Public health

Thailand

Basic minimum needs. A. Nondasuta and P. Piyarath.
il *World Health* p14-15 Je '87

United States

See Public health

West Africa

Victory in sight against 'river blindness'. D. D. Silva.
il *UN Chron* 24:75-6 My '87

West Virginia

See also
Williamson (W. Va.)—Public health

Zimbabwe

Popular technology beats schisto. P. Taylor. il *World
Health* p28-9 Jl '87
Zimbabwe: from supermarket to cafeteria. H. Anenden.
il *World Health* p21-3 Je '87

Public health and mass media *See* Mass media and public
health
Public Health Service *See* United States. Public Health
Service
Public housing projects *See* Housing projects
Public institutions

See also
Mentally handicapped—Institutional care

Public interest

See also
Whistle blowing (Public interest)

Public lands

See also
Homesteads—History
National parks and reserves
United States. Bureau of Land Management
Wilderness areas
Biodiversity and the public lands [cover story; special
section; with editorial comment by T. H. Watkins]
il maps *Wilderness* 50:10-38+ Spr '87
Of turbo boots and rooster tails: the ORV and the
public lands. R. Reinhardt. il *Wilderness* 50:28-36
Summ '87

Arizona
Photographs and photography
Arizona territories. D. Schicketanz. il *Wilderness* 50:41-9
Spr '87

Idaho

An about-face for the BLM [planting sagebrush] G.
Oakley. il *Sierra* 72:13-14 Ja/F '87

United States

See Public lands

Western States

Hunt the locked-up places. J. Zumbo. il *Outdoor Life*
180:90-1+ N '87
Shale shock on the western slope. S. M. Voynick. il
Sierra 72:29-31 My/Je '87

Wyoming

What price, hunting? [privatization of wildlife and public
lands access] L. Williamson. il *Outdoor Life* 180:38+
Ag '87

Public libraries *See* Libraries
Public offerings of stock *See* Stocks—Marketing
Public officers

See also
Black public officers
Bureaucracy
Conflict of interests (Public office)
Congressmen
Drugs and public officers
Governors
Politicians
Senators
United States—Executive departments
Women public officers
Top performances of '87 [special section] il *U S News
World Rep* 103:46-9+ D 21 '87

Anecdotes, facetiae, satire, etc.

Unsung heroes. M. Ivins. il *Progressive* 51:19 Ap '87

Appointment, qualifications, etc.

The help-wanted sign on the White House door. R.
Fly. *Bus Week* p41 F 2 '87
Who's who in the administration. See issues of The
Washington Monthly
The young pol's guide to the brave new world [grueling
confirmation hearings] D. Brooks. il *Natl Rev* 39:28-30+
Ap 10 '87

Biography

Judgment in hard-cover [books about B. Mulroney] P.
Gessell. il *Macleans* 100:17 N 2 '87

Dismissal

Firing is hard to do [reluctance of presidents to fire
officials and staff members] il *Time* 129:15 Mr 2
'87

Ethics

See Political ethics

Financial disclosure

How not to value a politician. L. Jereski. il *Forbes*
140 Sp Issue:352 O 26 '87

Protection

Notes and comment. *New Yorker* 63:33 N 23 '87

Resignation

Washington's shameful revolving door [lobbying by former government officials] R. Evans and R. D. Novak.
Read Dig 130:118-22 My '87

Salaries, allowances, etc.

Banning the free lunch [executive branch officials
prohibited from accepting free lunches] E. Clift. il
Newsweek 110:19 D 28 '87
More pay? 'Who, us?'. M. Greenfield. il *Newsweek* 109:80
F 9 '87
Pay dirt [D. Regan's role in federal pay raise recommen-
dation] F. Barnes. *New Repub* 196:12-14 F 2 '87
Washington may get a raise—but not without a fight.
D. Harbrecht. il *Bus Week* p36 F 2 '87

Sexual behavior

Author's life imitates his art [libel suit won by J. Archer
in Great Britain] A. Deming. il por *Newsweek* 110:62
Ag 3 '87
A Rocky horror shower scene looms large in the lusty
memoir Joan Braden wants to forget. W. Plummer.
il pors *People Wkly* 28:38-40 S 28 '87
Spare pennies [J. Archer wins libel suit against the Star]
W. R. Doerner. il por *Time* 130:31-2 Ag 3 '87

Canada

See also
Canada. Cabinet

United States

See Public officers

Public opinion

See also
AIDS (Disease)—Public opinion
Baseball, Professional—Public opinion
Developing countries—Foreign opinion—American
Football, Professional—Public opinion
Genetic research—Public opinion
Iran-contra affair—Public opinion
Israel—Foreign opinion—American
Japan—Foreign opinion—American
Nuclear warfare—Public opinion
Political attitudes
Public opinion polls
Reagan-Gorbachev summit conference, 1987—Public
opinion
Rumor
Soviet Union—Foreign opinion—American
Space research—Public opinion
Stock market crash, 1987—Public opinion

Public opinion—See also—*cont.*
   Surrogate mothers—Public opinion
   Tennis—Public opinion
   United States—Foreign opinion
The 19th annual Gallup poll of the public's attitudes toward the public schools. A. Gallup and D. L. Clark. *Phi Delta Kappan* 69:17-30 S '87
1987 readers' poll. L. Lague. il *People Wkly* 28:66-76 Jl 27 '87
Americans and their money: 1987 [survey] W. C. Banks. il *Money* 16:211-12+ N '87
Are schools a scandal? [results of survey] I. Groller. il *Parents* 62:33 N '87
Attitudes in black and white [results of Time poll] il *Time* 129:21 F 2 '87
Business week/Harris poll. See issues of Business Week
Crime in America: the shocking truth [results of survey] R. Hillhouse. *McCalls* 145:144 Mr '87
Differences between educators and the public on questions of education policy. S. M. Elam. il *Phi Delta Kappan* 69:294-6 D '87
Heroic proportions [most admired men and women polls; study by Tom W. Smith] A. H. Rosenfeld. il *Psychol Today* 21:15 Jl '87
Interpreting public opinion: five common fallacies. J. Doble. *Current* 294:20-5 Jl/Ag '87
Listening to the heartbeat [American public's perceptions of aviation] R. L. Collins. *Flying* 114:24+ My '87
The Money readers' poll. C. Rubenstein. il *Money* 16:194-7 F '87
Of many things [Inside America] G. W. Hunt. *America* 156:inside cover Je 13 '87
Popularity contest [results of poll on sources of pleasure or satisfaction] J. Queenan. *New Repub* 196:14-15 Mr 23 '87
The president, the public and the schools. *America* 157:259 O 24 '87
This just in: love is eternal [U.S. news-CNN poll] il *U S News World Rep* 102:10 F 23 '87
TV preachers and public trust [U.S. news-CNN poll] il *U S News World Rep* 102:15 Ap 13 '87
A U.S. news poll: echoes of Watergate [dismay over public morality] il *U S News World Rep* 102:56-7 F 23 '87
The ultimate screen test [poll on movie stars] il *People Wkly* 27:56-8+ F 9 '87
The view from Main Street: America is slipping. M. Doan. il *U S News World Rep* 102:20-1 F 2 '87
Canada
   See also
   Soviet Union—Foreign opinion—Canadian
Should the state kill? [cover story; special section; with editorial comment by Kevin Doyle] il *Macleans* 100:2, 14-20+ Je 29 '87
A turning away from politics [Maclean's/Decima poll; special section; with editorial comment by Kevin Doyle] il *Macleans* 100:2, 24-8+ Ja 5 '87
China
Think tanks come of age. M. Lord. il *U S News World Rep* 103:44 O 12 '87
Germany
   See also
   Great Britain—Foreign opinion—German
Great Britain
   See also
   United States—Foreign opinion—British
India
   See also
   United States—Foreign opinion—Indian (East Indian)
Italy
   See also
   United States—Foreign opinion—Italian
Japan
   See also
   United States—Foreign opinion—Japanese
Soviet Union
   See also
   United States—Foreign opinion—Russian
United States
   See Public opinion
Western Europe
   See also
   Nicaragua—Foreign opinion—European
   United States—Foreign opinion—European
Public opinion polls
Excuse me, what's the pollsters' big problem? [accuracy] S. Siwolop. il *Bus Week* p108 F 16 '87
Local opinion polling for educators. J. E. Walker. *Educ Dig* 53:26-9 D '87

Problems in the use of survey questions to measure public opinion. H. Schuman and J. Scott. bibl f il *Science* 236:957-9 My 22 '87
Public ownership *See* Government ownership
Public policy analysis *See* Policy sciences
Public prosecutors
   See also
   Giuliani, Rudolph W.
The high price of indictment [problems of public officials] T. Gest and D. Baer. il *U S News World Rep* 102:23-4 Je 8 '87
Whose trial is it anyway? [defense lawyers attacking victims and prosecutors in court] R. Lacayo. il *Time* 129:62 My 25 '87
Public radio broadcasting *See* Radio broadcasting, Public
Public records
FCC faces records meltdown. R. O'Brien. il *Channels* 7:11 Ja '87
Public relations
   See also
   Architectural firms—Public relations
   Banks and banking—Public relations
   Business—Public relations
   Motorcycle industry—Public relations
   Petroleum industry—Public relations
   Press releases
   Publicity
   Resorts—Public relations
   School and the community
   Sports—Public relations
   Women in public relations
A cracked morality play. J. Saltzman. *USA Today (Periodical)* 115:91 Mr '87
Japan
The sin of 'smelling Japanese' [trying to build a more American image] A. Miller. il *Newsweek* 109:55 Ap 27 '87
Public relations and politics
   See also
   Advertising, Political
   Government publicity
   Presidents—Public relations
The politics of blame: public policy and avoidance behavior. R. K. Weaver. *Current* 296:11-15 O '87
Public relations consultants
   See also
   Primetime (Firm)
   Anecdotes, facetiae, satire, etc.
Hard sell. T. C. Boyle. *Harpers* 275:17-20 D '87
   Fees
Is this article worth $19,260? [Primetime's charges to clients] J. Alter. il por *Newsweek* 109:77 Ap 20 '87
Public school and college cooperation *See* Educational cooperation
Public school teachers *See* Teachers
Public schools
   See also
   Education
   High schools
   Magnet schools
   Voucher plan in education
The 19th annual Gallup poll of the public's attitudes toward the public schools. A. Gallup and D. L. Clark. *Phi Delta Kappan* 69:17-30 S '87
Are schools a scandal? [results of survey] I. Groller. il *Parents* 62:33 N '87
Choice: the parents' perspective. V. D. Mueller. *Phi Delta Kappan* 68:761-2 Je '87
A continuing conundrum? [research on effectiveness of public vs. private schools] G. W. Bracey. il *Phi Delta Kappan* 69:74-5 S '87
Differences between educators and the public on questions of education policy. S. M. Elam. il *Phi Delta Kappan* 69:294-6 D '87
Local opinion polling for educators. J. E. Walker. *Educ Dig* 53:26-9 D '87
Preschool children in the public schools: good investment? Or bad? D. B. Strother. bibl f il *Phi Delta Kappan* 69:304-8 D '87
The president, the public and the schools. *America* 157:259 O 24 '87
Results and future prospects of state efforts to increase choice among schools. J. Nathan. bibl f il *Phi Delta Kappan* 68:746-52 Je '87
Should prekindergarten be public? F. Roberts. il *Parents* 62:58 F '87
The United States educational system [address, October 26, 1987] D. T. Kearns. *Vital Speeches Day* 54:150-3 D 15 '87

Public schools—*cont.*
What do you need to know? A close look at U.S. education [cover story; special issue] il *Sch Update* 120:1-8+ N 6 '87

Censorship
See Censorship

Desegregation
See also
Magnet schools
Blacks holding ground, Hispanics losing in desegregation. *Phi Delta Kappan* 68:406-7 Ja '87
Can a judge raise taxes? [R. G. Clark's attempt to end school segregation by ordering tax increases in Kansas City] J. Seligmann. il por *Newsweek* 110:98 O 12 '87
Ebony update: Ernest Green [central figure in 1957 desegregation case in Little Rock, Ark.] il pors *Ebony* 43:72+ D '87
The heirs of Oliver Brown: in Topeka, a landmark equality case is still before the courts [Brown v. Board of Education] J. E. White. il por *Time* 130:88-9 Jl 6 '87
A judge's breach of confidence [former law clerk P. Elman's revelations about F. Frankfurter and Brown v. Board of Education] R. Lacayo. il pors *Time* 129:71 Ap 6 '87
Kansas judge raises taxes to desegregate schools [Russell Clark] *Jet* 73:22 O 19 '87
Little Rock Nine return to school where violence erupted 30 years ago. W. Wofford, Jr. il *Jet* 73:14-16 N 9 '87

Finance
See Education—Finance

Medical care
Issues for school clinics. L. Edwards and N. Brent. *Educ Dig* 53:52-5 N '87

Segregation
Atlanta, Chicago schools among the most segregated. *Jet* 72:12 Ag 10 '87
Illinois leads U.S. with most school segregation. *Jet* 72:8 Mr 30 '87

Uniforms
See School uniforms

Public schools and business *See* Business and education
Public schools and religion
AAP joins in appeal of Tennessee textbook ruling. H. Fields. *Publ Wkly* 231:30 Mr 6 '87
Alabama board to appeal ban on 'humanist' texts. M. Yen. *Publ Wkly* 231:14 Mr 27 '87
Alabamboozle [secular humanist textbook ruling] E. Doerr. *Humanist* 47:39-40 My/Je '87
Back talk [discussion of February 1987 article, Censoring science] K. Stein. il *Omni* 9:12+ S '87
Bill Bennett's dilemma. D. Wagner. il *Natl Rev* 39:28-31+ Je 19 '87
Book ban overturned [Tennessee textbook case] *Christ Century* 104:745 S 9-16 '87
Books and schools [fundamentalists' attacks on books] *Nation* 244:705-6 My 30 '87
Can a state require public schools to allow a moment of silence? [New Jersey statute] H. Hagerman; R. L. Maddox. il *Christ Today* 31:52 N 20 '87
Celebrating Christmas in public schools. W. Bole. *Christ Today* 31:35-6 D 11 '87
Censoring science [fundamentalists] K. Stein. il *Omni* 9:42-4+ F '87
Challenging the private sector. M. E. Marty. *Christ Century* 104:871 O 7 '87
Curriculum in the public schools: can compromise be reached? C. L. Glenn. il *Christ Century* 104:441-3 My 6 '87
Defining the role of religion in the American classroom. J. W. McDermott. *Educ Dig* 52:14-17 Ap '87
Does religion belong in our public schools? E. Doerr. *USA Today (Periodical)* 116:48-50 S '87
Fundamentalists lose two textbook cases in federal appeals courts [Alabama and Tennessee cases] *Publ Wkly* 232:11 S 11 '87
God's right Hand [W. Brevard Hand's decision that secular humanism is a religion in Alabama textbook case] D. R. Carlin, Jr. il *Commonweal* 114:263-4 My 8 '87
Going back to the books [fundamentalists lose court cases in Tenn. and Ala.] R. Lacayo. il *Time* 130:60 S 7 '87
The humanist. E. Doerr. *Humanist* 47:2 N/D '87
Is 'humanism' a religion? [Judge W. Brevard Hand bans certain textbooks in Alabama] T. Gest. il *U S News World Rep* 102:10-11 Mr 16 '87

Mark of Darrow [fundamentalists lose textbook court battles in Tenn. and Ala.] il *U S News World Rep* 103:10 S 7 '87
Nondenominational humanism? [Alabama secular humanist textbook case] *Natl Rev* 39:19 Ap 10 '87
Not-so-good books [United States history texts slight the role of religion] J. L. Pasley. *New Repub* 196:20-2 Ap 27 '87
Other sides to the textbook controversy [discussion of May 6, 1987 articles, Voltaire arraigned in Alabama: the textbook humanism case and Curriculum in the public schools: can compromise be reached?] D. Underhill; C. L. Glenn. il *Christ Century* 104:631-2 Jl 15-22 '87
Paul Vitz on censorship [excerpts from Censorship: evidence of bias in our children's textbooks] P. C. Vitz. *Phi Delta Kappan* 68:453 F '87
Private prayer in the schools. E. W. Kelly. *Educ Dig* 53:34-5 S '87
Reassessing religion and public education. P. L. Shriver. *Educ Dig* 53:30-3 D '87
Religion in public education. E. Doerr. il *Humanist* 47:41-2 N/D '87
Religious bias [Judge W. Brevard Hand bans "secular humanist" textbooks from Alabama schools] il *Time* 129:66 Mr 16 '87
Religious literacy and public schools. *America* 157:123 S 12-19 '87
The right books [Paul Vitz's study of public school social studies texts] C. Williamson. *Natl Rev* 39:64 Ja 30 '87
Right-wing pressure. *USA Today (Periodical)* 116:11 D '87
Should government help kids attend private schools? J. H. DeDakis. il *Christ Today* 31:52-3 My 15 '87
Should public schools teach creation science? W. S. Morrow; J. Wiester. il *Christ Today* 31:50 S 18 '87
The significance of the decision in 'Scopes II' [fundamentalists vs. school system in Tennessee textbook case] E. B. Jenkinson. bibl f *Phi Delta Kappan* 68:445-50 F '87
Some thoughts on the Tennessee textbook case. T. J. Flygare. bibl f il *Phi Delta Kappan* 68:474-5 F '87
Striking down the textbook rulings. K. A. Lawton. il *Christ Today* 31:50-1 O 2 '87
Student clinics: a sexy issue [Catholic bishops condemn high school birth control clinics] D. Whitman. il *U S News World Rep* 103:12 N 30 '87
Students speak out against textbook censorship [Buffalo, N.Y.] F. Edwords. *Humanist* 47:23-6+ Mr/Ap '87
Supreme Court considers a second moment-of-silence law [New Jersey statute] *Christ Today* 31:56 N 6 '87
Supreme Court will rule on moment-of-silence law [New Jersey statute] B. Spring. il *Christ Today* 31:56+ Mr 20 '87
Textbook cases. T. C. Muck. *Christ Today* 31:17 Ap 17 '87
The textbook cases: secularism on appeal [cases in Tenn. and Ala.] P. A. Zirkel. bibl f *Phi Delta Kappan* 69:308-10 D '87
Textbook controversies: a 'disaster for public schools'? [fundamentalists vs. school system in Tennessee textbook case] C. L. Glenn. bibl f *Phi Delta Kappan* 68:451-5 F '87
Textbook ruling sparks concern [secular humanism ruling in Alabama] C. Holden. *Science* 235:1459 Mr 20 '87
Textbooks ignore religion in American history. *Educ Dig* 52:46-7 Mr '87
Textbooks on trial [Alabama decision banning textbooks from public schools because they promote secular humanism] *America* 156:265 Ap 4 '87
Tillich in an Alice-in-Wonderland world [court decisions pertaining to school textbooks and secular humanism] J. McBride. *Christ Century* 104:519-20 Je 3-10 '87
Voltaire arraigned in Alabama: the textbook humanism case. D. Underhill. *Christ Century* 104:438-40 My 6 '87
Why censor religion? Faiths and the textbooks. B. Vobejda. *Current* 296:30-2 O '87
Wins and losses [referenda on church-state issues and Tennessee textbook case] E. Doerr. *Humanist* 47:40+ Ja/F '87

Public sculpture *See* Public art
Public service advertising *See* Advertising, Public service
Public Service Co. of N. H.
A utility runs out of juice. K. H. Hammonds. il *Bus Week* p26 Ag 24 '87
"We are in a heap of trouble" [Seabrook nuclear plant] J. Attinger. il *Time* 130:114 O 26 '87

Public Service Co. of N. H.—*cont.*
Who says utilities can't be raider bait? [M. J. Whitman's play for Public Service of N.H. includes debt by Seabrook nuclear plant] C. Brown. il por *Bus Week* p112 N 23 '87

Public Service Co. of New Mexico
More power to 'em. T. Jaffe. il *Forbes* 139:194 Ap 6 '87

Public service television programs *See* Television broadcasting—Public service programs
Public services *See* Municipal services
Public speaking
See also
Rhetoric
And our next speaker is . . . drugged [using propranolol to treat stage fright] C. Schaeffer. il *Changing Times* 41:18 Ag '87
Fear of speaking [women] L. J. Nonkin. il *Vogue* 177:161+ My '87
Honing your speaking skills. L. Wiener. il *U S News World Rep* 102:56 Ja 12 '87
How to give a speech. W. Kiechel, III. il *Fortune* 115:179-80+ Je 8 '87
How to pick an exciting speaker. M. Olmstead. *Work Woman* 12:21 Mr '87
Merchants of inspiration [motivational speakers] J. Main. il *Fortune* 116:69-71+ Jl 6 '87
Never be nervous again [condensation]; ed. by Gaylen Moore. D. Sarnoff. *Read Dig* 131:27-8+ D '87
Perils of the platform. R. Lynes. il *Archit Dig* 44:42+ D '87
Speakers and the bottom line [address, August 7, 1987] R. Kelly. *Vital Speeches Day* 54:47-50 N 1 '87

Anecdotes, facetiae, satire, etc.
A few words about public speaking. D. Barry. il *Saturday Evening Post* 259:28 Ja/F '87

Study and teaching
The sounds of success. J. Sherman. *Work Woman* 12:72 D '87

Public television *See* Television broadcasting, Public
Public transportation *See* Local transit
Public utilities
See also
Electric utilities
Gas utilities
JWP Inc.
New York (N.Y.)—Public utilities
Northwest Harris County Municipal Utility District No. 19 (Tex.)
UtiliCorp United Inc.
Waterworks

Acquisitions and mergers
Building a powerhouse, one utility at a time [UtiliCorp's acquisitions] M. Ivey. il por *Bus Week* p81 F 2 '87

Laws and regulations
See also
Public utilities—Rates

Rates
New tax laws should lower your utility bills. *Consum Rep* 52:466 Ag '87

Securities
Utilities: they're still hot. M. C. Paulson. il *Changing Times* 41:88-94 Mr '87

Taxation
New tax laws should lower your utility bills. *Consum Rep* 52:466 Ag '87

Public welfare
See also
Child welfare
Day care—Federal aid
Legal Services Corporation
Old age assistance
Rent subsidies
Welfare hotels
Workfare
Back on the chain gang. il *Progressive* 51:7-8 Ag '87
Back to the drawing board. *Natl Rev* 39:18 Mr 27 '87
Black women leaders view needed reforms in welfare. *Jet* 73:15 O 26 '87
Caging the welfare monster. R. B. Carleson. il *Read Dig* 131:86-90 S '87
The Democrats are getting to work on welfare reform. S. B. Garland. il *Bus Week* p39 Ag 3 '87
Fixing welfare [need to reform Aid to Families with Dependent Children program] G. J. Church. il *Time* 129:18-21 F 16 '87
Gray works to save fed. programs cut by Reagan [Rep. W. Gray] *Jet* 71:4 Mr 9 '87
Is the time ripe for welfare reform? C. Holden. il *Science* 238:607-9 O 30 '87

The key to welfare reform. D. Whitman. il *Atlantic* 259:22-5 Je '87
The move to reform welfare. D. C. Ruffin. il *Black Enterp* 17:21 Ja '87
New efforts to help America's poor [special issue] il maps *Sch Update* 119:3-10+ Mr 23 '87
The NIMBY syndrome [not in my backyard rationale in objecting to placement of public facilities] *Commonweal* 114:310 My 22 '87
Poor laws and pauper policies [address, November 29, 1986] D. M. Stewart. *Vital Speeches Day* 53:245-8 F 1 '87
Reagan cuts cause many to slip through 'net'. *Jet* 73:28 S 28 '87
Rep. Ford gets backing for new welfare reform bill. por *Jet* 72:36 Ap 20 '87
Should the poor earn their keep? [Christian values and welfare policy] S. V. Monsma. il por *Christ Today* 31:28-31 Je 12 '87
Strong medicine. *America* 156:166-7 F 28 '87
Tough, tightfisted and traditional [D. Moynihan's proposal for reform] W. Shapiro. il por *Time* 130:19 Ag 3 '87
Welfare reform may finally be in the works. S. B. Garland. il *Bus Week* p108-9+ N 2 '87
A welfare reform mirage [D. Moynihan's proposal] M. Kaus. il por *Newsweek* 110:21 Ag 3 '87
The welfare strait. R. Kuttner. *New Repub* 197:20-1+ Jl 6 '87

History
Americans' changing views of the needy. I. Peck. il *Sch Update* 119:15-17 Mr 23 '87

California
California: an ambitious effort to give welfare recipients education and job skills. S. LaFee. il *Sch Update* 119:25 Mr 23 '87
A welfare mother's battle to clean up the Medicaid mess. S. B. Garland. il *Bus Week* p42 D 21 '87
Workfare [cover story] L. Udesky. il *Progressive* 51:14-17 D '87

Massachusetts
Have we seen the future? [M. Dukakis' program; cover story] A. Kopkind. il *Nation* 244:631+ My 16 '87
Letters [discussion of May 16, 1987 article, Have we seen the future?] A. Kopkind. *Nation* 244:872+ Je 27 '87
Massachusetts's ET program: workfare that stresses choices and child care. J. Krasner. *Sch Update* 119:24-5 Mr 23 '87
Public policies that perform. il *U S News World Rep* 103:18-19 Ag 10 '87

New York (State)
See also
New York (N.Y.)—Public welfare

Scandinavia
Scandinavia sours on welfare cost. R. Knight. il *U S News World Rep* 102:39 My 25 '87

United States
See Public welfare

Washington (D.C.)
See Washington (D.C.)—Public welfare

Washington (State)
Welfare-plus in Washington [Family Independence Program] H. G. Chua-Eoan. il *Time* 129:23 Ja 19 '87

Western Europe
Western Europe's safety net. P. M. Jones. il *Sch Update* 119:26-7 Mr 23 '87

Public works
See also
Dams
Water resources development
Capital spending suffers when public investment lags. G. Koretz and K. Pennar. il *Bus Week* p34 N 2 '87

Arizona
See also
Central Arizona Project

Publicists, Publishing *See* Books—Advertising
Publicity
See also
Advertising
Government publicity
Here's a new way to fame: just paint yourself into a big corner [Angelyne] il pors *People Wkly* 27:73 Je 22 '87
Indecent exposure: will too much hype spoil these rock stars? J. Pareles. il *Mademoiselle* 93:80+ D '87

Publicity, Political *See* Advertising, Political
Publishers and authors *See* Authors and publishers
Publishers and libraries *See* Libraries and publishers
Publishers and publishing
 See also
  Academy Chicago Publishers
  Addison-Wesley Publishing Co.
  Adler & Adler Publishers Inc.
  Alfred A. Knopf, Inc.
  Arbor House Publishing Company, Inc.
  Atlantic Monthly Press
  August House Inc.
  Authors and publishers
  Ballantine Books, Inc.
  Bantam, Doubleday, Dell Publishing Group
  Best sellers
  Betterway Publications Inc.
  Black Sparrow Press
  Books—Marketing
  Books—Prices
  Callaway Editions (Firm)
  Catalogs, Publishers'
  Celestial Arts Publishing Company
  Chronicle Books
  Chronicle Publications Inc.
  City Lights Books Inc.
  College teachers—Publications
  Collins Publishers Inc.
  Computers—Publishing use
  Contemporary Books, Inc.
  Crown Publishers Inc.
  Curbstone Press
  Dembner Books
  Doubleday & Company, Inc.
  Dover Publications, Inc.
  Ecco Press
  Editors and editing
  Edward L. Burlingame Books
  Facts on File, Inc.
  Farrar Straus & Giroux, Inc.
  Freundlich Books
  Friendly Press
  Grove Press, Inc.
  Gulf & Western, Inc.
  Harcourt Brace Jovanovich, Inc.
  Harper & Row Publishers, Inc.
  Health Communications Inc.
  Hearst Corporation
  Henry Holt and Company
  Hill & Wang, Inc.
  Houghton Mifflin Co.
  IBS Publishing (Firm)
  Information storage and retrieval systems—
   Publishing use
  Libraries and publishers
  Literary agencies and agents
  Little, Brown & Co. Inc.
  Longman Group U.S.A. Inc.
  Macmillan, Inc.
  McGraw-Hill, Inc.
  Medallion Books
  Mercury House Publishing
  Monthly Review Press
  New Society Publishers
  New York Times Company
  Newmarket Press
  Nick Lyons Books
  Ortho Books
  Oxmoor House Inc.
  Pantheon Books, Inc.
  Pelican Publishing Company Inc.
  Performing Arts Journal Publications
  Philosophical Library Inc.
  Pocket Books
  Printing industry
  Prometheus Books
  Publishing Hall of Fame
  Putnam Publishing Group
  Random House Inc.
  Reader's Digest Condensed Books
  Roberts Rinehart (Firm)
  Schocken Books Inc.
  Scholastic Inc.
  Scribner Book Companies, Inc.
  Self publishing
  Simon & Schuster Inc.
  Soho Press Inc.
  South End Press
  Stephen Greene Press
  Stewart, Tabori & Chang
  Stockton Press
  Summit Books
  Thomas Nelson, Inc.
  Ticknor & Fields
  Time Inc.
  University presses
  Viking Penguin Inc.
  Villard Books
  Warner Books Inc.
  Weidenfeld & Nicolson (New York, N.Y.)
  Western Publishing Co.
  William Morrow & Co., Inc.
  Women in publishing
  Writers & Readers Publishing Inc.

1986: looking back [special section] il *Publ Wkly* 231:35-7+ Ja 9 '87
1986: the year in review [special section] il *Publ Wkly* 231:16-33 Mr 13 '87
Another kind of censorship [reluctance of publishers and booksellers to deal with report of Pornography Commission] M. J. McManus. por *Publ Wkly* 231:70 Ja 23 '87
Beyond the big time [trade publishing] J. B. Adler. por *Publ Wkly* 232:67 S 11 '87
Esquire's guide to the literary universe [with introd. by Rust Hills] il *Esquire* 108:51-3+ Ag '87
The Fellowship in action [symposium on innovation sponsored by Oscar Dystel Fellowship] J. F. Baker. *Publ Wkly* 232:33 D 25 '87
Forgotten skills [specialized publishing] N. Lyons. por *Publ Wkly* 232:48 Ag 21 '87
Independent publishing. J. Barbato. See occasional issues of Publishers Weekly beginning October 23, 1987
The literary-industrial complex. T. Solotaroff. *New Repub* 196:28+ Je 8 '87
News of the week. M. Reuter and M. Yen. See issues of Publishers Weekly
The small time [small presses] S. Klawans. *Nation* 245:422-5 O 17 '87
The small time [small presses] S. Klawans. *Nation* 244:654-6 My 16 '87
Southern spotlight. B. Summer. See occasional issues of Publishers Weekly beginning January 20, 1984
Talk of the trade. L. Fleischer. See issues of Publishers Weekly
Tracking New York's literary ghosts [writers' and publishers' burial places] J. Culbertson and T. Randall. il *Publ Wkly* 232:27-9 Jl 17 '87
Trade news. J. Davis and W. Goldstein. See issues of Publishers Weekly
West watch. L. See. See occasional issues of Publishers Weekly beginning September 2, 1983
A worthy cause [S. Alyson's efforts to get the publishing community to produce a free book about fighting AIDS] L. Fleischer. *Publ Wkly* 232:40 Ag 21 '87
  Acquisitions and mergers
Anatomy of an acquisition (I). G. Feldman. il *Publ Wkly* 231:19-27 Je 26 '87
Anatomy of an acquisition (II). G. Feldman. il *Publ Wkly* 232:17-23 Jl 3 '87
Buying out the boss at CBS Magazines [P. Diamandis' group] D. Lieberman. il por *Bus Week* p30 Jl 27 '87
Congress is uninterested in examining industry consolidation. H. Fields. *Publ Wkly* 231:26 Je 12 '87
Falling off a limb at Harcourt [Salomon and Mutual Shares lost on convertible bond gamble] D. Zigas. por *Bus Week* p32 Jl 6 '87
Harper & Row gets $190 million offer from private investor [T. L. Cross] M. Reuter. il por *Publ Wkly* 231:10 Mr 20 '87
Harper & Row studies HBJ, Cross takeover bids. *Publ Wkly* 231:13 Mr 27 '87
HBJ sells units to Edgell group for $334.1 million. C. Reid. *Publ Wkly* 232:11 N 27 '87
HBJ shows the leveraged deal is alive and well [R. L. Edgell acquires magazine unit] G. DeGeorge. *Bus Week* p36-7 N 30 '87
Judge backs Harcourt in ruling on debentures. *Publ Wkly* 232:12 Jl 3 '87
Let's look much harder at mergers. I. Karp. por *Publ Wkly* 231:46 Ap 17 '87
Los Angeles financial firm is acquiring assets of Medallion Books. *Publ Wkly* 232:18 Ag 14 '87
McGraw-Hill purchases TDM. *Publ Wkly* 232:416 Ag 7 '87
Mergers, large and small, a Midwest habit too. T. Unsworth. *Publ Wkly* 232:74 Ag 14 '87
Peter Diamandis is finally working for himself [CBS Magazines] P. Finch. il por *Bus Week* p48 Ag 3 '87

Publishers and publishing—Acquisitions and mergers—*cont.*

Random buys Schocken for unit of Pantheon. *Publ Wkly* 232:101 Jl 24 '87

"We'll get back to you on that" [how Ziff-Davis magazines are faring at CBS and Murdoch group] R. Behar. il *Forbes* 139:42+ Ap 6 '87

What makes book publishing firms such enticing takeover targets? M. Yen. *Publ Wkly* 231:14-15 Ap 17 '87

Anecdotes, facetiae, satire, etc.

Merger, he wrote. R. Curtis. il *Publ Wkly* 231:46 Ja 9 '87

International aspects

Bantam's Vitale to head Doubleday-Dell trade group [changes in wake of Bertelsmann takeover] *Publ Wkly* 231:24 Ja 9 '87

Battle of the book barons [R. Maxwell's bid for Harcourt Brace Jovanovich] R. Henkoff. il por *Newsweek* 109:46 Je 1 '87

Bertelsmann's U.S. invasion may be just beginning. J. E. Pluenneke. il *Bus Week* p72-3 Ag 10 '87

A British press lord goes global [R. Maxwell seeks takeover of Harcourt Brace Jovanovich] P. Sherrid. il por *U S News World Rep* 102:49-50 Je 1 '87

Citizen Murdoch makes his mark in books and television [bid for Harper & Row] D. Pauly. il por *Newsweek* 109:47+ Ap 13 '87

A costly save at Harcourt [antitakeover measures against R. Maxwell's bid] P. Engardio. *Bus Week* p42 Je 8 '87

CVBC executives hail Random House takeover. V. Menkes. *Publ Wkly* 231:21 My 22 '87

Elsevier hunts for 'high margin' acquisitions in United States. H. R. Lottman. *Publ Wkly* 231:22 My 29 '87

HBJ rejects Maxwell's $1.7 billion bid. il por *Publ Wkly* 231:18 My 29 '87

Jovanovich charges Maxwell is 'unfit' [takeover controversy; with interview with R. Maxwell] M. Reuter. *Publ Wkly* 231:13-14 Je 5 '87

Jovanovich sees nothing friendly in Maxwell's bid. P. Engardio. il por *Bus Week* p47 Je 1 '87

Macmillan buys out Octopus to be sole owner of Pan for $36.5 million. V. Menkes. *Publ Wkly* 232:15 O 2 '87

Maxwell sues to block HBJ's $3 billion plan. *Publ Wkly* 231:23 Je 12 '87

Murdoch increases stake in Pearson conglomerate to 14.7%. V. Menkes. *Publ Wkly* 232:28 O 9 '87

Murdoch to sell half of Harper & Row to Collins, to become co-chairman. J. Mutter and V. Menkes. *Publ Wkly* 232:70 S 18 '87

Pearson in a pickle [R. Murdoch's stake in publishing operations of Pearson plc] S. Miller. *Bus Week* p60 O 12 '87

A press giant is set to pounce [Hachette eyes U.S. companies] F. J. Comes. *Bus Week* p54+ D 21 '87

Random House to acquire Chatto, Virago, Bodley and Cape group. *Publ Wkly* 231:114 My 15 '87

Rupert Murdoch to acquire Harper & Row for $65 a share. M. Reuter. il por *Publ Wkly* 231:16-17 Ap 10 '87

Simon & Schuster bids on stake in Britain's ABP. V. Menkes. *Publ Wkly* 231:10 Je 26 '87

Thomas and 13 others leave Harper & Row [reorganization in wake of takeover by News Corporation Ltd.] M. Reuter. il *Publ Wkly* 231:21-2 My 29 '87

Weidenfeld and Grove: a flying start. C. T. Anthony. il *Publ Wkly* 232:15-18 S 4 '87

Canada

Harrowsmith's leader cuts his roots [J. Lawrence sells out to Telemedia] A. Shortell. il por *Macleans* 100:30 Mr 30 '87

Saturday night fever [C. Black's purchase of Saturday night magazine] P. Young. por *Macleans* 100:55 Je 29 '87

Great Britain

Octopus to acquire ABP's trade publishing lines. V. Menkes. *Publ Wkly* 232:12 D 18 '87

Reed acquires Octopus, leads British publishing. V. Menkes. il *Publ Wkly* 232:11 Jl 17 '87

Netherlands

Kluwer battles Elsevier's hostile takeover attempt. H. R. Lottman. *Publ Wkly* 232:15 Jl 10 '87

Advertising

See Books—Advertising

Antitrust cases

Giving no ground, Avon and NCBA settle suit. M. Colin. *Publ Wkly* 232:9 N 13 '87

Art

Expanding your market with multiples [posters, prints, and reproductions based on paintings] M. S. Doherty. il *Am Artist* 51:52-9 My '87

Art literature

See also
Abbeville Press Inc.
Harry N. Abrams, Inc.
Hudson Hills Press Inc.

Divine inspiration [publication of Fra Angelico: the light of the soul and Rembrandt: the human form and spirit] E. P. Williams. il *Vogue* 177:112 F '87

A remarkable book from the 'greatest painter of flowers' [Knopf/Callaway publication of Georgia O'Keeffe: one hundred flowers] W. Goldstein. il *Publ Wkly* 232:27+ S 11 '87

Associations

See also
Association of American Publishers
Baltimore Publishers Association
Motovun Group
Publishers Marketing Association
Texas Publishers Association

Autobiography

Making book on Oliver North. S. Meredith. *Harpers* 274:54-5 Mr '87

Aviation literature

See also
Jane's Publishing Company Ltd.

Awards

See also
Carey-Thomas Awards

Herbert Bailey wins 'Ben' Award [Curtis Benjamin Award] il por *Publ Wkly* 231:18 Ap 17 '87

Backlist books

Looking harder at the backlist [children's books] C. C. Epstein. il *Publ Wkly* 232:119-21 Jl 24 '87

Black literature

Oxford to publish 19th century black women writers series. B. Levine. il *Publ Wkly* 231:48-9 Je 5 '87

Business literature

See also
AMACOM Book Division
American City Business Journals, Inc.
Commerce Clearing House, Inc.
Prentice-Hall, Inc. Business and Professional Division

Calendars

7,300 days . . . and counting [Sierra Club calendars] M. Olmstead. il *Sierra* 72:96-8+ N/D '87

Cartoons

'Best editorial cartoons' series: a southern perennial [published by Pelican] B. Summer. *Publ Wkly* 232:42 S 4 '87

Children's literature

See also
ABC-CLIO (Firm)
Checkerboard Press
Children's Book Press
Determined Productions (Firm)
Frederick Warne & Co. Ltd.
Joy Street Books
Ladybird Books Ltd.
Marvel Publishing (Firm)
Orchard Books
R & S Books
Walker Books Ltd.

Children's science fiction and fantasy grows up. L. E. Owen. il *Publ Wkly* 232:32+ O 30 '87

Fall 1987 children's books [special section] D. E. Roback and K. O. Fakih. il *Publ Wkly* 232:107-21+ Jl 24 '87

Making book on book-and-cassette packages. B. Stewart. il *Publ Wkly* 232:51-5 N 27 '87

Marketing on two fronts. A. Meeker. *Publ Wkly* 232:44-7 N 27 '87

A new era in Canadian children's books. F. Wishinsky. *Publ Wkly* 231:36 Mr 20 '87

Random House, Dell launch series for younger readers. il *Publ Wkly* 232:24 S 25 '87

Spring 1987 children's books [special section] D. E. Roback and K. O. Fakih. il *Publ Wkly* 231:93-137 F 27 '87

A start with babies [agent/publisher V. Lansky] T. Unsworth. *Publ Wkly* 232:38 D 11 '87

Comic books, strips, etc.

See also
Marvel Comics Group

Conferences

Book massification [The book as a mass commodity] M. Reuter and M. Yen. *Publ Wkly* 231:13-14 Ap 3 '87

Publishers and publishing—Conferences—*cont.*
Trade book publishing: state of the art [Association of American Publishers symposium] D. Maryles and others. *Publ Wkly* 232:12+ N 27 '87

Cookbooks
See also
HP Books

Dictionaries
The war of words. R. A. Carter. il *Publ Wkly* 232:27-8+ O 2 '87

Educational literature
See also
Publishers and publishing—Textbooks

Employees
See also
Strikes—Publishers and publishing
Women in publishing
People in motion: some notable job changes. il *Publ Wkly* 231:41 Ja 9 '87

Salaries, pensions, etc.
What some senior women earn. *Publ Wkly* 231:31 Ja 23 '87

Encyclopedias
New directions for encyclopedias. A. Hellemans. il *Publ Wkly* 232:40+ O 2 '87

Ethical aspects
How menacing is the Red menace? E. B. Claflin. il *Publ Wkly* 232:23-4 N 20 '87
When is a true story true? [dilemma of publishing W. Strieber's Communion as nonfiction] E. B. Claflin. il por *Publ Wkly* 232:23-6 Ag 14 '87

Facsimiles of manuscripts
See Manuscripts—Facsimiles

Fiction
Fiction's new look [trade paperbacks] T. Todd. il *Publ Wkly* 231:29-33 F 6 '87
Is there a short story boom? G. Feldman. il *Publ Wkly* 232:25-9 D 25 '87
Prestige and profits [quality fiction paperbacks] R. Givens. il *Newsweek* 110:59 Jl 27 '87
Who needs a blockbuster? Another way of publishing [university presses] C. Sternhell. il *N Y Times Book Rev* 92:40 O 11 '87

Finance
AAP endorses Senate bill to change educational block grants. H. Fields. *Publ Wkly* 232:20 Ag 14 '87
Commerce Dept. predicts 4.5% sales gain in 1987. H. Fields. *Publ Wkly* 231:25 Ja 9 '87
Communications media. A. B. Block. il *Forbes* 139:99-100 Ja 12 '87
Five-year forecast sees 9.1% annual growth. M. Reuter. il *Publ Wkly* 232:20-2 D 25 '87
Proposed budget has good and bad news. H. Fields. *Publ Wkly* 231:21 Ja 23 '87
U.K. publishers are sanguine after London market crash. V. Menkes. *Publ Wkly* 232:11 N 13 '87
Why 'big books' are essential. W. C. Hammond, III. por *Publ Wkly* 232:26 Jl 31 '87

Garden literature
See also
Ortho Books
The flowering of garden books. C. T. Anthony. il *Publ Wkly* 231:37-9+ F 20 '87

Graphic novels
Graphic novels: the latest word in illustrated books. B. Levine. bibl il *Publ Wkly* 231:45-7 My 22 '87

Guidebooks
See also
Global Travel Publishers
The widening world of travel books. G. Feldman. il *Publ Wkly* 231:31-2+ F 13 '87

Historical literature
Mediawatch [history on TV sells books in Great Britain] H. David. *Hist Today* 37:8-9 O '87
To picture the past [publishing books on Canadian history] G. Hildebrandt. il *Macleans* 100:62 O 12 '87

History
How the book trade survived the Great Depression [reprints from March 10, 1975 issue] C. B. Grannis. il *Publ Wkly* 232:19-22 N 20 '87
'The image' and publishing: 1962 [excerpt from The image] D. J. Boorstin. *Publ Wkly* 232:24 D 4 '87

Illustated books
See also
Harry N. Abrams, Inc.

International aspects
See also
Books—Export-import trade
Abbeville announces joint publishing program with the Soviets. *Publ Wkly* 232:24 S 4 '87

The international face of British publishing. G. Feldman. il *Publ Wkly* 232:19-20+ N 27 '87
International front. H. R. Lottman. See occasional issues of Publishers Weekly beginning May 27, 1983
Mikhail Gorbachev, author [interview with S. M. Bessie] A. P. Sanoff. il por *U S News World Rep* 103:73 O 12 '87
The Moscow protocols. J. F. Baker. *Publ Wkly* 232:23 O 16 '87
Our very own summit [Soviet-American Citizens' Summit] L. Fleischer. *Publ Wkly* 232:46 D 25 '87
Soviet delegation to U.S. proposes more copublishing ventures. il *Publ Wkly* 231:18 Je 19 '87
When freedom to read suffers [implications of decisions of McGraw-Hill and other publishing firms to terminate their South African operations] I. L. Horowitz. por *Publ Wkly* 232:38 Jl 17 '87

Large print books
Large-print for children: ABC-CLIO's two new lines. D. E. Roback. il *Publ Wkly* 232:23 S 25 '87

Laws and regulations
See also
Copyright
Son of Sam laws
Let's look much harder at mergers. I. Karp. por *Publ Wkly* 231:46 Ap 17 '87
Salinger and 'The bell jar': what do they mean to publishers? C. E. Rinzler. il *Publ Wkly* 231:20-2 Ap 24 '87
The year in Washington. H. Fields. il *Publ Wkly* 231:37 Ja 9 '87

Limited editions
See also
Alecto Historical Editions
Limited Editions Club

Motion picture literature
See also
Lone Eagle Press

Music
See also
SBK Entertainment World Inc.

Nature literature
See also
Voyageur Wilderness Books (Firm)

New Age literature
New Age. D. Tuller. il *Publ Wkly* 232:29-33 S 25 '87

Paperback books
See also
Avon Books (Firm)
Bantam Books, Inc.
Berkley Publishing Group
Dell Publishing Co., Inc.
Fireside Books
HP Books
Lynx Communications
Noonday Press
Pan Books Ltd.
Paperback books—Marketing
Penguin Books Inc.
Pocket Books
Traveller's Bookshelf (Firm)
Zebra Books
Fiction's new look [trade paperbacks] T. Todd. il *Publ Wkly* 231:29-33 F 6 '87
'Hamlet': a cause for indecision [examination of various editions] W. Goldstein and B. Levine. il *Publ Wkly* 232:25-6 N 6 '87
Prestige and profits [quality fiction paperbacks] R. Givens. il *Newsweek* 110:59 Jl 27 '87

Periodicals
See also
American City Business Journals, Inc.
CBS Inc. Magazines Division
Computers—Publishing use
Family Media, Inc.
Hearst Corporation
Johnson Publishing Company, Inc.
Knapp Communications Corp.
M. Shanken Communications
Magazine Development Corporation
Newhouse Broadcasting Corporation
Time Inc.
Weider Health & Fitness Corporation
Ziff-Davis Publishing Co.
Back-of-the-envelope philosopher [L. Solomon] D. Machan. il por *Forbes* 140:106-7 Ag 24 '87
Magazines for the hip. J. Schwartz. il *Newsweek* 109:46-7 Ap 6 '87
The small time [small presses] S. Klawans. *Nation* 244:263-4+ F 28 '87

Publishers and publishing—*cont.*

Photographic literature

Photo book publishers. A. Stone. *Petersens Photogr Mag* 16:44+ O '87

U.S.S.R. opens up to Day in the life crew [shooting of Collins Publishers' picture book] S. Bolle. il *Publ Wkly* 232:35-7 Ag 28 '87

Picture books

Photo book publishers. A. Stone. *Petersens Photogr Mag* 16:44+ O '87

Political literature

Left, but not left out. J. Mutter. il *Publ Wkly* 232:18-19 Jl 17 '87

South End Press: the long march continues [radical publisher seeks to influence political dialogue] R. Bongartz. il *Publ Wkly* 232:17+ Jl 17 '87

Quality control

Turning off youthful readers [high prices, shoddy production, and poor editorial quality of books] C. R. Larson. por *Publ Wkly* 232:49 N 20 '87

Religious literature

See also

Bible—Publication and distribution
Meyer Stone Books
Multnomah Press
Thomas Nelson, Inc.
Wolgemuth and Hyatt
Word Inc.
Zondervan Corp.

Christian book publishers face leaner times. D. D. Buss. il *Christ Today* 31:60-2 Mr 6 '87

Fall religious books [special section] il *Publ Wkly* 232:39-61 O 9 '87

Harper, San Francisco: experienced at weathering change. L. See. *Publ Wkly* 232:49 Jl 31 '87

Religious books. W. Griffin. See occasional issues of Publishers Weekly beginning July 29, 1983

Religious publishing. W. Griffin. See occasional issues of Publishers Weekly beginning July 18, 1986

Spring religious books [special section] il *Publ Wkly* 231:38-52+ Mr 6 '87

Reprints

See also

Comstock Editions Inc.
Mutual Publishing Company

Returns policy

Keeping a rein on returns. J. E. Holzer. por *Publ Wkly* 232:428 Ag 7 '87

Returns are born [reprint from March 10, 1975 issue] A. R. Leventhal. il *Publ Wkly* 232:20 N 20 '87

Returns: how high is too high? [roundtable discussion] il *Publ Wkly* 231:34-9 Mr 13 '87

Science fiction

Children's science fiction and fantasy grows up. L. E. Owen. il *Publ Wkly* 232:32+ O 30 '87

Scientific literature

See also

Plenum Publishing Corp.
Tempus Books

Securities

Bulls, bears and book publishers: assessing the damage [effects of crash] M. Reuter and C. Reid. il *Publ Wkly* 232:10-11 N 6 '87

PW Index underperformed. K. Gruneich. il *Publ Wkly* 231:36 Ja 9 '87

Short stories

See Publishers and publishing—Fiction

Spy stories

See also

Foreign Intelligence Press

Statistics

See also

Graphics Press

Book sales rise 5.8% to $10.5 billion in 1986. il *Publ Wkly* 231:12 Je 26 '87

First quarter sales: vigorous. J. P. Dessauer. il *Publ Wkly* 232:426 Ag 7 '87

Second quarter sales: solid. J. P. Dessauer. il *Publ Wkly* 232:40 O 16 '87

Slow finish to lackluster 1986. J. P. Dessauer. il *Publ Wkly* 231:24 Ap 3 '87

Title output level, prices stabilized. C. B. Grannis. il *Publ Wkly* 231:16-19 Mr 13 '87

U.S. book title output and average prices, final 1986 figures. C. B. Grannis. il *Publ Wkly* 232:45+ O 2 '87

Study and teaching

Publishing education in changing times. D. Tuller. il *Publ Wkly* 232:30-3 D 25 '87

Study guides

See also

Cliff's Notes Inc.

When less is more [Keynotes line of literary study guides devised by W. J. Campbell] L. Fleischer. il *Publ Wkly* 231:81 Ja 9 '87

Taxation

House unit urges textbook costs be deducted as they are incurred. H. Fields. *Publ Wkly* 232:15 Ag 21 '87

IRS and expenses: good news and bad news for publishers, authors. H. Fields; R. G. Stern. *Publ Wkly* 232:12 N 6 '87

New tax law: is a book the medium or the message? R. G. Stern. *Publ Wkly* 231:24-5 My 29 '87

Senators appear sympathetic to change in tax capitalization. H. Fields. *Publ Wkly* 232:18-19 Ag 14 '87

Task force campaigns to restore prepublication tax deductions. H. Fields. *Publ Wkly* 231:13 Mr 27 '87

Technical literature

See also

Howard W. Sams & Co.
Plenum Publishing Corp.
Tempus Books

Textbooks

College publishers and used books. D. C. Baker and J. Hileman. il *Publ Wkly* 232:18-21 D 11 '87

House unit urges textbook costs be deducted as they are incurred. H. Fields. *Publ Wkly* 232:15 Ag 21 '87

Japanese versus U.S. texts: Dept. of Ed. assessment. H. Fields. *Publ Wkly* 231:21 F 6 '87

Textbook controversy intensifies nationwide. C. Holden. il *Science* 235:19-20 Ja 2 '87

Textbook publishers plead their case to key congressional staffers. H. Fields. *Publ Wkly* 232:13 Jl 10 '87

Thesauri

The word according to Roget [Roget's international thesaurus] R. A. Carter. *Publ Wkly* 232:36 O 2 '87

Travel literature

See also

Traveller's Bookshelf (Firm)

Fearless spirits: tales of women explorers. L. Shapiro. il *Newsweek* 110:65 Ag 3 '87

Brazil

See also

Distribuidora Record de Servicos de Imprensa SA

Canada

See also

International Thomson Organisation Ltd.
McClelland & Stewart
Quebecor Inc.

Canada trade talks may end 'fire sales' of U.S. subsidiaries. H. Fields. *Publ Wkly* 232:12-13 O 23 '87

A new era in Canadian children's books. F. Wishinsky. *Publ Wkly* 231:36 Mr 20 '87

Publishing in French Canada. J. Poulin. il *Publ Wkly* 232:36+ Jl 31 '87

To picture the past [publishing books on Canadian history] G. Hildebrandt. il *Macleans* 100:62 O 12 '87

France

See also

Compagnie Européenne de Publication
Hachette (Librairie)
Librairie Arthème Fayard

Legally bound [publishers in France dismayed by red tape involved in selling rights to Americans] H. R. Lottman. *Publ Wkly* 231:34 Je 12 '87

Publishing cities: Paris. H. R. Lottman. il *Publ Wkly* 232:13-14+ N 13 '87

Germany (West)

See also

Bertelsmann AG

Munich. H. R. Lottman. il *Publ Wkly* 232:126-32 S 18 '87

Great Britain

See also

Alecto Historical Editions
Associated Book Publishers plc
Bloomsbury Publishing Ltd.
Chatto, Virago, Bodley Head & Jonathan Cape Ltd.
Frederick Warne & Co. Ltd.
Jane's Publishing Company Ltd.
Ladybird Books Ltd.
Octopus Publishing Group plc
Pan Books Ltd.
Reed International plc
Virago Press Ltd.
Walker Books Ltd.
William Collins plc

Publishers and publishing—Great Britain—*cont.*
British publishing [special section] il *Publ Wkly* 232:17+ N 27 '87
U.K. publishers are sanguine after London market crash. V. Menkes. *Publ Wkly* 232:11 N 13 '87
　　　　　Hawaii
See also
Mutual Publishing Company
　　　　　Israel
What's new in Jerusalem. H. R. Lottman. il *Publ Wkly* 231:26-35 F 20 '87
　　　　　Italy
See also
Mondadori Viaggi SpA
　　　　　Japan
See also
Nihon Keizai Shimbun, Inc.
　　　　　Netherlands
See also
Elsevier (Firm)
Kluwer NV
　　　　　Nicaragua
Managua's first book fair. H. Rohmer. il *Publ Wkly* 232:19-21 S 4 '87
　　　　　Soviet Union
The Moscow protocols. J. F. Baker. *Publ Wkly* 232:23 O 16 '87
The new look in Moscow. N. Perlman. *Publ Wkly* 232:11 O 16 '87
Our very own summit [Soviet-American Citizens' Summit] L. Fleischer. *Publ Wkly* 232:46 D 25 '87
Soviet delegation to U.S. proposes more copublishing ventures. il *Publ Wkly* 231:18 Je 19 '87
'They must not print books that nobody buys' [interview with M. Nenaschev] por *Publ Wkly* 232:30-1 O 16 '87
　　　　　Spain
International front. H. R. Lottman. *Publ Wkly* 232:31 N 6 '87
Revival in Barcelona. H. R. Lottman. il *Publ Wkly* 231:29-30+ My 22 '87
　　　　　Sweden
See also
R & S Books
　　　　　United States
See Publishers and publishing
Publishers Marketing Association
Publishers Marketing Association: a study in multiple strategies. L. See. il *Publ Wkly* 232:33-5 D 18 '87
Publishing *See* Publishers and publishing
Publishing Hall of Fame
John H. Johnson among the ten inducted into Publishing Hall of Fame. il pors *Jet* 73:12+ D 21 '87
Publishing Technology Inc.
Introducing ColorStone [prepress color system] J. P. Frank. il *Publ Wkly* 232:66-8 O 2 '87
Publius
The pursuit of happiness. il *New Leader* 70:12-13 O 5 '87
To form a more perfect union [with editorial comment] *New Leader* 70:2, 11-12 Jl 13-27 '87
To provide for the common defense. *New Leader* 70:12-14 N 16 '87
Puccini, Giacomo, 1858-1924
　　　　　about
La bohème [opera] Reviews
　Opera News il 51:20-1 Ja 3 '87. S. W. Shrader
　Opera News il 51:22-5 Ja 3 '87
Madama Butterfly [opera] Reviews
　New Yorker 63:82-3 Ap 13 '87. A. Porter
　Opera News il 51:20-3 Ja 17 '87
Manon Lescaut [opera] Reviews
　Opera News il 51:18-23 Ja 31 '87
A Puccini bouquet: in his works the composer cultivated floral imagery. K. Stern. il por *Opera News* 51:14-16 Ja 17 '87
Tosca [opera] Reviews
　Opera News il 52:26-8, 30 D 5 '87
Turandot [opera] Reviews
　N Y il 20:62+ Mr 30 '87. P. G. Davis
　New Yorker 63:104+ Mr 30 '87. A. Porter
　Opera News il 51:18-20, 22-3 Mr 28 '87
　Time il 129:92 Mr 23 '87. M. Walsh
Puccio, Thomas
　　　　　about
A gale of fresh air at Milbank Tweed. L. J. Tell. il pors *Bus Week* p102-4 Jl 20 '87
Pucillo, Anthony
　　　　　about
Laying down the PC law. C. O'Malley. il por *Pers Comput* 11:170-1 O '87

Pucillo and Jaynes
Laying down the PC law. C. O'Malley. il por *Pers Comput* 11:170-1 O '87
Puckett, Kirby
　　　　　about
Minny's mighty mite. R. Telander. il pors *Sports Illus* 66:46-9 Je 15 '87
The secret of my new success. J. Coplon. il pors *Sport Mag* 78:50-1+ N '87
Puddings
Thanksgiving puddings. K. Haedrich. il *Ctry J* 14:54-7 N '87
Puddington, Arch
Cambodia [discussion of April 1987 article, Pol Pot in retrospect] *Commentary* 84:14-15 Ag '87
Pol Pot in retrospect. *Commentary* 83:49-54 Ap '87
Pudu *See* Deer
Puebla (Mexico)
　　　　　Description
Puebla and Cholula. C. Hunt. il *Travel Holiday* 167:23-4+ Ap '87
Pueblo Indians
　　　See also
　Hopi Indians
　Petroglyphs National Monument (N.M.)
Ancient mansions of Chaco Canyon [work of the Hyde Exploring Expedition in excavating Anasazi artifacts] il *Nat Hist* 96:74-7 Mr '87
Cutting through a sacred forest [Ojo power line and sacred sites in the Jemez Mountains, N.M.] D. Gibson. il *Sierra* 72:135-6 Ja/F '87
No peace on the Pueblo [radioactive contamination from Los Alamos laboratories] T. Arrandale. il *Sierra* 72:30-3 Mr/Ap '87
Verna Williamson. R. Brown. il por *Ms* 16:102+ Jl/Ag '87
Puerto Mosquito (Vieques Island, Puerto Rico)
A million stars caught in the sea. W. C. Rice. *Sierra* 72:75-6 S/O '87
Puerto Rican cooking *See* Cooking, Puerto Rican
Puerto Ricans
　　　　　United States
　　　　　Crime
A boy and his dog in hell [illegal dog fighting with pit bull terriers in Philadelphia] M. Sager. il *Roll Stone* p36-7+ Jl 2 '87
　　　　　Education
Where high school kids learn to think [Pedro Albizu Campos High School, Chicago] M. Ervin. il *Progressive* 51:11 Je '87
Puerto Rico
　　　See also
　Astronomical observatories—Puerto Rico
　Caribbean National Forest (Puerto Rico)
　Puerto Ricans
　San Juan (Puerto Rico)
　Wildlife—Puerto Rico
　　　　　Industries
　　　See also
　Citrus fruit industry—Puerto Rico
　Liquor industry—Puerto Rico
Puett, Garnett
　　　　　about
Breaking out in hives. G. Henry. il *Art News* 86:174 F '87
Garnett Puett at Dart. S. Taylor. il *Art Am* 75:142-3 Mr '87
Puff pastry *See* Pastry
Puffins
Huffin' for puffins [rescuing young puffins on Heimaey, Iceland] il map *Natl Geogr World* 144:12-15 Ag '87
　　　　　Photographs and photography
Filling the bill. W. Wegner. il *Nat Hist* 96:76-7 Je '87
Puffs, Book *See* Books—Advertising
Puget Sound (Wash.)
　　　See also
　Marine pollution—Puget Sound (Wash.)
　　　　　Photographs and photography
Puget Sound: the maritime world of Wilhelm Hester [turn-of-the-century photographer] R. A. Weinstein. il *Am Hist Illus* 21:20-35 Ja '87
Puget Sound Power & Light Co.
Business helps the elderly [Gatekeeper Program] il *Futurist* 21:53 Mr/Ap '87
The waiting game. J. Cook. il por *Forbes* 140:130+ N 30 '87
Pugin, A. W. N. (Augustus Welby Northmore), 1812-1852
　　　　　about
Pugin & the medieval dream. N. Yates. bibl il *Hist Today* 37:33-40 S '87

Pugin, Augustus Welby Northmore *See* Pugin, A. W. N. (Augustus Welby Northmore), 1812-1852
Pugwash movement
Student Pugwash awarded major grants. R. Hart. *Phys Today* 40:110-11 O '87
Pujol, Annie
about
Filling in a big blank space, French Wheel of fortune fans elect a Vanna of their own. M. Dougherty. il pors *People Wkly* 28:98-9 Ag 3 '87
Pulitzer prizes
Blacks win Pulitzer prizes in drama, poetry categories [A. Wilson and R. Dove] pors *Jet* 72:9 My 4 '87
The march of power [award given to C. Krauthammer for commentary] A. Cockburn. *Nation* 244:564 My 2 '87
Philadelphia stories [3 Pulitzers awarded to Philadelphia inquirer] R. Zoglin. il *Time* 129:62 Ap 27 '87
Pullin, Diana
(jt. auth) *See* Madaus, George F., and Pullin, Diana
Pulls, Door *See* Doorknobs, pulls, etc.
Pulmonary emphysema *See* Emphysema
Pulmonary surfactants *See* Surface active substances
Pulp mills *See* Paper mills
Pulp wood industry *See* Wood pulp industry
Pulsars
Millisecond pulsar discovered in globular cluster [PSR1821-24] *Astronomy* 15:91 N '87
Millisecond pulsar PSR 1937+21: a highly stable clock. L. A. Rawley and others. bibl f il *Science* 238:761-5 N 6 '87
New-wave pulsars. N. E. White. il *Sky Telesc* 73:22-4 Ja '87
Pulsar sets new record [PSR 1937 + 21; work of James Imamura] *Sky Telesc* 74:231 S '87
Puzzling pulsar offers opportunities [millisecond pulsar] D. E. Thomsen. *Sci News* 132:7 Jl 4 '87
When will a pulsar in supernova 1987A be seen? F. C. Michel and others. bibl f il *Science* 238:938-40 N 13 '87
Pulse code modulation
A digital alternative [Toshiba DX-900 video recorder with built-in PCM adapter] C. J. Esse. il *High Fidel* 37:11 Ag '87
Pulse generators *See* Signal generators
Pulse techniques (Electronics)
See also
Pulse code modulation
Fast times in silicon circuits. I. Peterson. il *Sci News* 132:20 Jl 11 '87
Trigger pulses. R. Grossblatt. il *Radio-Electron* 58:121+ My '87
Pumas
Debate around the collar [collaring Florida panthers] B. Latoof. il *Sierra* 72:18+ Mr/Ap '87
Lions—mountain or mounted? [California cougar] K. Glass. il *Sierra* 72:12-13 Jl/Ag '87
Recovery plan focuses on panther survival [Florida panther] il *Natl Parks* 61:45 Mr/Ap '87
Pumping stations
Lake pumper [West Desert Pumping Project for Great Salt Lake] G. Davis. il *Pop Sci* 231:68-70 S '87
Pumpkin faces *See* Halloween
Pumpkin soup *See* Soups
Pumpkins
See also
Cooking—Vegetables
About pumpkins. S. Pacher. il *Mother Earth News* 107:24-31 S/O '87
The Babe Ruth of pumpkin growers [H. Dill] il por *50 Plus* 27:61 O '87
Introducing zunkins [zucchini-pumpkin hybrids] W. Bilozir. il por *Rodale's Org Gard* 34:88-9 O '87
Seed
Fighting stones with seeds [bladder stones] il *Prevention* 39:53 O '87
Pumps
See also
Heat pumps
Mine pumps
Sump pumps
Vacuum pumps
Water pumps
Punch (Beverage)
Flowing bowl. J. Mackin. il *Americana* 15:38-41 N/D '87
Party punches [fruit punches] il *Better Homes Gard* 65:171-2 Ap '87
Three mean punches. G. Waggoner. il *Esquire* 107:24+ Ja '87
Punch! [drama] *See* Shapiro, Leonardo

Punch bowls
The silver punch bowl. O. Bernier. il *Am Herit* 38:24-5 D '87
A tall order for Mr. Clay [400-serving Sweeney Punch Bowl in Wheeling, W. Va.] il *South Living* 22:73 Mr '87
Punching (Metal work)
See also
Taps and dies
Punctuality
See also
Tardiness
Punic Wars
How Carthage lost the sea [reconstruction of Punic warship] H. Frost. il maps *Nat Hist* 96:58-67 D '87
Punishment
See also
Amnesty
Capital punishment
Corporal punishment
Lynching
Pardon
Parole
Preventive detention
Prisons
School discipline
Torture
Considering the alternatives [punishment other than prison] R. Lacayo. il *Time* 129:60-1 F 2 '87
Making punishment fit white-collar crime. L. J. Tell. il *Bus Week* p84-5 Je 15 '87
Stiffer penalties needed [corporate fraud; views of W. Holder and Theodore Mock] *USA Today (Periodical)* 116:6 D '87
Punjab (India)
Hell on wheels [Sikh extremists murder Hindu bus travelers] il *Time* 130:50 Jl 20 '87
'Such a dance of death' [Sikh attacks against Hindus] F. Willey. il *Newsweek* 110:34 Jl 20 '87
Punk culture
Skinheads on the rampage [neo-Nazi youths in California] G. Hackett. il *Newsweek* 110:22 S 7 '87
Photographs and photography
Skinheads of Newcastle. C. Killip. il *Society* 24:84-6 Jl/Ag '87
Puns and punning
Onomatopoeias: the wily photo pun strikes again! H. Werran. il *Petersens Photogr Mag* 16:40-2 N '87
Puns and parodies pay off. S. Glasser. *Writer* 100:19-20+ Je '87
Punt, Neal
All are saved except. por *Christ Today* 31:43-4 Mr 20 '87
Pupil-teacher relationship *See* Teachers and students
Pupils, School *See* Students
Puppets and puppet plays
See also
Howdy Doody (Puppet)
Primitives (Puppets)
Wayang
Chivalry lives as Mike Manteo revives knights to remember [Papa Manteo's Life-Sized Marionettes] D. Grogan. il *People Wkly* 27:52-4 Je 1 '87
Twin cinema [work of T. and S. Quay] T. Rafferty. il *Atlantic* 259:74-6 Je '87
Therapeutic use
Puppets versus drugs [Mexico's Youth Integration Centres] E. Massün. il *World Health* p2-5 Je '87
Puppies *See* Dogs
Puppo, Alberto
The tree [story] il *Américas* 39:50-2 N/D '87
Puppo, Ethel
about
Gopher baroque. C. Bach. il por *Américas* 39:2-7+ S/O '87
Puppo, Giancarlo
about
Gopher baroque. C. Bach. il por *Américas* 39:2-7+ S/O '87
Purcell, Ann
(jt. auth) *See* Purcell, Carl, and Purcell, Ann
Purcell, Carl
Hanging around over Rio. il *Américas* 39:46-9 S/O '87
Purcell, Carl, and Purcell, Ann
Traveler's camera. *See* issues of Popular Photography
Purcell, Gillis, d. 1987
about
Obituary
Macleans il por 100:2 N 30 '87. K. Doyle

Purcell, Rosamond Wolff
　　about
　History in bits and pieces: body snatcher [interview]
　　D. Lessem. il *Omni* 10:82-9 D '87
Purcell, Susan Kaufman
　The choice in Central America. bibl f map *Foreign
　　Aff* 66:109-28 Fall '87
Purcell (Frank) Walnut Lumber Company *See* Frank Purcell
　　Walnut Lumber Company
Purchasing
　　See also
　　Boats and boating—Purchasing
　　Compulsive shopping
　　Consumption (Economics)
　　Motor boats—Purchasing
　　Sales
　　Shopping and shoppers
Purchasing, Government *See* Contracts, Government
Purchasing, Household
　　See also
　　Electronic shopping
　A course in supermarket savvy. *Prevention* 39:42+ F
　　'87
　The eater-friendly grocery list that makes shopping easy.
　　S. Burstein. il *Work Woman* 12:168+ My '87
　Say, brother [man's view of food shopping] N. G.
　　Nesmith. por *Essence* 17:8 Ja '87
　Touring the aisles on a budget. S. C. Finn. il *50 Plus*
　　27:82-3+ Ja '87
Purchasing, Industrial
　If orders are any clue, the quarter looks golden. J.
　　C. Cooper. il *Bus Week* p49-50 O 19 '87
Purchasing, Military *See* United States. Army—
　　Procurement; United States. Dept. of Defense—
　　Procurement
Purdy, Donald A.
　Walking slowly in circles. por *U S News World Rep*
　　102:7 Ap 6 '87
Purdy, Susan
　Luxurious lobster. il *Saturday Evening Post* 259:92-4
　　Jl/Ag '87
Purgatory (Colo.: Resort) *See* Resorts—Colorado
Purification of water *See* Water purification
Purifiers, Air *See* Air filters
Purim, Flora
　　about
　Flora Purim/Airto Moreira. M. Bourne. il pors *Down
　　Beat* 54:15 Ja '87
Puritan Revolution, 1642-1660 *See* Great Britain—History—
　　Puritan Revolution, 1642-1660
Puritans and puritanism
　Editorial. W. Garrett. il *Antiques* 131:598-9 Mr '87
　A republic of souls: puritanism and the American
　　presidency. R. Sennett. il *Harpers* 275:41-6 Jl '87
Purl, Linda
　　about
　Since the world of Matlock isn't her oyster, Linda Purl
　　is shucking the show. J. Stark. il pors *People Wkly*
　　27:67-9 My 18 '87
Purlin, Buck
　Housewrighting without headaches. il *Mother Earth News*
　　106:66-9 Jl/Ag '87
Purmort, Lou
　　about
　"Sailing was boring". B. Leonard. il por *Forbes* 140:50-1
　　Jl 27 '87
Purnick, Joyce, and Oreskes, Michael
　Jesse Jackson aims for the mainstream. il pors *N Y
　　Times Mag* p28-31+ N 29 '87
Pursell, Wallace G.
　A portable photographic platform. il *Astronomy* 15:91-3
　　Jl '87
Purses
　Purses & plumage. il *Harpers Bazaar* 121:52 D '87
Pursuit of happiness *See* Happiness
Purtan, Dick
　　about
　Thanks to a Detroit dee jay, even death hasn't stopped
　　Elvis from turning out more Presleys. il por *People
　　Wkly* 28:45 Jl 27 '87
Purves, Dale, and others
　Nerve terminal remodeling visualized in living mice
　　by repeated examination of the same neuron. bibl
　　f il *Science* 238:1122-6 N 20 '87
Puryear, Martin, 1941-
　　about
　Maverick sculptor makes good. M. Brenson. il por *N
　　Y Times Mag* p84+ N 1 '87
PUSH *See* People United to Serve Humanity (Organization)
Push processing (Photography) *See* Photography—Process-
　　ing

Pushkin Museum of Fine Arts (Moscow, Soviet Union)
　A surprise at the Pushkin [M. Chagall exhibit] S. Strasser.
　　il por *Newsweek* 110:87 S 14 '87
Put and call transactions
　　See also
　　Foreign exchange options
　　Interest rate options
　　Stock index options
　Fancy stuff [funds with sophisticated option strategies
　　and the market crash] W. Baldwin. il *Forbes* 140:185
　　N 30 '87
　Four ways to tame this bear market. J. Edgerton. il
　　Money 16:145-6 D '87
　How put options prop up mutual funds. P. Nulty. il
　　Fortune 116:174-5 D 21 '87
　A low-risk strategy with stocks [selling call options] J.
　　J. Curran. il *Fortune* 116:105-6 Jl 20 '87
　The lowdown on option income funds: their options
　　can imperil your income. E. Schurenberg and L. N.
　　Vreeland. il *Money* 16:25-7 Ap '87
　An options play conservatives can love [covered-call
　　writing] D. Zigas. *Bus Week* p172 S 14 '87
　Racing the market with options. J. Rachlin. il *U S
　　News World Rep* 103:75-6 S 21 '87
Put-downs *See* Invective
La puta vida trilogy [drama] *See* Povod, Reinaldo
Putnam, Pat
　Fateful date against Tate. pors *Sports Illus* 67:48-9 O
　　19 '87
　Gaining at last on the top guy. il por *Sports Illus* 66:40-1
　　Ap 27 '87
　Local boy makes good. il pors *Sports Illus* 66:59 Je
　　15 '87
　Loud left from a quiet champ. il pors *Sports Illus* 67:34-5
　　Jl 27 '87
　Once more with feeling. il pors *Sports Illus* 67:94+ O
　　26 '87
　Only one no. 1. il pors *Sports Illus* 67:20-3 Ag 10
　　'87
　The Orange has the juice. il *Sports Illus* 67:70-2 O
　　26 '87
　The Sioux came through. il *Sports Illus* 66:132+ Ap
　　6 '87
　Soaring to unseen heights. il por *Sports Illus* 66:24-5
　　Mr 9 '87
　Too good for his own good. il pors *Sports Illus* 67:89-90
　　N 30 '87
　You ready, Boom Boom? il por *Sports Illus* 66:96 My
　　11 '87
Putnam Publishing Group
　Peter Israel leaves Putnam; Phyllis Grann becomes CEO.
　　pors *Publ Wkly* 232:15 Ag 28 '87
Putt, M.
　(jt. auth) *See* Rivkin, Richard B., and Putt, M.
Putters (Golf clubs) *See* Golf clubs (Sticks)
Puttnam, David, 1941-
　　about
　Felled in Hollywood's 'killing fields'. J. Egan. por *U
　　S News World Rep* 103:82 S 28 '87
　He rode into Hollywood on a Chariot of fire, but David
　　Puttnam's job at Columbia went up in smoke. M.
　　Dougherty. il pors *People Wkly* 28:125-6+ N 16 '87
　A Hollywood outsider's exit. M. Reese and J. Foote.
　　il por *Newsweek* 110:65 S 28 '87
Puya
　Once in a lifetime [rare Puya raimondii blossoms 72
　　years early] R. Poole. il *Sierra* 72:12 Ja/F '87
Puzzles
　　See also
　　Anagrams
　　Crossword puzzles
　　Jigsaw puzzles
　　Rebuses
　　Rubik's Magic
　　Word games
　Algopuzzles: wherein trains of thought follow algorithmic
　　tracks to solutions. A. K. Dewdney. il *Sci Am*
　　256:128-31 Je '87
　Brain bogglers. M. Stueben. See issues of Discover
　　beginning November 1984 through September 1987
　Penny puzzlers. il *Natl Geogr World* 142:14-15 Je '87
　Puzzles in two and three dimensions, and ways to simplify
　　their solution. J. Walker. *Sci Am* 256:122-6 Je '87
Pyatt, Everett A.
　Streamlining the U.S. acquisition system. por *Aviat Week
　　Space Technol* 127:123 O 19 '87
Pye, A. Kenneth
　　about
　Is there life after football? P. Applebome. il *N Y Times
　　Mag* p73-4+ O 4 '87

Pyes, Craig
Neo-Nazi U. il *New Repub* 196:17-18+ Ja 19 '87
Pyfer, Jean
about
Making a difference. D. Young. il pors *South Living* 22:98+ Je '87
Pygmalion [drama] See Shaw, Bernard, 1856-1950
Pyle, Gerald F., and Patterson, K. David (Karl David), 1941-
The geography of influenza. il maps *Focus* 37:16-23 Fall '87
Pyles, Denise
Her goal: to help others trim down as she did. il pors *Prevention* 39:100+ My '87
Pymm Thermometer (Firm)
Playing with poison [mercury poisoning] K. Dobie and A. Goodman. il *Progressive* 51:19-23 F '87
Pyramid selling operations
Commodores' King arrested in L.A. investment scheme. por *Jet* 72:12 Ap 13 '87
Eternal pyramid: new looks for old scams. *Changing Times* 41:8 F '87
A scam as old as the pyramids. D. R. Katz. il *Esquire* 108:81-2 O '87
Pyramids
Egypt
Heirs to ancient air [plan to study sealed Egyptian crypt; cover story] R. Monastersky. il *Sci News* 132:172-3 S 12 '87
Herodotus's theory of how the pyramids were built gets a lift [views of Martin Isler] il *Discover* 8:8-9 Je '87
New tools for an ancient dig [pharaoh's wooden bark observed in sealed chamber at Great Pyramid] W. D. Marbach. il *Newsweek* 110:80-1 N 2 '87
Pharaoh's boat found in ancient pit [use of remote sensing] R. Monastersky. *Sci News* 132:295 N 7 '87
Probing the chambers of Cheops [video camera reveals wooden boat] D. S. Jackson. il *Time* 130:75 N 2 '87
A quest for ancient Egyptian air [use of remote sensing in archeological investigation] C. Holden. il *Science* 236:1419-20 Je 12 '87
Pyridine compounds
See also
MPTP (Drug)
Identification of an α subunit of dihydropyridine-sensitive brain calcium channels. M. Takahashi and W. A. Catterall. bibl f il *Science* 236:88-91 Ap 3 '87
Pyrotechnic devices
See also
Fireworks
Pythons
For sale: the Gloved One's cast-off main squeeze [Sherman Oaks, Calif. pet store owner L. de Borondy attempts to sell singer M. Jackson's former pet python] il por *People Wkly* 27:88 My 25 '87
Pytka, Joe
about
It's positively Pytka. A. Miller. il por *Newsweek* 110:59 S 14 '87
Pytka Productions
It's positively Pytka. A. Miller. il por *Newsweek* 110:59 S 14 '87
Pyxis (Constellation) See Constellations

Q

Q, Stacey
about
Rock wrap up. il por *Teen* 31:58 Mr '87
Q fever
Poker players, pneumonia and cat tales [Q fever rickettsia transmitted by cat] D. D. Edwards. *Sci News* 132:255 O 17 '87
Q-Med, Inc.
Watch Q-Med as it stalks a silent killer [portable EKG machine to detect silent ischemia] G. G. Marcial. il *Bus Week* p88 Ap 13 '87
Q.V. (New York, N.Y.: Restaurant) See New York (N.Y.)—Restaurants, nightclubs, bars, etc.
Q&A Write (Word processor program) See Word processors and processing—Programming
Qabbānī, Nizār
about
The silence in Arab culture. F. Ajami. *New Repub* 196:27-33 Ap 6 '87

Qabus bin Said, Sultan of Oman, 1940-
about
One dagger not aimed at America. J. Barnes. il por map *U S News World Rep* 102:52 Ap 27 '87
Qaddafi, Muammar al-, 1942-
about
Chad: Kaddafi on the run. F. Coleman. il map *Newsweek* 109:28 Ja 19 '87
Down and out in Faya-Largeau. J. Smolowe. il por map *Time* 129:42 Ap 6 '87
Gaddafi plays desert phantom—staying under wraps after that American death plot. il por *People Wkly* 27:36-7 Mr 9 '87
'How I bombed Qaddafi'. il *Pop Mech* 164:110-14+ Jl '87
Libya's Qaddafi: still in command? L. Anderson. bibl f *Curr Hist* 86:65-8+ F '87
A message for Kaddafi. N. Cooper. il *Newsweek* 109:35 Ja 5 '87
Muammar's mortification. F. Willey. il map *Newsweek* 109:35 Ap 6 '87
Pariah in the desert: the increasing isolation of Qadaffi. B. Slavin and J. P. Tarpey. por *Bus Week* p57 N 30 '87
Qadhafi magic: turning defeat to verbal victory. R. Z. Chesnoff. il por *U S News World Rep* 102:31 Ap 13 '87
'Reagan was the target'. il por *Newsweek* 110:59 O 5 '87
Target Qaddafi. S. M. Hersh. il *N Y Times Mag* p16-22+ F 22 '87
Washing Libya out of their hair. H. G. Chua-Eoan. il por *Time* 129:45 Je 1 '87
Qawi, Dwight Muhammad
about
Qawi's loss is a win when decision comes in. por *Jet* 72:51 Je 8 '87
Tuning up for Tyson. C. Gammon. il pors *Sports Illus* 67:48-50+ D 14 '87
QCD See Quantum chromodynamics
QE 2 See Queen Elizabeth 2 (Ship)
Qin Ben Li
about
China's trumpet of reform [interview] D. R. Shanor. il por *World Press Rev* 34:38 O '87
Quacks and quackery
See also
Museum of Medical Quackery (Saint Louis, Mo.)
Bogus health tests. P. L. Spencer. *Consum Res Mag* 70:2 Mr '87
A cure for doctors who are hazardous to health. F. Warshofsky. il *Read Dig* 130:70-4 Ja '87
Defrauding the desperate: quackery and AIDS. M. Segal. il *FDA Consum* 21:16-19 O '87
An 'F' for fake: wonder-drug science project gets bad grade from FDA [arthritis drug Dio-Hemo-2000 developed by 16 yr. old boy] A. Hecht. il *FDA Consum* 21:41-2 F '87
Luring consumers down the primrose path [evening primrose oil] C. Ballentine and S. Maifarth. il *FDA Consum* 21:34-5 N '87
Preying on AIDS patients. T. Monmaney. il *Newsweek* 109:52-4 Je 1 '87
Tell us it's new and improved—but keep health out of it [advertising] Z. Schiller and R. Rhein, Jr. il *Bus Week* p47 Ag 10 '87
Quadra Logic Technologies Inc.
A new drug deal with China. P. C. Newman. il *Macleans* 100:31 S 14 '87
Quadrantids (Meteors) See Meteors
Quadrex Holdings Inc.
Gary Klesch is no innocent abroad. S. Miller. il por *Bus Week* p144 S 14 '87
Quadriplegics See Paralytics
Quadruplets
"I had in vitro quadruplets"; ed. by Ann Schrader. D. Schock. il por *Redbook* 170:41+ D '87
Quaid, Dennis
about
Dennis Quaid. por *People Wkly* 28:52-3 D 28 '87-Ja 4 '88
Making it in Hollywood. D. Ansen. il *Newsweek* 110:69 S 7 '87
Young rascal. K. Dieckmann. pors *Roll Stone* p37-8+ S 24 '87
Quaij, Stephen, 1947-
about
The street of crocodiles [film] Reviews
Film Comment il 23:8 My/Je '87. A. Vogel
Twin cinema. T. Rafferty. il *Atlantic* 259:74-6 Je '87

Quaij, Timothy, 1947-
about
The street of crocodiles [film] Reviews
Film Comment il 23:8 My/Je '87. A. Vogel
Twin cinema. T. Rafferty. il *Atlantic* 259:74-6 Je '87
Quail salads See Salads
Quail shooting
A beginning [boy's quail hunt in California] B. Kahn. il *Field Stream* 91:64-5 Ja '87
Bob's bobwhites. B. Brister. il *Field Stream* 91:75+ Ja '87
Great day in the morning [hunting in Missouri] J. M. Vance. il *Field Stream* 92:14+ Jl '87
Legend of the Gambel [quail in Arizona] B. Tarrant. il *Field Stream* 92:148+ My '87
The ultimate quail [Mearns quail] R. B. Whitaker. il *Outdoor Life* 179:60-1+ Ja '87
Quails
Japanese quail can learn phonetic categories. K. R. Kluender and others. bibl f il *Science* 237:1195-7 S 4 '87
Quaker Oats Co.
Focusing on foods has fattened Quaker's stock. G. G. Marcial. il *Bus Week* p80 Mr 2 '87
Food fight! [General Mills to challenge Quaker Oats with Total Oatmeal] S. B. Weiner. il *Forbes* 140:86+ Jl 27 '87
Quakers See Society of Friends
Quality Books Inc.
Quality: selling small-press books into libraries. T. Unsworth. *Publ Wkly* 232:41 N 20 '87
Quality control
See also
Airplane industry—Quality control
Automobile equipment industry—Quality control
Automobile industry—Quality control
Electronic industries—Quality control
Guided missile industries—Quality control
Household appliances industry—Quality control
Munitions—Quality control
Publishers and publishing—Quality control
Meet a corporate Dr. No [R. Giovacchini, Gillette's vice president of product integrity] J. Strahinich. il por *Read Dig* 130:101-4 Mr '87
The pedagogy of competition. M. L. Weidenbaum. *Society* 25:46-54 N/D '87
The push for quality [cover story; special section] il *Bus Week* p130-6+ Je 8 '87
Japan
The American who saved Japan [W. E. Deming] P. M. Jones. por *Sch Update* 119:8 Ap 6 '87
How to make it right the first time [Taguchi method] O. Port. il *Bus Week* p142-3 Je 8 '87
Quality of life
Do we live as well as we used to? [cover story] S. Nasar. il *Fortune* 116:32-4+ S 14 '87
How many creatures? [discussion of October 1986 article, Cultural carrying capacity: a biological approach to human problems] G. J. Hardin. *BioScience* 37:246-7 Ap '87
A portrait of our environmental quality. il *Curr Health 2* 13:16-18 My '87
Quality of life [Environmental Quality Index] il *Natl Wildl* 25:40 F/Mr '87
Quality of products
See also
Quality control
Standardization
99 things that, yes, Americans make best. C. E. Trunzo. il *Money* 16:138-9 My '87
1988 buying guide issue. il *Consum Rep* 52:1-397 D '87
The push for quality [cover story; special section] il *Bus Week* p130-6+ Je 8 '87
Speaker for the house. J. Keely. See issues of Good Housekeeping
Quammen, David, 1948-
The keys to Kingdom Come. il *Roll Stone* p60-2+ Je 18 '87
Quantity cooking
A summer feast. K. Haedrich. il *Ctry J* 14:40-3+ S '87
Quantum chromodynamics
Asymptotic freedom [adaptation of address, April 1986] D. J. Gross. il *Phys Today* 40:39-44 Ja '87
Exploiting highly concurrent computers for physics. K. C. Bowler and others. bibl f il *Phys Today* 40:40-8 O '87
Quarks realistic and naive [discussion of January 1987 article, Asymptotic freedom] D. J. Gross. bibl *Phys Today* 40:112+ D '87

Quantum Corp.
Will Quantum take a leap? G. G. Marcial. *Bus Week* p136 N 30 '87
Quantum Fund
Frenzy feeds frenzy [G. Soros' The alchemy of finance] R. Phalon. por *Forbes* 139:44-5 My 18 '87
The master money manager [views of G. Soros] D. R. Katz. il por *Esquire* 108:67-8 D '87
Why Posner backed out of a bailout for Sharon Steel. P. Engardio. il por *Bus Week* p40 My 4 '87
World's champion bull rider [G. Soros] F. Ungeheuer. il por *Time* 129:75 My 4 '87
Quantum gravity
See also
Superstring theories (Physics)
New variables for quantum gravity [work of Abhay Ashtekar] M. M. Waldrop. *Science* 235:284-5 Ja 16 '87
Quantum mechanics See Quantum theory
Quantum Media, Inc.
Quantum leaps. J. A. Trachtenberg. il por *Forbes* 139:178-9 Je 1 '87
Quantum theory
See also
Energy levels (Quantum mechanics)
Exciton theory
Relativity (Physics)
Squeezed light
Statistical mechanics
Thermodynamics
Tunneling (Physics)
The coupled-cluster method. R. F. Bishop and H. Kümmel. bibl f il *Phys Today* 40:52-60 Mr '87
Do-it-yourself universes [research by Alan H. Guth and others] M. M. Waldrop. *Science* 235:845-6 F 20 '87
In the beginning was quantum mechanics [cover story] D. E. Thomsen. *Sci News* 131:346-7 My 30 '87
Interview [D. Bohm] J. Briggs and F. D. Peat. por *Omni* 9:68-70+ Ja '87
A midrash upon quantum mechanics. D. E. Thomsen. *Sci News* 132:26-7 Jl 11 '87
Quantized galaxy redshifts. W. G. Tifft and W. J. Cocke. il *Sky Telesc* 73:19-21 Ja '87
Quantized vortices in superfluid helium-4. W. I. Glaberson and K. W. Schwarz. bibl f il *Phys Today* 40:54-60 F '87
Quantum physics' world: now you see it, now you don't. J. S. Trefil. bibl (p144) il *Smithsonian* 18:66-70+ Ag '87
Superconductivity and quantum mechanics [views of E. Teller] D. E. Thomsen. *Sci News* 131:358 Je 6 '87
Quarks See Particles (Nuclear physics)
Quarrels
See also
Feuds
Arguing—gently—to win [views of Suzette Haden Elgin] C. Tavris. *Vogue* 177:178 Mr '87
Family feuds [results of survey] I. Groller. il *Parents* 62:32 Je '87
Family fights don't have to be fatal. D. Curran. il *U S Cathol* 52:22-9 S '87
Family quarrels: how to repair the fights nobody really wins. B.-J. Raphael. il *Glamour* 85:200-1 D '87
Fighting words: the shame of name-calling. D. Heyn. *Mademoiselle* 93:120 D '87
Fights can be positive force in a marriage. *Jet* 72:8 Ag 24 '87
The fine art of social argument. S. Jacoby. il *Glamour* 85:165+ Mr '87
How fighting can help a marriage [excerpt from Till death do us part] J. C. Lauer and R. H. Lauer. il *Ladies Home J* 104:42+ Jl '87
Temper tantrums and stony silences: is this any way to fight? *Glamour* 85:118 S '87
When friends fight, should you fix it? C. Rickey. *Mademoiselle* 93:160 Ag '87
Anecdotes, facetiae, satire, etc.
Fighting form. M. McNamara. il *Ms* 16:20+ O '87
How men win fights with women: ways to foil their sneaky, secret combat tricks. G. Schwartz. il *Glamour* 85:282-3+ O '87
Quarterbacks (Football players) See Football players
Quartermaine's terms [television program] See Television program reviews—Single works
Quartet for three actors [drama] See Deverell, Rex
Quartz
Asteroid impact gets more support [research by Bruce Bohor and others] R. A. Kerr. bibl il *Science* 236:666-8 My 8 '87

Quartz—*cont.*

Extinction upon impact? [research by Bruce F. Bohor and others] R. Monastersky. il *Sci News* 131:309-10 My 16 '87

Shock of impact [shocked quartz as evidence of asteroid impact with earth; work of Bruce F. Bohor and others] *Sci Am* 257:22-3 Jl '87

Shocked quartz in the Cretaceous-Tertiary boundary clays: evidence for a global distribution. B. F. Bohor and others. bibl f il map *Science* 236:705-9 My 8 '87

Who killed the dinosaurs? [impact-generated extinction theory] *Space World* X-8-284:9 Ag '87

Quasars

100 trillion clouds [research by Ralph L. Fiedler and others] il *Sky Telesc* 74:121-2 Ag '87

"Active nucleus" at a galaxy's edge? [quasar-like activity in radio galaxy PKS 2152-69] il *Sky Telesc* 73:603 Je '87

Binary quasar discovered [PKS 1145-071; work of Stanislav Djorgovski and others] *Astronomy* 15:90-1 O '87

Birth of a quasar [supercomputer model developed by Stuart Shapiro and Saul Teukolsky] A. Fisher. il *Pop Sci* 231:10 S '87

Bloated stars in quasars? [research by Richard C. Puetter] *Sky Telesc* 74:457-8 N '87

New satellite would extend VLBI into space [QUASAT] il *Astronomy* 15:76 F '87

Occult occulters [new type of interstellar object discovered by Ralph L. Fiedler and others] *Sci Am* 257:19+ Jl '87

Oodles of 'noodles' found in galaxy [research by Ralph L. Fiedler and others] D. E. Thomsen. *Sci News* 131:247 Ap 18 '87

Quasar cluster discovered [work of David Crampton and others] il *Sky Telesc* 73:483-4 My '87

Quasarlike activity discovered in fringes of radio galaxy [PKS 2152-69] il *Astronomy* 15:74-5 My '87

Quasars faster than the speed of light? [superluminals] *Astronomy* 15:79+ F '87

Quasars: the movie [work of Stuart Shapiro and Saul Teukolsky] il *Sky Telesc* 74:457 N '87

Something passing in the night [Extreme Scattering Events; research by R. Fiedler] G. L. Verschuur. il *Astronomy* 15:26-31 D '87

Star hopping to a quasar [3C 273] J. Mood. il *Astronomy* 15:49-52 Ap '87

Spectra and spectroscopy

Aging of primordial hydrogen clouds [work of Hugh S. Murdoch and others] *Sky Telesc* 74:235-6 S '87

Breaking the redshift-4 barrier. *Sci News* 132:254 O 17 '87

Bright infrared galaxies may be young quasars. il *Astronomy* 15:78-9 Ap '87

Color this quasar infrared [IRAS 13349+2438] *Astronomy* 15:79-80 Mr '87

Cosmic collisions [IRAS data] S. P. Maran. *Nat Hist* 96:22+ Ag '87

Exploring the Lyman-alpha forest [work of Wallace L. W. Sargent] M. M. Waldrop. *Science* 235:284 Ja 16 '87

IRAS and the quasars. R. Tresch-Fienberg. il *Sky Telesc* 73:13 Ja '87

The most distant "normal" galaxy [work of S. G. Djorgovski] il *Sky Telesc* 73:365-6 Ap '87

Probing the early universe with quasar light [Lyman alpha forest] B. M. Schwarzschild. bibl f il *Phys Today* 40:17-20 N '87

A quasar with rotating "fuzz" [3C 275.1] il *Sky Telesc* 73:599-600 Je '87

Quasars in the making? [link with infrared galaxies; research by David B. Sanders and others] il *Sky Telesc* 74:577-8 D '87

Seeing double. il *Sci News* 132:55 Jl 25 '87

Quasicrystals

Disorder in Al-Li-Cu and Al-Mn-Si icosahedral alloys. P. A. Heiney and others. bibl f il *Science* 238:660-3 O 30 '87

Icosahedral solids: a new phase of matter? P. J. Steinhardt. bibl f il *Science* 238:1242-7 N 27 '87

Quasiprogress. *Sci Am* 256:63+ Ja '87

Shaking up quasicrystals [work of Hartmut Zabel and others] I. Peterson. *Sci News* 131:152 Mr 7 '87

Quaternary period See Paleoclimatology—Quaternary

Quay, Stephen See Quaij, Stephen, 1947-

Quay, Timothy See Quaij, Timothy, 1947-

Quayle, Dan

Should Congress enact the Quayle amendments to the Bilingual Education Act? [excerpts from statement, June 5, 1986] *Congr Dig* 66:82+ Mr '87

Should the Levin-Nunn Amendment be approved? [excerpts from address, May 13, 1987] *Congr Dig* 66:269+ N '87

Quayle, Robert G.

(jt. auth) See Changery, Michael J., and Quayle, Robert G.

Quaytman, Harvey

about

Harvey Quaytman. K. Sofer. il *Art News* 86:159 Ap '87

Harvey Quaytman at David McKee. C. Little. *Art Am* 75:225-6 Ap '87

Québec (Province)

See also

Boisbriand (Québec)

Dance festivals—Québec (Province)

Finance—Québec (Province)

Fishing—Québec (Province)

Hunting—Québec (Province)

Labor laws and regulations—Québec (Province)

Montreal (Québec)

Motion picture festivals—Québec (Province)

Police—Québec (Province)

Québec (Québec)

Sherbrooke (Québec)

Commercial policy

Quebec's French connection [book imports] J. Poulin. il *Publ Wkly* 232:24 N 13 '87

Economic conditions

Land of hope and hustle. P. Stoler. il *Time* 130:37-8 O 5 '87

Foreign relations

France

See France—Foreign relations—Québec (Province)

Industries

See also

Maple sugar industry—Canada

Publishers and publishing—Canada

Languages

An echo of past battles [Quebec Court of Appeal decision declaring mandatory French-only signs illegal sparks vandalism] B. Wallace. il *Macleans* 100:14 Ja 12 '87

Language on trial [Court of Appeal rules against language charter requiring French-only commercial signs] B. Wallace. *Macleans* 100:8 Ja 5 '87

New fury over language. B. Wallace. il *Macleans* 100:16-17 N 9 '87

Nationalism

See also

Parti Rhinoceros

Breakthrough [agreement that will allow Quebec to sign the Constitution; cover story; special section] il *Macleans* 100:8-12+ My 11 '87

Canada's new deal [cover story; special section; with editorial comment by Kevin Doyle] il *Macleans* 100:2, 8-10+ Je 15 '87

Constitutional clouds [attempt to have Quebec sign the Constitution] M. Rose. il *Macleans* 100:10-11 Ap 27 '87

Debates on the morning after [constitutional breakthrough] M. Gee. il *Macleans* 100:12-13 My 18 '87

Facing a deadline [constitutional resolution and Quebec endorsement] M. Janigan. il *Macleans* 100:13 Jl 6 '87

A Liberal family feud [constitutional agreement] M. Rose. il *Macleans* 100:12+ My 25 '87

Mourning a patriot son [R. Lévesque; special section] il *Macleans* 100:10-12+ N 16 '87

Trudeau's power punch [denunciation of constitutional accord] M. Janigan. il por *Macleans* 100:10-11 Je 8 '87

Trudeau's star turn [criticism of the constitutional accord] M. Janigan. il por *Macleans* 100:14-16+ S 7 '87

Politics and government

See also

Parti québécois

Politics, Corruption in—Québec (Province)

Fortunately they forgot Quebec [rejection of capital punishment] A. Fotheringham. il *Macleans* 100:52 Jl 13 '87

The NDP's Quebec gamble. B. Wallace. il *Macleans* 100:20-1 D 14 '87

Quebec shows a new face. B. Simon. *World Press Rev* 34:39 Mr '87

Quebec's quiet welcome [visit of Queen Elizabeth] B. Wallace. il por *Macleans* 100:16 N 2 '87

Québec (Québec)

Description

A French-Canadian street-life ramble. M. Bricklin. il *Prevention* 39:82-4+ Mr '87

Québec (Québec)—Description—*cont.*
Paris without a passport: Quebec. B. Keating. il *50 Plus* 27:47-8+ Ap '87

Festivals
An exhilarating Rendez-Vous [highlights of NHL-Soviet hockey games at Quebec City festival] H. Quinn. il *Macleans* 100:50-1 F 23 '87
A multimillion-dollar Rendezvous [NHL All-stars vs. Soviet national team highlights Rendez-Vous 87 festival] H. Quinn. il *Macleans* 100:30-1 F 9 '87
A tenacious will for winning [Rendez-Vous 87 organizer M. Aubut] il por *Macleans* 100:30-1 D 28 '87

History
Siege, 1775-1776
Could Canada have ever been our Fourteenth Colony? [cover story] E. Park. bibl (p204) il map *Smithsonian* 18:40-9 D '87

Quebec Securities Commission
The Memotec affair [insider trading scandal] B. Wallace. il *Macleans* 100:38 O 5 '87

Quebecor Inc.
Front-page challenge [Sherbrooke daily, The record, sold to Quebecor Inc.] B. Wallace. *Macleans* 100:49 O 26 '87
Montreal's widening newspaper wars [P. Péladeau seeks to introduce English language daily] A. Wilson-Smith. il por *Macleans* 100:46 Mr 9 '87
Quebecor acquires Semline; names John Collins president. *Publ Wkly* 231:68 Ja 9 '87

Queen Charlotte Islands (B.C.)
See also
Forests and forestry—Queen Charlotte Islands (B.C.)
South Moresby National Park (B.C.)
Description and travel
Canada's Queen Charlotte Islands: homeland of the Haida. M. Johnston. il map *Natl Geogr* 172:102-27 Jl '87

Queen Elizabeth 2 (Ship)
Crossing the Atlantic in style. F. W. Rosen. il *Saturday Evening Post* 259:84-5+ S '87
A cruise that had the blues [problems on voyage of refurbished ship] il *Time* 129:57 My 18 '87
The Queen of ocean liners sails again. il *Pop Mech* 164:151 Ap '87

Queenan, Joe
Bio-tech. il *New Repub* 197:12-14 O 12 '87
Corporate comeback strategies. il *Commonweal* 114:340-1 Je 5 '87
Popularity contest. *New Repub* 196:14-15 Mr 23 '87
Puppy-Aid. *New Repub* 197:18 D 7 '87
Rag time. *New Repub* 196:13-14 Ap 6 '87

Queens (New York, N.Y.)
Crime
'Fat Cat' and the crack wars: brash young dealers muscle the drug establishment. P. Blauner. il por *N Y* 20:46-54 S 7 '87
'Sorry' for comment to white woman: Ward [Police Commissioner B. Ward] por *Jet* 72:28 Ag 24 '87
Criminal justice, Administration of
New York woman acquitted of killing her husband [battered woman, K. Straw] *Jet* 73:46 N 2 '87
Festivals
Greek Village. *New Yorker* 63:20 Ag 10 '87
Galleries and museums
See also
Queens Museum
Newspapers
See also
New York newsday (Newspaper)
Politics and government
'Dallas' on the Hudson [J. Zaccaro scandal] il pors *Newsweek* 110:10 O 26 '87
This congressman preaches in church every Sunday [interview with F. H. Flake] por *Christ Today* 31:58-9 Mr 20 '87
Race relations
See also
Howard Beach case

Queens Museum
New York City gets small [model on exhibit] B. Barol. il *Newsweek* 109:54 Je 29 '87

Queensland (Australia)
See also
Historic houses, sites, etc.—Queensland (Australia)
Description and travel
Cairns to Kuranda . . . short but scenic rail trip in Australia's tropical north. il map *Sunset* 178:94+ Ap '87

Quenching
Antiarthritic gold compounds effectively quench electronically excited singlet oxygen. E. J. Corey and others. bibl f il *Science* 236:68-9 Ap 3 '87

Why does gold help arthritics? [research by Elias J. Corey and others] *Sci News* 131:264 Ap 25 '87

Quennell, Peter, 1905-
Palladian retreat of a royal mistress. il *Archit Dig* 44:86+ My '87

Query letters (Authors to publishers) *See* Authors and publishers

Quest for Peace (Organization)
The other aid network. R. Nordland. il *Newsweek* 110:37 Jl 27 '87

Questioning
See also
Children's questions and answers
Police questioning
The fine art of asking smart questions [excerpt from Smart questions] D. Leeds. il *Work Woman* 12:132-3+ N '87
Slow down, you move too fast [wait time by teachers to allow students to answer questions; research by Kenneth Tobin] G. W. Bracey. *Phi Delta Kappan* 69:234 N '87
Smart questions to ask to get ahead in your job [excerpts from Smart questions] D. Leeds. il *Glamour* 85:116+ My '87

Queues (Waiting lines)
Mind if I cut in? V. Bozzi. il *Psychol Today* 21:67 Ap '87

Quiberon (Brittany, France: Resort) *See* Health resorts, watering places, etc.—France

Quick, Thomas L.
How picking favorites can improve performance [excerpt from Managing people at work desk guide] *Work Woman* 12:21 Ja '87
How to be a graceful winner [excerpt from Managing people at work desk guide] *Work Woman* 12:20 Ap '87
How to learn from your mistakes [excerpt from Managing people at work desk guide] *Work Woman* 12:27 My '87
How to make the grapevine work for you [excerpt from Managing people at work desk guide] *Work Woman* 12:23 S '87
How to motivate people. il *Work Woman* 12:15+ S '87
How to plug those time leaks [excerpt from Managing people at work desk guide] *Work Woman* 12:25 Je '87
How to turn bright ideas into solid results. il *Work Woman* 12:92-3+ Je '87
Keep an up-to-date file on yourself [excerpt from Managing people at work desk guide] *Work Woman* 12:23 D '87
Managing the excusaholic employee [excerpt from Managing people at work desk guide] *Work Woman* 12:15 Ag '87
Moving a key subordinate out of a rut [excerpt from Managing people at work desk guide] *Work Woman* 12:33 N '87
What to do when an employee turns down a promotion [excerpt from Managing people at work desk guide] *Work Woman* 12:18 Jl '87
What to do when you don't like your boss [excerpt from Managing people at work desk guide] *Work Woman* 12:27 O '87
When no decision is the best decision [excerpt from Managing people at work desk guide] *Work Woman* 12:18 Mr '87

Quick breads *See* Bread

Quiet Nacelle Corporation
Quiet Nacelle Corp. cleared to install hush kits on DC-8s. E. H. Kolcum. il *Aviat Week Space Technol* 126:96-7 Je 1 '87

Quiet rooms
Quiet rooms: concert promoters set aside a place for parents. D. Handelman. il *Roll Stone* p15+ Je 4 '87

Quigley, Robert Wellington, 1946-
about
After Arcadia. P. M. Sachner. il *Archit Rec* 175:138-49 Je '87

Quilting *See* Quilts and quilting

Quilts and quilting
Hawaii's prized quilts. A. Satterfield. il *Travel Holiday* 167:12-13 Ja '87
Keeping the Cardinals in stitches [baseball quilts by F. Claas and C. Rothmeier] J. E. Vader. il pors *Sports Illus* 67:44 O 26 '87
Kentucky country quilts to make. il *Good Housekeep* 204:146-9+ Ap '87
Notes and comment [C. Jones initiates AIDS memorial quilt] *New Yorker* 63:31-2 O 5 '87

Quilts and quilting—*cont.*
Pick-up-and-go crafts. J. Williams and J. Severson. il
Better Homes Gard 65:126-7+ Ag '87
Super simple Amish quilt. J. Williams and J. Severson.
il *Better Homes Gard* 65:33 Ja '87
Taking up needles and thread to honor the dead helps
AIDS survivors patch up their lives [C. Jones organizes
memorial quilt] C. Ruskin. il por *People Wkly* 28:42-4+
O 12 '87

Collectors and collecting
The newest quilt fad seems to be going like crazy [cover
story] J. A. Harriss. bibl (p184) il *Smithsonian*
18:114-16+ My '87
A passion for quilts—vintage & modern [collection of
Robert and Ardis James] R. Siegel. il pors *Am Craft*
47:49+ D '87/Ja '88
Quilts of central Pennsylvania. J. Lasansky. bibl f il
Antiques 131:288-99 Ja '87

Exhibitions
American textiles [First flowering: early Virginia quilts
at the DAR Museum, Washington, D.C.] S. B. Sherrill.
il *Antiques* 132:252+ Ag '87
Amish quilts in the Museum of American Folk Art.
E. V. Warren. bibl f il *Antiques* 132:514-23 S '87
D.A.R. Museum [First flowering: early Virginia quilts
exhibition] il *Antiques Collect Hobbies* 92:54 Ag '87
Homage to the quilt [exhibition at the American Craft
Museum; cover story] il *Am Craft* 47:42-8 D '87/Ja
'88
Quilt havens: new showcases [museums dedicated to
quilts] J. Tognini. il *Am Craft* 47:50-1 D '87/Ja '88
Quimby, Doug
about
Frankie and Doug Quimby sing songs of slavery to
keep alive the lore of their forebears. D. Grogan.
il pors *People Wkly* 28:129-31 O 12 '87
Quimby, Frankie
about
Frankie and Doug Quimby sing songs of slavery to
keep alive the lore of their forebears. D. Grogan.
il pors *People Wkly* 28:129-31 O 12 '87
Quimpo, Candy
Church and state in the Philippines. *Christ Century*
104:647 Jl 29-Ag 5 '87
Quin, Langdon
about
Langdon Quin at Robert Schoelkopf. L. Campbell. il
Art Am 75:158-9 D '87
Quinby, Brie P.
White nights: where to ski (and après-ski) this winter.
il *Mademoiselle* 93:174+ N '87
Quincy (Mass.)
Historic houses, sites, etc.
See also
Adams National Historic Site
Quindlen, Anna
The drive to excel. il pors *N Y Times Mag* p32+ F
22 '87
Facing widespread infertility, a generation presses the
limits of medicine and morality. il *Life* 10:23-6 Je
'87
The second child. il *Ladies Home J* 104:60+ S '87
Quinn, James Brian, 1928-, and others
Technology in services. il *Sci Am* 257:50-8 D '87
Quinn, Jane Bryant
[Column] See occasional issues of Newsweek
Quinn, John R.
Open letters to Archbishop John R. Quinn [discussion
of February 7, 1987 article, On the pastoral care of
homosexual persons] *America* 156:238-44 Mr 21 '87
Toward an understanding of the letter On the pastoral
care of homosexual persons. *America* 156:92-5+ F 7
'87
Quinn, John Robert
Mrs. Overholt's garden [poem] *Christ Century* 104:356
Ap 15 '87
Winter aconite [poem] *Christ Century* 104:245 Mr
11 '87
Quinn, Peter
The gathering gloom: is 1929 about to happen again?
America 157:105-9 Ag 29-S 5 '87
It's coming on Christmas. *Commonweal* 114:731-2 D
18 '87
Quinnett, Paul G., 1939-
Rural sprawl: of junked cars and spent refrigerators.
il *Ctry J* 14:68-71 N '87
Snowbound. il *Audubon* 89:30+ Ja '87
Quinoa
A supergrain for the future. P. E. Rogers. il *Americas*
39:36-8 My/Je '87

Quinoa Corporation
Transplant in the Rockies. B. London. il *Americas*
39:38-41 My/Je '87
Quinolinic acid
Animals yield clues to Huntington's disease. J. L. Marx.
il *Science* 238:1510-11 D 11 '87
Quinolones
See also
Ciprofloxacin
Bug busters. G. Bronson. il *Forbes* 140:212+ N 30 '87
Quinones
See also
Hydroquinones
Dianion stabilization by $(M(C_5(CH_3)_5)_2)^+$: theoretical
evidence for a localized ring in $(DDQ)^2$. J. S. Miller
and D. A. Dixon. bibl f il *Science* 235:871-3 F 20
'87
Quint, Barbara Gilder
More for your money. See issues of Glamour
Quinta da Bacalhoa (Portugal: Country estate) *See* Country
estates—Portugal
Quintana, Carmen Gloria
about
One woman's fiery ordeal. A. Finlayson. por *Macleans*
100:24 Mr 30 '87
Quintana, Patricia
A taste of Mexico. il *Americana* 15:56-9 My/Je '87
Quintanilla, Maria Aline Griffiths y Dexter *See* Aline,
Countess of Romanones
Quintets, Instrumental
See also
Compact discs—Quintets, Instrumental
Quintuplets
Five times blessed! [Gaither quintuplets] J. Ralston. il
McCalls 114:55-6+ Jl '87
Small wonders [condensed from Full house: the story
of the Anderson quintuplets]; ed. by Jo Robinson.
K. Anderson. il *Read Dig* 131:120-4 S '87
Quirk, John Patrick
about
Spying on the spooks pays off for a publisher. M. Frons.
il por *Bus Week* p107 My 11 '87
Quiroga G., Alberto
Dealing against illegal drugs. *Americas* 39:55 My/Je '87
Quito (Ecuador)
Description
Quito: a sense of history. M. L. Wilkinson. il *Americas*
39:42-7 Ja/F '87
Quitting (Psychology) *See* Resignation (Psychology)
Quitting of jobs *See* Employees—Resignation
Quixote, Don (Fictional character) *See* Don Quixote (Fic-
tional character)
Qumran scrolls *See* Dead Sea scrolls
Quotas, Employment *See* Blacks—Employment
Quotas, Import (U.S.) *See* United States—Commercial
policy
Quotations
See also
Allusions
Bible—Quotations
Points to ponder. See issues of Reader's Digest
Quotable quotes. See issues of Reader's Digest
Thoughts on the business of life. See issues of Forbes
Toward more picturesque speech. See issues of Reader's
Digest
The year in pictures '86 [special issue; with editorial
comment by Judith Daniels] il *Life* 10:5, 8-19+ Ja
'87
Quotations, Stock *See* Stock quotations
Qwelane, Jon
about
Getting the story (I). W. Finnegan. *New Yorker* 63:31-4+
Jl 13 '87
Getting the story (II). W. Finnegan. *New Yorker* 63:40-2+
Jl 20 '87
QWERTY keyboard *See* Keyboards

R

R & B phonograph records *See* Phonograph records—Rock
music
R & S Books
FSG to distribute R & S Books of Stockholm. il *Publ
Wkly* 232:30 Ag 28 '87
R. B. Pamplin Corporation
Bob Pamplin's second career. G. Eisler. il por *Forbes*
139:182 My 18 '87

R.D. Percy & Company
Beyond the people meter. M. Fritz. il por *Forbes* 140:248 D 14 '87
R. D. Smith & Company
Boom in the bust market. E. Linden. il *Time* 130:52 O 12 '87
R.E.M. (Musical group)
R.E.M. [cover story] S. Pond. il *Roll Stone* p46-8+ D 3 '87
R.E.M.'s new 'Document': a 'loose, weird' effort. A. DeCurtis. il *Roll Stone* p18 Ag 27 '87
R.H. Love Galleries, Inc.
An American cache at Chicago's R. H. Love Galleries. V. Lautman. il por *Archit Dig* 44:74+ S '87
R. H. Macy & Co., Inc.
The year's best sale at Macy's: itself. A. Dunkin. il por *Bus Week* p136-7 Ja 12 '87
R. J. Reynolds Industries, Inc.
See also
RJR Nabisco Inc.
R. J. Reynolds Tobacco Co.
Asbestos subpoena quashed. J. Raloff. *Sci News* 132:55 Jl 25 '87
Where there's no smoke . . . [smokeless cigarette] N. R. Gibbs. il *Time* 130:53 S 28 '87
R. M. Mills Bookstores (Nashville, Tenn.) *See* Booksellers and bookselling—Tennessee
R. R. Donnelley & Sons Co.
Tending to business. J. Andresky. il *Forbes* 140:120-1 N 16 '87
R. Twining & Co. Ltd.
Tea time in London means profits in the pot for the Twining family. J. Calio. il pors *People Wkly* 28:75+ S 7 '87
R&D (Research and development) *See* Industrial research; Research
Raab *See* Broccoli raab
Raab cooking *See* Cooking—Vegetables
Raban, Avner
Herod's great harbour. il *Courier* 40:30-1 N '87
Raban, Jonathan
about
PW interviews. M. Field. por *Publ Wkly* 231:76-7 F 13 '87
Rabbaniha, Sally
Shock among Arabs. il *World Press Rev* 34:18-19 Ja '87
Rabbis
See also
Schneerson, Menachem M.
Rabbit hunting
Hunting today's cottontails. M. Pearce. il *Outdoor Life* 180:45-7+ D '87
Rabbit Systems, Inc.
The Rabbit punch [R. Wright charges Rabbit Systems and MarketCorp Venture Associates with misappropriation of trade secrets] K. Healy. il por *Forbes* 140:175-6 S 21 '87
Rabbits
See also
Cooking—Game
Hares
Pikas
The ubiquitous bunny. D. Petersen. il *Mother Earth News* 104:70-3 Mr/Ap '87
What are the limits of love? [giving away pet rabbit] J. Glass. il *Glamour* 85:198 S '87
La Rabida Children's Hospital and Research Center (Chicago, Ill.) *See* Children—Hospitals
Rabies
Raccoons and rabies: an eastern urban threat. il *Mother Earth News* 103:69 Ja/F '87
Vaccines and vaccination
Low-dose rabies vaccine. *FDA Consum* 21:2-3 Mr '87
Raccoons and rabies. R. Cooke. il *Technol Rev* 90:15-16 My/Je '87
Rabin, Cedric
about
Stocks from the frozen North [interview] A. E. Serwer. il por *Fortune* 115:108 Mr 30 '87
Rabindranath Tagore *See* Tagore, Sir Rabindranath, 1861-1941
Rabinove, Samuel
Religious freedom for all: a Jewish perspective. il *USA Today (Periodical)* 116:32-5 N '87
Rabinovich, Abraham
Rampaging rabbis. *New Repub* 197:24-6 S 14-21 '87
Rabinovich, Itamar, 1942-
Syria and Lebanon. bibl f *Curr Hist* 86:61-4+ F '87

Rabinow, Jacob
about
One man's mousetraps. R. Kanigel. il por *N Y Times Mag* p48+ My 17 '87
Rabinowitz, Alan
about
Jaguars: why protect a killer? J. T. Bohlen. il map *Int Wildl* 17:4-11 Mr/Ap '87
Raboy, Marc
In the Hurrell style. il *Petersens Photogr Mag* 16:20-1 S '87
Raby, Rosie
about
Granny midwives: portrait of a timeless profession. E. I. M. Holland. il pors *Ms* 15:48-51+ Je '87
Raccoons
Backyard bandits. D. Petersen. il map *Mother Earth News* 103:66-9 Ja/F '87
Diseases and pests
Raccoons and rabies. R. Cooke. il *Technol Rev* 90:15-16 My/Je '87
Raccoons and rabies: an eastern urban threat. il *Mother Earth News* 103:69 Ja/F '87
Race *See* Ethnology
Race differences
Buoyancy basics [A. Campanis' remarks] D. Seligman. *Fortune* 116:102 Jl 20 '87
Race discrimination
See also
Apartheid
Blacks—Segregation
Discrimination in education
Discrimination in employment
Discrimination in housing
Discrimination in sports
International Day for the Elimination of Racial Discrimination
United Nations. Committee on the Elimination of Racial Discrimination
Assembly appeals for intensified activities to combat racism, condemns increased use of mercenaries. *UN Chron* 24:126 F '87
Black psychiatrists tell how racism hurts whites, too. il *Jet* 72:16-17 Jl 20 '87
Carter: racism could be inherent in all of us [views of J. Carter] il por *Jet* 71:15 Mr 9 '87
Ex-Education chief cites racism in Reagan staff [views of T. Bell] por *Jet* 73:38 N 9 '87
Full moons and white men [woman physician attempts to dispel bias that favors white males] S. P. Harwood. il *Ms* 16:103 O '87
My gloves are off, sisters [women's movement and racism] M. A. Gillespie. por *Ms* 15:19-20 Ap '87
The new racism: don't deny, ignore or accept it. il *Glamour* 85:102 S '87
Race for the bomb [television program] *See* Television program reviews—Single works
Race horses *See* Horses, Race
Race prejudice *See* Race discrimination
Race relations
See also
Alabama—Race relations
Alice Springs (Australia)—Race relations
Anchorage (Alaska)—Race relations
Arizona—Race relations
Asia—Race relations
Atlanta (Ga.)—Race relations
Boston (Mass.)—Race relations
Brazil—Race relations
Cardiff (Wales)—Race relations
Chicago (Ill.)—Race relations
Church and race relations
Church colleges and universities—Race relations
Colleges and universities—Race relations
Cumming (Ga.)—Race relations
Fiji—Race relations
Flint (Mich.)—Race relations
France—Race relations
Gage Park (Ill.)—Race relations
Gaithersburg (Md.)—Race relations
Glendale (Calif.)—Race relations
Greenwood (Miss.)—Race relations
High schools—Race relations
Indianapolis (Ind.)—Race relations
Interracial dating
Interracial marriage
Isola (Miss.)—Race relations
Japan—Race relations
Keysville (Ga.)—Race relations
Ku Klux Klan
Long Branch (N.J.)—Race relations

Race relations—See also—*cont.*
Los Angeles (Calif.)—Race relations
Louisiana—Race relations
Louisville (Ky.)—Race relations
Martin Luther King, Jr. Center for Nonviolent Social Change
Miami (Fla.)—Race relations
Mobile (Ala.)—Race relations
Montreal (Québec)—Race relations
Moody (Ala.)—Race relations
Nashville (Tenn.)—Race relations
New Hampshire—Race relations
New Orleans (La.)—Race relations
New York (N.Y.)—Race relations
North Carolina—Race relations
Portsmouth (Va.)—Race relations
Prisons—Race relations
Race discrimination
Richmond (Va.)—Race relations
Rome (Ga.)—Race relations
Rumford (Me.)—Race relations
San Diego (Calif.)—Race relations
San Jose (Calif.)—Race relations
Shaker Heights (Ohio)—Race relations
Southern States—Race relations
Tampa (Fla.)—Race relations
Tifton (Ga.)—Race relations
United States—Race relations
Virginia—Race relations
Warren (Mich.)—Race relations
Washington (D.C.)—Race relations
Western Europe—Race relations
Zimbabwe—Race relations

Race relations and the press
See also
Howard Beach case—Reporters and reporting

Race relations in television
In a shocker show, Cagney & Lacey tests limits with the most vicious racial slurs ever heard on TV [teleplay by S.-A. Williams] J. Hall. il por *People Wkly* 28:62-4 O 5 '87

Race tracks
Keeneland races with class. D. Young. il *South Living* 22:24+ Ap '87
Thoroughbred compost you can bet on [Nutra-Gro compost from Louisiana Downs spent stable bedding] F. Westergaard. il por *Rodale's Org Gard* 34:77-80 F '87

Buildings
Birmingham Turf Club. W. Schemmel. il *Travel Holiday* 168:8-10 Jl '87
The palace of kings [Sports Palace at Maryland's Laurel Race Course] J. Orsini. il *Travel Holiday* 167:36+ Ap '87

Employees
Loading the cannon [gate crew] J. Rolfe. il *Sport Mag* 78:92 O '87

Race tracks, Automobile *See* Speedways

Race walking
How to get slim hips and catcalls [aerobic walking] D. Brand. il *Time* 129:67 Je 1 '87
Life in the slow lane. C. Dilks. il *Nations Bus* 75:61-2 Mr '87

Races of man *See* Ethnology

Rachmaninoff, Sergei, 1873-1943
about
Rachmaninoff's lost chords. D. Neff. il pors *Christ Today* 31:63-4 D 11 '87

Rachwald, Arthur R.
The Polish road to the abyss. bibl f *Curr Hist* 86:369-72+ N '87

Racial differences *See* Race differences
Racial discrimination *See* Race discrimination
Racine (Wis.)
Buildings
Frank Lloyd Wright [traveling exhibition entitled Frank Lloyd Wright and the Johnson Wax buildings] S. B. Sherrill. il *Antiques* 131:950+ My '87

Racing
See also
Airplane racing
Automobile racing
Bicycle racing
Boat racing
Bobsled racing
Dog racing
Duck racing
Harness racing
Horse racing
Hurdle racing
Luge racing

Motor boat racing
Motor vehicle racing
Motorcycle racing
Mud racing
Pigeon racing
Sailboat racing
Ski racing
Swine racing
Yacht racing

Racing car models *See* Automobile models
Racing cars *See* Automobiles, Racing
Racing form *See* Daily racing form
Racing motorcycles *See* Motorcycles, Racing
Racing Strollers (Firm)
Merrily they roll along [P. and M. Baechler] R. Orr. il pors *Nations Bus* 75:65 N '87
Racing trucks *See* Trucks, Racing
Racism *See* Race discrimination
Racker, Efraim, 1913-
Structure, function, and assembly of membrane proteins. bibl f *Science* 235:959-61 F 27 '87
Racket sports
See also
Racquetball
Racketeer Influenced and Corrupt Organizations Act of 1970
Breaking the Teamsters. J. Schwartz. il *Newsweek* 109:43 Je 22 '87
High Court asked to rule on RICO bookstore case [adult bookstore in Indiana] *Publ Wkly* 232:10 N 13 '87
How Teamsters high command may be unhorsed. W. L. Chaze. il *U S News World Rep* 102:12-13 Je 22 '87
Reagan proposes RICO law based on Meese porno recommendations. H. Fields. *Publ Wkly* 232:13 D 4 '87
Why not try union democracy? [racketeering suit against Teamsters] J. Connolly. il *Nation* 245:192-4+ S 5 '87
Racketeering
See also
Mafia
Racketeer Influenced and Corrupt Organizations Act of 1970
Trials (Racketeering)
Rackets, Tennis *See* Tennis rackets
Racks, Car-top *See* Automobiles—Equipment
Racks, Magazine *See* Magazine stands, racks, etc.
Racks, Roof-top *See* Trucks—Equipment
Racks, Towel *See* Towel racks, rings, etc.
Racks and shelves *See* Shelves and racks
Racquetball
Nightmare in a box. L. Tabak. il *World Tennis* 34:48-9 Ja '87
The ratings game for rally sports [work of David Strauss] *Sci News* 132:269 O 24 '87
Radair, Inc.
Radair offers low-cost weather coverage for general aviation. il *Aviat Week Space Technol* 126:103 Je 29 '87
Radair's clearer picture [weather avoidance system for general aviation] J. M. McClellan. il *Flying* 114:82-3 O '87
Radakovich, Anka
Sarah Lemire: creating the "Cosby" look. il pors *Seventeen* 46:87-8+ Jl '87
Radar
See also
Optical radar
Transponders
Vital signs [radar detection of heartbeat and breathing] *Sci Am* 256:69-70 Ja '87
Antennas
Lockheed-Georgia seeking major role in ADI development [C-130 phased array antennas] E. H. Kolcum. il *Aviat Week Space Technol* 126:126-7 My 18 '87
Raytheon broadens application of Rotman lens technology. il *Aviat Week Space Technol* 126:105+ F 16 '87
Interference
See Radar interference
Meteorological use
See Radar meteorology
Military use
See also
Airplanes, Military—Radar equipment
Airplanes, Military transport—Radar equipment
Guided missiles—Radar equipment
Radar defense networks
Radar's growing vulnerability. S. Budiansky. il *Science* 238:1219-21 N 27 '87

Radar astronomy *See* Radar in astronomy
Radar defense networks

Administration disputes findings of U.S. visit to Soviet radar [Krasnoyarsk] P. Mann. il map *Aviat Week Space Technol* 127:26-8 S 14 '87

Air Force to phase in second sector of East Coast OTH/B radar system [over-the-horizon backscatter] K. J. Stein. il *Aviat Week Space Technol* 126:89+ F 2 '87

. . . and I'll show you mine [U.S. congressmen tour Krasnoyarsk radar facility in Siberia] il *Time* 130:28 S 21 '87

Army/USAF use diverse technologies to validate Joint STARS concepts. il *Aviat Week Space Technol* 126:84-5+ Mr 2 '87

Canada regards space-based radar as follow-on to North Warning System. il *Aviat Week Space Technol* 127:135+ S 28 '87

The challenge of space surveillance. J. A. Howell. il *Sky Telesc* 73:584-6+ Je '87

A close-up look at a secret Soviet radar [Krasnoyarsk] C. Norman. il map *Science* 237:1408-9 S 18 '87

Danes bristle at U.S. radar plans [phased-array radar planned for Thule, Greenland complicates ABM Treaty] M. Burcharth. il map *Bull At Sci* 43:11-13 Je '87

Defense Dept. official cites need for early decision on space-based radars as part of ADI surveillance network [Air Defense Initiative] *Aviat Week Space Technol* 126:25-6 Ap 13 '87

A dispute over Soviet ABM plans. C. Norman. *Science* 235:524-6 Ja 30 '87

Ground-based radar [SDI Terminal Imaging Radar experiment] il *Aviat Week Space Technol* 127:75 N 23 '87

Joint STARS intensifies reliance on software in development phase. E. H. Kolcum. il *Aviat Week Space Technol* 126:81-2+ F 23 '87

Long-range signals [Americans inspect Soviet radar complex in Krasnoyarsk] *Commonweal* 114:516-17 S 25 '87

Maine OTH-B radar achieves limited operational status [over-the-horizon-backscatter] *Aviat Week Space Technol* 127:26 D 14 '87

North Warning radar on schedule, but Phase 2 faces delays. il map *Aviat Week Space Technol* 127:132+ S 28 '87

Push for early SDI deployment could spur Air Defense Initiative. J. D. Morrocco. *Aviat Week Space Technol* 126:18-20 F 2 '87

Report from Krasnoyarsk [U.S. congressmen visit radar facility in Siberia] T. J. Downey and others. il *Bull At Sci* 43:11-14 N '87

SDI watch [Krasnoyarsk radar inspection by group of Democratic congressmen and staffers] *Natl Rev* 39:18-19 O 9 '87

Soviet Union accused of treaty violations [Antiballistic Missile Treaty] C. Norman. *Science* 235:1456-7 Mr 20 '87

Space-based radar [Air Defense Initiative] G. N. Tsandoulas. bibl f il map *Science* 237:257-62 Jl 17 '87

Space Command completes acquisition of Pave Paws warning radar installations. *Aviat Week Space Technol* 126:128-9 My 18 '87

The superpower dispute over radars [large phased-array radars and the ABM Treaty] J. P. Rubin. bibl f *Bull At Sci* 43:34-7 Ap '87

U.S./Canadian radar research questioned. *Aviat Week Space Technol* 126:22 Ap 20 '87

Unlocking the riddle of Krasnoyarsk [Americans visit Soviet radar complex] W. D. Marbach. map *Newsweek* 110:43 S 21 '87

What are 'they' up to? [Krasnoyarsk radar station inspected in the Soviet Union] W. F. Buckley. *Natl Rev* 39:62 N 6 '87

Radar detectors

Gotcha! [pocket-size radar detectors] R. Taylor. il *Pop Mech* 164:95-8 Jl '87

Micro magic boxes. C. Csere and D. Sherman. il *Car Driv* 32:53-5+ Ap '87

Smokey snooping at 40,000 feet [Navy's use of Whistler radar detectors] S. Wilkinson. il *Car Driv* 33:29 S '87

Radar in astronomy

Canada approves development of scaled-back Radarsat. T. M. Foley. il *Aviat Week Space Technol* 127:51+ Jl 13 '87

Magellan: around Venus for 240 days. R. Spangenburg and D. Moser. il *Space World* X-3-279:14-17 Mr '87

Pinpointing near-earth asteroids [radar studies; work of Donald Yeomans, Steven Ostro, and Paul Chodas] *Sky Telesc* 74:576 D '87

Radar in aviation

See also

Airplanes—Collision avoidance systems
Airplanes, Military—Radar equipment
Airplanes, Military transport—Radar equipment
Guided missiles—Radar equipment
Helicopters—Radar equipment
Radar meteorology

ASR-9 surveillance radar will track aircraft, weather simultaneously. K. J. Stein. il *Aviat Week Space Technol* 126:100-1+ Je 29 '87

Board examines radar's role in Cerritos midair collision [August 31, 1986 collision in California] *Aviat Week Space Technol* 127:127-8+ D 14 '87

Dole proposes upgrade of nine radar service areas to TCA status [airport terminal control areas] *Aviat Week Space Technol* 127:33 Ag 31 '87

The grand delusion. J. M. McClellan. il *Flying* 114:72-4 Je '87

Grounded grassroots [proposed Mode C rule] M. Phelps. il *Flying* 114:40 D '87

Mode S expected to reduce interference. *Aviat Week Space Technol* 126:100-1 Je 29 '87

New radar sectors improve metropolitan area traffic flow [New York Terminal Radar Control] *Aviat Week Space Technol* 127:119 Jl 6 '87

NTSB cites erroneous transponder code in near collision [two American Airlines Boeing 727s near O'Hare International Airport] *Aviat Week Space Technol* 126:82 Je 15 '87

Transponder a la Mode S. J. M. McClellan. il *Flying* 114:22-3 Je '87

Radar in meteorology *See* Radar meteorology
Radar in navigation

1988 buyer's guide: Lorans, radars, sat navs, plotters. G. West. il *Mot Boat Sail* 160:67+ D '87

Radar in traffic control

See also

Radar detectors

Flash a friend today [flashing headlights to warn other drivers of radar traps] B. W. Yates. il *Car Driv* 33:24 D '87

"We're not cops" [using police radar to record actual driving speeds in Texas] G. Baxter. il *Car Driv* 33:20 S '87

Radar interference

Italians develop RF memory for deception jammer system. il *Aviat Week Space Technol* 126:73 F 16 '87

Navy/USAF begin flight testing airborne self-protection jammer. *Aviat Week Space Technol* 126:91 F 9 '87

New materials promise low radar reflectance [retinyl Schiff base salts] il *Aviat Week Space Technol* 126:22-3 My 18 '87

Northrop leads U.S. production of airborne jamming equipment. il *Aviat Week Space Technol* 126:83+ F 16 '87

Raytheon broadens application of Rotman lens technology. il *Aviat Week Space Technol* 126:105+ F 16 '87

Soviet book describes techniques for jamming monopulse radars. *Aviat Week Space Technol* 126:61+ F 9 '87

Visions of an invisible aircraft [retinyl Schiff base salts; work of Robert R. Birge and others] il *Sci News* 132:137 Ag 29 '87

Radar meteorology

ASR-9 surveillance radar will track aircraft, weather simultaneously. K. J. Stein. il *Aviat Week Space Technol* 126:100-1+ Je 29 '87

Functional box-counting and multiple elliptical dimensions in rain. S. Lovejoy and others. bibl f il *Science* 235:1036-8 F 27 '87

Radair offers low-cost weather coverage for general aviation. il *Aviat Week Space Technol* 126:103 Je 29 '87

Radair's clearer picture [weather avoidance system for general aviation] J. M. McClellan. il *Flying* 114:82-3 O '87

Stormbusters [Sperry's LSZ-850 lightning sensor and Primus 870 turbulence-detecting radar] J. M. McClellan. il *Flying* 114:64-6+ Mr '87

U.S., Japan present plans for joint spacecraft mission [Tropical Rainfall Measuring Mission] il *Aviat Week Space Technol* 127:69+ O 26 '87

Unisys wins $60-million contract for Nexrad Doppler weather radar. *Aviat Week Space Technol* 127:35 D 7 '87

Radavich, David

In life, what's important is that you lose. por *U S News World Rep* 103:5 Ag 24 '87

Radcliff, Robert R.
Game figurines. il *Antiques Collect Hobbies* 92:32-3 D '87

Radeka, Lynn
Zone system (I). il *Petersens Photogr Mag* 16:34-6 Jl '87
Zone system (II). il *Petersens Photogr Mag* 16:27-9 Ag '87

Radeka, Vic
about
Attention, shoppers: check out the wedding special in aisle 2! L. Tielis. il pors *People Wkly* 28:143-5 O 26 '87

Rademacher, Tom
The sound of a miracle. il pors *Seventeen* 46:96-8 My '87

Rademakers, Fons
about
The assault [film] Reviews
Macleans 100:58 My 4 '87. L. O'Toole
N Y 20:77 F 16 '87. D. Denby
Time il 129:80 Ap 6 '87. R. Schickel

Radial keratotomy *See* Cornea—Surgery
Radial saws *See* Saws and sawing
Radial tires *See* Tires, Automobile
Radiation
See also
Cosmic background radiation
Cosmic rays
Electromagnetic waves
Integrated circuits, Effect of radiation on
Light
Luminescence
Materials, Effect of radiation on
Mössbauer effect
Scattering (Physics)
Semiconductors, Effect of radiation on
Solar radiation
Stars—Radiation
Synchrotron radiation
Ultraviolet rays
X rays

Measurement
See also
Radiation dosimeters and dosimetry
Seeing the light [solid state sensor] *Sci Am* 257:24 Ag '87

Physiological effects
See also
Electromagnetic waves—Physiological effects
Light—Physiological effects
National Association of Radiation Survivors
Ultraviolet rays—Physiological effects
A-bomb radiation doses reassessed. R. Weiss. *Sci News* 132:263 O 24 '87
America's human guinea pigs. R. C. Cowen. il *Technol Rev* 90:20-1 F/Mr '87
Atomic bomb doses reassessed. L. Roberts. il *Science* 238:1649-51 D 18 '87
Australia's nuclear graveyard [British nuclear tests in the outback during the 1950s and 1960s] R. Milliken. il map *Bull At Sci* 43:38-44 Ap '87
A battle against deadly dust [R. Gale and others treat radiation victims in Brazil] C. Gorman. il por *Time* 130:66 N 16 '87
A carnival of glittering poison [effects of discarded cesium-137 in Goiania, Brazil] S. Seibert. il *Newsweek* 110:55 O 19 '87
Chernobyl: a radiobiological perspective. M. Goldman. bibl f *Science* 238:622-3 O 30 '87
Chernobyl's high cost [interview with R. Gale] J. Bennett. il por *Macleans* 100:6-8 Jl 6 '87
Deadly glitter [poisoning caused by discarded cesium-137 in Goiania, Brazil] *Time* 130:38 O 19 '87
Evidence for increased somatic cell mutations at the glycophorin A locus in atomic bomb survivors. R. G. Langlois and others. bibl f il *Science* 236:445-8 Ap 24 '87
Interview [R. Gale] M. C. Smith. il pors *Omni* 10:110-12+ O '87
Living with fallout [effect of Chernobyl disaster on Italy] M. J. Salter. il *Atlantic* 259:30-2+ Ja '87
Oncogenes in radioresistant, noncancerous skin fibroblasts from a cancer-prone family. E. H. Chang and others. bibl f il *Science* 237:1036-9 Ag 28 '87
Playing with radiation [poisoning caused by discarded cesium-137 in Goiania, Brazil] A. Dwyer. il *Macleans* 100:44 N 2 '87
Radiation accident grips Goiânia. L. Roberts. il map *Science* 238:1028-31 N 20 '87

Radiation exposure: safe, eye on radon [report by the National Council on Radiation Protection and Measurements] B. Bower. *Sci News* 132:347 N 28 '87
The *raf* oncogene is associated with a radiation-resistant human laryngeal cancer. U. Kasid and others. bibl f il *Science* 237:1039-41 Ag 28 '87
Recalculating the cost of Chernobyl [anticipated cancer deaths; report by the Dept. of Energy] E. Marshall. il *Science* 236:658-9 My 8 '87
Rosalie Bertell. B. Lawren. *Omni* 9:96-7 S '87
"What has happened is incredible" [increased cancer incidence in Utah near site of 1950's atomic bomb tests]; ed. by Dena Kleiman. C. Peterson. il por *Redbook* 168:44+ Ja '87

Safety devices and measures
See also
Nuclear power plants—Safety devices and measures
Nuclear reactors—Safety devices and measures
Radioactive waste disposal

Therapeutic use
See Radiotherapy
Radiation dosimeters and dosimetry
Atomic bomb doses reassessed. L. Roberts. il *Science* 238:1649-51 D 18 '87
Radiation Technology, Inc.
No fried food in New Jersey [anti-irradiation activists] K. Terry. *Progressive* 51:25 S '87
Radiators
How to camouflage a radiator. il *Glamour* 85:264 S '87

Maintenance and repair
Preparing radiators for winter. J. Warde. il *Consum Res Mag* 70:22-3 D '87
Radical left (Political science) *See* Radicalism
Radical Party (Italy)
Letter from Rome [party member Cicciolina] A. Lee. *New Yorker* 63:133-6+ N 9 '87
Radical publishers *See* Publishers and publishing—Political literature
Radicalism
See also
Black militants
Black Panther Party
Neo-Nazis
Students for a Democratic Society
Weather Underground (Organization)
Youth movement
The ballot trap. R. Jahnkow. il *Progressive* 51:14-15 Ag '87
Dreams of the sixties. A. Brinkley. bibl f il *N Y Rev Books* 34:10+ O 22 '87
Extremist groups seek recruits in prisons. I. Suall. il *USA Today (Periodical)* 116:22-8 S '87
Jackson's challenge [J. L. Jackson; cover story] S. Muwakkil. il *Progressive* 51:16-19 Jl '87
Letters [discussion of September 19, 1987 article, Radicals in academia] R. Jacoby. *Nation* 245:434 O 24 '87
Radicals in academia [excerpt from The last intellectuals] R. Jacoby. il *Nation* 245:263-4+ S 19 '87
Resurrecting the new left. S. McConnell. *Commentary* 84:31-8 O '87
There's something happening here [new new left on campus] M. Margaronis. *Nation* 245:757 D 19 '87
They're back: stirrings on the left. J. Klein. il *N Y* 20:14+ Ag 31 '87

Anecdotes, facetiae, satire, etc.
Harry, Krishna, and me. P. J. O'Rourke. *New Repub* 197:16-18 N 2 '87

Italy
Decline of the Italian left. L. Rosenthal. il *Nation* 244:878-81 Je 27 '87
Radicals (Chemistry)
Atmospheric trends in methylchloroform and the global average for the hydroxyl radical. R. G. Prinn and others. bibl f il *Science* 238:945-50 N 13 '87
Bypass heart damage with vitamin E [free radical formation; research by Nicholas Cavarocchi] *Prevention* 39:11 O '87
Carbon tetrachloride at hepatotoxic levels blocks reversibly gap junctions between rat hepatocytes. J. C. Sáez and others. bibl f il *Science* 236:967-9 My 22 '87
Oxygen free radicals linked to many diseases. J. L. Marx. *Science* 235:529-31 Ja 30 '87
Radical dangers up in smoke [preventing free radical damage to fire victims; research by Thomas M. Lachocki and others] S. Weisburd. *Sci News* 132:169 S 12 '87

Radicals (Chemistry)—*cont.*
Radical therapy: drugs may combat brain damage by toxic oxygen free radicals. K. Wright. *Sci Am* 257:34 S '87

Radicals and radicalism *See* Radicalism

Radin, Victoria
Letter from London. il *Vogue* 177:114+ My '87
On the set. il *Vogue* 177:62+ My '87

Radio

Emergency use
See also
Radio beacons

History
The early days of radio (III). M. Clifford. il *Radio-Electron* 58:59-61+ Ap '87
The early days of radio (IV). M. Clifford. il *Radio-Electron* 58:52+ Jl '87
The early days of radio (V). M. Clifford. il *Radio-Electron* 58:64-6+ D '87
Inventors and inventions. R. D. Fitch. il *Radio-Electron* 58:86-7 Mr '87

Interference
See Radio interference

Radio, Military
See also
World War, 1914-1918—Communications
Court rules against challenge to Air Force GWEN towers [Ground Wave Emergency Network towers to be built in Maine] *Aviat Week Space Technol* 127:18-19 N 30 '87
The prospect of nuclear war in your back yard [Air Force GWEN towers] R. Riley. il *U S News World Rep* 103:36 D 7 '87
Signaling subs. T. A. Heppenheimer. il *Pop Sci* 230:44-8 Ap '87

Radio, Shortwave

Equipment
Short wave: get the word from around the world. J. W. Verity. il *Bus Week* p124 O 26 '87

Radio, Single sideband
See also
Radiotelephone on ships, boats, etc.

Radio advertising
See also
Advertising jingles
Books—Advertising
Joy Radio, Inc.
Commercial zapper for your radio. M. Rumreich. il *Radio-Electron* 58:45-7+ Ap '87
Radio days. M. Beauchamp. il *Forbes* 140:200+ N 30 '87
Radio marketing [address, September 16, 1987] C. C. Cox. *Vital Speeches Day* 54:88-92 N 15 '87
To be or not to be commercial?—That is the question [public broadcasting] R. L. Fischer. *USA Today (Periodical)* 116:89-91 S '87

Radio amplifiers *See* Amplifiers
Radio and blacks *See* Blacks and radio
Radio and history
Mediawatch [BBC's The cross and the crescent series on the Crusades] H. David. il *Hist Today* 37:4-5 Ap '87

Radio and politics
See also
Advertising, Political

Radio antennas
See also
Radio telescopes
The antenna problem. P. W. Mitchell. *Stereo Rev* 52:96-7 N '87
Marconi lucked out. H. Friedman. il *Radio-Electron* 58:82-4 Je '87
Replacing a radio antenna. M. Thompson. il *Fam Handyman* 37:82+ Jl/Ag '87

Tuning
Noise isn't always bad [Palomar Engineers Tuner-Tuner] H. Friedman. il *Radio-Electron* 58:44+ Mr '87

Radio astronomy
See also
Cosmic background radiation
Interstellar communication
Meteor burst communication
Radio sources (Astronomy)
Radio telescopes
Spacelab-2 plasma depletion experiments for ionospheric and radio astronomical studies. M. Mendillo and others. bibl f il *Science* 238:1260-4 N 27 '87
Tracing M81's spiral arms. M. Kaufman. il *Sky Telesc* 73:135-7 F '87

Radio beacons
A chirping 'bird' helps rescuers find planes that vanish [emergency locator transmitters] G. Williams. bibl (p183) il map *Smithsonian* 17:136-40+ Mr '87
EPIRBs: which ones can save your life? [Emergency Position Indicating Radio Beacon] D. Fales. il *Mot Boat Sail* 160:74+ Jl '87
The Starduster's last flight [M. Ryan rescued after plane crash with use of emergency locator transmitter] P. O. D'Aulaire and E. D'Aulaire. il *Read Dig* 131:75-80 Jl '87

Radio broadcasting
See also
Radio industry
Radio program reviews
Radio stations
Tape recordings—Radio programs
Women in the radio industry

Advertising
See Radio advertising

Archives
See also
Museum of Broadcasting (New York, N.Y.)

Astronomy programs
See Radio broadcasting—Science programs

Automobile repair programs
Tuning in, tuning up [Click and Clack, the Tappet Brothers] B. Barol. il pors *Newsweek* 109:68 Je 1 '87

Blues music
Military personnel get a taste of the blues [Armed Forces Radio] *Jet* 72:62 Ag 31 '87

Censorship
Blue boys of the airwaves [FCC broadens definition of indecency] R. H. Bork, Jr. il *U S News World Rep* 102:16-17 Ap 27 '87
The F.C.C. cleans up the airways. R. Corn. il *Nation* 245:679-81 D 5 '87
FCC doublespeak [indecency standard] L. P. Sheinfeld. il *Film Comment* 23:87-90 S/O '87
An indecent proposal [FCC's new definition of indecency] J. Saltzman. il *USA Today (Periodical)* 116:95 Jl '87
Radio daze [FCC issues warnings to radio stations for broadcasting obscene material] R. Stengel. il por *Time* 129:32 Ap 27 '87
Raunch 'n' roll radio is here to stay. J. Reed. il *U S News World Rep* 102:52 My 4 '87

Collectibles
Childhood memories are preserved in radio premiums. S. Bagdade and A. Bagdade. il *Antiques Collect Hobbies* 92:76-9 Mr '87

Comedy programs
Unforgettable Fred Allen. M. Zolotow. il *Read Dig* 131:55-6+ O '87

Conversation programs
Voices from behind the Iron Curtain [call-in program on Radio Free Europe] R. Reeves. il *Read Dig* 131:103-7 Jl '87

Anecdotes, facetiae, satire, etc.
Today's radio selections. J. Crane. il *Atlantic* 260:39 D '87

Frequency allocation
See Radio frequency allocation

Frequency modulation
See Radio frequency modulation

Government use
See also
Voice of America (Radio program)

History
See also
Society to Preserve and Encourage Radio Drama, Variety and Comedy

International aspects
See also
World Administrative Radio Conference

Jazz music
Commercial fair? W. R. Stokes. *Down Beat* 54:5+ S '87
Jazz on the air. C. Sarde and S. Zeloznicki. il *Down Beat* 54:6 Je '87
Philly Jazz goes national on NPR [Jazz impressions from Philadelphia] R. Woessner. *Down Beat* 54:60 S '87

Music
The invincible voice of Cape Ann [FCC's attempt to revoke license of WVCA, S. Geller's classical music station] R. J. Bidinotto. il por *Read Dig* 131:201-2+ O '87

New Age music
The Wave hits Los Angeles [rock station KMET becomes New Age station KTWV] *Newsweek* 109:68 Je 1 '87

Radio broadcasting—*cont.*
News
Footloose or screw loose? Sondra Lowell gives listeners all the news that's fit to tap. il por *People Wkly* 27:102-3 Ja 19 '87

Opera
Chicago on the air: a guide to Lyric Opera's 1987 broadcast season (I). il *Opera News* 51:25-9 My '87
Chicago on the air: a guide to Lyric Opera's 1987 broadcast season (II). il *Opera News* 51:37-42 Je '87
San Francisco on the air: a guide to the company's 1987 broadcast season (I). il *Opera News* 52:45-8 S '87
San Francisco on the air: a guide to the company's 1987 broadcast season (II). il *Opera News* 52:27-30+ O '87
San Francisco on the air: a guide to the company's 1987 broadcast season (III). il *Opera News* 52:43-6 N '87
Texaco-Metropolitan Opera radio network: 1987-88 season. *Opera News* 52:22 D 5 '87

Popular music
Radio romance. J. Updike. il *Esquire* 107:117-18 Je '87
Sinatra [broadcaster S. Mark] *New Yorker* 63:32-4 Ap 6 '87

Propaganda
See also
Radio Free Europe
Radio Liberty
Radio Marti
Radio Moscow
Voice of America (Radio program)

Religious programs
Dial down to Jesus [religious programming on public radio] P. Aufderheide. il *Technol Rev* 90:13-14 Ja '87
Radio marketing [address, September 16, 1987] C. C. Cox. *Vital Speeches Day* 54:88-92 N 15 '87

Rock music
KMET goes off the air [L.A. rocker replaced by New Age station] K. Loder. *Roll Stone* p13+ Ap 9 '87
Radio kills music, self. B. C. Sokolow. il *High Fidel* 37:56 Ag '87
The Wave hits Los Angeles [rock station KMET becomes New Age station KTWV] *Newsweek* 109:68 Je 1 '87
What's wrong with radio [1987 in review] S. Pond. il *Roll Stone* p85-7 D 17-31 '87

Science programs
A Texan with stars in her eyes [astronomy broadcaster D. Byrd] D. Young. il por *South Living* 22:94 D '87

Sports
Baseball on the radio? Hear, hear. G. Waggoner. il *Sport Mag* 78:86 My '87
Leonard rides wave of success to radio show [boxer S. R. Leonard] por *Jet* 72:48 Ag 3 '87
Sports around the clock [WFAN, 24 hour sports station in New York City] M. Bishop. il *Sports Illus* 67:91 Jl 27 '87
'Still very sweet indeed' [Baltimore Orioles' baseball announcer J. Miller] W. Taaffe. il pors *Sports Illus* 67:80 Jl 6 '87

Anecdotes, facetiae, satire, etc.
The voices of summer [announcers' goofs; excerpt from Baseball: a laughing matter] W. Fusselle. *Sport Mag* 78:65 Jl '87

Syndicated programs
Radio's new golden age. A. Miller. il *Newsweek* 110:41 Ag 3 '87

Transmission
See Radio transmission

Unauthorized use
FCC shuts hatch on pirate station [Radio New York International] R. Tannenbaum. il *Roll Stone* p32+ S 24 '87
Raiding the radio pirates of New York. il *Newsweek* 110:21 Ag 10 '87

Canada
See also
Canadian Broadcasting Corporation
Canadian Radio-Television and Telecommunications Commission

Cuba
See also
Radio Marti

Eastern Europe
See also
Radio Free Europe

Great Britain
Mediawatch [BBC's The cross and the crescent series on the Crusades] H. David. il *Hist Today* 37:4-5 Ap '87

Soviet Union
See also
Radio Moscow

Western Europe
VOA-Europe: message radio. N. Martin. *Nation* 244:848-52 Je 20 '87

Radio broadcasting, Public
See also
Minnesota Public Radio
National Public Radio (U.S.)
Dial down to Jesus [religious programming on public radio] P. Aufderheide. il *Technol Rev* 90:13-14 Ja '87

Radio broadcasting, Shortwave *See* Radio, Shortwave
Radio-Canada *See* Canadian Broadcasting Corporation
Radio Canada International *See* Canadian Broadcasting Corporation. Radio Canada International
Radio censorship *See* Radio broadcasting—Censorship
Radio clubs
Antique radio clubs. *Radio-Electron* 58:120 My '87
Radio commercials *See* Radio advertising
Radio communication, Military *See* Radio, Military
Radio communication in aviation *See* Radio in aviation
Radio control
See also
Automobile models—Control
Garage doors—Control
Radio critics and criticism
See also
Radio program reviews
Radio days [film] *See* Motion picture reviews—Single works
Radio direction finders
See also
Communications satellites—Direction finding use
Radio beacons
Radio direction finders [excerpt from The optimum sailboat] R. Florence. *Mot Boat Sail* 159:98 Je '87
Radio-electronics (Periodical)
Using the RE-BBS. *Radio-Electron* 58:122 My '87
Where is ComputerDigest going? B. C. Fenton. il *Radio-Electron* 58:4 D '87
Radio equipment
See also
Paging devices
Transponders
Radio filters
Think ferrite. H. Friedman. il *Radio-Electron* 58:127-8 My '87
Radio Free Europe
Jamming flim-flam [Soviet jamming] *Natl Rev* 39:16 Je 19 '87
Voices from behind the Iron Curtain [call-in program] R. Reeves. il *Read Dig* 131:103-7 Jl '87
Radio frequency allocation
Airlines criticize call to share exclusive aviation radio bands. P. J. Klass. *Aviat Week Space Technol* 126:28-9 Je 1 '87
High-definition's spectrum needs spur TV broadcasters to action [UHF vs. radio spectrum] S. Behrens. il *Channels* 7:16 Ap '87
New broadcast stations coming. *Radio-Electron* 58:4 Ap '87
Radio frequency converters *See* Frequency changers
Radio frequency interference *See* Radio interference
Radio frequency modulation
SCA/FM-stereo receiver (I) [cover story] R. F. Graf and W. Sheets. il *Radio-Electron* 58:39-44+ Ag '87
SCA/FM-stereo receiver (II). R. F. Graf and W. Sheets. il *Radio-Electron* 58:46+ S '87
Radio frequency waves *See* Electromagnetic waves
Radio frequency weapons *See* Electromagnetic weapons
Radio galaxies *See* Radio sources (Astronomy)
Radio in astronomy *See* Radio astronomy
Radio in aviation
See also
Airplanes—Radio equipment
Airplanes, Military—Radio equipment
Radio beacons
Golden age of radio. J. M. McClellan. il *Flying* 114:110-12+ S '87
The great communicator. R. L. Collins. il *Flying* 114:20 F '87
Straight talk. R. L. Collins. il *Flying* 114:58-60+ Ag '87
STS hand-held adds VOR nav. J. M. McClellan. *Flying* 114:84 O '87

Radio in navigation
> See also
>> Loran
>> Radio beacons
>> Radio direction finders
>> Radio in aviation

Radio industry
> See also
>> American Broadcasting Companies, Inc.
>> Malrite Guaranteed Broadcast Partners Limited Partnership
>> Mutual Broadcasting System, Inc.
>> National Broadcasting Co., Inc.
>> NBC Radio Network
>> Radio stations
>> RKO General, Inc.
>> Westwood One, Inc.
>> Women in the radio industry

A new age dawns as the ad market dims. L. Jay. *Channels* 7 Sp Issue:94 D '87

Radio's new golden age. A. Miller. il *Newsweek* 110:41 Ag 3 '87

The stakes get higher; the marketplace, tougher. N. Gunther. il *Channels* 7 Sp Issue:92-3 D '87

Acquisitions and mergers

From owner to manager. S. Behrens. *Channels* 7:50 Ap '87

Jumping Jack strikes again [J. Welch sells NBC Radio Network] P. Elmer-Dewitt. il *Time* 130:44 Ag 3 '87

Securities

Investors hear the call of radio. D. Lieberman. il *Bus Week* p118 S 28 '87

Radio interference

Image interference. H. Friedman. il *Radio-Electron* 58:94+ F '87

Jamming flim-flam [Soviet jamming of Radio Free Europe/Radio Liberty] *Natl Rev* 39:16 Je 19 '87

Think ferrite. H. Friedman. il *Radio-Electron* 58:127-8 My '87

Towed expendable RF decoy to defeat classified threats. *Aviat Week Space Technol* 127:23 S 21 '87

Voice of the Evil Empire [Radio Moscow can now be heard on AM radios throughout southern Florida] B. R. Johnson. *Natl Rev* 39:41 Ag 14 '87

Radio interferometry *See* Interferometers and interferometry

Radio Kings (Firm)

Radio Kings: ad rock. R. Buchanan. il *Roll Stone* p58 S 10 '87

Radio laws and regulations
> See also
>> Fairness Doctrine (Broadcasting)
>> Radio frequency allocation

Canada
> See also
>> Canadian Radio-Television and Telecommunications Commission

Radio Liberty

Jamming flim-flam [Soviet jamming] *Natl Rev* 39:16 Je 19 '87

Radio Marti

The phantom interview [R. Reagan interview staged by the National Security Council] A. Lopez-Muñoz. *New Repub* 196:11 Je 29 '87

Radio Moscow

Voice of the Evil Empire [Radio Moscow can now be heard on AM radios throughout southern Florida] B. R. Johnson. *Natl Rev* 39:41 Ag 14 '87

Radio New York International

FCC shuts hatch on pirate station. R. Tannenbaum. il *Roll Stone* p32+ S 24 '87

Raiding the radio pirates of New York. il *Newsweek* 110:21 Ag 10 '87

Radio news *See* Radio broadcasting—News

Radio observatories *See* Astronomical observatories

Radio program reviews

Single works

Click and Clack, the Tappet Brothers
> *Newsweek* il 109:68 Je 1 '87. B. Barol

The cross and the crescent
> *Hist Today* il 37:4-5 Ap '87. H. David

Jazz impressions from Philadelphia
> *Down Beat* 54:60 S '87. R. Woessner

A prairie home companion
> *Christ Century* 104:517-19 Je 3-10 '87. D. Heim
> *N Y* il 20:25 Je 15 '87. D. Galant
> *Newsweek* il 109:65-6 Je 15 '87. B. Barol
> *Publ Wkly* il 232:34-5 Ag 21 '87. D. E. Roback
> *Time* il 129:64-5 Je 29 '87. J. Skow
> *U S News World Rep* il 102:10 Je 22 '87. W. Kling

Star date
> *South Living* il 22:94 D '87. D. Young

Radio programs *See* Radio broadcasting

Radio receivers
> See also
>> Automobiles—Radio equipment
>> Radio, Shortwave—Equipment

The early days of radio (III). M. Clifford. il *Radio-Electron* 58:59-61+ Ap '87

The early days of radio (IV). M. Clifford. il *Radio-Electron* 58:52+ Jl '87

The early days of radio (V). M. Clifford. il *Radio-Electron* 58:64-6+ D '87

New life for old car radios (I) [conversion to home receiver] G. McClellan. il *Radio-Electron* 58:42-4 My '87

Portables [antique receivers] R. D. Fitch. il *Radio-Electron* 58:74-6+ Ja '87

Receivers. il *Stereo Rev* 52:72+ F '87

SCA/FM-stereo receiver (I) [cover story] R. F. Graf and W. Sheets. il *Radio-Electron* 58:39-44+ Ag '87

SCA/FM-stereo receiver (II). R. F. Graf and W. Sheets. il *Radio-Electron* 58:46+ S '87

Collectors and collecting

Antique radios. R. D. Fitch. See issues of Radio-Electronics beginning February 1985

Radio daze [collector P. Collins] R. Rapoport. il por *Americana* 15:49-52 N/D '87

Control

Commercial zapper for your radio. M. Rumreich. il *Radio-Electron* 58:45-7+ Ap '87

Maintenance and repair

Help wanted [Fisher Model 400 AM-FM receiver] il *Radio-Electron* 58:12+ F '87

Restoring a classic (I). R. D. Fitch. il *Radio-Electron* 58:80-1+ Je '87

Restoring a classic (II). R. D. Fitch. il *Radio-Electron* 58:39-40 N '87

Noise

Eliminating radio noise [cars] M. Thompson. il *Fam Handyman* 37:94 Mr '87

Tape recorder combination

Loud noise from little headphones [effect on hearing of Walkman-type radios and tape players] M. Dobbin. il *U S News World Rep* 103:77-8 O 12 '87

Testing

Walkabout stereos. il *Consum Rep* 52:408-11 Jl '87

Walkabout stereos. il *Consum Rep* 52:346-51 D '87

Testing

a/d/s/ R4 AM/FM stereo receiver. J. D. Hirsch. il *Stereo Rev* 52:84-8 D '87

Can a receiver equal separate components? J. D. Hirsch. il *Stereo Rev* 52:21-2 N '87

Denon DRA-75VR receiver. J. D. Hirsch. il *Stereo Rev* 52:49-50+ O '87

NAD 7175PE receiver. il *High Fidel* 37:42+ Ja '87

NAD Model 7600 receiver. J. D. Hirsch. il *Stereo Rev* 52:51+ N '87

Regency Informant scanning receiver. il *Radio-Electron* 58:16+ Ag '87

Sherwood S-2770RCP. J. D. Hirsch. il *Stereo Rev* 52:46+ Ag '87

Technics SA-590 AM/FM receiver. J. D. Hirsch. il *Stereo Rev* 52:37-8+ F '87

Tuning

Clearing the cobwebs. J. D. Hirsch. il *Stereo Rev* 52:24+ S '87

Harman Kardon Citation twenty-three tuner. J. D. Hirsch. il *Stereo Rev* 52:25+ N '87

How to buy a tuner. P. W. Mitchell. il *Stereo Rev* 52:93-7 N '87

Magnum Dynalab FT 101 FM tuner. J. D. Hirsch. il *Stereo Rev* 52:44+ My '87

NEC T-710 AM/FM tuner. J. D. Hirsch. il *Stereo Rev* 52:53-4 D '87

Perreaux TU-3 FM tuner. J. D. Hirsch. il *Stereo Rev* 52:53-4 Ja '87

Tuners. il *Stereo Rev* 52:108-9+ F '87

Radio reception

Diversity microphone transmission. H. Friedman. il *Radio-Electron* 58:26-7+ Ag '87

Radio Shack *See* Tandy Corp.

Radio sources (Astronomy)
> See also
>> Pulsars
>> Quasars

"Active nucleus" at a galaxy's edge? [quasar-like activity in radio galaxy PKS 2152-69] il *Sky Telesc* 73:603 Je '87

Radio sources (Astronomy)—*cont.*

Arcs, birth and a disk in the sky [discovery of radio galaxy 3C 326.1] M. D. Lemonick. il *Time* 129:59 Ja 19 '87

Birth announcements [disk of particles around Beta Pictoris; possible new radio galaxy 3C 326.1; luminous arcs encircling distant galaxies] *Sci Am* 256:60+ Mr '87

A cosmic birth announcement [nascent radio galaxy 3C 326.1] S. Begley. il *Newsweek* 109:55 Ja 19 '87

Galaxy in the making? [3C 326.1] il *Sky Telesc* 73:365 Ap '87

Gravitationally lensed giant galaxy [3C-324 radio galaxy] il *Sky Telesc* 73:482-3 My '87

Keeping up with Cygnus X-3. il *Sky Telesc* 73:272 Mr '87

New light on Cassiopeia A [research by Robert A. Fesen and others] il *Sky Telesc* 74:124 Ag '87

Quasarlike activity discovered in fringes of radio galaxy [PKS 2152-69] il *Astronomy* 15:74-5 My '87

Radio lobes revealed [galaxy 3C33; work of Klaus Meisenheimer and Hermann-Josef Röser] il *Sky Telesc* 73:25 Ja '87

Unexplained blazing objects [BL Lacertae objects] S. P. Maran. *Nat Hist* 96:78+ Mr '87

A very old galaxy that may be very young [3C326.1] D. E. Thomsen. *Sci News* 131:23 Ja 10 '87

Radio spectrum allocation *See* Radio frequency allocation

Radio stations

The invincible voice of Cape Ann [FCC's attempt to revoke license of WVCA, S. Geller's classical music station] R. J. Bidinotto. il por *Read Dig* 131:201-2+ O '87

KMET goes off the air [L.A. rocker replaced by New Age station] K. Loder. *Roll Stone* p13+ Ap 9 '87

Listen to your Mother [stations that carry Mother Earth news programming] il *Mother Earth News* 105:112+ My/Je '87

Racial jokes bring end of campus radio station [University of Michigan] *Jet* 71:33 Mr 23 '87

Sports around the clock [WFAN, 24 hour sports station in New York City] M. Bishop. il *Sports Illus* 67:91 Jl 27 '87

The stakes get higher; the marketplace, tougher. N. Gunther. il *Channels* 7 Sp Issue:92-3 D '87

The Wave hits Los Angeles [rock station KMET becomes New Age station KTWV] *Newsweek* 109:68 Je 1 '87

Radio stations, Black

Dorothy Brunson. K. Smikle. *Black Enterp* 17:45-6 Ap '87

Topping the charts [V. Green, general manager of Detroit radio station WJLB-FM] J. Chenault. il *Essence* 17:90+ Ja '87

Radio stations, Pirate *See* Radio broadcasting— Unauthorized use

Radio telephone *See* Radiotelephone

Radio telescopes

See also

Interferometers and interferometry

New radiotelescopes open era of submillimeter astronomy. W. Sweet. il *Phys Today* 40 pt1:65-7 Ag '87

New satellite would extend VLBI into space [QUASAT] il *Astronomy* 15:76 F '87

Radio images and planetaries' distances [observations by Very Large Array] Y. Terzian. il *Sky Telesc* 73:128 F '87

SN 1006's radio portrait [Very Large Array radio telescope] il *Sky Telesc* 73:480 My '87

The telescope that never sleeps [Very Large Array radio telescope] L. A. Shore. il *Astronomy* 15:14-22 Ag '87

Transportation

How to move a dish—carefully [Very Large Array] L. A. Shore. il *Astronomy* 15:17 Ag '87

Radio towers

Environmental aspects

Court rules against challenge to Air Force GWEN towers [Ground Emergency Network towers to be built in Maine] *Aviat Week Space Technol* 127:18-19 N 30 '87

The prospect of nuclear war in your back yard [Air Force GWEN towers] R. Riley. il *U S News World Rep* 103:36 D 7 '87

Radio tracking, Biological *See* Biotelemetry

Radio transmission

Diversity microphone transmission. H. Friedman. il *Radio-Electron* 58:26-7+ Ag '87

Marconi lucked out. H. Friedman. il *Radio-Electron* 58:82-4 Je '87

Radio transmitters

See also

Radio towers

Radio tubes

The early days of radio (IV). M. Clifford. il *Radio-Electron* 58:52+ Jl '87

Radio tuners *See* Radio receivers—Tuning

Radio waves *See* Electromagnetic waves

Radioactive dating

See also

Radiocarbon dating

Calcium-41 concentration in terrestrial materials: prospects for dating of Pleistocene samples. W. Henning and others. bibl f il *Science* 236:725-7 My 8 '87

Fission-track dating of Haughton Astrobleme and included biota, Devon Island, Canada. G. Omar and others. bibl f il map *Science* 237:1603-5 S 25 '87

Precise timing of the last interglacial period from mass spectrometric determination of thorium-230 in corals. R. L. Edwards and others. bibl f il *Science* 236:1547-53 Je 19 '87

Stone Age site gets pushed back in time [potassium-argon dating of Olorgesailie site; work of Bethany A. Bye and others] B. Bower. *Sci News* 132:199 S 26 '87

A younger universe is seen in the stars [thorium dating; work of Harvey R. Butcher] M. M. Waldrop. il *Science* 237:361-2 Jl 24 '87

Radioactive decay

See also

Beta decay

Radioactive fallout *See* Radioactive pollution

Radioactive pollution

See also

Radioactive space pollution

Radioactive waste disposal

Radon pollution

Uranium industry—Environmental aspects

Physiological effects

See Radiation—Physiological effects

Australia

Australia's nuclear graveyard [British nuclear tests in the outback during the 1950s and 1960s] R. Milliken. il map *Bull At Sci* 43:38-44 Ap '87

Brazil

See also

Goiania (Brazil)—Radioactive pollution

Germany (West)

West Germany pours hot milk [disposition of milk contaminated by Chernobyl] D. Egger. il *Nation* 244:392-4+ Mr 28 '87

Italy

Living with fallout [effect of Chernobyl disaster] M. J. Salter. il *Atlantic* 259:30-2+ Ja '87

Lapland

Lapp life after Chernobyl. S. Stephens. il map *Nat Hist* 96:32-41 D '87

The legacy of Chernobyl: disaster for the Lapps [reindeer meat contamination] R. Knight. il map *U S News World Rep* 102:36 Mr 23 '87

New Jersey

No fried food in New Jersey [anti-irradiation activists] K. Terry. *Progressive* 51:25 S '87

New Mexico

No peace on the Pueblo [radioactive contamination from Los Alamos laboratories] T. Arrandale. il *Sierra* 72:30-3 Mr/Ap '87

Oklahoma

Making fertilizer from what? [Kerr-McGee's conversion of radioactive waste to fertilizer at Sequoyah Falls plant] M. D. Lemonick. il *Time* 130:79 N 30 '87

Pacific Northwest

Hanford's radioactive tumbleweed. E. Marshall. il *Science* 236:1616-20 Je 26 '87

Sweden

Life after Chernobyl. J. Forssell and E. Forssell. il pors *Mother Earth News* 105:94-8+ My/Je '87

Ukraine

See also

Chernobyl nuclear disaster, 1986

Utah

"What has happened is incredible" [increased cancer incidence in Utah near site of 1950's atomic bomb tests]; ed. by Dena Kleiman. C. Peterson. il por *Redbook* 168:44+ Ja '87

Yugoslavia

Hard rain falls on Yugoslavia [effects of Chernobyl] S. Drakulich. il *Nation* 244:177-8+ F 14 '87

Radioactive space pollution

Cosmos 1402's uranium remains. J. Eberhart. *Sci News* 132:278-9 O 31 '87

Detection of uranium from Cosmos-1402 in the stratosphere [from nuclear reactor power supply] R. Leifer and others. bibl f il *Science* 238:512-14 O 23 '87

Radioactive space pollution—*cont.*
Nuclear power: how safe in space? P. Chien. il *Space World* X-9-285:11-13 S '87
RTGs—a plutonium crap-shoot? [Galileo spacecraft] *Space World* X-6-282:24 Je '87

Radioactive substances
See also
Radon
Tritium
Uranium

Radioactive tracers
See also
Nuclear medicine
Noninvasive transplant-rejection test? *Sci News* 131:282 My 2 '87
Visualization of viral clearance in the living animal. E. M. Verdin and others. bibl f il *Science* 236:439-42 Ap 24 '87

Radioactive waste disposal
Low-level nuclear waste: who makes it, who will take it. A. Stine. il *Sierra* 72:16-17 S/O '87
Thirty ways to temporize on waste. E. Marshall. il *Science* 237:591-2 Ag 7 '87

Laws and regulations
Delaying DOE's radwaste program. *Sci News* 131:106 F 14 '87
Fighting the nuke-waste shell game [cover story] D. Russell. il *Nation* 245:577+ N 21 '87
The greening of DOE. E. Marshall. *Science* 235:1315 Mr 13 '87
Laying nuclear waste to rest [cover story; special issue; with editorial comment by Gilbert F. White] il *Environment* 29:inside cover, 6-20+ O '87

Maine
Is Maine Yankee headed for the dump? [proposal to ban production of nuclear waste] J. Kriesberg. *Progressive* 51:12-13 N '87

South Dakota
The Sioux reject nuclear waste [Cheyenne River Sioux reservation] J. W. Wilson. *Progressive* 51:11-12 S '87

Great Britain
Nuclear prehistory [archeological finds in nuclear dump site, Lincolnshire] D. Byrne. *Hist Today* 37:3 Ag '87

Nevada
The politics and promises of nuclear waste disposal: the view from Nevada. R. H. Bryan. bibl f il maps *Environment* 29:14-17+ O '87

New Mexico
A nuclear dump springs a leak [New Mexico cave] S. Begley. il *Newsweek* 110:65 D 28 '87

South Carolina
Savannah River's $1-billion glassmaker [Defense Waste Processing Facility] E. Marshall. il *Science* 235:1314-17 Mr 13 '87

Sweden
The Swedish model for handling dangerous waste. il *Pop Mech* 164:107 S '87

Washington (State)
Hanford's radioactive tumbleweed. E. Marshall. il *Science* 236:1616-20 Je 26 '87

Western Europe
Nuclear waste disposal in Europe. *Environment* 29:41 O '87

Radioactive waste reprocessing *See* Reactor fuel reprocessing

Radioactivity
See also
Autoradiography

Physiological effects
See Radiation—Physiological effects

Radioautography *See* Autoradiography

Radiocarbon dating
C-14 dating for Shroud of Turin? J. Raloff. *Sci News* 131:265 Ap 25 '87
New dates from old bones [Old Crow site in Yukon Territory] W. N. Irving. map *Nat Hist* 96:8+ F '87
Shroud dating isn't ironed out. *Sci News* 132:302 N 7 '87
Tempting providence with the Turin Shroud? C. Chippindale. il *Hist Today* 37:5-6 S '87

Radiography
See also
Autoradiography
Contrast media
Tomography
Floral derangement [work of A. G. Richards] N. Guccione. il *Omni* 10:100-5 D '87

Radiography, Medical
See also
Magnetic resonance imaging—Medical use
Mammography
Tomography—Medical use

Making X-ray procedures safer [Omnipaque contrast agent] il *USA Today (Periodical)* 115:14-15 F '87
Medical physics. il *Phys Today* 40:S42-S45 Ja '87
New technique checks brain's blood supply [projection angiography] il *Radio-Electron* 58:4 Mr '87
Skull X-ray exams. *FDA Consum* 21:3-4 Ap '87
X rays: what's safe? P. Von Nostitz. il *Parents* 62:209-12 Ap '87

Radioisotopes
See also
Cesium—Isotopes
Radioactive tracers
Tritium
Accelerator mass spectrometry for measurement of long-lived radioisotopes. D. Elmore and F. M. Phillips. bibl f il *Science* 236:543-50 My 1 '87

Radioisotopes in medicine *See* Nuclear medicine

Radios *See* Radio receivers

Radiotelephone
See also
Cellular radio
Communications satellites—Radiotelephone use
A telephone, at last, for the hard to reach [digital radiotelephone in service to rural areas] W. J. Cook. il *U S News World Rep* 103:69 D 21 '87

Testing
Cordless phones. il *Consum Rep* 52:293-8 D '87

Radiotelephone in agriculture
Radio revolution replacing the dinner bell. D. Mowitz. il *Success Farm* 85:18AF Ap '87

Radiotelephone in business
Why one phone is stirring up the Big Board [broker W. J. Higgins' mobile phone] J. M. Laderman. il por *Bus Week* p123 Jl 20 '87

Radiotelephone on airplanes
A helping hand-held. M. Phelps. il *Flying* 114:76-7 D '87
A navcom in your palm [KX99] J. M. McClellan. il *Flying* 114:95 Je '87
Phoning at 40,000 feet. G. Eichler. il *Esquire* 107:40 Ja '87
STS hand-held adds VOR nav. J. M. McClellan. *Flying* 114:84 O '87

Radiotelephone on ships, boats, etc.
See also
Cellular radio on ships, boats, etc.
1988 buyer's guide: radios & cellular phones [VHFs and SSBs] G. West. il *Mot Boat Sail* 160:58-60+ N '87

Radiotherapy
See also
Cancer—Therapy
Lungs—Cancer—Therapy
Ovaries—Cancer—Therapy
Deep breath down under [sick people seeking radon cure in old Montana mines] M. Dobbin. il *U S News World Rep* 102:40 Ap 27 '87

Complications
Faulty therapy machines cause radiation overdoses [Therac-25 machines] R. C. Thompson. il *FDA Consum* 21:37-8 D '87/Ja '88

Radner, Gilda
Hooked on fame. il por *Ms* 15:56-7+ F '87

Radon
Deep breath down under [sick people seeking radon cure in old Montana mines] M. Dobbin. il *U S News World Rep* 102:40 Ap 27 '87

Radon detectors
Home radon monitor [At Ease Radon Monitor] S. Ashley. il *Pop Sci* 231:97 S '87
Radon detectors. il *Consum Rep* 52:440-7 Jl '87
Using people to screen for home radon [work of Richard E. Toohey] *Sci News* 132:105 Ag 15 '87

Radon pollution
See also
Radon detectors
Danger just downstairs. il *Time* 130:72 Ag 17 '87
Have that dream house checked for radon. J. Berger. il *Bus Week* p179 My 25 '87
Household hazards. G. Reiger. *Field Stream* 92:12+ Je '87
Making your home safe from radon. H. Manley. il *Good Housekeep* 204:148 Ja '87
Nowhere to run from radon. M. Galen. il *Nation* 244:180-2 F 14 '87
Radon. il *Mother Earth News* 107:50-3 S/O '87
Radon and the consumer [proposed national clearinghouse] P. S. Stern. *Environment* 29:2-3 Ja/F '87
Radon: EPA's biggest air pollutant . . . and its leading water pollutant. *Sci News* 132:105 Ag 15 '87

Radon pollution—*cont.*

Radon: identification and measurement. *Workbench* 43:66-8 Ja/F '87

Radon: reducing radon in the home. B. Gould. il *Workbench* 43:72-4 Mr/Ap '87

Radon revisited. V. E. Gilmore. il *Pop Sci* 231:92+ S '87

Radon roundup results [work of Douglas G. Mose and others] R. Monastersky. *Sci News* 132:335 N 21 '87

Radon: what to do about this invisible health threat. D. Groves. *McCalls* 114:106 Ja '87

A special report on radon. J. Vara. il *Ctry J* 14:16-19+ N '87

Toxic hazards in the home: sometimes the best thing to do is nothing. il *Money* 16:47 Mr '87

The truth about radon. J. Chapline. *Ctry J* 14:11 F '87

Why did my sister get lung cancer? C. SerVaas. il *Saturday Evening Post* 259:56-60+ Ja/F '87

Colorado

Colorado: the legacy of uranium mining. A. J. Hazle. il *Environment* 29:13+ Ja/F '87

Florida

Florida: working with the phosphate factor. J. D. Nash. bibl f il map *Environment* 29:13+ Mr '87

Maryland

See also

Mount Airy (Md.)—Radon pollution

New Jersey

New Jersey: involving the commercial sector. G. P. Nicholls and D. A. Deieso. bibl f il map *Environment* 29:12+ Mr '87

Pennsylvania

Pennsylvania: protecting the homefront. T. M. Gerusky. il map *Environment* 29:12+ Ja/F '87

Reporting on radon: the role of local newspapers. S. M. Friedman and others. *Environment* 29:4-5+ Mr '87

Rados, Bill

Protecting tots from drug poisonings. il *FDA Consum* 21:24-5 Mr '87

Radosh, Ronald

Feet people. *New Repub* 196:15-17 Mr 9 '87

Nicaragua revisited. *New Repub* 197:20-2 Ag 3 '87

Radovsky, Vicki Jo

Michelle Phillips—"I'm a proud Mama". il pors *Redbook* 169:12+ Ag '87

Radstone, Richard

Fluorescent landscapes. il *Petersens Photogr Mag* 15:30-2 Mr '87

Radtke, Richard L.

Brine shrimp: curious crustaceans. il *Sea Front* 33:128-33 Mr/Ap '87

Radziwill, Lee

Christmas thoughts. por *McCalls* 115:164 D '87

Raeburn, Paul

Can dogfish cure diabetes? il *Natl Wildl* 26:34-9 D '87/Ja '88

RAF *See* Great Britain. Royal Air Force

Rafe, Stephen C.

about

The 90-second heel. L. Mueller. il pors *Outdoor Life* 180:59+ N '87

How to be top dog. L. Mueller. il *Outdoor Life* 180:102-3+ S '87

Rafelski, Johann, and Jones, Steven E.

Cold nuclear fusion. bibl (p116) il *Sci Am* 257:84-9 Jl '87

Rafelson, Bob

about

Black widow [film] Reviews

Macleans 100:52 F 16 '87. L. O'Toole

N Y il 20:72 F 16 '87. D. Denby

New Repub 196:24-5 Mr 2 '87. S. Kauffmann

New Yorker 63:111-12 F 23 '87. P. Kael

Newsweek il 109:72 F 16 '87. D. Ansen

People Wkly il 27:6 Mr 2 '87. P. Travers

Roll Stone il p19+ Mr 12 '87. A. DeCurtis

Time il 129:76 F 16 '87. R. Corliss

Raffaele, Cathy

Hanging around in Borneo. il map *Natl Geogr World* 140:30-5 Ap '87

Raffel, Dawn

Dating games you can't win. il *Seventeen* 46:72+ Ja '87

Rafferty, Jean Bond

Christmas chic: Gallic galas. il *Harpers Bazaar* 121:80+ D '87

Rafferty, Terrence

Serious stars: Barbara Hershey. por *Vogue* 177:483+ Mr '87

Twin cinema. il *Atlantic* 259:74-6 Je '87

Raffi

about

Crown to launch books based on songs of popular singer. il por *Publ Wkly* 231:42 My 29 '87

Raffield, George, Jr.

about

The new kid. por *Time* 130:61 N 9 '87

Raffles *See* Lotteries

Rafsanjani, Hashemi

about

Iran: a mullah for all seasons. T. Stanger. por *Newsweek* 109:35 F 16 '87

Iran's smiling powerbroker. R. Wright. por *New Leader* 70:5-7 Ja 12-26 '87

Raft trips *See* Running rapids

Ragaini, Robert

Swan song for a jingle singer. por *Newsweek* 109:13 Ja 12 '87

The truth is not simple. il *N Y Times Mag* p38 Ja 11 '87

An unmarried couple. il *50 Plus* 27:55-7 N '87

Ragan, David

Health styles of the rich and famous. il *50 Plus* 27:92-4 Mr '87

Ragans, Justin

about

Accident victim's son, 2, awarded nearly $1.7 million. pors *Jet* 72:36 Ag 17 '87

Ragde, Haakon

about

For president or plain citizen, prostate problems come with age, says surgeon Haakon Ragde [interview] R. Sackett. il por *People Wkly* 27:72+ Ja 12 '87

Rage *See* Anger

Ragozin, Leonard

about

By the numbers. J. Coplon. por *New Yorker* 63:56+ D 21 '87

Rahal, Bobby

Trading places. il *Car Driv* 32:153+ Ap '87

about

This Bud's for Bear. P. Lyons. il pors *Car Driv* 32:158 Ap '87

Very much an Indy-vidual. S. Moses. il pors *Sports Illus* 66:46-8+ My 25 '87

Rahe, Jürgen

about

Inside the IHW: the professionals [interview] J. K. Beatty. pors *Sky Telesc* 73:256-7 Mr '87

Rahme, Amin J.

about

Will Minitel play deep in the heart of Texas? J. E. Davis. il por *Bus Week* p94 O 19 '87

Rail cycling

Ron Forster bikes off—way off—the beaten track. il por *People Wkly* 27:91 Je 22 '87

Railey, Walker

about

A cloud falls on a Dallas preacher. D. Pedersen. il por *Newsweek* 109:23 My 25 '87

Strangled in Dallas: an ungodly mystery. *Newsweek* 109:30 My 11 '87

A troubled minister's tale. S. Peterson. il por *U S News World Rep* 102:28 My 25 '87

Railguns

Bringing SDI down to earth. il *Pop Mech* 164:69 N '87

Electromagnetic guns. T. A. Heppenheimer. il *Pop Sci* 231:54-8 Ag '87

Ground-based hypervelocity guns [SDI program] il *Aviat Week Space Technol* 127:81 N 23 '87

SDI research railgun succeeds in rapid repetitive firing. il *Aviat Week Space Technol* 127:29 D 21 '87

SDIO to conduct hypervelocity firing of subscale Thunderbolt prototype. *Aviat Week Space Technol* 127:28-9 Ag 24 '87

Railroad accidents *See* Railroads—Accidents

Railroad holding companies

See also

CSX Corporation

Kansas City Southern Industries, Inc.

Santa Fe Southern Pacific Corporation

Soo Line Corp.

Acquisitions and mergers

See Railroads—Acquisitions and mergers

Railroad law

See also

United States. Federal Railroad Administration

"Open access". J. Cook. il *Forbes* 140:46+ S 21 '87

Railroad models
Photographs and photography
Meet the masters of railroad miniatures. B. Hurter. il *Petersens Photogr Mag* 16:54-8+ D '87
Railroad museums
See also
Gold Coast Railroad Museum
National Capital Trolley Museum
Ding, ding, ding [trolley lines and museums] K. Zimmermann. il *Americana* 15:58-60+ Mr/Ap '87
Railroad stations *See* Railroads—Stations
Railroad tramps *See* Homeless
Railroad travel
All aboard for an old-fashioned train ride! S. Birnbaum. il *Good Housekeep* 205:46+ Ag '87
Cairns to Kuranda . . . short but scenic rail trip in Australia's tropical north. il map *Sunset* 178:94+ Ap '87
Closely observed trains [steam trains around the world; cover story] J. Western. il *Focus* 37:10-17 Summ '87
A Housatonic holiday [Housatonic Railroad's excursion] C. La VO. il *Travel Holiday* 168:30+ S '87
Long train coming [Trans-Siberian] J.-C. Castelli. il *Esquire* 107:49+ Je '87
Passage to Bangkok: rail adventures through Southeast Asia. N. H. Belcher. il map *Travel Holiday* 168:42-7 D '87
See Europe by train [Eurailpass] il *Glamour* 85:170+ Je '87
States of Chihuahua & Sinaloa: Chihuahua al Pacifico RR. L. D. O'Connor. il *Saturday Evening Post* 259:70+ O '87
The unknown commuter [Metro-North commute between Connecticut and Grand Central Terminal] *New Yorker* 63:29 Mr 9 '87
Railroad workers
See also
Black railroad workers
Strikes—Railroad workers
Salaries, pensions, etc.
See also
British Rail Pension Fund
Collective bargaining—Railroads
The great train robbery [railroad retirement system] P. Longman. il *Wash Mon* 19:12-14+ D '87
Railroads
See also
Burlington Northern Inc.
Collective bargaining—Railroads
Consolidated Rail Corporation
Housatonic Railroad Company
Illinois Central Gulf RR. Co.
Light rail systems
Long Island Rr.
National Railroad Passenger Corp.
Norfolk Southern Corporation
Strikes—Railroad workers
Union Pacific Corp.
Venango River Corporation
Accidents
Body on the line [B. Willson run over by train while protesting against U.S. arms shipments to Central America] B. Kessler. *Nation* 245:329 O 3 '87
Legacy of a railroad disaster [January 1987 crash near Baltimore] D. Gates. il *Newsweek* 109:8 My 18 '87
Verdict on a disaster [head-on crash between CN freight train and Via Rail passenger train, February 1986] M. Clark. il *Macleans* 100:25 F 2 '87
Acquisitions and mergers
Can Santa Fe outrun the raiders? K. Deveny. il *Bus Week* p60-1 N 2 '87
The end of the line [Santa Fe Southern Pacific's plan to merge] A. A. Lappen. por *Forbes* 140:10 Jl 27 '87
Just when Kansas City Southern was ready to pounce . . . [hostile bid led by H. Kaskel] M. Ivey and C. Hawkins. *Bus Week* p26-7 Ag 24 '87
The raiders are eager to start splitting rails [Santa Fe Southern Pacific a target] J. N. Frank and S. Payne. *Bus Week* p36-7 Jl 13 '87
Riding on billions. J. Crudele. il *N Y* 20:14+ Jl 20 '87
Santa Fe's pursuers may have to settle for pieces. S. Toy. il *Bus Week* p74 D 28 '87-Ja 4 '88
Competitive transportation
CSX may have charted a treacherous course [purchase of Sea-Land] T. Ichniowski. il *Bus Week* p36+ F 16 '87
"Open access". J. Cook. il *Forbes* 140:46+ S 21 '87

Employees
See Railroad workers
Federal aid
See Railroads and state
Finance
Surface transportation. P. Fuhrman. il *Forbes* 139:210-11 Ja 12 '87
Freight service
See also
Piggyback transportation
History
Photographs and photography
Causing a Rau [discovery of photographs by W. Rau] S. Staggs. il *Art News* 86:37 N '87
International aspects
Closely observed trains [steam trains around the world; cover story] J. Western. il *Focus* 37:10-17 Summ '87
Models
See Railroad models
Photographs and photography
All for the love of trains. P. Barry. il *Petersens Photogr Mag* 15:32-7 Ja '87
Real estate operations
It may be time to hitch a ride on the Reading. J. M. Laderman. il *Bus Week* p82 Ja 26 '87
Riding on billions. J. Crudele. il *N Y* 20:14+ Jl 20 '87
Right of way
See also
Rails-to-Trails Conservancy
From old rails to new trails [Missouri River Trail] R. R. Pryor. il *Sierra* 72:77-8 S/O '87
"Open access". J. Cook. il *Forbes* 140:46+ S 21 '87
Safety devices and measures
A matter of rail safety. S. Shane. *Travel Holiday* 168:6 S '87
Securities
Arriving soon: the biggest-ever IPO [Conrail initial public offering] il *Fortune* 115:9 Mr 30 '87
Conrail sale aids bankers. M. A. Fortune. *Black Enterp* 17:22 Ap '87
The Conrail sale: how much is it worth? C. Hawkins and C. S. Eklund. il *Bus Week* p78+ Mr 23 '87
Is this any way to sell a railroad? [Conrail's public offering] L. Smith. il *Fortune* 115:91-2+ My 25 '87
The raiders are eager to start splitting rails [Santa Fe Southern Pacific a target] J. N. Frank and S. Payne. *Bus Week* p36-7 Jl 13 '87
Rail stocks are comin' round the mountain. A. E. Serwer. il *Fortune* 115:124 My 25 '87
Stations
See also
Pennsylvania Station (New York, N.Y.)
Conservation and restoration
All aboard for arts [Duluth's St. Louis County Heritage and Arts Center, The Depot] E. Beck. il *Horizon* 30:19-21 Ap '87
Track
See also
Rail cycling
Trains, Magnetic
See Magnetic levitation vehicles
Alaska
History
Kennecott's boom and bust. R. Churchill and K. Jones. il *Focus* 37:1-5 Fall '87
Australia
Cairns to Kuranda . . . short but scenic rail trip in Australia's tropical north. il map *Sunset* 178:94+ Ap '87
Canada
Verdict on a disaster [head-on crash between CN freight train and Via Rail passenger train, February 1986] M. Clark. il *Macleans* 100:25 F 2 '87
Mexico
States of Chihuahua & Sinaloa: Chihuahua al Pacifico RR. L. D. O'Connor. il *Saturday Evening Post* 259:70+ O '87
Siberia (Soviet Union)
Long train coming [Trans-Siberian] J.-C. Castelli. il *Esquire* 107:49+ Je '87
Southeast Asia
Passage to Bangkok: rail adventures through Southeast Asia. N. H. Belcher. il map *Travel Holiday* 168:42-7 D '87
United States
See Railroads
Western Europe
See Europe by train [Eurailpass] il *Glamour* 85:170+ Je '87

Railroads, Cable *See* Cable railroads
Railroads, Magnetic *See* Magnetic levitation vehicles
Railroads and state
    See also
      Consolidated Rail Corporation
      National Railroad Passenger Corp.
      United States. Federal Railroad Administration
        Canada
Revolution on the rails. D. Jenish. il *Macleans* 100:26-7
    S 14 '87
A short and angry strike [rail workers ordered back
    to work] M. Gee. il *Macleans* 100:22-3 S 7 '87
Rails (Birds)
Tales of two rails [Maryland's black rail and Michigan's
    yellow rail] W. G. Burt, III; R. McKee. il *Audubon*
    89:78-87 S '87
Rails-to-Trails Conservancy
New pleasures on old tracks. R. Riley. il *U S News*
    World Rep 103:69 D 21 '87
Rails to Trails. D. Murphy. il *Women's Sports Fitness*
    9:86-7 Mr '87
Rain and rainfall
    See also
      Acid rain
      Automobile driving—Storm hazards
      Droughts
      Floods
      Motorcycling—Storm hazards
      Runoff
      Walking—Storm hazards
Around the world—water, water almost everywhere .
    . . [1986] D. LeCompte. il *Weatherwise* 40:9-11 F
    '87
Functional box-counting and multiple elliptical dimen-
    sions in rain. S. Lovejoy and others. bibl f il *Science*
    235:1036-8 F 27 '87
How often does it rain where you live? N. J. Doesken
    and W. P. Eckrich. il maps *Weatherwise* 40:200-3
    Jl/Ag '87
Pesticidal rains. *Sci News* 131:360 Je 6 '87
Pray for rain [trout fishing in New York State] J.
    MacGregor. il *Field Stream* 92:46-7+ Ag '87
Raindrops keep falling on my track [calculating velocity
    and shape of raindrops] D. Simanaitis. il *Road Track*
    39:150 O '87
Rainy day blues and whites. M. Reed. il *Weatherwise*
    40:262-3 O '87
Real-time landslide warning during heavy rainfall. D.
    K. Keefer and others. bibl f il map *Science* 238:921-5
    N 13 '87
U.S., Japan present plans for joint spacecraft mission
    [Tropical Rainfall Measuring Mission] il *Aviat Week*
    Space Technol 127:69+ O 26 '87
        Terminology
Stotting polecats and pitchforks. M. Reed. *Weatherwise*
    40:213-14 Jl/Ag '87
Rain and rainfall, Artificial
Rain on the road [touring theater] M. Loeffler. il *Theatre*
    Crafts 21:23+ Ag/S '87
Rain clothing *See* Clothing, Waterproof
Rain forest crown canopy *See* Forest crown canopy
Rain forests
Battles and treaties for tropical forests. *Environment*
    29:21 Jl/Ag '87
Crisis in the rain forest. D. Schoonmaker. il map *Mother*
    Earth News 106:94-6+ Jl/Ag '87
Hunter-gatherers of the tropical forest. L. Palade. il maps
    Courier 40:20-2 Je '87
Peter Raven [tropical deforestation expert] B. Lawren.
    Omni 9:38+ S '87
We're killing our world [address, February 14, 1987]
    P. H. Raven. *Vital Speeches Day* 53:472-8 My 15
    '87
        Belize
In Belize, Coke goes better [Coca-Cola vs. rain forest]
    D. Voelker. il map *Sierra* 72:12 S/O '87
        Bolivia
Bolivia swaps debt for conservation. J. Walsh. map
    Science 237:596-7 Ag 7 '87
The deal is on in Bolivia . . . the deal is off in Nicaragua.
    M. Gaines. il *Sierra* 72:16-17 N/D '87
        Brazil
The last frontier [Amazon policy] B. Levin. il *Macleans*
    100:28 Ja 19 '87
Rubber and Amazon alliances. S. Schwartzman. il map
    Technol Rev 90:15-16 Ap '87
        Central America
Hamburgers are killing trees [boycott of fast-food outlets
    until they stop using Central American beef] il
    Newsweek 110:74 S 14 '87

One costly hamburger [importation of Central American
    beef contributes to tropical deforestation; views of
    Christopher Uhl] *Ctry J* 14:12-13 Ag '87
        Chile
Trees of the trembling earth [southern beech forest]
    T. T. Veblen. il *Nat Hist* 96:42-7 S '87
        Costa Rica
In the tropics, still rolling back the rain forest primeval.
    J. Omang. bibl (p182) il *Smithsonian* 17:56-60+ Mr
    '87
        Ecuador
    Photographs and photography
Jungle journey: taking photos in the Ecuadoran rain
    forest. C. Purcell and A. Purcell. il *Pop Photogr* 94:40+
    N '87
        French Guiana
Down to the treetops by balloon [exploring the tropical
    forest canopy; work of Francis Halle and others] il
    map *Natl Geogr World* 146:13-19 O '87
Out on a limb [exploring the tropical forest canopy
    by hot air balloon; work of Francis Halle and others]
    K. Brower. il *Omni* 9:56-64+ Ap '87
        Latin America
Buying debt, saving nature [offers to suspend debt pay-
    ments for tropical countries which protect forests] J.
    B. Copeland. il *Newsweek* 110:46 Ag 31 '87
Cutting the debt, saving the forest. D. Page. *Environment*
    29:4-5+ S '87
Exchanging debt for conservation [debt for nature scheme]
    A. L. Spitler. il *BioScience* 37:781 D '87
A golden deal: debt for nature. J. D. Hair. il *Int Wildl*
    17:30 S/O '87
        Nicaragua
The deal is on in Bolivia . . . the deal is off in Nicaragua.
    M. Gaines. il *Sierra* 72:16-17 N/D '87
        Panama
Kuna Indians: building a bright future [preservation of
    virgin rain forest] N. Myers. il map *Int Wildl* 17:18-24
    Jl/Ag '87
Trouble ahead for the Canal? [deforestation may cause
    water shortage] J. Borrell. il *Time* 129:63 Mr 2 '87
        Puerto Rico
    See also
      Caribbean National Forest (Puerto Rico)
        Venezuela
Apogeotropic roots in an Amazon rain forest. R. L.
    Sanford. bibl f il *Science* 235:1062-4 F 27 '87
When growing down isn't good enough [apogeotropic
    roots; study by Robert L. Sanford, Jr.] *Sci News* 131:188
    Mr 21 '87
Rainbow Acres (Organization)
There are no handicapped at Rev. Showers' Rainbow
    Acres. L. Rozen. il pors *People Wkly* 27:71-2+ My
    4 '87
Rainbow Band
Rainbow comes to Latin America. J. Robbins. il *Down*
    Beat 54:12 My '87
Rainbow Coalition *See* National Rainbow Coalition
Rainbow effect photography *See* Photography, Trick
Rainbow trout fishing *See* Trout fishing
Raincoats *See* Clothing, Waterproof
Raindrops *See* Rain and rainfall
Raine, Craig
Baize doors [poem] *Am Sch* 56:546-7 Aut '87
Rainer, Arnulf, 1929-
    about
Arnulf Rainer: self-exposures. D. B. Kuspit. bibl f il
    pors *Art Am* 75:170-9 Ap '87
Rainer, J. Kenyon, 1952-
First do no harm [condensation] il *Read Dig* 131:282-9+
    N '87
Raines, Howell
Thatcher's capitalist revolution [cover story] il pors *N*
    Y Times Mag p16-19+ My 31 '87
Raines, Tim
    about
The last laugh. D. Whitford. il pors *Sport Mag* 78:16-18+
    D '87
More bang for more bucks. S. Wulf. il pors *Sports*
    Illus 66:32-3 My 11 '87
Raines, Smith resemble black gold as N.L. stars. pors
    Jet 72:50 Ag 3 '87
Rainwater, Richard E.
    about
Creating value. J. Merwin. il *Forbes* 139 Ann Directory:57
    Ap 27 '87
Git along, little thrifts. T. Mason. il por *Bus Week*
    p33 O 26 '87

Rainwear *See* Clothing, Waterproof
Raised bed gardening *See* Gardens and gardening
Raises, Pay *See* Wages and salaries
A raisin in the sun [drama] *See* Hansberry, Lorraine, 1930-1965
Raising Arizona [film] *See* Motion picture reviews—Single works
Raisins
Advertising
Filmmaker Will Vinton and his feats of clay are giving animation a new raisin d'être. D. Van Biema. il pors *People Wkly* 27:76+ Mr 9 '87
Raisins [use of popular commercial to celebrate Festival of Claymation at the Metro Cinema in Manhattan] *New Yorker* 63:29 My 4 '87
Raitz, Karl B.
Kentucky Bluegrass [cover story] il map *Focus* 37:6-11 Fall '87
Rajathurai, Sribaskaran
about
Trying to make a new life. B. Wallace. il por *Macleans* 100:14 Ag 24 '87
Rajewsky, Klaus, and others
Evolutionary and somatic selection of the antibody repertoire in the mouse. bibl f il *Science* 238:1088-94 N 20 '87
Rajk, László
about
The sons of communism. M. T. Kaufman. il pors *N Y Times Mag* p50+ Mr 8 '87
Rakosy, Alex
about
Little drop of horrors. H. Wouk. il *Omni* 10:84-9 N '87
Rakove, Jack N., 1947-
'The great compromise' drafting the American Constitution, 1787 [cover story] bibl il *Hist Today* 37:19-25 S '87
Raleigh (N.C.)
Airports
American begins operations at new Raleigh hub complex [Raleigh/Durham Airport] C. A. Shifrin. il *Aviat Week Space Technol* 127:54+ Jl 6 '87
City planning
Preservation spawns downtown housing. il *South Living* 22:96 D '87
Galleries and museums
See also
North Carolina Museum of Art
Monuments, statues, etc.
Raleigh honors Vietnam vets. il *South Living* 22:53 O '87
Raleigh/Durham Airport *See* Raleigh (N.C.)—Airports
Rallies, Automobile *See* Automobile rallies
Rallies, Boat *See* Boat rallies
Rallies, Motor vehicle *See* Motor vehicle rallies
Rallies, Motorcycle *See* Motorcycle rallies
Rally cars *See* Automobiles, Racing
Rallycross racing *See* Automobile racing
Ralston, Anthony
Let them use calculators. il *Technol Rev* 90:30-1 Ag/S '87
Ralston, Dennis
A balancing act. il por *World Tennis* 34:41 F '87
Better your balance for consistency. il *World Tennis* 35:74 S '87
Flexibility. il *World Tennis* 34:31 Ap '87
Forewarned is forearmed. il *World Tennis* 35:31 Jl '87
Pick a pocket or two. il *World Tennis* 35:27 Ag '87
Reach up high. il *World Tennis* 35:65 O '87
Smash & recover. il pors *World Tennis* 35:17 D '87
Step back first. il *World Tennis* 35:25 N '87
Ralston, Jeannie
Five times blessed! il *McCalls* 114:55-6+ Jl '87
Would you spy on your man? Meet 8 women who did. il *Glamour* 85:266+ S '87
RAM *See* Random access memory
Ram Dass
about
Ram Dass, veteran guru and former LSD prophet, leads a new kind of vision quest. J. Sugden. il pors *People Wkly* 28:79-80+ S 28 '87
Rama Rao, N. T.
about
Pols of India. C. Das Gupta and J. Hoberman. il pors *Film Comment* 23:20-4 My/Je '87
Rama Rao, Nandamuri Taraka *See* Rama Rao, N. T.
Ramachandran, M. G.
about
Pols of India. C. Das Gupta and J. Hoberman. il pors *Film Comment* 23:20-4 My/Je '87

Ramada Inc.
Snake eyes. T. Jaffe. il *Forbes* 139:266 My 18 '87
Ramalingaswami, Vulimiri
How many doctors? il *World Health* p5-7 Ap '87
Ramanujan Aiyangar, Srinivasa, 1887-1920
about
The formula man. I. Peterson. il *Sci News* 131:266-7 Ap 25 '87
Remembering a "magical genius". G. Kolata. il por *Science* 236:1519-21 Je 19 '87
Ramaphosa, Cyril
about
Striking figure. J. Greenwald. il por *Time* 130:42+ S 14 '87
Rambo (Fictional character)
Is there life beyond Rambo? [Carolco] A. B. Block. il *Forbes* 139:88+ Je 1 '87
Zeal without understanding: reflections on Rambo and Oliver North. R. Jewett. il *Christ Century* 104:753-6 S 9-16 '87
Rameau, Jean Philippe
about
Les fêtes d'Hébé [opera] Reviews
Horizon il 30:42 Mr '87. P. J. Rosenwald
Ramey, Samuel
about
Giving the devil his due. M. Walsh. il pors *Time* 129:76 Je 8 '87
Ramirez, Maria Fiorini
about
Buying 30-year Treasuries is 'the last thing I would do right now'. D. Zigas. il por *Bus Week* p163 D 28 '87-Ja 4 '88
Ramírez Mercado, Sergio, 1942-
about
Poetry and power in Nicaragua. F. Goldman. il por *N Y Times Mag* p44-6+ Mr 29 '87
Sergio Ramirez: the view from Managua [interview] C. Dreifus. il por *Progressive* 51:19-20 S '87
Vice president and author [interview] A. Morales. il por *World Press Rev* 34:58 N '87
Ramis, Harold
about
Joke-buster. B. Roe. por *Vogue* 177:82 O '87
Ramoa, Ary S., and others
Transient morphological features of identified ganglion cells in living fetal and neonatal retina. bibl f il *Science* 237:522-5 Jl 31 '87
Ramos, Juan L., and others
Redesigning metabolic routes: manipulation of TOL plasmid pathway for catabolism of alkylbenzoates. bibl f il *Science* 235:593-6 Ja 30 '87
Rams, Hydraulic *See* Hydraulic rams
Ramsay, Ansil
Thailand: surviving the 1980's. bibl f *Curr Hist* 86:164-7+ Ap '87
Ramsay, Jack
about
Not getting older, just better. il por *Sports Illus* 67:16 S 14 '87
Ramses II, King of Egypt
about
Rameses the Great. il *USA Today (Periodical)* 115:8-9 Ap '87
Ramsey, Bennett
Books on the Americas. *America* 157:168+ S 26 '87
Ramsey, Charles C.
about
Bear Stearns: hitting its stride while others trip. D. Zigas. il por *Bus Week* p59-60 Ag 31 '87
Ramsey, Van Broughton
about
Period perfect: Van Broughton Ramsey costumes Horton Foote's Texas. R. Seidenberg. il *Theatre Crafts* 21:99-102 My '87
Ranada, David
Bits & pieces. See alternate issues of High Fidelity (New York, N.Y.) beginning January 1986
Scan lines. See alternate issues of High Fidelity (New York, N.Y.) beginning April 1986
(jt. auth) See Sarver, Carleton, and Ranada, David
Ranard, Donald A.
The last bus. il *Atlantic* 260:26-8+ O '87
Ranawat, Chitranjan S.
about
The bender mender. S. Shapiro. il *Discover* 8:22-3 O '87
Ranch houses
Architectural digest visits: Robert Wagner [Los Angeles ranch house designed by Cliff May] J. Allen. il pors *Archit Dig* 44:124-31+ My '87

Ranch houses—cont.

In the shadow of the Rockies: renewing the historic Cody Ranch in Wyoming [TE Ranch owned by Charles and Anne Duncan] M. M. Thomas. il *Archit Dig* 44:150-5+ S '87

La Quinta Norte: Douglas S. Cramer's ranch in the Santa Ynez Valley [decorated by Michael Taylor] L. Bernikow. il por *Archit Dig* 44:136-47 Ap '87

Ranch houses, Remodeled See Houses, Remodeled

Ranch life

See also

Cowboys

Ranches

See also

Rainbow Acres (Organization)

Alabama

See also

Big Oak Boys Ranch (Ala.)

California

La Quinta Norte: Douglas S. Cramer's ranch in the Santa Ynez Valley [decorated by Michael Taylor] L. Bernikow. il por *Archit Dig* 44:136-47 Ap '87

Rancho La Vista: western themes in California's Ojai Valley [western art collector V. Milner] M. Webb. il pors *Archit Dig* 44:112-19 D '87

Stonepine: sophisticated equestrian retreat in California's Carmel Valley. B. D. Colen. il *Archit Dig* 44 Archit Dig Travels:32-7+ O '87

Colorado

Planning pays off for rancher [Bob Chenoweth] D. Allen and G. Johnston. il *Success Farm* 85:12 Je '87

Idaho

White-water Idaho: riding the River of No Return. S. Robertson. il *Travel Holiday* 167:56-61 My '87

Montana

Derek's herd [White Galloway breeder D. Pruitt] R. Gavin. il por *Ctry J* 14:21-5 Jl '87

Texas

Deep in the heart of Texas [HK Ranch barbecues] J. Nathan. il *Mother Earth News* 106:54-9 Jl/Ag '87

How Ray Muzny doubled gross sales with little extra cost [cattle rancher] il *Success Farm* 85 no4:B20 F '87

Anecdotes, facetiae, satire, etc.

The call of the wild [Mayan Dude Ranch] M. Sorkin. il *Vogue* 177:356+ Mr '87

Wisconsin

See also

Rawhide Boys Ranch

Wyoming

Home on the range [summer job at Wyoming cattle ranch] A. Peterson. il *Seventeen* 46:268+ Ag '87

In the shadow of the Rockies: renewing the historic Cody Ranch in Wyoming [TE Ranch owned by Charles and Anne Duncan] M. M. Thomas. il *Archit Dig* 44:150-5+ S '87

Ranchhands

Home on the range [summer job at Wyoming cattle ranch] A. Peterson. il *Seventeen* 46:268+ Ag '87

Rancho Santa Fe (Calif.)

Restaurants, nightclubs, bars, etc.

Spécialités de la maison:

Mille Fleurs. C. Bates. il *Gourmet* 47:20+ S '87

Rancho Seco nuclear power plant (Calif.) See Nuclear power plants

Rand, A. Barry

about

Xerox moves Rand to top. M. A. Fortune. por *Black Enterp* 17:17 My '87

Rand, Abby

What's best in the ski resorts. il *Glamour* 85:272-5 N '87

Randall, Ariane

Survival at sea. il por map *Seventeen* 46:108-9+ D '87

Randall, Francis B.

Lost at sea. il pors map *N Y* 20:36-43 Ag 10 '87

Randall, Frederika

The heart & mind of a genius. il por *Vogue* 177:480-1+ Mr '87

Randall, Nellie Pike

My father's best gift. il *Read Dig* 130:11-16 Ja '87

Randall, Robert

Return of the Pleiades. il *Nat Hist* 96:42-53 Je '87

Randall, Ruth E.

The Minnesota dialogue on education. il *Phi Delta Kappan* 68:539-43 Mr '87

Randall, Tom, 1945-

(jt. auth) See Culbertson, Judi, and Randall, Tom, 1945-

Randall-Cutler, Roger

about

The Brit pack. R. Nicolson. il pors *Vogue* 177:80 D '87

Randi, James

about

Fleecing the flock. J. Tierney. il pors *Discover* 8:50-4+ N '87

Randolph, Bernard P.

about

Air Force's Randolph is tabbed for 4-star general. por *Jet* 72:22 My 11 '87

Bernard P. Randolph: the armed forces' only black four-star general. D. M. Cheers. il pors *Ebony* 43:154+ N '87

Randolph is the top black U.S. gen.; gets 4th star. il por *Jet* 72:6 Ag 17 '87

Randolph, Edmund Jennings, 1753-1813

about

The non-signers. C. L. Mee. pors *Am Herit* 38:78-9 S/O '87

Randolph, Laura B.

Vanessa Williams: now that the storm is over [cover story] il pors *Essence* 18:87-9+ Jl '87

Randolph, Marie Jackson- See Jackson-Randolph, Marie

Random access memory

A 16-megabit memory chip from Japan [dynamic random access memory] A. L. Robinson. il *Science* 235:1324-5 Mr 13 '87

The All Card AT1/M. J. Angel. il *Byte* 12:324-6 Ja '87

Awesome I/O card. R. Grehan. il *Byte* 12:101-2 D '87

Build your own 256K Amiga expansion RAM. R. F. Retter and A. N. Morelli, Jr. il *Byte* 12:129-32 F '87

Communicating . . . in the background [RAM-resident communications software] P. Honan. il *Pers Comput* 11:100-3+ Jl '87

Designer RAM. R. Grossblatt. il *Radio-Electron* 58:77-8+ D '87

Dynamic memory. R. Grossblatt. il *Radio-Electron* 58:26-7+ Jl '87

First PS/2 expansion board [RamQuest 50/60] R. Lockwood. il *Pers Comput* 11:276 N '87

Gofer finds what you've lost [RAM-resident utility] C. Bermant. il *Pers Comput* 11:294 D '87

High-speed memory boards for ATs. B. Nance. il *Byte* 12:124-8+ D '87

Lightning and Flash [disk cache programs] W. F. Bolton. il *Byte* 12:260+ Ap '87

Lotus Metro does it all [RAM-resident set of utilities] S. R. Reed. il *Pers Comput* 11:182 Ap '87

Memory-expansion boards for the IBM PC AT [BIX product focus] C. Franklin, Jr. il *Byte* 12:133-6 D '87

Nine PC AT multifunction cards. W. Rash, Jr. il *Byte* 12:318-20+ Ja '87

Non-volatile memory IC's. R. Grossblatt. il *Radio-Electron* 58:60-3 O '87

Orchid PC turbo 286e IBM-PC accelerator card. il *Radio-Electron* 58:24+ F '87

Packing more memory into silicon [dynamic random access memory] il *Sci News* 131:189 Mr 21 '87

A RAM-hungry Partner [RAM-resident set of utilities] R. Lockwood. *Pers Comput* 11:176 Jl '87

RAM-resident utilities. J. Edwards. il *Byte* 12 Sp Issue:103-8+ Summ '87

RAM residents for the enlightened. R. Nelson. il *Pers Comput* 11:81-5+ Mr '87

A shared network spreadsheet [virtual memory routines] P. R. Horton and M. D. Morris. *Byte* 12:185-6+ Jl '87

Static (RAM) at PC's Limited. A. C. Hixson. il *Pers Comput* 11:25 Ag '87

The submicron era may belong to the Japanese [dynamic random access memory chips] O. Port. il *Bus Week* p98 Mr 16 '87

Text and graphics: together at last [Inset 2 RAM-resident utility program] P. Honan. il *Pers Comput* 11:164 Mr '87

Turbo-Amiga: a peripheral for the Amiga 1000 that's actually another computer. W. Block. il *Byte* 12:235-8 Je '87

Which memory? R. Grossblatt. il *Radio-Electron* 58:123-4+ My '87

Random House Audiobooks

Random House Audio tries self-help with a health series [coproduced by A. Ulene's production firm Feeling Fine Programs] il *Publ Wkly* 231:39-40 My 1 '87

Random House dictionary of the English language See English language—Dictionaries

Random House Inc.

AAP and seven authors ask to join Random House in Salinger appeal [blocked publication of I. Hamilton's biography of J. D. Salinger] H. Fields. *Publ Wkly* 232:11 S 25 '87

AAP files amicus brief for Random House in appeal of Salinger decision [appeals court decision to bar publication of I. Hamilton's biography of J. D. Salinger] M. Yen. *Publ Wkly* 231:90 F 27 '87

After the un-Random showdown [hiring of J. Evans] M. Reuter. il pors *Publ Wkly* 232:11 O 30 '87

CVBC executives hail Random House takeover. V. Menkes. *Publ Wkly* 231:21 My 22 '87

Dick and Joni [bitter divorce battle between J. Evans and R. Snyder] J. Kasindorf. il pors *N Y* 20:60-4+ D 14 '87

Joni Evans leaves Simon & Schuster; to head imprint at Random House. J. Mutter. por *Publ Wkly* 232:10 S 4 '87

Joni Evans replaces Kaminsky at Random. *Publ Wkly* 232:11 O 23 '87

Once half of publishing's dynamic duo, Joni Evans is now throwing the book at her husband, Dick Snyder. M. Vespa. il pors *People Wkly* 28:149-50+ N 16 '87

Random buys Schocken for unit of Pantheon. *Publ Wkly* 232:101 Jl 24 '87

Random House buys Warner Audio for second audio line. il *Publ Wkly* 231:56-7 My 22 '87

Random House, Dell launch series for younger readers. il *Publ Wkly* 232:24 S 25 '87

Random House seeks review of Salinger decision [decision to bar publication of I. Hamilton's biography of J. D. Salinger] M. Yen. *Publ Wkly* 231:24 F 13 '87

Random House to acquire Chatto, Virago, Bodley and Cape group. *Publ Wkly* 231:114 My 15 '87

The rumble at Random House [J. Evans' arrival forces showdown between R. Bernstein and H. Kaminsky] J. Alter. il pors *Newsweek* 110:62 O 26 '87

A talk with Erroll McDonald, editor of the 1986 Nobel laureate for literature. G. Blooston. por *Publ Wkly* 231:86+ Mr 6 '87

When less is more [Keynotes line of literary study guides devised by W. J. Campbell] L. Fleischer. il *Publ Wkly* 231:81 Ja 9 '87

Whose words are they, anyway? [suit brought by J. D. Salinger] D. Margolick. il *N Y Times Book Rev* 92:1+ N 1 '87

Random number generators

Building a random-number generator [Pascal program] B. A. Wichmann and D. Hill. il *Byte* 12:127-8 Mr '87

Testing intrinsic random-number generators. D. T. Modianos and others. bibl il *Byte* 12:175-6+ Ja '87

Random numbers *See* Numbers, Random
Random processes *See* Stochastic processes
Randova, Eva

about

Touch of Venus. J. H. Sutcliffe. pors *Opera News* 51:34-5 Ja 17 '87

Rangefinder cameras *See* Cameras
Rangel, Charles B.

about

Rangel urges Congress to clear record of Garvey. *Jet* 72:22 Ap 20 '87

Rangers, Park *See* Park rangers
Ranges, Kitchen *See* Stoves
Ranges, Livestock *See* Livestock ranges
Ranges, Test *See* Proving grounds
Ranieri, Lewis S.

about

Salomon Brothers parts with a son. A. Bianco. *Bus Week* p60 Jl 27 '87

Ranke, Leopold von, 1795-1886

about

What Ranke meant. F. Gilbert. *Am Sch* 56:393-7 Summ '87

Rankin, Aimee

about

Aimée Rankin. D. Rubey. il *Art News* 86:145-6 S '87

Ranking of colleges and universities *See* Colleges and universities—Evaluation

Ranly, Donald

Effective nonfiction writing: seven C's plus one. *Writer* 100:19-21+ Ja '87

Ranney, Austin

Farewell to reform—almost. bibl *Society* 24:29-38 My/Je '87

Ranz des vaches *See* Folk songs, Swiss

Rao, K. R., and others

Phonon density of states and specific heat of forsterite, Mg_2SiO_4. bibl f il *Science* 236:64-5 Ap 3 '87

Rao, N. T. Rama *See* Rama Rao, N. T.
Rao, R. V. R. Chandrasekhar *See* Chandrasekhar Rao, R. V. R.
Rao, Veena N., and others

erg, a human *ets*-related gene on chromosome 21: alternative splicing, polyadenylation, and translation. bibl f il *Science* 237:635-9 Ag 7 '87

Rap music

See also

Phonograph records—Rap music

He's not lean but his rap is mean, so the trashers relate to Skatemaster Tate. il pors *People Wkly* 27:155-6 Je 8 '87

The kings of rap, together [Run-D.M.C. and the Beastie Boys] B. Barol. il *Newsweek* 109:71 Je 29 '87

A movie star goes to Watts to make sure the Bard gets a good rap [work of J. Agutter] K. Hubbard. il pors *People Wkly* 27:83-4 Je 29 '87

Moral and religious aspects

The Fat Boys say: 'Protect yourself' [rap song about condoms] *Harpers* 274:18 Je '87

Rapper L.L. Cool J charged with lewdness on Ga. stage. por *Jet* 72:53 Jl 13 '87

Rape

See also

Child molesting
Date rape
Trials (Rape)

The dark playground [male response to rape] D. Voll. il *N Y Times Mag* p86 O 4 '87

Ex-champ Pryor shot, held in Miami for rape [A. Pryor] por *Jet* 71:50 Mr 23 '87

Fingerprinting only black males in town sparks tension, fear [Homestead, Pa.] L. Ransom. il *Jet* 72:12-14+ S 21 '87

Homestead NAACP chided on fingerprint support. il *Jet* 73:7 S 28 '87

"I had no choice" [decision to have an illegal abortion in 1954 after being raped] S. Matulis. il por *Redbook* 168:38+ Mr '87

"I never thought it could happen to me" [rape in the suburbs] A. Fischer. il *Redbook* 169:120-2+ Je '87

Innocent man's eight-year prison ordeal [case of N. Walker in New Jersey] W. Leavy. il pors *Ebony* 42:86+ Mr '87

Learning how to cry rape. S. Nelton. il *Nations Bus* 75:67-8 Ja '87

Not in my town [problems of paroled rapist L. Singleton] il por *Time* 129:31 Je 1 '87

Packer receiver Lofton faces sex assault trial. por *Jet* 71:50 F 9 '87

Pryor gets no record in Miami kidnapping case [rape charges dropped against A. Pryor] *Jet* 72:52 S 14 '87

Pryor preps for battle on rape charge in Miami [A. Pryor] por *Jet* 72:51 Mr 30 '87

The psychological effects of rape. M. Sones. il *Glamour* 85:178+ Ag '87

Rape [personal account of victim] il *People Wkly* 27:40-3 My 4 '87

Rape prevention: Du Pont's model program. A. Hornaday. il *Ms* 15:31 Je '87

Rape strikes the suburbs. A. Fischer. il *Read Dig* 131:59-62 S '87

Rape: the macho view [study by Donald L. Mosher and Ronald D. Anderson] P. McCarthy. *Psychol Today* 21:12 Ap '87

Say, brother [rape of friend] M. W. Griffith. por *Essence* 18:10 S '87

The search for a rapist [blacks asked to submit to fingerprinting in Homestead, Pa.] il *Newsweek* 110:42 S 14 '87

Sexual and family violence: a growing issue for the churches [cover story] L. G. Livezey. il *Christ Century* 104:938-42 O 28 '87

'Sorry' for comment to white woman: Ward [New York Police Commissioner B. Ward] por *Jet* 72:28 Ag 24 '87

Then I had this day that was one rape after another [pediatric emergency room] P. Klass. il *Discover* 8:18+ Jl '87

Trying to trace a rapist [fingerprinting of blacks in Homestead, Pa.] F. Trippett. il *Time* 130:28 S 14 '87

Victims' psychological aftermath [views of Deborah Rose] il *USA Today (Periodical)* 116:15 D '87

We had to find our daughter's molester. S. Kraft. il *Read Dig* 130:147-51 My '87

Rape oil *See* Rapeseed oil
Rapeseed oil
Contamination
Spain's deadly elixir [toxic industrial rapeseed oil poisoning case] il *Macleans* 100:35 Ap 13 '87
Raphael, 1483-1520
about
Polished work, divine doodles. il *Newsweek* 110:77 N 30 '87
Raphael and his circle: Pierpont Morgan Library. M. E. Haus. il *Art News* 86:144 D '87
Raphael's drawings. A. C. Danto. *Nation* 245:765-7 D 19 '87
Raphael, Bette-Jane
Can this be love? See issues of Glamour
Can we change the people we love? il *Glamour* 85:222+ S '87
Family quarrels: how to repair the fights nobody really wins. il *Glamour* 85:200-1 D '87
Fear of entertaining. il *Glamour* 85:124+ D '87
Loving an unfaithful man. il *Glamour* 85:168+ My '87
Raphael, Chaim
Pagans, Christians, Jews. *Commentary* 84:39-44 O '87
Raphael, Maryanne
Should you keep a diary? *Writer* 100:30 Ja '87
Raphaelson, Joel
(ed) See Ogilvy, David, 1911-. Memos from an advertising man
Rapid Deployment Force (U.S.) *See* United States. Rapid Deployment Force
Rapid reading *See* Speed reading
Rapids, Running of *See* Running rapids
Rapini *See* Broccoli raab
Rapini cooking *See* Cooking—Vegetables
Rapists: can they be stopped? [television program] See Television program reviews—Single works
Rapoport, Roger
Radio daze. il por *Americana* 15:49-52 N/D '87
Rapp, Anthony
about
"Adventures in babysitting": the mad movie about the pitfalls of making pocket money. E. Miller. il pors *Seventeen* 46:71-2+ Jl '87
Rapp, Ellen
The herpes nobody knows. il *Mademoiselle* 93:80 Ja '87
Sex Rx: is your gynecologist good enough? il *Mademoiselle* 93:104+ O '87
Why you crave what you crave. il *Mademoiselle* 93:142 Ap '87
Why you want sex—and why you don't. *Mademoiselle* 93:176 S '87
(jt. auth) See Tanne, Janice Hopkins, and Rapp, Ellen
Rapp, Joel
The five best bloomers. il *Redbook* 169:72-3+ Ag '87
High standards. il *Redbook* 169:126-9+ My '87
Plants from the table. il *Redbook* 168:102-5 F '87
Rappaport, Roy A.
about
Letters [discussion of November 1986 article, Untrashing Margaret Mead] *Sci Am* 256:6 F '87
Rapping (Music) *See* Rap music
Rappoport, Ken
Football feuds—on the field and off. il *Saturday Evening Post* 259:24+ N '87
Rare animals
See also
Bison, American
Bobcats
Caribou
Cheetahs
Elephants
Endangered Species Act (1973)
Ferrets
Gorillas
Leopards
Llamas
Manatees
Otters
Pandas
Rhinoceros
Seals (Animals)
Tigers
Turtles
Whales
Wolves
Too many cooks. G. Reiger. il *Field Stream* 92:15-16+ N '87
What's new at the zoo? [breeding endangered species] D. M. Kennedy. il *Technol Rev* 90:66-73 Ap '87

Rare birds
See also
Condors
Parrots
Pelicans
Plovers
Storks
Woodpeckers
Protection
See Bird sanctuaries
Rare books
See also
Manuscripts
Decorating by the book [antique books being bought for display purposes] E. Felber. il por *Publ Wkly* 232:76 Ag 14 '87
Ed the collector, Jake the dentist and Beckett: a tale that ends in Texas. C. Lake. il *N Y Times Book Rev* 92:2 S 6 '87
The real things [description of signed first edition of H. James's The golden bowl from Christie's catalog] G. S. Johnston. *Harpers* 274:54-5 F '87
Rare earth metals
See also
Cesium
Ytterbium
Yttrium
Searching land and sea for the dinosaur killer. R. A. Kerr. il *Science* 237:856-7 Ag 21 '87
Rare plants
See also
Cactus
Endangered Species Act (1973)
Ginseng
Wildflowers
Ras Tafari movement
Va. fed. judge says 'Rasta' cons must eat prison food. *Jet* 72:12 Ag 3 '87
Räsänen, Matti E., and others
Fluvial perturbance in the western Amazon basin: regulation by long-term sub-Andean tectonics. bibl f il map *Science* 238:1398-401 D 4 '87
Rash, Steve
about
Can't buy me love [film] Reviews
People Wkly il 28:14 S 7 '87. T. Cunneff
Rashad, Ahmad
about
Phylicia and Ahmad Rashad: TV's super couple juggle careers and family [cover story] L. Norment. il pors *Ebony* 42:148-50+ My '87
TV's reigning mom, Phylicia Rashad, and her football hero, Ahmad, revel in a match made by Bill Cosby. J. Hall. il pors *People Wkly* 28:95-8+ N 16 '87
Rashad, Phylicia
about
Debbie Allen and Phylicia Rashad's mother Vivian Ayers talks about their fame [cover story] il pors *Jet* 72:54-5 My 18 '87
Phylicia and Ahmad Rashad: TV's super couple juggle careers and family [cover story] L. Norment. il pors *Ebony* 42:148-50+ My '87
Phylicia Rashad tells why she plays slave role in 'Uncle Tom's cabin' movie [cover story] L. Ransom. il pors *Jet* 72:24-5 Ag 3 '87
Sisters: Debbie Allen and Phylicia Rashad. S. Flatow. il pors *McCalls* 114:90-5 Jl '87
TV's reigning mom, Phylicia Rashad, and her football hero, Ahmad, revel in a match made by Bill Cosby. J. Hall. il pors *People Wkly* 28:95-8+ N 16 '87
Rasheed, Prentice
about
Prentice Rasheed jabs Florida's new gun law. il por *Jet* 73:18 O 19 '87
Rashid, Ahmed
Pakistanis want an Afghan peace. il *Nation* 244:110-12+ Ja 31 '87
The sting. *Nation* 244:241-2 F 28 '87
Rashid, Justin
about
For forager Justin Rashid, the woods are lovely, dark and deep—and filled with things that he can eat. M. Neill. il pors *People Wkly* 28:125-7 O 19 '87
Raskin, A. H.
A Labor Day warning. por *Newsweek* 110:7 S 7 '87
Raskin, Barbara
about
Barbara Raskin tackles menopause, malaise and a sexy coming of age in her raunchy new best-seller. A. Chambers. il pors *People Wkly* 28:149-51 D 14 '87

Raskin, Ilya, and others
Salicylic acid: a natural inducer of heat production in Arum lilies. bibl f il *Science* 237:1601-2 S 25 '87
Rasmussen, Susan McKinnon
The watercolor page. il por *Am Artist* 51:42-5+ My '87
Rasmussen's encephalitis
The miracle of Maranda [hemispherectomy] E. Sherman. il pors *Ladies Home J* 104:48+ N '87
Rasor, Dina
about
Dina Rasor: patriot with a purpose. A. Steinbach. il pors *McCalls* 114:52 F '87
Raspberries
Brambles: berries of the brier patch. L. B. Trigg. il *South Living* 22:68-71 F '87
Managing the unmanageable berries . . . in pots. il *Sunset* 178:52-3 Ja '87
Trellising brambles. J. Ruttle. il *Rodale's Org Gard* 34:72-3 N '87
Rasps *See* Files and rasps
Rasputin, Valentin Grigor'evich
about
Siberian writer Valentin Rasputin fears for the planet's fate. S. K. Reed. il pors *People Wkly* 27:127-8 Ap 6 '87
Rastafari movement *See* Ras Tafari movement
Ratchet wrenches *See* Wrenches
Ratcliff, Carter
Aestheticism then and now. il *Art Am* 75:90-103 F '87
Architectural digest visits: Andy Williams [cover story] il por *Archit Dig* 44:40-7+ Jl '87
Focus on feats of Klee. il *Harpers Bazaar* 120:198-99+ F '87
Images on the edge of abstraction. il por *Archit Dig* 44:52+ D '87
The Italian baroque paintings of Morton and Mary Jane Harris. il por *Archit Dig* 44:50+ My '87
Jan Mitchell—the varied tastes of a New York connoisseur. il por *Archit Dig* 44:298+ N '87
Kiefer's heart of darkness. il *Harpers Bazaar* 121:160-1+ D '87
Masters of the glum "eureka!". il *Art Am* 75:98-101 Ja '87
Max Neuhaus: aural spaces. il *Art Am* 75:154-63 O '87
Optimism and apocalypse. il por *Archit Dig* 44:44+ Ap '87
View points. il *Art Am* 75:96-103 Mr '87
Rate it X [film] See Motion picture reviews—Single works
Rates, Electric utility *See* Electric utilities—Rates
Rates, Freight *See* Freight rates
Rates, Gas *See* Gas utilities—Rates
Rates, Interest *See* Interest (Economics)
Rates, Postal *See* Postal rates
Rates, Public utility *See* Public utilities—Rates
Rates, Telephone *See* Telephone—Rates
Rates, Water *See* Water rates
Rath, Bernie
about
ABA's Rath addresses bookselling issues [interview] A. Symons. il por *Publ Wkly* 231:49-50 My 22 '87
Rathbone, Richard
Ghana: thirty years on. il *Hist Today* 37:5-7 Mr '87
Rather, Dan
about
Anchor away. il *Time* 130:55 S 28 '87
CBS News with Dan Rather. W. F. Buckley. *Natl Rev* 39:54-5 Je 5 '87
The cloud of seriousness. T. Teachout. *Natl Rev* 39:62-4+ O 23 '87
Dan Rather draws a blank. H. F. Waters. il por *Newsweek* 110:47-8 S 28 '87
Dan Rather's struggle. J. Alter. il por *Newsweek* 110:51 Ag 24 '87
The most trusted men in America. C. Kramer. il pors *McCalls* 114:128+ Jl '87
Rather strange. E. Diamond. il por *N Y* 20:28+ S 28 '87
Taking the heat for sagging ratings, CBS anchor Dan Rather is toughing it out in last place. J. Hall. por *People Wkly* 28:32-3 Ag 10 '87
Rather, John D. G.
about
Laser clones. B. Lawren. il *Omni* 9:24 Ja '87
Raths, Louis Edward
about
Teaching for thinking: Louis E. Raths revisited. S. Wassermann. bibl f il *Phi Delta Kappan* 68:460-6 F '87

Rating of air pilots *See* Air pilots—Rating
Rating of colleges and universities *See* Colleges and universities—Evaluation
Rating of employees *See* Employees—Rating
Rating of industrial development bonds *See* Bonds, Industrial development—Rating
Rating of motion pictures *See* Motion pictures—Ratings
Rating of municipal bonds *See* Municipal bonds—Rating
Rating of school superintendents and principals *See* School superintendents and principals—Rating
Rating of teachers *See* Teachers—Rating
Rating of television programs *See* Television broadcasting—Ratings
Rating of women executives *See* Women executives—Rating
Rational-emotive therapy *See* Psychotherapy
Rational expectations (Economics) *See* Economics
Rationalism
See also
Irrationalism (Philosophy)
Ratitae
See also
Ostriches
Ratner, Michael, and Lerner, David
A mini-C.I.A. *Nation* 245:113+ Ag 15-22 '87
Rats
Brain
See Brain
Ratt (Musical group)
Ratt: the rightt combination. E. Miller. il *Seventeen* 46:59-60+ Je '87
Ratteray, Joan Davis
Escape to freedom [address, March 6, 1987] *Vital Speeches Day* 53:497-8 Je 1 '87
Ratterman, Debra
Judicial determination of reasonable efforts. il *Child Today* 15:26+ N/D '86
Rattigan, Thomas J.
about
Commodore is anything but dead. G. Lewis. il por *Bus Week* p96-7 Mr 9 '87
Why did heads roll at Commodore? G. Lewis. il por *Bus Week* p114 My 11 '87
Rattle, Simon
about
Rattling the strings. N. Kenyon. il por *World Press Rev* 34:58-9 D '87
Rattlesnakes
Hidden life of the timber rattler. W. S. Brown. il map *Natl Geogr* 172:128-38 Jl '87
Snakeskin. W. Sloat. il *N Y Times Mag* p60 Ja 25 '87
Timber rattler. H. Middleton. il *South Living* 22:46+ Mr '87
Rattner, Selma
To save the world we built [interview with J. M. Fitch] il *Am Herit* 38:84-91 Ap '87
Rattner, Steven
A view from the trenches. il *Newsweek* 110:80 D 14 '87
Ratto, Trish
Smart shopping for vitamins. il *Women's Sports Fitness* 9:16 Ja '87
Ratushinskaya, Irina
Give me a nickname, prison [poem]; tr. by Frances Padorr Brent and Carol J. Avins. *Harpers* 274:28 My '87
Two poems from prison [poem]; tr. by Frances Padorr Brent and Carol Avins. *N Y Rev Books* 34:19 My 7 '87
about
Five poems that spelled danger. B. Wolfer. il *Commonweal* 114:107-11 F 27 '87
An interview with Irina Ratushinskaya. E. Kuryluk. il por *N Y Rev Books* 34:16-20 My 7 '87
Russia's "gift" to the West [interview] il por *Christ Today* 31:41 Je 12 '87
Ratzinger, Joseph, Cardinal
about
A classic case of consequentialism. E. W. Doherty. *Commonweal* 114:10-11 Ja 16 '87
Ratzinger's 'land mine'. *Christ Century* 104:1138 D 16 '87
The Vatican and bioethics [interview] H. Tincq. *World Press Rev* 34:58 Jl '87
Rau, William, 1855-1920
about
Causing a Rau. S. Staggs. il *Art News* 86:37 N '87

Raudsepp, Vivian
about
An Orthodox monk and a Lutheran pastor witness the
survival of faith in an atheistic state. M. Brower.
il pors *People Wkly* 27:110-13 Ap 6 '87
Rauh, Joseph L., 1911-
about
Nominating a hero for 1987. A. Fotheringham. il
Macleans 100:64 Ja 19 '87
Rault, Sterling
about
"Everyone's a victim in this". R. Woodbury. il por
Time 130:22 S 7 '87
Rausch, Thomas P.
Who speaks for the Church? *America* 156:344-6 Ap
25 '87
Rauschenberg, Robert, 1925-
about
All in the family. il por *Art News* 86:188 My '87
Raushenbush, Bret
Tennis for tennis's sake, please. il *World Tennis* 35:128
S '87
Raven, Peter H.
We're killing our world [address, February 14, 1987]
Vital Speeches Day 53:472-8 My 15 '87
about
Peter Raven. B. Lawren. *Omni* 9:38+ S '87
Ravenna Jazz Festival *See* Music festivals—Italy
Raver, Anne
Leaf magic. il *Read Dig* 131:9-10+ S '87
Ravioli
It's ravioli, and it's homemade! il *South Living* 22:192
O '87
Ravitch, Diane
Take a hike! il *Vogue* 177:248-9+ Je '87
Tot sociology: grade school history. *Current* 298:4-10
D '87
Tot sociology: or What happened to history in the grade
schools. *Am Sch* 56:343-54 Summ '87
What happened to history in the grade schools? *Educ
Dig* 53:7-9 O '87
Where have all the classics gone? You won't find them
in primers. il *N Y Times Book Rev* 92:46-7 My 17
'87
about
'What do our 17-year-olds know?' assesses the failure
of American high school education. *Publ Wkly* 232:134
S 18 '87
Ravven, Wallace
Lobster lust: Don Juans of the deep [with editorial
comment by Paul Hoffman] il por *Discover* 8:4, 34-40
D '87
Raw food *See* Food, Raw
Raw materials
See also
Commodity control
Mines and mineral resources
Raw materials haven't been bloodied much [no sign
of recession yet in commodity prices] G. Koretz. il
Bus Week p24 N 30 '87
Raw milk cheese *See* Cheese
Rawhide Boys Ranch
Wisconsin boys ranch says no to hiring homosexuals.
W. North. il *Christ Today* 31:48 Mr 6 '87
Rawl, Lawrence G.
about
"I love to step on toes". C. Leinster. il por *Fortune*
116:27-8 Ag 3 '87
Rawles, Richard
The dark side of The Force. il *Sierra* 72:58-62 S/O
'87
Rawley, L. A., and others
Millisecond pulsar PSR 1937+21: a highly stable clock.
bibl f il *Science* 238:761-5 N 6 '87
Rawley, Shane
about
Three men on a roll. F. Lidz. il pors *Sports Illus* 67:40-2+
Ag 24 '87
Rawlings, Jerry J.
about
Ghana's shift from radical populism. J. Kraus. *Curr
Hist* 86:205-8+ My '87
Rawlins, Stephen L.
(jt. auth) See Rogoff, Martin H., and Rawlins, Stephen
L.
Rawls, Charles Allen, d. 1987
about
Obituary
Jet por 71:8 F 23 '87

Rawls, Lou
about
Lou Rawls heads Parade of stars on telethon to benefit
black colleges. il pors *Jet* 73:24-5 D 28 '87-Ja 4 '88
Ray, Charles
about
Charles Ray: edgy, provocative presences. P. Clothier.
il por *Art News* 86:97-8 D '87
Ray, Elaine C.
Fun family getaways. il *Essence* 18:20+ Jl '87
How an M.B.A. makes a difference. il *Essence* 18:105-6
D '87
Ray, Gypsy
(jt. auth) See Rosett, Jane, and Ray, Gypsy
Ray, Satyajit
about
The last Bengali renaissance man. I. Buruma. bibl f
il *N Y Rev Books* 34:12+ N 19 '87
Ray family
about
Anatomy of a hate campaign [family burned out of
home because of fear of AIDS in Arcadia, Fla.] W.
Plummer. il *People Wkly* 28:32-7 S 14 '87
The castaways: fears about AIDS drive three boys from
home. M. Voboril. il *Life* 10:98-100 O '87
Ray Sykes Buick
Making it on driving ambition. L. Gite. il por *Black
Enterp* 17:96+ F '87
Raychem Corp.
Raychem: "faster, better, quicker". A. A. Lappen. il
por *Forbes* 140:200+ N 2 '87
Rayer, Thomas A.
The bicentennial and church-related schools. *America*
157:427-9+ D 5 '87
Rayl, A. J. S.
In search of Camelot. il *Omni* 9:24+ Mr '87
Rayman, Ronald
Albert Ruger and the bird's-eye view movement in
America, 1866-1891. il *Antiques Collect Hobbies* 92:74-9
Ag '87
Raymark Corporation
How Raytech means to sidestep Manville's fate [fear
of asbestos suits] J. R. Norman. il *Bus Week* p56+
Ag 24 '87
Raymo, Chet
A "yes" for the French space ring. *Sky Telesc* 74:5
Jl '87
Raymond, Barbara
"We will never, ever give up!" [with editorial comment
by Elizabeth Sloan] il pors *McCalls* 145:10, 66+ Mr
'87
(ed) See Keeton, Sharron. I lost 117 lbs. and won back
my husband
Raymond, Michael
about
The con man. M. A. Farber. il por *N Y Times Mag*
p34+ Je 21 '87
Raymonda [ballet] See Ballet reviews—Single works
Rayner, William P.
Stylish ease. il *House Gard* 159:80-9 Jl '87
Rayns, Tony
Model citizen: Bernardo Bertolucci on location in China
[cover story] il por *Film Comment* 23:31-2+ N/D
'87
Rayovac Corporation
Electrifying. S. B. Weiner. il *Forbes* 140:196+ N 30
'87
Rays (Fish)
Sexual behavior
See Sexual behavior—Fish
Raytech Corporation
How Raytech means to sidestep Manville's fate [fear
of asbestos suits] J. R. Norman. il *Bus Week* p56+
Ag 24 '87
Raytheon Co.
Advanced raster monitors provide quick, accurate color
ATC displays. D. Hughes. il *Aviat Week Space Technol*
127:109-10 N 9 '87
Flying on a wing and a half. R. Simon. il por *Forbes*
140:350+ Jl 13 '87
Raytheon broadens application of Rotman lens tech-
nology. il *Aviat Week Space Technol* 126:105+ F 16
'87
Raytheon wins contract to design new version of Standard
Missile. D. Hughes. il *Aviat Week Space Technol*
127:24-5 Ag 17 '87
Raytheon wins contracts for Stinger, Sparrow missiles.
Aviat Week Space Technol 127:29 O 5 '87
Revisions to fraud statute aid suit against Raytheon.
Aviat Week Space Technol 127:27 N 9 '87

Raywid, Mary Anne
Public choice, yes; vouchers, no! bibl f il *Phi Delta Kappan* 68:762-9 Je '87

Razors
The razor's edge. il *Pop Mech* 164:68 My '87
Collectors and collecting
Some scarce old safeties. P. Krumholz. il *Antiques Collect Hobbies* 91:40-3 Ja '87

R:Base (Data base management system) *See* Information storage and retrieval systems—Management

RCA Corp.
GE's gamble on American-made TVs. P. Petre. il *Fortune* 116:50-2+ Jl 6 '87
Red Seal revival. T. W. Libbey, Jr. il *High Fidel* 37:54 Je '87

RCAF *See* Canada. Royal Canadian Air Force

RDF *See* Radio direction finders

RDS (Respiratory distress syndrome) *See* Respiratory distress syndrome

Il re pastore [opera] See Mozart, Wolfgang Amadeus, 1756-1791

Rea, David K.
Windfalls of dust. il map *Nat Hist* 96:28+ F '87

Rea, Rupert Pennant- *See* Pennant-Rea, Rupert

Reaction time
A quicker response [improving video game response time in the elderly; research by Jane E. Clark] P. McCarthy. *Psychol Today* 21:23 O '87
Slow down, you move too fast [wait time by teachers to allow students to answer questions; research by Kenneth Tobin] G. W. Bracey. *Phi Delta Kappan* 69:234 N '87

Reactions, Chemical *See* Chemical reactions

Reactive armored tanks, Military *See* Tanks, Military

Reactor fuel reprocessing
DOD sees risks in plutonium trade. D. Charles. il *Science* 238:886 N 13 '87
Pakistan's bomb-making capacity [gas centrifuge enrichment plant at Kahuta] D. Albright. bibl f il *Bull At Sci* 43:30-3 Je '87
A plea to close defense reactors [plutonium manufacturing] E. Marshall. *Science* 238:886-7 N 13 '87
Plutonium recycling [discussion of March 27, 1987 article, Why recycle plutonium?] D. Albright and H. A. Feiveson. *Science* 237:707-8 Ag 14 '87
Stemming the spread of nuclear weapons. M. M. Miller. il *Technol Rev* 90:68-75 Ag/S '87
Why is D.O.E. for food irradiation? [justifying the extraction of plutonium from commercial nuclear wastes for use in nuclear weapons] K. Terry. il *Nation* 244:142+ F 7 '87
Why recycle plutonium? D. Albright and H. A. Feiveson. bibl f il *Science* 235:1555-6 Mr 27 '87

Reactors, Nuclear *See* Nuclear reactors

Read only memory
See also
CD-ROM (Compact disc-Read only memory)
IBM PC family BIOS comparison. J. Shiell. il *Byte* 12 no12 Sp Issue:173-4+ '87
The KEPROM: sinking the software pirates. J. Holtzman. il *Radio-Electron* 58 ComputerDigest:100-4 Je '87
Non-volatile memory IC's. R. Grossblatt. il *Radio-Electron* 58:60-3 O '87
RegionMaker [Macintosh program] H. Katz. il *Byte* 12:145-6+ Ja '87
A timing-independent BIOS. H. N. Cohen and J. Hanel. il *Byte* 12 no12 Sp Issue:219-20+ '87

Reader, John
Pitt Rivers Museum at Oxford offers a cultural cornucopia. il *Smithsonian* 18:108-14+ Jl '87

Readers (Books)
Ruffles and flourishes [oversimplification in basal readers] S. Ohanian. il *Atlantic* 260:20+ S '87
Where have all the classics gone? You won't find them in primers. D. Ravitch. il *N Y Times Book Rev* 92:46-7 My 17 '87

Readers and authors *See* Authors and readers

Reader's digest
Unforgettable DeWitt Wallace. C. W. Ferguson. il pors *Read Dig* 130:177-80+ F '87

Reader's Digest Condensed Books
After 36 years at Condensed Books, Zinsser looks back—and forward. C. T. Anthony. il por *Publ Wkly* 232:16 Ag 14 '87

Readiness Command (U.S.) *See* United States. Readiness Command

Readiness for school
All in good time. K. D. Fishman. il *N Y* 20:66-71 N 23 '87
Cutting it in kindergarten. *Harpers* 275:24 N '87

Getting a jump on schooling. G. W. Bracey. il *Phi Delta Kappan* 68:546 Mr '87
Kindergarten: ready or not? F. Roberts. *Parents* 62:54+ Ag '87
Why we skipped nursery school. L. Kotrosits. il *Parents* 62:68+ S '87

Reading
See also
Authors—Reading
Books and reading
Children's reading
Executives—Reading
Kwikscan reading system
Presidential candidates—Reading
Reading aloud
Speed reading
Television and reading
Women—Reading
Young adults' reading
'Boring' reading and nearsightedness [work of Josh Wallman and others] D. D. Edwards. *Sci News* 132:23 Jl 11 '87
Eyeing myopia [how reading could lead to nearsightedness; research by Josh Wallman] E. Collins. *Sci Am* 257:36 O '87
Local retinal regions control local eye growth and myopia [impoverished stimulus situation of reading; cover story] J. Wallman and others. bibl f il *Science* 237:73-7 Jl 3 '87
The workings of working memory. M. M. Waldrop. il *Science* 237:1564-7 S 25 '87
Study and teaching
See also
Literacy education
Readers (Books)
Reading comprehension
Deprogramming reading failure: giving unequal learners an equal chance. M. Carbo. bibl f il *Phi Delta Kappan* 69:197-202 N '87
Experiment at P.S. 192: Babar and Horton teach reading [Open Sesame experiment at Manhattan school] M. Reuter. il *Publ Wkly* 231:88-9 F 27 '87
Helping students become independent learners. H. L. Herber and J. Nelson-Herber. *Educ Dig* 53:12-15 D '87
Illiteracy starts too soon. N. Larrick. bibl f il *Phi Delta Kappan* 69:184-9 N '87
The maturing of phonics instruction. P. Groff. *Educ Dig* 52:42-4 Ja '87
Minorities do better at Catholic schools: study. *Jet* 72:24 Je 22 '87
Minorities in Catholic schools: why do they read better? V. Lee. *Educ Dig* 52:20-3 F '87
Reading styles research: 'What works' isn't always phonics. M. Carbo. bibl f il *Phi Delta Kappan* 68:431-5 F '87
Reforming reading instruction [elementary schools] W. T. Pink and R. E. Liebert. *Educ Dig* 52:24-7 Mr '87
Update on reading [special section; with editorial comment by Robert W. Cole] bibl f il *Phi Delta Kappan* 68:418, 424-55 F '87
Testing
A 15th-grade reading level for high school seniors? A. Whimbey. il *Phi Delta Kappan* 69:207 N '87
Reading level: a metaphor that shapes practice. K. Cadenhead. bibl f il *Phi Delta Kappan* 68:436-41 F '87

Reading (Pa.)
Economic conditions
Reading redux. J. Merwin. il *Forbes* 139:48-9+ Mr 9 '87
Stores
Reading redux. J. Merwin. il *Forbes* 139:48-9+ Mr 9 '87

Reading aloud
Where art and commerce coexist [public readings by authors] J. Eidus. por *Publ Wkly* 232:43 D 18 '87

Reading Company
It may be time to hitch a ride on the Reading. J. M. Laderman. il *Bus Week* p82 Ja 26 '87

Reading comprehension
How to help students in reading mathematics. D. E. Gullatt. *Educ Dig* 52:40-1 Ja '87
Reading comprehension: asking the right questions. D. Nessel. bibl il *Phi Delta Kappan* 68:442-5 F '87
Reading more, understanding less [speed reading and comprehension; research by Marcel Just and others] J. Meer. *Psychol Today* 21:12 Mr '87

Reading comprehension—*cont.*
Anecdotes, facetiae, satire, etc.
Reading comprehension [excerpt from Condensed book]
P. Cherches. *Harpers* 274:28+ Mr '87
Testing
See Reading—Testing
Reading disability
See also
Dyslexia
Reading laboratories
Starting the day with a good book [reading lab open
every day before school] L. Distad. *Phi Delta Kappan*
68:476-7 F '87
Reading lists
See also
Best sellers
Books and reading—Best books
Children's literature—Bibliography
Reading of newspapers *See* Newspaper reading
Reading of periodicals *See* Periodical reading
Reading Prong
Geology of the Reading Prong. D. Schutz. *Environment*
29:14-15 Mr '87
Ready Set Go (Desktop publishing program) *See* Desktop
publishing—Programming
Reagan, Maureen
about
Maureen Reagan meets Lincoln's ghost. il *Newsweek*
109:29 F 2 '87
Reagan, Michael
about
The second time around. L. Fleischer. il *Publ Wkly*
231:375 Ja 30 '87
Reagan, Nancy, 1923-
about
The big scare: Nancy Reagan's time comes. S. Findlay.
il por *U S News World Rep* 103:16 O 26 '87
Coffee or tea? il pors *Time* 130:33 D 14 '87
Confrontation of the superwives. M. Hornblower. il pors
Time 130:23 D 21 '87
Fighting drugs on ice. P. SerVaas. il pors *Saturday Evening
Post* 259:50 Ja/F '87
First Helpmate. A. McCarthy. il *Commonweal* 114:230-1
Ap 24 '87
The First Lady: a hang-up about Don Regan. G. Hackett.
por *Newsweek* 109:22-3 Mr 2 '87
The First Lady weathers the storm. K. T. Walsh. il
por *U S News World Rep* 103:21-2 Ag 31 '87
A frank talk with the First Lady. K. T. Walsh. por
U S News World Rep 103:38 S 28 '87
How Nancy Reagan protects her constituency. M.
McLoughlin. il pors *U S News World Rep* 102:20-3
Mr 9 '87
"I guess it's my turn". J. V. Lamar, Jr. por *Time* 130:36
O 26 '87
Irangate: stereotypes as side effects. L.-M. Delloff. *Christ
Century* 104:263-4 Mr 18-25 '87
Just say goodbye, Don. A. Wilentz. il pors *Time* 129:28+
Mr 9 '87
'Let's just hold hands' [special section] il pors *Newsweek*
110:28-31 O 26 '87
'Mommy' dearest. M. McDonald. il por *Macleans* 100:30
Mr 16 '87
My 35 years with Nancy [interview with R. Reagan]
pors *Good Housekeep* 204:113+ Mr '87
Nancy: no pardons. L. Howard. por *Newsweek* 110:7
N 30 '87
Nancy Reagan gets tough. M. J. Weiss. por *Ladies Home
J* 104:64+ Ag '87
Not necessarily the First Lady. J. Wiener. *Nation* 245:337
O 3 '87
Peephole on the presidency [excerpt from Behind the
scenes] M. K. Deaver. il pors *Life* 10:49-50+ D '87
President Nancy. F. Barnes. *New Repub* 196:11-13 Mr
23 '87
Raisa and Nancy: superpower struggle. il pors *Newsweek*
110:18-19 D 21 '87
The Reagans' latest battle. *Macleans* 100:32 O 26 '87
The Safire tirade. W. F. Buckley. *Natl Rev* 39:60-1 Ap
10 '87
Was this operation necessary? C. Wallis. il por *Time*
130:78 N 2 '87
Washington notebook. D. Schorr. il *New Leader* 70:3-4
Mr 23 '87
The Week of the Dragon. il por *Time* 129:24 Mr 16
'87
Who's in the kitchen with Nancy? G. Hackett. il por
Newsweek 109:22 Mr 16 '87
Words of assurance for a stricken First Lady. il por
People Wkly 28:48-50+ N 2 '87

Anecdotes, facetiae, satire, etc.
How Bess fired Douglas MacArthur. G. W. S. Trow.
New Yorker 63:27 Mr 30 '87
The Nancy gene. R. Baker. il *N Y Times Mag* p14
Mr 22 '87
Reagan, Ronald, 1911-
See also
Reagan-Gorbachev summit conference, 1986
Reagan-Gorbachev summit conference, 1987
29th report on Cyprus [message to the Congress, November 14, 1986] *Dep State Bull* 87:58 F '87
30th report on Cyprus [message to Congress, January
29, 1987] *Dep State Bull* 87:34 Ap '87
31st report on Cyprus [message to Congress, April 21,
1987] *Dep State Bull* 87:57 Jl '87
32d report on Cyprus [message to Congress, July 17,
1987] *Dep State Bull* 87:42 S '87
40th anniversary of the Marshall Plan [address, June
1, 1987] *Dep State Bull* 87:67-72 Ag '87
200th anniversary of the signing of the Constitution
[address, September 17, 1987] *Vital Speeches Day* 54:2-3
O 15 '87
750th anniversary of Berlin [proclamation, June 8, 1987]
Dep State Bull 87:25 Ag '87
Acid rain [statement, March 18, 1987] *Dep State Bull*
87:8 Je '87
Afghanistan Day, 1987 [proclamation, March 20, 1987]
Dep State Bull 87:87-8 Je '87
Aid to the Nicaraguan democratic resistance [address,
July 18, 1987] *Dep State Bull* 87:5-6 O '87
America's vision of the future [address, September 21,
1987] *Dep State Bull* 87:1-4 N '87
Baltic Freedom Day, 1987 [proclamation, June 13, 1987]
Dep State Bull 87:38 S '87
Captive Nations Week, 1987 [proclamation, July 17,
1987] *Dep State Bull* 87:36 O '87
Central American peace plan [address, August 22, 1987]
Dep State Bull 87:8 N '87
Compact of free association with Pacific Islands [text
of executive order, October 16, 1986] *Dep State Bull*
86:74-5 D '86
The current state of Soviet-American relations [address,
April 10, 1987] *Dep State Bull* 87:10-12 Je '87
Czechoslovak human rights initiative [statement, Decem-
ber 31, 1986] *Dep State Bull* 87:45 Ap '87
Economic assistance for Central America [message to
Congress, March 3, 1987] *Dep State Bull* 87:82-3 My
'87
Economic sanctions against South Africa [messages and
letter to Congress, September 25-29, 1986] *Dep State
Bull* 86:35-7 D '86
Energy security [message to Congress, May 6, 1987]
Dep State Bull 87:51-2 Jl '87
European economic summit meeting [address, June 15,
1987] *Vital Speeches Day* 53:546-8 Jl 1 '87
A forward strategy for peace and freedom [address, August
26, 1987] *Dep State Bull* 87:1-3 O '87
Germany's decision on proposed INF reductions [state-
ment, June 4, 1987] *Dep State Bull* 87:50 Ag '87
Helsinki Human Rights Day, 1987 [proclamation, July
31, 1987] *Dep State Bull* 87:37 O '87
Imports from the EEC [proclamation, January 21, 1987]
Dep State Bull 87:30 Ap '87
Independent counsel to investigate arms sales to Iran
[address, December 2, 1986] *Dep State Bull* 87:6 Mr
'87
INF extended session ends [statement, March 27, 1987]
Dep State Bull 87:18-19 My '87
INF talks resume [statement, April 23, 1987] *Dep State
Bull* 87:35 Je '87
Instructions to ambassadors on chain of command. *Dep
State Bull* 87:40 Mr '87
International agricultural trade reform [statement, July
6, 1987] *Dep State Bull* 87:33 S '87
Iran arms and contra aid controversy [address, March
4, 1987] *Dep State Bull* 87:1-2 My '87
The Iran-contra affair [address, August 12, 1987] *Vital
Speeches Day* 53:674-6 S 1 '87
Iran-contra controversy and president's goals [excerpts
from address, August 12, 1987] *Dep State Bull* 87:4-5
O '87
Iran-Iraq War [statements, January 23 and February
25, 1987] *Dep State Bull* 87:52 Ap '87
Kidnappings in Lebanon [statement, January 26, 1987]
Dep State Bull 87:51 Ap '87
Managing the global economy [address, September 29,
1987] *Dep State Bull* 87:5-8 N '87
The month in Congress [excerpts from address, January
27, 1987] *Congr Dig* 66:65-7+ Mr '87
News conference of March 19, 1987. *Dep State Bull*
87:2-6 My '87

Reagan, Ronald, 1911—— *cont.*

Nuclear and space arms talks close round six [statement, November 12, 1986] *Dep State Bull* 87:41 Ja '87

Nuclear and space arms talks open round eight [statement, May 4, 1987] *Dep State Bull* 87:24-6 Jl '87

Nuclear and space arms talks open round six [statement, September 17, 1986] *Dep State Bull* 86:39 D '86

Nuclear and space arms talks resume round seven [statement, January 12, 1987] *Dep State Bull* 87:36-7 Mr '87

Nuclear cooperation with EURATOM [letter to Congress, February 28, 1986] *Dep State Bull* 87:77 Je '87

Pan American Day and Week, 1987 [proclamation, April 9, 1987] *Dep State Bull* 87:86 Jl '87

Persian Gulf [remarks, May 29, 1987] *Dep State Bull* 87:81-2 Ag '87

Poland [statements, December 12, 1986 and February 19, 1987] *Dep State Bull* 87:33-4 Ap '87

President meets with arms negotiators [statement, March 6, 1987] il por *Dep State Bull* 87:17 My '87

President Reagan and General Secretary Gorbachev meet in Reykjavik. il pors *Dep State Bull* 86:1-21 D '86

President's response to the Tower Commission report [address, March 4, 1987] *Vital Speeches Day* 53:322-4 Mr 15 '87

President's visit to Canada. il pors map *Dep State Bull* 87:1-9 Je '87

Promoting freedom and democracy in Central America [address, May 3, 1987] *Dep State Bull* 87:1-4 Jl '87

A quest for excellence [excerpts from address, January 27, 1987] *Dep State Bull* 87:1-3 Ap '87

Ronald Reagan on rights, responsibilities and being frightened by footsteps. il por *Life* 10:24-5 O '87

SDI anniversary [statement, March 23, 1987] *Dep State Bull* 87:72 Je '87

Security at the U.S. embassy in Moscow [remarks and question-and-answer session, April 7, 1987] *Dep State Bull* 87:60-1 Je '87

Security Council calls for cease-fire in Iran-Iraq War [statement, July 20, 1987] *Dep State Bull* 87:76-7 S '87

Seventy-fifth anniversary year of the Department of Labor [proclamation, April 23, 1987] *Mon Labor Rev* 110:2 Je '87

Soviet foreign minister visits Washington. il pors *Dep State Bull* 87:34-40 N '87

Soviet noncompliance with arms control agreements [report to Congress, March 10, 1987] *Dep State Bull* 87:37-42 Je '87

State of the Union [address, January 27, 1987] *Vital Speeches Day* 53:258-61 F 15 '87

State of the Union address [excerpts from address, January 27, 1987] *Dep State Bull* 87:5-6 Mr '87

Trade with Japan. *Dep State Bull* 87:35-7 Jl '87

U.S. compliance with arms control agreements [report to Congress, February 17, 1987] *Dep State Bull* 87:42-7 Je '87

U.S. initiative to Iran [address, November 13, 1986] *Dep State Bull* 87:65-6 Ja '87

U.S.-Japan semiconductor trade [statement, June 8, 1987] *Dep State Bull* 87:55 Ag '87

U.S. proposes INF reductions [statement, September 14, 1987] *Dep State Bull* 87:25 N '87

U.S. relationship with Pacific Islands [statement, November 3, 1986] *Dep State Bull* 87:78 Ja '87

U.S.-Soviet nuclear and space arms negotiations [statement, May 8, 1987] *Dep State Bull* 87:25 Jl '87

U.S. tables draft INF Treaty [remarks, March 3, 1987] *Dep State Bull* 87:16-17 My '87

UN narcotics conference meets in Vienna [message, June 15, 1987] *Dep State Bull* 87:79 S '87

U.S. takes defensive action in Persian Gulf [statement, September 24, 1987] *Dep State Bull* 87:43-4 N '87

Vienna CSCE followup meeting resumes [statement, January 26, 1987] *Dep State Bull* 87:34 Ap '87

The view from the White House. pors *Forbes* 140:35-6 S 21 '87

Visit of Chad president [remarks, June 19, 1987] il por *Dep State Bull* 87:23 S '87

Visit of Costa Rican president [remarks, December 4, 1986] il por map *Dep State Bull* 87:56 Mr '87

Visit of French prime minister [remark, March 31, 1987] il por *Dep State Bull* 87:56 Jl '87

Visit of Gabon president [remarks, July 31, 1987] il por *Dep State Bull* 87:14-15 O '87

Visit of Guatemalan president [remarks, May 13, 1987] il por *Dep State Bull* 87:87 Ag '87

Visit of Israeli Prime Minister Peres [remarks, September 15, 1986] *Dep State Bull* 86:73 D '86

Visit of Israeli Prime Minister Shamir [remarks, February 17 and 18, 1987] il por *Dep State Bull* 87:49-51 Ap '87

Visit of Japanese Prime Minister Nakasone [remarks and text of joint statement, April 30-May 1, 1987] il por *Dep State Bull* 87:37-41 Jl '87

Visit of Kenyan president [remarks, March 12, 1987] il por *Dep State Bull* 87:28 Je '87

Visit of Philippines' President Aquino [remarks, September 17, 1986] il por map *Dep State Bull* 86:55-7 D '86

Visit of Prime Minister Thatcher [remarks, July 17, 1987] *Dep State Bull* 87:41 S '87

Visit of Swedish prime minister [remarks, September 9, 1987] il por *Dep State Bull* 87:40-2 N '87

Visit of West German Chancellor Kohl [remarks and joint statement, October 21, 1986] *Dep State Bull* 87:54-6 Ja '87

Visit of Zaire's president [remarks, December 9, 1986] il por *Dep State Bull* 87:15 Ap '87

Visit to the Holy See and West Germany. il pors *Dep State Bull* 87:22-6 Ag '87

World Food Day, 1986. *Dep State Bull* 86:66 D '86

World Trade Week, 1987 [proclamation, May 15, 1987] *Dep State Bull* 87:45 Jl '87

about

Advice from the third man. S. Talbott. il pors *Time* 130:18 N 30 '87

And now for Ronald Reagan's finale. R. Darman. il *U S News World Rep* 103:31 D 28 '87-Ja 4 '88

Backing away from Armageddon. D. Schorr. *New Leader* 70:3-4 D 28 '87

Bombshells. F. Barnes. *New Repub* 197:10+ D 14 '87

Can he be more like Ike? R. Watson. il pors *Newsweek* 109:27 Mr 2 '87

Can he recover? [Tower Commission report; special section] il pors *Time* 129:20-4+ Mr 9 '87

Can 'Operation Comeback' work? K. T. Walsh. il por *U S News World Rep* 102:18-20 Ja 26 '87

The case against glee. M. Kondracke. *New Repub* 196:16-17 Ja 26 '87

A change in the weather [cover story] L. Morrow. il *Time* 129:28-34+ Mr 30 '87

A chat with the commander in chief [interview] por *U S News World Rep* 103:22-3 S 21 '87

A conservative makes a final plea. P. Buchanan. il por *Newsweek* 109:23-6 Mr 30 '87

Constructing scandal. J. C. Alexander. *New Repub* 196:18+ Je 8 '87

Damning with faint praise [Tower Commission report; special section; with editorial comment by David Gergen] il pors *U S News World Rep* 102:14-24, 68 Mr 9 '87

Darkness on the edge of the shining city. J. Morley. il *New Repub* 196:20-3 Mr 23 '87

Dead duck. F. Barnes. *New Repub* 197:16-17 N 9 '87

A dubious world defies Reagan. H. Trewhitt. il por *U S News World Rep* 102:18-19 F 16 '87

Eight (years) is enough. G. F. Will. il *Newsweek* 110:92 N 23 '87

The emperor's new clothes. il *Progressive* 51:7-8 Jl '87

The final witness. *Nation* 245:109 Ag 15-22 '87

The Ford years. F. Barnes. *New Repub* 196:7-9 My 25 '87

The good soldier. J. V. Lamar, Jr. il pors map *Time* 129:30-1+ My 25 '87

The great pretender. S. Hoffmann. il *N Y Rev Books* 34:3-4+ My 28 '87

A growing, dreamy detachment [during Iran arms scandal] C. O'Connor. il por *Newsweek* 109:26 Ja 5 '87

The hard road ahead on the comeback trail [special section; with editorial comment by Mortimer B. Zuckerman] il pors *U S News World Rep* 102:16-20, 88 Mr 16 '87

Has Reagan changed? J. Alter. il por *Newsweek* 110:20 N 23 '87

His darkest hour? J. McLaughlin. *Natl Rev* 39:24 D 18 '87

How much damage? L. Walczak and others. il por *Bus Week* p24-5 Jl 27 '87

'I am for morality' [interview] por *U S News World Rep* 102:25 My 25 '87

'I had a plan . . . to deal from strength' [interview] D. Frost. il pors *U S News World Rep* 103:31-2 D 7 '87

Im——ch Reagan? *Commonweal* 114:339-41 Je 5 '87

The imperial temptation: Reagan's presidency succumbs. A. M. Schlesinger. *New Repub* 196:17 Mr 16 '87

Is he more out of touch than ever? G. J. Church. il por *Time* 129:16-17 Ja 26 '87

Reagan, Ronald, 1911- —about—cont.

Is Reagan conservative? C. Krauthammer. *New Repub* 197:12-14 Jl 27 '87

Is Reagan lying? [Iran-contra case] W. F. Buckley. *Natl Rev* 39:56-7 Jl 31 '87

Is there life after Tower? [Tower Commission report] B. Crozier. *Natl Rev* 39:26 Ap 10 '87

'It was my idea'. L. Martz. il pors *Newsweek* 109:16-19 My 25 '87

A land with "no limits" [interview] il por *Nations Bus* 75:74+ S '87

The last battles [struggle to reassert leadership] G. J. Church. il por *Time* 129:16-18 Ja 12 '87

Lessons for the president. D. Schorr. por *New Leader* 70:3-4 Ag 10-24 '87

Let's get to work, Mr. President. M. B. Zuckerman. il *U S News World Rep* 102:80 F 9 '87

Letter from Washington. E. Drew. *New Yorker* 63:140-6+ My 4 '87

Letter from Washington. E. Drew. *New Yorker* 62:95-102+ F 16 '87

Letter from Washington. E. Drew. *New Yorker* 63:111-19 Mr 30 '87

Letter from Washington. E. Drew. *New Yorker* 63:75-6+ Je 22 '87

Life after death. F. Barnes. *New Repub* 197:12-13 Ag 10-17 '87

The lonesome drifter. W. Greider. il *Roll Stone* p25-6 Mr 12 '87

Martin Marietta hosts Reagan SDI visit. T. M. Foley. il *Aviat Week Space Technol* 127:21-2 N 30 '87

Minority report. C. Hitchens. *Nation* 244:314 Mr 14 '87

The missing witness [Iran-contra case] T. Noah and M. Kaus. il por *Newsweek* 110:15 Ag 10 '87

My 35 years with Nancy [interview] pors *Good Housekeep* 204:113+ Mr '87

Never give up [effect of Iran-contra case] H. Sidey. il pors *Time* 130:14-15 Ag 24 '87

The new shape of American politics. W. Schneider. il *Atlantic* 259:39-48+ Ja '87

No confidence. M. Kaus. *New Repub* 196:15-16 Mr 23 '87

No method to his madness [parallels between his acting and political career; cover story] R. Schickel. il pors *Film Comment* 23:11-19 My/Je '87

No right-on for Reagan. G. J. Church. il *Time* 130:25 S 14 '87

Not with a bang [cover story; special section] il pors *Newsweek* 110:14-21 Jl 13 '87

Notes and comment [change in the political climate] *New Yorker* 63:25 F 23 '87

Notes and comment [loss of power to define the political agenda] *New Yorker* 62:25 F 16 '87

Notes and comment [Tower Commission report] *New Yorker* 63:25-6 Mr 9 '87

Peephole on the presidency [excerpt from Behind the scenes] M. K. Deaver. il pors *Life* 10:49-50+ D '87

Penguin rushes paperback of book on Reagan. *Publ Wkly* 231:74 Ap 10 '87

Politics after Reagan. R. J. Bresler. il *USA Today (Periodical)* 116:7 S '87

The presidency. H. Sidey. See issues of Time

President Reagan as political strategist. A. B. Wildavsky. *Society* 24:56-62 My/Je '87

Pride and power [Tower Commission report; special section; with editorial comment by Kevin Doyle] il pors *Macleans* 100:2, 16-22+ Mr 9 '87

Putting the presidency back to work. J. F. Stacks. il por *Time* 130:20 N 23 '87

A ray of light in arms control. H. Trewhitt. il por *U S News World Rep* 103:28-9 Ag 10 '87

Reagan: a valedictory for an old soldier? T. M. DeFrank. il por *Newsweek* 110:26-7 N 9 '87

Reagan: 'an old lion in winter'. M. McLoughlin. il por *U S News World Rep* 103:16-18 N 30 '87

Reagan at ground zero. K. T. Walsh. il por *U S News World Rep* 102:20-2 Ja 12 '87

The Reagan crisis: dreaming impossible dreams. P. Geyelin. *Foreign Aff* 65 Sp Issue:447-57 ['87]

Reagan: eyes right. T. Morganthau. il por *Newsweek* 109:20-1+ Mr 30 '87

Reagan, RIP? W. F. Buckley. *Natl Rev* 39:61 F 13 '87

Reagan, Star Wars, and American culture. J. Smith. bibl f il *Bull At Sci* 43:19-25 Ja/F '87

Reagan: what has gone wrong? *Natl Rev* 39:17 S 25 '87

Reagan: what next? *Natl Rev* 39:15-16 Mr 27 '87

Reagan's failure [Tower Commission findings; special section] il pors *Newsweek* 109:16-23+ Mr 9 '87

Reagan's no suicide. W. A. Rusher. *Natl Rev* 39:36 Je 5 '87

Reality? Just say no [denial syndrome] G. Sheehy. *New Repub* 196:16-18 Mr 30 '87

Red-baiting Ron. *Nation* 245:739-40 D 19 '87

Ronald Reagan. H. Sidey. il pors *People Wkly* 28:28-31 D 28 '87-Ja 4 '88

Ronald Reagan and the Supremes. V. S. Navasky. il *Esquire* 107:77-80+ Ap '87

Ronald Wilson Hoover? J. Klein. il por *N Y* 20:40-3 N 2 '87

The second time around [forthcoming biography by son M. Reagan] L. Fleischer. il *Publ Wkly* 231:375 Ja 30 '87

Snarls from the bedclothes. R. Brustein. *New Repub* 196:27-9 F 2 '87

The spirit of Buchanan. *Natl Rev* 39:20-1 My 8 '87

Ten myths about the Reagan debacle. W. Safire. il pors *N Y Times Mag* p20-6+ Mr 22 '87

Time of trial [special section] il por *Newsweek* 109:16-23+ My 11 '87

TRB from Washington. M. Kinsley. See issues of The New Republic beginning April 25, 1983

Trying to put it all behind him. G. Borger and K. T. Walsh. il por *U S News World Rep* 103:20-1 Ag 24 '87

Two more years. *Nation* 244:3-4 Ja 10 '87

Unfazed and a bit aloof [ignoring the Iran-contra hearings] K. T. Walsh. il por *U S News World Rep* 102:28 My 18 '87

Wake-up call. F. Barnes. *New Repub* 197:10-11 O 26 '87

The 'wall around the president' is beginning to crumble. P. Dwyer. il *Bus Week* p71 My 25 '87

Water torture. F. Barnes. *New Repub* 196:11-12 Je 8 '87

Who's in charge? [cover story; special section] il por *Time* 130:18-24+ N 9 '87

Why Reagan and Gorbachev need an arms agreement. M. I. Goldman. il por *Technol Rev* 90:18+ Jl '87

Why the Reagan era won't end in 1989. R. Fly and others. il por *Bus Week* p33 Jl 13 '87

Addresses, messages, etc.

Ash Wednesday: 'going forward' [response to the Tower Commission report] *America* 156:226 Mr 21 '87

The long road back [speech on Iran; special section] il pors *Newsweek* 109:18-22 Mr 16 '87

The president talks about AIDS. *America* 156:493-4 Je 20-27 '87

Reagan booed, Taylor cheered at AIDS benefit. *Jet* 72:7 Je 15 '87

Reagan flays racism during King observance. il por *Jet* 71:6 F 2 '87

Reagan lauds civil rights era at White House meet for minority businesses. *Jet* 72:12 Ag 3 '87

Reagan tells Tuskegee grads to choose black role models in sciences and professions. il pors *Jet* 72:13 My 25 '87

Reagan's de facto détente. D. Schorr. il *New Leader* 70:3-4 S 21 '87

The scandal that Reagan cannot kill [Irangate] I. Austen. il por *Macleans* 100:26 Ag 24 '87

Trying a comeback [special section] il pors *Time* 129:18-20+ Mr 16 '87

"We're still Jefferson's children". H. Sidey. il por *Time* 130:14 Jl 13 '87

Age

Irangate: stereotypes as side effects [stereotyping the Reagans harms women and the elderly] L.-M. Delloff. *Christ Century* 104:263-4 Mr 18-25 '87

Anecdotes, facetiae, satire, etc.

Addicted to Nicaragua. R. Baker. il *N Y Times Mag* p14 My 31 '87

The Gipper's changing gait. A. Fotheringham. il *Macleans* 100:56 Je 8 '87

The Great Communicator. *New Repub* 197:4+ S 7 '87

My and Ed's peace proposals. V. Geng. *New Yorker* 63:74 S 7 '87

Running on his rims. M. Ivins. il *Progressive* 51:17 My '87

True North. T. Southern. *Nation* 245:41-2 Jl 18-25 '87

What he didn't know. P. Slansky. *New Repub* 196:18+ Ja 5-12 '87

Archives

One loss for the Gipper [plans for Reagan library at Stanford cancelled] *Time* 129:84 My 4 '87

Too close for comfort? [Stanford University as site] G. Hackett. il *Newsweek* 109:30 F 23 '87

Reagan, Ronald, 1911——cont.

Assassination attempt, March 30, 1981

Black woman's 'murder wish' for Reagan is free speech, Supreme Court says [case of A. M. Jackson] il por *Jet* 72:30 Jl 13 '87

Covering up for a sick president. il por *Newsweek* 110:56 O 5 '87

Hinckley's hope [government blocks one day leave for J. Hinckley from St. Elizabeths Hospital] por *Time* 129:29 Ap 20 '87

Correspondence

Autopen presidency [abuse of presidential signature writing machine by C. Channell] M. Hosenball. *New Repub* 196:16-18 My 11 '87

Anecdotes, facetiae, satire, etc.

Trading letters [imaginary correspondence between R. Reagan and Y. Nakasone] R. Baker. il *N Y Times Mag* p14 My 10 '87

Health

"The circuits are overloaded". H. Sidey. por *Time* 129:24 Mr 9 '87

Prostate surgery and time for a cancer checkup. M. Clark. *Newsweek* 109:20 Ja 12 '87

Homes

FAA reports frequent violations of airspace over Reagan's ranch [near midair collision, August 13, 1987] map *Aviat Week Space Technol* 127:24-5 Ag 24 '87

Press conferences

Afterglow: all the president's men. A. Cockburn. *Nation* 244:422-3 Ap 4 '87

Letter from Washington [conference on the stock market] Cato. *Natl Rev* 39:14 N 20 '87

The president's performance [Iran-contra scandal news conference] M. McDonald. il por *Macleans* 100:20-1 Mr 30 '87

A star turn for the Gipper [answering Iran arms-contra aid questions] J. L. Sheler. il por *U S News World Rep* 102:8 Mr 30 '87

Well, he survived [answers questions about Iran arms-contra aid case] G. J. Church. il pors *Time* 129:20-3 Mr 30 '87

Anecdotes, facetiae, satire, etc.

A pugnacious policy. R. Baker. il *N Y Times Mag* p12 Jl 26 '87

Press relations

The Mick Jaggers of journalism. H. Sidey. il *Time* 130:28 O 5 '87

Newsman as predator [S. Donaldson] J. Alter. il pors *Newsweek* 109:58-9 Mr 2 '87

No popularity contest [resignation of spokesman L. Speakes] H. Sidey. il por *Time* 129:20 F 9 '87

The phantom interview [R. Reagan interview on Radio Marti staged by the National Security Council] A. Lopez-Muñoz. *New Repub* 196:11 Je 29 '87

The president's image. il *World Press Rev* 34:8 Ag '87

The Safire tirade. W. F. Buckley. *Natl Rev* 39:60-1 Ap 10 '87

Anecdotes, facetiae, satire, etc.

Reagan tells all. L. Grossberger. il *Roll Stone* p43-5 Jl 16-30 '87

Protection

From smoking gun to smoking dog: a 'Beat the devil' investigation [killing of dogs at Topeka's Forbes Field Airport before arrival of R. Reagan] A. Cockburn. map *Nation* 245:332-3 O 3 '87

'Reagan was the target' [threats from Libya] il por *Newsweek* 110:59 O 5 '87

Public relations

Come out of the wings, Mr. Reagan. J. McLaughlin. *Natl Rev* 39:24 D 4 '87

A critic's view of Reagan's tussles with the truth [interview with J. D. Barber] D. Grogan. il *People Wkly* 27:40-2 Mr 9 '87

The cynic route [Iran arms scandal] W. Schneider. *New Repub* 196:12-13 Ja 19 '87

A distinct sense of unease [results of survey on Iran-contra affair] il *U S News World Rep* 103:22-3 Jl 13 '87

A failure to communicate [Iran arms case] C. J. Matthews. il por *U S News World Rep* 102:27 Ja 26 '87

Jackson, Reagan confab suggests open door policy. il pors *Jet* 71:5-6 Mr 16 '87

Not yet a potted plant [Iran-contra hearings and resultant damage to credibility] E. Magnuson. il pors *Time* 130:12-13 Ag 10 '87

One-third say Reagan should consider resigning [fallout from Iran arms scandal] il *Newsweek* 109:21 Mr 9 '87

Pardon? [discussion of presidential pardon for J. Poindexter and O. North] F. Barnes. *New Repub* 196:13-15 Ja 5-12 '87

Politics and mood swings. M. Greenfield. il *Newsweek* 109:76 Je 29 '87

Reagan's public relations offensive. M. McDonald. il por *Macleans* 100:28-9 Mr 16 '87

A trouper plays America again. H. Sidey. il por *Time* 129:22 Ap 6 '87

Anecdotes, facetiae, satire, etc.

Uncivil liberties. C. Trillin. *Nation* 244:242 F 28 '87

Relations with Congress

Administration opposes House bill on offsets. P. Mann. *Aviat Week Space Technol* 126:26-7 Jl 6 '87

America's failure of nerve in Nicaragua [role of the Boland amendments] R. N. Perle. il *U S News World Rep* 103:32-3 Ag 10 '87

Bork in the balance. A. Press. il por *Newsweek* 110:38+ O 12 '87

Carterized [Reagan administration domestic legislative proposals floundering in wake of Iran arms scandal] F. Barnes. *New Repub* 196:14-15 Mr 16 '87

Congress and arms control. D. B. Fascell. bibl f *Foreign Aff* 65:730-49 Spr '87

Congress smells blood after Reagan's highway-bill defeat . . . R. Fly and D. Harbrecht. *Bus Week* p35 Ap 20 '87

Congress to provide $62.5 million for Landsat follow-on program, pending compromise with administration. T. M. Foley. *Aviat Week Space Technol* 127:29-30 Jl 6 '87

Congress tries again on arms control. J. D. Isaacs. il *Bull At Sci* 43:3-4 Je '87

Congress warns administration not to attempt Saudi arms sale. M. Mecham. *Aviat Week Space Technol* 127:28-9 O 5 '87

Congress will feed Reagan a tax increase—in small bites. D. Harbrecht. *Bus Week* p55 Je 1 '87

Despite a college try, the Gipper loses one [congressional override of highway bill veto] il *Newsweek* 109:23 Ap 13 '87

Facing down Congress. D. Schorr. *New Leader* 70:3 D 28 '87

Fandango over the budget [with interview with J. Miller] M. W. Karmin. il pors *U S News World Rep* 102:45-7 Ja 12 '87

Finally, some grudging budget compromises. P. Magnusson. *Bus Week* p39 Ag 3 '87

Flocking together on trade. G. J. Church. il *Time* 129:24 F 2 '87

The Gipper goes down [Congress overrides R. Reagan's highway legislation veto] A. Plattner. il *U S News World Rep* 102:22 Ap 13 '87

Going . . . going . . . [fails to win support for Supreme Court nominee R. Bork] G. Borger. il pors *U S News World Rep* 103:20-2 O 12 '87

Gone with the wind [failure to win support for Supreme Court nominee R. Bork] J. V. Lamar, Jr. il por *Time* 130:18-20 O 12 '87

If he would just get interested. H. Sidey. il *Time* 129:22 Ja 19 '87

In search of a trade bill Reagan won't veto. D. Harbrecht and B. Javetski. il *Bus Week* p26 Ag 3 '87

Just saying no [Reagan veto strategy] F. Barnes. *New Repub* 196:8+ My 11 '87

Now Congress gets its chance. R. Fly and D. Harbrecht. il por *Bus Week* p26-7 F 9 '87

Pie in the sky [trillion dollar budget] B. Rudolph. il *Time* 129:52-3 Ja 12 '87

The president [100th Congress] M. Christopher. il por *Sch Update* 119:7 Ja 12 '87

Reagan, Congress on collision course over treaty limits [SALT 2 and ABM restrictions] *Aviat Week Space Technol* 127:32 O 12 '87

Reagan's 1988 wish list: already 'D.O.A.' [budget] R. Thomas. il *Newsweek* 109:22-3 Ja 12 '87

Reagan's budget won't wash—but can Congress do better? H. Gleckman. il *Bus Week* p32 Ja 19 '87

Reagan's no-risk regimen. J. McLaughlin. *Natl Rev* 39:26 N 6 '87

Reagan's vow: never again [covert operations procedure] il por *U S News World Rep* 103:11 Ag 17 '87

Road warriors [Congress overrides R. Reagan's veto of highway bill] W. Shapiro. il por map *Time* 129:16-19 Ap 13 '87

Round II [selection of D. Ginsburg as nominee for Supreme Court] F. Barnes. *New Repub* 197:9-11 N 23 '87

Rules of the game: does Congress have the guts to go one-on-one with Reagan? [views of L. Hamilton] W. Greider. il *Roll Stone* p37-9 Je 18 '87

Sallies of a new Congress: first blood. J. M. Hildreth. il *U S News World Rep* 102:10 F 16 '87

Reagan, Ronald, 1911- —Relations with Congress—cont.

Senate leadership warns president against 'rushing' into Euromissile pact. P. Mann. *Aviat Week Space Technol* 126:40-1 Ap 27 '87

The skirmishing begins again [Reagan nominees to the Supreme Court] A. Press. por *Newsweek* 110:32 O 26 '87

So many issues, so little time. D. Harbrecht. il *Bus Week* p32-3 S 14 '87

Target practice [deficit target] F. Barnes. *New Repub* 196:10-11 Ap 13 '87

Trade policy: the White House may miss the boat. H. Gleckman and B. Javetski. *Bus Week* p57 F 23 '87

Vitriol in the Rose Garden [opposition to revised Gramm-Rudman] T. Gup. il por *Time* 130:21 O 12 '87

"We have reached breakpoint" [budget battle] R. Stengel. il por *Time* 129:12 Je 29 '87

The welfare strait. R. Kuttner. *New Repub* 197:20-1+ Jl 6 '87

Whose credibility? [congressional override of R. Reagan's veto of highway bill] W. F. Buckley. *Natl Rev* 39:61 My 8 '87

Religion

Reagan and the Disciples: a widening chasm. M. S. Lord. *Christ Century* 104:1055-6 N 25 '87

Speechwriters and speechwriting

Speechless [State of the Union address] F. Barnes. *New Repub* 196:8-10 F 16 '87

Staff

All the president's men [members of the administration in trouble] il *U S News World Rep* 103:16-17 Jl 27 '87

Baker breaks the fever [chief of staff] E. Magnuson. il por *Time* 129:24+ Mr 16 '87

The Baker regency [chief of staff H. H. Baker] *Nation* 244:311-12 Mr 14 '87

Baker's half-dozen. F. Barnes. *New Repub* 196:10-12 Mr 30 '87

Baker's mission. W. F. Buckley. *Natl Rev* 39:61 Ap 10 '87

Baker's recipe [H. Baker's input into AIDS testing policy] F. Barnes. *New Repub* 196:9-10 Je 29 '87

Can he rescue Reagan? [new chief of staff H. Baker] G. Borger and K. T. Walsh. por *U S News World Rep* 102:23 Mr 9 '87

Changing the guard [H. H. Baker appointed chief of staff] K. Scanlon. il por *Macleans* 100:22 Mr 9 '87

Damage control [Tower Commission report] R. Fly and others. il por *Bus Week* p38-9 Mr 9 '87

Ex-Education chief cites racism in Reagan staff [views of T. Bell] por *Jet* 73:38 N 9 '87

Executive suite. il por *Life* 10:100-1 Fall '87

Fall of the Californians. C. O'Connor. il *Newsweek* 110:19 Jl 27 '87

The First Lady: a hang-up about Don Regan. G. Hackett. por *Newsweek* 109:22-3 Mr 2 '87

Giving normalcy a good name [H. H. Baker] H. Sidey. il por *Time* 129:22 My 11 '87

Gunning for Baker. L. Howard. il por *Newsweek* 110:4 Jl 20 '87

"The Heifer" takes some hits [H. H. Baker] B. Seaman. il pors *Time* 130:16 O 19 '87

The help-wanted sign on the White House door. R. Fly. *Bus Week* p41 F 2 '87

How the new right is undermining Howard Baker. R. Fly. il por *Bus Week* p43 S 21 '87

Howard Baker: fighting the president's final battles [cover story] D. Eisenhower. il pors *N Y Times Mag* p18-21+ S 6 '87

Howard Baker's long, hot summer. L. Walczak and others. il por *Bus Week* p24-5 Ag 3 '87

Learning from Reagan's debacle [applying Iran arms scandal mistakes to business management] A. R. Dowd. il por *Fortune* 115:169-72 Ap 27 '87

A lesson in how not to pick a president's team. T. Jacoby. il *Newsweek* 110:16 Ag 10 '87

Letter from Washington [D. Regan resigns] Cato. *Natl Rev* 39:14 Mr 27 '87

Letter from Washington [role of H. Baker in R. H. Bork confirmation debacle] Cato. *Natl Rev* 39:14 N 6 '87

Look out for the ideolog! [media's use of ideologue to characterize personages struggling for influence in the Reagan White House] D. Seligman. il *Fortune* 116:169-70 D 21 '87

Morality among the supply-siders [Reagan administration members with ethical or legal charges against them] R. Stengel. il *Time* 129:18-20 My 25 '87

The mouse that roars. J. B. Judis. *New Repub* 197:23-5 Ag 3 '87

One for the Gipper: Baker signs on [new chief of staff] B. Barol. il pors *Newsweek* 109:22 Mr 9 '87

Pay dirt [D. Regan's role in federal pay raise recommendation] F. Barnes. *New Repub* 196:12-14 F 2 '87

The president's new men [H. Baker's recruits] W. Shapiro. il por *Time* 129:24 Ap 6 '87

Putting the president out front [work of H. Baker] G. Borger. il pors *U S News World Rep* 102:21-2 Ap 13 '87

Reagan breaks his fall [new arms proposal and H. Baker made chief of staff] R. Fly and others. il pors *Bus Week* p34-5 Mr 16 '87

Reagan's band of true believers [Iran-contra affair] F. FitzGerald. il *N Y Times Mag* p36-9+ My 10 '87

Reagan's kingpin [H. Baker] T. Jacoby. il pors *Newsweek* 110:15 Ag 24 '87

Reagan's no-risk regimen. J. McLaughlin. *Natl Rev* 39:26 N 6 '87

Regan bashing [Iran arms scandal] T. Morganthau. il por *Newsweek* 109:18-19 F 16 '87

The right man at the right time [H. Baker, new chief of staff] J. V. Lamar, Jr. il pors *Time* 129:27 Mr 9 '87

Sending in the clowns [Iran arms scandal] L. H. Lapham. *Harpers* 274:8+ F '87

Watch Baker [H. H. Baker] J. McLaughlin. *Natl Rev* 39:24 Ap 10 '87

The White House mess. K. T. Walsh. il *U S News World Rep* 103:22 N 23 '87

White House musical chairs. il *Newsweek* 109:4 F 2 '87

White House split [T. Griscom planning to leave] L. Howard. il por *Newsweek* 110:3 Jl 13 '87

White House vigilante [P. Buchanan] J. B. Judis. *New Repub* 196:17-18+ Ja 26 '87

Who's who in the administration. See issues of The Washington Monthly

Why business is bananas over Baker. il por *Fortune* 115:8 Mr 30 '87

Anecdotes, facetiae, satire, etc.

Unsung heroes. M. Ivins. il *Progressive* 51:19 Ap '87

Resignation

See also

Deaver, Michael K.—Conflict of interests case

The final days of Donald Regan. J. Alter. por *Newsweek* 109:23 Mr 9 '87

Just say goodbye, Don [N. Reagan's role in ouster of D. Regan] A. Wilentz. il pors *Time* 129:28+ Mr 9 '87

President Nancy [resignation of D. Regan] F. Barnes. *New Repub* 196:11-13 Mr 23 '87

Resignation—Anecdotes, facetiae, satire, etc.

The Nancy gene. R. Baker. il *N Y Times Mag* p14 Mr 22 '87

State of the Union messages

For Reagan, it will be a state of the presidency address. R. Fly. por *Bus Week* p47 Ja 26 '87

Going nowhere fast. L. Martz. il por *Newsweek* 109:24-5 F 9 '87

The month in Congress [excerpts from address, January 27, 1987] R. Reagan. *Congr Dig* 66:65-7+ Mr '87

A new call for free trade [reassurances to Canada included] I. Austen. il por *Macleans* 100:18 F 9 '87

Notes and comment. *New Yorker* 62:27-8 F 9 '87

Now Congress gets its chance. R. Fly and D. Harbrecht. il por *Bus Week* p26-7 F 9 '87

Of many things. G. W. Hunt. *America* 156:inside cover F 28 '87

A quest for excellence [excerpts from address, January 27, 1987] R. Reagan. *Dep State Bull* 87:1-3 Ap '87

Speechless. F. Barnes. *New Repub* 196:8-10 F 16 '87

The state of Reagan. G. J. Church. il por *Time* 129:16-18 F 9 '87

State of the Union. *Progressive* 51:10 Mr '87

State of the Union [address, January 27, 1987] R. Reagan. *Vital Speeches Day* 53:258-61 F 15 '87

State of the Union address [excerpts from address, January 27, 1987] R. Reagan. *Dep State Bull* 87:5-6 Mr '87

States of two unions [M. Gorbachev's speech at Party plenum contrasted with Reagan's State of the Union] *Nation* 244:129 F 7 '87

Sunset for a presidency? K. T. Walsh. il por *U S News World Rep* 102:22-3 F 9 '87

Anecdotes, facetiae, satire, etc.

Back to the future [year 2000] *Commonweal* 114:69-71 F 13 '87

Reagan, Ronald, 1911-—*cont.*
Visit to Canada, 1987
The biggest deal in history [free trade accord and upcoming visit; cover story; special section; with editorial comment by Kevin Doyle] il *Macleans* 100:2, 10-12+ Ap 6 '87
Fraternity at the top. il pors *Macleans* 100:12-13 Ap 20 '87
Getting together with a friend. G. Russell. il por *Time* 129:54 Ap 20 '87
President's visit to Canada. R. Reagan. il pors map *Dep State Bull* 87:1-9 Je '87
Reagan and Mulroney: the bloom is off the shamrock. M. Whitaker. il por *Newsweek* 109:34-5 Ap 6 '87
Reporters and reporting
Beat the devil. A. Cockburn. *Nation* 244:494-5 Ap 18 '87
Visit to Germany (West), 1987
Challenge from Berlin. B. Levin. il por *Macleans* 100:16-17 Je 22 '87
Visit to the Holy See and West Germany. R. Reagan. il pors *Dep State Bull* 87:22-6 Ag '87
Visit to the Vatican, 1987
Visit to the Holy See and West Germany. R. Reagan. il pors *Dep State Bull* 87:22-6 Ag '87
Visit to Western Europe, 1987
Back to the Wall [Venice summit] G. J. Church. il pors *Time* 129:18-20 Je 22 '87
For Reagan, missed opportunities at a soufflé summit. W. L. Chaze. il por *U S News World Rep* 102:20-1 Je 22 '87
Venice economic summit [cover story] il pors *Dep State Bull* 87:1-21 Ag '87
Waiting for Gorbachev [results of Venice economic summit] R. Watson. il pors *Newsweek* 109:18-19 Je 22 '87

Reagan, Ronald Prescott
about
If papa won't preach it, young Ron Reagan will, with a TV pitch promoting safe sex. S. Haller. il pors *People Wkly* 28:38-40 Jl 13 '87
Young Reagan makes a pitch for condoms. il por *Newsweek* 109:24 Je 22 '87

Reagan family
about
A feuding First Family. G. Borger. il *U S News World Rep* 103:22 Ag 31 '87

Reagan-Gorbachev summit conference, 1986
Arms control. J. B. Hehir. *Commonweal* 114:38-9 Ja 30 '87
Arms control: the Reagan legacy. R. J. Bresler. il *USA Today (Periodical)* 115:6-7 Ja '87
Getting over the summit. L. V. Sigal. il *Bull At Sci* 43:12-13 Ja/F '87
President Reagan and General Secretary Gorbachev meet in Reykjavik. R. Reagan; G. P. Shultz. il pors *Dep State Bull* 86:1-21 D '86
Revive the Reykjavik dynamism. U. Albrecht. il *Bull At Sci* 43:40-1 Mr '87
Reykjavik: a watershed in U.S.-Soviet relations [address, October 31, 1986] G. P. Shultz. *Dep State Bull* 86:22-5 D '86
Reykjavik and revelations: a turn of the tide? J. R. Schlesinger. *Foreign Aff* 65 Sp Issue:426-46 ['87]
Secretary's interview on "This week with David Brinkley" [interview with G. P. Shultz; transcript of program, October 5, 1986] *Dep State Bull* 86:32-4 D '86
A way out of Reykjavik. B. Scowcroft and others. il *N Y Times Mag* p40+ Ja 25 '87
Why the Soviets want an arms-control agreement, and why they want it now. E. V. Rostow. *Commentary* 83:19-26 F '87

Reagan-Gorbachev summit conference, 1987
126 VIPs chosen for historic White House dinner during summit. S. Booker. il *Jet* 73:4-6+ D 28 '87-Ja 4 '88
But will we still love him tomorrow? [cover story; special section] il *U S News World Rep* 103:20-8+ D 21 '87
Come out of the wings, Mr. Reagan. J. McLaughlin. *Natl Rev* 39:24 D 4 '87
Comrades in arms control [signing INF Treaty; special section] il *Bus Week* p34-7 D 21 '87
The dangers of Détente II. R. N. Perle. il *U S News World Rep* 103:37-8 N 23 '87
Dear Gorbo. F. Barnes. *New Repub* 197:14+ D 21 '87
Dear Ron. M. Kondracke. *New Repub* 197:10+ D 21 '87
Gorbachev's shrewd summitry. H. Smith. il *N Y Times Mag* p50-1+ D 6 '87
'He does not envy us' [cover story; special section] il *Newsweek* 110:18-25+ D 14 '87

History on the wing. *Nation* 245:737 D 19 '87
'The last chance we have' [cover story; special section] il *Newsweek* 110:14-20+ D 21 '87
Moscow touts an '87 summit. L. Howard. il *Newsweek* 109:6 Ja 12 '87
Next attraction: the Gipper and Gorby show. K. T. Walsh. il *U S News World Rep* 103:14-15 D 7 '87
A no-frills summit. E. Magnuson. il *Time* 130:50-1 N 9 '87
The odd couple [special section] il *Time* 130:14-18+ D 7 '87
On to the summit, as Star Wars waits. S. Budiansky and H. Trewhitt. il *U S News World Rep* 103:13-14 N 9 '87
The peace contest. I. Austen. il *Macleans* 100:22-3 D 14 '87
Put the right men in the right place . . . [cover story; special section] il *U S News World Rep* 103:22-7+ D 14 '87
Reagan/Gorbachev summit [special section; with editorial comment by Donald E. Fink] il *Aviat Week Space Technol* 127:11, 18-24 D 14 '87
Reagan-Gorbachev III. W. G. Hyland. *Foreign Aff* 66:7-21 Fall '87
Reagan on Gorbachev: "We can get along". H. Sidey. il *Time* 130:22 D 28 '87
Reagan's disarmament. G. F. Will. il *Newsweek* 110:78 D 21 '87
A rendezvous in Washington. S. Strasser. il *Newsweek* 110:26-9 D 7 '87
Reviving the 'spirit'. D. Schorr. *New Leader* 70:4 D 28 '87
The right wing opens fire [conservatives snipe at INF and the summit] R. Watson. il *Newsweek* 110:36-7 N 30 '87
The rocky path to a summit. il *Sch Update* 120:5 N 20 '87
Rocky road to the summit. J. Bierman. il *Macleans* 100:19 N 23 '87
A rush to the summit. R. Watson. il *Newsweek* 110:14-16 S 7 '87
Shifting toward a summit. *America* 157:347 N 14 '87
The spirit of Washington [special section] il *Time* 130:16-23+ D 21 '87
The summit. *Natl Rev* 39:12-13 D 31 '87
The summit: a few fine-tuning points. *Newsweek* 110:37 N 23 '87
The summit as symbol. *America* 157:491 D 26 '87
Summit breakthrough. I. Austen. il *Macleans* 100:18-19 N 9 '87
Summit gazing. *Commonweal* 114:723-4 D 18 '87
The summit: on again. R. Watson. il *Newsweek* 110:52-4 N 9 '87
A summit with style [cover story; special section; with editorial comment by Kevin Doyle] il *Macleans* 100:2, 24-9 D 21 '87
Waiting for Gorbachev. R. Watson. il pors *Newsweek* 109:18-19 Je 22 '87
Wary antagonists Reagan and Gorbachev reach out for peace with a handshake. il *People Wkly* 28:36-7 D 21 '87
We meet again [cover story; special section] il *Time* 130:16-21+ D 14 '87
Why Gorbachev is upping the summit ante. B. Javetski and others. il *Bus Week* p57 N 9 '87
Anecdotes, facetiae, satire, etc.
The great baby sit-in for peace [world leaders babysit during imagined summit conference] M. K. Blakely. il por *Ms* 16:83-5 D '87
Public opinion
High marks: a Newsweek poll. il *Newsweek* 110:22 D 21 '87
Reporters and reporting
The summit. il *World Press Rev* 34:4-5 D '87
Terminology
Smiles of a summit night. W. Safire. il *N Y Times Mag* p4+ D 27 '87

Reaganomics *See* United States—Economic policy
Real estate [drama] See Page, Louise
Real estate agencies and agents
　　See also
　　Black real estate agencies and agents
　　Centeq Cos.
　　Century 21 Real Estate Corp.
　　Patten Corporation
　　Women real estate agents
Local real estate agent best bet for rating dollar value of home improvements. H. Porter. *Fam Handyman* 37:12+ S '87

Real estate agencies and agents—*cont.*

Accounting

Old game, new twist [Patten Corp.'s bookkeeping] G. Morgenson. il *Forbes* 139:44-5+ Ja 12 '87

Commissions

Pay less to sell your house. T. Tilling. *Parents* 62:52+ Ap '87

Real estate auctions *See* Auctions

Real estate business

See also

Banks and banking—Real estate operations
Barnes-Connally Partnership
Cable television—Real estate programs
Cohen Brothers Realty Corporation
Colleges and universities—Real estate operations
Computers—Real estate use
Del E. Webb Corp.
Eastdil Realty Inc.
General Development Corp.
House buying
House selling
Information storage and retrieval systems—Real estate use
Irvine Co.
Kroh Brothers Development (Firm)
Landmark Land Company, Inc.
Lincoln Property Company
McCormick & Co. Inc.
Patten Corporation
Railroads—Real estate operations
Real estate agencies and agents
Saint Douglas Company
Savings and loan associations—Real estate operations
Timesharing (Real estate)

Building castles in the sky [D. Trump; cover story] M. Ryan. il pors *People Wkly* 28:52-7 D 7 '87

Citizen Trump [cover story] B. Powell and P. McKillop. il pors *Newsweek* 110:50-5+ S 28 '87

Commercial real estate—the worst is yet to come. R. L. Stern and H. Rudnitsky. il *Forbes* 139:64-8 Ja 26 '87

Down cycle. I. Chithelen. il *Forbes* 140:8 Ag 10 '87

Downhill racers [Colorado ski resorts] J. A. Conway. il *Forbes* 139:8 Ap 20 '87

For sale: the rich look [Blackhawk, Calif. homes] J. Adler. il *Newsweek* 109:80 Je 22 '87

Is the sun setting on Florida's overbuilding? G. DeGeorge. il *Bus Week* p102 O 12 '87

Outer Banks [problems brought by development] A. Bailey. *New Yorker* 63:94-104+ My 25 '87

The stars of brick and mortar: the builder as celebrity. J. Schwartz. il *Newsweek* 110:62 S 28 '87

Trump on Trump [excerpt from Trump; cover story] D. J. Trump. il pors *N Y* 20:50-64+ N 16 '87

Welcome to the capital of Texas [Austin] W. P. Barrett. il *Forbes* 140:188+ D 14 '87

"You get to play God" [billionaires] L. S. Richman. il por *Fortune* 116:138-9 O 12 '87

Acquisitions and mergers

International aspects

More than a yen [Nomura Securities buys interest in Eastdil Realty] J. Willoughby. il por *Forbes* 139:122 F 9 '87

Advertising

Guerrillas [street theater in New York advertising a real estate broker] *New Yorker* 63:31-2 N 30 '87

Anecdotes, facetiae, satire, etc.

Burgville marches on. R. Baker. il *N Y Times Mag* p20 Ag 23 '87

Taxation

Tax the Forbes 400! R. S. McIntyre. *New Repub* 197:15-17 Ag 31 '87

Canada

See also

Campeau Corporation
Leopold Property Consultants Inc.
Olympia & York Developments Ltd.
Triple Five Corporation

Real estate consultants

Meet real estate's new czars: the middlemen. T. Mason. il *Bus Week* p98-9+ O 5 '87

Real estate development *See* Real estate business

Real estate investment

See also

Cable television—Real estate programs
Hall Financial Group
Integrated Resources, Inc.
JMB Realty Trust
Texas Guaranty Investments

$1.1 mil. suit filed by athletes in Fla. land deal [legal malpractice against Holland & Knight] *Jet* 72:50 Je 8 '87

After tax reform, historic rehabs can still pay off. B. Hitchings. il *Bus Week* p123 Ap 6 '87

Against the odds [investor D. P. Lawrence; cover story] D. R. Squires. il pors *Black Enterp* 18:48-50+ O '87

Any pay dirt left in real estate? M. C. Paulson. il *Changing Times* 41:85-6+ Ja '87

The bright jewels in real estate. J. J. Curran. il *Fortune* 116 Sp Issue:24 Fall '87

Building a cozy tax shelter with historic rehabs [real estate limited partnership] T. Segal. il *Bus Week* p118 S 7 '87

Building the assets you live in [special section] il *Money* 16:70-4+ Je '87

Buy your North 40 while it's dirt-cheap [farmland] P. Houston. il *Bus Week* p92-3 Ap 20 '87

Buying to rent. L. Hazelton. il *Black Enterp* 18:85-6+ O '87

Commercial real estate—the worst is yet to come. R. L. Stern and H. Rudnitsky. il *Forbes* 139:64-8 Ja 26 '87

Don't rush in. S. E. Roulac. por *Forbes* 140:135 Ag 24 '87

Down cycle. I. Chithelen. il *Forbes* 140:8 Ag 10 '87

Farms: the bulls rush in. J. B. Quinn. il *Newsweek* 109:48 Je 22 '87

Farms without farmers. O. Davidson. il *Progressive* 51:25-7 Ag '87

Hitch 22 [tax credits intended to draw investment into housing for the poor] J. Novack. il *Forbes* 139:54 F 9 '87

How to make 25% a year in real estate—even with tax reform [views of J. T. Reed] C. E. Trunzo. il por *Money* 16:190 S '87

I'll take Manhattan—and Waikiki [Japanese investors] J. Castro. il *Time* 129:62 Mr 9 '87

Investors pick up low-priced land [farmland] *Success Farm* 85:18BH Ap '87

Is Texas losing its independence? [outsiders' investments] T. Mack. il *Forbes* 140:184+ D 14 '87

The Japanese buying binge [U.S. real estate] L. S. Richman. il *Fortune* 116:77+ D 7 '87

Judge: $115,000 Duvalier aide's condo in Miami belongs to Haiti Republic. *Jet* 71:6 Mr 2 '87

Low-effort real estate investing [cover story] M. C. Paulson. il *Changing Times* 41:22-6 Ag '87

Meet real estate's new czars: the middlemen. T. Mason. il *Bus Week* p98-9+ O 5 '87

More land sells, buyers pay cash, prices firm [farmland] *Success Farm* 85:19 My '87

A new look at ski-country real estate [Western States; with editorial comment by William Grout] K. Brizzolara. il *Skiing* 40:8, 126-7+ D '87

The next land boom [raw land syndicators] J. B. Quinn. il *Newsweek* 109:56 Mr 2 '87

No, it didn't crash—but its footing isn't exactly sure. T. Mason. il *Bus Week* p174+ D 28 '87-Ja 4 '88

Outflanked, outmaneuvered [Integrated Resources vs. Cohen Brothers Realty over 666 5th Ave., New York City] H. Rudnitsky. il *Forbes* 140:343-4 Jl 13 '87

The quake on Wall Street is rocking real estate. F. A. Miller. il *Bus Week* p184 N 16 '87

Real estate. See issues of Esquire beginning February 1985

Real estate action you can buy like stock [master limited partnerships] B. Hitchings. *Bus Week* p102 F 9 '87

Real estate deals that help ol' alma mater—and you. D. B. Moskowitz. il *Bus Week* p126 O 26 '87

Real estate: still a hands-on affair. M. Schiffres. il *Changing Times* 41:43+ N '87

Return on land investment improves. D. Allen. il *Success Farm* 85 no2:18A Ja '87

The Rising Sun on U.S. real estate [Japanese investment] il *Technol Rev* 90:80 Ag/S '87

Six bites from one apple [R. Campo sells Houston condo investors on desyndication deal] W. P. Barrett. il por *Forbes* 140:88+ S 7 '87

Tough new rules for rental real estate. R. Micheli. il *Money* 16:193-4+ Ap '87

Want a tax shelter—and a good conscience? [tax credits for investing in housing for the poor] C. Yang. *Bus Week* p130 O 5 '87

Anecdotes, facetiae, satire, etc.

Plan 10 from Zone R-3. P. Frost. *New Yorker* 63:28-9 Ap 13 '87

Belize

Fishing in muddy waters. W. P. Barrett. il *Forbes* 139:128+ My 4 '87

Real estate investment—*cont.*
Canada
Downfall of a schemer [W. Player's role in Toronto real estate fraud scandal] P. Best. il por *Macleans* 100:32 Jl 20 '87
Caribbean region
Sunspots. L. J. Gallagher. il *Esquire* 107:36 F '87
France
Buying a second house in Paris [experience of B. and C. Haber] C. Styles-McLeod. il pors *Archit Dig* 44 Archit Dig Travels:10+ O '87
Great Britain
Capital developments [Reichmann's take over London's Canary Wharf project] D. Jenish. il *Macleans* 100:28-9 Ag 24 '87
Ireland
A place in the soft rain. A. Jones. il *Forbes* 139:146+ Mr 23 '87
Mexico
Where the dollar still buys a hot property [Acapulco] A. Bard. il *Bus Week* p180 My 25 '87
United States
See Real estate investment
Real estate investment trusts
See also
Hotel Investors Trust
National Real Estate Stock Fund
Weingarten Realty, Inc.
Agonizing reappraisals [pension fund real estate holdings] H. Rudnitsky. *Forbes* 140:40 S 7 '87
Deep discounts in bricks and mortar. J. Mendes. *Fortune* 116:208+ N 23 '87
Look who's leaping into real estate. A. E. Serwer. il *Fortune* 116:198 O 12 '87
A realty fund primer. M. Kuntz. il *Forbes* 139:162-4 Mr 9 '87
REITs are looking rosy again . . . and gold is panning out [views of Bailard, Biehl & Kaiser] G. G. Marcial. *Bus Week* p88 Ap 13 '87
The renewed appeal of REITs [interview with K. Statz] M. McFadden. por *Fortune* 115:132 Ja 19 '87
Sweden
See also
Beväringen Company
Real estate management
See also
Wallace H. Campbell & Company
Real estate syndicates *See* Real estate investment
Real estate tax *See* Real property—Taxation
Real property
See also
Airspace (Law)
Deeds
Easements
Joint ownership
Land
Land tenure
Mechanics' liens
Mortgages
Real estate business
Real estate investment
Trespass
Taxation
See also
Assessment
Mortgages—Taxation
Rent—Taxation
Any pay dirt left in real estate? M. C. Paulson. il *Changing Times* 41:85-6+ Ja '87
Combating modern-day feudalism: land as God's gift. W. Rybeck and R. D. Pasquariello. il *Christ Century* 104:470-2 My 13 '87
Going it alone in the ghetto [South Central Los Angeles proposes property taxes to pay for police] J. D. Hull. il *Time* 129:22 Ap 13 '87
Home ownership. il *U S News World Rep* 103:80 D 7 '87
Keeping home expense records for the tax man. T. Tilling. *Parents* 62:52 Jl '87
L.A. kills anti-crime bill that would raise taxes. *Jet* 72:8 Je 22 '87
Making home fix-up pay [reducing taxable profit on home sale] L. Wiener. il *U S News World Rep* 103:53 Jl 13 '87
The new bottom line. H. J. Lehman. il *Changing Times* 41:121-4 Ja '87
New shocks at tax time [Montreal property tax] B. Wallace. il *Macleans* 100:56 Mr 30 '87
Rules change for the income tax game. H. Porter. il *Fam Handyman* 37:20 Ap '87

Selling a house? The IRS is watching. il *Consum Rep* 52:508-9 Ag '87
Tax protest pays off. H. Porter. *Fam Handyman* 37:26-7 Mr '87
Tax the Forbes 400! R. S. McIntyre. *New Repub* 197:15-17 Ag 31 '87
Trade down without tripping up [avoiding taxation on house sale profits] K. McCormally. il *Changing Times* 41:20 O '87
Vacation homes: how to cope with the new tax rules. M. Schiffres. il *Changing Times* 41:35-6+ Je '87
Vacation homes may cut your taxes. H. Porter. *Fam Handyman* 37:12+ Ja '87
What a difference a day makes [tax angles on vacation homes] L. Saunders. il *Forbes* 139:221-2 My 18 '87
Your home as a tax shelter. L. Wiener. il *U S News World Rep* 102:58 My 18 '87
Your home still offers you shelter. P. Philipps. il *Bus Week* p114 Ap 13 '87
Taxation for education
See Education—Finance
Valuation
See also
Assessment
Agonizing reappraisals [pension fund real estate holdings] H. Rudnitsky. *Forbes* 140:40 S 7 '87
Carting your upscale items to the auction block. L. Zinn. il *Bus Week* p162 N 30 '87
Home improvements that are money in the bank. M. C. Thomsett. il *Home Mech* 83:44-6 Ag '87
Local real estate agent best bet for rating dollar value of home improvements. H. Porter. *Fam Handyman* 37:12+ S '87
Money trees [landscaping enhances property values; views of Duane Durgee] il *USA Today (Periodical)* 116:7-8 D '87
Real-time data processing
Adding the moon to a real-time clock. R. W. Sinnott. il *Sky Telesc* 73:536-7 My '87
REAL Women (Organization)
The cold shoulder of equality. B. Amiel. il *Macleans* 100:5 F 23 '87
Realism in advertising
Telephone talk [AT&T's realism in TV advertising for small business phone systems] B. Kanner. il *N Y* 20:22+ Ap 27 '87
Realism in art
See also
Figurative art
Grand Central Art Galleries Educational Association
Photo-realism
Trompe-l'oeil
Exhibitions
Representing realist artists [views of gallery directors] P. Van Gelder. il *Am Artist* 51:64-9+ My '87
Realism in literature
Plotting the realistic detective novel. M. Muller. *Writer* 100:12-15+ Je '87
Stranger than fiction. R. Anscombe. por *Newsweek* 109:8-9 My 4 '87
Realism in television
Connect the dots. R. Pattison. il *Nation* 244:295-8 Mr 7 '87
Reality
See also
Relativity
Are you "driven crazy" by things you can't control? Learn how to accept . . . B. L. Stern. *Vogue* 177:477 O '87
Stranger than fiction. R. Anscombe. por *Newsweek* 109:8-9 My 4 '87
Realtors *See* Real estate agencies and agents
Reamer, Norton
about
Norton Reamer collects money management firms. A. Beam. il por *Bus Week* p114 My 18 '87
Reapportionment *See* Apportionment (Election law)
Reason
See also
Common sense
Wisdom
Reason in literature
Be reasonable—unless you're a writer. W. Kennedy. il *N Y Times Book Rev* 92:3 Ja 25 '87
Reasoning
See also
Inference
Problem solving
Thought and thinking

Reasoning—*cont.*
Study and teaching
Teaching reasoning. R. E. Nisbett and others. bibl f il *Science* 238:625-31 O 30 '87
Rebates
Buy your next appliance from your utility and you may just get a rebate! H. Porter. *Fam Handyman* 37:8 N '87
No-frills travel agents. R. Simon. il *Forbes* 139:140+ My 4 '87
Rebay, Hilla, 1890-1967
about
The sky line. B. Gill. *New Yorker* 63:49-50+ Je 8 '87
Rebecca's (Venice, Calif.: Restaurant) *See* Venice (Calif.)—Restaurants, nightclubs, bars, etc.
Rebek, Victoria
The roots of conflict in Sri Lanka. *Christ Century* 104:792-4 S 23 '87
Rebek, Julius, Jr.
Model studies in molecular recognition [cover story] il *Science* 235:1478-84 Mr 20 '87
Rebellions *See* Revolutions
Rebodied automobiles *See* Automobiles, Remodeled
Rebsamen, Werner A.
Today's pop-ups: more complex than ever. il *Publ Wkly* 231:72+ Mr 6 '87
Rebuses
The rebus treasury [excerpt] J. Marzollo. il *Parents* 62:205-8+ N '87
Recall (Psychology) *See* Memory
Recall of automobiles *See* Automobiles—Recall; Automobiles, Foreign—Recall
Recall of commercial products *See* Commercial products—Recall
Recapitalization
Home-equity loans, Wall Street style [takeover defense] J. Egan. il *U S News World Rep* 102:50-1 Je 22 '87
Now introducing son of greenmail [takeover defense] *Time* 129:62 Je 8 '87
Receivers (Football players) *See* Football players
Receptacles, Electric *See* Electric wire and wiring
Reception rooms
[Special issue on State Dept. Building] *Antiques* 132:118-87 Jl '87
Receptions, Wedding *See* Wedding receptions
Receptor sites (Biochemistry) *See* Binding sites (Biochemistry)
Receptors, Chemical *See* Chemoreceptors
Receptors, Drug *See* Drug receptors
Receptors, Hormone *See* Hormone receptors
Receptors, Neural *See* Sensory receptors
Receptors, Protein *See* Protein receptors
Receptors, Sensory *See* Sensory receptors
Receptors, Visual *See* Rods and cones
Recertification (Teachers) *See* Teachers—Certification
Recession, Business *See* Business depression
Rechargeable flashlights *See* Flashlights
Recidivists
Characterizing criminal careers. A. Blumstein and J. Cohen. bibl f il *Science* 237:985-91 Ag 28 '87
Prison versus probation [report of Joan Petersilia and Susan Turner] *Society* 24:3 My/Je '87
Recipe boxes, files, etc.
Sharing your favorite recipes: three ways to go. il *Sunset* 179:116-17 D '87
Recipes *See* Cooking
Reckoning [television program] See Television program reviews—Single works
Reclamation Bureau *See* United States. Bureau of Reclamation
Reclamation of land
See also
Irrigation
Can strip mining clean up its act? [failure to enforce Surface Mining Control and Reclamation Act] W. Marx. il *Read Dig* 130:121-5 Mr '87
Reclamation of waste water *See* Water reuse
Recluses
See also
Hermits
Recognition (Psychology)
See also
Kin recognition
Cells in temporal cortex of conscious sheep can respond preferentially to the sight of faces. K. M. Kendrick and B. A. Baldwin. bibl f il *Science* 236:448-50 Ap 24 '87
Old familiar voices [familiar-voice recognition] D. Van Lancker. il *Psychol Today* 21:12-13 N '87

So that's why they keep giving each other those sheepish looks [sheep temporal lobe facial recognition cells; work of K. M. Kendrick and B. A. Baldwin] il *Discover* 8:6 Jl '87
When looking sheepish counts as smarts. *Sci News* 131:313 My 16 '87
Recoil (Shooting) *See* Shooting
Recombinant DNA research *See* Genetic research
Recommendation, Letters of *See* Letters of recommendation
Reconciliation
Reconciliation rooms: I'd rather be kept in the dark. M. Scheiber. *U S Cathol* 52:30-2 Ap '87
Reconnaissance, Aerial *See* Aerial reconnaissance
Reconnaissance airplanes *See* Airplanes, Military
Reconnaissance satellites *See* Artificial satellites—Military use
Reconstruction (1939-1951)
Western Europe
See also
Marshall Plan
Reconstructive surgery *See* Surgery, Plastic
Record (Newspaper: Sherbrooke, Québec)
Front-page challenge [Sherbrooke daily, The record, sold to Quebecor Inc.] B. Wallace. *Macleans* 100:49 O 26 '87
Record changers *See* Phonograph—Turntables
Record Houses Awards *See* Architecture—Awards
Record industry *See* Phonograph record industry
Record Interiors Awards *See* Interior decoration—Awards
Record players *See* Phonograph
Recorders, Flight *See* Flight recorders
Recording equipment
Recorders and electrical and electronic apparatus. *Science* 235 pt2:G166-G168 F 27 '87
Recording heads (Videotape) *See* Videotape recorders and recording—Heads
Recording of music *See* Sound—Recording and reproducing
Recording studios *See* Sound—Recording and reproducing
Records
See also
Automobile speed records
Aviation records
Criminal records
Farm records
Garden records
Household records
Hunting records
Personnel records
Public records
Running records
School reports and records
Shooting records
Sports records
Tax records
Weather records
World records
Preservation
See Archives
Records, Phonograph *See* Phonograph records
Recovery of airplanes *See* Airplanes—Recovery
Recovery of petroleum *See* Petroleum engineering
Recreation
See also
Aged—Recreation
Blacks—Recreation
Boats and boating
Children—Recreation
College students—Recreation
Executives—Recreation
Hangouts
Hobbies
Leisure
Nursing home patients—Recreation
Outdoor life
Play
Playgrounds
Prisoners—Recreation
Sports
United States. President's Commission on Americans Outdoors
Youth—Recreation
For the fun of it. See issues of Changing Times
Private time. See issues of Glamour
Equipment
What's new in recreation. S. F. Brown. See issues of Popular Science beginning December 1985
Fees
See also
National parks and reserves—Fees

Recreation—*cont.*
New York (State)
See also
New York (N.Y.)—Recreation
United States
See Recreation
Recreation areas
California
See also
Golden Gate National Recreation Area (Calif.)
Kentucky
See also
Big South Fork National River and Recreation Area (Tenn. and Ky.)
Tennessee
See also
Big South Fork National River and Recreation Area (Tenn. and Ky.)
Recreation centers
See also
Sports facilities
Puerto Rico
See also
Roberto Clemente Sports City (Carolina, Puerto Rico)
Recreation rooms
See also
Children's rooms
Step up to a new rec room. il *Better Homes Gard* 65:69 Mr '87
Recreational therapy
See also
Puppets and puppet plays—Therapeutic use
Toys—Therapeutic use
Recreational vehicle industry
See also
Zimmer Corp.
The traffic jam building at RV dealers. S. Toy. il *Bus Week* p34 Mr 30 '87
Recreational vehicles
See also
All terrain vehicles
Automobile trailers
Campers, Truck
Snowmobiles and snowmobiling
Vans
RV review. J. Keebler. il *Pop Sci* 230:50+ Je '87
Sport vehicles. T. Opre. See issues of Outdoor Life
Take it to the street. T. Fegely. il *Outdoor Life* 179:62+ My '87
Equipment
Product update. D. Leathers. *Travel Holiday* 168:24-5 N '87
RV/camping products update. D. Leathers. *Travel Holiday* 167:30 My '87
Maintenance and repair
In tune for spring. T. Opre. il *Outdoor Life* 179:73-4+ My '87
Safety devices and measures
RV safety on the road. R. Dunlop. *Travel Holiday* 167:30-1 Je '87
Recruiting
See also
Basketball, College—Recruiting
Black colleges and universities—Student recruiting
Black executives—Recruiting
Brokers—Recruiting
College teachers—Recruiting
Colleges and universities—Student recruiting
Employees—Recruiting
Football, College—Recruiting
Government employees—Recruiting
Military service, Compulsory
Teachers—Recruiting
United States—Armed Forces—Recruiting, enlistment, etc.
Rectum
Cancer
See also
Colorectal cancer
Diseases
See also
Hemorrhoid Clinics of America
Recumbent bicycles *See* Human powered vehicles
Recycled buildings *See* Buildings, Remodeled
Recycling (Waste, etc.)
See also
Airplane junkyards
Automobile junkyards
Filling (Earthwork)
Motorcycle junkyards
Refuse as fuel

Water reuse
Burning trash: how it could work [cover story] A. Hershkowitz. il *Technol Rev* 90:26-34 Jl '87
Garbage: it isn't the other guy's problem anymore. T. Thompson and M. Bluestone. il *Bus Week* p150-1+ My 25 '87
Garden uses for old tires. G. Abraham and K. Abraham. il *Flower Gard* 31:32 Je/Jl '87
Give me your wretched refuse [beverage containers] F. Trippett. il *Time* 130:95 N 23 '87
Pit power [Lindsay Olive Growers' pit recycling schemes] J. K. Miller. il *Omni* 9:22 S '87
Recycling: coming of age. B. Goldoftas. il *Technol Rev* 90:28-35+ N/D '87
Japan
Garbage [views of Allen Hershkowitz] *New Yorker* 63:25-6 Je 1 '87
Tchaikovsky and toilet paper. M. Tharp. il *U S News World Rep* 103:62 D 14 '87
Red Bird, Calandra
about
Against all odds. R. Arias. il pors *People Wkly* 28:32-42+ O 26 '87
Red cabbage cooking *See* Cooking—Vegetables
Red cockaded woodpeckers *See* Woodpeckers
Red crabs *See* Crabs
Red Cross
The Red Cross [address, February 19, 1987] G. B. Weber. *Vital Speeches Day* 53:461-3 My 15 '87
Red foxes *See* Foxes
Red hair *See* Hair
Red kiss [film] *See* Motion picture reviews—Single works
Red noses [drama] *See* Barnes, Peter, 1931-
Red Sea
The rifting of continents. E. Bonatti. bibl (p128) il maps *Sci Am* 256:96-103 Mr '87
Red Seal phonograph records *See* Phonograph records
Red shift
Breaking the redshift-4 barrier. *Sci News* 132:254 O 17 '87
Density determines destiny of the universe [work of Edwin Loh and Earl Spillar] *Astronomy* 15:78 F '87
How starlight loses energy. il *Astronomy* 15:11 O '87
The large-scale streaming of galaxies. A. Dressler. bibl (p120) il *Sci Am* 257:46-54 S '87
The most distant "normal" galaxy [work of S. G. Djorgovski] il *Sky Telesc* 73:365-6 Ap '87
A new way of making spectral redshifts [theory of Emil Wolf] D. E. Thomsen. *Sci News* 132:22 Jl 11 '87
Probing cosmic geometry suggests the universe is flat [work of Edwin Loh and Earl Spillar] B. M. Schwarzschild. il *Phys Today* 40:17-20 My '87
Quantized galaxy redshifts. W. G. Tifft and W. J. Cocke. il *Sky Telesc* 73:19-21 Ja '87
Redshift theory may alter cosmic distances [research by Emil Wolf] il *Astronomy* 15:97-8 D '87
Ripples in the universal Hubble flow. P. H. Andersen. il *Phys Today* 40:17-19 O '87
Star formation and IRAS galaxies. D. A. Allen. il *Sky Telesc* 73:372-4 Ap '87
Red-shouldered hawks *See* Hawks
Red tape *See* Bureaucracy
Red tide
Deadly blooms and curious clocks [Gonyaulax; research by Donald M. Anderson and Bruce A. Keafer] *Sci News* 131:122 F 21 '87
Red wines *See* Wine
Red wolves *See* Wolves
REDCOM *See* United States. Readiness Command
Reddaway, Peter
Gorbachev the bold. bibl f il *N Y Rev Books* 34:21-5 My 28 '87
Reddicliffe, Steven
The new season: headed for another fall. il *Roll Stone* p32+ O 8 '87
Redding, Otis, 1941-1967
about
20 years later Otis Redding still buried in tomb on family's Ga. farm. il pors *Jet* 72:16-18 Jl 27 '87
Redding, Zelma
about
20 years later Otis Redding still buried in tomb on family's Ga. farm. il pors *Jet* 72:16-18 Jl 27 '87
Reddy, T. J.
She reminds [poem] *Essence* 17:121 Ap '87
Redecorating *See* House decoration
Redemption *See* Salvation
Redemption of bonds *See* Bonds—Redemption
Redemption of municipal bonds *See* Municipal bonds—Redemption

Redenbacher, Orville
about
Meet the presidents: Orville Redenbacher. C. P. Andersen. il por *Good Housekeep* 204:164+ My '87
Redfield, Robert, 1897-1958
Talk with a stranger. *Cent Mag* 20:51-7 My/Je '87
Redfish fisheries *See* Fisheries
Redfishes
See also
Cooking—Fish
Redgrave, Vanessa, 1937-
about
The clearing of Vanessa Redgrave. M. Heins. il *Nation* 245:713-15 D 12 '87
Reding, Andrew A.
Books on Latin America. *America* 156:252-4+ Mr 28 '87
Redistricting *See* Apportionment (Election law)
Redknap, Mark
(jt. auth) *See* Flemming, Nicholas, and Redknap, Mark
Redleaf, Andrew
Speed kills. il *Natl Rev* 39:43-7 N 20 '87
Redling, Edward T., and Gorman, Kevin
Executive pay: a slower rise. il *Nations Bus* 75:41-2 F '87
Redlining (Mortgages) *See* Discrimination in mortgages
Redmond, Michael
about
An American in Tokyo shows the Japanese he's got it at Go. il por *People Wkly* 28:63 Ag 24 '87
Redotex (Drug)
Dangerous diet drugs from south of the border [Mexican diet] R. C. Thompson. il *FDA Consum* 21:29-30 My '87
The Mexican way: easy but dangerous [Mexican diet] F. Gibney. *Newsweek* 109:76-7 F 2 '87
Redshift *See* Red shift
Redstone, Sumner
about
Now Redstone is a media giant. D. Lieberman and L. Therrien. il por *Bus Week* p42 Mr 16 '87
The redthroats [drama] *See* Cale, David
Reduced instruction set computers
The Archimedes A310. D. Pountain. il *Byte* 12:125-6+ O '87
Chipmakers are taking a gamble on RISC. R. Brandt. il *Bus Week* p104-5 Jl 20 '87
Hewlett-Packard may have come up with a winner. R. Brandt. il *Bus Week* p48 Je 1 '87
Instruction set strategies [cover story; special section] il *Byte* 12:141-6+ Ap '87
Reducing diet *See* Diet
Reducing preparations *See* Weight reducing preparations
Reduction, Chemical
See also
Bacteria, Sulfate reducing
Redware, American *See* Poetry, American
Redwine, Yvonne *See* Farouché
Redwood
Born of fire [prescribed burning for sequoia groves] W. C. Tweed. il *Natl Parks* 61:22-7+ Ja/F '87
Checkbooks stop chainsaws [increasing size of Sinkyone Wilderness State Park in Calif.] A. Alm. il *Sierra* 72:79-80 Mr/Ap '87
Razing the giant redwoods [Pacific Lumber Co.] P. Abramson. il por *Newsweek* 110:38 Jl 6 '87
Redworth, Glyn
Whatever happened to the English Reformation? bibl il *Hist Today* 37:29-36 O '87
Reebok International Ltd.
Keep on walking. M. Rowland. il *Work Woman* 12:87-8+ My '87
Lori McNeil accepts an apparel endorsement deal. por *Jet* 73:48 N 2 '87
Reebok's recent blisters seem to be healing. L. Helm. il por *Bus Week* p62 Ag 3 '87
Setting up shop in China: three paths to success. D. J. Yang. il *Bus Week* p74 O 19 '87
True grit [commercials] B. Kanner. il *N Y* 20:24+ S 7 '87
Walking [new line of walking shoes] *New Yorker* 62:27-9 F 16 '87
Reece, Chuck
Jan Kemp. il por *Ms* 15:44+ Ja '87
Reed, Alaina
about
'227' star fills man void with pricey toy. il por *Jet* 73:35 N 16 '87
Reed, Cordell
After Chernobyl: where do we go from here? il *USA Today (Periodical)* 116:48-51 N '87

Reed, David
Can this man save Africa? il por *Read Dig* 130:221-2+ My '87
High stakes in Nicaragua. il *Read Dig* 131:72-7 S '87
Kidnapped by Beloved Leader Comrade. il *Read Dig* 130:105-12 Mr '87
Maggie Thatcher: "She's all backbone". por *Read Dig* 131:213-14+ N '87
South Africa: glimmers of hope? il *Read Dig* 131:131-6 Ag '87
Will this man control the Panama Canal? por *Read Dig* 130:136-40 Ja '87
Reed, David
In praise of pins. il por *Americana* 15:30-4 My/Je '87
Reed, David, and Lasky, Jane E.
Business travel. il *Esquire* 108:201-7 O '87
The business traveler. il *Esquire* 107 Summ Traveler:T49-T52+ Ap '87
Reed, David Frederick, 1946-
about
Baroque expansions. T. Bell. bibl f il *Art Am* 75:126-9+ F '87
Reed, Fred
Games people play. *Harpers* 275:72-4 Jl '87
Reed, Gregory
about
Detroit man first black to chair Bar division. por *Jet* 72:22 My 11 '87
Reed, J. D.
Some ado about who was, or was not, Shakespeare. bibl (p187) il pors *Smithsonian* 18:155-8+ S '87
Reed, John, 1887-1920
about
John Reed: a centenary tribute. D. Lawson. *Humanist* 47:33-4 Mr/Ap '87
A kinswoman of famed journalist John Reed finds that Ten days still shakes the Soviet Union. S. K. Reed. il pors *People Wkly* 27:114+ Ap 6 '87
Reed, John C., and others
Regulation of *bcl*-2 proto-oncogene expression during normal human lymphocyte proliferation. bibl f il *Science* 236:1295-9 Je 5 '87
Reed, John S.
about
A brash and brainy "brat". G. M. Bock. il por *Time* 129:50 Je 1 '87
John Reed's bold stroke [cover story] J. Fierman. il por *Fortune* 115:26-30+ Je 22 '87
A stunner from the Citi. S. Bartlett. il por *Bus Week* p42-3 Je 1 '87
Taking stock: a talk with John Reed. S. Bartlett. il por *Bus Week* p45 N 9 '87
Teaching old banks new tricks. E. A. Finn, Jr. and J. Willoughby. il por *Forbes* 139:34-6 Je 15 '87
Three cheers for Citicorp's initiative. J. S. Henry. il *U S News World Rep* 102:48 Je 1 '87
Reed, John Shedd
about
The end of the line. A. A. Lappen. por *Forbes* 140:10 Jl 27 '87
Reed, John T.
about
How to make 25% a year in real estate—even with tax reform. C. E. Trunzo. il por *Money* 16:190 S '87
Reed, Kit, 1932-
What writers live on. por *Publ Wkly* 232:55 Ag 28 '87
Reed, Lillian Craig *See* Reed, Kit, 1932-
Reed, Lou
about
Lou Reed [interview] D. Fricke. por *Roll Stone* p292+ N 5-D 10 '87
Reed, Mary
A memorable Easter ice storm. il *Weatherwise* 40:78-83 Ap '87
Reed, Paul, 1956-, and Hinds, David
Writing for Celestial Arts. *Writer* 100:26-7 Ja '87
Reed, Rochelle
Castillo del Lago. il *House Gard* 159:204-14 My '87
Winter travel. il *N Y* 20:54-60+ O 12 '87
Reed, Sandra R.
View from the Valley. *See* issues of Personal Computing beginning June 1987
Reed, Stanley
Arafat makes another comeback. il *Nation* 244:137-41 F 7 '87
Hussein's game. *Nation* 244:839-40 Je 20 '87
Mubarak maneuver. *Nation* 244:421 Ap 4 '87
Why they hate us. *Nation* 244:168-9 F 14 '87

Reed, William, Jr.
about
Racing to the head of his class. F. Lidz. il pors *Sports Illus* 66:36-8 F 2 '87
Reed, William F.
The $5.7 million secret. il *Sports Illus* 67:82 N 23 '87
Reed, Willis
about
One on one [interview] L. Villarosa. pors *Health* 19:30 Jl '87
Reed International plc
Reed acquires Octopus, leads British publishing. V. Menkes. il *Publ Wkly* 232:11 Jl 17 '87
Reefs, Artificial
Enhancing coastal production [spiny lobster fishery in Mexico] L. Tangley. il *BioScience* 37:309-12 My '87
Oil rigs and sea life: a shotgun marriage that works. P. K. Driessen. il *Sea Front* 33:362-72 S/O '87
Recycling oil rigs. *Oceans* 20:69 Jl/Ag '87
A state's scheme to rig the reefs [Louisiana Rigs-to-Reefs project] C. R. Cotton. il *Sierra* 72:19 Jl/Ag '87
Sunk junk: new homes for sea life. il *Natl Geogr World* 139:26-31 Mr '87
Reefs, Fossil
Travels of an ancient reef. G. D. Stanley, Jr. il maps *Nat Hist* 96:36-43 N '87
Reel-to-reel tape recorders *See* Tape recorders and recording
Reels, Fishing *See* Fishing tackle
Reese, Thomas J.
Three years later: U.S. relations with the Holy See. *America* 156:29-35 Ja 17 '87
Reeve, Christopher
about
Christopher Reeve: it isn't easy being Superman! M. J. Bandler. il pors *McCalls* 114:53-4 S '87
Reeves, Daniel J.
Learning to teach art: an integrative process. *Des Arts Educ* 89:41-4 S/O '87
Reeves, Richard
The Palme obsession. il pors *N Y Times Mag* p20-4+ Mr 1 '87
The Paris Tribune at one hundred. il *Am Herit* 38:114-19 N '87
Voices from behind the Iron Curtain. il *Read Dig* 131:103-7 Jl '87
Reeves, Robert
Exploring the summer Milky Way. il *Astronomy* 15:99-102 S '87
Hidden images: dissecting bright nebulae. il *Astronomy* 15:72-5 Mr '87
Science at McDonald Observatory. il pors *Astronomy* 15:6-17 Jl '87
Reeves, Robert, and Hooley, Mace
Taming the Schmidt camera. il *Astronomy* 15:82-7 D '87
Reeves, William J.
(jt. auth) See Labianca, Dominick A., and Reeves, William J.
Reevis Mountain School of Self-Reliance
Reevis Mountain School of Self-Reliance. D. Petersen. il *Mother Earth News* 108:66-9 N/D '87
Refac Technology Development Corp.
A father of innovation [E. M. Lang] R. Thompson. il pors *Nations Bus* 75:61-2 Ap '87
Refco Group Ltd.
Trading machine. S. B. Weiner. il por *Forbes* 140:168+ N 30 '87
Refereeing of scientific literature *See* Scientific literature—Refereeing
Referees and refereeing (Sports) *See* Basketball, Professional—Refereeing; Boxing—Refereeing; Football, Professional—Officiating; Hockey, Professional—Refereeing; Sports officiating
Reference books
See also
CD-ROM (Compact disc-Read only memory)—Reference books
References, Employment *See* Employment references
Referendum
The environment wins in most state polls. *Environment* 28:22-4 D '86
Voting on the environment. D. D. Schmidt. il *Technol Rev* 90:15-16 Ag/S '87
Wins and losses [referenda on church-state issues and Tennessee textbook case] E. Doerr. *Humanist* 47:40+ Ja/F '87
Poland
Poles at the polls [referendum on proposed austerity plan] *New Repub* 197:4 D 21 '87
Thanks for asking, but no [referendum for economic reform] W. R. Doerner. il *Time* 130:43 D 14 '87

Reffalt, William C.
A shelter for refuges. *Wilderness* 50:60 Summ '87
Refineries *See* Petroleum refineries
Refining of petroleum *See* Petroleum—Refining
Refinishing of furniture *See* Furniture—Finishes and finishing
Reflecting telescopes *See* Telescopes
Reflection (Optics)
Gone in a flash [game spooked by reflective hunting gear] B. McRae. il *Field Stream* 92:68-9+ Jl '87
Reflections from a water surface display some curious properties. J. Walker. il *Sci Am* 256:120-4+ Ja '87
Reflections (Photography)
Poetic reflection [work of M. Jodice] S. Piperato. il por *Pop Photogr* 94:70-1 Ja '87
Reflections: where you want them. J. Zuckerman. il *Petersens Photogr Mag* 15:50-1+ Ap '87
Reflectometers and reflectometry
Finding cable faults [use of time-domain reflectometry] V. D. Martin. il *Radio-Electron* 58:66-70+ Mr '87
Test ban compliance: is seismology enough? [U.S. prefers Continuous Reflectometry for Radius versus Time Experiments] D. C. Morrison. il *Science* 236:383-6 Ap 24 '87
Reflectors (Heat)
Ray banners. P. L. Spencer. *Consum Res Mag* 70:2 F '87
Reflectors (Photography) *See* Photography—Light and lighting
Reflex (Data base management system) *See* Information storage and retrieval systems—Management
Reflexes
See also
Conditioned responses
Retina transplant restores rat reflex [pupillary reflex; work of Henry Klassen and Raymond D. Lund] R. Weiss. il *Sci News* 132:245 O 17 '87
Reforestation
See also
Forest reproduction
Replanting Mt. St. Helens. S. Kaveski. il *Technol Rev* 90:14-15 Ag/S '87
Reform Association of Canada
Filling a western vacuum. J. Howse. il *Macleans* 100:12 Je 1 '87
Reform Party of Canada
A party's labor pains. D. Smith. *Macleans* 100:17 N 16 '87
Reformation
The Reformation & the red light [medieval attitudes toward prostitution] N. Orme. il *Hist Today* 37:36-41 Mr '87
Historiography
Whatever happened to the English Reformation? G. Redworth. bibl il *Hist Today* 37:29-36 O '87
Reformed Church in America
RCA General Synod. *Christ Century* 104:584-5 Jl 1-8 '87
Reformed churches
South Africa
Afrikaner church needs 'critical solidarity' [Dutch Reformed Church] H. W. Turner. *Christ Century* 104:645-6 Jl 29-Ag 5 '87
A congregation divided [Dutch Reformed Church] C. Erasmus. *Macleans* 100:24 Jl 20 '87
Refracting telescopes *See* Telescopes
Refrigerator-freezers *See* Refrigerators
Refrigerators
Appliances: hard working and good looking. il *South Living* 22:122+ O '87
Refrigerator/freezers. il *Consum Rep* 52:25-9 D '87
Refrigerators. il *Consum Rep* 52:34-41 Ja '87
Energy usage
The most energy-efficient refrigerator-freezers. il *Consum Res Mag* 70:20-3 O '87
Maintenance and repair
Flood pain. C. Maxwell. il *Fam Handyman* 37:70-1 D '87
Marketing
GE is pulling out the stops at home [new line of refrigerators] Z. Schiller. il *Bus Week* p94 N 2 '87
Refueling of artificial satellites *See* Artificial satellites—Refueling
Refueling of jet airplanes *See* Airplane engines, Jet—Refueling
Refugee children
Christianity today talks to Steve Standiford [adopting refugee children] *Christ Today* 31:35 F 20 '87
Imprisonment
End of the road for littlest illegals. P. Dworkin. il *U S News World Rep* 102:23 Ap 13 '87

Refugees
See also
Asylum, Right of
Exiles
Refugee children
United Nations. Group of Governmental Experts on International Co-operation to Avert New Flows of Refugees
United Nations. High Commissioner for Refugees
United Nations Relief and Works Agency for Palestine Refugees in the Near East
World War, 1939-1945—Refugees
A fellowship of suffering. B. R. Thompson. il por maps *Christ Today* 31:24-9 F 20 '87
General Assembly calls for world-wide aid for refugees in adopting 9 resolutions. il *UN Chron* 24:112-16 F '87
New policy, new protests [Canada] M. Rose. il *Macleans* 100:14-16 My 18 '87
Perspectives on U.S. refugee programs [address, June 11, 1987; statement June 30, 1987] J. Moore. *Dep State Bull* 87:54-8 S '87
Proposed refugee admissions for FY 1988 [statement, September 23, 1987] J. Moore. il *Dep State Bull* 87:47-52 N '87
Refugees and foreign policy: immediate needs and durable solutions [address, April 6, 1987] J. Moore. *Dep State Bull* 87:70-4 Jl '87
A roof for refugees . . . A. Billard. il *World Health* p12-15 Jl '87
Saying no [Canada's refugee policy; cover story; special section] il map *Macleans* 100:8-17 Ag 24 '87
U.S. refugee policy and programs for FY 1987 [statements, September 16 and 26, 1986] J. Moore; R. L. Funseth. il *Dep State Bull* 86:78-81 D '86

Refugees, Afghan
Afghan refugees find help at the border [World Vision outreach program in Pakistan] il *Christ Today* 31:40-1 Ap 3 '87
Caught in the cross fire [Afghan refugees in Pakistan] K. Gannon. il *Progressive* 51:14 Ja '87

Refugees, African
Refugee situation in Southern Africa [statement, February 5, 1987] M. H. Armacost. map *Dep State Bull* 87:65-7 My '87

Refugees, Arab
See also
Palestinian Arabs
United Nations Relief and Works Agency for Palestine Refugees in the Near East

Refugees, Central American
See also
Proyecto Libertad
Casa Romero closes: where do they go from here? [INS closes Catholic Church-run shelter for refugees in Brownsville, Tex.] C. McElroy. il map *Focus* 37:28-9 Spr '87
Charges of break-ins and infiltration [FBI investigation of the sanctuary movement] J.-M. Andriote. il *Christ Today* 31:44-5 Ap 17 '87
Closing the door [refugees trying to get into Canada] A. Dwyer. *Nation* 244:384-5 Mr 28 '87
El Norte's sheltering arms [Supreme Court ruling on asylum cases] il *U S News World Rep* 102:13 Mr 23 '87
End of the road for littlest illegals. P. Dworkin. il *U S News World Rep* 102:23 Ap 13 '87
Fleeing to Canada. E. Gress. *Commonweal* 114:164-6 Mr 27 '87
Gimme shelter [Supreme Court requires INS to use more lenient standards in asylum cases] R. Lacayo. il *Time* 129:70 Mr 23 '87
Immigrants in an uneasy wait [refugees turned back at Canadian border] B. Wallace. il *Macleans* 100:8-10 Mr 9 '87
No refugees need apply [seekers of political asylum] C. Dreifus. il *Atlantic* 259:32-5 F '87
Ottawa shuts the gate. M. Gee. il *Macleans* 100:12 Mr 2 '87
Sanctuary: should parishes break the law for a stranger? R. McClory. il *U S Cathol* 52:32-8 My '87
Sister Darlene Nicgorski [sanctuary movement worker] R. Brown. il por *Ms* 15:54+ Ja '87

Refugees, Cuban
See also
Cubans—United States

Refugees, Dominican
Horror off Death's Head Beach [refugees bound for Puerto Rico attacked by sharks after shipwreck] W. R. Doerner. il *Time* 130:33 O 19 '87

Refugees, Guatemalan
A Guatemalan family's flight to sanctuary in the U.S. P. M. Jones. il *Sch Update* 119:18 Mr 9 '87
The happy birds move on [Guatemalan Indian refugees flee to Mexico] R. J. Stout. il *Christ Century* 104:222-3 Mr 4 '87

Refugees, Honduran
The comforts of 10 Lemp Alley [refugees, contras and U.S. soldiers in Honduras] M. McDonald. il *Macleans* 100:22-4 F 23 '87

Refugees, Indochinese
See also
Indochinese—United States

Refugees, Iranian
Refugees from Iran [Turkey] R. Laver. il *Macleans* 100:29-30 F 2 '87

Refugees, Kampuchean
See also
Kampucheans—United States
Beyond the killing fields. M. Kelly. *America* 156:172-3 F 28 '87
Donors pledge $8.7 million for Kampuchean relief [refugees in Thailand] il *UN Chron* 23:78 N '86
Donors pledge nearly $6.2 million for Kampuchean relief. *UN Chron* 23:16 Ja '86
Waiting in a cruel limbo [Cambodian refugees in Thailand camps] B. Barber. il *Macleans* 100:15-16 Ag 24 '87
Photographs and photography
Seeing is deceiving [work of B. Burke] S. Piperato. il por *Pop Photogr* 94:58-9 F '87

Refugees, Laotian
The last bus [attempt to resettle Thailand's Hmong refugees in the U.S.] D. A. Ranard. il *Atlantic* 260:26-8+ O '87

Refugees, Mozambican
Mozambicans in diaspora. W. L. Moser. *America* 156:440-1+ My 30 '87

Refugees, Nicaraguan
Feet people. R. Radosh. *New Repub* 196:15-17 Mr 9 '87

Refugees, Salvadoran
Along the Salvadoran pipeline. R. Symanski. il map *Focus* 36:2-11 Wint '86
The impact of Simpson-Rodino. P. Shiras. *Commonweal* 114:276-7 My 8 '87
Salvadoran developments [repatriation of refugees] *Christ Century* 104:994 N 11 '87
Twice blest [bill to allow Salvadoran refugees to remain in U.S.] *America* 157:76 Ag 15-22 '87

Refugees, South African
Fugitives from apartheid. L. Arditi. il *Progressive* 51:32-4 Ap '87

Refugees, Tamil
See also
Tamils—Canada

Refugees, Turkish
A decision to stem the refugee tide [Canadian policy] M. Gee. il *Macleans* 100:14 Ja 19 '87
Refugees at the door [Canada] B. Wallace. il *Macleans* 100:11 Ja 12 '87

Refugees, Vietnamese
See also
Vietnamese—United States
Refugees in Hong Kong. M. H. Kelleher. *America* 157:84-5 Ag 15-22 '87

Refugees and the church *See* Church and social problems
Refuges, Wildlife *See* Wildlife sanctuaries
Refunding (Bonds) *See* Bonds—Refunding
Refunding (Municipal bonds) *See* Municipal bonds—Refunding
Refunds for returned goods *See* Return of goods
Refuse and refuse disposal
See also
Arcata (Calif.)—Sanitary affairs
Asbestos—Disposal
Beaches—Sanitation
Chambers Development Company
Chicago (Ill.)—Sanitary affairs
Denver (Colo.)—Sanitary affairs
Hazardous substances—Disposal
Incineration and incinerators
Islip (N.Y.)—Sanitary affairs
Medical waste disposal
New York (State)—Sanitary affairs
Radioactive waste disposal
Refuse trucks
Saint Louis (Mo.)—Sanitary affairs
San Diego (Calif.)—Sanitary affairs
Trade waste—Disposal
Waste disposal in the ocean
Waste Management, Inc.

Refuse and refuse disposal—*cont.*

Another day older and deeper in trash. R. A. Taylor. il *U S News World Rep* 102:20-1 My 11 '87

The Disposable Society. J. S. Lang. il *U S News World Rep* 102:68 Je 1 '87

The economics of garbage. il *Futurist* 21:42-3 N/D '87

Garbage: it isn't the other guy's problem anymore. T. Thompson and M. Bluestone. il *Bus Week* p150-1+ My 25 '87

Municipal waste. P. H. Abelson. *Science* 236:1409 Je 12 '87

Tons and tons of trash and no place to put it. S. Budiansky. il *U S News World Rep* 103:58-62 D 14 '87

What to do with our waste. W. D. Marbach. il *Newsweek* 110:51-2 Jl 27 '87

Equipment

See also

Allwaste Inc.

Refuse disposers

Germany (West)

Dumping on science [plan to use fossil rich Grube Messel as a garbage dump] P. Shipman. il map *Discover* 8:60-6 D '87

Refuse as fuel

Garbage in, garbage out [waste-to-energy incinerators] C. Mann. il *Sierra* 72:20+ S/O '87

Garbage: it isn't the other guy's problem anymore. T. Thompson and M. Bluestone. il *Bus Week* p150-1+ My 25 '87

Garbage: to burn or not to burn? T. Davis. il *Technol Rev* 90:19 F/Mr '87

Refuse containers

Trash-can hideaway: build it yourself! il *Better Homes Gard* 65:22 Ag '87

Refuse disposers

Replace a kitchen disposer. M. Henkenius. il *Workbench* 43:82+ N/D '87

Refuse recycling *See* Recycling (Waste, etc.)

Refuse trucks

See also

Allwaste Inc.

Notes and comment [Ann Arbor, Mich. donates garbage truck to sister city Juigalpa, Nicaragua] *New Yorker* 63:15-16 Ag 17 '87

Refuseniks *See* Immigration and emigration—Soviet Union

Regal Theater (Chicago, Ill.) *See* New Regal Theater (Chicago, Ill.)

Regan, Donald T.

about

The final days of Donald Regan. J. Alter. por *Newsweek* 109:23 Mr 9 '87

The First Lady: a hang-up about Don Regan. G. Hackett. por *Newsweek* 109:22-3 Mr 2 '87

"It's very difficult to accept". J. V. Lamar, Jr. il pors *Time* 130:11 Ag 10 '87

Just say goodbye, Don. A. Wilentz. il pors *Time* 129:28+ Mr 9 '87

Letter from Washington. Cato. *Natl Rev* 39:14 Mr 27 '87

Pay dirt. F. Barnes. *New Repub* 196:12-14 F 2 '87

President Nancy. F. Barnes. *New Repub* 196:11-13 Mr 23 '87

Regan bashing. T. Morganthau. il por *Newsweek* 109:18-19 F 16 '87

Regan, Lynne, and others

Polypeptide sequences essential for RNA recognition by an enzyme. bibl f il *Science* 235:1651-3 Mr 27 '87

The regard of flight [drama] See Irwin, Bill

Regattas

See also

Rowing

Regazzoni, Enrico

(jt. auth) See Perrelli, Gianni, and Regazzoni, Enrico

Le Regence (New York, N.Y.: Restaurant) *See* New York (N.Y.)—Restaurants, nightclubs, bars, etc.

Regency Electronics, Inc.

A rock-bottom high-tech buy? G. G. Marcial. *Bus Week* p83 Ja 19 '87

Regency Theatre (New York, N.Y.) *See* Motion picture theaters

Regeneration (Biology)

See also

Wound healing

Astrocytes block axonal regeneration in mammals by activating the physiological stop pathway. F. J. Liuzzi and R. J. Lasek. bibl f il *Science* 237:642-5 Ag 7 '87

Behavioral recovery induced by applied electric fields after spinal cord hemisection in guinea pig. R. B. Borgens and others. bibl f il *Science* 238:366-9 O 16 '87

Chip nerves [reconnecting nerve fibers; work of Morton Grosser and Joseph M. Rosen] J. I. Mattill. il *Technol Rev* 90:15 O '87

Good connections? It's in the chips [reconnecting nerve fibers; work of Joseph M. Rosen and Morton Grosser] D. D. Edwards. il *Sci News* 131:86 F 7 '87

Human amnion membrane serves as a substratum for growing axons in vitro and in vivo. G. E. Davis and others. bibl f il *Science* 236:1106-9 My 29 '87

An in vitro neurite-promoting antigen functions in axonal regeneration in vivo. A. W. Sandrock, Jr. and W. D. Matthew. bibl f il *Science* 237:1605-8 S 25 '87

Lipoprotein uptake by neuronal growth cones in vitro. M. J. Ignatius and others. bibl f il *Science* 236:959-62 My 22 '87

The long and short of 'web legs' [webs made by spiders with regenerated legs; research by Fritz Vollrath] *Sci News* 132:72 Ag 1 '87

Neurons regenerate into spinal cord [work of Jerry Silver and Michel Kliot] R. Weiss. *Sci News* 132:324 N 21 '87

Repair shop [reconnecting nerve fibers] O. Davies. il *Omni* 10:140 N '87

Skin reborn from muscle [research by Ioannis Yannas] S. Weisburd. *Sci News* 132:164 S 12 '87

Regeneration (Botany)

See also

Forest reproduction

Reggae music

See also

Phonograph records—Reggae music

Reggae or not: jazz goes dread? N. Weinstein. il *Down Beat* 54:63 Mr '87

Reggae Sunsplash *See* Music festivals—Jamaica

Regier, Gail

Talking to the sun [story] il *Atlantic* 260:76-80 S '87

Regina (Ship)

Yo-ho-ho and a bottle of Mumm! Veteran diver Lee Spence toasts the treasure of the lost wreck Regina. N. Geeslin. il pors *People Wkly* 28:143-5 N 16 '87

Regina Co.

CU wins a round in fight to stay out of advertising [use of Consumers Union ratings in vacuum cleaner commercials] *Consum Rep* 52:526 S '87

Regina keeps cleaning up. G. G. Marcial. *Bus Week* p117 Ja 12 '87

Reginato, James

Nobel House: publisher Roger Straus just keeps on winning. il pors *N Y* 20:56-60+ N 9 '87

Regional airlines *See* Airlines—Local service

Regional Dance America (Organization)

Regional Dance America's New York office closed. M. Horosko and R. Philip. *Dance Mag* 61:8-9 N '87

Regional ileitis

Inflammatory bowel disease: recognizing the symptoms. P. A. Banks. por *McCalls* 114:108 Ja '87

Nutritional aspects

Curbing magnesium deficiency in Crohn's disease. *Prevention* 39:92 Mr '87

Regional marketing *See* Marketing

Regional planning

See also

Bioregionalism

City planning

Shopping centers

Suburbs

Lake Tahoe region (Calif. and Nev.)

Battle-weary Lake Tahoe combatants try compromise. J. Stuller. il *Audubon* 89:44-6+ My '87

Regional theater *See* Theater

Regionalism

National change and the regional conundrum. B. L. Weinstein and H. T. Gross. *Society* 25:55-61 N/D '87

Canada

See also

Canada. Dept. of Regional Industrial Expansion

Regional racism from sea to sea. A. Fotheringham. il *Macleans* 100:72 N 9 '87

Mexico

The five nations of Mexico. L. B. Casagrande. il map *Focus* 37:2-9 Spr '87

Regis, Edward, 1944-

The Exodus Institute. il *Omni* 9:20+ Mr '87

Registers of births, etc.
Louisiana woman losing her bid to be categorized white [S. Phipps] por *Jet* 71:36 Ja 12 '87
Registration of voters *See* Voter registration
Registry of ships *See* Ships—Registration and transfer
Registry of tankers *See* Tankers—Registration and transfer
Regnier, Fred E.
The role of protein structure in chromatographic behavior. bibl f *Science* 238:319-23 O 16 '87
Regulation of body temperature *See* Temperature, Animal and human
Regulation of industry by government *See* Industry and state
Regulators, Voltage *See* Voltage regulators
Regulatory agencies
Reagan's regulators are suddenly starting to crack down. S. Crock. il *Bus Week* p45 Ja 19 '87
Rehabilitation
See also
Drug abuse—Rehabilitation
Handicapped and animals
Occupational therapy
Prisoners—Rehabilitation
Rehabilitation centers
See also
Drug abuse—Rehabilitation
Southern States
See also
Healthsouth (Firm)
Rehe, Stephanie
about
Winning at beauty. il pors *Teen* 31:74-7 Jl '87
Rehnquist, William H.
Time [address, May 17, 1987] *Vital Speeches Day* 53:549-51 Jl 1 '87
about
Coup at the Court. R. Adler. il *New Repub* 197:37+ S 14-21 '87
Earth diary: Justice Rehnquist and the land. T. Turner. il *Mother Earth News* 103:112+ Ja/F '87
The Supreme Court with a smile. T. Gest. il por *U S News World Rep* 102:23 Ja 12 '87
Reich, Bernard
Israel's year of transition. bibl f *Curr Hist* 86:69-72+ F '87
Reich, Charles A.
The liberals' mistake [with discussion] por *Cent Mag* 20:49-59 Jl/Ag '87
Reich, Edith
about
"The most corrupt person". N. J. Perry. por *Fortune* 116:93 Ag 17 '87
Reich, Ilan
about
The seduction of Ilan. A. Smith. il *Esquire* 107:75-6 My '87
Reich, Lee
Grow figs anywhere. *Flower Gard* 31:29 F/Mr '87
Reich, Robert B.
Enterprise and double cross [excerpt from Tales of a new America] *Wash Mon* 18:13-19 Ja '87
The expanding economic vista. il *N Y Times Mag* p52-4+ S 13 '87
How nit-picking regulations get that way [excerpt from Tales of a new America] *Harpers* 274:18+ F '87
Of markets and myths. *Commentary* 83:38-42 F '87
The rise of techno-nationalism. il *Atlantic* 259:62-9 My '87
Secrets of his success. il *N Y Times Mag* p94-5 My 3 '87
about
Robert Reich takes on Rambo. T. J. Peters. *Wash Mon* 19:51-6 Mr '87
Reich, Steve
about
Reich's progress. P. G. Davis. il por *N Y* 20:110-11 N 23 '87
Reichek, Elaine, 1943-
about
Elaine Reichek at Carlo Lamagna and A.I.R. N. Princenthal. il *Art Am* 75:129 Jl '87
Reichmann brothers
about
Bloody Monday was a blessing in disguise for the Reichmanns. E. B. Terry. il *Bus Week* p56 D 21 '87
Capital developments. D. Jenish. il *Macleans* 100:28-9 Ag 24 '87
The expansive Reichmanns. D. Jenish. il *Macleans* 100:36 D 7 '87

The Reichmann touch: facing the toughest test yet. E. B. Terry. il *Bus Week* p96-7+ Mr 23 '87
Reichner, Henry F.
(jt. auth) See Zirkel, Perry A., and Reichner, Henry F.
Reichstag (Berlin, Germany: West)
Reichstag Museum and Museum of German History. I. R. Mitchell. il *Hist Today* 37:61 Ag '87
Reid, Angus
about
A heady new scent of coalition. P. C. Newman. il por *Macleans* 100:35 S 28 '87
Reid, Brenda Olcott- *See* Olcott-Reid, Brenda
Reid, Brian Holden
The tank and visions of future war [cover story] bibl il *Hist Today* 37:36-41 D '87
Reid, Daphne Maxwell
about
Tim Reid, Daphne Maxwell: how to work together and stay in love [cover story] C. Waldron. il pors *Jet* 72:26-8 S 14 '87
Reid, George
about
First black sheriff is elected in McCormick, S.C. por *Jet* 71:17 F 2 '87
Reid, J. R.
about
The biggest man on campus. C. Kirkpatrick. il pors *Sports Illus* 66:32-5 Mr 2 '87
Reid, James S., Jr.
about
A hero in the Rust Belt. B. D. Fromson. il por *Fortune* 115:103 Ja 5 '87
Reid, Lloyd Carew- *See* Carew-Reid, Lloyd
Reid, Tim
about
Tim Reid, Daphne Maxwell: how to work together and stay in love [cover story] C. Waldron. il pors *Jet* 72:26-8 S 14 '87
Reid, Vernon
about
Back in black: a group of musicians unites to reclaim the right to rock. D. Fricke. il pors *Roll Stone* p64+ S 24 '87
Blindfold test. G. Santoro. il por *Down Beat* 54:51 D '87
Reiger, George, 1939-
Conservation. See issues of Field & Stream
Reilly, Ann
Celebrate the bicentennial: create a Constitution garden. il *Flower Gard* 31:80-1 Ap/My '87
Tomorrow's good lawns are in the bag today (literally!). il *Flower Gard* 31:18-19 Ag/S '87
Reilly, Rick
Bad Tidings from 'Bama. por *Sports Illus* 66:78 Ja 19 '87
Biggest change in town. il pors *Sports Illus* 67 Sp Issue:76-8+ S 9 '87
Bowed but not broken. il pors *Sports Illus* 66:32-4+ Je 22 '87
The Broncos were boffo [cover story] il *Sports Illus* 67:26-8+ S 21 '87
Curse of the camera. por *Sports Illus* 66:85 Mr 2 '87
Guts, brains and glory. il *Sports Illus* 66:12-17 Ja 12 '87
Here's to happy days. il pors *Sports Illus* 66:47-8+ Ap 13 '87
How about it, Mr. Pete? Ten good reasons Denver deserves a major league team. por *Sports Illus* 67:90 Ag 24 '87
In search of trust [cover story] il pors *Sports Illus* 67:84-8+ N 23 '87
Mister T [cover story] il pors *Sports Illus* 67:30-2+ Ag 31 '87
One from the heart. il pors *Sports Illus* 66:44-6+ My 18 '87
One will be made whole. il pors *Sports Illus* 66:58-64+ Mr 30 '87
An Open and shut case [cover story] il pors *Sports Illus* 66:20-7 Je 29 '87
Quick, before you're 30: a checklist for the male sports fan who thinks he's with it. por *Sports Illus* 66:76 Je 22 '87
A ring and a prayer. il pors *Sports Illus* 67:88-92+ D 21 '87
Season for no reason. il *Sports Illus* 67:44-6+ N 30 '87
Seven ahead, nine to go, and then . . . il *Sports Illus* 66:62-6+ Je 15 '87
Sizzling rivals. il *Sports Illus* 67:14-17 S 7 '87

Reilly, Rick—*cont.*
Staying away in flocks. il *Sports Illus* 67:38-40+ N 9 '87
T.C. conquers L.A. in O.T. il por *Sports Illus* 66:22-4+ Mr 2 '87
The talk of the town. por *Sports Illus* 67:84 S 14 '87
These Bills stack up. il *Sports Illus* 67:66-7+ D 7 '87
Thirty pieces of silver: reflections on the not-so-great football strike of 1987. por *Sports Illus* 67:132 O 26 '87
Trapped by the past. il *Sports Illus* 67 Sp Issue:18-26+ S 9 '87
Unseen hands on my game. il map *Sports Illus* 67:66-70+ Ag 17 '87
Very British Open. il pors *Sports Illus* 67:18-23 Jl 27 '87
Welcome home, guys—maybe. il *Sports Illus* 67:42-4+ N 2 '87

Reilly, Robert T.
Good news or good snooze: what Catholics expect from a homily [cover story] il *U S Cathol* 52:6-13 S '87
Have Catholic colleges kept the faith? il *U S Cathol* 52:34-40 O '87
Who's got the last word on Catholic morality? il *U S Cathol* 52:54-8 Je '87

Reiman, Kathy
about
Investing in a confident style. J. Giambanco. il pors *Work Woman* 12:103-4+ D '87

Reimer, Judith A.
Getting bedtime right. il *Parents* 62:95-8 O '87
Picky-eater defeaters. il *Parents* 62:80-1+ S '87

Reims, Gordon A.
Finding a subject for short nonfiction. *Writer* 100:25-6 F '87

Reinarman, Craig
(jt. auth) See Levine, Harry, and Reinarman, Craig

Reincarnation
Walk like an Egyptian [excerpt from The search for Omm Sety] J. Cott. il *Omni* 9:66-8+ Jl '87

Reindeer
See also
Caribou

Reindeer meat contamination See Meat contamination

Reiner, Carl, 1922-
about
Summer school [film] Reviews
Macleans il 100:47 Jl 27 '87. P. Young
People Wkly 28:8 Ag 10 '87. T. Cunneff

Reiner, Rob
about
Prince Rob [interview] H. Jacobson. il por *Film Comment* 23:58+ S/O '87
The princess bride [film] Reviews
Glamour il 85:250 N '87. J. G. Boyum
Macleans il 100:58 O 5 '87. L. O'Toole
New Yorker 63:110-12 O 19 '87. P. Kael
Newsweek il 110:85 O 5 '87. D. Ansen
People Wkly 28:14 S 28 '87. P. Travers
Sch Update il 120:40 O 2 '87. D. Scheuer
Time il 130:74 S 21 '87. R. Corliss

Reinforced concrete See Concrete, Reinforced

Reinforcement (Psychology)
Using positive reinforcement. T. R. McDaniel. *Educ Dig* 53:36-9 O '87

Reingold, J. R.
An insider's look at federal youth programs. *Educ Dig* 53:34-5 N '87

Reinhardt, D. E.
An oddity with taste—asparagus pea. il *Flower Gard* 31:95 F/Mr '87

Reinhardt, Richard
Of turbo boots and rooster tails: the ORV and the public lands. il *Wilderness* 50:28-36 Summ '87
Starting again in San Francisco. il *Am Herit* 38:92-8 Ap '87

Reinhardt, Uwe E.
Reaganomics, R.I.P. *New Repub* 196:24+ Ap 20 '87

Reinhold, Brian
Weather regimes: the challenge in extended-range forecasting. bibl f il maps *Science* 235:437-41 Ja 23 '87

Reinhold, Toni
Linda Gray: "Why isn't life fair?". il pors *Redbook* 169:16+ My '87
Michael Landon: "My mother tried to stab me" [interview] il pors *Redbook* 169:59-60+ S '87

Reinke, Dean
Watch the world's best in Rome. il *Women's Sports Fitness* 9:58 Ag '87

Reinking, Ann
about
She's a brass band: Ann Reinking back on Broadway. K. Grubb. il pors *Dance Mag* 61:84-5 Mr '87

Reinstein, Fred
about
WallWalker wizard's washup wonder. G. Buchalter. il por *Forbes* 139:240 My 18 '87

Reinvestment of dividends See Dividend reinvestment

Reis, Donald J.
(jt. auth) See Saji, Makoto, and Reis, Donald J.

Reisman, Sol Simon
about
The 'best man for the job' [interview] M. Drohan. por *Macleans* 100:16-17 O 19 '87
Simon Reisman's way. M. Drohan. il por *Macleans* 100:22 O 5 '87

Reisman, Vivian
about
Baby Steps are the socks of choice for toddlers who don't want to hit the skids early. il *People Wkly* 28:183 N 16 '87

Reiss, Bob
Merv Larson's team takes nature to the animals. il por *Smithsonian* 17:106-8+ F '87

Reiss, Diana
about
Dolphin talk [interview] G. Hartwell. *Oceans* 20:62-3 Mr/Ap '87

Reiss, Howard
Gas-phase polymerization: ultraslow chemistry. bibl f il *Science* 238:1368-73 D 4 '87

Reiss, James
Castrati in Caesar's court [poem] *New Repub* 197:34 Jl 13-20 '87

Reissues of phonograph records See Phonograph records—Reissues

Reitan, Sandy
about
Darts. *New Yorker* 63:33-5 D 21 '87

Reiter, Carla
The mysterious magic of pollination. il *Natl Wildl* 25:14-17 Ag/S '87

Reiter, Mark
The smartest thing I did in my 60s. il *50 Plus* 27:24-7+ F '87

Reith, Kathryn M.
Indoor rowing: progress in place. il *Women's Sports Fitness* 9:80-1 D '87
Pulling your own oar. bibl il *Women's Sports Fitness* 9:24-8 Ag '87

Rejection (Organs, tissues, etc.) See Immunological tolerance

Rejection (Psychology)
Dumped: how I survived the first six months. C. Hope. il por *Glamour* 85:236+ Ap '87

Relational data base management systems See Information storage and retrieval systems—Management

Relatives See Family

Relativism See Relativity

Relativity
See also
Subjectivity
The philosopher and the everyday. T. Todorov. *New Repub* 197:34-7+ S 14-21 '87

Relativity (Physics)
See also
Field theory (Physics)
Gravity and gravitation
Lorentz transformations
Quantum gravity
Quantum theory
Space and time
Einstein and ether drift experiments. J. Stachel. bibl f *Phys Today* 40:45-7 My '87
Einstein and Michelson-Morley [discussion of August 1982 article, How I created the theory of relativity] A. I. Miller. bibl f il *Phys Today* 40:9+ My '87
The impact of special relativity on theoretical physics. J. D. Jackson. bibl f il *Phys Today* 40:34-42 My '87

Relaxation
Relaxation really works [stress reduction; study by Robert C. Peveler and Derek W. Johnston] C. Wood. *Psychol Today* 21:68 Ja '87
Stressed to excess? P. Rudolf. il *Redbook* 170:102-5 D '87
Takin' it easy: relax your way to body, job, diet success. S. Young. il *Glamour* 85:30 S '87

Relaxation methods (Mathematics)
An introduction to relaxation methods [solving physics problems] G. William. il *Byte* 12:111-14+ Ja '87

Reliability (Engineering)
See also
Quality control
Reliance Capital Group L. P.
The new order at Blair. J. F. Berry. il por *Channels*
7:53-6 Ap '87
Reliance Electric Co.
The little motor that couldn't [Exxon sells Reliance
Electric in a leveraged buyout] J. A. Conway. il *Forbes*
139:8 F 9 '87
Reliance Group Holdings, Inc.
An enfant terrible comes of age [S. Steinberg] il por
U S News World Rep 103:53 Jl 6 '87
Relics and reliquaries
See also
Holy Shroud
Relief work
See also
Evacuation of civilians
Feed the Children (Organization)
Hands Across America, 1986
Operation Get Down Food Co-op
United States. Federal Emergency Management
Agency
Blacks seek aid for big losses in Calif. quake. il *Jet*
73:14 N 16 '87
An evening with Trevor's dad [work with the homeless
of Philadelphia by T. and F. Ferrell] E. S. Vaughn.
il pors *Christ Today* 31:12-13 F 20 '87
Hands reach out to a hungry heartland. C. Tevis. il
Success Farm 85 no3:M1 F '87
John 3:16 Cook has saving words for Vegas losers.
K. Hubbard. il pors *People Wkly* 27:115-16+ My 11
'87
Matthew Weaver: helping the down-and-out in L.A. [food
relief] C. Lapin. por *Seventeen* 46:111 O '87
Old friends [New York City's Meals on Wheels program]
G. Greene. il *N Y* 20:10-11 Ja 12 '87
The strategy of humanitarian assistance. T. Kunugi. il
UN Chron 24:54-5 My '87
International aspects
See also
Catholic Relief Services
Food and Agriculture Organization of the United
Nations
Missions, Medical
Office of the United Nations Disaster Relief Co-
ordinator
Red Cross
UNICEF
United States. Agency for International Development
Food aid and food habits. J. Shoham and B. Stainier.
il *Courier* 40:32-4 My '87
General Assembly calls for world-wide aid for refugees
in adopting 9 resolutions. il *UN Chron* 24:112-16
F '87
The politics of hunger [food surplus keeps growing] W.
Greider. il *Roll Stone* p34-5 Jl 2 '87
Africa
See also
Live Aid concert, 1985
United Nations. Office of Emergency Operations
in Africa
USA for Africa
Appeal made for urgent and intensified international
efforts to meet Africa's emergency needs. *UN Chron*
24:47 F '87
From Africa, with love. L. Ullmann. il pors *Seventeen*
46:210-11+ Ap '87
Colombia
Assembly urges international support to alleviate effects
of Colombian volcanic eruption [Nevado del Ruiz]
il *UN Chron* 23:21-2 Ja '86
Developing countries
See also
Food for the Poor (Organization)
Child survival: an achievable goal in hunger relief [cover
story] T. Peterson. il *Christ Century* 104:594-5 Jl 1-8
'87
Hard times for foreign aid. J. Greenwald. il *Time* 129:38-9
F 9 '87
El Salvador
All states asked to provide emergency assistance to El
Salvador after devastating earthquake; President Duarte
addresses United Nations on earthquake assistance.
il por *UN Chron* 24:65 F '87
Ethiopia
Attacking the victims [Eritrean People's Liberation Front
cuts UN food supply lines] S. Seibert. il *Newsweek*
110:56 N 9 '87

Bootstrap time in a luckless land [D. Carlson and B.
Downing working in Ethiopia for Save the Children
Federation] J. Buckley. il pors map *U S News World
Rep* 103:88-90+ D 28 '87-Ja 4 '88
Does helping really help? [political situation interfering
with famine relief work] O. Friedrich. il *Time* 130:44-5
D 21 '87
Scandals in Catholic Relief [cover story] J. MacGuire.
il *Natl Rev* 39:26-30+ Jl 3 '87
The spectre of famine. A. Bilski. il map *Macleans*
100:18-19 D 7 '87
Tourists in hell [excerpt from Breakfast in hell] M.
Harris. *Harpers* 274:28-31 F '87
Haiti
Père Mahfood's Food for the Poor. A. Rodriguez-Soto.
America 156:153-4 F 21 '87
Latin America
Disaster preparedness in the Americas. C. de Ville de
Goyet. il *World Health* p20-2 O '87
Lebanon
Food aid to Lebanon [State Dept. statement, July 10,
1987] *Dep State Bull* 87:47 S '87
U.S. food aid program for Lebanon [State Dept. statement,
April 28, 1987] il *Dep State Bull* 87:61 Jl '87
Mexico
Follow-up meeting on Mexican relief held 30 October.
UN Chron 22:104 N/D '85
Middle East
See also
United Nations Relief and Works Agency for
Palestine Refugees in the Near East
Mozambique
Hunger and armed conflict threaten Mozambique. R.
Frame. il *Christ Today* 31:60-1 O 2 '87
Jet editor takes supplies to aid Africans. D. M. Cheers.
il map *Jet* 72:24-6+ Ap 6 '87
More than $200 million pledged for humanitarian as-
sistance to Mozambique. il *UN Chron* 24:29 My '87
The Renamo menace: hunger and carnage in Mozambique
[cover story; with editorial comment] A. R. Norton.
il *New Leader* 70:2, 5-8 N 16 '87
Nicaragua
See also
Evangelical Committee for Aid and Development
in Nicaragua
Quest for Peace (Organization)
The other aid network [humanitarian aid from U.S.]
R. Nordland. il *Newsweek* 110:37 Jl 27 '87
Pakistan
Afghan refugees find help at the border [World Vision
outreach program in Pakistan] il *Christ Today* 31:40-1
Ap 3 '87
Sudan
For Falwell: new job, new questions [questionable use
of funds donated for Sudanese famine relief] S. Emerson
and G. Witkin. il por *U S News World Rep* 102:60-1
Ap 6 '87
Thailand
Donors pledge $8.7 million for Kampuchean relief
[refugees in Thailand] il *UN Chron* 23:78 N '86
Donors pledge nearly $6.2 million for Kampuchean relief.
UN Chron 23:16 Ja '86
United States
See Relief work
Religion
See also
Aged—Religious life
AIDS (Disease)—Religious aspects
Architecture and religion
Art and religion
Arts and religion
Atheism
Australian aborigines—Religion and mythology
Baby boom generation—Religious life
Bahaism
Black women—Religious life
Blacks—Religious life
Cancer patients—Religious life
Catholic Church
Celebrities—Religious life
Children—Religious life
Chinese—Canada—Religious life
Christianity
Christianity and other religions
College students—Religious life
Corporal punishment—Religious aspects
Cults
Death—Religious aspects
Engineers—Religious life
Evangelicalism
Executives—Religious life

Bibliography

Books. See issues of The Christian Century
Books. See issues of Christianity Today
[Column] G. M. Costello. See issues of U.S. Catholic beginning January 1985
Favorite books and how they influence [cover story] il *Christ Century* 104:490-5 My 20-27 '87
Religious Book Week: critics' choices. il *Commonweal* 114:149-59 Mr 13 '87
Religious books: fall 1987. W. Griffin. il *Publ Wkly* 232:46-61 O 9 '87
Religious books: spring 1987. il *Publ Wkly* 231:45-52+ Mr 6 '87

History

Bibliography

Paperback history [twelfth and thirteenth centuries] H. Lawrence. *Hist Today* 37:57 Mr '87

Study and teaching

Three views from the trenches: teaching high school religion in the city [New York City] D. H. Powell. *America* 157:212-16 O 10 '87

Religion, Primitive

See also

Voodooism

Religion and agriculture

See also

Church work with farmers

Facing up to the farm crisis [Interreligious Conference on Rural Life; cover story] V. Rebeck. *Christ Century* 104:381-3 Ap 22 '87

The fate of the soil. R. Clapp. il *Christ Today* 31:14-15 O 2 '87

Religion and architecture *See* Architecture and religion
Religion and art *See* Art and religion
Religion and communism *See* Communism and religion
Religion and culture

See also

Christianity and culture

Religion and education *See* Church and education; Church schools; Public schools and religion

Religion and humor

Sola gratia in Lake Wobegon [cover story] W. L. Miller. il por *Christ Century* 104:526-8 Je 3-10 '87
What makes CT laugh? T. C. Muck. il *Christ Today* 31:11 D 11 '87

Religion and justice

God isn't fair (and I'm glad He isn't). P. Yancey. il *Christ Today* 31:72 N 20 '87
Justice without conscience is dead. J. T. Burtchaell. *Christ Today* 31:26 Je 12 '87
Moving Christian worship toward social justice. J. F. White. il *Christ Century* 104:558-60 Je 17-24 '87
Restorative justice: does it work? [conference in Guelph, Ont.] R. Rempel. *Christ Century* 104:156-7 F 18 '87

Religion and labor *See* Church and labor
Religion and language

See also

Bible—Language, style

Religion and law

Lawsuits: the great American plague. C. W. Colson. *Christ Today* 31:72 Mr 6 '87

Religion and medicine *See* Medicine and religion
Religion and motion pictures *See* Motion pictures—Moral and religious aspects; Motion pictures—Religious films

Religion and music

See also

Christian contemporary music
Rock music—Moral and religious aspects

Religion and nuclear warfare *See* Nuclear warfare and religion
Religion and nuclear weapons *See* Nuclear weapons—Moral and religious aspects

Religion and peace

See also

Church and disarmament

Catholic thought on war & peace [discussion of September 11 and September 25, 1987 articles, The heritage abandoned?] P. Steinfels. *Commonweal* 114:690+ D 4 '87
Expanding the peace movement [National Association of Evangelicals] R. J. Neuhaus. *Natl Rev* 39:46 F 27 '87
The heritage abandoned? (I) [G. Weigel's critique of the Catholic position on war and peace, Tranquillitas ordinis] P. Steinfels. *Commonweal* 114:487-92 S 11 '87
The heritage abandoned? (II) [G. Weigel's critique of the Catholic position on war and peace, Tranquillitas ordinis] P. Steinfels. il *Commonweal* 114:530-3 S 25 '87
Presbyterians: politics and responsibility. G. Telford. *Christ Century* 104:614-16 Jl 15-22 '87
The price of pacifism [discussion of October 22, 1986 article, A practical Christian pacifism] D. A. Hoekema. *Christ Century* 104:20-2 Ja 7-14 '87
Prophets and builders of peace. *America* 156:21 Ja 17 '87
Reclaiming the Catholic heritage [G. Weigel's Tranquillitas ordinis and M. Novak's Will it liberate?] A. R. Muggeridge. *Commentary* 84:39-44 S '87
Weaving a seamless garment out of peace, freedom, and security [National Association of Evangelicals guidelines on war and peace] R. Frame. il *Christ Today* 31:42-4 My 15 '87

Conferences

Mount Hiei day of prayer for peace [Japan] T. Michel. il *America* 157:475-7 D 19 '87

Religion and philosophy *See* Philosophy and religion
Religion and poetry *See* Poetry—Moral and religious aspects

Religion and politics

Religion and politics—See also—*cont.*
   Reagan, Ronald, 1911-—Religion
   Religion and peace
   Socialism and religion
Ambitions and strategies of the religious right [contenders for the 1988 Republican presidential nomination] M. Negri. *Humanist* 47:29-32 My/Je '87
The chains of religious freedom. W. H. Willimon. il por *Christ Today* 31:28-30 S 18 '87
A congressman who would be president [interview with J. Kemp] por *Christ Today* 31:40 Ap 3 '87
A convert's convictions [views of C. W. Colson] il por *Newsweek* 110:10 O 19 '87
Evangelical politicians defeat themselves. B. Hallman. il por *Christ Today* 31:12 N 6 '87
A farewell to harms. K. S. Kantzer. il *Christ Today* 31:14-15 D 11 '87
God and politics on television [PBS series] *America* 157:492-3 D 26 '87
Gospel or government? [National Association of Evangelicals' annual convention] H. Smith. il *Christ Today* 31:38-9 Ap 3 '87
Isn't it time we Christians made some things clear? P. Steinfels. *America* 157:181-2 O 3 '87
A Jerry-built coalition regroups. R. N. Ostling. il por *Time* 130:68-9 N 16 '87
The least you can do is vote [with readers' comments] M. O'Connell. *U S Cathol* 52:14-20 My '87
Listening to both sides of the 'divided kingdom' [B. Moyers' PBS series God and politics] J. M. Wall. *Christ Century* 104:1166-7 D 23-30 '87
Lost momentum [the religious right; interview with C. F. H. Henry] B. Spring. il por *Christ Today* 31:30-2 S 4 '87
Memphis churches back Rep. Ford with $100,000. il por *Jet* 72:7 Je 15 '87
No-fault prophecy. R. J. Neuhaus. *Natl Rev* 39:44 Ap 10 '87
Of many things [R. P. McBrien's Caesar's coin] G. W. Hunt. *America* 156:inside cover Mr 28 '87
Politics won't cure death. J. Garvey. il *Commonweal* 114:584-5 O 23 '87
Preacher-bashing and the public life [J. Bakker scandal and media overkill] J. M. Wall. *Christ Century* 104:347-8 Ap 15 '87
The Presbyterian moment. D. Ritchie. il *Natl Rev* 39:30-1 Jl 31 '87
The presidency and the power of suggestion. J. M. Wall. *Christ Century* 104:43 Ja 21 '87
Presidential candidates: preachers and pragmatists. J. M. Wall. *Christ Century* 104:1051-2 N 25 '87
A presidential straw poll [National Association of Evangelicals convention] *Christ Today* 31:39 Ap 3 '87
Principles & politics [views of Catholic theologian A. Dulles] J. B. Hehir. il *Commonweal* 114:169-70 Mr 27 '87
Prudence, humility and the Niebuhrian ethic. J. M. Wall. *Christ Century* 104:875-6 O 14 '87
The questions lawmakers ask about religion [views of C. Whittier] *Christ Today* 31:66 O 2 '87
The religious character of American patriotism. F. Edwords. il por *Humanist* 47:20-4+ N/D '87
Single-issue politics and the Church [Catholic Church] K. R. Himes. *America* 156:377-81 My 9 '87
Spying on Henry Hyde at Mass. C. W. Colson. il *Christ Today* 31:80 N 6 '87
Televangelist takeover. *Nation* 244:419-20 Ap 4 '87
The value of preacher-bashing [discussion of April 15, 1987 article, Preacher-bashing and the public life] J. M. Wall. *Christ Century* 104:532-4 Je 3-10 '87
The wall that never was [First Amendment] T. C. Muck. il *Christ Today* 31:16-17 Jl 10 '87

Bibliography
Books on religion and politics. J. H. Yoder. *America* 157:89-90 Ag 15-22 '87
Religion and psychology *See* Psychology, Religious
Religion and science
   See also
   American Scientific Affiliation
   Creation
   Evolution
   Nature—Religious interpretations
Cease-fire in the laboratory [cover story] T. Stafford. il *Christ Today* 31:17-21 Ap 3 '87
Darwinism defined: the difference between fact and theory. S. J. Gould. il *Discover* 8:64-5+ Ja '87
The godfather of disaster [cometary theory of W. Whiston] S. J. Gould. il *Nat Hist* 96:20+ S '87
Is human life only chemistry? J. F. Haught. *Current* 294:4-7 Jl/Ag '87

Justice Scalia's misunderstanding. S. J. Gould. il *Nat Hist* 96:14+ O '87
Religious groups join animal patent battle. M. Crawford. *Science* 237:480-1 Jl 31 '87
The return of the God-hypothesis. B. Durbin, Jr. il por *Christ Today* 31:22-3 Ap 3 '87
Science & the ways to God [views of S. L. Jaki] H. Rolston. *Commonweal* 114:313-16 My 22 '87
Science and religion: divided we stand? [surveys of college students by Robert W. Susher] R. Camer. *Psychol Today* 21:61 Je '87
Science: from the womb of religion [address, May 1987] S. L. Jaki. il *Christ Century* 104:851-4 O 7 '87
Science on the track of God. J. Gleick. il *N Y Times Mag* p22-3 Ja 4 '87
Two decades of ultimate dialogue [conference in Toronto on ultimate reality and meaning; work of T. Horvath] D. J. Leigh. *America* 157:504-5 D 26 '87
Religion and sex *See* Sex and religion
Religion and social problems *See* Church and social problems
Religion and socialism *See* Socialism and religion
Religion and sociology
   See also
   Sociology, Christian
Religion and sports
   See also
   Football, High school—Religious aspects
Religion and state *See* Church and state; Religious liberty
Religion and television *See* Television broadcasting—Moral and religious aspects
Religion and the arts *See* Arts and religion
Religion and the draft *See* Military service, Compulsory—Moral and religious aspects
Religion and the environment
Brother sun, sister moon [25th anniversary celebration at Assisi of the World Wildlife Fund] L. Harris. *New Yorker* 63:80-92+ Ap 27 '87
Dogs in the manger [Dean J. P. Morton's Theology of the earth at Saint John the Divine, New York City] D. K. Mano. *Natl Rev* 39:65-6 Ja 30 '87
Ecology and the church: theology and action. D. E. Sherwood and K. Franklin. *Christ Century* 104:472-4 My 13 '87
Teaching the eco-justice ethic: the parable of the Billerica Dam. J. R. Engel. il *Christ Century* 104:466-9 My 13 '87
Who in Solihull cares about dolphins? [Catholic theology] E. P. Echlin. *America* 157:15-17 Jl 4-11 '87
Religion and war *See* War and religion
Religion in literature
   See also
   Religious literature
The downward trajectory of John Updike. D. Mehl. *Natl Rev* 39:53-4+ F 13 '87
An interview with Mavis Gallant. P. H. Samway. *America* 156:485-7 Je 13 '87
Joseph Brodsky: scrutinizing the good. D. Heim. *Christ Century* 104:989-90 N 11 '87
Little shop of horrors [discussion of July 17, 1987 article] M. Z. Stange. *Commonweal* 114:546+ O 9 '87
Little shop of horrors [women in the fiction of A. Greeley; cover story] M. Z. Stange. il por *Commonweal* 114:412-17 Jl 17 '87
'The meaning is in you': Flannery O'Connor in her letters. J. P. Baumgaertner. *Christ Century* 104:1172-6 D 23-30 '87
Percy's syndrome [discussion of October 7, 1987 article, The Thanatos syndrome] J. L. Womack. *Christ Century* 104:1003-4 N 11 '87
The Thanatos syndrome: exciting, horrifying, disappointing [W. Percy's novel] R. C. Wood. il por *Christ Century* 104:857-8 O 7 '87
Religion in public schools *See* Public schools and religion
Religions *See* Religion
Religious advertising
Admen for heaven [Episcopal Ad Project] D. Neff. il pors *Christ Today* 31:12-13 S 18 '87
Religious architecture *See* Churches (Buildings)
Religious art, Christian *See* Christian art and symbolism
Religious books *See* Religious literature
Religious conferences
   See also
   Catholic Church. National Conference of Catholic Bishops
   Religion and peace—Conferences
   Synod of Bishops (1987)
Admiring what works [10th anniversary of Catholic Church's A call to action] A. McCarthy. *Commonweal* 114:73-4 F 13 '87

Religious conferences—*cont.*

The Holy Spirit and world evangelization [North American Congress on the Holy Spirit and World Evangelization] J. Duin. il *Christ Today* 31:44-5 S 4 '87

Mission possible [Urbana student missionary conferences] H. Smith. *Christ Today* 31:15 D 11 '87

Scholars say historical evidence buttresses the claims of Scripture [Jesus Christ: God and man conference] W. A. Durbin, Jr. il *Christ Today* 31:55+ Ja 16 '87

Great Britain

See also

World Conference on Church, Community, and State (1937)

Japan

See also

International Seminar on the Future of Mankind and Cooperation Among Religions

Singapore

Calling the next generation of Christian leaders [Singapore 87 conference] J. D. Douglas. *Christ Today* 31:39 Ag 7 '87

Switzerland

See also

Lausanne Committee for World Evangelization

Religious cooperation

See also

Ecumenical movement

Religious discrimination in employment *See* Discrimination in employment

Religious education

See also

Catechetics

Catholic Church—Education

Church colleges and universities

Church schools

Religion—Study and teaching

Sunday schools

Theology—Study and teaching

Religious faith *See* Faith

Religious films *See* Motion pictures—Religious films

Religious freedom *See* Religious liberty

Religious history *See* Church history

Religious journalism *See* Journalism, Religious

Religious liberty

See also

Church and state

Taxation, Exemption from

Between anarchy and fanaticism: religious freedom's challenge. E. B. Borowitz. il *Christ Century* 104:619-22 Jl 15-22 '87

The chains of religious freedom. W. H. Willimon. il por *Christ Today* 31:28-30 S 18 '87

Neutrality and religious freedom [Northwest Ordinance of 1787] M. E. Marty. *Christ Century* 104:580-1 Jl 1-8 '87

Psychology and religion in court—again [anticult theories of coercive persuasion] J. R. Lewis and J. G. Melton. *Christ Century* 104:914-16 O 21 '87

Religious freedom for all: a Jewish perspective. S. Rabinove. il *USA Today (Periodical)* 116:32-5 N '87

Va. fed. judge says 'Rasta' cons must eat prison food. *Jet* 72:12 Ag 3 '87

International aspects

UN official seeks data on repression of believers [A. Ribeiro of the Commission on Human Rights] B. Spring. *Christ Today* 31:34-5 F 6 '87

Iran

Holy terror [persecution of Bahais] F. M. Bordewich. il *Atlantic* 259:26+ Ap '87

Soviet Union

A new Russian revolution? *America* 157:371 N 21 '87

Taking a firm stand against faith [growing population of Muslims] R. N. Ostling. il *Time* 129:60 Ja 12 '87

Religious life *See* Christian life; Spiritual life

Religious literature

See also

Booksellers and bookselling—Religious literature

Christian literature

Publishers and publishing—Religious literature

Religion—Bibliography

Translators and translating

Edith Piaf among the pygmies [importance of translation in the passage of ideas from one civilization to another]; tr. by Helen R. Lane. O. Paz. il *N Y Times Book Rev* 92:1+ S 6 '87

Religious meditation *See* Meditation

Religious music

See also

Gospel music

Hymns

Andrew Lloyd Webber: from Superstar to Requiem [cover story; interview] D. Polkow. il por *Christ Century* 104:272-6 Mr 18-25 '87

Banjo and guitar picker John Michael Talbot gave up rock for a new role as a musical monk. C. A. Azizian. il pors *People Wkly* 27:145-6 Je 8 '87

The Big Singing [annual gathering in Benton, Ky. to sing from the Southern harmony songbook] W. White. il *New Yorker* 62:78-84+ Ja 19 '87

From songs of protest to hymns of praise [J. M. Talbot] L. K. Cook. por *Christ Century* 104:279-80+ Mr 18-25 '87

Rachmaninoff's lost chords [A. Antolini's quest for church choral piece] D. Neff. il pors *Christ Today* 31:63-4 D 11 '87

Religious news

See also

Church and the press

1987 and beyond. il *Christ Today* 31:41-3 Ja 16 '87

Cory Aquino: religious newsmaker no. 1. D. Peerman. *Christ Century* 104:3-4 Ja 7-14 '87

Debating school-based clinics and freemasonry. *Christ Today* 31:53-4 S 4 '87

A disturbing year past [1986] M. E. Marty. *Christ Century* 104:39 Ja 7-14 '87

Events and people. See issues of The Christian Century

My editorial governor. M. E. Marty. *Christ Century* 104:671 Jl 29-Ag 5 '87

Of many things [Catholic news events of 1987] G. W. Hunt. *America* 157:490 D 26 '87

Swaggart column nixed [Baton Rouge advocate charges plagiarism] *Christ Century* 104:552 Je 17-24 '87

The televangelist fiasco: top '87 religion story. *Christ Century* 104:1163-5 D 23-30 '87

There's no business like soul business. L. Cryderman. *Christ Today* 31:15 N 6 '87

The top 10 stories of 1987; Looking to 1988 and beyond. R. Frame. il *Christ Today* 31:34-6+ D 11 '87

The top ten stories of 1986. R. Frame. il *Christ Today* 31:38-9+ Ja 16 '87

Religious newspapers and periodicals

See also

Christian century (Periodical)

Christian Science monitor

Christianity today (Periodical)

Religious orders

See also

Communauté de Taizé

Franciscans

Jesuits

Religious psychology *See* Psychology, Religious

Religious radio programs *See* Radio broadcasting—Religious programs

Religious schools *See* Church schools

Religious societies

See also

Evangelical Theological Society

Religious television programs *See* Television broadcasting—Religious programs

Religious thought

See also

Puritans and puritanism

Religious tolerance *See* Religious liberty

Religious vocation *See* Vocation in religion

Relishes *See* Pickles and relishes

REM (Rapid eye movement) sleep *See* Sleep

Remainders (Books)

See also

Booksellers and bookselling—Remainders

Bridging the gap [publishers paying authors royalties on remainders] J. F. Baker. *Publ Wkly* 231:10 Mr 27 '87

Remarriage

See also

Stepparents and stepchildren

How to avoid "rerun" of failed first marriage [views of Susan Regas] il *USA Today (Periodical)* 115:1-2 Ap '87

"Memories are wrecking our marriage". L. Duncan. il *Ladies Home J* 104:10+ Ja '87

Now the bell for round two [second weddings] G. Waggoner. il *Esquire* 108:30 Ag '87

Reconciliation, remarriage: the trauma continues [children's behavior; study by D. M. Fergusson] P. Nicholas. *Psychol Today* 21:11 Ja '87

The special stresses of second marriages. B. Wein. *Redbook* 169:100-1+ Je '87

Remarriage—*cont.*

Writer Marjorie Holmes celebrates a marriage made in heaven and set to words and music in Pittsburgh. K. McMurran. il pors *People Wkly* 28:115-16+ N 2 '87

Your first, his second. M. A. Kellogg. *Harpers Bazaar* 120:138-9+ Jl '87

Remas, Theodora A.

Keeping guayabera cool. il *Américas* 39:32-7 Ja/F '87

Rembar, Charles

Debunking the 'reasonable man' rule. por *Publ Wkly* 231:16 Je 26 '87

Rembrandt Group Ltd.

An Afrikaans insider questions the system [industrialist J. Rupert] S. Mufson. il por *Bus Week* p80+ My 18 '87

Rembrandt Harmenszoon van Rijn, 1606-1669

about

Rembrandt: the unvarnished truth? [cover story] S. Hochfield. il pors *Art News* 86:102-11 D '87

'A wonderful, haunting picture'. R. W. Walker. il *Art News* 86:17 F '87

Tomb

Bones of contention. A. Steacy. por *Macleans* 100:66-7 D 7 '87

Remedial teaching

Life in remedial English: learning about teaching and learning [writing course at the City University of New York] L. Forstall. *Phi Delta Kappan* 68:796-7 Je '87

The realities of teaching remedial English in college. R. C. Reynolds. *Educ Dig* 52:58-60 F '87

Remer, Jane

Quo vadis arts education: a national agenda. *Des Arts Educ* 89:38-40 N/D '87

Remington, Robin Alison

Nation versus class in Yugoslavia. bibl f *Curr Hist* 86:365-8+ N '87

Remington Arms Co., Inc.

The charge of the green brigade [new guns] B. Brister. il *Field Stream* 91:99-101 Mr '87

Reminiscence Centre (London, England)

Articles of association: the Reminiscence Centre. T. Aldous. il *Hist Today* 37:61-2 D '87

Remnick, David

Fighting lady. il pors *Sports Illus* 66:62-6+ F 2 '87

Good news is no news. il pors *Esquire* 108:156-8+ O '87

Reggie at sunset. il pors *Esquire* 107:128-30+ Je '87

Still on the outside. il pors *Sports Illus* 67:44-7+ O 5 '87

True-life adventures of H. Ross Perot. por *Read Dig* 131:165-6+ S '87

Remodeled attics *See* Attics, Remodeled

Remodeled automobiles *See* Automobiles, Remodeled

Remodeled basements *See* Basements, Remodeled

Remodeled four wheel drive vehicles *See* Four wheel drive vehicles—Remodeled vehicles

Remodeled garages *See* Garages, Remodeled

Remodeled helicopters *See* Helicopters, Remodeled

Remodeled mills *See* Mills, Remodeled

Remodeled motorcycles *See* Motorcycles, Remodeled

Remodeled trucks *See* Trucks, Remodeled

Remodeling (Architecture)

See also

Apartments, Remodeled

Buildings, Remodeled

Houses, Remodeled

School buildings, Remodeled

Remorse *See* Repentance

Remote control

See also

Audio-visual equipment—Control

Camera shutters—Control

Computers—Control use

Garage doors—Control

Radio receivers—Control

Remotely piloted vehicles

Television receivers—Control

The automated house. P. Langdon. il *Atlantic* 260:93-6 O '87

Build a trainable infrared master controller. S. Ciarcia. il *Byte* 12:113-23 Mr '87

Build an infrared remote controller. S. Ciarcia. il *Byte* 12:101-10 F '87

Butler in a box [Butler-In-A-Box voice-recognition system] J. Schefter. il *Pop Sci* 230:62 Mr '87

A DTMF receiver [dual tone multi-frequency receiver] R. Grossblatt. il *Radio-Electron* 58:82-3 Mr '87

The home of the future. J. Seisler. il *Consum Res Mag* 70:34-7 F '87

The home of the future [Smart House] D. J. MacFadyen. il *Radio-Electron* 58:115-17 My '87

Houses with high IQs. P. E. Godwin. il *Changing Times* 41:103-4 S '87

Magic wand [RC-AV1 Unifier] S. A. Booth. il *Pop Mech* 164:46 Jl '87

The new unified remote controls. J. Cohen. il *Consum Res Mag* 70:29-30 D '87

Onkyo Unifier universal programmable remote control. il *Radio-Electron* 58:22-3+ S '87

An output decoder [DTMF transmitter-receiver] R. Grossblatt. il *Radio-Electron* 58:76-8 Ap '87

Phonlink interactive remote control (I). G. Roseth. il *Radio-Electron* 58:39-41 My '87

Phonlink interactive remote control (II). G. Roseth. il *Radio-Electron* 58:53-7 Je '87

Remote-control transmitter [DTMF system] R. Grossblatt. il *Radio-Electron* 58:82-4 Ja '87

Remote possibilities [all-in-one wireless remote controls] J. B. Meigs. il *Roll Stone* p155 Ap 23 '87

The smart house. il *Futurist* 21:52-3 S/O '87

SMT project: I-R remote on a keychain [surface-mount technology] F. M. Mims. il *Radio-Electron* 58:77-9 N '87

Remote control manipulators *See* Manipulators (Mechanism)

Remote sensing

See also

Artificial satellites—Earth sciences use

Artificial satellites—Oceanographic use

Geologist's hammer is joined by spectrometers [work of Gregg Vane] R. A. Kerr. *Science* 236:1625 Je 26 '87

Heirs to ancient air [plan to study sealed Egyptian crypt; cover story] R. Monastersky. il *Sci News* 132:172-3 S 12 '87

New tools for an ancient dig [pharaoh's wooden bark observed in sealed chamber at Great Pyramid at Giza] W. D. Marbach. il *Newsweek* 110:80-1 N 2 '87

On the edge between water and ice [Marginal Ice Zone Experiment] R. Monastersky. il *Sci News* 131:280 My 2 '87

Pharaoh's boat found in ancient pit. R. Monastersky. *Sci News* 132:295 N 7 '87

Probing the chambers of Cheops [video camera reveals wooden boat inside Great Pyramid] D. S. Jackson. il *Time* 130:75 N 2 '87

A quest for ancient Egyptian air [use of remote sensing in archeological investigation] C. Holden. il *Science* 236:1419-20 Je 12 '87

Remote sensing of the Fram Strait marginal ice zone. R. A. Shuchman and others. bibl f il *Science* 236:429-31 Ap 24 '87

They didn't carry out the trash [use of remote sensing to locate hut remains in Valley Forge National Historical Park; work of Jay Parrish] R. Monastersky. *Sci News* 132:319 N 14 '87

Remote viewing (Psychic ability) *See* Extrasensory perception

Remotely piloted vehicle engines

Nozzles

Israelis flight test jet-powered RPV fitted with thrust-vectoring nozzles. *Aviat Week Space Technol* 126:21 My 18 '87

Remotely piloted vehicles

Bell/Boeing team developing tilt-rotor Pointer RPV. B. M. Greeley, Jr. il *Aviat Week Space Technol* 126:58-9 Mr 9 '87

Can a plane fly forever? [microwave aircraft] M. Rogers. il *Newsweek* 110:42+ S 28 '87

Congressional pressure prompts order to revive anti-radar drone [Seek Spinner program] J. D. Morrocco. il *Aviat Week Space Technol* 127:84-5 Ag 3 '87

Expendable defenses [special section] il *Aviat Week Space Technol* 127:22-5 S 21 '87

Grumman refining naval multimission RPV concept [shipborne, vertical takeoff and landing remotely piloted vehicle] S. W. Kandebo. il *Aviat Week Space Technol* 126:117-18+ My 11 '87

International RPVs and drones [tables] il *Aviat Week Space Technol* 126:178 Mr 9 '87

The little airplane that could [Navy Pioneer mini-RPV based on Israel's Mastiff] P. Hellman. il *Discover* 8:78-87 F '87

Northrop mid-range RPV contender stresses operational flexibility [NV-144R remotely piloted vehicle] B. A. Smith. il *Aviat Week Space Technol* 126:326-7 Je 15 '87

A ride on Voyager's tail [drone aircraft designed for California Microwave Inc. by Burt Rutan] G. G. Marcial. *Bus Week* p117 Ja 12 '87

Remotely piloted vehicles—*cont.*
Skepticism, joint needs block larger role for RPVs. B. M. Greeley, Jr. il *Aviat Week Space Technol* 126:21-2 Je 1 '87
Stealthy robot planes [cover story] J. Schefter. il *Pop Sci* 231:64-8+ O '87
U.S. RPVs & drones [tables] il *Aviat Week Space Technol* 126:176-7 Mr 9 '87
USAF seeks new RPVs by 1993. J. D. Morrocco. *Aviat Week Space Technol* 126:17-18 F 16 '87

Optical equipment
Marines' remotely operated device will use aerial fiber-optic link. il *Aviat Week Space Technol* 126:73 F 2 '87

Recovery
Developmental Sciences tests parafoil recovery on Skyeye RPV. il *Aviat Week Space Technol* 126:92 Je 1 '87

Testing
Companies testing Long-EZ derivative for unmanned aerial vehicle market [California Microwave CM-44 designed by Burt Rutan] W. B. Scott. il *Aviat Week Space Technol* 126:128+ Ap 27 '87
Lockheed prepares Altair RPV for initial test flight. S. W. Kandebo. il *Aviat Week Space Technol* 127:63-5 Jl 20 '87
Navy begins final testing of Pioneer short-range RPV. J. D. Morrocco. *Aviat Week Space Technol* 127:93+ S 14 '87
Navy plans operational trials for Amber RPV in 1989. J. D. Morrocco. il *Aviat Week Space Technol* 127:25-6 D 14 '87
New vehicles mark Teledyne Ryan's strong return to RPV business. B. A. Smith. il *Aviat Week Space Technol* 127:53+ N 30 '87
Questions over operational tests delay Aquila production decision. *Aviat Week Space Technol* 127:20-1 O 19 '87
Soaring into history [microwave flight project] M. Gray. il *Macleans* 100:45 O 19 '87
Teledyne Ryan will begin testing long-duration RPV this month. B. A. Smith. il *Aviat Week Space Technol* 127:117+ O 12 '87

Egypt
New vehicles mark Teledyne Ryan's strong return to RPV business. B. A. Smith. il *Aviat Week Space Technol* 127:53+ N 30 '87

Israel
Israelis flight test jet-powered RPV fitted with thrust-vectoring nozzles. *Aviat Week Space Technol* 126:21 My 18 '87
The little airplane that could [Navy Pioneer mini-RPV based on Israel's Mastiff] P. Hellman. il *Discover* 8:78-87 F '87

Italy
Italian RPV wins $16-million bid for NATO missile range service [Mirach 100/Mizar remotely piloted vehicle] J. M. Lenorovitz. il *Aviat Week Space Technol* 126:52-3 F 23 '87
Mirach 100 entered in U.S. RPV competition. il *Aviat Week Space Technol* 126:97 Ap 27 '87

Western Europe
NATO, industry groups study use of RPVs for small ships. *Aviat Week Space Technol* 127:95+ S 14 '87

Rempel, Ron
Restorative justice: does it work? *Christ Century* 104:156-7 F 18 '87

Rempel, Sylvia
about
'I was brought up for work'. por *Macleans* 100:24-5 D 28 '87

Renaissance, Harlem *See* Harlem renaissance
Renaissance revival house decoration *See* House decoration, Renaissance revival
Renamo *See* Mozambique National Resistance Movement
Renault (Automobile) *See* Automobiles, Foreign
Renault (Regie Nationale des Usines Renault)
Hard driver at the wheel [R. Levy] S. Tully. por *Fortune* 116:51 Ag 3 '87
Renault climbs off the critical list. J. Rossant. il *Bus Week* p48 S 28 '87

Rendell, Ruth, 1930-
How do you learn to write? il *Writer* 100:7-10 N '87
about
A gift of reasonable terror. D. Lehman. il por *Newsweek* 110:77 S 21 '87

Rendering, Architectural *See* Architectural drawing
Rendez-vous [film] See Motion picture reviews—Single works

Rendezvous (Space) *See* Orbital rendezvous (Space flight)
Renehan, Edward
John Burroughs—philosopher, poet, literary naturalist. il *Conservationist* 41:3-6 Ja/F '87
Renewal of the church *See* Church renewal
Renfrew, Nita M.
Who started the war? *Foreign Policy* 66:98-108 Spr '87
Renfrew, Nita M., and Blauner, Peter
How a Macy's engineer and his pals became rogue American agents. il pors *N Y* 20:102-4+ D 7 '87
Renfro, William L.
The 100th Congress [address, October 5, 1987] *Vital Speeches Day* 54:95-6 N 15 '87
Future histories: a new approach to scenarios. il por *Futurist* 21:38-41 Mr/Ap '87
Renin
Direct demonstration of macula densa-mediated renin secretion. O. Skøtt and J. P. Briggs. bibl f il *Science* 237:1618-20 S 25 '87
Rennels, Glenn D., and Shortliffe, Edward H.
Advanced computing for medicine. bibl (p184) il *Sci Am* 257:154-61 O '87
Renner, Thomas C.
about
Taking the pulse of crime. A. O'Malley. por *Publ Wkly* 231:71-2 F 6 '87
Rennie, Susan
Breast cancer prevention: a controversial new diet program. il *Ms* 15:40-51+ Ap '87
Breast cancer: when chemotherapy works. il *Ms* 16:70-4 N '87
Reno, Dawn E.
Black American musical collectibles. il *Antiques Collect Hobbies* 92:63-5 D '87
Reno (Nev.)
Hotels, motels, etc.
See also
Casinos
Renoir, Jean, 1894-1979
about
First encounters. E. Sorel and N. C. Sorel. il *Atlantic* 260:73 S '87
La vie est à nous [film] Reviews
New Repub 196:26-7 Je 1 '87. S. Kauffmann
Renouf Corporation International
A drum, a drum, Renouf doth come [raid on Benequity Holdings] H. Rudnitsky. il *Forbes* 139:146+ My 18 '87
Rensselaer Polytechnic Institute. George M. Low Center for Industrial Innovation *See* George M. Low Center for Industrial Innovation
Rent
See also
Apartments—Leasing and renting
Farm rents
Houses—Leasing and renting
Landlord and tenant
Taxation
Real estate: still a hands-on affair. M. Schiffres. il *Changing Times* 41:43+ N '87
Tough new rules for rental real estate. R. Micheli. il *Money* 16:193-4+ Ap '87
Rent-A-Center, Inc.
Lender of last resort. D. Henry. por *Forbes* 139:73+ My 18 '87
Rent control *See* Rent laws
Rent laws
Rent stabilization: knowing your rights [New York City] J. Goldman. *N Y* 20:34 Je 22 '87
Where do the homeless come from? [rent control] W. Tucker. il *Natl Rev* 39:32+ S 25 '87
Rent stabilization laws *See* Rent laws
Rent subsidies
Housing solutions sought as federal subsidy agreements run out [projects that owners will have option of taking onto open market] J. Trewhitt. il *Archit Rec* 175:35 O '87
Renting of apartments *See* Apartments—Leasing and renting
Renting of automobiles *See* Automobiles—Leasing and renting
Renton, Paul
Electronic combination lock. il *Radio-Electron* 58:107-8+ N '87
Rentschler, Frederick B.
about
Getting top dollar for Beatrice's leftovers. L. Therrien. il por *Bus Week* p50-1 Jl 6 '87
Rentz, Mark D.
Diplomats in our backyard. por *Newsweek* 109:10 F 16 '87

Renwick Gallery
The contemporary crafts movement has come of age, and at the Renwick Gallery its prospects have never been brighter. R. M. Adams. *Smithsonian* 17:12 Ja '87

Reodica, Eminiano
about
Road to riches: cars for immigrants. J. Foote. il por *Newsweek* 110:48 S 7 '87

Reorganization of corporations *See* Corporations—Reorganization

Repair shops
See also
Automobile service stations

Repairing
See also
Electric lamps—Repairing
Houses—Maintenance and repair
Patching materials
Repairs improve your garden spirit. R. Rodale. il *Rodale's Org Gard* 34:14-15 My '87

Repairmen
See also
Camera repairmen

Reparation
See also
Son of Sam laws

Repatriation

El Salvador

Salvadoran developments [repatriation of refugees] *Christ Century* 104:994 N 11 '87

Repensek, Tom
(tr) *See* Daix, Pierre. Picasso's time of decisive encounters

Repentance
See also
Penance
The loving penance of Hu Bo [caring for former teacher after Cultural Revolution; condensed from After the nightmare] H. Liang and J. Shapiro. il *Read Dig* 130:104-9 Ap '87

Repentance [film] *See* Motion picture reviews—Single works

Replacements (Musical group)
Meet the misfits. D. Fricke. il *Roll Stone* p51-2 Jl 2 '87

Replication of viruses *See* Viruses—Reproduction

Report on America [television program] *See* Television program reviews—Single works

Reporters and reporting
See also
Afghanistan—Russian invasion, 1979- —Reporters and reporting
AIDS (Disease) and the press
Black journalists
Cable television—News
Challenger (Space shuttle) explosion, 1986—Reporters and reporting
Confidential communications—Press
Crime and the press
Environmental news
Foreign correspondents
Government and the press
Greece—History—Civil War, 1944-1949—Reporters and reporting
Holocaust, Jewish (1939-1945)—Reporters and reporting
Howard Beach case—Reporters and reporting
Interviewing
Iran-contra affair—Reporters and reporting
Iranian-Iraqi War, 1980- —Reporters and reporting
John Paul II, Pope, 1920- —Visit to the United States, 1987—Reporters and reporting
Journalists
Lebanon hostage cases, 1984- —Reporters and reporting
Libyan-American conflict, 1986—Reporters and reporting
Muckraking
News
Newspaper court reporting
Press and disarmament
Press and feminism
Press and politics
Radio broadcasting—News
Reagan-Gorbachev summit conference, 1987—Reporters and reporting
Space flight—Shuttle missions—Reporters and reporting
Sports journalism
Stark (Warship)—Iraqi missile attack, 1987—Reporters and reporting

Stock market crash, 1987—Reporters and reporting
Strikes—Television news
Television broadcasting—News
Terrorism and the press
United States—History—Civil War, 1861-1865—Reporters and reporting
Vietnamese War, 1957-1975—Reporters and reporting
Wine journalism
World War, 1939-1945—Reporters and reporting

Reports
See also
Corporation reports
Financial statements
Student themes and reports

Repos *See* Repurchase agreements

Reppert, Bertha
Caraway thyme. il *Rodale's Org Gard* 34:63 Jl '87
Costmary. il *Rodale's Org Gard* 34:55 D '87
Sweet cicely. il *Rodale's Org Gard* 34:32 Je '87

Representative government and representation
See also
Democracy
Proportional representation

Representatives, Congressional *See* Congressmen

Repression (Psychology)
Suppress now, obsess later [thought suppression; study by Daniel M. Wegner] J. F. Neath. il *Psychol Today* 21:10 D '87

Reprints, Unauthorized *See* Copyright infringement

Reproduction
See also
Artificial insemination, Human
Conception
Conjugation (Biology)
Embryology
Fertilization (Biology)
Fertilization in vitro
Fetus
Fish—Reproduction
Infertility
Insects—Reproduction
Menstruation
Parthenogenesis
Plants—Reproduction
Sea urchins—Reproduction
Sex determination and control
Spawning
Spontaneous generation
Viruses—Reproduction
Viviparity
The genetic effect. C. Marshall. *Vogue* 177:404+ O '87
The poisoned womb [views of John Elkington] *Futurist* 21:55 My/Je '87
Reproductive rights for today. L. Gordon. il *Nation* 245:230-2 S 12 '87
Surrogate motherhood and medical alternatives for childless couples. Z. Stern. *USA Today (Periodical)* 116:70-1 N '87

Caricatures and cartoons
Cartoonists take a look at reproductive technology. il *Christ Today* 31:56 N 20 '87

Moral and religious aspects
Diagnosing the Vatican 'Instruction' [Instruction on respect for human life in its origin and on the dignity of procreation] J. C. Harvey. *Commonweal* 114:238-9 Ap 24 '87
The ethics of human manufacture [Vatican document on artificial forms of procreation; cover story] C. Krauthammer. *New Repub* 196:17-21 My 4 '87
Is there a wrong way to make babies? [viewpoint of Catholic Church] M. Orth. il *Glamour* 85:272-3+ O '87
Lovemaking & babymaking. S. Callahan. il *Commonweal* 114:233-9 Ap 24 '87
Procreation, science and sin [Catholic Church pronouncement] J. Carey. il *U S News World Rep* 102:10 Mr 23 '87
Religious leaders respond to the Vatican's ban on artificial conception [Instruction on respect for human life in its origin and on the dignity of procreation] B. Spring. il *Christ Today* 31:41-2 Ap 17 '87
Roma locuta [Vatican's statement on issues of artificial reproduction] *Natl Rev* 39:19-20 Je 19 '87
Rules for making love and babies [Vatican pronouncement] K. L. Woodward. il *Newsweek* 109:42-3 Mr 23 '87
Taking it on the chin—for life: reflections on a Vatican instruction [On respect for human life and its origin and on the dignity of procreation] D. E. Pilarczyk. *America* 156:295-6 Ap 11 '87

Reproduction—Moral and religious aspects—*cont.*
Technology and the womb [Catholic Church denounces advances in reproductive technology] R. N. Ostling. il *Time* 129:58-9 Mr 23 '87
The Vatican and bioethics [interview with J. Ratzinger] H. Tincq. *World Press Rev* 34:58 Jl '87
The Vatican document on bioethics: two responses [with editorial comment] L. S. Cahill; R. A. McCormick. *America* 156:245-8 Mr 28 '87
The Vatican weighs in. C. Holden. *Science* 235:1455 Mr 20 '87
Vatican't. H. Hertzberg. *New Repub* 196:42 Ap 6 '87
What comes naturally [Vatican's Instruction on respect for human life in its origin and on the dignity of procreation] *Commonweal* 114:163-4 Mr 27 '87
What is sex for? [Vatican statement on human reproduction] S. Grenz. il por *Christ Today* 31:22-3 Je 12 '87

Reproduction, Asexual
See also
Clones (Biology)
Reproduction of photographs *See* Photography—Copying
Reproductions of American furniture *See* Furniture, American—Reproductions
Reproductions of works of art *See* Art—Reproductions
Reproductive organs
See also
Ovaries
Testicles
Vagina
Animals
Runaway sexual selection [diversity of male genitalia] W. G. Eberhard. *Nat Hist* 96:4+ D '87
Diseases
Women's medical tests: what your doctor may not tell you. P. Gadsby. il *Good Housekeep* 205:239-40 N '87
Surgery
See also
Sterilization reversal
The gentlest cut of all [gynecological laser surgery] J. Wilson. *Health* 19:57-8+ O '87
Husbands for safe blood [transfusions in the OB/GYN departments] C. SerVaas. il *Saturday Evening Post* 259:82+ N '87
Reproductive technology *See* Reproduction
Reptiles
See also
Age—Reptiles
Alligators
Iguanas
Lizards
Snakes
Turtles
Ecology
Suburban "hotbeds of sexual diversity" [New England reptile microhabitat study by M. Klemens] B. D. Stutz. il *Nat Hist* 96:80-3 S '87
Eggs
Cracks in the egg theory [turtles] *Sci News* 132:24 Jl 11 '87
Egg thieves of Playa Grande [leatherback turtle eggs] R. Hamm. il map *Sea Front* 33:27-33 Ja/F '87
Habits and behavior
See also
Sexual behavior—Reptiles
Reptiles, Fossil
See also
Dinosaurs
Pterosaurs
Avascular necrosis: occurrence in diving Cretaceous mosasaurs. B. Rothschild and L. D. Martin. bibl f il *Science* 236:75-7 Ap 3 '87
Before the dinosaurs [reconstruction of Placerias skeleton; work of R. A. Long] B. Weber. il pors *N Y Times Mag* p66 Ag 23 '87
Flying high on a basement fossil find [ichthyosaurs] *Sci News* 131:106 F 14 '87
Republic (Steamship)
Romancing the wreck. W. G. Flanagan. il *Forbes* 140:116 S 7 '87
Republic Pictures Corporation
Republic flies again [R. Goldsmith] L. Gubernick. il por *Forbes* 140:248 D 14 '87
Republican National Committee
The GOP's black eye [ballot integrity program backfires] H. Klingeman. *Natl Rev* 39:31 Ja 30 '87
Republican Party (U.S.)
A bad case of foot-in-mouth disease is alarming the Texas GOP [Governor W. P. Clements] T. Mason. por *Bus Week* p39 Ag 31 '87

Beware of Republicans bearing voting rights suits. M. Cooper. *Wash Mon* 19:11-15 F '87
Faithful on the move [P. Robertson supporters in Iowa] T. J. Curry. il *Commonweal* 114:727-9 D 18 '87
Fat and sassy. R. Kuttner. *New Repub* 196:21-3 F 23 '87
Going after white males [the South] T. Jacoby. il *Newsweek* 110:38+ S 14 '87
The gold mine is playing out [direct mail fund raising] J. Novack. il *Forbes* 139:146+ Ap 6 '87
The GOP smells more than gumbo in Louisiana [governorship up for grabs] R. Fly. il por *Bus Week* p56 O 26 '87
'A hard hit' for the Grand Old Party [effects of stock market crash] G. Borger. il *U S News World Rep* 103:24 N 2 '87
How to win in '88: meld the unmeldable. N. J. Ornstein. il *U S News World Rep* 103:31-2+ O 12 '87
Iran and the GOP. J. McLaughlin. *Natl Rev* 39:24 My 22 '87
Labels can be misleading [study by Warren E. Miller and M. Kent Jennings] il *USA Today (Periodical)* 116:12 D '87
Letter from Washington [campaign coffers] Cato. *Natl Rev* 39:13 Jl 31 '87
Life after the Red menace [conservatives' split] G. Borger. il *U S News World Rep* 103:41-2 D 21 '87
No more Mr. Nice guys [Senate Republicans] H. Klingeman. *Natl Rev* 39:40-1 Jl 17 '87
Rebuilding the parties [address, April 7, 1987] R. J. Dole. *Vital Speeches Day* 53:482-4 Je 1 '87
Red-baiting Ron [conservative criticism of INF Treaty] *Nation* 245:739-40 D 19 '87
A Republican looks at foreign policy. R. G. Lugar. *Foreign Aff* 66:249-62 Wint '87/'88
Senate minority could imperil treaty [arms control] J. D. Isaacs. il *Bull At Sci* 43:5-6 S '87
State-loving in the G.O.P. W. F. Buckley. *Natl Rev* 39:62 D 18 '87
When right isn't right. M. Greenfield. il *Newsweek* 109:88 My 4 '87
Where's the beef? [cover story] M. Kondracke. *New Repub* 197:16-18+ Jl 6 '87
Republican presidential candidates *See* Presidential candidates
Repurchase agreements
So you thought you'd seen the last of tax straddles [fraudulent repo straddles] D. Zigas. il por *Bus Week* p90 Je 15 '87
Repurchase of stocks *See* Stocks—Repurchase
Reputation
Choose wisely [address, August 14, 1987] B. Chiodo. *Vital Speeches Day* 54:40-2 N 1 '87
Requiems
See also
Compact discs—Requiems
Reruns, Syndicated *See* Television broadcasting—Syndicated programs
Res publica (Periodical)
Another country. A. Applebaum. *New Repub* 197:12-13 Ag 24 '87
Coming up from underground. J. Dobija. *Progressive* 51:13 N '87
Resale trade *See* Secondhand trade
Resch, Chico
about
Chico Resch. S. Fischler. il por *Sport Mag* 78:94-5 D '87
Rescue work
See also
Artificial satellites—Rescue work use
First aid in illness and injury
Helicopters in rescue work
Seals (Animals) in rescue work
United States. Coast Guard
19 hours in "Devil's Icebox" [rescue of D. Easter, pinned by boulder in Missouri mine] S. Kelly. il *Read Dig* 131:60-6 Ag '87
Alone in the shark-filled sea [W. Wyatt adrift after small plane crashes] P. Michelmore. il *Read Dig* 131:116-21 O '87
Baby Jessica [rescued from well] il por *People Wkly* 28:34-5 D 28 '87-Ja 4 '88
Boy, 9, clad in underwear, rescues 6 sisters, brothers from fire on 22-degree night [L. Davis] il por *Jet* 71:40 F 16 '87
A brave little girl [rescue of J. McClure from well in Midland, Tex.] G. Hackett. il por *Newsweek* 110:41 O 26 '87

Rescue work—*cont.*

Burning alive! [C. Marsh saves S. Moses from farm accident electrocution] S. Kelly. il *Read Dig* 131:95-9 S '87

Chain of circumstance [children saved from cold water drowning in Westbrook, Conn.] P. O. D'Aulaire and E. D'Aulaire. il *Read Dig* 131:143-8 D '87

The epic rescue of Jessica McClure [child removed from well; cover story] L. Hart and A. Maier. il pors *People Wkly* 28:42-7 N 2 '87

Five-year-old Rocky Lyons, son of the Jets' star, thought he could save his mom's life—and he did [traffic accident rescue] R. Arias. il pors *People Wkly* 28:169-70 D 14 '87

Girl, 12, rescued from freezing Philly sand pit [S. Bonelli] il por *Jet* 71:18 Mr 23 '87

Grain-bin 'lifeguards' [farm accidents] C. Tevis. il *Success Farm* 85:62R-62S O '87

"Help! My baby is drowning!"; ed. by Elaine Fein. C. Garcia. il por *Redbook* 169:26+ Je '87

Inferno on the interstate [fireman J. P. Sullivan saves five victims of traffic accident] S. Kelly. il *Read Dig* 130:106-11 Ja '87

Lost at sea [surviving a plane crash off Haiti] F. B. Randall. il pors map *N Y* 20:36-43 Ag 10 '87

A miraculous sky rescue [G. Robertson rescues fellow skydiver] il por *Time* 129:26 My 4 '87

Niagara rapids rescue [1918 breeches buoy rescue] *Sea Front* 33:145-6 Mr/Ap '87

One went right [rescue of J. McClure from Texas well] W. Shapiro. il pors *Time* 130:30-1 O 26 '87

Rescue in midair! [G. Robertson saves free-falling parachutist D. Williams] P. O. D'Aulaire and E. D'Aulaire. il *Read Dig* 131:100-5 N '87

Saving the babies [J. McClure rescued from a well in Midland, Tex.] il por *Macleans* 100:49 O 26 '87

Survival at sea [plane crash off Haiti] A. Randall. il por map *Seventeen* 46:108-9+ D '87

Research

See also

Advertising research
Agricultural research
Animal experimentation
Astronomical research
Aviation research
Biological research
Botanical research
Communication in science
Computers—Scientific use
Educational research
Environmental research
Genetic research industry
Historical research
Industrial research
Literary research
Market research
Materials research
Mathematical research
Medical research
Military research
National Science Foundation (U.S.)
Nuclear research
Pharmaceutical research
Psychiatric research
Psychological research
Sex research
Social science research

See also subhead Research under various subjects

Applied research: key to innovation. A. M. Clogston. bibl f *Science* 235:12-13 Ja 2 '87

Replies to progress [discussion of April 1986 article, Scientific progress: an interim report] D. E. Chubin. *BioScience* 37:108-9 F '87

Tips for readers of research [questionable bulimia statistics lead to warning to be wary of any research results] G. W. Bracey. il *Phi Delta Kappan* 69:236-7 N '87

Anecdotes, facetiae, satire, etc.

The DNA dragon 1. D. E. Koshland, Jr. *Science* 237:1397 S 18 '87

Ethical aspects

Doctored data [scientific fraud] *Sci Am* 256:68-9 Ap '87

Fraud in science. D. E. Koshland, Jr. *Science* 235:141 Ja 9 '87

Publish or perish—or fake it [scientists' publication of fraudulent data] D. S. Greenberg. il *U S News World Rep* 102:72-3 Je 8 '87

Scientists and lawyers look at fraud in science. J. Wrather. *Science* 238:813-14 N 6 '87

Tempests in a test tube. S. Begley. il *Newsweek* 109:64 F 2 '87

Federal aid

See also

Colleges and universities—Research—Federal aid
Research grants

Big versus little science in the federal budget. E. Marshall. il *Science* 236:249 Ap 17 '87

Budget details released. C. Norman. il *Science* 235:628 F 6 '87

A dose of reality for Reagan's science spree? E. Clark. il *Bus Week* p76 D 14 '87

FY 1988 budget: a predictable proposal. L. Tangley. il *BioScience* 37:251-6 Ap '87

FY '88 budget: scant details on proposed increases. J. Raloff. il *Sci News* 131:20-1 Ja 10 '87

Gramm-Rudman-Hollings strikes back. M. Crawford. *Science* 238:604 O 30 '87

R&D enriched by 1988 budget but science policy impoverished. I. Goodwin. il *Phys Today* 40:59-65 My '87

Research opportunities. *Futurist* 21:48 Ja/F '87

Science budget: more of the same. C. Norman. *Science* 235:151-3 Ja 9 '87

Science budgets fare well in House action. M. Crawford. *Science* 237:22 Jl 3 '87

Science budgets get lift from Senate. M. Crawford. *Science* 238:151 O 9 '87

A science tax on information? *Sci News* 131:57 Ja 24 '87

International aspects

America's seductive charms. D. Dickson. *Science* 237:1107 S 4 '87

Europe

Europe ends at the Iron Curtain: most "European" cooperation is strictly West European. D. Dickson. *Science* 237:1114 S 4 '87

Great Britain

The decline of the British science empire. R. Williams. il *Bull At Sci* 43:45-8 O '87

U.K. lifts veto on plans for EEC [Framework Program] D. Dickson. *Science* 237:126 Jl 10 '87

U.K. science: survival of the fittest—or fattest? D. Dickson. il *Science* 236:512-13 My 1 '87

Japan

Japan's inscrutable research budget. M. Sun. il *Science* 238:22 O 2 '87

Soviet Union

Soviet research to be self-directed. D. Dickson. *Science* 237:482 Jl 31 '87

Tibet

Science on the roof of the world. R. Lewin. il *Science* 236:910-12 My 22 '87

United States

See Research

Western Europe

See also

Eureka (Program)

EEC research program in jeopardy [Framework Program] D. Dickson. *Science* 235:158 Ja 9 '87

EEC: uniting to meet high-tech's challenge. D. Dickson. il *Science* 237:1103-4 S 4 '87

Euroscience lexicon. *Science* 237:1113 S 4 '87

Networking: better than creating new centers? D. Dickson. *Science* 237:1106-7 S 4 '87

Science and mutual self-interest. D. Dickson and C. Norman. il *Science* 237:1101-2 S 4 '87

With IT in the scientific jet set [EEC's Framework Program to promote scientific collaboration] F. Pearce. *World Press Rev* 34:55 Ja '87

Research, Freedom of *See* Science, Freedom of

Research and development *See* Industrial research; Research

Research and state *See* Research—Federal aid; Science and state

Research grants

See also

Presidential Young Investigators Awards

Howard Hughes moves into science education. B. J. Culliton. il *Science* 238:150 O 9 '87

Pilot program cuts red tape for federal grants [Florida Demonstration Project] D. Charles. *Science* 235:966 F 27 '87

Report blasts Human Development Office [report by the House Committee on Government Operations] C. Holden. *Science* 236:386-7 Ap 24 '87

Scientific philanthropy [Howard Hughes Medical Institute] T. Beardsley. *Sci Am* 257:22+ D '87

State control of universities. J. S. Fulda. *Cent Mag* 20:59 My/Je '87

Research institutions

See also

Franklin Institute (Philadelphia, Pa.)
Heritage Foundation (Washington, D.C.)

Research institutions—See also—*cont.*
    Industrial Technology Institute
    Institute for Theoretical Physics (Minn.)
    International Center for Development Policy
    International Institute for Applied Systems Analysis
    Lawrence Berkeley Laboratory
    Ortho Research Center
    SRI International
    University of Chicago. Center for Decision Research
    Urban Institute

Taxation
Hughes settles with IRS. B. J. Culliton. il *Science* 235:1318 Mr 13 '87

Canada
    See also
    Canadian Institute for Theoretical Astrophysics
    Plant Biological Institute (Canada)
Research laboratories *See* Laboratories
Research libraries
    Libraries and learning. O. Handlin. *Am Sch* 56:205-18 Spr '87
Research papers *See* Student themes and reports
Reservations, Airline *See* Airlines—Reservation systems
Reservations, Indian (American) *See* Indians of North America—Reservations
Reserve Officers' Training Corps (Navy) *See* United States. Navy. Reserve Officers' Training Corps
Reserves, Bank *See* Banks and banking—Reserves
Reserves, Helium *See* Helium—Reserves
Residences, Official *See* Official residences
Resident theater *See* Theater
Residential energy conservation *See* Energy conservation
Residential mobility *See* Migration, Internal
Residents, Medical *See* Interns (Medicine)
Resignation
    See also
    Employees—Resignation
    Executives—Resignation
    Public officers—Resignation
    Reagan, Ronald, 1911——Staff—Resignation
    Teachers—Resignation
Resignation (Psychology)
    Take this dream and shove it. M. Jacobson. il *Esquire* 108:53-4 N '87
Resistance, Bacterial *See* Bacteria—Resistance and sensitivity
Resistance to drugs *See* Drug resistance
Resistance to government *See* Government, Resistance to
Resistance to infection *See* Immunity
Resistance to pesticides *See* Pesticide resistance
Resnick, Lynda
    about
    Beaux arts in southern California. il *House Gard* 159:174-9+ D '87
Resolution (Optics)
    Across the lines [resolution of video monitors] C. Sarver. il *High Fidel* 37:55+ D '87
    Resolution results [discussion of July 1986 article, A daytime test of resolving power] R. W. Sinnott. il *Sky Telesc* 73:443 Ap '87
Resolving power (Optics) *See* Resolution (Optics)
Resonance, Magnetic *See* Magnetic resonance imaging
Resorption (Physiology) *See* Absorption (Physiology)
Resort timesharing (Real estate) *See* Timesharing (Real estate)
Resorts
    See also
    Grand Champions Resort Development Corporation
    Health resorts, watering places, etc.
    S-K-I Ltd.
    7 things to do at a ski resort. il *Glamour* 85:86 Mr '87
    The best cross-country ski havens. G. S. Bush. il *Better Homes Gard* 65:214+ N '87
    Changes of place. il *Esquire* 108:196-201 D '87
    Holiday getaways [tennis resorts] S. Stevenson. il *World Tennis* 35:48-9 D '87
    How to enjoy skiing with your kids. C. Walter. il *Skiing* 39:93-4+ Ja '87
    Mondo condo [ski area condominiums] A. H. Greenberg. *Skiing* 40:30 O '87
    See the U.S.A. [tennis resorts] B. Socolow. il *World Tennis* 35:64 Jl '87
    Skiing: all in the family. il *Saturday Evening Post* 259:66-8+ N '87
    Skiing out of a suitcase. D. P. Wiener. il *Fortune* 115:135-6+ Ja 19 '87
    Travel. S. Russell. See issues of Skiing beginning November 1985
    What's best in the ski resorts. A. Rand. il *Glamour* 85:272-5 N '87

White nights: where to ski (and après-ski) this winter. B. P. Quinby. il *Mademoiselle* 93:174+ N '87
    Environmental aspects
Cracks appear in the magic mountain [Switzerland's policy of shortchanging the mountains while favoring tourism] E. Beck. il *Sierra* 72:116-19 Ja/F '87
Hubris in the hills [ski resorts] R. Kimber. il *Ctry J* 14:52-6 Mr '87
Showdown in the Saddleback [proposal to enlarge the Saddleback Mountain ski area] il *Wilderness* 50:7+ Summ '87
    International aspects
    See also
    Club Méditerranée SA
Fit to be tried [tennis resorts offering a multi-sport experience] B. Socolow. il *World Tennis* 34:50-1 Mr '87
Hot spots for honeymooners. D. G. Salter. *Essence* 17:16+ F '87
Something for everyone [five star resorts for family vacations and tennis] B. Socolow. il *World Tennis* 35:38+ Je '87
Sunscape '87 [special section] il *Vogue* 177:286+ N '87
Winter travel. R. Reed. il *N Y* 20:54-60+ O 12 '87
    Marketing
Now Club Med wants an antidote for competition. A. Dunkin. il *Bus Week* p120-1 N 2 '87
    Public relations
The limits of '*glasnost*' [attitudes of ski areas towards publicizing avalanche dangers] A. H. Greenberg. *Skiing* 40:64-5+ N '87
    Alberta
Three by Banff [ski resorts] J. Skow. il *Skiing* 39:44-51 F '87
    Antigua (Antigua and Barbuda)
Paradise regained [Curtain Bluff Resort Hotel] E. Hunter. il *Vogue* 177:120+ Ja '87
    Argentina
August in the Andes [Valle de las Leñas] A. H. Greenberg. il *Skiing* 39:19-20 Spr '87
A summer place for skiers. G. M. Bock. il *Bus Week* p144 My 4 '87
    Arizona
Summer bargains at Tucson's desert-foothill resorts. il *Sunset* 179:35-7 Jl '87
    Australia
    See also
    Hamilton Island (Australia)
    Bahamas
There goes the neighborhood [Lyford Cay Club] R. King, Jr. il *Forbes* 140 Sp Issue:89-90+ O 26 '87
    British Columbia
Taking the pulse at Whistler. A. Fotheringham. il *Macleans* 100:56 Ja 12 '87
    British Virgin Islands
The British Virgin Islands. C. Lofting. il map *Travel Holiday* 167:38-43 Mr '87
    California
    See also
    Palm Springs (Calif.)
    Squaw Valley (Calif.)
Desert delights [tennis resorts] L.-M. Singer. il *World Tennis* 34:44-6+ Ja '87
    Canada
Boom times on the slopes [ski resorts] J. Barber. il *Macleans* 100:44 Mr 9 '87
    Caribbean region
A better place to be [tennis resorts] P. M. Coan. il *World Tennis* 35:54-6 O '87
The connoisseur's Caribbean. D. H. Dunn. il *Bus Week* p104-5 Ja 26 '87
A fabulous Caribbean season. il *Vogue* 177:288+ N '87
Island travel. L. Wolfe and J. Cecil. il *N Y* 20:64-6+ N 9 '87
Rooms with a view. il *Black Enterp* 17:51-2 My '87
    Catskill Mountains region (N.Y.)
Bungalow Colony [reunion of the East Pond Bungalow Colony] *New Yorker* 63:24-5 S 7 '87
    Colorado
    See also
    Aspen (Colo.)
    Snowmass Village (Colo.)
    Steamboat Springs (Colo.)
    Telluride (Colo.)
Downhill racers [ski resorts] J. A. Conway. il *Forbes* 139:8 Ap 20 '87
Pure Copper [Copper Mountain ski resort] A. Pospisil. il *Skiing* 40:216-20+ O '87
Purgatory [ski resort] A. H. Greenberg. il *Skiing* 39:61-4+ F '87

Resorts—Colorado—*cont.*
Ski again: a novice skier returns to the slopes [Keystone] S. Y. Lopez. il *Black Enterp* 17:144 F '87
Ski lodges that scale the heights of luxury. L. Friedland. il *Bus Week* p152 D 7 '87
Skiing the Creek [Beaver Creek] D. Ford. il *Skiing* 40:176+ N '87
Winter Park [ski resort] H. Barlow. il *Skiing* 39:46-52 Ja '87

Europe
Best buys in Europe [ski trips] C. Walter. il *Skiing* 40:196 S '87

Florida
See also
Miami Beach (Fla.)
All that Florida jazz. il *Vogue* 177:296+ N '87
Fort Wilderness: Disney World's "Hinterland". M. T. O'Keefe. il *Saturday Evening Post* 259:92-4+ Ja/F '87
Monkey Business Inc. [Turnberry Isle resort is home port to yacht made famous in G. Hart scandal] il *Newsweek* 109:48 Je 29 '87
Of the past, of the place [Seaside, Useppa Island, and Sea Oaks resorts] L. Joyner. il *South Living* 22:120-3 My '87
A slice of citrus [tennis resorts] P. M. Coan. il *World Tennis* 35:56+ N '87
Southern exposure [tennis resorts] il *World Tennis* 34:49-51 F '87
The white queen of the Gulf [Belleview Biltmore Resort and Spa, Clearwater] M. G. Stoddard. il *Saturday Evening Post* 259:94+ Ja/F '87

Florida Keys (Fla.)
The most exclusive resort in Florida [Ocean Reef] J. Clemans. il *Mot Boat Sail* 159:36-41+ Ap '87

France
See also
Val d'Isère (France)
The glamorous winter [Courchevel ski resort] R. Alleman. il *Vogue* 177:126+ Ja '87

Georgia
From summit to sea. J. A. Martin. il *Travel Holiday* 167:20+ F '87
Georgia on your mind [Sea Palms] E. Schmidt, Jr. il *World Tennis* 35:62-3 Ag '87

Hawaii
See also
Waikiki Beach (Honolulu, Hawaii)
Designer of all he surveys, Hawaii's Chris Hemmeter leis on the luxury to embellish his visions of paradise. M. Neill. il pors *People Wkly* 28:92-4 O 19 '87
Peacocks, geysers, marble stallions—Mr. Mega-Resort strikes again [C. Hemmeter] J. B. Levine. il por *Bus Week* p64-5 Mr 30 '87

Idaho
See also
Sun Valley (Idaho)

Maine
Showdown in the Saddleback [proposal to enlarge the Saddleback Mountain ski area] il *Wilderness* 50:7+ Summ '87
Sunday punch [Sunday River Ski Resort] D. Ford. il *Skiing* 40:132-4+ N '87

Mexico
See also
Acapulco (Mexico)
Mexico. P. Plawin. il *Changing Times* 41:95-8+ N '87
Villa Vera. M. Pennacchia. il *Travel Holiday* 168:8+ N '87

Montana
Big Sky ski sampler. R. C. Gildart. il *Travel Holiday* 168:26-9 N '87

New York (State)
See also
Lake Placid (N.Y.)
An Adirondack wilderness retreat [Elk Lake Lodge in North Hudson] D. G. Shekerjian. il *Travel Holiday* 168:34+ N '87

North America
Travel guide '88 [ski resorts; cover story] il *Skiing* 40:93-102+ O '87

North Carolina
Hit the slopes of North Carolina [Ski Beech] il *South Living* 22:10+ Ja '87

Pacific Northwest
Where the grizzlies go. L. S. Brady. il *Esquire* 107:33-4 Mr '87

Pacific region
Pacific perfect. il *Vogue* 177:306+ N '87

South Carolina
See also
Hilton Head Island (S.C.)

Switzerland
See also
Davos (Switzerland)
Grindelwald (Switzerland)
Gstaad (Switzerland)
Cracks appear in the magic mountain [policy of short-changing the mountains while favoring tourism] E. Beck. il *Sierra* 72:116-19 Ja/F '87

United States
See Resorts

Utah
Utah powder . . . where the locals ski. il map *Sunset* 178:56-8 F '87

Vermont
I skied Killington in March, April, May, and June. D. Ford. il *Skiing* 39:45-9 Spr '87
Journey to Jay [Jay Peak ski resort] E. Hanson. il *Skiing* 40:116-18+ D '87
A new look at Ascutney. A. H. Greenberg. il *Skiing* 39:54-7+ Ja '87
Snow job [snow making at Mt. Snow, Vt. ski resort] J. Vock. il *Skiing* 40:197-202 N '87
Stratton ho! [ski resort] L. Tejada-Flores. il *Skiing* 40:182-9 O '87

Western Europe
Skiing in Europe: the Alpine experience. L. Tejada-Flores. il *Skiing* 40:114+ O '87

Western States
A new look at ski-country real estate [with editorial comment by William Grout] K. Brizzolara. il *Skiing* 40:8, 126-7+ D '87

Wyoming
Jackson for purists [skiing] H. Barlow. il *Skiing* 40:198-202+ S '87
Jackson for tourists [skiing] P. Oliver. il *Skiing* 40:198-202+ N '87

Resorts International Inc.
Atlantic City action. L. Gubernick. il *Forbes* 139:170 F 23 '87
Atlantic City roulette [competition between M. Davis and D. Trump] J. Crudele. il pors *N Y* 20:24 My 18 '87
Donald Trump gets a $200 million Christmas gift [contract to manage Resorts International Atlantic City casino approved by New Jersey Casino Control Commission] L. J. Tell and S. Benway. il por *Bus Week* p76 D 28 '87-Ja 4 '88
He who eats last . . . [D. Trump and Tweedy, Browne buy interests in Resorts International] R. Phalon. il por *Forbes* 140:130+ D 14 '87

Resource management *See* Conservation of resources
Resource recovery *See* Recycling (Waste, etc.)
Resources, Conservation of *See* Conservation of resources
Resources, Natural *See* Natural resources
Respiration
See also
Apnea
Asphyxia
Breathing exercises
Vital signs [radar detection of heartbeat and breathing] *Sci Am* 256:69-70 Ja '87

Respirators
Don't pollute yourself: wear the right protective mask. A. Rooze. il *Fam Handyman* 37:8+ Mr '87

Respiratory distress syndrome

Therapy
Baby lung lube [pulmonary surfactants; work of T. Allen Merritt] O. Davies. il *Health* 19:19 Mr '87
Respiratory equipment *See* Oxygen equipment
Respiratory organs
See also
Lungs

Diseases
See also
Asthma
Cold (Disease)
Emphysema
Influenza
Legionnaires' disease
Lungs—Diseases
Pneumonia
Respiratory distress syndrome
Sinusitis

Respite care
Respite care: help goes both ways [church programs] J. B. Gehret. *Christ Century* 104:76-7 Ja 28 '87
Response, Frequency (Electric engineering) *See* Frequency response (Electric engineering)
Responsibility
See also
Assistance in emergencies

Responsibility—*cont.*

Abortion and his responsibility. C. L. Mithers. *Glamour* 85:180 Jl '87

Change what you can change [excerpt from Feel the fear and do it anyway] S. Jeffers. *Redbook* 168:82-3+ F '87

Easy consciences on Wall Street. J. M. Wall. *Christ Century* 104:179-80 F 25 '87

Raising a responsible child. C. Berman. il *Parents* 62:110-12+ O '87

A sense of responsibility [adolescents] J. P. Comer. il *Parents* 62:269 N '87

Taking your hide to the market [personal responsibility] H. Fehren. *U S Cathol* 52:41-3 Mr '87

Anecdotes, facetiae, satire, etc.

I was absent that day. K. Fury. il *Work Woman* 12:176 S '87

Responsibility (Corporate) *See* Business—Social aspects

Responsibility (Law) *See* Liability (Law)

Rest

See also
Bed rest
Relaxation
Sleep

Rest rooms *See* Public comfort stations

Restak, Richard M., 1942-

Glut responses. *Vogue* 177:325+ Ag '87

Restaurant critics and criticism *See* Food critics and criticism

Restaurant de la Tour Eiffel (New Orleans, La.) *See* New Orleans (La.)—Restaurants, nightclubs, bars, etc.

Restaurant decoration

"21" plus [Manhattan restaurant redecorated by C. Pfister] M. Filler. il *House Gard* 159:24+ S '87

For adults only [designer A. Tihany] D. Shaw. il por *N Y* 20:42 D 7 '87

Northern light [K. Blomstedt's redesign of Bulevardia restaurant, Helsinki; cover story] P. M. Sachner. il *Archit Rec* 175:120-5 Ag '87

Sam Lopata, the clown prince of restaurant designers, lets nothing interfere with atmosphere. E. Levin. il pors *People Wkly* 28:103-4+ N 23 '87

This year's remodels [New York City] J. Freiman. il *N Y* 20:15 Ja 12 '87

Restaurant employees

See also
Hotel Employees and Restaurant Employees International Union
Waiters and waitresses

Restaurant management

See also
Athletes in restaurant management
Fast food restaurant management
Women in restaurant management

Hot restaurants—how they get that way . . . [New York City] B. Kafka. il *Vogue* 177:338+ Mr '87

The trouble with Harry's: behind the coup at Cipriani [New York City] J. Taylor. il por *N Y* 20:62-7 O 19 '87

Restaurant signs

Italics [signs outside restaurants along Madison Avenue in Manhattan] *New Yorker* 63:30-1 Ap 27 '87

Restaurant Sofi (New York, N.Y.) *See* New York (N.Y.)—Restaurants, nightclubs, bars, etc.

Restaurants

See also
Art in restaurants
Cafeterias
Diners (Restaurants)
Fast food restaurants
Pizza restaurants
Salad bars

Best & worst brunch bets. il *Glamour* 85:316 O '87

Best & worst "first-date" restaurants. il *Glamour* 85:294 Ag '87

Best breakfasts. J. Stern and M. Stern. il *Harpers Bazaar* 120:102+ O '87

The best new bars and restaurants of 1987. J. F. Mariani. il *Esquire* 108:169-72+ N '87

The best waterfront restaurants. J. F. Mariani. il *Mot Boat Sail* 159:32 My '87

The dawn patrol [restaurants for power breakfasts] il *Harpers Bazaar* 120:26+ Ja '87

Dining out with a healthy appetite. il *FDA Consum* 21:18-23 Mr '87

Eat out and lose weight! E. Padus. il *Prevention* 39:68-74 Ag '87

Eating out: be $-wise in a good restaurant. il *Glamour* 85:268 F '87

Eating out . . . when you're on the road. il *Glamour* 85:192 Jl '87

The etiquette of eating out. L. Lufkin. il *Seventeen* 46:26+ My '87

Fed up to here [trendy food] L. Wells. il *N Y Times Mag* p133-4 D 6 '87

Getting rich on dinner [Zagat restaurant survey] L. Shapiro. il pors *Newsweek* 110:60 D 21 '87

Hanging out 101 [off-campus haunts] E. Wing. il *Roll Stone* p123-4+ Mr 26 '87

Haute hotel tables. J. F. Mariani. il *Harpers Bazaar* 121:162+ N '87

Holy cow! Steaks are high [steak houses] J. Stern and M. Stern. il *Harpers Bazaar* 120:72+ My '87

Home cooking. D. C. Craig. il *Life* 10:67+ Jl '87

In the world according to the Zagats, everyone's a critic. K. Johnson. il pors *People Wkly* 28:52-4 Jl 6 '87

It's a tropical heat wave [Caribbean-style restaurants] M. Sheraton. il *Time* 130:64 Ag 31 '87

Real Mexican, at last. C. Andrews. il *Harpers Bazaar* 120:108+ F '87

A room of one's own [restaurants owned by athletes] B. L. Ladson. il *Sport Mag* 78:85+ N '87

The six rudest restaurants in America. M. Willens. il *Money* 16:115-16+ O '87

Specialties of the house [most often ordered dishes] il *Ladies Home J* 104:104-5+ Mr '87

Square meals for a Sunday night [businessmen alone in new town] B. Harte. il *Fortune* 115:311+ Ap 27 '87

A table for one, please. H. Yorkshire. il *Work Woman* 12:132-4 S '87

"A table for one, please" [single diners] il *Glamour* 85:404 S '87

That cozy bookstore café. J. Bethune. il *Publ Wkly* 231:46-8 Ap 24 '87

What irks a restaurant most? il *Glamour* 85:320 My '87

Where to find that perfect Valentine's feast. T. Segal. il *Bus Week* p89 F 2 '87

Bibliography

America the bountiful—best eating guides. B. Kafka. il *Vogue* 177:133-4 Je '87

Chain and franchise operations

See also
Bombay Palace Restaurants Inc.
Cinema 'N' Drafthouse International Inc.
Denny's Inc.
Fast food restaurants
Hard Rock (Firm)
Horn & Hardart Co.
Lettuce Leaf Restaurants
Peasant Restaurants (Firm)
Pillsbury Co.
Sbarro, Inc.
Wendy's International Inc.

Chain restaurant smarts. il *Glamour* 85:240 Je '87

Directories

Let's eat out. See issues of Gourmet

Finance

Cutting the risks in the restaurant game [limited partnerships] T. Carson. il *Bus Week* p120-1 Ag 17 '87

History

Let's eat Chinese tonight. B. R. Johnson. il *Am Herit* 38:98-103+ D '87

Interior decoration

See Restaurant decoration

International aspects

Food in Vogue. B. Kafka. il *Vogue* 177:206 Ag '87

Management

See Restaurant management

Wine lists

See Wine lists

Wine service

See Wine service

Atlantic States

Keeping your fish simple [East Coast seafood restaurants] J. F. Mariani. il *Mot Boat Sail* 160:28 Jl '87

California

See also
Anaheim (Calif.)—Restaurants, nightclubs, bars, etc.
Berkeley (Calif.)—Restaurants, nightclubs, bars, etc.
Beverly Hills (Calif.)—Restaurants, nightclubs, bars, etc.
Glendale (Calif.)—Restaurants, nightclubs, bars, etc.
Irvine (Calif.)—Restaurants, nightclubs, bars, etc.
Los Angeles (Calif.)—Restaurants, nightclubs, bars, etc.
Malibu (Calif.)—Restaurants, nightclubs, bars, etc.
Mendocino (Calif.)—Restaurants, nightclubs, bars, etc.
Mountain View (Calif.)—Restaurants, nightclubs, bars, etc.

Restaurants—California—See also—*cont.*
  Newport Beach (Calif.)—Restaurants, nightclubs, bars, etc.
  Pasadena (Calif.)—Restaurants, nightclubs, bars, etc.
  Rancho Santa Fe (Calif.)—Restaurants, nightclubs, bars, etc.
  San Francisco (Calif.)—Restaurants, nightclubs, bars, etc.
  San Luis Obispo (Calif.)—Restaurants, nightclubs, bars, etc.
  Santa Barbara (Calif.)—Restaurants, nightclubs, bars, etc.
  Santa Monica (Calif.)—Restaurants, nightclubs, bars, etc.
  Tiburon (Calif.)—Restaurants, nightclubs, bars, etc.
  Venice (Calif.)—Restaurants, nightclubs, bars, etc.

China
From Peking to Canton. M. Sheraton. il *Time* 129:82-3+ Ap 13 '87

Colorado
  See also
  Aspen (Colo.)—Restaurants, nightclubs, bars, etc.
  Snowmass Village (Colo.)—Restaurants, nightclubs, bars, etc.

Europe
European dining. W. Schemmel. *Travel Holiday* 167:73-6 Mr '87

Finland
  See also
  Helsinki (Finland)—Restaurants, nightclubs, bars, etc.

Florida
  See also
  Tarpon Springs (Fla.)—Restaurants, nightclubs, bars, etc.

France
  See also
  Paris (France)—Restaurants, nightclubs, bars, etc.
Where stars don't matter [Normandy to Provence] A. Alvarez. il *House Gard* 159:30+ F '87

Georgia
  See also
  Atlanta (Ga.)—Restaurants, nightclubs, bars, etc.
  Cordele (Ga.)—Restaurants, nightclubs, bars, etc.

Great Britain
  See also
  London (England)—Restaurants, nightclubs, bars, etc.

Hawaii
Aloha dining. R. L. Balzer. il *Travel Holiday* 168:14-18 N '87

Kansas
  See also
  Lenexa (Kan.)—Restaurants, nightclubs, bars, etc.

Louisiana
  See also
  New Orleans (La.)—Restaurants, nightclubs, bars, etc.

Minnesota
  See also
  Minneapolis (Minn.)—Restaurants, nightclubs, bars, etc.

Nevada
  See also
  Las Vegas (Nev.)—Restaurants, nightclubs, bars, etc.

New York (State)
  See also
  Brooklyn (New York, N.Y.)—Restaurants, nightclubs, bars, etc.
  New York (N.Y.)—Restaurants, nightclubs, bars, etc.

North America
1988 Travel/Holiday guide to fine dining: United States, Canada, Mexico [cover story] R. L. Balzer. il *Travel Holiday* 168:83-116 D '87

Norway
  See also
  Oslo (Norway)—Restaurants, nightclubs, bars, etc.

Pennsylvania
  See also
  Philadelphia (Pa.)—Restaurants, nightclubs, bars, etc.
Marketing miniatures [baby vegetables for upscale restaurants raised at Overbrook Herb Farm] K. Pechter. il por *Rodale's Org Gard* 34:72-6 D '87

Soviet Union
  See also
  Moscow (Soviet Union)—Restaurants, nightclubs, bars, etc.

Spain
  See also
  Madrid (Spain)—Restaurants, nightclubs, bars, etc.
Foods and finos of Spain. T. Lydecker. il *Travel Holiday* 167:16+ F '87

Texas
Expect the unexpected in new southwestern cuisine. D. Lowery. il *South Living* 22:86-9, 146+ Je '87

Trinidad and Tobago
Twin islands cuisine. J. Nash and C. Cherry. il *Essence* 17:82-4+ Ap '87

United States
  See Restaurants

Washington (D.C.)
  See Washington (D.C.)—Restaurants, nightclubs, bars, etc.

Western States
  History
How good food and Harvey 'skirts' won the West. J. A. Cox. il *Smithsonian* 18:130-4+ S '87

Wisconsin
  See also
  Lake Geneva (Wis.)—Restaurants, nightclubs, bars, etc.

Restivo, Mary Ann
  about
Designer Mary Ann Restivo walks on fashion's mild side, which suits her working women fans just fine. M. Vespa. il pors *People Wkly* 28:149+ N 23 '87

Reston, James, 1909-
  about
The best journalist of his time. T. Griffith. il por *Time* 130:60 Ag 31 '87
James Reston steps down. *Natl Rev* 39:20 Ag 28 '87
A legend in his Times. por *Time* 130:55 Ag 17 '87
Protocol and peace. W. F. Buckley. *Natl Rev* 39:54 Je 5 '87
Pundit to pasture. A. Cockburn. *Nation* 245:114 Ag 15-22 '87

Reston, James, 1941-
The astronauts after Challenger. il *N Y Times Mag* p46-7+ Ja 25 '87

Restoration of books *See* Books—Conservation and restoration
Restoration of bronzes *See* Bronzes—Conservation and restoration
Restoration of buildings *See* Architecture—Conservation and restoration
Restoration of frescoes *See* Frescoes—Conservation and restoration
Restoration of mural painting and decoration *See* Mural painting and decoration—Conservation and restoration
Restoration of painting *See* Painting—Conservation and restoration
Restoration of sculpture *See* Sculpture—Conservation and restoration
Restoration of works of art *See* Art—Conservation and restoration
Restorative justice *See* Criminal justice, Administration of
Restored airplanes *See* Airplanes, Restored
Restored automobiles *See* Automobiles, Restored
Restored cottages *See* Cottages, Restored
Restored houses *See* Houses, Restored
Restored motorcycles *See* Motorcycles, Restored
Restored space vehicles *See* Space vehicles, Restored
Restored villages *See* Villages, Restored
Restraint of patients
Whose best interest? [use of restraints in nursing homes] B. Lindeman. il *50 Plus* 27:4 D '87
Restraint of trade
  See also
  Boycott
Résumés of employment *See* Job applications
Resurrection
  See also
  Jesus Christ—Resurrection and Ascension
A calendar of feasts [mother's growing frailty] R. A. Blake. il *America* 156:321-3 Ap 18 '87
Raising eyebrows and the dead [O. Roberts claims to raise the dead] R. N. Ostling. il por *Time* 130:55 Jl 13 '87
Saving souls—or a ministry? [O. Roberts claims that he can raise the dead] K. L. Woodward. il por *Newsweek* 110:52-3 Jl 13 '87
You shall live. M. K. Hellwig. *America* 156:inside back cover Mr 28 '87
Resuscitation
Computer heartthrobs [CPR training system developed by Actronics, Inc.] M. D. Brown. *Health* 19:22 F '87
CPR training: to save a life. il *Curr Health 2* 14:28-9 S '87
Investing in CPR [cardiopulmonary resuscitation vest] J. Silberner. *Sci News* 131:73 Ja 31 '87

Resuscitation—*cont.*

Neonatal resuscitation. P. A. Hillard. il *Parents* 62:150+ Je '87

RET (Rational-emotive therapy) *See* Psychotherapy

Retail trade

See also

Aca Joe (Firm)
Allied Stores Corp.
Associated Dry Goods Corp.
Big Bear, Inc.
Blacks in retail trade
Bloomingdale's
Cash business
Catalog showrooms
Christmas business
Clothestime Inc.
Clothing industry—Marketing
CML Group, Inc.
Consolidated Stores Corp.
Convenience stores
Dart Group Corporation
Dayton-Hudson Corp.
Department stores
Discount houses (Retail trade)
Display of merchandise
Door-to-door selling
Edison Brothers Stores, Inc.
F. W. Woolworth Co.
Franchise system
Interactive video—Retail trade use
J. C. Penney Company, Inc.
K Mart Corp.
Lands' End (Firm)
Limited, Inc.
Mail order business
Melville Corporation
Montgomery Ward & Co., Inc.
Nature Company
Nordstrom, Inc.
Petrie Stores Corp.
Price Co.
R. H. Macy & Co., Inc.
Rich's (Firm)
Sales
Sales personnel
Sears, Roebuck and Co.
Secondhand trade
Sharper Image (Firm)
Shopping centers
Stores
Supermarkets
Tuesday Morning Inc.
Wal-Mart Stores, Inc.
Wickes Companies, Inc.

Buying from "non-stores". *Futurist* 21:55-6 Jl/Ag '87

Acquisitions and mergers

At Zayre, the skies were just starting to clear [takeover threat by E. J. De Bartolo] C. Brown. *Bus Week* p59-60 O 19 '87

Edelman: a new Lucky strike? [A. Edelman's moves on Lucky Stores] K. M. Hafner. il por *Bus Week* p49 F 23 '87

The Hafts may mean it [bid for Dayton Hudson] M. J. Pitzer. il *Bus Week* p37 O 5 '87

The most feared family in retailing [Haft family] B. Saporito. il *Fortune* 115:65-6+ Je 22 '87

International aspects

Campeau's cash squeeze [R. Campeau's takeover of Allied Stores] T. Fennell. il por *Macleans* 100:26 Mr 2 '87

Is Campeau in over his head at Allied Stores? D. Cook. il *Bus Week* p52-3 F 9 '87

Canada

The Nor'westers' revenge [Hudson's Bay Co. sells off Northern Stores] P. C. Newman. il *Macleans* 100:42 My 11 '87

Retreat from the frontier [Hudson's Bay to sell off Northern Stores] A. Walmsley. il *Macleans* 100:26-7 F 16 '87

Banking services

Attention, savers! K Mart wants you [linkup with First Nationwide] J. B. Levine. il *Bus Week* p81-2 Ja 19 '87

Name recognition [Sears Savings scales back California operations] J. Heins. il *Forbes* 140:137 N 30 '87

Finance

Retailing. J. A. Trachtenberg. il *Forbes* 139:206-8 Ja 12 '87

Some growing pains—but nothing serious. A. Dunkin. il *Bus Week* p107 Ja 12 '87

Management

Power retailers [cover story] A. Dunkin and M. D. Oneal. il *Bus Week* p86-9+ D 21 '87

The supermen of specialty stores [billionaires] S. Smith. il por *Fortune* 116:142-3 O 12 '87

Securities

Correcting the Gap. T. Jaffe. *Forbes* 140:246 N 2 '87

Missed by the bulls: retailing stocks. J. Mendes. il *Fortune* 115:105 Mr 30 '87

Shock of the news [analysts overestimate earnings of the Gap and The Limited] J. Crudele. il *N Y* 20:19 O 5 '87

Tailing it out of retail. S. Lee. il *Forbes* 139:144 F 9 '87

Wholesale trouble for retail stocks. G. Weiss. il *Bus Week* p101 O 5 '87

Win one, lose one. A. A. Lappen. il *Forbes* 140:8 O 19 '87

Canada

See also

Hudson's Bay Co.
Zellers Inc.

Great Britain

See also

Marks & Spencer plc
Woolworth Holdings plc

Japan

See also

Marui Co. Ltd.

Sweden

See also

IKEA Svenska Forsaljnings AB

Retail trade catalogs *See* Catalogs, Commercial

Retail, Wholesale and Department Store Union

The lessons of Eaton's [1984-85 strike] S. D. Driedger. il *Macleans* 100:32-3 Jl 13 '87

Retail workers

See also

Retail, Wholesale and Department Store Union

Retaining walls

Retaining wall maintenance. G. Branson. il *Fam Handyman* 37:68-9 O '87

Retaliation against terrorists *See* Terrorism—Retaliation

Retallack, Gregory J., and Feakes, Carolyn R.

Trace fossil evidence for late Ordovician animals on land. bibl f il *Science* 235:61-3 Ja 2 '87

Retarded children *See* Mentally handicapped children

Retarded persons *See* Mentally handicapped

Retin-A *See* Retinoic acid

Retina

See also

Rods and cones
Visual purple

'Boring' reading and nearsightedness [work of Josh Wallman and others] D. D. Edwards. *Sci News* 132:23 Jl 11 '87

Corresponding spatial gradients of TOP molecules in the developing retina and optic tectum. D. Trisler and F. Collins. bibl f il *Science* 237:1208-9 S 4 '87

Eyeing myopia [how reading could lead to nearsightedness; research by Josh Wallman] E. Collins. *Sci Am* 257:36 O '87

Formation of retinal ganglion cell topography during prenatal development [cats] B. Lia and others. bibl f il *Science* 236:848-51 My 15 '87

Local retinal regions control local eye growth and myopia [impoverished stimulus situation of reading; cover story] J. Wallman and others. bibl f il *Science* 237:73-7 Jl 3 '87

Transient morphological features of identified ganglion cells in living fetal and neonatal retina. A. S. Ramoa and others. bibl f il *Science* 237:522-5 Jl 31 '87

Diseases and defects

See Eye—Diseases and defects

Transplantation

Retina transplant restores rat reflex [pupillary reflex; work of Henry Klassen and Raymond D. Lund] R. Weiss. il *Sci News* 132:245 O 17 '87

Retina cells *See* Nerve cells; Rods and cones

Retinoblastoma *See* Eye—Cancer

Retinoic acid

An anti-ageing cream with a new wrinkle: it may work [Retin-A] P. W. Moser. il *Discover* 8:72-6+ Ag '87

Antidote to all those wrinkles? [Retin-A] A. Toufexis. il *Time* 130:90+ D 14 '87

Baldness drug gets a boost. il *Prevention* 39:14 S '87

Form-fitting genes [identification of morphogen; research by Christina Thaller and Gregor Eichele] *Discover* 8:8+ S '87

Retinoic acid—*cont.*
Shape-inducing chemical identified [research by Christina Thaller and Gregor Eichele] R. Weiss. il *Sci News* 131:406 Je 27 '87

Retinol *See* Vitamins—Vitamin A

Retinyl Schiff base salts *See* Schiff base salts

Retired military personnel
The Marine's private army [Oliver North's use of former CIA agents and military officers in his covert operations] J. F. Stacks. il *Time* 130:32 Jl 13 '87

Employment
From top guns to corporate brass [former black officers] D. C. Ruffin. il *Black Enterp* 17:115-17+ F '87

Retirees *See* Aged

Retirement
See also
American Association of Retired Persons
Baseball managers—Retirement
Baseball players—Retirement
Boxers—Retirement
Clergy—Retirement
College teachers—Retirement
Congressmen—Retirement
Executives—Retirement
Police—Retirement
Senators—Retirement
Social security
Trade unions—Employees—Retirement
Lobbies rock the retirement boat [American Assoc. of Retired Persons vs. C. Pepper] C. Murphy. il *50 Plus* 27:13-14 Ja '87
Set free [early retirement] R. B. Elsberry. il *N Y Times Mag* p37 Ja 4 '87
Stranger in my house [retired husband] H. Sampson. il *Read Dig* 130:9-10 Ap '87
Workers rejecting incentives to stay on the job [views of Carolyn E. Paul on early retirement] il *USA Today (Periodical)* 115:16+ Ap '87

International aspects
Early retirement as a labor force policy: an international overview. B. A. Mirkin. bibl f il *Mon Labor Rev* 110:19-33 Mr '87

Retirement, Places of
Do we have a swamp for you! [Louisiana Cajun country] B. Keating. il *50 Plus* 27:55-9+ Jl '87
Snowbirds [migratory retirees descend on the Rio Grande Valley each winter] L. M. Keefe. il *Forbes* 139:117-18 Mr 23 '87
Some like it hot! [retirees in Hemet, Calif.] S. Angel. il *50 Plus* 27:54-8 Je '87

Retirement benefits
The crisis in health benefits. S. B. Garland. il *Bus Week* p36 Je 15 '87
Employer-sponsored health insurance for retirees: the need and the cost. *Mon Labor Rev* 110:38 My '87
Sick retirees could kill your company. J. Nielsen. il *Fortune* 115:98-9 Mr 2 '87
Unfunded, nonregulated, miscalculated [retiree health benefits] C. Murphy. il *50 Plus* 27:14+ O '87

Accounting
The silent killer [accounting treatment of employee health benefits] L. Jereski. il *Forbes* 139:112 F 23 '87

Taxation
Retirement help. il *U S News World Rep* 103:82+ D 7 '87
Tax reform changes retirement plans. D. Lamaute. il *Black Enterp* 18:41-2 S '87
Taxes for young retirees. L. Saunders. il *Forbes* 139 Ann Directory:71+ Ap 27 '87

Retirement communities
See also
Life care communities

Retirement income
See also
Individual retirement accounts
Pensions
Simplified employee pensions
Social security
How to beat the retirement clock. B. Siverd. il *Work Woman* 12:34+ Ja '87
In a big fix on a small fixed income [retiree George Littrell] E. Schurenberg. il *Money* 16:144-8 Ja '87
Investing for a brighter future [excerpt from 50 plus guide to retirement investing] W. W. David. il *50 Plus* 27:68+ Mr '87
On the road again [Airstream trailer couple Lueen and Howard Miller] R. Micheli. il *Money* 16:140-4 S '87
Retirees increasingly well off [views of Rita Ricardo-Campbell] *USA Today (Periodical)* 115:15 Ap '87
Want to quit early? It'll take a bundle. L. Wiener. il *U S News World Rep* 102:63-4 Je 8 '87

Retraining, Occupational
Job training: the Democrats are stealing the show. M. E. Recio. il *Bus Week* p53 Mr 9 '87
Retraining [Worker Adjustment Assistance Program proposed in 1988 budget] *Time* 129:23 Ja 19 '87
Retraining America's workers [American Society for Training and Development study] *Futurist* 21:43 Ja/F '87
Time to retrain the American farmer. L. C. Thurow. il *Technol Rev* 90:22-3 My/Je '87

Retrievers
Cable training for retrievers. L. Mueller. il *Outdoor Life* 179:126+ My '87
Fetch on faith and cripples first [M. Kellogg's methods of training for retrievers] L. Mueller. il por *Outdoor Life* 180:44-5 Ag '87
Grandpa and the kid [Chesapeake Bay retriever] D. Sisson. il *Field Stream* 92:51+ S '87
Grandpa and the kid [jumpshooting end of season ducks on the Umpqua River with a Chesapeake Bay retriever] D. Sisson. il *Field Stream* 91:49+ F '87
Instant underwater retriever training [Labrador retrievers] L. Mueller. il *Outdoor Life* 179:24-6 Ja '87
Kellogg's "arm extenders" [use of a slingshot in training dogs] L. Mueller. il pors *Outdoor Life* 180:52+ Jl '87
Making retrievers seaworthy. B. Tarrant. il *Field Stream* 92:174+ S '87
Retriever scent training. L. Mueller. il *Outdoor Life* 179:52+ Mr '87
A tale of turtles [Labrador retriever assists box turtle researchers C. and E. Schwartz] il pors *Natl Geogr World* 146:28-31 O '87

Retro training *See* Running

Retrovir *See* Azidothymidine

Retroviruses
See also
HIV viruses
HTLV viruses
Leukemia viruses
Tissue-specific expression of functionally rearranged λ1 Ig gene through a retrovirus vector. R. D. Cone and others. bibl f il *Science* 236:954-7 My 22 '87

Rettie, Allan E., and others
Cytochrome P-450-catalyzed formation of Δ⁴-VPA, a toxic metabolite of valproic acid. bibl f il *Science* 235:890-3 F 20 '87

Return of goods
Many happy returns: how to take back a purchase without the hassle. il *Glamour* 85:30 Ja '87

Returns policy in publishing *See* Publishers and publishing—Returns policy

Reuben, William A., and Norman, Carlos
The women of Lexington Prison. il *Nation* 244:881-4 Je 27 '87

Reubens, Paul *See* Herman, Pee-wee

Reunions, College *See* College reunions

Reunions, Family *See* Family reunions

Reunions, High school *See* High school reunions

Reupholstering *See* Upholstery

Reuss, Lloyd E.
Catalysts of genius, dealers in hope [address, October 14, 1986] *Vital Speeches Day* 53:173-6 Ja 1 '87

Reuter, Edzard
about
The banker behind the shakeup at Daimler-Benz. R. Ingersoll and R. Brady. il pors *Bus Week* p36-7 Jl 27 '87
Putsch and shove at Daimler-Benz. N. J. Perry. il por *Fortune* 116:92 Ag 17 '87

Reuter, Madalynne, and Yen, Marianne
News of the week. See issues of Publishers Weekly

Reuters Holdings plc
Reuters after the crash: slowing down to a gallop. M. Maremont. il *Bus Week* p114-15+ D 21 '87

Revco D.S., Inc.
Why going private didn't bring Sidney Dworkin happiness. Z. Schiller. *Bus Week* p43+ O 12 '87

Revelation
See also
Apocalyptic literature

Revenge
See also
Feuds
Revenge is sweet, but . . . S. Blotnick. il *Forbes* 139 Ann Directory:338 Ap 27 '87

Revenue Canada *See* Canada. Revenue Canada

Revenue sharing *See* Intergovernmental tax relations

Revenue stamps
DEC's 1987 migratory waterfowl print and stamp. il *Conservationist* 42:54 Jl/Ag '87

Reverse discrimination in employment *See* Discrimination in employment
Reverse glass painting *See* Glass painting and staining
Reverse mortgages *See* Home equity conversion
Reverse transcriptase *See* Transcriptases
Reverse transcription *See* Genetic transcription
Reves, Emery, 1904-1981
about
An art-filled villa finds a special setting in Texas. H. Dudar. il pors *Smithsonian* 17:50-9 Ja '87
Reves, Wendy Russell
about
An art-filled villa finds a special setting in Texas. H. Dudar. il pors *Smithsonian* 17:50-9 Ja '87
Reviews of ballet *See* Ballet reviews
Reviews of books *See* Book reviews and reviewing
Reviews of dance *See* Dance reviews
Reviews of motion pictures *See* Motion picture reviews
Reviews of musicals, revues, etc. *See* Musicals, revues, etc.—Reviews
Reviews of opera *See* Opera reviews
Reviews of operetta *See* Operetta reviews
Reviews of oratorios *See* Oratorio reviews
Reviews of plays *See* Theater reviews
Reviews of radio programs *See* Radio program reviews
Reviews of television programs *See* Television program reviews
Reviews of videodiscs *See* Videodisc reviews
Reviews of videotapes *See* Videotape reviews
Reviglio, Franco
about
Business recovery by the book. R. I. Kirkland, Jr. il por *Fortune* 116:42 Ag 3 '87
Revision of manuscripts *See* Authorship—Copy preparation
Revival houses (Motion picture theaters) *See* Motion picture theaters
Revlon Inc.
The battle of the curls [American Health and Beauty Aids Institute objects to Revlon racist statement about black consumers and black hair care manufacturers] K. Smikle. *Black Enterp* 17:18 Ja '87
Big investors on Wall Street [sparring over Salomon Inc.] pors *Fortune* 116:8 O 26 '87
Can Revlon repair its image? [black boycott] P. Wang and M. Malone. il *Newsweek* 109:53 F 23 '87
A gaffe at Revlon has the black community seething [disparaging black-owned hair-care companies] C. Dugas and K. Dreyfack. il *Bus Week* p36-7 F 9 '87
Has Perelman taken a shine to Sterling Drug? [R. O. Perelman] G. G. Marcial. il por *Bus Week* p101 Jl 13 '87
How Ron Perelman scared Gillette into shape. K. H. Hammonds. il *Bus Week* p40-1 O 12 '87
Make-over at Revlon. B. Kanner. il *N Y* 20:12-13 Ja 12 '87
Operation PUSH continues boycott of Revlon products. *Jet* 71:17 Ja 12 '87
The raider who runs Revlon [R. Perelman] A. Ramirez. il pors *Fortune* 116:56-8+ S 14 '87
Revlon must change package similar to Soft Sheen's. *Jet* 73:18 O 19 '87
Revlon's striving makeover man [R. Perelman] A. Ramirez. il por *Fortune* 115:54-5 Ja 5 '87
Salomon and Revlon: what really happened. A. Bianco. il pors *Bus Week* p156+ O 12 '87
A tale of our times [R. Perelman's deals] A. Sloan and L. Jereski. il *Forbes* 139:180 My 18 '87
Vernon Jordan named to board of Revlon. por *Jet* 73:39 O 26 '87
A white knight saves Salomon [W. Buffett outflanks R. Perelman] B. Powell. il por *Newsweek* 110:66 O 12 '87
White-knight time on Wall Street [W. Buffett saves Salomon Brothers from corporate raider R. Perelman] J. Egan. il pors *U S News World Rep* 103:60 O 12 '87
Revocable living trusts *See* Living trusts
Revocable trusts *See* Trusts and trustees
Revolution, Industrial *See* Industrial revolution
Revolutionary War (U.S.) *See* United States—History—Revolution, 1775-1783
Revolutionists
How-to book for revolutionists [work of Jay S. Mendell] il *Futurist* 21:44 Jl/Ag '87
Revolutions
See also
France—History—Revolution, 1789-1799
Haiti—History—Revolution, 1791-1804
Latin America—History—Wars of Independence, 1806-1830

National liberation movements
United States—History—Revolution, 1775-1783
A look at six types of revolution. J. Rose. il *Sch Update* 119:7-8 My 4 '87
Bibliography
Paperback history. R. Porter. *Hist Today* 37:55 Ag '87
Revolving houses *See* Houses, Rotating
Revson, Lyn
about
Lyn Revson's beaux-arts address. Suzy. il por *Archit Dig* 44:130-9+ N '87
Rewards, prizes, etc.
See also
American Black Achievement Awards
Certificates of merit
Literary prizes
Martin Luther King, Jr. Nonviolent Peace Prize
Nobel prizes
Salute to Greatness Awards
Anecdotes, facetiae, satire, etc.
An award-worthy guest column. S. MacLeod. por *Macleans* 100:52 Ag 17 '87
Dialogue [Omnibust award winners] *Omni* 9:12 Ja '87
Dubious achievements of 1986! il *Esquire* 107:55-8+ Ja '87
Rex, Betty
The tears—and rage—of a foster mother; ed. by Barbara Hanson Pierce. il por *Redbook* 169:34+ Jl '87
Rexnord Inc.
The next takeover artist you meet could be Jeff Steiner [Banner Industries takeover of Rexnord Inc.] Z. Schiller. il por *Bus Week* p33+ F 9 '87
Rey, Margret
about
Curious George and his literary mama, Margret Rey, celebrate a half-century of monkeyshines. il por *People Wkly* 27:98 Je 1 '87
Rey, Michel
A chance for every child. il *Courier* 40:13-15 Ag '87
Reyes, Elizabeth
Mauritius rises above the dodo. il *World Press Rev* 34:63 Ja '87
Reye's syndrome
As use of kids' aspirin drops, so do cases of Reye syndrome. D. Stehlin. il *FDA Consum* 21:20-1 O '87
Reykjavik summit, 1986 *See* Reagan-Gorbachev summit conference, 1986
Reynaud, Claude-Agnès
(jt. auth) See Weill, Jean-Claude, and Reynaud, Claude-Agnès
Reynolds, A. H.
Azania [poem] *Essence* 18:128 S '87
Ecstasy [poem] *Essence* 18:159 S '87
A woman fully grown [poem] *Essence* 18:124 S '87
Reynolds, Alan
Europe needs a tax cut. il *Natl Rev* 39:40-1+ F 27 '87
What scared the markets? il *Natl Rev* 39:47-9 N 20 '87
Reynolds, Burt
about
Burt Reynolds: why he needs Loni now. il por *McCalls* 114:13+ My '87
Loni Anderson: "Why are people so cruel to us?". L. Eisenberg. il pors *Redbook* 168:82+ Mr '87
Reynolds, Butch
about
Preparing a big move. K. Moore. il pors *Sports Illus* 67:36-8+ S 7 '87
Reynolds, C. P.
The Cotswolds. il map *Gourmet* 47:54-9+ S '87
Hermès. il *Gourmet* 47:42-7+ F '87
Paris journal. See occasional issues of Gourmet
Reynolds, Earle
about
Voyage of a peace activist. S. A. Wittman. il por *Progressive* 51:16 F '87
Reynolds, John E., III, and Wilcox, J. Ross
People, power plants, and manatees. il map *Sea Front* 33:263-9 Jl/Ag '87
Reynolds, Patrick T.
A river town that thrives on its history. il *Americana* 14:56-60 Ja/F '87
Reynolds, Peter C.
Imposing a corporate culture. il *Psychol Today* 21:32-4+ Mr '87
Reynolds, R. C.
The realities of teaching remedial English in college. *Educ Dig* 52:58-60 F '87

Reynolds, Steven H., and others
Activated oncogenes in B6C3F1 mouse liver tumors: implications for risk assessment. bibl f il *Science* 237:1309-16 S 11 '87
Reynolds, William Bradford
Power to the people. il *N Y Times Mag* p116-18+ S 13 '87

about

The High Court's unofficial arbiters. D. Baer. il pors *U S News World Rep* 103:23-4 N 23 '87
Reynolds (R. J.) Tobacco Co. *See* R. J. Reynolds Tobacco Co.
Reynolds Metals Co.
Reynolds hits pay dirt Down Under [gold in Australia] G. L. Miles. il *Bus Week* p99 Jl 13 '87
The rez sisters [drama] *See* Highway, Tomson
Rezzori, Beatrice von

about

A tower in Tuscany. B. Chatwin. il *House Gard* 159:78-85+ Ja '87
Rezzori, Gregor von

about

A tower in Tuscany. B. Chatwin. il *House Gard* 159:78-85+ Ja '87
RF (Radio frequency) weapons *See* Electromagnetic weapons
RF waves *See* Electromagnetic waves
Rh factor
The Rh factor. P. A. Hillard. il *Parents* 62:198+ O '87
Rhapsody Films
Putting jazz back into the picture. F. Davis. il *High Fidel* 37:71-2 Jl '87
Rhees (Rush) Library *See* Rush Rhees Library
Das Rheingold [opera] *See* Wagner, Richard, 1813-1883
Rhenium

Isotopes

Cosmic clock dates the universe [rhenium-osmium isotopes] R. Layne. *Pop Sci* 230:53 Mr '87
Rheology
True ZITs: can such things be? [anisotropies] D. E. Thomsen. *Sci News* 131:4-5 Ja 3 '87
Rhesus factor *See* Rh factor
Rhetoric
The halls still ring with the echoes of master orators [Congress] M. Dubrow and B. Lieber. il *People Wkly* 27:28-9 Mr 23 '87
Rheumatic fever
Mysterious return of a childhood scourge. J. Silberner. il *U S News World Rep* 103:64 Ag 31 '87
Rheumatic fever: down but not out. E. Zamula. il *FDA Consum* 21:26-8 Jl/Ag '87
Rheumatism

See also

Arthritis
Fibrositis
Rheumatoid arthritis *See* Arthritis
Rhine River
Rhine diary. M. G. Stoddard. il *Saturday Evening Post* 259:90+ S '87
Rhine River chemical spills, 1986
And toxic flows the Rhine! V. Abramov. il *World Health* p24-6 Mr '87
Beyond the spill on the Rhine. D. C. Marsh. il *World Press Rev* 34:50 Ja '87
A sadness on the Rhine. W. C. Clark. *Environment* 28:inside cover D '86
Washing the Rhine. *Progressive* 51:12 F '87
Rhinoceros
My close call with a rhino. F. Sunquist. il *Int Wildl* 17:16-17 Jl/Ag '87
New ZIP codes for resident rhinos in Nepal [restocking Bardia Wildlife Reserve with rhinos captured from Royal Chitawan National Park] H. R. Mishra and E. Dinerstein. il *Smithsonian* 18:66-73 S '87
The rhino wars [battling black rhino poachers in Zimbabwe] M. Vollers. il *Sports Illus* 66:60-8+ Mr 2 '87
The rhino's fatal flaw [horn trade in Africa and Asia] P. Jackson. il maps *Int Wildl* 17:4-11 Ja/F '87
A war to save the black rhino [battle against poachers in Zimbabwe] M. Vollers. il *Time* 130:62-3 S 7 '87
Rhinoceros, Fossil
The rise and fall of the American rhino. D. R. Prothero. il *Nat Hist* 96:26-33 Ag '87
Rhinoceros Party *See* Parti Rhinoceros
Rhinoplasty *See* Surgery, Plastic
Rhizobium
BioTechnica tests EPA review process [field test] M. Crawford. *Science* 235:840 F 20 '87
Rhizobium, the farmer's Mr. Fixit [Unesco program] E. J. DaSilva and others. il *Courier* 40:27-8 Mr '87

Rhoades, Lillian
Toward the 21st century. por *Essence* 17:114 Ja '87
Rhoads, George

about

Sculpture funhouse. R. Kostelanetz. il por *N Y Times Mag* p28-31 My 31 '87
Rhode Island
See also
Beaches—Rhode Island
Block Island (R.I.)
Crime and criminals—Rhode Island
Music festivals—Rhode Island
Rhodes, Dusty
Major League players. il *Horizon* 30:49-50 Ap '87
Rhodes, Frank H. T., 1926-
Let the student decide. il *U S News World Rep* 103:72-4 O 26 '87
Rhodes, Richard
Cupcake Land. il *Harpers* 275:51-7 N '87
A thin disguise. il *N Y Times Mag* p62 Jl 19 '87
A yield against the odds: harvest time on a Missouri farm. il *Harpers* 274:53-7 Ap '87
Rhodes, Steven L.
(jt. auth) *See* Wiley, Karen B., and Rhodes, Steven L.
Rhodes scholars and scholarships
Bermuda's 1st woman named Rhodes scholar [E. Robinson] *Jet* 72:33 My 18 '87
Two blacks among 32 U.S. Rhodes scholarship winners. il *Jet* 71:22 Ja 26 '87
Rhododendrons
See also
Azaleas
Hardy rhododendrons. D. G. Leach. il *Rodale's Org Gard* 34:62-6 N '87
Rhodopseudomonas
Molecular mechanisms of photosynthesis [cover story] D. C. Youvan and B. L. Marrs. bibl (p136) il *Sci Am* 256:42-8 Je '87
Rhodopsin *See* Visual purple
Rhodopsin, Bacterial *See* Pigments (Biology)
Rhone-Poulenc SA
Union Carbide sold to Rhone-Poulenc. *Success Farm* 85 no2:18T Ja '87
Rhubarb
See also
Cooking—Rhubarb
The first "fruit" of spring: rhubarb. A. W. Dominick. il *Flower Gard* 31:30 F/Mr '87
Rhubarb desserts *See* Desserts
Rhue, Madlyn

about

After years of lying, actress Madlyn Rhue reveals the truth about her multiple sclerosis [interview] L. Armstrong. il pors *People Wkly* 28:105+ N 16 '87
Rhus *See* Sumac
Rhythm
The beat goes on [social rhythms] C. A. Douglis. il *Psychol Today* 21:36-9+ N '87
Rhythm, Biological *See* Biological rhythms
Rhythm and BLU (Musical group)
Rhythm and BLU. M. Bourne. il *Down Beat* 54:15 F '87
Rhythm and blues phonograph records *See* Phonograph records—Rock music
Rhythm instruments *See* Percussion instruments
Rian, Jeffrey
Social science fiction [cover story; interview with R. Prince] il *Art Am* 75:86-95 Mr '87
Ribakov, Anatolii *See* Rybakov, Anatolii Naumovich
Ribavirin
Ribavirin antagonizes the effect of azidothymidine on HIV replication. M. W. Vogt and others. bibl f il *Science* 235:1376-9 Mr 13 '87
Risky business on AIDS [ICN's experience with ribavirin] J. Crudele. il *N Y* 20:16+ Ap 27 '87
Whither go the AIDS treatments? D. D. Edwards. *Sci News* 131:372 Je 13 '87
Ribbon loudspeakers *See* Loudspeakers
Ribbons
Bows & bands & braids [modeled by Connie Sellecca] il *Redbook* 168:10 Mr '87
Bows: for better or worse. il *Vogue* 177:134 Ja '87
Ribe, Neil M.
Atonal music and its limits. *Commentary* 84:49-54 N '87
Ribeiro, Angelo Vidal d'Almeida

about

UN official seeks data on repression of believers. B. Spring. *Christ Today* 31:34-5 F 6 '87

Riblet tape *See* Laminar flow
Ribollita *See* Soups
Ribonucleases
Identification and localization of mutations at the Lesch-Nyhan locus by ribonuclease A cleavage. R. A. Gibbs and C. T. Caskey. bibl f il *Science* 236:303-5 Ap 17 '87
Model substrates for an RNA enzyme. W. H. McClain and others. bibl f il *Science* 238:527-30 O 23 '87
Ribonucleic acid *See* RNA
Ribosomal RNA *See* RNA
Ribosomes
A complete mapping of the proteins in the small ribosomal subunit of Escherichia coli [neutron scattering data] M. S. Capel and others. bibl f il *Science* 238:1403-6 D 4 '87
A tunnel in the large ribosomal subunit revealed by three-dimensional image reconstruction. A. Yonath and others. bibl f il *Science* 236:813-16 My 15 '87
Riboud, Barbara Chase- *See* Chase-Riboud, Barbara, 1936-
Ribs, Barbecued *See* Barbecue cooking
Ricciuti, Edward R.
(jt. auth) See Wilson, R. L. (Robert Lawrence), 1939-, and Ricciuti, Edward R.
Rice, Anthony L.
The Christmas Island Phosphate Company. bibl il por map *Sea Front* 33:444-53 N/D '87
Rice, Donna
Donna Rice tells her story; ed. by James Grant. il *Life* 10:82-6+ Jl '87
about
Chronicle of a ruinous affair. M. Green. il pors *People Wkly* 27:104-8 Je 15 '87
Coming attractions. il pors *Time* 130:18 Ag 17 '87
Donna Fawn Hahn. pors *People Wkly* 28:62-3 D 28 '87-Ja 4 '88
Donna Rice: 'the woman in question'. A. Richman. il pors *People Wkly* 27:32-7 My 18 '87
Fall from grace [cover story; special section] il pors *Time* 129:16-20+ My 18 '87
The follies of 1987 [special section] il *World Press Rev* 34:32-4 Jl '87
My dinner with Donna. T. Schwartz. il por *N Y* 20:27 My 18 '87
The new seductress. N. Scovell. il pors *Mademoiselle* 93:244-7 N '87
On the springboard of notoriety. F. Trippett. il pors *Time* 130:64-5 O 12 '87
PAAF. *New Yorker* 63:31-2 My 18 '87
The sudden fall of Gary Hart [cover story; special section] il pors *Newsweek* 109:22-8+ My 18 '87
Anecdotes, facetiae, satire, etc.
A truly Hart-stopping chickadee. A. Fotheringham. il *Macleans* 100:56 My 18 '87
Rice, Elmer L., 1892-1967
about
Street scene [drama] Reviews
New Yorker 63:35-7 D 7 '87
Rice, Jackson *See* Lish, Gordon
Rice, Jerry
about
Rice is a breed apart. R. Wiley. il pors *Sports Illus* 67:40-3 S 28 '87
Rice, Jim
about
What's eating Jim Rice? R. Wetzsteon. il pors *Sport Mag* 78:40-1+ Je '87
Rice, Larry
America's unknown wildlands [cover story] il *Sierra* 72:44-53 Mr/Ap '87
Rice, Linda Johnson
about
Backstage. il por *Ebony* 42:26 S '87
Linda Johnson Rice gets MBA, named president of Johnson Publishing Co. il por *Jet* 72:6+ Jl 6 '87
A nice graduation present: Johnson Publishing. L. Therrien. por *Bus Week* p40 Jl 13 '87
Rice, Millard Millburn
The last stop [letter] *Harpers* 274:4-7 My '87
Rice
See also
Cooking—Rice
From our kitchen to yours. K. Adams. *South Living* 22:198-9 Mr '87
Breeding
Rice plants regenerated from protoplasts. J. L. Marx. il *Science* 235:31-2 Ja 2 '87
Export-import trade
A grain revolution: the impact of imported rice on millet-based African civilizations. T. Ndoye and M. M'Baye. il *Courier* 40:8-9 My '87

Rebel with a cause [Lion Petroleum's T. Sato's campaign against rice subsidies in Japan] A. Tanzer. il por *Forbes* 139:84+ Mr 23 '87
Prices
The rice plot [rice subsidies in Japan] J. M. Fallows. il *Atlantic* 259:22-6 Ja '87
Varieties
Not the same old rice [American adaptations of long-grain basmati rice] J. Pruess. il *N Y Times Mag* p49-50 S 6 '87
Rice paper
Using rice paper to transfer color. B. Senter. il *Am Artist* 51:60-3 My '87
Rich, Adrienne
Resisting amnesia [excerpt from address, February 1983] *Ms* 15:66-7 Mr '87
Rich, Alan
Opera's turn. il por *Opera News* 52:16-18+ D 5 '87
Rich, Beatrice R.
The eyes (I). il por *World Tennis* 34:36-7 Ap '87
The eyes (II). il *World Tennis* 34:42-3 My '87
Rich, Buddy, 1917-1987
about
Obituary
Down Beat il por 54:61+ Jl '87. W. Minor
Down Beat il por 54:11 Jl '87. J. McDonough
High Fidel il 37:54 Jl '87. A. Steele
New Yorker 63:80-1 Je 15 '87. W. Balliett
Rich, Dorothy
Let's not throw out the baby with the bath water [with reply by S. B. Heath and M. W. McLaughlin] bibl f *Phi Delta Kappan* 68:784-6 Je '87
Rich, Frank
The gay decades. il *Esquire* 108:87-92+ N '87
Rich, Frank, and Aronson, Lisa
He made the stage come alive. il por *N Y Times Mag* p52-4+ O 11 '87
Rich, John Martin
Teachers and immoral conduct. *Educ Dig* 52:6-8 Mr '87
Rich, Maria F.
Playing it safe. il *Opera News* 52:20+ N '87
Rich, Paul
The quest for Englishness. bibl il *Hist Today* 37:24-30 Je '87
Rich
See also
Billionaires
Children of the rich
Millionaires
Wealth
The aristobrats: they're young, they're rich, they're oh-so-shallow (could you be one of them?). D. Handelman. il *Mademoiselle* 93:230-1+ Ap '87
Art fever: the passion and frenzy of the ultimate rich man's sport [cover story] D. Smith. il *N Y* 20:34-43 Ap 20 '87
The Forbes four hundred [cover story; with editorial comment by Lawrence Minard and Malcolm Forbes] il *Forbes* 140 Sp Issue:6, 21, 106-7+ O 26 '87
The Forbes four hundred cost of living index. C. Brown. il *Forbes* 140 Sp Issue:54+ O 26 '87
Getting rich in America: men, money & the survival of capitalism [cover story; special issue; with editorial comment by Byron Dobell] il *Am Herit* 38:5, 34-51+ N '87
People are talking about money [special section] il *Vogue* 177:204-9+ Ja '87
Poor little rich girls [19th century American heiresses who married British nobility] C. M. Wallace. il *Forbes* 140 Sp Issue:62+ O 26 '87
The rich got poorer [effect of stock market crash on Forbes four hundred] P. Newcomb. il *Forbes* 140:41+ N 16 '87
What it takes to be rich in America [cover story; special section] il *Fortune* 115:22-9+ Ap 13 '87
Who's who in charity? C. Cox. il *Vogue* 177:396-9 N '87
Anecdotes, facetiae, satire, etc.
Oh yes you can (be too rich or too thin). K. Fury. il *Work Woman* 12:114 F '87
Crime
See also
Billionaire Boys Club
Education
Dropouts make good. B. Leonard. il *Forbes* 140 Sp Issue:76-7+ O 26 '87
Housing
For sale: the rich look [Blackhawk, Calif. homes] J. Adler. il *Newsweek* 109:80 Je 22 '87

Rich—*cont.*

Medical care

Should it cover millionaires? [Medicare] F. Greve. *50 Plus* 27:20+ My '87

Taxation

The bad new tax law. H. Gutmann. il *N Y Rev Books* 34:26-8 F 12 '87

The bad new tax law: an exchange [discussion of February 12, 1987 article] H. Gutmann. il *N Y Rev Books* 34:49-51 Jl 16 '87

Gentle persuasion for the rich [Canada] D. Francis. por *Macleans* 100:7 Je 15 '87

How to pull in revenues without gutting tax reform. P. C. Roberts. il *Bus Week* p14 Ag 10 '87

Tax the Forbes 400! R. S. McIntyre. *New Repub* 197:15-17 Ag 31 '87

Rich in television

Spoofing it: the TV rich are very different from the real rich. L. Robinson. por *Vogue* 177:207 Ja '87

Richard, Christopher W.

Weir urges direct negotiations. *Christ Century* 104:324-5 Ap 8 '87

Richard Hannay (Fictional character)

John Buchan's Richard Hannay [character modeled after E. Ironside, amateur spy among Germans and Boers in Southern Africa] G. Powell. bibl il pors map *Hist Today* 37:32-9 Ag '87

Richard II [drama] See Shakespeare, William, 1564-1616

Richard York Gallery

American themes at the Richard York Gallery. M. Weber. il por *Archit Dig* 44:162+ F '87

Richards, Albert G.

about

Floral derangement. N. Guccione. il *Omni* 10:100-5 D '87

Richards, Beah

about

Beah Richards. il pors *Ebony* 42:61+ O '87

Richards, David

about

David Richards. B. Anderson. il por *Sports Illus* 67:65 Ag 31 '87

Richards, Kay

Phantom fathers. il *Progressive* 51:34 Ag '87

Richards, Keith

about

Keith Richards [interview] K. Loder. il por *Roll Stone* p64-7 N 5-D 10 '87

Keith Richards set to record first solo LP. A. DeCurtis and K. Loder. il por *Roll Stone* p15 S 10 '87

Richards, Lloyd G.

about

Leaving his imprint on Broadway. S. G. Freedman. il pors *N Y Times Mag* p38+ N 22 '87

Richards, Melanie

about

Shy N.Y. lotto winner claims $12 million prize after waiting 3 months. il por *Jet* 71:30 Mr 9 '87

Richards, Rebekah

The secret to sexual satisfaction. *Redbook* 168:80-1+ Ja '87

Richardson, Ashley

about

The beauty buddy system: a supermodel (Ashley) shares her secrets. il pors *Mademoiselle* 93:232-7 N '87

Once nicknamed: 'the Stick', Ashley Richardson threw modeling some curves and rose to the top. M. Neill. il pors *People Wkly* 28:112-14 S 7 '87

Richardson, James, 1950-

The mind-body problem [poem] *New Repub* 197:36 D 7 '87

The mind-body problem [poem] *New Repub* 197:34 N 2 '87

Richardson, John

Custom of the country. il por *House Gard* 159:146-56 Ag '87

Eugenia Errazuriz. il por *House Gard* 159:76+ Ap '87

From old England to New England. il *House Gard* 159:214-21+ N '87

Givenchy grandeur. il *House Gard* 159:218-30 Ap '87

Picasso's apocalyptic whorehouse. bibl f il *N Y Rev Books* 34:40-7 Ap 23 '87

Picasso's secret love. il pors *House Gard* 159:174-83+ O '87

Rediscovering an early modern vision. il por *House Gard* 159:158-63+ F '87

Splendid sanctuary. il *House Gard* 159:104-7+ D '87

Richardson, Judy

We need a movement. por *Essence* 17:135 Mr '87

Richardson, Ken

Medley. See issues of High Fidelity (New York, N.Y.) beginning November 1986

Richardson, Micheal Ray

about

Banned NBAer files suit over his '86 drug relapse. *Jet* 72:50 My 25 '87

Richardson, Miles

about

The salvation of a homeland. il por *Macleans* 100:32-3 D 28 '87

Richardson, Miranda

about

Shanghai surprise. K. O'Shaughnessy. il por *Vogue* 177:74 D '87

Richardson, Richard C., and others

Graduating minority students: lessons from ten success stories. il *Change* 19:20-7 My/Je '87

Richardson, William

Should Congress adopt the House-passed "Gephardt Amendment"? [excerpts from debate, April 29, 1987] *Congr Dig* 66:184+ Je/Jl '87

Richardson, William

about

A bleak tale of riches to rags. D. Francis. il *Macleans* 100:7 Ag 10 '87

Richie, Kathleen M.

Lost and found [story] il *Américas* 39:49-51 My/Je '87

Richie, Lionel

about

Flying solo: stars take off alone. il pors *Teen* 31:80-1 My '87

Lionel Richie: superstar copes with crossover problems. C. Whitaker. il pors *Ebony* 42:135-6+ F '87

Richie rewards Miami student as 1st 'Scholar'. il pors *Jet* 72:56 Jl 20 '87

Richie splits with Kragen after six-year management. il pors *Jet* 71:17 Mr 2 '87

Richie talks about friend, fellow star Michael Jackson. il pors *Jet* 71:62 F 16 '87

Richie, Michael

The road to Veracruz. il *Américas* 39:22-5+ Mr/Ap '87

Richler, Mordecai, 1931-

Batman at midlife: or, The funnies grow up. il *N Y Times Book Rev* 92:35 My 3 '87

Cinéma vérité. il *N Y Times Mag* p16 Mr 8 '87

Richman, Alan

Calling on the reserves. il *Esquire* 107:22+ F '87

Richman, John Marshall, 1927-

about

Kraft, minus some extra baggage, is picking up speed. K. Dreyfack. il por *Bus Week* p74-5 Mr 9 '87

Richman, Sandy

about

Sandy Richman, stuntwoman. F. DiGiacomo. por *Seventeen* 46:232 Ag '87

Richmond, Peter

12 things no woman has the right to ask her man to give up. il *Glamour* 85:44+ Je '87

Creatures from the black cartoon. il por *Roll Stone* p79-80+ S 24 '87

How do men feel about their bodies? il *Glamour* 85:312-13+ Ap '87

How men really feel about condoms. il *Glamour* 85:304-5+ N '87

The sultan of spike. il pors *Roll Stone* p87+ Jl 16-30 '87

Richmond, Tim

about

Fit, fast and feisty. S. Moses. il pors *Sports Illus* 67:50+ Jl 20 '87

Richmond (Calif.)

Buildings

On the Pacific Rim [Ortho Research Center] G. Anderson. il *Archit Rec* 175:100-3 Jl '87

Richmond (Va.)

Cemeteries

Rural beauty of Hollywood. il *South Living* 22:39 My '87

Galleries and museums

See also

Virginia Museum of Fine Arts

Housing

Landlord in Richmond, Va. fined for racial remarks. *Jet* 72:4 Ap 20 '87

Monuments, statues, etc.

Washington didn't sleep in Richmond. il *Am Herit* 38:82-3 D '87

Richmond (Va.)—_cont._

Race relations

Interracial couple in Richmond, Va. fight to overcome racism [J. and M. Wicker] il pors *Jet* 73:52-5 D 28 '87-Ja 4 '88

Rich's (Firm)

Schools are my business [program for high school students in Atlanta] J. M. Zimmerman. por *Newsweek* 109:6-7 My 11 '87

Richter, Gerhard

about

Gerhard Richter. K. Sofer. il *Art News* 86:201 Summ '87

Richter, Klaus, and others

D-alanine in the frog skin peptide dermorphin is derived from L-alanine in the precursor. bibl f il *Science* 238:200-2 O 9 '87

Rickard, Robert J. M.

about

Look! Up in the sky! It's a bird! It's a fish! It's grist for oddity archivist Robert Rickard. R. Wolmuth. il pors *People Wkly* 27:55-6 My 18 '87

Ricketts, David

about

David and David, a couple of musical moralists who look at L.A. from down the up staircase. il pors *People Wkly* 27:71 Ja 12 '87

Rickettsia

See also

Q fever

Rickey, Carrie

Ready to wear. See issues of Mademoiselle beginning March 1985

What every single girl should know. See issues of Mademoiselle beginning September 1986 through August 1987

Ricklefs, Robert E.

Community diversity: relative roles of local and regional processes. bibl f il *Science* 235:167-71 Ja 9 '87

Rico, Carlos, 1950-

Mexico and Latin America: the limits of cooperation. bibl f *Curr Hist* 86:121-4+ Mr '87

RICO *See* Racketeer Influenced and Corrupt Organizations Act of 1970

Riddell, Rhoda

Everybody smiles at Santa. il *Ladies Home J* 104:134+ D '87

Ridder, P. Anthony

about

Tony Ridder could be just what the editor ordered. P. Engardio. por *Bus Week* p71 N 23 '87

Riddles, Libby

about

Arctic dreams. K. McCoy. il pors *Women's Sports Fitness* 9:22-7+ F '87

Riddles, Sally

The coloring advantage. il *Harpers Bazaar* 120:18+ Ag '87

Your redhead beauty guide. *Harpers Bazaar* 120:109+ Jl '87

Riddles

See also

Rebuses

Ride, Sally K.

Sally Ride on America's future in space. *Space World* X-9-285:25 S '87

about

Getting NASA back on track. A. Toufexis. il *Time* 130:56 Ag 31 '87

A mission to planet earth [interview] L. Sherr. il *Ms* 16:180-1 Jl/Ag '87

Ride panel calls for aggressive action to assert U.S. leadership in space [with editorial comment by Donald E. Fink] C. Covault. il *Aviat Week Space Technol* 127:11, 26-7 Ag 24 '87

Ride panel will urge lunar base, earth science as new space goals. C. Covault. il *Aviat Week Space Technol* 127:16-18 Jl 13 '87

Ride report: charting the nation's future course in space. I. Goodwin. por *Phys Today* 40:64-6 O '87

Ride report: the going, not the goal. J. Eberhart. *Sci News* 132:117 Ag 22 '87

Sally Ride to leave NASA orbit; exodus at NSF. I. Goodwin. *Phys Today* 40:45 Jl '87

Space program said to lack direction. C. Norman. il por *Science* 237:965 Ag 28 '87

Rider College

Salieri at Rider. K. Richardson. il *High Fidel* 37:56 Mr '87

Ridge, Tom

Should Congress adopt the House-passed "Gephardt Amendment"? [excerpts from debate, April 29, 1987] *Congr Dig* 66:180+ Je/Jl '87

Ridged fields *See* Terraces (Agriculture)

Ridgefield (Conn.)

Galleries and museums

See also

Aldrich Museum of Contemporary Art (Ridgefield, Conn.)

Ridgway, Rozanne L.

FY 1988 assistance requests for Europe [statements, February 3 and March 3, 1987] *Dep State Bull* 87:48-54 My '87

Recent developments in Europe [statement, June 18, 1987] *Dep State Bull* 87:65-7 Ag '87

Riding, Alan

Cocaine billionaires: the men who hold Colombia hostage. il map *N Y Times Mag* p26-32+ Mr 8 '87

Riding *See* Horsemanship

Riding mowers *See* Lawn mowers

Ridley, Layne

The 11 worst flying fears—and how they can't, won't or hardly ever come true [excerpt from White knuckles] il *Glamour* 85:112+ Je '87

Ridley turtles *See* Turtles

Riedel, Georgia

Back aid. il *World Tennis* 34:25-7 F '87

Riedel, Heimo, and others

A chimeric, ligan-binding v-erbB/EGF receptor retains transforming potential. bibl f il *Science* 236:197-200 Ap 10 '87

Riedel, Karen

Drill ship probes Indian Ocean mysteries. il *Oceans* 20:6-7 S/O '87

Riedel, Nora, and others

A subset of yeast snRNA's contains functional binding sites for the highly conserved Sm antigen. bibl f il *Science* 235:328-31 Ja 16 '87

Rieder, Jonathan

Inside Howard Beach. *New Repub* 196:17-19 F 9 '87

Rieder, William

A collection of eighteenth-century English furniture. il *Antiques* 131:1314-25 Je '87

Riedmiller, Josef

Threats to the UN. il *World Press Rev* 34:24-5 F '87

Rieff, David (David Sontag)

The second Havana. il *New Yorker* 63:65-9+ My 18 '87

Rielly, John E.

America's state of mind. il *Foreign Policy* 66:39-56 Spr '87

Riesener, Jean-Henri, 1734-1806

about

Jean-Henri Riesener: furniture maker to royalty. A. Bahar. il por *Antiques Collect Hobbies* 92:39-42 N '87

Rifkin, Paul

The God letters [excerpts] il *McCalls* 114:97-8 Ja '87

Rifle sights *See* Firearms—Sights

Rifles

See also

National Rifle Association of America

Caseless-cartridge rifle [G11 assault rifle] D. Scott. il *Pop Sci* 230:40 F '87

The guns of July. B. Woods. il *Mother Earth News* 106:46-9 Jl/Ag '87

The new middle class. D. E. Petzal. il *Field Stream* 91:86+ F '87

Reborn Model 70 and some great new shooting gear. J. Carmichel. il *Outdoor Life* 179:36+ Ap '87

Weight

The ultimate lightweight rifle. J. Carmichel. il *Outdoor Life* 180:21-2+ O '87

Rift Valley fever

Detection of Rift Valley fever viral activity in Kenya by satellite remote sensing imagery [vegetation measurement linked to flood conditions that produce mosquitoes] K. J. Linthicum and others. bibl f il maps *Science* 235:1656-9 Mr 27 '87

Rift Valley fever: long-distance diagnosis [vegetation measurement linked to floods and mosquitoes; study by Kenneth J. Linthicum and others] J. Silberner. *Sci News* 131:199 Mr 28 '87

Rifts (Geology) *See* Faults (Geology)

Riga, Peter J.

No benefit of appeal: registration & basic rights. *Commonweal* 114:582-4 O 23 '87

Rigden, John S.

about

Rigden is new physics director at AIP. por *Phys Today* 40:61-2 Jl '87

Rigdon, Kevin
about
The play's the thing. J. Dolan. il por *Theatre Crafts* 21:28-31+ F '87
Rigging *See* Hoisting equipment—Rigging
Riggs, B. Lawrence
about
The calcium controversy: an expert warns that supplements are not the cure-all for dowager's hump [interview] G. Breu. il pors *People Wkly* 27:69-70+ Ap 13 '87
Riggs, L. Spencer
Rosemeyer revisited [discussion of July 1987 article, The Silver Comet] *Car Driv* 33:16 N '87
The Silver Comet. il pors *Car Driv* 33:141-2+ Jl '87
Varzi's honor. il pors *Car Driv* 32:143-4+ Mr '87
about
Sultan of the Smith Corona. D. Sherman. il *Car Driv* 33:9 Jl '87
Riggs, Michael
Basically speaking. See issues of High Fidelity (New York, N.Y.) through January 1987
Front lines. See issues of High Fidelity (New York, N.Y.) beginning March 1987
Right (Political science) *See* Conservatism; Fascism
Right and left (Political science)
See also
Communism
Conservatism
Fascism
Liberalism
Radicalism
Socialism
Minority report [Second Thoughts Conference] C. Hitchens. *Nation* 245:511+ N 7 '87
The second thinkers [Second Thoughts Conference] A. Cockburn. *Nation* 245:475 O 31 '87
Washington diarist [Second Thoughts Conference] M. Peretz. *New Repub* 197:42 N 9 '87
Right- and left-handedness *See* Left- and right-handedness
Right of asylum *See* Asylum, Right of
Right of entry fees (Immigration) *See* Immigration and emigration—Right of entry fees
Right of privacy *See* Privacy, Right of
Right of way
See also
Railroads—Right of way
Right to die
See also
Euthanasia
Living wills
The Catholic tradition on the use of nutrition and fluids. J. J. Paris and R. A. McCormick. *America* 156:356-61 My 2 '87
Do patients have a "right to die"? M. Christopher. il *Sch Update* 119:21 Ap 20 '87
Is it wrong to cut off feeding? [comatose patients] R. N. Ostling. il *Time* 129:71 F 23 '87
Letters in reaction [discussion of May 2, 1987 article, The Catholic tradition on the use of nutrition and fluids] J. J. Paris and R. A. McCormick. *America* 156:449-52 My 30 '87
Life-defying acts. E. J. Larson and B. Spring. il por *Christ Today* 31:17-22 Mr 6 '87
The miraculous story of a coma survivor [J. Cole] J. R. Heilman. il por *Redbook* 169:90-1+ Jl '87
Right to life movement *See* Pro life movement
Rights, Civil *See* Civil rights
Rights of artists *See* Artists' rights
Rights of women *See* Women—Equal rights
Rigler, Lloyd E.
about
An angel's way . . . L. Kandell. il por *Opera News* 51:8-10 Ja 31 '87
Rigoletto [opera] *See* Verdi, Giuseppe, 1813-1901
Rijsttafel *See* Cooking, Indonesian
Riklis, Meshulam
about
The Guinness affair gets curiouser and curiouser. M. Maremont. *Bus Week* p59-60 My 25 '87
Riley, Alan
Is creative dance responsive to research? bibl f il *Des Arts Educ* 88:36-40 My/Je '87
Riley, Clayton
The color of power. por *Essence* 18:148 N '87
Riley, Jack
about
Rocket ride [cover story] R. L. Collins. il por *Flying* 114:32-6 O '87

Riley, Pat
about
Beers with [interview] J. Capouya. il por *Sport Mag* 78:19-21 Je '87
With a special home court advantage, L.A. Laker coach Pat Riley can't stop winning. N. Geeslin. il pors *People Wkly* 27:143-4+ My 4 '87
Rimsky-Korsakov, Nikolay, 1844-1908
about
Czar Saltan [opera] Reviews
New Yorker 63:107-8 My 18 '87. A. Porter
The golden cockerel [opera] Reviews
New Yorker 63:108-9 My 18 '87. A. Porter
Rinaldo Piaggio (Firm)
Advantage, Avanti. J. M. McClellan. il *Flying* 114:54-63 D '87
Beech, Piaggio weigh market for new business aircraft sales [Beech Starship 1 and Rinaldo Piaggio PD. 180 Avanti] D. A. Brown. il *Aviat Week Space Technol* 126:68-9+ Je 29 '87
Former Gates Learjet employees are assembling Avanti sections. il *Aviat Week Space Technol* 127:78 S 28 '87
Piaggio's Avanti combines jet-like handling with turboprop efficiency [cover story] B. M. Greeley, Jr. il *Aviat Week Space Technol* 127:118-20+ Ag 10 '87
Rinderpest in cattle *See* Cattle—Diseases and pests
Riney, Hal
about
America's hottest adman. F. Kessler. il por *Fortune* 115:110-11 Ja 5 '87
Riney (Hal) & Partners *See* Hal Riney & Partners
Ring (Periodical)
Muhammad Ali inducted to Ring's Hall of Fame. por *Jet* 72:50 S 14 '87
The ring of truth [television program] *See* Television program reviews—Single works
Ring systems (Astronomy)
See also
Uranus (Planet)—Ring system
The changing shape of planetary rings [cover story; with editorial comment by Richard Berry] L. W. Esposito. il *Astronomy* 15:6-17, 45 S '87
Ringelstein, Robert
Finance: business's outlay for plants and equipment holding its own. il *Archit Rec* 175:41+ Jl '87
Ringgold, Faith
about
Faith Ringgold. M. Moorman. il *Art News* 86:159-60 Ap '87
Faith Ringgold at Bernice Steinbaum. L. R. Lippard. il *Art Am* 75:184-5 My '87
Ringle, Ken
The gospel according to Pilkey. pors *Oceans* 20:18-22 Mr/Ap '87
Ringlights (Photography) *See* Photography—Flash equipment
Ringling Bros.-Barnum & Bailey Combined Shows, Inc.
Ladies and gentlemen, presenting—Kenneth Feld. M. E. Recio. il por *Bus Week* p76+ Je 8 '87
Theater. T. M. Disch. *Nation* 244:585 My 2 '87
Ringnecked pheasant shooting *See* Pheasant shooting
Ringoen, Richard
about
A passion for fine-tuning. R. McGough. il por *Forbes* 139:44 My 4 '87
Rings
See also
Wedding rings
Rings of trees *See* Tree rings
Ringwald, Molly
about
Molly Ringwald: a distinctive edge. il pors *Vogue* 177:747-53 S '87
Ringwood (N.J.)
Historic houses, sites, etc.
The moving spirits of Ringwood Manor. R. Lynes. il *Archit Dig* 44:27+ Jl '87
Ringworm
See also
Athlete's foot (Disease)
Rinks, Ice skating *See* Ice skating rinks
Rinzler, Carol Eisen
Does a working woman really need to be married? No. il *Work Woman* 12:60+ Ag '87
Dollars & sense. See isssues of Mademoiselle
For whom the blurbs toll: the most likely to be talked about this month. il *Vogue* 177:475-6 S '87
The greatest moments in a girl's life. il *Am Herit* 38:34-5 F/Mr '87

Rio de Janeiro (Brazil)
Description
Hanging around over Rio [hang gliding] C. Purcell. il
  Américas 39:46-9 S/O '87
Marvelous Rio. E. Newton. il *Black Enterp* 18:81-2
  Ag '87
Rio Grande Valley
In Texas, a grim new Appalachia. F. Gibney. il *Newsweek*
  109:27-8 Je 8 '87
Snowbirds [migratory retirees descend on the Rio Grande
  Valley each winter] L. M. Keefe. il *Forbes* 139:117-18
  Mr 23 '87
Riordan Freeman & Spogli
Sharp shoppers [B. Freeman specializes in leveraged
  buyouts of supermarkets] M. Fritz. il por *Forbes* 140:236
  N 30 '87
Ríos Montt, José Efraín
about
Ríos Montt: from president to full-time church elder.
  K. Piecuch. il por *Christ Today* 31:46-7 F 20 '87
Riots
See also
Prison riots
Belgium
See also
Brussels (Belgium)—Riots
California
See also
Hollister (Calif.)—Riots
Florida
See also
Tampa (Fla.)—Riots
Haiti
Death in the streets. M. Nichols. il *Macleans* 100:19
  Ag 10 '87
Nigeria
Did Muslims plan religious violence? *Christ Today* 31:43
  Jl 10 '87
Panama
See also
Panama (Panama)—Riots
Demonstration against U.S. embassy in Panama [State
  Dept. statement, July 1, 1987] *Dep State Bull* 87:82
  S '87
The general who won't go [M. A. Noriega; with interview]
  J. Smolowe. il por *Time* 130:36-8 Jl 20 '87
Philippines
Aquino: an end to innocence. N. Cooper. il *Newsweek*
  109:37 F 2 '87
'Bloody Thursday'. L. Neumann. il *Macleans* 100:55
  F 2 '87
Death in Manila [demonstrators shot by riot policemen]
  E. W. Desmond. il por *Time* 129:34-6 F 2 '87
New troubles for Aquino. W. A. Taylor. il por *U S
  News World Rep* 102:33-4 F 2 '87
Snapping at the revolution [massacre in Manila and
  aborted military coup] *New Repub* 196:5-6 F 16 '87
Saudi Arabia
See also
Mecca (Saudi Arabia)—Riots
South Africa
A bloody campaign trail. A. Bilski. il *Macleans* 100:26-7
  My 4 '87
Soviet Union
See also
Alma-Ata (Soviet Union)—Riots
Tibet
Fire at the top of the world. F. Willey. il map *Newsweek*
  110:50+ O 19 '87
Fire in a snowy land [pro-independence rioting] W. E.
  Smith. il map *Time* 130:26-7 O 19 '87
The monks' rebellion. M. Nichols. il *Macleans* 100:33
  O 19 '87
Tibet [special section] il *World Press Rev* 34:19-22 D
  '87
Tibetans rally to guard a culture. J. Elbert. *Christ Century*
  104:988-9 N 11 '87
A tinderbox in Tibet inflames U.S.-China relations. J.
  Becker and B. Javetski. il *Bus Week* p53 O 26 '87
Unrest rocks the calm of 'Shangri-La' [anti-Chinese
  demonstrations] il *U S News World Rep* 103:10 O
  19 '87
Riotta, Gianni
Italy. *Nation* 244:453+ Ap 11 '87
Ripken, Billy
about
Billy the Kid rides again. P. Gammons. il pors *Sports
  Illus* 67:18-19 Ag 3 '87

Ripken, Cal, Jr.
about
One rip-roaring family affair. H. Hersch. il pors *Sports
  Illus* 66:26-8+ Mr 9 '87
Send more Ripkens. T. Kirkjian. pors *Sport Mag* 78:57
  Ap '87
Ripken, Cal, Sr.
about
One rip-roaring family affair. H. Hersch. il pors *Sports
  Illus* 66:26-8+ Mr 9 '87
Send more Ripkens. T. Kirkjian. pors *Sport Mag* 78:57
  Ap '87
Ripoffs *See* Fraud
Ririe-Woodbury Dance Company
Reviews:
  Video visions program performed in Salt Lake City.
  L. Kumin. *Dance Mag* 61:27+ My '87
RISC *See* Reduced instruction set computers
Rise Technology Inc.
Rise Technology is earning its name. G. G. Marcial.
  Bus Week p136 My 11 '87
Risk
See also
Hedging (Finance)
Activated oncogenes in B6C3F1 mouse liver tumors:
  implications for risk assessment. S. H. Reynolds and
  others. bibl f il *Science* 237:1309-16 S 11 '87
Decision-making in the presence of risk. M. J. Machina.
  bibl f il *Science* 236:537-43 My 1 '87
The fantasy of life without risk. V. M. Earle, III. il
  por *Fortune* 115:113-14+ F 16 '87
Health hoax and a health scare [address, September
  22, 1987] E. M. Whelan. il *Vital Speeches Day* 54:57-61
  N 1 '87
Perspectives in risk [address, June 1987] M. R. Fox.
  Vital Speeches Day 53:730-2 S 15 '87
Risk assessment [special issue; with editorial comment
  by Daniel E. Koshland, Jr.] il *Science* 236:241, 267-300
  Ap 17 '87
The risks of risk studies. E. R. Shell. il *Atlantic* 260:114-15
  N '87
The signs of life: a guide to assessing your health risks.
  S. Goodman. il *Curr Health 2* 13:3-9 Ap '87
Risk taking (Psychology)
See also
Type T behavior
Fear-free! [women and sports] S. Cummings. il *Health*
  19:44-6+ N '87
Five ways to overcome fear. M. Dalloway. il *Women's
  Sports Fitness* 9:15 Je '87
Getting high on danger. J. Laughridge. *Harpers Bazaar*
  120:89-90+ Jl '87
How dare we? [cover story] R. Weiss. il *Sci News* 132:57-9
  Jl 25 '87
Risky relationships: how to live together when one of
  you wants to live at the edge. B.-J. Raphael. *Glamour*
  85:26 Je '87
A sense of drama [motorcyclist and young son] T.
  Simmons. il *N Y Times Mag* p130 S 13 '87
Some lessons come hard. H. Altman. il *Nations Bus*
  75:6 Jl '87
Were you born to be wild? [quiz] E. Kunes. il *Seventeen*
  46:155 Mr '87
Risotto *See* Cooking—Rice
Risse-Kappen, Thomas
Star Wars controversy in West Germany. *Bull At Sci*
  43:50-2 Jl/Ag '87
Rist, Marilee C.
Antismoking policies can work in schools. *Educ Dig*
  52:53-5 Ap '87
Rita Ford, Inc.
Music boxes and Maxilla & Mandible. H. Bridges. il
  Gourmet 47:28+ S '87
Rita, Sue and Bob too [film] *See* Motion picture
  reviews—Single works
Ritalin
Behavior pills [disciplining unruly kids] E. Salholz. il
  Newsweek 109:76 Ap 20 '87
Ritchie, Dan
The Presbyterian moment. il *Natl Rev* 39:30-1 Jl 31
  '87
Ritchie, Michael
about
The golden child [film] Reviews
  N Y 20:46 Ja 5 '87. D. Denby
  People Wkly il 27:10 Ja 12 '87. T. Cunneff
Rite Aid Corp.
The doctor is in. K. Hannon. il *Forbes* 140:426-7 Jl
  13 '87
Rite of spring [ballet] *See* Ballet reviews—Single works

Rites and ceremonies
    See also
    Circumcision
    Festivals
    Initiation rites
Rejoicing in rituals. S. Kanfer. il *Read Dig* 131:131-2 O '87
    Tahiti
Island fling [French traveler's description of 1903-4 ceremony; excerpt from Journal des îles] V. Segalen. il *Courier* 40:23 Ap '87
    Tonga
Festivities in the Friendly Islands [excerpt from Captain Cook's voyages of discovery] J. Cook. il *Courier* 40:12-13 Ap '87
Ritsko, Alan J.
    about
Made in the U.S.A. R. Koselka. il pors *Forbes* 139:80-1+ Je 15 '87
Ritt, Martin
    about
Nuts [film] Reviews
    America il 157:506 D 26 '87. R. A. Blake
    Macleans il 100:66 N 30 '87. L. O'Toole
    New Repub 197:23-4 D 14 '87. S. Kauffmann
    Newsweek il 110:83 N 23 '87. D. Ansen
    People Wkly il 28:14 N 23 '87. P. Travers
    Time il 130:104 N 30 '87. R. Corliss
Ritter, John
"I'm proud of my brother"; ed. by Jerry Buck. il pors *Redbook* 170:76+ N '87
    about
Maybe John Ritter is bitter about his canine co-star, but Hooperman won't be dropping Britches. il por *People Wkly* 28:82+ D 14 '87
Ritter, Tom
    about
"I'm proud of my brother"; ed. by Jerry Buck. J. Ritter. il pors *Redbook* 170:76+ N '87
Ritter-Murray, Jean
It's time for economic conversion. *Humanist* 47:30+ S/O '87
Rittereiser, Fredric
    about
Trying not to be a second First Jersey. C. Welles. il por *Bus Week* p44 Ja 12 '87
Rittereiser, Robert P.
    about
The fall of the House of Hutton. S. Bartlett. il pors *Bus Week* p98-9+ D 21 '87
Ritual *See* Rites and ceremonies
Ritz, Mary C., and others
Cocaine receptors on dopamine transporters are related to self-administration of cocaine. bibl f il *Science* 237:1219-23 S 4 '87
Le rivali concordi [opera] *See* Steffani, Agostino
Rivalry *See* Competition (Psychology)
Rivalry, Sibling *See* Siblings
Rivarola Matto, Juan Bautista
Soul brother [story]; tr. by Andrés Morales. il *Américas* 39:48-50 Mr/Ap '87
Rivas, Carlos Lehder *See* Lehder Rivas, Carlos
Rivas, Nazario
    about
A reluctant contra's struggle for survival. J. McPhaul. por *Sch Update* 119:16 Mr 9 '87
River blindness *See* Onchocerciasis
River boats *See* Steamships and steamboats
River Café (Brooklyn, N.Y.) *See* Brooklyn (New York, N.Y.)—Restaurants, nightclubs, bars, etc.
River ecology *See* Fresh water ecology
River otters *See* Otters
River pollution *See* Water pollution
River riding
Hot roadsters are breaking the peace [on the Black River] il *Newsweek* 109:27 Je 29 '87
River sediments *See* Sedimentation and deposition
River trips
    See also
    Running rapids
Adrift on the Amazon. W. Hamilton. il *House Gard* 159:64+ F '87
Attacking the Amazon. R. Blount. il pors *Sports Illus* 66:60-4+ Ap 13 '87
Big wheel, big river [Mississippi Queen excursion] C. Males. il map *Travel Holiday* 168:50-5 Jl '87
The great Amazonian expedition [M. S. Forbes and friends] C. T. Buckley. il pors map *Forbes* 140:193-8+ O 19 '87

Jet boating plus brunch or dinner . . . out of Grants Pass [Oregon's Rogue River] il *Sunset* 178:56-7 Je '87
Life on the Mississippi . . . [D. and S. Watson's attempt to run every river in North America] P. Whittell. il pors *Mot Boat Sail* 159:78-81+ F '87
Rhine diary. M. G. Stoddard. il *Saturday Evening Post* 259:90+ S '87
Riding the river with a Kentucky Belle [Ohio River] J. T. Black. il *South Living* 22:22+ Je '87
Steamboat on the upper Mississippi [Mississippi Queen] C. Davidson. il *Am Herit* 38:24+ Ap '87
Taming the Amazon [cruise on 148-ft. yacht Calliope] P. Whittell. il *Mot Boat Sail* 159:36-43+ My '87
Where jungle meets river [Zaire's Congo River] D. Jacobs. il *World Press Rev* 34:62 O '87
Rivera, Edgar
Death and resurrection in Matiguás. *America* 157:261-2 O 24 '87
Rivera, Geraldo
    about
He's tough, smart and honest—just ask him—but Geraldo Rivera wants something more: respect. A. Richman. il pors *People Wkly* 28:135-6+ D 7 '87
What makes Geraldo run? P. E. Bauer. il pors *Channels* 7:62-3 Je '87
Riverbanks Zoological Park (Columbia, S.C.)
Animals: handled with care at Riverbanks Zoo. il *South Living* 22:31-2 My '87
Riverbend Festival (Chattanooga, Tenn.) *See* Chattanooga, Tenn.)—Festivals
RiverPlace Athletic Club (Portland, Or.) *See* Health clubs
Riverport (Mo.)
Swamps, towns, and football downs [proposed St. Louis Cardinals stadium in the Missouri Bottoms] R. R. Pryor. il *Sierra* 72:136-7 Ja/F '87
Rivers, Caryl
Intimate enemies [fiction] il *Good Housekeep* 205:243-6+ S '87
Rivers, Joan, 1937-
    about
The Fox trot ends for Joan Rivers. J. Friedman. il pors *People Wkly* 27:28-31 Je 1 '87
Joan mourns Edgar. R. Meryman. il pors *People Wkly* 28:32-6 Ag 31 '87
Rupert Murdoch, can we talk? R. Grover. il por *Bus Week* p50 Je 1 '87
Rivers, Ulysses J.
K.K. Karanja: young chess champ on a mission. il pors *Ebony* 42:54+ F '87
Rivers, Valerie R.
Tom Lynch: Paris sketchbook. il por *Am Artist* 51:S7-S10 N '87
Rivers
    See also
    Black River (Ark. and Mo.)
    Columbia River
    Fox River (Wis.)
    Friends of the River (Organization)
    Housatonic River (Conn. and Mass.)
    Kings River (Calif.)
    Kissimmee River (Fla.)
    Mattole River (Calif.)
    Merced River (Calif.)
    Mississippi River
    Ohio River
    Rogue River (Or.)
    Sacramento River (Calif.)
    Saint Lawrence River
    Salmon River (Idaho)
    Santa Margarita River (Calif.)
    Savannah River (Ga. and S.C.)
    Smith River (Mont.)
    South Yuba River (Calif.)
    Verde River (Ariz.)
    Water pollution
    Wild and scenic rivers
    Yazoo River (Miss.)
        Regulation
    See also
    Dams
        Wading
    See Wading
        Africa
    See also
    Congo River
        Canada
White-water death trips. A. Steacy. *Macleans* 100:40-1 Ag 17 '87

Rivers—*cont.*
Great Britain
See also
Wye River (Wales and England)
Mexico
See also
New River (Mexico and Calif.)
North America
Life on the Mississippi . . . [D. and S. Watson's attempt to run every river in North America] P. Whittell. il pors *Mot Boat Sail* 159:78-81+ F '87
Sudan
Wadi Howar: paleoclimatic evidence from an extinct river system in the southeastern Sahara. H.-J. Pachur and S. Kröpelin. bibl f il map *Science* 237:298-300 Jl 17 '87
Venezuela
See also
Orinoco River (Venezuela)
Wales
See also
Wye River (Wales and England)
Western Europe
See also
Rhine River
River's edge [film] See Motion picture reviews—Single works
Riverside (Calif.)
Galleries and museums
See also
California Museum of Photography
Riverside (Ill.)
Religious institutions and affairs
Nothing big happened this year [Ascension Church] M. E. Marty. *Christ Century* 104:1191 D 23-30 '87
Riverside Book and Bible House Inc.
Earle Fitz's Bible blitz. R. Clapp. il por *Christ Today* 31:14-15 Ap 17 '87
Riverside Park (New York, N.Y.)
Riverside Drive [park activist S. Angevin] A. Jolles. il por *N Y* 20:30 Ag 24 '87
Riverside Records (Firm)
Riverside Records. C. Farran. il *Road Track* 38:70-2 Ja '87
Riverside Symphony
Musical events:
Alice Tully Hall program. A. Porter. *New Yorker* 63:139-40 O 26 '87
Riverside Telescope Makers Conference *See* Astronomy—Conferences
Rives, Chip
about
Toys for girls and boys. D. S. Looney. il pors *Sports Illus* 67:20-1 D 21 '87
Rivets and riveting
Now, a stapler can become a riveting tool [Xpando T-50XP] il *Consum Rep* 52:73 F '87
Riviera (France and Italy)
Description and travel
Roving the Italian Riviera. S. Weaver. il *Prevention* 39:114-16+ F '87
Rivière, Marie
about
Rohmer's obdurate angel. D. Mason. por *Vogue* 177:36 Ja '87
Rivkin, Richard B., and Putt, M.
Diel periodicity of photosynthesis in polar phytoplankton: influence on primary production. bibl f il *Science* 238:1285-8 N 27 '87
Rivlin, Gary
In Chicago a machine dies. il *Nation* 244:424-6 Ap 4 '87
Uncle Tom Sawyer. *Nation* 245:741 D 19 '87
Rix, Polly Stanoch
Life after high school. il *Teen* 31:24+ S '87
Scoliosis: one 'Teen model's battle. il por *Teen* 31:26+ Jl '87
To tell (or not) on a troubled friend. il *Teen* 31:48+ My '87
Riyadh (Saudi Arabia)
Hospitals
Saving sight in Saudi Arabia [King Khaled Eye Specialist Hospital] I. Badr. il *World Health* p23-4 My '87
Rizzo, Frank Lazarro
about
A fracas in Philadelphia. il pors *U S News World Rep* 103:20 N 16 '87
Philadelphia's bare-knuckled political brawl. T. E. Johnson. il pors *Newsweek* 110:59 N 2 '87
Wilson Goode, Frank Rizzo stump for mayor's seat in Philadelphia election. *Jet* 72:12 Je 8 '87

RJR Nabisco Inc.
The burning question at RJR: now what? [smokeless cigarette] S. Ticer. il *Bus Week* p28-9 S 28 '87
Coming from RJR: high-tech vegetables [joint venture with Biotechnica International] il *Bus Week* p44 O 5 '87
Handy guy with a razor [F. R. Johnson] B. Saporito. il por *Fortune* 116:53 Ag 3 '87
A knack for ending up on top [F. R. Johnson] M. McComas. il por *Fortune* 115:108 Ja 5 '87
RJR Nabisco may cut down on tobacco. G. G. Marcial. il *Bus Week* p116 F 23 '87
Ross Johnson. S. Ticer. por *Bus Week* Sp Issue:222 Ap 17 '87
A sudden exodus leaves Winston-Salem eating dust. S. Ticer. *Bus Week* p69 S 7 '87
Tainted tobacco could poison a hot market [exports cigarettes tainted by weed killer to Japan] N. Gross and S. Ticer. il *Bus Week* p45+ Je 15 '87
What smoke screen? [C. E. Hugel named non-executive chairman] N. J. Perry. il por *Fortune* 116:137-8 O 26 '87
RKO General, Inc.
Singing the company blues [R. Del Guidice's use of computers] M. Antonoff. il por *Pers Comput* 11:155+ O '87
Turning off RKO's licenses [FCC ruling] *Time* 130:42 Ag 24 '87
Will GenCorp bow out of broadcasting—or be pushed? [FCC decision threatens RKO's licenses] D. Lieberman and others. il *Bus Week* p25 Ag 24 '87
RNA
See also
Genetic code
Genetic transcription
Viroids
Apolipoprotein B-48 is the product of a messenger RNA with an organ-specific in-frame stop codon. S.-H. Chen and others. bibl f il *Science* 238:363-6 O 16 '87
Autoreactive epitope defined as the anticodon region of alanine transfer RNA. C. C. Bunn and M. B. Mathews. bibl f il *Science* 238:1116-19 N 20 '87
Cancer's genes and chemotherapy [research with P-glycoprotein mRNA by Ira Pastan and Michael M. Gottesman] *Sci News* 131:57 Ja 24 '87
Cellular localization of somatomedin (insulin-like growth factor) messenger RNA in the human fetus. V. K. M. Han and others. bibl f il *Science* 236:193-7 Ap 10 '87
The chemistry of self-splicing RNA and RNA enzymes. T. R. Cech. bibl f il *Science* 236:1532-9 Je 19 '87
Decreased TRH receptor mRNA activity precedes homologous downregulation: assay in oocytes. Y. Oron and others. bibl f il *Science* 238:1406-8 D 4 '87
Differential expression of c-myb mRNA in murine B lymphomas by a block to transcription elongation. T. P. Bender and others. bibl f il *Science* 237:1473-6 S 18 '87
Diurnal expression of transducin mRNA and translocation of transducin in rods of rat retina. M. R. Brann and L. V. Cohen. bibl f il *Science* 235:585-7 Ja 30 '87
Elevated levels of glucose transport and transporter messenger RNA are induced by *ras* or *src* oncogenes. J. S. Flier and others. bibl f il *Science* 235:1492-5 Mr 20 '87
The evolution of catalytic function. P. A. Sharp and D. Eisenberg. *Science* 238:729-30+ N 6 '87
The glucocorticoid receptor protein binds to transfer RNA. M. Ali and W. V. Vedeckis. bibl f il *Science* 235:467-70 Ja 23 '87
Herpes latency makes 'anti-sense'. D. D. Edwards. *Sci News* 132:356 D 5 '87
Identification of the human U7 snRNP as one of several factors involved in the 3′ end maturation of histone premessenger RNA's. K. L. Mowry and J. A. Steitz. bibl f il *Science* 238:1682-7 D 18 '87
Identification of the iron-responsive element for the translational regulation of human ferritin mRNA. M. W. Hentze and others. bibl f il *Science* 238:1570-3 D 11 '87
In vivo uncoating and efficient expression of foreign mRNAs packaged in TMV-like particles [tobacco mosaic virus] D. R. Gallie and others. bibl f il *Science* 236:1122-4 My 29 '87
Localization of amyloid β protein messenger RNA in brains from patients with Alzheimer's disease. S. Bahmanyar and others. bibl f il *Science* 237:77-80 Jl 3 '87

RNA—*cont.*

A mammalian mitochondrial RNA processing activity contains nucleus-encoded RNA. D. D. Chang and D. A. Clayton. bibl f il *Science* 235:1178-84 Mr 6 '87

Model substrates for an RNA enzyme. W. H. McClain and others. bibl f il *Science* 238:527-30 O 23 '87

Polypeptide sequences essential for RNA recognition by an enzyme. L. Regan and others. bibl f il *Science* 235:1651-3 Mr 27 '87

Reading frame selection and transfer RNA anticodon loop stacking. J. F. Curran and M. Yarus. bibl f il *Science* 238:1545-50 D 11 '87

RNA complementary to a herpesvirus α gene mRNA is prominent in latently infected neurons. J. G. Stevens and others. bibl f il *Science* 235:1056-9 F 27 '87

RNA satellites confer viral resistance [work of Bryan D. Harrison and others] R. Weiss. *Sci News* 132:133 Ag 29 '87

Saccharomyces cerevisiae has a U1-like small nuclear RNA with unexpected properties. P. G. Siliciano and others. bibl f il *Science* 237:1484-7 S 18 '87

A small viral RNA is required for in vitro packaging of bacteriophage φ29 DNA. P. Guo and others. bibl f il *Science* 235:690-4 My 8 '87

Splicing of messenger RNA precursors. P. A. Sharp. bibl f il *Science* 235:766-71 F 13 '87

Structurally distinct, stage-specific ribosomes occur in Plasmodium. J. H. Gunderson and others. bibl f il *Science* 238:933-7 N 13 '87

A subset of yeast snRNA's contains functional binding sites for the highly conserved Sm antigen. N. Riedel and others. bibl f il *Science* 235:328-31 Ja 16 '87

Tissue distribution and developmental expression of the messenger RNA encoding angiogenin. H. L. Weiner and others. bibl f il *Science* 237:280-2 Jl 17 '87

Roach, Alfred J.

The Caribbean Basin Initiative [address, November 17, 1986] *Vital Speeches Day* 53:317-18+ Mr 1 '87

Roach, John V.

about

The quotable John Roach [interview] J. Blackford and A. C. Hixson. il pors *Pers Comput* 11:121-3+ S '87

Roach, Max

about

Drummer Max Roach sets Shakespeare to jazz. por *Jet* 72:57 S 14 '87

Roach, Steve

about

Steve Roach. J. Diliberto. il por *Down Beat* 54:46-8 Mr '87

Roach (Hal) Studios Inc. *See* Hal Roach Studios Inc.

Road & track (Periodical)

Chevy wins one for the gyppers! [Manufacturers Challenge Cup] J. Dinkel. il *Road Track* 39:38-40 N '87

Fun and games at R&T [new staff members] J. Dinkel. il *Road Track* 39:31-4 S '87

How it all comes right [fan letter to Road & track addressed to the wrong editor] A. Girdler. il *Road Track* 39:24 N '87

Miscellaneous ramblings [graffiti on walls of Road & track offices] J. Dinkel. il *Road Track* 38:47-9 Je '87

Road & track 40th anniversary [special section; with editorial comment by Peter Egan] il *Road Track* 38:20, 72+ Je '87

Years ago. See issues of Road & Track

Road construction *See* Highway engineering

Road-killed animals *See* Automobile driving—Animal hazards

Road maps, guides, etc.

Driving by the glow of a screen [Etak Navigator and DriverGuide] P. Elmer-Dewitt. il *Time* 129:63 Ap 20 '87

Map storage on CD-ROM [digital street mapping] D. F. Cooke. *Byte* 12:129-30+ Jl '87

Road show [drama] *See* Schisgal, Murray, 1926-

Road shows *See* Theater, Traveling

Road signs *See* Billboards

The road to Mecca [drama] *See* Fugard, Athol

Roads

See also

   Express highways

   Highway engineering

   National forests—Roads

   Potholes (Pavements)

   Wilderness areas—Roads

The heartland highway [traveling U.S. 50 from Ocean City, Md. to Sacramento, Calif. in Porsche 911 Cabriolet] L. Griffin. il map *Car Driv* 32:84-7+ Ap '87

Federal aid

See Express highways—Federal aid

Finance

See also

   Toll roads

Guard fences

Life and death in the fast lane [highway dividers trap crossing animals] M. Kantor. il *Sierra* 72:14 S/O '87

California

A place to drive [Figueroa Mountain Road] P. Bedard. il *Car Driv* 33:148 Ag '87

Europe

The great transalpine routes. B. Parisi. il *Courier* 40:11-13 F '87

Great Britain

Roads to ruins [destruction of archeological sites by road crews] K. Nurse. il *Hist Today* 37:2 Mr '87

Philippines

A new road in the Philippines spurs development [project supported by World Bank loan] L. V. Coronel. il *UN Chron* 24:66-7 Ag '87

United States

See Roads

Wisconsin

Rustic roads. J. Chapline. il *Ctry J* 14:12 Mr '87

Roadside marketing

Farm fresh [Bay Area] il *Sunset* 179:10-11+ S '87

Roadside stands *See* Roadside marketing

Roaratorio, an Irish circus on Finnegans wake [dance] *See* Dance reviews—Single works

Roasting *See* Cooking—Meat

Roasts, Celebrity

Jump shots and free throws [Democrats roast B. Bradley] L. I. Barrett. il por *Time* 130:13 Jl 6 '87

Robb, David

Bush's covenants. *Nation* 245:616-17 N 28 '87

Robb, J. Wesley

Are scholarship and technology compatible? [address, May 10, 1986] *Vital Speeches Day* 53:220-2 Ja 15 '87

Robberies and assaults

See also

   Bank robberies

   Pillage

Management among thieves [interview with armed robber; excerpt from Bosses] J. A. Wall. *Harpers* 274:23-4 F '87

Robbins, Clyde

(jt. auth) *See* Leckel, John, and Robbins, Clyde

Robbins, Fred

Angie Dickinson is riding high [interview] por *50 Plus* 27:32-3+ Ap '87

Robbins, Jerome

about

Dance Collection names archive for Robbins, launches campaign. por *Dance Mag* 61:7 Ag '87

Fancy free [ballet] Reviews

   N Y il 20:92 Mr 30 '87. T. Tobias

In memory of . . . [ballet] Reviews

   Dance Mag 61:83 My '87. J. Gruen

Robbins, Jim

Burdensome bison. il *Audubon* 89:24+ Ja '87

Violating history. il *Natl Parks* 61:26-31 Jl/Ag '87

Robbins, Michael W.

Buy the beloved country: finding an affordable retreat. il *N Y* 20:48-56+ My 25 '87

Editorial. See issues of Oceans beginning July/August 1986

(jt. auth) *See* Cecil, Jennifer, and Robbins, Michael W.

Robert, Jacky

about

Knowing no boundary. B. Cost. il *N Y Times Mag* p69-70 Ap 19 '87

Robert A. M. Stern Architects

Postmodern paradox [offices in New York City] H. L. Smith, Jr. il *Archit Rec* 175:102-5 Je '87

Robert Halmi, Inc.

Big names, slim budgets—and hit TV movies. D. Lieberman. il *Bus Week* p88 My 25 '87

Robert Maynard Hutchins Center for the Study of Democratic Institutions

Donald McDonald—a career of commitment. P. McDonald. *Cent Mag* 20:18 S/O '87

Robert Mondavi Winery

Buy now, sip much later: these are wines to wait for [wine futures] *Money* 16:13 My '87

The Mondavi method. N. Hazelton. *Natl Rev* 39:60+ N 6 '87

Roberto Clemente Sports City (Carolina, Puerto Rico)

It's a dream come true. J. Kaplan. il por *Sports Illus* 67:95 O 5 '87

Robertovna, Aina
about
From Russia without love: Aina Robertovna's dream and how she got it. D. Blum. il pors *N Y* 20:46-50+ My 11 '87

Roberts, Cokie
about
Couples. M. Orth. il pors *Vogue* 177:388-9 F '87

Roberts, David, 1943-
Boston uncommon. il *Archit Dig* 44:156-9 S '87
Mexico's poet of the commonplace. il por *Archit Dig* 44:38+ My '87

Roberts, Diane
Common sense in the kitchen. il *World Health* p12-15 Mr '87

Roberts, Elizabeth
(jt. auth) See Roberts, Robert C., and Roberts, Elizabeth

Roberts, Francis
School days. See issues of Parents beginning January 1983

Roberts, Gary R.
Big-time college athletics: academic eligibility rules are elitist. il *USA Today (Periodical)* 116:68-70 Jl '87

Roberts, Isaac
about
Discovering M31's spiral shape. G. H. de Vaucouleurs. il por *Sky Telesc* 74:595-8 D '87

Roberts, J. N. (James Nelson)
about
J.N. Roberts: "what's a mother to do?". T. O'Connor. il pors *Cycle* 38:54-7+ Jl '87

Roberts, James Nelson See Roberts, J. N. (James Nelson)

Roberts, James R.
about
Drug money. J. Wynn. il por *Forbes* 139:254 Je 15 '87

Roberts, Jim
Robert Cray: the blues . . . and a little bit more. il pors *Down Beat* 54:23-5 Mr '87

Roberts, Joan
(jt. auth) See Villarosa, Linda, and Roberts, Joan

Roberts, Lee
about
Going topless and other sins. B. Kantrowitz and A. Murr. il *Newsweek* 110:79-80 O 26 '87

Roberts, Mel
about
Black managers face off first for pro baseball. *Jet* 72:49 Jl 20 '87

Roberts, Nancy, 1945-
Think you're too fat? [with introd. by Melody Trask] pors *McCalls* 114:34, 38-9 S '87

Roberts, Oral
about
Did Oral Roberts go too far? R. Frame. por *Christ Today* 31:43-5 F 20 '87
God and Oral. T. C. Muck. *Christ Today* 31:17 Mr 20 '87
A price tag on salvation. L. Black. *Macleans* 100:43 Mr 2 '87
Raising eyebrows and the dead. R. N. Ostling. il por *Time* 130:55 Jl 13 '87
Roberts: troubled healer. por *Time* 129:63 Ap 6 '87
Saving souls—or a ministry? K. L. Woodward. il por *Newsweek* 110:52-3 Jl 13 '87
What will Oral Roberts do next? M. Dobbin. il pors *U S News World Rep* 102:25 Mr 9 '87
Your money or his life. R. N. Ostling. *Time* 129:63 Ja 26 '87

Roberts, Paul Craig
Economic watch. See issues of Business Week beginning September 5, 1983
The unilateral disarmament of the American spirit [address, October 10, 1986] *Vital Speeches Day* 53:212-15 Ja 15 '87

Roberts, Richard Samuel, 1880-1936
about
Richard Samuel Roberts. J. Meyer. il *Art News* 86:35+ Mr '87

Roberts, Robert C., and Roberts, Elizabeth
Reconcilable differences. il pors *Christ Today* 31:17-20 Je 12 '87

Roberts, Roxanne
The truth about blushing. il *Teen* 31:46-7 N '87

Roberts, Roy S.
about
Can Roy Roberts rebuild the GM machine? [cover story] K. D. Thompson. il pors *Black Enterp* 18:57-60+ D '87
Roy Roberts gets top personnel post at GM. por *Jet* 72:27 Ap 27 '87

Roberts, Sam
Criminals, authors and criminal authors. il *N Y Times Book Rev* 92:1+ Mr 22 '87

Roberts, Shauna S.
1987 guide to biotechnology products and instruments. *Science* 235 pt2:G4, G23+ F 27 '87

Roberts, Steven V.
about
Couples. M. Orth. il pors *Vogue* 177:388-9 F '87

Roberts, Thomas M.
about
NRC's political meltdown. E. Marshall. il por *Science* 237:123-4 Jl 10 '87

Roberts, Vera Mowry
Every teacher an arts teacher. *Des Arts Educ* 88:25-7 Ja/F '87

Roberts, Willo Davis
Living with diabetes. il *Parents* 62:306+ N '87

Roberts Rinehart (Firm)
Unpublished work by H. L. Mencken coming from Roberts Rinehart [1926 Hatrack obscenity case] B. Levine. *Publ Wkly* 232:62 O 9 '87

Robertson, Donald F.
Cassini. il *Astronomy* 15:20-4 S '87
Soviet Phobos mission to probe moons of Mars. il *Astronomy* 15:29-32 N '87
U.S. Mars Observer seeks global picture. il *Astronomy* 15:33-7 N '87

Robertson, G. Philip
Nitrogen: regional contributions to the global cycle. bibl il *Environment* 28:16-20+ D '86

Robertson, Gregory
about
A miraculous sky rescue. il por *Time* 129:26 My 4 '87
Rescue in midair! P. O. D'Aulaire and E. D'Aulaire. il *Read Dig* 131:100-5 N '87

Robertson, Lanie
about
Lady Day at Emerson's Bar & Grill [drama] Reviews *Down Beat* il 54:13 Ja '87. M. Bourne

Robertson, Nan
about
'I'm one drink away from a drunk' [interview] B. Brophy. il por *U S News World Rep* 103:63 N 30 '87

Robertson, Pat
about
Again: character tests. il por *U S News World Rep* 103:8 O 19 '87
Con man of the cloth. W. A. Henry. il *Channels* 7:16 Ja '87
Faithful on the move. T. J. Curry. il *Commonweal* 114:727-9 D 18 '87
Getting out God's vote: Pat Robertson and the evangelicals [cover story] F. Edwords and S. McCabe. il *Humanist* 47:5-10+ My/Je '87
God's on his side. A. Kopkind. *Nation* 245:400-1 O 17 '87
His eyes have seen the glory. L. I. Barrett. il pors *Time* 130:22-3 S 28 '87
Kemp's surprising victory. L. Schiffren. *Natl Rev* 39:37+ Ap 10 '87
Letter from Washington. Cato. *Natl Rev* 39:14 Je 19 '87
The Pat Robertson effect. H. Fineman. il por *Newsweek* 110:29 S 28 '87
Pat Robertson: why he can't win. il por *U S News World Rep* 103:16 S 28 '87
The power and the preacher. H. Rainie. il por *U S News World Rep* 103:43-5 D 14 '87
Robertson ascendant. F. Barnes. *New Repub* 197:11-12 N 30 '87
Robertson running. *Christ Century* 104:817-18 S 30 '87
Those fractious Republicans. H. Smith. il *N Y Times Mag* p30+ O 25 '87
Unglad tidings. il por *Time* 130:25 O 12 '87
Wild oats. il por *Time* 130:21 O 19 '87
Will Pat run? B. Spring. il pors *Christ Today* 31:34-6 Ag 7 '87

Anecdotes, facetiae, satire, etc.
Beseeching the Great Decider. A. Fotheringham. il *Macleans* 100:72 D 7 '87
Pat Robertson's catalog essay for a new exhibition of paintings by David Salle. V. Geng. *N Y Rev Books* 34:34 N 19 '87

Robertson, R. Meldrum
(jt. auth) See Dumont, James P. C., and Robertson, R. Meldrum

Robertson, Richard Trafton
about
The world according to Lorimar-Telepictures [interview]
M. Brown and P. E. Bauer. il pors *Channels* 7:78-9
F '87
Robertson, Robbie
about
"The half-breed rides again". J. Cocks. il por *Time*
130:98 N 30 '87
Robbie Robertson [interview] M. Goldberg. por *Roll
Stone* p187-9 N 5-D 10 '87
Robbie Robertson's brilliant return. S. Pond. il por *Roll
Stone* p113-15 N 19 '87
The second coming of Robbie Robertson. M. Goldberg.
il pors *Roll Stone* p65+ N 19 '87
Songs of a native son. N. Jennings. il pors *Macleans*
100:52+ N 23 '87
Robertson, Sara
Chronology 1986. *Foreign Aff* 65 Sp Issue:653-96 ['87]
Robertson, Sheila
High noon at western haystacks. *Sierra* 72:28-9+ Ja/F
'87
White-water Idaho: riding the River of No Return. il
Travel Holiday 167:56-61 My '87
Robertson, Struan
about
High dives into a deep money pool. P. C. Newman.
il por *Macleans* 100:28 F 9 '87
Robertson, Colman & Stephens
Susan Harman: an instinct for high-tech success. P. Finch.
por *Bus Week* p81 F 9 '87
Robeson, Paul, 1898-1976
about
CSU kicks off season dedicated to Paul Robeson. por
Jet 72:53 S 14 '87
Robey
about
On TV's Friday the 13th, it's Robey who makes little
boys really howl. T. Cunneff. il pors *People Wkly*
28:87+ D 14 '87
Robichaud, Bonnie
about
No to sexual harassment. M. Clark. il por *Macleans*
100:44 Ag 10 '87
Robillard, Duke
about
Duke Robillard. J. Macnie. il por *Down Beat* 54:14
Jl '87
Robillard, Mark J.
Robotics. See issues of Radio-Electronics beginning July
1985 through March 1987
Robinette, Glenn A.
about
Dirty tricks again? L. Howard. il por *Newsweek* 110:6
Jl 6 '87
Secord agent. *Nation* 245:40-1 Jl 18-25 '87
Robins, Anthony W.
Top this one: the continuing saga of the tallest building
in the world. il *Archit Rec* 175:56-8+ Ja '87
Robins, Joan
My brother, Will [story] il *Parents* 62:137-40+ Ap
'87
Robins, Natalie S.
The defiling of writers [cover story] il *Nation* 245:367-70+
O 10 '87
Three lives [discussion of October 10, 1987 article, The
defiling of writers] *Nation* 245:666 D 5 '87
about
Two writers probe FBI surveillance of American authors.
W. Goldstein. *Publ Wkly* 232:38 O 30 '87
Robins (A. H.) Company, Inc. *See* A. H. Robins Company,
Inc.
Robinson, Andrea, and Schefer, Dorothy
Beautystyle. See issues of Vogue beginning July 1985
Robinson, Andrew
An elusive master [interview with V. S. Naipaul] por
World Press Rev 34:32-3 O '87
Robinson, Anthony B.
Deceiving ourselves about 'safe sex'. *Christ Century*
104:550 Je 17-24 '87
Robinson, Barbara
The wedding of Willard and what's her name [story]
il por *McCalls* 114:89-93 Je '87
Robinson, Bill
about
Mets coach Bill Robinson going for 'pilot's license'.
por *Jet* 72:50 Jl 20 '87
Robinson, Bishop
about
Baltimore police chief is new top cop for Maryland.
Jet 71:4 Mr 9 '87

Robinson, Britt
Doctors find a prescription for profits. il *Black Enterp*
17:70-2+ Mr '87
Robinson, Bruce
about
English director Bruce Robinson's astonishing debut. R.
Koenig. por *Vogue* 177:40+ Jl '87
Withnail and I [film] Reviews
Macleans 100:55 Jl 6 '87. L. O'Toole
New Repub 197:26-7 Jl 13-20 '87. S. Kauffmann
Vogue il 177:40 Jl '87. M. Haskell
Robinson, Bryan E., and others
The AIDS epidemic hits home. bibl (p65) il *Psychol
Today* 21:48-52 Ap '87
Robinson, David
about
Anchors aweigh. H. Hersch. il por *Sports Illus* 67:22
Jl 6 '87
David Robinson, Navy's top gun: he's NBA-shape, not
shipshape. J. Friedman. il pors *People Wkly* 27:85-6+
F 23 '87
Navy basketball star satisfied by compromise. il por
Jet 72:47 Ap 13 '87
Navy tackles McCallum, and checks Robinson. pors
Jet 72:50 My 11 '87
Robinson, David
AIDS & the law [discussion of October 1986 article,
Sodomy and the Supreme Court] *Commentary* 83:2+
F '87
Robinson, Donald
Mind over disease: your attitude can make you well.
il *Read Dig* 130:73-6 Ap '87
Robinson, Doug
Haute skiing. il *Natl Parks* 61:14-19 Ja/F '87
Robinson, Eddie
about
Sugar Ray Leonard, an Eddie Robinson fan, gifts $250G's
to Grambling. il pors *Jet* 72:50 Jl 13 '87
Robinson, Edward N.
The countryman's trailer. il *Ctry J* 14:25-7 My '87
Robinson, Emma
about
Bermuda's 1st woman named Rhodes scholar. *Jet* 72:33
My 18 '87
Robinson, Frank
about
In America's national pastime, says Frank Robinson,
white is the color of the game off the field. il pors
People Wkly 27:46+ Ap 27 '87
Robinson touted as next Baltimore Orioles GM. por
Jet 73:48 N 9 '87
Robinson, Gloria
(jt. auth) See Boyle, Joseph, and Robinson, Gloria
Robinson, Holly
about
A feisty straight-shooter, Holly Robinson puts the jump
in TV's 21 Jump Street. S. Spillman. il pors *People
Wkly* 28:75-6+ S 21 '87
Robinson, Jackie, 1919-1972
about
40 years after Jackie Robinson, baseball still has no
black managers. N. O. Unger. il pors *Jet* 72:48-51
My 4 '87
40th anniversary: biggest breakthrough in sports [excerpt
from Negro firsts in sports] A. S. Young. il pors
Ebony 42:66-8+ My '87
The fuse that lit the fire. G. F. Will. il *Newsweek* 109:88
Ap 13 '87
Remembering . . . Jackie Robinson. S. A. Robinson.
il pors *Essence* 17:49 Ap '87
Robinson, James A.
Taiwan's generation-long political evolution [address, June
1, 1987] *Vital Speeches Day* 53:633-7 Ag 1 '87
Robinson, James D., III
about
Fund raising in trying times. A. Gabor. il por *U S
News World Rep* 102:53 My 4 '87
Service starts with the man at the top. B. Saporito
and M. J. Williams. il pors *Fortune* 116:108 D 7
'87
Robinson, Jeffrey
Cary Grant: "I've lived my life". il pors *Redbook* 168:28+
Mr '87
Di's bad boy. il pors *Redbook* 169:88-9+ Je '87
London's Dolphin Brasserie. il *Gourmet* 47:60-1+ Ag
'87
The pubs of central London. il *Gourmet* 47:52-7+ Mr
'87
Small museums of London. il *Gourmet* 47:72-7+ D '87
Tea. il *Gourmet* 47:118+ N '87

Robinson, Jerry
about
Raiders' star Robinson facing Calif. drug charge. por *Jet* 72:50 Ag 10 '87
Robinson, Jo
(ed) See Anderson, Karen, 1945-. Small wonders
Robinson, John
about
Double dip for Daly City. K. Moore. il pors *Sports Illus* 67:106-10+ O 26 '87
Robinson, Julian, and others
Yellow rain: the story collapses. bibl f *Foreign Policy* 68:100-17 Fall '87
Robinson, Katherine
Fabric care that works [excerpt from The clothing care handbook] *Work Woman* 12:112 S '87
Robinson, Kathryn
Sweetening the season to be jolly. il *Américas* 39:2-7 N/D '87
Robinson, Linda S.
Peace plan problems. *Commonweal* 114:580-2 O 23 '87
Robinson, Lisa
Spoofing it: the TV rich are very different from the real rich. por *Vogue* 177:207 Ja '87
Robinson, Louie
Nancy Wilson: home on the range. il pors *Ebony* 43:116-18+ N '87
Robinson, Lucy C., and others
CDC25: a component of the RAS-adenylate cyclase pathway in Saccharomyces cerevisiae. bibl f il *Science* 235:1218-21 Mr 6 '87
Robinson, Marilynne
Beyond the pale with Edgar Allan Poe. il *N Y Times Book Rev* 92:11 F 8 '87
Language is smarter than we are. il *N Y Times Book Rev* 92:8 Ja 11 '87
Let's not talk down to ourselves. *N Y Times Book Rev* 92:11 Ap 5 '87
A nasty, empty, dangerous word. il *N Y Times Book Rev* 92:10-11 Mr 15 '87
Robinson, Michael
In a world of silken lines, touch must be exquisitely fine. bibl (p230) il *Smithsonian* 18:94-6+ O '87
Phenomena, comment and notes. il *Smithsonian* 17:30+ F '87
Robinson, Phil Alden
about
In the mood [film] Reviews
Newsweek il 110:77 S 28 '87. M. Reese
People Wkly il 28:12 O 12 '87. T. Cunneff
Robinson, Randall
about
TransAfrica: the black world's voice on Capitol Hill. D. M. Cheers. il pors *Ebony* 42:108+ Jl '87
Robinson, Ray
Big Bird's mother hen [cover story; interview with J. Cooney] il pors *50 Plus* 27:24-7 D '87
Robinson, Robert
about
Black man returns home after 47 years in Russia. S. Booker. il pors *Ebony* 42:67+ Je '87
Robinson, Rumeal
about
The waiting game is over. H. Hersch. il pors *Sports Illus* 67 Sp Issue:67 N 18 '87
Robinson, Sandra Longfellow
Kindergarten in America: five major trends. *Phi Delta Kappan* 68:529-30 Mr '87
Robinson, Sharon A.
Remembering . . . Jackie Robinson. il pors *Essence* 17:49 Ap '87
Robinson, Smokey
about
Smokey Robinson [interview] M. Goldberg. il por *Roll Stone* p61-2 N 5-D 10 '87
Smokey Robinson talks about new hit and a quiet divorce after 27-year marriage [cover story] A. Collier. il pors *Jet* 72:56-8 Jl 13 '87
Robinson, Sugar Ray
about
Bittersweet twilight for Sugar. R. Wiley. il pors *Sports Illus* 67:68-72+ Jl 13 '87
Champ Sugar Ray Robinson subject of TV mini-series. *Jet* 72:48 Je 15 '87
Robinson, Theodore, 1852-1896
about
American impressionist painting. S. B. Sherrill. il *Antiques* 132:662+ O '87
Robinson, Thomas W.
The new era in Sino-Soviet relations. *Curr Hist* 86:241-4+ S '87

Robinson-Shaw, Jill
The American Riviera. il *Vogue* 177:234+ My '87
Robinson Student Humanitarian Achievement Award
Students in public service: honoring those who care [interview with winners] F. Newman. il *Change* 19:19-27 Jl/Ag '87
Robinson's garden [film] See Motion picture reviews—Single works
Robison, Mary
Seizing control [story] *New Yorker* 63:35-6 My 25 '87
Robitaille, Luc
about
The King and his court. P. Fichtenbaum. il pors *Sport Mag* 78:61-2+ F '87
The Kings' crown princes. B. Anderson. il pors *Sports Illus* 66:58+ Ja 26 '87
Robles, Ruth
about
With a new line of suits, formal wear and even (ruff!) lingerie, any hound can put on the dog. il *People Wkly* 28:73 O 5 '87
RoboCop [film] See Motion picture reviews—Single works
Robot arms See Manipulators (Mechanism)
Robots
See also
Manipulators (Mechanism)
Baseball is for robots [study of pitching motion as applied to robotics] E. R. C. Capulong. *Pop Sci* 231:39 Ag '87
Build BERT, the Basic Educational Robot Trainer, (I). K. Brown. il *Byte* 12:113-18+ Ap '87
Build BERT, the Basic Educational Robot Trainer (II). K. Brown. il *Byte* 12:113-14+ My '87
Dextor, the willowy six-footer that bends at the waist [work of Lyman Petrosky] T. Dworetzky. il *Discover* 8:18 O '87
Here come the robots! il *Natl Geogr World* 138:18-21 F '87
Improving robot vision [work of Gerard Medioni] *USA Today (Periodical)* 115:10 Je '87
Invasion of the service robots. G. Bylinsky. il *Fortune* 116:81-2+ S 14 '87
Making a robot out of rubbish [CHICO project for Hispanic students sponsored by University of Maryland] il *Natl Geogr World* 141:25-9 My '87
Mondo-Tronics Space Wings robotics kit. il *Radio-Electron* 58:22-3 O '87
Putting on a robotic balancing act [research by Irving J. Oppenheim and Lyman Petrosky] *Sci News* 132:63 Jl 25 '87
R-E Robot (II). S. E. Sarns. il *Radio-Electron* 58:42-4+ Ja '87
R-E Robot (III). S. E. Sarns. il *Radio-Electron* 58:48-50 F '87
R-E Robot (IV). S. E. Sarns. il *Radio-Electron* 58:52-6 Mr '87
R-E Robot (V). S. E. Sarns. il *Radio-Electron* 58:39-44+ Ap '87
R-E Robot (VI). S. E. Sarns. il *Radio-Electron* 58:62-6 My '87
R-E Robot (VII). S. E. Sarns. il *Radio-Electron* 58:58-60+ Je '87
R-E Robot (VIII). S. E. Sarns. il *Radio-Electron* 58:44-6+ Jl '87
R-E Robot (IX). S. E. Sarns. il *Radio-Electron* 58:57-60+ Ag '87
R-E Robot (X). S. E. Sarns. il *Radio-Electron* 58:56+ S '87
R-E Robot (XI). S. E. Sarns. il *Radio-Electron* 58:56-9+ O '87
R-E Robot (XII). S. E. Sarns. il *Radio-Electron* 58:67-8+ D '87
The robot in the 21st century. I. Asimov. il *Radio-Electron* 58:99-101 My '87
Robotics. M. J. Robillard. See issues of Radio-Electronics beginning July 1985 through March 1987
Robots with a lot of nerve [eye-hand coordination; work of M. Kuperstein; cover story] I. Peterson. il *Sci News* 131:362-3 Je 6 '87
Tech update. il *Pop Mech* 164:96 Ag '87
The Wrights and their robot 'kids'. il pors *Ebony* 42:72+ Mr '87

Agricultural use
Coming: new dairy ideas from Europe and Israel. S. Spahr. il *Success Farm* 85:50 O '87

Art use
Portrait maker [Panasonic's robotic portrait maker] M. Gould. il *Pop Sci* 230:22-3 Je '87

Robots—*cont.*

Control

Coming: graceful robots? [ultrasonic motors] D. Stover. il *Pop Sci* 230:27 Ja '87

Exhibitions

"Ouch! Oooh! Cut it out!" [Robots and beyond at the Boston Museum of Science] J. M. Nash. il *Time* 129:78 F 9 '87

Horse racing use

I got the jock right here; he sure ain't Paul Revere. T. Dworetzky. il *Discover* 8:14 Je '87

Industrial use

See also
Bisiach & Carrù SpA

Limping along in robot land. G. Bock. il *Time* 130:46-7 Jl 13 '87

The revolution that wasn't. il *World Press Rev* 34:48 Ag '87

The risks of robotization. il *Futurist* 21:56 My/Je '87

Robot auto inspector [VICTER (Vision Inspection and Calibration Test by Robot)] D. Scott. il *Pop Sci* 230:66 F '87

Travelling robot to work in radiation-hardened IC lab [Sandia National Laboratories] *Radio-Electron* 58:4 N '87

Troubleshooting with robots [nuclear power plants] *USA Today (Periodical)* 115:14 Je '87

Laboratory use

Robot tackles chemistry's dirty side [work of Phil Fuchs and Gary Kramer] il *USA Today (Periodical)* 115:8-9 Je '87

Military use

See also
Autonomous land vehicles

The Blade runner blues [android soldiers] G. Fjermedal. *Omni* 9:78 Ja '87

Cyberwars. O. Davies. il *Omni* 9:76-8 Ja '87

Securities

Super stocks for tomorrow: robotics. J. Kosnett. il *Changing Times* 41:60-4 Ag '87

Space flight use

Factories in space: the role of robots [cover story] L. A. C. Weaver. il por *Futurist* 21:29-34 My/Je '87

First the robots [Soviet Mars exploration program] P. Jones. *Space World* X-5-281:29 My '87

Robots, Toy *See* Toys

Robots in motion pictures

Method acting [Number 5] B. Weber. il *N Y Times Mag* p86 D 20 '87

Robson, Britt

A quest for excellence [special section] il *Black Enterp* 17:273-4+ Je '87

Reaping high returns from social investments. il *Black Enterp* 18:86-8+ D '87

Robyns, Gwen

Fabulous Fergie flying high. il pors *Ladies Home J* 104:114-15+ F '87

Rocawich, Linda

Lock 'em up: America's all-purpose cure for crime [cover story] il *Progressive* 51:16-19 Ag '87

Tubal ligation. il *Progressive* 51:50 Ja '87

Rocha, Wanda

(jt. auth) See Cetron, Marvin J., and Rocha, Wanda

Rochas, Carole

about

Parisian exotic. J.-M. Baron. il por *House Gard* 159:130-9+ Jl '87

Rochas, François

about

Parisian exotic. J.-M. Baron. il por *House Gard* 159:130-9+ Jl '87

Roche, Anne *See* Muggeridge, Anne Roche, 1936-

Roche, George, 1935-

Good intentions aren't enough. por *U S News World Rep* 102:6 My 4 '87

Roche, Gerard R.

about

Hero hunter. N. J. Perry. il por *Fortune* 116:160+ N 9 '87

Roche, John Pearson, 1923-

From Reykjavik all roads led down. il *Natl Rev* 39:27-30 My 22 '87

Taming the NSC. *Natl Rev* 39:40-2 Mr 27 '87

Roche, Stephen

about

Score a big one for the Irish. A. Wolff. il por *Sports Illus* 67:22-3 Ag 3 '87

Rochelle, Wilbert D.

about

First black mayor serves as head of Jennings, La. *Jet* 72:9 Mr 30 '87

Rochester (Minn.)

Health facilities

See also
Mayo Clinic (Rochester, Minn.)

Rochester (N.Y.)

Dance

National Dance Week is April 26-May 2. H. M. Simpson. il *Dance Mag* 61:14-15 Ap '87

Galleries and museums

See also
International Museum of Photography at George Eastman House

Music

See also
Eastman Opera Theatre

Rochette, Anne

The post-Beaubourg generation. il *Art Am* 75:41-7+ Je '87

Rochette, Ed, 1927-

Numismatics. See issues of Antiques & Collecting Hobbies beginning March 1985

Numismatics. See issues of Hobbies through February 1985

Rochlin, Margy

The eccentric genius of "Crimes of the heart". il por *Ms* 15:12+ F '87

In search of self. il pors *Ms* 16:58-60 N '87

Janet Jackson: in control at last? il pors *Seventeen* 46:130-1+ Jl '87

Rochon, Donald

about

Black FBI agent sues bureau for harassment; white wife threatened. il por *Jet* 73:16 N 23 '87

Rock, Arthur

about

The best investors of our time. il pors *Money* Sp Issue:32-6+ Fall '87

Rock, Maxine

The first-year blues. *Harpers Bazaar* 120:138+ Jl '87

Rock, Victoria

about

Chronicle Books hires New York editor to start children's list. *Publ Wkly* 232:26+ O 30 '87

Rock & Roll Hall of Fame

The joint jumps again as rock 'n' roll's Hall of Fame pays homage to 15 pioneers. il *People Wkly* 27:119-20 F 9 '87

Rock and Roll Hall of Fame [special section] il *Roll Stone* p42-3+ F 12 '87

Rock 'n' roll legends are inducted into Hall of Fame. il *Jet* 71:52-3 F 16 '87

Second annual Rock Hall of Fame bash. M. Coleman. il *Roll Stone* p6-8 Mr 12 '87

Rock bands *See* Rock groups

Rock climbing *See* Mountaineering

Rock concert posters *See* Posters

Rock concerts

Doo-wop [concert at Symphony Space, New York City] *New Yorker* 63:27-8 Mr 2 '87

The Glass Spider tour: designer remedies for Bowie's theatre bug. M. Loeffler. il pors *Theatre Crafts* 21:38-41+ N '87

Live vs. studio. L. Berman. il *High Fidel* 37:55 My '87

Quiet rooms: concert promoters set aside a place for parents. D. Handelman. il *Roll Stone* p15+ Je 4 '87

Superstar acts hitting the road [summer tours] A. DeCurtis. *Roll Stone* p25+ Ap 23 '87

Superstar stadium concerts dominate summer season. J. Ressner. *Roll Stone* p24 S 24 '87

Touring: the road to ruin? [1987 in review] J. Ressner. il *Roll Stone* p81-2 D 17-31 '87

Tours de force [summer concerts] G. D. Garcia. il *Time* 130:70-1 Ag 17 '87

Benefit performances

See also
Bishop Tutu Peace Concert, 1987
Live Aid concert, 1985
Welcome Home concert, 1987

Concerts aim to end funds for contras. S. Pond. *Roll Stone* p15+ O 22 '87

Harry Chapin is gone, but friends carry his song in their hearts. il pors *People Wkly* 28:49-50 D 21 '87

Julian Bond hired to promote Paul Simon tour [Graceland U.S. tour] il por *Jet* 72:55 Je 1 '87

Voices of freedom rock London [benefit for Amnesty International] il *Roll Stone* p6-7 My 7 '87

Anecdotes, facetiae, satire, etc.

Puppy-Aid. J. Queenan. *New Repub* 197:18 D 7 '87

Rock concerts—*cont.*

Food service

Joy of cooking: the life of rock caterers. L. Fissinger. il *Roll Stone* p32+ Je 4 '87

Required: an espresso machine at every stop [rock musicians' contract riders concerning food service] L. Rozen. il *Seventeen* 46:100 Jl '87

History

Live! Twenty concerts that changed rock & roll [cover story; special section] D. Fricke. il *Roll Stone* p44-6 Je 4 '87

Stage lighting

Rock 'n' roll lighting control. S. Pollock. il *Theatre Crafts* 21:44+ Ap '87

Rock critics and criticism *See* Music critics and criticism

Rock drawings *See* Cave drawings and paintings

Rock fertilizers *See* Fertilizers and manures

Rock festivals *See* Music festivals

Rock groups

See also

Phonograph records—Rock music

Rock musicians

See also names of rock groups

Random notes. S. Rogers. See issues of Rolling Stone

Rock and roots: brave new bands. L. Robinson. il *Vogue* 177:54 Jl '87

Seeking pop's promised land [Canadian rock acts] R. Atherley. il *Macleans* 100:36-7 Jl 6 '87

Stricter visa rules could keep new acts out of U.S. [foreign rock bands] M. Goldberg. *Roll Stone* p25+ F 26 '87

Rock music

See also

Black Rock Coalition

Compact discs—Rock music

MTV Networks Inc.

Phonograph records—Rock music

Radio broadcasting—Rock music

Reggae music

Rock groups

Rock musicians

Videodiscs—Rock music

Videotapes—Rock music

Full-metal racket [heavy metal music] S. Pond. il *Roll Stone* p41+ Ag 13 '87

The heavy-metal frenzy. M. A. Lerner. il *Newsweek* 110:59 Ag 10 '87

How rock gives love a bad name [hostility towards women in lyrics] J. Pareles. il *Mademoiselle* 93:92+ My '87

Metallic rock that's designed to shock [speed metal] J. Podhoretz. il *U S News World Rep* 103:50-1 S 7 '87

Midlife music [40 yr. old can't keep up with contemporary rock] M. Goldensohn. il *N Y Times Mag* p48 Je 21 '87

Music yearbook 1987 [cover story; special issue] il *Roll Stone* p6-10+ D 17-31 '87

Pumping out the new sound of rock [accordion] N. Jennings. il *Macleans* 100:50 Ag 10 '87

Raw power [heavy metal] il *Seventeen* 46:54-5 Jl '87

Roadside rock [tourist attractions for rock music lovers] J. Barth and M. Wilkins. il *Roll Stone* p104-5+ Jl 16-30 '87

Rock goes gold [special section; with editorial comment by Kevin Doyle] il *Macleans* 100:2, 30-7 Mr 2 '87

Song '87. il *People Wkly* 27:62-3 Ja 5 '87

Synchronicity and the liberal arts. D. O'Brien. *Des Arts Educ* 88:42-5 Jl/Ag '87

When springtime comes to Philadelphia, even the robins sing Louie Louie [parade to celebrate song] il *People Wkly* 27:34-5 My 25 '87

Anecdotes, facetiae, satire, etc.

La Bamba Hot Line. B. A. Mason. *New Yorker* 63:27 S 7 '87

Golden oldies in the year 2017. C. Gordon. por *Macleans* 100:9 Ja 12 '87

Awards

See also

New York Music Awards

1986 Music Awards [Rolling Stone Readers and Critics Poll] il *Roll Stone* p9-10+ F 26 '87

Critics and criticism

See Music critics and criticism

Economic aspects

'Forbes': Springsteen is rock's top earner. F. Goodman. *Roll Stone* p21 O 22 '87

History

Art rock [excerpt from The art of rock] P. Grushkin. il *Roll Stone* p71-5 S 24 '87

Critics dispute Elvis as king of rock 'n' roll. il por *Jet* 72:53 Ag 31 '87

Rock style: 1967-1987 [cover story; special issue] il *Roll Stone* p74-7+ Ap 23 '87

Twentieth anniversary [Rolling stone; cover story; special issue] il *Roll Stone* p7+ N 5-D 10 '87

Moral and religious aspects

See also

Christian contemporary music

Parents' Music Resource Center

Biafra trial ends in hung jury [J. Biafra] J. Ressner. il por *Roll Stone* p22 O 8 '87

Caution: this music may be hazardous to your virtue. J. Pareles. il *Mademoiselle* 93:139+ N '87

Censorship or sales marketing? [Wal-Mart stops selling rock magazines] K. Henderson. *Seventeen* 46:86 Ja '87

Getting prissy: the new monogamy rock. J. Matheson. il *Glamour* 85:254 N '87

Misogyny and racism top the charts [views of Alix Dobkin] il *USA Today (Periodical)* 116:14-15 Ag '87

Raising kids in an X-rated society [views of T. Gore] F. Barnes. *Des Arts Educ* 89:47-8 N/D '87

Rockers: sending messages as well as music. S. Rubin. il *Teen* 31:36+ My '87

Rockin' with the First Amendment [J. Biafra of the Dead Kennedys acquitted on charges of distributing harmful matter to minors] S. Wishnia. il *Nation* 245:444-6 O 24 '87

Rock's lost God [XTC's Dear God] P. Crescenti. il *Christ Today* 31:64 D 11 '87

Traditional values? [G. Michael's I want your sex] M. E. Marty. *Christ Century* 104:775 S 9-16 '87

Periodicals

See also

Rolling stone (Periodical)

Censorship or sales marketing? [Wal-Mart stops selling rock magazines] K. Henderson. *Seventeen* 46:86 Ja '87

Writing

At work with a wizard of song [J. Vallance] N. Jennings. il por *Macleans* 100:38 Jl 6 '87

A songwriter's South African odyssey [interview with P. Simon] A. P. Sanoff. il por *U S News World Rep* 102:74 Mr 2 '87

Canada

The superstar [cover story; special section] il pors *Macleans* 100:32-8 Jl 6 '87

Germany (West)

Meanwhile, in East Berlin [youths clash with police while attempting to listen to concert in West Berlin] il *Time* 129:20 Je 22 '87

Prince in Europe: a preview of his new show. K. Loder. il pors *Roll Stone* p11-12+ Jl 2 '87

Great Britain

Yankee rock is a hit with Brits. R. Flans. il *Mademoiselle* 93:60 Je '87

Israel

Dylan stirs controversy in Israel. K. Loder. *Roll Stone* p15 O 22 '87

Japan

'Bad' Michael Jackson thrills Tokyo audience during Japan tour debut. il por *Jet* 73:4+ S 28 '87

Michael Jackson conquers Japan and continues his world tour [cover story] il pors *Jet* 73:54-7 N 9 '87

Michael's first epistle [M. Jackson tour; cover story] M. Small. il pors *People Wkly* 28:102-4+ O 12 '87

Soviet Union

Aquarium's leader rises to the surface [B. Grebenschikov] N. Traver. il por *People Wkly* 27:51 Ap 6 '87

Back in the U.S.S.R. M. R. Benson. *Nation* 244:824-6 Je 13 '87

Billy Joel's Russian roadshow. M. R. Benson. il pors *Roll Stone* p16 S 24 '87

Rock in Russia. M. R. Benson. il *Roll Stone* p15-16+ Mr 26 '87

Rock 'n' roll in Red. C. Redden. il *Macleans* 100:8+ S 7 '87

Stas Namin and Ludmila Senchina reign over the pop scene while rock's underground rumbles. S. K. Reed. il pors *People Wkly* 27:46-8+ Ap 6 '87

Rock musicians

See also

Children of rock musicians

Clothing and dress—Rock musicians

Phonograph records—Rock music

Rock & Roll Hall of Fame

Rock groups

USA for Africa

Women rock musicians

Rock musicians—*cont.*

See also names of rock musicians

The beat goes on [rock stars of the 1960s] il *People Wkly* 28:28-31 Ag 10 '87

Beauty and the beat [rock stars who marry models] J. Pareles. il *Mademoiselle* 93:60+ Je '87

The best beats in '87. J. Pareles. il *Mademoiselle* 93:74+ Ja '87

Indecent exposure: will too much hype spoil these rock stars? J. Pareles. il *Mademoiselle* 93:80+ D '87

Music makers on the move. il *Teen* 31:80 Ag '87

Pop rockers hitting a high note. il *Teen* 31:63 Je '87

Random notes. S. Rogers. See issues of Rolling Stone

Required: an espresso machine at every stop [rock musicians' contract riders concerning food service] L. Rozen. il *Seventeen* 46:100 Jl '87

The return of rock's dinosaurs. J. Pareles. il *Mademoiselle* 93:50+ Jl '87

The rock report. L. Fissinger. il *Seventeen* 46:45 Jl '87

Where are they now? [special section] il *Roll Stone* p52-6+ S 10 '87

Photographs and photography

Images 1967-1987 [reprints of original Rolling stone photographs] il *Roll Stone* p71-7+ N 5-D 10 '87

Political activities

Darkness on the edge of the shining city [B. Springsteen and the end of Reaganism] J. Morley. il *New Repub* 196:20-3 Mr 23 '87

Jackson Browne [interview] A. DeCurtis. por *Roll Stone* p157-8+ N 5-D 10 '87

Right rock [rock icons from the '60s turn to the right] J. L. Pasley. *New Repub* 196:22 Mr 23 '87

Rockers: sending messages as well as music. S. Rubin. il *Teen* 31:36+ My '87

Rock's new rebels with a cause. J. Pareles. il *Mademoiselle* 93:160+ S '87

Video vérité: Jackson Browne makes his point about U.S. policy in Central America. A. DeCurtis. il por *Roll Stone* p12 Ja 29 '87

Rock opera

See also

Phonograph records—Rock opera

Rock paintings *See* Cave drawings and paintings

Rock roses (Helianthemum) *See* Sun roses

Rock slides *See* Landslides

Rock songs *See* Rock music

Rockburne, Dorothea, 1934-

about

A beckoning stillness. J. Gruen. il por *Archit Dig* 44:40+ F '87

Röckenwagner (Venice, Calif.: Restaurant) *See* Venice (Calif.)—Restaurants, nightclubs, bars, etc.

Rocket engines

See also

Guided missiles—Propulsion systems

Space vehicles—Propulsion systems

Rocketdyne (Firm)

Rocketdyne proposes changes to improve shuttle engine. E. H. Kolcum. *Aviat Week Space Technol* 126:47+ Mr 2 '87

Rocketdyne selected to build SDI nuclear power demonstration units. *Aviat Week Space Technol* 127:28 D 21 '87

Rockets

See also

Guided missiles

So you wanna build a rocket [advice from R. Truax] il por *Omni* 9 Omni Exper:5+ Ap '87

Accidents and explosions

Launch score: nature 3, NASA 0 [lightning launches rockets at Wallops Island, Va.] J. Eberhart. *Sci News* 131:390 Je 20 '87

Lightning accidentally launches three rockets at Wallops Island. *Aviat Week Space Technol* 126:66 Je 15 '87

History

Last of the rocket team: a conversation with Georg von Tiesenhausen. F. I. Ordway. il por *Space World* X-6-282:29-32 Je '87

Specifications

International research rockets [tables] il *Aviat Week Space Technol* 126:161 Mr 9 '87

U.S. research rockets [tables] il *Aviat Week Space Technol* 126:160 Mr 9 '87

Testing

SDI science office plans to launch electrical space test in November [Spear, for Space Power Experiments Aboard Rockets] T. M. Foley. *Aviat Week Space Technol* 127:28-9 Ag 24 '87

SDI suborbital launch yields data for high-power platform design [Space Power Experiments Aboard Rocket] T. M. Foley. il *Aviat Week Space Technol* 127:26-7 D 21 '87

Rockfish

Food and feeding

See Fish—Food and feeding

Rockford (Ill.)

Bookstores

See Booksellers and bookselling—Illinois

Hospitals

Patients' best friend [pet room at the Swedish American Hospital] il *Prevention* 39:8 Ap '87

Rocking chairs *See* Chairs

Rocks

See also

Geology

Tors

Using small stones to create strong effects. il *Sunset* 179:144 Ag '87

Age

See Geological time

Rocks, Igneous

See also

Granite

Lava

Obsidian

Volcanic ash, tuff, etc.

Disruption of the Mauna Loa magma system by the 1868 Hawaiian earthquake: geochemical evidence. R. I. Tilling and others. bibl f il map *Science* 235:196-9 Ja 9 '87

Lateral isotopic discontinuity in the lower crust: an example from Antarctica. R. I. Kalamarides and others. bibl f il maps *Science* 237:1192-5 S 4 '87

Rocks, Sedimentary

Reading the rocks. K. Almy. il *Sierra* 72:92-4 N/D '87

Rocks in art

Tell the tooth! Dr. Joe Daugherty's rock repast may look filling, but it's a real jawbreaker [converting rocks into fake food] il por *People Wkly* 27:123 My 25 '87

Rockwell, John

Andrew Lloyd Webber: superstar [cover story] il pors *N Y Times Mag* p28-31+ D 20 '87

Music, every which way. il pors *N Y Times Mag* p32-3+ Ag 16 '87

Rockwell, Marian

about

West Pointers flip and fall for Marian Rockwell. L. Rozen. il pors *People Wkly* 27:65-7 Mr 23 '87

Rockwell International Corp.

Rockwell International begins work on replacement shuttle orbiter [OV-105] il *Aviat Week Space Technol* 127:24-5 Ag 10 '87

Rockwell International consolidates space, electronics divisions. *Aviat Week Space Technol* 127:68 Jl 20 '87

Rockwell International investigates production line damage on B-1Bs. W. B. Scott. *Aviat Week Space Technol* 127:29 Ag 17 '87

Rockwell predicts HLV will lower launch costs [recoverable heavy-lift vehicle] B. A. Smith. il *Aviat Week Space Technol* 126:24-5 F 2 '87

Rockwell probe determines causes of B-1B production line damage. *Aviat Week Space Technol* 127:24 S 7 '87

Rockwell sneaks up on the Stealth bomber [challenging Northrop] D. Griffiths. il *Bus Week* p96 Je 29 '87

Rockwell team demonstrates automatic construction of large composite wings. il *Aviat Week Space Technol* 126:333+ Je 15 '87

Rockwell to test space-based missile interceptor for SDI. M. A. Dornheim. il *Aviat Week Space Technol* 127:81+ S 14 '87

USAF, Rockwell strengthen B-1B against bird strikes. D. M. North. *Aviat Week Space Technol* 127:30 D 21 '87

Rockwell International Corp. Avionics Group

Automated military avionics factory reducing flaws in workmanship. il *Aviat Week Space Technol* 127:89-90+ O 26 '87

New automated factory to produce GPS equipment at significant savings [Global Positioning System/Navstar] P. J. Klass. il *Aviat Week Space Technol* 127:102-3+ O 5 '87

Rocky Mount (Piney Flats, Tenn.: Historic house) *See* Piney Flats (Tenn.)—Historic houses, sites, etc.

Rocky Mount Undergarment Co., Inc.

Danger zone. K. Hannon. il *Forbes* 140:54+ N 2 '87

Rocky Mountain Arsenal (Colo.)
Decontaminating federal facilities: the case of the Rocky Mountain Arsenal [with editorial comment by Wallace N. Quintrell] K. B. Wiley and S. L. Rhodes. bibl f il maps *Environment* 29:2-3, 16-20+ Ap '87

Rocky Mountain goats
A mountainous appetite [Olympic National Park] J. Burger. il *Natl Parks* 61:28-31 Ja/F '87

Rocky Mountain spotted fever
Vaccines and vaccination
Cloned gene of rickettsia rickettsii surface antigen: candidate vaccine for Rocky Mountain spotted fever. G. A. McDonald and others. bibl f il *Science* 235:83-5 Ja 2 '87
Spotted vaccine to follow? *Sci News* 131:41 Ja 17 '87

Rocky Mountains
Peak primer. E. Weiner. il *Flying* 114:44-6+ Mr '87
The unfinished wilderness. D. Zaslowsky. il map *Wilderness* 50:10-24 Summ '87

Rocky Mountains region
See also
Hunting—Rocky Mountains region
Wildlife management—Rocky Mountains region

Rococo furniture *See* Furniture, Rococo

Rodale, Robert
With the editor. See issues of Prevention (Emmaus, Pa.)
With the editor. See issues of Rodale's Organic Gardening

Rodale Research Center
Cover crop update [work at the Rodale Research Center] P. H. Johnson. il *Rodale's Org Gard* 34:32-3 O '87

Rodale's Organic gardening (Periodical) *See* Organic gardening (Periodical)

Rodchenko, H. A.
BlueJean-Luc Godard. il *Film Comment* 23:2+ N/D '87

Roddenberry, Gene, 1921-
about
Gene Roddenberry and Majel Barrett's most successful Enterprise isn't a starship; it's their 17-year marriage. N. Geeslin. il pors *People Wkly* 27:111-12+ Mr 16 '87

Rodeghier, Katherine
From Russia with *glasnost*. il *Travel Holiday* 168:60-6 Ag '87
Stratford, On-Tario. il *Travel Holiday* 167:56-61 Je '87

Rodent filth in food *See* Food contamination

Rodents
See also
Beavers
Embryology—Rodents
Eye—Rodents
Hearing—Rodents
Mice
Mutation—Rodents
Prairie dogs
Squirrels
Viscachas
Woodchucks

Rodeo Drive (Beverly Hills, Calif.)
Christmas shopping on the Drive. D. P. Marshall. il *Travel Holiday* 168:20-1+ D '87

Rodeos
Essence woman [L. Hudson, barrel racing champion] B. Taylor. il por *Essence* 17:30 Mr '87
For Houston, an oil-town bust, a cow-town boom [Livestock Show and Rodeo] S. Peterson. il *U S News World Rep* 102:26 Mr 9 '87
Roll out the barrel! When this coltish teen cuts corners, rodeo records fall [barrel racer C. James] il por *People Wkly* 28:139 O 12 '87
Round up for a rodeo [Dixie National Rodeo and Livestock Show in Jackson, Miss.] C. Griffith. il *South Living* 22:8-9+ F '87
Sitting atop a Tornado [bull rider F. Brown] W. K. Stratton. il por *Sports Illus* 66:89 My 25 '87
Photographs and photography
Rodeo! J. DeCindis. il *Petersens Photogr Mag* 16:26-8 My '87
Canada
Calgary's five-ring Stampede [indoor Olympic rodeo] J. Howse. il *Macleans* 100:26 Jl 20 '87

Roderick, David M.
about
A CEO as tough as steel. B. Saporito. il por *Fortune* 116:64 Ag 3 '87
Not in the next 30 days. J. Merwin. il por *Forbes* 140:72-5+ Jl 13 '87
Roderick's plan for an encore will not wow the Street. G. L. Miles. il por *Bus Week* p32 F 2 '87
Waterloo at USX. J. Castro. il por *Time* 129:51 Ja 19 '87

Rodger, Ian
Now Japan faces unemployment. *World Press Rev* 34:44-5 Mr '87

Rodgers, Frank A.
Causes of war and causes of peace [address, February 12, 1987] *Vital Speeches Day* 53:375-9 Ap 1 '87

Rodgers, Johnny, 1951-
about
Former Heisman winner Rodgers gets 6 months. il por *Jet* 71:24 Mr 23 '87

Rodgers, Marion
about
Rodgers and Haardt. L. Fleischer. il *Publ Wkly* 231:77 Ja 16 '87

Rodgers, Nile
about
Stevie Wonder, Nile Rodgers produce disc from 2 coasts. il pors *Jet* 71:56 Mr 23 '87

Rodgers Crossing dam project *See* Dams

Rodin (San Francisco, Calif.: Restaurant) *See* San Francisco (Calif.)—Restaurants, nightclubs, bars, etc.

Rodman, Letha
about
Her brilliant career. il por *Seventeen* 46:88 My '87

Rodman, Maia *See* Wojciechowska, Maia, 1927-

Rodney, Red
about
Blindfold test. M. Bourne. il *Down Beat* 11:45 N '87

Rodney M. Davis (Warship)
Navy commissions 1st war ship named for a black medal of honor winner [R. M. Davis] il por *Jet* 72:38 Je 1 '87

Rodri, Jack
about
Dickerson files $12 million suit vs. Norton's agency. il por *Jet* 72:48 Je 8 '87

Rodrigues, Charles
about
The winner of the Rodrigues Caption Contest. W. Livingstone. il *Stereo Rev* 52:14 Jl '87

Rodrigues Island (Mauritius)
Description and travel
Rodrigues. D. W. Gade. il maps *Focus* 37:34-5 Fall '87

Rodriguez, Chi Chi
about
At 51, Chi Chi's still laughing; now it's on his way to the bank. J. Friedman. il pors *People Wkly* 28:51-2 S 21 '87
Chi Chi has a last laugh. J. Diaz. il pors *Sports Illus* 67:38-40+ N 23 '87

Rodriguez, Hernan
Great expectations. il *World Press Rev* 34:20 Ap '87

Rodriguez, Nicolas, 1939-1986
about
Obituary
Am Craft por 47:71 Ap/My '87. K. Karnes

Rodriguez, Richard
Across the borders of history. il *Harpers* 274:42-9+ Mr '87
What is an American education? *Des Arts Educ* 89:44-6 N/D '87

Rodriguez Roque, Oswaldo, 1949-
Realism and idealism in Hudson River School painting. bibl f il *Antiques* 132:1096-109 N '87

Rodriguez-Soto, Ana
Père Mahfood's Food for the Poor. *America* 156:153-4 F 21 '87

Rodrique, Eustache
about
Ex-boyfriend beheads teen girl with samurai sword in New York. por *Jet* 72:17 Je 8 '87

Rodriquez, Johnette Frick
The ABC's of literacy. il *Ms* 16:74 D '87

Rods, Fishing *See* Fishing tackle

Rods and cones
Distribution of cones in human and monkey retina: individual variability and radial asymmetry [cover story] C. A. Curcio and others. bibl f il *Science* 236:579-82 My 1 '87
Diurnal expression of transducin mRNA and translocation of transducin in rods of rat retina. M. R. Brann and L. V. Cohen. bibl f il *Science* 235:585-7 Ja 30 '87
Divalent cations directly affect the conductance of excised patches of rod photoreceptor membrane. J. H. Stern and others. bibl f il *Science* 236:1674-8 Je 26 '87
How photoreceptor cells respond to light. J. L. Schnapf and D. A. Baylor. bibl (p128) il *Sci Am* 256:40-7 Ap '87

Rods and cones—*cont.*
Intracellular topography of rhodopsin bleaching [toads] C. L. Makino and others. bibl f il *Science* 238:1716-17 D 18 '87
The molecules of visual excitation. L. Stryer. bibl (p116) il *Sci Am* 257:42-50 Jl '87

Roe, Joann
Larsen of the Northwest Passage. il pors map *Oceans* 20:48-53+ N/D '87

Roe, Margie McCreless
As if in prayer [poem] *Christ Century* 104:997 N 11 '87

Roe v. Wade decision *See* United States. Supreme Court— Decisions—Abortion decisions

Roeg, Nicolas, 1928-
about
Castaway [film] Reviews
Time 130:69 S 28 '87. R. Schickel

Roel, Raymond A.
New options (positive) for the troubled Doubleday clubs [interview with P. von Puttkamer] il pors *Publ Wkly* 232:21-3 O 23 '87

Roessing, Walter
Amateur bowlers on a roll. il *Saturday Evening Post* 259:38-9+ O '87
Clint Eastwood: small-town mayor. il pors *Saturday Evening Post* 259:42-5 S '87
High hopes on the slopes. il *Saturday Evening Post* 259:64-5+ D '87
Talking is their game. il *Saturday Evening Post* 259:64-5+ Ap '87

Rogak, Lisa
Both sides now. il *World Tennis* 34:14-15 Mr '87
How to avoid cyclist's knee. il *Women's Sports Fitness* 9:11-12 Je '87
Is your body out of whack? il *Mademoiselle* 93:96 D '87
When mommy moves out: women who choose to give up custody of their children. il *N Y* 20:36-41 Ja 5 '87

Rogé, Pascal, 1951-
about
Rogé's Poulenc. R. Freed. il por *Stereo Rev* 52:141 D '87

Roger Tory Peterson Institute of Natural History
The Roger Tory Peterson Institute of Natural History. il *Conservationist* 42:55 Jl/Ag '87

Rogers, Adrian
about
Nine wins in a row. il por *Time* 129:57 Je 29 '87

Rogers, Barbara Radcliffe
Hanging the harvest. il *Ctry J* 14:73-5 O '87
Marvelous mustards. il *Ctry J* 14:28-31 Mr '87
Wreaths. il *Ctry J* 14:50-4 Ja '87

Rogers, Bernard W.
about
Can NATO survive an arms deal? J. Keegan. il *U S News World Rep* 103:30 Jl 27 '87
Generals can be right. W. F. Buckley. *Natl Rev* 39:56 Jl 31 '87
Memo to the Senate. *Natl Rev* 39:15 Jl 17 '87
NATO's shake-up: exit a European favorite. por *Newsweek* 109:44 Mr 9 '87
The need for nuclear arms [interview] R. Knight. por *U S News World Rep* 102:22-3 Je 22 '87
What's wrong with 'zero' [interview] J. Barry. por *Newsweek* 109:27 Ap 27 '87

Rogers, Carl R. (Carl Ransom), 1902-1987
about
Obituary
Sci News 131:122 F 21 '87

Rogers, Dorothy, 1882-1952
about
Ingenuity and genius: the Rogers Collection. A. Bahar. il *Antiques Collect Hobbies* 92:43-6 Jl '87

Rogers, Earl
about
Counsel for the indefensible. R. F. Snow. por *Am Herit* 38:96-7 F/Mr '87

Rogers, Elaine
You can visualize a new body. il *Women's Sports Fitness* 9:58-9 Je '87

Rogers, Fred
You can be a more sensitive parent. il por *Redbook* 168:88-9+ Ap '87

Rogers, Henry C., 1914-
You promoted a weak person? Here's how to set things right. *Work Woman* 12:15 Ag '87

Rogers, Jackie
Get started. *Good Housekeep* 204:88 My '87

Rogers, James B.
about
Gentleman's quarters: James Rogers' Beaux-Arts town-house in Manhattan. J. Taylor. il *Archit Dig* 44:76-83 F '87

Rogers, John, Jr.
about
A jock shows how to scout for small stocks that can score. D. M. Topolnicki. il por *Money* 16:224 My '87

Rogers, Kelly
about
Town manager fired, mayor quits in row over new black police chief in N.C. por *Jet* 72:8 Ap 6 '87

Rogers, Kenny, 1941-
"Christmas at my house". il pors *Redbook* 170:94-5 D '87
about
Friends. *New Yorker* 63:43-4 N 9 '87
On the road with Kenny Rogers. P. Battelle. il por *Ladies Home J* 104:42+ Ja '87
Photographs and photography
Shooting the shooter. G. Bernstein. il por *Petersens Photogr Mag* 16:39 Ag '87

Rogers, Linda
Regional report: Latin America. See issues of World Press Review beginning September 1986

Rogers, Louisa
Build a better body image. il *McCalls* 114:16 Ag '87

Rogers, Mimi
about
Mimi Rogers: "I used to think I was too normal to be a good actress". S. Drucker. il por *Vogue* 177:84 O '87
Now married to Mimi Rogers, Tom's Cruising days are over. pors *People Wkly* 27:83 My 25 '87

Rogers, Peggy Ellen
All that glitters [cover story] il *Américas* 39:8-13 Mr/Ap '87
Gathering the golden fleece. il *Américas* 39:34-9 S/O '87
A supergrain for the future. il *Américas* 39:36-8 My/Je '87

Rogers, Richard, 1933-
about
City of the future. W. Feaver. il *Art News* 86:44 Mr '87
Exhibition report: New architecture: Foster, Rogers, Stirling. H. Aldersey-Williams. *Archit Rec* 175:73+ Mr '87
London assurance. M. Filler. il *House Gard* 159:90-3+ Ja '87
Open house. D. Saatchi. il por *House Gard* 159:206-13+ N '87

Rogers, Roy, 1912-
about
Once estranged, Roy Rogers Jr. and Sr. see only happy trails from now on. K. Gross. il pors *People Wkly* 28:66-8 Ag 17 '87

Rogers, Roy, 1946-
about
Once estranged, Roy Rogers Jr. and Sr. see only happy trails from now on. K. Gross. il pors *People Wkly* 28:66-8 Ag 17 '87

Rogers, Sheila
Random notes. See issues of Rolling Stone

Rogers, Thomas F.
about
Tank land: a conversation with Thomas F. Rogers. T. Reichhardt. il por *Space World* X-8-284:27-30 Ag '87

Rogers, Trumbull
On the road to mediocrity. il *Publ Wkly* 232:42 D 4 '87

Rogers, Vincent
(jt. auth) See Gable, Robert, and Rogers, Vincent

Rogers (Millicent) Museum (Taos, N.M.) *See* Millicent Rogers Museum (Taos, N.M.)

Rogers (Will) Memorial *See* Will Rogers Memorial

Rogers Communications Inc.
Agitated airwaves [offer for Selkirk Communications] P. Best. il *Macleans* 100:38 O 26 '87

Rogin, Gilbert L.
From the editor. See issues of Discover through August 1987

Roginski, Jim
Fan club organized for Walter Brooks's 'Freddy' books. il *Publ Wkly* 231:105 F 27 '87
Meltzer awarded top honors at SCBW conference. *Publ Wkly* 232:42 D 25 '87

Rogoff, Martin H., and Rawlins, Stephen L.
Food security: a technological alternative: biotechnology can convert biomass into a stable food supply. bibl il *BioScience* 37:800-7 D '87
Rogue River (Or.)
Jet boating plus brunch or dinner . . . out of Grants Pass. il *Sunset* 178:56-7 Je '87
Roh, Tae Woo
about
A cautious victory. B. Levin. il por *Macleans* 100:16 Jl 13 '87
How to have it all: mix old stability with new freedom. M. Tharp. il por map *U S News World Rep* 103:42-4 D 28 '87-Ja 4 '88
Korea votes for economic stability. L. Nakarmi. il por *Bus Week* p69 D 28 '87-Ja 4 '88
Korea's 'Democratic coup' will start another scrap. L. Nakarmi. il por *Bus Week* p32 Jl 13 '87
Old friends. M. S. Serrill. il pors *Time* 129:40 Je 15 '87
Roh wins—but can he rule? [with interview] N. Cooper. il por *Newsweek* 110:22-4 D 28 '87
Roh's bloody victory. M. Nichols. il por *Macleans* 100:40-1 D 28 '87
South Korea's 'miracle' week. M. Whitaker. il por *Newsweek* 110:26-8 Jl 13 '87
A successor in his own image. B. Levin. il por *Macleans* 100:18 Jl 6 '87
Suddenly, a new day [with interview] W. R. Doerner. il pors *Time* 130:34-7 Jl 13 '87
An unlikely champion of South Korean democracy. L. Nakarmi. por *Bus Week* p62 S 14 '87
A vote for stability. J. Greenwald. il pors *Time* 130:28-31 D 28 '87
Rohan-Chabot, Joy de
about
Paris: painting the town. S. Drucker. il por *Vogue* 177:228-33+ Je '87
Rohatyn, Felix G., 1928-
The blight on Wall Street. il *N Y Rev Books* 34:21-3 Mr 12 '87
On the brink. il *N Y Rev Books* 34:3-4+ Je 11 '87
What next? il *N Y Rev Books* 34:3-5 D 3 '87
Rohmer, Harriet
Managua's first book fair. il *Publ Wkly* 232:19-21 S 4 '87
Rohr, Wendy Joi
Are you too concerned with being liked? *Teen* 31:22+ My '87
Best friends: why they're so special. il *Teen* 31:24+ O '87
Facial gestures: do you get the message? il *Teen* 31:20+ Ap '87
Mom-entos. il *Teen* 31:66-7 D '87
Pet peeves: when they drive you wild! il *Teen* 31:100-2 Je '87
Rohr Industries, Inc.
Cost pressures on airframe makers prompt rise in risk-sharing ventures. il *Aviat Week Space Technol* 127:157+ N 9 '87
Rohrer, Heinrich
about
Physics Nobel Prize. P. F. Schewe. bibl f *Phys Today* 40:S70 Ja '87
Physics Nobel Prize awarded for microscopies old and new. B. M. Schwarzschild. il pors *Phys Today* 40:17-21 Ja '87
Rohrig, Byron L.
Believing Thomas. il *Christ Century* 104:350-1 Ap 15 '87
January in the body. *Christ Century* 104:77-8 Ja 28 '87
The most uncomfortable day of the year. il *Christ Century* 104:180-1 F 25 '87
Saints of common place. *Christ Century* 104:934-5 O 28 '87
Röhrl, Walter
about
Perfection on Pikes Peak. L. Griffin. il pors *Car Driv* 33:146-8+ N '87
Roiphe, Anne Richardson, 1935-
"Don't worry!". il por *McCalls* 114:58-60 Ja '87
(jt. auth) See Roiphe, Herman, 1924-, and Roiphe, Anne Richardson, 1935-
Roiphe, Herman, 1924-
If your child goes to the hospital. *McCalls* 114:60 Ja '87
Roiphe, Herman, 1924-, and Roiphe, Anne Richardson, 1935-
Questions on child raising you'd be too embarrassed to ask. *McCalls* 114:77-9 S '87

Roitberg, Bernard D.
(jt. auth) See Mather, Monica H., and Roitberg, Bernard D.
Roitberg, Bernard D., and Prokopy, Ronald J.
Insects that mark host plants. il *BioScience* 37:400-6 Je '87
Roizman, Bernard, 1929-
(jt. auth) See Longnecker, Richard, and Roizman, Bernard, 1929-
Rojas, Fernando de, d. 1541
about
La tragicomedia de Calisto y Melibea [drama] Reviews
Nation 245:245-6 S 12 '87. T. M. Disch
Rojas-Mix, Miguel
The angel with the arquebus. il *Courier* 40:36-8 S '87
Rojo, F., and others
Assemblage of ortho cleavage route for simultaneous degradation of chloro- and methylaromatics. bibl f il *Science* 238:1395-8 D 4 '87
Roker, Al
about
Roker the rain king. L. Schulte. il por *N Y* 20:20 Ag 17 '87
Roland, Alex
We shouldn't build the space station now. il *Technol Rev* 90:22-3 Jl '87
Roldan, Juan Domingo
about
Fourth title for Thomas. R. Wiley. il pors *Sports Illus* 67:34-6 N 9 '87
Record fourth title win sets Hearns atop boxing. il pors *Jet* 73:46 N 16 '87
Role, Sex *See* Sex role
Role, Social *See* Social role
Role models *See* Social role
Role playing
See also
Simulation games in education
Rolfe, John
Muddy track, hopeless long shots . . . it's a living. il *Sport Mag* 78:98 Mr '87
Rolfe, John, and Demartini, Pablo
Uncrowned prince of the Triple Crown. il pors *Sport Mag* 78:63+ Je '87
Rolfe, Ronald S.
about
Two lawyers turning Cravath into a force in takeovers. M. Frons. pors *Bus Week* p103 Ja 26 '87
Rolland, Ian McKenzie
Business [address, November 25, 1986] *Vital Speeches Day* 53:253-6 F 1 '87
Rolle, Esther
about
'Raisin' doesn't typify black family life: Rolle. il por *Jet* 72:59 Ap 27 '87
Roller coasters
See also
Arrow Dynamics, Inc.
All aboard! K. Hannon. il por *Forbes* 140:96-8 Ag 10 '87
Killer coasters. T. H. Cole. il *Pop Mech* 164:56-9+ S '87
Walking the Cyclone [W. Williams, head repairman at the Coney Island Cyclone] *New Yorker* 63:28-9 S 14 '87
Roller skates
Skates on a roll. J. Skorupa and D. Burnside. il *Pop Mech* 164:83-5 D '87
Rolling, Walter A.
about
Black runs company that develops computer ware for Defense Department. *Jet* 72:23 My 4 '87
Rolling pins *See* Kitchen utensils and appliances
Rolling stone (Periodical)
1986 Music Awards [Readers and Critics Poll] il *Roll Stone* p9-10+ F 26 '87
'Rolling stone' history coming from Friendly Press. il *Publ Wkly* 231:251 My 15 '87
Twentieth anniversary [cover story; special issue] il *Roll Stone* p7+ N 5-D 10 '87
Rolling Stones
Keith Richards [interview] K. Loder. il por *Roll Stone* p64-7 N 5-D 10 '87
Mick Jagger [interview] M. Gilmore. il por *Roll Stone* p30-2+ N 5-D 10 '87
Mop-top pop. G. Santoro. *Down Beat* 54:44-5 S '87
The Rolling Stones. M. Moses. il *High Fidel* 37:70+ Ap '87
The Rolling Stones: U.S. tour, November-December 1969. D. Fricke. il *Roll Stone* p62-4 Je 4 '87

Rolling Stones—*cont.*
The Stones: is it all over now? K. Loder. *Roll Stone*
p9 My 7 '87
The Stones on CD. S. Simels. il *Stereo Rev* 52:88-9
Mr '87
Rollins, Barrett J., and others
A cell-cycle constraint on the regulation of gene expression
by platelet-derived growth factor. bibl f il *Science*
238:1269-71 N 27 '87
Rollins, Timothy
about
Tim Rollins & K.O.S. at Jay Gorney Modern Art. G.
Indiana. il *Art Am* 75:137-8 Mr '87
Rolls *See* Bread
Rolls-Royce Ltd.
Pratt & Whitney expands role in V2500 compressor
work; Rolls-Royce retains lead in IAE V2500 cold-
section development. *Aviat Week Space Technol*
126:32-3 Mr 16 '87
Rolls developing increased-thrust RB211 versions for
future transports. S. W. Kandebo. il *Aviat Week Space
Technol* 127:81-2 Ag 3 '87
Rolls examines development of RB211-700 engine for
future twinjet aircraft. *Aviat Week Space Technol* 127:23
Jl 20 '87
Rolls, GE propose engine versions to power A330. *Aviat
Week Space Technol* 126:36 Mr 30 '87
Rolls-Royce and Allison unite to pursue U.S. military
market. *Aviat Week Space Technol* 127:34 O 12 '87
Rolls-Royce commits to developing increased-thrust
RB211-524 version. *Aviat Week Space Technol* 127:36
Ag 24 '87
Rolls-Royce plans to join MTM390 engine program
[French and German program] *Aviat Week Space
Technol* 127:29 Ag 10 '87
Rolls-Royce tests XG-40 engine fuel system, afterburner
design. il *Aviat Week Space Technol* 126:63 Mr 2
'87
Rolls skeptical about early propfan service introduction.
il *Aviat Week Space Technol* 126:68-70 Ap 13 '87
Rolls will request government aid for V2500 SuperFan
development. D. A. Brown. *Aviat Week Space Technol*
126:36 Mr 2 '87
A spanner in the works [privatization of Rolls-Royce
endangered by V2500 setbacks] H. Banks. il *Forbes*
139:36-7 Je 1 '87
Rolls-Royce Motors Ltd.
How to buy a Rolls: follow your nose [scent strip ads]
il *Newsweek* 109:46 Je 22 '87
Rolltop desks *See* Desks
Rolston, Holmes, 1932-
Science & the ways to God. *Commonweal* 114:313-16
My 22 '87
Rolston, Matthew
Kim Basinger [cover story] il pors *Esquire* 108:203-9
D '87
The late show. il pors *Esquire* 107:82-5 F '87
ROM *See* Read only memory
Román, Agustín A.
about
Miami's bishop Agustin Roman defuses a human time
bomb to end the Cuban prison riots peacefully. R.
Arias. il pors *People Wkly* 28:104-6 D 21 '87
'This is a moment of peace'. *America* 157:468-9 D 19
'87
Roman amphoras *See* Amphoras
Roman Catholic Church *See* Catholic Church
Roman Catholics *See* Catholics
Roman Empire *See* Rome
Roman glass *See* Glassware
Roman law
Imagine, if you will, a time without any lawyers at
all. L. Casson. bibl (p230) il *Smithsonian* 18:122-4+
O '87
Roman sculpture *See* Sculpture, Roman
Romance
See also
Courtship
Dating (Social customs)
Alone together: the unromantic generation [cover story]
B. Weber. il *N Y Times Mag* p22-6+ Ap 5 '87
Baby love [parent-child relationship's role in development
of adult beliefs about romance; studies by Phillip
Shaver and Cindy Hazan] M. Roberts. *Psychol Today*
21:22 Mr '87
How romantic are you? [quiz] M. Rosen. il *Good
Housekeep* 204:58+ F '87
How to put romance back in your marriage. J. Brothers.
il por *Good Housekeep* 204:117+ F '87
In praise of fly-by-night romances. B. Hersey. il *Glamour*
85:302 O '87

Modern romance. H. Brubach. il *Vogue* 177:218+ Mr
'87
Romance wreckers. il *Teen* 31:60 S '87
Summer love: girls don't have to get burned. L. Darling.
Mademoiselle 93:80 Jl '87
Summer love: why it's so special. il *Teen* 31:12 Je
'87
Ten-boy summer. S. Nelson. il *Glamour* 85:44+ Jl '87
Romance fiction
Writing the short love story. I. Stewart. *Writer* 100:16-18+
Mr '87
Anecdotes, facetiae, satire, etc.
Ripping Clio's bodice—the chronicles of a sweet savage
hack. F. King. il *N Y Times Book Rev* 92:27+ My
3 '87
Romania
See also
Americans—Romania
Civil rights—Romania
Sexual behavior—Romania
Commerce
United States
See United States—Commerce—Romania
Commercial treaties and agreements
United States
See United States—Commercial treaties and agree-
ments—Romania
Description and travel
See also
Automobile touring—Romania
An American in Romania. G. McTigue. il *Travel Holiday*
167:60-3+ Ap '87
Foreign relations
Soviet Union
See Soviet Union—Foreign relations—Romania
Politics and government
'Down with the dictator'. F. Willey. il *Newsweek* 110:27+
D 28 '87
Romania in the age of *glasnost*. W. Fisher. il *New
Leader* 70:11-13 Je 29 '87
Religious institutions and affairs
See also
Church and state—Romania
Romanones, Aline Griffith *See* Aline, Countess of
Romanones
Romanow, Roy J.
about
Changing of the guard. D. Eisler. il por *Macleans* 100:10+
N 23 '87
Romanowski, Patricia
(ed) *See* White, Vanna. Vanna speaks
(ed) *See* White, Vanna. The world of Vanna
Romantic love *See* Love
Romanticism
Bibliography
Romantic originals. C. Rosen. bibl f il *N Y Rev Books*
34:22+ D 17 '87
Exhibitions
Sharing the poet's obsession [William Wordsworth and
the age of English Romanticism at the New York
Public Library] R. Hughes. il *Time* 130:95 D 14 '87
Words' worth [William Wordsworth and the age of English
Romanticism at the New York Public Library] K.
Larson. il *N Y* 20:140+ D 7 '87
Romanticism in poetry
The Romantics return. P. Pettingell. *New Leader* 70:14-16
Je 29 '87
Romberg, Alan D.
(jt. auth) *See* Gleysteen, William H., Jr., and Romberg,
Alan D.
Romberg, Sigmund, 1887-1951
about
The desert song [operetta] Reviews
N Y il 20:104 S 14 '87. P. G. Davis
Romberger, Judy
Body-beautiful diet guide. il *Teen* 31:16+ Je '87
Mom was mad for 'em (you will be too!). il *Teen*
31:22+ D '87
Rich kids: cashing in on happiness? il *Teen* 31:32+
Ag '87
Romboy homotopy *See* Homotopy
Rome
Bibliography
The Roman revolution? D. Braund. il *Hist Today* 37:49-52
Ap '87
Church history
See Church history—Primitive and early church
History, Naval
How Carthage lost the sea [reconstruction of Punic
warship] H. Frost. il maps *Nat Hist* 96:58-67 D '87

Rome—History, Naval—_cont._
The Madrague de Giens wreck [Roman freighter off coast of France] A. Tchernia. il *Courier* 40:11 N '87

Rome (Ga.)

Race relations
Broadcasting exec gets apology from organization following racial insult [X. Clayton snubbed by Rome, Ga. affiliate of National Federation of Business and Professional Women's Clubs] il por *Jet* 72:32 My 18 '87

Rome (Italy)
See also
Vatican City

Bookstores
See Booksellers and bookselling—Italy

Education
See also
American Academy in Rome

History
A drama of Rome [description of city in 1800] W. Weaver. il *Opera News* 52:24-5 D 5 '87
See also
Opera—Italy

Music

Street traffic
A traffic ban drives Rome crazy. *Newsweek* 109:47 Mr 16 '87

Rome Air Development Center
Forecast 2 programs may revolutionize USAF command, control technology. K. J. Stein. il *Aviat Week Space Technol* 126:68-9+ Mr 23 '87

Romeo and Juliet [ballet] *See* Ballet reviews—Single works

Romero, Curro
about
To fight or not to fight—bullfighter Curro Romero faces a dilemma with horns. W. Plummer. il pors *People Wkly* 28:38-9 Ag 3 '87

Romero, Oscar A. (Oscar Arnulfo), 1917-1980

Assassination
Grave encounters [J. N. Duarte links R. D'Aubuisson to murder] H. G. Chua-Eoan. il pors *Time* 130:32-4 D 7 '87

Romey, William D.
Baltic crafts. il map *Focus* 37:24-8 Fall '87

Romiti, Cesare, 1923-
about
Fiat's unsung Roman general. R. I. Kirkland, Jr. il por *Fortune* 115:64 Ja 5 '87
Steering to new records. R. I. Kirkland, Jr. il por *Fortune* 116:48 Ag 3 '87

Romm, Joseph J.
about
Goldin and Romm are selected to be Congressional Fellows. pors *Phys Today* 40:79 Jl '87

Romney, W. Mitt
about
Putting it on the line. L. Jereski. il por *Forbes* 140:240 N 30 '87

Romneya *See* Matilija poppies

Romualdez Marcos, Imelda *See* Marcos, Imelda

La ronde [ballet] *See* Ballet reviews—Single works

Rondthaler, Edward
Old-fashioned spelling is tuf and dum. por *U S News World Rep* 103:9 Jl 13 '87

Rong Yiren, 1916-
about
China's Mister Right. L. Kraar. il por *Fortune* 115:109 Ja 5 '87

Ronning, Astrid
The bride wore oven mitts. il *Gourmet* 48:80+ Je '87

Rood, Jon P.
Cheated cheetah. il *Nat Hist* 96:42-3 D '87

Rood, Steven
about
Bones of contention get buried in Doggy Court, where justice is tempered with mercy. il por *People Wkly* 27:135 My 11 '87

Roodt, Darrell
about
Place of weeping [film] Reviews
Commonweal 114:16-17 Ja 16 '87. T. O'Brien

Roof decks *See* Decks, patios, terraces, etc.

Roofs and roofing
See also
Shingles and shingling
Vaults (Architecture)
Above all . . . a good roof. S. Carmichael. il *Home Mech* 83:48-9 Ap '87
A monitor roof links two wings of the house. il *Sunset* 178:112 Je '87

Re-roofing? Add insulation. K. L. Herrington. il *Pop Sci* 231:68-9 Ag '87
Romance in the rooftops [condominiums] P. Langdon. il *Atlantic* 260:85-7 Jl '87
A roof under your feet. D. Osby. il *Mother Earth News* 107:22 S/O '87
Roofing: synthesizing design and craftsmanship. P. Green. il *Archit Rec* 175:136-41 F '87
Skylines of fabric. D. Stewart. il *Technol Rev* 90:60-7 Ja '87
Top choices for roofs. R. Barnhart. il *Home Mech* 83:50 Ap '87

Drainage
See House drainage

Maintenance and repair
How to remedy roof ice buildup. A. Rooze and G. Branson. il *Fam Handyman* 37:26-8+ D '87

Waterproofing
See Waterproofing

Rook, Edward Francis, 1870-1960
about
American impressionist painting. S. B. Sherrill. il *Antiques* 131:738+ Ap '87

Rooke, Leon
Pretty pictures [story] *Harpers* 275:31-2 Jl '87

Rookies, Baseball *See* Baseball players

Room air conditioners *See* Air conditioning equipment

Room dividers
Divide and conquer—with fabric. L. M. Dalsgaard. il *Home Mech* 83:66 Jl '87
Divider creates bedroom office. il *Sunset* 178:132 Mr '87
Instead of walls . . . three ways to divide a room. il *Sunset* 179:146 S '87
Room divider supplies privacy, storage. L. M. Dalsgaard. il *Home Mech* 83:16 Ag '87
Storage dividers—two easy-to-build styles. A. W. Lees. il *Pop Sci* 230:95-7 F '87

Room furnishings *See* Household furnishings

The room upstairs [television program] *See* Television program reviews—Single works

Rooms
See also
Alcoves
Bathrooms
Bedrooms
Children's rooms
Dens (Rooms)
Drawing rooms
Family rooms
Garden rooms
Guest rooms
House decoration
Kitchens
Living rooms
Locker rooms
Quiet rooms
Reception rooms
Recreation rooms
Sitting rooms
Spa rooms
Studies (Rooms)
Sun rooms
1,200-square-foot all-in-one room . . . trusses do it. il *Sunset* 178:171 Ap '87
Comfort! Rooms you love to come home to. S. Van Zante and others. il *Better Homes Gard* 65:107-17 O '87
Loom rooms with a view. il *Sunset* 179:124 N '87
Need more room? Build a dormer. G. Branson and C. J. De Groote. il *Fam Handyman* 37:62-3+ Jl/Ag '87
Small rooms. M. Hampton. il *House Gard* 159:118+ My '87
Small-space tactics [decorating] D. L. Caringer and R. E. Dittmer. il *Better Homes Gard* 65:74-81 Ag '87

Rooms, Clean *See* Clean rooms

Rooms, Outdoor *See* Decks, patios, terraces, etc.

Rooms, Remodeled *See* Houses, Remodeled

Rooms in art
Edmund C. Tarbell's paintings of interiors. T. J. Fairbrother. bibl f il *Antiques* 131:224-35 Ja '87
Johan Zoffany and the eighteenth-century interior [cover story] G. Jackson-Stops. bibl f il *Antiques* 131:1264-79 Je '87
Portraits in style: David Mode Payne's paintings of interiors. M. M. Thomas. il *Archit Dig* 44:196-201 Ap '87

Rooms in art—*cont.*
Exhibitions
Charles Sheeler's American interiors [exhibit at the Yale University Art Gallery] S. Fillin-Yeh. bibl f il *Antiques* 131:828-37 Ap '87
Rooney, Andrew A.
Running on empty. il *N Y Times Mag* p26 N 8 '87
Sugar City goes sour. il *Saturday Evening Post* 259:26 Ja/F '87
To kill a maple tree. il *Saturday Evening Post* 259:66-7 Ap '87
Rooney, Andy *See* Rooney, Andrew A.
Rooney, Patrick J.
about
Pat Rooney's back—and he hasn't changed a bit. A. Bianco. il por *Bus Week* p110-11 My 4 '87
Rooney, Rita
Isn't this what Christmas is all about? il *Good Housekeep* 205:120+ D '87
Like father, like daughter. il *Good Housekeep* 204:108-9+ Je '87
Rooney, Pace Group Inc.
Where were the cops? [broker J. A. Lugo] R. L. Stern and M. Fritz. il *Forbes* 139:60-2 Ap 6 '87
Roosevelt, Eleanor, 1884-1962
Christmas 1940 [story] il por *McCalls* 114:95-7 Ja '87
Roosevelt, Franklin D. (Franklin Delano), 1882-1945
about
The big leak. T. J. Fleming. il por *Am Herit* 38:64-71 D '87
FDR's own network: gentlemen spies. il por *U S News World Rep* 102:22 Ja 12 '87
Of many things. G. W. Hunt. *America* 157:74 Ag 15-22 '87
The Roosevelt precedent. por *Time* 129:26 Je 1 '87
Homes
The good neighbor in Warm Springs [Little White House] il *South Living* 22:22 D '87
The house at Hyde Park. G. C. Ward. il pors *Am Herit* 38:41-6+ Ap '87
Photographs and photography
FDR: the last photo. il por *Am Herit* 38:102-3 Jl/Ag '87
Roosevelt, James, 1907-
about
Geezer sleaze. C. Coulson. *New Repub* 196:21-3 Ap 20 '87
Roosevelt Committee draws heavy fire. R. Rosenblatt. il por *50 Plus* 27:14-16+ My '87
Roosevelt, Sara Delano
about
The house at Hyde Park. G. C. Ward. il pors *Am Herit* 38:41-6+ Ap '87
Roosevelt, Selwa
Diplomatic immunity and U.S. interests [statement, August 5, 1987] *Dep State Bull* 87:29-32 O '87
Roosevelt, Theodore, 1858-1919
Assassination attempt, October 14, 1912
1912. K. Ide. por *Am Herit* 38:110-11 S/O '87
Homes
Sagamore Hill: a visit to President Theodore Roosevelt's famous home on Long Island. N. A. Ruhling. il *Antiques Collect Hobbies* 92:38-9+ Je '87
Memorials
See also
Theodore Roosevelt Island (Washington, D.C.)
Roosevelt elk hunting *See* Elk hunting
Roosevelt Island (Washington, D.C.) *See* Theodore Roosevelt Island (Washington, D.C.)
Root, Lawrence S.
Britain's redundancy payments for displaced workers. bibl f il *Mon Labor Rev* 110:18-23 Je '87
Root, William Pitt, 1941-
Ordeal by devotion [poem] *Nation* 244:484 Ap 11 '87
Root cellars
Prefab root cellar [from old freezer] M. Bubel and N. Bubel. il *Mother Earth News* 107:22 S/O '87
Roots, Ivan
Prints, politics & people: The English satirical print, 1600-1832. il *Hist Today* 37:47-53 Mr '87
Roots
See also
Mycorrhiza
Apogeotropic roots in an Amazon rain forest. R. L. Sanford. bibl f il *Science* 235:1062-4 F 27 '87
When growing down isn't good enough [apogeotropic roots; study by Robert L. Sanford, Jr.] *Sci News* 131:188 Mr 21 '87

Roots [television program] *See* Television program reviews—Single works
Rootworms, Corn *See* Corn rootworms
Rope
See also
Knots and splices
Rope jumping
It's time to jump! [Skip Its, acrobatic rope skipping troupe] il *Natl Geogr World* 139:4-9 Mr '87
Jump to it! S. Johnson. il *Women's Sports Fitness* 9:34-8 Ag '87
Roper, Clyde F. E., 1937-
about
Around the Mall and beyond. E. Park. *Smithsonian* 18:28+ My '87
Roper, Lanning, 1912-1983
about
Transatlantic transplant. J. Brown. il por *House Gard* 159:90+ Je '87
Ropp, Steve C.
Panama's struggle for democracy. bibl f *Curr Hist* 86:421-4+ D '87
Roque, Oswaldo Rodriquez *See* Rodriguez Roque, Oswaldo, 1949-
Rorer Group Inc.
Buying into Chapter 11: the method in Rorer's madness [bid for A. H. Robins] C. S. Eklund. il *Bus Week* p73-4 Jl 20 '87
Rorschach test
Anecdotes, facetiae, satire, etc.
Last word. W. C. Mericle. il *Omni* 9:118 Mr '87
Rosa Luxemburg [film] *See* Motion picture reviews—Single works
Rosalind Newman and Dancers
Roz Newman forms a multi-national alliance [Canadian artist P. Hebert's designs for new dance] E. Zimmer. il por *Dance Mag* 61:4 F '87
Rosand, David
Faith in the flesh. il *New Repub* 196:29-33 F 9 '87
Rosario, Edwin
about
Too good for his own good. P. Putnam. il pors *Sports Illus* 67:89-90 N 30 '87
Rosas (Dance company)
On dance [performance of Elena's aria] L. A. Jacobs. *New Leader* 70:23 N 30 '87
Reviews:
Performances of Rosas danst Rosat at the Brooklyn Academy of Music. N. V. Dalva. *Dance Mag* 61:36-7 Ap '87
Woman's work [performance of Elena's aria at the Brooklyn Academy of Music] T. Tobias. il *N Y* 20:108-9 N 23 '87
Rosas danst Rosas [dance] *See* Dance reviews—Single works
Rosch, Leah
Modern-day mentors: five lessons in success. il *Work Woman* 12:55-9 Ag '87
Rose, Barbara
The great big little paintings of Georgia O'Keeffe. il por *House Gard* 159:160-1+ D '87
Rose, Ben
about
Rainbow strobo: a tribute to Ben Rose. D. Brooks. il *Petersens Photogr Mag* 16:16-20+ N '87
Rose, D. F., and others
Magnetoencephalography and epilepsy research. bibl f il *Science* 238:329-35 O 16 '87
Rose, Daniel Asa
Amnesia in Polynesia. il *Esquire* 108:47+ O '87
Cowboys and West Indians. il *Esquire* 107:20+ F '87
Nine lives in New Zealand. il *Esquire* 108:29-30 Ag '87
Rose, David John, 1922-1985
about
Obituary
Technol Rev por 90:4 Ag/S '87. J. I. Mattill
Rose, Dirk
about
Now you see it, now you don't. A. Sloan. il *Forbes* 140:136-7 S 7 '87
Rose, Frank
Pied Piper of the computer. il por *N Y Times Mag* p56+ N 8 '87
Rose, Jeanie C.
Scallops transplanted to algae-damaged beds. il *Oceans* 20:6 Ja/F '87
Rose, Julie
Mourning a miscarriage. por *Newsweek* 110:7 Ag 3 '87

Rose, Kathy
about
Metamorphosis. D. Towers. il *Dance Mag* 61:68-9 S '87
Rose, Kenneth D.
Climbing adaptations in the early Eocene mammal Chriacus and the origin of Artiodactyla. bibl f il *Science* 236:314-16 Ap 17 '87
Rose, Lloyd
about
American splendor [drama] Reviews
Nation 245:725 D 12 '87. T. M. Disch
Rose, Pete, 1941-
about
Pete has 'em seeing Red. H. Hersch. il *Sports Illus* 67:24-7 Ag 10 '87
Rose, Randall
about
Talmudist who would be king. il por *U S News World Rep* 103:51 Jl 13 '87
Rose, Stuart
about
From street kid to superstar? D. Cook. il por *Bus Week* p33 F 16 '87
Rose Bowl (Pasadena, Calif.: Stadium)
Rose Bowl. il *Sport Mag* 78:48-9 Ja '87
Rose Bowl Parade *See* Pasadena (Calif.)—Parades
Rose mallows *See* Hibiscus
Rosé wines *See* Wine
Roseland Dance City (New York, N.Y.)
In New York: celebrating an eternal prom. G. Jaynes. il *Time* 130:10 Ag 17 '87
Roseman, Lenny
about
Teaching s-e-x in school: the facts of life in Mrs. Roseman's class. D. Prince. il por *N Y* 20:56-8+ Ap 6 '87
Rosemeyer, Bernd
about
Rosemeyer revisited [discussion of July 1987 article, The Silver Comet] L. S. Riggs. *Car Driv* 33:16 N '87
The Silver Comet. L. S. Riggs. il pors *Car Driv* 33:141-2+ Jl '87
Rosemond, John K.
Parenting. See issues of Better Homes and Gardens beginning June 1985
Rosen, Anita L.
(jt. auth) See Meddin, Barbara J., and Rosen, Anita L.
Rosen, Benjamin M.
about
Two brief conversations with Ben Rosen. P. Lemmons. *Byte* 12:6 Ja '87
Rosen, Charles, 1927-
Romantic originals. bibl f il *N Y Rev Books* 34:22+ D 17 '87
Rosen, Charles, 1927-, and Zerner, Henri
The avant-garde and the academy: an exchange [discussion of February 26, 1987 article, The judgment of Paris] *N Y Rev Books* 34:48-9 Jl 16 '87
The judgment of Paris. il *N Y Rev Books* 34:21-5 F 26 '87
Rosen, Clare Mead
The eerie world of reunited twins. il *Discover* 8:36-42+ S '87
Rosen, David
(jt. auth) See Bradburn, Norman M., and Rosen, David
Rosen, Judith
Getting your WordsWorth. il *Publ Wkly* 232:419-22 Ag 7 '87
Rosen, Majorie
Confessions of a (failed) quiz show contender. *Glamour* 85:178+ S '87
Rosen, Marcia
Are you ready for marriage? [quiz] *Harpers Bazaar* 120:139+ Jl '87
How romantic are you? il *Good Housekeep* 204:58+ F '87
Rosen, Martin
about
Stacking [film] Reviews
Macleans 100:59 N 23 '87. B. D. Johnson
Rosen, Ora M.
After insulin binds. bibl f il *Science* 237:1452-8 S 18 '87
Rosen, Rick
Supafrost diffusion filters. il *Petersens Photogr Mag* 16:52-3 My '87
Rosen, Roy
Dear doctor. See issues of 'Teen beginning June 1984

Rosen, Zach
My father is my patient. il *Newsweek* 109:10-11 Mr 30 '87
Rosenbauer, Tom
A salmon delights in gaudy colors [cover story; with editorial comment by Les Line] il *Audubon* 89:4, 64-73 S '87
Rosenbaum, Bruce
about
Talk about slimy deals! Peanut butter wrestling is now in the mainstream! A. Fine. il por *People Wkly* 28:99-100 N 9 '87
Rosenbaum, Jean
Softer, safer, saner. il *Women's Sports Fitness* 9:60-1 Ag '87
Rosenbaum, Maj-Britt
Body and soul. See issues of Mademoiselle
Rosenbaum, Ron
Breaking the crack murders. il *N Y Times Mag* p44-6+ N 15 '87
Crack murder: a detective story. il pors *N Y Times Mag* p24-30+ F 15 '87
Movies. See issues of Mademoiselle
Rosenberg, Barbara Hatch
Updating the biological weapons ban. *Bull At Sci* 43:40-3 Ja/F '87
Rosenberg, Barr
about
Money men, California style. il por *Fortune* 116:34 Jl 20 '87
Rosenberg, David A.
The Philippines: Aquino's first year. bibl f *Curr Hist* 86:160-3+ Ap '87
Rosenberg, David Alan
U.S. nuclear strategy: theory vs. practice. bibl f *Bull At Sci* 43:20-6 Mr '87
Rosenberg, Edgar
about
Obituary
People Wkly il pors 28:32-6 Ag 31 '87. R. Meryman
Rosenberg, Evelyn
about
She's an artist whose explosives make a lasting impression. R. Wolkomir. il pors *Smithsonian* 18:166-8+ D '87
Rosenberg, Jan
Archie Bunker, roll over. *Commonweal* 114:470-2 S 11 '87
Rosenberg, John
Of salmon and sovereignty. *Christ Century* 104:428-9 My 6 '87
Rosenberg, Karen
Soviet science fiction: to the present via the future. bibl il *Technol Rev* 90:66-74 Jl '87
Rosenberg, Liz
After the death of a neighbor's child [poem] *New Yorker* 62:69 F 2 '87
Form and experimentation in poetry. *Writer* 100:17-18 F '87
Grant opportunities. por *Harpers Bazaar* 120:139+ Ag '87
In the country of dreamers [poem] *New Yorker* 63:32 Mr 2 '87
Lovesick [poem] *Nation* 245:318 S 26 '87
Rosenberg, Marjorie A.
Inventing the homosexual. *Commentary* 84:36-40 D '87
Rosenberg, Martin
about
Rosenberg and Abbott: giant steps in desktop publishing. P. Finch. il pors *Bus Week* p81 F 9 '87
Rosenberg, Richard M.
Banking in the 80s [address, November 5, 1986] *Vital Speeches Day* 53:232-5 F 1 '87
Rosenberg, Robert M.
about
Two doughnuts and a martini, please. K. Hannon. il por *Forbes* 139:128+ Mr 9 '87
Rosenberg, Rosalind, 1946-
about
Disparity or discrimination? [interview] D. Tell. *Society* 24:4-10 S/O '87
Rosenberg, Steven A.
about
Cancer M.D.'s clash over interleukin therapy. M. Bloom. il por *Science* 235:154-5 Ja 9 '87
Interleukin-2: an encouraging study. por *Newsweek* 109:74 Ap 20 '87
Rosenberg, Susan Lisa
about
The women of Lexington Prison. W. A. Reuben and C. Norman. il *Nation* 244:881-4 Je 27 '87

Rosenberg, Tina
Chile's student leaders under fire. il *Roll Stone* p97+ S 24 '87
Death watch in Mexico. il *Nation* 244:500-2+ Ap 18 '87
Smuggler's paradise. *New Repub* 196:14-16 Je 8 '87 (jt. auth) See Morley, Jefferson, and Rosenberg, Tina

Rosenberg Institutional Equity Management
Money men, California style. il por *Fortune* 116:34 Jl 20 '87

Rosenblatt, Bernard S.
A case for theory. bibl f *Des Arts Educ* 88:31-5 My/Je '87

Rosenblum, Robert
Art: the Boston school of painters. il *Archit Dig* 44:188-93 My '87
Art: tiny paintings. il *Archit Dig* 44:222-7 N '87

Rosencrantz & Guildenstern are dead [drama] See Stoppard, Tom

Rosendale, Don
A whistle-blower. il *N Y Times Mag* p56 Je 7 '87

Rosenfeld, Alan
about
Gruntal & Co. [interview] il por *Fortune* 116 Sp Issue:180-1 Fall '87

Rosenfeld, Anne H., and Stark, Elizabeth
The prime of our lives. bibl (p94) il *Psychol Today* 21:62-4+ My '87

Rosenfeld, Eric
Looking beyond. il *World Tennis* 34:44-6 My '87

Rosenfield, Israel
Neural Darwinism: an exchange [discussion of October 9, 1986 article, Neural Darwinism: a new approach to memory and perception] *N Y Rev Books* 34:44-5 Mr 12 '87

Rosenfield, James H.
about
Rosenfield to the rescue. R. Buck. il por *Channels* 7:14 Jl/Ag '87

Der Rosenkavalier [opera] See Strauss, Richard, 1864-1949

Rosenquist, James, 1933-
about
Advertisements for a mean utopia. H. Cotter. il *Art Am* 75:82-9 Ja '87
Photographs and photography
Being open to suggestions brings the best results. J. Loengard. il *Pop Photogr* 94:52 D '87

Rosenstein, Jeffrey M.
Neocortical transplants in the mammalian brain lack a blood-brain barrier to macromolecules. bibl f il *Science* 235:772-4 F 13 '87

Rosenthal, A. M.
AIDS: what must be done now. *Read Dig* 131:91-2 S '87
about
Abe speaks his mind. J. Alter. il por *Newsweek* 109:54 Mr 9 '87
The hugs of A. M. Rosenthal and the fear of cod. J. Gorman. il *Discover* 8:22+ My '87
Short-notice wisdom. T. Griffith. il por *Time* 129:62 F 9 '87
War and remembrance. L. Wieseltier. *New Repub* 196:50 F 9 '87

Rosenthal, Ceil
Workshops. See issues of Popular Photography beginning June 1986

Rosenthal, David
An English accent at Kentshire. il pors *Archit Dig* 44:78+ Mr '87
Pre-Columbian priority: rare treasures in a Manhattan apartment. il *Archit Dig* 44:140-4+ Ag '87

Rosenthal, Edward Cohen- See Cohen-Rosenthal, Edward

Rosenthal, Elisabeth
When pain is the only choice. il *Discover* 8:24 D '87

Rosenthal, Harold D., 1917-1987
about
Obituary
Opera News il por 52:30 Jl '87. G. H. H. L. Harewood, 7th Earl of

Rosenthal, Jack
The ring of untruth. il *N Y Times Mag* p12+ Ag 2 '87

Rosenthal, Lawrence
Decline of the Italian left. il *Nation* 244:878-81 Je 27 '87

Rosenthal, Manuel, 1904-
about
Rien de trop. D. Harris. por *Opera News* 51:10-11+ My '87

Rosenthal, Mike
Return of the leaper. il *Ctry J* 14:30-5 Jl '87

Rosenthal, Raymond
(tr) See Levi, Primo, 1919-1987. Beyond judgment

Rosenwald, Peter J.
Britain takes the stage. il *Horizon* 30:29-31 N '87

Rosenzweig, Anne
about
Once it was Jack and Charlie's and now it's Ken and Anne's, but is it still the 21 Club? A. Richman. il pors *People Wkly* 27:49-50 My 25 '87

Rosenzweig, Roy
American labor history: a conspiracy of silence? bibl f *Mon Labor Rev* 110:51-3 Ag '87

Roser, Steven M.
Head pain: could it be a TMJ disorder? por *McCalls* 115:82 O '87

Roses
Advice from the rose growers: don't baby the miniatures. il *Sunset* 178:251 Ap '87
Celebrating the rose. E. Henke. il *Saturday Evening Post* 259:46-7 Jl/Ag '87
A gift of roses—make it last! R. Haskell. il *Flower Gard* 31:8 F/Mr '87
Give roses a good start. il *South Living* 22:60 F '87
Meet 1987's crop of new roses. il *Sunset* 178:205 Mr '87
A riot of roses. C. McLaughlin. il *50 Plus* 27:66-9 Jl '87
A riot of roses [Pennsylvania rose garden of Dr. Joseph Kassab] C. Vogel. il *N Y Times Mag* p52-3 My 24 '87
Time to prune roses [excerpt from Basic gardening] M. MacCaskey. il *Flower Gard* 31:72-3 F/Mr '87
Welcome roses into the garden. T. A. Steadman. il *South Living* 22:54-5 S '87
Where has all the fragrance gone? M. Mohs. il *Discover* 8:90-1+ Je '87
All-America Selections
See Plants—All-America Selections
Anecdotes, facetiae, satire, etc.
Who said a rose is a rose!? M. G. Stoddard. il *Saturday Evening Post* 259:46-7 Ap '87

Roses, Sun See Sun roses

Roses, Wars of the, 1455-1485 See Great Britain—History—Wars of the Roses, 1455-1485

Roseth, Gene
Phonlink interactive remote control (I). il *Radio-Electron* 58:39-41 My '87
Phonlink interactive remote control (II). il *Radio-Electron* 58:53-7 Je '87

Rosett, Jane, and Ray, Gypsy
Facing AIDS. il *Ms* 16:64-9 S '87

Rosette (Nebula) See Nebulae

Rosewood Financial (Firm)
Mrs. Hunt's Rainwater [M. Hobbs] L. Gubernick. por *Forbes* 140:108 Ag 24 '87

Le Rosey (School) See Private schools—Switzerland

Rosi, Francesco
about
Rosi and the Italian film crisis. P. Lennon. por *World Press Rev* 34:56 Jl '87

Rosie's Cafe [drama] See Shiomi, R. A.

Rosin, Mark Bruce
Stepfathers & stepkids—can they get along? il *Parents* 62:221-2+ Ap '87

Roslansky, Roger D.
Saving energy. il *Nations Bus* 75:40 Ja '87

Rosomoff, Hubert L.
about
Hubert Rosomoff only hurts the back-pain patients he loves. D. Van Biema. il pors *People Wkly* 27:73-4+ My 18 '87

Rosovsky, Henry
Highest education. *New Repub* 197:13-14 Jl 13-20 '87

Rosovsky, Jay Martin, 1945-
about
Frying pan to fire. B. Leonard. il por *Forbes* 139:116+ Ap 6 '87

Ross, Aden
Tenure or The great chain of being. il *Change* 19:54-5 Jl/Ag '87

Ross, Albion
Public affairs journalism. *Cent Mag* 20:33-5 Mr/Ap '87

Ross, D. S. Carne- See Carne-Ross, D. S.

Ross, Daniel Charles
Detroit report. See issues of Motor Trend

Ross, Donald R.
Risk and reality: the AIDS crisis and insurance [address, July 14, 1987] *Vital Speeches Day* 53:681-4 S 1 '87

Ross, Ethel
about
A childhood of sorrows [excerpt from Call me Anna] P. Duke and K. Turan. il pors *People Wkly* 28:70-2+ Jl 13 '87
A troubled coming of age [excerpt from Call me Anna] P. Duke and K. Turan. il pors *People Wkly* 28:54-6+ Jl 20 '87

Ross, Gary N.
A blue future for Mexican indigo. il *Américas* 39:40-6 Jl/Ag '87

Ross, Glynn
about
Ringleader for opera. K. Milam. il por *Horizon* 30:48 My '87

Ross, Herbert
about
Dancers [film] Reviews
Dance Mag il 61:36-43 O '87. J. Gruen
New Repub 197:25-6 N 9 '87. S. Kauffmann
Newsweek il 110:86 O 26 '87. D. Ansen
Vogue il 177:220-3+ Jl '87. H. Brubach
'Giselle' goes to Hollywood. M. Pally. il por *Film Comment* 23:80+ S/O '87
The secret of my success [film] Reviews
Commonweal 114:318-19 My 22 '87. T. O'Brien
Macleans il 100:53-4 Ap 20 '87
N Y 20:126+ Ap 27 '87. D. Denby
New Repub 196:24 My 11 '87. S. Kauffmann
New Yorker 63:130+ My 4 '87. P. Kael
People Wkly il 27:8 Ap 27 '87. S. Haller
Time il 129:97 My 4 '87. R. Corliss
USA Today (Periodical) 116:43 Jl '87. K. R. Hey

Ross, Irwin, 1919-
In demand: Wall Street's liberals. il *Fortune* 115:187-8+ Ap 27 '87
A new drug that fights cholesterol. il *Read Dig* 131:91-4 D '87

Ross, Janice
Back to basics [cover story] il por *Dance Mag* 61:38-43 Ag '87

Ross, Jerrold
The Holmes Group: implications for arts education. bibl *Des Arts Educ* 89:19-24 S/O '87

Ross, John
about
A childhood of sorrows [excerpt from Call me Anna] P. Duke and K. Turan. il pors *People Wkly* 28:70-2+ Jl 13 '87
A troubled coming of age [excerpt from Call me Anna] P. Duke and K. Turan. il pors *People Wkly* 28:54-6+ Jl 20 '87

Ross, Justin
about
From chorus boy to producer: the many lives of Justin Ross. K. Grubb. il pors *Dance Mag* 61:88-9 Ja '87

Ross, Katharine
about
The unlikeliest movie star. L. Feldman. il pors *McCalls* 115:162+ N '87

Ross, Kevin
about
Kevin Ross' explosion ends in Chicago with new beginning in Calif. il pors *Jet* 72:14+ Ag 10 '87
Ross returns to Chicago to seek doctor's care. por *Jet* 72:48 Ag 31 '87

Ross, Lester
Environmental policy in post-Mao China [cover story] bibl f il map *Environment* 29:12-17+ My '87

Ross, Lloyd L.
about
Keep the customers waiting. L. M. Keefe. il por *Forbes* 140:74 S 21 '87

Ross, Malcolm
about
One teacher's prejudice. K. Harley. il pors *Macleans* 100:17 Ap 27 '87

Ross, Muriel D.
about
Inner ears and outer space. R. Spangenburg and D. Moser. il por *Space World* X-9-285:17-20 S '87

Ross, Roger
Book manufacturing in Spain. il *Publ Wkly* 232:47-8+ D 4 '87
Spanish printers cast glances at U.S. market. il *Publ Wkly* 232:44+ N 20 '87

Ross, Steven J.
about
The feud at Warner just keeps getting hotter. S. Benway. il pors *Bus Week* p76-8+ Je 29 '87

Ross gets a few dollars more. B. Dumaine. il pors *Fortune* 115:57-8+ Ap 13 '87
The Warner war: why Steve Ross and Herb Siegel can't get along [cover story] J. Taylor. il pors *N Y* 20:34-42 Jl 13 '87

Ross, Steven S.
Software reviews for architects. il *Archit Rec* 175:163+ N '87
Software reviews for architects. il *Archit Rec* 175:154-6+ O '87
Using your micro to specify [with editorial comment by Mildred F. Schmertz] il *Archit Rec* 175:9, 134-7 S '87

Ross, Thomas
Cairo's conflict between old and new. il *World Press Rev* 34:58-9 Mr '87

Ross, Tracey
about
Tracey Ross found out about sex by reading. por *Jet* 71:59 F 2 '87

Rossant, Colette
America entertains. See issues of McCall's beginning February 1987
An exotic pilgrimage. il *N Y Times Mag* p72-4 Ap 26 '87
The underground gourmet. See occasional issues of New York

Rossellini, Isabella
about
Personal style: the new moods of beauty. il pors *Harpers Bazaar* 120:146-53 F '87
Photographs and photography
Intensely Isabella. B. Weber. il pors *Vogue* 177:180-7 Je '87

Rosser, Eric
about
Whenever this peripatetic pianist feels like giving a concert, all he has to do is put on the brakes. T. Schlesinger. il por *People Wkly* 28:101-2 D 14 '87

Rossi, Aldo, 1931-
about
Aldo Rossi makes his American debut. K. D. Stein. il por *Archit Rec* 175:67 My '87

Rossi, Mario
Venice is shrinking. *World Press Rev* 34:58 Ja '87

Rossi, Peter Henry, 1921-
No good applied social research goes unpunished. *Society* 25:73+ N/D '87

Rossi, Peter Henry, 1921-, and others
The urban homeless: estimating composition and size. bibl f il *Science* 235:1336-41 Mr 13 '87

Rossi-Lemeni, Nicola Makedon, 1920-
about
Keepers of the flame. C. Battaglia. il pors *Opera News* 52:28-30+ N '87

Rossignol Production (Skis)
Going downhill. il *Time* 129:68 F 23 '87

Rossini, Gioacchino, 1792-1868
about
The barber of Seville [opera] Reviews
Nation 245:318-19 S 26 '87. E. W. Said
La Cenerentola [opera] Reviews
New Yorker 63:60 Jl 6 '87. A. Porter
La donna del lago [opera] Reviews
New Yorker 62:81-2 Ja 26 '87. A. Porter
Ermione [opera] Reviews
New Yorker 63:113-14 O 5 '87. A. Porter
Il viaggio a Reims [opera] Reviews
New Yorker 63:149-50 N 9 '87. A. Porter

Rossini Foundation
In quest of Rossini. C. Battaglia. il *Opera News* 52:30-1+ Ag '87

Rossini Opera Festival *See* Music festivals—Italy

Rossman, Parker, 1919-
Computer networking as a global-scale tool. *Futurist* 21:10-11 Mr/Ap '87

Rossner, Judith
I am Cinderella's stepmother and I know my rights. il *N Y Times Book Rev* 92:3 Ap 19 '87
about
No sequels. P. S. Nathan. *Publ Wkly* 232:27 Jl 31 '87

Rostenkowski, Dan
Should Congress adopt the House-passed "Gephardt Amendment"? [excerpts from debate, April 29, 1987] *Congr Dig* 66:173+ Je/Jl '87
about
Getting a trade bill is going to take a lot of trading. D. Harbrecht and B. Javetski. il por *Bus Week* p34 S 28 '87

Rostenkowski, Dan—about—*cont.*
It worked with the tax bill—and it just might with trade. H. Gleckman and D. Harbrecht. il por *Bus Week* p42 Mr 9 '87
Washington's odd couple shakes up taxes. A. R. Dowd. il pors *Fortune* 115:40-1 Ja 5 '87
Rostow, Eugene Victor, 1913-
The INF trap. *New Repub* 197:16-17 Ag 24 '87
The Soviet threat: Western schizophrenia. *Current* 295:25-9 S '87
Why the Soviets want an arms-control agreement, and why they want it now. *Commentary* 83:19-26 F '87
Rostow, W. W. (Walt Whitman), 1916-
On ending the cold war. *Foreign Aff* 65:831-51 Spr '87
Rostow, Walt Whitman *See* Rostow, W. W. (Walt Whitman), 1916-
Rostropovich, Mstislav, 1927-
about
Birthdays. T. W. Libbey, Jr. il *High Fidel* 37:55 My '87
Most happy cello. P. G. Davis. il por *N Y* 20:108-9 Mr 9 '87
Musical events:
60th birthday concerts. A. Porter. *New Yorker* 63:99-100 Ap 6 '87
Ongoing Dialogues. P. G. Davis. il *N Y* 20:82+ Ap 6 '87
To Slava with love. T. W. Libbey, Jr. il *High Fidel* 37:54 Jl '87
Rotary engines
New power to the props. F. Mackerodt. il *Pop Mech* 164:14 Ap '87
Norton Rotary Rocket. M. Oxley. il *Cycle* 38:64-9 D '87
Rotary rocket [Mazda RX-7 Turbo] T. Wilkinson. il *Pop Sci* 230:32+ Ja '87
Rotary International
Rotary action [Supreme Court ruling on admission of women] *Time* 129:62 My 18 '87
Rotary: women's turn comes round [Supreme Court decision] *U S News World Rep* 102:14 My 18 '87
Ruckus over Rotary women [Supreme Court ruling] J. Seligmann. il *Newsweek* 109:47 My 18 '87
Rotary tillers *See* Cultivators
Rotating houses *See* Houses, Rotating
Rotation
See also
Earth—Rotation
Precession
Rotation diet *See* Diet
Rotation of crops
He's squeezing the tillage out of corn/bean rotation. R. Fee. il *Success Farm* 85:18A My '87
Rethinking continuous cultivation in Amazonia. P. M. Fearnside. bibl f il *BioScience* 37:209-14 Mr '87
Yurimaguas technology [discussion of March 1987 article, Rethinking continuous cultivation in Amazonia] P. M. Fearnside. *BioScience* 37:638-40 O '87
Rotaviruses
Infant diarrhea in research spotlight [rotavirus-associated diarrhea] D. D. Edwards. *Sci News* 132:255 O 17 '87
The October-to-April trek of the 'stomach bug' [childhood diarrhea] J. Silberner. il *U S News World Rep* 103:90 N 9 '87
ROTC (Navy) *See* United States. Navy. Reserve Officers' Training Corps
Rotenberg, Jonathan
Who worries about 'the rest of us'? por *Pers Comput* 11:252 O '87
about
A different kind of computer whiz kid. A. Beam. il por *Bus Week* p97-8 Mr 9 '87
(jt. auth) *See* Klein, Susan, 1944-, and Rotenstreich, Susan
Roth, Faylene
Autumn leaves. il *Sierra* 72:96-9 S/O '87
Roth, Hal
Hal Roth: on to Bali. *Mot Boat Sail* 159:170+ Ja '87
Hal Roth: sailing to the Seychelles. *Mot Boat Sail* 159:158+ F '87
Roth, Henry, 1906-
about
Call it an awakening. M. Dickstein. il pors *N Y Times Book Rev* 92:1+ N 29 '87
PW interviews. P. Kaganoff. por *Publ Wkly* 232:67-8 N 27 '87

Roth, Irene Wydler- *See* Wydler-Roth, Irene
Roth, Kenneth
Prague & the perils of jazz. il *Commonweal* 114:351-4 Je 5 '87
Roth, Philip
Joe College: memories of a fifties education [cover story] il *Atlantic* 260:41-8+ D '87
My life as a boy. il pors *N Y Times Book Rev* 92:1+ O 18 '87
about
Defenders of the faith. R. Alter. *Commentary* 84:52-5 Jl '87
The varnished truths of Philip Roth. P. Gray. il pors *Time* 129:78-80 Ja 19 '87
'Writers have a third eye' [interview] A. P. Sanoff. il pors *U S News World Rep* 102:61-2 F 2 '87
Roth, Robert A.
Staffing methods that threaten the teaching profession. *Educ Dig* 52:18-21 Ja '87
Roth, Steven
about
Model Marla Hanson, showing the face of courage to a jury, helps convict the thug who maimed her. J. Wadler. il pors *People Wkly* 27:38-40+ Ja 5 '87
Roth, William George, 1938-
about
Anyone got a raft? K. Hannon. il *Forbes* 140:91-2 S 7 '87
Rothberg, Howard Perry
about
A deco discovery. A. Duncan. il *House Gard* 159:156-9+ My '87
Rothchild, John
Revenge in a hot place. *Wash Mon* 19:45-6+ D '87
The stock analysts. il *Wash Mon* 19:10-14+ O '87
Rothenberg, Marc E., and others
Eosinophils cocultured with endothelial cells have increased survival and functional properties. bibl f il *Science* 237:645-7 Ag 7 '87
Rothenberg, Randall
Why Bradley isn't running. il pors *N Y Times Mag* p28-31+ Ag 2 '87
Rothenberg, Randall, and Roy, Susan
Dive bums. il *Oceans* 20:38-45 Ja/F '87
Rothenberg, Susan
about
Images on the edge of abstraction. C. Ratcliff. il por *Archit Dig* 44:52+ D '87
Spectral light, anxious dancers. R. Hughes. il por *Time* 130:109 N 9 '87
Susan Rothenberg. J. Bell. il *Art News* 86:147 My '87
Rothenstein, Richard
Mommie barest. il *50 Plus* 27:84+ Je '87
Rotherhithe (London, England) *See* London (England)
Rothert, Matt R.
about
The man who put God's trust in your pocket! E. Rochette. il *Antiques Collect Hobbies* 92:80-1 Jl '87
Rothman, David H.
The electronic Peace Corps. *Natl Rev* 39:43-4 Mr 27 '87
Rothman, Jerry
about
When a child dies, a therapist warns, the grief of brothers and sisters may leave lasting scars [interview] C. Tamarkin. il por *People Wkly* 27:77-8+ Mr 23 '87
Rothman, Tony
The seven arrows of time. il *Discover* 8:62-4+ F '87
This is the way the world ends [cover story] il *Discover* 8:82-4+ Jl '87
A 'what you see is what you beget' theory [cover story] il *Discover* 8:90-6+ My '87
Rothman, Tony, and Ellis, George
Has cosmology become metaphysical? il *Astronomy* 15:6-22 F '87
Rothman, Tony, and Mereson, Amy
Fiddling with the future. il pors *Discover* 8:58-64+ S '87
Rothmeier, Clara
about
Keeping the Cardinals in stitches. J. E. Vader. il pors *Sports Illus* 67:44 O 26 '87
Rothmeier, Steven George
about
Steve Rothmeier's Northwest looks great—on paper. P. Houston. il por *Bus Week* p58-9 S 28 '87
Rothschild, Bruce, and Martin, Larry D.
Avascular necrosis: occurrence in diving Cretaceous mosasaurs. bibl f il *Science* 236:75-7 Ap 3 '87

Rothschild, David de
about
A hot new name in French banking: Rothschild. J. Rossant. il por *Bus Week* p142-3 Ja 12 '87
Rothschild, Emma
A European strategy for peace. il *N Y Times Mag* p48-9 Ap 5 '87
Rothschild, Guy de
about
Architectural digest visits: Baron and Baroness Guy de Rothschild: the evolution of the chalet at Ferrières. C. Aillaud. il pors *Archit Dig* 44:208-18+ Ap '87
Rothschild, Marie-Hélène de
about
Architectural digest visits: Baron and Baroness Guy de Rothschild: the evolution of the chalet at Ferrières. C. Aillaud. il pors *Archit Dig* 44:208-18+ Ap '87
Rothschild, Miriam
The flowering hayfield. il por *Archit Dig* 44:24+ Ja '87
about
Profiles. K. Fraser. il *New Yorker* 63:45-8+ O 19 '87
Rothschild, Norman
Offbeat. See issues of Popular Photography through September 1987
about
Pro challenge. il por *Pop Photogr* 94:60 S '87
Rothschild, Philippine de
about
Setting the stage: Baroness Philippine de Rothschild in Paris. C. Aillaud. il por *Archit Dig* 44:98-101 Ag '87
Rothschild (L.F.) Holdings Inc. See L.F. Rothschild Holdings Inc.
Rothschild & Associates Bank
A hot new name in French banking: Rothschild. J. Rossant. il por *Bus Week* p142-3 Ja 12 '87
Rothschild, House of See House of Rothschild
Rothstein, Edward
Edward Rothstein on music. See occasional issues of The New Republic beginning August 27, 1984
A fateful intellectual friendship. *Commentary* 84:41-9 D '87
Israel's alienated intellectuals. *Commentary* 83:53-7 F '87
Rotisserie League Baseball
In New York: major league fantasies. M. Walsh. il *Time* 129:10-11 My 4 '87
Star search: how to draft a dream team. P. Hirdt. il *Sport Mag* 78:83+ My '87
Rotman, Jeff
Optical marvels, fish eyes are visual feasts themselves. bibl (p271) il *Smithsonian* 18:172-7 N '87
Rotor aircraft
Army analysis of LHX program cites strengths of tilt-rotor. B. M. Greeley, Jr. *Aviat Week Space Technol* 126:22-3 Mr 23 '87
Navy to exploit V-22's VTOL, range in hunting Arctic subs. B. M. Greeley, Jr. *Aviat Week Space Technol* 126:30-1 Je 8 '87
Rotorcraft technology update [special section; with editorial comment by Donald E. Fink] il *Aviat Week Space Technol* 126:11, 45-51+ Ja 19 '87
Success of tilt-rotor service will require special heliports. il *Aviat Week Space Technol* 127:115-16 N 9 '87
Tilt-rotors may change the way you fly. il map *Pop Mech* 164:93 Ag '87
X-wing and tilt-rotor: hybrid aircraft that get up and go [cover story] S. F. Brown and S. Ashley. il *Pop Sci* 231:44-9+ Jl '87
Costs
Technological problems, rising costs force X-wing program to scale down. *Aviat Week Space Technol* 127:23 O 19 '87
Testing
Bell-Boeing schedules first flight of Pointer tilt-rotor demonstrator. S. W. Kandebo. il *Aviat Week Space Technol* 127:56 Ag 10 '87
Program delays spur NASA, DARPA to restructure X-wing flight tests. *Aviat Week Space Technol* 127:23-4 Ag 31 '87
Researchers urge further tests to improve rotorcraft models. W. B. Scott. il *Aviat Week Space Technol* 126:50-3+ Ap 20 '87
Rotors (Helicopters) See Helicopters—Rotors
Rotter, Pat
Fine lines [poem] *Good Housekeep* 205:193 Ag '87
What about rainbows? [poem] *Good Housekeep* 205:188 N '87

Rotus (Automobile) See Sports cars
Roud, Richard
about
70-millimeter nerves [interview] R. Corliss. por *Film Comment* 23:36+ S/O '87
Roudiez, Leon
(tr) See Kristeva, Julia, 1941-. AIDS and Eros
Roueché, Berton, 1911-
Pleasant and living. il *New Yorker* 63:121-5 F 23 '87
Roughgarden, Jonathan
(jt. auth) See Gaines, Steven D., and Roughgarden, Jonathan
Roulac, Stephen E.
Don't rush in. por *Forbes* 140:135 Ag 24 '87
Roulades
Florentine beef roulades. il *Redbook* 168:14 Ja '87
Round houses See Houses, Round
Round midnight [film] See Motion picture reviews—Single works
Round the world yacht races See Yacht racing
Roundup (Herbicide) See Herbicides
Rountree, Thomas D.
Windbirds by the bay [photographs] il *Audubon* 89:52-9 N '87
Rouse, Mikel
about
Music. G. Santoro. *Nation* 245:210-12 S 5 '87
Rousmaniere, John
Sailing on Shamrock. *Mot Boat Sail* 159:150+ F '87
Rousse, Georges
about
Georges Rousse at Farideh Cadot. E. Heartney. *Art Am* 75:130 Ja '87
Rousseve, Ronald J.
A black American youth torn between cultures [cover story] il por *Humanist* 47:5-8 Mr/Ap '87
Roussimoff, André See André the Giant
Rousso, Marc
about
Beware the stamp man. J. Clements. il por *Forbes* 139:232+ My 18 '87
Rout, Ettie A.
about
Condoms to the rescue: New Zealand's Ettie Rout "made vice safe" in World War I. J. Tolerton. il pors *Ms* 15:28-30 My '87
Route 50 See Roads
Router bits See Bits (Drilling and boring)
Routing machines
Basic router how-to. A. Rooze. il *Fam Handyman* 37:8+ O '87
Monster routers—why you need one. A. J. Hand. il *Pop Sci* 231:110-13 N '87
Stands, tables, etc.
See Machinery—Stands, tables, etc.
Roux, Annette
about
Can Beneteau fill its sails in the U.S. boat market? M. Resener. il por *Bus Week* p75 Ag 17 '87
Roux (Cooking)
From our kitchen to yours. K. Adams. il *South Living* 22:190 O '87
Rover Group plc
Shh! Please don't call this car a Rover [Sterling] M. Maremont. il *Bus Week* p59 Ja 12 '87
Rovin, Jeff
Joan Lunden: now she's got it all! il pors *Ladies Home J* 104:62+ Ap '87
Row covers for plants See Plants—Protection
Row houses
Redefining the row house. L. J. Gallagher. il *Esquire* 107:64 My '87
Rowan, Carl Thomas, 1925-
Words that give us strength. il pors *Read Dig* 130:49-50+ Ap '87
Rowan, Carl Thomas, 1925-, and Mazie, David M.
A walk through history. il *Read Dig* 131:20-5 O '87
Rowan Companies, Inc.
How two offshore drillers kept their heads above water. T. Vogel. il *Bus Week* p87-8 Ag 3 '87
Rowan Oak (Oxford, Miss.: Historic house) See Oxford (Miss.)—Historic houses, sites, etc.
Rowbotham, Sheila
'Commanding the heart': Edward Carpenter and friends. bibl il pors *Hist Today* 37:41-6 S '87
Rowe, Harmeen
AIDS behind bars—a prisoner's concern. il *U S News World Rep* 102:7 F 2 '87
Rowe, James W.
(jt. auth) See Abelson, Philip H., and Rowe, James W.

Rowe, John W.
about
Humble pie. J. Cook. il por *Forbes* 139:50-1 Ap 20 '87
Rowe, John W. (John Wallis), 1944-, and Kahn, Robert Louis, 1918-
Human aging: usual and successful. bibl f *Science* 237:143-9 Jl 10 '87
Rowe, Jonathan
I like Mike. *Wash Mon* 19:50-3 D '87
Zen and the art of cultural misappropriation. *Wash Mon* 19:49-52 My '87
Rowe, Katharine
Choreography and copyright. il *Dance Mag* 61:42-3 Mr '87
Rowe, Patrick J.
Infertility. il *World Health* p20-1 N '87
Rowe, Samuel
Closed-end mutual funds can be a bargain. il *Black Enterp* 18:31-2 Ag '87
Where to put your rainy day funds. il *Black Enterp* 17:87-9 Jl '87
Rowell, Galen A.
Baltistan. il map *Natl Geogr* 172:526-50 O '87
Mountain light. See issues of Petersen's Photographic Magazine beginning June 1987 through August 1987
The road to Shangri-La. il map *Int Wildl* 17:40-5 Ja/F '87
about
Team depth. B. Hurter. por *Petersens Photogr Mag* 16:10 Je '87
Rowen, John
Brook trout—an appreciation. il *Conservationist* 42:36-41 Jl/Ag '87
Rowing
Coxing her way to victory [Harvard coxswain] D. Mahony. il pors *N Y Times Mag* p44+ Ap 26 '87
Not just for galley slaves and preppies. J. Flynn. il *Bus Week* p161 My 18 '87
Oxford's U.S. rowers jump ship, leaving the varsity without all its oars in the water. W. Plummer. il *People Wkly* 27:38+ F 23 '87
Pulling your own oar. K. M. Reith. bibl il *Women's Sports Fitness* 9:24-8 Ag '87
Row, row, row your scull . . . or rowboat or canoe [California lakes] il *Sunset* 179:40+ O '87
Rowers snub South Boston club race that bans blacks. *Jet* 72:16 Je 8 '87
South Boston club ends it's ban against blacks [rowing club] *Jet* 72:4 Je 15 '87
The Sultans did swing [Harvard wins collegiate nationals] F. Lidz. il *Sports Illus* 66:57-8 Je 22 '87
Study and teaching
The fitness-goers [Florida Rowing Center] D. Halberstam. il por *Vogue* 177:234-5+ Jl '87
Rowing, Indoor
Indoor rowing: progress in place. K. M. Reith. il *Women's Sports Fitness* 9:80-1 D '87
The zaniest regatta [CRASH-B Sprints] C. Lambert. il *Women's Sports Fitness* 9:22 My '87
Rowland, Frank Sherwood
Can we close the ozone hole? il *Technol Rev* 90:50-8 Ag/S '87
Rowland, Mark, 1952-
Streets of steel. il *Esquire* 108:41-2 N '87
Rowland, Mary
13 ways tax reform will change your company. *Work Woman* 12:114-15 Ap '87
Rowland, Ross
about
Escape from New York. J. Clements. il por *Forbes* 140:126 S 7 '87
Rowland, Rowland W. *See* Rowland, Tiny
Rowland, Tiny
about
'Tiny' Rowland: pushing 70 and pushing harder than ever. R. A. Melcher. il por *Bus Week* p70+ O 12 '87
Rowles, Jimmy
about
Blindfold test. L. Feather. il pors *Down Beat* 54:51 Jl '87
Rowles, Stacy
about
Blindfold test. L. Feather. il pors *Down Beat* 54:51 Jl '87
Rowley, Charles Stoddard
about
Looking for the mysterious 'Mr. Roly'. il pors *Life* 10:119-20+ N '87

Rowley-Conwy, Peter A.
(jt. auth) See Legge, Anthony J., and Rowley-Conwy, Peter A.
Rowny, Edward L., 1917-
Advancing U.S.-Soviet relations: the challenge of arms control [address, September 9, 1987] *Dep State Bull* 87:24-5 N '87
Arms control: the East Asian and Pacific focus [address, December 30, 1986] *Dep State Bull* 87:37-9 Mr '87
Effective arms control demands a broad approach [address, April 27, 1987] *Dep State Bull* 87:22-4 Jl '87
New prospects for agreement in INF and START [address, March 20, 1987] *Dep State Bull* 87:33-6 Je '87
Rowse, A. L. (Alfred Leslie), 1903-
All booked up. il *House Gard* 159:54+ N '87
Rowse, Alfred Leslie *See* Rowse, A. L. (Alfred Leslie), 1903-
Rowse, David
about
Veryfine: oh, what a difference packaging makes. K. H. Hammonds. il por *Bus Week* p71 Ag 31 '87
Roxanne [film] *See* Motion picture reviews—Single works
Roxborough State Park (Colo.) *See* Colorado—Parks and reserves
Roxlo, C. B., and others
Edge surfaces in lithographically textured molybdenum disulfide. bibl f il *Science* 235:1629-31 Mr 27 '87
Roy, Ann
It wasn't the end of the world. il *Work Woman* 12:126-9+ Mr '87
Roy, Bernard
about
At the eye of a blistering storm. M. Rose. il pors *Macleans* 100:9 F 23 '87
Roy, Della M.
New strong cement materials: chemically bonded ceramics. bibl f il *Science* 235:651-8 F 6 '87
Roy, Gabrielle, 1909-1983
Roses for Yolande [condensed from Enchanted summer] il *Read Dig* 130:137-40 Ap '87
Roy, J. Stapleton
Administration supports New Zealand Preference Elimination Act [statements, September 22, 1987] *Dep State Bull* 87:46-7 N '87
South Pacific Nuclear Free Zone [statement, December 15, 1986] *Dep State Bull* 87:52-4 S '87
Roy, Matt
about
Slip-slidin' away to '88. W. Nack. il por *Sports Illus* 66:64-5 Mr 9 '87
Roy, Rustum
Ceramics by the solution-sol-gel route. bibl f il *Science* 238:1664-9 D 18 '87
Roy, Susan
(jt. auth) See Rothenberg, Randall, and Roy, Susan
Royal Astronomical Society
Amateurs, professionals unite in England. N. Henbest. *Sky Telesc* 74:536-8 N '87
Royal Ballet
Footwork. P. J. Rosenwald. il *Horizon* 30:36 N '87
Harvey's Royal stint: "like Fonteyn in overdrive". S. Greco. il por *Dance Mag* 61:4 Mr '87
Reviews:
Performance of Swan Lake. M. E. Willis. *Dance Mag* 61:178-9 Je '87
Royal Bank of Canada
A megamerger in the works [Wood Gundy and Royal Bank of Canada] P. C. Newman. il *Macleans* 100:46 My 4 '87
Royal Bardia Wildlife Reserve (Nepal) *See* Wildlife sanctuaries—Nepal
Royal Canadian Legion
Remembering Vimy Ridge [Canadian vets return to France for 70th anniversary of battle] il *Macleans* 100:10-11 Ap 20 '87
Royal Canadian Mounted Police
When women do men's work [guarding both male and female prisoners] B. Amiel. il *Macleans* 100:9 O 12 '87
Royal Chitawan National Park (Nepal) *See* National parks and reserves—Nepal
Royal Conservatory of Music (Toronto, Ont.)
A century of success. P. Young. il *Macleans* 100:58 F 16 '87
Royal Court Theatre
Foul play [controversy surrounding production of J. Allen's Perdition] D. Pryce-Jones. *New Repub* 196:15-17 Mr 2 '87

Royal Crown Cola Co.
Three sparkling turnarounds: can this really be Victor Posner? P. Engardio. il por *Bus Week* p56-7 Jl 27 '87

Royal Danish Ballet
Bournonville lives in oral memoirs [work of T. Tobias] por *Dance Mag* 61:108-9 Mr '87
More than make-believe [Royal Danish Ballet Festival] M. Hunt. il *Dance Mag* 61:58-60 O '87
Reviews:
    Performances of workshop program. E. Aschengreen. *Dance Mag* 61:21+ My '87

Royal Dornoch (Scotland: Golf course) *See* Golf courses— Scotland

Royal Dutch/Shell Group
Management by committee—it works [L. C. van Wachem] R. I. Kirkland, Jr. por *Fortune* 116:28 Ag 3 '87

Royal families of Western Europe *See* Western Europe— Royal families

Royal family of Great Britain *See* Great Britain—Royal family

Royal family of Laos *See* Laos—Royal family

Royal family of Monaco *See* Monaco—Royal family

Royal family of Thailand *See* Thailand—Royal family

Royal Hong Kong Jockey Club
A $40 million day at the races. D. J. Yang. il *Bus Week* p160 Mr 23 '87

Royal Ontario Museum
A glimpse of beauty past and present [Eye of the beholder exhibition] il *Macleans* 100:50-1 Ap 13 '87
Museum piece: the Chinese Collections, Royal Ontario Museum. P. Johnston. il *Hist Today* 37:60-2 Ap '87

Royal Opera House (London, England)
A creaky Covent Garden may be losing its last chance at change. J. Percival. il *Dance Mag* 61:31 Je '87
London. N. Goodwin. il *Opera News* 51:44-5 Mr 14 '87
Music [The barber of Seville] E. W. Said. *Nation* 245:318-20 S 26 '87
Seoul/Tokyo [six-week tour] N. Goodwin. *Opera News* 51:40-1 Ja 3 '87

Royal Ottawa Hospital *See* Ottawa (Ont.)—Hospitals

Royal Philharmonic Orchestra
Music [Carnegie Hall concert with V. Ashkenazy as conductor and performer] E. W. Said. *Nation* 244:336-8 Mr 14 '87
Record royalty. T. W. Libbey, Jr. il *High Fidel* 37:56 Ap '87

Royal Princess (Ship)
The majesty of an ocean-going Princess. M. C. Lehrer. il *USA Today (Periodical)* 116:36-43 N '87

Royal Shakespeare Company
Hey, Falstaff, can you spare a shilling? P. Sherrid. il *U S News World Rep* 103:64 Jl 20 '87

Royal Spanish National Ballet
Jose Antonio leads Spain's National Ballet back to the United States. L. Kumin. il *Dance Mag* 61:6 D '87

Royal spoonbills *See* Spoonbills

Royal Swedish Ballet
Reviews:
    Performances of Napoli at the Royal Opera House, Stockholm. L. Svedin. *Dance Mag* 61:34+ My '87

Royal Trustco Limited
Royal Trust challenges the banks. P. C. Newman. il por *Macleans* 100:25 Jl 27 '87

Royal Windsor Horse Show *See* Horse shows

Royal Winnipeg Ballet
Arnold Spohr to step down. P. Citron. il por *Dance Mag* 61:18 My '87
Reviews:
    Performance of Swan Lake. M. Crabb. il *Dance Mag* 61:18 D '87

Royalpar Industries, Inc.
A temp firm whose zip may not last. G. G. Marcial. *Bus Week* p126 Jl 20 '87

Royalties
Bridging the gap [publishers paying authors royalties on remainders] J. F. Baker. *Publ Wkly* 231:10 Mr 27 '87
Can you beat this? [ruling that J. Fedders is to receive share of profits from abused wife's book] L. Fleischer. *Publ Wkly* 232:56 N 13 '87
The fight over golden oldies [rock music] N. Jennings. il *Macleans* 100:36-7 Mr 2 '87
Little Richard sues over ownership of new hit song. por *Jet* 71:59 Mr 9 '87
Prince's sis says he stole lyrics from her. *Jet* 72:62 S 7 '87

The push to end blanket licensing hits a sour note with songwriters [music on television] P. E. Bauer. *Channels* 7:17 Ap '87

Royalty *See* Nobility

Royalty is royalty [drama] *See* Mitchell, W. O. (William Ormond), 1914-

Royalty Management Office (U.S.) *See* United States. Office of Royalty Management

Roybal, Maximiliano
    about
Santos by Roybal. N. C. Benson. il por *Americana* 15:45-8 Mr/Ap '87

Royce, Charles
    about
Small stocks to sock away. M. McFadden. il por *Fortune* 115:133 Mr 2 '87

Royer, Warren L.
A short perspective on educational administration. il *Phi Delta Kappan* 69:145-6 O '87

Royko, Mike, 1933-
That's outrageous! il *Read Dig* 130:74-8 F '87

Royston (Ga.)
    Education
The kids who saved a dying town [class project to upgrade town] B. B. Henderson. il *Read Dig* 131:42-6 S '87

    Municipal improvement
The kids who saved a dying town [class project to upgrade town] B. B. Henderson. il *Read Dig* 131:42-6 S '87

Royte, Elizabeth
The 8 biggest diet don'ts and how to deep-six them. il *Mademoiselle* 93:80+ F '87
How to keep your heart healthy. il *Mademoiselle* 93:90 F '87
Sweet dreams are made of this (how to get a good night's sleep). il *Mademoiselle* 93:82 Ja '87

Roza [musical] *See* Musicals, revues, etc.—Reviews—Single works

Rozek, Michael
Crash course. il *Natl Wildl* 25:20-3 F/Mr '87

Rozelle, Pete
    about
The not-so-super state of pro football [interview] il por *U S News World Rep* 102:68 Ja 26 '87
Rozelle says black coach is an NFL owners' problem. *Jet* 72:46 Jl 20 '87

Rozema, Patricia
    about
Exploration of a dreamer. il por *Macleans* 100:34-5 D 28 '87
I've heard the mermaids singing [film] Reviews
    Commonweal 114:498 S 11 '87. T. O'Brien
    Macleans il 100:48 S 28 '87. L. O'Toole
    Natl Rev 39:60-1 O 23 '87. J. Simon
    Time il 130:77 S 14 '87. R. Corliss
Murmurs of the heart. E. Trapunski. il por *Macleans* 100:48 S 28 '87

Rozen, Leah
Required: an espresso machine at every stop. il *Seventeen* 46:100 Jl '87

Rozhdestvenski, Gennadi
    about
Stravinsky's ballet music. R. Freed. il por *Stereo Rev* 52:150 D '87

RPVs (Remotely piloted vehicles) *See* Remotely piloted vehicles

RSC *See* Royal Shakespeare Company

RU-486 (Drug)
Abortion pill gets mixed response from physicians. *Jet* 71:28 Ja 19 '87
Abortion without surgery. A. Steacy. il *Macleans* 100:42 Ja 12 '87
RU-486: the unpregnancy pill. S. M. Halpern. il *Ms* 15:56+ Ap '87

Rubber checks *See* Checks, Fraudulent

Rubber industry
    See also
    Firestone Tire & Rubber Co.
    Goodyear Tire & Rubber Company
    Tire industry

    Brazil
Rubber and Amazon alliances. S. Schwartzman. il map *Technol Rev* 90:15-16 Ap '87

Rubber producing plants
Punching holes in a sticky defense [insect vein-cutting behavior counters plant latex defenses; research by David E. Dussourd and Thomas Eisner] D. D. Edwards. il *Sci News* 132:134 Ag 29 '87

Rubber producing plants—*cont.*
Vein-cutting behavior: insect counterploy to the latex defense of plants. D. E. Dussourd and T. Eisner. bibl f il *Science* 237:898-901 Ag 21 '87
Rubbermaid Incorporated
Why the bounce at Rubbermaid? A. L. Taylor, III. il *Fortune* 115:77-8 Ap 13 '87
Rubbia, Carlo
about
How to win a Nobel Prize. M. D. Lemonick. il por *Time* 129:55 F 9 '87
Rubbia in line to head CERN. D. Dickson. por *Science* 238:1223 N 27 '87
Ruben, George
Developments in industrial relations. See issues of Monthly Labor Review
Ruben, Joe
about
The stepfather [film] Reviews
N Y 20:107 My 25 '87. D. Denby
Nation 244:740-2 My 30 '87. T. Rafferty
New Yorker 62:92-3 F 9 '87. P. Kael
Newsweek 109:79 F 23 '87. D. Ansen
People Wkly 27:10 My 18 '87. P. Travers
Time 129:74 Je 15 '87
Rubenstein, Carin
Making time for love. il *Work Woman* 12:154+ O '87
The Money readers' poll. il *Money* 16:194-7 F '87
Rubenstein, Carin, and Tavris, Carol
Special survey results: 26,000 women reveal the secrets of intimacy. il *Redbook* 169:147-9+ S '87
Rubies
See also
Ruby mines and mining
Prices
"You die for sure" [smuggling rubies from Burma] L. Gubernick. il map *Forbes* 140 Sp Issue:94-6 O 26 '87
Rubik's Magic
Now there is Rubik's Magic, a new puzzle that provides a study in permutation operators. J. Walker. il *Sci Am* 257:170-3 O '87
Rubin, Barry
Drowning in the Gulf. *Foreign Policy* 69:120-34 Wint '87/'88
Rubin, Charlie
Magnum farce. il *Harpers Bazaar* 120:222+ Ap '87
Rubin, David M., and Hunter, Ralph E.
Bedform alignment in directionally varying flows [cover story] bibl f il *Science* 237:276-8 Jl 17 '87
Rubin, Ellis
about
Dilemma for the defense. M. A. Moore. il por *U S News World Rep* 102:24 Je 8 '87
Rubin, Greg
A wooden reindeer. il *Ctry J* 14:40 D '87
Rubin, Hanna
Help! I've been wait-listed. *Seventeen* 46:152+ Ap '87
One little résumé—and how it grew. *Work Woman* 12:100-2+ Ap '87
Rubin, Howard
about
Bond bombshell. il *Time* 129:53 My 11 '87
Merrill Lynch takes a bath. D. Pauly. il *Newsweek* 109:53 My 11 '87
Rubin, James P.
The superpower dispute over radars. bibl f *Bull At Sci* 43:34-7 Ap '87
Rubin, Karen
Caring about child care [cover story; with list of resources] bibl il *Ms* 15:31-6+, 60+ Mr '87
Rubin, Kyna
(tr) See Liu Binyan, 1925-. Delving into life—the Chinese writer's duty
Rubin, Larry
Lines for a dead sister, reawakening [poem] *America* 156:280 Ap 4 '87
Rubin, Louis Decimus, 1923-
about
Is it art yet? L. Fleischer. *Publ Wkly* 231:34 My 8 '87
Rubin, Nancy
Women behind bars. il *McCalls* 114:36+ Ag '87
Rubin, Sam
Rockers: sending messages as well as music. il *Teen* 31:36+ My '87
School rules: who makes 'em? Who breaks 'em? il *Teen* 31:72+ O '87
Rubin, Sylvia
High on the mountain. il pors *Women's Sports Fitness* 9:29-32 My '87

Racing sleek. il pors *Women's Sports Fitness* 9:38-41 O '87
Rubino, Carl A.
Alternative universes: literature, ethics and the American dream. *America* 157:332+ N 7 '87
Rubinshtein, Irina
about
Winning at beauty. il pors *Teen* 31:74-7 Jl '87
Rubinstein, Leslie
Oprah! Thriving on faith. il pors *McCalls* 114:136-8+ Ag '87
Rubio, Yvette
about
Exercising options in Florida. J. Giambanco. il pors *Work Woman* 12:105-6+ Je '87
Ruby, Walter
Among the refuseniks. il *World Press Rev* 34:56 S '87
Ruby mines and mining
Burma
"You die for sure" [smuggling rubies from Burma] L. Gubernick. il map *Forbes* 140 Sp Issue:94-6 O 26 '87
Ruck, Rob, 1950-
Swifter, higher, stronger around the hemisphere. il *Americas* 39:2-7 Jl/Ag '87
Rudeness See Courtesy
Ruder, David S.
about
How Ruder will steer the SEC. V. Cahan. *Bus Week* p29 Je 29 '87
The SEC's new boss. *Newsweek* 109:47 Je 29 '87
A way to stop a stock-market 'meltdown'? por *Newsweek* 110:60 O 19 '87
Rudman, William B.
Solar-powered animals [cover story] il *Nat Hist* 96:50-3 O '87
Rudney, Gabriel
(jt. auth) See Johnston, Denis, and Rudney, Gabriel
Rudnick, Joseph, and Gaspari, George
The shapes of random walks. bibl f il *Science* 237:384-9 Jl 24 '87
Rudolf, Patricia
Stressed to excess? il *Redbook* 170:102-5 D '87
Rudolph, Alan
about
Made in heaven [film] Reviews
New Yorker 63:145 N 16 '87. P. Kael
Newsweek 110:108 N 16 '87. D. Ansen
People Wkly 28:18 N 30 '87. P. Travers
Rudolph, Wilma
about
Olympian Wilma Rudolph gets DePauw college post. por *Jet* 71:52 F 2 '87
What makes Wilma coach? M. Goldberg. por *Women's Sports Fitness* 9:26 My '87
Ruether, Rosemary Radford
Invisible Palestinians: ideology and reality in Israel. il *Christ Century* 104:587-91 Jl 1-8 '87
Ruette, Jacky
about
Sumptuous sea fare. S. Ballard. il por *Sports Illus* 66:81 Je 15 '87
Ruff, Patsy
I can breathe again! il pors *Saturday Evening Post* 259:100-2+ D '87
Ruffed grouse cooking See Cooking—Game
Ruffelle, Frances
about
Broadway goes wild for London's little miss from Les miz. T. Cunneff. il pors *People Wkly* 28:115-16 Jl 6 '87
Ruffin, David C.
Washington page. See issues of Black Enterprise beginning April 1984
Ruffin, Frances E.
A delightful tour of Bordeaux and Cognac. il *Black Enterp* 18:109-10 O '87
Ruffner, Mason
about
Critics cry for Mason Ruffner's rock 'n' roll & Rimbaud gumbo. il por *People Wkly* 27:54 Je 29 '87
Ruffolo, Lisa
about
Turning computer babble into plain English. T. Engstrom. il pors *Work Woman* 12:61+ My '87
Rug and carpet industry
See also
V'Soske, Inc.

Rugelach *See* Cookies

Ruggera, Paul
about
Warming to the idea: heat research may help hearts, kidneys, and man's best friend. W. Grigg. il por *FDA Consum* 21:25-7 My '87

Ruggieri, George D.
about
Aquarium news. *New Yorker* 62:22-4 Ja 26 '87

Ruggiero, Vincent Ryan
Where has the time gone? [address, June 14, 1987] *Vital Speeches Day* 53:671-2 Ag 15 '87

Rugs and carpets
See also
Indian blankets, rugs, etc. (American)
Designer rugs from remnants. L. M. Dalsgaard. il *Home Mech* 83:70-2+ F '87
Care
See also
ZZZZ Best Company
Collectors and collecting
Antiques: art deco rugs. C. Bricker. il *Archit Dig* 44:160-5 S '87

Rugs and carpets, Miniature
Ingenuity and genius: the Rogers Collection. A. Bahar. il *Antiques Collect Hobbies* 92:43-6 Jl '87

Rugs and carpets, Oriental
Bonds are O.K., but you can't walk on them. P. Angiolillo. il *Bus Week* p106 Ja 26 '87
Exemplary antique and decorative Persian rugs [cover story] N. Mohaber. il *Antiques Collect Hobbies* 92:28-31 Ap '87

Ruh, Glen B.
How petals from the sea form these fragile blossoms. il por *Smithsonian* 17:106-10 Ja '87

Ruhlen, Merritt
Voices from the past. map *Nat Hist* 96:6+ Mr '87

Ruhling, Nancy A.
Back by popular demand: Shaker design. il *Antiques Collect Hobbies* 92:12-16 Mr '87
The curious house that Mark built. il por *Antiques Collect Hobbies* 92:80-2+ Mr '87
Sagamore Hill: a visit to President Theodore Roosevelt's famous home on Long Island. il *Antiques Collect Hobbies* 92:38-9+ Je '87
Tussie mussies. il *Antiques Collect Hobbies* 92:30-2 Ag '87

Ruhlman, Michael
A writer at his best. il por *N Y Times Mag* p60-1+ S 20 '87

Ruifen, Li
China's health food tradition. il *Courier* 40:24-7 My '87

Ruined cities *See* Cities and towns, Ruined, extinct, etc.

Ruise, Phillipe
about
Milliner for an unknown planet, Phillipe Ruise tests the limits of weird. C. Ruskin. il por *People Wkly* 27:100-2 Je 15 '87

Ruiz, Hilton
about
Eddie Palmieri/Hilton Ruiz/Papo Lucca. L. Birnbaum. il *Down Beat* 54:52-3 Ag '87
Hilton Ruiz. L. Birnbaum. il por *Down Beat* 54:15 S '87

Ruiz, Jesus F. Garcia *See* Garcia Ruiz, Jesus F.

Ruiz, L. Barcenas- *See* Barcenas-Ruiz, L.

Rule, Ann, 1934?-
about
Unmasking a murderous mother, crime writer Ann Rule closes the book on another psychopath. M. Brower. il pors *People Wkly* 28:125 S 14 '87

Rule of law
See also
Judicial review
The tenth justice (I) [role of the Solicitor General] L. Caplan. *New Yorker* 63:29-32+ Ag 10 '87
The tenth justice (II) [role of the Solicitor General] L. Caplan. *New Yorker* 63:30-2+ Ag 17 '87
Terrorism and the rule of law [address, April 23, 1987] L. P. Bremer, III. *Dep State Bull* 87:83-6 Ag '87

Rum
The best of the West Indies. W. Grimes. il *Esquire* 107:46 Je '87
More than piña coladas: the rums of Puerto Rico. E. Fried. il *Black Enterp* 17:45 My '87
The real McCoy [W. McCoy, rum runner during Prohibition] J. F. Mariani. il *Mot Boat Sail* 160:30 O '87
The spirits of Puerto Rico. R. L. Balzer. il *Travel Holiday* 168:10-11+ S '87

Rumania *See* Romania

Rumen, Artificial
Rusitec the cow [rumen simulation as part of project to analyse different feedstuffs] il *Courier* 40:26 Mr '87

Rumford (Me.)
Race relations
Saying no to the Klan. M. M. Fortune. *Christ Century* 104:958-9 N 4 '87

Ruminants
See also
Llamas

Rummel, Lynette
More about that visible cold front [discussion of July/August 1987 article, A visible cold front] il *Weatherwise* 40:301-2+ D '87
A "visible" cold front. il *Weatherwise* 40:183 Jl/Ag '87

Rumor
The buzz on Wall Street [rumors surround the insider trading scandal] B. Powell. *Newsweek* 109:49 Mr 9 '87
Now, rumortrage [Wall Street] J. Crudele. il *N Y* 20:16+ Je 15 '87
Psst! Wait till you hear this [views of J.-N. Kapferer] J. Leo. il *Time* 129:76 Mr 16 '87

Rumreich, Mark
Commercial zapper for your radio. il *Radio-Electron* 58:45-7+ Ap '87

Run-D.M.C. (Musical group)
The kings of rap, together. B. Barol. il *Newsweek* 109:71 Je 29 '87

Runaways
Former Reagan boy hero, 13, returns home from 'streetlife' [T. Ford] il por *Jet* 72:27 Ag 3 '87
The great escape. P. Theroux. il *Parents* 62:55-7 Jl '87

Runaways—24 hours on the street [television program] *See* Television program reviews—Single works

Runci, Matthew
Should the "Minimum Wage Restoration Act of 1987" be approved? [excerpts from testimony, July 23, 1987] *Congr Dig* 66:213+ Ag/S '87

Runcie, Robert
about
Anglicans in turmoil. K. L. Woodward. il pors *Newsweek* 110:57 D 21 '87
Death and the archbishop. R. N. Ostling. il pors *Time* 130:60 D 21 '87

Runcorn, S. K.
The moon's ancient magnetism [cover story] bibl (p158) il *Sci Am* 257:60-8 D '87

Rundgren, Todd, 1948-
about
Lost Beatles script to emerge. M. Jenkins. *Roll Stone* p14 Mr 12 '87

Runes, Dagobert David, 1902-1982
about
Philosophical Library redux. R. Larkin. il por *Publ Wkly* 232:26-8 Ag 21 '87

Running
See also
Cross country running
Hash House Harriers (Organization)
Hurdle racing
Marathon running
Track and field athletics
World Peace Run, 1987
Back into fitness [retro running] C. Schaeffer. il *Changing Times* 41:97 F '87
CEOs on the slow track [long slow distance running] N. J. Perry. il *Fortune* 116:167 D 7 '87
For women only [women's races] N. Kuscsik. il *Women's Sports Fitness* 9:70-1 F '87
He made the climb to fitness [S. Silva going for vertical mile record] il por *Sports Illus* 67:20 O 5 '87
Joggers: take a step backward [retro running] D. B. Moskowitz. il *Bus Week* p166 Mr 23 '87
Joggling—the whole-body workout. S. Morris. il *Omni* 9:136-7 My '87
Run, or diet? C. Schaeffer. *Changing Times* 41:18 Ag '87
The running debate [views of P. D. Wood] J. Poppy. il *Esquire* 107:49-50 Mr '87
Setbacks along the way [one legged runner S. Fonyo] R. Laver. il por *Macleans* 100:42 Mr 30 '87
Sisterhood on the run [Great Britain's Sisters Network] A. Turnbull. il *Women's Sports Fitness* 9:90 S '87
Super-fit climber Steve Silva is a new man since first he chose to aim for the stairs [attempt to set vertical mile record] il pors *People Wkly* 28:147-8 N 2 '87

Running—*cont.*

Economic aspects

Meat meet draws urban runners [10 km fitness run in Illinois] il *Success Farm* 85 no4:B24 F '87

Equipment

See also

Nike Inc.

Racing Strollers (Firm)

Running shoes

Photographs and photography

Don't settle for spectator status at international events [Bali 10K] C. Purcell and A. Purcell. il *Pop Photogr* 94:34 Ag '87

Physiological effects

Are you running into arthritis? *Prevention* 39:64 Mr '87

'Groucho running' saves knees [work of Thomas A. McMahon] il *Prevention* 39:8 D '87

A Harvard prof tells runners: on your Marx; get set; Groucho! [T. McMahon advocates jogging like Groucho] il *People Wkly* 28:85 S 21 '87

Highs and woes of runners' hormones [elevated ACTH and cortisol levels] D. D. Edwards. *Sci News* 131:325 My 23 '87

It's not how far you go [low calorie intake may contribute to amenorrhea in athletes] J. Venturino. il *Women's Sports Fitness* 9:20 S '87

Running the numbers [figuring calories burned while running] M. Brzycki. il *Women's Sports Fitness* 9:20 S '87

Should you jog in smog? P. McCarthy. il *Women's Sports Fitness* 9:15 N '87

This mayor elected to have a fitter future; ed. by Maria Mihalik. J. Daddona. il pors *Prevention* 39:81-2+ O '87

A young runner faces osteoporosis. E. Carson. il *Women's Sports Fitness* 9:58-9 Ja '87

The running man [film] See Motion picture reviews—Single works

Running rapids

Big drops and standing waves [whitewater rafting] R. Kimber. il *Ctry J* 14:36-41 Je '87

Kayaking the Amazon. P. Chmielinski. il pors map *Natl Geogr* 171:460-73 Ap '87

Let's go river rafting! S. Birnbaum. il *Good Housekeep* 204:56-7 Mr '87

River adventure [canoeing and kayaking with PGL Young Adventure on the Wye River, England] il map *Natl Geogr World* 142:24-9 Je '87

Tales from a river woman [raft trip guide on the Colorado River]; ed. by Deborah Whitford. G. Clark. il pors *Women's Sports Fitness* 9:38-41+ Ap '87

White-water Idaho: riding the River of No Return. S. Robertson. il *Travel Holiday* 167:56-61 My '87

White-water wear. W. Withers. il *Women's Sports Fitness* 9:56 Ap '87

Whitewater trout. N. Strung. il *Field Stream* 91:52+ Ap '87

Accidents

White-water death trips [Canada] A. Steacy. *Macleans* 100:40-1 Ag 17 '87

Running records

See also

Track and field athletics records

When is a record not a record? S. Stuller. il *Women's Sports Fitness* 9:92-3 Mr '87

Running shoes

Nike's high-stepping air force [Air Max shoes] J. Skorupa. il *Pop Mech* 164:33 Ag '87

The padded plus. K. S. Zimmeth. il *Health* 19:16 F '87

Running. M. Kort. il *Women's Sports Fitness* 9:58-60+ Mr '87

Running shoes. il *Consum Rep* 52:183-7 D '87

Running shoes make a leap into the space age [Dynacoil shoes by Kangaroo designed by space suit developer A. L. Gross] K. Dreyfack. il por *Bus Week* p70 Ja 19 '87

Walk before you run [Kangaroos' walking and running shoe designs] T. H. Cole. il *Pop Mech* 164:48 Mr '87

Runoff

Using tires to track pollution. R. Monastersky. *Sci News* 132:6 Jl 4 '87

World agriculture and soil erosion. D. Pimentel and others. bibl f il *BioScience* 37:2. 7-83 Ap '87

Runté, Terry

Last word. il *Omni* 9:126 F '87

Last word. il *Omni* 9:126 Jl '87

Last word. il *Omni* 9:142 Ap '87

Last word. il *Omni* 9:114 Ag '87

Runways (Air bases) *See* Air bases—Runways

Ruoff, Mary

Take it from the bank. il *Progressive* 51:13 D '87

Ruoslahti, Erkki, and Pierschbacher, Michael D.

New perspectives in cell adhesion: RGD and integrins. bibl f il *Science* 238:491-7 O 23 '87

Rupert, Johann P.

about

An Afrikaans insider questions the system. S. Mufson. il por *Bus Week* p80+ My 18 '87

Rupnik, Jacques

Borders of the mind. *New Repub* 196:17-19 Mr 9 '87

Gorbachev's profs. *New Repub* 197:10+ D 7 '87

Rupp, Becky

The American breakfast. il *Ctry J* 14:50-5 F '87

Rupp, Christy

about

Christy Rupp at P.P.O.W. H. Cotter. *Art Am* 75:130 Ja '87

Ruppe, Loret

First word. il *Omni* 9:6 Je '87

Ruptured disks *See* Spine—Abnormalities

Rural development programs *See* Rural planning

Rural education *See* Education, Rural

Rural industries

The challenge of the future [address, September 22, 1987] A. Harrigan. *Vital Speeches Day* 54:109-11 D 1 '87

Rural life *See* Country life; Farm life

Rural medical care *See* Medical care, Rural

Rural migration *See* Migration, Internal

Rural planning

A champion for developing rural areas [T. Coleman] *Success Farm* 85:49 Ag '87

International aspects

Jimmy Yen: crusader for mankind. J. Hersey. il por *Read Dig* 131:138-45+ O '87

New Hampshire

Rural hot spots . . . rural cold spots. B. Trebilcock. il *Ctry J* 14:32-5+ Je '87

Vermont

Our changing town. D. D. Sleeper. il *Ctry J* 14:14-15 N '87

Rural schools *See* Education, Rural

Rural telephone service

A telephone, at last, for the hard to reach [digital radiotelephone] W. J. Cook. il *U S News World Rep* 103:69 D 21 '87

Rusalka [opera] *See* Dvořák, Antonín, 1841-1904

Rusch, Kristine Kathryn

Expanding in Portland. il *Publ Wkly* 231:40-1+ Ja 23 '87

Rush, Bette, and Lebelson, Harry

Alaskan marine life and the Eskimo—through art. il por *Sea Front* 33:84-9 Mr/Ap '87

Rush, Jean C.

Research, the river, and the art education engineers. bibl f *Des Arts Educ* 88:21-6 My/Je '87

Rush, Tom

about

In New Hampshire: skid marks. J. Skow. il por *Time* 129:8-9 My 11 '87

Rush-Presbyterian-St. Luke's Medical Center (Chicago, Ill.) *See* Chicago (Ill.)—Hospitals

Rush Rhees Library

John A. Williams Archive established at university. por *Jet* 71:24 Ja 26 '87

Rushdie, Salman

Good advice is rarer than rubies [story] *New Yorker* 63:26-8 Je 22 '87

about

If it's Tuesday, this must be Managua. C. Lane. *Wash Mon* 19:48-51 Je '87

Rushdoony, Rousas John

about

The Armenian connection. R. Clapp. por *Christ Today* 31:22 F 20 '87

Rusher, William A., 1923-

Reagan's no suicide. *Natl Rev* 39:36 Je 5 '87

Rushing, Felder

about

Garden writers, classic and contemporary. B. Summer. *Publ Wkly* 231:40 Mr 20 '87

Rusk, Chris

about

A gripping invention. D. Marth. il por *Nations Bus* 75:82 My '87

Rusk, Rogers D., d. 1985

about

Obituary

Phys Today por 40:130+ F '87. J. R. Rusk

Ruska, Ernst, 1906-
about
Physics Nobel Prize. P. F. Schewe. bibl f *Phys Today* 40:S70 Ja '87
Physics Nobel Prize awarded for microscopies old and new. B. M. Schwarzschild. il pors *Phys Today* 40:17-21 Ja '87
Rusko Writing Company, Inc.
A gripping invention [Stetro pencil grippers invented by C. Rusk] D. Marth. il por *Nations Bus* 75:82 My '87
Russ Berrie & Co., Inc.
A bullish play on Snuggle Bears. il *Money* 16:8 Ap '87
Russel Davis Planetarium
Jackson, Miss., theater named for Ronald McNair. il *Jet* 71:37 F 2 '87
Russell, Amy
When you're born a 2.5. il *Glamour* 85:58+ O '87
Russell, Bill
about
Growing up with privilege and prejudice [cover story] K. K. Russell. il pors *N Y Times Mag* p22-8 Je 14 '87
The king at his new court. J. McCallum. il pors *Sports Illus* 67:36-9+ N 16 '87
Russell to coach Kings then become pres., owner. por *Jet* 72:48 My 18 '87
Russell, Charles
about
The Marine Corps says goodbye to Charles Russell, its last active-duty WW II combat vet. R. Arias. il pors *People Wkly* 28:159-60 N 23 '87
Russell, Chuck
about
A nightmare on Elm Street, part 3: Dream warriors [film] Reviews
New Leader 70:19-20 Mr 23 '87. J. Gardner
Russell, Clarence H.
(tr) See Halévy, Ludovic, 1834-1908. Breaking the rules
Russell, Conrad
England's last poll tax. il *Hist Today* 37:9-11 O '87
Russell, Dianne
The perfect country dog. il *Ctry J* 14:28-34 D '87
Russell, Dick
Fighting the nuke-waste shell game [cover story] il *Nation* 245:577+ N 21 '87
Russell, Dora Winifred Black Russell, Countess, 1894-1986
about
Dora who? [adaptation of address, June 1987] B. Earles. il pors *Humanist* 47:17-19+ N/D '87
Russell, Erk
about
Head man. D. S. Looney. il pors *Sports Illus* 67:98-100+ Ag 31 '87
Russell, Francis, 1910-
The case that will not close. bibl f il por *N Y Rev Books* 34:4+ N 5 '87
Russell, George
Can the Sandinistas still be stopped? *Commentary* 84:26-34 Jl '87
Russell, George
about
Indexing a success. S. W. Angrist. por *Forbes* 139:234+ My 18 '87
When George Russell talks, pension funds listen. H. Gleckman. il por *Bus Week* p134-5 N 30 '87
Russell, Herman J.
about
Atlanta City Hall to get facelift; black firm helps build new addition. il *Jet* 72:33 S 21 '87
Building up, spreading out. D. Marth. il pors *Nations Bus* 75:58-9 Ja '87
How Herman Russell built his business . . . brick by brick. N. McCall. il pors *Black Enterp* 17:176-80+ Je '87
Russell, Janice Valls- *See* Valls-Russell, Janice
Russell, Jeffrey Burton
about
Speak of the devil. J. J. Pelikan. *Commentary* 83:63-6 Ap '87
Russell, John, 1919-
Art. il *N Y Times Book Rev* 92:11-12 My 31 '87
Outdoor abstractions. il por *House Gard* 159:182-5+ F '87
Quest for a proper place to read. *Writer* 100:5-6 Mr '87
Russell, Karen K.
Growing up with privilege and prejudice [cover story] il pors *N Y Times Mag* p22-8 Je 14 '87

Russell, Ken, 1927-
about
Gothic [film] Reviews
America 156:445 My 30 '87. R. A. Blake
Newsweek il 109:79 Ap 27 '87. J. Kroll
People Wkly 27:14 Ap 20 '87. P. Travers
Time 129:76 Ap 20 '87. R. Corliss
Russell, Kimberly
about
Prime time profiles. pors *Teen* 31:66 Je '87
Russell, Mark
Making it on Main Street. il *Black Enterp* 18:66-8+ D '87
The push to make black business competitive. il *Black Enterp* 17:259-60+ Je '87
Russell, Michael K.
about
Demand-side journalism. R. McGough. il pors *Forbes* 139:68+ F 23 '87
What's black and white—and in the red? M. Ivey. il pors *Bus Week* p60 F 16 '87
Russell, Milton
Environmental protection for the 1990s and beyond. bibl f *Environment* 29:12-15+ S '87
Russell, Milton, and Gruber, Michael
Risk assessment in environmental policy-making. bibl f *Science* 236:286-90 Ap 17 '87
Russell, Robert
about
Release. *New Yorker* 63:28-32 S 28 '87
Russell, Sally
Travel. See issues of Skiing beginning November 1985
Russell, Sue
Pam Dawber: "I'm traditional about marriage" [interview] il pors *Redbook* 168:20+ Ap '87
Russell, Theresa
about
Russell's rhapsody. A. DeCurtis. por *Roll Stone* p19+ Mr 12 '87
Russell, Willy
about
Educating Rita [drama] Reviews
New Yorker 63:87 My 18 '87. E. Oliver
Time il 129:71 My 25 '87. W. A. Henry
Russell (Charles M.) National Wildlife Refuge (Mont.)
See Wildlife sanctuaries—Montana
Russell (Frank) Company *See* Frank Russell Company
Russell (H. J.) Construction Co., Inc. *See* H. J. Russell Construction Co., Inc.
Russia *See* Soviet Union
Russian architecture *See* Architecture, Russian
Russian art *See* Art, Russian
Russian artificial satellites *See* Artificial satellites, Russian
Russian authors *See* Authors, Russian
Russian commandos *See* Commandos, Russian
Russian cooking *See* Cooking, Russian
Russian defectors *See* Defectors, Political
Russian embassy buildings *See* Embassies (Buildings)
Russian exiles *See* Exiles
Russian fiction
Riding the bronze horse. J. Bayley. il *N Y Rev Books* 34:9-10 O 22 '87
Russian folk music *See* Folk music, Russian
Russian helicopters *See* Helicopters
Russian Jews *See* Jews—Soviet Union
Russian lacquerware *See* Lacquer and lacquering
Russian language
Notes and comment [how Russian words affect our feelings about the Soviet Union] *New Yorker* 63:21-2 Mr 30 '87
Russian literature
See also
Russian fiction
The burden of caring [women and Russian literature] B. Heldt. *Nation* 244:820-4 Je 13 '87
Progress on the margin. E. von Kuehnelt-Leddihn. *Natl Rev* 39:40 D 31 '87
Russian military assistance *See* Military assistance, Russian
Russian nuclear submarines *See* Nuclear submarines, Russian
Russian Orthodox Church *See* Orthodox Eastern Church, Russian
Russian painting *See* Painting, Russian
Russian photographers *See* Photographers, Russian
Russian propaganda *See* Propaganda, Russian
Russian Revolution *See* Soviet Union—History—Revolution, 1917-1921
Russian science fiction
Soviet science fiction: to the present via the future. K. Rosenberg. bibl il *Technol Rev* 90:66-74 Jl '87

Russian shuttle missions *See* Space flight—Shuttle missions, Russian
Russian space stations *See* Space stations, Russian
Russian space vehicles *See* Space vehicles, Russian
Russian spaceplane *See* Spaceplane, Russian
Russian studies *See* Soviet studies
Russian submarines *See* Submarines, Russian
Russians
Across a land of power and poetry [cover story; special issue] il map *People Wkly* 27:32-42+ Ap 6 '87
Afghanistan
See also
Afghanistan—Russian invasion, 1979-
Canada
Aftermath of a romance [K. Inwood of Toronto charged with assaulting his Russian wife and child] R. Corelli. il pors *Macleans* 100:58 S 28 '87
Cherishing new freedom [Soviet Army deserters from Afghanistan now living in Canada] S. Aikenhead. il *Macleans* 100:10 Ag 24 '87
Foreign countries
The Soviets abroad. L. Pochivalov. il *World Press Rev* 34:30-1 D '87
United States
Emigré teaching—mystique or method? [Russian teachers and coaches] M. Horosko. il *Dance Mag* 61:76-7 Mr '87
From Russia without love: Aina Robertovna's dream and how she got it. D. Blum. il pors *N Y* 20:46-50+ My 11 '87
From Russia—with real love [exiled writer V. Aksenov] J. Podhoretz. il por *U S News World Rep* 103:49-50 Ag 17 '87
The Kremlin in America. A. Wilson-Smith. il *Macleans* 100:29 D 21 '87
The long hard road to Moscow [émigrés return home from U.S.] J. Smolowe. il *Time* 129:47 Ja 12 '87
The man without a country [Soviet émigré writer E. Sevela] M. L. Grisanti. il pors *N Y* 20:38-43 Ja 12 '87
Orlov provides perspectives on Gorbachev's reforms [interview] W. Sweet. por *Phys Today* 40:79-82 My '87
The return of the prodigal Russians [émigrés return after living in the U.S.] *Newsweek* 109:31 Ja 12 '87
A Soviet emigre takes the 'A' Train [roots of Soviet feelings about America] V. P. Aksenov. il *N Y Times Mag* p60+ My 3 '87
Soviets at work: Moscow on the Potomac [M. Gorbachev's summit delegation] S. Strasser. il *Newsweek* 110:30-1 D 21 '87
The struggle to settle [refuseniks and returnees] C. Redden. il *Macleans* 100:33 Ja 19 '87
Russkies [film] *See* Motion picture reviews—Single works
Russwurm, John B.
about
Founders of the black press. L. Bennett. il pors *Ebony* 42:96+ F '87
Rust, Mathias
about
Audacious airman. il pors map *Life* 10:66-9 Ag '87
Destination Red Square. B. Levin. il *Macleans* 100:24 Je 8 '87
A folk hero in the slammer. N. Cooper. il por *Newsweek* 109:36 Je 15 '87
Four years for a "fun" flight. W. R. Doerner. il por *Time* 130:42 S 14 '87
Gaps in Soviet defenses? R. Kaylor. il *U S News World Rep* 102:30 Je 15 '87
A hard landing in Moscow. C. Redden. il por *Macleans* 100:22 S 14 '87
Joyride. W. F. Buckley. *Natl Rev* 39:56 Jl 17 '87
Kremlin prop wash. W. R. Doerner. il por *Time* 129:30-2 Je 15 '87
Red faces in Red Square. N. Cooper. il por *Newsweek* 109:36 Je 8 '87
Rust's unhappy landing. S. Seibert. il *Newsweek* 110:49 S 14 '87
Welcome to Moscow. J. Greenwald. il por *Time* 129:34-5 Je 8 '87
Rust *See* Corrosion and anticorrosives
Rustic furniture *See* Furniture, Rustic
Rustin, Bayard, 1910-1987
The King to come [adaptation of address, January 19, 1987] *New Repub* 196:19-21 Mr 9 '87
about
$1 million estate of Bayard Rustin, 77, left to son, 38, adopted in 1982. por *Jet* 73:4 O 12 '87
Obituary
Black Enterp por 18:24 N '87
Jet por 72:54 S 7 '87

Jet il por 73:4-5 O 19 '87
Natl Rev 39:20 S 25 '87
New Leader 70:2 S 7 '87
New Repub 197:10-11 S 28 '87
Rustlers, Cactus *See* Cactus—Theft
Rustlers, Sheep *See* Sheep—Theft
Rusz, Joe
About the sport. See issues of Road & Track
Rutan, Burt
about
Sketchy details. P. Garrison. il *Flying* 114:20-2 Jl '87
Rutan, Dick
about
Gallant victory for an odd bird. S. Moses. il pors *Sports Illus* 66:36-9 Ja 5 '87
Rutherford, Donald
Captain Scammon: the whaler who turned naturalist. il pors map *Sea Front* 33:18-26 Ja/F '87
Rutherford, Malcolm
Come the election . . . *World Press Rev* 34:12-13 My '87
Rutherfurd, Edward
about
PW interviews. S. S. Steinberg. por *Publ Wkly* 232:57-8 Ag 28 '87
Rutland, Robert Allen, 1922-
The battle to ratify. il *Life* 10:76 Fall '87
Rutledge, John
about
The saving of America. P. Brimelow. il por *Forbes* 139:71 Ap 20 '87
Rutledge Education System
Embodiment of the dream [G. Shinn] E. F. Cone. il por *Forbes* 140:72-3 N 30 '87
Rutsala, Vern
Traffic watch [poem] *Atlantic* 259:66 F '87
Ruttan, Susan
about
Playing the lovesick secretary on L.A. law has helped Susan Ruttan learn how not to handle men. D. Hutchings. il pors *People Wkly* 28:103-4+ N 2 '87
Ruttle, Jack
Well equipped. See issues of Rodale's Organic Gardening beginning May 1986 through July 1987
RVs *See* Recreational vehicles
Rwanda
See also
Crime and criminals—Rwanda
Trials—Rwanda
Ryan, Barbara B.
Pint-sized ship of state. il por *Am Hist Illus* 22:36-7+ S '87
Weaves of grass. il pors *Travel Holiday* 167:34-6 Mr '87
Ryan, David
about
A brash young investing champ gets rich by defying old rules. G. Anrig, Jr. il por *Money* 16:140 Ag '87
Ryan, Ed
about
Want a room with a view? This hotel has one of hell. M. Small. il por *People Wkly* 28:175-7 N 16 '87
Ryan, James W.
(jt. auth) See Enright, Joseph F., and Ryan, James W.
Ryan, Joan
One step to stardom. il pors *Women's Sports Fitness* 9:30-2 Je '87
U.S. Open: preview '87. il *Women's Sports Fitness* 9:65+ S '87
Ryan, John C.
about
Once a G-man, now a pacifist. T. E. Johnson. il por *Newsweek* 110:24 N 23 '87
Ryan, Kay
Caryatid [poem] *Commonweal* 114:618 N 6 '87
Les natures profondement bonnes sont toujours indecises [poem] *Am Sch* 56:548 Aut '87
The palm at the end of the mind [poem] *New Repub* 197:41 O 5 '87
Ryan, Kimberly
about
Coming back to life. F. M. Henley. il pors *Ladies Home J* 104:34+ Jl '87
Ryan, Martin
Transactions [poem] *Am Sch* 56:470 Aut '87
Ryan, Michael
Blood and money: the unsolved murder of a Long Island woman leads to a novel suit against her husband. il pors *N Y* 20:38-44 Je 8 '87
Ryan, Michael
Crossroads Inn [poem] *Nation* 245:766 D 19 '87

Ryan, Michael, d. 1987
about
A bloody rage in rural England. il *U S News World Rep* 103:11 Ag 31 '87
The market-day massacre. B. Levin. il *Macleans* 100:20 Ag 31 '87
They shoot only in America, don't they? por *Newsweek* 110:34 Ag 31 '87
Wednesday, bloody Wednesday. C. Ogden. il *Time* 130:27 Ag 31 '87
Ryan, Michael J. (Michael Joseph), 1953-, and Wagner, William E., Jr.
Asymmetries in mating preferences between species: female swordtails prefer heterospecific males. bibl f il *Science* 236:595-7 My 1 '87
Ryan, Mike
about
The Starduster's last flight. P. O. D'Aulaire and E. D'Aulaire. il *Read Dig* 131:75-80 Jl '87
Ryan, Patrick J.
The Word. See issues of America beginning November 21, 1987
Ryan, Victoria
A river changes. il map *Earth Sci* 39:15-17 Wint '86
Ryan Homes, Inc.
Pyrrhic possibilities [NV Homes' acquisition of Ryan Homes] K. Hannon. il por *Forbes* 139:94 Je 15 '87
Rybakov, Anatolii Naumovich
about
Beyond *glasnost*. W. Laqueur. *Commentary* 84:63-5 O '87
A compatriot's view from the homeland [interview] D. Stanglin. il por *U S News World Rep* 103:50 Ag 17 '87
Tales from a time of terror. J. O. Jackson. il pors *Time* 129:45-6 Ap 27 '87
Rybeck, Walter, and Pasquariello, Ronald D.
Combating modern-day feudalism: land as God's gift. il *Christ Century* 104:470-2 My 13 '87
Ryder, Michael L.
The evolution of the fleece. il *Sci Am* 256:112-19 Ja '87
Ryder System, Inc.
Tony Burns has Ryder's rivals eating dust. P. Engardio. il por *Bus Week* p104+ Ap 6 '87
U-Haul hits the skids. D. Pauly. il *Newsweek* 110:54-5 S 14 '87
Ryerson, André
Capitalism & selfishness [discussion of December 1986 article] *Commentary* 83:10-12+ Mr '87
Politics and "peace education". *Read Dig* 130:133-8 Je '87
Rykoff-Sexton Inc.
What's the hurry? E. Paris. il por *Forbes* 140:112+ N 2 '87
Rykwert, Joseph, 1926-
Historic architecture: Joseph Maria Olbrich: a jugendstil design at the Mathildenhöhe artists' colony. il por *Archit Dig* 44:180-5+ Ap '87
Louis Sullivan and the gospel of height. il *Art Am* 75:158-69+ N '87
A Russian teahouse: memories of St. Petersburg in Germany. il *Archit Dig* 44:164-7 Je '87
Ryland Group Inc.
Most improved. il *Forbes* 139:112 Ja 12 '87
Ryman, Chris
The turn shape/pole plant connection. il *Skiing* 40:185+ D '87
Ryokans (Inns) See Hotels, motels, etc.—Japan
Rypdal, Terje, 1947-
about
Terje Rypdal: sculptor in sound. B. Milkowski. il por *Down Beat* 54:20-2 O '87
Terje Rypdal's The curse—a guitar transcription. J. Dennison. il *Down Beat* 54:56 O '87

S

S. C. Johnson & Son, Inc.
Frank Lloyd Wright [traveling exhibition entitled Frank Lloyd Wright and the Johnson Wax buildings] S. B. Sherrill. il *Antiques* 131:950+ My '87
S corporations
Congress, spare us this reform. G. W. Padwe. il *Nations Bus* 75:58 Ag '87
Preserving fiscal years. il *Nations Bus* 75:10 O '87

S. D. Warren Co.
Warren introduces glare-free and lightweight gloss grades to book publishers. il *Publ Wkly* 231:254+ My 15 '87
S.G. Warburg Group plc
Why Warburg is proving to be such a survivor. R. A. Melcher. il *Bus Week* p164-5 N 2 '87
S-K-I Ltd.
Strap on your skis for this one. G. G. Marcial. *Bus Week* p114 Je 1 '87
Sa, Khun See Khun Sa
Saab (Automobile) See Automobiles, Foreign
Saab-Scania AB
The original Saab story. H. Rasmussen. il *Mot Trend* 39:104-5+ N '87
Switzerland's Crossair considers purchase of stretched Saab SF340. J. M. Lenorovitz. il *Aviat Week Space Technol* 126:42-3 Je 8 '87
Saad-Cook, Janet
about
Sun dancing. J. Bell. il *Omni* 10:34+ D '87
Saatchi, Charles
about
As advertised: the world's top sellers. M. Magnet. il pors *Fortune* 115:96 Ja 5 '87
The Saatchi factor. R. W. Walker. il por *Art News* 86:117-21 Ja '87
Saatchi, Doris
Open house. il por *House Gard* 159:206-13+ N '87
Saatchi, Maurice
about
As advertised: the world's top sellers. M. Magnet. il pors *Fortune* 115:96 Ja 5 '87
Saatchi & Saatchi Company plc
And now, the Saatchi & Saatchi bank? [attempt to merge with Midland Bank] M. Maremont. il *Bus Week* p92 S 28 '87
As advertised: the world's top sellers [M. and C. Saatchi] M. Magnet. il pors *Fortune* 115:96 Ja 5 '87
Bare knuckles on Madison Avenue [Saatchi & Saatchi takeover of Ted Bates] A. Kleiner. il por *N Y Times Mag* p34-9+ N 8 '87
Is the new, improved, giant economy-size Saatchi really better? R. A. Melcher and S. Benway. il *Bus Week* p60-2 D 21 '87
Saatchi Collection See Art—Collectors and collecting
Saavedra, Daniel Ortega See Ortega Saavedra, Daniel
Saba, Shoichi
about
The man Toshiba hung out to dry. A. Tanzer. il por *Forbes* 140:96+ S 7 '87
Saba (Netherlands Antilles)
See also
Americans—Saba (Netherlands Antilles)
Description and travel
Dive bums [American skin divers in Saba, Dutch West Indies] R. Rothenberg and S. Roy. il *Oceans* 20:38-45 Ja/F '87
Sabah, Saud Nasir al- See Al-Sabah, Saud Nasir
Sabatier, Patrick
Children of December. il *World Press Rev* 34:12-13 Mr '87
'The world's richest man'. il *World Press Rev* 34:49 N '87
Sabatier, Renee
The global costs of AIDS. il *Futurist* 21:19-21 N/D '87
Sabatini, Gabriela
about
Look out Steffi, Chris & Martina—Gabriela is gunning for you. R. Arias. il pors *People Wkly* 28:127-8+ S 7 '87
Sabbath
The ease of distraction [decline of a common cultural memory and rise of secularism, convenience, and distraction] J. Garvey. il *Commonweal* 114:520-1 S 25 '87
Sabel, Charles F., and others
How to keep mature industries innovative [cover story] il *Technol Rev* 90:26-35 Ap '87
Sabena Belgian World Airlines
European deregulation expected to lead to airline mergers [proposed SAS-Sabena merger] *Aviat Week Space Technol* 126:203+ Mr 9 '87
Europe's skies may be full of mergers [SAS and Sabena] J. Kapstein and others. il *Bus Week* p62 My 11 '87
SAS board authorizes merger talks with Sabena. *Aviat Week Space Technol* 126:34 My 4 '87

Saber saws *See* Saws and sawing
Saberhagen, Bret
        about
  Return of the Royal nonesuch. P. Gammons. il pors
    Sports Illus 66:28-9 Je 8 '87
Sabine Consolidated Inc.
  A death at work can put the boss in jail [homicide
    conviction] J. Tasini. *Bus Week* p37-8 Mr 2 '87
Sable (Aircraft carrier)
  The side-wheel carriers. G. C. Long. il *Am Herit* 38:104-7
    F/Mr '87
SAC *See* United States. Air Force. Strategic Air Command
Sacbé (Musical group)
  Mexico's jazz master. M. Holston. por *Américas* 39:58-60
    N/D '87
Saccharomyces *See* Yeasts
Sacerio-Garí, Enrique
  The other Borges: a precursor from the future. il por
    Christ Century 104:1026-9 N 18 '87
Sachs, Leo
  The molecular control of blood cell development. bibl
    f il *Science* 238:1374-9 D 4 '87
Sack, Albert
  Regionalism in early American tea tables. bibl f il *Antiques*
    131:248-63 Ja '87
Sack, Donald R.
  (jt. auth) *See* Louis, Peter A., and Sack, Donald R.
Sack, Harold
  The furniture. il *Antiques* 132:160-73 Jl '87
Sackler, Arthur M., 1913-1987
        about
  Dr. Arthur M. Sackler, for whom our new gallery is
    named, sought to link the arts and sciences with the
    humanities. R. M. Adams. il *Smithsonian* 18:10 O
    '87
Sackler (Arthur M.) Gallery (Washington, D.C.) *See* Arthur
    M. Sackler Gallery (Washington, D.C.)
Sackler Galleries for Asian Art *See* Metropolitan Museum
    of Art (New York, N.Y.). Sackler Galleries for Asian
    Art
Sacks, Oliver W.
  Tics. bibl il *N Y Rev Books* 34:37-41 Ja 29 '87
        about
  Oliver Sacks: "I began to think that wellness might
    be a disease, that one might suffer from chronic health
    in California". H. Brubach. il pors *Vogue* 177:230+
    N '87
      Anecdotes, facetiae, satire, etc.
  More clinical tales. R. Liebmann-Smith. *New Yorker*
    63:30-1 My 4 '87
Sacks, Oliver W., and Wasserman, Robert
  The case of the colorblind painter. bibl f il *N Y Rev
    Books* 34:25-34 N 19 '87
Sacks, Susan Riemer
  (jt. auth) *See* Travers, Eva Foldes, and Sacks, Susan
    Riemer
Sacks
  Custom-made sacks to hold gift bottles of wine. il *Sunset*
    179:102 D '87
Sacramento (Calif.)
        Art
  Public art with public transportation in Sacramento [light
    rail stations] il *Sunset* 179:58 S '87
        Crime
  Greg Withrow's neo-Nazi past returns to inflict the
    ultimate scourge: crucifixion. M. Green. il pors *People
    Wkly* 28:41-2+ S 21 '87
        Stations
  Public art with public transportation in Sacramento [light
    rail stations] il *Sunset* 179:58 S '87
Sacramento River (Calif.)
  Floating and fishing the big rivers [float fishing] S.
    Netherby. il *Field Stream* 92:97+ Jl '87
Sacraments
    See also
    Baptism
    Penance
  Empirical liturgy: the search for grace. A. M. Greeley.
    America 157:379-83+ N 21 '87
Le sacre du printemps [ballet] *See* Ballet reviews—Single
    works
Sacred books
    See also
    Bible
Sacred Congregation for the Doctrine of the Faith *See*
    Catholic Church. Congregation for the Doctrine of
    the Faith
Sacred Heart devotion
  The restful friendship of God. R. Kress. *America*
    156:501-5 Je 20-27 '87

Sacred music *See* Religious music
Sacrifice
    See also
    Santería (Cult)
SAD *See* Seasonal affective disorder
Sadar, Anthony J.
  The awesome aurora [cover story] il *Weatherwise* 40:76-7
    Ap '87
Sadasivam, Bharati
  Bombay's 'red-light' children. *World Press Rev* 34:54
    Jl '87
Sadat, Anwar, 1918-1981
        Assassination
  A hero falls [excerpt from A woman of Egypt] J. Sadat.
    il pors *People Wkly* 28:48-50+ Ag 17 '87
Sadat, Jehan
  A hero falls [excerpt from A woman of Egypt] il pors
    People Wkly 28:48-50+ Ag 17 '87
Saddleback (Me.: Resort) *See* Resorts—Maine
Saddoris, James
  Your professional organization [address, August 10, 1987]
    Vital Speeches Day 53:767-8 O 1 '87
Sadik, Nafis
        about
  A new era for UNFPA. M. Morain. *Humanist* 47:33
    N/D '87
Sadism
    See also
    Sadomasochism
Sadiya
        about
  Found: a new beauty. il pors *Vogue* 177:216 N '87
Sadkin, Alex
        about
  Obituary
    Roll Stone il por p25 S 24 '87. F. Goodman
Sadler, Charles A.
        about
  Diplomat wins $150,000 for job discrimination. *Jet* 72:16
    Jl 6 '87
Sadler's Wells Royal Ballet
  Ashley's "all-American" Aurora bemuses British bal-
    letomanes. M. E. Willis. il por *Dance Mag* 61:102
    S '87
  Footwork. P. J. Rosenwald. il *Horizon* 30:36 N '87
Sadness
    See also
    Depression, Mental
Sadoff, Ira
  At the jazz concert [poem] *New Repub* 196:41 Mr
    9 '87
Sadomasochism
  Rough sex gets real. M. F. Coburn. il *Mademoiselle*
    93:238-9+ My '87
Sadovsky, Anne
        about
  Against all odds. P. F. Stewart. il por *Ladies Home
    J* 104:148 O '87
Sadruddin Aga Khan *See* Aga Khan, Sadruddin, Prince,
    1933-
Saëns, Camille Saint- *See* Saint-Saëns, Camille, 1835-1921
Saëns, Charles Camille Saint- *See* Saint-Saëns, Camille,
    1835-1921
Sáez, J. C., and others
  Carbon tetrachloride at hepatotoxic levels blocks rever-
    sibly gap junctions between rat hepatocytes. bibl f
    il *Science* 236:967-9 My 22 '87
Safari Grill (New York, N.Y.) *See* New York (N.Y.)—
    Restaurants, nightclubs, bars, etc.
Safe Drinking Water Act
  Getting the lead out [EPA regulations concerning lead
    in the water supply] *Sci News* 132:269 O 24 '87
Safe sex [drama] *See* Fierstein, Harvey
SafeCard Services Inc.
  Cashing in on missing credit cards. J. Mendes. *Fortune*
    116:100+ Ag 17 '87
  Dangers for SafeCard. M. Schifrin. il *Forbes* 140:258-9
    N 30 '87
Safety, Industrial *See* Occupational health and safety
Safety belts
    See also
    Automobiles—Safety belts
    School buses—Safety belts
Safety clothing *See* Clothing, Protective
Safety devices and measures *See* Accidents—Prevention
Safety education
    See also
    Automobile driving—Study and teaching
    Aviation—Safety devices and measures
    Child Assault Prevention (Program)
    Cycling

Safety education—See also—*cont.*
    Drowning—Prevention
    Helping parents help their children [Girls Clubs of America's KID-ABILITY sexual abuse prevention program] *Child Today* 16:5 My/Je '87
    How to keep your kids safe [protection against sexual abuse] M. Jacobbi and R. Wright. *McCalls* 114:95-6 F '87
    Peer prevention [National Head and Spinal Injury Prevention Program] D. Zevin. il *Health* 19:16 My '87
    Safety for latchkey children. C. Loomis. il *Parents* 62:13 D '87
    Staying out of crime's way. S. Perry. il *Curr Health 2* 14:20-1 O '87
    Streetwise families. D. Bjorklund and B. Bjorklund. il *Parents* 62:267 N '87
Safety goggles *See* Goggles
Safety Harbor Spa and Fitness Center (Fla.: Resort) *See* Health resorts, watering places, etc.—Florida
Safety helmets *See* Helmets
Safety laws and regulations
    See also
    Occupational health and safety—Laws and regulations
Safety razors *See* Razors
Safety seats *See* Automobiles—Safety devices and measures
Safeway Stores, Inc.
    How to get in on the Safeway LBO [warrants] J. M. Laderman. *Bus Week* p100 Ap 27 '87
Saffo, Mary Beth
    New light on seaweeds [cover story] bibl il *BioScience* 37:654-64 O '87
Saffo, Paul
    Desktop publishing. See issues of Personal Computing beginning May 1987
Safford, Frances Gruber, and Caccavale, Ruth Wilford
    Japanesque silver by Tiffany and Company in the Metropolitan Museum of Art. bibl f il *Antiques* 132:808-19 O '87
Saffron
    See also
    Cooking—Herbs and spices
Safire, William
    Lincoln meets the press. il *N Y Times Mag* p28-9 Ag 23 '87
    On language. See issues of The New York Times Magazine
    Ten myths about the Reagan debacle. il pors *N Y Times Mag* p20-6+ Mr 22 '87
    Tug-of-war. il *N Y Times Mag* p61-2+ S 13 '87
        about
    From Nixon to Lincoln. L. Weymouth. il pors *N Y* 20:42-7 Ag 31 '87
    Lincoln: fiction & fact [interview] A. M. Schlesinger. il pors *Am Herit* 38:84-9 D '87
    A modern vote for Abraham Lincoln [interview] A. P. Sanoff. il por *U S News World Rep* 103:57 Ag 24 '87
    Safire on Lincoln and 'Freedom'. J. Kroll. il pors *Newsweek* 110:56-7 Ag 31 '87
    The Safire tirade. W. F. Buckley. *Natl Rev* 39:60-1 Ap 10 '87
    William Safire talks about 'Freedom,' his new novel. T. Todd. por *Publ Wkly* 231:49-50 My 29 '87
Safran, Claire
    Mystery of the buried amulet. il *Read Dig* 130:95-9 Je '87
    Secret exodus: the story of Operation Moses [excerpt] il *Read Dig* 130:96-104+ Ja '87
    You are what you think. il *Read Dig* 131:44-6 Ag '87
Safran, Nadav
    Reflagging folly. *New Repub* 197:10-11 Ag 3 '87
Sagal, Katey
        about
    As a laugh-getter, Katey Sagal is cleaning up in TV's dirtiest show, Married . . . with children. S. Spillman. il por *People Wkly* 27:67-8+ Je 22 '87
Sagamore Hill National Historic Site (N.Y.)
    Sagamore Hill: a visit to President Theodore Roosevelt's famous home on Long Island. N. A. Ruhling. il *Antiques Collect Hobbies* 92:38-9+ Je '87
Sagamore Hotel (Bolton Landing, N.Y.) *See* Bolton Landing (N.Y.)—Hotels, motels, etc.
Sagan, Carl, 1934-
    Why Star Wars is bad for astronomy. il *Sky Telesc* 74:340-1 O '87
Sagan, Dorion, 1959-
    Bioshelters. il *Omni* 9:54-9 Mr '87
Sagan, Dorion, 1959-, and Margulis, Lynn, 1938-
    Bacterial bedfellows. il *Nat Hist* 96:26+ Mr '87

Sagaponack (N.Y.)
        Historic houses, sites, etc.
    Literary lair: Freddy and George Plimpton in Sagaponack. G. Plimpton. il por *Archit Dig* 44:126-31 Je '87
Sagdeev, R. Z. *See* Sagdeyev, Roald Zinnurovich
Sagdeyev, Roald Zinnurovich
        about
    The wizard of IKI. D. Thompson. il por *Time* 130:69 O 5 '87
Sagdeyev, Roald Zinnurovich, and Galeev, Albert A.
    Comet Halley and the solar wind. il *Sky Telesc* 73:252-5 Mr '87
Sage, Sybil Adelman
    When his old flame reappeared: how I put out the fire. il *Glamour* 85:222+ Ap '87
Sage
        See also
    Salvia
Sage Analytics International Inc.
    Why Sage isn't disaster-proof. G. G. Marcial. *Bus Week* p106 O 5 '87
Sagebrush
    An about-face for the BLM [planting sagebrush in Idaho] G. Oakley. il *Sierra* 72:13-14 Ja/F '87
Sagendorph, Robb
        about
    Unforgettable Uncle Robb [condensed from The education of a Yankee] J. D. Hale. il por *Read Dig* 131:87-8+ N '87
Sager, Carole Bayer
        about
    Architectural digest visits: Burt Bacharach and Carole Bayer Sager. B. Gooch. il pors *Archit Dig* 44:128-33+ O '87
Sager, Mike
    A boy and his dog in hell. il *Roll Stone* p36-7+ Jl 2 '87
Sagitta (Constellation) *See* Constellations
Sagnier, Thierry
    Educating the 'most beautiful children in the world'. il *UN Chron* 24:74-5 N '87
Sagor, Richard
    Looking for peace in the war on drugs. *Educ Dig* 52:50-2 Ap '87
Saguaro *See* Cactus
Sahara
        See also
    Tuaregs
    Into Africa [testing Audis in the Algerian Sahara] P. Bingham. il map *Mot Trend* 39:118-23+ D '87
    Just desert [driving Audis through the Sahara in Algeria] J. Rusz. il *Road Track* 39:54-6 N '87
    Wadi Howar: paleoclimatic evidence from an extinct river system in the southeastern Sahara. H.-J. Pachur and S. Kröpelin. bibl f il map *Science* 237:298-300 Jl 17 '87
Sahatjian, Elizabeth
    Going with the grain. il *Esquire* 107:26 Ja '87
    Knee-deep in blackberries. il *Esquire* 108:20 Jl '87
    Nothing like a Thai grill. il *Esquire* 107:52+ Je '87
    The toast of Tuscany. il *Esquire* 108:52 O '87
    Waiter, what's that ribollita doing in my soup? il *Esquire* 108:38 N '87
Sahel
    Africa's Sahel: the stricken land [cover story] W. S. Ellis. il map *Natl Geogr* 172:140-79 Ag '87
    Report on reports: Continuing the commitment: agricultural development in the Sahel [Office of Technology Assessment report] L. Olsson. il *Environment* 29:25-7 Mr '87
Sahl, Mort
        about
    Not going gentle into that good night, caustic comic Mort Sahl gears up for a Broadway comeback. K. Gross. il pors *People Wkly* 28:134-6 O 12 '87
    Theater [Mort Sahl on Broadway] T. M. Disch. *Nation* 245:570 N 14 '87
    The theatre [Mort Sahl on Broadway!] M. Kramer. *New Yorker* 63:133-5 O 26 '87
Sahni, Julie
    Playing with fire. il *N Y Times Mag* p93-4 O 11 '87
Said, Edward W.
    Cairo recalled. il por *House Gard* 159:20+ Ap '87
    Interpreting Palestine. *Harpers* 274:19-22 Mr '87
        about
    Edward Said: an exile's exile [interview] M. Stevenson. il *Progressive* 51:30-4 F '87
Saigh, William
        about
    Tossing up a winner. G. Heiman. il por *Nations Bus* 75:76 D '87

Sail America Foundation
Rough sailing [M. Burnham] G. Buchalter. il por *Forbes* 140:452 Jl 13 '87

Sailboat racing
See also
Yacht racing
Repel all boarders! [world 18-foot skiff championship] D. Brantley. il *Sports Illus* 66:12 F 2 '87
The Tyniste twins of Estonia jibe as sailing's double threat. S. K. Reed. il pors *People Wkly* 27:108-9 Ap 6 '87

Sailboats
See also
Praus (Boats)
Yachts and yachting
The optimum boat. R. Florence. See issues of Motor Boating & Sailing beginning June 1986
Trends '88: sailboats. R. Marshall. il *Mot Boat Sail* 160:52-5 S '87
Purchasing
Second homes you can float. il *Money* 16:13-14 Ap '87
Testing
Ride the wind. C. Caswell. il *Pop Mech* 164:62-5 O '87

Sailing
See also
Cruising
Sailboat racing
Seamen
Voyages
Voyages around the world
Women in sailing
Yachts and yachting
Study and teaching
Come on aboard: the water's fine! D. Young. il *South Living* 22:22+ S '87
Sailing ships *See* Sailing vessels
Sailing vessels
See also
Praus (Boats)
You can sail on a tall ship [Pacific Coast cruises] il *Sunset* 178:48+ My '87
Photographs and photography
Puget Sound: the maritime world of Wilhelm Hester [turn-of-the-century photographer] R. A. Weinstein. il *Am Hist Illus* 21:20-35 Ja '87
Sailing yachts *See* Yachts and yachting
Sailors *See* Seamen
Sailors' songs *See* Sea songs
Sails
Choosing and using sails [excerpt from The optimum sailboat] R. Florence. *Mot Boat Sail* 159:161-2+ Ja '87
Controlling sails for maximum power [excerpt from The optimum sailboat] R. Florence. *Mot Boat Sail* 159:109+ F '87
Headsail helpers [roller furling systems] H. Halsted. il *Mot Boat Sail* 159:26 F '87
New mainsail systems. H. Halsted. il *Mot Boat Sail* 159:20 Ja '87

Saint, H. F. (Harry F.)
Memoirs of an invisible man [fiction] il *Money* 16:170-2+ Je '87
about
PW interviews. B. List. por *Publ Wkly* 231:53-4 Ap 24 '87
Saint, Harry F. *See* Saint, H. F. (Harry F.)
Saint (New York, N.Y.: Nightclub) *See* New York (N.Y.)— Restaurants, nightclubs, bars, etc.
Saint Andrews (N.B.)
Industries
Star-Kist's revival [reopening of plant] T. Fennell. il *Macleans* 100:34 S 28 '87
Saint-Aubin, Horace de *See* Balzac, Honoré de, 1799-1850
Saint Augustine (Fla.)
Churches (Buildings)
Flagler built this Florida church [Memorial Presbyterian Church] il *South Living* 22:50 N '87
Description
Confessions from St. Augustine. E. Von Jares. il *Saturday Evening Post* 259:98-9 Ja/F '87
Galleries and museums
See also
Lightner Museum
Historic houses, sites, etc.
History in houses: the Ximenez-Fatio House in Saint Augustine, Florida. W. Seale. il *Antiques* 131:426-31 F '87

Saint Barthelemy (Guadeloupe)
Description and travel
Gourmet holidays. D. Beal. il maps *Gourmet* 47:46-51+ Mr '87
Saint Bavon Cathedral (Ghent, Belgium)
A canary in an aquarium [Adoration of the mystic lamb altarpiece by J. and H. van Eyck] B. Grauman. il *Art News* 86:101-2 Ja '87
Saint Croix (Virgin Islands of the U.S.)
See also
Salt River Bay (Virgin Islands of the U.S.)
Saint Douglas Company
Against the odds [D. P. Lawrence; cover story] D. R. Squires. il pors *Black Enterp* 18:48-50+ O '87
Saint EOM *See* Martin, Eddie Owens, 1908-1986
Saint Eustatius (Netherlands Antilles)
Description and travel
The good life in St. Maarten and St. Eustatius. P. A. Jones. il *Black Enterp* 17:67-8 Ja '87
Gourmet holidays. D. Beal. il maps *Gourmet* 47:46-51+ Mr '87
Saint Francis National Forest (Ark.)
Crowley's Ridge, Arkansas. R. H. Mohlenbrock. il map *Nat Hist* 96:84-6 N '87
Saint Helena (Calif.)
Architecture
French flavor in Napa: Provence style for a California house and winery [home of Lloyd and Elaine Cunningham] J. Chatfield-Taylor. il *Archit Dig* 44:140-5+ Je '87
Saint James's Club (Paris, France)
The St. James's Club. C. Aillaud. il *Archit Dig* 44:164-7 D '87
Saint James's lilies *See* Jacobean lilies
Saint John's (Nfld.)
Newspapers
See also
Sunday express (Saint John's, Nfld.: Newspaper)
Saint Laurent, Yves
about
Gardens: Château Gabriel: Yves Saint Laurent and Pierre Bergé at Deauville [cover story] C. Aillaud. il *Archit Dig* 44:172-9+ My '87
Gardens: Majorelle remembered: Yves Saint Laurent and Pierre Bergé in Marrakesh. C. Aillaud. il pors *Archit Dig* 44:160-5 O '87
Le Maître: Yves Saint Laurent. C. Worthington. il *Harpers Bazaar* 120:188-91+ My '87
Saint Lawrence River
River of giant muskies. K. Schultz. il *Field Stream* 92:117-18 S '87
Saint Louis (Mo.)
Child welfare
Specialized foster care: families as treatment resources. S. S. Stepleton. il *Child Today* 16:27-31 Mr/Ap '87
City planning
See also
Riverport (Mo.)
Galleries and museums
See also
Museum of Medical Quackery (Saint Louis, Mo.)
Health facilities
Domestic terrorism: on the front line at an abortion clinic [work of clinic director J. Widdicombe in St. Louis] M. Kort. il por *Ms* 15:48-51+ My '87
Music
See also
Opera Theatre of Saint Louis
Protests, demonstrations, etc.
Domestic terrorism: on the front line at an abortion clinic [work of clinic director J. Widdicombe] M. Kort. il por *Ms* 15:48-51+ My '87
Sanitary affairs
Plastic pipe liner [Insitutube] D. Stover. il *Pop Sci* 230:49 F '87
Sports
No losers in St. Loo [hometown fans] F. Deford. il por *Sports Illus* 67:116 O 19 '87
Saint Lucia
See also
Pigeon Island National Historic Park (Saint Lucia)
Saint Martin
See also
Health resorts, watering places, etc.—Saint Martin
Description and travel
The good life in St. Maarten and St. Eustatius. P. A. Jones. il *Black Enterp* 17:67-8 Ja '87
Gourmet holidays. D. Beal. il map *Gourmet* 47:42-7+ Ja '87

Saint Martin—Description and travel—*cont.*
 Anecdotes, facetiae, satire, etc.
A day at the beach. G. Wolff. il *Esquire* 108:254-6+ D '87
Shapeful islands for a 'tied up' businessman. R. Wolkomir. il *Smithsonian* 17:192 Mr '87
Saint Matthias Islands (Papua New Guinea)
 Antiquities
Prehistoric Polynesian puzzle [origin of Lapita culture; cover story] B. Bower. il map *Sci News* 132:232-3 O 10 '87
Saint Michael's College
Helping dropouts drop in [Covenant House-St. Michael's College program] J. N. Baker. il *Newsweek* 110:63 Ag 3 '87
Saint Paul (Minn.)
 Bookstores
 See Booksellers and bookselling—Minnesota
 Music
 See also
 Minnesota Opera
Saint-Paul-de-Vence (France)
 Architecture
Architectural digest visits: James Baldwin. J. Baldwin. il pors *Archit Dig* 44:122-5 Ag '87
 Hotels, motels, etc.
Garden of earthly delights [La Colombe d'Or] S. Bolotin. il *Vogue* 177:544+ S '87
Saint Paul's College
Rebuilding lives: a college program for single parents and their kids. R. Brown. il *Ebony* 43:134+ D '87
Saint Petersburg (Fla.)
 Arts
 See also
 Bayfront Center (Saint Petersburg, Fla.)
 Health facilities
A 'New Start' with the Prevention Walking Club [program of the New Start Health Center] G. Maleskey. il *Prevention* 39:46+ Jl '87
Saint-Phalle, Niki de
 about
An artist throws the book at misinformation. il *Newsweek* 109:61 Je 15 '87
A garden of earthly delights. B. Rose. il pors *Vogue* 177:266-73+ D '87
House of cards: Niki de Saint Phalle's Tuscan fantasy [cover story] Michael, Prince of Greece. il por *Archit Dig* 44:124-31 S '87
Saint-Pierre (Martinique)
 Harbor
Saint-Pierre Bay: Mont Pelée's underwater graveyard [reminders of 1902 eruption] J. C. Fine. il *Sea Front* 33:288-95 Jl/Ag '87
Saint-Pol, Louis, of Luxembourg, comte de, 1418-1475
 about
A patriot for whom? The treason of Saint-Pol, 1474-75. S. H. Cuttler. bibl f il *Hist Today* 37:43-8 Ja '87
Saint-Saëns, Camille, 1835-1921
 about
Samson et Dalila [opera] Reviews
 N Y il 20:97-8 Ag 13 '87. P. G. Davis
 Opera News il 51:26-8, 30 Ap 11 '87
 Opera News il 51:34-7+ Ap 11 '87. J. Kestner
Saint-Saëns, Charles Camille *See* Saint-Saëns, Camille, 1835-1921
Saint Silicon
 about
Chip thrills: the joke of Silicon Valley. J. Stone. il *Discover* 8:54-6+ D '87
Saint Thomas (Ont.)
 Industries
One city's daily debate [impact of proposed free trade accord with the U.S.] S. Aikenhead. il *Macleans* 100:18-19 Ap 6 '87
Saint Thomas (Virgin Islands of the U.S.)
 See also
 Music festivals—Saint Thomas (Virgin Islands of the U.S.)
 Description and travel
Three for the road [traveling with a baby] S. Bolotin. il *Vogue* 177:138+ Je '87
Saint Valentine's Day *See* Valentine's Day
Saints
 See also
 All Saints' Day
 Augustine, Saint, Bishop of Hippo
 Beatification
 Cuthbert, Saint, 653?-687
 Peter, the Apostle, Saint
 Thérèse, de Lisieux, Saint, 1873-1897

Somebody up there likes me: what U.S. Catholic readers believe about the saints [cover story] J. Breig. il *U S Cathol* 52:6-15 N '87
 Art
 See also
 Santos (Art)
Sajak, Pat
 about
Pat Sajak: Vanna White and me. V. Scott. il pors *Good Housekeep* 205:34+ N '87
Saji, Makoto, and Reis, Donald J.
Delayed transneuronal death of substantia nigra neurons prevented by γ-aminobutyric acid agonist. bibl f il *Science* 235:66-9 Ja 2 '87
Sakamoto, Edward, 1940-
 about
The life of the land [drama] Reviews
 New Yorker 63:72 Je 15 '87. E. Oliver
Sake
 See also
 Morita & Company
Sakhai, Nedjatollah
 about
Frenchy and the Persians. C. Trillin. *New Yorker* 63:44+ Je 29 '87
Sakharov, Andreï Dmitrievich, 1921-
Of arms and reforms [adaptations of three addresses] il por *Time* 129:40-3 Mr 16 '87
On accepting a prize. il *N Y Rev Books* 34:49 Ag 13 '87
 about
Glasnost: 'There's no turning back' [interview] M. B. Zuckerman. il pors *U S News World Rep* 102:31 Ap 20 '87
Gorbachev's 'courageous' reform plan [interview] por *U S News World Rep* 102:13 F 16 '87
A hard bargain [special section] il pors *Newsweek* 109:12-23 Ja 5 '87
A meeting with Sakharov [interview] H. Feshbach. il pors *Phys Today* 40:7+ Ap '87
Moscow meeting—the *glasnost* menagerie. S. Frankel. il pors *Bull At Sci* 43:8-12 My '87
Picking up where he left off. J. Smolowe. il pors *Time* 129:53-4 Ja 5 '87
Raising the stakes in Soviet reform [with interview] S. Powell. il por *U S News World Rep* 102:30-1 Ja 12 '87
Sakharov and Gorky. M. A. Evangelista. *Bull At Sci* 43:21 Ap '87
Sakharov sends message to Vienna. C. Holden. *Science* 235:739 F 13 '87
Sakharov: the folly of SDI [interview] A. McGowan. *Harpers* 275:20 O '87
Sakharov's list. B. Keller. il por *N Y Times Mag* p34-7+ F 15 '87
Time for Sakharov's global dialogue. R. E. Marshak. il pors *Bull At Sci* 43:7-8 O '87
Sakharov, Elena Bonner *See* Bonner, Elena
Saks, Gene
 about
Brighton Beach memoirs [film] Reviews
 Glamour il 85:131 Ja '87. J. G. Boyum
 Macleans il 100:20 Ja 5 '87. L. O'Toole
 N Y il 20:77-8 Ja 19 '87. D. Denby
 New Repub 196:26-7 Ja 26 '87. S. Kauffmann
 New Yorker 62:74-5 Ja 26 '87. P. Kael
Saks, Michael J.
Accuracy v. advocacy. il *Technol Rev* 90:42-9 Ag/S '87
Salad bars
 See also
 Lettuce Leaf Restaurants
The salad-bar chef. L. Goldrich. il *Work Woman* 12:94+ F '87
 Sanitation
Salad bars: as good as they look? B. Hayton. il *Curr Health 2* 14:14-16 S '87
Salad burnet *See* Burnet
Salad dressings
Creamy salad dressings. il *Gourmet* 48:196 Je '87
Simple salad dressings. A. Bailey. il *Parents* 62:140+ Je '87
Salad greens *See* Greens, Edible
Saladin, Sultan of Egypt and Syria, 1137-1193
 about
Saladin's triumph over the crusader states: the Battle of Hattin, 1187 [cover story] N. Housley. bibl il map *Hist Today* 37:17-23 Jl '87
Saladino, John
 about
Classical collage. S. Stephens. il *House Gard* 159:138-45+ D '87

Saladino, John—about—*cont.*
Cultivating romance. E. Greene. il *House Gard* 159:166-73+ My '87
Salads
Appetizers and salads for two. il *South Living* 22:214-15 Ap '87
Bird in hand [Alfred Portale's roast-quail salad] B. Costikyan. il *N Y* 20:53 Mr 16 '87
Carbing up at the salad bowl. R. Schrambling. il *Work Woman* 12:140+ Je '87
Celebrate fall with a salad. il *South Living* 22:170 O '87
Colorful salad with black beans. il *Sunset* 178:154 Mr '87
Cool, crisp salads to beat the heat. B. E. Templeton. il *South Living* 22:144-5+ Jl '87
Cool, light salad: potatoes, mussels. il *Sunset* 178:188 My '87
Designer greens. C. Idone. il *Harpers Bazaar* 120:48+ Ag '87
Fresh asparagus in cool salads. il *Sunset* 179:176 D '87
Fresh summer salads. il *Better Homes Gard* 65:49-50 Jl '87
The freshest, prettiest salads. M. C. Agnew. il *South Living* 22:198-200 Ap '87
Gastronomie sans argent [entrée salads] il *Gourmet* 48:74-5+ Je '87
The golden age of salads. il *Sunset* 178:174-5+ Je '87
Great salads. J. Nash. il *Essence* 18:90 Je '87
How fat is your salad? B. Hayton. il *Curr Health 2* 14:16 S '87
If you crossed celery with licorice . . . fennel. il *Sunset* 178:192 Ap '87
It may remind you of grandma's salad [pea and roasted pecan slaw] il *Sunset* 178:106 Ja '87
Low-fat, high-style salads. il *Glamour* 85:186-8 Jl '87
Mexican vegetables and salads. E. L. Ortiz. il *Gourmet* 47:80-1+ My '87
Perfect potato salad [microwave recipe] J. B. Hurley. il *Prevention* 39:80 Mr '87
The perfect salad. J.-A. Heslin and A. B. Natow. il *Redbook* 169:79-82 Je '87
Potato salad. L. Colwin. il *Gourmet* 47:222+ O '87
Put a salad on the menu. il *South Living* 22:216-17 My '87
Quick teamwork: cheese and salad. il *Sunset* 179:186+ O '87
Recipe of the week [garden chicken salad] il *Jet* 72:37 Jl 13 '87
Recipe of the week [party egg salad appetizer] il *Jet* 73:38 D 21 '87
Salad days. B. Kafka. il *Vogue* 177:208 My '87
Salad days [C. Idone's salads] L. Wells. il *N Y Times Mag* p65-6 Je 28 '87
Salad surprises . . . corn and potatoes. il *Sunset* 179:126-7 Ag '87
A salad that looks like a rose. il *Sunset* 179:165 O '87
Salads! il *Good Housekeep* 205:128-38+ Jl '87
Salads from your pantry. il *South Living* 22:104 Ja '87
Salads that fit the season. il *South Living* 22:142 D '87
Spanish salads. il *Sunset* 179:182-3 S '87
Spinach, slaw, or mixed: when your holiday need is a crisp, green salad. il *Sunset* 179:169 N '87
Sprightly spring salads. J. R. Nyenhuis. il *Saturday Evening Post* 259:17-19 Ap '87
Squeeze salads. il *Sunset* 178:140+ F '87
Squid boat salad. il *Sunset* 179:200 N '87
Summer salmon salads, simple and quick. il *Sunset* 179:131 Jl '87
Supper salads. B. Greenwood. il *Better Homes Gard* 65:138-9 My '87
Sweet and sour spinach salad. il *Sunset* 178:218 Ap '87
Tangy, crunchy holiday salads [fruit salads] il *South Living* 22:84-5 N '87
Time for tuna. il *Saturday Evening Post* 259:28 My/Je '87
What a salad! il *South Living* 22:191 O '87
Winter's-end salad . . . shredded. il *Sunset* 178:142 Mr '87
Salamanders
Multidimensional analysis of an evolving lineage. D. B. Wake and A. Larson. bibl f il *Science* 238:42-8 O 2 '87
Salami
Salam-ease [venison salami] R. P. Stuart. il *Outdoor Life* 179:58-9+ Ja '87

Advertising
83 plus 17 [new Hebrew National advertising theme] *New Yorker* 63:35 O 19 '87
Salaries *See* Wages and salaries
Salas, Rafael M.
Cities. il map *Courier* 40:10-17 Ja '87
Urban population growth: blessing or burden? il *USA Today (Periodical)* 116:74-7 Jl '87
Sale, Kirkpatrick
Ecofeminism—a new perspective. il *Nation* 245:302-5 S 26 '87
Fictive techniques for nonfiction writing. *Writer* 100:16-18 Ap '87
Ill at ease in the fourth world. il *Nation* 245:592-4 N 21 '87
What is ecofeminism? [discussion of September 26, 1987 article, Ecofeminism—a new perspective] *Nation* 245:702+ D 12 '87
Where not to find new ideas. *Nation* 244:320-3 Mr 14 '87
Salenger, Meredith
about
Ones to watch. il pors *Teen* 31:60 O '87
Salerno-Sonnenberg, Nadja
about
Nadja Salerno-Sonnenberg [cover story] S. McHenry. il pors *Ms* 16:40 O '87
The showbiz fiddler. L. Shapiro. il por *Newsweek* 110:61 Jl 20 '87
The violinist from left field. J. McCollister. il pors *Saturday Evening Post* 259:30+ D '87
What becomes a virtuoso most? D. Denby. il por *Vogue* 177:184 S '87
Sales
See also
Auctions
Door-to-door selling
Line up early for the plant sale May 2 in Golden Gate Park. il *Sunset* 178:262 My '87
Sales & bargains. L. Fleischer. See issues of New York
Sales catalogs *See* Catalogs, Commercial
Sales personnel
See also
Automobile sales personnel
Booksellers and bookselling
Manufacturers' agents
Marketing
Telephone selling
America's best salesmen. M. J. Williams. il *Fortune* 116:122-4+ O 26 '87
Brainy is beautiful [successful Avon salespersons] il *McCalls* 114:118-21 Ja '87
Getting top performance from your sales force. H. Waldrop. il *Work Woman* 12:56 D '87
If only Willy Loman had used a laptop. J. B. Levine. il *Bus Week* p137 O 12 '87
Sexist sales [men receive more prompt service in department stores; study by Bette Ann Stead and George M. Zinkhan] V. Bozzi. *Psychol Today* 21:11 Jl '87
Tools of the sales trade. H. Fersko-Weiss. il *Pers Comput* 11:78-81+ Ag '87
Salaries, commissions, pensions, etc.
Women's history and EEOC v. Sears [sex discrimination case; special section] *Society* 24:4-16 S/O '87
Training
Listeners speak out [instructional tapes] J. Zinsser. *Publ Wkly* 232:57-60 O 2 '87
Sales policies
See also
Cash business
Return of goods
Sales promotion
See also
Coupons
Display of merchandise
Premiums
Prize contests
Samples (Merchandising)
Sales tax
See also
Value added tax
Mail order taxes? J. W. Merline. *Consum Res Mag* 70:38 D '87
Taxing news from the states for '88. J. Bodnar. *Changing Times* 41:8 D '87
Canada
Sales tax: the unknown factor. A. Shortell. il *M* 100:40-1 Je 29 '87

Sales tax—*cont.*

Florida

Advertisers fume, lawyers sue over new Florida tax. K. R. Sheets. *U S News World Rep* 102:45 My 11 '87

As Florida booms, its problems explode [proposal to tax almost all services] G. DeGeorge. il *Bus Week* p88-9 Ap 20 '87

Down on the levy [ad tax dampens Orlando TV market boom] M. Clary. il *Channels* 7:53-5 N '87

Florida's rookie governor is stuck in a slump [B. Martinez] G. DeGeorge. il por *Bus Week* p174+ O 12 '87

Florida's service tax sparks a revolt. G. DeGeorge. il *Bus Week* p49 Je 22 '87

Grappling with growth [tax on service industries] il *Time* 129:33 Ap 27 '87

Taxing patience on Madison Ave. [advertisers' opposition to sales tax on service industries] R. Hornik. il *Time* 129:52 Je 1 '87

Why Florida faces tax rebellion. A. L. Taylor, III. il *Fortune* 116:82-3 Jl 6 '87

Japan

Japan. *Bus Week* p53 Mr 2 '87

Tax reform: the stakes don't get much higher. B. Buell. il *Bus Week* p51+ Ap 6 '87

A whiff of blood in the water. B. Hillenbrand. il *Time* 129:35 Mr 23 '87

Sales training *See* Sales personnel—Training

Salesians

Missions

The gospel and the gold rush [Tucano Indians caught between Salesian missionaries and gold mining interests in Brazil] R. N. Ostling. il *Time* 129:64 Je 1 '87

Salesmanship *See* Selling

Salesmen *See* Sales personnel

Saleswomen *See* Sales personnel

Saletan, William

Sons of guns. *New Repub* 196:11-13 Mr 2 '87

Salgado, Sebastiao

An epic struggle for gold [photographs] il *N Y Times Mag* p34-41 Je 7 '87

about

The other Americas [photographs] C. Healy. il *Américas* 39:2-7 Mr/Ap '87

Salibello, Anna

about

Tiles with style: Terra Designs, Inc. W. Konrad. il pors *Work Woman* 12:137-8 N '87

Salicylic acid

Salicylic acid: a natural inducer of heat production in Arum lilies. I. Raskin and others. bibl f il *Science* 237:1601-2 S 25 '87

Salieri, Antonio, 1750-1825

about

Salieri at Rider. K. Richardson. il *High Fidel* 37:56 Mr '87

Salina (Italy)

See also

Ecology—Salina (Italy)

Salinas (Calif.)

Historic houses, sites, etc.

Steinbeck country. B. Golightly. il *Horizon* 30:62 Jl/Ag '87

Salinas de Gortari, Carlos

about

Continuity for Mexico. A. Landaburu. por *World Press Rev* 34:25 D '87

For De la Madrid, it's almost like being reelected. S. Baker. il por *Bus Week* p78-9 O 19 '87

Mexico chooses a new president. por *Newsweek* 110:52 O 12 '87

A professor's pupil makes good. J. Smolowe. por *Time* 130:37 O 19 '87

Saline water

See also

Sea water

Salinger, J. D. (Jerome David), 1919-

about

AAP and seven authors ask to join Random House in Salinger appeal. H. Fields. *Publ Wkly* 232:11 S 25 '87

AAP files amicus brief for Random House in appeal of Salinger decision. M. Yen. *Publ Wkly* 231:90 F 27 '87

Holden Caulfield goes to law school. A. Delbanco. *New Repub* 196:27-8+ Mr 9 '87

Random House seeks review of Salinger decision. M. Yen. *Publ Wkly* 231:24 F 13 '87

Return to sender. por *Time* 129:62 F 9 '87

Salinger and 'The bell jar': what do they mean to publishers? C. E. Rinzler. il *Publ Wkly* 231:20-2 Ap 24 '87

The Salinger file. P. Hoban. il pors *N Y* 20:36-42 Je 15 '87

Salinger then and now. T. Teachout. *Commentary* 84:61-4 S '87

Whose mail is it, anyway? A. Press. il pors *Newsweek* 109:58 F 9 '87

Whose words are they, anyway? D. Margolick. il *N Y Times Book Rev* 92:1+ N 1 '87

Salinger, Jerome David *See* Salinger, J. D. (Jerome David), 1919-

Salisbury, Wright

Mastering polished audiovisual presentations. il *Archit Rec* 175:29+ Ap '87

Salish Indians

The Salish-Kootenai comeback [environmental management of reservation lands] J. Bruggers. il *Sierra* 72:22-3+ Jl/Ag '87

Saliva

See also

Sputum

How much do you smoke? Spit it out [testing saliva levels of cotinine; research by David B. Abrams] *Sci News* 132:25 Jl 11 '87

Salivary glands

Diseases

See also

Sjögren's syndrome

Salizzoni, Frank L., 1938-

about

TW's numbers man throws caution to the winds. L. Baum. il por *Bus Week* p67-9 Ag 3 '87

Salk, Jonas, 1914-

about

The continuing search for a cure. il por *Fortune* 116:126 D 21 '87

A tough old soldier joins the fight against AIDS. S. Siwolop and R. Rhein, Jr. il por *Bus Week* p69-70 Jl 27 '87

Salk, Lee, 1926-

The child psychologist. See issues of McCall's beginning March 1986

Christmas under the new family tree. *Harpers Bazaar* 121:126+ D '87

about

Autumn on Sandbar Island: Dr. Lee Salk's retreat in Maine. C. T. Buckley. il por *Archit Dig* 44:134-9 O '87

Salkoff, Lawrence, and others

Genomic organization and deduced amino acid sequence of a putative sodium channel gene in Drosophila. bibl f il *Science* 237:744-9 Ag 14 '87

Salle, David

about

Art. A. C. Danto. *Nation* 244:302-4 Mr 7 '87

Artsmart. il *Harpers Bazaar* 120:164+ Ja '87

The big tease. K. Larson. il *N Y* 20:58-9 F 9 '87

Dipping into a grab bag of pop culture. C. McGuigan. il *Newsweek* 109:77 Mr 2 '87

The four brushmen of the apocalypse. L. Hirschberg. il pors *Esquire* 107:76-84+ Mr '87

How David Salle mixes high art and trash. P. Taylor. il por *N Y Times Mag* p26-9+ Ja 11 '87

Karole Armitage & David Salle. S. Allison. il pors *Life* 10:104-6+ N '87

Random bits from the image haze. R. Hughes. il *Time* 129:67-8 F 9 '87

The School of Bloomingdale's. M. Stevens. *New Repub* 196:25-8 My 18 '87

Secret codes on canvas. G. James. il *Macleans* 100:46 Ag 3 '87

Teasing images, hip estrangement. N. Grimes. il *Art News* 86:173 Ap '87

Anecdotes, facetiae, satire, etc.

Pat Robertson's catalog essay for a new exhibition of paintings by David Salle. V. Geng. *N Y Rev Books* 34:34 N 19 '87

Sallie Mae *See* Student Loan Marketing Association

Salloum, Habeeb

The uncommon artichoke. il *Saturday Evening Post* 259:20+ Ap '87

Salmansohn, Pete

Audubon ecology camp. il *Ctry J* 14:60-2 Je '87

Salmon, M. H.

about

The wind-splitters. L. Mueller. il por *Outdoor Life* 180:22+ D '87

Salmon
    See also
      Cooking—Fish
Along the Mattole, helping hands heal the watershed.
    il *Sierra* 72:62-3 Mr/Ap '87
Return of the leaper [Atlantic salmon] M. Rosenthal.
    il *Ctry J* 14:30-5 Jl '87
Salmon make a comeback, but what's ahead? il *Sunset*
    179:220 S '87
Throwing fish off the scent [acid water and salmon's
    sense of smell] S. Begley. il *Natl Wildl* 25:12 F/Mr
    '87
Salmon culture *See* Fish culture
Salmon fisheries (Commercial) *See* Fisheries
Salmon fishing
Death on the Miramichi [heat wave endangers salmon]
    K. Harley. il *Macleans* 100:41 Ag 3 '87
Fishing with the right stuff [fishing with C. Yeager]
    J. Zumbo. il por *Outdoor Life* 179:64-5+ Ap '87
Salmon: by land, sea, or air [British Columbia] J. Bashline.
    il *Field Stream* 91:46+ Ap '87
A salmon delights in gaudy colors [cover story; with
    editorial comment by Les Line] T. Rosenbauer. il
    Audubon 89:4, 64-73 S '87
Tradition unbound. J. Bashline. il *Field Stream* 91:68+
    Ja '87
The ultimate estuary [Alaska's Karluk Lagoon] B. Stearns.
    il *Field Stream* 92:100+ Jl '87
White nights, Red faces [U.S. anglers in Soviet Union]
    C. Gammon. il *Sports Illus* 67:76-8+ O 26 '87
        Anecdotes, facetiae, satire, etc.
Exit laughing [making cigarette TV commercials at a
    salmon fishing camp] E. Zern. il *Field Stream* 92:142
    Jl '87
Mr. Cool meets the king [father and teenage son go
    king salmon fishing] A. Liere. il *Field Stream* 92:47-8+
    My '87
Salmon poaching *See* Poaching
Salmon River (Idaho)
Idaho batholith. B. G. Norton. il map *Wilderness* 50:30-1
    Spr '87
White-water Idaho: riding the River of No Return. S.
    Robertson. il *Travel Holiday* 167:56-61 My '87
Salmon salads *See* Salads
Salmonella
Avoiding sick chicks [Chik Chek test for salmonella
    bacteria] M. Kemp. il *Discover* 8:20 O '87
Salmonellosis
Dangers of "miracle" drugs [antibiotic feed supplements]
    Futurist 21:51-2 Mr/Ap '87
Foul chickens. B. Costikyan. il *N Y* 20:44-8 Ag 10
    '87
It must have been something you ate. P. W. Moser.
    il *Discover* 8:94-100 F '87
Maybe it was something you ate (I). P. W. Moser.
    il *Saturday Evening Post* 259:62-3+ Ap '87
Maybe it was something you ate (II). P. W. Moser.
    il *Saturday Evening Post* 259:46-9 My/Je '87
Mourners felled by pasta poisoning. il *FDA Consum*
    21:41-2 Mr '87
New food poisoning alert. H. Manley. il *Good Housekeep*
    205:201 Jl '87
Risky shell game: pet turtles can infect kids. C. Lecos.
    il *FDA Consum* 21:19-21 D '87/Ja '88
Serving up salmonella for dinner. J. Carey. il *U S News*
    World Rep 102:60-1 Mr 9 '87
Watch out for food poisoning! P. W. Moser. il *Read*
    Dig 131:113-17 S '87
Salomon, Arthur K.
    about
Incident at Exit 20. M. Stone. il pors *N Y* 20:50-4+
    O 5 '87
Salomon Inc.
Big investors on Wall Street [sparring over Salomon
    Inc.] pors *Fortune* 116:8 O 26 '87
Can Salomon grow by shrinking? [shutting down
    municipal bond unit and laying off staff] A. Bianco.
    il *Bus Week* p30-1 O 26 '87
Falling off a limb at Harcourt [Salomon and Mutual
    Shares lost on convertible bond gamble] D. Zigas.
    por *Bus Week* p32 Jl 6 '87
No higher yields exist [survey on coins and stamps]
    Changing Times 41:126 N '87
Salomon and Revlon: what really happened. A. Bianco.
    il pors *Bus Week* p156+ O 12 '87
Salomon Brothers parts with a son [resignation of L.
    S. Ranieri] A. Bianco. *Bus Week* p60 Jl 27 '87
What color is your mail? [Salomon Brothers pays green-
    mail to Minerals & Resources Corp.] A. Sloan. il
    Forbes 140:36-7 O 19 '87

What's behind the profit squeeze at Salomon. A. Bianco.
    il por *Bus Week* p72-3 Ap 20 '87
A white knight saves Salomon [W. Buffett outflanks
    R. Perelman] B. Powell. il por *Newsweek* 110:66 O
    12 '87
White-knight time on Wall Street [W. Buffett saves
    Salomon Brothers from corporate raider R. Perelman]
    J. Egan. il pors *U S News World Rep* 103:60 O
    12 '87
Salon du Livre (Book fair) *See* Book fairs
Salón Internacional del Libro (Book fair) *See* Book fairs
Salone Internazionale del Mobile *See* Furniture, Italian—Ex-
    hibitions
Salonen, Esa-Pekka
    about
Applause! Applause! P. G. Davis. il por *N Y* 20:53-4
    Ja 12 '87
Musical events. A. Porter. *New Yorker* 62:99 Ja 12
    '87
Salons, Beauty *See* Beauty shops
Saloons *See* Bars and barrooms
Salpeter, Eliahu
Arms and the budget in Israel. il *New Leader* 70:5-6
    F 9-23 '87
Face-off in Israel [cover story] il *New Leader* 70:5-6
    Ap 20 '87
Israel without television. il *New Leader* 70:7-8 N 30
    '87
Triple trouble in Israel [with editorial comment] il *New*
    Leader 70:2, 5-7 Mr 23 '87
Salpingitis *See* Pelvic inflammatory disease
Salps
The see-through salp. M. D. Gottfried. il *Sea Front*
    33:427 N/D '87
Salsa music *See* Music, Latin American
Salt, Sir Titus, 1803-1876
    about
Titus Salt: enlightened entrepreneur. I. C. Bradley. bibl
    il por *Hist Today* 37:30-6 My '87
Salt
    See also
      Low sodium cooking
Salt of the earth. R. L. Bates. il *Earth Sci* 40:23-4
    Wint '87
A taste for salt. J. Lowenstein. il *Oceans* 20:72 Ja/F
    '87
        Physiological effects
    See Salt in the body
Salt deposits
    See also
      Salt domes
Salt domes
Salt tectonics. C. J. Talbot and M. P. A. Jackson. bibl
    (p116) il *Sci Am* 257:70-9 Ag '87
Salt in the body
    See also
      Osmoregulation
Direct demonstration of macula densa-mediated renin
    secretion. O. Skøtt and J. P. Briggs. bibl f il *Science*
    237:1618-20 S 25 '87
Salt-sensitive genes [research by Judy Z. Miller] V.
    DeBenedette. *Health* 19:23 My '87
Shaking the salt habit. C. Schaeffer. il *Changing Times*
    41:20 S '87
The sodium-hypertension connection [cover story] J.
    Schein. il *Consum Res Mag* 70:11-14+ O '87
Sweet news about sugar and salt. S. Schneider. il *Women's*
    Sports Fitness 9:19 Jl '87
Your diet: salt debates. J. S. Stern. *Vogue* 177:480 O
    '87
Salt Lake (Utah) *See* Great Salt Lake (Utah)
Salt Lake City (Utah)
        Criminal justice, Administration of
A Latter-Day forger [Mormon M. Hofmann pleads guilty
    to murder] A. Wilentz. il por *Time* 129:32 F 2 '87
        Religious institutions and affairs
    See also
      Mormons and Mormonism
        Social life and customs
Salt Lake City makeovers. il *Glamour* 85:296-9 O '87
Salt licks
Licking big game [finding big game at mineral licks]
    G. P. Michiel. il *Outdoor Life* 179:98-9+ My '87
Salt marsh ecology *See* Marsh ecology
Salt River Bay (Virgin Islands of the U.S.)
Caribbean landing point. R. H. Wauer. il *Natl Parks*
    61:20-1 Ja/F '87
St. Croix's Salt River Bay targeted for development.
    Natl Parks 61:40 Ja/F '87

SALT talks *See* Strategic Arms Limitation Talks
Salt water *See* Sea water
Salt water fishing
> *See also*
> Billfish fishing
> Bonefish fishing
> Casting (Fishing)
> Cod fishing
> Tarpon fishing

Global hotspots. P. B. Wright. il map *Mot Boat Sail* 160:50-1+ O '87
Hooked [Motor boating & sailing columnist P. B. Wright] P. A. Janssen. por *Mot Boat Sail* 160:11 O '87
Saltwater fishing. B. Stearns. See occasional issues of Field & Stream
To catch a fish [fishing from a cruiser] S. Stapleton. il *Mot Boat Sail* 159:118 Ap '87
The Wright stuff. P. B. Wright. See issues of Motor Boating & Sailing beginning October 1987
Saltaire (England)
> **History**

Titus Salt: enlightened entrepreneur. I. C. Bradley. bibl il por *Hist Today* 37:30-6 My '87
Salter, Mary Jo
Living with fallout. il *Atlantic* 259:30-2+ Ja '87
Salter, Stephanie
Softball dreamin'. il *Women's Sports Fitness* 9:28-9 Jl '87
Salts
> *See also*
> Schiff base salts

An answer to the sphinx's problem [salt damage] R. Monastersky. *Sci News* 132:301 N 7 '87
Imitating iron's magnetism [cover story] I. Peterson. il *Sci News* 131:252-3 Ap 18 '87
Salts, Marine *See* Sea water
Saltwort
Saltwort meadows needed by fishes [Florida salt marshes; research by Grant Gilmore and others] il *Sea Front* 33:461-3 N/D '87
Saltz, Hilde
Policy based on morality. il *World Press Rev* 34:14 S '87
Saltzman, Joe
The lively arts. See alternate issues of USA Today (Periodical)
Salute to Greatness Awards
'Salute to Greatness' program honors Black enterprise publisher [E. G. Graves] il pors *Jet* 71:4-6+ F 9 '87
Salvador *See* El Salvador
Salvador (Brazil)
> **Religious institutions and affairs**

Bahia's Candomblé. J. B. Harris. *Black Enterp* 18:82+ Ag '87
Salvadoran refugees *See* Refugees, Salvadoran
Salvadorans
> **United States**
> *Crimes against*

The death squads hit home: which side is the FBI on? [attacks against Salvadoran exiles in the U.S.] V. Bielski and others. il *Progressive* 51:15-19 O '87
Death squads invade California [threats to Salvadorans living in Los Angeles] C. Garcia. il *Time* 130:20-1 Ag 3 '87
Salvage (Ships)
> *See also*
> Archeology, Submarine
> Columbus-America Discovery Group
> Institut Français de Recherche pour l'Exploitation de la Mer
> Republic (Steamship)
> Ship junkyards
> Sub-Ocean Salvors International
> Treasure Salvors Inc.
> Treasure trove
Salvage (Waste)
> *See also*
> Airplane junkyards
> Automobile junkyards
> Great American Salvage Company
> Motorcycle junkyards
> Recycling (Waste, etc.)
Salvation
> *See also*
> Annihilationism (Theology)
> Universalism (Theology)

Cosmic groanings. R. Goetz. il *Christ Century* 104:1083-7 D 2 '87
Gateway to life. M. K. Hellwig. *America* 156:inside back cover My 2 '87

Gift of new life. M. K. Hellwig. *America* 156:inside back cover Je 20-27 '87
Joint Commission agrees on meaning of salvation [Anglican and Roman Catholic churches] il *Christ Today* 31:61 Mr 20 '87
This is God's Chosen One. M. K. Hellwig. *America* 156:inside back cover Ja 3-10 '87
Salvation Army
And joy [concert celebrating start of annual Christmas drive] *New Yorker* 63:38-9 D 7 '87
Salvator Rosa [opera] *See* Gomes, Antonio Carlos, 1836-1896
Salvatore Ferragamo SpA
Winning by a foot [W. Ferragamo] N. J. Perry. il por *Fortune* 116:137 O 26 '87
Salvia
Exuberantly colorful year after year . . . the perennial sages. il *Sunset* 178:198-9 Mr '87
Salvigsen, Stanley D.
> *about*

Fancying the Rust Belt and the oil patch [interview] A. E. Serwer. il por *Fortune* 116:112 Jl 20 '87
Knowing when to say 'when' made his fund no. 1. G. Weiss. il por *Bus Week* p160 D 28 '87-Ja 4 '88
Salwi, Dilip M.
Kavalur's stellar hermitage. il *Sky Telesc* 73:375-6 Ap '87
Salzberg, Charles
Postwritum depression, false stagnancy and other ills caused by writing books. il *N Y Times Book Rev* 92:3 Mr 8 '87
Sweetwater [excerpt from From set shot to slam dunk] il por *Sport Mag* 78:63 Jl '87
Salzburg Festival *See* Music festivals—Austria
Salzman, Jason
The genesis of New Zealand's ban. il *Bull At Sci* 43:45-6+ Jl/Ag '87
Kiwis just say 'no'. *Sierra* 72:32+ My/Je '87
Nuclear war as an environmental issue. *Environment* 29:4-5+ Ja/F '87
Salzman, Mark
One question. *Harpers* 275:24+ N '87
Sam and Dave (Musical group)
New 'Sam and Dave' duo can't use legendary name. *Jet* 72:62 Ag 31 '87
Samalin, Nancy
How to stop fighting with your kids [excerpt from Loving your child is not enough]; ed. by Martha Moraghan Jablow. il *Good Housekeep* 205:98+ S '87
"You make me so mad!"; ed. by Martha Moraghan Jablow. il *Parents* 62:53-7 Ja '87
Samalin, Nancy, and Jablow, Martha Moraghan
How to help when your child feels bad. il *Parents* 62:73-8 F '87
Samana Cay (Bahamas)
Retracing the path of Christopher Columbus. il *Sea Front* 33:307 Jl/Ag '87
La Samanna (Saint Martin: Resort) *See* Health resorts, watering places, etc.—Saint Martin
Samantha (Fictional character)
"The Samantha stories". D. E. Matter and R. M. Matter. il *Antiques Collect Hobbies* 91:48-50 Ja '87
Samaras, Lucas, 1936-
> *about*

Lucas Samaras at Pace. E. Heartney. il *Art Am* 75:182 My '87
Sambuca (Liqueur) *See* Liqueurs
Samcor (Firm)
Why black workers may say 'thanks, but no thanks' to Ford [partial worker ownership of Samcor] S. Mufson. il *Bus Week* p47 Jl 6 '87
Samis (European people) *See* Lapps
Sammy and Rosie get laid [film] *See* Motion picture reviews—Single works
Sammy Davis Jr. National Liver Institute
Sammy brings Broadway to Newark for fundraiser [S. Davis Jr.] il pors *Jet* 72:53 Je 8 '87
Samoan Islands
> *See also*
> Ethnology—Samoan Islands
Samoilov, Yuri
Some thought on bioethics [interview with L. Badalyan] *World Press Rev* 34:52 Ag '87
Samon, Katherine
Handling the overachiever. il *Work Woman* 12:24+ Mr '87
A thoroughly modern mistress. il *Mademoiselle* 93:246-7+ Ag '87

Sample, Billy
Some things I won't miss: a retired player loved baseball, but not every part of it. por *Sports Illus* 67:108 Jl 6 '87

Sample, Johnny
about
Former NFL star Sample has a passion for tennis. *Jet* 71:49 Ja 26 '87

Samplers
Antiques: samplers. J. A. Cuadrado. il *Archit Dig* 44:152-7 Je '87

Samples, John
Ferdinand Toennies: dark times for a liberal intellectual. bibl *Society* 24:65-8 S/O '87

Samples (Merchandising)
Freebies and cheapies. *Teen* 31:14+ Ja '87
'Teen classifieds. *Teen* 31:38+ Jl '87

Sampling (Statistics)
Another approach to data compression [Basic programs explore the Nyquist sampling theorem] R. J. Sciamanda. il *Byte* 12:137-8+ F '87
Statistical traps lurk in the fossil record [views of Carl Koch] R. Lewin. il *Science* 236:521-2 My 1 '87

Sampson, Anthony
Both ends against the middle. il *Newsweek* 109:30 Je 22 '87

Sampson, Hannah
Stranger in my house. il *Read Dig* 130:9-10 Ap '87

Sampson, Ralph
about
Ralph Sampson, bride miss wedding—already married. il pors *Jet* 72:57 Ag 3 '87
Ralph Sampson, wife may be headed for divorce. il pors *Jet* 72:12 S 14 '87
Sampson missed All-star game, may sit out season. *Jet* 71:47 F 23 '87
Sampson signs contract to stay with Rockets. por *Jet* 73:52 N 9 '87
Sampson soon to settle lifelong Rockets' pact. por *Jet* 72:50 Je 1 '87
Sampson, wife reconcile, divorce suit shelved. *Jet* 73:51 N 16 '87

Sams, Carl R.
about
The deerstalker. L. Line. il por *Audubon* 89:4 My '87
Sams (Howard W.) & Co. *See* Howard W. Sams & Co.
Samson et Dalila [opera] *See* Saint-Saëns, Camille, 1835-1921

Samsung Group
Tough comeback artist [Lee Byung-Chull] L. Kraar. por *Fortune* 116:53 Ag 3 '87

Samuel, Frank E., Jr.
Health care in America [address, December 4-5, 1986] *Vital Speeches Day* 53:335-7 Mr 15 '87

Samuels, Jonathan, and Balter, Lawrence
How useful are telephone consultation services for parents? bibl f il *Child Today* 16:27-30 My/Je '87

Samuelson, Robert J.
[Column on economic questions] *See* occasional issues of *Newsweek* beginning February 20, 1984

Samuelsson, Bengt, and others
Leukotrienes and lipoxins: structures, biosynthesis, and biological effects. bibl f il *Science* 237:1171-6 S 4 '87

Samway, Patrick H.
Eudora Welty's eye for the story [cover story] il *America* 156:417-20 My 23 '87
An interview with Mavis Gallant. *America* 156:485-7 Je 13 '87

San Andreas fault *See* Faults (Geology)
San Antonio (Tex.)
City planning
San Antonio: laying the foundation for the future. H. Cisneros. il *USA Today (Periodical)* 116:24-33 Jl '87
Economic conditions
San Antonio: laying the foundation for the future. H. Cisneros. il *USA Today (Periodical)* 116:24-33 Jl '87
Fortification
See also
Alamo (San Antonio, Tex.)
Galleries and museums
See also
San Antonio Museum of Art
Historic houses, sites, etc.
Stars mark the way in San Antonio [Texas Star Trail] il *South Living* 22:18 F '87
Monuments, statues, etc.
Empty tomb honors Alamo heroes [Alamo Cenotaph] il *South Living* 22:20-1 Je '87

Plazas
A possible dream [Plaza Guadalupe] M. Gaskie. il *Archit Rec* 175:128-33 O '87
Politics and government
San Antonio: putting family first [Mayor H. Cisneros declines race for governor; chooses to care for new son ailing from birth defects] D. Pedersen. il por *Newsweek* 110:8 S 14 '87
Religious institutions and affairs
Church/state: the first freedom [agreement between Archdiocese of San Antonio and Park Service to operate San Antonio National Historical Park] J. Freeman. il *Natl Parks* 61:18 Mr/Ap '87
Papa do preach [state of Hispanic Catholicism] A. Sullivan. *New Repub* 197:13-14+ O 5 '87
The Pope's visit to San Antonio. T. H. Stahel. *America* 157:147-9 S 26 '87
Stores
See also
La Villita Tortillas (Firm)
San Antonio Festival
Reviews:
Ballet Nacional de Mexico and other groups at the San Antonio Festival. J. Neal. *Dance Mag* 61:25+ Ja '87
San Antonio Missions National Historical Park (Tex.)
Church/state: the first freedom [agreement between Archdiocese of San Antonio and Park Service] J. Freeman. il *Natl Parks* 61:18 Mr/Ap '87
San Antonio Museum of Art
New, Mexican folk art gallery in Texas. *Américas* 39:58 Ja/F '87
San Bruno Mountain State and County Park (Calif.) *See* California—Parks and reserves
San Carlos de Bariloche (Argentina)
Description
Argentina's Switzerland. L. Vidal Rucabado. il *World Press Rev* 34:62 Ag '87
San Diego (Calif.)
Architecture
They found the views with a cherry picker . . . and went up for them. il *Sunset* 178:168-9 My '87
Crime
Calif. 'Big Spin' winner pleads guilty to theft [cocaine charge against T. Garrett dismissed] *Jet* 71:36 Ja 12 '87
Criminal justice, Administration of
Former Heisman winner Rodgers gets 6 months [J. Rodgers] il por *Jet* 71:24 Mr 23 '87
Racist gets prison term for harassing black family [M. E. Maas] *Jet* 72:5 Mr 30 '87
Description
Across the borders of history. R. Rodriguez. il *Harpers* 274:42-9+ Mr '87
The joys of San Diego. E. Paris. il *Forbes* 139:164-6 Je 1 '87
San Diego's lively new-and-old downtown. il maps *Sunset* 178:64-71 F '87
Galleries and museums
See also
Museum of Photographic Arts (San Diego, Calif.)
Hospitals
See also
Children's Hospital (San Diego, Calif.)
Police
Black who killed white cop, wounded others; acquitted [case of S. Penn] *Jet* 73:47 N 2 '87
Race relations
Racist gets prison term for harassing black family [M. E. Maas] *Jet* 72:5 Mr 30 '87
San Diego street named after King changed: blacks protest, urge boycott. il *Jet* 73:52 N 30 '87
Sanitary affairs
Sludge busters [water hyacinth sewage treatment system] R. Stayton. il *Pop Sci* 230:43-4 F '87
Stores
San Diego's lively new-and-old downtown [Horton Plaza shopping center] il maps *Sunset* 178:64-71 F '87
Streets
San Diego street named after King changed: blacks protest, urge boycott. il *Jet* 73:52 N 30 '87
San Diego Wild Animal Park (Escondido, Calif.)
Caring for the condor [California condor keeper D. J. Sterner] B. Weber. il por *N Y Times Mag* p106 O 4 '87
San Domenico Palace (Taormina, Italy: Hotel) *See* Taormina (Italy)—Hotels, motels, etc.

San Felipe Handicap *See* Horse racing
San Francisco (Calif.)

Architecture

See also

San Francisco (Calif.)—Buildings

Art

Artists sue over posters: San Francisco battle focuses on rights to psychedelic artwork from the sixties. M. Goldberg. *Roll Stone* p29 Ap 23 '87

Banks

See also

Bank of Canton of California
Wells Fargo Bank, National Association

Bookstores

See Booksellers and bookselling—California

Bridges

See also

Golden Gate Bridge (San Francisco, Calif.)

Buildings

In the great tradition [SunarHauserman showroom] C. K. Gandee. il *Archit Rec* 175:116-21 My '87

City planning

Parkmerced. B. Wallach. il *Focus* 36:12-15 Wint '86

Description

California idyll. N. Hazelton. *Natl Rev* 39:67-9 S 11 '87
Guided walks of historic San Francisco. *Sunset* 178:50 Je '87
SoMa [South Market district] il maps *Sunset* 179:102-5 N '87
Starting again in San Francisco. R. Reinhardt. il *Am Herit* 38:92-8 Ap '87

Earthquake and fire, 1906

Great quake body count. J. Silberner. *Sci News* 131:255 Ap 18 '87

Economic conditions

No longer number one [losing economic edge to Los Angeles] G. C. Lubenow. il *Newsweek* 109:28 Ap 13 '87

Galleries and museums

See also

California Academy of Sciences. Natural History Museum
Exploratorium
Jewish Community Museum (San Francisco, Calif.)
Kuromatsu (Firm)
National Maritime Museum (U.S.)
San Francisco Museum of Modern Art

San Francisco exhibits exceed photography's boundaries. L. Lufkin. il *Pop Photogr* 94:26+ Ja '87

Gardens and gardening

In just 425 square feet, a shady green retreat. il *Sunset* 179:157 O '87

Harbor

Dining along San Francisco's working waterfront. il map *Sunset* 178:68+ Ap '87

Health facilities

Profiles [L. and K. Looper run the Chateau, a board-and-care home for schizophrenics] B. Barich. il *New Yorker* 63:51-2+ O 12 '87

Historic houses, sites, etc.

Revitalizing a 10-story San Francisco landmark [Monadnock Building] il *Sunset* 179:50 O '87

History

See also

San Francisco (Calif.)—Earthquake and fire, 1906
Starting again in San Francisco. R. Reinhardt. il *Am Herit* 38:92-8 Ap '87

Hotels, motels, etc.

See also

Hotel Group of America
The butler does it [S. Bromley, manager of the Clift Hotel] P. Tyre. il por *N Y* 20:14 Ag 3 '87
Lifted lexicons [dictionaries at San Francisco's Stanford Court] *Time* 129:87 Ap 6 '87
Solidarity lives among hotel workers [Local 2 of Hotel and Restaurant Employees Union] P. Somlo. il *Progressive* 51:15 Mr '87

Housing

Is a San Francisco architect's plan to put the homeless in boxes humane or heartless? [D. MacDonald's city sleepers] il por *People Wkly* 28:95 Ag 31 '87
San Francisco housing complex ordered to pay black for discrimination [case of Robert Cannon] *Jet* 72:18 My 25 '87

Industries

Down and out in San Francisco. P. Dworkin. il *U S News World Rep* 102:46 Ja 19 '87

Medical care

AIDS stresses health care in San Francisco. D. M. Barnes. *Science* 235:964 F 27 '87

Music

See also

San Francisco Opera
San Francisco Symphony Orchestra

Newspapers

See also

San Francisco chronicle

Politics and government

Feinstein looks beyond San Francisco. por *Newsweek* 110:59 N 2 '87
An upstart mayor, a shaky future [new mayor A. Agnos] P. A. Witteman. il por *Time* 130:29-30 D 21 '87

Population

Latin legacy in the City by the Bay. S. E. Caldwell. il *Américas* 39:44-9 N/D '87

Public health

Volunteers, home care, and money: how San Francisco has mobilized [AIDS epidemic] J. O. Hamilton. il *Bus Week* p125 Mr 23 '87

Restaurants, nightclubs, bars, etc.

Dining along San Francisco's working waterfront. il map *Sunset* 178:68+ Ap '87
A side order of sea slugs [Chinese herbal cookery at Emperor Herbal Restaurant] L. Shapiro. il *Newsweek* 110:77 S 14 '87
Spécialités de la maison:
Le Castel, Rodin, Zuni Café & Grill. C. Bates. il *Gourmet* 47:20+ Mr '87
Fleur de Lys. C. Bates. il *Gourmet* 47:20+ Jl '87
Harry's Bar and American Grill, China Moon Cafe. C. Bates. il *Gourmet* 47:16+ Ja '87
Izzy's Steak & Chop House and Celadon. C. Bates. il *Gourmet* 47:48+ O '87
Masa's, Janot's, Golden Turtle. C Bates. il *Gourmet* 47:24+ My '87

Stations

Cut and recover [Forest Hill Station] D. Brenner. il *Archit Rec* 175:68-71 Ja '87

Stores

See also

Japonesque (Firm)
San Francisco shopping. G. Asher. il *Gourmet* 48:60-5+ Je '87

Terminals

See San Francisco (Calif.)—Stations

Theater

See also

Survival Research Laboratories (Group)

Transit systems

The bells still toll for San Francisco's hills. B. C. Lewis. il *Am Hist Illus* 22:36-43 Ap '87

Water supply

See also

Hetch Hetchy Water Supply Project
San Francisco Ballet
Back to basics [cover story] J. Ross. il por *Dance Mag* 61:38-43 Ag '87
Reviews:
Performances in Chicago. A. Barzel. *Dance Mag* 61:48-9 F '87
SFB's Val Caniparoli: sunrise for Caniparoli. il por *Dance Mag* 61:44-5 Ag '87

San Francisco Bay (Calif.)
Wings beneath the bay [vortex foils tested] *Oceans* 20:3 Mr/Ap '87

San Francisco Bay region (Calif.)

See also

Opera—San Francisco Bay region (Calif.)

Description and travel

Biking and birding around southern San Francisco Bay. il *Sunset* 178:10-11 Ja '87

Galleries and museums

See also

Bay Area Discovery Museum

Lighting

Big-scale and bright, architectural lighting makes a Bay Area comeback. il *Sunset* 179:14-15 D '87

Parks and reserves

Parks that say yes (and no) to dogs. il *Sunset* 179:47-8 N '87

San Francisco chronicle
The 'San Francisco chronicle' focuses on children's books. M. Colin. il *Publ Wkly* 231:39-40 My 29 '87

San Francisco Museum of Modern Art
Eager to raise the stakes for the SFMMA [new director J. R. Lane] K. Regan. por *Art News* 86:32+ Ap '87

San Francisco Opera
San Francisco. S. Von Buchau. *Opera News* 51:40-2 Mr 14 '87
San Francisco. S. Von Buchau. *Opera News* 51:35-7 Ja 3 '87

San Francisco Opera—*cont.*
San Francisco on the air: a guide to the company's 1987 broadcast season (I). il *Opera News* 52:45-8 S '87
San Francisco on the air: a guide to the company's 1987 broadcast season (II). il *Opera News* 52:27-30+ O '87
San Francisco on the air: a guide to the company's 1987 broadcast season (III). il *Opera News* 52:43-6 N '87

San Francisco Symphony Orchestra
New life for the invalid [premiere of J. Harbison's Symphony no. 2] M. Walsh. il por *Time* 129:71 Je 1 '87
Sound sense [performance at Carnegie Hall] P. G. Davis. il *N Y* 20:104-6 Mr 2 '87

San Jose (Calif.)
City planning
San Jose: seeking a soul in the Sun Belt. P. Dworkin. il *U S News World Rep* 103:20-1 Ag 10 '87
Historic houses, sites, etc.
Mystery mansion [Llanda Villa designed by S. Winchester] J. Ashbery. il por *House Gard* 159:148-53+ Mr '87
Race relations
San Jose blacks angered over white racist group's threat to black woman. *Jet* 72:4 Ag 31 '87

San Juan (Puerto Rico)
Hotels, motels, etc.
Death in a towering inferno [Dupont Plaza hotel] B. Levin. il *Macleans* 100:16-19 Ja 12 '87
In the wake of a tragic hotel fire, disaster attorneys seek compensation for the victims—and for themselves [Dupont Plaza] J. S. Kunen. il pors *People Wkly* 27:36-8 Ja 26 '87
"A New Year we'll never forget" [fire at Dupont Plaza] A. Wilentz. il map *Time* 129:19-20 Ja 12 '87
San Juan's towering inferno [Dupont Plaza hotel] G. Hackett. il *Newsweek* 109:24 Ja 12 '87

San Luis Obispo (Calif.)
Restaurants, nightclubs, bars, etc.
Creekside dining in San Luis Obispo. il *Sunset* 179:49 Ag '87

San Marino Grand Prix *See* Automobile racing—Italy
San Martín, José de, 1778?-1850
about
San Martín and the OAS. C. Godoy-García. il *Américas* 39:55-6 Jl/Ag '87

San Miguel Corp.
Andres Soriano's battle for San Miguel. M. Shao. il por *Bus Week* p54 S 28 '87

San Miguel de Allende (Mexico)
Architecture
Custom of the country [P. Glenville's house] J. Richardson. il por *House Gard* 159:146-56 Ag '87
Description
San Miguel de Allende's special appeal. A. R. Williams. il *Américas* 39:42-8 My/Je '87

San Pedro de Macoris (Dominican Republic)
From Michigan, with love [baseball gloves sent to Dominican Republic] N. Shine. il por *Read Dig* 130:134-8 My '87

San Simeon *See* Hearst-San Simeon State Historical Monument (Calif.)

Sanchez, Janet H.
Brassicas from abroad. il *Rodale's Org Gard* 34:42-5 N '87
Oriental beans. il *Rodale's Org Gard* 34:54+ Ja '87
Playing for keeps [cover story] il *Rodale's Org Gard* 34:38-42 S '87
Savor sprouting broccoli. il *Rodale's Org Gard* 34:46+ N '87

Sanchez, Nicolas
Bilingual education: a barrier to achievement. *Educ Dig* 53:42-3 D '87

Sanchez, Oscar Arias *See* Arias Sanchez, Oscar
Sanchez, Pedro A., and Benites, Jose R.
Low-input cropping for acid soils of the humid tropics. bibl f il *Science* 238:1521-7 D 11 '87

Sánchez Borbón, Guillermo
Panama fallen among thieves. il *Harpers* 275:57-67 D '87

Sanctions (International law)
See also
Embargo
United Nations. Intergovernmental Group to Monitor the Supply and Shipping of Oil and Petroleum Products to South Africa
AAUP opposes embargo on sales of books to South Africa. C. Reid. *Publ Wkly* 232:12 D 11 '87

Britain's assault on the Commonwealth [Britain refuses to agree to wider sanctions against South Africa] H. Mackenzie. il *Macleans* 100:24-5 O 26 '87
Economic sanctions against South Africa [messages and letter to Congress, September 25-29, 1986] R. Reagan. *Dep State Bull* 86:35-7 D '86
Gray pushes for sanctions against Ethiopia atrocity. *Jet* 73:4 O 12 '87
Ignoring both carrot and stick [effect of sanctions on South Africa] W. R. Doerner. il *Time* 130:36 O 5 '87
International aviation group discusses sanctions on supporters of terrorism. *Aviat Week Space Technol* 126:41 F 23 '87
Jaruzelski wins one with the end of U.S. sanctions. D. Stanglin. il por *U S News World Rep* 102:35 Mr 2 '87
New bill to ban Ethiopia. K. Jackson. il *Black Enterp* 17:18 Jl '87
Non-aligned at Harare call for sanctions [call for convening of the Security Council to impose sanctions against South Africa] *UN Chron* 23:46 N '86
Out of Africa [Comprehensive Anti-Apartheid Act] J. M. Woods. il *Black Enterp* 17:15 Ja '87
Pro and con [Secretary of State's Advisory Committee on South Africa urges sanctions] *Time* 129:58 F 23 '87
Sanctions and survival [South Africa and the 1986 nonaligned nations conference] R. Shaplen. il *New Yorker* 62:74-80+ F 2 '87
Sanctions in context [Catholic bishops reaffirm support for sanctions against South Africa] R. E. Lambert. *Commonweal* 114:166-7 Mr 27 '87
Security Council does not adopt text calling for selective mandatory sanctions against South Africa. il *UN Chron* 24:22-5 My '87
South African retaliation: a blessing in disguise? R. A. Evans and A. F. Evans. *Christ Century* 104:79-80 Ja 28 '87
Text calling for comprehensive mandatory sanctions against South Africa vetoed after discussion in eight meetings. il *UN Chron* 24:22-5 Ag '87
Text calling for mandatory selective sanctions against South Africa vetoed in Security Council. il *UN Chron* 23:3-5 Ja '86
The truth about sanctions. J. H. Wolfe. *USA Today (Periodical)* 115:9 Mr '87
Two questions about South Africa [efficacy of sanctions and Communist domination of African National Congress] D. Seligman. *Fortune* 115:122+ Mr 2 '87
U.S. takes measures against Syria [White House statement, November 14, 1986] *Dep State Bull* 87:79 Ja '87
Why deny the children? [effects of American publishers' boycott of South Africa] G. Miklowitz. por *Publ Wkly* 232:66 O 9 '87
Why sanctions are a failure. S. Jenkins. il *U S News World Rep* 103:40 S 21 '87
Why South Africa shrugs at sanctions. P. Brimelow. il *Forbes* 139:100-4 Mr 9 '87

Sanctuaries, Bird *See* Bird sanctuaries
Sanctuaries, Wildlife *See* Wildlife sanctuaries
Sanctuary (Law) *See* Asylum, Right of
Sanctuary movement (Refugee aid)
Charges of break-ins and infiltration [FBI investigation of the sanctuary movement] J.-M. Andriote. il *Christ Today* 31:44-5 Ap 17 '87
A Guatemalan family's flight to sanctuary in the U.S. P. M. Jones. il *Sch Update* 119:18 Mr 9 '87
Sanctuary: should parishes break the law for a stranger? R. McClory. il *U S Cathol* 52:32-8 My '87
Sister Darlene Nicgorski [sanctuary movement worker] R. Brown. il por *Ms* 15:54+ Ja '87
Western Europe
Europe's sanctuary movement: grappling with governments. M. McConnell. il *Christ Century* 104:1001-3 N 11 '87

Sand
Home on the grain [marine invertebrates that can colonize single grains of sand] D. D. Edwards. il *Sci News* 131:156-7 Mr 7 '87

Sand castles
If you are serious about sandcastling. il *Sunset* 179:68-9 Ag '87

Sand dollars *See* Sea urchins
Sandall, Roger
Beyond California. *Commentary* 83:56-60 Je '87
Sandbar Island (Me.)
See also
Historic houses, sites, etc.—Sandbar Island (Me.)

Sandberg, Peter Lars, 1934-
To have and to hold [story] il *Good Housekeep* 204:102-3+ Je '87
Sandblasting

Equipment
Workbench builds a sandblasting cabinet. P. McCafferty. il *Workbench* 43:88-93 S/O '87
Sandcastles *See* Sand castles
Sandeen, Michael

about
Michael Sandeen's Spinjammer is a new twist on an old disc. il por *People Wkly* 27:138-9 My 11 '87
Sandell, John G.
The plant rack. il *Rodale's Org Gard* 34:74-6 F '87
Sanden, John Howard
A painter looks at John Singer Sargent. il *Am Artist* 51:66-70+ Ja '87
Sander, Leonard M.
Fractal growth. bibl (p128) il *Sci Am* 256:94-100 Ja '87
Sanderlings *See* Sandpipers
Sanders, Ivan
The other Europeans. *Nation* 245:279-82 S 19 '87
Sanders, Scott R. (Scott Russell), 1945-
Death of a homeless man. il *Progressive* 51:50 Mr '87
Sanders, Sol W.
United States relations with Mexico [address, April 23, 1987] *Vital Speeches Day* 53:525-8 Je 15 '87
Sanders, Timothy Greenfield- *See* Greenfield-Sanders, Timothy
Sanders, Tom

about
Ex-Celtic Tom Sanders joins NBA front office. por *Jet* 72:50 Ag 24 '87
Sanders, W. J. (Walter Jeremiah), III

about
Silicon Valley's vale of tears. P. Dworkin. il por *U S News World Rep* 102:47 Mr 2 '87
Sanders, Walter Jeremiah *See* Sanders, W. J. (Walter Jeremiah), III
Sanders (Machinery) *See* Sanding and sanding equipment
Sanders Associates, Inc.
Sanders-GE team forms INEWS management structure [integrated electronic warfare system] *Aviat Week Space Technol* 126:78 F 16 '87
Sanderson, Susan Walsh
Mexico's agricultural policy. bibl f *Curr Hist* 86:109-12+ Mr '87
Sanderson, Wimp

about
How the Tide has turned. R. Wiley. il *Sports Illus* 66:32-4 F 2 '87
Sandia National Laboratories
Sandia develops nuclear-powered Falcon optical laser concept. T. M. Foley. *Aviat Week Space Technol* 127:24 O 19 '87
Travelling robot to work in radiation-hardened IC lab. *Radio-Electron* 58:4 N '87
Sandiford, Cedric

about
Survivor of racial attack in N.Y. wants special probe. il por *Jet* 71:4 Ja 19 '87
Sanding and sanding equipment
Belt sander basics (I). H. Wicks. il *Home Mech* 83:26 Ap '87
Belt sander basics (II). H. Wicks. il *Home Mech* 83:32 My '87
Boatkeeper's guide to scraping and sanding. B. Gladstone. il *Mot Boat Sail* 160:67-9 S '87
How to get a fine furniture finish. A. Rooze. il *Fam Handyman* 37:21-2 N '87
Sanding a hardwood floor. A. Rooze. il *Fam Handyman* 37:46-51 N '87
Sandinista government *See* Nicaragua—Politics and government
Sandino, Augusto César, 1895-1934

about
Sandinismo: the nationalist faith of Nicaragua. C. C. O'Brien. *Cent Mag* 20:31-4 Jl/Ag '87
The Sandinista heritage. C. Foster. il *Hist Today* 37:5-8 Ap '87
Sandke, Jordan

about
Randy and Jordan Sandke. C. Deffaa. il pors *Down Beat* 54:50-1 Mr '87
Sandke, Randy

about
Randy and Jordan Sandke. C. Deffaa. il pors *Down Beat* 54:50-1 Mr '87

Sandler, Herbert M., 1931-

about
Boring is better. J. Heins. il pors *Forbes* 140:167-8 N 16 '87
Sandler, Marion O.

about
Boring is better. J. Heins. il pors *Forbes* 140:167-8 N 16 '87
Sandler, Roberta
Blowing smoke. *Harpers* 275:15-16 Ag '87
Sandmaier, Marian
Doctor No: when M.D. spells trouble. *Mademoiselle* 93:174+ Mr '87
Don't mess with magic pills, darling: they're bad medicine. il *Mademoiselle* 93:128-9+ Jl '87
Sandmel, Ben
Allons danser. il *Atlantic* 260:88+ Jl '87
Sandpaper
How to get a fine furniture finish. A. Rooze. il *Fam Handyman* 37:21-2 N '87
Sandpaper basics. H. Wicks. il *Home Mech* 83:16 S '87
Sandpaper bins *See* Bins
Sandpipers

Photographs and photography
Brooding on the tundra [sanderlings of Jenny Lind Island] B. Lyon. il *Nat Hist* 96:84-7 D '87
Sandrock, Alfred W., Jr., and Matthew, William D.
An in vitro neurite-promoting antigen functions in axonal regeneration in vivo. bibl f il *Science* 237:1605-8 S 25 '87
Sandroff, Ronni
When the obstetrician says "no". il *Health* 19:52-4+ N '87
Who thrives in which job? il *Work Woman* 12:126-8+ N '87
Sands, Andrea
Do your clothes need help? il *Redbook* 168:106-9 Ap '87
Sands, Josefina
All-around achiever. il por *Essence* 18:102+ Je '87
Sands, Julian

about
Julian Sands's English macho. V. Radin. por *Vogue* 177:32 Ja '87
Sandstrom, Tomas

about
The lowdown on a high-sticking. il por *Sports Illus* 67:16 N 9 '87
Sandved, Kjell Bloch, 1922-

about
Around the Mall and beyond. E. Park. il por *Smithsonian* 18:24+ S '87
Sandweiss, Martha A.
An enduring grace: the photography of Laura Gilpin. il por *USA Today (Periodical)* 115:54-63 Mr '87
Sandwich (Mass.)

Education
Lawmakers—not lawbreakers [seventh graders lobby for tougher cigarette sales law] C. Lowrance. il *Good Housekeep* 204:96 Mr '87
Sandwich Islands *See* Hawaii
Sandwiches
Between the bread. il *Health* 19:64-6+ Mr '87
Brown-bag sandwiches. il *Better Homes Gard* 65:153-4 S '87
Every 'wich way. il *Seventeen* 46:156-7 O '87
Fish out of water [Gordon Naccarato's Chippewa salmon sandwich] B. Costikyan. il *N Y* 20:62 Je 8 '87
Hot sandwiches to satisfy. il *South Living* 22:230-1 N '87
Let's have high tea! [cress and mustard sprout sandwiches] W. E. Wooldridge. il *Flower Gard* 32:79 D '87/Ja '88
Sandwich fillings. il *Gourmet* 47:206 S '87
Sandwiches! B. Greenwood. il *Better Homes Gard* 65:84-5 Je '87
Sandwiches—a meal in themselves. J. Nash. il *Essence* 18:110 My '87
Soup and sandwich—a natural combo [microwave recipes] il *South Living* 22:106+ Ja '87
Super sandwiches. L. Hoppe. il *Better Homes Gard* 65:143 O '87
Super summer sandwiches. il *Ladies Home J* 104:102-3+ Je '87
Take a new look at sandwiches. B. E. Templeton. il *South Living* 22:204+ My '87

Anecdotes, facetiae, satire, etc.
Deliverance [memories of frozen sandwiches for school lunches] C. Murphy. il *Atlantic* 260:22+ N '87

Sandza, Richard
 A daughter's father. il *N Y Times Mag* p59 F 1 '87
SANE, Inc.
 See also
  SANE/FREEZE (Organization)
SANE/FREEZE (Organization)
 A nuclear FREEZE is a SANE proposal. H. A. Jack. *Christ Century* 104:1133-5 D 16 '87
Sanford, Adelaide L.
 about
 Making the system work [interview] D. A. Williams. por *Essence* 18:80+ S '87
Sanford, Fred Glenn
 about
 Redd Foxx does prison benefits in memory of his ex-con brother. il pors *Jet* 72:56-7 Mr 30 '87
Sanford, Liz
 about
 Staff notes [interview] il por *Seventeen* 46:252-3 Ag '87
Sanford, Robert L.
 Apogeotropic roots in an Amazon rain forest. bibl f il *Science* 235:1062-4 F 27 '87
Sanger, Sirgay, and Kelly, John, 1945-
 Could you be a better mother? [excerpt from The woman who works: the parent who cares] *Redbook* 169:94-5+ Je '87
 How to be a better (working) mother [excerpt from The modern mother] *Redbook* 168:94-5+ Mr '87
Sanitary napkins, tampons, etc. *See* Feminine hygiene products
Sanitation
 See also
  Arcata (Calif.)—Sanitary affairs
  Beaches—Sanitation
  Chicago (Ill.)—Sanitary affairs
  Denver (Colo.)—Sanitary affairs
  Food handling
  Food stores—Sanitation
  Hot tubs—Sanitation
  International Drinking Water Supply and Sanitation Decade, 1981-1990
  Islip (N.Y.)—Sanitary affairs
  New York (State)—Sanitary affairs
  Plumbing
  Public comfort stations
  Refuse and refuse disposal
  Saint Louis (Mo.)—Sanitary affairs
  Salad bars—Sanitation
  San Diego (Calif.)—Sanitary affairs
  Shellfish industry—Sanitation
  Space stations—Sanitation
  Swimming pools—Sanitation
  Telephone—Equipment—Sanitation
  Toilet seats—Sanitation
Sanjurjo de Casciero, Annick
 The abstract landscapes of Pacheco. il por *Américas* 39:14-17+ Ja/F '87
Sankai Juku (Dance company)
 Reviews:
  Performance of Tamago netsu in Ohya City, Japan. S. Ueno. il *Dance Mag* 61:20+ Mr '87
Sankara, Thomas
 Assassination
 Burkina Faso. il *World Press Rev* 34:46 D '87
 Upright down. por *Time* 130:52 O 26 '87
Sanneh, Lamin O.
 Christian missions and the Western guilt complex [cover story] il *Christ Century* 104:330-4 Ap 8 '87
Sanrio Co., Ltd.
 Mickey Mouse, meet Hello Kitty. M. Beauchamp and H. Katayama. il por *Forbes* 139:68+ My 18 '87
Sans Souci (Jamaica: Resort) *See* Health resorts, watering places, etc.—Jamaica
Sans Souci Palace (Haiti) *See* Palaces—Haiti
Sansevieria trifasciata *See* Snake plant
Santa Barbara (Calif.)
 Photographs and photography
 Time and Detroit . . . and New York . . . and Santa Barbara [then and now photographs] il *Am Herit* 38:100-5 Ap '87
 Restaurants, nightclubs, bars, etc.
 Spécialités de la maison:
  Michael's Waterside Inn, The Palace Cafe, Oysters. C. Bates. il *Gourmet* 47:24+ N '87
Santa Barbara (Calif.). University of California *See* University of California, Santa Barbara
Santa Barbara County (Calif.)
 Maps
 Where to hike and bike: guides to Santa Barbara County. il *Sunset* 179:38 N '87

Santa Clara (Calif.)
 Galleries and museums
 See also
  Triton Museum of Art
Santa Clara (Calif.). Triton Museum of Art *See* Triton Museum of Art
Santa Clara County (Calif.)
 Employees
 Affirmative action: after the debate, opportunity [Supreme Court decision] P. Dwyer. il *Bus Week* p37 Ap 13 '87
 Balancing act [Supreme Court expands affirmative action] R. Stengel. il *Time* 129:18-20 Ap 6 '87
 Court ruling affirmative [Supreme Court decides affirmative action case] J. C. Baker. *Black Enterp* 17:20 Jl '87
 Gender-based hiring and promotions approved [Supreme Court decision in affirmative action case] *Mon Labor Rev* 110:41-2 My '87
 Ladies' day [Supreme Court ruling in affirmative action case] *New Repub* 196:4+ Ap 20 '87
 Saying "yes" to affirmative action [Supreme Court ruling in Santa Clara case] M. Takas. *Vogue* 177:58 N '87
 The Supreme Court puts the mike in Diane Joyce's hands, giving feminists a major victory. W. Plummer. il pors *People Wkly* 27:49-50+ Ap 13 '87
 Tribal justice [Supreme Court majority opinion upholding the legality of Santa Clara, Calif. affirmative action plan] *Natl Rev* 39:17-18 Ap 24 '87
 A woman's day in court [Supreme Court decision in affirmative action case] A. Press. il *Newsweek* 109:58-9 Ap 6 '87
 The women win—again [Supreme Court decision in affirmative action case] T. Gest. il *U S News World Rep* 102:18-19 Ap 6 '87
Santa Claus
 Christmas shopping [with toddlers] J. T. Gibson. il *Parents* 62:194 D '87
 Does it damage children to deceive them about Santa Claus? Ho, ho, no, says Dr. Carl Anderson [interview] L. Armstrong. il pors *People Wkly* 28:45+ D 21 '87
 Everybody smiles at Santa [mentally retarded man] R. Riddell. il *Ladies Home J* 104:134+ D '87
 Santa lives [children's beliefs; study by Cyndy Scheibe and John Condry] V. Bozzi. il *Psychol Today* 21:12 D '87
 A Santa suit does not a Santa Claus make [excerpt from Seven stories of Christmas love] L. F. Buscaglia. il *Good Housekeep* 205:44+ D '87
 Why I believe in Santa Claus. M. Zolotow. il *McCalls* 115:138-40 D '87
 Collectibles
 A note from Santa Claus! [bank notes depicting Santa Claus] E. Rochette. il *Antiques Collect Hobbies* 92:80-1 D '87
Santa Fe (N.M.)
 Architecture
 Adobe blowup [Ron Robles remodels house] G. Winkel. il *House Gard* 159:122-5 Ja '87
 Arts
 Santa Fe/Taos [special section] il *Horizon* 30:41-59 O '87
 Description
 The adobe island. F. Eberstadt. il *Vogue* 177:324+ O '87
 Santa Fe/Taos [special section] il *Horizon* 30:41-59 O '87
 The Santa Fe blend. L. Banks. il *Travel Holiday* 168:64-8 S '87
 Historic houses, sites, etc.
 Southwest rhythms: restoring a Sante Fe adobe [home of M. Mahaffey] L. Bernikow. il por *Archit Dig* 44:130-5 F '87
 Markets
 See also
  Indian Market (Santa Fe, N.M.)
 Music
 See also
  Orchestra of Santa Fe
  Santa Fe Opera
  Santa Fe Symphony
Santa Fe Opera
 Opera in the desert. J. P. Forsthoffer. il por *Horizon* 30:57-9 O '87
 Santa Fe. H. E. Phillips. il *Opera News* 52:48+ D 5 '87
Santa Fe Southern Pacific Corporation
 Can Santa Fe outrun the raiders? K. Deveny. il *Bus Week* p60-1 N 2 '87
 The end of the line. A. A. Lappen. por *Forbes* 140:10 Jl 27 '87

Santa Fe Southern Pacific Corporation—*cont.*
The raiders are eager to start splitting rails. J. N. Frank and S. Payne. *Bus Week* p36-7 Jl 13 '87
Santa Fe's pursuers may have to settle for pieces. S. Toy. il *Bus Week* p74 D 28 '87-Ja 4 '88
Santa Fe Symphony
Point, counterpoint. J. P. Forsthoffer. il *Horizon* 30:44 O '87
Santa Margarita River (Calif.)
The Corps (Marine) and the only natural river [Camp Pendleton and proposed Santa Margarita dams] J. Sunila. il map *Audubon* 89:114-16+ S '87
Santa Maria (Calif.)
Santa Maria invites you for a rancher's barbecue. il *Sunset* 178:40 Je '87
Santa Maria (Ship)
　　　　　　Collectibles
Santa Maria boat [glass souvenir] M. Wollett and B. Wollett. il *Antiques Collect Hobbies* 92:42 Ap '87
Santa Maria del Carmine (Church: Florence, Italy)
True colors [restoration of frescoes in the Brancacci Chapel] G. Armstrong. il *Art News* 86:39+ Mr '87
Santa Monica (Calif.)
　　　　　Galleries and museums
Santa Monica & Venice: a guide to the galleries. map *Art Am* 75:90-1 My '87
　　　　Restaurants, nightclubs, bars, etc.
Spécialités de la maison:
　　Valentino. C. Bates. il *Gourmet* 47:42+ Ag '87
Santa Monica Bay (Calif.)
　　　　See also
Marine pollution—Santa Monica Bay (Calif.)
Santa Monica Partners
Terra incognita [L. Goldstein's pink sheet stock strategy] T. Jaffe. il por *Forbes* 140:38-40 D 28 '87
Santa Rosa Island (Calif.)
　　　　　Antiquities
Monument to a discoverer? [Santa Rosa Island stone linked to J. R. Cabrillo] B. McGinty. il *Am Hist Illus* 22:38-41 O '87
Santería (Cult)
Among the believers: converts to Santeria. T. Cochran. il *N Y* 20:33-4 O 12 '87
Santiago, Benito
　　　　　about
Benito finito at 34 games. F. Lidz. il por *Sports Illus* 67:26-7 O 12 '87
Santiago (Guatemala)
　　　　　Festivals
The pride that flies [giant kites] M. Cavallaro. il *Américas* 39:14-19 My/Je '87
Santo Domingo Pueblo (N.M.)
　　　　　Education
An enthusiasm to learn through video [Santo Domingo Indian children] B. Atencio. *Phi Delta Kappan* 68:632-3 Ap '87
Santorini (Greece) See Thera (Greece: Island)
Santoro, Gene
Bernard Edwards: hit man on the production line. il pors *Down Beat* 54:20-2 Je '87
Carlos Alomar: generating electric dreams. il pors *Down Beat* 11:20-2 N '87
David Murray. *Nation* 244:554-6 Ap 25 '87
Jazz. *Nation* 244:374-6 Mr 21 '87
JVC Jazz Festival New York. *Nation* 245:100-4 Ag 1-8 '87
Lyle Mays: catching a (sound) wave [interview; cover story] il pors *Down Beat* 54:16-19 Jl '87
Music. *Nation* 245:210-12 S 5 '87
Music. *Nation* 245:65-8 Jl 18-25 '87
Music. *Nation* 244:696-8 My 23 '87
Music. *Nation* 244:776-8 Je 6 '87
Music. *Nation* 244:481-2 Ap 11 '87
Music. *Nation* 245:351-3 O 3 '87
Santos, David Raimundo
　　　　　about
Letter from the Elysian Fields. J. Kramer. *New Yorker* 63:40-2+ Mr 2 '87
Santos, Jose
　　　　　about
Uncrowned prince of the Triple Crown. J. Rolfe and P. Demartini. il pors *Sport Mag* 78:63+ Je '87
Santos, Sherod, 1948-
The art of fiction [poem] *Nation* 244:194 F 14 '87
The children of paradise [poem] *Nation* 244:58 Ja 17 '87
Midsummer [poem] *New Yorker* 63:26 Ag 17 '87
The whelk [poem] *New Yorker* 63:112 O 19 '87

Santos (Art)
Santos by Roybal. N. C. Benson. il por *Americana* 15:45-8 Mr/Ap '87
Sanyo Securities Co. Ltd.
Small world [Sanyo Securities buys stake in Spear Financial Services] J. Heins. il *Forbes* 139:159+ My 4 '87
Sanzio, Raffaello See Raphael, 1483-1520
Saouma, Edouard
　　　　　about
The politics of food. H. Mackenzie. il por *Macleans* 100:25 N 23 '87
Saperstein, Marc
Books on the Holocaust. *America* 157:385-9 N 21 '87
Sapolsky, Robert M.
The case of the falling nightwatchmen: in behavorial biology, not all facts are created equal. il *Discover* 8:42-5 Jl '87
Sapolsky, Robert M., and others
Interleukin-1 stimulates the secretion of hypothalamic corticotropin-releasing factor. bibl f il *Science* 238:522-4 O 23 '87
Sapphire braces (Orthodontics) See Orthodontics
Sapphires
The kindest cut of all turns stone-broke Roy Whetstine's $10 buy into a million-buck rock of ages. K. Demaret. il pors *People Wkly* 27:79+ F 16 '87
Sapporo Olympics, 1972 See Olympic Games—1972—Winter Olympics
SAR (Firm)
Los Angeles financial firm is acquiring assets of Medallion Books. *Publ Wkly* 232:18 Ag 14 '87
Sara Lee Corp.
A week in the life of a CEO [J. H. Bryan] J. H. Dobrzynski. il pors *Bus Week* Sp Issue:46-50+ O 23 '87
Sarabeth's Kitchen
Foods with flair: Sarabeth's Kitchen [S. Levine] J. Ciabattari. il por *Work Woman* 12:134-6 N '87
Sarafina! [musical] See Musicals, revues, etc.—Reviews—Single works
Sarah, Duchess of York, 1959-
　　　　　about
Andrew and "Fergie": royalty's happiest, most unusual marriage [cover story] D. Keay. il pors *Good Housekeep* 204:130-1+ Ap '87
Connecticut Yankees court the Yorks [cover story] L. Rozen. il pors *People Wkly* 28:96-7+ S 21 '87
'Fabulous Fergie' [cover story; special section; with editorial comment by Kevin Doyle] il pors *Macleans* 100:2, 26-30+ Jl 27 '87
Fabulous Fergie flying high. G. Robyns. il pors *Ladies Home J* 104:114-15+ F '87
Fergie and Andrew do Niagara, and Canada falls. il pors *People Wkly* 28:36-7 Ag 3 '87
Fergie wins her wings and Andy's a backseat pilot. il por *People Wkly* 27:36 Mr 2 '87
How far will these girls go? P. Junor. il pors *McCalls* 115:14-16+ N '87
Jobs too frantic? City living just too much? Rent a cozy rural hideway like Andy and Fergie did. il por *People Wkly* 27:101 F 16 '87
No titters, you two, this is serious! B. Johnson and L. Rozen. il pors *People Wkly* 28:24-8+ Jl 20 '87
Roughing it in the bush. M. McIver. il pors *Macleans* 100:46 Ag 10 '87
Royal welcome in the West. M. Gray. il pors *Macleans* 100:36-7 Ag 3 '87
Snakes alive! When Fergie met this party animal in Greenwich, her skin just started to crawl. il pors *People Wkly* 28:100-1 O 5 '87
A triumphant transformation: Fergie's first year. J. Whitaker. il pors *McCalls* 114:32-4+ Je '87
When the critics get tough, Fergie's major defender, her dad, rides to the rescue [cover story; interview] F. Hauptfuhrer. il pors *People Wkly* 28:100-3 S 21 '87
Sarasota Opera Association
Sarasota. M. Fleming. *Opera News* 52:38-9 Ag '87
Saratoga National Historical Park (N.Y.)
Digging into history [amateur archeologists excavate Saratoga battlefield] J. E. Stevens. il *Americana* 14:41-4 Ja/F '87
Saratoga Springs (N.Y.)
　　　　　Galleries and museums
　　　　See also
National Museum of Dance (U.S.)
Sarcoma viruses See Oncogenic viruses
Sarda, Rajendra Kumar
Schisto comes to town. il *World Health* p27-9 Je '87
Sarde, Cliff, and Zeloznicki, Susan
Jazz on the air. il *Down Beat* 54:6 Je '87

Sarduy, Severo
The concrete poetry movement. il *Courier* 39:28 D '86
Sargent, Bill
The case of Cape Cod. *Oceans* 20:47 Mr/Ap '87
Sargent, John Singer, 1856-1925
about
Fragments of a lost world. B. B. Stretch. il pors *Art News* 86:122-9 Ja '87
John Singer Sargent: style and sensibility. P. Hills. il por *USA Today (Periodical)* 115:77-83 Mr '87
A painter looks at John Singer Sargent. J. H. Sanden. il *Am Artist* 51:66-70+ Ja '87
Sargent, Joseph
about
Jaws the revenge [film] Reviews
Macleans 100:49 Ag 3 '87. L. O'Toole
People Wkly il 28:12 Ag 3 '87. T. Cunneff
Sark (Channel Islands)
The Lord of Sark may not have serfs, but his pigeon rights are heir-tight [M. Beaumont] J. Cooper. il pors *People Wkly* 28:89-91 Jl 27 '87
Sarlos, Andy
about
Steady as it goes for the new year. P. C. Newman. il por *Macleans* 100:16 Ja 5 '87
Sarmiento, Domingo Faustino, 1811-1888
Dance-floor democracy [excerpt from Travels] il *Courier* 40:30 Ap '87
Sarney, José, 1930-
about
The beat of Brazil. C. Wood. il *World Press Rev* 34:24-6 Mr '87
Brazil woes: Sarney plays an Army card. C. A. Robbins. il por *U S News World Rep* 103:41 Jl 13 '87
Brazil's Cruzado Plan. E.-S. Pang and L. Jarnagin. bibl f *Curr Hist* 86:13-16+ Ja '87
Brazil's new beat [special section; with editorial comment by Kevin Doyle] il por map *Macleans* 100:2, 18-22+ Ja 19 '87
The debt crisis isn't Brazil's only liability. P. C. Roberts. il *Bus Week* p14 Ap 20 '87
In Brazil, the president and Congress jostle for power. J. Ryser. por *Bus Week* p62 Je 8 '87
That old-time inflation hits Brazil. R. A. Manning. il por *U S News World Rep* 102:36 Mr 2 '87
Sarni, Vincent A.
about
Vincent Sarni is shattering the old PPG. M. Schroeder. il por *Bus Week* p74-5 Ag 17 '87
Sarno, John E., 1923-
about
Ah, my non-aching back: a longtime sufferer finds it's all in the mind. T. Schwartz. il por *N Y* 20:44-8+ Mr 16 '87
Sarnoff, Dorothy
Never be nervous again [condensation]; ed. by Gaylen Moore. *Read Dig* 131:27-8+ D '87
Sarnoff (David) Research Center *See* David Sarnoff Research Center
Sarns, Steven E.
R-E Robot (II). il *Radio-Electron* 58:42-4+ Ja '87
R-E Robot (III). il *Radio-Electron* 58:48-50 F '87
R-E Robot (IV). il *Radio-Electron* 58:52-6 Mr '87
R-E Robot (V). il *Radio-Electron* 58:39-44+ Ap '87
R-E Robot (VI). il *Radio-Electron* 58:62-6 My '87
R-E Robot (VII). il *Radio-Electron* 58:58-60+ Je '87
R-E Robot (VIII). il *Radio-Electron* 58:44-6+ Jl '87
R-E Robot (IX). il *Radio-Electron* 58:57-60+ Ag '87
R-E Robot (X). il *Radio-Electron* 58:56+ S '87
R-E Robot (XI). il *Radio-Electron* 58:56-9+ O '87
R-E Robot (XII). il *Radio-Electron* 58:67-8+ D '87
Sarongs
Sexy wrapups: tie one on! il *Harpers Bazaar* 120:156-63 Ap '87
Sarpellon, Giovanni
The 'new poor'. il *Courier* 40:22-4 Ja '87
Sarrel, Lorna J.
(jt. auth) See Sarrel, Philip M., 1937-, and Sarrel, Lorna J.
Sarrel, Philip M., 1937-, and Sarrel, Lorna J.
Managing menopause. il *Work Woman* 12:150+ O '87
Sarsat (Satellite) *See* Artificial satellites—Rescue work use
Sarti, Giuseppe, 1729-1802
about
I due litiganti [opera] Reviews
New Yorker 63:100-1 Ap 6 '87. A. Porter
Sartre, Jean Paul, 1905-1980
about
Jean-Paul Sartre: an 'ethical compass' [interview with A. Cohen-Solal] R. Z. Chesnoff. il pors *U S News World Rep* 103:67 N 2 '87

No exit [drama] Reviews
Nation 245:350 O 3 '87. T. M. Disch
Bibliography
Summing up Sartre. J. Weightman. il *N Y Rev Books* 34:42-6 Ag 13 '87
Sarver, Carleton
Across the lines. il *High Fidel* 37:55+ D '87
Sarver, Carleton, and Ranada, David
True colors. il *High Fidel* 37:48-52 Mr '87
SAS
European deregulation expected to lead to airline mergers [proposed SAS-Sabena merger] *Aviat Week Space Technol* 126:203+ Mr 9 '87
Europe's skies may be full of mergers [SAS and Sabena] J. Kapstein and others. il *Bus Week* p62 My 11 '87
SAS bid for British Caledonian cleared by British government. *Aviat Week Space Technol* 127:36 D 21 '87
SAS board authorizes merger talks with Sabena. *Aviat Week Space Technol* 126:34 My 4 '87
SAS, British Airways boost bids for stake in British Caledonian. *Aviat Week Space Technol* 127:34 D 14 '87
SAS considers Boeing 767 to replace DC-10. *Aviat Week Space Technol* 126:34 My 4 '87
SAS gears for 1990s. D. E. Fink. *Aviat Week Space Technol* 126:15 My 11 '87
SAS seeks British Caledonian tie to boost international traffic. D. A. Brown. *Aviat Week Space Technol* 127:30-1 N 30 '87
SAS weighs fleet options following Boeing's 7J7 decision. *Aviat Week Space Technol* 127:30-1 Ag 31 '87
Saskatchewan
See also
Finance—Saskatchewan
Lakes—Saskatchewan
Wildlife—Saskatchewan
Commercial policy
Canadian-United States trade [address, September 14, 1987] G. Devine. *Vital Speeches Day* 54:76-9 N 15 '87
Devine's control zone [Saskatchewan enacts potash protectionist measures to counteract U.S. duties] D. Eisler. il *Macleans* 100:14-15 S 14 '87
Industries
See also
Potash Corporation of Saskatchewan
Politics and government
Changing of the guard [R. Romanow chosen leader of New Democrats] D. Eisler. il por *Macleans* 100:10+ N 23 '87
Sasquatch
Tracking the Sasquatch [work of G. Krantz] S. Begley. il por *Newsweek* 110:73 S 21 '87
Sass, Martin D.
about
Risk arbitrage for the little guy. G. G. Marcial. *Bus Week* p62 Ag 10 '87
Sass (M. D.) Institutional Arbitrage Partners *See* M. D. Sass Institutional Arbitrage Partners
Sasso, John
about
Debacle for the Duke. J. Klein. il por *N Y* 20:26+ O 12 '87
Duke of piety. S. Lehigh and F. J. Connolly. *New Repub* 197:13-15 O 26 '87
The dwarfs in disarray. G. J. Church. il pors *Time* 130:22+ O 12 '87
Now, a Dukakis fiasco. M. Kaus. il por *Newsweek* 110:40 O 12 '87
The price of deception. J. Bierman. *Macleans* 100:32 O 12 '87
Sasson, Albert
A challenge for the developing world. il *Courier* 40:29-33 Mr '87
SAT *See* Scholastic Aptitude Test
Satanism *See* Demonology
Satchmo: America's musical legend [musical] *See* Musicals, revues, etc.—Reviews—Single works
Satellite Broadcasting and Communications Association
Cable-satellite agreement boosts prospects for direct-to-home service. J. C. Lowndes. il *Aviat Week Space Technol* 126:145+ F 9 '87
Satellite solar power stations *See* Artificial satellites—Solar energy use
Satellite Television Industry Association
See also
Satellite Broadcasting and Communications Association

Satellites
> *See also*
> Artificial satellites
> Asteroids—Satellites
> Jupiter (Planet)—Satellites
> Mars (Planet)—Satellites
> Moon
> Pluto (Planet)—Satellites
> Saturn (Planet)—Satellites
> Uranus (Planet)—Satellites

Satire
> *See also*
> Caricatures and cartoons
> *See also* subhead Anecdotes, facetiae, satire, etc.
> under various subjects
> Prints, politics & people: The English satirical print, 1600-1832 [Chadwyck-Healey's seven volume collection of satirical prints] I. Roots. il *Hist Today* 37:47-53 Mr '87

Satisfaction
> *See also*
> Comfort
> Job satisfaction
> Popularity contest [results of poll on sources of pleasure or satisfaction] J. Queenan. *New Repub* 196:14-15 Mr 23 '87

Sato, Taiji
> *about*
> Rebel with a cause. A. Tanzer. il por *Forbes* 139:84+ Mr 23 '87

Satran, Pamela Redmond
> High-energy weight control: three real-life solutions. il *Work Woman* 12:86+ F '87
> Looking for the "perfect" man. il *Glamour* 85:216-17+ D '87
> No more rules. il *Work Woman* 12:145+ My '87
> Shop sharp: how to be a store trooper. *Mademoiselle* 93:186 Mr '87
> Short power. il *Work Woman* 12:98-100 Je '87

Satriano, John
> (tr) See Moravia, Alberto, 1907-. The terrorist aesthetic

Satter, David
> A test case. il por *N Y Rev Books* 34:3-4 F 12 '87

Satterfield, Archie
> A Canadian Christmas feast: bringing out the British. il *Travel Holiday* 168:66-9 N '87
> Hawaii's prized quilts. il *Travel Holiday* 167:12-13 Ja '87
> Lights, camera, aloha! On location in Hawaii. il map *Travel Holiday* 168:36-41 Ag '87
> Totem heritage. il *Travel Holiday* 167:82 Je '87

Saturday night (Periodical)
> The end of Fulford's era [resignation of editor] D. Fetherling. *Macleans* 100:53 Jl 6 '87
> Pages for the powerful. B. D. Johnson. il *Macleans* 100:62 Ja 19 '87
> Saturday night fever [C. Black's purchase] P. Young. por *Macleans* 100:55 Je 29 '87
> Telling tales on Saturday night. G. Bain. il *Macleans* 100:44 Jl 27 '87

Saturday night live [television program] See Television program reviews—Single works

Saturday review
> Guccione's unlikely new conquest. D. Lieberman. il por *Bus Week* p40 N 23 '87

Saturn, Bob
> A buyer's guide to selected sound products at AES. il *Theatre Crafts* 21:31+ Mr '87

Saturn (Planet)
> *See also*
> Space flight to Saturn
> **Satellites**
> From its shape, a look inside Mimas [work of Stanley Dermott and Peter Thomas] R. A. Kerr. *Science* 235:31 Ja 2 '87
> The many moons of Saturn. il *Sky Telesc* 73:638 Je '87

Saturn Corporation
> GM maps massive cutbacks. P. Lienert. *Road Track* 38:100+ F '87
> Now we're getting somewhere. D. C. Ross. il *Mot Trend* 39:18-19 Mr '87
> Whatever happened to Saturn Corporation? M. Keller. il *Mot Trend* 39:122 O '87
> Will Saturn ever leave the launchpad? W. J. Hampton. il *Bus Week* p107 Mr 16 '87

Sauces
> *See also*
> Ice cream toppings
> Marinades
> Mayonnaise

Soy sauce
> Best Birmingham barbecue sauce. B. R. Merims. il *Ctry J* 14:22-3 S '87
> Bravo! A delicious no-cook tomato sauce. il *Redbook* 169:16 Ag '87
> Dessert is easy with fruit sauces [microwaved] il *South Living* 22:110 Ag '87
> Easy sauces for everyday dishes. il *Redbook* 168:104-7 Mr '87
> The freshest tomato sauce [microwaved] J. B. Hurley. il *Prevention* 39:58-9 Jl '87
> High on the hog [barbecued spareribs and sauce] il *Esquire* 108:70-1 Jl '87
> Hollandaise and béarnaise. *Gourmet* 47:210 Ap '87
> The low-cholesterol meal [sauces to complement fish] S. Bashline. il *Field Stream* 92:31 Ag '87
> Microwave before you grill [with tangy barbecue sauce] J. B. Hurley. il *Prevention* 39:52 Je '87
> New uses, old wines. C. Claiborne and P. Franey. il *N Y Times Mag* p91-2 S 20 '87
> Picante sauce burns with flavor. D. G. Lowery. il *South Living* 22:72-3 S '87
> Recipe of the week [beer barbecue sauce] il *Jet* 72:37 Jl 6 '87
> Sauces and relishes for meat. il *Better Homes Gard* 65:175-6 O '87
> A sorcerer's sauce [Wizard Baldour's Hot Stuff] M. Oberlaender. il por *Nations Bus* 75:70 Ja '87
> Spareribs in a hot-sweet sauce. il *Sunset* 179:124 Ag '87
> Speedy pasta sauces. il *Ladies Home J* 104:94 O '87
> Spoon on sauces for flavor [vegetable sauces] il *South Living* 22:184-5 O '87

Saudi Arabia
> *See also*
> Agriculture—Saudi Arabia
> Americans—Saudi Arabia
> Civil rights—Saudi Arabia
> Investments, American—Saudi Arabia
> Mecca (Saudi Arabia)
> Red Sea
> Riyadh (Saudi Arabia)
> Women—Saudi Arabia
> **Commerce**
> *United States*
> *See* United States—Commerce—Saudi Arabia
> **Defenses**
> *See also*
> Guided missiles, Saudi Arabian
> **Foreign relations**
> *Iran*
> *See* Iran—Foreign relations—Saudi Arabia
> *Persian Gulf region*
> *See also*
> Iranian-Iraqi War, 1980- —Saudi Arabian participation
> *United States*
> *See* United States—Foreign relations—Saudi Arabia

Saudi Arabian military assistance *See* Military assistance, Saudi Arabian

Saul, John Ralston
> The war business. il *World Press Rev* 34:19-21 Je '87

Saul, Nigel
> Forget-me-nots: patronage in Gothic England. bibl il *Hist Today* 37:18-24 N '87

Saul [oratorio] *See* Handel, George Frideric, 1685-1759

Sauna
> Seija's sauna [cover story] M. Morris. il *Home Mech* 83:38-40+ S '87
> Taking the heat. J. R. Luoma. il *Audubon* 89:76-9 Ja '87

Saunders, Dero A.
> Flashbacks. See issues of Forbes

Saunders, Ernest Walter, 1935-
> *about*
> Britain's own Boesky case. R. I. Kirkland, Jr. il por *Fortune* 115:85-6 F 16 '87
> Downfall of a titan. T. Fennell. il por *Macleans* 100:28 My 25 '87
> How Guinness suddenly fell from grace. R. A. Melcher and M. Maremont. il pors *Bus Week* p44-6 F 9 '87
> Look who may take a fall in the Guinness scandal. M. Maremont. por *Bus Week* p48 O 26 '87
> The questions surrounding Guinness' U.S. connection. P. Dwyer and M. Maremont. il por *Bus Week* p36-7 Ap 27 '87
> The scandal at Guinness: will the chief fall? M. Maremont and R. A. Melcher. il por *Bus Week* p52 Ja 19 '87

Saunders, Fred
about
Fish, frogs and furniture. il por *Workbench* 43:96 N/D '87

Saunders, Jacqueline
about
Blind D.C. woman wins $1.2 million in lottery. *Jet* 71:7 Ja 19 '87
Woman dies of heart attack after $1.2 million lottery win. *Jet* 71:18 Mr 9 '87

Saunders, Raymond, 1934-
about
Raymond Saunders at Terry Dintenfass. R. G. Edelman. *Art Am* 75:146 F '87

Saunders, Richard
about
Obituary
Jet por 72:54 S 7 '87

Saunders, William S.
Architectural education: what kinds do practicing architects want? por *Archit Rec* 175:45 Jl '87

Sauro, Joan
Immortality [story] il *U S Cathol* 52:32-7 N '87

Sausage
See also
Cooking—Sausage
Frankfurters
Salami
From our kitchen to yours. K. Adams. *South Living* 22:223 N '87

Sauter, Van Gordon
Did Dan Rather get this story wrong? il *U S News World Rep* 102:72 Mr 23 '87
A TV man views the storm. il *U S News World Rep* 102:68 F 16 '87

Sauterne (Wine) *See* Wine

Sauvage, Leo
On stage. See issues of The New Leader

Sauvageot, Claude
about
Girls apart [film] Reviews
Nation 245:463-4 O 24 '87. M. Gevisser

Sava, Samuel G.
Holding on to student enthusiasm. *Educ Dig* 52:28-31 Mr '87

Savage, David G.
Combining categorical program services can make a major difference [discussion of April 1987 article, Why Chapter 1 hasn't made much difference] *Phi Delta Kappan* 68:787-8 Je '87
Watching a changing Court: will the center hold? *Phi Delta Kappan* 69:135-7 O '87
Why Chapter 1 hasn't made much difference. il *Phi Delta Kappan* 68:581-4 Ap '87

Savage, Gus
about
Rep. Savage heads group to examine industrial policy of United States. por *Jet* 71:32 F 2 '87
Savage heads up Black Caucus business trust. por *Jet* 72:40 Je 29 '87

Savage, Linette
about
Making a healthy business out of fitness. M. Kort. il pors *Ms* 15:14+ Ap '87

Savage, Richard
Competing for tickets. il *Travel Holiday* 168:22-3 Ag '87

Savan, Leslie
How to live rich on your salary. il *Mademoiselle* 93:222-3+ My '87

Savannah (Ga.)
Arts
Savannah [special section] il *Horizon* 30:33-46+ Ap '87
Description
Savannah [special section] il *Horizon* 30:33-46+ Ap '87
Education
Classrooms go to town [heritage education program] M. Wade. il *Horizon* 30:38-9 Ap '87
Galleries and museums
See also
Savannah Science Museum, Inc.
Historic houses, sites, etc.
Classrooms go to town [heritage education program] M. Wade. il *Horizon* 30:38-9 Ap '87
A diamond for the Girl Scouts [Juliette Gordon Low Birthplace] il *South Living* 22:18 Mr '87
Spectacular preservation efforts have made this gracious old city a national showplace. B. Golightly. il *Horizon* 30:33-5 Ap '87

Hotels, motels, etc.
Savor Savannah's historic inns. il *South Living* 22:52+ My '87

Savannah River (Ga. and S.C.)
Savannah's true pilot [S. Stevens] D. Young. il pors *South Living* 22:74 Ag '87

Savannah River Plant nuclear reactors *See* Nuclear reactors

Savannah Science Museum, Inc.
The natural side of Savannah. il *South Living* 22:36 Mr '87

Savannah State College
Savannah State faces loss of NROTC program. *Jet* 73:36 N 2 '87

Savant, Marilyn Mach Vos *See* Vos Savant, Marilyn Mach

Savant syndrome
Along with crippling retardation, Doris Walker finds in her students a baffling paradox—genius. M. Neill. il pors *People Wkly* 28:159-61 D 14 '87
They all have high hopes [arts education of mentally retarded at Hope University] E. M. Reingold. il por *Time* 129:61 Mr 2 '87

Save the Children Federation
Bootstrap time in a luckless land [D. Carlson and B. Downing working in Ethiopia] J. Buckley. il pors map *U S News World Rep* 103:88-90+ D 28 '87-Ja 4 '88
How to market good works. J. A. Conway. il *Forbes* 139:10 Mr 23 '87

Save Venice Inc.
Saving la dolce Venice. G. D. Garcia. il *Time* 130:72-3 S 14 '87

Savile Row tailors *See* Tailors—Great Britain

Savimbi, Jonas, 1934-
about
Can this man save Africa? D. Reed. il por *Read Dig* 130:221-2+ My '87
The right's last, best hope. M. Maren. il *Nation* 245:744-6 D 19 '87

Saving and savings
See also
Bank accounts
Finance, Personal
Investments
10 ways to save money if you've always failed before. B. G. Quint. il *Glamour* 85:146+ Ag '87
Are we saving? W. F. Buckley. *Natl Rev* 39:62-3 N 6 '87
A dozen painless ways to help a nest egg grow. P. M. Scherschel. il *U S News World Rep* 102:58+ Je 8 '87
Fighting the urge to splurge. S. Koepp. il *Time* 130:58-61 D 14 '87
Guarding your hard-won wealth. R. Eisenberg. il *Money* 16:62-4+ O '87
How to get Americans to sock away a bit more. B. Nussbaum. il *Bus Week* p86 Ap 13 '87
Kids and college: how to build a nest egg. B. G. Quint. il *Glamour* 85:180 Ap '87
Making the savings rate look good—with mirrors. L. Helm. il *Bus Week* p84 O 12 '87
Much ado about saving. G. P. Brockway. *New Leader* 70:13-14 Jl 13-27 '87
Radical way to save more [big year-end bonus; views of F. Thomas Juster] *USA Today (Periodical)* 116:10 Jl '87
Revisionist thoughts on savings. H. Banks. *Forbes* 140:27 S 7 '87
The safest places to park cash. A. Rock. il *Money* 16:89-90+ D '87
Saving for what future? [perception of nuclear threat and savings habits; study by Joel Slemrod] J. A. Natale. *Psychol Today* 21:16 Ag '87
The saving of America [views of J. Rutledge] P. Brimelow. il por *Forbes* 139:71 Ap 20 '87
Japan
Socking it away in Japan. B. Hillenbrand. il *Time* 130:60 D 14 '87

Savings accounts *See* Bank accounts

Savings and loan associations
See also
Black savings and loan associations
How reliable are savings and loan institutions? T. Tilling. il *Parents* 62:47 D '87
It may be time for S&Ls to just fade away. V. Cahan. il *Bus Week* p52 Je 1 '87
"We're the lifeblood" [regulators turn to money brokers for help with weak thrifts] M. Schifrin. il *Forbes* 140:43-4 Jl 27 '87
What the S&L crisis means to you. il *Money* 16:11 Je '87

Savings and loan associations—*cont.*
Accounting
Bargains and apparent bargains. R. King, Jr. il *Forbes* 140:46+ N 30 '87

Acquisitions and mergers
Bill Simon goes treasure-hunting in the Pacific. T. Carson and C. Debes. il por *Bus Week* p84-6 Mr 9 '87

Booby trap [S. Zell's investment in Freedom Savings & Loan Association] R. King, Jr. *Forbes* 140:48 N 30 '87

An empire rising in the West [work of W. E. Simon] T. McCarroll. il por *Time* 130:42 S 7 '87

Git along, little thrifts [plan for rounding up Texas' ailing S&Ls by M. H. Meyerson and R. E. Rainwater] T. Mason. il por *Bus Week* p33 O 26 '87

Going once, going twice . . . [W. Popejoy's plan for Financial Corp. of America] T. Carson. il por *Bus Week* p102 O 5 '87

Good-bye Peru, hello Peoria [Citicorp buys sick S&Ls] J. Heins. il *Forbes* 140:34-. 28 '87

How playing it safe worked for Great Western. T. Carson. il por *Bus Week* p70 S 7 '87

The king of the S&L's [P. Martin] R. Thomas. il por *Newsweek* 109:52-3 Mr 30 '87

One deal away from being Mr. Megathrift [A. M. Frank of First Nationwide wants Financial Corp. of America] J. B. Levine. il por *Bus Week* p103-4 O 26 '87

Psst! Wanna buy the big daddy of thrifts? [Federal Home Loan Bank Board looking for a buyer of Financial Corp. of America] T. Carson. *Bus Week* p36 Mr 30 '87

Sweet charity. A. A. Lappen. il *Forbes* 140:8 N 2 '87

There may be a buyer for FCA [Financial Corp. of America] T. Carson. *Bus Week* p38-9 Je 8 '87

White knights or black hats? J. Heins. il *Forbes* 140:386+ Jl 13 '87

Why the Bowery deal wasn't a ripoff. S. Bartlett. il *Bus Week* p105 O 19 '87

William Simon's Pacific overtures. L. J. Davis. il pors *N Y Times Mag* p14-17+ D 27 '87

Canada
Victory to the outsiders [Nova Scotia Savings & Loan takeover defense ruled illegal in court] C. Wood. il *Macleans* 100:28 F 16 '87

Federal aid
And you get to pick up the bill. J. Novack. il *Forbes* 139:32-3 My 4 '87

Bonds away at the Bank Board [new issues from The Financing Corp.] V. Cahan. *Bus Week* p102 O 5 '87

Feuding among the ruins of failed thrifts. J. B. Levine. il *Bus Week* p116 My 18 '87

Insurance
See also
Federal Savings and Loan Insurance Corporation

Laws and regulations
See Banks and banking—Laws and regulations

Real estate operations
Deep in the hole in Texas. R. E. Norton. il *Fortune* 115:61-2+ My 11 '87

Oil Patch thrifts are deep in gloom [guidelines for revaluing assets issued by Federal Home Loan Bank Board] T. Vogel. il *Bus Week* p47-8 F 23 '87

An S&L whodunit where everyone's a suspect [Independent American Savings & Loan] J. Weber, Jr. il por *Bus Week* p96-8 Jl 13 '87

The Wright man to see [J. Wright's efforts on behalf of Texas thrifts] R. Thomas and D. Pauly. il por *Newsweek* 109:44-5 Je 29 '87

Securities
Money in the bank. Z. Lazarevic. il *Forbes* 139:114 Je 29 '87

The overlooked bargains in S&L stocks. T. Carson. il *Bus Week* p116 Ja 12 '87

California
See also
Family Savings & Loan Association (Los Angeles, Calif.)
Financial Corp. of America
First Nationwide Financial Corp.
First Nationwide Savings, A Federal Savings & Loan Assoc.
Golden West Financial Corp.
Great Western Financial Corp.
Lincoln Savings & Loan Association

Name recognition [Sears Savings scales back California operations] J. Heins. il *Forbes* 140:137 N 30 '87

Canada
Downfall of a schemer [W. Player's role in Toronto real estate fraud scandal] P. Best. il por *Macleans* 100:32 Jl 20 '87

Florida
See also
Freedom Savings & Loan Association

Georgia
See also
Georgia Federal Bank, FSB

Kansas
See also
Franklin Savings Association

Maryland
See also
Second National Building & Loan Inc.

Massachusetts
See also
Home Owners Federal Savings & Loan Assn.

Nova Scotia
See also
Nova Scotia Savings & Loan Company

Texas
See also
Commodore Savings Association
Independent American Savings & Loan Association
Sunbelt Savings Association of Texas

Deep in the hole in Texas. R. E. Norton. il *Fortune* 115:61-2+ My 11 '87

Git along, little thrifts [plan for rounding up ailing S&Ls by M. H. Meyerson and R. E. Rainwater] T. Mason. il por *Bus Week* p33 O 26 '87

Oil Patch thrifts are deep in gloom [guidelines for revaluing assets issued by Federal Home Loan Bank Board] T. Vogel. il *Bus Week* p47-8 F 23 '87

S&Ls in Wright country [Texas thrifts and House Speaker J. Wright] *Natl Rev* 39:19-20 Ag 28 '87

Savings: the highs of Texas are nearly behind you. il *Money* 16:27 S '87

The Wright man to see [J. Wright's efforts on behalf of Texas thrifts] R. Thomas and D. Pauly. il por *Newsweek* 109:44-5 Je 29 '87

Virginia
See also
Dominion Federal Savings & Loan Assn.

Savings bank life insurance *See* Savings banks—Insurance

Savings banks
See also
Bowery Savings Bank
Carver Federal Savings Bank
College Savings Bank
ComFed Savings Bank
Firstrust Savings Bank
Savings and loan associations
Sears Savings Bank

Insurance
Insurance agents attack New York's savings bank life insurance. *Consum Rep* 52:331 Je '87

Savings bonds *See* Bonds, Government

Savory, Allan
about
In New Mexico: desert healer. G. Ehrlich. il por *Time* 130:10-11 D 7 '87

Savvy (Periodical)
Savvy [article submission policy] M. H. J. Farrell. il *Writer* 100:25 N '87

Saw tables *See* Machinery—Stands, tables, etc.

Sawbucks *See* Sawhorses

Sawhorses
The perfect sawhorse. J. Taylor. il *Ctry J* 14:33-5 O '87

Sawing *See* Saws and sawing

Saws and sawing
See also
Miter boxes, gages, etc.
Wood cutting

2 super scroll saws [Hegner Multimax-2 and RB Industries Hawk 220] J. Gaynor. il *Home Mech* 83:78+ D '87

Chainsaw alternatives. J. Vara. il *Ctry J* 14:19-20 Ag '87

The circular saw. il *Mother Earth News* 103:74-6+ Ja/F '87

Deep-throated scroll saw [Foley Belsaw Model 435] J. W. Hedden. il *Workbench* 43:14 Mr/Ap '87

Electronic radial-arm saw [Sears Craftsman] R. Capotosto. il *Pop Mech* 164:30 My '87

How to buy and use a portable circular saw. R. J. DeCristoforo. il *Home Mech* 83:66-8+ Ap '87

How to succeed on the radial arm saw. A. Rooze. il *Fam Handyman* 37:28+ S '87

Make yourself a panel saw. R. J. DeCristoforo. il *Pop Sci* 231:78-9+ D '87

A new slant on perfect angles: power miter saws. P. McCafferty. il *Pop Sci* 230:94-6 Mr '87

Saws and sawing—*cont.*
Outdoor power tools: buyers guide. M. Thompson. il *Fam Handyman* 37:54-6+ O '87
Power saw secrets [using a portable circular saw] R. Capotosto. il *Pop Mech* 164:85-9 F '87
Sabre saw for homeowners [JSE-60 saw] H. Wicks. il *Home Mech* 83:36 My '87
A saw that does it all—but not well [Wen All Saw 3700] il *Consum Rep* 52:407 Jl '87
Sears radial arm saw. A. Rooze. il *Fam Handyman* 37:66+ Ja '87
Train a table saw for accuracy. R. J. DeCristoforo. il *Workbench* 43:30-1 N/D '87
What to look for in a chain saw. il *Mother Earth News* 107:46-7 S/O '87
What? You don't own a band saw? R. J. DeCristoforo. il *Pop Sci* 230:68-71 My '87

Equipment
Guides, jigs and accessories that let you do more with your circular saw. R. J. DeCristoforo. il *Home Mech* 83:60-2+ Jl '87
Simple hold-down for your table saw. A. J. Hand. il *Pop Sci* 230:98 My '87

Safety devices and measures
Chainsaw safety and the curse of overconfidence. D. Thomas. il *Ctry J* 14:28-9 N '87
Safety first [circular saws] R. J. DeCristoforo. il *Home Mech* 83:70 Ap '87

Stands, tables, etc.
See Machinery—Stands, tables, etc.

Sawyer, Diane
My inspiration. il pors *Saturday Evening Post* 259:50-1 Ap '87

about
Diane Sawyer. por *Harpers Bazaar* 120:238, 358-9 S '87
Out of Africa with Diane Sawyer. M. G. Stoddard. il pors *Saturday Evening Post* 259:52-4+ Ap '87
The Sawyer exception. por *Newsweek* 109:41 Ja 12 '87
Weighed as a future anchor, Diane Sawyer joins TV's million-dollar men's club. J. Hall. il por *People Wkly* 27:30-1 Ja 19 '87

Sawyer, Eugene
about
Eugene Sawyer vows to continue reforms of Mayor Washington. R. E. Johnson. il pors *Jet* 73:4-6+ D 21 '87
Lakeside follies: a machine-made mayor for Chicago. M. Satchell. il por *U S News World Rep* 103:12 D 14 '87
Shaky start. por *Time* 130:36 D 14 '87
Uncle Tom Sawyer. G. Rivlin. *Nation* 245:741 D 19 '87
An unsettling victory. J. McCormick. il por *Newsweek* 110:52 D 14 '87

Sawyer, S. R., and others
Spectrophotometry of Pluto-Charon mutual events: individual spectra of Pluto and Charon. bibl f il *Science* 238:1560-3 D 11 '87

Sawyer-Miller Group
KYW's consultant coup. J. Malanowski. il *Channels* 7:22-3 S '87

Sax, Richard
Salmon-devilishly good. il *Work Woman* 12:159 Mr '87

Saxe, Adrian
about
Stylistic ensembles [cover story] J. B. Mays. il por *Am Craft* 47:42-9 O/N '87

Saxe, Dorothy
about
Glass of the 80s. R. Kehlmann. il pors *Am Craft* 47:32-9 Ap/My '87

Saxe, George
about
Glass of the 80s. R. Kehlmann. il pors *Am Craft* 47:32-9 Ap/My '87

Saxe (George and Dorothy) Collection *See* Glassware—Collectors and collecting

Saxophone music
See also
29th Street Saxophone Quartet
World Saxophone Quartet
Joe Henderson's solo on Song for my father—a tenor saxophone transcription. J. T. Cohen. il *Down Beat* 54:58-9 S '87
Steve Lacy's solo on Skippy—a soprano saxophone transcription. S. Griggs. il *Down Beat* 54:60-2 D '87

Saxophone players
See also
Berne, Tim

Blythe, Arthur
Brecker, Michael
Brötzmann, Peter
Carter, James
Coleman, Ornette
Coltrane, John, 1926-1967
G, Kenny
Garrett, Kenny
Gordon, Dexter
Henderson, Joe
Howard, George
Lacy, Steve
Marsalis, Branford
Mobley, Hank, 1930-1986
Morgan, Frank
Murray, David, 1955-
Parker, Charlie, 1920-1955
Parker, Evan
Smith, Tommy
Watanabe, Sadao

Sayão, Bidú, 1902-
about
Golden days. W. Seward. pors *Opera News* 51:20 F 28 '87

Sayed, Refaat el *See* El Sayed, Refaat
Sayings *See* Quotations
Sayle, Murray
The ballad of Ron and Yasu [cover story] *New Repub* 196:18-21 Je 15 '87

Sayles, Janice Ulm
The watercolor page. il por *Am Artist* 51:38-41+ Ag '87

Sayles, John, 1950-
The Halfway Diner [story] il *Atlantic* 259:59-68 Je '87
about
John Sayles mines new film territory. J. DeLynn. por *Harpers Bazaar* 120:382+ S '87
John Sayles's labor of love. S. G. Freedman. il pors *Roll Stone* p27-8 O 8 '87
Matewan [film] Reviews
Commonweal il 114:626-7 N 6 '87. T. O'Brien
Glamour 85:298 S '87. J. G. Boyum
Horizon il por 30:12-14 S '87. R. Seidenberg
Macleans 100:56 O 12 '87. L. O'Toole
Nation 245:427-8 O 17 '87. M. Margaronis
New Repub 197:24-5 S 7 '87. S. Kauffmann
Newsweek il 110:82 S 14 '87. D. Ansen
People Wkly il 28:12 S 21 '87. R. Novak
Theatre Crafts il 21:45-8 Ap '87. R. Seidenberg
Time il 130:77 S 14 '87. R. Corliss
Sayles talk. R. Seidenberg. il por *Horizon* 30:12-14 S '87

Sayre, Robert F.
The longest war. *Nation* 244:133 F 7 '87
Sayre, Roxanna, d. 1986
about
Obituary
Audubon 89:7 Mr '87. L. Line
SBA *See* United States. Small Business Administration
Sbarro, Inc.
Sbarro's juicy slice of the fast-food market. F. McCoy. il *Bus Week* p72-3 S 7 '87
SBK Entertainment World Inc.
A dealmaker decides there's no biz like show biz [S. C. Swid] M. Frons. il por *Bus Week* p107 My 11 '87
SBLI (Savings bank life insurance) *See* Savings banks—Insurance
SCA subcarriers *See* Radio frequency modulation
Scabs (Strikebreakers) *See* Strikebreakers
Scaffolding
A roof under your feet. D. Osby. il *Mother Earth News* 107:22 S/O '87
Scalapino, Robert A.
Asia's future. *Foreign Aff* 66:77-108 Fall '87
Scalds *See* Burns and scalds
Scales, Junius Irving
about
A southern ex-Communist remembers. B. Summer. *Publ Wkly* 231:55 My 29 '87
Scales, Maurice
about
Maurice Scales—brother of invention. il pors *Ebony* 42:51-2+ O '87
Scales, Peter
Sex, psychology and censorship: preserving the freedoms of the mind. il por *Humanist* 47:18-22+ S/O '87

Scales (Earth sciences) *See* Earth sciences—Measurement

Scales (Weighing instruments)

See also

Balances (Scales)

Scali, McCabe, Sloves, Inc.

C.E.O., TV [F. Perdue's television commercials] T. Whiteside. *New Yorker* 63:39-40+ Jl 6 '87

The sweet smell of success. B. Kanner. il *N Y* 20:16+ Je 1 '87

Scalia, Antonin, 1936-

about

Justice Scalia's misunderstanding. S. J. Gould. il *Nat Hist* 96:14+ O '87

Scallion, Mark

about

Mountie to the rescue. E. Burns. il por *Sports Illus* 66:84 Ja 12 '87

Scallop culture *See* Shellfish culture

Scalp

See also

Baldness

Dandruff

Down to the roots revival. il *Health* 19:41 D '87

Scalp shape-ups. S. Young. il *Glamour* 85:358 Ap '87

Scalping of tickets *See* Ticket selling—Ethical aspects

Scammon, Charles Melville, 1825-1911

about

Captain Scammon: the whaler who turned naturalist. D. Rutherford. il pors map *Sea Front* 33:18-26 Ja/F '87

Scams *See* Fraud

Scandals, Political *See* Politics, Corruption in

Scandinavia

See also

Copyright—Scandinavia

Denmark

Finland

Norway

Public welfare—Scandinavia

Sweden

Commerce

United States

See United States—Commerce—Scandinavia

Defenses

Scandinavians increase defense spending. *Aviat Week Space Technol* 126:96-7 Mr 9 '87

Industries

See also

Phonograph record industry—Scandinavia

SAS

Scandinavian Airlines System *See* SAS

Scandinavian house decoration *See* House decoration, Scandinavian

Scanlan, Tracy

The next generation: can we pull it off? por *Aviat Week Space Technol* 126:111+ Je 1 '87

Scanlon, Terrence M., 1939-

Spring clean up: safety in the yard. *Consum Res Mag* 70:25-7 My '87

Warming up to safe heating. *Consum Res Mag* 70:32-3 F '87

about

Crossing swords over consumer safety. J. P. Shapiro. il por *U S News World Rep* 103:28 O 26 '87

Scanners (Radio receivers) *See* Radio receivers

Scanning systems

See also

Optical scanners

Thermography

Tomography

Scanning X ray microscopes and microscopy *See* X ray microscopes and microscopy

Scarf, Maggie, 1932-

A marriage of fire and ice: a case history [excerpt from Intimate partners] il *Redbook* 168:124-5+ Mr '87

about

PW interviews. E. Gleick. por *Publ Wkly* 231:62-3 F 20 '87

Scarfiotti, Ferdinando

about

California in focus. D. Thomson. il por *House Gard* 159:140-5+ Ag '87

Scarlet gilia

On the benefits of being eaten [herbivory benefits plants; research by Ken Paige and Thomas Whitham] R. Lewin. il *Science* 236:519-20 My 1 '87

Scarves

Aerostich Wind Scarf and Wind Triangle [for motorcyclists] il *Cycle* 38:87 Mr '87

The muffler. J. Berendt. *Esquire* 107:18+ Ja '87

Sexy wrapups: tie one on! il *Harpers Bazaar* 120:156-63 Ap '87

The wrap-up on scarves. il *Mademoiselle* 93:74 Mr '87

Scattering (Physics)

A complete mapping of the proteins in the small ribosomal subunit of Escherichia coli [neutron scattering data] M. S. Capel and others. bibl f il *Science* 238:1403-6 D 4 '87

Neutrons clarify superconductors [ceramic oxides] A. L. Robinson. il *Science* 237:1115-17 S 4 '87

Scavullo, Francesco, 1929-

The character is back! il *Esquire* 107:97-101 Ap '87

Francesco Scavullo: flower photographer. por *Saturday Evening Post* 259:47-9 Jl/Ag '87

Picture perfectionist: my life as a photographer. il por *Saturday Evening Post* 259:50-3+ My/Je '87

SCCA *See* Sports Car Club of America

Scene designers *See* Set designers

Scene designing *See* Motion pictures—Setting and scenery; Opera—Stage setting and scenery; Television broadcasting—Setting and scenery; Theater—Stage setting and scenery

Scene of the crime [film] See Motion picture reviews—Single works

Scenery, Photographic *See* Photography—Setting and scenery

Scenery, Stage *See* Opera—Stage setting and scenery; Television broadcasting—Setting and scenery; Theater—Stage setting and scenery

Scenic rivers *See* Wild and scenic rivers

Scenic views *See* Views (Scenery)

Scent *See* Perfumes

Scent strips (Automobile advertising) *See* Automobile industry—Advertising

Scented plants *See* Plants, Fragrant

Schaap, Dick, 1934-

The death of an athlete. il *Sports Illus* 67:26-8+ Jl 27 '87

Schaap, William H.

The fight in Fiji. *Nation* 244:707 My 30 '87

Schachter, Bill

about

The sleuth who snoops for sloops. B. Rice. il por *50 Plus* 27:76-8+ Je '87

Schaefer, Ernest D.

about

GM's bootstrap battle: the factory-floor view. A. Gabor. il por *U S News World Rep* 103:52-3 S 21 '87

Schaefer, Faith

Sea secrets. See issues of Sea Frontiers beginning January/February 1986

Schaefer, George Anthony, 1928-

about

For Caterpillar, the metamorphosis isn't over. K. Deveny. il *Bus Week* p72-4 Ag 31 '87

George Schaefer. K. Deveny. il por *Bus Week* Sp Issue:258 Ap 17 '87

Schaefer, Jacob, and others

Aromatic cross-links in insect cuticle: detection by solid-state ^{13}C and ^{15}N NMR. bibl f il *Science* 235:1200-4 Mr 6 '87

Schaefer, Morris

Health principles of housing. il *World Health* p18-19 Jl '87

Schaeffer, Edith

Till death do us part. por *Christ Today* 31:20 Mr 6 '87

Schaeffer, Francis A. (Francis August)

about

Till death do us part. E. Schaeffer. por *Christ Today* 31:20 Mr 6 '87

Schaeffer, Pamela

Spirituality in abstract art [cover story] il *Christ Century* 104:819-22 S 30 '87

Schaeffer, Rebecca

about

A breath of fresh air: Rebecca Schaeffer. E. Miller. il pors *Seventeen* 46:61-2+ My '87

Schafer, Kevin

The real birdman of Alcatraz. il pors *Natl Wildl* 25:18-21 Ag/S '87

Schafer, Marilyn

Bay Area spirit. il *House Gard* 159:184-9 O '87

In a glass house. il *House Gard* 159:112-21 F '87

Pacific orientation. il por *House Gard* 159:160-5+ My '87

Second nature. il *House Gard* 159:156-61 Jl '87

Schaller, Jörg

When men and mountains meet. il map *Courier* 40:9-10 F '87

Schama, Simon
Holland's feast of life [excerpt from The embarrassment of riches] il *House Gard* 159:68+ Je '87
Schaper, Richard L.
Pastoral care for persons with AIDS and for their families. il *Christ Century* 104:691-4 Ag 12-19 '87
Schapiro, Mark, and Burnand, Eric
Keeping Faith. *Nation* 244:42 Ja 17 '87
Schapiro, Meyer, 1904-
about
Not just another summer painter. R. B. Woodward. il por *Art News* 86:18+ Summ '87
The scholar-artist: Meyer Schapiro. R. Storr. il por *Art Am* 75:172-3+ O '87
Schar, Dwight C.
about
Pyrrhic possibilities. K. Hannon. il por *Forbes* 139:94 Je 15 '87
Schatzberg, Jerry, 1927-
about
Street smart [film] Reviews
Glamour il 85:243-4 Ap '87. J. G. Boyum
Macleans il 100:54 Ap 20 '87
N Y il 20:89-90 Mr 30 '87. D. Denby
New Yorker 63:82-3 Ap 20 '87. P. Kael
People Wkly il 27:12 Mr 30 '87. P. Travers
Vogue il 177:62 Ap '87. M. Haskell
Schaub, George
Just out. See issues of Popular Photography beginning March 1986 through January 1987
Markets & careers. See issues of Popular Photography beginning February 1987
Schaufuss, Peter
about
Farther from Denmark: the two sides of Peter Schaufuss. M. E. Willis. il pors *Dance Mag* 61:56-9 D '87
Schechter, Bruce
Fractal fairy tales. il *Omni* 10:86-91 O '87
How to make your own superconductors. il *Omni* 10:72-4+ N '87
May the force be with you. il por *Omni* 9:36-8+ Mr '87
Schedules
See also
Airlines—Schedules
Scheduling (Management)
Digging out: what to do when you're snowed under with work. il *Glamour* 85:172 S '87
Scheele, Adele M.
You can get that raise. *Read Dig* 131:55-6+ N '87
Schefer, Dorothy
(jt. auth) See Robinson, Andrea, and Schefer, Dorothy
Schefflera
Scheffleras are old friends. il *South Living* 22:58 D '87
Scheiber, Dave
Muscling her way to the fore. il por *Sports Illus* 67:82 D 14 '87
Turning pain into gain. il pors *Sports Illus* 66:93-4 My 11 '87
Vinny's ship has come in [cover story] il pors *Sports Illus* 67:24-6+ Ag 3 '87
Scheiber, Matt
Advent: is there someone worth waiting for? *U S Cathol* 52:34-5 D '87
Reconciliation rooms: I'd rather be kept in the dark. *U S Cathol* 52:30-2 Ap '87
Scheible, John
Called to broaden my horizon. *Commonweal* 114:523-5 S 25 '87
Schein, Barbara
about
Barbara Schein finally gets a shot at walking the beat. A. Abrahams. il pors *People Wkly* 27:139-40 My 4 '87
Schein, Françoise
about
Françoise Schein at Bette Stoler. J. Crary. il *Art Am* 75:177-8 N '87
Scheina, Robert L.
The Titanic's legacy to safety. il *Sea Front* 33:200-9 My/Je '87
Scheinman, Pamela
Engineering light and movement. bibl f il *Am Craft* 47:22-9+ F/Mr '87
Schele, Linda
Reading Mayan images. il map *Américas* 39:38-43 Mr/Ap '87
Schell, Jessie
A new tradition [story] il *McCalls* 114:78+ Jl '87

Schell, Jonathan, 1943-
The bomb we never see. il *Progressive* 51:25-8 D '87
History in Sherman Park (I). *New Yorker* 62:35-6+ Ja 5 '87
History in Sherman Park (II). *New Yorker* 62:57-8+ Ja 12 '87
Schell, Maximilian, 1930-
about
Marlene [film] Reviews
Macleans il 100:48 Ja 12 '87. L. O'Toole
People Wkly 27:12 Ja 5 '87. P. Travers
USA Today (Periodical) il 115:96 Mr '87. K. R. Hey
Schell, Orville
Look, Mao—no pajamas! il *Women's Sports Fitness* 9:68+ Ag '87
Running dogs and credit cards: class struggle and a Chinese dictionary. il *N Y Times Book Rev* 92:3+ Je 7 '87
Schemmel, William
Birmingham Turf Club. il *Travel Holiday* 168:8-10 Jl '87
European dining. *Travel Holiday* 167:73-6 Mr '87
Gator riding in the Okefenokee. il *Travel Holiday* 168:90+ N '87
(jt. auth) See Bianco, Frank, and Schemmel, William
Schenley Industries, Inc.
The Guinness affair gets curiouser and curiouser [role of M. Riklis and sale of Schenley to Guinness] M. Maremont. *Bus Week* p59-60 My 25 '87
Schepisi, Fred
about
Roxanne [film] Reviews
America 157:66+ Ag 1-8 '87. R. A. Blake
Commonweal 114:387-8 Je 19 '87. T. O'Brien
Macleans il 100:48 Je 29 '87. L. O'Toole
N Y il 20:87+ Je 15 '87. D. Denby
Natl Rev 39:51-2 Jl 31 '87. J. Simon
New Repub 196:24-5 Je 29 '87. S. Kauffmann
New Yorker 63:77-8 Je 15 '87. P. Kael
Newsweek il 109:73 Je 22 '87. D. Ansen
People Wkly il 28:10 Jl 6 '87. P. Travers
Time il 129:74 Je 15 '87. R. Corliss
Scher, Laura S.
about
Laura Scher: doing good business helps good causes. M. Mallory. il por *Bus Week* p76 O 26 '87
Scherer, Barrymore Laurence
Academic questions. il *Opera News* 52:16-18+ N '87
Storyteller. il por *Opera News* 51:32+ Mr 14 '87
Scherer, Mike
New wrinkles in old clothing. il *Sierra* 72:120-4 Ja/F '87
Scherer, Roy See Hudson, Rock, 1925-1985
Schering-Plough Corp.
Devour thy tail. G. Bronson. il pors *Forbes* 140:85+ N 2 '87
Scherman, Tony
This man captured the true sounds of a whole world. il pors *Smithsonian* 18:110-12+ Ag '87
Schiavone Construction Company
"Give me back my reputation!" [ex-Labor Secretary R. Donovan] G. J. Church. il por *Time* 129:31 Je 8 '87
Schick, Kathrine
about
All-American Girl-talk. il por *Teen* 31:68 N '87
Schickel, Richard
No method to his madness [cover story] il pors *Film Comment* 23:11-19 My/Je '87
Schickel, William
about
William Schickel's 'Salvation suite'. J. W. Goetz. il *America* 157:304-5 O 31 '87
Schicketanz, Dale
Arizona territories [photographs] il *Wilderness* 50:41-9 Spr '87
Schiedermayer, David L.
Choices in plague time. il por *Christ Today* 31:20-2 Ag 7 '87
Schieven, G. H. Moriarty- See Moriarty-Schieven, G. H.
Schiff, András, 1953-
about
András Schiff's fresh-sounding Tchaikovsky. R. Freed. *Stereo Rev* 52:71 Mr '87
Schiff, Irwin, 1937-1987
about
The Fat Man: the life and high times of Irwin Schiff [cover story] M. Daly. il pors *N Y* 20:46-61 O 19 '87

Schiff base salts
New materials promise low radar reflectance [retinyl Schiff base salts] il *Aviat Week Space Technol* 126:22-3 My 18 '87
Visions of an invisible aircraft [retinyl Schiff base salts; work of Robert R. Birge and others] il *Sci News* 132:137 Ag 29 '87

Schiffren, Lisa
Kemp's surprising victory. *Natl Rev* 39:37+ Ap 10 '87

Schifrin, Bill
about
Not strictly all business. *New Yorker* 63:27-9 My 25 '87

Schifter, Richard
1986 human rights report released [statement, February 19, 1987] *Dep State Bull* 87:37-8 Ap '87
Human rights and U.S. foreign policy [address, May 18, 1987] *Dep State Bull* 87:75-7 Ag '87
The human rights issue in Korea [statement, May 6, 1987] *Dep State Bull* 87:77-8 Ag '87
Human rights progress in 1986 [address, December 10, 1986] *Dep State Bull* 87:67-9 F '87
Human rights, the Soviet Union, and the Helsinki process [address, January 28, 1987] *Dep State Bull* 87:42-8 Ap '87
The reality about human rights in the U.S.S.R. [address, February 16, 1987] *Dep State Bull* 87:38-41 Ap '87
The Soviet constitution: myth and reality [address, August 10, 1987] *Dep State Bull* 87:34-7 O '87

Schilit, Barry
[Month] weather. See issues of Southern Living

Schiller, F. C. S. (Ferdinand Canning Scott), 1864-1937
about
F.C.S. Schiller: an appreciation. D. Lawson. *Humanist* 47:35 S/O '87

Schiller, Ferdinand Canning Scott See Schiller, F. C. S. (Ferdinand Canning Scott), 1864-1937

Schiller, Herbert I., 1919-
Information: important issue for '88. *Nation* 245:1+ Jl 4-11 '87

Schiller, Riva Berleant- See Berleant-Schiller, Riva

Schiller, Ronald
Unlocking the amazing mystery of our continent. il map *Read Dig* 131:152-6+ S '87

Schilling, Phil
Editorial. See issues of Cycle

Schimmel, Paul
about
Mr. Personality. *New Yorker* 63:25-7 Ap 13 '87

Schindler, Alexander M.
Pursue not just the material [address, May 7, 1987] *Vital Speeches Day* 53:659-60 Ag 15 '87

Schine, Cathleen
A time for watches. il *N Y Times Mag* p14 F 15 '87

Schine, Cathleen, and Denby, David
Entertainment. See issues of McCall's beginning April 1986

Schinella, John R.
about
An auto designer at home. M. Ferrara. il pors *Home Mech* 83:68-9 Jl '87

Schineller, Peter
Learning from missionaries. *America* 156:249-51 Mr 28 '87

Schintzius, Dwayne
about
Big mouth from the South. F. Lidz. il por *Sports Illus* 67 Sp Issue:77 N 18 '87

Schirk, Heinz
about
The Wannsee Conference [film] Reviews
Commonweal 114:749 D 18 '87. T. O'Brien
Macleans 100:67 N 30 '87. L. O'Toole
N Y 20:152+ D 7 '87. D. Denby
Nation 245:767-8 D 19 '87. M. Pally
New Repub 197:26-7 D 7 '87. S. Kauffmann

Schirra, Wally
How to get America back into space. il *Pop Mech* 164:76-8+ Mr '87

Schisgal, Murray, 1926-
about
Road show [drama] Reviews
N Y 20:63 Je 1 '87. J. Simon
Nation 244:860 Je 20 '87. T. M. Disch
New Yorker 63:94 Je 1 '87. E. Oliver

Schistosomiasis
Popular technology beats schisto [Zimbabwe] P. Taylor. il *World Health* p28-9 Jl '87
Schisto comes to town. R. K. Sarda. il *World Health* p27-9 Je '87

Vaccines and vaccination
Immunity to schistosomes: progress toward vaccine. A. Capron and others. bibl f il *Science* 238:1065-72 N 20 '87
Parasite pacification. J. Schecter. map *Technol Rev* 90:10-11 O '87

Schizophrenia
Biological issues in schizophrenia. D. M. Barnes. bibl f il *Science* 235:430-3 Ja 23 '87
Her own mental illness behind her, a young doctor reaches out to the victims of schizophrenia; ed. by Giovanna Breu. C. S. North. il por *People Wkly* 28:127-8+ N 9 '87
Hushing the voices schizophrenics hear [work of Peter Bick and Marcel Kinsbourne] *Discover* 8:4-5 Ap '87
Profiles [L. and K. Looper run the Chateau, a board-and-care home for schizophrenics in San Francisco] B. Barich. il *New Yorker* 63:51-2+ O 12 '87
Viral exposure boosts schizophrenia risk [research by Sarnoff A. Mednick and others] B. Bower. *Sci News* 132:180 S 19 '87

Therapy
Low-dose caveat for schizophrenia [research by Stephen R. Marder and others] B. Bower. *Sci News* 131:374 Je 13 '87
Madness in the family. N. Harlow. il *Redbook* 169:130-1+ My '87
Sanity saver [clozapine; study by Herbert Y. Meltzer] M. Mintzer. il *Health* 19:17 S '87
Schizophrenia: new hope from an old drug [clozapine] B. Bower. *Sci News* 131:324 My 23 '87

Schlaerth, Katherine
Secrets of enormous families. il *Parents* 62:114-19+ D '87

Schlafly, Phyllis, and Weyrich, Paul
Disowning the Surgeon General. *Harpers* 275:16-17 Ag '87

Schlage Lock Co.
To catch a thief. E. Paris. il *Forbes* 140:92-3 Ag 24 '87

Schlatter, Thomas
Weather queries. See issues of Weatherwise

Schlechty, Phillip C., and Ingwerson, Donald W.
A proposed incentive system for Jefferson County teachers. il *Phi Delta Kappan* 68:585-90 Ap '87

Schlem, Paul
about
Paul Schlem uncorks a turnaround plan. J. O. Hamilton. il por *Bus Week* p102 S 28 '87

Schlenker, Karen
Frost boils. il *Ctry J* 14:71-4 Ap '87

Schlesinger, Arthur M., 1917-
A Democrat looks at foreign policy. *Foreign Aff* 66:263-83 Wint '87/'88
The imperial temptation: Reagan's presidency succumbs. *New Repub* 196:17 Mr 16 '87
Lincoln: fiction & fact [interview with W. Safire] il pors *Am Herit* 38:84-9 D '87
about
The Schlesinger thesis. K. S. Lynn. *Commentary* 83:46-52 Mr '87

Schlesinger, Helmut
about
The Bundesbank's hardliner has a change of heart. B. Riemer. il por *Bus Week* p32 D 14 '87

Schlesinger, Ibis
(jt. auth) See James, John, 1946-, and Schlesinger, Ibis

Schlesinger, James R.
Reykjavik and revelations: a turn of the tide? *Foreign Aff* 65 Sp Issue:426-46 ['87]
about
Bugproofing the embassy. il por *Time* 130:14 Jl 13 '87

Schlesinger, John, 1926-
about
The believers [film] Reviews
Newsweek 109:66 Je 29 '87. D. Ansen
People Wkly il 27:12 Je 22 '87. P. Travers
Time il 129:76 Je 22 '87. R. Schickel
Vogue il 177:36 Jl '87. M. Haskell

Schlessman, Mark A., 1952-
Gender modification in North American ginsengs. bibl f il *BioScience* 37:469-75 Jl/Ag '87

Schleswig-Holstein (Germany)
Politics and government
A deadly game of dirty tricks [suspicious circumstances surrounding death of U. Barschel] S. Seibert. il *Newsweek* 110:49 O 26 '87

Schley, Reeve
about
Reeve Schley III. M. Mathews-Berenson. il *Am Artist*
51:70-3+ N '87
Schloesser, Jeffrey
U.S. policy in the Persian Gulf. maps *Dep State Bull*
87:38-44 O '87
Schlöndorff, Volker
about
Black like Mich. A. Horton. il por *Film Comment* 23:8-9
Mr/Ap '87
Das Schloss [opera] See Laporte, André, 1931-
Schlossberg, Nancy K., 1929-
Taking the mystery out of change. bibl (p94-5) *Psychol
Today* 21:74-5 My '87
Schlozman, Kay L., and Verba, Sidney
Sending messages, getting replies. *Society* 24:48-55 My/Je
'87
Schlumberger Ltd.
Euan Baird. J. Rossant. il por *Bus Week* Sp Issue:264
Ap 17 '87
From Reds to riches—and now red ink. K. R. Sheets.
il *U S News World Rep* 102:44-5 Mr 9 '87
What the Fairchild fiasco signals for trade policy [Fujitsu
deal collapses] J. W. Wilson and S. J. Dryden. il
Bus Week p28 Mr 30 '87
Schmemann, Serge
Glasnost: between hope and history. il *N Y Times Book
Rev* 92:12-13 Ap 26 '87
Schmertz, Mildred F.
Editorial. See issues of Architectural Record beginning
October 1985
Schmid, Judith
Fit feet. il *Vogue* 177:246-7+ Je '87
Schmidgall, Gary
Can do [special section] il *Opera News* 52:12-16+ O
'87
Dramatic leanings. por *Opera News* 51:21-2 Ja 31 '87
Our favorite force of nature. il pors *Opera News* 52:20-2+
Jl '87
Schmidinger, Kim
about
The M & M kids. D. B. Witchel. il pors *Skiing* 39:137-8+
Ja '87
Schmidinger, Krista
about
The M & M kids. D. B. Witchel. il pors *Skiing* 39:137-8+
Ja '87
Schmidt, Edward, Jr.
Georgia on your mind. il *World Tennis* 35:62-3 Ag
'87
Schmidt, Helmut, 1918-
Europe should begin to assert itself. il *World Press
Rev* 34:21-3 F '87
The 'zero option'—a Western idea. il *World Press Rev*
34:28-30 Jl '87
Schmidt, J. M., and Smith, J. J. B.
Short interval time measurement by a parasitoid wasp.
bibl f il *Science* 237:903-5 Ag 21 '87
Schmidt, Mark T.
(jt. auth) See Hannibal, Joseph T., and Schmidt, Mark
T.
Schmidt, Michelle
Sunday brunch with friends. il *Work Woman* 12:82-4+
Ja '87
Schmidt, Mike, 1949-
about
Master of swat [cover story] G. Waggoner. il pors *Esquire*
107:139-40+ My '87
Schmidt, Peggy
Warning: men at work may be hazardous to your career.
il *Mademoiselle* 93:178-9+ D '87
Schmidt, Robert J., and others
Transposon tagging and molecular analysis of the maize
regulatory locus opaque-2. bibl f il *Science* 238:960-3
N 13 '87
Schmidt, Scott
about
Cliff jumper. E. Perlman. il por *Skiing* 40:34 O '87
Schmidt, Stuart, and Kipnis, David
The perils of persistence. bibl (p65) il *Psychol Today*
21:32+ N '87
Schmidt cameras *See* Cameras
Schmieler, George
about
Writer Marjorie Holmes celebrates a marriage made
in heaven and set to words and music in Pittsburgh.
K. McMurran. il pors *People Wkly* 28:115-16+ N 2
'87

Schmit, Randall
about
Randall Schmit at Tilden-Foley. M. E. Vetrocq. il *Art
Am* 75:145 Ja '87
Schmit, Robert
about
French virtuosity at Galerie Schmit. J. A. Cuadrado.
il por *Archit Dig* 44:86+ Je '87
Schmitt, Carl, 1888-1985
about
Legality, legitimacy, and Carl Schmitt. P. Gottfried. *Natl
Rev* 39:52-4 Ag 28 '87
Schmitt, Jack
(tr) See Neruda, Pablo, 1904-1973. Birds of a poet's
native land
Schmoke, Kurt
about
Baltimore may elect first black mayor, 37-year-old atty.
Kurt L. Schmoke. il por *Jet* 73:4 O 5 '87
Holy Schmoke! il por *Time* 130:25 S 28 '87
Kurt Schmoke takes oath as first black elected mayor
of Baltimore, Md. il por *Jet* 73:12 D 28 '87-Ja 4
'88
Schmugge, Fred
Campbell's primordial soup: spontaneous generation: a
danger in canned foods? *Harpers* 274:18 My '87
Schnabel, Artur, 1882-1951
about
Edward Rothstein on music. *New Repub* 197:26-8 Ag
10-17 '87
Schnabel, Julian
about
Art smart. il *Harpers Bazaar* 121:122 N '87
The artist as entrepreneur [cover story] R. Hughes. *New
Repub* 197:24-5+ D 14 '87
The four brushmen of the apocalypse. L. Hirschberg.
il pors *Esquire* 107:76-84+ Mr '87
The hunger artist. K. Larson. il *N Y* 20:88-9 N 30
'87
Julian Schnabel at Pace. P. Schjeldahl. il *Art Am* 75:129-30
Ja '87
A painter's pratfall. M. Stevens. il por *Newsweek* 110:115+
N 16 '87
Running on empty. M. Stevens. *New Repub* 196:25-8
Ja 19 '87
Schnapf, Julie L., and Baylor, Denis A.
How photoreceptor cells respond to light. bibl (p128)
il *Sci Am* 256:40-7 Ap '87
Schnarre, Monika
about
The super models [cover story; special section] il pors
Macleans 100:36-42+ Ap 13 '87
Supermodel Monika Schnarre. M. J. Coughlin. il pors
Seventeen 46:192-5 Ap '87
Schneerson, Menachem M.
about
'Farbrengen' my baby back home. M. Pally. il por *Film
Comment* 23:75-7 My/Je '87
Schneider, Dick, 1922-
Catherine Marshall remembered. il por *Saturday Evening
Post* 259:55+ Ap '87
Schneider, Elizabeth
A citrus sampler. il *Gourmet* 47:60-3+ Ja '87
Nutmeg. il *Gourmet* 47:86-7+ D '87
Schneider, Jason
Home on the solid-fuel range: an introduction to wood
and coal cookstoves. il *Ctry J* 14:36-41 O '87
Schneider, Marijo Despréaux
(tr) See Boulanger, Daniel. Short stories: weapons of
pessimists
Schneider, Mark L.
Health as a bridge for peace. il *World Health* p4-6
O '87
Schneider, Nicholas M., and others
Eclipse measurements of Io's sodium atmosphere. bibl
f il *Science* 238:55-8 O 2 '87
Schneider, Peter, 1940-
Hitler's shadow. il *Harpers* 275:49-54 S '87
The light at the end of the novel; tr. by Leigh Hafrey.
il *N Y Times Book Rev* 92:1+ Jl 26 '87
Lost innocents: the myth of missing children. il *Harpers*
274:47-53 F '87
Schneider, Phyllis
A new parenting style takes hold. *Work Woman* 12:117
D '87
What it's like to adopt. il por *Parents* 62:167-70+ N
'87
Schneider, Richard H. *See* Schneider, Dick, 1922-
Schneider, Stephen Henry
Climate modeling [cover story] il *Sci Am* 256:72-8+
My '87

Schneider, Susan
"I deserve a change". il pors *Redbook* 168:82-5 Ja '87
(ed) See Siegel, Bernie S. Three medical miracles: the
medicine was love
Schneider, William, 1944-
The cynic route. *New Repub* 196:12-13 Ja 19 '87
The Democrats in '88 [cover story] il *Atlantic* 259:37-44+
Ap '87
The new shape of American politics. il *Atlantic* 259:39-48+
Ja '87
The Republicans in '88. il *Atlantic* 260:58-62+ Jl '87
Schneier, Donna
about
Going for the gold in jewelry. M. I. Finney. il por
Nations Bus 75:71 Ja '87
Schneller, Johanna
Framed! il *Seventeen* 46:122-3+ O '87
Schnepper, Jeff A.
Money and taxes. il *USA Today (Periodical)* 115:69
Ja '87
Whither social security? il *USA Today (Periodical)* 116:21
N '87
Schnick, James
about
Auguries of innocence. L. Zuckerman. il por *Time* 130:21
O 19 '87
A shocking arrest breaks the case of a Missouri farm
family's murder—and rescues a boy's reputation. M.
Green. il pors *People Wkly* 28:101-2+ O 26 '87
Schnitzer, Rob
about
Managing the needs of others. P. Honan. il por *Pers
Comput* 11:164-5 O '87
Schnurnberger, Lynn
Eight days a week. il *N Y* 20:88-99 N 23 '87
Kids: what to do with them, where to do it. il *N
Y* 20:114+ Je 29-Jl 6 '87
The new rectangle. il *Glamour* 85:240+ N '87
Shopping without tears (or tantrums). il *Parents* 62:88-92
My '87
Stamina! How to get it, how to keep it. il *Ladies Home
J* 104:56+ O '87
Those terrific karate kids. il *Parents* 62:150-4 N '87
Weekend getaways. il *Parents* 62:227-9+ O '87
You can lead a kid to culture . . . il *Parents* 62:122-4+
D '87
Schnurr, Eileen
Tenants, anyone? il *Work Woman* 12:167+ N '87
Schock, Dixie
"I had in vitro quadruplets"; ed. by Ann Schrader.
il por *Redbook* 170:41+ D '87
Schocken Books Inc.
Random buys Schocken for unit of Pantheon. *Publ Wkly*
232:101 Jl 24 '87
Schoellhorn, Robert Albert
Medical technology [address, October 14, 1987] *Vital
Speeches Day* 54:122-5 D 1 '87
Schoemaker, Hubert J. P.
about
In treatment, Centocor is breaking new ground. C. S.
Eklund. il por *Bus Week* p91 Je 1 '87
Schoen, John W., and others
Last stronghold of the grizzly. il map *Nat Hist* 96:50-61
Ja '87
Schoen, William J.
about
Healthy profits. M. Fritz. il por *Forbes* 140:454 Jl 13
'87
Schoenberg, Arnold, 1874-1951
about
Atonal music and its limits. N. M. Ribe. *Commentary*
84:49-54 N '87
Schoener, Thomas W., 1943-, and Spiller, David A.
Effect of lizards on spider populations: manipulative
reconstruction of a natural experiment. bibl f il *Science*
236:949-52 My 22 '87
Schoenfield, Howard
about
Break point [interview] J. E. Loehr. il *World Tennis*
34:10-12 Ja '87
Schoenhut, Albert
about
Schoenhut's wooden animals. C. P. Hutton. il *Antiques
Collect Hobbies* 92:40-2+ Ag '87
Schoenstein, Ralph, 1933-
Who does know Marilyn? por *Publ Wkly* 231:82 Ja
9 '87
Schoenthal, Robert
about
The young turks making over L.F. Rothschild. C. Farrell.
il pors *Bus Week* p58-9 Ag 31 '87

Schofield, Norma Nixon
Caracas. il *Black Enterp* 17:35-6 My '87
Schofield, William
Beyond the purchase of friendship. *Society* 24:69-75
Mr/Ap '87
Scholarly publishing
See also
University presses
Scholarly publishing (Periodical)
The UPs' own journal. il *Publ Wkly* 231:38 Je 5 '87
Scholars
See also
Intellectuals and intellectual life
1837. K. Ide. il por *Am Herit* 38:107-8 Jl/Ag '87
Where would Emerson find his scholar now? [adaptation
of address, June 1987] A. Kazin. il *Am Herit* 38:93-6
D '87
Scholarship *See* Learning and scholarship
Scholarships and fellowships
See also
Lois Young-Thomas Scholarship and Leadership
Guild
National Urban Fellows
Rhodes scholars and scholarships
Science—Scholarships and fellowships
Thurgood Marshall Black Education Fund
30 super scholarships. I. Fiddler. *Seventeen* 46:120-1+
Ja '87
1988 scholarship guide [women athletes] il *Women's
Sports Fitness* 9:51-7+ D '87
Cleveland pays for its A's [Scholarship-in-Escrow
Program] il *Newsweek* 110:66 Ag 31 '87
Coca-Cola USA awards seven scholarships in Black
History sweepstakes [Black History Month "Share the
Dream" sweepstakes] il *Jet* 72:26-7 Jl 6 '87
Coming: student Nobelists [American Nobel Fellowships]
Sci News 131:57 Ja 24 '87
Democrats award King Scholarships to 5 youths. *Jet*
72:8 Mr 30 '87
Hidden money [sources for women] A. Simpson. il *Ms*
16:74 O '87
How to get a piece of the $21 billion scholarship pie.
R. E. McKinney. bibl il *Ebony* 43:124+ D '87
Perfect match [MVP Athletic Network links women
athletes with scholarships] il *Women's Sports Fitness*
9:58 F '87
Richie rewards Miami student as 1st 'Scholar' [Lionel
Richie Scholar] il pors *Jet* 72:56 Jl 20 '87
Scholarship fund honors Dr. Edith Irby Jones. *Jet* 72:12
Jl 20 '87
Scholarship update: hunting college cash? B. L. Phillips.
Seventeen 46:109 O '87
Scholarships given in honor of Daisy Bates and her
late husband. *Jet* 72:23 Ag 3 '87
Scholarships well worth a try. H. Manley. il *Good
Housekeep* 205:205 Jl '87
Sports: new path to college for women. il *Ebony* 42:27-8+
Ap '87
Tapping into "no need" scholarships [college money]
J. Yonan. il *Changing Times* 41:97-8+ O '87
Worlds of Curls present college scholarship awards. il
Jet 72:13 Ag 31 '87
Taxation
The IRS goes to college—to collect. G. W. Padwe. il
Nations Bus 75:70 Jl '87
Scholastic Aptitude Test
Are more blacks bound for college? [rising SAT scores]
il *U S News World Rep* 103:13 O 5 '87
Are the SATs unfair? C. Ingham. il *Seventeen* 46:142-3+
O '87
Black critics blast bias of SAT, ACT college test. *Jet*
71:40 Mr 9 '87
Blacks' scores still lag despite big rise, Stewart [views
of Donald M. Stewart] il *Jet* 73:36 O 12 '87
Coaching for SAT tests. M. Conroy. il *Better Homes
Gard* 65:105-6 N '87
Cramming for college [coaching courses to boost SAT
and ACT scores] K. McCormick. il *Changing Times*
41:61+ S '87
No mistake, these five kids have all the answers: they
scored perfect 1600s on their SAT exams. M. Small.
il *People Wkly* 27:63-4+ Je 8 '87
A rejection slip for the SAT. *Newsweek* 109:71 Ap 27
'87
The SAT pill [beta blockers quell anxiety] *Newsweek*
110:103 N 16 '87
SAT scores rise for black students. *Newsweek* 110:92
O 5 '87
SAT's, school by school. il *U S News World Rep* 103:90
O 26 '87

Scholastic Aptitude Test—*cont.*
Testing . . . testing [alleged sexism in scholastic testing] D. Seligman. il *Fortune* 115:153-4 My 11 '87
"This isn't school" [Princeton Review] B. Kallen. il por *Forbes* 140:246+ N 16 '87

Scholastic Awards
1987 Scholastic Writing Awards. *Sch Update* 119:TE9-TE11 My 18 '87

Scholastic Inc.
Scholastic to go private through $84 million buyout. *Publ Wkly* 231:10 Je 26 '87

Scholastic Lorimar (Firm)
Scholastic leaves Lorimar, sets up label at IVE. *Publ Wkly* 232:137-8 S 18 '87

Scholastic sports America [television program] See Television program reviews—Single works

Scholastic update (Periodical)
From the editor. D. Goddy. *Sch Update* 120:3 S 4 '87

Scholem, Gershom Gerhard, 1897-1982
about
A fateful intellectual friendship. E. Rothstein. *Commentary* 84:41-9 D '87

Scholer, Jeannette F.
A question of faith. *Christ Century* 104:237-8 Mr 11 '87

Scholz, Kenneth P., and Byrne, John H.
Long-term sensitization in Aplysia: biophysical correlates in tail sensory neurons. bibl f il *Science* 235:685-7 F 6 '87

Scholz, Uwe
about
Reviews:
Performances of works by U. Scholz. H. Koegler. *Dance Mag* 61:27-8 F '87

Schombert, James
Surveying the northern sky. il *Sky Telesc* 74:128-31 Ag '87

Schomburg Center for Research in Black Culture
Recovering black history [G. Parris; cover story] J. W. Donohue. *America* 157:35-7 Jl 18-25 '87

Schön, Nancy
about
Boston makes way for ducklings: the Mallard family in bronze. A. Meeker. il *Publ Wkly* 232:27 O 30 '87

Schönberg, Arnold See Schoenberg, Arnold, 1874-1951

School, Choice of
Choosing a preschool. M. Mohler. il *Ladies Home J* 104:86 My '87
The new common school. C. L. Glenn. il *Phi Delta Kappan* 69:290-4 D '87
[School choice; special section] bibl f il *Phi Delta Kappan* 68:746-69 Je '87

School, Readiness for See Readiness for school
School activities See Student activities
School administration See School management and organization

School administrators
See also
School superintendents and principals
Women school administrators
Standards are changing for school administrators [results of survey] R. P. Gousha and others. *Educ Dig* 53:25-7 S '87

School age
See also
Readiness for school
A national cutoff date for entering kindergarten. R. Lofthouse. *Educ Dig* 53:44-5 N '87
Public school for four-year-olds. J. L. Hymes. *Educ Dig* 53:47-9 O '87

School and social and economic problems
See also
Children of migrant laborers—Education
School children—Social and economic status
Socially handicapped children—Education
Character education and clinical intervention: a paradigm shift for U.S. schools. P. London. bibl f il *Phi Delta Kappan* 68:667-73 My '87

School and the community
See also
Colleges and universities—Public relations
Community education
School buildings—Extended use
Volunteer service
The 19th annual Gallup poll of the public's attitudes toward the public schools. A. Gallup and D. L. Clark. *Phi Delta Kappan* 69:17-30 S '87
Are schools a scandal? [results of survey] I. Groller. il *Parents* 62:33 N '87

Community as social capital: James S. Coleman on Catholic schools. A. M. Greeley. *America* 157:110-12 Ag 29-S 5 '87
Differences between educators and the public on questions of education policy. S. M. Elam. il *Phi Delta Kappan* 69:294-6 D '87
Local opinion polling for educators. J. E. Walker. *Educ Dig* 53:26-9 D '87
The Minnesota dialogue on education. R. E. Randall. il *Phi Delta Kappan* 68:539-43 Mr '87
One community's response to the dropout problem [Erwin, N.C.] G. H. Arnold and V. Biggers. *Phi Delta Kappan* 68:708-9 My '87
A reading program that works as a community effort [Reading Incentive Program at Samuel Bowles School in Springfield, Mass.] M. R. McGrath. il *Phi Delta Kappan* 68:475-6 F '87
State and local arts councils: what role? [special issue] bibl f *Des Arts Educ* 88:2-48 N/D '86

School and the home
See also
Home education
Parents' and teachers' associations
School management and organization—Parent participation
A,B,C, or F: test your child's school. V. Cobb. il *Parents* 62:138-42+ N '87
Child-custody issues and the schools. A. H. Hempe and W. Decker. *Educ Dig* 53:50-1 O '87
A child resource policy beyond school and family. S. B. Heath and M. W. McLaughlin. *Educ Dig* 53:19-21 O '87
A child resource policy: moving beyond dependence on school and family [cover story] S. B. Heath and M. W. McLaughlin. bibl f il *Phi Delta Kappan* 68:576-80 Ap '87
Children's math aptitude linked to mom's attitude. il *Jet* 71:39 F 9 '87
Choice: the parents' perspective. V. D. Mueller. *Phi Delta Kappan* 68:761-2 Je '87
Dealing with child's low grades. il *USA Today (Periodical)* 115:11 Ap '87
Helping your child with homework [excerpt from Your child's growing mind] J. M. Healy. il *Good Housekeep* 205:114 S '87
Learning begins at home. D. F. Bjorklund and B. Bjorklund. il *Parents* 62:214 O '87
Let's not throw out the baby with the bath water [discussion of April 1987 article, A child resource policy: moving beyond dependence on school and family] S. B. Heath and M. W. McLaughlin. bibl f *Phi Delta Kappan* 68:784-6 Je '87
A note for the teacher. S. Evans. il *Parents* 62:90-2 S '87
Parental separation and school problems. F. Roberts. *Parents* 62:53 D '87
Schools and single parents. J. Barney and J. Koford. *Educ Dig* 53:40-3 O '87
Teachers can help parents with educational choices. D. Elkind. *Educ Dig* 52:24-6 Ap '87
Tutoring: when parent and teacher disagree. F. Roberts. *Parents* 62:48+ Ja '87
"We have a problem". J. Marks. il *Parents* 62:60+ N '87
Why Johnny drops out [interview with J. S. Coleman] B. Leonard. il por *Forbes* 140:242+ N 16 '87
Why smart kids get bad grades and what parents can do about it. P. Krantz. il *Better Homes Gard* 65:62+ F '87

School architecture See School buildings
School art See Art—Study and teaching
School athletics
See also
Basketball, High school
College athletics
Football, High school
Physical education and training
Track and field athletics
The crisis in athletics [liability insurance crisis] F. Roberts. *Parents* 62:50+ My '87

Accidents and injuries
Mounting injury toll [high school athletes; views of National Athletic Trainers' Association] il *USA Today (Periodical)* 116:14-15 D '87

Ethical aspects
Anecdotes, facetiae, satire, etc.
Setting things right in school. G. V. Griffith. por *Newsweek* 110:16-17 S 21 '87

School attendance
See also
Dropouts

School attendance—*cont.*

Anecdotes, facetiae, satire, etc.

"Please ackuse me . . . " [absentees' excuses] D. Flynn. il *Seventeen* 46:178 S '87

School bands *See* Bands (Music)

School boards

ACLU sues to end school bd. appointments in Va. [black discrimination cited] *Jet* 73:37 N 2 '87

Arts education, the board of education, and you. W. B. Newman. *Des Arts Educ* 89:34-7 N/D '87

Black elected president of Cleveland school board [S. E. Tolliver] *Jet* 71:5 F 2 '87

State/local boards [special section] il *Phi Delta Kappan* 69:53-68 S '87

Superintendent-school board conflict: working it out. J. G. Hayden. *Educ Dig* 52:11-13 Ap '87

What makes an effective school board? *Educ Dig* 52:6-10 Ap '87

Why your school board needs you. R. Fletcher. il *Parents* 62:78+ O '87

School books *See* Textbooks

School buildings

See also

Classrooms

Designing schools for changing needs. B. A. Jilk. *Educ Dig* 53:12-13 N '87

A new season for schools [with introd. by Herbert L. Smith, Jr.] il *Archit Rec* 175:87-101 S '87

Perfect pitch [St. Thomas Choir School, New York City] P. M. Sachner. il *Archit Rec* 175:116-19 N '87

Community use

See School buildings—Extended use

Extended use

Project Day-care [views of E. F. Zigler] R. J. Trotter. bibl (p63) il pors *Psychol Today* 21:32-8 D '87

Laws and regulations

Asbestos: a back-to-school hazard. J. L. Sheler. *U S News World Rep* 103:33 S 14 '87

School buildings, Remodeled

Recycled schools [conversion into housing] M. Sinclair. *50 Plus* 27:17-18 Jl '87

Surplus schools can serve the community [housing for the elderly] K. Noyes. il *Aging* no356:13-16 '87

School buses

Safety belts

School bus safety—are seat belts necessary? F. Roberts. il *Parents* 62:67 Mr '87

Seats

Are kids better off backward on the bus? *Prevention* 39:21 Ja '87

School censorship *See* Censorship

School children

See also

Children, Gifted

High school students

Readiness for school

School phobia

Teachers and students

School days. F. Roberts. See issues of Parents beginning January 1983

Adjustment

Coping with the ways students cope with homework. T. N. Turner. *Educ Dig* 52:32-5 Ja '87

The first day of school. P. S. Guthrie. il *Ladies Home J* 104:47-50+ S '87

Helping biracial children adjust. T. J. Buttery. *Educ Dig* 52:38-41 My '87

Teaching "entry" behavior to elementary schoolers [approaching a play group] G. L. Macklem. *Educ Dig* 53:40-3 N '87

Health and hygiene

See also

Public schools—Medical care

An AIDS patient's fight for life [R. White] M. Nichols. il por *Sch Update* 119:4 Ap 20 '87

Do AIDS teens have a right to school? D. Sussman. il *Sch Update* 120:27 O 16 '87

No escaping the dilemma of kids with AIDS in school. M. Kaus. il *Newsweek* 110:52-3 S 7 '87

Threats stalk the victims of a plague [perceived danger of AIDS in the classroom] N. Underwood. il *Macleans* 100:50+ O 5 '87

Nutrition

See School lunches

Punishment

See School discipline

Reading

See Children's reading

Social and economic status

The social impact of ability grouping [research by Linda Grant and James Rothenberg] G. W. Bracey. il *Phi Delta Kappan* 68:701-2 My '87

Uniforms

See School uniforms

School children and drugs *See* Drugs and youth

School contests

See also

Odyssey of the Mind

School counseling *See* Educational counseling

School counselors *See* Educational counselors

School discipline

See also

Corporal punishment

Student suspension and expulsion

After-school discussion helps problem students [program at Central High School in Indianapolis] W. Bourke and R. D. Furniss. il *Phi Delta Kappan* 69:241-2 N '87

Antismoking policies can work in schools. M. C. Rist. *Educ Dig* 52:53-5 Ap '87

Behavior pills [disciplining unruly kids with Ritalin] E. Salholz. il *Newsweek* 109:76 Ap 20 '87

Dealing with youth gangs in the schools. D. Stover. *Educ Dig* 52:30-3 F '87

Discipline: what's the school's role? F. Roberts. il *Parents* 62:52 N '87

Educators and police working together. P. Blauvelt. *Educ Dig* 53:26-9 N '87

School enrollment

Mass production doesn't always work [providing smaller schools] J. LaBate. por *U S News World Rep* 103:5 S 14 '87

School equipment *See* School furniture, equipment, etc.

School evaluation *See* Education—Evaluation

School finance *See* Education—Finance

School furniture, equipment, etc.

Sprucing up the classroom [PTA projects] F. Roberts. il *Parents* 62:58 Ap '87

School gardens and gardening

How zucchini won 5th-grade hearts [Arizona program; cover story] D. Cavaliere. il *Child Today* 16:18-21 My/Je '87

'My favorite subject is gardening!' [California programs] G. Hanauer. il *Rodale's Org Gard* 34:42+ Ap '87

The wonders of gardening . . . in a saucer [kindergarten project] il *Sunset* 179:90-1 O '87

School grades *See* Grading and marking (Students)

School insurance *See* Insurance, School

School journalism *See* College and school journalism

School laws and regulations *See* Educational laws and regulations

School lunches

Packed with love: lunch-box food kids will eat. H. Garrison. il *Parents* 62:167-70+ S '87

Anecdotes, facetiae, satire, etc.

Deliverance [memories of frozen sandwiches for school lunches] C. Murphy. il *Atlantic* 260:22+ N '87

School management and organization

See also

Class size

Crisis management in education

School administrators

School boards

School discipline

School superintendents and principals

Women school administrators

Beating back the education 'blob'. L. Solórzano. il *U S News World Rep* 102:74 Ap 27 '87

A "culture of concern" for at-risk students. R. Valdivieso. *Educ Dig* 52:29-31 Ja '87

The human dimension of data-based decision making [interview with Newman Walker] D. B. Strother. il por *Phi Delta Kappan* 68:470-3 F '87

An inside view of change in schools. E. E. Eubanks and R. Parish. il *Phi Delta Kappan* 68:610-15 Ap '87

Is in loco parentis dead? P. A. Zirkel and H. F. Reichner. bibl f il *Phi Delta Kappan* 68:466-9 F '87

The paper chase [bureaucratic obstacles to obtaining a proper toilet paper dispenser for the teachers' restroom] S. Ohanian. il *Phi Delta Kappan* 69:153-5 O '87

School management and organization—*cont.*
A short perspective on educational administration. W. L. Royer. il *Phi Delta Kappan* 69:145-6 O '87
What education reform? [local reforms preferred over state mandates] P. Welsh. *Educ Dig* 52:6-9 F '87
Parent participation
Involving low-income parents in the schools: a role for policy? M. W. McLaughlin and P. M. Shields. bibl f il *Phi Delta Kappan* 69:156-60 O '87
Reauthorizing or restructuring Chapter 1? [parent involvement] A. C. Lewis. il *Phi Delta Kappan* 69:4-5 S '87
Why your school board needs you. R. Fletcher. il *Parents* 62:78+ O '87
Student participation
School rules: who makes 'em? Who breaks 'em? S. Rubin. il *Teen* 31:72+ O '87
Teacher participation
Bureaucracy and the neutering of teachers [study of urban teachers; cover story] J. R. Frymier. il *Phi Delta Kappan* 69:8-14 S '87
Raises, reform and respect. J. N. Baker. il *Newsweek* 110:92 O 5 '87
Restructuring teaching: a call for research. M. H. Futrell. *Educ Dig* 53:2-5 S '87
Something is missing from the education reform movement [lesson of open education] M. Henley. il *Phi Delta Kappan* 69:284-5 D '87
Teacher "professionalization" versus democratic control. L. Darling-Hammond. *Educ Dig* 53:15-17 S '87
Teachers are writing the ABCs of school reform. J. Tasini. il *Bus Week* p74-5 S 7 '87
Teachers fight for control of their own profession [School Improvement Project in Alexandria, Va.] P. Welsh. *Educ Dig* 53:18-21 S '87
Teaching reform in an active voice [role of teacher unions] S. M. Johnson and N. C. W. Nelson. bibl f il *Phi Delta Kappan* 68:591-8 Ap '87
School medical care *See* Public schools—Medical care
School music
See also
    Bands (Music)
    National Association of School Music Dealers
School newspapers *See* College and school journalism
School of American Ballet
Dressing up [workshop performances] T. Tobias. il *N Y* 20:64-5 Je 22 '87
Reviews:
    Annual workshop performances. M. Hunt. *Dance Mag* 61:79-81 D '87
    Stanley Williams [luncheon given in honor of ballet teacher] *New Yorker* 63:26-7 My 4 '87
    Suki Schorer takes the mystery out of mastery: caring. M. Hunt. il pors *Dance Mag* 61:54-7 F '87
School of Visual Arts (New York, N.Y.)
Take the SVA train [posters exhibited at the Cooper-Hewitt Museum] J. W. Graham. il *Horizon* 30:73 Jl/Ag '87
School organization *See* School management and organization
School phobia
Overcoming fear of school. H. R. Kennedy. *U S News World Rep* 103:81 S 21 '87
School prayer *See* Public schools and religion
School principals *See* School superintendents and principals
School reform *See* Education
School reports and records
See also
    Grading and marking (Students)
The graduate [B. Shields' transcript from Princeton] il por *Life* 10:24-5 Ag '87
School size *See* School enrollment
School subjects *See* Courses of study
School superintendents and principals
See also
    Black school superintendents and principals
    Council of Chief State School Officers
    Women school superintendents and principals
Help for principals in managing school crises. W. D. St. John. *Educ Dig* 52:36-9 Ap '87
How superintendents can work better with others. J. D. Abrams. *Educ Dig* 53:26-8 O '87
How valid are principals' judgments of teacher effectiveness? D. M. Medley and H. Coker. bibl f il *Phi Delta Kappan* 69:138-40 O '87
Murder hits home [murder of school principal W. H. Donahue of Highland Park, N.J.] S. G. Freedman. il *N Y Times Mag* p20+ My 31 '87
Not gunmen, but smarties [principal J. Greene at Redford High School in Detroit] B. Dolan. il por *Time* 129:85 Ap 27 '87

Superintendent-school board conflict: working it out. J. G. Hayden. *Educ Dig* 52:11-13 Ap '87
Support for beginning principals. J. C. Daresh. *Educ Dig* 52:10-13 Ja '87
Teacher evaluation: more than a game that principals play. A. B. Pigford. il *Phi Delta Kappan* 69:141-2 O '87
Dismissal
Fighting over a principal [movement to fire principal D. Littky in Winchester, N.H.] S. Doherty. il por *Newsweek* 109:76 My 25 '87
Rating
Evaluating elementary principals. P. L. White. il *Phi Delta Kappan* 69:143-4 O '87
Supply and demand
The school executive shortage: how serious is it? K. McCormick. *Educ Dig* 53:2-5 D '87
School supervision and supervisors
A checklist for instructional supervision. P. J. Wood. *Educ Dig* 52:46-7 Ap '87
Permitting access: teachers controlling supervision. A. Blumberg and R. S. Jonas. *Educ Dig* 53:22-5 N '87
School supplies *See* School furniture, equipment, etc.
School tax system *See* Education—Finance
School teachers *See* Teachers
School teaching *See* Teaching
School uniforms
Dress, right, dress [public schools] il *Time* 130:76 S 14 '87
Dressing to be successful [public schools] J. N. Baker. il *Newsweek* 110:62 N 30 '87
Kids and parents at a Baltimore grade school are uniformly opposed to costly kid fashions [uniforms at Cherry Hill public school] il *People Wkly* 28:133 O 12 '87
School violence
In Detroit, kids kill kids [searching students for weapons used in school-related attacks] E. Salholz. il *Newsweek* 109:74 My 11 '87
School volunteer programs *See* Volunteer workers in education
School-work plans *See* Business and education
School year
Inching toward more school [Los Angeles adopts year-round classes] J. N. Baker. il *Newsweek* 110:75-6 O 26 '87
School all year round. F. Roberts. il *Parents* 62:54 Ag '87
Anecdotes, facetiae, satire, etc.
The interminable term. R. Baker. il *N Y Times Mag* p42 S 20 '87
Notes and comment [Huck Finn at school during the summer] *New Yorker* 63:27 O 26 '87
Schooley, Bill Jaye
about
Jackson State Univ. names white to run Opera/South. *Jet* 72:25 Ag 31 '87
Schools
See also
    Art schools
    Catholic schools
    Church schools
    Correspondence schools and courses
    Education
    High schools
    Private schools
    Proprietary schools
    Public schools
    School buildings
    Summer schools
    Sunday schools
    Vocational-technical education
Spotlight on schools. il *Teen* 31:111 Ag '87
Schools, Medical *See* Medical colleges
Schools, Rural *See* Education, Rural
Schooners
See also
    Pride of Baltimore (Schooner)
Schopf, J. William, 1941-, and Packer, Bonnie M.
Early Archean (3.3-billion to 3.5-billion-year-old) microfossils from Warrawoona Group, Australia. bibl f il map *Science* 237:70-3 Jl 3 '87
Schorer, Suki
about
Suki Schorer takes the mystery out of mastery: caring. M. Hunt. il pors *Dance Mag* 61:54-7 F '87
Schorn, Ronald A.
Supernova 1987A and the press. il *Sky Telesc* 74:116 Ag '87
Schorr, Daniel, 1916-
April's spy scare. il *New Leader* 70:3-4 Ap 20 '87
Facing down Congress. *New Leader* 70:3 D 28 '87

Schorr, Daniel, 1916——_cont._
The Iran-contra hearings halfway. il _New Leader_ 70:3-4 Jl 1-15 '87
Lessons for the president. por _New Leader_ 70:3-4 Ag 10-24 '87
McFarlane's folly. _New Leader_ 70:3-4 F 9-23 '87
On the Bork front. _New Leader_ 70:5-6 O 19 '87
The public image of public figures. il _New Leader_ 70:3-4 N 16 '87
Reagan's de facto détente. il _New Leader_ 70:3-4 S 21 '87
Washington notebook. il _New Leader_ 70:3-4 Mr 23 '87
Schorske, Carl E.
Artist of angst. il _N Y Rev Books_ 33:20-2 Ja 15 '87
Schoyen, Warner O.
Amanda's garden [poem] il _Good Housekeep_ 204:194 Mr '87
Schrader, Ann
(ed) See Schock, Dixie. "I had in vitro quadruplets"
Schrader, Constance, 1933-
Feel & look your best! il _Harpers Bazaar_ 120:130-1+ Ja '87
Healthsmart. _Harpers Bazaar_ 121:94+ N '87
Healthsmart. _Harpers Bazaar_ 120:68+ Ag '87
Insights on eyesight. il _Harpers Bazaar_ 120:40+ Ap '87
Super body: tan and fit. il _Harpers Bazaar_ 120:54+ Je '87
(jt. auth) See Bihova, Diana, and Schrader, Constance, 1933-
Schrader, David
See a world in a grain of sand. il _Oceans_ 20:24-33 Mr/Ap '87
Schrader, Paul
about
Light of day [film] Reviews
  Christ Today il 31:66 My 15 '87. S. Ulstein
  Macleans il 100:46 F 9 '87. B. D. Johnson
  _N Y_ 20:102-3 Mr 2 '87. D. Denby
  Newsweek il 109:73 F 9 '87. D. Ansen
  People Wkly il 27:12 F 23 '87. P. Travers
  Roll Stone il por p25-6 Ja 15 '87. S. Pond
  Time il 129:74 F 9 '87. R. Corliss
Schrafft's (New York, N.Y.: Restaurants) _See_ New York (N.Y.)—Restaurants, nightclubs, bars, etc.
Schrag, Francis
Is high school the place to teach thinking? _Educ Dig_ 53:16-19 D '87
Schrambling, Regina
Carbing up at the salad bowl. il _Work Woman_ 12:140+ Je '87
New-wave fish. il _Work Woman_ 12:112-14 O '87
Some fry it hot. il _Esquire_ 108:48 D '87
Schramm, David N.
Why astronomers need the SSC. il _Sky Telesc_ 74:588 D '87
Schramm, Wilbur Lang, 1907-
Grandpa Hopewell and his flying tractor [story] il _Saturday Evening Post_ 259:42-5+ Ap '87
Grandpa Hopewell and his flying tractor [story] il _Saturday Evening Post_ 259:36+ My/Je '87
Schramsberg Vineyards Co.
Pardon their French, but the first of American bubbly boasts a champagne worthy of the name. E. Levin. il pors _People Wkly_ 28:113-14 D 21 '87
Schrecker, Ellen
about
The class struggle. T. Draper. _New Repub_ 196:29-36 Ja 26 '87
Oh, if I could only be a Communist. J. Hart. _Natl Rev_ 39:44 Je 19 '87
Schreiber, Jean-Jacques Servan- _See_ Servan-Schreiber, Jean-Jacques
Schreiner, Samuel Agnew
Why do we cry? il _Read Dig_ 130:141-4 F '87
Schrell, Wolfgang
about
Need a little blueblood to go? Does Germany's Wolfgang Schrell have a princess for you! M. Neill. il pors _People Wkly_ 28:159-60 D 7 '87
Schreyer, Edward
about
An attack on gay rights. _Macleans_ 100:11 Jl 27 '87
Schroeder, Barbet
about
Barfly [film] Reviews
  Film Comment il 23:53-4+ Jl/Ag '87. C. Hodenfield
  Macleans il 100:66 N 30 '87. L. O'Toole
  Mademoiselle il 93:108+ N '87. R. Rosenbaum
  _N Y_ il 20:114-15 O 26 '87. D. Denby
  Natl Rev 39:57-8+ D 4 '87. J. Simon
  New Yorker 63:137-40 N 2 '87. P. Kael

  Newsweek il 110:86 O 26 '87. D. Ansen
  People Wkly il 28:14 N 2 '87. P. Travers
Schroeder, Gertrude E.
The Soviet economy under Gorbachev. bibl f _Curr Hist_ 86:317-20+ O '87
Schroeder, Harry W., Jr., and others
Early restriction of the human antibody repertoire. bibl f il _Science_ 238:791-3 N 6 '87
Schroeder, Patricia
Is the administration approach to federal employee drug testing sound? [excerpts from testimony, September 16, 1986] _Congr Dig_ 66:139+ My '87
about
Can Pat Schroeder be more than 'the women's candidate'? D. Harbrecht and R. Fly. il por _Bus Week_ p35-6 O 5 '87
The fall of a contender. M. McDonald. il por _Macleans_ 100:30 O 5 '87
Her sound-bites draw blood. G. F. Will. il _Newsweek_ 110:76 Ag 17 '87
Leading roles: the stature of Schroeder & Nunn. J. B. Hehir. _Commonweal_ 114:645-6 N 20 '87
Letter from Washington. Cato. _Natl Rev_ 39:14 Jl 17 '87
Pat Schroeder's ambition to be First Lady in the Oval Office nears the moment of truth. M. Green. il pors _People Wkly_ 28:48-50 S 7 '87
"Run, Pat, run!". A. Stanley. il _Time_ 130:20 Ag 3 '87
Two in Congress debate U.S. defense [interview] J. Martin. pors _Sch Update_ 119:22 F 23 '87
Schroeder, William Ralph
Adventures in computerland. il _Consum Res Mag_ 70:24-7 Ap '87
Schruers, Fred
Glory day. il pors _Sport Mag_ 78:65-6+ D '87
Soldier's story. il por _Roll Stone_ p23-4+ Ja 29 '87
Schubert, Franz, 1797-1828
about
Edward Rothstein on music. _New Repub_ 197:26-8 Ag 10-17 '87
Musical events:
  Hundred and ninetieth birthday. A. Porter. _New Yorker_ 62:92-3 F 16 '87
Schubert, Martin
about
There goes the neighborhood. E. A. Finn, Jr. il por _Forbes_ 139:35-7 Je 29 '87
Schuck, Peter H.
What went wrong with the Voting Rights Act. _Wash Mon_ 19:51-5 N '87
Schudson, Michael
Colorization and authenticity. _Society_ 24:18-19 My/Je '87
Schueler, Donald G.
The Place. il _Audubon_ 89:110-14+ My '87
Schuessler, Raymond
A creek is worth the knowing. il _Conservationist_ 41:54-5 Mr/Ap '87
Who did what? Studying animals through their tracks. il _Conservationist_ 41:18-23 Ja/F '87
Schulberg, Budd
'Waterfront'—'more than a 90-minute movie'. il _N Y Times Book Rev_ 92:1+ Ap 26 '87
Schulein, Robert B.
Surround-sound attractions. il _High Fidel_ 37:49+ Je '87
Schulke, Flip
about
Flip Schulke's philosophy forms his photographic style. H. Chapnick. il por _Pop Photogr_ 94:28 Je '87
Schuller, Robert Harold
about
Dr. Robert Schuller: TV's minister of hope. D. De Dubovay. il pors _McCalls_ 114:44+ Ap '87
Problems for Schuller. _Christ Century_ 104:818 S 30 '87
Schullery, Paul
Sketches from nature. See issues of Country Journal beginning December 1986
Schulte, Rolf, 1949-
about
Musical events. A. Porter. _New Yorker_ 63:105-6 Mr 2 '87
Schultz, Deborah E.
What do you want to know late in the twentieth century? [address, January 26, 1987] _Vital Speeches Day_ 53:366-8 Ap 1 '87
Schultz, Dodi
(jt. auth) See Karlsrud, Katherine, and Schultz, Dodi

Schultz, Elfred
about
Ex-cop Lawrencia Bembenek claims she was wrongly convicted of murder in the case of the unsmoking gun. J. S. Kunen. il pors *People Wkly* 28:116-18+ D 7 '87

Schultz, Gregory S., and others
Epithelial wound healing enhanced by transforming growth factor-α and vaccinia growth factor. bibl f il *Science* 235:350-2 Ja 16 '87

Schultz, Mark
Activists take to the airwaves. il *Progressive* 51:13 S '87
Saying 'no' to psychiatry. il por *Progressive* 51:17 F '87

Schultz, Morton J.
Car clinic. See issues of Popular Mechanics

Schultz, Peter G.
(jt. auth) See Corey, D. R., and Schultz, Peter G.

Schultz, Peter H.
(jt. auth) See Grant, John A., and Schultz, Peter H.

Schultz, Richard D., 1929-
about
Mr. Clean comes to the NCAA. M. Ivey. il por *Bus Week* p51+ S 7 '87

Schultz, Ron
Interview [B. A. Smith] il pors *Omni* 9:66-8+ F '87
Silicosms. il *Omni* 9:52-7 Ag '87

Schultze, Quentin J.
The never-ending story. il por *Christ Today* 31:26-9 Ap 17 '87
The private lives of private eyes. il *Christ Today* 31:71 S 4 '87

Schultz, Christian Norberg- *See* Norberg-Schulz, Christian

Schulz, William F., Jr.
Fostering prejudice. il *Progressive* 51:15 Ja '87
The hunger artists. il *Progressive* 51:14-15 Je '87

Schulz-Keil, Wieland
Huston [cover story] il pors *Film Comment* 23:18-23 S/O '87

Schulze, E.-D., and others
Plant water balance. bibl f il *BioScience* 37:30-7 Ja '87

Schulzke, Margot Seymour
Anita Wolff's portraits and landscapes in pastel. il por *Am Artist* 51:60-3+ S '87

Schumacher, Joel
about
The Lost Boys [film] Reviews
Glamour il 85:199 Ag '87. J. G. Boyum
Macleans 100:49 Ag 3 '87. P. Young
Newsweek il 110:67 Ag 3 '87. D. Ansen
People Wkly 28:10 Ag 17 '87. J. Calio

Schuman, Howard, and Scott, Jacqueline
Problems in the use of survey questions to measure public opinion. bibl f il *Science* 236:957-9 My 22 '87

Schuman, William, 1910-
about
As American as Pittsburgh. E. Salzman. il por *Stereo Rev* 52:118 S '87

Schumer, Fran
A woman at old Exeter. il pors *N Y Times Mag* p98-101 O 11 '87

Schunk, Sharon
"My son was hit by lightning"; ed. by Lorene Hanley Duquin. il por *Redbook* 169:17+ Ag '87

Schupack, Andy
How to get your camera fixed. il *Petersens Photogr Mag* 16:53 Jl '87

Schurmann, Franz
Hu's not on first. *Nation* 244:100-1 Ja 31 '87

Schuster, Joseph
Hal Hempen's All-American dream. il *Sport Mag* 78:90 S '87
Wit and wisdom of Joe Magrane. il pors *Sport Mag* 78:73-4+ O '87

Schuyler, James
Horse-chestnut trees and roses [poem] *New Yorker* 63:32 Je 8 '87
Rain [poem] *New Yorker* 63:32 Ag 24 '87

Schuyler, Linda
about
Singing the puberty blues. P. Hluchy. il *Macleans* 100:54 Ja 19 '87

Schwab, Charles
about
How now, Chuck Schwab? J. Heins. il por *Forbes* 139:37-8 Je 15 '87
Schwab: bear markets have been very, very good to him. J. B. Levine. il por *Bus Week* p95 N 23 '87

Schwab: no R.I.P. for the IRA. por *Money* 16:67 Mr '87

Schwab (Charles) & Co., Inc. *See* Charles Schwab & Co., Inc.

Schwabe, Markus
United Nations at seabed. *World Press Rev* 34:44 O '87

Schwabsky, Barry
(tr) See Baudrillard, Jean, 1929-. Ads for ourselves

Schwahn, Linda
(jt. auth) See Paschal, John H., and Schwahn, Linda

Schwartz, Alvin
McKinley to Reagan: collecting U.S. presidents. il *Antiques Collect Hobbies* 92:79-80 S '87

Schwartz, Anne
Poisons in your home: a disposal dilemma. il *Audubon* 89:12-16 My '87
A woman's place. il *Americana* 15:30-2+ Mr/Ap '87

Schwartz, Benjamin I. (Benjamin Isadore), 1916-
The China syndrome. *New Repub* 196:15-16 F 9 '87

Schwartz, Bernard L.
about
Merci, Jimmy. S. N. Chakravarty. il por *Forbes* 139:114+ Je 15 '87

Schwartz, Brian B., 1938-
about
Schwartz of Brooklyn College is new APS education officer. por *Phys Today* 40:93 Mr '87

Schwartz, Charles Leon, 1931-
about
A physicist objects. J. J. Neuburger. il por *Progressive* 51:12-13 Jl '87

Schwartz, Charles Walsh
about
A tale of turtles. il pors *Natl Geogr World* 146:28-31 O '87

Schwartz, David M.
Should we beware the gourmet grouper? il *Int Wildl* 17:36-7 N/D '87
The termite connection. il por *Int Wildl* 17:38-42 Jl/Ag '87
Underachiever of the plant world. il *Audubon* 89:46-61 S '87

Schwartz, Elizabeth Reeder
about
A tale of turtles. il pors *Natl Geogr World* 146:28-31 O '87

Schwartz, Eric A.
Depolarization without calcium can release γ-aminobutyric acid from a retinal neuron. bibl f il *Science* 238:350-5 O 16 '87

Schwartz, Felice N.
Don't write women off as leaders. il por *Fortune* 115:185+ Je 8 '87

Schwartz, Gerald
about
Building a first for Canada. D. Jenish. il por *Macleans* 100:22+ Jl 27 '87
Can-do Canadian. L. Jereski. il por *Forbes* 140:124 S 7 '87

Schwartz, Gil
A boy's-eye view. See issues of Seventeen through July 1987
Him. See issues of Seventeen beginning August 1987
How men win fights with women: ways to foil their sneaky, secret combat tricks. il *Glamour* 85:282-3+ O '87

Schwartz, Herman, 1931-
The frantic reflagging of Bork [cover story] il *Nation* 245:253+ S 19 '87
New judicial activists. il *Nation* 244:361-2 Mr 21 '87
Rolling back the Constitution. il *Nation* 245:13-15 Jl 4-11 '87

Schwartz, Hillel, 1948-
Fantasiestücke 3. Ann Landers comes to me for advice [poem] *Commonweal* 114:357 Je 5 '87
about
Being thin isn't always being happy [interview] il por *U S News World Rep* 102:74 F 9 '87

Schwartz, Ira M.
(jt. auth) See AuClaire, Philip, and Schwartz, Ira M.

Schwartz, Jonathan
TRafalgar 6. il *N Y* 20:89 D 21-28 '87

Schwartz, Lynne Sharon
Let fiction change your life. *Writer* 100:14-17 N '87

Schwartz, Martha
about
Paradise lost. L. Smallwood. il *Art News* 86:57 O '87

Schwartz, Mindy Sue
about
Blood and money: the unsolved murder of a Long Island woman leads to a novel suit against her husband. M. Ryan. il pors *N Y* 20:38-44 Je 8 '87
Schwartz, Pat
Conscious of time and place. il por *World Press Rev* 34:61 O '87
Schwartz, Samuel
about
Blood and money: the unsolved murder of a Long Island woman leads to a novel suit against her husband. M. Ryan. il pors *N Y* 20:38-44 Je 8 '87
Schwartz, Sanford, 1946-
The art world. *New Yorker* 63:151-4 D 7 '87
Clement Greenberg—the critic and his artists. *Am Sch* 56:535-45 Aut '87
Schwartz, Stephen A.
about
Marketing. *New Yorker* 63:28-9 F 23 '87
Schwartz, Tony, 1952-
Ah, my non-aching back: a longtime sufferer finds it's all in the mind. il por *N Y* 20:44-8+ Mr 16 '87
Schwartz, Wendy
The secret that could not be kept. il *Progressive* 51:34 O '87
Schwartz, William A.
Drug addicts with dirty needles. il *Nation* 244:843-6 Je 20 '87
Schwartzberg, Neala S.
Bright, average, or slow? il *Parents* 62:106-8+ My '87
"Stuck on you!". il *Parents* 62:100-2+ O '87
What is my baby saying? il *Parents* 62:78-82 Jl '87
What TV does to kids. il *Parents* 62:100-4 Je '87
Schwarz, Gerard
about
Schwarz: masterly Prokofiev. D. Hall. por *Stereo Rev* 52:74 Ag '87
Schwarz, John H., 1941-
Superstrings. bibl f il *Phys Today* 40:33-40 N '87
Schwarz, Klaus W.
(jt. auth) See Glaberson, William I., and Schwarz, Klaus W.
Schwarz, Michael
Deadly traffic. il *N Y Times Mag* p54+ Mr 22 '87
Schwarz (F. A. O.) *See* F. A. O. Schwarz
Schwarzenegger, Arnold
about
Pex sell tix [cover story] D. Geringer. il pors *Sports Illus* 67:80-4+ D 7 '87
What makes Arnold run? C. McGuigan. il pors *Newsweek* 110:84-6 D 7 '87
Schwarzschild, Henry
about
Capital punishment: just or cruel? [interview] A. Kenney. pors *Sch Update* 119:13 F 9 '87
Schweickart, Russell L.
Our backs against the bomb, our eyes on the stars. il *Discover* 8:62+ Jl '87
Schweinhart, Lawrence J., and others
Policy options for preschool programs. bibl f il *Phi Delta Kappan* 68:524-9 Mr '87
Schweitzer, Gertrude, 1909-
Who is my love? [story] il *Good Housekeep* 204:124-5+ Mr '87
Schweitzer, John C.
Dating antique valentines. il *Antiques Collect Hobbies* 91:42-6 F '87
Schweitzer (Albert) Music Award *See* Albert Schweitzer Music Award
Schweizer, Peter, 1964-
(jt. auth) See Denton, James S., and Schweizer, Peter, 1964-
Schweizer Aircraft Corp.
Schweizer demonstrates SA 2-37A low-cost surveillance aircraft. P. Proctor. *Aviat Week Space Technol* 126:100-1 Je 1 '87
Schweizer will fly turbine helicopter before year-end [Model 330 Sky Knight] P. Proctor. il *Aviat Week Space Technol* 127:69 Jl 20 '87
Schweizer's super snooper [SA2-37A] N. Moll. il *Flying* 114:54-8 O '87
Sciascia, Leonardo
Bibliography
Tales of detection. J. Marcus. *Nation* 245:598-9 N 21 '87
Sciatic nerve
Adipsin: a circulating serine protease homolog secreted by adipose tissue and sciatic nerve. K. S. Cook and others. bibl f il *Science* 237:402-5 Jl 24 '87

Scicolone, Michele
Pasta: new sauces, new shapes. il *Ladies Home J* 104:122-3+ Ap '87
Science
See also
American Association for the Advancement of Science
Biology
Chaos (Science)
Communication in science
Computers—Scientific use
Information storage and retrieval systems—Scientific use
Islam and science
Lasers—Scientific use
Medicine
Music and science
National Science Week
Natural history
Physics
Radio broadcasting—Science programs
Religion and science
Scientists
Technology
War and science
The golden age of science is now. M. Brake. *Astronomy* 15:28 O '87
Science & technology. G. Bronson. See issues of Forbes beginning March 10, 1986
Awards
See also
National Medal of Science
Presidential Young Investigators Awards
Association awards presented at annual meeting in Chicago. J. Wrather. *Science* 235:1230-2 Mr 6 '87
New York Academy presents awards. *BioScience* 37:300 Ap '87
NSF honors Rabi and Witten, names Young Investigators [Vannevar Bush and Alan T. Waterman Awards] il *Phys Today* 40:95-6 S '87
Bibliography
Book reviews. See issues of Science
Books. See issues of Physics Today
Books. See issues of Science News
Books. P. Morrison. See issues of Scientific American
Conferences
See also
American Association for the Advancement of Science—Meetings
Dahlem Konferenzen
Gordon Research Conferences
Women in science and engineering is focus of conferences. *Science* 238:86 O 2 '87
Experiments
Anecdotes, facetiae, satire, etc.
What lies beyond the wildest dreams of science. J. Gorman. il *Discover* 8:20+ Mr '87
Fiction
See Science fiction
History
50 and 100 years ago. See issues of Scientific American
International aspects
See also
Exchanges, Literary and scientific
United Nations. Intergovernmental Committee on Science and Technology for Development
OECD to set rules for international science. D. Dickson. il *Science* 238:743 N 6 '87
Science and technology cooperation with Latin America [statement, July 30, 1987] J. Negroponte. *Dep State Bull* 87:50-2 O '87
Science and technology policies and priorities: a comparative analysis. L. L. Lederman. bibl f il *Science* 237:1125-33 S 4 '87
Juvenile literature
See Scientific literature for children
Miscellanea
Antimatter. See issues of Omni (New York, N.Y.)
Hidden wonders of your house [condensed from The secret house] D. Bodanis. *Read Dig* 130:126-8 F '87
They say a man's home is his castle, but David Bodanis' Secret house reveals the creepy truth. il pors *People Wkly* 27:133-5 Ap 20 '87
Periodicals
See also
Bulletin of the atomic scientists
Discover (Periodical)
Science news (Periodical)
Journal price increases [discussion of May 22, 1987 article, Libraries stunned by journal price increases] C. Holden. *Science* 238:597-8 O 30 '87

Science—Periodicals—cont.
Libraries stunned by journal price increases. C. Holden. *Science* 236:908-9 My 22 '87

Philosophy
See also
System theory
Soft sciences are often harder than hard sciences. J. M. Diamond. il *Discover* 8:34-5+ Ag '87

Political aspects
See Science and state

Religious aspects
See Religion and science

Research
See Research

Scholarships and fellowships
See also
Science Talent Search
AAAS summer fellows at work. L. A. Levey and S. Sauer. il *Science* 237:660-1 Ag 7 '87
Howard Hughes moves into science education. B. J. Culliton. il *Science* 238:150 O 9 '87
Scientific philanthropy [Howard Hughes Medical Institute] T. Beardsley. *Sci Am* 257:22+ D '87

Social aspects
Failing to recognize bias in science. D. Goleman. il *Technol Rev* 90:26-7 N/D '87
Raising the image of science in Britain. D. Dickson. il *Science* 235:1134-5 Mr 6 '87

Study and teaching
See also
Hands-On-Science Outreach Program
North Carolina School of Science and Mathematics
Science and the humanities—Study and teaching
Science students
Science teachers
Scientists as teachers
Are our universities rotten at the "core"? [adaptation of address, February 23, 1987] F. H. Westheimer. bibl f *Science* 236:1165-6 Je 5 '87
The core curriculum [discussion of June 5, 1987 article, Are our universities rotten at the core?] F. H. Westheimer. *Science* 237:474-5 Jl 31 '87
The drive to excel [D. Kuo, Chinese student at Bronx High School of Science] A. Quindlen. il pors *N Y Times Mag* p32+ F 22 '87
Inquiry in the undergraduate science classroom. C. D'Avanzo. *BioScience* 37:540 S '87
The need for science in a core curriculum. D. A. Labianca and W. J. Reeves. il *USA Today (Periodical)* 115:74-6 Mr '87
STS science teaching emphasizes problem solving [science/technology/society focus] R. E. Yager. *Educ Dig* 53:39-41 S '87
Subtle messages turn students off to science [views of David Suzuki] *Phi Delta Kappan* 68:714-15 My '87
What's right, what's wrong with U.S. science? [address, March 13, 1987] M. L. Goldberger. *Vital Speeches Day* 53:537-40 Je 15 '87
Who needs women? K. C. Cole. *Omni* 9:35 My '87
Why Johnny can't think. N. Lear. il *Omni* 9:30 F '87

Aids and devices
See also
National Geographic Kids Network
Magical tools for the 1980s [math and science software created by E. Goldstein] H.-J. Taferner. il por *Pers Comput* 11:173+ O '87
Science fiction . . . and facts [Science fare] il *Parents* 62:23 My '87

Federal aid
NSF undergrad programs upset scientists. I. Goodwin. il *Phys Today* 40:66-7 F '87
Upgrading basic science education. *Sci News* 131:106 F 14 '87

Projects
A little science, a little magic. V. Cobb. il *Parents* 62:97-100+ F '87

China
Modernizing science and technology in China. D. F. Simon. bibl f *Curr Hist* 86:249-52+ S '87

Developing countries
See also
United Nations. Intergovernmental Committee on Science and Technology for Development

France
Anecdotes, facetiae, satire, etc.
What science has done to the French, and vice versa. J. Gorman. il *Discover* 8:22+ Ap '87

Great Britain
Raising the image of science in Britain. D. Dickson. il *Science* 235:1134-5 Mr 6 '87

Japan
See also
Tsukuba Science City (Japan)

Latin America
Science and technology cooperation with Latin America [statement, July 30, 1987] J. Negroponte. *Dep State Bull* 87:50-2 O '87

Western Europe
Science in Europe [cover story; special section; with editorial comment by Daniel E. Koshland, Jr.] il *Science* 237:1093, 1101-14 S 4 '87

Science, Freedom of
The anti-space act of 1986 [restricting access to NASA tech briefs] J. Rhea. il *Space World* X-7-283:3 Jl '87
Coming: the big chill? [restrictions on unclassified data; cover story] J. Raloff. il *Sci News* 131:314-17 My 16 '87
Death of a data directive [automated databases] R. Chalk. il *Technol Rev* 90:13-14 Jl '87
Export controls and research results. *Sci News* 132:73 Ag 1 '87
Forbidden facts. P. Bagne. il *Omni* 9:18+ F '87
In rough waters, White House cancels controls on databases. I. Goodwin. *Phys Today* 40:66 My '87
Making waves: Poindexter sails into scientific databases. I. Goodwin. por *Phys Today* 40:51-2 Ja '87
National security and the environment. W. C. Clark. bibl *Environment* 29:inside cover+ Je '87
Stumbling on superconductors [U.S. science adviser's decision to exclude non-citizens from conference] E. Marshall and M. Sun. *Science* 237:477 Jl 31 '87
What is federal policy on scientific communication? D. R. Corson. *Phys Today* 40:144 Ja '87

Science and business *See* Science and industry

Science and civilization
Vastly improved scientific equipment raises the question: what is the contribution of technique to thought? R. M. Adams. bibl (p162) il *Smithsonian* 18:10 Ap '87

Science and ethics
See also
Bioethics
Research—Ethical aspects

Science and industry
See also
Industrial research
IUPAP and Corporate Associates meet in Washington. W. Sweet. il *Phys Today* 40:76-7 D '87
Physics applied to industry. *Phys Today* 40:S51-S55 Ja '87
Striking it rich in biotech [scientist-founders] S. Gannes. il *Fortune* 116:131-2+ N 9 '87
Tobacco science wars. E. Marshall. il *Science* 236:250-1 Ap 17 '87

Science and Islam *See* Islam and science
Science and literature *See* Literature and science
Science and music *See* Music and science
Science and politics *See* Science and state
Science and religion *See* Religion and science
Science and society *See* Science—Social aspects

Science and state
See also
Botanical research—Federal aid
National Science Foundation (U.S.)
Research—Federal aid
Science, Freedom of
Scientists—Political activities
Scientists in government
Technology and state
United States. Congress. House. Committee on Science, Space, and Technology
Agencies vie over human genome project. L. Roberts. il *Science* 237:486-8 Jl 31 '87
On Constitution's bicentennial, OTA examines effects of science [report entitled Science, technology and the Constitution] I. Goodwin. il *Phys Today* 40:43-5 N '87
Science and scientists in the public arena. E. A. Shils. *Am Sch* 56:185-202 Spr '87
Science policy programs progress. J. Walsh. *Science* 235:1320-1 Mr 13 '87
Science, scientists, and politics [symposium] *Cent Mag* 20:29-44 N/D '87
Washington reports. See issues of Physics Today beginning July 1983
Washington watch. See issues of BioScience beginning April 1983

Cuba
Castro's science. B. Lawren. il *Omni* 10:26+ O '87

Science and state—*cont.*
Great Britain
Britain centralizes science policy-making. D. Dickson. il *Science* 237:1562-3 S 25 '87
The decline of the British science empire. R. Williams. il *Bull At Sci* 43:45-8 O '87
U.K. science: survival of the fittest—or fattest? D. Dickson. il *Science* 236:512-13 My 1 '87
Hungary
Hungary seeks ways to live off its wits. D. Dickson. *Science* 236:770-1 My 15 '87
Japan
The U.S. has the advances, but Japan may have the advantage [superconductivity research] E. Clark. *Bus Week* p97 Ap 6 '87
Soviet Union
Science and technology. L. R. Graham. *Nation* 244:804-8 Je 13 '87
Soviet research to be self-directed. D. Dickson. *Science* 237:482 Jl 31 '87
United States
See Science and state
Science and the humanities
Study and teaching
The joys of science. R. T. Klose. por *Newsweek* 110:14-15 O 26 '87
Project on liberal education and the sciences receives funding. B. G. Walthall. *Science* 236:610 My 1 '87
Science and war *See* War and science
Science buildings, College *See* College architecture
Science cities
　　See also
　　Tsukuba Science City (Japan)
Science education *See* Science—Study and teaching
Science Fellows, Congressional *See* Scientists in government
Science fiction
　　See also
　　Canadian science fiction
　　Publishers and publishing—Science fiction
　　Russian science fiction
　　Space flight in literature
Mothers of invention [excerpt from The Media Lab] S. Brand. *Omni* 9:18+ Ag '87
Anthologies
Authors in search of a universe [shared world anthologies] P. S. Beagle. il *Omni* 10:40+ N '87
Authorship
Putting the science in science fiction [work of R. L. Forward] M. J. Mackowski. il por *Space World* X-1-277:32-3 Ja '87
The real Fahrenheit 451 [views of science fiction authors on censorship of their books] M. Long. il *Omni* 9:22 F '87
Science fiction today. I. Asimov. il *Writer* 100:7-10 F '87
The strange visions of J.G. Ballard [interview] J. Cott. il por *Roll Stone* p76+ N 19 '87
Awards
Hubbard awards, three years old, find sanction [Writers of the Future awards] R. Herbert. il *Publ Wkly* 231:22 My 22 '87
Bibliography
Science fiction. G. Jonas. il *N Y Times Book Rev* 92:30 Mr 8 '87
Science fiction. G. Jonas. il *N Y Times Book Rev* 92:18-19 Je 7 '87
Science fiction. G. Jonas. *N Y Times Book Rev* 92:29 Ap 26 '87
Science fiction. G. Jonas. il *N Y Times Book Rev* 92:25 Ag 2 '87
Science fiction. G. Jonas. il *N Y Times Book Rev* 92:18 D 20 '87
Science fiction. G. Jonas. il *N Y Times Book Rev* 92:36 O 18 '87
Collectibles
Monster trash [auction of duplicates from F. J. Ackerman's collection] B. Arbinger. il *Omni* 10:28+ D '87
Single works
　　See name of author for full entry
Adeste fideles. Pohl, Frederik, 1919-
The apotheosis of Isaac Rosen. Dann, Jack
Arachne. Mason, Lisa
Daddy's big girl. Le Guin, Ursula K., 1929-
Diner. Barrett, Neal, Jr.
E-ticket to Namland. Simmons, Dan
The evening and the morning and the night. Butler, Octavia E.
The fable of the farmer and fox. Brunner, John, 1934-
Forever yours, Anna. Wilhelm, Kate
God's hour. Bishop, Michael, 1945-
Hardware. Silverberg, Robert

Hide and seek. Klein, Gérard
Kingdom come. McAllister, Bruce
Lord of hosts. Willis, Connie
Night of the cooters. Waldrop, Howard
On golden seas. Clarke, Arthur C., 1917-
Palindrome. Disch, Thomas M.
Paper moon. Kilworth, Garry
Patterns. Cadigan, Pat
The pear-shaped man. Martin, George R. R.
Pictures made of stones. Shepard, Lucius
Quest's end. Zelazny, Roger
Rude awakening. Disch, Thomas M.
The sentinel. Clarke, Arthur C., 1917-
Stardust. Jacobs, Harvey
Thy sting. Broderick, Damien
The visitation. Bear, Greg, 1951-
Technique
How do you tell a good science fiction story? S. B. Weston. *Writer* 100:18-20 S '87
Science fiction film special effects *See* Motion pictures—Special effects
Science fiction films *See* Motion pictures—Science fiction films
Science in literature
　　See also
　　Science fiction
Science in television
　　See also
　　Television broadcasting—Science programs
Science information *See* Communication in science
Science journalism *See* Journalism, Scientific
Science literature *See* Scientific literature
Science museums
　　See also
　　La Cité des Sciences et de l'Industrie (Paris, France)
　　Exploratorium
　　Savannah Science Museum, Inc.
　　Southwest Museum of Science and Technology, The Science Place
Exploratorium influences science museums new and old. W. Sweet. il *Phys Today* 40:65-8 Mr '87
Volunteer workers
Science museums and AAAS members. P. S. Curlin. *Science* 237:1224 S 4 '87
Science news
　　See also
　　Journalism, Scientific
　　Medical news
After 1986, nowhere to go but up. *World Press Rev* 34:56 F '87
APS Star Wars study given prominent coverage in US press. W. Sweet. *Phys Today* 40:55-6 Je '87
Continuum. See issues of Omni (New York, N.Y.)
Five reasons to be cheerful. il *Esquire* 108:273-7 D '87
News from the world of science. See occasional issues of Reader's Digest
Phenomena, comment and notes. J. P. Wiley, Jr. See issues of Smithsonian
Physics news in 1986 [special section] P. F. Schewe. il *Phys Today* 40:S1-S70 Ja '87
Science. T. H. Cole. See issues of Popular Mechanics beginning July 1987
Science. D. Eskow. See issues of Popular Mechanics through June 1987
Science news of the year. il *Sci News* 132:400-6 D 19-26 '87
Science newsfront. A. Fisher. See issues of Popular Science
Search & discovery. See issues of Physics Today
Supernova 1987A and the press. R. A. Schorn. il *Sky Telesc* 74:116 Ag '87
Up front. See issues of Discover
Science news (Periodical)
Major awards to three SN writers. J. Greenberg. il *Sci News* 132:397 D 19-26 '87
Science Place (Museum) *See* Southwest Museum of Science and Technology, The Science Place
Science policy *See* Science and state
Science projects *See* Science—Study and teaching—Projects
Science students
　　See also
　　Science Talent Search
Foreigners in science [report from the National Science Foundation] C. Holden. il *Science* 237:970 Ag 28 '87
Student Pugwash awarded major grants. R. Hart. *Phys Today* 40:110-11 O '87
Science Talent Search
High school students honored for research. *Sci News* 131:56 Ja 24 '87
The rewards of student research. il *Sci News* 131:151 Mr 7 '87

Science Talent Search—*cont.*
STSers win MacArthurs. *Sci News* 131:390 Je 20 '87
When the Westinghouse Science Talent scouts dealt out their awards, they gave the Kuos a full house. M. Shaughnessy. il *People Wkly* 27:149-50 Je 8 '87
Science teachers
    See also
    Scientists as teachers
OSA expands programs for teachers [Optical Society of America] *Phys Today* 40:101 F '87
Teachers as scientists, scientists as teachers. *Futurist* 21:52-3 My/Je '87
    Certification
NSTA launches national certification program for science teachers. *Phi Delta Kappan* 68:409 Ja '87
Teacher certification program under way. J. Walsh. il *Science* 235:838-9 F 20 '87
Scientific associations *See* Scientific societies
Scientific conferences *See* Science—Conferences
Scientific creationism *See* Creation
Scientific criminology *See* Criminal investigation
Scientific education *See* Science—Study and teaching
Scientific equipment
    See also
    Astronomical equipment
    Balances (Scales)
    Biological equipment
    Medical equipment
    Physical equipment
    Psychological equipment
    Spectrograph
1987 guide to biotechnology products and instruments [with editorial comment] S. S. Roberts. *Science* 235 pt2:G4, G23+ F 27 '87
Products and materials. See issues of Science
Vastly improved scientific equipment raises the question: what is the contribution of technique to thought? R. M. Adams. bibl (p162) il *Smithsonian* 18:10 Ap '87
Scientific errors *See* Errors, Scientific
Scientific exchanges *See* Exchanges, Literary and scientific
Scientific expeditions
    See also
    Antarctic exploration
    Arctic exploration
    Earthwatch (Organization)
The business of selling adventure. S. Ocko. il *Technol Rev* 90:64-9+ F/Mr '87
Expedition to a 'lost' world [Cerro de la Neblina] A. Conover. il map *Int Wildl* 17:38-42 My/Je '87
The North Borneo Expedition of 1981 [college students collect samples of agricultural pests] C. Alexander. map *New Yorker* 63:39-44+ S 14 '87
Wildlife au naturel [expeditions sponsored by zoos] D. G. Gordon. *Travel Holiday* 168:30-1 Jl '87
Scientific freedom *See* Science, Freedom of
Scientific information *See* Communication in science
Scientific instruments *See* Scientific equipment
Scientific literature
    See also
    Science—Bibliography
    Science—Periodicals
Homage to speculation: putting fun back into science. S. B. Brandt and M. E. McDonald. *BioScience* 37:771 D '87
Integrity of research papers questioned [study by Walter W. Stewart and Ned Feder] B. J. Culliton. *Science* 235:422-3 Ja 23 '87
A long-disputed paper goes to press [Walter W. Stewart's and Ned Feder's critical study of publications by J. Darsee and coauthors] M. Murray. il *Sci News* 131:52-3 Ja 24 '87
Science writing: too good to be true? B. Coleman. il *N Y Times Book Rev* 92:1+ S 27 '87
A soap opera for science [study by Walter Stewart and Ned Feder] D. E. Chubin. bibl f *BioScience* 37:259-61 Ap '87
    Authorship
Doctored data [scientific fraud] *Sci Am* 256:68-9 Ap '87
Publish or perish—or fake it [scientists' publication of fraudulent data] D. S. Greenberg. il *U S News World Rep* 102:72-3 Je 8 '87
A weighty word processor [Lotus Manuscript] M. Antonoff. il *Pers Comput* 11:56 Ap '87
    Refereeing
The Matthew effect. D. Sobel. *Omni* 9:27 Ag '87
Scientific literature for children
The year of the "LRFO": Let's Read-and-Find-Out books in the '80s [series published by Harper & Row] K. O. Fakih. il *Publ Wkly* 231:38-9 Ja 23 '87

    Bibliography
A vacation trip for young readers around the world of science. P. Morrison and P. Morrison. *Sci Am* 257:148-57 D '87
Scientific research *See* Research
Scientific societies
    See also
    Academy of Sciences of the USSR
    Acoustical Society of America
    American Association for the Advancement of Science
    American Crystallographic Association
    American Institute of Physics
    American Physical Society
    American Scientific Affiliation
    American Vacuum Society
    Materials Research Society
    National Academy of Sciences (U.S.)
    National Council of Black Engineers and Scientists
    New York Academy of Sciences
    Optical Society of America
Toward an Academia Europaea? D. Dickson. *Science* 237:1102 S 4 '87
Scientists
    See also
    Biologists
    Engineers
    Inventors
    Minorities in science
    Physicists
    Women scientists
Six scientists who may save the world [special section] B. Lawren. il *Omni* 9:36-8+ S '87
    Political activities
    See also
    Federation of American Scientists
    Union of Concerned Scientists
About face [interview with antinuclear physicist T. B. Taylor] D. Sheff. il por *Roll Stone* p59+ S 24 '87
APS panel disowns council statement [statement that argued against early deployment of Strategic Defense Initiative] C. Norman. *Science* 238:155 O 9 '87
Cornell unit surveys some US Academy members on SDI. W. Sweet. *Phys Today* 40:72-3 Ja '87
Fasting for life [C. Hyder's hunger strike for disarmament] J. Cott. il por *Roll Stone* p33+ My 7 '87
The Hamburg disarmament proposals [excerpts from statement at the International Scientists' Peace Congress in Hamburg, West Germany, November 14-16, 1986] *Bull At Sci* 43:52 Ja/F '87
How eminent physicists have lent their names to a politicized report on strategic defense. A. M. Codevilla. *Commentary* 84:21-6 S '87
Leo Szilard: giving peace a chance in the nuclear age. B. J. Bernstein. il pors *Phys Today* 40:40-7 S '87
A matter of life and death [fast for disarmament; interview with C. Hyder] J. Cott. il por *Roll Stone* p48-9+ F 26 '87
Physicist Hyder fasts for peace. W. Sweet. il por *Phys Today* 40:68 Ap '87
A physicist objects [C. Schwartz stops teaching classes in higher physics at Berkeley] J. J. Neuburger. il por *Progressive* 51:12-13 Jl '87
Physicists report progress at Moscow disarmament forum. W. Sweet. il *Phys Today* 40:67-70 Ap '87
Reflections of a Japanese physicist. M. Kimura. il pors *Bull At Sci* 43:7-10 N '87
Science and scientists in the public arena [atomic scientists since WW II] E. A. Shils. *Am Sch* 56:185-202 Spr '87
Seismic politics. D. C. Morrison. il *Science* 236:385 Ap 24 '87
Star Wars lasers: a question of technical integrity. I. Peterson. *Sci News* 132:276 O 31 '87
    Psychology
Failing to recognize bias in science. D. Goleman. il *Technol Rev* 90:26-7 N/D '87
    Salaries, pensions, etc.
Salaries of scientists up modestly. E. L. Babco. *Science* 238:1426 D 4 '87
Scientists, Amateur
    See also
    Astronomers, Amateur
The amateur scientist. J. Walker. See issues of Scientific American
Scientists, American
    See also
    Federation of American Scientists
Scientists, German
NASA's Nazis. L. Hunt. *Nation* 244:671 My 23 '87

Scientists, Handicapped
Genius unbound [S. W. Hawking] R. Morais. il por *Forbes* 139:142 Mr 23 '87
'He loves life' [story behind S. W. Hawking's A brief history of time] L. Fleischer. *Publ Wkly* 232:56 O 16 '87
Programs provide services for scientists with disabilities. W. Sweet. *Phys Today* 40:57-8 Je '87

Scientists as teachers
Teachers as scientists, scientists as teachers. *Futurist* 21:52-3 My/Je '87

Scientists in government
Congressional Fellowship program gets good review. *Phys Today* 40 pt1:79 Ag '87
Goldin and Romm are selected to be Congressional Fellows. pors *Phys Today* 40:79 Jl '87
Science, scientists, and politics [symposium] *Cent Mag* 20:29-44 N/D '87
Wanted: technical expertise in government. R. R. Ropelewski. *Aviat Week Space Technol* 126:11 Mr 2 '87

Scientology
A defeat for Scientology [Canadian publication of Russell Miller's biography of L. R. Hubbard allowed] D. Todd. *Macleans* 100:54 D 14 '87

SCLC *See* Southern Christian Leadership Conference

Sclerosis, Amyotrophic lateral *See* Amyotrophic lateral sclerosis

Sclerosis, Multiple *See* Multiple sclerosis

Sclocchini, Lydia
about
For Scotty and Lida Sclocchini, a unique superpower detente begins at home in Irkutsk. J. W. Seymore. il pors *People Wkly* 27:42+ Ap 6 '87

Sclocchini, Silvio
about
For Scotty and Lida Sclocchini, a unique superpower detente begins at home in Irkutsk. J. W. Seymore. il pors *People Wkly* 27:42+ Ap 6 '87

SCM Corp.
Writing on the wall [chief executive L. Thompson] G. Slutsker. il por *Forbes* 140:106 Jl 27 '87

Scoble, Hubert A.
(jt. auth) See Biemann, Klaus, and Scoble, Hubert A.

Scofield, John
about
John Scofield: all shades of blue. B. Milkowski. il pors *Down Beat* 54:16-18+ Ja '87

Scofield, Michael, and Teich, Mark
Mind-bending music. il *Health* 19:69-70+ F '87

Scoggins, Tracy
about
Tracy's outside interests. il por *Health* 19:35 Ja '87

Scoliosis
Scoliosis: one 'Teen model's battle. P. S. Rix. il por *Teen* 31:26+ Jl '87

Scombroid poisoning
Red, hot and dangerous: scombroid-poisonous fishes. S. Scott. il *Sea Front* 33:280-5 Jl/Ag '87

Scooters
The summer of the scooter. il *Newsweek* 110:70 Ag 31 '87

Scooters, Motor *See* Motor scooters

Scopes, Jack
Grandpa's famous trial. il *Progressive* 51:34 Je '87

Scopes, John Thomas
about
Grandpa's famous trial. J. Scopes. il *Progressive* 51:34 Je '87

Scopes for firearms *See* Firearms—Sights

Scopes trial *See* Tennessee evolution controversy

Scoreboards
The Wall's inside story [Fenway Park] E. M. Swift. il *Sports Illus* 67:48-50 Jl 6 '87

Scores (Musicals, revues, etc.) *See* Musicals, revues, etc.—Scores

Scoring (Sports)
See also
Golf—Scoring
SportsTicker (Firm)

Scorpion fish *See* Scorpionfish

Scorpionfish
Scorpionfish: danger in disguise. D. Doubilet. il *Natl Geogr* 172:634-43 N '87

Scorsese, Martin
about
The color of money [film] Reviews
Film Comment il 23:72+ My/Je '87. J. McDonough

Scotch *See* Scots

Scotch Cap Lighthouse *See* Lighthouses—Aleutian Islands (Alaska)

Scotch whiskey *See* Whiskey

Scotland
See also
Barra Island (Scotland)
Crofters—Scotland
Festivals—Scotland
Fishery laws and regulations—Scotland
Glasgow (Scotland)
Golf courses—Scotland
Highlands (Scotland)
Historic houses, sites, etc.—Scotland
Hunting—Scotland
Investments, Scottish
Land tenure—Scotland
Motion picture festivals—Scotland
Scots
Sculpture gardens and parks—Scotland
Whithorn (Scotland)

Industries
See also
Baxters of Speyside Ltd.
Dawson International Ltd.
Investment advisers—Scotland

Scots

Canada
Anecdotes, facetiae, satire, etc.
Music for repressed Scotsmen [annual St. Andrew's Ball] A. Fotheringham. il *Macleans* 100:52 D 28 '87
History
'A family affair': colonising New Kincardineshire. M. Harper. bibl il map *Hist Today* 37:42-8 O '87
West Africa
History
Long nose, white skin and 'honey mouth' [visit to the king; excerpt from Travels into the interior of Africa] M. Park. por *Courier* 40:18+ Ap '87

Scott, Adrian
about
Ordeal by Disney. J. Scott. il pors *Film Comment* 23:52-4+ N/D '87

Scott, Barbara
Discovering my potential with pastel. il por *Am Artist* 51:56-7+ Jl '87

Scott, Brian
about
UFO update. J. Clark. il *Omni* 9:89 F '87

Scott, Calvin
about
Miami preacher convicted for selling heroin. *Jet* 72:10 Je 15 '87

Scott, Hal S.
Betrayal. *New Repub* 197:12-13 D 14 '87

Scott, J. Michael, and others
Species richness: a geographic approach to protecting future biological diversity [cover story] bibl f il map *BioScience* 37:782-8 D '87

Scott, Jack Denton, 1915-
For love of lobster. il *Read Dig* 130:91-4 Je '87
Texas longhorns on the comeback trail. il *Read Dig* 130:56-60 Ja '87
The tree of life. il *Read Dig* 131:43-4+ N '87

Scott, Jacqueline
(jt. auth) See Schuman, Howard, and Scott, Jacqueline

Scott, James *See* Monmouth, James Scott, Duke of, 1649-1685

Scott, Jane
about
Cleveland rock critic Jane Scott may be pushing 70, but she's still got the beat. K. Myers. il pors *People Wkly* 27:91-2 Je 8 '87

Scott, Joan
Ordeal by Disney. il pors *Film Comment* 23:52-4+ N/D '87

Scott, Kevin
Working women of the silver screen: do you know these celluloid executives? il *Work Woman* 12:66-7 Ag '87

Scott, Michael
A connoisseur's Callas. il pors *Opera News* 52:29-30+ S '87

Scott, Mike, 1955-
about
The anatomy of an at-bat. D. Granger. il pors *Sport Mag* 78:26-9 Jl '87
Mike Scott got a grip on the split-fingered fastball and threw his career a nice curve. P. Jordan. il pors *People Wkly* 28:45+ Jl 6 '87
No wonder he's hot. R. Fimrite. il pors *Sports Illus* 66:92-6+ Ja 12 '87

Scott, Monica
Southern exposure. il pors *Essence* 17:97-8+ Mr '87

Scott, Munroe
about
McClure [drama] Reviews
   Macleans 100:70 N 9 '87. K. Harley
Scott, Peter Dale
The secret team behind contragate. il *Nation* 244:97+
   Ja 31 '87
Scott, Peter Markham, 1909-
The Antarctic challenge. il pors *Natl Geogr* 171:538-43
   Ap '87
Scott, Ridley
about
Someone to watch over me [film] Reviews
   Macleans 100:63 O 26 '87. L. O'Toole
   N Y 20:95 N 2 '87. D. Denby
   Nation 245:461-2 O 24 '87. T. Rafferty
   New Yorker 63:140 N 2 '87. P. Kael
   People Wkly il 28:16 O 19 '87. P. Travers
   Time il 130:84 O 12 '87. R. Corliss
Scott, Robert F.
State of solid state. See issues of Radio-Electronics
Scott, Robert Falcon, 1868-1912
about
The Antarctic challenge. P. M. Scott. il pors *Natl Geogr*
   171:538-43 Ap '87
In the footsteps of Scott. R. Swan. il pors map *Natl
   Geogr* 171:544-55 Ap '87
Scott, Susan
Painting with pesticides: the controversial organotin
   paints. il *Sea Front* 33:414-21 N/D '87
Red, hot and dangerous: scombroid-poisonous fishes.
   il *Sea Front* 33:280-5 Jl/Ag '87
Scott, Tony
about
Beverly Hills cop II [film] Reviews
   Jet il 72:56-8 Je 15 '87
   Macleans il 100:55 Je 1 '87. L. O'Toole
   N Y il 20:95 Je 1 '87. D. Denby
   N Y 20:71-3 Je 22 '87. D. Denby
   New Repub 196:25 Je 29 '87. S. Kauffmann
   Newsweek il 109:69 Je 1 '87. D. Ansen
   People Wkly il 27:10 My 25 '87. P. Travers
   Roll Stone il p27-9 Jl 2 '87. D. Handelman
   Time il 129:73 Je 1 '87. R. Schickel
Scott, Vernon
The millionaire who made Vanna White a star. il pors
   Good Housekeep 204:66+ My '87
Pat Sajak: Vanna White and me. il pors *Good Housekeep*
   205:34+ N '87
Shelley Long. il pors *Good Housekeep* 204:89+ Ja '87
The triumph of Mikko Mayeda. il por *Good Housekeep*
   204:40 Mr '87
Scott, Walter, 1872-1954
about
Scotty's Castle [excerpt] S. W. Paher. il *Natl Parks* 61:46-7
   S/O '87
Scott, Walter D.
Acid rain monitor. il *Radio-Electron* 58:48-9+ Ap '87
Scott, Willard
about
Great Scott! E. Boddie. il pors *50 Plus* 27:30-1+ D
   '87
Great Scott! TV's favorite weatherman. E. Sherman.
   il pors *Ladies Home J* 104:62+ N '87
Scott, William P.
Berthe Morisot's experimental techniques and impres-
   sionist style. il *Am Artist* 51:42-7 D '87
Frank Trefny [cover story] il por *Am Artist* 51:52-7
   D '87
Scott (Dred) case *See* Dred Scott case
Scott (J. Robert) (Firm) *See* J. Robert Scott (Firm)
Scott Antarctic Expedition, 1910-1912 *See* Antarctic explora-
   tion
Scottish Highlands *See* Highlands (Scotland)
Scottish Opera
Glasgow. N. Goodwin. *Opera News* 51:41 Ja 17 '87
London/Glasgow. N. Goodwin. *Opera News* 51:39-40
   F 14 '87
Scottish terriers
Collectibles
See also
   Wee Scots (Organization)
Scotto, Renata, 1934-
about
Staged by Scotto [with editorial comment by Jane L.
   Poole] C. Battaglia. il pors *Opera News* 51:4, 10-13
   Ja 17 '87
Scotty's Castle (Calif.)
Scotty's Castle [excerpt] S. W. Paher. il *Natl Parks* 61:46-7
   S/O '87

Scouts and scouting
See also
   Boy Scouts of America
   Girl Scouts of the United States of America
Scovell, Jane
Domingo: giving his best [cover story] il pors *Opera
   News* 52:14-17 S '87
Scovell, Nell
The new seductress. il pors *Mademoiselle* 93:244-7 N
   '87
Scoville, Orlena
about
Quinta da Bacalhoa. J. Taboroff. il por *House Gard*
   159:180-5+ D '87
Scowcroft, Brent, and others
A way out of Reykjavik. il *N Y Times Mag* p40+
   Ja 25 '87
SCR (Silicon controlled rectifiers) *See* Thyristors
Scrabble (Game)
Masters of the tiles. B. Chamish. il *Atlantic* 259:54-8
   Je '87
Scrambled eggs *See* Cooking—Eggs
Scrambling systems (Telecommunication)
The General [General Instrument buys Video Cipher
   from M/A-Com] A. B. Block. il *Forbes* 139:38-9 Je
   29 '87
Pay TV's descrambling wars [suit against Network Produc-
   tions Inc.] C. Gerber. *Channels* 7:11 Je '87
Practical descrambling [M/A-COM scrambling system
   has been breached] B. Cooper, Jr. il *Radio-Electron*
   58:83-4 F '87
Tri-mode cable-TV scrambling. J. Coffell. il
   Radio-Electron 58:43-7+ F '87
TV signal descrambling (VII). W. Sheets and R. F.
   Graf. il *Radio-Electron* 58:53-6 Ja '87
TV signal descrambling (VIII). W. Sheets and R. F.
   Graf. il *Radio-Electron* 58:63-5 Mr '87
TV signal descrambling (IX). W. Sheets and R. F. Graf.
   il *Radio-Electron* 58:58-61+ Jl '87
Videocipher has been cracked. B. Cooper, Jr. il
   Radio-Electron 58:4+ Ja '87
What's next? [home-dish industry] B. Cooper, Jr. il
   Radio-Electron 58:74-5 D '87
Why Videocipher is dead. B. Cooper, Jr. il *Radio-Electron*
   58:78-9 Mr '87
The ZITS fraud [VideoCipher descrambling chip] B.
   Cooper, Jr. il *Radio-Electron* 58:76-7+ Je '87
Zombies, ZITS, and zowee! B. Cooper, Jr. il
   Radio-Electron 58:77-8+ My '87
Scranton (Pa.)
That championship season long past, author-actor Jason
   Miller tests the new weather in Scranton. K. Hubbard.
   il pors *People Wkly* 28:58-60+ N 23 '87
Scratchboard drawing
Techniques of scratchboard drawing [work of L. Farley]
   C. Farley. il *Am Artist* 51:62-5 Mr '87
Screen doors *See* Screens (Doors, windows, etc.)
Screen printing *See* Silk screen printing
Screened porches *See* Decks, patios, terraces, etc.
Screenplays *See* Motion picture scripts
Screens (Doors, windows, etc.)
Hanging a wooden screen door. H. Wicks. il *Home
   Mech* 83:52-4 Jl '87
Maintenance and repair
How to repair a patio screen door. R. Capotosto. il
   Pop Mech 164:135-7 Je '87
Screens (Fences) *See* Fences
Screens (Furniture)
Decorate a screen with decoupage! S. Wood. il *McCalls*
   145:162+ Mr '87
The screens and screen designs of Donald Deskey. M.
   Komanecky. bibl f il *Antiques* 131:1064-77 My '87
Screens by artists: revealing, concealing, anything but
   modest. il *Vogue* 177:336 Mr '87
Screenwriting *See* Motion picture authorship
Screw threads
Loctite thread repair [Form-A-Thread] B. Gould. il
   Workbench 43:21 My/Je '87
Screwdrivers
Quick-draw drill [Black & Decker cordless drill/
   screwdriver] R. Capotosto. il *Pop Mech* 164:48 Je
   '87
Screwdriver with a twist [Skil Twist cordless screwdriver]
   R. Capotosto. il *Pop Mech* 164:36 F '87
Screws
Screws. il *Mother Earth News* 105:38 My/Je '87
Screws. J. Truini. il *Pop Mech* 164:81-4 Ag '87
Scribble! (Word processor program) *See* Word processors
   and processing—Programming

Scribner Book Companies, Inc.
Charles Scribner's Sons [manuscript submission policy]
S. Kirk. *Writer* 100:24-5 Jl '87
Where's Papa? [criticism of T. Jenks's editing of E.
Hemingway's The garden of Eden] B. P. Solomon.
New Repub 196:30-4 Mr 9 '87
Script writing (Motion pictures) *See* Motion picture author-
ship
Script writing (Television) *See* Television authorship
Scripts, Motion picture *See* Motion picture scripts
Scroll saws *See* Saws and sawing
Scrushy, Richard
about
Turning health into wealth. M. Gill. il por *Esquire* 108:94
S '87
Scruton, Roger
about
Down with ignorance, long live ontology. A. Broyard.
il *N Y Times Book Rev* 92:12 Jl 26 '87
Scuba diving *See* Skin diving
Scull, Sudi
about
Still-life decorating. J. R. Provey. il por *Home Mech*
83:66-7 Ja '87
Sculley, John
Odyssey: John Sculley and the saga of the Macintosh
(I) [excerpt from Odyssey] il *Pers Comput* 11:182-5+
N '87
Odyssey: John Sculley and the saga of the Macintosh
(II) [excerpt from Odyssey] il *Pers Comput* 11:201-3+
D '87
Professionals and their computers. por *Pers Comput*
11:236 O '87
Sculley's lessons from inside Apple [excerpt from Odyssey]
il pors *Fortune* 116:108-11+ S 14 '87
about
Apple's comeback. K. M. Hafner. il por *Bus Week*
p84-9 Ja 19 '87
In the study of John Sculley. il por *Esquire* 107:86-7
Ap '87
The reshaping of Apple. A. C. Hixson. il por *Pers Comput*
11:119+ Ap '87
The world according to John Sculley. K. M. Hafner.
il por *Bus Week* p71+ S 28 '87
Scully, Vincent Joseph, 1920-
Architecture: David Sellers. il por *Archit Dig* 44:146-51+
Je '87
Vincent Scully. See occasional issues of Architectural
Digest beginning October 1985
Sculpture
See also
Alexandria (Va.)—Monuments, statues, etc.
Animals in art
Boston (Mass.)—Monuments, statues, etc.
Bronzes
Buddhas in art
Ceramic sculpture
Chicago (Ill.)—Monuments, statues, etc.
Dinosaurs in art
Figurines
Glass sculpture
Hamburg (Germany)—Monuments, statues, etc.
Inflatable art
Kinetic sculpture
Masks (Sculpture)
New York (N.Y.)—Monuments, statues, etc.
Newark (N.J.)—Monuments, statues, etc.
Nutley (N.J.)—Monuments, statues, etc.
Plaster casts (Sculpture)
Public art
Raleigh (N.C.)—Monuments, statues, etc.
Seattle (Wash.)—Monuments, statues, etc.
Sharks in art
Soap sculpture
Washington (D.C.)—Monuments, statues, etc.
Wood carving
Outdoor abstractions [work of E. Kelly] J. Russell. il
por *House Gard* 159:182-5+ F '87
Collectors and collecting
Buy what you love—but make sure it's first-rate [R.
Nasher] J. H. Dobrzynski. il por *Bus Week* p185
D 28 '87-Ja 4 '88
The collectors: a passion for sculpture: Patsy and
Raymond D. Nasher's Dallas residence and gardens.
J. Chatfield-Taylor. il *Archit Dig* 44:112-21 O '87
Just getting started [P. and R. Nasher] K. Gregor. il
pors *Art News* 86:59-60+ N '87

Conferences
See Art—Conferences
Conservation and restoration
Monumental corrosion [effect of acid rain on sculptures;
views of Robert Baboian] K. Rosenberg. il *Technol
Rev* 90:11-12 O '87
Exhibitions
Artsmart. il *Harpers Bazaar* 120:150+ Jl '87
A century of modern sculpture [Selections from the
Patsy and Raymond Nasher Collection at the National
Gallery of Art] il *USA Today (Periodical)* 116:8-9
Ag '87
Essen: Scenes; Münster: Sculptural projects. M. Hübl.
il *Art News* 86:200 O '87
Monte Carlo sculpture '87. C. Mosley. il *Art News* 86:201
O '87
Sighted in Münster [Skulptur projekte exhibition] E.
Heartney. il *Art Am* 75:140-3+ S '87
What isn't modern sculpture? [What is modern sculpture?
at the Pompidou Center, Paris] A. E. Elsen. il *Art
News* 86:144-7 Ja '87
Preservation
See Sculpture—Conservation and restoration
Sculpture, American
See also
Ahearn, John, 1951-
Barron, Slater
Biederman, James
Boehm, Edward Marshall
Capps, Kenneth
Dailey, Dan
Davis, Debby
Driscoll, Ellen
Dwight, Edward J., Jr.
Finster, Howard
Gillespie, Richard
Graves, Nancy, 1940-
Highstein, Jene, 1942-
Holden, Barry
Hollander, Richard
Huchthausen, David R.
Kelly, Ellsworth, 1923-
King, William Dickey, 1925-
Langlais, Bernard, 1921-1977
Lere, Mark, 1950-
MacQueen, Elizabeth
Mellon, Marc Richard
Oldenburg, Claes, 1929-
Otterness, Tom, 1952-
Paulson, Alan
Pavia, Phillip, 1912-
Pepper, Beverly, 1924-
Prescott, Ted
Puett, Garnett
Puryear, Martin, 1941-
Ray, Charles
Rhoads, George
Rosenberg, Evelyn
Rupp, Christy
Serra, Richard
Shapiro, Joel
Sheehan, Maura
Singer, Steven
Slavit, Ann
Smyth, Ned, 1948-
Sonfist, Alan, 1948-
Sonnier, Keith, 1941-
Sugarman, George
Tanner, James, 1941-
Truitt, Anne, 1921-
Ullberg, Kent, 1945-
Gabo's progeny [influence of N. Gabo's work on contem-
porary American sculptors] C. Nadelman. il por *Art
News* 86:123-7 D '87
Sculptors strengthen ties at landmark conference [National
Sculpture Conference: Works by Women] F. Grossen.
Am Craft 47:13 O/N '87
Sculpture, Argentine
See also
Fontana, Lucio, 1899-1968
Sculpture, Baroque
Sculpture, theatre of the sublime. F. Souchal. il *Courier*
40:20-2 S '87
Sculpture, Brazilian
See also
Lisboa, Antônio Francisco, 1730-1814
Sculpture, British
Britain's 'new generation'. J. Higgins. il *Art News*
86:118-22 D '87

Sculpture, British—*cont.*

Exhibitions

Site reading: British art in public spaces [TSWA 3D show] R. Cork. il *Art Am* 75:144-51 S '87

Sculpture, Canadian

See also

Bladen, Ronald, 1918-1988

Fafard, Joe

Malay, Rod

Sculpture, Classical

Six decades in exile [Statue of a Young Woman, originally called forgery, reclassified as genuine at Metropolitan] il *U S News World Rep* 103:53 Ag 10 '87

Sculpture, English

See also

Machin, Arnold

Moore, Henry, 1898-1986

Tucker, William, 1935-

Woodrow, Bill

Britain's 'new generation'. J. Higgins. il *Art News* 86:118-22 D '87

Exhibitions

Border lines [Juxtapositions: recent sculpture from England and Germany at P.S. 1] K. Larson. il *N Y* 20:66+ My 25 '87

Juxtapositions at P.S.1. E. Heartney. il *Art Am* 75:177 N '87

Sculpture, French

See also

Kirili, Alain, 1946-

Matisse, Henri

Poirier, Anne

Poirier, Patrick

Sculpture, German

See also

Lüpertz, Markus, 1941-

Exhibitions

Border lines [Juxtapositions: recent sculpture from England and Germany at P.S. 1] K. Larson. il *N Y* 20:66+ My 25 '87

Juxtapositions at P.S.1. E. Heartney. il *Art Am* 75:177 N '87

The perils of public sculpture [West Germany] D. Galloway. il *Art Am* 75:37-9+ D '87

Sculpture, Italian

See also

Bernini, Gian Lorenzo, 1598-1680

Melotti, Fausto, 1901-1986

Michelangelo Buonarroti, 1475-1564

Sculpture, Kinetic *See* Kinetic sculpture

Sculpture, Norwegian

See also

Breivik, Bard

Sculpture, Polish

See also

Abakanowicz, Magdalena

Sculpture, Roman

Buried treasure [restoration of Roman bronzes found in Marches region of Italy] G. Armstrong. il *Art News* 86:91-2 Ap '87

Sculpture, Russian

See also

Gabo, Naum, 1890-

Neizvestnyĭ, Ernst, 1926-

Sculpture, Scottish

See also

Finlay, Ian Hamilton, 1925-

Sculpture, Spanish

See also

Chillida, Eduardo, 1924-

Iglesias, Cristina, 1956-

Solano, Susana, 1946-

Sculpture, Zimbabwean

Romancing the stone [Shona sculpture] R. Wilkinson. il *Newsweek* 110:80 S 14 '87

Sculpture gardens and parks

France

In nature's shadow [park at the Kerguéhennec Estate in southwestern Brittany] K. Kertess. il *Art Am* 75:57-9 S '87

Great Britain

Figures in a landscape: sculpture in the British garden. G. Jackson-Stops. bibl f il *Antiques* 132:782-97 O '87

Italy

A garden of earthly delights [N. de Saint-Phalle's fantastical sculptures inspired by the Tarot] B. Rose. il pors *Vogue* 177:266-73+ D '87

House of cards: Niki de Saint Phalle's Tuscan fantasy [Garden of the Tarot; cover story] Michael, Prince of Greece. il por *Archit Dig* 44:124-31 S '87

Maine

An imaginative kingdom: sculptor Bernard Langlais' Maine legacy. A. Berman. il *Archit Dig* 44:174-7+ Je '87

New York (State)

See also

Isamu Noguchi Garden Museum

Scotland

Neoclassical rearmament [work of I. H. Finlay] C. Gintz. il *Art Am* 75:110-17 F '87

South Carolina

See also

Brookgreen Gardens

Texas

See also

Museum of Fine Arts (Houston, Tex.). Lillie and Hugh Roy Cullen Sculpture Garden

The collectors: a passion for sculpture: Patsy and Raymond D. Nasher's Dallas residence and gardens. J. Chatfield-Taylor. il *Archit Dig* 44:112-21 O '87

Sculpture in motion *See* Kinetic sculpture

Sculpture in the Environment, Inc. *See* SITE, Inc.

Scurvy

Saved by the Indians [antidote given to French explorers; excerpt from Voyages au Canada] J. Cartier. il *Courier* 40:12 Ap '87

SDI *See* Strategic Defense Initiative

SDS *See* Students for a Democratic Society

Sea-air interaction *See* Ocean-atmosphere interaction

Sea anemones

The anemone is not its enemy [clownfish] D. G. Fautin. il *Natl Wildl* 25:22-5 O/N '87

Sea birds

See also

Albatrosses

Murres

Terns

Suburbs close in on a seabird colony [proposed expansion of Kilauea National Wildlife Refuge] J. Yoshimoto and C. Proczka. il *Sierra* 72:69-70 My/Je '87

Sea birds, Fossil

Fossil skeleton sets seabird size record [pseudodontorn bound in South Carolina; work of Storrs L. Olson] B. Bower. *Sci News* 132:310 N 14 '87

Sea Breeze Awards *See* Youth—Awards

Sea captains *See* Shipmasters

Sea cows, Fossil *See* Sirenia, Fossil

Sea cucumber sexual behavior *See* Sexual behavior—Echinoderms

Sea festivals *See* Festivals

Sea floor *See* Ocean bottom

Sea frontiers (Periodical)

Crow's nest [results of reader survey] G. L. Voss. *Sea Front* 33:162-3 My/Je '87

Sea Grant Programs (U.S.) *See* United States. National Oceanic and Atmospheric Administration. Office of Sea Grant Programs

Sea horses

Fishy horses. il *Natl Geogr World* 138:30-3 F '87

Sea Island (Ga.)

See also

Architecture, Domestic—Sea Island (Ga.)

Sea Islands

See also

Blacks—Sea Islands

Description and travel

"Nowhere to lay down weary head". C. L. Blockson. il maps *Natl Geogr* 172:734-43+ D '87

Sea kayaking *See* Kayaks and kayaking

Sea-Land Corp.

CSX may have charted a treacherous course [purchase of Sea-Land] T. Ichniowski. il *Bus Week* p36+ F 16 '87

Sea law *See* Maritime law

Sea level changes

Chronology of fluctuating sea levels since the Triassic. B. U. Haq and others. bibl f il *Science* 235:1156-67 Mr 6 '87

"It can't happen to me". G. Reiger. il *Field Stream* 92:34+ Jl '87

Precise timing of the last interglacial period from mass spectrometric determination of thorium-230 in corals. R. L. Edwards and others. bibl f il *Science* 236:1547-53 Je 19 '87

Refining and defending the Vail sea level curve. R. A. Kerr. il *Science* 235:1141-2 Mr 6 '87

The rise and fall of Neptune's kingdom. C. T. Feazel. il *Sea Front* 33:4-11 Ja/F '87

Rising seas levels: predictions and plans [work of Tom M. L. Wigley and Sarah C. B. Raper] R. Monastersky. *Sci News* 132:326 N 21 '87

Sea level changes—*cont.*
Sea cycle clock [seismic stratigraphy; work of Peter R. Vail and others] S. Weisburd. il *Sci News* 131:154-5 Mr 7 '87
Sea life *See* Seafaring life
Sea Life Park (Waimanalo, Hawaii)
Fish's-eye views of Hawaii at Waikiki and Sea Life Park. il *Sunset* 179:82-3 N '87
Sea lions *See* Seals (Animals)
Sea monkeys *See* Brine shrimp
Sea monsters
What is that? [work of P. H. LeBlond] D. G. Gordon. il *Oceans* 20:44-9 Jl/Ag '87
Sea Oaks (Vero Beach, Fla.: Resort) *See* Resorts—Florida
Sea of Cortéz (Mexico) *See* Gulf of California (Mexico)
Sea Palms Resort (Saint Simons Island, Ga.) *See* Resorts—Georgia
Sea parrots *See* Puffins
Sea planes *See* Seaplanes
Sea rescues *See* Rescue work
Sea shells *See* Shells (Conchology)
Sea slugs
Deep colors [nudibranch] G. Martin. il *Oceans* 20:56+ Ja/F '87
Solar-powered animals [aeolid nudibranchs growing zooxanthellae inside their bodies; cover story] W. B. Rudman. il *Nat Hist* 96:50-3 O '87
　　　　Orientation
See Orientation
Sea snakes
A deadly business [Philippine divers collect venomous snakes for snakeskin trade; with photographs] H. Hall. il *Int Wildl* 17:12-15 Jl/Ag '87
Sea songs
Chantey sing in San Francisco. il *Sunset* 178:34 F '87
Sea stars *See* Starfish
Sea turtles *See* Turtles
Sea urchins
Diadema antillarum was not a keystone predator in cryptic reef environments. J. B. C. Jackson and K. W. Kaufmann. bibl f il *Science* 235:687-9 F 6 '87
Down under a sand dollar: world of the tiniest crab [Dissodactylus mellitae] J. L. Bell. il *Sea Front* 33:210-15 My/Je '87
The spangled reef. il *Sea Front* 33:183-5 My/Je '87
　　　　Embryology
See Embryology—Echinoderms
　　　　Reproduction
The existential decision of a sperm [research by Bennett Shapiro] il *Discover* 8:10-11 Ag '87
Sea water
Acantharian fluxes and strontium to chlorinity ratios in the North Pacific Ocean. R. E. Bernstein and others. bibl f il *Science* 237:1490-4 S 18 '87
Bacteria: link or sink? [discussion of May 16, 1986 article, Bacterioplankton: a sink for carbon in a coastal marine plankton community] H. W. Ducklow and others. *Science* 235:88-9 Ja 2 '87
Can microscale chemical patches persist in the sea? Microelectrode study of marine snow, fecal pellets. A. L. Alldredge and Y. Cohen. bibl f il *Science* 235:689-91 F 6 '87
Oxygen supersaturation in the ocean: biological versus physical contributions. H. Craig and T. Hayward. bibl f il *Science* 235:199-202 Ja 9 '87
Swept away: resuspension of bacterial mats regulates benthic-pelagic exchange of sulfur. J. Grant and U. V. Bathmann. bibl f il *Science* 236:1472-4 Je 12 '87
　　　　Pollution
See Marine pollution
　　　　Therapeutic use
See Thalassotherapy
Sea water powered hydraulic tools *See* Hydraulic tools
Sea waves *See* Waves
Sea Week (Horta, Azores) *See* Festivals—Azores
Seabass sexual behavior *See* Sexual behavior—Fish
Seabed mining *See* Ocean mining
Seabirds *See* Sea birds
Seaborg, Glenn T., and Loeb, Benjamin S., 1914-
Make the partial test ban comprehensive. *Bull At Sci* 43:3 My '87
Seabrook nuclear power plant (N.H.) *See* Nuclear power plants
Seabury, Jennifer
Up, up, and away. il *N Y* 20:36-42 Ag 3 '87
Seacat, Alysoun
　　　　about
Alysoun Seacat is number one in Nuka's heart—by a whisker. B. Rowes. il por *People Wkly* 28:110-11 Ag 10 '87

Seafaring life
See also
Voyages
　　　　History
A boy at sea [memories of life aboard a Pacific lumber schooner in 1915] R. B. Hope. il por *Am Hist Illus* 21:14-18 Ja '87
Seafirst Corporation
Banking in the 80s [address, November 5, 1986] R. M. Rosenberg. *Vital Speeches Day* 53:232-5 F 1 '87
Seafood
See also
Cooking—Seafood
Fish as food
Surimi
Seafood appetizers *See* Appetizers
Seafood Industry Museum (Biloxi, Miss.)
A taste of Biloxi's seafood heritage. il *South Living* 22:27 Ap '87
Seafood restaurants *See* Restaurants
Seaga, Edward P. G.
　　　　about
The locomotive needs help. A. D. Frank. por *Forbes* 139:100 Ja 26 '87
Seaga plays for time in Jamaica. P. Engardio. il por *Bus Week* p41 Ap 20 '87
Seaga under pressure. J. C. Baker. por *Black Enterp* 17:17 Ja '87
Seagate Technology
How Tom Mitchell lays out the competition. B. O'Reilly. il pors *Fortune* 115:90-3+ Mr 30 '87
Seagate goes East—and comes back a winner. R. Brandt. il por *Bus Week* p94 Mr 16 '87
Seagram Company Ltd.
Can the Bronfmans keep Seagram in the family? E. B. Terry. il *Bus Week* p60 Je 1 '87
A dynasty divided [Bronfman family] P. Best. il *Macleans* 100:41 My 18 '87
Seagull Energy Corp.
Sitting pretty. L. M. Keefe. il *Forbes* 140:172 O 5 '87
Seahorses *See* Sea horses
Seal, Kathy Shenkin
Can the beauty pageant be saved? il *Ms* 15:32 My '87
Sealand Aquarium (West Brewster, Mass.)
Strange pool-fellows [dolphin swim seminar] L. W. Kloss. il *Travel Holiday* 167:8+ Ap '87
Seale, William
History in houses: the Ximenez-Fatio House in Saint Augustine, Florida. il *Antiques* 131:426-31 F '87
Sealfon, Peggy
Electronics roundup. il *Petersens Photogr Mag* 16:12+ S '87
Sealing
Back to the killing field [hunt for harp and hooded seals off Labrador] C. Wood. il *Macleans* 100:22 Ap 6 '87
Is saving the seals killing the Eskimos? E. Wiedemann. il *World Press Rev* 34:35-7 Jl '87
Netting a solution [fur seals killed by entanglement in plastic netting at sea] L. Williamson. il *Outdoor Life* 180:38+ Jl '87
Sealing compounds
See also
Caulking
Loctite Corp.
Seals (Animals)
See also
Sealing
Balancing act at Point Reyes [cover story] K. Evans. il *Natl Parks* 61:16-21 Jl/Ag '87
Diving adaptations of the Weddell seal. W. M. Zapol. bibl (p136) il *Sci Am* 256:100-5 Je '87
Encounter under the ice [crabeater seals meet humans off coast of Antarctica] D. Allan. il *Int Wildl* 17:48-51 Mr/Ap '87
In the society of lions [Galapagos sea lions] T. De Roy. il *Int Wildl* 17:30-5 N/D '87
Netting a solution [fur seals killed by entanglement in plastic netting at sea] L. Williamson. il *Outdoor Life* 180:38+ Jl '87
Seals and their kin [cover story] R. L. Gentry. il supp (folded map) *Natl Geogr* 171:474-501 Ap '87
Seals under the sun [Galapagos fur seals] F. Trillmich. il *Nat Hist* 96:42-9 O '87
　　　　Food and feeding
PCB-polluted fishes cause seal decline [Waddenzee, Netherlands] *Sea Front* 33:305-6 Jl/Ag '87
Seal-salmon controversy escalates in B.C. [harbor seals] B. Obee. il *Oceans* 20:8-9 S/O '87

Seals (Animals)—*cont.*

Photographs and photography

Surf's up [San Nicolas Island sea lions] S. Leatherwood. il *Nat Hist* 96:76-7 Ag '87

Seals (Animals) in rescue work

Saved by a seal. il *Life* 10:158-9 N '87

Seals (Christmas) *See* Christmas seals

Seals (Numismatics)

Antiques: seals: assuring identity and privacy with style. S. Drummond. il *Archit Dig* 44:182-7 O '87

Delete slave ship from Chicago seal: aldermen. il *Jet* 72:4 S 21 '87

Sealy Incorporated

Mattress wars [Ohio Mattress acquires Sealy] J. Andresky. il *por Forbes* 139:41 Je 15 '87

Seaman, Barbara

about

How green was her valley. L. Fleischer. il *Publ Wkly* 231:89 F 13 '87

Seaman, Carl

about

Heir raising. B. Leonard. il *pors Forbes* 140:74+ S 7 '87

Seaman, Morton

about

Heir raising. B. Leonard. il *pors Forbes* 140:74+ S 7 '87

Seaman, Rosie

Ready, set, learn! 10 games to grow on [cover story] il *Parents* 62:84-6+ Jl '87

Seaman Furniture Co., Inc.

Heir raising. B. Leonard. il *pors Forbes* 140:74+ S 7 '87

Seamanship

See also

Boats and boating—Handling

Navigation

Seamanship. See alternate issues of Motor Boating & Sailing

Seamen

Auld mug's game [crews of Stars & Stripes and Kookaburra III] J. D. Reed. il *Time* 129:46-7 F 9 '87

Who was that mast man? [J. Barnitt, youngest crew member on Stars & Stripes] C. Neff. il *Sports Illus* 66:17 F 16 '87

Language

Crow's nest [proper use of sea terms] G. L. Voss. *Sea Front* 33:82-3 Mr/Ap '87

Paying the devil. D. Starr. il *N Y Times Mag* p6+ Mr 22 '87

Songs and music

See Sea songs

Seamen, Handicapped

On eye opening [blind sailor J. Dickson attempts to sail across the Atlantic alone] W. F. Buckley. *Natl Rev* 39:73 S 11 '87

Seamounts

Birth of an island [exploration of Loihi by submarine Alvin] J. C. Borg. il map *Oceans* 20:26-33 Jl/Ag '87

Seamount serendipity in the South Pacific [eruption of MacDonald Seamount] R. Monastersky. *Sci News* 132:262 O 24 '87

Submarine crew finds volcano, minerals and exotic animals [Alvin explores Loihi] il *Earth Sci* 40:7 Fall '87

Seaplanes

See also

Chalk's International Airlines

Northwest exploring by seaplane . . . cities, waterways, wild high country. il *Sunset* 178:66 Je '87

Piloting

High explosives [Cessna 206 floatplane with leaky fuel lines] W. Haines. il *Flying* 114:108-9 Jl '87

Search and rescue operations *See* Rescue work

Search for Extraterrestrial Intelligence *See* Interstellar communication

Searches and seizures

Bill Bolling: boarded, bothered and busted [arrested for interfering with Coast Guardsmen trying to board boat] P. Whittell. il *pors Mot Boat Sail* 159:66-9+ F '87

Boarding—with dignity [change in Coast Guard policy] P. A. Janssen. il *Mot Boat Sail* 159:11 My '87

Drugs, AIDS and the threat to privacy. Y. Kamisar. il *N Y Times Mag* p108-10+ S 13 '87

High Court splits on search of public employee's office [O'Connor v. Ortega] T. J. Flygare. *Phi Delta Kappan* 68:792-4 Je '87

In Detroit, kids kill kids [searching students for weapons used in school-related attacks] E. Salholz. il *Newsweek* 109:74 My 11 '87

Rambo & Rambo, attorneys-at-law [lawyers acting as prosecutors in trademark counterfeit cases] D. Fanning. *Forbes* 139:76 Ja 26 '87

Searching, On line *See* On line searching

Searls, Hank

Jaws—the revenge [fiction] il *Ladies Home J* 104:78+ Ag '87

about

Strictly Bush league. .. Fleischer. *Publ Wkly* 232:30 N 20 '87

Sears, John R., Jr.

about

John Sears has brought Norfolk change. D. Young. il *por South Living* 22:160+ Ap '87

Sears, Roebuck and Co.

The big store (I). D. R. Katz. il *Esquire* 108:107-8+ S '87

The big store (II). D. R. Katz. il *Esquire* 108:177-80+ O '87

Can Sears get sexier but keep the common touch? M. D. Oneal. il *por Bus Week* p93-5 Jl 6 '87

The good old days [prices of sporting goods in 1900 Sears catalog] E. B. Mann. il *Field Stream* 92:66-7+ Je '87

Lawyer in the lobby [black woman lawyer B. M. Girton of Washington, D.C. corporate governmental affairs office] N. A. Williams. il *por Essence* 18:113+ Jl '87

The rise of Discover. S. B. Weiner. il *Forbes* 139:46-7 My 4 '87

Sears: trimming the worst of the corporate fat. M. D. Oneal. *Bus Week* p39 Mr 16 '87

Women's history and EEOC v. Sears [sex discrimination case; special section] *Society* 24:4-16 S/O '87

Sears Savings Bank

Name recognition [scales back California operations] J. Heins. il *Forbes* 140:137 N 30 '87

Seascape photography *See* Marine photography

Seascapes *See* Marine painting

Seashore

See also

Beaches

Seashore ecology

See also

Intertidal ecology

Seashore photography *See* Marine photography

Seashore protection *See* Shore protection

Seasickness *See* Motion sickness

Seasonal affective disorder

Beating winter blahs. il *Vogue* 177:356 D '87

Can weather affect your mood? B. Levine. il *Seventeen* 46:166+ S '87

Those SAD winter days. il *Newsweek* 109:54 My 4 '87

Winter doldrums. il *Ms* 16:53 D '87

Therapy

Antidepressant and circadian phase-shifting effects of light. A. J. Lewy and others. bibl f il *Science* 235:352-4 Ja 16 '87

Cure for the winter blues [light therapy; work of Gary Sachs] S. J. Nadis. il *Technol Rev* 90:12-13 N/D '87

Winter depression: day for night [correction of melatonin production timing; research by Alfred J. Lewy and others] J. Meer. il *Psychol Today* 21:12 Je '87

Seasonal industries

See also

Construction industry

Seasonal labor

See also

Migrant labor

Seasonings

See also

Garlic

Herbs

Mustard, Prepared

Salt

Spices

Assertive seasoning pastes for barbecued seafood or meat. il *Sunset* 179:134 Ag '87

Seasons

See also

Autumn

Equinoxes

Spring

Summer

Winter

The importance of "tweety birds". S. Cook. il *Natl Wildl* 25:46-7 O/N '87

Seastar airplanes *See* Airplanes, Amphibious
Seat belts, Automobile *See* Automobiles—Safety belts
Seat belts, School bus *See* School buses—Safety belts
Seaton, Bruce *See* Seaton, Wilbur Bruston
Seaton, Wilbur Bruston
about
Train, ahoy! J. Cook. il por *Forbes* 139:60+ My 18 '87
Seats
See also
Airplanes, Jet—Seats
School buses—Seats
Toilet seats
Seats on commodity exchanges *See* Commodity exchanges—Membership
Seats on stock exchanges *See* Stock exchanges—Membership
Seattle (Wash.)
Architecture
An envelope of air around this house keeps it cool in summer, warm in winter. il *Sunset* 178:94-6 F '87
For the views and warmth, she lives mostly on the second floor. il *Sunset* 179:126+ N '87
Art
"Northwest impressions" at Henry Art Gallery. M. Kangas. *Art Am* 75:191+ My '87
Bookstores
See Booksellers and bookselling—Washington (State)
City planning
How not to design a park: Seattle settles on a Rouse project . . . [Westlake Center development] D. Gantenbein. il *Archit Rec* 175:63 Ag '87
Crime
Seattle's Gene Anderson throws the book at white-collar coke users who once knew no fear. M. Green. il por *People Wkly* 27:111-12 F 2 '87
Galleries and museums
See also
Museum of Flight (Seattle, Wash.)
Seattle Art Museum
Housing
Double identity [Doublehouse apartment house] D. Dietsch. il *Archit Rec* 175:94-7 mid-Ap '87
Monuments, statues, etc.
Paradise lost [M. Schwartz's sculptural environment in main entry plaza of new jail] L. Smallwood. il *Art News* 86:57 O '87
Music
See also
Seattle Opera
Police
Recycled as cyclists, Seattle's posse of bike-riding crime fighters put their mettle to the pedal. D. Chu. il *People Wkly* 28:53-4 N 9 '87
Religious institutions and affairs
Hunthausen reinstated. *Christ Century* 104:522 Je 3-10 '87
Hunthausen restored. *Commonweal* 114:372-3 Je 19 '87
Letter from Seattle [Catholic Church] J. Whelan. *America* 156:463-5+ Je 6 '87
Panel probe in Seattle [R. C. Hunthausen case] *Christ Century* 104:215 Mr 4 '87
Theater
See also
Intiman Theatre (Seattle, Wash.)
Transit systems
This summer, one more way to get to Victoria by water. il *Sunset* 179:34-5 Ag '87
Seattle Art Museum
'A tremendous opportunity' [appointment of P. Sims as new chief curator] L. Smallwood. por *Art News* 86:37-8 N '87
Seattle Opera
'Ring' of magic. P. G. Davis. il *N Y* 20:116-17 Ag 24 '87
Seattle [Ring cycle] D. Harris. il *Opera News* 52:36 D 19 '87
Seaver, Tom
about
Tom Seaver. P. Jordan. il por *Sport Mag* 78:95-7 D '87
Tom to the rescue. P. Gammons. il *Sports Illus* 66:54 Je 15 '87
Seawater *See* Sea water
Seaweed
See also
Kelp
New light on seaweeds [role of light harvesting pigments in depth zonation of seaweeds; cover story] M. B. Saffo. bibl il *BioScience* 37:654-64 O '87

Seaweed as food
Limu: a Hawaiian delicacy. C. Bates. il *Gourmet* 47:72-3+ S '87
Seawright, Toni
about
First black Miss Mississippi to compete for Miss America. por *Jet* 72:14-15 Ag 3 '87
Sebastopol (Calif.)
Historic houses, sites, etc.
Burbank's legacy [Goldridge Farm] J. Cox. il pors map *Rodale's Org Gard* 34:27-8+ S '87
SEC *See* United States. Securities and Exchange Commission
Sechler, Teena
A drummer's gift [story] il *Redbook* 170:60-1 D '87
Second Advent
See also
Millennium
No time for end times. H. Smith. *Christ Today* 31:15 O 2 '87
Second Committee (United Nations) *See* United Nations. Economic and Financial Committee
Second mortgages *See* Mortgages
Second National Building & Loan Inc.
A good niche is hard to find. J. Wynn. il por *Forbes* 139:90 Ja 26 '87
Second opinion, Medical *See* Surgery
Second wind (Athletics)
In search of the second wind. C. E. Lincoln. il *Sport Mag* 78:87-8 Jl '87
Secondary education *See* Education, Secondary
Secondhand books
See also
Booksellers and bookselling—Secondhand books
Secondhand cameras *See* Cameras, Used
Secondhand trade
See also
Flea markets
Are you buying used goods? H. R. Kennedy. *U S News World Rep* 103:75 D 14 '87
The town that transforms junk into treasure [Hohenwald, Tenn.] G. Witkin. il *U S News World Rep* 102:22 Mr 16 '87
Secord, Richard V.
about
"A man of many talents". R. Stengel. il por *Time* 129:16 My 11 '87
The man who ran the show. G. J. Church. il pors *Time* 129:34-6 My 18 '87
Ollie North's secret network. T. Morganthau. il pors *Newsweek* 109:32-7 Mr 9 '87
A patriot—or a profiteer? L. Martz. il por *Newsweek* 109:38-40+ My 18 '87
Patriots pursuing profits. E. Magnuson. il por *Time* 129:24-5 Je 8 '87
Reagan's secret government. *New Repub* 196:7-9 Je 1 '87
A 'sad and sordid' story. I. Austen. il por *Macleans* 100:18-19 My 18 '87
Secord agent. *Nation* 245:40-1 Jl 18-25 '87
The secret world of General Secord [cover story] R. Nordland. il pors *Newsweek* 109:20-2 My 11 '87
A shadowy figure behind the scenes. il por *Newsweek* 109:27 F 9 '87
Why it hurts: the murky worlds of Hart and Secord raise painful questions about what America expects of its leaders and institutions. R. Stengel. il *Time* 129:14-15 My 18 '87
Secrecy (Law)
See also
Confidential communications
Trade secrets
Secrecy in government *See* Classified information; Official secrets
Secret agents *See* Espionage
Secret bank accounts *See* Confidential communications—Banking
Secret codes *See* Cryptography
The secret garden [television program] *See* Television program reviews—Single works
The secret of my success [film] *See* Motion picture reviews—Single works
Secret service
See also
Intelligence service
Iranian-Iraqi War, 1980- —Secret service
United States. Central Intelligence Agency
World War, 1939-1945—Secret service

Secret service—*cont.*
Canada
See also
Royal Canadian Mounted Police
Chile
See also
Letelier, Orlando—Assassination
Israel
See also
Israel. Shin Bet
Soviet Union
See also
KGB
Secret societies
See also
Ku Klux Klan
Secretaries
See also
Administrative assistants
Professional Secretaries International
Don't call me honey [managing a secretary] S. Bing. il *Esquire* 108:49 Jl '87
How to work without a secretary. E. W. Allison and M. A. Allison. *Work Woman* 12:22 Ag '87
A male secretary. J. Finder. il *N Y Times Mag* p68 F 22 '87
My secretary, my ally. S. Y. Lopez. il *Black Enterp* 17:100 F '87
Secretaries (Furniture) *See* Desks
Secretaries of State (U.S.)
The president and the Secretary of State. T. C. Sorensen. *Foreign Aff* 66:231-48 Wint '87/'88
To quit or not to quit: did Shultz get it right? T. Jacoby. il *Newsweek* 110:19 Ag 3 '87
Secretions
See also
Endocrine glands
Gonadotropins
Melatonin
Mucus
Pheromones
Secrets, Official *See* Official secrets
Secrets, Personal *See* Personal secrets
Secrets, Trade *See* Trade secrets
Sectionalism *See* Regionalism
Sector funds *See* Investment trusts
Sects
See also
Amish
Jehovah's Witnesses
Mennonites
Mormons and Mormonism
Shakers
Unification Church
Secular humanism *See* Humanism
Secular humanism and Christianity *See* Christianity and humanism
Secularism
Our secular Constitution. E. Doerr. *Humanist* 47:43-4 Mr/Ap '87
The use and abuse of liberty. T. Eastland. il por *Christ Today* 31:28-30 Jl 10 '87
Secura Group
Fence jumper [W. M. Isaac] E. Giltenan. il por *Forbes* 140:224 O 5 '87
Securities
See also
American depositary receipts
Asset-backed financing
Banks and banking—Securities handling
Blind pools (Securities)
Brokers
Church securities
Convertible securities
Over-the-counter securities markets
Parking (Securities)
Pay-in-kind securities
Private placements (Securities)
Stock exchanges
Stocks
Street sweeps (Securities)
Treasury bills and notes
Under-the-counter securities
See also subhead Securities under various subjects
Best investment moves to make now. J. Bodnar. il *Changing Times* 41:24-9 Jl '87
Great investment portfolios [cover story] D. M. Kehrer. il *Changing Times* 41:24-36 S '87
Markets & investments. See issues of Business Week
Smart ways to invest in a risky market. W. L. Updegrave. il *Money* 16:44-8 O '87

Statistical spotlight. See issues of Forbes
Guaranty
See also
Financial Security Assurance
Laws and regulations
See also
Corporations—Acquisitions and mergers—Laws and regulations
United States. Securities and Exchange Commission
Are we hissing the wrong guys? G. J. Stigler. il *Forbes* 140:52-3+ Jl 13 '87
Ban program trading. *New Repub* 197:9 N 30 '87
Behind the crash probes. S. Waldman. il *Newsweek* 110:36-7 D 28 '87
The blight on Wall Street. F. G. Rohatyn. il *N Y Rev Books* 34:21-3 Mr 12 '87
Can't sue your broker? It's no big loss [Supreme Court decision upholds arbitration] D. Zigas. il *Bus Week* p128 Je 22 '87
Cranking up the reform machine [result of stock market crash] P. Elmer-Dewitt. il *Time* 130:42 N 9 '87
Crime wave [securities crime; cover story] R. L. Stern and M. Schifrin. il *Forbes* 139:67-70 Je 29 '87
Futures shock. D. Corn. *Nation* 245:509-10 N 7 '87
Government bond dealers: a bell is tolling. G. DeGeorge. *Bus Week* p63-4 My 25 '87
Insider trading's victims [investors rush to court] B. Powell and C. Friday. il *Newsweek* 109:40-1 Ap 6 '87
The lawyers to call when there's heat on the Street [attorneys who battle for accused insider traders] G. Weiss. il *Bus Week* p58+ Ap 6 '87
Maybe we just need a dictionary [proposals for an insider-trading definition] *Fortune* 116:14 S 14 '87
Must the panic get worse to spark reform? A. Bianco. il *Bus Week* p46-7 N 9 '87
No news is bad news [quicker corporate disclosure to discourage insider trading] J. Crudele. il *N Y* 20:20-1 Je 8 '87
Program previews. J. Crudele. *N Y* 20:16+ N 16 '87
Protecting your securities investment. *Consum Res Mag* 70:33-5 O '87
The Securities Act of 1988? P. Fuhrman. il *Forbes* 139:40-1 Mr 9 '87
Small investors and the crash. C. Friday. il *Newsweek* 110:50-1 D 21 '87
Stock wars: the longs vs. the shorts. C. Wells. il *Bus Week* p118-19+ My 11 '87
The Street is fretting over 'Street sweeps'. A. Bianco. il por *Bus Week* p71-2 Ag 3 '87
Strong medicine for the markets. M. Mayer. il *U S News World Rep* 103:34 N 2 '87
Sue your stockbroker? You can't, you know [upcoming Supreme Court ruling] S. Weiss. il *Bus Week* p75-6 Mr 2 '87
Wall Street's watchword: hire a watchdog [in-house legal staffs] L. J. Tell. il *Bus Week* p120+ O 5 '87
What happened and what's next [post crash reforms] A. L. Taylor, III. il *Fortune* 116:76-9+ N 23 '87
What is insider trading? An answer may be on the way. V. Cahan. il *Bus Week* p28 Je 29 '87
What next? F. G. Rohatyn. il *N Y Rev Books* 34:3-5 D 3 '87
What to do if your broker leads you astray. T. Segal. il *Bus Week* p90 F 2 '87
What Washington can do to clean up the Street. V. Cahan and others. il *Bus Week* p35 Mr 2 '87
Why stockbrokers sleep at night [Supreme Court upholds binding arbitration] M. Meyer. il *Money* 16:105-8+ Jl '87

International aspects
The global funny money game. H. M. Wachtel. il *Nation* 245:784-6+ D 26 '87-Ja 2 '88
The insider-trading dragnet is stretching across the globe. J. Templeman and W. Glasgall. il *Bus Week* p50-1 Mr 23 '87
Canada
See also
Ontario Securities Commission
Quebec Securities Commission
A strange way to run a company [questionable practices by Technigen Platinum Corp.] D. Francis. il *Macleans* 100:11 S 28 '87
The ugly face of markets [upcoming security fraud trials] T. Tedesco. il *Macleans* 100:30 S 14 '87
Who is watching the traders? [views of B. Steck] P. C. Newman. il por *Macleans* 100:42 O 26 '87
Great Britain
Britain's business elite takes a fall [Guinness affair] P. Sherrid. il *U S News World Rep* 102:47-8 F 2 '87

Securities—Laws and regulations—Great Britain—*cont.*
Britain's own Boesky case [Guinness affair] R. I. Kirkland, Jr. il por *Fortune* 115:85-6 F 16 '87
Downfall of a titan [E. W. Saunders' role in Guinness securities scandal] T. Fennell. il por *Macleans* 100:28 My 25 '87
Fearing that "muck will stick" [Guinness stock trading scandal] S. Holmes. il *Time* 129:61 Mr 9 '87
The Guinness affair gets curiouser and curiouser [role of M. Riklis and sale of Schenley to Guinness] M. Maremont. *Bus Week* p59-60 My 25 '87
How Guinness suddenly fell from grace. R. A. Melcher and M. Maremont. il pors *Bus Week* p44-6 F 9 '87
Look who may take a fall in the Guinness scandal. M. Maremont. por *Bus Week* p48 O 26 '87
The questions surrounding Guinness' U.S. connection [Washington lawyer T. J. Ward] P. Dwyer and M. Maremont. il por *Bus Week* p36-7 Ap 27 '87
Scandal at Guinness. R. Laver. il *Macleans* 100:62 F 2 '87
The scandal at Guinness: will the chief fall? [insider trading charges] M. Maremont and R. A. Melcher. il por *Bus Week* p52 Ja 19 '87

Sweden
Scandal in Sweden: how the Fermenta dream turned sour. J. Kapstein. il por *Bus Week* p68-9 Je 8 '87

Marketing
See also
Specialists (Stock exchange firms)
Deals of the year. D. P. Wiener. il *Fortune* 115:68-72+ F 2 '87

Mathematical models
A war of the generations [crash ignites feud between Wall Street old-timers and quants] B. Powell. il *Newsweek* 110:48-9 N 30 '87

Prospectuses
Required reading [muni prospectus] B. Weberman. il *Forbes* 139:183 Ap 6 '87

Short selling
Four ways to tame this bear market. J. Edgerton. il *Money* 16:145-6 D '87
Full throttle, damn the shorts [selling of Fountain Power-boats Industries] R. L. Stern. il por *Forbes* 139:80-1 Je 1 '87
How to sell Japan short [trading futures on Japan's Nikkei 225-stock index on the Singapore Stock Exchange] F. Rice. il *Fortune* 115:170+ Je 22 '87
Inside Wall Street: how bulls and bears are playing the crash. G. G. Marcial. il *Bus Week* p56 N 2 '87
Leveraging your mutual funds. B. Kallen. il *Forbes* 139:161-2 Ap 6 '87
Reaping from grim decline. D. R. Katz. il *Esquire* 107:33-4 F '87
Selling short: not for the faint of heart. R. Brady. il *Nations Bus* 75:63 Mr '87
Shelby could give the shorts a shock [Shelby Williams Industries] G. G. Marcial. *Bus Week* p165 O 12 '87
Short selling: what looks good now [recommendations of Michael Murphy] J. Egan. il *U S News World Rep* 102:51 Mr 9 '87
The shorts in AT&E: caught with their pants down? G. G. Marcial. il *Bus Week* p94 Mr 9 '87
Shortsellers in the bull market. B. D. Fromson. il *Fortune* 116:52-4+ Ag 31 '87
Spread on thick. K. L. Fisher. il *Forbes* 139 Ann Directory:334 Ap 27 '87
Stock wars: the longs vs. the shorts. C. Wells. il *Bus Week* p118-19+ My 11 '87
Tailing it out of retail. S. Lee. il *Forbes* 139:144 F 9 '87
This Symbol may be misinterpreted [short selling of Symbol Technologies Inc.] G. G. Marcial. *Bus Week* p73 Ag 24 '87
Trouble for the shorts in Zenith Labs? G. G. Marcial. il *Bus Week* p72 Ap 6 '87

Taxation
The breaks of buying on margin. B. Hitchings. il *Bus Week* p120 Je 1 '87
Make the taxman share the losses. W. Baldwin. *Forbes* 140:48+ N 16 '87
Worth less than the sum of its parts? G. W. Padwe. il *Nations Bus* 75:75 N '87

Yields
10 great ways to invest for income [cover story; special section] il *Money* 16:59-64+ Je '87
Tips from America's best income investor [B. Johnstone] J. E. Goodman. il por *Money* 16:81-4 Ja '87
Will the real yield please stand up. J. Bodnar. il *Changing Times* 41:125-6+ Ja '87

Australia
See also
Stock exchanges—Sydney exchange
Treasury bills and notes—Australia
Dateline: Sydney. T. Jaffe. *Forbes* 139:290-1 Ja 12 '87

Canada
See also
Brokers—Canada
Hard times for small stocks [new issues] A. Shortell. il *Macleans* 100:36-7 O 26 '87
Living with the crash [cover story; special section; with editorial comment by Kevin Doyle] il *Macleans* 100:2, 26-36+ N 2 '87
Profits from mortgages. A. Walmsley. il *Macleans* 100:26 Ja 12 '87
Stocks from the frozen North [interview with C. Rabin] A. E. Serwer. il por *Fortune* 115:108 Mr 30 '87

France
A choice menu from Jacques Chirac. M. McFadden. il *Fortune* 115:18-19 Ja 5 '87

Great Britain
See also
Bonds, Government—Great Britain
Adding to the wreckage [sale of British Petroleum shares] R. Laver. il *Macleans* 100:45 N 9 '87
British Airways value set at $1.36 billion. *Aviat Week Space Technol* 126:36 F 2 '87
Panmure Gordon & Co. [interview with M. Henderson] il por *Fortune* 116 Sp Issue:182-3 Fall '87
A spanner in the works [privatization of Rolls-Royce endangered by V2500 setbacks] H. Banks. il *Forbes* 139:36-7 Je 1 '87
Unloading British Airways. R. A. Melcher. *Bus Week* p48 F 9 '87

Indonesia
See also
Bonds, Government—Indonesia

Jamaica
See also
Stock exchanges—Jamaican exchange

Japan
See also
Bonds, Government—Japan
Brokers—Japan
Japan Fund, Inc.
Over-the-counter securities markets—Japan
Banzai, Nikkei? S. Lee. il *Forbes* 140:466 Jl 13 '87
How to say frenzy in Japanese. A. Rock. il *Money* 16:211-12 Je '87
How to sell Japan short [trading futures on Japan's Nikkei 225-stock index on the Singapore Stock Exchange] F. Rice. il *Fortune* 115:170+ Je 22 '87
Land of the rising stocks [cover story] H. Rudnitsky and P. Fuhrman. il *Forbes* 139:139-43 My 18 '87
'Shogun' bonds start to storm Japan. B. Buell and W. Glasgall. il *Bus Week* p73 F 9 '87
Sitting tight in Japan [interview with L. Biehl] A. E. Serwer. il por *Fortune* 115:306 Ap 27 '87
Time to go easy on Japanese stocks? J. P. Newport, Jr. il *Fortune* 116:97-8 Ag 31 '87
We'll send you VCRs—you send us stocks. M. Beauchamp and J. Heins. il *Forbes* 140:60-2 Ag 10 '87

Korea (South)
See also
Korea Fund Inc.

Norway
A couple of Norwegian dogs. T. Jaffe. il *Forbes* 139:109 My 4 '87

Western Europe
Global table talk [France, Italy and Spain] S. Lee. il *Forbes* 139:174 Mr 23 '87

Securities, Tax exempt
See also
Bonds, Industrial development
Mortgage bonds and notes
Municipal bonds
Stripped municipal bonds
Securities and Exchange Commission (U.S.) *See* United States. Securities and Exchange Commission
Securities Commission (Ont.) *See* Ontario Securities Commission
Securities Dealers, National Association of *See* National Association of Securities Dealers
Securities fraud *See* Fraud
Securities Groups
Pied Piper to the truly rich [C. Atkins indicted for tax evasion and securities fraud] F. Ungeheuer. il por *Time* 129:52 Ap 6 '87
Wall Street's prime-time crime drama [tax evasion and securities fraud charges against C. Atkins] D. Pauly. il por *Newsweek* 109:44 Ap 6 '87

Securities industry *See* Brokers
Securitization *See* Asset-backed financing
Security, Internal *See* Internal security
Security, Job *See* Job security
Security analysts *See* Investment advisers
Security and insecurity (Psychology)
Special spots. G. Hill. il *Field Stream* 92:21 Ag '87
Anecdotes, facetiae, satire, etc.
A surge of insecurity. R. Baker. il *N Y Times Mag*
p14 Je 21 '87
Thighs & whispers. B. Shacochis. *Vogue* 177:390+ F
'87
Security classification (Government documents) *See* Classified information
Security Council (United Nations) *See* United Nations.
Security Council
Security guards *See* Guards
Security systems
See also
ADT, Inc.
Airplanes, Business—Security measures
Alarms
Automated teller machines—Security measures
Automobiles—Audio systems—Security measures
Automobiles—Security measures
Boats and boating—Security measures
Booksellers and bookselling—Security measures
Buildings—Security measures
Cellular radio—Security measures
Computers—Security measures
Credit cards—Security measures
Electronic mail systems—Security measures
Embassies (Buildings)—Security measures
Information storage and retrieval systems—Security
measures
Libraries—Security measures
Military bases—Security measures
Nuclear power plants—Security measures
Schlage Lock Co.
Space centers—Security measures
Telecommunication—Security measures
Telephone—Security measures
The illusion of 'security'. M. Greenfield. il *Newsweek*
109:92 Ap 20 '87
Sedatives
See also
Tranquilizing drugs
Sedensky, Margaret M., and Meneely, Philip M.
Genetic analysis of halothane sensitivity in Caenorhabditis
elegans. bibl f il *Science* 236:952-4 My 22 '87
Sedge, Michael H.
Taking refuge on Elba. il *Travel Holiday* 167:36-8 F
'87
Sedgwick, John, 1954-
Lightning: nature's terrible swift sword. il *Read Dig*
131:23-5+ Ag '87
Sedimentary rocks *See* Rocks, Sedimentary
Sedimentation and deposition
See also
Marine sediments
Rocks, Sedimentary
Turbidity
Bedform alignment in directionally varying flows [cover
story] D. M. Rubin and R. E. Hunter. bibl f il *Science*
237:276-8 Jl 17 '87
Fluvial perturbance in the western Amazon basin: regulation
by long-term sub-Andean tectonics. M. E. Räsänen
and others. bibl f il map *Science* 238:1398-401 D
4 '87
Polychlorinated biphenyl dechlorination in aquatic sediments
[river sediments] J. F. Brown and others. bibl
f il *Science* 236:709-12 My 8 '87
Sedition
Foiling a revolt [white supremacists indicted] il *Time*
129:24 My 4 '87
Sedorova, Tanya
about
Aftermath of a romance. R. Corelli. il pors *Macleans*
100:58 S 28 '87
Seduction
The new seductress [D. Rice, F. Hall, and J. Hahn]
N. Scovell. il pors *Mademoiselle* 93:244-7 N '87
Sedum
Burro's-tail sedum. B. A. Branson. il *Flower Gard* 31:51+
O/N '87
See, Lisa
West watch. See occasional issues of Publishers Weekly
beginning September 2, 1983

Seed banks *See* Germplasm resources—Plants
Seed catalogs *See* Catalogs, Seed and plant
Seed germination *See* Germination
Seed industry
International aspects
The plant germplasm controversy [cover story; with reply
by H. G. Wilkes] J. Kloppenburg, Jr. and D. L.
Kleinman. bibl f il maps *BioScience* 37:190-8, 215-18
Mr '87
Seeds of struggle: the geopolitics of genetic resources.
J. Kloppenburg, Jr. and D. L. Kleinman. il map *Technol
Rev* 90:46-53 F/Mr '87
Marketing
New corn blight has little effect on seed marketing.
Success Farm 85:10 My '87
Seed companies abandon C cytoplasm [threat from
southern corn leaf blight] *Success Farm* 85:62I O '87
Seed mail order business *See* Mail order business
Seed production *See* Seed industry
Seed Savers Exchange
Kent Whealy's seedy operation provides garden variety
veggies from centuries past. N. Geeslin. il por *People
Wkly* 27:91-2 My 11 '87
Seed starting *See* Seeding
Seeding
See also
Flats, etc. (Horticulture)
Soybeans—Seeding
Wheat—Seeding
Get a jump on spring. T. Steadman. il *South Living*
22:70-1 Ja '87
Planting with nature. D. Bonta. il *Rodale's Org Gard*
34:65-6 F '87
Seed starting. A. C. Sinnes. il *Flower Gard* 31:52+ F/Mr
'87
Three tricks to speed seed sowing. il *Sunset* 178:192
Mr '87
Seeding machinery *See* Planters (Farm machines)
Seedlings
Start your own backyard nursery . . . A. Guttierrez
and R. Lorenz. il *Home Mech* 83:76-7+ O '87
Time to thin seedlings. il *South Living* 22:80 My '87
Seeds
See also
America the Beautiful Fund
Germination
Germplasm resources—Plants
Grasses—Seed
Pumpkins—Seed
Seed industry
Seed Savers Exchange
Soybeans—Seed
Vegetables—Seed
Save our seeds. K. Z. Peppler. il *Rodale's Org Gard*
34:38-41 D '87
Saving seeds. N. Bubel. il *Mother Earth News* 107:58-63
S/O '87
SOS—save our seeds! L. Ponte. il *Read Dig* 130:118-22
Je '87
Anecdotes, facetiae, satire, etc.
Wanted: old genetic furniture from the planet's attic.
J. Gorman. il *Discover* 8:24+ F '87
Seeds, Artificial
Artificial seed breakthrough [work of Dennis Gray] *USA
Today (Periodical)* 115:7 Je '87
Seeds, Effect of weightlessness on
LDEF's late tomatoes [Long Duration Exposure Facility]
B. Dickey. il *Space World* X-4-280:16 Ap '87
Seeing eye dogs *See* Guide dogs
Seeley, David
How to talk to a boy. il *Seventeen* 46:306-7+ Ag '87
Perfumed girls . . . how scents keep a man spellbound.
il *Mademoiselle* 93:150-1+ Je '87
The rush of the crush. il *Seventeen* 46:174-5+ N '87
Seeley, David S.
Education, dependence, and poverty. *Educ Dig* 52:6-9
Ja '87
Seelig, Anita
about
Career makeover: from newspaper sportswriter to computer
publications manager. il por *Glamour* 85:106
Je '87
Seelig, Mildred S., 1920-
about
More about magnesium [interview] R. Grindy. il por
Saturday Evening Post 259:50-3+ Jl/Ag '87
Seelig, Warren
Classic turn: the 13th Lausanne Biennial of Tapestry.
il *Am Craft* 47:26-33 O/N '87
Comment. *Am Craft* 47:20+ Ap/My '87

Seelig, Warren—*cont.*
A living journal: Francoise Grossen. il *Am Craft* 47:34-7 O/N '87
Seelinger, Kathy
The hamlet handicap. por *Newsweek* 109:10-11 My 18 '87
Seem-To-Be Players
The imagination express. M. Wade. il por *Horizon* 30:19-20 S '87
Sefton, Nancy
Rings on coral fingers. il *Sea Front* 33:134-5 Mr/Ap '87
What's in a cave? il *Sea Front* 33:404-13 N/D '87
Segal, Julius, 1924-, and Segal, Zelda
As they grow/5 and 6. See issues of Parents beginning July 1985
Segal, Lore Groszmann
An absence of cousins [story] *New Yorker* 63:22-9 Ag 17 '87
Segal, Marian
AIDS education [cover story] il *FDA Consum* 21:26-30 S '87
Defrauding the desperate: quackery and AIDS. il *FDA Consum* 21:16-19 O '87
A potpourri of consumers' questions about food. il *FDA Consum* 21:30-2 N '87
A progress report on AIDS research. il *FDA Consum* 21:8-12 O '87
Segal, Zelda
(jt. auth) See Segal, Julius, 1924-, and Segal, Zelda
Segalen, Victor, 1878-1919
Island fling [excerpt from Journal des îles] il *Courier* 40:23 Ap '87
Segall, Maurice
about
At Zayre, the skies were just starting to clear. C. Brown. *Bus Week* p59-60 O 19 '87
Segall, Paul
about
A clinically doggone beagle, medical miracle Miles is a former chilly dog back from the beyond. il *People Wkly* 27:85 Ap 20 '87
Segerson, Thomas P., and others
Thyroid hormone regulates TRH biosynthesis in the paraventricular nucleus of the rat hypothalamus. bibl f il *Science* 238:78-80 O 2 '87
Segovia, Andrés, 1893-1987
about
Obituary
High Fidel il 37:56 S '87. T. W. Libbey, Jr.
Macleans il por 100:50 Je 15 '87. P. Young
Newsweek il por 109:74-5 Je 15 '87. L. Shapiro
Time il por 129:69 Je 15 '87. M. Walsh
Segre, Dan Vittorio
My mother's conversion. *Commentary* 83:27-37 F '87
Segregation, Social
See also
Blacks—Segregation
Segregation in education See Colleges and universities—Segregation; Discrimination in education; Public schools—Segregation
Segregation in sports See Discrimination in sports
Seguin, Carl, and Hamer, Dean H.
Regulation in vitro of metallothionein gene binding factors. bibl f il *Science* 235:1383-7 Mr 13 '87
Seguso, Robert
about
It's doubles or nothing. R. Sullivan. il pors *Sports Illus* 67:60+ Ag 10 '87
Sehested, Ken
Public exorcism in Forsyth County. *Christ Century* 104:238-9 Mr 11 '87
Sehgal, Pravinkumar B., and others
Human β₂ interferon and B-cell differentiation factor BSF-2 are identical. bibl f *Science* 235:731-2 F 13 '87
Seibels, Cynthia
Restore iron and brass beds. il *Americana* 15:63-6 Mr/Ap '87
Seibert, Gary G.
The Word. See issues of America beginning July 4-11, 1987 through November 14, 1987
Seibu Group
'The world's richest man' [Y. Tsutsumi] P. Sabatier. il *World Press Rev* 34:49 N '87
Seid, Christopher
Owls [poem] *Ctry J* 14:73 My '87
Seidelman, Susan
about
Making Mr. Right [film] Reviews
Glamour il 85:154 Je '87. J. G. Boyum

Macleans 100:49 Ap 13 '87
Ms 15:22 My '87. S. Dworkin
N Y il 20:125-6 Ap 27 '87. D. Denby
N Y il 20:46-9 Mr 30 '87. A. Virshup
New Repub 196:26-7 My 4 '87. S. Kauffmann
Newsweek il 109:77-8 Ap 13 '87. J. Kroll
People Wkly il 27:8 Ap 27 '87. R. Novak
Time il 129:78 Ap 13 '87. R. Schickel
Susan Seidelman directs post-feminist fun. C. Krupp. il pors *Glamour* 85:224 My '87
Seideman, Tony
Video news and notes. See issues of Rolling Stone beginning September 12, 1985
Seidenberg, Robert
Matewan: Nora Chavooshian creates major miners. il *Theatre Crafts* 21:45-8 Ap '87
Period perfect: Van Broughton Ramsey costumes Horton Foote's Texas. il *Theatre Crafts* 21:99-102 My '87
Sayles talk. il por *Horizon* 30:12-14 S '87
Stranded: Michele Burke's friendly foreigners. il por *Theatre Crafts* 21:83-6 N '87
Seiff, Rita
Getting better all the time. il por *Ladies Home J* 104:20+ Jl '87
Seigel, Jerrold E.
Pilgrims in Paris. *New Repub* 197:30-4 S 28 '87
Seiken, Jeff
"Not a look of fear was seen" [cover story] il *Am Hist Illus* 22:12-15+ N '87
Seisler, Jeffrey
Window coverings to seal the cold out. il *Consum Res Mag* 70:14-16 D '87
Seismic detection of nuclear explosions See Nuclear weapons—Testing—Detection
Seismic waves
Chronology of fluctuating sea levels since the Triassic. B. U. Haq and others. bibl f il *Science* 235:1156-67 Mr 6 '87
Core questions [use of seismic tomography to probe earth's core] *Sci Am* 256:60-1 F '87
Getting a full view of the earth's innards [seismic surveys] R. A. Kerr. *Science* 235:433-4 Ja 23 '87
Global images of the earth's interior. A. M. Dziewonski and J. H. Woodhouse. bibl f il maps *Science* 236:37-48 Ap 3 '87
Journey to the center of the earth [seismic tomography studies] T. A. Heppenheimer. il map *Discover* 8:86-90+ N '87
Mountains and valleys are at earth's core mantle boundary [seismic tomography studies] *Earth Sci* 40:9 Summ '87
Opening doors to the core, and more. S. Weisburd. *Sci News* 131:9 Ja 3 '87
San Salvador: small quake, big problems [volcanic ash amplifies earthquake] J. Silberner. *Sci News* 131:212 Ap 4 '87
Sea cycle clock [seismic stratigraphy; work of Peter R. Vail and others] S. Weisburd. il *Sci News* 131:154-5 Mr 7 '87
Seeing bright spots in the middle crust. R. A. Kerr. *Science* 238:891 N 13 '87
Underwater earthquakes create devastating sea waves that can kill thousands and wash away towns. M. Hill. *Earth Sci* 40:38 Wint '87
Seismological research See Seismometers and seismometry
Seismometers and seismometry
See also
Earthquake prediction
Helioseismology
GAO finds fault with NSF award [earthquake engineering research center] J. Walsh. il *Science* 237:241-2 Jl 17 '87
Seitz, Frederick, and others
H. William Koch and AIP. *Phys Today* 40:144 Ap '87
Seitz, Michael H.
Film. See issues of The Progressive
Seitzer, Kevin
about
Kevin Seitzer. J. Garrity. por *Sports Illus* 67:48 Jl 13 '87
Seivold, Gary
about
Oh brother, here comes Carolina. D. Brantley. il pors *Sports Illus* 66:69-70 My 4 '87
Seivold, Joey
about
Oh brother, here comes Carolina. D. Brantley. il pors *Sports Illus* 66:69-70 My 4 '87
Seiyo, Ginza (Tokyo, Japan: Hotel) See Tokyo (Japan)—Hotels, motels, etc.

Seize the day [television program] See Television program reviews—Single works

Seizinger, Bernd R., and others
Common pathogenetic mechanism for three tumor types in bilateral acoustic neurofibromatosis. bibl f il *Science* 236:317-19 Ap 17 '87

Seizure of vessels and cargoes
See also
Pirates

Seizures (Medicine) See Convulsions

Seizures and searches See Searches and seizures

Seko, Mobutu Sese See Mobutu Sese Seko, 1930-

Sekuler, Robert, and Blake, Randolph
Sensory underload. il *Psychol Today* 21:48-51 D '87

Selbst, Stanton C.
about
Stanton Selbst: success with a school for stockbrokers. M. Frons. por *Bus Week* p103 Ja 26 '87

Selbst (Stanton C.) Inc. See Stanton C. Selbst Inc.

Selden, Richard F., and others
Implantation of genetically engineered fibroblasts into mice: implications for gene therapy. bibl f il *Science* 236:714-18 My 8 '87

Seldes, George, 1890-
about
Eye witness. E. Knoll. *Progressive* 51:4 Je '87

Selected American Shares, Inc.
Two new all-weathers. *Money* 16:39+ Jl '87

Selection, Natural See Natural selection

Selection of architects See Architects—Selection and appointment

Selection of teachers See Teachers—Selection and appointment

Selective service, Military See Military service, Compulsory

SelectQuote Insurance Services
Insurance on simpler terms. B. Kallen. il *Forbes* 140:108+ Ag 10 '87

Selenium
See also
Feeds—Selenium content
The case of the poisoned wildlife refuge [J. Claus discovers selenium at Kesterson National Wildlife Refuge] R. Fitzgerald. il por *Read Dig* 131:133-7 O '87
Fowl play [selenium pollution at Kesterson National Wildlife Refuge] C. Caufield. il *Omni* 9:22+ Je '87
Fungi: California's answer to selenium? [Kesterson National Wildlife Refuge] *Sci News* 132:8 Jl 4 '87
In situ X-ray absorption study of surface complexes: selenium oxyanions on α-FeOOH. K. F. Hayes and others. bibl f il *Science* 238:783-6 N 6 '87

Seles, Monika
about
The Baltic basher. N. Bollettieri. il por *World Tennis* 34:12 Mr '87

Seleznev, Gennady
about
That new word 'glasnost' [interview] B. Shelby. *World Press Rev* 34:16-17 Ap '87

Self, Jim
about
Self made man. G. Hyman. il pors *Horizon* 30:14-16 Mr '87

Self, Stephen
(jt. auth) See Francis, Peter, and Self, Stephen

Self
See also
Consciousness
Identity (Psychology)
Individuality
Mind and body
Personality
Ads for ourselves [New York City Marathon]; tr. by Barry Schwabsky. J. Baudrillard. *Harpers* 275:32 O '87
We reap what we sow [child rearing practices and adult ego development; study by Eric F. Dubow] S. Chollar. *Psychol Today* 21:12 D '87

Self (Philosophy)
Capitalism & selfishness [discussion of December 1986 article] A. Ryerson. *Commentary* 83:10-12+ Mr '87
"I sez to myself, sez I". D. F. Kinlaw. il *Christ Today* 31:11 Ap 17 '87

Self actualization See Self realization

Self awareness See Self perception; Self realization

Self blame
Let's be careful out there [crime victims] R. C. Davis. *Psychol Today* 21:10 Ag '87

Self care, Medical See Medical care

Self chilling beverage containers See Beverage containers

Self concept See Self perception

Self confidence
Beauty confidence: how to get it. il *Teen* 31:112 Ap '87
A sense of confidence [two year olds] B. Weissbourd. il *Parents* 62:204 S '87

Self consciousness
See also
Bashfulness
Embarrassment
Lost in the crowd [group size and composition can affect behavior; research by Brian Mullen] J. Goetz. il *Psychol Today* 21:60 Je '87

Self control
The age of self-control. R. Sennett. *Vogue* 177:362-3+ Ap '87
Secrets every achiever knows [self discipline; condensed from The 25-hour woman] S. Stanton. il *Read Dig* 131:63-6 S '87

Self criticism See Criticism, Personal

Self culture See Self improvement

Self deception
Failing to recognize bias in science. D. Goleman. il *Technol Rev* 90:26-7 N/D '87
On honesty and self-deception: 'you are the man'. L. Steffen. *Christ Century* 104:403-5 Ap 29 '87
Who are you kidding? [cover story] D. Goleman. bibl (p59) il *Psychol Today* 21:24-6+ Mr '87

Self defense
Doubts about self-defence [trial of Calgary, Alta. drugstore owner S. Kesler] M. Gray. il pors *Macleans* 100:45 Je 29 '87
Fear, arms and a verdict [S. Kesler acquitted of murder charges in Alberta] M. Gray. il por *Macleans* 100:48 Jl 6 '87
Florida's new crop of pistol packers [gun controls lifted] T. Gest. il *U S News World Rep* 103:16 O 12 '87
A lethal lucky charm [Florida gun laws] M. McIver. il *Macleans* 100:59-60 O 12 '87
Local gun controls bite the dust [Florida] T. Gest. il *U S News World Rep* 102:14-15 My 25 '87
'Make my day' laws—the impact. T. Gest. il *U S News World Rep* 102:12-13 Ap 20 '87
Pistol packers [Florida] C. Garcia. il *Time* 130:28 S 28 '87
Prentice Rasheed jabs Florida's new gun law. il por *Jet* 73:18 O 19 '87
The public fights back. T. Gest. il *U S News World Rep* 102:16-17 Je 29 '87
West Pointers flip and fall for Marian Rockwell. L. Rozen. il pors *People Wkly* 27:65-7 Mr 23 '87
Wyatt Earp comes to the Sunshine State [Florida gun law] *Newsweek* 110:42 O 12 '87

Self defense [drama] See Cacaci, Joe

Self defense for women
Fight, not flight [Model Mugging course] C. Cummins. il *Women's Sports Fitness* 9:20 D '87
Fighting back! [Model Mugging course] G. Levoy. il *Health* 19:18 S '87
Lisa Sliwa: brains over brawn. L. Van Buskirk. por *Seventeen* 46:105 Je '87
Rape prevention: Du Pont's model program. A. Hornaday. il *Ms* 15:31 Je '87
Staying safe: the smart woman's guide to self-defense [views of L. Sliwa] D. Ingber. il pors *McCalls* 145:138+ Mr '87
When you're driving alone. D. McCluggage. il *Essence* 18:112 S '87
Women fight sexual assault [Chimera method] A. J. Johnston. il *Progressive* 51:12-13 S '87

Self defense in animals See Defense mechanisms (Biology)

Self denial
Of slime, worms and bums. M. E. Marty. *Christ Century* 104:71 Ja 21 '87

Self dependence See Self reliance

Self destruction See Suicide

Self diagnosis See Diagnosis

Self discipline See Self control

Self disclosure
A republic of souls: puritanism and the American presidency. R. Sennett. il *Harpers* 275:41-6 Jl '87
Rewriting your romantic résumé. L. Dormen. il *Glamour* 85:316-17+ N '87
Skeletons in the closet should be locked away [study by Kenneth Sereno] il *USA Today (Periodical)* 115:11 My '87

Self education See Self improvement
Self employed
  See also
    Cottage industries
    Entrepreneurs
The dream job you create for yourself. D. E. Gumpert. il *Work Woman* 12:39-41 O '87
How to win the struggle to fit a mortgage lender's mold. H. Porter. il *Fam Handyman* 37:9+ D '87
Leaving the corporate nest. H. Bacas. il *Nations Bus* 75:14-16+ Mr '87
On their own: the self-employed and others in private business. S. E. Haber and others. bibl f il *Mon Labor Rev* 110:17-23 My '87
            Taxation
Deductions galore for the self-employed. C. Yang. *Bus Week* p139 N 23 '87
How to avoid a tax audit. il *Work Woman* 12:40 O '87
Profiting from losses. L. Wiener. il *U S News World Rep* 102:56 Ap 13 '87
Put the kids on the payroll and give yourself a break. P. Philipps. il *Bus Week* p154 Je 8 '87
Self esteem See Self respect
Self evaluation
  See also
    Criticism, Personal
    Self perception
Self examination of skin See Skin—Examination
Self examination of the breast See Breast—Examination
Self experimentation in medicine
The guinea pig closest at hand. il *U S News World Rep* 103:58-9 Jl 13 '87
Self fulfillment See Self realization
Self help
  See also
    Cable television—Self help programs
    Tape recordings—Self help use
    Videotapes—Self help use
Samuel Smiles: the gospel of self-help. A. Briggs. bibl il *Hist Today* 37:37-43 My '87
Self help groups
  See also
    Esalen Institute
In good company: workday weight-loss support systems. S. Johnson. il *Work Woman* 12:100+ F '87
Self-help for executives. *U S News World Rep* 102:68 F 9 '87
Self help literature
Self-help: a bargain? [views of Gerald M. Rosen] P. Chance. *Psychol Today* 21:17 Ag '87
Smart women, foolish books: can your love life be saved in ten chapters or less? A. Landi. *Mademoiselle* 93:180-1+ O '87
Some self-help books can be harmful [views of Judith Myers-Walls] il *USA Today (Periodical)* 115:12 Ap '87
Why is all the relationship-repair advice aimed at women? il *Glamour* 85:64 F '87
            Bibliography
Addicted to love. J. Maynard. il *Mademoiselle* 93:90+ Ag '87
Advice givers strike gold. L. Shapiro. il *Newsweek* 109:64-5 Je 1 '87
Women who read too much. S. Bolotin. il *Vogue* 177:246+ F '87
Self hypnosis therapy See Hypnotism—Therapeutic use
Self image See Self perception
Self improvement
Academy helps Army be all that it can be [report on human performance enhancement] C. Holden. *Science* 238:1501-2 D 11 '87
The me I didn't know [pretending to be someone else as a way to self improvement; research by Robert Hartley] P. Chance. *Psychol Today* 21:20 Ja '87
Self improvement literature See Self help literature
Self in motion pictures
Looking north at a world of self [watching W. Allen's movies in Latin America] M. Gallagher. *America* 157:82-3 Ag 15-22 '87
Self indulgence See Selfishness
Self insurance See Insurance—Self insurance
Self love See Narcissism; Self respect
Self perception
  See also
    Body image
Do you see yourself as others do? [quiz] T. Hartman. il *Teen* 31:16+ Mr '87
Do you take yourself seriously? New thoughts, questions about self-image. B. L. Stern. *Vogue* 177:240 Ja '87

The macho man behind the beard [study by Douglas Wood] V. Bozzi. il *Psychol Today* 21:20 My '87
Self portraits See Portraits
Self portraits, Photographic See Photography—Portraits
Self publishing
Hard to get [J. Kron to self publish Ms. Faux Pas's guide to glitterati manners] L. Fleischer. *Publ Wkly* 232:78 S 25 '87
Self realization
30 ways to feel good about yourself. A. Arnott. *McCalls* 114:130 S '87
Activity overload. D. Elkind. il *Parents* 62:271 N '87
The actualized worker [cover story] M. Sinetar. il por *Futurist* 21:21-2+ Mr/Ap '87
Affirmation. S. L. Taylor. il *Essence* 18:55 My '87
Are you at a turning point? S. P. Haven. *Glamour* 85:168+ N '87
Are you the one for me? [excerpt] J. James and I. Schlesinger. il *Glamour* 85:378-9+ S '87
Are you trapped by your image? C. Jakobson. il *Seventeen* 46:204-5+ Ap '87
Is it time for you to blossom? [excerpt from Attaining personal greatness] M. Brown. *Redbook* 169:74-5+ Ag '87
Taking flight. S. L. Taylor. il *Essence* 18:51 O '87
Time travel [imagining one's future as a therapeutic tool; work of J. Hart] B. Lawren. il *Omni* 10:20+ N '87
Self reliance
Becoming independent [two year olds] B. Weissbourd. il *Parents* 62:192 Ag '87
Control [teaching children how to take control in their lives] D. F. Bjorklund and B. Bjorklund. il *Parents* 62:156 Jl '87
Have you declared your independence? [quiz] J. Adams. *Essence* 18:95+ S '87
An old woman's victory garden [independence at home] M. K. Blakely. il por *Ms* 16:94+ S '87
The road to self-reliance [lesson of boarding school] M. Norman. il *N Y Times Mag* p82 D 13 '87
Streetwise families. D. Bjorklund and B. Bjorklund. il *Parents* 62:267 N '87
Self respect
  See also
    California. Task Force to Promote Self-Esteem, Personal and Social Responsibility
Alice Miller: the cost of parental tyranny [abusive child rearing practices deny children self respect] L. Van Gelder. il por *Ms* 16:82+ O '87
Body image and self-esteem. *Society* 25:7 N/D '87
Do you like yourself? [quiz] *Teen* 31:12 Jl '87
Encouraging self-esteem [children] J. P. Comer. il *Parents* 62:162 F '87
The esteem team. D. Seligman. *Fortune* 116:134+ S 14 '87
How to help your child develop self-esteem. L. Salk. il *McCalls* 145:59 Mr '87
Interview [A. Miller] D. Connors. por *Omni* 9:72-4+ Mr '87
Striking a balance between others' feelings and your own self-interests. B. L. Stern. *Vogue* 177:364 My '87
"We have a problem". J. Marks. il *Parents* 62:60+ N '87
Self revelation See Self disclosure
Self storage warehouses
Rent-a-closet. E. Paris. il *Forbes* 139:136 Je 15 '87
Self-service storage: what to know before you store. il *Glamour* 85:90 Mr '87
Self sufficiency See Self reliance
Selfishness
Bring back the sin of selfishness [with readers' comments] T. McGrath. *U S Cathol* 52:14-19 O '87
Capitalism & selfishness [discussion of December 1986 article] A. Ryerson. *Commentary* 83:10-12+ Mr '87
Seligman, Daniel
Keeping up. See issues of Fortune
Seligman, Martin E. P.
            about
Stop blaming yourself. R. J. Trotter. bibl (p64) il pors *Psychol Today* 21:30-2+ F '87
Seligmann, Werner
Le Corbusier as structural engineer. il *Archit Rec* 175:142-51 O '87
Seligson, Tom
Cybill Shepherd: "How can I handle twins?" [cover story; interview] il pors *Redbook* 169:16+ S '87
Selker, Eric U., and others
A portable signal causing faithful DNA methylation de novo in Neurospora crassa. bibl f il *Science* 238:48-53 O 2 '87

Selkirk Communications Limited
Agitated airwaves [Rogers Communications' offer for Selkirk Communications] P. Best. il *Macleans* 100:38 O 26 '87

Selkoe, Dennis J.
about
An expert says doctors still have no cure but are closing in on the causes of Alzheimer's [interview] G. Verner. il por *People Wkly* 27:83-4 Je 1 '87

Selkoe, Dennis J., and others
Conservation of brain amyloid proteins in aged mammals and humans with Alzheimer's disease [cover story] bibl f il *Science* 235:873-7 F 20 '87

Sellars, Peter
about
Don Juan in hell. P. G. Davis. il *N Y* 20:48-9 Ag 3 '87
PepsiCo Summerfare. M. Hodgson. *Nation* 245:208-10 S 5 '87

Selleck, Tom
about
Five questions you'd like to ask Tom Selleck. C. Kramer. il por *McCalls* 115:148+ N '87
In a Nevada chapel, under a veil of secrecy, Tom Selleck marries his kitten from Cats. il pors *People Wkly* 28:34-5 S 21 '87
Meet the new "Mr. Moms" [interview] K. Henderson. il pors *Redbook* 170:44+ N '87
Tom Selleck: what's next? T. Klein. il pors *Saturday Evening Post* 259:50-1+ Mr '87
Who is the father of this baby? [interview] il pors *Good Housekeep* 205:106+ N '87
Photographs and photography
Selleck by Trindl [interview with G. Trindl; cover story] B. Hurter. il pors *Petersens Photogr Mag* 15:20-1+ Ap '87

Sellers, David
about
Architecture: David Sellers. V. J. Scully. il por *Archit Dig* 44:146-51+ Je '87

Selling
See also
Direct selling
Marketing
Sales personnel
America's best salesmen. M. J. Williams. il *Fortune* 116:122-4+ O 26 '87
How to make sales calls that get business. M. Stevens. *Work Woman* 12:51-3 D '87
Selling by telephone *See* Telephone selling
Selling of small businesses *See* Small business, Sale of
Sellman, Zelda Hedden- *See* Hedden-Sellman, Zelda
Seltzer
See also
Original New York Seltzer (Firm)
The new taste in seltzers: is it the real thing? il *Newsweek* 109:50 F 16 '87
Old-time seltzer in new-fangled bottles [plastic squirt container] J. O. Hamilton. il por *Bus Week* p164 S 14 '87

Selzer, Richard
The elusive language of pleasure and pain. il *N Y Times Book Rev* 92:38-9 Ap 5 '87
A mask on the face of death. il por *Life* 10:58-64 Ag '87

Selznick, Philip, 1919-
The demands of the community [with discussion] por *Cent Mag* 20:33-54 Ja/F '87

Semahj, Heru Ankh-Ra
about
Designs on our cultural legacy. K. J. Halliburton. il por *Essence* 18:42 N '87

Sematech
Chip makers plan research center. E. Marshall. *Science* 235:1320 Mr 13 '87
Defense Science Board urges semiconductor consortium. B. D. Nordwall. *Aviat Week Space Technol* 126:94 Mr 2 '87
DOD is asked to aid semiconductor firms. J. Raloff. *Sci News* 131:117 F 21 '87
High-tech boondoggle? R. J. Samuelson. il *Newsweek* 109:50 Je 29 '87
National security and the semiconductor industry. D. G. Dallmeyer. il *Technol Rev* 90:46-52+ N/D '87
NSF lends a hand with DOD award. J. Walsh. il *Science* 238:748 N 6 '87
Semi-tough. M. Gladwell. *New Repub* 196:9-11 My 18 '87
Senate votes financial aid to semiconductor consortium. *Aviat Week Space Technol* 127:155 O 12 '87

Silicon Valley unfurls a flag: 'don't tread on me'. R. Brandt and O. Port. il *Bus Week* p62-3 Ag 31 '87
Weinberger cites need to boost chip industry. *Aviat Week Space Technol* 126:24 My 18 '87

Semenov, IÛlian Semenovich, 1931-
about
In Yulian Semyonov's thrillers the villains are CIA types—and some say the author works for the KGB. M. Brower. il pors *People Wkly* 27:81+ Ap 6 '87
The looking-glass spy. A. Wilson-Smith. il por *Macleans* 100:63 O 12 '87
Russia's big bestseller: a talk with Julian Semyonov. M. Berkley. il pors *Publ Wkly* 232:34-5 O 16 '87
Semiconductor industry *See* Electronic industries
Semiconductor Manufacturing Technology Institute *See* Sematech
Semiconductor Research Corporation
NSF lends a hand with DOD award [Sematech project] J. Walsh. il *Science* 238:748 N 6 '87

Semiconductors
See also
Charge coupled devices (Electronics)
Gallium arsenide
Germanium
Metal oxide semiconductors
Silicon
Thyristors
Transistors
Artificially structured thin-film materials and interfaces. V. Narayanamurti. bibl f il *Science* 235:1023-8 F 27 '87
Band-gap engineering: from physics and materials to new semiconductor devices. F. Capasso. bibl f il *Science* 235:172-6 Ja 9 '87
High-temperature cubic boron nitride P-N junction diode made at high pressure. O. Mishima and others. bibl f il *Science* 238:181-3 O 9 '87
Lasers light the way for computer links. S. Weisburd. *Sci News* 131:408 Je 27 '87
Optical materials. A. M. Glass. bibl f il *Science* 235:1003-9 F 27 '87
Putting the heat on new semiconductors [cubic boron nitride diode; work of Osamu Mishima and others] I. Peterson. *Sci News* 132:247 O 17 '87
State of solid state. R. F. Scott. See issues of Radio-Electronics
They may not be super, but semis are hot. S. Weisburd. *Sci News* 132:390 D 19-26 '87
Ultrahigh-power semiconductor diode laser arrays. P. S. Cross and others. bibl f il *Science* 237:1305-9 S 11 '87
What's new in solid state. R. F. Scott. il *Radio-Electron* 58:61-2+ Ja '87

Semiconductors, Effect of radiation on
Probing semiconductor-semiconductor interfaces [synchrotron radiation photoemission spectroscopy] R. S. Bauer and G. Margaritondo. bibl f il *Phys Today* 40:26-34 Ja '87

Seminarians
Choosing the impossible: seminary students speak out [roundtable discussion] *Christ Century* 104:131-6 F 4-11 '87
Students speak out; Presbytery responds [discussion of February 4-11, 1987 article, Choosing the impossible: seminary students speak out] *Christ Century* 104:384-5 Ap 22 '87
Seminaries *See* Theological seminaries
Seminars
See also
American Management Association
Cottage seminars
Getting better at your job—do seminars help? G. Hechinger. il *Glamour* 85:346+ Mr '87

Semline, Inc.
Quebecor acquires Semline; names John Collins president. *Publ Wkly* 231:68 Ja 9 '87

Semperverde (Firm)
How to steal an S&L—legally [Green family buyout of Firstrust Saving Bank] B. D. Fromson. il *Fortune* 116:57-8+ O 12 '87

Semprevivo, Philip C.
about
Updating a classic. B. Kanner. il pors *N Y* 20:19-20 Jl 13 '87
Semyonov, Yulian *See* Semenov, IÛlian Semenovich, 1931-
Sen, Amartya Kumar
about
Original Sen. A. B. Atkinson. il *N Y Rev Books* 34:41-4 O 22 '87

Sen, Sudhir
Development under siege. *Commonweal* 114:647-52 N 20 '87
Sena, Michael
(jt. auth) See Teicholz, Eric, and Sena, Michael
Senate (Canada) *See* Canada. Parliament. Senate
Senate (U.S.) *See* United States. Congress. Senate
Senatobia (Miss.)
Education
Student boycott ends in Senatobia, Miss. [hiring of black assistant superintendent] *Jet* 72:22 Ap 6 '87
Senatorial campaigns *See* Political campaigns
Senators
Anecdotes, facetiae, satire, etc.
Uncivil liberties. C. Trillin. *Nation* 244:136 F 7 '87
Ethics
See Political ethics
Press relations
Being newsworthy. S. Hess. *Society* 24:39-47 Ja/F '87
Retirement
Suddenly, Proxmire the gadfly looks more like a godsend. V. Cahan. *Bus Week* p47 S 14 '87
Will a new chairman polarize the Senate Budget Committee? [retirement of L. Chiles] D. Harbrecht. *Bus Week* p49 D 21 '87
Senchina, Ludmila
about
Stas Namin and Ludmila Senchina reign over the pop scene while rock's underground rumbles. S. K. Reed. il pors *People Wkly* 27:46-8+ Ap 6 '87
Sendak, Maurice
Where the Wild Things began. il *N Y Times Book Rev* 92:1+ My 17 '87
Sendero Luminoso (Guerrilla group)
Debt, democracy and terrorism in Peru. D. P. Werlich. bibl f *Curr Hist* 86:29-32+ Ja '87
Embattled in Peru. J. N. Montesinos. *World Press Rev* 34:39 My '87
Shining Path burns with a hotter flame. B. Durr. il *U S News World Rep* 102:35 My 25 '87
Senders, Cherri
El condor pasa. il *Omni* 9:98 Ag '87
Sénéchal, Michel, 1927-
about
Singer for life. T. Eckert, Jr. il por *Opera News* 51:26 F 28 '87
Senegal
See also
Keur Massar (Senegal)
Senegalese
Senegal and the United States
See also
Educational exchanges
Senegalese
United States
Out of Africa: the Senegalese peddlers of New York. P. Blauner. il *N Y* 20:42-6 F 16 '87
Senescence *See* Aging
Senez, Jacques C.
The new biotechnologies: promise and performance. il *Courier* 40:4-12 Mr '87
Senft, R. L., and others
Large herbivore foraging and ecological hierarchies. bibl il *BioScience* 37:789-95+ D '87
Senger, Trustman
Trial by fire. il *Roll Stone* p111-12+ S 24 '87
Senghaas, Dieter
Dismantle offense, strengthen defense. il *Bull At Sci* 43:9-11 D '87
Senigallia, Silvio F.
Italy gets a new government. por *New Leader* 70:3-4 Jl 13-27 '87
Italy's moot relay. il *New Leader* 69:8-9 D 29 '86
Italy's reaction to 'glasnost'. *New Leader* 70:7 Mr 23 '87
Senile dementia *See* Senility
Senility
See also
Alzheimer's disease
Panel urges dementia be diagnosed with care. G. Kolata. *Science* 237:725 Ag 14 '87
Senior centers
See also
Mobile senior centers
Getting the homebound out of the house [National Council of Jewish Women recreation program at senior center in Brooklyn, N.Y.] il *Aging* no355:22 '87
Senior Center becomes medical satellite to hospital in Pittsburgh [Vintage Senior Adult Center and West Penn Hospital] il *Aging* no355:29-30 '87

Senior citizens *See* Aged
Senior Citizens' Orchestra of Miami Beach
Second wind for a sassy band [excerpt from Alone in America] L. Bernikow. il *50 Plus* 27:72-5+ My '87
Senior Companion Program (U.S.)
Senior Companions, a vital connection for the rural elderly. il *Aging* no356:28-9 '87
Senior Olympics
Be an Olympian [women] il *Women's Sports Fitness* 9:56 Je '87
Seniority, Employee
See also
Promotions
Seniors, High school *See* High school students
Senna, Ayrton
about
A day in the life of the world's best race driver. R. Bulgin. il pors *Mot Trend* 39:115-18 Ag '87
Senna savvy [Monaco Grand Prix] R. Walker. il *Road Track* 39:136-8 S '87
Street smart in Motown. R. F. Jones. il pors *Sports Illus* 66:68-9 Je 29 '87
Taking an active role. R. Walker. il *Road Track* 39:130-4 O '87
Sennett, Richard, 1943-
The age of self-control. *Vogue* 177:362-3+ Ap '87
A cellar performance. il *Vogue* 177:248+ N '87
A republic of souls: puritanism and the American presidency. il *Harpers* 275:41-6 Jl '87
Sensation *See* Senses and sensation
Sense of humor *See* Humor
Sense organs
See also
Ear
Eye
Photoreceptors
Senses and sensation
Sensory receptors
Senses and sensation
See also
Brain
Hearing
Pain
Perception
Pleasure
Sensory stimulation
Smell
Synesthesia
Taste
Time perception
Touch
Vision
Sensory underload [aging and sensory loss] R. Sekuler and R. Blake. il *Psychol Today* 21:48-51 D '87
Sensing, Remote *See* Remote sensing
Sensitivity
Sensitivity or touchiness? G. F. Kreyche. *USA Today (Periodical)* 116:98 N '87
Where are the sensitive men? [views of Art Bohart] il *USA Today (Periodical)* 116:1-2 Ag '87
You can be a more sensitive parent. F. Rogers. il por *Redbook* 168:48-9+ Ap '87
Sensors *See* Detectors
Sensors, Biomedical *See* Biosensors
Sensors, Infrared *See* Detectors, Infrared
Sensory receptors
Global flexibility in a sensory receptor: a site-directed cross-linking approach. J. J. Falke and D. E. Koshland, Jr. bibl f il *Science* 237:1596-600 S 25 '87
Sensory tuning of lateral line receptors in Antarctic fish to the movements of planktonic prey [teleosts] J. C. Montgomery and J. A. Macdonald. bibl f il *Science* 235:195-6 Ja 9 '87
Sensory stimulation
Common scents [multi-sensory stimulation for comatose patients with head injuries] J. D. Schwartz. il *Health* 19:21 S '87
Superglut! [overstimulation] L. J. Nonkin. *Vogue* 177:324+ Ag '87
Sentences (Criminal justice) *See* Criminal justice, Administration of
Sentences (Grammar)
It was a lovely year for a bookstore [novelists' sentence writing techniques] A. Broyard. il *N Y Times Book Rev* 92:12 My 17 '87
Senter, Bill
Using rice paper to transfer color. il *Am Artist* 51:60-3 My '87

Sentosa Island (Singapore)
Description and travel
Sentosa Island [cover story] R. W. Cox. il *Travel Holiday* 168:12+ O '87
Senz, Laurie S.
The battle in your mouth. il *Saturday Evening Post* 259:22-3+ Mr '87
Giving teeth a face-lift. il *Saturday Evening Post* 259:30-1 O '87
Seoul (Korea)
Description
The Summer Games. J. Orsini. il *Travel Holiday* 168:9-11 D '87
Surprising Seoul. P. Plawin. il *Changing Times* 41:62-6+ O '87

Galleries and museums
See also
National Museum of Modern Art (Seoul, Korea)
Stadiums
See Stadiums—Korea (South)
Seoul Olympics, 1988 *See* Olympic Games—1988—Summer Olympics
Separation (Law)
See also
Children of separated parents
Strawberry, wife separate, await ruling on her suit. il por *Jet* 71:32 F 16 '87
Separation (Psychology)
See also
Maternal deprivation
Paternal deprivation
A divorce alternative. P. Booth. il *Harpers Bazaar* 120:141+ Ag '87
The gold watch [son's separation from parents] G. Jellinek. il *N Y Times Mag* p42 Je 28 '87
Headed for a painful breakup? Sociologist Diane Vaughan discusses the warning signs [interview] M. Wilhelm. il pors *People Wkly* 27:97-8+ Mr 2 '87
How not to go nuts when he goes away. B.-J. Raphael. *Glamour* 85:141 N '87
The long goodbye [failing relationships; cover story] D. Vaughan. il *Psychol Today* 21:36-8+ Jl '87
Separation anxiety [toddlers] J. T. Gibson. il *Parents* 62:146 F '87
We celebrate our wedding anniversaries apart. M. J. Weber. il *Glamour* 85:282 Ag '87
Separation (Technology)
See also
Chromatographic analysis
Cytology—Methodology
Electrophoresis
Separation of powers
See also
Executive privilege (Government information)
Judicial power
Judicial review
Presidents—Powers and duties
United States. Congress—Powers and duties
America—200 years on. E. Wright. il *Hist Today* 37:7-10 S '87
Fragmentation of powers: have the arguments preserved liberty or brought government to a stalemate? H. Sidey. il *Time* 130:36-7 Jl 6 '87
In order to form a more perfect union. P. McGrath and A. McDaniel. il *Newsweek* 109:50-2 My 25 '87
Sepkoski, J. John, Jr.
Environmental trends in extinction during the Paleozoic. bibl f il *Science* 235:64-6 Ja 2 '87
SEPs *See* Simplified employee pensions
September
Deliberate September [excerpt from Hal Borland's Twelve moons of the year] H. Borland. il *Audubon* 89:45 S '87
The September almanac. il *Atlantic* 260:16 S '87
September [film] See Motion picture reviews—Single works
Sepulchral monuments
See also
Epitaphs
Anecdotes, facetiae, satire, etc.
Tombstone in the kitchen. K. T. Windham. il *Mother Earth News* 107:72-5 S/O '87
Sepúlveda Amor, Bernardo
U.S.-Mexico Binational Commission meets [remarks, January 29, 1987] il por *Dep State Bull* 87:54-6 Ap '87
Sequent Computer Systems Inc.
Intel and Sequent kiss and make up [80386 microprocessors] J. W. Wilson. il *Bus Week* p120 My 25 '87

Sequentia (Musical group)
Musical events:
Medieval English music performed by Sequentia. A. Porter. *New Yorker* 63:90-1 Mr 9 '87
Sequestering agents
See also
Ethylenediamine tetraacetic acid
Sequoia and King's Canyon National Park (Calif.)
Born of fire [prescribed burning for sequoia groves] W. C. Tweed. il *Natl Parks* 61:22-7+ Ja/F '87
Get back to your manzanita berries! [new black bear policies] il *Sunset* 179:42 Ag '87
Sequoiadendron giganteum *See* Redwood
Serban, Andrei
about
Fragments of a Greek trilogy [drama] Reviews *N Y* il 20:64-5 F 2 '87. J. Simon
Serengeti Plain (Tanzania)
See also
Wildlife conservation—Serengeti Plain (Tanzania)
Serfaty, Simon
Lost illusions. *Foreign Policy* 66:3-19 Spr '87
Sergeant York gun system *See* Guns, Anti-aircraft
Serial murders *See* Murder
Serials, Television *See* Television serials
Serig, Howard W., Jr.
S.S. Birchglen. il map *Oceans* 20:46-55+ S/O '87
Ship graveyards. il *Oceans* 20:30-7 Ja/F '87
Serigraphy *See* Silk screen printing
Serine proteases *See* Proteases
Serious money [drama] *See* Churchill, Caryl
Serkin, Peter
about
Brahms first from Serkin and Shaw. D. Hall. por *Stereo Rev* 52:104 Je '87
Serkin, Rudolf, 1903-
about
Serkin's Reger. R. Freed. por *Stereo Rev* 52:141 Ja '87
Serlen, Bruce
What guys really think about their own looks. il *Seventeen* 46:164-6 Ap '87
Sermons
See also
Preaching
Good news or good snooze: what Catholics expect from a homily [cover story] R. T. Reilly. il *U S Cathol* 52:6-13 S '87
Men in the collar shouldn't speak off the cuff. R. E. Burns. *U S Cathol* 52:2 Ag '87
Serotonin
Arson: a chemical fire? [arsonists' lower levels of serotonin; research by Matti Virkkunen and Markku Linnoila] J. Fischman. *Psychol Today* 21:18 Jl '87
Increased numbers of ion channels promoted by an intracellular second messenger. R. Gunning. bibl f il *Science* 235:80-2 Ja 2 '87
Serotta, Edward
The cabbie wore red [story] il *Road Track* 39:58-60 D '87
Serra, Junípero, 1713-1784
about
A question of faith in California. il *U S News World Rep* 102:24 My 11 '87
So you want to be a saint. L. Gomez and W. Wynn. il pors *Life* 10:68-9+ S '87
Serra, Miguel José *See* Serra, Junípero, 1713-1784
Serra, Richard
about
A loss for Serra. G. Danto. il *Art News* 86:61 O '87
Richard Serra: Pace, Castelli. R. Bass. il *Art News* 86:143-4 D '87
Serra goes to court. A. Decker. *Art News* 86:29 Ap '87
Tilted arc goes to court. *Art Am* 75:168 F '87
Serums
Extended culture of mouse embryo cells without senescence: inhibition by serum. D. T. Loo and others. bibl f il *Science* 236:200-2 Ap 10 '87
A glycan-phosphatidylinositol-specific phospholipase D in human serum. M. A. Davitz and others. bibl f il *Science* 238:81-4 O 2 '87
SerVaas, Cory
Medical mailbox. See issues of The Saturday Evening Post
SerVaas, Paul
Fighting drugs on ice. il pors *Saturday Evening Post* 259:50 Ja/F '87
Pushing the panic button. il *Saturday Evening Post* 259:14+ Mr '87
Servadio, Gaia
(tr) See Levi, Primo, 1919-1987. Two poems

Servan-Schreiber, Jean-Jacques
about
Europe still fails the challenge. G. de Jonquieres. por *World Press Rev* 34:46-7 My '87
Servants *See* Household employees
Servants, Indentured *See* Indentured servants
Service, National *See* National service
Service, Volunteer *See* Volunteer service
Service contracts
See also
American Warranty Company
A buyer's guide to service contracts. R. Hillhouse and S. La Rosa. il *McCalls* 114:177 F '87
Service Credit Volunteer Program
A new kind of money. C. McLaughlin. il *50 Plus* 27:12+ Jl '87
Service industries
See also
Moving and storage companies
PHH Group Inc.
Trade unions—Service industries
The boom in service industries will not solve U.S. trade problems [report from the Office of Technology Assessment] E. Marshall. *Science* 237:243 Jl 17 '87
Chicken Little is wrong again [address, August 17, 1987] P. Laxalt. *Vital Speeches Day* 53:741-2 O 1 '87
Entrepreneurs find success in the service sector. il *Bus Week* p68 S 28 '87
Franchising: business services. B. Gatty. il *Nations Bus* 75:38-40 Mr '87
The myth of a post-industrial economy. S. S. Cohen and J. Zysman. il *Technol Rev* 90:54-60+ F/Mr '87
The shift to a service economy. il *Sch Update* 119:3 Ja 26 '87
Technology in services. J. B. Quinn and others. il *Sci Am* 257:50-8 D '87
Thank heaven for the service sector. J. L. Heskett. il *Bus Week* p22 Ja 26 '87
Where the customer is still king [five American companies] G. Russell. il *Time* 129:56-7 F 2 '87
Advertising
Playing in Peoria [local TV advertising] J. Vitale. il *Channels* 7:50-1 N '87
Employees
Accountants to zoologists. *Time* 129:52 F 2 '87
Industrial structure has little impact on jobless rate of experienced workers. R. M. Devens, Jr. bibl f il *Mon Labor Rev* 110:30-2 My '87
Low-paying service work is a "myth" [address, March 5, 1987] W. E. Brock. *Vital Speeches Day* 53:444-6 My 1 '87
The myth of 'McJobs'. *Natl Rev* 39:19-20 Ap 10 '87
Export-import trade
The bright future of service exports. R. I. Kirkland, Jr. il *Fortune* 115:32-4+ Je 8 '87
The service revolution. R. K. Shelp. *Society* 24:71-7 Ja/F '87
Finance
Industrial and office services. A. Snitzer. il *Forbes* 139:148+ Ja 12 '87
Presto! The convenience industry: making life a little simpler [cover story] S. Benway. il *Bus Week* p86-9+ Ap 27 '87
Services [1990s] K. Labich. il *Fortune* 115:37-8 F 2 '87
Statistics
The service 500 [cover story; special section] il *Fortune* 115:191-4+ Je 8 '87
Management
Productivity puzzle. S. Nasar. il *Fortune* 115:44 Je 8 '87
Service with a smile [productivity in the service sectors] S. Lee and C. Brown. *Forbes* 140:79 Ag 24 '87
Securities
An investor's guide to the convenience industry. il *Bus Week* p94 Ap 27 '87
Long on sizzle, short on steak. J. J. Curran. il *Fortune* 115:149+ Je 8 '87
Taxation
Advertisers fume, lawyers sue over new Florida tax. K. R. Sheets. *U S News World Rep* 102:45 My 11 '87
As Florida booms, its problems explode. G. DeGeorge. il *Bus Week* p88-9 Ap 20 '87
Down on the levy [ad tax dampens Orlando TV market boom] M. Clary. il *Channels* 7:53-5 N '87
Florida's rookie governor is stuck in a slump [B. Martinez] G. DeGeorge. il por *Bus Week* p174+ O 12 '87
Florida's service tax sparks a revolt. G. DeGeorge. il *Bus Week* p49 Je 22 '87

Grappling with growth [Florida] il *Time* 129:33 Ap 27 '87
Taxing patience on Madison Ave. [advertisers' opposition to sales tax in Fla.] R. Hornik. il *Time* 129:52 Je 1 '87
Why Florida faces tax rebellion. A. L. Taylor, III. il *Fortune* 116:82-3 Jl 6 '87
Japan
Can Japan keep its economy from hollowing out? A. Borrus. il *Bus Week* p52-5 Jl 13 '87
A homecoming lament [comparison with decline in American service] E. M. Reingold. *Time* 129:55 F 2 '87
Service Merchandise Co., Inc.
Catalog of woes. M. Kuntz. il por *Forbes* 139:75+ My 4 '87
Service Resources Corp.
Pat Rooney's back—and he hasn't changed a bit. A. Bianco. il por *Bus Week* p110-11 My 4 '87
Service stations, Airplane *See* Airplane service stations
Service stations, Automobile *See* Automobile service stations
ServiceMaster Industries Inc.
ServiceMaster: looking for new worlds to clean. M. D. Oneal. il pors *Bus Week* p60-1 Ja 19 '87
Servicemen
See also
AIDS (Disease) and servicemen
Children of servicemen
Trade unions—Servicemen
Pay, allowances, etc.
See United States. Army—Pay, allowances, etc.
Psychology
See Psychology, Military
Retirement
See Retired military personnel
Suits and claims
Supreme Court extends limits on suits by military personnel. M. Mecham. *Aviat Week Space Technol* 126:26 My 25 '87
Servicemen, Discharged *See* Veterans
Servicemen's families
Anchors aweigh: help for Navy families [stress of separations] H. Hall. il *Psychol Today* 21:16 Ap '87
Army families face financial hardships [study by Robert J. Thoresen] il *USA Today (Periodical)* 116:4-5 D '87
Servicewomen
Much too macho [sexist treatment of women in the Navy and the Marines] *Time* 130:28 S 28 '87
"Sergeant Mom" [Army sergeant has child with spina bifida] B. A. Kidwell. il por *Ladies Home J* 104:16+ Ja '87
Canada
Close encounter at sea [Canadian ships introduce women crew members] C. Wood. il *Macleans* 100:45 Je 1 '87
Serving trays *See* Trays
Servomechanisms
See also
Stepping motors
Sesame Street [television program] *See* Television program reviews—Single works
Seshadri, Vijay
A sketch from the campaign in the north [poem] *Nation* 245:244 S 12 '87
Sessions, William Steele
about
The FBI gets its man. M. Kaus. il por *Newsweek* 110:20 Ag 3 '87
Next chief of the FBI: a tall Texan. il por *U S News World Rep* 103:7 Ag 3 '87
Tough Texan. por *Time* 130:18 Ag 3 '87
Sessler, Stephen M.
Making the architect-engineer relationship work. *Archit Rec* 175:43 F '87
Sestanovich, Stephen
What Gorbachev wants [cover story] *New Repub* 196:20-3 My 25 '87
Set design *See* Motion pictures—Setting and scenery; Opera—Stage setting and scenery; Television broadcasting—Setting and scenery; Theater—Stage setting and scenery
Set designers
See also
Aronson, Boris
Crowley, Bob
Kokkos, Yannis
Lobel, Adrianne
Okun, Alexander
Rigdon, Kevin
Svoboda, Josef, 1920-

Set designers—See also—*cont.*
    United Scenic Artists
    Vychodil, Ladislav
    Walton, Tony
    Designers at work [cover story; special section] il *Theatre
        Crafts* 21:23-42+ My '87
Set photography
    Selleck by Trindl [interview with G. Trindl; cover story]
        B. Hurter. il pors *Petersens Photogr Mag* 15:20-1+
        Ap '87
Set theory
        See also
    Fractals
Sethi, Robbie Clipper
    The bride wore red [story] il *Mademoiselle* 93:154+
        Ap '87
SETI (Search for Extraterrestrial Intelligence) *See* Interstel-
    lar communication
Setsuko
        about
    Chalet Balthus. J. Leymarie. il por *House Gard* 159:108-17
        D '87
Setters (Dogs)
        See also
    English setters
    Gordon setters
Setting in fiction *See* Fiction—Setting
Settlement of land *See* Land settlement
Settlements, Squatter *See* Squatter settlements
Seuss, Dr.
        about
    Seuss on the loose. M. J. Bandler. il pors *Parents*
        62:116-18+ S '87
Sevela, Efraim
        about
    The man without a country. M. L. Grisanti. il pors
        N Y 20:38-43 Ja 12 '87
Seven days in May [television program] *See* Television
    program reviews—Single works
Seventeen (Periodical)
    Seventeen's greatest hits! [excerpts from interviews] il
        Seventeen 46:65-8 Jl '87
    Staff notes [interview with L. Sanford, fashion editor]
        il por *Seventeen* 46:252-3 Ag '87
Seventeen hundred and eighty-seven
    Newsclips: of sorcerers, pests and downright ugly matters
        in 1787. il *Life* 10:38-9 Fall '87
    The year in pictures: 1787. K. Emmons. il *Life* 10:28-34
        Fall '87
Seventeen year locusts *See* Cicadas
Severance pay
    Axed in an acquisition [finances of laid-off bank manager
        Mike Garbutt] S. Seixas. il *Money* 16:104-8 Mr '87
    What to do with your severance package. F. McCoy.
        il *Black Enterp* 17:63-4 Mr '87
Severy, Merle
    Shakespeare lives at the Folger. il *Natl Geogr* 171:244-59
        F '87
    The world of Süleyman the Magnificent [cover story]
        il map *Natl Geogr* 172:552-601 N '87
Sewage disposal
        See also
    International Drinking Water Supply and Sanitation
        Decade, 1981-1990
    Waste disposal in the ocean
Sewage purification
        See also
    Water reuse
Seward, Deborah
    Europe's vanishing storks. il *Int Wildl* 17:4-11 My/Je
        '87
Seward, William
    Golden days. pors *Opera News* 51:20 F 28 '87
Sewell, John W., and Contee, Christine E.
    Foreign aid and Gramm-Rudman. bibl f *Foreign Aff*
        65:1015-36 Summ '87
Sewer cleaning
        See also
    Insituform Group Ltd.
    Insituform of North America, Inc.
Sewer pipes
        Maintenance and repair
    Fixing the pipes [Insituform process] J. Novack. il *Forbes*
        140:70 Ag 24 '87
    Plastic pipe liner [Insitutube used in Saint Louis, Mo.]
        D. Stover. il *Pop Sci* 230:49 F '87
Sewing
        See also
    Dress forms
    Flashing (Sewing)
    Tailoring

Creative machine stitchery. J. Williams and J. Severson.
    il *Better Homes Gard* 65:46-9+ Ja '87
Dish-towel chic [towels made into clothing] il *Good
    Housekeep* 205:126-7 Jl '87
        Competitions
Sewin' off with show-off style [winners of Sew 'N Show
    contest] il *Teen* 31:70 Ja '87
Sewing machines
        See also
    Union Special Corp.
Sex (Biology)
        See also
    Conjugation (Biology)
    Plants, Sex in
    Reproduction
    Sex ratio
Evolution, sex, and sex allocation [special issue]
    BioScience 37:466-96+ Jl/Ag '87
Sex (Psychology) *See* Sexual behavior
Sex and fashion
    Early feminist fashion [views of designer E. Hawes]
        B. Berch. il por *Ms* 15:26 Mr '87
    Mergers & acquisitions: manstyle for women. il *Harpers
        Bazaar* 120:154-63 F '87
    Will sexy sell? [1988 spring fashions] C. Donovan. il
        N Y Times Mag p126-7 D 6 '87
Sex and law
        See also
    Prostitution
    Rape
Sex and religion
        See also
    Bishops—Sexual behavior
    Homosexuality and Christianity
    Priests—Sexual behavior
Appropriate vulnerability: a sexual ethic for singles. K.
    Lebacqz. il *Christ Century* 104:435-8 My 6 '87
A battle over sexual morals [Episcopal Church] J. Duin.
    il *Christ Today* 31:46-7 Ap 3 '87
Catholic authority, Catholic theology, Catholic identity
    [special section] *Commonweal* 114:43-51 Ja 30 '87
Charles E. Curran: a teaching moment continues [cover
    story; special issue; with editorial comment by George
    W. Hunt] il *America* 156:inside cover, 334-46+ Ap
    25 '87
Deceiving ourselves about 'safe sex'. A. B. Robinson.
    Christ Century 104:550 Je 17-24 '87
Father Charles Curran and Canon 812. R. M. Brown.
    Christ Century 104:100 F 4-11 '87
Great sex: reclaiming a Christian sexual ethic [cover
    story; special section] il *Christ Today* 31:23-46 O 2
    '87
Houston Catholics must refrain from sex to have gala
    church wedding. *Jet* 73:33 N 16 '87
Intimacy: our latest sexual fantasy. T. Stafford. il *Christ
    Today* 31:21-7 Ja 16 '87
Just say no to condom ads. J. Piper. il por *Christ
    Today* 31:16 S 4 '87
A plan for Catholic marriages [penalty for cohabitation
    in Houston] K. L. Woodward. il *Newsweek* 110:73
    D 14 '87
Renewal leaders issue a call to biblical morality [Episcopal
    Church] A. Hibbard. il *Christ Today* 31:42+ Je 12
    '87
Reuniting sexuality and spirituality. J. B. Nelson. il
    Christ Century 104:187-90 F 25 '87
Roman Catholic sexual ethics: a dissenting view [cover
    story] C. E. Curran. il *Christ Century* 104:1139-42
    D 16 '87
Rubber trees and valentines [Catholic reaction to National
    Research Council's report, Risking the future: adolescent
    sexuality, pregnancy and childbearing] *America* 156:1-2
    Ja 3-10 '87
Sex ed for grownups. T. C. Muck. *Christ Today* 31:15
    Je 12 '87
Sex education: a matter of body & soul [New York
    City program vs. Catholic Church] K. S. Smith. il
    Commonweal 114:206-10 Ap 10 '87
Sexual and family violence: a growing issue for the
    churches [cover story] L. G. Livezey. il *Christ Century*
    104:938-42 O 28 '87
Sexuality and vulnerability [discussion of May 6, 1987
    article, Appropriate vulnerability: a sexual ethic for
    singles] K. Lebacqz. *Christ Century* 104:596-8 Jl 1-8
    '87
Short-order sexuality. D. F. Kinlaw. *Christ Today* 31:11
    F 20 '87
Teen-age sexuality [special issue; with editorial comment
    by George W. Hunt] *America* 156:inside cover
    F 14 '87

Sex and religion—*cont.*
Teen-age sexuality and public morality. A. J. Moore. il *Christ Century* 104:747-50 S 9-16 '87
Witch hunts: the sex factor [Europe] A. Barstow. il *Ms* 16:85 N '87

Bibliography
Further reading. K. Cook and S. Grenz. *Christ Today* 31:46 O 2 '87

Sex attractants
See also
Pheromones
Sex behavior *See* Sexual behavior
Sex business *See* Sex oriented business
Sex change *See* Change of sex
Sex chromosome abnormalities *See* Chromosome abnormalities
Sex control *See* Sex determination and control
Sex crimes
See also
Child molesting
Incest
Prostitution
Rape
Sodomy
Sexual and family violence: a growing issue for the churches [cover story] L. G. Livezey. il *Christ Century* 104:938-42 O 28 '87

Canada
Anger over sex crimes. il *Macleans* 100:16 Ap 20 '87
Hockey as a cause [three Montreal Canadiens accused of sexual misconduct with minors] H. Quinn. il *Macleans* 100:50-1 Ap 27 '87

Denmark
Deception and propaganda. B. Kutchinsky. *Society* 24:21-4 Jl/Ag '87

Sex determination and control
Choosing baby's gender [research by Ronald Ericsson and Allan Abramovitch] N. Underwood. *Macleans* 100:66 N 9 '87
Discarding the females. il *World Press Rev* 34:5 Mr '87
Evolution, sex, and sex allocation [special issue] *BioScience* 37:466-96+ Jl/Ag '87
Gender choice a 'gross deception'. il *FDA Consum* 21:2 Ap '87
Gender kits—caveat emptor [FDA censures Gender Choice kit manufacturer] il *U S News World Rep* 102:12 F 9 '87
Is she or isn't she? [growing movement to end gender testing in the Olympics] L. Fink. il *Women's Sports Fitness* 9:71 D '87
Your next child will be a: boy, girl. R. Lewis. il *Health* 19:58-60+ Ja '87

Sex differences
See also
Androgyny (Psychology)
All in the family [views of E. Maccoby] E. Hall. il pors *Psychol Today* 21:54-8+ N '87
Assertiveness breeds contempt [male vs. female evaluations of assertive female managers; study by David L. Mathison] V. Bozzi. *Psychol Today* 21:15 S '87
Big plus for females [sports interest and math skills] J. E. Vader. por *Sports Illus* 67:100 N 23 '87
Boys' comedy, girls' comedy. D. Seeley. il *Seventeen* 46:113 N '87
Boys will be boys . . . [problems in raising non-sexist children] G. Witkin-Lanoil. il *Health* 19:6 Ag '87
Copper: what a difference sex makes [research by Meira Fields and others] J. Raloff. *Sci News* 131:70 Ja 31 '87
An emotional back burner. J. Stone. *Glamour* 85:52 Jl '87
Fatherese & motherese. P. Perry. il *Parents* 62:100-4 Mr '87
Female math anxiety on the wane. C. Holden. il *Science* 236:660-1 My 8 '87
Fragile communication between the sexes [views of Margaret L. McLaughlin] il *USA Today (Periodical)* 115:11 My '87
Girls and boys: how different? J. Segal and Z. Segal. il *Parents* 62:200 Ap '87
The great sports debate [men competing against women] L. Villarosa. il *Health* 19:27-30+ Jl '87
Interruptions: an equal-opportunity disturber [study by Kathryn Dindia] V. Bozzi. *Psychol Today* 21:15 S '87
Mathematics: a male advantage? [study by Camilla Persson Benbow] R. J. Trotter. *Psychol Today* 21:66-7 Ja '87

Ms. Right and Mr. Wrong [women athletes score higher than male athletes in tests of moral reasoning] L. Howard. il *Women's Sports Fitness* 9:45 O '87
Pink and blue: the power of suggestion [influence of color on strength; research by Jeffrey M. Smith] P. McCarthy. *Psychol Today* 21:24-5 Jl '87
Scaling the heights of passion [Passionate Love Scale developed by Elaine Hatfield and Susan Sprecher] G. Lowe. il *Psychol Today* 21:10 Jl '87
What are little boys (and girls) made of? D. F. Bjorklund. il *Parents* 62:88-91 F '87
Why do women live longer than men? C. Holden. il *Science* 238:158-60 O 9 '87

Animals
Animal gender benders [animal-gender associations; study by Steven Lash and James Polyson] il *Psychol Today* 21:8 D '87

Sex discrimination
See also
Black women—Employment
Discrimination in employment
Equal pay for equal work
United Nations. Committee on the Elimination of Discrimination against Women
Women—Employment
America's grandmother fixation [use of term to define women] S. W. Olds. il *Ms* 15:104 Ja '87
Full moons and white men [woman physician attempts to dispel bias that favors white males] S. P. Harwood. il *Ms* 16:103 O '87
Getting clubbed [men's clubs] *New Repub* 196:4+ Mr 16 '87
How wide is the gender gap? [women artists] E. Heartney. il *Art News* 86:139-45 Summ '87
Much too macho [sexist treatment of women in the Navy and the Marines] *Time* 130:28 S 28 '87
The parable of the cheek-turners and the cheek-smiters [feminist opposition to proposed revision of the Diagnostic and statistical manual of mental disorders] S. Boxer. il *Discover* 8:80-3 Ag '87
The politics of masochism [feminists challenge proposed revisions to Diagnostic and statistical manual of mental disorders] D. Franklin. il *Psychol Today* 21:52-7 Ja '87
Rotary action [Supreme Court ruling on admission of women] *Time* 129:62 My 18 '87
Rotary: women's turn comes round [Supreme Court decision] *U S News World Rep* 102:14 My 18 '87
Ruckus over Rotary women [Supreme Court ruling] J. Seligmann. il *Newsweek* 109:47 My 18 '87
Sexist sales [men receive more prompt service in department stores; study by Bette Ann Stead and George M. Zinkhan] V. Bozzi. *Psychol Today* 21:11 Jl '87
A small moral quandary [dining at men's club that bars women] O. Friedrich. il *Time* 129:94 Mr 16 '87
Tap, tap, tap on the clubhouse door [men-only clubs] L. Rosellini. il *U S News World Rep* 102:72+ My 11 '87
There ought to be a law [sexist rulings and remarks in courts] K. Burkett. il *Ms* 16:74 D '87
Threat to women's gyms [men sue for entry in San Francisco] il *Women's Sports Fitness* 9:18 Mr '87

Sex discrimination in advertising
No comment. See occasional issues of Ms.

Sex discrimination in education
Are the SATs unfair? C. Ingham. il *Seventeen* 46:142-3+ O '87
Extremism on campus: symbols of hate, symbols of hope [collegiate gay baiting] E. D. Howard. il *Christ Century* 104:625-7 Jl 15-22 '87
Get involved—write a letter! [restoration of Title IX to original strength to aid women's sports] *Women's Sports Fitness* 9:64 Je '87
Student aid: are women getting what they deserve? G. Hechinger. *Glamour* 85:206-7 Jl '87
Testing . . . testing [alleged sexism in scholastic testing] D. Seligman. il *Fortune* 115:153-4 My 11 '87
What's in the future for women's sports? [demise of gymnastics at Southwest Texas State University as an example of effects of weakened Title IX regulations] C. L. Hogan. il *Women's Sports Fitness* 9:42-7 Je '87

Sex discrimination in language
The battle of the lexicons [meeting of the Evangelical Theological Society titled Male and female in biblical and theological perspective] D. Neff. il *Christ Today* 31:44+ Ja 16 '87

Sex discrimination in language—*cont.*

The good news on 'man' [New American Bible dumps generic use of word 'man' when the Greek meaning is inclusive of both sexes] *Commonweal* 114:228-9 Ap 24 '87

Passion among Ivypersons [avoidance of sexist language by Yale daily news] W. F. Buckley. *Natl Rev* 39:63 Ap 24 '87

Sex discrimination in medicine

The female heart [difference in numbers of men and women referred for catheterization] il *U S News World Rep* 103:6 Ag 3 '87

Science discovers women [overlooked in medical research] R. Wolkomir and J. Wolkomir. *Omni* 10:37 O '87

Sex discrimination in sports

Sexism in "men-only" sports: why I'm not a victim. N. Lieberman. il por *Glamour* 85:64 Ag '87

Sex education

AIDS and education: the front line of prevention. D. D. Lenaghan and M. J. Lenaghan. il pors *Futurist* 21:17-19 N/D '87

AIDS education [cover story] M. Segal. il *FDA Consum* 21:26-30 S '87

Considering the way most of us learned about sex, it's a wonder we can do it, do it well or have any interest in doing it at all. C. L. Mithers. il *Glamour* 85:44+ Mr '87

A dangerous silence [views of E. C. Koop] A. C. Lewis. il *Phi Delta Kappan* 68:348-9 Ja '87

A fact of life: AIDS & explicit education. J. Garvey. il *Commonweal* 114:694-5 D 4 '87

Home sex ed: values 1, facts 0 [results of survey] V. Bozzi. *Psychol Today* 21:14 My '87

How to talk about sex. J. Conant. il *Newsweek* 109:68 F 16 '87

Koop and Bennett agree to disagree. B. Barol. il pors *Newsweek* 109:64 F 16 '87

Koop makes waves in his war on AIDS. C. O'Connor. por *Newsweek* 109:31 Mr 2 '87

A Mother's Day challenge [discussion of sex with teenage daughter] M. Cartledge-Hayes. il *Ms* 15:80 My '87

Responding to the AIDS crisis [advertising condoms on television and broadening sex education efforts] K. A. Lawton. il *Christ Today* 31:34-6 Ap 3 '87

'Safe sex' and the presence of the absence [Dartmouth College's safe sex kit] J. Hart. *Natl Rev* 39:43+ My 8 '87

Saying no [chastity in sex education] H. Smith. il *Christ Today* 31:12-13 F 6 '87

Sex ed for grownups. T. C. Muck. *Christ Today* 31:15 Je 12 '87

Sex education [Parents poll results] O. S. Nordberg. il *Parents* 62:30 F '87

Sex education: a matter of body & soul [New York City program vs. Catholic Church] K. S. Smith. il *Commonweal* 114:206-10 Ap 10 '87

Sex education for kids? L. F. Webb. il *Essence* 18:12+ O '87

Sex education in school. F. Roberts. il *Parents* 62:50 My '87

Should schools offer sex education? J. Leo. *Read Dig* 130:138-42 Mr '87

Should sex education teach more than abstinence? [interviews with D. Williams and F. Turpen] D. Williams; F. Forrest. il *Christ Today* 31:40 Ap 17 '87

Spreading the news about AIDS. J. Barber. il *Macleans* 100:50+ Mr 23 '87

Taking on teen pregnancy. A. Levine. il *U S News World Rep* 102:67-8 Mr 23 '87

Talking to kids about AIDS. C. Schaeffer. bibl *Changing Times* 41:23+ D '87

Talking to teens about sex and intimacy. L. Salk. il *McCalls* 114:81 My '87

Teach the children well [Catholic response to pending California legislation requiring AIDS prevention education] W. J. Wood. il *America* 156:397-400 My 16 '87

Teaching s-e-x in school: the facts of life in Mrs. Roseman's class [New York City] D. Prince. il por *N Y* 20:56-8+ Ap 6 '87

Teen-age sexuality [special issue; with editorial comment by George W. Hunt] *America* 156:inside cover, 117-18+ F 14 '87

Teen pregnancy: an issue for schools [cover story; with editorial comment by Robert W. Cole] A. M. Kenney. bibl f il *Phi Delta Kappan* 68:722, 728-36 Je '87

Teen pregnancy: it's time for the schools to tackle the problem [cover story] J. Buie. il *Phi Delta Kappan* 68:737-9 Je '87

Teenage pregnancy. M. C. McClellan. il *Phi Delta Kappan* 68:789-92 Je '87

Telling '80s kids about sex. E. E. Goode. bibl il *U S News World Rep* 103:83-4 N 16 '87

Virginity regained [excerpt from Sex respect] C. K. Mast. *Harpers* 274:20-2 Ap '87

Why Johnny can't abstain. W. J. Bennett. *Natl Rev* 39:36-8+ Jl 3 '87

Aids and devices

Rae Dawn Chong draws heat with an education film on sex and AIDS. il *People Wkly* 27:112 Ap 13 '87

Federal aid

Another muzzle for AIDS education? [Congress attacks comic book aimed at homosexuals] W. Booth. *Science* 238:1036 N 20 '87

More gay-bashing [congressional amendment to appropriations bill that will hamstring safer sex education programs aimed at gays] *Nation* 245:473 O 31 '87

Canada

Hard facts for children. J. Bennett. il *Macleans* 100:38 Ja 12 '87

Estonia

Sex education in Estonia—and the U.S.S.R.—focuses on the family [work of psychologist Marika Veisson] J. W. Seymore. il *People Wkly* 27:107 Ap 6 '87

Sex hormones *See* Hormones, Sex

Sex in advertising

See also

Nudity in advertising

Television: and now, the naked truth. A. Miller. il *Newsweek* 109:54 My 11 '87

Sex in art *See* Erotic art

Sex in business

Dealing with sexual harassment. P. A. Jones. *Black Enterp* 17:108+ F '87

Employee 'relations'. L. Grensing. il *Essence* 17:105+ F '87

Ending sexual harassment [M. Vinson case] C. E. Simmons. *Vogue* 177:70 S '87

The high cost of sexual harassment. W. Kiechel, III. il *Fortune* 116:147-8+ S 14 '87

No to sexual harassment [Canadian Supreme Court rules that employers under federal jurisdiction are responsible for acts of harassment their employees commit] M. Clark. il por *Macleans* 100:44 Ag 10 '87

Sexual harassment at Smyrna [Nissan plant] J. Junkerman. il *Progressive* 51:19 Je '87

Sexual harassment: one way out. B. Allen. il *Essence* 18:96+ Ag '87

Sex in dance

Reviews:

Sex & dance at P.S. 122 and Bessie Schönberg Theater, New York City. E. Zimmer. il *Dance Mag* 61:22+ Mr '87

Sex in motion pictures

See also

Pornography

'Angel' heart is rated X; likely to be edited for R. *Jet* 71:59 Mr 9 '87

An August heat wave. D. Ansen. il *Newsweek* 110:60-1 Ag 24 '87

Back to the boudoir [1987 films] L. Henricksson. il *Roll Stone* p147-8 D 17-31 '87

Chaste out of town? [Hollywood is preaching a new morality] M. Brower. il *People Wkly* 27:102-3+ My 11 '87

Film group to reconsider Bonet's 'Angel heart' film. il por *Jet* 71:16 Mr 2 '87

Killer bimbos & galactic gigolos star in video's grade Z future [low budget exploitation movies] D. Hutchings and D. Lindeman. il *People Wkly* 28:159-60+ S 7 '87

Panic attack? No. Sex with a new man can be funny if Gail Parent writes the script [Cross my heart] J. Powell. il por *Glamour* 85:250 N '87

Should sex rate an "X"? R. Rosenbaum. il *Mademoiselle* 93:46+ Je '87

Why Lisa Bonet of 'Cosby' fame made X-rated film. il pors *Jet* 71:60-1 Mr 16 '87

Sex in television

AIDS scare changes way stars make love on TV. il *Jet* 73:58-9 S 28 '87

Chaste out of town? [Hollywood is preaching a new morality] M. Brower. il *People Wkly* 27:102-3+ My 11 '87

Does Miami Vice's Sonny Crockett carry condoms? Is Dynasty's Alexis on the pill? Did Dallas's Jenna Wade wear a diaphragm? C. Krupp. il *Glamour* 85:232+ Mr '87

Less sex please—we're European. R. Laver. il *Macleans* 100:50 O 12 '87

Sex in television—*cont.*
Anecdotes, facetiae, satire, etc.
Help for the TV-shy. D. Owen. il *Atlantic* 260:18 S '87

Sex in television advertising *See* Sex in advertising
Sex in video games
Dominatrix on the desktop [MacPlaymate] J. Bell. il *Pers Comput* 11:255 Jl '87
Sex in videotapes
Bedroom eyes: erotic movies come home. E. Abeel. il *Mademoiselle* 93:194-5+ O '87
Is there too much sex in aerobics? K. Andes. il *Women's Sports Fitness* 9:60 Ja '87

Sex organs *See* Reproductive organs
Sex oriented business
See also
Pornography
Prostitution
Couch dancing. K. G. McWalter. il *N Y Times Mag* p138 D 6 '87

Sex pheromones *See* Pheromones
Sex Pistols (Musical group)
The Sex Pistols: Winterland, San Francisco, January 14th, 1978. D. Fricke. il *Roll Stone* p97+ Je 4 '87
Sex ratio
Hey, Pisces, what's your latitude? [silversides; research by David O. Conover and Stephen W. Heins] *Sci News* 131:232 Ap 11 '87
Labile sex ratios in wasps and bees. J. H. Werren. bibl f il *BioScience* 37:498-506 Jl/Ag '87
What do you suppose B-forces make? [high ratio of daughters to sons in fighter pilots exposed to high G-forces; research by Bertis Little] *Sci News* 132:377 D 12 '87

Sex relations *See* Sexual behavior
Sex research
A candid conversation with Dr. Mary Calderone. M. Fox. il por *Health* 19:75-6+ My '87
Sex role
See also
Androgyny (Psychology)
Avoiding sex-role stereotypes. J. Segal and Z. Segal. il *Parents* 62:200 D '87
Boys, toys . . . joys. J. Kelman. il *McCalls* 115:63-4 D '87
Boys will be boys, girls will be . . . [spotted hyenas may help answer questions about gender and aggression in humans] J. L. Hopson. bibl (p67) il *Psychol Today* 21:60-6 Ag '87
Calling all cousins—who connects the family [role of women] C. Tavris. *Vogue* 177:122 My '87
The chalice and the blade: an interview with Riane Eisler. F. P. Hosken. *Humanist* 47:26-30+ Jl/Ag '87
Christianity today talks to George Gilder. L. Neff. por *Christ Today* 31:35 Mr 6 '87
How three generations see women's roles [views of the Beste and Morrisroe families] E. Johnson. il *Sch Update* 119:19 My 18 '87
How working with women has made my life better [lone male teacher] H. S. Karlitz. il por *Work Woman* 12:100-1+ Jl '87
I've had it with he-men. B. G. Harrison. *Mademoiselle* 93:166 My '87
Liberty, equality, sexuality. A. D. Bloom. *Commentary* 83:24-30 Ap '87
Men in the eighties: multiplying roles: the next stage. D. Hellerstein. il *Ms* 16:48-50 O '87
Mother's moments: nonsexist toys? Forget it. D. Sobel. *Ladies Home J* 104:66+ D '87
An officer and a feminist. J. M. Dubik. por *Newsweek* 109:8-9 Ap 27 '87
Say, brother [man's view of food shopping] N. G. Nesmith. por *Essence* 17:8 Ja '87
Taking charge of change: how the new role definitions for women are created by women. J. Kagan. *Work Woman* 12:53-4 Ag '87
Test your views of U.S. women. il *Sch Update* 119:7 My 18 '87
Why smart men still want dumb women. R. Grant. il *Ladies Home J* 104:78+ S '87
Photographs and photography
The family of Nan [N. Goldin's "The ballad of sexual dependency"] M. Kozloff. il pors *Art Am* 75:38-9+ N '87
Nan Goldin [exhibit entitled The ballad of sexual dependency] E. Heartney. il por *Art News* 86:177+ Ap '87

Sex selection *See* Sex determination and control
Sex stereotypes *See* Sex role
Sex surgery *See* Reproductive organs—Surgery
Sex therapy
Interview with a sex therapist [C. Madanes] L. J. Nonkin. *Vogue* 177:128 My '87
Treating lost interest in sex [views of Douglas Sprenkle] il *USA Today (Periodical)* 116:6 Ag '87

Sexism *See* Sex discrimination
Sexist language *See* Sex discrimination in language
Sexl, Roman Ulrich, d. 1986
about
Obituary
Phys Today por 40:88 Jl '87. P. C. Aichelburg
Sextuplets
A half dozen miracles! England's sensational sextuplets [Walton sextuplets] A. Thompson. il *McCalls* 114:47 Ja '87

Sexual abuse of children *See* Child molesting
Sexual addiction
Taking life one night at a time. J. Seligmann. il *Newsweek* 110:48-9 Jl 20 '87

Sexual arousal *See* Sexual behavior
Sexual attraction *See* Interpersonal attraction
Sexual behavior
See also
Androgyny (Psychology)
Aphrodisiacs
Bisexuality
Bishops—Sexual behavior
Celibacy
Clergy—Sexual behavior
College students—Sexual behavior
Desire
Executives—Sexual behavior
Flirting
Handicapped—Sexual behavior
Homosexuality
Lesbianism
Married couples—Sexual behavior
Masculinity (Psychology)
Masochism
Masturbation
Monogamy
Orgasm
Politicians—Sexual behavior
Presidential candidates—Sexual behavior
Presidents—Sexual behavior
Priests—Sexual behavior
Prime ministers—Sexual behavior
Prisoners—Sexual behavior
Public officers—Sexual behavior
Sadomasochism
Seduction
Sex therapy
Sexual deviation
Sexual disorders
Sodomy
Women executives—Sexual behavior
Youth—Sexual behavior
5 wrong reasons to have sex [excerpt from Hidden bedroom partners] P. Garwood and F. Hajcak. il *Glamour* 85:250-1+ Ag '87
The 10 commonest questions about sex. M. Klein. *McCalls* 114:122+ Jl '87
. . . and Dworkin's treatise on intercourse [excerpt from Intercourse] A. Dworkin. il *Ms* 15:28 Ap '87
Bedroom eyes. B. M. Campbell. il *Essence* 18:78-80+ My '87
Body and soul. M.-B. Rosenbaum. See issues of Mademoiselle
A different take on the ol' bump and grind [women watching the Chippendales striptease revue] M. A. Gillespie. il por *Ms* 16:88+ O '87
The erotic art of undressing. J. P. Davis. il *Glamour* 85:206-7+ D '87
Friends and enemies of male sexuality. D. Foley. il *Prevention* 39:68-73 Je '87
High-risk sex studied in women, men. D. D. Edwards. *Sci News* 132:116 Ag 22 '87
How sex feels: a reverie. F. Conroy. il *Esquire* 107:205-6+ Je '87
How to ask about sex and get honest answers [randomized response method] G. Kolata. il *Science* 236:382 Ap 24 '87
How to find your body map to sexual pleasure. S. S. Cohen. il *Glamour* 85:298-9+ Ap '87
The intelligent woman's guide to sex. D. Heyn. See issues of Mademoiselle beginning December 1986
Is there sexy after 40? E. Jong. *Vogue* 177:304-5 My '87

Sexual behavior—*cont.*

Lying in bed: can you believe his pillow talk? B. Weber. *Mademoiselle* 93:72 Jl '87

Members only: what every guy wants a girl to know. J. McCabe. *Mademoiselle* 93:278-9+ Mr '87

Now here's a real headache for lovers [sex-induced headaches] il *Discover* 8:12+ F '87

Putting the romance back into sex [excerpt from I love you] D. S. Viscott. il *Good Housekeep* 205:148-9+ O '87

The secret to sexual satisfaction. R. Richards. *Redbook* 168:80-1+ Ja '87

Seven truths about sex [condensed from How to make love all the time] B. De Angelis. *Read Dig* 131:127-30 Ag '87

Sex. J. Liebmann-Smith. il *Ms* 15:78+ Ap '87

Sex & health. S. Zussman. See issues of Glamour beginning November 1986

Sex & the single-breasted woman [recovering from a mastectomy] L. Dackman. *Vogue* 177:420+ S '87

Sex, AIDS and pillow talk. S. Nelson. il *Glamour* 85:350-1+ S '87

Sex improves with age [views of Herant Katchadourian] il *USA Today (Periodical)* 116:11 S '87

Sexual health [questions and answers] L. F. Webb. See issues of Essence

The sexual revolution and the black middle class. R. Staples. il *Ebony* 42:56-8 Ag '87

Special survey results: 26,000 women reveal the secrets of intimacy. C. Rubenstein and C. Tavris. il *Redbook* 169:147-9+ S '87

The underrated power of scent [body odor] H. S. Kaplan. il por *Redbook* 169:38+ My '87

Understanding the reasons behind men's new sexual fears. S. S. Cohen. il *Glamour* 85:206-7+ Je '87

What men really want from women in bed. J. P. Davis. il *Glamour* 85:178-9+ Ja '87

Why men still yearn for "an experienced virgin". *Glamour* 85:162 Je '87

Women's headaches can be cured with sex. *Jet* 73:35 N 16 '87

Your sex switch: why do you turn off when you want to turn on? J. G. Patrick. *Redbook* 168:94-5+ Ap '87

Amphibia

Frog went a-courtin' [gray tree frog; work of Georg M. Klump and H. Carl Gerhardt] il *Sci Am* 256:28 Je '87

Anecdotes, facetiae, satire, etc.

In case you hadn't noticed . . . sex is over. I. Shoales. *Mademoiselle* 93:186-7+ Ag '87

Animals

After opening day [hunting whitetailed deer] G. Clancy. il *Outdoor Life* 180:75-7+ N '87

Boys will be boys, girls will be . . . [spotted hyenas may help answer questions about gender and aggression in humans] J. L. Hopson. bibl (p67) il *Psychol Today* 21:60-6 Ag '87

Changing of the guard [aging gelada baboon loses his harem to a younger male] R. I. M. Dunbar. il *Int Wildl* 17:30-3 Ja/F '87

Elephants in musth, lust [Kenya's Amboseli National Park] J. H. Poole. il *Nat Hist* 96:46-55 N '87

The ids of March [mating behavior of hares] T. Foote. il *Atlantic* 259:14+ Mr '87

Mild and woolly monkeys [male bonding and female dispersal in muriquis; research by Karen B. Strier] *Sci News* 132:334 N 21 '87

Mule deer metamorphoses. G. Webster. il *Field Stream* 92:53+ N '87

Runaway sexual selection [diversity of male genitalia] W. G. Eberhard. *Nat Hist* 96:4+ D '87

These are real swinging primates [muriqui monkeys] S. Brownlee. il map *Discover* 8:66-8+ Ap '87

'Til death (or whatever) do them part [monogamy] il *Natl Wildl* 25:44-50 F/Mr '87

Birds

Looking for Mr. Goodbird [relationship between garish plumage and parasite resistance; research by Andrew Read] il *Discover* 8:8 O '87

Mockingbird song aimed at mates, not rivals [research by Randall Breitwisch and George Whitesides] R. Lewin. il *Science* 236:1521-2 Je 19 '87

Why the old alibi just won't fly for these unfaithful penguins [work of Ann Bowles with emperor penguins] il *Discover* 8:13 Ja '87

Crustaceans

Getting to the heart of lobster love [work of J. Atema] D. Q. Haney. il por *Natl Wildl* 25:18-21 Ap/My '87

Lobster lust: Don Juans of the deep [research by J. Atema; with editorial comment by Paul Hoffman] W. Ravven. il por *Discover* 8:4, 34-40 D '87

You light up my life, Vargula [firefleas] il *Sci News* 131:282 My 2 '87

Echinoderms

Sex among the sessile [sea cucumbers] R. L. Shimek. il *Nat Hist* 96:60-3 Mr '87

Fish

Asymmetries in mating preferences between species: female swordtails prefer heterospecific males. M. J. Ryan and W. E. Wagner, Jr. bibl f il *Science* 236:595-7 My 1 '87

Differentiation and evolution of sex change in fishes. D. Y. Shapiro. bibl f il *BioScience* 37:490-7 Jl/Ag '87

The evolution of sexual patterns in the seabasses. E. A. Fischer and C. W. Petersen. bibl f il *BioScience* 37:482-9 Jl/Ag '87

Female fish fond of male's fiefdom [bluehead wrasse] S. Weisburd. *Sci News* 132:295 N 7 '87

Mating stingrays. A. J. Dugger. il *Sea Front* 33:352-4 S/O '87

Insects

Evolution of male pheromones in moths: reproductive isolation through sexual selection? P. L. Phelan and T. C. Baker. bibl f il *Science* 235:205-7 Ja 9 '87

Wasp pickup [thynnine wasp mating] B. A. Wells and A. G. Wells. il *Nat Hist* 96:84-5 Ap '87

Reptiles

Courtship in unisexual lizards: a model for brain evolution. D. Crews. bibl (p158) il *Sci Am* 257:116-21 D '87

Does pseudosex enhance virgin birth? [desert grassland whiptail lizard; research by David Crews] il *Discover* 8:5-6 Ap '87

Leaping lizards and male impersonators: are there hidden messages? [research by David Crews and others] D. D. Edwards. il *Sci News* 131:348-9 My 30 '87

Research

See Sex research

Canada

Sex in the eighties [special section; with editorial comment by Kevin Doyle] il *Macleans* 100:2, 30-6+ Ja 12 '87

Sex lives of Canadians [Maclean's/Decima poll] J. Barber. il *Macleans* 100:66+ Ja 5 '87

Egypt

Bedouin blues [Bedouin poetry] L. Abu-Lughod. il *Nat Hist* 96:24-33 Jl '87

India

Anecdotes, facetiae, satire, etc.

Gandhi's girls. A. Levine. il pors *Wash Mon* 19:25-7 Jl/Ag '87

Romania

The erotic stripped bare. L. Mizejewski. il *Harpers* 274:57-62 Mr '87

Sexual desire *See* Desire

Sexual deviation

See also

Sex crimes

The maneless lions. R. J. Neuhaus. *Natl Rev* 39:45 My 8 '87

Sexual diseases *See* Venereal diseases

Sexual disorders

See also

Impotence

Sexual addiction

Anti-baldness drug linked with sexual staying power [minoxidil] *Jet* 71:38 F 23 '87

Doctor reveals sexual addiction a growing problem [M. Lee] T. S. Moore. il pors *Jet* 72:24-5 Mr 30 '87

Dysaphrodisiacs [sexual dysfunction caused by prescribed drugs] E. Collins. *Sci Am* 257:42+ O '87

Not tonight, dear [lack of sexual desire] D. Gelman. il *Newsweek* 110:64-6 O 26 '87

A sexual turnoff [side effects of medications] *Redbook* 169:134+ My '87

When hormones go wrong [role of prenatal hormones in sexual development; views of John Money] *Psychol Today* 21:64 Ag '87

Sexual ethics

See also

Adultery

Monogamy

Prostitution

Sex and religion

Sex education

Virginity

AIDS and Eros; tr. by Leon Roudiez. J. Kristeva. *Harpers* 275:24-5 O '87

Sexual ethics—*cont.*

AIDS fear leads many singles to marriage. *Jet* 71:31 F 23 '87

AIDS, sexual oppression, and violence: a call for prevention. J. W. Prescott. il por *Humanist* 47:15-17+ Jl/Ag '87

Appropriate vulnerability: a sexual ethic for singles. K. Lebacqz. il *Christ Century* 104:435-8 My 6 '87

The big chill: fear of AIDS [special section] il *Time* 129:50-6+ F 16 '87

Cheating ain't cheap: the high cost of infidelity. D. Heyn. *Mademoiselle* 93:202 N '87

Don't get around much anymore [fear of AIDS] A. Edwards. *Essence* 18:77+ S '87

Exploring the kingdom of AIDS [heterosexual community] P. Davis. il *N Y Times Mag* p32-6+ My 31 '87

Grave new world. M. Jacobson. il *Esquire* 108:65+ S '87

Great sex: reclaiming a Christian sexual ethic [cover story; special section] il *Christ Today* 31:23-46 O 2 '87

Harvard researcher's study of sex between doctors and patients helps stir strong debate. *Jet* 73:24+ D 21 '87

Heterosexuals and AIDS. K. Leishman. il *Atlantic* 259:39-49+ F '87

Is it just lust? Or will he love you tomorrow? B. Weber. *Mademoiselle* 93:104 F '87

Loving an unfaithful man. B.-J. Raphael. il *Glamour* 85:168+ My '87

The maneless lions. R. J. Neuhaus. *Natl Rev* 39:45 My 8 '87

More couples live together; fear catching AIDS. *Jet* 72:37 S 14 '87

Never love a stranger. L. Darling. *Mademoiselle* 93:214 S '87

The new foreplay: how do you ask about AIDS? B. Weber. *Mademoiselle* 93:141 O '87

A new romance [getting tested for AIDS] M. Kramer. il *N Y Times Mag* p71 Ag 16 '87

The new sexual morality. il *Ebony* 43:52+ N '87

The new sexual realism. L. Wolfe. il *Ladies Home J* 104:58+ Ap '87

Reuniting sexuality and spirituality. J. B. Nelson. il *Christ Century* ·104:187-90 F 25 '87

Sex in the eighties [special section; with editorial comment by Kevin Doyle] il *Macleans* 100:2, 30-6+ Ja 12 '87

Sexual ethics. P. Grant. See issues of Glamour through March 1987

Sexual ethics. C. L. Mithers. See issues of Glamour beginning April 1987

Sexuality and vulnerability [discussion of May 6, 1987 article, Appropriate vulnerability: a sexual ethic for singles] K. Lebacqz. *Christ Century* 104:596-8 Jl 1-8 '87

To catch a guy, do you dare be a thief? D. Heyn. *Mademoiselle* 93:230 S '87

What it takes to "say no" [teenagers] K. McCoy. *Seventeen* 46:30+ N '87

Would you spy on your man? Meet 8 women who did. J. Ralston. il *Glamour* 85:266+ S '87

Sexual fantasy *See* Fantasy

Sexual harassment

See also

Sex discrimination in education

Sex in business

The dark side of love [cover story] J. S. Kunen. il *People Wkly* 28:88-90+ O 26 '87

Dear Betty Harragan [sexual harassment by religious employers] B. L. Harragan. il *Work Woman* 12:30+ Jl '87

The girl in 1-A: sexual harassment hits home. A. B. Eagan. il *Mademoiselle* 93:252-3+ Ap '87

Sex for shelter: when your landlord wants more than the rent. J. Bode. il *Glamour* 85:318-19+ N '87

Sexual maturity *See* Puberty

Sexual sterilization *See* Sterilization, Sexual

Sexuality *See* Sexual behavior

Seybold, Jonathan

about

Seybold on standards [interview] D. Needle. por *Pers Comput* 11:114 Ja '87

Seyfert galaxies *See* Galaxies

Seymour, Jane

about

The private lives of star moms [excerpt from Starring mothers] J. Barber. il pors *McCalls* 114:57+ My '87

Your skin's prime time [cover story] M. Fox. il pors *Health* 19:40-3 S '87

Seymour, John, ca. 1738-1818

about

John Seymour in Portland, Maine. L. F. Sprague. bibl f il *Antiques* 131:444-9 F '87

Seymour, Roy

about

Cultivating community spirit. P. H. Johnson. por *Rodale's Org Gard* 34:103-4 D '87

Seymour, William J.

about

Untold story of black founder of Pentecostal church body rocked by sex scandal of whites. S. Booker. il pors *Jet* 72:12-14+ My 18 '87

Seymour Island (Antarctic regions)

See also

Paleontology—Seymour Island (Antarctic regions)

Seymour Specialty Wire Company

What it takes to succeed [employee ownership] M. Daniel. il *U S News World Rep* 102:48 Je 8 '87

Sferrino, Alicia

about

A desperate search for a second life. M. Jacobbi and R. Wright. il pors *McCalls* 114:127-9 Je '87

SGS Ates Componeti Elettronici SpA

An Italian chipmaker shows the way [SGS's merger with Thomson] W. C. Symonds. il por *Bus Week* p134+ My 25 '87

Shabad, Steven

Regional report: the Soviet Union. See issues of World Press Review beginning October 1986

Shabalala, Joseph

about

Singing to the rhythm of dreams. J. Cocks. il por *Time* 130:37 Ag 10 '87

Shabazz, Betty

Remembering . . . Malcolm X. il pors *Essence* 17:61 F '87

Shaber, David

about

Bunker reveries [drama] Reviews

N Y 20:60-1 Ag 31 '87. J. Simon

New Yorker 63:67 Ag 31 '87. E. Oliver

Shachak, Moshe, and others

Herbivory in rocks and the weathering of a desert. bibl f il *Science* 236:1098-9 My 29 '87

Shachtman, Max

about

Trotsky's orphans. M. Massing. *New Repub* 196:18-20+ Je 22 '87

Shackelford, Lottie

about

Black woman elected mayor of Little Rock. por *Jet* 71:57 F 9 '87

Shackleton, Keith, 1923-

Icy realm of Antarctic birds. il *Int Wildl* 17:54-9 S/O '87

Shacochis, Bob

Forgotten son of the lost generation. il pors *Vogue* 177:190+ D '87

An island between seasons. il *Harpers* 274:57-60+ F '87

Thighs & whispers. *Vogue* 177:390+ F '87

Yesterday's revolution. il *Harpers* 275:41-4+ O '87

Shad, John S. R.

about

Banking on ethics. *Time* 129:79 Ap 13 '87

Ethics 101: can the good guys win? B. Brophy. il por *U S News World Rep* 102:54 Ap 13 '87

Harvard's $30 million windfall for ethics 101. J. A. Byrne. por *Bus Week* p40 Ap 13 '87

Shad the lawgiver. D. Seligman. il *Fortune* 115:154 My 11 '87

Shade gardens and gardening

Bulbs that are persistent even in shade. il *Sunset* 179:200-1 S '87

Shades (Automobiles) *See* Automobiles—Equipment

Shades (Window) *See* Window shades

Shades and shadows

Shadow bands explained. *Sky Telesc* 73:27-8 Ja '87

Photographs and photography

Shades of luck [photograph by G. Haller] S. Piperato. il por *Pop Photogr* 94:72-3 Je '87

Shadow matter (Astronomy) *See* Dark matter (Astronomy)

Shadows *See* Shades and shadows

Shaefer, Kim

about

A new mother's fitness plan. C. Straley. il pors *Parents* 62:134-5+ Mr '87

Shaevitz, Morton H.

His 'n hers fantasies [excerpt from Sexual static] il *Health* 19:74-6+ Ap '87

Shaevitz, Morton H.—*cont.*
Why men confuse the women they love [condensed from Sexual static] il *Read Dig* 131:65-6+ N '87
Why men won't help with housework [excerpt from Sexual static] il *Ladies Home J* 104:76+ Je '87

Shaffer, Richard A.
Industry watch. See issues of Personal Computing beginning January 1985

Shafton, Ken
about
A Mac on every drafting table. P. Honan. il por *Pers Comput* 11:185+ O '87

Shaggy mane mushroom cooking *See* Cooking—Mushrooms

Shah, Diane K.
Starting over [cover story] il pors *N Y Times Mag* p26-9+ O 25 '87

Shah, Iqbal, and Khanna, Jitendra
"Nature's contraceptive". il *World Health* p10-12 N '87

Shaham, Jacob
The oldest pulsars in the universe. bibl (p140) il *Sci Am* 256:50-6 F '87

Shahrouzi, Ali
about
The courage to adapt. P. Skinner. il por *Petersens Photogr Mag* 15:36-7+ Ap '87

Shaiken, Harley
Globalization and the worldwide division of labor. *Mon Labor Rev* 110:47 Ag '87
about
Wait 'til next year [interview] J. Flint. *Forbes* 139:112 Je 15 '87

Shaken child syndrome
Don't shake the baby! P. Von Nostitz. il *Parents* 62:31+ Jl '87

Shaker art *See* Art, Shaker

Shaker cooking *See* Cooking, Shaker

Shaker furniture
Back by popular demand: Shaker design. N. A. Ruhling. il *Antiques Collect Hobbies* 92:12-16 Mr '87
Pine dresser you build from plans. il *Home Mech* 83:84 F '87

Shaker Heights (Ohio)
Race relations
Controversy stirs around barricades in Cleveland. il *Jet* 72:6 Jl 13 '87

Shaker Village of Pleasant Hill (Harrodsburg, Ky.)
Spend a Shaker weekend. J. T. Black. il *South Living* 22:10-12 S '87

Shakers
The Shakers face their last amen; ed. by Cable Neuhaus. B. Lindsay. il pors *People Wkly* 27:78-81 Mr 2 '87
The simple life [film and book by K. and A. Burns; with editorial comment by Sandra Wilmot] D. Welebit. il *Americana* 15:3, 37-9 S/O '87

Shakes (Shingles) *See* Shingles and shingling

Shakespeare, William, 1564-1616
about
Bantam launching Shakespeare series. il *Publ Wkly* 232:24 N 6 '87
Boom time for the Bard. M. B. Zuckerman. il *U S News World Rep* 102:78 My 18 '87
"Canst thou not minister to a mind diseas'd?". C. C. Park. *Am Sch* 56:219-34 Spr '87
The comedy of errors [drama] Reviews
N Y il 20:91 Je 15 '87. J. Simon
Nation 245:31-2 Jl 4-11 '87. T. M. Disch
New Leader 70:20-1 Je 29 '87. L. Sauvage
New Repub 197:28 Jl 6 '87. R. Brustein
New Yorker 63:72 Je 15 '87. E. Oliver
Time il 129:70 Je 15 '87. W. A. Henry
'Hamlet': a cause for indecision. W. Goldstein and B. Levine. il *Publ Wkly* 232:25-6 N 6 '87
Henry IV, part 1 [drama] Reviews
N Y il 20:114 S 14 '87. J. Simon
New Yorker 63:93-4 S 7 '87. M. Kramer
A midsummer nights dream [drama] Reviews
Macleans 100:62 O 26 '87. J. Bemrose
Othello [drama] Reviews
Jet il 73:22 O 5 '87
Macleans il 100:50 Ag 17 '87. J. Bemrose
Richard II [drama] Reviews
N Y il 20:48-9 Jl 20 '87. J. Simon
Stocking up on Shakespeare. W. Goldstein and B. Levine. *Publ Wkly* 232:26 N 6 '87
The two gentlemen of Verona [drama] Reviews
America 157:88+ Ag 15-22 '87. G. G. Seibert
N Y il 20:64 Ag 17 '87. J. Simon
Nation 245:175 Ag 29 '87. T. M. Disch
New Yorker 63:59-60 Ag 10 '87. M. Kramer

Anecdotes, facetiae, satire, etc.
The Shakespeare number [Belles lettres magazine studies the question, Was Shakespeare gay?] C. Simmons. *Nation* 244:291-5 Mr 7 '87
Authorship
A fair shake for Oxford. J. Sobran. *Natl Rev* 39:54-6 N 6 '87
Some ado about who was, or was not, Shakespeare [Earl of Oxford theory] J. D. Reed. bibl (p187) il pors *Smithsonian* 18:155-8+ S '87
Study and teaching
A movie star goes to Watts to make sure the Bard gets a good rap [work of J. Agutter] K. Hubbard. il pors *People Wkly* 27:83-4 Je 29 '87

Shakespeare Festival (Stratford, Ont.) *See* Stratford Festival (Ont.)

Shakespeare festivals
See also
Alabama Shakespeare Festival
Stratford Festival (Ont.)

Shakey's Incorporated
A Shakey turnaround [chief executive G. Brown] L. M. Keefe. il por *Forbes* 140:184 O 19 '87

Shaklee Corp.
A distributor's "road of empty dreams". il *Money* 16:139 Je '87
Fruit-enriched vitamins? E. Paris. il por *Forbes* 140:56 O 5 '87

Shales, Tom
Is comedy making a comeback or what? [cover story] il *Esquire* 108:118-22+ O '87
Woody: the first fifty years [cover story] il pors *Esquire* 107:88-95 Ap '87
about
Who's afraid of Tom Shales? J. Traub. il por *Channels* 7:36-9+ F '87

Shalev-Gerz, Esther
about
Sinking feelings. M. Gibson. il *Art News* 86:105+ Summ '87

Shallhorn, Steve
Standing up to the United States. *Bull At Sci* 43:16-17 O '87

Shamans and shamanism
Andrews's sisters. R. M. Staubs. il por *Omni* 10:28 O '87

Shamberger, Raymond J., 1934-
about
Researcher accused of plagiarism resigns. C. Holden. *Science* 237:1098 S 4 '87

Shame
See also
Guilt
Shame and rage—the emotional chain reaction. C. Tavris. *Vogue* 177:198 Ap '87

Shamina, Zlata B.
(jt. auth) See Butenko, Raissa G., and Shamina, Zlata B.

Shamir, Yitzhak
Visit of Israeli Prime Minister Shamir [remarks, February 17 and 18, 1987] il por *Dep State Bull* 87:49-51 Ap '87
about
Destined for a dogfight. W. E. Smith. il pors *Time* 129:39 My 11 '87
Face-off in Israel [cover story] E. Salpeter. il *New Leader* 70:5-6 Ap 20 '87
A government at war over peace. B. Levin. il pors *Macleans* 100:18 My 25 '87
Israel: at war with itself. M. J. Kubic. il pors *Newsweek* 109:30 My 25 '87
Israel's year of transition. B. Reich. bibl f *Curr Hist* 86:69-72+ F '87
'Nothing to hide' [interview] il por *U S News World Rep* 102:16 F 23 '87
Peace-talks plan: push comes to shove in Israel. il *U S News World Rep* 102:16 My 25 '87
Shamir: "I think it will pass" [interview] J. McGeary. por *Time* 129:36 Ap 20 '87
So much for national unity. il por *Time* 129:50 My 25 '87

Visit to the United States, 1987
Shamir: weaving through the Washington jungle. P. R. Range. il por *U S News World Rep* 102:34 Mr 2 '87
The 'teflon country'. A. Deming. il por *Newsweek* 109:37 F 23 '87
Visit of Israeli Prime Minister Shamir [remarks, February 17 and 18, 1987] G. P. Shultz; Y. Shamir; R. Reagan. il por *Dep State Bull* 87:49-51 Ap '87

Shammas, Anton
Arab walls, reflecting change; tr. by Yael Lotan. *Harpers* 275:30+ N '87
Shampooing of hair *See* Hair—Care
Shampoos
Healthy hair [shampoo for color-treated hair] il *Prevention* 39:55 Jl '87
Safer ways to cope with head lice. il *Consum Rep* 52:595 O '87

Advertising
The girl next door becomes superwoman [Breck ad campaign] il *Newsweek* 110:64 Ag 17 '87
Shamrock Associates
Natalie Koether: the lady is a raider. P. Finch. il por *Bus Week* p118-19 F 23 '87
Shamrock Holdings, Inc.
Arb makes good [M. Buchsbaum's Holly Sugar Corp. attracts Shamrock Holdings] P. Berman and C. Brown. por *Forbes* 139:152 Je 1 '87
Shandling, Garry
about
The sitcom with turbopower. M. Pollan. il pors *Channels* 7:60-1 Ap '87
This is the article about Garry Shandling's show. L. Grossberger. il por *Roll Stone* p41-2 F 26 '87
Shane, Jay
TV troubleshooter's notebook: black vertical bars. il *Radio-Electron* 58:70+ Je '87
Shane, Scott, 1950-
Key West. il *Travel Holiday* 167:38-43+ Ja '87
Shanga excavations *See* Kenya—Antiquities
Shanghai (China)
Photographs and photography
Finding the past in modern Shanghai's afternoon light. J. Loengard. il *Pop Photogr* 94:60 N '87
Shanghai Metallurgical & Mining Machinery Mfg.
The factory that made a great leap forward. D. J. Yang. il *Bus Week* p145 N 2 '87
Shanken, Marvin R.
about
Liquid assets. B. Kanner. il por *N Y* 20:37-8+ D 7 '87
Shanken (M.) Communications *See* M. Shanken Communications
Shanks, Alan L.
The onshore transport of an oil spill by internal waves. bibl f il map *Science* 235:1198-200 Mr 6 '87
Shanley, Lorraine
Direct marketing success stories. il *Publ Wkly* 232:48-50 N 13 '87
Shannon, Claude Elwood, 1916-
about
Interview. A. Liversidge. il por *Omni* 9:60-2+ Ag '87
Shannon, Jacqueline
Crisis in child care. il *Health* 19:29-31+ O '87
Shannon, James A.
The National Institutes of Health: some critical years, 1955-1957. bibl f il *Science* 237:865-8 Ag 21 '87
Shannon, Joseph, 1933-
about
Fantastic voyages. J. Ashbery. il *Art Am* 75:148-9+ D '87
Shannon, Thomas A. (Thomas Anthony), 1940-
What the market will bear. il *Commonweal* 114:234-5 Ap 24 '87
Shannon, William H.
God is not elected but people are: reflections occasioned by NBC's news special "Report on America". *America* 157:136-8 S 12-19 '87
Shanor, Donald R.
Regional report: Europe. See issues of World Press Review beginning October 1986
Shanor, Karen
Are you afraid to be happy? il *Ladies Home J* 104:108+ Ap '87
Shape memory alloys
See also
Nitinol
Mondo-Tronics Space Wings robotics kit. il *Radio-Electron* 58:22-3 O '87
Shapedown (Program)
How can Lana lose? An overweight teen and her family reach for help [L. Areton] J. Mason. il pors *Life* 10:34-8+ F '87
Shapinsky, Harold
about
Harold Shapinsky. E. Turner. il *Art News* 86:49 My '87
Shapiro, Arthur M.
Holding (Peron's) hands in Argentina. il *New Leader* 70:5-7 Ag 10-24 '87

Shapiro, David
(jt. auth) See Shaw, Lois Banfill, and Shapiro, David
Shapiro, Douglas Y.
Differentiation and evolution of sex change in fishes. bibl f il *BioScience* 37:490-7 Jl/Ag '87
Shapiro, Ezra
Applications only. See issues of Byte beginning March 1986
Shapiro, Fred C.
Letter from Beijing. *New Yorker* 63:96-103 D 28 '87
Shapiro, Harold T., 1935-
about
A new kind of Tiger. por *Time* 129:77 My 11 '87
Shapiro, Harvey D.
Sale of the century. il *Channels* 7:48-52 Ap '87
Shapiro, Jane
Volpone [story] *New Yorker* 63:37-43 N 30 '87
Shapiro, Jerrold Lee
The expectant father. bibl (p63) il *Psychol Today* 21:36-9+ Ja '87
Shapiro, Joel
about
Joel Shapiro at Paula Cooper. N. Princenthal. il *Art Am* 75:141-2 F '87
Minimalism made human [cover story] R. Bass. il pors *Art News* 86:94-101 Mr '87
Shapiro, Judith, 1953-
Into the streets again: faith vs. frustration. il *Newsweek* 109:31+ Ja 5 '87
Surviving the hurricane. il *N Y Rev Books* 34:5-6+ Jl 16 '87
(jt. auth) See Liang, Heng, and Shapiro, Judith, 1953-
Shapiro, Judith, 1953-, and Liang, Heng
Letter from China—young writers test the limits. il *N Y Times Book Rev* 92:3+ Ja 11 '87
Shapiro, Leonardo
about
Punch! [drama] Reviews
Nation 244:774-5 Je 6 '87. T. M. Disch
Shapiro, Michael
Taiwan 11, USA 4. il *Sport Mag* 78:65-7 S '87
Shapiro, Steven
The bender mender. il *Discover* 8:22-3 O '87
Shapland, Robert
Should the financing of U.S. catastrophic health care emphasize private insurance methods? [excerpts from testimony, January 26, 1987] *Congr Dig* 66:112+ Ap '87
Shaplen, Robert, 1917-
Sanctions and survival. il *New Yorker* 62:74-80+ F 2 '87
The thin edge (I). *New Yorker* 63:43-6+ S 21 '87
The thin edge (II). *New Yorker* 63:63-74+ S 28 '87
Share, Jeff
about
A peace march starts a photographer's career. H. Chapnick. il por *Pop Photogr* 94:20 My '87
Shareholders *See* Stockholders
Shark Bay (Australia)
Shark Bay. J. Woods. il map *Sea Front* 33:324-33 S/O '87
Sharks
Australia's southern seas [great white sharks] R. Ellis. il map *Natl Geogr* 171:286-319 Mr '87
Balancing act at Point Reyes [cover story] K. Evans. il *Natl Parks* 61:16-21 Jl/Ag '87
Fiber-optic feeding frenzy [telephone cables attacked by sharks] *Time* 129:77 Je 22 '87
Great white shark behavior study [work of A. Peter Klimley] il *Sea Front* 33:146-8 Mr/Ap '87
Horror off Death's Head Beach [Dominican refugees bound for Puerto Rico attacked by sharks after shipwreck] W. R. Doerner. il *Time* 130:33 O 19 '87
Shark research at sea. J. F. Morrissey. bibl il map *Sea Front* 33:244-55 Jl/Ag '87
Why the shark bites [underwater telephone cables] B. D. Stutz. *Nat Hist* 96:94+ N '87
Sharks in art
Listen, if there are flying fish, there are bound to be accidents [B. Heine sticks shark sculpture into roof of his Headington, England home] il por *People Wkly* 27:66 Mr 2 '87
Sharks in motion pictures
Anecdotes, facetiae, satire, etc.
Jaws XIV—a shark-eating man. J. Keefauver. *Natl Rev* 39:40 N 20 '87
Sharma, Ravi
Assessing development costs in India [cover story] bibl f il *Environment* 29:6-11+ Ap '87

Sharma, Surendra, and others
Molecular cloning and expression of a human B-cell growth factor gene in Escherichia coli. bibl f il *Science* 235:1489-92 Mr 20 '87

Sharon, Ariel
about
The press on trial. R. M. Dworkin. bibl f il *N Y Rev Books* 34:27-37 F 26 '87

Sharon Steel Corp.
A shark gets bitten [V. Posner files for bankruptcy] J. A. Conway. il *Forbes* 139:8 My 18 '87
Why Posner backed out of a bailout for Sharon Steel [bailout from Quantum Fund] P. Engardio. il *por Bus Week* p40 My 4 '87

Sharp, Elliott
about
Elliott Sharp. B. Milkowski. il por *Down Beat* 54:47-8 O '87

Sharp, Jane M. O.
NATO's security dilemma. il *Bull At Sci* 43:42-4 Mr '87

Sharp, K., and others
Computer simulations of the diffusion of a substrate to an active site of an enzyme. bibl f il *Science* 236:1460-3 Je 12 '87

Sharp, Phillip A.
Splicing of messenger RNA precursors. bibl f il *Science* 235:766-71 F 13 '87

Sharp, Phillip A., and Eisenberg, David
The evolution of catalytic function. *Science* 238:729-30+ N 6 '87

Sharp, Rebecca
Your brilliant career. See issues of Mademoiselle beginning May 1987

Sharp, Saundra
This last piece of paper [poem] *Essence* 17:116 F '87

Sharp, William
about
Musical events:
W. Sharp wins the Carnegie Hall International American Music Competition for Vocalists. A. Porter. *New Yorker* 63:124 O 12 '87

Sharpe, Arlene H., and others
Retroviruses and mouse embryos: a rapid model for neurovirulence and transplacental antiviral therapy. bibl f il *Science* 236:1671-4 Je 26 '87

Sharpe, Genell J. Subak- See Subak-Sharpe, Genell J.

Sharpe, Kenneth E. (Kenneth Evan)
The real cause of Irangate. bibl f *Foreign Policy* 68:19-41 Fall '87

Sharpe, Rochelle
(jt. auth) See Gladwell, Malcolm, and Sharpe, Rochelle

Sharpe, Ronald M.
about
Pennsylvania gets first black state police major. por *Jet* 71:32 Mr 23 '87
Sharpe is 1st black tabbed to head Pa. state police. por *Jet* 72:8 Ag 31 '87
Sharpe is first black Pa. state police chief. por *Jet* 73:47 N 2 '87

Sharpe, Sterling
about
A pair extraordinaire. D. S. Looney. il *Sports Illus* 67:100+ N 9 '87

Sharpeners and sharpening
How to keep a cutting edge on your tools. A. Rooze. il *Fam Handyman* 37:12+ F '87
Sharpening cutlery. R. Capotosto. il *Pop Mech* 164:32 S '87
Stone your way to sharper tools. J. Vara. il *Ctry J* 14:16-17 My '87
Tool sharpening basics [cover story] P. Stone. il *Mother Earth News* 108:78-83 N/D '87

Sharper Image (Firm)
Of our time [president R. Thalheimer] *New Yorker* 62:22-4 Ja 12 '87

Sharpeville (South Africa)
Botha in the lions' den [visit to Sharpeville] S. Reiss. il por *Newsweek* 109:43 Je 15 '87

Sharples, Frances E.
Regulation of products from biotechnology. bibl f *Science* 235:1329-32 Mr 13 '87

Sharpshooters See Shooters (of arms)

Sharptailed grouse shooting See Grouse shooting

Shatraw, Harriet B.
Remembering John Burroughs (1837-1921). il *Conservationist* 41:8-13 Ja/F '87

Shaver, Alan Maclean, 1938-
about
Life in the outside lane. D. Machan. il pors *Forbes* 140:220+ O 5 '87

Shaver, Helen
about
The late show. M. Rolston. il pors *Esquire* 107:82-5 F '87

Shaving
See also
Razors

Shaw, Bernard, 1856-1950
about
Pygmalion [drama] Reviews
N Y il 20:82-3 My 11 '87. J. Simon
Nation 244:694-5 My 23 '87. M. Hodgson
New Leader 70:21 Ap 20 '87. L. Sauvage
New Yorker 63:80 My 11 '87. E. Oliver
Time il 129:107 My 4 '87. W. A. Henry

Shaw, Christopher A., and McDonald, H. Gregory
First record of giant anteater (Xenarthra, Myrmecophagidae) in North America. bibl f il map *Science* 236:186-8 Ap 10 '87

Shaw, Daniel
Scenes: the big idea this summer is escape. il *N Y* 20:42-6 Je 29-Jl 6 '87
Tribeca: on quiet streets, the ghosts of the Washington Market. il map *N Y* 20:96-8 My 4 '87

Shaw, Dereck
about
Suicide and satanism. C. Wood. il *Macleans* 100:54 Mr 30 '87

Shaw, E. Clay
Is the administration approach to federal employee drug testing sound? [excerpts from remarks, September 16, 1986] *Congr Dig* 66:140+ My '87

Shaw, George Bernard See Shaw, Bernard, 1856-1950

Shaw, Harry Alexander, III
about
Easy rider. K. Hannon. il por *Forbes* 140:304-5 N 16 '87

Shaw, Jill Robinson- See Robinson-Shaw, Jill

Shaw, John
Light of spring. il por *Pop Photogr* 94:38-45 My '87
Nature. See issues of Popular Photography beginning June 1987

Shaw, Linda
Richard Attenborough's 'Biko'. il *World Press Rev* 34:60 Je '87

Shaw, Lois Banfill, and Shapiro, David
Women's work plans: contrasting expectations and actual work experience. bibl f il *Mon Labor Rev* 110:7-13 N '87

Shaw, Phyllis C.
Multiple sclerosis: a riddle wrapped in a mystery. il *USA Today (Periodical)* 116:87-91 Jl '87

Shaw, Robert
about
Couples on the couch [interview] *Vogue* 177:387+ F '87

Shaw, Robert T.
about
ICH Corp.'s ascent from nowhere. C. J. Loomis. il por *Fortune* 115:50-2+ Ap 13 '87

Shaw, Robert W.
Air pollution by particles. bibl (p116) il *Sci Am* 257:96-103 Ag '87

Shaw Festival (Niagara-on-the-Lake, Ont.) See Drama festivals—Ontario

Shawls
Collectors and collecting
The paisley shawl: anecdotes and facts [cover story] F. Ames. il *Antiques Collect Hobbies* 92:32-6 S '87

Shawn, William
about
The fate of the earth. E. Diamond. il por *N Y* 20:12-13 Ja 26 '87
Fear and loathing at the New Yorker. M. Salter. il por *Macleans* 100:46 Ja 26 '87
Sha·vn with the wind. A. Gingold. il *New Repub* 196:10-12 F 9 '87
The squawk of the town. J. Alter. il pors *Newsweek* 109:83 Ja 26 '87
Still here at the New Yorker. B. Gill. il *N Y Times Book Rev* 92:1+ O 4 '87
The talk of the town. J. Kelly. il pors *Time* 129:69 Ja 26 '87

Shawnee National Forest (Ill.)
Garden of the Gods, Illinois. R. H. Mohlenbrock. il map *Nat Hist* 96:66-8 Je '87

A shayna maidel [drama] See Lebow, Barbara

Shays' Rebellion, 1786-1787
Shays' Rebellion: a black cloud that rose in the East. B. McGinty. il *Am Hist Illus* 21:10-13+ Ja '87
Shcherbitskii, V. V. (Vladimir Vasil'evich), 1918-
about
Shcherbitsky: the Politburo's untouchable. J. Barnathan. il map *Newsweek* 109:50 My 18 '87
Shcherbitskii, Vladimir Vasil'evich *See* Shcherbitskii, V. V. (Vladimir Vasil'evich), 1918-
Shea, John
A down-and-out disciple meets his match [story] il *U S Cathol* 52:27-9 Ap '87
Friends in high places [poem] il *U S Cathol* 52:47 Je '87
Pride: a legend in your own mind. il *U S Cathol* 52:7-8 Ag '87
about
Why Jesus was dying to save you [interview] il *U S Cathol* 52:18-25 Mr '87
Shea, Quinlan
about
Behind the lines in the information war. D. A. Demac. il *Progressive* 51:32 My '87
Shea, William M., 1935-
Our brother the Pope [discussion of November 7, 1986 article, The Pope, our brother] *Commonweal* 114:34+ Ja 30 '87
Shear, Jeff
A lawyer courts best-sellerdom. il por *N Y Times Mag* p54-5+ Je 7 '87
When anxiety comes to bat. il pors *N Y Times Mag* p72+ Mr 8 '87
Shear, William A.
Arilbred irises. il *Flower Gard* 31:46-7 Je/Jl '87
Sheard, Philip, and Jacobson, Marcus
Clonal restriction boundaries in Xenopus embryos shown with two intracellular lineage tracers. bibl f il *Science* 236:851-4 My 15 '87
Shearer, Gail
Should the financing of U.S. catastrophic health care emphasize private insurance methods? [excerpts from testimony, January 27, 1987] *Congr Dig* 66:111+ Ap '87
Shearing, George
about
Jazz. W. Balliett. *New Yorker* 63:126+ F 23 '87
Shearson Lehman/American Express Inc.
See also
Shearson Lehman Brothers Inc.
Shearson Lehman Brothers Inc.
Can Cohen the consolidator make Shearson-Hutton work? A. Bianco. il por *Bus Week* p96-8 D 21 '87
For sale: Wall Street giant [bid for E.F. Hutton] J. Schwartz. il *Newsweek* 110:64 D 7 '87
Hardball on Wall Street [R. A. Minicucci; cover story] J. Sterngold. il pors *N Y Times Mag* p22-7+ Ag 16 '87
It won't stop with the Shearson deal [Nippon Life Insurance buys stake] W. Glasgall and T. Aritake. il *Bus Week* p36 Ap 6 '87
The newest seer now predicts a bear market rally (what a relief!) [E. Garzarelli] G. Anrig, Jr. il por *Money* 16:232 D '87
A pair of prescient winners [E. Fried of Shearson Lehman wins Fortune's investment challenge] P. Nulty. il pors *Fortune* 116 Sp Issue:176-9 Fall '87
Shearson Lehman Brothers [interview with E. Fried] il por *Fortune* 116 Sp Issue:186-7 Fall '87
Shearson's summer stocks ['uncommon values' list] G. Weiss. *Bus Week* p124 Jl 20 '87
The stranger in the corner [broker H. Kirschner launches securities scam from Greenwich office] D. Fanning. *Forbes* 140:37-8 O 5 '87
Shearson Lehman Multiple Opportunities Portfolio *See* Multiple Opportunities Portfolio
Sheaths
PVC knife sheath. C. Holl. il *Field Stream* 91:120 F '87
Shebar, William
(jt. auth) *See* Barnes, Edward, and Shebar, William
Sheds
A backyard building for under $1,000. M. Morris. il *Home Mech* 83:40-3 Mr '87
Best outdoor projects [storage shed] il *Fam Handyman* 37:40 My/Je '87
Shop and shed. A. Gutierrez and G. Campbell. il *Home Mech* 83:62-6 Je '87
Simply . . . sheds. J. Vara. il *Ctry J* 14:24-7 S '87
Trash-can hideaway: build it yourself! il *Better Homes Gard* 65:22 Ag '87

Sheedy, Ally
Daughter/mother. il pors *Ms* 16:158-9 Jl/Ag '87
Sheehan, Maura
about
Fragments and frames. N. Princenthal. il *Art Am* 75:144-5 My '87
Sheehan, Patty
about
Bringing lives up to par. J. Diaz. il pors *Sports Illus* 67:28-9 D 21 '87
Sheehan, Peter M.
Geology in Milwaukee. il *Earth Sci* 39:18-19 Wint '86
Sheehy, Gail
Reality? Just say no. *New Repub* 196:16-18 Mr 30 '87
Sheeler, Charles, 1883-1965
about
American painting. S. B. Sherrill. il *Antiques* 132:632+ O '87
Charles Sheeler's American interiors. S. Fillin-Yeh. bibl f il *Antiques* 131:828-37 Ap '87
Landscapes of power. J. Colihan. il por *Am Herit* 38:86-91 N '87
Sheen, Charlie
about
Good-time Charlie Sheen puts the pow in Platoon. F. A. Bernstein. il pors *People Wkly* 27:48-50+ Mr 9 '87
Oliver's army. F. Schruers. il por *Roll Stone* p24 Ja 29 '87
Sheep
See also
Wool
Brain
See Brain
Breeding
The evolution of the fleece. M. L. Ryder. il *Sci Am* 256:112-19 Ja '87
Prenatal 'sex change' for a leaner ewe [research by John Klindt] *Sci News* 131:361 Je 6 '87
Theft
The last hired gun [Wyoming range detective E. Cantrell] J. Conaway. il por *Harpers* 275:58-63 Ag '87
Sheep, Wild *See* Mountain sheep
Sheep dogs
Training
The training of Nell. M. Barker. il *Mother Earth News* 107:32-4+ S/O '87
Sheep herding
See also
Sheep dogs
When a 500-pound pig hounds sheep and puts honest dogs out of work, it just doesn't seem kosher. il *People Wkly* 27:148-9 My 4 '87
Sheep rustlers *See* Sheep—Theft
Sheep shows *See* Livestock shows
Sheet films *See* Photography—Films
Sheet music
Collectors and collecting
Collecting sheet music. D. Stewart. il *Antiques Collect Hobbies* 92:69-72 Ag '87
Sheets, William
(jt. auth) *See* Graf, Rudolf F., and Sheets, William
Sheets, William, and Graf, Rudolf F.
TV signal descrambling (VII). il *Radio-Electron* 58:53-6 Ja '87
TV signal descrambling (VIII). il *Radio-Electron* 58:63-5 Mr '87
TV signal descrambling (IX). il *Radio-Electron* 58:58-61+ Jl '87
Sheets
Easy elegance [decorating ideas] D. L. Caringer and R. E. Dittmer. il *Better Homes Gard* 65:95-101 S '87
French dressing [use of sheets in bedroom decoration] il *Seventeen* 46:272-3 Mr '87
New ways to decorate with sheets. il *Good Housekeep* 205:150-3+ O '87
Sheet style! [sheets used in decoration at Mainstay Inn, Cape May, N.J.] S. Wood and E. Young. il *McCalls* 114:70-3+ My '87
Sheff, David
About face [interview with T. B. Taylor] il por *Roll Stone* p59+ S 24 '87
Sheila E. *See* E., Sheila
Sheinfeld, Lois P.
FCC doublespeak. il *Film Comment* 23:87-90 S/O '87
Sheinkman, Jack
Should the "Minimum Wage Restoration Act of 1987" be approved? [excerpts from testimony, July 23, 1987] *Congr Dig* 66:208+ Ag/S '87

Shekerjian, Denise G.
An Adirondack wilderness retreat. il *Travel Holiday* 168:34+ N '87
Shelburne Museum
American folk art [traveling exhibition entitled An American sampler: folk art from the Shelburne Museum] S. B. Sherrill. il *Antiques* 132:986 N '87
Taking to the road. J. Newcombe. il *Americana* 15:26-31 N/D '87
Shelby, Barry
Regional report: Africa. See issues of World Press Review beginning June 1986
Shelby, Carroll, 1923-
about
From checkered flag to checkered career, Carroll Shelby takes all of life's curves flat out. J. Kelley. il pors *People Wkly* 27:105-6+ Je 1 '87
Shelby Williams Industries, Inc.
Shelby could give the shorts a shock. G. G. Marcial. *Bus Week* p165 O 12 '87
Sheldon, Elisabeth
Are perennials for you? il *Flower Gard* 31:16-17+ Ap/My '87
Sheldon, Jeffrey G., and Anderson, Denton L.
Genetic engineering and the Patent Office. *BioScience* 37:679-81 O '87
Sheldon, Sidney, 1917-
Answers to questions on fiction writing. il *Writer* 100:9-11 Ap '87
The professional response. *Writer* 100:6 O '87
Sheldon National Antelope Refuge (Nev.) See Wildlife sanctuaries—Nevada
Shelekhov, Grigorii Ivanovich, 1747-1795?
A Russian on the coast of Alaska [excerpt from Peregrinations of the Russian merchant Grigori Shelikhov from Okhotsk to the coasts of America by the Eastern Ocean] il *Courier* 40:13-14 Ap '87
Shell, Ellen Ruppel
The new breast-cancer scare—should you say no to alcohol? il *Mademoiselle* 93:112 Ag '87
The risks of risk studies. il *Atlantic* 260:114-15 N '87
Snake oil. il *Atlantic* 260:74-5 Ag '87
Watch this space. il *Omni* 9:36-8+ Ag '87
Weather versus chemicals. il *Atlantic* 259:27-31 My '87
Your best breast defense: how to outsmart breast cancer. il *Mademoiselle* 93:246-7+ Ap '87
Shell craft See Shellwork
Shell Group See Royal Dutch/Shell Group
Shell Oil Company
Shell game [accused of using former church leader James Armstrong to neutralize religious opposition to Shell's South African activities] *Christ Century* 104:937 O 28 '87
Shelley, Mary Wollstonecraft, 1797-1851
The more evil monster [fiction] *Harpers* 275:43 S '87
Shellfish
See also
Clams
Crabs
Krill
Mollusks
Shellfish as food
See also
Cooking—Shellfish
Shellfish contamination
See also
Clams—Contamination
Crabs—Contamination
Consumers protected from unclean shellfish [New York] B. Hogan. il *Conservationist* 42:19 S/O '87
A deadly seafood mystery [Atlantic Canada contamination scare] M. Janigan. *Macleans* 100:22 D 21 '87
A discovery of poison [Atlantic Canada fisheries] M. Clark. *Macleans* 100:38 D 28 '87
Shellfish culture
See also
Snail farming
Westcott Bay Sea Farms
Mussel colonies thrive on oil platform legs. J. Stuller. il *Oceans* 20:6-7+ Ja/F '87
Scallops transplanted to algae-damaged beds [Long Island] J. C. Rose. il *Oceans* 20:6 Ja/F '87
International aspects
Do you want to get into shrimp? Try Grenada. *Success Farm* 85:66 Ag '87
Shellfish fisheries
An oysterman's battle to keep 'black mayonnaise' at bay [T. Backer works to clean up Long Island Sound] R. Mitchell. il *Bus Week* p98 O 12 '87

Photographs and photography
Blue grit [Long Island Sound lobstermen] T. Pich. il *Oceans* 20:28-35 S/O '87
Antarctic regions
Krill: food of the future? S. Nicol. il *Sea Front* 33:12-17 Ja/F '87
Azores
Traditional squid fishing in the Azores. R. T. Hanlon. il *Sea Front* 33:34-41 Ja/F '87
Canada
A deadly seafood mystery [Atlantic Canada contamination scare] M. Janigan. *Macleans* 100:22 D 21 '87
A discovery of poison [Atlantic Canada fisheries] M. Clark. *Macleans* 100:38 D 28 '87
Voices against the tide [Annapolis Tidal Power Plant on Bay of Fundy is accused of harming clam fishery] D. Holt. il *Macleans* 100:11-12 N 2 '87
Mexico
Enhancing coastal production [spiny lobster fishery] L. Tangley. il *BioScience* 37:309-12 My '87
Pacific region
The domestication of reef-dwelling clams [giant clams; cover story] G. A. Heslinga and W. K. Fitt. il *BioScience* 37:332-9 My '87
Shellfish industry
Sanitation
Cracking down on crab pickers [processors in Alabama] C. Carey and C. L. Hommel. il *FDA Consum* 21:33-4 S '87
Shellfish packing industry See Shellfish industry
Shellfish processing industry See Shellfish industry
Shells (Conchology)
See also
Chitin
Nautilus
Florida's great big treasure hunt. il *South Living* 22:12+ F '87
Shells (Projectiles) See Projectiles
Shellwork
How petals from the sea form these fragile blossoms [seashell flowers by J. Manoff] G. B. Ruh. il por *Smithsonian* 17:106-10 Ja '87
Shelp, Ronald Kent
A crossroads in U.S. trade policy [address, May 4, 1987] *Vital Speeches Day* 53:618-21 Ag 1 '87
The service revolution. *Society* 24:71-7 Ja/F '87
Shelters
See also
Garden houses, shelters, etc.
Shelters, Atomic bomb See Atomic bomb shelters
Shelters, Snow See Building, Ice and snow
Shelters, Tax See Tax shelters
Shelton, Ian
about
Discovery on a cosmic scale. il por *Macleans* 100:16-17 D 28 '87
Exploding star contains atoms of Elvis Presley's brain. J. Tierney. il pors maps *Discover* 8:46-7+ Jl '87
Spectacular death throes of a star. A. Steacy. il por *Macleans* 100:40+ Mr 9 '87
Supernova! E. Edelson. il por *Pop Sci* 231:60-4+ S '87
Shelton, Peter
about
Studio. P. Clothier. il por *Art News* 86:83-4 S '87
Shelton, Richard, 1933-
Summer's children [poem] *Atlantic* 260:74 D '87
Shelves and racks
See also
Bookcases
Magazine stands, racks, etc.
Colonial wall shelf. C. L. Widdicombe. il *Workbench* 43:32+ Mr/Ap '87
Cookie tin cabinet [storage rack] W. E. Burton. il *Workbench* 43:16-17 Ja/F '87
Fan shelf. J. G. Hick. il *Pop Mech* 164:155 Je '87
Foyer shelf. T. H. Jones. il *Fam Handyman* 37:92-5 Ap '87
The plant rack. J. G. Sandell. il *Rodale's Org Gard* 34:74-6 F '87
Room transition with high tech etagere. P. Pederson. il *Workbench* 43:74 N/D '87
Serving shelves for corners. il *Sunset* 179:154 O '87
Show off! [étagere] L. M. Dalsgaard. il *Home Mech* 83:62-5 Ja '87
Shemitz, Sylvan R.
Lighting the way. il *Archit Rec* 175:148-55 N '87
Shen, Sinyan
Acoustics of ancient Chinese bells. il map *Sci Am* 256:104-10 Ap '87

Shen, Susan
Biological diversity and public policy. il *BioScience* 37:709-12 N '87
Shenandoah National Park (Va.)
Shenandoah [excerpt] H. Crandell. il *Natl Parks* 61:54-5 Mr/Ap '87
Shenandoah NP battles against the gypsy moth. il *Natl Parks* 61:38 Jl/Ag '87
Shenker, Israel
At long last, Britain's Turner Bequest finds a proper home. bibl (p144) il por *Smithsonian* 18:50-8+ Ag '87
Denis Mahon and his 'old friends'. il por *Art News* 86:121-7 Mr '87
Doing away with all babble from the Tower of Babel. bibl (p132) il *Smithsonian* 17:112-23+ Ja '87
'I've never seen a dazzling rose': the bossy approach to garden writing. il por *N Y Times Book Rev* 92:15 My 31 '87
Marks & Spencer, the 'uniquely-British aunty'. il *Smithsonian* 18:142-6+ N '87
Shenon, Philip
Walsh makes his move. il por *N Y Times Mag* p46-7+ O 25 '87
Shenyang (China)
Economic policy
The Shenyang experiment. D. Elliott. il *Newsweek* 109:36 Mr 30 '87
Shenzhen (China)
Politics and government
A democratic experiment in Shenzhen. H. Anderson. il map *Newsweek* 109:30 Ja 12 '87
Shepard, Jim
Reach for the sky [story] *New Yorker* 63:28-9 S 7 '87
Shepard, Lorrie A.
(jt. auth) See Smith, Mary Lee, and Shepard, Lorrie A.
Shepard, Lucius
Pictures made of stones [fiction] il *Omni* 9:68-70+ S '87
Shepard, Roger N.
Toward a universal law of generalization for psychological science. bibl f il *Science* 237:1317-23 S 11 '87
Shepard, Sam, 1943-
True Dylan [text of drama] il *Esquire* 108:59-62+ Jl '87
Shepard, William
Is there an Islamic fundamentalism? *Christ Century* 104:85-7 Ja 28 '87
Shephard, Bruce D., 1944-
Today's prenatal testing. *McCalls* 114:88+ S '87
Update: the pill's risks—and benefits. il *McCalls* 114:85-6 S '87
Shepherd, Cybill
about
Behind the scenes at Moonlighting. E. Sherman. pors *Ladies Home J* 104:34+ Mr '87
Cybill marries her other Bruce. L. Armstrong and others. il pors *People Wkly* 27:98-9+ Mr 16 '87
Cybill Shepherd: "How can I handle twins?" [cover story; interview] T. Seligson. il pors *Redbook* 169:16+ S '87
Twinkle, twinkle, Cybill's stars [cover story] S. Toepfer. il pors *People Wkly* 28:30-5 D 21 '87
Shepherd, Gary K.
Eight modern myths. il por *Humanist* 47:15-17+ Mr/Ap '87
Shepherd, J. Barrie
Advent awakening [poem] *Christ Century* 104:1134 D 16 '87
March [poem] *Christ Century* 104:261 Mr 18-25 '87
Mary at the manger [poem] il *Christ Century* 104:1078-9 D 2 '87
Maundy Thursday: Thomas's testimony [poem] *Christ Century* 104:327-8 Ap 8 '87
Shepherd, Jack, 1937-
Poised on the brink. il *Atlantic* 260:26-31 Jl '87
Sheppard, Chris
about
Girls apart [film] Reviews
Nation 245:463-4 O 24 '87. M. Gevisser
Sherbrooke (Québec)
Newspapers
See also
Record (Newspaper: Sherbrooke, Québec)
Politics and government
A young and rising star [minister of state for youth J. Charest] M. Rose. il por *Macleans* 100:6-7 S 21 '87

Sheridan, Greg
How the Japanese beat us in school. il *World Press Rev* 34:32-3 My '87
Sheriffs
See also
Black sheriffs
Give us just one honest man . . . please [race for sheriff in McCormick County, S.C.] il *Newsweek* 109:31 F 9 '87
Sherlock, Patricia
To Meg, on becoming thirteen. il *Read Dig* 131:189-90 D '87
Sherlock Holmes (Fictional character)
'A chorus of groans,' notes Sherlock Holmes [reading the personals] J. Harkison. il *Smithsonian* 18:196 S '87
The enduring cult of Sherlock Holmes. D. Todd. il por *Macleans* 100:60-1 N 16 '87
The game is still afoot. S. Kanfer. il *Time* 130:76 Ag 17 '87
The game's still afoot [Sherlockian scholarship] C. Murphy. il *Atlantic* 259:58-62+ Mr '87
The greatest detective who never lived. F. Strebeigh. il *Read Dig* 130:41-2+ Mr '87
The sainted sleuth, still on the case [centenary of first appearance] A. Burgess. bibl il *N Y Times Book Rev* 92:1+ Ja 4 '87
Sherlock Holmes: here's a clue to how our sleuth has lived to be 100. il *People Wkly* 27:54-6+ F 2 '87
Sherlock's last case [drama] See Marowitz, Charles
Sherman, Andrew
Financing the franchise. il *Nations Bus* 75:41-4 O '87
Sherman, Cindy
about
Art. A. C. Danto. *Nation* 245:134-7 Ag 15-22 '87
Cindy Sherman. M. E. Haus. il *Art News* 86:167-8 O '87
Cindy Sherman at Metro Pictures and the Whitney Museum. S. Tillim. il *Art Am* 75:162-3 D '87
Photographer Cindy Sherman shoots her best model—herself. M. Small. il pors *People Wkly* 28:157-8+ N 30 '87
Who's that girl? K. Larson. il por *N Y* 20:52-3 Ag 3 '87
Sherman, Clayton
about
Coping with pain-in-the-neck employes [interview] il por *U S News World Rep* 103:74 D 14 '87
Sherman, Don
Editorial license. See issues of Car and Driver beginning November 1985
Sherman, Eric
What's hot. See issues of Ladies' Home Journal beginning March 1987
Sherman, Guy
about
Aural Fixation. S. Borey. il por *Theatre Crafts* 21:42+ O '87
Sherman, Jean
I took a turn on "Wheel of fortune". il pors *Seventeen* 46:24+ Jl '87
Sherman, Joe
Inspecting your house. il *Ctry J* 14:57-61 Mr '87
Sherman, Roger, 1721-1793
about
Bill of Rights draft found. *Am Hist Illus* 22:12 O '87
Connecticut Yankee Roger Sherman's draft of the Bill of Rights makes a surprise appearance in Washington. il por *People Wkly* 28:71 Ag 17 '87
Rights show their roots. por *Time* 130:25 Ag 10 '87
Sherman, Steve, 1938-
Horror spreads across the country. il *Publ Wkly* 232:26-8 D 4 '87
To catch a thief: what some booksellers do. il *Publ Wkly* 231:63-5 Je 12 '87
Sherman, William T. (William Tecumseh), 1820-1891
about
The new Sherman letters [cover story] J. H. Ewing. il pors *Am Herit* 38:24-7+ Jl/Ag '87
Sherman Oaks (Calif.)
Stores
For sale: the Gloved One's cast-off main squeeze [pet store owner L. de Borondy attempts to sell singer M. Jackson's former pet python] il por *People Wkly* 27:88 My 25 '87
Sherman tanks See Tanks, Military
Sherman's March [film] See Motion picture reviews—Single works
Sherr, Lynn
A mission to planet earth [interview with S. K. Ride] il *Ms* 16:180-1 Jl/Ag '87

Sherrill, Robert
Can Miami save itself? [cover story] il *N Y Times Mag* p18-24+ Jl 19 '87
Sherrill, Sarah B.
Current and coming. See issues of Antiques
For collectors and students. See issues of Antiques
What's where when. See issues of Antiques beginning August 1984
Sherry, Michael S., 1945-
Was 1945 a break in history? bibl f il *Bull At Sci* 43:12-15 Jl/Ag '87
Sherry, Susan
Number-crunching helps sell yuppie puppy food. il por *Work Woman* 12:40-1 Ja '87
Sherry *See* Wine
Sherwin, Duane O.
about
Psychiatrist gets reality therapy. *FDA Consum* 21:44 F '87
Sherwin, Jane
The perilous flight of Henry O'Grady [story] il por *McCalls* 114:102-4 Ag '87
Sherwood, Diane E., and Franklin, Kristin
Ecology and the church: theology and action. *Christ Century* 104:472-4 My 13 '87
Sherwood, Jerry Puckett
about
A tale of two Minnesota mothers: one seeks the truth behind their son's death, the other stands accused. D. Chu. il pors *People Wkly* 27:28-31 Mr 2 '87
Sherwood Investors Ltd.
Trying not to be a second First Jersey. C. Welles. il por *Bus Week* p44 Ja 12 '87
She's gotta have it [film] See Motion picture reviews—Single works
Sheshunoff, Alex
Why bankers must say no. il por *Fortune* 115:177-8+ Je 22 '87
about
Smiling all the way to the bank. S. W. Angrist. il por *Forbes* 140:48+ N 2 '87
Sheshunoff & Company
Smiling all the way to the bank. S. W. Angrist. il por *Forbes* 140:48+ N 2 '87
Shetland (Scotland)
See also
Wildlife—Shetland (Scotland)
Shetterley, Susan Hand
A slice of Down East. il map *50 Plus* 27:70-6 O '87
Shevardnadze, Eduard
Soviet foreign minister visits Washington. il pors *Dep State Bull* 87:34-40 N '87
about
Shevardnadze schmooze. F. Barnes. *New Repub* 197:10+ O 19 '87
Shewey, Don
America's new honky-tonk heroes. il *Harpers Bazaar* 120:238-9+ O '87
On a role: stars on the stage. il *Harpers Bazaar* 120:310-13 Mr '87
Shields, Brooke
about
Brooke Shields: getting back on the fitness track [cover story] A. K. Leopold. il pors *Vogue* 177:340-7+ D '87
Brooke Shields post-grad beauty book. il pors *Harpers Bazaar* 120:96-9+ Je '87
The graduate. il por *Life* 10:24-5 Ag '87
Those growls at Brooke's commencement weren't coming from the Princeton Tiger. il pors *People Wkly* 27:34-5 Je 22 '87
Shields, Patrick M.
(jt. auth) See McLaughlin, Milbrey Wallin, 1941-, and Shields, Patrick M.
Shifting cultivation
Pollen probe of early Maya farming [work of David J. Rue] *Sci News* 131:218 Ap 4 '87
Shih, Charles C.-Y., and Truitt, Robert L.
Downregulation of L3T4+ cytotoxic T lymphocytes by interleukin-2. bibl f il *Science* 238:344-7 O 16 '87
Shih, Stan
about
Stan Shih wants 'made in Taiwan' to mean first-rate. M. Shao. il por *Bus Week* p109+ Je 8 '87
Shiina, Takeo
about
Just when IBM was roaring back in Japan . . . A. Borrus. il por *Bus Week* p70-1 F 2 '87

Shiitake mushrooms *See* Mushrooms
Shiite Muslims *See* Muslims
Shiley, Inc.
Shiley ends sale of heart valve. *FDA Consum* 21:2 F '87
Shiller, Robert J.
The volatility of stock market prices. bibl f il *Science* 235:33-7 Ja 2 '87
Shilling, Dana
The art of the cold call. il pors *Work Woman* 12:50-3 D '87
How two owners handled the tax changes. il pors *Work Woman* 12:40-1 Mr '87
Shiloh, Battle of, 1862 *See* United States—History—Civil War, 1861-1865—Campaigns and battles
Shils, Edward Albert, 1911-
More at home than out of step. *Am Sch* 56:577-80+ Aut '87
Science and scientists in the public arena. *Am Sch* 56:185-202 Spr '87
Shilts, Randy
about
The appalling saga of Patient Zero. W. A. Henry. il pors *Time* 130:40+ O 19 '87
The making of an epidemic. J. Miller. il por *Newsweek* 110:91+ O 19 '87
'Patient Zero' and the AIDS virus. A. Steacy. il por *Macleans* 100:53 O 19 '87
Shiman, David A., and Mwiria, Kilemi
Struggling against the odds: Harambee secondary schools in Kenya. bibl f *Phi Delta Kappan* 68:369-72 Ja '87
Shimek, Ronald L.
Sex among the sessile. il *Nat Hist* 96:60-3 Mr '87
Shin, Sang Ok
Kidnapping
Kidnapped by Beloved Leader Comrade. D. Reed. il *Read Dig* 130:105-12 Mr '87
Shin Bet (Israel) *See* Israel. Shin Bet
Shin splints *See* Leg—Wounds and injuries
Shinano (Aircraft carrier)
The sinking of a supercarrier [American submarine attack on Japanese aircraft carrier] J. F. Enright and J. W. Ryan. il *Wash Mon* 19:13-18 My '87
Shine, Neal
From Michigan, with love. il por *Read Dig* 130:134-8 My '87
Shine, R. A., and others
White light sunspot observations from the solar optical universal polarimeter on Spacelab-2. bibl f il *Science* 238:1264-7 N 27 '87
Shiner, Lewis
Rebels [story] il *Omni* 10:64-6+ N '87
Shiners (Fish)
Going with the gold [golden shiners as bait for largemouth bass] J. Gibbs. il *Outdoor Life* 179:92-3+ My '87
Shingles and shingling
Don't shingle on top of foam board. E. R. C. Capulong. *Pop Sci* 231:104 S '87
The esoteric art of splitting (and fitting) wood shingles. D. Petersen. il *Mother Earth News* 105:56-9 My/Je '87
Red Cedar Shingle & Handsplit Shake Bureau 1987 Awards. il *Archit Rec* 175:81-3 O '87
Split personality [handsplit cedar shake roof] F. L. Wolff and J. Wolff. il *Pop Mech* 164:120-2+ Ap '87
Shining Path (Guerrilla group) *See* Sendero Luminoso (Guerrilla group)
Shinker, William M.
about
Burlingame to have imprint at Harper; Shinker is publisher. il pors *Publ Wkly* 232:14-15 O 16 '87
Shinn, Eugene A.
Sand castles from the past: Bahamian stromatolites discovered [cover story] il map *Sea Front* 33:334-43 S/O '87
Shinn, George
about
Embodiment of the dream. E. F. Cone. il por *Forbes* 140:72-3 N 30 '87
Shinn, Karen Geller- *See* Geller-Shinn, Karen
Shinn, Roger Lincoln
Cooperation among world religions. *America* 156:482-4 Je 13 '87
Great expectations and some apprehensions. *America* 157:399-402 N 28 '87
Shinnecock Hills (N.Y.) in art
Exhibitions
Dreams of summer [William Merritt Chase: summers at Shinnecock; cover story] M. Wade. il *Horizon* 30:35 S '87

Shinnecock Hills (N.Y.) in art—Exhibitions—*cont.*
William Merritt Chase at Shinnecock Hills [cover story]
N. Cikovsky. bibl f il *Antiques* 132:290-303 Ag '87
Shiomi, R. A.
about
Rosie's Cafe [drama] Reviews
New Yorker 63:130 O 26 '87. E. Oliver
Ship and boat models
Blueblood boating [Far Hills Yacht Club regatta for
yacht models] D. Wallace. il *Mot Boat Sail* 160:42-5+
Ag '87
Fair copies [replicas of ancient ships] il *Courier* 40:22-3
N '87
Santa Maria boat [glass souvenir] M. Wollett and B.
Wollett. il *Antiques Collect Hobbies* 92:42 Ap '87
Collectors and collecting
Antiques: ship models. L. Atwill. il *Archit Dig* 44:178-9
Mr '87
Ship building *See* Shipbuilding
Ship junkyards
Ship graveyards. H. W. Serig, Jr. il *Oceans* 20:30-7
Ja/F '87
Shipbuilding
See also
Collective labor agreements—Shipbuilding
General Dynamics Corp. Electric Boat Division
Tenneco Inc.
Ethical aspects
A defense case may break [witnesses get immunity in
General Dynamics ship probe] S. Payne. *Bus Week*
p40+ Mr 23 '87
The General Dynamics case sets a bad precedent [Justice
Dept. decides not to seek indictment] P. Dwyer and
S. Payne. il *Bus Week* p41 Je 8 '87
Probe scuttled [Justice Dept. drops inquiry of General
Dynamics] *Time* 129:51 Je 1 '87
Federal aid
Shipbuilders: caught in the wake of Navy cutbacks. S.
Payne. *Bus Week* p70 Ja 12 '87
Canada
See also
Versatile Corp.
Worldwide storms in the shipyards. D. Jenish. il *Macleans*
100:40-1 O 26 '87
Shipley, Don
Sprucing up with decorating franchises. il *Nations Bus*
75:40-1 Ag '87
Shipman, Bert
Dogs and deer. il *Ctry J* 14:17-20 Ap '87
Shipman, Dennis Khatib
Say, brother. por *Essence* 18:10 Je '87
Shipman, Pat
Dumping on science. il map *Discover* 8:60-6 D '87
The myths and perturbing realities of cannibalism. il
Discover 8:70-2+ Mr '87
The prehumans: our family tree. *Current* 290:4-8 F '87
Teaching to overcome technophobia. *Educ Dig* 52:18-19
Ap '87
Shipman, Wanda
Bowls of vigorous greens. il *Ctry J* 14:38-9 D '87
Country graphics. il *Ctry J* 14:70-5 My '87
Finger-lap firkin in original paint. il *Ctry J* 14:52-9
D '87
Listener. See issues of Country Journal beginning April
1987
Revolutionary corn. il *Ctry J* 14:51-3 Je '87
Shipmasters
Confessions: what yacht captains really think of owners.
C. Davis. il *Mot Boat Sail* 160:48-9+ N '87
Crow's nest [questions about authority and responsibility
of a ship's master] G. L. Voss. *Sea Front* 33:322-3
S/O '87
Shipment of goods
See also
Freight forwarders
Intermodal transportation
United Parcel Service of America, Inc.
Shipping
See also
American President Companies Ltd.
Collective labor agreements—Shipping
Freight forwarders
Freighters
Longshoremen
McLean Industries Inc.
Merchant marine
Panama Canal
Ports
Sea-Land Corp.
Tankers

Federal aid
Wharton by the sea [federal government spends millions
to train shipping executives at the U.S. Merchant
Marine Academy] S. Feinberg. il *Wash Mon* 19:29-30+
O '87
Will Congress rescue the listing merchant marine? S.
Payne. il *Bus Week* p39 Mr 2 '87
Finance
The shipping industry finally gets out of the doldrums.
S. Payne. il *Bus Week* p27 Ag 31 '87
International aspects
Chasing a dream on the high seas. P. Sherrid. il *U
S News World Rep* 103:54-5 D 14 '87
Taxation
The Soviet maritime threat [address, March 17, 1987]
F. Drozak. *Vital Speeches Day* 53:534-7 Je 15 '87
Canada
Worldwide storms in the shipyards. D. Jenish. il *Macleans*
100:40-1 O 26 '87
Great Lakes region
S.S. Birchglen. H. W. Serig, Jr. il map *Oceans* 20:46-55+
S/O '87
Sailors of the Fourth Coast try to look ahead [ore carrier
Columbia Star] M. Agar. il *Smithsonian* 18:116-20+
S '87
Indonesia
Plying the Java Sea [traditional wooden prahu; cover
story] S. P. Breslow. il map *Oceans* 20:20-7 S/O '87
Persian Gulf region
See also
Iranian-Iraqi War, 1980- —Economic aspects
Soviet Union
See also
Merchant marine—Soviet Union
Taiwan
See also
Evergreen Group
Shipping subsidies *See* Shipping—Federal aid
Shippingport nuclear power plant (Pa.) *See* Nuclear power
plants
Ships
See also
Container ships
Federalist (Ship)
Freighters
Ice breaking vessels
Lightships
Ocean liners
Prison ships
Sailing vessels
Shipwrecks
Steamships and steamboats
Submarines
Tankers
Tugboats
Warships
Yachts and yachting
Manufacture
See Shipbuilding
Officers
See Shipmasters
Registration and transfer
Malcom McLean's pirate ships. A. D. Frank. il por
Forbes 139:32-3 Mr 23 '87
Safety devices and measures
The Titanic's legacy to safety. R. L. Scheina. il *Sea
Front* 33:200-9 My/Je '87
Stability and stabilizers
A question of stability [Herald of Free Enterprise] J.
Lowenstein. il *Oceans* 20:72 Jl/Ag '87
Ships, Ancient
Fair copies [replicas of ancient ships] il *Courier* 40:22-3
N '87
Resurrector of wrecks [J. R. Steffy] M. Geannette. il
pors *Oceans* 20:36-41 N/D '87
Egypt
New tools for an ancient dig [pharaoh's wooden bark
observed in sealed chamber at Great Pyramid] W.
D. Marbach. il *Newsweek* 110:80-1 N 2 '87
Pharaoh's boat found in ancient pit [use of remote
sensing] R. Monastersky. *Sci News* 132:295 N 7 '87
Probing the chambers of Cheops [video camera reveals
wooden boat inside Great Pyramid] D. S. Jackson.
il *Time* 130:75 N 2 '87
Ships, Model *See* Ship and boat models
Shipwrecks
See also
Archeology, Submarine
Central America (Steamship)
Commodore (Ship)
Geldermalsen (Ship)

The boat that wouldn't sink [Coyote racer, scuttled by drug smugglers off Florida coast, floats to England] P. A. Janssen. il *Mot Boat Sail* 160:60-1 Jl '87
Historical maritime research widespread. *Oceans* 20:55 Jl/Ag '87
Horror off Death's Head Beach [Dominican refugees bound for Puerto Rico attacked by sharks after shipwreck] W. R. Doerner. il *Time* 130:33 O 19 '87
Ordeal on Bay Ledge Buoy [clam digger R. Curtis stranded] D. J. Snyder. il por *Read Dig* 130:112-17 My '87
Saint-Pierre Bay: Mont Pelée's underwater graveyard [reminders of 1902 eruption] J. C. Fine. il *Sea Front* 33:288-95 Jl/Ag '87
Ship graveyards. H. W. Serig, Jr. il *Oceans* 20:30-7 Ja/F '87
The turtles of Mona Island [shipwrecked ferry imperils turtles] R. Wild. il *Wash Mon* 19:35-8 Mr '87
Laws and regulations
The amphora war [looting of ancient shipwrecks] il *Courier* 40:25 N '87
Law and the underwater heritage. L. V. Prott and P. J. O'Keefe. *Courier* 40:24 N '87
Canada
Diving for dollars [special section] il *Macleans* 100:36-42 Ag 10 '87
Shipyards
　　See also
　　Shipbuilding
Shirai, Mitsuko
　　　　about
Voices of import. P. G. Davis. il por *N Y* 20:86 F 16 '87
Shiras, Peter
El Salvador: the new face of war. il *Commonweal* 114:275-8 My 8 '87
Shiratori, Rei, 1937-
Japan turns toward home. por *World Press Rev* 34:24 D '87
Shirk, Richard
　　　　about
Music for three pianos. R. Freed. pors *Stereo Rev* 52:132 O '87
Shirley, Craig
　　　　about
Republican dirty tricks. F. Barnes. *New Repub* 197:18+ Jl 27 '87
Shirley, George
　　　　about
A teacher pushes migrants' kids into college—and gets fired by his California school board. M. Green. il pors *People Wkly* 27:50+ F 2 '87
Shirts
　　See also
　　Cuffs (Clothing)
　　Custom Shop Shirtmakers Inc.
Dress shirts that suit you to a tee. T. Segal. il *Bus Week* p167 Je 22 '87
The formalities [men's evening shirts] R. La Ferla. il *N Y Times Mag* p52 N 1 '87
The Hawaiian shirt. J. Berendt. il *Esquire* 108:22+ Ag '87
Keeping guayabera cool [lightweight shirts worn in Latin America] T. A. Remas. il *Américas* 39:32-7 Ja/F '87
Paul Bunyan dons a giant T-shirt—are tall tails next? [Autotomy U.S.A. dresses statue in Bemidji, Minn.] il *People Wkly* 28:97 Ag 3 '87
Say Tees! il *Teen* 31:68-9 Mr '87
Shirt stuff [T-shirts with rock music logos] il *Roll Stone* p122 Ap 23 '87
Stanley DeSantis: turning 'my neuroses' into fashion [T shirt designer] K. Kelly. il por *Bus Week* p146 D 7 '87
Sweatshirt shenanigans. il *Sunset* 178:100-1 Je '87
T shirts that shout [worn by black South Africans] il *Time* 129:48 Ja 12 '87
Top priority: the bigshirt. il *Harpers Bazaar* 120:8-11 Jl '87
T's the hot tops. il *Harpers Bazaar* 120:214-21 Ap '87

Winners named in World T-shirt contest. il *Natl Geogr World* 138:22-9 F '87
Shiseido Company Ltd.
Will Shiseido's make-over leave it less glamorous? A. Borrus. il *Bus Week* p82 N 2 '87
Shish kabobs *See* Kabobs
Shityikov, Vladimir
　　　　about
Vladimir Shityikov mines 'black gold' (and the good life) in some of the world's harshest weather. M. Brower. il pors *People Wkly* 27:61+ Ap 6 '87
Shiver, Jube
Los Angeles: the growing metropolis on the coast. il *Black Enterp* 17:65-6+ My '87
Shizuru, Judith A., and others
Islet allograft survival after a single course of treatment of recipient with antibody to L3T4. bibl il *Science* 237:278-80 Jl 17 '87
Shlomo, Yoseph Ben- *See* Ben-Shlomo, Yoseph
Shneidman, Edwin
At the point of no return. bibl (p59) il *Psychol Today* 21:54-8 Mr '87
Shoales, Ian
In case you hadn't noticed . . . sex is over. *Mademoiselle* 93:186-7+ Ag '87
You didn't hear this from me, but . . . the sexiest man alive has cooties. il *Mademoiselle* 93:98-9+ Jl '87
Shock
　　See also
　　Electric shock
　　Toxic shock syndrome
　　Traumatism
Shock: the sneaky killer. il *Curr Health 2* 14:28-9 N '87
Shock absorbers
　　See also
　　Automobiles—Shock absorbers
Shock therapy
Caffeine jolt for ECT [work of C. Edward Coffey] J. Greenberg and B. Bower. *Sci News* 131:328 My 23 '87
Shock therapy's return to respectability. S. Squire. il *N Y Times Mag* p78-9+ N 22 '87
Shocks for snakebites. R. Herzberg. il *Outdoor Life* 179:55-7+ Je '87
Shock waves
　　See also
　　Sonic boom
SDI Delta intercept yields data on space collision shock waves. C. Covault. il *Aviat Week Space Technol* 126:26-7 Je 8 '87
Medical use
　　See also
　　Lithotripsy
Shoe industry
　　See also
　　Allen-Edmonds Shoe Corp.
　　Ballet Makers, Inc.
　　Cherokee Group
　　Kangaroos U.S.A. Inc.
　　Reebok International Ltd.
　　Two City Kids Intl Inc.
　　U.S. Shoe Corp.
　　Wolverine World Wide Inc.
Advertising
True grit [Reebok commercials] B. Kanner. il *N Y* 20:24+ S 7 '87
Export-import trade
Shoe wars: an angry American takes on Japan [J. Stollenwerk of Allen-Edmonds] *Newsweek* 109:38 Ja 26 '87
Finance
Apparel, shoes and textiles. E. Pomice. il *Forbes* 139:68-70 Ja 12 '87
Shoe inserts *See* Orthopedic equipment
Shoe repair stores
Anecdotes, facetiae, satire, etc.
"Any time I can be of service". D. Mayes. il *Read Dig* 130:9-10 F '87
Shoemaker, Bill
Han Bennink/Peter Brotzmann: first entrances and last exits [interview] il pors *Down Beat* 54:24-6 Ja '87
Shoemaker, Carolyn
　　　　about
Dark time. R. Preston. *New Yorker* 63:64+ O 26 '87
Shoemaker, Eugene Merle, 1928-
　　　　about
Dark time. R. Preston. *New Yorker* 63:64+ O 26 '87

Shoemaker, Willie, 1931-
about
Stride for stride with Willie Shoemaker. H. H. Broun. il por *50 Plus* 27:60-1+ My '87
Shoemakers *See* Shoe industry
Shoen, L. S.
about
King Lear. J. Parr. il *Forbes* 139:84 F 23 '87
Shoes, Aerobics *See* Aerobics—Equipment
Shoes, boots, rubbers, etc. *See* Footwear
Shoham, Jeremy, and Stainier, Bruno
Food aid and food habits. il *Courier* 40:32-4 My '87
Shomer, Enid
Tonight you dine on the water [poem] *America* 156:235 Mr 21 '87
Shona sculpture *See* Sculpture, Zimbabwean
Shone, Richard
Matisse: an intimate splendor. il pors *House Gard* 159:132-9+ Mr '87
Shook, Barbara Ingalls
about
A triumph of will/Barbara Shook. J. Kaplan. il por *Vogue* 177:454-5+ Mr '87
Shooters (of arms)
Health and hygiene
Shooting for safety [Gentex 1030 Active Hearing Protector] D. Geary. il *Pop Mech* 164:150 F '87
Shooting
See also
Ballistics
Biathlon
Decoys (Hunting)
Duck shooting
Game bird shooting
Goose shooting
Grouse shooting
Hunting
Mourning dove shooting
National Rifle Association of America
Partridge shooting
Pheasant shooting
Pigeon shooting
Quail shooting
Rifles
Snipe shooting
Target practice
Trapshooting
Water bird shooting
Woodcock shooting
Recoil in terror. D. E. Petzal. il *Field Stream* 92:76+ O '87
Shooting. B. Brister. See issues of Field & Stream
Shooting. J. Carmichel. See issues of Outdoor Life
Study and teaching
Shooting for tomorrow. P. W. Johnston. il *Field Stream* 91:59-60 Ap '87
Shooting in art *See* Hunting in art
Shooting preserves
The sporting life 'ADAPTs' their farm [John and Mary Jo Rouse farm in Missouri] J. Walter. il *Success Farm* 85 no4:27 F '87
What price, hunting? [privatization of wildlife and public lands access] L. Williamson. il *Outdoor Life* 180:38+ Ag '87
Shooting ranges
Teach your children well [lack of shooting ranges] L. Williamson. il *Outdoor Life* 180:82+ S '87
Trapshooting shells out the profit [Dale Stockdale's range in Iowa] C. Finck. il *Success Farm* 85:23 S '87
Shooting records
Past disasters, future folly [keeping logs] D. E. Petzal. il *Field Stream* 92:110+ My '87
Shooting stars *See* Meteors
Shooting stars (Flowers)
Alum Cove, Arkansas [French's shooting stars in Ozark National Forest] R. H. Mohlenbrock. il map *Nat Hist* 96:60-2 Ap '87
Shop windows *See* Show windows
Shoplifting
My shoplifter [girlfriend] M. S. Zurita. il *Glamour* 85:126+ Je '87
Shop'n Chek Inc.
The spy who came in from the cold cuts [C. D. Cherry] P. Finch. il por *Bus Week* p101 Jl 20 '87
Shopping and shoppers
See also
Bargains
Christmas shopping
Coupons
Electronic shopping
Haggling (Shopping)

Mail order business
Personal shoppers
Purchasing, Household
Return of goods
Sales
Secondhand trade
Stores
Warehouse clubs
Do you hate to shop? Here's how to look great anyway. *Glamour* 85:87 Mr '87
Little shopping horrors: getting your guy to buy. P. Mehlman. il *Mademoiselle* 93:170+ Ap '87
Shop sharp: how to be a store trooper. P. R. Satran. *Mademoiselle* 93:186 Mr '87
Shopping options: explore different kinds of stores to get the best value for your time and money. il *Glamour* 85:52 N '87
Shopping trip-ups: 11 spending traps to avoid. P. R. Satran. il *Mademoiselle* 93:178 My '87
Shopping without tears (or tantrums) [shopping with and for children] L. Schnurnberger. il *Parents* 62:88-92 My '87
International aspects
Bargaining in Bangkok. P. Plawin. *Changing Times* 41:72-4+ Ap '87
The ultimate shopping spree [special section] il *Harpers Bazaar* 120:54+ Jl '87
Bibliography
Shopping by the book. D. P. Marshall. il *Travel Holiday* 168:16-17 S '87
Psychological aspects
See also
Compulsive shopping
Attention, shoppers! [shopping with mom] R. Ascher. il *Seventeen* 46:235 Ag '87
Do malls seduce shoppers? il *USA Today (Periodical)* 116:8-9 Jl '87
The girl who showed too much [attractive woman shopping with possessive boyfriend] L. Darling. *Mademoiselle* 93:102 Je '87
Belgium
Bountiful Belgium. D. P. Marshall. il *Travel Holiday* 167:24-5+ Je '87
Hong Kong
Far-Eastern finds. D. G. Salter. il *Essence* 18:27-9+ S '87
Japan
Tokyo clothes and other buys. D. P. Marshall. il *Travel Holiday* 168:42-3 Jl '87
Singapore
Singapore: shop place of the world. D. P. Marshall. il *Travel Holiday* 168:18-21 Ag '87
Soviet Union
The main point of communism. D. Seligman. il *Fortune* 116:183-4+ D 7 '87
Shopping bag ladies *See* Homeless women
Shopping carts in advertising
An upstart is upsetting Actmedia's shopping carts [Cooperative Marketing Co.] R. Mitchell. il *Bus Week* p28-9 S 7 '87
Shopping centers
The American Riviera [mall culture of southern California] J. Robinson-Shaw. il *Vogue* 177:234+ My '87
The call of the mall [special section] il *Seventeen* 46:320-5+ Ag '87
Do malls seduce shoppers? il *USA Today (Periodical)* 116:8-9 Jl '87
Just shut up and shop [bans on public discourse; with editorial comment by Erwin Knoll] K. Peck. il *Progressive* 51:4, 23-5 O '87
Minority businesses open at new mall in Miami. *Jet* 72:23 My 4 '87
Off with their heads [Meret Inc.'s shopping center redesigns] S. B. Weiner. il *Forbes* 139:34-5 F 9 '87
On time in Bloomington [Ghermezian brothers complete deal to build Fashion Mall of America in Minnesota] D. Jenish. il *Macleans* 100:36 Ja 19 '87
San Diego's lively new-and-old downtown [Horton Plaza shopping center] il maps *Sunset* 178:64-71 F '87
Sushi and an oil change [auto repair malls] J. Parr. il *Forbes* 140:93-4 Ag 24 '87
Tiffany, the teenage mall flower who serenades the shoppers of America. L. Russell. il pors *People Wkly* 28:81+ S 14 '87
Welcome to a Carolina cotton mill [Brookstown Mill] il *South Living* 22:24-5 Ja '87
Shopping malls *See* Shopping centers
Shore, David
(jt. auth) See Nasmyth, Kim, and Shore, David

Shore, Dinah, 1920-
about
Architectural digest visits: Dinah Shore. B. D. Colen. il por *Archit Dig* 44:158-63+ D '87
Shore, Lys Ann
IUE: nine years of astronomy. il *Astronomy* 15:14-22 Ap '87
The telescope that never sleeps. il *Astronomy* 15:14-22 Ag '87
Shore birds
See also
Egrets
Herons
Plovers
Sandpipers
Sea birds
How fare the Audubon birds a century later? [wading birds] F. Graham. il *Audubon* 89:14-16+ Mr '87
Migration
Birds of a feather feed together [feeding on horseshoe crab eggs by migrating shore birds at Delaware Bay] W. P. Carty. il *Américas* 39:28-33+ S/O '87
Photographs and photography
Windbirds by the bay. T. D. Rountree. il *Audubon* 89:52-9 N '87
Shore erosion *See* Coast changes
Shore line changes *See* Coast changes
Shore photography *See* Marine photography
Shore protection
See also
Jetties
Our troubled coasts [cover story; special issue; with editorial comment by Michael W. Robbins] il *Oceans* 20:2, 8-53+ Mr/Ap '87
Conferences
Who is minding the coast? [Coastal Zone '87 symposium] R. M. Strickland. *Oceans* 20:7-8 Jl/Ag '87
Laws and regulations
The budget and the environment [funding the Coastal Zone Management Program] il *Oceans* 20:65 Mr/Ap '87
Connecticut
An oysterman's battle to keep 'black mayonnaise' at bay [T. Backer works to clean up Long Island Sound] R. Mitchell. il *Bus Week* p98 O 12 '87
Florida
Is the sun setting on Florida's overbuilding? G. DeGeorge. il *Bus Week* p102 O 12 '87
New Jersey
On the Jersey shore, business crumbles like a sand castle. E. T. Smith. il *Bus Week* p104 O 12 '87
Shorenstein Hays, Carole
about
Mending Fences. L. Garchik. por *Vogue* 177:118 O '87
Shorewood Packaging Corporation
How high is high? [stock price] T. Jaffe. *Forbes* 140:246 O 5 '87
Short, Ken
about
Corridos! Ken Short puts a revolution on a soundstage. G. Loney. il *Theatre Crafts* 21:85-8 O '87
Short, Lester L., and Horne, Jennifer F. M.
"I saw it!". il *Int Wildl* 17:22-3 Mr/Ap '87
Short, Martin
about
Couples. M. Orth. il pors *Vogue* 177:393 F '87
Martin Short: life after Ed Grimley. J. Powell. il por *Glamour* 85:136 Ja '87
Short bowel syndrome
Kentucky tot hospitalized three years goes home [case of T. Foster] il por *Jet* 72:36 Jl 13 '87
Short Brothers Ltd.
Short Brothers pushes Starstreak for U.S. Army air defense. D. A. Brown. il *Aviat Week Space Technol* 126:68-9 Ap 6 '87
Short people *See* Stature
Short selling *See* Securities—Short selling
Short stories
See also
Children's stories
Christmas stories
Detective and mystery stories
See name of author for full entry
The abduction. Oates, Joyce Carol, 1938-
An absence of cousins. Segal, Lore Groszmann
Absence of mercy. Stone, Robert, 1937-
Abundance. Dickinson, Charles, 1951-
Admirals. Chabon, Michael
After all these years. Kennedy, Daniel
All the men she loved and lost. Solwitz, Sharon
Almost the real thing. Cherry, Kelly

Alpha. Woiwode, Larry
Always room for one more. Dubus, Elizabeth Nell
Alzheimer's. Cherry, Kelly
The angel of the bridge. Cheever, John, 1912-1982
At the walls of Jericho. Hawkes, G. W.
At war with Amy. Hood, Ann
The awful secret of Monsieur Bonneval. Gallico, Paul, 1897-
Babel's children. Barker, Clive
The baby-sitter. Bache, Ellyn
Bears. Mattison, Alice
Bech in Czech. Updike, John
Best friends and other strangers. Mills, Lia
The blue room. Gopnik, Adam
Book of dreams. Grimm, Mary
The boy who wouldn't say his name. Nunes, Shirley
The bride wore red. Sethi, Robbie Clipper
Brother grasshopper. Updike, John
The Buddha of suburbia. Kureishi, Hanif
Bumblebees. Mason, Bobbie Ann
The burglar alarm. Updike, John
The catbird seat. Thurber, James, 1894-1961
A cautionary tale. Eisenberg, Deborah
Celebration. Lawler, Pat
Change of heart. Kaufman, Lynne
The child in time. McEwan, Ian
Children. Ford, Richard, 1944-
The circular library of stones. Emshwiller, Carol
City Sundays. Dowell, Coleman, 1925-1985
Closing night at the Zebra Lounge. Berle, Milton
A color television. Acosta, Luis Alberto
Come soar with me. McConnell, Jean
Conjunction. Updike, John
Cooker. Barthelme, Frederick
The countess and the devil. Colyton, Henry John
The courage of Millie Baldwin. Trueblood, Harriett
Creature comforts. Kumin, Maxine, 1925-
Cruise control. McWey, Michael
A cry for help. Love, John M.
The curfew. Gordon, Peter
A date with fate. Yellin, Linda Nell
A daughter's duty. Hudson, Helen
A death in Palestine. Hanniya, Akram
Déclassé. Gallant, Mavis
Dédé. Gallant, Mavis
Demonstration. Hoover, Paul, 1946-
Distances. Kinsella, W. P.
The double-edged knife. Oates, Joyce Carol, 1938-
A down-and-out disciple meets his match. Shea, John
The dream broker. Bliss, Corinne Demas, 1947-
The drinking club. Adams, Alice, 1926-
Driving. Franzen, Bill
The dying year. Drabble, Margaret, 1939-
Enlisting. Liu, M. E.
Epitaph. O'Brien, Edna
Errand. Carver, Raymond
Etheleen Grossberg takes stock. Ephron, Nora
An every-afternoon affair. Green, Jesse
Ex libris. Gilliatt, Penelope
The exiles. Havemann, Ernst
Family secrets. Lewis, Sara E.
Family sins. Trevor, William, 1928-
A farm at Raraba. Havemann, Ernst
Father. Dovlatov, Sergeï
A father's wish. Slater, Judith
Faux pas. Tallent, Elizabeth, 1954-
The first good-bye. Horan, Hillary
A foreign affair. Chabon, Michael
Forever. MacDuff, Lynn
Frau Messinger. Trevor, William, 1928-
Fryday. Summers, Barbara
Game farm. Gardiner, John Rolfe
Geometry. Troy, Judy
The ghost lemurs of Madagascar. Burroughs, William S., 1914-
Gold rings & orange blossoms. St. Clair, Joy
Good advice is rarer than rubies. Rushdie, Salman
Grandpa Hopewell and his flying tractor. Schramm, Wilbur Lang, 1907-
Half past four. Le Guin, Ursula K., 1929-
The Halfway Diner. Sayles, John, 1950-
Hannah's example. Tallent, Elizabeth, 1954-
Happy endings. Atwood, Margaret, 1939-
Helping. Stone, Robert, 1937-
Her secret. Bittle, Camilla R.
Hijacked heart. Bell, Alison
Hold tight, my love. Gerber, Merrill Joan
Hostess. Mangum, Donald
How do you do? May I marry you? Clayton, Sara
How to tell a true war story. O'Brien, Tim
Hurry up and love me. Coates, Ruth Allison

Short stories—*cont.*

"I love ya, baby". Gallico, Paul, 1897-
Ice cream at noon. Holmstrom, David
Imagine a day at the end of your life. Beattie, Ann
Immortality. Sauro, Joan
In hiding. Ehlenbeck, Steve
Inn Essence. Lombreglia, Ralph
Insider trading. Ephron, Nora
Jack's girl. Kadohata, Cynthia
January. Barthelme, Donald
Jaws. Barthelme, Donald
Jealousy. Michaels, Leonard
Joanna loves Jesus. Lampart, Jacob
Johnny Pye and the Fool-killer. Benét, Stephen Vincent, 1898-1943
Just what it says. Fuentes Millán, Hugo
Kafkas. Wiggins, Marianne
Kate and Allie and Kate. Painter, Pamela
Keeping count. Picoult, Jodi
A kind of dying. Barrett, Marvin
Kingdom of the heart. Ledbetter, Eve
Landscaping. Ephron, Nora
The laugh. Brodkey, Harold
Launching day, 1962. Johnson, Joyce, 1935-
Law of averages. Barthelme, Frederick
Leaving home. Keillor, Garrison
Let it pass. Gallant, Mavis
A letter from her past. Smolens, John
Lingo. Gilliatt, Penelope
A little holiday. O'Brien, Edna
A little tatter of sky. Heller, Peter
Live performance. Carden, Sarah
Long distance. Smiley, Jane
Look at Violet now! Dyer, Susan
Looking for love. Troy, Judy
The loser. MacDuff, Lynn
Lost and found. Richie, Kathleen M.
Love song. Cusack, Isabel Langis
Love the ones you're with. Smith, Lee, 1944-
Low rider. Daugherty, Tracy
The magical geranium. Jackson, Margaret Weymouth
The man he used to be. Bauer-Stuchly, Judy
The man who knew Belle Starr. Bausch, Richard, 1945-
The man who married Mom. Doig, D. T.
Maneuvers. Summers, Barbara
Marigolds. Kadohata, Cynthia
A matter of responsibility. Lawler, Pat
Meeting Mossie. Moore, Susan J.
The men in her life. Soman, Florence Jane
The messenger. Dickerson, Karle
Midnight magic. Mason, Bobbie Ann
The mission. Cave, Hugh B.
Mole. DeMarinis, Rick, 1934-
The mother next door. Ariail, Jacqueline
Ms. Grossberg's legs. Ephron, Nora
My father's son. Havemann, Ernst
The myth. Creech, Wendy Goodall
A new act. Berle, Milton
A new tradition. Schell, Jessie
No dogs allowed. Lull, Roderick
Office romance. Fleming, Thomas J., 1927-
Oh, what avails. Munro, Alice
On the deck. Barthelme, Donald
Optimists. Ford, Richard, 1944-
Parallel play. Ephron, Nora
A part of him revealed. Polizzi, Catherine
Penny Royal. Yaw, Yvonne
The perfect match. Stewart, Isobel
The perilous flight of Henry O'Grady. Sherwin, Jane
The place to be. Hazzard, Shirley, 1931-
Police dreams. Bausch, Richard, 1945-
Presents. Eisenberg, Deborah
Pretty pictures. Rooke, Leon
Pulitzer. Contou-Carrère, Enrique Jorge
The quality of mercy. Pennell, H. Barrett, Jr.
Reach for the sky. Shepard, Jim
Reach for tomorrow. Thomas, Rosie
Rebels. Shiner, Lewis
The red cocoon. Abé, Kobo
The red dress. Janecky, J. Y.
Research. Apple, Max
Reunion. McInerney, Jay
Revolutionaries. Abbott, Lee K.
Road stop. Picoult, Jodi
Running from love. Bache, Ellyn
The Ryans. Ford, Kathleen, 1945-
A salmon for the White House. Train, Arthur
A scrap of time. Fink, Ida
The seasons of love. Shyer, Marlene Fanta
Seizing control. Robison, Mary
The ship ahoy. Le Guin, Ursula K., 1929-

Shopping. Oates, Joyce Carol, 1938-
The silent speech of love. Ding Ling
Simple celebrations. Heffernan, Maryclare J.
Smoke. McInerney, Jay
Smorgasbord. Wolff, Tobias, 1945-
Snares. Erdrich, Louise
Sonata for two pianos. Pollitt, Katha
Sorry fugu. Boyle, T. Coraghessan
Soul brother. Rivarola Matto, Juan Bautista
State champions. Mason, Bobbie Ann
Stop that music! Mudd, E. J.
Story of my life. McInerney, Jay
Stranded. Mardon, Deirdre
The succession. Goodman, Allegra
Sugar. Byatt, A. S. (Antonia Susan), 1936-
Sylvia Smith-Smith's mixed-up masquerade. Nelson, Peter
Taking the road not taken. Ephron, Nora
Talking to the sun. Regier, Gail
Tangerine dreams. Prose, Francine, 1947-
Tennis or what. Newbound, Christopher
The terrorist. Hersey, John, 1914-
Think of wives in old China. Wolfe, Linda
Time to laugh again. Franco, Marjorie
To have and to hold. Sandberg, Peter Lars, 1934-
To vault over the moon. Mondeschein, Brian
Tomorrow's magic. Shyer, Marlene Fanta
Total immersion. Goodman, Allegra
Toussaint. Turner, Ronald F.
A train trip. Hemingway, Ernest, 1899-1961
The tree. Puppo, Alberto
A trinity. Trevor, William, 1928-
Two's a crowd. Dyer, Susan
Uncle Leopold. Dovlatov, Sergeï
The Valley. Burroughs, William S., 1914-
Violation. Gordon, Mary, 1949-
The violin of his mind. Cherry, Kelly
Vital statistics. Soman, Florence Jane
Voice from the grave. Powell, Padgett
Volpone. Shapiro, Jane
Way to the dump. Goldman, E. S.
A way with men. Franco, Marjorie
Wedding. Cravens, Gwyneth
The wedding of Willard and what's her name. Robinson, Barbara
What are friends for. Yellin, Linda Nell
What will be. Franco, Marjorie
Where I'd quit. Kauffman, Janet, 1945-
Who is my love? Schweitzer, Gertrude, 1909-
Why I live where I live. Cameron, Peter
The widow. Lordan, Beth
Wildlife. Updike, John
The winner's touch. Tiritilli, Patricia
Womb ward. Lessing, Doris May, 1919-
Women and children first. Prose, Francine, 1947-
World after dark. Gardiner, John Rolfe
The year of getting to know us. Canin, Ethan
Young people. Goodman, Allegra
The youngest old lady in the world. Zimmerman, Lisa Horton

Short story
　　See also
　　Fiction in periodicals and newspapers
The action of metaphor. L. Michaels. *Harpers* 274:30+ Ja '87
Before the beginning. R. DeMarinis. *Writer* 100:12-14 Ag '87
A failing grade for the present tense. W. H. Gass. il *N Y Times Book Rev* 92:1+ O 11 '87
The long and short of it. J. Lutz. *Writer* 100:11-13 D '87
Short stories: weapons of pessimists; tr. by Penny Million Pucelik and Marijo Despréaux Schneider. D. Boulanger. *Harpers* 275:40-1 N '87
Using images in fiction. M. J. Gerber. *Writer* 100:15-18 Ja '87
Writing short stories. P. Meinke. *Writer* 100:12-14 Ja '87

Bibliography
Brevity, soul and wit. A. Manguel. il *Macleans* 100:53-4 S 21 '87
Short story publishing *See* Publishers and publishing—Fiction
Short term dynamic psychotherapy *See* Psychotherapy
Short-Wing Piper Club
Short wings, big heart. G. Baxter. il *Flying* 114:103 Ap '87
Shortliffe, Edward H.
(jt. auth) See Rennels, Glenn D., and Shortliffe, Edward H.
Shorts (Clothing)
Fashion legwork. il *Teen* 31:76-9 Je '87

Shorts (Clothing)—*cont.*

The shorts story. C. Cummins. il *Women's Sports Fitness* 9:34-7+ Ap '87

Shortstops (Baseball players) *See* Baseball players

Shortt, Terence M.

about

Terry Shortt: a life's journey into nature. R. M. Peck. il por *Int Wildl* 17:4-11 Jl/Ag '87

Shortwave radio *See* Radio, Shortwave

Shostak, Seth

Where are the extraterrestrials hiding? il *Saturday Evening Post* 259:62-5 S '87

Shostakovich, Dmitrii Dmitrievich, 1906-1975

about

Beyond bombast: the intimate Shostakovich. R. R. Reilly. il *High Fidel* 37:61-2 Jl '87

Penderecki and Shostakovich: death affirms life. L. Mendes. *Christ Century* 104:287-8 Mr 18-25 '87

Shot

Getting the lead out [waterfowl poisoning from lead shot] M. Rosenthal. il *Ctry J* 14:10-11 O '87

The hazards of leadshot in soil. *Sci News* 131:233 Ap 11 '87

Steeling ourselves for the future (I) [steel shot for waterfowl] B. Brister. il *Field Stream* 92:66+ Ag '87

Steeling ourselves for the future (II) [steel shot for waterfowl] B. Brister. il *Field Stream* 92:129-30+ S '87

Shotblockers (Basketball players) *See* Basketball players

Shotgun shells *See* Cartridges

Shotguns

Double-barreled beauty [Hatfield shotgun] G. Norman. il *Esquire* 108:43-4 S '87

The guns of July. B. Woods. il *Mother Earth News* 106:46-9 Jl/Ag '87

Shotts, Cheryl Carter- *See* Carter-Shotts, Cheryl

Shoulder

The bolder shoulder: tips for baring all. il *Mademoiselle* 93:10 Jl '87

Sexy summer shoulders. il *Glamour* 85:33 Jl '87

Shoulder pads

Anecdotes, facetiae, satire, etc.

Shoulder high! or What Joan Crawford knew. F. Garmaise. il *Ms* 16:50 S '87

Shovels, spades, etc.

Moving snow by hand. R. Kimber. il *Ctry J* 14:10-13 Ja '87

Show business *See* Entertainment industry; Performing arts

Show jumping (Horsemanship) *See* Horsemanship

Show rooms *See* Showrooms

Show windows

Fish window [F. Lara's window displays at the Citarella Fish Company in Manhattan] *New Yorker* 63:23-5 Jl 6 '87

Gearing up for the holidays [Lord & Taylor Christmas windows] B. Weber. il *N Y Times Mag* p110 N 15 '87

Window-dressing [Bloomingdale's] B. Kanner. il *N Y* 20:12-13 Ag 17 '87

Showalter, Elaine

about

Literary feminism comes of age. E. Kolbert. il por *N Y Times Mag* p110+ D 6 '87

Shower baths

Closet becomes shower. il *Sunset* 178:187 Ap '87

Replace a leaky shower floor. M. Henkenius. il *Home Mech* 83:28+ Ap '87

River rock over old shower pan. il *Sunset* 178:180 Ap '87

Shower shudders [breathing toxins; research by Julian Andelman] G. Woolley. il *Sierra* 72:13-14 Jl/Ag '87

Shower curtains

The World [shower curtain with world map] *New Yorker* 63:24-5 Je 22 '87

Showers, Beverly

(jt. auth) See Joyce, Bruce R., and Showers, Beverly

Showers, Ralph K.

about

There are no handicapped at Rev. Showers' Rainbow Acres. L. Rozen. il pors *People Wkly* 27:71-2+ My 4 '87

Showker, Kay

A Caribbean for all seasons [special section] il *Travel Holiday* 167:69+ Ap '87

Cruising '88. il *Travel Holiday* 168:65-6+ O '87

Showrooms

See also

Catalog showrooms

Coleman-Karger Showroom

International Design Center New York

A little bit timeless [ICF showroom designed by M. Botta] P. M. Sachner. il *Archit Rec* 175:124-9 mid-S '87

To market we go. C. K. Gandee. il *Archit Rec* 175:105-21 My '87

Showscan Film Corporation

Chills and thrills on the big screen. G. G. Marcial. *Bus Week* p122 D 14 '87

Shparo, Dmitry

about

Over the Arctic ice cap. A. Steacy. il por *Macleans* 100:46-7 Ap 6 '87

Shrader, Steven W.

A critic's nightmare. por *Opera News* 51:20-1 Ja 3 '87

Shrady, Nicholas

Architecture: Ricardo Bofill. il *Archit Dig* 44:124-31+ Jl '87

Earth sheltered: blending with nature on the Costa Brava. il *Archit Dig* 44:90-5 Ja '87

Gardens: Villa Melzi: Count Gallarati Scotti's flowering hills on Lake Como. il *Archit Dig* 44:126-31 Ag '87

Spain's doyen of interiors. il por *Archit Dig* 44:246+ Ap '87

Shrager, Jeff, and others

Observation of phase transitions in spreading activation networks. bibl f il *Science* 236:1092-4 My 29 '87

Shragg, Bruce

A degree of detachment. il *N Y Times Mag* p48 Jl 26 '87

Shredders, Garden *See* Garden equipment

Shreveport (La.)

Description

A stroll in Shreveport. *South Living* 22:47 My '87

Shrimp

See also

Brine shrimp

Cooking—Shellfish

Shrimp culture *See* Shellfish culture

Shriner, Wil

about

Making a new Merv. B. Yagoda. il pors *Channels* 7:46-50 F '87

Shrines, War *See* War memorials

Shriver, Donald W.

What can liberals and evangelicals teach each other? il *Christ Century* 104:687-90 Ag 12-19 '87

Shriver, Eunice Kennedy

about

Eunice Shriver's Olympian friends. M. Green. il pors *People Wkly* 28:31-3 Ag 17 '87

Shriver, Pam

about

A delicate balance. C. Shmerler. il pors *World Tennis* 34:26-9+ Mr '87

Shriver, Peggy L.

Reassessing religion and public education. *Educ Dig* 53:30-3 D '87

Shrontz, Frank A.

about

Cool, calm, and lawyerly. A. Ramirez. il por *Fortune* 116:54 Ag 3 '87

Shroud, Holy *See* Holy Shroud

Shrubs

See also

Barberries

Boxwood

Cotoneasters

Hedges

Holly

Rhododendrons

Sagebrush

Spirea

Windbreaks

Notable natives [California shrubs] il *Sunset* 179:206-7 O '87

Pruning

See Pruning

Shrum, Robert

The Democrats' script for 1988. *Harpers* 275:14+ S '87

Shuchman, R. A., and others

Remote sensing of the Fram Strait marginal ice zone. bibl f il *Science* 236:429-31 Ap 24 '87

Shue, Elisabeth

about

"Adventures in babysitting": the mad movie about the pitfalls of making pocket money. E. Miller. il pors *Seventeen* 46:71-2+ Jl '87

Shue, Larry

about

The nerd [drama] Reviews

Nation 244:516+ Ap 18 '87. T. M. Disch

Shue, Larry—about—The nerd—*cont.*
   New Yorker 63:81 Ap 6 '87. E. Oliver
Shugart, Alan F.
                     about
Seagate goes East—and comes back a winner. R. Brandt.
   il por *Bus Week* p94 Mr 16 '87
Shugart, H. H.
Dynamic ecosystem consequences of tree birth and death
   patterns. bibl il *BioScience* 37:596-602 S '87
Shuger, Scott
What I learned in school today. il *Sport Mag* 78:60-1
   O '87
Shuler, Irene
What Sitkans say about Sitka. *Mother Earth News* 107:71
   S/O '87
Shulman, Lee S.
Assessment for teaching: an initiative for the profession.
   il *Phi Delta Kappan* 69:38-44 S '87
Shulman, Marshall D.
Four decades of irrationality: U.S.-Soviet relations [cover
   story] il *Bull At Sci* 43:15-25 N '87
Shulman, Martha Rose
The vegetarian good life [cover story] il *Health* 19:36-9+
   Jl '87
Shulman, Robert
                     about
The little drug company that could. J. Merwin. il por
   Forbes 139:72-3 Ja 26 '87
Shulman, Seth
Funding for biological weapons research grows amidst
   controversy. il *BioScience* 37:372-5 Je '87
Poisons from the Pentagon [cover story] il *Progressive*
   51:16-19 N '87
Shulton Group
The girl next door becomes superwoman [Breck ad
   campaign] il *Newsweek* 110:64 Ag 17 '87
The sweet smell of success [Old Spice] J. A. Trachtenberg.
   il *Forbes* 140:92-3 Ag 10 '87
Shultz, George Pratt, 1920-
40th anniversary of the Marshall Plan [address, May
   26, 1987] *Dep State Bull* 87:67-72 Ag '87
ASEAN: a model for regional cooperation [remarks, May
   27, 1987] *Dep State Bull* 87:10-13 Jl '87
Benefits of an INF agreement. *Dep State Bull* 87:17-18
   Jl '87
Correspondence from the Secretary of State. *Foreign
   Aff* 66:426-8 Wint '87/'88
The democratic future of South Africa [address, September
   29, 1987] *Dep State Bull* 87:9-12 N '87
The foreign affairs budget crisis: a threat to our vital
   interests [statement, January 23, 1987] il *Dep State
   Bull* 87:7-14 Mr '87
Human rights and Soviet-American relations [address,
   October 31, 1986] *Dep State Bull* 86:26-9 D '86
Instructions to ambassadors on chain of command. *Dep
   State Bull* 87:40-1 Mr '87
Iran and U.S. policy [statement; with text of question
   and answer session, December 8, 1986] *Dep State
   Bull* 87:22-33 F '87
Matching foreign policy resources with goals [statement,
   August 7, 1987] *Dep State Bull* 87:6-11 O '87
Meeting America's foreign policy challenges [address,
   February 20, 1987] *Dep State Bull* 87:5-8 Ap '87
Meeting the challenges of change in the Pacific [address,
   May 14, 1987] *Dep State Bull* 87:4-7 Jl '87
Meeting with Arab League delegation [remarks, May
   7, 1987] il por *Dep State Bull* 87:63 Jl '87
Monroe portrait unveiled [remarks, April 28, 1987] il
   por *Dep State Bull* 87:81 Jl '87
Narcotics: a global threat [address, May 4, 1987] *Dep
   State Bull* 87:45-6 Ag '87
News briefing of June 2, 1987. *Dep State Bull* 87:40-3
   Ag '87
News briefing of May 8, 1987. *Dep State Bull* 87:13-14
   Jl '87
News conference of April 8, 1987. *Dep State Bull* 87:24-7
   Je '87
News conference of August 6, 1987. *Dep State Bull*
   87:11-14 O '87
Nicaragua: the moral and strategic stakes [address,
   February 12, 1987] *Dep State Bull* 87:14-18 Mr '87
North Atlantic Council meets in Iceland [texts of final
   communique and news conference, June 12, 1987]
   Dep State Bull 87:59-63 Ag '87
Nuclear weapons, arms control, and the future of deter-
   rence [address, November 17, 1986] *Dep State Bull*
   87:31-5 Ja '87
Peace, democracy, and security in Central America [state-
   ment, September 10, 1987] *Dep State Bull* 87:13-16
   N '87

Peace, friendship, and U.S.-Canada relations [address,
   July 2, 1987] *Dep State Bull* 87:16-17 S '87
President Reagan and General Secretary Gorbachev meet
   in Reykjavik. il pors *Dep State Bull* 86:1-21 D '86
Promoting inter-American cooperation [address, Novem-
   ber 11, 1986] *Dep State Bull* 87:27-30 Ja '87
Public diplomacy in the information age [address, Septem-
   ber 15, 1987] *Dep State Bull* 87:16-18 N '87
Pursuing an effective foreign policy [statement, February
   3, 1987] *Dep State Bull* 87:11-14 Ap '87
Pursuing the promise of Helsinki [address, November
   5, 1986] *Dep State Bull* 87:47-50 Ja '87
A reply to Nixon and Kissinger. il por *Time* 129:40
   My 18 '87
Resolving the POW/MIA issue [address, July 18, 1987]
   Dep State Bull 87:18-19 S '87
Restoring the foreign affairs budget [address, November
   3, 1986] *Dep State Bull* 87:24-6 Ja '87
Reykjavik: a watershed in U.S.-Soviet relations [address,
   October 31, 1986] *Dep State Bull* 86:22-5 D '86
Secretary praises AID and comments on Iran [remarks,
   November 25, 1986] *Dep State Bull* 87:23 Ja '87
Secretary Shultz attends UN General Assembly [texts
   of news conferences, September 21-October 1, 1987]
   Dep State Bull 87:52-60 N '87
Secretary visits Asia. *Dep State Bull* 87:6-11 My '87
Secretary visits Bermuda and Africa [address, January
   8, 1987] maps *Dep State Bull* 87:23-8 Mr '87
Secretary visits Canada [text of joint press conference,
   November 21, 1986] *Dep State Bull* 87:45-8 F '87
Secretary's trip to Helsinki, Moscow, and Brussels. il
   por *Dep State Bull* 87:12-24 Je '87
Secretary's visit to Asia and the Pacific [statements and
   texts of press conferences, June 13-22, 1987] *Dep State
   Bull* 87:29-37 Ag '87
Security Council calls for cease-fire in Iran-Iraq War
   [statement, July 20, 1987] *Dep State Bull* 87:75-6 S
   '87
Southern Africa: American hopes for the future [address,
   December 4, 1986] *Dep State Bull* 87:36-40 F '87
Soviet foreign minister visits Washington. il pors *Dep
   State Bull* 87:34-40 N '87
U.S. and Mongolia establish diplomatic relations [texts
   of communique and remarks, January 27, 1987] il
   por *Dep State Bull* 87:41 Mr '87
U.S. business and the world economy [address, May
   11, 1987] *Dep State Bull* 87:43-5 Ag '87
U.S. interests in the Persian Gulf [statement, January
   27, 1987] *Dep State Bull* 87:19-20 Mr '87
U.S.-Mexico Binational Commission meets [remarks,
   January 29, 1987] il por *Dep State Bull* 87:54-6 Ap
   '87
Visit of Israeli Prime Minister Shamir [remarks, February
   17 and 18, 1987] il *Dep State Bull* 87:49-51 Ap '87
Visit of Japanese Prime Minister Nakasone [remarks
   and text of joint statement, April 30-May 1, 1987]
   il *Dep State Bull* 87:37-41 Jl '87
Working for peace and freedom [address, May 17, 1987]
   Dep State Bull 87:7-10 Jl '87
                     about
Breaking up is hard to do. por *Time* 129:22 F 2 '87
The CIA's 'cowboys': out of control? L. Martz. il por
   Newsweek 109:22-4 F 2 '87
The cost of Shultz. A. Brummer. map *World Press
   Rev* 34:14-15 F '87
An edge of anger [special section] il pors *Time* 130:12-17
   Ag 3 '87
George Shultz, wimp. R. M. Goolrick. il *Wash Mon*
   19:18-19 O '87
North Atlantic Council meets in Brussels [texts of final
   communique, declaration on conventional arms control,
   and press conference, December 12, 1986] *Dep State
   Bull* 87:42-6 Mr '87
Secretary meets with ANC leader Tambo [State Dept.
   statement, January 28, 1987] il pors *Dep State Bull*
   87:28 Mr '87
Secretary's interview on "Face the nation" [transcript
   of program, September 13, 1987] *Dep State Bull*
   87:19-21 N '87
Secretary's interview on "Meet the press" [transcript
   of program, January 18, 1987] *Dep State Bull* 87:20-3
   Mr '87
Secretary's interview on "Meet the press" [transcript
   of program, June 28, 1987] *Dep State Bull* 87:37-9
   Ag '87
Secretary's interview on "Meet the press" [transcript
   of program, October 19, 1986] *Dep State Bull* 86:29-32
   D '86
Secretary's interview on "This week with David Brinkley"
   [transcript of program, February 8, 1987] *Dep State
   Bull* 87:8-11 Ap '87

Shultz, George Pratt, 1920— about—*cont.*
Secretary's interview on "This week with David Brinkley" [transcript of program, October 5, 1986] *Dep State Bull* 86:32-4 D '86
Secretary's interview on "This week with David Brinkley" [transcript of program, September 21, 1987] *Dep State Bull* 87:21-3 N '87
Secretary's interview on "Worldnet" [interview; transcript of program, December 16, 1986] *Dep State Bull* 87:33-6 F '87
Shultz takes the stand. M. McDonald. il por *Macleans* 100:28 Ag 3 '87
Shultz's long war [special section] il pors *Newsweek* 110:14-19 Ag 3 '87
Shultz's way. R. Steel. il pors *N Y Times Mag* p14-21+ Ja 11 '87
A stand-up guy's disquieting tales. M. Healy. il por *U S News World Rep* 103:18 Ag 3 '87
Star Wars: Shultz's goal. il *Newsweek* 109:4 F 2 '87
Talking with terrorists [interview] por *U S News World Rep* 102:29 F 9 '87
Testing time for Shultz. H. Trewhitt. il por *U S News World Rep* 102:14-16 My 11 '87
    Visit to Africa, 1987
Probing for an Africa policy. P. R. Range. il por map *U S News World Rep* 102:32-3 Ja 19 '87
    Visit to Canada, 1986
Secretary visits Canada [text of joint press conference, November 21, 1986] G. P. Shultz; J. Clark. *Dep State Bull* 87:45-8 F '87
    Visit to China, 1987
Reading the fortune cookies. H. Trewhitt. il por *U S News World Rep* 102:37-8 Mr 16 '87
    Visit to East Asia, 1987
The great Pacific game. H. Trewhitt. il *U S News World Rep* 102:30-1 Mr 2 '87
Secretary visits Asia. G. P. Shultz. *Dep State Bull* 87:6-11 My '87
    Visit to Southeast Asia, 1987
Secretary's visit to Asia and the Pacific [statements and texts of press conferences, June 13-22, 1987] G. P. Shultz. *Dep State Bull* 87:29-37 Ag '87
    Visit to the Pacific region, 1987
Secretary's visit to Asia and the Pacific [statements and texts of press conferences, June 13-22, 1987] G. P. Shultz. *Dep State Bull* 87:29-37 Ag '87
    Visits to the Soviet Union, 1987
An arms tango in Moscow [meets with M. Gorbachev] A. Finlayson. il pors *Macleans* 100:18-19 Ap 27 '87
Confusion abounding. *Natl Rev* 39:18-19 N 20 '87
Dealing at last [M. Gorbachev's offer to cut back Euromissiles; cover story; special section] il pors map *Newsweek* 109:20-8+ Ap 27 '87
Failure in Moscow. B. Levin. il por *Macleans* 100:20-1 N 2 '87
A Gorbachev arms offer even Europe may not refuse. B. Javetski and P. Galuszka. il por *Bus Week* p53 Ap 27 '87
The Moscow agenda. T. Jacoby. il *Newsweek* 109:24 Ap 20 '87
Nearing a deal on Euromissiles. H. Trewhitt. il por *U S News World Rep* 102:48-9 Ap 27 '87
Now, super-zero? [M. Gorbachev's proposal to NATO] G. J. Church. il pors *Time* 129:20-3 Ap 27 '87
Secretary's trip to Helsinki, Moscow, and Brussels. G. P. Shultz. il por *Dep State Bull* 87:12-24 Je '87
Shultz in Moscow: ready to deal. R. B. Cullen. il por *Newsweek* 110:47 O 26 '87
Snuffing a summit [Soviets demand concession on SDI] J. Kohan. il por *Time* 130:56-7 N 2 '87
Waiting for the postman [Soviets use Star Wars as bargaining ploy] R. Watson. il por *Newsweek* 110:60-1+ N 2 '87
Shuptrine, Hubert
Home to Jericho [excerpts] il *South Living* 22:88-91 O '87
    about
The return of 'Jericho,' a southern classic. B. Summer. *Publ Wkly* 232:66 O 16 '87
Shuswap Indians
A girl's anger rouses her kinfolk from an alcoholic daze [work of A. and P. Chelsea in Alkali Lake, B.C.] M. Green. il pors *People Wkly* 27:83-4 Ja 26 '87
Shutdowns of airplane factories *See* Airplane factories—Shutdowns
Shutdowns of airports *See* Airports—Shutdowns
Shutdowns of automobile factories *See* Automobile factories—Shutdowns

Shutdowns of canneries *See* Canneries—Shutdowns
Shutdowns of factories *See* Factories—Shutdowns
Shutdowns of petroleum refineries *See* Petroleum refineries—Shutdowns
Shute House (Great Britain) *See* Historic houses, sites, etc.—Great Britain
Shutters
Custom-size plastic shutters. G. Sears. il *Pop Sci* 231:102-3 S '87
Vintage look returns to the window [plantation shutters] il *South Living* 22:114+ Jl '87
Shutters, Camera *See* Camera shutters
Shutters, Video camera *See* Video camera shutters
Shuttle, Space *See* Space vehicles
Shuttle missions *See* Space flight—Shuttle missions
Shuttle service, Airline *See* Airlines—Shuttle service
Shuttle service, Helicopter *See* Helicopter airlines—Shuttle service
Shuttle simulators *See* Space flight simulators
Shyer, Charles
    about
Baby boom [film] Reviews
  Commonweal 114:602 O 23 '87. T. O'Brien
  Glamour il 85:160 D '87. J. G. Boyum
  Glamour il 85:256+ N '87. C. Krupp
  Macleans il 100:63 O 26 '87. L. O'Toole
  N Y 20:91-2 O 12 '87. D. Denby
  New Repub 197:24-5 N 9 '87. S. Kauffmann
  New Yorker 63:109-10 O 19 '87. P. Kael
  Newsweek il 110:84 O 12 '87. D. Ansen
  People Wkly il 28:16 O 19 '87. R. Novak
  Time 130:85 O 12 '87
Shyer, Marlene Fanta
The seasons of love [story] il *Good Housekeep* 205:124-5+ Jl '87
Tomorrow's magic [story] il *Good Housekeep* 204:138-9 Ap '87
Shyness *See* Bashfulness
Sialic acid
Selective inactivation of influenza C esterase: a probe for detecting 9-O-acetylated sialic acids. E. A. Muchmore and A. P. Varki. bibl f il *Science* 236:1293-5 Je 5 '87
Siamese Imports, Inc.
When only the best will do [L. Maxym's imports of handpainted Russian lacquer boxes] R. Hotch. il por *Nations Bus* 75:78+ My '87
Siamese twins
Black surgeon works to separate Siamese twins [B. Carson's participation in separating Binder twins] il por *Jet* 73:8 S 28 '87
A chance to live apart [surgeons separate the Binder twins] M. Clark. il *Newsweek* 110:71-2 S 21 '87
An hour when life stood still [Binder twins separated at Johns Hopkins] C. Wallis. il *Time* 130:56-7 S 21 '87
"My Siamese twins have brought me joy" [Cady twins] M. L. S. Cady. il *Redbook* 168:32+ F '87
Siamese twins: from Ripley's to college. S. Begley. il *Newsweek* 110:72 S 21 '87
Twins joined at head enter Calif. college at age 38 [Yvonne and Yvette McCarther at Compton Community College] il *Jet* 72:6 My 18 '87
"Why my babies?" [surgical separation of the Taylor twins of Wisconsin] J. G. Hubbell. il *Read Dig* 131:117-22 N '87
Siberia (Soviet Union)
    See also
  Airlines—Routes—Siberia (Soviet Union)
  Bering Sea
  Coal mines and mining—Siberia (Soviet Union)
  Hunting—Siberia (Soviet Union)
  Investments, Canadian—Siberia (Soviet Union)
  Lake Baikal (Soviet Union)
  Railroads—Siberia (Soviet Union)
  Water pollution—Siberia (Soviet Union)
  Women—Siberia (Soviet Union)
    Description and travel
Long train coming [Trans-Siberian] J.-C. Castelli. il *Esquire* 107:49+ Je '87
    Industries
    See also
  Fur industry—Siberia (Soviet Union)
  Wood pulp industry—Siberia (Soviet Union)
Siblings
    See also
  Birth order
10 ways to help your kids become friends. M. Jacobbi. il *McCalls* 145:57 Mr '87

Siblings—*cont.*

And baby makes four: preparing your first child for the second. J. K. Rosemond. il *Better Homes Gard* 65:38 Ja '87

Blood brothers [pronghorn hunting in Montana] K. McCafferty. il *Field Stream* 92:44-5 D '87

Getting set for a sibling [program at Central Michigan Hospital in Mt. Pleasant] J. Smith. il *Good Housekeep* 205:132 S '87

Kids in the delivery room. C. Schaeffer. *Changing Times* 41:22-3 S '87

Making friends in the family [curing adult sibling rivalry] E. Keiffer. il *Read Dig* 130:77-80 Ja '87

My brother is an alcoholic. D. Madison. il *Seventeen* 46:174-5 Mr '87

My sister is in love . . . again. J. D. Pollack. il *Seventeen* 46:196+ Mr '87

Oh, brother! A sort of love story. J. Duveil. il *Mademoiselle* 93:182-3+ D '87

On his thirtieth birthday, my brother placed a hunting rifle in his mouth and pulled the trigger. J. M. Leder. il por *Glamour* 85:204+ N '87

Our breakfast club [coping with sibling rivalry] J. M. Guidry. il *Parents* 62:84+ D '87

The perils of comparisons [sibling rivalry] A. Faber and E. Mazlish. il *Parents* 62:82-6 My '87

Sibling sins: when you're punished too. M. Barbera-Hogan. il *Teen* 31:34+ Mr '87

Siblings without rivalry [black celebrities] il *Jet* 72:54-6 Jl 6 '87

Sister-friends. M. A. Gillespie. il por *Ms* 16:130+ Jl/Ag '87

Social security [Sibling-To-Be preparation class at St. Luke's-Roosevelt Hospital in Manhattan] M. Mintzer. il *Health* 19:22 O '87

"We have a problem" [child's acceptance of brother's death] J. Marks. il *Parents* 62:70+ Je '87

When a brother or sister is ill [parents' treatment of healthy children] C. Wallinga and others. *Psychol Today* 21:42-3 Ag '87

When a child dies, a therapist warns, the grief of brothers and sisters may leave lasting scars [interview with J. Rothman] C. Tamarkin. il por *People Wkly* 27:77-8+ Mr 23 '87

Anecdotes, facetiae, satire, etc.

Kid brothers and their practical application. P. F. McManus. il *Outdoor Life* 180:120+ Ag '87

Sicart, Francois

about

Companies that refused to rust. J. Egan. il *U S News World Rep* 103:50 Jl 27 '87

Sicilia, José Maria, 1954-

about

Five from Spain. J. Gambrell. il pors *Art Am* 75:160-71 S '87

The Sicilian [film] See Motion picture reviews—Single works

Sicilian Mafia *See* Mafia

Sicily

See also
Dance festivals—Sicily
Mount Etna (Sicily)
Opera—Sicily
Taormina (Italy)
Trials—Sicily

Description and travel

A ruin with a view. L. S. Brady. il *Esquire* 108:23-4 Jl '87

Sick, Gary, 1935-

Iran's quest for superpower status. bibl f *Foreign Aff* 65:697-715 Spr '87

Sick

See also
Hospital patients
Restraint of patients

He's feeling sick? Take two aspirin and watch out. B.-J. Raphael. *Glamour* 85:30 Jl '87

Civil rights

See also
Cancer patients—Civil rights

Family relationships

Are you taking care of someone who is sick or elderly? Help may be ahead for you. M. Engel. il *Glamour* 85:50+ My '87

"I'm allergic to my family"; ed. by Barbara Yost. B. Jorgensen. il por *Redbook* 168:42+ Ap '87

Anecdotes, facetiae, satire, etc.

Stomach flu & toddlers, too. M. Stevenson. il *Parents* 62:92-4 F '87

Psychology

See also
Medicine, Psychosomatic

If I've got it, it can't be that bad [downplaying the seriousness of an illness; study by John Jemmott] V. Bozzi. *Psychol Today* 21:18 Ja '87

Sick children

See also
Amanda the Panda, Inc.
Children—Hospital care
Children—Medical care
Children—Preparation for hospital and medical care

Daycare for sick children. D. M. Topolnicki. il *Good Housekeep* 205:245 N '87

For working parents with a sick child, hospital day care centers may spell instant relief [Sick Bay in Oak Park, Ill.] D. Grogan. il *People Wkly* 28:63+ Jl 13 '87

"Mommy, I feel sick". S. Evans. il *Parents* 62:120-2 O '87

A second home for sick kids [sick care centers] J. Shannon. *Health* 19:33 O '87

Sick at school [children of working parents] B. D. Colen. il *Health* 19:8 Ja '87

What happened to my daughter? [cerebral hemorrhage] M. T. Zimmermann. il por *Good Housekeep* 204:82+ Ap '87

When a brother or sister is ill [parents' treatment of healthy children] C. Wallinga and others. *Psychol Today* 21:42-3 Ag '87

When your child is seriously ill: lifelines for parents. S. Lowe. il *McCalls* 114:40-1 Je '87

Education

Educating the chronically ill child. J. Meer. *Psychol Today* 21:36-7 Ag '87

Psychology

A sound mind in an unsound body [chronically ill] D. Hurley. bibl (p67) il *Psychol Today* 21:34-8+ Ag '87

Sick leave

Smokers take more sick leave. *Prevention* 39:122 Ja '87

Sickle cell anemia

Delay time of hemoglobin S polymerization prevents most cells from sickling in vivo. A. Mozzarelli and others. bibl f il *Science* 237:500-6 Jl 31 '87

New sickle cell trait raises risk for blacks [risk of sudden death during strenuous exercise] *Jet* 73:14 N 2 '87

Sickle-cell alert [risk of sudden death during strenuous exercise] *Time* 130:61 O 5 '87

Sudden death tied to sickle-cell trait [risks of strenuous exercise] D. D. Edwards. *Sci News* 132:197 S 26 '87

Diagnosis

Health Institute urges sickle cell tests for all. *Jet* 72:31 My 18 '87

Panel urges newborn sickle cell screening. G. Kolata. *Science* 236:259-60 Ap 17 '87

Therapy

Texas Southern researchers find sickle cell treatment. il *Jet* 72:31 My 18 '87

Sickle cell anemia in fish *See* Fish—Diseases and pests

Sickness

See also
Diagnosis
Diseases
Sick

Health policy and chronic illness. A. L. Strauss. *Society* 25:33-9 N/D '87

Sid-Ahmed, Mohamed

Egypt: the Islamic issue. *Foreign Policy* 69:22-39 Wint '87/'88

Siddons, Anne Rivers

Winter's glory. il *Read Dig* 130:53-5 Ja '87

Side effects of drugs *See* Drugs—Physiological effects

Sideboards *See* Buffets, sideboards, etc. (Furniture)

Sidel, Victor W.

Medical technology and the poor. il *Technol Rev* 90:24-5 My/Je '87

Sidelines, Bookstore *See* Booksellers and bookselling—Sidelines

Sider, Ronald J.

about

With the religious right in disarray, two groups consider new opportunities [with interview] B. Spring. il por *Christ Today* 31:46, 48 Jl 10 '87

Sidereal time *See* Time measurement

Sidewalks

See also
Walk of Fame (Hollywood, Calif.)
Walk of Fame (Philadelphia, Pa.)

Sidey, Hugh
 The presidency. See issues of Time
 Ronald Reagan. il pors *People Wkly* 28:28-31 D 28
  '87-Ja 4 '88

Anecdotes, facetiae, satire, etc.
 The Great Communicator. *New Repub* 197:4+ S 7 '87
Sidikou, Hamidou A.
 The desert as a way of life. il *Courier* 40:16-19 Je
  '87
Siding (Building)
 Residing an older home. J. Drako. il *Workbench* 43:103-5
  Mr/Ap '87
 Siding: who needs it? J. Knudsen. *Changing Times* 41:18
  N '87

Maintenance and repair
 How to renew weathered wood siding. G. Branson. il
  Fam Handyman 37:66+ S '87
 Repair damaged siding. R. Barnhart. il *Home Mech*
  83:90-3 My '87
 Wood revival [use of Dekswood and Aquatrol] R. Barn-
  hart. il *Home Mech* 83:12 Jl '87
Sidney Janis Gallery
 Sidney Janis waiting a year for the blue. J. James.
  il por *Art News* 86:85-6 D '87
SIDS *See* Sudden infant death syndrome
Sieber, George
  about
 "I pray for cash and it comes in". S. Caminiti. il por
  Fortune 115:46 Ap 27 '87
Sieberling, John F., 1918-
 The national security bureaucracy [address, February
  6, 1987] *Vital Speeches Day* 53:362-5 Ap 1 '87
Siebert, Charles
 The girl with the silver gun. il pors *Mademoiselle*
  93:247-9+ Mr '87
 Say hey! Is Eric Davis the next . . . il pors *N Y*
  Times Mag p42+ My 3 '87
Sieg, Albert Louis
  about
 Straw in the wind? A. Tanzer. il por *Forbes* 139:122-3
  F 9 '87
Sieg, Theo. Le *See* Seuss, Dr.
Siegal, John
 The Dukakis design. il *New Leader* 70:10-13 Ag 10-24
  '87
Siegan, Bernard H.
  about
 New judicial activists. H. Schwartz. il *Nation* 244:361-2
  Mr 21 '87
 Rolling back the Constitution. H. Schwartz. il *Nation*
  245:13-15 Jl 4-11 '87
Siegel, Bernie S.
 Three medical miracles: the medicine was love; ed. by
  Susan Schneider. *Redbook* 170:84-5+ D '87
  about
 Dr. Bernie Siegel's prescription for cancer victims (and
  a best-seller): 'Patient, heal thyself'. K. Gross. il pors
  People Wkly 28:61+ S 21 '87
Siegel, Frederic R.
 Prospecting with plants. il *Earth Sci* 40:18-19 Fall '87
Siegel, Frederick F., 1945-
 Baby-boomerang: why the Democrats can't count on
  generational politics. *Commonweal* 114:442-5 Ag 14
  '87
 Cuomo's decision. *Commonweal* 114:133-6 Mr 13 '87
 The political marketplace. il *Commonweal* 114:113-16
  F 27 '87
Siegel, Herbert J.
  about
 The feud at Warner just keeps getting hotter. S. Benway.
  il pors *Bus Week* p76-8+ Je 29 '87
 Ross gets a few dollars more. B. Dumaine. il pors
  Fortune 115:57-8+ Ap 13 '87
 The Warner war: why Steve Ross and Herb Siegel can't
  get along [cover story] J. Taylor. il pors *N Y* 20:34-42
  Jl 13 '87
Siegel, Janis
  about
 Janis Siegel. M. Bourne. por *Down Beat* 54:14 O '87
Siegel, Jay P., and others
 The IL-2 receptor β chain (p70): role in mediating signals
  for LAK, NK, and proliferative activities. bibl f il
  Science 238:75-8 O 2 '87
Siegel, Martin A.
  about
 New arrests on Wall Street. D. Pauly. il por *Newsweek*
  109:48-50 F 23 '87
 A raid on Wall Street. G. Russell. il por *Time* 129:64-6
  F 23 '87

Siegel, Micki
 Tips from top cooks. il *Good Housekeep* 205:179-80+
  N '87
 (ed) See Maloney, Rita. A fair share
Siegel, Robert
 The hunt [poem] *America* 156:366 My 2 '87
 Straight at the blue [poem] *Christ Century* 104:783
  S 23 '87
 The very first dream of morning [poem] *Atlantic*
  259:43 Mr '87
Siegel, Roslyn
 A passion for quilts—vintage & modern. il pors *Am*
  Craft 47:49+ D '87/Ja '88
Siekevitz, Miriam, and others
 Activation of the HIV-1 LTR by T cell mitogens and
  the trans-activator protein of HTLV-I. bibl f il *Science*
  238:1575-8 D 11 '87
Siemens AG
 Gentle leader of a sluggish Goliath [K. Kaske] L. S.
  Richman. il por *Fortune* 116:45 Ag 3 '87
 Siemens testing new RWRs, Elint equipment for mul-
  tinational aircraft [radar warning receivers, electronic
  intelligence equipment and jam-resistant communica-
  tions systems] il *Aviat Week Space Technol* 126:71+
  F 16 '87
 Siemens über alles. R. Morais. il por *Forbes* 140:366+
  Jl 13 '87
Siemers, Linda
 Adventurous Victorians. il *Travel Holiday* 167:92 My
  '87
Siena (Italy)
Description
 Siena. A. M. Zwack. il *Gourmet* 47:54-9+ F '87
Social life and customs
  See also
  Palio di Siena (Italy)
Sierck, Detlef *See* Sirk, Douglas, 1900-1987
Sierra (Periodical)
 Beyond the mountaintops. J. F. King. *Sierra* 72:6 S/O
  '87
Sierra Club
 1988 spring trips. il *Sierra* 72:69-78 N/D '87
 7,300 days . . . and counting [calendars] M. Olmstead.
  il *Sierra* 72:96-8+ N/D '87
 Questions & answers. See issues of Sierra beginning
  March/April 1983
 Sierra Club 1988 foreign outings. il *Sierra* 72:63-70 Jl/Ag
  '87
 The Sierra Club difference. L. Downing and M. L. Fischer.
  Sierra 72:6 Jl/Ag '87
 Sierra Club financial report. il *Sierra* 72:69-71 Mr/Ap
  '87
 Sierra Club outings 1987. il *Sierra* 72:51-114 Ja/F '87
 Sierra notes. See issue of Sierra
Sierra Nevada Mountains (Calif. and Nev.)
 How to plan a Sierra horsepack trip. il maps *Sunset*
  178:78-80, 98-103 Ap '87
Sierra Nevada Mountains (Calif. and Nev.) in art
 Sierran souvenirs [reproductions of watercolor paintings]
  T. Foster. il *Sierra* 72:55-60 N/D '87
Sierra Photo Contest *See* Photography—Competitions
Siesta [film] See Motion picture reviews—Single works
Siffre, Michel
 The time of our lives: subterranean experiments on
  the rhythms imposed by the solar day. il *Courier*
  40:14-15 Je '87
Sigal, Leon V.
 Getting over the summit. il *Bull At Sci* 43:12-13 Ja/F
  '87
 INF deal faces conservative opposition. il *Bull At Sci*
  43:14-16 My '87
 Signs of a Soviet shift. bibl f il *Bull At Sci* 43:16-20
  D '87
Sigatoka disease *See* Bananas—Diseases and pests
Sigcau, Stella
  about
 First woman chosen leader of South African homeland.
  Jet 73:38 O 26 '87
Sight *See* Vision
Sight hounds *See* Gazehounds
Sighthounds *See* Gazehounds
Sights for firearms *See* Firearms—Sights
Sightseeing airplanes *See* Airplanes in sightseeing
Sightseeing boats
  See also
  Cap'n Sam's Riverboat Cruises
Food service
 Ahoy, all ye diners! Try a meal afloat. D. H. Dunn.
  il *Bus Week* p162 N 30 '87

Sigma Tek, Inc.
Honeywell's Sperry Group sells ARC product line. *Aviat Week Space Technol* 127:32 S 14 '87
Sigman, David S.
(jt. auth) See Chen, Chi-Hong B., and Sigman, David S.
Sigmatron Nova, Inc.
Electroluminescent thin-film panels developed for aircraft. K. J. Stein. *Aviat Week Space Technol* 126:83+ Ap 6 '87
Sigmund, Barbara

about
Tough hide/soft heart? L. Davis. *Vogue* 177:392 S '87
Sigmund Freud Museum (London, England)
Dr. Freud's last dream. M. Filler. il *House Gard* 159:176-81+ F '87
Sign o' the times [film] See Motion picture reviews—Single works
Sign of the dollar *See* Dollar sign
Signal Companies, Inc.
See also
Allied-Signal Inc.
Signal generators
See also
Oscillators
Commodore pulse generator. J. Barbarello. il *Radio-Electron* 58 ComputerDigest:96-100 O '87
Pattern generator NCM Model 871. il *Radio-Electron* 58:14-15+ N '87
Simple multi-tone generator. il *Radio-Electron* 58:31 N '87
SMT project: a business-card tone generator [surface mount technology] F. M. Mims. il *Radio-Electron* 58:85-6+ N '87
Sound-effects generator. E. B. Tupue. il *Radio-Electron* 58:40 Je '87
Tone generator IC's. R. F. Scott. il *Radio-Electron* 58:80-1 Ap '87
Signal processing
See also
Charge coupled devices (Electronics)
Waveform analysis
Audio/video synergy [surround sound processors] J. D. Hirsch. il *Stereo Rev* 52:23-4 Ap '87
Audio alchemy [Chace Stereo Surround Processor] G. Buchalter. il por *Forbes* 140:188 O 5 '87
Desktop DSP. D. Ranada. il *High Fidel* 37:17 S '87
A digital alternative [Toshiba DX-900 video recorder with built-in PCM adapter] C. J. Esse. il *High Fidel* 37:11 Ag '87
Electronic musical chairs [Yamaha digital sound field processor and graphic equalizers] F. Vizard. il *Pop Mech* 164:44+ S '87
NEC AVD-700E surround-sound processor. il *High Fidel* 37:37-8 Je '87
The resurgence of surround sound [DSP-1 Digital Sound Field Processor] L. Klein. il *Radio-Electron* 58:74-5+ My '87
Signal processors. L. Klein. il *Radio-Electron* 58:72-3 Ja '87
Signal processors. R. Long. il *High Fidel* 37:47 S '87
Sound Concepts SSD550 time-delay system. J. D. Hirsch. il *Stereo Rev* 52:39-40 O '87
Stereo TV decoder (I). T. T. Templin. il *Radio-Electron* 58:37-41 Ja '87
Stereo TV decoder (II). T. T. Templin. il *Radio-Electron* 58:51-4 F '87
Surround sound [processors and decoders] T. R. Gillett. il *Stereo Rev* 52:54-8 Ap '87
Surround-sound attractions. R. B. Schulein. il *High Fidel* 37:49+ Ag '87
Surround sound: music and movies with dazzling realism. M. C. Lehrer. il *USA Today (Periodical)* 116:86-8 S '87
System compatibility. J. D. Hirsch. il *Stereo Rev* 52:22+ F '87
VHSIC demonstrates significant benefits in performing signal processing functions [use in Flir imagery] *Aviat Week Space Technol* 127:98-9 S 7 '87
Video's new image. R. Jaccoma. il *Stereo Rev* 52:70-3 O '87
Signals and signaling
See also
Fog signals
Signature (Law)
Ill-informed buyer gets duped [unexpected second mortgage from signing document for home improvement loan] H. Porter. *Fam Handyman* 37:14+ Jl/Ag '87

Signature writing machines
Autopen presidency [abuse of presidential signature writing machine by C. Channell] M. Hosenball. *New Repub* 196:16-18 My 11 '87
Signs and signboards
See also
Billboards
Food store signs
Neon signs
Restaurant signs
Street signs
An echo of past battles [Quebec Court of Appeal decision declaring mandatory French-only signs illegal sparks vandalism] B. Wallace. il *Macleans* 100:14 Ja 12 '87
Language on trial [Quebec Court of Appeal rules against language charter requiring French-only commercial signs] B. Wallace. *Macleans* 100:8 Ja 5 '87
Stupid yellow sign on board [baby on board signs] A. Girdler. il *Road Track* 38:24 Je '87
Sigoloff, Sanford C.

about
The fix-up artist goes on the attack. B. O'Reilly. il pors *Fortune* 115:105 Ja 5 '87
Sanford Sigoloff. S. Toy. il por *Bus Week* Sp Issue:214 Ap 17 '87
Sigur, Gaston Joseph, 1924-
China policy today: consensus, consistence, stability [address, December 11, 1986] *Dep State Bull* 87:48-52 F '87
FY 1988 assistance requests for East Asia and the Pacific [statement, February 25, 1987] *Dep State Bull* 87:30-6 My '87
Korea: new beginnings [address, July 21, 1987] *Dep State Bull* 87:32-4 S '87
Korean politics in transition [address, February 6, 1987] *Dep State Bull* 87:19-21 Ap '87
The strategic importance of the emerging Pacific [address, September 29, 1986] *Dep State Bull* 86:75-8 D '86
The U.S. approach to East Asia and the Pacific [address, October 29, 1986] *Dep State Bull* 87:55-7 F '87
U.S. policy priorities for relations with China [address, April 22, 1987] *Dep State Bull* 87:41-3 Jl '87
Vitality and possibility on the Pacific Rim [address, December 3, 1986] *Dep State Bull* 87:52-4 F '87
Sigurdsson, Haraldur
A dead chief's revenge? il maps *Nat Hist* 96:44-9 Ag '87
Sihanouk *See* Norodom Sihanouk, Prince, 1922-
Sikes, Gini
Baby-sitting emergencies. *Seventeen* 46:246-7 Ag '87
Baby-sitting the brat. il *Seventeen* 46:184+ Mr '87
Profile of a New-Age date. *Mademoiselle* 93:187+ Ag '87
Worn in the USA: where big looks are born. il *Mademoiselle* 93:148-51+ D '87
Sikhs
Hell on wheels [Sikh extremists murder Hindu bus travelers] il *Time* 130:50 Jl 20 '87
'Such a dance of death' [attacks against Hindus] F. Willey. il *Newsweek* 110:34 Jl 20 '87
Canada
Charlesville's big boom [East Indian refugee landing site generates tourist trade] B. Hatfield. il *Macleans* 100:8 O 5 '87
Drawing a harder line on migrants. M. Janigan. il *Macleans* 100:10+ Ag 10 '87
A harrowing story. M. Janigan. il *Macleans* 100:10-11 Ag 17 '87
The newest boat people [voyage to Nova Scotia; special section] il *Macleans* 100:6-10 Jl 27 '87
A wary welcome for a human cargo. M. Janigan. il *Macleans* 100:18-19 Ag 3 '87
We say hello [refugees in Nova Scotia] il *Time* 130:47 Jl 27 '87
Sikorsky, Igor

about
The U.S. Business Hall of Fame. A. M. Louis. il por *Fortune* 115:107 Ap 13 '87
Sikorsky, Robert
Highway robbery: the scandal of auto repair in America. il por map *Read Dig* 130:90-9 My '87
Sikorsky Aircraft
Army developing helicopter derivatives for special operations missions. S. W. Kandebo. il *Aviat Week Space Technol* 127:47+ D 14 '87
Flight restrictions lifted for most Marine Corps CH-53Es [transmission problems] *Aviat Week Space Technol* 127:28-9 Jl 13 '87
Manufacturer details configurations of Navy/Coast Guard SH-60F derivatives. S. W. Kandebo. il *Aviat Week Space Technol* 126:96-7 My 18 '87

Sikorsky Aircraft—*cont.*
Navy restricts Sikorsky helicopter flights [defect in the transmission gear] *Aviat Week Space Technol* 126:27 F 23 '87
Program delays spur NASA, DARPA to restructure X-wing flight tests. *Aviat Week Space Technol* 127:23-4 Ag 31 '87
Sikorsky/Navy program to prolong service life of SH-3 helicopter. il *Aviat Week Space Technol* 126:100-1 My 18 '87
Sikorsky Aircraft assesses new H-76 armament pylon. il *Aviat Week Space Technol* 126:49 Mr 23 '87
Supreme Court weighs liability in military contractor suit [Boyle vs. Sikorsky over helicopter crash] M. Mecham. il *Aviat Week Space Technol* 127:81-2 O 26 '87

Siksika Indians
Forest Service steps on Blackfeet [struggling to save sacred land in Lewis and Clark National Forest] J. Bruggers. il *Progressive* 51:14 Ap '87
Wilderness and worship—or wells? [Lewis and Clark National Forest Plan vs. Blackfeet Indians] M. Kantor. il *Sierra* 72:67-8 My/Je '87

Silage
Silage beats hay as supplement to wheat pasture [cattle] *Success Farm* 85 no4:B13 F '87

Silas Marner [television program] See Television program reviews—Single works

Silber, Allan
about
Banking in the big leagues. P. C. Newman. il por *Macleans* 100:25 Ag 10 '87

Silber, John R.
Democracy and its heroes. *Current* 294:16-19 Jl/Ag '87

Silber, Mark B.
Successful supervisory secrets. il *USA Today (Periodical)* 116:92-4 Jl '87

Silberman, James H.
Summit Books. *Writer* 100:25 Jl '87

Silberman, Robert
David Huchthausen: controlled fragments [cover story] il por *Am Craft* 47:54-9 Ag/S '87
East meets West, postmodern style. il *Art Am* 75:13-15+ My '87
Outside report: Robert Frank. il *Art Am* 75:130-9 F '87

Silberstein, Gary B., and Daniel, Charles W.
Reversible inhibition of mammary gland growth by transforming growth factor-β. bibl f il *Science* 237:291-3 Jl 17 '87

Silden, Isobel
Doo Dah, Doo Dah. il *Travel Holiday* 168:66 D '87
Hollywood on Location. *Travel Holiday* 168:35 Ag '87

Silence
The Walkman cometh. M. A. Noll. il *Christ Today* 31:22-3 F 6 '87

Silent films *See* Motion pictures—Silent films
Silent heart attacks *See* Heart—Diseases
Siler, Todd
about
Todd Siler at Ronald Feldman Fine Arts. S. Westfall. il *Art Am* 75:175 S '87

Siliciano, Paul G., and others
Saccharomyces cerevisiae has a U1-like small nuclear RNA with unexpected properties. bibl f il *Science* 237:1484-7 S 18 '87

Silicon
Covalent group IV atomic clusters. W. L. Brown and others. bibl f il *Science* 235:860-5 F 20 '87
High-resolution electron microscopy and scanning tunneling microscopy of native oxides on silicon. A. H. Carim and others. bibl f il *Science* 237:630-3 Ag 7 '87
Limits on sensitivity of large silicon bolometers for solar neutrino detection. C. J. Martoff. bibl f il *Science* 237:507-9 Jl 31 '87
Raising a crop of transistors [use of silicon and tantalum; work of Brian M. Ditchek] il *Sci News* 132:25 Jl 11 '87
Silicon devices: LED there be light. S. Weisburd. il *Sci News* 131:294-5 My 9 '87

Silicon chip copyright *See* Copyright—Integrated circuits
Silicon chips *See* Integrated circuits
Silicon Compiler Systems Corporation
Do-it-yourself chips get easier. O. Port. *Bus Week* p92 Mr 30 '87

Silicon Compilers, Inc.
See also
Silicon Compiler Systems Corporation
It's cold out there. M. Beauchamp. il por *Forbes* 139:60+ F 23 '87

Silicon compilers (Computers)
CAD for building chips: silicon compilers and the automated building of VLSI circuits. S. Trimberger and J. Rowson. il *Byte* 12:217-18+ Je '87

Silicon compounds
See also
Polysilanes

Silicon controlled rectifiers *See* Thyristors
Silicon Design Labs, Inc.
See also
Silicon Compiler Systems Corporation

Silicon Valley electronic industries *See* Electronic industries
Silk, Joseph, 1942-
The formation of galaxies. bibl il *Phys Today* 40:28-35 Ap '87

Silk, Leonard Solomon, 1918-
The United States and the world economy. *Foreign Aff* 65 Sp Issue:458-76 ['87]
Volcker on the crash. il por *N Y Times Mag* p40+ N 8 '87

Silk, Mark
The hot History Department. il pors *N Y Times Mag* p42-3+ Ap 19 '87

Silk
Aristocrats of the genre—woven silks. J. Simpson. il *Archit Dig* 44:230+ O '87

Silk industry
China
China's silken success. H. Ahmad. il *World Press Rev* 34:49 D '87

Silk roads *See* Trade routes
Silk screen printing
Collectors and collecting
Searching for serigraphs. R. W. Williams. il *Am Artist* 51:68-71 S '87

Silkscreen printing *See* Silk screen printing
Sill, Gertrude Grace
Two rediscovered paintings by John Haberle. bibl f il por *Antiques* 132:1118-21 N '87

Sill, Kelly
about
How to become a house musician. M. Stryker. pors *Down Beat* 54:54+ F '87

Silla (Kingdom)
A lost dynasty revealed. G. Hesse. il *Travel Holiday* 167:24-7 Ja '87

Sills, Beverly
about
Architectural digest visits: Beverly Sills. J. Gruen. il pors *Archit Dig* 44:184-9 N '87
The executive superstar of the opera. K. Brady. il pors *Work Woman* 12:62-3+ Je '87

Sills, Beverly, and Linderman, Lawrence
Beverly! [excerpt] il pors *Ladies Home J* 104:30+ My '87

Silone, Ignazio, 1900-1978
about
Socialism and sensibility. I. Howe. *New Repub* 197:38-42 O 26 '87

Silva, Adroaldo Moura da
about
View from the middle [interview] E. A. Finn, Jr. il por *Forbes* 140:60+ N 16 '87

Silva, Anibal Cavaco *See* Cavaco Silva, Anibal, 1939-
Silva, Chris, 1962?-
about
Black swimmer resurfaces thanks to Campanis' slur. il por *Jet* 72:51 My 18 '87

Silva, Donatus De
Victory in sight against 'river blindness'. il *UN Chron* 24:75-6 My '87

Silva, Ozires
about
The Iacocca of Brazil. J. Barham. il por *Fortune* 116:60+ Ag 3 '87

Silva, Rea Ann
about
Eric Dickerson must pay pregnant ex-girlfriend. pors *Jet* 72:25 S 7 '87
White ex-girlfriend hits Dickerson with paternity and palimony lawsuits. pors *Jet* 72:52 Ag 3 '87

Silva, Steve
about
He made the climb to fitness. il por *Sports Illus* 67:20 O 5 '87
Super-fit climber Steve Silva is a new man since first he chose to aim for the stairs. il pors *People Wkly* 28:147-8 N 2 '87

Silva Xavier, Joaquín José da See Tiradentes, d. 1792
Silver, Diane
about
Producer Diane Silver and the making of "Native son". S. McHenry. por *Ms* 15:15-17 Mr '87
Silver, Horace
about
Blindfold test. F. Bouchard. il por *Down Beat* 54:48 S '87
Silver, Isidore, 1934-
The Meese factor: packing the lower courts. *Commonweal* 114:102 F 27 '87
Silver, Ken
Matisse's retour à l'ordre. bibl f il *Art Am* 75:110-23+ Je '87
The other fin de siècle. bibl f il *Art Am* 75:104-11+ D '87
Silver
See also
Silversmithing
Silverware
Silver as an investment
Stake a claim in the 'poor man's gold'. T. Segal. il *Bus Week* p164 My 11 '87
Silver as money
Yesterday's lemon is today's watermelon! [Panic of 1893 and issuance of watermelon notes] E. Rochette. il *Antiques Collect Hobbies* 92:71-2 Ap '87
Silver dollars See Coins
Silverberg, Robert
Hardware [fiction] il *Omni* 10:134-6+ O '87
Silverman, Jonathan
about
Would you hire this kid to impersonate you on Broadway? por *People Wkly* 27:113 Mr 30 '87
Silverman, Leonard
Corporate child care: playpens in the boardroom or productivity investment? il *USA Today (Periodical)* 115:67-9 My '87
Silverman, Mervyn
about
Mandatory tests for AIDS? [interview] pors *U S News World Rep* 102:62 Mr 9 '87
Silverman, Rachel
Being strong takes more than muscles. il por *Women's Sports Fitness* 9:60 O '87
Silverman, Robert B.
Whaling in the Azores. il *Sea Front* 33:174-82 My/Je '87
Silverman, Stephen
about
Judge blocks production of 'Amos 'n' Andy' musical. *Jet* 72:56 S 14 '87
Silvers, Phil, 1912-1985
Anecdotes, facetiae, satire, etc.
Uncivil liberties. C. Trillin. il *Nation* 245:778 D 26 '87-Ja 2 '88
Silversides
Hey, Pisces, what's your latitude? [research by David O. Conover and Stephen W. Heins] *Sci News* 131:232 Ap 11 '87
Silversmithing
William Gale & Son, New York silversmiths. R. A. Green. il *Antiques Collect Hobbies* 91:18-20 F '87
Silverstein, Ellen
about
Ellen Silverstein, photo stylist. J. Dolce. il por *Seventeen* 46:232 Ag '87
Silverstein, Olga
about
Couples on the couch [interview] *Vogue* 177:387+ F '87
The good mother [interview] *Vogue* 177:84+ Je '87
Silverware
See also
Silversmithing
Collectors and collecting
Antique silver. F. Donegan. il *Americana* 14:74-6 Ja/F '87
Do you know this . . . about silver and pewter? C. Thompson. il por *Antiques Collect Hobbies* 92:19-21 O '87
Silver and gold in the diplomatic reception rooms [State Dept. Building] J. F. Goldsborough. il *Antiques* 132:174-81 Jl '87
Silver futures [S. Wagstaff collection] N. F. Weber. il *House Gard* 159:42+ Mr '87
William Gale & Son, New York silversmiths. R. A. Green. il *Antiques Collect Hobbies* 91:18-20 F '87

Exhibitions
American silver [exhibition entitled A silver celebration at Greensboro Historical Museum, Greensboro, N. C.] S. B. Sherrill. il *Antiques* 131:958+ My '87
American silver [The silver of Tiffany & Company, 1850-1980 at the Museum of Fine Arts, Boston] S. B. Sherrill. il *Antiques* 132:400+ S '87
Japanesque silver by Tiffany and Company in the Metropolitan Museum of Art. F. G. Safford and R. W. Caccavale. bibl f il *Antiques* 132:808-19 O '87
Silver in Pennsylvania [exhibition entitled Chester County silver: heirlooms reflecting history in West Chester, Pa.] il *Antiques* 131:962 My '87
Triumphs of American silvermaking [exhibition at Metropolitan Museum of Art of Tiffany & Co. objects] il *USA Today (Periodical)* 116:8-9 D '87
Silverwork See Silversmithing
Silvis, Randall, 1950-
The writer's eye. *Writer* 100:7-8 O '87
Simanaitis, Dennis
Technical tidbits. See issues of Road & Track beginning January 1985
Simberloff, Daniel
A funny thing happend on the way to the taxidermist. il *Nat Hist* 96:50-5 Ag '87
Simcox, Carroll E.
The gift of aging. *Christ Century* 104:1090-2 D 2 '87
Petitionary prayer reconsidered. *Christ Century* 104:212-13 Mr 4 '87
Simels, Steve
(jt. auth) See Barter, Christie, and Simels, Steve
(jt. auth) See Nelson, Sara, and Simels, Steve
Simes, Dimitri K.
Gorbachev: a new foreign policy? bibl f *Foreign Aff* 65 Sp Issue:477-500 ['87]
Simi (Firm)
Zelma of Simi [Z. Long] N. Hazelton. *Natl Rev* 39:57-8 F 13 '87
Simian viruses
Pancreatic neoplasia induced by SV40 T-antigen expression in acinar cells of transgenic mice. D. M. Ornitz and others. bibl f il *Science* 238:188-93 O 9 '87
The role of individual cysteine residues in the structure and function of the v-*sis* gene product. N. A. Giese and others. bibl f il *Science* 236:1315-18 Je 5 '87
Unwinding of duplex DNA from the SV40 origin of replication by T antigen. M. Dodson and others. bibl f il *Science* 238:964-7 N 13 '87
Similarity mapping See Multidimensional scaling
Simkin, Susan M., and others
Markarian 348: a tidally disturbed Seyfert galaxy [cover story] bibl f il *Science* 235:1367-70 Mr 13 '87
Simmers, R. N., and others
Fragile sites at 16q22 are not at the breakpoint of the chromosomal rearrangement in AMMoL. bibl f il *Science* 236:92-4 Ap 3 '87
Simmons, Althea
about
Simmons, Jones mastermind move to dump Robert Bork. pors *Jet* 73:12 O 26 '87
Simmons, Amy
Hawks nest on Peace Board. *Progressive* 51:16 Mr '87
Simmons, Charles
The Shakespeare number. *Nation* 244:291-5 Mr 7 '87
Simmons, Charles, 1924-
about
PW interviews. J. F. Baker. por *Publ Wkly* 231:54-5 My 8 '87
Simmons, Connie E.
Ending sexual harassment. *Vogue* 177:70 S '87
Simmons, Dan
E-ticket to Namland [fiction] il *Omni* 10:108-10+ N '87
Simmons, Harold C.
about
Harold Simmons is set to roll another seven. G. G. Marcial. il por *Bus Week* p106 O 5 '87
Simmons, Heber, Jr.
Dental care for children: an expert's advice. *McCalls* 114:114+ F '87
Simmons, James C.
To the Marquesas. il map *Oceans* 20:20-5 Jl/Ag '87
Simmons, Jean
about
Now Perry Mason falls for the enduring charms of Jean Simmons. S. Adelson. il pors *People Wkly* 27:103-4+ Mr 2 '87
Simmons, Judy
The clock turns backwards [poem] *Essence* 17:118 Ap '87

Simmons, Maryanne
about
Playing by her own rules. A. Wolff. il por *Sports Illus* 67:38-9 Jl 6 '87
Simmons, Rosie S.
about
Bolivar County, Miss. gets black as circuit clerk. por *Jet* 72:6 S 14 '87
Simmons, Ted, 1949-
about
Playing by her own rules. A. Wolff. il por *Sports Illus* 67:38-9 Jl 6 '87
Simmons, Thomas
I'll sue—that's what I'll do! *Read Dig* 131:17-18 Ag '87
A sense of drama. il *N Y Times Mag* p130 S 13 '87
Simms, John
about
Banking on a "croakie". H. Rothman. il pors *Nations Bus* 75:81 My '87
Simms, Margaret
Looking toward international markets. il *Black Enterp* 18:39-40 O '87
Making human resources more competitive. il *Black Enterp* 17:37 Jl '87
Simms, Phil, 1955-
about
Glory day. F. Schruers. il pors *Sport Mag* 78:65-6+ D '87
Phil Simms, super-hero. B. Phillips. il por *Sch Update* 120:36-7 N 20 '87
Simon, Allen
A celebration of plenty. il *Saturday Evening Post* 259:18-19+ N '87
Christmas feast with an Oriental flavor. il *Saturday Evening Post* 259:18-20 D '87
Simon, Bernard
Quebec shows a new face. *World Press Rev* 34:39 Mr '87
Simon, Carly
about
After an onstage collapse and a six-year battle with stage fright, Carly Simon braves a comeback. J. Hall. il pors *People Wkly* 28:38-40 Ag 17 '87
The private lives of star moms [excerpt from Starring mothers] J. Barber. il pors *McCalls* 114:57+ My '87
Simon, Dennis F.
Modernizing science and technology in China. bibl f *Curr Hist* 86:249-52+ S '87
Simon, Francesca
The road [poem] *Essence* 18:149 S '87
Simon, Herbert Alexander, 1916-
about
Artificial intelligence: the rational optimist. C. Holden. *Current* 293:36-40 Je '87
Simon, Jeffrey D.
Misunderstanding terrorism. *Foreign Policy* 67:104-20 Summ '87
Simon, John
Film. See occasional issues of National Review
Quoth the maven 'evermore'. *New Leader* 69:5-7 D 1-15 '86
Theater. See issues of New York
Simon, Julian
Now (I think) I understand the ecologists better. il por *Futurist* 21:18-19 S/O '87
Simon, Neil
The Automat. il *N Y* 20:66-7 D 21-28 '87
about
Brighton Beach memoirs [drama] Reviews
   Theatre Crafts il 21:22-5+ F '87. M. LaRue
Broadway bound [drama] Reviews
   New Leader 69:17-18 D 29 '86. L. Sauvage
Simon, Nissa
Yum! Helping your kids to healthy food habits. il *Work Woman* 12:149-51 S '87
Simon, Paul, 1928-
about
'Bow-tie politics'. G. F. Will. il *Newsweek* 109:88 My 11 '87
Does Simon have a Pinocchio problem? M. Kramer. il pors *U S News World Rep* 103:25-6 N 30 '87
Is Paul Simon another McGovern? No, but he may be another Reagan. J. Klein. il pors *N Y* 20:50-4 D 7 '87
An old-fashioned senator on the move. M. McDonald. il pors *Macleans* 100:20-1 D 7 '87
Paul Simon: return of the liberal [cover story] A. Kopkind. *Nation* 245:665+ D 5 '87
Pee-Wee's big adventure [cover story] F. Barnes. il *New Repub* 197:25-7 O 5 '87

Scrutinizing 'Simon Pure'. E. Clift. il por *Newsweek* 110:28 N 30 '87
Some of that old-time religion. W. Shapiro. il pors *Time* 130:26+ N 16 '87
Work over welfare [interview] L. Neff. por *Christ Today* 31:30 Je 12 '87
Anecdotes, facetiae, satire, etc.
The character issue. *New Repub* 197:6+ O 26 '87
Simon, Paul, 1942-
about
The apostle of angst. J. Allen. il pors *Esquire* 107:210-12+ Je '87
Architectural digest visits: Paul Simon. J. Thurman. il por *Archit Dig* 44:108-115 S '87
'Graceland' in Africa. N. Cooper. il por *Newsweek* 109:45 F 23 '87
Julian Bond hired to promote Paul Simon tour. il por *Jet* 72:55 Je 1 '87
Paul Simon. G. Santoro. il por *Down Beat* 54:54 Jl '87
Paul Simon. F. Spotnitz. il por *Roll Stone* p36 Mr 26 '87
Paul Simon goes on tour with black South Africans. *Jet* 71:17 Mr 2 '87
Paul Simon's amazing Graceland tour [cover story] D. Fricke. il pors *Roll Stone* p42-4+ Jl 2 '87
Singer Paul Simon strikes sour chord with students at Howard U. over album. *Jet* 71:59 F 2 '87
A songwriter's South African odyssey [interview] A. P. Sanoff. il por *U S News World Rep* 102:74 Mr 2 '87
Tapping pop music's African roots. N. Jennings. il por *Macleans* 100:52-3 My 4 '87
UN forgives Paul Simon for 'Graceland' album. *Jet* 71:30 F 23 '87
UN group attacks Paul Simon: says 'Graceland' broke cultural boycott of South Africa. R. Tannenbaum. *Roll Stone* p11+ F 12 '87
Simon, Philipp
about
What's up, docs? Supercarrot is on the way. il pors *People Wkly* 27:40 Mr 16 '87
Simon, Roger Lichtenberg, 1943-
My week with Oleg 1: writers, detectives and the caviar Mafia. il *N Y Times Book Rev* 92:11 S 13 '87
Simon, William
Testing freedom and restraint. *Society* 24:27-30 Jl/Ag '87
Simon, William E., 1927-
Liberty to all [address, June 22, 1987] *Vital Speeches Day* 54:7-11 O 15 '87
about
Bill Simon goes treasure-hunting in the Pacific. T. Carson and C. Debes. il por *Bus Week* p84-6 Mr 9 '87
An empire rising in the West. T. McCarroll. il por *Time* 130:42 S 7 '87
William Simon's Pacific overtures. L. J. Davis. il pors *N Y Times Mag* p14-17+ D 27 '87
Simon & Schuster Inc.
The best kind of advertising [word of mouth makes M. S. Peck's The road less traveled into best seller] J. A. Trachtenberg. il por *Forbes* 139:91-2 Ap 20 '87
Dick and Joni [bitter divorce battle between J. Evans and R. Snyder] J. Kasindorf. il pors *N Y* 20:60-4+ D 14 '87
Joni Evans leaves Simon & Schuster; to head imprint at Random House. J. Mutter. por *Publ Wkly* 232:10 S 4 '87
Kaplan joins Simon & Schuster as special adviser to Snyder. pors *Publ Wkly* 231:16 Ja 16 '87
Kaplan moves to new post of S & S president. il por *Publ Wkly* 232:10 S 25 '87
Once half of publishing's dynamic duo, Joni Evans is now throwing the book at her husband, Dick Snyder. M. Vespa. il pors *People Wkly* 28:149-50+ N 16 '87
S & S buys bio of Knopf by Peter Prescott. *Publ Wkly* 231:87 F 27 '87
S & S juvenile division restructured. *Publ Wkly* 231:10 Ap 3 '87
Simon & Schuster bids on stake in Britain's ABP. V. Menkes. *Publ Wkly* 231:10 Je 26 '87
Simon & Schuster challenges N.Y. State 'Son of Sam' law [suit over application of statute to Wiseguy by Nicholas Pileggi] *Publ Wkly* 232:14 Ag 14 '87
Simon & Schuster Inc. Audio Publishing Division
'Instant' audios due from S & S, Nightingale-Conant. *Publ Wkly* 232:47-8 O 30 '87
S & S adds Nightingale-Conant audio line. *Publ Wkly* 231:57 My 22 '87

Simon & Schuster Inc. Audio Publishing Division — *cont.*
Simon & Schuster Audio launches Star trek series. il *Publ Wkly* 231:44-5 My 8 '87
Simon & Schuster Inc. Video Publishing Division
S&S tries video . . . again. *Publ Wkly* 231:50-1 Ja 23 '87
Simon & Schuster reaffirms commitment to video. il *Publ Wkly* 232:57-8 O 16 '87
Simoneau, Yves
about
In the shadow of the wind [film] Reviews
Macleans il 100:54 Ja 26 '87. M. Abley
Simons, Carol
Kyoiku mama: secret of Japan's schools. il *Read Dig* 131:117-20 Jl '87
They get by with a lot of help from their kyoiku mamas [cover story] bibl (p182) il *Smithsonian* 17:44-53 Mr '87
Simons, Kent
about
A value seeker says there's plenty left [interview] A. E. Serwer. il por *Fortune* 116:200 Ag 3 '87
Simons, Lewis M.
With new energy, Vietnam gets down to business. il *Smithsonian* 18:62-6+ Ap '87
Simons, Pamela Ellis- *See* Ellis-Simons, Pamela
Simons, Stefan
China still battles for Tibet. il *World Press Rev* 34:29-31 My '87
Simons, Thomas C., 1928-
about
Thank you, Tom Simons. J. Andresky. il por *Forbes* 139:99 Mr 23 '87
Simplified employee pensions
Self-employed? Check out a simplified employee plan. B. M. Stephens. *Black Enterp* 17:326+ Je '87
A shelter that's still standing. A. McGrath. il *U S News World Rep* 102:56 Ap 6 '87
Simplified spelling *See* Spelling
Simplot, Jack
about
Cashing in on food and drink. B. Saporito. il por *Fortune* 116:152-3 O 12 '87
Shootout at the OKC Corral. E. F. Cone. por *Forbes* 140:86+ D 14 '87
Simply Red (Musical group)
Simply Red's Mick Hucknall. E. Miller. il pors *Seventeen* 46:89-90+ S '87
Simpson, Alan K.
In the pit [excerpt from remarks] *Natl Rev* 39:30 Ap 10 '87
Should the proposed Product Liability Reform Act be approved? [excerpts from debate, September 23, 1986] *Congr Dig* 66:31 Ja '87
about
Nice guys do finish first—just ask Al Simpson. D. Harbrecht. por *Bus Week* p94 N 9 '87
Simpson, Anne
Hidden money. il *Ms* 16:74 O '87
Simpson, Don, 1945-
about
1+1=$935 million. M. Dougherty. il pors *Life* 10:96-8+ Ap '87
You don't know them—but they know moviegoers. R. Grover. il pors *Bus Week* p166+ My 25 '87
Simpson, Eileen B.
about
PW interviews. W. Smith. por *Publ Wkly* 232:49-50 Jl 3 '87
Simpson, Jeffrey
Canada roused by military plan. il *Bull At Sci* 43:9-10 O '87
Simpson, John, 1944-
Falling for a Warsaw Pact dame. il *Harpers* 274:58-62 Je '87
Simpson, John Alexander, 1916-
about
Lost Ulysses. D. Stewart. il *Omni* 9:20+ S '87
Simpson, Joy
about
Obituary
Jet por 72:58 Ap 13 '87
Philadelphia opera singer stricken in South Africa. *Jet* 72:62 Ap 6 '87
Simpson, Mary K.
What do I do while they're writing? *Educ Dig* 52:44-6 My '87
Simpson, Maylene
3 children who needed a medical miracle; ed. by Linda Lee. il por *Redbook* 168:110+ F '87

Simpson, Mimi Brown
Whales' new lease on life. il *Oceans* 20:57-8 S/O '87
Simpson, Mona
Somebody to talk about. il pors *N Y Times Mag* p40+ Mr 8 '87
about
Money, Meryl and a movie contract can't spoil acclaimed first novelist Mona Simpson. A. Chambers. il por *People Wkly* 27:62+ Mr 16 '87
Simpson, Orville
about
The world according to Orville. A. Fadiman. il por *Life* 10:15-16+ S '87
Simpson, Scott
about
An Open and shut case [cover story] R. Reilly. il pors *Sports Illus* 66:20-7 Je 29 '87
Simpson, Thomas
about
3 children who needed a medical miracle; ed. by Linda Lee. M. Simpson. il por *Redbook* 168:110+ F '87
Simpson, Wallis Warfield *See* Windsor, Wallis Warfield, Duchess of, 1896-1986
Sims, Calvin
Invasion of the patent pirates. il *Read Dig* 131:33-6 O '87
Sims, Jack
about
Reaching baby boomers in southern California. B. Bird. il por *Christ Today* 31:45-6 Ag 7 '87
Sims, Jacqueline
(jt. auth) *See* Käferstein, Fritz, and Sims, Jacqueline
Sims, Naomi, 1949-
about
Model firsts: pioneers in black beauty. B. Summers. il pors *Essence* 17:38-42+ Ja '87
Sims, Patterson
about
'A tremendous opportunity'. L. Smallwood. por *Art News* 86:37-8 N '87
Simscript (Computer language)
PC Simscript II. 5. Z. A. Karian. *Byte* 12:244-6 Jl '87
SimuFlite Training International, Inc.
Descent into disaster [microburst simulator profile] J. M. McClellan. *Flying* 114:100-1 Ag '87
SimuFlite wins bid to train Navy aircrews. *Aviat Week Space Technol* 127:29 N 2 '87
Simulation, Computer *See* Computer simulation
Simulation games in education
Role-playing in class: casting counts [friction caused by game in Glendale, Calif.] *Newsweek* 110:76 D 14 '87
Simulators
See also
Electromagnetic pulse simulators
Flight simulators
Management games
Space flight simulators
Weightlessness simulators
A most powerful X-ray machine [Saturn X-ray simulator] D. E. Thomsen. il *Sci News* 132:276 O 31 '87
A simulated goddess [Aurora nuclear blast simulator] D. Eskow. il *Pop Mech* 164:21 My '87
Simultaneous equations
Solving linear equations [discussion of June 14, 1985 article, Solving linear systems faster] G. Kolata. *Science* 236:461-3 Ap 24 '87
Sin
See also
Confession
Penance
The devil made me do it. H. Fehren. *U S Cathol* 52:38-40 Jl '87
No-fault prophecy. R. J. Neuhaus. *Natl Rev* 39:44 Ap 10 '87
Sin. P. Yancey. il *Christ Today* 31:30-4 Mr 6 '87
Sin, psychopathology and Father Brown [comparison with M. Mann's Manhunter] M. Horst. *Christ Century* 104:46-7 Ja 21 '87
Why the seven deadly sins are still tempting [cover story; special section] il *U S Cathol* 52:6-15 Ag '87
Sin in advertising
Anecdotes, facetiae, satire, etc.
You can have it all! [ads promoting the seven deadly sins] il *Harpers* 275:43-50 N '87
Sinaceur, Mohammed Allal
The city-builders of Islam. bibl f il *Courier* 40:20-4 Jl '87
Sinatra, Frank, 1915-
about
The first Mrs. Sinatra [excerpt from His way] K. Kelley. il pors *Ladies Home J* 104:72-3+ Jl '87

Sinatra, Frank, 1915-—about—*cont.*
Frank Sinatra. T. Teachout. il por *High Fidel* 37:75+ Ap '87
Frank Sinatra to receive NAACP achievement honor. *Jet* 71:16 Mr 23 '87
L.A. branch of NAACP gives Sinatra achievement award. il por *Jet* 72:56 Je 1 '87
Saint Francis of Hoboken. D. Okrent. il pors *Esquire* 108:211-16 D '87
Sammy and Frank treat L.A. to rare duo performances. il pors *Jet* 72:55 S 21 '87
Sammy Davis, Frank Sinatra, Dean Martin together again for historic concert tour. il pors *Jet* 73:36 D 21 '87
Sinatra. *New Yorker* 63:32-4 Ap 6 '87
When Frank Sinatra had a cold: a reflection on the cause of today's common journalism. G. Talese. il pors *Esquire* 108:161-6 N '87
Sinatra, Nancy Barbato
about
The first Mrs. Sinatra [excerpt from His way] K. Kelley. il pors *Ladies Home J* 104:72-3+ Jl '87
Sinbad
about
Sinbad the stand-up. R. Laermer. il por *N Y* 20:34 S 14 '87
Sinclair, Ward
Keeping soil down on the farm. il *Sierra* 72:26-9 My/Je '87
Sineno, John
about
Out of the fire and into the frying pan. il *Newsweek* 109:58 Mr 9 '87
Singapore
See also
Birth rate—Singapore
Historic houses, sites, etc.—Singapore
Sentosa Island (Singapore)
Shopping and shoppers—Singapore
Stores—Singapore
Youth—Singapore
Economic conditions
Singapore: a tiny nation with one very rich resource—people. L. Hopping. il *Sch Update* 119:11 Ap 6 '87
Religious institutions and affairs
See also
Religious conferences—Singapore
Social policy
The government as a matchmaker. A. Peters. il *World Press Rev* 34:58 F '87
Singapore Stock Exchange *See* Stock exchanges—Singapore exchange
Singer, Daniel
From Public TV to 'Dallasty'. *Nation* 245:482+ O 31 '87
The lessons of defeat. *Nation* 245:81-4 Ag 1-8 '87
On recapturing the Soviet past. il *Nation* 245:716-18 D 12 '87
Top down or bottom up? il *Nation* 244:756-8 Je 6 '87
Singer, Howard
Conservative Judaism [discussion of December 1986 article, The Judaism born in America] *Commentary* 83:6-8+ Ap '87
Interfaith dialogue [discussion of May 1987 article, The rise & fall of interfaith dialogue] *Commentary* 84:4-6+ S '87
The rise & fall of interfaith dialogue. *Commentary* 83:50-5 My '87
Singer, Ira D.
AIDS in the workplace. il *Nations Bus* 75:36-9 Ag '87
Singer, June Flaum
about
A new agent and a new publisher for June Flaum Singer. *Publ Wkly* 232:24 Jl 31 '87
Singer, Mark
Profiles [W. G. Arader] il *New Yorker* 63:44-6+ N 30 '87
Singer, Max
Can the contras win? *Natl Rev* 39:30-4 F 13 '87
Cory Aquino and the psychology of bubbles. il *Natl Rev* 39:34-8 Ag 14 '87
Unclean elections. *New Repub* 197:9-10 Ag 3 '87
Singer, S. Fred
Lowering the gloom. por *Newsweek* 110:12 S 14 '87
Singer, S. Fred, and Crandall, Candace
Assessing the threat to the ozone [cover story] il *Consum Res Mag* 70:11-14 Jl '87

Singer, Steven
about
Steven Singer at Bernice Steinbaum. G. Henry. il *Art Am* 75:154-5 D '87
Singer Company
Paul Bilzerian still don't get no respect. P. Engardio. il por *Bus Week* p62+ N 23 '87
Ripe enough for Pickens [T. B. Pickens stalks Singer] R. Mitchell. il *Bus Week* p23 Ag 24 '87
Singers
See also
Opera singers
Women singers
Singh, Nagendra
Fortieth anniversary message: 'developing the rule of law' [excerpts from address, October 25, 1985] *UN Chron* 22:101 N/D '85
Singh, Usha
about
The road back to El Morocco: Usha Singh and the $2-million gamble. W. Norwich. il por *N Y* 20:48-51 Ap 27 '87
Singh, Vishwanath Pratap
about
Singh a song of discord. F. Willey. il por *Newsweek* 110:28 Ag 3 '87
Singher, Martial
about
Beau idéal. Q. Eaton. il pors *Opera News* 51:10-14 Ap 11 '87
Singing
See also
Yodeling
The Big Singing [annual gathering in Benton, Ky. to sing from the Southern harmony songbook] W. White. il *New Yorker* 62:78-84+ Ja 19 '87
Competitions
Musical events:
W. Sharp wins the Carnegie Hall International American Music Competition for Vocalists. A. Porter. *New Yorker* 63:124 O 12 '87
Study and teaching
Academic questions [opera training] B. L. Scherer. il *Opera News* 52:16-18+ N '87
A joyful noise [views of New York City teachers of operatic singing; with editorial comment by Jane L. Poole] C. Battaglia. il *Opera News* 51:4, 10-15 Ja 3 '87
Our favorite force of nature [B. Nilsson's master classes for opera singers at the Manhattan School of Music] G. Schmidgall. il pors *Opera News* 52:20-2+ Jl '87
Sharing the music [interview with opera voice coach and accompanist J. Wustman] J. W. Freeman. il pors *Opera News* 52:16-18+ Jl '87
Singing teachers
Attitudes
A joyful noise [views of New York City teachers of operatic singing; with editorial comment by Jane L. Poole] C. Battaglia. il *Opera News* 51:4, 10-15 Ja 3 '87
Singing Wind Bookshop (Ariz.) *See* Booksellers and bookselling—Arizona
Singlaub, John
about
Singlaub's new mission. B. Levin. il por *Macleans* 100:20 Mr 2 '87
Taking the stand. T. Brewster. il pors *Life* 10:28-32 Ag '87
Talk show. *Nation* 244:750-1 Je 6 '87
Single fathers
"Am I old enough to be a parent?"; ed. by Kate Manning. M. Gallagher. il por *Redbook* 169:34+ My '87
Say, brother. C. Powell. por *Essence* 18:10 Ag '87
Solo fathers. B. Anderson. il *Essence* 18:108+ N '87
Teen fathers: the other side of the story. M. Barbera-Hogan. *Teen* 31:32+ Jl '87
When fathers have custody. R. B. McCall. il *Parents* 62:211 Ag '87
Single issue interest groups *See* Special interest groups
Single-lens reflex cameras *See* Cameras, Single-lens reflex
Single men
See also
Divorced fathers
Divorcees
10 'perfect 10' men. L. Hirschberg. il *Harpers Bazaar* 120:64+ My '87
Bachelors for 1987 [black men] il *Ebony* 42:116-18+ Je '87
Black men more likely to wed than black women. *Jet* 72:36 Ap 20 '87

Single men—*cont.*

A good woman is hard to find: the sad saga of an eligible man. E. Weiner. il *Mademoiselle* 93:122-3+ Jl '87

Has the black male shortage spoiled black men? il *Ebony* 42:116+ My '87

Is this man taken? How to tell at first sight. C. Rickey. *Mademoiselle* 93:202 Mr '87

Looking for Ms. Right: the black male side of the dating game. C. Whitaker. il *Ebony* 42:128+ S '87

Men for sale [bachelor auctions for charity] L. Darling. *Mademoiselle* 93:138 O '87

A neighborhood. G. Pollock. il *N Y Times Mag* p104 N 8 '87

Why wed? The ambivalent American bachelor. T. Gabriel. il *N Y Times Mag* p24-9+ N 15 '87

Anecdotes, facetiae, satire, etc.

Is he marriage material? 74 sneaky ways to separate the possibilities from the deadbeats. L. Dormen and M. Zussman. il *Glamour* 85:226-7+ F '87

Your basic bachelor [excerpt from The bachelor home companion] P. J. O'Rourke. il *Mademoiselle* 93:156-7+ Je '87

Single mothers

See also
Church work with single mothers

'Don't you talk about my mama!' [adaptation of address, 1987] J. Jordan. *Essence* 18:53+ D '87

Holidays and single moms. V. Gallman. il *Essence* 18:102 D '87

Phantom fathers. K. Richards. il *Progressive* 51:34 Ag '87

Economic conditions

Slum community saves itself [efforts of single mothers to insure survival of low cost housing in Pittsburgh] R. Kahn. *Ms* 15:32 Je '87

A teenage mother's battle to raise her child and pay the bills [Marielle Nelson] M. Maran. il *Sch Update* 119:6 Mr 23 '87

Education

The case for separate schools for pregnant teenagers. J. Buie. *Educ Dig* 53:50-2 D '87

Fort Worth, Texas: a high school that helps teenage mothers shape new lives [New Lives Center] L. Chandler. il *Sch Update* 119:24 Mr 23 '87

Rebuilding lives: a college program for single parents and their kids [Saint Paul's College] R. Brown. il *Ebony* 43:134+ D '87

Employment

Black Boston TV anchor goes public on pregnancy [L. Walker] por *Jet* 72:32 Jl 6 '87

Routes to self-sufficiency: teenage mothers and employment. D. F. Polit. bibl f il *Child Today* 16:6-11 Ja/F '87

Vocational-technical education

Aid for unwed teens [job training program in Norfolk, Va. subsidized by Systems Management American Corp.] S. S. Harrison. *Black Enterp* 17:17 Mr '87

Single parent families

Can one parent be as good as two? B. Spock. *Redbook* 168:17 Ap '87

Single parents and the school *See* School and the home

Single people

See also
Dating (Social customs)
Divorcees
Museums and single people
Unmarried couples

AIDS fear leads many singles to marriage. *Jet* 71:31 F 23 '87

The coming of the singles society. E. S. Cornish. il *Futurist* 21:2+ Jl/Ag '87

How to be happily single [excerpt from The joy of being single] J. Harayda. *Essence* 18:61-2 O '87

Living alone and loving it [cover story; special section] il *U S News World Rep* 103:52-60 Ag 3 '87

"A table for one, please" [single diners in restaurants] il *Glamour* 85:404 S '87

U.S. may become society of singles, expert says [views of Edward Cornish] *Jet* 72:16 Ag 17 '87

Economic conditions

Financing the single way of life. A. McGrath. il *U S News World Rep* 103:56-7 Ag 3 '87

Poverty linked with living alone [aged] M. Hodge. il *50 Plus* 27:17-18 Mr '87

Anecdotes, facetiae, satire, etc.

Raw meat for the accountant. B. Staples. il *N Y Times Mag* p38-9 Mr 15 '87

Housing

If you can buy, you should. A. McGrath. il *U S News World Rep* 103:58-9 Ag 3 '87

Religious life

See also
Church work with single people

Travel

A vacation for one. J. Rachlin. il *U S News World Rep* 103:58-9 Ag 3 '87

Single premium life insurance *See* Insurance, Life

Single sideband radiotelephone on boats *See* Radiotelephone on ships, boats, etc.

Single-source research (TV audience research)

And now, BuyerGraphics. S. Behrens. il *Channels* 7:21 S '87

Single women

See also
Divorced mothers
Divorcees
Widows

25 ways to find a good man. il *Ebony* 42:146+ Mr '87

Bachelorettes for 1987 [black women] il *Ebony* 42:36-8+ Jl '87

Betting on myself [staying single] P. Giddings. *Essence* 17:55+ F '87

The Census Bureau's good news for single women. M. Engel. il *Glamour* 85:276+ F '87

The current state of affairs [single women and married men] E. B. Fein. *Mademoiselle* 93:247+ Ag '87

If you live alone: 9 ways to deal with emergencies. il *Glamour* 85:99 Ap '87

The marriage trap [criticism of various studies] S. Faludi. il *Ms* 16:62+ Jl/Ag '87

Stress and the single girl (having it all—and surviving it). J. M. Toal. il *Mademoiselle* 93:293-5+ S '87

A thoroughly modern mistress. K. Samon. il *Mademoiselle* 93:246-7+ Ag '87

What every single girl should know. G. Blair. See issues of Mademoiselle beginning September 1987

What every single girl should know. C. Rickey. See issues of Mademoiselle beginning September 1986 through August 1987

Working girl by day/party animal by night. S. Orlean. il *Mademoiselle* 93:132-3+ F '87

Anecdotes, facetiae, satire, etc.

If you're free Friday night, read this. S. Parriott. il *Mademoiselle* 93:232-3+ My '87

Lips like Kim Basinger's and other fantasies of single women. D. Stillman. il *Mademoiselle* 93:174-5+ O '87

What makes single girls tingle [views of C. Heimel] D. Maychick. il por *Mademoiselle* 93:38 Je '87

Economic conditions

An anesthetist seeks to invest her profit sharing [Louise Weizer] D. Harris. il *Money* 16:185-6 S '87

Making big bucks from the Big Bang [American A. Berkowitch working for Booz, Allen & Hamilton in London] N. Seixas. il pors *Money* 16:161-2+ My '87

Singlehanded cruising *See* Cruising

Singlehanded yacht racing *See* Yacht racing

Singles bars *See* Bars and barrooms

Singles market

Japan

James Baker, meet the dokushin kizoku [Marui Co.'s appeal to Japan's singles] A. Tanzer. il por *Forbes* 139:46-8 Ap 20 '87

Singleton, Henry E.

about
The brilliant Dr. S. T. Jaffe. por *Forbes* 139:178 Mr 9 '87

Singleton, Lawrence

about
Not in my town. il por *Time* 129:31 Je 1 '87

Singleton, William Dean

about
Beneath the mogul, paradox. N. J. Perry. il por *Fortune* 116:191-2 O 12 '87

Dean Singleton: the making of a media baron. T. Mason and others. il por *Bus Week* p29 S 28 '87

Extra: Texan builds newspaper empire. J. Schwartz. il por *Newsweek* 110:48 S 28 '87

Forget about art and cars. L. Zuckerman. il por *Time* 130:55 S 28 '87

Is Dean Singleton a media king in the making? Check his papers. V. Balfour. il pors *People Wkly* 28:47-8 O 5 '87

Sinhalese

A disputed homeland [civil war between Tamils and Sinhalese] S. K. Hennayake and J. S. Duncan. il map *Focus* 37:20-7 Spr '87

An orgy of killing. K. Scanlon. il *Macleans* 100:34-5 O 19 '87

Sinhalese—*cont.*
The roots of conflict in Sri Lanka. V. Rebeck. *Christ Century* 104:792-4 S 23 '87
Sri Lanka: a nation disintegrates [cover story] S. R. Weisman. il map *N Y Times Mag* p34-8+ D 13 '87

Sinkler, Becky
about
Lucky, plucky Becky Sinkler. D. Hurford. il por *50 Plus* 27:50+ Ag '87

Sinks
Bright new looks for sinks and accessories [kitchen sinks] il *South Living* 22:148+ O '87

Sinkyone Wilderness State Park (Calif.) *See* California—Parks and reserves

Sinnott, Roger W.
Astronomical computing. See issues of Sky and Telescope beginning April 1984
Gleanings for ATM's. See issues of Sky and Telescope

Sino-Soviet relations *See* Soviet Union—Foreign relations—China

Sinopoli, Giuseppe
about
Doctor in the house. P. G. Davis. il por *N Y* 20:63 Je 8 '87

Sint Maarten *See* Saint Martin

Sinusitis
Break out of the sinus blockade. M. Mihalik. *Prevention* 39:28+ S '87
Sound savers [ear care, sinusitis and air travel] E. S. Orzac. il *Travel Holiday* 168:30 Ag '87

Sinyavsky, Andrey, 1925-
about
What Yevgeny knew. D. Jameson. *New Repub* 196:39-41 Je 22 '87

Sioux Indians *See* Dakota Indians

Sir John Soane's Museum (London, England)
An architectural kaleidoscope: Sir John Soane's Museum in London. P. Thornton. bibl f il *Antiques* 131:264-77 Ja '87

Sirenia
See also
Manatees

Sirenia, Fossil
Sea cow family reunion. D. P. Domning. il *Nat Hist* 96:64+ Ap '87

Sirius (Star) *See* Stars, Double

Sirk, Douglas, 1900-1987
about
Obituary
New Repub 196:25 F 16 '87. S. Kauffmann

Sirkin, Elliott
My son, Larry Hagman. il pors *Good Housekeep* 205:111+ Jl '87

Sisk, John P.
Cowboy. *Am Sch* 56:400-6 Summ '87

Siskel, Gene
about
"It stinks!" "You're crazy!". R. Zoglin. il pors *Time* 129:64 My 25 '87
Siskel on Ebert—Ebert on Siskel [interview] *Omni* 9:52+ Je '87

Siskiyou County (Calif.)
Politics and government
Calif.'s first black-elected sheriff: humble and proud [C. Byrd] por *Jet* 71:30 F 23 '87

Sisson, Dan
Grandpa and the kid. See alternate issues of Field & Stream beginning September 1983

Sister chromatid exchange *See* Crossing over (Genetics)

Sister Cities International
Twisted sisters. J. L. Pasley. *New Repub* 196:14+ Je 22 '87

Sisterhoods
See also
Carmelites
Convents
Missionaries of Charity
Nuns

Sisters *See* Siblings

Sisters and brothers *See* Siblings

Sisters of Forgiveness—Together Against AIDS
A time for forgiveness. C. SerVaas. il *Saturday Evening Post* 259:50-5+ N '87

Sistine Chapel *See* Vatican. Cappella Sistina

Sistrand, Andrew
about
Overloaded. *New Yorker* 62:28-31 F 9 '87

Sitcoms (Programs) *See* Television broadcasting—Comedy programs

SITE, Inc.
Out of the commonplace [display system of mutable floating walls for Museum of the Borough of Brooklyn] M. Gaskie. il *Archit Rec* 175:162-5 mid-S '87

Sites, Historic *See* Historic houses, sites, etc.

Sites, Industrial *See* Location in business and industry

Sitka region (Alaska)
Description and travel
Alaska's Sitka district. S. Pacher. il map *Mother Earth News* 107:64-71 S/O '87

Sitkovetsky, Dmitry
about
For pianist Bella Davidovich, Dmitry Sitkovetsky is more than just 'my son, the violinist'. D. Chu. il pors *People Wkly* 27:107-9 F 2 '87

Sitler, Linn
Sleuthing around on Easter Island. il *Travel Holiday* 167:62-3 Ja '87

Sitting *See* Posture

Sitting rooms
An Englishman's house in France. D. Bogarde. il por *Archit Dig* 44:22+ F '87
In comfort and style [family sitting rooms; cover story] C. Engle. il *South Living* 22:78-83 N '87

Situation comedy programs *See* Television broadcasting—Comedy programs

Six dances [dance] See Dance reviews—Single works

Six Day War, 1967 *See* Israel-Arab Wars, 1967-

Sixth Committee (United Nations) *See* United Nations. Legal Committee

Sixth force (Physics)
Evidence for new force—may be no. 6. R. Monastersky. *Sci News* 132:388 D 19-26 '87
Tower study hints at a "sixth force". M. Basgall. il *Science* 238:1654-5 D 18 '87

Sixties (Decade) *See* Nineteen hundred and sixties

Size
See also
Clothing and dress—Size
Plants, Size of

Size of body *See* Body size

Size of crowds *See* Crowds

Sizemore, Ralph
about
"Snitty". K. McCafferty. il *Field Stream* 91:44+ Ja '87

Sjöberg, Patrik
about
Sneaking up on the eight-foot barrier. por *Newsweek* 110:49 Jl 13 '87
Sweden's new royal highness. K. Moore. il por *Sports Illus* 67:26-7 Jl 13 '87

Sjögren's syndrome
A new look at dry eyes. J. Tarail. il *McCalls* 115:84 O '87

Skafte, Dianne
Facing fear on the mountain. il *Women's Sports Fitness* 9:78 Ap '87

Skaggs, Robert
about
Robert Skaggs at Jan Cicero. S. Taylor. il *Art Am* 75:143 Ja '87

Skalka, Patricia
Blood: the river of life [cover story] bibl il *Curr Health 2* 14:3-9 D '87
Diane Clark: the mayor of Peace City. il pors *McCalls* 114:134 Ap '87
A doctor's prize catch. il *Read Dig* 130:128-32 Mr '87
Mr. Davis builds his dream house. il por *Read Dig* 131:100-4 S '87

Skall, Terry
Italy's chic showcase. il map *Travel Holiday* 168:50-7 S '87

Skantze, Lawrence A.
B-1B: a timely lesson in risk management. *Aviat Week Space Technol* 126:11 Mr 23 '87

Skateboards and skateboarding
He's not lean but his rap is mean, so the trashers relate to Skatemaster Tate. il pors *People Wkly* 27:155-6 Je 8 '87
Rolling thunder. T. Gabriel. il *Roll Stone* p73-6 Jl 16-30 '87
Teenager Tony Hawk soars above everybody in the scary sport of skateboarding. B. Manning. il pors *People Wkly* 27:48-9 Mr 23 '87
Trouble in paradise [Vancouver's skateboarders] J. O'Hara. il *Macleans* 100:48 Ap 6 '87

Skatemaster Tate
about
He's not lean but his rap is mean, so the trashers relate to Skatemaster Tate. il pors *People Wkly* 27:155-6 Je 8 '87

Skates, Roller *See* Roller skates
Skating
  See also
  Figure skating
  Ice skating
  Speed skating
Skeels, Janet
  (jt. auth) See Daly, Bridget, and Skeels, Janet
Skeet shooting *See* Trapshooting
Skeeter, Brent R.
  (jt. auth) See Cerveny, Randall S., and Skeeter, Brent R.
Skeletal muscle *See* Muscle
Skeleton
  See also
  Maxilla & Mandible (Firm)
  Skull
  We have an obligation to return the Indian skeletal remains in our collections to tribal descendants. R. M. Adams. *Smithsonian* 18:12 My '87
Skewer cooking *See* Barbecue cooking
Skewes, Wilson
    about
  Night lights. S. M. L. Aronson. il *House Gard* 159:56+ F '87
Ski Beech (N.C.: Resort) *See* Resorts—North Carolina
Ski bindings *See* Skis and skiing—Equipment
Ski boots *See* Skis and skiing—Equipment
Ski camping *See* Camping
Ski camps *See* Camps
Ski clothes *See* Clothing and dress—Sports clothes
Ski coaches
  Don't settle for mediocre ski lessons [Interski XIII at Banff, Alta.] W. Grout. il *Skiing* 40:6 O '87
  Killy the instructor. A. H. Greenberg. *Skiing* 39:42 F '87
Ski houses *See* Vacation houses
Ski journalism *See* Sports journalism
Ski jumping
  Cliff jumper [S. Schmidt] E. Perlman. il por *Skiing* 40:34 O '87
  Jump, shoot, ski . . . win [Nordic World Ski Championships silver medalists K. Lynch and J. Thompson] B. Koch. il por *Skiing* 40:42+ S '87
    Study and teaching
  Skiing without snow [Olympic Ski Jump Complex, Lake Placid, N.Y.; cover story] il *Natl Geogr World* 142:3-7 Je '87
Ski lifts
  Uneasy rider. W. Grout. *Skiing* 39:4 F '87
  Up, up, and away! C. Mohler. il *Skiing* 39:70-3 F '87
  Uphill racers. B. Most. il *Pop Mech* 164:57-9 Ja '87
Ski poles *See* Skis and skiing—Equipment
Ski racing
    See also
  Biathlon
  The 10 percent dilemma: coaches say U.S. nordic skiers are too fat. il *Women's Sports Fitness* 9:72 D '87
  Adwoman of the mountain [Grey Advertising account executive and professional ski racer L. Feinberg] J. Seabury. il por *N Y* 20:22 Mr 16 '87
  Canada's long glide to gold [national cross-country ski team; with editorial comment by Kevin Doyle] D. Keefler. il *Macleans* 100:2, 46-7 My 25 '87
  Golden Girl [D. Golden, amputee ski racer] P. Miller. il pors *Skiing* 40:44+ N '87
  A grand slam for the Swiss [World Cup competition] A. H. Greenberg; N. Howe. il *Skiing* 40:236-8+ S '87
  High hopes on the slopes [America's female ski racers] W. Roessing. il *Saturday Evening Post* 259:64-5+ D '87
  Inside racing. C. Cooper. See issues of Skiing beginning September 1985
  Jump, shoot, ski . . . win [Nordic World Ski Championships silver medalists K. Lynch and J. Thompson] B. Koch. il por *Skiing* 40:42+ S '87
  The M & M kids [twins K. and K. Schmidinger] D. B. Witchel. il pors *Skiing* 39:137-8+ Ja '87
  On the edge of greatness: Olympian Pirmin Zurbriggen [cover story] T. Gabriel. il pors *N Y Times Mag* p10-13+ D 27 '87
  Preparing for snowless slopes [Mount Allan as site for 1988 Olympic downhill and slalom races] D. Keefler. il *Macleans* 100:42 Mr 2 '87
  A pro forma year. R. Kahl. il *Skiing* 40:260+ S '87
  Real life on the pro tour. T. Cerkovnik; T. Ahola. il *Skiing* 40:152-3+ D '87
  Rec racing revs up. P. Oliver. il *Skiing* 39:102+ Ja '87

Record-breakers [speed skiing] D. B. Witchel. il *Skiing* 40:272 S '87
Skating into skiing's future [Nordic World Ski Championships in Oberstdorf, West Germany] D. Keefler. il *Macleans* 100:32 Mr 9 '87
Skiing scene. See issues of Skiing
Slouching towards Stowe [Stowe Derby cross country race] P. Knize. il *Skiing* 40:58-9 D '87
Swish went the Swiss [Alpine World Championships] W. O. Johnson. il *Sports Illus* 66:26-30 F 16 '87
Uphill in the downhill [B. Johnson] W. O. Johnson. il pors *Sports Illus* 67:66-8+ D 21 '87
'We do it our way' [pro racing] C. Adgate. il *Skiing* 39:58-60 Spr '87
The world championships [preview] A. H. Greenberg. il *Skiing* 39:84-6 F '87
The World Cup after Lang. A. H. Greenberg. *Skiing* 40:16 S '87
Z-man is a real he-man [P. Zurbriggen clinches third World Cup title] W. O. Johnson. il pors *Sports Illus* 66:42-3 Mr 23 '87
    Economic aspects
Life on the fast track [World Cup skiing circuit] D. Keefler. il *Macleans* 100:34-5 Mr 23 '87
    History
1936: Garmisch-Partenkirchen. N. Howe. il *Skiing* 40:56+ S '87
1956: Cortina D'Ampezzo. N. Howe. il *Skiing* 40:24+ O '87
1968: Grenoble. N. Howe. il *Skiing* 40:24-5+ N '87
1972: Sapporo. N. Howe. il *Skiing* 40:42+ D '87
The race for gold [Olympic champions] W. Bingham. il *Sports Illus* 67:41+ N 23 '87
    Study and teaching
  See Skis and skiing—Study and teaching
Ski racks, Automobile *See* Automobiles—Equipment
Ski resorts *See* Resorts
Ski touring *See* Skis and skiing
Ski tuning *See* Skis and skiing—Maintenance and repair
Skibo, Charles Michael, 1938-
    about
Sprint's new chief has a lot of wires to untangle. M. Ivey. il por *Bus Week* p29 Jl 27 '87
Skidding of automobiles *See* Automobiles—Skidding
Skiers
    See also
  Johnson, Bill
  Lynch, Kerry
  Zurbriggen, Pirmin
Skiing people. See issues of Skiing beginning September 1986
    Accidents and injuries
  See Skis and skiing—Accidents and injuries
    Health and hygiene
It goes to your head [mountain sickness] S. Festa. il *Women's Sports Fitness* 9:10 O '87
    Nutrition
The 10 percent dilemma: coaches say U.S. nordic skiers are too fat. il *Women's Sports Fitness* 9:72 D '87
    Training
Building from the ground up [U.S. Ski Team junior regional program] C. Cooper. *Skiing* 40:26-7 N '87
Power training for explosive turns. R. C. Farentinos. il *Skiing* 40:253-5 O '87
Shape up for the slopes. C. Schaeffer. il *Changing Times* 41:23 D '87
Skiing tip for recreational racers: Circuit training. H. Kashiwa. il *Skiing* 40:48 S '87
Skiing *See* Skis and skiing
Skijaks
Skijak zealot David Kiner has big feet, a dream and at least one oar in the water. il *People Wkly* 28:65 Jl 27 '87
Skill-based pay
Pay-for-knowledge compensation plans: hypotheses and survey results. N. Gupta and others. bibl f il *Mon Labor Rev* 110:40-3 O '87
Skill cranes (Games)
Quarter-eaters. *New Yorker* 63:25-6 S 7 '87
Skilled labor
The great jobs mismatch [need for skilled labor and rise in unskilled workers] R. J. Shapiro. il *U S News World Rep* 103:42-3 S 7 '87
Help wanted [cover story] A. Bernstein. il *Bus Week* p48-53 Ag 10 '87
Jobs without people and people without jobs: the coming mismatch in the information society. W. H. Kolberg. il *USA Today (Periodical)* 116:18-20 Jl '87
Skillet cooking
    See also
  Stir-frying

Skillet cooking—*cont.*
Cook-and-serve skillet set. il *McCalls* 114:149-50+ F '87
Fast & light. il *Redbook* 169:137-42+ My '87
Skillets *See* Kitchen utensils and appliances
Skills, Life *See* Life skills
Skilton, Dave
Onions from seed. il *Rodale's Org Gard* 34:60-1 Ja '87
Skin

> *See also*
> Birthmarks
> Moles (Dermatology)
> Sunburn
> Suntan

Expression of an exogenous growth hormone gene by transplantable human epidermal cells. J. R. Morgan and others. bibl f il *Science* 237:1476-9 S 18 '87
Identification of a T3-associated γδ T cell receptor on Thy-1+ dendritic epidermal cell lines. F. Koning and others. bibl f il *Science* 236:834-7 My 15 '87
New clues to the immune system [photophoresis treatment of lymphatic cancer and immunologic function of skin] S. Squire. il por *N Y Times Mag* p32-3+ F 1 '87

Amphibia

The case of the frog that healed leads Dr. Michael Zasloff to a medical leap ahead. M. Brower. il por *People Wkly* 28:34-5 Ag 17 '87
D-alanine in the frog skin peptide dermorphin is derived from L-alanine in the precursor. K. Richter and others. bibl f il *Science* 238:200-2 O 9 '87
Frog defense: make snakes yawn [neurotoxins in skin of African clawed frogs; research by George T. Barthalmus and William J. Zielinski] S. Weisburd. *Sci News* 132:215 O 3 '87
Frogs get the jump on microbes [research by Michael Zasloff] S. Weisburd. *Sci News* 132:85 Ag 8 '87
Frog's gift to man [Michael Zasloff discovers natural antibiotic in frog skin] il *U S News World Rep* 103:6 Ag 10 '87
Ribbiting evidence [anti-infection peptides in skin of African clawed frog; work of Michael Zasloff] il *Time* 130:31 Ag 10 '87
Skin of frog . . . [natural antibiotic found by Michael Zasloff] T. Beardsley. il *Sci Am* 257:36+ O '87

Cancer

I was too young for skin cancer [melanoma] C. M. Antley. por *Ladies Home J* 104:22+ Je '87
What are your chances of developing skin cancer? *Glamour* 85:160 Jl '87

Causes

> *See also*
> Suntan

Ozone and skin cancer. *Consum Res Mag* 70:13 Jl '87

Diagnosis

Spotting skin cancer before it's too late. I. Pave. il *Bus Week* p82 Jl 27 '87

Prevention

> *See also*
> Suntan products

Saying SCRAM to the sun [Skin Cancer Risk Assessment on Microcomputer] M. Fox. *Health* 19:14 Ag '87

Surgery

Maimed by skin cancer, this onetime sun worshipper paid a painful price for the perfect tan [nose surgery and reconstruction] J. Caprio. il pors *People Wkly* 28:87-8+ Ag 10 '87

Therapy

If you do get skin cancer. F. Lunzer. *Forbes* 139:242 Je 15 '87

Vaccines and vaccination

Taking a shot at melanoma. D. D. Edwards. *Sci News* 132:267 O 24 '87

Care and hygiene

> *See also*
> Cosmetics

Active skin care. G. N. Tusler. il *Good Housekeep* 205:96 O '87
After-sun skin savers. il *Glamour* 85:158-61 Jl '87
Ageproofing our skin: the latest achievements. C. Morris. il *Essence* 18:72-3+ Ag '87
An anti-ageing cream with a new wrinkle: it may work [Retin-A] P. W. Moser. il *Discover* 8:72-6+ Ag '87
Anti-aging beauty: the myths, the facts. S. Sommers. il *Ladies Home J* 104:68+ N '87
Antidote to all those wrinkles? [Retin-A] A. Toufexis. il *Time* 130:90+ D 14 '87
Beautiful skin for life. il *Harpers Bazaar* 120:186-9+ Ap '87
Behind every great face . . . the abc's of beauty control. il *Mademoiselle* 93:184-9 D '87

The bolder shoulder: tips for baring all. il *Mademoiselle* 93:10 Jl '87
Coming clean. il *Seventeen* 46:73-4 Mr '87
Coping with oily skin. il *Glamour* 85:410 S '87
The doctors' guide to guarding your sensitive skin. il *Prevention* 39:33+ O '87
Dry skin, limp hair: fight-back winter beauty strategies. il *Mademoiselle* 93:16 F '87
Facing up! Skin boosters. il *Harpers Bazaar* 120:82 F '87
Facing up to spring. S. Rose. il *Work Woman* 12:96 Mr '87
Fast-track facial. il *Good Housekeep* 205:141 O '87
Flawless skin. il *Harpers Bazaar* 120:130+ Ag '87
Is your skin too touchy? il *Redbook* 168:90-3 Ap '87
Just your type. il *Seventeen* 46:136-9 O '87
Large pores: what you can and can't do about them. S. Young. il *Glamour* 85:326 My '87
Let's glow to the videotape. il *Seventeen* 46:108-11 Ja '87
McCall's guide to skin care. M. Clarke. il *McCalls* 114:27-9 Ap '87
New ways to get rid of wrinkles. S. Berkman. il *Good Housekeep* 204:151 Ja '87
Pamper your working face. H. McCrum. il *Work Woman* 12:114 S '87
Peak performance: skincare [men] il *Harpers Bazaar* 120:30 My '87
Perfect skin: the clean sweep. C. Duhé. il *Harpers Bazaar* 120:214-19+ O '87
The right soap can change your skin. il *Redbook* 170:116-17 N '87
Sexy summer shoulders. il *Glamour* 85:33 Jl '87
Skin care in home spas [use of saunas, whirlpool baths and facial steaming machines] P. Boyer. il *Prevention* 39:58+ Ag '87
Skin-care news you can use right now. il *Glamour* 85:302-3 N '87
Skin in the workplace [special section] il *Vogue* 177:156-61+ Ja '87
Skin progress [special section] il *Vogue* 177:456-61+ Mr '87
Smooth talk. il *Seventeen* 46:167 Ap '87
Solving the beauty and health problems of dry winter air. S. Young. il *Glamour* 85:26 F '87
Stop wrinkles in a wink! P. Boyer. il *Prevention* 39:54+ Je '87
Sun girls' guide to skin care. il *Teen* 31:104-5 My '87
Time out for super skin. il *Teen* 31:60-1 Ja '87
Wash and wear. *FDA Consum* 21:22 Jl/Ag '87
Young skin for life. See issues of Prevention (Emmaus, Pa.) beginning April 1987
Your best look for '87. il *Glamour* 85:166-7 Ja '87
Your diet: clear-skin nutrition. J. S. Stern. *Vogue* 177:362 My '87
Your skin problems solved! C. Straley. il *Parents* 62:105-8 F '87
Your skin's prime time [J. Seymour's regimen; cover story] M. Fox. il pors *Health* 19:40-3 S '87

Diseases

> *See also*
> Acne
> Dandruff
> Psoriasis
> Schistosomiasis
> Warts

Contagious skin diseases: things that go itch in the night. J. Moss. il *Curr Health 2* 14:22-3 S '87
Itchy, scratchy rashes [allergic contact dermatitis] P. Von Nostitz. il *Parents* 62:214+ My '87
Life-saving screening prescribed [skin symptoms of adult-onset diabetes; views of Carl S. Korn] *USA Today (Periodical)* 115:12-13 F '87
Skin deep. E. D. Thomas. il *Outdoor Life* 180:14+ D '87

Therapy

Skin [lumps, bumps, and eruptions] G. Hartzmark. il *Ms* 15:74+ Ap '87

Examination

Skin cancer self-exam. il *Glamour* 85:160-1 Jl '87

Surgery, Plastic

See Surgery, Plastic

Wounds and injuries

> *See also*
> Burns and scalds

Skin, Artificial
Test-tube skin and other high-tech treatments for burns. D. Farley. il *FDA Consum* 21:28-31 Je '87

Skin care products *See* Cosmetics
Skin care products industry *See* Cosmetics industry
Skin diving

Cruising underwater [scuba diving] S. Stapleton. il *Mot Boat Sail* 159:30 My '87

A deadly business [Philippine divers collect venomous snakes for snakeskin trade; with photographs] H. Hall. il *Int Wildl* 17:12-15 Jl/Ag '87

Dive bums [American skin divers in Saba, Dutch West Indies] R. Rothenberg and S. Roy. il *Oceans* 20:38-45 Ja/F '87

Diving for horseshoe crabs. il *Natl Geogr World* 141:20-3 My '87

Encounter under the ice [crabeater seals meet humans off coast of Antarctica] D. Allan. il *Int Wildl* 17:48-51 Mr/Ap '87

Great places to see underseas [snorkeling] L. N. Vreeland. il *Money* 16:76-8+ Mr '87

In deep water [scuba diving off Grand Cayman] J. Mills. il *Women's Sports Fitness* 9:45-9 Jl '87

In the lair of the lusca [Bahamian blue holes] R. Palmer. il *Nat Hist* 96:42-7 Ja '87

The siren of scuba: a top diver bubbles about life at the bottom [S. Earle] D. E. Haupt. il pors *Life* 10:46-51 Je '87

Take a dive [scuba diving] G. Norman. il *50 Plus* 27:32-6 S '87

Vancouver Island's undersea kaleidoscope: a diver's paradise. L. Wood. il *Sea Front* 33:97-104 Mr/Ap '87

Equipment

If you're 20 fathoms down and out of oxygen, the answer is Larry Williamson's Spare Air. il por *People Wkly* 27:65 My 18 '87

Scuba scooter. J. Free. il *Pop Sci* 231:102 N '87

Skin grafting
　See also
　Skin, Artificial

Future 'patchwork' cure for hemophilia? D. D. Edwards. *Sci News* 131:168 Mr 14 '87

Long-term skin graft survival [use of cyclosporin with cadaver skin grafts; work of Bruce Achauer] *USA Today (Periodical)* 115:13 F '87

Test-tube skin and other high-tech treatments for burns. D. Farley. il *FDA Consum* 21:28-31 Je '87

Tolerance induced by thymic epithelial grafts in birds. H. Ohki and others. bibl f il *Science* 237:1032-5 Ag 28 '87

Skin patches *See* Transdermal patches
Skin pigmentation *See* Color of man
Skin regeneration *See* Regeneration (Biology)
Skin tags (Papillomas) *See* Tumors (Benign)
Skinheads *See* Punk culture
Skinner, B. F. (Burrhus Frederic), 1904-

A humanist alternative to A.A.'s twelve steps. *Humanist* 47:5 Jl/Ag '87

Programmed instruction revisited. *Educ Dig* 52:12-16 Mr '87

Skinner, Burrhus Frederic *See* Skinner, B. F. (Burrhus Frederic), 1904-
Skinner, Don Covill

A visit from Rosa Parks: power of the ordinary. *Christ Century* 104:300-1 Ap 1 '87

Skinner, Jeffrey

For Stuart Porter, who asked for a poem that would not depress him further [poem] *Atlantic* 260:54 D '87

The maple keys [poem] *Commonweal* 114:541 S 25 '87

Prayer to cottonmouth blocking the road to the pond [poem] *Commonweal* 114:176 Mr 27 '87

Prayer to sparrow in two seasons [poem] *Atlantic* 259:72 Ja '87

Skinner, Karen J.

(jt. auth) See Young, Frank E., and Skinner, Karen J.

Skinner, Peter

The courage to adapt. il por *Petersens Photogr Mag* 15:36-7+ Ap '87

Return to the Sea of Cortez: following in the wake of John Steinbeck. il map *Petersens Photogr Mag* 15:36-40 F '87

Skinner, Tom

about

Skinner chides youths' ignorance of King legacy. il pors *Jet* 71:16 F 9 '87

Skinning of game *See* Game, Dressing of
Skins *See* Hides and skins
Skipping rope *See* Rope jumping
Skirts (Clothing)

The continuing hemline saga. C. Donovan. il *N Y Times Mag* p58-61 Je 7 '87

Don't let this happen to you [problems encountered wearing miniskirts] il *Glamour* 85:134 N '87

Everyone can wear a mini. il *Ladies Home J* 104:100 O '87

Finally, let there be legs! [miniskirts] M. Smilgis. il *Time* 129:76-7 My 18 '87

Hold on to those hems [miniskirts] J. Conant. il *Newsweek* 109:69-70 Ap 27 '87

How short is too short? The best length for your legs. il *Mademoiselle* 93:52 O '87

How to wear a miniskirt. L. Mosedale. il pors *Glamour* 85:192-3+ D '87

The mini [informal survey on the miniskirt] *New Yorker* 63:23-5 Je 8 '87

Short, sassy, sexy and stylish [miniskirt] A. Steacy. il *Macleans* 100:46-7 Jl 6 '87

Short stuff: skirting the issue . . . *Vogue* 177:166-7 Jl '87

A skirt for all seasons. il *Vogue* 177:330 O '87

Why short is chic. C. Donovan. il *N Y Times Mag* p70-1 Ap 26 '87

Anecdotes, facetiae, satire, etc.

Skinny on the mini. il *People Wkly* 27:111-13 Je 29 '87

Skis and skiing
　See also
　Evolution USA (Firm)
　Helicopters in skiing
　National Brotherhood of Skiers
　Ski lifts
　Skijaks
　Skis and skiing, Children's
　Water skis and skiing

The absolute, pluperfect, most exciting, sublime ski runs in America. Period. il *Esquire* 108:134-8+ N '87

Cross-country skiing . . . changing even faster. il *Sunset* 179:70-3 D '87

Dual-action hummers [sport/racing models] B. Glenne. il *Skiing* 40:168-70+ N '87

Get the perfect fit [women's skis] M. Bhonslay. il *Women's Sports Fitness* 9:23-4+ N '87

Good sports [sport all-around skis] B. Glenne. il *Skiing* 40:232-6+ O '87

Good sports for women. B. Glenne. il *Skiing* 40:168-70+ D '87

How 'standard' are our test skis? B. Glenne. il *Skiing* 40:48 D '87

Inside Skiing. W. Grout. See issues of Skiing beginning September 1986

Making tracks [cross-country] J. B. Harris. il *Black Enterp* 17:145 F '87

The new GS skis. B. Glenne. il *Skiing* 40:142-4+ N '87

Of tykes and patriarchs. A. H. Greenberg. *Skiing* 40:40-1 D '87

Over the river and through the woods [cross country skiing] J. Dostal. bibl il *Women's Sports Fitness* 9:40-4 D '87

Should ski writers ski? A. H. Greenberg. il *Skiing* 39:28+ Ja '87

Skate skiing [cross country technique] R. Hutter. il *Health* 19:18 N '87

Ski the backcountry [national parks] K. Sferra. il *Natl Parks* 61:12-13+ Ja/F '87

Skiing out of a suitcase. D. P. Wiener. il *Fortune* 115:135-6+ Ja 19 '87

Skiing scene. See issues of Skiing

Skis for skating [cross country models] B. Glenne. il *Skiing* 39:142-4 Ja '87

Skis for the quick [slalom models] B. Glenne. il *Skiing* 40:204-6+ O '87

Skis: light, lively, lustrous. B. Glenne. il *Skiing* 40:92-6+ S '87

Snow job [H. Higdon promotes skiing for older people] B. Lindeman. il *50 Plus* 27:6 F '87

Travel. S. Russell. See issues of Skiing beginning November 1985

Update on women's skis. B. Glenne. il *Skiing* 39:35-6 F '87

X-C equipment: a skater's market. I. Devlin. il *Skiing* 40:159-60+ S '87

Accidents and injuries

　See also
　Snowblindness

Skis and skiing—Accidents and injuries—*cont.*
The iron courage of Joni Dunn [victim of serious skiing accident becomes triathlon champion] J. G. Hubbell. il pors *Read Dig* 130:39-44 Ja '87

Clothing and dress
See Clothing and dress—Sports clothes

Competitions
See also
Ski racing
Flying high! [U.S. wins freestyle World Cup] D. B. Witchel. il *Skiing* 40:266+ S '87
The free and the brave [U.S. freestyle team] M.-C. Wrenn. il *Life* 10:97-8 D '87

Economic aspects
Ski discount cards. C. Walter. *Skiing* 40:184+ N '87

Equipment
See also
Rossignol Production (Skis)
1991 and beyond [binding and boot design] C. Ettlinger. il *Skiing* 39:95-7 Spr '87
Accessories: the new wave. D. White. il *Skiing* 40:136-40+ S '87
Bindings report:
The versatile Ess. C. Ettlinger. il *Skiing* 39:81-3 F '87
Bindings: smarter and safer. C. Ettlinger. il *Skiing* 40:125-6+ S '87
Boots: more bang for the buck. C. Meader. il *Skiing* 40:112-16+ S '87
Boots that feel good! [women's gear] M. Bhonslay. il *Women's Sports Fitness* 9:28+ N '87
A cold sun can cook your skin. il *Esquire* 108:132 N '87
Eight boots for the fast lane. C. Meader. il *Skiing* 40:158-60+ O '87
Eight boots to grow on. C. Meader. il *Skiing* 40:150-2+ N '87
The Fit System [proper boot fit] D. Killham. il *Skiing* 39:91-3 Spr '87
The gifted skier. D. White. il *Skiing* 40:138-41 D '87
Glasses for sport. D. White. il *Skiing* 39:53-7 Spr '87
Junior bindings: ins and outs. C. Ettlinger. il *Skiing* 39:120+ Ja '87
Junior boots: how to fit growing feet. R. Kahl. il *Skiing* 39:116-18 Ja '87
Kids' bindings get better. C. Ettlinger. il *Skiing* 40:199-200+ D '87
Marker's Twincam Series [bindings] C. Ettlinger. il *Skiing* 40:225+ O '87
The new Looks [bindings] C. Ettlinger. il *Skiing* 40:211-12+ N '87
Poles: high-tech, high-toned. P. Gordon. il *Skiing* 40:132+ S '87
Space-age bindings [women's gear] M. Bhonslay. il *Women's Sports Fitness* 9:32+ N '87
Sport bindings: ease of entry and exit. C. Ettlinger. il *Skiing* 40:200 O '87
We test six recreational bindings for boot-binding compatibility. C. Ettlinger. il *Skiing* 40:56 D '87
A woman's choice [boots] C. Meader. il *Skiing* 40:104-6+ D '87

Maintenance and repair
Tuning in to your tuner. W. Grout. il *Skiing* 40:6 S '87
Tuning tip:
How should your edges be sharpened? J. Deines. il *Skiing* 40:142 D '87
How to talk to your ski technician. J. Deines. *Skiing* 40:53 S '87
A physical exam for ski bases. J. Deines. *Skiing* 40:41 O '87

Photographs and photography
Linde Waidhofer [interview] M. Corbett. il por *Natl Parks* 61:32-3 Ja/F '87
Shooting the slopes. G. Schaub. il *Pop Photogr* 94:60-7 Ja '87

Resorts
See Resorts

Safety devices and measures
Skiing tip:
Where to stop. P. Jones. il *Skiing* 39:36 Ja '87

Social aspects
The boys of winter. F. Morton. il *N Y Times Mag* p54 Mr 1 '87
Skiing with the guys. C. Ettlinger. il *Work Woman* 12:76-9 F '87

Study and teaching
See also
Ski coaches
Skiers—Training
Sun Valley Trekking (Firm)

Accelerating out of a turn: myth or reality? [racing turns] O. Larsson and B. Glenne. il *Skiing* 39:90-2 F '87
First cousins: V1 and marathon [skating strokes for cross country skiers] B. Koch. il *Skiing* 40:50 O '87
For steep uphills: the diagonal V [skating stroke for cross country skiers] B. Koch. il *Skiing* 40:40 N '87
How to get the most from summer ski camp. C. Cooper. *Skiing* 39:77-8 Spr '87
Offensive or defensive. P. Jones. il *Skiing* 39:145-7 Ja '87
Rx for weak turns [special section] il *Skiing* 40:121-3+ N '87
The secret to long, strong turns. J. Warren. il *Skiing* 39:98-100 Spr '87
Ski-do! [women's ski weeks] J. O'Grady. il *Women's Sports Fitness* 9:15 O '87
Skiing clinic:
A cure for excessive banking; ed. by Doug Smith. D. Larsh. il *Skiing* 40:91 N '87
Needed: more steering of the feet and legs; ed. by Doug Smith. M. Porter. il por *Skiing* 40:48 O '87
Stubborn stems; ed. by Doug Smith. G. Briner. il *Skiing* 40:218 D '87
Skiing tip:
Coping with catwalks. L. Tejada-Flores. il *Skiing* 40:52 O '87
Coping with deep-snow disasters. L. Tejada-Flores. il *Skiing* 40:38 N '87
Coping with flat light. L. Tejada-Flores. il *Skiing* 40:52 D '87
Handling the ice [recreational racing] H. Kashiwa. il *Skiing* 39:32 Ja '87
In bumps, add weight to your pole plants. S. Singleton. il *Skiing* 39:133 Ja '87
Racing drills to sharpen your skills [recreational racing] H. Kashiwa. il *Skiing* 39:26 Spr '87
Taking advantage of ruts [recreational racing] H. Kashiwa. il *Skiing* 39:41 F '87
Skiing tip for recreational racers:
Follow the leader to learn the line. H. Kashiwa. il *Skiing* 40:23 O '87
Mental imagery and position at the gate. H. Kashiwa. il por *Skiing* 40:166 D '87
A pre-race checklist. H. Kashiwa. *Skiing* 40:48+ N '87
Summer ski camps '87. *Skiing* 39:82-7 Spr '87
Switching [skating stroke for cross country skiers] B. Koch. il *Skiing* 40:227 D '87
The turn shape/pole plant connection. C. Ryman. il *Skiing* 40:185+ D '87

Training
See Skiers—Training

Tuning
See Skis and skiing—Maintenance and repair

Alberta
Three by Banff. J. Skow. il *Skiing* 39:44-51 F '87

Antarctic regions
Ski Antarctica. E. Perlman. il *Skiing* 40:32 S '87

Arctic regions
Over the Arctic ice cap [D. Shparo proposes Soviet-Canadian ski expedition] A. Steacy. il por *Macleans* 100:46-7 Ap 6 '87
Solo to the Pole [interview with J.-L. Etienne] il pors *Courier* 40:30-2 Je '87

Argentina
August in the Andes [Valle de las Leñas] A. H. Greenberg. il *Skiing* 39:19-20 Spr '87

Austria
The boys of winter. F. Morton. il *N Y Times Mag* p54 Mr 1 '87

British Columbia
Cat tracks [snowcat skiing] C. Mohler. il *Skiing* 39:52-9 F '87
First tracks in the Gothics [heli-skiing] J. Skow. il *Skiing* 40:224-9+ S '87
Skiing with the guys. C. Ettlinger. il *Work Woman* 12:76-9 F '87

California
See also
Squaw Valley (Calif.)
Haute skiing [ski touring the Sierra High Route in comparison to Europe's Haute Route] D. Robinson. il *Natl Parks* 61:14-19 Ja/F '87

Colorado
See also
Aspen (Colo.)
Snowmass Village (Colo.)
Steamboat Springs (Colo.)
Telluride (Colo.)

Skis and skiing—Colorado—*cont.*
Pure Copper [Copper Mountain ski resort] A. Pospisil. il *Skiing* 40:216-20+ O '87
Purgatory. A. H. Greenberg. il *Skiing* 39:61-4+ F '87
Ski again: a novice skier returns to the slopes [Keystone resort weekend] S. Y. Lopez. il *Black Enterp* 17:144 F '87
Skiing the Creek [Beaver Creek resort] D. Ford. il *Skiing* 40:176+ N '87
Snowcat skiing high in Colorado. il *Sunset* 178:43 F '87
Winter Park. H. Barlow. il *Skiing* 39:46-52 Ja '87
France
See also
Val d'Isère (France)
Variations on a Grand Traverse [Jura Mountains trip] A. Pospisil. il *Skiing* 40:161-4+ N '87
Germany (West)
Gourmet holidays: cross-country skiing from Baden-Baden. P. J. Wade. il map *Gourmet* 47:48-53+ F '87
Idaho
See also
Sun Valley (Idaho)
Maine
Sunday punch [Sunday River Ski Resort] D. Ford. il *Skiing* 40:132-4+ N '87
New York (State)
See also
Lake Placid (N.Y.)
New Zealand
Skiing in dreamland. L. Tejada-Flores. il *Skiing* 39:30-6 Spr '87
North Carolina
Hit the slopes of North Carolina [Ski Beech] il *South Living* 22:10+ Ja '87
Switzerland
See also
Davos (Switzerland)
Grindelwald (Switzerland)
Gstaad (Switzerland)
Utah
Utah powder . . . where the locals ski. il map *Sunset* 178:56-8 F '87
Vermont
I skied Killington in March, April, May, and June. D. Ford. il *Skiing* 39:45-9 Spr '87
Journey to Jay [Jay Peak ski resort] E. Hanson. il *Skiing* 40:116-18+ D '87
A new look at Ascutney. A. H. Greenberg. il *Skiing* 39:54-7+ Ja '87
Stratton ho! L. Tejada-Flores. il *Skiing* 40:182-9 O '87
Western Europe
Haute skiing [ski touring the Sierra High Route in comparison to Europe's Haute Route] D. Robinson. il *Natl Parks* 61:14-19 Ja/F '87
Western States
Cat tracks [snowcat skiing] C. Mohler. il *Skiing* 39:52-9 F '87
Wyoming
Jackson for purists. H. Barlow. il *Skiing* 40:198-202+ S '87
Jackson for tourists. P. Oliver. il *Skiing* 40:198-202+ S '87
Skis and skiing, Children's
'Go, Dad, go'. W. Grout. il *Skiing* 39:4 Ja '87
How to enjoy skiing with your kids. C. Walter. il *Skiing* 39:93-4+ Ja '87
Junior bindings: ins and outs. C. Ettlinger. il *Skiing* 39:120+ Ja '87
Junior boots: how to fit growing feet. R. Kahl. il *Skiing* 39:116-18 Ja '87
Junior skis: blazing boards. B. Gleene. il *Skiing* 39:110+ Ja '87
Kidd's page. B. Kidd. See issues of Skiing beginning September 1984
Kids' bindings get better. C. Ettlinger. il *Skiing* 40:199-200+ D '87
Of tykes and patriarchs. A. H. Greenberg. *Skiing* 40:40-1 D '87
Skiing tip:
Follow-the-leader. E. P. Foster. il *Skiing* 39:38 Ja '87
Winter sports for kids. C. Loomis. il *Parents* 62:284+ N '87
Skiwear *See* Clothing and dress—Sports clothes
Sklar, Ellen, and Carlson, Cathy M.
Foster grandparents go inside prison walls. il *Aging* no356:20-3 '87
Sklute, Ken
about
Pro challenge. il por *Pop Photogr* 94:45 F '87

Skoglund, Sandy, 1946-
about
Sandy Skoglund. il *Life* 10:122-3 O '87
Skolnik, Richard
Test your money smarts [excerpt from Money talks] *Good Housekeep* 204:204 F '87
Skorupa, Joe
Outdoors. See issues of Popular Mechanics beginning July 1987
Skøtt, Ole, and Briggs, Josephine P.
Direct demonstration of macula densa-mediated renin secretion. bibl f il *Science* 237:1618-20 S 25 '87
Skoug, Kenneth N., Jr.
Cuba's growing crisis [address, May 27, 1987] *Dep State Bull* 87:85-90 S '87
A spotlight on Cuba [address, October 22, 1986] *Dep State Bull* 86:81-4 D '86
Skousen, W. Cleon (Willard Cleon), 1913-
about
In God we trust. il por *Time* 129:26 F 9 '87
A word from the right on rights. A. T. Podesta. il por *Progressive* 51:13-14 Jl '87
Skousen, Willard Cleon *See* Skousen, W. Cleon (Willard Cleon), 1913-
Skow, John
"Negative biography": a Who's who for who's not. il *Smithsonian* 18:172 Ap '87
Skowron, Bill, 1930-
Memoirs of a Moose; ed. by Bill Shaw. il pors *People Wkly* 28:103-4+ S 14 '87
Skowron, Moose *See* Skowron, Bill, 1930-
Skreslet, Paula
The prizes of first grade. por *Newsweek* 110:8 N 30 '87
Skrine, Peter
An age of exuberance, drama and disenchantment. il *Courier* 40:4-9 S '87
Skull
Hominoid lineages and keystone clues [Robert B. Eckhardt's challenge to Todd R. Olson's nasal bone theory] B. Bower. il *Sci News* 132:71 Ag 1 '87
Measurement
See Craniometry
Radiography
See Radiography, Medical
Skulme, Džemma, 1925-
about
Comrade artist. A. Stille. il por *Art News* 86:10+ Ja '87
Skunk works (Term)
Murder board at the skunk works. W. Safire. il *N Y Times Mag* p18+ O 11 '87
Skunks
Summer skunks. E. Hoagland. *Nation* 245:149 Ag 29 '87
Anecdotes, facetiae, satire, etc.
The skunked hunt. J. B. Middleton. il *Outdoor Life* 180:86-7+ N '87
Skutch, Alexander Frank, 1904-
about
Indefatigable watcher of nesting birds. il *Audubon* 89:128+ N '87
Škvorecký, Josef
Huckleberry Finn: or, Something exotic in Czechoslovakia. *N Y Times Book Rev* 92:47-8 N 8 '87
Sky
See also
Constellations
Eye on the sky. R. Burnham. See issues of Astronomy beginning May 1986
Summer reverie with Cygnus overhead. J. J. Falout. il *Astronomy* 15:24+ Je '87
Photographs and photography
Astrophotography without a telescope. J. Baumgardt. il *Astronomy* 15:46-51 Ja '87
Photographing the southern sky [cover story] S. Tsang. il por *Astronomy* 15:58-63 Jl '87
Sensational star traces. R. S. Harris. il *Petersens Photogr Mag* 16:62-5+ N '87
Sky photography near the Arctic circle [work of P. Parviainen] D. Di Cicco. il *Sky Telesc* 73:343-5 Mr '87
Spacious sky: double printing makes it always glorious. R. T. Stephens. il *Petersens Photogr Mag* 16:44-6 N '87
Sky and telescope (Periodical)
Bits and bytes [new computer subscription fulfillment system] il *Sky Telesc* 73:427 Ap '87
Who the heck are you, anyway? [subscribers] J. K. Beatty. il *Sky Telesc* 74:572 D '87

Sky charts *See* Astronomy—Charts, diagrams, etc.
Skydiving *See* Parachuting
Skye, Ione
about
Donovan's kid, Ione Skye, gets her feet wet in River's edge. il por *People Wkly* 28.54 Ag 3 '87
New star style! il pors *Harpers Bazaar* 121:178-97 N '87
Ones to watch. il pors *Teen* 31:60 O '87
Skyfox airplanes *See* Airplanes, Training
Skyjacking *See* Airplane hijacking
Skylab missions *See* Space stations—Skylab missions
Skylights
Install your own skylight. R. N. Hoffman. il *Workbench* 43:43-7 S/O '87
Let the sun shine in with a skylight. il *Good Housekeep* 204:224 Ap '87
Let the sun—and stars—shine in. S. Woolley. il *Bus Week* p172 S 14 '87
Reach for the sun. T. O. Bakke. il *Pop Sci* 230:76-9+ Je '87
Simple daylight for a small room. il *Sunset* 178:173 Ap '87
Skylight condensation problem licked. il *Workbench* 43:12 S/O '87
Skylight designs that eliminate common problems. G. Branson. il *Fam Handyman* 37:74+ S '87
A skylight for all seasons [Roto-Lids] D. Stover. il *Pop Sci* 231:70-2 Jl '87
The skylight that's also a table. il *Sunset* 178:178 Ap '87
Skylights: best ways to let the light in. il *Changing Times* 41:16+ Ag '87
Skylights everywhere. il *Sunset* 178:118-19 My '87
Skylights on the floor? il *Sunset* 178:123 F '87
The ultimate "open house". il *Mother Earth News* 104:104-7 Mr/Ap '87
Welcome a slice of sky. il *Mother Earth News* 103:38+ Ja/F '87
Skyscrapers
Protecting skyscrapers against earthquakes [use of fiber reinforced concrete called SIFCON; work of Antoine E. Naaman] *USA Today (Periodical)* 115:3 Je '87
Fires and fire prevention
A net plus for safety, Ralph Baker's Life Chute may save lives in high-rise fires. J. Calio. il por *People Wkly* 28:107-8 Jl 13 '87
History
Top this one: the continuing saga of the tallest building in the world. A. W. Robins. il *Archit Rec* 175:56-8+ Ja '87
Skytrader Corporation
Skytrader develops light utility STOL transport for military use. *Aviat Week Space Technol* 126:27 Ap 6 '87
Slack, Kenneth
London letter. See occasional issues of The Christian Century through October 28, 1987
about
Obituary
Christ Century 104:1053-4 N 25 '87. T. Beeson
Christ Century 104:933 O 28 '87
Slacks *See* Pants
Slam dance [film] *See* Motion picture reviews—Single works
Slamon, Dennis J., and others
Human breast cancer: correlation of relapse and survival with amplification of the HER-2/*neu* oncogene. bibl f il *Science* 235:177-82 Ja 9 '87
Slaney, Mary Decker
about
Back on top? il por *Vogue* 177:132 O '87
Worldclass mom. L. Kramer. il pors *Women's Sports Fitness* 9:28-31 Ap '87
Slang
See also
Jargon
Words, Obscene
Slansky, Paul
Iran-'contra' nostalgia quiz. *New Repub* 197:24-5 Ag 31 '87
Iran-contra quiz. *New Repub* 196:7-9 My 18 '87
What he didn't know. *New Repub* 196:18+ Ja 5-12 '87
Slansky, Rudolf
about
The sons of communism. M. T. Kaufman. il pors *N Y Times Mag* p50+ Mr 8 '87
The Slap Maxwell story [television program] *See* Television program reviews—Single works

Slapton Sands (England)
Monuments, statues, etc.
Requiem for a fiasco [Englishman K. Small's crusade to honor Americans killed in World War II landing maneuvers] M. Brower. il pors *People Wkly* 28:60-5 N 30 '87
Slash-and-burn agriculture *See* Shifting cultivation
Slate tile laying *See* Tile laying
Slater, Helen
about
Making the big screen scene. il pors *Teen* 31:77 Ag '87
Why Helen Slater won't be out-foxed. D. Maychick. il pors *Mademoiselle* 93:72 My '87
Slater, John
History and controversy in the classroom. il *Hist Today* 37:6-7 Ja '87
Slater, Judith
A father's wish [story] il *Redbook* 169:48-50 Jl '87
Slater, Rodney
about
Black appointed to Ark. Highway Commission, hired by Arkansas State Univ. *Jet* 72:15 Ap 13 '87
Rodney Slater, 32, Ark. gov's ex-staffer, gets university post. por *Jet* 72:30 My 18 '87
Slater, Shirley
(jt. auth) *See* Basch, Harry, and Slater, Shirley
Slatkin, Montgomery
Gene flow and the geographic structure of natural populations. bibl f il *Science* 236:787-92 My 15 '87
Slatta, Richard W., 1947-
ScholarNet: the beginning of a world academic community. il por *Futurist* 21:17-19 Mr/Ap '87
Slaughter, Carolyn
The veld. il *Seventeen* 46:101+ D '87
Slaughter, D. French, Jr.
Should the financing of U.S. catastrophic health care emphasize private insurance methods? [excerpts from statement, February 4, 1987] *Congr Dig* 66:108+ Ap '87
Slaughter, Jane, 1941-
A beaut of a shiner. il *Progressive* 51:50 My '87
Mexican auto workers resist cuts. *Progressive* 51:12-13 O '87
Which side are they on? The AFL-CIO tames Guatemala's unions. il *Progressive* 51:32-5 Ja '87
Slaughter, Paul
Your first trip to India. il *Petersens Photogr Mag* 16:26-31 D '87
Slave labor camps *See* Concentration camps
Slave trade
Delete slave ship from Chicago seal: aldermen. il *Jet* 72:4 S 21 '87
Zanzibar
When the music in our parlors brought death to darkest Africa [19th century use of ivory for piano keys] R. Conniff. il *Audubon* 89:76-93 Jl '87
Slavery
See also
Dred Scott case
Slave trade
Celebrating the Constitution: a dissent [excerpt from address, May 6, 1987] T. Marshall. *Harpers* 275:17-19 Jl '87
The Constitution [discussion of May 1987 article, Why blacks, women & Jews are not mentioned in the Constitution] R. A. Goldwin. *Commentary* 84:2+ O '87
The Constitution [excerpt from address, May 6, 1987] T. Marshall. por *Essence* 18:166 S '87
The Constitution and the people left out: a study in original intent. R. A. Goldwin. *Current* 295:4-10 S '87
A failure of nerve? [debate at the Constitutional Convention of 1787] J. Alter. il *Newsweek* 109:65 My 25 '87
Isaac Jefferson: the slave who remembered. B. McGinty. il por *Am Hist Illus* 21:32-3 F '87
Justice Marshall's minority report [asserting that the Constitution helped entrench slavery] T. Gest. il por *U S News World Rep* 102:12-13 My 18 '87
Marshall cites faults of Constitution at 200th year. por *Jet* 72:12 My 25 '87
Public backs Marshall in his views on Constitution [Supreme Court Justice T. Marshall] por *Jet* 72:32 Je 1 '87
The real meaning of the Constitution bicentennial [address, May 6, 1987] T. Marshall. il pors *Ebony* 42:62+ S '87

Slavery—*cont.*

Why blacks, women & Jews are not mentioned in the Constitution. R. A. Goldwin. *Commentary* 83:28-33 My '87

Emancipation

See also

Emancipation Proclamation (1863)

Family and freedom: black families in the American Civil War. I. Berlin and others. bibl f il *Hist Today* 37:8-15 Ja '87

Fugitive slaves

See also

Underground railroad

Songs and music

Frankie and Doug Quimby sing songs of slavery to keep alive the lore of their forebears. D. Grogan. il pors *People Wkly* 28:129-31 O 12 '87

United States

See Slavery

Slavery in insects *See* Insects—Habits and behavior

Slavery in literature

'Five years of terror' [interview with T. Morrison] M. Horn. por *U S News World Rep* 103:75 O 19 '87

The ghosts of 'sixty million and more' [T. Morrison's Beloved] W. Clemons. il *Newsweek* 110:75 S 28 '87

Telling how it was [S. Foote's The Civil War and T. Morrison's Beloved] G. C. Ward. il *Am Herit* 38:14+ D '87

Slavic art *See* Art, Slavic

Slavic civilization *See* Civilization, Slavic

Slavic studies

See also

American Association for the Advancement of Slavic Studies

Slavick, Susanne

about

Susanne Slavick at Struve. M. Bonesteel. il *Art Am* 75:190 O '87

Slavin, Maeve

The birth of a business. il pors *Work Woman* 12:31-3 Ag '87

Slavin, Robert E.

Making Chapter 1 make a difference. bibl f il *Phi Delta Kappan* 69:110-19 O '87

Slavit, Ann

about

Fe fi fo fum! Ann Slavit's boot is a ticket seller's chum. il por *People Wkly* 28:69 D 21 '87

Sled dog racing *See* Dog racing

Sledding *See* Sleds and sledding

Sleds and sledding

See also

Bobsled racing

Dog sleds and sledding

Luge racing

Easy game sled [use of mini-boggans for game transportation] N. Strung. *Field Stream* 92:110 O '87

Old at seventeen. D. Vecsey. il *N Y Times Mag* p50 D 20 '87

Sliding on snow [cover story] R. Kimber. il *Ctry J* 14:76-9 D '87

Snow speedster [toboggan] A. Capotosto. il *Pop Mech* 164:86-9+ D '87

The yearlong search for a perfect sled to ride down Jumbo. P. Stark. il por *Smithsonian* 18:138-42+ D '87

Sleep

See also

Dreams

Insomnia

Nightmares

Snoring

Wakening from sleep

The A to ZZZ of better sleep. L. J. Brown and P. Gadsby. il *Good Housekeep* 204:146-7 Ja '87

All through the night? Not quite [getting children to sleep] E. Klavan. il *Parents* 62:80-4 F '87

Asleep in the cosmos [astronauts] S. J. Nadis. il *Omni* 9:26+ Je '87

Bedtime battles [toddlers] J. T. Gibson. il *Parents* 62:201 My '87

"But I don't want to go to bed!" [children's problems] A. E. Nourse. il *Good Housekeep* 205:134+ S '87

Can toddlers have nap schedules? J. T. Gibson. il *Parents* 62:110 Ja '87

Feeling sleepy? Shhh! Bacteria at work. il *Discover* 8:12 Ap '87

For too many, life is just a snore. S. N. Wellborn. il *U S News World Rep* 102:56-7 Je 15 '87

From yawn to dawn: the science of sweet sleep. il *Prevention* 39:34-6+ Jl '87

Getting bedtime right. J. A. Reimer. il *Parents* 62:95-8 O '87

How to get the kids to go to bed and stay there. J. K. Rosemond. il *Better Homes Gard* 65:109-10 N '87

Nap-time strategies that work. V. Lansky. il *Parents* 62:343-4 N '87

REM sleep: pilot light of the mind? L. Miller. il *Psychol Today* 21:8+ S '87

Sleeping better. *Vogue* 177:474 O '87

The sleepless sportsman. J. Poppy. il *Esquire* 108:71-2 O '87

Sweet dreams are made of this (how to get a good night's sleep). E. Royte. il *Mademoiselle* 93:82 Ja '87

What is this thing called sleep? M. E. Long. il *Natl Geogr* 172:786-821 D '87

Whose bed is it anyway? [children sleeping in parents' bed] L. G. Katz. il *Parents* 62:188 Mr '87

Anecdotes, facetiae, satire, etc.

To sleep, perchance—. M. G. Stoddard. il *Saturday Evening Post* 259:50-1 O '87

Sleep apnea *See* Apnea

Sleep capsules (Modules) *See* Sleeping modules

Sleep positions

An exercise in sleep. il *Natl Geogr* 172:792-5 D '87

Sleep-wake cycles *See* Biological rhythms

Sleeper, Jim

The resegregation of America. il *Commonweal* 114:619-23 N 6 '87

The sleeping beauty [ballet] *See* Ballet reviews—Single works

Sleeping garments *See* Sleepwear

Sleeping modules

See also

Space stations—Sleeping quarters

Is a San Francisco architect's plan to put the homeless in boxes humane or heartless? [D. MacDonald's city sleepers] il por *People Wkly* 28:95 Ag 31 '87

Sleeplessness *See* Insomnia

Sleepwear

The greatest of ease [men's robes and pajamas] il *N Y Times Mag* p42 Mr 15 '87

Sleepy Hollow Educational Centers

Where there's a will: from anger to action [M. Jackson-Randolph's life after losing her children in a fire] B. M. Campbell. il pors *Essence* 18:57-8+ D '87

Sleet, Moneta

about

The artistry of Moneta Sleet Jr. il por *Ebony* 42:66-8+ Ja '87

Sleight of hand [drama] *See* Pielmeier, John

Slesin, Louis

Power lines and cancer: the evidence grows. il *Technol Rev* 90:52-9 O '87

Zapped? *Nation* 244:313 Mr 14 '87

Slicers, Food *See* Food slicers

Slide films *See* Photography—Films

Slide fire escapes *See* Fire escapes

Slide projectors *See* Projectors

Slide shows *See* Slides (Photography)—Projection

Slidell (La.)

Stores

Cross the lake to Slidell. il *South Living* 22:37 Jl '87

Slides (Photography)

Captions

Captions give slides an edge in a competitive marketplace. G. Schaub. il *Pop Photogr* 94:28 My '87

Copying

Improving astrophotos by copying. T. B. Hunter. il *Sky Telesc* 74:326-8 S '87

Editing

Culling the shots: how to edit your marketable photographs. G. Schaub. il *Pop Photogr* 94:30 Ap '87

Processing

A Cibachrome primer [making color prints from slides] W. Levin. il *Petersens Photogr Mag* 15:28-31 F '87

Equipment

Grouper steals the show! A special-effects system incorporates 16 images on just one slide! J. Drafahl and S. Drafahl. il *Petersens Photogr Mag* 15:42-4 Mr '87

High-quality slide-making [ImageMaker] S. R. Reed. il *Pers Comput* 11:156 F '87

Projection

See also

Projectors

Mastering polished audiovisual presentations [client presentations by architects] W. Salisbury. il *Archit Rec* 175:29+ Ap '87

Slides (Photography)—Projection—*cont.*
Producing single-projector slide shows. J. Drafahl and S. Drafahl. il *Petersens Photogr Mag* 15:66-8+ Mr '87
Projecting the past: Lorie Novak portrays memory by projecting slides from her past in empty rooms. S. Piperato. il *Pop Photogr* 94:48-53 Je '87

Storage
Order of business: a step-by-step guide to filing slides. G. Schaub. il *Pop Photogr* 94:18 S '87
Slide rules: tips for storing and protecting your images. G. Schaub. il *Pop Photogr* 94:38 O '87
Ultimate slide management [SlideScribe System] K. Geller-Shinn. il *Petersens Photogr Mag* 15:20 Mr '87

Trimming, mounting, etc.
Who says you should never crop your prints or slides? N. Rothschild. il *Pop Photogr* 94:24 Jl '87

Slides (Water) *See* Water slides
Sliding doors *See* Doors
Slim minnow lures *See* Fishing lures, flies, etc.
Slime feather duster worms *See* Annelids
Slime molds
Antisense RNA inactivation of myosin heavy chain gene expression in Dictyostelium discoideum [cover story] D. A. Knecht and W. F. Loomis. bibl f il *Science* 236:1081-6 My 29 '87
Cell-autonomous determination of cell-type choice in Dictyostelium development by cell-cycle phase. R. H. Gomer and R. A. Firtel. bibl f il *Science* 237:758-62 Ag 14 '87
Cracking the mold [gene targeting and anti-sense techniques used in Dictyostelium myosin research] *Sci Am* 257:26 Ag '87
Disruption of the Dictyostelium myosin heavy chain gene by homologous recombination. A. De Lozanne and J. A. Spudich. bibl f il *Science* 236:1086-91 My 29 '87
Is it a plant? Is it an animal? il *Natl Geogr World* 143:19-23 Jl '87
"Switching" in yeast and slime molds [research by David Soll and others] il *Science* 236:30 Ap 3 '87
Slingshots and slingshooting
Kellogg's "arm extenders" [use of a slingshot in training dogs] L. Mueller. il pors *Outdoor Life* 180:52+ Jl '87
Slip covers *See* Slipcovers
Slipcovers
Reupholster or slipcover a sofa. il *Glamour* 85:310 My '87
Slipped disks *See* Spine—Abnormalities
Slippers *See* Footwear
Slips of the tongue *See* Errors, Speech
Sliwa, Curtis
about
Shapers: a marriage of city-bred Angels. D. O. Relin. il pors *Sch Update* 120:13 D 4 '87
Sliwa, Lisa
about
Lisa Sliwa: brains over brawn. L. Van Buskirk. por *Seventeen* 46:105 Je '87
Shapers: a marriage of city-bred Angels. D. O. Relin. il pors *Sch Update* 120:13 D 4 '87
Staying safe: the smart woman's guide to self-defense. D. Ingber. il pors *McCalls* 145:138+ Mr '87
Sloan, Clifford
Death row clerk. *New Repub* 196:18+ F 16 '87
Sloan, Elizabeth
From our editor. See issues of McCall's beginning March 1986
Sloan, Harry Evans
about
High drama from the folks who brought you Godzilla '85. R. Grover. il pors *Bus Week* p30 S 7 '87
Sloan, John E.
The American folly of courting "Europeanization" [address, September 1, 1987] *Vital Speeches Day* 54:29-32 O 15 '87
A reasonable appeal to reason [address, October 7, 1986] *Vital Speeches Day* 53:168-71 Ja 1 '87
Sloan, Ronald R.
about
A boardroom drama as time ran out for Amfac's CEO. J. B. Levine. il pors *Bus Week* p59 D 7 '87
Sloan-Kettering Cancer Center *See* Memorial Sloan-Kettering Cancer Center
Sloan School of Management
Now Sloan's MBAs will be masters of technology [new dean, L. Thurow] L. Helm. il por *Bus Week* p64 Ap 13 '87

Sloane, Carol
about
Profiles. W. Balliett. pors *New Yorker* 63:72-4+ Ap 6 '87
Sloane, Jeanne Vibert
A Duncan Phyfe bill and the furniture it documents. bibl f il *Antiques* 131:1106-13 My '87
Sloane Rangers
Tayee, Kemo Sabe. W. Safire. *N Y Times Mag* p18 Ag 30 '87
Sloat, Warren
Snakeskin. il *N Y Times Mag* p60 Ja 25 '87
Slocum, George Sigman, 1940-
about
Can Transco wriggle out of the 'take-or-pay' mess? J. E. Davis. il por *Bus Week* p66-7 S 28 '87
Slocum, Milton Jonathan
House calls 2000. *Omni* 9:27 Jl '87
Slogans
Words still matter [advertising slogans] J. A. Trachtenberg. il *Forbes* 139:142 My 4 '87
Slone, Beth
New solutions to old problems. il *Publ Wkly* 232:36 N 13 '87
Slope planting *See* Hillside gardens and gardening
Sloppiness *See* Messiness
Slot machines *See* Gambling machines
Sloth *See* Laziness
Sloths
Oh, it's so nice to have a sloth around the house. J. Hoke. il *Smithsonian* 18:88-92+ Ap '87
Slotkin, Richard, 1942-
about
The Iran arms scandal, says a historian, shows how the power of myth can cloud a president's mind [interview] D. Van Biema. il pors *People Wkly* 27:97-8+ Ja 19 '87
Slotnick, Barry Ivan
about
Slotnick for the defense. P. McKillop. por *Newsweek* 109:62 My 4 '87
Subway shooter Bernhard Goetz is the latest defendant to hire the hottest legal gun in town—Barry Slotnick. K. Gross. il pors *People Wkly* 27:115-16+ My 4 '87
Slovakia (Czechoslovakia)
Description and travel
Slovakia's spirit of survival. Y. Momatiuk and J. Eastcott. il map *Natl Geogr* 171:120-46 Ja '87
Slovenes
The Alpine culture of Slovenia. M. Kmecl. il *Courier* 40:18+ F '87
Slovenia (Yugoslavia)
Civilization
The Alpine culture of Slovenia. M. Kmecl. il *Courier* 40:18+ F '87
Slovic, Paul, 1938-
Perception of risk. bibl f il *Science* 236:280-5 Ap 17 '87
Slovik, Eddie, 1920-1945
about
The example of Private Slovik. B. B. Kimmelman. il pors *Am Herit* 38:97-104 S/O '87
Sloviter, Robert, 1950-
Decreased hippocampal inhibition and a selective loss of interneurons in experimental epilepsy. bibl f il *Science* 235:73-6 Ja 2 '87
Epilepsy hypothesis [discussion of January 2, 1987 article, Decreased hippocampal inhibition and a selective loss of interneurons in experimental epilepsy] bibl f *Science* 238:1292-3 N 27 '87
Slovo, Joe
about
The Red and the black. W. R. Doerner. il por *Time* 129:36 Mr 2 '87
Uncle Joe. S. Mufson. *New Repub* 197:20-3 S 28 '87
Slow learning children
See also
Learning disabilities
Education
Preparing disenchanted students to succeed in society. R. C. Smith. il *USA Today (Periodical)* 116:87-9 N '87
Slower learners need a slower and steady pace. K. Weber. *Educ Dig* 52:51-3 Mr '87
Sloyan, Patrick J.
Iranamok and OPEC. *New Repub* 197:19-21 N 9 '87
SLR cameras *See* Cameras, Single-lens reflex
Slugs
Fight, fight, fight, fight, banana slugs, banana slugs [mascot for University of California, Santa Cruz] J. Stuller. il *Audubon* 89:128-30+ Mr '87

Slugs—*cont.*

Anecdotes, facetiae, satire, etc.

Does creepiness recapitulate phylogeny? J. Gorman. il *Discover* 8:30+ O '87

Control

Snail strategy and sympathy. *Sunset* ' 8:180 Mr '87

Slugs, Sea *See* Sea slugs

Sluka, James P., and others

Synthesis of a sequence-specific DNA-cleaving peptide. bibl f il *Science* 238:1129-32 N 20 '87

Slumber parties *See* Entertaining

Slums

See also

Squatter settlements

"His slum, not mine" [Manila] E. A. R. Ouano. il *World Health* p10-11 Jl '87

The slum behind the Sheraton. J. DeParle. il *Wash Mon* 19:32-44 D '87

Slye, Leonard Franklin *See* Rogers, Roy, 1912-

SM *See* Sadomasochism

Smale, John Gray, 1927-

about

Luv that market. B. Saporito. il por *Fortune* 116:56 Ag 3 '87

Parks, Smale feted at annual UNCF gala held in New York City. il pors *Jet* 72:12-13 Ap 6 '87

Small, Deborah

about

Deborah Small. L. Goldman. il *Art News* 86:33 Mr '87

Small, G. J.

(jt. auth) See Jankowiak, R., and Small, G. J.

Small, Ken

about

Requiem for a fiasco. M. Brower. il pors *People Wkly* 28:60-5 N 30 '87

Small, Linda Lee

Home-based business—a moving experience. il pors *Ms* 16:76+ S '87

Small, Stephen, d. 1987

Kidnapping

Kidnappers: the 'dumb' and deadly. il por *U S News World Rep* 103:14 S 21 '87

Small, W. Clem

Certification for electronics technicians. il *Radio-Electron* 58:52-4 Ag '87

Small business

See also

Cottage industries

Entrepreneurs

Franchise system

Incubators (Entrepreneurship)

Minority business enterprises

National Business League

Self employed

Women entrepreneurs

Computerizing your business [special section] il *Work Woman* 12:33+ S '87

Computers in small business [tables] P. Honan. il *Pers Comput* 11:277 S '87

Enterprise. See issues of Working Woman beginning September 1983

Enterprise. G. D. Wallace. See issues of Business Week beginning July 27, 1987

How to delegate when there's no one to delegate to [small businesses using outside service contractors] E. Alvarez. il *Work Woman* 12:51-2 F '87

Keeping up in the fast lane. N. L. Croft. il *Nations Bus* 75:24-6 Jl '87

A reasonable appeal to reason [address, October 7, 1986] J. E. Sloan. *Vital Speeches Day* 53:168-71 Ja 1 '87

Small business report. See issues of Nation's Business beginning February 1984

Start-up help for your business. R. R. Roha. il *Changing Times* 41:73-4+ Je '87

Tapping a growth market [cooperation between small and large firms; views of David Birch] il *Nations Bus* 75:14 Jl '87

Winning your own game [cover story] R. Thompson. il *Nations Bus* 75:16-17+ Jl '87

Accounting

New niche for accountants [part-time controller service] il *Nations Bus* 75:12 Ja '87

Taking off by the numbers. M. Leepson. il *Nations Bus* 75:48-50 Ag '87

Advertising

See Advertising

Directories

Hot growth companies [cover story; special section] il *Bus Week* p82-6+ My 25 '87

List of opportunity? [200 best small companies in America] P. Newcomb. il *Forbes* 140:194-5+ N 16 '87

Export-import trade

Helping small firms compete [Small Business Trade Competitiveness and Innovation Act] *Nations Bus* 75:12 Je '87

Sell abroad; you can collect [use of factoring agents] S. Golob. il *Nations Bus* 75:44+ N '87

Federal aid

See also

United States. Small Business Administration

Blueprint for competitiveness [Making America work again: jobs, small business and the international challenge] il *Nations Bus* 75:12 My '87

Finance

See also

Small business investment companies

Venture capital

Business outlook '87 [special issue] il *Nations Bus* 75:16-17+ Ja '87

The economy according to small business. H. S. Braun. il *Nations Bus* 75:42-4+ My '87

Finding a capital way to finance your company. B. Robson. il *Black Enterp* 17:274 Je '87

How healthy is your business? M. Stevens. il *Work Woman* 12:39-42 Ja '87

How to find under $1 million [cover story] R. Thompson. il *Nations Bus* 75:14-16+ N '87

Keeping your business afloat [avoiding bankruptcy] N. L. Croft. il *Nations Bus* 75:16-18+ F '87

A new bond for small business [Citytrust Capital Market industrial development bonds] R. W. King. *Bus Week* p109 Je 1 '87

Small-business confidence: looking good at home. H. S. Braun. il *Nations Bus* 75:32-3+ N '87

The year of living dangerously [first year for start-ups] D. Harris. il *Money* 16:162-6 F '87

Statistics

Hot growth companies [cover story; special section] il *Bus Week* p82-6+ My 25 '87

List of opportunity? [200 best small companies in America] P. Newcomb. il *Forbes* 140:194-5+ N 16 '87

Little giants. J. H. Dobrzynski. il *Bus Week* Sp Issue:38+ Ap 17 '87

Information services

Small business on a recharge [Statistics Canada's Small Business Database] D. Cohen. por *Macleans* 100:9 Ap 27 '87

Laws and regulations

The American folly of courting "Europeanization" [address, September 1, 1987] J. E. Sloan. *Vital Speeches Day* 54:29-32 O 15 '87

Heeding Equal Access [Equal Access to Justice Act] il *Nations Bus* 75:12 D '87

Small business and Congress [lobbying priorities] R. Thompson. il *Nations Bus* 75:9+ Mr '87

Taxation

The 10 most asked tax reform questions. M. Moktarian. il *Nations Bus* 75:28-9+ Ag '87

Estimated tax trauma. G. W. Padwe. *Nations Bus* 75:44 Je '87

For entrepreneurs. il *U S News World Rep* 103:82 D 7 '87

The new tax law: what it means for your business. M. Stevens. il *Work Woman* 12:39-42 Mr '87

Paperwork burden grows. *Nations Bus* 75:102-3 S '87

There are 100 ways to raise your taxes—and Congress is looking at all of them. il *Nations Bus* 75:80 O '87

When tax reform clobbers small business [interest rates may soar on industrial development bond loans] L. Helm. il *Bus Week* p41 My 4 '87

Year-end tax strategies for smalls. J. C. Szabo. il *Nations Bus* 75:42-3 D '87

Canada

Small business on a recharge [Statistics Canada's Small Business Database] D. Cohen. por *Macleans* 100:9 Ap 27 '87

Hawaii

The aloha spirit of enterprise. S. Nelton. il *Nations Bus* 75:6 Ag '87

Slow and steady wins the race [C. K. Nishioka] R. Thompson. il pors *Nations Bus* 75:63-4 Ag '87

Latin America

Do-gooders who really do good [Accion International] P. Duggan. il *Forbes* 140:117-18 N 30 '87

Western Europe

Europe's new entrepreneurs. R. I. Kirkland, Jr. il *Fortune* 115:253+ Ap 27 '87

Small business, Sale of
Just merged [cover story] K. Berney. il *Nations Bus* 75:30-2+ D '87
Small Business Administration (U.S.) *See* United States. Small Business Administration
Small business brokers
See also
Geneva Business Services, Inc.
Small business investment companies
Finding capital in the tax reform era [minority enterprise small business investment companies] M. King. il *Black Enterp* 17:60-5 Ap '87
Small business lobby *See* Lobbyists and lobbying
Small cell cancer of the lung *See* Lungs—Cancer
Small claims courts
How to succeed in small-claims court. T. Hauser. il *McCalls* 114:64 Je '87
Small farms *See* Farms, Small
Small Press Expo *See* Book fairs
Small presses *See* Publishers and publishing
Small schools *See* School enrollment
Small town life *See* Village life
Small Waters (Firm)
Getting your feet wet. G. Norman. il *Esquire* 107:28 My '87
Smallmouth bass fishing *See* Bass fishing
Smallpox
Smallpox: never again! [cover story; special issue] il *World Health* p1-25 Ag/S '87
Vaccines and vaccination
Smallpox showed the world the way. J. F. Wickett. il *World Health* p26-7 Ja/F '87
Smalls, Charlie, 1943-1987
about
Obituary
Jet 72:56 S 21 '87
Smalltalk (Computer language)
Smalltalk/V release 1.2. M. Davis. *Byte* 12:256+ Je '87
Smallwood, Christopher, and Cassidy, John
The world after Volcker. il *World Press Rev* 34:44-5 Ag '87
Smallwood, Joseph R., 1900-
about
Support for a legend. *Macleans* 100:25 F 2 '87
Smardo, Frances A.
Helping children adjust to moving. bibl f il *Child Today* 16:10-13 My/Je '87
Smart, Jean
about
Those remarkable Designing women. H. Yorkshire. il pors *McCalls* 115:78-9+ N '87
Smart, Keith
about
How Indiana got Smart. B. Newman. il pors *Sports Illus* 67 Sp Issue:14-16 N 18 '87
Smart shot. S. Krasnow. il por *Sport Mag* 78:9 D '87
Smart cards *See* Memory cards
Smart houses *See* Computers—Home use
Smart machines *See* Computers
Smart modems *See* Modems
Smeal, Eleanor
The ERA: should we eat our words? *Ms* 16:170+ Jl/Ag '87
about
A new battlefield for NOW's fearless leader. por *Newsweek* 110:30-1 Jl 20 '87
Smell
See also
Aroma therapy
Odors
Are we led by the nose? T. Monmaney. il *Discover* 8:48-54+ S '87
Isolation of an olfactory cDNA: similarity to retinol-binding protein suggests a role in olfaction. K.-H. Lee and others. bibl f il *Science* 235:1053-6 F 27 '87
Maternal scents [mothers most likely to recognize new-borns by smell] E. Comte. *Health* 19:26 N '87
Mmmmm . . . the emotional sense. K. Levine. il *Parents* 62:106-10 Je '87
New routes to early memories [split brain research] D. Kucharski and W. G. Hall. bibl f il *Science* 238:786-8 N 6 '87
Nosy readers [results of survey] K. McKinney. il *Omni* 9:18 My '87
Pheromone components and active spaces: what do moths smell and where do they smell it? C. E. Linn, Jr. and others. bibl f il *Science* 237:650-2 Ag 7 '87
Retriever scent training. L. Mueller. il *Outdoor Life* 179:52+ Mr '87

Scents of encounter [special section] il *Vogue* 177:322-9+ My '87
Smell and tell [odor and memory; studies by Trygg Engen] H. Hall. *Psychol Today* 21:11 Ag '87
The smell of fear [rats; research by Michael Fanselow] P. Chance. *Psychol Today* 21:16 Jl '87
The smell results: survey. A. N. Gilbert and C. J. Wysocki. il *Natl Geogr* 172:514-25 O '87
Throwing fish off the scent [acid water and salmon's sense of smell] S. Begley. il *Natl Wildl* 25:12 F/Mr '87
Smelters
Environmental aspects
The death of Ducktown [desert created in Tennessee 100 years ago when copper smelter fumes killed vegetation] W. Barnhardt. il map *Discover* 8:34-6+ O '87
Smetana, Bedřich, 1824-1884
about
Prague's Smetana Museum. J. F. Lee. il *Travel Holiday* 167:84 Ja '87
Smetana Museum (Prague, Czechoslovakia)
Prague's Smetana Museum. J. F. Lee. il *Travel Holiday* 167:84 Ja '87
Smikle, Ken
Chicago: the Second City pushes to be no. 1. il *Black Enterp* 17:60-2 My '87
Smil, Vaclav
China's standing in the developing world. bibl f il *Curr Hist* 86:245-8+ S '87
Smile [musical] *See* Musicals, revues, etc.—Reviews—Single works
Smiles, Samuel, 1812-1904
about
Samuel Smiles: the gospel of self-help. A. Briggs. bibl il *Hist Today* 37:37-43 My '87
Smiles
The enigmatic smile. M. Konner. il *Psychol Today* 21:42-4+ Mr '87
The first smile [excerpt from The first six months] P. Leach. il *Good Housekeep* 205:120 S '87
Put a smile on your face. S. Perry. il *Curr Health 2* 14:14-15 O '87
Smile if you want to find this funny [research by Fritz Strack] *Discover* 8:18-19 N '87
Smiley, Daniel
about
A man ahead of his time. M. Winerip. il por *Natl Wildl* 25:10 F/Mr '87
Smiley, Jane
Long distance [story] il *Atlantic* 259:68-75 Ja '87
Smith, Adam, 1930-
Passage at Cape Horn. il pors *Esquire* 107:88-90+ Mr '87
Unconventional wisdom. See issues of Esquire
Smith, Agnes M.
The first Mormon mission to Britain. bibl il *Hist Today* 37:24-31 Jl '87
Smith, Albert E.
about
Dr. A.E. Smith installed as S.C. State president; Sammy Davis gives speech. il pors *Jet* 72:29 Mr 30 '87
Smith, Allen B.
The photogenic art of dance in the studio and on the stage. il *Petersens Photogr Mag* 16:32-3+ Ag '87
Smith, Allison
about
Off-screen with Allison Smith. R. N. Thomas. il pors *Teen* 31:78-9 Jl '87
Smith, Andrew V.
AIDS: a corporate attitude [address, October 14, 1987] *Vital Speeches Day* 54:113-15 D 1 '87
Smith, Antony
Storm window [poem] il *America* 157:480 D 19 '87
Smith, Arthur
The least of things [poem] *New Yorker* 63:30 Jl 6 '87
Smith, Arthur E.
about
Venice-on-the-Hudson. P. Warner. il por *Archit Dig* 44:140-7+ N '87
Smith, Blackwell
Priorities in a military culture. il *Bull At Sci* 43:9-10 Je '87
Smith, Bob, 1917-
I remember Howdy; ed. by Cable Neuhaus. il pors *People Wkly* 28:149-50+ N 30 '87
Smith, Bradford A.
about
Interview. R. Schultz. il pors *Omni* 9:66-8+ F '87

Smith, Brian Abel- *See* Abel-Smith, Brian
Smith, Bubba
about
Ex-NFL star Bubba Smith wants to own Balt. team. por *Jet* 72:46 Ag 24 '87
Smith, Cassandra L., and others
A physical map of the Escherichia coli K12 genome. bibl f il *Science* 236:1448-53 Je 12 '87
Smith, Charles
"The children I could never forget"; ed. by Maria Karazianis. il pors *Redbook* 170:30+ N '87
Smith, Charles A.
Nurturing kindness through storytelling. *Educ Dig* 53:53-5 S '87
Smith, Charlie, 1947-
The holly tree [poem] *Nation* 245:387 O 10 '87
Indistinguishable from the darkness [poem] *New Yorker* 63:42 My 11 '87
Smith, Christopher J.
The geography of drinking. il map *Focus* 36:16-23 Wint '86
Smith, Craig R.
Should Congress approve the Fairness Doctrine? [excerpts from testimony, March 18, 1987] *Congr Dig* 66:251+ O '87
Smith, Dave, 1942-
Crab house [poem] *Atlantic* 260:76 N '87
New Year's Day [poem] *Nation* 245:659 N 28 '87
Smith, Dave, 1955-
about
Tossed on the waves. A. Keteyian. il por *Sports Illus* 67:36 D 14 '87
Smith, David Jeddie *See* Smith, Dave, 1942-
Smith, David Lionel
New books on black music. il *Black Enterp* 18:37 Ag '87
Smith, David R.
Your move, General Lee. il *Americana* 14:66-9 Ja/F '87
Smith, Debbi Kempton- *See* Kempton-Smith, Debbi
Smith, Dinitia
Art fever: the passion and frenzy of the ultimate rich man's sport [cover story] il *N Y* 20:34-43 Ap 20 '87
'Hey, bro'er!' It's William F. Buckley Jr. il pors *N Y* 20:36-42 Jl 27 '87
The Raj duet. il pors *N Y* 20:58-60+ O 5 '87
Tough guys make movie. il pors *N Y* 20:32-5+ Ja 12 '87
Smith, Doug
(ed) *See* Briner, Gordon. Stubborn stems
(ed) *See* Larsh, Don. A cure for excessive banking
(ed) *See* Porter, Mike. Needed: more steering of the feet and legs
Smith, Douglas H., and others
Blocking of HIV-1 infectivity by a soluble, secreted form of the CD4 antigen. bibl f il *Science* 238:1704-7 D 18 '87
Smith, Dustin Beall
A promise of renewal. il *N Y Times Mag* p52 F 15 '87
Smith, E. G.
about
E.G. Smith, sockmeister. L. Grunwald. il pors *Esquire* 107:F41+ Mr '87
Smith, Eleanor, 1954-
How flexible should you be? il *Women's Sports Fitness* 9:10 S '87
Life search. il *Omni* 9:32 Je '87
Windows on the mind. il *Omni* 9:92-6 My '87
Winter in Antarctica: health despite discomfort. il *Psychol Today* 21:60-1 Mr '87
Smith, Emmitt
about
Growing up fast. R. Telander. il pors *Sports Illus* 67:44-6+ N 16 '87
Smith, Etta Louise
about
Etta Smith's inspiration cost her four days in jail. J. Kelley. il por *People Wkly* 27:33 My 25 '87
Smith, Frederick W., 1944-
about
The man in the pilot's seat. il por *Fortune* 116:35 Ag 17 '87
Why Federal Express has overnight anxiety. D. Foust. il *Bus Week* p62+ N 9 '87
Smith, Gary
A bout against doubt. il pors *Sports Illus* 66:76-80+ Je 8 '87
The corner man. il pors *Sports Illus* 67:92-6+ N 2 '87

The fiesta in the town of ghosts. il *Sports Illus* 67:76-80+ O 5 '87
Joe Biden in the crunch. il pors *Life* 10:78-80+ O '87
Smith, Gavin
Post-mod squad. il por *Film Comment* 23:24-9 N/D '87
Smith, George P., II
Jimmy Carter's judges [excerpt from The judges war] il *Natl Rev* 39:44+ O 23 '87
Smith, George Williams
about
Check six, George. M. Trahan. *Flying* 114:104 F '87
Smith, Geri
Brasília: shapes of the future. il *Américas* 39:31-7 N/D '87
Smith, Grub
Assaults on the British novel. *New Leader* 70:17-18 D 14 '87
Literary London. *New Leader* 70:20-1 My 4-18 '87
Smith, Hal
Deer ranching: do fallow deer offer hope for struggling farms? il *Ctry J* 14:48-53 N '87
Smith, Hanna
Don't forget them after Christmas. por *U S News World Rep* 103:5 D 21 '87
Smith, Hedrick
Gorbachev's shrewd summitry. il *N Y Times Mag* p50-1+ D 6 '87
Those fractious Republicans. il *N Y Times Mag* p30+ O 25 '87
Smith, Henry
about
Dream comes true for St. Louis man who won $2 million in lottery. il por *Jet* 72:6 S 21 '87
Smith, Henry C.
Islands in the sun. il *World Health* p21-2 Ja/F '87
Smith, Henry Nash, 1906-1986
about
The American studies of Henry Nash Smith. R. Bridgman. *Am Sch* 56:259-68 Spr '87
Smith, Herbert L., Jr.
(tr) *See* Bekaert, Geert. An unexpected surprise
Smith, Hughie Lee- *See* Lee-Smith, Hughie
Smith, Ilan Mitchell- *See* Mitchell-Smith, Ilan
Smith, J. J. B.
(jt. auth) *See* Schmidt, J. M., and Smith, J. J. B.
Smith, Jackie
Reflections of a peer mentor. *Child Today* 16:21 Jl/Ag '87
Smith, Jackie L., 1940-
about
The whole game in their hands. D. Whitford. il por *Sport Mag* 78:25-8 F '87
Smith, Jaclyn
about
Black earth bounty. P. H. Johnson. il por *Rodale's Org Gard* 34:38-40+ F '87
Smith, James
about
Bonecrusher says he is immune to Mike 'Tysonitis'. il por *Jet* 71:50 Mr 2 '87
Boning up for a battle. C. Gammon. il pors *Sports Illus* 66:46-9 Mr 2 '87
First college graduate becomes a boxing champion. N. O. Unger. il pors *Jet* 71:51-3 Ja 19 '87
New champs' date with destiny promises action; Loss least of woes for Tim Witherspoon. il pors *Jet* 71:48 Ja 12 '87
They could have danced all night . . . il pors *Sports Illus* 66:20-1 Mr 16 '87
Tip from Ali helped Smith survive onslaught of Tyson, who cracked his ribs. il pors *Jet* 72:48 Mr 30 '87
Tyson wins 2nd crown, works harder at party. il pors *Jet* 71:52-4 Mr 23 '87
Smith, James Todd *See* L. L. Cool J
Smith, Jaynie
Getting set for a sibling. il *Good Housekeep* 205:132 S '87
Smith, Jeff
about
Feasting on herbs in the midst of love: a conversation with Jeff Smith. P. P. Allen. por *Christ Century* 104:1087-90 D 2 '87
Preaching the word about food. L. Shapiro. il por *Newsweek* 109:58+ My 9 '87
With two best-sellers, a hot show and a happy home, frugal gourmet Jeff Smith is cooking on all burners. N. Geeslin. il pors *People Wkly* 27:101-2 F 23 '87
Smith, Jeff
Ministering to the collective soul amid the arms race. il *Christ Century* 104:17-20 Ja 7-14 '87

Smith, Jeff—*cont.*
Reagan, Star Wars, and American culture. bibl f il *Bull At Sci* 43:19-25 Ja/F '87
Smith, Joan Liebmann- *See* Liebmann-Smith, Joan
Smith, Joe
about
Joe Smith named head of Capitol/EMI. A. DeCurtis. *Roll Stone* p11+ F 12 '87
Smith, John H.
about
Prichard, Ala.'s Smith is black mayors' leader. por *Jet* 72:24 My 18 '87
Smith, Joshua L.
about
California college boss quits; blames red tape. *Jet* 72:38 S 14 '87
Smith, Julia Woodel
about
One day in August. R. E. Parrott. *Christ Century* 104:679-80 Ag 12-19 '87
Smith, June
about
Woman bites dog. E. Giltenan. il por *Forbes* 140:198 S 21 '87
Smith, Karen Sue
Imprisoned in limbo. *Commonweal* 114:552-3 O 9 '87
Sex education: a matter of body & soul. il *Commonweal* 114:206-10 Ap 10 '87
What's become of the pastoral? il *Commonweal* 114:742-7 D 18 '87
Smith, Kate, 1909-1986
about
For Kate Smith, death alone isn't grounds for burial. il por *People Wkly* 27:77 Je 15 '87
Pygmalion. *New Yorker* 63:33-5 O 19 '87
Smith, Kathy, and Coufal, James E.
Wanakena—the New York State Ranger School. il *Conservationist* 42:42-5 S/O '87
Smith, Keith
about
Keith Smith, gold's raging bull. R. A. Melcher. il por *Bus Week* p70-1 Je 22 '87
Smith, Lee, 1944-
Love the ones you're with [story] il *Redbook* 169:48+ Ag '87
Smith, Lee
Goodbye consensus: divisiveness in Japan. *Current* 294:30-3 Jl/Ag '87
Smith, Lee N., 1951-
about
Lee Smith at Contemporary Arts Museum. S. Kalil. il *Art Am* 75:145 Mr '87
Smith, Leila, d. 1987
about
Obituary
Jet 71:52 Mr 2 '87
Smith, Leon Polk, 1906-
about
Leon Polk Smith at Ruth Siegel. R. G. Edelman. il *Art Am* 75:218-19 Ap '87
Smith, Libby
A focus on oil and hazardous materials spills. il *Conservationist* 41:46-9 Ja/F '87
Smith, Libby, and Stegemann, Eileen
Cleaner waters pay off in better fishing. il *Conservationist* 41:6-15 Mr/Ap '87
Smith, Linda Brown
about
The heirs of Oliver Brown: in Topeka, a landmark equality case is still before the courts. J. E. White. il por *Time* 130:88-9 Jl 6 '87
Smith, Liz
Dawn Steel: the most powerful woman in Hollywood [interview] por *Vogue* 177:210-11+ Ja '87
Elaine Stritch: "I've decided the reason I work well with Woody Allen is that he's got my number" [interview] il por *Vogue* 177:174+ D '87
Scoop du jour [interview with N. Collins] il por *Vogue* 177:352-3+ Ap '87
Smith, Lloyd Mason
Automated DNA sequence analysis. bibl f *Science* 235 pt2:G89 F 27 '87
Smith, Lonnie
about
Royals promote Smith, but he's no millionaire. *Jet* 72:48 Ag 3 '87
Smith, Lorin
Say, brother. por *Essence* 18:10+ Jl '87

Smith, Mandy
about
Her first Stone casts teen model Mandy Smith into the limelight. por *People Wkly* 27:105 F 23 '87
Smith, Marcia S.
Lessons unlearned: space policy after Challenger. il *Space World* X-10-286:21-3 O '87
Smith, Marjorie
A matter of interpretation. por *Newsweek* 110:9 D 14 '87
Smith, Martin Cruz
Interview [R. Gale] il pors *Omni* 10:110-12+ O '87
Smith, Mary C.
The gardening secrets of a glad man. il *Flower Gard* 31:10+ Je/Jl '87
Smith, Mary Lee, and Shepard, Lorrie A.
What doesn't work: explaining policies of retention in the early grades. bibl f il *Phi Delta Kappan* 69:129-34 O '87
Smith, Melba
(jt. auth) See McRae, Dianne, and Smith, Melba
Smith, Michael
about
Common name, uncommon talent. J. Garrity. il por *Sports Illus* 67 Sp Issue:83 N 18 '87
Smith, Mikki
Playing the egg game. il *Mother Earth News* 108:22 N/D '87
Smith, Nate
about
Pittsburgh's Nate Smith shot in hip near diner. por *Jet* 72:10 Ag 31 '87
Smith, Owen
about
A one-man recycling program. P. H. Johnson. por *Rodale's Org Gard* 34:94-5 S '87
Smith, Ozzie
about
No.1 in his field. R. Fimrite. il pors *Sports Illus* 67:60-9 S 28 '87
Raines, Smith resemble black gold as N.L. stars. pors *Jet* 72:50 Ag 3 '87
The secret of my new success. J. Coplon. il pors *Sport Mag* 78:50-1+ N '87
Smith, Patrick
about
The boss said no. B. Leonard. il por *Forbes* 139:94+ F 9 '87
Smith, Patrick J., 1932-
. . . Uncle Sam's way. il *Opera News* 51:10-12 Ja 31 '87
Smith, Patti
about
Patti Smith, Patty Smyth: how to tell them apart. J. Powell. pors *Glamour* 85:158 Je '87
Patti Smith: songs from a marriage. L. Robinson. por *Vogue* 177:130 Mr '87
Smith, Paul
about
Mr. Smith comes to New York. B. Boehlert. il por *N Y* 20:28 Ap 20 '87
Smith, Paul H.
Terminal culture? "The British Edge". il *Art Am* 75:36-9+ S '87
Smith, Paul J.
American craft: poetry of the physical. il *USA Today (Periodical)* 116:74-85 S '87
about
Consummate connoisseur. R. Kehlmann. il por *Am Craft* 47:50-5 O/N '87
Paul Smith named director emeritus of museum. *Am Craft* 47:6 Je/Jl '87
Smith, Peter H.
Uneasy neighbors: Mexico and the United States. bibl f *Curr Hist* 86:97-100+ Mr '87
Smith, Philip
Exploring Patagonia's ranges. il map *Américas* 39:8-15 Jl/Ag '87
Smith, Preston
Washington report. See issues of Successful Farming beginning April 1987
Smith, R. C.
Preparing disenchanted students to succeed in society. il *USA Today (Periodical)* 116:87-9 N '87
Smith, Rachel Richardson
Swordplay in Sunday school. por *Newsweek* 110:9 D 21 '87
Smith, Richard A.
about
The new show at Neiman-Marcus. J. P. Newport, Jr. il por *Fortune* 115:103-4+ Ap 27 '87

Smith, Richard A. (Richard Allan), 1951-, and others
Water-quality trends in the nation's rivers. bibl f il maps *Science* 235:1607-15 Mr 27 '87
Smith, Richard Liebmann- *See* Liebmann-Smith, Richard, 1942-
Smith, Robert
about
The Cure's Robert Smith likes his music to shake you up. E. Miller. il por *Seventeen* 46:88+ Ap '87
Smith, Robert A.
about
London journal. J. Bainbridge. il *Gourmet* 47:28+ My '87
Smith, Roger B.
about
The $750 million muzzle. D. Sherman. il *Car Driv* 32:7 Mr '87
Detroit. P. Lienert. il pors *Road Track* 38:110 Mr '87
General Motors: what went wrong. W. J. Hampton and J. R. Norman. il *Bus Week* p102-8+ Mr 16 '87
It's no fun running no. 1 when you're taking heat. A. L. Taylor, III. il por *Fortune* 116:26-7 Ag 3 '87
Roger Smith. W. J. Hampton. il por *Bus Week* Sp Issue:232 Ap 17 '87
Roger Smith speaks out. J. Flint. il por *Forbes* 140:33 Ag 24 '87
The shadow of Mr. Sloan. il pors *Forbes* 139:10-11 Ja 26 '87
Smith, Ron
Leaving forever [poem] *Nation* 244:264 F 28 '87
Smith, Ronald L.
Johnny Carson: his private worlds [excerpt from Johnny Carson] il pors *McCalls* 114:141-4 S '87
Smith, Roy A.
A teacher's view on cooperative learning. il *Phi Delta Kappan* 68:663-6 My '87
Smith, Sally Ann, d. 1986
about
Obituary
Sierra 72:9 Mr/Ap '87
Smith, Samantha
about
East-west misunderstanding. J. M. McClellan. il *Flying* 114:20-2 My '87
Smith, Samuel Stanhope, 1750-1819
about
An universal freckle. S. J. Gould. il por *Nat Hist* 96:14+ Ag '87
Smith, Selwyn
about
Doctor under examination. A. Finlayson. *Macleans* 100:5 Ja 12 '87
Smith, Shirley A. Harris- *See* Harris-Smith, Shirley A., d. 1987
Smith, Sinjin
about
For outdoor volleyball ace Sinjin Smith, going to work is a day at the beach. K. Hubbard. il pors *People Wkly* 28:39-40 Ag 31 '87
Smith, Stephen B. Wall- *See* Wall-Smith, Stephen B.
Smith, Steve
about
S.C. State, UAPB name new men's basketball coaches. *Jet* 72:51 Ap 27 '87
Smith, Susan
about
Turning computer babble into plain English. T. Engstrom. il pors *Work Woman* 12:61+ My '87
Smith, Sylvanus
about
730-lb. man trying Dick Gregory's formula to aid in weight loss. il pors *Jet* 72:52 My 4 '87
Smith, Terry M.
(jt. auth) See Barnes, Robert, and Smith, Terry M.
Smith, Thomas G. (Thomas Graham), 1938-
Reel illusions. il *Omni* 9:70-9 Je '87
Smith, Tommy
about
Tommy Smith. C. Wright. il por *Down Beat* 54:44-5 O '87
Smith, Truman E.
Tree ivy. il *Flower Gard* 32:45 D '87/Ja '88
Smith, Wayne S.
Lies about Nicaragua. *Foreign Policy* 67:87-103 Summ '87
Smith, Wendy, 1956-
Glenn Thompson: breaking down barriers. il pors *Publ Wkly* 232:19-22 S 11 '87
Smith, Wes
Welcome to the real world! [excerpt] il *Read Dig* 131:15-16 O '87

Smith, Wesley J.
The client's bill of rights: conduct you deserve from your lawyer [excerpt from The lawyer book] *McCalls* 115:170+ N '87
Smith, Will, b. 1877
about
Florida man celebrates his 110th birthday. il por *Jet* 72:12 Je 22 '87
Smith, Willi
about
Obituary
Essence por 18:49 Jl '87
Jet por 72:9 My 4 '87
Spider-man bride wears Willi Smith's last design. il *Jet* 72:53 Je 22 '87
WilliWear partner talks about future of WilliWear. por *Jet* 72:52 My 25 '87
Smith, William T.
about
Once more to the well. J. Willoughby. il por *Forbes* 140:194 S 21 '87
Smith (E. G.) Color Socks (Firm) *See* E. G. Smith Color Socks (Firm)
Smith (R. D.) & Company *See* R. D. Smith & Company
Smith & Wesson
A raider's new world [G. Hutchings' bid] M. Maremont. il por *Bus Week* p49-50 Je 15 '87
Smith Barney, Harris Upham & Co. Incorporated
For Smith Barney, the go-go years have just begun [takeover by Primerica Corp.] R. Mitchell. il por *Bus Week* p39-40 Je 8 '87
A Wall Street broker's story [S. Blair] D. O. Relin. il por *Sch Update* 120:5 D 18 '87
Smith College. Museum of Art
Small towns, big art. T. Bross. il *Travel Holiday* 167:29-31 Ja '87
Smith-Corona Marchant Corp. *See* SCM Corp.
Smith-Harrison Museum
George and Martha in Alabama. il pors *South Living* 22:51 N '87
Smith River (Mont.)
Float to wild trout [Montana] E. A. Bauer. il *Outdoor Life* 180:58-9+ Ag '87
Smithers, Jan
about
Altared states: Brolin & Co. B. Goodwin. pors *Harpers Bazaar* 120:136-7 Jl '87
Smithfield ham *See* Ham
SmithKline Beckman Corp.
SmithKline: sprinting just to stay in place. S. Benway. il por *Bus Week* p74+ Ag 31 '87
Smiths Industries plc
Lear Siegler sells subsidiary companies to Smiths Industries. *Aviat Week Space Technol* 127:32 Ag 3 '87
Smithsonian (Periodical)
Around the Mall and beyond [selling posters of Smithsonian illustrations] E. Park. il *Smithsonian* 18:30+ N '87
Smithsonian Institution
Around the Mall and beyond. E. Park. See issues of Smithsonian
Behind the scenes at the Smithsonian. D. Young. il *South Living* 22:173-4+ N '87
Musical chairs at NASA and Smithsonian. I. Goodwin. *Phys Today* 40:66 O '87
Smithsonian horizons. R. M. Adams. See issues of Smithsonian beginning October 1984
Smithsonian Institution. Anacostia Neighborhood Museum *See* Anacostia Neighborhood Museum (Washington, D.C.)
Smithsonian Institution. Archives of American Art *See* Archives of American Art
Smithsonian Institution. Arthur M. Sackler Gallery *See* Arthur M. Sackler Gallery (Washington, D.C.)
Smithsonian Institution. Center for African, Near Eastern and Asian Cultures
Underneath a garden [cover story] M. F. Schmertz. il *Archit Rec* 175:112-21 S '87
Smithsonian Institution. Conservation and Research Center
Around the Mall and beyond [Wildlife Conservation and Management Training Program] E. Park. *Smithsonian* 18:26+ O '87
Smithsonian Institution. Cooper-Hewitt Museum *See* Cooper-Hewitt Museum
Smithsonian Institution. Cultural Education Committee
Four blacks on Smithsonian Cultural Education Board. *Jet* 71:22 F 2 '87
Smithsonian Institution. Enid A. Haupt Garden *See* Enid A. Haupt Garden (Washington, D.C.)

Smithsonian Institution. Information Center
Around the Mall and beyond. E. Park. *Smithsonian* 18:20+ Ap '87
Smithsonian Institution. Museum Support Center
Around the Mall and beyond [tick collection] E. Park. il *Smithsonian* 17:22+ Ja '87
Smithsonian Institution. National Museum of African Art *See* National Museum of African Art (U.S.)
Smithsonian Institution. National Museum of American Art *See* National Museum of American Art (U.S.)
Smithsonian Institution. National Museum of American History *See* National Museum of American History (U.S.)
Smithsonian Institution. National Museum of Natural History *See* National Museum of Natural History (U.S.)
Smithsonian Institution. Renwick Gallery *See* Renwick Gallery
Smits, Jimmy

about
Jimmy Smits, a soon-to-be divorced dad, hopes the L.A. law lightning will strike again on film. J. Grant. il pors *People Wkly* 27:105-7 Je 22 '87
Smog

See also
   Los Angeles (Calif.)—Air pollution
High noon for smog control. D. S. Strait and R. E. Ayres. bibl f *Environment* 29:43-5 S '87
Missing the deadline on ozone. M. D. Uehling. il *Natl Wildl* 25:34-7 O/N '87
New clues to smog's effects on lungs. J. Raloff. *Sci News* 132:86 Ag 8 '87
Smog-ozone policy shift. J. Raloff. *Sci News* 131:244 Ap 18 '87
Smoke

See also
   Soot
Lung cancer and indoor air pollution in Xuan Wei, China [burning of smoky coal] J. L. Mumford and others. bibl f il map *Science* 235:217-20 Ja 9 '87
Radical dangers up in smoke [preventing free radical damage to fire victims; research by Thomas M. Lachocki and others] S. Weisburd. *Sci News* 132:169 S 12 '87
Smoke detectors *See* Fire detectors
Smoked food *See* Food, Smoked
Smokehouses
A smoker for sportsmen. il *Field Stream* 92:105-6 Je '87
Smokeless cigarettes
The burning question at RJR: now what? S. Ticer. il *Bus Week* p28-9 S 28 '87
Desperately seeking smokers. *Sci News* 132:204 S 26 '87
Where there's no smoke . . . [R. J. Reynolds' smokeless cigarette] N. R. Gibbs. il *Time* 130:53 S 28 '87
Smokeless tobacco

See also
   Chewing tobacco
Fighting student use of smokeless tobacco. C. E. Koop. *Educ Dig* 53:53-5 D '87
Needed: a cure for curing snuff [research by William J. Chamberlain and others] S. Weisburd. *Sci News* 132:169 S 12 '87

Laws and regulations
"Pre-emptive ban" sought against smokeless tobacco by world experts. il *World Health* p30 O '87
Smokestack industries *See* Manufacturing industries
Smoking

See also
   Cigarettes
   Matchcovers
The advice is basic: don't smoke [lung disease] J. Carey and J. Silberner. il *U S News World Rep* 103:63-4 Ag 17 '87
The assault on smoking. R. J. Samuelson. il *Newsweek* 109:41 Mr 23 '87
The best bet yet for worried smokers [excerpt from The smoker's book of health] T. Ferguson. il *Prevention* 39:74-80 Je '87
Blowing smoke. R. Sandler. *Harpers* 275:15-16 Ag '87
Cigarette ads and the press [symposium] il *Nation* 244:283-8 Mr 7 '87
Cigarettes smoked outstrip population growth [third world] il *World Health* p30 Mr '87
Don't bet against cigarette makers. D. Seligman. il *Fortune* 116:70-2+ Ag 17 '87
Exchange [discussion of March 7, 1987 article, Cigarette ads and the press] *Nation* 244:526+ Ap 25 '87
How much do you smoke? Spit it out [testing saliva levels of cotinine; research by David B. Abrams] *Sci News* 132:25 Jl 11 '87

How smoking kills you. M. Callahan. il *Parents* 62:209-11+ D '87
How to quit without gaining weight [views of John B. Morrison] il *USA Today (Periodical)* 115:13-14 Ap '87
Kicking a habit. A. Steacy. il *Macleans* 100:29 Je 22 '87
Less colitis among smokers. *Sci News* 131:213 Ap 4 '87
Lung cancer in perspective [address, May 10, 1987] C. A. LeMaistre. *Vital Speeches Day* 53:564-6 Jl 1 '87
New Year's resolution to quit smoking [views of Stephen Tiffany] *USA Today (Periodical)* 116:5 D '87
Nicotine slowdown [effect on thinking; study by George J. Spilich] J. C. Horn. il *Psychol Today* 21:24 D '87
No butts [food cravings of ex-smokers; research by Neil E. Grunberg] D. Tonnessen. il *Health* 19:10 Je '87
'No smoking' sweeps America [cover story; special section] il *Bus Week* p40-3+ Jl 27 '87
Non-smokers: time to clear the air [dangers of passive smoking] C. E. Koop. por *Read Dig* 130:110-13 Ap '87
Pushing the panic button [nicotine chewing gum] P. SerVaas. il *Saturday Evening Post* 259:14+ Mr '87
Smoke and non-smokers. J. W. Merline. *Consum Res Mag* 70:38 F '87
Smoke-free forever? [kicking the habit] K. Freifeld. il *Health* 19:12+ N '87
Smoke screened by vitamin E. *Prevention* 39:14 F '87
Smoking-related diseases: free with every puff. J. Cassidy. il *Curr Health 2* 14:13-15 N '87
Smoking under fire. L. J. Brown and P. Gadsby. il map *Good Housekeep* 204:253 Ap '87
Tobacco science wars. E. Marshall. il *Science* 236:250-1 Ap 17 '87
Tobacco's toll [leading cause of preventable deaths] *Newsweek* 110:62 N 9 '87
Weed economics. D. Seligman. il *Fortune* 116:96 Ag 31 '87

History
Smoke through the ages. M. Gray. il *Macleans* 100:32 Je 22 '87

Laws and regulations
Ban cigarette advertising? il *Consum Rep* 52:565-9 S '87
Caveat fumator [rulings in favor of Liggett & Myers and American Brands in product liability cases] J. Castro. il *Time* 130:43 S 7 '87
Eyes on the lies [black leaders team up with tobacco industry in fight against New York City's smoking ban as a civil rights issue] S. Milligan. il *Wash Mon* 19:39-42 Je '87
Frank Fat's napkin: how the trial lawyers (and the doctors!) sold out to the tobacco companies [California] P. Glastris. il *Wash Mon* 19:19-25 D '87
Hands up and butts out! [ban on smoking in Beverly Hills restaurants] M. Smilgis. il *Time* 129:78 Ap 27 '87
Hazards of tobacco advertising [report by William L. Weis and Chauncey Burke] *Society* 24:2 S/O '87
A judicial smoke alert [pro-industry rulings in Liggett & Myers Tobacco Co. cases] il *U S News World Rep* 103:12 S 7 '87
The new prohibition. B. D. Colen. il *Health* 19:8+ D '87
Tobacco goes on trial. P. B. Gray. *Read Dig* 131:225-6+ O '87
Tobacco wins one in court [ruling that warning labels on cigarettes shielded Liggett & Myers from liability claim] D. Pauly. il *Newsweek* 110:44 S 7 '87
Tough times for tobacco lobby. A. Plattner. il *U S News World Rep* 102:17 F 23 '87
Where there's smoke [legislation banning public smoking] O. Friedrich. il *Time* 129:22-3 F 23 '87

Anecdotes, facetiae, satire, etc.
Huffing—not puffing—at the back. A. Fotheringham. il *Macleans* 100:56 F 23 '87
Smoke in Cambridge. R. Baker. il *N Y Times Mag* p26 Mr 29 '87

Canada
Crackdown on smoking [cover story; special section; with editorial comment by Kevin Doyle] il *Macleans* 100:2, 24-32 Je 22 '87
Ottawa's message to smokers: butt out [sweeping anti-smoking policy] M. Gray. il *Macleans* 100:50-1 My 4 '87
Taking the tobacco war too far [Canadian plan to ban cigarette advertising] D. Francis. il *Macleans* 100:11 N 30 '87

Smoking—Laws and regulations—*cont.*
Switzerland
Smoking ban at WHO HQ. il *World Health* p30 My '87

Psychological aspects
Hot boxes for ex-smokers. F. E. Zimring. por *Newsweek* 109:12 Ap 20 '87
Smoke and stress: a double whammy [effect on heart rate; research by Kenneth A. Perkins] G. Lowe. *Psychol Today* 21:19 My '87

Smoking accessories
See also
Tobacco pipes

Smoking and blacks
Eyes on the lies [black leaders team up with tobacco industry in fight against New York City's smoking ban as a civil rights issue] S. Milligan. il *Wash Mon* 19:39-42 Je '87

Smoking and employment
Cold turkey [USG forbids employees to smoke at work or at home] *Time* 129:32 F 2 '87
A crusader who helps offices go smoke-free [R. Addison] P. Finch. il por *Bus Week* p105 Mr 23 '87
No smoking on the job. M. Salter. il *Macleans* 100:71 F 2 '87
A sign of the times: smokers need not apply. J. O. Hamilton. il *Bus Week* p42-3 Jl 27 '87
Smoke-free work sites growing world-wide. il *World Health* p30 Ag/S '87
Smokers take more sick leave. *Prevention* 39:122 Ja '87
Smoking can stunt your career. il *Prevention* 39:12 My '87
Thou shalt not smoke. B. Rudolph. il *Time* 129:58-9 My 18 '87
Three ways to handle smoking in the office. J. Sherman. *Work Woman* 12:24-5 S '87
Will smoking hinder you in a job search? il *Glamour* 85:110 D '87

Smoking and women
Smoking. L. Van Gelder. il *Ms* 15:37-8 F '87
Smoking raises female heart attack risk [research by Walter C. Willett and others] S. Eisenberg. *Sci News* 132:341 N 28 '87
Smoking, the pill, and coronary disease [lowered prostacyclin levels; studies by Jerry L. Nadler] il *USA Today (Periodical)* 115:4 F '87

Smoking and youth
Antismoking policies can work in schools. M. C. Rist. *Educ Dig* 52:53-5 Ap '87
Kids and smoking: informed consent? [study by Howard Leventhal] B. L. Benderly. *Psychol Today* 21:24 D '87
Lawmakers—not lawbreakers [seventh graders from Sandwich, Mass. lobby for tougher cigarette sales law] C. Lowrance. il *Good Housekeep* 204:96 Mr '87
Tobacco-free youth. *Futurist* 21:52 Mr/Ap '87

Smoking on airplanes
Clear the smoke screen. D. E. Fink. *Aviat Week Space Technol* 126:11 Mr 16 '87
Flying high and feeling low. J. Venturino. il *Women's Sports Fitness* 9:19 S '87
Transportation Dept. to study need for airline smoking ban. *Aviat Week Space Technol* 127:39 O 12 '87

Smoky Mountains National Park (N.C. and Tenn.) *See* Great Smoky Mountains National Park (N.C. and Tenn.)

Smolen, Michael
about
Michael Smolen, senior editor. W. Livingstone. il por *Stereo Rev* 52:8 Mr '87

Smolens, John
A letter from her past [story] il *Redbook* 170:62+ N '87

Smoller, Jordan W.
Can childhood be cured? A research evaluation. *Educ Dig* 52:56-9 Ap '87

Smoot, Jane
Death in the mountains. il *South Living* 22:100 N '87

Smooth muscle *See* Muscle

Smorgasbord
"Try a little of many dishes". il *Sunset* 179:80-1, 170+ D '87

Smothering *See* Asphyxia

SMPS *See* Society for Marketing Professional Services

SMU *See* Southern Methodist University

Smucker, Paul H.
about
Of jams and a family. A. H. Malcolm. il por *N Y Times Mag* p82-3+ N 15 '87

Smucker (J. M.) Co. *See* J. M. Smucker Co.

Smuggling
See also
Narcotics trade
Arms for Marcos? L. Howard. il por *Newsweek* 110:5 D 21 '87
As Stockholm lays siege to Nobel . . . [arms smuggling charges] J. Kapstein. il *Bus Week* p46 S 21 '87
'Irangate' unfolds in Italy [arms smuggling charges against F. Borletti] W. C. Symonds. *Bus Week* p46 S 21 '87
Nobody here but us tamales [smuggling unsafe clams across Baja border] il *FDA Consum* 21:40-1 Mr '87
The real McCoy [W. McCoy, rum runner during Prohibition] J. F. Mariani. il *Mot Boat Sail* 160:30 O '87
Smuggler's paradise [Paraguay] T. Rosenberg. *New Repub* 196:14-16 Je 8 '87
The spectator in solitary [former CIA agent E. P. Wilson convicted of selling guns to Libyan terrorists] F. Trippett. il por *Time* 129:19 Je 15 '87
"You die for sure" [smuggling rubies from Burma] L. Gubernick. il map *Forbes* 140 Sp Issue:94-6 O 26 '87

Smurfit, Michael
about
An Irishman feasts on American trees. K. Labich. il por *Fortune* 116:62-4+ Jl 20 '87

Smuts, Barbara
What are friends for? il *Nat Hist* 96:36-45 F '87

Smyre, Calvin
about
Georgia leader urges AME delegates to fight crime. *Jet* 73:32 S 28 '87

Smyth, Deborah
My first job was my worst job. il *Seventeen* 46:52 Je '87

Smyth, Frank
AFL-CIO is Spanish for union busting. *Wash Mon* 19:24-7 S '87
Duarte's secret friends. il *Nation* 244:316-18 Mr 14 '87
El Salvador's forgotten war. il *Progressive* 51:22-4 Ag '87

Smyth, Kermit C., and Miller, J. Houston
Chemistry of molecular growth processes in flames. bibl f il *Science* 236:1540-6 Je 19 '87

Smyth, Ned, 1948-
about
Ned Smyth. E. Turner. il *Art News* 86:46+ My '87
On the waterfront. N. Princenthal. il *Art Am* 75:210-11+ Ap '87

Smyth, Patty
about
The lone rocker. K. Dieckmann. por *N Y* 20:24 Mr 23 '87
Patti Smith, Patty Smyth: how to tell them apart. J. Powell. pors *Glamour* 85:158 Je '87
Rock's supergirl stars. pors *Teen* 31:58 O '87

Smyth, Rencie
Savannah: a new cultural vision. il *Horizon* 30:40-6+ Ap '87

Snacks
See also
Lance, Inc.
Potato chips
100 snacks under 100 calories. il *Ladies Home J* 104:130-2+ S '87
Goody-goodies! [children's snacks] il *Redbook* 169:200+ S '87
The great snack exchange. L. Bellini-Gergley. *Mademoiselle* 93:144 Ap '87
How to survive a snack attack. D. Eller. il *Mademoiselle* 93:222 O '87
Long-lasting snacks: dried vegetables, fruit, yogurt. il *Sunset* 178:196+ My '87
Return to vendor [healthy treats] il *Seventeen* 46:216 S '87
Secret eating—how to stop snacking on the sly. N. Malkin. il *Mademoiselle* 93:260 Ap '87
Snacks-from-the-box. il *McCalls* 115:48 D '87
Snacks in a flash [microwaving] il *Redbook* 169:87+ O '87
Snacks to keep you cheering. il *South Living* 22:102 Ja '87
Social grazes [light party treats] M. Fox. il *Health* 19:42-4+ Je '87
Super snacks to bake and take. C. Wapner. il *Good Housekeep* 205:102+ O '87
Treats from the freezer. il *South Living* 22:118 Ag '87
TV snack attacks. il *Seventeen* 46:123-4 Ja '87

Snail farming

California escargot [European brown snail as pest and gourmet treat] C. Wilvert. il *Focus* 37:28-30 Summ '87

His stock moves slowly, but Fresno's Ralph Tucker is America's most avid snailman. M. Neill. il por *People Wkly* 28:71-2 Jl 6 '87

Snail fever *See* Schistosomiasis

Snails

See also

Slugs

Control

California escargot [European brown snail as pest and gourmet treat] C. Wilvert. il *Focus* 37:28-30 Summ '87

Snail strategy and sympathy. *Sunset* 178:180 Mr '87

Diseases and pests

Vertical distribution of an estuarine snail altered by a parasite. L. A. Curtis. bibl f il *Science* 235:1509-11 Mr 20 '87

Food and feeding

See Mollusks—Food and feeding

Snails, Edible

See also

Cooking—Snails

California escargot [European brown snail as pest and gourmet treat] C. Wilvert. il *Focus* 37:28-30 Summ '87

Snake plant

Kind words for the mother-in-law's tongue. H. W. Christopher. il *Flower Gard* 31:47 O/N '87

Snake venom

Crossing paths with a snake. E. Hale. il map *FDA Consum* 21:14-19 Jl/Ag '87

Shocks for snakebites. R. Herzberg. il *Outdoor Life* 179:55-7+ Je '87

Snakebite *See* Snake venom

Snakes

See also

Boa constrictors

Pythons

Rattlesnakes

Sea snakes

Snakes under pressure [circulatory system adapts to the demands of gravity; cover story] H. B. Lillywhite. il *Nat Hist* 96:58-67 N '87

Photographs and photography

One picture . . . [red-shouldered hawk and garter snake] J. McDonald. il *Audubon* 89:80-1 Ja '87

Snakes, Fear of *See* Fear of snakes

Snapper, Clifford M., and Paul, William E.

Interferon-γ and B cell stimulatory factor-1 reciprocally regulate Ig isotype production. bibl f il *Science* 236:944-7 My 22 '87

Snapshots *See* Photographs

Snarey, John R., 1948-

A question of morality. il *Psychol Today* 21:6+ Je '87

Snead, Sam

Nixon: the fairway tapes [excerpt from Slammin' Sam] *Harpers* 274:28 Ja '87

Sneakers *See* Footwear

Sneakers, Running *See* Running shoes

Sneakers, Tennis *See* Tennis shoes

Snedaker, Robert Hume, Jr.

about

Sprint's new chief has a lot of wires to untangle. M. Ivey. il por *Bus Week* p29 Jl 27 '87

Sneddon, Sharon K.

Using your car as a mobile blind. il *Petersens Photogr Mag* 16:44-6 Ag '87

Sneezing

Who 'nose' how to sneeze? *Prevention* 39:14 F '87

Snell, Dixie

[Month] in the South. See issues of Southern Living through January 1987

Snider, Tim

A wallpaper primer. il *Ctry J* 14:46-51 Mr '87

Snipe shooting

Anecdotes, facetiae, satire, etc.

Exit laughing. E. Zern. il *Field Stream* 92:138 O '87

Snobs and snobbishness

The aristobrats: they're young, they're rich, they're oh-so-shallow (could you be one of them?). D. Handelman. il *Mademoiselle* 93:230-1+ Ap '87

Le snob appeal [Paris] C. Worthington. il *Harpers Bazaar* 120:172+ O '87

Snoring

The darker side of snoring [sleep apnea] *Consum Rep* 52:137 Mr '87

Surgery that could put snoring to rest. D. B. Moskowitz. il *Bus Week* p154 Je 8 '87

Unbearable snoring. G. Grant. il *Essence* 18:19+ Ag '87

Wake up! Snoring can be dangerous. L. Rosenthal. il *McCalls* 114:143 Jl '87

Snorkeling *See* Skin diving

Snow, Carlos

about

Growing up fast. R. Telander. il pors *Sports Illus* 67:44-6+ N 16 '87

Snow, Ray

Mount Rainier [excerpt] il *Natl Parks* 61:46-7 N/D '87

Snow

See also

Avalanches

Building, Ice and snow

Snowstorms

Snowfall—below average [1985/86 season] D. M. Ludlum. il *Weatherwise* 40:41-4 F '87

Snow and ice climbing

Steep freeze. il *Natl Geogr World* 137:3-7 Ja '87

Snow and ice removal

How to remedy roof ice buildup. A. Rooze and G. Branson. il *Fam Handyman* 37:26-8+ D '87

Snow blowers, throwers, etc.

Never shovel again. J. Anthony. *Changing Times* 41:20 D '87

New way to throw snow [Toro CCR-2000] M. Morris. il *Home Mech* 83:84 Ja '87

Outdoor power tools: buyers guide. M. Thompson. il *Fam Handyman* 37:54-6+ O '87

Powerful new snowthrowers. il *Workbench* 43:63 N/D '87

Snow removal equipment. S. Nesbitt. il *Flower Gard* 32:74-5 D '87/Ja '88

Throw that snow. T. O. Bakke. il *Pop Sci* 230:92-4 F '87

What to look for in a snow thrower. M. Ferrara. il *Home Mech* 83:87-8 N '87

Maintenance and repair

Let it snow! D. Sprockett. il *Flower Gard* 32:75-6 D '87/Ja '88

Snow fences

Instant living snow fence. J. Walter. il *Success Farm* 85 no4:8 F '87

Snow goose shooting *See* Goose shooting

Snow leopards *See* Leopards

Snow making

Preparing for snowless slopes [Mount Allan as site for 1988 Olympic downhill and slalom races] D. Keefler. il *Macleans* 100:42 Mr 2 '87

Snow job [Mt. Snow, Vt. ski resort] J. Vock. il *Skiing* 40:197-202 N '87

Snow-on-the-mountain (Plant)

A surprising white cools the garden. il *South Living* 22:56 Ag '87

Snow removal equipment

See also

Snow blowers, throwers, etc.

Snow shovels *See* Shovels, spades, etc.

Snow slides *See* Avalanches

Snow storms *See* Snowstorms

Snow surveys

Snow testers. C. Miller. *Ctry J* 14:21-3 D '87

When adventure is a snow job. R. Wolkomir and J. Wolkomir. il *Natl Wildl* 25:50-1 F/Mr '87

Snow throwers *See* Snow blowers, throwers, etc.

Snow trails (Animal tracks) *See* Animal tracks and trails

Snow White (Fictional character)

Disney's enduring masterpiece [cover story] E. Oxford. il por *Am Hist Illus* 22:30-9 D '87

The lost Snow White: working sketches reveal how Disney's fairy tale came true. M. Dougherty. il *Life* 10:52-4+ Ap '87

Snow White speaks. A. Caselotti. il *People Wkly* 27:102-4+ My 18 '87

Some day my prince will come and other lies Snow White told us. il *Glamour* 85:78 Ag '87

Tots in tow, the stars turn out for Snow White's semicentennial. il *People Wkly* 28:57 Jl 27 '87

Unforgettable Snow White. J. Culhane. il *Read Dig* 131:114-19 D '87

Anecdotes, facetiae, satire, etc.

Snow White & Seven Dwarfs, Inc. (or Even a princess has to work). J. Viorst. il *Redbook* 170:36+ N '87

Snow White and the seven dwarfs [film] *See* Motion picture reviews—Single works

Snowbirds (Flight squadron)

'Snowbirds rolling . . . now!'. il *Natl Geogr World* 138:12-17 F '87

Snowblindness

Snowblind! W. Grout. *Skiing* 39:4 Spr '87

Snowboarding
Hangin' ten on the ski slopes. G. M. Bock. il *Bus Week* p91 F 2 '87
Snowboarders invade the slopes. M. Smilgis. il *Time* 129:85 Mr 9 '87
Snow's up! Skiers take the plunge as surfing on slopes becomes the hottest fad of the winter. il *People Wkly* 27:118-19 Mr 16 '87
Snurf's up! B. Stepko. il *Seventeen* 46:87 Ja '87
Snowcat skiing *See* Skis and skiing
Snowcats (Machines)
Mothers, don't raise your sons to drive snow-cats [driver D. deKoevend] A. Pospisil. il *Skiing* 40:220 O '87
Snowden, Joan Baratz- *See* Baratz-Snowden, Joan
Snowdon, Antony Armstrong-Jones, Earl of, 1930-
about
The misfortunes of a princess. A. Steacy. il pors *Macleans* 100:34 N 9 '87
Snowfall *See* Snow
Snowmass Village (Colo.)
Restaurants, nightclubs, bars, etc.
Game for a good meal? [Krabloonik restaurant] B. Newman. il *Sports Illus* 66:93 Mr 9 '87
Snowmobiles and snowmobiling
Iceland
Icelandic snowmobiling and ice-fishing adventure. S. Netherby. *Field Stream* 91:98 Ja '87
Snowshoes and snowshoeing
Snowshoeing: making tracks. Y. Prater. il por *Women's Sports Fitness* 9:78-9 D '87
Snowslides *See* Avalanches
Snowstorms
See also
Aviation—Storm hazards
April snows of yesteryear. D. M. Ludlum. *Ctry J* 14:24 My '87
The blizzard of '88. P. E. Hughes. il *Weatherwise* 40:312-14+ D '87
The blizzard of '88 in historical perspective. D. M. Ludlum. *Weatherwise* 40:319 D '87
The great blizzard of '88. L. Ponte. il *Read Dig* 131:11-12+ D '87
Man and machine forecast big snow [Washington, D.C.] R. A. Kerr. il *Science* 235:1460-1 Mr 20 '87
Notes and comment [New York City] *New Yorker* 63:23-4 Mr 2 '87
Notes and comment [remembering the snowstorm of 1947] *New Yorker* 63:34-5 D 28 '87
Notes and comment [unseasonal snowstorm in Dutchess County, N.Y.] *New Yorker* 63:31 O 19 '87
Winter's glory. A. R. Siddons. il *Read Dig* 130:53-5 Ja '87
Anecdotes, facetiae, satire, etc.
Snowbound. P. G. Quinnett. il *Audubon* 89:30+ Ja '87
Snowy owls *See* Owls
Snuffy Smith (Comic strip) *See* Comic books, strips, etc.
Snug Harbor Cultural Center
A Snug Harbor for Vinoly [renovation of Staten Island's Music Hall] M. LaRue. il *Theatre Crafts* 21:14 O '87
Snyder, Adam
Dick Clark grows up [cover story] il pors *Channels* 7:28-31+ My '87
Snyder, Alan
about
An unending quest for value [interview] A. E. Serwer. il por *Fortune* 115:114 Mr 16 '87
Snyder, Cory
about
The Erie sensation. G. Macnow. il por *Sport Mag* 78:37-43 My '87
Pow! Wow! R. Fimrite. il pors *Sports Illus* 66:74-6+ Ap 6 '87
Snyder, Don J.
Ordeal on Bay Ledge Buoy. il por *Read Dig* 130:112-17 My '87
Snyder, Joan
about
Bullish on calves and sheep. H. Zelinsky. il por *Ms* 15:23 Ap '87
Snyder, Joan, 1940-
about
Painting from the heart. S. Gill. il por *Art News* 86:128-35 Ap '87
Snyder, Richard E.
about
Dick and Joni. J. Kasindorf. il pors *N Y* 20:60-4+ D 14 '87
Kaplan joins Simon & Schuster as special adviser to Snyder. pors *Publ Wkly* 231:16 Ja 16 '87

Once half of publishing's dynamic duo, Joni Evans is now throwing the book at her husband, Dick Snyder. M. Vespa. il pors *People Wkly* 28:149-50+ N 16 '87
Snyder, Robbie
about
A tornado took away his world. J. Grazier. il pors *McCalls* 114:130-2 Je '87
Snyder Capital Management (Firm)
An unending quest for value [interview with A. Snyder] A. E. Serwer. il por *Fortune* 115:114 Mr 16 '87
Snyder-Stone, Lisa
(jt. auth) *See* Stone, Larry, and Snyder-Stone, Lisa
Soames, Richard M.
about
Lights! Camera! Completion bond! R. Grover. il por *Bus Week* p50 Ag 24 '87
Soane, Sir John, 1753-1837
about
Soane country. M. Filler. il por *House Gard* 159:172-9+ N '87
Soane's Ealing home. C. Robinson. il *Hist Today* 37:6-7 O '87
Soane's Museum (London, England) *See* Sir John Soane's Museum (London, England)
Soap
Perfect skin: the clean sweep. C. Duhé. il *Harpers Bazaar* 120:214-19+ O '87
The right soap can change your skin. il *Redbook* 170:116-17 N '87
Soap's up! [unusual soap shapes made by Twincraft] il *Natl Geogr World* 144:24-8 Ag '87
Soap box derbies
The All-American Soap Box Derby. C. Jensen. il *Car Driv* 33:153-4+ D '87
Soap bubbles and films
Bubbles. P.-G. De Gennes. il *Phys Today* 40:7+ Jl '87
Dew drops on a bathroom mirror. C. F. Bohren. il *Weatherwise* 40:102-6 Ap '87
A metal's many faces [research by John W. Cahn and Jean E. Taylor] I. Peterson. il *Sci News* 131:76-7 Ja 31 '87
Music and ammonia vapor excite the color pattern of a soap film. J. Walker. il *Sci Am* 257:104-7 Ag '87
Soap bubble meteorology. M. J. Iacono and D. C. Blanchard. il *Weatherwise* 40:141-2 Je '87
Soap industry
See also
Colgate-Palmolive Co. (Delaware)
Procter & Gamble Co.
Twincraft Company
Advertising
Alan Klimpke's career as a singer is running hot and cold [winner of Coast-to-Coast Shower Sing-Off] il por *People Wkly* 28:79 N 30 '87
Marketing
A case of malpractice—in market research? [Beecham sues Yankelovich over research on new detergent] M. Rothman. *Bus Week* p28-9 Ag 10 '87
Soap operas *See* Television serials
Soap sculpture
Cut it out. il *Natl Geogr World* 140:19 Ap '87
Soares, Cecilia
(jt. auth) *See* Isaacs, Susan, and Soares, Cecilia
Soaring (Aviation) *See* Gliding and soaring
Sobel, Dava
AIDS: what you should know! What you should tell your children! il *Good Housekeep* 204:71-5 Je '87
Common injuries and what to do about them. il *Good Housekeep* 204:91-4 Mr '87
Mother's moments: nonsexist toys? Forget it. *Ladies Home J* 104:66+ D '87
Sobel, David S. (David Stuart)
(jt. auth) *See* Ornstein, Robert Evans, and Sobel, David S. (David Stuart)
Sobering compounds *See* Alcohol antagonists
Soberón Acevedo, Guillermo
Health manpower out of balance. il *World Health* p16-17 Ap '87
Sobran, Joseph
Howard Beach: the use and abuse of race. il *Natl Rev* 39:28-30+ Mr 27 '87
Le nouveau canard. *Natl Rev* 39:44-5+ F 13 '87
(jt. auth) *See* Waller, J. Michael, and Sobran, Joseph
SOCATA
European air forces interested in Socata/Mooney TBM 700 [single-engine business turboprop as transport aircraft for military officials] *Aviat Week Space Technol* 127:147 O 12 '87

Soccer, College
Kicking with both his heels [North Carolina men's and women's teams under A. Dorrance] J. Diaz. il por *Sports Illus* 67:80 N 23 '87
Soccer, Indoor (Professional) *See* Soccer, Professional
Soccer, Professional
The big D stands for destiny [Dallas beats Tacoma for MISL championship] M. Bishop. il *Sports Illus* 66:75-6 Je 29 '87
Toe-to-toe for the title [Tacoma vs. Dallas for MISL championship] C. Gammon. il *Sports Illus* 66:54 Je 22 '87

Ethical aspects
The centennial of a troubled game [English Football League] A. Collie. il *Macleans* 100:36-7 Ag 17 '87
Soccer: old riot, new riot [Belgian trial for British fans over 1985 riot in Brussels] T. Clifton and R. Marshall. il *Newsweek* 110:8 S 21 '87
A suspicion of bribery [Canadian national team members under investigation] G. Ferzoco. il *Macleans* 100:37 Ag 17 '87

Canada
A suspicion of bribery [Canadian national team members under investigation] G. Ferzoco. il *Macleans* 100:37 Ag 17 '87

Great Britain
The centennial of a troubled game [English Football League] A. Collie. il *Macleans* 100:36-7 Ag 17 '87
Soccer coaches
See also
Dorrance, Anson
Soccer fans
Soccer: old riot, new riot [Belgian trial for British fans over 1985 riot in Brussels] T. Clifton and R. Marshall. il *Newsweek* 110:8 S 21 '87
Soccer players
See also
Tatu
Sochurek, Howard
Medicine's new vision. il *Natl Geogr* 171:2-41 Ja '87
Medicine's new wonder machines. il *Read Dig* 130:193-8 My '87
Social action
See also
Church and social problems
Social agencies

Cooperation
Developing partnerships between families and service providers in rural Vermont [work of the Milton Family Community Center] L. Horel. il *Child Today* 16:17-19 Ja/F '87
Social behavior of animals *See* Animals—Habits and behavior
Social behavior of insects *See* Insects—Habits and behavior
Social change
See also
Social Darwinism
The Columbus argument. D. C. Stove. *Commentary* 84:57-8 D '87
What's next? G. F. Kreyche. *USA Today (Periodical)* 115:98 Mr '87
Social classes
See also
Elite (Social sciences)
Labor
Middle classes
Poor
Upper classes
You can go home—sort of [tweeners] B. O'Reilly. por *Newsweek* 110:14-15 D 7 '87
Great Britain
Classes and the masses in Victorian England. G. Crossick. bibl il *Hist Today* 37:29-35 Mr '87
Social conditions
See also
Civilization
Peace
Quality of life
Women—Social conditions
Social conflict
See also
Culture conflict
Social Darwinism
Social Credit Party (B.C.)
Revolution on the right [privatization] J. Pifer. il por *Macleans* 100:28 Ag 31 '87
Vander Zalm's bold plans. J. O'Hara. il por *Macleans* 100:14-16 N 2 '87
Social Darwinism
Herbert Spencer and 'inevitable' progress. R. M. Young. bibl il por *Hist Today* 37:18-22 Ag '87

Social Democratic Party (Germany: West)
Brandt steps down. *Natl Rev* 39:20 Ap 24 '87
Too long at the table [W. Brandt retires] A. Nagorski. il por *Newsweek* 109:39 Ap 6 '87
Social Democratic Party (Great Britain)
A bad stumble for a man in a hurry [D. Owen] por *Newsweek* 110:32 Ag 17 '87
Both ends against the middle. A. Sampson. il *Newsweek* 109:30 Je 22 '87
Merger in the middle [proposed merger of the Social Democratic Party and the Liberals] R. Laver. il *Macleans* 100:22 Ag 17 '87
The rise and fall of Britain's neoliberals. P. Toynbee. il *Wash Mon* 19:22-8 N '87
Social Democrats, U.S.A.
Trotsky's orphans. M. Massing. *New Repub* 196:18-20+ Je 22 '87
Social Development Commission (United Nations) *See* United Nations. Commission for Social Development
Social development of children *See* Children—Growth and development
Social diseases *See* Venereal diseases
Social drinking *See* Drinking customs
Social ecology *See* Human ecology
Social education
See also
Moral education
Peace studies
Social sciences—Study and teaching
"Caring from the heart" [teaching children to help the homeless] S. Lapinski. il *Ladies Home J* 104:26+ Mr '87
The fourth R? [social decision making; study by John Clabby and Maurice Elias] J. Meer. *Psychol Today* 21:68-9 F '87
Nurturing kindness through storytelling. C. A. Smith. *Educ Dig* 53:53-5 S '87
Teaching selflessness in a selfish society. T. J. Lasley. bibl f il *Phi Delta Kappan* 68:674-8 My '87
Teaching young people to help others in crises. W. W. Crowder. *Educ Dig* 53:46-9 S '87
Social evolution *See* Social change
Social forecasting
The coming of the singles society. E. S. Cornish. il *Futurist* 21:2+ Jl/Ag '87
Ervin Laszlo. B. Lawren. *Omni* 9:96 S '87
Families and children in the year 2000. A. J. Norton. il *Child Today* 16:6-9 Jl/Ag '87
Retroactive prophets. D. E. Koshland, Jr. *Science* 238:727 N 6 '87
U.S. may become society of singles, expert says [views of Edward Cornish] *Jet* 72:16 Ag 17 '87
Social groups *See* Groups (Sociology)
Social history
See also
Baltimore (Md.)—Social history
Boston (Mass.)—Social history
Brooklyn (New York, N.Y.)—Social history
Castile (Spain)—Social history
Chicago (Ill.)—Social history
Great Britain—Social history
Hollywood (Calif.)—Social history
Netherlands—Social history
Paris (France)—Social history
Social, Humanitarian and Cultural Committee (United Nations) *See* United Nations. Social, Humanitarian and Cultural Committee
Social insurance *See* Social security
Social interaction
Are you (no! not me!) boring? B. Levine. il *Seventeen* 46:82+ My '87
Focus on: social studies [special section] il *Seventeen* 46:120-1 My '87
Social isolation
See also
Alienation (Social psychology)
Loneliness
All by their lonesome [views of J. Diamond] S. Budiansky. il *U S News World Rep* 102:71 My 4 '87
Fighting teacher isolation. J. B. Davis. *Educ Dig* 52:27-9 My '87
Social justice *See* Justice
Social policy
See also
United States—Social policy
Social problems
See also
Alcoholics and alcoholism
Church and social problems
Cost and standard of living
Crime and criminals

Social problems—See also—*cont.*
    Discrimination
    Divorce
    Drug abuse
    Family
    Family size
    Homeless
    Juvenile delinquents and delinquency
    Migrant labor
    Muckraking
    Poor
    Prejudice
    Prostitution
    School and social and economic problems

Social problems in literature
Delving into life—the Chinese writer's duty [excerpts from address, November 9, 1979]; tr. by Perry Link and Kyna Rubin. Liu Binyan. por *N Y Times Book Rev* 92:3+ F 22 '87

Social progress *See* Social change

Social psychology
    See also
    Alienation (Social psychology)
    Behavior (Psychology)
    Competition (Psychology)
    Crowding stress
    Crowds
    Empathy
    Ethnopsychology
    Family
    Helping behavior
    Human relations
    Leadership
    Morale, National
    NIMBY syndrome
    Obedience
    Political psychology
    Prison psychology
    Public opinion
    Social role
    Stereotype (Psychology)
    Violence
The beat goes on [social rhythms] C. A. Douglis. il *Psychol Today* 21:36-9+ N '87

Social research *See* Social science research

Social revolution
    See also
    Counterculture
How-to book for revolutionists [work of Jay S. Mendell] il *Futurist* 21:44 Jl/Ag '87

Social role
    See also
    Sex role
Athletes or role models? Demanding higher standards from players is unrealistic. J. Papanek. por *Sports Illus* 66:84 Je 15 '87
Modern-day mentors: five lessons in success [role models] L. Rosch. il *Work Woman* 12:55-9 Ag '87
Positive primary education for young black males. S. H. Holland. *Educ Dig* 53:56-8 N '87
Role models [for men's fashions] R. La Ferla. il *N Y Times Mag* p128 D 6 '87
What would ALF say? [role models] J. W. Yates, II. por *Christ Today* 31:33 S 4 '87

Social science research
    See also
    Evaluation research
No good applied social research goes unpunished. P. H. Rossi. *Society* 25:73+ N/D '87
Resolute ignorance: social science and affirmative action. W. R. Beer. *Society* 24:63-9 My/Je '87

Social sciences
    See also
    Economics
    Policy sciences
    Political science
    Power (Social sciences)
    Sociology
Prophets with tenure [views of M. Walzer] R. J. Neuhaus. *Commentary* 84:49-52 Jl '87

History
A quarter-century of social science [special section] *Society* 25:15-61 N/D '87

Research
See Social science research

Study and teaching
    See also
    Intercultural education
Tot sociology: grade school history. D. Ravitch. *Current* 298:4-10 D '87

Tot sociology: or What happened to history in the grade schools. D. Ravitch. *Am Sch* 56:343-54 Summ '87
What happened to history in the grade schools? D. Ravitch. *Educ Dig* 53:7-9 O '87
The world as seen by students in Accelerated Christian Education schools [with reply by Ronald E. Johnson] D. B. Fleming and T. C. Hunt. bibl f il *Phi Delta Kappan* 68:518-23 Mr '87

Textbooks
Paul Vitz on censorship [excerpts from Censorship: evidence of bias in our children's textbooks] P. C. Vitz. *Phi Delta Kappan* 68:453 F '87
The right books [Paul Vitz's study of public school social studies texts] C. Williamson. *Natl Rev* 39:64 Ja 30 '87
Social studies texts need a global perspective. C. E. Cortés and D. B. Fleming. *Educ Dig* 52:42-5 Mr '87

Social security
    See also
    National Committee to Preserve Social Security and Medicare
Administration cancels cuts in welfare benefits. *Jet* 73:18 N 2 '87
The budget's sacred cow. *Time* 130:24 N 9 '87
The coming social security surplus. M. J. Boskin. il *Fortune* 115:111+ Mr 30 '87
Controversy over SSA service and reliability. M. Sinclair. *50 Plus* 27:20-1 O '87
An exchange on social security [with reply by Michael Kinsley] J. Tobin. *New Repub* 196:20+ My 18 '87
How to win on social security [repeal earnings penalty] M. S. Forbes, Jr. il *Forbes* 140:27 D 28 '87
Retirees are about to see a healthier boost in benefits . . . but U.S. children are slipping past the safety net. G. Koretz. il *Bus Week* p26+ O 12 '87
The right's free lunch [reform proposals of P. S. Du Pont and N. Gingrich] M. Kaus. *New Repub* 196:14 Mr 9 '87
The war between the generations. L. Smith. il *Fortune* 116:78-80+ Jl 20 '87
Warning: social security: do not touch. W. F. Buckley. *Natl Rev* 39:62 D 4 '87
Whither social security? J. A. Schnepper. il *USA Today (Periodical)* 116:21 N '87
Working after you retire. *Black Enterp* 18:42 S '87

Cost of living adjustments
Social security: have COLAs lost their fizz? M. Hodge. il *50 Plus* 27:28-9 D '87

Taxation
Replace social security with a stable, permanent retirement system. N. Gingrich. il *USA Today (Periodical)* 116:22-3 Jl '87
Will tax reform bite into your social security? M. Hodge. il *50 Plus* 27:39-40+ Je '87

United States
See Social security

Social security taxes *See* Social security—Taxation

Social status
    See also
    School children—Social and economic status
    Social classes

Social stratification *See* Social classes

Social studies *See* Social sciences

Social welfare *See* Economic assistance, Domestic; Public welfare

Social work
    See also
    Family social work
    Public welfare
    Social agencies
    Social workers

New York (State)
    See also
    Nassau County (N.Y.)—Social work

Vermont
    See also
    Milton (Vt.)—Social work

Social work with youth
An insider's look at federal youth programs. J. R. Reingold. *Educ Dig* 53:34-5 N '87
Social services in American high schools. E. Farrar and R. L. Hampel. il *Phi Delta Kappan* 69:297-303 D '87

Social workers
Salaries, pensions, etc.
The high price of low pay. M. Piturro. il por *Work Woman* 12:157-8 Mr '87

Socialism
    See also
    Communism
    Utopias

Socialism—*cont.*

A death much exaggerated. R. J. Neuhaus. *Natl Rev* 39:44 Ag 28 '87

Socialism as the teflon dream. R. J. Neuhaus. *Natl Rev* 39:52 Ja 30 '87

Great Britain

'Commanding the heart': Edward Carpenter and friends. S. Rowbotham. bibl il pors *Hist Today* 37:41-6 S '87

Thatcher's third term target. N. Gelb. il *New Leader* 70:6-7 Je 29 '87

Soviet Union

Cats and bears: practicing left politics in the Soviet Union [interview with B. Kagarlitsky] A. Cockburn. *Nation* 245:706-7 D 12 '87

The Soviet new left [interview with B. Kagarlitsky] A. Cockburn. *Nation* 245:618-19 N 28 '87

United States

Bibliography

The New York intellectuals & the socialist legacy. J. Hart. *Natl Rev* 39:58+ S 11 '87

Western Europe

The lessons of defeat. D. Singer. *Nation* 245:81-4 Ag 1-8 '87

Socialism and education

The academy [discussion of October 1986 article, The tenured left] S. H. Balch and H. I. London. *Commentary* 83:11-12 Ja '87

Socialism and religion

Stewart Headlam and the Christian Socialists [Victorian England] E. Norman. bibl il por *Hist Today* 37:27-32 Ap '87

Socialism and the arts

The dialectics of dissent [excerpt from The velvet prison] M. Haraszti. *Harpers* 275:28+ D '87

The seduction of censorship. M. Haraszti. *New Repub* 197:32-4+ N 23 '87

Socially handicapped children

See also

National Resource Center for Children in Poverty

Against all odds [lives of three poor American children] R. Arias. il pors *People Wkly* 28:32-42+ O 26 '87

Hard knocks [head injuries of inner city children; work of George E. Locke and others] *Sci Am* 256:30 Je '87

Improving the chances of our weakest underdogs—poor children. A. S. Blinder. por *Bus Week* p20 D 14 '87

Land of the unfree [report by Committee for Economic Development] *America* 157:147 S 26 '87

Education

See also

Compensatory education

I Have a Dream Foundation

Another 'What works' due from ED. *Phi Delta Kappan* 68:636+ Ap '87

The burgeoning educational underclass. M. Horn. il *U S News World Rep* 102:66-7 My 18 '87

Business leaders urge more aid for poor kids. K. D. Thompson. il *Black Enterp* 18:30 D '87

Differential treatment in preschool [research by Lorene Quay and Olga Jarrett] G. W. Bracey. il *Phi Delta Kappan* 68:703-4 My '87

Education, dependence, and poverty. D. S. Seeley. *Educ Dig* 52:6-9 Ja '87

Involving low-income parents in the schools: a role for policy? M. W. McLaughlin and P. M. Shields. bibl f il *Phi Delta Kappan* 69:156-60 O '87

Preparing disenchanted students to succeed in society. R. C. Smith. il *USA Today (Periodical)* 116:87-9 N '87

What schools can do to help disadvantaged children. *Educ Dig* 53:14-18 O '87

Sociedade de Turismo e Diversões de Macau

Macau's casino king gets set to play with Beijing [S. Ho] M. Shao. il por *Bus Week* p98-9 Ja 19 '87

Societas Sacerdotalis Sanctae Crucis *See* Opus Dei (Society)

Société Astronomique de France

Amateurs triumph in Paris [colloquium celebrating the 100th anniversary] S. J. O'Meara. il *Sky Telesc* 74:481-3 N '87

Société de Construction d'Aviations Tourismes et d'Affairs *See* SOCATA

Société Nationale Elf Aquitaine *See* Elf Aquitaine

Société Radio-Canada *See* Canadian Broadcasting Corporation

Societies

See also

Literary clubs and societies

Scientific societies

Wine societies

Society, Primitive

See also

Cannibalism

Hunters and gatherers

Man, Prehistoric

Nomads

Society (Periodical)

Looking backward and lurching forward. I. L. Horowitz. *Society* 25:9-12 N/D '87

Society and architecture *See* Architecture—Social aspects

Society and art *See* Art—Social aspects

Society and computers *See* Computers and civilization

Society and literature *See* Literature and society

Society and music *See* Music—Social aspects

Society and psychiatry *See* Psychiatry and society

Society and science *See* Science—Social aspects

Society and the church *See* Church and the world

Society and the telephone *See* Telephone—Social aspects

Society for Marketing Professional Services

Change in the blink of an eye [roundtable] J. Capelin. il *Archit Rec* 175:45+ F '87

Society for Psychical Research (Great Britain)

Physics and psychics [discussion of May 1986 article, Physics and psychic research in Victorian and Edwardian England] J. Oppenheim. *Phys Today* 40:144-5 My '87

Society for Worldwide Interbank Financial Telecommunications *See* SWIFT

Society of American Foresters

Foresters receive awards. *BioScience* 37:163 F '87

Society of Children's Book Writers

Meltzer awarded top honors at SCBW conference. J. Roginski. *Publ Wkly* 232:42 D 25 '87

Society of Dance History Scholars

Dance historians honor Duncan. S. J. Cohen. por *Dance Mag* 61:6-7 Jl '87

Society of Friends

Friends United Meeting: a new beginning. C. Fager. *Christ Century* 104:742-3 S 9-16 '87

Society of Jesus *See* Jesuits

Society of North American Goldsmiths

The American way: metalsmiths meet at Cranbrook. M. Schick. il *Am Craft* 47:16-17 O/N '87

Society of St. Francis de Sales *See* Salesians

Society of Woman Geographers

S.W.G. *New Yorker* 63:21-2 Je 22 '87

Society to Preserve and Encourage Radio Drama, Variety and Comedy

They're tuned in to the 'thrilling days of yesteryear'. L. Maltin. bibl (p182) il *Smithsonian* 17:70-9 Mr '87

Sociolinguistics

Baby Faith [black family's involvement with language and creativity] M. Wallace. il por *Ms* 16:154+ Jl/Ag '87

In so many words . . . language & society 1500-1900 (I) [special section; with introd. by Penelope Corfield] il *Hist Today* 37:16-29 Ja '87

In so many words . . . language & society 1500-1900 (II) [special section] bibl il *Hist Today* 37:30-42 F '87

In so many words . . . language & society 1500-1900 (III). il *Hist Today* 37:29-35 Mr '87

Sociologists

See also

Blumer, Herbert, 1900-1987

Mannheim, Karl, 1893-1947

Ossowski, Stanisław

Toennies, Ferdinand

Sociology

See also

Anthropology

Community

Educational sociology

Groups (Sociology)

Human ecology

Human relations

Individualism

Intercultural research

Man—Influence of environment

Social psychology

Sociolinguistics

Disenthralling sociology. I. L. Horowitz. bibl f *Society* 24:48-55 Ja/F '87

Disenthralling sociology [discussion of January/February 1987 article] I. L. Horowitz. *Society* 24:3-5 Jl/Ag '87

Sociology, Christian

See also

Christianity and economics

Church and industry

Church and social problems

Church work

Sociology, Christian—See also—*cont.*
    Liberation theology
Decadence American style [responding to R. N. Bellah's Habits of the heart] K. S. Kantzer. il *Christ Today* 31:12-13 Ag 7 '87
What would ALF say? [role models] J. W. Yates, II. por *Christ Today* 31:33 S 4 '87
Sociology, Rural
    See also
    Village life
Sociology and literature *See* Literature and society
Socket wrenches *See* Wrenches
Socks *See* Hosiery
Socolow, Elizabeth Anne
The saints' wives [poem] *Ms* 15:12 Mr '87
SOD (Superoxide dismutase) *See* Superoxide dismutase
Söderström, Elisabeth, 1927-
                    about
Reaching the heart. D. J. Soria. il pors *Opera News* 51:8-12+ F 14 '87
Saying it all. P. G. Davis. *Opera News* 51:12 F 14 '87
Sodium
    See also
    Low sodium cooking
Eclipse measurements of Io's sodium atmosphere. N. M. Schneider and others. bibl f il *Science* 238:55-8 O 2 '87
Sodium bicarbonate
Soda loading [used to improve athletic performance] D. Groves. il *Women's Sports Fitness* 9:68 D '87
Sodium chloride *See* Salt
Sodium nitrite *See* Nitrites
Sodium transport *See* Biological transport
Sodomy
AIDS & the law [discussion of October 1986 article, Sodomy and the Supreme Court] D. Robinson. *Commentary* 83:2+ F '87
Soeharto, 1921-
                    about
Invisible Indonesia. D. K. Emmerson. bibl f map *Foreign Aff* 66:368-87 Wint '87/'88
Sofaer, Abraham David, 1938-
                    about
Administration wrong on ABM Treaty. C. Levin. il *Bull At Sci* 43:30-3 Ap '87
George Shultz's feisty lawyer. B. Van Voorst. por *Time* 129:31 Ap 6 '87
Minority report. C. Hitchens. *Nation* 244:103 Ja 31 '87
Sofas
Futon sofa bed. K. Collier. il *Fam Handyman* 37:76-80 O '87
Sofer, David
                    about
The British connection. A. Miller. il por *Newsweek* 109:39 Mr 23 '87
The insider scandal travels abroad. S. Koepp. il por *Time* 129:51 Mr 23 '87
Sofi (New York, N.Y.: Restaurant) *See* New York (N.Y.)— Restaurants, nightclubs, bars, etc.
Sofia, Sabatino
(jt. auth) *See* Chan, Kwing L., and Sofia, Sabatino
Soft contact lenses *See* Contact lenses
Soft drink industry
    See also
    A&W Brands Inc.
    Allegheny Beverage Corp.
    Coca-Cola Bottling Co. Consolidated
    Coca-Cola Bottling Company of Philadelphia
    Coca-Cola Company
    Double Cola Co.-USA
    Pepsico, Inc.
    Royal Crown Cola Co.
                Advertising
Foot and Falconetti are TV's most popular penguin pitchmen, and it serves them right. il por *People Wkly* 28:50 Ag 24 '87
Max Headroom speaks the dreaded 'P-word' [Coke's new ads] S. Ticer. il *Bus Week* p40-1 Mr 16 '87
Michael Jackson to get about $10M for Pepsi ads. *Jet* 71:22 F 9 '87
                Marketing
Pepsi and Coca-Cola: the all-American worldwide war. S. Caminiti. il *Fortune* 116:56 O 26 '87
Soda war [American National Beverage fights trademark dispute with Anheuser-Busch] R. L. Stern. il *Forbes* 139:82-3 My 4 '87
These guys don't blink [C. Ware and C. Morrison of Coca-Cola] A. Edmond, Jr. il pors *Black Enterp* 17:310-12+ Je '87

                Cuba
Cuba libre, sans Coke. G. García Márquez. *World Press Rev* 34:34 N '87
                India
The mouse that roared at Pepsi [Double-Cola] S. Tefft. il *Bus Week* p42 S 7 '87
                South Africa
    See also
    Amalgamated Beverage Industries Pty. Ltd.
Soft-focus lenses *See* Lenses, Photographic
Soft kill weapons
All stuck up, no way to go [use against tanks and helicopters; views of S. A. Hoenig] S. Budiansky. il *U S News World Rep* 103:62 Jl 20 '87
Soft Sheen Products
Revlon must change package similar to Soft Sheen's. *Jet* 73:18 O 19 '87
Softball
    See also
    King and His Court (Softball team)
The 1½-ton softball machine [Ohio's Men of Steele] L. Griggs. il *Time* 130:62 Ag 3 '87
Faster than a speeding bullet [woman pitcher M. Granger] M. Kort. il por *Ms* 16:90 N '87
Play ball! F. E. Halpert. bibl il *Women's Sports Fitness* 9:30-5 Jl '87
Softball dreamin'. S. Salter. il *Women's Sports Fitness* 9:28-9 Jl '87
Softball immortality. J. F. Clarity. il *N Y Times Mag* p52 Mr 22 '87
Woman to watch: Michele Granger. por *Women's Sports Fitness* 9:25 My '87
                Study and teaching
Getting to first base [batting tips] R. Schuessler. il *Women's Sports Fitness* 9:58 Ap '87
                Tournaments
Almost untouchable [M. Granger leads U.S. women's team in the Pan Am Games] H. Hersch. il pors *Sports Illus* 67:24 Ag 24 '87
Software *See* Computer programming
Software industry *See* Computer service industries
Software Resource (Firm)
Turning computer babble into plain English [S. Smith and L. Ruffolo] T. Engstrom. il pors *Work Woman* 12:61+ My '87
Software stores *See* Computer stores
Software Toolworks Inc.
Heeeere's Les Crane—and he's talking software. P. Finch. il por *Bus Week* p101 Jl 20 '87
Sohappy, David
                    about
Of salmon and sovereignty. J. Rosenberg. *Christ Century* 104:428-9 My 6 '87
Sohmer, Stephen T.
                    about
PW interviews. W. Brisick. por *Publ Wkly* 232:51-2 N 20 '87
SoHo (New York, N.Y.)
SoHo: downtown boomtown. P. Gardner. il *Art News* 86:128-33 Mr '87
Soho Press Inc.
First list. L. Fleischer. *Publ Wkly* 231:48 Mr 20 '87
Soil *See* Soils
Soil acidity
Low-input cropping for acid soils of the humid tropics. P. A. Sanchez and J. R. Benites. bibl f il *Science* 238:1521-7 D 11 '87
Soil amendments *See* Soil conditioners
Soil blocks (Seed starters) *See* Flats, etc. (Horticulture)
Soil conditioners
What about those new soil polymers? il *Sunset* 178:252-4 Ap '87
Soil conservation
    See also
    Contour farming
    Terraces (Agriculture)
    United States. Soil Conservation Service
Managing the soils of Sub-Saharan Africa. R. Lal. bibl f il maps *Science* 236:1069-76 My 29 '87
Soil [Environmental Quality Index] il *Natl Wildl* 25:39 F/Mr '87
Tax break for composters. S. O. Daniels. il *Rodale's Org Gard* 34:7-8 O '87
                Laws and regulations
    See also
    United States. Dept. of Agriculture. Conservation Reserve Program
Soil Conservation Service (U.S.) *See* United States. Soil Conservation Service

Solar system—*cont.*

Glimpses of solar systems in the making [Beta Pictoris, HL Tauri, and T Tauri] M. M. Waldrop. il *Science* 235:971-2 F 27 '87

Interview [B. A. Smith] R. Schultz. il pors *Omni* 9:66-8+ F '87

Were Titius and Bode right? il *Sky Telesc* 73:371 Ap '87

Young solar systems around other stars [HL Tauri and Beta Pictoris] il *Astronomy* 15:76-7 Ap '87

Exploration

See Space flight

Motion in space

The E-M method of polar alignment [equatorial mounts] B. Gordon. *Sky Telesc* 73:454 Ap '87

An odd figure 8 [analemma] T. D. Nicholson. il *Nat Hist* 96:76-9 D '87

That amazing analemma. G. Lovi. il *Sky Telesc* 73:519-20 My '87

Solar ventilators *See* Ventilators

Solar wind

See also

Heliosphere

Comet Halley and the solar wind. R. Z. Sagdeyev and A. A. Galeev. il *Sky Telesc* 73:252-5 Mr '87

Solariums *See* Sun rooms

Solarization (Photography) *See* Photography—Processing

Solarization of soil *See* Soils, Effect of solar radiation on

Solarquest (Game)

Film and game. K. McMains. *Space World* X-8-284:36 Ag '87

Solc, Charles K., and others

Single-channel and genetic analyses reveal two distinct A-type potassium channels in Drosophila. bibl f il *Science* 236:1094-8 My 29 '87

Die Soldaten [opera] *See* Zimmermann, Bernd Alois, 1918-1970

Solder and soldering

EPA bans lead solder. il *Home Mech* 83:86 Ag '87

Hand-soldering SMC's [surface mount components] F. M. Mims. il *Radio-Electron* 58:71-2+ N '87

Soldering: old techniques & new technology. V. D. Martin. il *Radio-Electron* 58:47-50 My '87

Soldering: small skill saves big bill. M. Henkenius. il *Home Mech* 83:66+ Ag '87

Equipment

Have iron, will travel [cordless soldering irons] P. McCafferty. il *Pop Sci* 230:80-1 Ja '87

Soldiers, Black *See* United States. Army—Blacks

Soldiers Delight (Md.) *See* Natural areas—Maryland

Soleirolia *See* Baby's-tears (Plant)

Soliciting donations *See* Fund raising

Solicitor General (U.S.) *See* United States. Dept. of Justice. Office of the Solicitor General

Solid helium *See* Helium, Solid

Solid rocket boosters for space vehicles *See* Space vehicles—Propulsion systems

Solid state devices *See* Semiconductors

Solidarity (Trade union)

A bitter anniversary [fifth anniversary of the declaration of martial law] *America* 156:1 Ja 3-10 '87

From a U.S. mole: inside story of what might have been [views of R. Kuklinski] R. Z. Chesnoff and D. Stanglin. il por *U S News World Rep* 102:32-3 Ap 20 '87

Gorbachev: the view from Warsaw [interview with J. Kuron] H. Luczywo and N. Gardels. *Harpers* 275:26-7 Jl '87

Lech's secret project [autobiography] L. Howard. il por *Newsweek* 109:6 Ap 27 '87

Lunch with Lech. N. Bethell. *New Repub* 197:13-14 N 2 '87

A new deal in Poland? A. Brumberg. bibl f il *N Y Rev Books* 33:32-6 Ja 15 '87

Poland [statements, December 12, 1986 and February 19, 1987] R. Reagan. *Dep State Bull* 87:33-4 Ap '87

Poland's plucky activist [A. Michnik] M. T. Kaufman. il por *N Y Times Mag* p38+ Ap 26 '87

Solidarity forsaken. *New Repub* 196:7-9 Ja 5-12 '87

Top down or bottom up? D. Singer. il *Nation* 244:756-8 Je 6 '87

A worker's tale [L. Walesa's autobiography] W. Svoboda. il por *Time* 129:70 My 4 '87

Solids

See also

Exciton theory

Disordered materials: a survey of amorphous solids. Y.-T. Cheng and W. L. Johnson. bibl f il *Science* 235:997-1002 F 27 '87

Hole-burning spectroscopy and relaxation dynamics of amorphous solids at low temperatures. R. Jankowiak and G. J. Small. bibl f il *Science* 237:618-25 Ag 7 '87

Icosahedral boron-rich solids. D. Emin. bibl f il *Phys Today* 40:55-62 Ja '87

Solien, T. L.

about

T. L. Solien. E. Heartney. il *Art News* 86:212+ Summ '87

Solitude

See also

Loneliness

Everyone needs a quiet place. D. Aprill. il *Conservationist* 42:56 Jl/Ag '87

Me and my cocoon. M. E. Marty. *Christ Century* 104:1071 N 25 '87

Why solo vacations are my secret salvation. C. Bickley. il *Glamour* 85:28+ Ag '87

Soloff, Lew

about

Lew Soloff: big band brass man. M. Bourne. il pors *Down Beat* 54:24-6 S '87

Solomon, Anthony M.

A declining dollar is just one piece in the puzzle. il *Bus Week* p20 Ap 13 '87

Financial markets [address, June 9, 1987] *Vital Speeches Day* 53:725-9 S 15 '87

Solomon, Barbara Probst

Art in post-Franco Spain. il *Art News* 86:120-4 O '87

Where's Papa? *New Repub* 196:30-4 Mr 9 '87

Solomon, Deborah

The art behind the dots. il por *N Y Times Mag* p42-6+ Mr 8 '87

Last of a breed. il *Harpers Bazaar* 121:88+ D '87

A Stellar performer. il *Harpers Bazaar* 120:378-9+ S '87

Woman of steel. il por *Art News* 86:112-17 D '87

Solomon, Frank

What myosin might do. bibl f *Science* 236:1043-4 My 29 '87

Solomon, Lee David, 1927-

about

Back-of-the-envelope philosopher. D. Machan. il por *Forbes* 140:106-7 Ag 24 '87

Solomon, Michael R.

Standard issue. bibl (p63) il *Psychol Today* 21:30-1 D '87

Solomon, Nancy

(jt. auth) See Pitts, Terence, and Solomon, Nancy

Solomon, Steve

My search for better broccoli. il *Rodale's Org Gard* 34:36-40 N '87

Symphilid solutions. il *Rodale's Org Gard* 34:80+ O '87

Solomon R. Guggenheim Museum

A far, far better thing: the Guggenheim and Whitney redesign their expansion schemes. il *Archit Rec* 175:45+ Ap '87

Growing pains [new expansion plans] M. Filler. il *Art Am* 75:14-19 Jl '87

Heir heads [proposed additions] K. Larson. il *N Y* 20:94-5 Mr 30 '87

The sky line [design by F. L. Wright] B. Gill. *New Yorker* 63:49-50+ Je 8 '87

Somewhere, Wright is smiling. M. Stevens. il *Art News* 86:238 N '87

Whose Chagall is it, anyway? [suit against R. Lubell for recovery of a purportedly stolen Marc Chagall gouache] A. Decker. *Art News* 86:21 D '87

Solomon's seal (Plant)

Japanese solomon's-seal. J. L. Creech. il *Flower Gard* 31:46+ Ap/My '87

Solotaroff, Ted, 1928-

The literary-industrial complex. *New Repub* 196:28+ Je 8 '87

Solow, Robert M.

about

Lyrics of loss, theories of gain. P. Gray; P. Elmer-DeWitt. il pors *Time* 130:80 N 2 '87

Nobel Prize for theory of economic growth. E. Marshall. il por *Science* 238:754-5 N 6 '87

Solti, Sir Georg, 1912-

about

The exuberant Solti at 75. A. Rich. il por *Newsweek* 110:93 O 19 '87

Solti. W. Livingstone. il pors *Stereo Rev* 52:76-8 O '87

Soltner, André
about
A chef's Easter. M. Burros. il *N Y Times Mag* p75-6 Ap 12 '87
Solunar theory *See* Fishing
Solution (Chemistry)
See also
Colloids
Diffusion
Solvents
Ceramics by the solution-sol-gel route. R. Roy. bibl f il *Science* 238:1664-9 D 18 '87
Free energy calculations by computer simulation. P. A. Bash and others. bibl f il *Science* 236:564-8 My 1 '87
Solvents
See also
Cleaning compositions
DMSO
Methylene chloride
Rotation and solvation of ammonium ion. C. L. Perrin and R. K. Gipe. bibl f il *Science* 238:1393-4 D 4 '87
Solwitz, Sharon
All the men she loved and lost [story] il *Mademoiselle* 93:162+ N '87
Solzhenitsyn, Aleksandr, 1918-
about
Solzhenitsyn's October 1916: a preview. J. M. Curtis. il por *USA Today (Periodical)* 115:90-2 Ja '87
Solzhenitsyn, Ignat
about
Solzhenitsyn's son Ignat starts his own career—as a pianist. C. Neuhaus. il por *People Wkly* 28:91 Jl 20 '87
Soman, Florence Jane
The men in her life [story] il *Good Housekeep* 205:128+ O '87
Vital statistics [story] il *Good Housekeep* 204:62+ Je '87
Somatomedins
Cellular localization of somatomedin (insulin-like growth factor) messenger RNA in the human fetus. V. K. M. Han and others. bibl f il *Science* 236:193-7 Ap 10 '87
Somatosensory cortex *See* Brain
Somatostatin *See* Hypothalamic hormones
Somatotropin *See* Pituitary hormones
Somatotypes
The many shapes of sport [women's bodies] K. Delhagen. il *Women's Sports Fitness* 9:28-31 F '87
Which sport will you excel in? [clues from women's body shapes] J. Mattera. il *Glamour* 85:122+ O '87
Sombke, Laurence
For gringos only. il *Esquire* 107:38 Ap '87
Some kind of wonderful [film] *See* Motion picture reviews—Single works
Someone to watch over me [film] *See* Motion picture reviews—Single works
Somers, Emmanuel
Transboundary pollution and environmental health [cover story] il *Environment* 29:6-9+ Je '87
Somers, Jane *See* Lessing, Doris May, 1919-
Somers (Conn.)
Prisons and reformatories
Laurel and Hardy in the big house [Somers Prison chapter of Sons of the Desert folds] D. M. Kimmel. il pors *Film Comment* 23:2+ Jl/Ag '87
Somerset, Anne, 1955-
Badminton House: the Duke and Duchess of Beaufort in Avon. il *Archit Dig* 44:48-55+ Jl '87
Somerville, Mary, 1780-1872
about
The education of Mary Somerville. K. Weitzenhoffer. por *Sky Telesc* 73:138-9 F '87
Something wild [film] *See* Motion picture reviews—Single works
Somlo, Patty
Solidarity lives among hotel workers. il *Progressive* 51:15 Mr '87
Somme, Battle of the, 1916
Echoes and voices summoned from a half-hour in hell [Royal Newfoundland Regiment casualties at the Battle of the Somme] J. D. Atwater. bibl (p271) il map *Smithsonian* 18:196-200+ N '87
Sommer, Alfred
Blinding malnutrition. il *World Health* p20-2 My '87
Sommer, Francine
about
A cigar-chomping venture capitalist named Francine. P. Finch. por *Bus Week* p101 Jl 20 '87

Sommer, Mark, and Feller, Gordon
Independent initiatives: an alternative peace process. *Current* 292:36-9 My '87
Sommers, Susan
Anti-aging beauty: the myths, the facts. il *Ladies Home J* 104:68+ N '87
Son of Sam laws
Crime and publishing. M. Garbus. il *Publ Wkly* 232:20-2 D 4 '87
Crime doesn't pay after all: a blow to crook books. A. Press. il *Newsweek* 110:48 Ag 24 '87
Criminals, authors and criminal authors. S. Roberts. il *N Y Times Book Rev* 92:1+ Mr 22 '87
Simon & Schuster challenges N.Y. State 'Son of Sam' law [suit over application of statute to Wiseguy by Nicholas Pileggi] *Publ Wkly* 232:14 Ag 14 '87
The wages of sin [S. Barrows permitted to keep profits from sale of book] *Time* 129:77 Mr 23 '87
Sonar
See also
Echolocation (Physiology)
Dredging for dollars [sonar used to find sunken sidewheel steamer Central America] W. J. Cook. il *U S News World Rep* 103:48 Ag 3 '87
Ocean dynamics and acoustic fluctuations in the Fram Strait marginal ice zone. I. Dyer and others. bibl f il *Science* 236:435-6 Ap 24 '87
Sonar suspension [Nissan system] J. Schefter. il *Pop Sci* 231:62+ D '87
Whales and walruses as tillers of the sea floor [side-scan sonar studies of the Bering Sea] C. H. Nelson and K. R. Johnson. il maps *Sci Am* 256:112-17 F '87
Sonar (Herbicide) *See* Herbicides
Sonata and sonatas
See also
Compact discs—Sonatas
Sondheim, Stephen
about
Company [musical] Reviews
New Yorker 63:148 N 16 '87. M. Kramer
Into the woods [musical] Reviews
America 157:458 D 12 '87. G. G. Seibert
N Y il 20:50-1 S 21 '87. R. D. Story
N Y il 20:109-10 N 16 '87. J. Simon
N Y il 20:74-6+ S 28 '87. E. Pooley
Nation 245:726-7 D 12 '87. T. M. Disch
New Leader 70:18-19 D 28 '87. L. Sauvage
New Repub 197:29-30 D 21 '87. R. Brustein
New Yorker 63:147-8 N 16 '87. M. Kramer
Newsweek il 110:106-7 N 16 '87. J. Kroll
Time il 130:96-7 N 16 '87. W. A. Henry
Master of the musical. W. A. Henry. il por *Time* 130:80-2 D 7 '87
Starshine for Sondheim. il por *Harpers Bazaar* 121:162-3 D '87
Sones, Melissa
The psychological effects of rape. il *Glamour* 85:178+ Ag '87
Sonfist, Alan, 1948-
about
Alan Sonfist at Diane Brown. E. Heartney. il *Art Am* 75:128-9 Jl '87
A forest grows in Manhattan. P. Hagan. il *Sierra* 72:16+ Mr/Ap '87
Song writing *See* Rock music—Writing
Songbooks
The Big Singing [annual gathering in Benton, Ky. to sing from the Southern harmony songbook] W. White. il *New Yorker* 62:78-84+ Ja 19 '87
Songs
See also
Children's songs
Compact discs—Songs
Hymns
Phonograph records—Songs
Popular music
Rock music
Sea songs
Songbooks
Songs, American
See also
Star spangled banner (Song)
State songs
Songs of birds *See* Birds—Song
Songs on a shipwrecked sofa [musical] *See* Musicals, revues, etc.—Reviews—Single works
Sonic boom
Strategic Air Command bombs out [Minnesota residents block low-altitude bomber training flights] M. Helmberger. il *Progressive* 51:11-12 Ag '87

Sonic Youth (Musical group)
Sonic Youth. J. Macnie. il *Down Beat* 54:14 Mr '87
La sonnambula [ballet] See Ballet reviews—Single works
Sonnenberg, Nadja Salerno- *See* Salerno-Sonnenberg, Nadja
Sonnier, Keith, 1941-
about
Keith Sonnier at Nature Morte. S. Ellis. il *Art Am* 75:149-50 Je '87
Sonograms, Medical *See* Ultrasonic waves—Medical use
Sonoluminescence
Sounding out chemical hot spots [ultrasonic irradiation of liquid; research by Kenneth S. Suslick] I. Peterson. *Sci News* 132:229 O 10 '87
Sonoma County (Calif.)
Description and travel
The September-glorious Mendocino-Sonoma coast. il map *Sunset* 179:60-5 S '87
Sonoma Valley (Calif.)
Wine industry
See Wine industry
Sonora (Mexico: State)
Description
On the 300-year-old trail of Father Kino. il map *Sunset* 179:52+ O '87
Sonoran Desert
For the desert toad, rain starts a race to metamorphosis [spadefoot toads] D. Cornejo. il *Smithsonian* 17:98-105 Mr '87
Lizards that take to the desert like ducks to water. B. Gilbert. bibl (p145) il *Smithsonian* 18:78-84+ Ag '87
Sons
Photographs and photography
Like father, like son [look alikes] il *Good Housekeep* 205:84-5 S '87
Like father, like son [look alikes] il *Good Housekeep* 205:70 Ag '87
Sons and parents *See* Parent-child relationship
Sons-in-law
The son-in-law watcher. M. Lazarus. il *N Y Times Mag* p94 Ap 5 '87
Sons of the Desert (Organization)
Laurel and Hardy in the big house [Somers Prison chapter folds in Connecticut] D. M. Kimmel. il pors *Film Comment* 23:2+ Jl/Ag '87
Sontag, Susan, 1933-
Pilgrimage. *New Yorker* 63:38-48+ D 21 '87
The pleasure of the image. il *Art Am* 75:122-31 N '87
Sony Corp.
Born in the U.S.A., sold to Japan [Sony acquires CBS Records] S. Koepp. il *Time* 130:66 N 30 '87
CBS Records: if you can't beat 'em, sell [sold to Sony Corp.] il *Newsweek* 110:53 N 30 '87
A solid gold record deal [Sony acquires CBS Records] D. Lieberman and W. J. Holstein. il *Bus Week* p36 N 30 '87
Sony's challenge [cover story] L. Armstrong. il pors *Bus Week* p64-9 Je 1 '87
Soo Line Corp.
So Soo me [stock price] T. Jaffe. il *Forbes* 140:138 Ag 24 '87
Soot
Chemistry of molecular growth processes in flames. K. C. Smyth and J. H. Miller. bibl f il *Science* 236:1540-6 Je 19 '87
Sophistication
Class makes a comeback: the return of the lady. K. Heller. il *Mademoiselle* 93:214-15+ My '87
Sorbet *See* Ice cream, ices, etc.
The sorcerer [operetta] See Sullivan, Sir Arthur, 1842-1900
Sorcery *See* Witchcraft
Sore throat *See* Throat—Diseases
Sorel, Edward, 1929-, and Sorel, Nancy Caldwell
First encounters. See alternate issues of The Atlantic
Sorel, Nancy Caldwell
(jt. auth) See Sorel, Edward, 1929-, and Sorel, Nancy Caldwell
Soren, David
about
Carthage. *New Yorker* 63:36-7 D 14 '87
Sorensen, Theodore C.
The president and the Secretary of State. *Foreign Aff* 66:231-48 Wint '87/'88
Sorenson, Laurel
Becoming an entrepreneur—overnight. il pors *Work Woman* 12:37+ Jl '87
Five ways to a fatter paycheck. *Work Woman* 12:102-3 Je '87
Tending friendships (even when work gets in the way). il *Work Woman* 12:108-10+ O '87

(jt. auth) See Ward, John L., and Sorenson, Laurel
Sorg Incorporated
Back on track. A. A. Lappen. il por *Forbes* 140:12 Jl 13 '87
Sorg Printing Co.
See also
Sorg Incorporated
Soria, Dorle J.
Reaching the heart. il pors *Opera News* 51:8-12+ F 14 '87
Treasures and trifles. il *Opera News* 52:24-6+ S '87
Soriano, Andres, III
about
Andres Soriano's battle for San Miguel. M. Shao. il por *Bus Week* p54 S 28 '87
Sorkin, Michael, 1948-
The call of the wild. il *Vogue* 177:356+ Mr '87
Sorman, Steven, 1948-
about
Steven Sorman at Thomson. R. Silberman. il *Art Am* 75:143-4 Mr '87
Sorohan, Erica Gordon
AIBS news. See occasional issues of BioScience
Sororities, College *See* College sororities
Soros, George
A global new deal. il *N Y Rev Books* 34:52-3 Ag 13 '87
about
Are stocks too high? [cover story] J. J. Curran. il pors *Fortune* 116:28-30+ S 28 '87
Frenzy feeds frenzy. R. Phalon. por *Forbes* 139:44-5 My 18 '87
The master money manager. D. R. Katz. il por *Esquire* 108:67-8 D '87
World's champion bull rider. F. Ungeheuer. il por *Time* 129:75 My 4 '87
Sorrell, Martin S.
about
Hang on, Madison Avenue, Martin Sorrell isn't finished. R. A. Melcher and M. N. Vamos. il por *Bus Week* p80-1 Jl 13 '87
Sorrell Ridge (Firm)
Natural instincts. I. C. Selinger. il por *Work Woman* 12:54-5 Mr '87
Sorrow
See also
Grief
Sorting (Computers)
The output side of data bases. C. O'Malley. *Pers Comput* 11:89+ Jl '87
Search and destroy [book index program] D. Pountain. il *Byte* 12:257-60 Ag '87
Sorting out the sorts [book index program] D. Pountain. il *Byte* 12:275-6+ Jl '87
Sosa & Associates
Learning to say 'buy' in Spanish. D. Graff. il *Channels* 7:17 S '87
Sosniak, Lauren A.
Gifted education boondoggles: a few bad apples or a rotten bushel? bibl f il *Phi Delta Kappan* 68:535-8 Mr '87
Sosnoff, Martin
about
My wife, the Comtesse. D. Machan. il por *Forbes* 139 Ann Directory:119-20 Ap 27 '87
Sotheby Parke Bernet & Co.
See also
Sotheby's (Firm)
Sotheby's (Firm)
Marketing masterpieces department-store style. M. Horn. il *U S News World Rep* 103:56 N 23 '87
Next time, ask [drawings sold as Piranesis at Sotheby's returned due to questionable authenticity] R. W. Walker. *Art News* 86:25-6 O '87
Refinishing & preserving fine furniture heirlooms [work of John Stair] R. Lorenz. il *Fam Handyman* 37:54-7 Ja '87
Sotheby's art market trends. See issues of Forbes beginning November 2, 1987
Soto, Ana Rodriguez- *See* Rodriguez-Soto, Ana
Soto, Hernando de
about
In defense of the black market; tr. by Alfred J. MacAdam. M. Vargas Llosa. il *N Y Times Mag* p28-31+ F 22 '87
Souchal, François
Sculpture, theatre of the sublime. il *Courier* 40:20-2 S '87
Soufflés
Make a soufflé to brag about [three-egg cheese soufflé] il *South Living* 22:182-3 O '87

Soukhanov, Anne H.
Word watch. See issues of The Atlantic beginning January 1987

Soul
Lost souls: a meditation. R. Kirk. il *Natl Rev* 39:30-2 D 31 '87

Soul food *See* Cooking, Black

Soul music phonograph records *See* Phonograph records—Black music

Sound
See also
   Acoustics, Architectural
   Audio engineering
   Noise
   Psychoacoustics
   Television sound
   Theater—Electronic sound control

Recording and reproducing
See also
   Audio systems
   Compact disc players
   Digital audio tape recorders and recording
   Phonograph records—Recording
   Pulse code modulation
   Tape recorders and recording
   Videotape recorders and recording—Sound quality

American hot wax [digital recording studios; cover story] S. Dupler. il *Pop Mech* 164:79-81+ N '87

Basically speaking. M. Riggs. See issues of High Fidelity (New York, N.Y.) through January 1987

Bits & pieces. D. Ranada. See alternate issues of High Fidelity (New York, N.Y.) beginning January 1986

The digital revolution. I. Masters. il *Stereo Rev* 52:58-62+ O '87

The digital revolution: why is rock falling behind? M. Walker. *Roll Stone* p15+ My 21 '87

Live vs. recorded. R. Hodges. il *Stereo Rev* 52:200 D '87

Psychoacoustics and stereo imagery. L. Klein. il *Radio-Electron* 58:80-1 Mr '87

Scan lines. D. Ranada. See alternate issues of High Fidelity (New York, N.Y.) beginning April 1986

Science serving art [digital recording] S. A. Booth. il *Pop Mech* 164:29-31 Ag '87

When stereo isn't stereo [releasing early non-stereo Beatles albums on stereo compact discs] M. Riggs. il *High Fidel* 37:5 D '87

Why stereo doesn't work. L. Klein. il *Radio-Electron* 58:68+ Ap '87

Equipment
See Sound equipment

Sound designers
See also
   LeBrecht, James
   Sherman, Guy
   Splet, Alan

Sound editing (Motion pictures) *See* Motion pictures—Sound editing

Sound effects (Television advertising) *See* Television advertising—Sound effects

Sound effects decoders *See* Sound equipment

Sound engineering *See* Audio engineering

Sound equipment
See also
   Amplifiers
   Headphones
   Loudspeakers
   Microphones
   Phonograph
   Sonar
   Tape recorders and recording

Audio/video synergy [surround sound processors] J. D. Hirsch. il *Stereo Rev* 52:23-4 Ap '87

Audio alchemy [Chace Stereo Surround Processor] G. Buchalter. il por *Forbes* 140:188 O 5 '87

A buyer's guide to selected sound products at AES. B. Saturn. il *Theatre Crafts* 21:31+ Mr '87

NEC AVD-700E surround-sound processor. il *High Fidel* 37:37-8 Je '87

Pro shop. See issues of Down Beat

Seduced by the pure music of Virgin Commies [use of vacuum tubes] W. Biddle. il *Discover* 8:68-75 My '87

Sound Concepts SSD550 time-delay system. J. D. Hirsch. il *Stereo Rev* 52:39-40 O '87

Stereo TV decoder (I). T. T. Templin. il *Radio-Electron* 58:37-41 Ja '87

Stereo TV decoder (II). T. T. Templin. il *Radio-Electron* 58:51-4 F '87

Surround sound [processors and decoders] T. R. Gillett. il *Stereo Rev* 52:54-8 Ap '87

Surround-sound attractions. R. B. Schulein. il *High Fidel* 37:49+ Je '87

Surround sound: music and movies with dazzling realism. M. C. Lehrer. il *USA Today (Periodical)* 116:86-8 S '87

Sound generators *See* Signal generators

Sound in art
Max Neuhaus: aural spaces. C. Ratcliff. il *Art Am* 75:154-63 O '87

Sculpture funhouse [audiokinetic sculptor G. Rhoads] R. Kostelanetz. il por *N Y Times Mag* p28-31 My 31 '87

Sound laboratories
General Dynamics begins tests in new anechoic chamber [cover story] C. A. Shifrin. *Aviat Week Space Technol* 127:51-2 O 19 '87

Sound measurement
See also
   Decibels

Sound pattern recognition
Picture this [work of C. A. Pickover; cover story] I. Peterson. il *Sci News* 131:392-5 Je 20 '87

Sound perception
See also
   Psychoacoustics
   Speech perception

Sound production by animals *See* Animal sounds

Sound production by fish *See* Fish sounds

Sound waves
See also
   Acoustic levitation
   Helioseismology
   Ultrasonic waves

Noise zapper [selective sound wave cancellation] J. Free. il *Pop Sci* 230:76-7+ Ja '87

Industrial use
Cleaning up with a smokestack's siren song [use of acoustic agglomeration to control particle emissions from coal-fired power plants] I. Peterson. *Sci News* 131:342 My 30 '87

Sounders *See* Depth indicators

Sounding and soundings
See also
   Depth indicators

Soundproofing
Listening room [keep sound from traveling to the rest of the house] J. Gaynor. il *Home Mech* 83:82 Ag '87

Sound isolation. R. Hodges. il *Stereo Rev* 52:116 Jl '87

Unwanted sounds. L. Klein. il *Radio-Electron* 58:78-9+ Je '87

Soundtrack recordings *See* Compact discs—Motion picture music; Phonograph records—Motion picture music

Soups
See also
   Bisques (Cooking)
   Campbell Soup Company
   Chowder
   Stocks (Cooking)

3 breads & 3 soups in 3 hours. B. Greenwood. il *Better Homes Gard* 65:128-31+ O '87

A 30-minute chill chaser [potato leek soup in bread bowls] il *Glamour* 85:325 Mr '87

Among other things, cheese smooths soup. il *Sunset* 178:190 Ap '87

Chicken cloud and egg crêpe: they're light and mild Chinese soups. il *Sunset* 179:145 D '87

Cool soups for warm days: avocado, carrot, or watercress. il *Sunset* 179:110 Ag '87

Glorious soups. il *Mademoiselle* 93:204-5+ Ag '87

The green leaves of summer [David Shack's coriander soup] B. Costikyan. il *N Y* 20:101 S 14 '87

Hearty soups in a hurry. A. Bailey. il *Parents* 62:158+ Mr '87

In the soup [fish] S. Bashline. il *Field Stream* 91:78 Mr '87

Is soup good food? [canned, frozen and dried] il *Consum Rep* 52:178-83 Mr '87

Light but rich . . . French vegetable bouillon. il *Sunset* 179:180 S '87

Low-calorie soups to beat winter's chill. J. Rogers. il *Prevention* 39:66-8+ Ja '87

Make extra soup, and freeze it [vegetable soup] il *South Living* 22:137 Je '87

Mediterranean soup: pasta, beans, vegetables. il *Sunset* 178:104 Ja '87

Potage provençal [Antoine Bouterin's cream-of-garlic soup] B. Costikyan. il *N Y* 20:57 Ja 26 '87

Pumpkin soup in tiny pumpkins. il *Sunset* 179:199 O '87

Soups—*cont.*

Recipe of the week [quick Italian soup] il *Jet* 72:30 S 7 '87

Slow-cooker soups. il *Better Homes Gard* 65:89-90 Ja '87

Soup & stew cookbook. il *Ladies Home J* 104:110-13+ F '87

Soup and sandwich—a natural combo [microwave recipes] il *South Living* 22:106+ Ja '87

Soups. il *Consum Rep* 52:364-8 D '87

Spanish soup: fresh clams and dry fava beans. il *Sunset* 178:170 Mr '87

Spring soups from the garden. R. Haskell. il *Flower Gard* 31:24+ Ap/My '87

Super soup in a hurry [microwave mushroom soup] J. B. Hurley. il *Prevention* 39:70 Ja '87

Tastes fresh . . . but you start with canned tomato purée. il *Sunset* 179:178 N '87

Ten all-American soups. il *Saturday Evening Post* 259:82-5 Ja/F '87

Waiter, what's that ribollita doing in my soup? E. Sahatjian. il *Esquire* 108:38 N '87

Whole-meal soup: lamb, vegetables. il *Sunset* 178:161 Je '87

Sour cream

See also

Cooking—Sour cream

Source Perrier SA

Perrier's unquenchable U.S. thirst [acquiring Arrowhead Drinking Water Co.] J. Rossant. *Bus Week* p46 Je 29 '87

Sourdough bread *See* Bread

Sous-vide cooking *See* Food pouches

Sousa, Jan Hart

Who will get our child? il *Parents* 62:72+ D '87

South *See* Southern States

South Africa

See also

Arts—South Africa

Boxing—South Africa

British—South Africa

Capital punishment—South Africa

Children—South Africa

Christian contemporary music—South Africa

Colleges and universities—South Africa

Educational laws and regulations—South Africa

Employee ownership—South Africa

Foreign correspondents—South Africa

Government and the press—South Africa

Household employees—South Africa

Housing—South Africa

Industry and state—South Africa

Investments, American—South Africa

Investments, British—South Africa

Investments, Canadian—South Africa

Investments, Foreign—South Africa

Iran-contra affair—South African participation

Johannesburg (South Africa)

Labor laws and regulations—South Africa

Loans, Bank—South Africa

Marriage law—South Africa

Medical care—South Africa

Political prisoners—South Africa

Popular music—South Africa

Riots—South Africa

Sharpeville (South Africa)

South Africans

Sports—South Africa

Strikes—Miners—South Africa

Strikes—South Africa

Television broadcasting—South Africa

Transkei (South Africa)

United Nations—South Africa

United States—Diplomatic and consular service—South Africa

Youth—South Africa

Commerce

See also

United Nations. Intergovernmental Group to Monitor the Supply and Shipping of Oil and Petroleum Products to South Africa

Britain's assault on the Commonwealth [Britain refuses to agree to wider sanctions against South Africa] H. Mackenzie. il *Macleans* 100:24-5 O 26 '87

Non-aligned at Harare call for sanctions [call for convening of the Security Council to impose sanctions] *UN Chron* 23:46 N '86

Sanctions and survival [South Africa and the 1986 nonaligned nations conference] R. Shaplen. il *New Yorker* 62:74-80+ F 2 '87

Security Council does not adopt text calling for selective mandatory sanctions against South Africa. il *UN Chron* 24:22-5 My '87

Strict implementation of 1977 arms embargo against South Africa asked by Council. *UN Chron* 24:46 F '87

Text calling for comprehensive mandatory sanctions against South Africa vetoed after discussion in eight meetings. il *UN Chron* 24:22-5 Ag '87

Text calling for mandatory selective sanctions against South Africa vetoed in Security Council. il *UN Chron* 23:3-5 Ja '86

Why sanctions are a failure. S. Jenkins. il *U S News World Rep* 103:40 S 21 '87

Canada

See Canada—Commerce—South Africa

Great Britain

See Great Britain—Commerce—South Africa

Israel

See Israel—Commerce—South Africa

United States

See United States—Commerce—South Africa

Cultural relations

United States

See United States—Cultural relations—South Africa

Diplomatic and consular service

Canada

An awkward visit [South African ambassador to Canada G. Babb invited to Peguis Indian reservation] D. Smith. il por *Macleans* 100:20 Mr 23 '87

Economic conditions

Ignoring both carrot and stick [effect of sanctions] W. R. Doerner. il *Time* 130:36 O 5 '87

Why South Africa shrugs at sanctions. P. Brimelow. il *Forbes* 139:100-4 Mr 9 '87

Economic relations

Southern Africa

Children on the frontline. M. A. Fortune. il *Black Enterp* 17:16 My '87

Congress seeks $800 mil. for new front-line states shipping ports, routes. *Jet* 72:4 Mr 30 '87

South African retaliation: a blessing in disguise? R. A. Evans and A. F. Evans. *Christ Century* 104:79-80 Ja 28 '87

A truly constructive step: helping South Africa's neighbors. E. Weiner and S. Mufson. map *Bus Week* p48 Mr 2 '87

Foreign relations

Angola

The Canadian connection [South Africa using Canadian-designed weaponry in Angola] A. Bilski. il map *Macleans* 100:36 O 19 '87

The right's last, best hope [J. Savimbi's UNITA] M. Maren. il *Nation* 245:744-6 D 19 '87

Security Council again condemns South Africa for 'un-provoked aggression' against Angola. il *UN Chron* 22:12-13 N/D '85

Canada

See Canada—Foreign relations—South Africa

Mozambique

Mozambicans in diaspora. W. L. Moser. *America* 156:440-1+ My 30 '87

Southern Africa

South Africa and its neighbors. R. E. Lambert. map *America* 156:148-52 F 21 '87

Struggle for Southern Africa. R. G. Mugabe. *Foreign Aff* 66:311-27 Wint '87/'88

United States policy in Southern Africa. P. H. Baker. bibl f *Curr Hist* 86:193-6+ My '87

United States

See United States—Foreign relations—South Africa

Zambia

Botha's defiant show of force [raid on Zambia] S. Reiss. il *Newsweek* 109:34 My 4 '87

Industries

See also

Amalgamated Beverage Industries Pty. Ltd.

Anglo American Corp. of South Africa, Ltd.

Black business enterprises—South Africa

Gold mines and mining—South Africa

Rembrandt Group Ltd.

Samcor (Firm)

Native peoples

See also

Zulus

Politics and government

See also

Apartheid

Communist Party (South Africa)

Elections—South Africa

South Africa—Politics and government—See also—*cont.*
Inkatha movement (South Africa)
Political campaigns—South Africa
South Africa. Parliament
306 solutions to a baffling problem [views of L. Louw and F. Kendall] B. W. Nelan. il pors *Time* 129:36 Mr 23 '87
Campaign of the iron fist [crackdown on protesters backfires] W. E. Smith. il *Time* 129:36-7 Ap 27 '87
Democracy in South Africa. R. Brookhiser. *Natl Rev* 39:34-6 Jl 31 '87
The democratic future of South Africa [address, September 29, 1987] G. P. Shultz. *Dep State Bull* 87:9-12 N '87
Fantasies about South Africa. P. L. Berger and B. Godsell. *Commentary* 84:35-40 Jl '87
Is South Africa invulnerable? J. Keegan. il map *U S News World Rep* 102:30-3 Mr 23 '87
Jockeying for the right corner. B. W. Nelan. il *Time* 129:38 Je 1 '87
Mandela's ANC fights for a foothold. J. Jones. il *U S News World Rep* 103:36 S 7 '87
A search for harmony [Zulu leaders propose new province of KwaNatal] il *U S News World Rep* 102:30 My 11 '87
South Africa [discussion of July 1987 article, Fantasies about South Africa] P. L. Berger and B. Godsell. *Commentary* 84:11-12+ O '87
South Africa: coercion and demands for change. K. W. Grundy. bibl f *Curr Hist* 86:197-200+ My '87
South Africa embattled. J. De St. Jorre. bibl f *Foreign Aff* 65 Sp Issue:538-63 ['87]
South Africa: the Afrikaner angst. P. H. Baker. *Foreign Policy* 69:61-79 Wint '87/'88
Subtle changes in South Africa? M. Dönhoff, Gräfin. il *World Press Rev* 34:26-8 My '87
Race relations
See also
Apartheid
Religious institutions and affairs
See also
Church and race relations—South Africa
Methodist Church—South Africa
Reformed churches—South Africa
Territories and possessions
See also
Namibia
South Africa. Parliament. House of Assembly
Arch foe of apartheid [H. Suzman] V. Butler. por *Read Dig* 130:157-62 Mr '87
Profiles [member H. Suzman] E. J. Kahn. por *New Yorker* 63:50-1+ Ap 20 '87
South Africa and the United States
See also
Educational exchanges
South Africa in literature
See also
Apartheid in literature
South Africa in motion pictures
See also
Apartheid in motion pictures
South Africa in television
See also
Apartheid in television
South African refugees *See* Refugees, South African
South African students in the United States *See* Foreign students—United States
South Africans
See also
Afrikaners
United States
Fugitives from apartheid. L. Arditi. il *Progressive* 51:32-4 Ap '87
South America
See also
Agriculture—South America
Amazon River Valley
Andes
Argentina
Brazil
Chile
Colombia
Paraguay
Peru
Uruguay
Venezuela
Wildlife conservation—South America
Description and travel
The High Andes: South America's islands in the sky. L. McIntyre. il maps *Natl Geogr* 171:422-59 Ap '87

Native peoples
See Indians of South America
Politics and government
See Latin America—Politics and government
South American Indians *See* Indians of South America
South Americans *See* Latin Americans
South Asia
See also
Economic assistance, American—South Asia
Foreign relations
United States
See United States—Foreign relations—South Asia
South Atlantic region
See also
United Nations—South Atlantic region
South Australia (Australia)
Description and travel
Australia's southern seas. R. Ellis. il map *Natl Geogr* 171:286-319 Mr '87
South Carolina
See also
Courts—South Carolina
Fishing—South Carolina
Francis Marion National Forest (S.C.)
Hilton Head Island (S.C.)
Little Wambaw Swamp (S.C.)
McCormick County (S.C.)
Paleontology—South Carolina
Radioactive waste disposal—South Carolina
Sea Islands
Vegetable gardens and gardening—South Carolina
Capitol
A long time building [South Carolina State House in Columbia] G. D. Ford. il *South Living* 22:86-7 N '87
Description and travel
South Carolina's golden coast. G. D. Ford. il map *South Living* 22:114-21 Ap '87
Legislature
S.C. rep. Juanita White elected to committee post. por *Jet* 72:24 Ag 24 '87
Politics and government
See also
South Carolina—Legislature
Social life and customs
The road visitor. E. Wakefield. il *South Living* 22:94 O '87
South Carolina State College
Dr. A.E. Smith installed as S.C. State president; Sammy Davis gives speech. il pors *Jet* 72:29 Mr 30 '87
South-Central Booksellers Association
237 heed SCBA's summons to Memphis. B. Summer. *Publ Wkly* 232:30 N 6 '87
South Coast Repertory
Script for success. J. P. Forsthoffer. il *Horizon* 30:53-4 Ja/F '87
South Dakota
See also
Agriculture—South Dakota
Black Hills (S.D. and Wyo.)
Education—South Dakota
Hell Canyon (S.D.)
Hunting—South Dakota
Radioactive waste disposal—Laws and regulations—South Dakota
Wind Cave National Park (S.D.)
Industries
See also
Gold mines and mining—South Dakota
Strip mining—South Dakota
South End Press
South End Press: the long march continues [radical publisher seeks to influence political dialogue] R. Bongartz. il *Publ Wkly* 232:17+ Jl 17 '87
South Hadley (Mass.)
Galleries and museums
See also
Mount Holyoke College. Art Museum
South Korea *See* Korea (South)
South Moresby National Park (B.C.)
Agreeing to a new park. J. Barber. *Macleans* 100:35 Jl 20 '87
Canada's South Moresby: the price of a new park. il map *Natl Parks* 61:36-7 Jl/Ag '87
The salvation of a homeland [M. Richardson, leader of the Haida people] il por *Macleans* 100:32-3 D 28 '87
South Moresby hailed as newest Canadian park. il *Natl Parks* 61:37 S/O '87
South Pacific [musical] *See* Musicals, revues, etc.—Reviews—Single works

South Padre Island (Tex.)
    Social life and customs
Spring break at South Padre Island. R. Woodbury. il
    Time 129:87 Ap 6 '87
South Pole
    See also
    Antarctic exploration
South Sea Islands *See* Oceania
South Yuba River (Calif.)
A nonrenewable river [proposed hydroelectric dams on
    the South Yuba] D. Carter. il *Sierra* 72:66-7 My/Je
    '87
Southampton (N.Y.)
    Architecture
Stylish ease [home of C. Di Montezemolo] W. P. Rayner.
    il *House Gard* 159:80-9 Jl '87
Southdown, Inc.
Is Southdown heading north? T. Jaffe. il *Forbes* 140:480
    Jl 13 '87
Southeast Asia
    See also
    ASEAN
    Burma
    City planning—Southeast Asia
    Geology—Southeast Asia
    Investments, American—Southeast Asia
    Kampuchea
    Narcotics trade—Southeast Asia
    Railroads—Southeast Asia
    Thailand
    United Nations—Southeast Asia
    Vietnam
    Bibliography
Book reviews. *Curr Hist* 86:176 Ap '87
    Commerce
    United States
    See United States—Commerce—Southeast Asia
    Description and travel
Back to ethnics. A. Hulbert. *New Repub* 197:12-13 O
    5 '87
Passage to Bangkok: rail adventures through Southeast
    Asia. N. H. Belcher. il map *Travel Holiday* 168:42-7
    D '87
    Foreign relations
    United States
    See United States—Foreign relations—Southeast
Asia
    Politics and government
Back to ethnics. A. Hulbert. *New Repub* 197:12-13 O
    5 '87
Peace, stability and co-operation in South-East Asia
    discussed by Assembly. map *UN Chron* 23:18-19 Ja
    '86
Southeast Asia [special issue] bibl f map (inside back
    cover) *Curr Hist* 86:145-86 Ap '87
The voting fields. il *New Repub* 197:7-9 Ag 10-17 '87
Southeast Asian cooking *See* Cooking, Southeast Asian
Southeast Banking Corporation
Credit where credit is due [L. Carlin sues Southeast
    Banking Corp. over credit rating dispute] il por *50
    Plus* 27:16+ S '87
Southeastern Baptist Theological Seminary
Southeastern Seminary: fundamentalists move in. W.
    H. Willimon. *Christ Century* 104:1020-1 N 18 '87
Southeastern Booksellers Association
SEBA stages showcase for authors, forum for issues.
    A. Symons. il *Publ Wkly* 232:28-30 N 6 '87
Southeastern States
    See also
    Theater—Southeastern States
    Industries
    See also
    Wine industry
Southeastern Universities Research Association
SURA gets new president from DOE: NSF loses two
    computer chiefs. I. Goodwin. *Phys Today* 40:60-1 D
    '87
Southern, Terry
True North. *Nation* 245:41-2 Jl 18-25 '87
Southern Africa
    See also
    Angola
    Botswana
    Child welfare—Southern Africa
    Economic assistance, American—Southern Africa
    Espionage, British—Southern Africa
    Namibia
    South Africa
    Swaziland
    United Nations—Southern Africa
    Women—Southern Africa

    Zimbabwe
    Description and travel
    See also
    Automobile touring—Southern Africa
    Economic relations
    South Africa
    See South Africa—Economic relations—Southern
Africa
    Foreign relations
    Mozambique
    See Mozambique—Foreign relations—Southern
Africa
    South Africa
    See South Africa—Foreign relations—Southern
Africa
    United States
    See United States—Foreign relations—Southern
Africa
    Politics and government
Refugee situation in Southern Africa [statement, February
    5, 1987] M. H. Armacost. map *Dep State Bull* 87:65-7
    My '87
South Africa and its neighbors. R. E. Lambert. map
    America 156:148-52 F 21 '87
South Africa: toward peace and stability [address, Decem-
    ber 1, 1986] C. A. Crocker. *Dep State Bull* 87:40-2
    F '87
United States policy in Southern Africa. P. H. Baker.
    bibl f *Curr Hist* 86:193-6+ My '87
    Bibliography
Before the revolution. L. M. Thompson. il *N Y Rev
    Books* 34:20+ Je 11 '87
Southern Baptist Convention *See* Baptists—United States
Southern Bell Telephone & Telegraph Co.
Florida woman wins suit against Southern Bell, who
    must pay $3.5 million [M. A. Vance] *Jet* 72:29 My
    4 '87
Southern California Booksellers Association
Carrying the torch for children's books in California
    [advertising efforts] L. See. il *Publ Wkly* 231:104 F
    27 '87
Southern Christian Leadership Conference
The dreams of Martin Luther King. C. V. Woodward.
    bibl f il pors *N Y Rev Books* 33:3+ Ja 15 '87
Southern cooking *See* Cooking, American
Southern furniture *See* Furniture, American
Southern Furniture Market *See* Furniture—Exhibitions
Southern Garden History Society
Reflowering Dixie. W. L. Hunt. por *Rodale's Org Gard*
    34:95-6 N '87
Southern harmony songbook *See* Songbooks
Southern Illinois University at Carbondale
United, SIU Carbondale seek more black pilots. *Jet*
    72:16 Ag 3 '87
Southern living (Periodical)
Life at Southern living. G. E. McCalla. See issues of
    Southern Living
Southern Methodist University
Dallas station refuses to flinch as it topples a gridiron
    power [WFAA takes on SMU scandal] D. Holder.
    il *Channels* 7:13 My '87
"Death" to S.M.U. football. *Time* 129:72 Mr 9 '87
Is there life after football? P. Applebome. il *N Y Times
    Mag* p73-4+ O 4 '87
Payoff, hike! [Gov. W. Clements' involvement in illegal
    payments to football players] E. Magnuson. il *Time*
    129:34 Mr 16 '87
Playing for pay in Texas [Gov. W. Clements admits
    involvement in football scandal] T. E. Johnson. por
    Newsweek 109:32 Mr 16 '87
Shame on you, SMU [NCAA suspends football program]
    R. Sullivan and C. Neff. il *Sports Illus* 66:18-21+
    Mr 9 '87
SMU [football program suspended] S. Bayless. il *Sport
    Mag* 78:98 D '87
SMU football is called for illegal motion. il *Newsweek*
    109:55 Mr 9 '87
Southern Oscillation
Historical coral [El Niño-Southern Oscillation events and
    cadmium levels in Galapagos coral; research by Glen
    T. Shen] *Sci News* 132:168 S 12 '87
Link between earthquakes and El Niños? [research by
    Daniel A. Walker] R. Monastersky. *Sci News* 132:373-4
    D 12 '87
Warming up to an El Niño. S. Weisburd. *Sci News*
    131:55 Ja 24 '87
Southern States
    See also
    Architecture—Southern States
    Architecture, Domestic—Southern States
    Blacks—Southern States

Southern States—See also—*cont.*
    Colleges and universities—Southern States
    Education—Southern States
    Gardens and gardening—Southern States
    Gulf States (U.S.)
    Historic houses, sites, etc.—Southern States
    Vegetable gardens and gardening—Southern States
[Month] in the South. J. Noles. See issues of Southern
    Living beginning February 1987
[Month] in the South. D. Snell. See issues of Southern
    Living through January 1987

Bibliography
Books about the South. See issues of Southern Living

Climate
[Month] weather. B. Schilit. See issues of Southern Living

Collectibles
Pink flamingos & Presleyana: the strange obsessions of
    Ole Miss Prof. Charles Wilson. K. Hubbard. il pors
    People Wkly 28:107-8+ D 14 '87

Description and travel
Southern sampler. F. Bianco and W. Schemmel. il *Travel
    Holiday* 167:79-88 Mr '87
Travel South. See issues of Southern Living

History
    See also
    United States—History—Civil War, 1861-1865
    Confederate States of America
    Slavery

Industries
Pay in synthetic fibers manufacturing in the southern
    region. il *Mon Labor Rev* 110:35-6 F '87

Politics and government
    See also
    Presidential primaries—Southern States
Dixie fix: can the Democrats win the South? F. Barnes.
    New Repub 197:10+ N 2 '87
Getting the black vote [Nathan Group targets radio
    commercials] M. Eaton. il por *Black Enterp* 17:20
    F '87
Going after white males. T. Jacoby. il *Newsweek* 110:38+
    S 14 '87
Southern attitudes and world affairs [Main Street America
    and the third world] J. H. Wolfe. *USA Today
    (Periodical)* 115:9 Ja '87

Race relations
    See also
    Ku Klux Klan
Beyond Forsyth [new civil rights activism] M. Eaton.
    Black Enterp 17:62 Je '87

Social life and customs
Southern journal. See issues of Southern Living
Southern States in art
Home to Jericho [excerpts] H. Shuptrine. il *South Living*
    22:88-91 O '87
Southerners
Southerners. See issues of Southern Living
Southgate, Martha
Between two worlds. por *Essence* 18:54-5+ Ag '87
Southland Corp.
7-Eleven wants out of the glare [leveraged buyout] J.
    Weber, Jr. il *Bus Week* p78 Jl 20 '87
Going private. A. A. Lappen. il *Forbes* 140:10 Jl 27
    '87
A junk-bond belly flop [Thompson family leveraged
    buyout] J. Weber, Jr. *Bus Week* p35 N 23 '87
Thank heaven for 7-Eleven. L. Gubernick. il *Forbes*
    139:52+ Mr 23 '87
Southmayd, William
    about
First aid for the fitness fanatic. P. Angiolillo. il por
    Bus Week p68 S 28 '87
Southwest Airlines Co.
Where 'frill' is a four-letter word. J. Weber, Jr. il por
    Bus Week p58+ S 21 '87
Southwest Ballet
Southwest Ballet intends to reflect its region. N. Plett.
    il *Dance Mag* 61:5 N '87
Southwest Museum (Los Angeles, Calif.)
Museum piece: the Southwest Museum, Los Angeles,
    California. K. Brinkley. il *Hist Today* 37:60-1 F '87
**Southwest Museum of Science and Technology, The Science
Place**
A new place for science in Dallas. il *South Living* 22:28
    S '87
Southwest Voter Registration Education Project
'All these guys owe Willie' [W. Velásquez] D. Pedersen.
    il por *Newsweek* 109:30+ Mr 16 '87
Southwestern cooking *See* Cooking, American
Southwestern States
    See also
    Crime and criminals—Southwestern States

Water supply—Southwestern States

Description and travel
    See also
    Automobile touring—Southwestern States
Desert sojourn. C. Haas. il *Esquire* 108:136-43 O '87
The land of the Navajo and the Hopi [cover story]
    il maps *Sunset* 178:96-109 My '87

History
Southwestward: the great American space. A. Kazin.
    il map *Am Herit* 38:52-61 Ap '87

Photographs and photography
An enduring grace: the photography of Laura Gilpin.
    M. A. Sandweiss. il por *USA Today (Periodical)*
    115:54-63 Mr '87
Following the sun to the scenic, spectacular Southwest.
    C. Purcell and A. Purcell. il *Pop Photogr* 94:38+ S
    '87

Politics and government
    See also
    Southwest Voter Registration Education Project
Southwestern States in art

Exhibitions
"Empowered painting" at the Santa Fe Museum of Fine
    Arts. D. Bell. *Art Am* 75:143+ Ja '87
Southwick, Edward E., and Heldmaier, Gerhard
Temperature control in honey bee colonies. bibl f il
    BioScience 37:395-9 Je '87
Souvenirs (Keepsakes)
    See also
    Baseball, Professional—Collectibles
    Black collectibles
    John Paul II, Pope, 1920-—Visit to the United
    States, 1987—Collectibles
Milestones [family memorabilia] P. Theroux. il *Parents*
    62:72+ Mr '87
Tomorrow's antiques [views of Charles J. Jordan] il
    Futurist 21:57 Jl/Ag '87
Souza, Tárik de
Music, the pulse of a people. il *Courier* 39:29-32 D
    '86
Sova, Dawn
Ways to get your money back. il *Read Dig* 130:25-6
    Ja '87
Sovereignty
    See also
    Treaties of guaranty
Soviet Academy of Sciences *See* Academy of Sciences of
    the USSR
Soviet Cultural Foundation
The Soviet Culture Fund: "setting this up is an amazing
    thing". M. Esterow. il *Art News* 86:108-9 O '87
Soviet embassy buildings *See* Embassies (Buildings)
Soviet photo (Periodical)
The state of photography behind the Iron Curtain [60th
    anniversary exhibition] A. Goldsmith. il por *Pop
    Photogr* 94:15 F '87
Soviet studies
    See also
    American Association for the Advancement of Slavic
    Studies
The cosmokremlinologists [American experts on Soviet
    space program] L. Dorr, Jr. il *Space World*
    X-10-286:28-30+ O '87
Gorbachev's profs. J. Rupnik. *New Repub* 197:10+ D
    7 '87
Iron curtain raising on campus. E. Bowen. il *Time* 130:65
    O 12 '87

Anecdotes, facetiae, satire, etc.
Glasnost TV-guide. E. Alterman. *New Repub* 197:12-13
    D 21 '87
Soviet Union
    See also
    Agriculture—Soviet Union
    AIDS (Disease)—Soviet Union
    Air traffic control—Soviet Union
    Alcoholics and alcoholism—Soviet Union
    Alma-Ata (Soviet Union)
    Americans—Soviet Union
    Anti-nuclear movement—Soviet Union
    Anti-Semitism—Soviet Union
    Art and state—Soviet Union
    Art trade—Soviet Union
    Arts and state—Soviet Union
    Authors' conferences—Soviet Union
    Automobile racing—Soviet Union
    Aviation—Soviet Union
    Baseball—Soviet Union
    Birds—Soviet Union
    Blacks—Soviet Union
    Books and reading—Soviet Union
    Censorship—Soviet Union

Soviet Union—See also—*cont.*
Chernobyl nuclear disaster, 1986
Civil rights—Soviet Union
Concentration camps—Soviet Union
Copyright—Soviet Union
Costume—Soviet Union
Criminal justice, Administration of—Soviet Union
Dance—Soviet Union
Dance schools—Soviet Union
Drug abuse—Soviet Union
Education—Soviet Union
Environmental policy—Soviet Union
Espionage, American—Soviet Union
Estonia
Fishing—Soviet Union
Food supply—Soviet Union
Foreign correspondents—Soviet Union
Freedom of information—Soviet Union
Gardens and gardening—Soviet Union
Germans—Soviet Union
Government and the press—Soviet Union
Hotels, motels, etc.—Soviet Union
Housing—Soviet Union
Immigration and emigration—Soviet Union
Investments, American—Soviet Union
Investments, Foreign—Soviet Union
Irkutsk (Soviet Union)
Jazz music—Soviet Union
Jews—Soviet Union
Kazakhstan (Soviet Union)
Lake Baikal (Soviet Union)
Leningrad (Soviet Union)
Liquor laws and regulations—Soviet Union
Literature and state—Soviet Union
Magadan (Soviet Union)
Marriage customs and rites—Soviet Union
Medical care—Soviet Union
Medical research—Soviet Union
Minorities—Soviet Union
Moscow (Soviet Union)
Motion picture festivals—Soviet Union
Motion pictures—Soviet Union
Music and state—Soviet Union
Music festivals—Soviet Union
Narcotics laws and regulations—Soviet Union
Narcotics trade—Soviet Union
Natural areas—Soviet Union
Nuclear research—Soviet Union
Oceanography—Soviet Union
Palaces—Soviet Union
Physics—Soviet Union
Political clubs and associations—Soviet Union
Political prisoners—Soviet Union
Psychiatry—Soviet Union
Public health—Soviet Union
Religious liberty—Soviet Union
Research—Soviet Union
Rock music—Soviet Union
Science and state—Soviet Union
Shopping and shoppers—Soviet Union
Siberia (Soviet Union)
Space research—Soviet Union
Technology—Soviet Union
Technology and state—Soviet Union
Television advertising—Soviet Union
Television broadcasting—Soviet Union
Tennis—Soviet Union
Theater—Soviet Union
Tractor factories—Soviet Union
Trials—Soviet Union
Underground literature—Soviet Union
United Nations—Soviet Union
United States—Diplomatic and consular service—Soviet Union
Uzbekistan (Soviet Union)
Videotapes—Soviet Union
Water pollution—Soviet Union
Women—Soviet Union
Youth—Soviet Union
Across a land of power and poetry [cover story; special issue] il map *People Wkly* 27:32-42+ Ap 6 '87
Regional report: the Soviet Union. S. Shabad. See issues of World Press Review beginning October 1986

Armed Forces
See also
Commandos, Russian
Military bases, Russian
Soviet Union—Army
Gorbachev takes on the generals. J. Trimble. il por *U S News World Rep* 102:29-30 Je 15 '87

Marching orders. R. Watson. il pors *Newsweek* 109:34-6 Je 15 '87
Plenty of guns, no politics for Gorbachev's generals. J. Trimble. il por *U S News World Rep* 102:32 My 11 '87
The two faces of Soviet military power. D. R. Jones. bibl f *Curr Hist* 86:313-16+ O '87

Forces in Afghanistan
See also
Afghanistan—Russian invasion, 1979-

Forces in East Asia
Arms control: the East Asian and Pacific focus [address, December 30, 1986] E. L. Rowny. *Dep State Bull* 87:37-9 Mr '87

Forces in the Pacific
Arms control: the East Asian and Pacific focus [address, December 30, 1986] E. L. Rowny. *Dep State Bull* 87:37-9 Mr '87
Moscow in the Pacific. S. Cropsey. *Natl Rev* 39:28-30 Je 5 '87
Red herring in the Pacific. W. M. Arkin. *Bull At Sci* 43:6-7 Ap '87

Forces in Vietnam
Soviets extend air, sea power with buildup at Cam Ranh Bay. B. M. Greeley, Jr. il *Aviat Week Space Technol* 126:76-7 Mr 2 '87

Army
U.S. inspects Soviet military exercise [State Dept. statement and report, September 22, 1987] *Dep State Bull* 87:44-6 N '87

Commerce
See also
Merchant marine—Soviet Union
High-tech shopping Moscow style. il *U S News World Rep* 103:12 N 2 '87

China
Soviet Union seeks to renew industry relations with China [Aviation Expo/China] *Aviat Week Space Technol* 127:29 O 26 '87

Developing countries
Russia: arms merchant to the world. P. Gupte. il *Forbes* 140:168+ N 2 '87

Japan
The battle over Toshiba [U.S.-Japan trade relations strained by Toshiba's sale of high tech goods to Soviets] J. B. Copeland. il *Newsweek* 110:40 Jl 13 '87
Beware of machines in disguise [conspiracy behind Toshiba's sales to the Soviets] S. Koepp. il *Time* 130:53 S 21 '87
Bright lights, big MITI [Toshiba's sale of top-security technology to the Soviets] C. Chandler. *New Repub* 197:11-13 Ag 31 '87
The case of the not-so-simple machine tools [Toshiba's sale of top-secret technology to the Soviet Union] M. I. Goldman. il *Technol Rev* 90:20+ O '87
Congress wants Toshiba's blood [diversion of high tech to Russia provokes U.S. punitive measures] S. J. Dryden. *Bus Week* p46-7 Jl 6 '87
How Toshiba is beating American sanctions [furor over illegal sale to Moscow dies down] S. J. Dryden. il *Bus Week* p58 S 14 '87
An illegal deal's noisy repercussions [Soviet deal with Toshiba and Kongsberg for milling machines to make submarine propellers] W. J. Cook. il *U S News World Rep* 102:42 Je 15 '87
Japan's bow of contrition [apologizing for Toshiba scandal] J. B. Copeland. il *Newsweek* 110:44 Jl 27 '87
A leak that could sink the U.S. lead in submarines [illegal sales to Soviet Union by Norway's KV and Japan's Toshiba] J. Kapstein. il *Bus Week* p65-6 My 18 '87
Making amends [Toshiba products banned in U.S. following sale of submarine technology to Soviets] *Time* 130:49 Jl 13 '87
Punish Toshiba? W. F. Buckley. *Natl Rev* 39:62-3 D 18 '87
Run silent, run to Moscow [sale of submarine technology to the Soviets by Toshiba and Kongsberg] G. Bock. il *Time* 129:45 Je 29 '87
Tackling Toshiba [U.S. reaction to high tech sale to Soviets] J. McLaughlin. *Natl Rev* 39:24 Ag 14 '87
Tora! Tora! Angry lawmakers torpedo Toshiba [U.S. seeks to punish company for illegal trade with Soviets] *U S News World Rep* 103:42 Jl 13 '87
Toshiba ban spurs review of technology export controls [U.S. reaction to Japan's high tech sale to Soviets] *Aviat Week Space Technol* 127:27 Jl 6 '87
The Toshiba scandal: anatomy of a betrayal [illegal sales to Soviet Union] R. K. Bennett. *Read Dig* 131:95-100 D '87

Soviet Union—Commerce—Japan—*cont.*

The Toshiba scandal has exporters running for cover [technology sale to Soviets] L. Armstrong and N. Gross. il *Bus Week* p86-7 Jl 20 '87

Toshiba vs. the U.S.: a Japanese view. *World Press Rev* 34:18 Ag '87

Welcome to Moscow on the Ginza [sale of submarine technology to the Soviets by Toshiba and Kongsberg] R. N. Perle. il *U S News World Rep* 102:31-2 Je 29 '87

Nicaragua

Nicaragua [oil shipments] *Bus Week* p49 Jl 6 '87

Norway

An illegal deal's noisy repercussions [Soviet deal with Toshiba and Kongsberg for milling machines to make submarine propellers] W. J. Cook. il *U S News World Rep* 102:42 Je 15 '87

A leak that could sink the U.S. lead in submarines [illegal sales to Soviet Union by Norway's KV and Japan's Toshiba] J. Kapstein. il *Bus Week* p65-6 My 18 '87

Run silent, run to Moscow [sale of submarine technology to the Soviets by Toshiba and Kongsberg] G. Bock. il *Time* 129:45 Je 29 '87

Such good friends: an old alliance under pressure [U.S. anger at Norway over illegal high tech sale to the Soviets] P. Sherrid. il *U S News World Rep* 103:42 O 5 '87

Welcome to Moscow on the Ginza [sale of submarine technology to the Soviets by Toshiba and Kongsberg] R. N. Perle. il *U S News World Rep* 102:31-2 Je 29 '87

United States

See United States—Commerce—Soviet Union

Western Europe

See also

Coordinating Committee on Multilateral Export Controls

Commercial policy

Comrade capitalists, come make money in the Soviet Union. K. R. Sheets. il *U S News World Rep* 102:39 Ja 19 '87

Ivan starts learning the capitalist ropes [joint ventures] R. Lewald. il *Bus Week* p154 N 2 '87

Letting Western business in [joint ventures] P. Galuszka and others. *Bus Week* p40 Ap 20 '87

Opening the Soviet hothouse: how far can Gorbachev go? M. I. Goldman. il por *Technol Rev* 90:18+ Ja '87

The twain are meeting—and cutting deals [U.S.-Soviet joint ventures] R. W. King and P. Galuszka. il *Bus Week* p88 D 7 '87

Western business may get a piece of *perestroika*. P. Galuszka and others. il *Bus Week* p70 D 28 '87-Ja 4 '88

Cultural policy

A dance for détente [M. Baryshnikov invited to dance in Moscow] P. Young. il por *Macleans* 100:74 F 2 '87

The four Soviet cultures. L. Steinmetz. *Natl Rev* 39:32+ O 23 '87

Mother Russia's new Red carpet [M. Baryshnikov and others invited to perform in their homeland] por *U S News World Rep* 102:10 F 2 '87

Reforming Soviet culture/Retrieving Soviet history. N. P. Condee and V. Padunov. il *Nation* 244:815-20 Je 13 '87

Siren songs from Moscow [M. Baryshnikov and other Soviet defectors invited to perform] M. S. Serrill. il por *Time* 129:46 F 2 '87

Cultural relations

From Russia with hope. B. Kaufman. il por *50 Plus* 27:29-31 Jl '87

Moscow calling [international peace forum] K. V. Heuvel. *Nation* 244:277 Mr 7 '87

Wooing the West [notables invited to a Moscow conference] J. Greenwald. il *Time* 129:22-4 Mr 2 '87

United States

See United States—Cultural relations—Soviet Union

Defenses

See also

Airplanes, Military—Soviet Union
Aviation, Military—Soviet Union
Chemical and biological weapons
Guided missiles, Russian
Korean Air Lines Flight 007 disaster, 1983
Military bases, Russian
Nuclear submarines, Russian
Nuclear weapons
Soviet Union—Armed Forces

Soviet Union—Army
Soviet Union—Navy
Strategic Arms Limitation Talks
Strategic Arms Reduction Talks
Submarines, Russian
Tanks, Military—Soviet Union
Warsaw Treaty Organization
Weapons

America has five years left. R. Jastrow. *Natl Rev* 39:42-3 F 13 '87

CIA, DIA at odds over Soviet threat. M. Krepon. *Bull At Sci* 43:6-7 My '87

Developing Soviet forces. L. Gouré. *Society* 24:50-5 Jl/Ag '87

Gaps in Soviet defenses? [West German, M. Rust, lands plane in Moscow] R. Kaylor. il *U S News World Rep* 102:30 Je 15 '87

Joint Chiefs chairman counsels long-term strategic view of Soviets [views of W. J. Crowe] il *Aviat Week Space Technol* 126:117+ Je 15 '87

NORAD, Space Command request system for surveillance of Soviet weapons. C. Covault. *Aviat Week Space Technol* 126:73+ Ap 6 '87

Offense-defense strategic balance in the 1990s [address, May 6, 1987] M. Wallop. *Vital Speeches Day* 53:610-13 Ag 1 '87

The secrets of Soviet Star Wars. W. J. Broad. il map *N Y Times Mag* p22+ Je 28 '87

Soviet ground lasers threaten U.S. geosynchronous satellites. J. D. Morrocco. *Aviat Week Space Technol* 127:27 N 2 '87

Soviet industrial espionage. P. Hanson. bibl f il *Bull At Sci* 43:25-9 Ap '87

Soviet strategic defense technology. E. Stubbs. bibl f il map *Bull At Sci* 43:14-19 Ap '87

Soviet strategic force upgrade paces U.S. modernization effort. J. D. Morrocco. il *Aviat Week Space Technol* 126:31-3+ Mr 9 '87

Soviets may not copy Star Wars [views of Matthew Evangelista] *USA Today (Periodical)* 116:15 Ag '87

The zap gap [Soviet edge in development of radio frequency weapons] C. De Caro. il *Atlantic* 259:24+ Mr '87

Description and travel

Enter this house and let the ice melt. R. Rosenblatt. il *Time* 130:94-6+ O 26 '87

From Riga to Siberia: the reforms outside Moscow. J. Trimble. il map *U S News World Rep* 103:50-5 O 19 '87

Moscow revisited. J. Woll. il *New Leader* 70:7-9 F 9-23 '87

Soviet specimens. W. Goodman. il *New Leader* 70:7-8 N 2 '87

Travel. N. Traver. il *People Wkly* 27:14 Ap 6 '87

Diplomatic and consular service

France

All for love [French expel Soviet diplomats in spy scandal] il *Time* 129:53 Ap 13 '87

France expels Soviets for spying on Ariane. D. Dickson. *Science* 236:142 Ap 10 '87

Israel

The Red flag is hoisted in Israel. il *U S News World Rep* 103:9 Jl 27 '87

A Soviet pilgrimage to Israel. F. Willey. il *Newsweek* 110:36 Jl 27 '87

United States

Expelled! How we ousted 80 Soviet spies. R. K. Bennett. il *Read Dig* 130:47-52 Ja '87

U.S.-Soviet agreement on embassy construction in Washington [statement, May 19, 1987] R. I. Spiers. *Dep State Bull* 87:34-5 Jl '87

Economic conditions

See also

Agriculture—Soviet Union
Food supply—Soviet Union
Underground economy—Soviet Union

Economic policy

Are America's liberals to the left of Gorbachev? P. C. Roberts. il *Bus Week* p14 S 7 '87

Can the Russians reform? J. K. Galbraith. *Harpers* 274:52-5 Je '87

The curtain rises on Gorbachev's Act II [economic reform] S. Bialer. il *U S News World Rep* 103:36-7 Jl 13 '87

A dirty word [profit] D. Seligman. il *Fortune* 116:203 Ag 3 '87

Gorbachev has planted the seeds, but will they grow? P. Galuszka and others. il por *Bus Week* p44-5 F 2 '87

Gorbachev is making a bold bid to get his reforms moving. P. Galuszka. il *Bus Week* p49 Je 29 '87

Soviet Union—Economic policy—*cont.*

Gorbachev reforms declare a dividend. il *U S News World Rep* 102:12 Ap 6 '87

Gorbachev: upping the ante [new economic mechanism] M. Whitaker. il por *Newsweek* 110:28 Jl 6 '87

Gorbachev's bottom line. P. G. Peterson. bibl f il *N Y Rev Books* 34:29-33 Je 25 '87

Gorbachev's Das kapitalism. B. Javetski and J. Pearson. il por *Bus Week* p30-1 Jl 13 '87

Gorbachev's gamble. P. Taubman. il por *N Y Times Mag* p28-9+ Jl 19 '87

Gorbachev's move. S. Bialer. *Foreign Policy* 68:59-87 Fall '87

Gorbachev's new challenge [economic reforms] por *Macleans* 100:19 Jl 6 '87

Gorbachev's uncertain reformation. J. W. Hahn. il *Commonweal* 114:586-8+ O 23 '87

Gorby's new economics. *Natl Rev* 39:16-17 Jl 31 '87

Inching down the capitalist road. J. O. Jackson. il *Time* 129:42 My 4 '87

Is it reform or rhetoric? Gorbachev and the Soviet economy. E. A. Hewett. *Current* 291:21-7 Mr/Ap '87

The left in the Soviet Union: the politics of *perestroika* [interview with B. Kagarlitsky] A. Cockburn. *Nation* 245:672-3 D 5 '87

Moscow stalling. A. B. Ulam. *New Repub* 197:12-14 D 7 '87

Promise and pain for a stagnant economy. W. L. Chaze. il *U S News World Rep* 103:38-40 O 19 '87

Reforming the economy. E. A. Hewett. *Nation* 244:802-4 Je 13 '87

Reforming the Soviet economy [cover story] P. Galuszka and B. Javetski. il *Bus Week* p76-80+ D 7 '87

Russia: where Gorbanomics is leading. R. I. Kirkland, Jr. il por *Fortune* 116:82-4+ S 28 '87

The second revolution. C. Redden. il por *Macleans* 100:19-20+ N 9 '87

"The Soviet economy is in a grave state" [interview with L. Abalkin] P. Fuhrman. il pors *Forbes* 140:106+ O 19 '87

The Soviet economy under Gorbachev. G. E. Schroeder. bibl f *Curr Hist* 86:317-20+ O '87

Soviets interested in study on economic conversion. M. Crawford. *Science* 235:1133 Mr 6 '87

Soviets pin economic hopes on technology. M. Crawford. *Science* 238:1644 D 18 '87

Economic relations

See also
Economic assistance, Russian
Soviet Union—Commerce

Foreign opinion

Foreign correspondents on Soviet changes. il *World Press Rev* 34:30-2 Je '87

The Soviet anniversary. il *World Press Rev* 34:5 D '87

American

Are America's liberals to the left of Gorbachev? P. C. Roberts. il *Bus Week* p14 S 7 '87

Gorbo talks. *Nation* 245:703-4 D 12 '87

A Soviet-American poll. il *Newsweek* 110:27 D 14 '87

A Soviet assessment [evaluating an American journalist's views]; tr. by Gretchen Trimble. D. Biryukov. il por *U S News World Rep* 103:54 O 19 '87

American—Anecdotes, facetiae, satire, etc.

The *glasnost* drapes. R. Baker. il *N Y Times Mag* p30 O 4 '87

Canadian

A growing fear of total war [Maclean's/Decima poll] B. Levin. il *Macleans* 100:50+ Ja 5 '87

Foreign relations

See also
Economic assistance, Russian
Espionage, Russian
Military assistance, Russian

America's chance. C. W. Maynes. *Foreign Policy* 68:88-99 Fall '87

Barriers in the fast lane for Moscow. J. Trimble. il por *U S News World Rep* 102:20 F 16 '87

Bothered, bewildered and in some cases bewitched. P. R. Range. il pors *U S News World Rep* 102:28-9 Ap 13 '87

From Russia with style. A. Wilson-Smith. il *Macleans* 100:23 S 28 '87

Gorbachev: a new foreign policy? D. K. Simes. bibl f *Foreign Aff* 65 Sp Issue:477-500 ['87]

The latest myths about the Soviet Union [S. Bialer's The Soviet paradox] N. Eberstadt. *Commentary* 83:17-27 My '87

Moscow's rubber Marx. R. V. Daniels. il *New Leader* 70:5-7 D 28 '87

'New thinking' in foreign policy. M. A. Evangelista. *Nation* 244:795-9 Je 13 '87

Removing Gorbachev's edge. M. Svec. il *Foreign Policy* 69:148-65 Wint '87/'88

Should the West help? M. Tatu. il *World Press Rev* 34:12+ Ap '87

The Soviet threat: Western schizophrenia. E. V. Rostow. *Current* 295:25-9 S '87

Staunch allies? [comparing Soviet support of allies to U.S. and British policies] B. Crozier. *Natl Rev* 39:26 Ap 24 '87

Step by step [address, May 2, 1987] J. A. Courter. *Vital Speeches Day* 53:581-5 Jl 15 '87

U.S.S.R. foreign relations [address, October 1, 1987] M. Gorbachev. *Vital Speeches Day* 54:130-3 D 15 '87

U.S.-Soviet relations: testing Gorbachev's "new thinking" [address, July 1, 1987] M. H. Armacost. *Dep State Bull* 87:36-41 S '87

What Gorbachev wants [cover story] S. Sestanovich. *New Repub* 196:20-3 My 25 '87

History

From World War to cold war. T. Garton Ash. bibl f il *N Y Rev Books* 34:44-50 Je 11 '87

Afghanistan

See also
Afghanistan—Russian invasion, 1979-

Angola

Birth of a Soviet satellite. B. Amiel. il *Macleans* 100:9 Ag 17 '87

Central America

A study in contrast: Central America & the Persian Gulf [competing Soviet and U.S. interests] J. B. Hehir. il *Commonweal* 114:439 Ag 14 '87

China

Beijing plays coy with Moscow. M. Hopkins. il *New Leader* 70:8-9 Ag 10-24 '87

The new era in Sino-Soviet relations. T. W. Robinson. *Curr Hist* 86:241-4+ S '87

To the north: a cautious thaw? il *Sch Update* 120:29 S 18 '87

Cuba—History

See also
Cuban Missile Crisis, 1962

Czechoslovakia

See also
Gorbachev, Mikhail—Visit to Czechoslovakia, 1987

Great expectations. H. Rodriguez. il *World Press Rev* 34:20 Ap '87

Developing countries

Moscow's third world game. H. Anderson. il *Newsweek* 109:34 Mr 23 '87

U.S.-Soviet relations: coping with conflicts in the third world [address, September 26, 1986] M. H. Armacost. *Dep State Bull* 86:57-61 D '86

East Asia

Moscow turns east. G. Perkovich. il *Atlantic* 260:30+ D '87

Soviet policy in East Asia. R. C. Horn. bibl f *Curr Hist* 86:321-4+ O '87

Eastern Europe

European drift: this time the wolf is at the door. H. Trewhitt. il *U S News World Rep* 102:22-4 Je 22 '87

Glasnost on the road, to mixed review. J. L. Galloway. il por *U S News World Rep* 102:34 Je 8 '87

Gorbachev and Eastern Europe. C. Gati. *Foreign Aff* 65:958-75 Summ '87

A new deal for Eastern Europe. A. J. McAdams. *Nation* 244:799-800+ Je 13 '87

A new era, comrade, when missiles go. J. Wallace. il map *U S News World Rep* 103:44+ D 7 '87

New kid on the bloc: Gorbachev's reforms spill into Eastern Europe. S. H. Loory. il *Progressive* 51:21-3 Je '87

Reform? Few fans in East bloc. D. Stanglin. il *U S News World Rep* 102:26 F 23 '87

Skeptical satellites. J. Bugajski. *New Repub* 196:15-16 My 4 '87

Soviet policy toward East Europe. M. Kraus. bibl f il *Curr Hist* 86:353-6+ N '87

Top down or bottom up? D. Singer. il *Nation* 244:756-8 Je 6 '87

Worried and nervous neighbors. S. Allis. il *Time* 129:51 Mr 9 '87

Eastern Europe—History

See also
Yalta Conference (1945)

Soviet Union—Foreign relations—*cont.*
France

See also
Chirac, Jacques, 1932——Visit to the Soviet Union, 1987
Soviet Union—Diplomatic and consular service—France

Germany (West)

German 'togetherness' could cause trouble for East and West. F. A. Miller. il *Bus Week* p41 Ap 20 '87
Moscow's arms-control offer has Kohl in a corner. J. E. Pluenneke and F. Thelen. il *Bus Week* p69 My 18 '87
Softening up the Germans [Soviet INF proposals] E. Galbraith. il *Natl Rev* 39:34-5 My 22 '87

Iran

After the Ayatollah. S. T. Hunter. *Foreign Policy* 66:77-97 Spr '87
Faking the red menace [Reagan administration's invention of a Soviet threat to Iran] *Nation* 244:65 Ja 24 '87
Study finds Rapid Deployment Force could thwart Soviet attack on Iran [study by Joshua M. Epstein of the Brookings Institution] P. Mann. il map *Aviat Week Space Technol* 126:85+ Ja 12 '87

Iran—Anecdotes, facetiae, satire, etc.

Poindexter file [disinformation supplied to Iran and Iraq concerning Soviet threat] R. R. Lingeman. *Nation* 244:68-9 Ja 24 '87

Israel

See also
Soviet Union—Diplomatic and consular service—Israel
Battle of Jericho [Soviet objection to Israeli Jericho II missiles] *Time* 130:22 Ag 10 '87
Israel. *Bus Week* p53 Ap 27 '87

Italy

Italy's reaction to 'glasnost'. S. F. Senigallia. *New Leader* 70:7 Mr 23 '87

Japan

Can Gorbachev break a 40-year deadlock with Japan? N. Gross and others. il *Bus Week* p57 O 5 '87

Middle East

Gorbachev's Middle East strategy. G. Golan. bibl f *Foreign Aff* 66:41-57 Fall '87
Mideast: Moscow on a roll. J. L. Galloway. il *U S News World Rep* 102:32-3 My 18 '87
Rx: a conference. A. Vasilyev. *World Press Rev* 34:13-14 Jl '87
Welcoming back the Bear. W. E. Smith. il *Time* 130:38-9 Jl 13 '87

Pakistan

Hot pursuit [Soviet-backed Afghan air force strikes at Pakistan] *Time* 129:42 Ap 6 '87

Persian Gulf region

See also
Iranian-Iraqi War, 1980- —Russian participation
Gorbachev's Gulf game. M. Whitaker. il por *Newsweek* 110:32-3 Jl 20 '87
High drama in the Persian Gulf. R. Evans and R. D. Novak. il map *Read Dig* 131:133-6 D '87
A mugging by Moscow. H. Trewhitt. il *U S News World Rep* 103:22 Ag 17 '87
A study in contrast: Central America & the Persian Gulf [competing Soviet and U.S. interests] J. B. Hehir. il *Commonweal* 114:439 Ag 14 '87
Superpowers in the Gulf. S. Pope. il *World Press Rev* 34:39 Ag '87

Poland

From a U.S. mole: inside story of what might have been [views of R. Kuklinski] R. Z. Chesnoff and D. Stanglin. il por *U S News World Rep* 102:32-3 Ap 20 '87
Gorbachev may be setting the stage for more unrest in Poland. W. Echikson. il *Bus Week* p53 Ja 19 '87
Gorbachev: the great counter-reformer, tr. by Pat Hunt and Jonathan Kozol. A. Michnik. *Harpers* 275:19-20 N '87
Gorbachev: the view from Warsaw [interview with J. Kuron] H. Luczywo and N. Gardels. *Harpers* 275:26-7 Jl '87

Romania

See also
Gorbachev, Mikhail—Visit to Romania, 1987
Romania in the age of glasnost. W. Fisher. il *New Leader* 70:11-13 Je 29 '87

Syria

Assad and his allies: irreconcilable differences? C. Dickey. bibl f *Foreign Aff* 66:58-76 Fall '87

United States

See United States—Foreign relations—Soviet Union

Western Europe

Advantage Gorbachev [gains in Europe due to Iran arms scandal] S. Sullivan. il por *Newsweek* 109:38 Mr 9 '87
Caution and doubt in Europe. L. Freedman. il *World Press Rev* 34:15-16 N '87
Exploiting the Soviet "threat" to Europe [European Defense Initiative] M. A. Evangelista. bibl f *Bull At Sci* 43:14-16+ Ja/F '87
Finlandizing Europe. J. McLaughlin. *Natl Rev* 39:20 D 31 '87
Gorbachev is making nice—and that makes NATO nervous. J. Templeman. il *Bus Week* p37 D 21 '87
The missile treaty is only a 3% solution. B. Javetski and D. Griffiths. il *Bus Week* p24 S 7 '87
Soviet aims in Europe. D. S. Yost. *Society* 24:72-9 Jl/Ag '87
A thunderclap [proposal that all nuclear missiles be removed from European soil] E. von Kuehnelt-Leddihn. *Natl Rev* 39:44 Jl 17 '87
Why Gorbachev's arms offer gives NATO the jitters. D. Griffiths. il *Bus Week* p49 Mr 30 '87

History
20th century

Remembering [the past as a fundamental problem] W. Pfaff. *New Yorker* 63:140-6+ D 7 '87

1917-

The Bolshevik Revolution turns 70. W. Leonhard. *Foreign Aff* 66:388-409 Wint '87/'88
Document: the Revolution and *perestroika* [excerpts from address, November 2, 1987] M. Gorbachev. *Foreign Aff* 66:410-25 Wint '87/'88
Lifting the veil on history [address by M. Gorbachev] T. A. Sancton. il por *Time* 130:45+ N 16 '87
On recapturing the Soviet past. D. Singer. il *Nation* 245:716-18 D 12 '87
Revising Lenin's legacy [imaginary debate between two brothers] F. M. Burlatskii. *Harpers* 275:27-8+ N '87

1917- —Photographs and photography

The state of photography behind the Iron Curtain [Soviet photo's 60th anniversary exhibition] A. Goldsmith. il por *Pop Photogr* 94:15 F '87

Revolution, 1917-1921

A kinswoman of famed journalist John Reed finds that Ten days still shakes the Soviet Union. S. K. Reed. il pors *People Wkly* 27:114+ Ap 6 '87
Time passes, but not the memories [recollections of October Revolution survivors] il *U S News World Rep* 103:47-8 O 19 '87

Revolution, 1917-1921—Historiography

'Glasnost' and the Russian Revolution [cover story] P. Dukes. il *Hist Today* 37:11-14 O '87

1925-1953

Beyond *glasnost* [A. N. Rybakov's Children of the Arbat] W. Laqueur. *Commentary* 84:63-5 O '87
A compatriot's view from the homeland [interview with A. Rybakov] D. Stanglin. il por *U S News World Rep* 103:50 Ag 17 '87
The ghost of an old Bolshevik [N. Bukharin] N. Cooper. pors *Newsweek* 110:76 N 16 '87
The ghost of Stalin [cover story] K. M. Campbell. il *New Leader* 70:9-14 N 2 '87
Tales from a time of terror [publication of A. Rybakov's Children of the Arbat] J. O. Jackson. il pors *Time* 129:45-6 Ap 27 '87

1925-1953—Historiography

Gaps in history. S. Shabad. *World Press Rev* 34:42 O '87
A new revolution in consciousness. D. Murarka. il *Nation* 245:486-8+ O 31 '87
Recovering the buried Stalin years [cover story] D. Murarka. il *Nation* 245:433+ O 24 '87

Historiography

Klyuchevsky and the course of Russian history. P. Dukes. il por *Hist Today* 37:51-4 Jl '87

Industries

See also
Airplane industry—Soviet Union
Clothing industry—Soviet Union
Helicopter industry—Soviet Union
Motion picture industry—Soviet Union
Petroleum industry—Soviet Union
Publishers and publishing—Soviet Union

Intellectual life

Gorbachev's disillusioned intellectuals. F. Coleman. il por *Newsweek* 110:37 N 30 '87

Soviet Union—*cont.*

Merchant marine
See Merchant marine—Soviet Union

Military policy
See also
Soviet Union—Defenses

Gorbachev's next move. M. A. Evangelista. il *Harpers* 274:24+ Ja '87

"New thinking" in the Kremlin. F. Griffiths. bibl f *Bull At Sci* 43:20-4 Ap '87

The Ogarkov factor [Soviet arms control proposals linked to views of N. Ogarkov] B. Crozier. *Natl Rev* 39:22 Je 5 '87

The Soviet debate on missile defense. B. Parrott. bibl f il *Bull At Sci* 43:9-12 Ap '87

The U.S.S.R. in the 1990's [address, April 17, 1987] R. F. Staar. *Vital Speeches Day* 53:487-90 Je 1 '87

Why the Soviets want an arms-control agreement, and why they want it now. E. V. Rostow. *Commentary* 83:19-26 F '87

Why the Soviets want arms control. M. K. MccGwire. il *Technol Rev* 90:36-45 F/Mr '87

Nationalism
Myth and memory in Soviet society. N. Tumarkin. *Society* 24:69-72 S/O '87

Navy
See also
Navy yards and naval stations, Russian

Superpower arms race at sea [cover story; special section] bibl f il *Bull At Sci* 43:13-28+ S '87

Forces in the Arctic
U.S. maritime strategy: a dangerous game. B. R. Posen. bibl f map *Bull At Sci* 43:24-8 S '87

Photographs and photography
A day in the life . . . [cover story; excerpts] il *Time* 130:54-9+ O 26 '87

Face to face. il *Newsweek* 110:28-9+ D 14 '87

U.S.S.R. opens up to Day in the life crew [shooting of Collins Publishers' picture book] S. Bolle. il *Publ Wkly* 232:35-7 Ag 28 '87

Politics and government
See also
Communism—Soviet Union
Communist Party (Soviet Union)
Political attitudes—Soviet Union
Politics, Corruption in—Soviet Union
Socialism—Soviet Union

10 days that shook the Kremlin [with interview with A. Yakolev; editorial comment by Mortimer B. Zuckerman] H. Trewhitt. il por *U S News World Rep* 103:51-2, 92 N 16 '87

70 years after Lenin [cover story; special section] il pors *U S News World Rep* 103:30-42+ O 19 '87

The Bolshevik Revolution turns 70. W. Leonhard. *Foreign Aff* 66:388-409 Wint '87/'88

The call to reform. W. R. Doerner. il pors *Time* 129:28-30 F 9 '87

Can anybody fix the Soviet system? M. I. Goldman. il por *U S News World Rep* 102:38-9 F 9 '87

Can Moscow control restive minorities? S. Powell. il map *U S News World Rep* 102:40-2 F 2 '87

Challenging abroad, opening up at home [M. Gorbachev] J. O. Jackson. por *Time* 129:36 Ja 5 '87

Coming to terms with Gorbachev. B. Amiel. il *Macleans* 100:7 Ap 13 '87

Conspicuous by his absence [M. Gorbachev] il por *Newsweek* 110:42 O 5 '87

Coping with Gorbachev. H. Trewhitt. il pors *U S News World Rep* 102:26-8 Ap 13 '87

Countering Gorbachev [*glasnost* campaign] M. Whitaker. il por *Newsweek* 109:32-3 F 23 '87

Document: the Revolution and *perestroika* [excerpts from address, November 2, 1987] M. Gorbachev. *Foreign Aff* 66:410-25 Wint '87/'88

Downfall of a folk hero [B. Yeltsin] C. Redden. il por *Macleans* 100:21 N 23 '87

Editor Gorbo. D. Kimelman. *New Repub* 197:13-14 S 7 '87

Faltering America, or Russia? B. Crozier. *Natl Rev* 39:22 D 31 '87

Foreign correspondents on Soviet changes. il *World Press Rev* 34:30-2 Je '87

From Stalin's grim legacy, new weapons for reform. D. Stanglin. il por *U S News World Rep* 103:36 Ag 10 '87

Future shock in Moscow. A. Toffler. *Cent Mag* 20:59-60 S/O '87

The ghost of Stalin [cover story] K. M. Campbell. il *New Leader* 70:9-14 N 2 '87

Glasnost [address, March 11, 1987] V. Bukovsky. *Vital Speeches Day* 53:596-600 Jl 15 '87

Glasnost: 'There's no turning back' [interview with A. Sakharov and E. Bonner] M. B. Zuckerman. il pors *U S News World Rep* 102:31 Ap 20 '87

The Gorbachev era [cover story; special section] il pors *Time* 130:28-34+ Jl 27 '87

Gorbachev: faster, faster [reform] R. A. Manning. il *U S News World Rep* 102:25-6 F 23 '87

Gorbachev: going slow. R. Watson. il por *Newsweek* 110:74-6 N 16 '87

Gorbachev: no time to relax [with interview with A. Yakovlev] J. L. Galloway. il por *U S News World Rep* 102:36-8 Je 1 '87

Gorbachev on the high wire. H. Trewhitt. il por *U S News World Rep* 102:36-7 F 9 '87

The Gorbachev regime after two years. J. Cracraft. bibl f *Bull At Sci* 43:31-3 My '87

Gorbachev: risking all for reform [with editorial comment by Mortimer B. Zuckerman] S. Bialer. il por *U S News World Rep* 102:50-1, 79-80 Ap 27 '87

Gorbachev talks tough [excerpts from address, June 19, 1986] M. Gorbachev. *Time* 129:54 Ja 5 '87

Gorbachev the bold. P. Reddaway. bibl f il *N Y Rev Books* 34:21-5 My 28 '87

Gorbachev: the great counter-reformer; tr. by Pat Hunt and Jonathan Kozol. A. Michnik. *Harpers* 275:19-20 N '87

Gorbachev: the man with a nice smile and iron teeth. R. Evans and R. D. Novak. por *Read Dig* 131:90-5 O '87

Gorbachev: the rest of the story. M. B. Zuckerman. il *U S News World Rep* 103:84-5 D 21 '87

Gorbachev: the view from Warsaw [interview with J. Kuron] H. Luczywo and N. Gardels. *Harpers* 275:26-7 Jl '87

Gorbachev's bottom line. P. G. Peterson. bibl f il *N Y Rev Books* 34:29-33 Je 25 '87

Gorbachev's 'courageous' reform plan [interview with A. Sakharov] por *U S News World Rep* 102:13 F 16 '87

Gorbachev's dilemma. E. H. Methvin. *Natl Rev* 39:42+ D 4 '87

Gorbachev's disillusioned intellectuals. F. Coleman. il por *Newsweek* 110:37 N 30 '87

Gorbachev's gamble [cover story; special section] por *World Press Rev* 34:9-12+ Ap '87

Gorbachev's move. S. Bialer. *Foreign Policy* 68:59-87 Fall '87

Gorbachev's opposition. R. Watson. il por *Newsweek* 109:48-50 My 18 '87

Gorbachev's progress. *Macleans* 100:20 Mr 2 '87

Gorbachev's revolution [special section] il pors *U S News World Rep* 103:68-72+ N 9 '87

Gorbachev's Soviet Union: after two years [cover story; special issue; with editorial comment] bibl il *Nation* 244:785-6, 792-800+ Je 13 '87

Gorbachev's tomatoes. M. B. Zuckerman. il *U S News World Rep* 102:76 Ap 20 '87

Gorbachev's uncertain reformation. J. W. Hahn. il *Commonweal* 114:586-8+ O 23 '87

Gorbo talks. *Nation* 245:703-4 D 12 '87

Gorbo's other woman [role of Soviet leader's wife] G. Freidin. *New Repub* 197:15-16 D 28 '87

Harper & Row to ship book by Gorbachev in early November. B. Levine. *Publ Wkly* 232:41-2 O 16 '87

"I am very guilty" [B. Yeltsin forced to resign as head of Moscow Communist Party] W. R. Doerner. il pors *Time* 130:34 N 23 '87

Kissinger: how to deal with Gorbachev. H. Kissinger. il pors *Newsweek* 109:39-40+ Mr 2 '87

The latest myths about the Soviet Union [S. Bialer's The Soviet paradox] N. Eberstadt. *Commentary* 83:17-27 My '87

Lenin to the rescue [letter attributed to Lenin bolsters Gorbachev's policies] B. Crozier. *Natl Rev* 39:26 S 11 '87

Lifting the veil on history [address by M. Gorbachev] T. A. Sancton. il por *Time* 130:45+ N 16 '87

Madcap Mik [M. Gorbachev] H. Hertzberg. *New Repub* 196:4 Mr 2 '87

Mikhail Gorbachev. il por *People Wkly* 28:32-3 D 28 '87-Ja 4 '88

Mikhail's year of living dangerously. J. Trimble. il por *U S News World Rep* 102:12 Mr 2 '87

The Moscow/Peking dilemma. B. Crozier. *Natl Rev* 39:26 D 18 '87

Moscow calling [international peace forum] K. V. Heuvel. *Nation* 244:277 Mr 7 '87

Moscow politics percolates in public [case of B. Yeltsin] J. Trimble. il por *U S News World Rep* 103:10-11 N 30 '87

Soviet Union—Politics and government—*cont.*
Moscow stalling. A. B. Ulam. *New Repub* 197:12-14 D 7 '87
Moscow's man in a hurry [M. Gorbachev] J. Smolowe. il por *Time* 130:16 Jl 6 '87
A new Russian revolution? *America* 157:371 N 21 '87
A new style First Lady [R. Gorbachev] M. Blyth. il pors *Ladies Home J* 104:98+ S '87
Not just another pretty face [A. Yakovlev appointed to Politburo] J. O. Jackson. por *Time* 130:39 Jl 13 '87
On recapturing the Soviet past. D. Singer. il *Nation* 245:716-18 D 12 '87
One step forward [M. Gorbachev's speech on anniversary of the Revolution] *Nation* 245:544-5 N 14 '87
A poet's view of *glasnost*. Y. A. Yevtushenko. il pors *Time* 129:32-3 F 9 '87
Red star blazes on [M. Gorbachev's tactics] B. Crozier. *Natl Rev* 39:26 Ag 14 '87
Rehab job [B. Yeltsin appointed to new government position] *Time* 130:37 N 30 '87
Round 2: Gorbachev vs. the hard-liners [career of Moscow party chief B. Yeltsin] J. Trimble and D. Stanglin. il por *U S News World Rep* 102:29-30 Je 29 '87
The second revolution. C. Redden. il por *Macleans* 100:19-20+ N 9 '87
Slowing down *glasnost*. C. Redden. il por *Macleans* 100:30-1 N 16 '87
The Soviet anniversary. il *World Press Rev* 34:5 D '87
The Soviet system today. P. M. Kennedy. il *Current* 296:16-26 O '87
The Soviet Union, 1987 [special issue] bibl f il map (inside back cover) *Curr Hist* 86:305-47 O '87
The Soviet Union at seventy. R. V. Daniels. il *New Leader* 70:11-13 O 19 '87
Sovieticus. S. F. Cohen. See issues of The Nation
Straight talk [M. Gorbachev interviewed by Italian Communist newspaper] por *Time* 129:43 Je 1 '87
Testing *glasnost*: an exile visits his homeland [cover story] A. Goldfarb. il pors *N Y Times Mag* p46-9+ D 6 '87
There are two fundamental questions. M. S. Forbes, Jr. il *Forbes* 140:25 N 30 '87
A touch of democracy. *Newsweek* 109:42 F 9 '87
Troubled waters [Kremlin infighting] B. Crozier. *Natl Rev* 39:24 Ag 28 '87
Two crossroads of reform. J. Kohan. il *Time* 130:66-8+ N 9 '87
The U.S.S.R. in the 1990's [address, April 17, 1987] R. F. Staar. *Vital Speeches Day* 53:487-90 Je 1 '87
Welcome back, Comrade Gorbachev. J. Trimble. il *U S News World Rep* 103:31 D 21 '87
'We're in an entirely new era' [interview with A. Hartman] por *U S News World Rep* 102:39 F 2 '87
What Gorbachev is up against. P. M. Kennedy. il *Atlantic* 259:29-38+ Je '87
What Gorbachev wants [cover story] S. Sestanovich. *New Repub* 196:20-3 My 25 '87
When to call off the cold war. C. Krauthammer. *New Repub* 197:18-21 N 16 '87
Wooing the West. J. Greenwald. il *Time* 129:22-4 Mr 2 '87
The year of Mikhail Gorbachev. il *Newsweek* 109:14-15 Ja 5 '87
The Yeltsin affair. *Natl Rev* 39:17 D 18 '87
Yeltsin walks the plank. R. Watson. por *Newsweek* 110:37 N 23 '87
Yevtushenko feels a fresh wind blowing [cover story; interview] K. Vanden Heuvel. il pors *Progressive* 51:24-31 Ap '87

Population
See also
Tatars

Religious institutions and affairs
See also
Christians—Soviet Union
Church and state—Soviet Union
Muslims—Soviet Union
Orthodox Eastern Church, Russian
Gorbachev facing faith & nationality. E. von Kuehnelt-Leddihn. *Natl Rev* 39:48 Mr 27 '87
Religion and atheism in the Soviet Union [special section] *Humanist* 47:5-24+ Ja/F '87

Social conditions
See also
Communism—Soviet Union
Women—Soviet Union

Social policy
The collapse of the Soviet welfare state. M. S. Bernstam. *Natl Rev* 39:40-1 N 6 '87

Strains in the welfare state. M. Walker. il *World Press Rev* 34:24-6 O '87

Study and teaching
See Soviet studies

Soviet Union. Academy of Sciences *See* Academy of Sciences of the USSR

Soviet Union. Constitution
All power to the party. M. S. Serrill. il *Time* 130:96 Jl 6 '87
The Soviet constitution: myth and reality [address, August 10, 1987] R. Schifter. *Dep State Bull* 87:34-7 O '87

Soviet Union. Copyright Agency
Abbeville announces joint publishing program with the Soviets. *Publ Wkly* 232:24 S 4 '87
Mikhail Gorbachev, author [interview with S. M. Bessie] A. P. Sanoff. il por *U S News World Rep* 103:73 O 12 '87

Soviet Union and the United States
See also
Exchanges, Literary and scientific
Soviet Union—Foreign opinion—American
Student exchange programs
United States—Foreign opinion—Russian
Entries in a détente diary. A. Hammer. il pors *Life* 10:40-1+ Ja '87
Glasnost comes to upstate New York [meetings between Soviets and Americans in Chautauqua, N.Y.] R. B. Cullen. il *Newsweek* 110:16 S 7 '87
Gorbachev's prairie pals [J. Chrystal and D. Andreas] T. Jacoby. il pors *Newsweek* 109:31 Ap 6 '87
The great dialogue [the Chautauqua conferences] D. Seligman. *Fortune* 116:188+ S 28 '87
Moscow bound [Chautauqua Soviet-American meeting] *Natl Rev* 39:17 S 25 '87
Notes and comment [how Russian words affect our feelings about the Soviet Union] *New Yorker* 63:21-2 Mr 30 '87
The ties don't always bind. M. Greenfield. il *Newsweek* 110:92 D 14 '87
U.S.-Soviet relations: background and prospects [address, September 15, 1986] J. F. Matlock, Jr. *Dep State Bull* 86:61-5 D '86

Soviet Union-Great Britain air agreements *See* Aviation—International aspects

Soviet Union in literature
How menacing is the Red menace? E. B. Claflin. il *Publ Wkly* 232:23-4 N 20 '87
My say [writers need to temper depiction of Soviet Union as always evil] R. D. Zimmerman. por *Publ Wkly* 231:39 Je 19 '87
Solzhenitsyn's October 1916: a preview. J. M. Curtis. il por *USA Today (Periodical)* 115:90-2 Ja '87

Soviet Union in motion pictures
Bold signal: a film confronts Stalin's legacy [Repentance] il *Newsweek* 109:20-1 Ja 5 '87
Christ meets Stalin in Soviet-made film [T. Abuladze's Repentance] J. Forest. *Christ Century* 104:676-7 Ag 12-19 '87
A "tragic phantasmagoria" [Soviet film Repentance opens in the U.S.] T. A. Sancton. il *Time* 130:54 D 14 '87

Soviet Union in television
ABC's Amerikan dream. H. F. Waters. il *Newsweek* 109:21-2 F 16 '87
Amerika: it can't happen here [ABC miniseries] A. Kopkind. *Nation* 244:165+ F 14 '87
Amerika the controversial. R. Zoglin. il *Time* 129:72-3 F 9 '87
Better red than dud [ABC's miniseries Amerika] N. Atkins. il *Roll Stone* p29-30 F 12 '87
A celluloid war of credibility [Platoon and Amerika] F. Bruning. por *Macleans* 100:7 Mr 16 '87
The Hitler in ourselves [ABC's Amerika] W. F. Buckley. *Natl Rev* 39:62-3 Mr 27 '87
Loyal Amerikans [ABC's Amerika] *Natl Rev* 39:18 Mr 13 '87
Made in Amerika [UN protests] J. Vitale. *Channels* 7:18 F '87
A new miniseries imagines Amerika's future—if the Soviets won World War III. D. Scheuer. il *Sch Update* 119:23 Ja 26 '87
Only in 'Amerika': the mini-series everyone loves to hate. P. Hoban. il *N Y* 20:36-41 Ja 26 '87
Remember, it's only a movie [ABC's Amerika] M. Bosc. il *U S News World Rep* 102:15 Ja 19 '87
Situation Commie [ABC's Amerika] J. Maslin. *New Repub* 196:25-7 F 23 '87
A TV man views the storm [Amerika broadcast] V. G. Sauter. il *U S News World Rep* 102:68 F 16 '87

Soviet Union in television—*cont.*

Will bad Russians make good ratings? [Amerika] A. P. Sanoff. il *U S News World Rep* 102:66-7 F 16 '87

Sow bugs *See* Sowbugs

Sowbugs

Control

Sowbugs, pillbugs. W. S. Moore. il *Flower Gard* 31:33 F/Mr '87

Sowell, Thomas, 1930-

about

A man alone. P. Brimelow. il por *Forbes* 140:40-1+ Ag 24 '87

Soweto Day *See* International Day of Solidarity with the Struggling Peoples of South Africa

Sowing *See* Seeding

Soy sauce

Amaranth: the color of soy sauce. *Prevention* 39:53-4 O '87

Soybean industry

Profiles [D. O. Andreas, chief executive officer of Archer-Daniels-Midland Co.] E. J. Kahn. por *New Yorker* 62:41-2+ F 16 '87

Export-import trade

Tofu-quality beans earn 40¢ premium for Illinois growers. *Success Farm* 85 no2:18 Ja '87

Soybean oil

Soybean ink could print more profits for farmers. *Success Farm* 85:62P O '87

Soybean products

See also

Cooking—Soybean products

Tofu

Soybeans

See also

Feeds—Soybeans

The prodigious soybean [cover story] F. Hapgood. il map *Natl Geogr* 172:66-91 Jl '87

Cultivation

Add fertilizer, subtract herbicide. M. Holmberg. il *Success Farm* 85 no1:26P Ja '87

Beans in wheat . . . and weeds in both [relay intercropping] D. Ohrtman. il *Success Farm* 85 no4:18AH F '87

'I can't afford perfect weed control'. M. Holmberg. il *Success Farm* 85 no1:26I Ja '87

Diseases and pests

Prefab clues for soybean disease sleuths [computer program] il *Success Farm* 85 no1:26V Ja '87

Field experiments

Bottom-line tillage trials [Minnesota demonstration plots] R. Fee. il *Success Farm* 85 no4:18P F '87

Prices

The charts like soybeans. G. Johnston. il *Success Farm* 85:7 My '87

A triple threat trade [soybean complex futures market] S. W. Angrist. il *Forbes* 139 Ann Directory:340 Ap 27 '87

Seed

The catch-22 with '87 bean seed. M. Holmberg. il *Success Farm* 85 no4:18AD F '87

Feverish soybeans in summer mean poor-quality seeds. *Success Farm* 85:70F Ag '87

Seeding

A boot-toe guide to replanting. M. Holmberg. il *Success Farm* 85:34B Je '87

Yield

A boot-toe guide to replanting. M. Holmberg. il *Success Farm* 85:34B Je '87

Soyinka, Akinwande Oluwole *See* Soyinka, Wole

Soyinka, Wole

about

Death and the king's horseman [drama] Reviews

N Y 20:58-9 Mr 16 '87. J. Simon

New Leader 70:21 Mr 9 '87. L. Sauvage

New Yorker 63:71 Mr 16 '87. E. Oliver

Nobel laureate Wole Soyinka [interview] W. Brown. por *Essence* 18:35 Ag '87

Nobel winner will accept a Morehouse degree only. il por *Jet* 72:28 Ap 27 '87

Wole Soyinka: Nobel laureate. P. Garland. il pors *Ebony* 42:141-2+ Ap '87

Soyuz flights *See* Space flight—Soyuz flights

Spa rooms

Skin care in home spas [use of saunas, whirlpool baths and facial steaming machines] P. Boyer. il *Prevention* 39:58+ Ag '87

Spa tubs *See* Hot tubs

Space, Outer

Art

See Space flight in art

Exploration

See Space flight; Space research

International aspects

See also

United Nations. Committee on the Peaceful Uses of Outer Space

Space, Personal *See* Personal space

Space (Architecture)

Experiencing places (I) [space and environment in architecture] T. Hiss. *New Yorker* 63:45-9+ Je 22 '87

Experiencing places (II) [space and environment in architecture] T. Hiss. *New Yorker* 63:73-80+ Je 29 '87

Space and time

See also

Hyperspace

Relativity (Physics)

Time travel

The geometry of space and time [cover story] J. C. LoPresto. il map *Astronomy* 15:6-19 O '87

New variables for quantum gravity [work of Abhay Ashtekar] M. M. Waldrop. *Science* 235:284-5 Ja 16 '87

Space astronomy

See also

Artificial satellites—Astronomical use

After Challenger: astronomical angst. R. T. Fienberg. *Sky Telesc* 74:29 Jl '87

New directions for space astronomy. R. A. Brown and R. Giacconi. bibl f *Science* 238:617-19 O 30 '87

Space biology

See also

Seeds, Effect of weightlessness on

Weightlessness

Weightlessness simulators

Lives of the cell [Lifesat] A. R. Oberg. il *Omni* 9:20+ Ag '87

Space centers

See also

Ames Research Center

George C. Marshall Space Flight Center

Hugh L. Dryden Flight Research Center

John F. Kennedy Space Center

Langley Research Center (U.S.)

Lyndon B. Johnson Space Center

National Space Technology Laboratories (U.S.)

Space vehicles—Launching pads, sites, etc.

White Sands Missile Range (N.M.)

Defense Dept. cancels shuttle planning complex. *Aviat Week Space Technol* 126:29 F 9 '87

NASA panel urges U.S. control of space station operations. T. M. Foley. *Aviat Week Space Technol* 126:341-2+ Je 15 '87

Employees

A year later [effects of Challenger disaster at Kennedy Space Center] B. Dickey. il *Space World* X-1-277:14-17 Ja '87

Security measures

Security tightens at space center [Guiana Space Center] il *Aviat Week Space Technol* 127:18 S 21 '87

Australia

Proposal deadline nears for Australian spaceport. il *Aviat Week Space Technol* 127:71 O 26 '87

China

Ancient and modern China blend at Xichang launch facilities. il *Aviat Week Space Technol* 127:130-1 Jl 13 '87

China evaluates benefits, intelligence value of Landsat [cover story] C. Covault. il *Aviat Week Space Technol* 127:42-5 O 5 '87

Chinese expand launch facilities to attract satellite customers. C. Covault. il *Aviat Week Space Technol* 127:120-1+ Jl 13 '87

Chinese facility combines capabilities to produce Long March boosters, ICBMs. C. Covault. il *Aviat Week Space Technol* 127:50-3 Jl 27 '87

Eosat will market Landsat data from Chinese ground stations. il *Aviat Week Space Technol* 127:52-3 Jl 20 '87

Third Chinese launch pad signals aerospace growth in Pacific Basin [Pacific Basin international symposium on space] C. Covault. *Aviat Week Space Technol* 126:66-7 Je 15 '87

French Guiana

Ariane launch teams complete training. il *Aviat Week Space Technol* 127:67 N 2 '87

Space centers—French Guiana—*cont.*
French install system to provide warning of lightning activity [Safir system at Kourou] il *Aviat Week Space Technol* 126:104-5 My 18 '87
Security tightens at space center. il *Aviat Week Space Technol* 127:18 S 21 '87

Great Britain

See also
National Space Center (Great Britain)

Italy

Italy proposes building, operating Columbus mission control center. *Aviat Week Space Technol* 127:135 Jl 13 '87

Space chemistry *See* Astrochemistry

Space colonies
See also
Lunar bases
Space [address, October 12, 1987] J. C. Fletcher. *Vital Speeches Day* 54:66-8 N 15 '87
"Special interest" colonies for oceans and space. *Futurist* 21:42-3 Ja/F '87
Terradreaming [terraforming Mars; excerpts from remarks, March 25, 1987] J. C. Fletcher. por *Space World* X-7-283:36 Jl '87

Space Command (Air Force) *See* United States. Air Force. Space Command

Space communication *See* Interstellar communication

Space constitution
A constitution for 2087. L. Frazer. il *Space World* X-5-281:32-4 My '87
Sending the Constitution into outer space [views of Carl Q. Christol] *USA Today (Periodical)* 115:3-4 Je '87

Space construction
Assembling the space station. P. Chien. il *Space World* X-12-288:16-17+ D '87
Canadian MSC to provide essential station assembly, docking capability [Mobile Servicing Center] T. M. Foley. il *Aviat Week Space Technol* 126:48-50 My 25 '87
McDonnell Douglas team will plan assembly of key elements in space [space station] il *Aviat Week Space Technol* 127:22-3 D 7 '87
Space station EVA simulation demonstrates orbital assembly. C. Covault. il *Aviat Week Space Technol* 126:60-1+ Ja 26 '87

Space Defense Operations Center *See* North American Aerospace Defense Command. Space Defense Operations Center

Space Defense Operations Center (Air Force) *See* United States. Air Force. Space Command. Space Defense Operations Center

Space Division (Air Force) *See* United States. Air Force. Space Division

Space flight
See also
Astronauts
Computers—Space flight use
Image processing—Space flight use
Information storage and retrieval systems—Space flight use
Insurance, Space flight
Lasers—Space flight use
Orbital rendezvous (Space flight)
Planets—Exploration
Robots—Space flight use
Space stations
Space stations—Skylab missions
United States. National Aeronautics and Space Administration
Fast Forward: a conversation with Robert L. Forward. R. M. Powers. il por *Space World* X-1-277:30-6 Ja '87
The long voyage from home [cover story] R. P. Burruss. il por *Futurist* 21:29-33 S/O '87
Lost wilderness. T. E. Bell. por *Space World* X-9-285:40 S '87
Star trek (I). D. J. Darling. il *Astronomy* 15:94-9 Mr '87
Star trek (II). D. J. Darling. il *Astronomy* 15:94-9 Ap '87
Van Allen visits [J. Van Allen's criticism of manned flight] S. Jochums. *Space World* X-8-284 Space Advocate:3-4 Ag '87

Accidents

See also
Challenger (Space shuttle) explosion, 1986
NASA panel would withhold accident witness accounts [Space Flight Safety Panel] il *Aviat Week Space Technol* 127:128-9 S 7 '87

Asteroid missions

Future Soviet space exploration to focus on Mars, asteroids. B. A. Smith. il *Aviat Week Space Technol* 126:81+ Je 22 '87

Cometary missions

A bunch of little comets—but just a little bunch [Voyager 2 data] J. Eberhart. *Sci News* 132:132 Ag 29 '87
Comet rendezvous—the next step [Comet Rendezvous Asteroid Flyby mission] M. Neugebauer. il *Sky Telesc* 73:266+ Mr '87
Evidence for chain molecules enriched in carbon, hydrogen, and oxygen in Comet Halley [Giotto data] D. L. Mitchell and others. bibl f il *Science* 237:626-8 Ag 7 '87
First polymer in space identified in Comet Halley [Giotto data] W. F. Huebner. bibl f il *Science* 237:628-30 Ag 7 '87
NASA and Halley: the road not taken. J. M. Logsdon. il *Sky Telesc* 73:268 Mr '87
Playing cometary tag. R. Farquhar. il *Sky Telesc* 73:267 Mr '87
Processed images detail comet's surface [Giotto probe] il *Aviat Week Space Technol* 127:60-1 Jl 27 '87
Proposed Caesar comet encounter vies for ESA authorization. il *Aviat Week Space Technol* 126:128 F 9 '87
Search for the primitive [cover story] R. Berry. il *Astronomy* 15:6-22 Je '87

Economic aspects

See also
American Rocket Company
Challenger (Space shuttle) explosion, 1986—Economic aspects
Conatec, Inc.
Eosat (Firm)
Orbital Sciences Corporation
Space Industries, Inc.
Space Services, Inc.
Spacehab, Inc.
Amroc official cites resistance to space commercialization [views of William R. Claybaugh] *Aviat Week Space Technol* 126:79 My 4 '87
Are the profits really there? [satellite launching business] W. W. Crook, III. il *Space World* X-7-283:34 Jl '87
Big dumb rockets. G. Easterbrook. il *Newsweek* 110:46-50+ Ag 17 '87
Blast-off for profits [satellite-launching business] J. Castro. il *Time* 129:44-5 Mr 2 '87
The broken promise of commercial space. T. M. Foley. *Aviat Week Space Technol* 127:15 S 14 '87
Commerce Dept. will buy ELVs from private sector [National Oceanic and Atmospheric Administration] *Aviat Week Space Technol* 126:24-5 Mr 23 '87
Commercial Delta 2 to be priced lower than international competitors. T. M. Foley. *Aviat Week Space Technol* 126:23-4 F 2 '87
Commercial space companies brief government on policies, prospects. T. M. Foley. *Aviat Week Space Technol* 127:47-8 O 5 '87
Commercial space firms propose booster, free-flier [Mars Observer] il *Aviat Week Space Technol* 126:76 Ap 6 '87
Company offers to buy NASA a rocket [Titan 3] M. M. Waldrop. *Science* 235:1568 Mr 27 '87
ELV manufacturers charge USAF with decision delays [expendable launch facilities] *Aviat Week Space Technol* 126:27 My 11 '87
First U.S. commercial sales of ELVs expected in 1987 [expendable launch vehicles] T. M. Foley. il *Aviat Week Space Technol* 126:113-14 Mr 9 '87
Getting into orbit—the non-NASA way. J. Eberhart. *Sci News* 131:326 My 23 '87
Governments must strive to make private enterprise work in space. R. Gibson. por *Aviat Week Space Technol* 127:91-2 N 2 '87
The iceman inspireth [entrepreneur F. Tudor as role model for creating a commercial space industry] J. Rhea. il *Space World* X-6-282:3 Je '87
Industry group criticizes Air Force draft agreement on ELVs [expendable launch vehicles and commercial launch industry] *Aviat Week Space Technol* 126:23 F 16 '87
Larceny at the launch pad. G. Easterbrook. il *Read Dig* 131:209-16 D '87
Launcher companies sign first commercialization agreements. *Aviat Week Space Technol* 127:26-7 Ag 10 '87
McDonnell Douglas Astronautics receives nine $50,000 deposits for commercial satellite launches [Delta 2s] *Aviat Week Space Technol* 126:29 Ap 13 '87
NASA issues five directives on commercial space policy. *Aviat Week Space Technol* 127:52-4 Jl 20 '87

Space flight—Economic aspects—*cont.*

NASA reaffirms strong support for space commercialization. C. Covault. *Aviat Week Space Technol* 127:31 O 5 '87

NASA revamps commercial policies, lifts ban on industry agreements. T. M. Foley. *Aviat Week Space Technol* 127:28-9 N 2 '87

NASA selects seven new Centers for Commercial Development of Space. *Aviat Week Space Technol* 127:31 Ag 3 '87

No business like space business. G. R. Graf. il *Space World* X-5-281:21-3 My '87

OSC offers to finance Titan 34D for Mars Observer [Orbital Sciences Corp.] *Aviat Week Space Technol* 126:24-5 Mr 23 '87

Payloads. W. H. Ganoe. See issues of Space World beginning June 1987

President's message. B. Bova. il *Space World* X-8-284 Space Advocate:8 Ag '87

Private launch prospects improve. M. M. Waldrop. il *Science* 236:766-8 My 15 '87

Proton marketing team finds U.S. interest, opposition [Soviet booster] il *Aviat Week Space Technol* 126:20-1 My 25 '87

Rockwell predicts HLV will lower launch costs [recoverable heavy-lift vehicle] B. A. Smith. il *Aviat Week Space Technol* 126:24-5 F 2 '87

Russki business [attempt to market Proton booster] L. Dorr, Jr. il *Space World* X-7-283:31-4 Jl '87

Satellite builders want change in U.S. anti-Proton policy. T. M. Foley. *Aviat Week Space Technol* 127:138-9 S 28 '87

Shuttle payload policy counters effort to attract private station suppliers. *Aviat Week Space Technol* 127:62 S 7 '87

Soviets offer three boosters for commercial launch services. il *Aviat Week Space Technol* 126:94-5 Ja 12 '87

Space shuttle a waste of money? [views of James Bennett and Philip Salin] il *USA Today (Periodical)* 115:2-3 Je '87

The space station launching a thousand contracts. S. Payne. il *Bus Week* p126-7+ N 23 '87

Space: the next business sector. M. Baldrige. por *Aviat Week Space Technol* 126:111 Je 1 '87

Starship enterprise: chasing NASA's unfinished business. S. Payne. il *Bus Week* p98-9+ N 9 '87

State Dept. denies license to export U.S. satellites to the Soviet Union [use of Proton] *Aviat Week Space Technol* 127:59 Jl 27 '87

U.S. space program urged to support international commercial competitiveness. C. Covault. *Aviat Week Space Technol* 127:55+ N 2 '87

Wealth from space: a rebuttal [discussion of August 1987 article, President's message] B. Bova. il *Space World* X-11-287:40 N '87

Why we mustn't create an "industrial policy" in space. A. Crawford. il *USA Today (Periodical)* 115:21-5 Ja '87

Extravehicular activity

EVA performed to dock Kvant module to Mir [astrophysics module] il *Aviat Week Space Technol* 126:21 Ap 20 '87

Of space walks and wolves: the incredible flight of Voskhod 2. W. W. Cook, III. il *Space World* X-1-277:11-13 Ja '87

Soviets planning to launch new module to Mir station [extravehicular activity airlock] *Aviat Week Space Technol* 127:22-3 O 12 '87

Space station EVA simulation demonstrates orbital assembly. C. Covault. il *Aviat Week Space Technol* 126:60-1+ Ja 26 '87

Two EVAs allow Mir cosmonauts to install third solar array. *Aviat Week Space Technol* 126:35 Je 22 '87

Food problems

Astrocrops [Controlled Ecological Life Support System] R. Wolkomir. il *Omni* 9:16+ Jl '87

Doing the dishes. D. Pine. *Space World* X-5-281:15 My '87

Seeding space [Closed Ecological Life Support System; cover story] B. Dickey. il *Space World* X-4-280:14-15+ Ap '87

Spin-off from space travel [hazard analysis critical control point in preventing food associated diarrheal diseases] S. Michanie and F. L. Bryan. il *World Health* p26-7 Ag/S '87

History

See also
Space flight—Voskhod flights

Historical analogies. B. Stites. *Space World* X-11-287 Space Advocate:5-6 N '87

The legacy of Sputnik [cover story; special issue; with editorial comment by John Rhea] il *Space World* X-10-286:3, 7-32+ O '87

Space firsts [quiz] M. R. Chartrand. *Space World* X-11-287:34 N '87

Sputnik 1 plus 30 years: the long and the short of it. J. Eberhart. *Sci News* 132:231 O 10 '87

Lightning hazards

Another launch failure [loss of Atlas rocket] J. Eberhart. *Sci News* 131:215 Ap 4 '87

Atlas accident inquiry board finds violation of launch commit criteria. C. Covault. il *Aviat Week Space Technol* 126:25-7 My 18 '87

Atlas failure analysis focuses on lightning. *Aviat Week Space Technol* 126:21 My 4 '87

Atlas launch follies. D. E. Fink. *Aviat Week Space Technol* 126:11 My 18 '87

French install system to provide warning of lightning activity [Safir system at Kourou, French Guiana] il *Aviat Week Space Technol* 126:104-5 My 18 '87

Kennedy lightning program yielding data to increase safety in launches. il *Aviat Week Space Technol* 127:70-1 D 7 '87

Launch score: nature 3, NASA 0 [lightning launches rockets at Wallops Island, Va.] J. Eberhart. *Sci News* 131:390 Je 20 '87

Lightning strikes twice at NASA [Atlas-Centaur accident] E. Marshall. *Science* 236:903 My 22 '87

Lightning studied in Atlas launch failure. *Aviat Week Space Technol* 126:31 Ap 13 '87

U.S./French lightning studies resume. *Aviat Week Space Technol* 127:20 Jl 20 '87

Military use

See also
Air Force Space Technology Center (U.S.)
Artificial satellites—Military use
Space stations—Military use
Space stations—Starlab missions
Space warfare
Spaceplane
Spaceplane, Russian
Strategic Defense Initiative
United States. Unified Space Command

Air Force awards contracts for Phase 1 ALS studies [advanced launch system] M. A. Dornheim. il *Aviat Week Space Technol* 127:25 Jl 20 '87

Defense Dept. cancels shuttle planning complex. *Aviat Week Space Technol* 126:29 F 9 '87

Defense Dept. developing range of launch vehicle concepts. B. A. Smith. il *Aviat Week Space Technol* 126:115+ Mr 9 '87

DOD revises its space policy. *Sci News* 131:189 Mr 21 '87

Letter from Washington. Cato. *Natl Rev* 39:15 Mr 13 '87

NASA may be forced to take minor role in heavy launcher. T. M. Foley. *Aviat Week Space Technol* 126:56-7 Mr 23 '87

New policy will increase similarity of U.S., Soviet military space efforts. il *Aviat Week Space Technol* 126:25 Je 1 '87

Pentagon usurps civilian space program. G. E. Brown, Jr. il *Bull At Sci* 43:26-31 N '87

Pentagon warns of Soviet space buildup. *Aviat Week Space Technol* 127:28-9 O 12 '87

Race into space: the Pentagon overtakes NASA by a missile length [Air Force's expendable launcher] S. Budiansky. il *U S News World Rep* 103:10 Ag 17 '87

USAF seeks industry responses for advanced launch system. *Aviat Week Space Technol* 126:26 My 11 '87

Physiological aspects

See also
Life support systems (Space environment)
Space medicine
Weightlessness

How to make space livable. il *Futurist* 21:56 Mr/Ap '87

The human factor: a conversation with Dr. Arnauld Nicogossian. T. Reichhardt and J. Rhea. il por *Space World* X-3-279:8-13 Mr '87

When the doctor is 200 miles away [proposed Health Maintenance Facility for the space station; cover story] L. Dorr, Jr. il *Space World* X-3-279:33-6 Mr '87

Pioneer flights

Goodbye, Pioneer 9. *Sci News* 131:166 Mr 14 '87

Pioneer data support theory of tenth planet. *Aviat Week Space Technol* 127:32 Jl 6 '87

Space flight—*cont.*

Reporters and reporting

See also
Challenger (Space shuttle) explosion, 1986—Reporters and reporting
Television broadcasting—Space broadcasts

Shuttle missions

See also
Challenger (Space shuttle) explosion, 1986
Space stations—Spacelab missions
Space stations—Starlab missions

Ariane, shuttle delayed again. D. Dickson. *Science* 236:1056-7 My 29 '87

Astronaut's diary [excerpt] J. A. Hoffman. il *Omni* 10:32+ O '87

Booster test equipment delays pose threat to shuttle schedule. E. H. Kolcum. *Aviat Week Space Technol* 127:31 O 26 '87

Defense Dept. cancels shuttle planning complex. *Aviat Week Space Technol* 126:29 F 9 '87

In charge at Mission Control: a conversation with Michele Brekke. M. Register. il por *Space World* X-4-280:33-6 Ap '87

NASA agreement with 3M sets precedent for large commercial space commitments. T. M. Foley. *Aviat Week Space Technol* 126:102-3 Ja 12 '87

NASA assigns launch dates to shuttle science missions. il *Astronomy* 15:82-3 Ja '87

NASA denies shuttle launch to commercial space firm [Spacehab, Inc.] T. M. Foley. *Aviat Week Space Technol* 127:26-8 S 7 '87

NASA nears key shuttle tests, changes initial payload schedule. C. Covault. *Aviat Week Space Technol* 127:28-9 Jl 6 '87

NASA reviews shuttle launch date, military station. *Aviat Week Space Technol* 126:27 My 25 '87

NASA sets shuttle launch dates, investigates main engine trouble. E. Marshall. *Science* 238:610 O 30 '87

New assessment slips shuttle launch to September, 1988. *Aviat Week Space Technol* 126:28-9 Ap 13 '87

New shuttle launch procedures may result in countdown scrubs. C. Covault. il *Aviat Week Space Technol* 126:64-5+ Mr 16 '87

New space launch manifest integrates shuttle, expendable booster missions. *Aviat Week Space Technol* 127:30-1 O 26 '87

On the road back. P. Chien. il *Space World* X-9-285:6-7 S '87

Satellites on a string [tethered satellite system] R. G. Nichols. il *Sky Telesc* 73:383-5 Ap '87

Shuttle delays force cutbacks in small research payloads. *Aviat Week Space Technol* 127:110 O 12 '87

Shuttle flight: 10 months and counting. il *U S News World Rep* 103:10 Ag 17 '87

Shuttle mission 26 will extend 3M materials experimentation. *Aviat Week Space Technol* 127:110+ O 12 '87

Shuttle payload policy counters effort to attract private station suppliers. *Aviat Week Space Technol* 127:62 S 7 '87

Shuttle, station disruptions slow U.S. civil space program. C. Covault. il *Aviat Week Space Technol* 126:111-12 Mr 9 '87

Space shuttle manifest [chart] *Space World* X-1-277:41 Ja '87

Space shuttle program managers concerned about staffing levels for three-orbiter processing. *Aviat Week Space Technol* 127:75 D 21 '87

Space station crew time extended to cut dependence on shuttle. T. M. Foley. *Aviat Week Space Technol* 127:30-1 Ag 3 '87

Spacebound again: the mixing of the fleet [cover story] J. Eberhart. il *Sci News* 132:330-1 N 21 '87

Photographs and photography

Astronauts discover new planet! P. Jones. il *Space World* X-3-279:18-20 Mr '87

Reporters and reporting

The story of the century [NASA's Journalist in Space program] C. Wise. il *Space World* X-4-280:22-5 Ap '87

Shuttle missions, Japanese

The other shuttles. J. Schefter. il *Pop Sci* 230:72-6 Mr '87

Shuttle missions, Russian

Energia heavy booster to double as Soviet shuttle propulsion system. il *Aviat Week Space Technol* 126:18-19 Je 8 '87

The other shuttles. J. Schefter. il *Pop Sci* 230:72-6 Mr '87

Soviets demonstrate flight readiness with firing of heavy-lift booster. il *Aviat Week Space Technol* 126:20-1 Mr 16 '87

Soviets fly jet-powered space shuttle testbed. il *Aviat Week Space Technol* 127:22-5 O 12 '87

Solar energy use

Efficient thin-film solar cells revive interest in space uses. B. D. Nordwall. *Aviat Week Space Technol* 126:105+ Je 29 '87

Two EVAs allow Mir cosmonauts to install third solar array. *Aviat Week Space Technol* 126:35 Je 22 '87

Soyuz flights

Case history: Vladimir Vasyutin [illness on Soyuz T-14 flight] L. Dorr. il por *Space World* X-3-279:36 Mr '87

Soviet long-duration crew activates Mir space station. C. Covault. il *Aviat Week Space Technol* 126:19-20 F 16 '87

Soviets conduct unusual manned, unmanned activities. C. Covault. *Aviat Week Space Technol* 127:29-30 S 7 '87

Soviets prepare to place cosmonaut crew on Mir for long-duration station flight. il *Aviat Week Space Technol* 126:28-9 Ja 26 '87

Thousand Astronomical Unit missions

Long day's journey. M. Bartusiak. il *Omni* 10:40 D '87

Oort cloud or bust. *Sky Telesc* 73:151 F '87

Star tracks. D. E. Thomsen. il *Sci News* 131:140-2 F 28 '87

Voskhod flights

Of space walks and wolves: the incredible flight of Voskhod 2. W. W. Cook, III. il *Space World* X-1-277:11-13 Ja '87

Voyager flights

Aiming for Neptune [Voyager's trajectory] C. E. Kohlhase. il *Astronomy* 15:6-15 N '87

Bound for the crown of Neptune [Voyager 2] J. Eberhart. *Sci News* 131:183 Mr 21 '87

A bunch of little comets—but just a little bunch [Voyager 2 data] J. Eberhart. *Sci News* 132:132 Ag 29 '87

Electroglow explained [Uranus glows in ultraviolet light] *Sky Telesc* 73:274 Mr '87

Interview [B. A. Smith] R. Schultz. il pors *Omni* 9:66-8+ F '87

JPL alters Voyager 2 controls to improve imaging of Neptune [Jet Propulsion Laboratory] *Aviat Week Space Technol* 127:131 Ag 10 '87

The moons of Uranus. T. V. Johnson and others. il *Sci Am* 256:48-60 Ap '87

Planetary probes double as space telescopes. il *Sky Telesc* 74:456 N '87

The rings of Uranus [Voyager 2 findings] J. N. Cuzzi and L. W. Esposito. bibl (p116) il *Sci Am* 257:52-4+ Jl '87

Uranus. A. P. Ingersoll. il *Sci Am* 256:38-45 Ja '87

Space flight centers *See* Space centers

Space flight in art

For the City of Light, a Ring of Light that's out of this world [space structure to mark the 100th anniversary of the Eiffel Tower] il *Discover* 8:6 F '87

France's Ring of Light [space structure to mark 100th anniversary of the Eiffel Tower] P. Lewis. il *Macleans* 100:22 Ja 5 '87

Lunar fantasies [work of C. Bonestell and F. Freeman for Collier's magazine] R. Miller and F. C. Durant. il *Omni* 9:50-5 F '87

Sky graffiti. S. J. Nadis. il *Omni* 10:24+ O '87

Starman [1950's sketches by W. von Braun for Collier's magazine] G. Williams. il *Omni* 9:86-93 Jl '87

Twinkle, twinkle, great big bauble [proposed Ring of Light to mark 100th anniversary of the Eiffel Tower] G. Taubes. il *Discover* 8:60-2+ N '87

A "yes" for the French space ring. C. Raymo. *Sky Telesc* 74:5 Jl '87

Space flight in literature

Astronauts by gaslight [cover story] R. Miller. il *Space World* X-9-285:26-9 S '87

Space flight in motion pictures

Lights! Camera! NASA! L. Suid. il *Space World* X-6-282:16-20 Je '87

Space flight simulators

See also
Weightlessness simulators

New space systems test facilities to cost $7 billion [Strategic Defense Initiative and National Aerospace Plane] il *Aviat Week Space Technol* 126:85 Ap 27 '87

Space station EVA simulation demonstrates orbital assembly. C. Covault. il *Aviat Week Space Technol* 126:60-1+ Ja 26 '87

Technologies merge in fantasy simulators [Star Tours at Disneyland and Toronto's Tour of the Universe] il *Pop Mech* 164:65 Je '87

Space flight to Jupiter
Galileo mission to Jupiter will involve more travel time, additional scientific data. B. A. Smith. il *Aviat Week Space Technol* 127:115-16 D 14 '87
Galileo's twenty year journey [cover story] R. Spangenburg and D. Moser. il *Space World* X-6-282:22-6 Je '87
Jupiter orbiter to launch in 1989 [Galileo] S. Eisenberg. il *Sci News* 132:373 D 12 '87
Project Galileo: the phoenix rises [cover story] M. W. Carroll. il *Sky Telesc* 73:359-61 Ap '87
Return to Jupiter [Galileo] G. L. Bennett. il *Astronomy* 15:6-15 Ja '87
Revving up for new voyages [NASA announces Galileo mission and space station] W. R. Doerner. il *Time* 130:65 D 14 '87

Space flight to Mars
Amassing momentum for Mars. J. Eberhart. *Sci News* 131:197 Mr 28 '87
Boland, NASA at odds over launch of Mars Observer. M. M. Waldrop. por *Science* 235:743 F 13 '87
The case against Mars. R. Grasshoff. *Astronomy* 15:28+ F '87
Close encounter [Phobos mission] M. M. Waldrop. il *Science* 236:1428 Je 12 '87
Commercial space firms propose booster, free-flier [Mars Observer] il *Aviat Week Space Technol* 126:76 Ap 6 '87
Company offers to buy NASA a rocket [Titan 3] M. M. Waldrop. *Science* 235:1568 Mr 27 '87
Destination Mars: a conversation with Michael Collins. T. Reichhardt and I. Gilman. il pors *Space World* X-7-283:16-20 Jl '87
The devastating delay [postponement of the Mars Observer] T. J. Frieling. il *Space World* X-7-283:27-30 Jl '87
Exploring deserts [Viking images of Mars compared to the Western Desert of Egypt] T. A. Maxwell. il *Earth Sci* 39:12-14 Wint '86
French offer balloon platform for use on Soviet Mars mission. J. M. Lenorovitz. il *Aviat Week Space Technol* 127:63+ Ag 3 '87
Future Soviet space exploration to focus on Mars, asteroids. B. A. Smith. il *Aviat Week Space Technol* 126:81+ Je 22 '87
International Mars mission proposed to energize U.S. space program; Lengthy manned Mars trip envisioned. R. G. O'Lone. *Aviat Week Space Technol* 126:73 Ja 26 '87
Let's save Mars first. J. Loudon. il *Sky Telesc* 74:228 S '87
Life search [proposed Mars Network Mission] E. Smith. il *Omni* 9:32 Je '87
Man's inevitable trip to Mars. S. N. Wellborn. il *U S News World Rep* 103:46-8 Ag 3 '87
Mars next? G. Woodcock. por *Space World* X-10-286:36 O '87
Mars-struck [Mars Observer] il *Sci Am* 256:63+ Ap '87
The Martian Metro [Mars Cycler envisioned by E. E. Aldrin] F. Braun and O. Davies. il *Omni* 10:52-4+ N '87
Medical hazards of Mars mission [views of William DeCampli] il *USA Today (Periodical)* 115:4 Je '87
Mission to Mars. il *Natl Geogr World* 137:27-31 Ja '87
More momentum for Mars—and Martians. J. Eberhart. *Sci News* 132:68-9 Ag 1 '87
NASA begins work on Mars mission to rejuvenate U.S. space program. C. Covault. il *Aviat Week Space Technol* 126:24-6 Mr 16 '87
NASA briefs contractors on Mars rover/sample return mission. M. A. Dornheim. il *Aviat Week Space Technol* 126:22-3 Ap 6 '87
NASA forms office to study manned lunar base, Mars missions. il *Aviat Week Space Technol* 126:22-3 Je 8 '87
Orbital Sciences, Space Agency disagree on cost of using transfer orbit stage as upper stage for the Mars Observer. *Aviat Week Space Technol* 126:27 My 11 '87
OSC offers to finance Titan 34D for Mars Observer [Orbital Sciences Corp.] *Aviat Week Space Technol* 126:24-5 Mr 23 '87
President's message. B. Bova. il *Space World* X-6-282 Space Advocate:8 Je '87
Probing the Phobian storehouse. M. Gould. por *Space World* X-12-288:39 D '87
The race is on: U.S., Soviet plans for Mars exploration [International Conference on Solar System Exploration] il *Astronomy* 15:86-7 O '87
Return to Mars [special section] il *Astronomy* 15:26-37 N '87

Seize the Mars initiative. D. E. Fink. *Aviat Week Space Technol* 126:11 Mr 16 '87
Settle cislunar space before heading to Mars. R. J. Erikson. por *Aviat Week Space Technol* 126:87 Je 22 '87
Soviet Mars mission will use modular propulsion system. *Aviat Week Space Technol* 127:81 N 2 '87
Soviet scientists present details of Mars exploration program. B. A. Smith. *Aviat Week Space Technol* 126:22 My 25 '87
Soviets advance definition work on 1990s unmanned Mars mission. J. M. Lenorovitz. il *Aviat Week Space Technol* 127:72-3 O 26 '87
Soviets consider possible Mars rover, sample return missions. C. A. Shifrin. *Aviat Week Space Technol* 126:26-7 Mr 23 '87
Soviets propose relay role for Mars Observer mission. C. Covault. il *Aviat Week Space Technol* 127:21-2 D 21 '87
Soviets will use international experts to help plan future science missions. J. M. Lenorovitz. il *Aviat Week Space Technol* 127:110-11 O 19 '87
Task force urges NASA to adopt manned Mars goal. *Aviat Week Space Technol* 126:263 Mr 9 '87
Terradreaming [terraforming Mars; excerpts from remarks, March 25, 1987] J. C. Fletcher. por *Space World* X-7-283:36 Jl '87
Tsander's dream. P. Pesavento. il por *Space World* X-5-281:28-31 My '87
U.S./Soviet teleconference highlights Mars exploration program objectives. B. A. Smith. *Aviat Week Space Technol* 127:61+ Ag 3 '87
View from Sri Lanka . . . and California; SDI "breakthroughs". *Space World* X-1-277:5-6 Ja '87
Viking images spark interest in future mission to Mars. *Aviat Week Space Technol* 127:64 O 12 '87

Space flight to Neptune
See also
Space flight—Voyager flights

Space flight to Pluto
A mission to Pluto. K. Croswell. il *Space World* X-9-285:22-4 S '87

Space flight to Saturn
Cassini. D. F. Robertson. il *Astronomy* 15:20-4 S '87

Space flight to the moon
See also
Lunar vehicles
Japan plans lunar mission in 1990. il *Aviat Week Space Technol* 126:63 F 23 '87
Lunar fantasies [work of C. Bonestell and F. Freeman for Collier's magazine] R. Miller and F. C. Durant. il *Omni* 9:50-5 F '87

Apollo 11 flight
The first men on the moon [remarks made after setting foot on moon, July 1969] N. Armstrong and E. E. Aldrin. il *Courier* 40:10 Ap '87

Space flight to the sun
Lost Ulysses [work of J. A. Simpson] D. Stewart. il *Omni* 9:20+ S '87
Voyage into the third dimension [Ulysses mission] G. L. Bennett. il *Astronomy* 15:14-22 My '87

Space flight to Uranus
See also
Space flight—Voyager flights

Space flight to Venus
Magellan: around Venus for 240 days. R. Spangenburg and D. Moser. il *Space World* X-3-279:14-17 Mr '87

Space heaters *See* Heaters

Space Industries, Inc.
Commercial space firms propose booster, free-flier. il *Aviat Week Space Technol* 126:76 Ap 6 '87
NASA will consider use of commercial space facility [Industrial Space Facility] *Aviat Week Space Technol* 127:55 N 2 '87
Westinghouse unit prepared to buy space module hardware [Industrial Space Facility] *Aviat Week Space Technol* 127:28-9 S 7 '87

Space laboratories *See* Space stations

Space law
See also
Space constitution
United Nations. Committee on the Peaceful Uses of Outer Space

Space manufacturing *See* Space processing

Space Master Enterprises Inc.
Prefab pokeys: when prison space is tight. D. Foust. il por *Bus Week* p86 N 2 '87

Space medicine
Astro docs [views of William M. DeCampli] D. Sobel. il *Omni* 9:22 Ap '87

Space medicine—*cont.*
The human factor: a conversation with Dr. Arnauld Nicogossian. T. Reichhardt and J. Rhea. il por *Space World* X-3-279:8-13 Mr '87

Space museums
See also
Kansas Cosmosphere and Space Center

Space perception
See also
Orientation
Experiencing places (I) [space and environment in architecture] T. Hiss. *New Yorker* 63:45-9+ Je 22 '87
Experiencing places (II) [space and environment in architecture] T. Hiss. *New Yorker* 63:73-80+ Je 29 '87

Space physics *See* Astrophysics
Space platforms *See* Space stations
Space policy *See* Space research

Space pollution
See also
Radioactive space pollution
Century 21: the age of space junk? S. Van den Bergh. il *Sky Telesc* 74:4 Jl '87
Debris danger zone. il *Nat Hist* 96:6 N '87
Hubble trouble? [possibility of damage from collisions with other satellites and space debris] il *Sky Telesc* 73:31 Ja '87
The impending crisis of space debris. J. A. Lovece. il *Astronomy* 15:6-13 Ag '87
SDI Delta intercept yields data on space collision shock waves. C. Covault. il *Aviat Week Space Technol* 126:26-7 Je 8 '87
Space debris: more than meets the eye. D. J. Kessler. il *Sky Telesc* 73:587 Je '87
Trashing space. map *Sci Am* 257:14+ Ag '87

Space processing
Aeritalia will develop microgravity facility for use on Spacelab [bubble drop and particle unit] *Aviat Week Space Technol* 127:54 Jl 20 '87
The broken promise of commercial space. T. M. Foley. *Aviat Week Space Technol* 127:15 S 14 '87
Chinese will launch French payload [Matra piggyback microgravity payload carried on board a Chinese satellite to be launched by a Long March 2] *Aviat Week Space Technol* 126:23 My 4 '87
Commercial space companies brief government on policies, prospects. T. M. Foley. *Aviat Week Space Technol* 127:47-8 O 5 '87
Congress to postpone station funding if NASA constrains materials science. *Aviat Week Space Technol* 127:29 O 12 '87
Destination: lunar industrial base [proposal by W. F. Mitchell] W. H. Ganoe. il *Space World* X-9-285:39 S '87
Europe seeks additional opportunities for microgravity space experiments. J. M. Lenorovitz. il *Aviat Week Space Technol* 127:133-5 Jl 13 '87
Expendable experiments [commercial space recovery vehicles developed for microgravity research] W. H. Ganoe. il *Space World* X-8-284:39 Ag '87
Factories in space: the role of robots [cover story] L. A. C. Weaver. il por *Futurist* 21:29-34 My/Je '87
Industrial space: the modeler [work of A. Cutler] W. H. Ganoe. il *Space World* X-7-283:35 Jl '87
Microgravity Task Force recommends sweeping changes to NASA program. T. M. Foley. il *Aviat Week Space Technol* 127:50-1 Jl 20 '87
NASA agreement with 3M sets precedent for large commercial space commitments [shuttle research] T. M. Foley. *Aviat Week Space Technol* 126:102-3 Ja 12 '87
NASA delays space station contracts as industrial research interest grows. C. Covault. il *Aviat Week Space Technol* 127:30-1 N 9 '87
NASA issues five directives on commercial space policy. *Aviat Week Space Technol* 127:52-4 Jl 20 '87
NASA will consider use of commercial space facility [Space Industries' Industrial Space Facility] *Aviat Week Space Technol* 127:55 N 2 '87
Report urges shift in microgravity effort. *Aviat Week Space Technol* 126:28 F 9 '87
Shuttle mission 26 will extend 3M materials experimentation. *Aviat Week Space Technol* 127:110+ O 12 '87
Shuttle payload policy counters effort to attract private station suppliers. *Aviat Week Space Technol* 127:62 S 7 '87
Soviets offer Mir for experiments, commercial space processing. il *Aviat Week Space Technol* 126:23 Je 22 '87
Support for lunar base grows among non-aerospace firms. il *Aviat Week Space Technol* 127:109-10 O 12 '87

Westinghouse unit prepared to buy space module hardware [Industrial Space Facility] *Aviat Week Space Technol* 127:28-9 S 7 '87
Why we mustn't create an "industrial policy" in space. A. Crawford. il *USA Today (Periodical)* 115:21-5 Ja '87

Space program (U.S.) *See* United States. National Aeronautics and Space Administration
Space programs *See* Space research
Space propulsion *See* Space vehicles—Propulsion systems

Space rescue work
See also
Artificial satellites—Rescue work use

Space research
See also
Air Force Space Technology Center (U.S.)
Jet Propulsion Laboratory (U.S.)
National Commission on Space (U.S.)
Planets—Exploration
Space flight
Space Studies Institute
Spacecause
Spacepac
United States. Congress. House. Committee on Science, Space, and Technology
United States. National Aeronautics and Space Administration
AAS adopts resolution on space science. W. Sweet. *Phys Today* 40:70-1 Ap '87
Adulthood. T. Reichhardt. il *Space World* X-9-285:4 S '87
America grounded [cover story; special section] il *Newsweek* 110:34-7+ Ag 17 '87
America in space: where next? [cover story] L. David. il *Sky Telesc* 74:23-9 Jl '87
Crippled birds in search of wings [U.S. program] O. Friedrich. il *Time* 130:72-3 O 5 '87
Disaster and indecision could cost U.S. entire generation of space scientists. il *USA Today (Periodical)* 115:1-2 Je '87
The future of science in space. P. M. Banks and D. C. Black. bibl f *Science* 236:244-5 Ap 17 '87
Getting NASA back on track [report by S. Ride] A. Toufexis. il *Time* 130:56 Ag 31 '87
Have we given up on our space program? R. P. MacLeod. il *USA Today (Periodical)* 115:14-16 My '87
Historical analogies. B. Stites. *Space World* X-11-287 Space Advocate:5-6 N '87
How to get America back into space. W. Schirra. il *Pop Mech* 164:76-8+ Mr '87
Lessons unlearned: space policy after Challenger. M. S. Smith. il *Space World* X-10-286:21-3 O '87
NASA selects seven new Centers for Commercial Development of Space. *Aviat Week Space Technol* 127:31 Ag 3 '87
Outlook for space science: conversations with Burt Edelson and Lennard Fisk. M. Freeman; T. Reichhardt. pors *Space World* X-11-287:26-31 N '87
Picking up the space banner. D. E. Fink. *Aviat Week Space Technol* 127:11 O 19 '87
A president for space. J. Muncy. *Space World* X-7-283 Space Advocate:4-5 Jl '87
President's message [presidential campaign] B. Bova. il *Space World* X-11-287 Space Advocate:8 N '87
Report identifies early science work for space station. T. M. Foley. *Aviat Week Space Technol* 126:84-5 Mr 30 '87
Ride panel calls for aggressive action to assert U.S. leadership in space [with editorial comment by Donald E. Fink] C. Covault. il *Aviat Week Space Technol* 127:11, 26-7 Ag 24 '87
Ride report: charting the nation's future course in space. I. Goodwin. por *Phys Today* 40:64-6 O '87
Ride report: the going, not the goal. J. Eberhart. *Sci News* 132:117 Ag 22 '87
Sally Ride on America's future in space. S. K. Ride. *Space World* X-9-285:25 S '87
Science and the space station. E. Marshall. il *Science* 236:1176-9 Je 5 '87
Settle cislunar space before heading to Mars. R. J. Erikson. por *Aviat Week Space Technol* 126:87 Je 22 '87
Shuttle, station disruptions slow U.S. civil space program. C. Covault. il *Aviat Week Space Technol* 126:111-12 Mr 9 '87
Space leadership void. D. E. Fink. *Aviat Week Space Technol* 127:9 Jl 27 '87
Space program said to lack direction [report by S. Ride] C. Norman. il por *Science* 237:965 Ag 28 '87
Space research: at a crossroads. F. B. McDonald. bibl f *Science* 235:751-4 F 13 '87

Space research—cont.

Space scuttle [need for coherent policy] R. Bazell. New Repub 197:11-12 O 12 '87

Space, the political imperative. C. Covault. Aviat Week Space Technol 127:9 N 30 '87

Two steps forward . . . T. Beardsley. Sci Am 257:18 S '87

U.S. space program: struggling to recover [special section; with editorial comment by Donald E. Fink] il Aviat Week Space Technol 127:11, 18-27 Ag 10 '87

U.S. space science program in jeopardy [views of the American Astronomical Society] il Astronomy 15:77-8 Ap '87

Washington orbit. See issues of Space World

What does he know and when does he know it? [proposed National Aeronautics and Space Council] J. Rhea. il Space World X-1-277:3 Ja '87

What's wrong with America's space program. S. Budiansky. il U S News World Rep 103:32-4 D 28 '87-Ja 4 '88

White House space policy review generates concern among agencies. C. Covault. Aviat Week Space Technol 127:28-9 Jl 27 '87

Anecdotes, facetiae, satire, etc.

Space exploration: 1957-1987. C. Colombo. il Space World X-4-280:3 Ap '87

International aspects

See also

International Astronautical Federation
International Space Year, 1992
Space stations—Spacelab missions
United Nations. Committee on the Peaceful Uses of Outer Space

Aggressive foreign space programs forcing U.S. strategic reassessment. C. Covault. Aviat Week Space Technol 127:28-30 O 12 '87

American-Soviet space pact. Sky Telesc 74:11 Jl '87

Defense Dept. backs down on international station demands. T. M. Foley. il Aviat Week Space Technol 126:42-3 Ap 27 '87

International cooperation to share expense [Soviet-U.S. space programs; views of Roald Sagdeev] il USA Today (Periodical) 116:8-9 D '87

No nation can be an island in science. R. C. Cowen. il Technol Rev 90:20+ My/Je '87

Political, technological needs spur new national launch strategies. C. Covault. il Aviat Week Space Technol 126:262-3+ Je 15 '87

Soviets propose relay role for Mars Observer mission. C. Covault. il Aviat Week Space Technol 127:21-2 D 21 '87

Space station policy problems [special section; with editorial comment by Donald E. Fink] il Aviat Week Space Technol 126:11, 18-24 Ap 20 '87

Space station—round 2. D. E. Fink. Aviat Week Space Technol 126:25 Ap 27 '87

Station talks conclude without firm commitments [Canadian, Japanese and European partners] T. M. Foley. Aviat Week Space Technol 127:32 O 26 '87

Superpower pact links initial Mars missions. S. Cole. il Astronomy 15:26-8 N '87

Technology transfer is the issue in space cooperation. M. M. Waldrop. Science 236:1430 Je 12 '87

U.S./Soviet teleconference highlights Mars exploration program objectives. B. A. Smith. Aviat Week Space Technol 127:61+ Ag 3 '87

U.S., Japan present plans for joint spacecraft mission [Tropical Rainfall Measuring Mission] il Aviat Week Space Technol 127:69+ O 26 '87

U.S. proposal would restrict European, Japanese station use. T. M. Foley. il Aviat Week Space Technol 126:23-5 F 16 '87

U.S.-Soviet space pact signed. J. Eberhart. Sci News 131:260 Ap 25 '87

U.S., Soviets to cooperate on September launch of biosatellite [Vostok biological satellite] il Aviat Week Space Technol 127:18-19 Jl 13 '87

Who will lead the world's next age of discovery? T. O. Paine. por Aviat Week Space Technol 127:43+ S 21 '87

Whose space is the space station? P. Marsh. il World Press Rev 34:51 My '87

Public opinion

President's message [Space Policy Survey] B. Bova. il Space World X-7-283 Space Advocate:8 Jl '87

The soap merchants [promoting space research] J. D. Kirwan. Space World X-11-287 Space Advocate:6-7 N '87

Who are we? G. Woodcock. por Space World X-6-282:36 Je '87

Brazil

Brazil's space program remains dynamic despite fiscal woes. il Aviat Week Space Technol 127:75+ Ag 24 '87

Canada

Canada would quit station if Pentagon demands prevail. P. Mann. Aviat Week Space Technol 126:20-2 Ap 20 '87

Canadian conundrum [participation in the space station] K. Day. por Space World X-8-284:40 Ag '87

Canadian MSC to provide essential station assembly, docking capability [Mobile Servicing Center] T. M. Foley. il Aviat Week Space Technol 126:48-50 My 25 '87

Canadians making early effort to organize for station use. T. M. Foley. Aviat Week Space Technol 126:24-5 My 11 '87

Compromise eludes U.S., Canada in space station negotiations. T. M. Foley. Aviat Week Space Technol 127:145 S 28 '87

Chile

Shuttle contingency landing site built by Chile on Easter Island. Aviat Week Space Technol 127:77 Ag 24 '87

China

China developing technology for future manned space flight. C. Covault. il Aviat Week Space Technol 126:22-3 Je 29 '87

France

See also

Centre National d'Études Spatiales (France)

French offer balloon platform for use on Soviet Mars mission. J. M. Lenorovitz. il Aviat Week Space Technol 127:63+ Ag 3 '87

Liberte! Egalite! Spatiale! W. H. Ganoe and J. Rhea. il Space World X-1-277:8-10 Ja '87

Great Britain

Thatcher reneges on pre-election promise to boost expenditures on British space projects. Aviat Week Space Technol 127:31 Ag 3 '87

Japan

Advanced technology moves Japan toward launcher market. il Aviat Week Space Technol 126:132-3 Mr 9 '87

Blast-off: Japan Inc. is joining the space race. B. Buell. il Bus Week p84+ Ag 24 '87

Japan in space. J. D. Kirwan. il Technol Rev 90:11-12 Ja '87

Japan plans lunar mission in 1990. il Aviat Week Space Technol 126:63 F 23 '87

Japanese commission outlines space program funding needs. il Aviat Week Space Technol 127:20 Jl 13 '87

Japan's blossoming space science. M. Oda and Y. Tanaka. il map Sky Telesc 73:7-11 Ja '87

Land of the rising rockets. M. Lord. il U S News World Rep 102:79 Je 8 '87

What do we learn from space? Space science in Japan. M. Oda. bibl il Phys Today 40:26-33 D '87

Pacific region

Third Chinese launch pad signals aerospace growth in Pacific Basin [Pacific Basin international symposium on space] C. Covault. Aviat Week Space Technol 126:66-7 Je 15 '87

Soviet Union

See also

Glavkosmos
Space flight—Soyuz flights
Space flight—Voskhod flights

American-Soviet space pact. Sky Telesc 74:11 Jl '87

A bold agenda for Soviet astrophysics. il Sky Telesc 74:601 D '87

Future Soviet space exploration to focus on Mars, asteroids. B. A. Smith. il Aviat Week Space Technol 126:81+ Je 22 '87

International cooperation to share expense [Soviet-U.S. space programs; views of Roald Sagdeev] il USA Today (Periodical) 116:8-9 D '87

The legacy of Sputnik [cover story; special issue; with editorial comment by John Rhea] il Space World X-10-286:3, 7-32+ O '87

Pentagon warns of Soviet space buildup. Aviat Week Space Technol 127:28-9 O 12 '87

The race is on: U.S., Soviet plans for Mars exploration [International Conference on Solar System Exploration] il Astronomy 15:86-7 O '87

Soviet Phobos mission· to probe moons of Mars. D. F. Robertson. il Astronomy 15:29-32 N '87

Soviet scientists present details of Mars exploration program. B. A. Smith. Aviat Week Space Technol 126:22 My 25 '87

Space research—Soviet Union—*cont.*
Soviet space advances [International Space Future Forum; special section; with editorial comment by Donald E. Fink] il *Aviat Week Space Technol* 127:15, 22-7 O 12 '87
Soviet space advances [special section] il *Aviat Week Space Technol* 127:110-12+ O 19 '87
Soviet space initiatives. D. E. Fink. *Aviat Week Space Technol* 126:11 My 25 '87
Soviet space records mark opening of international forum; USSR offers several missions as cooperative space flights [Space Future Forum] C. Covault. il *Aviat Week Space Technol* 127:26-7 O 5 '87
Soviet space science missions challenge U.S. leadership. C. Covault. il *Aviat Week Space Technol* 126:20-1 Mr 2 '87
Soviet space science opens to the West. M. M. Waldrop. il *Science* 236:1427-31 Je 12 '87
Soviet Union takes lead in manned space operations. *Aviat Week Space Technol* 126:129-30+ Mr 9 '87
Soviets advance definition work on 1990s unmanned Mars mission. J. M. Lenorovitz. il *Aviat Week Space Technol* 127:72-3 O 26 '87
Soviets consider possible Mars rover, sample return missions. C. A. Shifrin. *Aviat Week Space Technol* 126:26-7 Mr 23 '87
Soviets expected to consolidate space program activities in 1987. J. M. Lenorovitz. il *Aviat Week Space Technol* 126:97+ Ja 12 '87
Soviets propose relay role for Mars Observer mission. C. Covault. il *Aviat Week Space Technol* 127:21-2 D 21 '87
Sputnik's heirs: what the Soviets are doing in space [cover story] P. Pesavento. il *Technol Rev* 90:26-35 O '87
Surging ahead [Soviet space program; cover story; special section] il *Time* 130:64-70+ O 5 '87
Tsander's dream [flight to Mars] P. Pesavento. il por *Space World* X-5-281:28-31 My '87
U.S.-Soviet space pact signed. J. Eberhart. *Sci News* 131:260 Ap 25 '87
World series of space [International Space Future Forum] *Space World* X-11-287:33 N '87

United States
See Space research

Western Europe
See also
European Space Agency
Europe seeks additional opportunities for microgravity space experiments. J. M. Lenorovitz. il *Aviat Week Space Technol* 127:133-5 Jl 13 '87
New Mir astrophysics module to include European experiments. *Aviat Week Space Technol* 126:21 F 16 '87

Space Research Corporation
The Canadian connection [South Africa using Canadian-designed weaponry in Angola] A. Bilski. il map *Macleans* 100:36 O 19 '87

Space sciences
See also
Astronomy
Astrophysics
Videotapes—Space sciences use
NASA refocusing strategy for space science efforts. il *Aviat Week Space Technol* 127:20-1 Ag 10 '87
Outlook for space science: conversations with Burt Edelson and Lennard Fisk. M. Freeman; T. Reichhardt. pors *Space World* X-11-287:26-31 N '87
Science funding steady despite limited flights. il *Aviat Week Space Technol* 126:118-19+ Mr 9 '87

Bibliography
Reviews. See issues of Space World beginning February 1986

Conferences
Dates and data. See issues of Space World beginning February 1986
Live from L.A. [National Space Society/National Commission on Space Symposium] *Space World* X-1-277:37-8 Ja '87
Nanotechnology [Space Development Conference] J. Rhea. il *Space World* X-6-282:8-9 Je '87
President's message [Space Development Conference] B. Bova. il *Space World* X-3-279:40 Mr '87
Soviet space advances [International Space Future Forum; special section; with editorial comment by Donald E. Fink] il *Aviat Week Space Technol* 127:15, 22-7 O 12 '87
Soviet space records mark opening of international forum; USSR offers several missions as cooperative space flights [Space Future Forum] C. Covault. il *Aviat Week Space Technol* 127:26-7 O 5 '87

Space Development Conference. *Space World* X-2-278:37-8 F '87
Space development in Pittsburgh [Space Development Conference] W. H. Ganoe. il *Space World* X-6-282 Space Advocate:1-3 Je '87
World series of space [International Space Future Forum] *Space World* X-11-287:33 N '87

Study and teaching
See also
International Space University
Bullish on space [Univ. of Colorado] E. Truitt. il *Space World* X-1-277:24 Ja '87
Space 101: NASA hits the classroom. S. E. Sutphin. il *Space World* X-12-288:27-34 D '87
The space educator. D. Diehl. See issues of Space World beginning June 1987
Space summer '87. G. Chitwood. il *Space World* X-4-280:38-9 Ap '87
Spaced-out students [program at Toronto high school] R. Atherley. il *Macleans* 100:64 O 19 '87
Teaching space science. G. Lovi. il *Sky Telesc* 73:291-2 Mr '87

Bibliography
Reviews. See issues of Space World beginning February 1986

Space sciences as a profession
What color is your spacecraft? [getting a job with NASA; cover story] M. J. Dyson. il *Space World* X-12-288:9-11 D '87
Your career in space. P. H. Diamandis and K. H. Sunshine. il *Space World* X-4-280:8-13 Ap '87

Space Services, Inc.
Houston power company invests in Space Services, Inc. *Aviat Week Space Technol* 126:59 F 23 '87

Space shuttle *See* Space vehicles
Space shuttle missions *See* Space flight—Shuttle missions
Space shuttle missions, Japanese *See* Space flight—Shuttle missions, Japanese
Space shuttle missions, Russian *See* Space flight—Shuttle missions, Russian
Space shuttle simulators *See* Space flight simulators
Space societies
See also
International Astronautical Federation
NASA Alumni League
National Space Society (U.S.)

Space stations
See also
Space colonies
Canadian conundrum [participation in the space station] K. Day. por *Space World* X-8-284:40 Ag '87
Canadians making early effort to organize for station use. T. M. Foley. *Aviat Week Space Technol* 126:24-5 My 11 '87
Company seeks funds for orbiting laboratory [External Tanks Corp. proposing to take over shuttle external tanks in orbit and convert them] il *Aviat Week Space Technol* 126:102-3 Ja 12 '87
Compromise eludes U.S., Canada in space station negotiations. T. M. Foley. *Aviat Week Space Technol* 127:145 S 28 '87
Defense Dept. backs down on international station demands. T. M. Foley. il *Aviat Week Space Technol* 126:42-3 Ap 27 '87
Europeans disagree on future station negotiation plans. J. M. Lenorovitz. *Aviat Week Space Technol* 126:43-5 Ap 27 '87
First word. S. N. McDonnell. por *Omni* 9:4 Jl '87
The future of science in space. P. M. Banks and D. C. Black. bibl f *Science* 236:244-5 Ap 17 '87
Limited occupancy [two phase plan] *Sci Am* 256:25 Je '87
NASA panel urges U.S. control of space station operations. T. M. Foley. *Aviat Week Space Technol* 126:341-2+ Je 15 '87
President's message [excerpts from testimony, March 10, 1987] B. Bova. il *Space World* X-4-280:40 Ap '87
Reagan endorses a two-phase space station. M. M. Waldrop. il *Science* 236:143 Ap 10 '87
Report identifies early science work for space station. T. M. Foley. *Aviat Week Space Technol* 126:84-5 Mr 30 '87
Revving up for new voyages [NASA announces Galileo mission and space station] W. R. Doerner. il *Time* 130:65 D 14 '87
Science and the space station. E. Marshall. il *Science* 236:1176-9 Je 5 '87
The sixth mission: a space station diary. N. McAleer. il *Space World* X-5-281:12-19 My '87

Space stations—*cont.*

Space station back on track after year of policy disarray. T. M. Foley. il *Aviat Week Space Technol* 126:277-8+ Je 15 '87

Space station crew time extended to cut dependence on shuttle. T. M. Foley. *Aviat Week Space Technol* 127:30-1 Ag 3 '87

Space station: cut back to go ahead. J. Eberhart. *Sci News* 131:230 Ap 11 '87

Space station policy problems [special section; with editorial comment by Donald E. Fink] il *Aviat Week Space Technol* 126:11, 18-24 Ap 20 '87

Space station—round 2. D. E. Fink. *Aviat Week Space Technol* 126:25 Ap 27 '87

Station talks conclude without firm commitments [Canadian, Japanese and European partners] T. M. Foley. *Aviat Week Space Technol* 127:32 O 26 '87

Tank land: a conversation with Thomas F. Rogers. T. Reichhardt. il por *Space World* X-8-284:27-30 Ag '87

U.S., Europe seek to conclude station talks at final bilateral meeting. *Aviat Week Space Technol* 127:28 S 7 '87

U.S. proposal would restrict European, Japanese station use. T. M. Foley. il *Aviat Week Space Technol* 126:23-5 F 16 '87

U.S. space station controversy grows. J. Eberhart. *Sci News* 131:293 My 9 '87

Walden lost [critics of program] J. Rhea. il *Space World* X-8-284:3 Ag '87

Whose space is the space station? P. Marsh. il *World Press Rev* 34:51 My '87

Costs

A $30-billion space station? [report by the National Academy of Sciences and the National Academy of Engineering] E. Marshall. *Science* 237:1403 S 18 '87

Congress to postpone station funding if NASA constrains materials science. *Aviat Week Space Technol* 127:29 O 12 '87

Congressmen support man-tended station [William Proxmire and Ed Boland] *Aviat Week Space Technol* 126:85 Mr 30 '87

Fiscal 1988 station funding faces battle in Senate. *Aviat Week Space Technol* 127:21-2 Ag 31 '87

The flying I-beam [cover story; with editorial comment by Tony Reichhardt] J. Rhea. il *Space World* X-5-281:3, 9-11 My '87

House subcommittee trims funding for space station by $50 million. T. M. Foley. *Aviat Week Space Technol* 126:35 Je 22 '87

An inflatable U.S. $pace $tation. J. Eberhart. il *Sci News* 132:37 Jl 18 '87

Military uses and rising costs jeopardize space station. W. Sweet. *Phys Today* 40:71 Ap '87

NASA apologizes for illegal lobbying to preserve budget, space station. T. M. Foley. *Aviat Week Space Technol* 127:20-1 Ag 31 '87

NASA delays space station contracts as industrial research interest grows. C. Covault. il *Aviat Week Space Technol* 127:30-1 N 9 '87

NASA, industry managers assess rise in station cost estimates. T. M. Foley. *Aviat Week Space Technol* 126:28-9 Ja 19 '87

NASA seeks to block massive reductions in station budget. *Aviat Week Space Technol* 127:29 D 14 '87

OMB says budget cuts will postpone station. *Aviat Week Space Technol* 127:32 O 26 '87

Panel doubts NASA can hold to space station R&D budget [National Research Council team] T. M. Foley. *Aviat Week Space Technol* 127:18-20 Jl 13 '87

President's message [cutbacks] B. Bova. il *Space World* X-1-277:40 Ja '87

Reagan to consider additional funding for station program. C. Covault. *Aviat Week Space Technol* 126:260-1 Mr 9 '87

Rep. Nelson criticizes administration space station funding estimate. T. M. Foley. *Aviat Week Space Technol* 126:27-8 Ap 13 '87

Severe budget cuts affect space station project. *Aviat Week Space Technol* 127:23 D 21 '87

Shuttle external tanks offer U.S. a shortcut to large space stations. E. Meyers. por *Aviat Week Space Technol* 127:60-1+ Jl 27 '87

Space station cost estimates double. M. M. Waldrop. il *Science* 235:965 F 27 '87

Space station costs up—again . . . but Bova warns of cuts. *Space World* X-4-280:4 Ap '87

Space station faces possible two-year deployment delay. T. M. Foley. *Aviat Week Space Technol* 126:28-30 F 9 '87

Space station: more study = more money. J. Eberhart. *Sci News* 132:183 S 19 '87

Space station price climbs higher. E. Marshall. *Science* 237:242-3 Jl 17 '87

We shouldn't build the space station now. A. Roland. il *Technol Rev* 90:22-3 Jl '87

White House delays action on new station cost estimates. T. M. Foley. *Aviat Week Space Technol* 126:26-7 Mr 2 '87

Design

Assembling the space station. P. Chien. il *Space World* X-12-288:16-17+ D '87

The flying I-beam [cover story; with editorial comment by Tony Reichhardt] J. Rhea. il *Space World* X-5-281:3, 9-11 My '87

How to make space livable. il *Futurist* 21:56 Mr/Ap '87

NASA advisor urges overhaul of space station design [views of Peter Banks] *Aviat Week Space Technol* 126:28 Mr 30 '87

NASA cites strengths, weaknesses of space station contract bids. *Aviat Week Space Technol* 127:23-4 D 21 '87

NASA issues station RFPs after agreeing to changes mandated by Congress [requests for proposals for space station hardware] *Aviat Week Space Technol* 126:26 My 4 '87

NASA seeks major role in developing heavy launcher. T. M. Foley. *Aviat Week Space Technol* 126:25-6 Ap 6 '87

NASA will proceed with scaled-back space station. T. M. Foley. il *Aviat Week Space Technol* 126:26-7 Mr 30 '87

NASA's next stop in space. W. D. Marbach. il *Newsweek* 109:52-3 Ja 19 '87

The next small step [T. L. Keller's Space M*A*X space station construction simulation program] S. Ditlea. il *Omni* 10:22 D '87

Panel backs space station design, but warns of flaws in program. T. M. Foley. *Aviat Week Space Technol* 127:28-9 S 21 '87

Profits into orbit [Space M*A*X and EOS: earth orbit station system] J. L. Wilson. *Space World* X-6-282:21 Je '87

Project Bluestar [zero gravity think tank space station] il *Futurist* 21:29-32 Ja/F '87

Rockwell engineer faults NASA design of space station [views of Oliver P. Harwood] *Aviat Week Space Technol* 126:27 Je 1 '87

Shuttle, station disruptions slow U.S. civil space program. C. Covault. il *Aviat Week Space Technol* 126:111-12 Mr 9 '87

Six aerospace firms compete to build space station hardware. T. M. Foley. il *Aviat Week Space Technol* 127:26-7 Jl 27 '87

Space station contracts [special section; with editorial comment by Donald E. Fink] il *Aviat Week Space Technol* 127:11, 18-23 D 7 '87

The space station: how elaborate will it be? il *Discover* 8:40-1+ Ja '87

The space station launching a thousand contracts. S. Payne. il *Bus Week* p126-7+ N 23 '87

Space station research program spurs key technological advances. T. M. Foley. il *Aviat Week Space Technol* 127:42-3+ Jl 27 '87

Space station will be revamped. T. H. Cole. *Pop Mech* 164:56+ Jl '87

Suddenly last spring [space station contracts] L. Garver and P. Chien. *Space World* X-6-282:5 Je '87

When the doctor is 200 miles away [proposed Health Maintenance Facility; cover story] L. Dorr, Jr. il *Space World* X-3-279:33-6 Mr '87

Earth sciences use

Soviets launch massive earth survey platform. C. Covault. il *Aviat Week Space Technol* 127:27-8 Ag 3 '87

Escape devices

NASA to seek design concepts for station crew escape vehicle. C. Covault. il *Aviat Week Space Technol* 127:30 Ag 17 '87

Soviets studying development of emergency capsules for Mir. il *Aviat Week Space Technol* 127:75 O 26 '87

Industrial use

See Space processing

Leasing and renting

NASA will consider use of commercial space facility [Space Industries' Industrial Space Facility] *Aviat Week Space Technol* 127:55 N 2 '87

Maintenance and repair

Canadian MSC to provide essential station assembly, docking capability [Mobile Servicing Center] T. M. Foley. il *Aviat Week Space Technol* 126:48-50 My 25 '87

Space stations—Maintenance and repair—*cont.*
Space station EVA simulation demonstrates orbital assembly. C. Covault. il *Aviat Week Space Technol* 126:60-1+ Ja 26 '87

Military use
Defense Dept. backs down on international station demands. T. M. Foley. il *Aviat Week Space Technol* 126:42-3 Ap 27 '87
Defense Dept. stands by demand for unrestricted space station use. *Aviat Week Space Technol* 126:283 Je 15 '87
Defense officials express concern over Soviet military space work. *Aviat Week Space Technol* 127:28 Jl 27 '87
Military uses and rising costs jeopardize space station. W. Sweet. *Phys Today* 40:71 Ap '87
NASA reviews shuttle launch date, military station. *Aviat Week Space Technol* 126:27 My 25 '87
Pentagon describes possible military station experiments. T. M. Foley. *Aviat Week Space Technol* 126:25-6 My 4 '87
Space station policy problems [special section; with editorial comment by Donald E. Fink] il *Aviat Week Space Technol* 126:11, 18-24 Ap 20 '87
Space station—round 2. D. E. Fink. *Aviat Week Space Technol* 126:25 Ap 27 '87
Weinberger firm on military uses for space station. *Aviat Week Space Technol* 127:32 S 21 '87
Weinberger objects to bill limiting military station use. T. M. Foley. *Aviat Week Space Technol* 126:27-8 My 18 '87

Physics use
EVA performed to dock Kvant module to Mir [astrophysics module] il *Aviat Week Space Technol* 126:21 Ap 20 '87
The high-flying Kvant module. J. K. Beatty. il *Sky Telesc* 74:599-601 D '87
New Mir astrophysics module to include European experiments. *Aviat Week Space Technol* 126:21 F 16 '87
Soviet Kvant astrophysics module to observe deep space targets. il *Aviat Week Space Technol* 126:80-1 My 4 '87
Soviets launch astrophysics module to Mir. *Aviat Week Space Technol* 126:24 Ap 6 '87

Power supply
Mir electrical power shortage affects orbital science activity. C. Covault. *Aviat Week Space Technol* 126:24 Je 1 '87
SDI science office plans to launch electrical space test in November [Spear, for Space Power Experiments Aboard Rockets] T. M. Foley. *Aviat Week Space Technol* 127:28-9 Ag 24 '87
SDI suborbital launch yields data for high-power platform design [Space Power Experiments Aboard Rocket] T. M. Foley. il *Aviat Week Space Technol* 127:26-7 D 21 '87

Safety devices and measures
See also
Space stations—Escape devices
Safety on the space station. M. J. Mackowski. il *Space World* X-3-279:22-4 Mr '87

Sanitation
Zero-g bathroom. D. Pine. *Space World* X-5-281:14 My '87

Skylab missions
Skylab/space station differences. il *Space World* X-12-288:18-19 D '87

Sleeping quarters
Bedrooms. *Space World* X-5-281:16 My '87

Spacelab missions
See also
Space stations—Starlab missions
Aeritalia will develop microgravity facility for use on Spacelab [bubble drop and particle unit] *Aviat Week Space Technol* 127:54 Jl 20 '87
Inner ears and outer space [work of M. D. Ross on utricular macula cell morphology] R. Spangenburg and D. Moser. il por *Space World* X-9-285:17-20 S '87
Scientists predict long-term damage from Spacelab mission cutbacks. T. M. Foley. il *Aviat Week Space Technol* 126:125+ F 9 '87
Spacelab-2 plasma depletion experiments for ionospheric and radio astronomical studies. M. Mendillo and others. bibl f il *Science* 238:1260-4 N 27 '87
Ultraviolet observations of solar fine structure. K. P. Dere and others. bibl f il *Science* 238:1267-9 N 27 '87
White light sunspot observations from the solar optical universal polarimeter on Spacelab-2. R. A. Shine and others. bibl f il *Science* 238:1264-7 N 27 '87

Stability and stabilizers
Soviets use new gyros to stabilize Mir station. J. M. Lenorovitz. il *Aviat Week Space Technol* 127:79-80 N 2 '87

Starlab missions
SDI's Starlab shuttle mission will test laser tracking system. *Aviat Week Space Technol* 127:25 O 19 '87
Starlab to engage satellites, rockets, ground-based laser. T. M. Foley. il *Aviat Week Space Technol* 127:58-9 O 26 '87

Transportation
NASA evaluates transportation of large space station payloads [C-5A modifications] B. A. Smith. il *Aviat Week Space Technol* 127:47+ Ag 10 '87

Space stations, European
See also
Space stations—Spacelab missions
Europe seeks additional opportunities for microgravity space experiments. J. M. Lenorovitz. il *Aviat Week Space Technol* 127:133-5 Jl 13 '87
Europeans approve development of Ariane 5, Hermes, Columbus. J. M. Lenorovitz. *Aviat Week Space Technol* 127:22-4 N 16 '87
Europeans disagree on future station negotiation plans. J. M. Lenorovitz. *Aviat Week Space Technol* 126:43-5 Ap 27 '87
Italy proposes building, operating Columbus mission control center. *Aviat Week Space Technol* 127:135 Jl 13 '87
Logica will manage software definition for Columbus module. *Aviat Week Space Technol* 126:24 Mr 23 '87
Space station partners resolve key issue on polar platform. *Aviat Week Space Technol* 127:28 D 14 '87
U.K. space chief resigns over funding; ESA reevaluates impact on polar platform. J. M. Lenorovitz. il *Aviat Week Space Technol* 127:26-7 Ag 10 '87

Space stations, Russian
CNES discusses Hermes-Mir compatibility with Soviets. *Aviat Week Space Technol* 126:25 My 11 '87
Defense officials express concern over Soviet military space work. *Aviat Week Space Technol* 127:28 Jl 27 '87
EVA performed to dock Kvant module to Mir [astrophysics module] il *Aviat Week Space Technol* 126:21 Ap 20 '87
Foreign cosmonauts train for flights on Mir space station. *Aviat Week Space Technol* 126:105 My 11 '87
The high-flying Kvant module. J. K. Beatty. il *Sky Telesc* 74:599-601 D '87
Inside Mir. T. Furniss. il *Space World* X-5-281:24-5 My '87
Large manned station, free-fliers foreseen in Soviet space program. il *Aviat Week Space Technol* 127:73 O 26 '87
The making of Mir Watch. E. S. Wynn. il *Space World* X-10-286:31-2 O '87
Mir electrical power shortage affects orbital science activity. C. Covault. *Aviat Week Space Technol* 126:24 Je 1 '87
Mir: has full-time occupancy begun? J. Eberhart. *Sci News* 131:103 F 14 '87
Mir mockup reveals docking hub for vehicle expansion. il *Aviat Week Space Technol* 127:38-9 Jl 27 '87
New Mir astrophysics module to include European experiments. *Aviat Week Space Technol* 126:21 F 16 '87
Soviet Kvant astrophysics module to observe deep space targets. il *Aviat Week Space Technol* 126:80-1 My 4 '87
Soviet long-duration crew activates Mir space station. C. Covault. il *Aviat Week Space Technol* 126:19-20 F 16 '87
Soviets conduct space tanker flight tests [docking maneuvers with Mir] *Aviat Week Space Technol* 127:25 N 16 '87
Soviets conduct unusual manned, unmanned activities. C. Covault. *Aviat Week Space Technol* 127:29-30 S 7 '87
Soviets developing plans for year-long mission [Mir space station] *Aviat Week Space Technol* 127:26 O 12 '87
Soviets exhibit full-scale model of Mir complex at Paris Air Show. il *Aviat Week Space Technol* 127:58-60 Jl 20 '87
Soviets launch astrophysics module to Mir. *Aviat Week Space Technol* 126:24 Ap 6 '87
Soviets launch massive earth survey platform. C. Covault. il *Aviat Week Space Technol* 127:27-8 Ag 3 '87
Soviets offer Mir for experiments, commercial space processing. il *Aviat Week Space Technol* 126:23 Je 22 '87

Space stations, Russian—*cont.*
Soviets planning to launch new module to Mir station [extravehicular activity airlock] *Aviat Week Space Technol* 127:22-3 O 12 '87
Soviets prepare to place cosmonaut crew on Mir for long-duration station flight. il *Aviat Week Space Technol* 126:28-9 Ja 26 '87
Soviets studying development of emergency capsules for Mir. il *Aviat Week Space Technol* 127:75 O 26 '87
Soviets use new gyros to stabilize Mir station. J. M. Lenorovitz. il *Aviat Week Space Technol* 127:79-80 N 2 '87
Two EVAs allow Mir cosmonauts to install third solar array. *Aviat Week Space Technol* 126:35 Je 22 '87
Space Studies Institute
The Exodus Institute. E. Regis. il *Omni* 9:20+ Mr '87
Space suits *See* Spacesuits
Space technology
> *See also*
> Technology transfer
NASA will begin $1.7-billion program to revitalize space technology base. il *Aviat Week Space Technol* 127:28-9 N 9 '87
Space station research program spurs key technological advances. T. M. Foley. il *Aviat Week Space Technol* 127:42-3+ Jl 27 '87
A strategic initiative for NASA's future [Civil Space Technology Initiative] J. Rhea. il *Space World* X-3-279:30-2 Mr '87
Space Telescope (Satellite) *See* Artificial satellites—Astronomical use
Space travel *See* Space flight
Space Van *See* Space vehicles
Space vehicle models
ESA shows full-scale mockup of Hermes manned spaceplane [Paris Air Show] il *Aviat Week Space Technol* 127:95 Jl 6 '87
Mir mockup reveals docking hub for vehicle expansion. il *Aviat Week Space Technol* 127:38-9 Jl 27 '87
Mockup shows differences between shuttle, spaceplane [Hermes] il *Aviat Week Space Technol* 127:86 Jl 6 '87
Soviets exhibit full-scale model of Mir complex at Paris Air Show. il *Aviat Week Space Technol* 127:58-60 Jl 20 '87
Space vehicle tires *See* Tires, Space vehicle
Space vehicles
> *See also*
> Artificial satellites
> Lunar vehicles
> Space centers
> Space stations
> Space vehicles, Restored
> Spaceplane
Alms for an orbiter [budget authority to fund construction of a replacement orbiter] T. J. Frieling. il *Space World* X-2-278:29-31 F '87
Orbital express [possible shuttle successors] T. Reichhardt. il *Space World* X-6-282:27-8 Je '87
Space shuttle a waste of money? [views of James Bennett and Philip Salin] il *USA Today (Periodical)* 115:2-3 Je '87

Accidents and explosions
> *See also*
> Challenger (Space shuttle) explosion, 1986
Atmospheric entry
Infrared imaging system will record flow fields during shuttle reentry. il *Aviat Week Space Technol* 127:65+ D 7 '87

Crews
See Astronauts
Design
Fixing the shuttle. E. Marshall. *Science* 235:527 Ja 30 '87
The Martian Metro [Mars Cycler envisioned by E. E. Aldrin] F. Braun and O. Davies. il *Omni* 10:52-4+ N '87
Private shuttle may fly in the 1990s [Space Van] il *Pop Mech* 164:65 My '87
Rockwell International begins work on replacement shuttle orbiter [OV-105] il *Aviat Week Space Technol* 127:24-5 Ag 10 '87
Shuttle plan faulted. E. Marshall. *Science* 235:425 Ja 23 '87

Electronic equipment
Video helmet [LCD display on astronauts' visors] M. Costello. il *Omni* 9:103 Ja '87

Engines
See Space vehicles—Propulsion systems
Equipment
> *See also*
> Life support systems (Space environment)
Escape devices
Escaping the shuttle. B. Nolley. *Space World* X-3-279:24 Mr '87
Malfunction, parts shortage affect shuttle escape system development. C. Covault. il *Aviat Week Space Technol* 127:125+ S 7 '87
NASA nears key shuttle tests, changes initial payload schedule. C. Covault. *Aviat Week Space Technol* 127:28-9 Jl 6 '87
New exits [space shuttle] A. R. Oberg. il *Omni* 9:28 My '87
Shuttle escape system. L. L. Kofler. il *Space World* X-11-287:8 N '87

Fuel systems
See Space vehicles—Propulsion systems
Fuel tanks
Access platform damages Centaur; NASA inquiry team assesses impact on next Atlas launch. il *Aviat Week Space Technol* 127:27 Jl 20 '87
Company seeks funds for orbiting laboratory [External Tanks Corp. proposing to take over shuttle external tanks in orbit and convert them] il *Aviat Week Space Technol* 126:102-3 Ja 12 '87
Shuttle external tanks offer U.S. a shortcut to large space stations. E. Meyers. por *Aviat Week Space Technol* 127:60-1+ Jl 27 '87
Tank land: a conversation with Thomas F. Rogers. T. Reichhardt. il por *Space World* X-8-284:27-30 Ag '87
Insulation
NASA to begin rebonding Discovery tiles. E. H. Kolcum. il *Aviat Week Space Technol* 126:105 Ja 12 '87
Landing and recovery
Expendable experiments [commercial space recovery vehicles developed for microgravity research] W. H. Ganoe. il *Space World* X-8-284:39 Ag '87
ISO: Liberty Bell [plan by C. Newport to salvage Mercury space capsule] T. Reichhardt. il por *Space World* X-1-277:25-8 Ja '87
NASA to conduct initial low-speed tests of shuttle groundroll arresting system. *Aviat Week Space Technol* 126:20 Je 8 '87
New shuttle site [Trans Atlantic Abort site at Ben Gurir, Morocco] *Space World* X-9-285:7 S '87
Shuttle contingency landing site built by Chile on Easter Island. *Aviat Week Space Technol* 127:77 Ag 24 '87
Launchers
See Space vehicles—Propulsion systems
Launching
> *See also*
> Artificial satellites—Launching
Launchlog '87: inching back into space [NASA's plans] J. Eberhart. *Sci News* 131:22 Ja 10 '87
NASA assigns launch dates to shuttle science missions. il *Astronomy* 15:82-3 Ja '87
NASA reviews shuttle launch date, military station. *Aviat Week Space Technol* 126:27 My 25 '87
New assessment slips shuttle launch to September, 1988. *Aviat Week Space Technol* 126:28-9 Ap 13 '87
New shuttle launch procedures may result in countdown scrubs. C. Covault. il *Aviat Week Space Technol* 126:64-5+ Mr 16 '87
New space launch manifest integrates shuttle, expendable booster missions. *Aviat Week Space Technol* 127:30-1 O 26 '87
Political, technological needs spur new national launch strategies. C. Covault. il *Aviat Week Space Technol* 126:262-3+ Je 15 '87
Space shuttle manifest [chart] *Space World* X-1-277:41 Ja '87
Spacebound again: the mixing of the fleet [cover story] J. Eberhart. il *Sci News* 132:330-1 N 21 '87
Launching pads, sites, etc.
> *See also*
> United States. Air Force. Eastern Test Range
Access platform damages Centaur; NASA inquiry team assesses impact on next Atlas launch. il *Aviat Week Space Technol* 127:27 Jl 20 '87
Construction of new orbiter at Vandenberg assessed. *Aviat Week Space Technol* 126:61 Mr 23 '87
NASA modifying shuttle launch pad for safety, efficiency. E. H. Kolcum. *Aviat Week Space Technol* 127:76 D 7 '87
Oil rigs near Vandenberg concern USAF. *Aviat Week Space Technol* 126:110 My 11 '87

Space vehicles—*cont.*

Maintenance and repair

Committee identifies shuttle contract issues [processing contract with Lockheed analyzed by Estess Committee] *Aviat Week Space Technol* 126:89 Mr 30 '87

Kennedy refining shuttle processing to resolve pre-accident shortcomings. E. H. Kolcum. *Aviat Week Space Technol* 126:77 Ja 26 '87

Quality gains new emphasis after shuttle processing review. E. H. Kolcum. *Aviat Week Space Technol* 126:85+ Mr 30 '87

Shuttle processing resumes after 18-month hiatus. E. H. Kolcum. *Aviat Week Space Technol* 127:29 Ag 3 '87

Space shuttle program managers concerned about staffing levels for three-orbiter processing. *Aviat Week Space Technol* 127:75 D 21 '87

Manipulators

See Manipulators (Mechanism)

Power supply

Gone with fission [views of George Chapline] D. E. Thomsen. *Sci News* 132:205 S 26 '87

Los Alamos eyes restarting nuclear propulsion work. *Aviat Week Space Technol* 126:34 My 11 '87

Nuclear power: how safe in space? P. Chien. il *Space World* X-9-285:11-13 S '87

RTGs—a plutonium crap-shoot? [Galileo spacecraft] *Space World* X-6-282:24 Je '87

Propulsion systems

See also

Space vehicles—Solar energy use

Advanced technology moves Japan toward launcher market. il *Aviat Week Space Technol* 126:132-3 Mr 9 '87

Ariane launch teams complete training. il *Aviat Week Space Technol* 127:67 N 2 '87

Ariane, shuttle delayed again. D. Dickson. *Science* 236:1056-7 My 29 '87

Ariane success boosts Europe's hopes. D. Dickson. *Science* 237:1561 S 25 '87

Ariane V19 launches dual satellite payload [with editorial comment by Donald E. Fink] J. M. Lenorovitz. il *Aviat Week Space Technol* 127:11, 18-20 S 21 '87

Challenger's legacy [expendable launch vehicle development program] D. E. Fink. *Aviat Week Space Technol* 126:13 Ja 26 '87

Chinese make inroads on commercial launch market. *Aviat Week Space Technol* 126:134 Mr 9 '87

Commerce Dept. will buy ELVs from private sector [National Oceanic and Atmospheric Administration] *Aviat Week Space Technol* 126:24-5 Mr 23 '87

Commercial Delta 2 to be priced lower than international competitors. T. M. Foley. *Aviat Week Space Technol* 126:23-4 F 2 '87

Company offers to buy NASA a rocket [Titan 3] M. M. Waldrop. *Science* 235:1568 Mr 27 '87

Computer simulates multi-spacecraft deployment from Ariane 4 launcher. il *Aviat Week Space Technol* 126:70-1 F 2 '87

Defense Dept. seeks launcher for SDI in supplemental budget. *Aviat Week Space Technol* 126:21 Ja 5 '87

ELV manufacturers charge USAF with decision delays [expendable launch facilities] *Aviat Week Space Technol* 126:27 My 11 '87

Europeans prepare TVSat 1 for launch on Ariane V20 [direct broadcast satellite] K. F. Mordoff. il *Aviat Week Space Technol* 127:65+ N 2 '87

Eutelsat weighs candidates for alternate launcher. *Aviat Week Space Technol* 126:101 Ja 12 '87

First U.S. commercial sales of ELVs expected in 1987 [expendable launch vehicles] T. M. Foley. il *Aviat Week Space Technol* 126:113-14 Mr 9 '87

General Dynamics cites launch candidates for Atlas G/Centaur. il *Aviat Week Space Technol* 126:25 Mr 23 '87

GM wants to use Soviet launchers. E. Marshall. *Science* 238:23 O 2 '87

Industry group criticizes Air Force draft agreement on ELVs [expendable launch vehicles and commercial launch industry] *Aviat Week Space Technol* 126:23 F 16 '87

Land of the rising rockets [plans to launch H-1 rocket] M. Lord. il *U S News World Rep* 102:79 Je 8 '87

Launcher companies sign first commercialization agreements. *Aviat Week Space Technol* 127:26-7 Ag 10 '87

Leaving the shuttle can be a hard trip [Cosmic Background Explorer] J. Eberhart. *Sci News* 132:166 S 12 '87

The light stuff: laser propulsion. N. McAleer. il *Space World* X-7-283:9-11 Jl '87

'Major step' on the stairway to orbit [Titan 3B launch] J. Eberhart. *Sci News* 131:116-17 F 21 '87

Martin pursuing 15 additional Titan launch contracts. T. M. Foley. *Aviat Week Space Technol* 126:66+ Ap 20 '87

Martin signs contract to launch Intelsat 6 satellites on Titan 3s. *Aviat Week Space Technol* 127:22 Ag 17 '87

McDonnell Douglas Astronautics receives nine $50,000 deposits for commercial satellite launches [Delta 2s] *Aviat Week Space Technol* 126:29 Ap 13 '87

McDonnell Douglas receives firm commercial Delta launch orders [Hughes Aircraft to purchase for launch of British Satellite Broadcasting spacecraft] *Aviat Week Space Technol* 127:24 Jl 20 '87

McDonnell plans rapid buildup of Delta launcher fleet. B. A. Smith. il *Aviat Week Space Technol* 126:114-15 F 16 '87

NASA plans other baskets for its eggs [expendable launch vehicles] J. Eberhart. *Sci News* 131:341 My 30 '87

New Chinese heavy rocket spurs effort to win commercial launch contracts. C. Covault. il *Aviat Week Space Technol* 126:22-3 My 4 '87

New space launch manifest integrates shuttle, expendable booster missions. *Aviat Week Space Technol* 127:30-1 O 26 '87

NOAA to hold competition to buy GOES launchers [Geostationary Operational Environmental Satellites] *Aviat Week Space Technol* 126:24 Ja 19 '87

OSC offers to finance Titan 34D for Mars Observer [Orbital Sciences Corp.] *Aviat Week Space Technol* 126:24-5 Mr 23 '87

Political, technological needs spur new national launch strategies. C. Covault. il *Aviat Week Space Technol* 126:262-3+ Je 15 '87

Priming the ELV business [E-Prime Aerospace Corporation] W. H. Ganoe. il *Space World* X-12-288:38 D '87

Proton marketing team finds U.S. interest, opposition [Soviet booster] il *Aviat Week Space Technol* 126:20-1 My 25 '87

Race into space: the Pentagon overtakes NASA by a missile length [Air Force's expendable launcher] S. Budiansky. il *U S News World Rep* 103:10 Ag 17 '87

Russki business [attempt to market Proton booster] L. Dorr, Jr. il *Space World* X-7-283:31-4 Jl '87

Satellite builders want change in U.S. anti-Proton policy. T. M. Foley. *Aviat Week Space Technol* 127:138-9 S 28 '87

Starship enterprise: chasing NASA's unfinished business. S. Payne. il *Bus Week* p98-9+ N 9 '87

State Dept. denies license to export U.S. satellites to the Soviet Union [use of Proton] *Aviat Week Space Technol* 127:59 Jl 27 '87

U.S. Air Force Titan launch restarts heavy booster flights [KH-11 imaging reconnaissance satellite launched] C. Covault. il *Aviat Week Space Technol* 127:24-5 N 2 '87

USAF Titan 34D launches missile warning satellite. E. H. Kolcum. il *Aviat Week Space Technol* 127:30-1 D 7 '87

Design

Air Force awards contracts for Phase 1 ALS studies [advanced launch system] M. A. Dornheim. il *Aviat Week Space Technol* 127:25 Jl 20 '87

Amroc pursues SDI as first paying customer. il *Aviat Week Space Technol* 127:24-5 O 19 '87

Arianespace moves to cut costs, improve management of boosters. J. M. Lenorovitz. il *Aviat Week Space Technol* 127:63-4 O 12 '87

Big dumb rockets. G. Easterbrook. il *Newsweek* 110:46-50+ Ag 17 '87

British offer Ariane deployment system for use on Titan 3 [Spelda dual satellite deployment system] il *Aviat Week Space Technol* 126:32-3 Ja 12 '87

China defines family of improved Long March launchers. il *Aviat Week Space Technol* 127:79 O 26 '87

Chinese facility combines capabilities to produce Long March boosters, ICBMs. C. Covault. il *Aviat Week Space Technol* 127:50-3 Jl 27 '87

Committee calls for SRB alternatives [shuttle solid rocket booster] *Aviat Week Space Technol* 126:24-5 Je 29 '87

Congress approves additional ALS funds [advanced launch system] *Aviat Week Space Technol* 127:21 Jl 13 '87

Congress, booster manufacturers criticize joint redesign program [Thiokol design for shuttle booster] C. Covault. il *Aviat Week Space Technol* 126:116-17 F 9 '87

Space vehicles—Propulsion systems—Design—*cont.*

Defense Dept. developing range of launch vehicle concepts. B. A. Smith. il *Aviat Week Space Technol* 126:115+ Mr 9 '87

Design changes tighten timetable for launch of Japan's H-2 booster. J. M. Lenorovitz. *Aviat Week Space Technol* 127:47-8 N 16 '87

Easing of shuttle weight limits key to new USAF upper stage [Adaptable Space Propulsion System] B. A. Smith. *Aviat Week Space Technol* 126:25-7 My 18 '87

Europeans approve development of Ariane 5, Hermes, Columbus. J. M. Lenorovitz. *Aviat Week Space Technol* 127:22-4 N 16 '87

Japan will develop new 3-stage booster. *Aviat Week Space Technol* 127:24 Jl 20 '87

Larceny at the launch pad. G. Easterbrook. il *Read Dig* 131:209-16 D '87

Martin converts USAF Titan 2 to launch vehicle for placing defense payloads into polar orbit. il *Aviat Week Space Technol* 127:18-19 Ag 10 '87

Martin evaluates bids on Titan launch adapter [Titan 3 dual satellite adapter] *Aviat Week Space Technol* 126:62-3 Je 22 '87

Martin Marietta selects Dornier to build Titan component. *Aviat Week Space Technol* 127:27 O 19 '87

Martin's ALS booster design uses multiple strap-on motors [advanced launch system] B. A. Smith. il *Aviat Week Space Technol* 127:29-30 S 21 '87

McDonnell Douglas studies larger payload assist modules. *Aviat Week Space Technol* 127:136 Ag 10 '87

NASA deputy endorses heavy-lift launch vehicle [views of Dale Myers] E. H. Kolcum. il *Aviat Week Space Technol* 126:60-1 Mr 23 '87

NASA may be forced to take minor role in heavy launcher. T. M. Foley. *Aviat Week Space Technol* 126:56-7 Mr 23 '87

NASA may seek proposals for shuttle-derived booster. T. M. Foley. *Aviat Week Space Technol* 126:24-5 Je 29 '87

NASA proceeds with shuttle-derived booster study. il *Aviat Week Space Technol* 127:24-5 Ag 10 '87

NASA seeks major role in developing heavy launcher. T. M. Foley. *Aviat Week Space Technol* 126:25-6 Ap 6 '87

New Hercules plant to cut solid rocket cost. il *Aviat Week Space Technol* 126:117 Ap 27 '87

Orbital Sciences, Space Agency disagree on cost of using transfer orbit stage as upper stage for the Mars Observer. *Aviat Week Space Technol* 126:27 My 11 '87

Reinventing the space truck [cargo vehicle to launch heavy loads] E. Marshall. il *Science* 238:266-8 O 16 '87

Research Council critiques NASA's booster redesign [space shuttle] M. M. Waldrop. il *Science* 237:122 Jl 10 '87

Rocketdyne proposes changes to improve shuttle engine. E. H. Kolcum. *Aviat Week Space Technol* 126:47+ Mr 2 '87

Rockwell predicts HLV will lower launch costs [recoverable heavy-lift vehicle] B. A. Smith. il *Aviat Week Space Technol* 126:24-5 F 2 '87

SDI considers cluster booster to launch Zenith Star spacecraft. C. Covault. il *Aviat Week Space Technol* 127:20-1 N 30 '87

Shuttle booster redesign, tests raise schedule delay concerns. C. Covault. *Aviat Week Space Technol* 126:26-7 Ja 26 '87

Soviet Mars mission will use modular propulsion system. *Aviat Week Space Technol* 127:81 N 2 '87

Tomorrow's rockets: a conversation with Franklin Chang-Diaz [plasma propulsion system] M. Freeman. il pors *Space World* X-9-285:14-16 S '87

Tracking the shuttle's path(s) to orbit. J. Eberhart. *Sci News* 131:54 Ja 24 '87

U.S. to bolster its capability in small space launch vehicles. C. Covault. il *Aviat Week Space Technol* 127:73+ D 7 '87

USAF awards McDonnell Douglas contract to build, operate MLVs [medium launch vehicles] B. A. Smith. *Aviat Week Space Technol* 126:20-1 Ja 26 '87

USAF narrows contractors for new upper stage. *Aviat Week Space Technol* 126:25 My 4 '87

USAF seeks industry responses for advanced launch system. *Aviat Week Space Technol* 126:26 My 11 '87

USAF seeks technology to cut heavy-lift launch costs; USAF prepares program to procure heavy-lift vehicles. *Aviat Week Space Technol* 126:24-5 Ja 26 '87

Failure

Access platform damages Centaur; NASA inquiry team assesses impact on next Atlas launch. il *Aviat Week Space Technol* 127:27 Jl 20 '87

Another launch failure [loss of Atlas rocket] J. Eberhart. *Sci News* 131:215 Ap 4 '87

Atlas accident inquiry board finds violation of launch commit criteria. C. Covault. il *Aviat Week Space Technol* 126:25-7 My 18 '87

Atlas failure analysis focuses on lightning. *Aviat Week Space Technol* 126:21 My 4 '87

Atlas launch follies. D. E. Fink. *Aviat Week Space Technol* 126:11 My 18 '87

FBI investigating fraud charges against Morton Thiokol in manufacture of shuttle solid rocket motors. *Aviat Week Space Technol* 126:41-2 Ap 27 '87

FltSatCom lost when Atlas Centaur launch fails [Fleet Satellite Communications spacecraft] *Aviat Week Space Technol* 126:20 Mr 30 '87

Lightning strikes twice at NASA [Atlas-Centaur accident] E. Marshall. *Science* 236:903 My 22 '87

Lightning studied in Atlas launch failure. *Aviat Week Space Technol* 126:31 Ap 13 '87

Morton Thiokol will forfeit $10 million in lieu of contract penalty. *Aviat Week Space Technol* 126:28 Mr 2 '87

NASA committee investigates cause of Atlas Centaur failure amid criticism of launch decision. E. H. Kolcum. *Aviat Week Space Technol* 126:23-4 Ap 6 '87

NASA nears decision to end Atlas Centaur program. *Aviat Week Space Technol* 127:21 Ag 31 '87

New factors cited in Challenger accident [undetected wind shear and a weakened attach ring that holds boosters to external tank] C. Covault. il *Aviat Week Space Technol* 126:21-2 F 23 '87

Severe drop in satellite orders follows 1986 launch failures. T. M. Foley. *Aviat Week Space Technol* 126:19-21 Je 8 '87

Soviet Proton booster fails; reconnaissance satellite explodes. C. Covault. il *Aviat Week Space Technol* 126:26-7 F 9 '87

Soviets lose Proton booster, payload in launch failure. *Aviat Week Space Technol* 126:24 My 4 '87

Inspection

NASA opts to use human inspector to examine stacked solid booster [space shuttle] E. H. Kolcum. il *Aviat Week Space Technol* 127:74-5 D 21 '87

Insulation

Titan 34D tests show aging not a factor in insulation bonds. *Aviat Week Space Technol* 126:266 Mr 9 '87

Maintenance and repair

Fixes to space shuttle hardware, management reach critical stage. E. H. Kolcum. *Aviat Week Space Technol* 126:77+ My 4 '87

Launch of Ariane V21 postponed. il *Aviat Week Space Technol* 127:23 N 16 '87

Titan mission success based on tighter heavy booster standards. W. B. Scott. *Aviat Week Space Technol* 127:25-6 N 2 '87

Photographs and photography

Close-up views reveal details of Soviet heavy-lift booster [Energia booster] il *Aviat Week Space Technol* 126:72-3 Je 8 '87

Soviets offer three boosters for commercial launch services. il *Aviat Week Space Technol* 126:94-5 Ja 12 '87

Specifications

International launch vehicles [tables] il *Aviat Week Space Technol* 126:154 Mr 9 '87

U.S. launch vehicles [tables] il *Aviat Week Space Technol* 126:158-9 Mr 9 '87

Testing

Aerojet completes tests of engine for adaptable space propulsion system [Transtar] R. G. O'Lone. il *Aviat Week Space Technol* 127:130-1 Ag 10 '87

American Rocket negotiating for suborbital test flight of hybrid launch vehicle. M. A. Dornheim. il *Aviat Week Space Technol* 126:67-8 Mr 16 '87

Boost for the booster [space shuttle redesign] il *Time* 130:67 S 14 '87

Booster test equipment delays pose threat to shuttle schedule. E. H. Kolcum. *Aviat Week Space Technol* 127:31 O 26 '87

Delta 181 mission has key SDI flight test objectives. C. Covault. il *Aviat Week Space Technol* 127:30-1 N 23 '87

Disassembled SRM field joint shows no damage after test [space shuttle solid rocket motor] *Aviat Week Space Technol* 127:34 S 14 '87

Energia heavy booster to double as Soviet shuttle propulsion system. il *Aviat Week Space Technol* 126:18-19 Je 8 '87

Space vehicles—Propulsion systems—Testing—*cont.*
First test-firing for redesigned shuttle booster rocket. il *Sci News* 132:151 S 5 '87
Fixes to space shuttle hardware, management reach critical stage. E. H. Kolcum. *Aviat Week Space Technol* 126:77+ My 4 '87
Ground test problems delay resumption of Ariane launches. *Aviat Week Space Technol* 126:25 F 16 '87
Kennedy moves ahead with plans for wet countdown demonstration test [space shuttle] *Aviat Week Space Technol* 126:110 My 11 '87
Morton Thiokol hot-fires redesigned space shuttle solid rocket motor joint. il *Aviat Week Space Technol* 127:23 Ag 10 '87
NASA, contractors weigh options for orbiter flight readiness firing [Discovery shuttle] *Aviat Week Space Technol* 126:27 F 9 '87
NASA managers debate need for flight readiness firing test [space shuttle main engines] E. H. Kolcum. *Aviat Week Space Technol* 126:23-4 F 23 '87
SDI Delta intercept yields data on space collision shock waves. C. Covault. il *Aviat Week Space Technol* 126:26-7 Je 8 '87
Shuttle booster redesign, tests raise schedule delay concerns. C. Covault. *Aviat Week Space Technol* 126:26-7 Ja 26 '87
The Soviets blast out in front [Energia rocket] M. D. Lemonick. il map *Time* 129:58 Je 1 '87
Soviets demonstrate flight readiness with firing of heavy-lift booster. il *Aviat Week Space Technol* 126:20-1 Mr 16 '87
Soviets fly jet-powered space shuttle testbed. il *Aviat Week Space Technol* 127:22-5 O 12 '87
Soviets test massive new booster for station, shuttle missions [Energia booster] C. Covault. il *Aviat Week Space Technol* 126:18-20 My 25 '87
Static firing of solid rocket motor clears USAF Titan 34Ds for launch. W. B. Scott. il *Aviat Week Space Technol* 127:26-7 Jl 20 '87
Thiokol begins full-diameter tests of redesigned SRB field joint [shuttle solid rocket booster] M. A. Dornheim. il *Aviat Week Space Technol* 126:119+ F 9 '87
Thiokol evaluates first full-scale test of redesigned shuttle booster. il *Aviat Week Space Technol* 127:26-7 S 7 '87
Thiokol test fires shuttle motor, reinstates old O-ring material. M. A. Dornheim. il *Aviat Week Space Technol* 126:26 Je 1 '87
A time of testing for the shuttle [solid rocket boosters] S. Butler-Hannifin. il *Space World* X-6-282:10-15 Je '87

Reentry
See Space vehicles—Atmospheric entry

Safety devices and measures
See also
Space vehicles—Escape devices
NASA may need $350-million fund boost to restore shuttle to safe flight status. *Aviat Week Space Technol* 126:28-9 Ap 13 '87
Review team urges close scrutiny of critical shuttle components. *Aviat Week Space Technol* 126:75 Ja 26 '87

Shielding (Heat)
Infrared imaging system will record flow fields during shuttle reentry. il *Aviat Week Space Technol* 127:65+ D 7 '87

Solar energy use
USAF pursues development of solar-powered rocket. W. B. Scott. il *Aviat Week Space Technol* 127:119-20 O 19 '87

Specifications
International spacecraft [tables] il *Aviat Week Space Technol* 126:157 Mr 9 '87
U.S. spacecraft [tables] il *Aviat Week Space Technol* 126:156 Mr 9 '87

Testing
NASA nears key shuttle tests, changes initial payload schedule. C. Covault. *Aviat Week Space Technol* 127:28-9 Jl 6 '87
Shuttle flight: 10 months and counting. il *U S News World Rep* 103:10 Ag 17 '87

Tires
See Tires, Space vehicle

Space vehicles, Chinese
China defines family of improved Long March launchers. il *Aviat Week Space Technol* 127:79 O 26 '87
Chinese facility combines capabilities to produce Long March boosters, ICBMs. C. Covault. il *Aviat Week Space Technol* 127:50-3 Jl 27 '87

Chinese make inroads on commercial launch market. *Aviat Week Space Technol* 126:134 Mr 9 '87
New Chinese heavy rocket spurs effort to win commercial launch contracts. C. Covault. il *Aviat Week Space Technol* 126:22-3 My 4 '87

Space vehicles, French
See also
Spaceplane, French

Space vehicles, Japanese
See also
Spaceplane, Japanese
Advanced technology moves Japan toward launcher market. il *Aviat Week Space Technol* 126:132-3 Mr 9 '87
Design changes tighten timetable for launch of Japan's H-2 booster. J. M. Lenorovitz. *Aviat Week Space Technol* 127:47-8 N 16 '87
Eastern shuttle. D. Stewart. il *Omni* 9:14 Ja '87
Japan will develop new 3-stage booster. *Aviat Week Space Technol* 127:24 Jl 20 '87
Land of the rising rockets [plans to launch H-1 rocket] M. Lord. il *U S News World Rep* 102:79 Je 8 '87
UFO update [August 12, 1986 cloud formed by liquid fuel released from Japanese rocket] J. E. Oberg. il *Omni* 9:83 Ja '87

Space vehicles, Restored
Restoring America's space treasures [Kansas Cosmosphere and Space Center] J. R. Vacca. il *Space World* X-8-284:10-13 Ag '87

Space vehicles, Russian
See also
Spaceplane, Russian
Earth station, can you read me? [monkey onboard Soviet space vehicle frees arm from restraints] il *Time* 130:36 O 19 '87
GM wants to use Soviet launchers. E. Marshall. *Science* 238:23 O 2 '87
Monkey business in orbit [rhesus monkey launched by Soviets] M. Gray. il *Macleans* 100:54 O 19 '87
Pentagon warns of Soviet space buildup. *Aviat Week Space Technol* 127:28-9 O 12 '87
Proton marketing team finds U.S. interest, opposition [Soviet booster] *Aviat Week Space Technol* 126:20-1 My 25 '87
Russki business [attempt to market Proton booster] L. Dorr, Jr. il *Space World* X-7-283:31-4 Jl '87
Satellite builders want change in U.S. anti-Proton policy. T. M. Foley. *Aviat Week Space Technol* 127:138-9 S 28 '87
Soviet Mars mission will use modular propulsion system. *Aviat Week Space Technol* 127:81 N 2 '87
Soviet space initiatives. D. E. Fink. *Aviat Week Space Technol* 126:11 My 25 '87
Soviets will offer space launch insurance at competitive prices. *Aviat Week Space Technol* 127:138-9 S 28 '87
State Dept. denies license to export U.S. satellites to the Soviet Union [use of Proton] *Aviat Week Space Technol* 127:59 Jl 27 '87
A Texas lawyer markets Soviet rockets [A. Dula] D. Pedersen. il por *Newsweek* 110:58 Ag 17 '87

Photographs and photography
Close-up views reveal details of Soviet heavy-lift booster [Energia booster] il *Aviat Week Space Technol* 126:72-3 Je 8 '87
Soviets offer three boosters for commercial launch services. il *Aviat Week Space Technol* 126:94-5 Ja 12 '87

Testing
Energia heavy booster to double as Soviet shuttle propulsion system. il *Aviat Week Space Technol* 126:18-19 Je 8 '87
Soviet Proton booster fails; reconnaissance satellite explodes. C. Covault. il *Aviat Week Space Technol* 126:26-7 F 9 '87
The Soviets blast out in front [Energia rocket] M. D. Lemonick. il map *Time* 129:58 Je 1 '87
Soviets demonstrate flight readiness with firing of heavy-lift booster. il *Aviat Week Space Technol* 126:20-1 Mr 16 '87
Soviets fly jet-powered space shuttle testbed. il *Aviat Week Space Technol* 127:22-5 O 12 '87
Soviets lose Proton booster, payload in launch failure. *Aviat Week Space Technol* 126:24 My 4 '87
Soviets test massive new booster for station, shuttle missions [Energia booster] C. Covault. il *Aviat Week Space Technol* 126:18-20 My 25 '87

Space walks *See* Space flight—Extravehicular activity
Space warfare
See also
Anti-satellite weapons

Space warfare—See also—*cont.*
　Artificial satellites—Military use
　Kinetic kill vehicles
　North American Aerospace Defense Command. Space
　　Defense Operations Center
　Railguns
　Strategic Defense Initiative
　United States. Air Force. Space Command
　United States. Air Force. Space Division
　United States. Unified Space Command
The empire strikes back [proposed Dept. of the Defense
　Force] R. C. Kirkwood. *Natl Rev* 39:41 Jl 17 '87
Pentagon usurps civilian space program. G. E. Brown,
　Jr. il *Bull At Sci* 43:26-31 N '87
Space and national strategy [address, May 15, 1987]
　E. C. Aldridge. *Vital Speeches Day* 53:614-16 Ag 1
　'87
Space weapons *See* Space warfare
Space world (Periodical)
The postman rings—frequently [letters] J. Rhea. il *Space
　World* X-12-288:4 D '87
President's message. B. Bova. il *Space World* X-12-288
　Space Advocate:8 D '87
Spaceballs [film] *See* Motion picture reviews—Single works
Spacecause
Space politics forum. G. P. Wilson. See issues of Space
　World beginning December 1987
Spacecraft *See* Space vehicles
Spacehab, Inc.
NASA denies shuttle launch to commercial space firm.
　T. M. Foley. *Aviat Week Space Technol* 127:26-8 S
　7 '87
Spacelab missions *See* Space stations—Spacelab missions
Spacemen *See* Astronauts
Spacepac
Space politics forum. G. P. Wilson. See issues of Space
　World beginning December 1987
Spaceplane
Aero-Space Plane project chief named [R. R. Barthelemy]
　Aviat Week Space Technol 127:28 O 5 '87
New space systems test facilities to cost $7 billion
　[Strategic Defense Initiative and National Aerospace
　Plane] il *Aviat Week Space Technol* 126:85 Ap 27
　'87
Teledyne Brown defines reusable spaceplane concept.
　Aviat Week Space Technol 127:141 Ag 10 '87
Three contractors win bids to continue X-30 development
　[National Aero-Space Plane] *Aviat Week Space Technol*
　127:35 O 12 '87
Will the aerospace plane work? [with editorial comment
　by John I. Mattill] S. Korthals-Altes. il *Technol Rev*
　90:2, 42-51 Ja '87
X-30 proceeds. il *Space World* X-10-286:5 O '87
X-30 research narrowing hypersonic design options
　[National Aerospace Plane] C. Covault. il *Aviat Week
　Space Technol* 126:32-3 Ap 27 '87
　　　　　　　　Cabins
Students propose interior designs for hypersonic travel
　[Art Center College of Design in Pasadena, Calif.]
　il *Aviat Week Space Technol* 126:328 Je 15 '87
　　　　　　　　Cockpits
Hermes flight deck combines cockpit technology concepts.
　il *Aviat Week Space Technol* 127:84 Jl 6 '87
　　　　　　　　Doors
Contraves seeks production contract for Hermes
　spaceplane bay doors. il *Aviat Week Space Technol*
　126:58-9 F 23 '87
Spaceplane, French
CNES discusses Hermes-Mir compatibility with Soviets.
　Aviat Week Space Technol 126:25 My 11 '87
Contraves seeks production contract for Hermes
　spaceplane bay doors. il *Aviat Week Space Technol*
　126:58-9 F 23 '87
ESA shows full-scale mockup of Hermes manned
　spaceplane [Paris Air Show] il *Aviat Week Space
　Technol* 127:95 Jl 6 '87
Europeans approve development of Ariane 5, Hermes,
　Columbus. J. M. Lenorovitz. *Aviat Week Space Technol*
　127:22-4 N 16 '87
Hermes flight deck combines cockpit technology concepts.
　il *Aviat Week Space Technol* 127:84 Jl 6 '87
Mockup shows differences between shuttle, spaceplane
　[Hermes] il *Aviat Week Space Technol* 127:86 Jl 6
　'87
The other shuttles. J. Schefter. il *Pop Sci* 230:72-6 Mr
　'87
Panel calls for interim manned capsule [Assn. for
　European Astronauts comment on Hermes program]
　Aviat Week Space Technol 127:48-9 Jl 27 '87

Spaceplane, Japanese
Japanese commission outlines space program funding
　needs. il *Aviat Week Space Technol* 127:20 Jl 13
　'87
Japanese panel recommends spaceplane development.
　Aviat Week Space Technol 127:31 Jl 6 '87
Spaceplane, Russian
Soviets near flight test of small manned spaceplane.
　C. Covault. *Aviat Week Space Technol* 126:23 Mr
　30 '87
Spacesuits
Off to see the wizard. G. R. Graf. il *Space World*
　X-4-280:26-9 Ap '87
Soviets display space suits similar to those used on
　Mir. il *Aviat Week Space Technol* 127:112 O 19 '87
Suiting up for space. il *Natl Geogr World* 143:6-13 Jl
　'87
Spacewatch [television program] *See* Television program
　reviews—Single works
Spackling compounds
Spackling compounds. il *Consum Rep* 52:229-31 D '87
Spackling compounds. il *Consum Rep* 52:433-5 Jl '87
Spadefoot toads *See* Toads
Spader, James
　　　　　　　　about
James Spader. E. Miller. il por *Seventeen* 46:100 N
　'87
Spaepen, Frans
The art and science of microstructural control. bibl f
　il *Science* 235:1010-14 F 27 '87
Spaeth, Robert L.
Individualism vs. liberal arts education [address, Septem-
　ber 8, 1987] *Vital Speeches Day* 54:22-6 O 15 '87
Spafford, Michael, 1934-
　　　　　　　　about
Politics outlives art. L. Smallwood. il *Art News* 86:28
　D '87
Spain, Tom
Audio/video plus. See issues of Publishers Weekly begin-
　ning May 9, 1986
Spain
　　　　See also
　　Art—Spain
　　Barcelona (Spain)
　　British—Spain
　　Bullfights—Spain
　　Castile (Spain)
　　Catalonia (Spain)
　　Dance—Spain
　　Dance festivals—Spain
　　Escorial (San Lorenzo, Spain)
　　Estremadura (Spain)
　　Industry and state—Spain
　　Investments, American—Spain
　　Investments, Foreign—Spain
　　Jerez (Spain)
　　Jews—Spain
　　La Rioja (Spain)
　　Lake Cisó (Spain)
　　Madrid (Spain)
　　Opera—Spain
　　Pamplona (Spain)
　　Public health—Spain
　　Restaurants—Spain
　　Student protests, demonstrations, etc.—Spain
　　Trials—Spain
　　　　　　　Commerce
　　　　　　United States
　　See United States—Commerce—Spain
　　　　　　　Defenses
　　　See also
　　North Atlantic Treaty Organization
　　United States—Armed Forces—Forces in Spain
　　United States. Air Force—Forces in Spain
　　　　　Description and travel
Don Quixote's Spain. M. Picchi. il *World Press Rev*
　34:61 N '87
　　　　　　Foreign opinion
　　　　　　　British
Donkey business and asinine journalism [British mass
　circulation dailies' coverage of false Spanish donkey
　abuse story fed them by an animal rights group] J.
　Valls-Russell. il *New Leader* 70:5-7 Ap 6 '87
Spanish grill [British newspapers' anti-Hispanic bias] R.
　Alan. *New Leader* 70:9 O 5 '87
　　　　　　　History
　　　　　　711-1516
The Cid of history and the history of The Cid. P.
　Linehan. bibl il *Hist Today* 37:26-32 S '87

Spain—History—cont.
> *House of Austria, 1516-1700*
> See also
> Mexico—History—Spanish colony, 1540-1810
> *Philip II, 1556-1598*
Philip II's grand design for the glory of God and empire. R. Wernick. bibl (p205) il pors *Smithsonian* 18:152-6+ D '87
> *19th century*
> See also
> Latin America—History—Wars of Independence, 1806-1830
> *Civil War, 1936-1939—Literature and the war*
The barricades and beyond. O. Paz. *New Repub* 197:26-30 N 9 '87
The Spanish tragedy. B. M. W. Knox. il *N Y Rev Books* 34:21-8 Mr 26 '87
'The Spanish tragedy': an exchange [discussion of March 26, 1987 article] B. M. W. Knox. il *N Y Rev Books* 34:52-3 Je 25 '87
> **History, Naval**
Securing the Spanish Main [cover story] W. Houk. il map *Américas* 39:8-13+ My/Je '87
Tales of sunken gold and hunters of the depths [Spanish galleons] B. S. Walker. bibl (p132) il map *Smithsonian* 17:96-102+ Ja '87
> **Industries**
> See also
> Compania Telefonica Nacional de Espana SA
> Printing industry—Spain
> Publishers and publishing—Spain
> **Kings and rulers**
> See also
> Philip II, King of Spain, 1527-1598
> **Languages**
> See also
> Spanish language in Spain
> **Nationalism**
The bullfight and Spanish national decadence. C. Graña. *Society* 24:33-7 Jl/Ag '87
> **Politics and government**
Offering retirement to the ETA. J. Valls-Russell. il *New Leader* 70:9-10 N 30 '87

Spam
Local lunch meat makes good, and Austin, Minnesota pays homage with a fond 'Play it again, Spam'. il *People Wkly* 28:53 Jl 20 '87

Spangehl, Stephen D.
The push to assess. il *Change* 19:35-9 Ja/F '87

Spangenburg, Ray, 1939-, and Moser, Diane, 1944-
A question of gravity. il *Space World* X-2-278:8-11 F '87

Spangler, Rudolph, and others
Activation of adenovirus promoters by the adenovirus E1A protein in cell-free extracts. bibl f il *Science* 237:1044-6 Ag 28 '87

Spaniards
> See also
> Basques

Spanish American architecture *See* Architecture, Spanish American

Spanish American house decoration *See* House decoration, Spanish American

Spanish art *See* Art, Spanish

Spanish Civil War *See* Spain—History—Civil War, 1936-1939

Spanish cooking *See* Cooking, Spanish

Spanish International Communications Corporation
The feud that toppled a TV empire [sold to Hallmark Cards] G. Critser. il pors *Channels* 7:24-31 Ja '87

Spanish language
> See also
> Government publications—Translations into Spanish
> Motion pictures—Spanish language films
> **Study and teaching**
Se habla español [language proficiency of former students of Spanish; study by Harry Bahrick] J. Meer. *Psychol Today* 21:12 My '87

Spanish language in Spain
> **History**
Hidalgo and pechero in Castile. I. A. A. Thompson. bibl f il *Hist Today* 37:23-9 Ja '87

Spanish language press
> See also
> El diario-La prensa (New York, N.Y.)

Spanish language programs *See* Television broadcasting—Spanish language programs

Spanish Main
Securing the Spanish Main [cover story] W. Houk. il map *Américas* 39:8-13+ My/Je '87

Spanish moss
Our Southland's silver cloak. H. Middleton. il *South Living* 22:57+ My '87

Spanish painting *See* Painting, Spanish

Spanish Sahara conflict, 1975- *See* Western Sahara conflict, 1975-

Spanish speaking people (U.S.) *See* Hispanic Americans

Spanish wines *See* Wine

Spanking *See* Corporal punishment

Spar, Ira
> about
Business, B.C. B. Weber. il por *N Y Times Mag* p114 N 22 '87

Spare time *See* Leisure

Spark, Muriel
Gardens: plotting an alpine cliffhanger: the Bagatti Valsecchi villa above Lake Como. il por *Archit Dig* 44:124-9+ F '87

Spark plugs
Spark plug do's and don'ts [automobiles] M. Ferrara. il *Home Mech* 83:16 Je '87

Sparks, Colin
> about
King's Road ransom. V. Becker. il pors *House Gard* 159:76+ My '87

Sparks, Glenn G.
How were children affected by the space shuttle disaster? *Educ Dig* 52:55-7 F '87

Sparks, Samuel S., d. 1987
> about
Obituary
> *Jet* por 71:14 Ja 26 '87

Sparks, Electric *See* Electric sparks

Sparks Steak House (New York, N.Y.) *See* New York (N.Y.)—Restaurants, nightclubs, bars, etc.

Sparling, Peter
> about
Peter Sparling: new positions. J. Gruen. il pors *Dance Mag* 61:66-9 Ap '87

Sparrow, Rory
> about
Building a basis for dreams. J. McCallum. il pors *Sports Illus* 67:22-3 D 21 '87

Sparrow (Missile) *See* Guided missiles

Sparrows
> **Photographs and photography**
Green mansion [house sparrow nest in traffic light, Tucson, Ariz.] C. A. Morgan. il *Nat Hist* 96:108-9 N '87

Spas *See* Health resorts, watering places, etc.

Spatial perception *See* Space perception

Spatter work (Craft)
Frame pictures with granite? [spatter-finished mat board] D. Hastings. il *South Living* 22:84 Ag '87

Spaulding, Norman W., d. 1987
> about
Obituary
> *Jet* por 72:55 Ag 10 '87

Spawning
In a tizzy over tommy cod [ice fishing for spawning tommycod in Quebec's Ste.-Anne River] S. Homer. il *Int Wildl* 17:18-24 Ja/F '87
A small misunderstanding [interest in salmon spawning on Scotland's Endrick River] R. Holland. il *Audubon* 89:62-3 S '87

SPE *See* Sucrose polyesters

Speakers *See* Loudspeakers

Speakers (Persons) *See* Public speaking

Speakers of the House of Representatives *See* United States. Congress. House—Speakers

Speakes, Larry Melvin
> about
No popularity contest. H. Sidey. il por *Time* 129:20 F 9 '87
Reagan admin. spawns two books: memoir and novel. *Publ Wkly* 232:81 Ag 14 '87

Speaking *See* Speech; Voice

Speaking, Public *See* Public speaking

Speaking in tongues
New policies on divorce and speaking in tongues [Southern Baptists] *Christ Today* 31:51+ S 18 '87

Spear, Laurinda
> about
Bernardo Fort-Brescia and Laurinda Spear: the iconoclasts. B. Dumaine. il pors *Fortune* 115:152-3 Je 22 '87

Spear Financial Services, Inc.
Small world [Sanyo Securities buys stake in Spear Financial Services] J. Heins. il *Forbes* 139:159+ My 4 '87

Spears, Monroe K.
Big bad Wolfe? il *N Y Rev Books* 34:34-7 S 24 '87

Special Clothes (Firm)
For kids who can use an assist, Judi Emens designs clothing that doesn't add to their handicaps. L. Rozen. il pors *People Wkly* 28:59+ S 28 '87

Special Committee against Apartheid *See* United Nations. Special Committee against Apartheid

Special Committee to Investigate Organized Crime in Interstate Commerce *See* United States. Congress. Senate. Special Committee to Investigate Organized Crime in Interstate Commerce

Special education
See also
Blind—Education
Children, Gifted—Education
Handicapped—Education
Mentally handicapped children—Education
Problem children—Education
Slow learning children—Education
Visually handicapped—Education

Preventive preschool programming that works [Ypsilanti, Mich.] J. A. Harper. il *Phi Delta Kappan* 69:81-2 S '87

Special effects *See* Motion pictures—Special effects; Theater—Special effects; Videotape recorders and recording—Special effects

Special effects (Photography) *See* Photography, Trick

Special Forces (U.S. Armed Forces) *See* United States—Armed Forces—Special Forces

Special Forces (U.S. Army) *See* United States. Army. Special Forces

Special interest groups
See also
Anti-nuclear movement
Citizens for Sensible Control of Acid Rain
Lobbyists and lobbying
Moral Majority
National Education Association of the United States
National Rifle Association of America
Political action committees

Can the Court be swayed? [amicus briefs before the Supreme Court; study by Karen O'Connor] *USA Today (Periodical)* 116:11-12 Ag '87

Single-issue politics and the Church [Catholic Church] K. R. Himes. *America* 156:377-81 My 9 '87

Special needs adoption *See* Adoption and adopted children

Special Olympics
Eunice Shriver's Olympian friends. M. Green. il pors *People Wkly* 28:31-3 Ag 17 '87

Heroism, hugs and laughter. J. Skow. il *Time* 130:60 Ag 17 '87

Rock elves from Sting to Springsteen give the Special Olympics A very Special Christmas. M. Green. il por *People Wkly* 28:157-9 N 2 '87

They came up roses. E. M. Swift. il *Sports Illus* 67:38-40+ Ag 17 '87

Special Operations Division (Army) *See* United States. Army. Special Operations Division

Special Political Committee (United Nations) *See* United Nations. Special Political Committee

Special prosecutors *See* Government investigations

Special Session on Disarmament: 1988 *See* United Nations. General Assembly (Special Session on Disarmament: 1988)

Specialists (Stock exchange firms)
The markets: some 'heavy tinkering' ahead [inadequacy of market makers in coping with trading by large institutional investors] C. Welles. il *Bus Week* p40+ N 9 '87

Two key questions: was program trading to blame . . . and did the specialists do their jobs? il *Bus Week* p51 N 2 '87

Specialty clothing stores *See* Clothing stores

Species
See also
Evolution
Natural selection
Phylogeny
Variation (Biology)

Asymmetries in mating preferences between species: female swordtails prefer heterospecific males. M. J. Ryan and W. E. Wagner, Jr. bibl f il *Science* 236:595-7 My 1 '87

How big can a species be? [research by John Eadie and others] R. Lewin. *Science* 237:1117 S 4 '87

On the rescue gene and the origin of species [work of Michael Ashburner and Pierre Hutter] *Discover* 8:6-7 Ag '87

The process whereby species originate [cover story] H. L. Carson. bibl il por *BioScience* 37:715-20 N '87

Specific heat
Phonon density of states and specific heat of forsterite, Mg_2SiO_4. K. R. Rao and others. bibl f il *Science* 236:64-5 Ap 3 '87

Specifications
See also
Standardization

Specimens, Zoological *See* Zoological specimens

Speckle interferometry *See* Interferometers and interferometry

Specktor, Mordecai
The Arctic adventures of Ann Bancroft. il pors *McCalls* 114:101 Ja '87

Spectacles *See* Eyeglasses

Spectator (Periodical)
Villains, and victims of AIDS [A. Waugh's pieces in The spectator] G. Bain. il *Macleans* 100:44 Ap 20 '87

Specter, Arlen
Should the Levin-Nunn Amendment be approved? [excerpts from address, May 13, 1987] *Congr Dig* 66:275+ N '87

about
A case of rank vs. privilege. T. Gup. il *Time* 130:29 S 14 '87

Spectinomycin
Belligerent bug makes Korean debut [spectinomycin-resistant Neisseria gonorrhoeae; research by John W. Boslego and others] *Sci News* 132:94 Ag 8 '87

Spector, Leonard S.
Nuclear proliferation: who's next? bibl f il *Bull At Sci* 43:17-20 My '87

Pakistani smuggling riles Congress. il *Bull At Sci* 43:3-4 O '87

Spectra-Physics, Inc.
A promise comes of age [Ciba-Geigy takes over Spectra-Physics] R. Addis. il *Forbes* 140:8 Ag 24 '87

Spectre, Jay
about
Going public. C. Vogel. il por *N Y Times Mag* p64-5 Mr 22 '87

Spectrograph
A simple slit spectrograph. B. Sorensen. il *Sky Telesc* 73:98-100 Ja '87

Spectrometers
Geologist's hammer is joined by spectrometers [work of Gregg Vane] R. A. Kerr. *Science* 236:1625 Je 26 '87

Spectrometry *See* Spectrum analysis

Spectroscopy *See* Spectrum analysis

Spectrum analysis
See also
Comets—Spectra and spectroscopy
Galaxies—Spectra and spectroscopy
Halley's comet—Spectra and spectroscopy
Hydrogen—Spectra and spectroscopy
Magnetic resonance imaging
Myoglobin—Spectra and spectroscopy
Nebulae—Spectra and spectroscopy
Proteins—Spectra and spectroscopy
Quasars—Spectra and spectroscopy
Stars—Spectra and spectroscopy
Sun—Spectra and spectroscopy

Accelerator mass spectrometry for measurement of long-lived radioisotopes. D. Elmore and F. M. Phillips. bibl f il *Science* 236:543-50 My 1 '87

Characterization by tandem mass spectrometry of structural modifications in proteins. K. Biemann and H. A. Scoble. bibl f il *Science* 237:992-8 Ag 28 '87

Focal points in mass spectrometry. W. N. Delgass and R. G. Cooks. bibl f il *Science* 235:545-53 Ja 30 '87

Hand of man seen in birds [tandem particle accelerator mass spectrometry used in dating; research by Storrs Olson and others] R. Lewin. *Science* 236:1522 Je 19 '87

Hole-burning spectroscopy and relaxation dynamics of amorphous solids at low temperatures. R. Jankowiak and G. J. Small. bibl f il *Science* 237:618-25 Ag 7 '87

In situ X-ray absorption study of surface complexes: selenium oxyanions on α-FeOOH. K. F. Hayes and others. bibl f il *Science* 238:783-6 N 6 '87

Laser spectroscopy of trapped atomic ions. W. M. Itano and others. bibl f il *Science* 237:612-17 Ag 7 '87

Picosecond holographic-grating spectroscopy. D. A. Wiersma and K. Duppen. bibl f il *Science* 237:1147-54 S 4 '87

Precise timing of the last interglacial period from mass spectrometric determination of thorium-230 in corals. R. L. Edwards and others. bibl f il *Science* 236:1547-53 Je 19 '87

Spectrum analysis—*cont.*

Probing semiconductor-semiconductor interfaces [synchrotron radiation photoemission spectroscopy] R. S. Bauer and G. Margaritondo. bibl f il *Phys Today* 40:26-34 Ja '87

Spectroscopy and light measurements. *Science* 235 pt2:G169-G178 F 27 '87

Spectrum analyzers

ADC Sound Shaper SS-525X equalizer/analyzer. il *High Fidel* 37:27-8+ S '87

AVCOM PSA-35A portable spectrum analyzer. il *Radio-Electron* 58:15+ Jl '87

Speculation

See also
Arbitrage
Commodity futures
Hedging (Finance)
Interest rate futures
Investments
Parking (Securities)
Real estate investment
Risk
Stocks

The biggest bull market. R. J. Samuelson. il *Newsweek* 109:57 Ap 20 '87

The blight on Wall Street. F. G. Rohatyn. il *N Y Rev Books* 34:21-3 Mr 12 '87

The contrarian. D. N. Dreman. See alternate issues of Forbes

Economic Armageddon [address, January 29, 1987] R. J. Buckley. *Vital Speeches Day* 53:347-9 Mr 15 '87

The end of the rich man's boom. L. Cawley. il *Nation* 245:675-6+ D 5 '87

Fair-weather genius [speculative mania in mutual funds] K. L. Fisher. il *Forbes* 140:304 S 7 '87

The global funny money game. H. M. Wachtel. il *Nation* 245:784-6+ D 26 '87-Ja 2 '88

Hey Wall Street, wanna buy the Brooklyn Bridge? [takeover hoax surrounding Dayton Hudson shows market's vulnerability to rumor] G. Weiss. il por *Bus Week* p31 Jl 6 '87

How Japan is beating the profit squeeze [zaitech financing] A. Borrus. il *Bus Week* p60-1 My 11 '87

Insights. S. Blotnick. See issues of Forbes beginning July 28, 1986

Japan writes a new definition of zaitech: 'investor beware'. B. Buell. *Bus Week* p45 S 21 '87

Must the panic get worse to spark reform? A. Bianco. il *Bus Week* p46-7 N 9 '87

Mutual-fund madness. P. Wang and D. Pauly. il *Newsweek* 110:40-1 Ag 31 '87

Now, rumortrage. J. Crudele. il *N Y* 20:16+ Je 15 '87

The perils of trading money for money. Y. Messarovitch. *World Press Rev* 34:46-7 Jl '87

Seeing value in stocks that few investors will touch [contrarians] J. E. Goodman and E. Schurenberg. il *Money* 16:8 D '87

Speed kills. A. Redleaf. il *Natl Rev* 39:43-7 N 20 '87

Suddenly, it's fashionable to go against the grain [contrarians] J. M. Laderman. il *Bus Week* p108-9 D 7 '87

Taking a flyer on companies that are still in the cellar. G. G. Marcial. il *Bus Week* p134-5 D 28 '87-Ja 4 '88

Wall Street's outrageous fortunes. A. Smith. il *Esquire* 107:73-4 Ap '87

Speculum Musicae (Musical group)

Musical events:
American premieres of works by Kurtág, Ruders and Birtwistle. A. Porter. *New Yorker* 62:96+ F 9 '87

The real thing [performance of H. Birtwistle's Secret theater] P. G. Davis. *N Y* 20:89-90 F 9 '87

Speech

See also
Accents
Air pilots—Language
Children—Language
Conversation
Language and languages
Men—Language
Public speaking
Voice

Refined speech the key to being thoroughly modern? [research by Philip Lieberman and others] R. Lewin. *Science* 236:670 My 8 '87

Origin
See Language and languages—Origin

Speech, Freedom of *See* Freedom of speech

Speech defects

See also
Stuttering

Speech errors *See* Errors, Speech

Speech perception

Japanese quail can learn phonetic categories. K. R. Kluender and others. bibl f il *Science* 237:1195-7 S 4 '87

Speech perception takes precedence over nonspeech perception. D. H. Whalen and A. M. Liberman. bibl f il *Science* 237:169-71 Jl 10 '87

Speech processing systems

See also
Computerphones
Vocoders

"Audiocruise: this is your driver speaking". N. J. Freundlich. il *Pop Sci* 230:86-7 Ja '87

Butler in a box [Butler-In-A-Box voice-recognition system] J. Schefter. il *Pop Sci* 230:62 Mr '87

"Car of the future" obeys voice commands [Votan system] il *Radio-Electron* 58:4 F '87

Crouzet, Bendix will develop voice command system [military aircraft] *Aviat Week Space Technol* 127:77 Jl 20 '87

High tech [VocaLink, voice-activated dialing for cellular phones] D. Sweeney. il *Car Driv* 32:38 Je '87

Its master's voice [R. Kurzweil's Voice works] D. Lander. il por *Pop Mech* 164:69-71 O '87

Release [blind author R. Russell and his talking word processor] *New Yorker* 63:28-32 S 28 '87

Talk may be cheap, but Ray Kurzweil stands to make millions by yakking to his voice computer. L. Rozen. il pors *People Wkly* 27:113-14 Mr 9 '87

Two phones that dial by voice [Voice Dialer 1000 and Command Dialer II] il *Consum Rep* 52:406 Jl '87

Speeches, addresses, etc.

See also
Baccalaureate addresses
Presidential candidates—Addresses, messages, etc.

Speechwriters and speechwriting

See also
Bush, George, 1924——Speechwriters and speechwriting
Presidential candidates—Speechwriters and speechwriting
Reagan, Ronald, 1911——Speechwriters and speechwriting

No heavy lifting [plagiarism] W. Safire. il *N Y Times Mag* p12+ S 27 '87

'Nobody ever throws fruit at the speechwriter' [corporate speechwriters] J. A. Byrne. il *Bus Week* p112-13+ O 12 '87

Speed

See also
Automobiles—Speed
Automobiles, Experimental—Speed
Computers—Speed
Fishing boats—Speed
Modems—Speed
Motorcycles—Speed

Zoom factor. P. Egan. il *Road Track* 38:28 Ag '87

Speed boats *See* Motor boats

Speed control equipment *See* Automobiles—Speed control

Speed indicators

See also
Speedometers
Tachometers

Speed limits *See* Traffic regulations

Speed metal music *See* Rock music

Speed of light *See* Light—Speed

Speed reading

Reading more, understanding less [speed reading and comprehension; research by Marcel Just and others] J. Meer. *Psychol Today* 21:12 Mr '87

Speed records

See also
Airplane speed records
Automobile speed records
Boat speed records
Land speed records
Motorcycle speed records

Speed skating

Competitions

The price of glory [World Cup competition tests Canadian skaters] J. Howse. il por *Macleans* 100:40-2 D 14 '87

Speed skating—Competitions—*cont.*
Sprinting to Calgary [U.S. performance at the World Sprint Speed Skating Championships] D. S. Looney. il *Sports Illus* 66:166 F 9 '87

History
Bobsleigh, luge and speed skating [U.S. Olympic competitors] W. Bingham. il *Sports Illus* 67:51+ D 14 '87

Speed skiing *See* Ski racing
Speed traps, Radar *See* Radar in traffic control
Speeding tickets *See* Traffic tickets
Speedometers
Digital speedometer for your car. R. Ortman. il *Radio-Electron* 58:47-51+ Jl '87
Needless needles. B. W. Yates. il *Car Driv* 32:20 Mr '87
What to do about a broken speedometer. P. Weissler. il *Home Mech* 83:73-7 D '87
Speedways
Miscellaneous ramblings [Watkins Glen] J. Dinkel. il *Road Track* 38:35 F '87
Ten best corners [racetracks] L. Griffin. *Car Driv* 32:47 Ja '87

Great Britain
A Brooklands birthday. M. Jordan. il *Cycle* 38:56-60+ D '87
Speenburgh, Gertrude
Louis C. Tiffany—the painter [excerpt from The arts of the Tiffanys] il *Antiques Collect Hobbies* 91:60-2 Ja '87
Speer, Roy M.
about
The rise and rise of HSN. M. Gill. il pors *Esquire* 107:70 Ap '87
Spelling
How to be a better speller. G. Hechinger. il *Glamour* 85:278+ F '87
Old-fashioned spelling is tuf and dum [simplified spelling] E. Rondthaler. por *U S News World Rep* 103:9 Jl 13 '87

Competitions
Spelling for dollars [school Spell-a-Thon] M. J. Valentine. *Phi Delta Kappan* 69:312-13 D '87

Study and teaching
Help for a bad speller. F. Roberts. *Parents* 62:60-1 F '87
Spelling bees *See* Spelling—Competitions
Spelling checker programs *See* Word processors and processing—Programming
Spelman College
'The Cosby show' goes to Spelman College for the season finale. D. M. Cheers. il *Jet* 72:28-30 My 11 '87
Johnnetta B. Cole: Spelman's "sister" president [interview] P. Giddings. il por *Essence* 18:34+ N '87
Johnnetta Cole: serving by example [interview with new president] A. Bernstein. il pors *Change* 19:46-55 S/O '87
Spelman College gets its first "sister president" [J. B. Cole] S. McHenry. il por *Ms* 16:58-61+ O '87
Spelman College names 1st black woman president [J. Cole] *Jet* 72:7 My 11 '87
Spence, Annette
Why does your body bloat? il *Redbook* 170:114-15+ N '87
Spence, David S.
Rethinking the role of vocational education. *Educ Dig* 52:48-51 F '87
Spence, Lee
about
Yo-ho-ho and a bottle of Mumm! Veteran diver Lee Spence toasts the treasure of the lost wreck Regina. N. Geeslin. il pors *People Wkly* 28:143-5 N 16 '87
Spence, Michael, 1952-
The right way to escape from a sinking ship [poem] *Am Sch* 56:328-9 Summ '87
Spence, Piers
(tr) See Levi, Primo, 1919-1987. Weightless
Spencer, Brian
about
The case against Brian Spencer. P. Dexter. il *Sports Illus* 66:98-102+ My 11 '87
A hockey player's victory in court. M. Gray. il pors *Macleans* 100:46-7 O 26 '87
Spencer, Duncan
A curfew for Karin. il *N Y Times Mag* p26 Jl 5 '87
Spencer, Edson W.
Buying health care in the new era of medicine [address, April 28, 1987] *Vital Speeches Day* 53:713-16 S 15 '87

Spencer, Henrietta C.
How to conquer food cravings. il *Ladies Home J* 104:69-70+ Ap '87
Spencer, Herbert, 1820-1903
about
Herbert Spencer and 'inevitable' progress. R. M. Young. bibl il por *Hist Today* 37:18-22 Ag '87
Spencer, Joel
about
How to become a house musician. M. Stryker. pors *Down Beat* 54:54+ F '87
Spencer, LaVyrle
The gamble [fiction] il por *Good Housekeep* 204:163-6+ Mr '87
Spencer, Paula
Big shots. *Health* 19:73-4+ N '87
The gift of sight [with editorial comment by Bard Lindeman] il pors *50 Plus* 27:4, 24-7+ Je '87
Her joints are jumping. il pors *50 Plus* 27:44-50 Ja '87
Spencer, Peter L.
A college financial aid primer. il *Consum Res Mag* 70:19-23 Ap '87
Spencer, Peter S., and others
Guam amyotrophic lateral sclerosis-Parkinsonism-dementia linked to a plant excitant neurotoxin [cover story] bibl f il map *Science* 237:517-22 Jl 31 '87
Spencer, Samuel R.
The courts and the colleges [address, December 8, 1986] *Vital Speeches Day* 53:310-14 Mr 1 '87
Spending *See* Consumption (Economics)
Spenser: for hire [television program] *See* Television program reviews—Single works
SPERDVAC *See* Society to Preserve and Encourage Radio Drama, Variety and Comedy
Spergel, D. N., and others
A simple model for neutrino cooling of the Large Magellanic Cloud supernova. bibl f il *Science* 237:1471-3 S 18 '87
Sperlich, Harold K.
1988: a year of reckoning for Detroit [address, September 8, 1987] *Vital Speeches Day* 54:92-5 N 15 '87
Sperling, George
(jt. auth) See Weichselgartner, Erich, and Sperling, George
Sperlonga (Italy)
Description
Letter from Sperlonga. W. Murray. *New Yorker* 63:94-103 Mr 30 '87
Sperm *See* Spermatozoa
Sperm donors *See* Artificial insemination, Human
Spermatozoa
Electrical responses of eggs to acrosomal protein similar to those induced by sperm. M. Gould and J. L. Stephano. bibl f il *Science* 235:1654-6 Mr 27 '87
The existential decision of a sperm [sea urchin research by Bennett Shapiro] il *Discover* 8:10-11 Ag '87
New option for infertile couples [sperm washing] il *USA Today (Periodical)* 115:11-12 F '87
'Precancer' gene localized in embryo, sperm [int-1 expression] il *Sci News* 132:68 Ag 1 '87
Sequence-specific packaging of DNA in human sperm chromatin. J. M. Gatewood and others. bibl f il *Science* 236:962-4 My 22 '87
Stopping sperm may block AIDS [virus penetration of HLA-DR tagged cells; research by Ellyn Ashida and Virginia Scofield] *Discover* 8:11+ O '87
Washing away infertility [sperm washing] J. Pratt. il *Health* 19:21 Ap '87
Spermicides
Spermicides for safer sex? M. Karpen. *Health* 19:25 Ag '87
Spero, Gena
about
Exercising her right to madness, accused killer Gena Spero poses a legal problem without a solution. J. S. Kunen. il pors *People Wkly* 28:115-16+ O 5 '87
Sperry Corp.
See also
Unisys Corp.
Sperry Flight Systems
Honeywell's Sperry Group sells ARC product line. *Aviat Week Space Technol* 127:32 S 14 '87
Spethmann, Dieter
about
Advice from father. L. S. Richman. il por *Fortune* 116:66 Ag 3 '87
Spetsnaz *See* Commandos, Russian
Spherical projection
Fun with stereographic projections [computer program] R. A. Mulford. il *Sky Telesc* 74:407-8 O '87

Sphinxes
An answer to the sphinx's problem [salt damage] R. Monastersky. *Sci News* 132:301 N 7 '87

Sphygmomanometers
Blood-pressure monitors. il *Consum Rep* 52:314+ My '87
Monitoring your blood pressure at home. J. Schein. il *Consum Res Mag* 70:31-5 D '87
Pressure testers. P. L. Spencer. *Consum Res Mag* 70:2 Ja '87

Spice industry
Marketing
Shaking up the spice industry. D. Tuller. il *Work Woman* 12:78+ O '87
Grenada
Nutmeg. E. Schneider. il *Gourmet* 47:86-7+ D '87

Spices
See also
Cooking—Herbs and spices
Curry
McCormick & Co. Inc.
Spice industry
The life of spice. P. G. McWilliams. il *Ctry J* 14:47-9+ Ag '87

The spider game [film] See Motion picture reviews—Single works

Spider Man (Fictional character)
Spider-man bride wears Willi Smith's last design. il *Jet* 72:53 Je 22 '87

Spider mites *See* Mites

Spider veins
Zap spider veins. il *Ladies Home J* 104:28 S '87

Spider webs
Crosshairs from spider web. R. W. Sinnott. il *Sky Telesc* 73:97 Ja '87
In a world of silken lines, touch must be exquisitely fine [Argiope spiders and their webs] M. Robinson. bibl (p230) il *Smithsonian* 18:94-6+ O '87
The long and short of 'web legs' [webs made by spiders with regenerated legs; research by Fritz Vollrath] *Sci News* 132:72 Ag 1 '87
Anecdotes, facetiae, satire, etc.
First, find your spider [renovating old brass filar micrometer] S. D. Ringwood. il *Astronomy* 15:28+ Ja '87

Spiders
Chemical mimicry: bolas spiders emit components of moth prey species sex pheromones. M. K. Stowe and others. bibl f il *Science* 236:964-7 My 22 '87
Complex dynamics link islands' predators [research by Thomas Schoener and David Spiller] R. Lewin. *Science* 236:917 My 22 '87
Effect of lizards on spider populations: manipulative reconstruction of a natural experiment. T. W. Schoener and D. A. Spiller. bibl f il *Science* 236:949-52 My 22 '87
In a world of silken lines, touch must be exquisitely fine [Argiope spiders and their webs] M. Robinson. bibl (p230) il *Smithsonian* 18:94-6+ O '87
Spider's perfume fatal for moths [research by Mark K. Stowe and others] S. Weisburd. il *Sci News* 131:340 My 30 '87
Food and feeding
See Arachnids—Food and feeding

Spiegel, Penina
Penina Spiegel, a Steinberg client, remembers a strange dinner with the lawyer and his daughter. por *People Wkly* 28:47 N 23 '87

Spiegel, Thomas
about
The thrift that junk bonds built. T. Carson. il por *Bus Week* p86 Je 29 '87

Spiegel, Inc.
Wall Street isn't buying Spiegel's high-gloss look. M. D. Oneal. il *Bus Week* p62 O 19 '87

Spiegelman, Art
Mauschwitz [excerpt from Maus, part II] il *Esquire* 107:67-9+ Mr '87
about
Comics and catastrophe. A. Gopnik. il *New Repub* 196:29-34 Je 22 '87

Spielberg, Steven, 1947-
about
The color purple [film] Reviews
Harpers 274:29 Ja '87
N Y Rev Books 34:17-20 Ja 29 '87. D. Pinckney
Empire of the sun [film] Reviews
Macleans il 100:65 D 14 '87. L. O'Toole
N Y il 20:86-7 D 14 '87. D. Denby
New Yorker 63:93-5 D 28 '87. P. Kael
Newsweek il 110:82-3 D 14 '87. D. Ansen

Time il 130:79 D 7 '87. R. Corliss
Steven Spielberg: too cute for words. R. Rosenbaum. il *Mademoiselle* 93:146+ S '87

Spielman, Chris
about
Chris Spielman. A. Murphy. il por *Sports Illus* 67:75 Ag 31 '87

Spielvogel, Carl
about
Nice guy finishes first. B. Kanner. il por *N Y* 20:29-31 S 14 '87

Spier, Dave
Shooting from a mobile blind. il *Conservationist* 41:44-7 Mr/Ap '87

Spiers, Ronald I.
Challenges facing the Foreign Service [address, May 1, 1987] *Dep State Bull* 87:30-4 Jl '87
Countering today's security challenges [statement, April 23, 1987] *Dep State Bull* 87:52-4 Je '87
The fiscal threat to U.S. foreign policy [address, October 15, 1986] *Dep State Bull* 86:47-50 D '86
Managing diplomacy: problems and issues [address, August 6, 1987] *Dep State Bull* 87:20-3 O '87
Toward a more representative Foreign Service [address, October 3, 1986] *Dep State Bull* 86:50-1 D '86
U.S.-Soviet agreement on embassy construction in Washington [statement, May 19, 1987] *Dep State Bull* 87:34-5 Jl '87
Underfunding and undermining our foreign policy infrastructure [statements, February 26 and March 4, 1987] *Dep State Bull* 87:23-7 My '87

Spies *See* Espionage
Spies, Industrial *See* Business intelligence

Spike, Paul, 1947-
Goldfingers. il *House Gard* 159:114+ Ap '87

Spillane, Mickey, 1918-
Murder never dies. il *Harpers Bazaar* 120:152-3+ Ja '87

Spiller, David A.
(jt. auth) See Schoener, Thomas W., 1943-, and Spiller, David A.

Spin, Airplane *See* Airplanes—Spinning
Spin, Molecular *See* Molecular spin
Spin, Nuclear *See* Nuclear spin
Spin-casting *See* Casting (Fishing)

Spina bifida
A burden gallantly borne [hockey player B. Bourne's son] A. Murphy. il pors *Sports Illus* 67:26-7 D 21 '87
"Sergeant Mom" [Army sergeant has child with spina bifida] B. A. Kidwell. il por *Ladies Home J* 104:16+ Ja '87
Zachary [son born with spina bifida] N. Lund. il por *Parents* 62:117-18+ Ag '87

Spinach salads *See* Salads

Spinal cord
Newly identified 'glutamate interneurons' and their role in locomotion in the lamprey spinal cord. J. T. Buchanan and S. Grillner. bibl f il *Science* 236:312-14 Ap 17 '87
Inflammation
See Myelitis
Surgery
Behavioral recovery induced by applied electric fields after spinal cord hemisection in guinea pig. R. B. Borgens and others. bibl f il *Science* 238:366-9 O 16 '87
A dancer's nightmare [S. Lavery] L. Leivick. il pors *N Y Times Mag* p66+ N 8 '87
Wounds and injuries
Neurons regenerate into spinal cord [work of Jerry Silver and Michel Kliot] R. Weiss. *Sci News* 132:324 N 21 '87

Spine
See also
Backache
Abnormalities
See also
Scoliosis
Spina bifida
Back from the past [colchicine used to alleviate disk disease] J.-B. Shoemaker. il *Health* 19:21 F '87
Surgery
Fast comeback for a quarterback with a bad back [return of J. Montana after spinal disk surgery] il *Discover* 8:14 Ja '87
New disk treatment given a whirl [suction diskectomy] *Prevention* 39:10 S '87
Wounds and injuries
See also
Paralytics

Spine—Wounds and injuries—*cont.*

Nightmare in the hayfield [T. Argrave run over by tractor and drags himself out of field] P. Michelmore. il *Read Dig* 130:64-9 Je '87

Spinjammer (Game)

Michael Sandeen's Spinjammer is a new twist on an old disc. il por *People Wkly* 27:138-9 My 11 '87

Spinks, Leon

about

Leon Spinks is suspended after loss; he won't quit. il *Jet* 71:51 F 9 '87

Stripped of his title, not of his heart, Michael Spinks fights Gerry Cooney, but looks out for Leon. J. Friedman. il pors *People Wkly* 27:38-40 Je 15 '87

Spinks, Michael

about

Boxing champ Spinks to debut in next 'Rambo' film. por *Jet* 71:46 Mr 16 '87

Michael Spinks wrecks car, faces DUI charge. *Jet* 72:46 Ap 6 '87

Say good night, Gerry. W. Nack. il pors *Sports Illus* 66:22-3 Je 22 '87

Spinks cleared to fight, but Cooney camp is quiet. por *Jet* 72:47 Ap 13 '87

Spinks-Cooney 'title' fight boasts equal opportunity. *Jet* 72:46 Je 1 '87

Spinks loses round one in bid to fight Cooney. por *Jet* 71:48 Ja 19 '87

Spinks says victory tells little guys to stand tall. il por *Jet* 72:48 Jl 6 '87

Spinks still feels like champion despite ruling. *Jet* 71:49 Mr 23 '87

Stripped of his title, not of his heart, Michael Spinks fights Gerry Cooney, but looks out for Leon. J. Friedman. il pors *People Wkly* 27:38-40 Je 15 '87

Tyson schedule so full Spinks may wait a year. pors *Jet* 72:48 Jl 20 '87

Why Cooney can't win . . . J. Ryan. il pors *Sport Mag* 78:13 Jl '87

Spinner baits *See* Fishing lures, flies, etc.

Spinoffs (Corporate) *See* Corporations—Divestiture

Spinoffs (Technology) *See* Technology transfer

Spiral galaxies *See* Galaxies

Spirea

Spireas are almost too simple. S. Bender. il *South Living* 22:124-7 My '87

Spirit communication *See* Spiritualism

Spirit Novelties (Firm)

The foam finger. A. D. Frank. il por *Forbes* 139:136+ My 4 '87

Spiritism *See* Spiritualism

Spiritual directors *See* Pastoral counseling

Spiritual healing *See* Faith cure

Spiritual life

See also

Christian life

Meditation

Soul

Spirituality

Call me Four Eyes. G. K. Brushaber. il *Christ Today* 31:11 Jl 10 '87

[Column] H. Fehren. See issues of U.S. Catholic

"Tell us," they asked, "what is God like?" An appreciation of Tony de Mello, S.J. [cover story] T. H. Stahel. *America* 157:446-50 D 12 '87

The Year of the Setback? H. Smith. *Christ Today* 31:13 Ag 7 '87

Spiritualism

See also

Channelers

Good heavens, Shirley! [beliefs of S. MacLaine] K. Garfield. por *Ladies Home J* 104:31+ O '87

Isness is her business [S. MacLaine] M. Gardner. il *N Y Rev Books* 34:16-19 Ap 9 '87

Otherworldly believers from the past. il *People Wkly* 27:34-5 Ja 26 '87

She's having the time of her lives [S. MacLaine] por *People Wkly* 27:28-9 Ja 26 '87

Spiritual glitz. B. G. Harrison. *Ms* 16:72+ Jl/Ag '87

Was she ever a housewife in Mesopotamia? [S. MacLaine] S. Nelson. por *Glamour* 85:210 S '87

Study and teaching

Going even farther out on that limb [S. MacLaine's seminars] B. Kantrowitz. il pors *Newsweek* 110:46-7 Jl 27 '87

Shirley's best performance [S. MacLaine's seminars] M. Harris. il por *Money* 16:160-2+ S '87

Spirituality

See also

Mysticism

Eugene Peterson: a monk out of habit [interview] R. Clapp. il pors *Christ Today* 31:24-8 Ap 3 '87

Growing together in spirituality: pastor and parish have a check-up. A. C. Krass. il *Christ Century* 104:311-14 Ap 1 '87

Shake the universe [spirituality of women] M. L'Engle. il *Ms* 16:182-4+ Jl/Ag '87

Spirituality: an African view [interview with C. E. Glover, Jr.] J. D. Simmons. por *Essence* 18:61+ D '87

Spirituality in abstract art [The spiritual in art: abstract painting 1890-1985; cover story] P. Schaeffer. il *Christ Century* 104:819-22 S 30 '87

Spiro, Stanley

about

In Florida: from molars to Moonglow. G. Jaynes. il por *Time* 129:12-13 F 9 '87

Spiro (Stan) and the Townsmen Orchestra *See* Stan Spiro and the Townsmen Orchestra

Spirochetes

See also

Borrelia

Spirodela *See* Duckweeds

Spiroplasmas

A defined medium for a fastidious spiroplasma. K. J. Hackett and others. bibl f il *Science* 237:525-7 Jl 31 '87

Spitz, Bob

Is collusion the name of the game? il *N Y Times Mag* p22-3+ Jl 12 '87

Spitzmiller, Walt

about

L.L. Bean vs. the preppified pooch. il por *Newsweek* 109:53 Mr 16 '87

Splet, Alan

about

Sound by Splet. S. Gowin. il *Theatre Crafts* 21:71-2 F '87

Spletzer-Newman, Michelle

about

After the baby: shedding 25 inches and 25 pounds. See issues of Glamour beginning June 1987 through December 1987

Splicing of genes *See* Genetic research

Split brain

New routes to early memories. D. Kucharski and W. G. Hall. bibl f il *Science* 238:786-8 N 6 '87

Splitfingered fastball *See* Pitching (Baseball)

Splitters, Log *See* Wood cutting equipment

Splitting of stocks *See* Stocks—Splitting

Splitting of wood *See* Wood cutting

Spock, Benjamin, 1903-

Are your kid's friends bad influences? por *Redbook* 169:22 Je '87

Can one parent be as good as two? *Redbook* 168:17 Ap '87

Every child should have a chore. por *Redbook* 169:30+ O '87

Happy birthday, Dr. Spock! il *Redbook* 169:19-20 My '87

How on-screen violence hurts your kids. il *Redbook* 170:26+ N '87

Is your child too dependent on you? il *Redbook* 169:28 Jl '87

Teaching children to give. il por *Redbook* 170:34+ D '87

What are you teaching your child about love & marriage? por *Redbook* 169:40 S '87

Spoerli, Heinz

about

Swan Lake [ballet] Reviews

Dance Mag il 61:74-5 Mr '87. I. Wydler-Roth

Spohr, Arnold

about

Arnold Spohr to step down. P. Citron. il por *Dance Mag* 61:18 My '87

Spoiling of children *See* Children—Management and training

Spokane Ballet

Aponte makes Spokane's dream come true. S. English. pcr *Dance Mag* 61:8-9 Ap '87

Sponge fisheries (Commercial) *See* Fisheries

Sponges

Better to cut, than hook, sponges. *Sea Front* 33:383 S/O '87

Interocean differences in size and nutrition of coral reef sponge populations [cover story] C. R. Wilkinson. il *Science* 236:1654-7 Je 26 '87

Sponsors, Advertising See Television advertising
Spontaneous abortion See Miscarriage
Spontaneous generation
   Campbell's primordial soup: spontaneous generation: a
   danger in canned foods? F. Schmugge. *Harpers* 274:18
   My '87
Spontaneous human combustion
          Anecdotes, facetiae, satire, etc.
   A blaze of glory. C. Murphy. il *Atlantic* 259:16+ Ap
   '87
Spontini, Gasparo, 1774-1851
          about
   Agnes von Hohenstaufen [opera] Reviews
     Opera News 51:40 Mr 28 '87. M. A. Zaccaria
Spoonbills
   The royal spoonbill [Australian study] M. P. Kahl. il
   map *Natl Geogr* 171:280-4 F '87
Spoons
   Now thanks to Suzanna Goodin, pets can clean the
   bowl—and then eat the spoon that feeds them. il
   por *People Wkly* 27:119 Mr 9 '87
Spoons (Fishing lures) See Fishing lures, flies, etc.
Spoor, William Howard
          about
   A CEO bake-off at Pillsbury. B. Dumaine. il pors *Fortune*
   116:109+ N 23 '87
Spores
     See also
   Fungal spores
Sporkin, Elizabeth
   Tina Turner: her most candid interview. por *Ladies
   Home J* 104:34+ Ap '87
Sport See Sports
Sport aviation [film] See Motion picture reviews—Single
   works
Sport fishing See Fishing
Sport fishing boats See Fishing boats
Sporting clays (Shooting) See Trapshooting
Sporting goods
     See also
   Aquatic sports—Equipment
   Bowling—Equipment
   Football—Equipment
   Mountaineering—Equipment
   Skis and skiing—Equipment
   Tennis—Equipment
   2001 a sports odyssey. K. Delhagen. il *Women's Sports
   Fitness* 9:32-3 Ag '87
   Athletic specs: the eyes have it. S. Krasnow. il *Sport
   Mag* 78:97+ Ag '87
   Check out this good sport! [sporting gear identification
   game] il *Natl Geogr World* 144:17-18 Ag '87
   For the fan who has everything [sports-oriented gifts]
   il *Sport Mag* 78:79-80+ Ja '87
   Great gear. il *Women's Sports Fitness* 9:76-7 D '87
   What's new in recreation. S. F. Brown. See issues of
   Popular Science beginning December 1985
          Exhibitions
   Live from Atlanta: it's all Super. P. Sikowitz. il *World
   Tennis* 34:60-1+ Ap '87
   SHOT '87: an embarrassment of riches [Shooting, Hunt-
   ing, and Outdoor Trade Show] B. Brister. il *Field
   Stream* 91:91-2+ Ap '87
          Prices
   The good old days [prices of sporting goods in 1900
   Sears catalog] E. B. Mann. il *Field Stream* 92:66-7+
   Je '87
Sporting goods, Used
   The short end of the stick [advocating a program to
   send used sports equipment to the third world] D.
   O'Connell. il *World Tennis* 35:80+ O '87
Sporting goods industry
     See also
   Drew Pearson Enterprises
   Evolution USA (Firm)
   Life-Link International, Inc.
   Nike Inc.
   Pederson Custom Golf Clubs Inc.
   Wilson Sporting Goods Co.
          France
     See also
   Rossignol Production (Skis)
Sporting goods stores
     See also
   All American SportsClub Inc.
   L. L. Bean, Inc.
   Mitchell & Ness Sporting Goods
   Oshman's Sporting Goods, Inc.
Sports
     See also
   Aged—Sports

AIDS (Disease) and sports
Alcohol and sports
Amateurism (Sports)
Amputees—Sports
Aquatic sports
Arbitration, Sports
Athletes
Black celebrities—Sports
Blind—Sports
Business and sports
Cable television—Sports
Celebrities—Sports
Children—Sports
Coed sports
College athletics
Computers—Sports use
Deaf—Sports
Discrimination in sports
Drugs and sports
Electronics in sports
Ex-convicts—Sports
Executives—Sports
Handicapped—Sports
Lasers—Sports use
Physical education and training
Priests—Sports
Prisoners—Sports
Radio broadcasting—Sports
Recreation
School athletics
Sex discrimination in sports
Television broadcasting—Sports
Track and field athletics
Videotapes—Sports
Winter sports
Women—Sports
Yuppies—Sports
   See also names of sports
Can you go the distance? [endurance sports] G. Bakoulis.
   il *Health* 19:34-6+ O '87
[Column] P. Axthelm. See occasional issues of Newsweek
For the record. See issues of Sports Illustrated
Moments of pure delight [victory celebrations in 1987]
   S. Wulf. il por *Sports Illus* 67:104 D 21 '87
Most of '86. il *Time* 129:66 Ja 5 '87
Of heroes, hellions and homer hankies [1987 highlights]
   R. Fimrite. il *Sports Illus* 67:14-17 D 28 '87-Ja 4
   '88
Scorecard. See issues of Sports Illustrated
Sport quiz. See issues of Sport Magazine
Sport talk. See issues of Sport Magazine
A sporting chance . . . N. O. Unger. See issues of
   Jet beginning December 31, 1984-January 7, 1985
   through January 26, 1987
Sports clinic. See issues of Esquire
Sun & games. il *Seventeen* 46:93-6 Je '87
That was the year that will be [sports in 1988] M.
   Lupica. il *Esquire* 108:81-2 D '87
Ultimate fitness [cover story; special section] il *Esquire*
   107:113-16+ My '87
What's in a nickname? [college and professional sports
   teams] J. Leo. il *Time* 129:82 Ja 19 '87
          Accidents and injuries
     See also
   Aquatic sports—Accidents and injuries
   Automobile racing—Accidents and injuries
   Baseball, Professional—Accidents and injuries
   Basketball, Professional—Accidents and injuries
   Boxing—Accidents and injuries
   Football, High school—Accidents and injuries
   Football, Professional—Accidents and injuries
   Hockey, Professional—Accidents and injuries
   Parachuting—Accidents and injuries
   School athletics—Accidents and injuries
   Skis and skiing—Accidents and injuries
   Tennis—Accidents and injuries
   Track and field athletics—Accidents and injuries
The best eyewear for your sport. il *Glamour* 85:37 Jl
   '87
Breaks of the game [injuries to children] S. Findlay.
   il *U S News World Rep* 103:75-7 O 5 '87
Read a chapter a day [advice of James G. Garrick]
   R. B. Taylor. il *Women's Sports Fitness* 9:14 Jl '87
Sport specs: play it safe! H. Platt. il *Harpers Bazaar*
   120:44+ Ap '87
          Anecdotes, facetiae, satire, etc.
Wake me when it's over. J. McCallum. por *Sports Illus*
   67:112 D 14 '87
What's going on here? [foreign athletes overshadowing
   Americans] J. McCallum. por *Sports Illus* 67:74 S
   28 '87

Sports—cont.

Awards

See also
Boxing—Awards
Flo Hyman Memorial Award
Football, College—Awards
Sullivan Award winner Jackie Joyner-Kersee is best amateur athlete. il por *Jet* 71:46 Mr 16 '87
Survey says nation's kids favor Bulls' Jordan, Bears [Outstanding Male Athlete Award] *Jet* 72:50 Ap 13 '87

Competitions

See also
Aerobics—Competitions
Diving—Competitions
Figure skating—Competitions
Gay Games
Junior Olympics
Olympic Games
Pan American Games
Pentathlon
Senior Olympics
Skis and skiing—Competitions
Special Olympics
Speed skating—Competitions
Triathlon
U.S. Olympic Festival

Economic aspects

See also
Arena football—Economic aspects
Athletes—Salaries, pensions, etc.
Boxing—Economic aspects
Football, Professional—Economic aspects
Hockey, Professional—Economic aspects
Running—Economic aspects
Sports agencies and agents
Women athletes—Salaries, pensions, etc.

Equipment

See Sporting goods

Ethical aspects

See also
Baseball, Professional—Ethical aspects
Basketball, College—Ethical aspects
Basketball, High school—Ethical aspects
Basketball, Professional—Ethical aspects
Blood boosting
Boxing—Ethical aspects
College athletics—Ethical aspects
Drugs and sports
Football, College—Ethical aspects
Football, Professional—Ethical aspects
Harness racing—Ethical aspects
Hockey—Ethical aspects
Hockey, Professional—Ethical aspects
Horse racing—Ethical aspects
Motor boat racing—Ethical aspects
School athletics—Ethical aspects
Soccer, Professional—Ethical aspects
Tennis—Tournaments—Ethical aspects
Track and field athletics—Ethical aspects
Violence in sports
Controversial 'blood doping' revisited. *Sci News* 131:344 My 30 '87
Endurance by the pint [blood doping] D. Pine. il *Women's Sports Fitness* 9:56 Jl '87
Gloating in the locker room [phony showmanship] C. Gordon. por *Macleans* 100:60 O 5 '87
On cooling a beef [recommendation that pro athletes use the body punch in arguments during games] P. Berger. il *Sport Mag* 78:79-80 S '87

International aspects

See also
Olympic Games
Pan American Games

Officiating

See Sports officiating

Organization and administration

Jesse vs. the big leagues. A. Edmond, Jr. il por *Black Enterp* 17:16 Jl '87
Minority hiring issue faces increased focus. il *Jet* 73:47 D 21 '87

Periodicals

See also
Sports illustrated (Periodical)
A guide to the other sports magazines. J. Millman. il *Sport Mag* 78:83+ F '87
Sports, recreation, conservation, and outdoors magazines. *Writer* 100:33-42 Ja '87

Photographs and photography

Making the photo play. D. Levine. il *Sport Mag* 78:95+ Ag '87

Meet the masters [W. Iooss] F. Cameron. il *Petersens Photogr Mag* 16:16-19+ O '87
Pictures '87 [special issue] il *Sports Illus* 67:14-26+ D 28 '87-Ja 4 '88

Psychological aspects

See also
Baseball, Professional—Psychological aspects
Golf—Psychological aspects
Tennis—Psychological aspects
Track and field athletics—Psychological aspects
Commonsense competition. C. Schaeffer. *Changing Times* 41:97-8 F '87
Interview [B. Ogilve] P. Weintraub and M. Teich. por *Omni* 9:80-2+ S '87
Mind over muscle [use of meditation techniques to boost athlete performance] L. Brummell and B. Weisbrot. il *Women's Sports Fitness* 9:60 My '87
Playing new mind games. S. Aikenhead. il *Macleans* 100:44-5 D 14 '87
Psychologists can conquer athletes' fears. il *USA Today (Periodical)* 116:11 Jl '87
Time machine psychology [M. E. P. Seligman's study of athletes' explanatory styles] il *Psychol Today* 21:36-7 F '87

Public relations

'Have I got a story!' [p.r. man J. Goldstein] D. S. Looney. il pors *Sports Illus* 66:58-60+ My 18 '87

Securities

Psst . . . wanna buy the Boston Celtics? [investing in teams] G. Weiss. il *Bus Week* p106 Mr 2 '87
Sports investing: the money pit? W. Strugatch. *Sport Mag* 78:86+ O '87

Social aspects

See also
Baseball, Professional—Social aspects
Bowling—Social aspects
Skis and skiing—Social aspects
Arthur Ashe raps role sports plays in society. por *Jet* 72:29 Ap 27 '87
Evening the score [society's concepts of justice reflected in sports] M. M. Mark and J. Greenberg. bibl (p63) il *Psychol Today* 21:44-50 Ja '87
Fitness times two. H. Platt. *Harpers Bazaar* 120:132+ Ja '87
'A little lower than the angels' [athletes who help others; cover story; special section; with introd. by Frank Deford] il *Sports Illus* 67:12-31 D 21 '87

Africa

Africans return to form at track championships [World Championships in Rome] *Jet* 73:47 S 28 '87

Australia

See also
Automobile racing—Australia

Austria

See also
Automobile racing—Austria

Belgium

See also
Automobile racing—Belgium
Motorcycle racing—Belgium

Brazil

See also
Automobile racing—Brazil

California

See also
Irwindale (Calif.)—Sports
Los Angeles (Calif.)—Sports
A Californian's lament: the Raiders and Lakers are not laid-back, thank you. R. Fimrite. il por *Sports Illus* 66:108 Je 1 '87
Everything under the sun. L. Montville. il *Sports Illus* 67:66-8+ S 7 '87

Photographs and photography

California dreamin' [cover story] il *Sports Illus* 67:50-65 S 7 '87

Canada

See also
Football, Professional—Canada
Hockey
Polo—Canada
Ski racing
Soccer, Professional—Canada
Speed skating
Revealing secret dreams [Maclean's/Decima poll] H. Quinn. il *Macleans* 100:56 Ja 5 '87

Colorado

See also
Denver (Colo.)—Sports

Sports—*cont.*

Developing countries

The short end of the stick [advocating a program to send used sports equipment to the third world] D. O'Connell. il *World Tennis* 35:80+ O '87

Dominican Republic

See also

Baseball—Dominican Republic

Florida

See also

Daytona Beach (Fla.)—Sports
Jacksonville (Fla.)—Sports
Palm Beach (Fla.)—Sports

France

See also

Automobile racing—France
Bicycle racing—France

Germany (West)

See also

Automobile racing—Germany (West)

Great Britain

See also

Automobile racing—Great Britain
Cricket (Sport)—Great Britain
Motorcycle racing—Great Britain
Soccer, Professional—Great Britain

Hungary

See also

Automobile racing—Hungary

Indiana

See also

Indianapolis (Ind.)—Sports
Milan (Ind.)—Sports

Italy

See also

Automobile racing—Italy
Basketball, Professional—Italy
Motorcycle racing—Italy

Japan

See also

Baseball, Professional—Japan

Korea (North)

Gold-medal diplomacy [North Korean demand to cohost 1988 Olympics] B. Wallace. il *Macleans* 100:21 Ag 17 '87
North Korea: games across the border [1988 Olympics] *Newsweek* 109:45 F 23 '87
Pyongyang's Olympic game [North Korea's desire to cohost the Olympics] F. Willey. il *Newsweek* 110:43 O 5 '87

Latin America

See also

Indians of South America—Sports

Massachusetts

See also

Boston (Mass.)—Sports

Mexico

See also

Automobile racing—Mexico
Bullfights—Mexico
Wrestling, Professional—Mexico

Missouri

See also

Saint Louis (Mo.)—Sports

Monaco

See also

Automobile racing—Monaco

Oregon

See also

Hood River (Or.)—Sports

Portugal

See also

Automobile racing—Portugal

South Africa

See also

Boxing—South Africa

South Africa's sports isolation. G. Behrens. *World Press Rev* 34:57 Ap '87
Track's longest-running win streak [South African middle distance runner J. Fourie banned from international competition] il por *Sports Illus* 67:16 Jl 27 '87

Soviet Union

See also

Baseball—Soviet Union
Tennis—Soviet Union

Spain

See also

Bullfights—Spain

Taiwan

See also

Baseball, Children's—Taiwan

Western Europe

See also

Automobile racing—Western Europe
Motorcycle racing—Western Europe

Wisconsin

See also

Green Bay (Wis.)—Sports

Sports afield (Periodical)

Sports afield [article submission policy] T. Paugh. il *Writer* 100:26 S '87

Sports agencies and agents

See also

IMG International Management Group
World Sports & Entertainment, Inc.

Bob Woolf: the man behind the $8 million man. L. Therrien. il por *Bus Week* p125-6 Ap 27 '87
Count Dracula [I. Tiriac, former player and current tennis agent and mentor] C. Kirkpatrick. il pors *Sports Illus* 66:60-4+ Je 22 '87

Ethical aspects

Agents of turmoil [N. Walters and L. Bloom accused of wooing blue chip college athletes with cash] C. Neff. il pors *Sports Illus* 67:34-40+ Ag 3 '87
Agents of violence? [dealings of N. Walters and L. Bloom] B. Selcraig. il por *Sports Illus* 66:25 Ap 6 '87
Agents: what's the deal? [special section] il *Sports Illus* 67:74-8+ O 19 '87
Buckeyes Carter sues agents for $4 million. por *Jet* 73:50 O 5 '87
Dickerson files $12 million suit vs. Norton's agency. il por *Jet* 72:48 Je 8 '87
Kareem fights English's suit with one of his own. *Jet* 72:48 Ap 6 '87
Payton's agent could pose a problem with NFL plans [plans to own team could be hindered by conduct of P. Holmes] *Jet* 72:50 Jl 13 '87

Sports and business *See* Business and sports

Sports arenas *See* Stadiums

Sports bars

Where you can belly up for the big games. P. Angiolillo. il *Bus Week* p101 F 9 '87

Sports bras *See* Brassieres

Sports broadcasters *See* Cable television—Sports; Radio broadcasting—Sports; Television broadcasting—Sports

Sports Car Club of America

Summer stock [SCCA Showroom Stock racing] R. Titus. il *Mot Trend* 39:108-13+ Mr '87

Sports car racing *See* Automobile racing

Sports cars

See also

Convertibles (Automobiles)
Midwestern Council of Sports Car Clubs
New Avanti Motor Corp.
Sports Car Club of America

Ali's car in demand before plant is built. il por *Jet* 71:46 Ja 19 '87
Driving well is the best revenge. M. Knepper. il *50 Plus* 27:30-3+ N '87
Luxury never sleeps [Jaguar, Lotus and BMW] il *Road Track* 39:102+ O '87
Mitsubishi Starion/Chrysler Conquest, Nissan 300ZX and Toyota Supra [owner surveys] P. Bohr. il *Road Track* 38:154-8+ My '87
Owner survey: Toyota MR 2. D. C. Ross. il *Mot Trend* 39:79-80 Ag '87
Two for the road [two-seaters] P. Bedard. il *Esquire* 107:31-2 Ap '87
Will the Ali car ever come out of its corner? M. E. Recio. il por *Bus Week* p133 Ja 12 '87

Anecdotes, facetiae, satire, etc.

Dinner in Milano, or: We drive the Paisano V-11. G. Baxter. il *Car Driv* 32:29 Je '87

Collectors and collecting

Ferrarimania [classic car market] il *Fortune* 116:9-10 S 28 '87

Design

Alfa's fresh-faced sedan and 150-mph sportster. P. Bingham. il *Mot Trend* 39:40 Je '87
Basics to the back [mid-engine 1988 Honda CRX] J. Thompson. il *Road Track* 38:44-6 F '87
British sports car revival [Panther Solo and AC Ace] *Mot Trend* 39:35 Jl '87
Corvette survey: the results. il *Road Track* 38:48-9 My '87
CRX survey: the results [Honda] il *Road Track* 38:70-2 Jl '87
Exclusive: Porsche's secret new price fighter. P. Bingham. il *Mot Trend* 39:17 Jl '87
Favorite Ferrari to be replaced [348 GTB] P. Bingham. il *Mot Trend* 39:18 S '87

Sports cars—Design—*cont.*

Ferrari F40 [cover story] D. Simanaitis. il *Road Track* 39:44-9 O '87

Ferrari futurity [cover story] J. Thompson. il *Road Track* 38:38-41 Ap '87

Ferrari's F40 tops them all! M. Cotton. il *Mot Trend* 39:16-17 O '87

Ford's new AC sportster. M. Cotton. il *Mot Trend* 39:16 Ja '87

A high-tech V-6 for the 300ZX [Nissan 300ZR] J. K. Yamaguchi. il *Road Track* 38:92+ F '87

Lamborghini Portofino takes the stand. M. Cotton. il *Mot Trend* 39:17 D '87

More Porsche crystal ball [redesigned 911] P. Frère. il *Road Track* 38:84+ Ag '87

Porsche perfects [Porsche 961 and 911] P. Bingham. il *Mot Trend* 39:13 Ap '87

Super Vette [1991 LT-5 Corvette; cover story] D. C. Ross. il *Mot Trend* 39:36-40 O '87

Super Vette [future Corvettes] J. Rusz. il *Road Track* 38:54-8+ Je '87

Exhibitions
See Automobiles—Exhibitions

Four wheel drive
Porsche 959. C. Csere. il *Car Driv* 33:116-18+ N '87

History
Aston Martin DB4GT Zagato [1962 model] T. Assenza. il *Car Driv* 33:91+ S '87

The Berkeley. J. F. Woods. il *Road Track* 39:104-6 N '87

Ponies old and new. A. Girdler. il *Road Track* 39:50-2 S '87

Rags to riches with the plastic fantastic [Corvette] A. Girdler. il *Road Track* 38:194 Je '87

Vettes in view [Corvettes] D. C. Ross. il *Mot Trend* 39:40+ O '87

When the future drove down Main Street [Jaguar XK-120] A. Girdler. il *Road Track* 38:68 Je '87

Prices
Supercars. J. Flint. il *Forbes* 140:206-7 N 2 '87

Speed
A gathering of eagles [AMG Hammer, Callaway Corvettes, Ferrari Testarossa, Keith Black Camaro, Motorsport Design Porsche 911 Turbo and Norwood Ferrari-Chevrolet GTO; cover story] R. Ceppos. il *Car Driv* 33:42-51 D '87

The world's fastest cars [AMG Hammer, Ferrari GTO and Testarossa, Isdera Imperator 108i, Koenig/RS, Lamborghini Countach, Porsche 959 and Ruf Twin-Turbo; cover story] P. Egan. il *Road Track* 38:50-61 Jl '87

Springs and suspension
Lotus active suspension [comparison of normal suspension Lotus Excel with active suspension version] D. Nye. il *Road Track* 38:60-4 F '87

Vette variations [base, Z51 and Z52 suspensions for Corvette] C. Csere. il *Car Driv* 32:109-10+ Je '87

Steering gear
4WS Fiero. D. McCosh. il *Pop Sci* 231:17 N '87

Testing
300ZX Turbo [Nissan] R. Grable. il *Mot Trend* 39:83-4+ Je '87

1988 Porsche 944 Turbo. R. Titus. il *Mot Trend* 39:86-7+ D '87

AC Ace. R. Hutton. il *Car Driv* 32:33 Mr '87

America's car to America's Cup (I) [driving a Corvette from Melbourne to Perth] J. R. Nerad. il *Mot Trend* 39:34-7+ Mr '87

America's car to America's Cup (II) [driving a Corvette from Melbourne to Perth] J. R. Nerad. il map *Mot Trend* 39:86-92 Ap '87

Autokraft beyond Cobra [Ace] J. Lamm. il *Road Track* 38:54-5 Mr '87

Beauty & the beast: Vette vs. Cobra: 25 years of performance history; cover story. R. Titus. il *Mot Trend* 39:46-9+ Jl '87

Chevrolet Corvette at 35,000 miles. il *Road Track* 39:66-8 O '87

Decisions, decisions . . . [Porsche 924S, 944, 944S and 944 Turbo; cover story] il *Road Track* 39:44-53 N '87

Domestic dynamite [Buick Regal Grand National, Chevy Camaro IROC 350 Z, Corvette, Dodge Daytona Turbo, Ford Mustang GT and Thunderbird Turbo Coupe and Pontiac Firebird GTA; cover story] R. Grable. il *Mot Trend* 39:44-51 Ag '87

Dream machines [Ruf Porsche Turbo and Autokraft AC Mk IV; cover story] il *Road Track* 38:40-7 My '87

Dueling Renaults: Alliance vs. GTA. M. Brockman. il *Mot Trend* 39:58-61 Ja '87

Europe's fastest of the fast [Ferrari Testarossa, Lamborghini Countach, Lotus Esprit Turbo and Porsche 928S 4] R. Grable. il *Mot Trend* 39:28-35 Ja '87

Ferrari F40 [cover story] D. Sherman. il *Car Driv* 33:40-3+ N '87

Ferrari Mondial & Ducati Paso [cover story] R. Grable. il *Mot Trend* 39:50-6+ N '87

Ferrari Mondial 3.2. D. Sherman. il *Car Driv* 33:109+ O '87

Ferrari Testarossa Quad Turbo. R. Grable. il *Mot Trend* 39:57-9+ Je '87

Fiero Formula vs MR2 Supercharged [Pontiac vs. Toyota] il *Road Track* 39:50-7 O '87

Fiero vs. Fiero at the Glen [racing GTP car vs. production GT] R. Grable. il *Mot Trend* 39:76-83 Ja '87

Four factory hot rods [Chevrolet Camaro IROC-Z and Pontiac Firebird Trans Am GTA vs Toyota Supra and Nissan 300ZX 2 + 2] il *Road Track* 38:158-64+ Ap '87

Four sporty cars [Acura Integra, Toyota Corolla FX16, Nissan Pulsar NX, Renault GTA] il *Consum Rep* 52:448-55 Jl '87

Good sports [best two-seaters] P. J. O'Rourke. il *House Gard* 159:108+ O '87

Honda Civic CRX Si. L. Griffin. il *Car Driv* 33:83-5 N '87

Honda CRX Si. il *Road Track* 39:68-72 D '87

Hot coupes [Toyota MR2 and Celica All-Trac Turbo] D. McCosh. il *Pop Sci* 231:71 D '87

Isdera Imperator 108i. P. L. Albrecht. il *Road Track* 38:176-8+ My '87

Life with Corvette [long term test] A. St. Antoine. il *Car Driv* 32:75-7 F '87

A lot of cars. See occasional issues of Road & Track beginning June 1986

Mazda RX-7 Turbo II. R. Titus. il *Mot Trend* 39:88-9+ S '87

Nissan 200SX SE. R. Ceppos. il *Car Driv* 32:123-5 Mr '87

Pontiac Fiero GT [long term test] R. Titus. il *Mot Trend* 39:62+ Ja '87

Porsche 928S 4. il *Road Track* 38:62-4+ Mr '87

Porsche 928S 4. R. Grable. il *Mot Trend* 39:61-2+ My '87

Porsche 928S 4. J. Rusz. il *Road Track* 38:86-7 Ja '87

Porsche 928S 4. D. Sherman. il *Car Driv* 32:67+ My '87

Porsche 944S. L. Griffin. il *Car Driv* 33:59+ Ag '87

Road & track's 10 best cars by value and passion [cover story] il *Road Track* 39:46-57 D '87

Rotary rocket [Mazda RX-7 Turbo] T. Wilkinson. il *Pop Sci* 230:32+ Ja '87

The Rotus Seven [roadster based on the Lotus Seven] P. Egan. il *Road Track* 38:74-5 Ja '87

Speed thrills [Chevrolet's Callaway Corvette and Buick's Regal GNX] M. Allen. il *Pop Mech* 164:63-6+ Mr '87

Stopping and going [Mazda RX-7 with anti-lock brakes and Mercedes-Benz 190 2.6] il *Road Track* 38:88-9 F '87

Supercar showdown [Aston Martin Vantage Zagato vs. Ferrari 288 GTO; cover story] P. Bingham. il *Mot Trend* 39:46-51+ D '87

Ten best cars. D. Sherman. il *Car Driv* 32:36-41 Ja '87

Ten best performers. C. Csere. il *Car Driv* 32:48-50 Ja '87

Toyota Celica All-Trac Turbo & MR2 Supercharged. D. Fuller. il *Mot Trend* 39:82-3+ N '87

Toyota MR2 1600G-Limited. Y. Ishiwatari. il *Car Driv* 32:27 Ja '87

Toyota MR2 Supercharged. N. Bissoon Dath. il *Car Driv* 33:55-8+ D '87

Update: long-term tests [Acura Legend Coupe L, Ford Taurus and Porsche 944 Turbo] il *Road Track* 39:64 D '87

Update: long-term tests [Chevrolet Corvette, Saab 9000 and Ford Taurus] il *Road Track* 38:130 Ap '87

Update: long-term tests [Chevrolet Corvette, Saab 9000 and Toyota MR2] il *Road Track* 38:134 Je '87

Update: long-term tests [Chevrolet Corvette, Toyota MR2 and Ford Taurus] il *Road Track* 38:74 F '87

Update: long-term tests [Ford Taurus, Saab 9000 and Toyota MR2] il *Road Track* 39:53 S '87

Update: long-term tests [Porsche 944 Turbo, Ford Taurus and Toyota MR2] il *Road Track* 39:62 N '87

Sports cars—Testing—*cont.*

The world's fastest cars [AMG Hammer, Ferrari GTO and Testarossa, Isdera Imperator 108i, Koenig/RS, Lamborghini Countach, Porsche 959 and Ruf Twin-Turbo; cover story] P. Egan. il *Road Track* 38:50-61 Jl '87

Tires

See Tires, Automobile

Sports cars, Racing *See* Automobiles, Racing

Sports cars, Remodeled *See* Automobiles, Remodeled

Sports cars, Used *See* Automobiles, Used

Sports clothes *See* Clothing and dress—Sports clothes

Sports Club. LA *See* Health clubs

Sports clubs

See also

Hash House Harriers (Organization)
National Brotherhood of Skiers

Executives & health leaders: how to get your people walking! M. Bricklin. il *Prevention* 39:92 Ap '87

Hong Kong

See also

Royal Hong Kong Jockey Club

Sports collectibles

See also

Spirit Novelties (Firm)

Sports equipment *See* Sporting goods

Sports facilities

See also

College sports facilities

Working out [with introd. by Deborah Dietsch] il *Archit Rec* 175:89-105 Ag '87

Puerto Rico

See also

Roberto Clemente Sports City (Carolina, Puerto Rico)

Sports fans

See also

Automobile racing fans
Baseball fans
Basketball fans
Football fans
Soccer fans
Tennis fans

Jilted at the altar of sports. F. Bruning. por *Macleans* 100:9 F 16 '87

Make up, stand up and cheer [Team Colors makeup kits by Bonne Bell] il *Sports Illus* 67:16 S 21 '87

No losers in St. Loo. F. Deford. il por *Sports Illus* 67:116 O 19 '87

Play ball: how to stay in love with a sports fanatic. *Glamour* 85:110 My '87

Stars until the tape runs out [sports fans and other spectators viewing themselves on videotape] C. Gordon. il *Macleans* 100:37 My 18 '87

Anecdotes, facetiae, satire, etc.

Quick, before you're 30: a checklist for the male sports fan who thinks he's with it. R. Reilly. por *Sports Illus* 66:76 Je 22 '87

Sports halls of fame

See also

Canadian Baseball Hall of Fame
Collegiate Tennis Hall of Fame
International Tennis Hall of Fame
Naismith Memorial Basketball Hall of Fame
National Baseball Hall of Fame and Museum
National Wrestling Hall of Fame
Pro Football Hall of Fame
Women's Sports Hall of Fame

Sports illustrated (Periodical)

Letter from the publisher. D. J. Barr. See issues of Sports Illustrated beginning December 9, 1985

Meet the masters [W. Iooss] F. Cameron. il *Petersens Photogr Mag* 16:16-19+ O '87

Sports in art

See also

Baseball in art
Hunting in art

Collectors and collecting

The art of sport: beyond Neiman. W. Grimes. il *Sport Mag* 78:93-4 Ap '87

Sports in literature

See also

Baseball in literature
Boxing in literature

A boy's own author [J. R. Tunis] J. Epstein. *Commentary* 84:50-6 D '87

Sports in motion pictures

See also

Wrestling in motion pictures

Home movies: sports films to go. A. Mancuso. il *Sport Mag* 78:88 N '87

Sports journalism

See also

Baseball players—Press relations

All in the game. *Nation* 245:289 S 26 '87

Assignment: sports [discrimination against women sportswriters in the men's locker rooms] J. Lannin. il *Women's Sports Fitness* 9:77-9+ Mr '87

A breath of fresh air [sportswriters on TV] W. Taaffe. il por *Sports Illus* 67:97 N 23 '87

Injunction withdrawn [dispute over Maclean's plans for special edition on Calgary Olympics] il *Macleans* 100:51 N 23 '87

Notes and comment [American journalists ignore Canada Cup hockey tournament] *New Yorker* 63:27-8 S 28 '87

An Olympian struggle [Maclean's and Olympic organizers heading for confrontation in the courts over a special issue of the magazine] *Macleans* 100:59 N 9 '87

You must remember this [32 years of covering sports] W. Bingham. por *Sports Illus* 66:94 Ap 27 '87

Sports literature

See also

Baseball literature
Fishing literature

Jock lit [books by and about sports personalities] J. McCallum. il *Sports Illus* 67:80-4+ S 21 '87

Sports locker rooms *See* Locker rooms

Sports management *See* Sports—Organization and administration

Sports medicine

See also

Motorcyclists—Health and hygiene
Second wind (Athletics)
Skis and skiing—Accidents and injuries
Tennis—Accidents and injuries

Arthritis Institute tackles sports. W. Booth. il *Science* 237:846-7 Ag 21 '87

Sports medicine. J. Ullyot. See issues of Women's Sports & Fitness

Sports medicine centers

See also

Sports Medicine Systems Inc.

Sports Medicine Drug Identification Laboratory

"High" hurdle. R. Callahan. il *Saturday Evening Post* 259:32-3 Jl/Ag '87

Sports Medicine Systems Inc.

First aid for the fitness fanatic. P. Angiolillo. il por *Bus Week* p68 S 28 '87

Sports News Network

A super stat service for your PC. D. Levine. il *Sport Mag* 78:85-6 My '87

Sports officiating

See also

Baseball, Professional—Umpiring
Basketball, Professional—Refereeing
Boxing—Judging
Boxing—Refereeing
Football, Professional—Officiating
Hockey, Professional—Refereeing
Instant replay (Sports)
Tennis—Tournaments—Officiating

Curse of the camera [TV replays can go too far] R. Reilly. por *Sports Illus* 66:85 Mr 2 '87

Sports on postage stamps *See* Postage stamps

Sports records

See also

Baseball records
Boat speed records
Football records
High jumping records
Hunting records
Long jumping records
Running records
Shooting records
Track and field athletics records
Triple jumping records

Where the women are [comparison with men's records] J. Ullyot. il *Women's Sports Fitness* 9:56 Je '87

Sports shoes *See* Footwear

Sports tickets

See also

Football, College—Tickets

Scalping

See Ticket selling—Ethical aspects

Sports uniforms

See also

Baseball, Professional—Uniforms

Sports writing *See* Sports journalism
Sportscasters *See* Cable television—Sports; Radio broadcasting—Sports; Television broadcasting—Sports
Sportsmanship
　　　　See also
　　　　Football, Professional—Ethical aspects
　　　　Tennis—Tournaments—Ethical aspects
Sportsmen *See* Athletes; Fishermen; Hunters
SportsTicker (Firm)
　　A whole new ballgame [P. Bavasi] E. F. Cone. il por *Forbes* 139:162 My 4 '87
Sportswomen *See* Women athletes
Sportswriting *See* Sports journalism
Spot removal (Laundry) *See* Laundry
Spot satellites *See* Artificial satellites—Earth sciences use
Spotted fever *See* Rocky Mountain spotted fever
Spotted owls *See* Owls
Spotted owls in art *See* Owls in art
Spouse murder *See* Murder
Spradlin, Byron
　　We can love Israel too much. il por *Christ Today* 31:14 Jl 10 '87
Spragens, John, Jr.
　　Computer programs for photographers. il *Petersens Photogr Mag* 15:32-4 F '87
Sprague, Laura Fecych
　　John Seymour in Portland, Maine. bibl f il *Antiques* 131:444-9 F '87
Sprague Technologies Inc.
　　This Penn Central spinoff may soar. G. G. Marcial. *Bus Week* p61 Ag 31 '87
Sprang, Stephen, and others
　　Structure of the nucleotide activation switch in glycogen phosphorylase a. bibl f il *Science* 237:1012-19 Ag 28 '87
　　The three-dimensional structure of Asn^{102} mutant of trypsin: role of Asp^{102} in serine protease catalysis. bibl f il *Science* 237:905-9 Ag 21 '87
Spray painting *See* Paint spraying and sprayers
Spraying and dusting
　　　　See also
　　　　Airplanes in insect control
　　　　Herbicides
　　　　Pesticides
　　Better apples the low-spray way [use of botanical insecticides] J. Ruttle. il *Rodale's Org Gard* 34:48-52 Ag '87
Spraying equipment
　　　　See also
　　　　Glue guns
　　　　Nozzles
　　　　Paint spraying and sprayers
　　　　Pressure washers
　　Cures for sprayer problems. C. Finck. il *Success Farm* 85 no3:18AI F '87
　　Direct injection takes to the field [agricultural sprayers] D. Mowitz. il *Success Farm* 85 no2:24-5 Ja '87
　　How to build a safe ATV sprayer. C. Finck. il *Success Farm* 85 no5:26AD Mr '87
　　Misapplication: still a 'billion dollar blunder' [pesticides] *Success Farm* 85 no3:17 F '87
　　Twist-and-turn sprayers. D. Mowitz. il *Success Farm* 85 no2:22-3 Ja '87
　　Weed & insect control issue [special section] il *Success Farm* 85 no1:19-26+ Ja '87
　　Weed warriors for all seasons. D. Mowitz and C. Finck. il *Success Farm* 85:16-18+ My '87
Sprays, Nasal *See* Nasal sprays
Spread spectrum communications
　　All about spread spectrum communications. J. E. McDermott. il *Radio-Electron* 58:55-8 Ap '87
Spreads (Food)
　　　　See also
　　　　Butter
　　　　Fruit butter
　　Breakfast spread: honey and nuts. il *Sunset* 178:98 Ja '87
　　A cheese-and-date delight. il *South Living* 22:124 D '87
Spreadsheets (Computer programs)
　　The all-purpose environment. M. Antonoff. il *Pers Comput* 11:101-3+ O '87
　　Both sides may win this war [market war between Lotus and Microsoft] A. Field. il *Bus Week* p104-5 O 19 '87
　　Lotus' dream-come-true: a sweet deal with IBM [1-2-3/M spreadsheet] A. Field and A. Beam. il *Bus Week* p116 My 25 '87
　　Lotus takes the offensive: targets 1-2-3 clones; add-in market. il *Pers Comput* 11:29-30 Mr '87

Pencil shrink gives way to computer shrink [spreadsheet to figure shrinkage when marketing slaughter-weight cattle] C. Peterson, Jr. il *Success Farm* 85 no4:B21 F '87
A shared network spreadsheet [virtual memory routines] P. R. Horton and M. D. Morris. *Byte* 12:185-6+ Jl '87
Spreadsheets. See issues of Personal Computing beginning July 1987
Spreadsheets: the computer's crystal ball. G. Vincent. il *Success Farm* 85:F1 My '87
Will Excel excel? S. R. Reed. il *Pers Comput* 11:33 N '87
　　　　Anecdotes, facetiae, satire, etc.
The spreadsheet follies [gambling program] D. Seligman. il *Fortune* 115:100 Mr 30 '87
　　　　Errors
Spreadsheets can be hazardous to your health. S. Ditlea. il *Pers Comput* 11:60-1+ Ja '87
　　　　Testing
Excel challenges the spreadsheet standard [cover story; with editorial comment by Fred Abatemarco] M. Antonoff. il *Pers Comput* 11:102-7+ D '87
Mastering macros in Lotus 1-2-3 [Macropac's 101 Macros for Lotus 1-2-3] S. R. Reed. il *Pers Comput* 11:160 Mr '87
Mostly Mac [Trapeze] E. Shapiro. *Byte* 12:296+ My '87
Spreadsheet add-ons. S. Quigley. il *Pers Comput* 11:137-9+ Mr '87
Spreadsheet and text processing [Words & Figures] H.-J. Taferner. il *Pers Comput* 11:56 F '87
Spreadsheet rivals [cover story] M. Antonoff and S. R. Reed. il *Pers Comput* 11:113-15 D '87
A spreadsheet smooth as Silk. H.-J. Taferner. *Pers Comput* 11:198+ S '87
Spreadsheets. R. Malloy. il *Byte* 12 Sp Issue:68-75 Summ '87
SuperCalc made better. P. Honan. il *Pers Comput* 11:190+ S '87
Three new spreadsheets [Microsoft's Windows Excel, Borland's Quattro, and WordPerfect's PlanPerfect] E. Shapiro. il *Byte* 12:119-21 N '87
Word wrapping in Lotus 1-2-3 [4Word] M. Antonoff. il *Pers Comput* 11:232 Je '87
Sprecher, Stanley Addison
　　Four score (and more) Christmas seals. il *Antiques Collect Hobbies* 92:26-30 D '87
Sprekelia formosissima *See* Jacobean lilies
Sprick, Daniel
　　　　　　about
　　Daniel Sprick. P. Eichner-Dixon. il por *Am Artist* 51:32-7 Ag '87
Spring, K. R.
　　(jt. auth) See Strange, K., and Spring, K. R.
Spring
　　　　See also
　　　　April
　　　　June
　　　　May
　　　　Vernal equinox
　　Focus on spring! [special section] il *Seventeen* 46:142-3 Ap '87
　　Up with spring. E. Hoagland. *Nation* 244:751 Je 6 '87
　　　　Anecdotes, facetiae, satire, etc.
　　You know spring is here when . . . T. Stratton. il *McCalls* 114:158 Ap '87
　　　　Photographs and photography
　　Warming to an Arctic spring. B. Milne. il *Int Wildl* 17:30-4 My/Je '87
Spring break *See* College students—Recreation
Spring dinners *See* Dinners and dining
Spring training (Baseball) *See* Baseball, Professional
Spring vacations *See* Vacations
Springboks
　　　　Photographs and photography
　　Back off, springbok! [pesky plover] il *Natl Geogr World* 146:10-11 O '87
Springer, Sally P., 1947-
　　Left brain, right brain: do we educate both? *Educ Dig* 53:22-5 O '87
Springfield (Ill.)
　　　　Politics and government
　　Blacks in Springfield, Ill. win voting rights case. *Jet* 71:17 F 2 '87
　　Judge in Springfield, Ill. to decide on voting issue. *Jet* 72:12 Je 8 '87
　　Judge orders Springfield, Ill. to vote on new government. *Jet* 72:4 Ap 20 '87
　　Pact reached in voting issue at Springfield, Ill. *Jet* 72:30 Jl 13 '87

Springfield (Mass.)
Arts
Springfield, Pioneer Valley [special section] il *Horizon*
30:41-8 N '87
Description
Springfield, Pioneer Valley [special section] il *Horizon*
30:41-8 N '87
Education
A reading program that works as a community effort
[Reading Incentive Program at Samuel Bowles School]
M. R. McGrath. il *Phi Delta Kappan* 68:475-6 F
'87
Galleries and museums
Binding ties. K. Simmons. il *Horizon* 30:43 N '87
Theater
See also
StageWest
Springfield (Or.)
This town fought TCI and won—well, sort of [cable
TV] K. M. Hafner. il *Bus Week* p91 O 26 '87
Crime
Unmasking a murderous mother, crime writer Ann Rule
closes the book on another psychopath [case of D.
Downs] M. Brower. il pors *People Wkly* 28:125 S
14 '87
Springfield Symphony Orchestra (Mass.)
Orchestra outreach. K. Simmons. il *Horizon* 30:43 N
'87
Springs
See also
Hot springs
Geoquiz. J. V. O'Connor. il *Earth Sci* 40:25 Wint '87
Springs (Mechanism)
See also
Automobiles—Springs and suspension
Springsteen, Bruce
about
Artist of the year. A. DeCurtis. il pors *Roll Stone* p9-10
F 26 '87
Bruce live set slips. M. Goldberg. *Roll Stone* p9 My
7 '87
Bruce looks down the long road. D. Fricke. il por *Roll
Stone* p50-2 Ja 15 '87
Bruce Springsteen [interview] M. Gilmore. il por *Roll
Stone* p22-4+ N 5-D 10 '87
Bruce Springsteen and The E Street Band: The Bottom
Line, New York City, August 13th-17th, 1975. D.
Fricke. il pors *Roll Stone* p89-90 Je 4 '87
Bruce's hard look at love. S. Pond. il por *Roll Stone*
p77-9 D 3 '87
Darkness on the edge of the shining city. J. Morley.
il *New Repub* 196:20-3 Mr 23 '87
How Bruce got glory-bound. G. Sikes. por *Mademoiselle*
93:112 Ap '87
Is Bruce a good boss? D. Handelman. *Roll Stone* p17
S 10 '87
Low-key start for 'Tunnel of love'. F. Goodman. il
por *Roll Stone* p15 N 19 '87
Making a loud noise. J. Miller. il pors *Newsweek* 109:74-5
Ap 13 '87
'Myths keep us strangers'. B. Barol. il pors *Newsweek*
110:76-8 N 2 '87
New paths for the trailblazing Boss. N. Jennings. il
por *Macleans* 100:54 O 12 '87
No home-video release likely for Springsteen footage.
A. DeCurtis. *Roll Stone* p34 Mr 26 '87
On the Springsteen scene: one Boss Club. E. Byron.
il por *Mademoiselle* 93:52 Je '87
Songs for the witching season. J. Cocks. il por *Time*
130:92 O 12 '87
'Tunnel of love' LP due from Springsteen. K. Loder.
Roll Stone p15 S 24 '87
Springtails
Control
What's the diagnosis? W. S. Moore. il *Flower Gard*
32:44 D '87/Ja '88
Sprinkel, Beryl W.
Anecdotes, facetiae, satire, etc.
Dear Doctor Lekachman . . . R. Lekachman. il *Nation*
244:390-2 Mr 28 '87
Sprinklers
See also
Fire sprinklers
Automatic sprinkler systems [lawn sprinklers] il *Flower
Gard* 31:56-7+ Ag/S '87
In-ground sprinklers: more green, less work. S. Advocate.
il *Home Mech* 83:68+ Je '87
Thou shalt not covet thy neighbor's lawn, so grab a
papal sprinkler and let us spray [lawn sprinklers in
the likeness of the Pope] il pors *People Wkly* 27:123
Je 8 '87

Sprinting *See* Track and field athletics
Sprizzo, Marianne
about
Wild in the streets. D. Frost. il pors *Women's Sports
Fitness* 9:33-6 My '87
Sprock, Fred
The latest academic fad. por *Newsweek* 109:8 Je 1 '87
Sprockett, Doc
Let it snow! il *Flower Gard* 32:75-6 D '87/Ja '88
Sprouse, Stephen
about
Fashion. W. Goodman. il por *N Y* 20:138-9 S 21 '87
Sprouting *See* Germination
Sprouts
Let's have high tea! [cress and mustard sprout sandwiches]
W. E. Wooldridge. il *Flower Gard* 32:79 D '87/Ja
'88
Sprung, Guy
about
A national dreamer in the spotlight. J. Bemrose. il por
Macleans 100:61-2 O 26 '87
Spry, Robin
about
Keeping track [film] Reviews
Macleans il 100:55 Ap 6 '87. B. D. Johnson
Spudich, James A.
(jt. auth) See De Lozanne, Arturo, and Spudich, James
A.
Spuds MacKenzie (Advertising character)
Break out the suds for Spuds: contrary to rumors, he's
alive—and not only that, he's a she! il *People Wkly*
28:62-4 S 14 '87
Frothing anti-drink forces set out to nip Spuds in the
Bud [objections to appeal to children] il *People Wkly*
28:87 O 26 '87
Spuds, you dog: 'party animal' faces bust. il *Newsweek*
110:68 D 14 '87
Top dog. B. Kanner. il *N Y* 20:20+ S 28 '87
Spurges
See also
Snow-on-the-mountain (Plant)
The perennials of tomorrow? il *Sunset* 178:248-50 My
'87
Sputnik (Artificial satellites) *See* Artificial satellites, Russian
Sputum
Getting a lung well [sputum test called Novacyte]
Prevention 39:12 Je '87
Spy (Periodical)
Annoying, appalling . . . hilarious. J. Cocks. il *Time*
130:84 N 2 '87
Puck's bad boys. E. Diamond. il *N Y* 20:16+ Jl 27
'87
Spy films *See* Motion pictures—Spy films
Spy planes *See* Airplanes, Military
Spy satellites *See* Artificial satellites—Military use
Spy stories
Authorship
The spy as a modern Everyman [interview with D.
Ignatius] A. P. Sanoff. por *U S News World Rep*
103:69 D 7 '87
Spying *See* Espionage
SQL (Structured Query Language) *See* Structured Query
Language (Computer language)
Squalor in literature
To squalor, with love. A. Broyard. il *N Y Times Book
Rev* 92:11 Ag 30 '87
Square dance [film] *See* Motion picture reviews—Single
works
Square one [television program] *See* Television program
reviews—Single works
Squares (Carpentry equipment) *See* Carpenters' squares
Squash (Sport)
The hustle [artist F. Stella's enthusiasm for the sport]
New Yorker 63:30-1 N 30 '87
Squash: the court of appeal. M. Paley. il *Harpers Bazaar*
120:130+ O '87
Squash blossom cooking *See* Cooking—Flowers
Squashes
See also
Cooking—Vegetables
An abundant harvest of squash. N. Bubel. il *Ctry J*
14:23-5 O '87
Introducing zunkins [zucchini-pumpkin hybrids] W.
Bilozir. il por *Rodale's Org Gard* 34:88-9 O '87
A taste of the Orient. D. S. Wechsler. il *Rodale's Org
Gard* 34:28-30 D '87
Try marrow . . . if you're tired of zucchini. W. E.
Wooldridge. il *Flower Gard* 31:26 Je/Jl '87

Squatter settlements
Little house on the prairie ["cabin" built by homeless family in New York City] P. Weber. il *N Y* 20:40 D 14 '87
Scenes from the squatting life [New York City owned buildings inhabited by squatters] P. Weber. il *Natl Rev* 39:28-32 F 27 '87

Squaw Valley (Calif.)
The Squaw Valley challenge. L. Tejada-Flores. il *Skiing* 40:92-6+ N '87

Squaw Valley Olympics, 1960 *See* Olympic Games—1960—Winter Olympics

Squeeze (Musical group)
Squeeze finally gets its hit. M. Coleman. il *Roll Stone* p26+ D 3 '87

The squeeze [film] *See* Motion picture reviews—Single works

Squeezed light
Still more squeezing of optical noise. B. G. Levi. bibl f il *Phys Today* 40:20-2 Mr '87

Squibb Corp.
Squibb's Rx for success: find a need and fill it. S. Benway. il *Bus Week* p80 O 5 '87
A tough act to follow [captopril] K. Hannon. il por *Forbes* 139:88+ Je 15 '87

Squid
See also
Cooking—Shellfish
Around the Mall and beyond [work of C. Roper with squid and blue-ringed octopus] E. Park. *Smithsonian* 18:28+ My '87

Squid fisheries *See* Shellfish fisheries

Squid salads *See* Salads

SQUIDs (Superconducting quantum interference devices)
Painting with superconductors [use of oxide compounds] il *Sci News* 131:293 My 9 '87

Squiers, Carol, 1948-
Diversionary (syn)tactics. il por *Art News* 86:76-85 F '87

Squire, Susan
Family-style: the Lattanzis have built a restaurant dynasty on anti-chic. il *N Y* 20:90-2+ Ag 24 '87
How to handle a picky boyfriend. il *Seventeen* 46:206-7+ S '87
New clues to the immune system. il por *N Y Times Mag* p32-3+ F 1 '87
Shock therapy's return to respectability. il *N Y Times Mag* p78-9+ N 22 '87

Squire-Buresh, Anne
Saints are not born to it [poem] *Christ Century* 104:431 My 6 '87

Squires, David R.
Against the odds [cover story] il pors *Black Enterp* 18:48-50+ O '87

Squirrel hunting
Farm squirrel bonanza. R. Spomer. il *Outdoor Life* 180:96-7+ S '87

Squirrels
See also
Ground squirrels
Mount Graham, Arizona. R. H. Mohlenbrock. il map *Nat Hist* 96:88-90 Mr '87
Prisoner of geography [Kaibab squirrels] G. Turbak. il *Natl Wildl* 25:14-17 F/Mr '87
Control
Squirrel-proof your bird feeder. K. Childers. il *Fam Handyman* 37:32-3 D '87

Sragow, Michael
Rocky Mountain 'hi'. *Film Comment* 23:6+ N/D '87

SRI International
GE gift-wraps a landmark lab [donating the David Sarnoff Research Center to SRI International] O. Port. il *Bus Week* p35 F 16 '87

Sri Lanka
See also
Dams—Sri Lanka
Terrorism—Sri Lanka
Antiquities
Still waters run deep [remains of earth embankment dam found] A. Bingham. il *Hist Today* 37:5-6 O '87
See also
Defenses
India—Army—Forces in Sri Lanka
Foreign relations
India
See India—Foreign relations—Sri Lanka
Politics and government
The battle for Jaffna [Indian troops mount assault on Tamil stronghold] T. A. Sancton. il *Time* 130:52 O 26 '87

Bearing gifts [Indian support of Tamil rebels] *Time* 129:40 Je 15 '87
Behind the haste in Sri Lanka. G. Jain. *World Press Rev* 34:49 O '87
A disputed homeland [civil war between Tamils and Sinhalese] S. K. Hennayake and J. S. Duncan. il map *Focus* 37:20-7 Spr '87
Giving peace a chance: India and Sri Lanka forge a Tamil compromise. F. Willey. il *Newsweek* 110:43 Ag 10 '87
A grisly scene on Gasworks Street [Tamil terrorists accused of planting bomb] N. R. Gibbs. il map *Time* 129:39 My 4 '87
If this is peace . . . [agreement signed by India and Sri Lanka] E. W. Desmond. il map *Time* 130:18-20 Ag 10 '87
The long agony of a city under siege [Indian troops fight Tamil rebels in Jaffna] B. Barber. il map *Macleans* 100:22-3 N 2 '87
Mother India intervenes [Air Force drops food to Tamils] R. Nordland. il *Newsweek* 109:38 Je 15 '87
A murderous backlash [assassination attempt on J. Jayawardene] K. Hall. *Macleans* 100:21 Ag 31 '87
Narrow escape [attempt to assassinate J. Jayewardene] *Time* 130:27 Ag 31 '87
An orgy of killing. K. Scanlon. il *Macleans* 100:34-5 O 19 '87
Paradise destroyed. J. Barber. il map *Macleans* 100:20-2 My 4 '87
Peace flexes its muscle [Tamil rebels surrender arms in Sri Lanka] H. G. Chua-Eoan. il *Time* 130:42 Ag 17 '87
Resolving the Sri Lankan conflict [statement, March 12, 1987] R. A. Peck. *Dep State Bull* 87:68-71 My '87
The roots of conflict in Sri Lanka. V. Rebeck. *Christ Century* 104:792-4 S 23 '87
Row over the airdrop [Indian airdrop of relief supplies to Tamils] A. Bilski. il *Macleans* 100:27 Je 15 '87
The siege of Jaffna. N. Cooper. il map *Newsweek* 110:67 N 2 '87
The siege of Jaffna. K. Scanlon. il map *Macleans* 100:33 O 26 '87
Sri Lanka: a nation disintegrates [cover story] S. R. Weisman. il map *N Y Times Mag* p34-8+ D 13 '87
Sri Lanka: a reluctant slaughter [Indian troops move against Tamils] *Newsweek* 110:49 O 26 '87
Sri Lanka: an Asian Lebanon? F. Willey. il map *Newsweek* 109:32 My 4 '87
Sri Lanka: no taming the 'Tigers'. W. A. Taylor. il map *U S News World Rep* 103:28-9 Jl 27 '87
Taming the Tigers [Tamils] M. Ispahani. *New Repub* 197:14+ Jl 27 '87
A troubled peace plan [India and Sri Lanka] K. Hall. il *Macleans* 100:20 Ag 10 '87
Wrong side, wrong war, for India [fighting between Indian troops and Tamil rebels] W. A. Taylor. il *U S News World Rep* 103:38 O 26 '87
Yes, politics makes strange bedfellows [India's help in subduing Tamil rebels] W. A. Taylor. il *U S News World Rep* 103:8 Ag 10 '87
Religious institutions and affairs
See also
Christians—Sri Lanka
Church and social problems—Sri Lanka

SSC *See* Superconducting Super Collider

SST (Supersonic transport) *See* Airplanes, Supersonic

St. Andrews (N.B.) *See* Saint Andrews (N.B.)

St. Antoine, Arthur
For your information. See issues of Car and Driver

St. Aubin, Helen
This mother could hit; ed. by Todd Gold. il pors *People Wkly* 28:77-8+ Ag 17 '87

St. Augustine (Fla.) *See* Saint Augustine (Fla.)

St. Augustine's College
Saint Augustine's College still 'gate of opportunity'. il *Jet* 72:18 Ap 27 '87

St. Barthélemy (Guadeloupe) *See* Saint Barthélemy (Guadeloupe)

St. Clair, Joy
Gold rings & orange blossoms [story] il *Teen* 31:42+ Jl '87

St. Elizabeths Hospital (Washington, D.C.) *See* Hospitals, Psychiatric—Washington (D.C.)

St. Elsewhere [television program] See Television program reviews—Single works

St. Eustatius (Netherlands Antilles) *See* Saint Eustatius (Netherlands Antilles)

St George-Hyslop, Peter H., and others
Absence of duplication of chromosome 21 genes in familial and sporadic Alzheimer's disease. bibl f il *Science* 238:664-6 O 30 '87
The genetic defect causing familial Alzheimer's disease maps on chromosome 21. bibl f il *Science* 235:885-90 F 20 '87

St. George's University School of Medicine
The outcasts from the Caribbean [offshore medical school graduates] J. Langone. il *Discover* 8:68-70+ Je '87

St. Helena (Calif.) *See* Saint Helena (Calif.)

St. James, Lyn
Car smarts. See occasional issues of Seventeen beginning February 1987
about
Introducing race-car champion Lyn St. James [interview] J. Pincus. por *Seventeen* 46:84 F '87

St. John, David, 1949-
The Kama Sutra according to Fiat [poem] *Harpers* 275:27 Ag '87

St. John, Walter D.
Help for principals in managing school crises. *Educ Dig* 52:36-9 Ap '87

St. Johns River City Band
Sundays in the park. K. Simmons. il *Horizon* 30:52 D '87

St. Laurent, Yves *See* Saint Laurent, Yves

St. Louis (Mo.) *See* Saint Louis (Mo.)

St. Louis County Heritage and Arts Center (Duluth, Minn.)
All aboard for arts. E. Beck. il *Horizon* 30:19-21 Ap '87

St. Luke in the Fields Church (New York, N.Y.)
Requiem and jubilate [restoration] D. Brenner. il *Archit Rec* 175:130-7 Je '87

St. Luke's-Roosevelt Hospital Center (New York, N.Y.)
Social security [Sibling-To-Be preparation class] M. Mintzer. il *Health* 19:22 O '87

St. Martin *See* Saint Martin

St. Paul Companies, Inc.
St. Paul may be doing too well [Alleghany's stake] M. J. Pitzer. il *Bus Week* p41-2 D 21 '87

St. Petersbourg (New York, N.Y.: Restaurant) *See* New York (N.Y.)—Restaurants, nightclubs, bars, etc.

St. Petersburg (Fla.) *See* Saint Petersburg (Fla.)

St. Pierre, Brian
Nature's mellow canvas. il map *50 Plus* 27:62-6+ O '87
Stop and smell the rosé [cover story] il map *50 Plus* 27:31-8 Je '87

St. Schell, Jozef
Transgenic plants as tools to study the molecular organization of plant genes. bibl f *Science* 237:1176-83 S 4 '87

St. Thomas (Virgin Islands of the U.S.) *See* Saint Thomas (Virgin Islands of the U.S.)

Staar, Richard Felix, 1923-
The U.S.S.R. in the 1990's [address, April 17, 1987] *Vital Speeches Day* 53:487-90 Je 1 '87
The Warsaw Treaty Organization. bibl f il *Curr Hist* 86:357-60+ N '87

Staatsoper (Austria) Ballet *See* Ballet—Austria
Staatsoper (Germany: West) *See* Opera—Germany (West)
Stabat mater [dance] *See* Dance reviews—Single works
Stability of ships *See* Ships—Stability and stabilizers
Stable, Marifeli Perez- *See* Perez-Stable, Marifeli
Stables *See* Barns and stables
Stables, Converted *See* Houses, Remodeled
Stacey Q *See* Q, Stacey

Stachel, John
Einstein and ether drift experiments. bibl f *Phys Today* 40:45-7 My '87

Stackhouse, Max L.
Tensions beset Church of South India. *Christ Century* 104:743-4 S 9-16 '87

Stacking [film] See Motion picture reviews—Single works

Stacy, Don
about
The $5-billion man [interview] J. O'Hara. il por *Macleans* 100:41 My 4 '87

Stacy, Roy A.
FY 1988 assistance requests for Sub-Saharan Africa [statement, March 12, 1987] *Dep State Bull* 87:11-16 My '87

Stade, George
The big chiller. *Nation* 244:258-62 F 28 '87

Stadiums
See also
Boston Garden (Mass.: Arena)
Fenway Park (Boston, Mass.)
Hubert H. Humphrey Metrodome (Minneapolis, Minn.)
Los Angeles Coliseum
Meadowlands Sports Complex
Polo Grounds (New York, N.Y.)
Rose Bowl (Pasadena, Calif.: Stadium)
Tiger Stadium (Detroit, Mich.)
Wrigley Field (Chicago, Ill.)
Build an arena now, get a team later—maybe. M. E. Recio. il *Bus Week* p90 Ap 20 '87
A bush-league Baedeker [ten great minor league ballparks] C. Warner. il *Sport Mag* 78:77+ Je '87
A new game plan for stadiums. il *Fortune* 116:9 Ag 31 '87
The next wave [projects on the drawing board] J. Rolfe. il map *Sport Mag* 78:76-7 Ag '87
Rx for cities: build a dome. P. Axthelm. il *Newsweek* 110:21 D 28 '87

Concessions (Food, etc.)
No bad hops with Wally [W. McNeil, top beer seller at Metrodome baseball games] F. Lidz. il pors *Sports Illus* 67:54+ Jl 6 '87

Employees
Photographs and photography
Before the roar [Tiger Stadium] D. Walberg. il *Sport Mag* 78:62-5+ O '87

Environmental aspects
Swamps, towns, and football downs [proposed St. Louis Cardinals stadium in the Missouri Bottoms] R. R. Pryor. il *Sierra* 72:136-7 Ja/F '87

Canada
Anecdotes, facetiae, satire, etc.
The heights of mediocrity. A. Fotheringham. il *Macleans* 100:56 My 25 '87

Japan
See also
Hiroshima Stadium (Japan)

Korea (South)
Cable domes [arenas for the 1988 Olympic Games in Seoul] J. Free. il *Pop Sci* 231:88-9 N '87

Staehle, Wolfgang
about
Wolfgang Staehle at Daniel Newburg. P. McGrath. il *Art Am* 75:125-6 Jl '87

Stafford, John Marshall
about
A CEO bake-off at Pillsbury. B. Dumaine. il pors *Fortune* 116:109+ N 23 '87

Stafford, Nancy
about
Playing by ear, Nancy Stafford finds the key to TV's Matlock. S. Adelson. il pors *People Wkly* 28:119-20+ N 16 '87

Stafford, Tim
Intimacy: our latest sexual fantasy. il *Christ Today* 31:21-7 Ja 16 '87

Stafford, William Edgar, 1914-
The writer's compass. *Writer* 100:5-6 S '87

Staffordshire pottery *See* Pottery, English
Stage *See* Theater
Stage costume *See* Costume, Theatrical
Stage designers *See* Set designers

Stage fright
And our next speaker is . . . drugged [using propranolol to treat stage fright] C. Schaeffer. il *Changing Times* 41:18 Ag '87

Stage lighting *See* Opera—Stage lighting; Rock concerts—Stage lighting; Theater—Stage lighting

Stage managers
Administration [work of the company manager and stage manager in touring theater] M. Loeffler. il *Theatre Crafts* 21:21+ Ag/S '87
The stage manager: Off-Broadway or on, the buck stops here [A. Hall, manager of Smile] R. Conniff. il pors *Smithsonian* 17:92-4+ F '87
Steven Zweigbaum minds Me and my girl. A. M. Hale. il por *Theatre Crafts* 21:88+ N '87

Stage scenery *See* Opera—Stage setting and scenery; Television broadcasting—Setting and scenery; Theater—Stage setting and scenery

Stager, Curt
Silent death from Cameroon's killer lake. il map *Natl Geogr* 172:404-20 S '87

StageWest
Innovative productions garner national attention for StageWest. M. Auerbach. il *Horizon* 30:41 N '87

Staggerlee [musical] *See* Musicals, revues, etc.—Reviews—Single works

Stahel, Thomas H.
"Tell us," they asked, "what is God like?" An appreciation of Tony de Mello, S.J. [cover story] *America* 157:446-50 D 12 '87

Stahl, Franklin William, 1929-
Genetic recombination. il *Sci Am* 256:90-101 F '87
Stain removal (Laundry) *See* Laundry
Stained glass *See* Glass painting and staining
Stainier, Bruno
(jt. auth) See Shoham, Jeremy, and Stainier, Bruno
Stains, Larry
Your money and your life. See issues of Prevention (Emmaus, Pa.) beginning February 1987
Stains, Laurence R. *See* Stains, Larry
Stains and staining
See also
Gilding
Graining
Coloring concrete. R. Day. il *Pop Sci* 231:108-9 N '87
Exterior paint and stain. K. Childers. il *Fam Handyman* 37:76-7 Mr '87
House paints & stains. il *Consum Rep* 52:365-74 Je '87
House paints and stains. il *Consum Rep* 52:207-20 D '87
Using oil stains. H. Wicks. il *Home Mech* 83:6+ D '87
Stains and staining (Microscopy)
See also
Fluorescent indicators in biological research
Stair machines *See* Exercising equipment
Staircases *See* Stairways
Stairways
See also
Garden steps
How to install a spiral staircase. M. Thompson. il *Fam Handyman* 37:40+ O '87
Materials are ordinary, the results are surprising. il *Sunset* 179:86 Jl '87
Quiet a squeaky step. M. Thompson. il *Fam Handyman* 37:41 Ap '87
Repair wood steps. G. Branson. il *Fam Handyman* 37:72-3 O '87
Stairwell gives them play area and storage. il *Sunset* 179:152-3 O '87
Staiti, Paul J., and Watson, Wendy M., 1948-
American art in the Mount Holyoke College Art Museum. il *Antiques* 132:1122-31 N '87
Stakeout [film] *See* Motion picture reviews—Single works
Staley, Delbert C.
about
How NYNEX' Bud Staley is dialing for dollars. J. J. Keller. il por *Bus Week* p84-6 Jl 6 '87
Staley Continental Inc.
Did Drexel bully takeover candidates? C. Welles. *Bus Week* p43-4 Mr 9 '87
Stalin, Joseph, 1879-1953
about
Beyond *glasnost.* W. Laqueur. *Commentary* 84:63-5 O '87
A compatriot's view from the homeland [interview with A. Rybakov] D. Stanglin. il por *U S News World Rep* 103:50 Ag 17 '87
The ghost of an old Bolshevik. N. Cooper. pors *Newsweek* 110:76 N 16 '87
The ghost of Stalin [cover story] K. M. Campbell. il *New Leader* 70:9-14 N 2 '87
A new revolution in consciousness. D. Murarka. il *Nation* 245:486-8+ O 31 '87
Recovering the buried Stalin years [cover story] D. Murarka. il *Nation* 245:433+ O 24 '87
Tales from a time of terror. J. O. Jackson. il pors *Time* 129:45-6 Ap 27 '87
Stalinism *See* Communism—Soviet Union
Staller, Eric
about
A vision in high visibility, Eric Staller believes in traveling lit. M. Small. il por *People Wkly* 28:137-9 O 19 '87
Stallone, Sylvester
about
Sly says bye, bye, Brigitte, and so a rocky marriage ends with a split decision. A. Richman. il pors *People Wkly* 28:38-9 Jl 27 '87
The Stallones: sex on the Sly? [cover story] J. Ash and others. pors *People Wkly* 28:48-9 Ag 10 '87
Stalls, Airplane *See* Airplanes, Jet—Stalling
Stambler, Lyndon
The shy guy tells all (finally!). il *Teen* 31:18+ N '87
Teens & AIDS: what you should know. *Teen* 31:92-3+ Je '87
Stamina *See* Endurance
Stamp collecting *See* Postage stamps—Collectors and collecting

Stamps, David
What was the Star of Bethlehem? il *Natl Wildl* 26:18-19 D '87/Ja '88
Stamps, Jeffrey
(jt. auth) See Lipnack, Jessica, and Stamps, Jeffrey
Stamps, Postage *See* Postage stamps
Stamps, Revenue *See* Revenue stamps
Stan Spiro and the Townsmen Orchestra
In Florida: from molars to Moonglow. G. Jaynes. il por *Time* 129:12-13 F 9 '87
Stancioff, Nadia
Gourmet holidays. il maps *Gourmet* 47:64-9+ My '87
Stand-alone (Term)
I'll stand alone. W. Safire. il *N Y Times Mag* p12+ O 25 '87
Standard Brands Paint Company
Painted into a corner. M. Beauchamp. il *Forbes* 139:72 Je 29 '87
Shareholders as losers. A. A. Lappen. il *Forbes* 140:8 D 14 '87
Standard of living *See* Cost and standard of living
Standard Oil Co. (Ohio)
See also
Standard Oil Company
Standard Oil Co. of California
See also
Chevron Corporation
Standard Oil Company
Why BP is going all out for all of Standard Oil. S. Miller. il *Bus Week* p50 Ap 13 '87
Standard Products Company (Ohio)
A hero in the Rust Belt [J. S. Reid] B. D. Fromson. il por *Fortune* 115:103 Ja 5 '87
Standard shift transmission *See* Automobiles—Transmission
Standardization
The importance and impact of standards [address, December 17, 1986] J. D. Michaels. *Vital Speeches Day* 53:441-4 My 1 '87
Standardized educational tests *See* Educational tests and measurements
Standards of measurement *See* Measurement
Standen, Nika *See* Hazelton, Nika
Standiford, Steven, 1953-
about
Christianity today talks to Steve Standiford. *Christ Today* 31:35 F 20 '87
Stands (Furniture)
See also
Book stands
Plant stands, flower stands, etc.
Stands (Machine) *See* Machinery—Stands, tables, etc.
Stands (Motorcycles) *See* Motorcycles—Equipment
Stands (Roadside) *See* Roadside marketing
Standup Shakespeare [musical] *See* Musicals, revues, etc.—Reviews—Single works
Stanek, Edward J.
about
Belter style. R. Christian. il pors *Americana* 15:46-50 S/O '87
Stanfill, Francesca
American heritage: Yankee art, western vistas. il pors *Vogue* 177:340-7+ Ap '87
Stanford, Dennis J.
The Ginsberg experiment. il *Nat Hist* 96:10+ S '87
Stanford, L. R.
Conduction velocity variations minimize conduction time differences among retinal ganglion cell axons. bibl f il *Science* 238:358-60 O 16 '87
Stanford, Leland, 1824-1893
about
Biggest of the four. R. F. Snow. il por *Am Herit* 38:90-1 D '87
Stanford (Ky.)
Historic houses, sites, etc.
Where Kentucky racing was born [William Whitley House State Historic Site] il *South Living* 22:20 Ag '87
Stanford Court (San Francisco, Calif.: Hotel) *See* San Francisco (Calif.)—Hotels, motels, etc.
Stanford University
B is for billion [fund raising drive] *Time* 129:61 F 16 '87
Band on the run [marching band] J. B. Meigs. il *Roll Stone* p86-9+ S 24 '87
Biggest of the four [founder L. Stanford] R. F. Snow. il por *Am Herit* 38:90-1 D '87
Computing gets an overhaul at Stanford University. J. N. Shurkin. il *Pers Comput* 11:179-81+ D '87
Distributed processing: the state of the art [Carnegie-Mellon's MACH and Stanford's V] W. A. Mason. il *Byte* 12:291-7 N '87

Stanford University—*cont.*
One loss for the Gipper [plans for Reagan library cancelled] *Time* 129:84 My 4 '87
Stanford psychiatrist resigns under a cloud [P. A. Berger] C. Holden. por *Science* 237:479-80 Jl 31 '87
Too close for comfort? [site for Reagan library] G. Hackett. il *Newsweek* 109:30 F 23 '87
Totem and taboo at Stanford. T. Bethell. *Natl Rev* 39:42+ O 9 '87
When historians judge their own [historian N. Davies sues Stanford University over denial of professorship because of his views on Jews] J. Wiener. il *Nation* 245:584-6+ N 21 '87

Stange, Eric
Millions of books are turning to dust—can they be saved? *N Y Times Book Rev* 92:3+ Mr 29 '87

Stange, Mary Zeiss
Little shop of horrors [cover story] il por *Commonweal* 114:412-17 Jl 17 '87
Little shop of horrors [discussion of July 17, 1987 article] *Commonweal* 114:546+ O 9 '87

Stanhope, Lawrence
about
Larry's magic garden. B. Dickey. *Space World* X-4-280:19 Ap '87

Stanislaus River (Calif.)
For the rivers, come hell or high water [work of M. Dubois] K. Crist. il pors *Sierra* 72:61-5 My/Je '87

Stanislaw, Richard J.
A trendy voice. il por *Christ Today* 31:72 S 4 '87

Stanislawski, Howard
Japan's Israel problem. *New Repub* 196:11-12 Mr 9 '87

Stankard, Paul J.
about
Natural wonders: the lampwork of Paul J. Stankard. P. Hollister. il *Am Craft* 47:36-43 F/Mr '87

Stanley, Bob
about
The mourning after. T. Balf. il pors *Sport Mag* 78:32-4 Mr '87

Stanley, George D., Jr.
Travels of an ancient reef. il maps *Nat Hist* 96:36-43 N '87

Stanley, John R.
about
Jack Stanley's 30-year oil feud is sizzling. J. R. Norman. il *Bus Week* p58-9 Ap 13 '87

Stanley, Julian C.
State residential high schools for mathematically talented youth. bibl f il *Phi Delta Kappan* 68:770-3 Je '87

Stanley, Sir William, 1548-1630
about
A patriot for whom? Stanley, York and Elizabeth's Catholics. S. Adams. bibl il *Hist Today* 37:46-50 Jl '87

Stanley Cup *See* Hockey, Professional
Stansberry, Kent
about
Star Wars: does it help or hurt arms-control efforts? [interview] J. Scarlott. il por *Sch Update* 120:20-1 N 20 '87

Stanton, Maura
At Hemingway's house [poem] *Am Sch* 56:502 Aut '87

Stanton, Sybil
Secrets every achiever knows [condensed from The 25-hour woman] il *Read Dig* 131:63-6 S '87

Stanton, Will
Chester's Christmas surprise [story] il *McCalls* 115:154+ D '87

Stanton C. Selbst Inc.
Stanton Selbst: success with a school for stockbrokers. M. Frons. por *Bus Week* p103 Ja 26 '87

Stanway, Alfred
about
What would ALF say? J. W. Yates, II. por *Christ Today* 31:33 S 4 '87

Stanwood, Les
Headaches [cover story] il *Curr Health 2* 13:3-9 My '87

Stap, Don
From a photograph [poem] *Am Sch* 56:406 Summ '87

Stapen, Candyce H.
Marriage & loneliness. il *Parents* 62:87-91 Ag '87

Stapen, Nancy
Art in Boston: an overview. il *Art News* 86:75+ Summ '87

Staphylococcal diseases
See also
Toxic shock syndrome

Staphylococci
Loosening bacteria's hold on implants [preventing staphylococci from adhering to polymers; research by Bernd Jansen] S. Weisburd. *Sci News* 132:190 S 19 '87

Staple guns *See* Staples and stapling machines
Staples, Brent
August Wilson. por *Essence* 18:50-1+ Ag '87
A commercial overture. il *N Y Times Mag* p106 S 20 '87
Paint it black. il *N Y Times Mag* p22 N 15 '87
Raw meat for the accountant. il *N Y Times Mag* p38-9 Mr 15 '87
Where are the black fans? il *N Y Times Mag* p26-32+ My 17 '87

Staples, Oceola, d. 1987
about
Obituary
Jet il por 73:25 O 26 '87

Staples, Robert
The sexual revolution and the black middle class. il *Ebony* 42:56-8 Ag '87

Staples, Inc.
Ballpoint pens "R" Us. B. Leonard. il por *Forbes* 139:172 Ap 6 '87

Staples and stapling machines
Now, a stapler can become a riveting tool [Xpando T-50XP] il *Consum Rep* 52:73 F '87
Pop goes the stapler [Pop 2000 staple gun] R. Capotosto. il *Pop Mech* 164:19 Ag '87

Staples Area Vocational Technical Institute
Staples Institute: a launching pad for photo lab technicians. G. Schaub. il *Pop Photogr* 94:46 N '87

Stapleton International Airport *See* Denver (Colo.)—Airports

Star (Johannesburg, South Africa: Newspaper)
Getting the story (I) [J. Qwelane, black reporter] W. Finnegan. *New Yorker* 63:31-4+ Jl 13 '87
Getting the story (II) [J. Qwelane, black reporter] W. Finnegan. *New Yorker* 63:40-2+ Jl 20 '87

Star (London, England: Newspaper)
New standards of vulgarity. R. Laver. il *Macleans* 100:39 O 19 '87

Star charts *See* Astronomy—Charts, diagrams, etc.
Star clusters *See* Stars—Clusters
Star date [radio program] *See* Radio program reviews—Single works
Star-Kist Foods, Inc.
Star-Kist's revival [reopening of St. Andrews, N.B. plant] T. Fennell. il *Macleans* 100:34 S 28 '87

Star maps *See* Astronomy—Charts, diagrams, etc.
Star of Bethlehem
Mars and Jupiter pair together. il *Sky Telesc* 73:455 Ap '87
What was the Star of Bethlehem? D. Stamps. il *Natl Wildl* 26:18-19 D '87/Ja '88

Star search [television program] *See* Television program reviews—Single works
Star spangled banner (Song)
The banner yet waves [condensed from Star of wonder] D. M. Epstein. il *Read Dig* 131:114-16 Jl '87

Star trek
Gene Roddenberry and Majel Barrett's most successful Enterprise isn't a starship; it's their 17-year marriage. N. Geeslin. il pors *People Wkly* 27:111-12+ Mr 16 '87
Simon & Schuster Audio launches Star trek series. il *Publ Wkly* 231:44-5 My 8 '87

Star trek: the next generation [television program] *See* Television program reviews—Single works
Star Wars defense program *See* Strategic Defense Initiative
Star wars motion picture series *See* Motion pictures—Science fiction films

Starch
See also
Amyloses

Starck, Philippe, 1950?-
about
Designing for people. M.-F. Leclère. il *World Press Rev* 34:60 N '87
The hot seat in France belongs to brash designer Philippe Starck. N. Geeslin. il por *People Wkly* 27:95-6 Ja 26 '87
The world according to Starck [interview] K. D. Stein. il por *Archit Rec* 175:102-7 mid-S '87

Stardust [musical] *See* Musicals, revues, etc.—Reviews—Single works

Starfind (Firm)
Inventor proposes locator system using one geosynchronous satellite. il *Aviat Week Space Technol* 126:89+ Je 22 '87
Starfish
Stars with thousands of feet [cover story] R. C. Anderson and J. E. Vanderwerff. bibl il *Sea Front* 33:422-6 N/D '87
Thyca: underarm and underfoot [starfish parasite] T. Bratcher. il *Sea Front* 33:286-7 Jl/Ag '87
Stark, Arlynne
Health: American Dance Therapy Association, a kinesthetic approach. il *Dance Mag* 61:56-7 N '87
Stark, Craig
(jt. auth) See Hirsch, Julian D., and Stark, Craig
about
Faces of middle class America: architect Craig Stark puts his hope in the future of Miami. il pors *Ebony* 42:144-5 Ag '87
Stark, Elizabeth
Forgotten victims: children of alcoholics. bibl (p63) il *Psychol Today* 21:58-62 Ja '87
The making of a manager. il *Psychol Today* 21:28-32 Ag '87
(jt. auth) See Rosenfeld, Anne H., and Stark, Elizabeth
Stark, Peter
A weather eye. il *Read Dig* 130:118-20 Mr '87
Stark, Peter
The yearlong search for a perfect sled to ride down Jumbo. il por *Smithsonian* 18:138-42+ D '87
Stark (Warship)
Upgrading Stark: will it prevent a tragedy? il *Pop Mech* 164:115 O '87
Iraqi missile attack, 1987
Antiquated rules of engagement. R. R. Ropelewski. *Aviat Week Space Technol* 126:11 Je 1 '87
Blacks among 37 sailors killed in attack on Stark. il *Jet* 72:14 Je 8 '87
Credibility Gulf. L. Ackland. *Bull At Sci* 43:2 Jl/Ag '87
The deadly mistake. W. Lowther. il *Macleans* 100:18-19 Je 1 '87
Engulfed. *Nation* 244:749-50 Je 6 '87
House Committee faults tactics instead of equipment in Stark attack. M. Mecham. *Aviat Week Space Technol* 126:32-3 Je 22 '87
Missile attack, Kuwaiti pact could draw U.S. into Gulf war. J. D. Morrocco. il map *Aviat Week Space Technol* 126:23-5 My 25 '87
On the Stark front. W. F. Buckley. *Natl Rev* 39:58-9 Jl 3 '87
Persian Gulf shooting gallery. D. E. Fink. *Aviat Week Space Technol* 126:11 My 25 '87
Policy at sea. *Time* 129:25 Je 15 '87
Stark choices. *New Repub* 196:11 Je 8 '87
Stark military doubts. *Natl Rev* 39:15-16 Je 19 '87
A tragedy in the Gulf [cover story; special section] il map *Newsweek* 109:16-26 Je 1 '87
The tragic cost of commitment. P. R. Range. il map *U S News World Rep* 102:16-18 Je 1 '87
The U.S. in the Gulf: a bigger role—and bigger risks. S. J. Dryden and others. il *Bus Week* p63 Je 1 '87
U.S.S. Stark hit by Iraqi missiles. il *Dep State Bull* 87:58-63 Jl '87
What happened on the Stark? T. Morganthau. il *Newsweek* 109:24-5 Je 29 '87
"Why did this happen?" [cover story; special section] il maps *Time* 129:16-22 Je 1 '87
Reporters and reporting
The Gulf. il *World Press Rev* 34:8 Jl '87
Starker, Joan
(jt. auth) See Abbott, Carl, and Starker, Joan
Starkey, David
Privy secrets: Henry VIII and the Lords of the Council [cover story] bibl il pors *Hist Today* 37:23-31 Ag '87
Starkman, Monica
Repeat after me: some hard facts about hypnosis. il *Vogue* 177:112+ S '87
Starkweather, Kendall N.
Technology education: its status and opportunities. *Educ Dig* 52:36-9 Mr '87
Starlab missions *See* Space stations—Starlab missions
Starlight Express [musical] *See* Musicals, revues, etc.—Reviews—Single works
Starling, Marlon
about
Breland knocked out of boxing unbeaten ranks. il pors *Jet* 72:52 S 14 '87
Off the mark. il por *Sports Illus* 67:13 Ag 31 '87

Starling, Roy
What one teacher learned becoming an undergraduate. *Educ Dig* 53:30-3 S '87
Starman [television program] See Television program reviews—Single works
Starn Twins
about
The art of double exposure. K. Ames. il *Newsweek* 109:68 Je 29 '87
The Starn Twins: "Making art flows through both of us. It's like a conversation". K. Larson. il *Vogue* 177:458+ S '87
Starr, Douglas
Paying the devil. il *N Y Times Mag* p6+ Mr 22 '87
Starr, Douglas
The calorie room. il *Health* 19:8 Ap '87
Heat wave. il *Natl Wildl* 25:22-4 Ag/S '87
How to protect the ozone layer. il *Natl Wildl* 26:26-8 D '87/Ja '88
Starr, Roger
The best woman in the hall. il por *N Y Times Mag* p30+ O 18 '87
The fat man's garden and other landmarks. il *N Y Times Book Rev* 92:34+ N 22 '87
Starrett, Cam
about
Cam Starrett. S. McHenry. *Ms* 16:52 N '87
Stars
See also
Astrology
Astronomy
Black holes (Astronomy)
Constellations
Galaxies
Herbig-Haro objects
Magellanic clouds
Neutron stars
Occultations
Stellar winds
Strange stars
Sun
Bloated stars in quasars? [research by Richard C. Puetter] *Sky Telesc* 74:457-8 N '87
Deep-sky wonders. W. S. Houston. See issues of Sky and Telescope
Looking for a few good stars [cover story] K. Croswell. il *Space World* X-7-283:12-15 Jl '87
Stars and spikes [finding stellar diffraction patterns for different telescope types; computer program] R. W. Sinnott. il *Sky Telesc* 74:294-6 S '87
Age
The oldest pulsars in the universe. J. Shaham. bibl (p140) il *Sci Am* 256:50-6 F '87
Stellar old-timers [search for Population III stars] S. P. Maran. *Nat Hist* 96:80+ F '87
White dwarfs and the age of the universe [research by Donald E. Winget and others] il *Sky Telesc* 74:347-8 O '87
Atlases
Big eye on the sky [Palomar Sky Survey] T. Dickinson. il *Pop Mech* 164:60-3+ S '87
The making of Uranometria 2000.0. K. R. Majdacic. il *Astronomy* 15:24+ Jl '87
New charts for the deep sky [Uranometria 2000.0 star atlas] G. Lovi. il *Sky Telesc* 73:611-13 Je '87
North view [pictorial star atlas by A. Jamieson] G. Lovi. il *Sky Telesc* 73:175-6 F '87
Norton's star atlas. R. Burnham. *Astronomy* 15:37-8 Je '87
Surveying the northern sky [new Palomar Sky Survey] J. Schombert. il *Sky Telesc* 74:128-31 Ag '87
Which star atlas is best for you? il *Astronomy* 15:66-7 Mr '87
Brightness
See Stars—Magnitudes
Charts, diagrams, etc.
See Astronomy—Charts, diagrams, etc.
Clusters
See also
Pleiades
A binocular Hyades variable [HU Tauri] il *Sky Telesc* 74:512 N '87
Clusters' first stand. T. D. Nicholson. il *Nat Hist* 96:72+ Ap '87
Curious cluster. il *Sky Telesc* 74:345-6 O '87
Globular clusters in the Coma cluster of galaxies [CCD observations by William E. Harris] il *Sky Telesc* 74:346-7 O '87
Lithium casts doubt on galactic history [Hyades cluster] il *Sky Telesc* 73:28 Ja '87

Stars—Clusters—*cont.*

New distance to the Hyades [work of Deane M. Peterson and Richard Solensky] *Sky Telesc* 73:28-9 Ja '87

Simulating clusters on your computer. T. B. Woods. il *Astronomy* 15:63-7 S '87

Photographs and photography

Tips for shooting clusters and nebulae. M. F. Willson. il *Astronomy* 15:56-9 Ag '87

Distances

New distance to the Hyades [work of Deane M. Peterson and Richard Solensky] *Sky Telesc* 73:28-9 Ja '87

Visit the nearest stars. K. Croswell. il *Astronomy* 15:16-22 Ja '87

Evolution

See also

Pulsars

The bare facts of stellar evolution. il *Sky Telesc* 74:356 O '87

The birth of neutron stars and black holes [cover story] A. Burrows. bibl f il *Phys Today* 40:28-37 S '87

Bubbles from a dying star [OH 231.8+4.2; work by Bo Reipurth] il *Astronomy* 15:77 Je '87

Deuterium, dust, and infant stars [study of Kleinmann-Low nebula; work of Malcolm Walmsley and others] *Sky Telesc* 74:236 S '87

Fossil stellar shell stumps astronomers [R Coronae Borealis] il *Astronomy* 15:76-7 Mr '87

Not with a bang . . . [evolution through mass loss] *Sci Am* 256:24-5 Je '87

R Cor Bor's cold nebula. il *Sky Telesc* 73:369-70 Ap '87

Star formation and IRAS galaxies. D. A. Allen. il *Sky Telesc* 73:372-4 Ap '87

Star formation in W49A: gravitational collapse of the molecular cloud core toward a ring of massive stars. W. J. Welch and others. bibl f il *Science* 238:1550-5 D 11 '87

Star-forming globule [Bok globule; research by D. J. King] il *Sky Telesc* 74:461-2 N '87

Stellar mass-loss theory spells trouble [work of Lee Anne Willson and others] *Sky Telesc* 73:154-5 F '87

Touring the stellar cycle. E. Fortier. il *Astronomy* 15:49-53 Mr '87

Granulation

Stellar granulation. R. A. Schorn. il *Sky Telesc* 74:247 S '87

Magnitudes

White Sirian stars: class A. J. B. Kaler. il *Sky Telesc* 73:491-4 My '87

Mass

Bubbles from a dying star [OH 231.8+4.2; work by Bo Reipurth] il *Astronomy* 15:77 Je '87

Finding Beta Lyrae's mass. il *Sky Telesc* 74:355 O '87

Not with a bang . . . [evolution through mass loss] *Sci Am* 256:24-5 Je '87

Stellar mass-loss theory spells trouble [work of Lee Anne Willson and others] *Sky Telesc* 73:154-5 F '87

Motion

Lambda Orionis' molecular ring [work of Ronald J. Maddalena and Mark Morris] il *Sky Telesc* 74:455 N '87

Star motions may alter view of galaxy [Lick Northern Proper Motion program] D. E. Thomsen. *Sci News* 132:69 Ag 1 '87

Orbits

The orbit of a binary star [computer program] M. P. Greaney. il *Sky Telesc* 74:71-2 Jl '87

Signs of Nemesis: meteors, magnetism. D. E. Thomsen. *Sci News* 131:100 F 14 '87

Oscillations

The birth of stellar seismology. D. H. Smith. *Sky Telesc* 74:475 N '87

Parallax

See Parallax

Radiation

Keeping up with Cygnus X-3. il *Sky Telesc* 73:272 Mr '87

Ugly ducklings redux [cygnets from Cygnus X-3] D. E. Thomsen. *Sci News* 131:8 Ja 3 '87

Why do stars emit X rays? E. N. Parker. bibl f il *Phys Today* 40:36-42 Jl '87

Spectra and spectroscopy

See also

A stars

B stars

F stars

O stars

Lithium casts doubt on galactic history [Hyades cluster] il *Sky Telesc* 73:28 Ja '87

The solar-stellar connection. M. S. Giampapa. il *Sky Telesc* 74:142-6 Ag '87

Temperature

A simple model for neutrino cooling of the Large Magellanic Cloud supernova. D. N. Spergel and others. bibl f il *Science* 237:1471-3 S 18 '87

Stars, Double

See also

Stars, Eclipsing binary

An 11-minute binary? [4U1820-30] *Astronomy* 15:85-6 Ja '87

Deep-sky wonders. W. S. Houston. *Sky Telesc* 73:683-5 Je '87

How many stars are binary? [work of Harold A. McAlister and others] *Sky Telesc* 74:8-9 Jl '87

Interferometer measures angular diameter of Sirius [amplitude technique used by John Davis and William J. Tango] *Astronomy* 15:78-9 F '87

Keeping up with Cygnus X-3. il *Sky Telesc* 73:272 Mr '87

The orbit of a binary star [computer program] M. P. Greaney. il *Sky Telesc* 74:71-2 Jl '87

The true nature of stormy XY Leonis [observations by Samuel Barden] il *Sky Telesc* 73:600-1 Je '87

Ugly ducklings redux [cygnets from Cygnus X-3] D. E. Thomsen. *Sci News* 131:8 Ja 3 '87

Ultrafast binary star [4U 1820-30] *Sky Telesc* 73:154 F '87

Very high energy gamma-ray binary stars. R. C. Lamb and T. C. Weekes. bibl f il *Science* 238:1528-34 D 11 '87

Stars, Dwarf

A 'brown dwarf' in the heavens [discovery by Benjamin Zuckerman and Eric Becklin] il *U S News World Rep* 103:15 N 23 '87

Extrasolar planets, maybe—but brown dwarfs, no. M. M. Waldrop. il *Science* 236:1623-4 Je 26 '87

Faint stars and brown dwarfs [research by Neil Reid] *Sky Telesc* 74:461 N '87

Signs of a 'something' circling a star [possible brown dwarf circling white dwarf Giclas 29-38; work of Benjamin Zuckerman and Eric E. Becklin] J. Eberhart. *Sci News* 132:327 N 21 '87

The strange case of the disappearing star—or was that a planet? [VB 8B] il *Discover* 8:9-10 Ja '87

VB 8B or not VB 8B? [brown dwarfs] M. Murray. il *Space World* X-3-279:27-9 Mr '87

VB 8B's vanishing act [brown dwarf] R. A. Schorn. il *Sky Telesc* 74:139 Ag '87

White dwarfs and the age of the universe [research by Donald E. Winget and others] il *Sky Telesc* 74:347-8 O '87

White dwarfs: fossil stars. S. D. Kawaler and D. E. Winget. il *Sky Telesc* 74:132-5 Ag '87

Stars, Eclipsing binary

A binocular Hyades variable [HU Tauri] il *Sky Telesc* 74:512 N '87

The strange case of Beta Lyrae. J. Tomkin and D. L. Lambert. il *Sky Telesc* 74:354-7 O '87

Stars, Giant

Betelgeuse. D. H. Levy and P. Jedicke. il *Astronomy* 15:6-13 Ap '87

Families of giant stars [use of speckle interferometry] *Sky Telesc* 73:25-6 Ja '87

White Sirian stars: class A. J. B. Kaler. il *Sky Telesc* 73:491-4 My '87

Stars, New

Nova Andromedae 1986. il *Sky Telesc* 73:181 F '87

T Pyxidis outburst due. il *Sky Telesc* 73:180 F '87

Stars, Variable

See also

Supernovas

Finding variable stars by fishhooks, lampshades, and candlesticks. G. Dyck. il *Sky Telesc* 73:658-9 Je '87

Fossil stellar shell stumps astronomers [R Coronae Borealis] il *Astronomy* 15:76-7 Mr '87

FU Orionis and its ilk [work of Lee W. Hartmann and Scott J. Kenyon] il *Sky Telesc* 73:272-3 Mr '87

Mira nears maximum [Omicron Ceti] il *Sky Telesc* 73:72 Ja '87

R Cor Bor's cold nebula. il *Sky Telesc* 73:369-70 Ap '87

The splendor of Eta Carinae. D. Malin. il *Sky Telesc* 73:14-18 Ja '87

The temperate F stars [Cepheids] J. B. Kaler. il *Sky Telesc* 73:131-4 F '87

The true nature of stormy XY Leonis [observations by Samuel Barden] il *Sky Telesc* 73:600-1 Je '87

Two short-period variables [CX and CY Aquarii] A. MacRobert. il *Sky Telesc* 74:398-9 O '87

Variable star day at Leiden. J. A. Mattei. il *Sky Telesc* 74:535-6 N '87

Stars in religion, folklore, etc.
See also
Star of Bethlehem
Starship (Musical group)
Rockers: then & now. il pors *Teen* 31:62-3 O '87
Starship: it's not over yet. S. Pond. il *Roll Stone* p28 S 24 '87
Starship airplanes *See* Airplanes, Business
START talks *See* Strategic Arms Reduction Talks
Starting, Automobile *See* Automobiles—Starting
Starvation
See also
Anorexia nervosa
Famines
Fasting
Malnutrition
Starzyk, Ruth M., and others
Evidence for dispensable sequences inserted into a nucleotide fold. bibl f il *Science* 237:1614-18 S 25 '87
Stasio, Marilyn
Crime in every hamlet. il *N Y Times Book Rev* 92:1+ Ag 2 '87
Stassinopoulos, Arianna
about
Mr. Peepers's nights: Mrs. Huffington entertains. il *N Y* 20:37-8 Ap 27 '87
State (Political science)
State-loving in the G.O.P. W. F. Buckley. *Natl Rev* 39:62 D 18 '87
State advertising
The taxman tries a little hype [states use ads to aid in tax collection] A. Miller. il *Newsweek* 109:55-6 F 23 '87
State aid to education *See* Education—State aid
State and art *See* Art and state
State and church *See* Church and state
State and dance *See* Dance and state
State and education *See* College education and state; Education and state
State and environment *See* Environmental policy
State and federal relations *See* Federal and state relations
State and industry *See* Industry and state
State and literature *See* Literature and state
State and medicine *See* Medical policy
State and music *See* Music and state
State and science *See* Science and state
State and technology *See* Technology and state
State and the arts *See* Arts and state
State Ballet of Missouri
Reviews:
Performances at Brooklyn College. L. Garafola. *Dance Mag* 61:94-5 O '87
State Bar of Michigan
Detroit man first black to chair Bar division [G. Reed] por *Jet* 72:22 My 11 '87
State Botanical Garden of Georgia *See* Botanical gardens—Georgia
State colleges and universities *See* Colleges and universities
State Dept. (U.S.) *See* United States. Dept. of State
State Dept. Building (Washington, D.C.)
[Special issue on State Dept. Building] *Antiques* 132:118-87 Jl '87
State employees
See also
Tennessee—Employees
Salaries, allowances, etc.
State and local government pay increases outpace five-year rise in private industry. R. Schumann. il *Mon Labor Rev* 110:18-20 F '87
State-federal tax relations *See* Intergovernmental tax relations
State finance
See also
Finance—California
Finance—Texas
Finance—West Virginia
Taxation, State
E pluribus . . . ulcers. H. Banks. il *Forbes* 139:35 My 18 '87
States and cities won't be building up the economy. G. Koretz. il *Bus Week* p24 Ag 17 '87
State fossils
Alabama and Colorado choose an ancient whale and a 150-million-year-old dinosaur as state fossils [letters] il *Earth Sci* 40:4 Spr '87
State governments
See also
Governors
National Forum of State Leaders

Beware of state takeover laws. J. W. Bartlett. il *Fortune* 116:179+ N 9 '87
States vs. raiders: will Washington step in? V. Cahan. il *Bus Week* p56-7 Ag 31 '87
Why states can do what Uncle can't. J. P. Shapiro. il *U S News World Rep* 103:35+ D 28 '87-Ja 4 '88
State historical societies *See* Historical societies
State legislators, Women *See* Women legislators
State legislatures
See also
California—Legislature
Georgia—Legislature
Michigan—Legislature
National Black Caucus of State Legislators
National Conference of State Legislatures
Ohio—Legislature
South Carolina—Legislature
Texas—Legislature
State lotteries *See* Lotteries
State officers
See also
Black state officers
State ownership *See* Government ownership
State police *See* Police
State rights *See* Federal and state relations
State sales tax *See* Sales tax
State songs
Blacks want new lyrics for 'racist' Va. state song [Carry me back to old Virginia] *Jet* 73:7 N 30 '87
State taxation *See* Taxation, State
State troopers *See* Police
Staten Island (New York, N.Y.)
Architecture
The Wright people [house designed by F. L. Wright] S. Staggs. il *Art News* 86:9-10 Ja '87
Arts
See also
Snug Harbor Cultural Center
Historic houses, sites, etc.
The high summer of Alice Austen. O. Jensen. il pors *House Gard* 159:94-9+ Ag '87
States, Ideal *See* Utopias
States (U.S.)
See also
State governments
U.S. in focus. il *Sch Update* 119:13-17 Ja 26 '87
Statesmen
See also
Heads of state
Requiem for the "establishment" [The wise men] H. J. Kaplan. *Commentary* 83:37-48 Ap '87
"The wise men" [discussion of April 1987 article, Requiem for the establishment] H. J. Kaplan. *Commentary* 84:10-12 Jl '87
Correspondence
History without letters [trend towards electronic communication reduces sources for historians] W. Isaacson. il *Time* 130:65-6 Ag 31 '87
Stathoplos, Demmie
But Jate, why so late? il *Sports Illus* 67:69-70 Jl 27 '87
Getting her point across. il pors *Sports Illus* 66:54-6 Mr 9 '87
Good to the last drop. il *Sports Illus* 67:56-7 S 28 '87
Gulch's Wood, but the Demon could. il *Sports Illus* 66:36-7 Ap 27 '87
Make way for superbug. il por *Sports Illus* 67:91 Jl 13 '87
Our women in Havana. il *Sports Illus* 66:46-7 Je 29 '87
A stake in the future. il *Sports Illus* 66:70-1 Mr 9 '87
This is no joyride. il map *Sports Illus* 67:50-3 S 14 '87
Three to get ready and . . . il *Sports Illus* 66:26-8+ Ap 13 '87
Station wagons
Four wheel drive
See also
Station wagons, Foreign—Four wheel drive
Family cars that go in snow, mud and rain. D. Chaikin. il *Home Mech* 83:44-6+ My '87
Testing
Ford Taurus LX Wagon. P. Bedard. il *Car Driv* 33:101+ Ag '87
Mid-size wagons. E. Henry. il *Changing Times* 41:58-62 Je '87

Station wagons, Foreign
Four wheel drive
Subaru's 4WD Turbo Wagon. B. Kilpatrick. il *Field Stream* 91:93-4 F '87
Testing
Mercedes-Benz 300TD. il *Road Track* 38:56-8 Ja '87
Mid-size wagons. E. Henry. il *Changing Times* 41:58-62 Je '87
Peugeot 505 Turbo Wagon [long term test] R. Titus. il *Mot Trend* 39:124+ My '87
Toyota Camry: making a good car better. D. Chaikin. il *Home Mech* 83:64-5 Ag '87
Station wagons, Remodeled *See* Automobiles, Remodeled
Stationery
See also
Booksellers and bookselling—Stationery
Stations, Railroad *See* Railroads—Stations
Stations of the Cross in art
Exhibitions
Symbols of the sacred [Montreal exhibition of contemporary art entitled Stations] G. James. il *Macleans* 100:49 Ag 31 '87
Statistical Commission (United Nations) *See* United Nations. Statistical Commission
Statistical mechanics
Small systems: when does thermodynamics apply? H. Feshbach. il *Phys Today* 40:9+ N '87
Statistical methods
See also
Graphic methods
Sampling (Statistics)
Stochastic processes
How to ask about sex and get honest answers [randomized response method] G. Kolata. il *Science* 236:382 Ap 24 '87
Statistical short-term earthquake prediction. Y. Y. Kagan and L. Knopoff. bibl f il *Science* 236:1563-7 Je 19 '87
Statistics
See also
Computers—Statistical use
Economic statistics
See also subhead Statistics under various subjects
Harper's index. See issues of Harper's
Vital statistics. See issues of U.S. News & World Report beginning August 3, 1987
Statue of Liberty (New York, N.Y.)
A colossus remodeled [visitor facilities] G. Anderson. il *Archit Rec* 175:98-103 Ap '87
The Statue of Liberty project: lessons learned from a Lady. I. Peterson. *Current* 292:4-8 My '87
Centennial celebration, 1986
Lady's day. il *Life* 10:47-8+ Ja '87
Fees
Setting Liberty free. S. Shane. *Travel Holiday* 168:4 Jl '87
Statues
See also
Bemidji (Minn.)—Monuments, statues, etc.
Kao-hsiung (Taiwan)—Monuments, statues, etc.
King, Martin Luther, 1929-1968—Statues, portraits, etc.
Philadelphia (Pa.)—Monuments, statues, etc.
Plaster casts (Sculpture)
Statuettes *See* Figurines
Stature
Dear Betty Harragan [short woman having problems supervising fellow chemists] B. L. Harragan. il *Work Woman* 12:46+ N '87
Do short men make better lovers? J. V. Iovine. il *Mademoiselle* 93:92 N '87
Help for slow-growing children [synthetic growth hormone] M. Vogel. il *FDA Consum* 21:14-17 Mr '87
The prejudice of height [link between intelligence and height in children; research by Darrell Wilson] S. Vandershaf. *Psychol Today* 21:14 Mr '87
A short (guy) love story. H. Dlugozima. il *Seventeen* 46:134 My '87
Short power [women executives] P. R. Satran. il *Work Woman* 12:98-100 Je '87
Sizes [a tall and a short reporter visit the van Gogh exhibit at the Metropolitan Museum of Art] *New Yorker* 63:28-30 Ap 27 '87
The surprising truth about children's height. D. Edmondson. il *Parents* 62:133-6+ S '87
Tall [women] M. B. Nelson. il *Ms* 15:60+ Ap '87
Statz, Kenneth
about
The renewed appeal of REITs [interview] M. McFadden. por *Fortune* 115:132 Ja 19 '87

Staub, August W.
Higher education as a fine irritant. *Des Arts Educ* 88:12-14 Ja/F '87
Staubs, Rose Marie
Andrews's sisters. il por *Omni* 10:28 O '87
Stautberg, Susan Schiffer
Choosing your child's pediatrician. *Work Woman* 12:94+ Jl '87
Hard choices: the tough decisions women must make today. il *Ladies Home J* 104:96-7+ Ja '87
Kids and drugs. il *Ladies Home J* 104:74+ My '87
Stave, Bruce M.
Prepare an oral history. il *Americana* 15:14+ N/D '87
Stavis, Benedict
China. *Nation* 244:466-8 Ap 11 '87
Stayton, Richard
Hopper's return from the edge. por *Harpers Bazaar* 120:381+ S '87
Steadfastness *See* Perseverance
Steak cooking *See* Cooking—Meat
Steak houses *See* Restaurants
Stealing
See also
Art thefts
Automobiles—Theft
Boats and boating—Theft
Burglary and burglars
Cactus—Theft
Credit card crimes
Embezzlement
Employee theft
Jewelry—Theft
Manuscripts, American—Theft
Milk crates—Theft
Photographs—Theft
Poaching
Robberies and assaults
Sheep—Theft
Shoplifting
Violin—Theft
Wallets—Theft
Fighting the school for scoundrels [New York City Transit Police Pickpocket Squad] T. Cochran. il *N Y* 20:25 My 25 '87
Guilty of theft, Bethea awaits sentencing in Va. [L. Bethea] *Jet* 71:49 Ja 19 '87
Stealth airplanes *See* Airplanes, Military
Steam baths
See also
Sauna
Home steam baths: turn a tub into a spa. il *Better Homes Gard* 65:46 O '87
Steam irons *See* Irons
Steam railroads *See* Railroads
Steam ships *See* Steamships and steamboats
Steamboat Springs (Colo.)
Steamboat. N. Howe. il *Skiing* 40:144-8+ D '87
Steamboats *See* Steamships and steamboats
Steamers (Ships) *See* Steamships and steamboats
Steaming (Cooking)
See also
Wok cooking
Steamship lines
See also
Alexander & Baldwin, Inc.
Carnival Cruise Lines Inc.
United States Lines, Inc.
Cruising '88. K. Showker. il *Travel Holiday* 168:65-6+ O '87
Floating resorts. R. Behar. il *Forbes* 139:62-3 Ja 26 '87
Steamships and steamboats
See also
Belle of Louisville (Steamboat)
Birchglen (Steamship)
Central America (Steamship)
Mississippi Queen (Steamboat)
Ocean liners
Yellow Stone (Steamboat)
The side-wheel carriers [steamers converted to aircraft carriers Wolverine and Sable for World War II service] G. C. Long. il *Am Herit* 38:104-7 F/Mr '87
Photographs and photography
Steamboats on the Mississippi [late 19th century photographer H. C. Norman] J. W. Gandy and T. H. Gandy. il *Am Hist Illus* 22:36-49 Mr '87
Steardo, Luca, and Nathanson, J. A. (James A.), 1947-
Brain barrier tissues: end organs for atriopeptins. bibl f il *Science* 235:470-3 Ja 23 '87

Stearman, David W.
Looking for trouble in medical devices. il *FDA Consum* 21:18-23 S '87
Stearns, Bob
Boating. See alternate issues of Field & Stream
Saltwater fishing. See occasional issues of Field & Stream
Stearns, Laurie
The importance of copy editing. il *Publ Wkly* 232:48 Jl 10 '87
Stechert, Kathryn
Are you an optimist or a pessimist? il *Glamour* 85:148+ S '87
How to survive the stress points in your marriage. il *Better Homes Gard* 65:87+ N '87
Strategic budgeting in good times and bad. il *Work Woman* 12:88-90+ Je '87
What's new for American families in '87. il *Better Homes Gard* 65:15+ Ja '87
Steck, Brian
about
Who is watching the traders? P. C. Newman. il por *Macleans* 100:42 O 26 '87
Stedman, Lawrence C.
It's time we changed the effective schools formula [with reply by W. B. Brookover] bibl f il *Phi Delta Kappan* 69:215-27 N '87
Stedman, Nancy
How to exercise without really exercising (almost). il *Redbook* 168:70-3 Ja '87
Steel, Danielle
Fine things [fiction] il por *Good Housekeep* 204:181-4+ F '87
about
Danielle Steel: her toughest challenge. E. Sherman. por *Ladies Home J* 104:84 Je '87
Steel, David, 1938-
about
Two Davids and Goliath. R. Watson. il pors *Newsweek* 109:26-7 My 25 '87
Steel, Dawn
about
Dawn Steel: the most powerful woman in Hollywood [interview] L. Smith. por *Vogue* 177:210-11+ Ja '87
Not just another pretty face. N. J. Perry. il por *Fortune* 116:167+ D 7 '87
Steel, Ronald
Shultz's way. il pors *N Y Times Mag* p14-21+ Ja 11 '87
Steel bands (Music)
Pan-demonium [National Steelband Music Festival, Trinidad] H. Mandel. *Down Beat* 54:13 Ja '87
Steel castings
Can advanced technology save the U.S. steel industry? J. Szekely. il *Sci Am* 257:34-41 Jl '87
Steel construction
See also
American Institute of Steel Construction
Steel furniture *See* Furniture, Metal
Steel industry
See also
Bayou Steel (Firm)
Bethlehem Steel Corp.
Birmingham Steel Corp.
Brenner Tank Company
Chaparral Steel Company
Collective labor agreements—Steel industry
Inland Steel Industries, Inc.
Kaiser Steel Corp.
Lone Star Technologies Inc.
National Intergroup Inc.
Sharon Steel Corp.
Steel workers
Strikes—Steel workers
United Steelworkers of America
USX Corporation
Weirton Steel Corporation
Can advanced technology save the U.S. steel industry? J. Szekely. il *Sci Am* 257:34-41 Jl '87
Acquisitions and mergers
Why Posner backed out of a bailout for Sharon Steel [bailout from Quantum Fund] P. Engardio. il por *Bus Week* p40 My 4 '87
Export-import trade
Two big mistakes. J. Merwin. il *Forbes* 140:76 Jl 13 '87
Finance
Cancel the funeral—steel is on the mend. G. L. Miles. il *Bus Week* p74+ O 5 '87
Is steel's revival for real? I. Ross. il *Fortune* 116:96-9 O 26 '87
Metals. J. Merwin. il *Forbes* 139:162-3 Ja 12 '87

One more chorus of the Steelyard blues. G. L. Miles. il *Bus Week* p81 Ja 12 '87
Steel: singing a new tune. D. Pauly. il *Newsweek* 110:76+ O 5 '87
Management
Performance of multifactor productivity in the steel and motor vehicles industries. M. K. Sherwood. bibl f il *Mon Labor Rev* 110:22-31 Ag '87
Steelmakers want to make teamwork an institution. A. Bernstein and M. Rothman. il *Bus Week* p84 My 11 '87
Canada
See also
Dofasco Inc.
Germany (West)
See also
Thyssen AG
Steel magnolias [drama] *See* Harling, Robert, 1910-
Steel shot *See* Shot
Steel workers
See also
Strikes—Steel workers
United Steelworkers of America
Making a career of it [unemployed steel worker becomes professional peace worker] L. Evans. il *Progressive* 51:34 D '87
Salaries, pensions, etc.
Bonuses for steelworkers? [National Intergroup] S. W. Angrist. il por *Forbes* 139 Ann Directory:126 Ap 27 '87
A laid-off steelworker's continuing bout with unemployment [Dominic Tardio] B. Perris. il *Sch Update* 119:7 Mr 23 '87
Two big mistakes. J. Merwin. il *Forbes* 140:76 Jl 13 '87
Who's going to pay steel's pensions? G. L. Miles. il *Bus Week* p115+ N 2 '87
Steele, Jonathan
Limits of American 'glasnost'. il *World Press Rev* 34:64 Ag '87
Rebirth of political activity. *World Press Rev* 34:38-9 N '87
Steelhead trout fishing *See* Trout fishing
Steen, Alann
Kidnapping
Video plea. por *Time* 129:41 Ap 6 '87
Steen, Lynn Arthur, 1941-
Mathematics education: a predictor of scientific competitiveness. bibl f *Science* 237:251-2+ Jl 17 '87
Points of stress in mathematics education. *Educ Dig* 52:36-9 Ja '87
Steeplechases (Horse races) *See* Horse racing
Steering gear
See also
Automobiles—Steering gear
Boats and boating—Steering gear
Stefan, Jon
Beverly Hills bride [poem] *Natl Rev* 39:39 Je 19 '87
Stefanidis, John
about
Country house in town: a designer's residence on the Thames. E. Lambert. il por *Archit Dig* 44:110-17+ My '87
Steffani, Agostino
about
Le rivali concordi [opera] Reviews
New Yorker 63:91-2 My 25 '87. A. Porter
Steffen, Lloyd
On honesty and self-deception: 'you are the man'. *Christ Century* 104:403-5 Ap 29 '87
Steffy, J. Richard
about
Resurrector of wrecks. M. Geannette. il pors *Oceans* 20:36-41 N/D '87
Stegemann, Eileen
(jt. auth) See Smith, Libby, and Stegemann, Eileen
Steger, Catherine B.
10 good money resolutions to make for 1988. il *Work Woman* 12:84-5+ D '87
Stegmaier, Mark E.
Allan R. Banks [cover story] il por *Am Artist* 51:42-7+ Ag '87
Howard Terpning. il por *Am Artist* 51:66-71+ D '87
Stegner, Wallace Earle, 1909-
The function of aridity. il *Wilderness* 51:14-18 Fall '87
Who are the Westerners? il *Am Herit* 38:34-41 D '87
about
PW interviews. J. F. Baker. por *Publ Wkly* 232:85-6 S 25 '87

Stegner, Wallace Earle, 1909——about—cont.
Typewritten on both sides: the conservation career of Wallace Stegner. T. H. Watkins. il por *Audubon* 89:88-90+ S '87
Stegosaurus *See* Dinosaurs
Stehlin, Dori
As use of kids' aspirin drops, so do cases of Reye syndrome. il *FDA Consum* 21:20-1 O '87
Erasing wrinkles: easier said than done [cover story] il *FDA Consum* 21:20-2 Jl/Ag '87
Stehno, Sandra M.
Kaleidoscope's Youth Development Program: a last chance for youth "aging out" of foster care. il *Child Today* 16:29-33 S/O '87
Steichen, Joanna T.
Jacqueline Picasso and me: the widow-of-the-great-man syndrome. il por *Ms* 15:76 Mr '87
Steidtmann, Nancy
Oakland: Alameda County [special section] il *Horizon* 30:33-46+ Ja/F '87
Steif, William
The careful Communists. il *Progressive* 51:24-7 F '87
Steig, William, 1907-
about
Steig: nobody is grown-up. S. Kroll. *N Y Times Book Rev* 92:26 Je 28 '87
William Steig at 80. D. Allender. il por *Publ Wkly* 232:116-18 Jl 24 '87
Steigerwaldt, Donna Wolf
about
Meet the presidents: Donna Steigerwaldt. C. P. Andersen. il por *Good Housekeep* 205:64+ Ag '87
Stein, Benjamin, 1944-
Analyzing the cost. il *N Y Times Mag* p22 O 25 '87
Blowing up the 60's. il *N Y Times Mag* p14 F 22 '87
Life with Trixie. il *N Y Times Mag* p48 Ap 19 '87
Talk about a buyout! il *N Y Times Mag* p50+ Mr 1 '87
Stein, Edith, 1891-1942
about
Blessed Edith Stein. *America* 156:354-5 My 2 '87
Edith Stein's early years. J. W. Donohue. *America* 156:7-9+ Ja 3-10 '87
A martyr of Auschwitz. S. M. Batzdorff. por *N Y Times Mag* p52-5+ Ap 12 '87
Saintly passions. D. Brand. por *Time* 129:82-3 My 4 '87
Stein, Elliott
25th New York Film Festival. il *Film Comment* 23:60-1+ N/D '87
Miami nice. *Film Comment* 23:6+ Jl/Ag '87
Nieto's show. il *Film Comment* 23:4+ Ja/F '87
Stein, Herbert, 1916-
Is the dismal science really a science? il *Discover* 8:96-9 N '87
A somewhat baffling budget. il *Fortune* 115:121-2 Ap 13 '87
Stein, Howard
about
Has the lion been tamed? R. L. Stern. il por *Forbes* 140:76+ S 21 '87
Stein, Jeff
It's closing time. il *Progressive* 51:28 My '87
Stein, Kathleen
Back talk [discussion of February 1987 article, Censoring science] il *Omni* 9:12+ S '87
Censoring science. il *Omni* 9:42-4+ F '87
Last rights [cover story] il *Omni* 9:58-60+ S '87
Life and death [discussion of September 1987 article, Last rights] *Omni* 10:18 D '87
Stein, Mary Dunlap
The facts on fat vacuuming. *McCalls* 114:41+ Je '87
Stein-Novack, Phyllis
The shape of you to come: how fast can you get fit? il *Mademoiselle* 93:144+ N '87
Steinbach, Alice
Dina Rasor: patriot with a purpose. il pors *McCalls* 114:52 F '87
"If we don't take them, who will?". il por *McCalls* 115:135-7 D '87
Steinbach, Haim
about
Material boys. K. Larson. il *N Y* 20:78-9 My 11 '87
Steinbeck, John, 1902-1968
about
Return to the Sea of Cortez: following in the wake of John Steinbeck. P. Skinner. il map *Petersens Photogr Mag* 15:36-40 F '87
Steinbeck country. B. Golightly. il *Horizon* 30:62 Jl/Ag '87

Steinberg, Elizabeth, d. 1987
Child abuse case
A tragic life and death. M. Gray. il pors *Macleans* 100:50 N 23 '87
A wicked rage claims a child. K. Gross. il pors *People Wkly* 28:44-9 N 23 '87
Steinberg, Gayfryd
about
Mr. Peepers: PEN goes the way of all flesh. il *N Y* 20:29-30 Ap 13 '87
Steinberg, Janet
Getting into travel writing. *Writer* 100:14-15+ My '87
Steinberg, Joel
about
A tragic life and death. M. Gray. il pors *Macleans* 100:50 N 23 '87
A wicked rage claims a child. K. Gross. il pors *People Wkly* 28:44-9 N 23 '87
Steinberg, Laurence D., 1952-
Bound to bicker. il *Psychol Today* 21:36-9 S '87
(jt. auth) See Greenberger, Ellen, and Steinberg, Laurence D., 1952-
Steinberg, Saul P.
about
An enfant terrible comes of age. il por *U S News World Rep* 103:53 Jl 6 '87
The new order at Blair. J. F. Berry. il por *Channels* 7:53-6 Ap '87
Saul Steinberg sees dollar signs in Hispanic TV. R. Grover. il *Bus Week* p34-5 Ja 19 '87
Steinberg may have trouble making money in Spanish. R. Barker. il *Bus Week* p29+ Ag 10 '87
Steinbrenner, George M. (George Michael), 1930-
about
'Actions' aren't racist Yankee boss tells NAACP. *Jet* 73:48 O 12 '87
Yankees owner points to 'black boy' in office as affirmative action. *Jet* 72:52 Jl 20 '87
Steinem, Gloria
Dolly Parton. il por *Ms* 15:66+ Ja '87
Humanism and the second wave of feminism. il por *Humanist* 47:11-15+ My/Je '87
If moral decay is the question, is a feminist ethic the answer? il *Ms* 16:57-9+ S '87
Looking to the future. *Ms* 16:55-7 Jl/Ag '87
Marilyn Monroe [excerpt from Marilyn] il pors *Redbook* 168:102-3+ Ja '87
Old movies through new eyes: sexual politics at your video store. il *Ms* 16:46 Jl/Ag '87
What the U.S. has to learn . . . il *Ms* 16:162 Jl/Ag '87
about
A close watch on feminism [interview] J. Davis. il por *Macleans* 100:52 N 16 '87
Steiner, Elaine B.
Gardens: Dans la Forêt: Japanese inspiration in Pennsylvania. il *Archit Dig* 44:118-23+ Jl '87
Steiner, Jeffrey J.
about
The next takeover artist you meet could be Jeff Steiner. Z. Schiller. il por *Bus Week* p33+ F 9 '87
Steinfeld, Jake
about
Jake Steinfeld: master of motivation. L. Kleinmann. por *Health* 19:60 F '87
Steinfels, Margaret O'Brien
about
A change of editors. *Commonweal* 114:693 D 4 '87
Steinfels, Peter
Catholic thought on war & peace [discussion of September 11 and September 25, 1987 articles, The heritage abandoned?] *Commonweal* 114:690+ D 4 '87
The heritage abandoned? (I). *Commonweal* 114:487-92 S 11 '87
The heritage abandoned? (II). il *Commonweal* 114:530-3 S 25 '87
Isn't it time we Christians made some things clear? *America* 157:181-2 O 3 '87
about
A change of editors. *Commonweal* 114:693 D 4 '87
Steingraber, Fred G.
Competitiveness [address, July 21, 1987] *Vital Speeches Day* 53:758-62 O 1 '87
Steinhardt, Michael
about
The best investors of our time. il pors *Money* Sp Issue:32-6+ Fall '87
Homer nods. J. Crudele. *N Y* 20:16+ D 14 '87
Steinhardt, Paul J.
Icosahedral solids: a new phase of matter? bibl f il *Science* 238:1242-7 N 27 '87

Steinhardt Partners
Homer nods [effect of crash on M. Steinhardt] J. Crudele. *N Y* 20:16+ D 14 '87
Steinhart, Peter
Essay. See issues of Audubon
Steinkuhler, Dean
about
A former Husker fesses up. A. Keteyian. il por *Sports Illus* 66:24 Ja 5 '87
Steinmetz, Leon
The four Soviet cultures. *Natl Rev* 39:32+ O 23 '87
Steir, Pat, 1940-
about
Pat Steir. S. Gill. il *Art News* 86:202+ Summ '87
The self in parts. N. Princenthal. il *Art Am* 75:170-1+ N '87
Steitz, Joan A.
(jt. auth) See Mowry, Kimberly L., and Steitz, Joan A.
Stella, Frank
about
Art. A. C. Danto. *Nation* 245:602-6 N 21 '87
Art. K. Larson. il por *N Y* 20:64-5 S 21 '87
Beyond abstract art? R. Kimball. *Commentary* 83:53-8 Mr '87
Frank Stella's serious fun. M. Stevens. il *Newsweek* 110:82-3 O 19 '87
The grand maximalist. R. Hughes. il por *Time* 130:83-4 N 2 '87
The hustle. *New Yorker* 63:30-1 N 30 '87
Stella performance. K. Larson. il *N Y* 20:123-4+ O 26 '87
A Stellar performer. D. Solomon. il *Harpers Bazaar* 120:378-9+ S '87
Stella's flying ships [cover story] L. Weschler. il por *Art News* 86:92-9 S '87
Stella, Joseph, 1877-1946
about
Stella stars at auction. R. W. Walker. *Art News* 86:17-18 F '87
Stellafane Convention *See* Astronomy—Conferences
Stellar interferometry *See* Interferometers and interferometry
Stellar magnitudes *See* Stars—Magnitudes
Stellar parallax *See* Parallax
Stellar spectra and spectroscopy *See* Stars—Spectra and spectroscopy
Stellar winds
The shaping of planetary nebulae. B. Balick. il *Sky Telesc* 73:125-7+ F '87
Stellenbosch University *See* University of Stellenbosch
Stempel, Robert C.
about
Bumps ahead for a car guy. A. L. Taylor, III. il por *Fortune* 116:105-6+ S 28 '87
The engineer who aims to tune up GM. J. B. Treece. il por *Bus Week* p38 Je 8 '87
It's time for a tune-up at GM. J. B. Treece. il por *Bus Week* p22-3 S 7 '87
A troubleshooter moves in at flabby GM. K. R. Sheets. *U S News World Rep* 102:45 Je 8 '87
Stemple, Jane H. Yolen *See* Yolen, Jane
Stems (Plants)
Cherry stems [how to tie a cherry stem into a knot inside your mouth] *New Yorker* 63:27 Je 1 '87
Stencil work
18 fast country crafts. il *Redbook* 170:127-32 N '87
Arkansas stencilers [work of S. Kittrell and R. Witsell] T. Kazas. il pors *Americana* 15:35-9 My/Je '87
Color your floors bright [stenciled doormat and painted floor cloth] V. Hahn. il *Parents* 62:147-8+ Ag '87
Country graphics. W. Shipman. il *Ctry J* 14:70-5 My '87
Stenciling step by step. L. Swercinski. il *Workbench* 43:44-5 My/Je '87
Collectors and collecting
The pochoir prints of Charles Rahn Fry. J. Gruen. il por *Archit Dig* 44:94+ Ap '87
Stenlund, Arne, and others
A promoter with an internal regulatory domain is part of the origin of replication in BPV-1. bibl f il *Science* 236:1666-71 Je 26 '87
Stensgaard, Niels
The AIDS bomb is ticking. *World Press Rev* 34:50 S '87
Stents, Arterial *See* Arteries—Diseases—Therapy
Stepchildren *See* Stepparents and stepchildren
The stepfather [film] *See* Motion picture reviews—Single works

Stephanie, Princess of Monaco
about
Hey, Prince Rainier, guess who's coming to the palace! Stephanie's latest beau, what's-his-name. il pors *People Wkly* 27:90-2 Mr 23 '87
Stephano, José Luis
(jt. auth) See Gould, Meredith, and Stephano, José Luis
Stephen Greene Press
E. J. Kahn book about 'New Yorker' to be published by Stephen Greene. *Publ Wkly* 232:76 O 2 '87
Stephen J. Cannell Productions
Go north, young man [interview with S. J. Cannell] P. E. Bauer. il pors *Channels* 7:70-1 Jl/Ag '87
Syndicating a success. G. Buchalter. il por *Forbes* 139:92 Ja 26 '87
Stephens, Gene
Crime and punishment: forces shaping the future. il por *Futurist* 21:18-26 Ja/F '87
Stephens, J. T.
about
East meets Little Rock. S. W. Angrist. il por *Forbes* 139:168+ Ap 6 '87
Stephens, Jackson *See* Stephens, J. T.
Stephens, Ken
(jt. auth) See Couch, Frank, and Stephens, Ken
Stephens, R. T.
Photodrawings. il *Petersens Photogr Mag* 15:38-40 Ja '87
Spacious sky: double printing makes it always glorious. il *Petersens Photogr Mag* 16:44-6 N '87
Stephens, Sharon
Lapp life after Chernobyl. il map *Nat Hist* 96:32-41 D '87
Stephens, Simone
about
Simone Stephens is 1st black 'Miss California'. il por *Jet* 72:53 Jl 6 '87
Stephens, Suzanne, 1942-
The buildings in close-up. il *Art Am* 75:152-5 My '87
Classical collage. il *House Gard* 159:138-45+ D '87
Rating the new American museums. il *House Gard* 159:62+ O '87
A vitrine for art. il *House Gard* 159:172-5 S '87
Stephens, Woody
about
A high-stakes dream. B. Weber. il por *N Y Times Mag* p62 Ag 2 '87
Triple Crown showdown. P. Axthelm. il pors *Newsweek* 109:86+ Je 8 '87
Stephens Inc.
East meets Little Rock. S. W. Angrist. il por *Forbes* 139:168+ Ap 6 '87
Epitaph for a trader [suicide of broker J. Markle] W. P. Barrett. il por *Forbes* 140:121 D 14 '87
A power lunch at the Blue Plate Special? W. P. Barrett. il *Forbes* 139:104+ My 18 '87
Stephenson, D. Grier, Jr.
John Marshall and the evolution of judicial review. il por *USA Today (Periodical)* 116:37-9 Jl '87
Stephenson, F. Richard (Francis Richard), 1941-
Computer dating. il *Nat Hist* 96:24+ Ja '87
Stephenson, Francis Richard *See* Stephenson, F. Richard (Francis Richard), 1941-
Stephenson, Marilyn
Meeting America's 1990 nutrition goals: we'll need a strong finish. il *FDA Consum* 21:15-17 S '87
Stepko, Barbara
Have surfboard, will drown. il *Seventeen* 46:225 Ag '87
I won't dance—don't ask me! il *Seventeen* 46:126 Ap '87
Stepleton, Susan S.
Specialized foster care: families as treatment resources. il *Child Today* 16:27-31 Mr/Ap '87
Stepparents and stepchildren
Prepping to be a stepparent [stepparent counseling] I. Pave. il *Bus Week* p149 Mr 16 '87
Stepfathers & stepkids—can they get along? M. B. Rosin. il *Parents* 62:221-2+ Ap '87
Stepparents have rights . . . but not many. R. R. Roha. il *Changing Times* 41:62-4+ Ap '87
"We have a problem" [child's guilt caused by wishing for the death of stepfather's family] J. Marks. il *Parents* 62:62+ F '87
When you like your stepparent too much. L. Dormen. il *Seventeen* 46:152-3+ O '87
Yours, mine, and ours: can stepfamilies ever blend? R. Greene. il *U S Cathol* 52:31-7 Jl '87
Steppenwolf (Musical group)
Computing is just a song [J. Kay's use of computers] C. Bermant. il por *Pers Comput* 11:182-3 O '87

Stepping motors
Tracking comets with a stepping motor. E. Everhart. il por *Sky Telesc* 73:208-12 F '87
Stepping out [drama] *See* Harris, Richard
Stepping out [musical] *See* Musicals, revues, etc.—Reviews—Single works
Steps *See* Stairways
Steps, Garden *See* Garden steps
Stereo headphones *See* Headphones
Stereo loudspeakers *See* Loudspeakers
Stereo receivers *See* Radio receivers
Stereo review (Periodical)
Special interests. L. G. Boundas. il *Stereo Rev* 52:4 My '87
Stereo Review's Record of the Year Awards *See* Phonograph records—Awards
Stereo sound recording and reproducing *See* Sound—Recording and reproducing
Stereo sound systems *See* Audio systems
Stereo television sound *See* Television sound
Stereochemistry
See also
Conformational analysis
Isomers and isomerism
Stereographic projection *See* Spherical projection
Stereoscopic television *See* Television, Stereoscopic
Stereotype (Psychology)
See also
Ageism
Sex role
Are you trapped by your image? C. Jakobson. il *Seventeen* 46:204-5+ Ap '87
A Californian's lament: the Raiders and Lakers are not laid-back, thank you. R. Fimrite. il por *Sports Illus* 66:108 Je 1 '87
Irangate: stereotypes as side effects [stereotyping the Reagans harms women and the elderly] L.-M. Delloff. *Christ Century* 104:263-4 Mr 18-25 '87
The Mafia mystique [Italian American stereotypes] J. Giordano. por *U S News World Rep* 102:6 F 16 '87
Stergiopoulos, Peter
Location car shoot. il *Petersens Photogr Mag* 15:48-9 Ap '87
Sterility in humans *See* Infertility
Sterilization, Sexual
See also
Sterilization reversal
Birth control that really works. J. Carey. il *U S News World Rep* 102:79-80 Mr 16 '87
Rising popularity. M. Morain. *Humanist* 47:33 My/Je '87
Psychological aspects
Sterilization and its discontents. P. McCarthy. il *Psychol Today* 21:10+ O '87
Sterilization (Birth control) *See* Sterilization, Sexual
Sterilization reversal
Sterilization and its discontents. P. McCarthy. il *Psychol Today* 21:10+ O '87
Sterling (Automobile) *See* Automobiles, Foreign
Sterling and Francine Clark Art Institute
Small towns, big art. T. Bross. il *Travel Holiday* 167:29-31 Ja '87
Sterling Drug Inc.
Has Perelman taken a shine to Sterling Drug? [R. O. Perelman] G. G. Marcial. il por *Bus Week* p101 Jl 13 '87
Sterling Lord Literistic Inc.
Sterling Lord and Literistic agencies merge for international clout. *Publ Wkly* 231:11 Mr 20 '87
Sterling Motor Cars
Shh! Please don't call this car a Rover. M. Maremont. il *Bus Week* p59 Ja 12 '87
Sterling Software, Inc.
Sam Wyly: will the hunter become the hunted? T. Mason. il pors *Bus Week* p110 Jl 13 '87
Stern, Barbara Lang
Your well-being. *See* issues of Vogue
Stern, Bert
about
Meet the masters. J. Cornfield. il *Petersens Photogr Mag* 16:22-4+ S '87
Stern, Cathy
Once removed [poem] *New Repub* 196:40 Ap 20 '87
Stern, D. F., and others
Construction of a novel oncogene based on synthetic sequences encoding epidermal growth factor. bibl f il *Science* 235:321-4 Ja 16 '87

Stern, Fritz Richard, 1926-
Einstein and Germany [discussion of February 1986 article] *Phys Today* 40:15+ Jl '87
Remembering the uprising [address, June 17, 1987; with introd. by Timothy Garton Ash] il por *N Y Rev Books* 34:14-16+ D 3 '87
Stern, Gary
A black Gandhi. il *Horizon* 30:37-8 N '87
Tony Walton at the Beaumont [cover story] il por *Theatre Crafts* 21:16-21+ Mr '87
Stern, Gerald
For once [poem] *Nation* 244:374 Mr 21 '87
My favorite farewell [poem] *Nation* 244:372 Mr 21 '87
Stopping Schubert [poem] *Nation* 244:372 Mr 21 '87
Stern, Howard
about
Radio daze. R. Stengel. il por *Time* 129:32 Ap 27 '87
Stern, J. H., and others
Divalent cations directly affect the conductance of excised patches of rod photoreceptor membrane. bibl f il *Science* 236:1674-8 Je 26 '87
Stern, Jack I., and Carroll, David, 1942-
22 top health hot lines [excerpt from Home medical handbook] il *Good Housekeep* 204:217 Je '87
Digestive distress! Signals of a system in trouble. il *Redbook* 169:90-1+ Ag '87
Stern, Jacques
about
Can a turnaround wizard make Honeywell Bull work? T. Peterson. il por *Bus Week* p84-5 Ap 20 '87
Stern, Jane
about
PW interviews. K. Harmon. pors *Publ Wkly* 232:59-60 Jl 31 '87
A road not often taken. M. Burros. il pors *N Y Times Mag* p67-8 Mr 8 '87
Roadfood. K. Haedrich. il pors *Ctry J* 14:14-18 Jl '87
Stern, Jane, and Stern, Michael, 1946-
Best breakfasts. il *Harpers Bazaar* 120:102+ O '87
Buddies. *New Yorker* 63:78+ S 21 '87
Elvis world [excerpts] il *Ladies Home J* 104:53-6 Ag '87
Holy cow! Steaks are high. il *Harpers Bazaar* 120:72+ My '87
Stern, Judith S.
Your diet. *See* issues of Vogue beginning October 1984
Stern, Kenneth
In defense of embellishment. il *Opera News* 51:18-21 F 14 '87
A Puccini bouquet: in his works the composer cultivated floral imagery. il por *Opera News* 51:14-16 Ja 17 '87
Stern, Leni
about
Leni Stern. B. Milkowski. il por *Down Beat* 54:14 F '87
Stern, Leonard
about
From birdseed to the Meadowlands. N. J. Perry. il por *Fortune* 116:122 S 28 '87
Stern, Michael, 1946-
(jt. auth) *See* Stern, Jane, and Stern, Michael, 1946-
about
PW interviews. K. Harmon. pors *Publ Wkly* 232:59-60 Jl 31 '87
A road not often taken. M. Burros. il pors *N Y Times Mag* p67-8 Mr 8 '87
Roadfood. K. Haedrich. il pors *Ctry J* 14:14-18 Jl '87
Stern, Mike
about
Mike Stern's new lease on life. B. Milkowski. il pors *Down Beat* 54:28-30 Ag '87
Stern, Richard Martin, 1915-
How well do you know your characters? *Writer* 100:9-11 Je '87
Stern, Robert A. M., 1939-
An architect's impressions of France. il por *Archit Dig* 44:234+ Je '87
about
Robert A.M. Stern: the scholar. B. Dumaine. il por *Fortune* 115:162-3 Je 22 '87
Stern, Robert G.
New tax law: is a book the medium or the message? *Publ Wkly* 231:24-5 My 29 '87
Stern, William
See also
Baby M case

Stern, Zev
Surrogate motherhood and medical alternatives for child-less couples. *USA Today (Periodical)* 116:70-1 N '87
Stern (Robert A. M.) Architects *See* Robert A. M. Stern Architects
Stern drive engines *See* Motor boat engines
Sternberg, Paul
about
Worm watching: the case of the suicidal sex cell. G. Montgomery. il por *Discover* 8:44-6+ O '87
Sternberg, Robert J.
Teaching critical thinking: eight easy ways to fail before you begin. il *Phi Delta Kappan* 68:456-9 F '87
about
A different kind of love triangle. M. Golin. il *Prevention* 39:80-2+ Jl '87
Sterner, Donald J.
about
Caring for the condor. B. Weber. il por *N Y Times Mag* p106 O 4 '87
Sternfeld, Joel, 1944-
In search of America. il *N Y Times Mag* p32-5 Mr 15 '87
about
Lovelorn tracts, minced wilderness. R. Lacayo. il *Time* 129:84 Ap 20 '87
Sterngold, James
Hardball on Wall Street [cover story] il pors *N Y Times Mag* p22-7+ Ag 16 '87
Sternhell, Carol
Nadine Gordimer: choosing to be a white African. il pors *Ms* 16:28+ S '87
Who needs a blockbuster? Another way of publishing. il *N Y Times Book Rev* 92:40 O 11 '87
Sternlieb, George
Planning, American style. *Society* 25:21-3 N/D '87
Steroids
See also
Corticosterone
Hormones, Sex
Lipids
Testosterone
Athletes and steroids: playing a deadly game. R. W. Miller. il *FDA Consum* 21:16-21 N '87
Athletes and steroids: the bad bargain. V. S. Cowart. il *Saturday Evening Post* 259:56-9 Ap '87
Bosworth faces the music [casualty of the NCAA's steroid crackdown] C. Neff. il pors *Sports Illus* 66:20-2+ Ja 5 '87
Calcium for steroid users. il *Prevention* 39:8+ Ja '87
Confessions of a steroid user [interview with anonymous female body builder] D. Barrilleaux. il *Women's Sports Fitness* 9:84 N '87
For athletes and dealers, black market steroids are risky business. D. Stehlin. il *FDA Consum* 21:24-5 S '87
Jailed [J. Bradshaw convicted of illegally distributing steroids] il *FDA Consum* 21:31 My '87
Neurosteroids: cytochrome P-450$_{scc}$ in rat brain. C. Le Goascogne and others. bibl f il *Science* 237:1212-15 S 4 '87
Of muscles and mania [steroid induced psychosis among bodybuilders: study by Harrison G. Pope Jr. and David L. Katz] E. Grant. il *Psychol Today* 21:12 S '87
A star flunks his test [B. Bosworth found using steroids] P. Axthelm. il por *Newsweek* 109:48-9 Ja 5 '87
Steroidogenesis-activator polypeptide isolated from a rat Leydig cell tumor. R. C. Pedersen and A. C. Brownie. bibl f il *Science* 236:188-90 Ap 10 '87
Steroids and teens. P. Gadsby. il *Good Housekeep* 205:269 S '87
Steroids: the stuff of synthetic supermen? [anabolic steroids] M. S. Kreiter. il *Curr Health 2* 14:14-16 D '87
Sterols
See also
Cholesterol
Stetter, Karl O., and others
Isolation of extremely thermophilic sulfate reducers: evidence for a novel branch of archaebacteria. bibl f il *Science* 236:822-4 My 15 '87
Steuben Glass
Susan King: a stone thrower who moved into a glass house. M. Mallory. il por *Bus Week* p59 Ag 17 '87
Steven Holl, Architects
Magnificent obsession. K. D. Stein. il *Archit Rec* 175:90-101 mid-S '87
Stevens, Carl
about
An heiress vs. a pastor. G. Hackett. por *Newsweek* 109:33 Ap 20 '87

Stevens, Douglas
Ethiopian landscapes. il *Commonweal* 114:652-4 N 20 '87
Stevens, Ernest L.
about
A visit with Ernest L. Stevens. P. Malvern and M. Malvern. il por *Antiques Collect Hobbies* 92:48-9+ Ag '87
Stevens, J. G., and others
RNA complementary to a herpesvirus α gene mRNA is prominent in latently infected neurons. bibl f il *Science* 235:1056-9 F 27 '87
Stevens, Joseph E.
Digging into history. il *Americana* 14:41-4 Ja/F '87
Stevens, Mark
about
Scooped. L. Gubernick. il por *Forbes* 139:107 Je 29 '87
Stevens, Mark, 1947-
How healthy is your business? il *Work Woman* 12:39-42 Ja '87
How to make sales calls that get business. *Work Woman* 12:51-3 D '87
The new tax law: what it means for your business. il *Work Woman* 12:39-42 Mr '87
Six small-business problems computers can solve. il *Work Woman* 12:33+ S '87
Stevens, Mark, 1951-
Somewhere, Wright is smiling. il *Art News* 86:238 N '87
Stevens, Marshall
about
Old-fashioned service. J. C. Johnson. il por *Nations Bus* 75:48-9 Je '87
Stevens, Melanie Chadwick
Details! Details! *Redbook* 169:82-3 Ag '87
Stevens, Phillip
about
Give it back to the Indians? T. Jacoby. il pors *Newsweek* 110:47 D 7 '87
Stevens, Risë, 1913-
about
Irreplaceable. W. Price. il pors *Opera News* 51:8-12 Mr 14 '87
Stevens, Samuel
about
Savannah's true pilot. D. Young. il pors *South Living* 22:74 Ag '87
Stevens, Sinclair
about
Conflicts and credibility gaps. G. Bain. il *Macleans* 100:52 D 21 '87
Harsh lessons from an inquiry. G. Bain. il *Macleans* 100:44 Ag 24 '87
Wrapping up an inquiry. S. Aikenhead. il *Macleans* 100:13 Mr 2 '87
'Wrong by any measure'. M. Rose. il por *Macleans* 100:12-14 D 14 '87
Stevens, Trisha
about
Shooting star. R. Cody. il pors *Women's Sports Fitness* 9:42-4+ Ap '87
Stevens, Wallace, 1879-1955
about
Wallace Stevens: poet of the secular imagination. D. Lawson. *Humanist* 47:35-6 My/Je '87
Stevens Institute of Technology
From campus to business [D. Patnaude's use of computers while a student] J. Schwartz. il por *Pers Comput* 11:189+ O '87
Stevenson, Alexandra
about
Mother of a pearl. S. Stevenson. il pors *World Tennis* 34:38-41+ Ap '87
Stevenson, George
about
Selling your business: frequently asked questions [interview] il por *Nations Bus* 75:34 D '87
Stevenson, James, 1929-
Fossil news. il *New Yorker* 63:36-7 My 11 '87
Post-season knucklers. il *New Yorker* 63:33 O 26 '87
The self once seen: reflective images in time. il *New Yorker* 63:26-7 Ag 31 '87
about
PW interviews. K. O. Fakih. por *Publ Wkly* 231:148-9 F 27 '87
Stevenson, Matthew
Edward Said: an exile's exile [interview] il *Progressive* 51:30-4 F '87
Stevenson, Melody
Stomach flu & toddlers, too. il *Parents* 62:92-4 F '87

Stevenson, Robert G., and Powers, Harry L.
How to handle death in the school. *Educ Dig* 52:42-3
My '87
Stevenson, Samantha
Bjorn again! [cover story] il pors *World Tennis* 35:18-24
D '87
A celebration of life. il *World Tennis* 35:38-42 O '87
Holiday getaways. il *World Tennis* 35:48-9 D '87
Mother of a pearl. il pors *World Tennis* 34:38-41+ Ap
'87
Stew
Bourride: bouillabaisse's country cousin [Provençal fish
stew] il *Sunset* 179:188-9 N '87
Burgoo and Brunswick stew. P. Y. Cordell. il *South
Living* 22:92-4 Ja '87
Marvelous no-meat stew [vegetarian couscous] il *McCalls*
145:123-4 Mr '87
One-pot meals. J. Nash. il *Essence* 18:96 N '87
Quick or Southwest? [pozole] il *Sunset* 179:206+ N '87
Savory stew! J. Taylor. il *Better Homes Gard* 65:184
N '87
Soup & stew cookbook. il *Ladies Home J* 104:110-13+
F '87
Splurge stew: oysters and artichokes. il *Sunset* 179:196
O '87
Stew pour vous [bistro beef stew and accompaniments]
il *Seventeen* 46:125-6 D '87
Stewing over winter. J. F. Mariani. il *Mot Boat Sail*
159:28 Ja '87
Steward, Rufus
about
Detroit man gets $1 million in police brutality case.
Jet 72:29 My 4 '87
Steward, Ruth
Dorsal, an embryonic polarity gene in Drosophila, is
homologous to the vertebrate proto-oncogene, c-rel.
bibl f il *Science* 238:692-4 O 30 '87
Stewardesses, Air *See* Airlines—Flight attendants
Stewardship, Christian
The fate of the soil. R. Clapp. il *Christ Today* 31:14-15
O 2 '87
On the stewardship of property. S. A. Portaro. *Christ
Century* 104:846-7 O 7 '87
Stewart, Barbara
Making book on book-and-cassette packages. il *Publ
Wkly* 232:51-5 N 27 '87
Stewart, Bill, d. 1985
about
One from the heart. R. Reilly. il pors *Sports Illus* 66:44-6+
My 18 '87
Stewart, D. Michael
Poor laws and pauper policies [address, November 29,
1986] *Vital Speeches Day* 53:245-8 F 1 '87
Stewart, Dave
about
The A's new Stew can do. R. Fimrite. il pors *Sports
Illus* 67:69-70 O 5 '87
Stewart, Don
The auto, love & advertising. il *Antiques Collect Hobbies*
92:75-9 Ap '87
Collecting sheet music. il *Antiques Collect Hobbies*
92:69-72 Ag '87
Collecting wood type. il *Antiques Collect Hobbies* 92:60-2
My '87
Matchbook cover collecting. il *Antiques Collect Hobbies*
92:74-8 Je '87
Stewart, Donald M.
Good writing [address, April 6, 1987] *Vital Speeches
Day* 53:630-3 Ag 1 '87
about
College board prexy says Reagan's ed. policy hurts
minority students most. por *Jet* 72:8 Ap 27 '87
Stewart, Doug
Eastern shuttle. il *Omni* 9:14 Ja '87
Higher education. il *Omni* 10:26+ N '87
Lost Ulysses. il *Omni* 9:20+ S '87
One shutterbug wears more than meets the eye [cover
story] il pors *Smithsonian* 18:108-12+ O '87
Skylines of fabric. il *Technol Rev* 90:60-7 Ja '87
Stewart, Isobel
Bless the child [story] il *Good Housekeep* 205:80+
D '87
Home for Christmas [story] il *Ladies Home J*
104:100+ D '87
The perfect match [story] il *Good Housekeep*
204:118-19+ F '87
Writing the short love story. *Writer* 100:16-18+ Mr '87
Stewart, Jackie
about
"Behind the wheel with Jackie Stewart". M. Anson.
il pors *Mot Trend* 39:130+ My '87

Upon the fyne arte of flying the coupe. T. West. il
Road Track 38:22 F '87
Stewart, James E.
about
Battling for survival in the concrete jungle. J. R. Norman.
il por *Bus Week* p66-7+ S 14 '87
Stewart, Jimmy
about
Jimmy Stewart. S. Yanow. il por *Down Beat* 54:48-50
Mr '87
Jimmy Stewart: It's a wonderful life. S. Granger. il
pors *Ladies Home J* 104:142-3+ D '87
Stewart, Lane
Passion in the piazza [photographs] il *Sports Illus* 67:42-9
Jl 20 '87
Stewart, Linda McK.
Jamaica Inn: Caribbean idyll. il *Harpers Bazaar* 120:139
My '87
Stewart, Martha
about
Wedding fair at Bookworks. B. List. il *Publ Wkly* 232:45-6
Ag 21 '87
Stewart, Pamela Rae
about
The ordeal of Pamela Rae Stewart. A. Bonavoglia. il
pors *Ms* 16:92-5+ Jl/Ag '87
Stewart, Paul
about
Whistling a new tune. M. Bishop. il pors *Sports Illus*
67:72-4+ N 30 '87
Stewart, Payne
about
One from the heart. R. Reilly. il pors *Sports Illus* 66:44-6+
My 18 '87
Stewart, Susan
The summer before the moon [poem] *Harpers* 275:34
Jl '87
Stewart, Walter
A case against the Crown [excerpts from Uneasy lies
the head] il *Macleans* 100:44-6+ My 11 '87
Stewart, Zan
Clarinetist for all seasons: Eddie Daniels. il pors *Down
Beat* 54:23-4+ Je '87
George Howard: in the groove. il por *Down Beat* 54:24-6
My '87
Stewart, Tabori & Chang
Tour of Louvre from Stewart Tabori & Chang. il *Publ
Wkly* 231:250 My 15 '87
Stick shift transmission *See* Automobiles—Transmission
Stickers
Stickers—for fun (and learning) [Stick & Learn series]
il *Parents* 62:21 S '87
Stickney, Michael
The way to quality venison. il *Conservationist* 42:44-7
N/D '87
Stickney, Phyllis
about
Phyllis Stickney stopped seeing herself as an outcast
when she found It's a different world. il por *People
Wkly* 28:111 Jl 13 '87
Stiefel, Herbert
about
Zipper man. *New Yorker* 63:34-6 D 14 '87
Stigler, George Joseph, 1911-
Are we hissing the wrong guys? il *Forbes* 140:52-3+
Jl 13 '87
Stigler, Stephen M., and Wagner, Melissa J.
A substantial bias in nonparametric tests for periodicity
in geophysical data. bibl f il *Science* 238:940-5 N
13 '87
Stilbestrols
DES update. P. A. Hillard. il *Parents* 62:186+ Ap '87
Still, Karin
about
Teddy Pendergrass starts new life with new wife [cover
story] il pors *Jet* 72:26-7 Jl 20 '87
Still life drawing
William A. Berry [colored pencil still lifes] B. S. Goldman.
il por *Am Artist* 51:68-73+ F '87
Still life painting
Daniel Sprick. P. Eichner-Dixon. il por *Am Artist* 51:32-7
Ag '87
Four objects, four interpretations. T. Bolt. il *Am Artist*
51:28-31 Jl '87
Jane Frey. B. S. Goldman. il por *Am Artist* 51:44-9
S '87
The watercolor page. J. U. Sayles. il por *Am Artist*
51:38-41+ Ag '87

Still life painting—*cont.*
Exhibitions
Still lifes in the Golden Anniversary National Art Exhibition [with introd. by John Stuart Ingle] il *Am Artist* 51:40-5 Je '87
Still life photography *See* Photography—Still life
Still video cameras *See* Video cameras
Stillbirth
No heartbeat. M. Atkinson. *Parents* 62:134-5 Ap '87
Stillbirth. P. A. Hillard. il *Parents* 62:142+ Jl '87
Religious aspects
A pastoral and theological response to losses in pregnancy. J. S. Peterman. *Christ Century* 104:750-3 S 9-16 '87
Stille, Alexander
Primo Levi: reconciling the man and the writer. por *N Y Times Book Rev* 92:5 Jl 5 '87
Stille, Ugo
The four crises of Irangate. *World Press Rev* 34:12-13 S '87
Stillman, Alan
about
Out of the cellar. F. J. Prial. il por *N Y Times Mag* p56 N 29 '87
Stillman, Deanne
Lips like Kim Basinger's and other fantasies of single women. il *Mademoiselle* 93:174-5+ O '87
Visit from mom. il *Mademoiselle* 93:202-3+ O '87
Stillman, Diane
7 ways to turn a TV-kid on to reading. il *McCalls* 115:61 O '87
Stillwater National Wildlife Management Area (Nev.) *See* Wildlife sanctuaries—Nevada
Stimpson, Catharine R.
The "F" word. *Ms* 16:80+ Jl/Ag '87
Stimson, Paul
Malice aforethought. il *Art Am* 75:114-17 Ja '87
Stimulants
See also
Amphetamines
Caffeine
Cocaine
Coffee
Stimulation (Physiology)
See also
Brain—Innervation
Electricity—Physiological effects
Electronic behavior control
Electrophysiology
Sensory stimulation
Stimulus and response
See also
Reaction time
Reflexes
Stinchecum, Amanda Mayer
Osaka: a lesson in Japanese character. il *Travel Holiday* 167:64-8 Ap '87
Ryokan: the Japanese inn. il map *Travel Holiday* 168:60-5 N '87
Sting
about
Sting [interview] D. Fricke. il por *Roll Stone* p297-8 N 5-D 10 '87
Well Stung. L. Robinson. por *Vogue* 177:94 D '87
Stingers (Guided missiles) *See* Guided missiles
Stinging jellyfish *See* Jellyfish
Stingray, Joanna
about
From L.A. to Russia with love: promoter Joanna Stingray says 'Da' to her Soviet rocker. il pors *People Wkly* 28:68-70 N 30 '87
Stingray sexual behavior *See* Sexual behavior—Fish
Stings, Insect *See* Insect bites and stings
Stinnett, Nick, and DeFrain, John
Six secrets of strong families [condensed from Secrets of strong families] il *Read Dig* 131:132-5 N '87
Stir-frying
See also
Wok cooking
Italian stir-fry? [tortellini with broccoli and gorgonzola] il *Sunset* 179:190+ O '87
No-chop stir-frys. B. Greenwood. il *Better Homes Gard* 65:138-9 Ap '87
Pork & scallops with crisp ginger. il *Good Housekeep* 204:38 Je '87
Stir-fry: fast and fabulous! il *Prevention* 39:50 Ap '87
Stir-fry to keep calories low. B. E. Templeton. il *South Living* 22:186+ Mr '87
Stirling, James Frazer
about
City of the future. W. Feaver. il *Art News* 86:44 Mr '87

Do we need another hero? S. Jones. il *Hist Today* 37:3-4 My '87
Exhibition report: New architecture: Foster, Rogers, Stirling. H. Aldersey-Williams. *Archit Rec* 175:73+ Mr '87
The homecoming [cover story] D. Dietsch. il *Archit Rec* 175:104-13 Jl '87
Stitches (Surgery) *See* Sutures
Stites, Bradley
Historical analogies. *Space World* X-11-287 Space Advocate:5-6 N '87
Stitt, Milan
Entr'acte. See occasional issues of Horizon (Tuscaloosa, Ala.) beginning July/August 1984
Stochastic processes
The orderly pursuit of pure disorder. K. McKean. il *Discover* 8:72-6+ Ja '87
Stock averages *See* Stocks—Price indexes and averages
Stock brokers *See* Brokers
Stock buybacks *See* Stocks—Repurchase
Stock car racing *See* Automobile racing
Stock dividends *See* Dividends
Stock exchanges
See also
Brokers
Computers—Investment use
Over-the-counter securities markets
Stock market crash, 1987
American exchange
The battle of the exchanges. J. A. Conway. il *Forbes* 139:8 My 4 '87
Frankfurt exchange
The Japanese are firing up Frankfurt. J. E. Pluenneke. il *Bus Week* p40 Ap 20 '87
Hong Kong exchange
The pall in Hong Kong may not lift soon. M. Shao. il *Bus Week* p81-2 N 16 '87
Ronald Li: as freewheeling as his stock exchange. M. Shao. il por *Bus Week* p76+ O 12 '87
International aspects
Are you ready to go global? [foreign stocks] J. Mendes. il *Fortune* 116 Sp Issue:71-2+ Fall '87
Black Monday: a world view. il *Sch Update* 120:14 D 18 '87
Dutch uncles [foreign reaction to budget deficit agreement] J. Crudele. il *N Y* 20:26+ D 7 '87
Global traders head for home. R. I. Kirkland, Jr. and L. Kraar. il *Fortune* 116:53-4+ D 7 '87
Going global [special section] il *Money* 16:50-2+ My '87
Strong currencies signal hot spots for trading. B. Riemer. il *Bus Week* p148-50 D 28 '87-Ja 4 '88
There are still some bargains left in foreign stocks. J. Templeman. il *Bus Week* p62 Jl 6 '87
Trading on foreign soil. D. R. Katz. il *Esquire* 107:39-40 Ja '87
Ups and downs in the global village [effect of stock market crash] E. W. Desmond. il *Time* 130:45+ N 9 '87
Where your bucks should stop over there [foreign securities] P. A. Dreyfus. il *Money* 16:131-2+ Ja '87
A world investor's favorite markets [interview with N. Fachler] J. Mendes. il por *Fortune* 116:130 S 14 '87
Jamaican exchange
Jamaicans fuel a skyrocketing market. A. McKenzie. il por map *Black Enterp* 18:93-4+ D '87
Laws and regulations
See Securities—Laws and regulations
London exchange
Big bust [Big Bang aftermath] R. L. Stern and D. Henry. il *Forbes* 140:64-5 Ag 24 '87
The City of London wanted competition—but not this much. R. A. Melcher. il *Bus Week* p37 Ag 10 '87
Instant relic: the new exchange floor [computers] R. A. Melcher. il *Bus Week* p60 Ja 12 '87
Thatcher after the crash: carry on, then. R. A. Melcher. il *Bus Week* p80-1 N 16 '87
Membership
Exchange seats are hot commodities. S. Weiss. il *Bus Week* p107 Je 1 '87
Mexico exchange
¿No mañana? L. Minard. *Forbes* 140:134 Ag 10 '87
Midwest exchange
The Midwest Exchange puts itself on the map. J. N. Frank. il *Bus Week* p112 My 4 '87
Montreal exchange
Taking stock of the QSSP [Quebec Stock Savings Plan] B. Wallace. il *Macleans* 100:30 N 23 '87
New York exchange
The ABC's of a frantic market. R. F. Black and K. R. Sheets. il *U S News World Rep* 103:32 N 9 '87

Stock market crash, 1987—*cont.*

Bulls, bears and book publishers: assessing the damage. M. Reuter and C. Reid. il *Publ Wkly* 232:10-11 N 6 '87

Bursting the supply-side bubble. G. P. Brockway. il *New Leader* 70:15-16 N 30 '87

Calm before a storm? [markets battered by weakening dollar] W. Glasgall. il *Bus Week* p30-2 D 14 '87

A clear warning to Washington. D. Francis. il *Macleans* 100:9 N 16 '87

Coming home to roost. S. Lee. il *Forbes* 140:312-13 N 16 '87

Computer-age correction? A. C. Brown. il *Forbes* 140:250 N 30 '87

Computers amplify Black Monday. M. M. Waldrop. il *Science* 238:602-4 O 30 '87

Crash diet. W. Greider. il *Roll Stone* p138-40+ D 17-31 '87

The crash of '87: how the stock market affects you [cover story; special issue] il *Sch Update* 120:2-15 D 18 '87

The day the market crashed. R. D. Hylton. il *Black Enterp* 18:29 D '87

Déjà vu all over again. R. L. Stern. il *Forbes* 140:35-6 N 30 '87

Diary of a decision: a week in the life of Amax [A. Born's struggle to buoy his company's stock] J. R. Norman. il por *Bus Week* p118+ N 9 '87

Diary of a money manager. K. L. Fisher. il *Forbes* 140:316 N 16 '87

Discounting the cuts [budget cuts and the stock market] J. Crudele. il *N Y* 20:16 N 30 '87

Don't be rash. D. N. Dreman. il *Forbes* 140:136 D 28 '87

Down, but hardly out [fund companies and the crash] R. Simon. il *Forbes* 140:81 N 30 '87

The dreamer awakes [Reaganomics and the stock market crash] *New Repub* 197:4 N 9 '87

Easy pickings? [market crash and arbitrage stocks] A. Sloan. il *Forbes* 140:36 N 30 '87

End of the comfort factor [effect on mutual funds] N. R. Gibbs. il *Time* 130:60 N 16 '87

The end of the rich man's boom. L. Cawley. il *Nation* 245:675-6+ D 5 '87

Fancy stuff [funds with sophisticated option strategies and the market crash] W. Baldwin. il *Forbes* 140:185 N 30 '87

Fishing season? T. Jaffe. il *Forbes* 140:322 N 16 '87

Futures shock. D. Corn. *Nation* 245:509-10 N 7 '87

Global traders head for home. R. I. Kirkland, Jr. and L. Kraar. il *Fortune* 116:53-4+ D 7 '87

Gurus who called the crash—or fell on their faces. P. Finch and M. Frons. il *Bus Week* p124-6+ N 30 '87

Heading off hard times [cover story; special section] il *Newsweek* 110:24-8+ N 9 '87

Holmes a Court's fortunes are sinking Down Under. C. Debes. il por *Bus Week* p142-4 D 7 '87

Homer nods [effect of crash on M. Steinhardt] J. Crudele. *N Y* 20:16+ D 14 '87

How an educated guess is paying off for George Keane [Common Fund's manager calls the crash] G. G. Marcial. il por *Bus Week* p106 D 21 '87

How bad? [cover story; special section] il *Bus Week* p42-54+ N 2 '87

How Citicorp landed in an Irish stew [trading gaffe in Dublin] R. A. Melcher. *Bus Week* p40-1 D 21 '87

How corporate America is coping with the aftershocks. C. Power. il *Bus Week* p105+ N 16 '87

How to read Wall Street's scrambled messages. A. S. Blinder. por *Bus Week* p28 N 16 '87

Hurry up please, it's time. But time for what? A. Cockburn. *Nation* 245:474-5 O 31 '87

If you think New York has it bad, take a look at Chicago. M. E. Kreca and J. M. Laderman. il *Bus Week* p132-3 N 30 '87

In the rubble. J. Crudele. il *N Y* 20:16+ N 9 '87

Investment challenge: surveying the damage. J. Mendes. il *Fortune* 116:176+ D 7 '87

IPOs: now only the best and the brightest need apply [case of Javelin Software Corp.] K. H. Hammonds. il *Bus Week* p37-8 N 30 '87

Irv Jacobs is still spooked. G. G. Marcial. *Bus Week* p136 N 30 '87

Is Alan Greenspan really such a hero? S. Zucker. por *Bus Week* p35 D 14 '87

It's time for America to wake up [cover story; special section] il *Bus Week* p158-61+ N 16 '87

Johnny one-note sings again. A. Bladen. il *Forbes* 140:317 N 16 '87

The knife must fall. S. Koepp. il *Time* 130:48-50 N 23 '87

Letter from Washington. Cato. *Natl Rev* 39:14 D 18 '87

Letter from Washington [R. Reagan's press conference] Cato. *Natl Rev* 39:14 N 20 '87

Letter from Washington [way the crash affects the Republican presidential candidates] Cato. *Natl Rev* 39:14 D 4 '87

Living with the crash [cover story; special section; with editorial comment by Kevin Doyle] il *Macleans* 100:2, 26-36+ N 2 '87

Looking back at Black Monday [cover story; special section] il *Natl Rev* 39:43-50+ N 20 '87

The losing hand [Washington's response] M. B. Zuckerman. il *U S News World Rep* 103:78 D 14 '87

Market collapse will increase operating pressures on airlines. P. Proctor. *Aviat Week Space Technol* 127:42 O 26 '87

The market crash batters corporate balance sheets [corporate debt] G. Koretz. il *Bus Week* p24 D 7 '87

Market crash makes minor impact on bookstore sales. *Publ Wkly* 232:44 N 13 '87

The market for Dole. F. Barnes. *New Repub* 197:9-11 N 16 '87

Massacre [new issues] R. Stern and C. M. Bartlett, Jr. il *Forbes* 140:56-7+ D 14 '87

Maybe it's 1928 again [interview with P. A. Fisher] T. Jaffe. por *Forbes* 140:126+ N 30 '87

Measuring consumer confidence. J. C. Szabo. il *Nations Bus* 75:10 D '87

The minority view: Bloody Monday staved off recession; The crash jolts a shifting job market. G. Koretz. il *Bus Week* p33 N 16 '87

Money and the moral vacuum. B. Amiel. il *Macleans* 100:9 N 9 '87

Money managers after the crash. J. P. Newport, Jr. il *Fortune* 116:71-2 D 7 '87

More greed than common sense. P. C. Newman. il *Macleans* 100:40 N 2 '87

Notes and comment [visiting the Exchange the day the market crashed] *New Yorker* 63:33-4 N 2 '87

Now what? [cover story; special section] il *World Press Rev* 34:9-18 D '87

Of many things. G. W. Hunt. *America* 157:314 N 7 '87

The pall in Hong Kong may not lift soon. M. Shao. il *Bus Week* p81-2 N 16 '87

Pick a forecast, any forecast. K. Pennar. il *Bus Week* p30-2 N 30 '87

Picking up the pieces [cover story; special section; with editorial comments by James W. Michaels, Malcolm Forbes and Malcolm Forbes Jr.] il *Forbes* 140:6, 17-18, 24-5+ N 16 '87

Prescription for a slump. W. C. Peterson. *New Leader* 70:14 N 30 '87

Program previews. J. Crudele. *N Y* 20:16+ N 16 '87

PW business survey: plunging stocks boost books. S. Bolle and others. il *Publ Wkly* 232:24+ D 18 '87

The quake on Wall Street is rocking real estate. F. A. Miller. il *Bus Week* p184 N 16 '87

Raiders of the cheap buck [foreign raiders after the crash] D. Pauly. il *Newsweek* 110:51 N 30 '87

Reagan's 'correction'. *New Repub* 197:7-9 N 16 '87

Reuters after the crash: slowing down to a gallop. M. Maremont. il *Bus Week* p114-15+ D 21 '87

Small investors and the crash. C. Friday. il *Newsweek* 110:50-1 D 21 '87

Staring into the abyss [cover story; special section; with editorial comment by Mortimer B. Zuckerman] il *U S News World Rep* 103:18-26+, 88 N 2 '87

Starting over [cover story; special section] il *Bus Week* p31-40+ N 9 '87

The stock market is a lousy economic forecaster. J. Willoughby. il *Forbes* 140:32-4 N 30 '87

Suddenly, it's fashionable to go against the grain [contrarians] J. M. Laderman. il *Bus Week* p108-9 D 7 '87

Suffering from ticker shock [presidential candidates' reactions] W. Shapiro. il *Time* 130:58-9 N 2 '87

Tell us again, Mr. Stone [views of J. Stone] L. Jereski. il por *Forbes* 140:232+ N 30 '87

Thanks, professor. D. N. Dreman. il *Forbes* 140:314-15 N 16 '87

Thatcher after the crash: carry on, then. R. A. Melcher. il *Bus Week* p80-1 N 16 '87

Think it's bargain-hunting time? Take it slow. J. M. Laderman. il *Bus Week* p178-9 N 16 '87

Tough options: an investor who hedged himself out of a bundle. J. M. Laderman. *Bus Week* p133 N 30 '87

Stock market crash, 1987—*cont.*

U.K. publishers are sanguine after London market crash. V. Menkes. *Publ Wkly* 232:11 N 13 '87

Van Peebles makes most of stock market crash. il por *Jet* 73:6 N 9 '87

Volcker on the crash. L. S. Silk. il por *N Y Times Mag* p40+ N 8 '87

Wall Street gets ready for Black Christmas. J. Egan. il *U S News World Rep* 103:10-11 D 14 '87

The Wall Street guessing game. B. Powell. il *Newsweek* 110:65 D 14 '87

Wall Street's credibility gap [cover story; special section] il *Bus Week* p92-5+ N 23 '87

A war of the generations [crash ignites feud between Wall Street old-timers and quants] B. Powell. il *Newsweek* 110:48-9 N 30 '87

The watchword after Bloody Monday: diversify. D. Zigas. *Bus Week* p142 N 9 '87

We better keep them happy [Japanese investment in the U.S.; interview with R. D. Hormats] A. D. Frank. il por *Forbes* 140:37-8 N 30 '87

What next? F. G. Rohatyn. il *N Y Rev Books* 34:3-5 D 3 '87

What to do? *Natl Rev* 39:19 N 20 '87

'What went wrong with what?'. J. Klein. il *N Y* 20:24+ N 9 '87

Where did it all go? J. K. Glassman. *New Repub* 197:11+ N 9 '87

Where to invest in 1988 [cover story; special section] il *Bus Week* p95-9+ D 28 '87-Ja 4 '88

Who's in charge? [cover story; special section] il por *Time* 130:18-24+ N 9 '87

Why a depression isn't in the cards. G. S. Becker. por *Bus Week* p22 N 9 '87

Why politicians don't matter on Wall Street. A. J. Glass. il *New Leader* 70:3-4 N 2 '87

Why the market crash won't cause a recession [cover story] S. Lee and C. Brown. il *Forbes* 140:120-4 N 30 '87

Why the worst may still be ahead [special section] il *U S News World Rep* 103:24-30+ N 9 '87

Wild in the Street [special section] il *N Y* 20:34-43 N 2 '87

Will the Democrats be able to seize the moment? L. Walczak and others. il *Bus Week* p67 N 2 '87

You thought Monday was bad? G. Bock. il *Time* 130:44 N 30 '87

Anecdotes, facetiae, satire, etc.
Puppy-Aid. J. Queenan. *New Repub* 197:18 D 7 '87

Wall Street's new bull market: jokes. G. Parshall. *U S News World Rep* 103:16 N 9 '87

Moral and religious aspects
A bear market and an overweight camel. J. M. Wall. il *Christ Century* 104:987 N 11 '87

Black Monday aftershocks [effect of crash on church investments] *Christ Century* 104:992 N 11 '87

Psychological aspects
An A+ on the stress test. il *Fortune* 116:16 N 23 '87

The burned, the baffled, the calm: tales of eight investors [post crash assessment] M. Frons. il *Bus Week* p102+ N 23 '87

The market on the couch. il *Newsweek* 110:33 N 2 '87

Psyching out the crash [Harvard study] J. Crudele. il *N Y* 20:16 N 23 '87

The psychology of stock buying. A. Shortell. il *Macleans* 100:26-7 N 2 '87

A theory of the panic. R. Rosenblatt. il *Time* 130:112 N 9 '87

Public opinion
Black Monday wasn't so black [views of suburban St. Louis residents] H. Rainie. il *U S News World Rep* 103:29-30 N 9 '87

Business week/Harris poll. il *Bus Week* p36 N 9 '87

The confidence gap: a poll. il *Newsweek* 110:20 N 2 '87

The confident consumer [results of Maclean's/Decima poll] D. Jenish. il *Macleans* 100:44 N 9 '87

Coping with the crash [results of Time poll] il *Time* 130:59 N 2 '87

Reporters and reporting
Beware good times. *Natl Rev* 39:14-15 D 31 '87

Crash reporting. E. Diamond. il *N Y* 20:30+ N 9 '87

Wake up, Business week! *Natl Rev* 39:18-19 D 18 '87

Terminology
What happened to the market? W. Safire. il *N Y Times Mag* p18+ N 8 '87

Stock market newsletters *See* Investment newsletters

Stock option contracts *See* Put and call transactions

Stock ownership, Employee *See* Employees as stockholders

Stock purchase options

GM: the bonus days are over [scrapping bonuses in favor of stock option plan] J. Schwartz. il *Newsweek* 109:53 Ap 27 '87

Millions lost, but who's counting? [effects of stock market crash] J. A. Byrne. il *Bus Week* p66+ N 16 '87

Accounting
"Better than free". L. Jereski. il *Forbes* 139:224 Je 15 '87

Stock purchase warrants

Arresting new warrants [British Petroleum] S. Miller. il *Bus Week* p126 My 25 '87

How to get in on the Safeway LBO. J. M. Laderman. *Bus Week* p100 Ap 27 '87

Stock quotations

See also
    Telerate, Inc.

How's the Dow? Check it on your PC [stock quote services and software] B. Hitchings. il *Bus Week* p105 Ja 26 '87

New tools for the armchair investor. B. Kallen. il *Forbes* 139:150 Mr 23 '87

Stock ranges *See* Livestock ranges

Stock splitting *See* Stocks—Splitting

Stock tenders *See* Stocks—Tender offers

Stockbrokers *See* Brokers

Stocker, Roland, and others

Bilirubin is an antioxidant of possible physiological importance. bibl f il *Science* 235:1043-6 F 27 '87

Stocker, Terry

Why were the Aztecs and Mayas stuck in the Stone Age? Obsidian, a kind of volcanic glass, may be the answer. *Earth Sci* 40:32 Summ '87

Stockey, Gregg

This country life [photographs] il *Ctry J* 14:80 Jl '87

Stockhausen, Karlheinz, 1928-
           about

Unfinished symphonies. C. Clay. il pors *Esquire* 107:106-9 My '87

Stockholders

See also
    Black stockholders
    Employees as stockholders
    Proxies

Are shareholders cheated by LBOs? G. Hector. il *Fortune* 115:98-100+ Ja 19 '87

The battle for corporate control [cover story] B. Nussbaum and J. H. Dobrzynski. il *Bus Week* p102-9 My 18 '87

Battling your broker gets harder [Supreme Court upholds arbitration] D. P. Wiener. il *U S News World Rep* 102:51 Je 22 '87

The burned, the baffled, the calm: tales of eight investors [post crash assessment] M. Frons. il *Bus Week* p102+ N 23 '87

Can't sue your broker? It's no big loss [Supreme Court decision upholds arbitration] D. Zigas. il *Bus Week* p128 Je 22 '87

Did you agree not to sue? [use of arbitration to settle broker-stockholder disputes] *U S News World Rep* 103:45 N 9 '87

Educating the managers [shareholder challenges at Union Enterprises Ltd. and Bow Valley Industries Ltd. of Canada] A. Shortell. il *Macleans* 100:28-9 S 28 '87

How to avoid a rogue broker. D. R. Katz. il *Esquire* 108:39-40 Ag '87

How to settle a beef with your broker. *Money* 16:13 Ap '87

If you want to know, just ask [seeking information from corporations] M. Schiffres. il *U S News World Rep* 102:55 Ap 13 '87

Insider trading's victims [investors rush to court] B. Powell and C. Friday. il *Newsweek* 109:40-1 Ap 6 '87

Insights. S. Blotnick. See issues of Forbes beginning July 28, 1986

Is it safe to go back in the boardroom? [exempting directors from liability] B. Powell. il *Newsweek* 109:45-6 My 4 '87

Keeping your broker under control. M. Hodge. il *50 Plus* 27:50-2 S '87

A lifeboat, just in case: what to do if the market collapses. L. Wiener. il *U S News World Rep* 103:61 Ag 31 '87

Pen pals. *New Yorker* 63:25-7 Mr 2 '87

Protecting your securities investment. *Consum Res Mag* 70:33-5 O '87

Stockholders—*cont.*

Riding the wild bull [successful individual investors] S. Koepp. il *Time* 130:50-2 Jl 27 '87

The SEC rattles its saber: trying to give small stockholders a break. C. Yang. *Bus Week* p96 S 28 '87

A shareholder revolt at Telecom. B. Dumaine. il por *Fortune* 115:58-60 Mr 2 '87

Shareholders aren't just rolling over anymore. C. Power. il *Bus Week* p32-3 Ap 27 '87

Small investors and the crash. C. Friday. il *Newsweek* 110:50-1 D 21 '87

Sue your stockbroker? You can't, you know [upcoming Supreme Court ruling] S. Weiss. il *Bus Week* p75-6 Mr 2 '87

Tales of bull market geniuses [cover story] M. Sivy. il *Money* 16:50-6+ Ap '87

This shareholder uprising may give Pan Am a tailwind. G. G. Marcial. por *Bus Week* p130 My 25 '87

The U.S. news 100: market bonanzas [cover story; special section] il *U S News World Rep* 103:48-57+ Jl 6 '87

We wuz robbed [arbitration in broker-customer cases] R. L. Stern. il *Forbes* 140:60-1 D 28 '87

What to do if your broker leads you astray. T. Segal. il *Bus Week* p90 F 2 '87

When you're burned by your broker. il *Changing Times* 41:77-80+ Ap '87

Why stockbrokers sleep at night [Supreme Court upholds binding arbitration] M. Meyer. il *Money* 16:105-8+ Jl '87

Stockholm (Sweden)

Galleries and museums

A new home for the Wasa. J. Richards-Williams. il *Hist Today* 37:2-3 Ja '87

Hotels, motels, etc.

Smooth sailing in Stockholm [Victory Hotel] G. McTigue. il *Travel Holiday* 168:18 D '87

Stocking of streams, lakes, etc. *See* Fish culture

Stockpiling

See also

Helium—Reserves

Stocks

See also

Banks and banking—Securities handling

Brokers

Colleges and universities—Investments

Dividends

Penny stocks

Preferred stocks

Speculation

Stock exchanges

Stockholders

Television broadcasting—Financial programs

See also subhead Securities under various subjects

100 U.S.-traded foreign stocks. il *Forbes* 140:158+ Jl 27 '87

Choosing dividends or price. L. Wiener. il *U S News World Rep* 103:60-1 S 7 '87

How the stock market works. L. Eskin. il *Sch Update* 120:6-7 D 18 '87

How to buy foreign stocks. P. Sherrid. il *U S News World Rep* 102:54+ My 11 '87

Inside Wall Street. G. G. Marcial. See issues of Business Week

Insights. S. Blotnick. See issues of Forbes beginning July 28, 1986

Reflections of an individual investor. P. D. Nigro. il *USA Today (Periodical)* 116:27-8 N '87

Streetwalker. See issues of Forbes

That rare thing, an investment book worth reading [views of M. Talley] R. Brady. il por *Nations Bus* 75:76 N '87

To win, be willing to make mistakes [interview with M. D. Talley] il por *U S News World Rep* 103:58 Ag 10 '87

Trading on foreign soil. D. R. Katz. il *Esquire* 107:39-40 Ja '87

Wall Street letter. See issues of Money through December 1987

Buybacks

See Stocks—Repurchase

Dollar cost averaging

It can pay to buy stock a bit at a time. G. Weiss. il *Bus Week* p156-7 My 18 '87

Taking the plunge: a plan for all seasons. M. Brill. il *Changing Times* 41:31-2 Ap '87

Insider trading

See Insider trading

Laws and regulations

See Securities—Laws and regulations

Margin buying

The bottom line on margins [views of A. Frank] D. R. Katz. il por *Esquire* 108:45-6 Jl '87

The breaks of buying on margin. B. Hitchings. il *Bus Week* p120 Je 1 '87

Here's how they work. *U S News World Rep* 103:34 N 9 '87

Leveraging your mutual funds. B. Kallen. il *Forbes* 139:161-2 Ap 6 '87

Marketing

See also

Specialists (Stock exchange firms)

Stocks—Repurchase

Arriving soon: the biggest-ever IPO [Conrail initial public offering] il *Fortune* 115:9 Mr 30 '87

A baby boom in stocks [initial public offerings] J. B. Quinn. il *Newsweek* 110:61 S 14 '87

The banks head for the Street. S. Bartlett. il *Bus Week* p98 Jl 13 '87

Blair's Morty Davis: the prince of going public. P. Finch. il por *Bus Week* p176+ N 2 '87

Carnival Cruise Lines is making waves. G. DeGeorge. il *Bus Week* p34 Jl 6 '87

Conrail sale aids bankers. M. A. Fortune. *Black Enterp* 17:22 Ap '87

The Conrail sale: how much is it worth? C. Hawkins and C. S. Eklund. il *Bus Week* p78+ Mr 23 '87

Dick Clark grows up [cover story] A. Snyder. il pors *Channels* 7:28-31+ My '87

Don't leap at these reverse LBOs [new public offerings] il *Money* 16:13 Jl '87

Entrepreneurs are cashing in while the price is right [initial public offerings] K. R. Sheets. *U S News World Rep* 102:42 Je 22 '87

Fast-cash express [initial public offering market] A. Miller and C. Friday. il *Newsweek* 109:36-7 Ja 12 '87

Gambling on initial public offerings. J. P. Newport, Jr. il *Fortune* 116:187-8+ O 26 '87

Hard times for small stocks [new issues in Canada] A. Shortell. il *Macleans* 100:36-7 O 26 '87

IPOs: it can pay to have second thoughts first [initial public offerings] S. Weiss. il *Bus Week* p112 Ap 13 '87

IPOs: now only the best and the brightest need apply [case of Javelin Software Corp.] K. H. Hammonds. il *Bus Week* p37-8 N 30 '87

Is this any way to sell a railroad? [Conrail's public offering] L. Smith. il *Fortune* 115:91-2+ My 25 '87

Lorenzo turns to terra firma [Jet Capital sale] por *Bus Week* p34 S 7 '87

Massacre [new issues] R. Stern and C. M. Bartlett, Jr. il *Forbes* 140:56-7+ D 14 '87

The never-sleeping precedent setter [Citicorp stock issue] il *Fortune* 116:7 S 14 '87

New issues: who's hot, who's not. R. L. Stern and Z. Lazarevic. il *Forbes* 139:82-4+ Mr 9 '87

Pinker than the pinks? [E. McLaughlin's stock strategy concentrates on busted initial public offerings and pink sheet stocks] por *Forbes* 140:146-7 D 28 '87

The price of quick riches [J. Bildner & Sons venture into new issues market] R. Simon. il por *Forbes* 140:112+ S 21 '87

A random walk through Euclid [spinoff subsidiaries in the new issues market] R. Phalon. il *Forbes* 140:170+ S 21 '87

Schwab's stock offering looks like a winner . . . G. Weiss. il *Bus Week* p77 Ag 17 '87

A surprise welcome for bank issues [new issues] F. A. Miller. il *Bus Week* p93 S 28 '87

The thrills and chills of new issues. G. Weiss. il *Bus Week* p82-3 Ag 10 '87

The unlikely kings of IPOs [closed-end funds] G. Weiss. il *Bus Week* p60 Jl 27 '87

Wall Street isn't buying Spiegel's high-gloss look. M. D. Oneal. il *Bus Week* p62 O 19 '87

New issues

See Stocks—Marketing

Over-the-counter trading

See Over-the-counter securities markets

Price-earnings ratios

Back in sync? [Treasury bond yields and price-earnings ratios] E. A. Finn, Jr. *Forbes* 140:34-5 N 16 '87

Big, medium or small cap? D. N. Dreman. il *Forbes* 140:215 O 19 '87

A cellar of stocks now ripe for buying [views of T. Hitschler] G. G. Marcial. il por *Bus Week* p114 D 7 '87

Stocks—Price-earnings ratios—*cont.*

The cheapest stocks in the world. J. Edgerton and J. E. Goodman. il *Money* 16:7 N '87

A cloud over stock prices [corporate profits] D. Pauly. il *Newsweek* 109:50 Mr 16 '87

Compared to what? [small company growth stocks] M. Kuntz. il *Forbes* 139:154 F 23 '87

Contingency plan. D. N. Dreman. il *Forbes* 139:120-1 Ap 20 '87

Fifty nifties. S. Lee. il *Forbes* 140:172 Jl 27 '87

Growth stocks the market left behind. A. E. Serwer. il *Fortune* 116:174 N 9 '87

High time. M. Ozanian. il *Forbes* 139:178 Ap 6 '87

Japan's newest import: U.S. equities. P. Fuhrman. il *Forbes* 139:43 Ja 12 '87

New issues: who's hot, who's not. R. L. Stern and Z. Lazarevic. il *Forbes* 139:82-4+ Mr 9 '87

A not-so-modest confession [low-P/E strategy] D. N. Dreman. il *Forbes* 139:118 Je 29 '87

Placing your bets on earnings surprises. J. Edgerton and J. E. Goodman. il *Money* 16:7 Ap '87

Price-earnings ratios: what may not meet the eye. T. Segal. il *Bus Week* p84 Ag 10 '87

The price of growth. M. Ozanian. il *Forbes* 140:232+ O 5 '87

Stock prices: getting scary. J. J. Curran. il *Fortune* 116:125-6 S 14 '87

Stocks: IBM, CBS, RJR and 37 other top earners for 1988. il *Money* 16:30 D '87

Upward bias. M. Ozanian. il *Forbes* 139:186+ Je 1 '87

What's propelling the market? Big, fat earnings. J. M. Laderman. il *Bus Week* p59-61 Jl 6 '87

What's your multiple? [mutual funds] M. Kuntz. il *Forbes* 139:190 Je 1 '87

When to pull the plug. il *Fortune* 116 Sp Issue:16 Fall '87

Price forecasting

The 2% rule. K. L. Fisher. il *Forbes* 140:258 D 14 '87

Ace analyst Robert Prechter says when skirts rise, so does the stock market—no bull [Elliott Wave theorist newsletter] L. Aitken. il pors *People Wkly* 27:42-4 My 11 '87

After the panic: what to do about stocks now. F. W. Frailey. il *Changing Times* 41:63-4+ D '87

Après nous le déluge. M. Hulbert. il *Forbes* 140:242 N 2 '87

Are any stocks still worth buying? [interview with J. Farrell] A. E. Serwer. il por *Fortune* 116:100 Ag 31 '87

Are you ready to go global? [foreign stocks] J. Mendes. il *Fortune* 116 Sp Issue:71-2+ Fall '87

As risky as a crapshoot [buying stock in a bankrupt firm] A. Gabor. il *U S News World Rep* 102:65 Ap 27 '87

Back to basics. K. L. Fisher. il *Forbes* 139:148 F 9 '87

Bear? Or bull? [Dow Theory] M. Hulbert. il *Forbes* 140:256 N 30 '87

The bears aren't in charge—yet. G. Weiss and J. M. Laderman. il *Bus Week* p109 Je 1 '87

Being quite contrary could make your garden grow [growth stocks] C. Farrell. il *Bus Week* p127+ D 28 '87-Ja 4 '88

Best investment moves to make now. J. Bodnar. il *Changing Times* 41:24-9 Jl '87

The best stocks for the tricky year ahead. P. A. Dreyfus. il *Money* 16:87-8+ Ja '87

Betting on a better mousetrap [influence of new products on company stocks] J. Crudele. il *N Y* 20:16+ S 28 '87

Big is beautiful. T. Jaffe. il *Forbes* 139 Ann Directory:330 Ap 27 '87

A big new plus for small stocks. P. Nulty. il *Fortune* 116:173-4 D 21 '87

The big portfolios. S. Lee. See issues of Forbes beginning July 2, 1984

The biggest bull market. R. J. Samuelson. il *Newsweek* 109:57 Ap 20 '87

Bird-in-hand theory [dividend discount valuation] M. Ozanian. il *Forbes* 139:104+ F 23 '87

Bottom fishing for value when all else fails. A. E. Serwer. il *Fortune* 116:103 Jl 6 '87

A brash young investing champ gets rich by defying old rules [D. Ryan] G. Anrig, Jr. il por *Money* 16:140 Ag '87

Bright prospects for shadow stocks. J. Edgerton and others. il *Money* 16:7 Ag '87

Bull in bull markets. K. L. Fisher. il *Forbes* 139:186 Ap 6 '87

The bull market may be in for a correction—but not a crash [views of James R. Solloway] G. Koretz. il *Bus Week* p22 Ap 27 '87

The bull turns 5—and roars on. J. Egan. il *U S News World Rep* 103:54-5 Ag 10 '87

Catching the upswing in domestic manufacturing. J. E. Goodman and W. L. Updegrave. il *Money* 16:7 Mr '87

Caution and portfolio pruning [post-crash strategies] il *U S News World Rep* 103:33-4 N 9 '87

The champion market forecaster [R. Prechter's Elliott Wave theorist] M. A. Elliott. il por *Fortune* 115:75 Ja 5 '87

Champions of cost cutting [bottom line growth stocks] J. Edgerton and others. il *Money* 16:7 My '87

Chartists [R. Prechter's Elliott Wave theorist] J. K. Glassman. *New Repub* 196:8-10 Ap 6 '87

Cheapskates in a pricey stock market [value investing] B. D. Fromson. il *Fortune* 116 Sp Issue:41-2+ Fall '87

A checklist for stock market prognosticators [cover story] G. Morgenson. il *Forbes* 139:110-14 My 4 '87

The contrarian. D. N. Dreman. See alternate issues of Forbes

Danger points. J. Crudele. il *N Y* 20:24+ O 26 '87

Defensive investing in an overwrought market. J. Edgerton and others. *Money* 16:7 F '87

Don't climb off the bull yet. J. J. Curran. il *Fortune* 116:195-6+ Ag 3 '87

The doom merchants. J. Crudele. il *N Y* 20:19+ Ag 31 '87

Even in good times, it pays to be cautious. R. Brady. il *Nations Bus* 75:55 Ap '87

A fan of smokestack America [interview with C. Clough] A. E. Serwer. il por *Fortune* 116:192 O 26 '87

Fancying the Rust Belt and the oil patch [interview with S. Salvigsen] A. E. Serwer. il por *Fortune* 116:112 Jl 20 '87

Fear of heights. S. Blotnick. il *Forbes* 139:174 Mr 9 '87

Fire that computer. P. Newcomb and M. Ozanian. il *Forbes* 140:122-3 Ag 10 '87

The forces driving stocks ever higher. J. J. Curran. il *Fortune* 115:54-8+ Mr 30 '87

The Fortune investment challenge: who can make the most of $100,000? il *Fortune* 116 Sp Issue:175-91 Fall '87

Four ways to tame this bear market. J. Edgerton. il *Money* 16:145-6 D '87

Fred Alger is high on the 'one-world' economy. G. G. Marcial. il por *Bus Week* p83 Ja 19 '87

The game isn't over for stocks. M. Meyer. il *Money* 16:97-8+ D '87

Giving stocks a 'rational value' [views of Charles C. Hickox and Parry v. S. Jones of Ashland Management] G. G. Marcial. *Bus Week* p136 My 11 '87.

Going hunting for sitting ducks [takeover targets] J. Edgerton and J. E. Goodman. il *Money* 16:7 Je '87

A Grahamite finds value in the rubble [interview with M. Gabelli] J. P. Newport, Jr. il por *Fortune* 116:212 N 23 '87

Growth stocks prosper in the new year [interview with portfolio manager L. Wang of Equitable Life Assurance] A. E. Serwer. il por *Fortune* 115:114 F 2 '87

Guarding against a 24% decline. M. Sivy. il *Money* 16:51-2 Jl '87

A guru gives the bear just a 'few months' to live [views of J. Templeton] G. G. Marcial. por *Bus Week* p188 N 16 '87

The guru who saw a 2000 Dow [R. Prechter's Elliott Wave theorist newsletter] A. Miller. il por *Newsweek* 109:40+ Ja 19 '87

Has the bull market hit its peak? J. Rachlin and D. P. Wiener. il *U S News World Rep* 102:48-9 Je 15 '87

Hidden gems in a high market [interview with P. Hoffmann] A. E. Serwer. il por *Fortune* 115:126 My 25 '87

His time horizon is long [interview with R. Foulkes of World International Growth Portfolio] M. McFadden. il por *Fortune* 115:20 Ja 5 '87

A hot seer sees the Dow at 3000 [views of A. Gray] G. G. Marcial. *Bus Week* p62 Ag 10 '87

How do you make money in a runaway market? (Very carefully) [cover story; special section] il *Money* 16:48-52+ Mr '87

How healthy is the bull? M. Hulbert. por *Forbes* 140:308 S 7 '87

How high the bull? R. D. Hylton. il *Black Enterp* 18:49-50+ N '87

Stocks—Price forecasting—*cont.*

How ripe for a crash? S. Koepp. il *Time* 130:44-6 O 5 '87

How to evaluate a stock tip. L. Meisler. il *Work Woman* 12:40 F '87

How to tell if the bear is back. M. Schiffres. il *Changing Times* 41:67+ N '87

If a correction comes, it may be short and sweet. J. M. Laderman. il *Bus Week* p71 Ap 6 '87

Inside Wall Street: how bulls and bears are playing the crash. G. G. Marcial. il *Bus Week* p56 N 2 '87

Inside Wall Street: these pros have already started betting on a rebound [stock market crash] G. G. Marcial. il por *Bus Week* p44 N 9 '87

Investment challenge: surveying the damage. J. Mendes. il *Fortune* 116:176+ D 7 '87

Is Dean LeBaron worried? A little. A. Beam. il por *Bus Week* p128 My 25 '87

Is this the beginning of the end for the bull? R. Brady. il *Nations Bus* 75:72 Jl '87

It looks like a year for long-distance runners. J. M. Laderman. il *Bus Week* p116-18 D 28 '87-Ja 4 '88

It's a hit and miss business [forecaster J. E. Granville] il por *U S News World Rep* 103:84 S 28 '87

It's all relative [using relative yield as forecasting tool; views of R. Newell] J. Heins. il por *Forbes* 140:54-5 Jl 27 '87

A jock shows how to scout for small stocks that can score [J. Rogers] D. M. Topolnicki. il por *Money* 16:224 My '87

Judging whether stocks are overvalued. J. Rachlin. il *U S News World Rep* 102:60-1 Mr 23 '87

Lagging laggards [losers-will-be-winners theory] M. Ozanian and T. Quinn. il *Forbes* 139:40-1 Ja 12 '87

Learning to live with the bear [post crash outlook] J. J. Curran. il *Fortune* 116:66-8 N 23 '87

Little big stocks [obscure stocks] J. Crudele. il *N Y* 20:19+ S 7 '87

Losers you can love. J. Kosnett. il *Changing Times* 41:35-8+ N '87

The market may be set for a pause that refreshes. S. Weiss. il *Bus Week* p90 Mr 9 '87

The market tries to find a bottom. J. Egan. il *U S News World Rep* 103:72 D 14 '87

Maybe it's 1928 again [interview with P. A. Fisher] T. Jaffe. por *Forbes* 140:126+ N 30 '87

Medium is beautiful [stocks with medium market capitalizations] K. L. Fisher. il *Forbes* 140:134 Ag 24 '87

A message from Ben Graham. M. Schifrin. *Forbes* 140:258 N 30 '87

New kick in the bull market. J. J. Curran. il *Fortune* 115:157-8+ My 11 '87

The newest seer now predicts a bear market rally (what a relief!) [E. Garzarelli] G. Anrig, Jr. il por *Money* 16:232 D '87

No 1929 in sight [views of J. E. Maack] R. Brady. il por *Nations Bus* 75:86 O '87

An open guessing game. R. Brady. il *Nations Bus* 75:61+ Ja '87

A patient card player's picks [interview with H. Hutzler] J. P. Newport, Jr. il por *Fortune* 116:176 N 9 '87

Pinker than the pinks? [E. McLaughlin's stock strategy concentrates on busted initial public offerings and pink sheet stocks] por *Forbes* 140:146-7 D 28 '87

Pirouetting ahead of the market [interview with M. Straus] A. E. Serwer. por *Fortune* 115:158 Je 8 '87

Placing your bets in '87. J. B. Quinn. il *Newsweek* 109:44 Ja 5 '87

Profiting from neglected growth stocks. J. Edgerton and others. il *Money* 16:7 O '87

Promising industries for investors. B. Dumaine. il *Fortune* 116 Sp Issue:136-8+ Fall '87

A promising posse of Lone Star stocks. J. Mendes. *Fortune* 116:128 S 14 '87

Putting his money where the trends are [interview with N. Miller of Chase Manhattan's Intermediate Cap Growth Fund] A. E. Serwer. il por *Fortune* 115:174 Je 22 '87

Rating the new market timers [money managers timing the market with mutual funds] J. Edgerton. il *Money* 16:117-20+ Mr '87

Regressing to the mean? [A. Frank's picks for Prudent speculator] M. Hulbert. il *Forbes* 140:262 D 14 '87

Revival in the Rust Belt. J. Edgerton. il *Money* 16:77-8+ Jl '87

Scary times on Wall Street. R. Brady. il *Nations Bus* 75:63-4 F '87

Sectors that still may surge. J. J. Curran. il *Fortune* 116:99-100 Ag 17 '87

The see-sawing Dow doesn't scare Peter Lynch. G. G. Marcial. por *Bus Week* p108 O 26 '87

Seeing value in stocks that few investors will touch [contrarians] J. E. Goodman and E. Schurenberg. il *Money* 16:8 D '87

"Sell," they say [technical analysis] P. Brimelow. il *Forbes* 140:44+ D 14 '87

Shares to make your money bloom [Greg Smith's picks] J. Egan. il *U S News World Rep* 102:51 Ja 12 '87

Shearson's summer stocks ['uncommon values' list] G. Weiss. *Bus Week* p124 Jl 20 '87

Smaller companies could take off—at last [inflation adjusted] J. Mendes. il *Fortune* 115:110+ Mr 16 '87

Sounds good . . . [theory that small company stocks outperform large company stocks in the long term] R. Simon. il *Forbes* 140:168 Jl 27 '87

A spate of earnings surprises. J. Egan. il *U S News World Rep* 102:63 My 18 '87

Sticking with big-company stocks [interview with P. Anderson] A. E. Serwer. por *Fortune* 116:200 O 12 '87

The stock market catches a big wave [R. Prechter's Elliott Wave theorist] il por *Discover* 8:12 Mr '87

Stock pros reveal their best ways to tell when to sell. *Money* 16:13 My '87

Stock trends. A. C. Brown. See issues of Forbes

Stocks even a skeptic can love [views of S. M. Black of Delphi Management] C. Farrell. *Bus Week* p69 F 2 '87

Stocks for a difficult market [interview with S. Einhorn] A. E. Serwer. il por *Fortune* 116:176 D 21 '87

Stocks have started to stumble. J. J. Curran. il *Fortune* 116 Sp Issue:12-14+ Fall '87

Stocks that still look good. J. J. Curran. il *Fortune* 115:105-6+ F 16 '87

Strictly by the numbers [Disciplined Investment Advisors Inc.] C. Siler. il por *Forbes* 140:184+ N 2 '87

Strong currencies signal hot spots for trading. B. Riemer. il *Bus Week* p148-50 D 28 '87-Ja 4 '88

A successful balancing act [interview with P. Bannan] A. E. Serwer. il por *Fortune* 116:180 D 7 '87

Suddenly, it's fashionable to go against the grain [contrarians] J. M. Laderman. il *Bus Week* p108-9 D 7 '87

Summer rally? M. Hulbert. por *Forbes* 140:470 Jl 13 '87

Taking a flyer on companies that are still in the cellar. G. G. Marcial. il *Bus Week* p134-5 D 28 '87-Ja 4 '88

Tales of bull market geniuses [cover story] M. Sivy. il *Money* 16:50-6+ Ap '87

A talk with Philip Fisher. T. Jaffe. *Forbes* 140:41+ O 19 '87

Ten favorites. M. Ozanian and S. Ramos. il *Forbes* 140:94+ D 28 '87

Ten terrible calls in 1986. J. J. Curran. il *Fortune* 115:123-4+ Ja 19 '87

There are still some bargains left in foreign stocks. J. Templeman. il *Bus Week* p62 Jl 6 '87

Think it's bargain-hunting time? Take it slow. J. M. Laderman. il *Bus Week* p178-9 N 16 '87

This bull sees Japanese cash driving up the Dow to 3500 [views of J. Feshbach] R. McNatt. il por *Money* 16:186 O '87

This early bear is catching worms [views of W. L. Twiste] G. G. Marcial. *Bus Week* p118 N 23 '87

This moneyman isn't yelling 'sell' [T. B. Kelley] G. G. Marcial. *Bus Week* p98 S 28 '87

This stock picker just follows a few homespun rules. G. G. Marcial. por *Bus Week* p113 My 4 '87

Three experts who buck the bears [views of Robert Prechter, Joseph Barthel and Mark Leibovit] G. G. Marcial. *Bus Week* p130 My 25 '87

Time to get out of the market? [cover story; special section] il *U S News World Rep* 103:56-61 Ag 31 '87

To win in this uncertain year, go for total return. W. L. Updegrave. il *Money* 16:54-7 Ja '87

An unending quest for value [interview with A. Snyder] A. E. Serwer. il por *Fortune* 115:114 Mr 16 '87

Updating the investment challenge: five out of six players lead the S&P 500. M. McFadden. il *Fortune* 115:110-11 F 16 '87

Updating the investment challenge: for no. 1 Shearson, a big jump on the market. T. Paré. il *Fortune* 115:166-7 My 11 '87

Updating the investment challenge: who has made $100,000 grow most. T. Paré. il *Fortune* 116:104-5 Ag 17 '87

Stocks—Price forecasting—*cont.*

A value seeker says there's plenty left [interview with K. Simons] A. E. Serwer. il por *Fortune* 116:200 Ag 3 '87

Venturing abroad [data bases tracking foreign stocks] il *Forbes* 139:112 Ap 20 '87

Wall Street ponders the continuing dearth of dividends . . . and wonders how long the merger boom can carry the ball. G. Koretz. il *Bus Week* p16+ Ag 3 '87

Wall Street's new pet: the big corporate kitty. B. Nussbaum. il *Bus Week* p109+ D 7 '87

Watching the bull through a technician's eyes [technical analysts] J. M. Laderman. il *Bus Week* p88-9 S 28 '87

Weathering the slump with Fred Adler. D. Machan. il pors *Forbes* 140:228+ N 30 '87

What goes up . . . K. L. Fisher. il *Forbes* 139:266 Je 15 '87

What the Boesky scandal means to you and your money [takeover stocks] J. Edgerton. il *Money* 16:64-7 Ja '87

When to invest in a battered stock. il *Bus Week* p162-3 Je 22 '87

Where Kidder's brokers bet [secondary stocks] G. G. Marcial. *Bus Week* p78 Ag 3 '87

Where pros are fishing in the wake of the crash [takeover stocks] G. G. Marcial. il *Bus Week* p136 N 30 '87

Where your bucks should stop over there [foreign securities] P. A. Dreyfus. il *Money* 16:131-2+ Ja '87

Which blue chips look best now. A. E. Serwer. il *Fortune* 116:205+ N 23 '87

Who needs a one-way ticket? [market timing letters] M. Hulbert. il *Forbes* 140:244 O 5 '87

A world investor's favorite markets [interview with N. Fachler] J. Mendes. il por *Fortune* 116:130 S 14 '87

Price indexes and averages

See also
> Index funds
> Program trading (Securities)
> Stock index futures
> Stock index options
> Stock market crash, 1987

Are bonds calling a turn? J. Crudele. il *N Y* 20:16+ My 11 '87

As the Dow go-gos over 2,000. J. Rachlin. il *U S News World Rep* 102:48+ Ja 19 '87

A bad case of nerves [April's market jolts] S. Bartlett. il *Bus Week* p30-2 Ap 27 '87

A bang-bang birthday [fifth anniversary of bull market] G. J. Church. il *Time* 130:36-8 Ag 24 '87

The bears may be taking the wrong trail. J. M. Laderman. il *Bus Week* p100-1+ O 19 '87

Bull market stampede. T. Tedesco. il *Macleans* 100:26 F 9 '87

The bull market takes a hit [effect of rising interest rates] J. M. Laderman. il *Bus Week* p143 S 14 '87

The bull tops 2000 [Dow Jones average] G. Russell. il *Time* 129:48-50 Ja 19 '87

Bulls: the pause that refreshes? D. P. Wiener. il *U S News World Rep* 103:12 S 14 '87

A case of the jitters [financial markets] L. Martz. il *Newsweek* 109:18-22+ My 4 '87

Casino Royale [January 23, 1986] J. J. Cramer. *New Repub* 196:10-11 F 16 '87

Coping with the markets [April jitters] B. Powell. il *Newsweek* 109:54 Ap 27 '87

The correction may be just what the doctor ordered. J. M. Laderman. il *Bus Week* p43 My 11 '87

Death wishes [executive health and stock market analysis] J. Crudele. il *N Y* 20:14 Jl 27 '87

An effect-ive stock strategy [stock market in January] il *Money* 16:12 D '87

Facts stranger than fiction [interview with P. E. Erdman] il por *U S News World Rep* 102:52 F 9 '87

The Fearless Fosdicks just won't quit [rising Dow] J. Egan. il *U S News World Rep* 103:10 Ag 24 '87

The Forbes/Wilshire 5000 review. See issues of Forbes

Hemlines, headlines, holidays: Wall Street's odd indicators. G. Weiss. il *Bus Week* p116-17 S 7 '87

How does the Street spell relief? G-r-e-e-n-s-p-a-n. S. Weiss. il por *Bus Week* p122-3 Je 22 '87

How the bull market has enriched the economy. J. Berger and N. Jonas. il *Bus Week* p54-5 Ag 10 '87

How to read the stock tables. L. Eskin. il *Sch Update* 120:6-7 D 18 '87

How's the market? It depends on the yardstick. J. M. Laderman. il *Bus Week* p124-5 S 21 '87

The incredible bull market just won't quit. J. Egan. il *U S News World Rep* 102:44-5 Ap 13 '87

Is the Fed behind the stock boom? D. Pauly. il *Newsweek* 109:36-7 Ja 26 '87

Is the party almost over? [cover story; special section] il *Newsweek* 110:50-6+ O 26 '87

Is Wall Street right? [difference of opinion with government officials over state of the economy] J. Egan. il *U S News World Rep* 103:20-1 O 26 '87

Kabuki theater on Wall Street. J. Egan. il *U S News World Rep* 103:41-2 Ag 17 '87

Looking at Japan's stock market through Japanese eyes . . . casts light on Wall Street's raging bull. G. Koretz. il *Bus Week* p26 S 14 '87

The manic stock market. M. Schiffres. il *U S News World Rep* 102:53 F 2 '87

The market's latest bull run. J. Schwartz. il *Newsweek* 110:32 Ag 24 '87

The next panic: fear and trembling on Wall Street. L. J. Davis. il *Harpers* 274:35-9+ My '87

Now that's a bull market. il *Changing Times* 41:44-5 Ap '87

The panic on Wall Street. T. Fennell. il *Macleans* 100:36-8 O 26 '87

A pig market? *Newsweek* 109:49 F 2 '87

Playing politics on Wall Street. J. Crudele. il *N Y* 20:16+ Ag 10 '87

The rampaging bull on Wall Street. T. Tedesco. il *Macleans* 100:32 Ag 24 '87

Riding the wild bull [successful individual investors] S. Koepp. il *Time* 130:50-2 Jl 27 '87

The sayonara scenario: worry over a Japanese pullout. J. Crudele. il *N Y* 20:37 S 21 '87

The setting sun [effect of Japanese market collapse] D. N. Dreman. il *Forbes* 140:130 Ag 24 '87

The shrug market [reaction to Iranian arms scandal] J. K. Glassman. *New Repub* 196:15-16 Ja 5-12 '87

Statistical spotlight. See issues of Forbes

The stock market's breathtakingly rapid rise. M. S. Forbes, Jr. il *Forbes* 140:25 S 7 '87

Stocks. il *Money* 16:46+ F '87

A storm in the markets. il *Macleans* 100:28-9 Ap 13 '87

Sunrise, sunset. *Nation* 244:455-6 Ap 11 '87

That crazy stock market [Dow Jones average] G. Russell. il *Time* 129:58 F 2 '87

This gender gap bodes well for Wall Street [spread between male and female unemployment as stock market indicator; research by Peter L. Bernstein] G. Koretz. il *Bus Week* p34 My 18 '87

Time to split the Dow? D. Pauly. il *Newsweek* 109:55 Mr 2 '87

Wall Street's happy new year may have just begun [January rally] J. M. Laderman. il *Bus Week* p78-9 Ja 19 '87

Wall Street's October massacre. G. Bock. il *Time* 130:32-3 O 26 '87

The way we were at 1000 [1972] il *Time* 129:50 Ja 19 '87

What the rally really means [massive revaluation of corporate assets; special section] il *Bus Week* p58-63 F 2 '87

What's behind day-end stock rises? [views of Lawrence Harris] il *USA Today (Periodical)* 116:7 D '87

What's making the market swing so wildly [program traders using the Major Market Index] J. M. Laderman and J. N. Frank. il *Bus Week* p72-3 F 9 '87

Why New York's eyes are glued to the Tokyo market. J. M. Laderman. il *Bus Week* p70-1 Ag 3 '87

Why the bad news wasn't bad for the market [insider trading scandal] G. Weiss. il *Bus Week* p31 Mr 2 '87

Why the bull is such a long-distance runner. J. M. Laderman. il *Bus Week* p71 Ag 24 '87

The yen to spend [Japanese dumping of U.S. equity sends Dow down] P. Fuhrman. *Forbes* 139:126 Ap 20 '87

Price-sales ratios

Betting on the Dow—partly. K. L. Fisher. il *Forbes* 139:170 Mr 9 '87

How to take—and keep—unfair advantage. K. L. Fisher. il *Forbes* 140 Sp Issue:400 O 26 '87

A market Prophet who ignores profits [interview with PSR prophet editor M. Brill] A. E. Serwer. il por *Fortune* 116:106 Ag 17 '87

Prices

See also
> Stocks—Dollar cost averaging

The 100 cheapest foreign stocks. il *Forbes* 140:112-14 Jl 27 '87

Are stocks too high? [cover story] J. J. Curran. il pors *Fortune* 116:28-30+ S 28 '87

Stocks—Prices—*cont.*

Bag a bargain. K. L. Fisher. il *Forbes* 139:300 Ja 12 '87

The best and worst stocks of 1986. J. Mendes. il *Fortune* 115:78-81 F 2 '87

Conglomerate stocks that measure up. M. McFadden. il *Fortune* 115:132 Mr 2 '87

Going global [special section] il *Money* 16:50-2+ My '87

Growth at bargain rates [emerging growth stocks] J. E. Goodman and A. Rock. il *Money* 16:7 Ja '87

Higher fliers among the 500. A. E. Serwer. il *Fortune* 115:291+ Ap 27 '87

How to spot a cheap stock. M. Sivy. il *Money* 16:131-2 Ag '87

The irrational stock market [views of Robert J. Shiller] *Sci Am* 256:60 Mr '87

A market for little guys. J. B. Quinn. il *Newsweek* 109:53 F 16 '87

Not bad [portfolio based on 1982 Forbes four hundred list] I. Chithelen. il *Forbes* 140 Sp Issue:386 O 26 '87

The stock you wish you had bought. P. Tai. il *Money* Sp Issue:12-13 Fall '87

The volatility of stock market prices. R. J. Shiller. bibl f il *Science* 235:33-7 Ja 2 '87

Public offerings
See Stocks—Marketing
Repurchase
See also
Greenmail

Buy-in. M. Ozanian. il *Forbes* 140:89 Ag 24 '87

Diary of a decision: a week in the life of Amax [A. Born's struggle to buoy his company's stock] J. R. Norman. il por *Bus Week* p118+ N 9 '87

Farewell buybacks, hello dividends. J. J. Curran. il *Fortune* 115:129-31 Mr 2 '87

Today's rejects, tomorrow's buys [strategy of W. F. Harnisch] G. G. Marcial. *Bus Week* p120 My 18 '87

Short selling
See Securities—Short selling
Splitting

How to double your shares without spending a dime. G. Weiss. il *Bus Week* p122 Mr 9 '87

Time to split the Dow? D. Pauly. il *Newsweek* 109:55 Mr 2 '87

Stop orders

Put a stop to those big losses. J. Egan. il *U S News World Rep* 102:61 Mr 23 '87

Stop orders: they are cleavers, not scalpels, but they cut losses. M. Meyer. il *Money* 16:233 N '87

Taxation
See Securities—Taxation
Tender offers

The Street is fretting over 'Street sweeps'. A. Bianco. il por *Bus Week* p71-2 Ag 3 '87

Under-the-counter trading
See Under-the-counter securities
Valuation
See Corporations—Valuation
Yields

Double damned. K. L. Fisher. il *Forbes* 140:238 O 5 '87

It's all relative [using relative yield as forecasting tool; views of R. Newell] J. Heins. il por *Forbes* 140:54-5 Jl 27 '87

The low-risk path to a high-income portfolio. G. G. Marcial. il *Bus Week* p120+ D 28 '87-Ja 4 '88

Many happy returns. F. W. Frailey. il *Changing Times* 41:108-9 O '87

Mutual funds: how to figure your real return. J. Bodnar. il *Changing Times* 41:69-70 Ap '87

A neglected clue to profits [return on equity] A. E. Serwer. il *Fortune* 116 Sp Issue:55-6+ Fall '87

Sustainable yield. W. Baldwin. il *Forbes* 140:204 D 14 '87

Will Rogers was right. K. L. Fisher. il *Forbes* 140:129 Ag 10 '87

Stocks, Gun *See* Gunstocks
Stocks (Cooking)

A stock portfolio. A. Meyer. il *Mother Earth News* 103:70-3 Ja/F '87

Vegetable stocks. T. Ney. il *Rodale's Org Gard* 34:86-8+ Ja '87

Your options in soup stocks. K. Haedrich. il *Ctry J* 14:24-7 D '87

Stocksdale, Bob, 1913-
about

World-class turner. R. La Trobe-Bateman. il *Am Craft* 47:30-5 D '87/Ja '88

Stockton Press

$550 'Dictionary of economics' announced by Stockton Press [The new Palgrave] *Publ Wkly* 232:63 O 9 '87

Stockwell, Dean, 1935-
about

Dean Stockwell, the comeback champ, puts his unique brand on the movies for the third time. L. Rozen. il pors *People Wkly* 27:63-4 Je 15 '87

Stoddard, Alexandra

Make the most of your day! *McCalls* 114:76 Jl '87

Stoddart, Veronica Gould

Art. See issues of Américas

Stodden, John R.

Market focus. See issues of Aviation Week & Space Technology beginning December 1, 1986

Stoga, Alan J.

For bilateralism. *Cent Mag* 20:57 Ja/F '87

Stokes, Carl
about

Carl Stokes considering comeback in Cleveland. por *Jet* 72:24 Jl 6 '87

Stokes, Louis
about

Rep. Stokes heads House Intelligence Committee. por *Jet* 71:7 Ja 12 '87

Stokes lectures Col. North, nation on law and America. il pors *Jet* 72:28-9 Ag 3 '87

Stokes, Trudy Gallant- *See* Gallant-Stokes, Trudy
Stokes, W. Royal

Commercial fair? *Down Beat* 54:5+ S '87

Vermont and all that jazz. il *Travel Holiday* 168:14+ Ag '87

Stolle, Fred

Attack the lefty forehand. il *World Tennis* 35:20 Je '87

Be offensive. il *World Tennis* 35:31 Ag '87

Direct your delivery. il *World Tennis* 34:47 Ja '87

Elbow in for sound strokes. il *World Tennis* 35:58 S '87

Less is more. il *World Tennis* 35:36 Jl '87

Punch that door open! il por *World Tennis* 35:47 D '87

Scouting. il *World Tennis* 34:30 Ap '87

Use your whole body. il *World Tennis* 35:34 N '87

Stollenwerk, John Joseph, 1940-
about

Shoe wars: an angry American takes on Japan. *Newsweek* 109:38 Ja 26 '87

Stoller, Bryan Michael
about

Gaining exposure with funny shorts, Bryan Stoller now pants for a feature film. il por *People Wkly* 28:147 D 14 '87

Stoller, Ezra, 1916?-
about

Ezra Stoller: the architectural landscape. il *Art News* 86:160-6 N '87

Stoller, Gary

Get your reward! il *Essence* 17:22 Mr '87

Stolley, Richard B.

Sentiment straight from the saddle. il *Life* 10:19-21 Jl '87

The tales of four hunters. il *Fortune* 115:31-4 Mr 2 '87

Twin boxers: it wasn't twice the fun. il *Sports Illus* 66:77 F 2 '87

Stoltz, Eric
about

Eric Stoltz: "I've been the flavor of the week". S. Drucker. por *Vogue* 177:36 Jl '87

Eric Stoltz plays the classmate you'd most like to go out with in Some kind of wonderful. E. Miller. por *Seventeen* 46:68 F '87

Stomach
See also
Digestion
Diseases
See also
Dyspepsia
Peptic ulcers
Surgery

Stomach 'bubble': diet device not without risks. E. Zamula. il *FDA Consum* 21:28-31 Ap '87

Stomach exercises *See* Exercise
Stomach ulcers *See* Peptic ulcers
Stommen, Joan

Getting the most from substitute teachers. *Educ Dig* 52:43-5 Ap '87

Stone, Amy

Contemporary design. il *Petersens Photogr Mag* 16:38-40 Jl '87

Stone, Amy—*cont.*
Quick & easy studio portraiture. il *Petersens Photogr Mag* 15:50-3 Mr '87
Soligor 35-300mm lens. il *Petersens Photogr Mag* 16:46-7 Je '87
Starblitz flash. il *Petersens Photogr Mag* 15:64-7 F '87

Stone, Brian
Models of kingship: Arthur in medieval romance. il *Hist Today* 37:32-8 N '87

Stone, Carl
Roots of violence will remain. *World Press Rev* 34:23 O '87

Stone, Doris M., 1918-
Fields of color. il *House Gard* 159:68-77+ Ag '87

Stone, Elizabeth, 1946-
The Vatican goes to Hell. il *Omni* 9:24 S '87

Stone, Geoffrey R.
Repeating past mistakes. *Society* 24:30-2 Jl/Ag '87

Stone, I. F. (Isidor Feinstein), 1907-
Binge: end of a profligate era [cover story] *Nation* 245:469+ O 31 '87
Covert loophole. *Nation* 245:184-5 S 5 '87
Gulf—or abyss? *Nation* 244:838-9 Je 20 '87
More glazed than *glasnost. Nation* 244:240-1 F 28 '87
A new deterrent. *Nation* 244:598-9 My 9 '87
Papal metaphysics. *Nation* 245:292-3 S 26 '87
Star Wars block. *Nation* 245:508-9 N 7 '87
Wedded by hate. *Nation* 244:492-3 Ap 18 '87
Weinberger's war. *Nation* 245:364-5 O 10 '87

Stone, Isidor Feinstein *See* Stone, I. F. (Isidor Feinstein), 1907-

Stone, James
about
Tell us again, Mr. Stone. L. Jereski. il por *Forbes* 140:232+ N 30 '87

Stone, James C.
How camping helps children grow. *Educ Dig* 52:47-9 My '87

Stone, John, 1936-
A trenta-sei for John Ciardi [poem] *Am Sch* 56:203-4 Spr '87

Stone, Judith
AIDS volunteers. il *Glamour* 85:288-9+ Mr '87
Jane Pauley's charmed life. il por *McCalls* 114:152+ Ap '87
On your own. See issues of Glamour beginning February 1987

Stone, Katharine
How and why I sued my boss for sex discrimination. *Glamour* 85:228-9+ Je '87

Stone, Larry, and Snyder-Stone, Lisa
A very special home for the elderly. il *McCalls* 114:68-9 Jl '87

Stone, Laurie
Narratives: the Doris Lessing standard. il *Ms* 16:29-30+ Jl/Ag '87
The woman behind Argentina's new film hit [interview with M. L. Bemberg] *Ms* 15:14+ F '87

Stone, Lawrence
The century of revolution. il *N Y Rev Books* 34:38-43 F 26 '87
about
The hot History Department. M. Silk. il pors *N Y Times Mag* p42-3+ Ap 19 '87

Stone, Lisa Snyder- *See* Snyder-Stone, Lisa

Stone, Lois
Getting zapped by technology. por *U S News World Rep* 103:7 S 7 '87

Stone, Michael
The Algonquin faces life. il *N Y* 20:52-4+ N 2 '87
Incident at Exit 20. il pors *N Y* 20:50-4+ O 5 '87
New York Hospital on the spot: three baffling deaths jolt a proud institution. il pors *N Y* 20:40-7 Je 22 '87
Q and A on AIDS. il *N Y* 20:34-43 Mr 23 '87
Strokes of genius: Steffi Graf peaks for the U.S. Open. il pors *N Y* 20:48-52 Ag 31 '87
Trying to raise children in the city. il *N Y* 20:26-33 F 2 '87

Stone, Oliver
My brilliant career. il por *Time* 129:60 Ja 26 '87
about
The ballad of a haunted soldier. G. Peary. il por *Macleans* 100:61-2 Mr 30 '87
For his look back in anger at Vietnam, Platoon's Oliver Stone is bombarded with Oscar nominations. A. Richman. il por *People Wkly* 27:82-3+ Mr 2 '87
Oliver Stone: "I love women; they're pretty. Except some actresses are too neurotic". M. Orth. por *Vogue* 177:166+ D '87

Oliver Stone's Platoon buddies recall the war 20 years later. il por *People Wkly* 27:81-4+ My 11 '87
Platoon [film] Reviews
Am Herit il 38:12+ Jl/Ag '87. G. C. Ward
America 156:159+ F 21 '87. R. A. Blake
Christ Century 104:60-1 Ja 21 '87. J. M. Wall
Commonweal 114:17-18 Ja 16 '87. T. O'Brien
Forbes il 139:170 Ap 6 '87. A. B. Block
Forbes il 140:33 Ag 10 '87. W. Harris
Humanist il 47:41 My/Je '87. H. M. Geduld
Macleans il 100:7 Mr 16 '87. F. Bruning
Mademoiselle il 93:96+ Ap '87. R. Rosenbaum
N Y 20:78+ Ja 19 '87. D. Denby
Nation 244:54-6 Ja 17 '87. T. Rafferty
Natl Rev 39:54-7 Mr 13 '87. J. Simon
New Leader 70:22-3 Mr 9 '87. J. Gardner
New Repub 196:4+ Mr 9 '87
New Repub 196:24-5 Ja 19 '87. S. Kauffmann
New Yorker 62:94-6 Ja 12 '87. P. Kael
Newsweek il 109:57 Ja 5 '87. D. Ansen
Newsweek il 110:56 N 23 '87
People Wkly il 27:101-2+ Ap 20 '87. W. Terry
People Wkly il 27:48-50+ Mr 9 '87
People Wkly il 27:8 Ja 19 '87. R. Novak
Time il 129:54-61 Ja 26 '87. R. Corliss
U S News World Rep 102:78 Mr 2 '87. H. Evans
USA Today (Periodical) il 115:94-5 Mr '87. K. R. Hey
Point man [interview] P. McGilligan. il pors *Film Comment* 23:11-14+ Ja/F '87
Soldier's story. F. Schruers. il por *Roll Stone* p23-4+ Ja 29 '87
Wall Street [film] Reviews
Bus Week il p38-9 D 21 '87. C. Welles
Macleans il 100:46 D 28 '87. P. C. Newman
Macleans il 100:61 D 21 '87. L. O'Toole
N Y 20:87-8 D 14 '87. D. Denby
Newsweek il 110:78-9 D 14 '87. C. McGuigan
Newsweek il 110:80 D 14 '87. S. Rattner
Time il 130:76-7 Jl 20 '87. G. D. Garcia
Time il 130:82-3 D 14 '87. R. Corliss
Time il 130:53 N 2 '87

Stone, Robert, 1937-
Absence of mercy [story] il *Harpers* 275:61-8 N '87
Helping [story] *New Yorker* 63:28-38+ Je 8 '87

Stone, Roger W.
about
"They thought we were a little crazy". R. Simon. il por *Forbes* 140:50-1 S 21 '87

Stone, Sly
about
Rocker Sly Stone jailed for parole violation. *Jet* 72:17 Je 22 '87

Stone
See also
Marble
Rocks

Stone Age
See also
Stone implements and weapons

America
A Mesolithic camp in Denmark [Vaenget Nord excavation] T. D. Price and E. B. Petersen. il maps *Sci Am* 256:112-19+ Mr '87

France
The myths and perturbing realities of cannibalism. P. Shipman. il *Discover* 8:70-2+ Mr '87

Syria
Gazelle killing in Stone Age Syria [emergence of agriculture at Tell Abu Hureyra] A. J. Legge and P. A. Rowley-Conwy. il map *Sci Am* 257:88-95 Ag '87
Letters [discussion of August 1987 article, Gazelle killing in Stone Age Syria] A. J. Legge and P. A. Rowley-Conwy. *Sci Am* 257:8+ N '87

Western Europe
Early farming in northwestern Europe [Neolithic period] J. M. Howell. il map *Sci Am* 257:118-24+ N '87

Stone Center for Developmental Services and Studies *See* Wellesley College. Stone Center for Developmental Services and Studies

Stone construction
See also
Stone houses
Architecture [work of Rev. J. P. Morton at Cathedral of St. John the Divine] C. Wiseman. il *N Y* 20:122-3 S 21 '87

Stone construction—*cont.*
Design awards/competitions: Building Stone Institute 1987 Tucker Architectural Awards. il *Archit Rec* 175:76-7 N '87
Stone: new technology and design. B. Donaldson. il *Archit Rec* 175:136-45 Jl '87
Stone Container Corp.
"They thought we were a little crazy". R. Simon. il por *Forbes* 140:50-1 S 21 '87
Stone houses
Out-island builder [Eleuthera] J. B. Gans. il map *Mother Earth News* 104:48-55 Mr/Ap '87
Stone implements and weapons
Discoveries in Africa are clues to early humans. il *Earth Sci* 40:8-9 Spr '87
Earlier appearance of humans in New World [work of Barbara Purdy] il *USA Today (Periodical)* 115:12 Je '87
The first technology. N. Toth. bibl (p128) il map *Sci Am* 256:112-21 Ap '87
Flakes, breaks and the first Americans [controversy over date of human migration to North America] B. Bower. il *Sci News* 131:172-3 Mr 14 '87
Seeking hidden messages in stone tool technology [research by Harold Dibble] R. Lewin. il *Science* 236:669-70 My 8 '87
Uncovering life by an ancient lake [Olorgesailie lake basin in Kenya] B. Bower. *Sci News* 131:264 Ap 25 '87
Stone Mountain Memorial (Ga.)
A terraced tribute [Memorial Plaza] il *South Living* 22:36 N '87
Stone-Sweet, Alec
Simply delicious la belle cuisine. il por *Harpers Bazaar* 120:292+ S '87
Stone tools *See* Stone implements and weapons
Stone top tables *See* Tables
Stonecipher, Harland C.
about
Ready, fire, aim. R. Thompson. il por *Nations Bus* 75:77-8 N '87
Stonecrops *See* Sedum
Stonegate Winery
Stonegate Winery's spectacular wines: slow aging and intimations of greatness. M. Gersh. *Vogue* 177:110 Ja '87
Stonehenge (England)
The longest day. C. Murphy. il *Atlantic* 259:14+ Je '87
Stonehenge in Missouri [half-scale model at Univ. of Missouri-Rolla] il *Sky Telesc* 74:83 Jl '87
Stonemasonry *See* Stone construction
Stonepine (Carmel Valley, Calif.: Ranch) *See* Ranches—California
Stonework *See* Stone construction
Stookey, John Hoyt, 1930-
about
Why National Distillers went on the wagon. C. Power. il por *Bus Week* p78+ S 14 '87
Stop orders (Stocks) *See* Stocks—Stop orders
Stoppard, Tom
Going to bat for Britain. il por *House Gard* 159:22+ N '87
about
Rosencrantz & Guildenstern are dead [drama] Reviews *N Y I* il 20:62-3 Je 1 '87. J. Simon
Stops, Gervase Jackson- *See* Jackson-Stops, Gervase
Storace, Patricia
Song of salt and pepper [poem] *New Yorker* 63:34 Mr 9 '87
Southern hospitality [poem] *N Y Rev Books* 34:4 Ap 9 '87
Storage
See also
Food—Storage
Sheds
Videotape recorders and recording—Storage
Storage batteries
Acid trip [airplane battery overheats] D. Hayes. il *Flying* 114:99 Je '87
Nickel-hydrogen: a better battery? E. R. C. Capulong. il *Pop Sci* 231:67 N '87
Repairing/replacing battery cables [automobiles] M. Thompson. il *Fam Handyman* 37:66 F '87
Charging
Build a trickle charger [car battery] T. J. Byers. il *Mother Earth News* 103:97 Ja/F '87
Maintenance and repair
Getting a full life from your battery. *Pop Mech* 164:118 My '87
Preventing battery brownouts [automobiles] P. Stenquist. il *Pop Mech* 164:111-14 Ag '87

Testing
Batteries [automobiles] il *Consum Rep* 52:103-7 F '87
Car batteries. il *Consum Rep* 52:82-6 D '87
Storage bins *See* Bins
Storage in the home
See also
Cabinets (Furniture)
Closets
Drawers
Kitchen cabinets
Kitchen utensils and appliances—Storage
Shelves and racks
Storage walls
Create storage. il *Workbench* 43:72-80 N/D '87
Get your life organized! D. Freedman. il *Better Homes Gard* 65:118+ N '87
Make your kitchen store more! G. G. Butler and D. S. Johnson. il *Better Homes Gard* 65:120-1 Mr '87
More storage and more light [walk-in closet transformed into storage unit] il *Sunset* 178:126 Mr '87
Neat storage systems. D. Anderson. il *Home Mech* 83:135 O '87
Put it away! M. Morris. il *Home Mech* 83:54-8 F '87
The race for inner space. J. Hayes. il *Saturday Evening Post* 259:30-1 Mr '87
Squeezing in kitchen storage. il *Sunset* 178:154 Je '87
Stairwell gives them play area and storage. il *Sunset* 179:152-3 O '87
Storage at the sink. A. W. Lees. il *Pop Sci* 230:130 F '87
Store it so you can find it [kitchens] il *South Living* 22:134+ O '87
When are you going to clean up this mess? M. D. Glass. il *Ladies Home J* 104:88-91 Ja '87
Storage Technology Corp.
Were STC's optical disks just a mirage? [suit brought by limited partnership investors] M. Ivey. il *Bus Week* p67 Je 15 '87
Storage walls
Off the wall. il *Redbook* 168:120 Ap '87
Side-wall storage in narrow garage. il *Sunset* 178:152+ My '87
Storat, Richard E.
about
Richard Storat succeeds Norman Pace at API. por *Publ Wkly* 232:45 S 4 '87
Store decoration
Clothes make the man [interior design and Esprit] C. K. Gandee. il por *Archit Rec* 175:120-3 mid-S '87
Setting the proper scene [interiors of men's stores] R. La Ferla. il *N Y Times Mag* p60-1+ Jl 19 '87
Store windows *See* Show windows
Stores
See also
Airports—Stores
Audio equipment stores
Candy stores
Catalog showrooms
Christmas stores
Clothing stores
Convenience stores
Department stores
Electronics stores
Fish markets
Food stores
Furniture stores
Hardware stores
Liquor stores
Museum stores
Pet stores
Phonograph record stores
Retail trade
Shoe repair stores
Shopping centers
Video stores
Belgium
See also
Brussels (Belgium)—Stores
California
See also
Berkeley (Calif.)—Stores
Beverly Hills (Calif.)—Stores
Castro Valley (Calif.)—Stores
Emeryville (Calif.)—Stores
San Diego (Calif.)—Stores
San Francisco (Calif.)—Stores
Sherman Oaks (Calif.)—Stores
The American Riviera [mall culture of southern California] J. Robinson-Shaw. il *Vogue* 177:234+ My '87

Stores—*cont.*

China

See also

Benxi (China)—Stores

Florida

See also

Miami (Fla.)—Stores

France

See also

Paris (France)—Stores

Germany (West)

See also

Berlin (Germany: West)—Stores

Great Britain

See also

London (England)—Stores

India

See also

New Delhi (India)—Stores

Italy

See also

Florence (Italy)—Stores

Milan (Italy)—Stores

Japan

See also

Tokyo (Japan)—Stores

Louisiana

See also

New Orleans (La.)—Stores

Slidell (La.)—Stores

Minnesota

See also

Bloomington (Minn.)—Stores

New York (State)

See also

Ithaca (N.Y.)—Stores

New York (N.Y.)—Stores

North Carolina

See also

Winston-Salem (N.C.)—Stores

Pennsylvania

See also

Reading (Pa.)—Stores

Singapore

Singapore: shop place of the world. D. P. Marshall. il *Travel Holiday* 168:18-21 Ag '87

South Carolina

See also

Columbia (S.C.)—Stores

Tennessee

See also

Hohenwald (Tenn.)—Stores

Thailand

See also

Bangkok (Thailand)—Stores

Washington (D.C.)

See Washington (D.C.)—Stores

Stores, Secondhand *See* Secondhand trade

Storey, Peter John

about

Peter Storey: hope for South Africa. W. H. Willimon. *Christ Century* 104:1109-11 D 9 '87

Storey, Raymond

about

The last bus [drama] Reviews

Macleans il 100:55 F 23 '87. M. Schoenberg

Stories, Children's *See* Children's stories

Stork Club (New York, N.Y.: Nightclub) *See* New York (N.Y.)—Restaurants, nightclubs, bars, etc.

Storks

Europe's vanishing storks. D. Seward. il *Int Wildl* 17:4-11 My/Je '87

Storlien, Leonard H., and others

Fish oil prevents insulin resistance induced by high-fat feeding in rats. bibl f il *Science* 237:885-8 Ag 21 '87

Storm, Jackie

Is there too much yeast in your diet? il *Women's Sports Fitness* 9:10-11 Jl '87

Should you worry about sulfites? il *Women's Sports Fitness* 9:12 Ap '87

Stressed out? Good food can help. il *Women's Sports Fitness* 9:54-5 O '87

The sweet truth. il *Women's Sports Fitness* 9:12+ D '87

Storm windows *See* Windows

Storms

See also

Automobile driving—Storm hazards

Aviation—Storm hazards

Boats and boating—Storm hazards

Cyclones

Hunting—Storm conditions

Hurricanes

Ice storms

Motorcycling—Storm hazards

Snowstorms

Thunderstorms

Tornadoes

United States. National Severe Storms Forecast Center

Walking—Storm hazards

Lake acidification [effect of Big Blow of November 25, 1950 on Adirondack lakes; with reply by A. H. Johnson, D. F. Charles, and S. B. Andersen] J. E. Dobson and others. bibl f il *Environment* 29:2-5 Je '87

Storr, Robert

Realm of the senses. bibl f il *Art Am* 75:132-45+ N '87

The scholar-artist: Meyer Schapiro. il por *Art Am* 75:172-3+ O '87

Unmaking history at the Costume Institute. bibl f il *Art Am* 75:15-17+ F '87

Storrs (Conn.)

Birds

See Birds—Connecticut

Story, Joseph, 1779-1845

about

"Pledged to religion, liberty, and law". M. A. Noll. por *Christ Today* 31:20 Jl 10 '87

Story, Richard David

The buildings New Yorkers love to hate [cover story] il *N Y* 20:30-5 Je 15 '87

Story of a marriage [television program] *See* Television program reviews—Single works

Story telling

Baby Faith [black family's involvement with language and creativity] M. Wallace. il por *Ms* 16:154+ Jl/Ag '87

Have we got a great tale for you. M. Horn. il *U S News World Rep* 103:65-6 N 2 '87

Nurturing kindness through storytelling. C. A. Smith. *Educ Dig* 53:53-5 S '87

Once upon a time . . . [storytellers Connie Regan-Blake and Barbara Freeman] M. Bartlett. il *Good Housekeep* 204:78 Ap '87

Told from the heart [storyteller J. O'Callahan] P. Mandell. il por *Americana* 15:38-40+ Jl/Ag '87

True stories [use of real events to teach values] F. K. Lord. il *Parents* 62:81-2+ Ag '87

Therapeutic use

Storytelling in therapy and counseling. E. Wynne. bibl f il *Child Today* 16:11-15 Mr/Ap '87

Storytelling *See* Story telling

Stott, John R. W.

God on the gallows [excerpt from The cross of Christ] il por *Christ Today* 31:28-30 Ja 16 '87

Stotts, Stuart

about

Easing the city squeeze. K. Martin. il pors *Rodale's Org Gard* 34:78+ Ap '87

Stoughton, Cecil

Cocktails at Camelot. il pors *Life* 10:66-7+ Je '87

Stout, Cathi

about

Run in place and Praise the Lord. il *Newsweek* 109:63 Je 1 '87

Stout, Mary

Lifting the Vietnam stigma. por *U S News World Rep* 103:10 N 16 '87

Stout, Robert Joe

The happy birds move on. il *Christ Century* 104:222-3 Mr 4 '87

Stovall, Robert H.

about

Twenty-First Securities [interview] il por *Fortune* 116 Sp Issue:190-1 Fall '87

Stovall/Twenty-First Advisers Inc.

Twenty-First Securities [interview with R. Stovall] il por *Fortune* 116 Sp Issue:190-1 Fall '87

Stove, D. C. (David Charles)

The Columbus argument. *Commentary* 84:57-8 D '87

Stove, David Charles *See* Stove, D. C. (David Charles)

Stover, Dawn

What's new: products/technology. See issues of Popular Science beginning January 1987

Stover, Del

Dealing with youth gangs in the schools. *Educ Dig* 52:30-3 F '87

Stover, Jim
about
Eaton sees its future—and it's on the ground. S. Phillips. il por *Bus Week* p113+ N 16 '87

Stoves
See also
Wood stoves
Appliances: hard working and good looking. il *South Living* 22:122+ O '87
Electric ranges. il *Consum Rep* 52:8-12 D '87
Electric ranges. il *Consum Rep* 52:272-8 My '87
Gas ranges. il *Consum Rep* 52:12-15 D '87
Gas ranges. il *Consum Rep* 52:623-7 O '87
Home on the solid-fuel range: an introduction to wood and coal cookstoves. J. Schneider. il *Ctry J* 14:36-41 O '87

Maintenance and repair
How to troubleshoot gas and electric ranges. M. J. Schultz. il *Pop Mech* 164:145-8 F '87

Stowe, Ernest
about
The rustic furniture of Ernest Stowe. C. Gilborn. bibl f il *Antiques* 132:550-7 S '87

Stowe, Mark K., and others
Chemical mimicry: bolas spiders emit components of moth prey species sex pheromones. bibl f il *Science* 236:964-7 My 22 '87

Straddles, Tax *See* Tax straddles

Stradivarius violin *See* Violin

Strahinich, John
Meet a corporate Dr. No. il por *Read Dig* 130:101-4 Mr '87

Strain gages
Strain-gage transducers. C. M. Wood. il *Radio-Electron* 58:61-3+ D '87

Strains and stresses
See also
Strain gages
Tension structures
F-actin and microtubule suspensions as indeterminate fluids. R. E. Buxbaum and others. bibl f il *Science* 235:1511-14 Mr 20 '87
Foam structures with a negative Poisson's ratio. R. Lakes. bibl f il *Science* 235:1038-40 F 27 '87
Is the San Andreas weak at heart? R. A. Kerr. il *Science* 236:388-9 Ap 24 '87
New evidence on the state of stress of the San Andreas fault system. M. D. Zoback and others. bibl f il maps *Science* 238:1105-11 N 20 '87
Putting the squeeze on foam [research by Roderic Lakes] I. Peterson. il *Sci News* 131:166 Mr 14 '87
Squeeze me [work of Roderic S. Lakes with foams] *Sci Am* 256:62+ My '87
Stressed-out holograms [study of earthquake producing stresses] R. Monastersky. il *Sci News* 132:396 D 19-26 '87

Strait, Donald S., and Ayres, Richard E.
High noon for smog control. bibl f *Environment* 29:43-5 S '87

Stranahan, Susan Q.
Living in the shadow of poisonous air. il *Natl Wildl* 25:30-3 Ag/S '87
Many happy returns for wildlife. il *Natl Wildl* 25:50-1 Ap/My '87

Stranahan House (Fort Lauderdale, Fla.) *See* Fort Lauderdale (Fla.)—Historic houses, sites, etc.

Strand, Mark, 1934-
The famous scene [poem] *New Yorker* 63:30 Mr 30 '87
Grete Samsa's letter to H. [poem] *New Repub* 196:38 Mr 2 '87
Luminism [poem] *New Repub* 197:41 S 28 '87

Strand, Paul, 1890-1976
about
Photo-gloss: on Paul Strand's "Cristo with thorns". J. Masheck. bibl f il *Art Am* 75:104-13 Mr '87

Strand, Tom
Work dramatization. il *Petersens Photogr Mag* 16:66-7 Je '87

Stranded [film] See Motion picture reviews—Single works

Strange, K., and Spring, K. R.
Absence of significant cellular dilution during ADH-stimulated water reabsorption. bibl f il *Science* 235:1068-70 F 27 '87

Strange, Michael
How to get rid of asbestos. il *Consum Res Mag* 70:29-32 Ap '87

Strange stars
Strange stars don't glitch [quarks] *Sky Telesc* 74:580 D '87

Stranger Partnership Fund
Rating Mr. Deal Rater. *Money* 16:13 Ag '87

Strangulation
A cloud falls on a Dallas preacher [attack on wife of W. Railey] D. Pedersen. il por *Newsweek* 109:23 My 25 '87
Strangled in Dallas: an ungodly mystery [Rev. W. Railey held in attack on his wife] *Newsweek* 109:30 My 11 '87
A troubled minister's tale [strangulation of W. Railey's wife] S. Peterson. il por *U S News World Rep* 102:28 My 25 '87

Strasberg, Murray
about
Acoustical Society appoints Strasberg new secretary. por *Phys Today* 40:59 Je '87

Strasfogel, Ian
The other side of the churchyard wall. il pors *Opera News* 51:30-2+ My '87

Strat-O-Matic Baseball (Game)
Strat-O-Matic vs. APBA: a tough call. A. Kim. *Sport Mag* 78:84+ S '87

Strategic Air Command *See* United States. Air Force. Strategic Air Command

Strategic Arms Limitation Talks
About arms control [discussion of June 6, 1986 article, Rethinking arms control and June 20, 1986 article, SALT free] *Commonweal* 114:2+ Ja 16 '87
The administration's disarray. L. Ackland. *Bull At Sci* 43:2 Ja/F '87
Aspin believes INF unworkable without SALT 2 compliance. M. Mecham. *Aviat Week Space Technol* 127:135 O 12 '87
Congressional leaders outline terms of arms control agreement [dropping references to ABM and SALT 2 treaties] *Aviat Week Space Technol* 127:24-5 N 23 '87
Explaining Soviet compliance. G. Duffy. *Society* 24:66-72 Jl/Ag '87
Missile begets new charge [Soviet deployment of SS-24s cited as violation of SALT] *Bull At Sci* 43:2 O '87
Reagan, Congress on collision course over treaty limits [SALT 2 and ABM restrictions] *Aviat Week Space Technol* 127:32 O 12 '87

Strategic Arms Reduction Talks
The big problems restarting START. H. Trewhitt. il *U S News World Rep* 103:26-8 D 21 '87
Heading toward a 4% solution [need for strategic arms reductions beyond those gained through INF negotiations] S. Talbott. il *Time* 130:28-9 S 21 '87
Mobile missile verification slows START negotiators. P. J. Klass. *Aviat Week Space Technol* 127:24-5 D 21 '87
Negotiations on Strategic Arms Reductions. *Dep State Bull* 87:16-18 O '87
A new nuclear balance? T. Jacoby. il *Newsweek* 110:28 D 21 '87
New prospects for agreement in INF and START [address, March 20, 1987] E. L. Rowny. *Dep State Bull* 87:33-6 Je '87
Soviets retreat on START/SDI link, reveal new arms surveillance capacity. il *Aviat Week Space Technol* 127:18 D 14 '87
Strategic Arms: elements of a deal. T. Jacoby. il *Newsweek* 110:25 D 14 '87

Strategic Defense Initiative
ABM must go. W. F. Buckley. *Natl Rev* 39:62 Ap 24 '87
ABM, SDI, SOS. *Natl Rev* 39:16-17 Ap 10 '87
The ABM Treaty and the Soviets. *Bull At Sci* 43:2 Ap '87
The ABM Treaty controversy. *Congr Dig* 66:257-88 N '87
Abrahamson asks contractors to gear up for mass production of SDI components. T. M. Foley. *Aviat Week Space Technol* 126:22-3 Ja 26 '87
Aerojet develops missile radome cooling technique for SDIO. *Aviat Week Space Technol* 127:76 Ag 17 '87
Air Force labs concentrate on SDI research [Air Force Space Technology Center] *Aviat Week Space Technol* 127:50 N 2 '87
America has five years left. R. Jastrow. *Natl Rev* 39:42-3 F 13 '87
Amroc pursues SDI as first paying customer. il *Aviat Week Space Technol* 127:24-5 O 19 '87
The APS Council and the DEW study [letters] *Phys Today* 40:9+ O '87
APS on SDI: too soon to decide. D. E. Thomsen. *Sci News* 131:276 My 2 '87

Strategic Defense Initiative—*cont.*

APS panel disowns council statement [statement that argued against early deployment] C. Norman. *Science* 238:155 O 9 '87

APS releases report on directed-energy weapons [special section] bibl f il *Phys Today* 40:S1-S16 My '87

APS report on SDI [discussion of May 1, 1987 article, Doubt cast on laser weapons] C. Norman. *Science* 236:1411-12 Je 12 '87

APS Star Wars study given prominent coverage in US press. W. Sweet. *Phys Today* 40:55-6 Je '87

Arms Control Agency challenges Nunn's contention on legality of testing kinetic systems [ABM Treaty restrictions] *Aviat Week Space Technol* 126:29 Mr 23 '87

Arms control and SDI. *Natl Rev* 39:20-1 F 27 '87

Arms control protests force delay in next stage of SDI research [risking abrogation of the Antiballistic Missile Treaty] P. Mann. *Aviat Week Space Technol* 126:16-17 F 16 '87

Army expedites demonstration program for neutral particle beam technology; McDonnell displays engineering mockup of SDI integrated space experiment. P. J. Klass. il *Aviat Week Space Technol* 127:26-7 Ag 17 '87

Army missile test demonstrates FLAGE guidance [flexible lightweight agile guided experiment] J. D. Morrocco. il *Aviat Week Space Technol* 126:22-3 Je 1 '87

Ball Aerospace will test ground-based laser element [Relay Mirror Experiment] B. A. Smith. il *Aviat Week Space Technol* 127:99+ O 19 '87

Ballistic missiles and SDI [address, November 13, 1986] K. L. Adelman. *Vital Speeches Day* 53:181-4 Ja 1 '87

Bringing SDI down to earth [rail guns] il *Pop Mech* 164:69 N '87

British researchers seek SDI funds. D. Dickson. il *Science* 235:736-7 F 13 '87

Budget jeopardizes SDI timetable; research efforts scaled back. T. M. Foley. *Aviat Week Space Technol* 127:25-6 N 9 '87

Business versus Star Wars. A. M. Cunningham. il *Technol Rev* 90:17 My/Je '87

Can SDI survive house arrest? *Sci Am* 256:59 Ja '87

Chemical laser destroys target drone. *Aviat Week Space Technol* 127:22 O 5 '87

Collision in space [SDI deployment and compliance with ABM Treaty] R. English and S. Daggett. *New Repub* 196:11-13 Je 29 '87

The confused course of SDI. P. Clausen and M. Brower. il *Technol Rev* 90:60-5+ O '87

Congress balks at proposal to speed space-based antimissile defense. P. Mann. *Aviat Week Space Technol* 126:22-4 Ja 26 '87

Congress questions wisdom, savings of expanded antimissile tests [broad interpretation of the ABM Treaty] P. Mann. *Aviat Week Space Technol* 126:18-19 Mr 2 '87

Congressional defense leaders, White House agree on SDI tests [compromise on ABM Treaty compliance] *Aviat Week Space Technol* 127:24-5 N 16 '87

Congressional leaders outline terms of arms control agreement [dropping references to ABM and SALT 2 treaties] *Aviat Week Space Technol* 127:24-5 N 23 '87

Cornell unit surveys some US Academy members on SDI. W. Sweet. *Phys Today* 40:72-3 Ja '87

Dangers of limited SDI. G. E. Marsh. *Bull At Sci* 43:13-14 Mr '87

The dark side of SDI. C. Norman. *Science* 235:962-3 F 27 '87

The dark side of The Force. R. Rawles. il *Sierra* 72:58-62 S/O '87

Debate on APS directed-energy weapons study. G. H. Canavan and others. bibl f pors *Phys Today* 40:48-53 N '87

Debate over SDI enters new phase. C. Norman. il *Science* 235:277-80 Ja 16 '87

Defense Dept. releases report on SDI spinoffs. *Aviat Week Space Technol* 126:35 My 11 '87

Defense Dept. seeks launcher for SDI in supplemental budget. *Aviat Week Space Technol* 126:21 Ja 5 '87

Defense is the best defense. E. Teller. il *N Y Times Mag* p47-8 Ap 5 '87

Delta 181 mission has key SDI flight test objectives. C. Covault. il *Aviat Week Space Technol* 127:30-1 N 23 '87

DOD Science Board finds SDI Phase I reasonable but 'sketchy'. I. Goodwin. il *Phys Today* 40:54-6 S '87

The door SDI won't shut [inadequate air defenses] C. Hammer. il *Wash Mon* 19:21-4 Mr '87

Doubt cast on laser weapons [report by the American Physical Society] C. Norman. il *Science* 236:509-10 My 1 '87

Draw the line at Star Wars. H. Brown. *Bull At Sci* 43:3 Ja/F '87

The earthly origins of Star Wars [cover story] G. Herken. bibl f il *Bull At Sci* 43:20-8 O '87

Exploiting the Soviet "threat" to Europe [European Defense Initiative] M. A. Evangelista. bibl f *Bull At Sci* 43:14-16+ Ja/F '87

Former SDI scientist believes gains in defensive capabilities could achieve limited nuclear attack protection [G. Yonas] *Aviat Week Space Technol* 126:20 F 2 '87

From Star Wars to smart rocks [ABM Treaty threatened by SDI] B. Van Voorst. il *Time* 129:27 F 23 '87

The hardware of early deployment. S. Budiansky. il *U S News World Rep* 102:28-9 F 23 '87

Heading toward a 4% solution [need for strategic arms reductions beyond those gained through INF negotiations] S. Talbott. il *Time* 130:28-9 S 21 '87

Holes in the impenetrable shield. D. C. Waller and J. T. Bruce. *Bull At Sci* 43:5-6 O '87

How eminent physicists have lent their names to a politicized report on strategic defense. A. M. Codevilla. *Commentary* 84:21-6 S '87

How Kemp may harden the GOP line on Star Wars. D. Griffiths and B. Javetski. *Bus Week* p71 My 25 '87

Hurry up please its time. *Natl Rev* 39:17-18 F 13 '87

In defense of ABM—and Star Wars. S. D. Drell. *Harpers* 274:21-3 Je '87

In defense of Strategic Defense [address, August 16, 1987] J. L. Piotrowski. *Vital Speeches Day* 53:742-5 O 1 '87

Industry officials optimistic about early SDI deployment. *Aviat Week Space Technol* 126:30 Mr 23 '87

Interpreting the ABM Treaty [address, April 1, 1987] P. H. Nitze. *Dep State Bull* 87:31-3 Je '87

Japan, U.S. agree on SDI participation. *Aviat Week Space Technol* 127:23 Jl 27 '87

Judd appointed SDI chief scientist at a time of program uncertainties. I. Goodwin. il por *Phys Today* 40:59-60 D '87

The Kremlin's new cards [Soviets tie INF agreement to SDI] J. V. Lamar, Jr. il *Time* 130:30 Jl 20 '87

Latest ABM ploy—old is new [dispute over legality of kinetic weapons] T. K. Longstreth. il *Bull At Sci* 43:3-4 D '87

Lockheed developing ERIS interceptor vehicle [exoatmospheric reentry-vehicle interceptor system] il *Aviat Week Space Technol* 126:73 Mr 16 '87

Los Alamos begins work on NPB test accelerator [Neutral Particle Beam Ground Test Accelerator] T. M. Foley. il *Aviat Week Space Technol* 127:93-4+ O 19 '87

Major SDI tests—compliance with alternative treaty regimes [ABM Treaty] il *Aviat Week Space Technol* 127:31 S 14 '87

Martin lab halves time needed to retarget space-based laser. B. A. Smith. il *Aviat Week Space Technol* 127:28-9 S 14 '87

Martin, Lockheed, TRW win work on SDI Zenith Star laser. T. M. Foley. *Aviat Week Space Technol* 127:32-3 O 12 '87

Martin Marietta selected to design potential nuclear SDI systems [nuclear-powered X-ray laser platform and nuclear hypervelocity pellet system] T. M. Foley. *Aviat Week Space Technol* 127:113-14 Ag 10 '87

Martin studies space-based KKV concept [kinetic kill vehicle] il *Aviat Week Space Technol* 127:20 Ag 31 '87

Mathematicians and SDI: a quandary. il *Discover* 8:14 F '87

McDonnell Douglas team to test neutral-particle beam accelerator in orbit. *Aviat Week Space Technol* 126:27 Je 8 '87

Medium-range missile cuts pose unclear impact on ABM research [Soviet proposal] P. Mann. *Aviat Week Space Technol* 126:262 Mr 9 '87

Mightier than the SDI [report issued by the American Physical Society] *Commonweal* 114:261-2 My 8 '87

Moral rhetoric, moral confusion in the Star Wars debate. E. T. Linenthal. il *Christ Century* 104:1058-61 N 25 '87

The Moscow agenda [visit to Russia by G. Shultz] T. Jacoby. il *Newsweek* 109:24 Ap 20 '87

Murdering SDI [suspicious murders and suicides of Europeans connected with SDI] J. S. Denton and P. Schweizer. *Natl Rev* 39:37-9 Jl 31 '87

Strategic Defense Initiative—*cont.*

National Test Bed facility demonstrates initial capability. T. M. Foley. *Aviat Week Space Technol* 127:22-3 O 5 '87

New space systems test facilities to cost $7 billion [Strategic Defense Initiative and National Aerospace Plane] il *Aviat Week Space Technol* 126:85 Ap 27 '87

Nine SDI tests planned in 1988-89 amid ABM debate over 'exotic' weapons. P. Mann. *Aviat Week Space Technol* 126:28 Ap 6 '87

Notes and comment [bargaining on Star Wars] *New Yorker* 63:35 D 7 '87

The nuclear opening. Sir S. Zuckerman. bibl f il *N Y Rev Books* 34:42-6 My 7 '87

Nuclear shysters [early deployment of SDI and the ABM Treaty] *New Repub* 196:7-8 Mr 9 '87

Nunn affirms 1972 ABM pact, finding kinetic tests illegal. P. Mann. *Aviat Week Space Technol* 126:21-3 Mr 16 '87

Nunn threatens INF pact with link to ABM Treaty. P. Mann. *Aviat Week Space Technol* 126:30 My 11 '87

Offense-defense strategic balance in the 1990s [address, May 6, 1987] M. Wallop. *Vital Speeches Day* 53:610-13 Ag 1 '87

On to the summit, as Star Wars waits. S. Budiansky and H. Trewhitt. il *U S News World Rep* 103:13-14 N 9 '87

O'Neill leaves SDI after Senate dust-up. I. Goodwin. *Phys Today* 40:57 S '87

Panel disputes SDI timetable [American Physical Society] *Aviat Week Space Technol* 126:37 Ap 27 '87

Pentagon will develop defense against Soviet tactical missiles [antitactical ballistic missile defense] J. D. Morrocco. *Aviat Week Space Technol* 126:22 Ja 19 '87

Permitted and prohibited activities under the ABM Treaty [address, October 31, 1986] P. H. Nitze. *Dep State Bull* 87:39-40 Ja '87

Physicists assess laser lethality for ballistic missile defense role [American Physical Society] P. J. Klass. *Aviat Week Space Technol* 126:104-5 My 18 '87

The political trials of SDI. R. N. Perle. il *U S News World Rep* 103:45-6 S 14 '87

Presidential memo. W. F. Buckley. *Natl Rev* 39:62-3 D 4 '87

Pro-SDI panel forecasts $121-billion antimissile costs, excluding research. *Aviat Week Space Technol* 126:133 F 9 '87

Push for early SDI deployment could spur Air Defense Initiative. J. D. Morrocco. *Aviat Week Space Technol* 126:18-20 F 2 '87

Reagan, Congress on collision course over treaty limits [SALT 2 and ABM restrictions] *Aviat Week Space Technol* 127:32 O 12 '87

The Reagan method. M. Kondracke. *New Repub* 197:12-14 N 30 '87

Reagan still has a shot at arms control—but it's a long one. B. Javetski. il *Bus Week* p63 F 23 '87

Reaganites at war over Star Wars. M. Healy and D. Mullin. il *U S News World Rep* 102:30 F 9 '87

Reagan's highest folly. Sir S. Zuckerman. bibl f il *N Y Rev Books* 34:35-41 Ap 9 '87

The real Star Wars threat. J. Galtung. *Nation* 244:248-50 F 28 '87

Refocusing the SDI debate. R. L. Garthoff. il *Bull At Sci* 43:44-50 S '87

Revive the Reykjavik dynamism. U. Albrecht. il *Bull At Sci* 43:40-1 Mr '87

Rocketdyne selected to build SDI nuclear power demonstration units. *Aviat Week Space Technol* 127:28 D 21 '87

Rockwell to test space-based missile interceptor for SDI. M. A. Dornheim. il *Aviat Week Space Technol* 127:81+ S 14 '87

Round one on Star Wars goes to the naysayers. P. R. Range. il *U S News World Rep* 102:28-9 F 23 '87

Rushing Star Wars could send it right back to earth. D. Griffiths and E. Clark. il *Bus Week* p43 Mr 2 '87

Sakharov: the folly of SDI [interview] A. McGowan. *Harpers* 275:20 O '87

Sandia develops nuclear-powered Falcon optical laser concept. T. M. Foley. *Aviat Week Space Technol* 127:24 O 19 '87

Scientists find corporate support building for deployment of SDI. J. D. Morrocco. il *Aviat Week Space Technol* 126:81 Ap 27 '87

Scientists shoot down Star Wars [American Physical Society] W. Sweet. *Bull At Sci* 43:7-9 Jl/Ag '87

Scientists urge new stance on SDI testing in U.S.-Soviet arms talks. T. M. Foley. *Aviat Week Space Technol* 127:30 S 14 '87

SDI anniversary [statement, March 23, 1987] R. Reagan. *Dep State Bull* 87:72 Je '87

SDI attempts to zap APS directed-energy weapons report. I. Goodwin. il *Phys Today* 40:43-6 Je '87

SDI budget constraints likely to foil new Army contract awards. *Aviat Week Space Technol* 127:22 N 2 '87

SDI death watch. *Natl Rev* 39:16-17 D 18 '87

An SDI defense: a Maginot Line in space [with discussion] R. Garwin. il por *Cent Mag* 20:45-53 N/D '87

SDI Delta intercept yields data on space collision shock waves. C. Covault. il *Aviat Week Space Technol* 126:26-7 Je 8 '87

SDI director denies covert shift of ABM research to deployment. P. Mann. il *Aviat Week Space Technol* 126:24-5 Ap 13 '87

SDI experts clash on nuclear satellites [views of Lowell Wood] C. Norman. il *Science* 238:883-4 N 13 '87

SDI finds staged deployment would inhibit Soviet attack. B. M. Greeley, Jr. il *Aviat Week Space Technol* 126:35-7 Ap 27 '87

SDI goes on the offensive. *Sci Am* 256:58+ Mr '87

SDI in the sky. M. Kondracke. *New Repub* 196:9-10+ Ap 20 '87

SDI: incentive for arms control [with discussion] F. J. Gaffney, Jr. *Cent Mag* 20:33-8 S/O '87

SDI: losing momentum over what is affordable and possible. I. Goodwin. il *Phys Today* 40:47-51 Ja '87

SDI National Test Facility to aid in recording ICBM signature data. il *Aviat Week Space Technol* 126:39 Ap 27 '87

SDI obfuscation. D. E. Fink. *Aviat Week Space Technol* 126:9 F 16 '87

SDI: paper pile grows on APS study. K. Hartley. *Sci News* 132:38 Jl 18 '87

SDI programs face delays due to fiscal 1988 cutbacks. T. M. Foley. *Aviat Week Space Technol* 127:28 Ag 17 '87

SDI report to Congress [White House statement, May 20, 1987] *Dep State Bull* 87:82 Ag '87

SDI research is critical. W. E. Morrow, Jr. il *Technol Rev* 90:24-5+ Jl '87

SDI research railgun succeeds in rapid repetitive firing. il *Aviat Week Space Technol* 127:29 D 21 '87

SDI science office plans to launch electrical space test in November [Spear, for Space Power Experiments Aboard Rockets] T. M. Foley. *Aviat Week Space Technol* 127:28-9 Ag 24 '87

SDI stakes initial deployment on success of four programs. T. M. Foley. *Aviat Week Space Technol* 127:30-1 O 12 '87

SDI suborbital launch yields data for high-power platform design [Space Power Experiments Aboard Rocket] T. M. Foley. il *Aviat Week Space Technol* 127:26-7 D 21 '87

SDI testing may ignite antisatellite race. M. Crawford. *Science* 237:482 Jl 31 '87

SDI watch. See issues of National Review beginning February 13, 1987

SDI zapped [American Physical Society study] *Sci Am* 256:18 Je '87

SDIO assesses energy storage for FEL defense [free electron lasers utilizing superconducting magnetic energy storage] *Aviat Week Space Technol* 126:29 Ap 6 '87

SDIO continues research across broad technology base. B. M. Greeley, Jr. il *Aviat Week Space Technol* 126:38-9+ Mr 9 '87

SDIO investigates shootback ability to protect orbiting strategic weapons. T. M. Foley. il *Aviat Week Space Technol* 127:65-6 D 21 '87

SDIO on verge of producing kinetic kill vehicle. *Aviat Week Space Technol* 126:24 F 9 '87

SDIO seeks funds to maintain full-scale development timetable. B. M. Greeley, Jr. *Aviat Week Space Technol* 126:26-7 Ja 12 '87

SDIO seeks integration contractor to serve as systems engineer. T. M. Foley. *Aviat Week Space Technol* 127:26 S 21 '87

SDIO selects five U.S./allied teams for phase 2 missile defense studies. *Aviat Week Space Technol* 127:28 Ag 3 '87

SDIO to conduct hypervelocity firing of subscale Thunderbolt prototype. *Aviat Week Space Technol* 127:28-9 Ag 24 '87

SDI's Starlab shuttle mission will test laser tracking system. *Aviat Week Space Technol* 127:25 O 19 '87

Strategic Defense Initiative—*cont.*

A secret plan to speed up SDI? C. Norman. *Science* 236:253 Ap 17 '87

Secretary's interview on "This week with David Brinkley" [interview with G. P. Shultz; transcript of program, February 8, 1987] *Dep State Bull* 87:8-11 Ap '87

The secrets of Soviet Star Wars. W. J. Broad. il map *N Y Times Mag* p22+ Je 28 '87

A shield against arms control [C. Weinberger calls for early deployment] S. Talbott. il por *Time* 129:25 F 2 '87

Showdown nears on ABM Treaty. C. Norman. il *Science* 238:147-9 O 9 '87

Six SDI programs win approval of Defense Acquisition Board. T. M. Foley. *Aviat Week Space Technol* 127:28-9 Ag 10 '87

Slow down S.D.I. *Nation* 244:562 My 2 '87

Snuffing a summit [Soviets demand concession on SDI] J. Kohan. il por *Time* 130:56-7 N 2 '87

The Soviet debate on missile defense. B. Parrott. bibl f il *Bull At Sci* 43:9-12 Ap '87

Soviets may not copy Star Wars [views of Matthew Evangelista] *USA Today (Periodical)* 116:15 Ag '87

Soviets retreat on START/SDI link, reveal new arms surveillance capacity. il *Aviat Week Space Technol* 127:18 D 14 '87

Space and national strategy [address, May 15, 1987] E. C. Aldridge. *Vital Speeches Day* 53:614-16 Ag 1 '87

Space race [C. W. Weinberger's push for early deployment] F. Barnes. *New Repub* 196:10-12 F 23 '87

Speeding up Star Wars. I. Austen. il *Macleans* 100:20+ F 16 '87

Speeding up Star Wars. R. Watson. il *Newsweek* 109:28-9 F 16 '87

Stage two for Star Wars. il *Time* 130:16 S 28 '87

Stanford/TRW team demonstrates potential lethality increase of space-based free-electron lasers. *Aviat Week Space Technol* 126:23 Mr 16 '87

Star Wars and the rhetoric of make-believe. M. E. Thompson. il *USA Today (Periodical)* 115:16-20 Ja '87

Star Wars block. I. F. Stone. *Nation* 245:508-9 N 7 '87

Star Wars controversy in West Germany. T. Risse-Kappen. *Bull At Sci* 43:50-2 Jl/Ag '87

Star Wars: does it help or hurt arms-control efforts? [with interviews with K. Stansberry and P. C. Warnke] J. Scarlott. il por *Sch Update* 120:20-1 N 20 '87

Star Wars fell on Alabama [Huntsville] D. Charles. il *Nation* 245:748-50 D 19 '87

Star Wars for starters. *Commonweal* 114:69 F 13 '87

Star Wars' hollow promise. D. Brand. il *Time* 130:17-18+ D 7 '87

Star Wars in Orogrande [laser testing site] F. Gibney. il map *Newsweek* 110:42 O 19 '87

Star Wars is coming, but where is it going? W. J. Broad. il *N Y Times Mag* p80+ D 6 '87

Star Wars lasers: a question of technical integrity. I. Peterson. *Sci News* 132:276 O 31 '87

Star Wars revives civil defense. J. Leaning. il *Bull At Sci* 43:42-6 My '87

Star Wars: Shultz's goal [bargaining chip in arms talks] il *Newsweek* 109:4 F 2 '87

Star Wars: the dream diminished [ERIS and HEDI interceptor systems] W. Biddle. il *Discover* 8:26-30+ Jl '87

Starlab to engage satellites, rockets, ground-based laser. T. M. Foley. il *Aviat Week Space Technol* 127:58-9 O 26 '87

Stop early SDI deployment. S. D. Drell. *Bull At Sci* 43:3 Ap '87

Strategic defense [special section] il *Aviat Week Space Technol* 127:19-23 N 30 '87

Strategic defense and directed-energy weapons. C. K. N. Patel and N. Bloembergen. il map *Sci Am* 257:39-45 S '87

The Strategic Defense Initiative and arms control [cover story; special section] il *Cent Mag* 20:4-24 My/Je '87

Strategic Defense Initiative: blueprint for a layered defense [cover story; special section] il *Aviat Week Space Technol* 127:48-9+ N 23 '87

Stretching the syllogism. W. F. Buckley. *Natl Rev* 39:63 Mr 13 '87

The summit: on again. R. Watson. il *Newsweek* 110:52-4 N 9 '87

Super-scientists to Reagan: SDI may not fly. S. Budiansky. il *U S News World Rep* 102:12-13 My 4 '87

A superpowers' October surprise [SDI blocks summit and arms treaty] H. Trewhitt. il *U S News World Rep* 103:36-7 N 2 '87

The Surprise Defense Initiative. M. Krepon. il *Bull At Sci* 43:5-6 Jl/Ag '87

A tactical defense initiative for Western Europe? I. H. Daalder. bibl f il *Bull At Sci* 43:34-9 My '87

Thoughts of a retiring APS president. S. D. Drell. il *Phys Today* 40 pt1:56-62 Ag '87

Triumph at Pad 17 [successful test of ICBM defense system] R. K. Bennett. il *Read Dig* 131:59-64 Jl '87

U.S., Israel to test Arrow antitactical missile. *Aviat Week Space Technol* 127:26-7 D 21 '87

Uncapping Star Wars [C. W. Weinberger's push for early deployment] *Nation* 244:201 F 21 '87

Uncertainties in building a strategic defense. C. A. Zraket. bibl f *Science* 235:1600-6 Mr 27 '87

USAF Center develops lightweight projectiles for SDI applications [Lightweight Exoatmospheric Projectile program] T. M. Foley. il *Aviat Week Space Technol* 127:46-7 N 2 '87

View from Sri Lanka . . . and California; SDI "breakthroughs". *Space World* X-1-277:5-6 Ja '87

Voodoo treaty-reading [ABM Treaty and the Strategic Defense Initiative] *Commonweal* 114:131-2 Mr 13 '87

Waiting for the postman [Soviets use Star Wars as bargaining ploy in meetings with G. Shultz] R. Watson. il por *Newsweek* 110:60-1+ N 2 '87

Weapons designers challenge SDI report [criticism of American Physical Society study] W. Booth. *Science* 237:127 Jl 10 '87

Weinberger approves SDI test program. *Aviat Week Space Technol* 127:32 S 28 '87

Weinberger endorses phased deployment of SDI. *Aviat Week Space Technol* 126:22-3 Ja 19 '87

Weinberger foresees no technical blocks to first-phase SDI deployment. R. G. O'Lone. *Aviat Week Space Technol* 126:103 My 11 '87

What price Star Wars? Sir S. Zuckerman. bibl f il *N Y Rev Books* 34:8+ Ap 23 '87

What the ABM Treaty means. S. Talbott. il *Time* 129:15 Mr 23 '87

When Nunn speaks . . . C. Norman. il por *Science* 235:1457 Mr 20 '87

Who's conservative now? W. F. Buckley. *Natl Rev* 39:62 Mr 27 '87

Why astronomers should love SDI. S. P. Worden. *Sky Telesc* 74:340 O '87

Why Gorbachev is upping the summit ante. B. Javetski and others. il *Bus Week* p57 N 9 '87

Why I quit. D. Parnas. *Cent Mag* 20:56-7 Ja/F '87

Why offense needs defense. C. W. Weinberger. *Foreign Policy* 68:3-18 Fall '87

Why Star Wars is bad for astronomy. C. Sagan. il *Sky Telesc* 74:340-1 O '87

Will Star Wars fly? il *World Press Rev* 34:17-20 Mr '87

Would a test ban strengthen SDI? S. Fetter. il *Bull At Sci* 43:40-1 N '87

Social aspects

How S.D.I. will change our culture. P. S. Boyer. il *Nation* 244:1+ Ja 10 '87

Reagan, Star Wars, and American culture. J. Smith. bibl f il *Bull At Sci* 43:19-25 Ja/F '87

Return technology to human hands. J. Manley. il *Bull At Sci* 43:7-8 D '87

Strategic planning, Business *See* Business planning

Strategy, Military *See* Military art and science; World War, 1939-1945—Strategy

Stratford (Va.)

Historic houses, sites, etc.

See also

Stratford Hall Plantation, Robert E. Lee Memorial Association (Stratford, Va.)

Stratford Festival (Ont.)

Stratford, On-Tario. K. Rodeghier. il *Travel Holiday* 167:56-61 Je '87

Stratford's cavalcade. J. Bemrose. il *Macleans* 100:54-5 Je 22 '87

Stratford Hall Plantation, Robert E. Lee Memorial Association (Stratford, Va.)

Imposing, enduring Stratford Hall. C. Engle. il *South Living* 22:86-7 D '87

Stratigraphic geology *See* Geology, Stratigraphic

Stratosphere *See* Atmosphere, Upper

Stratton, Frederick Prescott, 1939-
about

Man on the bull's eye. J. A. Conway. il por *Forbes* 139:8 My 4 '87

Stratton, Tom
You know spring is here when . . . il *McCalls* 114:158 Ap '87
Stratton, W. K.
Sitting atop a Tornado. il por *Sports Illus* 66:89 My 25 '87
Stratton (Vt.: Resort) *See* Resorts—Vermont
Stratus Computer, Inc.
Mixed blessings [marketing arrangement with IBM] K. K. Wiegner. il por *Forbes* 140:70+ S 21 '87
Straus, Jack B., Jr.
The Zambian debt dilemma: a just repayment plan. *Christ Century* 104:855-6 O 7 '87
Straus, Melville
about
Pirouetting ahead of the market [interview] A. E. Serwer. por *Fortune* 115:158 Je 8 '87
Straus, Roger W.
about
Nobel House: publisher Roger Straus just keeps on winning. J. Reginato. il pors *N Y* 20:56-60+ N 9 '87
Strausberg, Randy
about
Better late than never. B. Weberman. il por *Forbes* 139:282-3 Ja 12 '87
Strauss, Anselm L.
Health policy and chronic illness. *Society* 25:33-9 N/D '87
Strauss, Bob
Cinema summit. il *Film Comment* 23:37-8 My/Je '87
Strauss, Johann, 1825-1899
about
Die Fledermaus [operetta] Reviews
N Y il 20:43 Ja 5 '87. P. G. Davis
Time il 129:71 Ja 5 '87. M. Walsh
Strauss, Josef
about
To get an impactful feel for how upsetting . . . M. S. Forbes, Jr. il por *Forbes* 140:25 Ag 24 '87
Strauss, Leo
about
The cult of Leo Strauss. J. Weisberg. il por *Newsweek* 110:61 Ag 3 '87
Strauss, Richard, 1864-1949
about
A luminous carousel. G. R. Marek. il pors *Opera News* 51:14-17 F 14 '87
Der Rosenkavalier [opera] Reviews
Opera News il 51:28-31 F 14 '87
Strauss, Robert S.
about
What to do about Japan [interview] por *U S News World Rep* 102:46-7 Ap 13 '87
Strauss, William M., and others
Measuring the human T cell receptor γ-chain. bibl f il *Science* 237:1217-19 S 4 '87
Stravinsky, Igor, 1882-1971
about
Citing copyright infringement, judge halts Stravinsky biography. J. Mutter. *Publ Wkly* 232:14 Ag 21 '87
Dancing:
M. Hodson's reconstruction of Le sacre du printemps. A. Croce. *New Yorker* 63:140-2+ N 23 '87
Straw, Karen
about
New York woman acquitted of killing her husband. *Jet* 73:46 N 2 '87
Straw, Ronnie
(jt. auth) See Hilton, Margaret, and Straw, Ronnie
Straw hats
Hats on! [for men] R. La Ferla. il *N Y Times Mag* p36 Jl 5 '87
Strawberries
See also
Cooking—Fruit
Alpine strawberries. J. Ruttle. il *Rodale's Org Gard* 34:47-9 Jl '87
Strawberry strategies [cover story] N. Eggleston. il *Rodale's Org Gard* 34:74-6 Ap '87
Strawberry, Darryl
about
Strawberry, wife separate, await ruling on her suit. il por *Jet* 71:32 F 16 '87
Taking the rap. S. Wulf. il pors *Sports Illus* 67:20-3 Jl 13 '87
Would you trade this man? [cover story] P. Hirdt. il *Sport Mag* 78:41 Ap '87

Strawberry desserts *See* Desserts
Stream, Matilda
about
Casa de las Mil Flores: Harold and Matilda Stream in Guatemala. C. T. Buckley. il *Archit Dig* 44:108-15 Ag '87
Stream ecology *See* Fresh water ecology
Stream fishing *See* Fishing
Streams *See* Brooks, creeks, etc.
Streater, Donald
about
An ex-con's journey to the right side of the law. L. B. Randolph. il pors *Ebony* 42:38-40+ O '87
Streb, Elizabeth
about
Mean machine. L. Friedman. il por *Vogue* 177:212 S '87
Strebeigh, Fred
The greatest detective who never lived. il *Read Dig* 130:41-2+ Mr '87
Pleasure in creation. bibl il *Am Herit* 38:82-9 Jl/Ag '87
Streep, Meryl
about
Meryl [cover story] B. Darrach. il pors *Life* 10:72-4+ D '87
Street, James H.
Mexico's development crisis. bibl f *Curr Hist* 86:101-4+ Mr '87
Street art and artists
The sidewalks of new art. D. Grant. *Am Artist* 51:10+ Jl '87
Street cars *See* Trolleys
Street gangs *See* Gangs
Street legal [television program] See Television program reviews—Single works
Street maps *See* Road maps, guides, etc.
Street music and musicians
Moondog [New York City street celebrity] G. Talese. il *N Y* 20:76 D 21-28 '87
Mr. Personality [P. Schimmel, clarinet player in New York City subways] *New Yorker* 63:25-7 Ap 13 '87
Whenever this peripatetic pianist feels like giving a concert, all he has to do is put on the brakes [E. Rosser entertains from the back of his bus] T. Schlesinger. il por *People Wkly* 28:101-2 D 14 '87
The street of crocodiles [film] See Motion picture reviews—Single works
Street photography *See* Photography, Documentary
Street scene [drama] See Rice, Elmer L., 1892-1967
Street signs
Street sign [B. Breeden arrested for stealing street sign named to honor J. Poindexter in Odon, Indiana] *Progressive* 51:4 Ag '87
Street smart [film] See Motion picture reviews—Single works
Street sweeps (Securities)
The Street is fretting over 'Street sweeps'. A. Bianco. il por *Bus Week* p71-2 Ag 3 '87
Street theater
Guerrillas [street theater in New York advertising a real estate broker] *New Yorker* 63:31-2 N 30 '87
Street trades
See also
Street art and artists
Out of Africa: the Senegalese peddlers of New York. P. Blauner. il *N Y* 20:42-6 F 16 '87
Sections [S. Bronsky sells discarded sections of the Sunday New York times on Manhattan sidewalk] *New Yorker* 62:24 Ja 26 '87

China
Beijing's popcorn entrepreneur [excerpt from Chinese lives] Zhang Xinxin. *Harpers* 275:35-6+ N '87
Street traffic *See* City traffic
Street trash [film] See Motion picture reviews—Single works
Street vendors *See* Street trades
Streetcars *See* Trolleys
Streisand, Barbra
about
Cute 22 acres for only $18 million—contact owner, Barbra Streisand. il *People Wkly* 28:103 O 5 '87
The Streisand specials. C. Albertson. por *Stereo Rev* 52:121 My '87
Streisand's show. R. Hemming. il por *Stereo Rev* 52:98 S '87
Strenger, Hermann-Josef
about
The breadth of a salesman. L. S. Richman. il por *Fortune* 116:50 Ag 3 '87

Strength exercises *See* Exercise
Strength of muscles *See* Muscle strength
Strep throat *See* Throat—Diseases
Streptococcus
Vaccination against tooth decay. H. Donoghue. il *World Press Rev* 34:52 My '87
Streptokinase
Drugs for heart attacks [FDA ruling] *FDA Consum* 21:7 S '87
Stress

See also
Anxiety
Crisis management (Psychology)
Crowding stress
Job stress
Plants, Effect of stress on
TMJ syndrome
Traumatism
Trees, Effect of stress on

39 ways to destress your home life. il *Prevention* 39:34-6+ S '87
Ah, my non-aching back: a longtime sufferer finds it's all in the mind [work of J. Sarno] T. Schwartz. il por *N Y* 20:44-8+ Mr 16 '87
The biofeedback way to starve stress. M. Golin. *Prevention* 39:30-2 Je '87
Blinding stress [central serous chorioretinopathy; research by Gary S. Gelber and Howard Schatz] P. Chance. *Psychol Today* 21:22-3 Jl '87
Busy, busy bees [stress on young children] L. G. Katz. il *Parents* 62:154 F '87
Complex characters handle stress better [study by Patricia W. Linville] D. Schechter. *Psychol Today* 21:26 O '87
Coping with stress [teenagers] D. Elkind. il *Parents* 62:202 Ag '87
Death by stress? [sudden cardiac arrest; research by Robert Eliot] G. Hanauer. il *Omni* 9:22+ Ag '87
Diabetes and stress: a Type A connection? [research by Brian Stabler and Richard S. Surwit] M. Roberts. *Psychol Today* 21:22 Jl '87
Do we push our kids too hard? [excerpt from The hurried child] D. Elkind. il *Good Housekeep* 205:117-19 S '87
Don't let go of your racket [controlling tennis match stress] J. E. Loehr. il *World Tennis* 35:10+ O '87
Eye of the (emotional) storm [central serous chorioretinopathy; research by Gary S. Gelber and Howard Schatz] *Sci News* 131:40 Ja 17 '87
Five ways to fight family stress [condensed from Stress and the healthy family] D. Curran. il *Read Dig* 130:169-70+ F '87
Getting tough: can people learn to have disease-resistant personalities? [hardiness training; work of Salvatore Maddi] J. Fischman. bibl (p63) il *Psychol Today* 21:26-8 D '87
Glut responses. R. M. Restak. *Vogue* 177:325+ Ag '87
The hardy heart [research by Richard J. Contrada] C. Wood. *Psychol Today* 21:22 Ja '87
Holiday stress busters. P. A. Toussaint. il *Essence* 18:95-6 D '87
How to avoid Christmas stress [views of Wallace Denton] *USA Today (Periodical)* 116:4 D '87
The hurricane hour [end-of-day family stress] K. W. Wiley. il *Health* 19:54-8 Ag '87
Hypertension, hostility, and race [study by Neil Schneiderman] *USA Today (Periodical)* 115:9 My '87
I learned to "think" stress away—and so can you. M. F. Hoyt. il pors *Good Housekeep* 204:50+ Je '87
June madness [stress of weddings] G. Witkin-Lanoil. il *Health* 19:90 Je '87
Keeping cool when traffic heats up. B. Brophy. il *U S News World Rep* 103:26-7 S 7 '87
Living with trouble that won't go away and learning how to keep it from dominating your life [chronic stress caused by illness or other problems] S. Jacoby. il *Glamour* 85:266-7+ My '87
Mind over disease: Warning! Daily hassles are hazardous. N. Peterson. il *Read Dig* 130:76-8 Ap '87
Miseducation. D. Elkind. il *Parents* 62:124-8+ O '87
New-baby blues [role of stress in maternal postpartum depression; research by Carolyn E. Cutrona and Beth R. Troutman] S. Vandershaf. il *Psychol Today* 21:18 Ap '87
Pressure points . . . active answers [special section] il *Vogue* 177:352-9+ Ag '87
Relaxation really works [study by Robert C. Peveler and Derek W. Johnston] C. Wood. *Psychol Today* 21:68 Ja '87
The smell of fear [rats; research by Michael Fanselow] P. Chance. *Psychol Today* 21:16 Jl '87

Smoke and stress: a double whammy [effect on heart rate; research by Kenneth A. Perkins] G. Lowe. *Psychol Today* 21:19 My '87
The sneaky signs of stress. S. Young. il *Glamour* 85:336 Mr '87
Step away from stress. M. Spilner. il *Prevention* 39:54+ N '87
Stress & disease. B. G. Barley. *Ladies Home J* 104:38+ My '87
Stress and the silent heart attack [research by Leisa J. Freeman and others] M. Roberts. *Psychol Today* 21:7 Ag '87
Stress and the single girl (having it all—and surviving it). J. M. Toal. il *Mademoiselle* 93:293-5+ S '87
Stress can be painful [research by Thomas F. Lundeen] *Prevention* 39:13 Je '87
Stress in the modern world. L. Levi. il *Courier* 40:27-30 Je '87
Stress-management tapes. J. Zinsser. il *Publ Wkly* 232:413-17 Ag 7 '87
Stress, pressure, and peak performance [cover story; special section] il *Ms* 15:37-9+ My '87
Stress stoppers. *Vogue* 177:524 Mr '87
Stress survival manual: how faith can help your family cope [cover story] D. Curran. il *U S Cathol* 52:6-13 Ap '87
Stress: the no.1 beauty enemy. D. Blumenthal. il *Ladies Home J* 104:92-5 Ja '87
Sudden refugee death [Southeast Asians] *Nat Hist* 96:4+ O '87
The taming of stress. T. Osborne. il *Curr Health 2* 14:22-3 O '87
Tough times for teens [views of Cynthia Baum] il *USA Today (Periodical)* 116:9-10 S '87
A tour of the stress circuit. *Psychol Today* 21:59 Ap '87
Turning stress into profits [P. G. Hanson's The joy of stress] D. Francis. por *Macleans* 100:9 Je 1 '87
When you're really hassled [mothers of toddlers] J. T. Gibson. il *Parents* 62:148 Jl '87
Winter in Antarctica: health despite discomfort [positive stress; study by Lawrence A. Palinkas] E. Smith. il *Psychol Today* 21:60-1 Mr '87
Worried sick: hassles and herpes [research by Susan Kennedy and others] R. Weiss. *Sci News* 132:360 D 5 '87
Yuletide strife [family conflict; views of Sidney Russak] il *USA Today (Periodical)* 116:16 D '87

Anecdotes, facetiae, satire, etc.
Aunt Lucy's country cure [holiday stress] J. Taylor. il *Mother Earth News* 108:144 N/D '87
Stress: marriage vs. jail term. M. G. Stoddard. il *Saturday Evening Post* 259:46-7 S '87

Nutritional aspects
High-cadmium diet: recipe for stress? [increased alcohol consumption in rats; research by Jack R. Nation and others] B. Bower. *Sci News* 132:101-2 Ag 15 '87
Keeping stress at bay the nutritious way. B. Hayton. il *Curr Health 2* 14:16-19 O '87
Serene cuisine: foods to battle frazzle and fight fat. P. Bozic. il *Mademoiselle* 93:202 D '87
Stressed out? Good food can help. J. Storm. il *Women's Sports Fitness* 9:54-5 O '87
Stress fractures *See* Fractures
Stress reducing exercises *See* Exercise
Stresses *See* Strains and stresses
Stretch, Bonnie Barrett
Artists' materials. il *Art News* 86:147+ O '87
Fragments of a lost world. il pors *Art News* 86:122-9 Ja '87
Stretch (Physiology)
How flexible should you be? E. Smith. il *Women's Sports Fitness* 9:10 S '87
Stretching exercises
Body be limber. il *Good Housekeep* 204:114 My '87
Fast relief for tension: 4 easy stretches. il *Parents* 62:24 D '87
Fitness. il *Health* 19:44-5 D '87
Stretch and tone! il *McCalls* 114:78-81 Je '87
Stretch out to shape up. D. Graves. il *Harpers Bazaar* 120:168-71+ My '87
Undercover exercise. K. Martin. il *Ms* 15:52-5 Ap '87
Strick, Lisa Wilson
The good old days. il *Good Housekeep* 205:82+ Ag '87
Strickland, Dan
Nantucket: the faraway land [cover story] il map *Oceans* 20:14-23 My/Je '87
Strickland, Edward
What Coltrane wanted. il por *Atlantic* 260:100-2 D '87
Strickland, Richard M., 1950-
The way of the coast. il *Oceans* 20:8-17 Mr/Ap '87

Strickland, Richard M., 1950——cont.
Who is minding the coast? *Oceans* 20:7-8 Jl/Ag '87
Strickland, Richard M., 1950-, and Bevan, Laurie
A new oyster for all seasons. *Oceans* 20:7-8 S/O '87
Strickler, Susan E., and Walsh, Judith C.
Technique in American watercolors from the Worcester Art Museum, Worcester, Massachusetts. bibl f il *Antiques* 131:412-25 F '87
Strieber, Whitley
What 'Communion' really said. por *Publ Wkly* 232:72 O 2 '87

about

Invasion of the Strieber snatchers. T. Cochran. il por *N Y* 20:26 Mr 30 '87
Making Communion with another world. M. Green. il pors *People Wkly* 27:34-9 My 11 '87
UFO update. J. Clary. il *Omni* 9:111 Ap '87
When is a true story true? E. B. Claflin. il por *Publ Wkly* 232:23-6 Ag 14 '87

Anecdotes, facetiae, satire, etc.

The village alien. T. M. Disch. il *Nation* 244:328-34+ Mr 14 '87
Striga *See* Witchweed
Strikebreakers
The life of a $725,000 scab [M. Gastineau] B. Saporito. il por *Fortune* 116:91-2+ O 26 '87
QB Vince Evans benefits from breaking NFL strike. por *Jet* 73:46 N 9 '87
The strikers strike out [scabs replace paper mill workers and football players] M. Satchell. il *U S News World Rep* 103:41-2 O 26 '87
What goes up comes down [NFL strikebreaker J. DeForest] W. Nack. il pors *Sports Illus* 67:68+ D 14 '87
Strikeout records *See* Baseball records
Strikes

See also

Collective labor agreements
Hunger strikes
Picketing
Strikebreakers

Air traffic controllers (Persons)

To rehire or not to rehire? B. Cohn. il *Newsweek* 110:55 N 23 '87

Airline employees

Back to work [TWA ordered to reinstate former strikers from the ranks of Independent Federation of Flight Attendants] D. Bensman. *Nation* 244:875 Je 27 '87
Northwest suit charges nine with organizing job slowdown. *Aviat Week Space Technol* 127:34 S 21 '87
Vicki Frankovich [Independent Federation of Flight Attendants' strike against TWA] C. Doudna. por *Ms* 15:74-6+ Ja '87

Canada

Grounding Air Canada. C. Barrett. il *Macleans* 100:15 D 7 '87
Not-so-friendly skies [Air Canada strike] D. Jenish. il *Macleans* 100:31 D 21 '87
Strike forces Air Canada to halt flight operations. *Aviat Week Space Technol* 127:35 D 7 '87

Automobile industry workers

Mexico

Mexican auto workers resist cuts [strike against Volkswagen] J. Slaughter. *Progressive* 51:12-13 O '87

Basketball players

'Save up,' says Magic, as NBA strike looms. *Jet* 73:48 N 2 '87

Department store employees

Canada

The lessons of Eaton's [1984-85 strike] S. D. Driedger. il *Macleans* 100:32-3 Jl 13 '87

Farm labor

A lawsuit could ruin the Farmworkers' Union [damages for violence in a 1979 strike] J. Flynn. il *Bus Week* p42 Mr 23 '87

Food industry workers

Victory on Cannery Row [settlement of strike at Watsonville Canning] R. Erlich. il *Progressive* 51:26-7 Jl '87

Football players

A big loss on the play. H. Quinn. il *Macleans* 100:45 O 26 '87
The cost of a free agent [NFL strike] A. Wilson-Smith. *Macleans* 100:48 O 5 '87
Dodging eggs and insults, N.Y. Jet Mark Gastineau lines up against his old union and his team. A. Richman. il por *People Wkly* 28:50-2 O 12 '87
Gridlock in the NFL. P. Axthelm. il *Newsweek* 110:74 O 5 '87
'It's our strike' [picketing outside Veterans Stadium, Philadelphia] J. Lieber. il *Sports Illus* 67:46+ O 12 '87

Left with an empty feeling [scab games] P. Zimmerman. il *Sports Illus* 67:38-40+ O 12 '87
The life of a $725,000 scab [M. Gastineau] B. Saporito. il por *Fortune* 116:91-2+ O 26 '87
The line crumbles. il *Time* 130:140 O 26 '87
Men in motion. il *U S News World Rep* 103:16 O 12 '87
New formation: odd man out [aftermath of strike] T. Callahan. il *Time* 130:86 N 9 '87
NFL owners may have fumbled away their victory. A. Bernstein. il *Bus Week* p162 N 2 '87
On the outside looking in [strike ends with no contract] P. Zimmerman. il *Sports Illus* 67:54-6+ O 26 '87
Once again, time out for the fans [strike issue of free agency] A. P. Sanoff. il *U S News World Rep* 103:30-1 O 5 '87
The penalties for delay of game. T. Callahan. il *Time* 130:59-60 O 5 '87
QB Vince Evans benefits from breaking NFL strike. por *Jet* 73:46 N 9 '87
So little gain for the pain. R. Mix. il *Sports Illus* 67:54-6+ O 19 '87
Sorry surrender in the NFL. P. Axthelm. il *Newsweek* 110:68 O 26 '87
The strikers strike out [scabs replace football players] M. Satchell. il *U S News World Rep* 103:41-2 O 26 '87
Striking while the owners are cool. T. Callahan. il *Time* 130:73 O 19 '87
A test of unity and loyalty [Dallas Cowboys] J. Lieber. il *Sports Illus* 67:41-3 O 5 '87
Thirty pieces of silver: reflections on the not-so-great football strike of 1987. R. Reilly. por *Sports Illus* 67:132 O 26 '87
Time to heal the wounds [49ers after strike] J. Lieber. il *Sports Illus* 67:86+ N 2 '87
Upshaw claims racism influences NFL strike. por *Jet* 73:49 O 19 '87
Welcome back to the NFL [season in wake of strike] P. Zimmerman. il *Sports Illus* 67:62-3 O 26 '87
What goes up comes down [strikebreaker J. DeForest] W. Nack. il pors *Sports Illus* 67:68+ D 14 '87
When push came to shove. P. Zimmerman. il *Sports Illus* 67:38-41 O 5 '87
Why the owners can't scuttle free agents. J. Hoerr. il *Bus Week* p42 O 5 '87

Helicopter industry

Workers strike at Bell Helicopter, De Havilland plants. *Aviat Week Space Technol* 126:27 Je 29 '87

Miners

South Africa

Black labor power. *Nation* 245:183-4 S 5 '87
Digging out to avoid a cave-in [strike settled] B. W. Nelan. il *Time* 130:32 S 7 '87
S. African mines hit hard with 'big' strike. il *Jet* 72:4 Ag 24 '87
South Africa: a clash of wills. S. Reiss. il *Newsweek* 110:28-9 Ag 24 '87
South Africa: lessons of a bitter strike. S. Reiss. il *Newsweek* 110:35 S 7 '87
South African miners test political clout. M. August. il *Black Enterp* 18:19-20 N '87
South Africa's whites face a new reality. J. Jones. il *U S News World Rep* 103:29 Ag 24 '87
A strike at a nation's heart. il *Macleans* 100:23 Ag 24 '87
This miners' strike may hit political pay dirt. A. Fine. il *Bus Week* p35 Ag 24 '87
Trouble from belowground. W. E. Smith. il *Time* 130:33 Ag 24 '87

Motion picture directors

Hollywood directors: lights, camera, walkout? R. Grover. il *Bus Week* p66 My 25 '87
Make money, not war. A. Gibney and A. Thompson. il *Film Comment* 23:17-18+ N/D '87

Paper industry workers

The strikers strike out [scabs replace paper mill workers] M. Satchell. il *U S News World Rep* 103:41-2 O 26 '87

Postal employees

Canada

Anger on the postal picket line. M. Clark. il *Macleans* 100:26+ O 19 '87
A bitter confrontation. M. Gee. il *Macleans* 100:10-11 Je 29 '87
A bitter return to work. M. Clark. il *Macleans* 100:27 O 26 '87
Drawing the battle lines [postal strike; cover story; special section; with editorial comment by Kevin Doyle] il *Macleans* 100:2, 10-14+ O 12 '87

Strikes—Postal employees—Canada—cont.
Post office showdown [impending strike by Canadian Union of Postal Workers] M. Clark. il *Macleans* 100:24-5 O 5 '87
Violence on the lines; The heart of the matter. M. Clark. il *Macleans* 100:10-11 Jl 6 '87

Publishers and publishing
Canada
An internal affair [Maclean's employees strike] K. Doyle. il *Macleans* 100:2 Ap 13 '87

Railroad workers
Canada
A short and angry strike [rail workers ordered back to work] M. Gee. il *Macleans* 100:22-3 S 7 '87
France
The rail strike may break—or make—Chirac. J. Rossant. il *Bus Week* p50 Ja 19 '87

Steel workers
It's a no-win situation for both sides at USX. M. Rothman and G. L. Miles. il *Bus Week* p55-6 Ja 19 '87
Steel workers on the line [strike against Brenner Tank Company] M. Wettstein, Jr. and J. Gormican. *Progressive* 51:15-16 Ja '87

Teachers
State's first teacher strike in Little Rock. il *Jet* 73:22 O 19 '87

Television news
Walking slowly in circles [writers' strike] D. A. Purdy. por *U S News World Rep* 102:7 Ap 6 '87
Israel
Israel enjoys silent airwaves. M. R. Halton. il *Christ Century* 104:1111-12 D 9 '87
Israel without television. E. Salpeter. il *New Leader* 70:7-8 N 30 '87

Television workers
Sammy Davis refuses to cross line of pickets [National Assn. of Broadcast Employees and Technicians] *Jet* 72:10 Ag 31 '87
France
Dark time in the City of Light. M. Whitaker. il por *Newsweek* 109:27 Ja 19 '87
Great Britain
History
Keeping the peace? Policing strikes 1906-26. B. Weinberger. bibl il *Hist Today* 37:29-35 D '87
Italy
Season of strikes and discontent. M. Johnson. il *Time* 130:35 D 7 '87
Korea (South)
Korean labor. A. Giarelli. il *World Press Rev* 34:48 O '87
Out on the street. *Time* 130:33 Ag 24 '87
South Korea: labor pains. N. Cooper. il *Newsweek* 110:26-7 Ag 31 '87
South Korea's days of danger. J. Dreyfuss. il *Fortune* 116:101+ O 12 '87
Sputtering back to life [Hyundai strike settled; others continue] H. G. Chua-Eoan. il *Time* 130:30 Ag 31 '87
Will labor unrest wreck Korea's economic boom? L. Nakarmi. il *Bus Week* p40-1 Ag 31 '87
Panama
The battle for 50th Street [opposition to M. A. Noriega] N. Cooper. il por *Newsweek* 110:42-3 Ag 10 '87
The general went to work [opposition to M. A. Noriega] J. Smolowe. il por *Time* 130:21 Ag 10 '87
South Africa
Botha's defiant show of force. S. Reiss. il *Newsweek* 109:34 My 4 '87
Labor: now it's showdown time. S. Mufson. il *Bus Week* p48 My 4 '87
United States
See Strikes
Yugoslavia
Striking at the system. il *Macleans* 100:21 Ap 13 '87

String ensembles
See also
Compact discs—String ensemble music
String quartets
See also
Compact discs—String quartet music
Juilliard String Quartet
Kronos Quartet
Orford String Quartet
String Trio of New York
String Trio of New York: a decade of perseverance. K. Whitehead. il *Down Beat* 11:26-8 N '87
Stringed instruments
See also
Violin

Stringer, Howard
about
"If Howard had known . . . " [cover story] M. Gordon. il pors *Channels* 7:60-6 O '87
Lessons in job leveraging from the CBS shake-up. J. Ciabattari. por *Work Woman* 12:67 F '87
News by the numbers. R. Corliss. por *Time* 129:64 Mr 16 '87
Stringer, Omer
about
From woods to Roots. D. Cumming. por *Macleans* 100:6 Ja 19 '87
Strings (Cosmic) See Cosmic strings
Strings (Tennis rackets) See Tennis rackets—Strings
Strip cropping
How the strip-croppers are polishing their act. M. Holmberg. il *Success Farm* 85 no6:18AF Mr '87
Native grass buffer strips [modified contour strip-cropping] J. Walter. il *Success Farm* 85 no5:26AJ Mr '87
Strip mined land, Reclamation of See Reclamation of land
Strip mining
Laws and regulations
See also
United States. Office of Surface Mining, Reclamation, and Enforcement
Can strip mining clean up its act? [failure to enforce Surface Mining Control and Reclamation Act] W. Marx. il *Read Dig* 130:121-5 Mr '87
South Dakota
More precious than gold [opposition to open pit gold mining] J. W. Wilson. il *Progressive* 51:11 N '87
Striped bass culture See Fish culture
Striped bass fishing See Bass fishing
Striper fishing See Bass fishing
Stripped municipal bonds
A new way to prepare for that rainy day. A. McGrath. il *U S News World Rep* 102:65 F 9 '87
A tax-exempt muni that's good college material. B. Hitchings. *Bus Week* p106 Ja 26 '87
Striptease, Male See Male striptease
Stritch, Elaine
about
Elaine Stritch: "I've decided the reason I work well with Woody Allen is that he's got my number" [interview] L. Smith. il por *Vogue* 177:174+ D '87
Strobe units (Photography) See Photography—Flash equipment
Strobel, Gary A.
about
Bozeman chain saw massacre. W. E. Brock. il pors *Discover* 8:78-82+ N '87
Montana State's troublesome elms. M. D. Lemonick. il por *Time* 130:67 S 14 '87
MSU faults Strobel for Dutch elm test. L. Roberts. *Science* 237:1286 S 11 '87
New questions in Strobel case. L. Roberts. *Science* 237:1097-8 S 4 '87
Researcher flouts gene-splicing rules. M. Crawford. *Science* 237:838-9 Ag 21 '87
Strober Organization (Firm)
Soaring sales, stalled stock. F. Rice. *Fortune* 116:172+ N 9 '87
Stroessner, Alfredo
about
Paraguay's Stroessner: losing control? J. H. Williams. bibl f *Curr Hist* 86:25-8+ Ja '87
Smuggler's paradise. T. Rosenberg. *New Repub* 196:14-16 Je 8 '87
Trying to ignore the winds of change [special section] il *World Press Rev* 34:26-8 D '87
Stroetzel, Diana
(jt. auth) See Stroetzel, Donald S., and Stroetzel, Diana
Stroetzel, Donald S., and Stroetzel, Diana
Should you join an HMO? *Read Dig* 131:91-5 Ag '87
Stroff, Stephen M.
Music memorabilia. See issues of Antiques & Collecting Hobbies beginning February 1986
Stroger, John H., Jr.
about
Honor King's birthday with vote drive, says Chicago commissioner. il por *Jet* 71:14 Ja 26 '87
Stroke See Cerebrovascular disease
Stroll, Ted
Travelers' respite. il *Natl Parks* 61:14-15 My/Je '87
Stromatolites
Sand castles from the past: Bahamian stromatolites discovered [cover story] E. A. Shinn. il map *Sea Front* 33:334-43 S/O '87

Stromberg-Carlson Corp.
Plessey's new face in the U.S. J. J. Keller. il *Bus Week* p32 Ap 20 '87
Strong, Maurice F.
about
Maurice Strong: reviving a valley with beer and religion. S. D. Atchison. il por *Bus Week* p146 D 7 '87
What happened to utopia? [interview] N. Myers. il *Int Wildl* 17:36-7 Jl/Ag '87
Strong, William S.
Legal shadings. *Society* 24:19-21 My/Je '87
Strontium in sea water *See* Sea water
Stroud, Betsy Dillard
Kay Polk: combining pastels and watercolors to paint portraits. il *Am Artist* 51:60-3 O '87
Roger Winter. il *Am Artist* 51:52-5 Jl '87
Strouse, Jean
Tycoon taste. il por *House Gard* 159:94+ My '87
Structural engineering
See also
Strains and stresses
Tension structures
Le Corbusier as structural engineer. W. Seligmann. il *Archit Rec* 175:142-51 O '87
Structural failures
See also
Building failures
Structural geology *See* Geology
Structured Query Language (Computer language)
Connecting to data bases. M. Liskin. il *Pers Comput* 11:79-80+ S '87
Why most of us need to learn to speak SQL. E. Esber, Jr. por *Pers Comput* 11:224 O '87
Struggle for existence *See* Competition (Biology)
The struggles for Poland [television program] See Television program reviews—Single works
Strum, Shirley
The "Gang" moves to a strange new land. il por map *Natl Geogr* 172:676-90 N '87
Strummer, Joe
about
Combat rocker [interview] G. Fuller. il pors *Film Comment* 23:45-6+ Jl/Ag '87
Struthers, Sally
about
Coming back big: Sally Struthers' lucky streak. N. Gittelson. il pors *McCalls* 114:12-13+ Je '87
Struve Gallery
High style in the heartland. S. Winckler. il *House Gard* 159:98+ Ap '87
Stryer, Lubert
The molecules of visual excitation. bibl (p116) il *Sci Am* 257:42-50 Jl '87
Stryker, Mark
How to become a house musician. pors *Down Beat* 54:54+ F '87
Stryper (Musical group)
Stryper: a holy hit. S. Pond. il *Roll Stone* p32 F 26 '87
Stuart, Floyd C.
The salt marsh. il *Atlantic* 260:70-6 O '87
Stuart, Jan
A queer kind of film. *Film Comment* 23:4+ N/D '87
Stuart, Michelle
about
Melancholy mapping. S. Westfall. il *Art Am* 75:104-9 F '87
Stuart, Otis
McBride gets to the pointe. por *Harpers Bazaar* 120:139+ Ag '87
New faces at the New York City Ballet: future indicative. il *Dance Mag* 61:70-3 Ja '87
Stepping out. il *Harpers Bazaar* 120:152+ O '87
Vancouver's Ballet British Columbia: staking a claim. il *Dance Mag* 61:50-1 Ag '87
Stuart, Richard B., and Jacobson, Barbara
Danger! Marriage can make you fat [excerpt from Weight, sex and marriage] il *Redbook* 169:92-3+ Ag '87
Stuart Brent Books (Chicago, Ill.: Bookstore) *See* Booksellers and bookselling—Illinois
Stuart-James Company Inc.
Poison wine in new bottles. D. Henry. il *Forbes* 140:32-4 O 5 '87
Stubbins, Hugh, 1912-
about
Hugh Stubbins and the life of architecture. R. Kimball. il *Archit Rec* 175:61+ Ap '87
Stubblefield, Sara P., and others
Fossil mycorrhizae: a case for symbiosis. bibl f il *Science* 237:59-60 Jl 3 '87

Stubbs, Eric
Soviet strategic defense technology. bibl f il map *Bull At Sci* 43:14-19 Ap '87
Stubbs, Ken
Rackets '87. il *World Tennis* 34:53-5 My '87
about
String break [interview] A. Beck. *World Tennis* 35:37+ N '87
Stubbs, Levi
about
Though green to film, Levi Stubbs of the Four Tops turns offscreen scene-stealer in Little shop of horrors. N. Geeslin. il pors *People Wkly* 27:105-6 Mr 9 '87
Stubbs, Phyllis E.
(jt. auth) See Phillips, Margaret G., and Stubbs, Phyllis E.
Stucco
How to stucco over concrete block. G. Branson. il *Fam Handyman* 37:49-52 S '87
Stuchly, Judy Bauer- *See* Bauer-Stuchly, Judy
Stud farms *See* Horses—Breeding
Student achievements
See also
Accountability (Education)
Educational tests and measurements
National Assessment of Educational Progress
Are Asian-American kids really smarter? F. Butterfield. il *Read Dig* 130:87-90 Ja '87
Chapter 1 students score higher than other disadvantaged students. *Phi Delta Kappan* 68:638+ Ap '87
"Demanding families" and black student achievement. C. R. Wharton. *Educ Dig* 52:18-20 My '87
Kids' views of school success. F. Roberts. *Parents* 62:61 Ap '87
The new whiz kids [Asian Americans; cover story] D. Brand. il *Time* 130:42-6+ Ag 31 '87
No boys allowed: a smart solution? [girls attending single-sex Catholic high schools do better academically; research by Valerie E. Lee and Anthony S. Bryk] S. Vandershaf. il *Psychol Today* 21:68 F '87
Small is beautiful—and effective [research by Sid Bourke] G. W. Bracey. il *Phi Delta Kappan* 68:703 My '87
"We have a problem". J. Marks. il *Parents* 62:60+ N '87
Student activities
See also
College and school drama
College and school journalism
College athletics
College students—Political activities
Drill teams
Proms (Dances)
Activity overload. D. Elkind. il *Parents* 62:271 N '87
No-pass/no-play hurts minorities more than whites [high school students] il *Phi Delta Kappan* 68:561 Mr '87
Student aid
See also
ConSern Program
I Have a Dream Foundation
Scholarships and fellowships
Student Loan Marketing Association
The bad business of student loans [defaults] G. Witkin. il *U S News World Rep* 103:32 S 14 '87
College board prexy says Reagan's ed. policy hurts minority students most [views of D. M. Stewart] por *Jet* 72:8 Ap 27 '87
A college financial aid primer. P. L. Spencer. il *Consum Res Mag* 70:19-23 Ag '87
Cuts in aid has drastic effect on black students. *Jet* 72:32 Ap 20 '87
A dream come true [followup on students of P.S. 121 in East Harlem helped by E. M. Lang] M. deC. Hinds. il por *N Y Times Mag* p32-6 Ap 26 '87
Education Dept. warns student loan defaulters. *Jet* 72:23 Ag 3 '87
Graduation-contingent student aid: fighting the high costs of dropping out. F. J. Fischer. il *Change* 19:40-7 N/D '87
Here's a course in paying for college. J. Bodnar. *Changing Times* 41:11 N '87
How to get a piece of the $21 billion scholarship pie. R. E. McKinney. bibl il *Ebony* 43:124+ D '87
Income contingent loans. J. P. Merisotis. il *Change* 19:10-11 Mr/Ap '87
Mike Hayes learns that tuition is just common cents [plea for pennies to finance education] il por *People Wkly* 28:154 N 16 '87
Needy kids, perpetual aid [A. Fogelman subsidizes college tuition for Memphis students] por *Time* 130:70 N 30 '87

Student aid—*cont.*

A 'pay up or else' ultimatum from William Bennett [threatening to withhold federal aid from colleges with 20% student loan default rate] R. A. Taylor. il *U S News World Rep* 103:16 N 16 '87

Plea for pennies turns up $14,000 for college student attending U. of Illinois [M. Hayes] *Jet* 73:24 O 26 '87

Revenge of the nerds [federal employee wages excluded from student loan collection efforts] F. Zakaria. *New Repub* 197:16-17 S 14-21 '87

Student aid: are women getting what they deserve? G. Hechinger. *Glamour* 85:206-7 Jl '87

Student-loan rules may hurt black schools. il *Jet* 73:4 D 7 '87

Taking on Secretary Bennett [issue of college costs and student aid] M. P. McPherson and P. Korshin. pors *U S News World Rep* 102:6 Je 29 '87

Ticker tape scholars selected for '87-'88 [students having financial trouble] il *Jet* 72:23-4 Jl 27 '87

Tuition aid 1980s style. J. B. Quinn. il *Newsweek* 110:74 O 12 '87

Canada

The artful dodgers [student loan defaults] M. McIver. il *Macleans* 100:61-3 O 5 '87

Student art *See* Children's art

Student clubs and societies
See also
Just Say No (Organization)

Student demonstrations *See* Student protests, demonstrations, etc.

Student dropouts *See* Dropouts

Student employment *See* Youth—Employment

Student exchange programs

Andover's mission to Moscow [exchange of high school students] J. N. Baker. il *Newsweek* 110:102-3 N 16 '87

I was a teen-age cosmonaut [Young Astronauts-Young Cosmonauts exchange] K. McMains. il *Space World* X-2-278:32-3+ F '87

The 'Kids for Peace' reach out [Moorestown, N.J. Friends School exchange program with East Germany] D. Dahlke. il *World Press Rev* 34:45 Ap '87

Semester abroad—at home [Washington Semester Program and Simmons Semester in Boston] il *Glamour* 85:206-7 Jl '87

The 'uglification' of hospitality [lack of host families for foreign students] J. Lurie. por *U S News World Rep* 103:8 O 12 '87

Student guidance *See* Educational counseling

Student Loan Marketing Association

Young, clever and filthy rich. J. Egan. il *U S News World Rep* 103:48 N 30 '87

Student loans *See* Student aid

Student militants
See also
Students for a Democratic Society

Student mobility
See also
Children of migrant laborers—Education

Student movement

There's something happening here [new new left on campus] M. Margaronis. *Nation* 245:757 D 19 '87

History

The real 'Big chill' in Michigan [reunion of 1960s Ann Arbor activists] E. Frank. il *Nation* 245:480-2 O 31 '87

China

History

Into the streets again: faith vs. frustration. J. Shapiro. il *Newsweek* 109:31+ Ja 5 '87

Proud legacy of youthful protest. il *Time* 129:52 Ja 5 '87

Student newspapers *See* College and school journalism

Student opinion *See* Students—Attitudes

Student participation in school administration *See* School management and organization—Student participation

Student performance *See* Student achievements

Student protests, demonstrations, etc.

Amy Carter and Abbie Hoffman win acquittal, but they want to keep the C.I.A. on trial. F. A. Bernstein. il pors *People Wkly* 27:57-8+ My 4 '87

Amy Carter gets probation for Brown apartheid protest. *Jet* 72:22 Mr 30 '87

Amy's day [A. Carter acquitted in protest against CIA campus recruiting] J. Nocera. *New Repub* 196:11-13 My 11 '87

Back to the future: Columbia replays the battles of '68 [eviction battles and racial tensions] P. Blauner. il *N Y* 20:30-3 My 18 '87

Campus controversy [racial tension at Columbia University] S. McConnell. *New Repub* 196:13-14 My 25 '87

Closing argument [protest against CIA campus recruitment; closing remarks to jury, April 15, 1987] A. Hoffman. *Nation* 244:562-3 My 2 '87

The future is yours (still) [closing remarks to jury, April 15, 1987] A. Hoffman. *Harpers* 275:21+ Jl '87

No longer in the White House, a young Carter rediscovers the importance of being Amy. D. Chu. il por *People Wkly* 27:36-7 Ja 5 '87

Not guilty by necessity [A. Carter acquitted in protest against CIA recruiting on campus] por *Time* 129:71 Ap 27 '87

On trial: cheers and jeers for Amy Carter. por *Newsweek* 109:33 Ap 20 '87

Yale anti-apartheid protest. il *Jet* 72:15 Je 15 '87

International aspects

New generation in the streets. W. Svoboda. il *Time* 129:62 F 23 '87

Chile

Chile's student leaders under fire. T. Rosenberg. il *Roll Stone* p97+ S 24 '87

China

Children of December. P. Sabatier. il *World Press Rev* 34:12-13 Mr '87

China. B. Stavis. *Nation* 244:466-8 Ap 11 '87

The China syndrome. B. I. Schwartz. *New Repub* 196:15-16 F 9 '87

China's ghastly tragedy. *Natl Rev* 39:16-17 F 13 '87

China's new math. S. Leys. *New Repub* 196:13 Mr 2 '87

China's student protests. il *World Press Rev* 34:19 F '87

China's student rebels are playing into Deng's hands. M. Shao. il por *Bus Week* p48-9 Ja 19 '87

Free speech Chinese style [special section] il por *Newsweek* 109:30-1+ Ja 5 '87

More wintry days of discontent. W. R. Doerner. il *Time* 129:38 Ja 12 '87

The new thunder out of China—what it means. R. A. Manning. il *U S News World Rep* 102:12 Ja 12 '87

Opening the windows. A. Bilski. il *Macleans* 100:19 Ja 12 '87

Rumblings. *New Repub* 196:7-9 Ja 19 '87

There's a dragon out there [government reaction] M. S. Serrill. il *Time* 129:45 Ja 19 '87

Thinking about home [reaction of Chinese students in the U.S.] il *Time* 129:45 F 2 '87

The threat of the gulag. M. Achiron. il *Newsweek* 109:33 Ja 19 '87

"We will march!". M. S. Serrill. il *Time* 129:50-2 Ja 5 '87

'You cannot arrest us'. D. Elliott. il *Newsweek* 109:28-30 Ja 12 '87

France

France. D. Ireland. *Nation* 244:464-6 Ap 11 '87

Student protests block university changes. D. Dickson. il *Science* 235:24-5 Ja 2 '87

Italy

Italy. G. Riotta. *Nation* 244:453+ Ap 11 '87

Korea (South)

The battle of Seoul. B. Levin. il *Macleans* 100:16-17 Jl 6 '87

Brinkmanship in South Korea. R. Watson. il por *Newsweek* 110:26-7 Jl 6 '87

Chun's hard line can only deepen Korea's unrest. L. Nakarmi and B. Javetski. il *Bus Week* p49 Jl 6 '87

Chun's option: to crush or concede. M. Lord. il map *U S News World Rep* 102:26-8 Je 29 '87

Crisis in Korea [cover story] R. Watson. il map *Newsweek* 109:28-35 Je 29 '87

Dark days of rage. B. Levin. il *Macleans* 100:28 Je 29 '87

"Down with dictatorship". il *Time* 129:40 Je 22 '87

Korea: a bloody fall term? New riots overshadow a constitutional accord. B. Martin. il *Newsweek* 110:48 S 14 '87

Korea divided. *Nation* 245:3-4 Jl 4-11 '87

Korea's boom times are keeping rebellion at bay—so far. L. Nakarmi and J. Becker. il *Bus Week* p42-3 Je 29 '87

Korea's endless surprises. T. Walkom. il *World Press Rev* 34:20-2 Ag '87

Onslaughts of force and fury. J. Greenwald. il *Time* 129:50-1 Mr 16 '87

Rage builds in South Korea. il *U S News World Rep* 102:18 Je 22 '87

South Korea. J. Brill. *Nation* 244:469-70 Ap 11 '87

The struggle gains its martyr [death of student protester] W. R. Doerner. il *Time* 130:43 Jl 20 '87

Student protests, demonstrations, etc.—Korea (South)—
cont.

Talk and fight [Chun Doo Hwan makes concessions to opposition] W. R. Doerner. il por *Time* 130:14-15 Jl 6 '87

Terror in the streets. P. McGill. il *Macleans* 100:18-19 Je 22 '87

Two steps forward, one back: free elections are scheduled and new violence breaks out. J. Greenwald. il *Time* 130:41 S 14 '87

Under siege [cover story; special section] il map *Time* 129:20-4+ Je 29 '87

A volcano of unrest. W. R. Doerner. il *Time* 129:46-7 My 25 '87

Years of dictatorship, days of destruction. F. Willey. il *Newsweek* 109:32+ Je 22 '87

Mexico

Mexico. W. A. Orme, Jr. *Nation* 244:468-9 Ap 11 '87

Spain

Spain. G. Jackson. il *Nation* 244:470-1 Ap 11 '87

Spain's students test the government [special section] il *World Press Rev* 34:29-31 Ap '87

Student publications *See* College and school journalism

Student records *See* School reports and records

Student recruiting *See* Black colleges and universities—Student recruiting; Colleges and universities—Student recruiting

Student reports *See* Student themes and reports

Student rights *See* Students—Civil rights

Student selection *See* Colleges and universities—Admission

Student suspension and expulsion

Blacks more likely to be suspended, punished in nation's public schools. *Jet* 72:32 Ap 20 '87

Sarabeth Eason [interview with 11 year old expelled from Toledo Catholic school for supporting abortion free choice] C. Grant. il pors *Ms* 15:60-1+ Ja '87

Student teachers

Internships in Alberta. T. McConaghy. *Phi Delta Kappan* 68:794-5 Je '87

Student themes and reports

The cheating industry [services selling term papers to lazy students] D. K. Mano. *Natl Rev* 39:50+ Je 5 '87

Student violence *See* School violence

Student volunteers *See* Volunteer service

Students

See also

Black students
Clothing and dress—Students
College students
Foreign students
High school students
High school students, Gifted
Law students
School children
School management and organization—Student participation
Science students
Seminarians
Women college students

Is in loco parentis dead? P. A. Zirkel and H. F. Reichner. bibl f il *Phi Delta Kappan* 68:466-9 F '87

Attitudes

American schools rate a "B" [survey of children] *USA Today (Periodical)* 116:5 Ag '87

Child likes [children's images of the future; study by Ruthanne Kurth-Schai] D. Sobel. il *Omni* 10:30+ N '87

Children's visions of the future [Weekly reader survey] L. Johnson. il por *Futurist* 21:36-40 My/Je '87

Kids' views of school success. F. Roberts. *Parents* 62:61 Ap '87

Cheating

See Cheating in school work

Civil rights

School rules: who makes 'em? Who breaks 'em? S. Rubin. il *Teen* 31:72+ O '87

Employment

See Youth—Employment

Ethics

See also

Cheating in school work
College graduates—Ethics

Grading

See Grading and marking (Students)

Psychology

How to handle death in the school. R. G. Stevenson and H. L. Powers. *Educ Dig* 52:42-3 My '87

Unemployment

See Unemployment

Volunteer service

See Volunteer service

Students and drugs *See* Drugs and youth

Students and teachers *See* Teachers and students

Students for a Democratic Society

Don't follow leaders [cover story] P. Berman. il *New Repub* 197:28-35 Ag 10-17 '87

Dreams of the sixties. A. Brinkley. bibl f il *N Y Rev Books* 34:10+ O 22 '87

Resurrecting the new left. S. McConnell. *Commentary* 84:31-8 O '87

Still idealists after all these years. W. L. Chaze. il *U S News World Rep* 102:60-2 Je 15 '87

Students' vocabularies *See* Vocabulary

Studer, Robert

about

The big cheese in London banking could be Swiss. J. Templeman. il *Bus Week* p37 Jl 27 '87

Studies (Rooms)

In the study of John Sculley [chairman of Apple Computer] il por *Esquire* 107:86-7 Ap '87

Now it's a study. il *South Living* 22:173 My '87

Studio apartments *See* Apartments

Studios

See also

Artists' studios
Dance studios

Materials are ordinary, the results are surprising. il *Sunset* 179:86 Jl '87

Studios, Recording *See* Sound—Recording and reproducing

Study

See also

Homework

Cram at your own risk. W. Coffey. il *Seventeen* 46:48+ My '87

Study guides

See also

Cliff's Notes Inc.

Publishers and publishing—Study guides

Study-work plans *See* Business and education

Stueben, Michael

Brain bogglers. See issues of Discover beginning November 1984 through September 1987

Stuffing (Food)

Easy corn-bread stuffing [microwaved] J. B. Hurley. il *Prevention* 39:94 N '87

Stuffing: a confession [turkey stuffing] L. Colwin. il *Gourmet* 47:120+ N '87

Stuller, Jay

Battle-weary Lake Tahoe combatants try compromise. il *Audubon* 89:44-6+ My '87

The littlest Marine. il pors *Read Dig* 131:123-7 Jl '87

Mussel colonies thrive on oil platform legs. il *Oceans* 20:6-7+ Ja/F '87

Stuller, Stuart

The last big dam? *Wilderness* 51:34-6 Fall '87

When is a record not a record? il *Women's Sports Fitness* 9:92-3 Mr '87

Stummer, Helen M.

Ordinary miseries. il *Society* 24:83-7 Mr/Ap '87

Stunkard, Albert J., 1922-

Family fat; ed. by Bill Lawren. il *Health* 19:8 F '87

Stunt flying *See* Aviation—Stunt flying

Stunt men and women

Sandy Richman, stuntwoman. F. DiGiacomo. por *Seventeen* 46:232 Ag '87

Stunt motorcycling *See* Motorcycling—Stunt cycling

Stunts

Photographs and photography

Pedal, Georg, but don't look back! Something might be gainin' on ya! [shot engineered by photographer G. Lukas in West Germany] il por *People Wkly* 28:137 D 14 '87

Stupidity

The stupid things we do. J. Bernard. il *Seventeen* 46:60 Mr '87

Stupple, Donna-Marie

Helping literature students learn about suicide. *Educ Dig* 53:56-8 D '87

Sturbridge (Mass.)

Historic houses, sites, etc.

See also

Old Sturbridge Village

Sturbridge Village *See* Old Sturbridge Village

Sturc, John H.

Illegal insider trading [address, October 17, 1986] *Vital Speeches Day* 53:404-9 Ap 15 '87

Sturgeon fishing
Fun with "alligators" on the Columbia River. P. Barrett. il *Field Stream* 91:82+ F '87
Sturgeons
See also
Caviar
Sturtevant, Roger
about
In Oakland, the architectural photography of Roger Sturtevant. il por *Sunset* 178:34 Ja '87
Stuttering
Rule no. 1 if your child stutters: relax. C. Tuzzolino. il *Bus Week* p206 N 2 '87
Stuttgart (Germany)
Music
See also
Opera—Germany (West)
Stuttgart Ballet
Reviews:
Performances of Sleeping beauty in Stuttgart. H. Koegler. il *Dance Mag* 61:20 Ag '87
Stutz, Bruce D.
Why the shark bites. *Nat Hist* 96:94+ N '87
Stutz, Geraldine
Buster of Bendel's. il *N Y* 20:68 D 21-28 '87
about
The battle of Bendel's. J. Kornbluth. il pors *N Y* 20:26-33 F 23 '87
Reshaping a corner of Connecticut. K. Whiteside. il *House Gard* 159:152-5+ Jl '87
Stüwe, Michael
(jt. auth) See Grodinsky, Caroline, and Stüwe, Michael
Style, Artistic
When artists change styles. D. Grant. *Am Artist* 51:22+ D '87
Style, Literary
Ripening desire and the muse of middle age [excerpt from Voicelust] M. Apple. il *N Y Times Book Rev* 92:1+ Mr 1 '87
That great blank page, the screen [questioning the concept of cinematic fiction] T. McDonough. il *N Y Times Book Rev* 92:1+ N 15 '87
Style, Personal *See* Fashion
Styles-McLeod, Catherine
The art of Count Bernard de Clavière d'Hust. il *Archit Dig* 44:208-15+ My '87
Buying a second house in Paris. il pors *Archit Dig* 44 Archit Dig Travels:10+ O '87
Eugene Viollet-le-Duc: restorer of France's architectural legacy. il por *Archit Dig* 44:172+ Ag '87
Styling, Automobile *See* Automobiles—Design
Styrene
A bizarre bezoar tale [research by Eckard W. Hellmuth] S. Weisburd. *Sci News* 132:190 S 19 '87
Styron, William, 1925-
Jimmy in the house. por *N Y Times Book Rev* 92:30 D 20 '87
A Tidewater morning [fiction] il *Esquire* 108:85-96 Ag '87
Su, Adrienne
Waking up. il por *Humanist* 47:20-1+ Mr/Ap '87
Suall, Irwin
Extremist groups seek recruits in prisons. il *USA Today (Periodical)* 116:22-8 S '87
Suard, Pierre
about
Now that CGE is a heavyweight, it will have to fight like one. T. Peterson and F. J. Comes. il por *Bus Week* p98+ My 18 '87
Sub-Ocean Salvors International
Romancing the wreck. W. G. Flanagan. il *Forbes* 140:116 S 7 '87
Subak-Sharpe, Genell J.
Common winter ailments and their cures. il *Ladies Home J* 104:102+ D '87
"Mommy, I don't feel good . . ." Kids' symptoms not to ignore. il *Ladies Home J* 104:82+ N '87
Women's symptoms not to ignore. *Ladies Home J* 104:31-2 Ap '87
Subaru (Automobile) *See* Automobiles, Foreign
Subaru of America, Inc.
It's tough, but it isn't doomsday. R. Phalon. il *Forbes* 139:53+ My 4 '87
Subchapter S corporations *See* S corporations
Subconsciousness
See also
Dreams
Hypnotism
Subliminal projection
The cognitive unconscious. J. F. Kihlstrom. bibl f *Science* 237:1445-52 S 18 '87

Subduction (Geology)
All's not quiet on the northwestern front [work of Thomas H. Heaton and Stephen H. Hartzell] map *Discover* 8:9-10 Je '87
Coastal ups and downs point to a big quake. R. A. Kerr. *Science* 235:166 Ja 9 '87
Earthquake hazards on the Cascadia subduction zone. T. H. Heaton and S. H. Hartzell. bibl f il maps *Science* 236:162-8 Ap 10 '87
The Juan de Fuca plate: a sticky situation [Cascadia subduction zone] R. Monastersky. il map *Sci News* 132:42-3 Jl 18 '87
Subiela, Eliseo
about
Man facing southeast [film] Reviews
Américas 39:60-1 N/D '87. J. Mosier
Commonweal 114:243-4 Ap 24 '87. T. O'Brien
Macleans il 100:49 Ap 13 '87
New Repub 196:26 Ap 6 '87. S. Kauffmann
Subjectivism *See* Subjectivity
Subjectivity
The tyranny of subjectivism [address, September 18, 1987] G. Leonard. *Vital Speeches Day* 54:50-7 N 1 '87
Subliminal projection
I like Harper's! [subliminal message tapes] *Harpers* 274:22 Ja '87
Submarine archeology *See* Archeology, Submarine
Submarine blasting *See* Blasting, Submarine
Submarine cables *See* Cables, Submarine
Submarine diving *See* Diving, Submarine
Submarine geology
See also
Marine sediments
Ocean bottom
Ocean Drilling Program
Seamounts
Horizontal plate motion: a key allocyclic factor in the evolution of the Great Barrier Reef. P. J. Davies and others. bibl f il map *Science* 238:1697-700 D 18 '87
Present at the birth of an ore deposit [Salton Sea area] R. A. Kerr. il *Science* 238:890-1 N 13 '87
Submarine mines *See* Mines, Submarine
Submarine photography *See* Photography, Submarine
Submarine research vehicles *See* Oceanographic submersibles
Submarine thermal springs *See* Hot springs
Submarine warfare
See also
Anti-submarine warfare
Guided missiles—Launching from submarines
World War, 1939-1945—Submarine operations
Enter the 'silent service' [submarine simulation video games] *U S News World Rep* 102:42 Je 15 '87
How to stop a Russian 'surge' [interview with T. Clancy] W. J. Cook and R. Kaylor. il por *U S News World Rep* 102:43 Je 15 '87
Submarines
See also
Nuclear submarines
Oceanographic submersibles
Submarine warfare
Deadly game of hide-and-seek [cover story; special section] il *U S News World Rep* 102:36-43 Je 15 '87
Communication systems
Signaling subs. T. A. Heppenheimer. il *Pop Sci* 230:44-8 Ap '87
Submarines, Atomic powered *See* Nuclear submarines
Submarines, Russian
An illegal deal's noisy repercussions [Soviet deal with Toshiba and Kongsberg for milling machines to make submarine propellers] W. J. Cook. il *U S News World Rep* 102:42 Je 15 '87
A leak that could sink the U.S. lead in submarines [illegal sales to Soviet Union by Norway's KV and Japan's Toshiba] J. Kapstein. il *Bus Week* p65-6 My 18 '87
Making amends [Toshiba products banned in U.S. following sale of submarine technology to Soviets] *Time* 130:49 Jl 13 '87
Run silent, run to Moscow [sale of submarine technology to the Soviets by Toshiba and Kongsberg] G. Bock. il *Time* 129:45 Je 29 '87
Submersibles, Oceanographic *See* Oceanographic submersibles
Subrahmanyam, K.
Eradicate the nuclear cult. il *Bull At Sci* 43:36-9 Mr '87

Subscriptions, Periodical *See* Periodicals—Subscriptions
Subsidences (Earth movements)
　Slowly sinking in the West [Arizona and New Mexico]
　　F. Turner. il *Wilderness* 51:47-50 Fall '87
Subsidiaries (Corporations) *See* Corporations—Subsidiaries
Subsidiaries (Foreign) *See* Corporations, International
Subsidiary Communications Authorization subcarriers *See*
　Radio frequency modulation
Subsidiary rights (Books) *See* Copyright
Subsidies
　　　See also
　　Agricultural administration
　　Airlines—Federal aid
　　Economic assistance, Domestic
　　Rent subsidies
Substance P
　Substance P activation of rheumatoid synoviocytes: neural
　　pathway in pathogenesis of arthritis. M. Lotz and
　　others. bibl f il *Science* 235:893-5 F 20 '87
Substitute products
　　　See also
　　Food substitutes
　　Sugar substitutes
Substitute teachers
　Getting the most from substitute teachers. J. Stommen.
　　Educ Dig 52:43-5 Ap '87
Subtitles (Opera) *See* Opera—Titling
Suburban crimes
　"I never thought it could happen to me" [rape] A.
　　Fischer. il *Redbook* 169:120-2+ Je '87
　Rape strikes the suburbs. A. Fischer. il *Read Dig*
　　131:59-62 S '87
Suburban life
　Return to suburbia. M. Johnson. il *Glamour* 85:72+
　　Mr '87
Suburbs
　The boom towns [megacounties] G. J. Church. il maps
　　Time 129:14-17 Je 15 '87
　City flight and suburb blight [views of Jon Teaford]
　　il *Futurist* 21:49 Jl/Ag '87
　Urban youth lose jobs to suburbs. A. F. Brimmer. il
　　Black Enterp 18:45 S '87
　　　Anecdotes, facetiae, satire, etc.
　Burgville marches on. R. Baker. il *N Y Times Mag*
　　p20 Ag 23 '87
Subversive activities
　　　See also
　　Espionage
　　Internal security
　　Terrorism
Subway stations
　　　See also
　　Boston (Mass.)—Stations
　　Brussels (Belgium)—Stations
　　Cambridge (Mass.)—Stations
　　New York (N.Y.)—Stations
　　　Conservation and restoration
　Eager beaver [restoration and improvement of Astor
　　Place Station New York City] G. Anderson. il *Archit
　　Rec* 175:80-3 Ja '87
Subways
　　　See also
　　London (England)—Subways
　　Los Angeles (Calif.)—Subways
　　New York (N.Y.)—Subways
　　　Fires and fire prevention
　Escalator to an inferno [London] J. Smolowe. il *Time*
　　130:30-1 N 30 '87
　Flaming horror in London's subway. A. Bilski. il *Macleans*
　　100:44 N 30 '87
　An inferno in the London underground. il *Newsweek*
　　110:46 N 30 '87
Subwoofers (Loudspeakers) *See* Loudspeakers
Success
　　　See also
　　Ambition
　　Failure (Psychology)
　　Fear of success
　　Life skills
　　Self realization
　　Wealth
　Can you see yourself as successful? *Glamour* 85:319
　　Ap '87
　Career on hold: the big stall. M. Willens. il *Harpers
　　Bazaar* 120:160+ O '87
　Career workshop [special section] il *Work Woman*
　　12:79-82+ Je '87
　The finer points of power building [excerpt from Company
　　manners] L. Wyse. il *Work Woman* 12:78-80+ Ja '87
　How to get what you want—nicely. A. Gottlieb. *McCalls*
　　114:54-5 Ja '87

How to succeed in corporate America [black executives]
　L. Norment. il *Ebony* 42:51-2+ Ag '87
Is it time for you to blossom? [excerpt from Attaining
　personal greatness] M. Brown. *Redbook* 169:74-5+ Ag
　'87
It's your move! [black women executives] S. Chassler.
　Essence 17:47+ Mr '87
The making of a top manager. B. Insel. il *Work Woman*
　12:105-8+ My '87
Managing nine critical career turning points [results of
　survey] J. Ciabattari. il *Work Woman* 12:87-90+ O
　'87
Modern-day mentors: five lessons in success [role models]
　L. Rosch. il *Work Woman* 12:55-9 Ag '87
The price of success [blacks] A. F. Poussaint. il por
　Ebony 42:76+ Ag '87
Secrets every achiever knows [self discipline; condensed
　from The 25-hour woman] S. Stanton. il *Read Dig*
　131:63-6 S '87
The smartest thing I did in my 60s. M. Reiter. il *50
　Plus* 27:24-7+ F '87
The so-so salesman who told millions how to make
　it big [D. Carnegie] R. Conniff. bibl (p230) il por
　Smithsonian 18:82-6+ O '87
Some lessons come hard. H. Altman. il *Nations Bus*
　75:6 Jl '87
Success: the Zen commandments: a doer's guide for
　dreamers (not schemers). S. Chassler. il *Work Woman*
　12:68-9 F '87
Ten steps to success before 40. M. Korda. il *Read
　Dig* 131:111-13 D '87
What makes top managers different? R. Jelinek. *Work
　Woman* 12:109 My '87
What successful people have in common [condensed
　from The great American success story] G. Gallup
　and A. Gallup. *Read Dig* 130:110-12 Je '87
What traits bring success? il *Glamour* 85:150 N '87
Who is the right man for a woman like you? [excerpt
　from The Type E woman] H. B. Braiker. il *Work
　Woman* 12:72-4+ Ja '87
Winning at life [examples of women athletes] L. T.
　Bessone. il *Women's Sports Fitness* 9:46-50 S '87
You get ahead, he gets mad . . . will success spoil
　your romance? M. F. Coburn. *Mademoiselle* 93:186-7+
　O '87
　　　Anecdotes, facetiae, satire, etc.
Of Ivy and success. R. Baker. il *N Y Times Mag* p20
　Ag 30 '87
Sequences. P. F. McManus. il *Outdoor Life* 179:126+
　Je '87
Successful farming (Periodical)
Across the editor's desk [integration of livestock sections]
　R. Krumme. il *Success Farm* 85:3 Ag '87
Across the editor's desk [ADAPT 100 conference] R.
　Krumme. il *Success Farm* 85 no1:4 Ja '87
Succoth *See* Sukkoth
Succulent plants
　　　See also
　　Aloe
　　Cactus
　　Sedum
It's fun to grow succulents from seeds. L. E. Giddings.
　il *Flower Gard* 31:74-5 O/N '87
Sucherman, Stuart F.
Old enough to get its act together. il *Channels* 7:68-70
　O '87
Suckling
Batmom's daily nightmare [Mexican free-tailed bat mater-
　nity colonies] G. F. McCracken and M. K. Gustin.
　il map *Nat Hist* 96:66-73 O '87
Sucrose polyesters
Dieters delight—P&G asks O.K. for no-cal fat additive
　[olestra] K. R. Sheets. *U S News World Rep* 102:47
　My 18 '87
Fake fat. N. Eurman. il *Health* 19:8 O '87
Fast food freaks, this will do your heart good [Procter
　& Gamble's fat substitute olestra] T. Dworetzky. il
　Discover 8:12 Ag '87
Fat without calories [synthetic fat substitute olestra] A.
　Steacy. il *Macleans* 100:49-50 Je 8 '87
Will fake fat yield plump profits? [Procter & Gamble's
　fat substitute olestra] G. M. Bock. il *Time* 129:57
　My 25 '87
Suction diskectomy *See* Spine—Surgery
Suction lipectomy *See* Surgery, Plastic
Sudan
　　　See also
　　Children—Sudan
　　Economic assistance, American—Sudan
　　Education—Sudan
　　Paleontology—Sudan

Sudan—See also—*cont.*
Relief work—Sudan
Rivers—Sudan
Trade routes—Sudan
Foreign relations
A view from Khartoum. A. M. Lesch. bibl f map *Foreign Aff* 65:807-26 Spr '87
United States
See United States—Foreign relations—Sudan
Politics and government
A view from Khartoum. A. M. Lesch. bibl f map *Foreign Aff* 65:807-26 Spr '87

Sudarkasa, Niara
about
Lincoln's 1st woman prexy is ready to lead school into the 21st century. *Jet* 72:12 Ap 27 '87

Sudden cardiac arrest *See* Heart—Diseases—Mortality

Sudden infant death syndrome
Blood imbalance detected in SIDS victims. J. Greenberg. *Sci News* 131:292 My 9 '87
Crib death clue [hemoglobin F] N. Eurman. il *Health* 19:25 N '87
Explaining SIDS. B. D. Colen. il *Health* 19:80 Mr '87

Südhof, Thomas C., and others
A synaptic vesicle protein with a novel cytoplasmic domain and four transmembrane regions. bibl f il *Science* 238:1142-4 N 20 '87

Sudia, Cecelia
Preventing out-of-home placement of children: the first step to permanency planning. il *Child Today* 15:4-5 N/D '86

Suenens, Léon Joseph, 1904-
about
Cardinal Suenens calls for a new Pentecost [interview] J. Catoir. *America* 156:457-9 Je 6 '87

Suffering
See also
Grief
Sober hope: some themes in Protestant theology today. G. Fackre. *Christ Century* 104:790-2 S 23 '87

Suffering of God
God on the gallows [excerpt from The cross of Christ] J. R. W. Stott. il por *Christ Today* 31:28-30 Ja 16 '87

Suffocation *See* Asphyxia

Suffolk, Charles Brandon, Duke of, d. 1545
about
Power and the early-Tudor courtier's house. M. Howard. bibl il por *Hist Today* 37:44-50 My '87

Suffolk, Henrietta Hobart Howard, Countess of, 1681-1767
about
Palladian retreat of a royal mistress. P. Quennell. il *Archit Dig* 44:86+ My '87

Suffolk (England)
Description and travel
Cycling in Suffolk. P. J. Wade. il maps *Gourmet* 48:54-9+ Je '87

Suffrage
See also
Voter registration
Voting
Woman suffrage

Sufi poetry
The mystic way [excerpt from Book of affliction] F. al-D. 'Aṭār. il *Courier* 40:26 Ap '87

Sugar
See also
Molasses
Physiological effects
See Sugar in the body
Prices
See also
Agricultural administration

Sugar City (Colo.)
Sugar City goes sour. A. A. Rooney. il *Saturday Evening Post* 259:26 Ja/F '87

Sugar in the body
β1-6 branching of Asn-linked oligosaccharides is directly associated with metastasis. J. W. Dennis and others. bibl f il *Science* 236:582-5 My 1 '87
Refined sugars can polish off chromium. *Prevention* 39:113 S '87
A study of sugar stirs up a sweet-and-sour reaction [FDA report] J. Carey. il *U S News World Rep* 102:66 Ja 19 '87
Sugar only harms teeth, gums. *FDA Consum* 21:6 F '87
Sugar squabble [report of FDA's Sugars Task Force] M. Teich. il *Health* 19:53-4 O '87
Sweet news about sugar and salt. S. Schneider. il *Women's Sports Fitness* 9:19 Jl '87

Your diet: sweet talk. J. S. Stern. *Vogue* 177:262 Jl '87

Sugar industry
See also
Holly Sugar Corp.
Acquisitions and mergers
Arb makes good [M. Buchsbaum's Holly Sugar Corp. attracts Shamrock Holdings] P. Berman and C. Brown. por *Forbes* 139:152 Je 1 '87
Sweetening the pot at Holly Sugar [bid by Brookehill Equities] M. Ivey. il *Bus Week* p34 Je 29 '87
Export-import trade
U.S. foreign agricultural policy and the sugar program [address, February 24, 1987] D. W. McMinn. *Dep State Bull* 87:40-3 My '87
The unsweetened truth about sugar subsidies. T. K. Billington. *Read Dig* 131:51-4 Ag '87
What do Cory Aquino, cocaine addicts, and American consumers have in common? They are all victims of the U.S. sugar program. R. Karaim. *Wash Mon* 19:17-21 N '87
Hawaii
See also
Alexander & Baldwin, Inc.

Sugar maple *See* Maple

Sugar price supports *See* Agricultural administration

Sugar substitutes
A new sweetener? [Acesulfame K] B. T. Hunter. il *Consum Res Mag* 70:8-9 My '87
Sugar alternatives for weight control. B. T. Hunter. il *Consum Res Mag* 70:8-9 Ag '87
Sweet nothing? [aspartame] M. Fox. il *Health* 19:10+ D '87
Sweet talk [aspartame] *Sci Am* 257:16 Jl '87
The sweet truth. J. Storm. il *Women's Sports Fitness* 9:12+ D '87
Your diet: sweet talk. J. S. Stern. *Vogue* 177:262 Jl '87

Sugarless gum *See* Chewing gum

Sugarman, Burt
about
What's his line? A. B. Block. il por *Forbes* 139:70-1 Ja 26 '87

Sugarman, Carole
New foods for your microwave. il *Consum Res Mag* 70:24-5 Mr '87

Sugarman, George
about
George Sugarman's maximal, musical sculpture. J. Gruen. il por *Art News* 86:138-43 Ja '87

Sugarmann, Josh
The NRA is right. il *Wash Mon* 19:11-15 Je '87

Sugars
See also
Fructose
Oligosaccharides

Suggestion
See also
Brainwashing
Hypnotism
Subliminal projection
Pink and blue: the power of suggestion [influence of color on strength; research by Jeffrey M. Smith] P. McCarthy. *Psychol Today* 21:24-5 Jl '87

Suggestion systems
See also
Ideas in business

Suharto *See* Soeharto, 1921-

Suicide
See also
Right to die
Suttee
Bergenfield's tragic foursome [teen suicides] il *U S News World Rep* 102:11 Mr 23 '87
Black and white cops duel in lovers' quarrel; he is critical and she is dead [J. Hill shoots John Kopek in New York City] *Jet* 73:8 N 2 '87
By their own hands [teenagers] S. R. Arbetter. il *Curr Health 2* 14:18-21 S '87
Can faith survive a suicide in the family? J. Davidson. il *U S Cathol* 52:16-21 N '87
Clergy malpractice [suit over suicide of K. Nally] *Christ Century* 104:850 O 7 '87
Commerce's Harold Jones found shot; ruled suicide. il *Jet* 73:17 N 16 '87
The copycat suicides [teenagers in Bergenfield, N.J.] L. Martz. il *Newsweek* 109:28-9 Mr 23 '87
A Cowboy's long way home [football player L. Bethea] G. Norman. il pors *Sport Mag* 78:79-80+ D '87

Suicide—*cont.*

Death takes a holiday [holiday suicide patterns; study by David P. Phillips and John S. Wills] J. Folkenberg. *Psychol Today* 21:22 N '87

Denied promotion, woman shoots supervisors and kills self in Atlanta [suicide of M. Dansby] *Jet* 72:25 My 18 '87

The ecology of suicide [teen suicide] *Natl Rev* 39:18-19 Ap 24 '87

Elizabeth Hartman. M. Ryan. il pors *People Wkly* 28:135-7+ S 7 '87

Epitaph for a trader [suicide of broker J. Markle] W. P. Barrett. il por *Forbes* 140:121 D 14 '87

First word [teenage suicides] H. Pardes. il *Omni* 9:6 Ja '87

Flint blacks angered by youth's 'suicide' probe [death of J. Carter] L. Ransom. il pors *Jet* 72:51-3 Ag 24 '87

Haitian sets self afire in protest of nation's strife [A. Thurel] *Jet* 72:4 S 21 '87

"I wanted to die" [teen suicide] il *Read Dig* 131:93-6 Jl '87

In the journals. il *Child Today* 16:5 Jl/Ag '87

Iranscam's near tragedy [R. McFarlane attempts suicide] G. J. Church. il por *Time* 129:25 F 23 '87

Joan mourns Edgar [E. Rosenberg's death] R. Meryman. il pors *People Wkly* 28:32-6 Ag 31 '87

Luther Vandross' drummer killed in 17-story leap [Y. Horton] il por *Jet* 72:53 Je 29 '87

My son tried to kill himself [17 year old] il *Good Housekeep* 204:30+ My '87

On his thirtieth birthday, my brother placed a hunting rifle in his mouth and pulled the trigger. J. M. Leder. il por *Glamour* 85:204+ N '87

On its 50th birthday, a survivor celebrates his victory over the Golden Gate Bridge [suicide leap by K. Baldwin] W. Plummer. il pors *People Wkly* 27:110-12 My 25 '87

Police questioned in Indianapolis homicide [suspicious suicide of Michael Taylor] *Jet* 73:46 N 2 '87

The self-imposed death sentence [jail suicide] A. K. Hess. bibl (p56) il *Psychol Today* 21:50-3 Je '87

Suicide: a future boom for baby boomers? [study by Dan G. Blazer] J. Folkenberg. *Psychol Today* 21:22 S '87

Suicide among American Indian youth: a look at the issues. P. A. May. bibl f il *Child Today* 16:22-5 Jl/Ag '87

Teen suicide. F. M. Eckman. *McCalls* 115:71-4 O '87

Teen suicide [Bergenfield, N.J.] A. Wilentz. il *Time* 129:12-13 Mr 23 '87

Teen suicide: the sobering facts. M. Mohler. *Ladies Home J* 104:106+ N '87

'Too much money, too much time': the life and death of Sandy Marsh [cover story] P. Morrisroe. il *N Y* 20:42-51 S 14 '87

Too young to die [teenagers; cover story] D. Eble. il por *Christ Today* 31:19-24 Mr 20 '87

Under pressure, a Marine loses control [attempted suicide of R. C. McFarlane] B. Barol. il pors *Newsweek* 109:22-4 F 23 '87

A Washington power trip to the edge and back [R. McFarlane's suicide attempt] S. Powell. il por *U S News World Rep* 102:11 F 23 '87

What teen suicide means. H. R. Kohl. il *Nation* 244:603-4+ My 9 '87

Whispering hope [suicide of M. Dansby, woman denied promotion by the Georgia Power Co.] R. Weems. il *Ms* 16:40-1 D '87

Prevention

At the point of no return. E. Shneidman. bibl (p59) il *Psychol Today* 21:54-8 Mr '87

Groping to cope with teen suicide. G. Witkin. il *U S News World Rep* 102:12 Mr 30 '87

Helping literature students learn about suicide [teenagers] D.-M. Stupple. *Educ Dig* 53:56-8 D '87

It can be prevented [teen suicide] S. L. Englebardt. *Read Dig* 131:97-8 Jl '87

Magnesium, a suicide-prevention mineral? *Prevention* 39:57 My '87

Mitch Anthony's war. D. Eble. por *Christ Today* 31:20 Mr 20 '87

Preventing teenage suicide. *Futurist* 21:55-6 S/O '87

Recognizing the signs of suicide [teenagers] S. R. Arbetter. il *Curr Health 2* 13:12-13 Mr '87

Canada

Suicide and satanism [case of 16 yr. old D. Shaw in Canada] C. Wood. il *Macleans* 100:54 Mr 30 '87

Great Britain

Anglicans in turmoil [G. V. Bennett's suicide after attacks on R. Runcie] K. L. Woodward. il pors *Newsweek* 110:57 D 21 '87

Death and the archbishop [G. Bennett commits suicide following publication of his critical essay on R. Runcie] R. N. Ostling. il pors *Time* 130:60 D 21 '87

Suicide in literature

Helping literature students learn about suicide [teenagers] D.-M. Stupple. *Educ Dig* 53:56-8 D '87

Teaching about teen suicide using young-adult novels. P. S. Berger. *Educ Dig* 52:48-9 Ap '87

Suicide in the Bible

Suicide and the silence of Scripture. T. D. Kennedy. il *Christ Today* 31:22-3 Mr 20 '87

Suid, Lawrence

Lights! Camera! NASA! il *Space World* X-6-282:16-20 Je '87

Suinn, Richard M.

about

Mind control. M. Teich and G. Dodeles. il *Omni* 10:53-60 O '87

Suitcases *See* Luggage

Suites (Music)

See also

Compact discs—Suites (Music)

Suitland (Md.)

Crime

D.C. police seek black van linked to murdered women. *Jet* 71:17 F 2 '87

Suits (Clothing) *See* Clothing and dress

Suits (Law) *See* Actions and defenses

Sukkoth

Raising the harvest home [Sukkah Jewish Community Museum, San Francisco] il *Archit Rec* 175:100-3 F '87

Suleiman I, Sultan of the Turks, 1495-1566

about

The Age of Sultan Suleyman the Magnificent. E. Atil. il *USA Today (Periodical)* 116:78-86 Jl '87

A golden trove fit for a sultan. C. McGuigan. il *Newsweek* 109:66-7 F 2 '87

His sultanic majesty's bequest. J. Perl. il *Vogue* 177:74 Ap '87

Sultan Suleyman courts America. M. Horn and C. Fenyvesi. il *U S News World Rep* 102:72 F 9 '87

A sultan's collection. E. Stein. *Horizon* 30:68 Ja/F '87

Topkapi treasures. O. Bernier. il *House Gard* 159:186-94 F '87

The world of Süleyman the Magnificent [cover story] M. Severy. il map *Natl Geogr* 172:552-601 N '87

Suleiman I, Sultan of the Turks, 1495-1566 *See* Suleiman I, Sultan of the Turks, 1495-1566

Sulfate reducing bacteria *See* Bacteria, Sulfate reducing

Sulfates

See also

Copper sulfate

Disulfate ion as an intermediate to sulfuric acid in acid rain formation. S. G. Chang and others. bibl f il *Science* 237:756-8 Ag 14 '87

Sulfides

See also

Hydrogen sulfide

Methyl sulfide

Edge surfaces in lithographically textured molybdenum disulfide. C. B. Roxlo and others. bibl f il *Science* 235:1629-31 Mr 27 '87

Symbiosis in the deep sea [sulfide based ecosystem at hydrothermal vents] J. J. Childress and others. il *Sci Am* 256:114-20 My '87

Sulfites

Should you worry about sulfites? J. Storm. il *Women's Sports Fitness* 9:12 Ap '87

What's being done about sulfites. C. Kitch. il *Good Housekeep* 204:205 F '87

Wines and sulfites: a necessary marriage. *Sci News* 131:409 Je 27 '87

Sulfoxides

See also

DMSO

Sulfur

Biogenic sulfur and the acidity of rainfall in remote areas of Canada. J. O. Nriagu and others. bibl f il *Science* 237:1189-92 S 4 '87

Sulfur that doesn't stay put [Canadian study by Jerome O. Nriagu and others] *Sci News* 132:204 S 26 '87

Sulfur compounds

See also

Thionates

Sulfur fluorides
A new method for analyzing powder diffraction patterns: confirmation of a predicted phase of SF_6 [neutron diffraction experiments] L. S. Bartell and others. bibl f il *Science* 236:1463-5 Je 12 '87
Sulfur oxidizing bacteria *See* Bacteria, Sulfur oxidizing
Sulfuric acid aerosols *See* Aerosols
Sulich, Vassili
about
Vassili Sulich's desert song. M. Veljkovic. il pors *Dance Mag* 61:66-9 Ja '87
Sullivan, Sir Arthur, 1842-1900
about
HMS Pinafore [operetta] Reviews
Macleans 100:58 N 23 '87. J. Bemrose
The Mikado [operetta] Reviews
Dance Mag 61:24+ Ap '87. M. U. West
N Y il 20:133 Ap 27 '87. P. G. Davis
New Yorker 63:86 Ap 13 '87. E. Oliver
The sorcerer [operetta] Reviews
N Y il 20:133-4 Ap 27 '87. P. G. Davis
Very model records of the major Gilbert & Sullivan. P. Kresh. il pors *High Fidel* 37:56-8 Je '87
Sullivan, Bill, 1942-
about
Bill Sullivan at G. W. Einstein. T. Towle. il *Art Am* 75:217-18 Ap '87
Sullivan, Brendan V.
about
'I'm not a potted plant'. A. Press. il pors *Newsweek* 110:21-2 Jl 20 '87
Sparring partners. J. V. Lamar, Jr. il pors *Time* 130:23 Jl 20 '87
Sullivan, Danny
about
Fast company: rich & racy. H. Minetree. il pors *Harpers Bazaar* 120:22-5+ My '87
Sullivan, Deidre
(ed) See Budz, Sherry. "I've kept my secret for too long"
Sullivan, Jerry
Of dumps, Chicago politics & herons. il *Audubon* 89:122-6 Mr '87
Sullivan, Jerry
Dallas does LA—in seven. il *Sport Mag* 78:33 My '87
Sullivan, Jim
about
Atlanta probes murder mystery of black wife of white millionaire. D. M. Cheers. il pors *Jet* 72:24-7 My 25 '87
Sullivan, John Patrick
about
Inferno on the interstate. S. Kelly. il *Read Dig* 130:106-11 Ja '87
Sullivan, Kevin
about
Anne of Green Gables grows up [cover story; special section; with editorial comment by Kevin Doyle] il pors *Macleans* 100:2, 46-8+ D 7 '87
Sullivan, Leon Howard, 1922-
The U.S. and apartheid. *Current* 297:11-17 N '87
about
Commandments without Moses. W. E. Smith. il por *Time* 129:34 Je 15 '87
Pull out of S. Africa in 9 months, Sullivan urges. por *Jet* 72:4 Je 22 '87
South Africa: why Leon Sullivan gave up his 'principles'. R. A. Manning. il por *U S News World Rep* 102:10-11 Je 15 '87
'Sullivan principles' deadline draws near. por *Jet* 71:14 Ja 12 '87
Sullivan says divest. F. D. Brown and D. C. Ruffin. il por *Black Enterp* 18:17 Ag '87
Sullivan's principles. L. Waldorf. *New Repub* 197:14-16 S 7 '87
Sullivan, Lita McClinton, d. 1987
about
Atlanta probes murder mystery of black wife of white millionaire. D. M. Cheers. il pors *Jet* 72:24-7 My 25 '87
Sullivan, Louis H., 1856-1924
about
Architectural decoration. S. B. Sherrill. il *Antiques* 131:534+ Mr '87
Form celebrates function. A. Betsky. *Horizon* 30:67 Ja/F '87
Louis Sullivan and the gospel of height. J. Rykwert. il *Art Am* 75:158-69+ N '87
Bibliography
The master builder. M. Filler. il *N Y Rev Books* 34:30-4 Ja 29 '87

Sullivan, Marc
about
Pop in his bat, or in his corner? J. McCallum. il pors *Sports Illus* 66:24-5 Mr 23 '87
Sullivan, Mark
about
Once more with feeling. P. Putnam. il pors *Sports Illus* 67:94+ O 26 '87
Sullivan, Maxine, 1911-1987
about
Obituary
Jet il por 72:58 Ap 27 '87
Sullivan, Robert
It's doubles or nothing. il pors *Sports Illus* 67:60+ Ag 10 '87
Keep Walden Pond open: Thoreau's watering hole should remain a public domain. por *Sports Illus* 67:86 Ag 17 '87
Mac gets a new Mr. Fix-it. il pors *Sports Illus* 67:26-7 Ag 17 '87
Time to play Foote ball? il *Sports Illus* 67:58-60+ D 21 '87
Woes of the wunderkind. il pors *Sports Illus* 67:38-9 D 14 '87
Sullivan, Robert, and Neff, Craig
Shame on you, SMU. il *Sports Illus* 66:18-21+ Mr 9 '87
Sullivan, Sharon
Guarding the monarch's kingdom [cover story] il map *Int Wildl* 17:4-11 N/D '87
Sullivan, Timothy
about
Tomorrow and tomorrow [opera] Reviews
Macleans por 100:51 Ap 13 '87
Sullivan, Walter
Curtains of light, horsemen of night. il map *Audubon* 89:40-51 Ja '87
Sullivan, Walter F.
Lay ministers won't put priests out of business. *U S Cathol* 52:22-3 N '87
Sullivan, William L.
Blazing a New Oregon Trail [cover story] il map *Sierra* 72:54-60 My/Je '87
Sullivan & Cromwell
A top law firm feels the heat [G. C. Kern charged by SEC with violating disclosure rules during Campeau's bid on Allied Stores] C. Friday. *Newsweek* 110:40-1 Jl 13 '87
Sullivan Award *See* Sports—Awards
Sullivan Code *See* Labor laws and regulations—South Africa
Sulloway, Frank J.
The metaphor and the rock. il *N Y Rev Books* 34:37-40 My 28 '87
Sultan, Donald K., 1951-
about
Dark poetry [cover story] G. Henry. il pors *Art News* 86:104-11 Ap '87
Sultanate of Oman *See* Oman
Sumac, Yma
about
Manhattan Inca. A. Feinstein. por *Vogue* 177:52 Je '87
Watch the crystal chandeliers! Incan Yma Sumac, the five-octave phenom of the '50s, is back in camp. D. Hutchings. il pors *People Wkly* 27:85-6+ Mr 16 '87
Sumac
Are you ready for sumac? [zahtar] il *Sunset* 179:185 N '87
Sumerian tablets *See* Tablets, Ancient
Sumitomo Bank, Ltd.
A Japanese survivor leads the charge on world banking [K. Komatsu] J. Dreyfuss. por *Fortune* 115:60-1 Ja 5 '87
Sumlin, Hubert
about
Hubert Sumlin. M. Point. il por *Down Beat* 54:14 D '87
Summary proceedings
From jury selection to verdict—in hours [summary jury trials] L. J. Tell. il *Bus Week* p48 S 7 '87
A push for 'quick justice' has GE squirming [summary trial in suit over Zimmer nuclear plant] Z. Schiller. *Bus Week* p31-2 S 21 '87
Summer, Bob
Southern spotlight. See occasional issues of Publishers Weekly beginning January 20, 1984
Summer
See also
August
Hot weather
July

Summer—See also—*cont.*

June

Great hometown adventures [summer fun] T. Hartman. il *Teen* 31:28+ Je '87

June-becoming-July [excerpt from Hal Borland's Twelve moons of the year] H. Borland. il *Audubon* 89:43 Jl '87

Kids and summer: when plans create a problem. L. Salk. il *McCalls* 114:54 Je '87

Old roses and birdsong [summer in New Hampshire] D. Hall. il *Harpers* 275:35-41 Ag '87

Splashdown to summer! [Malibu U.; cover story; special section] il *Teen* 31:98-111 My '87

Summer at Windmill Point [Lake George] M. C. Davis. il *Conservationist* 42:2-5 Jl/Ag '87

Summer pleasures [New York City; cover story; special issue] il *N Y* 20:21-36+ Je 29-Jl 6 '87

Summer safety & first aid. C. L. Carney. il *Parents* 62:96-8+ Jl '87

When summers were free [Brooklyn in the 1940's] P. Hamill. il *Read Dig* 131:72-4 Jl '87

Photographs and photography

"No season such delight can bring" [cover story] il *Conservationist* 42:28-35 Jl/Ag '87

Summer camps *See* Camps
Summer cocktails *See* Cocktails
Summer cooking *See* Cooking
Summer drinks *See* Beverages
Summer entertaining *See* Entertaining
Summer flounders *See* Flounders
Summer heat [film] See Motion picture reviews—Single works
Summer houses *See* Vacation houses
Summer in art

"No season such delight can bring" [cover story] il *Conservationist* 42:28-35 Jl/Ag '87

Summer jobs for students *See* Youth—Employment
Summer night [film] See Motion picture reviews—Single works
Summer resorts *See* Resorts
Summer romance *See* Romance
Summer school [film] See Motion picture reviews—Single works
Summer schools

Summer school: for singles, couples and families [learning vacations] G. Hechinger. il *Glamour* 85:364+ Ap '87

Summer with a preschooler. F. Roberts. *Parents* 62:59-60 Je '87

Summer simmer index

The summer simmer index. J. W. Pepi. il *Weatherwise* 40:143-5 Je '87

Summer vacations *See* Vacations
Summerall, Pat

about

The voice is familiar . . . W. Taaffe. il pors *Sports Illus* 66:52-4+ Ja 26 '87

Summerfare (Festival) *See* PepsiCo Summerfare
Summers, Barbara

Fryday [story] il *Essence* 18:68-70+ N '87

Maneuvers [story] il *Essence* 17:55-6+ Mr '87

Model firsts: pioneers in black beauty. il pors *Essence* 17:38-42+ Ja '87

Summers, Carol, 1925-

about

Hacienda La Trinidad: artists' retreat near Guanajuato, Mexico. S. Cadwallader. il *Archit Dig* 44:126-31 Ja '87

Summers, Harry G.

Nuts, bolts, & death. *Wash Mon* 18:51-2 Ja '87

Summers, Joan Ward

about

Hacienda La Trinidad: artists' retreat near Guanajuato, Mexico. S. Cadwallader. il *Archit Dig* 44:126-31 Ja '87

Summers, Lawrence H.

A few good taxes. *New Repub* 197:14-16 N 30 '87

Summers, Mary

The front-runner. *Nation* 245:621-4+ N 28 '87

Summit Books

Summit Books [manuscript submission policy] J. H. Silberman. *Writer* 100:25 Jl '87

Summitt, Pat Head

about

Dynasty! P. L. Hudson. *Women's Sports Fitness* 9:26 My '87

Sumner, Gordon *See* Sting
Sump pumps

Water-powered sump pump. S. F. Brown. il *Pop Sci* 231:86 S '87

Sun

See also
Eclipses, Solar
Solar activity
Solar cycle
Solar radiation
Solar system
Space flight to the sun
Sunspots
Ultraviolet rays

The fate of the sun. il *Time* 129:65 Mr 23 '87

In defense of the sun. W. Jolly. il *Sky Telesc* 73:356 Ap '87

The solar-stellar connection. M. S. Giampapa. il *Sky Telesc* 74:142-6 Ag '87

The sun, moon, and planets this month. D. Byrd. See issues of Sky and Telescope beginning August 1985

When the sun swallows the earth [research by Jeff Goldstein] il *Sky Telesc* 74:575 D '87

Atmosphere

See also
Sun—Corona

Corona

See also
Solar wind

Heating the sun's corona: still a mystery? il *Sky Telesc* 74:231-2 S '87

Distance

Calculating the distance to the sun by observing the trail of a meteor. J. Walker. il *Sci Am* 256:122-6 Mr '87

Influence on weather

See Sun and meteorology

Internal structure

See also
Global Oscillation Network Group

Solar spheres may affect climate [work of Edward J. Rhodes] *USA Today (Periodical)* 115:6-7 Je '87

Magnetic properties

See also
Alfvén waves
Heliosphere

The sun's hidden magnetism [research by David Moss] il *Sky Telesc* 74:343-4 O '87

Oscillations

See also
Global Oscillation Network Group
Helioseismology

Exciting solar oscillations [work of Ken Libbrecht] il *Sky Telesc* 73:276 Mr '87

Solar irradiance change and special longitudes due to r-modes. C. L. Wolff and J. R. Hickey. bibl f il *Science* 235:1631-3 Mr 27 '87

Photographs and photography

Photographing our nearest star. R. Dilsizian. il *Astronomy* 15:38-43 My '87

Prominences

See also
Solar flares

Old and new views of solar prominences. W. C. Livingston and others. il *Astronomy* 15:18-22 Jl '87

Spectra and spectroscopy

Ultraviolet observations of solar fine structure. K. P. Dere and others. bibl f il *Science* 238:1267-9 N 27 '87

Sun and meteorology

The climate connection [work of Elizabeth Ribes] il *Sky Telesc* 73:590 Je '87

Solar cycle linked to weather [work of Karin Labitzke and Harry van Loon] R. Monastersky. *Sci News* 132:388-9 D 19-26 '87

Solar spheres may affect climate [work of Edward J. Rhodes] *USA Today (Periodical)* 115:6-7 Je '87

Solar-system rhythms in our climate [computer program] A. Blackadar. il *Weatherwise* 40:209-12 Jl/Ag '87

Sunspot-weather correlation found [work of Karin Labitzke and Harry van Loon] R. A. Kerr. il *Science* 238:479-80 O 23 '87

Weather and sites. J. Anderson. map *Sky Telesc* 74:22 Jl '87

Sun dials *See* Sundials
Sun glasses *See* Sunglasses
Sun-heated houses *See* Solar houses
Sun House Museum (Ukiah, Calif.)

Pomo baskets and portraits at Ukiah's Sun House. il *Sunset* 178:84 Ap '87

Sun Ice Ltd.

'I was brought up for work' [founder S. Rempel] por *Macleans* 100:24-5 D 28 '87

Sun Microsystems Inc.
A network for all computers. S. R. Reed. il *Pers Comput* 11:217 Ag '87
Sun's sizzling race to the top. S. Gannes. il *Fortune* 116:88-91 Ag 17 '87

Sun rooms
Adding a room? Try bringing the outdoors in. T. Segal. il *Bus Week* p180 Jl 20 '87
Adding a sunspace—fast. J. Horst. il *Pop Sci* 230:80-2 Je '87
Dazzling sunrooms [excerpt from Living under glass] S. Cliff and J. Tresidder. il *Redbook* 169:114-19 Je '87
Greenhouse or sunroom? il *Flower Gard* 31:18-24 O/N '87
New sun-catcher for this 1926 house. il *Sunset* 179:150 O '87
Our editors build a sun-room. G. D. Cook. il *Better Homes Gard* 65:69-73 Ag '87
Pavilion opens to garden and sky. il *Sunset* 178:104 F '87
Solarium planned for entertaining. il *South Living* 22:159 My '87
They added a functional but friendly solar room. il *Sunset* 178:162-3 Ap '87
Two decks and a sunroom make the difference. il *Sunset* 179:90-1 Ag '87

Sun roses
Bright ground covers from Europe . . . the sunroses. il *Sunset* 178:238 Ap '87

Sun screens (Cosmetics) *See* Suntan products
Sun shades (Automobiles) *See* Automobiles—Equipment
Sun spots *See* Sunspots
Sun-times (Chicago, Ill.) *See* Chicago sun-times (Newspaper)
Sun Valley (Idaho)
Sun Valley. G. S. Bush. il *Skiing* 39:38-44 Spr '87

Sun Valley Trekking (Firm)
Hut-one, hut-two . . . J. Maxwell. il *Esquire* 108:43-4 D '87

Sun Ying
about
A dancer on the bronze phoenix terrace [dance] Reviews *Dance Mag* il 61:18-19 D '87. J.-P. Ou

SunarHauserman (Firm)
In the great tradition [showroom in San Francisco] C. K. Gandee. il *Archit Rec* 175:116-21 My '87

Sunbaths
See also
Suntan

Sunbelt *See* Southern States; Southwestern States
Sunbelt Savings Association of Texas
Getting savers to take a shine to Sunbelt. J. Weber, Jr. il pors *Bus Week* p74+ N 9 '87

Sunbow Foundation
Al Capone's landladies [negative publicity affects funding after broadcast of The mystery of Al Capone's vaults] D. Gates. il *Newsweek* 109:4 Ja 5 '87

Sunburn
Sun smarts [dangers of exercising with a sunburn] A. Ranard. *Vogue* 177:372 Ag '87
The sunburn survival guide. L. Keegan. il *Mademoiselle* 93:62 Jl '87
Therapy
Burned again! K. Freifeld. il *Health* 19:6 Jl '87

Sundaes *See* Ice cream, ices, etc.
Sunday express (Saint John's, Nfld.: Newspaper)
A challenge to big-city dailies. G. Bain. il *Macleans* 100:44 Je 22 '87

Sunday in the park with George [musical] *See* Musicals, revues, etc.—Reviews—Single works
Sunday River Ski Resort (Me.) *See* Resorts—Maine
Sunday schools
Collectibles
"Little's Cross and Crown System": Sunday school awards from the early twentieth century. D. E. Matter and R. M. Matter. il *Antiques Collect Hobbies* 92:82-3 D '87

Sunday supplements *See* Newspapers—Magazine sections
Sundborn (Sweden)
Historic houses, sites, etc.
Carl Larsson's home—a Swedish legacy [Lilla Hyttnäs] M. Kluger. il *Gourmet* 47:56-9+ Jl '87

Sundials
Sundials on walls [computer program] W. S. Maddux. il *Sky Telesc* 74:646-8 D '87
Watching earth move with the shadow clock. B. McClure. il *Astronomy* 15:32-5 Ag '87

Sundiata, Sekou
Forsaken sea [poem] *Essence* 18:142 Je '87

Sundin, Daniel R., and others
A G1 glycoprotein epitope of La Crosse virus: a determinant of infection of Aedes triseriatus. bibl f il *Science* 235:591-3 Ja 30 '87

Sundried tomatoes *See* Tomatoes—Drying
Sunfish fishing
Basic truths. K. Cowgill. il *Field Stream* 92:95+ My '87

Sunflowers, Mexican *See* Mexican sunflowers
Sung, Sophia
about
Miss Muse. *New Yorker* 63:29-31 S 14 '87

SunGard Data Systems (Firm)
Blue-chip backup. R. Koselka. il *Forbes* 139:80-1 Ja 26 '87

Sunglass Hut of America Inc.
Sunglass Huts: thriving in nooks and crannies. A. Fins. il *Bus Week* p77 Jl 27 '87

Sunglasses
See also
Sunglass Hut of America Inc.
A cold sun can cook your skin [recommendations for skiers] il *Esquire* 108:132 N '87
Cool in the shade. C. Cummins. il *Women's Sports Fitness* 9:20 Jl '87
Eye care for the summer. M. Hopkins. il *Consum Res Mag* 70:11-14 Je '87
Five steps to a better pair of sunglasses. *Prevention* 39:106 Je '87
Glasses for sport. D. White. il *Skiing* 39:53-7 Spr '87
Helmet sunglasses [for motorcyclists] il *Cycle* 38:39 N '87
Keeping an eye out. A. P. Farah. il *Health* 19:14 Ag '87
Polafocus Fisherman's Bifocals. D. Brooks. il *Petersens Photogr Mag* 16:14 N '87
Serengeti Drivers sunglasses. il *Cycle* 38:76 Ja '87
Shades of greatness [sunglasses for tennis] P. M. Coan. il *World Tennis* 35:48-9 Ag '87
Sun specs. il *Teen* 31:88-9 Je '87
Sunglass savvy: hot fashions, flattering looks. il *Glamour* 85:102 My '87
Anecdotes, facetiae, satire, etc.
Cool in the shades. M. Musto. il *Harpers Bazaar* 120:32+ Ap '87

Sunila, Joyce
The Corps (Marine) and the only natural river. il map *Audubon* 89:114-16+ S '87

Sunken treasure *See* Treasure trove
Sunkist Growers, Inc.
Sunset in the groves? E. Paris. il *Forbes* 139:35-6 Mr 23 '87

Sunlight
See also
Photosynthesis
Physiological effects
See Ultraviolet rays—Physiological effects
Sunlight in art
David Jenks. D. C. Hines. il pors *Am Artist* 51:54-9+ S '87
Sun dancing [sun drawings of J. Saad-Cook] J. Bell. il *Omni* 10:34+ D '87

Sunni Muslims *See* Muslims
Sunquist, Fiona
My close call with a rhino. il *Int Wildl* 17:16-17 Jl/Ag '87

Sunrooms *See* Sun rooms
Sunroses *See* Sun roses
Sunscreens (Cosmetics) *See* Suntan products
Sunset
Photographs and photography
Bidding the day adieu. il *Sky Telesc* 74:680 D '87

Sunset (Periodical)
A living encyclopedia of southern California horticulture [work of panel of garden experts] il *Sunset* 178:196 F '87

Sunset [dance] *See* Dance reviews—Single works
Sunshine, Kenneth H.
(jt. auth) *See* Diamandis, Peter H., and Sunshine, Kenneth H.

Sunshine Skyway (Tampa, Fla.: Bridge) *See* Tampa Bay (Fla.)—Bridges
Sunsight New Age Books & Gifts (Minneapolis, Minn.)
See Booksellers and bookselling—Minnesota

Sunspots
See also
Solar flares
How the sun faded even as its sunspots did [research by Peter Foukal and Judith Lean] R. A. Kerr. il *Science* 236:1624-5 Je 26 '87

Sunspots—*cont.*

A more complex solar cycle. D. E. Thomsen. il *Sci News* 131:39 Ja 17 '87

Solar cycle linked to weather [work of Karin Labitzke and Harry van Loon] R. Monastersky. *Sci News* 132:388-9 D 19-26 '87

The sun also surprises. S. P. Maran. il *Nat Hist* 96:88-91 N '87

The sunspot cycle: tip of the iceberg. L. J. Robinson. il *Sky Telesc* 73:589-91 Je '87

Sunspot-weather correlation found [work of Karin Labitzke and Harry van Loon] R. A. Kerr. il *Science* 238:479-80 O 23 '87

White light sunspot observations from the solar optical universal polarimeter on Spacelab-2. R. A. Shine and others. bibl f il *Science* 238:1264-7 N 27 '87

Suntan

See also
Sunburn

After-sun skin savers. il *Glamour* 85:158-61 Jl '87

Avoiding the sun's dangers. il *USA Today (Periodical)* 116:11 Jl '87

Be safe in the sun. S. L. Englebardt. il *Read Dig* 130:173-4+ Je '87

Beach chic. il *Good Housekeep* 204:84 My '87

Burning issues. il *Seventeen* 46:54 Je '87

Having your sun—and a safe tan, too. J. Lewis. il *Curr Health 2* 13:10-11 Ap '87

How to live safely in the sun. D. Foley. il *Prevention* 39:86+ Ap '87

How to prevent skin cancer. *Ladies Home J* 104:26 Je '87

Out of the bronzed age [skin cancer risk; cover story] R. C. Thompson. il *FDA Consum* 21:20-3 Je '87

Smart sunning guide: how healthy are your sun habits? il *Glamour* 85:214-17 Je '87

Solar power. il *Mademoiselle* 93:186-93 My '87

Sunshine: every little bit hurts [automobile drivers' exposure] il *Prevention* 39:8+ Je '87

Test your sun savvy [quiz] C. Straley. il *Parents* 62:113-16 Jl '87

What a gorgeous tan! il *Redbook* 169:12 Je '87

Psychological aspects

Tanorexia: when girls just gotta have sun. S. Orlean. il *Mademoiselle* 93:166-7+ Je '87

Suntan products

Bronze, don't burn. D. White. *Skiing* 39:55 Spr '87

A cold sun can cook your skin [recommendations for skiers] il *Esquire* 108:132 N '87

The fake-tan plan. il *Mademoiselle* 93:14 Je '87

Fight back against photoaging [use of sunscreens] P. Boyer. il *Prevention* 39:50+ Jl '87

Golden protection: tan-smart sun guide. il *Harpers Bazaar* 120:180-3+ My '87

Have your day in the sun—but painlessly. T. Segal. il *Bus Week* p152 Je 8 '87

Out of the bronzed age [skin cancer risk; cover story] R. C. Thompson. il *FDA Consum* 21:20-3 Je '87

A place in the sun. L. Wells. il *N Y Times Mag* p88-98 My 17 '87

Potions for sun lovers. F. Lunzer. il *Forbes* 139:238+ Je 15 '87

Skin and sun. S. Lord. il *Vogue* 177:52 Ap '87

Summer skin care: staying safe in the danger zone. G. Bakoulis. *Work Woman* 12:128 Je '87

The sun and our skin [black women] il *Essence* 18:44 Jl '87

Sunless tanning: the best of both worlds [lotions] P. Boyer. il *Prevention* 39:76-8 Ja '87

Super body: tan and fit. C. Schrader. il *Harpers Bazaar* 120:54+ Je '87

This sunscreen's a scream [Le Zink] il *Prevention* 39:14 Ja '87

Suny, Ronald Grigor

The nationality question. il *Nation* 244:808-10 Je 13 '87

Sunyar, Andrew William, 1920-1986

about

Obituary
Phys Today il por 40:112 My '87. P. D. Bond

Super Bowl *See* Football, Professional—Super Bowl

Super Tuesday *See* Presidential primaries—Southern States

Superchargers

See also
Airplane engines—Superchargers
Automobile engines—Superchargers
Automobiles, Racing—Engines—Superchargers
Diesel engines, Automotive—Superchargers
Diesel engines, Marine—Superchargers

Supercomputers

Advanced computing for manufacturing. A. M. Erisman and K. W. Neves. bibl (p184) il *Sci Am* 257:162-9 O '87

Birth of a quasar [supercomputer model developed by Stuart Shapiro and Saul Teukolsky] A. Fisher. il *Pop Sci* 231:10 S '87

Cray supercomputer axed, superstar departs. M. M. Waldrop. il por *Science* 237:1558-9 S 25 '87

Do orbits change in 100 million years? [Project Longstop] R. W. Sinnott. il *Sky Telesc* 74:182-3 Ag '87

Foreseeing failure [computers that predict problems may make nuclear plants safer] *Futurist* 21:42 Ja/F '87

High-tech treachery [arrest of Ivan Batinic and others for attempting to sell supercomputer technology to the Soviets] *Newsweek* 110:56 N 2 '87

The hungry pack nipping at Cray's heels. J. W. Verity and O. Port. il *Bus Week* p110+ O 26 '87

A look at Apple's Cray simulation engine. *Byte* 12:37-8 S '87

NASA uses supercomputer for aerodynamic simulation [Numerical Aerodynamic Simulator] il *Aviat Week Space Technol* 126:264-5 Mr 9 '87

Now, Cray is only way ahead. M. J. Pitzer. il *Bus Week* p109 Jl 13 '87

NSF supercomputer centers plan for next leap into research. I. Goodwin. il map *Phys Today* 40:61-4 O '87

Silicosms [Numerical Aerodynamic Simulator] R. Schultz. il *Omni* 9:52-7 Ag '87

Solving unsolvable puzzles with supercomputers. A. Fisher. il *Pop Sci* 230:48-53 My '87

Staying on top in supercomputing [Society for Industrial and Applied Mathematics report] *Sci News* 132:335 N 21 '87

Street smarts: the supercomputer becomes a stock strategist. J. W. Verity. il *Bus Week* p84-5 Je 1 '87

A super-supercomputer [Numerical Aerodynamic Simulator] *Sci News* 131:166 Mr 14 '87

Superconducting magnets *See* Magnets

Superconducting quantum interference devices *See* SQUIDs (Superconducting quantum interference devices)

Superconducting Super Collider

$4.4 b Super Collider gets go-ahead. J. Raloff. *Sci News* 131:84 F 7 '87

Academies select panel to judge ideal SSC site. I. Goodwin. *Phys Today* 40 pt1:52 Ag '87

And the winner in the super atom smasher derby is . . . L. Therrien. il *Bus Week* p36 S 14 '87

DOE submits 36 SSC site bids while House seeks to micro-manage project. I. Goodwin. map *Phys Today* 40:45-6 O '87

Experimenting with 40 trillion electron-volts [cover story] D. E. Thomsen. *Sci News* 132:314-16 N 14 '87

Generalizing the SSC decision. J. D. Bjorken. *Phys Today* 40:136 Mr '87

The lure of subatomic violence. S. N. Welborn. il *U S News World Rep* 102:78 Ap 27 '87

Quark barrel politics. R. Bazell. *New Repub* 196:9-10 Je 22 '87

Race for the ring: DOE reacts to Congress's anxieties on SSC. I. Goodwin. il *Phys Today* 40 pt1:47-50 Ag '87

Reagan endorses the SSC, a colossus among colliders. I. Goodwin. il *Phys Today* 40:47-9 Mr '87

Reagan okays the Supercollider. M. Crawford. *Science* 235:625 F 6 '87

Science committee okays Supercollider. M. Crawford. *Science* 238:477 O 23 '87

Siting the SSC: criteria and procedure. D. E. Thomsen. *Sci News* 131:119 F 21 '87

SSC: an iffy proposition in Congress. D. E. Thomsen. *Sci News* 132:374 D 12 '87

SSC, fusion machine hit a roadblock [funding] M. Crawford. *Science* 237:1559 S 25 '87

SSC: lord of the rings. map *Time* 129:70 My 11 '87

SSC sites narrowed. *Sci News* 132:247 O 17 '87

The SSC's price tag troubles Congress. M. Crawford. il *Science* 235:837-8 F 20 '87

States race SSC site-proposal deadline. D. E. Thomsen. *Sci News* 132:167 S 12 '87

Super Collider given presidential blessing. *Astronomy* 15:78 My '87

Super Collider: steps to reality. D. E. Thomsen. il *Sci News* 132:103 Ag 15 '87

Super cyclotron. M. Kaku and J. Trainer. il *Omni* 9:20 F '87

Super push for a Supercollider. J. S. DeMott. il *Time* 129:19 Ap 13 '87

Supercollider faces budget barrier. M. Crawford. il *Science* 236:246-8 Ap 17 '87

Superconducting Super Collider—*cont.*

The Supercollider sweepstakes. E. Marshall. *Science* 237:1288 S 11 '87

Superconducting superscramble. D. E. Thomsen. il *Sci News* 131:364-5 Je 6 '87

Superscramble for a Supercollider [state bids for construction] il *U S News World Rep* 103:11 S 14 '87

Supersite. *Sci Am* 256:66 Ap '87

When protons—and politics—collide. W. D. Marbach. il *Newsweek* 110:44-5 Jl 6 '87

Why astronomers need the SSC. D. N. Schramm. il *Sky Telesc* 74:588 D '87

Will high T$_c$ stop the SSC? [letters] bibl f *Phys Today* 40:13+ N '87

Will high-T$_c$ superconductivy affect the SSC's design? I. Goodwin. il *Phys Today* 40 pt1:50-2 Ag '87

The world's biggest machine. A. Fisher. il *Pop Sci* 230:56-61+ Je '87

Superconductors and superconductivity
   See also
      Consortium for Superconducting Materials and Instrumentation
      Josephson junctions
      Superfluidity

The 1987 Nobel Prize for Physics [awarded to J. G. Bednorz and K. A. Muller] M. M. Waldrop. il pors *Science* 238:481-2 O 23 '87

Advances in superconductivity challenge APS communications. il *Phys Today* 40:82-3 My '87

Antiferromagnetism observed in La$_2$CuO$_4$ [research by David Johnston and others] A. L. Robinson. *Science* 236:780 My 15 '87

Bednorz and Müller win Nobel Prize for new superconducting materials [ceramic oxides] A. Khurana. il pors *Phys Today* 40:17-19 D '87

The chemistry of superconductivity [use of ceramic oxides] J. Raloff. il *Sci News* 131:247 Ap 18 '87

Current news about superconductors [use of ceramic oxides] D. E. Thomsen. *Sci News* 131:308 My 16 '87

The discovery of a class of high-temperature superconductors [ceramic oxides] K. A. Müller and J. G. Bednorz. bibl f il *Science* 237:1133-9 S 4 '87

Dreams into reality [use of ceramic oxides] *Time* 129:61 My 25 '87

An electrifying discovery [ceramic oxide material] J. Gleick. *Read Dig* 131:131 Jl '87

Electrifying progress [use of cermaic oxides] il *U S News World Rep* 102:15 Mr 2 '87

Even lanthanum copper oxide is superconducting. A. Khurana. bibl f il *Phys Today* 40:17-22 S '87

Fast-food physics [use of ceramic oxides] il *Life* 10:38-9+ S '87

Getting warmer [use of ceramic oxides] T. Beardsley. il *Sci Am* 257:32+ O '87

Getting warmer . . . [use of ceramic oxides] M. Rogers. il *Newsweek* 110:42-3 Jl 6 '87

High-powered discussions on high-temperature superconductivity [use of ceramic oxides] K. Hartley. *Sci News* 132:359 D 5 '87

High-school students make YBa$_2$Cu$_3$O$_{7-x}$ [Gilroy, Calif. class produces superconducting material] W. Sweet. il *Phys Today* 40:111-12 O '87

High T$_c$ may not need phonons; supercurrents increase. A. Khurana. bibl f il *Phys Today* 40:17-21 Jl '87

High-temperature superconductivity: what's here, what's near and what's unclear [use of ceramic oxides; cover story] K. Hartley. *Sci News* 132:106-7+ Ag 15 '87

High-temperature superconductor hints [use of ceramic oxides] A. L. Robinson. *Science* 236:1431 Je 12 '87

Hot questions in superconductivity [use of ceramic oxides; research by Paul C. W. Chu and others] S. Weisburd. *Sci News* 131:164-5 Mr 14 '87

How to make your own superconductors [use of ceramic oxides] B. Schechter. il *Omni* 10:72-4+ N '87

IBM superconductor leaps current hurdle. A. L. Robinson. *Science* 236:1189 Je 5 '87

In the trenches of science [use of ceramic oxides; work of Ching-Wu (Paul) Chu] J. Gleick. il *N Y Times Mag* p28-31+ Ag 16 '87

Keeping current with cosmic strings [research by Edward Witten and others] M. M. Waldrop. il *Science* 235:283-4 Ja 16 '87

The microstructure of high-critical current superconducting films. P. Chaudhari and others. bibl f il *Science* 238:342-4 O 16 '87

More superconductivity questions than answers [special section] A. L. Robinson. il *Science* 237:248-50 Jl 17 '87

Neutrons clarify superconductors [ceramic oxides] A. L. Robinson. il *Science* 237:1115-17 S 4 '87

A new electrical revolution [use of ceramic oxides] W. D. Marbach. il *Newsweek* 109:74 My 25 '87

New evidence at Wayne State for superconductivity at 240 K [use of ceramic oxides] A. L. Robinson. *Science* 236:28 Ap 3 '87

New heights in superconductivity [use of ceramic oxides] I. Peterson. *Sci News* 131:23 Ja 10 '87

A new route to oxide superconductors. A. L. Robinson. *Science* 236:1526 Je 19 '87

The new superconductivity [use of ceramic oxides] il *Sci Am* 256:32-3 Je '87

No resistance to superconductivity. K. Hartley. *Sci News* 132:84-5 Ag 8 '87

Nobel prizes: physics [use of ceramic oxides] J. Horgan. *Sci Am* 257:46 D '87

'Our life has changed' [cover story; special section] il *Bus Week* p94-100 Ap 6 '87

Oxygen isotope effect in high-temperature oxide superconductors. H.-C. Zur Loye and others. bibl f il *Science* 238:1558-60 D 11 '87

An oxygen key to the new superconductors [special section] A. L. Robinson. il *Science* 236:1063-5 My 29 '87

Putting superconductors to work—superfast [use of ceramic oxides] E. T. Smith. il *Bus Week* p124-6 My 18 '87

Record high-temperature superconductors claimed [use of ceramic oxides] A. L. Robinson. il *Science* 235:531-3 Ja 30 '87

Research on high-T$_c$ superconductivity in Japan [use of ceramic oxides] S. Tanaka. bibl il *Phys Today* 40:53-7 D '87

The resonating valence bond state in La$_2$CuO$_4$ and superconductivity. P. W. Anderson. bibl f il *Science* 235:1196-8 Mr 6 '87

Seeking the perfect wire [use of ceramic oxides] W. J. Cook. il *U S News World Rep* 102:66-71 My 11 '87

Signs of a new high in ceramic superconductivity [work of Ahmet Erbil] I. Peterson. *Sci News* 132:356 D 5 '87

Superconduction possible at room temperatures? [use of ceramic oxides] il *Radio-Electron* 58:5 Jl '87

Superconductive barriers surpassed [use of ceramic oxides] S. Weisburd. *Sci News* 131:116-17 F 21 '87

Superconductivity: a hard frost [use of ceramic oxides] D. E. Thomsen. *Sci News* 131:215 Ap 4 '87

Superconductivity: a physics rush [use of ceramic oxides] D. E. Thomsen. il *Sci News* 131:196-7 Mr 28 '87

Superconductivity and quantum mechanics [views of E. Teller] D. E. Thomsen. *Sci News* 131:358 Je 6 '87

Superconductivity at 40 K in the oxygen-defect perovskites La$_{2-x}$Sr$_x$CuO$_{4-y}$. J. M. Tarascon and others. bibl f il *Science* 235:1373-6 Mr 13 '87

Superconductivity at 52.5 K in the lanthanum-barium-copper-oxide system. C.-W. Chu and others. bibl f il *Science* 235:567-9 Ja 30 '87

Superconductivity glimpsed near 300 K [use of ceramic oxides] D. E. Thomsen. *Sci News* 132:4 Jl 4 '87

A superconductivity happening [use of ceramic oxides] A. L. Robinson. il *Science* 235:1571 Mr 27 '87

Superconductivity heats up [use of ceramic oxides] M. D. Lemonick. il *Time* 129:62 Mr 2 '87

Superconductivity: hype vs. reality [use of ceramic oxides] G. Maranto. il *Discover* 8:22-4+ Ag '87

Superconductivity in alkaline earth-substituted La$_2$CuO$_{4-y}$. J. G. Bednorz and others. bibl f il *Science* 236:73-5 Ap 3 '87

Superconductivity seen above the boiling point of nitrogen [use of ceramic oxides; cover story] A. Khurana. bibl f il *Phys Today* 40:17-23 Ap '87

Superconductor claim raised to 94 K [use of ceramic oxides] A. L. Robinson. *Science* 235:1137-8 Mr 6 '87

Superconductor frenzy [use of ceramic oxides] A. Fisher. il *Pop Sci* 231:54-8+ Jl '87

Superconductor race heats up. A. L. Robinson. *Science* 236:664 My 8 '87

Superconductors! [use of ceramic oxides] M. D. Lemonick. il *Read Dig* 131:13-14+ N '87

Superconductors! [use of ceramic oxides; cover story] M. D. Lemonick. il *Time* 129:64-70+ My 11 '87

Superconductors: a dimpled beauty [neutron diffraction of ceramic oxides] D. E. Thomsen. *Sci News* 131:327 My 23 '87

Superconductor's critical current at a new high [use of ceramic oxides] M. M. Waldrop. il *Science* 238:1655-6 D 18 '87

Superconductors: early visions [use of ceramic oxides] T. H. Cole. il *Pop Mech* 164:16 Ag '87

Superconductors and superconductivity—*cont.*
Superconductors: facing reality [use of ceramic oxides] T. H. Cole. il *Pop Mech* 164:32 N '87
Superconductors gain [use of ceramic oxides] A. Fisher. il *Pop Sci* 231:10 Ag '87
Superconductors get into business. A. Ramirez. il *Fortune* 115:114-16+ Je 22 '87
Superconductors heat up [use of ceramic oxides] *Sci Am* 256:64-5 Mr '87
Superconductors heat up [use of ceramic oxides] M. Gray. il *Macleans* 100:44 Ap 6 '87
Superconductors' promise [use of ceramic oxides] *World Press Rev* 34:54 S '87
Venture capital's new gold rush. J. B. Levine. *Bus Week* p66+ O 5 '87
Yb or not Yb? That is the question [mistake in element listing in publishing of Paul Chu's ceramic oxide formula] G. Kolata. il *Science* 236:663-4 My 8 '87

Anecdotes, facetiae, satire, etc.
Exit laughing [superconductors used in fishing tackle] E. Zern. il *Field Stream* 92:138 Je '87

Aviation use
Aerospace agencies foster research, application studies on superconductors. D. Hughes. il *Aviat Week Space Technol* 127:89-90+ N 23 '87
Superconductivity consortium pursues aerospace applications. il *Aviat Week Space Technol* 127:59+ N 16 '87

Conferences
Stumbling on superconductors [U.S. science adviser's decision to exclude non-citizens from conference] E. Marshall and M. Sun. *Science* 237:477 Jl 31 '87

Data transmission use
A superconductivity dream comes true. *Newsweek* 110:98 O 12 '87

Federal aid
Berkeley lab marshals superconductor research in Bay Area [Lawrence Berkeley Laboratory] *Aviat Week Space Technol* 127:92 N 23 '87
Frenzied hunt for the right stuff. J. Greenwald. il *Time* 130:26+ Ag 10 '87
A helping hand from Washington: how much is too much? E. Clark. *Bus Week* p125 My 18 '87
Reagan hails new age of superconductivity at 'pep rally'. I. Goodwin. il *Phys Today* 40:51-4 S '87
White House spotlights new superconductors. M. Crawford. il *Science* 237:593-4 Ag 7 '87

Military use
Aerospace agencies foster research, application studies on superconductors. D. Hughes. il *Aviat Week Space Technol* 127:89-90+ N 23 '87
Pentagon boosts research spending to develop practical superconductors. D. Hughes. il *Aviat Week Space Technol* 127:57-9 N 16 '87
SDIO assesses energy storage for FEL defense [free electron lasers utilizing superconducting magnetic energy storage] *Aviat Week Space Technol* 126:29 Ap 6 '87

Periodicals
Covering superconductivity. I. Goodwin. *Phys Today* 40:54 S '87

Supercritical fluid chromatography See Chromatographic analysis

Superfluidity
Quantized vortices in superfluid helium-4. W. I. Glaberson and K. W. Schwarz. bibl f il *Phys Today* 40:54-60 F '87
Vortices in rotating superfluid He³. P. Hakonen and O. V. Lounasmaa. bibl f il *Phys Today* 40:70-8 F '87

Superfood See Nutrition
Superfund for waste cleanup See Trade waste—Disposal—Laws and regulations
Superintendents, School See School superintendents and principals
Superior children See Children, Gifted
Superior National Forest (Minn.)
Old adversaries guard the woods [protest against proposed Minnesota National Guard training facility] M. Helmberger. il *Sierra* 72:81-2 Mr/Ap '87
Superluminal quasars See Quasars
Superman (Fictional character)
Fifty [anniversary] *New Yorker* 63:25-6 Je 8 '87
Superman IV [film] See Motion picture reviews—Single works
Supermarkets
See also
Big Bear, Inc.
Collective labor agreements—Supermarkets
Computers—Grocery trade use
Delchamps, Inc.
Food Lion Inc.

Great Atlantic & Pacific Tea Company, Inc.
J. Bildner & Sons
Kroger Co.
Lucky Stores Inc.
Safeway Stores, Inc.
Salad bars
Supermarkets General Corp.
Vons Grocery Co.
Attention, shoppers: check out the wedding special in aisle 2! [D. Francis and V. Radeka marry at Florida supermarket where they met] L. Tielis. il pors *People Wkly* 28:143-5 O 26 '87
Designs for shopping. C. Kummer. il *Atlantic* 259:84-5 My '87
A new generation of don't-miss markets in and around Los Angeles. il *Sunset* 179:98-101 O '87
Supermarkets take up the challenge. R. Gold. il *Work Woman* 12:177-8+ My '87

Acquisitions and mergers
How to get in on the Safeway LBO [warrants] J. M. Laderman. *Bus Week* p100 Ap 27 '87
Sharp shoppers [B. Freeman specializes in leveraged buyouts of supermarkets] M. Fritz. il por *Forbes* 140:236 N 30 '87
Will Dart bag a grocer this time? [Supermarkets General] T. Ichniowski. *Bus Week* p35-6 Mr 23 '87

Advertising
See also
Supermarkets—In-store advertising

Book departments
California plan puts quality children's books in supermarkets. M. Colin. *Publ Wkly* 232:28 O 30 '87

Finance
Food distributors. R. King, Jr. il *Forbes* 139:130+ Ja 12 '87

In-store advertising
An upstart is upsetting Actmedia's shopping carts [Cooperative Marketing Co.] R. Mitchell. il *Bus Week* p28-9 S 7 '87

Produce departments
Pesticide protection [California markets test produce] J. Adler. il *Newsweek* 110:69+ N 9 '87

Securities
It pays to mind the store. M. Ozanian. il *Forbes* 140:462 Jl 13 '87

Supermarkets General Corp.
Will Dart bag a grocer this time? T. Ichniowski. *Bus Week* p35-6 Mr 23 '87
Supernatural
See also
Ghosts
Miracles
Parapsychology
Supernatural in literature
See also
Horror tales
Supernovas
Bang: the supernova of 1987. D. Helfand. bibl il *Phys Today* 40 pt1:24-32 Ag '87
A burst of discovery: the first days of supernova 1987A. R. Talcott. il *Astronomy* 15:90-5 Je '87
CCD images of supernova remnants. il *Sky Telesc* 73:27 Ja '87
A cosmic birth announcement [Cassiopeia A observations] S. Begley. il *Newsweek* 109:55 Ja 19 '87
Desperately seeking supernovae [cover story] R. N. Kahn. il *Sky Telesc* 73:594-7 Je '87
Discovery on a cosmic scale [1987A discoverer I. Shelton] il por *Macleans* 100:16-17 D 28 '87
Echoing supernova; A supernova remnant around a pulsar. *Sci News* 132:361 D 5 '87
Exploding star contains atoms of Elvis Presley's brain [discovery of 1987A by I. Shelton] J. Tierney. il pors maps *Discover* 8:46-7+ Jl '87
Follow that star! il *Life* 10:123 D '87
Follow that supernova [1987A; cover story] D. E. Thomsen. il *Sci News* 132:122-3 Ag 22 '87
The great supernova of 1987. il *Sky Telesc* 73:524-5 My '87
Guest stars are always welcome. F. R. Stephenson. *Nat Hist* 96:72+ S '87
A hint of gamma rays; Blank about Mont Blanc [supernova 1987A] D. E. Thomsen. *Sci News* 132:286 O 31 '87
Large Magellanic explosion: supernova 1987A is nature's most spectacular blast [cover story] D. E. Thomsen. *Sci News* 132:380-1 D 12 '87
Letters [discussion of June 1987 article, Desperately seeking supernovae] R. N. Kahn. *Sky Telesc* 74:229-30 S '87

Supernovas—*cont.*

NASA initiates flights to obtain supernova data. *Aviat Week Space Technol* 127:28 N 9 '87

Nature of Supernova 1987A, mysterious companion discussed at AAS meeting. il *Astronomy* 15:74-5 S '87

Neutrino astronomy born in a supernova [1987A] D. E. Thomsen. *Sci News* 131:180 Mr 21 '87

Neutrino physics after the supernova [explosion of 1987A] D. E. Thomsen. *Sci News* 131:231 Ap 11 '87

Neutrinos from hell [detected from supernova 1987A] R. A. Schorn. il *Sky Telesc* 73:477-9 My '87

New light on Cassiopeia A [research by Robert A. Fesen and others] il *Sky Telesc* 74:124 Ag '87

On supernovae. D. H. Levy. *Space World* X-9-285:21 S '87

'Out, damned spot'; Doing the pulsar twist [1987A] D. E. Thomsen. *Sci News* 132:268 O 24 '87

A quick and dirty supernova expedition [1987A] S. J. Edberg. *Astronomy* 15:28+ Jl '87

A revisit to the guest star of A.D. 185. Y.-L. Huang and G. H. Moriarty-Schieven. bibl f il *Science* 235:59-60 Ja 2 '87

Scientists, 'boxed in', scramble after supernova, find neutrinos [1987A] D. E. Thomsen. *Sci News* 131:165 Mr 14 '87

Scientists size up the supernova [1987A] D. E. Thomsen. *Sci News* 132:229 O 10 '87

Searching for supernovae: the discovery in M-99. C. Pennypacker. il *Astronomy* 15:74-9 Ag '87

Seeking supernovas systematically. D. E. Thomsen. *Sci News* 132:156-7 S 5 '87

Sighting of a supernova [1987A] M. M. Waldrop. il *Science* 235:1143 Mr 6 '87

A simple model for neutrino cooling of the Large Magellanic Cloud supernova. D. N. Spergel and others. bibl f il *Science* 237:1471-3 S 18 '87

Sky watch on a dying giant [supernova 1987A] il *U S News World Rep* 102:10 Mr 9 '87

SN 1006's radio portrait [Very Large Array radio telescope] il *Sky Telesc* 73:480 My '87

SN 1987A: watching and waiting. R. A. Schorn. il *Sky Telesc* 74:14-15 Jl '87

Spectacle of cosmic surprises [1987A] D. Thompson. il *Time* 129:53 Je 29 '87

Spectacular death throes of a star. A. Steacy. il por *Macleans* 100:40+ Mr 9 '87

A star explodes. il *Natl Geogr World* 141:16-19 My '87

Star sheds galaxy of light on scientists' theories [Supernova 1987A] il *Earth Sci* 40:8-9 Fall '87

A star's subatomic message [neutrinos spit out by 1987A] S. Budiansky. il *U S News World Rep* 102:75 Mr 23 '87

Supernova! [1987A] il *Sci Am* 256:54+ My '87

Supernova! [1987A] E. Edelson. il por *Pop Sci* 231:60-4+ S '87

Supernova! [discovery of 1987A; cover story] M. D. Lemonick. il *Time* 129:60-3+ Mr 23 '87

Supernova 1987A: a mysterious stranger. M. M. Waldrop. il *Science* 237:25-6 Jl 3 '87

Supernova 1987A after 200 days. R. A. Schorn. il *Sky Telesc* 74:477-9 N '87

Supernova 1987A and the press. R. A. Schorn. il *Sky Telesc* 74:116 Ag '87

Supernova 1987A: astronomers' luck. D. E. Thomsen. il *Sci News* 131:148 Mr 7 '87

Supernova 1987A: notes from all over [special section] M. M. Waldrop. il *Science* 236:522-3 My 1 '87

Supernova 1987A on center stage. M. M. Waldrop. il *Science* 238:1038-41 N 20 '87

The supernova 1987A shows a mind of its own—and a burst of neutrinos. M. M. Waldrop. il *Science* 235:1322-3 Mr 13 '87

Supernova 1987A's fading glory. R. A. Schorn. il *Sky Telesc* 74:258-9 S '87

Supernova: high on understanding [1987A] D. E. Thomsen. il *Sci News* 131:279 My 2 '87

A supernova in our backyard [SN 1987A] R. A. Schorn. il *Sky Telesc* 73:382 Ap '87

Supernova in the LMC. R. Berry. *Astronomy* 15:37 My '87

Supernova neutrinos [1987A] il *Sci Am* 256:18+ Je '87

Supernova neutrinos at IMB [explosion of 1987A] M. M. Waldrop. *Science* 235:1461 Mr 20 '87

Supernova update [1987A] il *Astronomy* 15:68-9 Jl '87

Supernova X-rays: too little too soon [1987A] D. E. Thomsen. *Sci News* 132:263 O 24 '87

A surprising supernova [1987A] R. A. Schorn. il *Sky Telesc* 73:582-3 Je '87

Were the supernova's neutrinos pulsed? [1987A; work of Martin Harwit and others] D. E. Thomsen. *Sci News* 132:117 Ag 22 '87

When will a pulsar in supernova 1987A be seen? F. C. Michel and others. bibl f il *Science* 238:938-40 N 13 '87

A wonder in the southern sky [supernova 1987A] M. D. Lemonick. il *Time* 129:70-1 Mr 9 '87

Spectra and spectroscopy

Double trouble [1987A] *Sci Am* 257:18-19 Jl '87

Helium-rich supernovas. J. C. Wheeler and R. P. Harkness. bibl (p150) il *Sci Am* 257:50-8 N '87

IUE satellite observes supernova in ultraviolet [International Ultraviolet Explorer] il *Aviat Week Space Technol* 126:260-1 Mr 9 '87

Supernova prologue [observation of Supernova 1984E before it blew up; work of C. Martin Gaskell and William C. Keel] il *Sky Telesc* 74:234 S '87

Supernova shines on [1987A; cover story] R. A. Schorn. il *Sky Telesc* 73:470-5 My '87

Superoxide dismutase

Computer simulations of the diffusion of a substrate to an active site of an enzyme. K. Sharp and others. bibl f il *Science* 236:1460-3 Je 12 '87

Superphénix nuclear power plant (France) *See* Nuclear power plants—France

Superscreen television *See* Television projection

Supersonic airplanes *See* Airplanes, Supersonic

Superstition

    See also
    Demonology
    Magic
    Medicine men
    Occult sciences
    Thirteen (The number)
    Voodooism
    Witchcraft

Superstring theories (Physics)

Superstrings. J. H. Schwarz. bibl f il *Phys Today* 40:33-40 N '87

A theory of everything [work of E. Witten; cover story] K. C. Cole. il pors *N Y Times Mag* p20-6+ O 18 '87

To the Big Bang and beyond. S. Odenwald. il *Astronomy* 15:90-5 My '87

Supervisors

    See also
    School supervision and supervisors

Don't promote "one of the boys". M. E. Moore. por *Nations Bus* 75:4 Mr '87

Suppers

    See also
    Buffet meals

Country suppers [microwaving] il *Good Housekeep* 204:75-6 Mr '87

Hearty soup and salad suppers. il *Gourmet* 47:66-8+ F '87

Indian-summer suppers [microwaving] il *Good Housekeep* 205:177-8 S '87

A midnight supper. il *Gourmet* 47:74-82 Ja '87

Summer suppers [special section] il *South Living* 22:69+ Jl '87

Supplementary employment

Moonlighting: a key to differences in measuring employment growth. J. F. Stinson, Jr. bibl f il *Mon Labor Rev* 110:30-1 F '87

Supply and demand

    See also
    Productivity, Industrial

Are we saving? W. F. Buckley. *Natl Rev* 39:62-3 N 6 '87

Bursting the supply-side bubble. G. P. Brockway. il *New Leader* 70:15-16 N 30 '87

The indisputable victory of supply-side economics. P. C. Roberts. il *Bus Week* p34 D 28 '87-Ja 4 '88

Is Jack Kemp fumbling his presidential bid? R. Fly. il por *Bus Week* p90+ Ap 13 '87

Reaganomics, R.I.P. U. E. Reinhardt. *New Repub* 196:24+ Ap 20 '87

Still more reasons to mistrust supply siders [Stefan Welzk's study of German tax loopholes and parallel decline in capital investments] R. Kuttner. por *Bus Week* p22 O 26 '87

Supply and demand have rarely been so out of sync. J. C. Cooper. il *Bus Week* p23-4 Ag 31 '87

Supply side economics *See* Supply and demand

Support (Domestic relations)

    See also
    Alimony

Support (Domestic relations)—*cont.*
Carson's son claims AIDS to make girlfriend abort baby: judge nixes test [child support suit against C. Carson] il por *Jet* 72:13-14 Ag 3 '87
The children who get cut out. D. Whitman. il *U S News World Rep* 103:24+ O 12 '87
Collecting child support—why Uncle Sam won't help. M. Takas. *Vogue* 177:58 N '87
Crackdown on defaulters [Ontario pursues support payment defaulters] J. Bennett. *Macleans* 100:48 Jl 6 '87
If you can't rely on the child-support system, what's a mother to do? *Glamour* 85:104 N '87
Johnny Carson to face queries on son's support. *Jet* 72:4 Jl 6 '87
Johnny Carson's son must pay support for black child who was living on welfare. il por *Jet* 72:52-3 Ap 13 '87
A new deal for the children of divorce [new child support guidelines] S. B. Garland. il *Bus Week* p32 S 7 '87
Phantom fathers. K. Richards. il *Progressive* 51:34 Ag '87
Wisconsin: getting tough on wayward fathers. D. Stoeffler. il *Sch Update* 119:23-4 Mr 23 '87
Wisconsin's child-support experiment. R. J. Margolis. il *New Leader* 70:14-16 O 19 '87
Support groups *See* Self help groups
Suppressor mutation *See* Mutation
Suprachiasmatic nucleus *See* Hypothalamus
Supremacy of the civil authority *See* Civil supremacy over the military
Supreme Court (Canada) *See* Canada. Supreme Court
Supreme Court (U.S.) *See* United States. Supreme Court
Supreme Court judges *See* United States. Supreme Court
Supreme Life Insurance Company
Supreme Life sales mgr. wins prestigious honor [T. Cole] il pors *Jet* 72:36 Ap 6 '87
Supremes (Musical group)
Judge OKs Mary Wilson's use of the name 'Supremes'. por *Jet* 71:56 Ja 26 '87
Surf fishing *See* Salt water fishing
Surface active substances
Baby lung lube [pulmonary surfactants; work of T. Allen Merritt] O. Davies. il *Health* 19:19 Mr '87
Surface area *See* Surfaces—Areas and volumes
Surface chemistry
Catalysis: new perspectives from surface science. D. W. Goodman and J. E. Houston. bibl f il *Science* 236:403-9 Ap 24 '87
Chemical coat helps semiconductor prospects. A. L. Robinson. il *Science* 238:27-9 O 2 '87
Edge surfaces in lithographically textured molybdenum disulfide. C. B. Roxlo and others. bibl f il *Science* 235:1629-31 Mr 27 '87
Surface Design Association (U.S.)
Surface Design reaches out [national conference] P. Dandignac. il *Am Craft* 47:68 Ag/S '87
Surface effect vehicles *See* Air cushion vehicles
Surface Mining, Reclamation, and Enforcement Office (U.S.) *See* United States. Office of Surface Mining, Reclamation, and Enforcement
Surface Mining Control and Reclamation Act *See* Strip mining—Laws and regulations
Surface mounting (Electronics)
Surface-mount components. E. Poe. il *Radio-Electron* 58:32 N '87
Surface-mount technology [special section] F. M. Mims. il *Radio-Electron* 58:57-79+ N '87
Surface phenomena *See* Surface chemistry
Surface tension
See also
Soap bubbles and films
Surfaces
See also
Interfaces
Thin films
Electrons and ions at the helium surface. A. J. Dahm and W. F. Vinen. bibl f il *Phys Today* 40:43-50 F '87
A metal's many faces [research by John W. Cahn and Jean E. Taylor] I. Peterson. il *Sci News* 131:76-7 Ja 31 '87
The surface of crystalline helium-4. H. J. Maris and A. F. Andreev. bibl f il *Phys Today* 40:25-30 F '87
Areas and volumes
Calculating the area of an irregular shape. R. Stolk and G. Ettershank. il *Byte* 12:135-6 F '87

Surfactants *See* Surface active substances
Surfcasting *See* Casting (Fishing)
Surfing
See also
Boardsailing
Ice surfing
Chairman of the board: Tom Curren. K. Nunn. il pors *Roll Stone* p81-4 Jl 16-30 '87
Queen of the surf [F. Zamba] D. Geringer. il pors *Sports Illus* 67:60-3 Jl 27 '87
Anecdotes, facetiae, satire, etc.
Have surfboard, will drown. B. Stepko. il *Seventeen* 46:225 Ag '87
Surge (Electricity) *See* Transients (Electricity)
Surgeon-General's Office (U.S.) *See* United States. Surgeon-General's Office
Surgeons
See also
American College of Surgeons
Bethune, Norman, d. 1939
Cooley, Denton A., 1920-
Duke, James
Hughes, Allen
Mirhoseini, Mahmood
Nolen, William A., 1928-1986
Choosing a plastic surgeon. *Vogue* 177:520 Mr '87
Surgery
See also
Anesthesia and anesthetics
Cesarean section
Children—Surgery
Cryosurgery
Dissection
Infants—Surgery
Infants, Newborn—Surgery
Microsurgery
Surgeons
Sutures
Transplantation of organs, tissues, etc.
See also subhead Surgery under names of organs and regions of the body
Bouncing back from surgery. E. Alvarez and S. Fuchs. il *Health* 19:49-50+ Mr '87
Day surgery. F. Lunzer. il *Forbes* 140:105+ Ag 10 '87
Surgery: always get a second opinion. A. Fischer. *Redbook* 168:94-5+ Ja '87
Surgery, Cosmetic *See* Surgery, Plastic
Surgery, Plastic
3 children who needed a medical miracle [hemangioma removed from two year old's nose]; ed. by Joan Rodman Goulianos. C. Dougan. il *Redbook* 168:112+ F '87
"An accident destroyed my face" [case of L. N. Farmer] A. Fischer. il pors *Redbook* 169:36+ O '87
Blind piano prodigy, age 4, gets free facial surgery [J. Gardner] il por *Jet* 72:24 S 14 '87
Changing the look of mental retardation. il *Psychol Today* 21:45 S '87
Cosmetic surgery: is it for you? il *Read Dig* 131:67-71 Jl '87
Cosmetic surgery today. N. Gallo. il *Better Homes Gard* 65:94+ Ap '87
Eye-opening cosmetic surgery. P. Boyer. il *Prevention* 39:42+ S '87
The facts on fat vacuuming. M. D. Stein. *McCalls* 114:41+ Je '87
Fat loss [suction lipectomy] M. S. Dolan. *Consum Res Mag* 70:2 S '87
Getting better all the time [three generations of women have surgery] R. Seiff. il por *Ladies Home J* 104:20+ Jl '87
Good-bye thunder thighs [suction lipectomy for dancers] M. Horosko. il *Dance Mag* 61:114-15 My '87
Lunch-hour operations [small skin flaws] il *Redbook* 169:174-5 S '87
Maimed by skin cancer, this onetime sun worshipper paid a painful price for the perfect tan [nose surgery and reconstruction] J. Caprio. il pors *People Wkly* 28:87-8+ Ag 10 '87
Miracle cure for saddlebags: does it really work and is it safe? [suction lipectomy] R. B. Pearce. il *Women's Sports Fitness* 9:38-9 Jl '87
Plastic surgery: what to know before you try it. L. Rosch. il *Glamour* 85:138+ Je '87
Sizing up breast implants [Mentor-Becker Expander/ Mammary Prosthesis] G. Carden. il *Health* 19:23 Ag '87
Snip, suction, stretch and truss [cosmetic surgery] M. Smilgis. il *Time* 130:70 S 14 '87

Surgery, Plastic—*cont.*

To be whole again: mastectomy treated Peggy McCann's cancer, but breast reconstruction made her well. D. E. Haupt. il pors *Life* 10:78-83+ My '87

Vanity fair. P. Dranov. il *Health* 19:65-6+ My '87

Whose breasts are they, anyway? [models and breast implants] J. Kaufman. il *Mademoiselle* 93:70 Ag '87

Will your face-lift be a letdown? S. McConnell. *Harpers Bazaar* 120:97+ Ag '87

Women warned of dangers of fat recycling technique [suction lipectomy] *Jet* 72:29 Jl 6 '87

Worried about wrinkles, wattles and thunder thighs? Here's a complete guide to overhauling yourself. il *People Wkly* 28:45-7 Ag 24 '87

Surgical centers, Ambulatory *See* Health facilities
Surgical equipment
See also
    Adhesives—Medical use
    Lasers—Medical use
Surgical gloves *See* Gloves
Surhoff, B. J.

about

B. J. Surhoff. T. Hanlon. por *Sports Illus* 67:48+ Jl 13 '87

Surimi

Completely adulterated seafood. L. Shapiro. il *Newsweek* 109:64-5 F 23 '87

Suro, Roberto

Going undercover for art's sake. il *N Y Times Mag* p42-3+ D 13 '87

Surplus products, Agricultural

The politics of hunger [food surplus keeps growing] W. Greider. il *Roll Stone* p34-5 Jl 2 '87

Subsidies, science more powerful than demand [views of Dennis Avery] *Success Farm* 85 no1:27 Ja '87

Why big feedlots feel 'PIKed' on. B. Eftink. il *Success Farm* 85 no2:B4+ Ja '87

A worldwide glut of food. M. Drohan. il *Macleans* 100:37-8 N 9 '87

Surrealism

Clothed in magic [fashion, art, and surrealism] B. Adams. il *Harpers Bazaar* 120:240-1 O '87

Meet the masters [photographer R. Gibson] F. Cameron. il *Petersens Photogr Mag* 15:28-30 Ja '87

The surreal life of Edward James. A. Cockburn. il por *House Gard* 159:198-206+ Je '87

Exhibitions

A hat is a rose is a chicken [Fashion and surrealism at Fashion Institute of Technology] J. Conant. il *Newsweek* 110:85+ N 30 '87

The interpretive link. H. Drohojowska. il *Art News* 86:29+ F '87

Toddling toward modernism [Interpretive link exhibit] J. Perl. il *Vogue* 177:106 Mr '87

Surrender [film] See Motion picture reviews—Single works
Surrogate law *See* Probate law and practice
Surrogate mothers

And baby makes four: for the first time a surrogate bears a child genetically not her own. B. Johnson. il por *People Wkly* 27:95-6+ My 4 '87

The modifiers of mother [terminology] W. Safire. il *N Y Times Mag* p10+ My 10 '87

Motherly love works a miracle [P. Anthony is surrogate for her daughter; cover story] E. Levin. il pors *People Wkly* 28:38-43 O 19 '87

No other hope for having a child. D. Shapiro. il *Newsweek* 109:50-1 Ja 19 '87

On surrogate motherhood. L. McDowell-Head. por *Essence* 18:136 Jl '87

The rent-a womb dilemma. C. Kocol. il por *Humanist* 47:37 Jl/Ag '87

Science and surrogacy. N. Cutner. il *Life* 10:36-8+ Je '87

Surrogate motherhood [special section] *McCalls* 114:55-8+ Je '87

Womb for rent. K. R. Lawrence. *Vogue* 177:84 Jl '87
Legal status, laws, etc.
See also
    Baby M case

Baby M winner [surrogate matchmaker N. P. Keane] M. Gladwell and R. Sharpe. *New Repub* 196:15-16+ F 16 '87

Birth-marketing. *Commonweal* 114:692 D 4 '87

Childless couples seeking surrogate mothers call Michigan lawyer Noel Keane—he delivers. J. S. Kunen. il pors *People Wkly* 27:93+ Mr 30 '87

A split decision [custody suit filed by surrogate mother A. Muñoz] il *Time* 129:66 Mr 9 '87

Surrogacy—what's legal? M. Asnes. *Vogue* 177:84+ Jl '87

Surrogate motherhood: a legal labyrinth. E. W. Clayton. il *USA Today (Periodical)* 116:68-9 N '87

Womb to let. M. Gallagher. il *Natl Rev* 39:27-30 Ap 24 '87

Moral and religious aspects

The battle over Baby M. J. M. Wall. *Christ Century* 104:99-100 F 4-11 '87

Buying & selling babies. M. Novak. il *Commonweal* 114:406-7 Jl 17 '87

Contracting anguish. J. Garvey. il *Commonweal* 114:232 Ap 24 '87

Hagar & her sisters: precedent for conduct [surrogate motherhood in the Bible] J. Gaffney. il *Commonweal* 114:240-2 Ap 24 '87

How not to have a baby. D. Neff. il *Christ Today* 31:14-15 Ap 3 '87

Surrogate-gate [Baby M case] *Commonweal* 114:35-6 Ja 30 '87

Surrogate motherhood: an ethical and moral dilemma. G. F. Kreyche. il *USA Today (Periodical)* 116:66-7 N '87

Surrogate mothers: right or wrong? R. Wright and M. Jacobbi. il *Ladies Home J* 104:91-2+ Jl '87

What Baby M is telling us. *America* 156:90-1 F 7 '87

What is the future for surrogate motherhood? B. Spring. il *Christ Today* 31:42-3+ Mr 6 '87

What the market will bear. T. A. Shannon. il *Commonweal* 114:234-5 Ap 24 '87

Wombs shouldn't be for rent [with readers' comments] M. Meehan. *U S Cathol* 52:16-21 S '87
Public opinion

Is surrogate motherhood okay? [results of survey] I. Groller. il *Parents* 62:28 O '87

This is what you thought: 71% say surrogate parenting should be allowed [results of survey] *Glamour* 85:135 O '87

Surry Opera Company

Barnyard diplomacy [Surry Opera Company from Maine tours U.S.S.R.] M. Baldwin. il *Opera News* 52:38-9 Jl '87

From a Maine barn to a Soviet stage, Walter Nowick's opera company raises the Iron Curtain to promote harmony. L. Aitken. il por *People Wkly* 27:93-4 Ja 12 '87

Surtees, John

about

John Surtees. C. Fox. il pors *Cycle* 38:68-71+ My '87

Surtitles (Opera) *See* Opera—Titling
Surtsey (Iceland)

All quiet on the Surtsey front. il *Nat Hist* 96:2+ Ag '87

Surveillance, Electronic *See* Electronics in criminal investigation, espionage, etc.
Surveillance, Laser *See* Lasers in criminal investigation, espionage, etc.
Surveillance satellites, Military *See* Artificial satellites—Military use
Surveying

How to find your property lines. il *Sunset* 178:136+ Je '87

Property surveys: preventive medicine for border disputes. H. Porter. *Fam Handyman* 37:14 O '87

Territorial prerogatives. H. J. Lehman. *Changing Times* 41:12+ F '87

Surveys
See also
    Public opinion polls
    Snow surveys

Answering autobiographical questions: the impact of memory and inference on surveys. N. M. Bradburn and others. bibl f il *Science* 236:157-61 Ap 10 '87

Survival, Wilderness *See* Wilderness survival
Survival and emergency equipment

If you're 20 fathoms down and out of oxygen, the answer is Larry Williamson's Spare Air. il por *People Wkly* 27:65 My 18 '87

Out in the cold [emergency camping gear] S. Netherby. il *Field Stream* 92:75-6 Ag '87

Survival kits *See* Survival and emergency equipment
Survival Research Laboratories (Group)

Cyber-punk: performance art on the furthest edge. S. Zakin. il *Vogue* 177:98 D '87

Masters of the universe. M. Weisang. il *Theatre Crafts* 21:28-9+ Ja '87

Survival skills

Survival: life in extreme conditions [cover story; special issue; with editorial comment by Edouard Glissant] il maps *Courier* 40:3-34 Je '87

Susann, Jacqueline, 1921-1974
about
How green was her valley. L. Fleischer. il *Publ Wkly* 231:89 F 13 '87
Sushi
When it comes to stylish sushi, it's safer to be square. E. Zamula. il *FDA Consum* 21:18-21 F '87
Süskind, Patrick
Amnesia in litteris. il *Harpers* 274:71-3 Mr '87
Suspect [film] See Motion picture reviews—Single works
Suspenders
Brace yourself. E. Pomice. il *Forbes* 139:117-18 F 9 '87
Suspenders. J. Berendt. il *Esquire* 107:42+ Je '87
Suspense stories See Detective and mystery stories
Suspension, Automobile See Automobiles—Springs and suspension
Suspension, Motorcycle See Motorcycles—Springs and suspension
Suspension, Student See Student suspension and expulsion
Susskind, Charles M., 1921-
Alvin W. Trivelpiece: AAAS Executive Officer. il por *Science* 236:377 Ap 24 '87
Sussman, Gerald Jay
(jt. auth) See Hut, Piet, 1952-, and Sussman, Gerald Jay
Sutcliffe, James Helme
Birthdays in Berlin (I). il *Opera News* 51:32-5 F 14 '87
Birthdays in Berlin (II). il *Opera News* 51:32-5+ Mr 28 '87
Touch of Venus. pors *Opera News* 51:34-5 Ja 17 '87
Sutherland, Donald, 1934-
Sutherland's folly. il por *House Gard* 159:184-9+ Je '87
about
Making a legend [cover story; special section; with editorial comment by Kevin Doyle] il pors *Macleans* 100:2, 26-34 Ag 10 '87
Sutherland, Joan, 1926-
about
Dead from Lincoln Center. S. Lipman. *Commentary* 83:59-63 My '87
Music. P. G. Davis. *N Y* 20:72 Ja 26 '87
The Sutherland/Pavarotti anniversary gala. il pors *Opera News* 51:40-1 F 28 '87
Suttee
Fire and faith [R. Kanwar revives custom in Deorala] *Time* 130:41 S 28 '87
Sutter, Joseph F., 1921-
about
Sutter's lucky sevens. N. Moll. por *Flying* 114:35 My '87
Sutter family
about
Hockey's big brother act. J. Mills. il *N Y Times Mag* p64-5+ Mr 29 '87
Sutton, Joe
about
As it is in heaven [drama] Reviews
Nation 244:585 My 2 '87. T. M. Disch
Sutton, Percy E.
about
Percy Sutton lauded; past year's battles celebrated at NAACP confab in N.Y. il por *Jet* 72:4-5 Jl 27 '87
Sutton, Remar
about
Car buying without fear [interview] J. Thornton. il por *U S News World Rep* 103:74-6 O 12 '87
The rebuilding of Remar Sutton. A. Toufexis. pors *Time* 129:72 Ap 6 '87
Yeah, but can he keep it off? B. Barol. pors *Newsweek* 109:70 Ap 27 '87
Sutton, Robert
about
Minus centimillionaire no more. L. Jereski. por *Forbes* 140 Sp Issue:8 O 26 '87
Sutton, Roger
Yooks, zooks and the bomb. *N Y Times Book Rev* 92:22 F 22 '87
Sutton, Tex
about
This man can make a horse fly. D. Young. il pors *South Living* 22:158+ Ap '87
Sutton, Walter L., Jr.
about
Walter Sutton Jr. named head of Bar Association. *Jet* 72:55 S 7 '87
Sutton (H.E. "Tex") Horse Charters See H.E. "Tex" Sutton Horse Charters

Sutures
How an old crab could keep you in stitches [use of chitin from discarded crabshells; work of Paul Austin] T. Dworetzky. il *Discover* 8:16 F '87
New life for crab shells [use of chitin for sutures; work of Paul Austin] *Oceans* 20:3-4 Mr/Ap '87
Suva, L. J., and others
A parathyroid hormone-related protein implicated in malignant hypercalcemia: cloning and expression. bibl f il *Science* 237:893-6 Ag 21 '87
Suzdak, Peter D., and others
Seizures in drug-treated animals [discussion of December 5, 1986 article, A selective imidazobenzodiazepine antagonist of ethanol in the rat (Ro15-4513)] bibl f *Science* 235:1127-8 Mr 6 '87
Suzman, Helen
about
Arch foe of apartheid. V. Butler. por *Read Dig* 130:157-62 Mr '87
Profiles. E. J. Kahn. por *New Yorker* 63:50-1+ Ap 20 '87
Suzuki Motor Company Ltd.
Buy two, they're cheap [advertising the Suzuki Samurai] J. Flint. il *Forbes* 140:193+ N 2 '87
SV40 virus See Simian viruses
Svarney, Patricia Barnes- See Barnes-Svarney, Patricia
Svec, Milan
Removing Gorbachev's edge. il *Foreign Policy* 69:148-65 Wint '87/'88
Svendsen, Elisabeth D.
about
In a seaside hee-haw haven, 1,700 donkeys bray each day for Elisabeth Svendsen. M. Neill. il pors *People Wkly* 27:84-7 My 25 '87
Svoboda, Josef, 1920-
about
Svoboda & Vychodil: Czechoslovakia's two master scenographers. J. M. Burian. il *Theatre Crafts* 21:34-7+ O '87
Svoray, Yaron
The making of a terrorist. *Natl Rev* 39:57-9 Je 19 '87
Swafford-Choyce, Alice
Sync [poem] *Essence* 17:121 F '87
Swaggart, Jimmy Lee
about
Divided Pentecostals: Bakker vs. Swaggart. E. L. Blumhofer. *Christ Century* 104:430-1 My 6 '87
Offering the hope of heaven. R. N. Ostling. il por *Time* 129:69 Mr 16 '87
Swaggart column nixed. *Christ Century* 104:552 Je 17-24 '87
Swaggart: singing crusader. por *Time* 129:63 Ap 6 '87
Swaggart swings through El Salvador. P. Lacefield. il por *Commonweal* 114:279-80+ My 8 '87
War of the evangelists: unfunny reflections. T. H. Stahel. *America* 156:293 Ap 11 '87
Swags (Draperies) See Curtains and draperies
Swahili (African people)
The Swahili corridor [Shanga excavations in Kenya] M. Horton. il maps *Sci Am* 257:86-8+ S '87
Swaim, Bob
about
Half Moon Street [film] Reviews
Mademoiselle il 93:66+ Ja '87. R. Rosenbaum
Swaim, Paul
(jt. auth) See Podgursky, Michael, and Swaim, Paul
Swain, Joseph P.
An apology for the hymn. *America* 156:421-3 My 23 '87
Swallows
Bank swallows [Cape Cod] R. Finch. il *Ctry J* 14:76-80 My '87
Swaminathan, Monkombu Sambasivan
about
Scientists: their rewards and humanity. R. D. Havener. *Science* 237:1281 S 11 '87
Swamps See Marshes
Swan, Matthew
about
"We thought our faith could save our son". K. Delaney. il pors *Redbook* 168:104-6 Ja '87
Swan, Michael
about
Soap star computes. il por *Pers Comput* 11:282 S '87
Swan, Robert
In the footsteps of Scott. il pors map *Natl Geogr* 171:544-55 Ap '87
Swan, Tony
Car repairs: where can you go? Whom can you trust? il *Better Homes Gard* 65:98-9+ My '87
Swan Lake [ballet] See Ballet reviews—Single works

Swanke, Hayden, Connell Architects
Sales reps or service reps: what do architects need from them? W. F. Koelling. il por *Archit Rec* 175:16-17 D '87
Swann, Christopher
Offshore outpost. il *Oceans* 20:42-7 N/D '87
Swans
Poisoning the trumpeters. P. Byrnes. il *Wilderness* 51:42-3 Wint '87

Photographs and photography
Swan song. il *Natl Wildl* 25:4-5 F/Mr '87
Swanson, Austin D., and Zhang Zhian
Education reform in China. bibl f il *Phi Delta Kappan* 68:373-8 Ja '87
Swanson, Joel A., and McNeil, Paul L.
Nuclear reassembly excludes large macromolecules. bibl f il *Science* 238:548-50 O 23 '87
Swanson, Robert A.

about

The man who could make biotechnology profitable—at last. G. Bylinsky. il por *Fortune* 115:101 Ja 5 '87
Robert Swanson. J. O. Hamilton. il por *Bus Week* Sp Issue:242 Ap 17 '87
Swanson, Robert K.

about

Fast-track stumble. J. A. Conway. il *Forbes* 139:8 Ap 6 '87
Swanson, Wil

about

Reviews:
Performances at the Bessie Schönberg Theater, New York City. L. Garafola. *Dance Mag* 61:37-8 Ja '87
Swanson (Wil) and Dancers *See* Wil Swanson and Dancers
Swap financing
Battered bonds? Try swapping them. D. Zigas. *Bus Week* p182 O 12 '87
Bolivia swaps debt for conservation. J. Walsh. map *Science* 237:596-7 Ag 7 '87
The brave new world of swaps [Norwest Bank's dealings in Brazil] P. Sherrid. il *U S News World Rep* 103:41 Ag 31 '87
Buying debt, saving nature [offers to suspend debt payments for tropical countries which protect forests] J. B. Copeland. il *Newsweek* 110:46 Ag 31 '87
Cashing in on debt [Latin debt-to-equity swaps] T. Tedesco. il *Macleans* 100:34-5 O 5 '87
The Citi squeezes its lemons [move to clean up third world debt with debt for equity swaps] S. Bartlett. il *Bus Week* p31 Je 15 '87
Cutting the debt, saving the forest. D. Page. *Environment* 29:4-5+ S '87
Exchanging debt for conservation [debt for nature scheme] A. L. Spitler. il *BioScience* 37:781 D '87
Fast bucks in Latin loan swaps [debt-equity swaps] J. Fierman. il *Fortune* 116:91-2+ Ag 3 '87
A golden deal: debt for nature. J. D. Hair. il *Int Wildl* 17:30 S/O '87
Here comes the repo man [debt-equity swaps in Latin America] W. Curtis. *Nation* 244:570+ My 2 '87
Swap a bond, save a buck. L. Wiener. il *U S News World Rep* 103:79 O 5 '87
Swapping bonds: the best revenge for paper losses. D. Zigas. *Bus Week* p164 Je 22 '87
There goes the neighborhood [M. Schubert's mastery of Latin loan swaps] E. A. Finn, Jr. il por *Forbes* 139:35-7 Je 29 '87
Third world debt: a flawed solution [debt-equity swaps] R. Kuttner. il *Bus Week* p18 Je 19 '87
"This is war" [Brazilian debt; interview with M. Colasuonno] L. Minard. il por *Forbes* 139:50 Je 29 '87
Swapping *See* Barter
Swarthmore College
Infill to the nth [Tarble Student Center] il *Archit Rec* 175:106-11 Mr '87
Swartz, Harvie

about

Harvie Swartz's Urban Earth. F. Bouchard. il por *Down Beat* 54:56 Je '87
Swartz, Steven L., and Jones, Mary Lou
Gray whales at play in Baja's San Ignacio Lagoon. il maps *Natl Geogr* 171:754-71 Je '87
Swavely, Mike
The significance of the Micro Channel. por *Pers Comput* 11:258 O '87
Swayze, Patrick

about

Dirty dancing's Patrick Swayze: not just the hunk of the month. J. Powell. il *Glamour* 85:202 Ag '87

Swaziland

Kings and rulers
See also
Mswati III, King of Swaziland
Politics and government
In the kingdom of "Fire Eyes" [Mswati] W. E. Smith. il *Time* 130:34 S 7 '87
Swearing
Teachers can be ousted for swearing at students [case of Midland College professor J. D. Martin] *Jet* 71:23 F 23 '87
Swearingen, John E.

about

Still drifting after all these years. J. N. Frank. il *Bus Week* p130+ My 11 '87
Sweat *See* Perspiration
Sweaters
See also
Neuma Inc.
Closely knit [men's sweaters] R. La Ferla. il *N Y Times Mag* p78 N 15 '87
Designer Lisa Nichols can't make a stitch but she's a great knit-picker. K. Johnson. il por *People Wkly* 27:98-9 F 16 '87
Easy to knit! Summer blues. il *Good Housekeep* 204:114-17+ Je '87
The Fair Isle sweater. J. Berendt. il *Esquire* 107:30 Mr '87
How to wear a sweater to work. J. Mattera. il *Glamour* 85:146 N '87
Knit one, hunt too [sweaters for the outdoorsman] K. Etling. bibl il *Outdoor Life* 180:96-7+ N '87
Make our sweetheart sweaters. il *Good Housekeep* 204:134-7+ F '87
The new denim-look crew [knitting instructions] il *Redbook* 169:89-90 My '87
Quick! Appliqué a designer sweater. il *Redbook* 169:43-4+ S '87
Quick-to-knit sweaters. J. Williams and J. Severson. il *Better Homes Gard* 65:62-3 Ja '87
Take a sweater and make it sparkle [knitting instructions] il *Good Housekeep* 205:144-7+ O '87
Sweatshirts *See* Shirts
Sweatshops
The return of the sweat shop. J. Mazur. il *USA Today (Periodical)* 115:31-3 Mr '87
Sweatt, Heman

about

UT-Austin names campus to honor black student. por *Jet* 72:38 S 14 '87
Sweden
See also
Environmental policy—Sweden
Industry and state—Sweden
Investments, Swedish
Organic farming—Sweden
Radioactive pollution—Sweden
Radioactive waste disposal—Sweden
Securities—Laws and regulations—Sweden
Stockholm (Sweden)
Sundborn (Sweden)
Traffic regulations—Sweden
Air Force
Swedish Air Force declares two Base 90 facilities operational. il *Aviat Week Space Technol* 126:56-7 My 11 '87
Swedish Air Force seeks backing for increased Gripen production. D. A. Brown. il *Aviat Week Space Technol* 126:18-20 My 4 '87
Swedish Air Force's challenge. D. E. Fink. *Aviat Week Space Technol* 126:15 My 11 '87
Antiquities
See also
Kronan (Ship)
Commerce
Iran
See Iran—Commerce—Sweden
Switzerland
Switzerland's Crossair considers purchase of stretched Saab SF340. J. M. Lenorovitz. il *Aviat Week Space Technol* 126:42-3 Je 8 '87
United States
See United States—Commerce—Sweden
Defenses
See also
Airplanes, Military—Sweden
Sweden—Air Force
Sweden scraps aggressive defense spending plan. *Aviat Week Space Technol* 126:30 Ja 19 '87

Sweden—*cont.*
Description and travel
Canoe-exploring the canals, rivers, and lakes of southwest Sweden. il *Sunset* 178:68 My '87
Economic relations
See also
Economic assistance, Swedish
Foreign relations
See also
Economic assistance, Swedish
Industries
See also
Beväringen Company
Bofors Nobel AB
Corporations—Acquisitions and mergers—Sweden
Ericsson Radio Systems AB
Fermenta AB
IKEA Svenska Forsaljnings AB
L.M. Ericsson Telephone Co.
Saab-Scania AB
Swedish Match AB
Swedish Space Corporation
Wallenberg Group
Religious institutions and affairs
See also
Church camps—Sweden
Swedish American Hospital (Rockford, Ill.) *See* Rockford (Ill.)—Hospitals
Swedish cooking *See* Cooking, Swedish
Swedish Match AB
A financial gambler tries to trump the Wallenbergs again [E. Penser's moves on Swedish Match] J. Kapstein. *Bus Week* p50+ Ja 19 '87
Swedish Space Corporation
Swedish firm develops lightweight airborne system for sea surveillance. *Aviat Week Space Technol* 127:101 S 21 '87
Swedish tennis players *See* Tennis players
Sweeney, David J.
Apply for a patent. bibl il *Radio-Electron* 58:48-52+ Ja '87
Learning about Loran. il maps *Radio-Electron* 58:51-2+ My '87
Sweeney, John A. H.
John Dickinson's Poplar Hall, Kent County, Delaware. il *Antiques* 132:820-7 O '87
Sweeney, Kevin
about
No longer Gary Hart's spokesman, Kevin Sweeney ponders his fate while waiting tables at Lily's. R. Arias. il pors *People Wkly* 28:103+ N 9 '87
Sweeney, Terrance A.
about
Sweeney agonistes. *America* 156:413-14 My 23 '87
Sweeney responds [discussion of May 23, 1987 article, Sweeney agonistes] *America* 157:22 Jl 4-11 '87
Sweeps (Securities) *See* Street sweeps (Securities)
Sweepstakes *See* Lotteries
Sweepstakes Clearing House
No consolation from this prize [using credit vouchers as prizes] il *Consum Rep* 52:270 My '87
Sweet, Alec Stone- *See* Stone-Sweet, Alec
Sweet, Jeffrey, 1950-
Roles in collision: a play begins. il *Writer* 100:16-18 My '87
Sweet, Leonard I.
Pearlygate satires are weak on substance. *Christ Century* 104:644-5 Jl 29-Ag 5 '87
Sweet, William
Scientists shoot down Star Wars. *Bull At Sci* 43:7-9 Jl/Ag '87
Sweet alyssum
Sweet alyssum gives the finishing touch. K. Piper. il *Flower Gard* 31:41 F/Mr '87
Sweet cicely
Sweet cicely. B. Reppert. il *Rodale's Org Gard* 34:32 Je '87
Sweet corn *See* Corn
Sweet Honey in the Rock (Musical group)
Sweet Honey in the Rock. I. Young. il *Essence* 18:92-4+ My '87
Sweet peppers *See* Peppers
Sweet potato pie *See* Pie
Sweet potatoes
See also
Cooking—Potatoes
Sweet Sue [drama] See Gurney, A. R. (Albert Ramsdell), 1930-
Sweet Victory Café (New York, N.Y.) *See* New York (N.Y.)—Restaurants, nightclubs, bars, etc.

Sweeteners
See also
Sugar substitutes
Xylitol
Swelling (Physiology)
Why does your body bloat? A. Spence. il *Redbook* 170:114-15+ N '87
Swenson, Edward E.
Memories of his master's voice [interview with R. K. Anderson] il por *High Fidel* 37:56-9 My '87
Swenson, Kari
Kidnapping
A made-for-television movie brings biathlete Kari Swenson face-to-face with her past. M. Neill. il pors *People Wkly* 27:76-8+ Mr 16 '87
Swenson, Loyd S., Jr.
Michelson and measurement. bibl il *Phys Today* 40:24-30 My '87
Swenson, May, 1919-
Strawberrying [poem] *Atlantic* 259:52 Mr '87
Swerdlow, Joel L.
Washington. See issues of Channels (New York, N.Y.: 1986) beginning May 1986
Swick, Thomas R.
Letter from Madrid: a view from the street. *Am Sch* 56:407-14 Summ '87
Swid, Stephen Claar
about
A dealmaker decides there's no biz like show biz. M. Frons. il por *Bus Week* p107 My 11 '87
Swidler, Arlene
Bring back women deacons. *U S Cathol* 52:30-1 Ag '87
Swidler, Leonard
Human rights & Catholic rights. *Commonweal* 114:485-6 S 11 '87
Swift, David
Manna from Amana. il *Mother Earth News* 107:54-7 S/O '87
Swift, E. M.
All that glittered was gold. il *Sports Illus* 66:63-5 F 16 '87
A belated Christmas gift. il *Sports Illus* 66:16-17 Ja 5 '87
The best and the brightest. il *Sports Illus* 67:40-5 Ag 31 '87
Carol and her big lug. il pors *Sports Illus* 66:88-91+ F 9 '87
Countdown to the cowtown hoedown. il map *Sports Illus* 66:72-8+ Mr 9 '87
The Cup runneth overlong. il por *Sports Illus* 66:88 Ap 13 '87
Détente on ice. il *Sports Illus* 66:12-19 F 23 '87
The Flyers forever. il *Sports Illus* 67:90-2+ O 12 '87
How they bore us in the Norris. il *Sports Illus* 66:36-9 Ja 19 '87
King of the seven seas. il por *Sports Illus* 66:74-5 My 18 '87
Manager on a red-hot seat. il *Sports Illus* 66:48-52+ Ap 6 '87
The NHL isn't so tough. il por *Sports Illus* 67:122 O 12 '87
Notre Dame is golden again. il *Sports Illus* 67:26-8+ N 9 '87
The Penguins are percolating. il por *Sports Illus* 67:20-1 D 14 '87
The pit bull: friend and killer [cover story] il *Sports Illus* 67:72-8+ Jl 27 '87
Pow! Pow! Pow! il *Sports Illus* 66:42-4+ Je 1 '87
Reprieve for the Browns. il *Sports Illus* 66:26-9 Ja 12 '87
They came up roses. il *Sports Illus* 67:38-40+ Ag 17 '87
Thou swell, thou Witt-y. il pors *Sports Illus* 66:20-3 Mr 23 '87
Three sevens on one roll. il *Sports Illus* 66:34-6+ My 11 '87
The triumph of skill: by beating Philly, the Oilers struck a blow for finesse. il por *Sports Illus* 66:96 Je 8 '87
The Wall's inside story. il *Sports Illus* 67:48-50 Jl 6 '87
Swift, Margaret *See* Drabble, Margaret, 1939-
SWIFT
The safety of the world's funds [address, September 10, 1987] W. D. Mulholland. *Vital Speeches Day* 54:86-8 N 15 '87
Swift Independent Holding Corporation
A meat-packing magnate gets boxed in [E. L. Cox] J. Weber, Jr. il por *Bus Week* p50+ Je 22 '87

Swimmer's ear *See* Ear—Diseases
Swimming
See also
Diving
A cold swim to promote warm U.S.-U.S.S.R. ties [Bering Strait crossing planned by L. Cox] il pors *Discover* 8:8+ Jl '87
Lynne Cox comes in from the cold [Bering Strait swim] R. L. Graham. il *Women's Sports Fitness* 9:12-13 N '87
Lynne Cox's brave swim across the frigid Bering Strait breaks the ice with the Russians. K. Hubbard. il pors *People Wkly* 28:32-4 Ag 24 '87
Splash! [latest tools, techniques, and exercises to aid swimmers] H. Casabona. il *Women's Sports Fitness* 9:27-9 Je '87
Swim for fitness. D. Steinman. *Women's Sports Fitness* 9:10 O '87
Swim for strong bones. L. Fink. il *Women's Sports Fitness* 9:19 Ag '87
The swim solution: workouts that lap up fat. il *Mademoiselle* 93:168-71 Je '87
Swimmer Lynne Cox braces for an ice water ordeal, a dire crossing in the Bering Strait. J. Friedman. il por *People Wkly* 27:46-7 My 4 '87
Swimming builds stronger bones [study by Eric S. Orwoll] il *Prevention* 39:6 S '87
Swimming for fitness. C. Schaeffer. *Changing Times* 41:16-17 My '87
The swimming postman [letters delivered in Amazon region by Indian swimmers in 1802] A. Humboldt, Freiherr von. il *Courier* 40:14 Ap '87
Swimming vs. weight loss. *Vogue* 177:474 O '87
Taking the plunge: how a fitness dabbler learned to love the open water. K. Coleman. il por *Women's Sports Fitness* 9:23-6 Je '87

Competitions
America's new golden girl [J. Evans' performance at the U.S. championships] B. Anderson. il pors *Sports Illus* 67:28-30+ Ag 10 '87
Black swimmer resurfaces thanks to Campanis' slur [C. Silva] il por *Jet* 72:51 My 18 '87
Graduating with honors [NCAA men's championship] C. Neff. il pors *Sports Illus* 66:52+ Ap 13 '87
Marie Wilcox, 65. M. Kort. il por *Women's Sports Fitness* 9:18 O '87
Texas pooled its talent [victory over University of Florida] H. Hersch. il *Sports Illus* 66:60 F 2 '87
Woman to watch: Sandy Neilson. il pors *Women's Sports Fitness* 9:54 Jl '87

Safety devices and measures
See Drowning—Prevention

Study and teaching
One with water [program for aquaphobes by Paul Lennon] D. Groves. il *Health* 19:16 Ja '87
Swimming (Animal locomotion) *See* Animal locomotion
Swimming pools

Sanitation
Little tub of horrors: pools and hot tubs can make you sick. J. C. Johnson. il *Mademoiselle* 93:74 Je '87

Swimming pools, Home
Backyard cool. il *Changing Times* 41:10+ My '87
Backyard pools—how to avoid going off the deep end. J. Rachlin. il *U S News World Rep* 102:50-1 Ap 13 '87
For the hillside pool, a wall of falls, tile, lights. il *Sunset* 178:150 My '87
How to choose a pool and someone to build it [interview with J. Garasich] R. Cogan. il por *Fam Handyman* 37:76-7 My/Je '87
Keeping the pool cool [planting around swimming pools] B. Damrosch. il *Esquire* 108:24 Jl '87
Landscaped by nature . . . or you. il *Sunset* 179:56-9 Ag '87
Pooling your resources. M. Morris. il *Home Mech* 83:40-2+ Je '87
Removing the pool from center stage. il *South Living* 22:97 My '87
Shaped by man, graced by nature [Virginia pool carved into rock] S. Bender. il *South Living* 22:68-9 Ag '87
This pool is an extension of the house. il *South Living* 22:48 Ag '87
Vinyl-lined pools: one-third the cost, but how do they look and last? il *Sunset* 178:150-1 Je '87
Swimming to Cambodia [film] *See* Motion picture reviews—Single works
Swimnastics *See* Water exercises
Swimsuits *See* Bathing suits
Swinburne, Stephen R.
Capturing the birds on film. il *Ctry J* 14:47-9 F '87

Swindlers and swindling *See* Fraud
Swine
Can you believe the pig report? [USDA statistics] G. Johnston. il *Success Farm* 85 no6:18T Mr '87
Hogs. G. Johnston. See issues of Successful Farming through May 1987
Pig at the Pacific! [Kevin Feaster and his pet pig Wilbur] il *Natl Geogr World* 143:15-17 Jl '87
When a 500-pound pig hounds sheep and puts honest dogs out of work, it just doesn't seem kosher. il *People Wkly* 27:148-9 My 4 '87

Anecdotes, facetiae, satire, etc.
My beef about micro pig, and your stake—or chop—in it. J. Gorman. il *Discover* 8:24+ Ja '87
On the trail of the micro pig and the macro trout. J. Gorman. il *Discover* 8:22+ Jl '87
Pigs. P. F. McManus. il *Outdoor Life* 179:164+ My '87

Carcasses
What is a good hog worth? [work of John Forrest] G. Johnston. il *Success Farm* 85:44 S '87

Care
Mix and move baby pigs. K. Coble. il *Success Farm* 85:46 N '87

Confinement methods
Cramped pigs. G. Johnston. il *Success Farm* 85 no6:18AN Mr '87

Diseases and pests
Vaccines and vaccination
Gene-altered hog vaccine causes stir for USDA [Omnivac pseudorabies vaccine] *Success Farm* 85 no6:18AZ Mr '87
Swine pseudorabies on the way out? D. Ohrtman. il *Success Farm* 85:69 Ag '87

Feeding
See also
Swine feedlots
The facts behind those amazing growth hormones [porcine growth hormone] *Success Farm* 85:H6-H7 Ap '87
Feeding hogs whole beans may beat soybean meal. *Success Farm* 85 no3:18T F '87
High-speed pork [use of porcine somatotropin and beta adrenergic agonists] K. Coble. il *Success Farm* 85:42 N '87
How you can stop biting the dust; Acid test for pig starters; How to run on-farm feed trials. il *Success Farm* 85:H2 Ap '87
Introducing the skinny pig [porcine somatotropin] R. Rhein, Jr. il *Bus Week* p37 Mr 23 '87

Identification
Smart ID tags coming for U.S. cows and sows. il *Success Farm* 85:70 Ag '87

Prices
1987 update: raise hogs for $30. G. Johnston. il *Success Farm* 85 no3:H1 F '87
Can livestock bubble continue to rise? G. Johnston. il *Success Farm* 85:62 Ag '87
How to make feeder pigs a sure bet for 1987. G. Johnston. il *Success Farm* 85 no1:7 Ja '87

Weight and measurements
See also
Swine—Carcasses
Swine breeding industry *See* Swine industry
Swine contracts *See* Contracts, Agricultural
Swine farm management
Chores don't end in hog house for Iowa brothers [Steve and Don Hanson] D. Allen and G. Johnston. il *Success Farm* 85:12-13 Je '87
Feeder-pig profit factory. G. Johnston. il *Success Farm* 85 no3:H2+ F '87
Old and new meet on 25,000-head hog farm [cover story] G. Johnston. il *Success Farm* 85:H6-H7 My '87
On-farm records beginning to tell what works, and doesn't. G. Johnston. il *Success Farm* 85:H2 My '87
A year on records yields paper plug for profit leaks. B. Freese. il *Success Farm* 85:H4 Ap '87
Swine feedlots
'Contracting is here to stay'. B. Freese. il *Success Farm* 85:50A Ag '87
Feeder-pig profit factory. G. Johnston. il *Success Farm* 85 no3:H2+ F '87
How to make feeder pigs a sure bet for 1987. G. Johnston. il *Success Farm* 85 no1:7 Ja '87
Swine flu *See* Influenza
Swine houses
See also
Swine—Confinement methods
Heating and ventilation
Heat exchangers. B. Freese. il *Success Farm* 85:H5 Ap '87

Swine in television
Mayor and pig [filming of public television program in New York City with E. Koch and Piggy-Wiggy] *New Yorker* 63:16-18 Ag 10 '87

Swine industry
See also
Beeler's Meat Market and Bakery
Pigs a poppin. K. Coble. il *Success Farm* 85:30 O '87
The top 20 hog ideas for 1987. G. Johnston and B. Freese. il *Success Farm* 85 no3:H4-H5 F '87

Swine racing
Pigs dash for the mash. il *Natl Geogr World* 145:21-4 S '87

Swinson, Ginny
How I (and the taxman) won $27,000 in prizes on Wheel of fortune!; ed. by Peter Haines. il pors *Good Housekeep* 204:72+ My '87

Swiss
Brazil
Pilgrims of the southern cross. E. Gardaz. *Courier* 39:8 D '86

Swiss folk songs *See* Folk songs, Swiss

Swissair AG
Lufthansa, Swissair introduce full-simulator pilot training [Futura] K. F. Mordoff. il *Aviat Week Space Technol* 127:38-9+ Ag 10 '87
Swiss, U.S. exchange access to Atlanta for check-in rights. *Aviat Week Space Technol* 127:34 Jl 27 '87

Swit, Loretta
about
Loretta Swit. N. Gittelson. il pors *McCalls* 114:10-11+ Jl '87

Switches, Electric *See* Electric switches
Switching, Optical *See* Optical switching

Switzer, Ellen
Blaming the victim. *Vogue* 177:782-3+ S '87
The hormone mysteries: what we know now. *Vogue* 177:236+ Mr '87
Medicine: the new enigma. il *Vogue* 177:220+ N '87
My husband doesn't want a baby. il *Ladies Home J* 104:12+ S '87
My husband lied to me. *Ladies Home J* 104:14+ Je '87
"We have nothing in common". il *Ladies Home J* 104:12+ F '87

Switzerland
See also
Air pollution—Switzerland
Alps
Architecture, Domestic—Switzerland
Art galleries and museums—Switzerland
Banks and banking—Switzerland
Bronze Age—Switzerland
Country estates—Switzerland
Davos (Switzerland)
Forests and forestry—Switzerland
Geneva (Switzerland)
Grindelwald (Switzerland)
Gstaad (Switzerland)
Industrial research—Switzerland
Investments, Swiss
Jura Mountains (France and Switzerland)
Money—Switzerland
Music festivals—Switzerland
Opera—Switzerland
Private schools—Switzerland
Smoking—Laws and regulations—Switzerland
Swiss
Ticino (Switzerland)
United States—Diplomatic and consular service—Switzerland
Zurich (Switzerland)
Commerce
Sweden
See Sweden—Commerce—Switzerland
Description and travel
Switzerland by gypsy wagon: a one-horsepower Jura tour. R. E. Baronas. il *Travel Holiday* 167:52-5+ My '87
Industries
See also
Belland AG
Ciba-Geigy AG
Contraves AG
Crossair AG
Jet Aviation (Firm)
Nestle SA
Swissair AG
Venture capital companies—Switzerland
Watch industry—Switzerland

Switzerland-United States air agreements *See* Aviation—International aspects

Swizzle sticks
Swizzle dazzlers [unusual designs] il *Time* 130:88 O 5 '87

Swordfish
See also
Cooking—Fish

Swordtails
Sexual behavior
See Sexual behavior—Fish

Sy, Mommadou
about
In Paris: designing men. C. Mongo. il pors *Essence* 18:43 O '87

Sybron Corp.
Behind the scenes at a leveraged buyout. E. Spragins. il *Bus Week* p120-2 Jl 20 '87

Sycamore Canyon (Ariz.)
Sycamore Canyon, Arizona. R. H. Mohlenbrock. il map *Nat Hist* 96:16-18 S '87

Sydenham, Michael
(jt. auth) *See* Cormack, William S., and Sydenham, Michael

Sydney (N.S.)
Criminal justice, Administration of
Exploring an injustice [inquiry into murder conviction of D. Marshall] M. Gee. *Macleans* 100:29 O 19 '87
Strange and contradictory testimony [testimony of R. N. Ebsary at inquiry into murder conviction of D. Marshall] M. Gee. il pors *Macleans* 100:23 S 21 '87

Sydney Futures Exchange
Commodity exchange [chief executive L. Hosking] S. W. Angrist. il por *Forbes* 140:126 S 7 '87

Sydney Stock Exchange *See* Stock exchanges—Sydney exchange

Sykes, Lynn R., and Davis, Dan M.
The yields of Soviet strategic weapons. bibl (p128) il map *Sci Am* 256:29-37 Ja '87

Sykes, Mark V., and others
IRAS serendipitous survey observations of Pluto and Charon. bibl f il *Science* 237:1336-40 S 11 '87

Sykes, Ray
about
Making it on driving ambition. L. Gite. il por *Black Enterp* 17:96+ F '87

Sykes (Ray) Buick *See* Ray Sykes Buick

Sylvester, David
Alechinsky's realm: the artist's house and studios near Paris. il pors *Archit Dig* 44:138-43+ Mr '87
The texture of a dream. il por *Archit Dig* 44:54+ Mr '87

Sylvia Hotel (Vancouver, B.C.) *See* Vancouver (B.C.)—Hotels, motels, etc.

Symanski, Richard
Along the Salvadoran pipeline. il map *Focus* 36:2-11 Wint '86
A sidelong look at The Alice. il map *Focus* 37:22-7 Summ '87

Symbiosis
See also
Mycorrhiza
The anemone is not its enemy [clownfish] D. G. Fautin. il *Natl Wildl* 25:22-5 O/N '87
Bacterial bedfellows [symbiotic theory of evolution] D. Sagan and L. Margulis. il *Nat Hist* 96:26+ Mr '87
The domestication of reef-dwelling clams [giant clams; cover story] G. A. Heslinga and W. K. Fitt. il *BioScience* 37:332-9 My '87
Down under a sand dollar: world of the tiniest crab [Dissodactylus mellitae] J. L. Bell. il *Sea Front* 33:210-15 My/Je '87
Mussels munch methane [research by James Childress] il *Technol Rev* 90:18 F/Mr '87
Red pond [Lake Cisó evidence for L. Margulis' theory of evolution by symbiosis] B. Lawren. il *Omni* 9:20 Ja '87
Solar-powered animals [aeolid nudibranchs growing zooxanthellae inside their bodies; cover story] W. B. Rudman. il *Nat Hist* 96:50-3 O '87
Symbiosis in the deep sea [sulfide based ecosystem at hydrothermal vents] J. J. Childress and others. il *Sci Am* 256:114-20 My '87

Symbol Technologies Inc.
This Symbol may be misinterpreted [short selling] G. G. Marcial. *Bus Week* p73 Ag 24 '87

Symbolism (Psychology)
Kids suddenly gain in grasp of symbols [research by Judy S. DeLoache] B. Bower. *Sci News* 132:389 D 19-26 '87
Rapid change in the symbolic functioning of very young children. J. S. DeLoache. bibl f il *Science* 238:1556-7 D 11 '87

Symbolism in art
> *See also*
> Christian art and symbolism

Symbolism in literature
Symbolism and meaning. J. M. Auel. *Writer* 100:13 O '87

Symbolism in medicine
Emblems of medicine: serpents that bear no evil. A. Brown. il *Curr Health 2* 14:12-13 S '87

Symbolism of numbers
Friendship: it's in the mail [picking pen pals by numerology] il *Teen* 31:56 F '87
Mathematics and magic. M. W. Browne. il *N Y Times Mag* p24 O 18 '87

Symbols
> *See also*
> Britannia (British national symbol)
> John Bull (British national symbol)
> Uncle Sam (Symbol)

Symmetry
Asymmetry of lineages and the direction of evolutionary time. S. J. Gould and others. il *Science* 236:1437-41 Je 12 '87
Double takes [paired images; work of G. Thorp] J. Hughes. il *Pop Photogr* 94:62-7 Ap '87

Symmetry (Biology)
> *See also*
> Laterality
Both sides now [effect of body imbalance on playing tennis] L. Rogak. il *World Tennis* 34:14-15 Mr '87
Is your body out of whack? L. Rogak. il *Mademoiselle* 93:96 D '87

Symmetry (Physics)
> *See also*
> Fractals
> Quasicrystals
Gürsey receives Wigner Medal for symmetry work. por *Phys Today* 40:89 Ja '87
Holes and loose ends in particle physics [adaptation of address, July 1986] S. Weinberg. por *Phys Today* 40:7+ Ja '87

Symms, Steven
65 mph: the time has come. *Car Driv* 32:27 My '87

Symonds, Steve
> *about*
Bedford, Texas runs the flag out of town, causing a flap. K. Demaret. il por *People Wkly* 27:53-4 My 11 '87

Symonette, Netica
> *about*
Success in the sun. J. C. McAdams and J. Simmons. il pors *Essence* 17:101-2+ Ap '87

Symons, Allene
Marketing. See occasional issues of Publishers Weekly beginning October 16, 1987

Symons, Allene, and Bolle, Sonja
Bookselling & merchandising. See issues of Publishers Weekly

Sympathy
> *See also*
> Empathy
Corporate compassion: striking the balance between personal pain and company policy. P. R. Satran. il *Work Woman* 12:105 Mr '87
Sympathy and cooperation [2 yr. olds] B. Weissbourd. il *Parents* 62:194 Ap '87

Symphilids *See* Garden symphylans

Symphonic poems
> *See also*
> Compact discs—Symphonic poems
> Phonograph records—Symphonic poems

Symphonie du nouveau monde [ballet] *See* Ballet reviews—Single works

Symphonies
> *See also*
> Compact discs—Symphonies
> Phonograph records—Symphonies
> Tape recordings—Symphonies

Symphony orchestras *See* Orchestras

Symptoms *See* Diagnosis

Synapses
> *See also*
> Nerve endings
Concanavalin A alters synaptic specificity between cultured Aplysia neurons. S. S. Lin and I. B. Levitan. bibl f il *Science* 237:648-50 Ag 7 '87
The dynamics of free calcium in dendritic spines in response to repetitive synaptic input. E. Gamble and C. Koch. bibl f il *Science* 236:1311-15 Je 5 '87

New connections may be memorable [Aplysia learning associated circuit formation; research by Craig Bailey and others] R. Weiss. *Sci News* 132:342 N 28 '87
A physiological basis for a theory of synapse modification. M. F. Bear and others. bibl f il *Science* 237:42-8 Jl 3 '87
Synapses that compute motion [study of ganglion cells] T. Poggio and C. Koch. il *Sci Am* 256:46-52 My '87
A synaptic vesicle protein with a novel cytoplasmic domain and four transmembrane regions. T. C. Südhof and others. bibl f il *Science* 238:1142-4 N 20 '87

Synaptic transmission *See* Electrophysiology

Synchro-Energizer *See* Psychological equipment

Synchrotron radiation
New opportunities in synchrotron X-ray crystallography. C. T. Prewitt and others. bibl f il *Science* 238:312-19 O 16 '87
Synchrotron radiation. H. Winick. il *Sci Am* 257:88-93+ N '87

Synchrotrons *See* Accelerators (Electrons, etc.)

Syndaktylia
Born with deformed hands and feet, an anchorwoman overcomes TV's obsession with perfect looks; ed. by Kristin McMurran. B. Walker. il pors *People Wkly* 28:117-18+ N 30 '87

Syndicated columns (Newspapers) *See* Newspapers—Sections, columns, etc.

Syndicated radio programs *See* Radio broadcasting—Syndicated programs

Syndicated television programs *See* Television broadcasting—Syndicated programs

Syndicates (Finance)
> *See also*
> Blind pools (Securities)

Syndicates (Real estate) *See* Real estate investment

Syndromes
> *See also*
> AIDS (Disease)
> Bloom's syndrome
> Chronic fatigue syndrome
> Lesch-Nyhan syndrome
> Reye's syndrome
> Shaken child syndrome
> Sudden infant death syndrome
> TMJ syndrome
> Tourette syndrome
> Toxic shock syndrome

Synesthesia
The sound of purple [colors associated with music; study by Robert A. Cutietta and Kelly J. Haggerty] A. H. Rosenfeld. *Psychol Today* 21:18-19 D '87

Synod of Bishops (1987)
Don't call us, we'll call you: what the synod said to women. A. McCarthy. il *Commonweal* 114:695-6 D 4 '87
A letter from Rome: on the Synod of Bishops. P. R. Divarkar. *America* 157:349-50 N 14 '87
Of many things [views of R. G. Weakland on women and the Catholic Church] G. W. Hunt. *America* 157:258 O 24 '87
Roman holiday. *Commonweal* 114:692-3 D 4 '87
Was this trip necessary? [vague statement on the status of women] R. N. Ostling. il *Time* 130:89 N 9 '87
What we have heard and what we will say [1987 World Synod of Bishops on The vocation and mission of the laity] J. L. May and others. *America* 157:102-4 Ag 29-S 5 '87

Synods of bishops
The bishops seek a voice: are the synods a sham? K. L. Woodward. il *Newsweek* 110:83+ D 7 '87

Syntex Corp.
Struggling with addiction. E. Paris. il *Forbes* 140:89+ N 30 '87

Synthases
Atomic structure of thymidylate synthase: target for rational drug design. L. W. Hardy and others. bibl f il *Science* 235:448-55 Ja 23 '87
Designer therapeutics [structure of thymidylate synthase; work of Larry W. Hardy and others] il *Sci Am* 256:69-70 Ap '87

Synthesis
> *See also*
> Amino acids—Synthesis
> Olefins—Synthesis
> Peptides—Synthesis
> Propellanes—Synthesis
> Proteins—Synthesis
Cages, cavities and clefts [molecular traps; cover story] I. Peterson. il *Sci News* 132:90-3 Ag 8 '87

Synthesis—*cont.*
Crafting a miniature pagoda [synthesis of pagodane by Wolf-Dieter Fessner and others] il *Sci News* 132:104 Ag 15 '87
Synthetases
Bloom's enzyme identified [DNA ligase] *Sci News* 131:72 Ja 31 '87
Evidence for dispensable sequences inserted into a nucleotide fold. R. M. Starzyk and others. bibl f il *Science* 237:1614-18 S 25 '87
Polypeptide sequences essential for RNA recognition by an enzyme. L. Regan and others. bibl f il *Science* 235:1651-3 Mr 27 '87
Synthetic fibers industry workers *See* Textile workers
Synthetic food *See* Food substitutes
Synthetic growth hormone *See* Pituitary hormones, Synthetic
Syphilis
Bad news bear [prehistoric syphilis] il *Discover* 8:8 D '87
Prehistoric syphilis [found in bear bones] *Sci News* 132:205 S 26 '87
Syphilis makes a sneak attack. *U S News World Rep* 103:13 Jl 20 '87
Syphilis on the rise. D. D. Edwards. *Sci News* 132:23 Jl 11 '87
Who spread syphilis? [Indiana bear fossil found to have had disease] *Newsweek* 110:73 S 21 '87
Therapy
AIDS may affect course of syphilis [research by Donna Felsenstein and others] R. Weiss. *Sci News* 131:391 Je 20 '87
Syracuse (N.Y.)
Music
See also
Syracuse Opera Company
Syracuse Opera Company
Syracuse. W. D. West. *Opera News* 51:35 F 28 '87
Syria
See also
Palaces—Syria
Stone Age—Syria
Antiquities
See also
Ugarit (Ancient city)
Gazelle killing in Stone Age Syria [emergence of agriculture at Tell Abu Hureyra] A. J. Legge and P. A. Rowley-Conwy. il map *Sci Am* 257:88-95 Ag '87
Letters [discussion of August 1987 article, Gazelle killing in Stone Age Syria] A. J. Legge and P. A. Rowley-Conwy. *Sci Am* 257:8+ N '87
Armed Forces
Forces in Lebanon
Assad's Lebanese quagmire. R. Nordland. il *Newsweek* 109:34 Mr 2 '87
The battle for Beirut: a close shave [Syria's war on beards] C. Dickey and S. Issa. il *Newsweek* 109:47 Mr 16 '87
Beirut spring [presence of Syrian troops and expected clash with PLO] *New Repub* 196:7-8 Ap 6 '87
Beirut's fragile peace. J. Muir. il *Macleans* 100:22 Mr 23 '87
Bloody battle for West Beirut. M. S. Serrill. il *Time* 129:26 Mr 2 '87
Can Syria clean up Lebanon? N. Cooper. il *Newsweek* 109:40-1 Mr 9 '87
The new battle for Lebanon. J. Vidal-Hall. il *World Press Rev* 34:28-9 Je '87
Saving a city from itself [Syrians move into West Beirut] W. E. Smith. il *Time* 129:48-9 Mr 9 '87
Syria scowls at Shiites while hostages simmer. J. L. Sheler. il *U S News World Rep* 103:16 Jl 13 '87
Syrian bullets impose Beirut peace—for now. P. R. Range. il pors *U S News World Rep* 102:32-3 Mr 9 '87
Foreign relations
Assad and his allies: irreconcilable differences? C. Dickey. bibl f *Foreign Aff* 66:58-76 Fall '87
An overture from Assad [with interview] C. Dickey. il por *Newsweek* 110:32-3 S 28 '87
Iran
See Iran—Foreign relations—Syria
Lebanon
See Lebanon—Foreign relations—Syria
Middle East
Can Syria's Assad keep his footing? J. P. Tarpey and B. Javetski. *Bus Week* p161 N 2 '87
The Middle East's man in the middle [interview with H. Assad] K. Graham and others. *Newsweek* 110:32-3 S 28 '87

Soviet Union
See Soviet Union—Foreign relations—Syria
United States
See United States—Foreign relations—Syria
Politics and government
Opening the road to Damascus. H. G. Chua-Eoan. il por *Time* 130:46 Jl 20 '87
Syria and Lebanon. I. Rabinovich. bibl f *Curr Hist* 86:61-4+ F '87
Syrian cooking *See* Cooking, Syrian
Syrian Social Nationalist Party
Behind the terror. E. Ya'ari. il *Atlantic* 259:18-22 Je '87
Syrian terrorists *See* Terrorists, Syrian
Syringes
Drug addicts with dirty needles [AIDS connection] W. A. Schwartz. il *Nation* 244:843-6 Je 20 '87
The new panic in Needle Park: AIDS [heroin addicts] T. Morganthau. il *Newsweek* 109:63 Ap 13 '87
System Industries, Inc.
Riding DEC's coattails [R. Duncan] I. Chithelen. il por *Forbes* 140:225 N 2 '87
System theory
A Buckminster Fuller dictionary. E. J. Applewhite. il pors *Futurist* 21:24-8 S/O '87
Systematics, Inc.
The back office boys. S. W. Angrist. il *Forbes* 139:62+ Je 15 '87
Systemic lupus erythematosus *See* Lupus erythematosus
Systemp (Firm)
'Tekkie' temps have this firm thriving. J. M. Laderman. *Bus Week* p98 Je 15 '87
Systems analysis
See also
International Institute for Applied Systems Analysis
Mathematical optimization
Systems Management American Corporation
Aid for unwed teens [job training program in Norfolk, Va.] S. S. Harrison. *Black Enterp* 17:17 Mr '87
Systems theory *See* System theory
Syverson, Dick
about
Planning a ceramic tile project [interview] B. Colglazier. il pors *Home Mech* 83:12+ F '87
Syzygy (Astronomy) *See* Conjunctions (Astronomy)
Syzygy [dance] *See* Dance reviews—Single works
Szamuely, George
The imperial Congress. *Commentary* 84:27-32 S '87
Szegedy-Maszak, Marianne
How the homeless bought a Rolls for Cornelius Pitts. il por *Wash Mon* 19:11-15 Jl/Ag '87
The twenty-five cent stamp: why it's here and why it shouldn't be. il *Wash Mon* 19:39-42 N '87
Szekely, Julian, 1934-
Can advanced technology save the U.S. steel industry? il *Sci Am* 257:34-41 Jl '87
Szilard, Leo
about
Leo Szilard: giving peace a chance in the nuclear age. B. J. Bernstein. il pors *Phys Today* 40:40-7 S '87
Szostak, Jack W.
(jt. auth) See Murray, Andrew W., and Szostak, Jack W.

T

T, Mr. *See* Mr. T
T-45 airplanes *See* Airplanes, Training
T cells *See* Lymphocytes
T. Eaton Co. Ltd.
The lessons of Eaton's [1984-85 strike] S. D. Driedger. il *Macleans* 100:32-3 Jl 13 '87
T. Rowe Price Capital Appreciation Fund
A three-way approach puts Rich Fontaine's new fund on top. R. A. Lynch. il por *Money* 16:210 F '87
T. Rowe Price New Era Fund Inc.
An antidote to inflation. il *Money* 16:35 O '87
T. Rowe Price New Horizons Mutual Fund Inc.
Compared to what? M. Kuntz. il *Forbes* 139:154 F 23 '87
T-shirts *See* Shirts
T4 antigens *See* Antigens and antibodies
TA Associates of Boston
Foreign affairs of a venture capitalist [P. Brooke] A. Ramirez. il pors *Fortune* 115:84-6+ F 2 '87

Taaffe, Philip, 1955-
about
Philip Taaffe. E. Heartney. il *Art News* 86:131-2 S '87
Taaffe, William
It's bottom-line time. il *Sports Illus* 67:50-2+ O 12 '87
'Still very sweet indeed'. il pors *Sports Illus* 67:80 Jl 6 '87
TV/radio. See occasional issues of Sports Illustrated
The voice is familiar . . . il pors *Sports Illus* 66:52-4+ Ja 26 '87
Tabak, Lawrence
Nightmare in a box. il *World Tennis* 34:48-9 Ja '87
Taber, Anthony
The last page. See issues of Audubon
Tabernacles, Feast of *See* Sukkoth
Table decoration
24 quick tips for holiday parties. J. Williams and others. il *Better Homes Gard* 65:74-9 D '87
Christmas takes the cake [centerpiece cakes] S. West. il *Ladies Home J* 104:138-41+ D '87
Living flowers for your table [cover story] D. Hastings. il *South Living* 22:116-17 Mr '87
Ring in the new: set a festive table [New Year's Eve party] S. Wood. il *McCalls* 114:29+ Ja '87
A wedding party. J. Williams and J. Severson. il *Better Homes Gard* 65:70-3+ Je '87
Table linen
See also
Tablecloths
The versatility of skirted tables. il *South Living* 22:108 D '87
Table manners *See* Etiquette
Table mats, tiles, etc.
Painting backward is one good way to make place mats. il *Sunset* 179:145 N '87
Table saws *See* Saws and sawing
Table setting
Beautiful holiday table settings. il *Good Housekeep* 205:156-9 D '87
A host of easy tips and ideas for imaginative table settings. J. Williams and J. Severson. il *Better Homes Gard* 65:24+ S '87
Setting the table. M. Hampton. il *House Gard* 159:34+ S '87
Table skirts *See* Table linen
Tablecloths
Pick-up-and-go crafts [crocheted] J. Williams and J. Severson. il *Better Homes Gard* 65:126-7+ Ag '87
Tables
3 nested tables. A. Hontoir. il *Workbench* 43:100-2 Mr/Ap '87
Antiques: transformation tables: ingenious designs with multiple uses. S. Birmingham. il *Archit Dig* 44:160-5 My '87
Big table slips over the firepit. il *Sunset* 179:148 O '87
Classic furniture series [Chippendale tilt-top table] G. Derzinski. il *Workbench* 43:66-9+ N/D '87
The classic look of stone. il *South Living* 22:146+ F '87
Contemporary glass top table [coffee table] R. Mateer. il *Workbench* 43:73-5 Ja/F '87
An easy-to-make folding table. A. Hontoir. il *Workbench* 43:66-7 Jl/Ag '87
Fine dining [mahogany dining table] R. Capotosto. il *Pop Mech* 164:110-15 N '87
Husky outdoor table . . . with drop-in cooktop. il *Sunset* 179:100+ Ag '87
Regionalism in early American tea tables. A. Sack. bibl f il *Antiques* 131:248-63 Ja '87
Slab-top coffee table. E. Waltner. il *Workbench* 43:32-4 My/Je '87
Social grace [classic mahogany butler's tray table] N. Barrett, Jr. il *Pop Mech* 164:88-91 My '87
Splayed-leg coffee table. J. Olivari. il *Workbench* 43:62-3 S/O '87
Sturdy table/bench yard set. M. Landis. il *Workbench* 43:40-1 Jl/Ag '87
A table for camping. M. C. Toth. il *Outdoor Life* 180:38 S '87
Table with a view [coffee table] L. M. Dalsgaard. il *Home Mech* 83:78-80 N '87
Tables for every setting. L. M. Dalsgaard. il *Home Mech* 83:48-50+ Ag '87
A tackle table [collapsible hobby table] M. C. Toth. il *Outdoor Life* 180:56 N '87
Take-apart trestle dining table. M. Kraft. il *Workbench* 43:24-6 My/Je '87
Traditional round oak table can be made expandable. R. Wonderlich. il *Workbench* 43:111-12+ Mr/Ap '87

Very contemporary furniture for kids. J. Thom. il *Workbench* 43:46-50 N/D '87
Tablets, Ancient
Business, B.C. [work of Assyriologist I. Spar] B. Weber. il por *N Y Times Mag* p114 N 22 '87
Lumps of clay that gave birth to numbers [Sumerian tablets; work of Denise Schmandt-Besserat] il *Discover* 8:7-8 Mr '87
Tablets (Medicine) *See* Pills
Tableware
See also
Spoons
Table setting
Design
Profiles [E. Zeisel] S. Lessard. il *New Yorker* 63:36-40+ Ap 13 '87
Tableware mail order business *See* Mail order business
Tabloid reading *See* Newspaper reading
Taboroff, June
Quinta da Bacalhoa. il por *House Gard* 159:180-5+ D '87
Tabuchi, Yoshihisa
about
'Making money, winning fame'. *U S News World Rep* 102:63-4 My 11 '87
Nomura: land of the rising young. B. Buell. il por *Bus Week* p51-2 N 30 '87
Tachometers
Digital tachometer for your car [cover story] R. Ortman. il *Radio-Electron* 58:45-9 Je '87
Tackle, Fishing *See* Fishing tackle
Tackle boxes, cases, etc. *See* Fishing tackle—Storage
Tactile perception *See* Touch
Taddeo, Mario
about
A murder mystery. L. Van Dusen. por *Macleans* 100:19-20 D 21 '87
Tadiran Israel Electronics Industries Ltd.
Tadiran-General Dynamics team will compete as second-source for Army Sincgars radios. *Aviat Week Space Technol* 127:28 Jl 13 '87
Tae Woo Roh *See* Roh, Tae Woo
Taft, Dudley S.
about
Taft Broadcasting may become a Carl Lindner production. D. Cook. il por *Bus Week* p37-8 Ap 27 '87
Taft Broadcasting Co.
A little UHF group tries a great big gamble [TVX buys stations from Taft Broadcasting] C. S. Eklund. il por *Bus Week* p84+ F 2 '87
Taft Broadcasting may become a Carl Lindner production. D. Cook. il por *Bus Week* p37-8 Ap 27 '87
Tag lines *See* Fishing tackle
Taganka Theater (Moscow, Soviet Union) *See* Moscow (Soviet Union)—Theater
Tager, Sally
Burnt sugar. il *Gourmet* 47:110-11+ N '87
Tagging of birds *See* Bird banding
Tagliarino, Peggy
about
At-home professionalism. P. Kripke. il por *Work Woman* 12:106-7 Mr '87
Tagore, Sir Rabindranath, 1861-1941
An Indian poet visits an English parson [excerpt from A Tagore reader] il por *Courier* 40:32 Ap '87
Taguchi, Genichi
about
How to make it right the first time. O. Port. il *Bus Week* p142-3 Je 8 '87
Taheri, Amir
about
Islamic terrorism: a growing peril [interview] D. Bombardier. il *World Press Rev* 34:17-19 My '87
Tahiti
See also
French—Tahiti
Rites and ceremonies—Tahiti
Tahoe National Forest (Calif.)
Just 2 miles from Interstate 80, wild but accessible Grouse Lakes. il map *Sunset* 179:38+ Jl '87
Tailgate picnics *See* Picnics
Taillevent (Paris, France: Restaurant) *See* Paris (France)—Restaurants, nightclubs, bars, etc.
Tailoring
Alterations: they can save you money by updating your wardrobe, keeping it in perfect shape. il *Glamour* 85:210 Ag '87
Passing through customs [made-to-order clothes] G. B. Boyer. il *Esquire* 108:218-20+ S '87
To sew a fine seam [hand tailoring of men's suits] R. La Ferla. il *N Y Times Mag* p50+ Je 7 '87

Tailors

Great Britain

Tailored for success [Savile Row tailors] R. La Ferla. il *N Y Times Mag* p68+ Ap 5 '87

Taiwan

See also

Baseball, Children's—Taiwan
Environmental movement—Taiwan
Investments, Japanese—Taiwan
Investments, Taiwanese
Kao-hsiung (Taiwan)
Money—Taiwan
Protests, demonstrations, etc.—Taiwan

Commerce

See also

Balance of trade—Taiwan

China

See China—Commerce—Taiwan

United States

See United States—Commerce—Taiwan

Commercial policy

Taiwan woos American business. H. Eason. il *Nations Bus* 75:64 Je '87
Where sanctions against Japan are really working. S. J. Dryden. il *Bus Week* p61-2 My 11 '87
Why Taiwan's doors should swing wide open. M. Shao. il *Bus Week* p41 Ag 3 '87

Economic conditions

Taiwan: prosperity for an island China. L. Hopping. il *Sch Update* 119:10 Ap 6 '87

Foreign relations

China

See China—Foreign relations—Taiwan

Industries

See also

Automobile industry—Taiwan
Evergreen Group
Multitech Industrial Corp.

Politics and government

See also

Elections—Taiwan

A dissident turned back [Hsu Hsin-liang] J. Motavalli. il por *Progressive* 51:14-15 F '87
A new voice is heard [interview with A. Chiang] D. R. Shanor. il por *World Press Rev* 34:21 N '87
Quiet victories in Taipei [opposition to martial law] E. W. Desmond. il *Time* 129:43 Je 1 '87
Taiwan begins to bend to the new reality. D. Doder. il *U S News World Rep* 103:51-2 N 9 '87
Taiwan's generation-long political evolution [address, June 1, 1987] J. A. Robinson. *Vital Speeches Day* 53:633-7 Ag 1 '87
Thirty-eight years later . . . [martial law lifted] H. G. Chua-Eoan. il *Time* 130:47 Jl 27 '87
Tiptoeing toward democracy? C. Goldstein. il *World Press Rev* 34:19-20 N '87

Treaties

United States

See United States—Treaties—Taiwan

Taizé Community *See* Communauté de Taizé

Takacs, Tibor

about

The gate [film] Reviews
People Wkly il 27:10 Je 8 '87. T. Cunneff

Takahashi, Masami, and Catterall, William A.

Identification of an α subunit of dihydropyridine-sensitive brain calcium channels. bibl f il *Science* 236:88-91 Ap 3 '87

Takahashi, Takami

about

An oasis in Bangkok: abstract art defines a penthouse apartment. L. Bernikow. il *Archit Dig* 44:60-7 Ja '87

Takano, Bokuichiro

Correlation of volcanic activity with sulfur oxyanion speciation in a crater lake [cover story] bibl f il map *Science* 235:1633-5 Mr 27 '87

Takas, Marianne

Eat right, stay off your feet—or go to jail. *Vogue* 177:148 My '87

Take-off of airplanes *See* Airplanes, Jet—Take-off

Take or pay contracts (Gas) *See* Pipeline companies—Laws and regulations

Takeshita, Noboru

about

A back-room man steps forward. H. G. Chua-Eoan. il por *Time* 130:65 N 2 '87
A black-belt prime minister. A. Bilski. por *Macleans* 100:28 N 30 '87
Can Japan still afford the politics of waiting? J. Wallace. il por *U S News World Rep* 103:42-3 N 2 '87

Japan: a change of style. il por *Newsweek* 110:66 N 2 '87
Japan turns toward home. R. Shiratori. por *World Press Rev* 34:24 D '87
A talk with Japan's new P.M. B. Martin. *Newsweek* 110:56 N 9 '87
Welcome to the hot seat, Mr. Prime Minister. A. Borrus. il por *Bus Week* p152-3 N 2 '87

Talbert, Bill *See* Talbert, William F., 1918-

Talbert, William F., 1918-

about

12 who mattered: Bill Talbert. C. Shmerler. por *World Tennis* 35:69 S '87

Talbot, Christopher J., and Jackson, Martin P. A.

Salt tectonics. bibl (p116) il *Sci Am* 257:70-9 Ag '87

Talbot, John Michael

about

Banjo and guitar picker John Michael Talbot gave up rock for a new role as a musical monk. C. A. Azizian. il pors *People Wkly* 27:145-6 Je 8 '87
From songs of protest to hymns of praise. L. K. Cook. por *Christ Century* 104:279-80+ Mr 18-25 '87

Talbott, Strobe

A toast for a composer's widow in Tashkent [poem] *New Yorker* 62:30-1 Ja 12 '87

Talcott, Richard

A burst of discovery: the first days of supernova 1987A. il *Astronomy* 15:90-5 Je '87
Possible planetary systems discovered. il *Astronomy* 15:18-19 S '87

Talent *See* Ability

Talent agents *See* Theatrical agencies and agents

Talented children *See* Children, Gifted

Tales from the Hollywood Hills [television program] *See* Television program reviews—Single works

Tales of Hans Christian Andersen [ballet] *See* Ballet reviews—Single works

The tales of Hoffmann [opera] *See* Offenbach, Jacques, 1819-1880

Talese, Gay

Chronicles of a [New York] brownstone (I). il por *Archit Dig* 44:44+ N '87
Chronicles of a New York brownstone (II). il por *Archit Dig* 44:28+ D '87
Moondog. il *N Y* 20:76 D 21-28 '87
Wartime Sunday. il *Esquire* 107:95-8+ My '87
When Frank Sinatra had a cold: a reflection on the cause of today's common journalism. il pors *Esquire* 108:161-6 N '87

Talese family

about

Wartime Sunday. G. Talese. il *Esquire* 107:95-8+ My '87

Taliaferro, Robert

about

The best prison paper in the U.S.—bar none—turns 100. J. Kaufman. il por *People Wkly* 28:66+ O 5 '87

Talk *See* Conversation; Speech

Talk radio [drama] *See* Bogosian, Eric

Talk shows *See* Radio broadcasting—Conversation programs; Television broadcasting—Conversation programs

Talking books

See also

Audio Renaissance Tapes (Firm)
Bantam Audio Publishing
Booksellers and bookselling—Talking books
Brilliance Corporation
Caedmon Audio (Firm)
Feeling Fine Programs (Firm)
Listen for Pleasure (Firm)
Newman Communications
Nightingale-Conant Corp.
Random House Audiobooks
Simon & Schuster Inc. Audio Publishing Division
Audio/video plus. T. Spain. See issues of Publishers Weekly beginning May 9, 1986
Audio preview: bestsellers on the way. il *Publ Wkly* 232:53-5 Jl 31 '87
Audio reviews: celebrity autobiographies. *Publ Wkly* 231:58-9 My 29 '87
Celebrity autobiographies on audio. A. Postman. il *Publ Wkly* 231:56-7 My 29 '87
Children's audio goes mass market [Toy Fair] *Publ Wkly* 231:93 Mr 6 '87
Commercial fiction on tape. A. Postman. il *Publ Wkly* 232:27-30+ S 4 '87
Fall audio cassettes. J. Zinsser and T. Spain. il *Publ Wkly* 232:33-4+ Ag 14 '87

Talking books—*cont.*
In their own voices [author readings] A. Postman. il *Publ Wkly* 232:33-7+ N 6 '87
Making book on book-and-cassette packages [children's market] B. Stewart. il *Publ Wkly* 232:51-5 N 27 '87
McGraw-Hill gets serious about audio. il *Publ Wkly* 232:36-7 Jl 17 '87
Spring audiocassettes. J. Zinsser and T. Spain. il *Publ Wkly* 231:40+ F 6 '87
Testing the waters. J. Zinsser. *Publ Wkly* 232:35-6 O 23 '87
Word-for-word [unabridged fiction] J. Zinsser. il *Publ Wkly* 231:52+ F 20 '87

Exhibitions
Around the booths: audio and video [American Booksellers convention] il *Publ Wkly* 231:225+ My 15 '87

Marketing
Bantam, General Mills schedule audio promotion. il *Publ Wkly* 232:69-70 O 9 '87
Bantam mixed-media promotions feature audio, paperbacks. il *Publ Wkly* 231:31-2 Mr 27 '87
Direct-mail audio line due from Prentice Hall. il *Publ Wkly* 232:70 O 9 '87

Talking computers *See* Speech processing systems
Talking dolls *See* Dolls
Talking Heads (Musical group)
Are four Heads better than one? D. Handelman. il por *Roll Stone* p34-6+ Ja 15 '87
Tall people *See* Stature
Tall ships *See* Sailing vessels
Talla, Michael
about
You don't need a great body at L.A.'s cushiest health club, but a big name and fat wallet help. S. K. Reed. il pors *People Wkly* 28:113-14 N 30 '87
Talladega College
Mrs. Eunice W. Johnson returns for Talladega to give reunion address. il pors *Jet* 72:14-16 Ag 24 '87
Tallchief, Maria
about
Cottage by the sea: Maria Tallchief and Henry D. Paschen on Martha's Vineyard. J. Allen. il *Archit Dig* 44:170-5+ O '87
Tallent, Elizabeth, 1954-
Faux pas [story] *New Yorker* 63:36-9 Ap 6 '87
Hannah's example [story] *New Yorker* 63:28-34 Je 15 '87
Taller de Arquitectura (Firm)
Architecture: Ricardo Bofill. N. Shrady. il *Archit Dig* 44:124-31+ Jl '87
Talley, M. Kirby, Jr.
Michelangelo rediscovered [cover story] il *Art News* 86:159-70 Summ '87
Talley, Madelon DeVoe
about
That rare thing, an investment book worth reading. R. Brady. il por *Nations Bus* 75:76 N '87
To win, be willing to make mistakes [interview] il por *U S News World Rep* 103:58 Ag 10 '87
Tallgrass Prairie National Preserve (Kan. and Okla.)
A budding prairie preserve. J. Hamilton. il *Sierra* 72:83-4 Jl/Ag '87
New hope arises for Tallgrass Preserve. L. Gilbert. *Natl Parks* 61:10 N/D '87
Tale of the tallgrass. E. Docekal. il map *Sierra* 72:76-9 My/Je '87
Tallgrass Prairie. B. G. Norton. il map *Wilderness* 50:33-4 Spr '87
Tallmer, Jerry
Off Broadway. il *N Y* 20:73 D 21-28 '87
Tamago netsu [dance] *See* Dance reviews—Single works
Tamales *See* Cooking, Mexican
Tamayo, Rufino, 1899-
about
Present primeval. I. Borger. il por *Archit Dig* 44:56+ S '87
Rufino Tamayo. L. Goldman. il *Art News* 86:27-8 F '87
Tambo, Oliver
about
Freedom's friend or freedom's foe? S. Powell. il por *U S News World Rep* 102:12 F 9 '87
Oliver Tambo's war cry. H. Mackenzie. il por *Macleans* 100:25 S 7 '87
Secretary meets with ANC leader Tambo [State Dept. statement, January 28, 1987] il pors *Dep State Bull* 87:28 Mr '87
South Africa: it takes two to Tambo. il por *Newsweek* 109:43 F 9 '87
Tambo on tour. *Nation* 244:167-8 F 14 '87

Tambo visit centers U.S. focus on S. Africa fight. il pors *Jet* 71:7 F 16 '87
Tambo's risky game. M. Whitaker. il por *Newsweek* 109:34-5 F 2 '87
Tango with Tambo. *Natl Rev* 39:19 F 27 '87
Tambopata Wildlife Reserve (Peru) *See* Wildlife sanctuaries—Peru
Tambs, Lewis A., 1927-
The future belongs to the free [address, February 14, 1987] *Vital Speeches Day* 53:379-81 Ap 1 '87
An overview of U.S.-Latin American relations [address, December 1986] *Vital Speeches Day* 53:279-81 F 15 '87
The tamer tamed [drama] *See* Fletcher, John, 1579-1625
Tamils
The battle for Jaffna [Indian troops mount assault on Tamil stronghold] T. A. Sancton. il *Time* 130:52 O 26 '87
Bearing gifts [Indian support of Tamil rebels in Sri Lanka] *Time* 129:40 Je 15 '87
Behind the haste in Sri Lanka. G. Jain. *World Press Rev* 34:49 O '87
A disputed homeland [civil war between Tamils and Sinhalese] S. K. Hennayake and J. S. Duncan. il map *Focus* 37:20-7 Spr '87
Giving once a chance: India and Sri Lanka forge a Tamil compromise. F. Willey. il *Newsweek* 110:43 Ag 10 '87
A grisly scene on Gasworks Street [Tamil terrorists accused of planting bomb] N. R. Gibbs. il map *Time* 129:39 My 4 '87
If this is peace . . . [agreement signed by India and Sri Lanka] E. W. Desmond. il map *Time* 130:18-20 Ag 10 '87
The long agony of a city under siege [Indian troops fight Tamil rebels in Jaffna] B. Barber. il map *Macleans* 100:22-3 N 2 '87
Mother India intervenes [Air Force drops food to Tamils in Sri Lanka] R. Nordland. il *Newsweek* 109:38 Je 15 '87
An orgy of killing. K. Scanlon. il *Macleans* 100:34-5 O 19 '87
Paradise destroyed [Sri Lanka] J. Barber. il map *Macleans* 100:20-2 My 4 '87
Peace flexes its muscle [Tamil rebels surrender arms in Sri Lanka] H. G. Chua-Eoan. il *Time* 130:42 Ag 17 '87
Resolving the Sri Lankan conflict [statement, March 12, 1987] R. A. Peck. *Dep State Bull* 87:68-71 My '87
The roots of conflict in Sri Lanka. V. Rebeck. *Christ Century* 104:792-4 S 23 '87
Row over the airdrop [Indian airdrop of relief supplies to Tamils in Sri Lanka] A. Bilski. il *Macleans* 100:27 Je 15 '87
The siege of Jaffna. N. Cooper. il map *Newsweek* 110:67 N 2 '87
The siege of Jaffna. K. Scanlon. il map *Macleans* 100:33 O 26 '87
Sri Lanka: a nation disintegrates [cover story] S. R. Weisman. il map *N Y Times Mag* p34-8+ D 13 '87
Sri Lanka: a reluctant slaughter [Indian troops move against Tamils] *Newsweek* 110:49 O 26 '87
Sri Lanka: an Asian Lebanon? F. Willey. il map *Newsweek* 109:32 My 4 '87
Sri Lanka: no taming the 'Tigers'. W. A. Taylor. il map *U S News World Rep* 103:28-9 Jl 27 '87
Taming the Tigers. M. Ispahani. *New Repub* 197:14+ Jl 27 '87
A troubled peace plan [India and Sri Lanka] K. Hall. il *Macleans* 100:20 Ag 10 '87
Wrong side, wrong war, for India [fighting between Indian troops and Tamil rebels] W. A. Taylor. il *U S News World Rep* 103:38 O 26 '87
Yes, politics makes strange bedfellows [India's help in subduing Tamil rebels in Sri Lanka] W. A. Taylor. il *U S News World Rep* 103:8 Ag 10 '87
Canada
Trying to make a new life [S. Rajathurai] B. Wallace. il por *Macleans* 100:14 Ag 24 '87
Tammany Hall
New York 1865 [W. M. Tweed] G. Dallas. bibl il *Hist Today* 37:17-22 D '87
Tamoxifen
Preventing recurrence of breast cancer [research by Douglass Tormey] *USA Today (Periodical)* 115:7 F '87

Tampa (Fla.)
Airports
Blacks fly with Marriott [concessionary business at Tampa International Airport] R. Baker. il *Black Enterp* 17:22 Ap '87
Arts
See also
Tampa Bay Performing Arts Center
Buildings
Tampa tower gives dance a boost [Tampa Ballet's dance studio in Ashley Tower] H. Ostlere. il *Dance Mag* 61:14-15 F '87
Police
Choke-hold death of black sparks violence in Tampa. *Jet* 71:15 Mr 9 '87
Fla. race issue clouds Dwight Gooden arrest. il pors *Jet* 71:46-7 Ja 12 '87
The good Doctor has a bad scrape [baseball player D. Gooden's confrontation with police] W. Nack. il pors *Sports Illus* 66:28-30+ Ja 5 '87
Police sue Mets' Gooden, seek $3 million award. por *Jet* 73:50 O 26 '87
White cop cleared in choke hold death of black man [D. D'Agresta] *Jet* 72:33 Ap 27 '87
Race relations
Fla. race issue clouds Dwight Gooden arrest. il pors *Jet* 71:46-7 Ja 12 '87
Riots
Choke-hold death of black sparks violence in Tampa. *Jet* 71:15 Mr 9 '87
Streets
Stretch your legs on the world's longest sidewalk [Bayshore Boulevard] G. Maleskey. il *Prevention* 39:48 Ag '87
Tampa Ballet
Tampa tower gives dance a boost [dance studio in Ashley Tower] H. Ostlere. il *Dance Mag* 61:14-15 F '87
Tampa Bay (Fla.)
Bridges
Inside the Sunshine Skyway [longest concrete span in the Western Hemisphere] D. Stover. il *Pop Sci* 231:50-3 Jl '87
Tampa Bay Performing Arts Center
Tampa Bay Performing Arts Center. M. LaRue. il *Theatre Crafts* 21:38-9+ D '87
Tampa Bay Performing Arts Center: the miracle works. H. Ostlere. il *Dance Mag* 61:68 N '87
Tampa International Airport *See* Tampa (Fla.)—Airports
Tampons *See* Feminine hygiene products
Tampopo [film] See Motion picture reviews—Single works
Tamu-tamu [opera] *See* Menotti, Gian Carlo, 1911-
Tan, Amy
Fish cheeks. il *Seventeen* 46:99 D '87
Tan (Suntan) *See* Suntan
Tanaka, Shoji
Research on high-T_c superconductivity in Japan. bibl il *Phys Today* 40:53-7 D '87
Tanaka, Yasuo
(jt. auth) See Oda, Minoru, and Tanaka, Yasuo
Tandem Computers Inc.
How Jim Treybig whipped Tandem back into shape. J. B. Levine. il por *Bus Week* p124-6 F 23 '87
How Jimmy Treybig turned tough. B. O'Reilly. il por *Fortune* 115:102-4 My 25 '87
Tandem mass spectroscopy *See* Spectrum analysis
Tandem mirror reactors *See* Nuclear reactors
Tandy Brands, Inc.
The big money in Raffles tables. E. F. Cone. il *Forbes* 140:68-9+ D 28 '87
Tandy Corp.
High-tech at a low price. il *Money* 16:8 O '87
IBM and Tandy turn up the heat [personal computers] il *Fortune* 116:12 Ag 31 '87
Resurgence at Tandy. R. A. Shaffer. il *Pers Comput* 11:35 Ap '87
The Tandy anniversary product explosion [cover story] R. Malloy and others. il *Byte* 12:100-6 O '87
Tandy finds a cold, hard world outside the Radio Shack [struggling to land business clients] T. Mason. il *Bus Week* p68+ Ag 31 '87
Tandy wants to be your computer company—can they be? [cover story; special section] il *Pers Comput* 11:102-9+ S '87
Tons and tons of little stuff. T. Mack. il *Forbes* 140:408+ Jl 13 '87
Tanenbaum, Marc H.
A revolution in mutual esteem. por *U S News World Rep* 103:9 S 21 '87
Tange, Kenzo
about
An elegant sweep toward heaven. K. Andersen. il por *Time* 129:81 Mr 30 '87

Tangier (Morocco)
Historic houses, sites, etc.
Legation in Tangier. il *Dep State Bull* 87:13 S '87
Tanglewood Music Festival *See* Music festivals—Massachusetts
Tango apasionado [musical] See Musicals, revues, etc.—Reviews—Single works
Tangorra, Joanne
Audio and video: the bookseller's perspective. *Publ Wkly* 231:102-3 Je 19 '87
Working a niche that works. il *Publ Wkly* 231:52+ Ja 16 '87
Tanii, Akio
about
Smooth strokes from a late bloomer. F. H. Katayama. il por *Fortune* 116:37 Ag 3 '87
Tank, David W.
(jt. auth) See Hopfield, John J., and Tank, David W.
Tank, David W., and Hopfield, John J.
Collective computation in neuronlike circuits. il *Sci Am* 257:104-8+ D '87
Tank airplanes
KC-135 provides microgravity testbed. il *Aviat Week Space Technol* 126:61 F 23 '87
McDonnell Douglas will develop expanded aerial refueling system for USAF KC-10s. il *Aviat Week Space Technol* 126:72 Je 22 '87
Tank ships *See* Tankers
Tank warfare
See also
Anti-tank weapons
Tankers
Registration and transfer
Collision course? [U.S. flags to protect Kuwaiti oil tankers in Persian Gulf] L. Howard. il *Newsweek* 109:5 My 25 '87
Democrats cite risk in Kuwaiti reflagging [report by Democratic Study Group] P. Mann. *Aviat Week Space Technol* 126:33 Je 22 '87
Missile attack, Kuwaiti pact could draw U.S. into Gulf war. J. D. Morrocco. il map *Aviat Week Space Technol* 126:23-5 My 25 '87
Piloting the camel [U.S. reflagging commitment to Kuwait] M. B. Zuckerman. il *U S News World Rep* 103:76 Jl 6 '87
Reflagging folly [U.S. plan to flag Kuwaiti ships and reinforce American military presence] N. Safran. *New Repub* 197:10-11 Ag 3 '87
Rough seas and new names [Kuwaiti tankers flying under American flag] J. V. Lamar, Jr. il map *Time* 129:13 Je 29 '87
U.S. policy in the Persian Gulf and Kuwaiti reflagging [statement, June 16, 1987] M. H. Armacost. *Dep State Bull* 87:78-81 Ag '87
Anecdotes, facetiae, satire, etc.
Reflagging: the secret NSC agenda. D. Halberstein. il *New Repub* 197:11 Ag 24 '87
Tanks
See also
Brenner Tank Company
Oil tanks
Water tanks
Tanks, Military
The first Chrysler bail-out: the M-1 tank. R. A. Mendel. il *Wash Mon* 19:17-23 F '87
Strategic surprise [reactive armored tanks] J. Flint. il map *Forbes* 139:94+ Je 29 '87
That California rumble is no quake: it's only the Alegre family, all tanked up and out for a drive [purchase of Sherman tank] il *People Wkly* 27:43 Ja 26 '87
History
The tank and visions of future war [views of J. F. C. Fuller; cover story] B. H. Reid. bibl il *Hist Today* 37:36-41 D '87
Soviet Union
Army modifies TOW missile to counter recent advances in Soviet reactive armor. *Aviat Week Space Technol* 127:23 Jl 27 '87
Tanne, Janice Hopkins
AIDS: to test or not to test? il *N Y* 20:40-6 S 28 '87
Diet warm-up: how to get ready to lose. il *Mademoiselle* 93:194-5+ My '87
Fighting AIDS. il *N Y* 20:22-31 Ja 12 '87
Tanne, Janice Hopkins, and Rapp, Ellen
Tips on conquering paralyzing anxiety: fearing the worst. il *N Y* 20:44-9 F 9 '87
Tannenbaum, Rob
The wizard of odd. il por *Roll Stone* p69-70+ Ap 23 '87

Tanner, James, 1941-
about
James L. Tanner/Maurine Littleton Gallery. J. W. Larson. il *Am Craft* 47:74-5 D '87/Ja '88
Tannhäuser [opera] *See* Wagner, Richard, 1813-1883
Tannin (Ala.)
City planning
Guidelines for a large-scale suburban development. J. Barnett. il *Archit Rec* 175:122-3 Jl '87
Tanning, Dorothea, 1913-
about
Dorothea Tanning at Kent. J. Rian. il *Art Am* 75:223 Ap '87
Romance to the Max. L. Liebmann. il por *Vogue* 177:200 My '87
Tanning (Suntan) *See* Suntan
Tanning (Suntan) products *See* Suntan products
Tanselle, G. Thomas (George Thomas), 1934-
about
Top 1987 APHA awards to Tanselle, Antiquarian Society. por *Publ Wkly* 231:76 F 6 '87
Tanselle, George Thomas *See* Tanselle, G. Thomas (George Thomas), 1934-
Tansey, Mark
about
Wrinkles in time. D. Joselit. il *Art Am* 75:106-11+ Jl '87
Tantalum
Raising a crop of transistors [use of silicon and tantalum; work of Brian M. Ditchek] il *Sci News* 132:25 Jl 11 '87
Tanzania
See also
Agriculture—Tanzania
Missions, Medical—Tanzania
National parks and reserves—Tanzania
Paleontology—Tanzania
Public health—Tanzania
Wildlife—Tanzania
Tanzi, Rudolph E., and others
Amyloid β protein gene: cDNA, mRNA distribution, and genetic linkage near the Alzheimer locus. bibl f il *Science* 235:880-4 F 20 '87
The amyloid β protein gene is not duplicated in brains from patients with Alzheimer's disease. bibl f il *Science* 238:666-9 O 30 '87
Taormina (Italy)
Hotels, motels, etc.
A ruin with a view [San Domenico Palace Hotel] L. S. Brady. il *Esquire* 108:23-4 Jl '87
Taormina (New York, N.Y.: Restaurant) *See* New York (N.Y.)—Restaurants, nightclubs, bars, etc.
Taos (N.M.)
Architecture
Architecture: Antoine Predock [home of Nat and Connie Troy] R. Morris. il por *Archit Dig* 44:90-7+ Ag '87
Arts
Santa Fe/Taos [special section] il *Horizon* 30:41-59 O '87
Description
Santa Fe/Taos [special section] il *Horizon* 30:41-59 O '87
Galleries and museums
See also
Millicent Rogers Museum (Taos, N.M.)
Historic houses, sites, etc.
Russian folk in Taos [home of N. Fechin] M. Morse. il *House Gard* 159:198-203 Ap '87
Taos (N.M.) in art
Art: Taos landscapes. A. Berman. il *Archit Dig* 44:158-63 Mr '87
Tap dance
See also
National Tap Dance Company of Canada
Footloose or screw loose? Sondra Lowell gives listeners all the news that's fit to tap. il por *People Wkly* 27:102-3 Ja 19 '87
Study and teaching
Technique: tap, tapping, and tappers [manuals, videos, and recordings] M. J. Brown. il *Dance Mag* 61:56-7 Ag '87
Tapas
In Spain, bar snacks are an art form. J. Rossant. il *Bus Week* p104 Mr 30 '87
Spanish short subjects. R. Sokolov. il *Nat Hist* 96:98+ O '87
Tapas. il *Good Housekeep* 205:108 Jl '87
Tapas: delicious little dishes of Spain. J. R. Nyenhuis. il *Saturday Evening Post* 259:18+ Ja/F '87

Tape
See also
Adhesive tape
Tape, Cassette *See* Tape, Magnetic
Tape, Magnetic
See also
Data tapes
Blank tape buying guide. W. Burton and others. il *Stereo Rev* 52:65-8 Mr '87
Longer audiotape [taping compact discs] F. Vizard. il *Pop Mech* 164:42+ N '87
The perfect match [tape's characteristics must match the deck's] P. W. Mitchell. il *High Fidel* 37:44-6 F '87
Super formats sharpen the video picture [Super VHS] E. Stecker. il *Pop Photogr* 94:71-2 S '87
Tape tracks. R. Long. See issues of High Fidelity (New York, N.Y.) beginning May 1986
Standards
8mm vs. VHS [camcorders] S. Sweetow. il *Petersens Photogr Mag* 15:54-5+ Ja '87
Aspects of camcorder choice. D. Ranada. il *High Fidel* 37:20 F '87
Format furor. P. Hoban. il *N Y* 20:14-15 F 16 '87
Format wars [VHS vs. 8mm] J. B. Meigs. il *Roll Stone* p43-4 Ja 15 '87
Korea ups the ante [4mm format] S. A. Booth. il *Pop Mech* 164:57 My '87
Palm-sized camcorder—smallest unit yet is a complete VCR, too [Samsung 4mm unit] W. J. Hawkins. il *Pop Sci* 230:47+ My '87
Video wars: the camcorder revolution. M. C. Lehrer. il *USA Today (Periodical)* 115:66-8 Ja '87
Why 8mm? [video] D. Ranada. il *High Fidel* 37:47-8+ F '87
Testing
Magnetic personalities [cover story] R. Long. il *High Fidel* 37:40-7+ Ag '87
Now hear this [BASE study of people's tape preferences] S. A. Booth. il *Pop Mech* 164:12+ N '87
Video tapes. il *Consum Rep* 52:327-9 D '87
What's in a name brand? R. Long. il *High Fidel* 37:24 F '87
Tape, Video (Magnetic) *See* Tape, Magnetic
Tape Data Media (Firm)
McGraw-Hill purchases TDM. *Publ Wkly* 232:416 Ag 7 '87
TDM, Caedmon end year-old distribution deal. *Publ Wkly* 231:50 Ap 24 '87
Tape decks *See* Tape recorders and recording
Tape recorders and recording
See also
Digital audio tape recorders and recording
Personics Corporation
Radio receivers—Tape recorder combination
Tape recordings
Videotape recorders and recording
Cassette decks. R. Long. *High Fidel* 37:44-5 S '87
The magic of tape. M. Riggs. il *High Fidel* 37:4 Ag '87
Open-reel recording. C. Stark. il *Stereo Rev* 52:122-4 N '87
The perfect match [tape's characteristics must match the deck's] P. W. Mitchell. il *High Fidel* 37:44-6 F '87
Tape decks buying guide. W. Burton and others. il *Stereo Rev* 52:69-77 Jl '87
Tape tracks. R. Long. See issues of High Fidelity (New York, N.Y.) beginning May 1986
Twelve tips on choosing a tape deck. W. Burton. il *Stereo Rev* 52:48-52 Mr '87
Anecdotes, facetiae, satire, etc.
The Walkman cometh. M. A. Noll. il *Christ Today* 31:22-3 F 6 '87
Design
How Sony keeps the copycats scampering [Walkman products] A. Borrus. il *Bus Week* p69 Je 1 '87
Maintenance and repair
Getting the most from your cassette deck. I. Masters. il *Stereo Rev* 52:81-4 O '87
Noise
Those pesky curves. R. Long. il *High Fidel* 37:22 Mr '87
Which silence is goldener (I). R. Long. il *High Fidel* 37:24 Ag '87
Which silence is goldener (II). R. Long. il *High Fidel* 37:20 S '87
Testing
Akai GX-8 cassette deck. il *High Fidel* 37:29-30 F '87
Akai GX-R70EX cassette deck. il *High Fidel* 37:34-5+ Ag '87

Tape recorders and recording—Testing—*cont.*

B&O Beocord 5500 cassette deck. il *High Fidel* 37:35-7 F '87

Denon DR-M14HX cassette deck. il *High Fidel* 37:29-30+ Ag '87

Kyocera D-811 cassette deck. C. Stark. il *Stereo Rev* 52:33-5 Mr '87

Luxman K-106 cassette deck. il *High Fidel* 37:38-9 Ag '87

NAD 6300 cassette deck. il *High Fidel* 37:27-9 Ag '87

NAD 6300 cassette deck. C. Stark. il *Stereo Rev* 52:37+ Je '87

Onkyo TA-2058 cassette deck. il *High Fidel* 37:37-8+ F '87

Teac V-770 cassette deck. il *High Fidel* 37:32+ Mr '87

Technics RS-B905 cassette deck. C. Stark. il *Stereo Rev* 52:45-6+ D '87

Tape recordings

See also

Bonneville Media Communications
Oral history
Talking books
Videotapes
Warner Audio Publishing

Audio/video plus. T. Spain. See issues of Publishers Weekly beginning May 9, 1986

Cassette singles emerge as 45s fade. M. Walker. *Roll Stone* p29+ Mr 26 '87

Enter, speaker right [audio drama] A. McIntyre. il *Publ Wkly* 232:39-41 D 11 '87

Now hear this [BASE study of people's tape preferences] S. A. Booth. il *Pop Mech* 164:12+ N '87

The shape of things to come [preview 1988] il *High Fidel* 37:61-71 S '87

Spring audiocassettes. J. Zinsser and T. Spain. il *Publ Wkly* 231:40+ F 6 '87

Through the hourglass. R. D. Darrell. il *High Fidel* 37:54-6+ F '87

Amateur recordings

Labels split on in-store taping [Personics System allows recording of customized tapes] N. Arnett and A. DeCurtis. *Roll Stone* p14+ Jl 2 '87

Starmaker machinery [Panasonic RQ-84 Karaoke-Songmate] M. Coleman. il *Roll Stone* p73+ Je 18 '87

Taping at retail [Personics System] C. J. Esse. il *High Fidel* 37:14 S '87

Under the boardwalk [Sing a Song Studio in Greenwich Village where amateur singers can make music tapes] *New Yorker* 63:26-7 Je 1 '87

Aviation use

See also

Flight recorders

Business use

A better way to communicate [audio cassettes in Entrepreneur Program at USC] S. Nelton. il *Nations Bus* 75:68 Jl '87

Listeners speak out [instructional tapes for sales personnel] J. Zinsser. *Publ Wkly* 232:57-60 O 2 '87

Children's use

Children's audio goes mass market [Toy Fair] *Publ Wkly* 231:93 Mr 6 '87

Making book on book-and-cassette packages. B. Stewart. il *Publ Wkly* 232:51-5 N 27 '87

Take a gander at Mother Goose's newest champions, Pam Beall and Susan Nipp of Wee Sing. A. Chambers. il pors *People Wkly* 28:66+ S 14 '87

Comedy

Comedy on cassette. J. Zinsser. il *Publ Wkly* 232:31+ D 4 '87

Concertos

Berg, Alban: Chamber concerto for violin, piano, and 13 wind instruments; Concerto for violin and orchestra. R. D. Darrell. il *High Fidel* 37:64 My '87

Editing

Confessions of a disinformationist. R. Long. il *High Fidel* 37:28 Ja '87

No-splice editing. R. Long. il *High Fidel* 37:20 N '87

Educational use

See also

Tape Data Media (Firm)

What can tapes teach you? More than just leg lifts. G. Hechinger. il *Glamour* 85:328-9 O '87

Exhibitions

Around the booths: audio and video [American Booksellers convention] il *Publ Wkly* 231:225+ My 15 '87

Filing systems

Tape filing: losers weepers. R. Long. il *High Fidel* 37:18 O '87

Health use

See also

Feeling Fine Programs (Firm)

Horror tales

Horror fiction on audio. A. Postman. bibl il *Publ Wkly* 232:33-6+ Jl 3 '87

Language study use

Teaching in tongues. D. Masello. il *Publ Wkly* 232:31-3 Jl 10 '87

Marketing

See also

Booksellers and bookselling—Tape recordings

Demise of the 45 [new cassette singles] P. Newcomb. il *Forbes* 139:91 Je 29 '87

Musical accompaniment

Is it live or Memorex? [performing live to taped accompaniment] B. Mikowski. *Down Beat* 54:6+ Ap '87

New Age movement

New Age on tape. il *Publ Wkly* 232:65+ S 25 '87

New media for a New Age. il *Publ Wkly* 232:60-1 S 25 '87

Orchestral music

Honegger, Arthur: Orchestral works. R. D. Darrell. *High Fidel* 37:82-3 Ja '87

Parent education use

HP Books to try audio under Knight-Ridder imprint this spring [birth and childcare audiocassettes] il *Publ Wkly* 231:70 F 13 '87

Piano music

Haydn, Joseph: Sonatas for piano (3) [Alfred Brendel] R. D. Darrell. il *High Fidel* 37:62 Je '87

Psychological use

Stress-management tapes. J. Zinsser. il *Publ Wkly* 232:413-17 Ag 7 '87

Radio programs

Comedy on cassette. J. Zinsser. il *Publ Wkly* 232:31+ D 4 '87

Self help use

See also

Audio Renaissance Tapes (Firm)
Nightingale-Conant Corp.
Positive Communications Inc.

I like Harper's! [subliminal message tapes] *Harpers* 274:22 Ja '87

Word How-To Library offers spiritual perspective. il *Publ Wkly* 232:40 N 20 '87

Symphonies

Roussel, Albert Charles Paul: Symphonies: no. 1 ("Le poème de la forêt"); no. 3, in G minor. R. D. Darrell. *High Fidel* 37:66 My '87

Unauthorized recording

Interrupted melody [CBS Copy Code system; cover story] D. Ranada. il *High Fidel* 37:44-7+ Jl '87

Labels split on in-store taping [Personics System allows recording of customized tapes] N. Arnett and A. DeCurtis. *Roll Stone* p14+ Jl 2 '87

Vespers (Music)

Handel, George Frideric: Roman vespers. R. D. Darrell. il *High Fidel* 37:82 Ja '87

Violin music

Berg, Alban: Chamber concerto for violin, piano, and 13 wind instruments; Concerto for violin and orchestra. R. D. Darrell. il *High Fidel* 37:64 My '87

Wind quintets

Mozart, Wolfgang Amadeus: Quintet for winds, in C minor [Ensemble Wien-Berlin] R. D. Darrell. *High Fidel* 37:84 Ja '87

Tapestry

Exhibitions

Classic turn: the 13th Lausanne Biennial of Tapestry. W. Seelig. il *Am Craft* 47:26-33 O/N '87

Tapia, Andrés

High-risk ministry. il por *Christ Today* 31:15-19 Ag 7 '87

Tapie, Bernard

about

'Seduction' is name of the game. P. Sherrid. il por *U S News World Rep* 103:39-40 Jl 27 '87

Tàpies, Antoni, 1923-

about

An art of constant renewal. M. Peppiatt. il por *Archit Dig* 44:40+ Ag '87

Tappan, David Stanton, Jr.

about

After the frying pan, what? M. Beauchamp. il por *Forbes* 139:60+ Mr 9 '87

Tapply, H. G.

Tap's tips. See issues of Field & Stream

Taps and dies

Using taps and dies. M. Thompson. il *Fam Handyman* 37:16+ Ja '87

Tarascon, J. M., and others
Superconductivity at 40 K in the oxygen-defect perovskites La$_{2-x}$Sr$_x$CuO$_{4-y}$. bibl f il *Science* 235:1373-6 Mr 13 '87

Tarawa, Battle of, 1943
The tide at Tarawa [computer program] D. W. Olson. il map *Sky Telesc* 74:526-8 N '87

Tarbell, Edmund Charles, 1862-1938
about
Edmund C. Tarbell's paintings of interiors. T. J. Fairbrother. bibl f il *Antiques* 131:224-35 Ja '87

Tardiness
Better late than clever? [employees] L. Washer. *Work Woman* 12:24 My '87
My husband was never on time. il *Good Housekeep* 204:26+ F '87
Never late is better [teenagers] J. Dolce. il *Seventeen* 46:115 N '87

Target practice
Hearing where the bullet will hit [Penn State research device lets you listen to your shooting faults] H. Berger. il *Outdoor Life* 180:126+ N '87
Laser bull's-eye. W. Siuru. il *Pop Sci* 231:126 N '87

Target ranges *See* Shooting ranges

Tariff
See also
Free trade and protection
General Agreement on Tariffs and Trade

Canada
Anger over a tree tax [protesting Ottawa's decision to impose a tariff on Christmas trees imported from United States] M. Clark. il *Macleans* 100:11 F 9 '87
Canada lifts tariff on books; publishing industry rejoices. B. Slopen. *Publ Wkly* 231:29 Mr 6 '87
Counting the cost of protectionism [GATT ruling against Canadian beer and wine tariffs] M. Janigan. il *Macleans* 100:14 N 23 '87
Nailing the consumer [Canadian lumber in the U.S.] M. Alexander and others. il *Consum Res Mag* 70:26-9 Mr '87
A new storm over trade [Canada-U.S. dispute over softwood lumber exports] M. Rose. il *Macleans* 100:10-11 Ja 12 '87
Ottawa's trade offensive [softwood lumber accord with the U.S.] M. Drohan. il por *Macleans* 100:10-11 Ja 19 '87
Talking tough on trade [U.S.-Canada softwood lumber accord; with editorial comment by Kevin Doyle] M. Drohan. il *Macleans* 100:2, 12+ Ja 26 '87

United States
See also
U.S. Customs Service
AAP protests to U.S. Customs Service over 'user fee' on imported books. H. Fields. *Publ Wkly* 231:87 F 27 '87
America vs. Japan: a no-win game [special section] il por *Bus Week* p30-4 My 4 '87
Canadians fear study will lead to import duties [beef] *Success Farm* 85 no2:B8 Ja '87
Chip wars [U.S. tariffs on Japanese semiconductors] *Natl Rev* 39:20-1 Ap 24 '87
Devine's control zone [Saskatchewan enacts potash protectionist measures to counteract U.S. duties] D. Eisler. il *Macleans* 100:14-15 S 14 '87
Explaining the war of the chips [U.S. tariff imposed on Japanese products] il *World Press Rev* 34:48 Je '87
Fighting the trade tilt [tariffs on Japanese electronics products] S. Koepp. il *Time* 129:50-1 Ap 6 '87
Firing up a new potash war [U.S. duty on Saskatchewan potash] D. Eisler. il *Macleans* 100:32-3 S 7 '87
Fixing a tariff blooper [U.S. tariff on Japanese electronic products] G. Lewis. *Bus Week* p35 D 14 '87
Harley-Davidson: ready to ride on its own [asking to end import restraints against Japan] *Newsweek* 109:50 Mr 30 '87
High-tech tariffs boomerang on the U.S. G. Lewis. il *Bus Week* p26-7 S 7 '87
Imports from the EEC [proclamation, January 21, 1987] R. Reagan. *Dep State Bull* 87:30 Ap '87
It's more than a trade brawl [U.S.-Japan relationship] P. R. Range. il *U S News World Rep* 102:20-2 My 4 '87
Japan may be listening, but it's not about to change [U.S. imposes tariffs on electronic products] A. Borrus. il *Bus Week* p35-6 Ap 13 '87
Let's not bash the Japanese. L. Smith. il *Fortune* 115:175-6 Ap 27 '87
Neo-protectionism [address, November 6, 1986] D. R. Peterson. *Vital Speeches Day* 53:230-1 F 1 '87

No more Mr. Nice Guy [tariffs on Japanese imports] D. Pauly. il *Newsweek* 109:42 Ap 6 '87
The peril of pushing Japan. J. Dreyfuss. il *Fortune* 115:113-14+ My 11 '87
Punishing Japan: Reagan walks a fine line [imposition of tariffs for failure to uphold semiconductor pact] B. Javetski and others. il *Bus Week* p34-5 Ap 13 '87
Reagan fires a shot across Tokyo's bow. W. L. Chaze. il *U S News World Rep* 102:16-17 Ap 27 '87
Rules for the game [imposition of tariffs on Japanese products] *America* 156:355 My 2 '87
Semi-tough [federal action to help American semiconductor companies] M. Gladwell. *New Repub* 196:9-11 My 18 '87
Sky wars over Airbus [U.S. threatening to slap duties on its U.S. sales] F. J. Comes. *Bus Week* p48 F 16 '87
Soothing talks, troubled times [defusing trade tensions between U.S. and Japan] B. Rudolph. il *Time* 129:74 My 4 '87
A talk with Shintaro Abe: the U.S. is 'going too far'. R. J. Dowling and L. Armstrong. por *Bus Week* p37 Ap 20 '87
Tariffs aren't great, but quotas are worse. J. Berger. il *Bus Week* p64 Mr 16 '87
Trade wars: Reagan plays with fire [duties imposed on European agricultural products] *Natl Rev* 39:21-2 Ja 30 '87
Trade with Japan [tariff on semiconductors] R. Reagan. *Dep State Bull* 87:35-7 Jl '87
Trade with Romania, Hungary, and China [most-favored-nation tariff status; White House statement, June 2, 1987] *Dep State Bull* 87:57 Ag '87
Tradeamok [cutting federal budget deficit] *New Repub* 196:7-9 Ap 27 '87
Transatlantic showdown [U.S.-European Community agricultural trade war] P. Lewis. il *Macleans* 100:30 Ja 19 '87
U.S. international trade [White House statement, December 30, 1986] *Dep State Bull* 87:32-3 Ap '87
U.S.-Japan semiconductor trade [statement, June 8, 1987] R. Reagan. *Dep State Bull* 87:55 Ag '87
We've met the enemy, and they are us? [effect of proposed tariffs on multinationals] E. A. Finn, Jr. and K. Healy. il *Forbes* 139:78+ F 9 '87
Yasu, the chips are down [effect of tariffs on Japanese exports on Y. Nakasone's popularity] H. G. Chua-Eoan. il por *Time* 129:38 Ap 27 '87

Western Europe
See also
European Economic Community

Tariff, Exemption from *See* Duty free importation

Tarkovsky, Andrei
about
Tarkovsky. H. Kennedy. il por *Film Comment* 23:44-6 My/Je '87

Taronga Zoo
Around the Mall and beyond. E. Park. *Smithsonian* 18:22+ Je '87

Tarot in art
Exhibitions
A garden of earthly delights [N. de Saint-Phalle's fantastical sculptures inspired by the Tarot] B. Rose. il pors *Vogue* 177:266-73+ D '87
House of cards: Niki de Saint Phalle's Tuscan fantasy [Garden of the Tarot; cover story] Michael, Prince of Greece. il por *Archit Dig* 44:124-31 S '87

Tarpon fishing
Going deep [getting lures deep for tarpon] B. Stearns. il *Field Stream* 92:78-9 Ag '87
Troubled times for the tarpon. B. Stearns. il *Field Stream* 92:80+ N '87

Tarpon Springs (Fla.)
Restaurants, nightclubs, bars, etc.
Sample Greek culture in Tarpon Springs. C. Griffith. il *South Living* 22:36+ Ag '87

Tarr, Peter
Aquino's first year. il *Nation* 244:353-7 Mr 21 '87

Tarragon
Russian is bland, French is aromatic . . . know the tarragons. il *Sunset* 179:150 Jl '87

Tarrant, Bill
Gun dogs. See issues of Field & Stream

Tarrant County Housing Finance Corporation
Three notches down [bonds] B. Weberman. il *Forbes* 140:171 Jl 27 '87

Tarses, Jay
about
Jay Tarses [interview] M. Christensen. il por *Roll Stone* p168+ D 17-31 '87

Tartikoff, Brandon
The quest for cable-resilience. il *Channels* 7:71 O '87
about
The man who turns on America. L. Hirschberg. il pors *Roll Stone* p59-60+ O 22 '87
The perils of a programmer. W. A. Henry. il *Channels* 7:56 N '87

Tarts
After quiche [open-faced tarts] P. Wells. il *N Y Times Mag* p61-2 O 4 '87
Basil-cheese tart. *South Living* 22:193 My '87
Dark victory [Thomas Keller's warm chocolate tart] B. Costikyan. il *N Y* 20:119 Ap 27 '87
Pies and tarts from the garden [made with fruits] R. Haskell. il *Flower Gard* 31:16+ Je/Jl '87

Tartuffe [drama] See Molière, 1622-1673

Tartufo *See* Ice cream, ices, etc.

Tash, Martin E.
about
Fish or cut bait. F. Meeks. il por *Forbes* 139:57+ Je 15 '87

Task Force to Promote Self-Esteem, Personal and Social Responsibility (Calif.) *See* California. Task Force to Promote Self-Esteem, Personal and Social Responsibility

Task forces in industry
Dear Betty Harragan [task force assignments reflect sex discrimination] B. L. Harragan. il *Work Woman* 12:26+ F '87

Tass, Nadia
about
Making Malcolm. W. Harris. il pors *Theatre Crafts* 21:73-4 F '87

TASS (Soviet Union)
Negative phenomena come to Nexis [current terms used by Tass] D. Seligman. il *Fortune* 115:166 Je 22 '87

Tassel, Janet
Return to Barcelona. il *Opera News* 52:41-2 S '87

Tassili-n-Ajjer cave drawings *See* Cave drawings and paintings

Taste
Odd and unusual tastes [conference at Saint Anthony's College, Oxford, England] R. Sokolov. il *Nat Hist* 96:104-7 N '87

Taste testing of wine *See* Wine tasting

Tata, J. R. D.
about
Millions for expansion but not one cent for tribute. S. N. Chakravarty. il por *Forbes* 140:46+ O 5 '87

Tata Sons Ltd.
Millions for expansion but not one cent for tribute. S. N. Chakravarty. il por *Forbes* 140:46+ O 5 '87

Tatara, Toshio, and others
SCAN: providing preventive services in an urban setting. il *Child Today* 15:17-22 N/D '86

Tatars
Testing the limits of *glasnost* [Crimean Tatars demonstrate in Red Square] S. Thomas. il *Time* 130:22 Ag 10 '87

Tate, David A.
Survivor's debt. il *N Y Times Mag* p38 Ag 30 '87

Tate, Frank
about
Fateful date against Tate. P. Putnam. pors *Sports Illus* 67:48-9 O 19 '87

Tate Gallery. Clore Wing
At long last, Britain's Turner Bequest finds a proper home. I. Shenker. bibl (p144) il por *Smithsonian* 18:50-8+ Ag '87
Do we need another hero? [J. Stirling's design for the Clore Wing] S. Jones. il *Hist Today* 37:3-4 My '87
Gallery for a 'wayward genius' [Turner Bequest] W. Feaver. il *Art News* 86:107-8 Summ '87
The homecoming [J. F. Stirlings design; cover story] D. Dietsch. il *Archit Rec* 175:104-13 Jl '87
London journal. J. Bainbridge. il *Gourmet* 47:36+ N '87

Tateho Chemical Industries Co. Ltd.
Japan writes a new definition of zaitech: 'investor beware' [financial speculation] B. Buell. *Bus Week* p45 S 21 '87

Tattooing
Overloaded [astrologer D. Hayes' tatoos applied by A. Sistrand] *New Yorker* 62:28-31 F 9 '87

Tatu
about
The shirtless wonder. J. Diaz. il pors *Sports Illus* 66:66+ Mr 9 '87

Tatu, Michel
Should the West help? il *World Press Rev* 34:12+ Ap '87

Tatum, Billy Joe
about
The American scene. E. Jones. il *Gourmet* 47:62+ F '87

Tatum, Cheryl
about
Woman fired for cornrows sues Hyatt hotel in Virginia. il por *Jet* 73:36 O 19 '87

TAU *See* Space flight—Thousand Astronomical Unit missions

Tauber, Peter
Notes on a brief campaign. il *N Y Times Mag* p48-50+ My 31 '87

Taubes, Gary
about
How to win a Nobel Prize. M. D. Lemonick. il por *Time* 129:55 F 9 '87

Taubman, Philip
Gorbachev's gamble. il por *N Y Times Mag* p28-9+ Jl 19 '87
The USSR and the press. *Current* 291:28-33 Mr/Ap '87

Taung skull *See* Man, Prehistoric

Taunton (Mass.)
Education
Racial slur in yearbook, sparks Mass. school probe [Taunton High School] *Jet* 72:16 Je 15 '87

Taurine
Myocardial failure in cats associated with low plasma taurine: a reversible cardiomyopathy [cover story] P. D. Pion and others. bibl f il *Science* 237:764-8 Ag 14 '87

Tavernier, Bertrand
about
Round midnight [film] Reviews
Down Beat il 54:22-3 Ja '87. H. Mandel

Taverns *See* Bars and barrooms

Taviani, Paolo, 1931-
about
Good morning, Babylon [film] Reviews
N Y 20:64-5 Jl 27 '87. D. Denby
New Repub 197:26-7 Ag 24 '87. S. Kauffmann
New Yorker 63:70-1 Ag 10 '87. P. Kael
Newsweek 110:68 Ag 3 '87. D. Ansen

Taviani, Vittorio, 1929-
about
Good morning, Babylon [film] Reviews
N Y 20:64-5 Jl 27 '87. D. Denby
New Repub 197:26-7 Ag 24 '87. S. Kauffmann
New Yorker 63:70-1 Ag 10 '87. P. Kael
Newsweek 110:68 Ag 3 '87. D. Ansen

Tavoulareas, William P.
about
Triple reverse. por *Time* 129:70 Mr 23 '87

Tavris, Carol
Mind health. See issues of Vogue
(jt. auth) See Rubenstein, Carin, and Tavris, Carol

Tawana, Kea
about
Grass-roots art seeks a haven. H. Metz. il por *Progressive* 51:14 O '87

Tax auditing
How to avoid a tax audit [self employed] il *Work Woman* 12:40 O '87
How to avoid an IRS audit. P. M. Scherschel. il *U S News World Rep* 102:63 Mr 2 '87
How to survive a tax audit. J. A. Harb. il *Consum Res Mag* 70:21-3 Mr '87
Is your return audit bait? W. L. Updegrave. il *Money* 16:119-20+ F '87
Just keep repeating 'only 3% are audited . . . . '. P. Philipps. il *Bus Week* p134 Ap 27 '87
What to do if you're audited. L. Wiener. il *U S News World Rep* 102:67 Ap 27 '87
Anecdotes, facetiae, satire, etc.
Your audit: a guide for the perplexed. R. H. Bell. il *Commonweal* 114:196-7 Ap 10 '87

Tax collection
See also
Canada. Revenue Canada
Tax penalties
United States. Internal Revenue Service
Congress wants a fierce IRS the public will love [Taxpayers' Bill of Rights] C. Yang. il *Bus Week* p35 O 26 '87
Making the IRS accountable [Taxpayers' Bill of Rights] A. Holzinger. il *Nations Bus* 75:38-9 D '87
Public policies that perform [Massachusetts] il *U S News World Rep* 103:18-19 Ag 10 '87

Tax collection—*cont.*

Reining in the tax man [proposed Omnibus Taxpayer Bill of Rights Act] S. Dentzer. il *Newsweek* 110:41 Jl 13 '87

The scariest dunner [Taxpayers' Bill of Rights] L. Saunders. il *Forbes* 140:76+ N 2 '87

The taxman tries a little hype [states use ads to aid in collection] A. Miller. il *Newsweek* 109:55-6 F 23 '87

Watch out for 'little brother' [federal-state cooperation] L. Wiener. il *U S News World Rep* 103:47 Jl 27 '87

Why we need to enact a Taxpayers' Bill of Rights. il *Nations Bus* 75:71 Je '87

You can't hide [state tax collectors] L. Saunders. il *Forbes* 140:124+ N 16 '87

Tax consultants

See also

   H & R Block, Inc.

The best tax practitioners. G. Anrig, Jr. and S. Ballen. il *Money* Sp Issue:113-14+ Fall '87

Advertising

Block, Block, fizz, fizz [Alka-Seltzer and H&R Block join advertising forces] S. D. Atchison. il *Bus Week* p36 Mr 30 '87

Tax courts

Suing the IRS—and winning. G. W. Padwe. *Nations Bus* 75:70 Jl '87

Tax credits

See also

   Investment tax credit

Fresh-start blues [tax credit for property-casualty insurers] J. Andresky. il *Forbes* 140:212 D 14 '87

Tax cuts *See* Income tax

Tax deductions *See* Income tax—Deductions

Tax evasion

See also

   Tax penalties

   Underground economy

After 20 months behind bars, a chastened Albert Nipon is trying to sew up the dress market again. B. Johnson. il pors *People Wkly* 28:91-2 Ag 31 '87

The eternal promoter [W. A. Kilpatrick] A. A. Lappen. il por *Forbes* 140:8 Ag 10 '87

Getty 'improprieties' attract IRS scrutiny [investigation into donations of works of art to the J. Paul Getty Museum] A. Decker. *Art News* 86:31-2 My '87

How 'tax-free' are these bonds? [munis underwritten by Matthews & Wright] D. Zigas. *Bus Week* p122 Ag 17 '87

Irving's taxing battle [Revenue Canada vs. Irving Oil over Bermudan tax shelter] C. Wood. il por *Macleans* 100:34 Ag 3 '87

Making crime pay [gasoline bootlegging] J. Cook. il *Forbes* 140:56+ Jl 27 '87

The never-say-die promoter [tax shelter promoter W. Kilpatrick] J. A. Conway. por *Forbes* 139:8 Ap 6 '87

Pearl picks up the pieces [P. Nipon] M. Rowland. il pors *Work Woman* 12:114-17 My '87

Pied Piper to the truly rich [C. Atkins indicted for tax evasion and securities fraud] F. Ungeheuer. il por *Time* 129:52 Ap 6 '87

The promoter who never quits [tax shelter operator W. A. Kilpatrick] A. A. Lappen. il por *Forbes* 139:60-1 F 9 '87

Riding for a fall [English jockey L. Piggott convicted] il por *Sports Illus* 67:24 N 2 '87

Sidney Poitier and others linked to tax shelter scam [case against C. Atkins] *Jet* 72:14 Ap 13 '87

So you thought you'd seen the last of tax straddles [fraudulent repo straddles] D. Zigas. il por *Bus Week* p90 Je 15 '87

Squeal [tax informers] L. Saunders. il *Forbes* 139:62-3 My 4 '87

Stain on a shining record [R. Anderson pleads guilty] por *Time* 129:52 Ap 6 '87

Tax troubles hound Gotham hotel queen Leona Helmsley, whom subjects call a royal pain. K. McMurran. il pors *People Wkly* 27:32-5 Ja 5 '87

Taxes: fairness first [tax reform and cheating; study by Amitai Etzioni] V. Bozzi. *Psychol Today* 21:12 Ap '87

Taxing a gambler's loss [Canadian embezzler B. Molony] D. Jenish. il por *Macleans* 100:34+ D 14 '87

Wall Street's prime-time crime drama [tax evasion and securities fraud charges against C. Atkins] D. Pauly. il por *Newsweek* 109:44 Ap 6 '87

Tax exemption *See* Taxation, Exemption from

Tax forms *See* Tax returns

Tax fraud *See* Tax evasion

Tax havens

A Eurobond bombshell [U.S. ends tax treaty with Netherlands Antilles] R. Brady and V. English. *Bus Week* p100 Jl 13 '87

Fund havens. R. Phalon. il *Forbes* 140:140+ S 7 '87

Innocent victims [multinational corporations getting caught in trap set for tax haven abusers] L. Saunders. il *Forbes* 140:64+ O 5 '87

Luxembourg: color it green [cover story] E. A. Finn, Jr. il *Forbes* 139:42-5 Ap 20 '87

The sun isn't setting on this tax haven [Netherlands Antilles] G. DeGeorge. il *Bus Week* p57-8 Ag 31 '87

A tempest hits the Treasury [cancels Antilles tax treaty] D. Zigas and V. English. il *Bus Week* p124 Jl 20 '87

Tight little islands [Channel Islands face social consequences of being a tax haven] R. Phalon. il *Forbes* 140:40-1 Jl 27 '87

Tax informers *See* Informers

Tax laws and regulations *See* Income tax; Taxation

Tax penalties

The IRS's match game. L. Wiener. il *U S News World Rep* 102:51 F 23 '87

Tax time. J. W. Merline. il *Consum Res Mag* 70:38 Mr '87

Tax preparers *See* Tax consultants

Tax records

Keeping home expense records for the tax man. T. Tilling. *Parents* 62:52 Jl '87

The simple science of keeping records. R. McNatt. il *Money* 16:197-8+ Mr '87

Tax reduction *See* Income tax

Tax reform *See* Income tax; Taxation

Tax refunds

Check a box, do some good [state tax checkoffs to fund worthy causes] L. Wiener. il *U S News World Rep* 103:82 O 12 '87

Tax relations, Intergovernmental *See* Intergovernmental tax relations

Tax returns

See also

   Computers—Tax return use

Before you sign a joint return—. L. Wiener. il *U S News World Rep* 102:71 Mr 30 '87

Figuring what to pay Uncle Sam. il *U S News World Rep* 102:60-1 Mr 2 '87

Filing taxes late [extension] il *Black Enterp* 17:24 My '87

Just one more form . . . [home mortgage interest deduction] M. Kaus. il *Newsweek* 110:21 Ag 24 '87

Meet the new, slimmed-down W-4. L. Wiener. il *U S News World Rep* 102:67 Mr 16 '87

Meet the new tax forms. J. Gilbert. il *Money* 16:60-2+ S '87

The smart taxpayer's guide. L. Wiener. il *U S News World Rep* 102:50-1+ Mr 2 '87

The taxman goes on-line [electronic filing] H. Fersko-Weiss. il *Pers Comput* 11:82-3 Ap '87

Those W-4s: help, Henry! B. Powell. il *Newsweek* 109:49 F 16 '87

What if you just happen to be 'far away' on Apr. 15? G. Weiss. il *Bus Week* p111 Ap 13 '87

You'll love filing this 1040 [1040X] G. Weiss. *Bus Week* p141 My 4 '87

Your 1986 return: what's new on the 1040 and what you can still do to reduce your tax bill. *Money* 16:114 F '87

Your '86 return: how to avoid expensive mistakes. B. G. Quint. *Glamour* 85:180+ Mr '87

Your taxes: up or down? il *Consum Rep* 52:164-71 Mr '87

Auditing

See Tax auditing

Tax shelter fraud *See* Tax evasion

Tax shelters

See also

   Gifts to minors

   Securities Groups

   Tax havens

   Tax straddles

After tax reform, historic rehabs can still pay off. B. Hitchings. il *Bus Week* p123 Ap 6 '87

Any pay dirt left in real estate? M. C. Paulson. il *Changing Times* 41:85-6+ Ja '87

Tax shelters—*cont.*

Building a cozy tax shelter with historic rehabs [real estate limited partnership] T. Segal. il *Bus Week* p118 S 7 '87

Equipment leasing faces trial by tax reform. G. Weiss. il *Bus Week* p114-15 Ja 12 '87

How to make 25% a year in real estate—even with tax reform [views of J. T. Reed] C. E. Trunzo. il por *Money* 16:190 S '87

Limited partnerships that like tax reform [capital equipment leasing] A. E. Serwer. il *Fortune* 116:102 Ag 17 '87

A 'PIG' can help with tax-shelter losses [passive income generators] B. Hitchings. *Bus Week* p94 Ap 20 '87

Propping up paper losses [passive income generators] H. Wheelwright. *Money* 16:159 Jl '87

Vacation homes may cut your taxes. H. Porter. *Fam Handyman* 37:12+ Ja '87

Whatever became of tax shelters? E. C. Baig. il *Fortune* 116 Sp Issue:101-2+ Fall '87

What's left of tax shelters. L. Marsa. il *Black Enterp* 17:324+ Je '87

Your home as a tax shelter. L. Wiener. il *U S News World Rep* 102:58 My 18 '87

Your home still offers you shelter. P. Philipps. il *Bus Week* p114 Ap 13 '87

Tax straddles

So you thought you'd seen the last of tax straddles [fraudulent repo straddles] D. Zigas. il por *Bus Week* p90 Je 15 '87

Taxation

See also

Advertising—Taxation
Aged—Taxation
Air travel—Taxation
Airplanes in business—Taxation
Americans—Foreign countries—Taxation
Annuities—Taxation
Artists—Taxation
Assessment
Authors—Taxation
Blacks—Taxation
Boats and boating—Taxation
Business consultants—Taxation
Business entertaining—Taxation
Business travel—Taxation
Capital gains tax
Cash business—Taxation
Children—Taxation
Cigarettes—Taxation
Closely held corporations—Taxation
Construction industry—Taxation
Corporations—Taxation
Corporations, International—Taxation
Dancers—Taxation
Deferred taxation
Divorcees—Taxation
Employees as stockholders—Taxation
Entertainers—Taxation
Entertainment industry—Taxation
Eskimos—Industries—Taxation
Estate planning
Excise tax
Executives—Taxation
Farmers—Taxation
Foster home care—Taxation
Foundations, Charitable and educational—Taxation
Gambling—Taxation
Gasoline—Taxation
Income tax
Industrial equipment leases—Taxation
Information services—Taxation
Inheritance tax
Insurance, Health—Taxation
Insurance, Life—Taxation
Insurance companies—Taxation
Intangible assets—Taxation
Interest (Economics)—Taxation
Intergovernmental tax relations
Inventories—Taxation
Investment trusts—Taxation
Investments—Taxation
Limited partnership—Taxation
Loans, Personal—Taxation
Local taxation
Mail order business—Taxation
Master limited partnership—Taxation
Mortgages—Taxation
Nonprofit institutions—Taxation
Partnership—Taxation
Pensions—Taxation

Petroleum industry—Taxation
Poll tax
Profit sharing—Taxation
Public utilities—Taxation
Publishers and publishing—Taxation
Real estate business—Taxation
Real property—Taxation
Rent—Taxation
Research institutions—Taxation
Retirement benefits—Taxation
Rich—Taxation
S corporations
Sales tax
Scholarships and fellowships—Taxation
Securities—Taxation
Self employed—Taxation
Service industries—Taxation
Shipping—Taxation
Social security—Taxation
Trade waste—Disposal—Taxation
Trusts and trustees—Taxation
United States. Dept. of the Treasury
United States. Internal Revenue Service
Value added tax
Venture capital companies—Taxation
Withholding tax
Women—Taxation
Women executives—Taxation

Con game. *Natl Rev* 39:18-19 D 4 '87

Congress will feed Reagan a tax increase—in small bites. D. Harbrecht. *Bus Week* p55 Je 1 '87

The Democrats may be losing a game of chicken on the budget. P. Magnuson and D. Harbrecht. il *Bus Week* p43 O 26 '87

Don't let a tax increase ruin a chance to whittle debt. P. C. Roberts. il *Bus Week* p21 Mr 23 '87

Don't raise taxes [detrimental to balancing the budget] W. T. Brookes. il *Read Dig* 131:163-6 O '87

A few good taxes. L. H. Summers. *New Repub* 197:14-16 N 30 '87

For your tax file. G. W. Padwe. See issues of Nation's Business beginning July 1983

Life after tax reform [cover story] C. T. Clotfelter. il *Change* 19:12-18 Jl/Ag '87

The OMB is digging in its heels on the budget. H. Gleckman. por *Bus Week* p41 F 9 '87

The outspoken Speaker has Democrats in a cold sweat [tax hike pronouncements by J. Wright] D. Harbrecht and R. Fly. por *Bus Week* p49 Mr 23 '87

Partisan budget. *Natl Rev* 39:17+ Jl 17 '87

Plain talk about the dreaded 'T' word. A. S. Blinder. il *Bus Week* p20 S 21 '87

The politics of austerity. B. Powell. il *Newsweek* 110:18-19 N 23 '87

Selling higher taxes [Democrats] R. Kuttner. *New Repub* 197:23-5 Ag 24 '87

A tax calendar for '87. L. Wiener. il *U S News World Rep* 102:57 Ja 12 '87

Tax hike pressures mount. il *Nations Bus* 75:14 My '87

Tax reform as environmental policy. B. Blackwelder and D. Campbell. *Sierra* 72:33-6 Mr/Ap '87

Taxes raise their ugly head [views of House Speaker Jim Wright] K. R. Sheets. *U S News World Rep* 102:49 Mr 16 '87

Taxing matters. See issues of Forbes

Taxing patience. *Natl Rev* 39:20 Ag 14 '87

The tough choices Washington can no longer dodge. M. McNamee and P. Magnusson. il *Bus Week* p47 N 2 '87

'Vindicated'—not gloating [W. F. Mondales's views] D. Gates. il por *Newsweek* 110:6 N 23 '87

Visiting the anti-tax side. W. F. Buckley. *Natl Rev* 39:63 D 4 '87

Collection

See Tax collection

International aspects

Taxes abroad: pressures for tax reform. J. A. Pechman. il *Current* 295:30-8 S '87

Australia

Call it a seminar [writing off business entertainment as seminars] G. Buchalter. il *Forbes* 139:42 Ja 12 '87

California

See also

Los Angeles (Calif.)—Taxation

Canada

See also

Canada. Revenue Canada

Income tax—Canada

Taxation—Canada—*cont.*
Cautious reform [special section] il *Macleans* 100:34-41 Je 29 '87
A personal tax touch. D. Jenish. il *Macleans* 100:38-9 My 11 '87
Standing firm on tax reform. M. Drohan. il *Macleans* 100:28 S 14 '87

Georgia
Carpetbaggers [Georgia objects to tax reform restrictions on tax-exempt status of municipal bonds] *Time* 130:63 S 14 '87

Germany (West)
See also
Income tax—Germany (West)
Still more reasons to mistrust supply siders [Stefan Welzk's study of German tax loopholes and parallel decline in capital investments] R. Kuttner. por *Bus Week* p22 O 26 '87

Great Britain
See also
Income tax—Great Britain
Poll tax—Great Britain

Hungary
Reform adjusts to realities. K. W. Banta. il *Time* 130:40 O 5 '87

Kansas
See also
Kansas City (Mo.)—Taxation

Massachusetts
Public policies that perform. il *U S News World Rep* 103:18-19 Ag 10 '87

New York (State)
See also
Income tax—New York (State)
New York (N.Y.)—Taxation

Ohio
State effort to tax transient business aircraft raises concern. *Aviat Week Space Technol* 127:56 Jl 27 '87

Québec (Province)
See also
Montreal (Québec)—Taxation

United States
See Taxation

Western Europe
See also
Value added tax—Western Europe
Europe needs a tax cut. A. Reynolds. il *Natl Rev* 39:40-1+ F 27 '87

Taxation, Double
See also
Americans—Foreign countries—Taxation
A taxing issue [taxes imposed on money paid to American authors by foreign publishers] R. Curtis. por *Publ Wkly* 231:52 Mr 20 '87

Taxation, Exemption from
Angel of death loophole [proposal to tax capital gains at death] *New Repub* 197:4 Jl 13-20 '87
Legal attack by bishops [National Conference of Catholic Bishops has asked the Supreme Court to overturn an order demanding that the bishops relinquish church files to critics of their stand on abortion] *Christ Century* 104:881-2 O 14 '87
Loopholes at large. R. S. McIntyre. *New Repub* 196:12+ Je 15 '87
Personalized taxes. L. Saunders. il *Forbes* 139:84+ Je 1 '87
Taking yet another look at television evangelism [congressional hearings] il por *Christ Today* 31:48-9+ S 18 '87
TV ministries and taxation. B. Spring. il *Christ Today* 31:36+ N 6 '87
TV preachers to testify. *Newsweek* 110:64 Ag 31 '87
Taxation, Municipal *See* Local taxation
Taxation, State
See also
Sales tax
And now, son of tax reform. G. Russell. map *Time* 129:55 Ja 12 '87
Bait and tax [personal income tax rates] J. Novack. il *Forbes* 140:52+ S 7 '87
Check a box, do some good [state tax checkoffs to fund worthy causes] L. Wiener. il *U S News World Rep* 103:82 O 12 '87
Many happy returns for wildlife [state income tax checkoffs] S. Q. Stranahan. il *Natl Wildl* 25:50-1 Ap/My '87
The nasty surprises in state taxes. H. Wheelwright. il *Money* 16:131-2 F '87
Nowhere to go but up. T. Smart. il *Bus Week* p24-5 Je 29 '87

The taxman tries a little hype [states use ads to aid in collection] A. Miller. il *Newsweek* 109:55-6 F 23 '87
You can't hide [state tax collectors] L. Saunders. il *Forbes* 140:124+ N 16 '87
Taxation for education *See* Education—Finance
Taxation of works of art
The delicate art of donating art. T. Segal. il *Bus Week* p167 Je 22 '87
The fine art of donating fine art. L. Wiener. il *U S News World Rep* 103:104 S 28 '87
Getty 'improprieties' attract IRS scrutiny [investigation into donations of works of art to the J. Paul Getty Museum] A. Decker. *Art News* 86:31-2 My '87
Tax breaks for a Picasso. M. Malone. il *Newsweek* 109:39-40 Ja 5 '87
Taxicab drivers

Training
New Orleans cabbies were making the Big Easy queasy, so the city has sent them to charm school [Jazzy Cabby course] J. Greene. il *People Wkly* 28:115-16 O 19 '87
Taxicabs
See also
New Orleans (La.)—Taxicabs
Taxidermy

Anecdotes, facetiae, satire, etc.
My best stuff. A. Liere. il *Field Stream* 91:21-3 F '87
Taxonomy *See* Biology—Classification; Botany—Classification; Fish—Classification
Taylor, Barry N.
(jt. auth) See Cohen, E. Richard, and Taylor, Barry N.
Taylor, Clarice
about
Clarice Taylor calls Cosby her son on TV but finds sassier fun as Moms Mabley. T. Cunneff. il pors *People Wkly* 28:79-80 O 26 '87
Taylor, Delores L.
Understanding lupus. *Essence* 18:18+ Je '87
Taylor, Elizabeth, 1932-
about
Elizabeth Taylor: act II. A. T. Fleming. pors *Vogue* 177:434-41+ O '87
Elizabeth Taylor in her prime [cover story] M. Blyth. il pors *Ladies Home J* 104:150-1+ N '87
Elizabeth Taylor's crusade against AIDS [cover story; interview] H. G. Miller. il pors *Saturday Evening Post* 259:52-3+ S '87
The fight against AIDS. E. Sherman. il por *Ladies Home J* 104:90+ S '87
Queen of diamonds. B. Darrach. il pors *People Wkly* 27:28-33 Ap 27 '87

Photographs and photography
An audience with the queen. G. Bernstein. il por *Petersens Photogr Mag* 16:24 D '87
Taylor by Bernstein [interview with G. Bernstein] F. Cameron. il por *Petersens Photogr Mag* 15:20-2 Ja '87
Taylor, Frank C.
Blues singer Alberta Hunter: the forgotten years [excerpt from Alberta Hunter]; ed. by Gerald Cook. por *Ms* 15:46-8+ Mr '87
Taylor, Henry, 1942-
The strength of words [address, April 26, 1987] *Vital Speeches Day* 53:600-2 Jl 15 '87
about
Virginia's Pulitzer-winning poet. D. Young. il pors *South Living* 22:133-4 S '87
Taylor, J. Wolfred
Aldo Leopold—a celebration of the land ethic. il pors *Conservationist* 42:12-15 N/D '87
Taylor, Jack A.
The gap between music research and music teaching. *Des Arts Educ* 88:27-30 My/Je '87
Taylor, Jay C.
The autophile. See occasional issues of High Fidelity (New York, N.Y.) beginning February 1985
Taylor, Jeff
Aunt Lucy's country cure. il *Mother Earth News* 108:144 N/D '87
Taylor, Jeffrey
The perfect sawhorse. il *Ctry J* 14:33-5 O '87
Taylor, Jennifer
Drive in U.K. to push children's books. *Publ Wkly* 231:38 Mr 20 '87
Julia MacRae moves to Walker U.K. *Publ Wkly* 232:48 N 27 '87
Updated Beatrix Potter brews a storm in Britain. il *Publ Wkly* 232:26 O 30 '87

Taylor, Joan
Books. See issues of The Conservationist
Taylor, Joan Chatfield- See Chatfield-Taylor, Joan
Taylor, John, 1955-
'Down with M.B.A.'s!'. il *N Y* 20:34-7 N 2 '87
Gentleman's quarters: James Rogers' Beaux-Arts town-house in Manhattan. il *Archit Dig* 44:76-83 F '87
A matter of symmetry. il *Archit Dig* 44:182-90 S '87
Milestones: charting the stages in a child's emotional development. il *N Y* 20:34-9 N 23 '87
Romantic modernism: a New York apartment to refresh the senses. il *Archit Dig* 44:132-5 Ag '87
The shadow [cover story] il maps *N Y* 20:40-8 O 5 '87
Tranquilla: an Italianate palazzo on Biscayne Bay [cover story] il pors *Archit Dig* 44:148-55 Ap '87
The trouble with Harry's: behind the coup at Cipriani. il por *N Y* 20:62-7 O 19 '87
The Warner war: why Steve Ross and Herb Siegel can't get along [cover story] il pors *N Y* 20:34-42 Jl 13 '87
about
Between the lines. pors *N Y* 20:9 Jl 13 '87
Taylor, John M.
The prodigal son. il pors *Am Hist Illus* 22:10-21 Mr '87
Taylor, John William Ransom
about
The gentlemen of Jane's. por *World Press Rev* 34:28-30 O '87
Taylor, Judy, 1932-
about
Brightening up Beatrix. K. O. Fakih. il pors *Publ Wkly* 232:25-6 S 25 '87
Taylor, Keith B.
Doctor's notes [discussion of May 1987 article, What's shaped like a bean and acts like a screen?] por *50 Plus* 27:6 Ag '87
This gland is your gland. il *50 Plus* 27:64-7 S '87
What older Americans need to know about A.I.D.S. *50 Plus* 27:45-50 N '87
What's shaped like a bean and acts like a screen? il *50 Plus* 27:80+ My '87
Taylor, Lawrence
about
Invincible? No, just real mean. J. Lieber. il por *Sports Illus* 66:36-8+ Ja 26 '87
NFL MVP Taylor reveals trap of drugs caught him. por *Jet* 72:51 Ap 6 '87
Taylor, Lawrence, and Falkner, David
LT: living on the edge [excerpt; cover story] il pors *Sport Mag* 78:68-72+ S '87
Taylor, Liba
Children-power in Mexico. il *World Health* p24-5 Ja/F '87
Taylor, Mark C., 1945-
Descartes, Nietzsche and the search for the unsayable. il *N Y Times Book Rev* 92:3+ F 1 '87
Taylor, Markland
Pioneer Valley: a creative legacy. il *Horizon* 30:45-8 N '87
Taylor, Michael
about
In the light of the Bay. L. H. Bucklin. il por *House Gard* 159:124-33+ S '87
Taylor, Nick
Heart to heart: can a chimp transplant save human life? il *N Y* 20:44-8 Jl 13 '87
The sins of the father: a mobster's past shadows his sons' football stardom. il *N Y* 20:42-4+ Ja 26 '87
Taylor, Paul
How David Salle mixes high art and trash. il por *N Y Times Mag* p26-9+ Ja 11 '87
Taylor, Paul
Popular technology beats schisto. il *World Health* p28-9 Jl '87
Taylor, Paul, 1930-
about
Kith and kin [dance] Reviews
N Y il 20:100 My 18 '87. T. Tobias
Paul Taylor, pace maker: those who can, do. E. Zimmer. il *Dance Mag* 61:36-40 S '87
Sunset [dance] Reviews
New Yorker 63:75 Jl 6 '87. A. Croce
zygy [dance] Reviews
N Y 20:77 My 11 '87. T. Tobias
lor and York to show a decade's collaboration. S. iter. por *Dance Mag* 61:6 Ap '87
r-made design. S. Flatow. il *Theatre Crafts* 21:24-5+ 87

Taylor, Paul D.
Expanding freedom: a formula for growth in the Americas. il *Dep State Bull* 87:79-84 F '87
Taylor, Peggy Ann
Harlem hospitality. il *Essence* 18:18+ O '87
Taylor, Philip Andrew, 1984-
about
The child custody murder. P. Maas. il pors *Good Housekeep* 205:154-5+ O '87
Legacy of a mother's murder. P. Maas. il pors *N Y Times Mag* p40-4+ Ap 12 '87
Winning back a child. P. Maas. il por *N Y Times Mag* p42+ Je 7 '87
Taylor, Richard, 1919-
A fulfillment. il *N Y Times Mag* p62 Mr 29 '87
Taylor, Susan L.
Essence. *Writer* 100:22 My '87
In the spirit. See issues of Essence
Taylor, Theodore B.
Third-generation nuclear weapons. bibl (p128) il *Sci Am* 256:30-9 Ap '87
about
About face [interview] D. Sheff. il por *Roll Stone* p59+ S 24 '87
Taylor, W. Thomas
Claire Van Vliet's Janus Press. il por *Am Craft* 47:52-9+ F/Mr '87
The Iowa Center for the Book. il *Am Craft* 47:26-33 Je/Jl '87
Taylor twins See Siamese twins
TCA (Terminal control areas) See Air traffic control
TCAS (Traffic alert and collision avoidance systems) See Airplanes—Collision avoidance systems
Tchernia, André
The Madrague de Giens wreck. il *Courier* 40:11 N '87
Tchudi, Stephen N., 1942-
Hidden agendas in writing across the curriculum. *Educ Dig* 52:33-5 Ap '87
TCOM Systems, Inc.
In dubious battle. J. Novack. il *Forbes* 139:72 My 18 '87
Tea (Beverage)
See also
Teas
The perfect pot of tea. T. Foley. il *Work Woman* 12:143 S '87
The pleasures of herbal tea. S. Rose. il *Work Woman* 12:160 Ap '87
Tea. J. Robinson. il *Gourmet* 47:118+ N '87
Twining's ten tips for tea lovers. il *People Wkly* 28:78 S 7 '87
Winter day antidote: a perfect cup of coffee or tea. il *Glamour* 85:58 F '87
Tea cake See Cake
Tea houses
A Russian teahouse: memories of St. Petersburg in Germany [built in Russia and moved to Kronberg over a century ago] J. Rykwert. il *Archit Dig* 44:164-7 Je '87
Tea industry
Export-import trade
International tea party [Argentina's tea exporters] P. Gupte. il *Forbes* 140:108+ N 16 '87
Argentina
International tea party [Argentina's tea exporters] P. Gupte. il *Forbes* 140:108+ N 16 '87
Great Britain
See also
R. Twining & Co. Ltd.
Tea pots See Teapots
Tea services, Miniature
Children's tea sets. K. M. McClinton. il *Antiques Collect Hobbies* 92:18-21 Jl '87
Tea sets, Miniature See Tea services, Miniature
Tea tables See Tables
Teacher accountability See Accountability (Education)
Teacher education See Teachers—Education
Teacher of the Year award See Teachers—Awards
Teacher opinion See Teachers—Attitudes
Teacher participation in school management See School management and organization—Teacher participation
Teacher-pupil relationship See Teachers and students
Teacher Recognition Week
Trickle-down recognition. R. W. Cole, Jr. *Phi Delta Kappan* 68:650 My '87
Teacher shortage See Teachers—Supply and demand
Teacher supervision See School supervision and supervisors
Teachers
See also
Academic freedom
Art teachers

Teachers—See also—*cont.*
    Artists as teachers
    Arts teachers
    Black teachers
    Collective bargaining—Teachers
    Collective labor agreements—Teachers
    College teachers
    Dance teachers
    Educators
    Exercise teachers
    Latin teachers
    Medical teachers
    Music teachers
    National Education Association of the United States
    School and the home
    School management and organization—Teacher participation
    Science teachers
    Scientists as teachers
    Strikes—Teachers
    Substitute teachers
    Teaching
    Theater teachers
    Trade unions—Teachers
America's future teaching force: predictions and recommendations [survey of high school seniors] R. E. Kemper and J. N. Mangieri. bibl f *Phi Delta Kappan* 68:393-5 Ja '87
A complaint and a prediction [teachers as focus of school reform efforts] C. M. Breinin. il *Phi Delta Kappan* 69:15-16 S '87
How a male teacher sees early childhood education. W. Ayers. *Educ Dig* 52:27-9 Ap '87
How working with women has made my life better [lone male teacher] H. S. Karlitz. il por *Work Woman* 12:100-1+ Jl '87
Learning from the giants. G. F. Will. il *Newsweek* 110:96 S 14 '87
Men and child care: the plot thickens [child molesting accusations] S. Miller. il por *Ms* 16:54-6 O '87
On teaching [special section; with editorial comment by Robert W. Cole, Jr.] il *Phi Delta Kappan* 68:570, 585-618 Ap '87
Restructuring teaching: a call for research. M. H. Futrell. *Educ Dig* 53:2-5 S '87
Teacher "professionalization" versus democratic control. L. Darling-Hammond. *Educ Dig* 53:15-17 S '87
Teachers are writing the ABCs of school reform. J. Tasini. il *Bus Week* p74-5 S 7 '87
Teachers' hours, bankers' hours? [research by Brad Chissom] G. W. Bracey. il *Phi Delta Kappan* 69:73-4 S '87
Understanding what it means to be a teacher [observing in a public elementary school] D. L. Duke. *Educ Dig* 52:20-3 Mr '87
Unlocking school reform: uncertainty as a condition of professionalism. C. D. Glickman. bibl f il *Phi Delta Kappan* 69:120-2 O '87
When teaching excellence does not pay off. V. McCormick. *Educ Dig* 52:14-15 F '87

Anecdotes, facetiae, satire, etc.
Raising chair awareness. A. McCarroll. il *Saturday Evening Post* 259:22 S '87

Assignments
See Teaching assignments

Attitudes
Experienced teachers share their insights. S. Lynn. *Educ Dig* 52:16-17 F '87
Public or independent schools: does where you teach make a difference? [results of survey] P. Kane. il *Phi Delta Kappan* 69:286-9 D '87
Teacher survey. J. W. Merline. il *Consum Res Mag* 70:38 Ag '87
What teachers think about their evaluations. R. R. Turner. *Educ Dig* 52:40-3 F '87
Why do teachers choose rural schools? W. A. Matthes and R. V. Carlson. *Educ Dig* 52:27-9 F '87

Awards
1987 Teacher of the Year [D. Oliver] M. S. Miller. il por *Good Housekeep* 204:144+ My '87
Five teachers who breathe life into our national charter ['Constitution in the Classroom' Bicentennial Awards'] E. Dzik. il *Sch Update* 120:24-5 S 4 '87
Introducing: "Teacher of the Year" Donna Oliver. il pors *Ebony* 43:148+ N '87

Certification
Alternative certification and urban schools. M. Haberman. *Educ Dig* 52:22-5 Ja '87
Geologists and lawyers needn't apply [question of teacher certification for professionals] L. Solórzano. il *U S News World Rep* 103:58 Jl 27 '87

Retooling teachers: the New York experience [replenishing supply of science and math teachers] B. S. Cooper. il *Phi Delta Kappan* 68:606-9 Ap '87
Staffing methods that threaten the teaching profession. R. A. Roth. *Educ Dig* 52:18-21 Ja '87
Teacher testing [special section] bibl f il *Phi Delta Kappan* 69:31-52 S '87

Crime
Ex-teacher in D.C. gets 52-155 yrs. for sex abuse [J. B. Crawford] *Jet* 72:36 Jl 27 '87

Dismissal
AIDS tests for teachers [teacher V. Chalk fights to regain position in Orange County, Calif.] J. N. Baker. por *Newsweek* 110:81 O 19 '87
Black TB victim in Fla. wins fight for her job [G. Arline case decided by Supreme Court] *Jet* 72:39 Mr 30 '87
Kentucky teacher hits The wall with Pink Floyd [J. Fowler fights dismissal for showing R-rated movie] T. J. Flygare. il *Phi Delta Kappan* 69:237-8 N '87
A teacher pushes migrants' kids into college—and gets fired by his California school board [case of G. Shirley at Alisal High in East Salinas] M. Green. il pors *People Wkly* 27:50+ F 2 '87

Education
See also
    Field work (Teacher training)
    Student teachers
Able students going into teaching: AACTE. il *Phi Delta Kappan* 68:636 Ap '87
Alternative programs are a workable option for teacher training. *Phi Delta Kappan* 68:715-16 My '87
Higher education: innovator or inhibitor? [arts education; special issue] bibl f *Des Arts Educ* 88:2-40 Ja/F '87
Lessons for teacher education from corporate practice. W. R. Houston. bibl f il *Phi Delta Kappan* 68:388-92 Ja '87
An overview of the Holmes Group. L. Olson. *Phi Delta Kappan* 68:619-21 Ap '87
Reflective teachers [research by Terry Wildman and Jerome Niles] G. W. Bracey. il *Phi Delta Kappan* 69:233-4 N '87
Strengths and weaknesses of the Holmes Group report. J. Pietig. *Educ Dig* 52:32-5 Mr '87
Teacher education and the liberal arts. E. F. Travers and S. R. Sacks. *Educ Dig* 53:9-11 D '87
Too bright to be a teacher? P. Woodring. il *Phi Delta Kappan* 68:617-18 Ap '87

Education in service
Changing teaching practices: what school-college collaboration is all about. B. DeMott. *Change* 19:36 S/O '87
Increasing teachers' understanding of mathematical ideas through inservice training. T. L. Good and D. A. Grouws. bibl f il *Phi Delta Kappan* 68:778-83 Je '87
A reform strategy for education: employer-sponsored teacher internships. G. G. Gold. il *Phi Delta Kappan* 68:384-7 Ja '87
Retooling teachers: the New York experience [replenishing supply of science and math teachers] B. S. Cooper. il *Phi Delta Kappan* 68:606-9 Ap '87
Teaching teachers about testing: another mismatch? G. W. Bracey. il *Phi Delta Kappan* 68:546-7 Mr '87

Evaluation
See Teachers—Rating

Examinations
Teacher testing [special section] bibl f il *Phi Delta Kappan* 69:31-52 S '87
Teachers fail Georgia test [competency testing] A. Press. il *Newsweek* 110:65 S 7 '87

Professional ethics
Teachers and immoral conduct. J. M. Rich. *Educ Dig* 52:6-8 Mr '87

Psychology
Fighting teacher isolation. J. B. Davis. *Educ Dig* 52:27-9 My '87
How teachers can cope with greater demands. E. Hallowell. *Educ Dig* 52:20-3 Ap '87

Qualifications
See also
    Teachers—Certification

Rating
See also
    School supervision and supervisors
    Teachers—Certification
    Teachers—Examinations
Assessment for teaching: an initiative for the profession [Teacher Assessment Project] L. S. Shulman. il *Phi Delta Kappan* 69:38-44 S '87
Critical attributes of teacher evaluation systems. D. T. Conley. *Educ Dig* 53:32-5 O '87

Teachers—Rating—*cont.*

How valid are principals' judgments of teacher effectiveness? D. M. Medley and H. Coker. bibl f il *Phi Delta Kappan* 69:138-40 O '87

Teacher evaluation: more than a game that principals play. A. B. Pigford. il *Phi Delta Kappan* 69:141-2 O '87

Teacher evaluations need to be custom made. *Phi Delta Kappan* 68:408-9 Ja '87

Testing students may raise legal issues for reformers [St. Louis lawsuit over evaluating teachers partly on the basis of how their students perform on competency tests] *Phi Delta Kappan* 68:481-3 F '87

What teachers think about their evaluations [results of poll] R. R. Turner. *Educ Dig* 52:40-3 F '87

Recertification

See Teachers—Certification

Recruiting

Researcher urges ROTC-style programs to recruit teachers. il *Phi Delta Kappan* 68:559-61 Mr '87

Resignation

Career makeover: high school teacher to high-tech sales [F. Monteleon, computer components distributer] il por *Glamour* 85:156 Mr '87

Salaries, pensions, etc.

See also

Teachers Insurance and Annuity Association

Am I a loser if I don't earn big bucks? B. Patrick. il *Glamour* 85:222 D '87

I teach for love—I'm too smart to be in it for the money. R. M. Olmsted. il *Glamour* 85:50 S '87

Model portfolio [teacher Jo Anne Rosenbaum's malpractice settlement] R. McNatt. il *Money* 16:223-4 Ap '87

A proposed incentive system for Jefferson County teachers [bonus point system] P. C. Schlechty and D. W. Ingwerson. il *Phi Delta Kappan* 68:585-90 Ap '87

Raises, reform and respect. J. N. Baker. il *Newsweek* 110:92 O 5 '87

Selection and appointment

Effective teacher selection. A. E. Wise and others. *Educ Dig* 53:14-18 N '87

Statistics

Teachers work long hours for low pay: Center for Statistics [survey] *Phi Delta Kappan* 68:408 Ja '87

Supply and demand

Controversial report says teacher supply keeping pace with demand [study by Emily Feistritzer] *Phi Delta Kappan* 68:479+ F '87

Higher entry standards and higher pay may help ease teacher shortage. *Phi Delta Kappan* 68:557-8 Mr '87

Prospective teachers: career choices. il *Change* 19:31-4 Mr/Ap '87

There is no shortage of teachers, Labor Department researcher contends. *Phi Delta Kappan* 68:558 Mr '87

Teachers, Part time

See also

College teachers, Part time

Teachers and students

See also

Classroom management

College teachers and students

Child abuse and neglect: prevention and reporting. B. J. Meddin and A. L. Rosen. *Educ Dig* 52:52-5 Ja '87

In praise of teachers. M. H. Medoff. pors *Read Dig* 130:69-73 F '87

The loving penance of Hu Bo [caring for former teacher after Cultural Revolution; condensed from After the nightmare] H. Liang and J. Shapiro. il *Read Dig* 130:104-9 Ap '87

One man's kids. D. Meier. il *N Y Times Mag* p56 N 1 '87

Professor Honda [high school teacher uses his motorcycle to relate to students] M. Miller. il *Cycle* 38:20 N '87

Student exams: accentuating the positive [communication between teachers and students] M. McMullen-Pastrick and M. G. Weimer. *Educ Dig* 52:14-17 My '87

Talk about teachers! J. Barth. il *Read Dig* 130:61-6 Mr '87

That special teacher. J. F. Bond. il *South Living* 22:128 F '87

A touching story [children's need for physical reassurance from teachers] P. Chance. il *Psychol Today* 21:14 My '87

When good intentions aren't enough [culture conflict between student and teacher] S. S. Wineburg. il *Phi Delta Kappan* 68:544-5 Mr '87

Teachers in television

The TV teacher trivia test. E. J. Nowicki. il *Phi Delta Kappan* 69:69-70 S '87

Teachers Insurance and Annuity Association

Clifton R. Wharton Jr.: the nation's highest-paid black executive. il pors *Ebony* 42:29-30+ S '87

Wharton to head fund. P. A. Jones. por *Black Enterp* 17:16 Ja '87

Teachers' unions *See* Trade unions—Teachers

Teaching

See also

Academic freedom

Class size

Classroom management

Education

Indoctrination

Remedial teaching

School discipline

Teachers

See also subhead Study and teaching under various subjects

Does "What works" work in the classroom? [criticism of Dept. of Education publication] A. Franza. *Educ Dig* 52:10-13 F '87

Slow down, you move too fast [wait time by teachers to allow students to answer questions; research by Kenneth Tobin] G. W. Bracey. *Phi Delta Kappan* 69:234 N '87

Teacher-centered instruction versus education reform. L. Cuban. *Educ Dig* 52:2-5 F '87

When research does not help teachers. M. Myers. *Educ Dig* 52:14-17 Ja '87

Aids and devices

See also

Audio-visual instruction

Computers—Educational use

Educational technology

Motion pictures in education

Tape recordings—Educational use

Television in education

Videodiscs—Educational use

Videotapes—Educational use

History

See Education—History

Teaching assignments

Staffing methods that threaten the teaching profession. R. A. Roth. *Educ Dig* 52:18-21 Ja '87

Teaching machines

See also

Computers—Educational use

Programmed instruction revisited. B. F. Skinner. *Educ Dig* 52:12-16 Mr '87

Teaching office of the Catholic Church *See* Catholic Church—Teaching office

Teachman Gerner, Goody

Growing pains. il por *Macleans* 100:36-7 S 7 '87

Teachout, Terry

Justice to John P. Marquand. *Commentary* 84:54-9 O '87

Pornography [discussion of August 1987 article, The pornography report that never was] *Commentary* 84:14-15+ N '87

The pornography report that never was. *Commentary* 84:51-7 Ag '87

Salinger then and now. *Commentary* 84:61-4 S '87

Teague, Bill

Focus on photography books. il por *Publ Wkly* 232:50-2 Jl 31 '87

Teak

Handily done [Manhattan apartment designed by Mark Simon] C. Vogel. il *N Y Times Mag* p59-61 F 8 '87

Teale, Edwin Way, 1899-1980

Children of the sun [excerpts from Grassroot jungles] il *Audubon* 89:63-71 Jl '87

Team learning *See* Group work in education

Team work in industry

Dear Betty Harragan [misuse of term "teamwork"] B. L. Harragan. il *Work Woman* 12:44+ Ap '87

Detroit vs. the UAW: at odds over teamwork. A. Bernstein and W. Zellner. il *Bus Week* p54-5 Ag 24 '87

GM's bootstrap battle: the factory-floor view [E. Schaefer brings team management to Van Nuys plant] A. Gabor. il por *U S News World Rep* 103:52-3 S 21 '87

Motivating the teams on your staff. G. Bakoulis. *Work Woman* 12:23+ D '87

Should we move to Milpitas? [Decision Pad software] E. Dyson. il *Forbes* 140:102 Ag 10 '87

Software catches the team spirit [groupware] L. S. Richman. il *Fortune* 115:125+ Je 8 '87

Team work in industry—*cont.*
Steelmakers want to make teamwork an institution. A. Bernstein and M. Rothman. il *Bus Week* p84 My 11 '87

Teamsters for a Democratic Union
Why not try union democracy? J. Connolly. il *Nation* 245:192-4+ S 5 '87

Teamsters Union *See* International Brotherhood of Teamsters, Chauffeurs, Warehousemen and Helpers of America

Teapots
Ceramic teapots, pitchers recalled [Dutch pottery] il *FDA Consum* 21:6 S '87

Collectors and collecting
Eighteenth-century teapots. F. Archambault. bibl il *Antiques Collect Hobbies* 91:27-9 Ja '87

Tearaway [film] *See* Motion picture reviews—Single works

Tears
See also
Crying

Teas
See also
Tea (Beverage)
Afternoon tea. il *Gourmet* 47:76-8+ Mr '87
Afternoon tea in New York. A. R. Gochman. il *Gourmet* 47:92-7+ N '87
Fuel for thought [excerpt from Having tea] T. Foley. il *Work Woman* 12:142-3+ S '87
Spécialités de la maison: Citrus, "three for tea" [Los Angeles] C. Bates. il *Gourmet* 47:42+ D '87

Tease (Musical group)
Levert and Tease sell the sizzle. C. Rogers and M. Moore. il *Essence* 17:24 F '87

Teatro Colón (Buenos Aires, Argentina) *See* Opera houses
Teatro dell'Opera (Rome, Italy) *See* Opera—Italy
Teatro Lirico Nacional La Zarzuela *See* Opera—Spain
Teatro Regio di Torino *See* Opera—Italy

Tech-Sym Corp.
The deals ahead in defense. G. G. Marcial. *Bus Week* p122 Mr 16 '87

Téchiné, André
about
Rendez-vous [film] Reviews
Nation 244:154-6 F 7 '87. T. Rafferty
Scene of the crime [film] Reviews
Macleans il 100:53 Ap 20 '87
N Y il 20:56-7 F 2 '87. D. Denby
Nation 244:154-6 F 7 '87. T. Rafferty

Technical assistance
See also
United Nations Development Programme

Technical assistance, American
Developing countries
The electronic Peace Corps. D. H. Rothman. *Natl Rev* 39:43-4 Mr 27 '87
Guyana
The last brickmaker in America [G. Black] C. Kuralt. il *Read Dig* 130:53-6 My '87
Latin America
See also
Alliance for Progress

Technical assistance, Dutch
Bangladesh
They stopped the sea [dam construction] H. van Duivendijk. il *Natl Geogr* 172:92-101 Jl '87

Technical education *See* Vocational-technical education
Technical literature
Translations into English
Japanese scientific and technological literature information: the demand in the U.S. remains low. M. Sun. il *Science* 238:1032-3 N 20 '87

Technical Support Services Inc.
"I was an incredibly wild child" [president T. McLaughlin] B. Leonard. il por *Forbes* 140:56-7 Ag 24 '87

Technical writing *See* Scientific literature—Authorship
Technicians, Electronic *See* Electronic technicians
Technigen Platinum Corporation
A strange way to run a company. D. Francis. il *Macleans* 100:11 S 28 '87

Technique (Art) *See* Painting—Technique
Technological change *See* Technological innovations
Technological forecasting
2001: electronics in the next century [cover story; special section; with editorial comment by Brian C. Fenton] il *Radio-Electron* 58:4, 79-119 My '87
The next computer revolution [cover story; special issue] bibl (p183-4) il *Sci Am* 257:56-64+ O '87
When robots rule the world [views of Carl Hewitt and George Williams] G. Fjermedal. il *Omni* 10:24 N '87

Technological innovations
See also
Agricultural innovations
Computers
Technology transfer
Applied research: key to innovation. A. M. Clogston. bibl f *Science* 235:12-13 Ja 2 '87
How to keep mature industries innovative [cover story] C. F. Sabel and others. il *Technol Rev* 90:26-35 Ap '87
Innovation vs. invention [interview with R. E. Gomory] W. J. Cook. por *U S News World Rep* 103:55 D 14 '87
Making brawn work with brains. O. Port. il *Bus Week* p56-8+ Ap 20 '87
Now Sloan's MBAs will be masters of technology [Sloan School of Management's new dean, L. Thurow] L. Helm. il por *Bus Week* p64 Ap 13 '87
Scientific innovations. il *Bus Week* p126-7 Ja 12 '87
Speeding new ideas to market. B. Uttal. il *Fortune* 115:62-4+ Mr 2 '87
Star tech. See issues of Omni (New York, N.Y.) beginning October 1986
Summer reading. L. G. Boundas. il *Stereo Rev* 52:4 Jl '87
The technical enterprise [views of Herbert I. Fusfeld] *Futurist* 21:41-2 Ja/F '87
Technology [address, September 9, 1987] H. L. Adams. *Vital Speeches Day* 54:83-5 N 15 '87
Trying to transcend copycat science [Japan] G. Bylinsky. il *Fortune* 115:42-4+ Mr 30 '87

Technological research *See* Industrial research
Technological unemployment *See* Unemployment
Technology
See also
Art and technology
Educational technology
Engineering
Inventions
Medical technology
Nanotechnology
Space technology
Science & technology. G. Bronson. See issues of Forbes beginning March 10, 1986
Star tech. P. Hoban. See issues of New York beginning September 24, 1984
Technology update. See issues of Popular Mechanics
Awards
See also
National Medal of Technology
Economic aspects
Can advanced technology save the U.S. steel industry? J. Szekely. il *Sci Am* 257:34-41 Jl '87
A century of struggle [trade unions and technology] bibl f il *Mon Labor Rev* 110:41-7 Ag '87
Commerce sees the future; says industry practices must change. M. Crawford. *Science* 237:20 Jl 3 '87
High-tech workers: do unions have a future? S. Early and R. Wilson. *Current* 292:24-31 My '87
Hope or hyperbole? High tech and economic development. E. J. Malecki. il *Technol Rev* 90:44-51 O '87
Lyrics of loss, theories of gain [Nobel Prize awarded to R. Solow for economics] P. Gray; P. Elmer-DeWitt. il pors *Time* 130:80 N 2 '87
New technologies good for employment [report by the National Academy of Sciences] C. Holden. *Science* 236:1622 Je 26 '87
Nobel Prize for theory of economic growth [theories of R. M. Solow] E. Marshall. il por *Science* 238:754-5 N 6 '87
R&D and productivity: measurement issues and econometric results. Z. Griliches. bibl f il *Science* 237:31-5 Jl 3 '87
The rise of techno-nationalism. R. B. Reich. il *Atlantic* 259:62-9 My '87
Successful worker training programs help ease impact of technology. S. Deutsch. bibl f *Mon Labor Rev* 110:14-20 N '87
Technological change. *Mon Labor Rev* 110:2 Jl '87
Technological change and employment: some results from BLS research. J. A. Mark. il *Mon Labor Rev* 110:26-9 Ap '87
Technology. See issues of Fortune beginning March 5, 1984
Technology and global industry. P. H. Abelson. *Science* 236:1609 Je 26 '87
Technology and the wealth of nations. J. R. Opel. *Society* 24:51-4 S/O '87
Technology in services. J. B. Quinn and others. il *Sci Am* 257:50-8 D '87

Technology—Economic aspects—*cont.*

Technology: songs the sirens sing. G. Bronson. il *Forbes* 140:234+ Jl 13 '87

A weakness in process technology. L. C. Thurow. bibl f *Science* 238:1659-63 D 18 '87

History

See also

Industrial revolution

50 and 100 years ago. See issues of Scientific American

Information services

See also

United States. National Technical Information Service

International aspects

See also

United Nations. Intergovernmental Committee on Science and Technology for Development

Academy panel blasts U.S. export controls [report by the National Academy of Sciences and the National Academy of Engineering] C. Norman. il *Science* 235:424-5 Ja 23 '87

The aerospace challenge. D. E. Fink. *Aviat Week Space Technol* 126:53 Je 15 '87

The anti-space act of 1986 [restricting access to NASA tech briefs] J. Rhea. il *Space World* X-7-283:3 Jl '87

Balancing US-Japan technology flow [discussion of February 1987 article, Equalizing US-Japan technology flow] W. C. Norris. *Phys Today* 40 pt1:11+ Ag '87

The ban that boomeranged [export of American technology to Soviet Union] T. H. Naylor. *Nation* 245:755-6 D 19 '87

The battle over Toshiba [U.S.-Japan trade relations strained by Toshiba's sale of high tech goods to Soviets] J. B. Copeland. il *Newsweek* 110:40 Jl 13 '87

Beware of machines in disguise [conspiracy behind Toshiba's sales to the Soviets] S. Koepp. il *Time* 130:53 S 21 '87

Bright lights, big MITI [Toshiba's sale of top-security technology to the Soviets] C. Chandler. *New Repub* 197:11-13 Ag 31 '87

The case of the not-so-simple machine tools [Toshiba's sale of top-secret technology to the Soviet Union] M. I. Goldman. il *Technol Rev* 90:20+ O '87

CoCom tightening high technology export controls. *Aviat Week Space Technol* 127:33 Ag 3 '87

Coming: the big chill? [restrictions on unclassified data; cover story] J. Raloff. il *Sci News* 131:314-17 My 16 '87

Congress readies trade bill to ease export controls [Trade and International Policy Reform Act of 1987] M. Mecham. il *Aviat Week Space Technol* 126:315-16+ Je 15 '87

Congress wants Toshiba's blood [diversion of high tech to Russia provokes U.S. punitive measures] S. J. Dryden. *Bus Week* p46-7 Jl 6 '87

Death of a data directive [automated databases] R. Chalk. il *Technol Rev* 90:13-14 Jl '87

Defense, Commerce Departments clash again over export controls. *Aviat Week Space Technol* 126:28-9 F 16 '87

Easing the high-tech sales ban: U.S. firms can now sell oil equipment to Moscow. J. B. Copeland. il *Newsweek* 109:38 Ja 26 '87

Equalizing US-Japan technology flow. W. C. Norris. *Phys Today* 40:168 F '87

Export controls and research results. *Sci News* 132:73 Ag 1 '87

Export controls of high-technology goods. P. H. Abelson. *Science* 235:1297 Mr 13 '87

Export controls: the political winds are shifting. *Bus Week* p31 F 16 '87

Forbidden facts. P. Bagne. il *Omni* 9:18+ F '87

France expels Soviets for spying on Ariane. D. Dickson. *Science* 236:142 Ap 10 '87

High-tech shopping Moscow style. il *U S News World Rep* 103:12 N 2 '87

High-tech treachery [arrest of Ivan Batinic and others for attempting to sell supercomputer technology to the Soviets] *Newsweek* 110:56 N 2 '87

High technology export controls [White House announcement, March 18, 1987] *Dep State Bull* 87:56 Je '87

Hobbling high-tech [report of panel of the National Academy of Sciences and the National Academy of Engineering] *Sci Am* 256:58 Mr '87

How Japan picks America's brains. J. Dreyfuss. il *Fortune* 116:79-80+ D 21 '87

How Toshiba is beating American sanctions [furor over illegal sale to Moscow dies down] S. J. Dryden. il *Bus Week* p58 S 14 '87

An illegal deal's noisy repercussions [Soviet deal with Toshiba and Kongsberg for milling machines to make submarine propellers] W. J. Cook. il *U S News World Rep* 102:42 Je 15 '87

In rough waters, White House cancels controls on databases. I. Goodwin. *Phys Today* 40:66 My '87

Japan's bow of contrition [apologizing for Toshiba scandal] J. B. Copeland. il *Newsweek* 110:44 Jl 27 '87

A leak that could sink the U.S. lead in submarines [illegal sales to Soviet Union by Norway's KV and Japan's Toshiba] J. Kapstein. il *Bus Week* p65-6 My 18 '87

Making amends [Toshiba products banned in U.S. following sale of submarine technology to Soviets] *Time* 130:49 Jl 13 '87

Making deals that won't give technology away. R. Neff. il *Bus Week* p62-3 Ap 20 '87

Making waves: Poindexter sails into scientific databases. I. Goodwin. por *Phys Today* 40:51-2 Ja '87

National security and the semiconductor industry. D. G. Dallmeyer. il *Technol Rev* 90:46-52+ N/D '87

NATO armaments programs hinge on technology transfer benefits. M. A. Dornheim. il *Aviat Week Space Technol* 126:220-2+ Je 15 '87

NSC and Ocean Drilling [Soviet participation] J. A. Knauss. *Environment* 29:2-3 Jl/Ag '87

Panel would reform U.S. export controls [study by the National Academy of Sciences] J. Raloff. *Sci News* 131:55 Ja 24 '87

Punish Toshiba? W. F. Buckley. *Natl Rev* 39:62-3 D 18 '87

Report on scientific and technological activities [message to Congress, June 17, 1987] R. Reagan. *Dep State Bull* 87:61-2 S '87

Report suggests further easing of controls on exports to China. *Aviat Week Space Technol* 127:28 Jl 13 '87

The rise of techno-nationalism. R. B. Reich. il *Atlantic* 259:62-9 My '87

Run silent, run to Moscow [sale of submarine technology to the Soviets by Toshiba and Kongsberg] G. Bock. il *Time* 129:45 Je 29 '87

Sanctions [U.S. actions against Toshiba for high tech sale to Soviets] L. G. Boundas. il *Stereo Rev* 52:8 N '87

Science and technology exchanges with the Soviet Union [statement, June 25, 1987] J. Negroponte. *Dep State Bull* 87:58-61 S '87

Science and technology policies and priorities: a comparative analysis. L. L. Lederman. bibl f il *Science* 237:1125-33 S 4 '87

Science panel urges lead export role for Commerce [study by National Academy of Sciences] P. Mann. *Aviat Week Space Technol* 126:20 Ja 19 '87

Shoot-out at tech gap [feud over export controls] S. Koepp. il *Time* 130:50-1 O 12 '87

Soviet industrial espionage. P. Hanson. bibl f il *Bull At Sci* 43:25-9 Ap '87

Soviet-ODP partnership on or off? [Ocean Drilling Program] S. Weisburd. *Sci News* 131:280 My 2 '87

Soviets disinvited to join Drilling Program [objections by the Dept. of Defense] C. Norman. il *Science* 236:659-60 My 8 '87

Strains in U.S.-Japan exchanges. M. Sun. il *Science* 237:476-8 Jl 31 '87

Strategic technology export controls [White House statement, September 18, 1987] *Dep State Bull* 87:33 N '87

Such good friends: an old alliance under pressure [U.S. anger at Norway over illegal high tech sale to the Soviets] P. Sherrid. il *U S News World Rep* 103:42 O 5 '87

Tackling Toshiba [U.S. reaction to high tech sale to Soviets] J. McLaughlin. *Natl Rev* 39:24 Ag 14 '87

Taking the cuffs off exports to the East bloc [rules on high tech] S. J. Dryden. il *Bus Week* p48-9 Je 1 '87

Tapping new secrets [government initiatives to control database information] M. McIver. il *Macleans* 100:60-1 S 28 '87

The technobandits [U.S. export controls] N. R. Gibbs. il *Time* 130:42-4 N 30 '87

Technology and the wealth of nations. J. R. Opel. *Society* 24:51-4 S/O '87

Tora! Tora! Angry lawmakers torpedo Toshiba [U.S. seeks to punish company for illegal trade with Soviets] *U S News World Rep* 103:42 Jl 13 '87

Toshiba ban spurs review of technology export controls [U.S. reaction to Japan's high tech sale to Soviets] *Aviat Week Space Technol* 127:27 Jl 6 '87

Technology—International aspects—*cont.*

The Toshiba scandal: anatomy of a betrayal [illegal sales to Soviet Union] R. K. Bennett. *Read Dig* 131:95-100 D '87

The Toshiba scandal has exporters running for cover [technology sale to Soviets] L. Armstrong and N. Gross. il *Bus Week* p86-7 Jl 20 '87

Toshiba vs. the U.S.: a Japanese view. *World Press Rev* 34:18 Ag '87

Tracking a technobandit [C. J. McVey captured for illegal sales of computer equipment to the Soviet Union] D. Pauly. il por *Newsweek* 110:66 D 7 '87

Tussle over high technology [major study attacks U.S. export restrictions] J. Castro. il *Time* 129:48 Ja 26 '87

Welcome to Moscow on the Ginza [sale of submarine technology to the Soviets by Toshiba and Kongsberg] R. N. Perle. il *U S News World Rep* 102:31-2 Je 29 '87

What is federal policy on scientific communication? D. R. Corson. *Phys Today* 40:144 Ja '87

Moral aspects
See Technology and ethics

Political aspects
See Technology and state

Securities
See also
Alliance Technology Fund

Hard times may be over for the high techs. G. G. Marcial. il *Bus Week* p120 My 18 '87

High tech: big returns from small stocks [interview with R. Coons] J. Mendes. il por *Fortune* 116:128 S 28 '87

How H&Q picks the Apples of tomorrow [Hambrecht & Quist] G. G. Marcial. il *Bus Week* p76 Ap 20 '87

Picking small high-tech winners [views of W. H. Duncan] G. G. Marcial. *Bus Week* p72 Ap 6 '87

A surprising boom in high-tech stocks. P. Dworkin. il *U S News World Rep* 102:54 Je 1 '87

Technology takes off. J. Edgerton and others. il *Money* 16:7-8 F '87

Social aspects
The case for a cheap dog [folly of putting your trust in things] C. Gordon. por *Macleans* 100:39 Je 15 '87

Future technology [address, June 4, 1987] T. Logsdan. *Vital Speeches Day* 53:716-22 S 15 '87

The great transformation. E. S. Cornish. il *Futurist* 21:2 Mr/Ap '87

Return technology to human hands. J. Manley. il *Bull At Sci* 43:7-8 D '87

The year the warning lights flashed on [technological disasters] T. Ferris. il *Life* 10:67-8+ Ja '87

Anecdotes, facetiae, satire, etc.
Hey you! Make way for my technology! [rudeness and consumer technology] D. Lyon. il *Technol Rev* 90:28-9 Ag/S '87

Study and teaching
See also
Stevens Institute of Technology

Reading, 'riting, 'rithmetic—and now tech ed. M. Bluestone. il *Bus Week* p114+ O 19 '87

Teaching to overcome technophobia. P. Shipman. *Educ Dig* 52:18-19 Ap '87

Technology education: its status and opportunities. K. N. Starkweather. *Educ Dig* 52:36-9 Mr '87

Canada
The future now [cover story; special section; with editorial comment by K. Doyle] il *Macleans* 100:2, 34-43 Ap 20 '87

China
High-tech expansion in China. il *Futurist* 21:51 My/Je '87

Modernizing science and technology in China. D. F. Simon. bibl f *Curr Hist* 86:249-52+ S '87

Report suggests further easing of controls on exports to China. *Aviat Week Space Technol* 127:28 Jl 13 '87

Developing countries
See also
United Nations. High Level Committee on the Review of Technical Co-operation among Developing Countries
United Nations. Intergovernmental Committee on Science and Technology for Development

Man and machine. T. Land. *New Leader* 69:4 D 29 '86

Eastern Europe
Nudging the East into high technology. M. Dau. *World Press Rev* 34:51 Je '87

Japan
Balancing US-Japan technology flow [discussion of February 1987 article, Equalizing US-Japan technology flow] W. C. Norris. *Phys Today* 40 pt1:11+ Ag '87

Equalizing US-Japan technology flow. W. C. Norris. *Phys Today* 40:168 F '87

How Japan picks America's brains. J. Dreyfuss. il *Fortune* 116:79-80+ D 21 '87

Japanese scientific and technological literature information: the demand in the U.S. remains low. M. Sun. il *Science* 238:1032-3 N 20 '87

Strains in U.S.-Japan exchanges. M. Sun. il *Science* 237:476-8 Jl 31 '87

Trying to transcend copycat science. G. Bylinsky. il *Fortune* 115:42-4+ Mr 30 '87

Soviet Union
Soviet industrial espionage. P. Hanson. bibl f il *Bull At Sci* 43:25-9 Ap '87

Soviets pin economic hopes on technology. M. Crawford. *Science* 238:1644 D 18 '87

United States
See Technology

Western Europe
Europe still fails the challenge. G. de Jonquieres. por *World Press Rev* 34:46-7 My '87

Technology and art *See* Art and technology

Technology and civilization
See also
Computers and civilization

Conscious technology: uniting the technocrat and the mystic. J. C. Glenn. *Futurist* 21:60 My/Je '87

Does improved technology mean progress? L. Marx. il *Technol Rev* 90:32-41+ Ja '87

A good technologist is a noble work. S. C. Florman. il *Technol Rev* 90:16 Ja '87

Anecdotes, facetiae, satire, etc.
The good old days [technology taking over household appliances] L. W. Strick. il *Good Housekeep* 205:82+ Ag '87

Technology and education *See* Educational technology

Technology and ethics
Are scholarship and technology compatible? [address, May 10, 1986] J. W. Robb. *Vital Speeches Day* 53:220-2 Ja 15 '87

Bibliography
The ethics of science & technology studies. C. Mitcham. il *Commonweal* 114:202-3 Ap 10 '87

Technology and society *See* Technology—Social aspects

Technology and state
Managing technology. P. H. Abelson. *Science* 235:265 Ja 16 '87

Needed: a consistent, long-term policy governing technology. R. J. Kuntz. por *Aviat Week Space Technol* 126:155-6+ Ap 27 '87

The rise of techno-nationalism. R. B. Reich. il *Atlantic* 259:62-9 My '87

Who will protect us from our protectors? P. W. Huber. il *Forbes* 140:56+ Jl 13 '87

The year of living competitively. D. Grossman. il *Technol Rev* 90:16 N/D '87

Canada
Learning to compete [address, April 23, 1987] D. R. Peterson. *Vital Speeches Day* 53:528-31 Je 15 '87

Great Britain
See also
Greater London Enterprise Board

Japan
What all of America's Japan-bashing can't change. L. Armstrong. *Bus Week* p63 Ag 31 '87

Soviet Union
Science and technology. L. R. Graham. *Nation* 244:804-8 Je 13 '87

Western Europe
See also
Eureka (Program)

Technology review
Forecasting the headlines. J. I. Mattill. il *Technol Rev* 90:4 O '87

A tribute to our sponsors. J. I. Mattill. il *Technol Rev* 90:4 Jl '87

Technology transfer
See also
Products, New
Refac Technology Development Corp.
Technology—International aspects

Cosmic tech. C. P. Weinstock. il *Omni* 9:32+ My '87

Defense Dept. releases report on SDI spinoffs. *Aviat Week Space Technol* 126:35 My 11 '87

President's message. B. Bova. il *Space World* X-8-284 Space Advocate:8 Ag '87

Technology transfer—*cont.*

Running shoes make a leap into the space age [Dynacoil shoes by Kangaroo designed by space suit developer A. L. Gross] K. Dreyfack. il por *Bus Week* p70 Ja 19 '87

SDIO offers unclassified spinoff program [database describing technology developed under SDI sponsorship] *Aviat Week Space Technol* 127:84 N 23 '87

Technology for sale. *Sci Am* 256:62 My '87

Technology transfer is the issue in space cooperation. M. M. Waldrop. *Science* 236:1430 Je 12 '87

Wealth from space: a rebuttal [discussion of August 1987 article, President's message] B. Bova. il *Space World* X-11-287:40 N '87

Technostress *See* Stress

Teck Corp.

An ambitious venture in Alaska. P. C. Newman. il por *Macleans* 100:34 Ag 24 '87

Critical mass . . . and momentum. J. Cook. il *Forbes* 140:68+ N 2 '87

Tectonics *See* Geology

Tecumseh (Neb.)

Description

ABC's Amerika raised hackles, but the citizens of Tecumseh, Nebraska got a unique thrill. il *People Wkly* 27:34-7 F 23 '87

Tecumseh Club

The Tecumseh Club. D. P. Moynihan. il *N Y* 20:96 D 21-28 '87

Ted Bates Worldwide, Inc.

See also

Backer Spielvogel Bates Worldwide

Bare knuckles on Madison Avenue [Saatchi & Saatchi takeover of Ted Bates] A. Kleiner. il por *N Y Times Mag* p34-9+ N 8 '87

Teddy & Alice [musical] *See* Musicals, revues, etc.—Reviews—Single works

Teddy bears

Anecdotes, facetiae, satire, etc.

Last word [Teddy Rescue, the hostage negotiator talking bear] M. Wilkins. il *Omni* 9:134 Je '87

Teele, Arthur E., Jr.

about

NBL's Teele launches bid to become Miami's mayor. por *Jet* 72:28 Ag 10 '87

'Teen (Periodical)

Great Model Search 1987: meet the finalists. il *Teen* 31:30-1 Jl '87

Great Model Search '87 [special section] il pors *Teen* 31:82-91 O '87

Sewin' off with show-off style [winners of Sew 'N Show contest] il *Teen* 31:70 Ja '87

Teenage birth control *See* Birth control

Teenage birth control clinics *See* Birth control clinics

Teenage business *See* Youth and business

Teenage curfew *See* Curfew

Teenage drinking *See* Alcohol and youth

Teenage drivers *See* Automobile drivers

Teenage employment *See* Youth—Employment

Teenage fathers, Unmarried *See* Single fathers

Teenage friendship *See* Friendship

Teenage literature *See* Young adults' literature

Teenage models (Persons) *See* Models (Persons)

Teenage obesity *See* Obesity

Teenage parties *See* Entertaining

Teenage pregnancy

Abortion law complications [parental notification argument before the Supreme Court] *Christ Today* 31:47+ D 11 '87

"Am I old enough to be a parent?" [single father; ed. by Kate Manning. M. Gallagher. il por *Redbook* 169:34+ My '87

At last—it's a boy! [couple witnesses birth of child they hope to adopt] M. Grant. il *Life* 10:28-34 Je '87

Can states restrict a minor's access to abortion? [upcoming Supreme Court decision] *Christ Today* 31:44+ Ap 3 '87

Caring for children [special section] bibl f *Society* 24:5-52 Mr/Ap '87

The case for separate schools for pregnant teenagers. J. Buie. *Educ Dig* 53:50-2 D '87

Fort Worth, Texas: a high school that helps teenage mothers shape new lives [New Lives Center] L. Chandler. il *Sch Update* 119:24 Mr 23 '87

How to prevent teenage pregnancy [excerpt from Families in peril] M. W. Edelman. il pors *Ebony* 42:60+ Jl '87

In San Francisco, teacher Robert Valverde fights teen pregnancy with flour power. D. Gorgan. il por *People Wkly* 27:34-5 Ap 27 '87

Is teenage pregnancy epidemic a myth? [views of Maris A. Vinovskis] il *USA Today (Periodical)* 116:3-4 Ag '87

Kids and contraceptives. B. Kantrowitz. il *Newsweek* 109:54-8+ F 16 '87

Mom, I want to have the baby. M. C. Funk. il por *Ladies Home J* 104:22+ N '87

My teenage daughter was pregnant. il *Good Housekeep* 204:24+ Mr '87

Numbers versus principles: moral realism and teen-age pregnancies. J. R. Kelly. *America* 156:130-6 F 14 '87

Parents also have rights. R. Gunnerson. por *Newsweek* 109:10-11 Mr 2 '87

Pregnant teens: no easy answers. M. Barbera-Hogan. il *Teen* 31:28+ F '87

Religious groups denied federal funds to prevent teen pregnancy. P. P. Wong. *Christ Today* 31:41-2 Jl 10 '87

Return of the shotgun wedding? [study by P. Lindsay Chase-Lansdale and Maris A. Vinovskis] P. Chance. il *Psychol Today* 21:14 S '87

Routes to self-sufficiency: teenage mothers and employment. D. F. Polit. bibl f il *Child Today* 16:6-11 Ja/F '87

Rubber trees and valentines [Catholic reaction to National Research Council's report, Risking the future: adolescent sexuality, pregnancy and childbearing] *America* 156:1-2 Ja 3-10 '87

Saying no [chastity in sex education] H. Smith. il *Christ Today* 31:12-13 F 6 '87

Social agenda [National Research Council report] *Sci Am* 256:85-6 F '87

Study reveals why 'shotgun weddings' last longer. il *Jet* 72:12-13 Je 1 '87

Taking on teen pregnancy. A. Levine. il *U S News World Rep* 102:67-8 Mr 23 '87

Teen fathers: the other side of the story. M. Barbera-Hogan. *Teen* 31:32+ Jl '87

Teen pregnancy: an issue for schools [cover story; with editorial comment by Robert W. Cole] A. M. Kenney. bibl f il *Phi Delta Kappan* 68:722, 728-36 Je '87

Teen pregnancy: it's time for the schools to tackle the problem [cover story] J. Buie. il *Phi Delta Kappan* 68:737-9 Je '87

A teenage mother's battle to raise her child and pay the bills [Marielle Nelson] M. Maran. il *Sch Update* 119:6 Mr 23 '87

Teenage pregnancy. M. C. McClellan. il *Phi Delta Kappan* 68:789-92 Je '87

Teenage pregnancy: the crisis in America [special section; with introd. by Lindsy Van Gelder and Pam Brandt] il *McCalls* 114:83-6+ My '87

Teenagers and abortion [parental consent] B. Kantrowitz. *Newsweek* 110:81 O 12 '87

Teens back birth control clinics, Reagan against it. *Jet* 71:28 Ja 19 '87

Three generations of love [Foster Grandparents work in child care center for teenage parents in Detroit, Mich.] N. Walls. il *Aging* no355:2-5 '87

Young and pregnant. J. P. Comer. il *Parents* 62:196 Mr '87

Teenage prostitution *See* Prostitution

Teenage reading *See* Young adults' reading

Teenage sex *See* Youth—Sexual behavior

Teenage smoking *See* Smoking and youth

Teenage suicide *See* Suicide

Teenage suicide in literature *See* Suicide in literature

Teenage unemployment *See* Unemployment

Teenage volunteers *See* Volunteer service

Teenagers *See* Adolescence; Black youth; Young men; Young women; Youth

Teenagers and parents *See* Parent-child relationship

Teenagers' group homes *See* Group homes for children

Teeth

See also

Dentistry

Dentists

Gums

Abnormalities

See also

Malocclusion

Animals

Michel Jutras doesn't win any trophies for cleaning hippo teeth, but he does get plenty of plaque. il por *People Wkly* 27:123 Je 15 '87

Care and hygiene

See also

Indians of North America—Dental care

Toothbrushes

Toothpastes, powders, etc.

Teeth—Care and hygiene—*cont.*
The battle in your mouth. L. S. Senz. il *Saturday Evening Post* 259:22-3+ Mr '87
Dental alert: how pregnancy affects your teeth and gums. D. Burden. *Work Woman* 12:140 O '87
Getting a grip on gum damage [proper grip on toothbrush] il *Prevention* 39:12 D '87
Michel Jutras doesn't win any trophies for cleaning hippo teeth, but he does get plenty of plaque. il por *People Wkly* 27:123 Je 15 '87
Mighty mouth [food and oral hygiene] S. Baker. il *Health* 19:55-6 Ja '87
Open wide! D. Edmondson. il *Parents* 62:112-16+ Mr '87
The painless way to healthy teeth. L. Washer. *Work Woman* 12:152 Ap '87
Smile, America: a special dental health-care section. il *McCalls* 114:107-8+ F '87
Super solutions for tooth decay. D. Born. il *Saturday Evening Post* 259:16+ Ja/F '87
Terrific teeth. il *Teen* 31:92-3 N '87
Terrific teeth. R. Lewis. il *Health* 19:74-9 Je '87
Word of mouth. il *Seventeen* 46:160 Mr '87
Your brightest, whitest smile: the newest ways to get it. il *Glamour* 85:302-5 Mr '87

Diseases
See also
Dental caries

Wounds and injuries
Tooth or consequences: what to do in a dental emergency. D. Born. il *Saturday Evening Post* 259:26-7 Ap '87
When having fun ends with broken teeth. B. M. Campbell. *Essence* 18:99 Je '87

Teeth, Artificial *See* Dentures
Teeth, Fossil
An age-old question: why did the human lineage survive? P. Shipman. il *Discover* 8:60-4 Ap '87
Debate over emergence of human tooth pattern. R. Lewin. il *Science* 235:748-50 F 13 '87
Early ancestors less human-like [work of B. Holly Smith] *USA Today (Periodical)* 115:11 Je '87
Hominid growth slows to an ape's pace [work of B. Holly Smith] B. Bower. *Sci News* 131:255 Ap 18 '87
Hominid headway [use of tomography to study Taung skull] B. Bower. *Sci News* 132:408-9 D 19-26 '87
Telltale teeth [prehistoric Indians] C. G. Turner, II. maps *Nat Hist* 96:6+ Ja '87

Teets, John W.
about
Can Greyhound leave the dog days behind? S. Toy. il por *Bus Week* p72+ Je 8 '87

Tefera
about
An angel from Tennessee. J. L. McCoy. il pors *McCalls* 114:132-4 Je '87

Tefft, Sheila, and others
Why the U.S. is trying harder to make friends with India. il *Bus Week* p61 Ja 12 '87

Tegucigalpa (Honduras)
Description
Tegucigalpa: a taste of colonial times. A. Fernández. il *Américas* 39:38-43 N/D '87

Teheran (Iran) *See* Tehran (Iran)
Tehran (Iran)
See also
Iranian seizure of United States embassy, 1979-1981
Description
The 'apex of civilization'. V. Pellizzari. il *World Press Rev* 34:54 D '87

Teich, Mark
Good, clean fun? il *Health* 19:67-8+ D '87
The saga of a bad back. il *Health* 19:11-12+ O '87
Sugar squabble. il *Health* 19:53-4 O '87
(jt. auth) See Scofield, Michael, and Teich, Mark

Teich, Mark, and Dodeles, Giselle
Mind control. il *Omni* 10:53-60 O '87

Teicholz, Eric, and Sena, Michael
In facility management, there are opportunities and pitfalls for architects. il *Archit Rec* 175:23+ Ja '87

Tejada, Susan Mondshein
Staying afloat: subsistence fishery in the Philippines. il map *Oceans* 20:46-53 Ja/F '87

Tejada-Flores, Lito
Global flora: new research links alpine wildflowers around the world. il *Natl Parks* 61:26-9 S/O '87

Tekno, Inc.
Fabulous studio fantasies. D. Brooks. il *Petersens Photogr Mag* 15:42-4 Ap '87

Tektites
Tektites and lunar volcanoes. *Sky Telesc* 73:481 My '87

Telander, Rick
Another border war. il *Sports Illus* 67:24-9 O 19 '87
Boom and doom [cover story] il *Sports Illus* 67:20-5 N 30 '87
The 'Canes were very able [cover story] il *Sports Illus* 67:28-30+ O 12 '87
Chicago's weighty issue [cover story] il pors *Sports Illus* 67:28-32+ Ag 24 '87
C'mon, Tony, lighten up. il pors *Sports Illus* 67:58-60+ N 2 '87
A game worth playing: college football taught this ex-player lasting lessons. por *Sports Illus* 67:130 Ag 31 '87
Getting there the hard way. il *Sports Illus* 66:14-20 Ja 19 '87
Growing up fast. il pors *Sports Illus* 67:44-6+ N 16 '87
A high time for the Huskers. il *Sports Illus* 67:62-5 S 21 '87
Linebacker music. il pors *Sports Illus* 67 Sp Issue:64+ S 9 '87
Minny's mighty mite. il pors *Sports Illus* 66:46-9 Je 15 '87
Rootin' from the roofs. il *Sports Illus* 67:82-4 Jl 6 '87
Shamefully lily-white: NFL head-coach opening? Blacks need not apply. il por *Sports Illus* 66:80 F 23 '87
Shuffling off to hibernation. il *Sports Illus* 66:18-21 Ja 12 '87
Tough guy in the clutch. il pors *Sports Illus* 66:30-3 Ja 26 '87

Telang, G. M.
Compromising moves. il *World Press Rev* 34:16+ Ja '87

Tele-Communications, Inc.
Cable's biggest leaguer. B. Powell. il por *Newsweek* 109:40-1 Je 1 '87
The king of cable TV [J. Malone; cover story] M. Ivey. il por *Bus Week* p88-92+ O 26 '87
Make way for John Malone. H. Rudnitsky and E. F. Cone. il pors *Forbes* 139:124-6+ Ap 6 '87
Making deals shrewdly [B. Magness] il por *U S News World Rep* 103:56-7 Jl 6 '87
What a performance [sale of United Artists Communications to Tele-Communications and spinoff of Todd-AO] A. B. Block. il *Forbes* 139:136 Ap 6 '87

Telecom Plus International, Inc.
A shareholder revolt at Telecom. B. Dumaine. il por *Fortune* 115:58-60 Mr 2 '87

Telecommunication
See also
American Telephone & Telegraph Co.
Communications Satellite Corp.
Communications satellites
Compaq Telecommunications Corporation
Computer networks
Data transmission systems
Executone/Long Island, Inc.
Integrated services digital network
ITT Corporation
MCI Communications Corp.
Scrambling systems (Telecommunication)
Spread spectrum communications
Telecom Plus International, Inc.
Telecommuting
Teleconferencing
Telephone
Television broadcasting
UNC Inc.
Western Union Corporation
1988 field guide to the electronic environment [cover story] il *Channels* 7 Sp Issue:10-12+ D '87
Communications corner. H. Friedman. See issues of Radio-Electronics
Communications in 2001—the third age of video. C. N. Judice. il *Radio-Electron* 58:102-5 My '87
Interview [C. E. Shannon] A. Liversidge. il por *Omni* 9:60-2+ Ag '87

Acquisitions and mergers
Comsat is left in the lurch [Contel backs out of proposed merger] S. Payne. *Bus Week* p38-9 Ap 27 '87
The Drexel connection [potential partners in Western Union takeover offer scared off by Pacific Asset's dealings with Drexel] J. Crudele. *N Y* 20:24 Ap 20 '87
'You'll see alliances you won't believe'. F. Seghers. il *Bus Week* p99 D 7 '87

Telecommunication—Acquisitions and mergers—*cont.*
International aspects
More rabbits, please, Signor De Benedetti [Olivetti's linkup with AT&T] S. Solomon. por *Forbes* 139:114+ Mr 9 '87

Canada
A buyer for Teleglobe [Memotec Data Inc.] *Macleans* 100:38 F 23 '87
A giant charts its future [Bell Canada Enterprises buys stake in Memotec Data] B. Wallace. il *Macleans* 100:26-7 My 25 '87
The Memotec affair [insider trading scandal] B. Wallace. il *Macleans* 100:38 O 5 '87
Memotec's tangled roots [takeover of Teleglobe Canada] T. Fennell. il *Macleans* 100:42+ Mr 23 '87

Italy
A failed merger blows Italy's shot at the big time [Italtel and Telettra] W. C. Symonds. il *Bus Week* p52+ N 23 '87

Antitrust cases
George Shultz, wimp [role in ITT antitrust case] R. M. Goolrick. il *Wash Mon* 19:18-19 O '87

Export-import trade
Data General gets the call [deal with Japan's NTT] L. Helm and N. Gross. il *Bus Week* p96 O 19 '87

Finance
As the big get bigger, the small may disappear. J. J. Keller. il *Bus Week* p90 Ja 12 '87
Telecommunications. K. Healy. il *Forbes* 139:212-13 Ja 12 '87

International aspects
See also
World Administrative Radio Conference

Laws and regulations
See also
Telephone companies—Laws and regulations
United States. Federal Communications Commission
The telecommunications jungle. D. Caruso. il *Pers Comput* 11:89-90 Je '87

Security measures
The national guards. D. Goldberg. il *Omni* 9:44-6+ My '87

Social aspects
Telecommunications and computers: whither privacy policy? J. E. Katz. *Society* 25:81-6 N/D '87

Terminology
Meaning behind the buzzwords. *Channels* 7 Sp Issue:130-1 D '87

Canada
See also
Bell Canada Enterprises Inc.
Bell-Northern Research Ltd.
Canadian Radio-Television and Telecommunications Commission
Maritime Telegraph & Telephone Co., Ltd.
Memotec Data Inc.
Teleglobe Canada

France
See also
Compagnie Générale d'Électricité

Germany (West)
See also
Siemens AG

Great Britain
See also
British Telecom plc

Italy
See also
Italtel (Firm)
Telettra Telefonia Elettronica e Radio SpA

Japan
See also
Nippon Telegraph & Telephone Corporation

Sweden
See also
L.M. Ericsson Telephone Co.

Telecommunication in business
New directions in telecommunications. M. Harper. il *Nations Bus* 75:38-40 Ap '87
Seven business reasons to turn to telecommunications. T. Engstrom. il *Work Woman* 12:44+ Ag '87
Sprint's chance to gallop [contract to supply network services to GM] J. J. Keller. il *Bus Week* p33 Je 15 '87

Telecommunications and Finance Subcommittee *See* United States. Congress. House. Committee on Energy and Commerce. Subcommittee on Telecommunications and Finance

Telecommuting
Bringing the office home [telecommuter M. Crampton] R. Lockwood. il por *Pers Comput* 11:176-7 O '87

Close to home [telecommuting program for blacks in Watts] J. Koblenz. il *Black Enterp* 17:22 F '87
Three views of working at home. J. Schwartz. il *Pers Comput* 11:87-9+ F '87

Teleconferencing
Computer networking as a global-scale tool. P. Rossman. *Futurist* 21:10-11 Mr/Ap '87
Face-to-face or not to face [discussion of September 1986 article, College credits through telecommunication] P. Lemmons. il *Byte* 12:186-8+ F '87
The quiet revolution [electronic university] B. N. Meeks. *Byte* 12:183-4+ F '87
Rising above trade rivalry [BizNet teleconference on U.S.-Japanese trade] il *Nations Bus* 75:45-6 Ap '87
U.S./Soviet teleconference highlights Mars exploration program objectives. B. A. Smith. *Aviat Week Space Technol* 127:61+ Ag 3 '87

Teleconverter lenses *See* Lenses, Photographic

Telecredit, Inc.
What checkless society? K. K. Wiegner. il *Forbes* 140:8 S 21 '87

Teledyne, Inc.
The brilliant Dr. S. [H. Singleton] T. Jaffe. por *Forbes* 139:178 Mr 9 '87
New vehicles mark Teledyne Ryan's strong return to RPV business. B. A. Smith. il *Aviat Week Space Technol* 127:53+ N 30 '87
Teledyne Brown defines reusable spaceplane concept. *Aviat Week Space Technol* 127:141 Ag 10 '87
Teledyne Ryan will begin testing long-duration RPV this month. B. A. Smith. il *Aviat Week Space Technol* 127:117+ O 12 '87

Telefilm Canada
High drama behind the screen. A. Shortell. il *Macleans* 100:50+ O 26 '87
High drama in the world of film [dispute between Telefilm Canada and R. Lantos over adult soap series Mont Royal] B. Amiel. il *Macleans* 100:7 S 14 '87

Telegence Corporation
New use for your phone. A. A. Lappen. *Forbes* 139:132 F 23 '87

Teleglobe Canada
A buyer for Teleglobe [Memotec Data Inc.] *Macleans* 100:38 F 23 '87
The Memotec affair [insider trading scandal] B. Wallace. il *Macleans* 100:38 O 5 '87
Memotec's tangled roots [takeover of Teleglobe Canada] T. Fennell. il *Macleans* 100:42+ Mr 23 '87

Telegraph
See also
Military telegraph

Telegraphic Agency of the Soviet Union *See* TASS (Soviet Union)

Telemarketing *See* Telephone selling

Telemedia Inc.
Harrowsmith's leader cuts his roots [J. Lawrence sells out to Telemedia] A. Shortell. il por *Macleans* 100:30 Mr 30 '87

Telemetry, Biological *See* Biotelemetry

Telemundo Group Inc.
The new order at Blair. J. F. Berry. il por *Channels* 7:53-6 Ap '87
Saul Steinberg sees dollar signs in Hispanic TV. R. Grover. il *Bus Week* p34-5 Ja 19 '87
Steinberg may have trouble making money in Spanish. R. Barker. il *Bus Week* p29+ Ag 10 '87
Targeting the nation in its own tongue. D. Bollier. il *Channels* 7 Sp Issue:83 D '87

Teleosts
Nervous system
See Nervous system—Fish

Telepanel Inc.
Russian-dressing roulette. W. J. Hawkins. il *Pop Sci* 231:14 D '87

Telephone
See also
Cellular radio
Computerphones
Picturephones
Radiotelephone
Rural telephone service
Phone watch. See occasional issues of Business Week
Telephones get smart. J. Castro. il *Time* 129:50-1 Mr 30 '87
Telephones: what's next. H. Manley. il *Good Housekeep* 204:252 Ap '87

Anecdotes, facetiae, satire, etc.
Last laugh. il *Mother Earth News* 103:128 Ja/F '87

Telephone—*cont.*

Directories

See Telephone directories

Emergency use

Emergency aid that works—enhanced. P. Michelmore. il *Read Dig* 131:165-8 N '87

Equipment

See also

Telephone answering machines

Telephone equipment industry

A phone shaped like a Colt .45 has its critics up in arms. il por *People Wkly* 27:38 F 16 '87

Telephones. il *Consum Rep* 52:290-3 D '87

Voices from the past: kit built telephones have antique look and pushbutton electronics. il *Workbench* 43:70-1 Ja/F '87

Maintenance and repair

Can't anyone out there repair this phone? [getting the runaround from AT&T] B. Willis. por *U S News World Rep* 103:12 N 9 '87

Do you need phone-wire insurance? il *Consum Rep* 52:465 Ag '87

How to repair telephones. M. J. Schultz. il *Pop Mech* 164:99-102 O '87

Sanitation

A new way to cash in on 'dirty phone calls' [OliverShields] il *Newsweek* 110:55 N 30 '87

Government use

Hello? This is Uncle Sam. Where's my phone system? F. Seghers. il *Bus Week* p102 S 7 '87

Installation

TFH's no-nonsense guide to understanding phone installation. M. Thompson. il *Fam Handyman* 37:52+ Jl/Ag '87

Anecdotes, facetiae, satire, etc.

Ma Bell's revenge. E. Lax. il *N Y Times Mag* p2 Mr 15 '87

Long distance service

See also

Long Distance America Inc.

Are the feds hobbling AT&T's rivals? [FCC-ordered rate cut] F. Seghers. *Bus Week* p33-4 Ja 19 '87

AT&T is eating 'em alive. J. J. Keller. il *Bus Week* p28-9 F 16 '87

Dial up savings on long distance phone bill. H. Porter. *Fam Handyman* 37:8+ N '87

The long-distance wars get hotter. J. J. Keller. il *Bus Week* p150-4+ Mr 23 '87

More distance. R. Coorsh. *Consum Res Mag* 70:4 Mr '87

Phone rates: cheaper calls for the new year. il *Newsweek* 109:42 Ja 12 '87

Watch out for this dial-a-deal [flat rates] *Consum Rep* 52:75 F '87

Why the FCC wants to cap rates instead of profits [overhauling AT&T price regulations] F. Seghers. il *Bus Week* p88 Ag 17 '87

Private branch exchanges

See Telephone exchanges

Rates

Are the feds hobbling AT&T's rivals? [FCC-ordered rate cut] F. Seghers. *Bus Week* p33-4 Ja 19 '87

Dial up savings on long distance phone bill. H. Porter. *Fam Handyman* 37:8+ N '87

Facts on phones. M. S. Evans. *Consum Res Mag* 70:3 Ap '87

Hang on—phone rates are falling again. *Changing Times* 41:8 Mr '87

More distance. R. Coorsh. *Consum Res Mag* 70:4 Mr '87

Phone rates: cheaper calls for the new year. il *Newsweek* 109:42 Ja 12 '87

Telephone talk. A. Arnott. il *McCalls* 114:95-6 My '87

Watch out for this dial-a-deal [flat rates for long distance calls] *Consum Rep* 52:75 F '87

Why the FCC wants to cap rates instead of profits [overhauling AT&T price regulations] F. Seghers. il *Bus Week* p88 Ag 17 '87

Security measures

How the Soviets are bugging America. D. P. Moynihan. il map *Pop Mech* 164:102-5 Ap '87

Social aspects

The newest dating game [party lines] J. A. Seamonds. il *U S News World Rep* 102:80 Je 8 '87

Phone frictions: how to understand the pitfalls of sharing a phone with a man. B.-J. Raphael. *Glamour* 85:26 Mr '87

Romancing the phone. A. L. Ball. il *Mademoiselle* 93:132-3+ Je '87

Since he got Connie Powers' number, long-distance operator Scott Luczak is hearing a steady aisle tone. il pors *People Wkly* 27:57 Mr 30 '87

Switching systems

See Telephone switching systems, Electronic

Wiretapping

See Wiretapping

Telephone and children

Reach out and touch someone [limiting access of children to dial-a-porn] R. Lacayo. il *Time* 130:58 D 21 '87

Suing Ma Bell over dirty language [parents sue over child's access to dial-a-porn] *Newsweek* 110:47 D 7 '87

Telephone and youth

Teen telephone talk. il *Teen* 31:96 Ap '87

Telephone answering machines

Answering machines with new talents. R. Farmanfarmaian. il *Work Woman* 12:114 Je '87

The Complete Answering Machine. N. Baran. il *Byte* 12:100-1 D '87

Telephone books *See* Telephone directories

Telephone cables

See also

Cables, Submarine

Jeno Paulucci's dream: bring fiber optics home [residential phones for Heathrow, Fla.] S. Ticer. il por *Bus Week* p34-5 S 21 '87

Telephone calls

When a stranger calls: how to handle annoyance calls. J. B. Wyatt. il *Seventeen* 46:143 S '87

Rates

See Telephone—Rates

Telephone centers, nooks, etc.

Phone station. D. Watson. il *Fam Handyman* 37:60 F '87

Telephone companies

See also

ALC Communications Corporation

Alltel Corp.

American Telephone & Telegraph Co.

Bell Atlantic Corp.

Contel Corp.

GTE Corp.

Long Distance America Inc.

MCI Communications Corp.

New York Telephone Co.

Nynex Corporation

Pacific Bell

Southern Bell Telephone & Telegraph Co.

US Sprint Communications Inc.

As the big get bigger, the small may disappear. J. J. Keller. il *Bus Week* p90 Ja 12 '87

The long-distance wars get hotter. J. J. Keller. il *Bus Week* p150-4+ Mr 23 '87

Telecommunications. K. Healy. il *Forbes* 139:212-13 Ja 12 '87

Accounting

A telephonic Tower of Babel. J. Andresky. il *Forbes* 139:92 Ap 6 '87

Acquisitions and mergers

Can GTE keep foiling the raiders? J. R. Norman. il por *Bus Week* p100-1 Ap 6 '87

Advertising

Telephone talk [AT&T's realism in TV advertising for small business phone systems] B. Kanner. il *N Y* 20:22+ Ap 27 '87

Antitrust cases

Info gridlock [U.S. lagging in videotex due to breakup of AT&T] *New Repub* 196:4 Ja 26 '87

Employees

See Telephone workers

Laws and regulations

Are the Baby Bells busting out all over? F. Seghers. il *Bus Week* p86 Jl 6 '87

Are the feds hobbling AT&T's rivals? F. Seghers. *Bus Week* p33-4 Ja 19 '87

Deregulating Europe's phones: the talk so far is just static. T. Peterson. il *Bus Week* p153 N 2 '87

Further freeing of the Bell Seven. *Fortune* 115:9 Mr 2 '87

More heat for Judge Greene [opinion blocks regional Bell holding companies from moving into equipment manufacturing and long-distance] il por *Fortune* 116:9+ O 12 '87

Sorry, wrong policy. H. Banks. *Forbes* 140:29 D 28 '87

Static on the line—the Baby Bells are calling. W. J. Cook. il *U S News World Rep* 102:60-1 Mr 30 '87

Securities

Hot wires [views of M. Gabelli] T. Jaffe. *Forbes* 140 Sp Issue:402 O 26 '87

Telephone companies—*cont.*

Suits and claims

How one guy beat the system [small claims suit brought by Bhaichand Patel against New York Telephone] *Consum Rep* 52:74 F '87

Canada

See also

Maritime Telegraph & Telephone Co., Ltd.

Great Britain

See also

British Telecom plc

Japan

See also

Nippon Telegraph & Telephone Corporation

Spain

See also

Compania Telefonica Nacional de Espana SA

Western Europe

Deregulating Europe's phones: the talk so far is just static. T. Peterson. il *Bus Week* p153 N 2 '87

Telephone crimes

See also

Cellular radio crimes

Telephone—Security measures

The Blue Box and Ma Bell. H. Friedman. il *Radio-Electron* 58:49-52+ N '87

Confessions of a heat merchant [bucket shop investment scams] W. G. Flanagan. il *Forbes* 140:190+ S 21 '87

Côte de Fraud [boiler room scam operators in Orange County, Calif.] M. Beauchamp. il *Forbes* 140:32-3 N 2 '87

Dial-a-dupe on Con Man's Coast [boiler room phone scams in Orange County, Calif.] P. Cary. il *U S News World Rep* 103:62-3 D 21 '87

Poison lures at the end of the line [investment fraud] J. Rachlin. il *U S News World Rep* 103:47 Jl 20 '87

Telefraud: they've got your number [boiler room investment scams] il *Consum Rep* 52:289-93 My '87

Wrong number! [boiler room scams] P. Glastris. *Read Dig* 130:161-4 Je '87

Telephone dialing systems

See also

Dual-tone multifrequency signalling

High tech [VocaLink, voice-activated dialing for cellular phones] D. Sweeney. il *Car Driv* 32:38 Je '87

Hotline: dialing for speed. S. R. Reed. *Pers Comput* 11:236 Je '87

Two phones that dial by voice [Voice Dialer 1000 and Command Dialer II] il *Consum Rep* 52:406 Jl '87

Telephone directories

Invasion of the yellow pages. J. Castro. il *Time* 130:52 O 5 '87

Telephone employees *See* Telephone workers

Telephone equipment industry

Acquisitions and mergers

International aspects

Plessey's new face in the U.S. [Stromberg-Carlson purchase in 1982] J. J. Keller. il *Bus Week* p32 Ap 20 '87

The Swedes give AT&T, and the U.S., painful black eyes [L. M. Ericsson captures piece of Compagnie Générale de Constructions Téléphoniques] T. Peterson and F. J. Comes. il *Bus Week* p44-5 My 4 '87

Canada

See also

Northern Telecom Ltd.

France

See also

Compagnie Générale de Constructions Téléphoniques

Sweden

See also

L.M. Ericsson Telephone Co.

Telephone exchanges

"Thank you for using Westinghouse" [private corporate networks] K. Healy. il *Forbes* 140:206+ N 30 '87

Telephone in astronomy

Telephone "hotlines". *Sky Telesc* 74 Sky Telesc Handb:21 S '87

Telephone in business

See also

Telephone selling

Voice mail systems

Mitchell rigs 'hot line' for black firm contracts. *Jet* 73:38 O 12 '87

"Thank you for using Westinghouse" [private corporate networks] K. Healy. il *Forbes* 140:206+ N 30 '87

When it comes to the phone, managers have a lot of hang-ups. W. Konrad. *Work Woman* 12:23 Je '87

Anecdotes, facetiae, satire, etc.

Giving good phone. S. Bing. il *Esquire* 107:68 My '87

Telephone in counseling

How useful are telephone consultation services for parents? [NYU Warmline] J. Samuels and L. Balter. bibl f il *Child Today* 16:27-30 My/Je '87

Telephone in gardening

Garden gate [Rodale's organic gardening hotline] S. O. Daniels. il *Rodale's Org Gard* 34:4-5 Jl '87

Telephone in medical care

22 top health hot lines [excerpt from Home medical handbook] J. I. Stern and D. Carroll. il *Good Housekeep* 204:217 Je '87

Crimes of the heart [Phone-In Program of Marvin Mordkoff] B. Prescott. il *Health* 19:23 S '87

The lone ranger of cancer care [P. McGrady] E. Kiester. il pors *50 Plus* 27:88-94 Ap '87

A 'PIP' of a heart program [Phone-In Program of Marvin Mordkoff] il *Prevention* 39:16 Ap '87

Take heart—the doctor's on call [heart monitored via telephone] il *Prevention* 39:10 N '87

Telephone in service to the aged

An AAA, Bell Tel and United Way set up 24-hour I & R system. *Aging* no355:30-1 '87

Putting their caring on the line [telephone support network for families caring for Alzheimer's patients] C. C. Goodman. il *Aging* no355:20-1 '87

A voice for the frail elderly [Coalition of Advocates for the Rights of the Infirm Elderly] J. Alwang. il *Aging* no355:10-13 '87

Telephone information service

See also

Toll-free telephone service

Dialing 1-900 for dollars. J. Schwartz. il *Newsweek* 109:40 Mr 23 '87

Anecdotes, facetiae, satire, etc.

La Bamba Hot Line. B. A. Mason. *New Yorker* 63:27 S 7 '87

Telephone lines

See also

Telephone cables

Photographs and photography

Those dreaded utility lines. A. Baget. il *Petersens Photogr Mag* 16:34-5 Ag '87

Telephone numbers

See also

Toll-free telephone service

TRafalgar 6 [New York City] J. Schwartz. il *N Y* 20:89 D 21-28 '87

Telephone pornography

Reach out and touch someone [limiting access of children to dial-a-porn] R. Lacayo. il *Time* 130:58 D 21 '87

Suing Ma Bell over dirty language [parents sue over child's access to dial-a-porn] *Newsweek* 110:47 D 7 '87

Telephone selling

"Hello, you have won a wonderful prize". il *McCalls* 114:74 Jl '87

How to say no (or yes) to your broker. J. Kosnett. il *Changing Times* 41:77-81 Mr '87

Many, many are called—by pro and rookie alike [calls by brokers] M. Schifrin. il *Forbes* 139:140-1 F 23 '87

Telephone switching systems, Electronic

See also

Telephone exchanges

Now that CGE is a heavyweight, it will have to fight like one [System 12 switch] T. Peterson and F. J. Comes. il por *Bus Week* p98+ My 18 '87

Telephone workers

Florida woman wins suit against Southern Bell, who must pay $3.5 million [M. A. Vance] *Jet* 72:29 My 4 '87

Training

Cooperative training in telecommunications: case studies [Communications Workers of America and American Telephone and Telegraph] M. Hilton and R. Straw. bibl f *Mon Labor Rev* 110:32-6 My '87

Telephoto lenses *See* Lenses, Photographic

Telepictures Corp.

See also

Lorimar-Telepictures Corporation

Telerate, Inc.

A whole new ballgame [P. Bavasi] E. F. Cone. il por *Forbes* 139:162 My 4 '87

Telescope guiding *See* Telescopes—Control

Telescope lenses *See* Lenses

Telescope mountings *See* Telescopes—Mounting

Telescopes

See also

Radio telescopes

Adler Planetarium introduces 20-inch telescope. il *Astronomy* 15:64-5 Ag '87

Telescopes—*cont.*

The art of planetary observing (I). D. C. Parker and T. A. Dobbins. il *Sky Telesc* 74:370-2 O '87

The art of planetary observing (II). D. C. Parker and T. A. Dobbins. il *Sky Telesc* 74:603-7 D '87

Astronomy's 1987 guide to telescopes [special section; with editorial comment by Richard Berry] il *Astronomy* 15:33, 46-53+ O '87

Breaking 'aperture fever'. W. Russell. *Astronomy* 15:26 O '87

Building fun telescopes for less than $10. R. Monaghan. il *Astronomy* 15:46-9 My '87

Building the most powerful telescope [Columbus Project] il *USA Today (Periodical)* 115:10-11 Je '87

Gleanings for ATM's. R. W. Sinnott. See issues of Sky and Telescope

How I built a real live telescope [Dobsonian] E. C. Doleman. il *Astronomy* 15:63-6 Ja '87

Kavalur's stellar hermitage [Vainu Bappu Observatory's 2.3-meter reflector in India] D. M. Salwi. il *Sky Telesc* 73:375-6 Ap '87

Meridian-circle astronomy. il *Sky Telesc* 74:245 S '87

Monster telescopes for the 1990's. L. J. Robinson. il *Sky Telesc* 73:495-6 My '87

A new generation of giant eyes gets ready to probe the universe [cover story] S. P. Maran. il *Smithsonian* 18:40-53 Je '87

Riverside Telescope Maker's Conference. R. Berry. il *Astronomy* 15:34-6 S '87

Spying on the stars. K. M. Miller. il *Esquire* 108:15+ Jl '87

Taking the measure of the stars [optical interferometry] D. E. Thomsen. *Sci News* 131:10-11 Ja 3 '87

A telescope worth every penny. K. Korczak. il *Astronomy* 15:28+ Je '87

The top 10 telescope ideas of 1987 [Stellafane, Riverside and the Texas Star Party] il *Sky Telesc* 74:590-4 D '87

Two new major observatories: Powell Observatory's 30-inch reflector. T. J. Martinez. il *Sky Telesc* 73:545 My '87

Control

The ATI "CAT": the wave of the future? [Computer Aided Telescope] D. J. Eicher. il *Astronomy* 15:66-71 D '87

Hassle-free astrophotography [precision sidereal-rate clock drive kit] R. Berry. il *Astronomy* 15:38-9 O '87

Observing with the CAT [Computer Aided Telescope] G. H. East. il *Sky Telesc* 74:484-6 N '87

Regulating the voltage of a DC motor [astrophotography; with comments by Roger W. Sinnott] A. Kremers. il *Sky Telesc* 74:198-201 Ag '87

Tracking comets with a stepping motor. E. Everhart. il por *Sky Telesc* 73:208-12 F '87

Equipment

Build a heated dew cap for less than $10. H. Hammond. il *Astronomy* 15:72-4 N '87

Crosshairs from spider web. R. W. Sinnott. il *Sky Telesc* 73:97 Ja '87

Filter reveals fascinating solar detail [T-Scanner, H-alpha solar filter system] D. Trombino. il *Astronomy* 15:46-7 D '87

Getting the picture in the infrared [infrared array detectors] D. E. Thomsen. il *Sci News* 131:295 My 9 '87

Imagery comes to infrared astronomy [infrared array detector] M. M. Waldrop. il *Science* 236:1525-6 Je 19 '87

A motorized observing chair. E. C. Larr. il *Sky Telesc* 74:665-7 D '87

A way to make big focusers. A. C. Heslop. il *Sky Telesc* 73:95-6 Ja '87

Anecdotes, facetiae, satire, etc.

First, find your spider [renovating old brass filar micrometer] S. D. Ringwood. il *Astronomy* 15:28+ Ja '87

History

Perfecting the modern reflector [work of J. B. L. Foucault] W. Tobin. il por *Sky Telesc* 74:358-9 O '87

Lenses

See Lenses

Maintenance and repair

Caring for optics. A. MacRobert. il *Sky Telesc* 73:380-1 Ap '87

The scientific and cultural heritage of Allegheny Observatory [restoration of Fitz/Clark 13-inch refractor] T. R. Jones. *Astronomy* 15:28+ Ap '87

The wandering stars of Allegheny [addition of Multichannel Astrometric Photometer to 30-inch Thaw refractor; cover story] R. W. Sinnott. il *Sky Telesc* 74:360-3 O '87

Mirrors

At the diffraction limit [use of speckle interferometry with the Multiple Mirror Telescope] il *Sky Telesc* 74:236 S '87

Big telescopes on a roll. D. E. Thomsen. il *Sci News* 132:170-1 S 12 '87

A digital Foucault tester [for telescope mirrors] F. L. Redburn. il *Sky Telesc* 73:439-42 Ap '87

The mirror maker [R. Angel] M. M. Waldrop. il pors *Discover* 8:78-84+ D '87

New telescope for old [Multiple Mirror Telescope] D. E. Thomsen. *Sci News* 131:40 Ja 17 '87

Notes on movable primary mirrors. R. Gebelein. il *Sky Telesc* 73:555 My '87

Progress and panic at Puimichel. L. Vanhoeck. il pors *Sky Telesc* 74:543-6 N '87

A quest for the perfect refractor. J. Gregory. il *Sky Telesc* 73:662-7 Je '87

Seeing a vampire in the mirror. P. Ceravolo. *Astronomy* 15:28 O '87

Spinning scopes [spin-cast telescope mirrors; work of R. Angel] A. Fisher. il pors *Pop Sci* 231:76-9+ O '87

Will future astronomers observe with liquid mirrors? P. H. Andersen. il *Phys Today* 40:23 Je '87

Mounting

Aquatic astronomy [floating telescope] T. Beardsley. il *Sci Am* 257:38-9 N '87

The E-M method of polar alignment [equatorial mounts] B. Gordon. *Sky Telesc* 73:454 Ap '87

How to "steady" a rooftop telescope. A. Wagner and P. J. Stiles. il *Sky Telesc* 74:314-16 S '87

Telescopes on airplanes *See* Airplanes in astronomy

Teleshopping *See* Electronic shopping

Telethons

See also

Comic Relief (Project)

I stayed up with Jerry [J. Lewis telethon] B. Barol. il pors *Newsweek* 110:66-8 S 21 '87

Lou Rawls heads Parade of stars on telethon to benefit black colleges. il pors *Jet* 73:24-5 D 28 '87-Ja 4 '88

Sammy Davis and Jerry Lewis star on telethon to fight muscular dystrophy [cover story] il pors *Jet* 72:60-1 S 7 '87

Telettra Telefonia Elettronica e Radio SpA

A failed merger blows Italy's shot at the big time [Italtel and Telettra] W. C. Symonds. il *Bus Week* p52+ N 23 '87

Televangelism *See* Television broadcasting—Religious programs

Television

See also

High definition television

Interactive video

Scrambling systems (Telecommunication)

United Nations and television

Video art

Transmitters and transmission

See Television transmission

Television, Cable *See* Cable television

Television, Stereoscopic

3-D maker [system invented by Li Chang] W. J. Hawkins. il *Pop Sci* 231:20 O '87

3-D TV comes home. J. B. Meigs. il *Pop Mech* 164:66-9+ Ag '87

Television actors and actresses *See* Television performers

Television adaptations

Anne of Green Gables grows up [cover story; special section; with editorial comment by Kevin Doyle] il pors *Macleans* 100:2, 46-8+ D 7 '87

Big books, small screen [miniseries based on books] L. See. il *Publ Wkly* 231:26-30+ Ap 3 '87

Rights. P. S. Nathan. See issues of Publishers Weekly

Tube power [miniseries based on books and their influence on bookstore sales] L. See. il *Publ Wkly* 231:49-50+ Je 12 '87

The year in rights. P. S. Nathan. *Publ Wkly* 231:42 Ja 9 '87

Television advertising

See also

Action for Children's Television

Advertising, Political

Advertising jingles

Animals in advertising

Automobile industry—Advertising

Books—Advertising

Brewing industry—Advertising

Brokers—Advertising

Computer industry—Advertising

Condoms—Advertising

Contraceptives—Advertising

Television advertising—See also—*cont.*
    Drug industry—Advertising
    Fast food restaurants—Advertising
    Insurance companies—Advertising
    Music in advertising
    Poultry industry—Advertising
    Pytka Productions
    Raisins—Advertising
    Sex in advertising
    Shoe industry—Advertising
    Soft drink industry—Advertising
    Telephone companies—Advertising
    Voiceovers (Advertising)
Advertising. il *Bus Week* p131 Ja 12 '87
Cosby ranks highest in TV ad 'believability,' too. *Jet* 71:28 Mr 9 '87
Lying with a smile on Madison Avenue. B. Lippert. il *U S News World Rep* 102:58 F 23 '87
The people's choice [Video Storyboard Tests] B. Kanner. il *N Y* 20:21-2 Ap 20 '87
They may seem driven, but pupils of commercial king Randy Kirby would settle for 30 seconds of work. K. Hubbard. il pors *People Wkly* 28:173-6 N 30 '87
To be or not to be commercial?—That is the question [public broadcasting] R. L. Fischer. *USA Today (Periodical)* 116:89-91 S '87
Cooperative advertising
Joint TV commercials: it's two, two, two ads in one. R. Grover. il *Bus Week* p27 Jl 6 '87
Costs
Is less really more? C. Marshall. il *Forbes* 140:196 N 2 '87
Where the money goes. A. B. Block. il *Forbes* 140:178+ S 21 '87
Costume
The shopper [designer D. Zaccaro] B. Kanner. il por *N Y* 20:21-3 Je 22 '87
Sound effects
You can't (hum) ignore (hum) that ad. S. Siwolop. il *Bus Week* p56 S 21 '87
Time purchasing
    See also
    Single-source research (TV audience research)
Advertising dollars from abroad pouring into U.S. television. M. Schrage. il *Channels* 7:13 Jl/Ag '87
And now the Super Bowl lineup: Seiko, McDonald's, Pepsi . . . C. Dugas. il *Bus Week* p35 F 2 '87
The books go electronic. S. Behrens. il *Channels* 7:15 O '87
A finer grind from the ratings mill. S. Behrens. il *Channels* 7 Sp Issue:10-12+ D '87
Local TV's ad battles [special section] il *Channels* 7:45-8+ N '87
Low-rent late-night getting gentrified. W. Dana. il *Channels* 7:9 Mr '87
The networks' big headache [people meters] D. Lieberman. il *Bus Week* p26-8 Jl 6 '87
The networks' revenge: how high will it go? J. Mandese. il *Channels* 7 Sp Issue:39-40 D '87
New season blues? M. Brown. il *Channels* 7:22 Je '87
The oracles of Madison Avenue. J. Traub. il *Channels* 7:36-9 My '87
The ten-most-aired commercials of late '86. S. Behrens. il *Channels* 7:64 My '87
TV: the vanishing viewer. B. Powell. il *Newsweek* 109:60 My 18 '87
TV's bright picture. il *Fortune* 116:9 N 9 '87
Where the biggest brands spend their ad dollars. il *Channels* 7:72 Jl/Ag '87
Who's gypping whom in TV ads? [effect of people meter] B. Dumaine. il *Fortune* 116:78-9 Jl 6 '87
China
Guess what they watch in China on Sunday nights? [Y.-S. Kan's One world series] D. J. Yang. il por *Bus Week* p91 Ja 19 '87
France
BlueJean-Luc Godard. H. A. Rodchenko. il *Film Comment* 23:2+ N/D '87
Japan
Japanese yearnings. J. M. Fallows. il *Atlantic* 259:16-18 Je '87
Soviet Union
TV advertising Russian style. J. A. Trachtenberg. il *Forbes* 140:107-8 S 7 '87
Television and blacks *See* Blacks and television
Television and business *See* Business and television
Television and children
    See also
    Action for Children's Television
    Cable television—Children's programs
    Television broadcasting—Children's programs

Case of the missing kids [ratings down for animated shows] S. Behrens. il *Channels* 7:21 Jl/Ag '87
Helping children deal with the news. J. Segal and Z. Segal. il *Parents* 62:265 N '87
How on-screen violence hurts your kids. B. Spock. il *Redbook* 170:26+ N '87
Marie Winn and Penguin designate November 'No TV Month' [forthcoming publication of Unplugging the plug-in drug] *Publ Wkly* 231:49-50 Je 5 '87
Television viewing and homework [study by the National Assessment of Education Progress] il *Consum Res Mag* 70:36 Ag '87
This is what you thought: 88% say TV violence makes kids violent [results of survey] *Glamour* 85:89 F '87
TV & family life: do they mix? [results of survey] I. Groller. il *Parents* 62:32 My '87
TV cold turkey. J. Gaylin. il *Parents* 62:102-4 S '87
Ugly stuff for kids. E. Crow. il *Parents* 62:6 Ja '87
Violent family hour. *Society* 24:2 Ja/F '87
What TV does to kids. N. S. Schwartzberg. il *Parents* 62:100-4 Je '87
Television and copyright *See* Copyright—Broadcasting rights
Television and history
Mediawatch [British TV] H. David. il *Hist Today* 37:6-8 Jl '87
Mediawatch [British documentaries on the Jarrow Crusade and the Titanic] H. David. il *Hist Today* 37:4-5 Ja '87
Mediawatch [history on TV sells books in Great Britain] H. David. il *Hist Today* 37:8-9 O '87
Poland's 20th-century struggles [series The struggles for Poland; cover story] N. Ascherson. il *Hist Today* 37:44-9 Je '87
TV: show business or education? J. Yardley. *Des Arts Educ* 88:46-7 Jl/Ag '87
Television and literature
    See also
    Television adaptations
    Television and reading
Television and motion pictures *See* Motion pictures and television
Television and politics
    See also
    Advertising, Political
    Cable television and politics
    Presidential debates
    Television broadcasting—Election results
    Television broadcasting—Government use
    United Nations and television
ABC's Amerikan dream. H. F. Waters. il *Newsweek* 109:21-2 F 16 '87
Amerika: it can't happen here [ABC miniseries] A. Kopkind. *Nation* 244:165+ F 14 '87
Amerika the controversial. R. Zoglin. il *Time* 129:72-3 F 9 '87
Better red than dud [ABC's miniseries Amerika] N. Atkins. il *Roll Stone* p29-30 F 12 '87
Blabscam: TV's rigged political talk shows. C. Hitchens. *Harpers* 274:75-6 Mr '87
But will he, she or it play in Peoria? P. D. Zimmerman. il *U S News World Rep* 103:22 Jl 27 '87
A celluloid war of credibility [Platoon and Amerika] F. Bruning. por *Macleans* 100:7 Mr 16 '87
The culture of criticism. H. Sidey. il *Time* 129:30 Je 1 '87
The curse of sound bites [comparison of British and American coverage] T. Griffith. il *Time* 130:68 Jl 20 '87
Free time is not the answer. E. O. Fritts. por *U S News World Rep* 102:8 Je 1 '87
Gorbo talks. *Nation* 245:703-4 D 12 '87
The Hitler in ourselves [ABC's Amerika] W. F. Buckley. *Natl Rev* 39:62-3 Mr 27 '87
In the telly's eye: an American-style British campaign. R. Knight. il pors *U S News World Rep* 102:10-11 Je 15 '87
Its ugly head [charges that 60 minutes is out to "get" J. L. Jackson] A. Cockburn. *Nation* 245:8 Jl 4-11 '87
Loyal Amerikans [ABC's Amerika] *Natl Rev* 39:18 Mr 13 '87
Masters of babble [McLaughlin Group] L. Wainwright. il *Life* 10:26 D '87
The medium and its message: from Nixon and Kennedy to Beirut. il *U S News World Rep* 103:20-1 Jl 27 '87
The Mick Jaggers of journalism [overbearing TV network correspondents] H. Sidey. il *Time* 130:28 O 5 '87
The monster's spell. A. McCarthy. il *Commonweal* 114:616-17 N 6 '87

Television and politics—*cont.*

More professional, less human. T. Griffith. il *Time* 130:95 N 16 '87

A new miniseries imagines Amerika's future—if the Soviets won World War III. D. Scheuer. il *Sch Update* 119:23 Ja 26 '87

Newsman as predator [S. Donaldson] J. Alter. il pors *Newsweek* 109:58-9 Mr 2 '87

Of many things [S. Donaldson] G. W. Hunt. *America* 156:inside cover My 9 '87

Only in 'Amerika': the mini-series everyone loves to hate. P. Hoban. il *N Y* 20:36-41 Ja 26 '87

Pushiness we can respect [S. Donaldson] J. Powell. *Wash Mon* 19:55-6 F '87

Quick-fix news [MacNeil/Lehrer] R. K. Manoff. il *Progressive* 51:15 Jl '87

Remember, it's only a movie [ABC's Amerika] M. Bosc. il *U S News World Rep* 102:15 Ja 19 '87

The selling of the president in '88. P. Sellers. il *Fortune* 116:131-2+ D 21 '87

Situation Commie [ABC's Amerika] J. Maslin. *New Repub* 196:25-7 F 23 '87

A TV man views the storm [Amerika broadcast] V. G. Sauter. il *U S News World Rep* 102:68 F 16 '87

TV news as political kingmaker [race for the Democratic nomination] V. Kamber. por *U S News World Rep* 102:8 Je 15 '87

TV's week: of gab and *glasnost*. R. Zoglin. il por *Time* 130:67-8 D 14 '87

When worlds collide [interview with M. Gorbachev and presidential candidates' debate] J. Klein. il por *N Y* 20:35-6+ D 14 '87

Will bad Russians make good ratings? [Amerika] A. P. Sanoff. il *U S News World Rep* 102:66-7 F 16 '87

Anecdotes, facetiae, satire, etc.

Presidential illusions. R. Baker. *N Y Times Mag* p12 Jl 5 '87

What if TV had been there? Imagining how the framers might fare in the media age. W. Shapiro. il *Time* 130:62-3 Jl 6 '87

Great Britain

The curse of sound bites [comparison of British and American coverage] T. Griffith. il *Time* 130:68 Jl 20 '87

Politics American style. G. C. Lubenow. il *Newsweek* 109:41 Je 8 '87

Nicaragua

CBS News with Dan Rather [distortions on Nicaragua] W. F. Buckley. *Natl Rev* 39:54-5 Je 5 '87

Television and reading

1987 Reading rainbow selections. *Publ Wkly* 231:106 F 27 '87

Au flair [French TV's Apostrophes] J. Bernstein. *Am Sch* 56:167-70+ Spr '87

The Carson of the literary set [Apostrophes host B. Pivot] L. Zuckerman. il por *Time* 130:64 Jl 13 '87

Mediawatch [history on TV sells books in Great Britain] H. David. *Hist Today* 37:8-9 O '87

A nation of readers [influence of B. Pivot's Apostrophes on best seller list in France] B. Murphy. il *Atlantic* 260:21-5 Ag '87

Putting reading in its proper place. D. F. Martia. por *U S News World Rep* 102:6 F 9 '87

Television and the environment

A naturalist's guide to prime time [excerpt from The untamed garden and other personal essays] D. R. Wallace. *Harpers* 274:32-4 Ap '87

Television and youth

At Fox, the quarry is teenagers. W. A. Henry. il *Channels* 7:65 Jl/Ag '87

Couch potatoes need exercise [research by Larry Tucker] P. McCarthy. *Psychol Today* 21:13 Ag '87

Television & adolescents. J. P. Comer. il *Parents* 62:159 Jl '87

Television audiences

See also

Couch potatoes

Fox's new network goes after the baby boomers. R. Grover. *Bus Week* p41+ Ap 6 '87

How to win friends and influence TV [viewers lobbying networks] P. E. Bauer. il *Channels* 7:69 Ja '87

Tubeless wonders [nonviewers; study by Robert E. Lee Roberts] P. McCarthy. *Psychol Today* 21:11 D '87

TV: the vanishing viewer. B. Powell. il *Newsweek* 109:60 My 18 '87

Zapping the TV networks: channel flippers give today's programmers the willies. A. P. Sanoff. il *U S News World Rep* 102:56-7 Je 1 '87

Monitoring

See also

People meters (TV audience research)

Single-source research (TV audience research)

Television authorship

A case of bigamy [partnership of author and J. Falsey] J. Brand. il *N Y Times Mag* p100 My 17 '87

Dave's kids: the twisted minds behind the Letterman show. E. Pooley. il por *N Y* 20:36-45 Ja 19 '87

Dreaming up questions to choke on, The new Newlywed game writers never quit making whoopee. M. Dougherty. il *People Wkly* 28:44-6+ Ag 3 '87

In a shocker show, Cagney & Lacey tests limits with the most vicious racial slurs ever heard on TV [teleplay by S.-A. Williams] J. Hall. il por *People Wkly* 28:62-4 O 5 '87

Terry Louise Fisher: how she dreamed up the women of "L.A. law". M. Kort. por *Ms* 15:38-9+ Je '87

Television awards

See also

Emmy Awards

Golden Globe Awards

Peabody Awards

Television broadcasting

See also

American Broadcasting Companies, Inc.

Cats in television

CBS Inc.

Characters in television

Communications satellites—Television broadcasting use

Computers—Television broadcasting use

Dogs in television

Fox Broadcasting Company

National Broadcasting Co., Inc.

Realism in television

Swine in television

Television adaptations

Television program reviews

Television stations

Television transmission

Videotapes—Television programs

Is television getting better? A. P. Sanoff. il *U S News World Rep* 103:62-4 D 7 '87

Television in the year 2000 [views of George Vinovich] *USA Today (Periodical)* 116:7 D '87

Advertising

See Television advertising

Anecdotes, facetiae, satire, etc.

Last word. M. Coleman and D. Jaffe. il *Omni* 9:138 My '87

Archives

See also

Museum of Broadcasting (New York, N.Y.)

Art programs

Watching the artist watch nature [J. Arnosky's Drawing from nature TV series] K. O. Fakih. il por *Publ Wkly* 231:43-4 My 29 '87

Arts programs

The arts, Sunday morning, and Charles Kuralt. M. Rhodes. il por *Horizon* 30:6 Je '87

Audiences

See Television audiences

Cartoons

See also

DIC Enterprises

Hanna-Barbera Productions, Inc.

Babe in Toyland [DIC Enterprises' cartoons tied into toy advertising] P. E. Bauer. il pors *Channels* 7:48-51 Jl/Ag '87

Case of the missing kids [ratings down] S. Behrens. il *Channels* 7:21 Jl/Ag '87

Look out, kids! The TV shoots back [interactive toys] A. Levine. il *U S News World Rep* 103:72 O 5 '87

Shooting the messenger [interactive toys and TV show Captain Power and the soldiers of the future] V. Ross. il *Macleans* 100:71 O 5 '87

TV's new toys send critics scrambling for their guns. J. Hall. il *People Wkly* 27:34-6+ Mr 23 '87

Zap, zap! You're dead, Lord Dread! [interactive toys] S. Koepp. il *Time* 129:52 F 9 '87

Censorship

Looser, yes, but still the deans of discipline [divisions of standards and practices] L. J. Davis. il *Channels* 7:32-5+ Jl/Ag '87

Children's programs

See also

Cable television—Children's programs

Children's Television Workshop

Television broadcasting—Cartoons

Television broadcasting—Children's programs—*cont.*

Harlequin [Pee-wee's playhouse] K. Leishman. il *Atlantic* 259:20-2 My '87

I remember Howdy; ed. by Cable Neuhaus. B. Smith. il pors *People Wkly* 28:149-50+ N 30 '87

Multiple fun on Square one [PBS mathematics series] R. Zoglin. il *Time* 129:86 F 23 '87

The Pee-wee perplex. T. Gertler. il pors *Roll Stone* p36-8+ F 12 '87

Pee-wee, the E.T. of comedy. C. Schine. il por *Vogue* 177:114+ F '87

Pee-wee's future playhouse. M. Long. *Omni* 10:62 D '87

Suffer the little children: the FCC does it again. R. L. Fischer. il *USA Today (Periodical)* 115:84-6 Ja '87

The weird world of Pee-wee. H. F. Waters. il pors *Newsweek* 109:83-4 My 18 '87

Zapping back at children's TV. R. Zoglin. il *Time* 130:99-100 N 30 '87

Comedy programs

See also

Cable television—Comedy programs

The agony and the ecstasy: live television comedy. J. Saltzman. il *USA Today (Periodical)* 116:90-2 N '87

Checkerboard gamble [syndication's new first-run comedies] S. Behrens. il *Channels* 7:58-9 F '87

Dawn of the 'dramedy'. H. F. Waters. il *Newsweek* 110:98-9 D 7 '87

Jay Tarses [interview] M. Christensen. il por *Roll Stone* p168+ D 17-31 '87

Not playing it for laughs [dramedy] R. Zoglin. il *Time* 130:96 N 9 '87

Will checkerboarding survive? [NBC stations' campaign to promote fall lineup of checkerboard sitcoms] P. Ellis-Simons. *Channels* 7:10 Je '87

Conversation programs

Arsenio Hall makes it big on late night TV talk show. il pors *Jet* 73:58-9 N 9 '87

Blabscam: TV's rigged political talk shows. C. Hitchens. *Harpers* 274:75-6 Mr '87

Chat show host Emma Freud, Sigmund's great-granddaughter, gets the lowdown by lying down [host of British show Pillow talk] M. Neill. il pors *People Wkly* 28:155-6 D 7 '87

The Fox trot ends for Joan Rivers. J. Friedman. il pors *People Wkly* 27:28-31 Je 1 '87

Making a new Merv [Group W grooms W. Shriner] B. Yagoda. il pors *Channels* 7:46-50 F '87

Anecdotes, facetiae, satire, etc.

A writer's 'TV block'. R. Baker. il *N Y Times Mag* p12 Ja 11 '87

Cooking programs

Preaching the word about food [J. Smith, The frugal gourmet] L. Shapiro. il por *Newsweek* 109:58+ Mr 9 '87

Costume

See Costume, Theatrical

Court proceedings

See Television broadcasting—Trials

Crime programs

Murder never dies. M. Spillane. il *Harpers Bazaar* 120:152-3+ Ja '87

Prime-time crime war. H. F. Waters. il *Newsweek* 110:74 N 2 '87

Docudramas

How they got that story. P. Noglows. il *Channels* 7:29-30+ N '87

Documentary programs

The once and future documentary. L. Brown. il *Channels* 7:15 Mr '87

Drama

Dawn of the 'dramedy'. H. F. Waters. il *Newsweek* 110:98-9 D 7 '87

Hallmark Hall of Fame. R. Buck. il *Channels* 7:47-8 O '87

Not playing it for laughs [dramedy] R. Zoglin. il *Time* 130:96 N 9 '87

Election results

The right not to know [universal poll-closing time bill] D. Olin. *New Repub* 197:18-19 Ag 10-17 '87

Environmental aspects

See Television and the environment

Festivals

See Television festivals

Financial programs

See also

American Business Network

Cable television—Financial programs

Are TV business shows headed the way of Mr. Ed? D. Lieberman. *Bus Week* p32-3 Ap 20 '87

The boom in business TV. il *Nations Bus* 75:29-32 Mr '87

Wall Street weak [new network business shows] J. F. Berry. il *Channels* 7:60-1 Mr '87

Game shows

Confessions of a (failed) quiz show contender [tryout for Wheel of fortune] M. Rosen. *Glamour* 85:178+ S '87

Dreaming up questions to choke on, The new Newlywed game writers never quit making whoopee. M. Dougherty. il *People Wkly* 28:44-6+ Ag 3 '87

Filling in a big blank space, French Wheel of fortune fans elect a Vanna of their own [A. Pujol] M. Dougherty. il pors *People Wkly* 28:98-9 Ag 3 '87

Game shows take off. E. Sherman. il *Ladies Home J* 104:74 Mr '87

How I (and the taxman) won $27,000 in prizes on Wheel of fortune!; ed. by Peter Haines. G. Swinson. il pors *Good Housekeep* 204:72+ My '87

How to ride TV's wheel of fortune. M. Schiffres. il *U S News World Rep* 102:54-5 F 2 '87

I took a turn on "Wheel of fortune". J. Sherman. il pors *Seventeen* 46:24+ Jl '87

The millionaire who made Vanna White a star. V. Scott. il pors *Good Housekeep* 204:66+ My '87

Pat Sajak: Vanna White and me. V. Scott. il pors *Good Housekeep* 205:34+ N '87

Quiz show kids: cashing in on their smarts. C. R. DeBevoise. il *Teen* 31:70+ N '87

Sorry, girls, Mom keeps house for Jeopardy! host Alex Trebek. M. Dougherty. il pors *People Wkly* 28:79-80+ O 12 '87

What a deal! H. F. Waters. il pors *Newsweek* 109:62-8 F 9 '87

Government use

Bring on the backbenchers [TV coverage of Canadian House of Commons] A. Fotheringham. il *Macleans* 100:48 Jl 27 '87

Hear no evil [Iran-contra hearings] C. Schine. il *Vogue* 177:114 Ag '87

Move over, Sam Ervin [Iran-contra hearings] W. Shapiro. il *Time* 129:21 My 11 '87

North displays talent for television politics. J. M. Wall. il *Christ Century* 104:611-12 Jl 15-22 '87

Ollie North, the movie. D. Denby. il *New Repub* 197:7-9 Ag 3 '87

Television's blinding power [O. L. North's testimony; cover story] M. McLoughlin. il pors *U S News World Rep* 103:18-21 Jl 27 '87

A TV viewer's guide [Iran-contra hearings] J. Alter. il *Newsweek* 109:23+ My 11 '87

International aspects

See also

World Administrative Radio Conference

Beyond the American screen. A. Snyder. il *Channels* 7 Sp Issue:24-5+ D '87

Jazz music

Blues for TV jazz. R. C. Walls. il *High Fidel* 37:53 F '87

Laugh tracks

Electric screams. S. Gillis. il *Seventeen* 46:112 N '87

Laws and regulations

See Television laws and regulations

Licenses

See Television laws and regulations

Lottery results

Langhart is fired after refusing TV lottery job [J. Langhart] por *Jet* 72:40 Jl 13 '87

Medical programs

Homespun doc James 'Red' Duke preaches what he practices—and inspires a new TV show. A. Maier. il pors *People Wkly* 27:65+ Je 29 '87

Meteorological programs

See also

Television broadcasting—Weather forecasts

Miniseries

Big books, small screen [miniseries based on books] L. See. il *Publ Wkly* 231:26-30+ Ap 3 '87

The Roots of the problem. D. Bianculli. il *Channels* 7:32-3 Ja '87

Tube power [miniseries based on books and their influence on bookstore sales] L. See. il *Publ Wkly* 231:49-50+ Je 12 '87

Moral and religious aspects

See also

Paulist Productions

Sex in television

Television broadcasting—Religious programs

Violence in television

Television broadcasting—Moral and religious aspects—*cont.*

The ease of distraction [decline of a common cultural memory and rise of secularism, convenience, and distraction] J. Garvey. il *Commonweal* 114:520-1 S 25 '87

The never-ending story [soap operas vs. a Christian view of life] Q. J. Schultze. il por *Christ Today* 31:26-9 Ap 17 '87

The private lives of private eyes [hedonism in Moonlighting] Q. J. Schultze. il *Christ Today* 31:71 S 4 '87

Motion picture criticism programs

Cinema Berraté: Yogi at the movies. T. N. Dawidoff. il por *Sports Illus* 67:10 D 21 '87

Reviewing the reviewers. J. Jarvis. il *People Wkly* 27:9 Ja 12 '87

Motion pictures

Coming attractions [TV movies about D. Rice and O. L. North] il pors *Time* 130:18 Ag 17 '87

The made-for-TV movie malady. D. Thorburn. il *Channels* 7:67-8 Ja '87

Midnight in London is 4 p.m. in L.A. [made for TV movies from Britain] L. Brown. il *Channels* 7:20 F '87

Music

See also
Phonograph records—Television music

The push to end blanket licensing hits a sour note with songwriters. P. E. Bauer. *Channels* 7:17 Ap '87

News

See also
Cable News Network
Cable television—News
Homeless and the press
Israel-Arab Wars, 1967- —Reporters and reporting
Libyan-American conflict, 1986—Reporters and reporting
Reagan-Gorbachev summit conference, 1987—Reporters and reporting
Strikes—Television news
Television and politics
Television broadcasting—Election results
Television broadcasting—Trials
Terrorism and the press
Vietnamese War, 1957-1975—Reporters and reporting

America's Q&A man [T. Koppel; cover story] J. Alter. il pors *Newsweek* 109:50-3+ Je 15 '87

Anchor away [D. Rather walks off CBS News] il *Time* 130:55 S 28 '87

The bad news hits home [layoffs at CBS News] D. Fitzpatrick. por *Newsweek* 109:8 Mr 23 '87

Baltimore's favorite anchorman returns despite serious malady [J. Turner of WJZ] S. Salmans. il por *Channels* 7:8 Je '87

Black Boston TV anchor goes public on pregnancy [L. Walker] por *Jet* 72:32 Jl 6 '87

Born with deformed hands and feet, an anchorwoman overcomes TV's obsession with perfect looks; ed. by Kristin McMurran. B. Walker. il pors *People Wkly* 28:117-18+ N 30 '87

Capitol spat over TV news. il *U S News World Rep* 102:10 My 11 '87

Cease-fire line [Laurence Tisch's view of news operations at CBS] F. Dannen. il *Channels* 7:32 F '87

The changing face of news graphics [computer graphics for television news] C. C. Cortes. il *Technol Rev* 90:10+ F/Mr '87

A close-up look at *glasnost* [CBS special Seven days in May] J. Alter. il *Newsweek* 109:62 Je 29 '87

The cloud of seriousness [CBS evening news] T. Teachout. *Natl Rev* 39:62-4+ O 23 '87

Connecticut's on-air authority [anchorwoman J. Peckinpaugh] J. Giambanco. il pors *Work Woman* 12:91-2+ Ja '87

Dan Rather draws a blank [anchor walks off telecast] H. F. Waters. il por *Newsweek* 110:47-8 S 28 '87

Dan Rather's struggle. J. Alter. il por *Newsweek* 110:51 Ag 24 '87

Days of turbulence, days of change [cutbacks in network news] J. Kelly. il *Time* 129:62-4 Mr 16 '87

Did Dan Rather get this story wrong? [effect of budget cuts on CBS News broadcasts] V. G. Sauter. il *U S News World Rep* 102:72 Mr 23 '87

The face of the news [retiring CBC anchorman K. Nash] J. Bennett. il por *Macleans* 100:10+ D 21 '87

Friends in high places [M. Frankel, L. Grossman, R. Wald and R. Arledge of Columbia's Class of 1952] B. Yagoda. il pors *Channels* 7:54-61 Ja '87

Hard times at a "can-do" network [CBS News] R. Zoglin. il *Time* 129:75 Mr 23 '87

Hardware outlays may rise in support of the news. B. McKernan. il *Channels* 7 Sp Issue:88-9 D '87

Helping children deal with the news. J. Segal and Z. Segal. il *Parents* 62:265 N '87

"If Howard had known . . . " [CBS News president H. Stringer; cover story] M. Gordon. il pors *Channels* 7:60-6 O '87

It's take two for former teacher Leona Morris as she starts another career on Baltimore TV. il por *People Wkly* 27:84 Ap 27 '87

KYW's consultant coup [Sawyer-Miller Group helps revive Philadelphia station] J. Malanowski. il *Channels* 7:22-3 S '87

Lessons in job leveraging from the CBS shake-up [case of H. Stringer] J. Ciabattari. por *Work Woman* 12:67 F '87

'Lines straight out of my life' [network news producer's views on film Broadcast news] C. Gould. il por *Newsweek* 110:50 D 28 '87

Medium, message. *Nation* 244:383-4 Mr 28 '87

The most trusted men in America [anchormen T. Brokaw, P. Jennings, and D. Rather] C. Kramer. il pors *McCalls* 114:128+ Jl '87

Moyers and Mudd: seers or soreheads? W. A. Henry. il por *Channels* 7:57 Ap '87

The National's new man [P. Mansbridge to anchor CBC's flagship news show] P. Young. il pors *Macleans* 100:58 N 23 '87

NBC's catalytic anchor [interview with T. Brokaw] pors *Channels* 7:62-3 My '87

NBC's crack (of dawn) news anchor, Deborah Norville, shoots for a spot as the next morning star. J. Hall. il pors *People Wkly* 28:79-80 Jl 27 '87

The networks' evening blues. G. F. Will. il *Newsweek* 109:86 Mr 30 '87

News by the numbers [McKinsey & Co.'s analysis of NBC News] E. Diamond. il *N Y* 20:20-1 My 25 '87

News meltdown hits L.A. [KCBS-TV] R. Adler. il *Channels* 7:70-1 F '87

The newsroom's revolving door [news directors] J. Vitale. il *Channels* 7:46-8 S '87

Nightly news update [CBS falters] il *Fortune* 116:16 Ag 3 '87

Pam Zekman [head of WBBM-TV's investigative unit] J. Vitale. il pors *Channels* 7:31-2 O '87

Quick-fix news [MacNeil/Lehrer] R. K. Manoff. il *Progressive* 51:15 Jl '87

Rather strange [D. Rather] E. Diamond. il por *N Y* 20:28+ S 28 '87

Rethinking TV news in the age of limits. J. Alter. il *Newsweek* 109:78+ Mr 16 '87

Rhetoric vs. real issues in the network news cutbacks. D. Lieberman. il *Bus Week* p33 Mr 30 '87

Robert Heinecken at the Art Institute [Television/source/subject] A. Slaton. il *Art Am* 75:165-6 D '87

Sad news at Black Rock, good news from the field. J. Vitale. il *Channels* 7 Sp Issue:36-7 D '87

Stay tuned for the evening news: the networks downsize. E. Diamond. il *N Y* 20:30-3 Mr 16 '87

Sweeps surrender [news ratings battle] B. Kanner. il *N Y* 20:12-13 F 9 '87

Taking the heat for sagging ratings, CBS anchor Dan Rather is toughing it out in last place. J. Hall. por *People Wkly* 28:32-3 Ag 10 '87

Tampering with the nervous system [CBS News] L. Brown. il map *Channels* 7:24 My '87

Tape at 11:00 [when you encounter a news event, keep the camcorder running] E. Stecker. il *Pop Photogr* 94:98-9 D '87

Tisch, Tisch, Tisch . . . [cutbacks at CBS News] E. Diamond. il por *N Y* 20:22+ Mr 30 '87

Up from 'Club Thirteen': the rise and rise of Peter Jennings. D. Blum. il *N Y* 20:50-6 N 30 '87

Walter Cronkite [interview] J. Alter. il por *Roll Stone* p87+ N 5-D 10 '87

The way it is for the network news [cutbacks] A. P. Sanoff. il *U S News World Rep* 102:51+ Mr 16 '87

Weighed as a future anchor, Diane Sawyer joins TV's million-dollar men's club. J. Hall. il por *People Wkly* 27:30-1 Ja 19 '87

Welcome to the Rustbelt [cutbacks by CBS News] *New Repub* 196:4+ Mr 30 '87

Who cares about indie news? M. Hoyt. *Channels* 7:49 Ja '87

You can go home again [network correspondents return to local anchor desks] W. A. Henry. il *Channels* 7:41-3 S '87

Television broadcasting—News—cont.
Anecdotes, facetiae, satire, etc.
Cautionary tales. L. H. Lapham. *Harpers* 274:12-13 Ja '87

Opera
Dead from Lincoln Center [L. Pavarotti-J. Sutherland gala, January 11, 1987] S. Lipman. *Commentary* 83:59-63 My '87

Performers
See Television performers

Periodicals
See also
KCET magazine
TV guide (Periodical)

Plots, themes, etc.
See also
Aged in television
AIDS (Disease) in television
Apartheid in television
Automobiles in television
Blacks in television
Boston (Mass.) in television
Business in television
Family in television
Handicapped in television
Hispanic Americans in television
Homeless in television
Homosexuality in television
Montreal (Québec) in television
Psychiatry in television
Race relations in television
Rich in television
Soviet Union in television
Teachers in television
Vietnamese War, 1957-1975, in television
Women in television
Yuppies in television
Television's untouchables. W. A. Henry. il *Channels* 7:57 Mr '87

Political programs
See Television and politics

Production and direction
See Television production and direction

Programming
Fall season 87 [special section] il *Channels* 7:51+ S '87
Hollywood's midseason deficits. L. Margulies. il *Channels* 7:11-12 Ja '87
How to win friends and influence TV [viewers lobbying networks] P. E. Bauer. il *Channels* 7:69 Ja '87
Independents' day. J. B. Grillo. il *Channels* 7:47-50 Ja '87
The man who turns on America [NBC's B. Tartikoff] L. Hirschberg. il pors *Roll Stone* p59-60+ O 22 '87
The perils of a programmer [NBC's B. Tartikoff] W. A. Henry. il *Channels* 7:56 N '87
A quantity of quality. L. Brown. il *Channels* 7:20 Je '87
The quest for cable-resilience. B. Tartikoff. il *Channels* 7:71 O '87
Soft spots in the networks' schedules. il *Channels* 7:80 Je '87
When bossy was boss [Indianapolis TV stations struggle to get time zones straight] J. B. Grillo. il *Channels* 7:71-2 Je '87
Who needs friends? [off-network series going to cable] L. Brown. il *Channels* 7:20 O '87
Zapping the TV networks: channel flippers give today's programmers the willies. A. P. Sanoff. il *U S News World Rep* 102:56-7 Je 1 '87
Anecdotes, facetiae, satire, etc.
A head full of bees [weekend-daytime TV] M. Markoe. il pors *Roll Stone* p31-2 Jl 2 '87

Psychological aspects
Soap opera addiction: what's the attraction? il *Teen* 31:36-8 Mr '87
Television: idle comfort [study by Robert W. Kubey] J. Goetz. il *Psychol Today* 21:10 Je '87

Public service programs
Hype in a good cause [work of J. Wishnow and M. Umansky] L. Brown. il por *Channels* 7:26 Jl/Ag '87
Making localism count [KARE of Minneapolis-St. Paul] J. B. Grillo. il *Channels* 7:58-9 Je '87
The trade-off that may bring back TV's public-service standard [dismantling comparative renewal] M. Frankel. *Channels* 7:15 Ap '87

Ratings
See also
A. C. Nielsen Co.
People meters (TV audience research)
R.D. Percy & Company

Single-source research (TV audience research)
Black viewers turn to NBC. il *Channels* 7:64 N '87
Case of the missing kids [ratings down for animated shows] S. Behrens. il *Channels* 7:21 Jl/Ag '87
Close-up view of the migrating audience. S. Behrens. il *Channels* 7:80 O '87
A finer grind from the ratings mill. S. Behrens. il *Channels* 7 Sp Issue:10-12+ D '87
How do you spell pain? ABC, NBC, and CBS. D. Lieberman. il *Bus Week* p128+ D 7 '87
Sweeps surrender [news ratings battle] B. Kanner. il *N Y* 20:12-13 F 9 '87
Tamper-proof sweeps? M. Couzens. il *Channels* 7:8 N '87
The trouble with CBS' stations. C. Capuzzi. il *Channels* 7:9 Je '87
TV: the vanishing viewer. B. Powell. il *Newsweek* 109:60 My 18 '87

Religious programs
See also
Christian Broadcasting Network, Inc.
PTL Network
As the spiritual soap opera plays on, an expert assesses how Jim Bakker's fall could change television preaching [interview with J. K. Hadden] J. S. Podesta. il pors *People Wkly* 27:44-6 Ap 13 '87
The Bakker tragedy [danger of mixing television and ministry] T. C. Muck. il por *Christ Today* 31:14-15 My 15 '87
British television's Catholic pioneer [mime H. Pepler] M. E. Evans. il *America* 157:501-3 D 26 '87
Christianity today surveys the top TV preachers. il *Christ Today* 31:46, 48-9 O 16 '87
Enterprising evangelism [effects of PTL scandal] R. N. Ostling. il *Time* 130:50-3 Ag 3 '87
Evangelists in Babylon. H. Fairlie. *New Repub* 196:22-4 Ap 27 '87
The fall of the House of Bakker [TV evangelists] J. M. Wall. *Christ Century* 104:323-4 Ap 8 '87
False profits [televangelists] T. McNichol. *New Repub* 196:11-12 Ap 13 '87
Falwell says media ministers need more accountability. por *Christ Today* 31:42 Jl 10 '87
Flacking in the fields of the Lord [Archbishop J. Foley's work for the Vatican] J. Ferullo. il pors *Channels* 7:45-8 Mr '87
God and money [TV evangelists; cover story; special section] il pors *Newsweek* 109:16-23 Ap 6 '87
God's green acres: at home with the televangelist. R. Healy and D. E. Haupt. il *Life* 10:54-8+ Je '87
The gospel according to the free market [shakeout among TV evangelists] T. Mason and S. Ticer. il por *Bus Week* p43-4 Ap 6 '87
Heads, you lose—tails, I win [Christian networks] M. Porrata. por *U S News World Rep* 102:11 Ap 27 '87
Hellfire, brimstone—and a TV scandal [J. Bakker sex scandal] B. Levin. il pors *Macleans* 100:42-3 Ap 6 '87
Is TV appropriate for mass evangelism? P. Crouch; W. Arn. il *Christ Today* 31:50 O 16 '87
Preacher-bashing and the public life [J. Bakker scandal and media overkill] J. M. Wall. *Christ Century* 104:347-8 Ap 15 '87
Searching for God in the soul of Man [CBC's Man alive] P. Young. il *Macleans* 100:53-4 Ja 12 '87
The state of Christian broadcasting. R. Frame. il *Christ Today* 31:48-50 Mr 20 '87
Taking yet another look at television evangelism [congressional hearings] il por *Christ Today* 31:48-9+ S 18 '87
Televangelist takeover. *Nation* 244:419-20 Ap 4 '87
This is what you thought: 97% say TV preachers are too concerned with raising money [results of survey] *Glamour* 85:135 S '87
TV evangelists: what a heavenly mess. B. G. Harrison. *Mademoiselle* 93:208 N '87
TV ministries and taxation. B. Spring. il *Christ Today* 31:36+ N 6 '87
TV preachers and public trust [U.S. news-CNN poll] il *U S News World Rep* 102:15 Ap 13 '87
TV preachers to testify. *Newsweek* 110:64 Ag 31 '87
An unholy war in the TV pulpits [cover story; special section; with editorial comment by David R. Gergen] il *U S News World Rep* 102:58-66, 72 Ap 6 '87
The value of preacher-bashing [discussion of April 15, 1987 article, Preacher-bashing and the public life] J. M. Wall. *Christ Century* 104:532-4 Je 3-10 '87
What profits a preacher? [televangelists] K. L. Woodward. il *Newsweek* 109:68 My 4 '87

Television broadcasting—Religious programs—*cont.*
Will those cards and letters keep coming? [televangelists]
A. Press. il *Newsweek* 109:72 My 11 '87

Science fiction programs

See also
Star trek

Science programs

Science on the air. See occasional issues of Science
News
Sir David Attenborough. L. J. Fisher. il por map *Earth
Sci* 40:11-12 Fall '87

Setting and scenery

See also
Hollywood on Location (Firm)
At the movies [special section; with editorial comment
by Scott Shane] il *Travel Holiday* 168:8+ Ag '87
Corridos! Ken Short puts a revolution on a soundstage.
G. Loney. il *Theatre Crafts* 21:85-8 O '87
Pee-wee's playhouse. D. F. Sisk. il *Theatre Crafts* 21:67-70
F '87

Soap operas

See Television serials

Social aspects

See also
Television and children
Television and youth
Television broadcasting—Psychological aspects
Connect the dots. R. Pattison. il *Nation* 244:295-8 Mr
7 '87
Is your love life going down "the tube"? N. Combs.
il *Read Dig* 131:146-8 O '87
The Lone Driver rides again. T. Gitlin. il *Progressive*
51:36-40 F '87
The monster's spell. A. McCarthy. il *Commonweal*
114:616-17 N 6 '87
A subtler kind of violence. J. Rosen. il *Channels* 7:58
My '87
Tubal ligation [living without a television] L. Rocawich.
il *Progressive* 51:50 Ja '87
Tubeless wonders [nonviewers; study by Robert E. Lee
Roberts] P. McCarthy. *Psychol Today* 21:11 D '87
TV's distorted window on the world. C. Dunkley. *World
Press Rev* 34:64 Ap '87
Watching TV promotes racial, sexual equality. *Jet* 72:36
Ap 20 '87

Anecdotes, facetiae, satire, etc.

The last segment. I. Frazier. *New Yorker* 63:23-4 Jl
13 '87

Sound transmission

See Television sound

Space broadcasts

Spacewatch [pilot for a proposed series about space]
L. L. Kofler. *Space World* X-10-286 Space Advocate:A2
O '87

Spanish language programs

See also
Spanish International Communications Corporation
Telemundo Group Inc.
Targeting the nation in its own tongue. D. Bollier. il
Channels 7 Sp Issue:83 D '87

Special effects

See also
Broadcast Arts (Firm)

Sports

See also
Big East Conference Television Network
Cable television—Sports
Instant replay (Sports)
And now for the real Superbowl [views of G. Klein
on professional football TV contracts] J. A. Trachten-
berg. il por *Forbes* 139:122 F 9 '87
And now the Super Bowl lineup: Seiko, McDonald's,
Pepsi . . . [TV ads] C. Dugas. il *Bus Week* p35
F 2 '87
Baseball clinic from ABC [World Series coverage] W.
Taaffe. il *Sports Illus* 67:113 N 2 '87
The big money battle [ABC wins TV broadcast rights
to Calgary Winter Olympics] P. Young. il *Macleans*
100:36-7 Mr 23 '87
Black football conference signs historic TV package
[Central Intercollegiate Athletic Assn.] *Jet* 72:46 Jl
20 '87
Bouncing the Canadian Open [U.S. TV] *Macleans* 100:28
Jl 20 '87
Bowling for moolah [Pro bowlers tour on ABC] W.
Taaffe. il *Sports Illus* 66:67 Ja 26 '87
A breath of fresh air [sportswriters on TV] W. Taaffe.
il por *Sports Illus* 67:97 N 23 '87
Bringing the Games to the world [Winter Olympics]
J. Howse. il *Macleans* 100:60-1 D 7 '87

The course jester of CBS [golf telecaster G. McCord]
W. Taaffe. il por *Sports Illus* 66:93 Je 8 '87
Dallas station refuses to flinch as it topples a gridiron
power [WFAA takes on SMU scandal] D. Holder.
il *Channels* 7:13 My '87
Daring to tackle the home team [Dallas sportscaster
D. Hansen breaks story of SMU's latest football scandal]
W. Taaffe. il por *Sports Illus* 66:22 Mr 9 '87
Ex-gridder Hill moves to ABC after CBS stint [J. Hill]
por *Jet* 72:23 Ag 10 '87
Eye of the storm [coverage of tennis at the U.S. Open]
N. Amdur. il *World Tennis* 35:50-2 S '87
Flipped out in Fresno [V. Jacobs, punk sportscaster
on KMPH news] W. Taaffe. il por *Sports Illus* 67:65
Ag 3 '87
A golden boy gets axed [ABC sportscaster J. Lampley]
W. Taaffe. il *Sports Illus* 67:67 Jl 13 '87
Gumbel to become NBC's Seoul man for Olympics.
por *Jet* 72:46 Jl 20 '87
Here's a bold new show [Monday sportsnite] W. Taaffe.
il *Sports Illus* 66:67 Je 29 '87
It's bottom-line time [networks cutting costs in program-
ming] W. Taaffe. il *Sports Illus* 67:50-2+ O 12 '87
Jazz, pizzazz and razzmatazz [NCAA basketball tour-
nament] W. Taaffe. il *Sports Illus* 66:38 Mr 23 '87
Look lively, lubbers, it's the America's Cup [to be
broadcast on ESPN] W. O. Johnson. il *Sports Illus*
66:74 Ja 19 '87
Monday man [D. Dierdorf joins Monday night football]
W. Taaffe. il pors *Sports Illus* 67 Sp Issue:124-7+
S 9 '87
NBC was strikingly superior [coverage of football strike]
W. Taaffe. il *Sports Illus* 67:43 O 5 '87
The NFL's big game. il *Fortune* 115:14 Mr 2 '87
Pans for the Pan Ams. W. Taaffe. il *Sports Illus* 67:87
Ag 24 '87
Pigskin English [language of pro football broadcasters]
R. MacNeil. il por *Sport Mag* 78:46-7 F '87
Pinch-hitting for Harry [guest celebs spelling Harry Caray
in the Cubs booth] W. Taaffe. il por *Sports Illus*
66:117 Ap 20 '87
Racist, sexist comment by CBS sports anchors riles
nation's women's groups [comments by B. Packer about
J. Gillom during Pan Am Games] il por *Jet* 72:54
S 14 '87
The rules of the game [interview with B. Costas] J.
Vitale. il pors *Channels* 7:61-2 N '87
T.V. listings [tennis] *World Tennis* 34:26-7+ Ja '87
Talking is their game [sportscasters] W. Roessing. il
Saturday Evening Post 259:64-5+ Ap '87
Tennis for tennis's sake, please [CBS coverage of the
U.S. Open] B. Raushenbush. il *World Tennis* 35:128
S '87
There is no hiding from Heidi. W. Taaffe. il *Sports
Illus* 67:80-1 D 21 '87
TV hoops: technical foul [pro basketball broadcasts] D.
Herndon. il *Sport Mag* 78:66-7 F '87
The voice is familiar . . . [broadcaster P. Summerall]
W. Taaffe. il pors *Sports Illus* 66:52-4+ Ja 26 '87
Wimbledon: hold the berries. W. A. Henry. il *Channels*
7:75 Je '87

Anecdotes, facetiae, satire, etc.

More teletrash, please. C. Kirkpatrick. por *Sports Illus*
67:78 S 7 '87
The voices of summer [announcers' goofs; excerpt from
Baseball: a laughing matter] W. Fusselle. *Sport Mag*
78:65 Jl '87

Syndicated programs

See also
King World Productions, Inc.
Lorimar-Telepictures Corporation
Give-backs to ailing stations causing new syndication
woes. P. E. Bauer. il *Channels* 7:14 Ap '87
Going back to basics [fall season] J. Vitale. il *Channels*
7:58 S '87
The state of syndication. il *Channels* 7:72-3 F '87
Syndication's brave new world. M. Brown. il *Channels*
7:26 S '87
There's Cosby and Boss and then everybody else. J.
Flinn. il *Channels* 7 Sp Issue:75-6+ D '87
Who's hot at NATPE [special section; with editorial
comment by Les Brown] il *Channels* 7:4, 45-51+ F
'87
Will checkerboarding survive? [NBC stations' campaign
to promote fall lineup of checkerboard sitcoms] P.
Ellis-Simons. *Channels* 7:10 Je '87
Wishful thinking by the numbers [accounting methods
and syndication revenues] L. Jereski. *Forbes* 140:67
O 19 '87

Trials

Courting the TV ratings. *50 Plus* 27:96 F '87

Television broadcasting—Trials—_cont._

Invasion of the law shows. A. Press. il *Newsweek* 110:95 N 16 '87

Reality shows: the syndicated bench. M. Pollan. il *Channels* 7:52-4 Jl/Ag '87

War news

See also

Vietnamese War, 1957-1975—Reporters and reporting

Weather forecasts

Clever weather clowns [Canada] M. Gray. il *Macleans* 100:45-6 Mr 16 '87

Live at five! [coverage of November 18, 1986 Arizona tornado] R. Norman, Jr. and R. C. Balling, Jr. il pors *Weatherwise* 40:36-7 F '87

Pretty cool cat [Bob the Weather Cat at KATU-TV, Portland, Or.; cover story] il *Natl Geogr World* 144:3-5 Ag '87

Putting a new face on weather reports. J. M. Mitchell. il *Weatherwise* 40:330-2 D '87

Roker the rain king [New York City weatherman A. Roker] L. Schulte. il por *N Y* 20:20 Ag 17 '87

Africa

TV's shortcomings in Africa. I. McLellan. *World Press Rev* 34:60-1 Ja '87

Canada

See also

Canadian Broadcasting Corporation

Canadian Radio-Television and Telecommunications Commission

Clever weather clowns. M. Gray. il *Macleans* 100:45-6 Mr 16 '87

Local heroes and imported fantasies. P. Hluchy. il *Macleans* 100:61-2 O 12 '87

Singing the puberty blues [Canadian producers L. Schuyler and K. Hood's series Degrassi Junior High] P. Hluchy. il *Macleans* 100:54 Ja 19 '87

Television. See occasional issues of Maclean's

France

Au flair [French TV's Apostrophes] J. Bernstein. *Am Sch* 56:167-70+ Spr '87

The Carson of the literary set [Apostrophes host B. Pivot] L. Zuckerman. il por *Time* 130:64 Jl 13 '87

Filling in a big blank space, French Wheel of fortune fans elect a Vanna of their own [A. Pujol] M. Dougherty. il pors *People Wkly* 28:98-9 Ag 3 '87

A nation of readers [influence of B. Pivot's Apostrophes on best seller list] B. Murphy. il *Atlantic* 260:21-5 Ag '87

Great Britain

See also

BBC

Channel Four (Television station: London, England)

Chat show host Emma Freud, Sigmund's great-granddaughter, gets the lowdown by lying down [host of British show Pillow talk] M. Neill. il pors *People Wkly* 28:155-6 D 7 '87

Mediawatch. H. David. il *Hist Today* 37:6-8 Jl '87

Mediawatch [documentaries on the Jarrow Crusade and the Titanic] H. David. il *Hist Today* 37:4-5 Ja '87

Mediawatch [history on TV sells books] H. David. *Hist Today* 37:8-9 O '87

TV's distorted window on the world. C. Dunkley. *World Press Rev* 34:64 Ap '87

Italy

Isiah Thomas' life story a series for Italian TV. por *Jet* 72:46 Ag 24 '87

Japan

Japan's closed television world. H. D. Shapiro. il *Channels* 7:12 O '87

Kenya

Kenya uses soap opera to stem high birth rate. *Jet* 72:62 Ag 31 '87

Working together in the third world [soap opera promotes family planning] M. Morain. il por *Humanist* 47:33-4 S/O '87

South Africa

American TV's mixed message to Pretoria. J. Von Herrmann. il *Channels* 7:8 Mr '87

Soviet Union

Stirring up the comrades [P. Donahue's broadcasts] R. Zoglin. il por *Time* 129:79 F 16 '87

Western Europe

Starring on the world stage [U.S. programs] L. Brown. il *Channels* 7:18 N '87

Television broadcasting, Public

See also

Corporation for Public Broadcasting

Public Broadcasting Service

Old enough to get its act together. S. F. Sucherman. il *Channels* 7:68-70 O '87

Finance

An institution on hold recalls its great hopes. J. J. Yore. il *Channels* 7 Sp Issue:85 D '87

To be or not to be commercial?—That is the question. R. L. Fischer. *USA Today (Periodical)* 116:89-91 S '87

Television broadcasting, Subscription

See also

Cable television

Television cabinets *See* Cabinets (Furniture)

Television cameramen

Black cameramen lose their $3.5 mil. suit against ABC. *Jet* 72:22 Ag 24 '87

Television cameras

See also

Film-to-video transfer system

Video cameras

Television cartoons *See* Television broadcasting—Cartoons

Television censorship *See* Television broadcasting—Censorship

Television characters *See* Blacks in television; Characters in television; Women in television

Television City (New York, N.Y.)

Koch to Trump to Koch: drop dead. J. R. Norman. il por *Bus Week* p98-9 Jl 20 '87

Television commercials *See* Television advertising

Television consultants

See also

Sawyer-Miller Group

Television costume *See* Costume, Theatrical

Television critics and criticism

See also

Shales, Tom

Television program reviews

Television directors

The newsroom's revolving door [news directors] J. Vitale. il *Channels* 7:46-8 S '87

Television display systems *See* Information display systems

Television editing

Non-linear nuances: Ediflex is cutting up Hollywood. C. Eller. il *Theatre Crafts* 21:89-90+ O '87

Television equipment

See also

Television projection

Television receivers

Television stations—Equipment

Videotape recorders and recording

Testing

Hands-on: Multivision [digital adapter] J. B. Meigs. il *Pop Mech* 164:46 F '87

Multivision 1.1 Digital Video Controller. il *High Fidel* 37:46-7 N '87

Multivision 3.1 digital TV tuner. il *High Fidel* 37:36+ Mr '87

MultiVision = multimagic. W. J. Hawkins. il *Pop Sci* 230:36 My '87

Product of the Year Award. D. Ranada. il *High Fidel* 37:50-4 D '87

Television equipment industry

See also

Rabbit Systems, Inc.

Zenith Electronics Corp.

Ethical aspects

The Rabbit punch [R. Wright charges Rabbit Systems and MarketCorp Venture Associates with misappropriation of trade secrets] K. Healy. il por *Forbes* 140:175-6 S 21 '87

Marketing

Are TVs still in GE's big picture? K. Dreyfack. il *Bus Week* p37 Mr 2 '87

GE's gamble on American-made TVs. P. Petre. il *Fortune* 116:50-2+ Jl 6 '87

Sharp and super: a new VCR's got the picture. D. Lachenbruch. il *Channels* 7 Sp Issue:124-5 D '87

This year's buzzword: digital, digital, digital. J. Kaminsky. il *Channels* 7 Sp Issue:126 D '87

Zenith is sticking its neck out in a cutthroat market. L. Therrien. il *Bus Week* p72-3 Ag 17 '87

Television festivals

California

M.O.B. rule [early work of W. Allen featured at the L.A. Television Festival] M. Mancini. il por *Film Comment* 23:76-7 Jl/Ag '87

Television frequency allocation

High-definition's spectrum needs spur TV broadcasters to action [UHF vs. radio spectrum] S. Behrens. il *Channels* 7:16 Ap '87

Television games *See* Video games

Television in agriculture

See also

Cable television—Agricultural programs

Television in agriculture—See also—*cont.*
   Direct broadcast satellite services—Agricultural programs
Television in counseling
   See also
   Cable television in counseling
Reality shows: the syndicated couch. J. Vitale. il *Channels* 7:56-7 Jl/Ag '87
Television in education
   See also
   Videotapes—Educational use
Television literacy programs for gifted children. R. Abelman. *Educ Dig* 52:30-2 My '87
TV: show business or education? J. Yardley. *Des Arts Educ* 88:46-7 Jl/Ag '87
Television in military art and science
Northrop developing tactical infrared focal plane array. il *Aviat Week Space Technol* 127:82-3 N 2 '87
Television in politics *See* Television and politics
Television industry
   See also
   American Broadcasting Companies, Inc.
   Blacks in the television industry
   Cable News Network
   Cable television
   Carson Productions
   CBS Inc.
   Children's Television Workshop
   Christian Broadcasting Network, Inc.
   Chuck Barris Productions Inc.
   Coca-Cola Television (Firm)
   Collective bargaining—Television industry
   DIC Enterprises
   Dick Clark Productions Inc.
   East Texas Television Network
   Fox Broadcasting Company
   Fox Inc.
   Gillett Group Inc.
   Golden Groove Productions
   Group W Productions
   GTG Entertainment (Firm)
   Hill Broadcasting Inc.
   King World Productions, Inc.
   Lifetime (Firm)
   Lorimar-Telepictures Corporation
   Low power television
   Malrite Guaranteed Broadcast Partners Limited Partnership
   National Association of Broadcasters
   National Association of Television Program Executives
   National Broadcasting Co., Inc.
   Newhouse Broadcasting Corporation
   Paramount Pictures Corp. Television Group
   Paulist Productions
   RKO General, Inc.
   Stephen J. Cannell Productions
   Television equipment industry
   Television production and direction
   Television stations
   Tribune Entertainment Company
   TVX Broadcast Group Inc.
   Unitel Video, Inc.
   Universal Television
   Viacom International Inc.
   Women in the television industry
The business side. M. Brown. See issues of Channels (New York, N.Y.: 1986) beginning January-February 1986
Hollywood Inc. P. E. Bauer. See issues of Channels (New York, N.Y.: 1986) beginning September 1986
Who needs friends? [off-network series going to cable] L. Brown. il *Channels* 7:20 O '87

Accounting
What's a flop worth? [Capital Cities earnings accounting] S. N. Chakravarty. *Forbes* 140:82 D 28 '87
Wishful thinking by the numbers [accounting methods and syndication revenues] L. Jereski. *Forbes* 140:67 O 19 '87

Acquisitions and mergers
   See also
   Cable television—Acquisitions and mergers
Big deals of '87. M. Brown. il *Channels* 7:18 Mr '87
Coveting thy neighbor's system. J. Vitale. il *Channels* 7 Sp Issue:51 D '87
An exception to Murphy's Law? [Capital Cities/ABC] S. N. Chakravarty. il por *Forbes* 140:36-8 Ag 10 '87
The feud that toppled a TV empire [Spanish International Communications Corp. sold to Hallmark Cards] G. Critser. il pors *Channels* 7:24-31 Ja '87

A little UHF group tries a great big gamble [TVX buys stations from Taft Broadcasting] C. S. Eklund. il por *Bus Week* p84+ F 2 '87
Marvin Davis wants back into Tinseltown [run at Lorimar] R. Grover. por *Bus Week* p64 D 7 '87
Not ready for prime time? [Capital Cities/ABC] G. Fabrikant. il pors *N Y Times Mag* p30+ Ap 12 '87
Psst! Wanna buy a station? M. Gordon. il *Channels* 7:38-40 Ja '87
Taft Broadcasting may become a Carl Lindner production. D. Cook. il por *Bus Week* p37-8 Ap 27 '87
What's his line? [B. Sugarman of Giant Group buys Chuck Barris Productions] A. B. Block. il por *Forbes* 139:70-1 Ja 26 '87
Who owns broadcasting? [cover story; special section] il *Channels* 7:47-56 Ap '87

Advertising
   See also
   Broadcast Promotion and Marketing Executives
KYW's consultant coup [Sawyer-Miller Group helps revive Philadelphia station] J. Malanowski. il *Channels* 7:22-3 S '87
Local TV fights back in Palm Beach. M. Clary. il map *Channels* 7:21-2 Ap '87
Twin ads: a case of mistaken identity [Michelob and ABC Sports run commercials using song Everybody have fun tonight by Wang Chung] *Newsweek* 110:37 Ag 24 '87
Will checkerboarding survive? [NBC stations' campaign to promote fall lineup of checkerboard sitcoms] P. Ellis-Simons. *Channels* 7:10 Je '87
WSMV's damage control [Nashville station promotions] R. Buck. il map *Channels* 7:21-2 My '87
   Awards
The copycat factor [Broadcast Promotion and Marketing Executives awards] R. Buck. il *Channels* 7:17-18 Je '87

Employees
   See Television workers
Ethical aspects
   See also
   Cable television—Ethical aspects
Export-import trade
American TV's mixed message to Pretoria. J. Von Herrmann. il *Channels* 7:8 Mr '87
Ending TV's isolationism. J. L. Swerdlow. il *Channels* 7:58 Mr '87
Midnight in London is 4 p.m. in L.A. [made for TV movies from Britain] L. Brown. il *Channels* 7:20 F '87
The path once taken [American-style commercial TV] L. Brown. il *Channels* 7 Sp Issue:20-1 D '87
Starring on the world stage [U.S. programs in Western Europe] L. Brown. il *Channels* 7:18 N '87
Watch out, here come more cheap imports [Lionheart Television International] A. B. Block. il por *Forbes* 139:150 Mr 9 '87

Finance
The Channels achievers [cover story; special section; with editorial comment by Les Brown] il *Channels* 7:4, 25-6+ Je '87
Communications media. A. B. Block. il *Forbes* 139:99-100 Ja 12 '87
Days of turbulence, days of change [cutbacks in network news] J. Kelly. il *Time* 129:62-4 Mr 16 '87
Down with trickle down. L. Brown. il *Channels* 7:16 Mr '87
For TV profits, the picture is gloomy. R. Grover. il *Bus Week* p100 Ja 12 '87
Give-backs to ailing stations causing new syndication woes. P. E. Bauer. il *Channels* 7:14 Ap '87
Hollywood's midseason deficits. L. Margulies. il *Channels* 7:11-12 Ja '87
How do you spell pain? ABC, NBC, and CBS. D. Lieberman. il *Bus Week* p128+ D 7 '87
It's bottom-line time [networks cutting costs in sports programming] W. Taaffe. il *Sports Illus* 67:50-2+ O 12 '87
Network prophets and the bottom line [views of Robert Wussler, Fred Silverman and Van Gordon Sauter] W. A. Henry. il *Channels* 7:59 My '87
The networks' big headache [people meters] D. Lieberman. il *Bus Week* p26-8 Jl 6 '87
Rethinking TV news in the age of limits. J. Alter. il *Newsweek* 109:78+ Mr 16 '87
Sizing up a down market. il *Channels* 7:58-9 Ap '87
Splashing new realities onto an old Hollywood [production scene] N. Koch. il *Channels* 7 Sp Issue:32-3 D '87
Stay tuned for the evening news: the networks downsize. E. Diamond. il *N Y* 20:30-3 Mr 16 '87

Television industry—Finance—*cont.*
Target practice: the networks under the gun. J. Baker. il *Channels* 7 Sp Issue:64-6 D '87
The tug-of-war behind your TV screen [networks vs. affiliates] D. Lieberman. il *Bus Week* p104+ Ap 13 '87
TV's bright picture. il *Fortune* 116:9 N 9 '87
The way it is for the network news [cutbacks] A. P. Sanoff. il *U S News World Rep* 102:51+ Mr 16 '87
Will temptation undo the tie that binds [networks questioning affiliate compensation] S. Behrens. il *Channels* 7:41-3 My '87

International aspects
The empire builders. P. Ainslie and R. Buck. il *Channels* 7:36-41 Ap '87

Management
$alary review [special section] il *Channels* 7:59-64 Jl/Ag '87
Help wanted: the old networks need an infusion of new blood. R. Buck. il *Channels* 7:8 My '87

Marketing
The maturing of marketing. J. Baker. il *Channels* 7:18 O '87
What's hot in marketing [special section] il *Channels* 7:57-63 Je '87

Securities
For glamour—and risk—try TV producers' stocks. G. Weiss. il *Bus Week* p120 F 16 '87
Hurt on the Street [views of media analyst Richard MacDonald] il *Channels* 7:57 My '87
The schizoid life of the media analyst. J. F. Berry. il *Channels* 7:62-8 F '87
What the market thinks. il *Channels* 7:33 Je '87

Suits and claims
Suing the bosses who bounced her, a bitter Valerie Harper fights to save her reputation. D. Hutchings. il pors *People Wkly* 28:46-8 O 19 '87

Canada
See also
CTV (Network)
Telefilm Canada
Anne of Green Gables grows up [cover story; special section; with editorial comment by Kevin Doyle] il pors *Macleans* 100:2, 46-8+ D 7 '87
Delightful, lovable chaos [Vancouver TV station CKVU] A. Fotheringham. il *Macleans* 100:52 Jl 20 '87
Go north, young man [interview with S. J. Cannell] P. E. Bauer. il pors *Channels* 7:70-1 Jl/Ag '87
The little TV station that grew [entrepreneur M. Znaimer] P. C. Newman. il por *Macleans* 100:32 Ap 20 '87

France
'Chirac's Yalta': the selling of French TV. J. Rossant. il *Bus Week* p48 F 16 '87
From Public TV to 'Dallasty'. D. Singer. *Nation* 245:482+ O 31 '87

Great Britain
See also
BBC
Channel Four (Television station: London, England)
Lionheart Television International
Midnight in London is 4 p.m. in L.A. [made for TV movies from Britain] L. Brown. il *Channels* 7:20 F '87

Western Europe
The coming profits from European TV. P. Sherrid. il *U S News World Rep* 102:52-3 My 25 '87
The empire builders. P. Ainslie and R. Buck. il *Channels* 7:36-41 Ap '87
The media barons battle to dominate Europe. J. Rossant and R. A. Melcher. il *Bus Week* p158+ My 25 '87
Outfoxing the establishment [S. Berlusconi] P. Sherrid. il por *U S News World Rep* 103:40-1 Jl 27 '87
The path once taken [American-style commercial TV] L. Brown. il *Channels* 7 Sp Issue:20-1 D '87
U.S.-style TV turns on Europe. S. Tully. il *Fortune* 115:96-8 Ap 13 '87

Television journalism *See* Television broadcasting—News

Television laws and regulations
See also
Fairness Doctrine (Broadcasting)
A compromise that could clear the static over the airwaves. F. Seghers. il *Bus Week* p28 Jl 6 '87
Congress and TV: hurry up and wait. J. L. Swerdlow. *Channels* 7:16+ F '87
Down with trickle down. L. Brown. il *Channels* 7:16 Mr '87
The trade-off that may bring back TV's public-service standard [dismantling comparative renewal] M. Frankel. *Channels* 7:15 Ap '87

Canada
See also
Canadian Radio-Television and Telecommunications Commission
The fight to rule the airwaves. M. Janigan. il *Macleans* 100:49-50 Jl 20 '87

France
From Public TV to 'Dallasty'. D. Singer. *Nation* 245:482+ O 31 '87

Television news *See* Television broadcasting—News

Television performers
See also names of television performers
The 10 most handsome men on TV [results of survey] il *Good Housekeep* 204:124-5 F '87
25 prettiest hairdos for spring [modeled by TV stars] il *Good Housekeep* 204:114-23+ Mr '87
Because Eight is enough wasn't enough, Dick Van Patten and his TV brood get together one last time. J. Stark. il *People Wkly* 28:60-2 Jl 27 '87
The celebrity wheel of fortune. J. Saltzman. *USA Today (Periodical)* 115:41 My '87
Crossing over in Hollywood [TV stars in movies] M. Reese. il *Newsweek* 109:76-7+ My 11 '87
Here's a gallery to dye for [blond performers] il *People Wkly* 27:95-7+ Mr 16 '87
Making the stars shine [work of hair and makeup expert Jeff Jones] S. Lee. il *Redbook* 170:10 D '87
Second to none [supporting casts] M. McWilliams. il *Roll Stone* p49+ Ap 23 '87

Photographs and photography
The group is a balanced equation [photographing the cast of Bustin' loose] G. Bernstein. il *Petersens Photogr Mag* 16:10 S '87

Television photography
Exhibitions
Robert Heinecken at the Art Institute [Television/source/subject] A. Slaton. il *Art Am* 75:165-6 D '87

Television picture enlargers *See* Television projection

Television producers
See also
Cannell, Stephen J.
Cerre, Mike
Goldberg, Gary David
Hampton, Henry
Hood, Kit
Paltrow, Bruce
Walker, Chet
Moving in on the big boys. P. E. Bauer. il *Channels* 7:65 S '87
Splashing new realities onto an old Hollywood. N. Koch. il *Channels* 7 Sp Issue:32-3 D '87

Television production and direction
See also
Television directors
Television producers
Television studios
ABC's Amerika raised hackles, but the citizens of Tecumseh, Nebraska got a unique thrill. il *People Wkly* 27:34-7 F 23 '87
Dark side of the Moon [Moonlighting's production delays] D. Handelman. il pors *Roll Stone* p52+ Mr 26 '87
Even career girls get the blues [The days and nights of Molly Dodd] M. Christensen. il *Roll Stone* p63+ My 21 '87
Excellence '87 [special section; with editorial comment by Merrill Brown] il *Channels* 7:4, 25-7+ O '87
A family's binding ties [making of Family ties] B. D. Johnson. il *Macleans* 100:44-5 F 9 '87
A labor of wanderlust [M. and G. Cerre, producers of GEO] L. S. Brady. il pors *Esquire* 107:48 Ja '87
The man they love to hate [agent M. Hurwitz] J. Traub. il pors *Channels* 7:66-70 Je '87
Mayor and pig [filming of public television program in New York City with E. Koch and Piggy-Wiggy] *New Yorker* 63:16-18 Ag 10 '87
Michael Mann [interview] L. Hirschberg. il por *Roll Stone* p163-4 D 17-31 '87
Moonlighting on the edge [production problems] R. Zoglin. il *Time* 129:79 Mr 30 '87
Taken for Granted [M. and J. Tinker, producers of St. Elsewhere] B. Zehme. il pors *Roll Stone* p33-5 Je 18 '87

Television program reviews
The best and the worst of the fall TV lineup. B. Allen. il *Ms* 16:36+ O '87
Best of '86. il *Time* 129:78 Ja 5 '87
Excellence '87 [special section; with editorial comment by Merrill Brown] il *Channels* 7:4, 25-7+ O '87
Fall season 87 [special section] il *Channels* 7:51+ S '87

Television program reviews—cont.

My favorite genres [fall season] C. Schine. il *Vogue* 177:206 S '87

New recruits in the war for ratings. H. Robertson. il *Macleans* 100:69-70 O 5 '87

The new season: headed for another fall. S. Reddicliffe. il *Roll Stone* p32+ O 8 '87

On television. M. Kitman. See occasional issues of The New Leader

People picks & pans. See issues of People Weekly

Private eye. W. A. Henry. See issues of Channels (New York, N.Y.: 1986)

The revolution will not be televised: Fox on the fritz. C. Schine. il *Vogue* 177:64 Jl '87

Spotlight. E. Miller. See issues of Seventeen

Television. See issues of Film Comment

Television [1987] J. Leonard. il *N Y* 20:107-8+ D 21-28 '87

Television [fall season] J. Leonard. il *N Y* 20:62-3 S 21 '87

Television. J. Leonard. See issues of New York beginning November 28, 1983

Tube [fall previews] il *People Wkly* 28:66+ Ag 31 '87

Tube '87. il *People Wkly* 27:46+ Ja 5 '87

TV tips. D. Scheuer. *Sch Update* 119:14 Ap 20 '87

What's new on the tube [fall line-up] il *Teen* 31:80-1 S '87

Yup, yup and away! [fall season] R. Zoglin. il *Time* 130:89-90 O 5 '87

Single works

60 minutes
 Ladies Home J il 104:46+ O '87. E. Sherman
 Nation 245:8 Jl 4-11 '87. A. Cockburn

227
 Ebony il 42:128+ Je '87. A. Collier
 Jet il 72:56-8 Ag 24 '87
 Vogue il 177:64 Jl '87. L. Robinson

The Adams chronicles
 Sch Update il 120:46-7 S 18 '87. D. Scheuer

Agatha Christie's Miss Marple
 N Y il 20:91 D 14 '87. J. Leonard

Agnes, the indomitable de Mille
 Dance Mag il 61:66 S '87. J. Gruen

ALF
 Channels il 7:65 Ja '87. W. A. Henry
 Channels il 7:15-16 N '87. N. Gunther

Amen
 Jet il 73:58-60 N 23 '87. A. Collier

America by design
 Archit Rec il 175:89 O '87. R. Kimball
 Nation 245:354-5 O 3 '87. J. H. Kay

Amerika
 Channels 7:18 F '87. J. Vitale
 Macleans il 100:57 F 16 '87. B. D. Johnson
 Macleans il 100:7 Mr 16 '87. F. Bruning
 N Y il 20:36-41 Ja 26 '87. P. Hoban
 N Y il 20:80+ F 16 '87. J. Leonard
 Nation 244:165+ F 14 '87. A. Kopkind
 Natl Rev 39:62-3 Mr 27 '87. W. F. Buckley
 Natl Rev 39:18 Mr 13 '87
 Natl Rev 39:57-8 F 27 '87. T. Teachout
 New Repub 196:25-7 F 23 '87. J. Maslin
 Newsweek il 109:21-2 F 16 '87. H. F. Waters
 People Wkly il 27:9 F 16 '87. J. Jarvis
 People Wkly il 27:34-7 F 23 '87
 Roll Stone il p29-30 F 12 '87. N. Atkins
 Sch Update 119:23 Ja 26 '87. D. Scheuer
 Time il 129:72-3 F 9 '87. R. Zoglin
 U S News World Rep il 102:66-7 F 16 '87. A. P. Sanoff
 U S News World Rep il 102:15 Ja 19 '87. M. Bosc
 U S News World Rep il 102:68 F 16 '87. V. G. Sauter
 Vogue il 177:114 F '87. T. Rafferty

Anne of Green Gables—the sequel
 Macleans il 100:46-8+ D 7 '87. B. D. Johnson

Antony Tudor
 Dance Mag il 61:106 Mr '87. J. Gruen

Apartheid
 Vogue il 177:100 D '87. C. Schine

Apostrophes
 Am Sch 56:167-70+ Spr '87. J. Bernstein
 Atlantic il 260:21-5 Ag '87. B. Murphy
 Time il 130:64 Jl 13 '87. L. Zuckerman

At mother's request
 Time il 129:78 Ja 5 '87. R. Zoglin

Beauty and the beast
 Newsweek il 110:58 D 28 '87. H. F. Waters

Billionaire Boys Club
 N Y il 20:117 N 9 '87. J. Leonard

Bluebell
 Dance Mag il 61:84 Ap '87. J. Gruen

Breaking silence
 Ms 15:21 Mr '87. S. McHenry

The Bretts
 N Y 20:72+ O 5 '87. J. Leonard
 Vogue il 177:114 O '87. C. Schine

Bustin' loose
 Black Enterp il 18:25 S '87. S. Herbert
 Jet il 73:58-60 N 2 '87
 Petersens Photogr Mag il 16:10 S '87. G. Bernstein

Cagney & Lacey
 Ms il 15:40-1+ Ja '87. M. Gordon
 People Wkly il 28:62-4 O 5 '87. J. Hall

Captain Power and the soldiers of the future
 Macleans il 100:71 O 5 '87. V. Ross

Casanova
 N Y 20:113-14 Mr 2 '87. J. Leonard

Celebrating Gershwin
 Vogue il 177:100 D '87. A. De Lorenzo

A child's Christmas in Wales
 Macleans il 100:53 D 21 '87. J. Bemrose

The Colbys
 Vogue il 177:207 Ja '87. L. Robinson

The conservatives
 Natl Rev 39:63-5 Ja 30 '87. T. Teachout

Conspiracy: the trial of the Chicago 8
 N Y il 20:94-5 My 18 '87. J. Leonard

Corridos!
 Theatre Crafts il 21:85-8 O '87. G. Loney

The Cosby show
 Jet il 72:28-30 My 11 '87. D. M. Cheers
 Jet il 72:38 Ag 31 '87
 Jet 72:32 Je 1 '87
 Jet il 72:58-60 S 21 '87

Crime story
 Channels il 7:65 Ja '87. W. A. Henry
 Harpers Bazaar il 120:124+ Ap '87. J. Cameron
 Newsweek il 110:74 N 2 '87. H. F. Waters
 Vogue il 177:90 My '87. C. Schine

Dance in America
 Dance Mag il 61:74-5 F '87. J. Gruen
 Dance Mag il 61:83 My '87. J. Gruen

The days and nights of Molly Dodd
 Roll Stone il p63+ My 21 '87. M. Christensen
 Time il 130:50 Ag 10 '87. R. Zoglin
 Vogue il 177:126 N '87. C. Schine

Death of the heart
 N Y 20:114+ My 4 '87. J. Leonard

Degrassi Junior High
 Macleans il 100:54 Ja 19 '87. J. Bemrose
 Sch Update il 120:17 D 18 '87. D. Scheuer

Designing women
 McCalls il 115:78-9+ N '87. H. Yorkshire
 People Wkly il 27:63-4+ Ap 20 '87. F. A. Bernstein
 Vogue il 177:144 Mr '87. C. Schine

A different world
 Jet il 73:54-5 O 26 '87

Dolly
 N Y 20:95 O 12 '87. J. Leonard
 Newsweek il 110:73-4 N 23 '87. C. Leerhsen

Donahue
 Time il 129:79 F 16 '87. R. Zoglin

Double dare
 People Wkly il 28:135 O 19 '87

Drawing from nature
 Publ Wkly il 231:43-4 My 29 '87. K. O. Fakih

The ebony tower
 N Y il 20:93-4 F 9 '87. J. Leonard

Eight is enough
 People Wkly il 28:60-2 Jl 27 '87. J. Stark

Elvis
 Roll Stone il p53-4+ Je 4 '87. D. Fricke

L'enfant et les sortilèges
 Dance Mag 61:66-7 S '87. J. Gruen

Escape from Sobibor
 N Y il 20:92-3 Ap 13 '87. J. Leonard
 Vogue il 177:114 Ap '87. C. Schine

Essence: the television program
 Essence il 18:34 My '87
 Essence il 18:38 O '87. P. Johnson

Eyes on the prize
 America 156:165-6 F 28 '87
 Channels il 7:48-50 O '87. J. Rosen
 Essence il 17:22 Ja '87. A. White
 N Y il 20:68 Ja 26 '87. J. Leonard
 Nation 244:120-2 Ja 31 '87. F. Powledge
 Time il 129:24 Ja 19 '87. R. Zoglin
 U S News World Rep il 102:58-9 Mr 9 '87. L. J. Lord
 Vogue il 177:44+ Ja '87. C. Schine

Television program reviews—Single works—_cont._

Family ties
  Macleans il 100:44-5 F 9 '87. B. D. Johnson
  McCalls il 114:61-4+ Ag '87
Farmers . . . entrepreneurs
  Success Farm il 85 no6:18AW Mr '87. C. Tevis
The Father Clements story
  Jet il 73:30-2 D 14 '87. C. Waldron
  _N Y_ 20:91-2 D 14 '87. J. Leonard
The first Eden: the Mediterranean world and man
  Earth Sci il 40:11-12 Fall '87. L. J. Fisher
  _N Y_ il 20:100 N 2 '87. J. Leonard
First frontier
  Theatre Crafts il 21:103-5 My '87. B. Kuerten
First person singular
  Macleans il 100:63 Mr 30 '87. J. Bemrose
Foxfire
  Sch Update il 120:TE8 D 4 '87. S. Linnea
  Sch Update il 120:TE8 N 20 '87. S. Linnea
Frank's Place
  Jet il 72:26-8 S 14 '87. C. Waldron
The frugal gourmet
  Newsweek il 109:58+ Mr 9 '87. L. Shapiro
A gathering of old men
  Film Comment il 23:8-9 Mr/Ap '87. A. Horton
GEO
  Esquire il 107:48 Ja '87. L. S. Brady
Getting into history
  Macleans il 100:63 Mr 30 '87. J. Bemrose
Ghost of a chance
  Jet il 72:56-7 My 11 '87. A. Collier
God and politics
  America 157:492-3 D 26 '87
  Christ Century 104:1166-7 D 23-30 '87. J. M. Wall
The golden girls
  50 Plus il 27:28-30 S '87. J. Porcino
Hallmark Hall of Fame
  Channels il 7:47-8 O '87. R. Buck
Heaven on earth
  Macleans il 100:51 Mr 2 '87. J. Bemrose
Hill Street Blues
  People Wkly il 27:44-5 My 4 '87. J. Jarvis
  Time il 129:89 Ap 27 '87. R. Zoglin
Hollywood's favorite heavy: businessmen on prime time TV
  Channels 7:16 F '87. J. Rosen
Hooperman
  _N Y_ il 20:124 S 28 '87. J. Leonard
  People Wkly il 28:82+ D 14 '87
The Howdy Doody show
  People Wkly il 28:149-50+ N 30 '87. B. Smith
I'll take Manhattan
  _N Y_ il 20:113 Mr 2 '87. J. Leonard
In love and war
  _N Y_ il 20:66 Mr 16 '87. J. Leonard
Intimate contact
  _N Y_ il 20:94-5 O 12 '87. J. Leonard
It was twenty years ago today
  Roll Stone p11 Mr 12 '87
It's Garry Shandling's show
  Channels il 7:60-1 Ap '87. M. Pollan
  Roll Stone il p41-2 F 26 '87. L. Grossberger
Kate & Allie
  _N Y_ il 20:115 O 19 '87. J. Leonard
Kids like these
  _N Y_ il 20:117-18 N 9 '87. J. Leonard
Kojak: the price of justice
  _N Y_ il 20:121-2 F 23 '87. J. Leonard
L.A. law
  Macleans il 100:53-4 F 23 '87. B. D. Johnson
  _Ms_ il 15:38-9+ Je '87. M. Kort
  Newsweek il 110:84-8+ N 16 '87. H. F. Waters
  People Wkly il 27:76-8+ F 2 '87. J. Hall
Late night with David Letterman
  _N Y_ il 20:36-45 Ja 19 '87. E. Pooley
  People Wkly il 28:165-7 D 7 '87
The late show
  People Wkly il 27:28-31 Je 1 '87. J. Friedman
Laurier
  Macleans il 100:48 Je 22 '87. P. Young
LBJ: the early years
  _N Y_ il 20:66 F 2 '87. J. Leonard
  People Wkly il 27:34-5 F 2 '87
The life and loves of a she devil
  Vogue il 177:40 Je '87. C. Schine
Life with Lucy
  Channels il 7:75 F '87. W. A. Henry
Lily Tomlin
  _N Y_ il 20:72 O 5 '87. J. Leonard
Long gone
  Sports Illus il 66:66 Je 1 '87. R. W. Creamer

Lost empires
  _N Y_ 20:68-9 Ja 26 '87. J. Leonard
Love among thieves
  _N Y_ il 20:121 F 23 '87. J. Leonard
Lovelaw
  Vogue 177:90 My '87. C. Schine
MacNeil/Lehrer newshour
  Progressive il 51:15 Jl '87. R. K. Manoff
Man alive
  Macleans il 100:53-4 Ja 12 '87. P. Young
The man who broke 1,000 chains
  _N Y_ 20:100-1 N 2 '87. J. Leonard
Mandela
  Film Comment il 23:11-12+ N/D '87. A. White
  Jet il 73:58-60 O 5 '87
  _N Y_ il 20:112 S 14 '87. J. Leonard
  Nation 245:462-3 O 24 '87. M. Massing
  Time il 130:80 S 21 '87. D. Worrell
Married . . . with children
  _N Y_ 20:83 Ap 20 '87. J. Leonard
Max Headroom
  Newsweek il 109:55 Ap 6 '87. H. F. Waters
Mayflower Madam
  _N Y_ 20:117+ N 16 '87. J. Leonard
  Vogue il 177:114 O '87. C. Schine
The McLaughlin Group
  Life il 10:26 D '87. L. Wainwright
Miami Vice
  Jet il 73:58-9 O 12 '87. T. S. Moore
  People Wkly il 28:132-7 N 23 '87. R. Sanders
  Pop Mech il 164:85-9+ Jl '87. C. Gromer
  Pop Mech il 164:156 Jl '87. T. H. Cole
Monday sportsnite
  Sports Illus il 66:67 Je 29 '87. W. Taaffe
Moonlighting
  Christ Today il 31:71 S 4 '87. Q. J. Schultze
  Ladies Home J il 104:34+ Mr '87. E. Sherman
  Roll Stone il p52+ Mr 26 '87. D. Handelman
  Time il 129:79 Mr 30 '87. R. Zoglin
More than the news
  Progressive il 51:13 S '87. M. Schultz
The morning program
  Time il 129:70 Ja 26 '87. R. Zoglin
  Time il 130:91 O 12 '87. L. Zuckerman
Moyers: in search of the Constitution
  Sch Update il 119:29 My 18 '87. L. Kravitz
Moyers: report from Philadelphia
  Sch Update il 119:29 My 18 '87. L. Kravitz
The mystery of Al Capone's vaults
  Newsweek il 109:4 Ja 5 '87. D. Gates
Napoleon and Josephine: a love story
  _N Y_ il 20:116-17 N 16 '87. J. Leonard
The new Newlywed game
  People Wkly il 28:44-6+ Ag 3 '87. M. Dougherty
Nightline
  Newsweek il 109:50-3+ Je 15 '87. J. Alter
Norman Rockwell's Breaking home ties
  _N Y_ 20:74-5 N 30 '87. J. Leonard
Nutcracker: money, madness, murder
  _N Y_ il 20:68-9 Mr 23 '87. J. Leonard
One life to live
  _N Y_ il 20:70-2+ My 18 '87. E. Hopkins
Out on a limb
  Christ Century 104:182-3 F 25 '87. C. V. Anderson
  _N Y_ 20:69 Ja 26 '87. J. Leonard
  N Y Rev Books il 34:16-19 Ap 9 '87. M. Gardner
  Vogue il 177:44 Ja '87. C. Schine
Pack of lies
  Sch Update il 119:34 Ap 20 '87. S. Linnea
Pee-wee's playhouse
  Atlantic il 259:20-2 My '87. K. Leishman
  _N Y_ il 20:14 Ja 19 '87. B. Donofrio
  Newsweek il 109:83-4 My 18 '87. H. F. Waters
  Omni 10:62 D '87. M. Long
  Roll Stone il p36-8+ F 12 '87. T. Gertler
  Theatre Crafts il 21:67-70 F '87. D. F. Sisk
  Vogue il 177:114+ F '87. C. Schine
The people's court
  50 Plus il 27:94+ F '87. R. Schoenstein
Poor little rich girl: the Barbara Hutton story
  McCalls il 115:186-8 N '87. M. J. Bandler
  _N Y_ 20:120 N 16 '87. J. Leonard
Prison mother, prison daughter
  Macleans il 100:54 Ja 12 '87. J. Bemrose
Private eye
  _N Y_ il 20:60-1 S 21 '87. J. Leonard
  Newsweek il 110:74 N 2 '87. H. F. Waters
  Roll Stone il p41-2 S 24 '87. M. Christensen
  Vogue il 177:126 N '87. C. Schine
Quartermaine's terms
  _N Y_ 20:95 My 18 '87. J. Leonard

Television program reviews—Single works—*cont.*
Race for the bomb
 Macleans 100:74 F 2 '87. J. Bemrose
Rapists: can they be stopped?
 Macleans il 100:54 F 23 '87. H. Robertson
Reckoning
 Macleans il 100:64 N 9 '87. B. D. Johnson
Report on America
 America 157:136-8 S 12-19 '87. W. H. Shannon
The ring of truth
 Astronomy 15:39-40 O '87. J. Kanipe
 Phys Today il 40:119-20 O '87. G. F. Wheeler
The room upstairs
 N Y 20:66-7 F 2 '87. J. Leonard
Roots
 Jet il 71:36-7 F 16 '87
Runaways—24 hours on the street
 Macleans il 100:63 S 7 '87. B. D. Johnson
Saturday night live
 Newsweek il 109:70 Ap 13 '87. H. F. Waters
 USA Today (Periodical) 116:90-2 N '87. J. Saltzman
Scholastic sports America
 Sch Update 120:20 N 6 '87. B. Phillips
The secret garden
 N Y il 20:74 N 30 '87. J. Leonard
Seize the day
 N Y il 20:114 My 4 '87. J. Leonard
 Time il 129:98 My 4 '87. R. Zoglin
Sesame Street
 N Y il 20:48-53 N 23 '87. P. Hellman
Seven days in May
 Newsweek il 109:62 Je 29 '87. J. Alter
Silas Marner
 Vogue il 177:144 Mr '87. C. Schine
The Slap Maxwell story
 N Y il 20:124-5 S 28 '87. J. Leonard
 Roll Stone il p39-40+ N 19 '87. B. Zehme
 Sports Illus il 67:66 N 16 '87. J. McCallum
Spacewatch
 Space World X-10-286 Space Advocate:A2 O '87.
 L. L. Kofler
Spenser: for hire
 Ebony il 42:62+ Ap '87. F. White, III
 Newsweek il 109:54 Ap 13 '87
Square one
 Time il 129:86 F 23 '87. R. Zoglin
St. Elsewhere
 Channels il 7:26-7+ O '87. L. Margulies
 Roll Stone il p33-5 Je 18 '87. B. Zehme
Star search
 Vogue 177:114 Ap '87. C. Schine
Star trek: the next generation
 People Wkly il 28:63-5 Ag 31 '87. M. Dougherty
 Roll Stone il p42 D 3 '87. B. Svetkey
Starman
 Sch Update il 119:TE8 F 23 '87. M. Ronan
Story of a marriage
 N Y il 20:87-8 Ap 6 '87. J. Leonard
 Theatre Crafts il 21:99-102 My '87. R. Seidenberg
Street legal
 Macleans il 100:53-4 F 23 '87. B. D. Johnson
The struggles for Poland
 Hist Today il 37:44-9 Je '87. N. Ascherson
Tales from the Hollywood Hills
 Time il 130:95 N 16 '87. R. Zoglin
thirtysomething
 Newsweek il 110:59 D 21 '87. H. F. Waters
 Roll Stone il p41-2 D 3 '87. T. Minsky
Today
 People Wkly il 27:22-5 Mr 2 '87. D. Waggoner
 Vogue il 177:352-3+ Ap '87. L. Smith
Tour of duty
 Channels il 7:76 O '87. W. A. Henry
 Jet 72:22 Ag 24 '87
The Tracey Ullman show
 N Y il 20:83-4 Ap 20 '87. J. Leonard
 Newsweek il 110:48 Jl 13 '87. H. F. Waters
Trying times
 Film Comment il 23:78-9 N/D '87. T. Carson
 N Y il 20:165 O 26 '87. J. Leonard
 Roll Stone il p40 N 19 '87. J. Martel
Uncle Tom's cabin
 Jet il 72:24-5 Ag 3 '87. L. Ransom
Waiting for the moon
 N Y il 20:62-3 Je 15 '87. J. Leonard
We are the children
 America 156:inside cover Mr 14 '87. J. W. Donohue
 N Y 20:66-7 Mr 16 '87. J. Leonard
Wheel of fortune
 Glamour 85:178+ S '87. M. Rosen
 Good Housekeep il 204:66+ My '87. V. Scott

 Good Housekeep il 204:72+ My '87
 Good Housekeep il 205:34+ N '87. V. Scott
 Newsweek il 109:62-8 F 9 '87. H. F. Waters
 Seventeen il 46:24+ Jl '87. J. Sherman
A year in the life
 Roll Stone p41-2 D 3 '87. T. Minsky
 Vogue il 177:206 S '87. C. Schine
Young Harry Houdini
 Sch Update il 119:28 Mr 9 '87. D. Scheuer
Your show of shows
 USA Today (Periodical) 116:90-2 N '87. J. Saltzman
Television programming *See* Cable television—Programming; Television broadcasting—Programming
Television programs *See* Television broadcasting
Television projection
Laser TV. M. Berger. il *Pop Sci* 231:22+ Ag '87
Progress in projection TV. D. Ranada. il *High Fidel* 37:18 D '87
Sight and sound: the big picture. H. Fantel. il *Opera News* 51:30-1 Ja 3 '87
Tiny circuit sharpens giant TV [Novabeam 100 projection TV monitor] J. Free. *Pop Sci* 230:59 Mr '87
Tune in to the big picture. P. Plawin. il *Changing Times* 41:39-42 My '87
Television ratings *See* Television broadcasting—Ratings
Television receivers
Heavyweight contender; Featherweight class [Mitsubishi 37 inch set and Heathkit's 9 inch model] S. A. Booth. il *Pop Mech* 164:14 S '87
In case you tuned in late [new features] P. Elmer-Dewitt. il *Time* 130:59 D 21 '87
The maxi-boom in mini-TVs. D. Levine. il *Sport Mag* 78:85 F '87
Microtip TV [flat-screen display] N. J. Freundlich. il *Pop Sci* 231:60-1+ Ag '87
Screen gems. J. B. Meigs. il *Roll Stone* p83+ O 22 '87
This year's buzzword: digital, digital, digital. J. Kaminsky. il *Channels* 7 Sp Issue:126 D '87
Toshiba non-interlaced TV and digital VCR [CZ2697 and DX-900] D. O'Neill. il *Petersens Photogr Mag* 16:9 Ag '87
True colors. C. Sarver and D. Ranada. il *High Fidel* 37:48-52 Mr '87
TV's for ears as well as eyes. il *U S News World Rep* 103:93-4+ N 9 '87
Video and the digital revolution. G. Brockhouse. il *High Fidel* 37:51+ N '87
Video to go. W. J. Hawkins. il *Pop Sci* 231:40-2 N '87

Collectors and collecting
Pre-war television sets: today's collectible. S. F. Hofer. il *Antiques Collect Hobbies* 92:79-80 My '87
Components
 See also
 Video monitors
Control
Universal wireless remote control and stereo TV tuner. il *Radio-Electron* 58:24-6 My '87
Maintenance and repair
Service clinic. J. Darr. See issues of Radio-Electronics through September 1987
TV troubleshooter's notebook: black vertical bars. J. Shane. il *Radio-Electron* 58:70+ Je '87
Manufacture
 See Television equipment industry
Testing
19- and 20-inch TV's. il *Consum Rep* 52:330-7 D '87
A guide to TVs. il *Consum Rep* 52:142-53 Mr '87
Tuning
Hands-on: Multivision. J. B. Meigs. il *Pop Mech* 164:46 F '87
Multivision 3.1 digital TV tuner. il *High Fidel* 37:36+ Mr '87
MultiVision = multimagic. W. J. Hawkins. il *Pop Sci* 230:36 My '87
Proton VT-210 monitor/receiver. il *High Fidel* 37:35-7 Jl '87
Universal wireless remote control and stereo TV tuner. il *Radio-Electron* 58:24-6 My '87
Television relay systems
 See also
 Cable television
Television reporters *See* Television broadcasting—News
Television scenery *See* Television broadcasting—Setting and scenery
Television script writing *See* Television authorship
Television serials
Behind the soapy scenes of 'One life to live': endless loves. E. Hopkins. il *N Y* 20:70-2+ My 18 '87

Television serials—*cont.*

Kenya uses soap opera to stem high birth rate. *Jet* 72:62 Ag 31 '87

The never-ending story [soap operas vs. a Christian view of life] Q. J. Schultze. il por *Christ Today* 31:26-9 Ap 17 '87

Soap opera addiction: what's the attraction? il *Teen* 31:36-8 Mr '87

The soaps clean up. E. Sherman. il *Ladies Home J* 104:48 O '87

Why do we love the queens of evil? J. Collins. il por *Redbook* 168:62+ F '87

Working together in the third world [Kenya soap opera promotes family planning] M. Morain. il por *Humanist* 47:33-4 S/O '87

Anecdotes, facetiae, satire, etc.

Modern-day gloom. R. Baker. il *N Y Times Mag* p16 My 24 '87

Uncivil liberties. C. Trillin. *Nation* 244:38 Ja 17 '87

Television sets *See* Television receivers

Television sound

Audio/video synergy [surround sound processors] J. D. Hirsch. il *Stereo Rev* 52:23-4 Ap '87

Audio alchemy [Chace Stereo Surround Processor] G. Buchalter. il por *Forbes* 140:188 O 5 '87

Broadcasters are waiting with both ears cocked [stereophonic TV] A. Snyder. il *Channels* 7 Sp Issue:86 D '87

Luxman LV-105 audio-video integrated amplifier. il *High Fidel* 37:56-7 Ja '87

NEC AVD-700E surround-sound processor. il *High Fidel* 37:37-8 Je '87

Stereo TV decoder (I). T. T. Templin. il *Radio-Electron* 58:37-41 Ja '87

Stereo TV decoder (II). T. T. Templin. il *Radio-Electron* 58:51-4 F '87

Surround sound [processors and decoders] T. R. Gillett. il *Stereo Rev* 52:54-8 Ap '87

Surround-sound attractions. R. B. Schulein. il *High Fidel* 37:49+ Je '87

Universal wireless remote control and stereo TV tuner. il *Radio-Electron* 58:24-6 My '87

Yamaha AVC-50 integrated audio/video amplifier. J. D. Hirsch. il *Stereo Rev* 52:43-4+ Ja '87

Television stage setting *See* Television broadcasting—Setting and scenery

Television stations

See also

Cable television

Low power television

Baltimore's favorite anchorman returns despite serious malady [J. Turner of WJZ] S. Salmans. il por *Channels* 7:8 Je '87

The changing indie landscape [special section; with editorial comment by Les Brown] il *Channels* 7:4, 35+ Ja '87

Coveting thy neighbor's system. J. Vitale. il *Channels* 7 Sp Issue:51 D '87

Dallas station refuses to flinch as it topples a gridiron power [WFAA takes on SMU scandal] D. Holder. il *Channels* 7:13 My '87

Delightful, lovable chaos [Vancouver TV station CKVU] A. Fotheringham. il *Macleans* 100:52 Ja 20 '87

Give-backs to ailing stations causing new syndication woes. P. E. Bauer. il *Channels* 7:14 Ap '87

Having it both ways [network affiliates] A. B. Block. il *Forbes* 140:42-3 Jl 27 '87

Home rule comes to a former O&O [Viacom's KMOV, St. Louis] R. Buck. il *Channels* 7:14 Jl/Ag '87

Indies' happy days may be here again. J. B. Grillo. il *Channels* 7 Sp Issue:72-3 D '87

KYTV [Springfield, Missouri's NBC affiliate] J. McGuire. il *Channels* 7:34-5+ O '87

KYW's consultant coup [Sawyer-Miller Group helps revive Philadelphia station] J. Malanowski. il *Channels* 7:22-3 S '87

L.A.'s major TV stations dominated by white men. *Jet* 72:22 Jl 20 '87

A little UHF group tries a great big gamble [TVX buys stations from Taft Broadcasting] C. S. Eklund. il por *Bus Week* p84+ F 2 '87

Local TV fights back in Palm Beach [ad campaign] M. Clary. il map *Channels* 7:21-2 Ap '87

Local TV's ad battles [special section] il *Channels* 7:45-8+ N '87

Loughlin's lament [J. Loughlin, manager of Chicago's WGN] J. B. Grillo. il por *Channels* 7:66-7 Jl/Ag '87

The loyal opposition [affiliates] J. B. Grillo. il *Channels* 7 Sp Issue:68 D '87

Making localism count [KARE of Minneapolis-St. Paul] J. B. Grillo. il *Channels* 7:58-9 Je '87

Must-carry's poster children [effect of regulation on independent WTZA-TV, Hudson Valley, N.Y.] C. Capuzzi. *Channels* 7:17 Ja '87

News meltdown hits L.A. [KCBS-TV] R. Adler. il *Channels* 7:70-1 F '87

Pam Zekman [head of WBBM-TV's investigative unit] J. Vitale. il pors *Channels* 7:31-2 O '87

The trouble with CBS' stations. C. Capuzzi. il *Channels* 7:9 Je '87

True grit in Amarillo [KVII] J. B. Grillo. il por *Channels* 7:74-5 O '87

The tug-of-war behind your TV screen [networks vs. affiliates] D. Lieberman. il *Bus Week* p104+ Ap 13 '87

TV's troubled independents. A. Miller. il *Newsweek* 109:50 F 16 '87

When bossy was boss [Indianapolis TV stations struggle to get time zones straight] J. B. Grillo. il *Channels* 7:71-2 Je '87

Who owns broadcasting? [cover story; special section] il *Channels* 7:47-56 Ap '87

Will temptation undo the tie that binds [networks questioning affiliate compensation] S. Behrens. il *Channels* 7:41-3 My '87

The Windy City's 'little indy that could' reaches for the stars [WPWR] P. J. Bednarski. il *Channels* 7:16 S '87

WSMV's damage control [Nashville station promotions] R. Buck. il map *Channels* 7:21-2 My '87

Equipment

Hardware outlays may rise in support of the news. B. McKernan. il *Channels* 7 Sp Issue:88-9 D '87

Television stations, Black

See also

East Texas Television Network

Battle rages for control of Detroit TV station [WGPR] il *Jet* 72:4 Jl 13 '87

Clarence McKee takes helm of $365 million TV station. por *Jet* 72:36-7 Ag 24 '87

McKee, Gillett Co. buy $365 mil. Fla. TV station. por *Jet* 72:6 Mr 30 '87

A trailblazer's trip to the top [J. B. Llewellyn] F. McCoy. il por *Bus Week* p129+ N 16 '87

Television studios

A TV studio guide. E. Belson. il *Travel Holiday* 168:27-9 Ag '87

Television transmission

See also

High definition television

Scrambling systems (Telecommunication)

Sight and sound: a hopeless wodge: unscrambling the international TV picture. C. Fuselli. *Opera News* 52:36+ Ag '87

True colors. C. Sarver and D. Ranada. il *High Fidel* 37:48-52 Mr '87

Television viewers *See* Television audiences

Television workers

See also

Strikes—Television workers

Salaries, pensions, etc.

$alary review [special section] il *Channels* 7:59-64 Jl/Ag '87

Television writing *See* Television authorship

Televisions *See* Television receivers

Televison and the United Nations *See* United Nations and television

Teleworking *See* Telecommuting

Telex Corporation

How to compete with IBM. S. W. Angrist. il por *Forbes* 139:145 F 23 '87

Telfair Academy of Arts and Sciences

An elegant home for art. K. Milam. il *Horizon* 30:36-7 Ap '87

Telford, George

Presbyterians: politics and responsibility. *Christ Century* 104:614-16 Jl 15-22 '87

Tell, David

Differences and inequality [interview with A. Kessler-Harris] *Society* 24:10-16 S/O '87

Disparity or discrimination? [interview with R. Rosenberg] *Society* 24:4-10 S/O '87

Tell Abu Hureyra excavations *See* Syria—Antiquities

Teller

See also

Penn & Teller

Teller, Edward, 1908-

Defense is the best defense. il *N Y Times Mag* p47-8 Ap 5 '87

about

Superconductivity and quantum mechanics. D. E. Thomsen. *Sci News* 131:358 Je 6 '87

Tendons—Wounds and injuries—*cont.*
Man down on the field [football player D. Dawson attempts comeback after Achilles injury] J. D. Miller. il *Sport Mag* 78:102 Ag '87
Teng, Hsiao-p'ing *See* Deng Xiaoping, 1904-
Tennant, Anthony M.
about
Guinness' new boss starts plugging the holes. M. Maremont. il por *Bus Week* p51 O 5 '87
Tennant, Colin *See* Glenconner, Colin Christopher Paget Tennant, 3rd Baron
Tennant, Raymond W., and others
Prediction of chemical carcinogenicity in rodents from in vitro genetic toxicity assays. bibl f il *Science* 236:933-41 My 22 '87
Tenneco Inc.
Plowing different fields [J. L. Ketelsen] P. Nulty. il por *Fortune* 116:62+ Ag 3 '87
Tennesen, Michael
Putting the sting on poachers. il *Natl Wildl* 25:26-8 O/N '87
Tennessee
See also
Big South Fork National River and Recreation Area (Tenn. and Ky.)
Blacks—Tennessee
Booksellers and bookselling—Tennessee
Child welfare—Tennessee
Country estates—Tennessee
Cumberland County (Tenn.)
Educational laws and regulations—Tennessee
Fishing—Tennessee
Great Smoky Mountains National Park (N.C. and Tenn.)
Employees
Tenn. reps urge their gov. to hire more blacks. *Jet* 72:13 Jl 6 '87
Industries
See also
Copper mines and mining—Tennessee
Politics and government
See also
Politics, Corruption in—Tennessee
Tennessee's new governor finds good fortune in a cookie [N. McWherter] il por *People Wkly* 27:75 F 2 '87
Tennessee. National Guard
Operation scare-the-pants-off-'em [mock invasions of high schools to promote patriotism] *Harpers* 274:22-3 Ap '87
Tennessee evolution controversy
Grandpa's famous trial [Scopes Monkey Trial] J. Scopes. il *Progressive* 51:34 Je '87
William Jennings Bryan's last campaign. S. J. Gould. il por *Nat Hist* 96:16+ N '87
Tennessee-Tombigbee Waterway
The Tenn-Tom: chronicle of a waterway. H. Middleton. il map *South Living* 22:42+ N '87
Tennis
See also
Collegiate Tennis Hall of Fame
International Tennis Hall of Fame
Advantage: Gardnar Mulloy. L. Lindeman. il pors *50 Plus* 27:68-70+ Ja '87
And now, the good news [solidarity of the game at both the pro and amateur levels] J. T. Fogarty. il *World Tennis* 34:64 Mr '87
Around the world. See issues of World Tennis
Blazing racquets! The day the legends met [Billie Jean King, Martina Navratilova, Chris Evert, and Pam Shriver play benefit doubles match] F. E. Halpert. il *Women's Sports Fitness* 9:64 Jl '87
A celebration of life [senior tennis] S. Stevenson. il *World Tennis* 35:38-42 O '87
Challenge of the tennis champions [benefit doubles match to be played by Billie Jean King, Martina Navratilova, Chris Evert, and Pam Shriver] *Women's Sports Fitness* 9:74 Ap '87
Mother of a pearl [6-year-old player A. Stevenson] S. Stevenson. il pors *World Tennis* 34:38-41+ Ap '87
My love affair with tennis. R. Barry. il *World Tennis* 34:88 My '87
Ones to watch. il *World Tennis* 34:17 Ja '87
Planned playerhood. C. Evert. il *World Tennis* 34:22-3 Ja '87
Accidents and injuries
See also
Epicondylitis
After the fall [life after a back ailment ends junior career at age 16] L. Hadge. il *World Tennis* 35:26+ Jl '87

The agony of de-feet. J. E. McNerney. il *World Tennis* 34:8-9 F '87
Getting the massage. B. Norris. il *World Tennis* 34:6-7 Ja '87
Head-to-toe treatments. B. Norris. il *World Tennis* 35:14-15 Je '87
Incredible journey [comeback of injury prone H. Lloyd] J. E. Loehr. il por *World Tennis* 34:16-17 Ap '87
Prevention's the best medicine [foot injuries] J. E. McNerney. il *World Tennis* 35:16-17 Jl '87
Smart tennis moves. C. Schaeffer. il *Changing Times* 41:16 Je '87
Who will stop the pain [overcoming injuries through positive imagery] K. Porter and J. Foster. il *World Tennis* 35:28-30 Jl '87
Anecdotes, facetiae, satire, etc.
The lobber baron. W. Walden. il *World Tennis* 34:18-19 Mr '87
Who can serve better, Crabs or Scorpios? D. D. Jackson. il *Smithsonian* 18:162 Je '87
Awards
WT's 1987 collegiate tennis awards. il *World Tennis* 35:102 S '87
Bibliography
Book review. *World Tennis* 34:27+ Ja '87
Economic aspects
Can Arthur Ashe put this idea over the net? [minority player development] B. Welling. il por *Bus Week* p120 S 21 '87
Equipment
See also
Tennis balls
Tennis rackets
Tennis shoes
Industry preview. P. Sikowitz and B. Socolow. il *World Tennis* 34:24-6 Ja '87
Live from Atlanta: it's all Super. P. Sikowitz. il *World Tennis* 34:60-1+ Ap '87
Shades of greatness [sunglasses] P. M. Coan. il *World Tennis* 35:48-9 Ag '87
Periodicals
See also
World tennis (Periodical)
Psychological aspects
Break point [pressures of junior tennis; interview with H. Schoenfield] J. E. Loehr. il *World Tennis* 34:10-12 Ja '87
The chemistry of doubles. J. E. Loehr. il *World Tennis* 35:18-19 Jl '87
Danger: big point ahead. J. E. Loehr. il *World Tennis* 35:12+ N '87
Don't let go of your racket [controlling match stress] J. E. Loehr. il *World Tennis* 35:10+ O '87
Emotional rescue [controlling temper] M. Navratilova. il *World Tennis* 35:86 S '87
Here comes that sinking feeling! [conquering nervousness] J. E. Loehr. il *World Tennis* 34:16-17 Mr '87
Looking beyond [college player who did not choose a pro career] E. Rosenfeld. il *World Tennis* 34:44-6 My '87
Mac says: overcome the mental challenge. J. McEnroe. il por *World Tennis* 35:58 Jl '87
The mental game [special section] il *World Tennis* 35:25-9 D '87
Motivation. N. Bollettieri. il *World Tennis* 34:35 Ap '87
The painful, lonely search for success [life on the satellite tour] N. Amdur. il *World Tennis* 34:22-3 Mr '87
That period of adjustment [accepting the loss of number 1 ranking] P. Gonzalez. il por *World Tennis* 35:80 Ag '87
Underdog. N. Bollettieri. il *World Tennis* 35:88+ S '87
The 'ups' and 'downs' of emotionalism. J. E. Loehr. il *World Tennis* 35:12+ Ag '87
What would you have done? [playing under pressures like the ones that faced the U.S. Davis Cup team in Paraguay] J. E. Loehr. il *World Tennis* 35:12-13 Je '87
When the balls come tumbling down [managing stress in junior tennis] J. E. Loehr. il *World Tennis* 35:14+ S '87
Whither the warrior? [mental toughness] J. E. Loehr. il *World Tennis* 34:12-13 F '87
Who will stop the pain [overcoming injuries through positive imagery] K. Porter and J. Foster. il *World Tennis* 35:28-30 Jl '87
Public opinion
And the winners are . . . [reader poll results] A. Beck. il *World Tennis* 35:70+ S '87
Rules
Courts of appeal. N. Powel. See issues of World Tennis

Tennis—Rules—cont.

Anecdotes, facetiae, satire, etc.

There oughta be a law. N. Powel. il *World Tennis* 35:50+ Je '87

Study and teaching

See also

Nick Bollettieri Tennis Academy (Bradenton, Fla.)
Tennis coaches

101 winning tips: crown jewels to help you close out points, games, sets and matches [cover story] il *World Tennis* 35:21-30 O '87

All-star instruction [special section] il *World Tennis* 34:28-35 Ap '87

Anticipation. J. L. Groppel. *World Tennis* 35:56 Jl '87

Ashe hopes tennis clinic will erase lazy players. por *Jet* 72:51 S 21 '87

Attack the lefty forehand [serving] F. Stolle. il *World Tennis* 35:20 Je '87

A balancing act [groundstrokes] D. Ralston. il por *World Tennis* 34:41 F '87

Be offensive [lobbing] F. Stolle. il *World Tennis* 35:31 Ag '87

Better your balance for consistency [serving] D. Ralston. il *World Tennis* 35:74 S '87

The camp spirit: bring it home. J. E. Loehr. il *World Tennis* 34:32-3 Ja '87

Climb every mountain: how to neutralize your male opponent. C. Evert. il *World Tennis* 34:22-4 F '87

Design your own diary [match diary] I. Lendl. il *World Tennis* 34:20-1 F '87

Direct your delivery [serving] F. Stolle. il *World Tennis* 34:47 Ja '87

Directory [tennis camps] il *World Tennis* 34:38-40+ Ja '87

Don't be a clay pigeon! C. Evert. il por *World Tennis* 34:48-50 My '87

Dynamic duos [improving doubles play] M. Navratilova. il *World Tennis* 34:40-1 Mr '87

Elbow in for sound strokes. F. Stolle. il *World Tennis* 35:58 S '87

Forewarned is forearmed [the volley] D. Ralston. il *World Tennis* 35:31 Jl '87

Formidable forehand: a frame-by-frame look at Lendl's championship stroke. J. L. Groppel. il pors *World Tennis* 35:30-1 D '87

Getting the most out of your game. il *World Tennis* 34:42-8 F '87

Golf and tennis schools. M. C. Lewis. il *Travel Holiday* 167:18+ Je '87

The half volley. il *World Tennis* 34:28-31 Ja '87

Hands. P. Gonzalez. il *World Tennis* 35:28-9 Je '87

How I developed my volley. C. Evert. il por *World Tennis* 35:30-1 N '87

Instinctively yours; ed. by Cindy Shmerler. H. Mandlikova. il por *World Tennis* 34:32-3 My '87

Less is more [the block return of serve] F. Stolle. il *World Tennis* 35:36 Jl '87

The magic touch [volleying] J. L. Groppel. il *World Tennis* 34:52-4 F '87

On the ball [winter drills] R. Schuessler. il *Women's Sports Fitness* 9:58 F '87

Patterned play: a lost art. J. Nogrady. il *World Tennis* 35:76 S '87

Pick a pocket or two [forehand return of serve] D. Ralston. il *World Tennis* 35:27 Ag '87

Punch that door open! [forehand volley] F. Stolle. il por *World Tennis* 35:47 D '87

Raise the level of your backhand down-the-line. il *World Tennis* 35:78-81 S '87

Raise the level of your game: 35s, 45s, 55s. il *World Tennis* 35:30-3 Je '87

Raise the level of your game: strategy. il *World Tennis* 34:34-7 My '87

Raise the level of your inside out forehand. il *World Tennis* 35:32-5 Jl '87

Raise the level of your mixed doubles. il *World Tennis* 35:26-9 N '87

Reach up high [backhand volley] D. Ralston. il *World Tennis* 35:65 O '87

Ready, set . . . [improvement of timing] J. L. Groppel. il *World Tennis* 35:60 S '87

The second serve. il *World Tennis* 34:30-3 Mr '87

Smash & recover [the overhead] D. Ralston. il pors *World Tennis* 35:17 D '87

Stay back to get ahead [playing the baseline] T. Tinling. il *World Tennis* 35:80 Je '87

Step back first [forehand volley] D. Ralston. il *World Tennis* 35:25 N '87

To skip or hop? [service delivery] P. Cohen. il *World Tennis* 35:82-3 S '87

The U.S. talent drought: it's elementary [skills of young players not being properly honed] W. Van Horn. *World Tennis* 34:64 Ja '87

Use your whole body [serving] F. Stolle. il *World Tennis* 35:34 N '87

Aids and devices

Taped crusaders [instructional videos] P. Stites. il *World Tennis* 35:12-13 D '87

Tournaments

And the surfer ate the shark [A. Gomez's victory in the Shearson Lehman Brothers Tournament of Champions] J. Diaz. il por *Sports Illus* 66:73 My 18 '87

Ashe, Gibson raise funds for tennis, UNCF on yacht. il pors *Jet* 72:8 Ag 10 '87

Australia had the Pat hand [victory over Sweden clinches Davis Cup] R. Yallop. il por *Sports Illus* 66:26-7 Ja 5 '87

Backstage at Wimbledon. S. Bayless. il *Sport Mag* 78:33-6+ Jl '87

Big Cat on the prowl [M. Mecir's victory in WCT Finals] J. Diaz. il por *Sports Illus* 66:91-2 Ap 20 '87

Boris's blunder [B. Becker defeated by P. Doohan at Wimbledon] C. Kirkpatrick. il pors *Sports Illus* 67:21 Jl 6 '87

Building blocks or stumbling blocks? [E. Nagel's views on the collegiate system] S. Flink. il *World Tennis* 35:16-17 O '87

Cash scales the heights [Wimbledon] S. Flink. il *World Tennis* 35:108+ S '87

Continental divide [new crop of American players to compete in Davis Cup] K. Cunningham. il *World Tennis* 34:46-8 Mr '87

Davis Cup [U.S. vs. West Germany] K. Cunningham. *World Tennis* 35:67 O '87

Davis Cup '86: credit for Cash. S. Flink. il por *World Tennis* 34:54-5 Mr '87

Davis Cup: a proposal. N. Amdur. il *World Tennis* 35:4 O '87

Davis Cup dilemma: what it means. N. Amdur. il *World Tennis* 34:4 My '87

Deutsche treat [Federation Cup] M. Witherell. il *World Tennis* 35:66-7 O '87

Diary of a rookie tour. A. Agassi. il pors *World Tennis* 35:32-6+ D '87

Easter Bowl: through her eyes [junior tournament organizer S. Hamilton] C. Shmerler. il por *World Tennis* 34:24+ Ap '87

Fire and rain at the Lipton. K. Cunningham. il *World Tennis* 34:68-9+ My '87

Germany shows a pair of aces [B. Becker and S. Graf at Wimbledon] T. Callahan. il pors *Time* 129:58-60 Je 29 '87

Getting fed to the Dawgs [University of Georgia hosts NCAA tournament] J. Diaz. il *Sports Illus* 66:68+ Je 1 '87

A golden opportunity for tennis [1988 Olympics] N. Amdur. il *World Tennis* 35:4 Jl '87

Good as Gould [Stanford University tennis coach] L.-M. Singer. il por *World Tennis* 35:41-3 D '87

Inside Wimbledon 1987 [special section] il *World Tennis* 35:38-44+ Jl '87

Ivan Lendl: master of the universe [winner of the Nabisco Masters] S. Flink. il por *World Tennis* 34:56-7 F '87

Lendl/Navratilova reign remains [U.S. Open; with editorial comment by Neil Amdur] S. Flink. il *World Tennis* 35:4, 66-9 N '87

Look who's on top again [M. Navratilova takes U.S. Open title] F. Deford. il por *Sports Illus* 67:40-3 S 21 '87

Look who's on top still [I. Lendl takes U.S. Open title] F. Deford. il por *Sports Illus* 67:44+ S 21 '87

Lori McNeil challenges tennis elite at US Open. il por *Jet* 73:51 S 28 '87

Mac gets a new Mr. Fix-it [adviser S. Daeshik at the Volvo International] R. Sullivan. il pors *Sports Illus* 67:26-7 Ag 17 '87

No place to go but up [rising young American and Soviet players at the U.S. Open] F. Deford. il por *Sports Illus* 67:59-60 S 14 '87

Olympic tennis: a bad idea. B. Colson. por *Sports Illus* 66:96 Je 29 '87

On and up with Steffi [S. Graf wins Virginia Slims Championships] J. Diaz. il por *Sports Illus* 67:92 N 30 '87

Score one more for Steffi [S. Graf beats M. Navratilova in French Open] F. Deford. il pors *Sports Illus* 66:38-42 Je 15 '87

Secrets of success [I. Lendl's match diary] K. Cunningham. il *World Tennis* 34:18-21 F '87

Tennis—Tournaments—*cont.*

Seventeen's Tennis Tournament of Champions. M. Lukens. il *Seventeen* 46:175+ Ap '87

She's no. 2 with a bullet [S. Graf's victory in the Lipton Players Championships] D. S. Looney. il pors *Sports Illus* 66:34-6+ Mr 16 '87

Slims Championship: Martina marches on. C. Shmerler. il por *World Tennis* 34:57+ F '87

Smash acts on centre court [Wimbledon] C. Kirkpatrick. il pors *Sports Illus* 67:28-30+ Jl 13 '87

A strange new tennis racket [Stakes Match] A. Wolff. il *Sports Illus* 67:24-7 D 7 '87

Strokes of genius: Steffi Graf peaks for the U.S. Open. M. Stone. il pors *N Y* 20:48-52 Ag 31 '87

Sweet inspiration [45 year old competitor] S. Bowden. il *World Tennis* 34:22-3 Ap '87

Too much too soon [revamping junior tennis] J. E. Loehr. il *World Tennis* 35:14+ D '87

Tournament report. See issues of World Tennis

U.S. Open '87 [special section] il *World Tennis* 35:31-8+ S '87

U.S. Open: preview '87. J. Ryan. il *Women's Sports Fitness* 9:65+ S '87

An uncompromising position [pursuing excellence in the men's 35s] F. Olmsted. il *World Tennis* 34:14-15 F '87

Vive la différence [women's matches are currently more exciting than men's matches] S. Flink. il *World Tennis* 35:20-1 Ag '87

Who's hot, and who's not [French Open] S. Flink. il *World Tennis* 35:66+ Ag '87

Why tennis is such a drag [Wimbledon] P. Axthelm. il *Newsweek* 109:55 Je 29 '87

Yankee flameout in Hartford [West Germany defeats U.S. in Davis Cup play] F. Lidz. il pors *Sports Illus* 67:20-1 Ag 3 '87

Year of challenge: 1986. il *World Tennis* 34:18-21 Ja '87

Anecdotes, facetiae, satire, etc.

Notes and comment. *New Yorker* 63:32 O 5 '87

Economic aspects

12 who mattered [promoter G. M. Heldman] C. Shmerler. il por *World Tennis* 35:64 N '87

Advantage, sponsors [French Open] F. J. Comes. *Bus Week* p58 Je 8 '87

Cigarettes anyone? Tennis and smoking [Virginia Slims tournaments sponsored by Philip Morris] R. Doar. *Wash Mon* 19:40 Je '87

The color of money [growth of college tennis spurred by corporate sponsorship] B. Socolow. il *World Tennis* 34:47-9 Ap '87

Count Dracula [I. Tiriac, former player and current tennis agent and mentor] C. Kirkpatrick. il pors *Sports Illus* 66:60-4+ Je 22 '87

Ethical aspects

The flag first! [defense of American behavior during Davis Cup play against West Germany] K. Flach. il *World Tennis* 35:49+ O '87

McEnroe's on a roll [behavior at WCT Finals in Dallas] K. Cunningham. il por *World Tennis* 35:12+ Jl '87

Nasty but necessary. W. Kalyn. il *World Tennis* 34:72 F '87

Out of control [Davis Cup] N. Amdur. il *World Tennis* 35:26-7 Je '87

Out of control [U.S. Open behavior] H. Mandlikova. il por *World Tennis* 35:72 D '87

What price victory? [boorish behavior of American players during Davis Cup play against West Germany] K. Cunningham. il *World Tennis* 35:48+ O '87

History

A 10 year salute to the U.S. Open. il *World Tennis* 35:61+ S '87

A complete history of the world rankings [1953-1985 World tennis rankings] il *World Tennis* 34:33-9 F '87

A monkey on the back [major titles that have eluded great players] S. Flink. il *World Tennis* 35:16-17 Je '87

Redheads have more fun [recollections of D. Budge and R. Laver] S. Flink. il pors *World Tennis* 35:18+ S '87

Officiating

Chief arbiter [interview with Wimbledon referee A. Mills] N. Amdur. il por *World Tennis* 35:50+ Jl '87

Organization and administration

Keeper of the flame [interview with Wimbledon chairman R. E. H. Hadingham] C. Gould. il pors *World Tennis* 35:46+ Jl '87

A letter to Lendl [advising tennis star not to play Davis Cup for the U.S.] S. Flink. il *World Tennis* 35:10-11 D '87

Qualifiers deserve a break. F. Weiss. il *World Tennis* 35:80 N '87

Psychological aspects

See Tennis—Psychological aspects

Television broadcasting

See Television broadcasting—Sports

Tickets

This summer, see Wimbledon . . . live. V. Phillips. il *Sport Mag* 78:93-4 Mr '87

Volunteer workers

12 who mattered: volunteers. K. Cunningham. il *World Tennis* 35:61 O '87

Soviet Union

No place to go but up [rising young American and Soviet players at the U.S. Open] F. Deford. il por *Sports Illus* 67:59-60 S 14 '87

Tennis associations

See also

United States Tennis Association

Tennis balls

Flight of the ball. P. Sikowitz and A. Beck. il *World Tennis* 35:50 Ag '87

Tennis camps *See* Camps

Tennis clothes *See* Clothing and dress—Sports clothes

Tennis coaches

See also

Gould, Dick

Massman, Bea

Tiriac, Ion

Back to school [instructional programs for teachers] B. Socolow. il *World Tennis* 35:32-3 N '87

My family, my team [serving as parent-coach to five children] W. A. Washington. il *World Tennis* 35:18+ O '87

Tennis courts

He built a clay court with 46 tons of sand. il *Sunset* 178:149 Je '87

Tennis elbow *See* Epicondylitis

Tennis etiquette *See* Tennis—Tournaments—Ethical aspects

Tennis fans

Patron saints [perennial U.S. Open attendees] P. M. Coan. il *World Tennis* 35:53 S '87

Tennis leagues

Team up with team tennis. J. E. Loehr. il *World Tennis* 34:26-7 My '87

Tennis players

See also

Amritraj, Vijay

Ashe, Arthur

Becker, Boris

Borg, Björn, 1956-

Budge, Don, 1915-

Cash, Pat

Chang, Michael

Cheney, Dodo

Connors, Jimmy, 1952-

Doohan, Peter

Edberg, Stefan

Evert, Chris

Fendick, Patty

Flach, Ken

Garrison, Zina

Gibson, Althea, 1927-

Gomez, Andres

Gonzalez, Pancho, 1928-

Graf, Steffi

King, Billie Jean

Kramer, Jack, 1921-

Laver, Rod

Leconte, Henri

Lendl, Ivan

Leschly, Jan

Lloyd, Holly

McEnroe, John

McNeil, Lori

Mecir, Miloslav

Mulloy, Gardnar, 1913-

Nagel, Ed

Navratilova, Martina, 1956-

Noah, Yannick

Pernfors, Mikael

Rehe, Stephanie

Sabatini, Gabriela

Schoenfield, Howard

Seguso, Robert

Seles, Monika

Shaefer, Kim

Shriver, Pam

Talbert, William F., 1918-

Tennis players—*cont.*

And the winners are . . . [picks for men's and women's all-time top ten] S. Flink. il *World Tennis* 34:16-17 F '87

Around the world. See issues of *World Tennis*

Arthur Ashe seeks cure for U.S. tennis malaise [development of black players] por *Jet* 72:49 Ag 31 '87

Can Arthur Ashe put this idea over the net? [minority player development] B. Welling. il por *Bus Week* p120 S 21 '87

A complete history of the world rankings [1953-1985 World tennis rankings] il *World Tennis* 34:33-9 F '87

Continental divide [new crop of American players to compete in Davis Cup] K. Cunningham. il *World Tennis* 34:46-8 Mr '87

A double fault for U.S. tennis. R. Wetzsteon. il *Sport Mag* 78:64-7 Ja '87

Endless summer [USTA Junior Boys' Davis Cup program] R. Brooks. il *World Tennis* 35:80 Jl '87

The eyes (I) [psychic analyzes top men players] B. R. Rich. il por *World Tennis* 34:36-7 Ap '87

The eyes (II) [psychic analyzes top women players] B. R. Rich. il *World Tennis* 34:42-3 My '87

Heirs to the throne? [who will be the next great American male player?] *World Tennis* 35:56 S '87

Hot shots [best stroke production] S. Flink. il *World Tennis* 35:34-7+ O '87

It ain't all glamour [women tennis stars] C. Shmerler. il *World Tennis* 35:22-5+ Je '87

Love-40 for the Stars and Stripes [lack of new American players] L. Rosellini. il *U S News World Rep* 102:58 Je 29 '87

A master plan for American tennis [proposals for changes in the structure of junior tennis] S. Flink. il *World Tennis* 35:16-17 N '87

The Midas touch [turning casual players into tennis buffs] G. M. Heldman. il *World Tennis* 35:38-9+ Ag '87

Newcomers to watch [U.S. Open] C. Shmerler. il *World Tennis* 35:48 S '87

No place to go but up [rising young American and Soviet players at the U.S. Open] F. Deford. il por *Sports Illus* 67:59-60 S 14 '87

Others sure to win, place or show [French Open competitors] il *World Tennis* 35:58-9 Je '87

Out of this world [1986 World tennis rankings] S. Flink. il por *World Tennis* 34:28-31 F '87

Pro tennis seeks black players for USA's future. *Jet* 72:48 Ap 13 '87

Studying the Swedes. L. Bergelin. il *World Tennis* 34:80 Ap '87

Traveling men [proposal for an amateur junior touring team] N. Bollettieri. il *World Tennis* 34:24+ My '87

Winning is only half the battle [problems of black women tennis players Z. Garrison and L. McNeil] M. Witherell. il pors *World Tennis* 34:38-41+ My '87

Accidents and injuries
See Tennis—Accidents and injuries

Awards
See Tennis—Awards

Clothing and dress
See Clothing and dress—Sports clothes

Health and hygiene

Altered states for mind & body [Trager method of massage] N. Amdur. il *World Tennis* 34:22+ My '87

Both sides now [effect of body imbalance on playing tennis] L. Rogak. il *World Tennis* 34:14-15 Mr '87

A lesson in extension. P. Stites. il *World Tennis* 35:22-3 S '87

Spring refresher [special section] il *World Tennis* 34:43-6 Ap '87

Sweat: how sweet it is! K. Cunningham and P. Stites. il *World Tennis* 34:60+ My '87

Nutrition

Best bites for '87. J. J. Kenney. il *World Tennis* 34:36-7 Ja '87

Grand Slam menus. L. C. Carrett. il *World Tennis* 35:34-5 Je '87

Smart eats. J. J. Kenney. il *World Tennis* 34:42-5 Mr '87

Winning dishes. M. Navratilova. il *World Tennis* 34:56-7 My '87

Photographs and photography

Perfect angles: never-published peeks at players caught in the act of being themselves. il *World Tennis* 35:42-3 Je '87

Psychology
See Tennis—Psychological aspects

Salaries, pensions, etc.

Black pro tennis stars are courting 'net' profits. *Jet* 72:48 My 25 '87

Black tennis stars winning big bucks but snubbed for commercials. pors *Jet* 72:48 Jl 20 '87

Player pensions: a creed of greed? S. Flink. il *World Tennis* 34:20-1 Mr '87

Training

Agility: learn to respond quickly to the ball. J. L. Groppel. il *World Tennis* 35:36 Ag '87

Fitness for your strokes. B. Brett. il *World Tennis* 34:34-5 Ja '87

Going for the gold [U.S. Junior Wightman Cup team visits the USTA Sport Science Camp] J. L. Groppel. il *World Tennis* 35:14-15 O '87

A new mother's fitness plan [K. Shaefer] C. Straley. il pors *Parents* 62:134-5+ Mr '87

Raise the level of your workout. N. Bollettieri. il *World Tennis* 35:32-4 Ag '87

Travelers advisory [staying in shape on the road] C. Evert. il *World Tennis* 35:96-7+ S '87

Tennis rackets

1987 racket almanac [special section] *World Tennis* 35:35+ N '87

Is lighter better? P. Sikowitz. *World Tennis* 35:98 S '87

Just smashing! T. Imbimbo. il *Women's Sports Fitness* 9:45-7 Ap '87

Racket man [J. Kramer signature rackets] B. Greene. il por *Esquire* 108:35-7 Ag '87

Racket reviews. il *World Tennis* 35:36-7 Je '87

Racket reviews. il *World Tennis* 35:44-5 O '87

Racket reviews. il *World Tennis* 35:52-4 Ag '87

Racket reviews. il *World Tennis* 35:100 S '87

Racket reviews. il *World Tennis* 35:62-3 Jl '87

Rackets '87. K. Stubbs. il *World Tennis* 34:53-5 My '87

Radical rackets [Dynaspot] P. Sikowitz. il *World Tennis* 35:43-4 O '87

Tennis rackets with a personal touch. T. Segal. il *Bus Week* p122 F 16 '87

Strings

String break [interview with K. Stubbs] A. Beck. *World Tennis* 35:37+ N '87

Tennis resorts See Resorts

Tennis shoes

Shocking news. J. L. Groppel and T. Clarke. il *World Tennis* 34:50-2 Ap '87

Shoe guide (I). J. E. McNerney. il *World Tennis* 34:53-4+ Ap '87

Shoe guide (II). J. E. McNerney. il *World Tennis* 35:55-8+ Ag '87

Shoe guide (III). J. E. McNerney. il *World Tennis* 35:51-3 O '87

Tennis. M. Kort. il *Women's Sports Fitness* 9:52-4+ Mr '87

Tennstedt, Klaus, 1926-

about

Tennstedt's poetic Mahler. D. Hall. il por *Stereo Rev* 52:89-90 O '87

Tennyson, Alfred Tennyson, Baron, 1809-1892

about

Passion and humdrum. R. B. Martin. il *N Y Rev Books* 34:17-19 O 22 '87

Tension (Psychology) See Stress

Tension headaches See Headache

Tension structures

Skylines of fabric. D. Stewart. il *Technol Rev* 90:60-7 Ja '87

Tent meeting [drama] See Larson, Larry

Tent structures See Tension structures

Tents

See also

Yurts

The joy of tents. B. McKeown. il *Outdoor Life* 179:56+ My '87

Survival tent. M. DiChristina. il *Pop Sci* 231:141 N '87

Tenure, Academic See College teachers—Tenure

Tenure, Land See Land tenure

Tenuta, Judy

about

Stand-up comic Tenuta is a Judy with punch. R. Arias. il por *People Wkly* 28:146-7 N 16 '87

Terada, Chiyono

about

Making it in a man's world. P. Sherrid. il por *U S News World Rep* 103:41 Jl 27 '87

Terauchi, Kenju
about
Through the Alaskan darkness Kenju Terauchi, a 747 pilot, is pursued by a UFO—or so he claims. D. Chu. il por *People Wkly* 27:74+ Ja 26 '87
Teresa, Mother, 1910-
"I've found God". il por *Saturday Evening Post* 259:16 Jl/Ag '87
about
Love in action and contemplation. J. D. Lynch. *Christ Century* 104:260-1 Mr 18-25 '87
Mother Teresa's work of grace. C. Tower. il pors *Read Dig* 131:163-75+ D '87
Teresa Benedicta, of the Cross See Stein, Edith, 1891-1942
Term insurance See Insurance, Life
Term papers See Student themes and reports
Terminal care
See also
  Hospices
  Living wills
Caring for the chronically ill. H. R. Kennedy. *U S News World Rep* 103:89 N 16 '87
Death in the mountains [terminal home care for old man] J. Smoot. il *South Living* 22:100 N '87
Deathwatch [child dying of cancer] P. Klass. il *Discover* 8:26+ O '87
Dying in character: the myth of the impish chuckle. P. Klass. il *Discover* 8:20+ F '87
Last rights [redefining death; cover story] K. Stein. il *Omni* 9:58-60+ S '87
Life and death [discussion of September 1987 article, Last rights] K. Stein. *Omni* 10:18 D '87
My father's last year [death from Lou Gehrig's disease] L. Cherry. il *Glamour* 85:300-1+ O '87
Terminal control areas See Air traffic control
Terminal radar approach control See Radar in aviation
Terminals (Computer) See Computer terminals
Terminals (Transportation)
See also
  Airports
  Cambridge (Mass.)—Stations
  New York (N.Y.)—Stations
  San Francisco (Calif.)—Stations
In transit [local transit stations; with introd. by Douglas Brenner] il *Archit Rec* 175:67 Ja '87
Termination of pension plans See Pensions—Termination
Terminology
See also
  Jargon
Termites
The termite connection [atmospheric methane; work of P. Zimmerman] D. M. Schwartz. il por *Int Wildl* 17:38-42 Jl/Ag '87
Control
No time for termites [EPA forces end to production of Termide] *Time* 130:46 Ag 24 '87
That gnawing sensation. J. Anthony. il *Changing Times* 41:20 D '87
When to call the exterminator [interview with A. M. Katz] P. Easton. il por *Home Mech* 83:14-15 Ap '87
Ternary system
A ternary state of affairs. R. T. Kurosaka. il *Byte* 12:319-20+ F '87
Terns
Closely watched terns. J. Page. il *Oceans* 20:65 N/D '87
Terpenes
See also
  Forskolin
Terpning, Howard, 1927-
about
Howard Terpning. M. E. Stegmaier. il por *Am Artist* 51:66-71+ D '87
Terpsicore [ballet] See Ballet reviews—Single works
Terra, Daniel
about
Daniel J. Terra. D. Kazanjian. il por *House Gard* 159:46+ My '87
Terra Designs, Inc.
Tiles with style: Terra Designs, Inc. [A. Salibello] W. Konrad. il pors *Work Woman* 12:137-8 N '87
Terra Museum of American Art (Chicago, Ill.)
Art times two. M. Wade. il *Horizon* 30:58-61 My '87
Daniel J. Terra. D. Kazanjian. il por *House Gard* 159:46+ My '87
The heart of the seasons [American impressionist paintings; cover story] E. Hardwick. il *House Gard* 159:122-31+ My '87
How to start a museum. R. Hughes. il *Time* 130:48-50 Ag 10 '87

New museum of American art [inaugural exhibit entitled A proud heritage: two centuries of American art] S. B. Sherrill. il *Antiques* 131:926+ My '87
Soft sell. P. M. Sachner. il *Archit Rec* 175:112-15 N '87
Terra's noble passion. S. Taylor. il *Art News* 86:36 S '87
Terraces (Agriculture)
10 ways to fertilize ridges. M. Holmberg. il *Success Farm* 85:18AJ-18AK Ap '87
Ridge planting on a roll. D. Mowitz and C. Finck. il *Success Farm* 85 no6:10-13 Mr '87
Ridging lets them cut chemical costs. R. Fee. il *Success Farm* 85 no1:26AG Ja '87
Terraces (Landscape gardening)
Adding a porch [terraced landing designed by Earle Barnhart and Hilde Maingay] il *Rodale's Org Gard* 34:54-6 N '87
Conquering a California hillside [work of architect Paul Gray, landscape architect Isabelle Greene, and owner] W. B. Logan. il *House Gard* 159:90-9+ Jl '87
Terracing a steep slope. il *Rodale's Org Gard* 34:50-2 S '87
Terraces (Outdoor living areas) See Decks, patios, terraces, etc.
Terracotta
Terra cotta: past to present. D. Rastorfer. il *Archit Rec* 175:110-17 Ja '87
Terraforming
Terradreaming [terraforming Mars; excerpts from remarks, March 25, 1987] J. C. Fletcher. por *Space World* X-7-283:36 Jl '87
Terranova, Giovanna
about
Jailed Mafia men face the wrath of Sicilian widows. il pors *People Wkly* 27:40-2+ My 18 '87
Terranova, Joe
Beyond the off-ramp [photographs] il *Cycle* 38:72-4 Mr '87
Big Apple bikes [photographs] il *Cycle* 38:75-9 N '87
Terrell, Dorothy
about
Dorothy Terrell. L. Gite. il por *Black Enterp* 17:46+ Ap '87
Terrell, Ernie
about
Ex-champ Ernie Terrell training Foreman's foe. *Jet* 71:50 Mr 2 '87
Terrell, Jack
about
A memo to Reagan. il pors *Newsweek* 110:7 S 21 '87
Mercenary with a cause. B. Connie and D. Bernstein. *Progressive* 51:13 Ag '87
Terres, John K.
Building a better home. il *Natl Wildl* 25:42-9 Ap/My '87
Hitchhikers in the sky. il *Natl Wildl* 25:38-40 O/N '87
Where would a bird be without its bill? il *Natl Wildl* 25:42-51 Ag/S '87
Terrestrial magnetism See Magnetism, Terrestrial
Terrine cooking
It's a wonderful loaf [Andy D'Amico's eggplant terrine] B. Costikyan. il *N Y* 20:50 Jl 13 '87
Territorial waters
See also
  Convention on the Law of the Sea (1982)
  Exclusive Economic Zone
  United Nations. Preparatory Commission for the International Sea-Bed Authority and the International Tribunal for the Law of the Sea
An epic Arctic journey [expedition retracing Inuit migration and demonstrating Canadian Arctic sovereignty; special section; with editorial comment by Kevin Doyle] il map *Macleans* 100:2, 20-8+ My 11 '87
Heating up the cod war [Newfoundland angry over Franco-Canadian fishing agreement] C. Barrett. il *Macleans* 100:13 F 23 '87
Larsen of the Northwest Passage [1940's voyage to bolster Canadian claims to sovereignty] J. Roe. il pors map *Oceans* 20:48-53+ N/D '87
Navigation rights and the Gulf of Sidra. map *Dep State Bull* 87:69-70 F '87
Rites of the fishermen [Newfoundland fishermen angered at agreement with France] M. Clark. il map *Macleans* 100:12 F 9 '87
Standing up to the United States [Canadian sovereignty in the Arctic] S. Shallhorn. *Bull At Sci* 43:16-17 O '87
Storm clouds over the Aegean [Greece-Turkey dispute] J. Bierman. il map *Macleans* 100:26-7 Ap 6 '87

Territorial waters—cont.

Threats to the North [U.S. threat to Canadian sovereignty in the Arctic and dispute over Arctic National Wildlife Refuge] M. Janigan. il map *Macleans* 100:10-11 Ja 26 '87

Uncle Sam's sovereignty promise [agreement on sovereignty in the Canadian Arctic between Ottawa and Washington] P. C. Newman. il *Macleans* 100:33 Mr 30 '87

Territoriality (Zoology)

The bird that farms the dell [relationship between bell miners, psyllids, and eucalyptus dieback] R. H. Loyn. il *Nat Hist* 96:54-60 Je '87

Terrorism

See also
Airplane hijacking
Assassination
Hostages

Gaddafi's goons [Chicago's El Rukn gang members convicted of terrorism] il *Time* 130:27 D 7 '87

Bibliography

The riddle of terrorism. S. Bakhash. il *N Y Rev Books* 34:12-16 S 24 '87

International aspects

See also
Letelier, Orlando—Assassination

Compromising moves. G. M. Telang. il *World Press Rev* 34:16+ Ja '87

Coping with terrorism. C. C. O'Brien. il por *Cent Mag* 20:45-9 Mr/Ap '87

Delle Chiaie: from Bologna to Bolivia [cover story] G. Black. il *Nation* 244:525+ Ap 25 '87

Disaster in the skies [bomb suspected in downing of Korean Air Lines Flight 858] A. Bilski. il *Macleans* 100:24 D 14 '87

A French turnabout on terrorism [cooperating with other countries] *Newsweek* 109:36 Je 8 '87

The future course of international terrorism. B. M. Jenkins. il por *Futurist* 21:8-13 Jl/Ag '87

International terrorism. R. B. Oakley. *Foreign Aff* 65 Sp Issue:611-29 ['87]

Islamic terrorism: a growing peril [interview with A. Taheri] D. Bombardier. il *World Press Rev* 34:17-19 My '87

Misunderstanding terrorism. J. D. Simon. *Foreign Policy* 67:104-20 Summ '87

The mystery of Flight 858 [North Koreans suspected of planting bomb on Korean Air Lines plane] *Time* 130:46 D 14 '87

Narcotics: terror's new ally [cover story; special section] M. Satchell. il map *U S News World Rep* 102:30-7 My 4 '87

The poisoned flight of KAL [possible North Korean involvement in bombing of Flight 858] il *U S News World Rep* 103:12 D 14 '87

A shattered dream [excerpt from The sorrow and the terror: the haunting legacy of the Air India tragedy] C. Blaise and B. Mukherjee. il pors *Macleans* 100:42-5 My 25 '87

Syrian support for international terrorism: 1983-86. *Dep State Bull* 87:73-6 F '87

Terrorism and the rule of law [address, April 23, 1987] L. P. Bremer, III. *Dep State Bull* 87:83-6 Ag '87

Terrorism: the challenge and the response [address, December 10, 1986] J. C. Whitehead. *Dep State Bull* 87:70-3 F '87

Uniting against terrorism [address, January 20, 1987] G. Bush. *Dep State Bull* 87:3 Ap '87

Who destroyed Korean Air 858? M. Liu. il *Newsweek* 110:61 D 14 '87

Philosophy

The terrorist aesthetic; tr. by John Satriano. A. Moravia. *Harpers* 274:37-9+ Je '87

Prevention

See also
Olympic Games—1988—Winter Olympics—Security measures
Air travel—Security measures
Airplanes, Business—Security measures
Airports—Security measures
Embassies (Buildings)—Security measures
G. Gordon Liddy Academy of Corporate Security and Private Investigation
Military bases—Security measures

The hostages & the moral question; A strategy for hostages. W. F. Buckley. *Natl Rev* 39:62-3 Mr 13 '87

How much security is enough? [address, January 22, 1987] R. E. Lamb. *Dep State Bull* 87:27-9 My '87

Measures to prevent terrorism, protection of diplomats discussed in Legal Committee. *UN Chron* 22:100+ N/D '85

Missions held hostage. S. Mumper. il *Christ Today* 31:37+ S 18 '87

Practical measures for dealing with terrorism [address, January 22, 1987] L. P. Bremer, III. il por *Dep State Bull* 87:1-4 Mr '87

Retaliation

See also
Libyan-American conflict, 1986

International aviation group discusses sanctions on supporters of terrorism. *Aviat Week Space Technol* 126:41 F 23 '87

Next: a rescue command. il *U S News World Rep* 102:10 F 16 '87

The sound of spinning wheels [Special Operations Forces] S. Emerson and R. A. Manning. il *U S News World Rep* 102:21 Mr 23 '87

A sting on the Mediterranean [FBI traps hijacker F. Yunis] S. Seibert. il por *Newsweek* 110:36 S 28 '87

Terrorism and intelligence [address, May 26, 1987] L. P. Bremer, III. *Vital Speeches Day* 53:578-81 Jl 15 '87

Egypt

See also
Sadat, Anwar, 1918-1981—Assassination

France

France's turnabout on terror [verdict against G. I. Abdallah] H. Anderson. il por *Newsweek* 109:42 Mr 9 '87

The French nab an Iranian 'sleeper cell'. R. Z. Chesnoff. il *U S News World Rep* 102:10 Ap 6 '87

A French turnabout on terrorism [cooperating with other countries] *Newsweek* 109:36 Je 8 '87

In France, when a terrorist needs a lawyer, Jacques Vergès usually gets the call [defense lawyer for G. I. Abdallah] P. Andriotakis. il pors *People Wkly* 27:109-10 Mr 9 '87

A Paris court stands firm [terrorist G. Abdallah sentenced to life in prison] K. Brady. il por *Time* 129:53 Mr 9 '87

Terrorism on trial [G. I. Abdallah given life sentence in Paris] A. Bilski. il *Macleans* 100:31 Mr 9 '87

Germany (West)

Disco bombers [possible involvement of H. Lummer in bombing of La Belle discothéque in West Berlin] N. Birnbaum. *Nation* 244:312-13 Mr 14 '87

A Lebanon-Iran link [Iran-backed terror network] il *Newsweek* 109:7 F 9 '87

Haiti

Blood at the ballot boxes. B. Levin. il *Macleans* 100:25+ D 14 '87

Blood in the ballot box. J. Smolowe. il *Time* 130:38-40 D 14 '87

Bloodshed blocks a ballot. J. Greenwald. il *Time* 130:34 D 7 '87

Cry Haiti. M. S. Hooper. *Nation* 245:740-1 D 19 '87

Haiti: democracy derailed. D. Peerman. *Christ Century* 104:1135-6 D 16 '87

Haiti robbed of hope [cover story] C. Cleaver. il *New Leader* 70:8-10 D 28 '87

How the U.S. miscalculated in Haiti. C. A. Robbins. il *U S News World Rep* 103:36-7 D 14 '87

Terror keeps Haiti in line. N. Cooper. il *Newsweek* 110:54-5 D 14 '87

Violence stops the vote. N. Cooper. il *Newsweek* 110:57 D 7 '87

What not to do in Haiti. *Commonweal* 114:724 D 18 '87

Iran

See also
Iranian seizure of United States embassy, 1979-1981

Israel

Death from the skies [Palestinian guerrilla attacks Israeli soldiers from hang glider] il *Time* 130:36 D 7 '87

Torture in Israel [Shin Bet counterterrorist torture] *New Repub* 197:7 N 23 '87

Italy

Delle Chiaie: from Bologna to Bolivia [cover story] G. Black. il *Nation* 244:525+ Ap 25 '87

Korea (South)

See also
Choi, Un Hui—Kidnapping
Shin, Sang Ok—Kidnapping

Lebanon

See also
Beirut airplane hijacking, 1985
Lebanon hostage cases, 1984-

Council members ask urgent measures for UNIFIL security [Shiites clash with French troops] *UN Chron* 23:58 N '86

Terrorism—Lebanon—*cont.*

Security Council condemns attacks against UNIFIL as 'criminal', calls for end to 'any military presence' unacceptable to Lebanon [Shiites clash with French troops] il *UN Chron* 23:59-62 N '86

A sting on the Mediterranean [FBI traps hijacker F. Yunis] S. Seibert. il por *Newsweek* 110:36 S 28 '87

U.S. policy, not militia gunfire, drives missionary teacher Nancie Wingo out of Lebanon. M. Avrech. il pors *People Wkly* 27:32-4+ Mr 16 '87

Middle East

A bloody Christmas. J. Turnbull. il map *Newsweek* 109:34 Ja 5 '87

The long shadow of Tehran. W. E. Smith. il map *Time* 129:56 Ja 5 '87

A who's who [Shiite terrorist organizations] S. Emerson and C. Fenyvesi. il *U S News World Rep* 102:26-7 F 9 '87

New Zealand

See also

Greenpeace bombing incident, 1985

Northern Ireland

The carnage in Enniskillen. G. C. Lubenow. il *Newsweek* 110:42 N 23 '87

An Ulster blast heard in Boston [Enniskillen bombing] M. Satchell. il *U S News World Rep* 103:14 N 23 '87

Philippines

The day of the sparrow [U.S. airmen murdered near Clark Air Base] H. Anderson. il *Newsweek* 110:54 N 9 '87

Portugal

Letter from Europe [O. Carvalho, leader of 1974 revolution, convicted of terrorism] J. Kramer. *New Yorker* 63:105-20 N 30 '87

Sri Lanka

A grisly scene on Gasworks Street [Tamil terrorists accused of planting bomb] N. R. Gibbs. il map *Time* 129:39 My 4 '87

Paradise destroyed. J. Barber. il map *Macleans* 100:20-2 My 4 '87

Resolving the Sri Lankan conflict [statement, March 12, 1987] R. A. Peck. *Dep State Bull* 87:68-71 My '87

Sri Lanka: an Asian Lebanon? F. Willey. il map *Newsweek* 109:32 My 4 '87

Sri Lanka: no taming the 'Tigers'. W. A. Taylor. il map *U S News World Rep* 103:28-9 Jl 27 '87

Sweden

See also

Palme, Olof, 1927-1986—Assassination

Turkey

The Istanbul synagogue massacre: an investigation. J. Miller. il *N Y Times Mag* p14-20+ Ja 4 '87

United States

See Terrorism

Western Europe

Murdering SDI [suspicious murders and suicides of Europeans connected with SDI] J. S. Denton and P. Schweizer. *Natl Rev* 39:37-9 Jl 31 '87

Terrorism and the press

Terrorism and the media [address, June 25, 1987] L. P. Bremer, III. *Dep State Bull* 87:72-5 S '87

Terrorists

See also

Weather Underground (Organization)

Terrorists, Arab

See also

Beirut airplane hijacking, 1985

Palestine Liberation Organization

France's turnabout on terror [verdict against G. I. Abdallah] H. Anderson. il por *Newsweek* 109:42 Mr 9 '87

The French nab an Iranian 'sleeper cell'. R. Z. Chesnoff. il *U S News World Rep* 102:10 Ap 6 '87

In France, when a terrorist needs a lawyer, Jacques Vergès usually gets the call [defense lawyer for G. I. Abdallah] P. Andriotakis. il pors *People Wkly* 27:109-10 Mr 9 '87

The Istanbul synagogue massacre: an investigation. J. Miller. il *N Y Times Mag* p14-20+ Ja 4 '87

The making of a terrorist. Y. Svoray. *Natl Rev* 39:57-9 Je 19 '87

A Paris court stands firm [terrorist G. Abdallah sentenced to life in prison] K. Brady. il por *Time* 129:53 Mr 9 '87

Terrorism on trial [G. I. Abdallah given life sentence in Paris] A. Bilski. il *Macleans* 100:31 Mr 9 '87

Terrorists, French

The Direct Action bust: a farmhouse coup. il *Newsweek* 109:42 Mr 9 '87

Jailing "Bonnie and Clyde" [4 members of Action Directe arrested] il *Time* 129:53 Mr 9 '87

Terrorists, Iranian

A costly exchange [suspected Iranian terrorist freed following release of French hostages in Lebanon] R. Laver. il *Macleans* 100:31 D 14 '87

A French terrorist-for-hostage deal? [Iranian terror suspect set free after two French hostages in Lebanon were freed] il *Newsweek* 110:61 D 14 '87

Furtive swap [suspected Iranian terrorist set free by France and French hostages released by Iran] *Time* 130:51 D 14 '87

A Lebanon-Iran link [Iran-backed terror network based in West Germany] il *Newsweek* 109:7 F 9 '87

Terrorists, Irish

See also

Irish Republican Army

A different kind of terror [organized crime] M. S. Serrill. *Time* 130:45 O 12 '87

Terrorists, Italian

Delle Chiaie: from Bologna to Bolivia [cover story] G. Black. il *Nation* 244:525+ Ap 25 '87

Terrorists, Libyan

'Reagan was the target'. il por *Newsweek* 110:59 O 5 '87

The spectator in solitary [former CIA agent E. P. Wilson convicted of selling guns] F. Trippett. il por *Time* 129:19 Je 15 '87

Terrorists, Peruvian

See also

Sendero Luminoso (Guerrilla group)

Terrorists, South African

See also

African National Congress

Terrorists, Syrian

See also

Syrian Social Nationalist Party

Syrian support for international terrorism: 1983-86. *Dep State Bull* 87:73-6 F '87

U.S. takes measures against Syria [White House statement, November 14, 1986] *Dep State Bull* 87:79 Ja '87

Terry, Ken

No fried food in New Jersey. *Progressive* 51:25 S '87

Why is D.O.E. for food irradiation? il *Nation* 244:142+ F 7 '87

Terry, Ralph, 1936-

about

A new line of play for an ex-Yankee. il por *Sports Illus* 66:20 My 18 '87

Terry, Robert J., d. 1987

about

Obituary

Jet por 73:8 O 12 '87

Terry, Steve

Entertainment industry standards. *Theatre Crafts* 21:22-3 O '87

Terry, Wallace

about

An angry Vietnam war correspondent charges that black combat soldiers are Platoon's M.I.A.s [interview] M. Wilhelm. il pors *People Wkly* 27:101-2+ Ap 20 '87

Terwilliger, Elizabeth

about

Meet 'Grandmother Nature'. M. McRae. il pors *50 Plus* 27:25-8 Jl '87

Terwilliger Nature Education Center

Meet 'Grandmother Nature' [E. Terwilliger] M. McRae. il pors *50 Plus* 27:25-8 Jl '87

Terzani, Tiziano

Behind Japanese superiority. il *World Press Rev* 34:27-8 Mr '87

Tesich, Steve, 1942-

about

Division Street [drama] Reviews

N Y il 20:92 F 16 '87. J. Simon

New Yorker 62:91 F 16 '87. E. Oliver

Tesinsky, William John, d. 1986

about

The photographer who got too close. J. G. Mitchell. il *Audubon* 89:28+ Mr '87

Tesoro Petroleum Corp.

Why is Tesoro so popular? T. Vogel. il *Bus Week* p40 D 21 '87

Tessellations (Mathematics)

Pieces of a polyomino puzzle [work of K. A. Dahlke] I. Peterson. il por *Sci News* 132:310 N 14 '87

Rectangles within rectangles [proof of tiling theorem] *Sci News* 132:187 S 19 '87

Test bans (Nuclear weapons) *See* Nuclear weapons—Testing—Suspension

Test discs *See* Compact discs—Test discs
Test driving (Automobiles) *See* Automobiles—Testing
Test pilots *See* Air pilots
Test tube babies *See* Fertilization in vitro
Testaverde, Vinny
about
This gun for hire. G. Myers. il por *Sport Mag* 78:26
Ja '87
Vinny's ship has come in [cover story] D. Scheiber.
il pors *Sports Illus* 67:24-6+ Ag 3 '87
Testes *See* Testicles
Testicles
A novel thyroid hormone receptor encoded by a cDNA
clone from a human testis library. D. Benbrook and
M. Pfahl. bibl f il *Science* 238:788-91 N 6 '87
Cancer
Steroidogenesis-activator polypeptide isolated from a rat
Leydig cell tumor. R. C. Pedersen and A. C. Brownie.
bibl f il *Science* 236:188-90 Ap 10 '87
Testimonials in advertising *See* Advertising—Testimonials
Testimony *See* Witnesses
Testing
See also
Aptitude tests
Educational tests and measurements
Employment tests
Examinations
Psychological tests
See also subhead Testing under various subjects
Testing—one, two, three. *Nation* 244:489 Ap 18 '87
Testing equipment
See also
Calibrators
Dynamometers
Electric meters
Oscilloscopes
Signal generators
Audible logic tester. P. L. Kane. il *Radio-Electron* 58:32-3
S '87
Build the Circuit Cellar IC tester (I). S. Ciarcia. il *Byte*
12:303-6+ N '87
Build the Circuit Cellar IC tester (II). S. Ciarcia. il
Byte 12:283-8 D '87
Diagnostic tools for diesels [marine engines] E. Dennis.
il *Mot Boat Sail* 159:70 Mr '87
A digital Foucault tester [for telescope mirrors] F. L.
Redburn. il *Sky Telesc* 73:439-42 Ap '87
The g-analyst: the driver's lie detector. R. Titus. il *Mot
Trend* 39:114 O '87
If I had my life to live over, I'd live over a Formula
1 garage [technicalities encountered in testing Benetton
B186 F1] D. Simanaitis. il *Road Track* 38:164 Mr
'87
In-circuit digital IC tester (I). B. Green. il *Radio-Electron*
58:43-8 N '87
In-circuit digital IC tester (II). B. Green. il *Radio-Electron*
58:55-8 D '87
Microchip mechanic [Buick's Computerized Automotive
Maintenance System] T. Swan. il *Pop Sci* 231:73-4+
Jl '87
Testing equipment industry
Securities
Testing, testing. T. Jaffe. *Forbes* 140:221 S 21 '87
Testing grounds *See* Proving grounds
Testorf, Helga
about
Heavily hyped Helga. J. Updike. *New Repub* 197:27-30
D 7 '87
The Helga pictures. A. Thorson. il *Art News* 86:193
O '87
Helgamania goes on the road. pors *U S News World
Rep* 102:13 Je 1 '87
Too much of a medium-good thing. R. Hughes. il *Time*
129:77 Je 1 '87
Wyeth paintings and the Helga controversy [cover story]
M. S. Doherty. il pors *Am Artist* 51:10-11 My '87
Wyeth's world: how a woman named Helga came to
haunt the art of America's foremost realist. R.
Meryman. il pors *Life* 10:72-6+ Je '87
Anecdotes, facetiae, satire, etc.
Vickie Lou's letters from Long Island [exhibit of A.
Wyeth's Helga paintings] il *Am Artist* 51:18+ S '87
Testosterone
An energy boost for menopause [research by Barbara
Sherwin] il *Prevention* 39:6 N '87
Prenatal 'sex change' for a leaner ewe [research by John
Klindt] *Sci News* 131:361 Je 6 '87
Testrake, John
about
A hero pilot's new flight plan. D. Gates. il por *Newsweek*
110:6 N 23 '87

A triumph over terror [interview] il pors *Christ Today*
31:46-7 Je 12 '87
Tetanus
Vaccines and vaccination
See also
DPT vaccine
Tete-a-tete [drama] See Burdman, Ralph
Tethered artificial satellites *See* Artificial satellites—
Tethered satellites
Tetley, Glen
about
Alice [ballet] Reviews
Dance Mag 61:36-8 F '87. C. Hardy
Macleans il 100:44 Jl 13 '87. M. Crabb
La ronde [ballet] Reviews
Macleans il 100:65 N 30 '87. P. Hluchy
Teton Valley (Idaho)
Description and travel
Two couples over the hill (from Jackson). D. Swift.
il *Mother Earth News* 106:45 Jl/Ag '87
Tetrahydroaminoacridine *See* THA (Drug)
Tevatron accelerator *See* Accelerators (Electrons, etc.)
Tevis, Cheryl
Joint venture. See issues of Successful Farming beginning
September 1984
Tevis Cup (Race) *See* Horse racing
Tex-Mex cooking *See* Cooking, Tex-Mex
Texaco Inc.
Bankruptcy court for Texaco: the lesser evil—barely.
T. Thompson and others. il *Bus Week* p102-3+ Ap
27 '87
Behind the scenes at Texaco's settlement [Pennzoil
agreement] J. R. Norman and T. Vogel. il *Bus Week*
p66-8 D 28 '87-Ja 4 '88
Bonds: the safest play on Texaco. G. G. Marcial. *Bus
Week* p124 Je 8 '87
A break in the action [Texaco files for Chapter 11]
J. Castro. il *Time* 129:52-3 Ap 27 '87
Carl Icahn deals himself in [controls 12% of Texaco]
J. R. Norman. il por *Bus Week* p38 D 14 '87
Chapter 11 for Texaco. D. Pauly. il *Newsweek* 109:52
Ap 20 '87
David Boies: the ace litigator playing Texaco's hand.
L. J. Tell. il por *Bus Week* p79 Ap 20 '87
Et tu, Pennzoil? [Texaco-Pennzoil case] *New Repub* 196:4+
My 4 '87
The gambler who refused $2 billion [Pennzoil's J. H.
Liedtke's fight with Texaco; cover story] S. P. Sherman.
il pors *Fortune* 115:50-4+ My 11 '87
Gushing money [Texas court rules in favor of Pennzoil
in takeover dispute with Texaco] *Newsweek* 109:56
F 23 '87
Icahn thickens the Texaco plot. *Newsweek* 110:66 D
7 '87
Is Holmes a Court trying to lasso Texaco? T. Thompson.
il por *Bus Week* p59 Jl 27 '87
Jaws: the Australian [accumulation of stock by R. Holmes
à Court] J. Castro. il por *Time* 130:53 Jl 27 '87
Knocked down in round 2 [Texas court upholds judgment
against Texaco] il *Time* 129:67 F 23 '87
Let 'Icahn do your work for you' [buying TWA stock
to get in on Texaco-Pennzoil deal] G. G. Marcial.
Bus Week p106 D 21 '87
Meet Larry Tribe, Pennzoil's hole card [bested Texaco
in Supreme Court] L. Helm and P. Dwyer. il por
Bus Week p78-9 Ap 20 '87
On tap: a $3 billion solution? [settlement in Pennzoil
vs. Texaco] K. R. Sheets and W. J. Cook. *U S News
World Rep* 103:16 D 21 '87
Paying the price for Getty [J. W. Kinnear] P. Nulty.
il por *Fortune* 116:34 Ag 3 '87
The shootout at Texaco corral [petition for Chapter
11] J. Egan. il *U S News World Rep* 102:62+ Ap
27 '87
A small price to pay [settlement of Texaco-Pennzoil
case] G. Bock. il *Time* 130:63 D 28 '87
Stalker of wounded game [R. Holmes à Court's interest
in Texaco stock] T. Jaffe. il por *Forbes* 139:38+ Je
15 '87
Stalking Texaco [stock purchase by R. Holmes à Court]
Time 129:52 Je 1 '87
Texaco skids on an oil slick. W. J. Cook. il *U S News
World Rep* 102:45 Mr 9 '87
Texaco starts a new life [bankruptcy] J. B. Copeland.
il *Newsweek* 109:50 Ap 27 '87
Texaco takes a knockdown punch [Supreme Court sends
Pennzoil case back to Texas] T. Thompson. il *Bus
Week* p27 Ap 20 '87
Texaco vs. Pennzoil: next stop, Washington [Texas
Supreme Court refuses to review judgment won by
Pennzoil] T. Vogel. il *Bus Week* p68 N 16 '87

Texaco Inc.—*cont.*

Texaco's $3 billion deal with Pennzoil. *Newsweek* 110:52 D 21 '87

Texaco's big gamble [bankruptcy gambit] T. Tedesco. il *Macleans* 100:42 Ap 27 '87

Texaco's last stand [negotiations over Pennzoil settlement] T. Tedesco. il *Macleans* 100:43 D 28 '87

Texaco's last stand in Texas [judgment won by Pennzoil] J. E. Davis and T. Vogel. il *Bus Week* p36 Mr 2 '87

Texaco's star falls. J. Castro. il *Time* 129:50-2 Ap 20 '87

Triumph of the sore-back lawyer [J. Jamail's skills in Texaco-Pennzoil battle] T. Mack. il por *Forbes* 139:33-4 My 4 '87

Will Aussie raider deliver coup de grace to crippled Texaco? [plans of R. Holmes à Court] K. R. Sheets. *U S News World Rep* 102:43 Je 1 '87

Will he, or won't he? Australia keeps Texaco on edge [R. Holmes à Court plans to boost holdings] K. R. Sheets. *U S News World Rep* 103:37 Jl 27 '87

Texans

My life as a Texan [oil bust] J. Nocera. *New Repub* 196:19-23 Ap 13 '87

Texas

    See also

    Architecture, Domestic—Texas

    Art—Texas

    Banks and banking—Texas

    Beaches—Texas

    Big Thicket National Preserve (Tex.)

    Caves—Texas

    Courts—Texas

    Criminal justice, Administration of—Texas

    Davis Mountains (Tex.)

    Finance—Texas

    Housing—Texas

    Law—Texas

    Music festivals—Texas

    Northwest Harris County Municipal Utility District No. 19 (Tex.)

    Paleontology—Texas

    Poor—Texas

    Prisons—Texas

    Ranches—Texas

    Rio Grande Valley

    San Antonio Missions National Historical Park (Tex.)

    Savings and loan associations—Texas

    Sculpture gardens and parks—Texas

    South Padre Island (Tex.)

    Traffic regulations—Texas

    Trails—Texas

Description and travel

Hills in the heart of Texas [with editorial comment by G. E. McCalla] L. Thomas. il map *South Living* 22:6, 110-17 My '87

Economic conditions

Collectors cotton to Texas bargains [auctions] B. Kallen. il *Forbes* 139:144+ Mr 9 '87

An economic uptick in the oil patch. S. A. Peterson. il *U S News World Rep* 103:23 Ag 3 '87

Is Texas losing its independence? [outsiders' investments] T. Mack. il *Forbes* 140:184+ D 14 '87

John Connally goes belly up after betting big on a Texas oil economy that ran out of gas [personal and partnership bankruptcy] W. Plummer. il pors *People Wkly* 28:36-7 Ag 17 '87

My life as a Texan [oil bust] J. Nocera. *New Repub* 196:19-23 Ap 13 '87

History

Finding a lost colony [Robertson's Colony; research by M. D. McLean] L. Thomas. il por *South Living* 22:136 S '87

Industries

    See also

    Petroleum industry

    Real estate business

A promising posse of Lone Star stocks. J. Mendes. *Fortune* 116:128 S 14 '87

Legislature

    Anecdotes, facetiae, satire, etc.

The Lege has a taxing session. M. Ivins. il *Nation* 245:120-2 Ag 15-22 '87

Missions

    See also

    San Antonio Missions National Historical Park (Tex.)

Politics and government

    See also

    Texas—Legislature

A bad case of foot-in-mouth disease is alarming the Texas GOP [Governor W. P. Clements] T. Mason. por *Bus Week* p39 Ag 31 '87

The battle-ax of the republic [P. Gramm] P. Magnusson. il por *Bus Week* p78-9 Ag 31 '87

Letter from Washington [Texas delegation in the House of Representatives] Cato. *Natl Rev* 39:14 Jl 17 '87

Payoff, hike! [Gov. W. Clements' involvement in illegal payments to football players at SMU] E. Magnuson. il *Time* 129:34 Mr 16 '87

Playing for pay in Texas [Gov. W. Clements admits involvement in SMU football scandal] T. E. Johnson. por *Newsweek* 109:32 Mr 16 '87

Social conditions

Sons of guns [love of guns] W. Saletan. *New Repub* 196:11-13 Mr 2 '87

There will always be a Texas. M. Ivins. il *Ms* 16:82-4 Jl/Ag '87

Texas A & I University

Presidential perspectives on university writing requirements [address, March 7, 1987] S. Altman. *Vital Speeches Day* 53:494-6 Je 1 '87

Texas A & M University System. Prairie View A & M University *See* Prairie View A & M University

Texas Air Corp.

Air fares you won't believe—until you hear the catch. K. R. Sheets. *U S News World Rep* 102:46 F 9 '87

Can United afford Texas Air's low fares? J. E. Ellis. il *Bus Week* p34 F 16 '87

Frank Lorenzo. J. E. Davis. il por *Bus Week* Sp Issue:228 Ap 17 '87

Is this any way to run an airline? [with interview with F. Lorenzo] G. Bock. il *Time* 130:55-6 N 23 '87

The new master of the skies [F. Lorenzo] K. Labich. il por *Fortune* 115:72-3 Ja 5 '87

People Express, New York Air merging under Continental umbrella. C. Preble. *Aviat Week Space Technol* 126:32-3 Ja 19 '87

Shareholders fail to block Texas Air's Continental buy. *Aviat Week Space Technol* 126:32 F 16 '87

Texas Air buys commuter aircraft for affiliates' use. *Aviat Week Space Technol* 127:43 S 14 '87

Texas Air, Continental agree on stock price. *Aviat Week Space Technol* 126:40 F 2 '87

Texas Air Corp. fare initiatives spur summer traffic demand. J. Ott. il *Aviat Week Space Technol* 126:30-1 Je 1 '87

Texas Air stockholders back management team, growth record. W. B. Scott. *Aviat Week Space Technol* 126:48 Je 1 '87

Texas Air unit charges American with restraining CRS business [computer reservation systems] C. A. Shifrin. *Aviat Week Space Technol* 127:51 D 7 '87

Texas Air will maintain Eastern's identity. *Aviat Week Space Technol* 126:32 Ja 19 '87

Who will be Sky King? [fare wars between Texas Air and American Airlines] A. Miller. il pors *Newsweek* 109:54 Mr 2 '87

Texas cooking *See* Cooking, American

Texas Eastern Corp.

Blue flame, black gunk [PCB-laced oil buried along Texas Eastern's pipelines] J. Egginton. il map *Audubon* 89:106-12 S '87

Cleanup target: 10,000 miles of toxic soup [PCBs dumped along pipeline] map *U S News World Rep* 103:16 N 23 '87

Mopping up the PCB mess. J. Castro. il *Time* 130:50 N 23 '87

Texas Guaranty Investments

J. R. McConnell: the ballad of a Texas tornado. T. Vogel. il por *Bus Week* p80+ N 9 '87

Texas Instruments Incorporated

The chip behind TI's smart weapons [Lisp chip] T. Mason. il *Bus Week* p104-6 Mr 9 '87

Playing hardball [doing business in Japan] il *U S News World Rep* 103:42-3 Ag 24 '87

Texas Instruments targets airlines for its AI products. *Aviat Week Space Technol* 127:43 O 19 '87

TI uses broad technology base to expand role in EW programs [electronic warfare] il *Aviat Week Space Technol* 126:53-4+ F 16 '87

Texas Medical Center (Houston, Tex.)

Wildcatters in the laboratory. T. Mack. il *Forbes* 140:258+ N 16 '87

Texas Publishers Association

Lone Star State's publishers: not so lonesome. B. Summer. *Publ Wkly* 231:36 Je 19 '87

Texas Southern University

Texas Southern University resolves urban woes. *Jet* 72:15 Ap 27 '87

Texas Star Party *See* Astronomy—Conferences
Texas Star Trail (San Antonio, Tex.) *See* Trails—Texas
Texas Tech University
Bridging the gap between a public school system and a university [Texas Tech faculty members adopt school classes in Lubbock] R. E. Ishler and E. C. Leslie. *Phi Delta Kappan* 68:615-16 Ap '87
Text editors (Computer programs) *See* Word processors and processing—Programming
Text processing (Computer science)
See also
Hypertext
WordCruncher [text indexing and retrieval program] R. Rabinovitz. *Byte* 12:216+ N '87
Textbooks
See also
Astronomy—Textbooks
Physics—Textbooks
Political science—Textbooks
Psychiatry—Textbooks
Publishers and publishing—Textbooks
Readers (Books)
Social sciences—Textbooks
United States—History—Textbooks
Teaching the great issues of the future. D. B. Fleming. il por *Futurist* 21:27-8 Ja/F '87
Two textbook studies differ on their impact on education. H. Fields. *Publ Wkly* 232:72 S 18 '87
Authorship
Writing textbooks isn't child's play. H. Billings. por *U S News World Rep* 103:6 Jl 27 '87
Binding
See Bookbinding
Censorship
AAP joins in appeal of Tennessee textbook ruling. H. Fields. *Publ Wkly* 231:30 Mr 6 '87
Alabama board to appeal ban on 'humanist' texts. M. Yen. *Publ Wkly* 231:14 Mr 27 '87
Alabamboozle [secular humanist textbook ruling] E. Doerr. *Humanist* 47:39-40 My/Je '87
Back talk [discussion of February 1987 article, Censoring science] K. Stein. il *Omni* 9:12+ S '87
Book ban overturned [Tennessee textbook case] *Christ Century* 104:745 S 9-16 '87
Books and schools [fundamentalists' attacks on public school books] *Nation* 244:705-6 My 30 '87
Censored! F. Roberts. il *Parents* 62:53 S '87
Censoring science [fundamentalists] K. Stein. il *Omni* 9:42-4+ F '87
Fundamentalists lose two textbook cases in federal appeals courts [Alabama and Tennessee cases] *Publ Wkly* 232:11 S 11 '87
God's right Hand [W. Brevard Hand's decision that secular humanism is a religion in Alabama textbook case] D. R. Carlin, Jr. il *Commonweal* 114:263-4 My 8 '87
Going back to the books [fundamentalists lose court cases in Tenn. and Ala.] R. Lacayo. il *Time* 130:60 S 7 '87
The humanist. E. Doerr. *Humanist* 47:2 N/D '87
Is 'humanism' a religion? [Judge W. Brevard Hand bans certain textbooks in Alabama] T. Gest. il *U S News World Rep* 102:10-11 Mr 16 '87
Mark of Darrow [fundamentalists lose textbook court battles in Tenn. and Ala.] il *U S News World Rep* 103:10 S 7 '87
Nondenominational humanism? [Alabama secular humanist textbook case] *Natl Rev* 39:19 Ap 10 '87
Other sides to the textbook controversy [discussion of May 6, 1987 articles, Voltaire arraigned in Alabama: the textbook humanism case and Curriculum in the public schools: can compromise be reached?] D. Underhill; C. L. Glenn. il *Christ Century* 104:631-2 Jl 15-22 '87
People for the American Way [interview with A. T. Podesta] R. Love. il por *Seventeen* 46:237 Ag '87
Religious bias [Judge W. Brevard Hand bans "secular humanist" textbooks from Alabama schools] il *Time* 129:66 Mr 16 '87
Right-wing pressure. *USA Today (Periodical)* 116:11 D '87
The significance of the decision in 'Scopes II' [fundamentalists vs. school system in Tennessee textbook case] E. B. Jenkinson. bibl f *Phi Delta Kappan* 68:445-50 F '87
Some thoughts on the Tennessee textbook case. T. J. Flygare. bibl f il *Phi Delta Kappan* 68:474-5 F '87
Striking down the textbook rulings. K. A. Lawton. il *Christ Today* 31:50-1 O 2 '87
Students speak out against textbook censorship [Buffalo, N.Y.] F. Edwords. *Humanist* 47:23-6+ Mr/Ap '87

Textbook cases. T. C. Muck. *Christ Today* 31:17 Ap 17 '87
The textbook cases: secularism on appeal [cases in Tenn. and Ala.] P. A. Zirkel. bibl f *Phi Delta Kappan* 69:308-10 D '87
Textbook controversies: a 'disaster for public schools'? [fundamentalists vs. school system in Tennessee textbook case] C. L. Glenn. bibl f *Phi Delta Kappan* 68:451-5 F '87
Textbook controversy intensifies nationwide. C. Holden. il *Science* 235:19-20 Ja 2 '87
Textbook ruling sparks concern [secular humanism ruling in Alabama] C. Holden. *Science* 235:1459 Mr 20 '87
Textbooks on trial [Alabama decision banning textbooks from public schools because they promote secular humanism] *America* 156:265 Ap 4 '87
This is what you thought: 92% worried about textbook censorship [results of survey] *Glamour* 85:137 Ap '87
Tillich in an Alice-in-Wonderland world [court decisions pertaining to school textbooks and secular humanism] J. McBride. *Christ Century* 104:519-20 Je 3-10 '87
Voltaire arraigned in Alabama: the textbook humanism case. D. Underhill. *Christ Century* 104:438-40 My 6 '87
Wins and losses [referenda on church-state issues and Tennessee textbook case] E. Doerr. *Humanist* 47:40+ Ja/F '87
Specifications
See also
Advisory Commission on Textbook Specifications
Textile arts *See* Textile crafts
Textile Conservation Workshop (South Salem, N.Y.)
Textile tending. E. Greene. il por *House Gard* 159:87-8+ Mr '87
Textile crafts
Engineering light and movement [work of J. Crain] P. Scheinman. bibl f il *Am Craft* 47:22-9+ F/Mr '87
Exhibitions
See also
Artweave Textile Gallery
Interlacing: the elemental fabric [exhibit at the American Craft Museum] B. Freudenheim. il *Am Craft* 47:42-9 Ap/My '87
A living journal: Francoise Grossen. W. Seelig. il *Am Craft* 47:34-7 O/N '87
Study and teaching
Comment. W. Seelig. *Am Craft* 47:20+ Ap/My '87
Textile design
See also
Surface Design Association (U.S.)
Weaving
Exhibitions
See Textile fabrics—Exhibitions
Textile exhibits *See* Textile fabrics—Exhibitions
Textile fabrics
See also
Chiffon
Chintz
Denim
Marine canvas work
Photographs on cloth
Plaid
Silk
Tapestry
Weaving
The beasts at bay [animal prints in house decoration] C. Vogel. il *N Y Times Mag* p66-7 N 1 '87
Country weaves, pastoral scenes. J. Simpson. il *Archit Dig* 44:268+ Je '87
Detachable fabric panels. il *South Living* 22:126 Jl '87
Everything's coming up roses [Paris spring couture features floral prints] il *Vogue* 177:240 My '87
The fashion world heeds the call of the wild: animal prints. il *People Wkly* 28:128-9 O 5 '87
The feel of fabric [study by Andrea Gwosdow and Larry Berglund] H. Hall. *Psychol Today* 21:25 Jl '87
Golden threads [English dealer J. Hope] S. M. L. Aronson. il por *House Gard* 159:20+ O '87
Imitation of life [animal prints] L. Wells. il *N Y Times Mag* p62-5 N 1 '87
Porter's: the photo fabric store. K. Geller-Shinn. il *Petersens Photogr Mag* 16:10 N '87
A spontaneous charm [Paris home of designers M. and Y. Halard] C. de Liagre. il por *House Gard* 159:126-33+ D '87
Conservation and restoration
See also
Textile Conservation Workshop (South Salem, N.Y.)

Textile fabrics—*cont.*
Exhibitions
European textiles [Cooper-Hewitt Museum exhibition entitled Color by the yard: printed fabric 1760-1860] S. B. Sherrill. il *Antiques* 132:990+ N '87

Textile fabrics, Fireproof
Fireproof kids' clothes. C. Loomis. il *Parents* 62:13 Jl '87

Textile fabrics, Waterproof
What the terms mean [fabrics for skiwear] H. Brooks. *Skiing* 40:178+ S '87

Textile fiber crafts *See* Textile crafts

Textile fibers
   See also
      Cotton
      Wool
Back to natural fibers. M. Rowland. il *Work Woman* 12:101+ N '87

Textile industry
   See also
      Burlington Industries, Inc.
      Coated Sales Inc.
      Dan River Inc.
      Graniteville Co.
      Guilford Mills, Inc.
      Infinite Creations, Inc.
      J.E. Morgan Knitting Mills, Inc.
      Parkdale Mills, Inc.
      R. B. Pamplin Corporation
      Unifi Inc.
      Wool industry
Apparel, shoes and textiles. E. Pomice. il *Forbes* 139:68-70 Ja 12 '87
Inspiration and imitation. P. Berman. *Forbes* 140:64 N 2 '87
Acquisitions and mergers
International aspects
Burlington almost invited Edelman to attack [bid by A. B. Edelman and Dominion Textile] D. Foust. il por *Bus Week* p50+ My 11 '87
Dominion's unraveling bid [bid for Burlington Industries] D. Foust. *Bus Week* p49-50 Je 1 '87
Export-import trade
Consumer protection? [Textile Apparel Trade Act] J. W. Merline. il *Consum Res Mag* 70:38 O '87
Marketing
Back to natural fibers. M. Rowland. il *Work Woman* 12:101+ N '87
Canada
   See also
      Dominion Textile Inc.
Great Britain
   See also
      Courtaulds plc
      ICI Fibres (Firm)
Japan
   See also
      Toray Industries, Inc
Scotland
   See also
      Dawson International Ltd.

Textile machinery industry
   See also
      Barber-Colman Co.
Suits and claims
Record $3.8 million awarded S.C. black in liability case [award to Clarence Barnwell in suit against Barber-Colman Co.] il *Jet* 72:28 Jl 6 '87
Germany (West)
How to keep mature industries innovative [Baden-Wurttemberg; cover story] C. F. Sabel and others. il *Technol Rev* 90:26-35 Ap '87

Textile Museum (Washington, D.C.)
One man's romance with fiber created the Textile Museum. M. McWilliam. il por *Smithsonian* 17:108-10+ Mr '87

Textile painting
Custom-made sacks to hold gift bottles of wine. il *Sunset* 179:102 D '87

Textile workers
Salaries, pensions, etc.
Occupational wages in textile manufacturing, June 1985. il *Mon Labor Rev* 110:33-5 F '87
Pay in synthetic fibers manufacturing in the southern region. il *Mon Labor Rev* 110:35-6 F '87

Textiles *See* Textile fabrics

Textron Inc.
Is Textron in Ford's future? The pros think so. G. G. Marcial. il *Bus Week* p61 Jl 27 '87
Royal Little: the conglomerator. D. A. Saunders. il pors *Forbes* 140:264+ Jl 13 '87

Texture (Photography)
The function of texture in the act of imagemaking. F. Patterson. il *Petersens Photogr Mag* 16:38-9 S '87
Texture screens in photography *See* Photography—Processing—Equipment

Teyber, Edward, and Hoffman, Charles D.
Missing fathers. bibl (p65) il *Psychol Today* 21:36-9 Ap '87

THA (Drug)
Alzheimer's drug trial put on hold. J. L. Marx. il *Science* 238:1041-2 N 20 '87
Palliative [Alzheimer's disease; work of William Summers] *Sci Am* 256:72 Ja '87
THA trials suspended, research probed. R. Weiss. *Sci News* 132:292 N 7 '87

Thacker, Floyd O., d. 1987
   about
Obituary
      Black Enterp il por 18:20 Ag '87. M. Eaton

Thai Airways International Ltd.
MD-11, A340 competition gains momentum at Thai International. R. G. O'Lone. *Aviat Week Space Technol* 126:30-1 Mr 16 '87

Thai cooking *See* Cooking, Thai
Thai House Cafe (New York, N.Y.) *See* New York (N.Y.)—Restaurants, nightclubs, bars, etc.
Thai Taste (New York, N.Y.: Restaurant) *See* New York (N.Y.)—Restaurants, nightclubs, bars, etc.

Thailand
   See also
      Agriculture—Thailand
      Bangkok (Thailand)
      Immigration and emigration—Thailand
      Public health—Thailand
      Relief work—Thailand
      Thais
Air Force
Thai Air Force upgrades fleet to meet Vietnamese threat. R. G. O'Lone. il *Aviat Week Space Technol* 126:92-3 Mr 30 '87
Defenses
   See also
      Airplanes, Military—Thailand
Foreign relations
Vietnam
Thai Air Force upgrades fleet to meet Vietnamese threat. R. G. O'Lone. il *Aviat Week Space Technol* 126:92-3 Mr 30 '87
Industries
   See also
      Thai Airways International Ltd.
Kings and rulers
   See also
      Thailand—Royal family
Politics and government
Thailand: a booming nation of farmers moves to democracy. L. Hopping. il *Sch Update* 119:12-13 Ap 6 '87
Thailand: surviving the 1980's. A. Ramsay. bibl f *Curr Hist* 86:164-7+ Ap '87
Uncertainty in the 'Golden Paradise'. D. Van Praagh. il *Macleans* 100:10 O 5 '87
Royal family
How I became a Royal White Elephant, Third Class [tutor to the Thai royal family] R. Eberhart. il por *Am Herit* 38:44-7 F/Mr '87

Thais
United States
How I became a Royal White Elephant, Third Class [tutor to the Thai royal family] R. Eberhart. il por *Am Herit* 38:44-7 F/Mr '87

Thalassotherapy
In Quiberon, a pleasure spa. F. du P. Gray. *Vogue* 177:180+ D '87

Thalheimer, Richard
   about
Of our time. *New Yorker* 62:22-4 Ja 12 '87

Thalidomide
Thalidomide: is there a silver lining? [graft-versus-host disease; research by Georgia B. Vogelsang] D. D. Edwards. *Sci News* 131:198 Mr 28 '87
The thalidomide tragedy—25 years ago. W. Grigg. il *FDA Consum* 21:14-17 F '87

Thampi, Venu
   about
A shattered dream [excerpt from The sorrow and the terror: the haunting legacy of the Air India tragedy] C. Blaise and B. Mukherjee. il pors *Macleans* 100:42-5 My 25 '87

Thampi, Vijaya, 1957-1985
about
A shattered dream [excerpt from The sorrow and the terror: the haunting legacy of the Air India tragedy] C. Blaise and B. Mukherjee. il pors *Macleans* 100:42-5 My 25 '87
Thanatology *See* Death
Thanksgiving Day
Notes and comment [remembering Thanksgivings past] *New Yorker* 63:33-4 D 14 '87
Thanksgiving dinners
A celebration of plenty. A. Simon. il *Saturday Evening Post* 259:18-19+ N '87
Dazzling Thanksgiving dinners [contributed by five top chefs] il *Redbook* 170:91-5+ N '87
An elegant Thanksgiving made easy. L. Hoppe. il *Better Homes Gard* 65:148-53+ N '87
A formal Thanksgiving. il *Gourmet* 47:156-62+ N '87
Gathering together [Yankee food recipes by Jasper White] C. Claiborne and P. Franey. il *N Y Times Mag* p74-6+ N 15 '87
Glorious gluttony. J. Miller. il *Ms* 16:36 N '87
McCall's Thanksgiving game & bird cookbook. il *McCalls* 115:115-20+ N '87
Our Thanksgiving family favorites. H. Garrison. il *Parents* 62:219-22+ N '87
The potluck Thanksgiving. il *Sunset* 179:212-14+ N '87
A southwestern Thanksgiving. il *Gourmet* 47:114-16+ N '87
Thanksgiving harvest. C. Lyons. il *Ebony* 43:122-4+ N '87
Thanksgiving puddings *See* Puddings
Thapar, Karan
Rajiv Gandhi's honeymoon is over. il por *World Press Rev* 34:40-1 Je '87
Tharp, Twyla
about
Ballare [dance] Reviews
   N Y il 20:110 Mr 2 '87. T. Tobias
Companies in transition. L. A. Jacobs. il *New Leader* 70:21-2 Mr 23 '87
Dance. M. Aloff. *Nation* 244:410-12 Mr 28 '87
Dancing:
   Twyla Tharp Dance Company's appearance at the Brooklyn Academy occasions thoughts on relationship of modern dance and ballet. A. Croce. *New Yorker* 63:118-20 F 23 '87
In the upper room [dance] Reviews
   N Y il 20:123 F 23 '87. T. Tobias
Reviews:
   Performances at the Brooklyn Academy of Music. J. R. Acocella. *Dance Mag* 61:194-6+ Je '87
Tharp regroups. S. Reiter. il por *Dance Mag* 61:4 N '87
Twyla Tharp's return. H. Brubach. il *Atlantic* 259:86+ Mr '87
Tharp (Twyla) Dance Company *See* Twyla Tharp Dance Company
That Petrol Emotion (Musical group)
That Petrol Emotion's rebel rock. R. Tannenbaum. il *Roll Stone* p24 O 22 '87
Thatcher, Carol
Thatcher on Gorbachev [cover story] il pors *Life* 10:32-4 O '87
Thatcher, Margaret
Visit of Prime Minister Thatcher [remarks, July 17, 1987] *Dep State Bull* 87:41-2 S '87
about
Aiming for three straight. C. Ogden. il por *Time* 129:44 My 18 '87
All revved up [with interview] D. Brand. il pors *Time* 129:34-8 Je 22 '87
Britain: Lords a-leaping. N. Cooper. il *Newsweek* 110:46 N 30 '87
Britain's cheesy campaign [cover story] F. Barnes. il *New Repub* 196:22-5 Je 22 '87
Campaigning for a record. P. C. Winslow. il por *Macleans* 100:20+ My 25 '87
Elections loom in Thatcher's future. K. Slack. *Christ Century* 104:183-4 F 25 '87
The empire's last nervous twitch. C. C. Mann. *Commonweal* 114:582-5 O 9 '87
Headed for the finish line. C. Ogden. il por *Time* 129:39 Je 15 '87
In the telly's eye: an American-style British campaign. R. Knight. il pors *U S News World Rep* 102:10-11 Je 15 '87
The long reign of Britain's 'Maggie III'. R. Knight. il por *U S News World Rep* 102:14 Je 22 '87
Maggie Thatcher: "She's all backbone". D. Reed. por *Read Dig* 131:213-14+ N '87

Maggie's revolution on the line. A. Lejeune. *Natl Rev* 39:32+ Je 19 '87
Minority report. C. Hitchens. *Nation* 244:752 Je 6 '87
Mrs. Thatcher's election prospects [interview with R. Pennant-Rea] A. Balk. il por *World Press Rev* 34:30-3 Ja '87
No slacking. A. Lejeune. *Natl Rev* 39:38 Jl 17 '87
Now at center stage, NATO's leading lady. S. Jenkins. il por *U S News World Rep* 102:33 Ap 6 '87
Now the other Britain needs Thatcher's attention. R. A. Melcher. il por *Bus Week* p43 Je 29 '87
Off and running. F. Painton. il por *Time* 129:34-6 Je 1 '87
On the stump with the Iron Lady. B. Amiel. il *Macleans* 100:9 Je 22 '87
One determined lady. R. Laver. il por *Macleans* 100:20 Je 22 '87
Power in the name of ideas. G. F. Will. il *Newsweek* 109:84 Je 22 '87
A search for 'respect'. R. Laver. il por *Macleans* 100:30 Mr 9 '87
Tea with Margaret Thatcher. J. Goodwin. *Ladies Home J* 104:135+ N '87
Thatcher after the crash: carry on, then. R. A. Melcher. il *Bus Week* p80-1 N 16 '87
Thatcher is looking more like a three-time winner. R. A. Melcher. il *Bus Week* p53 Ap 13 '87
Thatcher on dangerous ground. N. Gelb. il *New Leader* 70:5-6 N 2 '87
Thatcher pushes ahead [cover story; special section] il *World Press Rev* 34:11-16 My '87
Thatcher reneges on pre-election promise to boost expenditures on British space projects. *Aviat Week Space Technol* 127:31 Ag 3 '87
Thatcher wins again. K. Slack. *Christ Century* 104:581-2 Jl 1-8 '87
Thatcher's capitalist revolution [cover story] H. Raines. il pors *N Y Times Mag* p16-19+ My 31 '87
Thatcher's revolution: act III. R. A. Melcher. il por *Bus Week* p72-4 My 25 '87
Thatcher's third term target. N. Gelb. il *New Leader* 70:6-7 Je 29 '87
Thatcher's two Britains. M. Whitaker. il por *Newsweek* 109:28-30 Je 22 '87
Two Davids and Goliath. R. Watson. il pors *Newsweek* 109:26-7 My 25 '87
Two Margarets on Maggie [interview with M. Drabble] M. Atwood. por *Ms* 16:65-6 N '87
What Maggie has wrought. R. I. Kirkland, Jr. il pors *Fortune* 115:91-2 Je 8 '87
What Maggie hath wrought. R. Knight and others. il pors *U S News World Rep* 102:30-2 Ap 6 '87
                    Visit to the Soviet Union, 1987
Campaigning in Moscow. R. Cornwell. *World Press Rev* 34:11-12 My '87
Giving better than she got. W. R. Doerner. il pors *Time* 129:50 Ap 13 '87
Thatcher on Gorbachev [cover story] C. Thatcher. il pors *Life* 10:32-4 O '87
A visit from the Iron Lady. il por *Macleans* 100:16-17 Ap 13 '87
                    Visit to the United States, 1987
Visit of Prime Minister Thatcher [remarks, July 17, 1987] R. Reagan; M. Thatcher. *Dep State Bull* 87:41-2 S '87
Thatcher, Mark
about
Mark Thatcher bridles. il pors *People Wkly* 27:26-7 Mr 2 '87
Thatcher, R. W., and others
Human cerebral hemispheres develop at different rates and ages. bibl f il *Science* 236:1110-13 My 29 '87
Thate, Jeremiah
                    Kidnapping
After four agonizing months, a Maryland couple are reunited with their kidnapped baby. M. Brower. il pors *People Wkly* 28:69-70+ N 16 '87
Thaw, Frances
about
The bulb broker. K. Harby. il por *Nations Bus* 75:58 Mr '87
Thaxton, Judy
about
June and Judy Thaxton: twins in engineering. F. White, III. il pors *Ebony* 42:116+ Mr '87
Thaxton, June
about
June and Judy Thaxton: twins in engineering. F. White, III. il pors *Ebony* 42:116+ Mr '87

Thay Sam
about
One refugee's story: "sometimes I'm okay". B. R. Thompson. por *Christ Today* 31:26 F 20 '87
Thayer, Paul
about
Picking up the pieces. W. P. Barrett. il por *Forbes* 140:113 Ag 10 '87
Thayer, Scofield, d. 1982
about
Rediscovering an early modern vision. J. Richardson. il por *House Gard* 159:158-63+ F '87
Thayer, W. Paul *See* Thayer, Paul
Theater
See also
Actors and actresses
Christmas pageants
Drama
Drama festivals
Mime
Motion picture theaters
Playbills
Puppets and puppet plays
Women in the theater
All the country's a stage [regional theater] B. Harte. il *Fortune* 115:117-18+ Mr 30 '87
News. See issues of Theatre Crafts
Opportunities for today's playwrights [list of 33 theaters] *Writer* 100:24-7 D '87
Advertising
The press release. C. Boneau. il *Theatre Crafts* 21:92+ N '87
Awards
See also
Tony Awards
Bibliography
Books. See issues of Theatre Crafts
Theater on the shelf. M. Stitt. il *Horizon* 30:9 Mr '87
Censorship
Charlottetown and the F-word [uproar over drama festival's censorship of play about Elvis Presley in Prince Edward Island] A. Fotheringham. il *Macleans* 100:60 My 4 '87
Costume
See Costume, Theatrical
Economic aspects
Hey, Falstaff, can you spare a shilling? [Royal Shakespeare Company] P. Sherrid. il *U S News World Rep* 103:64 Jl 20 '87
Electronic sound control
AES report [annual convention] S. Pollock. *Theatre Crafts* 21:31-4 Mr '87
Aural Fixation [work of sound designer G. Sherman] S. Borey. il por *Theatre Crafts* 21:42+ O '87
A buyer's guide to selected sound products at AES. B. Saturn. il *Theatre Crafts* 21:31+ Mr '87
James LeBrecht [sound designer at Berkeley Rep] A. M. Hale. il por *Theatre Crafts* 21:34-5+ F '87
Retrofitting the sixties: rethinking your intercom system. R. Long. il *Theatre Crafts* 21:84-7 D '87
Sound [touring theater] A. M. Hale. il *Theatre Crafts* 21:22+ Ag/S '87
Employees
See also
Set designers
Stage managers
Exhibitions
Prague Quadrennial '87: America throws its process into the international design ring. M. Sommers. il *Theatre Crafts* 21:18 My '87
The United States wins Prague Quadrennial. E. Fielding. il *Theatre Crafts* 21:32-3+ O '87
History
20 years ago. M. LaRue. il *Theatre Crafts* 21:10-11+ My '87
International aspects
See also
International Organization of Scenographers, Theatre Architects and Technicians
Theater and the individual talent [Actors Equity prohibition on foreign actors] R. Brustein. *New Repub* 197:28-9 Ag 3 '87
Management
See Theater management
Moral and religious aspects
See also
A.D. Players
Political aspects
The agitprop players [Standin' the Gaff, international festival of leftist political theater in Sydney, N.S.] C. Wood. il *Macleans* 100:55 Je 8 '87

Production and direction
See also
College and school drama
Computers—Theatrical use
Musicals, revues, etc.—Production and direction
United States Institute for Theatre Technology
1987 new product buyers guide. B. Burns and M. Loeffler. il *Theatre Crafts* 21:39+ Ag/S '87
Are directors necessary? M. Stitt. il *Horizon* 30:12 My '87
A Christmas carol [various productions of C. Dickens' work] B. Burns. il *Theatre Crafts* 21:38-41+ O '87
Director without a country [Soviet exile Y. Lyubimov of Moscow's Taganka Theater] R. B. Cullen. il por *Newsweek* 109:60 Ja 19 '87
Glitz! D. Harris. il *Vogue* 177:318-19+ D '87
The Mahabharata [special section] il *Theatre Crafts* 21:27-31+ N '87
Producing [touring theater] M. Sommers. il *Theatre Crafts* 21:20+ Ag/S '87
Product news. See issues of Theatre Crafts
Russian dressing: concocting the recipe for Wild honey. M. Sommers. il *Theatre Crafts* 21:26-7+ Ja '87
Bibliography
Product literature directory. S. Nielsen and S. Alexander. *Theatre Crafts* 21:16+ Ja '87
Directories
Directory 1987/88 [special issue] R. Smith. il *Theatre Crafts* 21:6-10+ Je/Jl '87
Social aspects
Cracked theatrical mirrors. R. J. Pentzell. *Society* 24:78-82 Ja/F '87
Sound systems
See Theater—Electronic sound control
Special effects
Broadway's new phenomenon: F/X musicals. K. Grubb. il *Dance Mag* 61:54-5 Jl '87
Fog . . . foggier . . . foggiest [machines and fluids] A. Brightman. il *Theatre Crafts* 21:28-9+ Mr '87
Rain on the road [touring theater] M. Loeffler. il *Theatre Crafts* 21:23+ Ag/S '87
Stage lighting
See also
Lighting designers
Architectural lighting control. S. Pollock. il *Theatre Crafts* 21:43+ O '87
Computer-assisted lighting controllers. D. F. Sisk. il *Theatre Crafts* 21:36-41 F '87
Lighting to sculpt shadows [work of P. Jenkins] C. Eller. il *Theatre Crafts* 21:26-7+ Mr '87
Lights [touring theater] A. M. Hale. il *Theatre Crafts* 21:24-5+ Ag/S '87
Load your own: software to turn your PC into a lighting controller. *Theatre Crafts* 21:38+ Ag/S '87
New York area lighting rental houses. D. F. Sisk. *Theatre Crafts* 21:14+ Ja '87
Retrofitting the sixties: upgrading your lighting booth. M. Mell. il *Theatre Crafts* 21:32+ D '87
Speed lighting: Paul Gallo prefers the fast track [cover story] A. M. Hale. il por *Theatre Crafts* 21:34-9+ Ap '87
USITT dimmer standards. D. F. Sisk. *Theatre Crafts* 21:16+ F '87
Stage setting and scenery
See also
Ballet—Stage setting and scenery
Dance—Stage setting and scenery
Musicals, revues, etc.—Stage setting and scenery
Opera—Stage setting and scenery
Set designers
Twin City Scenic Studio
An artist sets the stage [M. Levine] R. Everett-Green. il por *Macleans* 100:53 Ap 6 '87
Brighton Beach memoirs. M. LaRue. il *Theatre Crafts* 21:22-5+ F '87
Build scale models. C. Wong. il *Theatre Crafts* 21:90+ Ap '87
Emotional spaces [work of A. Okun] M. Sommers. il por *Theatre Crafts* 21:44-7+ N '87
Greek-born designer decorates Paris stage [Y. Kokkos] E. Lampert. il *Theatre Crafts* 21:18 N '87
He made the stage come alive [B. Aronson] F. Rich and L. Aronson. il por *N Y Times Mag* p52-4+ O 11 '87
Josie Caruso: modeling a career. B. Burns. il por *Theatre Crafts* 21:18 O '87
Les liaisons dangereuses [B. Crowley's production design; cover story] M. Sommers. il por *Theatre Crafts* 21:26-31+ Ag/S '87
The play's the thing [work of designer K. Rigdon] J. Dolan. il por *Theatre Crafts* 21:28-31+ F '87

Theater—Stage setting and scenery—*cont.*
Retrofitting the sixties: rigging & rigging control. J. O. Glerum. il *Theatre Crafts* 21:26-7+ F '87
Retrofitting the sixties: turntables, lifts, and other stage machinery. D. F. Sisk. il *Theatre Crafts* 21:30+ Mr '87
Scene painting. R. Long. il *Theatre Crafts* 21:44-6+ O '87
Svoboda & Vychodil: Czechoslovakia's two master scenographers. J. M. Burian. il *Theatre Crafts* 21:34-7+ O '87
Tony Walton at the Beaumont [sets for The house of blue leaves and The front page; cover story] G. Stern. il por *Theatre Crafts* 21:16-21+ Mr '87

Study and teaching
See also
Frohman Academy for Musical Theatre Education
Yale University. School of Drama
A case for theory. B. S. Rosenblatt. bibl f *Des Arts Educ* 88:31-5 My/Je '87
Eight questions for higher education [preparation of high school theater teachers] W. Waack. *Des Arts Educ* 88:32-5 Ja/F '87

Arizona
See also
Arizona Theatre Company

Brazil
Black theatre, black consciousness. A. V.-B. da Mota. *Courier* 39:18 D '86

California
See also
Oakland (Calif.)—Theater
Take the freeway to Broadway [imports from California] R. Alleman. il *Vogue* 177:128 O '87

Canada
An artist sets the stage [M. Levine] R. Everett-Green. il por *Macleans* 100:53 Ap 6 '87
Theatre. See occasional issues of Maclean's

China
Fantastick voyage [bringing The fantasticks to China] B. R. Marriott. il *Horizon* 30:64-5 O '87

Connecticut
See also
Goodspeed Opera House

Czechoslovakia
Svoboda & Vychodil: Czechoslovakia's two master scenographers. J. M. Burian. il *Theatre Crafts* 21:34-7+ O '87

France
See also
Paris (France)—Theater

Great Britain
See also
English Shakespeare Company
London (England)—Theater
Royal Court Theatre
Royal Shakespeare Company
Snarls, continued [British conquest of Broadway] R. Brustein. *New Repub* 196:27-8+ My 4 '87

Java (Indonesia)
Shadow world of the Javanese [wayang performances] W. Keeler. il *Nat Hist* 96:68-72+ N '87

New Mexico
See also
New Mexico Repertory Theatre

New York (State)
See also
New York (N.Y.)—Theater

South Africa
See also
Johannesburg (South Africa)—Theater

South Carolina
See also
Charleston (S.C.)—Theater

Southeastern States
Southeast style. M. Sommers. il *Theatre Crafts* 21:22-5+ Mr '87

Soviet Union
See also
Moscow (Soviet Union)—Theater
Cultural exchange within the global village. M. Rhodes. por *Horizon* 30:9 D '87

Ukraine
History
Les Kurbas, founder of Ukrainian theatre. N. Kornienko. il por *Courier* 40:32-3 O '87

Washington (D.C.)
See Washington (D.C.)—Theater

Theater, Amateur
See also
American Association of Community Theatres

Theater, Black
See also
AMAS Repertory Theatre, Inc.
Black drama
Negro Ensemble Company
New Regal Theater (Chicago, Ill.)
Black theatre, black consciousness [Brazil] A. V.-B. da Mota. *Courier* 39:18 D '86
A conversation with . . . [G. Moses] D. Armstrong. il por *Essence* 17:26 Ja '87
Leaving his imprint on Broadway [L. Richards] S. G. Freedman. il pors *N Y Times Mag* p38+ N 22 '87
Risky business [black musicals created from operettas] S. Flatow. il *Opera News* 51:18-20+ My '87

Theater, Children's
See also
Seem-To-Be Players
Children and theater. il *Futurist* 21:38 N/D '87

Theater, Experimental
See also
Fiji Theater Company
Survival Research Laboratories (Group)
Wooster Group

Theater, Hispanic American
See also
La Compañia de Teatro de Albuquerque

Theater, Indian (American)
Legends on the stage [Canadian native theater] D. Taylor. il *Macleans* 100:69 O 19 '87

Theater, Open-air
See also
Street theater

Theater, Traveling
See also
Cornerstone Theater Company
Geese Company
Getting your show on the road [special section] il *Theatre Crafts* 21:19-25+ Ag/S '87
How does Broadway play in Peoria? W. A. Henry. il *Time* 130:86-7 S 14 '87
In Iowa: rolling toward Peoria [touring cast of On the Twentieth Century] R. Coniff. il *Time* 129:11-13 Ap 20 '87

Theater and politics *See* Theater—Political aspects
Theater and the aged
Street scene [reactions to performance of E. Rice play] *New Yorker* 63:35-7 D 7 '87
Theater and the blind
The eyes and ears have it in DC [Audio Description narration service] S. Green. il *Theatre Crafts* 21:41+ Ap '87
Theater and the handicapped
See also
National Theater Workshop of the Handicapped
Retrofitting the sixties: making your theatre accessible. A. M. Hale. il *Theatre Crafts* 21:40-1+ Ap '87
Theater buildings
Architecture 87 [cover story; special section] il *Theatre Crafts* 21:37-54+ D '87
Retrofitting the sixties: wear, tear and the way we were. P. MacKay. il *Theatre Crafts* 21:34-5+ Ja '87

Conservation and restoration
A full Circle [Circle Theatre, Indianapolis] B. Golightly. il *Horizon* 30:23 Je '87
Grand palaces [Oakland, Calif.] il *Horizon* 30:36 Ja/F '87
Renovation [renovation of Brooklyn's Majestic for The Mahabharata] M. Sommers. il *Theatre Crafts* 21:28-31+ N '87
Retrofitting the sixties: taking the temperature of your theatre. R. Davis. il *Theatre Crafts* 21:36-9 Ja '87
A Snug Harbor for Vinoly [renovation of Staten Island's Music Hall] M. LaRue. il *Theatre Crafts* 21:14 O '87

Theater critics and criticism *See* Drama critics and criticism
Theater decoration
Fe fi fo fum! Ann Slavit's boot is a ticket seller's chum [air-filled sculpture on Martin Beck Theatre, New York City] il por *People Wkly* 28:69 D 21 '87
Theater festivals *See* Drama festivals
Theater management
Administration [work of the company manager and stage manager in touring theater] M. Loeffler. il *Theatre Crafts* 21:21+ Ag/S '87
Theater models
Build scale models [use in scenic design] C. Wong. il *Theatre Crafts* 21:90+ Ap '87
Josie Caruso: modeling a career. B. Burns. il por *Theatre Crafts* 21:18 O '87

Theater museums
    See also
      Theatre Museum (London, England)
Theater reviews
  Anticipated communications. M. Stitt. il *Horizon* 30:10
    O '87
  Best of '86. il *Time* 129:79 Ja 5 '87
  Bright lights, Big Apple. L. Black. il *Macleans* 100:69-70
    D 7 '87
  Cue: a complete entertainment guide for the week. See
    issues of New York
  Entr'acte. M. Stitt. See occasional issues of Horizon
    (Tuscaloosa, Ala.) beginning July/August 1984
  Goings on about town. See issues of The New Yorker
  On stage. L. Sauvage. See issues of The New Leader
  Robert Brustein on theater. R. Brustein. See occasional
    issues of The New Republic
  Theater. See occasional issues of The Nation
  Theater. J. Simon. See issues of New York
  The theatre. M. Kramer. See issues of The New Yorker
    beginning June 8, 1987
  The theatre. E. Oliver. See issues of The New Yorker
    beginning February 16, 1987
Single works

    See name of author for full entry
  1984. Kohout, Pavel
  All my sons. Miller, Arthur, 1915-
  All the king's men. Hall, Adrian
  Almost by chance a woman: Elizabeth. Fo, Dario
  American splendor. Rose, Lloyd
  April snow. Linney, Romulus, 1930-
  Are you lonesome tonight? Bleasdale, Alan
  As is. Hoffman, William M.
  As it is in heaven. Sutton, Joe
  Asinamali! Ngema, Mbongeni
  The Bacchae. Euripides, ca. 485-ca. 406 B.C.
  Barometer rising. Ouzounian, Richard
  Beautiful city. Walker, George F.
  Beirut. Bowne, Alan
  Blithe spirit. Coward, Noel
  Bloody poetry. Brenton, Howard, 1942-
  Bodies, rest, and motion. Hedden, Roger
  Bouncers. Godber, John
  Breaking the code. Whitemore, Hugh
  Brighton Beach memoirs. Simon, Neil
  Broadway. Dunning, Philip
  Broadway bound. Simon, Neil
  Bunker reveries. Shaber, David
  Burn this. Wilson, Lanford, 1938-
  The casting of Kevin Christian. Holt, Stephen
  The CIVIL warS. Wilson, Robert, 1941-
  Claptrap. Friedman, Ken
  Coastal disturbances. Howe, Tina
  The colored museum. Wolfe, George C.
  The comedy of errors. Shakespeare, William, 1564-1616
  The common pursuit. Gray, Simon James Holliday, 1936-
  The coyote cycle. Mednick, Murray
  Crime and punishment. Lyubimov, Yuri
  Danger: memory! Miller, Arthur, 1915-
  Death and the king's horseman. Soyinka, Wole
  Detaining Mr. Trotsky. Fothergill, Robert
  Division Street. Tesich, Steve, 1942-
  Driving Miss Daisy. Uhry, Alfred
  Educating Rita. Russell, Willy
  El Salvador. Lima, Rafael
  A feast in the plague-time. Lyubimov, Yuri
  Fences. Wilson, August
  Fire. Ledoux, Paul
  Fragments of a Greek trilogy. Serban, Andrei
  Frankie and Johnny in the Clair de Lune. McNally,
    Terrence, 1939-
  The front page. Hecht, Ben, 1894-1964
  The garden of earthly delights. Clarke, Martha, 1944?-
  Groucho: a life in revue. Marx, Arthur
  Happy days. Beckett, Samuel, 1906-
  Hard times. Jeffreys, Stephen
  Henry IV, part 1. Shakespeare, William, 1564-1616
  Holy Ghosts. Linney, Romulus, 1930-
  House arrest. Bozzone, Bill
  The hunger artist. Clarke, Martha, 1944?-
  Hunting cockroaches. Głowacki, Janusz
  I am yours. Thompson, Judith, 1939-
  The importance of being earnest. Wilde, Oscar, 1854-1900
  It's a man's world. Mehrten, Greg
  Jerker. Chesley, Robert, 1943-
  The Jew of Malta. Marlow, Christopher, 1564-1593
  Joe Turner's come and gone. Wilson, August
  Lady Day at Emerson's Bar & Grill. Robertson, Lanie
  The last bus. Storey, Raymond
  Laughing wild. Durang, Christopher, 1949-
  Les liaisons dangereuses. Hampton, Christopher, 1946-

  The life of the land. Sakamoto, Edward, 1940-
  Little murders. Feiffer, Jules
  The Lucky Spot. Henley, Beth
  The maderati. Greenberg, Richard
  The Mahabharata. Brook, Peter, 1925-
  A man for all seasons. Bolt, Robert
  The marriage of Figaro. Beaumarchais, Pierre Augustin
    Caron de, 1732-1799
  McClure. Scott, Munroe
  Melody farm. Mitchell, Ken
  A midsummer nights dream. Shakespeare, William,
    1564-1616
  The milk train doesn't stop here anymore. Williams,
    Tennessee, 1911-1983
  Moms. Childress, Alice, 1920-
  A month of Sundays. Larbey, Bob
  Moonchildren. Weller, Michael
  The musical comedy murders of 1940. Bishop, John,
    1929-
  My darling Judith. Foster, Norm, 1949-
  My Gene. Gelb, Barbara
  The nerd. Shue, Larry
  No exit. Sartre, Jean Paul, 1905-1980
  Old business. Cacaci, Joe
  On the verge. Overmyer, Eric
  Only you. Mason, Timothy
  Othello. Shakespeare, William, 1564-1616
  Pass the blutwurst, bitte (The Egon Schiele story). Kelly,
    John
  Perdition. Allen, Jim
  Pericles Prince of Tyre by William Shakespeare. Dubois,
    René-Daniel
  Peter Pan. Barrie, J. M. (James Matthew), 1860-1937
  Philistines. Gorky, Maksim, 1868-1936
  A place with the pigs. Fugard, Athol
  Pride & prejudice. Pownall, David, 1938-
  Psycho beach party. Busch, Charles
  Punch! Shapiro, Leonardo
  La puta vida trilogy. Povod, Reinaldo
  Pygmalion. Shaw, Bernard, 1856-1950
  Quartet for three actors. Deverell, Rex
  A raisin in the sun. Hansberry, Lorraine, 1930-1965
  Real estate. Page, Louise
  Red noses. Barnes, Peter, 1931-
  The redthroats. Cale, David
  The regard of flight. Irwin, Bill
  The rez sisters. Highway, Tomson
  Richard II. Shakespeare, William, 1564-1616
  Road show. Schisgal, Murray, 1926-
  The road to Mecca. Fugard, Athol
  Rosencrantz & Guildenstern are dead. Stoppard, Tom
  Rosie's Cafe. Shiomi, R. A.
  Royalty is royalty. Mitchell, W. O. (William Ormond),
    1914-
  Safe sex. Fierstein, Harvey
  Self defense. Cacaci, Joe
  Serious money. Churchill, Caryl
  A shayna maidel. Lebow, Barbara
  Sherlock's last case. Marowitz, Charles
  Sleight of hand. Pielmeier, John
  Steel magnolias. Harling, Robert, 1910-
  Stepping out. Harris, Richard
  Street scene. Rice, Elmer L., 1892-1967
  Sweet Sue. Gurney, A. R. (Albert Ramsdell), 1930-
  Talk radio. Bogosian, Eric
  The tamer tamed. Fletcher, John, 1579-1625
  Tartuffe. Molière, 1622-1673
  Tent meeting. Larson, Larry
  Tete-a-tete. Burdman, Ralph
  Three men on a horse. Holm, John Cecil, 1904-1981
  La tragicomedia de Calisto y Melibea. Rojas, Fernando
    de, d. 1541
  Trash, the city and death. Fassbinder, Rainer Werner,
    1946-1982
  Two gentlemen of Verona. Shakespeare, William,
    1564-1616
  Waiting for Lefty. Odets, Clifford, 1906-1963
  A walk in the woods. Blessing, Lee
  The Widow Claire. Foote, Horton
  Wild blue. Pintauro, Joseph
  Wild honey. Frayn, Michael
  Zangezi. Khlebnikov, Velimir, 1885-1922
  Zastrozzi. Walker, George F.
Theater teachers
Certification

  Drama/theatre education: what K-12 teachers need to
    know and be able to do. K. A. Wheetley. bibl f
    Des Arts Educ 89:36-40 S/O '87

Theaters *See* Theater buildings
Theatre Museum (London, England)
Stage or stepping stone? J. Earl. il *Hist Today* 37:5-7 Ag '87
Theatrical agencies and agents
See also
Affiliate Artists, Inc.
Black theatrical agencies and agents
Cosmic Contact Psychic Services
International Creative Management (Firm)
Josephson International Inc.
Triad Artists, Inc.
Richie splits with Kragen after six-year management. il pors *Jet* 71:17 Mr 2 '87
Suits and claims
Jury selection under way in Eddie Murphy dispute. *Jet* 71:16 Mr 23 '87
Kim Fields sues ex-agent in a contract dispute. *Jet* 72:56 Ap 27 '87
Kim Fields sues ex-agent in a contract dispute [reprint from April 27, 1987 issue] *Jet* 72:24 My 11 '87
Murphy settles battle with ex-manager out of court [E. Murphy's suit] il por *Jet* 72:54 Ap 6 '87
Todd Bridges and mom sue managers for $2 million. *Jet* 72:15 Ap 13 '87
Yo, Broder! Eddie Murphy has to pay the King's ransom. K. Gross. il pors *People Wkly* 27:103-4+ Ap 13 '87
Germany (West)
Need a little blueblood to go? Does Germany's Wolfgang Schrell have a princess for you! M. Neill. il pors *People Wkly* 28:159-60 D 7 '87
Theatrical costume *See* Costume, Theatrical
Theatrical designers *See* Set designers
Theatrical directors
See also
Abbott, George
Bennett, Michael
Brook, Peter, 1925-
Lyubimov, Yuri
Ouzounian, Richard
Serban, Andrei
Sprung, Guy
Wilson, Robert, 1941-
Are directors necessary? M. Stitt. il *Horizon* 30:12 My '87
Theatrical directors, Handicapped
Paralyzed after a near-fatal accident, director Jack Hofsiss stages a dramatic comeback; ed. by Bonnie Johnson. J. Hofsiss. il pors *People Wkly* 28:131-2+ S 14 '87
Theatrical production and direction *See* Theater—Production and direction
Thebes (Egypt: Ancient city)
See also
Temple of Luxor
Theft *See* Shoplifting; Stealing
Theme [film] See Motion picture reviews—Single works
Theme parks *See* Amusement parks
Theobald, Gillian
about
Gillian Theobald. L. Goldman. il *Art News* 86:52 My '87
Theobald, Thomas
about
Ten on the Richter scale. C. Siler. il por *Forbes* 140:96-7 N 30 '87
Tom Theobald has second thoughts. N. J. Perry. il por *Fortune* 116:92 Ag 31 '87
Tom Theobald's big question. J. N. Frank. por *Bus Week* p28 Ag 10 '87
Theocracy
See also
Christian Reconstruction movement
Theodore Roosevelt Island (Washington, D.C.)
'Walking the dog' is a fortuitous excuse to wander the woods and marshes of an island memorial to a naturalist president. J. P. Wiley, Jr. *Smithsonian* 17:30+ Ja '87
Theologians
See also
Augustine, Saint, Bishop of Hippo
Curran, Charles E.
Dulles, Avery Robert, 1918-
Hauerwas, Stanley, 1940-
Küng, Hans, 1928-
Liguori, Alfonso Maria de', Saint, 1696-1787
Moltmann, Jürgen
Niebuhr, Reinhold, 1892-1971
Tillich, Paul, 1886-1965
Anecdotes, facetiae, satire, etc.
The divine deli. il *Christ Today* 31:27 S 18 '87

Theological education *See* Theology—Study and teaching
Theological seminaries
See also
Boston University. School of Theology
Concordia Seminary (Saint Louis, Mo.)
Fuller Theological Seminary
Howard University. School of Divinity
Seminarians
Southeastern Baptist Theological Seminary
Wesley Theological Seminary
Theological education 1987 [special issue] il *Christ Century* 104:100-4+ F 4-11 '87
Curriculum
Seminary, ministry and social responsibility. J. F. Fishburn. *Christ Century* 104:100-2 F 4-11 '87
Enrollment
Anecdotes, facetiae, satire, etc.
The latest academic fad. F. Sprock. por *Newsweek* 109:8 Je 1 '87
Theological students *See* Seminarians
Theology
See also
Annihilationism (Theology)
Black theology
Catechetics
Catholic Church. Congregation for the Doctrine of the Faith
Christian ethics
Christianity
Covenants (Theology)
Election (Theology)
Eschatology
Evangelical Theological Society
Faith
God
Good and evil
Good works (Theology)
Grace (Theology)
Heresy
Incarnation
Kingdom of God
Law (Theology)
Liberation theology
Love (Theology)
Mary, Blessed Virgin, Saint—Theology
Mysticism
Orthodoxy
Prayer
Process theology
Religion
Resurrection
Salvation
Secularism
Sermons
Soul
Truth
Universalism (Theology)
Word of God (Theology)
Catholic authority, Catholic theology, Catholic identity [special section] *Commonweal* 114:43-51 Ja 30 '87
Finding a place for emotions in Christian theology. G. S. Clapper. il *Christ Century* 104:409-11 Ap 29 '87
Moral theology and public dissent: a temporary compromise [Catholic Church] J. L. Lombardi. *America* 156:100-1+ F 7 '87
Scripture and dogma today [Catholic doctrine] R. E. Brown. *America* 157:286-9 O 31 '87
Sober hope: some themes in Protestant theology today. G. Fackre. *Christ Century* 104:790-2 S 23 '87
Study and teaching
See also
Theological seminaries
America and theological education [Catholic theology; address] G. W. Hunt. *America* 157:6-8 Jl 4-11 '87
Charles E. Curran: a teaching moment continues [cover story; special issue; with editorial comment by George W. Hunt] il *America* 156:inside cover, 334-46+ Ap 25 '87
Public and private theologians [lack of theology students in public institutions] M. E. Marty. *Christ Century* 104:703 Ag 12-19 '87
Theological education 1987 [special issue] il *Christ Century* 104:100-4+ F 4-11 '87
Theology and the environment *See* Religion and the environment
Theonomy
See also
Christian Reconstruction movement
Theos Software Corporation
Susan Catalano: software keeps her on her toes. P. Finch. il por *Bus Week* p58 Ap 27 '87

Theotokopoulos, Domenikos *See* El Greco, 1541-1614
Thera (Greece: Island)
Ice traces of catastrophe: Chernobyl . . . and the ancient volcano Thera. *Sci News* 132:121 Ag 22 '87
Therapeutics
See also
Acupuncture
Aroma therapy
Bed rest
Dance therapy
Electrotherapy
Gene therapy
Home remedies
Intravenous therapy
Occupational therapy
Psychotherapy
Radiotherapy
Thalassotherapy
See also subheads Therapeutic use; Therapy under various subjects
Beyond the limits of traditional medicine [alternative therapies] L. J. Moore. il *U S News World Rep* 102:54-5 Je 29 '87
Complementary medicine. S. Fulder. il *Courier* 40:16-19 Ag '87
When medical treatment takes an alternate route. J. Lewis. il *Curr Health 2* 13:22-3 Mr '87
Complications
See also
Iatrogenic diseases
Therborn, Göran
Migration and Western Europe: the old world turning new. bibl f il *Science* 237:1183-8 S 4 '87
Thérèse, de Lisieux, Saint, 1873-1897
about
Love in action and contemplation. J. D. Lynch. *Christ Century* 104:260-1 Mr 18-25 '87
'Thérèse': a second opinion. J. W. Donohue. *America* 156:137-8+ F 14 '87
Thérèse [film] See Motion picture reviews—Single works
Thermal energy storage *See* Heat storage
Thermal imaging *See* Thermography
Thermal protection tiles, Space shuttle *See* Space vehicles—Insulation
Thermal radiation *See* Heat—Radiation and absorption
Thermal springs *See* Hot springs
Thermal underwear *See* Underwear
Thermal window shades *See* Window shades
Thermedics Inc.
The chemical nose. W. Baldwin. il *Forbes* 140:278 N 16 '87
From making hearts to winning them [drug delivery skin patches redesigned to release fragrances] C. Brown. il *Bus Week* p153+ N 16 '87
Thermo Electron Corp.
Serendipity. W. Baldwin. il por *Forbes* 140:274+ N 16 '87
Thermodynamics
See also
Entropy
Free energy
Statistical mechanics
Small systems: when does thermodynamics apply? H. Feshbach. il *Phys Today* 40:9+ N '87
Thermoelectric equipment
See also
Thermo Electron Corp.
Thermography
Engines: how hot? [motorcycle engines measured with Probeye infrared system] P. Gordon. il *Cycle* 38:33-8 S '87
Medical use
Is the pain real? B. Kevles. il *Women's Sports Fitness* 9:20 Je '87
Thermolysin
Calculation of the relative change in binding free energy of a protein-inhibitor complex. P. A. Bash and others. bibl f il *Science* 235:574-6 Ja 30 '87
Evaluation of intrinsic binding energy from a hydrogen bonding group in an enzyme inhibitor. P. A. Bartlett and C. K. Marlowe. bibl f il *Science* 235:569-71 Ja 30 '87
Structures of two thermolysin-inhibitor complexes that differ by a single hydrogen bond. D. E. Tronrud and others. bibl f il *Science* 235:571-4 Ja 30 '87
Thermometers, Clinical
New urinary thermometers may streamline temperature taking. *Prevention* 39:32 F '87
Thermometers and thermometry
See also
Calorimeters and calorimetry

Thermonuclear reactions *See* Nuclear fusion
Thermophilic bacteria *See* Bacteria, Thermophilic
Thermoplastics
Wash-away plastics [developed by Belland AG] S. Ashley. il *Pop Sci* 230:45+ Je '87
Thermoregulatory behavior *See* Temperature, Animal and human
Thermostats
Electronic thermostats: setback and relax. N. Cooper. il *Home Mech* 83:26 F '87
Thernstrom, Abigail M., 1936-
about
What went wrong with the Voting Rights Act. P. H. Schuck. *Wash Mon* 19:51-5 N '87
Theroux, Alexander, 1939-
Caution: geniuses at work and play. il *Read Dig* 131:215-18+ O '87
Theroux, Paul
Salad days. il *N Y Times Mag* p22 N 22 '87
Theroux, Phyllis
First-person parent. See issues of Parents beginning December 1984
Thesauri
See also
Publishers and publishing—Thesauri
Thesaurus word processor programs *See* Word processors and processing—Programming
Thian, Raphael P.
about
He saved the South's money. il *South Living* 22:24 Jl '87
Thiemann, Ronald F.
Making theology central in theological education. *Christ Century* 104:106-8 F 4-11 '87
Thigh exercises *See* Exercise
Thin films
Artificially structured thin-film materials and interfaces. V. Narayanamurti. bibl f il *Science* 235:1023-8 F 27 '87
Efficient thin-film solar cells revive interest in space uses. B. D. Nordwall. *Aviat Week Space Technol* 126:105+ Je 29 '87
IBM superconductor leaps current hurdle. A. L. Robinson. *Science* 236:1189 Je 5 '87
Interference patterns on garage door windows. C. F. Bohren. il *Weatherwise* 40:266-70 O '87
Think tanks *See* Research institutions
Thinking *See* Thought and thinking
Thinness *See* Weight (Physiology)
Thiokol Corp.
See also
Morton Thiokol, Inc.
Thionates
Correlation of volcanic activity with sulfur oxyanion speciation in a crater lake [cover story] B. Takano. bibl f il map *Science* 235:1633-5 Mr 27 '87
Third Committee (United Nations) *See* United Nations. Social, Humanitarian and Cultural Committee
Third Reich *See* National socialism
Third world *See* Developing countries
Thirteen (The number)
Triskaidekaphobia. il *Discover* 8:16 N '87
Triskaidekaphobia can strike when you're most expecting it. P. Hoffman. il *Smithsonian* 17:122-4+ F '87
Thirty Years' War, 1618-1648
Deutschlands truebste Zeit: the calamity of 1648. C. E. Kraft. il *Antiques Collect Hobbies* 92:79-81 Je '87
thirtysomething [television program] See Television program reviews—Single works
Thistles
Control
Clean up a thistle patch with a $200 sack of bugs [musk thistle weevil] *Success Farm* 85 no1:26 Ja '87
Thitchener, Carl
The condom conundrum: a sermon on AIDS to raise the conscience of our times. il pors *Humanist* 47:11-14+ Jl/Ag '87
about
The condom preacher—and his pantless past. il por *Newsweek* 109:69 Mr 2 '87
Minister gives condoms to stop AIDS, starts a controversy on subject. il por *Jet* 71:10 F 23 '87
Tholen, David J., and others
Improved orbital and physical parameters for the Pluto-Charon system. bibl f il *Science* 237:512-14 Jl 31 '87
Thomas, the Apostle, Saint
about
Easter meditation:
Believing Thomas. B. L. Rohrig. il *Christ Century* 104:350-1 Ap 15 '87

Thomas, the Apostle, Saint—about—*cont.*
Lenten meditation:
Maundy Thursday: Thomas's testimony. J. B. Shepherd. *Christ Century* 104:327-8 Ap 8 '87
Thomas, Arthur E.
CSU's Thomas visits Senegal and forms socio-economic tie. il por *Jet* 71:21 Mr 2 '87
Thomas, Bob
The Angela Lansbury story. il pors *Good Housekeep* 204:132-3+ Mr '87
Thomas, Brooks
about
Thomas and 13 others leave Harper & Row. M. Reuter. il *Publ Wkly* 231:21-2 My 29 '87
Thomas, Caitlin
about
From Dylan Thomas' widow, Caitlin, comes a portrait of the poet as a (mad) young dog. D. Grogan. il pors *People Wkly* 28:79+ Jl 6 '87
PW interviews. M. Field. por *Publ Wkly* 231:56-7 Mr 20 '87
Thomas, Clarence
about
EEOC chair weds labor lawyer in D.C. ceremony. il pors *Jet* 72:30 Je 29 '87
EEOC's Thomas wants blacks in high-paying fed. jobs. por *Jet* 73:38 O 12 '87
A question of fairness. J. Williams. il pors *Atlantic* 259:70-5+ F '87
Thomas, David A.
Life among Mexico's ruins: ancient cities, modern inns. il map *Travel Holiday* 167:51-5+ F '87
Thomas, Debi
about
Cool on ice. A. Engeler. por *Vogue* 177:102+ Ag '87
Debi Thomas: on the cutting edge. J. Kaufman. il pors *Seventeen* 46:258-9+ Mr '87
Debi Thomas: skater extraordinaire. M. Kort. pors *Ms* 15:32-3 F '87
Fire on ice. E. Greenspan. il pors *Women's Sports Fitness* 9:22-5+ Mr '87
Thomas, Dennis
about
Day Gleeson and Dennis Thomas at A & P. T. Cokes. il *Art Am* 75:139-40 Ja '87
Thomas, Derrel
about
Black managers face off first for pro baseball. *Jet* 72:49 Jl 20 '87
Derrel Thomas fired as minor league manager. por *Jet* 72:50 Ag 17 '87
Ex-Dodger Thomas named to manage 'Class A' team. por *Jet* 72:46 Jl 6 '87
Thomas, Dirk
Cutting brush [cover story] il *Ctry J* 14:58-63 My '87
Rotary tillers. il *Ctry J* 14:21-7 Ap '87
Thomas, Dylan, 1914-1953
about
From Dylan Thomas' widow, Caitlin, comes a portrait of the poet as a (mad) young dog. D. Grogan. il pors *People Wkly* 28:79+ Jl 6 '87
PW interviews [C. Thomas] M. Field. por *Publ Wkly* 231:56-7 Mr 20 '87
Thomas, Elizabeth Marshall, 1931-
about
PW interviews. S. S. Steinberg. por *Publ Wkly* 231:70-1 Ja 9 '87
Thomas, Evan
Marshall arts. *Wash Mon* 19:54-5 Jl/Ag '87
Thomas, George Henry, 1816-1870
about
GAR tumbler: Gen. George H. Thomas. M. Wollett and B. Wollett. il *Antiques Collect Hobbies* 92:53 Mr '87
Thomas, Graham Stuart
about
Rare species. H. Mitchell. il por *House Gard* 159:56+ O '87
Thomas, Isiah
about
Demand for crime fighter Isiah is Piston's problem. por *Jet* 71:51 Ja 12 '87
Detroit's Thomas sees Bird in black & white. pors *Jet* 72:50 Je 22 '87
'I have got to do right'. W. Nack. il pors *Sports Illus* 66:60-4+ Ja 19 '87
Isiah & Bernhard. J. Morley. *Nation* 245:4-5 Jl 4-11 '87
Isiah Thomas' life story a series for Italian TV. por *Jet* 72:46 Ag 24 '87

Isiah's graduation day surprises Mother Thomas. il pors *Jet* 72:48 Je 1 '87
There's just no doubting Thomas [cover story] J. McCallum. il pors *Sports Illus* 66:30-2+ My 18 '87
Thomas, Jon R.
A long campaign. *Cent Mag* 20:55 Ja/F '87
Thomas, Kathleen J.
Videocassette tapes: a source directory. *Am Artist* 51:62+ Jl '87
Thomas, Maria
A state of permanent revolution. il *Harpers* 274:53-6+ Ja '87
Thomas, Mary
about
Isiah's graduation day surprises Mother Thomas. il pors *Jet* 72:48 Je 1 '87
Thomas, Maxine F.
about
Order judge to take 2-month leave after complaints of behavior. il por *Jet* 73:36 N 30 '87
Thomas, Maynell A.
about
The business of show biz. S. Herbert. il por *Essence* 18:116+ S '87
Thomas, Michael M.
How G.M. bought itself a lemon. il *Nation* 244:108-9 Ja 31 '87
Money managing in a bell jar. il *Nation* 244:318-20 Mr 14 '87
Why this is 1929 all over again. *Nation* 244:641-2+ My 16 '87
Thomas, Michael Tilson, 1944-
about
Beethoven, Ludwig van: Symphonies no. 8 and 9. T. Hathaway. il por *High Fidel* 37:84 N '87
Thomas, N. Gordon
A more perfect union. il *USA Today (Periodical)* 116:16-19 S '87
Thomas, Patricia O'Flynn
about
Black press organization names 1st woman president. por *Jet* 72:31 Jl 27 '87
Thomas, Philip Michael
about
5 of 6 charges dismissed against 'Miami Vice' star. *Jet* 72:28 Je 22 '87
Frisco judge dismisses Thomas libel lawsuit. por *Jet* 72:32 Je 8 '87
Philip Michael Thomas and Olivia Brown sizzle in 'Miami Vice' [cover story] T. S. Moore. il pors *Jet* 73:58-9 O 12 '87
Thomas, Philippe
about
Philippe Thomas at the Centre Pompidou. D. Soutif. *Art Am* 75:191+ O '87
Thomas, Pinklon
about
Iron Mike passes a test. R. Wiley. il pors *Sports Illus* 66:26-7 Je 8 '87
Tyson taps ex-champ Thomas as his next foe. *Jet* 72:48 Ap 13 '87
Thomas, Regina Y.
about
Programmed for success. M. Whigham. il por *Essence* 17:103+ F '87
Thomas, Robert Joseph *See* Thomas, Bob
Thomas, Rosie
Reach for tomorrow [story] il *Good Housekeep* 205:200-1+ S '87
Thomas, Ross, 1926-
about
Wide world of intrigue. D. Lehman. il por *Newsweek* 110:89 O 19 '87
With his 21st thriller, writer Ross Thomas just might hit it big—not that he hasn't been trying. M. Donovan. il pors *People Wkly* 28:109-10 N 30 '87
Thomas, Sam, Jr.
about
In Louisiana: "We got the hook in 'em now, Bubba". G. Jaynes. il por *Time* 130:11 S 28 '87
Thomas, Virginia Lamp
about
EEOC chair weds labor lawyer in D.C. ceremony. il pors *Jet* 72:30 Je 29 '87
Thomas-Bailey, Jane
How to keep the pro-life movement small. *Commonweal* 114:308-9 My 22 '87
Thomas Nelson, Inc.
Jeremiad on Bible manufacture in the United States [turning to foreign manufacturing] W. Griffin. *Publ Wkly* 232:24 Ag 21 '87

Thomas Nelson, Inc.—*cont.*
The problems at the 'big three'. D. D. Buss. il *Christ Today* 31:60-1 Mr 6 '87
Thomas Wolfe Society
Of time and the railroad. *New Yorker* 63:41-3 N 9 '87
Thompson, Allison
"Dear friends and gentle hearts". il pors *Am Hist Illus* 22:44-9 Ap '87
Thompson, Anne
The 12th annual grosses gloss. il *Film Comment* 23:62-4+ Mr/Ap '87
Oscar 'tout sheet'. il *Film Comment* 23:52-5 Ja/F '87
Rise and shine [interview with M. Medavoy] il por *Film Comment* 23:54-6+ My/Je '87
(jt. auth) See Gibney, Alex, and Thompson, Anne
Thompson, Antony Worrall- *See* Worrall-Thompson, Antony
Thompson, Barbara R.
A fellowship of suffering. il por maps *Christ Today* 31:24-9 F 20 '87
Thompson, Bill
'So you want your author on the radio . . . '. il por *Publ Wkly* 232:42 O 30 '87
Thompson, Caroline
How I found the child in me I thought was lost forever. il *Glamour* 85:178 Jl '87
Thompson, Catherine C., and others
Identification of a novel thyroid hormone receptor expressed in the mammalian central nervous system. bibl f il *Science* 237:1610-14 S 25 '87
Thompson, Chuck
Do you know this . . . about silver and pewter? il por *Antiques Collect Hobbies* 92:19-21 O '87
Thompson, Daley
about
'World's greatest athlete' favors American baseball. por *Jet* 72:46 My 25 '87
Thompson, Darryll
about
Avenging a murder. D. O. Relin. il por *Sch Update* 120:7 D 4 '87
Thompson, Dianne
"Our 'nice' neighbor was sexually abusing our daughter. *McCalls* 114:93-5 F '87
Thompson, Dick
about
Two Iowa farmers sow the seeds of change. C. Isenhart. il pors *Sierra* 72:79-82 N/D '87
Thompson, E. P. (Edward Palmer), 1924-
The peace movement's next task [cover story] *Nation* 245:701+ D 12 '87
Thompson, Edward Anthony *See* Lejeune, Anthony, 1928-
Thompson, Edward Palmer *See* Thompson, E. P. (Edward Palmer), 1924-
Thompson, Era Bell, d. 1986
about
Obituary
Ebony por 42:25 Mr '87
Jet por 71:6-7 Ja 19 '87
Thompson, Glenn
about
Glenn Thompson: breaking down barriers. W. Smith. il pors *Publ Wkly* 232:19-22 S 11 '87
Thompson, Hunter S.
about
Hunter S. Thompson [interview] P. J. O'Rourke. il por *Roll Stone* p230-2 N 5-D 10 '87
Thompson, I. A. A.
Hidalgo and pechero in Castile. bibl f il *Hist Today* 37:23-9 Ja '87
Thompson, John M.
Seven strategies for gaining the competitive edge. il *Work Woman* 12:56+ O '87
Thompson, Josephine
Using medical radiation from the inside out. il *FDA Consum* 21:10-13 Jl/Ag '87
Thompson, Josh
about
Jump, shoot, ski . . . win. B. Koch. il por *Skiing* 40:42+ S '87
Ready, aim . . . medal! J. Lieber. il por *Sports Illus* 66:54-5 F 23 '87
Thompson, Judith, 1939-
about
I am yours [drama] Reviews
Macleans 100:65 N 30 '87. J. Bemrose
Thompson, Kenneth W., 1921-
From illusions to norms in international relations. *Society* 25:15-20 N/D '87
Words and deeds in foreign policy. *Society* 24:24-8 My/Je '87

Thompson, Lea
about
Now playing. pors *Teen* 31:52 Mr '87
Thompson, Lee
about
Writing on the wall. G. Slutsker. il por *Forbes* 140:106 Jl 27 '87
Thompson, Leonard Monteath
Before the revolution. il *N Y Rev Books* 34:20+ Je 11 '87
Thompson, Liz
about
Dance Magazine Awards 1987. il pors *Dance Mag* 61:44-6 F '87
Thompson, Mark
Fast fixes. See issues of The Family Handyman beginning July/August 1986
Home & shop improvements. See issues of The Family Handyman beginning September 1986
The new Family handyman garage. See issues of The Family Handyman beginning July/August 1987
Thompson, Mark E.
Star Wars and the rhetoric of make-believe. il *USA Today (Periodical)* 115:16-20 Ja '87
Thompson, Parke
about
Jet-sitters. il pors *Life* 10:91-4 My '87
Kings of the road. B. Rice. il pors *50 Plus* 27:22-5+ Mr '87
The race to visit every country on earth. B. Rice. il *50 Plus* 27:17 Ap '87
Thompson, Ramona Joan
about
Kidnapped! E. Fein. il pors *Ladies Home J* 104:46+ Je '87
Thompson, Richard C.
A 'complaint department' for medical devices. il *FDA Consum* 21:10-13 Mr '87
Dangerous diet drugs from south of the border. il *FDA Consum* 21:29-30 My '87
Faulty therapy machines cause radiation overdoses. il *FDA Consum* 21:37-8 D '87/Ja '88
Out of the bronzed age [cover story] il *FDA Consum* 21:20-3 Je '87
Playing hide and seek with FDA. il *FDA Consum* 21:36-7 Ap '87
Thompson, Richard Frederick, 1930-
The cerebellum and memory storage [discussion of August 29, 1986 article, The neurobiology of learning and memory] *Science* 238:1728-30 D 18 '87
Thompson, Roger
Defending our shores. il *Oceans* 20:34-41 Mr/Ap '87
Thompson, Sharon
about
Two Iowa farmers sow the seeds of change. C. Isenhart. il pors *Sierra* 72:79-82 N/D '87
Thompson, William F.
about
The Hollywood superstar no one's ever heard of. G. Geipel. il por *Bus Week* p98-9 Ja 26 '87
Thompson (J. Walter) Company *See* J. Walter Thompson Company
Thompson Bousquet Gold Mines Ltd.
The chase for leftover fortunes [T. Howes' discovery of unclaimed Thompson Bousquet Gold Mines stock] D. Francis. il *Macleans* 100:5 Jl 27 '87
Thompson family
about
7-Eleven wants out of the glare. J. Weber, Jr. il *Bus Week* p78 Jl 20 '87
Going private [Southland Corp.] A. A. Lappen. il *Forbes* 140:10 Jl 27 '87
A junk-bond belly flop [leveraged buyout of Southland] J. Weber, Jr. *Bus Week* p35 N 23 '87
Thomson, David, 1941-
California in focus. il por *House Gard* 159:140-5+ Ag '87
Gray ghost. il pors *Film Comment* 23:26+ Mr/Ap '87
Thomson, David Kenneth Roy
about
All in the family. T. Tedesco. il por *Macleans* 100:35 Je 15 '87
Thomson, Patrick
A baseball for dad. il *Read Dig* 130:13-14+ Mr '87
Thomson, Richard M.
about
A maverick in the big bankers. P. C. Newman. il por *Macleans* 100:41 O 12 '87
Thomson, Robert
Three for tomorrow. il por *World Press Rev* 34:23 D '87

Thomson, Virgil, 1896-
about
Four saints in three acts [opera] Reviews
Theatre Crafts il 21:14 My '87. R. Smith
Thomson-C S F
French developing systems for combat aircraft [electronic
warfare systems] il *Aviat Week Space Technol* 126:65-6
F 16 '87
Millimeter-wave radar may enhance safety of helicopter
flights. *Aviat Week Space Technol* 127:103 Jl 6 '87
Thomson-CSF develops simulator, test range to support
EW development. il *Aviat Week Space Technol* 126:80-1
F 9 '87
Thomson McKinnon Inc.
Requiem for a heavyweight [bank broker C. H. Howard]
L. Jereski. il *Forbes* 140:152 N 30 '87
Thomson McKinnon [interview with H. Zisson] il por
Fortune 116 Sp Issue:188-9 Fall '87
Thomson SA
And then there was one [GE sells consumer electronics
division to Thomson SA] J. B. Copeland. il *Newsweek*
110:36 Ag 3 '87
An Italian chipmaker shows the way [SGS's merger
with Thomson] W. C. Symonds. il por *Bus Week*
p134+ My 25 '87
Jumping Jack strikes again [J. Welch sells GE's consumer
electronics division] P. Elmer-Dewitt. il *Time* 130:44
Ag 3 '87
Overnight, Thomson has the stuff to take on the titans
[purchase of GE's consumer electronics business] T.
Peterson. il *Bus Week* p36-7 Ag 10 '87
A sweet swap for GE and Thomson. *Fortune* 116:8
Ag 17 '87
Thorburn, David
The made-for-TV movie malady. il *Channels* 7:67-8
Ja '87
Thoreau, Henry David, 1817-1862
about
Keep Walden Pond open: Thoreau's watering hole should
remain a public domain. R. Sullivan. por *Sports Illus*
67:86 Ag 17 '87
Teaching the eco-justice ethic: the parable of the Billerica
Dam. J. R. Engel. il *Christ Century* 104:466-9 My
13 '87
Thoreau the thorough impressionist [excerpt from address,
July 12, 1986] J. Barzun. *Am Sch* 56:250-8 Spr '87
Thoreau walks the Cape. J. J. Thorndike. il *Am Herit*
38:70-5 Ap '87
Thoreau's book of life. G. O'Brien. il *N Y Rev Books*
33:46-51 Ja 15 '87
Walden lost. J. Rhea. il *Space World* X-8-284:3 Ag
'87
Thorgeirsson, S. S., and others
Expression of the multidrug-resistant gene in hepatocar-
cinogenesis and regenerating rat liver. bibl f il *Science*
236:1120-2 My 29 '87
Thorium dating *See* Radioactive dating
Thorndike, John
Gasconade Farm: where apprentice farmers learn their
trade. il *Ctry J* 14:27-30+ Ag '87
Thorndike, Joseph Jacobs, 1913-
Thoreau walks the Cape. il *Am Herit* 38:70-5 Ap '87
Thorndike, Nick
After reading the Detroit news [poem] *Christ Century*
104:47 Ja 21 '87
Tomatoes of the Lord [poem] *Christ Century* 104:549
Je 17-24 '87
Thorne, Mike
Common sense investing. *Antiques Collect Hobbies*
92:51-2 S '87
Thorne, Robert
Building bridges: George Godwin and architectural jour-
nalism. bibl il por *Hist Today* 37:11-17 Ag '87
Thornhill, Arthur H., Jr.
about
Arthur Thornhill looks back on 39 years at Little, Brown.
R. Herbert. il por *Publ Wkly* 231:18+ F 6 '87
Thornton, Donna Selby
about
Retarded couple face the new year with a baby boy.
pors *Jet* 71:8 Ja 12 '87
Thornton, John
about
Six years after PATCO's crash, fired air controller John
Thornton helps a new union get off the ground. D.
Chu. il por *People Wkly* 28:38-9 S 14 '87
Thornton, Peter, 1925-
An architectural kaleidoscope: Sir John Soane's Museum
in London. bibl f il *Antiques* 131:264-77 Ja '87

Thornton, Ricardo
about
Retarded couple face the new year with a baby boy.
pors *Jet* 71:8 Ja 12 '87
Thornton family
about
Donald Thornton's magnificent dream. J. Coudert. il
por *Read Dig* 130:121-5 F '87
Thoroughbred horse auctions *See* Auctions
Thoroughbred horses *See* Horses, Race
Thorp, Gregory
about
Double takes. J. Hughes. il *Pop Photogr* 94:62-7 Ap
'87
Thorson, Bruce
about
Two pros overcome handicaps for successful careers.
H. Chapnick. il pors *Pop Photogr* 94:20 F '87
Thought, Visual *See* Visualization
Thought and language *See* Psycholinguistics
Thought and thinking
See also
Artificial intelligence
Attention
Cognition
Cognitive therapy
Common sense
Creativity
Memory
Mind
Problem solving
Reasoning
A Buckminster Fuller dictionary. E. J. Applewhite. il
pors *Futurist* 21:24-8 S/O '87
"I sez to myself, sez I" [Pascal's definition of thinking
as an inner dialogue] D. F. Kinlaw. il *Christ Today*
31:11 Ap 17 '87
Nicotine slowdown [effect on thinking; study by George
J. Spilich] J. C. Horn. il *Psychol Today* 21:24 D
'87
Suppress now, obsess later [thought suppression; study
by Daniel M. Wegner] J. F. Neath. il *Psychol Today*
21:10 D '87
Thinking like Christopher [child's thoughts] C. R. Fitz-
gerald. il *Parents* 62:102-4 Ap '87
What kind of thinker are you? [quiz; condensed from
The stressless home] R. M. Bramson and S. Bramson.
il *Read Dig* 131:149-52 D '87
Study and teaching
Can colleges teach thinking? [reflective judgment or critical
thinking] E. Bowen. il *Time* 129:61 F 16 '87
"Critical thinking" programs: why they won't work. M.
J. Adler. *Educ Dig* 52:9-11 Mr '87
High road, low road, end of the road for CAI and
programming? G. W. Bracey. il *Phi Delta Kappan*
68:547-8 Mr '87
How to think like an innovator. D. Waitley and R.
B. Tucker. il *Futurist* 21:9-15 My/Je '87
If not golden, silence may be helpful [critical thinking;
research by Bryce Hudgins and Sybil Edelman] G.
W. Bracey. il *Phi Delta Kappan* 68:398-9 Ja '87
Is high school the place to teach thinking? F. Schrag.
Educ Dig 53:16-19 D '87
Making kids smarter. L. J. Greene. il *Parents* 62:94-8+
D '87
A potpourri of computers [influence on children's thinking
skills] G. W. Bracey. il *Phi Delta Kappan* 69:235-6
N '87
Teaching critical thinking: eight easy ways to fail before
you begin. R. J. Sternberg. il *Phi Delta Kappan* 68:456-9
F '87
Teaching for thinking: Louis E. Raths revisited. S. Wasser-
mann. bibl f il *Phi Delta Kappan* 68:460-6 F '87
Who is accountable for 'thoughtfulness'? R. Brown. bibl
f il *Phi Delta Kappan* 69:49-52 S '87
Thouron, Sir John
about
Fields of color. D. M. Stone. il *House Gard* 159:68-77+
Ag '87
Thousand Astronomical Unit missions *See* Space flight—
Thousand Astronomical Unit missions
Thousand Oaks (Calif.)
Ordinances
Little horse, big deal—protestors cry 'There goes the
neighborhood' [P. Fairchild fights to keep her miniature
horse] il pors *People Wkly* 27:96-7 Je 1 '87
Thread cutting
See also
Taps and dies

Threadgill, Henry
about
Music. G. Santoro. *Nation* 245:65-8 Jl 18-25 '87
Threadgill (Henry) Sextett *See* Henry Threadgill Sextett
Threads, Screw *See* Screw threads
Threats
See also
Extortion
Three amigos [film] *See* Motion picture reviews—Single works
Three dimensional computer graphics *See* Computer graphics
Three dimensional television *See* Television, Stereoscopic
Three for the road [film] *See* Motion picture reviews—Single works
Three men and a baby [film] *See* Motion picture reviews—Single works
Three men on a horse [drama] *See* Holm, John Cecil, 1904-1981
Three Mile Island nuclear power plant (Pa.) *See* Nuclear power plants
Three postcards [musical] *See* Musicals, revues, etc.—Reviews—Single works
Three Rivers (Calif.)
Description
Jazz and turtles just outside Sequoia. il *Sunset* 178:56-7 Ap '87
Three wheel automobiles *See* Automobiles, Three wheel
Three wheel motor vehicles *See* Motor vehicles, Three wheel
Threshold Test Ban Treaty *See* Nuclear weapons—Testing—Suspension
Thresholds *See* Doorways
Thrift
See also
Finance, Personal
Anecdotes, facetiae, satire, etc.
Last laugh. il *Mother Earth News* 105:128 My/Je '87
Thrift institutions
See also
Savings and loan associations
Savings banks
Banks and thrifts. T. Pouschine. il *Forbes* 139:74-7 Ja 12 '87
Thrips
Control
Gladiolus thrips. W. S. Moore. il *Flower Gard* 31:43 Je/Jl '87
Throat
See also
Esophagus
Larynx
Nasopharynx
Pharynx
Diseases
Diagnosis
Dangers of undetected strep. il *Parents* 62:15 N '87
Therapy
Sure-to-soothe cold and sore-throat remedies [excerpt from Cold cures] M. Castleman. *Prevention* 39:99+ D '87
Thrombin
See also
Antithrombin
Thromboplastin
Blood clot agent's genes are read [tissue factor; work of Ronald Bach and others] *Sci News* 132:104 Ag 15 '87
Thrombosis
See also
Anticoagulants
Thrombospondin
Thrombospondin promotes cell-substratum adhesion. G. P. Tuszynski and others. bibl f il *Science* 236:1570-3 Je 19 '87
Throw momma from the train [film] *See* Motion picture reviews—Single works
Thrower, James, 1936-
Some reflections on religion in the U.S.S.R. il por *Humanist* 47:21-3+ Ja/F '87
Throwers, Snow *See* Snow blowers, throwers, etc.
Throwing
See also
Ball throwing
Anecdotes, facetiae, satire, etc.
Throwing stuff. P. F. McManus. il *Outdoor Life* 179:130+ Ja '87
Thull (Pakistan)
Social conditions
"Friend by day, enemy by night" [blood feuds] R. L. Keiser. il *Nat Hist* 96:8+ N '87

Thunderbirds *See* United States. Air Force. Thunderbirds
Thunderstorms
See also
Automobile driving—Storm hazards
Aviation—Storm hazards
Lightning
Motorcycling—Storm hazards
Walking—Storm hazards
Inside the storm. E. Havill. il *Ctry J* 14:40-6 Ag '87
Rapid pressure changes near thunderstorms, directional lightning. T. Schlatter. il *Weatherwise* 40:99-100 Ap '87
Thunderstorm vaults. T. Schlatter. il *Weatherwise* 40:216-17 Jl/Ag '87
Thunderstorms: an important mechanism in the transport of air pollutants. R. R. Dickerson and others. bibl f il *Science* 235:460-5 Ja 23 '87
Thurber, James, 1894-1961
The catbird seat [story] il *Read Dig* 131:138-44 Ag '87
Thurel, Antoine, d. 1987
about
Haitian sets self afire in protest of nation's strife. *Jet* 72:4 S 21 '87
Thurgood Marshall Black Education Fund
New Thurgood Marshall Fund awards scholarships. il *Jet* 71:4-5 F 23 '87
Thurman, Judith, 1946-
Architectural digest visits: Paul Simon. il por *Archit Dig* 44:108-115 S '87
Thurman, Robert A. F.
(jt. auth) *See* Gere, Richard, and Thurman, Robert A. F.
Thurow, Lester C.
[Column] *See* alternate issues of Technology Review beginning July 1984
A surge in inequality. bibl (p128) il *Sci Am* 256:30-7 My '87
A weakness in process technology. bibl f *Science* 238:1659-63 D 18 '87
about
Now Sloan's MBAs will be masters of technology. L. Helm. il por *Bus Week* p64 Ap 13 '87
When Lester Thurow talks, Democrats listen. A. Kupfer. il pors *Fortune* 116:88-90+ Jl 20 '87
Thurow, Lester C., and Tyson, Laura D'Andrea, 1947-
The economic black hole. bibl f *Foreign Policy* 67:3-21 Summ '87
Thyca
Thyca: underarm and underfoot [starfish parasite] T. Bratcher. il *Sea Front* 33:286-7 Jl/Ag '87
Thylefors, Björn
"Foresight prevents blindness". il *World Health* p3-5 My '87
Thyme
Caraway thyme. B. Reppert. il *Rodale's Org Gard* 34:63 Jl '87
Thymic lymphocytes *See* Lymphocytes
Thymidine
See also
Azidothymidine
Thymidylate synthase *See* Synthases
Thymus-derived lymphocytes *See* Lymphocytes
Thymus gland
Transplantation
Tolerance induced by thymic epithelial grafts in birds. H. Ohki and others. bibl f il *Science* 237:1032-5 Ag 28 '87
Thyristors
Using Triacs and SCR's. R. Marston. il *Radio-Electron* 58:64-8 S '87
Working with Triacs and SCR's. R. Marston. il *Radio-Electron* 58:64-7+ O '87
Testing
Testing semiconductors (IV). T. J. Byers. il *Radio-Electron* 58:59-61 My '87
Thyroid hormone receptors *See* Hormone receptors
Thyroid hormones
A cure for PMS? *Women's Sports Fitness* 9:60 My '87
Therapy by mimicry [thyromimetic SK&F L-94901 reduces blood cholesterol without increasing heart rate] *Sci Am* 256:88 F '87
Thyroid hormone regulates TRH biosynthesis in the paraventricular nucleus of the rat hypothalamus. T. P. Segerson and others. bibl f il *Science* 238:78-80 O 2 '87
Thyrotropin releasing factor
Arginine vasopressin as a thyrotropin-releasing hormone. M. D. Lumpkin and others. bibl f il *Science* 235:1070-3 F 27 '87

Thyrotropin releasing factor—*cont.*

New treatment approach [thyrotropin releasing hormone therapy for neuromuscular diseases; work of W. King Engel] il *USA Today (Periodical)* 115:8 F '87

Thyroid hormone regulates TRH biosynthesis in the paraventricular nucleus of the rat hypothalamus. T. P. Segerson and others. bibl f il *Science* 238:78-80 O 2 '87

Thyrotropin releasing hormone receptors *See* Hormone receptors

Thyssen AG

Advice from father [D. Spethmann] L. S. Richman. il por *Fortune* 116:66 Ag 3 '87

Thyssen-Bornemisza, Hans Heinrich, Baron, 1921-
about

The baron thinks twice. E. Beck. il por *Art News* 86:45 N '87

Spirited composition on Chester Square: the London house of Baron and Baroness Thyssen-Bornemisza. J. J. Norwich. il por *Archit Dig* 44:104-11 O '87

Thyssen-Bornemisza, Tita, Baroness
about

Spirited composition on Chester Square: the London house of Baron and Baroness Thyssen-Bornemisza. J. J. Norwich. il por *Archit Dig* 44:104-11 O '87

Thyssen-Bornemisza Collection *See* Art—Collectors and collecting

TIAA *See* Teachers Insurance and Annuity Association

Tia's Doll Emporium

All-American Girl-talk [winner T. Hunnicutt] il pors *Teen* 31:46 Jl '87

Toying with success [proprietress T. Hunnicutt] il por *Teen* 31:68+ Ja '87

Tibet

See also

Airlines—Routes—Tibet
French—Tibet
Geology—Tibet
Polyandry—Tibet
Research—Tibet
Riots—Tibet

Tibet. M. LeVasseur. il map *Focus* 37:34-5 Spr '87

Defenses

See also

Airplanes, Military—Tibet
Aviation, Military—Tibet

Description and travel

A Christmas card in Tibet. V. Kilgour. por *Newsweek* 110:7 D 28 '87

A journey to Lhasa. J. Bernstein. map *New Yorker* 63:47-50+ D 14 '87

Nomads' land: a journey through Tibet. S. Wilby. il pors map *Natl Geogr* 172:764-85 D '87

Foreign relations

China

See China—Foreign relations—Tibet

History

A journey to Lhasa. J. Bernstein. map *New Yorker* 63:47-50+ D 14 '87

Native peoples

Tibetan nomads: 'high' living . . . combined with low blood pressure [Phala nomads] *Sci News* 131:312 My 16 '87

Religious institutions and affairs

See also

Buddhism—Tibet
Dalai Lama XIV, 1935-

China still battles for Tibet. S. Simons. il *World Press Rev* 34:29-31 My '87

Tiburon (Calif.)

Restaurants, nightclubs, bars, etc.

Spécialités de la maison:
Guaymas. C. Bates. *Gourmet* 47:20+ Jl '87

Tic

See also

Tourette syndrome

Tics. O. W. Sacks. bibl il *N Y Rev Books* 34:37-41 Ja 29 '87

Ticino (Switzerland)

See also

Architecture—Ticino (Switzerland)

Description and travel

Letter from the Ticino. W. Murray. *New Yorker* 63:61+ Je 1 '87

Ticket scalping *See* Ticket selling—Ethical aspects

Ticket selling

Ethical aspects

Scalping [Yankee Stadium] D. K. Mano. *Natl Rev* 39:54 Ag 28 '87

Tickets

See also

Football, College—Tickets
Tennis—Tournaments—Tickets

Ticknor & Fields

Editor Katrina Kenison of Ticknor & Fields. G. Blooston. il por *Publ Wkly* 231:64+ F 13 '87

Ticks

Around the Mall and beyond [tick collection at Smithsonian's Museum Support Center] E. Park. il *Smithsonian* 17:22+ Ja '87

Tick attack [manual removal of ticks] L. W. Smith. il *Outdoor Life* 180:110 Jl '87

Vision

See Vision—Arachnids

Ticks as carriers of infection

See also

Babesiosis
Lyme disease
Rocky Mountain spotted fever

A novel mode of arbovirus transmission involving a nonviremic host. L. D. Jones and others. bibl f il *Science* 237:775-7 Ag 14 '87

Tidal power *See* Tide power

Tidal waves

Tsunami! F. H. Forrester. il *Weatherwise* 40:84-9 Ap '87

Tsunamis generated by eruptions from Mount St. Augustine volcano, Alaska [cover story] J. Kienle and others. il maps *Science* 236:1442-7 Je 12 '87

Tide power

Modeling tidal power [tidal power dam in the Bay of Fundy would raise tide levels in the Gulf of Maine] D. A. Greenberg. il maps *Sci Am* 257:128-128C+ N '87

Voices against the tide [Annapolis Tidal Power Plant on Bay of Fundy is accused of harming clam fishery] D. Holt. il *Macleans* 100:11-12 N 2 '87

Tides

See also

Intertidal ecology

Lunar and solar alignments caused high tides on earth [syzygy] *Earth Sci* 40:8-9 Summ '87

The moon's irresistible pull. H. Middleton. il *South Living* 22:30+ O '87

The tide at Tarawa [computer program] D. W. Olson. il map *Sky Telesc* 74:526-8 N '87

Tie-dyeing *See* Dyes and dyeing

Tienda, Marta

(jt. auth) See Borjas, George J., and Tienda, Marta

Tierney, John

Exploding star contains atoms of Elvis Presley's brain. il pors maps *Discover* 8:46-7+ Jl '87

Stephen Jay Gould [interview] il por *Roll Stone* p38-9+ Ja 15 '87

Tierney, Paul E., Jr.
about

The trio that humbled Allegis. S. P. Sherman. il pors *Fortune* 116:52-4+ Jl 20 '87

Ties (Neckwear) *See* Neckties

Tiesenhausen, Georg von, 1914-
about

Last of the rocket team: a conversation with Georg von Tiesenhausen. F. I. Ordway. il por *Space World* X-6-282:29-32 Je '87

Tiffany
about

Tiffany, the teenage mall flower who serenades the shoppers of America. L. Russell. il pors *People Wkly* 28:81+ S 14 '87

Tiffany, Charles Lewis, 1812-1902
about

Charles Tiffany's 'fancy goods' shop and how it grew. D. Cohen. bibl (p204) il por *Smithsonian* 18:52-6+ D '87

Tiffany, Louis Comfort, 1848-1933
about

Louis C. Tiffany—the painter [excerpt from The arts of the Tiffanys] G. Speenburgh. il *Antiques Collect Hobbies* 91:60-2 Ja '87

Tiffany & Co.

American silver [The silver of Tiffany & Company, 1850-1980 at the Museum of Fine Arts, Boston] S. B. Sherrill. il *Antiques* 132:400+ S '87

Birthday at Tiffany's. H. Brubach. il *Vogue* 177:454-5+ O '87

Charles Tiffany's 'fancy goods' shop and how it grew. D. Cohen. bibl (p204) il por *Smithsonian* 18:52-6+ D '87

Tiffany & Co.—*cont.*
Japanesque silver by Tiffany and Company in the Metropolitan Museum of Art. F. G. Safford and R. W. Caccavale. bibl f il *Antiques* 132:808-19 O '87
'My deah, have you heard the news on Fifth Avenue?'. A. Garbor. il *U S News World Rep* 103:44 Ag 3 '87
Sesquicentennial sparkle. D. G. Lowe. il *House Gard* 159:204-7+ O '87
Temping at Tiffany's. B. Kanner. il *N Y* 20:24+ D 14 '87
Tiffany and Company—celebrating 150 years. J. Loring. il *Archit Dig* 44:34+ O '87
A Tiffany gift. il *Am Herit* 38:90-5 S/O '87
Tiffany toasts its 150th. M. Smilgis. il *Time* 130:72-3 S 28 '87
The Tiffany touch: a wealth of riches. D. Harris. il *Harpers Bazaar* 120:206+ S '87
Tiffany's, past and present. H. Bridges. il *Gourmet* 47:54+ D '87
Triumphs of American silvermaking [exhibition at Metropolitan Museum of Art] il *USA Today (Periodical)* 116:8-9 D '87
Tifft, William G., and Cocke, W. John
Quantized galaxy redshifts. il *Sky Telesc* 73:19-21 Ja '87
Tifton (Ga.)
Race relations
Black student 'outraged' after she is fired from white pharmacy in Georgia [T. F. Bateman] il por *Jet* 72:30 Ag 31 '87
Tiger hunting
Jim Corbett: the reluctant executioner. G. C. Ward. il por maps *Audubon* 89:44-9+ Jl '87
Tiger Stadium (Detroit, Mich.)
Free speech and the 'bleacher creatures' [efforts to curb fans' bad behavior] il *Newsweek* 110:38 S 21 '87
Who are the 'moderates'? [ACLU objects to Detroit Tigers' attempt to curb fans' vulgarity] G. F. Will. il *Newsweek* 110:100 O 12 '87
Photographs and photography
Before the roar. D. Walberg. il *Sport Mag* 78:62-5+ O '87
Tigers
A contemptuous tiger's loss of innocence [man-eating tiger in Corbett National Park] G. C. Ward. il *Audubon* 89:50-1 Jl '87
India's intensifying dilemma: can tigers and people coexist? G. C. Ward. bibl (p269) il *Smithsonian* 18:52-62+ N '87
The state of the tiger. J. R. Luoma. il map *Audubon* 89:61-3 Jl '87
Tightrope walking *See* High wire walking
Tihany, Adam D., 1948?-
about
For adults only. D. Shaw. il por *N Y* 20:42 D 7 '87
Tijuana (Mexico)
Description
Across the borders of history. R. Rodriguez. il *Harpers* 274:42-9+ Mr '87
Tile industry
See also
Terra Designs, Inc.
Export-import trade
The high price of complacency [ceramic tile] A. A. Lappen. il *Forbes* 140:356+ Jl 13 '87
Tile laying
Dress up a planter with tile. J. Drako. il *Workbench* 43:62-3 My/Je '87
Fireplace hearth: update it with new tile! [ceramic tile] D. Kassler. il *Workbench* 43:88-9 Ja/F '87
Friendly footing [floor tile] P. Barrett. il *Pop Mech* 164:126-8+ Ap '87
How to install slate flooring. P. Barrett. il *Pop Mech* 164:125-8 D '87
Planning a ceramic tile project [interview with D. Syverson] B. Colglazier. il pors *Home Mech* 83:12+ F '87
Remodel with tile [bathroom] B. Sanders. il *Workbench* 43:80-4 Mr/Ap '87
Tiles
Today's ceramic tiles warm the hearth. il *Better Homes Gard* 65:27 O '87
Tiles, Space shuttle *See* Space vehicles—Insulation
Tilia *See* Linden
Tiling (Mathematics) *See* Tessellations (Mathematics)
Tillage
See also
Contour farming
Terraces (Agriculture)
Bottom-line tillage trials [Minnesota demonstration plots] R. Fee. il *Success Farm* 85 no4:18P F '87

He's squeezing the tillage out of corn/bean rotation. R. Fee. il *Success Farm* 85:18A My '87
'Incorporate' chemicals in no-till [herbicide impregnated on dry bulk fertilizer] R. Fee. il *Success Farm* 85 no1:26Z Ja '87
Make your soil smile. P. H. Johnson. il *Rodale's Org Gard* 34:88-92 Mr '87
Tillage cuts found in new crop survey [South Dakota] *Success Farm* 85:70J Ag '87
Weird weeds [conservation tillage] B. Freese. il *Success Farm* 85:18U My '87
Tillers, Imants, 1950-
about
Imants Tillers at Bess Cutler. J. Rian. il *Art Am* 75:178-9 O '87
Tillers *See* Cultivators
Tillers, Boat *See* Boats and boating—Steering gear
Tillich, Paul, 1886-1965
about
Tillich in an Alice-in-Wonderland world. J. McBride. *Christ Century* 104:519-20 Je 3-10 '87
Tillim, Sidney
Criticism and culture, or Greenberg's doubt. *Art Am* 75:122-7+ My '87
Tilling, Robert I., and others
Disruption of the Mauna Loa magma system by the 1868 Hawaiian earthquake: geochemical evidence. bibl f il map *Science* 235:196-9 Ja 9 '87
Tilling, Thomas
Family finance. See issues of Parents beginning July 1986
Tillou, Peter H.
about
Peter H. Tillou's American flair. C. D. B. Bryan. il por *Archit Dig* 44:64+ Je '87
Tilt-rotor aircraft *See* Rotor aircraft
Tilt-top tables *See* Tables
Timber
See also
Lumber industry
Timber clearcutting *See* Clearcutting
Timber cutting *See* Lumbering
Timber rattlesnakes *See* Rattlesnakes
Timber wolves *See* Wolves
Timbuk 3 (Musical group)
Timbuk 3, two Texas tunesmiths who hope their future's so bright they'll have to wear shades. il *People Wkly* 27:93 F 16 '87
Timbuktu (Mali)
History
Into the heart of Africa [Frenchman's visit in the 1820s; excerpt from Journal d'un voyage à Temboctou et à Jenné] R. Caillé. il *Courier* 40:35-6 Ap '87
Time
See also
Biological rhythms
Geological time
Past
Reaction time
Space and time
The seven arrows of time. T. Rothman. il *Discover* 8:62-4+ F '87
Systems and standards
See also
Daylight saving
International date line
A matter of time [leap second] E. Marshall. il *Science* 238:1641-3 D 18 '87
When bossy was boss [Indianapolis TV stations struggle to get time zones straight] J. B. Grillo. il *Channels* 7:71-2 Je '87
Time (Periodical)
Covering Time's Men of the Year [exhibit at the National Portrait Gallery] C. Bond. il *Smithsonian* 17:188 Mr '87
A letter from the publisher. J. A. Meyers. See issues of Time through February 2, 1987
A letter from the publisher. R. L. Miller. See issues of Time beginning February 9, 1987
The press on trial [R. Adler's book on Westmoreland v. CBS and Sharon v. Time] R. M. Dworkin. bibl f il *N Y Rev Books* 34:27-37 F 26 '87
The readers speak: 1986's mail. il *Time* 129:16 F 16 '87
'Time' will tell [book department editor S. Kanfer] por *Publ Wkly* 231:26-7 Ap 10 '87
Time [musical] *See* Musicals, revues, etc.—Reviews—Single works
Time balls
The bygone era of time balls. I. R. Bartky. il *Sky Telesc* 73:32-5 Ja '87

Time capsules
Oh, well. A. Bergesen. il *Atlantic* 260:16+ Jl '87
Time domain reflectometers and reflectometry *See* Reflectometers and reflectometry
Time exposure (Photography) *See* Photography—Exposure
Time Inc.
Can Time's new deal bring the ads back? D. Lieberman and M. N. Vamos. il *Bus Week* p30 S 28 '87
Discover is headed for a new family [Family Media] D. Lieberman. il *Bus Week* p40 Je 8 '87
A new chieftain for Time Inc. [J. McManus] J. Alter. il por *Newsweek* 109:63 Ap 27 '87
Nick Nicholas. D. Lieberman. por *Bus Week* Sp Issue:238 Ap 17 '87
Their Time [chairman N. Nicholas and editor-in-chief J. McManus] E. Diamond. il pors *N Y* 20:29-31 O 12 '87
Time's Nick & Dick show [N. J. Nicholas and J. R. Munro; cover story] B. Nussbaum. il pors *Bus Week* p54-7+ Ag 3 '87
Time management
Beat the clock in your home and shop. G. Williams. il *Home Mech* 83:48-50+ F '87
Being there [parents and children] P. Theroux. il *Parents* 62:56+ O '87
Best beauty boosts: 12 ways to save time & 8 luxurious ways to spend it. il *Glamour* 85:210-15 D '87
Digging out: what to do when you're snowed under with work. il *Glamour* 85:172 S '87
Do you spend too much time in meetings? [excerpt from Effective listening] K. J. Murphy. *Work Woman* 12:30 D '87
Don't let time management be a waste of time. J. A. Byrne. il *Bus Week* p144 My 4 '87
Get organized! C. Straley. il *Parents* 62:213-16 N '87
Getting organized for 1987. K. V. Brailsford. il *Black Enterp* 17:54-6 Ja '87
How to manage the staff procrastinator. C. Golden. *Work Woman* 12:31 N '87
How to plug those time leaks [excerpt from Managing people at work desk guide] T. L. Quick. *Work Woman* 12:25 Je '87
Making the most of time [writers] S. A. Keller. *Writer* 100:22-3 Jl '87
Making time to work out. L. L. Griffith and D. Pine. *Women's Sports Fitness* 9:28-33 S '87
Managing your work time. B. Nivens. il *Essence* 18:110 D '87
Not enough time for kids? R. B. McCall. il *Parents* 62:172 F '87
Quality time—what's that? K. Levine. il *Parents* 62:76+ N '87
The theory of the busy class. M. Harris. il *Money* 16:202-6+ Ap '87
Thirteen ways to procrastinate efficiently and gain control of your time. C. R. Hobbs. *Work Woman* 12:96-7 O '87
Time [address, May 17, 1987] W. H. Rehnquist. *Vital Speeches Day* 53:549-51 Jl 1 '87
Where has the time gone? [address, June 14, 1987] V. R. Ruggiero. *Vital Speeches Day* 53:671-2 Ag 15 '87
Where to find more time for yourself [excerpt from Organize yourself!]; ed. by Kate Kelly. R. Eisenberg. il *Redbook* 168:74-5+ Ja '87
You survived a cutback—now, make the most of it. J. A. Byrne. il *Bus Week* p131 D 14 '87
You're probably working too hard. F. S. Worthy. il *Fortune* 115:133+ Ap 27 '87
Time measurement
See also
Chronograph
Clocks
Sundials
Time—Systems and standards
Watches
Watches, Electronic
Hassle-free astrophotography [precision sidereal-rate clock drive kit] R. Berry. il *Astronomy* 15:38-9 O '87
Parasitic wasps keep on ticking [research by Jonathan M. Schmidt and J. J. B. Smith] R. Weiss. *Sci News* 132:134 Ag 29 '87
Short interval time measurement by a parasitoid wasp. J. M. Schmidt and J. J. B. Smith. bibl f il *Science* 237:903-5 Ag 21 '87
What time is it? [sidereal time program] R. C. Walter, Jr. il *Astronomy* 15:38-40 F '87
Time perception
An image in time [child's concept; research by William Friedman] S. Vandershaf. il *Psychol Today* 21:20 Jl '87

Who thrives in which job? R. Sandroff. il *Work Woman* 12:126-8+ N '87
Time release drugs *See* Drugs—Dosage forms
Time sharing (Real estate) *See* Timesharing (Real estate)
A time to die [film] *See* Motion picture reviews—Single works
Time travel
Time travel [imagining one's future as a therapeutic tool; work of J. Hart] B. Lawren. il *Omni* 10:20+ N '87
Time zones *See* Time—Systems and standards
Timerbaev, Roland
A Soviet official on verification. *Bull At Sci* 43:8-10 Ja/F '87
Timerman, Jacobo, 1923-
Under the dictator; tr. by Robert Cox. *New Yorker* 63:47-50+ N 2 '87
Timers *See* Timing devices
Timers, Darkroom *See* Photography—Processing—Equipment
Times (New York, N.Y.) *See* New York times
Times (Washington, D.C.) *See* Washington times
Times Square (New York, N.Y.)
Lights dim on the Great White Way. V. Muse. il *Life* 10:84-7+ D '87
The Marriott Marquis: Renaissance on Broadway. il *USA Today (Periodical)* 115:34-44 Mr '87
The sky line [redevelopment plans] B. Gill. *New Yorker* 63:113-18+ N 9 '87
Timesharing (Real estate)
Splitting a second home four ways [quarter-sharing] J. Wynn. il *Bus Week* p112 Je 29 '87
Timidity
See also
Bashfulness
Timing belts (Automobiles) *See* Automobile engines—Belts
Timing devices
See also
Delay devices
Automatic timers: smart products, imaginative uses. il *Glamour* 85:96-7 Ap '87
High-performance software analysis on the IBM PC [high-resolution timer] B. Sheppard. il *Byte* 12:157-8+ Ja '87
Installing a light timer. G. Branson. il *Fam Handyman* 37:86 My/Je '87
Long-time timer [ZN1034E] R. F. Scott. il *Radio-Electron* 58:129-30 My '87
Versatile digital timer. R. Ortman. il *Radio-Electron* 58:45-7 Ag '87
When the gardener's away [automatic water timers] J. Ruttle. il *Rodale's Org Gard* 34:50-2+ My '87
Timmerman, Kenneth R.
Europe's arms pipeline to Iran. *Nation* 245:47-8+ Jl 18-25 '87
Timmons, Shirlene
about
The empty crib. L. A. Walker. il por *Ladies Home J* 104:76+ Mr '87
Tin
See also
International Tin Council
Tin compounds
See also
Tributyltin
Tin containers
Cookie tin cabinet [storage rack] W. E. Burton. il *Workbench* 43:16-17 Ja/F '87
Tin men [film] *See* Motion picture reviews—Single works
Tin toys *See* Toys
Tincq, Henri
The Vatican and bioethics [interview with J. Ratzinger] *World Press Rev* 34:58 Jl '87
Tinker, Grant
about
Behind the McTelevision show. N. J. Perry. il pors *Fortune* 116:122 S 28 '87
Grant's back & Gannett's got him. J. Baker. il por *Channels* 7:40-3 Jl/Ag '87
How CBS landed Grant Tinker. M. Brown. il por *Channels* 7:26 Ap '87
Starting over [cover story] D. K. Shah. il pors *N Y Times Mag* p26-9+ O 25 '87
Taken for Granted. B. Zehme. il pors *Roll Stone* p33-5 Je 18 '87
Tinker's CBS deal. A. D. Frank. il por *Forbes* 140:184+ O 19 '87
Tinker, John
about
Taken for Granted. B. Zehme. il pors *Roll Stone* p33-5 Je 18 '87

Tinker, Mark

about

Taken for Granted. B. Zehme. il pors *Roll Stone* p33-5 Je 18 '87

Tinling, Teddy

Stay back to get ahead. il *World Tennis* 35:80 Je '87

Tinnitus

Tinnitus: when the ringing in your ears won't stop. P. C. Smith. il *McCalls* 115:84+ O '87

When noise is more than irritating. Z. Qinghua. il *Bus Week* p152 F 23 '87

Tinsley, Marion

about

Checker king 'Two-Ton' Tinsley jumps for joy—and victory. A. Richman. il pors *People Wkly* 28:53+ S 7 '87

Tinware

See also
Tin containers

Tippet, Clark

about

Enough said [ballet] Reviews
New Yorker 63:75-6 Jl 6 '87. A. Croce

Tipping

Paying the bill: who to tip and how much. il *Glamour* 85:328 Mr '87

Power tipping. F. Eberstadt. il *Vogue* 177:148+ D '87

Tipping takes a trip [China] il *Time* 130:32 Ag 3 '87

Tipton, Jennifer

about

Taylor-made design. S. Flatow. il *Theatre Crafts* 21:24-5+ Ja '87

Tiradentes, d. 1792

about

Tiradentes: a vision vindicated. por *Dep State Bull* 87:77 Mr '87

Tirami su (Dessert) *See* Desserts

Tire chains

Getting a grip on ice and snow. R. Kimber. il *Ctry J* 14:74-6 N '87

Tire factories

Italy

Rubber revelations [visit to Firestone's International Technical Center in Rome] T. Assenza. il *Car Driv* 33:22 Ag '87

Tire industry

See also
Cooper Tire & Rubber Company
Firestone Tire & Rubber Co.
GenCorp Inc.
Goodyear Tire & Rubber Company
Uniroyal Goodrich Tire Co.

Acquisitions and mergers

GenCorp feels the pincers [Wagner & Brown-AFG team] T. Carson and Z. Schiller. *Bus Week* p33-4 Mr 30 '87

Canada

See also
Canadian Tire Corp., Ltd.
Michelin Canada Ltd.

France

See also
Michelin et Cie

Japan

See also
Bridgestone Corp.

Tire pressure gages

Tire-pressure gauges. il *Consum Rep* 52:95-7 D '87

Tire-pressure gauges. il *Consum Rep* 52:108-9 F '87

Tiredness *See* Fatigue

Tirelli, Umberto

about

Dressing dreams: costumier Umberto Tirelli's residences in Rome and Capri. C. Aillaud. il por *Archit Dig* 44:140-5 O '87

Tires

Recycling

See Recycling (Waste, etc.)

Tires, Automobile

See also
Tire factories
Tire pressure gages

Aedes albopictus in North America: probable introduction in used tires from northern Asia. W. A. Hawley and others. bibl f il *Science* 236:1114-16 My 29 '87

Bridgestone debuts new performance radial. R. Grable. il *Mot Trend* 39:38 Ag '87

Finally—high-performance tires that go in rain, shine, or snow [cover story] J. Keebler. il *Pop Sci* 231:55-9 D '87

Hold that tiger: a very tiresome pursuit [probable introduction of Asian tiger mosquitoes in used tires from northern Asia; research by Paul Reiter] il map *Discover* 8:8-9 Ag '87

Hot rubber [high performance tires] R. Taylor. il *Pop Mech* 164:82-5+ Ap '87

Okay to mix radials, bias-ply tires? il *Mot Trend* 39:34 S '87

Using tires to track pollution. R. Monastersky. *Sci News* 132:6 Jl 4 '87

Anecdotes, facetiae, satire, etc.

The big fix. P. F. McManus. il *Outdoor Life* 179:144+ F '87

Fires and fire prevention

The radial-ply inferno [Hudson, Colo.] il *Newsweek* 109:26 Je 22 '87

Grading and standardization

A little dark reading. S. Harrison. il *Mot Trend* 39:94+ Ap '87

Testing

Designer treads [tires for Corvette] K. Reynolds. il *Road Track* 38:142-6+ Ap '87

Slippin' and slidin' [traction and braking of different types of tires] D. Simanaitis. il *Road Track* 39:172-3 D '87

Tires, Motorcycle

Waterskiing [riding in the rain] K. Cameron. il *Cycle* 38:17 S '87

Testing

Michelin foam tubes [flatproof tire/mousse combination] il *Cycle* 38:94+ Je '87

Sporting tires. il *Cycle* 38:66-71 Ag '87

Sporting tires. il *Cycle* 38:55-60 S '87

Tires, Rubber

See also
Tire pressure gages

Tires, Space vehicle

Testing

NASA tests shuttle tires to improve wear, steering. il *Aviat Week Space Technol* 127:78 D 21 '87

Tires, Truck

Replacement tires. S. L. White. il *Field Stream* 92:64+ D '87

Tiriac, Ion

about

Count Dracula. C. Kirkpatrick. il pors *Sports Illus* 66:60-4+ Je 22 '87

Tirió Indians *See* Trio Indians

Tiritilli, Patricia

The winner's touch [story] il *Teen* 31:26+ My '87

Tisch, Jonathan M.

about

Jon's room is at the top of Loews Hotels. M. Frons. il por *Bus Week* p54-5 Ap 13 '87

Tisch, Laurence A.

about

A bear hug for CBS. A. L. Taylor, III. il por *Fortune* 115:35 Ja 5 '87

Laurence Tisch. D. Lieberman. il por *Bus Week* Sp Issue:220 Ap 17 '87

Nice cop, tough cop. E. Diamond. pors *N Y* 20:14+ F 9 '87

O.K., Larry and Bill, take your places. It's showtime. D. Lieberman and M. N. Vamos. il por *Bus Week* p36-7 Ja 26 '87

A Tisch is still a Tisch. F. Dannen. il pors *Channels* 7:28-33 F '87

Tisch, Tisch, Tisch . . . E. Diamond. il por *N Y* 20:22+ Mr 30 '87

Tsk, tsk, Larry Tisch. il por *Fortune* 116:118 O 26 '87

Tisch, Preston Robert, 1926-

about

Can Bob Tisch get the mail moving? F. Seghers. il *Bus Week* p29 Ag 3 '87

Tisch, Steve

about

Steve hits it big in a risky business. R. Grover. *Bus Week* p55+ Ap 13 '87

Tisch family

about

The first-rate careers of the second-generation Tisches [special section] il *Bus Week* p54-5+ Ap 13 '87

The sons also rise in the dynasty at Loews. il *U S News World Rep* 103:54-5 Jl 6 '87

Tisdale, Sallie

We do abortions here: a nurse's story. *Harpers* 275:66-70 O '87

Tisher, Bill

about

The master trailbuilder of Lake Tahoe. J. P. Jeffries. il por map *Sierra* 72:79-82 Jl/Ag '87

Tissue factor *See* Thromboplastin

Tissue plasminogen activator *See* TPA (Drug)

Tissues

See also

Adipose tissues

Bone

Cells

Connective tissues

Fetal tissue

Ligaments

Muscle

Nerve tissue

Plant cells and tissues

Culture

Cell culture, fusion, manipulation, and tissue culture. *Science* 235 pt2:G35-G36 F 27 '87

Preservation

See Preservation of organs, tissues, etc.

Titan (Launch vehicle) *See* Space vehicles—Propulsion systems

Titan (Missile) *See* Guided missiles

Titan II Missile Museum (Ariz.)

Arizona's atomic attraction. L. Banks. il *Travel Holiday* 168:92 Ag '87

Titanic (Steamship)

1912. K. Ide. *Am Herit* 38:111 Ap '87

Down to the great ship. W. F. Buckley. il por *N Y Times Mag* p40-1+ O 18 '87

Epilogue for Titanic. R. D. Ballard. il *Natl Geogr* 172:454-63 O '87

Excavating the Titanic [L. Weicker's bill barring importation of artifacts] W. F. Buckley. *Natl Rev* 39:65 S 25 '87

A man with Titanic vision [R. D. Ballard] F. Golden. il pors *Discover* 8:50-3+ Ja '87

Mediawatch [British TV documentaries on the Jarrow Crusade and the Titanic] H. David. il *Hist Today* 37:4-5 Ja '87

Reminders of a tragedy. B. Wallace. il *Macleans* 100:58 N 9 '87

Tempest over the Titanic [French salvage expedition] M. D. Lemonick. il *Time* 130:56 Ag 3 '87

Titanic bound; Lingering questions; Down to the Titanic. W. F. Buckley. *Natl Rev* 39:70-1 O 9 '87

The Titanic's legacy to safety. R. L. Scheina. il *Sea Front* 33:200-9 My/Je '87

Treasure quest in a tomb [French salvage mission] A. Steacy. *Macleans* 100:42 Ag 3 '87

Treasures of the Titanic [cover story] S. Rubin. il *Pop Mech* 164:64-9 D '87

Treasures reclaimed from the deep. M. D. Lemonick. il *Time* 130:70-2 N 2 '87

Titanic (Steamship) in motion pictures

Nearer my wreck to thee. H. M. Geduld. *Humanist* 47:45 Jl/Ag '87

Titanium

Titanium: for when you care enough to use the very best. J. R. Chiles. bibl (p184) il *Smithsonian* 18:86-90+ My '87

Titanium dental materials *See* Dental materials

Tithonia *See* Mexican sunflowers

Title IX regulations *See* United States. Dept. of Education

Titles, Job *See* Job descriptions

Titles of address *See* Forms of address

Titles of books, stories, etc.

The day New York became harmless [academic books] A. Broyard. il *N Y Times Book Rev* 92:11 O 4 '87

Titles of honor and nobility

London journal [R. A. Smith, auctioneer of English titles] J. Bainbridge. il *Gourmet* 47:28+ My '87

Titling (Motion pictures) *See* Motion pictures—Titling

Titling (Opera) *See* Opera—Titling

Tivnan, Edward

Homosexuals and the churches. il *N Y Times Mag* p84-6+ O 11 '87

Tizzard, Tom

about

A phone shaped like a Colt .45 has its critics up in arms. il por *People Wkly* 27:38 F 16 '87

Tkac, Debora

Are you a shopaholic? il *Prevention* 39:62-5 Ap '87

New-wave fitness. il *Prevention* 39:100-3 Ja '87

TK!Solver (Computer program) *See* Computer programming

TLC Group Inc.

Black investor realizes mammoth 90-to-1 return [R. F. Lewis] por *Jet* 72:6 Jl 27 '87

Buying into the big time [R. Lewis's TLC Group purchase BCI International Food Company] J. M. Horowitz. il por *Time* 130:42 Ag 24 '87

Reg Lewis hits the big time—and takes it in stride [acquisition of BCI International Food Co.] P. Finch. il por *Bus Week* p27+ Ag 24 '87

Reg to riches [R. F. Lewis] N. J. Perry. il por *Fortune* 116:122-3 S 14 '87

Reginald Lewis cuts the big deal [cover story; with editorial comment by Earl G. Graves] A. Edmond, Jr. il pors *Black Enterp* 18:9, 42-6 N '87

TLC deal signals new era for black business [acquisition of Beatrice International] K. D. Thompson. por *Black Enterp* 18:21-2 O '87

When Wall Street began to take blacks seriously. R. H. Bork, Jr. il por *U S News World Rep* 103:44 Ag 31 '87

TME, Inc.

From medical breakthrough to health-care tool. D. Holder. il por *Work Woman* 12:69-70 My '87

TMJ syndrome

Head pain: could it be a TMJ disorder? S. M. Roser. por *McCalls* 115:82 O '87

Joint venture [arthroscopy to treat TMJ syndrome] J. Carpi. *Health* 19:26 Je '87

TMJ—jawbone pain that's all too common. D. Born. il *Saturday Evening Post* 259:26-7 D '87

TNF (Tumor necrosis factor) *See* Cachectin

Toads

For the desert toad, rain starts a race to metamorphosis [spadefoot toads] D. Cornejo. il *Smithsonian* 17:98-105 Mr '87

Embryology

See Embryology—Amphibia

Eye

See Eye—Amphibia

Ova

See Ova

Photographs and photography

Buried alive! [desert spadefoot toads] T. A. Wiewandt. il *Natl Wildl* 25:18-19 F/Mr '87

Treatment

Guiding toads to safe sex can cause a case of tunnel vision [protective measures taken in England and France] il *People Wkly* 27:154-5 Ap 13 '87

Toads [tunnels built to protect road-crossing toads in Great Britain] *New Yorker* 63:16-18 Ag 17 '87

Toal, Jeanne M.

Can you think yourself healthy? il *Mademoiselle* 93:164+ S '87

Stress and the single girl (having it all—and surviving it). il *Mademoiselle* 93:293-5+ S '87

Summer power: diet and exercise for hot times. il *Mademoiselle* 93:54+ Jl '87

Supervaccines. il *Omni* 9:20+ Jl '87

You can't drink like a man—the latest word on women and alcohol. il *Mademoiselle* 93:104+ My '87

Toaster ovens *See* Kitchen utensils and appliances

Toasters

Toasters. *Consum Rep* 52:61-3 D '87

Tobacco

See also

Chewing tobacco

Nicotine

Smokeless tobacco

Smoking

Curing

Needed: a cure for curing snuff [research by William J. Chamberlain and others] S. Weisburd. *Sci News* 132:169 S 12 '87

Tobacco industry

See also

American Brands, Inc.

Cigarette industry

Culbro Corp.

Liggett & Myers Tobacco Company

Philip Morris, Inc.

R. J. Reynolds Tobacco Co.

Tobacco science wars. E. Marshall. il *Science* 236:250-1 Ap 17 '87

Federal aid

Bob Dole and the tobacco connection. D. Corn. il *Nation* 244:381+ Mr 28 '87

Finance

Beverages and tobacco. H. Seneker. il *Forbes* 139:78+ Ja 12 '87

Big tobacco's fortunes are withering in the heat [antismoking onslaught] S. Ticer. il *Bus Week* p47-9+ Jl 27 '87

Don't bet against cigarette makers. D. Seligman. il *Fortune* 116:70-2+ Ag 17 '87

Tobacco industry—*cont.*

Suits and claims

Asbestos subpoena quashed [request by the R. J. Reynolds Tobacco Co.] J. Raloff. *Sci News* 132:55 Jl 25 '87

Caveat fumator [rulings in favor of Liggett & Myers and American Brands in product liability cases] J. Castro. il *Time* 130:43 S 7 '87

Frank Fat's napkin: how the trial lawyers (and the doctors!) sold out to the tobacco companies [California] P. Glastris. il *Wash Mon* 19:19-25 D '87

A judicial smoke alert [pro-industry rulings in Liggett & Myers Tobacco Co. cases] il *U S News World Rep* 103:12 S 7 '87

Tobacco goes on trial. P. B. Gray. *Read Dig* 131:225-6+ O '87

Tobacco wins one in court [ruling that warning labels on cigarettes shielded Liggett & Myers from liability claim] D. Pauly. il *Newsweek* 110:44 S 7 '87

Canada

The growers' despair. N. Underwood. il *Macleans* 100:30-1 Je 22 '87

Tobacco industry lobby *See* Lobbyists and lobbying

Tobacco mosaic virus *See* Viruses, Plant

Tobacco pipes

Pipe dreams [free-form custom-carved pipes] C. Caiati. il *Pop Mech* 164:72-3+ Ja '87

Tobacco tokens *See* Tokens

Tobacco workers

Salaries, pensions, etc.

Occupational pay structure in cigarette manufacturing plants. il *Mon Labor Rev* 110:36-8 My '87

Toback, James

about

The pick-up artist [film] Reviews

N Y 20:93 O 12 '87. D. Denby

New Yorker 63:92-3 O 5 '87. P. Kael

Newsweek 110:77 S 28 '87. D. Ansen

People Wkly 28:12 O 12 '87. T. Cunneff

Time il 130:69 S 28 '87. R. Corliss

Tobias, Andrew P.

My troubles with the taxman. il *N Y Times Mag* p40+ Ja 18 '87

Your 10 best investments for 1988 (slightly revised). il por *Money* 16:135-6+ D '87

about

To win, play by the rules [interview] por *U S News World Rep* 103:86 N 16 '87

Tobias, Sheila

(jt. auth) *See* Goudinoff, Peter, and Tobias, Sheila

Tobias, Tobi

Dance. *See* issues of New York

Travels with Coppélia. il *Dance Mag* 61:52-3 F '87

about

Bournonville lives in oral memoirs. por *Dance Mag* 61:108-9 Mr '87

Tobin, James

about

A lawyer justified. A. A. Lappen. il por *Forbes* 139:8 Je 29 '87

Tobin, James, 1918-

An exchange on social security [with reply by Michael Kinsley] *New Repub* 196:20+ My 18 '87

Tobin, Mary Luke

about

American nuns: are they still a class act? [interview] por *U S Cathol* 52:27-34 Ja '87

Female and Catholic: please don't bring me flowers anymore [interview] il *U S Cathol* 52:20-6 Ap '87

Tobin, William

Perfecting the modern reflector. il por *Sky Telesc* 74:358-9 O '87

Toboggans and tobogganning *See* Sleds and sledding

Toby jugs *See* Pitchers (Pottery, glass, etc.)

Tocopherol *See* Vitamins—Vitamin E

Tocqueville Fund

Companies that refused to rust. J. Egan. il *U S News World Rep* 103:50 Jl 27 '87

Today [television program] *See* Television program reviews—Single works

Todd, Alden

Research tips to help you write. *Writer* 100:22-4+ N '87

Todd, James A., 1928-

about

Help wanted: Stakhanovites only. J. Flint. il por *Forbes* 140:82+ S 7 '87

Todd, Mabel Loomis, 1856-1932

about

Amorous in Amherst. R. Craft. bibl f pors *N Y Rev Books* 34:18-21 Ap 23 '87

Todd, Trish

Fiction's new look. il *Publ Wkly* 231:29-33 F 6 '87

William Safire talks about 'Freedom,' his new novel. por *Publ Wkly* 231:49-50 My 29 '87

Todd-AO Corp.

What a performance [sale of United Artists Communications to Tele-Communications and spinoff of Todd-AO] A. B. Block. il *Forbes* 139:136 Ap 6 '87

Toddlers *See* Children

Todorov, Tzvetan, 1939-

The philosopher and the everyday. *New Repub* 197:34-7+ S 14-21 '87

Stalled thinkers. *New Repub* 196:26-7 Ap 13 '87

Toe lock *See* Foot—Wounds and injuries

Toennies, Ferdinand

about

Ferdinand Toennies: dark times for a liberal intellectual. J. Samples. bibl *Society* 24:65-8 S/O '87

Toffler, Alvin

Future shock in Moscow. *Cent Mag* 20:59-60 S/O '87

Tofu

See also

Cooking—Soybean products

Mr. Yogurt takes a chance on tofu [J. E. Metzger] F. McCoy. il por *Bus Week* p115 Jl 20 '87

Tognini, Joyce

Contemporary craft at the Met. il *Am Craft* 47:50-5 Ap/My '87

Toher, Jennifer

(jt. auth) *See* Hanks, David A., and Toher, Jennifer

Toilet seats

Sanitation

Women are lining up for Lore Harp's Le Funelle. P. Finch. il por *Bus Week* p80 Je 8 '87

Women take a stand in public restrooms [Le Funelle] *Prevention* 39:12 F '87

Toilets

Water efficiency in the house. il *Sunset* 179:154+ S '87

Maintenance and repair

Noisy toilet. G. Branson. il *Fam Handyman* 37:55 F '87

Reseating a toilet. R. Barnhart. il *Home Mech* 83:84 Ag '87

Toilets, Public *See* Public comfort stations

Tokamaks

SSC, fusion machine hit a roadblock [funding] M. Crawford. *Science* 237:1559 S 25 '87

U.S.S.R. eyes role in U.S. Compact Tokamak Ignition experiment. M. Crawford. il *Science* 238:1035 N 20 '87

Tokarev, Vladimir V.

My American dream. il *Newsweek* 110:49 D 14 '87

Tokens

Tobacco tokens may prove to be your lucky strike! E. Rochette. il *Antiques Collect Hobbies* 92:80-1 O '87

Tokuyama, Jiri

Insecurely secure. *World Press Rev* 34:17-18 Ag '87

Tokyo (Japan)

Art

A confusion of realms [Tokyo: form and spirit at the IBM Gallery] K. Larson. il *N Y* 20:55+ Ja 12 '87

East meets West, postmodern style [traveling exhibit entitled Tokyo: form and spirit] R. Silberman. il *Art Am* 75:13-15+ My '87

Haiku to high tech [Tokyo: form and spirit exhibit] il *Sunset* 178:50 Mr '87

Hotels, motels, etc.

An oasis in the Ginza [Seiyo, Ginza] A. Tanzer. il *Forbes* 140:98-9 Jl 27 '87

Markets

A gourmet at large [Tsukiji market] F. Ferretti. il *Gourmet* 48:44+ Je '87

Music

See also

Opera—Japan

Stores

Tokyo bazaar. D. Takahashi. il *Harpers Bazaar* 120:60+ Jl '87

Tokyo clothes and other buys. D. P. Marshall. il *Travel Holiday* 168:42-3 Jl '87

Tokyo Audio Fair *See* Audio systems—Exhibitions

Tokyo Shibaura Electric Company, Ltd. *See* Toshiba Corporation

Tokyo Stock Exchange *See* Stock exchanges—Tokyo exchange

Tolbert, Margaret, and Lippman, Richard E.

Are your contact lenses as safe as you think? il *FDA Consum* 21:16-19 Ap '87

Tolbert, Margaret A., and others
Reaction of chlorine nitrate with hydrogen chloride and water at Antarctic stratospheric temperatures. bibl f il *Science* 238:1258-60 N 27 '87

Tolchin, Martin, and Gerth, Jeff
The contradictions of Bob Dole. il pors *N Y Times Mag* p62-5+ N 8 '87

Tolchin, Martin, and Tolchin, Susan
Foreign money, U.S. fears. il *N Y Times Mag* p63-4+ D 13 '87

Tolchin, Susan
(jt. auth) See Tolchin, Martin, and Tolchin, Susan

Toledo (Ohio)

Education

Sarabeth Eason [interview with 11 year old expelled from Catholic school for supporting abortion free choice] C. Grant. il pors *Ms* 15:60-1+ Ja '87

History

Writing great-grandfather's biography [S. M. Jones, Toledo's turn of the century mayor] M. Jones. *Am Sch* 56:519-34 Aut '87

Tolerance, Immunological *See* Immunological tolerance
Tolerance, Religious *See* Religious liberty
Tolerance to drugs *See* Drugs—Physiological effects
Toleration
Beyond tolerance to equal rights. J. M. Wall. *Christ Century* 104:395-6 Ap 29 '87

Tolerton, Jane
Condoms to the rescue: New Zealand's Ettie Rout "made vice safe" in World War I. il pors *Ms* 15:28-30 My '87

Toll, Marie-Pierre
(jt. auth) See Toll, Roger C., and Toll, Marie-Pierre

Toll, Roger C., and Toll, Marie-Pierre
Woven in Oaxaca. il *House Gard* 159:102+ My '87

Toll-free telephone service
1-800 . . . [use of service by consumers of packaged goods] B. Wallraff. il *Atlantic* 260:18+ O '87
Busy signals [customers' inability to get through to brokers and funds on toll free numbers during the crash] M. Schifrin. il *Forbes* 140:38+ N 16 '87
Call 1-800-227-3988 [Women's Sports Foundation service] il *Women's Sports Fitness* 9:52 Ja '87
Fine furniture by phone—cheap. *U S News World Rep* 103:111 N 9 '87
Low-cost life insurance: finding the best deals by phone. *Better Homes Gard* 65:52 N '87
Toll-free expertise. il *Home Mech* 83:16 D '87
Toll-free help. *Consum Rep* 52:75 F '87
Toll-free woes [opposition groups clogging J. Falwell's toll-free phone lines] *Time* 129:63 Ja 26 '87
Where to call to ask questions about food [food manufacturers' hot lines] *Sunset* 179:158 D '87

Toll roads
Freeway privatization [address, April 10, 1987] R. W. Poole. *Vital Speeches Day* 53:553-6 Jl 1 '87

Tolleson, Robin
Steve Morse: guitar power. il pors *Down Beat* 54:16-18+ Ap '87

Tolley, Ray
Making it as a free-lance writer-photographer. il *Petersens Photogr Mag* 15:51-3 Ja '87

Tolliday, William

about

Castle Lizzardo. A. Bahar. il por *Antiques Collect Hobbies* 92:48-52 Mr '87

Tolliver, Stanley E.

about

Black elected president of Cleveland school board. *Jet* 71:5 F 2 '87

Tolomeo [opera] *See* Handel, George Frideric, 1685-1759

Tolson, Ed
Taming the circus of TSR software. por *Pers Comput* 11:228 O '87

Tom Petty and the Heartbreakers (Musical group)
Tom Petty and the Heartbreakers [concert at Arizona State University] S. Hochman. il *Roll Stone* p28-9 Jl 16-30 '87
Tom Petty's new LP: back to basics [Let me up] A. DeCurtis. il por *Roll Stone* p10 My 7 '87

Tomahawk (Missile) *See* Guided missiles

Tomalonis, Alexandra
First decade for Washington Ballet: the company that just happened. il *Dance Mag* 61:64-5 Ap '87

Tomasson, Helgi

about

Back to basics [cover story] J. Ross. il por *Dance Mag* 61:38-43 Ag '87

Tomasz, Maria, and others
Isolation and structure of a covalent cross-link adduct between mitomycin C and DNA. bibl f il *Science* 235:1204-8 Mr 6 '87

Tomato Bob

about

Tomato Bob. *New Yorker* 63:36-8 O 12 '87

Tomato sauce *See* Sauces
Tomato soups *See* Soups
Tomatoes

See also

Cooking—Vegetables
1987: the year of the tomato. il *Flower Gard* 31:34-5+ Ap/My '87
About tomatoes. il *Mother Earth News* 105:22-4+ My/Je '87
Don't miss out on fall tomatoes. il *South Living* 22:51 Jl '87
Supercharge your tomatoes [cover story] K. Martin. il *Rodale's Org Gard* 34:34-7 Ag '87
Tomato Bob. *New Yorker* 63:36-8 O 12 '87
Tomato tips. il *South Living* 22:102 My '87

Diseases and pests

Curing curly top. R. Flint and S. Flint. il map *Rodale's Org Gard* 34:70-3 Ag '87

Drying

Sundried tomatoes. J. B. Hurley. il *Rodale's Org Gard* 34:47 Ag '87

Preservation

Preserving summer-fresh tomatoes. il *Better Homes Gard* 65:121 Ag '87

Tomb robberies *See* Body snatching
Tombaugh, Clyde, 1906-

about

Clyde Tombaugh: planetary observer and telescope maker. D. H. Levy. il por *Sky Telesc* 73:88-9 Ja '87

Le tombeau de Couperin [ballet] *See* Ballet reviews—Single works

Tombs

See also

Epitaphs
For Kate Smith, death alone isn't grounds for burial [controversy with local Catholic Church over plans to build mausoleum in Lake Placid, N.Y.] il por *People Wkly* 27:77 Je 15 '87
Remove Jackie Wilson from unmarked grave; fans buy a mausoleum. il pors *Jet* 72:22-3 Je 29 '87

Argentina

See also

Perón, Juan Domingo, 1895-1974—Tomb

China

Treasures from an ancient Chinese tomb [Duke of Qin Tomb No. 1] Wen Ruitang. il *Courier* 40:32-3 Ja '87

Netherlands

See also

Rembrandt Harmenszoon van Rijn, 1606-1669—Tomb

Wales

See also

Arthur, King—Tomb

Tombstone epitaphs *See* Epitaphs
Tombstones *See* Sepulchral monuments
Tomic, Milan T., and others
Structure of a psoralen cross-linked DNA in solution by nuclear magnetic resonance. bibl f il *Science* 238:1722-5 D 18 '87

Tomita, Isao

about

Tomita. B. Milkowski. *Down Beat* 54:52 Mr '87

Tomkin, Jocelyn, and Lambert, David L.
The strange case of Beta Lyrae. il *Sky Telesc* 74:354-7 O '87

Tomkins, Alan J.
Psychology and the Constitution. bibl (p58) *Psychol Today* 21:48-50 S '87

Tomkins, Calvin, 1925-
The art world. See occasional issues of The New Yorker
Profiles [J. M. Brealey] por *New Yorker* 63:44-6+ Mr 16 '87
Profiles [R. Bernier] por *New Yorker* 62:38-40+ Ja 19 '87

Tomkins (F. H.) plc *See* F. H. Tomkins plc
Tomlin, Elaine

about

Free lance photog who worked for Jet has her life's work stolen. *Jet* 72:22 S 14 '87

Tommy Lasorda's Ribs and Pasta (Los Angeles, Calif.: Restaurant) *See* Los Angeles (Calif.)—Restaurants, nightclubs, bars, etc.

Tommy Tang's (New York, N.Y.: Restaurant) *See* New York (N.Y.)—Restaurants, nightclubs, bars, etc.

Tommycod fishing *See* Cod fishing

Tomography
See also
Microtomography

Agricultural use
You say tomato, they say tomography. R. Weiss. il *Sci News* 132:164 S 12 '87

Archeological use
Mummy dearest [studying Egyptian mummies with CT scan] S. Allison. il *Life* 10:106-9 O '87

Geological use
Core questions [use of seismic tomography to probe earth's core] *Sci Am* 256:60-1 F '87
Journey to the center of the earth [seismic tomography studies] T. A. Heppenheimer. il map *Discover* 8:86-90+ N '87
Mountains and valleys are at earth's core mantle boundary [seismic tomography studies] *Earth Sci* 40:9 Summ '87

Medical use
Brain pics [PET scans; work of Monte S. Buchsbaum] L. Marsa. il *Omni* 9:14+ Jl '87
Hip graphics. B. Weber. il *N Y Times Mag* p110 D 13 '87
Images of obsession [positron emission tomography; cover story] B. Bower. il *Sci News* 131:236-7 Ap 11 '87
Mapping human brain monoamine oxidase A and B with [11]-labeled suicide inactivators and PET. J. S. Fowler and others. bibl f il *Science* 235:481-5 Ja 23 '87
Plaque hemorrhage linked to stroke [scanning carotid arteries; research by Antonio Culebras and others] S. Weisburd. il *Sci News* 131:167 Mr 14 '87
Scanning your bones: can these tests do any good? [computerized tomography or dual photon absorptiometry] S. Festa. il *Women's Sports Fitness* 9:18 Jl '87

Oceanographic use
Greenland Sea Project uses tomography. *Sea Front* 33:143 Mr/Ap '87

Paleontological use
Hominid headway [use of tomography to study Taung skull] B. Bower. *Sci News* 132:408-9 D 19-26 '87

Physics use
Quantitative three-dimensional optical tomographic imaging of supersonic flows. G. W. Faris and R. L. Byer. bibl f il *Science* 238:1700-2 D 18 '87

Tomorrow and tomorrow [opera] *See* Sullivan, Timothy

Tompane (A.B.) & Company *See* A.B. Tompane & Company

Tompkins, Doug
about
Clothes make the man. C. K. Gandee. il por *Archit Rec* 175:120-3 mid-S '87
The spirit of Esprit! M. Altman. il *Seventeen* 46:83-4+ Je '87

Tompkins, Susie
about
The spirit of Esprit! M. Altman. il *Seventeen* 46:83-4+ Je '87
Susie Tompkins: the spirit in Esprit [interview] E. Klensch. il por *Vogue* 177:344-7+ Ag '87

Tompkins, Warwick
about
Tompkins's big chance. J. Lowenstein. il *Oceans* 20:72 S/O '87

Tomsun Foods International Inc.
Mr. Yogurt takes a chance on tofu [J. E. Metzger] F. McCoy. il por *Bus Week* p115 Jl 20 '87

Tonality
See also
Atonality

Tonawanda, Jackie
about
Lady boxing champ seeks $10,000,000 court victory. il por *Jet* 72:52 Je 29 '87

Tone dialing *See* Dual-tone multifrequency signalling

Tone generators *See* Signal generators

Tonegawa, Susumu, 1939-
about
Antibody research garners Nobel Prize. J. L. Marx. il por *Science* 238:484-5 O 23 '87
Hard chargers find the keys to glory. S. Budiansky. il por *U S News World Rep* 103:12-13 O 26 '87
Medicine, chemistry, physics Nobels announced. S. Eisenberg. il por *Sci News* 132:244 O 17 '87
Nobel prizes: physiology or medicine. K. Wright. *Sci Am* 257:45-6 D '87

Tonelson, Alan
Give 'em hell. *New Repub* 197:20-1+ O 5 '87

Toner, Gerald R.
Caroling on command [story] il *Saturday Evening Post* 259:42-5+ D '87

Tong, Margaret
(ed) *See* Albee, George W. A country wok

Tong, Miren
about
The "modern style": furniture by Miren Tong. A. Bahar. il por *Antiques Collect Hobbies* 91:44-7 Ja '87

Tonga
See also
Rites and ceremonies—Tonga

Discovery and exploration
Festivities in the Friendly Islands [excerpt from Captain Cook's voyages of discovery] J. Cook. il *Courier* 40:12-13 Ap '87

Tongass National Forest (Alaska)
The Forest Service's road to nowhere [timber contracts and roadbuilding projects] K. E. Franklin. il *Progressive* 51:12 Je '87
Paradise in peril [clearcutting] R. Robotham. il map *Life* 10:92-6 N '87
Trashing the Tongass. G. Laycock. il maps *Audubon* 89:110-12+ N '87

Tongue
See also
Taste

Tongues, Speaking in *See* Speaking in tongues

Toning tables *See* Exercising equipment

Tonka Corp.
Is Tonka toying with trouble? [acquisition of Kenner Parker toys] G. G. Marcial. *Bus Week* p165 O 12 '87

Tony Awards
Broadway's hit play 'Fences' is nominated for six Tonys. *Jet* 72:55 Je 1 '87
'Fences,' Jones, grab top Tonys for drama. il pors *Jet* 72:54 Je 22 '87
Show folk face off for the most competitive Tony Awards in years. il *People Wkly* 27:45-6 Je 22 '87

Tony Godwin Memorial Award *See* Editors and editing—Awards

Too many girls [musical] *See* Musicals, revues, etc.—Reviews—Single works

Too outrageous! [film] *See* Motion picture reviews—Single works

Toobin, Jeffrey
Viva Miranda. *New Repub* 196:11-12 F 16 '87

Tool and dye industry
The decline of the master craftsman. S. Gilbert. il *Forbes* 139:288-9 Ja 12 '87

Tool boxes, racks, etc.
Bucket power: carry cord, tools. il *Sunset* 178:139 My '87
Carpenter's tool box. C. Self. il *Workbench* 43:62-4 Jl/Ag '87
Garden tool caddy. il *Home Mech* 83:24 S '87

Tool industry
See also
Black & Decker Corp.

Toolan, David
Religions of the one God [interview with H. Küng] *Commonweal* 114:143+ Mr 13 '87

Tooley, Reva B.
Turning trials into triumph. il por *Work Woman* 12:66-8+ Ja '87

Tools
See also
Bone implements and weapons
Chisels
Files and rasps
Garden equipment
Hammers
Levels (Tools)
Paint and varnish removers
Painting, Industrial and practical—Equipment
Planes and planing
Screwdrivers
Stone implements and weapons
Tool and dye industry
Wood cutting equipment
Wrenches

9 new auto-care aids. P. Weissler. il *Home Mech* 83:102+ O '87
Annual tool roundup. il *Workbench* 43:56+ Ja/F '87
Basic tool kit for fall spruce-ups. il *Glamour* 85:100-1 S '87
Better tools for homeowners. J. R. Provey. il *Home Mech* 83:5 O '87
The boatkeeper's basic tool kit. B. Gladstone. il *Mot Boat Sail* 159:73-5 Je '87

Tools—*cont.*
Fill 'er up: gutsy gas tools [cordless tools from Ryobi] P. McCafferty. il *Pop Sci* 231:72-3 D '87
Frozen tools [use of deep-cryogenic processing; cover story] V. E. Gilmore. il *Pop Sci* 230:64-7+ Je '87
High-speed problem solvers [compact power tools] M. Thompson. il *Fam Handyman* 37:12+ My/Je '87
Modular power tools; Variable-speed Moto-Tool. R. Capotosto. il *Pop Mech* 164:26 Ap '87
New for car-care enthusiasts. P. Weissler. il *Home Mech* 83:76+ My '87
Three tools driven by one engine [Solo MultiMot system] M. Ferrara. il *Home Mech* 83:102 My '87
Tool tests. See issues of Popular Mechanics beginning January 1986
Toolmakers cut the cord. H. Wicks. il *Home Mech* 83:68+ Ja '87
Tools of the trade [auto tools and service manuals] il *Pop Mech* 164:150-1+ My '87
Using tools. See issues of The Family Handyman
What's new in tools. V. E. Gilmore. See issues of Popular Science
Your first lathe tools. il *Workbench* 43:64 S/O '87

Leasing and renting
Renting the "rightest" tools. J. Vara. il *Ctry J* 14:19-20 Jl '87

Safety devices and measures
Pro tips to avoid accidents. A. Rooze. il *Fam Handyman* 37:10+ Jl/Ag '87
Workshop safety devices [Shopsmith safety tools] H. Wicks. il *Home Mech* 83:92 Ja '87

Sharpening
See Sharpeners and sharpening

Storage
See also
Tool boxes, racks, etc.

Toomer, Ronald
about
All aboard! K. Hannon. il por *Forbes* 140:96-8 Ag 10 '87

Toomre, Alar
about
Cosmic mergers. S. J. Nadis. il *Omni* 9:24+ Ag '87

Toon, Al
about
Singing a new Toon. R. Hoerburger. il pors *Sport Mag* 78:41-7 N '87

Tooth decay *See* Dental caries
Tooth decay prevention *See* Teeth—Care and hygiene
Toothbrushes
Baffled by brushes. D. Born. il *Saturday Evening Post* 259:18-19+ My/Je '87
Is your toothbrush making you sick? C. Loomis. il *Parents* 62:17 Mr '87

Toothpastes, powders, etc.
Toothpastes. *Consum Rep* 52:196-8 D '87
Topeka (Kan.)

Airports
From smoking gun to smoking dog: a 'Beat the devil' investigation [killing of dogs at Forbes Field Airport before arrival of R. Reagan] A. Cockburn. map *Nation* 245:332-3 O 3 '87

Education
The heirs of Oliver Brown: in Topeka, a landmark equality case is still before the courts [Brown v. Board of Education] J. E. White. il por *Time* 130:88-9 Jl 6 '87

Politics and government
Bugg tabbed as top ranked black city exec. in Topeka [R. Bugg] por *Jet* 73:36 N 9 '87

Toperoff, Sam
Open season in Pittsburgh. il pors *Sports Illus* 67 Sp Issue:96-100+ S 9 '87
An ugly feeling. il *N Y Times Mag* p64 O 25 '87

Topex (Satellite) *See* Artificial satellites—Oceanographic use

Topham, Marva
about
An audible impact. S. Moore. il por *Essence* 18:118 O '87

Topić, Ante *See* Mimara, Ante Topić, 1898-1987
Topoff, Howard
Ant wars. il *Nat Hist* 96:62-6+ Ja '87
Topographic maps
See also
Contours (Cartography)
Topology
See also
Homotopy
Mappings (Mathematics)
Poincaré conjecture

Topping, Seymour
Thaw and freeze and thaw again: the cultural weather in China. *N Y Times Book Rev* 92:3+ D 27 '87
Toppings, Ice cream *See* Ice cream toppings
Toradze, Alexander
about
Music for three pianos. R. Freed. pors *Stereo Rev* 52:132 O '87
Toray Industries, Inc
The joys of having patient stockholders. A. Tanzer. il *Forbes* 140:84+ Jl 13 '87
Torbet, Laura
(jt. auth) See Gittelson, Bernard, and Torbet, Laura
Torches
See also
Olympic torch
Toretto, Eleanore
Food for (uninterrupted) thought. il *Work Woman* 12:86 Ag '87
Torgov, Morley
A fear of lawyers. il *N Y Times Mag* p64 N 15 '87
Tories, American *See* American loyalists
Tormé, Mel, 1925-
about
Mel Tormé. C. Albertson. il por *Stereo Rev* 52:96 Mr '87
Torn, David
about
David Torn. B. Milkowski. il por *Down Beat* 54:48+ F '87
Tornado airplanes *See* Airplanes, Military
Tornadoes
Day of the killer tornadoes [condensed from Tornado watch #211] J. G. Fuller. il map *Read Dig* 130:152-61+ My '87
A disaster in Edmonton. J. Howse. il *Macleans* 100:8-9 Ag 10 '87
Edmonton after the storm [July tornado] J. Howse. *Macleans* 100:12 O 26 '87
The "fist" of a tornado? [Concord N. H.; letter] M. D. Hill. il *Weatherwise* 40:69-70 Ap '87
Inside a Texas tornado [McKinney, Tex.; reprint from June 1951 issue] R. S. Hall. *Weatherwise* 40:72-5 Ap '87
Live at five! [television coverage of November 18, 1986 Arizona tornado] R. Norman, Jr. and R. C. Balling, Jr. il pors *Weatherwise* 40:36-7 F '87
Pain and hope after the killer winds [aftermath of tornado in Edmonton, Alta.] M. Gray. il *Macleans* 100:39-40 Ag 17 '87
Possible tornado-like tracks on Mars. J. A. Grant and P. H. Schultz. bibl f il maps *Science* 237:883-5 Ag 21 '87
Tornado! P. Miller. il map *Natl Geogr* 171:690-715 Je '87
Tornadoes: fewest fatalities on record [1986] E. W. Ferguson and others. il maps *Weatherwise* 40:28-35 F '87
Twisters on the red planet? [research by John A. Grant and Peter H. Schultz] il *Sky Telesc* 74:579-80 D '87
Visit Mars in the off-season [possible tornadoes; research by John Grant and Peter Schultz] il *Discover* 8:10+ N '87
Toronto (Ont.)

Banks
See also
Toronto Dominion Bank
Stakes in metropolitan power [proposal to make Canadian cities international banking centers overlooks Toronto] S. Aikenhead. il *Macleans* 100:34 Ja 26 '87

Bookstores
See Booksellers and bookselling—Ontario

Crime
Aftermath of a romance [K. Inwood charged with assaulting his Russian wife and child] R. Corelli. il pors *Macleans* 100:58 S 28 '87
Downfall of a schemer [W. Player's role in real estate fraud scandal] P. Best. il por *Macleans* 100:32 Jl 20 '87

Education
Spaced-out students [high school space sciences program] R. Atherley. il *Macleans* 100:64 O 19 '87

Galleries and museums
Toronto's group of five: museums as varied as Canada. H. Loverseed. il *Travel Holiday* 168:44-50 O '87

Health facilities
Conscience over duty [policeman D. Packer refuses to guard abortion clinic] C. Barrett. *Macleans* 100:24 S 21 '87

Toronto (Ont.)—cont.
Music
See also
Opera Atelier (Ont.)
Police
Conscience over duty [D. Packer refuses to guard abortion clinic] C. Barrett. Macleans 100:24 S 21 '87
Religious institutions and affairs
Barred from the church altar [S. Bernier prohibited from serving as altar girl] M. McIver. por Macleans 100:45 Jl 6 '87
Social life and customs
Going nowhere in the fast lane. C. Gordon. il Macleans 100:52 S 7 '87
Waterfront
Battles on the waterfront. M. Nichols. il Macleans 100:20 Ag 24 '87
Warring factions on the waterfront. M. Gray. il Macleans 100:53-4 N 2 '87
Toronto Dominion Bank
A maverick in the big bankers [R. Thomson] P. C. Newman. il por Macleans 100:41 O 12 '87
Toronto Free Theatre. Centre Stage
A national dreamer in the spotlight [G. Sprung] J. Bemrose. il por Macleans 100:61-2 O 26 '87
Toronto Stock Exchange See Stock exchanges—Toronto exchange
Toronto Sun Publishing Corp.
A new voice for business [purchase of the Financial post] P. Best. il Macleans 100:37-8 O 12 '87
Partners for the Post [Financial post venture to include London's Financial times] P. Best. por Macleans 100:40 O 19 '87
Torque
Torque and horsepower. R. Grable. il Mot Trend 39:106-7 S '87
Torrence, Charles
about
The heart of Canton, Ohio. H. Hurt. Read Dig 130:49-52 Mr '87
Torres, Alejandrina
about
The women of Lexington Prison. W. A. Reuben and C. Norman. il Nation 244:881-4 Je 27 '87
Torres, José
The Palladium. il N Y 20:99 D 21-28 '87
Torres-García, Joaquín, 1874-1949
about
Joaquín Torres-García. E. Turner. Art News 86:57 Ja '87
Order and symbol: Torres-García's constructivism. V. G. Stoddart. il Américas 39:57-8 Ja/F '87
Torresi, Enzo N.
This is the year of non-confusion. por Pers Comput 11:254 O '87
Torrey, Joanna
Add a power surge. il Women's Sports Fitness 9:34-7 O '87
Torrey, Theodore C.
about
Ted Torrey interview. J. Lowe. il por Flower Gard 32:48+ D '87/Ja '88
Torri, Dave
about
Dave Torri. M. Bishop. por Sports Illus 67:110 Ag 31 '87
Tors
Lions lurk and cowboys ride in rounded rock heaps that form underground from rotting blocks of granite. M. Hill. il Earth Sci 40:38 Fall '87
Torte See Cake
Tortillas See Cooking, Mexican
Torts
See also
Wrongful life
The liability crisis isn't over yet. J. L. Gattuso. il map Consum Res Mag 70:15-19 O '87
Megatort mania. E. A. Finn, Jr. il Forbes 139:114+ Je 1 '87
Solving the liability crisis. B. Gatty. il Nations Bus 75:39-40+ Je '87
The time has come for tort reform. R. K. Willard. il USA Today (Periodical) 115:48-9 Mr '87
Tort reform. M. B. Zuckerman. il U S News World Rep 103:68 S 7 '87
Tort reform scores significant victories [reforms that affect architects and engineers] C. K. Hoyt. il Archit Rec 175:35 N '87
Tort reform—bit by bit. J. A. Conway. il Forbes 139 Ann Directory:10 Ap 27 '87

Torture
See also
Amnesty International
Convention against Torture and Other Cruel, Inhuman, or Degrading Treatment or Punishment (1984)
The fight to stop torture. J. D. Barber. il USA Today (Periodical) 116:29-31 N '87
A miracle, a universe (I) [involvement of Presbyterian minister J. Wright and Cardinal Arns in project to document torture by Brazilian military governments, 1964-1979] L. Weschler. New Yorker 63:69-84+ My 25 '87
A miracle, a universe (II) [involvement of Presbyterian minister J. Wright and Cardinal Arns in project to document torture by Brazilian military governments, 1964-1979] L. Weschler. New Yorker 63:72-80+ Je 1 '87
Stop the torture! [South African youth] B. F. Chavis. por Essence 18:146 O '87
Torture in Israel [Shin Bet counterterrorist torture] New Repub 197:7 N 23 '87
Torture Victims Protection Act (Proposed)
Torture prevention: dragging our heels. M. D. Wilde. Christ Century 104:616-17 Jl 15-22 '87
Torvill, Jayne
about
Fighting drugs on ice. P. SerVaas. il pors Saturday Evening Post 259:50 Ja/F '87
Torvill & Dean: so nice on ice. D. Chase. il pors Saturday Evening Post 259:48-9+ Ja/F '87
Tory Party (Great Britain) See Conservative Party (Great Britain)
Tosca [opera] See Puccini, Giacomo, 1858-1924
Toscanini, Arturo, 1867-1957
about
Beethoven, Ludwig van: Symphonies no. 8 and 9. T. Hathaway. il por High Fidel 37:84 N '87
Misunderstanding Toscanini. T. Hathaway. il pors High Fidel 37:63-5 Ag '87
Tosco Corp.
Waiting game. M. Beauchamp. il Forbes 140:130+ N 16 '87
Tosh, Peter, 1944-1987
about
More intrigue involved in Peter Tosh's murder. por Jet 73:32 O 26 '87
Obituary
Down Beat 54:11 D '87. B. Beuttler
High Fidel il 37:63 D '87. L. Jaffee
Reggae great Peter Tosh murdered. M. Goldberg. por Roll Stone p24+ O 22 '87
Reggae star Peter Tosh fatally shot in Jamaica. por Jet 73:62 S 28 '87
Toshiba Corporation
After the scandal [J. Aoi] F. H. Katayama. por Fortune 116:60 Ag 3 '87
How Toshiba is beating American sanctions. S. J. Dryden. il Bus Week p58 S 14 '87
The man Toshiba hung out to dry [S. Saba] A. Tanzer. il por Forbes 140:96+ S 7 '87
Punish Toshiba? W. F. Buckley. Natl Rev 39:62-3 D 18 '87
Samurais for hire [Toshiba lobbying Congress] G. Witkin. il U S News World Rep 103:50 O 5 '87
Toshiba Machine Co. Ltd.
The battle over Toshiba [U.S.-Japan trade relations strained by Toshiba's sale of high tech goods to Soviets] J. B. Copeland. il Newsweek 110:40 Jl 13 '87
Beware of machines in disguise [conspiracy behind Toshiba's sales to the Soviets] S. Koepp. il Time 130:53 S 21 '87
Bright lights, big MITI [sale of top-security technology to the Soviets] C. Chandler. New Repub 197:11-13 Ag 31 '87
The case of the not-so-simple machine tools [sale of top-secret technology to the Soviet Union] M. I. Goldman. il Technol Rev 90:20+ O '87
Congress wants Toshiba's blood [diversion of high tech to Russia provokes U.S. punitive measures] S. J. Dryden. Bus Week p46-7 Jl 6 '87
How Toshiba is beating American sanctions [furor over illegal sale to Moscow dies down] S. J. Dryden. il Bus Week p58 S 14 '87
An illegal deal's noisy repercussions [Soviet deal with Toshiba and Kongsberg for milling machines to make submarine propellers] W. J. Cook. il U S News World Rep 102:42 Je 15 '87
Japan's bow of contrition [apologizing for Toshiba scandal] J. B. Copeland. il Newsweek 110:44 Jl 27 '87

Toshiba Machine Co. Ltd.—*cont.*
A leak that could sink the U.S. lead in submarines [illegal sales to Soviet Union] J. Kapstein. il *Bus Week* p65-6 My 18 '87
Making amends [Toshiba products banned in U.S. following sale of submarine technology to Soviets] *Time* 130:49 Jl 13 '87
Punish Toshiba? W. F. Buckley. *Natl Rev* 39:62-3 D 18 '87
Run silent, run to Moscow [sale of submarine technology to the Soviets] G. Bock. il *Time* 129:45 Je 29 '87
Sanctions [U.S. actions against Toshiba for high tech sale to Soviets] L. G. Boundas. il *Stereo Rev* 52:8 N '87
Tackling Toshiba [U.S. reaction to high tech sale to Soviets] J. McLaughlin. *Natl Rev* 39:24 Ag 14 '87
Tora! Tora! Angry lawmakers torpedo Toshiba [U.S. seeks to punish company for illegal trade with Soviets] *U S News World Rep* 103:42 Jl 13 '87
Toshiba ban spurs review of technology export controls [U.S. reaction to Japan's high tech sale to Soviets] *Aviat Week Space Technol* 127:27 Jl 6 '87
The Toshiba scandal: anatomy of a betrayal [illegal sales to Soviet Union] R. K. Bennett. *Read Dig* 131:95-100 D '87
The Toshiba scandal has exporters running for cover [technology sale to Soviets] L. Armstrong and N. Gross. il *Bus Week* p86-7 Jl 20 '87
Toshiba vs. the U.S.: a Japanese view. *World Press Rev* 34:18 Ag '87
Welcome to Moscow on the Ginza [sale of submarine technology to the Soviets] R. N. Perle. il *U S News World Rep* 102:31-2 Je 29 '87
Tostadas *See* Cooking, Mexican
TOTAL-Compagnie Française des Pétroles
A diplomat turned businessman [F.-X. Ortoli] S. Tully. il por *Fortune* 116:66 Ag 3 '87
Total Flood Corporation
Halon provides extinguishing gains. il *Aviat Week Space Technol* 126:137 F 9 '87
Totalitarianism
See also
Fascism
Cultural control [with discussion] L. Nader. il por *Cent Mag* 20:50-9 Mr/Ap '87
Margaret Atwood [address] M. Atwood. il *Humanist* 47:5-7+ S/O '87
The regime within [interview with V. Havel]; tr. by A. G. Brain. E. Blair. *Harpers* 274:24+ Je '87
Search for the human dimension [interview with V. Havel] E. Blair. il por *World Press Rev* 34:24-5 My '87
Tote bags *See* Bags
Totem poles
Ketchikan's three big totem collections . . . easy to get to. il *Sunset* 179:40-1 Ag '87
Totem heritage. A. Satterfield. il *Travel Holiday* 167:82 Je '87
Toth, Nicholas
The first technology. bibl (p128) il map *Sci Am* 256:112-21 Ap '87
Toth, Steve
Appliance clinic. See issues of Popular Mechanics
Toth, Susan Allen
The importance of being remembered. il *N Y Times Book Rev* 92:1+ Je 28 '87
Life in the slow lane. *Vogue* 177:246 N '87
Touaregs *See* Tuaregs
Touch
The feel of fabric [study by Andrea Gwosdow and Larry Berglund] H. Hall. *Psychol Today* 21:25 Jl '87
Physiological evidence for serial processing in somatosensory cortex. T. P. Pons and others. bibl f il *Science* 237:417-20 Jl 24 '87
The touchables. il *Mademoiselle* 93:164-7 O '87
Touching: why simple physical contact can heal, give you a lift. B. L. Stern. *Vogue* 177:384 Ap '87
Touch and go [film] See Motion picture reviews—Single works
Touch-tone dialing *See* Dual-tone multifrequency signalling
Touchscreen displays *See* Information display systems
Tougaloo College
J. Herman Blake, Tougaloo College president, resigns. por *Jet* 72:22 Ap 6 '87
Tough guys don't dance [film] See Motion picture reviews—Single works
Toulmin, Stephen Edelston
The conscientious spy. bibl f il *N Y Rev Books* 34:54-60 N 19 '87

Toulon (France)
History
Counter-revolution? Toulon, 1793. W. S. Cormack and M. Sydenham. bibl il *Hist Today* 37:49-55 O '87
Tour brochures *See* Travel literature
Tour de France (Race) *See* Bicycle racing—France
Tour of duty [television program] See Television program reviews—Single works
Tour of the universe (Space shuttle simulation) *See* Space flight simulators
Tourette syndrome
Fighting the enemy within [baseball player J. Eisenreich] R. Demak. il pors *Sports Illus* 66:40-3 Je 22 '87
Tics. O. W. Sacks. bibl il *N Y Rev Books* 34:37-41 Ja 29 '87
Tourette's sufferers can't help but say what's on their minds—even when it hurts; ed. by Giovanna Breu. S. Lubaroff. il pors *People Wkly* 27:95+ Mr 23 '87
When anxiety comes to bat [baseball player J. Eisenreich] J. Shear. il pors *N Y Times Mag* p72+ Mr 8 '87
Touring, Automobile *See* Automobile touring
Touring theater *See* Theater, Traveling
Tourism *See* Tourist trade
Tourist trade
See also
National Tourism Week
Resorts
Travel—Economic aspects
Travel agencies and agents
Consumer watch. See issues of Travel Holiday beginning July 1987
Getting your gripe heard [dealing with travel operators] B. Bauer. il *U S News World Rep* 103:105 N 9 '87
I love New York, L.A., Hawaii . . . [young Japanese tourists] B. Buell. il *Bus Week* p54 Mr 23 '87
Environmental aspects
Another country, another world [journalists discuss tourism, ecology, and development in Yugoslavia] P. C. Pritchard. *Natl Parks* 61:5 S/O '87
The four-percent solution [increase in national park visitors] P. C. Pritchard. *Natl Parks* 61:5 N/D '87
Ethical aspects
Anatomy of a travel scam. H. Gieseking. *Travel Holiday* 168:77-8 S '87
How to avoid being fare game. L. Laurence. il *Money* 16:183-4+ Ap '87
How to turn a dream vacation into a nightmare. il *Consum Rep* 52:269 My '87
Stopping travel scams. S. Shane. *Travel Holiday* 168:5 N '87
Too good to be true. R. Corelli. il *Macleans* 100:40 Ag 24 '87
Travel scams: a costly trip. D. Pauly. il *Newsweek* 109:48-9 Ap 27 '87
Travel scams: don't start packing yet. A. Fins and P. Engardio. il *Bus Week* p33 Jl 6 '87
An unbelievable vacation bargain? Hang up that phone! il *Money* 16:12 D '87
Watch out for these travel scams. H. Manley. il *Good Housekeep* 204:211 Je '87
International aspects
Travel briefs. W. G. Flanagan. il *Forbes* 139:101 Je 29 '87
Travel tomorrow [cover story] M. J. Cetron and W. Rocha. il pors *Futurist* 21:29-34 Jl/Ag '87
Study and teaching
Spotlight on schools. *Teen* 31:110 N '87
Arctic regions
Polar daredevils. M. Nichols. il *Macleans* 100:28 My 11 '87
British Columbia
A B.C. tourism gamble [refitting Victoria-Seattle ferries with gambling casinos] il *Macleans* 100:29 Ap 20 '87
California
The hyping of Napa Valley. P. Abramson and A. Miller. il *Newsweek* 110:51 Ag 10 '87
Canada
Canada calling. J. A. Conway. il *Forbes* 139:8 Ap 20 '87
China
Tipping takes a trip. il *Time* 130:32 Ag 3 '87
Italy
Agriturismo [vacationing on Italian farms] D. Morneau. il *Ctry J* 14:14-15 Ja '87
Japan
Do you have the yen to travel? H. Katayama. il *Forbes* 139:222+ My 18 '87
New Jersey
On the Jersey shore, business crumbles like a sand castle. E. T. Smith. il *Bus Week* p104 O 12 '87

Tourist trade—*cont.*

Nicaragua

A Sandinista holiday. M. McDonald. *Macleans* 100:6+ N 16 '87

Nova Scotia

See also

Charlesville (N.S.)—Tourist trade

Western Europe

Destination: Europe. J. Castro. il *Time* 129:42-3 Je 29 '87

Europe welcomes a peaceful invasion. M. Gray. il *Macleans* 100:40 Jl 27 '87

This summer, Paris should sizzle [American tourists] W. C. Symonds. il *Bus Week* p66 My 18 '87

The time has come for American travelers to return to Europe. M. Mercouri. il *USA Today (Periodical)* 115:70-3 My '87

"Welcomed at your convenience". B. Kallen. il *Forbes* 139:149+ My 4 '87

Tourmalines

Maine's tourmaline gems. il *Earth Sci* 40:14-16 Wint '87

Tournament of Roses *See* Pasadena (Calif.)—Parades

Tournaments

See also

Baseball—Tournaments

Baseball, Children's—Tournaments

Baseball, College—Tournaments

Basketball—Tournaments

Basketball, College—Tournaments

Bowling—Tournaments

Checkers (Game)—Tournaments

Crossword puzzles—Tournaments

Darts (Game)—Tournaments

Golf—Tournaments

Hockey—Tournaments

Hockey, College—Tournaments

Softball—Tournaments

Tennis—Tournaments

Volleyball, College—Tournaments

Tours, Art *See* Art tours

Tours, Garden *See* Garden tours

Tousignant, Claude

about

Claude Tousignant at 49th Parallel. W. Thompson. il *Art Am* 75:179-80 O '87

Toussaint, Eddy

about

Reviews:

Performances at Place des Arts. L. Howe-Beck. *Dance Mag* 61:35+ Ja '87

Symphonie du nouveau monde [ballet] Reviews *Dance Mag* 61:181-3 Je '87. L. Howe-Beck

Toussaint, Eugenio

about

Mexico's jazz master. M. Holston. por *Américas* 39:58-60 N/D '87

TOW (Tube-launched, optionally tracked, wire-guided) missiles *See* Guided missiles

Towboats *See* Tugboats

Towel racks, rings, etc.

Floor-to-ceiling towel rack. F. Stepney. il *Home Mech* 83:104 F '87

Towels

Dish-towel chic [towels made into clothing] il *Good Housekeep* 205:126-7 Jl '87

Terry-fied on the beach. A. Polakov. il *Harpers Bazaar* 120:20+ Jl '87

Wringing profits out of towels [B. Pope's innovative beach towels] M. S. Goodman and D. Harris. il por *Money* 16:164-6 F '87

Tower, Courtney

Mother Teresa's work of grace. il pors *Read Dig* 131:163-75+ D '87

Tower, Jeremiah

about

Restaurateur Jeremiah Tower cooks by the book—his own. L. Rozen. il pors *People Wkly* 27:95-6 Ap 13 '87

Tower, John

about

Placing truth above loyalty, John Tower delivers a tough verdict on Reagan's men. M. Wilhelm. il por *People Wkly* 27:38-9 Mr 9 '87

Tower cranes

Power lifters. D. Meyer. il *Pop Mech* 164:82-5+ N '87

Tower Records (Firm)

The Tower phenomenon. M. Kimmelman. il *U S News World Rep* 102:60 My 18 '87

Towers, Deirdre

Dancevideo. See issues of Dance Magazine beginning November 1984

Instructional video directory. il *Dance Mag* 61:44-50 Mr '87

Towers

See also

Eiffel Tower (Paris, France)

Observation towers

Pagodas

Radio towers

A tower in Tuscany [home of G. and B. von Rezzori] B. Chatwin. il *House Gard* 159:78-85+ Ja '87

Towers, Perrin, Forster & Crosby Inc.

A specialist slips into big-league consulting. J. A. Byrne. il por *Bus Week* p73+ Jl 27 '87

Towing

See also

Automobile trailers—Towing

Automobiles—Towing

Boats and boating—Towing

Tow it. J. Dunne. il *Pop Mech* 164:78-80 My '87

Towles, Dorothea

about

Model firsts: pioneers in black beauty. B. Summers. il pors *Essence* 17:38-42+ Ja '87

Town & Country Jewelry Mfg. Co.

The jewel in the town [stock price] T. Jaffe. il *Forbes* 140:246 O 5 '87

Town gates *See* City gates

Town life *See* City and town life

Town planning *See* City planning

Townecraft (Firm)

Townecraft sells the fear of frying [safety questions] il *Consum Rep* 52:474 Ag '87

Townhouse decoration *See* House decoration

Townhouses, Remodeled *See* Houses, Remodeled

Towns *See* Cities and towns

Towns, Restored *See* Villages, Restored

Townsend, Daniel S.

Fatherhood in frogdom. il *Nat Hist* 96:28-35 My '87

Townsend, Francis Everett, 1867-1960

about

Finding wealth on the wings of Mercury. E. Rochette. il *Antiques Collect Hobbies* 91:81-2 F '87

Townsend, Robert

about

Class clowns. A. White. il *Film Comment* 23:11-14 Mr/Ap '87

Hollywood shuffle [film] Reviews

Essence il 18:28 My '87. H. Als

Macleans 100:55 Je 1 '87. L. O'Toole

Mademoiselle 93:46-7+ Jl '87. R. Rosenbaum

N Y il 20:90-1 Ap 6 '87. D. Denby

New Repub 196:26 My 4 '87. S. Kauffmann

Time il 129:79 Ap 27 '87. R. Corliss

In Hollywood shuffle comic actor Robert Townsend wields his wit against movie industry racism. D. Donoloe. il pors *People Wkly* 27:61-2 My 18 '87

Robert Townsend. B. Allen. pors *Essence* 18:88-90+ S '87

Robert Townsend explains why he produced hit comedy film, 'Hollywood shuffle'. C. Waldron. il pors *Jet* 72:58-60 Je 1 '87

Robert Townsend: Hollywood 'shuffling' to the top. M. Marshall. il pors *Ebony* 42:54D Jl '87

Waking up rich and famous. il pors *Ebony* 42:36+ S '87

Townsend-Greenspan & Company

Forecasting's dim prognosis. S. Dentzer and R. Thomas. il por *Newsweek* 110:42 Jl 27 '87

Townsend pension plan

Finding wealth on the wings of Mercury [F. E. Townsend's 1933 request for dime contributions] E. Rochette. il *Antiques Collect Hobbies* 91:81-2 F '87

Townshend, Pete

about

Pete Townshend [interview] D. Fricke. il pors *Roll Stone* p179-80+ N 5-D 10 '87

Towson (Md.)

Historic houses, sites, etc.

See also

Hampton National Historic Site (Towson, Md.)

Toxic shock syndrome

Is "Thucydides syndrome" back? [toxic shock as complication of flu] C. Wallis. il *Time* 129:62 Mr 30 '87

New mean team: flu and toxic shock. *Sci News* 131:169 Mr 14 '87

Tampon absorbency, not material, increases TSS risk. *FDA Consum* 21:2 N '87

Toxic shock syndrome—*cont.*

Toxic shock: it's still with us, and the mystery lingers. il *Glamour* 85:202+ Jl '87

The toxic shock puzzle [tampon absorbency] D. Todd. il *Macleans* 100:8 S 21 '87

Toxic substances *See* Poisons and poisoning

Toxic trade waste disposal *See* Trade waste—Disposal

Toxic waste disposal *See* Hazardous substances—Disposal

Toxins and antitoxins

See also

Psoralens

Red tide

The bad seed [connection between neurotoxins in food and brain disease; research by Peter S. Spencer and others] K. Wright. *Sci Am* 257:44 O '87

Environmental hypothesis for brain diseases strengthened by new data [plant toxins] R. Lewin. il *Science* 237:483-4 Jl 31 '87

Frog defense: make snakes yawn [neurotoxins in skin of African clawed frogs; research by George T. Barthalmus and William J. Zielinski] S. Weisburd. *Sci News* 132:215 O 3 '87

Genetic ablation: targeted expression of a toxin gene causes microphthalmia in transgenic mice. M. L. Breitman and others. bibl f il *Science* 238:1563-5 D 11 '87

Guam amyotrophic lateral sclerosis-Parkinsonism-dementia linked to a plant excitant neurotoxin [cover story] P. S. Spencer and others. bibl f il map *Science* 237:517-22 Jl 31 '87

Lymphotoxin is an important T cell-derived growth factor for human B cells. J. H. Kehrl and others. bibl f il *Science* 238:1144-6 N 20 '87

Mapping the main immunogenic region and toxin-binding site of the nicotinic acetylcholine receptor. T. Barkas and others. bibl f il *Science* 235:77-80 Ja 2 '87

Moulds that can kill. R. V. Bhat. il *World Health* p20-2 Mr '87

Mutations in diphtheria toxin separate binding from entry and amplify immunotoxin selectivity. L. Greenfield and others. bibl f il *Science* 238:536-9 O 23 '87

New clue [effect of quinolinic acid on brain cells in Huntington's disease; work of Dennis Choi and others] *USA Today (Periodical)* 115:9 F '87

Plant at the root of neural disorders [research by Peter S. Spencer and others] *Sci News* 132:94 Ag 8 '87

Redesigning nature's poisons to create anti-tumor reagents [immunotoxins] E. S. Vitetta and others. bibl f il *Science* 238:1098-104 N 20 '87

Should we beware the gourmet grouper? [ciguatera] D. M. Schwartz. il *Int Wildl* 17:36-7 N/D '87

Toxoplasmosis

Animal rightists raid USDA lab [interruption of research at Animal Parasitology Institute] C. Holden. *Science* 237:1099 S 4 '87

Letting cats out of the lab: a cautionary tale [animal activists' interruption of toxoplasmosis research at the Animal Parasitology Institute] P. Gadsby. il *Discover* 8:22 N '87

Toy and game industry

See also

Blacks in the toy and game industry

Coleco Industries, Inc.

Determined Productions (Firm)

Harrison/Erickson (Firm)

Hasbro Inc.

International Black Toy Manufacturers Association

International Playthings, Inc.

IQ Foundation (Firm)

Kenner Parker Toys Inc.

Mattel Inc.

Ohio Art Company

Tonka Corp.

View-Master Ideal Group Inc.

Worlds of Wonder Inc.

Future toys. J. Maxwell. il *Omni* 10:60-2+ D '87

In Playland, Secrets 'R Us [technology used to make interactive toys] *Time* 129:52 F 9 '87

Acquisitions and mergers

Another toymaker may be in play [New World Pictures to go after Mattel] G. G. Marcial. *Bus Week* p108 S 21 '87

Can Monopoly find happiness in Spiderman's arms? [Kenner Parker Toys weighs bid from New World Pictures] K. H. Hammonds. il *Bus Week* p34 Ag 3 '87

High drama from the folks who brought you Godzilla '85 [New World's play for Kenner] R. Grover. il pors *Bus Week* p30 S 7 '87

Is Tonka toying with trouble? [acquisition of Kenner Parker toys] G. G. Marcial. *Bus Week* p165 O 12 '87

Advertising

Babe in Toyland [DIC Enterprises' cartoons tied into toy advertising] P. E. Bauer. il pors *Channels* 7:48-51 Jl/Ag '87

Lego wars: a Christmas tale [Ohio Art's Zaks vs. Lego construction toys] il *Newsweek* 110:40-1 D 28 '87

Look out, kids! The TV shoots back [interactive toys] A. Levine. il *U S News World Rep* 103:72 O 5 '87

Shooting the messenger [interactive toys and TV show Captain Power and the soldiers of the future] V. Ross. il *Macleans* 100:71 O 5 '87

TV's new toys send critics scrambling for their guns. J. Hall. il *People Wkly* 27:34-6+ Mr 23 '87

Zap, zap! You're dead, Lord Dread! [interactive toys] S. Koepp. il *Time* 129:52 F 9 '87

Marketing

Marketing [views of Hasbro vice president S. Schwartz] *New Yorker* 63:28-9 F 23 '87

Toymakers could wake up to coal-filled stockings. K. H. Hammonds. il *Bus Week* p131 O 12 '87

Video games make a Christmas comeback. il *Fortune* 116:8 D 7 '87

Securities

Picking toy stocks: it's not child's play. T. Segal. il *Bus Week* p148-9 Mr 16 '87

Denmark

See also

LEGO System AS

Germany

Early German tin toy autos 1900-1925. C. Dinelli and J. Dinelli. il *Antiques Collect Hobbies* 92:55-8+ O '87

Japan

See also

Nintendo Co. Ltd.

Toy boxes *See* Toy chests

Toy catalogs *See* Catalogs, Commercial

Toy chests

Very contemporary furniture for kids. J. Thom. il *Workbench* 43:46-50 N/D '87

Toy houses *See* Doll houses

Toy soldiers *See* Military miniatures

Toy stores

See also

Chad's Rainbow, Inc.

Child World, Inc.

F. A. O. Schwarz

Penny Whistle Toys (Firm)

Toys R Us Inc.

Waldenkids (Firm)

Toynbee, Polly

The rise and fall of Britain's neoliberals. il *Wash Mon* 19:22-8 N '87

Toynton, Norman, 1939-

about

Norman Toynton. D. Bonetti. il *Art News* 86:52+ Ja '87

Toyoda, Shoichiro

about

"Slow decision, quick action". J. Dreyfuss. il por *Fortune* 116:35 Ag 3 '87

Toyota (Automobile) *See* Automobiles, Foreign; Sports cars

Toyota Motor Corporation

It has 400 HP, costs $40,000—and comes from Toyota? [Turbo Supra race car] J. O. Hamilton. il *Bus Week* p39 Ap 27 '87

The NUMMI experience [joint venture between Toyota and General Motors] M. Keller. il *Mot Trend* 39:126-7 Mr '87

"Slow decision, quick action" [S. Toyoda] J. Dreyfuss. il por *Fortune* 116:35 Ag 3 '87

Toys

See also

Balloons, Toy

Dolls

Playgrounds, Home—Equipment

Scooters

Teddy bears

Toy and game industry

Yo-yos

The best new toys for brighter kids [Christmas presents] J. Oppenheim. il *Redbook* 170:30+ D '87

Child's wheelbarrow. R. E. Markarian. il *Workbench* 43:43-4 Mr/Ap '87

Etch a future [Etch A. Sketch] G. Slutsker. il por *Forbes* 139:72 Mr 23 '87

Far-out toy facts. il *Natl Geogr World* 148:16-17 D '87

Fun tractor. il *Home Mech* 83:30-1+ S '87

Toys—*cont.*

Good, clean fun? [safe, educational toys for Christmas] M. Teich. il *Health* 19:67-8+ D '87

High flyers [toys designed by Norman Marshall] K. Collier. il *Fam Handyman* 37:58-63 N '87

High-tech toys. B. Kantrowitz. il *Newsweek* 110:71+ N 2 '87

High-tech toys and simpler delights. A. Steacy. il *Macleans* 100:52-3 D 14 '87

Hot this year: yakety dolls and TV guns [Christmas toys] il *U S News World Rep* 103:66 N 30 '87

It walks, talks and falls asleep, and so animal lovers must ask—is it live or is it Robopet? [B. Gillard's robotic dogs] il *People Wkly* 28:97 D 7 '87

The joys of toys. C. Loomis and R. Butler. il *Parents* 62:193-8+ N '87

Kidcorder [Fisher-Price camcorder] W. J. Hawkins. il *Pop Sci* 231:59 Ag '87

Look out, kids! The TV shoots back [interactive toys] A. Levine. il *U S News World Rep* 103:72 O 5 '87

Mitey maze. il *Mother Earth News* 108:96+ N/D '87

Mother's moments: nonsexist toys? Forget it. D. Sobel. *Ladies Home J* 104:66+ D '87

Now even Lego is going high-tech [linkage with Logo to make programmable toys] P. Angiolillo and M. Bluestone. il *Bus Week* p40 Ag 17 '87

Shooting the messenger [interactive toys and TV show Captain Power and the soldiers of the future] V. Ross. il *Macleans* 100:71 O 5 '87

Starting with a clean slate, old masters of Etch A Sketch make marketable art in a new medium. M. Small. il *People Wkly* 27:93+ Ja 19 '87

Toymakers come to a disarming decision [realistic toy guns] il *Newsweek* 110:104 D 7 '87

TV's new toys send critics scrambling for their guns. J. Hall. il *People Wkly* 27:34-6+ Mr 23 '87

Wooden spoke wheels. H. Wicks. il *Home Mech* 83:12 Je '87

Working toys [wooden bulldozer, grader and flatbed truck] A. Rooze. il *Fam Handyman* 37:72-7+ Jl/Ag '87

You call these toys? [elaborate and expensive playthings] N. Gibbs. il *Time* 130:42-3 D 7 '87

Zap, zap! You're dead, Lord Dread! [interactive toys] S. Koepp. il *Time* 129:52 F 9 '87

Collectors and collecting

Antiques: toys in transit [toy vehicles] J. S. Wamsley. il *Archit Dig* 44:168-73 D '87

Children's tea sets. K. M. McClinton. il *Antiques Collect Hobbies* 92:18-21 Jl '87

Early German tin toy autos 1900-1925. C. Dinelli and J. Dinelli. il *Antiques Collect Hobbies* 92:55-8+ O '87

The everlasting appeal of American tin toys. M. Jailer. il *Antiques Collect Hobbies* 91:36-8+ Ja '87

Gail Haley never grew up. J. T. Black. il pors *South Living* 22:105 Jl '87

Miniature machinery business booms [farm toys] C. Finck. il *Success Farm* 85 no5:26N-26O Mr '87

Noah's ark: the history of a toy. A. Bahar. il *Antiques Collect Hobbies* 92:43-7 Ap '87

Peaceful toy soldiers [non-military figures by Britains Ltd.] P. Bordan. il *Antiques Collect Hobbies* 92:40-2 Jl '87

Schoenhut's wooden animals. C. P. Hutton. il *Antiques Collect Hobbies* 92:40-2+ Ag '87

Some said Mary Mace had bats in her belfry, until she proved who made the toys in the basement [Berkshire Museum discovery of painted wooden toys created by A. Calder] il por *People Wkly* 27:53 Ja 26 '87

Toy power [clockwork toys] M. Jailer. il *Antiques Collect Hobbies* 92:83-5 N '87

Toy trains and how they grew. M. Jailer. il *Antiques Collect Hobbies* 92:38-41 Mr '87

Exhibitions

Dolls and toys at home for Christmas. M. Jailer. il *Antiques Collect Hobbies* 92:34-8 D '87

For toymakers, business is a slimy game [American International Toy Fair] il *Newsweek* 109:52 F 23 '87

The "interactive" generation [American International Toy Fair] B. Cornfeld. il *Ms* 16:79-81 D '87

Toy Fair report: children's video seeks broader market. T. Spain. il *Publ Wkly* 231:92-4 Mr 6 '87

Toy treasures: more and more waiting for discovery. M. Jailer. il *Antiques Collect Hobbies* 91:38-41 F '87

Toying around [F. A. O. Schwarz buyers at the American International Toy Fair in New York] B. Kanner. il *N Y* 20:22+ Mr 9 '87

Photographs and photography

Toybot. K. McKinney. il *Omni* 9:52-7 Ja '87

Safety devices and measures

Toy safety starts at home. C. Loomis. il *Parents* 62:13 O '87

Therapeutic use

Chad's dad [D. Brandon uses toys to treat son's autism]; ed. by John Grossmann. D. Brandon. il *Health* 19:79-80 Ap '87

Toys, Miniature

Vintage toys and Golden Oak [work of B. Burkey] A. Bahar. il por *Antiques Collect Hobbies* 92:46-9 S '87

Toys and Soldiers Museum (Vicksburg, Miss.)

The tiny troops of Vicksburg. il por *South Living* 22:17-18 Ag '87

Toys R Us Inc.

Toys 'R' Us goes overseas—and finds that toys 'R' them, too. M. Maremont. il *Bus Week* p71-2 Ja 26 '87

TPA (Drug)

After the battle, tPA declared a winner. D. D. Edwards. *Sci News* 132:325 N 21 '87

Biotech's bid to build a better mouse [transferring human genes into mice to make human proteins] R. Rhein, Jr. il *Bus Week* p102 N 9 '87

Birth of a blockbuster: how Genentech delivered the goods [FDA approves TPA] J. O. Hamilton. il *Bus Week* p138-40+ N 30 '87

Drugs for heart attacks [FDA ruling] *FDA Consum* 21:7 S '87

An experimental wonder drug awaits approval. J. P. Shapiro. il *U S News World Rep* 103:68 S 21 '87

FDA puts new heart drug on hold. M. Sun. il *Science* 237:16-18 Jl 3 '87

Genentech takes a tumble [FDA's adverse ruling on TPA] D. Pauly. il *Newsweek* 109:48 Je 15 '87

Go-ahead for a wonder drug [FDA approval] il *Time* 130:68 N 23 '87

Help's arrived for heart-attack victims. S. Findlay. il *U S News World Rep* 103:109-11 D 28 '87-Ja 4 '88

Minimizing heart attack damage [research by Condon VanderArk] *USA Today (Periodical)* 115:4 F '87

A nasty shock for Genentech [FDA rejects TPA] J. O. Hamilton and R. Rhein, Jr. *Bus Week* p37 Je 15 '87

New data clinch heart drug approval. M. Sun. il *Science* 238:1031 N 20 '87

Picking up the pieces at Genentech [FDA denies marketing approval] G. Bylinsky. il *Fortune* 116:60-1 Jl 6 '87

Robert Swanson. J. O. Hamilton. il por *Bus Week* Sp Issue:242 Ap 17 '87

TPA and PDQ. D. E. Koshland, Jr. *Science* 237:341 Jl 24 '87

Will tPA force changes in cardiac care? D. D. Edwards. *Sci News* 132:376 D 12 '87

Patents

Companies vie over new heart drug [Genentech vs. Wellcome] M. Sun. il *Science* 237:120-2 Jl 10 '87

Genentech takes another hit [Britain rejects TPA patent] J. O. Hamilton and M. Maremont. *Bus Week* p75 Jl 20 '87

Ruling on heart drug may boost research [British court's ruling] M. Sun. il *Science* 237:244 Jl 17 '87

Traber, Wendy

about

A survivor's bout with cancer. M. Maran. il por *Sch Update* 119:4-5 Ap 20 '87

Trace elements

Contamination

Trace mineral supplement also had traces of lead [Nutramin Preferred Formula Trace Minerals] *FDA Consum* 21:32 Jl/Ag '87

Trace fossils

Dry run [trace fossils evidence for late Ordovician land animals in Pennsylvania; work of Gregory J. Retallack and Carolyn R. Feakes] *Sci Am* 256:64-5 My '87

Landing the earliest plants and animals [Pennsylvania] *Sci News* 131:41 Ja 17 '87

Microbial trace-fossil formation, biogenous, and abiotic weathering in the Antarctic cold desert. E. I. Friedmann and R. Weed. bibl f il *Science* 236:703-5 My 8 '87

Trace fossil evidence for late Ordovician animals on land [Pennsylvania] G. J. Retallack and C. R. Feakes. bibl f il *Science* 235:61-3 Ja 2 '87

Trace gases *See* Gases

Tracers, Radioactive *See* Radioactive tracers

The Tracey Ullman show [television program] *See* Television program reviews—Single works

Trachtenberg, Stephen Joel

Morality and education [address, January 27, 1987] *Vital Speeches Day* 53:333-5 Mr 15 '87

Trachtman, Michael G.

What you don't sign can still hurt you [excerpt from What every executive better know about the law] *Work Woman* 12:26+ Je '87

Track and field athletics

See also

Heptathlon

High jumping

Hurdle racing

Long jumping

Triple jumping

Africans return to form at track championships [World Championships in Rome] *Jet* 73:47 S 28 '87

Barred from track again, Gault settles on football. por *Jet* 72:48 Ap 20 '87

Blacks dominate for U.S. in track championships [World Championships in Rome] il *Jet* 73:46-7 S 28 '87

Bursting from the shadows [100-meter record holder B. Johnson] K. Moore. il pors *Sports Illus* 67:94-8+ N 30 '87

Carl Lewis runs record 200 after attending dad's funeral. il por *Jet* 72:50 Je 1 '87

Dash and crash on an Indy track [World Indoor Championships] K. Moore. il *Sports Illus* 66:22-4+ Mr 16 '87

A double with trouble [J. Joyner-Kersee wins long jump and 100 meter hurdles at the Pepsi Invitational] C. Neff. il por *Sports Illus* 66:69 My 25 '87

Flash out of the blocks [stellar sprint field at the Vitalis/ U.S. Olympic Invitational] C. Neff. il *Sports Illus* 66:56-7 F 23 '87

The gift of power [track star V. Brisco; cover story] M. Kort. pors *Women's Sports Fitness* 9:40-3 N '87

Joyner-Kersee's record leads U.S. Pan Am team. il por *Jet* 72:50+ Ag 31 '87

NBA star Dantley aids Hershey track program. *Jet* 72:48 Ag 3 '87

Number one at the gun [sprinter L. McRae] H. Hersch. il pors *Sports Illus* 66:64+ My 18 '87

On top of the worlds [World Track and Field Championships; cover story] K. Moore. il pors *Sports Illus* 67:18-23 S 14 '87

Pluck of the Irish [E. Coghlan wins Wanamaker Mile] C. Neff. il pors *Sports Illus* 66:158+ F 9 '87

Preparing a big move [B. Reynolds, Ohio State 400 meter man] K. Moore. il pors *Sports Illus* 67:36-8+ S 7 '87

Racing to the head of his class [high school quarter-miler W. Reed] F. Lidz. il pors *Sports Illus* 66:36-8 F 2 '87

The road to Rome [USA/Mobil Outdoor Track & Field Championships] K. Moore. il *Sports Illus* 67:20-1 Jl 6 '87

Soaring to unseen heights [TAC USA/Mobil Indoor Track & Field Championships] P. Putnam. il por *Sports Illus* 66:24-5 Mr 9 '87

Sprinting to find your stride and joy. C. Pesmen. il *Sport Mag* 78:75+ Ja '87

Track's longest-running win streak [South African middle distance runner J. Fourie banned from international competition] il por *Sports Illus* 67:16 Jl 27 '87

Watch the world's best in Rome [preview of women's events in the World Championships] D. Reinke. il *Women's Sports Fitness* 9:58 Ag '87

Worldclass mom [runner M. Slaney; cover story] L. Kramer. il pors *Women's Sports Fitness* 9:28-31 Ap '87

Accidents and injuries

Back on top? [M. Slaney] il por *Vogue* 177:132 O '87

Economic aspects

A bad deal for track: it's time for the top runners to start racing one another. K. Moore. il por *Sports Illus* 67:70 Jl 20 '87

Ethical aspects

Head winds and scandals. H. Quinn. *Macleans* 100:39 Ag 31 '87

Psychological aspects

A life on the run [distance runner G. Lindgren] K. Moore. il pors *Sports Illus* 66:76-80+ My 18 '87

Track and field athletics records

See also

High jumping records

Long jumping records

Triple jumping records

Bravos for a Roman candle [B. Johnson breaks 100 meter record in the World Championships] K. Moore. il por *Sports Illus* 67:18-21 S 7 '87

Chasing '68. T. Kertes. il *Sport Mag* 78:61-3 S '87

Giants on the earth [B. Beamon's long jump record and L. Evans' 400 meters record, set at 1968 Olympics, still stand] K. Moore. il pors *Sports Illus* 66:48-50+ Je 29 '87

Head winds and scandals [B. Johnson] H. Quinn. *Macleans* 100:39 Ag 31 '87

It was the best of times [B. Johnson sets 100m record] H. Quinn. il por *Macleans* 100:46 S 14 '87

When is a record not a record? [running events] S. Stuller. il *Women's Sports Fitness* 9:92-3 Mr '87

Track and field coaches

See also

Blunt, Russell

Rudolph, Wilma

Track lighting fixtures *See* Lighting fixtures

Tracked vehicles

See also

Bulldozers (Machines)

Tanks, Military

Tractors

Tracking (Education) *See* Ability grouping in education

Tracking and trailing

See also

Animal tracks and trails

Biotelemetry

Home on the range [habits of whitetail deer] H. Buck. il *Field Stream* 92:58-9+ N '87

Tracks International Inc.

The gay market has put this CPA on the fast Track [N. J. Feinstein] P. Finch. il por *Bus Week* p58 Ap 27 '87

Tracon (Terminal radar approach control) *See* Radar in aviation

Traction (Automobiles) *See* Automobiles—Traction

Traction (Motor vehicles) *See* Motor vehicles—Traction

Tractor factories

Soviet Union

A tractor factory tries to pull its own weight [A. A. Zhadanov Vladimir Tractor Works] P. Galuszka. il *Bus Week* p79 D 7 '87

Tractor industry

See also

Caterpillar Inc.

Tractor factories

Tractor pulling

Pull right up, please. N. Mayersohn. il *Pop Mech* 164:44 Jl '87

Tractors

Can a Magnum gun down a Deere? D. Mowitz and C. Finck. il *Success Farm* 85:6 N '87

Rubber tracks dig into farm market [Caterpillar tractor] il *Success Farm* 85 no3:18A F '87

Equipment

$250 and old tractor makes floater [flotation sprayer] C. Finck. il *Success Farm* 85 no1:26Q Ja '87

Taking care of business at both ends [front-mount equipment] C. Finck and D. Mowitz. il *Success Farm* 85:14-17 Ap '87

Throw water weight around with caddies. D. Mowitz. il *Success Farm* 85:18T-18U Ap '87

Four wheel drive

Techno-tractors [Honda RT5000 and Kubota PX-2100] J. Schefter. il *Pop Sci* 230:87-8 Je '87

Maintenance and repair

Care for your investment [lawn tractors] H. Wicks. il *Home Mech* 83:52 Mr '87

Testing

F&G's annual tractor round-up. il *Flower Gard* 31:56-7+ F/Mr '87

Lawn tractors: we test the best. M. Ferrara. il *Home Mech* 83:44-8+ Mr '87

Multi-task tiller/tractor. E. F. Lindsley. il *Pop Sci* 230:80 My '87

New-breed garden tractor [SunStar] T. O. Bakke. il *Pop Sci* 231:105 S '87

Performance! D. Mowitz and C. Finck. il *Success Farm* 85 no3:9-15 F '87

Tractors for all reasons [garden tractors] S. Willson. il *Pop Mech* 164:74-8+ S '87

What'll it be . . . riding mower or garden tractor? [Gravely model 8179-G] A. C. Sinnes. il *Flower Gard* 31:48-51 F/Mr '87

Tractors, Toy *See* Toys

Tracy, Robert

Metaphors for the world. il por *Archit Dig* 44:72+ O '87

Trade *See* Commerce

Trade, Balance of *See* Balance of trade

Trade and Development Conference (United Nations) *See* United Nations Conference on Trade and Development

Trade and professional associations
Your professional organization [address, August 10, 1987]
J. Saddoris. *Vital Speeches Day* 53:767-8 O 1 '87
Trade conferences *See* Economic conferences
Trade deficits *See* Balance of trade
Trade marks and trade names
See also
Corporations—Names
Wine—Names
Amelia Batchler: for 51 years she's carried the torch
for Columbia [model for motion picture logo] A.
Batchler. il por *People Wkly* 27:48-9 F 9 '87
Ceasing and desisting [Winter Olympics trademark protec-
tion effort in Canada] H. Quinn. il *Macleans* 100:61
D 7 '87
Is it real? Counterfeit goods are a big business—how
to avoid getting ripped off. il *Glamour* 85:210 My
'87
Nipper and his friends [phonograph label trademarks;
cover story] J. L. Poole. il *Opera News* 52:8-12 Ag
'87
OCO's symbolic victory [Olympic lapel pin distributor
B. Hipson taken to court over trademark rights in
Calgary] H. Quinn. il por *Macleans* 100:40 Je 8 '87
The prisoner of Seventh Avenue: how Halston lost the
right to his own name. L. Belkin. il pors *N Y Times
Mag* p16-22+ Mr 15 '87
Rambo & Rambo, attorneys-at-law [lawyers acting as
prosecutors in trademark counterfeit cases] D. Fanning.
Forbes 139:76 Ja 26 '87
Revlon must change package similar to Soft Sheen's.
Jet 73:18 O 19 '87
Soda war [American National Beverage fights trademark
dispute with Anheuser-Busch] R. L. Stern. il *Forbes*
139:82-3 My 4 '87
SoHo skirmish [American Natural Beverage wins
trademark dispute with Anheuser-Busch] J. A. Conway.
il *Forbes* 139:8 Je 29 '87
Thomas Dolby settles suit over name. M. Coleman.
Roll Stone p10 My 7 '87
What really is in a name? J. Schwartz. il *Newsweek*
110:55 N 30 '87
Trade names *See* Trade marks and trade names
Trade publishing *See* Publishers and publishing
Trade routes
China
Riding the Silk Road in China [cover story] G. Woodcock.
il *New Leader* 70:10-15 S 21 '87
East Africa
The Swahili corridor. M. Horton. il maps *Sci Am*
257:86-8+ S '87
Sudan
North to Cairo along the scorching Way of the Forty
[camel drive from Sudan to Egypt] L. Werner. il map
Smithsonian 17:120-4+ Mr '87
Trade secrets
In Playland, Secrets 'R Us [technology used to make
interactive toys] *Time* 129:52 F 9 '87
The Rabbit punch [R. Wright charges Rabbit Systems
and MarketCorp Venture Associates with misappropria-
tion of trade secrets] K. Healy. il por *Forbes* 140:175-6
S 21 '87
Trade union leaders *See* Trade unions—Officials
Trade unions
See also
AFL-CIO
Boycott
Collective bargaining
Collective labor agreements
Communications Workers of America
Industrial relations
International Brotherhood of Teamsters, Chauffeurs,
Warehousemen and Helpers of America
International Longshoremen's and Warehousemen's
Union
Laborers' International Union of North America
Picketing
Strikes
United Automobile, Aerospace and Agricultural
Implement Workers of America
United Food and Commercial Workers International
Union
The best & the worst of American unions [cover story]
S. Waldman. il *Wash Mon* 19:28-32+ Jl/Ag '87
Comparing Canadian and American unions. S. M. Lipset.
bibl *Society* 24:60-70 Ja/F '87
Labor month in review. See issues of Monthly Labor
Review
Mega mergers [address, September 7, 1987] R. H. Guest.
Vital Speeches Day 54:20-2 O 15 '87

Merger phobia has unions wheeling and dealing. Z.
Schiller. il *Bus Week* p118+ Mr 23 '87
The recent decline of unionization in the United States.
H. S. Farber. bibl f il *Science* 238:915-20 N 13 '87
Actors and actresses
See also
Actors' Equity Association
Air pilots
See also
Air Line Pilots Association
Air traffic controllers (Persons)
See also
National Air Traffic Controllers Association
Air-traffic controllers: getting organized again? S. B.
Garland. il *Bus Week* p52 My 18 '87
Airline employees
See also
Association of Flight Attendants International
Independent Federation of Flight Attendants
International Association of Machinists and
Aerospace Workers
Pan Am union coalition attempts buyout. *Aviat Week
Space Technol* 127:32 Jl 27 '87
Anecdotes, facetiae, satire, etc.
Bottom-line days. R. Baker. il *N Y Times Mag* p14
S 6 '87
Authors
See also
Writers Guild of America
Automobile industry workers
Canada
See also
National Automobile, Aerospace and Agricultural
Implement Workers Union of Canada
Benefit funds
Protecting workers in the marketplace: new union benefit
privileges. R. Denison. *Mon Labor Rev* 110:39-40 Ag
'87
Blacks
The black labor movement and the fight for social
advance. W. H. Harris. *Mon Labor Rev* 110:37-8 Ag
'87
Black serves as marshall of N.Y. Labor Day Parade
[P. J. Ottley] *Jet* 72:55 S 21 '87
Forging a partnership between blacks and unions. N.
Hill. *Mon Labor Rev* 110:38-9 Ag '87
Brewery workers
A long-brewing boycott ends at Coors [AFL-CIO wins
right to try to organize workers] *Newsweek* 110:46
Ag 31 '87
Will labor's Joe Sixpack come back to Coors? [union
boycott ends as AFL-CIO wins right to organize] S.
D. Atchison. il *Bus Week* p29 S 7 '87
Corporate campaigns
"Publish and be damned" [interview with C. R. Perry]
J. Novack. por *Forbes* 140:380+ Jl 13 '87
Elections
A setback for labor [Michelin workers in Nova Scotia
vote against joining the Canadian Auto Workers union]
D. Jones. il *Macleans* 100:14 Ja 26 '87
Electronics workers
High-tech workers: do unions have a future? S. Early
and R. Wilson. *Current* 292:24-31 My '87
Employees
Retirement
A retirement offer they couldn't refuse [United Steelwor-
kers employees] il *Newsweek* 109:44 Je 22 '87
Farm labor
See also
United Farm Workers of America
Financial services
Perks for the rank and file. B. Cohn. *Newsweek* 109:42
Ap 6 '87
Fish industry workers
See also
United Seafood Workers, Smoked Fish and Cannery
Union
Fishermen
Canada
Unions fighting unions [R. Cashin switches Newfoundland
fishermen's union affiliation from United Food and
Commercial Workers to Canadian Auto Workers] D.
Jenish. il *Macleans* 100:41-2 Ap 27 '87
History
A century of struggle [cover story; special section] bibl
f il *Mon Labor Rev* 110:32-40 Ag '87
Hotel workers
See also
Hotel Employees and Restaurant Employees Inter-
national Union

Trade unions—*cont.*

International aspects

See also

International Labour Organisation

Journalism

See Journalism, Labor

Membership

See also

Trade unions—Blacks

Trade unions—Women

How union members and nonmembers view the role of unions. C. Keegan. *Mon Labor Rev* 110:50-1 Ag '87

New data on workers belonging to unions, 1986. *Mon Labor Rev* 110:36 My '87

Membership drives

See also

Trade unions—Corporate campaigns

High-tech workers: do unions have a future? S. Early and R. Wilson. *Current* 292:24-31 My '87

Life at Nissan: paradise lost? [UAW's new drive to unionize Smyrna, Tenn. plant] B. Turque and J. B. Copeland. il *Newsweek* 110:50 Ag 10 '87

A long-brewing boycott ends at Coors [AFL-CIO wins right to try to organize workers] *Newsweek* 110:46 Ag 31 '87

A novel union role: picketing for the boss [Ohio supermarkets enlist workers in push against nonunion rivals] S. Phillips. il *Bus Week* p80 D 28 '87-Ja 4 '88

Perks for the rank and file. B. Cohn. *Newsweek* 109:42 Ap 6 '87

Will labor's Joe Sixpack come back to Coors? [union boycott ends as AFL-CIO wins right to organize] S. D. Atchison. il *Bus Week* p29 S 7 '87

Metal workers

Germany (West)

Weakened labor is still talking tough. J. E. Pluenneke and F. Thelen. *Bus Week* p60 Ja 12 '87

Miners

See also

United Mine Workers of America

South Africa

See also

National Union of Mineworkers (South Africa)

Motion picture industry employees

Make money, not war. A. Gibney and A. Thompson. il *Film Comment* 23:17-18+ N/D '87

Union shopping. A. B. Block. il *Forbes* 139:106+ Je 15 '87

Officials

Blue collars in the boardroom: putting business first. J. Hoerr. il *Bus Week* p126+ D 14 '87

Salaries, pensions, etc.

How much top labor leaders made in 1986. J. Tasini. il *Bus Week* p96 My 4 '87

Organizing activities

See Trade unions—Membership drives

Organizing drives

Labor-saving devices [cover story] D. Kusnet. il *Commonweal* 114:526-9 S 25 '87

Political activities

See also

Trade unions and communism

For labor: a newer deal. *Nation* 245:181 S 5 '87

Labor & Nicaragua [urging condemnation of aid to the contras] *Nation* 245:472-3 O 31 '87

Labor's best candidate may be no candidate at all. R. Fly and S. B. Garland. il *Bus Week* p59 My 11 '87

Politics: a change of Hart [G. Hart courts union support] C. O'Connor. il por *Newsweek* 109:27 F 23 '87

Postal employees

Canada

See also

Canadian Union of Postal Workers

Restaurant employees

See also

Hotel Employees and Restaurant Employees International Union

Retail workers

See also

Retail, Wholesale and Department Store Union

Service industries

Technological change and unionization in the service sector. C. B. Costello. bibl f *Mon Labor Rev* 110:45-6 Ag '87

Servicemen

Great Britain—History

Troops & trade unions, 1919. D. Englander. il *Hist Today* 37:8-13 Mr '87

Steel workers

See also

United Steelworkers of America

Teachers

See also

National Education Association of the United States

Teaching reform in an active voice. S. M. Johnson and N. C. W. Nelson. bibl f il *Phi Delta Kappan* 68:591-8 Ap '87

Canada

See also

British Columbia Teachers' Federation

Television workers

See also

National Association of Broadcast Employees and Technicians

Theater

See also

Actors' Equity Association

United Scenic Artists

Women

Williams 1st woman on UAW Local 249 exec. bd. [B. Williams] *Jet* 72:30 Ag 24 '87

Canada

See also

Confédération des Syndicats Nationaux

Comparing Canadian and American unions. S. M. Lipset. bibl *Society* 24:60-70 Ja/F '87

Labor's fight to survive [cover story; special section; with editorial comment by Kevin Doyle] il *Macleans* 100:2, 28-35 Jl 13 '87

Some lessons for American labor. M. Lynk. il *Nation* 245:374-6 O 10 '87

El Salvador

AFL-CIO is Spanish for union busting [U.S. efforts to destroy independent labor movement] F. Smyth. *Wash Mon* 19:24-7 S '87

Duarte's secret friends [U.S. efforts to divide and destroy new independent labor movement] F. Smyth. il *Nation* 244:316-18 Mr 14 '87

'If Americans knew . . .' [visit to U.S. by representatives of El Salvador's independent labor unions] K. E. Bean. il *Progressive* 51:24 Ag '87

Germany (West)

Unexpected ally for the dollar? [labor leader E. Breit] L. Minard. por *Forbes* 139:158+ Mr 23 '87

Great Britain

British trade union blues. N. Gelb. il *New Leader* 70:6-7 O 5 '87

History—Historiography

The Webbs: working on trade union history. C. Wrigley. bibl il pors *Hist Today* 37:51-5 My '87

Guatemala

Which side are they on? The AFL-CIO tames Guatemala's unions. J. Slaughter. il *Progressive* 51:32-5 Ja 87

Japan

How are Japanese unions responding to microelectronics-based automation? W. E. Klay. bibl f *Mon Labor Rev* 110:39-40 Mr '87

Korea (South)

What kind of Korea will the new labor movement build? L. Nakarmi. il *Bus Week* p56-7 O 12 '87

Latin America

See also

American Institute for Free Labor Development

Mexico

See also

Mexican Workers Confederation

The dilemma of Mexican labor. J. Bortz. *Curr Hist* 86:105-8+ Mr '87

Middle East

Force for change in the West Bank [Palestinian labor movement] J. R. Hiltermann. il *Nation* 245:338-40 O 3 '87

Poland

See also

Solidarity (Trade union)

South Africa

See also

Congress of South African Trade Unions

United States

See Trade unions

Trade unions and communism

History

Troops & trade unions, 1919 [Great Britain] D. Englander. il *Hist Today* 37:8-13 Mr '87

Trade unions and the church *See* Church and labor

Trade unions and the family

Archie Bunker, roll over. J. Rosenberg. *Commonweal* 114:470-2 S 11 '87

Trade waste
Disposal
See also

American Toxxic Control (Firm)
Citizen's Clearinghouse for Hazardous Wastes, Inc.
Love Canal case
Waste disposal in the ocean
Waste Management, Inc.

Biology's answer to toxic dumps [microbes] J. J. Holbrook. *Sierra* 72:24-5+ Ja/F '87
Black areas often used for toxic waste dumps. *Jet* 72:36 My 11 '87
Chemical cleanup [EPA cleanup at closed facilities of Arkansas Chemical Co. in Newark, N.J.] B. Weber. il *N Y Times Mag* p42 D 27 '87
Cleaning up. B. Leonard. il *Forbes* 139:52-3 Je 1 '87
Cleaning up after industry's slobs. E. Pomice. il *Forbes* 139:90 Ap 20 '87
Discovering microbes with a taste for PCBs. L. Roberts. il *Science* 237:975-7 Ag 28 '87
Hazardous waste: prevention vs. cure [Office of Technology Assessment report] *Futurist* 21:47 Mr/Ap '87
Toxic wastes? A little fungus may help. S. Budiansky. il *U S News World Rep* 103:85 N 9 '87
Waste dump wanted [desirability of low level dumps in Calif.] il *Time* 130:70 Jl 20 '87
Waste reduction: a new strategy to avoid pollution. K. U. Oldenburg and J. S. Hirschhorn. bibl f il *Environment* 29:16-20+ Mr '87
Insurance
See Insurance, Pollution liability
Laws and regulations
Environmental crime: putting offenders behind bars. D. Wann. bibl f il *Environment* 29:5+ O '87
Hazardous waste: where to put it? M. Crawford. il *Science* 235:156-7 Ja 9 '87
The new debate over Superfund: how clean is clean enough? T. Smart. il *Bus Week* p34 Jl 13 '87
The toxic waste battle is boiling over [Westinghouse's court fight with insurers] M. Schroeder. il *Bus Week* p73-4 Ag 3 '87
The unrealized potential of SARA: mobilizing new protection for natural resources [superfund; with editorial comment by Alan McGowan] T. Atkeson and R. C. Dower. bibl f *Environment* 29:2, 6-8+ My '87
Taxation
From those wonderful folks who brought you the new W-4 . . . G. W. Padwe. il *Nations Bus* 75:54-5 Ap '87
Western Europe
See also

Rhine River chemical spills, 1986
Trademarks *See* Trade marks and trade names
Trader Vic's (Los Angeles, Calif.: Restaurant) *See* Los Angeles (Calif.)—Restaurants, nightclubs, bars, etc.
Trades *See* Occupations
Trading *See* Barter
Trading cards
See also

Baseball cards
Trading companies
See also

Siamese Imports, Inc.

Most U.S. companies are innocents abroad. il *Bus Week* p168-9 N 16 '87
Sell abroad; you can collect [use of factoring agents] S. Golob. il *Nations Bus* 75:44+ N '87
U.S. exporters need first-rate global banking networks. H. R. Heller. il *Bus Week* p20 Je 8 '87
Germany (West)
The mark puts a stranglehold on exporters. F. A. Miller. il *Bus Week* p60 F 23 '87
Hong Kong
See also

Jardine Matheson & Co., Ltd.
Japan
See also

Mitsui & Co., Ltd
Western Europe
Taking the sting out of the plunging dollar [European companies exporting from U.S. subsidiaries] B. Riemer and F. J. Comes. il *Bus Week* p72-3 D 7 '87
Tradition
The idea of tradition in American art criticism [R. Cortissoz and C. Greenberg] H. Kramer. *Am Sch* 56:319-27 Summ '87
The importance of family ties. J. Brothers. il pors *Good Housekeep* 205:96+ S '87
Rejoicing in rituals. S. Kanfer. il *Read Dig* 131:131-2 O '87

Tradition [address, September 10, 1986] J. Ledbetter. *Vital Speeches Day* 53:189-90+ Ja 1 '87
Traffic *See* City traffic
Traffic, Air freight service *See* Air freight service—Traffic
Traffic, Airline *See* Airlines—Traffic
Traffic accidents
See also

Alcohol and automobile drivers
Cycling—Accidents and injuries
"An accident destroyed my face" [case of L. N. Farmer] A. Fischer. il pors *Redbook* 169:36+ O '87
Accident victim's son, 2, awarded nearly $1.7 million [son of traffic accident victim H. Fisher] pors *Jet* 72:36 Ag 17 '87
Ben Vereen's daughter killed in car accident. il pors *Jet* 73:28 D 21 '87
Car phone users: we've got your number. D. C. Ross. il *Mot Trend* 39:158 Je '87
"Drivin' my life away" [epidemiology of fatal motor vehicle crashes] maps *Sci Am* 257:28+ Ag '87
Forensic physics of vehicle accidents [cover story] A. C. Damask. bibl f il *Phys Today* 40:36-44 Mr '87
In a crash, bigger is better [report by the Highway Loss Data Institute] il *U S News World Rep* 103:106 S 28 '87
Now, the 'seat belt defense' [Michigan case] *Newsweek* 109:69 F 16 '87
Rebuilt and running, but not by the book [repairing Honda CBR600 Hurricane] M. Lindemann. il *Cycle* 38:54-6+ N '87
A roar of tearing metal [car accident while driving and tending child in back seat] S. M. Flanagan. *Read Dig* 130:145 Ja '87
The safest cars, the least costly cars [report by the Highway Loss Data Institute] il *Consum Res Mag* 70:14-17 N '87
The scandal of killer trucks. K. Labich. il *Fortune* 115:85-7 Mr 30 '87
Totalled or not: no easy answer [totalling vs. repairing Honda 600 Hurricane] T. Carrithers. il *Cycle* 38:47-9 N '87
Trucking safety on the rise. il *Consum Res Mag* 70:32 My '87
Turning highway rights into wrongs [young drivers injured in accidents] D. Hochberg. por *U S News World Rep* 103:6 N 30 '87
We got our son back for Christmas [automobile accident victim E. Erwig] J. L. Block. il por *Good Housekeep* 205:111-13 D '87
What to do if your car hits deep water. D. McCluggage. *Glamour* 85:144+ Je '87
When an accident is unavoidable. D. Chaikin. il *Home Mech* 83:32 F '87
Rescue work
See Rescue work
Bermuda
Love and hate on one leg [leg fractured in traffic accident] K. Bonnell. il por *Glamour* 85:73-4 O '87
Canada
Of tragedy and triumph [4 players on Swift Current Bronco hockey team killed in bus accident] R. Corelli. il *Macleans* 100:48-50+ Mr 30 '87
One very close call [crash on icy road in Audi 5000] C. Csere. *Car Driv* 33:71 Jl '87
Northern Ireland
Matthew Broderick ends a holiday in a tragic crash that claims two lives. il por *People Wkly* 28:53 Ag 24 '87
Matthew Broderick leaves behind the grieving Irish town that charges him with two lost lives. A. Richman. il por *People Wkly* 28:92-4 S 28 '87
Traffic accidents in art
Exhibitions
On the road [A. Paulson's Highway to heaven sculpture on Route 15, Pa.] S. Staggs. il por *Art News* 86:15-16 O '87
Traffic alert and collision avoidance systems *See* Airplanes—Collision avoidance systems
Traffic circles
Traffic circle sanity . . . D. Chaikin. il *Home Mech* 83:21 Je '87
Traffic congestion
Gunfire in traffic [shooting on Los Angeles freeways] A. Steacy. il *Macleans* 100:41 Ag 17 '87
Gunplay on the freeway [shootings in Los Angeles] M. Kaus. il *Newsweek* 110:18 Ag 10 '87
Highway to homicide [freeway shootings in Los Angeles area] F. Trippett. il *Time* 130:18 Ag 17 '87
How to handle on-the-road hostility. D. McCluggage. il *Glamour* 85:120+ N '87

Traffic congestion—*cont.*

Jam sessions [cover story; special section] C. P. Work. il *U S News World Rep* 103:20-6 S 7 '87

Mayhem on the freeways [drivers' responses to congestion] A. Lobue. por *U S News World Rep* 103:9 S 28 '87

Rambo's brothers cruise clogged expressways [Los Angeles freeway shootings] T. Gest. il *U S News World Rep* 103:6 Ag 10 '87

Trapped behind the wheel. M. Smilgis. il *Time* 130:64-5 Jl 20 '87

Traffic control, Airway *See* Air traffic control
Traffic control, Radar *See* Radar in traffic control
Traffic engineering

See also
Radar in traffic control

Traffic in arms *See* Munitions—Export-import trade
Traffic jams *See* Traffic congestion
Traffic regulations

See also
Traffic tickets

65 mph: America steps on the gas [Congress votes to change rural speed limit] il *U S News World Rep* 102:12 Mr 30 '87

65 mph: the time has come. S. Symms. *Car Driv* 32:27 My '87

65—its for real! [speed limit] T. Orme. il *Mot Trend* 39:44 Jl '87

Contrived concrete evidence! [55-mph speed limit] J. Dinkel. *Road Track* 39:40 O '87

Fast talk [CNN debate with Rep. J. Howard on 55-mph speed limit] R. Ceppos. il *Car Driv* 33:26-7 Jl '87

Speed-limit tutelage: is 65 enough? *Natl Rev* 39:18 Je 19 '87

Step on it [Congress votes to increase the speed limit on rural interstate highways] *Time* 129:26 Mr 30 '87

War stories [encounters with traffic police over 55mph speed limit] P. Bedard. il *Car Driv* 33:164 Jl '87

Wooden nickels [repeal of 55 mph speed limit] R. Ceppos. il *Car Driv* 32:22 Ap '87

Anecdotes, facetiae, satire, etc.

Ten best cop stories. D. Coulter. il *Car Driv* 32:85-7 Ja '87

California
Anecdotes, facetiae, satire, etc.

Mail your junkers [Cycle staff's speeding tickets] P. Schilling. il *Cycle* 38:13 Je '87

Canada

A bright idea? [laws in Canada and Sweden requiring driving with headlights on] J. Dinkel. *Road Track* 38:34-6 Ja '87

Sweden

A bright idea? [laws in Canada and Sweden requiring driving with headlights on] J. Dinkel. *Road Track* 38:34-6 Ja '87

Texas

"We're not cops" [using police radar to record actual driving speeds] G. Baxter. il *Car Driv* 33:20 S '87

"You can't do this to me . . ." [weak drunk driving laws] G. Baxter. il *Car Driv* 33:28 D '87

Traffic safety

See also
Automobile driving
Cycling
Motorcycling
Roads—Guard fences
United States. National Highway Traffic Safety Administration

Laws and regulations
See Traffic regulations

Traffic tickets

A Chicago sting: CEO scofflaws, beware [company cars ticketed] *Newsweek* 109:52 F 9 '87

How to beat a speeding ticket [videotape] il *Cycle* 38:56 Ap '87

Anecdotes, facetiae, satire, etc.

Mail your junkers [Cycle staff's speeding tickets] P. Schilling. il *Cycle* 38:13 Je '87

Traffic violations

See also
Traffic tickets

When everyone else is speeding . . . D. Chaikin. il *Home Mech* 83:22 S '87

La tragicomedia de Calisto y Melibea [drama] *See* Rojas, Fernando de, d. 1541

Trahey, Meg, and McCormick, Frank

A cytoplasmic protein stimulates normal N-*ras* p21 GTPase, but does not affect oncogenic mutants. bibl f il *Science* 238:542-5 O 23 '87

Trailers

See also
Automobile boat trailers
Automobile trailers

Go-go grain carts. D. Mowitz. il *Success Farm* 85:62N O '87

Trailers, Motion picture *See* Motion picture industry—Advertising
Trailing spouse problem *See* Executives—Relocation
Trails

See also
Rails-to-Trails Conservancy
WalkWays Center (Organization)

Atlantic States
See also
Appalachian Trail

California

Biking and birding around southern San Francisco Bay. il *Sunset* 178:10-11 Ja '87

Scrambling trail over Marin headlands. il *Sunset* 178:74 Ap '87

Kauai (Hawaii)

Paradise beyond road's end [Kalalau Trail] M. Freeman. il *Sierra* 72:64-7 S/O '87

Lake Tahoe region (Calif. and Nev.)

The master trailbuilder of Lake Tahoe [work of B. Tisher] J. P. Jeffries. il por map *Sierra* 72:79-82 Jl/Ag '87

Missouri

From old rails to new trails [Missouri River Trail] R. R. Pryor. il *Sierra* 72:77-8 S/O '87

Oregon

See also
New Oregon Trail (Or.)

Texas

Stars mark the way in San Antonio [Texas Star Trail] il *South Living* 22:18 F '87

Utah

See also
Burr Trail (Utah)

Trailways Inc.

All aboard [Greyhound to buy Trailways] il *Time* 129:46 Je 29 '87

Leave the driving to Fred Currey [plan for fusing Greyhound and Trailways] J. Weber, Jr. il por *Bus Week* p62-3 Ag 24 '87

Unhappy Trails [Greyhound to acquire Trailways] *Newsweek* 109:49 Je 29 '87

Train, Arthur

A salmon for the White House [story] il *Saturday Evening Post* 259:64-8+ My/Je '87

A salmon for the White House [story] il *Saturday Evening Post* 259:36+ Jl/Ag '87

Train travel *See* Railroad travel
Trainer, Jennifer

(jt. auth) *See* Kaku, Michio, and Trainer, Jennifer

Training, Occupational *See* Vocational-technical education
Training airplanes *See* Airplanes, Training
Training camps, Military *See* Military training camps
Training devices *See* Simulators
Training films, Corporate *See* Motion pictures in industry
Training of children *See* Children—Management and training
Training of dogs *See* Dogs—Training
Training of fruit trees *See* Fruit trees—Training
Trains (Magnetic) *See* Magnetic levitation vehicles
Trains (Toy) *See* Toys
Trajectories

Aiming for Neptune [Voyager's trajectory] C. E. Kohlhase. il *Astronomy* 15:6-15 N '87

Tranaeus, Jarl

The poorest had most to gain. il *World Health* p14-15 Ag/S '87

Tranquilizing drugs

See also
Buspirone
Clozapine
Phenobarbital

Awake at the wheel [nonsedating drugs] F. Lunzer. *Forbes* 139:102 Je 29 '87

Don't mess with magic pills, darling: they're bad medicine. M. Sandmaier. il *Mademoiselle* 93:128-9+ Jl '87

Lag time [participation in study testing effectiveness of triazolam in treating jet lag] K. Lautman. il *Omni* 9:16 Ja '87

Seizures in drug-treated animals [discussion of December 5, 1986 article, A selective imidazobenzodiazepine antagonist of ethanol in the rat (Ro15-4513)] P. D. Suzdak and others. bibl f *Science* 235:1127-8 Mr 6 '87

Trans-Siberian Railroad *See* Railroads—Siberia (Soviet Union)

Trans World Airlines Inc.

Back to work [ordered to reinstate former strikers from the ranks of Independent Federation of Flight Attendants] D. Bensman. *Nation* 244:875 Je 27 '87

Carl Icahn is at it again [bid for USAir] C. Hawkins. *Bus Week* p42+ Mr 16 '87

Carl Icahn may soon be back in the raiding business [taking TWA private] C. Hawkins and C. Power. *Bus Week* p29-30 Ag 3 '87

For Carl Icahn, the flight path never ends [takeover bid for USAir] por *Newsweek* 109:50 Mr 16 '87

How USAir cut Icahn out [plan to buy Piedmont] S. Payne. il por *Bus Week* p35 Mr 23 '87

Icahn proposes merger that could make TWA a private company. *Aviat Week Space Technol* 127:32 Jl 27 '87

Icahn's juggle: TWA, USX, SEC. C. J. Loomis. il por *Fortune* 115:81-2 My 11 '87

Let 'Icahn do your work for you' [buying TWA stock to get in on Texaco-Pennzoil deal] G. G. Marcial. *Bus Week* p106 D 21 '87

The raider who kept TWA flying [C. Icahn] J. Nielsen. il por *Fortune* 115:63 Ja 5 '87

Standing up to Carl Icahn [Independent Federation of Flight Attendants and Machinists Union] C. Friday and J. Schwartz. il *Newsweek* 109:54 Ap 13 '87

Taking over the controls [C. Icahn plans to take TWA private] pors *Time* 130:43 Ag 3 '87

TWA discussing aircraft order with McDonnell Douglas, Boeing. C. Preble. *Aviat Week Space Technol* 126:38-9 Mr 30 '87

TWA pilots extend current contract. *Mon Labor Rev* 110:42 Mr '87

Vicki Frankovich [Independent Federation of Flight Attendants' strike against TWA] C. Doudna. por *Ms* 15:74-6+ Ja '87

TransAfrica (Organization)

Apartheid fighters zero in on presidential race. *Jet* 71:14 Mr 23 '87

TransAfrica: the black world's voice on Capitol Hill. D. M. Cheers. il pors *Ebony* 42:108+ Jl '87

Transamerica Computer Corporation *See* Transamerica Corp.

Transamerica Corp.

Stalking Transamerica. E. Paris. il por *Forbes* 140:55 S 21 '87

TransAmerican Natural Gas Corporation

Jack Stanley's 30-year oil feud is sizzling [Coastal Corp's O. Wyatt stages hostile takeover of TransAmerican Natural Gas in bankruptcy court] J. R. Norman. il *Bus Week* p58-9 Ap 13 '87

Transatlantic airline service *See* Airlines—Routes—Transatlantic

Transatlantic balloon flights *See* Balloon ascensions

Transatlantic cables *See* Cables, Submarine

Transatlantic flights *See* Aviation—Transatlantic flights

Transatlantic Trophy series *See* Motorcycle racing—Great Britain

Transatlantic voyages *See* Voyages

Transatmosphere vehicle *See* Spaceplane

Transbrasil SA-Linhas Aéreas

Transbrasil seeks U.S. routes following domestic growth. il *Aviat Week Space Technol* 127:48+ Ag 31 '87

TransCanada PipeLines Limited

Always a bridesmaid [bid for Dome Petroleum] A. Walmsley. il por *Macleans* 100:42 My 4 '87

A bidding war shapes up for debt-ridden Dome. E. B. Terry. il *Bus Week* p50 Ap 27 '87

Dome's trans-Canadian vision [bid by TransCanada PipeLines] T. Fennell. il *Macleans* 100:45 Ap 27 '87

Transco Energy Co.

Can Transco wriggle out of the 'take-or-pay' mess? J. E. Davis. il por *Bus Week* p66-7 S 28 '87

Transcriptases

Expression and processing of the AIDS virus reverse transcriptase in Escherichia coli. W. G. Farmerie and others. bibl f il *Science* 236:305-8 Ap 17 '87

Inactivation

Characterization and clinical association of antibody inhibitory to HIV reverse transcriptase activity. J. Laurence and others. bibl f il *Science* 235:1501-4 Mr 20 '87

Transcription (Genetics) *See* Genetic transcription

Transcripts, School *See* School reports and records

Transdermal patches

From making hearts to winning them [Thermedics drug delivery skin patches redesigned to release fragrances] C. Brown. il *Bus Week* p153+ N 16 '87

Hot flash! [use of clonidine transdermal patches to counter menopausal flashes] P. McCarthy. *Health* 19:29 N '87

More about estrogen skin patches. C. SerVaas. il *Saturday Evening Post* 259:52-4+ Ja/F '87

Transducers

Strain-gage transducers. C. M. Wood. il *Radio-Electron* 58:61-3+ D '87

Temperature transducer. R. F. Scott. il *Radio-Electron* 58:84 Mr '87

Transducer installations—the right way [small boats] B. Stearns. il *Field Stream* 91:83+ Ja '87

Transducin

Diurnal expression of transducin mRNA and translocation of transducin in rods of rat retina. M. R. Brann and L. V. Cohen. bibl f il *Science* 235:585-7 Ja 30 '87

The molecules of visual excitation. L. Stryer. bibl (p116) il *Sci Am* 257:42-50 Jl '87

Transfer factor

Transfer factor and AIDS. J. Silberner. *Sci News* 131:153 Mr 7 '87

Transfer of funds

See also

Clearinghouse (Banking)

Computers—Banking use

Debit cards

Attention, swappers [trade-in time for funds] G. Weiss. il *Bus Week* p180 N 16 '87

More is not better [switching of mutual funds] M. Hulbert. il *Forbes* 140:216 O 19 '87

Rolling with new rollover rules [rolling over pension money into an IRA] A. Rock. *Money* 16:74-5 Mr '87

Switching mutual funds. M. Rowland. il *Work Woman* 12:60+ N '87

Transfer of technology *See* Technology transfer

Transfer RNA *See* RNA

Transferases

The molecular basis of the sparse fur mouse mutation [ornithine transcarbamylase] G. Veres and others. bibl f il *Science* 237:415-17 Jl 24 '87

Transferrin

A chicken transferrin gene in transgenic mice escapes X-chromosome inactivation. M. A. Goldman and others. bibl f il *Science* 236:593-5 My 1 '87

Transfiguration of Christ *See* Jesus Christ—Transfiguration

Transformation, Genetic *See* Gene transfer

Transformation (Computers)

Word ladders and a Tower of Babel lead to computational heights defying assault. A. K. Dewdney. il *Sci Am* 257:108-11 Ag '87

Transformations (Mathematics)

See also

Fourier transformation

Homotopy

Lorentz transformations

Measurement scales on the continuum. R. D. Luce and L. Narens. bibl f il *Science* 236:1527-32 Je 19 '87

Transforming growth factor *See* Growth regulators

Transfusion of blood *See* Blood—Transfusion

Transients (Electricity)

In search of electrical surges. I. Peterson. il *Sci News* 132:378-9 D 12 '87

Transistors

See also

Metal oxide semiconductors

Thyristors

Ballistic electrons in semiconductors. M. Heiblum and L. F. Eastman. il *Sci Am* 256:102-11 F '87

Chemical coat helps semiconductor prospects. A. L. Robinson. il *Science* 238:27-9 O 2 '87

Closing the biosensor gap [molecular-based transistor; work of Mark S. Wrighton] S. Weisburd. *Sci News* 132:214 O 3 '87

Gallium arsenide transistors. W. R. Frensley. bibl (p116) il *Sci Am* 257:80-7 Ag '87

Making news—39 years ago. il *Radio-Electron* 58:63 Ja '87

Raising a crop of transistors [use of silicon and tantalum; work of Brian M. Ditchek] il *Sci News* 132:25 Jl 11 '87

Shrinking silicon chips down to size [work of George Sai-Halasz and others] S. Weisburd. il *Sci News* 132:132-3 Ag 29 '87

Transistor amplifier design. J. Cunkelman. il *Radio-Electron* 58:55-6+ Ag '87

Specifications

Understanding data sheets of RF power transistors. N. E. Dye. il *Radio-Electron* 58:109-12+ N '87

Testing

Testing semiconductors (I) [bipolar transistors] T. J. Byers. il *Radio-Electron* 58:58-60+ F '87

Transistors—Testing—cont.
Testing semiconductors (II) [field-effect transistors] T. J. Byers. il *Radio-Electron* 58:71-2+ Mr '87
Testing semiconductors (V). T. J. Byers. il *Radio-Electron* 58:61-3+ Je '87
Transit police (New York, N.Y.) *See* New York (N.Y.)—Police
Transit systems *See* Local transit
Transition metals
Electronic theory for materials science. H. Ehrenreich. bibl f *Science* 235:1029-35 F 27 '87
Transits (Astronomy)
See also
Mercury (Planet)—Transits
Pluto (Planet)—Transits
Transkei (South Africa)
Politics and government
First woman chosen leader of South African homeland [S. Sigcau] *Jet* 73:38 O 26 '87
Translations *See* Translators and translating
Translators (Computer programs)
Advantage C + + and Guidelines C + +. M. Mallett. il *Byte* 12:229-30+ O '87
The Cheetah Adapter/386 [translator card] J. Shiell. il *Byte* 12:135-7 Ap '87
Translators and translating
See also
Bible—Versions
Government publications—Translations into Spanish
Machine translating
Religious literature—Translators and translating
Technical literature—Translations into English
Faces of middle class America: Bonnie Jenkins is single and living in Washington D.C. [FBI translator] il pors *Ebony* 42:146+ Ag '87
From the editors [translators for World press review] il *World Press Rev* 34:4 N '87
A matter of interpretation [translating's role in international relations] M. Smith. por *Newsweek* 110:9 D 14 '87
Anecdotes, facetiae, satire, etc.
Uncivil liberties. C. Trillin. il *Nation* 245:330 O 3 '87
Translocation of chromosomes *See* Chromosome abnormalities
Transmission, Automobile *See* Automobiles—Transmission; Automobiles, Foreign—Transmission
Transmission, Helicopter *See* Helicopters—Transmission
Transoceanic cables *See* Cables, Submarine
Transoceanic voyages *See* Voyages
Transpacific airline service *See* Airlines—Routes—Transpacific
Transpacific voyages *See* Voyages
Transparencies
See also
Slides (Photography)
Transplantation of organs, tissues, etc.
See also
Adrenal glands—Transplantation
Brain—Transplantation
Cornea—Transplantation
Donation of organs, tissues, etc.
Fetal tissue—Transplantation
Heart—Transplantation
Immunological tolerance
Kidneys—Transplantation
Knee—Transplantation
Liver—Transplantation
Lungs—Transplantation
Marrow—Transplantation
Muscle—Transplantation
Nerve tissue—Transplantation
Ova—Transplantation
Pancreas—Transplantation
Preservation of organs, tissues, etc.
Retina—Transplantation
Thymus gland—Transplantation
Xenografts
The cutting edge. il *Newsweek* 110:10 D 7 '87
Girl, 3, fights odds after multiple organ transplant [T. Foster] il por *Jet* 73:8 N 16 '87
Herpes virus transplanted with organs? [genital herpesvirus in contaminated organs; research by Jesse L. Goodman] D. D. Edwards. *Sci News* 132:255 O 17 '87
Spare-parts people: the future of transplants. E. S. Cornish. il *Futurist* 21:2+ My/Je '87
The transplant revolution [cover story; special section; with editorial comment by Kevin Doyle] il *Macleans* 100:2, 34-6+ N 23 '87
Transplants come of age. G. Bronson. il *Forbes* 139 Ann Directory:86+ Ap 27 '87

Ethical aspects
A death, a life [anencephalic baby kept alive to keep organs healthy for transplantation] il *Time* 130:76 N 2 '87
The flesh peddlers [fetal tissue transplants] *Progressive* 51:9-10 O '87
Help from the unborn [cell implants from aborted fetuses] J. Levine. il *Time* 129:62 Ja 12 '87
A life-giving death [anencephalic baby kept alive to serve as organ donor] N. Underwood. il *Macleans* 100:45 N 2 '87
Should medicine use the unborn? [fetal tissue implants] M. Clark. il *Newsweek* 110:62-3 S 14 '87
Who deserves transplants? B. D. Colen. il *Health* 19:6+ O '87
Transplanting
See also
Tree planting
Transponders
Grounded grassroots [proposed Mode C rule] M. Phelps. il *Flying* 114:40 D '87
Mode S expected to reduce interference. *Aviat Week Space Technol* 126:100-1 Je 29 '87
Transponder a la Mode S. J. M. McClellan. il *Flying* 114:22-3 Je '87
Transport, Biological *See* Biological transport
Transport airplanes *See* Airplanes, Jet
Transportation
See also
Airports—Transportation
Bus lines
Commuters
Ferries
Freight forwarders
Intermodal transportation
Local transit
Pack transportation
Piggyback transportation
Railroads
Shipping
Space stations—Transportation
United States. Dept. of Transportation
Waterways
Wine—Transportation
Acquisitions and mergers
CSX may have charted a treacherous course [purchase of Sea-Land] T. Ichniowski. il *Bus Week* p36+ F 16 '87
From two used trucks to a $1.2-billion deal [Overnite Transportation's H. Cochrane sells out to Union Pacific Corp.] A. B. Rea. il por *Fortune* 115:67 Ja 5 '87
Piedmont is in play—and Norfolk Southern is flying. C. S. Eklund and S. Ticer. il *Bus Week* p37 F 9 '87
Laws and regulations
Tilting at the windmills of transportation policy [address, May 27, 1987] R. V. Delaney. *Vital Speeches Day* 53:627-30 Ag 1 '87
New Jersey
See also
Port Authority of New York and New Jersey
New York (State)
See also
Port Authority of New York and New Jersey
Pacific States
Light rail hits the West . . . again. il *Sunset* 178:58+ My '87
Transportation, Automotive
See also
Piggyback transportation
Transportation, High speed
See also
Magnetic levitation vehicles
Transportation, Military
See also
Airlines—Military use
Airplanes, Military transport
United States. Air Force. Military Airlift Command
United States. Civil Reserve Air Fleet
Transportation and state
See also
United States. Dept. of Transportation
Transportation Dept. (U.S.) *See* United States. Dept. of Transportation
Transportation industry *See* Transportation
Transposons
Discovery of transposable element activity among progeny of tissue culture-derived maize plants. V. M. Peschke and others. bibl f il *Science* 238:804-7 N 6 '87

Transposons—*cont.*

Heritable somatic excision of a Drosophila transposon. G. J. Bryan and others. bibl f il *Science* 235:1636-8 Mr 27 '87

Hybrid dysgenesis in D. melanogaster is not a general release mechanism for DNA transpositions. R. C. Woodruff and others. bibl f il *Science* 237:1206-8 S 4 '87

Hybrid particle mimics AIDS virus [retrotransposons] D. D. Edwards. *Sci News* 132:151 S 5 '87

Jumping genes—nature's secret agents. L. Ponte. *Read Dig* 130:132-6 Ap '87

The maize transposable element Ds is spliced from RNA. S. R. Wessler and others. bibl f il *Science* 237:916-18 Ag 21 '87

Transposition of gram-positive transposon Tn916 in Acholeplasma laidlawii and Mycoplasma pulmonis. K. Dybvig and G. H. Cassell. bibl f il *Science* 235:1392-4 Mr 13 '87

Transposon tagging and molecular analysis of the maize regulatory locus opaque-2. R. J. Schmidt and others. bibl f il *Science* 238:960-3 N 13 '87

Transsexualism *See* Change of sex

Transuranium elements

Chemistry at periodic table's edge [element 105] *Sci News* 132:236 O 10 '87

Transworld Corp.

See also

TW Services Inc.

Trap-Ease Inc.

Instead of just squeaking by, retiree Mel Melton snaps at the chance to easily trap the common mouse. il por *People Wkly* 27:114 F 2 '87

Trap shooting *See* Trapshooting

Trapnell, Jane

about

Visual intrigue. S. M. L. Aronson. il pors *Archit Dig* 44:228-32+ N '87

Trappers

The American dreamer [boy trappers] G. Hill. il *Field Stream* 92:10 D '87

Traps

See also

Mousetraps

A garden varmint trap. M. Haight. il por *Mother Earth News* 106:34+ Jl/Ag '87

Trapshooting

Lessons from sporting clays. B. Brister. il *Field Stream* 92:80+ Je '87

Trapshooting shells out the profit [Dale Stockdale's range in Iowa] C. Finck. il *Success Farm* 85:23 S '87

Competitions

Sporting clays. il *Outdoor Life* 180:138 S '87

Study and teaching

A shotgun education [Orvis Shooting School] V. Klinkenborg. il *Esquire* 107:36 Ap '87

Trash cans *See* Refuse containers

Trash containers *See* Refuse containers

Trash, the city and death [drama] *See* Fassbinder, Rainer Werner, 1946-1982

Traska, Thomas W.

Discover the Bahamas [special section] il *Travel Holiday* 168:67-8+ Ag '87

Trass, Eddie

about

Selling the home advantage. S. Herbert. il pors *Black Enterp* 18:90-2 O '87

Trass, Ray

about

Selling the home advantage. S. Herbert. il pors *Black Enterp* 18:90-2 O '87

Traub, James

The Katzenjammer Falcon: an elaborate government sting gets fouled up in Reagan's Iranscam. il por *N Y* 20:36-42 F 9 '87

The lords of Hell's Kitchen. il pors *N Y Times Mag* p38+ Ap 5 '87

Two on the isles. il *Vogue* 177:234+ Ap '87

Trauma care units

Trauma in the emergency room. M. Clark. il *Newsweek* 109:76-7 F 16 '87

Trauma centers *See* Trauma care units

Traumatism

See also

Shock

Coping with trauma [preschoolers] L. G. Katz. il *Parents* 62:210 O '87

Travel

See also

Aged—Travel

Air travel

Art tours

Artists—Travel

Authors—Travel

Automobile touring

Black women—Travel

Bus travel

Business travel

Cardiacs—Travel

Children—Travel

Cruising

Guidebooks

Hotels, motels, etc.

John Paul II, Pope, 1920——Travel

Luggage

Ocean travel

Packing of luggage

Railroad travel

Single people—Travel

Time travel

Tourist trade

Vacations

Voyages

Voyages around the world

Women—Travel

Youth—Travel

The active traveler. See issues of Prevention (Emmaus, Pa.) beginning April 1986 through February 1988

Architectural digest travels [special section] il *Archit Dig* 44 Archit Dig Travels:1+ O '87

The Esquire traveler, summer 1987 [special section] il *Esquire* 107 Summ Traveler:T1+ Ap '87

How to get the most from your trip. See issues of Glamour

The rewards of travel. J. Crane. *Focus* 36:1 Wint '86

Summer travel planner. S. Shane. *Travel Holiday* 167:8 Je '87

The travel advisor. H. Gieseking. See issues of Travel Holiday

Travel complaints: how to get what you want. *Glamour* 85:101 N '87

Travel digest. See issues of Travel Holiday

Travel news. S. Birnbaum. See issues of Good Housekeeping

Travel now. R. Alleman. See issues of Vogue

Travel poll results. H. Gieseking and A. Gist. *Travel Holiday* 167:85-6 My '87

Travel tips. *Better Homes Gard* 65:86-7 Mr '87

Travel tomorrow [cover story] M. J. Cetron and W. Rocha. il pors *Futurist* 21:29-34 Jl/Ag '87

TravelBazaar. See issues of Harper's Bazaar

What's new, what's news in travel. il *Glamour* 85:140-2 Ja '87

What's new, what's news in travel: 52 weekend getaways. il *Glamour* 85:116-19 Jl '87

Wildlife au naturel [expeditions sponsored by zoos] D. G. Gordon. *Travel Holiday* 168:30-1 Jl '87

Winter travel '87 [special section] il *Esquire* 108:136-55+ O '87

Bibliography

Travel. E. Newby. il *N Y Times Book Rev* 92:48-9 My 31 '87

Travel and adventure. D. Ackerman. il *N Y Times Book Rev* 92:17 D 6 '87

Walks on the wild side. L. Shapiro. il *Newsweek* 110:64-5 Ag 3 '87

Economic aspects

See also

Airlines—Fares

Hotels, motels, etc.—Rates

Buying a wonderful time (wish you were here!). L. Stains. il *Prevention* 39:68-9 Mr '87

Consumer watchdog [dispute between travel company and clients concerning a nonrefundable deposit] H. Gieseking. *Travel Holiday* 167:76-8 Ja '87

Credit cards offer new incentives for travelers. il *Black Enterp* 17:30 Ap '87

The dollar: No, garçon, I ordered a Big Mac, not a cognac [tables] il *Money* 16:40 Ap '87

Don't go abroad without your trusty cash card. D. Zigas. il *Bus Week* p179 Jl 20 '87

Hidden bargains in the Caribbean. T. Grossinger. il map *Better Homes Gard* 65:198+ O '87

How far the dollar goes in far-flung places. D. H. Dunn. il *Bus Week* p149 O 19 '87

How to stretch your vacation dollar. il *Good Housekeep* 204:276-7 My '87

If it's Tuesday, this must be Transylvania [package tours] P. Plawin. il *Changing Times* 41:71-6 Mr '87

It's not too late to go to Europe. B. Bauer. il *U S News World Rep* 103:46-7 Jl 27 '87

Travel—Economic aspects—*cont.*

Look before you leap at a vacation bargain. S. Payne. il *Bus Week* p150 F 23 '87

Too expensive now to go to Europe? Guess again. B. Bauer. il *U S News World Rep* 102:48-9 Ap 6 '87

Equipment

Going my way. R. La Ferla. il *N Y Times Mag* p74 D 20 '87

Traveling in style. D. Weidner. il *Travel Holiday* 168:70-3 N '87

Health aspects

Be a healthy traveller. R. F. Davies. il *World Health* p8-9 Mr '87

Coping with turista [diarrhea] F. Lunzer. il *Forbes* 139:136 F 23 '87

Don't forget first-aid kit [vacation supplies; views of Patty Gerou] il *USA Today (Periodical)* 116:15 Ag '87

Summer vacation destination: health. A. Brown. il *Curr Health 2* 13:14-15 My '87

Travel health. E. S. Orzac. See alternate issues of Travel Holiday

Travel injuries abroad—who's responsible? H. Gieseking. *Travel Holiday* 167:71-2 Je '87

Travelers advisory [staying in shape on the road] C. Evert. il *World Tennis* 35:96-7+ S '87

Travelers' advisory: malaria still threatens much of globe. E. Zamula. il *FDA Consum* 21:8-13 My '87

Ways to go [Amazon adventure] R. O'Hanlon. *Harpers* 274:23 Je '87

Your diet: smart vacation eating. J. S. Stern. *Vogue* 177:448 N '87

Periodicals

See also

Travel & leisure (Periodical)

Safety devices and measures

Traveling safely. A. S. Blask. il *Travel Holiday* 168:88-90+ S '87

Taxation

See also

Air travel—Taxation

Tax reform: the bottom line. H. Gieseking. il *Travel Holiday* 167:95-6 F '87

Travel & leisure (Periodical)

Travel & leisure [manuscript submission policy] P. Fiori. il *Writer* 100:30-1 Ap '87

Travel agencies and agents

See also

Eastern River Expeditions (Firm)

Overseas Adventure Travel (Firm)

Sun Valley Trekking (Firm)

Consumer watchdog [dispute between travel company and clients concerning a nonrefundable deposit] H. Gieseking. *Travel Holiday* 167:76-8 Ja '87

Don't let your travel agent take you for a ride. A. Keefe. il *50 Plus* 27:56-7 O '87

Commissions

Bargain flights for summer nights. il *Fortune* 115:10 Je 8 '87

Getting less for less [discount agents and fares] G. Eichler. il *Esquire* 107:62 Ap '87

No-frills travel agents. R. Simon. il *Forbes* 139:140+ My 4 '87

Suits and claims

Travel injuries abroad—who's responsible? H. Gieseking. *Travel Holiday* 167:71-2 Je '87

Travel assistance services

Easy visas [visa service companies] A. S. Blask. *Travel Holiday* 168:41+ Jl '87

Travel advisories [nonpolitical service offered by the Bureau of Consular Affairs] *Dep State Bull* 87:19 O '87

Vis-à-visas: how to cut the red tape [visa services] G. Eichler. il *Esquire* 108:72 N '87

What if you break your leg in Karachi? F. S. Chapman. il *U S News World Rep* 102:51-2 Je 15 '87

Travel clubs

See also

Travelers' Century Club

Travel consultants *See* Travel agencies and agents

Travel folders *See* Travel literature

Travel literature

See also

Guidebooks

Publishers and publishing—Travel literature

Travel—Bibliography

Travellers' tales [cover story; special issue; with editorial comment by Edouard Glissant] bibl il *Courier* 40:3-38 Ap '87

Authorship

Getting into travel writing. J. Steinberg. *Writer* 100:14-15+ My '87

Having minimalist time, wish you were here. A. Broyard. il *N Y Times Book Rev* 92:13 Mr 22 '87

Specifics in nonfiction writing. C. Wakefield. *Writer* 100:23-4 Mr '87

Travels with my father: what we learned from working together. R. J. Christmas. il por *Ms* 15:66+ Mr '87

Using your vacation for article ideas. J. Watlington. *Writer* 100:19-21 Ag '87

Collectors and collecting

Art: travel books of the 19th century. J. J. Norwich. il *Archit Dig* 44:102-7 Ag '87

Travel operators *See* Tourist trade

Travel photography

A behind-the-scenes look at some great vacation pictures. C. Begole. il *Glamour* 85:134+ Je '87

Photo tours. M. Kiwak. *Petersens Photogr Mag* 16:66+ N '87

Photo tours. L. Nielsen. il *Petersens Photogr Mag* 16:70-1 My '87

Travel in focus. M. Grimm and T. Grimm. See alternate issues of Travel Holiday

Travel photographer Sam Abell seeks out "solemn beauty". H. Chapnick. il por *Pop Photogr* 94:30 S '87

Traveler's camera. C. Purcell and A. Purcell. See issues of Popular Photography

Traveling with color. G. Schaub and B. Schwalberg. il *Pop Photogr* 94:50-3 Ag '87

Travel regulations

See also

Passports

U.S. Customs Service

International aspects

When Americans land in foreign jails. G. Breitstein. il *Sch Update* 119:14 F 9 '87

Travel with children

Adventures: kids in the capital [Washington, D.C.] A. K. Horowitz. il *Publ Wkly* 231:144-5 My 15 '87

Off on a business trip? Don't forget the diapers. S. D. Atchison. il *Bus Week* p79+ N 30 '87

On the road. J. P. Comer. il *Parents* 62:166 Je '87

On the road with kids. B. Bauer. bibl il *U S News World Rep* 102:56-9 My 25 '87

A roar of tearing metal [car accident while driving and tending child in back seat] S. M. Flanagan. *Read Dig* 130:145 Ja '87

Three for the road [traveling to St. Thomas with a baby] S. Bolotin. il *Vogue* 177:138+ Je '87

Traveling with a preschooler. L. G. Katz. il *Parents* 62:160 Je '87

A view from the back seat. A. J. Packer. *U S News World Rep* 102:59 My 25 '87

Weekend getaways. L. Schnurnberger. il *Parents* 62:227-9+ O '87

Travel with pets

Traveling with Rover. H. R. Kennedy. *U S News World Rep* 103:79 D 21 '87

Travelers' Century Club

For the consummate traveler. J. Kraus. *Travel Holiday* 167:32+ Ja '87

Jet-sitters [globetrotting contest among C. D. Buckley, J. Clouse, and P. Thompson] il pors *Life* 10:91-4 My '87

Kings of the road [J. Clouse and P. Thompson] B. Rice. il pors *50 Plus* 27:22-5+ Mr '87

The race to visit every country on earth [competition between J. Clouse and P. Thompson] B. Rice. il *50 Plus* 27:17 Ap '87

Travelers checks

See also

American Express Co.

Travelers Corp.

Bringing the office home [telecommuter M. Crampton] R. Lockwood. il por *Pers Comput* 11:176-7 O '87

Travelers' insurance *See* Insurance, Travelers'

Traveling salesman problem

Netting a better sales route [elastic net algorithm; work of Richard Durbin and David Willshaw] I. Peterson. *Sci News* 131:262 Ap 25 '87

Traveling theater *See* Theater, Traveling

Traveller's Bookshelf (Firm)

Warner initiates 'Traveller's Bookshelf' this spring. *Publ Wkly* 232:30-1 O 23 '87

Travers, Eva Foldes, and Sacks, Susan Riemer

Teacher education and the liberal arts. *Educ Dig* 53:9-11 D '87

Travers Stakes See Horse racing

Traverse, Alfred
Pollen and spores date origin of rift basins from Texas to Nova Scotia as early late Triassic. bibl f il map *Science* 236:1469-72 Je 12 '87

La traviata [opera] See Verdi, Giuseppe, 1813-1901

Travis, Randy

about

The making good of Randy Ray. J. Cocks. il por *Time* 129:72 Je 22 '87

Randy Travis. A. Nash. por *Stereo Rev* 52:95 S '87

Trawls and trawling
Build a troll-aid. N. Strung. il *Field Stream* 92:123 Je '87

Trolling for bass. K. Schultz. il *Field Stream* 92:73+ My '87

Equipment

Lowdown on downriggers. K. Schultz. il *Field Stream* 91:82+ Ap '87

Tray tables See Tables

Trays

See also

Lazy Susans

Lap desk or bed tray . . . sturdy but lightweight. il *Sunset* 179:114-17 O '87

Tray magnifique. L. M. Dalsgaard. il *Home Mech* 83:56-8 Jl '87

Treadmills (Exercising equipment) See Exercising equipment

Treason

See also

Sedition

A patriot for whom? The treason of Saint-Pol, 1474-75. S. H. Cuttler. bibl f il *Hist Today* 37:43-8 Ja '87

Treasure Salvors Inc.
A fabulous lady from Spain [cover story] R. A. Green. il por *Antiques Collect Hobbies* 92:30-4 My '87

Treasure trove

See also

Central America (Steamship)
Geldermalsen (Ship)
Mary Rose (Ship)
Nuestra Señora de Atocha (Ship)
Regina (Ship)
Republic (Steamship)
Titanic (Steamship)
Whidah (Ship)

8 great buried treasures. L. Gomez. il *Life* 10:28-36+ Mr '87

Ciphernauts [search for treasure buried by T. J. Beale in the 1820's in Virginia] P. Hoffman. il *Omni* 9:26+ My '87

Diving for dollars [special section] il *Macleans* 100:36-42 Ag 10 '87

Tales of sunken gold and hunters of the depths [Spanish galleons] B. S. Walker. bibl (p132) il map *Smithsonian* 17:96-102+ Ja '87

Treasury bills and notes
Back in sync? [Treasury bond yields and price-earnings ratios] E. A. Finn, Jr. *Forbes* 140:34-5 N 16 '87

Bearish on stocks, bullish on bonds [interview with R. Kelly] B. Weberman. *Forbes* 140:54+ N 16 '87

The bears may be taking the wrong trail. J. M. Laderman. il *Bus Week* p100-1+ O 19 '87

Buying 30-year Treasuries is 'the last thing I would do right now' [views of M. F. Ramirez] D. Zigas. il por *Bus Week* p163 D 28 '87-Ja 4 '88

Buying a piece of Uncle Sam. L. Wiener. il *U S News World Rep* 103:48 Jl 20 '87

Costly zeros [life insurance wrapped around Treasury zeros] B. Weberman. il *Forbes* 140:131 D 28 '87

Empty shelves [inventory shortage] B. Weberman. il *Forbes* 140:249 N 30 '87

Government bond dealers: a bell is tolling. G. DeGeorge. *Bus Week* p63-4 My 25 '87

Government minus [misrepresentation of government bond fund yields] B. Weberman. il *Forbes* 139:117 Ap 20 '87

How the bond market is forcing the Fed's hand. S. Bartlett. il *Bus Week* p42 My 11 '87

How the spike in interest rates snagged First Boston [Treasury bond options] D. Zigas. *Bus Week* p30-1 Je 29 '87

How Wall Street is driving the mortgage market. C. Farrell. il *Bus Week* p108-9 My 4 '87

In Japan we (must) trust [Japanese investments in U.S. Treasuries affect interest rates] E. A. Finn, Jr. il *Forbes* 140:32-4 S 21 '87

An investor the U.S. can't afford to lose [Japan in Treasury bond market] W. Glasgall. il *Bus Week* p32 My 4 '87

New Treasury Direct program makes it easy to buy T-bills. il *Consum Rep* 52:654 N '87

Treasuries go high-tech [Treasury Direct] M. McNamee. il *Bus Week* p203 N 2 '87

Treasuries: to buy them takes a bit of know-how. M. Meyer. il *Money* 16:225-6 D '87

Treasury how-tos. B. Weberman. il *Forbes* 140:303 S 7 '87

The U.S. gets foreign aid [Treasury bond sale] J. B. Copeland. il *Newsweek* 109:58 My 18 '87

Yankee, stay home. B. Weberman. il *Forbes* 140:127 Ag 10 '87

Australia

Head Down Under for double-digit bond yields. T. Segal. *Bus Week* p126 S 21 '87

Treasury Dept. (U.S.) See United States. Dept. of the Treasury

Treaties

See also

Alliances
Antarctic Treaty (1959)
Treaties of guaranty
United States—Treaties

Treaties, Disarmament See Disarmament

Treaties of guaranty
Treaties of guarantee. J. H. Wolfe. il *USA Today (Periodical)* 116:63 Jl '87

Treatment of prisoners See Prisoners—Treatment

Trebek, Alex

about

Sorry, girls, Mom keeps house for Jeopardy! host Alex Trebek. M. Dougherty. il pors *People Wkly* 28:79-80+ O 12 '87

Trebelhorn, Tom

about

Ten wins and therefore no ties. T. Callahan. il *Time* 129:66 Ap 27 '87

Trebes, James E., and others
Demonstration of X-ray holography with an X-ray laser. bibl f il *Science* 238:517-19 O 23 '87

Trebilcock, Bob
The barn builder. il pors *Ctry J* 14:34-40 Mr '87
Rural hot spots . . . rural cold spots. il *Ctry J* 14:32-5+ Je '87
This land is my land. il *Ctry J* 14:50-5 S '87

Tree, Anne
Fantasy bestowed on form. il *House Gard* 159:190-7+ Ap '87
Partners with the past: Lady Anne and Michael Tree at Shute House. il *Archit Dig* 44:168-73 Je '87

Tree, Marietta
Life at Heron Bay: Palladian pavilion on the island of Barbados [cover story] il *Archit Dig* 44:54-9+ Ag '87

Tree Climbers International
New sport: go climb a tree. M. Vogel. il por *Natl Wildl* 25:36 Je/Jl '87

Tree climbing

See also

Tree Climbers International

Tree death
Tree death: cause and consequence [cover story; special issue] il *BioScience* 37:542-6+ S '87

Tree felling
Maple euthanasia. J. D. Randolph. il *Ctry J* 14:4+ Jl '87
Mr. T chops down trees on his property; angers his neighbors in suburb. por *Jet* 72:57 Je 8 '87
Mr. T suffers backlash after tree-cutting spree. il por *Jet* 72:54 Je 15 '87
Open-face felling. D. Johnson. il *Ctry J* 14:24-7 N '87
Suburb plans to legally axe Mr. T.'s tree-chopping. por *Jet* 72:33 Je 22 '87

Anecdotes, facetiae, satire, etc.

To kill a maple tree. A. A. Rooney. il *Saturday Evening Post* 259:66-7 Ap '87

Tree frogs See Frogs

Tree houses
They built their own tree house. il *Sunset* 178:110-11 My '87

Tree ivy See Fatshedera

Tree mallows
Lavatera is kind of a laid-back hollyhock. il *Sunset* 178:252 My '87

Tree peonies See Peonies

Tree planting

See also

Reforestation

Foolproof planting. J. Ruttle. il *Rodale's Org Gard* 34:62+ S '87

Tree planting—cont.
Now's the time to move a camellia. il *Sunset* 179:252 N '87
Start your own backyard nursery . . . A. Guttierrez and R. Lorenz. il *Home Mech* 83:76-7+ O '87
Transplanting trees and shrubs in the fall. P. M. White. il *Ctry J* 14:32-4 N '87

Tree rings
Dating earthquakes [work of Gordon Jacoby and others] J. Silberner. *Sci News* 131:255 Ap 18 '87
Dead trees tell tales. S. Thybony. il *Natl Wildl* 25:40 Ag/S '87

Tree stands (Hunting) *See* Hunting—Equipment

Trees
　　　See also
　　Bark
　　Christmas trees
　　Forest crown canopy
　　Forest ecology
　　Forests and forestry
　　Fruit trees
　　Hedges
　　Tree felling
　　Tree planting
　　Windbreaks
　　Woodlots
　　　See also names of trees
Centering yourself in a zone of trees. R. Rodale. il *Rodale's Org Gard* 34:110-12 Mr '87
Earth almanac. A. Leopold. il *Conservationist* 42:54-5 N/D '87
　　　　　　Care
Care and maintenance of older trees. il *Conservationist* 41:37 Mr/Ap '87
　　　　Diseases and pests
　　See also
　　Elm—Diseases and pests
　　Gypsy moths
　　Maple—Diseases and pests
　　　　　Planting
　　See Tree planting
　　　　　Pruning
　　See Pruning
　　　　　Training
　　See also
　　Espaliers
　　　　Wounds and injuries
Stubs, knobs and bulges. J. M. Haller. il *Flower Gard* 31:14 Ap/My '87

Trees, Dwarf
　　　See also
　　Bonsai
　　Fruit trees, Dwarf
Elfin Forest, Puerto Rico. R. H. Mohlenbrock. il map *Nat Hist* 96:20-2 D '87

Trees, Effect of air pollution on
Acid rain in Europe [cover story; special section; with editorial comment by Leen Hordijk] bibl f il maps *Environment* 29:inside cover, 4-15+ N '87
The forest decline enigma. D. Hinrichsen. il *BioScience* 37:542-6 S '87
Forests are dying but is acid rain really to blame? J. R. Luoma. il map *Audubon* 89:36-8+ Mr '87
Green devolution [West Germany] il map *Natl Parks* 61:17 S/O '87
Life, the great chemistry experiment [State of the earth 1987] S. Postel. il *Nat Hist* 96:41-8 Ap '87
Searching for a breath of Clean Air. I. Peterson. map *Sci News* 132:340 N 28 '87
Sounding taps for the sugar maple. J. W. Edwards. il *Natl Wildl* 25:20 O/N '87
Turning off the maples. P. A. A. Berle. *Audubon* 89:6 S '87

Trees, Effect of climate on
Modeling the climate dynamics of tree death. P. J. Michaels and B. P. Hayden. bibl il maps *BioScience* 37:603-10 S '87

Trees, Effect of ozone on *See* Plants, Effect of ozone on

Trees, Effect of stress on
Characteristics of trees predisposed to die. R. H. Waring. bibl il *BioScience* 37:569-74 S '87

Trees, Historic
Eighteen acres of harmony [trees on the White House grounds] H. Sidey. il *Time* 130:25 S 28 '87
Join the search for champion trees [cover story] K. Wilson. il *Rodale's Org Gard* 34:66+ Mr '87
New York's famous and historic trees. C. Wiedemann. il *Conservationist* 41:32-7 Mr/Ap '87

TreeSweet Products Co.
A juice maker squeezes itself dry. J. E. Davis. il por *Bus Week* p42 Ag 10 '87

Trefethen, Florence
The poet's workshop. See alternate issues of The Writer through May 1987

Trefil, J. S. (James S.), 1938-
Quantum physics' world: now you see it, now you don't. bibl (p144) il *Smithsonian* 18:66-70+ Ag '87

Trefil, James S. *See* Trefil, J. S. (James S.), 1938-

Trefny, Frank, 1948-
　　　　　about
Frank Trefny [cover story] W. P. Scott. il por *Am Artist* 51:52-7 D '87

Trehan, Madhu P.
India's Merchant with a view. por *World Press Rev* 34:60 My '87

Trekking *See* Hiking

Trelford, Donald
　　　　　about
'U.S. motivation is benign, but often misguided' [interview] J. R. Moskin. por *World Press Rev* 34:27-8 N '87

Trellises
Big sweep of a trellis, made with plastic pipe. il *Sunset* 178:167 My '87
A Eugene gardener may have designed the perfect bean trellis. il *Sunset* 178:240+ Ap '87
Rock-steady trellises. M. Maltas. il *Rodale's Org Gard* 34:56-7 My '87
Super-trellis did it. il *Sunset* 178:98-9 Je '87
Trellis and screen for front-yard privacy. il *Sunset* 179:138-9 O '87
Trellising brambles. J. Ruttle. il *Rodale's Org Gard* 34:72-3 N '87
Up the trellis go fuchsias or cherry tomatoes. il *Sunset* 178:282 My '87
Wisteria and children are both welcome. il *Sunset* 179:128 O '87
Zigzag trellis takes the chaos out of berries. il *Sunset* 178:188 F '87

Trematodes
Vertical distribution of an estuarine snail altered by a parasite. L. A. Curtis. bibl f il *Science* 235:1509-11 Mr 20 '87

Tremblay, Michel, 1942-
　　　　　about
Peering into the soul of French Canada. il por *Macleans* 100:46 Ap 13 '87

Tremont Nail Company
Visit to a nail foundry. B. Gould. il *Workbench* 43:80 My/Je '87

Tremors (Geology) *See* Earthquakes

Trenchcoats *See* Coats

Trencher, Reed
　　　　　about
Is this article worth $19,260? J. Alter. il por *Newsweek* 109:77 Ap 20 '87

Trenet, Charles, 1913-
　　　　　about
Charles Trenet. *New Yorker* 63:40-1 N 9 '87

Trent, Dan, and Trent, Lynda
High society [fiction] il pors *Good Housekeep* 204:229-32+ Ap '87

Trento, Joseph J., 1947-
　　　　　about
Lost in space. G. Easterbrook. *Wash Mon* 19:48-54 Ap '87

Trenton, Battle of, 1776
Trenton and Princeton. R. F. Snow. il *Am Herit* 38:26+ D '87

Trescott, Pamela
(jt. auth) *See* Ashman, Charles R., and Trescott, Pamela

Tresidder, Jane
(jt. auth) *See* Cliff, Stafford, and Tresidder, Jane

Trespass
Hunt the locked-up places. J. Zumbo. il *Outdoor Life* 180:90-1+ N '87
Passwords to posted signs [getting hunting permission on posted lands] J. Weiss. il *Outdoor Life* 180:74-5+ Jl '87
Posted: sign of the times. J. Walter. il *Success Farm* 85:61 N '87
This land is my land [posting of private land] B. Trebilcock. il *Ctry J* 14:50-5 S '87

Trestle tables *See* Tables

Tretinoin *See* Retinoic acid

Treu, Tiziano
Italian labor relations: a system in transition. *Mon Labor Rev* 110:37-9 Mr '87

Treverton, Gregory F.
Covert action and open society. bibl f *Foreign Aff* 65:995-1014 Summ '87
Trevino, Lee
about
'Like a Rembrandt'. J. Diaz. il por *Sports Illus* 67:26-7 D 7 '87
Trevor, William, 1928-
Family sins [story] *New Yorker* 63:28-38 Jl 6 '87
Frau Messinger [story] *New Yorker* 63:30-9 Mr 2 '87
A trinity [story] *New Yorker* 63:38-48 My 11 '87
Treybig, James G.
about
How Jim Treybig whipped Tandem back into shape. J. B. Levine. il por *Bus Week* p124-6 F 23 '87
How Jimmy Treybig turned tough. B. O'Reilly. il por *Fortune* 115:102-4 My 25 '87
TRH (Thyrotropin releasing hormone) *See* Thyrotropin releasing factor
Tri-Star Pictures Inc.
At Columbia, things might go better with Tri-Star [Coca-Cola merging two studios] R. Grover. il por *Bus Week* p74-5 N 30 '87
Triacs *See* Thyristors
Triad America Company
Khashoggi's connections. D. Jenish. il por *Macleans* 100:34-6 Ja 19 '87
Triad Artists, Inc.
In her own image [office of R. Gomez, literary agent for Triad Artists] F. Greenberg. il por *Work Woman* 12:76-7 D '87
Trial by jury *See* Jury
Trial reporting *See* Newspaper court reporting
Trials
See also
Actions and defenses
Jury
Justice, Miscarriage of
Legal procedure
Mock jury
Newspaper court reporting
Summary proceedings
Television broadcasting—Trials
War crime trials
Witnesses
Media megatrials: why they go on and on . . . and on. T. Gest. il *U S News World Rep* 102:10 My 11 '87
Alberta
Doubts about self-defence [trial of Calgary, Alta. drugstore owner S. Kesler] M. Gray. il pors *Macleans* 100:45 Je 29 '87
Fear, arms and a verdict [S. Kesler acquitted of murder charges] M. Gray. il por *Macleans* 100:48 Jl 6 '87
Argentina
The dirty war's dirty laundry [human rights trials] F. Willey. il por *Newsweek* 109:40 F 23 '87
Time out or time's up [R. Alfonsin's request for legislation that would free most of the military officers currently up on charges of human rights abuse] P. Lacefield. *Commonweal* 114:375-7 Je 19 '87
Torturers saved by the bell, almost [R. Alfonsin signs bill stopping initiation of human rights abuse cases] D. L. Boroughs. il *Progressive* 51:13 Ap '87
Belgium
Soccer: old riot, new riot [Belgian trial for British fans over 1985 riot in Brussels] T. Clifton and R. Marshall. il *Newsweek* 110:8 S 21 '87
California
Judge Wapner's favorite cases [excerpt from A view from the bench] J. A. Wapner. il pors *Good Housekeep* 205:50+ O '87
Canada
A questionable witness to abuse [bill would eliminate need for corroboration of unsworn testimony of a child in sexual abuse cases] B. Amiel. il *Macleans* 100:9 Ja 26 '87
The ugly face of markets [upcoming security fraud trials] T. Tedesco. il *Macleans* 100:30 S 14 '87
Central African Republic
Former emperor Bokassa is sentenced to death. *Jet* 72:9 Je 29 '87
Grenada
Some fell slow and some fell fast [trial of M. Bishop's murderers] G. Wagner. *Natl Rev* 39:32-3 Je 5 '87
Yesterday's revolution [trial of M. Bishop's murderers] B. Shacochis. il *Harpers* 275:41-4+ O '87
Israel
A case of treason [trial of M. Vanunu] A. Bilski. il por *Macleans* 100:25 S 14 '87

A right to disobedience? [trial of M. Vanunu] S. Seibert. il por *Newsweek* 110:41 S 7 '87
Poland
See also
Popieluszko, Jerzy—Murder case
Rwanda
Rwandan justice: a show of pomp and circumstantial evidence [trial in absentia of American W. McGuire for murder of Dian Fossey] B. A. Borst. il *Discover* 8:45 F '87
Sicily
Hard time: 2,665 years in jail [Mafia trial] il *Newsweek* 110:31 D 28 '87
Hitting back [Mafia members sentenced] il *Time* 130:34 D 28 '87
Soviet Union
Four years for a "fun" flight [sentencing of German pilot, M. Rust, for landing plane in Moscow] W. R. Doerner. il por *Time* 130:42 S 14 '87
A hard landing in Moscow [M. Rust sentenced to 4 yrs. in Soviet labor camp] C. Redden. il por *Macleans* 100:22 S 14 '87
Judgment at Chernobyl [trial of nuclear plant officials] J. Greenwald. il *Time* 130:44-5 Jl 20 '87
Rust's unhappy landing [sentenced to a labor camp for flying small plane into Red Square] S. Seibert. il *Newsweek* 110:49 S 14 '87
Ten years in stir for Chernobyl's scapegoats. *Newsweek* 110:47 Ag 10 '87
Spain
Spain's deadly elixir [toxic industrial rapeseed oil poisoning case] il *Macleans* 100:35 Ap 13 '87
Trials (Espionage)
See also
Walker family espionage case
Secrets storm [R. W. Pelton sentenced to life imprisonment] *Nation* 244:4-5 Ja 10 '87
Trials (Malpractice)
Clergy malpractice [suit over suicide of K. Nally] *Christ Century* 104:850 O 7 '87
Trials (Military) *See* Courts martial and courts of inquiry
Trials (Murder)
The Billionaire Boy—and the missing body [trial of J. Hunt] por *Newsweek* 109:61 My 4 '87
Black doctor sentenced to life for death of white woman patient in Georgia [V. D. Mallory] il por *Jet* 73:33 O 26 '87
Black who killed white cop, wounded others; acquitted [case of S. Penn] *Jet* 73:47 N 2 '87
Court orders new trial for Steven Linscott. il por *Christ Today* 31:68+ S 4 '87
Deaf mute cleared of murdering Ala. woman [case of J. Green] *Jet* 73:36 O 19 '87
Doubts about self-defence [trial of Calgary, Alta. drugstore owner S. Kesler] M. Gray. il pors *Macleans* 100:45 Je 29 '87
Ex-cop Lawrencia Bembenek claims she was wrongly convicted of murder in the case of the unsmoking gun. J. S. Kunen. il pors *People Wkly* 28:116-18+ D 7 '87
Fear, arms and a verdict [S. Kesler acquitted of murder charges in Alberta] M. Gray. il por *Macleans* 100:48 Jl 6 '87
Georgia murder conviction overturned: black jurors struck for racial reasons [case of W. Gamble] *Jet* 72:40 Ag 3 '87
A hockey player's victory in court [B. Spencer acquitted of killing M. Dalfo] M. Gray. il pors *Macleans* 100:46-7 O 26 '87
Murder and intrigue California-style [Billionaire Boys' Club trial] M. Gray. por *Macleans* 100:44 F 16 '87
New York woman acquitted of killing her husband [battered woman, K. Straw] *Jet* 73:46 N 2 '87
Rwandan justice: a show of pomp and circumstantial evidence [trial in absentia of American W. McGuire for murder of Dian Fossey] B. A. Borst. il *Discover* 8:45 F '87
Twilight Zone: the verdict. *Time* 129:69 Je 8 '87
The 'Twilight Zone' verdict: not guilty. por *Newsweek* 109:83 Je 8 '87
Trials (Obscenity)
Biafra trial ends in hung jury [J. Biafra] J. Ressner. il por *Roll Stone* p22 O 8 '87
Rockin' with the First Amendment [J. Biafra of the Dead Kennedys acquitted on charges of distributing harmful matter to minors] S. Wishnia. il *Nation* 245:444-6 O 24 '87
Trials (Racketeering)
Busting the godfathers [Mafia dons convicted in New York City] E. Magnuson. il *Read Dig* 130:92-6 Ap '87

Trials (Racketeering)—cont.

The "Dapper Don" beats a rap [J. Gotti acquitted in Brooklyn] J. S. DeMott. il por *Time* 129:18 Mr 23 '87

A jury sides with 'the Dapper Don' [J. Gotti trial in Brooklyn] *Newsweek* 109:30 Mr 23 '87

Twilight of the dons [Mafia chiefs sentenced in New York City] N. Underwood. il *Macleans* 100:40 Ja 26 '87

Trials (Rape)

Packers' Cade is found guilty of raping aunt. il por *Jet* 72:33 Ag 17 '87

Packers win one, lose one in Green Bay sex cases [J. Lofton and M. Cade] il pors *Jet* 72:49 Je 15 '87

Triana, Jorge Ali *See* Ali Triana, Jorge

Triangle Industries, Inc.

Who's getting the deal in the Triangle shuffle? [N. Peltz and P. W. May construct deal to sell Triangle to its affiliate CJI Industries Inc.] C. Power. il por *Bus Week* p78 N 23 '87

Triassic period *See* Geology, Stratigraphic—Triassic; Paleobotany—Triassic; Paleontology—Triassic

Triathlon

Bob Jordan: tops in news and health. il pors *Ebony* 42:145-6+ F '87

If at last you would succeed, triathlon. C. Schaeffer. il *Changing Times* 41:150 Ja '87

The iron courage of Joni Dunn [victim of serious skiing accident becomes triathlon champion] J. G. Hubbell. il pors *Read Dig* 130:39-44 Ja '87

Joy is back [J. Hansen recovers from a breakdown] J. Mills. por *Women's Sports Fitness* 9:46 O '87

Not getting older, just better [J. Ramsay, basketball coach and triathlete] il por *Sports Illus* 67:16 S 14 '87

Racing sleek [K. Hanssen] S. Rubin. il pors *Women's Sports Fitness* 9:38-41 O '87

Running to extremes [B. Whitman] M.-C. Wrenn. il pors *Life* 10:46-8+ F '87

Starting at the finish line. D. Wright. il por *Work Woman* 12:132 Je '87

A triple triumph: taking on the triathlon challenge. S. Festa. il *Work Woman* 12:130+ Je '87

Triumph for Pigg power [Bud Light U.S. Triathlon Series] C. Neff. il *Sports Illus* 67:62-3 O 5 '87

Triazolam *See* Tranquilizing drugs

Tribal Assets Management

A new band of Tribal tycoons. F. Ungeheuer. il *Time* 129:56+ Mr 16 '87

Tribbia, Joseph J., and Anthes, Richard A.

Scientific basis of modern weather prediction. bibl f il map *Science* 237:493-9 Jl 31 '87

Tribble, Brian Lee

about

Bias' friend Tribble glad 'system did not fail me'. pors *Jet* 72:48 Je 22 '87

Tribe, Laurence H.

The final say. il *N Y Times Mag* p68-70+ S 13 '87

about

The effort to intimidate Reagan. W. F. Buckley. *Natl Rev* 39:57 Jl 31 '87

The High Court's unofficial arbiters. D. Baer. il pors *U S News World Rep* 103:23-4 N 23 '87

Meet Larry Tribe, Pennzoil's hole card. L. Helm and P. Dwyer. il por *Bus Week* p78-9 Ap 20 '87

Tribeca (New York, N.Y.)

Tribeca: on quiet streets, the ghosts of the Washington Market. D. Shaw. il map *N Y* 20:96-8 My 4 '87

Triboluminescence *See* Luminescence

Tribune Entertainment Company

What makes Geraldo run? [G. Rivera's marketing savvy] P. E. Bauer. il pors *Channels* 7:62-3 Je '87

Tributyltin

No safe harbor for marine life [TBT based paint and the marine environment] A. J. Mitteldorf and J. S. Weis. il *Sierra* 72:27+ S/O '87

Painting with pesticides: the controversial organotin paints. S. Scott. il *Sea Front* 33:414-21 N/D '87

Tricentrol plc

A squall over oil whips up the North Sea [British independents scurrying for white knights] S. Miller. il *Bus Week* p89-90 D 28 '87-Ja 4 '88

Trichloroethylene

Atmospheric trends in methylchloroform and the global average for the hydroxyl radical. R. G. Prinn and others. bibl f il *Science* 238:945-50 N 13 '87

Shower shudders [breathing toxins; research by Julian Andelman] G. Woolley. il *Sierra* 72:13-14 Jl/Ag '87

Trichogrammatids *See* Wasps

Trick photography *See* Photography, Trick

Tricks

See also
Conjuring
Jugglers and juggling

Tricyanic acid *See* Cyanuric acid

Tricycles, Recumbent *See* Human powered vehicles

Trident (Missile) *See* Guided missiles—Launching from submarines

Trieste (Italy)

Historic houses, sites, etc.

Decoration for a dynasty [19th century Tripcovich-Banfield house redecorated by Emilio Carcano] W. Weaver. il *House Gard* 159:100-11+ F '87

Triethylamines *See* Ethylamines

Trietley, Harry L., 1943-

All about A-to-D converters. il *Radio-Electron* 58:71-7 F '87

Trigg, Oliver A., Jr.

about

Chairman acquires control of Family Savings & Loan has assets of $144 mil. *Jet* 72:6 Ag 24 '87

S&L eyes black support. M. Bernstein. por *Black Enterp* 18:22 N '87

Triglycerides *See* Glycerides

Trillin, Abigail

Coastal retreat. il *Seventeen* 46:250+ Ag '87

Trillin, Calvin

Frenchy and the Persians. *New Yorker* 63:44+ Je 29 '87

Uncivil liberties. See occasional issues of The Nation

Trillmich, Fritz

Seals under the sun. il *Nat Hist* 96:42-9 O '87

Trimble, Virginia

Gravity waves: a progress report. il *Sky Telesc* 74:364-9 O '87

Trimm, H. Wayne

about

Wayne Trimm receives Ernest F. Trad Award. il por *Conservationist* 41:56 Mr/Ap '87

Trindl, Gene

about

Selleck by Trindl [interview; cover story] B. Hurter. il pors *Petersens Photogr Mag* 15:20-1+ Ap '87

Trinidad and Tobago

See also
Bird sanctuaries—Trinidad and Tobago
Carnival (Pre-Lenten festival)—Trinidad and Tobago
Music festivals—Trinidad and Tobago
Natural history—Trinidad and Tobago
Nature centers—Trinidad and Tobago
Restaurants—Trinidad and Tobago
Women—Trinidad and Tobago

Description and travel

Dazzling: Trinidad and Tobago! [special section] il *Essence* 17:77-8+ Ap '87

Trinity

See also
Holy Spirit

Compassionate and gracious. M. K. Hellwig. *America* 156:back cover Je 6 '87

Trinity and unity [discussion of April 15, 1987 article, The Trinity and women's experience] B. Brown Zikmund. *Christ Century* 104:534-6 Je 3-10 '87

The Trinity and women's experience. B. Brown Zikmund. *Christ Century* 104:354-6 Ap 15 '87

Trinity Broadcasting Network

They're not the Bakkers [P. and J. Crouch] K. L. Woodward. il pors *Newsweek* 110:61 Ag 31 '87

Trintex Inc.

Are IBM and Sears crazy? Or canny? B. Saporito. il *Fortune* 116:74-5+ S 28 '87

Trio Indians

Dr. Plotkin's jungle pharmacy: an ethnobotanist goes native for science [work among the Tirió tribe in Suriname] A. Fadiman. il pors *Life* 10:15-17 Je '87

Triple Crown (Horse racing) *See* Horse racing

Triple Five Corporation

On time in Bloomington [Ghermezian brothers complete deal to build Fashion Mall of America in Minnesota] D. Jenish. il *Macleans* 100:36 Ja 19 '87

Triple jumping

Ties that bind [J. Joyner-Kersee and brother A. Joyner] K. Moore. il pors *Sports Illus* 66:76-80+ Ap 27 '87

Triple jumping records

Soaring to unseen heights [M. Conley sets indoor triple jump record at the TAC USA/Mobil Indoor Track & Field Championships] P. Putnam. il por *Sports Illus* 66:24-5 Mr 9 '87

Triple witching hour (Securities) *See* Program trading (Securities)

Triplets
It's a girl . . . and a girl . . . and a girl! [financial implications of raising triplets for Bill and Eileen Lund] S. Seixas. il *Money* 16:80-3+ N '87
Motherly love works a miracle [P. Anthony is surrogate for her daughter; cover story] E. Levin. il pors *People Wkly* 28:38-43 O 19 '87

Triplett, Betty, and others
Moving toward family preservation services in Kentucky. *Child Today* 15:8-11 N/D '86

Triploidy *See* Chromosomes

Tripods, Camera *See* Camera tripods

Tripp, James T. B., and others
Equity and ozone protection. bibl f *Environment* 29:43-5 Jl/Ag '87

Trips *See* Travel

TriQuarterly (Periodical)
Optimistic tragedies [special issue entitled From South Africa] R. Nixon. *Nation* 245:453-4 O 24 '87

Triremes
An Athenian legend sails the Aegean once more. L. Rosellini. il *U S News World Rep* 103:54-5 Ag 17 '87
The Athenian trireme. P. Lipke. il *Oceans* 20:8-10 N/D '87
The glory that was Greece. A. Toufexis. il *Time* 130:73 Ag 17 '87
Rho, rho, rho, your boat. il *Discover* 8:8 N '87

Trisha Brown Dance Company
Off the beaten path [City Center season] T. Tobias. il *N Y* 20:104+ O 5 '87
Trisha Brown's empty flashes [performances at the City Center in N.Y.] L. A. Jacobs. *New Leader* 70:22 O 5 '87

Triskaidekaphobia *See* Thirteen (The number)

Trisler, David, and Collins, Frank
Corresponding spatial gradients of TOP molecules in the developing retina and optic tectum. bibl f il *Science* 237:1208-9 S 4 '87

Tristan (Accelerator) *See* Accelerators (Electrons, etc.)

Tristan und Isolde [opera] See Wagner, Richard, 1813-1883

Tritium
Neutrino mass: a tritium disagreement. D. E. Thomsen. *Sci News* 131:342 My 30 '87

Triton Museum of Art
A dazzling new home for the Triton Museum in Santa Clara. il *Sunset* 179:49 D '87

Trivelpiece, Alvin W.
Soviet science and technology at the Boston meeting. *Science* 238:1631 D 18 '87
about
Alvin Trivelpiece of DOE is named new executive officer of AAAS. B. J. Culliton. por *Science* 235:840 F 20 '87
Alvin W. Trivelpiece: AAAS Executive Officer. C. M. Susskind. il por *Science* 236:377 Ap 24 '87

Trivia
Star-track trivia. M. Ehrman. il *Teen* 31:40 Ag '87
Trivia quiz. See issues of National Geographic World beginning September 1985
Trivia trek [national parks] T. Kilpatrick. il *Natl Parks* 61:22-3+ Jl/Ag '87
The TV teacher trivia test. E. J. Nowicki. il *Phi Delta Kappan* 69:69-70 S '87

Trockadero Gloxinia Ballet Company
Off the beaten path [performance at La Mama] T. Tobias. il *N Y* 20:104+ O 5 '87

Troetshler, Ruth
How to solarize your soil. il *Flower Gard* 31:58-9 Je/Jl '87

Trogdon, William *See* Least Heat Moon, William

Trois etudes pour Alexandre [ballet] *See* Ballet reviews—Single works

Trolley buses *See* Trolleys

Trolley museums *See* Railroad museums

Trolleys
See also
National Capital Trolley Museum
Ding, ding, ding [trolley lines and museums] K. Zimmermann. il *Americana* 15:58-60+ Mr/Ap '87
Trolleys—by any other name. C. Skrzycki. il *U S News World Rep* 102:46 Ap 6 '87

Trolling *See* Trawls and trawling

Troma, Inc.
The Troma-tic experience. J. Schwartz. il *Newsweek* 109:48 Je 29 '87

Trombonists
See also
Turre, Steve

Trompe-l'oeil
Another Haberle rediscovery [resurfacing of Torn in transit] E. H. Gustafson. il *Antiques* 132:1080 N '87
Fabulous fakery [R. L. Neas uses trompe l'oeil to create French atmosphere in Long Island cottage] E. Greene. il *House Gard* 159:134-43 S '87
Going with the grain of tradition [decorative painting techniques; work of L. Pardon] S. Wood. il por *Home Mech* 83:62-3 Mr '87
Painting a world [decorative artist S. Gemberling] E. Greene. il por *House Gard* 159:40+ D '87
Paris: painting the town [J. de Rohan-Chabot] S. Drucker. il por *Vogue* 177:228-33+ Je '87
Suggesting a plausible fantasy [work of R. Haas] J. Gruen. il por *Archit Dig* 44:154+ Jl '87
Two rediscovered paintings by John Haberle [Imitation and Japanese corner] G. G. Sill. bibl f il por *Antiques* 132:1118-21 N '87

Tronrud, Dale E., and others
Structures of two thermolysin-inhibitor complexes that differ by a single hydrogen bond. bibl f il *Science* 235:571-4 Ja 30 '87

Trooper Tom *See* Emonds, Tom

Trophies, Sport
See also
Fishing trophies
Hunting trophies

Tropical Agricultural Research and Training Center *See* Centro Agronómico Tropical de Investigación y Enseñanza

Tropical diseases *See* Tropical medicine

Tropical forests, Dry *See* Forests and forestry

Tropical fruit industry *See* Fruit industry

Tropical medicine
Ways to go [Amazon adventure] R. O'Hanlon. *Harpers* 274:23 Je '87

Tropical rain forests *See* Rain forests

Tropics
See also
Agriculture—Tropics
Amazon River Valley
Food supply—Tropics
Wildlife conservation—Tropics
Climate
U.S., Japan present plans for joint spacecraft mission [Tropical Rainfall Measuring Mission] il *Aviat Week Space Technol* 127:69+ O 26 '87

Tropism
See also
Geotropism

Trost, Carlisle A. H., 1930-
Antisubmarine warfare [address, May 20, 1987] *Vital Speeches Day* 53:551-3 Jl 1 '87

Trotsky, Leon, 1879-1940
about
Trotsky's orphans. M. Massing. *New Repub* 196:18-20+ Je 22 '87

Trotta, Geri
City dining: New Orleans. il *Gourmet* 47:48+ My '87
Williamstown: culture in the country. il *Gourmet* 47:56-9+ Ag '87

Trotta, Margarethe von
about
Rosa Luxemburg [film] Reviews
Ms 15:22-3 My '87. L. Stone
N Y 20:96-7 Je 1 '87. D. Denby
Nation 244:546-9 Ap 25 '87. D. Egger
New Repub 196:24-5 My 18 '87. S. Kauffmann

Trotter, Robert J.
The play's the thing. bibl (p63) il pors *Psychol Today* 21:26-34 Ja '87
Stop blaming yourself. bibl (p64) il pors *Psychol Today* 21:30-2+ F '87
You've come a long way, baby. *Current* 295:11-16 S '87
You've come a long way, baby. bibl (p94) il *Psychol Today* 21:34-6+ My '87

Trousers *See* Pants

Trout, Emerson
Homecoming. il *Ctry J* 14:26-7 Mr '87

Trout
See also
Cooking—Fish
The lake trout returns to Lake Ontario. J. E. Marsden. il *Conservationist* 41:10-13 My/Je '87

Trout culture *See* Fish culture

Trout fishing
See also
Char fishing
Grayling fishing

Trucks—*cont.*
Ford's new-look pickups [F-series] T. Opre. il *Outdoor Life* 179:32+ Ja '87
Lord LUV a truck [Chevy LUV pickup truck] D. Sherman. il *Car Driv* 32:7 F '87
New pickups: power and class. T. Opre. il *Outdoor Life* 179:62-4+ F '87
Surviving 18-wheelers. D. Chaikin. il *Home Mech* 83:36 Ap '87

Accidents
See Traffic accidents

Camping equipment
See also
Campers, Truck

Equipment
Custom roof rack. il *Field Stream* 91:81+ Ja '87
Custom storage box. il *Field Stream* 92:137-9 S '87
Multipurpose truck accessory [Deck Slider] M. Ferrara. il *Home Mech* 83:95 Mr '87
Pickup bed protection [Duraliner and Durabox] R. Barnhart. il *Home Mech* 83:80 Jl '87

Four wheel drive
The better breed [Chevy and GMC trucks] S. L. White. il *Field Stream* 92:82+ N '87
I love my wife, but oh you pickup [Chevrolet C/K series and Mazda 4x4] R. Sessions and S. Murray. il *Road Track* 38:102+ My '87
PM long-term car tests: Nissan SE Pickup, Ford Taurus LX, Oldsmobile Delta 88. W. Hoyt and M. Allen. il *Pop Mech* 164:78+ Jl '87

History
The legendary Dodge Power Wagon. D. McCaig. il *Ctry J* 14:28-33 My '87

Laws and regulations
When the dinosaur hit Lodi, Ohio [overweight truck stopped by police] J. Paris. il *Read Dig* 130:145-8 Ap '87

Leasing and renting
See also
Ryder System, Inc.
U-Haul International, Inc.

Maintenance and repair
Anecdotes, facetiae, satire, etc.
It's the principle. A. Girdler. il *Road Track* 38:24-5 Jl '87

Safety devices and measures
The scandal of killer trucks. K. Labich. il *Fortune* 115:85-7 Mr 30 '87
Trucking safety on the rise. il *Consum Res Mag* 70:32 My '87

Testing
Brand new pickups [Chevy line-up] T. Opre. il *Outdoor Life* 179:24+ Je '87
Chevrolet Pickup. D. C. Ross. il *Mot Trend* 39:109-11 Ap '87
Chevy's all-new full-size pickups. M. Thompson. il *Fam Handyman* 37:84 Jl/Ag '87
F-Troop [Ford's F-Series pickups] L. Emanuelson. il *Mot Trend* 39 no12 Sp Issue:84-9 '87
Ford Ranger STX. M. Thompson. il *Fam Handyman* 37:68 N '87
Ford's F-Series [pickups] B. Kilpatrick. il *Field Stream* 92:86 Je '87
Pick of the pickups—how much truck do you need? [Ford F-150, Jeep Comanche, Dodge Dakota LE, and Chevrolet Cheyenne 1500] J. Keebler. il *Pop Sci* 230:26-8+ Je '87
Ranger STX [pickup truck] M. Brockman. il *Mot Trend* 39 no12 Sp Issue:38-41 '87
Road tests of pickup trucks [Dodge Dakota, Chevrolet S-10, Ford Ranger, and Jeep Comanche] il *Consum Rep* 52:344-51 Je '87
Thunder trucks! [Chevrolet C-1500, Ford F-150 and Dodge D-100 pickups] il *Pop Mech* 164:59-63 D '87

Weight and size regulations
See Trucks—Laws and regulations

Trucks, Foreign
Four wheel drive
See Trucks—Four wheel drive

Testing
P'UP with bark [Isuzu P'UP] H. Wicks. il *Home Mech* 83:37 My '87

Trucks, Racing
Testing
SST [Showroom Stock Truck pro racing series] J. Rusz. il *Road Track* 38:162-5 My '87

Trucks, Remodeled
See also
Vans, Remodeled
We have a winner! [Customize-This-Truck contest] il *Pop Mech* 164:99-101 Jl '87

Wrenches and welders take to the fields [field service trucks] D. Mowitz. il *Success Farm* 85 no6:18V Mr '87
Trucks, Toy *See* Toys
Trucks in advertising
Spiels on wheels. N. L. Croft. il *Nations Bus* 75:14 F '87
Trucks in business
Truck fever [cover story] J. Candler. il *Nations Bus* 75:14-16+ O '87
Trudeau, G. B., 1948-
about
'Doonesbury' in Arizona. il *Newsweek* 110:41 S 14 '87
Trudeau, Garry B. *See* Trudeau, G. B., 1948-
Trudeau, Jane Pauley *See* Pauley, Jane
Trudeau, Pierre Elliott
about
Enduring magnetism. B. Wallace. il pors *Macleans* 100:18-19 S 7 '87
Trudeau's power punch. M. Janigan. il por *Macleans* 100:10-11 Je 8 '87
Trudeau's star turn. M. Janigan. il por *Macleans* 100:14-16+ S 7 '87
True, Michael
about
Superintendent found guilty of slander for teacher recommendation. T. J. Flygare. il *Phi Delta Kappan* 68:629-30 Ap '87
True stories [film] *See* Motion picture reviews—Single works
Trueblood, Harriett
The courage of Millie Baldwin [story] il *Redbook* 168:42+ Mr '87
Trueson, John
(jt. auth) *See* Carlson, John, and Trueson, John
Truffles
Of truffles and lavender [harvesting and Provençal recipes] L. Forbes. il *House Gard* 159:42+ S '87
Raising American truffles. L. Korn. il *Rodale's Org Gard* 34:24+ O '87
Truitt, Anne, 1921-
about
Anne Truitt at André Emmerich. N. Princenthal. *Art Am* 75:142 F '87
Truitt, Ed
Rocky Mountain high-tech. il *Space World* X-1-277:22-4 Ja '87
Truitt, Robert L.
(jt. auth) *See* Shih, Charles C.-Y., and Truitt, Robert L.
Trülzsch, Holger
about
Her bold looks made her a standout in the '60s, but now Veruschka paints herself into the background. M. Small. il pors *People Wkly* 27:88-90 F 16 '87
Truman, Bess Wallace, 1885-1982
Anecdotes, facetiae, satire, etc.
How Bess fired Douglas MacArthur. G. W. S. Trow. *New Yorker* 63:27 Mr 30 '87
Truman, Harry S., 1884-1972
about
Notes and comment. *New Yorker* 63:33 N 23 '87
Correspondence
"Equally bizarre, but somewhat different" [further notes on how the Washington post was scooped on Truman's letter to music critic P. Hume] M. S. Forbes. *Forbes* 140:18-19 Ag 10 '87
Here's how the Washington post was scooped on Truman's letter [letter to music critic P. Hume over review of daughter Margaret's singing] M. S. Forbes. il *Forbes* 139:18 Je 29 '87
Trumbull, John, 1756-1843
about
Mystery lady. I. B. Jaffe. il pors *Art News* 86:34-5 Mr '87
Trumbull, Sarah, d. 1824
about
Mystery lady. I. B. Jaffe. il pors *Art News* 86:34-5 Mr '87
Trump, Donald J.
Trump on Trump [excerpt from Trump; cover story] il pors *N Y* 20:50-64+ N 16 '87
about
Atlantic City roulette. J. Crudele. il pors *N Y* 20:24 My 18 '87
Building castles in the sky [cover story] M. Ryan. il pors *People Wkly* 28:52-7 D 7 '87
Citizen Trump [cover story] B. Powell and P. McKillop. il pors *Newsweek* 110:50-5+ S 28 '87
Donald Trump. il por *People Wkly* 28:79 D 28 '87-Ja 4 '88

Trump, Donald J.—about—*cont.*

Donald Trump gets a $200 million Christmas gift. L. J. Tell and S. Benway. il por *Bus Week* p76 D 28 '87-Ja 4 '88

Donald Trump: what's behind the hype? [cover story] J. R. Norman. il pors *Bus Week* p92-5+ Jl 20 '87

Donald Trump's mystery. J. Schwartz. il por *Newsweek* 109:46 Je 29 '87

For Bally, dumping Trump raises the ante. M. D. Oneal. il *Bus Week* p45 Mr 9 '87

He who eats last . . . R. Phalon. il por *Forbes* 140:130+ D 14 '87

'I'm just an investor'. *U S News World Rep* 102:61 Ap 27 '87

Trump for president? G. Hackett. il por *Newsweek* 110:41 S 14 '87

Trump lands in Red Square. J. Barnathan. il por *Newsweek* 110:41 Jl 20 '87

Trump vs. Wynn: 'giant egos on the line'. R. Grover. il por *Bus Week* p31-2 Jl 27 '87

Two deal-makers. *New Repub* 197:4+ D 28 '87

Trump, Ivana

about

Ivana, the 'Queen of the Castle'. A. Miller. il por *Newsweek* 110:54 S 28 '87

Trumpet music

See also

Fanfares

Phonograph records—Trumpet music

Videotapes—Trumpet music

Miles Davis' solo on Tutu—a trumpet transcription. B. Bergstein. il *Down Beat* 54:51 My '87

Trumpeter swans *See* Swans

Trumpeters

See also

Brown, Clifford, 1930-1956

Davis, Miles

Drayton, Leslie

Gillespie, Dizzy, 1917-

Little, Booker, 1938-1961

Marsalis, Wynton

Masekela, Hugh

McGhee, Howard, 1918-1987

Rodney, Red

Sandke, Jordan

Sandke, Randy

Soloff, Lew

Trump's Castle Hotel and Casino

Ivana, the 'Queen of the Castle'. A. Miller. il por *Newsweek* 110:54 S 28 '87

Trungpa, Chogyam, 1939-1987

about

In search of tradition. C. Wood. il por *Macleans* 100:15+ My 4 '87

In Vermont: a spiritual leader's farewell. G. Jaynes. il *Time* 129:10+ Je 22 '87

Truss, Orian

about

Medical disputes you should know about. G. Williams. *Ladies Home J* 104:56+ Mr '87

Trussardi, Nicola

about

Traces of the future's past: Nicola Trussardi's palazzo in Bergamo. G. Y. Dryansky. il por *Archit Dig* 44:152-9 My '87

Trusses

1,200-square-foot all-in-one room . . . trusses do it. il *Sunset* 178:171 Ap '87

Trust departments of banks *See* Banks and banking—Trust departments

Trust for Public Land (U.S.)

The Trust for Public Land [donating conservation easements to land trusts] il *Mother Earth News* 104:64-6 Mr/Ap '87

Trust funds *See* Trusts and trustees

Trust Territory of the Pacific Islands *See* Pacific Islands (Trust territory)

Trustees of Reservations (Mass.)

Banking land. R. R. Payne. il *House Gard* 159:56+ S '87

Trusteeship Council (United Nations) *See* United Nations. Trusteeship Council

Trusthouse Forte Ltd.

The trouble with Harry's: behind the coup at Cipriani. J. Taylor. il por *N Y* 20:62-7 O 19 '87

Trusts, Industrial

J.P. Morgan: the agglomerator. J. Merwin. il por *Forbes* 140:275+ Jl 13 '87

Law

See Antitrust law

Trusts, Investment *See* Investment trusts

Trusts and trustees

See also

Banks and banking—Trust departments

Living trusts

Keeping a rein on your assets [revocable trusts] A. McGrath. il *U S News World Rep* 102:66 Mr 16 '87

Suits and claims

Heir-tight. D. Fanning. il *Forbes* 140 Sp Issue:353+ O 26 '87

Taxation

Of death and taxes [putting life insurance into an irrevocable trust] L. R. Walbert. il *Forbes* 140:460 Jl 13 '87

Saving for college: one scheme has survived [minor's Section 2503(c) trust] P. Philipps. il *Bus Week* p147 Ja 12 '87

Thinking about setting up a trust? Better think twice. P. Philipps. il *Bus Week* p182 My 25 '87

Trusts that tax reform didn't topple. C. Yang. il *Bus Week* p148-9 O 19 '87

Truth

See also

Reality

Answering Pilate: truth and the postliberal church. W. H. Willimon. *Christ Century* 104:82-5 Ja 28 '87

A challenge to Willimon's postliberalism [discussion of January 28, 1987 article, Answering Pilate: truth and the postliberal church] W. H. Willimon. *Christ Century* 104:306-10 Ap 1 '87

Truthfulness

See also

Honesty

Lying

TRW Inc.

Can they keep it up? J. Flint. il por *Forbes* 139:46+ F 9 '87

Matra wins Telecom 2 contest, resolves constraints on TRW for Intelsat bid. *Aviat Week Space Technol* 127:24-5 N 30 '87

Money for nothing [TRW Credentials' marketing of credit information] A. Snitzer. il *Forbes* 139:212+ My 18 '87

Stanford/TRW team demonstrates potential lethality increase of space-based free-electron lasers. *Aviat Week Space Technol* 126:23 Mr 16 '87

Take control of your credit [TRW Credentials program] il *Consum Rep* 52:412 Jl '87

TRW's air-bag business looks ready to balloon. S. Phillips. il *Bus Week* p74+ N 2 '87

Trying times [television program] *See* Television program reviews—Single works

Trypanosomes

Identification and isolation of a variant surface glycoprotein from Trypanosoma vivax. P. R. Gardiner and others. bibl f il *Science* 235:774-7 F 13 '87

Similarity of cruzin, an inhibitor of Trypanosoma cruzi neuraminidase, to high-density lipoprotein. R. P. Prioli and others. bibl f il *Science* 238:1417-19 D 4 '87

Trypsin

See also

Antitrypsin

The catalytic role of the active site aspartic acid in serine proteases. C. S. Craik and others. bibl f il *Science* 237:909-13 Ag 21 '87

Mutants of bovine pancreatic trypsin inhibitor lacking cysteines 14 and 38 can fold properly. C. B. Marks and others. bibl f il *Science* 235:1370-3 Mr 13 '87

The three-dimensional structure of Asn[102] mutant of trypsin: role of Asp[102] in serine protease catalysis. S. Sprang and others. bibl f il *Science* 237:905-9 Ag 21 '87

Tryptophan

Blood pressure bows to tryptophan. *Prevention* 39:17-18 D '87

Tsai, Gerald, Jr.

about

For Smith Barney, the go-go years have just begun. R. Mitchell. il por *Bus Week* p39-40 Je 8 '87

Jerry Tsai listens to his mother. C. Leinster. il por *Fortune* 116:82-4+ Ag 17 '87

Tsakos, Paul

about

Marketing miniatures. K. Pechter. il por *Rodale's Org Gard* 34:72-6 D '87

Tsander, Fridrikh Arturovich, 1887-1933
about
Tsander's dream. P. Pesavento. il por *Space World* X-5-281:28-31 My '87
Tsandoulas, G. N.
Space-based radar. bibl f il map *Science* 237:257-62 Jl 17 '87
Tsang, Simon
Photographing the southern sky [cover story] il por *Astronomy* 15:58-63 Jl '87
Tse, Bernard K.
about
And the last shall be first. K. K. Wiegner. il por *Forbes* 140:100+ N 16 '87
Tsipis, Kosta
Arms control pacts can be verified. il maps *Discover* 8:79-93 Ap '87
The uncommon ground of security debate. *Bull At Sci* 43:10-11 Jl/Ag '87
TSR (Terminate and stay resident) programming *See* Computer programming
TSS *See* Toxic shock syndrome
Tsuji, Shintaro
about
Mickey Mouse, meet Hello Kitty. M. Beauchamp and H. Katayama. il por *Forbes* 139:68+ My 18 '87
Tsukamoto, Koichi
about
Western wear. H. Katayama. il por *Forbes* 140:305 N 16 '87
Tsukiji (Tokyo, Japan: Market) *See* Fish markets—Japan
Tsukuba Science City (Japan)
Tsukuba: science city. *World Press Rev* 34:16 Ag '87
Tsunamis *See* Tidal waves
Tsutsumi, Yoshiaki
about
'The world's richest man'. P. Sabatier. il *World Press Rev* 34:49 N '87
Tsvetaeva, Marina Ivanovna, 1892-1941
about
Poet of the air. J. Bayley. il *N Y Rev Books* 34:20+ O 8 '87
Tuaregs
African Noel [excerpt from An African journey] M. Patinkin. il *Omni* 10:26+ D '87
Tub caulking *See* Caulking
Tubb, Barry
about
Posing bareback in Sweet Sue, Texas-bred actor Barry Tubb has landed a seat on Broadway. D. Hutchings. il pors *People Wkly* 27:127-8+ Ap 20 '87
Tube feeding
Moral and religious aspects
The Catholic tradition on the use of nutrition and fluids. J. J. Paris and R. A. McCormick. *America* 156:356-61 My 2 '87
Christian nursing center adopts life-support policy [Crista Ministries in Seattle] E. J. Larson. *Christ Today* 31:59 O 16 '87
Do patients have a "right to die"? M. Christopher. il *Sch Update* 119:21 Ap 20 '87
Is it wrong to cut off feeding? [comatose patients] R. N. Ostling. il *Time* 129:71 F 23 '87
Letters in reaction [discussion of May 2, 1987 article, The Catholic tradition on the use of nutrition and fluids] J. J. Paris and R. A. McCormick. *America* 156:449-52 My 30 '87
Tube-launched, optically tracked, wire-guided missiles *See* Guided missiles
Tuberculosis
Black TB victim in Fla. wins fight for her job [G. Arline case decided by Supreme Court] *Jet* 72:39 Mr 30 '87
Vaccines and vaccination
Toward a TB vaccine and a leprosy link. *Sci News* 131:264 Ap 25 '87
Tubers
See also
Potatoes
Tubes
See also
Vacuum tubes
Tubes, Plastic
Make a CPVC support frame for your boat cover. E. Morrissey. il *Home Mech* 83:98-100 O '87
Tubin, Eduard, 1905-1982
about
Coming to terms with an Estonian symphonist. R. R. Reilly. il por *High Fidel* 37:78-9 Ja '87

Tubs, Bath *See* Bathtubs
Tubs, Hot *See* Hot tubs
Tubulin
Aluminum: a high price for a surrogate? [research by Timothy L. MacDonald and others] D. D. Edwards. il *Sci News* 131:245 Ap 18 '87
Promotion of tubulin assembly by aluminum ion in vitro. T. L. MacDonald and others. bibl f il *Science* 236:183-6 Ap 10 '87
Tubulin transport *See* Biological transport
Tucano Indians
The gospel and the gold rush [caught between Salesian missionaries and gold mining interests in Brazil] R. N. Ostling. il *Time* 129:64 Je 1 '87
Tucci, Mario
about
Out of the cellar. F. J. Prial. il por *N Y Times Mag* p56 N 29 '87
Tuchman, Barbara Wertheim
A nation in decline? il *N Y Times Mag* p52+ S 20 '87
Tucker, Dorothy
Guess who's coming to dinner now? il *Essence* 17:45-6+ Ap '87
Tucker, Michael
about
Jill Eikenberry and Michael Tucker: L.A. law's . . . perfect match. J. Buck. il pors *McCalls* 114:10-12 Ag '87
L.A. law's closest couple. K. Koontz. il pors *Health* 19:34 Je '87
Tucker, Ralph
about
His stock moves slowly, but Fresno's Ralph Tucker is America's most avid snailman. M. Neill. il por *People Wkly* 28:71-2 Jl 6 '87
Tucker, Richard H.
about
Charting the southern sky. J. Lankford. il pors *Sky Telesc* 74:243-6 S '87
Tucker, Robert B.
(jt. auth) See Waitley, Denis, and Tucker, Robert B.
Tucker, Tony
about
Only one no. 1 [cover story] P. Putnam. il pors *Sports Illus* 67:20-3 Ag 10 '87
Tucker, Walter B., III
(jt. auth) See Gow, Anthony J., and Tucker, Walter B., III
Tucker, William, 1935-
about
William Tucker at David McKee. W. Saunders and A. Rochette. *Art Am* 75:154 D '87
Tucker, William, 1942-
Where do the homeless come from? il *Natl Rev* 39:32+ S 25 '87
Why farm subsidies have come a cropper. il *Read Dig* 130:81-6 Ja '87
Tucker, Anthony & R. L. Day, Inc.
Investing in a confident style [broker K. Reiman] J. Giambanco. il pors *Work Woman* 12:103-4+ D '87
Tucson (Ariz.)
Arts
Tucson [special section] il *Horizon* 30:41-54+ My '87
Description
Old Tucson [movie location] C. Buhl. il *Travel Holiday* 168:10+ Ag '87
Tucson [special section] il *Horizon* 30:41-54+ My '87
Galleries and museums
See also
Old Pueblo Museum (Tucson, Ariz.)
Tucson Museum of Art
Resorts
See Resorts—Arizona
Tucson (Ariz.) in motion pictures
Old Tucson [movie location] C. Buhl. il *Travel Holiday* 168:10+ Ag '87
Tucson Museum of Art
Art pioneers. M. Wade. il *Horizon* 30:46-7 My '87
Tucson Symphony Orchestra
Musical progressions. K. Milam. il *Horizon* 30:45 My '87
Tudor, Antony, 1909-1987
about
Antony Tudor: master provocateur. M. Hunt. il pors *Dance Mag* 61:36-41 My '87
De Mille on Tudor [address, December 6, 1986] A. De Mille. *Dance Mag* 61:42 My '87
Obituary
Dance Mag il pors 61:18-19 Ag '87. O. Maynard *Dance Mag* 61:19 Ag '87. G. Parks

Tudor, Antony, 1909-1987—about—Obituary—*cont.*
  N Y 20:101 My 18 '87. T. Tobias
  New Yorker 63:70+ Jl 6 '87. A. Croce
  Pillar of fire [ballet] Reviews
    Dance Mag il por 61:54-9 S '87
Tudor, Frederic, 1783-1864
                about
  The iceman inspireth. J. Rhea. il *Space World* X-6-282:3
    Je '87
Tudor-Craig, Pamela
  Painting in medieval England: the wall-to-wall message.
    bibl il *Hist Today* 37:39-45 N '87
Tudor England *See* Great Britain—History—Tudors, 1485-
  1603
Tudor Fund
  Pirouetting ahead of the market [interview with M. Straus]
    A. E. Serwer. por *Fortune* 115:158 Je 8 '87
Tudor Investment Corporation
  Hot commodity [P. T. Jones] D. Machan. il por *Forbes*
    139:282 Ja 12 '87
Tuesday Morning Inc.
  Keep the customers waiting. L. M. Keefe. il por *Forbes*
    140:74 S 21 '87
Tufte, Edward R., 1942-
                about
  Publish and prosper. W. Baldwin. il por *Forbes* 139:121-3
    My 18 '87
Tufts University
  Satellites for the classroom [joint U.S.-U.S.S.R. course
    on the nuclear arms race] S. Begley. il *Newsweek*
    110:103 N 16 '87
Tugboats
  Like his father before him, a brave tugboat skipper
    battles wind and sea to bring great ships to port
    [P. Mahoney] D. Grogan. il pors *People Wkly* 28:88-9+
    O 12 '87
Tugman, Tony
                about
  A pair of prescient winners. P. Nulty. il pors *Fortune*
    116 Sp Issue:176-9 Fall '87
Tugwell, Maurice
  The threat from a failed system. *Vital Speeches Day*
    53:645-7 Ag 15 '87
Tuition, College *See* College education—Costs
Tuition payment programs (Business) *See* Business and
  education
Tukano Indians *See* Tucano Indians
Tulip Time Festival (Holland, Mich.) *See* Holland (Mich.)—
  Festivals
Tuller, David
  New Age. il *Publ Wkly* 232:29-33 S 25 '87
  Publishing education in changing times. il *Publ Wkly*
    232:30-3 D 25 '87
Tully, Alice, 1902-
                about
  Alice Tully. *New Yorker* 63:32-4 O 5 '87
Tully, John
  Popcorn man [poem] *America* 156:384 My 9 '87
Tully, Judd
  Dana Van Horn. il por *Am Artist* 51:42-7+ F '87
  Sidney and Frances Lewis—the quest for the best in
    art. il pors *Smithsonian* 18:84-8+ N '87
Tully (Alice) Hall (New York, N.Y.) *See* Alice Tully Hall
  (New York, N.Y.)
Tulsa (Okla.)
                Courts
  Harris is youngest judge ever appointed in Okla. [J.
    Harris] por *Jet* 71:27 Ja 19 '87
                Hospitals
    See also
  City of Faith Medical and Research Center (Tulsa,
    Okla.)
            Politics and government
  NAACP hits Tulsa with voting rights suit. *Jet* 72:29
    Ag 10 '87
Tulsa Ballet Theatre
  Second comings [performance of Mozart violin concerto]
    T. Tobias. il *N Y* 20:60-1+ F 9 '87
Tumarkin, Nina
  Myth and memory in Soviet society. *Society* 24:69-72
    S/O '87
Tumblers *See* Drinking vessels
Tumbling
  Utah's tiny Derrick Gibson is a dervish who makes
    bigger tumblers bounce up and take notice. il por
    People Wkly 28:121 Jl 6 '87
Tumor angiogenesis factor *See* Growth regulators
Tumor cells (Malignant) *See* Cancer cells
Tumor inhibiting substances *See* Cancer inhibiting sub-
  stances

Tumor necrosis factor *See* Cachectin
Tumor producing substances *See* Cancer—Causes
Tumor viruses *See* Oncogenic viruses
Tumors (Benign)
    See also
  Cysts
  Fibroid tumors
  Neurofibromatosis
  Sleuthing to prevent cancer [skin tags help identify persons
    at risk for colon polyps] C. SerVaas. il *Saturday Evening
    Post* 259:98+ Jl/Ag '87
                Surgery
  3 children who needed a medical miracle [hemangioma
    removed from two year old's nose]; ed. by Joan
    Rodman Goulianos. C. Dougan. il *Redbook* 168:112+
    F '87
  A dancer's nightmare [S. Lavery] L. Leivick. il pors
    N Y Times Mag p66+ N 8 '87
Tumors (Malignant) *See* Cancer
Tuna canneries *See* Canneries
Tuna fish
    See also
  Cooking—Fish
  Test tank for fast fish [researching body temperature
    regulation and swimming dynamics of warm-blooded
    albacore tuna] *Oceans* 20:5 My/Je '87
                Prices
  Fish story [Japan's rising importation of U.S. tuna] P.
    Fuhrman. il *Forbes* 140:38-9 Ag 10 '87
Tuna fisheries (Commercial) *See* Fisheries
Tuna fishermen *See* Fishermen
Tuna fishing
              Competitions
    See Fishing—Competitions
Tuna salads *See* Salads
Tune, Ray
                about
  In Missouri: outdoor work, very heavy lifting. S. Hubbell.
    il por *Time* 130:12+ Ag 24 '87
Tune ups, Automobile *See* Automobile engines—Main-
  tenance and repair
Tunicates
    See also
  Salps
Tunick, David, 1943-
                about
  Drawn to the masters—David Tunick. J. Kornbluth.
    il por *Archit Dig* 44:74+ My '87
Tuning, Radio *See* Radio receivers—Tuning
Tuning equipment
    See also
  Radio antennas—Tuning
  Radio receivers—Tuning
  Television receivers—Tuning
Tunis, John R., 1889-1975
                about
  A boy's own author. J. Epstein. *Commentary* 84:50-6
    D '87
Tunisia
    See also
  United Nations—Tunisia
              Antiquities
    See also
  Carthage (Ancient city)
            Foreign relations
                Israel
    See Israel—Foreign relations—Tunisia
          Politics and government
  Defeat of the supreme combatant [H. Bourguiba ousted
    by Z. A. Ben Ali] M. S. Serrill. por *Time* 130:48
    N 16 '87
  Punishing the pious [sentencing of fundamentalists for
    plotting to overthrow H. Bourguiba] M. S. Serrill.
    il por *Time* 130:42 O 12 '87
  Sidelining of a legend [H. Bourguiba ousted] *Macleans*
    100:24 N 16 '87
  'The worst has been avoided'. S. Seibert. il por *Newsweek*
    110:52 O 12 '87
      Religious institutions and affairs
    See also
  Muslims—Tunisia
Tunnel (New York, N.Y.: Discotheque) *See* New York
  (N.Y.)—Restaurants, nightclubs, bars, etc.
Tunneling (Physics)
  Electron tunneling paths in proteins. A. Kuki and P.
    G. Wolynes. bibl f il *Science* 236:1647-52 Je 26 '87
  Hole-burning spectroscopy and relaxation dynamics of
    amorphous solids at low temperatures. R. Jankowiak
    and G. J. Small. bibl f il *Science* 237:618-25 Ag 7
    '87

Tunneling microscopes, Scanning See Electron microscopes and microscopy
Tunnels and tunneling
See also
New York (N.Y.)—Tunnels and tunneling
Tunnels and tunneling, Underwater
Western Europe
See also
English Channel tunnel
Tuolumne River (Calif.)
See also
Hetch Hetchy Water Supply Project
Tupperware International
Party animal. K. Hannon. il Forbes 140:262+ N 16 '87
Turan, Kenneth
(jt. auth) See Duke, Patty, and Turan, Kenneth
Turandot [opera] See Puccini, Giacomo, 1858-1924
Turback, Michael
about
Made in New York. New Yorker 63:36-7 D 28 '87
Turbak, Gary
Prisoner of geography. il Natl Wildl 25:14-17 F/Mr '87
Shy survivor. il Natl Wildl 26:12-16 D '87/Ja '88
Working their magic on ducks. il Int Wildl 17:24-8 Mr/Ap '87
Turbidity
Turbidity current activity in a British Columbia fjord. D. B. Prior and others. bibl f il map Science 237:1330-3 S 11 '87
Turbina, Nika
about
Russian poetry finds a prodigy in 12-year-old Nika Turbina. M. Brower. il por People Wkly 27:67 Ap 6 '87
Turbine airplane engines See Airplane engines, Jet
Turbines
See also
Gas turbines, Automotive
Turbo-Union, Ltd.
Decision near in West Germany on EFA interim engine [European fighter aircraft] Aviat Week Space Technol 127:27 S 28 '87
GE, Turbo-Union allowed to rebid on EFA interim engine [European fighter aircraft program] Aviat Week Space Technol 126:24 F 23 '87
Turbo-Wash (Firm)
WallWalker wizard's washup wonder [creator F. Reinstein] G. Buchalter. il por Forbes 139:240 My 18 '87
Turbochargers See Airplane engines—Superchargers; Automobile engines—Superchargers; Automobiles, Racing—Engines—Superchargers; Diesel engines, Automotive—Superchargers; Diesel engines, Marine—Superchargers
Turbofan airplane engines See Airplane engines, Jet
Turboprop airplane engines See Airplane engines, Jet
Turbulence
Time-resolved three-dimensional concentration measurements in a gas jet. B. Yip and others. bibl f il Science 235:1209-11 Mr 6 '87
Why a fluid flows faster when the tube is pinched. J. Walker. il Sci Am 257:104-7 Jl '87
Turco, Lewis, 1934-
The kite [poem] Nation 244:300 Mr 7 '87
Turgeon, Pierre
about
Great expectations. C. Warner. il pors Sport Mag 78:70-2+ Mr '87
Turin, Shroud of See Holy Shroud
Turin (Italy)
Music
See also
Opera—Italy
Turin Master, fl. ca. 1420
See also
Eyck, Hubert van, ca. 1366-1426
Turing machines
The Turing machine. I. Malitz. bibl il Byte 12:345-6+ N '87
Turkana (African people)
Beating the odds in arid Africa [Turkana of Kenya] J. T. McCabe and J. E. Ellis. il map Nat Hist 96:32-41 Ja '87
Turkey
See also
Bodrum (Turkey)
Iranians—Turkey
Istanbul (Turkey)
Jews—Turkey
Military assistance, American—Turkey
Terrorism—Turkey

Turks
Defenses
See also
Airplanes, Military—Turkey
Foreign relations
Cyprus
See Cyprus
Greece
See Greece—Foreign relations—Turkey
Western Europe
The Turks are coming! E. von Kuehnelt-Leddihn. Natl Rev 39:42 F 27 '87
History
Ottoman Empire, 1288-1918
The world of Süleyman the Magnificent [cover story] M. Severy. il map Natl Geogr 172:552-601 N '87
Industries
See also
Tusas Aerospace Industries, Inc.
Politics and government
Ankara's search for identity [with interview with T. Ozal] J. P. Shapiro. il pors U S News World Rep 102:35-6 F 16 '87
A remote but bitter war [Kurds vs. Turks] T. Jacoby. il map Newsweek 109:45 Mr 30 '87
Religious institutions and affairs
See also
Orthodox Eastern Church—Turkey
Turkey calling See Bird calling
Turkey cooking See Cooking—Poultry
Turkey decoys See Decoys (Hunting)
Turkey hunting
Bowbag a gobbler. J. E. Churchill. il Outdoor Life 179:90-1+ My '87
Dismal day gobblers. K. Etling. il Outdoor Life 179:62-3+ Mr '87
Duel at dawn [roosting turkeys] M. Pearce. il Outdoor Life 179:62-3+ Ap '87
It could happen to you [safety for turkey hunters] W. H. Gross. il Outdoor Life 179:64-5+ Je '87
Let the turkeys come to you. B. W. Dalrymple. il Field Stream 92:62-3+ S '87
My hunting comrade, Pete [live turkey as decoy; reprint from January 1900 issue] J. Gordon. il Field Stream 91:60-1 F '87
Seven faces of old Tom. J. Trout, Jr. il Outdoor Life 179:45-7+ F '87
Sit tight for turkeys. D. Painter. il Field Stream 92:82-3 My '87
Thunder gobbler. T. Weddle. il Outdoor Life 180:70-1+ O '87
Training to be a spring-turkey detective. B. W. Dalrymple. il Field Stream 91:59+ Mr '87
A wild turkey for Thanksgiving [New York] W. Hollister. il Conservationist 42:2-9 S/O '87
Turkey industry See Poultry industry
Turkey stuffing See Stuffing (Food)
Turkey vultures
Why vultures make good neighbors [photographs] J. L. Ferrara. il Natl Wildl 25:16-21 Je/Jl '87
Turkeys
See also
Cooking—Poultry
Turkeys, Frozen
Frozen turkey. il Consum Rep 52:369-72 D '87
Talking turkey. il Consum Rep 52:600-5 O '87
Turkeys, Wild
Photographs and photography
Duel at dawn. M. Biggs. il Field Stream 91:64-5 Mr '87
Shooting
See Turkey hunting
Turkington, Carol
Help for the worried well. il Psychol Today 21:44-8 Ag '87
Special talents. il Psychol Today 21:42-6 S '87
Turkish art See Art, Turkish
Turkish cooking See Cooking, Turkish
Turkish refugees See Refugees, Turkish
Turks
Canada
A decision to stem the refugee tide. M. Gee. il Macleans 100:14 Ja 19 '87
Refugees at the door. B. Wallace. il Macleans 100:11 Ja 12 '87
Turks and Caicos Islands
Foreign relations
Canada
See Canada—Foreign relations—Turks and Caicos Islands

Turks and Caicos Islands—*cont.*
Politics and government
Canada's fantasy islands [with editorial comment by Kevin Doyle] P. Gessell. il map *Macleans* 100:2, 10-12 Mr 30 '87
Turley, Keith L., 1923-
about
Overload? J. Heins. il por *Forbes* 140:124+ D 14 '87
Turlington, Christy
about
Christy Turlington. D. A. Keeps. pors *Harpers Bazaar* 120:260, 368-71 S '87
Turnberry Isle Yacht and Racquet Club (Miami, Fla.: Resort) *See* Resorts—Florida
Turnbull, Alison
Sisterhood on the run. il *Women's Sports Fitness* 9:90 S '87
Turner, Christy G., II
Telltale teeth. maps *Nat Hist* 96:6+ Ja '87
Turner, David L.
about
Profile of a hurricane pilot. il por *Weatherwise* 40:132 Je '87
Turner, Frederick, 1943-
Literature lost in the thickets. il *N Y Times Book Rev* 92:1+ F 15 '87
Rethinking the university: design for a new academy. *Current* 290:22-6 F '87
The saguaro cactus. il *Ctry J* 14:31-4+ Ag '87
Slowly sinking in the West. il *Wilderness* 51:47-50 Fall '87
Turner, Harold W.
Afrikaner church needs 'critical solidarity'. *Christ Century* 104:645-6 Jl 29-Ag 5 '87
Turner, Ike
about
Ike Turner arrested again for cocaine possession. por *Jet* 72:65 S 7 '87
Turner pleads innocent to cocaine charges. por *Jet* 71:61 Ja 26 '87
Turner, J. M. W. (Joseph Mallord William), 1775-1851
about
At long last, Britain's Turner Bequest finds a proper home. I. Shenker. bibl (p144) il por *Smithsonian* 18:50-8+ Ag '87
Gallery for a 'wayward genius'. W. Feaver. il *Art News* 86:107-8 Summ '87
London journal. J. Bainbridge. il *Gourmet* 47:36+ N '87
Turner, Jack
about
Casket on steps evokes apology from judge who denounced King's memory. *Jet* 71:4 F 16 '87
Turner, Jerry
about
Baltimore's favorite anchorman returns despite serious malady. S. Salmans. il por *Channels* 7:8 Je '87
Turner, John
about
The great Liberal divide. P. Gessell. il por *Macleans* 100:12 Je 8 '87
John Turner's public struggle. P. Gessell. il por *Macleans* 100:20-1 S 7 '87
Turner strikes back. P. Gessell and H. Mackenzie. il por *Macleans* 100:10-11 Ag 31 '87
Turner's counteroffensive plan [with interview] H. Mackenzie. il por *Macleans* 100:10-11 S 14 '87
Turner's troubles. M. Clark. *Macleans* 100:19 Ag 24 '87
The war among the Liberals. M. Rose. il *Macleans* 100:12-13 Je 22 '87
Anecdotes, facetiae, satire, etc.
Dog days and snakes in a sponge. A. Fotheringham. il *Macleans* 100:60 S 14 '87
Turner, Joseph Mallord William *See* Turner, J. M. W. (Joseph Mallord William), 1775-1851
Turner, Kathleen
about
Joining ranks with Garbo and Gish, Kathleen Turner proves that playing Camille is not a dying art. il por *People Wkly* 27:70-1+ Ja 5 '87
Turner, Lana
about
Essence woman. M. Southgate. il por *Essence* 17:28 Ap '87
Turner, Pete, 1934-
about
Meet the masters [cover story] F. Cameron. il por *Petersens Photogr Mag* 16:20-5 My '87
Turner, R. E.
(jt. auth) See Abernethy, Y., and Turner, R. E.

Turner, Rebecca R.
What teachers think about their evaluations. *Educ Dig* 52:40-3 F '87
Turner, Rodney
about
Man poses as 14-year-old for chance at education. il por *Jet* 72:8 Je 1 '87
Turner, Ronald F.
Toussaint [story] *Harpers* 275:41-2 N '87
Turner, Ted, 1938-
about
Atlanta NAACP targets Turner's Hawks, Braves. *Jet* 73:48 D 14 '87
Growing up is hard to do [cover story] J. Traub. il por *Channels* 7:22-7 N '87
Ted Turner passes the hat around. S. Ticer. il *Bus Week* p38 Ja 26 '87
The Ted Turner show: shorter reins, but a steadier ride. S. Ticer. por *Bus Week* p96 O 26 '87
Turner's windless sails. B. Powell. il pors *Newsweek* 109:46-7 F 9 '87
TV's boldest gambler bets the plantation. S. P. Sherman. il por *Fortune* 115:104 Ja 5 '87
Turner, Thomas N.
Coping with the ways students cope with homework. *Educ Dig* 52:32-5 Ja '87
Turner, Tina
about
Lisa, it's for you . . . it's Tina Turner! [interview] L. Robinson. il *Vogue* 177:94 My '87
Rockers: then & now. il pors *Teen* 31:62-3 O '87
Tina Turner [Madison Square Garden concert] A. DeCurtis. il por *Roll Stone* p18 O 8 '87
Tina Turner considering move from U.S. to Britain and won't change name. por *Jet* 71:23 F 9 '87
Tina Turner: her most candid interview. E. Sporkin. por *Ladies Home J* 104:34+ Ap '87
Tina Turner talks about her final concert tour [cover story] il pors *Jet* 73:58-60 O 19 '87
Tina will write 2nd book but will leave Ike out. por *Jet* 73:37 S 28 '87
Turner, Tom
Earth diary. See issues of The Mother Earth News beginning January/February 1987
Of gold fever and brown rivers. il *Sierra* 72:30-3 Jl/Ag '87
Turner Broadcasting System, Inc.
At Ted's right hand [W. C. Bevins] C. Capuzzi. por *Channels* 7:54 Je '87
Growing up is hard to do [cover story] J. Traub. il por *Channels* 7:22-7 N '87
Is NBC getting hooked up to cable? [deal with Disney Channel and Turner Broadcasting] D. Lieberman. il por *Bus Week* p73 D 28 '87-Ja 4 '88
Southern exposure [X. Clayton of WTBS, Atlanta] M. Scott. il pors *Essence* 17:97-8+ Mr '87
Ted Turner passes the hat around [soaring debt] S. Ticer. il *Bus Week* p38 Ja 26 '87
The Ted Turner show: shorter reins, but a steadier ride. S. Ticer. por *Bus Week* p96 O 26 '87
Turner's windless sails. B. Powell. il pors *Newsweek* 109:46-7 F 9 '87
TV's boldest gambler bets the plantation [T. Turner] S. P. Sherman. il por *Fortune* 115:104 Ja 5 '87
Turner Communications Corporation
See also
Turner Broadcasting System, Inc.
Turning (Machine work)
See also
Lathes
Turn a rolling pin. E. Waltner. il *Workbench* 43:62-4 Mr/Ap '87
World-class turner [wooden bowls of B. Stocksdale] R. La Trobe-Bateman. il *Am Craft* 47:30-5 D '87/Ja '88
Turning Heads (Firm)
Peggy's still Turning Heads [owner P. Dillard] R. Houston. il *Essence* 18:50+ N '87
Turnover of labor *See* Labor turnover
Turnovers *See* Pastry
Turntables
See also
Phonograph—Turntables
Turocy, Catherine
about
Terpsicore [ballet] Reviews
Nation 244:624-6 My 9 '87. M. Aloff
Turow, Scott
about
Agent Gail Hochman's role in the ascent of 'Presumed innocent'. A. O'Malley. il por *Publ Wkly* 231:35-6 Ap 3 '87

Turow, Scott—about—cont.
Investigating Scott Turow. *Time* 130:73 D 14 '87
A lawyer courts best-sellerdom. J. Shear. il por *N Y Times Mag* p54-5+ Je 7 '87
PW interviews. W. Goldstein. por *Publ Wkly* 232:52-3 Jl 10 '87
Turpen, Forrest
Should sex education teach more than abstinence? [interview] il por *Christ Today* 31:40 Ap 17 '87
Turre, Steve
about
Steve Turré: trombone straight from the hip. M. Bourne. il pors *Down Beat* 54:28-30 D '87
Turrell, James, 1943-
about
Dream space. S. Gablik. il *Art Am* 75:132-3+ Mr '87
Roden's eye. F. Hapgood. il por *Atlantic* 260:46-52 Ag '87
Turtle Wax (Firm)
Simonizing poetic. R. Ceppos. il *Car Driv* 32:22-3 Ja '87
Turtles
Egg thieves of Playa Grande [leatherback turtle eggs] R. Hamm. il map *Sea Front* 33:27-33 Ja/F '87
The ins and outs of turtles. il *Natl Geogr World* 137:18-23 Ja '87
Leatherback deep dives. il *Sea Front* 33:304-5 Jl/Ag '87
Not the best way to save turtles [proposed experiment to study the impact of underwater explosions on endangered sea turtles] il *Oceans* 20:69 N/D '87
A tale of turtles [Labrador retriever assists box turtle researchers C. and E. Schwartz] il pors *Natl Geogr World* 146:28-31 O '87
The turtles of Mona Island [shipwrecked ferry imperils turtles] R. Wild. il *Wash Mon* 19:35-8 Mr '87
USAF to the rescue [Atlantic loggerhead turtle nest sites at Eglin Air Force Base] *Oceans* 20:4-5 N/D '87
Yertle: 1; Orca: 0 [deep diving by leatherback turtles; research by Scott A. Eckert] il *Discover* 8:14 S '87
Age
See Age—Reptiles
Eggs
See Reptiles—Eggs
Migration
The Kemp's ridley puzzle. T. Andersen. il *Oceans* 20:42-9 My/Je '87
The legacy of Tortuguero [work of A. Carr on sea turtle migration] il *Nat Hist* 96:2+ Je '87
Turtle tracks [Kemp's ridleys; work of Anne B. Meylan] il *Nat Hist* 96:4+ My '87
Turtles, Fossil
Modern turtle origins: the oldest known cryptodire [northeastern Arizona discovery] E. S. Gaffney and others. bibl f il *Science* 237:289-91 Jl 17 '87
Turtles as carriers of infection *See* Animals as carriers of infection
Turturro, John, 1957?-
about
John Turturro's bad-guy blues. P. Tyre. il por *N Y* 20:32 O 5 '87
Tusas Aerospace Industries, Inc.
Joint venture to build aircraft modernization installation in Turkey. J. D. Morrocco. il *Aviat Week Space Technol* 126:70-1 Ap 6 '87
Tuscany (Italy)
Description and travel
Spa Italian style [Bagni de Lucca] A. Alvarez. il *House Gard* 159:74+ O '87
Tushinsky, Joseph S.
about
The power of prayer. J. A. Conway. por *Forbes* 139:8 Mr 9 '87
Tuskegee Institute
See also
Tuskegee University
Tuskegee University
Reagan tells Tuskegee grads to choose black role models in sciences and professions. il pors *Jet* 72:13 My 25 '87
Tusks, Fossil
Prehistoric tusk: early boomerang? [mammoth tusk found in Polish cave; research by Pawel Valde-Nowak and others] B. Bower. *Sci News* 132:215 O 3 '87
Tussie mussies
Tussie mussies. N. A. Ruhling. il *Antiques Collect Hobbies* 92:30-2 Ag '87
Tuszynski, George P., and others
Thrombospondin promotes cell-substratum adhesion. bibl f il *Science* 236:1570-3 Je 19 '87

Tuthill, Charles
about
Charles Tuthill: a legend in cut and intaglio glass. B. Boggess and L. Boggess. il *Antiques Collect Hobbies* 92:14-18 Ap '87
Tutors and tutoring
See also
Gakkyusha (Firm)
Princeton Review, Ltd.
Coaching for SAT tests. M. Conroy. il *Better Homes Gard* 65:105-6 N '87
Cramming for college [coaching courses to boost SAT and ACT scores] K. McCormick. il *Changing Times* 41:61+ S '87
Expanding the use of cross-age/peer tutoring. D. Hedin. *Educ Dig* 53:39-41 D '87
How I became a Royal White Elephant, Third Class [tutor to the Thai royal family] R. Eberhart. il por *Am Herit* 38:44-7 F/Mr '87
Tutoring: when parent and teacher disagree. F. Roberts. *Parents* 62:48+ Ja '87
Tuttle, Liza
(jt. auth) See Culhane, Brien, and Tuttle, Liza
Tuttleton, James W.
Literacy at the barricades. *Commentary* 84:45-8 Jl '87
Tutu, Desmond
about
Bishop Tutu calls for dismantling of apartheid system, beginning of dialogue with blacks. por *UN Chron* 22:17 N/D '85
Tutwiler (Miss.)
Poor
The healing of soul and body [work of Sister Anne Brooks] L. Lindeman. il pors *50 Plus* 27:20-3+ D '87
Sister Anne Brooks, doctor and nun, practices without preaching to the poor. B. Shaw. il pors *People Wkly* 27:82-3+ Mr 23 '87
TV guide (Periodical)
TV guide takes on all comers. J. F. Berry. il *Channels* 7:15 Jl/Ag '87
Warning: manipulation ahead [rebuke of TV guide for using author's picture in full page N.Y. times ad] W. F. Buckley. *Natl Rev* 39:63 F 27 '87
Tvedten, Steve
about
Safety first. P. H. Johnson. il por *Rodale's Org Gard* 34:82-4+ D '87
TVX Broadcast Group Inc.
A little UHF group tries a great big gamble [TVX buys stations from Taft Broadcasting] C. S. Eklund. il por *Bus Week* p84+ F 2 '87
TW Services Inc.
TWA without the wings and woes. J. Main. *Fortune* 116:196+ O 12 '87
TW's numbers man throws caution to the winds [F. L. Salizzoni buys Denny's] L. Baum. il por *Bus Week* p67-9 Ag 3 '87
TWA *See* Trans World Airlines Inc.
Twain, Mark, 1835-1910
Mark Twain on the safest sex. *Harpers* 275:22-3 O '87
about
The curious house that Mark built. N. A. Ruhling. il por *Antiques Collect Hobbies* 92:80-2+ Mr '87
Huckleberry Finn: or, Something exotic in Czechoslovakia. J. Škvorecký. *N Y Times Book Rev* 92:47-8 N 8 '87
Twain (Mark) Memorial (Hartford, Conn.) *See* Mark Twain Memorial (Hartford, Conn.)
Tway, Bob
about
The golfing machine. P. De Jonge. por *N Y Times Mag* p88+ Ap 5 '87
Here's to happy days. R. Reilly. il pors *Sports Illus* 66:47-8+ Ap 13 '87
Tweed, William C.
Born of fire. il *Natl Parks* 61:22-7+ Ja/F '87
Tweed, William Marcy, 1823-1878
about
New York 1865. G. Dallas. bibl il *Hist Today* 37:17-22 D '87
Tweed Museum of Art (Duluth, Minn.)
Joining a winner. E. Beck. il *Horizon* 30:15 Ap '87
Tweedsmuir, John Buchan, Baron *See* Buchan, John, 1875-1940
Tweedy, Browne Inc.
He who eats last . . . [D. Trump and Tweedy, Browne buy interests in Resorts International] R. Phalon. il por *Forbes* 140:130+ D 14 '87

Twentieth century
What really mattered [10 most important headlines of the twentieth century] O. Friedrich. il *Time* 130:94 O 12 '87

Twentieth Century-Fox Film Corp.
Fun and profits at Beverly Hills High [deal with Twentieth Century-Fox Film Corp.] il *Newsweek* 110:45 Ag 31 '87

Twentieth Century Insurance Company *See* 20th Century Insurance Company

Twenty-first century
The 21st century economy. W. V. D. Wishard. il por *Futurist* 21:23-8 My/Je '87
Challenges for the twenty-first century. W. V. D. Wishard. *Futurist* 21:60 S/O '87
Marvin Cetron says he's seen the future, and it's high-tech joy [interview] B. Cornell. il *People Wkly* 27:84-6 Ja 12 '87

Twickenham (London, England)
Historic houses, sites, etc.
Palladian retreat of a royal mistress [H. Howard, countess of Suffolk] P. Quennell. il *Archit Dig* 44:86+ My '87

Twig furniture *See* Furniture, Rustic
Twin Cities *See* Minneapolis (Minn.)
Twin City Scenic Studio
Memorable memorabilia. il *Theatre Crafts* 21:19+ Ap '87

Twincraft Company
Soap's up! il *Natl Geogr World* 144:24-8 Ag '87

Twining, Sam
about
Tea time in London means profits in the pot for the Twining family. J. Calio. il pors *People Wkly* 28:75+ S 7 '87

Twining (R.) & Co. Ltd. *See* R. Twining & Co. Ltd.
Twins
See also
Siamese twins
16 matchless makeovers [eight sets of identical twins] il *Good Housekeep* 205:118-23+ Ag '87
All about twins [cover story] S. Begley. il *Newsweek* 110:58-62+ N 23 '87
Body doubles: the twin mystique. B. G. Harrison. *Mademoiselle* 93:76 Jl '87
Cybill Shepherd: "How can I handle twins?" [cover story; interview] T. Seligson. il pors *Redbook* 169:16+ S '87
Drew U. medical study focuses on 75 twins [heart research] il *Jet* 72:36 Ap 13 '87
The eerie world of reunited twins [Minnesota study] C. M. Rosen. il *Discover* 8:36-42+ S '87
Exploring the traits of twins [study by the Minnesota Center for Twin and Adoption Research] J. Leo. il *Time* 129:63 Ja 12 '87
Genes and behavior: a twin legacy [Minnesota study by Thomas J. Bouchard] C. Holden. il *Psychol Today* 21:18-19 S '87
The genetics of personality. C. Holden. il *Science* 237:598-601 Ag 7 '87
Growing up: Del and Rey, Johnny and Jimmy [experiments carried out on twins in the early 1930's] il *Sci Am* 257:30-2 Jl '87
Happiness is a reunited set of twins. J. S. Lang. il *U S News World Rep* 102:63-6 Ap 13 '87
June and Judy Thaxton: twins in engineering. F. White, III. il pors *Ebony* 42:116+ Mr '87
The M & M kids [ski racing twins K. and K. Schmidinger] D. B. Witchel. il pors *Skiing* 39:137-8+ Ja '87
Sins and twins. R. Bazell. *New Repub* 197:17-18 D 21 '87
To the manner born. W. Gallagher. il *Roll Stone* p56+ N 19 '87
Twinkle, twinkle, Cybill's stars [C. Shepherd's babies; cover story] S. Toepfer. il pors *People Wkly* 28:30-5 D 21 '87
Twins. S. Harper. il *Seventeen* 46:122-3+ Je '87
Twins attend reunion of once-frail babies [L. and J. Foster] il pors *Jet* 72:32 Je 29 '87
The Tyniste twins of Estonia jibe as sailing's double threat. S. K. Reed. il pors *People Wkly* 27:108-9 Ap 6 '87
When Güher and Süher Pekinel take the stage, classical piano buffs savor a twin Turkish delight. D. Grogan. il pors *People Wkly* 27:48+ Mr 16 '87

Twiste, Walter LeRoy
about
This early bear is catching worms. G. G. Marcial. *Bus Week* p118 N 23 '87

Two career couples *See* Married couples—Employment
Two City Kids Intl Inc.
Sole mates [shoe designers R. and M. Evins] J. Roberts. il pors *N Y* 20:28 Mr 9 '87
Two family houses
Family business [Salasky/Sedel house, Virginia Beach, Va.] K. D. Stein. il *Archit Rec* 175:86-93 mid-Ap '87
Two Forks Project (Colo.) *See* Dams
Two gentlemen of Verona [drama] *See* Shakespeare, William, 1564-1616
Two-stroke engines *See* Automobile engines
Two thousand (Year)
AIDS and the year 2000 [cover story; special section; with editorial comment by Edward Cornish] il *Futurist* 21:2+ 9-21 N/D '87
Business in the year 2000 [predictions by Barbara Chrispin] *USA Today (Periodical)* 115:10 My '87
Families and children in the year 2000. A. J. Norton. il *Child Today* 16:6-9 Jl/Ag '87
The Middle East in the year 2000 [address, April 24, 1987] A. Ghandour. *Vital Speeches Day* 53:450-5 My 15 '87
Projections 2000 [special section] bibl f il *Mon Labor Rev* 110:3-63 S '87
Television in the year 2000 [views of George Vinovich] *USA Today (Periodical)* 116:7 D '87
Anecdotes, facetiae, satire, etc.
Back to the future [year 2000] *Commonweal* 114:69-71 F 13 '87
Two thousand one (Year)
2001: electronics in the next century [cover story; special section; with editorial comment by Brian C. Fenton] il *Radio-Electron* 58:4, 79-119 My '87
A night at the movies [seven directors describe movies they'd like to do in 2001; cover story] M. Long. il *Omni* 9:44-6+ Je '87
Two thousand seven (Year)
Canada at 120: future shocks. M. Nichols. il *Macleans* 100:42-4 Jl 6 '87
The seers' catalog. M. Long. il *Omni* 9:36-8+ Ja '87
Two thousand seventeen (Year)
Anecdotes, facetiae, satire, etc.
Golden oldies in the year 2017. C. Gordon. por *Macleans* 100:9 Ja 12 '87
Two-tier contracts *See* Collective labor agreements
Two-way radio *See* Radiotelephone
Two-year colleges *See* Community and junior colleges
Twycross, Stephen, ca. 1745-ca. 1822
about
Federal Bostonians and their London jeweler, Stephen Twycross. M. G. Fales. bibl f il *Antiques* 131:642-9 Mr '87
Twyla Tharp Dance Company
Companies in transition [Brooklyn Academy of Music performances] L. A. Jacobs. il *New Leader* 70:21-2 Mr 23 '87
Dance [performances at the Brooklyn Academy of Music] M. Aloff. *Nation* 244:410-12 Mr 28 '87
Dancing:
Twyla Tharp Dance Company's appearance at the Brooklyn Academy occasions thoughts on relationship of modern dance and ballet. A. Croce. *New Yorker* 63:118-20 F 23 '87
Fighting-mad [performance of In the upper room at the Brooklyn Academy of Music] T. Tobias. il *N Y* 20:123-4 F 23 '87
Reviews:
Performances at the Brooklyn Academy of Music. J. R. Acocella. *Dance Mag* 61:194-6+ Je '87
Stepping out [performance of Ballare at the Brooklyn Academy of Music] T. Tobias. il *N Y* 20:110 Mr 2 '87
Tharp regroups. S. Reiter. il por *Dance Mag* 61:4 N '87
Twyla Tharp's return. H. Brubach. il *Atlantic* 259:86+ Mr '87
Tye, Barbara Benham, 1942-
The deep structure of schooling. il *Phi Delta Kappan* 69:281-4 D '87
Tylenol poisoning case, 1982
The Tylenol mystery. il *Newsweek* 110:10 O 12 '87
Tyler, Gus
Looking back to the 'Forward'. il *New Leader* 70:9-10 Ap 20 '87
Tyler, Kathie
about
Scoliosis: one 'Teen model's battle. P. S. Rix. il por *Teen* 31:26+ Jl '87

Tyler, Ralph Winfred, 1902-
Education reforms. il *Phi Delta Kappan* 69:277-80 D '87

Tyll, Ed
about
Atlanta NAACP is fuming over white talk show host's calling Lewis 'Buckwheat'. il pors *Jet* 72:22 Ag 10 '87

Tynan, Kathleen
about
Kathleen Tynan: "Ken constantly surprised and confused me . . . I had to find out about him". E. Soames. il pors *Vogue* 177:242 N '87

Tynan, Kenneth, 1927-1980
about
Kathleen Tynan: "Ken constantly surprised and confused me . . . I had to find out about him". E. Soames. il pors *Vogue* 177:242 N '87
Tynanosaurus rex. R. Brustein. *New Repub* 197:23-5 N 16 '87

Tynan, William
Front lines. See issues of High Fidelity (New York, N.Y.) through January 1987

Tyniste, Toomas
about
The Tyniste twins of Estonia jibe as sailing's double threat. S. K. Reed. il pors *People Wkly* 27:108-9 Ap 6 '87

Tyniste, Tynu
about
The Tyniste twins of Estonia jibe as sailing's double threat. S. K. Reed. il pors *People Wkly* 27:108-9 Ap 6 '87

Type A behavior
Competitive women risk heart attacks [findings of Carl Thoresen] il *USA Today (Periodical)* 116:8 S '87
Diabetes and stress: a Type A connection? [research by Brian Stabler and Richard S. Surwit] M. Roberts. *Psychol Today* 21:22 Jl '87
Smile your way to a longer life [work of Meyer Friedman] L. Vaughn. il *Prevention* 39:87-90+ Ag '87
Type A: affairs of the heart [research by Michael J. Strube] J. Goetz. *Psychol Today* 21:20 My '87
Type A and coronary artery disease [research by Jeffrey P. Kahn and others] S. Eisenberg. *Sci News* 132:293 N 7 '87
Type A on trial. J. Fischman. bibl (p64) il *Psychol Today* 21:42-4+ F '87
Young Type A's: the heartbreak kids [views of Carl Thoresen] J. Fischman. *Psychol Today* 21:10-11 Ja '87

Anecdotes, facetiae, satire, etc.
Life in the slow lane. C. Murphy. il *Read Dig* 130:47-8 Ap '87
The Type A vacation (or The case for staying home). K. Fury. il *Work Woman* 12:104 Jl '87

Type and typefounding
A personal type [type designer M. Carter] A. Ward. il pors *N Y Times Mag* p146 S 20 '87

Collectors and collecting
Collecting wood type. D. Stewart. il *Antiques Collect Hobbies* 92:60-2 My '87

Type E behavior
Who is the right man for a woman like you? [excerpt from The Type E woman] H. B. Braiker. il *Work Woman* 12:72-4+ Ja '87

Type T behavior
The big thrill [views of F. H. Farley] C. Zweig. il *Omni* 9:26+ Ap '87
Risk takers. C. Skrzycki. il *U S News World Rep* 102:60-7 Ja 26 '87

Types, Psychological *See* Typology (Psychology)

Typesetting
See also
Computers—Printing use

Typewriter industry
See also
SCM Corp.

Typewriters
Keyboards
See Keyboards

Typewriters, Electronic
Electronic typewriters. il *Consum Rep* 52:683-91 N '87
Those bleeping high-tech typewriters. N. Henderson. il *Changing Times* 41:43-4+ Je '87
Write of passage. M. T. Winter. il *Writer* 100:5-6 D '87

Typewriting
Hands on the home row. R. Nelson. il *Pers Comput* 11:57-8 N '87

Study and teaching
Aids and devices
Typing tutors [computer software] N. Henderson and M. Schiffres. il *Changing Times* 41:76 Ag '87

Typhoid fever
Vaccines and vaccination
Typhoid vaccine declared a success. *Sci News* 132:301 N 7 '87

Typing *See* Typewriting
Typographical errors *See* Errors, Typographical
Typology (Psychology)
See also
Myers-Briggs Type Indicator
Love your job! [determining your work personality] K. Koontz. il *Health* 19:29-33 Je '87

Tyre, Peg
Flatbush: touches of the Dutch and turn-of-the-century grandeur. il map *N Y* 20:64-6 My 4 '87
Witness stand. il *N Y* 20:14-15 Mr 16 '87

Tyrosine kinase *See* Kinases
Tyson, Cicely
Cry freedom. il pors *Ebony* 43:60-2+ D '87

Tyson, Gerald P., 1942-, and others
Fit to print. *Des Arts Educ* 88:13-16 Jl/Ag '87

Tyson, Laura D'Andrea, 1947-
(jt. auth) See Thurow, Lester C., and Tyson, Laura D'Andrea, 1947-

Tyson, Mike
about
Beers with . . . [interview] J. Price. il por *Sport Mag* 78:25-6 My '87
Iron Mike passes a test. R. Wiley. il pors *Sports Illus* 66:26-7 Je 8 '87
Kid Dynamite. J. C. Oates. il pors *Life* 10:64-6+ Mr '87
Larry Holmes agrees to fight Mike Tyson in '88. *Jet* 73:48 O 26 '87
Mike Tyson and Robin Givens: champ talks about their romance and his rise from street gangs to success [cover story] R. E. Johnson. il pors *Jet* 73:58-60 D 28 '87-Ja 4 '88
Mike Tyson faces assault and battery rap; tried to kiss girl, hit her boss. il por *Jet* 72:51 Jl 27 '87
Mike Tyson wins fight; KO's Biggs in the 7th. il pors *Jet* 73:51 N 2 '87
Mike Tyson: youngest heavyweight champion ever. M. Marshall. il pors *Ebony* 42:71+ F '87
Movie companies compete for the Mike Tyson story. por *Jet* 71:50 Ja 26 '87
New champs' date with destiny promises action; Loss least of woes for Tim Witherspoon. il pors *Jet* 71:48 Ja 12 '87
Only one no. 1 [cover story] P. Putnam. il pors *Sports Illus* 67:20-3 Ag 10 '87
Second boxing award impresses even Tyson. por *Jet* 71:49 F 16 '87
They could have danced all night . . . il pors *Sports Illus* 66:20-1 Mr 16 '87
Tip from Ali helped Smith survive onslaught of Tyson, who cracked his ribs. il pors *Jet* 72:48 Mr 30 '87
Tyson cleared in assault of LA parking employee. por *Jet* 73:48 O 19 '87
Tyson crowned champ during a $1/4 million coronation ceremony. R. E. Johnson. il pors *Jet* 72:51+ Ag 17 '87
Tyson lives up to billing, stars help him celebrate. il pors *Jet* 72:52 Je 15 '87
Tyson meets Thomas for title, then to get award. il por *Jet* 72:46 Je 1 '87
Tyson says he's 'a nobody' and not ready for marriage. il por *Jet* 72:29 S 7 '87
Tyson schedule so full Spinks may wait a year. pors *Jet* 72:48 Jl 20 '87
Tyson taps ex-champ Thomas as his next foe. *Jet* 72:48 Ap 13 '87
Tyson wins 2nd crown, works harder at party. il pors *Jet* 71:52-4 Mr 23 '87
Tyson's road to title is paved with hard work. *Jet* 71:50 Mr 9 '87
Very tough night at the office. W. Nack. il pors *Sports Illus* 67:64+ O 26 '87

Tysons Corner (Va.)
City planning
The new American downtown: Tyson's Corner as a case study. R. L. Miller. il *Archit Rec* 175:79+ S '87

Street traffic
Jammed up in Virginia, smooth sailing in Texas. W. J. Cook. il *U S News World Rep* 103:24-5 S 7 '87

U

U-Haul International, Inc.
King Lear [founder L. S. Shoen] J. Parr. il *Forbes* 139:84 F 23 '87
U-Haul hits the skids. D. Pauly. il *Newsweek* 110:54-5 S 14 '87

U.S. 50 *See* Roads

U.S. Bancorp
Buy or be bought. J. Heins. il por *Forbes* 139:48 My 18 '87

U.S. Committee in Solidarity with the People of El Salvador
Varelli: in from the cold [involvement in FBI spying on Committee in Solidarity with the People of El Salvador] D. R. Gordon. *Nation* 244:273+ Mr 7 '87

U.S. Consumer Product Safety Commission
Crossing swords over consumer safety [controversial chief T. M. Scanlon] J. P. Shapiro. il por *U S News World Rep* 103:28 O 26 '87
Is the CPSC being recalled? J. R. Provey. il *Home Mech* 83:6 S '87

U.S. Customs Service
Lockheed to supply P-3 AEW aircraft to Customs Service. B. A. Smith. *Aviat Week Space Technol* 126:29-30 Je 8 '87
A matter of customs. D. P. Marshall. *Travel Holiday* 168:74-6 N '87
A question of fees [fees on international airline tickets to cover the rising costs of inspections] S. Shane. *Travel Holiday* 167:39 F '87
Shell game at the docks [U.S. Customs not enforcing antidumping restrictions] G. Slutsker. il *Forbes* 139:34-5 Je 29 '87

U.S. Fish and Wildlife Service
A shelter for refuges [National Wildlife Refuge System] W. C. Reffalt. *Wilderness* 50:60 Summ '87

U.S. Fitness Academy
Why we need the new U.S. Fitness Academy. G. Allen. il por *Prevention* 39:94-6 Ap '87

U.S. Holocaust Memorial Museum
A go-ahead for "bad manners" [controversy over J. I. Freed's design] K. Andersen. il por *Time* 129:65 Je 29 '87

U.S. Home Corp.
U.S. Home: a cozy investment? [views of George Putnam III] G. G. Marcial. *Bus Week* p74 Mr 30 '87

U.S. Horse Cavalry Association
In Kansas: echoing hoofbeats. J. Skow. il *Time* 130:12-13+ N 23 '87

U.S. Jet
Charter company expanding medevac operations with BK. 117 fleet. P. Proctor. il *Aviat Week Space Technol* 126:83+ Ja 26 '87

U.S. news & world report (Periodical)
A message to our readers. F. Drasner. il *U S News World Rep* 103:3 Ag 3 '87

U.S. Nuclear Regulatory Commission
The case of the dissenting commissioner [J. Asselstine] A. Stine. il pors *Sierra* 72:46-50 My/Je '87
Controversy over nuclear evacuation planning. J. Raloff. *Sci News* 131:100 F 14 '87
Holes in the U.S. nuclear safety net. D. Utroska. bibl f il *Bull At Sci* 43:36-40 Jl/Ag '87
Legality of new NRC rule is challenged [licensing of nuclear power plants] R. Weiss. *Sci News* 132:309 N 14 '87
NRC to vote on new evacuation rule. R. Weiss. *Sci News* 132:279 O 31 '87
NRC's political meltdown. E. Marshall. il por *Science* 237:123-4 Jl 10 '87
NRC's research program comes under fire [National Academy of Sciences report] J. Raloff. *Sci News* 131:38 Ja 17 '87
Nuclear licensing on hold. *Sci News* 131:150 Mr 7 '87
Nuclear-power industry gets a wake-up call [NRC shuts down Peach Bottom plant in Pa.] R. A. Taylor. il *U S News World Rep* 102:14 Ap 13 '87
Nuclear reactor safety assailed in report [GAO report] R. Weiss. *Sci News* 132:213 O 3 '87
The safety goals of the U.S. Nuclear Regulatory Commission. D. Okrent. bibl f il *Science* 236:296-300 Ap 17 '87

U.S. Olympic Festival
An Olympic warmup in North Carolina. *South Living* 22:45 Je '87

U.S. Shoe Corp.
U.S. Shoe isn't dragging its feet. G. G. Marcial. *Bus Week* p101 Jl 13 '87

U.S. Trust Co. of New York
Dressing in the rich tradition [banker E. Patterson] W. Konrad. il pors *Work Woman* 12:83-4+ Jl '87

U.S. Videotel Inc.
Will Minitel play deep in the heart of Texas? J. E. Davis. il por *Bus Week* p94 O 19 '87

U2 (Musical group)
Band on the run [cover story] J. Cocks. il pors *Time* 129:72-7 Ap 27 '87
Bono. il por *People Wkly* 28:66-7 D 28 '87-Ja 4 '88
Bono [cover story; interview] D. Breskin. il pors *Roll Stone* p42-5+ O 8 '87
Bono [interview] D. Breskin. por *Roll Stone* p282-4 N 5-D 10 '87
A Celebration: U2 fans join the club. S. Hochman. il *Roll Stone* p16-17 Jl 2 '87
From street punks to rock idealists. N. Jennings. il *Macleans* 100:62-3 N 2 '87
An Irish Pied Piper of rock. C. McGuigan. il *Newsweek* 109:87 Ap 20 '87
On the road with U2. S. Pond. il por *Roll Stone* p15-16+ My 21 '87
Truths and consequences [cover story] A. DeCurtis. il pors *Roll Stone* p26-8+ My 7 '87
U2. D. Sussman. il *Sch Update* 120:25 D 4 '87
U2 [concert at Giants Stadium] J. Guterman. il *Roll Stone* p18 N 19 '87
U2: finding what they're looking for. il por *Teen* 31:86 S '87
U2 releases 'The Joshua tree'. A. DeCurtis. il *Roll Stone* p29+ Mr 26 '87
U2 rises to the occasion [release of Joshua tree] S. Pond. il por *Roll Stone* p71-2 Ap 9 '87
U2 tour film, LP planned for spring. il *Roll Stone* p15 D 3 '87

UAL Inc.
See also
Allegis Corporation
Can UAL and its Hilton wing fly in formation? J. E. Ellis. il *Bus Week* p45 Ja 12 '87

UAW *See* United Automobile, Aerospace and Agricultural Implement Workers of America

Ubiquinone *See* Coenzyme Q

Ubiquitin
Ubiquitin is a component of paired helical filaments in Alzheimer's disease. H. Mori and others. bibl f il *Science* 235:1641-4 Mr 27 '87

Uccel Corporation
Computer Associates buys its way to the top [acquisition of Uccel] A. Field. il *Bus Week* p68 Je 15 '87
Running room at Uccel. G. G. Marcial. por *Bus Week* p100 F 16 '87

Uchida, Mitsuko
about
Musical events. A. Porter. *New Yorker* 63:105-6 Mr 2 '87

UCLA *See* University of California, Los Angeles

UCLA diet *See* Diet

UCSB *See* University of California, Santa Barbara

UCSC *See* University of California, Santa Cruz

Udall, James R.
Just add water marketing. *Sierra* 72:37-8+ Mr/Ap '87
Polar opposites. il map *Sierra* 72:40-8 S/O '87

Udall, Morris K.
Arctic schemes. *Wilderness* 50:60 Spr '87
Staking out the last frontier. il por *Natl Parks* 61:16-17 N/D '87

Ude, Chema
Hidebound [poem] *Essence* 18:139 N '87
Moon waters back home [poem] *Essence* 18:157 S '87
Underdeveloped criminals [poem] *Essence* 18:139 O '87

Udesky, Laurie
Workfare [cover story] il *Progressive* 51:14-17 D '87

UDF *See* United Democratic Front (South Africa)

Ueberroth, Peter
about
Citizen Ueberroth [interview] R. B. Cramer. il pors *Esquire* 107:69-72+ F '87
Edwards and Ueberroth, classmates now teammates. pors *Jet* 72:51 Je 29 '87
Minorities in his office a priority, Ueberroth says. *Jet* 72:50 S 7 '87
Peter principles. por *Sports Illus* 66:72-3 Ap 27 '87
Ueberroth vows baseball will lead in hiring. *Jet* 72:47 Ag 17 '87

Uehling, Mark D.
Missing the deadline on ozone. il *Natl Wildl* 25:34-7 O/N '87

Ueltschi, Albert L.
about
Still flying high. J. A. Conway. por *Forbes* 139:8 Je 15 '87
UFCW *See* United Food and Commercial Workers International Union
UFOs
See also
Mutual UFO Network
Closer encounters. E. Dolnick. *New Repub* 197:15-16 Ag 10-17 '87
Invasion of the Strieber snatchers [W. Strieber's encounters with extraterrestrial aliens] T. Cochran. il por *N Y* 20:26 Mr 30 '87
Making Communion with another world. M. Green. il pors *People Wkly* 27:34-9 My 11 '87
Secret sharers [UFO abductees; cover story] P. Weintraub. il *Omni* 10:52-6+ D '87
Strange encounter over Alaska [sighting aboard Japan Air Lines flight 1628] map *Newsweek* 109:26 Ja 12 '87
Through the Alaskan darkness Kenju Terauchi, a 747 pilot, is pursued by a UFO—or so he claims. D. Chu. il por *People Wkly* 27:74+ Ja 26 '87
UFO update. See issues of Omni (New York, N.Y.)
What 'Communion' really said. W. Strieber. por *Publ Wkly* 232:72 O 2 '87
What's behind our UFO mania? E. Ziegler. *Read Dig* 131:113-17 Ag '87
When is a true story true? [dilemma of publishing W. Strieber's Communion as nonfiction] E. B. Claflin. il por *Publ Wkly* 232:23-6 Ag 14 '87
Anecdotes, facetiae, satire, etc.
The village alien [W. Strieber] T. M. Disch. il *Nation* 244:328-34+ Mr 14 '87
Conferences
Anecdotes, facetiae, satire, etc.
Sightings [UFO convention in New York City] *New Yorker* 63:25 Jl 6 '87
Uganda
History
Starting over. R. D. Kaplan. il *Atlantic* 259:18-21+ Ap '87
Politics and government
Alice's army on the march [rebel followers of A. Lakwena] M. A. Fitzgerald. il por *Macleans* 100:24 N 2 '87
Goodbye, Mama Alice [rebel leader] W. R. Doerner. il por *Time* 130:38 N 23 '87
Starting over. R. D. Kaplan. il *Atlantic* 259:18-21+ Ap '87
Ugarit (Ancient city)
Syria's disappearing palace. T. Mirabelli. il *Hist Today* 37:4-5 Ag '87
Ugarte, Augusto Pinochet *See* Pinochet Ugarte, Augusto
Ugliness, Physical *See* Homeliness
Ugolnik, Anthony
Finland's New Valamo: orthodoxy meets culture. il *Christ Century* 104:1176-8 D 23-30 '87
UHF *See* Television transmission
UHF (Ultrahigh frequency) television stations *See* Television stations
Uhlenberg, Peter
Reinforcing the fragile family. il por *Christ Today* 31:31-3 Ja 16 '87
Uhlig, Mark A.
From Hazelwood to the High Court. il *N Y Times Mag* p100-7 S 13 '87
Uhry, Alfred
about
Driving Miss Daisy [drama] Reviews
Commonweal 114:750 D 18 '87. G. Weales
N Y il 20:122 My 4 '87. J. Simon
Nation 245:459-60 O 24 '87. T. M. Disch
New Repub 197:28-30 S 28 '87. R. Brustein
New Yorker 63:73 Ap 27 '87. E. Oliver
Time il 129:71 My 25 '87. W. A. Henry
Vogue 177:70 Jl '87. S. Bolotin
Uilleann bagpipe *See* Bagpipe
Ukiah (Calif.)
Galleries and museums
See also
Sun House Museum (Ukiah, Calif.)
Ukraine
See also
Chernobyl nuclear disaster, 1986
Firefighters—Ukraine
Political prisoners—Ukraine
Theater—Ukraine
Description and travel
Ukraine. M. Edwards. il maps *Natl Geogr* 171:594-631 My '87

Politics and government
Shcherbitsky: the Politburo's untouchable. J. Barnathan. il map *Newsweek* 109:50 My 18 '87
Religious institutions and affairs
See also
Catholic Church—Ukraine
Ukrainian war criminals *See* World War, 1939-1945—War criminals
Ulam, Adam B., 1922-
Moscow stalling. *New Repub* 197:12-14 D 7 '87
Ulcerative colitis *See* Colitis
Ulcers
See also
Peptic ulcers
Ulene, Art
about
Random House Audio tries self-help with a health series. il *Publ Wkly* 231:39-40 My 1 '87
Ullberg, Kent, 1945-
about
Kent Ullberg's monumental sculptures [cover story] M. S. Doherty. il pors *Am Artist* 51:48-53 N '87
Ullman, Leslie
Heat [poem] *New Yorker* 63:28 Jl 20 '87
Ullman, Tracey
about
British wit Tracey Ullman says some nice things about America. C. Krupp. por *Glamour* 85:154 Je '87
Foxy lady. B. Zehme. il por *Roll Stone* p39-41+ Ag 27 '87
Tracey Ullman. il por *People Wkly* 28:70-1 D 28 '87-Ja 4 '88
Tracey Ullman goes back to the future of TV comedy [cover story] M. Kort. il pors *Ms* 16:18+ S '87
Will the real Tracey please stand up. H. F. Waters. il por *Newsweek* 110:48 Jl 13 '87
Ullmann, Linn
From Africa, with love. il pors *Seventeen* 46:210-11+ Ap '87
Ulloa, Jane
about
With a new line of suits, formal wear and even (ruff!) lingerie, any hound can put on the dog. il *People Wkly* 28:73 O 5 '87
Ullyot, Joan, 1940-
Sports medicine. See issues of Women's Sports & Fitness
Ulmer, James
Crabbing for blue-claws [poem] *New Yorker* 63:48 N 2 '87
Ulrich, Allan
Fournet—à la française. il por *Opera News* 51:38-9+ Ap 11 '87
Ulstein, Stefan
Is education going to the technicians? il por *Christ Today* 31:28 S 4 '87
Ultra Violet
Ultra Violet on Andy [excerpt from Ultra Violet remembers Andy Warhol] il pors *N Y* 20:46-7 Mr 9 '87
Ultrahigh bypass ratio engines *See* Airplane engines, Jet
Ultrahigh frequency television stations *See* Television stations
Ultrahigh frequency television transmission *See* Television transmission
Ultrasonic waves
See also
Sonoluminescence
Chemical use
Sound waves for activating nickel [research by Kenneth S. Suslick and Dominick J. Casadonte] I. Peterson. *Sci News* 131:388 Je 20 '87
Industrial use
Coming: graceful robots? [ultrasonic motors] D. Stover. il *Pop Sci* 230:27 Ja '87
Medical use
Prostate manograms on the MaleMobile. C. SerVaas. il *Saturday Evening Post* 259:106+ Ja/F '87
Sound advice on ultrasound: sonograms found to reduce cesarean rates. L. Piepenbrink. il *Health* 19:23 S '87
Ultrasound *See* Ultrasonic waves
Ultraviolet astronomy
See also
Artificial satellites—Astronomical use
Electroglow explained [Uranus glows in ultraviolet light] *Sky Telesc* 73:274 Mr '87
The extreme ultraviolet: a promising new window on the universe. J. K. Davies. il *Astronomy* 15:82-7 Jl '87
Planetary probes double as space telescopes. il *Sky Telesc* 74:456 N '87

Ultraviolet astronomy—*cont.*
Ultraviolet observations of solar fine structure. K. P. Dere and others. bibl f il *Science* 238:1267-9 N 27 '87

Ultraviolet photography
Fluorescent landscapes. R. Radstone. il *Petersens Photogr Mag* 15:30-2 Mr '87

Ultraviolet rays
Physiological effects
See also
Seasonal affective disorder
Sunburn
Suntan
Keep your sunny side up [benefits of exercising in the sun] P. Cowan. il *Women's Sports Fitness* 9:13 Ag '87
A rusty path to life's origin [effect of ultraviolet rays on ferrous carbonate; work of Gustaf Arrhenius] I. Peterson. *Sci News* 131:152 Mr 7 '87
Specs shield eyes from UV. il *Prevention* 39:14 Ap '87
Traveling through time [benefits of outdoor light in jet lag therapy] M. DuHamel. il *Women's Sports Fitness* 9:17 D '87

Ulysses (Greek mythology) *See* Odysseus (Greek mythology)
Uma *See* Lizards
Umansky, Martin
about
Hype in a good cause. L. Brown. il por *Channels* 7:26 Jl/Ag '87

Umberg, Günter
about
Gunter Umberg at Lorence Monk. E. Saxon. il *Art Am* 75:187-8 O '87

Umbilical cord
Prolapse
Umbilical cord prolapse. P. A. Hillard. il *Parents* 62:178+ Mr '87

Umbilical diving *See* Diving, Submarine
Umbrellas
The New York Flower Show and Uncle Sam Umbrella Shop. H. Bridges. il *Gourmet* 47:42+ Mr '87
You and your umbrella: how to make the relationship last. il *Glamour* 85:199 Mr '87

Umbria Jazz Festival *See* Music festivals—Italy
Umpires and umpiring (Sports) *See* Baseball, Professional—Umpiring
Umstadter, Kristen
about
Pennsylvania gothic. G. Hackett. il por *Newsweek* 110:27 Ag 17 '87
Primed to kill, an angry young man shoots his dead sister's boyfriend, leaving two families in ruins. J. Hammer. il *People Wkly* 28:159-60+ N 16 '87

Umstadter, Travis
about
Primed to kill, an angry young man shoots his dead sister's boyfriend, leaving two families in ruins. J. Hammer. il *People Wkly* 28:159-60+ N 16 '87

UMW *See* United Mine Workers of America
UN *See* United Nations
Un-American Activities Committee *See* United States. Congress. House. Committee on Un-American Activities
Una Donna, Ltd.
Going for the gold in jewelry. M. I. Finney. il por *Nations Bus* 75:71 Ja '87

Unanue, Emil R., and Allen, Paul M.
The basis for the immunoregulatory role of macrophages and other accessory cells. bibl f il *Science* 236:551-7 My 1 '87

UNC Inc.
A successful decontamination. K. Hannon. il por *Forbes* 140:68 Ag 24 '87

UNCITRAL *See* United Nations. Commission on International Trade Law
Unclaimed estates *See* Estates, Unclaimed
Uncle Sam (Symbol)
Collectibles
Our most noted relative: Uncle Sam [postcards] S. S. Carver. il *Antiques Collect Hobbies* 92:64-8 Jl '87

Uncle Tom's cabin [television program] *See* Television program reviews—Single works
Unconsciousness *See* Coma; Subconsciousness
UNCTAD *See* United Nations Conference on Trade and Development
Under-the-counter securities
Pinker than the pinks? [E. McLaughlin's stock strategy concentrates on busted initial public offerings and pink sheet stocks] por *Forbes* 140:146-7 D 28 '87
Terra incognita [L. Goldstein's pink sheet stock strategy] T. Jaffe. il por *Forbes* 140:38-40 D 28 '87

Underclass *See* Poor
Undercofler, James F.
An argument for a new college arts education curriculum. *Des Arts Educ* 88:30-1 Ja/F '87

Underdeveloped areas *See* Developing countries
Underground economy
Italy
The Italian miracle begins underground. J. Algañaraz. *World Press Rev* 34:50-1 Je '87
Peru
In defense of the black market [work of H. de Soto]; tr. by Alfred J. MacAdam. M. Vargas Llosa. il *N Y Times Mag* p28-31+ F 22 '87
Soviet Union
Inching down the capitalist road. J. O. Jackson. il *Time* 129:42 My 4 '87

Underground houses *See* Houses, Earth sheltered
Underground literature
Hungary
'Informing on ourselves'. G. Konrád. *Nation* 244:237+ F 28 '87
Poland
Another country. A. Applebaum. *New Repub* 197:12-13 Ag 24 '87
Publishing in Poland. A. Husarska. il *New Leader* 69:21-4 D 1-15 '86
Soviet Union
'Exodus' in samizdat: still popular and still subversive. E. McDowell. il *N Y Times Book Rev* 92:13 Ap 26 '87

Underground nuclear testing *See* Nuclear weapons—Testing
Underground Opera (Opera company)
Musical events:
La virtù de' strali d'Amore by P. F. Cavalli. A. Porter. *New Yorker* 63:62-3 Ag 24 '87

Underground railroad
The underground railroad. C. L. Blockson. il *Essence* 17:43+ F '87

Underhill, David
Other sides to the textbook controversy [discussion of May 6, 1987 article, Voltaire arraigned in Alabama: the textbook humanism case] il *Christ Century* 104:631-2 Jl 15-22 '87
Voltaire arraigned in Alabama: the textbook humanism case. *Christ Century* 104:438-40 My 6 '87

Underprivileged children *See* Socially handicapped children
Undersea mining *See* Ocean mining
Undertakers and undertaking
See also
Black undertakers and undertaking
Laws and regulations
Charles Diggs wins back his mortuary license. por *Jet* 73:39 O 26 '87

Underwater archeology *See* Archeology, Submarine
Underwater art
He's unknown now, but the world's top underwater artist is waiting for his reputation to surface [J. Verheylewegen] il pors *People Wkly* 28:147 N 30 '87

Underwater blasting *See* Blasting, Submarine
Underwater cables *See* Cables, Submarine
Underwater cave diving *See* Skin diving
Underwater drilling
See also
Ocean Drilling Program
Underwater hotels, motels, etc.
Scuba hotel [Jules' Undersea Lodge in Key Largo, Fla.] A. Ferber. il *Women's Sports Fitness* 9:16 Ag '87
Sleep tight, underwater [Jules' Undersea Lodge off Key Largo] B. Barol. il *Newsweek* 109:56 Ap 6 '87

Underwater photography *See* Photography, Submarine
Underwater research *See* Oceanography
Underwater Systems Australia Ltd.
A yellow submarine pops up from Down Under [C'Cat] C. Debes. il *Bus Week* p104 S 28 '87

Underwater treasure *See* Treasure trove
Underwater villages
"Special interest" colonies for oceans and space. *Futurist* 21:42-3 Ja/F '87

Underwear
Boxer shorts. J. Berendt. il *Esquire* 108:44+ S '87
Frilly—and very feminine [lingerie] A. Steacy. il *Macleans* 100:34-5 F 9 '87
How to dress better from the inside out. il *Glamour* 85:93-6 Ja '87
Little lace luxuries [lingerie] il *Harpers Bazaar* 120:66+ O '87
No longer in hiding. C. Donovan. il *N Y Times Mag* p86-7 My 3 '87
A short guide to long johns [ski underwear] E. Perlman. il *Skiing* 39:87-9 F '87

Underwear—*cont.*
Slip into the past [lingerie] J. Conant. il *Newsweek* 109:51 Ja 5 '87
Under it all [thermal underwear] K. Etling. il *Outdoor Life* 180:80-1+ O '87
Understatements. W. Goodman. il *N Y* 20:46-50 Ja 19 '87
Underwear industry
See also
　Fruit of the Loom, Inc.
　J.E. Morgan Knitting Mills, Inc.
　Jockey International, Inc.
　Maidenform, Inc.
　Natori Company
　Rocky Mount Undergarment Co., Inc.
Japan
See also
　Wacoal Corp.
Underweight *See* Weight (Physiology)
Underwood, James H., and others
X-ray photographs of a solar active region with a multilayer telescope at normal incidence. bibl f il *Science* 238:61-4 O 2 '87
Underwood, John, 1934-
Bo's two-way stretch. il *pors Life* 10:93-4+ O '87
UNDOF (United Nations Disengagement Observer Force)
See United Nations—Armed Forces—Forces in the Middle East
UNDP *See* United Nations Development Programme
UNDRO *See* Office of the United Nations Disaster Relief Co-ordinator
Unemployment
See also
　Layoffs
Behind the help-wanted signs [coexistence of labor shortages and high unemployment rates] G. J. Church. il *Time* 130:55 Jl 20 '87
How low can we go? S. Nasar. il *Fortune* 115:64 Mr 16 '87
Job loss from wage hike. il *Nations Bus* 75:103 S '87
Jobs without people and people without jobs: the coming mismatch in the information society. W. H. Kolberg. il *USA Today (Periodical)* 116:18-20 Jl '87
Surviving unemployment. J. Malveaux. il *Essence* 18:108 D '87
The tragic impact of joblessness. R. A. Oswald. il *USA Today (Periodical)* 115:28-30 Mr '87
Unemployment lines: shorter every day. J. C. Cooper. il *Bus Week* p50 O 19 '87
Urban youth lose jobs to suburbs. A. F. Brimmer. il *Black Enterp* 18:45 S '87
Psychological aspects
Unemployed hubby [black man] G. G. Grant. il *Essence* 18:14 Jl '87
Relief measures
See also
　Full employment
　Retraining, Occupational
　Unemployment benefits
　Workfare
The failure of federal job training programs. J. Bovard. il *USA Today (Periodical)* 116:12-17 Jl '87
The jobs conundrum. *New Repub* 197:7-9 N 30 '87
Worker dislocation report. *Mon Labor Rev* 110:2 F '87
Statistics
Decline in youth population does not lead to lower jobless rates. T. J. Nardone. bibl f il *Mon Labor Rev* 110:37-41 Je '87
Industrial structure has little impact on jobless rate of experienced workers. R. M. Devens, Jr. bibl f il *Mon Labor Rev* 110:30-2 My '87
The pulse of economic change: displaced workers of 1981-85. F. W. Horvath. bibl f il *Mon Labor Rev* 110:3-12 Je '87
This gender gap bodes well for Wall Street [spread between male and female unemployment as stock market indicator; research by Peter L. Bernstein] G. Koretz. il *Bus Week* p34 My 18 '87
Time spent unemployed: a new look at data from the CPS. M. W. Horrigan. bibl f il *Mon Labor Rev* 110:3-15 Jl '87
Great Britain
Beat the devil [Thatcher election victory] A. Cockburn. *Nation* 244:876-7 Je 27 '87
Britain's redundancy payments for displaced workers. L. S. Root. bibl f il *Mon Labor Rev* 110:18-23 Je '87
Japan
Japanese unemployment: BLS updates its analysis. C. Sorrentino. bibl f il *Mon Labor Rev* 110:47-53 Je '87

Japan's newest import: U.S.-style layoffs. L. Armstrong. il *Bus Week* p57-8 Mr 9 '87
Land of rising unemployment. *Fortune* 115:10+ F 2 '87
Now Japan faces unemployment. I. Rodger. *World Press Rev* 34:44-5 Mr '87
Shame and a growing crisis for Japan. M. Gray. il *Macleans* 100:42-3 Je 8 '87
Massachusetts
Down and out in the midst of Boston's boom. K. H. Hammonds. il *Bus Week* p53 Ag 10 '87
Ohio
A laid-off steelworker's continuing bout with unemployment [Dominic Tardio] B. Perris. il *Sch Update* 119:7 Mr 23 '87
United States
See Unemployment
Western Europe
European unemployment: the challenge of the '80s. R. Dornbusch. il *Current* 289:25-31 Ja '87
Unemployment benefits
See also
　Insurance, Unemployment
Britain's redundancy payments for displaced workers. L. S. Root. bibl f il *Mon Labor Rev* 110:18-23 Je '87
Health insurance loss: the case of the displaced worker. M. Podgursky and P. Swaim. bibl f il *Mon Labor Rev* 110:30-3 Ap '87
Unemployment compensation *See* Insurance, Unemployment
Unemployment insurance *See* Insurance, Unemployment
Unesco
Four prizes awarded on International Literacy Day. *UN Chron* 23:20 N '86
Mainstreaming Unesco? *Christ Century* 104:956-7 N 4 '87
Rhizobium, the farmer's Mr. Fixit. E. J. DaSilva and others. il *Courier* 40:27-8 Mr '87
A scientist back at the helm of Unesco? [nomination of F. Mayor] D. Dickson. por *Science* 238:473-4 O 23 '87
Unesco and drugs. il *Courier* 40:6-7 Jl '87
UNESCO asks states considering withdrawal to 'reconsider their position'. *UN Chron* 23:83-4 Ja '86
UNESCO board appeals for protection of cultural sites in war-torn areas. *UN Chron* 24:74 Ag '87
UNESCO Board considers organizational reforms, plans for zero-growth budget for 1988-1989. *UN Chron* 24:98 F '87
Unesco. Man and the Biosphere Programme *See* Man and the Biosphere Programme
UNFICYP (United Nations Peace-Keeping Force in Cyprus)
See United Nations—Armed Forces—Forces in Cyprus
UNFPA *See* United Nations Fund for Population Activities
Ungar, Sanford J.
Life goes on under Pinochet's yoke. il *U S News World Rep* 103:40 N 30 '87
Unchaining South Korean journalists. il *U S News World Rep* 103:31 Ag 10 '87
Unger, Norman O.
Baseball's black millionaires. il *Ebony* 42:92+ My '87
Ebony update: George Foreman. il pors *Ebony* 42:92+ Je '87
A sporting chance . . . See issues of Jet beginning December 31, 1984-January 7, 1985 through January 26, 1987
Sugar Ray Leonard: why I am fighting again [cover story] il *Ebony* 42:92-4+ Ap '87
Unger, Roberto M.
Bibliography
The professor of smashing. S. Holmes. *New Repub* 197:30-8 O 19 '87
Ungulates
Why the deer and the antelope play. J. A. Byers. il *Nat Hist* 96:54-61 My '87
UNHCR *See* United Nations. High Commissioner for Refugees
UNICEF
1987 State of world's children: 'the silent emergencies'. il *UN Chron* 24:64-7 My '87
Belafonte succeeds Kaye as UNICEF ambassador. pors *Jet* 71:30 Mr 23 '87
Belafonte testifies on behalf of UNICEF. *Jet* 72:59 Ap 27 '87
Child-abuse charges rock UNICEF. *Newsweek* 110:33 Jl 6 '87
Declaration affirming commitment to immunization of all the world's children by 1990 signed at headquarters. il *UN Chron* 22:107 N/D '85
Lessons for UNICEF. P. Valley. il por *World Press Rev* 34:53-4 Mr '87

UNICEF—*cont.*
UNICEF at forty. il *Courier* 40:34 Ja '87
UNICEF board reviews strategies on child survival, women, communications. il *UN Chron* 24:69 Ag '87
UNICEF's new trick: giving on the fly [raising money from air travelers] *Newsweek* 110:43 Jl 27 '87

Unicorns in art
Unicorn mailbag [children's drawings] il *Natl Geogr World* 147:24-5 N '87

Unicorp Canada Corporation
Unicorp fuels a fight [sale of Palm Dairies blocked by Competition Act tribunal] T. Fennell. il *Macleans* 100:14-15 Ja 5 '87

Unidentified flying objects *See* UFOs

UNIDO *See* United Nations. Industrial Development Organization

Unifi Inc.
Polyprofitable. T. Jaffe. *Forbes* 140:270 D 14 '87

Unification Church
Moonie journalism [Washington times] T. McNichol. *Wash Mon* 19:23-8 O '87
Notes & asides [editorial controversy at the Washington times] W. F. Buckley. il *Natl Rev* 39:20+ My 22 '87
Psychology and religion in court—again [anticult theories of coercive persuasion] J. R. Lewis and J. G. Melton. *Christ Century* 104:914-16 O 21 '87
Underdog to an 800-pound gorilla [ownership of Washington times] L. Zuckerman. il por *Time* 129:64-5 Je 15 '87
War of independence [charges of editorial interference at Washington times] *Newsweek* 109:63 Ap 27 '87

Unified Space Command (U.S.) *See* United States. Unified Space Command

UNIFIL (United Nations Interim Force in Lebanon) *See* United Nations—Armed Forces—Forces in Lebanon

Uniforce Temporary Personnel, Inc.
Will success be merely temporary? F. McCoy. il por *Bus Week* p86 My 25 '87

Uniforms
See also
Baseball, Professional—Uniforms
Girl Scouts of the United States of America—Uniforms
Military uniforms
School uniforms
United States. Air Force—Uniforms
Standard issue [employees in uniform] M. R. Solomon. bibl (p63) il *Psychol Today* 21:30-1 D '87

UNILAW *See* United Law Network

Unilever NV
Pulling together a two-part company [F. A. Maljers and M. Angus] R. I. Kirkland, Jr. il pors *Fortune* 116:40 Ag 3 '87

Union agreements *See* Collective labor agreements

Union Bank of Switzerland
The big cheese in London banking could be Swiss [proposed buyout of Hill Samuel Group plc] J. Templeman. il *Bus Week* p37 Jl 27 '87

Union Carbide Agricultural Products Co., Inc.
Union Carbide sold to Rhone-Poulenc. *Success Farm* 85 no2:18T Ja '87

Union Carbide Corp.
See also
Bhopal poisonous gas disaster, India, 1984
Endgame for a corporate moonwalker. J. Merwin. il *Forbes* 139:130-2+ My 18 '87
Strategic planning [address, March 18, 1987] R. D. Kennedy. *Vital Speeches Day* 53:624-7 Ag 1 '87

Union Carbide poisonous gas leak, Bhopal, India, 1984
See Bhopal poisonous gas disaster, India, 1984

Union catalogs *See* Catalogs, Union

Union Enterprises Ltd.
Educating the managers [shareholder challenges] A. Shortell. il *Macleans* 100:28-9 S 28 '87

Union membership *See* Trade unions—Membership

Union of Concerned Scientists
Scientists urge new stance on SDI testing in U.S.-Soviet arms talks. T. M. Foley. *Aviat Week Space Technol* 127:30 S 14 '87

Union of Soviet Socialist Republics *See* Soviet Union

Union Pacific Corp.
From two used trucks to a $1.2-billion deal [Overnite Transportation's H. Cochrane sells out to Union Pacific Corp.] A. B. Rea. il por *Fortune* 115:67 Ja 5 '87

Union Special Corp.
A stitch in time. J. Parr. il por *Forbes* 140:172+ N 16 '87

Union Underwear Co.
See also
Fruit of the Loom, Inc.

Unions, Labor *See* Trade unions

Unipod camera supports *See* Camera supports

Unique Mobility (Firm)
Unique Mobility [development of electric cars] R. Grable. il *Mot Trend* 39:90-5 My '87

Uniroyal, Inc.
See also
Uniroyal Goodrich Tire Co.

Uniroyal Goodrich Tire Co.
What's deflating Uniroyal Goodrich. Z. Schiller. il *Bus Week* p35 N 30 '87

Unisys Corp.
Globesat designing satellite for Unisys. *Aviat Week Space Technol* 127:29 O 19 '87
Unisys: so far, so good—but the real test is yet to come. R. Mitchell. il por *Bus Week* p84+ Mr 2 '87
Unisys wins $60-million contract for Nexrad Doppler weather radar. *Aviat Week Space Technol* 127:35 D 7 '87

Unit photography *See* Set photography

UNITA *See* National Union for the Total Independence of Angola

UNITAR *See* United Nations Institute for Training and Research

Unitarian Universalist Association
Unitarians. A. H. Fowlie, Jr. il por *Cent Mag* 20:15-17 S/O '87
UUA resolves. *Christ Century* 104:617 Jl 15-22 '87

United Aerospace Defense Systems
Joint venture to bid on LOS-F-H portion of FAADs [line of sight-forward heavy portion of the Army's forward area air defense system] *Aviat Week Space Technol* 126:29 Ap 20 '87

United Air Lines, Inc.
Air pockets around United [pilots propose employee buyout] G. M. Bock. il *Time* 129:52-3 Ap 20 '87
The Allegis experiment turns into a bonanza. J. E. Ellis. *Bus Week* p123+ N 9 '87
Boeing financing of United orders reflects stiffening competition. *Aviat Week Space Technol* 126:29-30 My 18 '87
Can United afford Texas Air's low fares? J. E. Ellis. il *Bus Week* p34 F 16 '87
Collins: United Airlines must hire more blacks. *Jet* 71:8 Mr 23 '87
Friendly guy, unfriendly skies [United's pilots choose W. R. Howard as the executive to help them buy the company] N. J. Perry. il por *Fortune* 116:122 S 14 '87
Lighting the way [lighting at United Airlines Terminal at O'Hare Airport] S. R. Shemitz. il *Archit Rec* 175:148-55 N '87
Pilots' offer to buy United meets company, union opposition. J. Ott. *Aviat Week Space Technol* 126:32-3 Ap 20 '87
PS/2's United Airline [automated reservation system] S. Makrias. il *Pers Comput* 11:34 N '87
The temple of marketing [H. Jahn's terminal at Chicago's O'Hare Airport] H. Muschamp. il *New Repub* 197:25-8 O 26 '87
UAL's pilots may put the airline into play [employee ownership offer] J. E. Ellis. il *Bus Week* p25 Ap 20 '87
United Airlines increases flights at Washington Dulles. *Aviat Week Space Technol* 126:49 Ja 26 '87
United conducts total training of MAC C-5 crews. il *Aviat Week Space Technol* 127:112 Jl 6 '87
United finds a new friend [Allegis' deal with Boeing] J. B. Copeland. il *Newsweek* 109:38 My 25 '87
United names Wolf, shares CRS codes with British Airways. *Aviat Week Space Technol* 127:35 D 14 '87
United, SIU Carbondale seek more black pilots. *Jet* 72:16 Ag 3 '87
United's pilots are inching closer to a coup [employee ownership] J. E. Ellis. il por *Bus Week* p32-3 Ag 31 '87
United's pilots get a captain and cash [mounting a buyout] *Newsweek* 110:32 Ag 24 '87
What's keeping new airports from getting off the ground [Stapleton Airport] M. Ivey. il *Bus Week* p32 Jl 27 '87

United Arab Emirates
Industries
See also
Emirates (Firm)

United Artists Communications, Inc.
What a performance [sale of United Artists Communications to Tele-Communications and spinoff of Todd-AO] A. B. Block. il *Forbes* 139:136 Ap 6 '87

United Artists Corp.
"Don't woo with words—show me" [films in production] *Film Comment* 23:36 Ja/F '87

United Asset Management Corporation
Norton Reamer collects money management firms. A. Beam. il por *Bus Week* p114 My 18 '87

United Automobile, Aerospace and Agricultural Implement Workers of America
Can GM afford this deal? *Newsweek* 110:63 O 19 '87
Collision course. J. Schwartz. il *Newsweek* 109:52 F 23 '87
Continuing education for blue-collar workers [UAW-Ford Employee Development and Training Program] P. H. Abelson. *Science* 238:875 N 13 '87
Deere contract protects employees against layoffs. *Mon Labor Rev* 110:56-7 Ap '87
Detroit vs. the UAW: at odds over teamwork. A. Bernstein and W. Zellner. il *Bus Week* p54-5 Ag 24 '87
A different sort of victory for the UAW [agreement with Ford] *Newsweek* 110:65 S 28 '87
Ford-UAW contract bolsters job security. il *Mon Labor Rev* 110:31-3 N '87
A Ford vehicle doomed to stall at General Motors [UAW contract] J. A. Seamonds. il *U S News World Rep* 103:16 S 28 '87
General Motors' new uphill course. J. A. Seamonds. il *U S News World Rep* 103:9 O 19 '87
GM may be off the hook: the Ford talks leave plenty of loopholes. A. Bernstein and W. Zellner. il *Bus Week* p26-7 S 28 '87
GM's not-so-radical proposal [productivity of each plant to determine wage increases and job security] *Fortune* 116:10 S 14 '87
How GM and the UAW kept from butting heads. W. Zellner. il *Bus Week* p32 O 26 '87
Life at Nissan: paradise lost? [UAW's new drive to unionize Smyrna, Tenn. plant] B. Turque and J. B. Copeland. il *Newsweek* 110:50 Ag 10 '87
Mack Trucks, Auto Workers settle. *Mon Labor Rev* 110:44 Jl '87
One down, tougher one to go [UAW settles with Ford] J. Castro. il *Time* 130:52 S 28 '87
Program guarantees 100-percent job security. *Mon Labor Rev* 110:72-3 S '87
Rough bargaining ahead. G. Bock. il *Time* 130:63 S 14 '87
Smiling fender to fender [Ford's UAW contract] W. Zellner and A. Bernstein. il *Bus Week* p39 O 5 '87
U.A.W. backs the wrong team. E. Mann. il *Nation* 244:171-2+ F 14 '87
The UAW faces a plant-by-plant struggle. W. Zellner. il *Bus Week* p25 Ag 10 '87
The UAW gears up for tough talks. il *Fortune* 116:8 Jl 6 '87
The UAW sees a smoother road at Ford. W. Zellner. il *Bus Week* p125+ S 14 '87
What the Auto Workers are up against. A. Bernstein. il *Bus Week* p83-4 Ap 27 '87
Williams 1st woman on UAW Local 249 exec. bd. [B. Williams] *Jet* 72:30 Ag 24 '87

United Church of Christ
Choosing sites [selection of headquarters] *Christ Century* 104:104 F 4-11 '87
Osei 1st black to head UCC conference in D.C. *Jet* 72:38 Jl 27 '87
UCC delays site choice. *Christ Century* 104:617 Jl 15-22 '87

United Coastal Insurance
Life after death [after asbestos claims litigation scares off insurers, Acmat Corp. forms own company to write liability policies] B. Leonard. il por *Forbes* 139:132-3 My 4 '87

United Democratic Front (South Africa)
The fall of the Front. S. Mufson. *New Repub* 196:17-19 Mr 23 '87

United Design Corporation
Itty Bitty monster hits. J. Culpepper and S. Dark. il pors *Nations Bus* 75:58 Jl '87

United Farm Workers of America
Farmworkers out on the line again [proposed UFW grape boycott] A. Stine. il *Sierra* 72:14+ Jl/Ag '87
A lawsuit could ruin the Farmworkers' Union [damages for violence in a 1979 strike] J. Flynn. il *Bus Week* p42 Mr 23 '87
Wooing the migrant farmer [growers' campaign to explain Immigration Reform and Control Act] J. B. Copeland. il *Newsweek* 109:47 Je 29 '87

United Farmers Organization
A harvest of struggle. Y. Moore. il *Black Enterp* 17:64 Je '87

United Financial Operations Inc.
The promoter who never quits [tax shelter operator W. A. Kilpatrick] A. A. Lappen. il por *Forbes* 139:60-1 F 9 '87

United Food and Commercial Workers International Union
Grocery store settlements. il *Mon Labor Rev* 110:56-7 Ag '87
Kroger workers forgo bonus plan to save jobs. *Mon Labor Rev* 110:42-3 Mr '87
A novel union role: picketing for the boss [Ohio supermarkets enlist workers in push against nonunion rivals] S. Phillips. il *Bus Week* p80 D 28 '87-Ja 4 '88
Unions fighting unions [R. Cashin switches Newfoundland fishermen's union affiliation from United Food and Commercial Workers to Canadian Auto Workers] D. Jenish. il *Macleans* 100:41-2 Ap 27 '87

United Healthcare Corp.
HMO survivor? J. Parr. il por *Forbes* 139 Ann Directory:126 Ap 27 '87

United Law Network
A spirited defense by local lawyers. L. J. Tell. il *Bus Week* p134 N 2 '87

United Media
Kartes licenses Peanuts from sister company [arrangement for home video rights] il *Publ Wkly* 231:50+ Ap 24 '87

United Methodist Church
　See also
　　Southern Methodist University
Black Methodist minister heads white Texas church [J. D. Phillips of St. Andrew's United Methodist Church in Killeen] por *Jet* 72:22 Jl 13 '87
Contract not renewed [faculty member E. Bettenhausen charges sexism in dispute with Boston University School of Theology] *Christ Century* 104:936 O 28 '87
Hymnal completed. *Christ Century* 104:993 N 11 '87
Methodist maneuvers [issues relating to homosexuality and sexism] il *Time* 130:64 D 28 '87
A Methodist on trial [trial of lesbian clergywoman R. Denman in Dover, N.H.] M. Starr. il por *Newsweek* 110:62 S 7 '87
Murder in Mozambique [attack on United Methodist mission station] *Christ Century* 104:850 O 7 '87
'The things that make for peace' [pastoral In defense of creation] W. H. Willimon. *Christ Century* 104:453-4 My 6 '87
Willimon hollering at bishops? [discussion of May 6, 1987 article, The things that make for peace] W. H. Willimon. *Christ Century* 104:632-4 Jl 15-22 '87
　　Employees
　　Salaries, pensions, etc.
Methodists will cut some stocks linked to S. Africa. *Jet* 72:14 S 14 '87

United Methodist Church and birth control *See* Birth control—Moral and religious aspects

United Mine Workers of America
The UMW won't hit much pay dirt this time. M. Schroeder. il *Bus Week* p99+ N 2 '87

United Nations
　See also
　　International Day for the Elimination of Racial Discrimination
The 38th floor. J. Pérez de Cuellar. See issues of UN Chronicle
"More than a map . . ." [emblem] il *UN Chron* 24:78 N '87
October news in pictures. il *UN Chron* 22:110 N/D '85
Pledges to World Disarmament Campaign total $360,000. *UN Chron* 22:83 N/D '85
Reform and renewal in the United Nations. *UN Chron* 24:43 Ag '87
The strategy of humanitarian assistance. T. Kunugi. il *UN Chron* 24:54-5 My '87
"What a legacy for our children!" [interview with S. Aga Khan] P. Gupte. il por *Forbes* 139:100+ Je 15 '87
　　Armed Forces
　　Forces in Cyprus
Security Council extends mandate of Cyprus force until 15 December 1987. il *UN Chron* 24:28-32 Ag '87
Security Council extends mandate of Cyprus Force until 15 June 1987. il map *UN Chron* 24:75-8 F '87
　　Forces in Lebanon
Lebanon peace force [special section] il *UN Chron* 23:54-64 N '86
Security Council approves security measures, financial arrangements on UNIFIL proposed by Secretary-General. il *UN Chron* 24:51-3 F '87

United Nations—Armed Forces—Forces in Lebanon—*cont.*
Security Council extends UNIFIL mandate until 31
January 1988, reiterates support for Lebanon's territorial
integrity. il *UN Chron* 24:52-3 N '87
Security Council extends UNIFIL mandate until 31 July
1987, reiterates support for Lebanon's territorial integrity. il *UN Chron* 24:15-16+ My '87
UNIFIL mandate extended for six months; Council
reiterates support for Lebanese sovereignty and ter-
ritorial integrity. il *UN Chron* 22:10-11 N/D '85
Forces in the Middle East
Mandate of UNDOF unanimously extended through May
1987. *UN Chron* 24:53 F '87
Mandate of UNDOF unanimously extended through
November 1987. il *UN Chron* 24:21 Ag '87
Mandate of United Nations force in Golan Heights
extended until 31 May 1986. il *UN Chron* 23:7 Ja
'86
Budget
See United Nations—Finance
Employees
See also
United Nations. Group of High-level Intergovernmen-
tal Experts to Review the Efficiency of the
Administrative and Financial Functioning of the
United Nations
Finance
See also
United Nations. Group of High-level Intergovernmen-
tal Experts to Review the Efficiency of the
Administrative and Financial Functioning of the
United Nations
Assembly decides economy measures should continue
to counter $85 million shortfall. *UN Chron* 24:26
F '87
Contributions, 1984. *UN Chron* 23:59 Ja '86
FY 1988 assistance requests for organizations and
programs [statement, April 1, 1987] A. Keyes. *Dep
State Bull* 87:88-91 Je '87
General Assembly approves reforms to improve or-
ganization's functioning and efficiency. il *UN Chron*
24:17-25 F '87
General Assembly considers item on financial emergency.
UN Chron 24:27 F '87
Reform at the U.N.: why Washington won't take 'yes'
for an answer [budgetary reform] R. Pearson and B.
Javetski. il *Bus Week* p51 F 9 '87
Secretary-General comments on 'most severe financial
crisis in UN history'. *UN Chron* 23:15 N '86
Threats to the UN. J. Riedmiller. il *World Press Rev*
34:24-5 F '87
UN administration and finances [statement, October 15,
1986] V. A. Walters. *Dep State Bull* 87:77-8 F '87
Non-governmental organizations
See also
United Nations. Committee on Non-Governmental
Organizations
Meeting on NGO involvement in combating drug use
held in Sweden. *UN Chron* 23:108 N '86
NGOs: 'partners with governments' in the fight against
drug abuse. il *UN Chron* 24:vii My '87
Partners in eye health. R. Pararajasegaram. il *World
Health* p6-8 My '87
Palestinian question
See United Nations—Middle East
Publications
Bibliography
Documents. See issues of UN Chronicle
Afghanistan
Arrangements for implementing settlement relating to
Afghanistan completed, issue of withdrawal time-frame
remains. *UN Chron* 24:72 F '87
Assembly urges political solution for situation relating
to Afghanistan. il *UN Chron* 24:69-72 F '87
Gap on time-frame for withdrawal of troops narrowed
to less than a year. il *UN Chron* 24:42 My '87
Gap on time-frame for withdrawal of troops shortened
but not bridged. *UN Chron* 24:54 N '87
Political solution urged by Assembly for situation relating
to Afghanistan. map *UN Chron* 23:12-14 Ja '86
Search for political solution on two tracks—Geneva
process and intra-Afghan discussion. *UN Chron* 24:32
Ag '87
Situation in Afghanistan [statement, November 4, 1986]
H. S. Okun. *Dep State Bull* 87:84-6 Ja '87
Talks held in Geneva on situation relating to Afghanistan;
Under-Secretary-General to continue efforts. *UN Chron*
23:76 N '86
Africa
See also
United Nations. Economic Commission for Africa

United Nations. Office of Emergency Operations
in Africa
Appeal made for urgent and intensified international
efforts to meet Africa's emergency needs. *UN Chron*
24:47 F '87
Secretary-General establishes Steering Committee to help
implement African recovery programme. il *UN Chron*
23:94 N '86
Antarctic regions
Question of Antarctica reviewed for fourth time; Assembly
adopts three texts. il *UN Chron* 24:94 F '87
Asia
See also
United Nations. Economic and Social Commission
for Asia and the Pacific
Canada
The politics of food [re-election of E. Saouma to head
Food and Agriculture Organization] H. Mackenzie.
il por *Macleans* 100:25 N 23 '87
Caribbean region
See also
United Nations. Economic Commission for Latin
America and the Caribbean
Central America
Assembly urges support for Contadora efforts towards
negotiated settlement in Central America. map *UN
Chron* 24:59-61 F '87
More action on Central America: follow-up to January
mission. *UN Chron* 24:10 My '87
Secretary-General reaffirms support for Contadora efforts
after four-day peace mission to region. il pors *UN
Chron* 24:7-10 My '87
Security Council considers Nicaraguan complaint of
'serious incidents' in Central America. il *UN Chron*
24:64 F '87
Colombia
Assembly urges international support to alleviate effects
of Colombian volcanic eruption [Nevado del Ruiz]
il *UN Chron* 23:21-2 Ja '86
Comoros
Sovereignty of Comoros over island of Mayotte reaffirmed
by Assembly. *UN Chron* 24:82 F '87
Cyprus
See also
United Nations—Armed Forces—Forces in Cyprus
Security Council extends mandate of Cyprus force until
15 December 1987. il *UN Chron* 24:28-32 Ag '87
Security Council extends mandate of Cyprus Force until
15 June 1987. il map *UN Chron* 24:75-8 F '87
Developing countries
See also
United Nations. Committee for Development Plan-
ning
United Nations. High Level Committee on the
Review of Technical Co-operation among
Developing Countries
United Nations. Industrial Development Organization
United Nations Development Programme
United Nations Pledging Conference for Development
Activities
Assembly reaches consensus on approach to external
debt of developing countries. *UN Chron* 24:109 F
'87
Is the international community a myth? R. J. Dupuy.
il *Courier* 40:4-8 Ja '87
Low-cost irrigation project interests other developing
countries [drip irrigation] Wan Qinghua. il *UN Chron*
24:65 Ag '87
Nairobi Safe Motherhood Conference reviews concerns,
activities to help pregnant women and mothers. il
UN Chron 24:63-4 My '87
El Salvador
All states asked to provide emergency assistance to El
Salvador after devastating earthquake; President Duarte
addresses United Nations on earthquake assistance.
il por *UN Chron* 24:65 F '87
Ethiopia
Attacking the victims [Eritrean People's Liberation Front
cuts UN food supply lines] S. Seibert. il *Newsweek*
110:56 N 9 '87
Europe
See also
United Nations. Economic Commission for Europe
Falkland Islands
Assembly asks Argentina and United Kingdom to initiate
negotiations on Falklands (Malvinas). *UN Chron* 24:81
F '87
Call for negotiations for peaceful, definitive resolution
of Falklands (Malvinas) issue. map *UN Chron* 23:8-10
Ja '86

United Nations—*cont.*

France

Secretary-General mediates successfully in 'Rainbow Warrior' affair; France, New Zealand to abide by ruling. *UN Chron* 23:75 N '86

Sovereignty of Comoros over island of Mayotte reaffirmed by Assembly. *UN Chron* 24:82 F '87

Iran

'Profound concern' over Iran-Iraq situation expressed by Security Council members. *UN Chron* 24:69 F '87

Secretary-General calls for moratorium by Iran and Iraq on attacks on civilian areas. *UN Chron* 23:77-8 N '86

Secretary-General discusses 'outline plan' during trip to Teheran, Baghdad. il pors *UN Chron* 24:16-18 N '87

Secretary-General suggests Security Council ministerial-level meeting to explore Iran-Iraq situation. il *UN Chron* 24:12-14 My '87

Secretary-General's 26 November report on Iran-Iraq. *UN Chron* 24:68-9 F '87

Secretary Shultz attends UN General Assembly [texts of news conferences, September 21-October 1, 1987] G. P. Shultz. *Dep State Bull* 87:52-60 N '87

Security Council again calls for immediate cease-fire, cessation of all hostilities, withdrawal of forces to international boundaries without delay. map *UN Chron* 24:66-8 F '87

Security Council calls for cease-fire in Iran-Iraq War [statements; with text of resolution, July 20, 1987] G. P. Shultz; R. Reagan. *Dep State Bull* 87:75-7 S '87

Security Council demands immediate cease-fire as first step towards negotiated settlement of Iran-Iraq War. il *UN Chron* 24:19-22 N '87

Security Council members condemn use of chemical weapons in Iran-Iraq conflict. *UN Chron* 24:33-4 Ag '87

Iraq

'Profound concern' over Iran-Iraq situation expressed by Security Council members. *UN Chron* 24:69 F '87

Secretary-General calls for moratorium by Iran and Iraq on attacks on civilian areas. *UN Chron* 23:77-8 N '86

Secretary-General discusses 'outline plan' during trip to Teheran, Baghdad. il pors *UN Chron* 24:16-18 N '87

Secretary-General suggests Security Council ministerial-level meeting to explore Iran-Iraq situation. il *UN Chron* 24:12-14 My '87

Secretary-General's 26 November report on Iran-Iraq. *UN Chron* 24:68-9 F '87

Secretary Shultz attends UN General Assembly [texts of news conferences, September 21-October 1, 1987] G. P. Shultz. *Dep State Bull* 87:52-60 N '87

Security Council again calls for immediate cease-fire, cessation of all hostilities, withdrawal of forces to international boundaries without delay. map *UN Chron* 24:66-8 F '87

Security Council calls for cease-fire in Iran-Iraq War [statements; with text of resolution, July 20, 1987] G. P. Shultz; R. Reagan. *Dep State Bull* 87:75-7 S '87

Security Council demands immediate cease-fire as first step towards negotiated settlement of Iran-Iraq War. il *UN Chron* 24:19-22 N '87

Security Council members condemn use of chemical weapons in Iran-Iraq conflict. *UN Chron* 24:33-4 Ag '87

Israel

Credentials Committee reports adopted [General Assembly action] il *UN Chron* 24:16 F '87

Security Council 'vigorously' condemns Israeli 'aggression' against Tunisian territory. il *UN Chron* 22:3-6 N/D '85

Kampuchea

Assembly endorses four principal components of a settlement to the situation in Kampuchea. il *UN Chron* 23:15-17 Ja '86

Assembly endorses four principal components of settlement of situation in Kampuchea. il *UN Chron* 24:79-80 F '87

Donors pledge $8.7 million for Kampuchean relief [refugees in Thailand] il *UN Chron* 23:78 N '86

Donors pledge nearly $6.2 million for Kampuchean relief. *UN Chron* 23:16 Ja '86

Situation in Cambodia [statement, October 20, 1986; with text of General Assembly resolution] V. A. Walters. *Dep State Bull* 87:80-2 Ja '87

Latin America

See also

United Nations. Economic Commission for Latin America and the Caribbean

Lebanon

See also

United Nations—Armed Forces—Forces in Lebanon

Security Council expresses concern over continuing situation in Lebanon. il *UN Chron* 24:17 My '87

Libya

General Assembly condemns April 1986 attack against Libyan Arab Jamahiriya. il *UN Chron* 24:73 F '87

Libya [statement, November 19, 1986] L. Pressler. *Dep State Bull* 87:87-90 Ja '87

Mexico

Follow-up meeting on Mexican relief held 30 October. *UN Chron* 22:104 N/D '85

Middle East

See also

United Nations—Armed Forces—Forces in the Middle East

United Nations. Committee on the Exercise of the Inalienable Rights of the Palestinian People

Assembly adopts seven resolutions on Middle East and Palestine issues; calls for comprehensive settlement under UN auspices. il *UN Chron* 24:48-50 F '87

Assembly says Israeli breaches of Geneva Convention constitute 'war crimes'. *UN Chron* 24:54-5 F '87

IAEA asked to consider measures to ensure Israel does not attack 'peaceful nuclear facilities' [General Assembly resolution prompted by Israel's attack on the Tammuz nuclear reactor in Iraq] *UN Chron* 23:11 Ja '86

Secretary-General finds increased interest in Middle East peace conference 'encouraging'. *UN Chron* 24:20 Ag '87

Security Council considers situation in Middle East, takes no action. il *UN Chron* 22:7-9 N/D '85

Security Council reaffirms that 1949 Geneva Convention applies to Israeli-occupied territories. *UN Chron* 24:56 F '87

Special Political Committee says Israel's 'grave breaches' of Geneva Convention are 'war crimes and an affront to humanity'. il *UN Chron* 23:51-3 Ja '86

Morocco

Secretary-General discusses Western Sahara with King Hassan of Morocco. *UN Chron* 23:76 N '86

Mozambique

More than $200 million pledged for humanitarian assistance to Mozambique. il *UN Chron* 24:29 My '87

Namibia

See also

International Conference for the Immediate Independence of Namibia

United Nations Council for Namibia

General Assembly demands action for immediate implementation of Namibian independence plan, comprehensive sanctions and South African withdrawal from the territory. il *UN Chron* 23:37-46 N '86

Namibia! Namibia! E. von Kuehnelt-Leddihn. *Natl Rev* 39:26 My 22 '87

The United Nations plan for Namibian independence. *UN Chron* 23:33 N '86

New Caledonia

Assembly decides New Caledonia is non-self-governing territory. *UN Chron* 24:131 F '87

New Zealand

Secretary-General mediates successfully in 'Rainbow Warrior' affair; France, New Zealand to abide by ruling. *UN Chron* 23:75 N '86

Nicaragua

Security Council considers Nicaraguan complaint against United States, takes no action. il *UN Chron* 23:79-82 N '86

Security Council does not adopt text calling for compliance with International Court ruling regarding Nicaraguan case. il *UN Chron* 24:62-3 F '87

Security Council does not adopt text calling for full compliance with International Court ruling in case of 'military and paramilitary activities in and against Nicaragua'. il *UN Chron* 23:83-8 N '86

North Africa

Libyan occupation of northern Chad [statement, November 18, 1986] H. S. Okun. *Dep State Bull* 87:87 Ja '87

Security Council hears Chad complaint against Libya, takes no action. *UN Chron* 23:74 F '87

Pacific Islands (Trust territory)

Visiting mission to Micronesia reports desire for quick end to trusteeship status. *UN Chron* 22:99-100 N/D '85

United Nations—*cont.*

Pacific region
See also
United Nations. Economic and Social Commission for Asia and the Pacific

Pakistan
Gap on time-frame for withdrawal of troops narrowed to less than a year [Afghanistan] il *UN Chron* 24:42 My '87

Search for political solution on two tracks—Geneva process and intra-Afghan discussion. *UN Chron* 24:32 Ag '87

Talks held in Geneva on situation relating to Afghanistan; Under-Secretary-General to continue efforts. *UN Chron* 23:76 N '86

Palau
Trusteeship Council recommends early completion of process of approval of compact for Palau. il *UN Chron* 24:37-9 Ag '87

Trusteeship Council sends mission to Palau. *UN Chron* 24:132 F '87

Visiting mission reports on plebiscite in Palau. il *UN Chron* 24:41-2 My '87

Visiting mission to Palau observes plebiscite. *UN Chron* 24:55 N '87

South Africa
See also
United Nations. Intergovernmental Group to Monitor the Supply and Shipping of Oil and Petroleum Products to South Africa
United Nations. Special Committee against Apartheid

Apartheid: a study in black and white [role of transnational corporations] il *UN Chron* 22:26-8 N/D '85

Assembly urges Security Council to impose mandatory oil embargo against South Africa: thirteen texts adopted on apartheid, Namibia issues. il *UN Chron* 24:40-4 F '87

Bishop Tutu calls for dismantling of apartheid system, beginning of dialogue with blacks. por *UN Chron* 22:17 N/D '85

Comprehensive study outlines post-independence national development strategies for Namibia. il *UN Chron* 23:34-5 N '86

Council commemorates Week of Solidarity with Namibians, SWAPO [U.N. Council for Namibia] il *UN Chron* 22:16 N/D '85

Council for Namibia calls for decisive action for territory's independence. il *UN Chron* 24:26 Ag '87

Council for Namibia president asks body to work for earliest independence for territory. *UN Chron* 23:32 N '86

'End apartheid by 1 January 1987', Panel of Eminent Persons asks; details world programme for action by TNCs. il *UN Chron* 22:18-20 N/D '85

Execution of ANC member deplored and condemned [B. Moloise] por *UN Chron* 22:14 N/D '85

Fifty-two witnesses present testimony during four days of hearings [role of transnational corporations] il *UN Chron* 22:21-5 N/D '85

General Assembly demands action for immediate implementation of Namibian independence plan, comprehensive sanctions and South African withdrawal from the territory. il *UN Chron* 23:37-46 N '86

International Conference for Independence of Namibia calls for mandatory sanctions against South Africa. il map *UN Chron* 23:21-32 N '86

Non-aligned at Harare call for sanctions [call for the Council to impose sanctions] *UN Chron* 23:46 N '86

Security Council does not adopt text calling for selective mandatory sanctions against South Africa. il *UN Chron* 24:22-5 My '87

Solemn meetings mark twentieth anniversary of start of Namibian liberation struggle. *UN Chron* 23:36 N '86

Strict implementation of 1977 arms embargo against South Africa asked by Council. *UN Chron* 24:46 F '87

Text calling for comprehensive mandatory sanctions against South Africa vetoed after discussion in eight meetings. il *UN Chron* 24:22-5 Ag '87

Text calling for mandatory selective sanctions against South Africa vetoed in Security Council. il *UN Chron* 23:3-5 Ja '86

The United Nations plan for Namibian independence. *UN Chron* 23:33 N '86

South Atlantic region
Assembly declares South Atlantic as zone of peace and co-operation. *UN Chron* 24:81 F '87

Southeast Asia
Peace, stability and co-operation in South-East Asia discussed by Assembly. map *UN Chron* 23:18-19 Ja '86

Southern Africa
Security Council again condemns South Africa for 'unprovoked aggression' against Angola. il *UN Chron* 22:12-13 N/D '85

Soviet Union
Assembly urges political solution for situation relating to Afghanistan. il *UN Chron* 24:69-72 F '87

Look who's playing peacekeeper now. J. Trimble. il *U S News World Rep* 103:47 N 2 '87

Political solution urged by Assembly for situation relating to Afghanistan. map *UN Chron* 23:12-14 Ja '86

Situation in Afghanistan [statement, November 4, 1986] H. S. Okun. *Dep State Bull* 87:84-6 Ja '87

Tunisia
Security Council 'vigorously' condemns Israeli 'aggression' against Tunisian territory. il *UN Chron* 22:3-6 N/D '85

United States
Alan Keyes resigns State Dept. post; charges racism. por *Jet* 73:4 O 5 '87

FY 1988 assistance requests for organizations and programs [statement, April 1, 1987] A. Keyes. *Dep State Bull* 87:88-91 Je '87

General Assembly condemns April 1986 attack against Libyan Arab Jamahiriya. il *UN Chron* 24:73 F '87

Inhuman rights [U.S. forces U.N. to omit footage of New York City's homeless from documentary] *Nation* 244:36-7 Ja 17 '87

Let it sink [cover story] C. Krauthammer. *New Repub* 197:18-23 Ag 24 '87

Libya [statement, November 19, 1986] L. Pressler. *Dep State Bull* 87:87-90 Ja '87

Reform at the U.N.: why Washington won't take 'yes' for an answer [budgetary reform] R. Pearson and B. Javetski. il *Bus Week* p51 F 9 '87

Rep. Crockett appointed to United Nations post. por *Jet* 72:8 S 7 '87

Security Council considers Nicaraguan complaint against United States, takes no action. il *UN Chron* 23:79-82 N '86

Security Council does not adopt text calling for compliance with International Court ruling regarding Nicaraguan case. il *UN Chron* 24:62-3 F '87

Security Council does not adopt text calling for full compliance with International Court ruling in case of 'military and paramilitary activities in and against Nicaragua'. il *UN Chron* 23:83-8 N '86

U.S. payment shortfall threatens cutback in ICAO operations. J. Ott. *Aviat Week Space Technol* 127:43 N 2 '87

UN administration and finances [statement, October 15, 1986] V. A. Walters. *Dep State Bull* 87:77-8 F '87

The United States vs. the World Court [report of the Independent Commission on Respect for International Law] *Cent Mag* 20:59-62 My/Je '87

West Africa
Victory in sight against 'river blindness'. D. D. Silva. il *UN Chron* 24:75-6 My '87

Western Sahara
Secretary-General discusses Western Sahara with King Hassan of Morocco. *UN Chron* 23:76 N '86

United Nations. Ad Hoc Committee on the Drafting of an International Convention against the Recruitment, Use, Financing and Training of Mercenaries
Continued work on draft convention against mercenaries recommended. il *UN Chron* 24:85 My '87

United Nations. Ad Hoc Committee on the Indian Ocean
Ad hoc committee continues preparations for conference on Indian Ocean. *UN Chron* 24:51 N '87

Ad Hoc Committee on Indian Ocean concludes first session of 1987. *UN Chron* 24:53 My '87

Indian Ocean Committee calls for convening of conference by 1988. *UN Chron* 23:73 N '86

United Nations. Commission for Social Development
Commission for Social Development adopts 16 texts; homeless, family, youth among its concerns. il *UN Chron* 24:58-9 My '87

United Nations. Commission on Human Rights
Human Rights Commission appoints special rapporteur on mercenaries, considers religious freedom, acts for first time on human rights situation in Sri Lanka. il *UN Chron* 24:30-8 My '87

UN official seeks data on repression of believers [A. Ribeiro] B. Spring. *Christ Today* 31:34-5 F 6 '87

United Nations. Commission on Human Settlements
Commission on Human Settlements stresses need for global strategy for shelter to year 2000. *UN Chron* 24:47 Ag '87

United Nations. Commission on International Trade Law
UNCITRAL adopts draft Convention on International Bills of Exchange, Legal guide on contracts. *UN Chron* 24:71 N '87

United Nations. Commission on Narcotic Drugs
Assembly adopts three texts on issues to combat drug abuse and illicit trafficking. il *UN Chron* 24:110-12 F '87

Commission recommends priority for drug control activities, continues work on new drug convention. il *UN Chron* 24:43-4 My '87

Draft declaration on drug control priorities recommended for adoption by world drug conference. il *UN Chron* 24:45 My '87

United Nations. Commission on the Status of Women
Commission on Status of Women acts to implement Nairobi Strategies to aid women. il *UN Chron* 24:60-2 My '87

United Nations. Commission on Transnational Corporations
Apartheid: a study in black and white [role of transnational corporations] il *UN Chron* 22:26-8 N/D '85

Commission discusses role of TNCs in South Africa, status of code of conduct. il *UN Chron* 24:60-2 Ag '87

'End apartheid by 1 January 1987', Panel of Eminent Persons asks; details world programme for action by TNCs. il *UN Chron* 22:18-20 N/D '85

Fifty-two witnesses present testimony during four days of hearings [role of transnational corporations] il *UN Chron* 22:21-5 N/D '85

United Nations. Committee for Development Planning
Development under siege. S. Sen. *Commonweal* 114:647-52 N 20 '87

United Nations. Committee for Programme and Co-ordination
Committee for Programme and Co-ordination cautions against 'negative impact' on programmes worldwide. *UN Chron* 24:42 Ag '87

United Nations. Committee on Information
Committee on Information adopts 48 recommendations after considering two sets of proposals. il *UN Chron* 24:66-7 N '87

Committee on Information adopts 57 recommendations after considering three sets of proposals. il *UN Chron* 23:110-12 N '86

Committee on Information adopts work programme for 1987, elects new chairman. *UN Chron* 24:72 My '87

United Nations. Committee on Natural Resources
Question of water resources primary focus of Natural Resources Committee. il *UN Chron* 24:70 Ag '87

United Nations. Committee on Non-Governmental Organizations
NGO Committee reviews reports, grants consultative status to 53 organizations. il *UN Chron* 24:71-2 My '87

United Nations. Committee on the Elimination of Discrimination against Women
Women's rights body reviews reports from 8 states. *UN Chron* 24:46 Ag '87

United Nations. Committee on the Elimination of Racial Discrimination
Committee on Racial Discrimination curtails August session due to financial troubles. *UN Chron* 24:68 N '87

Racial Discrimination Committee reviews reports on 26 nations. *UN Chron* 24:39 My '87

United Nations. Committee on the Exercise of the Inalienable Rights of the Palestinian People
Palestine Solidarity Day observed on 29 November. *UN Chron* 23:6 Ja '86

Palestinian Rights Committee elects officers, approves work programme. il *UN Chron* 24:21 My '87

United Nations. Committee on the Peaceful Uses of Outer Space
Assembly adopts 15 principles on remote sensing; states urged to prevent outer space arms race. il *UN Chron* 24:95-6 F '87

Outer space sub-committees discuss use of nuclear power sources on space vehicles. il *UN Chron* 24:48-52 My '87

United Nations committee calls for strengthened co-operation in exploration and peaceful use of outer space. *UN Chron* 24:35-6 Ag '87

United Nations. Conference on Disarmament
1986 Conference on Disarmament sees 'positive and substantive' developments, in-depth discussions held. il *UN Chron* 23:66-70 N '86

Conference on Disarmament resumes 1987 session on 9 June in Geneva. il *UN Chron* 24:19 Ag '87

Further progress on chemical weapons ban, other "promising developments", reported. il *UN Chron* 24:48-50 N '87

Work in 1987 Conference on Disarmament begins, five ad hoc committees in operation. il *UN Chron* 24:46-7 My '87

United Nations. Declaration of the Rights of the Child
See Declaration of the Rights of the Child

United Nations. Decolonization Committee
Assembly adopts 20 texts on decolonization issues, reviews status of 14 territories. il *UN Chron* 24:127-30 F '87

Fourth Committee focuses on foreign economic interests and military activities impeding decolonization. *UN Chron* 22:98 N/D '85

Fourth Committee takes action on Western Sahara, small territories, other decolonization issues. *UN Chron* 23:77-80 Ja '86

United Nations. Disarmament Commission
Verification, naval disarmament discussed by 1987 Disarmament Commission. il *UN Chron* 24:16-17 Ag '87

United Nations. Division of Narcotic Drugs
Heads of drug law enforcement agencies throughout world meet in Vienna. *UN Chron* 23:108 N '86

United Nations. Economic and Financial Committee
Assembly acts on key issues related to trade, food, housing and other development matters. il *UN Chron* 24:99-108 F '87

Reports on trade, finance among issues considered in Second Committee in October. il *UN Chron* 22:90-1 N/D '85

Second Committee continues review of development issues in November discussion. *UN Chron* 23:57-9 Ja '86

Wide-ranging agenda item on development and international co-operation discussed in Second Committee. il *UN Chron* 22:88-90 N/D '85

World economic issues and deterioration of economies of developing nations discussed in general debate. il *UN Chron* 22:86-8 N/D '85

United Nations. Economic and Social Commission for Asia and the Pacific
Asia-Pacific industry and technology ministers meet in Bangkok. il *UN Chron* 23:113 N '86

Review of 'geological risks' in ESCAP urban areas planned. *UN Chron* 23:22 Ja '86

United Nations. Economic and Social Council
Economic and development policy is focus of Economic and Social Council at second 1986 session. il *UN Chron* 23:95-100 N '86

Economic and Social Council holds 1987 organizational session. il *UN Chron* 24:56 My '87

Economic and Social Council reviews regional economic conditions. il *UN Chron* 23:101 N '86

Economic and Social Council reviews world economic and social policy, calls for measures to combat AIDS. il *UN Chron* 24:59-62 N '87

General Assembly elects members to two councils. il *UN Chron* 22:83 N/D '85

Human rights and measures to help the homeless among main concerns of Economic and Social Council. il *UN Chron* 24:56-8 Ag '87

United Nations. Economic and Social Council. Commission for Social Development *See* United Nations. Commission for Social Development

United Nations. Economic and Social Council. Committee on Non-Governmental Organizations *See* United Nations. Committee on Non-Governmental Organizations

United Nations. Economic and Social Council. Population Commission *See* United Nations. Population Commission

United Nations. Economic and Social Council. Statistical Commission *See* United Nations. Statistical Commission

United Nations. Economic Commission for Africa
African leaders meet in Nigeria, review United Nations Programme of Action for African Economic Recovery. *UN Chron* 24:63 Ag '87

United Nations. Economic Commission for Europe
ECE seminar in Greece considers East-West trade prospects. *UN Chron* 23:113 N '86

United Nations. Economic Commission for Latin America and the Caribbean
ECLAC special conference discusses ways to ensure economic recovery and growth in Latin America and Caribbean. il *UN Chron* 24:11 My '87
United Nations. First Committee *See* United Nations. Political and Security Committee
United Nations. Food and Agriculture Organization *See* Food and Agriculture Organization of the United Nations
United Nations. Fourth Committee *See* United Nations. Decolonization Committee
United Nations. General Assembly (40th session: 1985)
Assembly affirms confidence in IAEA, urges co-operation regarding peaceful uses of nuclear energy. *UN Chron* 23:10 Ja '86
Assembly calls for steps to combat illicit traffic in cultural property. il *UN Chron* 23:19-20 Ja '86
Assembly endorses four principal components of a settlement to the situation in Kampuchea. il *UN Chron* 23:15-17 Ja '86
Assembly urges international support to alleviate effects of Colombian volcanic eruption [Nevado del Ruiz] il *UN Chron* 23:21-2 Ja '86
Call for negotiations for peaceful, definitive resolution of Falklands (Malvinas) issue. map *UN Chron* 23:8-10 Ja '86
General Assembly elects members to two councils [Security Council and the Economic and Social Council] il *UN Chron* 22:83 N/D '85
General Assembly invites Security Council to recommend procedures to settle disputes peacefully. *UN Chron* 23:9 Ja '86
Global strategy for youth endorsed at conclusion of World Conference on International Youth Year (1985). il *UN Chron* 23:23-6 Ja '86
IAEA asked to consider measures to ensure Israel does not attack 'peaceful nuclear facilities' [resolution prompted by Israel's attack on the Tammuz nuclear reactor in Iraq] *UN Chron* 23:11 Ja '86
The nations speak: general debate, 1985. il *UN Chron* 22:29-81 N/D '85
Peace, stability and co-operation in South-East Asia discussed by Assembly. map *UN Chron* 23:18-19 Ja '86
Political solution urged by Assembly for situation relating to Afghanistan. map *UN Chron* 23:12-14 Ja '86
United Nations. General Assembly (41st session: 1986)
All states asked to provide emergency assistance to El Salvador after devastating earthquake; President Duarte addresses United Nations on earthquake assistance. il *por UN Chron* 24:65 F '87
Appeal made for urgent and intensified international efforts to meet Africa's emergency needs. *UN Chron* 24:47 F '87
Assembly acts on key issues related to trade, food, housing and other development matters. il *UN Chron* 24:99-108 F '87
Assembly acts on wide range of social concerns. *UN Chron* 24:117 F '87
Assembly adopts 15 principles on remote sensing; states urged to prevent outer space arms race. il *UN Chron* 24:95-6 F '87
Assembly adopts 20 texts on decolonization issues, reviews status of 14 territories. il *UN Chron* 24:127-30 F '87
Assembly adopts declaration on protection and welfare of children; also acts on diplomats' safety, host country relations. il *UN Chron* 24:133-6 F '87
Assembly adopts Declaration on Right to Development, acts on wide range of issues related to human rights. il *UN Chron* 24:119-25 F '87
Assembly adopts seven resolutions on Middle East and Palestine issues; calls for comprehensive settlement under UN auspices. il *UN Chron* 24:48-50 F '87
Assembly adopts three texts on issues to combat drug abuse and illicit trafficking. il *UN Chron* 24:110-12 F '87
Assembly appeals for intensified activities to combat racism, condemns increased use of mercenaries. *UN Chron* 24:126 F '87
Assembly asks Argentina and United Kingdom to initiate negotiations on Falklands (Malvinas). *UN Chron* 24:81 F '87
Assembly calls for action to improve international peace and security. il *UN Chron* 24:93 F '87
Assembly calls for co-operation in a new world information and communication order. *UN Chron* 24:96-7 F '87
Assembly calls for priority measures to improve status of women. *UN Chron* 24:118 F '87

Assembly decides economy measures should continue to counter $85 million shortfall. *UN Chron* 24:26 F '87
Assembly decides New Caledonia is non-self-governing territory. *UN Chron* 24:131 F '87
Assembly declares South Atlantic as zone of peace and co-operation. *UN Chron* 24:81 F '87
Assembly endorses four principal components of settlement of situation in Kampuchea. il *UN Chron* 24:79-80 F '87
Assembly lauds agreement on pioneer investment formula [sea law] *UN Chron* 24:82 F '87
Assembly reaches consensus on approach to external debt of developing countries. *UN Chron* 24:109 F '87
Assembly says Israeli breaches of Geneva Convention constitute 'war crimes'. *UN Chron* 24:54-5 F '87
Assembly urges co-operation with IAEA to promote peaceful use of nuclear energy. il *UN Chron* 24:83-5 F '87
Assembly urges political solution for situation relating to Afghanistan. il *UN Chron* 24:69-72 F '87
Assembly urges Security Council to impose mandatory oil embargo against South Africa: thirteen texts adopted on apartheid, Namibia issues. il *UN Chron* 24:40-4 F '87
Assembly urges support for Contadora efforts towards negotiated settlement in Central America. map *UN Chron* 24:59-61 F '87
Credentials Committee reports adopted. il *UN Chron* 24:16 F '87
Disarmament issues, especially nuclear matters, acted on by General Assembly. il *UN Chron* 24:87-92 F '87
Forty-first General Assembly lays foundation for a 'better United Nations for a better world'. il *UN Chron* 24:8-14 F '87
General Assembly appeals for high safety standards in nuclear plants, approves 1987 conference plans. *UN Chron* 24:86 F '87
General Assembly approves reforms to improve organization's functioning and efficiency. il *UN Chron* 24:17-25 F '87
General Assembly calls for world-wide aid for refugees in adopting 9 resolutions. il *UN Chron* 24:112-16 F '87
General Assembly condemns April 1986 attack against Libyan Arab Jamahiriya. il *UN Chron* 24:73 F '87
General Assembly considers item on financial emergency. *UN Chron* 24:27 F '87
General Assembly demands action for immediate implementation of Namibian independence plan, comprehensive sanctions and South African withdrawal from the territory. il *UN Chron* 23:37-46 N '86
Governments asked to make 'most generous efforts' to meet needs of Palestine refugee agency. il *UN Chron* 24:57-8 F '87
The nations speak: general debate, 1986. il *UN Chron* 24:28-39 F '87
Question of Antarctica reviewed for fourth time; Assembly adopts three texts. il *UN Chron* 24:94 F '87
Revitalization of the international system, resolving financial crisis are 1986 priorities. il *UN Chron* 23:7-15 N '86
Secretary-General appointed to a second five-year term. il *por UN Chron* 24:4-5 F '87
Sovereignty of Comoros over island of Mayotte reaffirmed by Assembly. *UN Chron* 24:82 F '87
UN General Assembly review for 1986. *Dep State Bull* 87:52-5 Mr '87
United Nations. General Assembly (42nd session: 1987)
America's vision of the future [address, September 21, 1987] R. Reagan. *Dep State Bull* 87:1-4 N '87
Forty-second General Assembly opens in hopeful atmosphere of increasing multilateral co-operation. il *UN Chron* 24:7-15 N '87
Secretary Shultz attends UN General Assembly [texts of news conferences, September 21-October 1, 1987] G. P. Shultz. *Dep State Bull* 87:52-60 N '87
United Nations. General Assembly (Special Session on Disarmament: 1988)
Preparatory body for third Assembly session on disarmament approves provisional agenda. *UN Chron* 24:18 Ag '87
United Nations. Group of Governmental Experts on International Co-operation to Avert New Flows of Refugees
Assembly asks member states to respect results of study on refugees flows. il *UN Chron* 24:115 F '87

United Nations. Group of High-level Intergovernmental Experts to Review the Efficiency of the Administrative and Financial Functioning of the United Nations
'Group of 18' on UN efficiency and financing makes 71 recommendations on organization's functioning. il *UN Chron* 23:17-20 N '86

United Nations. High Commissioner for Refugees
Refugee questions subject of Third Committee scrutiny in November. il *UN Chron* 23:64-9 Ja '86

United Nations. High Level Committee on the Review of Technical Co-operation among Developing Countries
Developing countries asked to continue to strive for collective self-reliance. *UN Chron* 24:64 Ag '87

United Nations. Human Rights Committee
Human Rights Committee meets in Geneva. *UN Chron* 23:109 N '86
Human Rights Committee reviews reports of four states, considers individual complaints. *UN Chron* 24:45 Ag '87
Human Rights Committee reviews reports of four states, considers individual complaints. *UN Chron* 24:68 N '87
Reports of three European countries considered in Geneva. *UN Chron* 23:76 Ja '86

United Nations. Industrial Development Organization
UNIDO board defers decision on financial crisis. *UN Chron* 24:80 My '87

United Nations. Intergovernmental Committee on Science and Technology for Development
High priority asked for projects to increase capabilities for dealing with natural disasters. *UN Chron* 24:65 N '87
Science and technology body meets in Brazil [Advisory Committee meeting] *UN Chron* 24:78 My '87

United Nations. Intergovernmental Group to Monitor the Supply and Shipping of Oil and Petroleum Products to South Africa
Group to monitor supply of oil and petroleum products to South Africa holds first meeting. *UN Chron* 24:23 My '87

United Nations. International Labour Organisation *See* International Labour Organisation

United Nations. International Law Commission
International Law Commission advances work on draft codes. *UN Chron* 24:71 N '87

United Nations. International Narcotics Control Board *See* International Narcotics Control Board

United Nations. Legal Committee
Measures to prevent terrorism, protection of diplomats discussed in Legal Committee. *UN Chron* 22:100+ N/D '85
Sixth Committee acts on wide variety of legal issues: protection of children, detained persons, among them. il *UN Chron* 23:81-2 Ja '86

United Nations. Office of Emergency Operations in Africa
Acute emergency conditions afflict 14 million in Africa. *UN Chron* 23:93 N '86
Rain, good harvests, but African emergency continues. *UN Chron* 23:60 Ja '86
Rain promises some respite, better harvests, cash still needed to buy food for deficit areas. *UN Chron* 22:104 N/D '85

United Nations. Office of the Disaster Relief Co-ordinator *See* Office of the United Nations Disaster Relief Co-ordinator

United Nations. Office of the High Commissioner for Refugees *See* United Nations. High Commissioner for Refugees

United Nations. Political and Security Committee
First Committee's disarmament debate: towards fewer weapons, more hope. il *UN Chron* 23:43-50 Ja '86
Political and Security Committee holds special meeting to observe Disarmament Week to highlight need for arms control. il *UN Chron* 22:82-3 N/D '85

United Nations. Population Commission
Population Commission recommends continued monitoring of world population trends and policies. il *UN Chron* 24:68-9 My '87

United Nations. Preparatory Commission for the International Sea-Bed Authority and the International Tribunal for the Law of the Sea
Assembly lauds agreement on pioneer investment formula. *UN Chron* 24:82 F '87
Preparatory commission agrees on procedures for registering pioneer investors in deep sea-bed mining. il *UN Chron* 23:89-91 N '86
Sea-bed commission postpones registration of pioneer investors. il *UN Chron* 24:40-1 Ag '87
Sea law commission registers India as first pioneer investor. il *UN Chron* 24:56-8 N '87

United Nations. Preparatory Committee for the International Conference on the Relationship between Disarmament and Development
Draft for disarmament and development conference agreed on. *UN Chron* 24:18 Ag '87

United Nations. Second Committee *See* United Nations. Economic and Financial Committee

United Nations. Security Council
General Assembly elects members to two councils. il *UN Chron* 22:83 N/D '85
General Assembly invites Security Council to recommend procedures to settle disputes peacefully. *UN Chron* 23:9 Ja '86

United Nations. Security Council (Meetings: 1985)
Mandate of United Nations force in Golan Heights extended until 31 May 1986. il *UN Chron* 23:7 Ja '86
Security Council again condemns South Africa for 'unprovoked aggression' against Angola. il *UN Chron* 22:12-13 N/D '85
Security Council considers situation in Middle East, takes no action. il *UN Chron* 22:7-9 N/D '85
Security Council 'vigorously' condemns Israeli 'aggression' against Tunisian territory. il *UN Chron* 22:3-6 N/D '85
Text calling for mandatory selective sanctions against South Africa vetoed in Security Council. il *UN Chron* 23:3-5 Ja '86
UNIFIL mandate extended for six months; Council reiterates support for Lebanese sovereignty and territorial integrity. il *UN Chron* 22:10-11 N/D '85

United Nations. Security Council (Meetings: 1986)
Lebanon peace force [special section] il *UN Chron* 23:54-64 N '86
Mandate of UNDOF unanimously extended through May 1987. *UN Chron* 24:53 F '87
'Profound concern' over Iran-Iraq situation expressed by Security Council members. *UN Chron* 24:69 F '87
Security Council again calls for immediate cease-fire, cessation of all hostilities, withdrawal of forces to international boundaries without delay [Iranian-Iraqi War] map *UN Chron* 24:66-8 F '87
Security Council approves security measures, financial arrangements on UNIFIL proposed by Secretary-General. il *UN Chron* 24:51-3 F '87
Security Council considers Nicaraguan complaint against United States, takes no action. il *UN Chron* 23:79-82 N '86
Security Council considers Nicaraguan complaint of 'serious incidents' in Central America. il *UN Chron* 24:64 F '87
Security Council does not adopt text calling for compliance with International Court ruling regarding Nicaraguan case. il *UN Chron* 24:62-3 F '87
Security Council does not adopt text calling for full compliance with International Court ruling in case of 'military and paramilitary activities in and against Nicaragua'. il *UN Chron* 23:83-8 N '86
Security Council extends mandate of Cyprus Force until 15 June 1987. il map *UN Chron* 24:75-8 F '87
Security Council hears Chad complaint against Libya, takes no action. *UN Chron* 24:74 F '87
Security Council reaffirms that 1949 Geneva Convention applies to Israeli-occupied territories. *UN Chron* 24:56 F '87
Strict implementation of 1977 arms embargo against South Africa asked by Council. *UN Chron* 24:46 F '87

United Nations. Security Council (Meetings: 1987)
Mandate of UNDOF unanimously extended through November 1987. il *UN Chron* 24:21 Ag '87
Security Council calls for cease-fire in Iran-Iraq War [statements; with text of resolution, July 20, 1987] G. P. Shultz; R. Reagan. *Dep State Bull* 87:75-7 S '87
Security Council demands immediate cease-fire as first step towards negotiated settlement of Iran-Iraq War. il *UN Chron* 24:19-22 N '87
Security Council does not adopt text calling for selective mandatory sanctions against South Africa. il *UN Chron* 24:22-5 My '87
Security Council expresses concern over continuing situation in Lebanon. il *UN Chron* 24:17 My '87
Security Council extends mandate of Cyprus force until 15 December 1987. il *UN Chron* 24:28-32 Ag '87
Security Council extends UNIFIL mandate until 31 January 1988, reiterates support for Lebanon's territorial integrity. il *UN Chron* 24:52-3 N '87

United Nations. Security Council (Meetings: 1987) —
cont.

Security Council extends UNIFIL mandate until 31 July
1987, reiterates support for Lebanon's territorial integrity. il *UN Chron* 24:15-16+ My '87

Security Council members condemn use of chemical
weapons in Iran-Iraq conflict. *UN Chron* 24:33-4 Ag
'87

Text calling for comprehensive mandatory sanctions
against South Africa vetoed after discussion in eight
meetings. il *UN Chron* 24:22-5 Ag '87

United Nations. Sixth Committee *See* United Nations. Legal
Committee

**United Nations. Social, Humanitarian and Cultural Commit-
tee**

Assembly adopts three texts on issues to combat drug
abuse and illicit trafficking. il *UN Chron* 24:110-12
F '87

Assembly asked to condemn 'wanton killing' in South
Africa, other aspects of racism throughout the world.
il *UN Chron* 22:96-7 N/D '85

Measures to implement women's 'forward-looking
strategies' called for in Third Committee. il *UN Chron*
23:70-1 Ja '86

Refugee questions subject of Third Committee scrutiny
in November. il *UN Chron* 23:64-9 Ja '86

Wide range of social concerns—crime, the aging,
disabled—acted on Third Committee. il *UN Chron*
23:72-5 Ja '86

**United Nations. Special Commission of the Economic and
Social Council on the In-depth Study of the United
Nations Intergovernmental Structure and Functions in
the Economic and Social Fields**

Special commission to study United Nations functions
and structure in economic and social fields. il *UN
Chron* 24:57 My '87

Special commission on UN work in economic and social
fields meets in New York. *UN Chron* 24:64 N '87

Commission studying United Nations functions and structure in economic and social fields continues work.
UN Chron 24:44 Ag '87

United Nations. Special Committee against Apartheid

Anti-apartheid notes. *UN Chron* 24:69-70 N '87

Anti-apartheid notes. *UN Chron* 24:27-8 My '87

Anti-apartheid notes. il *UN Chron* 24:44-5 F '87

Anti-apartheid notes. il *UN Chron* 23:47-9 N '86

Anti-apartheid notes. *UN Chron* 24:27 Ag '87

Committee condemns attempts to curb South African
press coverage. *UN Chron* 23:6 Ja '86

Day of Solidarity with South African and Namibian
Women observed. il *UN Chron* 23:36 N '86

Day of Solidarity with South African Political Prisoners
observed; immediate release of all such detainees asked.
il *UN Chron* 22:14-15 N/D '85

Special meetings mark 27th anniversary of Sharpeville
massacre. il *UN Chron* 24:26-7 My '87

UN group attacks Paul Simon: says 'Graceland' broke
cultural boycott of South Africa. R. Tannenbaum.
Roll Stone p11+ F 12 '87

United Nations. Special Committee on Decolonization *See*
United Nations. Special Committee on the Situation
with Regard to the Implementation of the Declaration
on the Granting of Independence to Colonial Countries
and Peoples

**United Nations. Special Committee on Enhancing the Effec-
tiveness of the Principle of the Non-Use of Force
in International Relations**

Committee on Non-Use of Force completes work on
draft declaration. *UN Chron* 24:82-3 My '87

**United Nations. Special Committee on the Charter of the
United Nations and on the Strengthening of the Role
of the Organization**

Charter Committee considers maintenance of international
peace and security, dispute settlement, rationalization
of United Nations procedures. il *UN Chron* 24:84-5
My '87

**United Nations. Special Committee on the Situation with
Regard to the Implementation of the Declaration on
the Granting of Independence to Colonial Countries
and Peoples**

Decolonization committee concludes 1986 session,
considers Namibia, non-self-governing territories. il *UN
Chron* 23:50-3 N '86

Decolonization Committee makes statement on New
Caledonia, discusses Namibia, other territories. il *UN
Chron* 24:40 My '87

United Nations. Special Political Committee

Bishop Tutu calls for dismantling of apartheid system,
beginning of dialogue with blacks. por *UN Chron*
22:17 N/D '85

Governments asked to make 'most generous efforts' to
meet needs of Palestinian refugee agency. il *UN Chron*
23:54-7 Ja '86

Opposition to nuclear testing in the Pacific voiced; action
on refugees and peace-keeping taken. il *UN Chron*
22:84-5 N/D '85

Special Political Committee says Israel's 'grave breaches'
of Geneva Convention are 'war crimes and an affront
to humanity'. il *UN Chron* 23:51-3 Ja '86

United Nations. Statistical Commission

Expert group meets on 1990 World Population and
Housing Census Programme. *UN Chron* 23:85 Ja '86

Statistical Commission reviews problems of least
developed countries, other data-oriented work. *UN
Chron* 24:70 My '87

United Nations. Third Committee *See* United Nations.
Social, Humanitarian and Cultural Committee

United Nations. Trusteeship Council

Trusteeship Council recommends early completion of
process of approval of compact for Palau. il *UN Chron*
24:37-9 Ag '87

Trusteeship Council sends mission to Palau. *UN Chron*
24:132 F '87

Visiting mission reports on plebiscite in Palau. il *UN
Chron* 24:41-2 My '87

Visiting mission to Micronesia reports desire for quick
end to trusteeship status. *UN Chron* 22:99-100 N/D
'85

Visiting mission to Palau observes plebiscite. *UN Chron*
24:55 N '87

United Nations. War Crimes Commission

Nazi trail [UN opens files] il *Time* 130:36 D 7 '87

United Nations. World Food Council *See* World Food
Council

United Nations and television

Made in Amerika. J. Vitale. *Channels* 7:18 F '87

**United Nations Conference for the Promotion of Inter-
national Co-operation in the Peaceful Uses of Nuclear
Energy**

General Assembly appeals for high safety standards in
nuclear plants, approves 1987 conference plans. *UN
Chron* 24:86 F '87

Harnessing the peaceful atom: past performance and
future challenges [address, March 23, 1987] R. T.
Kennedy. *Dep State Bull* 87:76-80 Je '87

World conference on peaceful uses of nuclear energy
unable to agree on key political issues. il *UN Chron*
24:10-15 Ag '87

United Nations Conference on the Human Environment

What happened to utopia? [interview with M. Strong]
N. Myers. il *Int Wildl* 17:36-7 Jl/Ag '87

United Nations Conference on Trade and Development

Economic and environmental crises cause a 'significant
deterioration' in LDC economies. il *UN Chron* 22:92-5
N/D '85

Revitalizing growth and development must be a worldwide co-operative effort, UNCTAD reports. *UN Chron*
24:77-8 My '87

Seventh UNCTAD adopts final act by consensus. il
UN Chron 24:29-37 N '87

Thanks, Dennis [U.S. delegate D. Goodman] L. Gubernick. il por *Forbes* 140:126+ S 7 '87

Trade and Development Board recommends UNCTAD
VII be held in July 1987 in Geneva. *UN Chron* 23:102
N '86

UNCTAD committee assesses impact of commodity crisis
on developing countries [Committee on Commodities]
UN Chron 24:79 My '87

UNCTAD: still North vs. South. *World Press Rev* 34:47
S '87

United Nations Council for Namibia

Anti-apartheid notes. *UN Chron* 24:69-70 N '87

Anti-apartheid notes. *UN Chron* 24:27 Ag '87

Council commemorates Week of Solidarity with
Namibians, SWAPO. il *UN Chron* 22:16 N/D '85

Council for Namibia calls for decisive action for territory's
independence. il *UN Chron* 24:26 Ag '87

Council for Namibia president asks body to work for
earliest independence for territory. *UN Chron* 23:32
N '86

Solemn meetings mark twentieth anniversary of start
of Namibian liberation struggle. *UN Chron* 23:36 N
'86

United Nations Day

'A recognition of the interdependence of nations'. J.
Pérez de Cuellar. *UN Chron* 22:2 N/D '85

United Nations Day observed on 24 October. il *UN
Chron* 24:15 F '87

United Nations Decade of Disabled Persons, 1983-1992

Society and the disabled. il *UN Chron* 24:63 N '87

United Nations Development Programme
A global search yields affordable water. D. Kinley. il *UN Chron* 24:71-2 Ag '87
UNDP chief Bradford Morse to retire. il por *UN Chron* 23:62 Ja '86
UNDP Governing Council approves 28 new programmes. il *UN Chron* 24:73-4 My '87
UNDP Governing Council approves new Africa programme. *UN Chron* 24:63 Ag '87
United Nations Disarmament Week *See* Disarmament Week
United Nations Disengagement Observer Force *See* United Nations—Armed Forces—Forces in the Middle East
United Nations Educational, Scientific and Cultural Organization *See* Unesco
United Nations Environment Programme
World Environment Day observed by 10,000 at headquarters. il *UN Chron* 24:59 Ag '87
United Nations Fund for Population Activities
10 billion by the year 2087? [1987 State of world population report; special section] il *UN Chron* 24:42-7 N '87
Leadership from abroad. M. Morain. il por *Humanist* 47:31-2 Mr/Ap '87
A new era for UNFPA [new executive director N. Sadik] M. Morain. *Humanist* 47:33 N/D '87
Population Fund anticipated reduction in contributions. il *UN Chron* 23:107 N '86
United Nations Institute for Training and Research
Board discusses restructuring of UNITAR, asks for 'positive assessment' by Secretary-General. *UN Chron* 24:64 Ag '87
United Nations Interim Force in Lebanon *See* United Nations—Armed Forces—Forces in Lebanon
United Nations International Atomic Energy Agency *See* International Atomic Energy Agency
United Nations International Children's Fund *See* UNICEF
United Nations International Conference for the Immediate Independence of Namibia *See* International Conference for the Immediate Independence of Namibia
United Nations International Conference on Drug Abuse and Illicit Trafficking *See* International Conference on Drug Abuse and Illicit Trafficking
United Nations International Conference on the Relationship between Disarmament and Development *See* International Conference on the Relationship between Disarmament and Development
United Nations International Year of Peace, 1986 *See* International Year of Peace, 1986
United Nations Peace-Keeping Force in Cyprus *See* United Nations—Armed Forces—Forces in Cyprus
United Nations Peace-Keeping Force in Lebanon *See* United Nations—Armed Forces—Forces in Lebanon
United Nations Pledging Conference for Development Activities
$1.1 billion pledged to development activities. *UN Chron* 24:101 F '87
$740 million pledged for UN development activities. *UN Chron* 23:62 Ja '86
United Nations Relief and Works Agency for Palestine Refugees in the Near East
Governments asked to make 'most generous efforts' to meet needs of Palestinian refugee agency. il *UN Chron* 23:54-7 Ja '86
Governments asked to make 'most generous efforts' to meet needs of Palestine refugee agency. il *UN Chron* 24:57-8 F '87
UNRWA: what it is, how it works. *UN Chron* 24:58 F '87
United Nations University
How unique is UNU? K. Mushakoji. il por *UN Chron* 23:114-15 N '86
United Negro College Fund
Lou Rawls heads Parade of stars on telethon to benefit black colleges. il pors *Jet* 73:24-5 D 28 '87-Ja 4 '88
Parks, Smale feted at annual UNCF gala held in New York City. il pors *Jet* 72:12-13 Ap 6 '87
Trained as animal doctor, Medal of Freedom winner Patterson founded UNCF. il por *Jet* 72:22 Jl 27 '87
UNCF approves withdrawal of $600,000 by Bishop. *Jet* 72:12 Ag 10 '87
UNCF founder Patterson to get presidential honor [F. D. Patterson] por *Jet* 72:24 My 11 '87
UNCF seeks support of federal employees. il *Jet* 72:38 S 14 '87
United Nuclear Corporation
    See also
  UNC Inc.
United Parcel Service of America, Inc.
UPS introduces 757 freighters to expand service, constrain noise. M. Mecham. il *Aviat Week Space Technol* 127:49+ S 14 '87

United Precious Metals (Firm)
That's a lot of bullion [G. R. Fox convicted of investment fraud] F. Greve. il *50 Plus* 27:18-19 Jl '87
United Scenic Artists
USA all the way. C. Eller. *Theatre Crafts* 21:14-15+ Mr '87
United Sciences of America Inc.
The eyes of Texas (and FDA) were upon them. D. Farley. il *FDA Consum* 21:29-31 O '87
In failing health. J. A. Conway. *Forbes* 139:8 Mr 9 '87
USA: the strange rise and fall of one MLM. il *Money* 16:140 Je '87
United Seafood Workers, Smoked Fish and Cannery Union
Fishy business [Fulton Fish Market and the Mafia] A. A. Lappen. il *Forbes* 140:8 N 16 '87
United States
    See also
  Americans
  Counties (U.S.)
  Gulf States (U.S.)
  Middle Western States
  Pacific Northwest
  Patriotism
  Southern States
  Southwestern States
  States (U.S.)
  Western States
            Antiquities
    See also
  Indians of North America—Antiquities
        Appropriations and expenditures
    See also
  Budget
  Grants-in-aid
  Intergovernmental fiscal relations
  Pork barrel legislation
  Research grants
  United States. Congress. House. Committee on the Budget
  United States. Congress. Senate. Committee on the Budget
How Congress creates a deficit [ten wasteful programs] D. Lambro. il *Read Dig* 131:39-40+ Jl '87
The latest idea in Washington [big spending] D. Seligman. il *Fortune* 115:109-10 Ap 13 '87
A new issue for Congress to consider: "the morality of government spending". il *Nations Bus* 75:76 F '87
On the problem of America's policy myopia [address, October 22, 1986] E. H. Crane. *Vital Speeches Day* 53:184-8 Ja 1 '87
A painless way to slash the deficit [shifting public services to the private sector] R. Fitzgerald. *Read Dig* 130:79-82 Mr '87
Priorities in a military culture. B. Smith. il *Bull At Sci* 43:9-10 Je '87
The public's agenda [results of Time poll] il *Time* 129:37 Mr 30 '87
Spending smarter. *New Repub* 196:5-7 F 2 '87
Testing the theory of less government, more prosperity. G. Koretz. il *Bus Week* p22+ F 2 '87
            Armed Forces
    See also
  Servicemen
  United States. Air Force
  United States. Air National Guard
  United States. Army
  United States. Coast Guard
  United States. Congress. House. Committee on Armed Services
  United States. Dept. of Defense
  United States. Marine Corps
  United States. Navy
Inside the nation's military machine: people and policies. J. Martin. il *Sch Update* 119:18-20 F 23 '87
Nuts, bolts, & death [budget cuts undermine readiness] H. G. Summers. *Wash Mon* 18:51-2 Ja '87
        Anecdotes, facetiae, satire, etc.
Humor in uniform. See occasional issues of Reader's Digest
        Appropriations and expenditures
    See United States. Dept. of Defense—Appropriations and expenditures
            Bands
    See Bands (Music)
            Blacks
From top guns to corporate brass [former black officers] D. C. Ruffin. il *Black Enterp* 17:115-17+ F '87

United States—Armed Forces—_cont._

Day care

See Day care and the military

Forces in Bolivia

Exporting the drug war [U.S. efforts against cocaine trade] T. Molnar. _Natl Rev_ 39:38 My 22 '87

Forces in Europe

Ike was right [reducing deployment of our troops in Europe] J. Chace. il _Atlantic_ 260:39-41 Ag '87

Make 'em pay [getting America's allies to shoulder more of the burden for their own defense] M. Kondracke. _New Repub_ 197:15-17 O 12 '87

Forces in foreign countries

The end of an era for U.S. global power? W. J. Holstein. il _Bus Week_ p170+ N 16 '87

Forces in Greece

Greece's balancing act [U.S. bases and nuclear weapons] W. M. Arkin. _Bull At Sci_ 43:11-12 Mr '87

Papandreou's 'whipping boy'. N. Cooper. il por _Newsweek_ 110:35 Jl 27 '87

Forces in Grenada

See also

Grenada—Invasion, 1983

Forces in Honduras

The comforts of 10 Lemp Alley [refugees, contras and U.S. soldiers in Honduras] M. McDonald. il _Macleans_ 100:22-4 F 23 '87

Forces in Korea

See also

Korean War, 1950-1953—American participation

Korean tripwire [possibility of nuclear war] P. Hayes and others. _Nation_ 245:256-7 S 19 '87

Forces in Spain

Spain, U.S. at an impasse over troop reduction issue. J. D. Morrocco. _Aviat Week Space Technol_ 126:28-9 Mr 23 '87

Forces in the Persian Gulf region

Study finds Rapid Deployment Force could thwart Soviet attack on Iran [study by Joshua M. Epstein of the Brookings Institution] P. Mann. il map _Aviat Week Space Technol_ 126:85+ Ja 12 '87

Forces in the Philippines

AIDS near U.S. bases. _Christ Century_ 104:11 Ja 7-14 '87

The bigger the bases, the bigger the trouble [Clark and Subic Bay] J. M. Fallows. il _U S News World Rep_ 103:32 N 23 '87

Testing an ally's resolve [future of bases] W. L. Chaze. il por map _U S News World Rep_ 103:73-5 S 28 '87

U.S. bases spread AIDS virus. C. D. Brubaker. il _Progressive_ 51:14 F '87

Forces in Vietnam

See also

Vietnamese War, 1957-1975—American participation

Management

See also

United States. President's Commission on Defense Management

Maneuvers

See Military maneuvers

Medical and sanitary affairs

See also

AIDS (Disease) and servicemen

Civilian Health and Medical Program of the Uniformed Services

Officers

The colonels' coup [involvement of military officers in Iran arms scandal] F. Zakaria. _New Repub_ 197:15 Jl 13-20 '87

Procurement

See United States. Dept. of Defense—Procurement

Public relations

See also

National Committee for Employer Support of the Guard and Reserve (U.S.)

Recruiting, enlistment, etc.

See also

Military service, Compulsory

Recruiters for peace [counter-recruiters] O. Davidson. _Nation_ 244:175-7 F 14 '87

Research

See Military research

Reserves

See also

National Committee for Employer Support of the Guard and Reserve (U.S.)

Retirement

See Retired military personnel

Special Forces

Defense Dept. establishes Special Operations Command. B. M. Greeley, Jr. il _Aviat Week Space Technol_ 126:61 Ap 20 '87

Next: a rescue command. il _U S News World Rep_ 102:10 F 16 '87

A small war [nomination of K. Berquist to head special operations] il _Newsweek_ 109:7 Je 1 '87

The sound of spinning wheels [Special Operations Forces] S. Emerson and R. A. Manning. il _U S News World Rep_ 102:21 Mr 23 '87

Special operations forces [special section] il _Aviat Week Space Technol_ 127:47+ D 14 '87

Women

See Servicewomen

Capital

Leaving Washington behind. W. B. Meyer. il _Am Herit_ 38:102-3 F/Mr '87

Census

Big-city mayors want blacks counted accurately in 1990 census report. il _Jet_ 72:8 Ag 17 '87

Census a public burden? [changes proposed by the Office of Management and Budget] C. Holden. _Science_ 237:839 Ag 21 '87

Changing America. J. W. Merline. _Consum Res Mag_ 70:38 Ap '87

Dymally pushing for fair black count in 1990 census. por _Jet_ 73:34 N 30 '87

Sparks are already flying over the 1990 census. S. B. Garland. _Bus Week_ p47 S 14 '87

Time spent unemployed: a new look at data from the CPS. M. W. Horrigan. bibl f il _Mon Labor Rev_ 110:3-15 Jl '87

Centennial celebrations, etc.

Collectibles

Centennial inkwell [1876] M. Wollett and B. Wollett. il _Antiques Collect Hobbies_ 92:27 Jl '87

Civil defense

See Civil defense

Civilization

See also

Morale, National

Social change

United States—Popular culture

United States—Social conditions

America as utopia: the city upon a hill. R. A. Nisbet. _Current_ 293:4-8 Je '87

The Civil War and American destiny. T. J. Fleming. il _Natl Rev_ 39:48+ N 6 '87

Cultural failure: the American preoccupation. W. F. Gavin. _Current_ 293:16-19 Je '87

In defense of our common culture. W. J. Bennett. il por _USA Today (Periodical)_ 115:45-7 Mr '87

Myth America. M. Lerner. _New Repub_ 197:11-13 S 7 '87

A nation in decline? B. W. Tuchman. il _N Y Times Mag_ p52+ S 20 '87

Notebook. L. H. Lapham. See issues of Harper's

Outside history. L. Weschler. _Harpers_ 274:16-18 Ja '87

Anecdotes, facetiae, satire, etc.

A country sage looks back. J. J. Kilpatrick. il por _Nations Bus_ 75:50-1 S '87

Climate

Almanac. D. M. Ludlum. See issues of Country Journal beginning October 1986

The climythology of America. D. M. Ludlum. il map _Weatherwise_ 40:255-9 O '87

Extreme fluctuations characterize recent winters. D. H. Hickcox. _Focus_ 36:31-2 Wint '86

In the United States—flash floods and drought [1986] D. Le Comte. il _Weatherwise_ 40:12-16 F '87

U.S. weather waxing cloudy. _Sci News_ 131:200 Mr 28 '87

Weatherwatch. D. M. Ludlum. See issues of Weatherwise

Commerce

See also

Balance of trade

Export-Import Bank of the United States

Investments, American

Merchant marine

Shipping

Taking on the world [special section] il _Time_ 130:46-50+ O 19 '87

United States trade [Dept. of Commerce report] P. H. Abelson. _Science_ 235:829 F 20 '87

Argentina

International tea party [Argentina's tea exporters] P. Gupte. il _Forbes_ 140:108+ N 16 '87

United States—Commerce—*cont.*
Australia
An alliance unbalanced. A. Lyons. *America* 157:373-4 N 21 '87
Australian Boeing order exploits greater domestic competition. J. Ott. *Aviat Week Space Technol* 127:36-7 O 12 '87
Brazil
Brazil's independent computer strategy [cover story] A. J. J. Botelho. il maps *Technol Rev* 90:36-45 My/Je '87
Canada
Anger over a tree tax [protesting Ottawa's decision to impose a tariff on Christmas trees imported from United States] M. Clark. il *Macleans* 100:11 F 9 '87
Beat the devil [R. Reagan's visit to Canada] A. Cockburn. *Nation* 244:494-5 Ap 18 '87
Big hug from Uncle Sam [historic trade pact] G. Bock. il *Time* 130:50 O 19 '87
The biggest deal in history [free trade accord and upcoming Reagan visit; cover story; special section; with editorial comment by Kevin Doyle] il *Macleans* 100:2, 10-12+ Ap 6 '87
Canada lifts tariff on books; publishing industry rejoices. B. Slopen. *Publ Wkly* 231:29 Mr 6 '87
A Canadian opportunity. C. M. Aho and M. Levinson. *Foreign Policy* 66:143-55 Spr '87
Canadian-United States trade [address, September 14, 1987] G. Devine. *Vital Speeches Day* 54:76-9 N 15 '87
Canadians fear study will lead to import duties [beef] *Success Farm* 85 no2:B8 Ja '87
The case for a free trade accord [U.S.-Canada talks] D. Francis. il *Macleans* 100:13 S 7 '87
Caught in the cross-fire [Canadian defense industry threatened by U.S. protectionism] M. Drohan. il *Macleans* 100:15 Mr 9 '87
Celebrations for the 'win-win' deal [final text of free trade agreement between Canada and the U.S.] M. Drohan. il *Macleans* 100:18-19 D 21 '87
A 'devil in the detail' [Senate passes sweeping protectionist trade bill] I. Austen. il *Macleans* 100:30-1 Ag 3 '87
Devine's control zone [Saskatchewan enacts potash protectionist measures to counteract U.S. duties] D. Eisler. il *Macleans* 100:14-15 S 14 '87
Division in the house [free trade debate dominates First Ministers' meeting] M. Drohan. il *Macleans* 100:10-12 D 7 '87
Emotional divisions [Canadian debate over trade agreement with U.S.] M. Janigan. il *Macleans* 100:21 N 16 '87
Fertilizer trade wars [Saskatchewan potash in the U.S.] T. Tedesco. il *Macleans* 100:35 Mr 9 '87
Fighting words on trade [C. Yeutter's views on protecting Canadian cultural industries] M. Gee. *Macleans* 100:16 F 16 '87
Firing up a new potash war [U.S. duty on Saskatchewan potash] D. Eisler. il *Macleans* 100:32-3 S 7 '87
Free trade: a historic midnight deal. P. Gessell. il *Macleans* 100:22-5 O 12 '87
A free trade advance. D. Jenish. il *Macleans* 100:38-9 My 18 '87
The free trade countdown. M. Drohan. il *Macleans* 100:15-16 S 28 '87
A free-trade milestone. E. B. Terry and others. il *Bus Week* p52-3 O 19 '87
From dollars to danger signals. P. C. Newman. il *Macleans* 100:42 My 18 '87
Getting together with a friend [possible free trade pact] G. Russell. il por *Time* 129:54 Ap 20 '87
Going public on trade [B. Mulroney pushes for free trade agreement with U.S.] M. Janigan. il por *Macleans* 100:16+ Mr 23 '87
Hard lines on trade. I. Austen. il *Macleans* 100:34 Ag 17 '87
How the free-trade talks are clobbering Canada's Tories. E. B. Terry. il *Bus Week* p61 Mr 9 '87
In search of a trade deal. M. Drohan. il *Macleans* 100:8-9 Jl 20 '87
Industry's surprising revival north of the border. E. B. Terry and others. il *Bus Week* p38-9 Jl 27 '87
A landmark trade treaty. *Newsweek* 110:71 O 12 '87
Nailing the consumer [Canadian lumber in the U.S.] M. Alexander and others. il *Consum Res Mag* 70:26-9 Mr '87
Neo-protectionism [address, November 6, 1986] D. R. Peterson. *Vital Speeches Day* 53:230-1 F 1 '87
A new call for free trade [reassurances to Canada included in Reagan State of the Union message] I. Austen. il por *Macleans* 100:18 F 9 '87

A new storm over trade [Canada-U.S. dispute over softwood lumber exports] M. Rose. il *Macleans* 100:10-11 Ja 12 '87
Nothing to fear but the fearful [free trade accord] D. Francis. il *Macleans* 100:13 O 19 '87
'One hell of a fight' [Canada-U.S. free trade agreement] M. Drohan. il *Macleans* 100:26-7 O 26 '87
Ottawa's trade offensive [softwood lumber accord] M. Drohan. il por *Macleans* 100:10-11 Ja 19 '87
The ownership issue [Canada-U.S. free trade negotiations] D. Jenish. il *Macleans* 100:40+ Je 1 '87
Personalities enter the trade talks [Canadian-U.S. negotiators] M. Janigan. il *Macleans* 100:18-19 D 14 '87
Potential victims of a trade pact [protectionist sentiment in Canada] M. Drohan. il *Macleans* 100:22-3 Ag 10 '87
Preparing for a real election [upcoming federal election in Canada seen to be focused on free trade issue] C. Gordon. il *Macleans* 100:41 N 2 '87
The pull of the American dream [free trade agreement-in-principle between Ottawa and Washington] P. C. Newman. il *Macleans* 100:42 O 19 '87
Redrawing the nation [trade accord; cover story; special section; with editorial comment by Kevin Doyle] il *Macleans* 100:2, 14-23 O 19 '87
A revolt over energy [controversy over Canada-U.S. free trade pact] M. Rose. il *Macleans* 100:15 N 23 '87
Stop signs for the competition [U.S. trade bills and Canada] D. Jenish. il *Macleans* 100:36-8 S 21 '87
The sweep of free trade. P. Gessell. il *Macleans* 100:24-5 Mr 16 '87
Talking tough on trade [U.S.-Canada softwood lumber accord; with editorial comment by Kevin Doyle] M. Drohan. il *Macleans* 100:2, 12+ Ja 26 '87
Temperatures rising [free trade debate in Canada] M. Janigan. il *Macleans* 100:10-12 N 9 '87
Tension in talking. D. Jenish. il *Macleans* 100:30-1 Je 29 '87
Toward the final hurdles [free trade accord discussed at First Ministers' meeting in Canada] M. Drohan. il *Macleans* 100:36-7 D 28 '87
Trade: a Canadian view. M. Drohan. *World Press Rev* 34:47 D '87
Trade bill addresses 'dumping' and Canada's bar to investment. H. Fields. *Publ Wkly* 232:19 Ag 14 '87
Trumpets of free trade. M. Rose. il *Macleans* 100:16 Mr 30 '87
The U.S.-Canada trade pact is already springing leaks. E. B. Terry and others. il *Bus Week* p75 D 7 '87
Uneasy over free trade [Maclean's/Decima poll] M. Rose. il *Macleans* 100:38-9 Ja 5 '87
Walkout from the talks [cover story; special section; with editorial comment by Kevin Doyle] il *Macleans* 100:2, 14-20+ O 5 '87
A warmer embrace of Canada? H. Eason. il *Nations Bus* 75:24+ F '87
What's at stake in the Canada talks. B. Javetski and H. Gleckman. *Bus Week* p39 Mr 2 '87
Whose power to which people? [B. C. Hydro's plans for hydroelectric dam for export on the Peace River] J. Baker. il *Sierra* 72:22-4 Ja/F '87
Why Brian Mulroney is up against a trade wall. E. B. Terry and others. il *Bus Week* p44-5 Je 15 '87
Canada—Anecdotes, facetiae, satire, etc.
Free trade? It will not happen. A. Fotheringham. il *Macleans* 100:64 O 26 '87
Caribbean region
See also
Caribbean American Chamber of Commerce and Industry
Caribbean Basin Initiative, 1983-
Chile
U.S. parts embargo grounds Chilean Air Force F-5 fleet. il *Aviat Week Space Technol* 127:73+ Ag 24 '87
China
Air Force issues RFPs for Chinese F-8-2 avionic upgrade kits. *Aviat Week Space Technol* 126:19 Mr 23 '87
Bernice Williams will lead trade group to China. por *Jet* 72:37 S 7 '87
The China bubble bursts. L. Kraar. il *Fortune* 116:86-9 Jl 6 '87
Report suggests further easing of controls on exports to China. *Aviat Week Space Technol* 127:28 Jl 13 '87
Y-7-100 instrument panel houses displays for U.S.-built systems [Chinese passenger aircraft] il *Aviat Week Space Technol* 127:58-9 D 21 '87
Developing countries
Agriculture on the high seas. J. C. Webster. il *Nations Bus* 75:49-50 D '87

United States—Commerce—Developing countries—*cont.*

Disaster for sale [pesticides exported from the United States] P. A. A. Berle. *Audubon* 89:6 My '87

Export increases rely on developing markets [grain] T. White. il *Success Farm* 85 no4:7 F '87

The export of U.S. toxic wastes [cover story] A. Porterfield and D. Weir. il *Nation* 245:325+ O 3 '87

East Asia

Gas for the lamps of Seoul? [Alaskan gas] L. Minard. map *Forbes* 139:34-5 Mr 23 '87

Trade progress may face its biggest obstacle in Asia [U.S. trade balance and exploding imports from the Asian Tigers] G. Koretz. il *Bus Week* p26 N 23 '87

A weaker dollar may blunt Asia's trade claws . . . and send more U.S. goods to the Pacific. G. Koretz. il *Bus Week* p22 Mr 16 '87

France

Delivery of C-130s expands French military airlift capability. il *Aviat Week Space Technol* 127:29 D 14 '87

McDonnell Douglas offers F/A-18 for French Navy's carrier air fleet. J. D. Morrocco. *Aviat Week Space Technol* 127:33-5 S 7 '87

Germany (West)

Readers respond to German businessman's query: "What does the U.S. make that a sensible European would buy?". *Forbes* 139 Ann Directory:38 Ap 27 '87

Great Britain

Britain-U.S. export pact protects AWACS technology. *Aviat Week Space Technol* 126:263 Mr 9 '87

British Airways places orders for 14 Boeing transports. *Aviat Week Space Technol* 127:36 Ag 24 '87

E-3 offsets expected to reach $2 billion [Boeing's agreement with Britain] *Aviat Week Space Technol* 127:25 O 26 '87

Midnight in London is 4 p.m. in L.A. [made for TV movies from Britain] L. Brown. il *Channels* 7:20 F '87

Shh! Please don't call this car a Rover [Sterling] M. Maremont. il *Bus Week* p59 Ja 12 '87

Watch out, here come more cheap imports [Lionheart Television International] A. B. Block. il por *Forbes* 139:150 Mr 9 '87

Wings West commuter orders 10 British Advanced Turboprops. *Aviat Week Space Technol* 127:37 S 28 '87

Wings West orders 15 Jetstream 31 commuters. *Aviat Week Space Technol* 127:36 O 19 '87

Haiti

Crates of fresh poison [EDB levels in mangoes] R. Caplan. *Harpers* 275:58-9 O '87

Honduras

Proposed sale of F-5s to Honduras [statement, May 19, 1987] E. Abrams. *Dep State Bull* 87:87-9 Jl '87

Hungary

Hungary: hybrid of the East. H. Eason. il *Nations Bus* 75:26+ Mr '87

India

The big money in cheap rock [India's Jains dominate U.S. market for low-priced diamonds] P. Gupte. il *Forbes* 140:64+ Ag 10 '87

Shamianas, anyone? [S. Pennathur's linkup with Indian artisans] P. Gupte. il pors *Forbes* 140:190+ O 5 '87

Iran

Message to Iran [U.S. bans imports] il *Time* 130:42 O 12 '87

Israel

Navy evaluates Israeli R&D programs for use on U.S. weapon systems. M. Mecham. *Aviat Week Space Technol* 126:20-1 Je 1 '87

Italy

New vroom [Alfa Romeo tackles U.S. market] P. Berman. il *Forbes* 139:79 Ja 26 '87

Young tells Italians he can be businessman and pastor [Mayor A. Young] il *Jet* 72:40 Je 29 '87

Jamaica

The locomotive needs help [apparel industry] A. D. Frank. por *Forbes* 139:100 Ja 26 '87

Japan

America vs. Japan: a no-win game [special section] il por *Bus Week* p30-4 My 4 '87

The battle over Toshiba [U.S.-Japan trade relations strained by Toshiba's sale of high tech goods to Soviets] J. B. Copeland. il *Newsweek* 110:40 Jl 13 '87

The big switch. *New Repub* 196:5-7 Je 15 '87

Bright lights, big MITI [Toshiba's sale of top-security technology to the Soviets] C. Chandler. *New Repub* 197:11-13 Ag 31 '87

The case of the not-so-simple machine tools [Toshiba's sale of top-secret technology to the Soviet Union] M. I. Goldman. il *Technol Rev* 90:20+ O '87

A cautionary tale [LaPine Technology's joint venture with Kyocera] K. K. Wiegner. il por *Forbes* 140:52-3 Ag 10 '87

Chip wars [tariffs on semiconductors] *Natl Rev* 39:20-1 Ap 24 '87

Clobbering car buyers [U.S. auto industry calls for new limits on Japanese imports] R. J. Samuelson. il *Newsweek* 110:69 D 14 '87

The coming U.S.-Japan crisis. G. R. Packard. bibl f *Foreign Aff* 66:348-67 Wint '87/'88

Congress wants Toshiba's blood [diversion of high tech to Russia provokes U.S. punitive measures] S. J. Dryden. *Bus Week* p46-7 Jl 6 '87

Congressman Merv Dymally leads trade mission to Japan and Seoul, Korea. il por *Jet* 72:37 My 18 '87

Data General gets the call [deal with Japan's NTT] L. Helm and N. Gross. il *Bus Week* p96 O 19 '87

Debate over F-15 derivative clouds selection of Japanese FS-X fighter. il *Aviat Week Space Technol* 126:178+ Je 15 '87

The end of innocence. J. W. Dower. il *Nation* 245:224-6+ S 12 '87

Exim Bank backs 767 sale to All Nippon to foil Airbus bid. *Aviat Week Space Technol* 126:31 Je 29 '87

Explaining the war of the chips [U.S. tariff imposed on Japanese products] il *World Press Rev* 34:48 Je '87

Fighting off the suitcase brigade [Japanese violations of semiconductor trade pact] P. Elmer-Dewitt. il *Time* 129:49 Mr 2 '87

Fighting the trade tilt [tariffs on Japanese electronics products] S. Koepp. il *Time* 129:50-1 Ap 6 '87

Fish story [Japan's rising importation of U.S. tuna] P. Fuhrman. il *Forbes* 140:38-9 Ag 10 '87

Fixing a tariff blooper [U.S. tariff on Japanese electronic products] G. Lewis. *Bus Week* p35 D 14 '87

From dollars to danger signals. P. C. Newman. il *Macleans* 100:42 My 18 '87

Harley-Davidson: ready to ride on its own [asking to end import restraints against Japan] *Newsweek* 109:50 Mr 30 '87

High-tech tariffs boomerang on the U.S. G. Lewis. il *Bus Week* p26-7 S 7 '87

A hot American car may hit Japan: the Honda [strong yen could prompt Japanese carmakers to reexport from the U.S.] W. J. Hampton and others. il *Bus Week* p50 Ja 26 '87

How to beat the Japanese at home. J. Dreyfuss. il *Fortune* 116:80-3 Ag 31 '87

How to beat the Japanese: five U.S. companies rise to the challenge [cover story; special section] C. P. Work and others. il *U S News World Rep* 103:38-45 Ag 24 '87

How Toshiba is beating American sanctions [furor over illegal sale to Moscow dies down] S. J. Dryden. il *Bus Week* p58 S 14 '87

"I know I sound protectionistic" [LSI Logic's W. Corrigan] K. K. Wiegner. il por *Forbes* 139:54+ Je 29 '87

It's more than a trade brawl. P. R. Range. il *U S News World Rep* 102:20-2 My 4 '87

It's tough, but it isn't doomsday [Japanese import share of U.S. new car market] R. Phalon. il *Forbes* 139:53+ My 4 '87

Japan and the Pacific Rim: economic challenge to America [cover story; special issue] il *Sch Update* 119:2-24 Ap 6 '87

Japan can't make a quick yen in the U.S. any more [consumer electronics] K. Dreyfack. il *Bus Week* p120-1 F 23 '87

Japan: hopes, but no gains [better relationship between Japan and black American consumers] D. C. Ruffin. il *Black Enterp* 18:22 Ag '87

Japan is building a cozy lead in laptops. L. Armstrong. il *Bus Week* p128+ F 23 '87

Japan is winning friends in the Rust Belt [midwesterners becoming less protectionist as a result of Japanese auto plant locations] W. J. Holstein. il *Bus Week* p54 O 19 '87

Japan may be listening, but it's not about to change [U.S. imposes tariffs on electronic products] A. Borrus. il *Bus Week* p35-6 Ap 13 '87

Japan to purchase foreign aircraft to ease balance of trade [helicopter imports] *Aviat Week Space Technol* 127:22 Jl 6 '87

Japan vs. the U.S. *World Press Rev* 34:8-9 My '87

Japanese challenge—American response [address, March 5, 1987] P. Cannon. *Vital Speeches Day* 53:503-9 Je 1 '87

The Japanese go on a mail-order shopping spree. T. Holden. il *Bus Week* p44 S 7 '87

United States—Commerce—Japan—cont.

Japan's bow of contrition [apologizing for Toshiba scandal] J. B. Copeland. il *Newsweek* 110:44 Jl 27 '87

Japan's case of malaise. R. J. Samuelson. il *Newsweek* 109:47 My 4 '87

Japan's defense agency selects F-16 as basis for FS-X aircraft [General Dynamics chosen] *Aviat Week Space Technol* 127:22-3 O 26 '87

Japan's pump-priming won't do much for U.S. exports. B. Buell. il *Bus Week* p49 Ap 27 '87

Just what the U.S. needs: an even smaller car from Japan [Daihatsu's Charade] S. Toy. il *Bus Week* p26 Ap 20 '87

Let's not bash the Japanese [U.S. tariff action] L. Smith. il *Fortune* 115:175-6 Ap 27 '87

Made in America: the Japanese auto cartel. A. T. Denzau. *Society* 24:30-5 S/O '87

Making amends [Toshiba products banned in U.S. following sale of submarine technology to Soviets] *Time* 130:49 Jl 13 '87

Maybe this time . . . [Detroit hangs on against imports and immigrant autos] J. Flint. il *Forbes* 140:34 S 7 '87

A meeting for the books [R. Reagan and Y. Nakasone] il por *Fortune* 115:8 My 25 '87

Morris the Cat is learning Japanese [U.S. cat food exports] B. Buell. il *Bus Week* p82 Je 15 '87

The myths of a trade war. B. Powell. il *Newsweek* 109:40-2 Ap 13 '87

News briefing of May 8, 1987. G. P. Shultz. *Dep State Bull* 87:13-14 Jl '87

No more Mr. Nice Guy [U.S. tariffs on Japanese imports] D. Pauly. il *Newsweek* 109:42 Ap 6 '87

The peril of pushing Japan. J. Dreyfuss. il *Fortune* 115:113-14+ My 11 '87

Playing by different rules. J. M. Fallows. il *Atlantic* 260:22+ S '87

Playing it cool [Y. Nakasone visits the U.S.] J. Greenwald. il por *Time* 129:32-3 My 11 '87

Punish Toshiba? W. F. Buckley. *Natl Rev* 39:62-3 D 18 '87

Punishing Japan: Reagan walks a fine line [imposition of tariffs for failure to uphold semiconductor pact] B. Javetski and others. il *Bus Week* p34-5 Ap 13 '87

Reagan fires a shot across Tokyo's bow. W. L. Chaze. il *U S News World Rep* 102:16-17 Ap 27 '87

'The real cause' of the U.S. trade deficit. M. Ishizuka. *World Press Rev* 34:45 Mr '87

Rising above trade rivalry [BizNet teleconference on U.S.-Japanese trade] *Nations Bus* 75:45-6 Ap '87

The rites of spring [Japanese autos in U.S. market] M. Keller. il *Mot Trend* 39:110 F '87

Rules for the game [imposition of tariffs on Japanese products] *America* 156:355 My 2 '87

Samurais for hire [Toshiba lobbying Congress] G. Witkin. il *U S News World Rep* 103:50 O 5 '87

Sanctions [U.S. actions against Toshiba for high tech sale to Soviets] L. G. Boundas. il *Stereo Rev* 52:8 N '87

Semi-tough [federal action to help American semiconductor companies] M. Gladwell. *New Repub* 196:9-11 My 18 '87

Shoe wars: an angry American takes on Japan [J. Stollenwerk of Allen-Edmonds] *Newsweek* 109:38 Ja 26 '87

Soothing talks, troubled times [defusing trade tensions between U.S. and Japan] B. Rudolph. il *Time* 129:74 My 4 '87

Tackling Toshiba [U.S. reaction to high tech sale to Soviets] J. McLaughlin. *Natl Rev* 39:24 Ag 14 '87

Tainted tobacco could poison a hot market [RJR Nabisco exports cigarettes tainted by weed killer] N. Gross and S. Ticer. il *Bus Week* p45+ Je 15 '87

A talk with Shintaro Abe: the U.S. is 'going too far'. R. J. Dowling and L. Armstrong. por *Bus Week* p37 Ap 20 '87

Tofu-quality beans earn 40¢ premium for Illinois growers. *Success Farm* 85 no2:18 Ja '87

Tokyo opens a southern trade route [Japanese factories in Mexico] S. L. Hawkins. il map *U S News World Rep* 103:40+ Ag 3 '87

Tokyo's end run around its 'trade problem'. N. Gross. il *Bus Week* p54-5 Jl 13 '87

Tora! Tora! Angry lawmakers torpedo Toshiba [U.S. seeks to punish company for illegal trade with Soviets] *U S News World Rep* 103:42 Jl 13 '87

Toshiba ban spurs review of technology export controls [U.S. reaction to Japan's high tech sale to Soviets] *Aviat Week Space Technol* 127:27 Jl 6 '87

The Toshiba scandal has exporters running for cover [technology sale to Soviets] L. Armstrong and N. Gross. il *Bus Week* p86-7 Jl 20 '87

Toshiba vs. the U.S.: a Japanese view. *World Press Rev* 34:18 Ag '87

Toward a trade war [semiconductor wars] W. Hutton. *World Press Rev* 34:19 Ag '87

Trade face-off [U.S.-Japan confrontation over semiconductor trade; cover story; special section] il *Time* 129:28-32+ Ap 13 '87

The trade wars. il *World Press Rev* 34:7 Je '87

Trade with Japan [tariff on semiconductors] R. Reagan. *Dep State Bull* 87:35-7 Jl '87

The truce in the chip war may be temporary. J. W. Wilson. *Bus Week* p46-7 F 23 '87

The U.S. and Japan: trying to head off a slump. B. Powell. il por *Newsweek* 109:50+ My 11 '87

The U.S. is getting Japan hooked on plastic. A. Borrus. il *Bus Week* p100+ My 25 '87

U.S.-Japan semiconductor trade [statement, June 8, 1987] R. Reagan. *Dep State Bull* 87:55 Ag '87

U.S.-Japan trade relations [address, April 13, 1987] W. A. Wallis. *Dep State Bull* 87:54-8 Je '87

The United States-Japan economic Olympics [address, December 11-12, 1986] R. A. Morse. *Vital Speeches Day* 53:409-11 Ap 15 '87

Visit of Japanese Prime Minister Nakasone [remarks and text of joint statement, April 30-May 1, 1987] R. Reagan; Y. Nakasone; G. P. Shultz. il por *Dep State Bull* 87:37-41 Jl '87

A war between friends [protectionist frenzy unleashed during Y. Nakasone's visit] M. McDonald. il por *Macleans* 100:32-3 My 11 '87

What all of America's Japan-bashing can't change. L. Armstrong. *Bus Week* p63 Ag 31 '87

What's wrong with Japan bashing. R. Darman. il *U S News World Rep* 103:53-4 O 5 '87

Where cigarettes and spirits are still booming. L. Armstrong. il *Bus Week* p94 S 14 '87

Why we'll sell more beef to Japan in coming years. G. Johnston. il *Success Farm* 85:68 Ag '87

Will Lotus overrun Microsoft's Japanese garden? B. Buell. il por *Bus Week* p76 Ap 13 '87

The winds of trade war [with interviews with R. Strauss and K. Kato] R. H. Bork, Jr. il *U S News World Rep* 102:46-7 Ap 13 '87

Yasu, the chips are down [effect of U.S. tariffs on Y. Nakasone's popularity] H. G. Chua-Eoan. il por *Time* 129:38 Ap 27 '87

Japan—Anecdotes, facetiae, satire, etc.

Trading letters [imaginary correspondence between R. Reagan and Y. Nakasone] R. Baker. il *N Y Times Mag* p14 My 10 '87

Korea (South)

Congressman Merv Dymally leads trade mission to Japan and Seoul, Korea. il por *Jet* 72:37 My 18 '87

Hyundai computers are stuck in the slow lane. G. Lewis. il *Bus Week* p50 Je 15 '87

Korea's new corporate bosses: made in America. L. Nakarmi and W. J. Holstein. il *Bus Week* p58-9 F 23 '87

The road most traveled [Hyundai] S. B. Weiner. il *Forbes* 140:60+ O 19 '87

Taiwan and Korea should be praised, not punished. G. S. Becker. il *Bus Week* p22 My 25 '87

Those rich Koreans are going on a U.S. shopping trip. J. B. Treece. il *Bus Week* p58 Mr 9 '87

The top of the wish list [appeal of low-priced Korean cars] M. Keller. il *Mot Trend* 39:130 Ap '87

Where sanctions against Japan are really working. S. J. Dryden. il *Bus Week* p61-2 My 11 '87

Latin America

Blues south of the border. H. Eason. il *Nations Bus* 75:35-6 Jl '87

Middle East

Export controls imposed on chemical weapons substances [State Dept. statement, July 31, 1987] *Dep State Bull* 87:49 O '87

Netherlands

The perils of protectionism [address, May 19, 1987] P. F. Dobbelmann. *Vital Speeches Day* 53:590-4 Jl 15 '87

Pacific region

Japan and the Pacific Rim: economic challenge to America [cover story; special issue] il *Sch Update* 119:2-24 Ap 6 '87

Vitality and possibility on the Pacific Rim [address, December 3, 1986] G. J. Sigur. *Dep State Bull* 87:52-4 F '87

United States—Commerce—_cont._

Pakistan

The nuclear caper [arrest of Arshad Pervez in Philadelphia on charges of trying to illegally export materials for Pakistan's weapons program] I. Austen. il _Macleans_ 100:19 Jl 27 '87

Pakistani smuggling riles Congress [nuclear smuggling] L. S. Spector. il _Bull At Sci_ 43:3-4 O '87

A rock and a hard place [Pakistan caught trying to illegally import maraging steel intended for bomb program] R. Nordland. il _Newsweek_ 110:30+ Jl 27 '87

Wanted: the bomb [possible cutoff of military aid after Pakistan's attempt buy steel alloy for nuclear weapons] il _U S News World Rep_ 103:8 Jl 27 '87

Persian Gulf region

U.S. companies are back in force in the Gulf. B. Slavin. il _Bus Week_ p79 O 19 '87

Philippines

Arms for Marcos? [smuggling case] L. Howard. il por _Newsweek_ 110:5 D 21 '87

Poland

Jaruzelski wins one with the end of U.S. sanctions. D. Stanglin. il por _U S News World Rep_ 102:35 Mr 2 '87

Romania

Trade with Romania, Hungary, and China [most-favored-nation tariff status; White House statement, June 2, 1987] _Dep State Bull_ 87:57 Ag '87

Saudi Arabia

Administration cancels missile sale; Congress critical of Middle East policy [proposed sale of 1,600 Maverick antitank missiles to Saudi Arabia] M. Mecham. _Aviat Week Space Technol_ 126:70-1 Je 15 '87

Administration to cite Saudi involvement in Gulf as justification for arms sale. M. Mecham. _Aviat Week Space Technol_ 127:31 Ag 24 '87

Congress moves to block sale of Mavericks to Saudis. M. Mecham. _Aviat Week Space Technol_ 126:23-4 Je 8 '87

Congress warns administration not to attempt Saudi arms sale. M. Mecham. _Aviat Week Space Technol_ 127:28-9 O 5 '87

Proposed Saudi sale spurs review of arms export controls. M. Mecham. _Aviat Week Space Technol_ 126:69+ Mr 30 '87

Scandinavia

SAS considers Boeing 767 to replace DC-10. _Aviat Week Space Technol_ 126:34 My 4 '87

South Africa

AAUP opposes embargo on sales of books to South Africa. C. Reid. _Publ Wkly_ 232:12 D 11 '87

American TV's mixed message to Pretoria. J. Von Herrmann. il _Channels_ 7:8 Mr '87

Economic sanctions against South Africa [messages and letter to Congress, September 25-29, 1986] R. Reagan. _Dep State Bull_ 86:35-7 D '86

Ignoring both carrot and stick [effect of sanctions] W. R. Doerner. il _Time_ 130:36 O 5 '87

Out of Africa [Comprehensive Anti-Apartheid Act] J. M. Woods. il _Black Enterp_ 17:15 Ja '87

Pro and con [Secretary of State's Advisory Committee on South Africa urges sanctions] _Time_ 129:58 F 23 '87

The truth about sanctions. J. H. Wolfe. _USA Today (Periodical)_ 115:9 Mr '87

Two questions about South Africa [efficacy of sanctions and Communist domination of African National Congress] D. Seligman. _Fortune_ 115:122+ Mr 2 '87

Why deny the children? [effects of American publishers' boycott] G. Miklowitz. por _Publ Wkly_ 232:66 O 9 '87

Why South Africa shrugs at sanctions. P. Brimelow. il _Forbes_ 139:100-4 Mr 9 '87

Southeast Asia

United States policy in Southeast Asia. E. Colbert. bibl f _Curr Hist_ 86:145-7+ Ap '87

Soviet Union

See also

Coordinating Committee on Multilateral Export Controls

The ban that boomeranged [export of American technology to Soviet Union] T. H. Naylor. _Nation_ 245:755-6 D 19 '87

Business as usual . . . but not with the Soviets? [GeoSpectra hesitant to handle Soviet satellite photographs] _Space World_ X-12-288:7-8 D '87

Easing the high-tech sales ban: U.S. firms can now sell oil equipment to Moscow. J. B. Copeland. il _Newsweek_ 109:38 Ja 26 '87

'Eefningwear' for America [Soviet designer V. Zaitsev's fashions to be licensed in the U.S.] A. Miller. il por _Newsweek_ 110:64 O 19 '87

Gorbachev opens the border for Jews—with good reason [trying to win support of U.S. Jews for relaxation of the Jackson-Vanik trade terms] J. Pearson. il _Bus Week_ p28 Ap 20 '87

Gorbachev's prairie pals [J. Chrystal and D. Andreas] T. Jacoby. il pors _Newsweek_ 109:31 Ap 6 '87

"The most corrupt person" [fabricating fraudulent Soviet orders for goods made by Dayco; case of E. Reich] N. J. Perry. por _Fortune_ 116:93 Ag 17 '87

One good subsidy merits another [U.S. subsidizes wheat sale to Soviet Union] _Newsweek_ 109:61 My 11 '87

Panel would reform U.S. export controls [study by the National Academy of Sciences] J. Raloff. _Sci News_ 131:55 Ja 24 '87

Proton marketing team finds U.S. interest, opposition [Soviet booster] il _Aviat Week Space Technol_ 126:20-1 My 25 '87

Russki business [attempt to market Proton booster] L. Dorr, Jr. il _Space World_ X-7-283:31-4 Jl '87

Satellite builders want change in U.S. anti-Proton policy. T. M. Foley. _Aviat Week Space Technol_ 127:138-9 S 28 '87

State Dept. denies license to export U.S. satellites to the Soviet Union [use of Proton] _Aviat Week Space Technol_ 127:59 Jl 27 '87

A Texas lawyer markets Soviet rockets [A. Dula] D. Pedersen. il por _Newsweek_ 110:58 Ag 17 '87

Tracking a technobandit [C. J. McVey captured for illegal sales of computer equipment to the Soviet Union] D. Pauly. il por _Newsweek_ 110:66 D 7 '87

Tussle over high technology [major study attacks U.S. export restrictions] J. Castro. il _Time_ 129:48 Ja 26 '87

Spain

Spain: Europe's sun belt. H. Eason. map _Nations Bus_ 75:28 Mr '87

Sweden

Fairchild delivers Metro 3 AEW testbed to Sweden [airborne early warning] C. A. Shifrin. il _Aviat Week Space Technol_ 127:127+ O 19 '87

Taiwan

Taiwan and Korea should be praised, not punished. G. S. Becker. il _Bus Week_ p22 My 25 '87

Taiwan woos American business. H. Eason. il _Nations Bus_ 75:64 Je '87

Where sanctions against Japan are really working. S. J. Dryden. il _Bus Week_ p61-2 My 11 '87

Western Europe

All's fair in the airliner war. A. Faujas. _World Press Rev_ 34:49-50 Je '87

Can Chrysler make a comeback in Europe, too? J. B. Treece. il _Bus Week_ p168-9 N 16 '87

Eurofighter bidding rules may bar U.S. companies. M. Feazel. _Aviat Week Space Technol_ 126:18-19 Ja 19 '87

Europeans criticize U.S. subsidy charges at Airbus A320 rollout. J. M. Lenorovitz. il _Aviat Week Space Technol_ 126:30-1 F 23 '87

Europeans will enter ATR42 in U.S. STOL competition [military cargo version] il _Aviat Week Space Technol_ 126:28-9 F 23 '87

Europe's credit-card market is ripe for invasion, too. F. A. Miller. il _Bus Week_ p104 My 25 '87

"Eye for eye, tooth for tooth" [U.S. trade dispute with European Economic Community] G. Russell. il _Time_ 129:54 Ja 12 '87

France orders Boeing E-3s; Britain signs formal contract. _Aviat Week Space Technol_ 126:27 Mr 2 '87

Imports from the EEC [proclamation, January 21, 1987] R. Reagan. _Dep State Bull_ 87:30 Ap '87

Italy, West Germany examine upgrading Allison engines [helicopters] _Aviat Week Space Technol_ 126:72 F 23 '87

More Chevys may be cruising the Autobahn. J. E. Pluenneke. il _Bus Week_ p55 Mr 16 '87

NATO pushes the 'eject' button on U.S. contractors [replacement program for F-16 fighters] J. Kapstein. _Bus Week_ p50 F 2 '87

Northwest's A330/A340 choice fuels aircraft subsidy debate. J. Ott. il _Aviat Week Space Technol_ 126:38-9 Ap 13 '87

The perils of protectionism [address, May 19, 1987] P. F. Dobbelmann. _Vital Speeches Day_ 53:590-4 Jl 15 '87

Secretary's joint news conference after meeting with EC ministers [text of press conference, December 12, 1986] _Dep State Bull_ 87:59-62 F '87

United States—Commerce—Western Europe—*cont.*

Sky wars over Airbus [U.S. threatening to slap duties on its U.S. sales] F. J. Comes. *Bus Week* p48 F 16 '87

Starring on the world stage [U.S. TV programs] L. Brown. il *Channels* 7:18 N '87

Taking the sting out of the plunging dollar [European companies exporting from U.S. subsidiaries] B. Riemer and F. J. Comes. il *Bus Week* p72-3 D 7 '87

A time for cool heads [dispute over subsidies to Europe's Airbus Industrie civil transport programs] D. E. Fink. *Aviat Week Space Technol* 126:11 F 23 '87

Trade wars: Reagan plays with fire [U.S. duties imposed on European agricultural products] *Natl Rev* 39:21-2 Ja 30 '87

Transatlantic showdown [U.S.-European Community agricultural trade war] P. Lewis. il *Macleans* 100:30 Ja 19 '87

U.S.-EC relations and the international trading system [address, October 8, 1986] W. A. Wallis. *Dep State Bull* 87:43-7 Ja '87

U.S., Europe agree on agenda for aircraft financing talks. D. A. Brown. *Aviat Week Space Technol* 127:36 N 2 '87

U.S., Europe seek rapid cure in Airbus subsidy dispute. M. Mecham. *Aviat Week Space Technol* 127:35+ O 26 '87

U.S., Europeans clash over Airbus subsidies. D. A. Brown. il *Aviat Week Space Technol* 126:18-20 F 9 '87

Commercial policy

See also

Balance of trade

Coordinating Committee on Multilateral Export Controls

Export-Import Bank of the United States

Tariff—United States

United States—Commercial treaties and agreements

United States. Dept. of Commerce

United States. Office of the U.S. Trade Representative

Academy panel blasts U.S. export controls [report by the National Academy of Sciences and the National Academy of Engineering] C. Norman. il *Science* 235:424-5 Ja 23 '87

Administration opposes House bill on offsets. P. Mann. *Aviat Week Space Technol* 127:26-7 Jl 6 '87

The ban that boomeranged [export of American technology to Soviet Union] T. H. Naylor. *Nation* 245:755-6 D 19 '87

The big switch. *New Repub* 196:5-7 Je 15 '87

Can we put U.S. agriculture on the road to recovery? D. Amstutz. il *USA Today (Periodical)* 116:18-20 N '87

A Canadian opportunity. C. M. Aho and M. Levinson. *Foreign Policy* 66:143-55 Spr '87

Clobbering car buyers [U.S. auto industry calls for new limits on Japanese imports] R. J. Samuelson. il *Newsweek* 110:69 D 14 '87

The competitiveness craze [cover story] R. Kuttner. *New Repub* 197:22+ N 2 '87

Competitiveness in America: is protectionism the answer? [address, May 27, 1987] D. W. McMinn. *Dep State Bull* 87:56-9 Ag '87

The competitiveness problem [address, September 14, 1987] G. M. Keller. *Vital Speeches Day* 54:61-4 N 1 '87

Congress readies trade bill to ease export controls [Trade and International Policy Reform Act of 1987] M. Mecham. il *Aviat Week Space Technol* 126:315-16+ Je 15 '87

Consumer protection? [Textile Apparel Trade Act] J. W. Merline. il *Consum Res Mag* 70:38 O '87

Copyright official challenges linking of copyright to trade negotiators. H. Fields. *Publ Wkly* 231:16 Ap 3 '87

A crossroads in U.S. trade policy [address, May 4, 1987] R. K. Shelp. *Vital Speeches Day* 53:618-21 Ag 1 '87

Dealing with Congress [protectionist sentiment clouds U.S.-Canada free trade accord] I. Austen. il *Macleans* 100:17 Ap 6 '87

Defense, Commerce Departments clash again over export controls. *Aviat Week Space Technol* 126:28-9 F 16 '87

A 'devil in the detail' [Senate passes sweeping protectionist trade bill] I. Austen. il *Macleans* 100:30-1 Ag 3 '87

Don't let the Grinch steal Christmas. G. F. Gilder. il *Natl Rev* 39:40-4 Ap 24 '87

Easing the high-tech sales ban: U.S. firms can now sell oil equipment to Moscow. J. B. Copeland. il *Newsweek* 109:38 Ja 26 '87

Export controls imposed on chemical weapons substances [State Dept. statement, July 31, 1987] *Dep State Bull* 87:49 O '87

Export controls of high-technology goods. P. H. Abelson. *Science* 235:1297 Mr 13 '87

Export controls: the political winds are shifting. *Bus Week* p31 F 16 '87

Finance and free trade. G. P. Brockway. il *New Leader* 70:10-11 F 9-23 '87

Flocking together on trade. G. J. Church. il *Time* 129:24 F 2 '87

Foreign trade policy. *Congr Dig* 66:163-92 Je/Jl '87

Free trade is no free lunch. W. R. Hawkins. *Natl Rev* 39:38-9 Ag 28 '87

Get ready for the trade act of 1987. A. C. Isgrò. il *Fortune* 115:83-4 Mr 2 '87

Getting a trade bill is going to take a lot of trading. D. Harbrecht and B. Javetski. il por *Bus Week* p34 S 28 '87

Gorbachev opens the border for Jews—with good reason [trying to win support of U.S. Jews for relaxation of the Jackson-Vanik trade terms] J. Pearson. il *Bus Week* p28 Ap 20 '87

Hard lines on trade [Canada-U.S. free trade talks] I. Austen. il *Macleans* 100:34 Ag 17 '87

Helping small firms compete [Small Business Trade Competitiveness and Innovation Act] *Nations Bus* 75:12 Je '87

High technology export controls [White House announcement, March 18, 1987] *Dep State Bull* 87:56 Je '87

Hobbling high-tech [report of panel of the National Academy of Sciences and the National Academy of Engineering] *Sci Am* 256:58 Mr '87

Horse-trading on Capitol Hill [trade bill subjected to pork barrel politics] T. Noah. il *Newsweek* 110:71 O 12 '87

How not to write a trade law. R. H. Bork, Jr. il *U S News World Rep* 103:48-50 O 5 '87

How to solve the trade problem [auctionable quota plan] R. Thomas. il *Newsweek* 109:40 Ja 12 '87

Howdy, I'm Dick Gephardt—trade warrior. D. Harbrecht. il por *Bus Week* p98-9 My 4 '87

In search of a trade bill Reagan won't veto. D. Harbrecht and B. Javetski. il *Bus Week* p26 Ag 3 '87

Industry presses congressional review of marketing cost ban. M. Mecham. *Aviat Week Space Technol* 127:77 N 2 '87

International competitiveness [address, June 8, 1987] H. Goldfeder. *Vital Speeches Day* 53:722-5 S 15 '87

International trade [address, January 13, 1987] J. Heinz, III. *Vital Speeches Day* 53:277-9 F 15 '87

Invasion of the patent pirates [foreign companies] C. Sims. il *Read Dig* 131:33-6 O '87

It worked with the tax bill—and it just might with trade [role of D. Rostenkowski] H. Gleckman and D. Harbrecht. il por *Bus Week* p42 Mr 9 '87

More problems with protectionism [effect on major banks] il *Fortune* 116:10 S 28 '87

The myths of a trade war [U.S.-Japan relationship] B. Powell. il *Newsweek* 109:40-2 Ap 13 '87

National security and the semiconductor industry. D. G. Dallmeyer. il *Technol Rev* 90:46-52+ N/D '87

'New protectionism' to fit the times. R. H. Bork, Jr. il *U S News World Rep* 102:44-5 Ap 6 '87

"No more Mr. Nice Guy". H. Banks. il *Forbes* 139:84-7 F 9 '87

No pain, no gain [self-defeating, protectionist trade bill] M. B. Zuckerman. il *U S News World Rep* 103:110 S 28 '87

Panel would reform U.S. export controls [study by the National Academy of Sciences] J. Raloff. *Sci News* 131:55 Ja 24 '87

Patent pirates may soon be walking the plank [infringement by foreign companies] R. Rhein, Jr. il *Bus Week* p62-3 Je 15 '87

Pentagon reviews trade pacts to standardize joint projects. J. D. Morrocco. il *Aviat Week Space Technol* 127:45+ O 19 '87

The perils of protectionism [address, May 19, 1987] P. F. Dobbelmann. *Vital Speeches Day* 53:590-4 Jl 15 '87

Political battles over trade wars [conflicting views of G. Hart and R. Gephardt] W. Shapiro. il pors *Time* 129:24 My 4 '87

Protectionism [address, January 29, 1987] C. K. Yeutter. *Vital Speeches Day* 53:290-3 Mr 1 '87

Protectionism can't protect jobs. M. McFadden. il *Fortune* 115:121+ My 11 '87

The protectionists may have spent their fury [House vote on Gephardt Amendment] D. Harbrecht and H. Gleckman. il *Bus Week* p44 My 11 '87

Real-world trade policies are making a comeback. R. Kuttner. il *Bus Week* p18 Mr 16 '87

United States—Commercial policy—*cont.*

Reversing America's decline in international trade. L. Kirkland. il *USA Today (Periodical)* 115:25-7 Mr '87

Say no to tariffs: why protectionism doesn't pay. R. Z. Lawrence and R. E. Litan. il *Current* 298:18-23 D '87

Science panel urges lead export role for Commerce [study by National Academy of Sciences] P. Mann. *Aviat Week Space Technol* 126:20 Ja 19 '87

Seeing through the rhetoric on 'fair' trade. G. S. Becker. il *Bus Week* p22 Jl 20 '87

Senators will load the trade bill with goodies. D. Harbrecht. *Bus Week* p58 My 25 '87

Shaping America's future competitiveness [address, September 30, 1986] J. F. Beré. *Vital Speeches Day* 53:208-10 Ja 15 '87

Shoot-out at tech gap [feud over export controls] S. Koepp. il *Time* 130:50-1 O 12 '87

State Dept. faulted for poor control of munitions exports [Office of Munitions Control] *Aviat Week Space Technol* 127:30 S 21 '87

Stop signs for the competition [trade bills and Canada] D. Jenish. il *Macleans* 100:36-8 S 21 '87

Taiwan and Korea should be praised, not punished. G. S. Becker. il *Bus Week* p22 My 25 '87

Talking tough [rising protectionism] *New Repub* 196:4 Ap 13 '87

Tariffs aren't great, but quotas are worse. J. Berger. il *Bus Week* p64 Mr 16 '87

The technobandits [U.S. export controls] N. R. Gibbs. il *Time* 130:42-4 N 30 '87

This trade bill just may fly. D. Harbrecht and others. il *Bus Week* p31 F 16 '87

Tougher talk on trade. B. Javetski. il *Bus Week* p28-9 Ja 19 '87

Trade. M. S. Forbes, Jr. il *Forbes* 140:25 D 14 '87

Trade bill addresses 'dumping' and Canada's bar to investment. H. Fields. *Publ Wkly* 232:19 Ag 14 '87

A trade bill gets a bum's rush. R. H. Bork, Jr. il *U S News World Rep* 103:25 Jl 6 '87

Trade: debate over protection. H. Eason. il *Nations Bus* 75:30+ Ja '87

Trade policy: the White House may miss the boat. H. Gleckman and B. Javetski. *Bus Week* p57 F 23 '87

Trade: the Democrats come out swinging—at one another. D. Harbrecht and B. Javetski. il *Bus Week* p41 Mr 30 '87

The trade wars. il *World Press Rev* 34:7 Je '87

Trading places on trade [Republicans and Democrats] *Fortune* 115:10 Ap 13 '87

The true cost of trade protection. H. Banks. *Forbes* 139 Ann Directory:49-50 Ap 27 '87

Turning the trade bill into a 'Christmas tree'. D. Harbrecht. il *Bus Week* p70 Jl 20 '87

Tussle over high technology [major study attacks U.S. export restrictions] J. Castro. il *Time* 129:48 Ja 26 '87

U.S. business and the world economy [address, May 11, 1987] G. P. Shultz. *Dep State Bull* 87:43-5 Ag '87

U.S. import rights: going once, going twice . . . [auctioning quotas] A. S. Blinder. il *Bus Week* p27 Mr 9 '87

U.S. international trade [White House statement, December 30, 1986] *Dep State Bull* 87:32-3 Ap '87

U.S.-Japan trade relations [address, April 13, 1987] W. A. Wallis. *Dep State Bull* 87:54-8 Je '87

U.S. must understand the link between R&D and the economy. R. S. Ames. por *Aviat Week Space Technol* 127:149-50 O 12 '87

U.S. trade policy and the trade deficit [statement, February 10, 1987; with appendix] C. K. Yeutter. il *Dep State Bull* 87:22-30 Ap '87

A war between friends [protectionist frenzy unleashed during Y. Nakasone's visit] M. McDonald. il por *Macleans* 100:32-3 My 11 '87

Washington outlook: protectionism fires burn cooler. D. Harbrecht and B. Javetski. il *Bus Week* p49 N 9 '87

Welcome to Moscow on the Ginza. R. N. Perle. il *U S News World Rep* 102:31-2 Je 29 '87

What am I bid for this fine quota? [proposal to auction off import rights] S. Koepp. il *Time* 129:59 Mr 16 '87

What can America sell? *New Repub* 196:5-7 My 25 '87

What's at stake in the Canada talks. B. Javetski and H. Gleckman. *Bus Week* p39 Mr 2 '87

What's wrong with Japan bashing. R. Darman. il *U S News World Rep* 103:53-4 O 5 '87

Why banks fear Congress' help [trade bill restrictions on Japanese banks and brokers in the U.S.] M. McNamee. il *Bus Week* p35 S 14 '87

The winds of trade war [with interviews with R. Strauss and K. Kato] R. H. Bork, Jr. il *U S News World Rep* 102:46-7 Ap 13 '87

Commercial treaties and agreements
Romania

Romania could lose its trade status because of rights abuses. *Christ Today* 31:37 Jl 10 '87

Constitutional law

See also
Committee on the Constitutional System (U.S.)
Judicial power
Separation of powers
United States. Congress—Powers and duties
United States. Supreme Court

A call for reform. J. M. Burns. il *Life* 10:126 Fall '87

The Constitution 1787-1987 [special section; with editorial comment by Byron Dobell] il *Am Herit* 38:7, 30-51+ My/Je '87

The Constitution and the Court: could Meese be right? S. Levinson. *Current* 292:32-5 My '87

The Constitution, the courts, and judicial competence. M. Cuomo. por *USA Today (Periodical)* 116:34-6 Jl '87

Government by lawyers & judges. W. Berns. *Commentary* 83:17-24 Je '87

The great voyage: two hundred years of the Constitution [cover story; special issue] il *N Y Times Mag* p14+ S 13 '87

Judicial review [discussion of June 1987 article, Government by lawyers & judges] W. Berns. *Commentary* 84:6+ N '87

New judicial activists. H. Schwartz. il *Nation* 244:361-2 Mr 21 '87

Ordered liberty [address, July 29, 1987] C. Mathias. *Vital Speeches Day* 53:706-10 S 15 '87

Our Constitution: after 200 years, the great experiment continues [cover story; special issue] il maps *Sch Update* 120:4-26 S 4 '87

Reasons and arguments in the Constitution [views expressed in The founders' Constitution] M. A. Noll. il *Christ Century* 104:499-500+ My 20-27 '87

A republic, if you can keep it [cover story; special section] il map *Newsweek* 109:44-52+ My 25 '87

Rolling back the Constitution [nomination of B. H. Siegan to U.S. Court of Appeals] H. Schwartz. il *Nation* 245:13-15 Jl 4-11 '87

Saving the Constitution [cover story; special section] il *Natl Rev* 39:30-7+ Jl 17 '87

The United States Constitution today [views of the American Assembly] *Cent Mag* 20:60-1+ S/O '87

Unraveling the Constitution. S. D. Pollack. bibl *Society* 24:56-9 Ja/F '87

Unraveling the Constitution: a rule of law. S. D. Pollack. *Current* 297:18-21 N '87

What am I? A potted plant? [strict constructionism] R. A. Posner. *New Repub* 197:23-5 S 28 '87

What hope for the courts? [23rd national meeting of the Philadelphia Society] L. Bridges. *Natl Rev* 39:36-7+ Ag 28 '87

Your Constitution. See issues of Scholastic Update (Teachers' edition) beginning September 22, 1986

Courts

See Courts

Cultural relations

See also
Artistic Ambassador Program (U.S.)
United States. Information Agency

U.S. culture, worldwide fans. S. Flack. il *Sch Update* 120:37 O 2 '87

Canada

Fighting words on trade [C. Yeutter's views on protecting Canadian cultural industries] M. Gee. *Macleans* 100:16 F 16 '87

Hollywood goes to war [Canada's plan to give Canadians larger share of movie distribution business] I. Austen. il *Macleans* 100:53-4 Je 22 '87

A question of identity [Maclean's/Decima poll] il *Macleans* 100:42 Ja 5 '87

Skepticism in the arts [reaction to U.S.-Canada free trade accord] V. Ross. il *Macleans* 100:21 O 19 '87

The survival of Canadian culture. B. Amiel. il *Macleans* 100:9 Ap 20 '87

China

China's odd couple [exhibit cancelled after Chinese refuse to include portraits of Douglas MacArthur and Golda Meir] il *U S News World Rep* 103:10 Jl 27 '87

United States—Cultural relations—China—*cont.*
Fantastick voyage [bringing The fantasticks to China] B. R. Marriott. il *Horizon* 30:64-5 O '87
Politically incorrect [Beijing exhibit of American portraits canceled after Chinese insisted that paintings of Golda Meir and General Douglas MacArthur be removed] D. Lanchner. il *Art News* 86:71 O '87

France
Warrant for Lee's arrest dropped [dispute between French government and former Cleveland Museum of Art director S. E. Lee over the export of a N. Poussin painting] R. W. Walker. *Art News* 86:30 Summ '87

Latin America
The unity and diversity of the Americas. F. Hodsoll. *Américas* 39:52-3 Ja/F '87

Mongolia
Out of Mongolia [visiting troupe of traditional Mongolian singers and dancers] *New Yorker* 63:28-30 O 26 '87

South Africa
'Graceland' in Africa [controversy surrounding P. Simon's album] N. Cooper. il por *Newsweek* 109:45 F 23 '87
Paul Simon goes on tour with black South Africans. *Jet* 71:17 Mr 2 '87
Paul Simon's amazing Graceland tour [cover story] D. Fricke. il pors *Roll Stone* p42-4+ Jl 2 '87
Singer Paul Simon strikes sour chord with students at Howard U. over album [Graceland] *Jet* 71:59 F 2 '87
Tapping pop music's African roots [P. Simon's Graceland album and tour] N. Jennings. il por *Macleans* 100:52-3 My 4 '87
UN forgives Paul Simon for 'Graceland' album. *Jet* 71:30 F 23 '87
UN group attacks Paul Simon: says 'Graceland' broke cultural boycott of South Africa. R. Tannenbaum. *Roll Stone* p11+ F 12 '87

Soviet Union
See also
Student exchange programs
Barnyard diplomacy [Surry Opera Company from Maine tours U.S.S.R.] M. Baldwin. il *Opera News* 52:38-9 Jl '87
Comrade artist [D. Skulme, head of Latvian Artists League] A. Stille. il por *Art News* 86:10+ Ja '87
Cultural exchange within the global village. M. Rhodes. por *Horizon* 30:9 D '87
From a Maine barn to a Soviet stage, Walter Nowick's opera company raises the Iron Curtain to promote harmony. L. Aitken. il por *People Wkly* 27:93-4 Ja 12 '87
Glasnost rock: American and Russian musicians rock & roll for disarmament at Moscow festival. M. R. Benson. il *Roll Stone* p15-16+ Ag 27 '87
Madame ambassador [literary agent M. McBride to address Soviet-American Dialogue in Moscow] L. Fleischer. *Publ Wkly* 232:153 S 18 '87
Trailblazers of the US/USSR dance exchange. H. Breazeale. il *Dance Mag* 61:70-2 Ap '87
"We're Stateniks!" The cult of America in the U.S.S.R. [condensed from In search of melancholy baby] V. P. Aksenov. il *Read Dig* 131:171-2+ Ag '87

Culture
See United States—Civilization

Culture, Popular
See United States—Popular culture

Defense policy
See United States—Military policy

Defenses
See also
Air defenses
Airplanes, Military
Artificial satellites—Military use
Chemical and biological weapons
Civil defense
Classified information
Guided missiles
North American Aerospace Defense Command
Nuclear submarines
Nuclear weapons
Strategic Arms Limitation Talks
Strategic Arms Reduction Talks
Strategic Defense Initiative
United States—Armed Forces
United States. Air Force
United States. Air National Guard
United States. Army
United States. Coast Guard
United States. Dept. of Defense
United States. Marine Corps
United States. Navy
Weapons

General Nutting and the invaders. W. M. Arkin. *Bull At Sci* 43:6-7 Ja/F '87
Offense-defense strategic balance in the 1990s [address, May 6, 1987] M. Wallop. *Vital Speeches Day* 53:610-13 Ag 1 '87
The perilous politics of defense [Democratic candidates' positions] H. Rainie. il *U S News World Rep* 103:29 O 5 '87
Protecting America's interests: defense and foreign aid [special issue] il maps *Sch Update* 119:6-16+ F 23 '87
Soviet strategic force upgrade paces U.S. modernization effort. J. D. Morrocco. il *Aviat Week Space Technol* 126:31-3+ Mr 9 '87
To provide for the common defense. Publius. *New Leader* 70:12-14 N 16 '87
Whose business is defense? [address, January 16, 1987] J. R. Munro. *Vital Speeches Day* 53:360-2 Ap 1 '87

Description and travel
See also
Automobile touring
Railroad travel
City lights U S A. il *Glamour* 85:262-4+ Ap '87
Cream of the country. S. Pacher. See issues of The Mother Earth News beginning September/October 1986
Destination U.S.A.: America's surprising cities. il *Better Homes Gard* 65:186+ My '87
Family adventure vacations. il *Better Homes Gard* 65:183-4+ Ap '87
Five great American walking weekends. map *Prevention* 39:60-1+ S '87
From sea to shining sea [Plymouth Pride in America Road Rally in which participants depend on the generosity of strangers] M. Neill. il map *People Wkly* 28:28-33 S 21 '87
Magical American islands. S. Birnbaum. il *Good Housekeep* 204:64+ Ap '87
Rediscover America [cover story; special issue; with editorial comment by Timothy C. Forbes] il *Am Herit* 38:6-7, 29-31+ Ap '87
Road shows. E. Henry and J. Yonan. il *Changing Times* 41:88-90+ S '87
Roadside rock [tourist attractions for rock music lovers] J. Barth and M. Wilkins. il *Roll Stone* p104-5+ Jl 16-30 '87
Take your dream vacation now! il *Ebony* 42:128+ My '87
Ten best wonders of the U.S.A. P. Bedard. il *Car Driv* 32:65-9 Ja '87
Weekends European-style. N. Berkowitz. il *Harpers Bazaar* 120:42+ Je '87
What's happening—and where. il *U S News World Rep* 102:60-2 My 25 '87

Diplomatic and consular service
How much security is enough? [address, January 22, 1987] R. E. Lamb. *Dep State Bull* 87:27-9 My '87
Instructions to ambassadors on chain of command. G. P. Shultz; R. Reagan. *Dep State Bull* 87:40-1 Mr '87
Our new Moscow embassy—bungled and bugged [failure of Foreign Buildings Office to get properly built embassies] J. Barron. *Read Dig* 130:100-4 Je '87

Austria
A Vienna success [R. S. and J. C. Lauder decorate ambassador's residence] T. Lessing. il por *House Gard* 159:100-5+ Jl '87

Czechoslovakia
Open house in Prague [Petschek Palace functions as U.S. embassy] W. W. Luers. il pors *House Gard* 159:150-5+ My '87

Iran
See also
Iranian seizure of United States embassy, 1979-1981

Japan
Aurelia Brazeal gets major U.S. embassy post in Japan. *Jet* 71:4 F 16 '87

Lebanon
Beirut: an embassy in hiding. R. Nordland. il *Newsweek* 109:36 F 9 '87

Mauritius
The untold story of black ambassador who weds Asian princess [R. D. Palmer weds Princess Intan in Mauritius] S. Booker. il pors *Jet* 73:12+ O 12 '87

Mongolia
U.S. and Mongolia establish diplomatic relations [texts of communique and remarks, January 27, 1987] G. P. Shultz. il por *Dep State Bull* 87:41 Mr '87

Morocco
A correspondence with the Secretary of State. *Forbes* 139:18 Ap 6 '87
Legation in Tangier. il *Dep State Bull* 87:13 S '87

United States—Diplomatic and consular service—*cont.*

Panama

Demonstration against U.S. embassy in Panama [State Dept. statement, July 1, 1987] *Dep State Bull* 87:82 S '87

South Africa

New man in the townships [black U.S. ambassador E. Perkins] B. W. Nelan. il por *Time* 129:58 F 23 '87

Perkins makes 1st public protest against S. Africa [U.S. ambassador E. J. Perkins] por *Jet* 72:24 My 11 '87

Quiet sting [views of U.S. Ambassador E. J. Perkins] W. R. Doerner. il por *Time* 130:50 D 21 '87

S. Africa banquet fails to invite speaker—Perkins. *Jet* 72:18 Ap 20 '87

Soviet Union

The battle of the bugs [Soviet and American embassies; special section] il map *Newsweek* 109:18-22 Ap 20 '87

Black Marine's parents cry their son is a 'scapegoat' in sex for secrets case [A. Bracy's family] il por *Jet* 72:5 Ap 20 '87

Booze, brawls and skirt chasing [U.S. Marine guard spy scandal at Moscow embassy] E. Magnuson. il *Time* 129:20+ Ap 13 '87

Bugproofing the embassy [plan to salvage part of U.S. embassy in Moscow] il por *Time* 130:14 Jl 13 '87

The case of espionage in the embassy. B. Duffy. il *U S News World Rep* 102:18-20 Ap 13 '87

Challenges facing the Foreign Service [address, May 1, 1987] R. I. Spiers. *Dep State Bull* 87:30-4 Jl '87

Charges of espionage and seduction [Marine guards in the Soviet Union] il *Macleans* 100:20 Ap 20 '87

Countering today's security challenges [statement, April 23, 1987] R. I. Spiers. *Dep State Bull* 87:52-4 Je '87

Crawling with bugs [Moscow embassy spy scandal; cover story; special section] il *Time* 129:14-18+ Ap 20 '87

Deep in the Bear's den [R. Helms leads investigation into security breaches at U.S. embassy in Moscow] H. Sidey. il por *Time* 129:14 Je 29 '87

An expert says tear down our bugged embassy in Moscow [interview with J. Bamford] M. Ryan. il por *People Wkly* 27:91+ Ap 27 '87

Fallout from the scandal [Marine guard spy case] il *Time* 129:22-3 Ap 27 '87

The fiasco in Moscow [security breach at U.S. embassy] L. Martz. il *Newsweek* 109:20-2 Ap 13 '87

From Russia with love and espionage [charges against C. Lonetree and A. Bracy, Marine guards at U.S. embassy in Moscow] il pors *Macleans* 100:18-19 Ap 13 '87

Holes in a spy scandal [Moscow embassy case] S. W. Cloud. il por *Time* 130:31 Jl 20 '87

The honey-trap spy case widens [charges against C. Lonetree and A. Bracy, Marine guards at the U.S. Embassy in Moscow] il pors *U S News World Rep* 102:12 Ap 6 '87

How to protect U.S. embassies. W. L. Chaze. il *U S News World Rep* 102:18-20 Ap 20 '87

Innocent man [charges against A. Bracy dropped] por *Time* 129:23 Je 22 '87

Is the Marine spy case unraveling? G. Witkin. il *U S News World Rep* 102:14 My 4 '87

A Marine and his "swallow" [security guard at U.S. Embassy in Moscow accused of spying] B. Duffy. il por *U S News World Rep* 102:25 Ja 26 '87

The Marine case falls apart [charges dropped against A. Bracy] M. Kaus. il por *Newsweek* 109:23 Je 22 '87

The Marine spy scandal: "It's a biggie" [Moscow embassy guards C. Lonetree and A. Bracy] A. Wilentz. il pors *Time* 129:21-2 Ap 6 '87

The Marine traitors. *Natl Rev* 39:18 Ap 24 '87

Military justice comes to attention [Marine guard spy case] R. Lacayo. il por *Time* 129:62 My 18 '87

The mission in Moscow. G. F. Kennan. por *Newsweek* 110:7 Jl 13 '87

Moonlighting in Moscow? [Marine guards C. Lonetree and A. Bracy charged with espionage] R. Watson. il pors *Newsweek* 109:32-3 Ap 6 '87

News conference of April 8, 1987. G. P. Shultz. *Dep State Bull* 87:24-7 Je '87

No entry [C. Lonetree denies allowing Soviets into Moscow embassy] il por *Time* 130:22 N 23 '87

Notes and comment [security breaches in the U.S. embassy in Moscow] *New Yorker* 63:25-6 My 4 '87

President meets with Foreign Intelligence Advisory Board [White House statement, July 14, 1987] *Dep State Bull* 87:31 S '87

Security at the U.S. embassy in Moscow [remarks and question-and-answer session, April 7, 1987] R. Reagan. *Dep State Bull* 87:60-1 Je '87

Semper fie [Marine security guard C. Lonetree arrested for spying] por *Time* 129:19 Ja 26 '87

Spy charges against black Marine dropped [case of A. Bracy] por *Jet* 72:9 Je 29 '87

Spy woes [testimony retracted in Marine guard spy case] *Time* 129:22 My 11 '87

Trying to undo the damage [State Dept. admits role in embassy security lapses] M. Santini. il *U S News World Rep* 102:23 My 25 '87

U.S.-Soviet agreement on embassy construction in Washington [statement, May 19, 1987] R. I. Spiers. *Dep State Bull* 87:34-5 Jl '87

Washington diarist [vilification of A. Hartman over neglect of security of American embassy in Moscow] L. Wieseltier. *New Repub* 196:42 My 11 '87

Where Moscow embassy went awry. C. M. Perkins. por *U S News World Rep* 102:8 My 18 '87

Why Moscow is winning [with interview with A. Hartman] W. L. Chaze. il *U S News World Rep* 102:36-8 Ap 27 '87

Soviet Union—Anecdotes, facetiae, satire, etc.

Uncivil liberties [bugging of U.S. embassy in Moscow] C. Trillin. *Nation* 244:674 My 23 '87

Switzerland

Keeping Faith [role of F. R. Whittlesey and other U.S. diplomats in promoting the contra cause] M. Schapiro and E. Burnand. *Nation* 244:42 Ja 17 '87

The petty inquisitors. M. Charen. il *Natl Rev* 39:36+ D 18 '87

Discovery and exploration
See United States—Exploring expeditions

Economic conditions

See also

Business conditions
Business depression
Business forecasting
Consumption (Economics)
Cost and standard of living
Debts, Public
Economic forecasting
Economic indicators
Economic statistics
Free enterprise
Income
Inflation (Finance)
Labor
Poor
Prices
Rich
Underground economy
Unemployment
United States—Industries

American enterprise: then, now and tomorrow: 75th anniversary issue [cover story; special issue] il *Nations Bus* 75:10-12+ S '87

Can the shifting economy keep on an even keel? K. Pennar. il *Bus Week* p27-8 Jl 27 '87

The economic consequences of immigration. G. J. Borjas and M. Tienda. bibl f il *Science* 235:645-51 F 6 '87

Economic diary. See issues of Business Week

Major problem with the American economy: hypochondria. M. S. Forbes, Jr. il *Forbes* 139:33 Mr 9 '87

Topsy-turvy times [1986] S. Koepp. il *Time* 129:60-2 Ja 5 '87

U.S. affairs annual: jobs and the economy [special issue] il *Sch Update* 119:2-12+ Ja 26 '87

Economic history

See also

Business depression, 1837
Business depression, 1893
Business depression, 1929-1939
Slavery

American enterprise: then, now and tomorrow: 75th anniversary issue [cover story; special issue] il *Nations Bus* 75:10-12+ S '87

America's love-hate view of competition. J. Rose. il *Sch Update* 119:18-20 Ja 26 '87

The expanding economic vista [commerce clause of the Constitution] R. B. Reich. il *N Y Times Mag* p52-4+ S 13 '87

Flashbacks. D. A. Saunders. See issues of Forbes

Getting rich in America: men, money & the survival of capitalism [cover story; special issue; with editorial comment by Byron Dobell] il *Am Herit* 38:5, 34-51+ N '87

Here we go again [corporate mergers and restructurings in the last 100 years; special section] il *Forbes* 140:242-6+ Jl 13 '87

United States—Economic history—*cont.*

How 200 words created our framework for free enterprise. T. Osborne. il *Sch Update* 120:19-20 S 4 '87

No one is safe [Forbes top 100 companies over the last 70 years] P. Newcomb. il *Forbes* 140:121-3+ Jl 13 '87

The price of money (II). W. Greider. *New Yorker* 63:68-72+ N 16 '87

The way we were at 1000 [1972] il *Time* 129:50 Ja 19 '87

Economic policy

See also
    Council of Economic Advisers (U.S.)
    Economic assistance, Domestic
    Energy policy
    Federal Reserve System (U.S.)
    Full employment
    Industry and state
    Inflation (Finance)
    Taxation
    United States—Appropriations and expenditures
    Wage-price policy

1987 need not become 1929 [cover story; special section] il *Fortune* 116:46-8+ N 23 '87

After the fall. il *Progressive* 51:7-8 D '87

After the fall. *Commonweal* 114:611-12 N 6 '87

After the fall [stock market crash; cover story; special section] il *Time* 130:20-6+ N 2 '87

After the meltdown of '87 [stock market crash; cover story; special section] il *Newsweek* 110:14-25+ N 2 '87

As Washington fiddles . . . G. Borger. il *U S News World Rep* 103:20-2 N 23 '87

Beware the deadly endive. L. H. Lapham. *Harpers* 274:8-10 Ap '87

Beyond our means [views of A. Malabre] A. Bladen. il *Forbes* 140:178 Jl 27 '87

Binge: end of a profligate era [cover story] I. F. Stone. *Nation* 245:469+ O 31 '87

Black Monday and beyond: a talk with Bill Bradley. L. Weymouth. il pors *N Y* 20:56-9 D 14 '87

The boom: coming or going? D. Gergen. il *U S News World Rep* 102:80 F 16 '87

Bursting the supply-side bubble. G. P. Brockway. il *New Leader* 70:15-16 N 30 '87

Can anyone compete? [Business week's cover story] *Natl Rev* 39:18-19 My 8 '87

Crash diet [stock market crash] W. Greider. il *Roll Stone* p138-40+ D 17-31 '87

The dangerous storm clouds over Reaganomics. R. J. Shapiro. il *U S News World Rep* 102:38-40 Je 29 '87

A deficit on the trail [positions of presidential candidates] W. Shapiro. il *Time* 130:30-1 N 9 '87

The dismal science. G. P. Brockway. See issues of The New Leader

The dreamer awakes [Reaganomics and the stock market crash] *New Repub* 197:4 N 9 '87

An economic bill of rights. il *Nations Bus* 75:54 Ag '87

The end of the rich man's boom. L. Cawley. il *Nation* 245:675-6+ D 5 '87

Floundering in Washington [stock market crash] P. Magnusson and M. McNamee. il *Bus Week* p32-4 N 9 '87

Glass houses [criticism in The economist] *Natl Rev* 39:20-1 O 9 '87

A handicapper's guide to Reaganomics. A. S. Blinder. il *Bus Week* p18 F 9 '87

Heading off hard times [stock market crash; cover story; special section] il *Newsweek* 110:24-8+ N 9 '87

The hidden issues facing America [address, January 6, 1987] W. E. Hoadley. *Vital Speeches Day* 53:270-3 F 15 '87

Hoovernomics is no cure for Reaganomics. R. Kuttner. por *Bus Week* p22 N 23 '87

How to talk about economic strategy [Catholic bishops' pastoral letter and Democratic Leadership Council's conference in Williamsburg] A. Cockburn and R. Pollin. il *Nation* 244:245-7 F 28 '87

Hurry up please, it's time. But time for what? [market collapse] A. Cockburn. *Nation* 245:474-5 O 31 '87

In search of leadership. I. Austen. il *Macleans* 100:22-3 N 16 '87

The indisputable victory of supply-side economics. P. C. Roberts. il *Bus Week* p34 D 28 '87-Ja 4 '88

Is Wall Street right? [difference of opinion with government officials over state of the economy] J. Egan. il *U S News World Rep* 103:20-1 O 26 '87

It's time for America to wake up [cover story; special section] il *Bus Week* p158-61+ N 16 '87

Jalopy road [scaling down the economy] *Progressive* 51:11-12 Ja '87

The knife must fall. S. Koepp. il *Time* 130:48-50 N 23 '87

Living beyond our means [condensed from Beyond our means] A. L. Malabre. *Read Dig* 131:123-6 N '87

Looking back at Black Monday [cover story; special section] il *Natl Rev* 39:43-50+ N 20 '87

Losing control of our economy. M. Moffitt. *Harpers* 275:22+ D '87

The losing hand [Washington's response to the stock market crash] M. B. Zuckerman. il *U S News World Rep* 103:78 D 14 '87

The man and the myth [J. A. Baker] M. B. Zuckerman. il *U S News World Rep* 102:68 Je 15 '87

Managing the global economy [address, September 29, 1987] R. Reagan. *Dep State Bull* 87:5-8 N '87

Memo to the chief [post crash options] M. Hammond. il *Sch Update* 120:12-13 D 18 '87

The morning after [cover story] P. G. Peterson. il *Atlantic* 260:43-50+ O '87

No pain, no gain: how America can grow again. N. Jonas. il *Bus Week* p68-9 Ap 20 '87

Now what? [cover story; special section] il *World Press Rev* 34:9-18 D '87

Observations. A. Bladen. See occasional issues of Forbes

Of many things [views of A. L. Malabre in Beyond our means] G. W. Hunt. *America* 156:inside cover Ap 18 '87

On the brink. F. G. Rohatyn. il *N Y Rev Books* 34:3-4+ Je 11 '87

Playing politics on Wall Street. J. Crudele. il *N Y* 20:16+ Ag 10 '87

A quiz for the candidates. A. Bladen. il *Forbes* 140:260 D 14 '87

A ray of light in arms control [R. Reagan attempts to boost weakened status] H. Trewhitt. il por *U S News World Rep* 103:28-9 Ag 10 '87

Reaganomics: bad press or no, it works. P. C. Roberts. il *Bus Week* p24 Ja 26 '87

Reaganomics, R.I.P. U. E. Reinhardt. *New Repub* 196:24+ Ap 20 '87

Reaganomics with a human face [neoliberalism; excerpt from Visions and nightmares] R. Lekachman. *Harpers* 274:24+ Mr '87

Reagan's 'correction' [post crash assessment] *New Repub* 197:7-9 N 16 '87

Robert Reich takes on Rambo [Tales of a new America] T. J. Peters. *Wash Mon* 19:51-6 Mr '87

Ronald Wilson Hoover? [effect of stock market crash] J. Klein. il por *N Y* 20:40-3 N 2 '87

A search for leadership [post stock market crash] B. Levin. il *Macleans* 100:46-8 N 9 '87

Sound as a dollar [Reaganism] *Nation* 244:99-100 Ja 31 '87

Stagnation and the nation. il *Progressive* 51:7-8 Je '87

Staring into the abyss [stock market crash; cover story; special section; with editorial comment by Mortimer B. Zuckerman] il *U S News World Rep* 103:18-26+, 88 N 2 '87

A Texas tornado hits the Senate [P. Gramm] E. H. Methvin. il por *Read Dig* 130:17-18+ Ap '87

There's no panacea for six years of bad policy. R. Kuttner. il *Bus Week* p28 My 11 '87

Tight money and loose fiscal policy. A. S. Blinder. bibl *Society* 24:80-3 Jl/Ag '87

Toward a socialist strategy [discussion of February 28, 1987 article, How to talk about economic strategy] A. Cockburn and R. Pollin. *Nation* 244:748+ Je 6 '87

The unilateral disarmament of the American spirit [address, October 10, 1986] P. C. Roberts. *Vital Speeches Day* 53:212-15 Ja 15 '87

The view from the White House. R. Reagan. pors *Forbes* 140:35-6 S 21 '87

Washington on hold. D. Gergen. il *U S News World Rep* 102:84 Je 8 '87

What if the winner keeps his promises? [1988 presidential candidates] P. Magnusson and R. Fly. il *Bus Week* p102 D 28 '87-Ja 4 '88

What next? F. G. Rohatyn. il *N Y Rev Books* 34:3-5 D 3 '87

What to do? [stock market crash] *Natl Rev* 39:19 N 20 '87

'What went wrong with what?' [stock market crash] J. Klein. il *N Y* 20:24+ N 9 '87

When Lester Thurow talks, Democrats listen. A. Kupfer. il pors *Fortune* 116:88-90+ Jl 20 '87

Where the candidates stand. L. Smith. il *Fortune* 116:129-30+ D 7 '87

United States—Economic policy—*cont.*

Who's in charge? [stock market crash; cover story; special section] il por *Time* 130:18-24+ N 9 '87

Why politicians don't matter on Wall Street. A. J. Glass. il *New Leader* 70:3-4 N 2 '87

Why the worst may still be ahead [stock market crash; special section] il *U S News World Rep* 103:24-30+ N 9 '87

Will the Democrats be able to seize the moment? L. Walczak and others. il *Bus Week* p67 N 2 '87

A year of benign neglect from Washington. M. McNamee. il *Bus Week* p98-9 D 28 '87-Ja 4 '88

Anecdotes, facetiae, satire, etc.

Dear Doctor Lekachman . . . R. Lekachman. il *Nation* 244:390-2 Mr 28 '87

History

See United States—Economic history

Economic relations

See also

Economic assistance, American

United States—Commerce

All eyes on the U.S. Y. Messarovitch. *World Press Rev* 34:25-6 N '87

The budget compromise isn't traveling well. M. McNamee. il *Bus Week* p58 D 7 '87

Dutch uncles [foreign reaction to budget deficit agreement] J. Crudele. il *N Y* 20:26+ D 7 '87

Financial markets [address, June 9, 1987] A. M. Solomon. *Vital Speeches Day* 53:725-9 S 15 '87

For bilateralism. A. J. Stoga. *Cent Mag* 20:57 Ja/F '87

A global new deal. G. Soros. il *N Y Rev Books* 34:52-3 Ag 13 '87

The growing foreign role in U.S. policy. K. N. Johnson. il por *Fortune* 116:36-8 Jl 6 '87

Is America going to the dogs? J. McLaughlin. *Natl Rev* 39:22 Jl 31 '87

Of many things [views of P. M. Kennedy on the decline of America] G. W. Hunt. *America* 157:98 Ag 29-S 5 '87

The (relative) decline of America [cover story] P. M. Kennedy. il *Atlantic* 260:29-34+ Ag '87

The U.S. as world leader: the (relative) decline of America. P. M. Kennedy. il *Current* 298:30-8 D '87

The United States and the world economy. L. S. Silk. *Foreign Aff* 65 Sp Issue:458-76 ['87]

A world called to account [stock market crash] P. Best. il *Macleans* 100:34-5 N 2 '87

Canada

World money wars. D. Jenish. il *Macleans* 100:60-1 F 2 '87

Developing countries

It's up to Germany and Japan to ease the trade trauma . . . but emerging economies could be the wild card. G. Koretz. il *Bus Week* p24+ My 4 '87

Germany (West)

Between competitiveness and co-operation [address, March 26, 1987] O. von Lambsdorff. *Vital Speeches Day* 53:455-60 My 15 '87

Can Germany withstand the heat from abroad this time? J. Templeman. il *Bus Week* p50-1 O 5 '87

Dollar wars: waiting for the Germans. D. Pauly. il *Newsweek* 109:53 F 9 '87

German roulette? P. Fuhrman and R. Morais. il *Forbes* 139:34-5 Je 1 '87

How to read Wall Street's scrambled messages. A. S. Blinder. por *Bus Week* p28 N 16 '87

Is a cutting loose by Germany a real possibility? M. S. Forbes. *Forbes* 140:17-18 N 30 '87

Kohl's second term: Washington may feel a chilly breeze. F. A. Miller and J. E. Pluenneke. il por *Bus Week* p48 F 9 '87

The risks of a free-fall [plunging dollar] B. Riemer and W. Glasgall. il *Bus Week* p28-9 F 2 '87

The United States can't solve the crisis by itself. R. J. Samuelson. il *Newsweek* 110:38+ N 9 '87

Where will the buck stop? B. Powell. il *Newsweek* 109:37 Ja 26 '87

Japan

The ballad of Ron and Yasu [effects of high yen; cover story] M. Sayle. *New Repub* 196:18-21 Je 15 '87

Double-talk on the dollar [plunging dollar] R. Thomas. il *Newsweek* 109:45 F 2 '87

Economic imbalances and world politics. C. F. Bergsten. bibl f *Foreign Aff* 65:770-94 Spr '87

How to read Wall Street's scrambled messages. A. S. Blinder. por *Bus Week* p28 N 16 '87

In Japan we (must) trust. E. A. Finn, Jr. il *Forbes* 140:32-4 S 21 '87

Japan's drive to pre-eminence. R. A. Morse. *Foreign Policy* 69:3-21 Wint '87/'88

Japan's expanding role [address, September 25, 1987] Y. Kashiwagi. *Vital Speeches Day* 54:79-83 N 15 '87

The nichibei economy could lead to future shock. N. Jonas. il *Bus Week* p108 O 5 '87

The political rivals jockeying for Japan's top job. B. Buell. il *Bus Week* p36-7 Ap 20 '87

The risks of a free-fall [plunging dollar] B. Riemer and W. Glasgall. il *Bus Week* p28-9 F 2 '87

'Shogun' bonds start to storm Japan. B. Buell and W. Glasgall. il *Bus Week* p73 F 9 '87

Strong, silent Japan starts to speak up. B. Buell. il *Bus Week* p50-1 N 30 '87

Structural adjustment, dialogue, and U.S.-Japan economic relations [address, February 16, 1987] W. A. Wallis. *Dep State Bull* 87:36-40 My '87

The trade deficit. P. H. Abelson. *Science* 236:653 My 8 '87

The U.S., Japan, and Asian Pacific security in perspective [address, May 29, 1987] M. H. Armacost. *Dep State Bull* 87:51-6 Ag '87

U.S.-Japan subcabinet meets [statement, October 31, 1986] W. A. Wallis. *Dep State Bull* 87:42-3 Ja '87

The United States can't solve the crisis by itself. R. J. Samuelson. il *Newsweek* 110:38+ N 9 '87

Vitality and possibility on the Pacific Rim [address, December 3, 1986] G. J. Sigur. *Dep State Bull* 87:52-4 F '87

Where will the buck stop? B. Powell. il *Newsweek* 109:37 Ja 26 '87

Latin America

U.S. business and the world economy [address, May 11, 1987] G. P. Shultz. *Dep State Bull* 87:43-5 Ag '87

Pacific region

Meeting the challenges of change in the Pacific [address, May 14, 1987] G. P. Shultz. *Dep State Bull* 87:4-7 Jl '87

The Pacific Basin's challenge to America: myth and reality. C. Johnson. il *USA Today (Periodical)* 115:20-4 Mr '87

Saudi Arabia

See also

United States-Saudi Arabia Joint Economic Commission

Educational policy

See College education and state; Education and state

Energy policy

See Energy policy

Environmental policy

See Environmental policy

Executive departments

Federal agencies involved [product liability legislation] *Congr Dig* 66:5+ Ja '87

Who's who in the administration. See issues of The Washington Monthly

Expenditures

See United States—Appropriations and expenditures

Exploring expeditions

See also

Lewis and Clark Expedition

Ancient mansions of Chaco Canyon [work of the Hyde Exploring Expedition in excavating Anasazi artifacts] il *Nat Hist* 96:74-7 Mr '87

Foreign economic policy

See United States—Economic relations

Foreign opinion

The follies of 1987 [special section] il *World Press Rev* 34:32-4 Jl '87

The world affairs annual 1987-88 [cover story; special issue] il *Sch Update* 120:4-10+ O 2 '87

British

The British view [U.S. Constitution] O. Wright. il *Am Herit* 38:90-3 My/Je '87

A British view of the contras. I. Hilton. il *World Press Rev* 34:17 S '87

Glass houses [criticism of U.S. economic policy in The economist] *Natl Rev* 39:20-1 O 9 '87

"The most-hated man in America" [1842 visit of C. Dickens] E. L. Abel. bibl il pors *Am Hist Illus* 22:10-15+ D '87

'U.S. motivation is benign, but often misguided' [interview with D. Trelford] J. R. Moskin. por *World Press Rev* 34:27-8 N '87

European

Advantage Gorbachev [Soviet Union gains in Europe due to Iran arms scandal] S. Sullivan. il por *Newsweek* 109:38 Mr 9 '87

Editorial. W. Garrett. il *Antiques* 131:411 F '87

United States—Foreign opinion—European—*cont.*

Erosion of U.S. power [effect of Iran arms scandal in Europe] J. Amalric. il *World Press Rev* 34:12-13 F '87

How Europeans viewed the United States and its people. R. Fanuzzi. il *Sch Update* 120:8-10 O 2 '87

Iranscam couldn't happen there [European reaction] J. Bonfante. il *Time* 129:36 Ja 26 '87

Love and hate across the Atlantic. N. Gelb. il *New Leader* 70:3-4 N 30 '87

Why Europeans support the Sandinistas. M. Falcoff. *Commentary* 84:61-5 Ag '87

Indian (East Indian)

An Indian view of the contras. B. S. Gupta. il *World Press Rev* 34:15-16 S '87

Italian

Indiana killer, Italian martyr [Italians show support for juvenile killer P. Cooper] G. Hackett. il por *Newsweek* 110:37 S 21 '87

Japanese

America-bashing: a new Japanese sport. J. B. Copeland. il *Newsweek* 109:42 Ap 13 '87

The end of innocence. J. W. Dower. il *Nation* 245:224-6+ S 12 '87

Russian

Communist view. See issues of World Press Review

Gotta have Hart [Moscow's reaction to G. Hart's sudden fall from electoral grace] J. E. Oberg. *Natl Rev* 39:40 Jl 17 '87

A Soviet-American poll. il *Newsweek* 110:27 D 14 '87

A Soviet emigre takes the 'A' Train [roots of Soviet feelings about America] V. P. Aksenov. il *N Y Times Mag* p60+ My 3 '87

"We're Stateniks!" The cult of America in the U.S.S.R. [condensed from In search of melancholy baby] V. P. Aksenov. il *Read Dig* 131:171-2+ Ag '87

What the Soviets think about American liberals. D. D'Souza. *Natl Rev* 39:39-41+ Ja 30 '87

Foreign policy

See United States—Foreign relations

Foreign relations

See also

Council on Foreign Relations
Economic assistance, American
Espionage, American
Military assistance, American
National Endowment for Democracy
Secretaries of State (U.S.)
Sister Cities International
United Nations—United States
United States—Economic relations
United States—Treaties
United States. Congress. Senate. Committee on Foreign Relations
United States. Dept. of State
United States. Information Agency
United States. National Security Council

Al Gore hits a Democratic sore spot [depicting rivals as indecisive] T. Jacoby. il por *Newsweek* 110:33 O 26 '87

America and the world 1986. bibl f *Foreign Aff* 65 Sp Issue:423-696 ['87]

America's state of mind. J. E. Rielly. il *Foreign Policy* 66:39-56 Spr '87

America's vision of the future [address, September 21, 1987] R. Reagan. *Dep State Bull* 87:1-4 N '87

Budgetary resources and foreign policy [statement, March 19, 1987] E. J. Derwinski. *Dep State Bull* 87:84-7 Je '87

The chains of liberty [address, September 17, 1987] E. S. Muskie. *Vital Speeches Day* 54:4-7 O 15 '87

The CIA and American foreign policy. R. M. Gates. bibl f *Foreign Aff* 66:215-30 Wint '87/'88

"Citty upon a hill". T. R. Davis and S. M. Lynn-Jones. bibl f *Foreign Policy* 66:20-38 Spr '87

Correspondence from the Secretary of State. G. P. Shultz. *Foreign Aff* 66:426-8 Wint '87/'88

Democracy and Colonel North. L. Wieseltier. *New Repub* 196:22-5 Ja 26 '87

A Democrat looks at foreign policy. A. M. Schlesinger. *Foreign Aff* 66:263-83 Wint '87/'88

The Democrats' zero options. P. Osterlund. *Natl Rev* 39:36+ Je 19 '87

Diplomacy for democracy [Reagan administration policy] W. Lowther. il *Macleans* 100:18 Jl 27 '87

Disease of distrust [presidential and congressional duties in foreign policy] D. Gergen. il *U S News World Rep* 103:64 Jl 27 '87

Don't underrate isolationism. B. Kauffman. il *Nation* 244:758-60 Je 6 '87

A dubious world defies Reagan. H. Trewhitt. il por *U S News World Rep* 102:18-19 F 16 '87

The fiscal threat to U.S. foreign policy [address, October 15, 1986] R. I. Spiers. *Dep State Bull* 86:47-50 D '86

Foreign affairs and the Constitution. L. Henkin. bibl f *Foreign Aff* 66:284-310 Wint '87/'88

The foreign affairs budget crisis: a threat to our vital interests [statement, January 23, 1987] G. P. Shultz. il *Dep State Bull* 87:7-14 Mr '87

Foreign policy crossroads [special section] il *World Press Rev* 34:11-16+ Ja '87

The four pillars. R. J. Barnet. *New Yorker* 63:76-84+ Mr 9 '87

Global intervention and a new imperial presidency. T. G. Carpenter. il *USA Today (Periodical)* 115:10-18 Mr '87

Hidden commitments. T. L. Deibel. *Foreign Policy* 67:46-63 Summ '87

How to deal with countries gone mad. C. Krauthammer. il *Time* 130:82 S 21 '87

Human rights and U.S. foreign policy [address, May 18, 1987] R. Schifter. *Dep State Bull* 87:75-7 Ag '87

The imperial Congress. G. Szamuely. *Commentary* 84:27-32 S '87

The imperial temptation: Reagan's presidency succumbs. A. M. Schlesinger. *New Repub* 196:17 Mr 16 '87

Is America going to the dogs? J. McLaughlin. *Natl Rev* 39:22 Jl 31 '87

It's time for nations to behave like adults. M. Ruby. il *U S News World Rep* 103:22-3 D 28 '87-Ja 4 '88

Lost illusions. S. Serfaty. *Foreign Policy* 66:3-19 Spr '87

Maintaining the momentum in U.S. foreign policy [address, February 25, 1987] J. C. Whitehead. *Dep State Bull* 87:35-6 Ap '87

Matching foreign policy resources with goals [statement, August 7, 1987] G. P. Shultz. *Dep State Bull* 87:6-11 O '87

A matter of interpretation [translating's role in international relations] M. Smith. por *Newsweek* 110:9 D 14 '87

Meeting America's foreign policy challenges [address, February 20, 1987] G. P. Shultz. *Dep State Bull* 87:5-8 Ap '87

Morality and foreign policy: a sketch of the issues. J. B. Hehir. il *America* 156:64-8 Ja 31 '87

New risks for old friends. P. R. Range. il map *U S News World Rep* 102:31-2 My 25 '87

News briefing of June 2, 1987. G. P. Shultz. *Dep State Bull* 87:40-3 Ag '87

News conference of August 6, 1987. G. P. Shultz. *Dep State Bull* 87:11-14 O '87

Noam Chomsky: an American dissident [interview; excerpt from The Chomsky reader] J. Peck. il *Progressive* 51:22-5 Jl '87

Others as we see them. il *Society* 24:2 My/Je '87

Parable in the jungle [role of public will and knowledge of foreign cultures in formulating policy] H. Evans. il *U S News World Rep* 102:78 Mr 2 '87

The politics of empire [Reagan presidency] N. Birnbaum. il *Nation* 244:9-12 Ja 10 '87

The price of power [relationship of democracy to foreign policy] C. Krauthammer. *New Repub* 196:23-5 F 9 '87

Public diplomacy in the information age [address, September 15, 1987] G. P. Shultz. *Dep State Bull* 87:16-18 N '87

Purposeful leaks [congressional foreign policy leaks] *Natl Rev* 39:20 S 11 '87

Pursuing an effective foreign policy [statement, February 3, 1987] G. P. Shultz. *Dep State Bull* 87:11-14 Ap '87

A ray of light in arms control [R. Reagan attempts to boost weakened status] H. Trewhitt. il por *U S News World Rep* 103:28-9 Ag 10 '87

A Republican looks at foreign policy. R. G. Lugar. *Foreign Aff* 66:249-62 Wint '87/'88

Restoring the foreign affairs budget [address, November 3, 1986] G. P. Shultz. *Dep State Bull* 87:24-6 Ja '87

The Schlesinger thesis [A. M. Schlesinger's The cycles of American history] K. S. Lynn. *Commentary* 83:46-52 Mr '87

Secretary's interview on "Meet the press" [G. P. Shultz; transcript of program, June 28, 1987] *Dep State Bull* 87:37-9 Ag '87

Secretary's interview on "Worldnet" [interview with G. P. Shultz; transcript of program, December 16, 1986] *Dep State Bull* 87:33-6 F '87

United States—Foreign relations—*cont.*

See no evil, hear no evil, speak no evil [O. L. North, J. M. Poindexter, and U.S. foreign policy] M. Kramer. il *U S News World Rep* 103:12 Jl 27 '87

Shultz's way. R. Steel. il pors *N Y Times Mag* p14-21+ Ja 11 '87

Too good for this world [foreign policies of Democratic presidential candidates] M. Kondracke. *New Repub* 197:17-18+ O 26 '87

U.S. foreign policy achievements and challenges [address, October 18, 1986] M. H. Armacost. *Dep State Bull* 87:61-4 Ja '87

U.S. human rights policy: origins and implementation [address, May 26, 1987] G. Lister. *Dep State Bull* 87:73-5 Ag '87

Underfunding and undermining our foreign policy infrastructure [statements, February 26 and March 4, 1987] R. I. Spiers. *Dep State Bull* 87:23-7 My '87

Understanding human rights [address, October 10, 1987] M. Decter. *Vital Speeches Day* 54:139-42 D 15 '87

Who's in charge here? [Congress's role in foreign policy] T. Jacoby. il *Newsweek* 110:18 Jl 27 '87

Why State can't lead. D. L. Clarke. bibl f *Foreign Policy* 66:128-42 Spr '87

Words and deeds in foreign policy. K. W. Thompson. *Society* 24:24-8 My/Je '87

Anecdotes, facetiae, satire, etc.

To my dearest enemy . . . R. Baker. il *N Y Times Mag* p16 My 17 '87

Anti-Communist measures

The arms race—intervention link. D. Cortright. *Cent Mag* 20:58-9 My/Je '87

Debate over the U.S. role in foreign wars. J. Martin. il *Sch Update* 119:11-12 My 4 '87

The democracy syndrome, cont'd. B. Crozier. *Natl Rev* 39:26 Je 19 '87

Guerrilla warfare: morality and the Reagan Doctrine. C. Krauthammer. *Current* 290:32-40 F '87

Maximum feasible containment. J. Muravchik. *New Repub* 196:23-5 Je 1 '87

Staunch allies? [comparing Soviet support of allies to U.S. and British policies] B. Crozier. *Natl Rev* 39:26 Ap 24 '87

The two faces of the Reagan administration's foreign policy approach [Reagan Doctrine] C. W. Kegley and E. R. Wittkopf. il *USA Today (Periodical)* 115:10-15 Ja '87

The world crisis and American responsibility [address, March 26, 1987] E. W. Lefever. *Vital Speeches Day* 53:518-20 Je 15 '87

History

American hubris: from Truman to the Persian Gulf. T. Draper. bibl f il *N Y Rev Books* 34:40-8 Jl 16 '87

Reagan's junta. T. Draper. bibl f il *N Y Rev Books* 34:5+ Ja 29 '87

Reagan's junta [discussion of January 29, 1987 article] T. Draper. *N Y Rev Books* 34:47-8 Ap 23 '87

Requiem for the "establishment" [The wise men] H. J. Kaplan. *Commentary* 83:37-48 Ap '87

"The wise men" [discussion of April 1987 article, Requiem for the establishment] H. J. Kaplan. *Commentary* 84:10-12 Jl '87

Afghanistan

See also
Afghanistan Day

Bear in a briarpatch: prospects for a Soviet pullout. G. Perkovich. il *Commonweal* 114:725-6 D 18 '87

Africa

See also
Shultz, George Pratt, 1920——Visit to Africa, 1987

The human rights dimension in Africa [address, November 6, 1986] C. W. Freeman. *Dep State Bull* 87:42-5 F '87

OAU leader meets with black politicos in D.C. to cement U.S. African ties [I. Oumarou] il por *Jet* 72:14 Je 1 '87

Angola

Ideological contradictions in U.S. policy toward Angola. R. A. Fangmeier. il *Christ Century* 104:1061-3 N 25 '87

Arab countries

Shock among Arabs. S. Rabbaniha. il *World Press Rev* 34:18-19 Ja '87

Argentina—History

Kissinger and the 'dirty war' [human rights violations during the 1970s] M. Andersen. il *Nation* 245:477-80 O 31 '87

Australia

An alliance unbalanced. A. Lyons. *America* 157:373-4 N 21 '87

Austria

See also
United States—Diplomatic and consular service—Austria

The case against Waldheim [Justice Dept. denies entry to the U.S.] N. Cooper. il pors *Newsweek* 109:40 My 11 '87

Haunted by ghosts of a Nazi past [K. Waldheim barred from entering U.S.] S. Masterman. il por *Macleans* 100:36 My 11 '87

Kurt Waldheim: persona non grata [Justice Dept. report leads to denial of entry into the U.S.] M. Doan and C. Fenyvesi. il por *U S News World Rep* 102:8-9 My 11 '87

Removing the welcome mat [K. Waldheim barred from the U.S.] W. R. Doerner. il por *Time* 129:38-9 My 11 '87

The Waldheim case limps on. E. von Kuehnelt-Leddihn. *Natl Rev* 39:46 Je 19 '87

Bolivia

How to lose the coke war [U.S.-Bolivian campaign] D. Kline. il *Atlantic* 259:22-7 My '87

Canada

See also
Canada—Diplomatic and consular service—United States
Reagan, Ronald, 1911——Visit to Canada, 1987
Shultz, George Pratt, 1920——Visit to Canada, 1986

Acid rain [statement, March 18, 1987] R. Reagan. *Dep State Bull* 87:8 Je '87

The acid test [acid rain] *Commonweal* 114:100-1 F 27 '87

Attempts to clear the air. I. Austen. il *Macleans* 100:18-19 Mr 30 '87

Canada's view on acid rain. M. Mardon. il *Sierra* 72:20-2 Jl/Ag '87

Cool criticism from Washington [Canadian plan to purchase fleet of nuclear-powered submarines] I. Austen. il *Macleans* 100:17 My 18 '87

Downfall of 'The Acid Rainmaker' [M. K. Deaver indicted on perjury counts] M. McDonald. il por *Macleans* 100:22-3 Mr 30 '87

An epic Arctic journey [expedition retracing Inuit migration and demonstrating Canadian Arctic sovereignty; special section; with editorial comment by Kevin Doyle] il map *Macleans* 100:2, 20-8+ My 11 '87

Keeping the word [Supreme Court rules that 3 Canadian films are propaganda] *Time* 129:49 My 11 '87

Nominating a hero for 1987 [J. Rauh's suit against CIA mind control experiments performed on Canadians] A. Fotheringham. il *Macleans* 100:64 Ja 19 '87

Peace, friendship, and U.S.-Canada relations [address, July 2, 1987] G. P. Shultz. *Dep State Bull* 87:16-17 S '87

Standing up to the United States [Canadian sovereignty in the Arctic] S. Shallhorn. *Bull At Sci* 43:16-17 O '87

Threats to the North [U.S. threat to Canadian sovereignty in the Arctic and dispute over Arctic National Wildlife Refuge] M. Janigan. il map *Macleans* 100:10-11 Ja 26 '87

A turning point in U.S.-Canadian relations. A. Bromke and K. R. Nossal. *Foreign Aff* 66:150-69 Fall '87

U.S./Canadian radar research questioned. *Aviat Week Space Technol* 126:22 Ap 20 '87

U.S.-Canada relations. *Dep State Bull* 87:8-9 Je '87

Uncle Sam's sovereignty promise [agreement on sovereignty in the Canadian Arctic between Ottawa and Washington] P. C. Newman. il *Macleans* 100:33 Mr 30 '87

When a good neighbor forgets. S. MacLeod. il *Macleans* 100:84 Ja 5 '87

Caribbean region

Partners in conflict. A. F. Lowenthal. il maps *Commonweal* 114:265-72+ My 8 '87

Central America

See also
National Bipartisan Commission on Central America (U.S.)

And what of the contras now? [Central American peace plans] *America* 157:75-6 Ag 15-22 '87

Another useful tool [discussion of April 18, 1987 article, Democrats and the Arias plan] L. Annunziata. *Nation* 244:565 My 2 '87

Apocalypse soon [effect of Central American peace plan on contra aid] J. Smolowe. il *Time* 130:34-6 S 21 '87

The Arias plan. J. B. Hehir. il *Commonweal* 114:521-2 S 25 '87

The battle of the isthmus [Reagan administration opposition to Central American peace plan] il *Progressive* 51:8-9 O '87

United States—Foreign relations—Central America—*cont.*

Central America: what are the alternatives? [address, April 21, 1987] E. Abrams. *Dep State Bull* 87:83-7 Jl '87

Central America: why peace talks aren't just talk. B. Javetski. il *Bus Week* p41 Ag 24 '87

Central America: will it be peace now? C. A. Robbins. il *U S News World Rep* 103:39-40 O 5 '87

A Central American Yalta? [peace agreement] M. Kramer. il *U S News World Rep* 103:13 Ag 24 '87

The choice in Central America [peace plans] S. K. Purcell. bibl f map *Foreign Aff* 66:109-28 Fall '87

Costa Rican initiative [Arias plan; statement, March 6, 1987] E. Abrams. *Dep State Bull* 87:90-1 My '87

Could it be? [ceasefire peace initiative] W. F. Buckley. *Natl Rev* 39:72-3 S 11 '87

Cursed are the peacemakers [plans for Nicaragua] M. S. Serrill. il *Time* 130:30-1 Ag 24 '87

Democrats and the Arias plan [cover story] L. Annunziata. il *Nation* 244:489+ Ap 18 '87

Echoes of Watergate [break-ins and surveillance campaign against critics of U.S. Central American policy] B. Levin. il *Macleans* 100:22+ F 16 '87

Elliott Abrams: the teflon Assistant Secretary. E. Alterman. por *Wash Mon* 19:19-22+ My '87

The end of the affair? [Central American peace plans and contra aid] J. Chace. bibl f il *N Y Rev Books* 34:24-6+ O 8 '87

Give 'em hell. A. Tonelson. *New Repub* 197:20-1+ O 5 '87

The glimmer [Central American peace initiative] J. Klein. il *N Y* 20:16+ S 14 '87

How credible is the proposal on Nicaragua? J. M. Wall. *Christ Century* 104:675-6 Ag 12-19 '87

The Jim Wright shuffle [Central American peace plan] J. Morley. *Nation* 245:185+ S 5 '87

A lean chain of hope [Central American peace proposal signed in Guatemala City on August 7] *Commonweal* 114:469 S 11 '87

Letter from Washington [effect of Central American peace initiative on contra aid] Cato. *Natl Rev* 39:15 S 11 '87

Litmus test [1988 presidential campaign issue] *Nation* 244:528-9 Ap 25 '87

New steps to Central American peace. M. Nichols. il *Macleans* 100:18-19 Ag 17 '87

Nicaragua: the moral and strategic stakes [address, February 12, 1987] G. P. Shultz. *Dep State Bull* 87:14-18 Mr '87

Not just one peace plan for Nicaragua, but two: Reagan and Central Americans unveil proposals. E. Magnuson. il *Time* 130:14-15 Ag 17 '87

On the battle fronts [Central America and the Persian Gulf] D. Schorr. *New Leader* 70:6 O 19 '87

Oscar's Nobel [Arias peace plan] M. Kondracke. *New Repub* 197:14-16 N 9 '87

Partners in conflict. A. F. Lowenthal. il maps *Commonweal* 114:265-72+ My 8 '87

Peace, democracy, and security in Central America [statement, September 10, 1987] G. P. Shultz. *Dep State Bull* 87:13-16 N '87

Peace plan problems [Arias plan] L. S. Robinson. *Commonweal* 114:580-2 O 23 '87

Peace scare. *New Repub* 197:4+ S 28 '87

Peaced off [Reagan-Wright plan upstaged by Central American peace proposal] F. Barnes. *New Repub* 197:10-11 Ag 31 '87

The phony peace [Reagan peace plan for Central America] *Nation* 245:147-8 Ag 29 '87

Potholes on the road to peace [U.S. delays Central American summit meeting; with interview with O. Arias Sánchez] J. Smolowe. il por *Time* 129:34+ Je 29 '87

The price of peace [Central American peace plan] M. Kempton. *N Y Rev Books* 34:46 S 24 '87

'Pricing the contras' [Central American peace initiative's effect on contra aid] H. Anderson. il *Newsweek* 110:24-5 Ag 24 '87

Promoting freedom and democracy in Central America [address, May 3, 1987] R. Reagan. *Dep State Bull* 87:1-4 Jl '87

Puzzling out a peace plan. H. Rainie. il *U S News World Rep* 103:19 S 7 '87

Reagan isn't calling the shots in Central America anymore. B. Javetski and others. il *Bus Week* p65 O 12 '87

Reagan peace plan: a win if it fails? J. Wallace. il *U S News World Rep* 103:24-5 Ag 17 '87

Revolution in Central America? C. Krauss. *Foreign Aff* 65 Sp Issue:564-81 ['87]

Rival plans, rival goals [Central American peace plans] B. Crozier. *Natl Rev* 39:30 S 25 '87

The rule of reason [Central American peace plan] *Commonweal* 114:549 O 9 '87

Should the Sandinistas be trusted? [peace plans] H. Anderson. il *Newsweek* 110:28+ Ag 31 '87

Slipping and sliding around peace [plans for Nicaragua] J. Smolowe. il *Time* 130:28+ S 7 '87

Speaking his peace [O. Arias Sanchez addresses Congress] J. Smolowe. il por *Time* 130:34-5 O 5 '87

A study in contrast: Central America & the Persian Gulf [competing Soviet and U.S. interests] J. B. Hehir. il *Commonweal* 114:439 Ag 14 '87

A 'successful' failure. I. Austen. por *Macleans* 100:20 Ag 17 '87

A twisting road to peace. C. Wood. il *Macleans* 100:19 Ag 31 '87

U.S. obsession with Central America [views of Abraham Lowenthal] il *USA Today (Periodical)* 116:14 D '87

U.S. policies in Central America: choices on Nicaragua. R. W. Fontaine. *Current* 291:34-40 Mr/Ap '87

United States policy in Central America. E. Kenworthy. bibl f *Curr Hist* 86:401-4+ D '87

What's at stake in Central America: U.S. influence under fire [special issue] il map *Sch Update* 119:4-25 Mr 9 '87

Who wants peace? [Arias plan; cover story] M. Kondracke. *New Repub* 197:16-19 S 28 '87

Whose peace plan is it anyway? J. Smolowe. por *Time* 130:34 S 28 '87

Will Ortega play for peace—or play for time? [Central American peace agreement] J. L. Galloway. il por *U S News World Rep* 103:30-1 Ag 24 '87

Will peace break out? [initiatives by R. Reagan and Central American governments] H. Anderson. il *Newsweek* 110:16-18 Ag 17 '87

Will the Arias peace plan work? *World Press Rev* 34:22-3 O '87

Central America—History

The war-torn roots of today's turmoil. J. Rose. il *Sch Update* 119:19-21 Mr 9 '87

Chad

See also

Habre, Hissene—Visit to the United States, 1987

Chile

Getting away with murder. H. Evans. il *U S News World Rep* 102:80 Mr 23 '87

The inverse law. B. Crozier. *Natl Rev* 39:26-7 My 8 '87

No, no Noriega [Reagan administration moves] M. Kondracke. *New Repub* 197:4 O 5 '87

Situation in Chile [statement, July 21, 1987] E. Abrams. *Dep State Bull* 87:63-6 O '87

Chile—History

See also

Letelier, Orlando—Assassination

China

See also

Shultz, George Pratt, 1920-—Visit to China, 1987

China policy today: consensus, consistence, stability [address, December 11, 1986] G. J. Sigur. *Dep State Bull* 87:48-52 F '87

China-U.S. friendship doesn't depend on our being nice. M. S. Forbes. *Forbes* 139:17 My 4 '87

A tinderbox in Tibet inflames U.S.-China relations. J. Becker and B. Javetski. il *Bus Week* p53 O 26 '87

U.S. policy priorities for relations with China [address, April 22, 1987] G. J. Sigur. *Dep State Bull* 87:41-3 Jl '87

China—History

Changing images: the U.S. & China. B. Howard. il *Sch Update* 120:20+ S 18 '87

Communist countries

Congress's Red Army [pro-Communist Democrats; cover story] J. M. Waller and J. Sobran. il *Natl Rev* 39:25-8 Jl 31 '87

Costa Rica

See also

Arias Sanchez, Oscar—Visit to the United States, 1986

Arias Sanchez, Oscar—Visit to the United States, 1987

Leaning on Arias. M. Honey and T. Avirgan. *Nation* 245:220-1 S 12 '87

Cuba

Cuba's declining fortunes. J. M. Del Aguila. bibl f *Curr Hist* 86:425-8+ D '87

Fantasy island. *New Repub* 196:4 My 18 '87

Pentagon banking on Castro phobia. W. M. Arkin. *Bull At Sci* 43:4-5 My '87

Cuba—History

See also

Cuba—History—Invasion, 1961

United States—Foreign relations—Cuba—History—See also
—cont.
> Cuban Missile Crisis, 1962
> > *Czechoslovakia*
> > See also
> > > United States—Diplomatic and consular service—
> > > Czechoslovakia
> > *Denmark*
> Danes bristle at U.S. radar plans [phased-array radar planned for Thule, Greenland complicates ABM Treaty] M. Burcharth. il map *Bull At Sci* 43:11-13 Je '87
> > *Developing countries*
> U.S. policy toward the third world [address, October 17, 1986] M. H. Armacost. *Dep State Bull* 87:56-60 Ja '87
> U.S.-Soviet relations: coping with conflicts in the third world [address, September 26, 1986] M. H. Armacost. *Dep State Bull* 86:57-61 D '86
> > *East Asia*
> > See also
> > > Shultz, George Pratt, 1920—Visit to East Asia, 1987
> The U.S. approach to East Asia and the Pacific [address, October 29, 1986] G. J. Sigur. *Dep State Bull* 87:55-7 F '87
> > *Eastern Europe*
> European drift: this time the wolf is at the door. H. Trewhitt. il *U S News World Rep* 102:22-4 Je 22 '87
> The U.S. and Eastern Europe. W. H. Luers. *Foreign Aff* 65:976-94 Summ '87
> > *Egypt*
> Egypt: the Islamic issue. M. Sid-Ahmed. *Foreign Policy* 69:22-39 Wint '87/'88
> > *El Salvador*
> > See also
> > > U.S. Committee in Solidarity with the People of El Salvador
> AFL-CIO is Spanish for union busting [U.S. efforts to destroy independent labor movement] F. Smyth. *Wash Mon* 19:24-7 S '87
> Duarte's secret friends [U.S. efforts to divide and destroy new independent labor movement in El Salvador] F. Smyth. il *Nation* 244:316-18 Mr 14 '87
> Honduran sting [aid to contras funneled through Ilopango air base] *Time* 129:29 Ap 6 '87
> 'If Americans knew . . .' [visit to U.S. by representatives of El Salvador's independent labor unions] K. E. Bean. il *Progressive* 51:24 Ag '87
> A visit to Salvador. M. Kondracke. *New Repub* 197:10-12 Ag 10-17 '87
> > *Ethiopia*
> Gray pushes for sanctions against Ethiopia atrocity. *Jet* 73:4 O 12 '87
> New bill to ban Ethiopia. K. Jackson. il *Black Enterp* 17:18 Jl '87
> > *Europe*
> Recent developments in Europe [statement, June 18, 1987] R. L. Ridgway. *Dep State Bull* 87:65-7 Ag '87
> > *Fiji*
> The fight in Fiji [questions about U.S. involvement in coup] W. H. Schaap. *Nation* 244:707 My 30 '87
> > *France*
> > See also
> > > Chirac, Jacques, 1932—Visit to the United States, 1987
> France, USAF discuss joint efforts on Project Forecast 2 technologies. *Aviat Week Space Technol* 126:78-9 Je 1 '87
> > *Gabon*
> > See also
> > > Bongo, Omar—Visit to the United States, 1987
> > *Germany (West)*
> > See also
> > > Kohl, Helmut, 1930—Visit to the United States, 1986
> > > Reagan, Ronald, 1911—Visit to Germany (West), 1987
> Deutschland uber allies. C. Layne. *New Repub* 197:12-14 S 28 '87
> Germany's Chancellor Kohl isn't charisma-less. M. S. Forbes. il por *Forbes* 140:17 Ag 24 '87
> Star Wars controversy in West Germany. T. Risse-Kappen. *Bull At Sci* 43:50-2 Jl/Ag '87
> > *Great Britain*
> > See also
> > > Thatcher, Margaret—Visit to the United States, 1987
> If Labour wins. W. B. Messmer. *Foreign Policy* 67:137-53 Summ '87
> Neil in the 'lion's den' [N. Kinnock's U.S. visit] M. White. il *World Press Rev* 34:13-14 My '87

> > *Great Britain—History*
> The Roosevelt precedent [decision to provide Britain with destroyers in 1940] por *Time* 129:26 Je 1 '87
> > *Greece*
> Papandreou's 'whipping boy'. N. Cooper. il por *Newsweek* 110:35 Jl 27 '87
> > *Grenada*
> > See also
> > > Grenada—Invasion, 1983
> > *Guatemala*
> > See also
> > > Cerezo Arévalo, Vinicio—Visit to the United States, 1987
> Going it alone. J. A. Briggs. il *Forbes* 139:172-4 My 18 '87
> > *Haiti*
> > See also
> > > Namphy, Henri, 1932—Visit to the United States, 1986
> Cry Haiti. M. S. Hooper. *Nation* 245:740-1 D 19 '87
> Haiti: democracy derailed. D. Peerman. *Christ Century* 104:1135-6 D 16 '87
> Haiti: the new violence. M. Massing. il *N Y Rev Books* 34:45-52 D 3 '87
> How the U.S. miscalculated in Haiti. C. A. Robbins. il *U S News World Rep* 103:36-7 D 14 '87
> Pondering chaos. *Commonweal* 114:517-18 S 25 '87
> Promoting democracy in Haiti. R. N. Holwill. map *Dep State Bull* 87:60-2 O '87
> Should the U.S. intervene? il *Time* 130:40 D 14 '87
> Terror keeps Haiti in line. N. Cooper. il *Newsweek* 110:54-5 D 14 '87
> What not to do in Haiti. *Commonweal* 114:724 D 18 '87
> > *Honduras*
> Honduran sting [aid to contras] *Time* 129:29 Ap 6 '87
> > *India*
> An aid package for Pakistan stirs up India's Yankee-bashers. V. Tenorio. il *Bus Week* p54 Je 15 '87
> "We don't have the bomb" [interview with R. Gandhi] P. Gupte. il pors *Forbes* 139:156+ My 18 '87
> Why the U.S. is trying harder to make friends with India. S. Tefft and others. il *Bus Week* p61 Ja 12 '87
> > *Iran*
> > See also
> > > Iran-contra affair
> > > Iranian seizure of United States embassy, 1979-1981
> After the Ayatollah. S. T. Hunter. *Foreign Policy* 66:77-97 Spr '87
> America's nemesis. R. Watson. il *Newsweek* 110:28-31 Ag 17 '87
> Assistant Secretary Murphy's interview on "Meet the press" [transcript of program, August 23, 1987] R. W. Murphy. *Dep State Bull* 87:44-8 O '87
> An attack in the Gulf [Navy attack on Iranian ship laying mines] M. Nichols. il map *Macleans* 100:26-8 O 5 '87
> The broader picture. B. Crozier. *Natl Rev* 39:28+ N 6 '87
> Buying revolutions. G. Dyer. *World Press Rev* 34:15 F '87
> Can't anybody here play this game? [U.S. unpreparedness in Persian Gulf] M. Kramer. il *U S News World Rep* 103:11 Ag 10 '87
> Caught in the act [U.S. captures Iranians laying mines in the Persian Gulf] E. Magnuson. il map *Time* 130:20-3 O 5 '87
> A chain of violence. il *Macleans* 100:17 Ag 10 '87
> Chin to chin in a sea of trouble [Iranian missiles hit Kuwaiti tanker sailing under U.S. flag] B. Duffy. il map *U S News World Rep* 103:25 O 26 '87
> Combined U.S. forces defeat Iranian mine-laying mission. B. M. Greeley, Jr. il map *Aviat Week Space Technol* 127:32-3 S 28 '87
> Convoy to a minefield [mine blast hits Kuwaiti tanker under American escort] B. Levin. il *Macleans* 100:20-1 Ag 3 '87
> Coping with the unfathomable. J. V. Lamar, Jr. il *Time* 130:39 Ag 17 '87
> The dangers deepen, and so do the doubts [special section] il map *U S News World Rep* 103:18-23 Ag 17 '87
> The dangers of taking sides. L. C. Wilson. *USA Today (Periodical)* 116:47 N '87
> A direct hit in reply [U.S. warships destroy Iranian oil installation] A. Bilski. il *Macleans* 100:25 N 2 '87
> Dreams of the Great Satan [A. Khashoggi's statements alleging a U.S. assassination plot against Khomeini and an Egyptian involvement in Iranscam] A. Cockburn. *Nation* 245:186 S 5 '87

United States—Foreign relations—Iran—cont.

Drowning in the Gulf. B. Rubin. *Foreign Policy* 69:120-34 Wint '87/'88

Engulfed. *Commonweal* 114:467-8 S 11 '87

F-14 crew fires at Iranian jet to defend Navy Gulf patrol. B. M. Greeley, Jr. il *Aviat Week Space Technol* 127:22-3 Ag 17 '87

The Gulf [cover story; special section] il *World Press Rev* 34:13-16+ O '87

The Gulf: an important success [trapping Iran in minelaying operations] *Natl Rev* 39:20 O 23 '87

Here a mine, there a mine [Persian Gulf] J. Greenwald. il *Time* 130:24-7 Ag 24 '87

In deeper in the Gulf [special section] il *Newsweek* 110:14-17 Ag 31 '87

Into rough water [U.S./Kuwaiti tankers encounter mines in the Persian Gulf] W. Isaacson. il *Time* 130:8-10 Ag 10 '87

Just war in the Gulf. *New Repub* 197:10-11 N 9 '87

Khomeini's Iran: a case study of hatred toward the U.S. L. Hopping. il *Sch Update* 120:27-8 O 2 '87

Losing patience with Iran. *Natl Rev* 39:18 S 11 '87

Lost empires. *Nation* 245:111-12 Ag 15-22 '87

The mines of August. R. Watson. il map *Newsweek* 110:22-4 Ag 24 '87

The mining episode . . . and more to come? [U.S.-flagged tanker Bridgeton hits mine in Persian Gulf] il maps *U S News World Rep* 103:26-7 Ag 3 '87

More blood in the Gulf [U.S. helicopters shoot it out with Iranian gunboats] R. Watson. il map *Newsweek* 110:44-5 O 19 '87

On the battle fronts [Central America and the Persian Gulf] D. Schorr. *New Leader* 70:6 O 19 '87

Perseverance pays. M. Kondracke. *New Repub* 197:13-14+ S 14-21 '87

Powder-keg politics. R. Laver. il map *Macleans* 100:14-15 Ag 31 '87

Pressing the attack [U.S. presses Iran] K. Scanlon. il *Macleans* 100:31-2 O 19 '87

Punch, counterpunch [U.S. attacks Iranian oil-loading platforms] M. S. Serrill. il *Time* 130:62-4 N 2 '87

Running the gauntlet [U.S.-flagged Kuwaiti tanker hits Iranian mine in the Persian Gulf] W. E. Smith. il map *Time* 130:24-7 Ag 3 '87

A salvo for Teheran [U.S. destroyers fire on Iranian oil rig] A. Deming. il map *Newsweek* 110:63+ N 2 '87

Saying no to Iran [request by Teheran for talks] L. Howard. il *Newsweek* 110:6 O 12 '87

Shoot-out in the Gulf, echoes on Capitol Hill [American helicopter gunships vs. Iranian gunboats] J. L. Galloway. il *U S News World Rep* 103:8 O 19 '87

Shunning Uncle Sam in the Gulf. W. L. Chaze. il *U S News World Rep* 103:39-40 N 2 '87

Silkworm's sting [Iranian missile attack on Kuwaiti tanker sailing under American flag] M. S. Serrill. il map *Time* 130:42-3 O 26 '87

A sting in the Gulf [mine blast hits Kuwaiti tanker under American escort] H. Anderson. il map *Newsweek* 110:24-6 Ag 3 '87

Swept up in the tides of the Gulf. H. Anderson. il *Newsweek* 110:40-2 Ag 10 '87

Time bombs in the ocean [mines in the Persian Gulf] A. Bilski. il *Macleans* 100:24 Ag 24 '87

Time for sweeping gestures [mines in the Persian Gulf] M. S. Serrill. *Time* 130:26 Ag 31 '87

A U.S. ambush in the Gulf [trapping Iran in the act of laying mines] R. Watson. il map *Newsweek* 110:24-7 O 5 '87

U.S. destroyers bombard Iranian oil platform. *Aviat Week Space Technol* 127:34 O 26 '87

The U.S. may face a long war of nerves. D. F. Graham and J. P. Tarpey. il *Bus Week* p34 Ag 17 '87

U.S. takes defensive action in Persian Gulf [statement, September 24, 1987] R. Reagan. *Dep State Bull* 87:43-4 N '87

U.S. will attack Iranian missile sites if hostile intent is evident. P. Mann. *Aviat Week Space Technol* 127:29-30 Jl 20 '87

Waiting for Iran [U.S. capture of Iranian mine laying vessels; with editorial comment by Mortimer B. Zuckerman] W. L. Chaze. il map *U S News World Rep* 103:22-4, 88 O 5 '87

War games in the Gulf. A. Wilson-Smith. il map *Macleans* 100:16-17 Ag 17 '87

"We engaged" [Iranians shoot at U.S. helicopters] E. Magnuson. il map *Time* 130:12-14 O 19 '87

Weinberger's war. I. F. Stone. *Nation* 245:364-5 O 10 '87

Why Reagan pulled his punch in the Persian Gulf [retaliating against Iran for missile attack on a U.S.-flagged tanker] B. Javetski and D. Griffiths. il *Bus Week* p161 N 2 '87

Will Reagan hit back at Iran? [retaliation for missile strike against U.S.-flagged tanker] N. Cooper. il *Newsweek* 110:42-3 O 26 '87

Iraq

See also

Stark (Warship)—Iraqi missile attack, 1987

Back Iraq. D. Pipes and L. Mylroie. *New Repub* 196:14-15 Ap 27 '87

Israel

See also

Peres, Shimon, 1923——Visit to the United States, 1986

Shamir, Yitzhak—Visit to the United States, 1987

Byzantine bedfellows. Y. Karny. *New Repub* 196:23-5 F 2 '87

Ending the 20-year war. M. Viorst. il *Newsweek* 109:10 Je 15 '87

Israel and Pollard [spy case] *World Press Rev* 34:36-7 My '87

Israelamok [Iranamok and the Pollard affair] *New Repub* 196:9 Mr 30 '87

Life for an Israeli spy [J. Pollard case] H. Anderson. il por *Newsweek* 109:26+ Mr 16 '87

Official rogues [Israeli government coverup of J. Pollard espionage case] G. Carver. *New Repub* 196:12-15 Ap 13 '87

One step ahead, two backward [J. Pollard case] J. Branegan. il por *Time* 129:53 Ap 13 '87

Spying between friends [J. Pollard sentenced to life imprisonment] W. E. Smith. il por *Time* 129:44+ Mr 16 '87

Spying between friends: Pollard case simmers on. S. Powell. il por *U S News World Rep* 102:12 Mr 16 '87

Triple trouble in Israel [with editorial comment] E. Salpeter. il *New Leader* 70:2, 5-7 Mr 23 '87

Uproar over a spy [J. Pollard case] W. E. Smith. il *Time* 129:30-2 Mr 23 '87

Israel—History

The Kissinger covenant and other reasons Israel is in trouble [excerpt from Sands of sorrow; cover story] M. Viorst. por map *Wash Mon* 19:23-9+ Je '87

Italy

Of cookies, convoys and Cassandra [address, January 10, 1987] U. Nordio. *Vital Speeches Day* 53:439-41 My 1 '87

Japan

See also

Japan—Diplomatic and consular service—United States

Nakasone, Yasuhiro—Visit to the United States, 1987

United States—Diplomatic and consular service—Japan

The coming U.S.-Japan crisis. G. R. Packard. bibl f *Foreign Aff* 66:348-67 Wint '87/'88

Jesse Jackson reports on trip to Japan and Korea. D. M. Cheers. il pors *Jet* 71:28-32 Ja 12 '87

Make 'em pay [getting America's allies to shoulder more of the burden for their own defense] M. Kondracke. *New Repub* 197:15-17 O 12 '87

The U.S., Japan, and Asian Pacific security in perspective [address, May 29, 1987] M. H. Armacost. *Dep State Bull* 87:51-6 Ag '87

Welcome to the hot seat, Mr. Prime Minister [N. Takeshita] A. Borrus. il por *Bus Week* p152-3 N 2 '87

The white peril [G. Vidal's comments on decline of U.S. and rise of Japan] J. M. Fallows. il *Atlantic* 259:18+ My '87

Kampuchea

The Cambodian issue [statement, March 11, 1987] J. C. Monjo. *Dep State Bull* 87:29-30 My '87

Kenya

See also

Moi, Daniel Arap—Visit to the United States, 1987

Korea

See also

Korean War, 1950-1953—American participation

Korea (South)

The burden of omnipotence. J. M. Fallows. il *Atlantic* 260:20-1+ O '87

Dateline South Korea: a divided Seoul. S. S. Harrison. bibl f *Foreign Policy* 67:154-75 Summ '87

Deciding when to switch. H. Trewhitt. il *U S News World Rep* 103:33 Jl 13 '87

United States—Foreign relations—Korea (South)—cont.
Jesse Jackson reports on trip to Japan and Korea. D.
M. Cheers. il pors *Jet* 71:28-32 Ja 12 '87
Korea: Asian paradox. W. H. Gleysteen, Jr. and A.
D. Romberg. *Foreign Aff* 65:1037-54 Summ '87
Korea counseling. *New Repub* 197:7-9 Jl 13-20 '87
Korea divided. *Nation* 245:3-4 Jl 4-11 '87
Korea: new beginnings [address, July 21, 1987] G. J.
Sigur. *Dep State Bull* 87:32-4 S '87
Korean politics in transition [address, February 6, 1987]
G. J. Sigur. *Dep State Bull* 87:19-21 Ap '87
Ties that bind: why South Korea matters. il map
Newsweek 109:30 Je 29 '87
What can the U.S. do? F. Willey. il *Newsweek* 109:35
Je 29 '87

Kuwait

A balance sheet in the Gulf. N. Cooper. il *Newsweek*
110:59 N 9 '87
Collision course? [U.S. flags to protect Kuwaiti oil tankers
in Persian Gulf] L. Howard. il *Newsweek* 109:5 My
25 '87
Democrats cite risk in Kuwaiti reflagging [report by
Democratic Study Group] P. Mann. *Aviat Week Space
Technol* 126:33 Je 22 '87
Kuwait shies away from confronting Iran [interview with
S. N. al-Sabah] L. Lief. il *U S News World Rep*
103:40 N 2 '87
Missile attack, Kuwaiti pact could draw U.S. into Gulf
war. J. D. Morrocco. il map *Aviat Week Space Technol*
126:23-5 My 25 '87
An offer spurned [U.S. turns down offer of offshore
naval facility inside Kuwait's waters] L. Howard. il
Newsweek 110:7 D 7 '87
Piloting the camel [U.S. reflagging commitment to Kuwait]
M. B. Zuckerman. il *U S News World Rep* 103:76
Jl 6 '87
Reflagging folly [U.S. plan to flag Kuwaiti ships and
reinforce American military presence] N. Safran. *New
Repub* 197:10-11 Ag 3 '87
Rough seas and new names [Kuwaiti tankers flying under
American flag] J. V. Lamar, Jr. il map *Time* 129:13
Je 29 '87
Supersap [U.S. effort to protect access to Persian Gulf
oil results in price rise] *New Repub* 197:4 Ag 31
'87
U.S. policy in the Persian Gulf and Kuwaiti reflagging
[statement, June 16, 1987] M. H. Armacost. *Dep State
Bull* 87:78-81 Ag '87

Laos

Resolving the POW/MIA issue [address, July 18, 1987]
G. P. Shultz. *Dep State Bull* 87:18-19 S '87
U.S.-Lao POW/MIA consultations held in Vientiane [joint
statement, August 12, 1987] *Dep State Bull* 87:23
O '87

Latin America
See also
National Year of the Americas (1987)
Pan American Day and Week
Democracy in Latin America and the Caribbean: the
promise and the challenge. il *Dep State Bull* 87:58-89
Mr '87
Needed: a new hemispheric policy. *America* 157:443-4
D 12 '87
An overview of U.S.-Latin American relations [address,
December 1986] L. A. Tambs. *Vital Speeches Day*
53:279-81 F 15 '87
Promoting inter-American cooperation [address, Novem-
ber 11, 1986] G. P. Shultz. *Dep State Bull* 87:27-30
Ja '87
South of the border. E. von Kuehnelt-Leddihn. *Natl
Rev* 39:28 O 9 '87
Strengthening Latin American democracy. A. F. Lowen-
thal. *Commonweal* 114:268 My 8 '87
The United States and Latin America [with discussion]
C. Fuentes. il por *Cent Mag* 20:4-19 Ja/F '87
United States relations with South America. H. J. Wiarda.
Curr Hist 86:1-4+ Ja '87

Latin America—History
See also
Monroe Doctrine
Collective security and the inter-American system. D.
S. Painter. il *Dep State Bull* 87:56-8 Ap '87

Lebanon
See also
United States—Diplomatic and consular service—
Lebanon
U.S. passports invalid for travel to Lebanon [statement,
January 28, 1987] *Dep State Bull* 87:51 Mr '87

Libya
See also
Libyan-American conflict, 1986

'Reagan was the target' [threats from Libya] il por
Newsweek 110:59 O 5 '87

Mauritius
See also
United States—Diplomatic and consular service—
Mauritius

Mexico

The CIA sizes up the Mexican domino. *Harpers* 274:21
My '87
The machine and the tiger. M. Kondracke. *New Repub*
196:16-21 F 23 '87
Mexico: the presidential problem. A. Aguilar Zinser.
bibl f *Foreign Policy* 69:40-60 Wint '87/'88
Mexico-United States relations [address, November 12,
1986] M. Comacho Solis. *Vital Speeches Day* 53:222-4
Ja 15 '87
U.S.-Mexico Binational Commission meets [remarks,
January 29, 1987] G. P. Shultz; B. Sepulveda Amor.
il *Dep State Bull* 87:54-6 Ap '87
Uneasy neighbors: Mexico and the United States. P.
H. Smith. bibl f *Curr Hist* 86:97-100+ Mr '87
United States relations with Mexico [address, April 23,
1987] S. W. Sanders. *Vital Speeches Day* 53:525-8
Je 15 '87

Micronesia

U.S. relationship with Pacific Islands [statement, November 3, 1986] R. Reagan. *Dep State Bull* 87:78 Ja
'87

Middle East
See also
United States—Foreign relations—Persian Gulf re-
gion
Arabs anonymous [National Association of Arab
Americans sponsorship of essay contest on America's
Middle East policy] J. L. Pasley. *New Repub* 197:17-18
Ag 10-17 '87
Can Washington repair its frayed Mideast ties? S. J.
Dryden. il *Bus Week* p59 Mr 23 '87
Is 'peace' at hand? [proposed conference to settle West
Bank question] M. Kramer. il *U S News World Rep*
102:14 Je 29 '87
Middle East activities [statement, July 28, 1987] R. W.
Murphy. *Dep State Bull* 87:45-8 S '87
Middle East developments [statement, April 21, 1987]
R. W. Murphy. *Dep State Bull* 87:70-2 Je '87
The Middle East in the year 2000 [address, April 24,
1987] A. Ghandour. *Vital Speeches Day* 53:450-5 My
15 '87
Middle East: time for negotiations. J. Carter. il por
Time 129:38-9 Ap 20 '87
Myths about Palestinians. K. Christison. bibl f *Foreign
Policy* 66:109-27 Spr '87
Peace nix [S. Peres's proposal for an international con-
ference on the Mideast] M. Kondracke. il *New Repub*
196:20-2 Je 8 '87
The Reagan administration and the Middle East. R.
E. Hunter. *Curr Hist* 86:49-52+ F '87
Supporting U.S. interests in the Middle East [statement,
October 8, 1986] R. W. Murphy. *Dep State Bull* 86:70-2
D '86
Working for peace and freedom [address, May 17, 1987]
G. P. Shultz. *Dep State Bull* 87:7-10 Jl '87

Mongolia
See also
United States—Diplomatic and consular service—
Mongolia

Morocco
See also
United States—Diplomatic and consular service—
Morocco

Morocco—History
Long-time friends: early U.S.-Moroccan relations, 1777-87.
S. B. Wells. bibl f il *Dep State Bull* 87:1-15 S '87

Mozambique
Notes and comment [policy regarding Renamo] *New
Yorker* 63:35-6 N 16 '87
U.S. policy toward Mozambique [statement, June 24,
1987] C. A. Crocker. *Dep State Bull* 87:19-22 S '87

Nepal—History
Chronology of relations between the United States and
Nepal, 1947-87. E. Duncan. il *Dep State Bull* 87:63-7
S '87

New Zealand
Administration supports New Zealand Preference Elimina-
tion Act [statements, September 22, 1987] J. S. Roy.
Dep State Bull 87:46-7 N '87
The genesis of New Zealand's ban. J. Salzman. il *Bull
At Sci* 43:45-6+ Jl/Ag '87
Kiwis just say 'no' [anti-nuclear stand] J. Salzman. *Sierra*
72:32+ My/Je '87

United States—Foreign relations—New Zealand—*cont.*
Minority report. C. Hitchens. *Nation* 244:600 My 9 '87
New Zealand paying for nuclear ban. K. P. Clements. bibl f il *Bull At Sci* 43:41-4 Jl/Ag '87
New Zealand's antinuclear stand. K. P. Clements. il *Bull At Sci* 43:32-4 Mr '87

Nicaragua
See also
Ortega Saavedra, Daniel—Visit to the United States, 1987
After the contra war: time for peacemaking. M. D. Wilde. *Christ Century* 104:45 Ja 21 '87
Central American peace plan [address, August 22, 1987] R. Reagan. *Dep State Bull* 87:8 N '87
Development of U.S.-Nicaragua policy [statements, February 5, 1987] E. Abrams; P. C. Habib. *Dep State Bull* 87:75-82 My '87
How democratic is the Sandinista government? [debate at the Carter Presidential Center of Emory University] B. Spring. il *Christ Today* 31:48+ Ja 16 '87
Lies about Nicaragua. W. S. Smith. *Foreign Policy* 67:87-103 Summ '87
Little steps. *Natl Rev* 39:20-1 O 23 '87
Money, drugs and the contras [cover story] J. Kwitny. il *Nation* 245:145+ Ag 29 '87
Nicaragua: the moral and strategic stakes [address, February 12, 1987] G. P. Shultz. *Dep State Bull* 87:14-18 Mr '87
Of drugs, money and contras [discussion of August 29, 1987 article, Money, drugs and the contras] J. Kwitny. *Nation* 245:254+ S 19 '87
Pas de scandale à gauche [congressional Democrats' relations with the Sandinistas] *Natl Rev* 39:17 Je 19 '87
Peace and the Central American drama. *America* 157:395-6 N 28 '87
Positive containment in Nicaragua. V. P. Vaky. *Foreign Policy* 68:42-58 Fall '87
Reagan's secret wars and missed opportunities [revelations from B. Woodward's Veil] J. M. Wall. *Christ Century* 104:907-8 O 21 '87
U.S. initiative for peace in Central America. *Dep State Bull* 87:54-6 O '87
U.S. policies in Central America: choices on Nicaragua. R. W. Fontaine. *Current* 291:34-40 Mr/Ap '87
You decide the next U.S. moves toward Nicaragua. S. Manning. *Sch Update* 119:9 Mr 9 '87

Nicaragua—Anecdotes, facetiae, satire, etc.
Addicted to Nicaragua. R. Baker. il *N Y Times Mag* p14 My 31 '87

Nicaragua—History
The Sandinista heritage. C. Foster. il *Hist Today* 37:5-8 Ap '87

Norway
Such good friends: an old alliance under pressure [U.S. anger at Norway over illegal high tech sale to the Soviets] P. Sherrid. il *U S News World Rep* 103:42 O 5 '87

Pacific region
See also
Shultz, George Pratt, 1920——Visit to the Pacific region, 1987
Challenges to U.S. power in the Pacific. P. M. Jones. il *Sch Update* 119:20-2 Ap 6 '87
Meeting the challenges of change in the Pacific [address, May 14, 1987] G. P. Shultz. *Dep State Bull* 87:4-7 Jl '87
Nothing fishy about new tuna treaty. D. G. Knibb. il *Oceans* 20:6-7 Jl/Ag '87
A nuclear free Pacific: enlisting U.S. support [South Pacific Nuclear Free Zone Treaty] R. A. Evans. *Christ Century* 104:373-4 Ap 22 '87
Red herring in the Pacific. W. M. Arkin. *Bull At Sci* 43:6-7 Ap '87
South Pacific Nuclear Free Zone [statement, December 15, 1986] J. S. Roy. *Dep State Bull* 87:52-4 S '87
South Pacific regional fisheries treaty signed [State Dept. statement, April 2, 1987] *Dep State Bull* 87:82 Je '87
The strategic importance of the emerging Pacific [address, September 29, 1986] G. J. Sigur. *Dep State Bull* 86:75-8 D '86
The U.S. approach to East Asia and the Pacific [address, October 29, 1986] G. J. Sigur. *Dep State Bull* 87:55-7 F '87

Pakistan
The great game. S. R. Weisman. *New Repub* 197:20-3 Ag 10-17 '87
Pakistan and the nuclear issue [statement, July 22, 1987] R. W. Murphy. *Dep State Bull* 87:53-4 O '87

Panama
See also
United States—Diplomatic and consular service—Panama
Backing away from a Latin dictator [M. A. Noriega] T. Gup. il por *Time* 130:21 S 7 '87
Cracking down on Panama's general [M. A. Noriega] C. A. Robbins. il por *U S News World Rep* 103:30 Ag 10 '87
"Everyone wants us". A. D. Frank. il *Forbes* 139:37-8 F 23 '87
Latin America and the Caribbean: the paths to democracy [address, June 30, 1987] E. Abrams. *Dep State Bull* 87:81-5 S '87
No, no Noriega [Reagan administration moves] M. Kondracke. *New Repub* 197:4 O 5 '87
Panama: disaster or democracy. R. Arias Calderón. bibl f *Foreign Aff* 66:328-47 Wint '87/'88
Panama's struggle for democracy. S. C. Ropp. bibl f *Curr Hist* 86:421-4+ D '87
Sending Reagan a message. F. Willey. il por *Newsweek* 110:30 Jl 13 '87
Twilight for a dictator? [M. A. Noriega] J. L. Galloway. il por map *U S News World Rep* 103:29-31 Jl 20 '87
U.S. and Panama—push comes to shove. J. L. Galloway. il por *U S News World Rep* 103:17 Jl 13 '87
Will this man control the Panama Canal? [M. A. Noriega] D. Reed. por *Read Dig* 130:136-40 Ja '87

Persian Gulf region
Iran-Iraq War [statements, January 23 and February 25, 1987] R. Reagan. *Dep State Bull* 87:52 Ap '87
The Persian Gulf: stakes and risks [statement, May 29, 1987] R. W. Murphy. *Dep State Bull* 87:64-7 Jl '87
The real stakes in the Persian Gulf. R. N. Perle. il *U S News World Rep* 103:26+ O 26 '87
U.S. interests in the Persian Gulf [statement, January 27, 1987] G. P. Shultz. *Dep State Bull* 87:19-20 Mr '87
U.S. policy in the Persian Gulf. J. Schloesser. maps *Dep State Bull* 87:38-44 O '87
U.S. policy in the Persian Gulf [White House statement, June 30, 1987] *Dep State Bull* 87:46 S '87
You decide the U.S. response to a crisis. L. Kravitz. map *Sch Update* 119:14 F 23 '87

Philippines
See also
Aquino, Corazon—Visit to the United States, 1986
Aquino under fire. T. Jacoby. il *Newsweek* 110:40 O 5 '87
Aquino's Philippines: the center holds. S. Burton. *Foreign Aff* 65 Sp Issue:524-37 ['87]
A brave woman's fight to heal a troubled U.S. ally [C. Aquino] J. Martin. il pors *Sch Update* 119:14-15 Ap 6 '87
The Cory myth. A. Cockburn. *Nation* 245:258-9 S 19 '87
Democracy in the Philippines [statement, September 10, 1987] D. F. Lambertson. *Dep State Bull* 87:27-9 N '87
The foiling of Ferdinand [Marcos' plot to overthrow Aquino] H. Anderson. il por *Newsweek* 110:35 Jl 20 '87
Manila fudge [views of W. Chapman and R. Bonner] J. M. Fallows. *Wash Mon* 19:53-6 S '87
Marcos at bay. F. Barnes. *New Repub* 196:9-11 Mr 2 '87
The Philippines and the United States [address, October 6, 1986] M. H. Armacost. *Dep State Bull* 86:52-5 D '86
Testing an ally's resolve. W. L. Chaze. il por map *U S News World Rep* 103:73-5 S 28 '87
The U.S. in the Philippines: damned if it helps, damned if it doesn't. M. Shao and B. Javetski. il *Bus Week* p57 D 14 '87
Visa denied [U.S. denies visa to anti-Marcos activist E. B. Olaguer] W. Steif. il *Progressive* 51:27 F '87

Poland
Poland [statements, December 12, 1986 and February 19, 1987] R. Reagan. *Dep State Bull* 87:33-4 Ap '87

Saudi Arabia
Pressing the Saudis. *New Repub* 197:9 Ag 24 '87
Simmering about the Saudis [U.S. wants support in the Persian Gulf] H. Anderson. il *Newsweek* 109:40 Je 15 '87
Washington is protecting much more than Kuwaiti tankers. B. Javetski and others. il *Bus Week* p89 Jl 20 '87

Senegal
See also
Diouf, Abdou—Visit to the United States, 1987

United States—Foreign relations—*cont.*
South Africa
See also
United States—Diplomatic and consular service—South Africa
Apartheid fighters zero in on presidential race [TransAfrica] *Jet* 71:14 Mr 23 '87
CBC pushes for new African agenda [Congressional Black Caucus] G. McKinney. il *Black Enterp* 17:19 My '87
The democratic future of South Africa [address, September 29, 1987] G. P. Shultz. *Dep State Bull* 87:9-12 N '87
Fantasies about South Africa. P. L. Berger and B. Godsell. *Commentary* 84:35-40 Jl '87
Freedom's friend or freedom's foe? [O. Tambo visits the U.S.] S. Powell. il por *U S News World Rep* 102:12 F 9 '87
Gray calls on Reagan to help S. African detainees. por *Jet* 72:12 Ag 31 '87
The inverse law. B. Crozier. *Natl Rev* 39:26-7 My 8 '87
Probing for an Africa policy. P. R. Range. il por map *U S News World Rep* 102:32-3 Ja 19 '87
Sanctions in context. R. E. Lambert. *Commonweal* 114:166-7 Mr 27 '87
Secretary meets with ANC leader Tambo [State Dept. statement, January 28, 1987] il pors *Dep State Bull* 87:28 Mr '87
South Africa [discussion of July 1987 article, Fantasies about South Africa] P. L. Berger and B. Godsell. *Commentary* 84:11-12+ O '87
South Africa embattled. J. De St. Jorre. bibl f *Foreign Aff* 65 Sp Issue:538-63 ['87]
South Africa: it takes two to Tambo [O. Tambo's visit to the U.S.] il por *Newsweek* 109:43 F 9 '87
South Africa: the Afrikaner angst. P. H. Baker. *Foreign Policy* 69:61-79 Wint '87/'88
South Africa: toward peace and stability [address, December 1, 1986] C. A. Crocker. *Dep State Bull* 87:40-2 F '87
Southern Africa: American hopes for the future [address, December 4, 1986] G. P. Shultz. *Dep State Bull* 87:36-40 F '87
Struggle for Southern Africa. R. G. Mugabe. *Foreign Aff* 66:311-27 Wint '87/'88
Talking with Tambo. H. Anderson. il *Newsweek* 109:26 Ja 19 '87
Tambo on tour [U.S. visit] *Nation* 244:167-8 F 14 '87
Tambo visit centers U.S. focus on S. Africa fight. il pors *Jet* 71:7 F 16 '87
Tambo's risky game [talks between African National Congress and Washington] M. Whitaker. il por *Newsweek* 109:34-5 F 2 '87
Tango with Tambo. *Natl Rev* 39:19 F 27 '87
The U.S. and apartheid. L. H. Sullivan; P. Duignan. *Current* 297:11-17 N '87
U.S. policy toward Southern Africa [address, December 1, 1986] C. A. Crocker. *Vital Speeches Day* 53:197-9 Ja 15 '87
Zambia president Kaunda urges Reagan to support efforts to end apartheid. il pors *Jet* 73:4 N 2 '87
South Asia
South Asia and the United States: an evolving partnership [address, April 29, 1987] M. H. Armacost. map *Dep State Bull* 87:75-80 Jl '87
Southeast Asia
See also
Shultz, George Pratt, 1920——Visit to Southeast Asia, 1987
United States policy in Southeast Asia. E. Colbert. bibl f *Curr Hist* 86:145-7+ Ap '87
The voting fields. il *New Repub* 197:7-9 Ag 10-17 '87
Southern Africa
CBC pushes for new African agenda [Congressional Black Caucus] G. McKinney. il *Black Enterp* 17:19 My '87
South Africa and its neighbors. R. E. Lambert. map *America* 156:148-52 F 21 '87
Southern Africa: American hopes for the future [address, December 4, 1986] G. P. Shultz. *Dep State Bull* 87:36-40 F '87
Struggle for Southern Africa. R. G. Mugabe. *Foreign Aff* 66:311-27 Wint '87/'88
The U.S. and Southern Africa: a current appraisal [address, June 15, 1987] M. H. Armacost. *Dep State Bull* 87:47-50 Ag '87
U.S. policy toward Southern Africa [address, December 1, 1986] C. A. Crocker. *Vital Speeches Day* 53:197-9 Ja 15 '87
United States policy in Southern Africa. P. H. Baker. bibl f *Curr Hist* 86:193-6+ My '87

Soviet Union
See also
Daniloff-Zakharov espionage case, 1986
Disarmament
Korean Air Lines Flight 007 disaster, 1983
Reagan-Gorbachev summit conference, 1986
Reagan-Gorbachev summit conference, 1987
Shultz, George Pratt, 1920——Visits to the Soviet Union, 1987
Soviet Union—Diplomatic and consular service—United States
Strategic Arms Limitation Talks
Strategic Arms Reduction Talks
United States—Diplomatic and consular service—Soviet Union
Advancing U.S.-Soviet relations: the challenge of arms control [address, September 9, 1987] E. L. Rowny. *Dep State Bull* 87:24-5 N '87
Advice from the third man [R. Nixon's mediation between R. Reagan and M. Gorbachev] S. Talbott. il pors *Time* 130:18 N 30 '87
America's chance. C. W. Maynes. *Foreign Policy* 68:88-99 Fall '87
The beginning of the big thaw? B. Javetski and D. Griffiths. il *Bus Week* p32-3 O 5 '87
The broader picture. B. Crozier. *Natl Rev* 39:28+ N 6 '87
Containment then and now. G. F. Kennan. *Foreign Aff* 65:885-90 Spr '87
Countering Gorbachev [*glasnost* campaign] M. Whitaker. il por *Newsweek* 109:32-3 F 23 '87
The current state of Soviet-American relations [address, April 10, 1987] R. Reagan. *Dep State Bull* 87:10-12 Je '87
Détente, 1987 style. J. Fromm. il *U S News World Rep* 103:35-6 O 5 '87
Faltering America, or Russia? B. Crozier. *Natl Rev* 39:22 D 31 '87
A forward strategy for peace and freedom [address, August 26, 1987] R. Reagan. *Dep State Bull* 87:1-3 O '87
Glasnost [address, March 11, 1987] V. Bukovsky. *Vital Speeches Day* 53:596-600 Jl 15 '87
Glasnost and us. *Nation* 244:785-6 Je 13 '87
Gorbachev: a new foreign policy? D. K. Simes. bibl f *Foreign Aff* 65 Sp Issue:477-500 ['87]
Gorbachev and 'Iragua'. B. Crozier. *Natl Rev* 39:28 F 13 '87
Gorbachev's bottom line. P. G. Peterson. bibl f il *N Y Rev Books* 34:29-33 Je 25 '87
How the cold war might end. J. L. Gaddis. il *Atlantic* 260:88-92+ N '87
Human rights and Soviet-American relations [address, October 31, 1986] G. P. Shultz. *Dep State Bull* 86:26-9 D '86
International views of the superpowers [cover story; special section; with editorial comment by Len Ackland] il *Bull At Sci* 43:2, 28-47 Mr '87
Is the real aim the status quo? G. A. Arbatov. il *World Press Rev* 34:14-15 N '87
Kissinger: how to deal with Gorbachev. H. Kissinger. il pors *Newsweek* 109:39-40+ Mr 2 '87
The latest myths about the Soviet Union [S. Bialer's The Soviet paradox] N. Eberstadt. *Commentary* 83:17-27 My '87
A mellower Moscow. R. Watson. il *Newsweek* 110:42-4 S 21 '87
Moscow's rubber Marx. R. V. Daniels. il *New Leader* 70:5-7 D 28 '87
Reagan's de facto détente. D. Schorr. il *New Leader* 70:3-4 S 21 '87
Reagan's rosy talk [relations following the Washington summit] L. Howard. il *Newsweek* 110:5 D 28 '87
The red queen. L. H. Lapham. *Harpers* 275:10-12 Jl '87
Removing Gorbachev's edge. M. Svec. il *Foreign Policy* 69:148-65 Wint '87/'88
Secretary's interview on "Meet the press" [interview with G. P. Shultz; transcript of program, October 19, 1986] *Dep State Bull* 86:29-32 D '86
Secretary's news conference in Vienna [November 6, 1986] G. P. Shultz. *Dep State Bull* 87:51-4 Ja '87
Should the West help Gorbachev? M. B. Zuckerman. il *U S News World Rep* 103:57-8 O 19 '87
Soviet foreign minister visits Washington [agreement on establishing Nuclear Risk Reduction Centers] R. Reagan; E. Shevardnadze; G. P. Shultz. il *Dep State Bull* 87:34-40 N '87
The Soviet threat: Western schizophrenia. E. V. Rostow. *Current* 295:25-9 S '87
Sovieticus. S. F. Cohen. *Nation* 244:789 Je 13 '87

United States—Foreign relations—Soviet Union—*cont.*
Soviets will pay U.S. for risk center equipment. P. Mann. *Aviat Week Space Technol* 127:31 S 21 '87
Still the 'Evil Empire'? M. Binyon. il *World Press Rev* 34:15 Ap '87
A streak of sanity. K. Kolenda. il *Humanist* 47:38-9 N/D '87
Stretching the syllogism. W. F. Buckley. *Natl Rev* 39:63 Mr 13 '87
Students who focus debate on U.S.-Soviet relations. il *Sch Update* 120:16-17 N 20 '87
A study in contrast: Central America & the Persian Gulf [competing Soviet and U.S. interests] J. B. Hehir. il *Commonweal* 114:439 Ag 14 '87
Superpowers in sync. M. Mandelbaum. il *U S News World Rep* 103:22-5 D 21 '87
There are two fundamental questions. M. S. Forbes, Jr. il *Forbes* 140:25 N 30 '87
Travelers to a changing land [delegation from the Council on Foreign Relations] J. Greenwald. il *Time* 129:34-5 F 16 '87
The U.S.-Soviet bilateral relationship [address, February 25, 1987] M. R. Parris. *Dep State Bull* 87:45-8 My '87
The U.S.-Soviet conflict: concert through decompression. G. Liska. *Current* 289:32-40 Ja '87
U.S.-Soviet move toward risk reduction. J. Borawski. bibl f *Bull At Sci* 43:16-18 Jl/Ag '87
U.S.-Soviet relations [address, March 5, 1987] J. C. Whitehead. *Dep State Bull* 87:43-5 My '87
U.S.-Soviet relations: coping with conflicts in the third world [address, September 26, 1986] M. H. Armacost. *Dep State Bull* 86:57-61 D '86
U.S.-Soviet relations: testing Gorbachev's "new thinking" [address, July 1, 1987] M. H. Armacost. *Dep State Bull* 87:36-41 S '87
U.S., Soviet Union to establish Nuclear Risk Reduction Centers [White House statement, May 5, 1987] *Dep State Bull* 87:21-2 Jl '87
United States-Soviet relations and arms control. L. T. Caldwell. bibl f *Curr Hist* 86:305-8+ O '87
Voice of the Evil Empire [Radio Moscow can now be heard on AM radios throughout southern Florida] B. R. Johnson. *Natl Rev* 39:41 Ag 14 '87
Wedded by hate. I. F. Stone. *Nation* 244:492-3 Ap 18 '87
What Yevgeny knew [Y. Yevtushenko's claim that the CIA helped the Soviets muzzle the writers A. Sinyavsky and I. Daniel] D. Jameson. *New Repub* 196:39-41 Je 22 '87
When to call off the cold war. C. Krauthammer. *New Repub* 197:18-21 N 16 '87
Where interests converge [U.S.-Soviet interest in ending Iranian-Iraqi War] M. J. Gart. il *Time* 130:14 O 19 '87
Where is linkage? W. F. Buckley. *Natl Rev* 39:59 Ag 28 '87
Will the cold war fade away? W. Isaacson. il *Time* 130:40-2+ Jl 27 '87
Soviet Union—History
See also
Cuban Missile Crisis, 1962
Yalta Conference (1945)
Another "low dishonest decade" on the left. P. Collier and D. Horowitz. *Commentary* 83:17-24 Ja '87
Containment: 40 years later [special section] bibl f *Foreign Aff* 65:827-90 Spr '87
The dangers of Détente II. R. N. Perle. il *U S News World Rep* 103:37-8 N 23 '87
The Dellums record [discussion of January 1987 article, Another "low dishonest decade" on the left] D. Horowitz and P. Collier. *Commentary* 84:2-3+ Jl '87
Four decades of irrationality: U.S.-Soviet relations [cover story] M. D. Shulman. il *Bull At Sci* 43:15-25 N '87
When in Moscow . . . [American presidents and officials in Moscow] H. Sidey. il *Time* 129:24 Ap 20 '87
Sudan
A view from Khartoum. A. M. Lesch. bibl f map *Foreign Aff* 65:807-26 Spr '87
Sweden
See also
Carlsson, Ingvar, 1934-—Visit to the United States, 1987
Switzerland
See also
United States—Diplomatic and consular service—Switzerland

Syria
No help for Glass [Syria declines to use its power in Lebanon to free American C. Glass] *Newsweek* 110:32 Jl 6 '87
Opening the road to Damascus. H. G. Chua-Eoan. il por *Time* 130:46 Jl 20 '87
Syria: forgive and forget? [role in release of hostage C. Glass] B. Hewitt. il por *Newsweek* 110:31 Ag 31 '87
U.S. takes measures against Syria [White House statement, November 14, 1986] *Dep State Bull* 87:79 Ja '87
Vietnam
Missing [Vietnamese War missing in action; cover story] M. C. Hickey and others. il *Life* 10:110-14+ N '87
Resolving the POW/MIA issue [address, July 18, 1987] G. P. Shultz. *Dep State Bull* 87:18-19 S '87
U.S. policy toward Vietnam [statement, September 30, 1987] D. F. Lambertson. il *Dep State Bull* 87:32-3 N '87

Vietnam—History
See also
Vietnamese War, 1957-1975—American participation
Western Europe
See also
North Atlantic Treaty Organization
Reagan, Ronald, 1911-—Visit to Western Europe, 1987
Atlanticism without NATO. C. Layne. bibl f *Foreign Policy* 67:22-45 Summ '87
Europe should begin to assert itself. H. Schmidt. il *World Press Rev* 34:21-3 F '87
The Europeans and the Americans. *America* 156:226-7 Mr 21 '87
Nuclear cooperation with EURATOM [letter to Congress, February 28, 1986] R. Reagan. *Dep State Bull* 87:77 Je '87
Of cookies, convoys and Cassandra [address, January 10, 1987] U. Nordio. *Vital Speeches Day* 53:439-41 My 1 '87
VOA-Europe: message radio. N. Martin. *Nation* 244:848-52 Je 20 '87
Zaire
See also
Mobutu Sese Seko, 1930-—Visit to the United States, 1986
Zambia
See also
Kaunda, Kenneth D. (Kenneth David), 1924-—Visit to the United States, 1987
Government
See United States—Politics and government
Government publications
See Government publications
Historic houses, sites, etc.
See Historic houses, sites, etc.
History
See also
Frontier and pioneer life
Slavery
United States—Economic history
United States—Foreign relations—History
United States—Social history
United States. Declaration of Independence
Put yourself to the test [quiz] K. Levine. il *Read Dig* 130:145-6+ Je '87
The sampler: a selection of previews, reviews, sundries, and suggestions. See issues of Americana
The time machine. See issues of American Heritage
Colonial period, ca. 1600-1775
See also
Puritans and puritanism
Another look at colonial religion [P. Bonomi's Under the cope of heaven] M. E. Marty. *Christ Century* 104:314-15 Ap 1 '87
French and Indian War, 1755-1763
The French and Indian War in Pittsburgh: a memoir. A. Dillard. il por *Am Herit* 38:49-53 Jl/Ag '87
Revolution, 1775-1783
See also
American loyalists
Classicism and the American Revolution. S. Andrews. bibl f il *Hist Today* 37:37-42 Ja '87
Editorial. W. Garrett. *Antiques* 132:775 O '87
The plot to kill Washington. B. C. Fenwick. il por *Am Hist Illus* 21:8-12 F '87
Revolution, 1775-1783—Campaigns and battles
See also
Québec (Québec)—History—Siege, 1775-1776
Princeton, Battle of, 1777
Saratoga National Historical Park (N.Y.)
Trenton, Battle of, 1776

United States—History—*cont.*
Revolution, 1775-1783—Causes
See also
Boston Tea Party, 1773
Revolution, 1775-1783—French participation
An American's attempt to rescue Lafayette [rescue attempt by F. Huger; cover story] A. L. Levin. il por *Am Hist Illus* 22:16-20+ O '87
Confederation, 1783-1789
See also
United States. Constitutional Convention (1787)
Designing a ship of state [special section] il *Life* 10:19-24+ Fall '87
A troubled league. il *Am Hist Illus* 22:18-23 Summ '87
1801-1809
See also
Lewis and Clark Expedition
War of 1812—Naval operations
See also
Niagara (Ship)
"The most remarkable series of naval tactics and maneuvers ever known". E. S. Maclay. il *Am Hist Illus* 22:16-17 N '87
"Not a look of fear was seen" [USS Constitution vs. HMS Guerrière; cover story] J. Seiken. il *Am Hist Illus* 22:12-15+ N '87
Civil War, 1861-1865
See also
Confederate States of America
Civil War, 1861-1865—Art and the war
Lost cause art [prints the North published for the South; Confederate image exhibit] M. E. Neely, Jr. and others. il *Americana* 15:59-62 Jl/Ag '87
Civil War, 1861-1865—Blacks
Family and freedom: black families in the American Civil War. I. Berlin and others. bibl f il *Hist Today* 37:8-15 Ja '87
Civil War, 1861-1865—Campaigns and battles
See also
Appomattox Campaign, 1865
Cedar Mountain, Battle of, 1862
Gettysburg, Battle of, 1863
Gettysburg National Military Park (Pa.)
1862 [Shiloh] K. Ide. il *Am Herit* 38:109-10 Ap '87
Blue and Gray Virginia: commemorating battles of a nation divided. C. B. Hayes. il map *Travel Holiday* 167:52-5+ Je '87
How men feel in battle. S. H. M. Byers. il *Am Hist Illus* 22:10-17 Ap '87
Civil War, 1861-1865—Collectibles
GAR tumbler: Gen. George H. Thomas [Grand Army of the Republic] M. Wollett and B. Wollett. il *Antiques Collect Hobbies* 92:53 Mr '87
Civil War, 1861-1865—Fiction
From Nixon to Lincoln [W. Safire] L. Weymouth. il pors *N Y* 20:42-7 Ag 31 '87
Lincoln: fiction & fact [interview with W. Safire] A. M. Schlesinger. il pors *Am Herit* 38:84-9 D '87
A modern vote for Abraham Lincoln [interview with W. Safire] A. P. Sanoff. il por *U S News World Rep* 103:57 Ag 24 '87
Safire on Lincoln and 'Freedom'. J. Kroll. il pors *Newsweek* 110:56-7 Ag 31 '87
Telling how it was [S. Foote's The Civil War and T. Morrison's Beloved] G. C. Ward. il *Am Herit* 38:14+ D '87
William Safire talks about 'Freedom,' his new novel. T. Todd. por *Publ Wkly* 231:49-50 My 29 '87
Civil War, 1861-1865—Literature and the war
The Civil War and American destiny. T. J. Fleming. il *Natl Rev* 39:48+ N 6 '87
Civil War, 1861-1865—Naval operations
See also
Monitor (Ironclad)
Civil War, 1861-1865—Peace
Meeting at the McLean House. R. G. Wilson. il pors *Am Hist Illus* 22:46-9 S '87
Civil War, 1861-1865—Personal narratives
How men feel in battle. S. H. M. Byers. il *Am Hist Illus* 22:10-17 Ap '87
With Lee at Appomattox [cover story] E. P. Alexander. il pors map *Am Hist Illus* 22:40-5+ S '87
Civil War, 1861-1865—Refugees
See also
Fraternidade Descendencia Americana
Civil War, 1861-1865—Reporters and reporting
Lincoln meets the press [imaginary conference with Lincoln's responses based on actual statements] W. Safire. il *N Y Times Mag* p28-9 Ag 23 '87

The new Sherman letters [cover story] J. H. Ewing. il pors *Am Herit* 38:24-7+ Jl/Ag '87
1901-1909—Fiction
Making McKinley sexy [G. Vidal's Empire] S. Waldman. *Wash Mon* 19:45-6+ S '87
The rise and fall of the American empire. A. P. Sanoff. por *U S News World Rep* 103:62 Jl 13 '87
1933-1945
See also
New Deal, 1933-1939
1945-1953
Tommy the Cork: the secret world of Washington's first modern lobbyist [T. Corcoran] A. J. Lichtman. il por *Wash Mon* 19:41-9 F '87
Korean War, 1950-1953
See Korean War, 1950-1953—American participation
Bibliography
The challenge of children's history: making it vivid, getting it right. P. Maier. il *N Y Times Book Rev* 92:42-3 My 17 '87
History bookshelf. See issues of American History Illustrated beginning September 1984
National Geographic books on American history. il *Am Hist Illus* 22:6 D '87
Exploring expeditions
See United States—Exploring expeditions
Pictorial works
J.L.G. Ferris. B. J. Mitnick. il por *Am Hist Illus* 21:14-21 F '87
Shaker village views. R. P. Emlen. il *Nat Hist* 96:48-57 S '87
Study and teaching
101 more things every college graduate should know about American history. J. A. Garraty. il *Am Herit* 38:49-53+ D '87
American history is falling down. B. A. Weisberger. il *Am Herit* 38:26-32 F/Mr '87
How do you compare? [quiz] D. O. Relin. il *Sch Update* 120:5+ N 6 '87
The (non) teaching of American history: U.S. history is falling down. B. A. Weisberger. *Current* 293:20-7 Je '87
Teaching history—alive and well [Lincoln Log Cabin project in Illinois] H. Malehorn. il *Phi Delta Kappan* 69:166-8 O '87
Textbooks
Maxine Waters blocks controversial text in California legislature [racist charges levelled against The making of America] *Jet* 72:5 Ap 6 '87
Not-so-good books [United States history texts slight the role of religion] J. L. Pasley. *New Repub* 196:20-2 Ap 27 '87
Racism charge by Brown prompts Calif. gov. to probe new history text. *Jet* 71:28 Mr 23 '87
Textbooks ignore religion in American history. *Educ Dig* 52:46-7 Mr '87
Why censor religion? Faiths and the textbooks. B. Vobejda. *Current* 296:30-2 O '87
A word from the right on rights [controversial textbook The making of America] A. T. Podesta. il por *Progressive* 51:13-14 Jl '87
History, Military
How the U.S. met five major challenges. C. McHugh. il *Sch Update* 119:11-13 F 23 '87
History, Naval
See also
United States—History—War of 1812—Naval operations
Industrial policy
See Industry and state
Industries
See also
United States—Commerce
39th annual report on American industry [special issue] il *Forbes* 139:61-78+ Ja 12 '87
America's leanest and meanest [cover story] G. D. Wallace. il *Bus Week* p78-82+ O 5 '87
The basics come back. il *Fortune* 116:8 Ag 31 '87
The boom in service industries will not solve U.S. trade problems [report from the Office of Technology Assessment] E. Marshall. *Science* 237:243 Jl 17 '87
Business outlook '87 [special issue] il *Nations Bus* 75:16-17+ Ja '87
Can America compete? [growth crisis; cover story; special section] il *Bus Week* p44-9+ Ap 20 '87
Can American industry make it? G. de Jonquieres and A. Kaletsky. il *World Press Rev* 34:22-6 Jl '87
Can anyone compete? [Business week's cover story] *Natl Rev* 39:18-19 My 8 '87

United States—Industries—*cont.*

Can we make U.S. industry competitive again? H. A. Poling. il *USA Today (Periodical)* 116:22-4 N '87

The challenge of global competition [address, September 17, 1987] G. H. Conrades. *Vital Speeches Day* 54:125-8 D 1 '87

The challenge to U.S. competitiveness. R. M. White. *Science* 236:1041 My 29 '87

Commerce sees the future; says industry practices must change. M. Crawford. *Science* 237:20 Jl 3 '87

Competitiveness [address, July 21, 1987] F. G. Steingraber. *Vital Speeches Day* 53:758-62 O 1 '87

The competitiveness challenge [address, August 21, 1987] J. J. Melone. *Vital Speeches Day* 54:100-4 D 1 '87

Competitiveness: getting it back. S. Nasar. il *Fortune* 115:217-18+ Ap 27 '87

Endgame strategy [interview with K. R. Harrigan] J. Willoughby. il por *Forbes* 140:181-2 Jl 13 '87

How to keep mature industries innovative [cover story] C. F. Sabel and others. il *Technol Rev* 90:26-35 Ap '87

In this corner, Uncle Sam [lower dollar helps American industry] D. Pauly. il *Newsweek* 110:61-2 D 7 '87

Industry outlook [special section] il *Bus Week* p65-72+ Ja 12 '87

The last iceman [companies doing well in declining industries] J. Willoughby. il *Forbes* 140:183+ Jl 13 '87

Making American industry competitive again [address, April 16, 1987] J. Weaver. *Vital Speeches Day* 53:560-2 Jl 1 '87

The myth of a post-industrial economy. S. S. Cohen and J. Zysman. il *Technol Rev* 90:54-60+ F/Mr '87

The nonsense of a "post-industrial society" [address, January 15, 1987] R. A. Lutz. *Vital Speeches Day* 53:330-3 Mr 15 '87

Old-line industry shapes up. T. Moore. il *Fortune* 115:22-6+ Ap 27 '87

The pedagogy of competition. M. L. Weidenbaum. *Society* 25:46-54 N/D '87

Promising industries for investors. B. Dumaine. il *Fortune* 116 Sp Issue:136-8+ Fall '87

The protean corporation [cover story] S. Lee and C. Brown. il *Forbes* 140:76-9 Ag 24 '87

Revival in the Rust Belt. J. Edgerton. il *Money* 16:77-8+ Jl '87

The smokestacks steam again. H. J. Steinbreder. il *Fortune* 116:47-8 D 21 '87

The smokestacks won't tumble. B. Saporito. il *Fortune* 115:30-2 F 2 '87

Special report on corporate restructuring: rebuilding to survive. il *Time* 129:44-8 F 16 '87

Taking on the world [special section] il *Time* 130:46-50+ O 19 '87

Technology and global industry. P. H. Abelson. *Science* 236:1609 Je 26 '87

Unbinding Gulliver [address, April 9, 1987] R. A. Voell. *Vital Speeches Day* 53:661-5 Ag 15 '87

A weakness in process technology. L. C. Thurow. bibl f *Science* 238:1659-63 D 18 '87

What the forecast means for 16 industries. B. Dumaine. il *Fortune* 116:46-8 Jl 20 '87

What the forecast means for 16 industries. J. Nielsen and F. Rice. il *Fortune* 115:76+ Ja 19 '87

Will the U.S. stay number one? [with interview with P. Drucker] M. W. Karmin. il *U S News World Rep* 102:18-23 F 2 '87

Intellectual life

1837 [R. W. Emerson's Phi Beta Kappa speech] K. Ide. il por *Am Herit* 38:107-8 Jl/Ag '87

Are student heads full of emptiness? [books by A. Bloom and E. D. Hirsch] E. Bowen. il *Time* 130:56-7 Ag 17 '87

A best-seller's puzzling sizzle [A. Bloom's The closing of the American mind] F. Bruning. por *Macleans* 100:7 Ag 31 '87

Bloom and doom [views of A. Bloom] W. Greider. il *Roll Stone* p39-40 O 8 '87

Campus 1987 [A. Bloom's views on college education; cover story; special section; with editorial comment by Richard Vigilante] *Natl Rev* 39:34-8+ O 9 '87

A cathode ray tube is [cultural literacy; views of E. D. Hirsch] J. Coyne. il *Glamour* 85:118+ Ag '87

Chicago philosophy professor Allan Bloom warns that America's universities are crumbling [interview] S. K. Reed. il por *People Wkly* 28:141-2+ S 14 '87

The civilized barbarian reader. S. Bellow. il *N Y Times Book Rev* 92:1+ Mr 8 '87

The closing of the American mind [views of A. D. Bloom] R. K. Bennett. *Read Dig* 131:81-4 O '87

Conservatism [discussion of October 1986 article, Our conservatism and theirs] B. Berger and P. L. Berger. *Commentary* 83:6-8+ F '87

Cultural 'keep-away'. D. R. Carlin, Jr. *Commonweal* 114:408-9 Jl 17 '87

Cultural literacy: what every American needs to know [condensation] E. D. Hirsch. *Read Dig* 131:79-83 D '87

Down with ignorance, long live ontology. A. Broyard. il *N Y Times Book Rev* 92:12 Jl 26 '87

A dunce cap for America [views of E. D. Hirsch and A. D. Bloom] D. Gates. il pors *Newsweek* 109:72-4 Ap 20 '87

If you can read this, says E.D. Hirsch, you may still be illiterate [interview] J. Cramer. il por *People Wkly* 28:69-71+ Ag 10 '87

The importance of Sidney Hook. H. Kramer. *Commentary* 84:17-24 Ag '87

Letters [discussion of September 19, 1987 article, Radicals in academia] R. Jacoby. *Nation* 245:434 O 24 '87

Literacy at the barricades [E. D. Hirsch's Cultural literacy and H. J. Graff's The legacies of literacy] J. W. Tuttleton. *Commentary* 84:45-8 Jl '87

A nation that has lost its intellectual bearings [interview with A. Bloom] A. P. Sanoff. il por *U S News World Rep* 102:78 My 11 '87

Philosophy & faith [discussion of August 1987 article, The importance of Sidney Hook] H. Kramer. *Commentary* 84:2+ N '87

A pop quiz on cultural literacy [book entitled Cultural literacy: what every American needs to know] L. Solórzano. il *U S News World Rep* 102:15 Ap 13 '87

Radicals in academia [excerpt from The last intellectuals] R. Jacoby. il *Nation* 245:263-4+ S 19 '87

Sex and drugs and Heidegger [views of A. D. Bloom] J. Weisberg. *Wash Mon* 19:49-53 S '87

Stalled thinkers. T. Todorov. *New Repub* 196:26-7 Ap 13 '87

Story behind the bestseller: Allan Bloom's 'The closing of the American mind'. W. Goldstein. il por *Publ Wkly* 232:25-7 Jl 3 '87

Undemocratic vistas [views of A. Bloom] M. C. Nussbaum. bibl f il *N Y Rev Books* 34:20-6 N 5 '87

What Americans should know [cover story] A. P. Sanoff. bibl il *U S News World Rep* 103:86-8+ S 28 '87

Where are all the young brains? [views of R. Jacoby] E. Bowen. il por *Time* 130:70 N 30 '87

Where would Emerson find his scholar now? [adaptation of address, June 1987] A. Kazin. il *Am Herit* 38:93-6 D '87

Writing to sell in the MTV era [A. D. Bloom's The closing of the American mind] A. Smith. il *Esquire* 108:87+ D '87

Labor policy

See also

Labor laws and regulations

United States. Dept. of Labor

United States. National Labor Relations Board

Wage-price policy

Jobilism, or, Is the world really flat? R. B. McKenzie. il *Forbes* 140:68-70 Jl 13 '87

Labor & the limits of the market place. *Commonweal* 114:3-4 Ja 16 '87

Low-paying service work is a "myth" [address, March 5, 1987] W. E. Brock. *Vital Speeches Day* 53:444-6 My 1 '87

Making the case for full employment. M. Hope and J. Young. *Christ Century* 104:715-18 Ag 26-S 2 '87

The state of the workforce [address, October 6, 1987] W. E. Brock. *Vital Speeches Day* 54:37-40 N 1 '87

Languages

See also

English language

Maps

Collectors and collecting

Albert Ruger and the bird's-eye view movement in America, 1866-1891. R. Rayman. il *Antiques Collect Hobbies* 92:74-9 Ag '87

Medical policy

See Medical policy

Merchant marine

See Merchant marine

Military history

See United States—History, Military

Military policy

See also

Military assistance, American

Strategic Defense Initiative

United States—Defenses

United States. Dept. of Defense

United States—Military policy—*cont.*

Ambiguous war: the United States and low-intensity conflict. M. Miller. il *Technol Rev* 90:60-7 Ag/S '87

Blundering into disaster [address, February 17, 1987] R. S. McNamara. *Vital Speeches Day* 53:390-4 Ap 15 '87

Computer combat [technological revolution in conventional warfare; cover story] E. A. Cohen. *New Repub* 196:15-17 Ap 20 '87

The dangers of quick launch. R. N. Lebow. bibl f il *Bull At Sci* 43:36-9 N '87

The empire strikes back [proposed Dept. of the Defense Force] R. C. Kirkwood. *Natl Rev* 39:41 Jl 17 '87

Equitable arms control [secure deterrence; address, February 19, 1987] A. M. Haig. *Vital Speeches Day* 53:387-90 Ap 15 '87

The game of perceptions in arms racing [with discussion] S. Kull. por *Cent Mag* 20:43-57 S/O '87

In the House, an abrasive defender of defense [L. Aspin] D. Griffiths. por *Bus Week* p53 Ag 24 '87

Joint Chiefs chairman counsels long-term strategic view of Soviets [views of W. J. Crowe] il *Aviat Week Space Technol* 126:117+ Je 15 '87

The military underpinnings of diplomacy [address, September 21, 1987] C. W. Weinberger. *Vital Speeches Day* 54:34-7 N 1 '87

Nuclear weapons, arms control, and the future of deterrence [address, November 17, 1986] G. P. Shultz. *Dep State Bull* 87:31-5 Ja '87

Nuke City: wake up, America, to another sunny doomsday in Washington, District of Catastrophe. M. Amis. il *Esquire* 108:97-100+ O '87

Of many things [views of P. M. Kennedy on the decline of America] G. W. Hunt. *America* 157:98 Ag 29-S 5 '87

Off with their heads: how Zbigniew Brzezinski hawked the doctrine of nuclear decapitation. M. Kaku and D. Axelrod. il *Progressive* 51:29-31 Ja '87

Protecting America's interests: defense and foreign aid [special issue] il maps *Sch Update* 119:6-16+ F 23 '87

The (relative) decline of America [cover story] P. M. Kennedy. il *Atlantic* 260:29-34+ Ag '87

Sam Nunn is sticking to his guns. D. Griffiths. il por *Bus Week* p52-3 Ag 24 '87

Thinking strategically [competitive strategies doctrine] P. Mann. *Aviat Week Space Technol* 127:13 Jl 6 '87

The U.S. as world leader: the (relative) decline of America. P. M. Kennedy. il *Current* 298:30-8 D '87

U.S. formulates strategic doctrine for high technology [competitive strategies doctrine] P. Mann. il map *Aviat Week Space Technol* 126:110-11+ Je 15 '87

U.S. nuclear strategy: theory vs. practice. D. A. Rosenberg. bibl f *Bull At Sci* 43:20-6 Mr '87

The uncommon ground of security debate. K. Tsipis. *Bull At Sci* 43:10-11 Jl/Ag '87

Why offense needs defense. C. W. Weinberger. *Foreign Policy* 68:3-18 Fall '87

Monetary policy

See Federal Reserve System (U.S.); Money

Moral conditions

See also

Violence

America as utopia: the city upon a hill. R. A. Nisbet. *Current* 293:4-8 Je '87

Before you lambast this generation [address, October 19, 1987] B. H. Alexander. *Vital Speeches Day* 54:70-2 N 15 '87

Caulking while Rome burns. P. Yancey. il *Christ Today* 31:64 F 20 '87

Decadence American style [responding to R. N. Bellah's Habits of the heart] K. S. Kantzer. il *Christ Today* 31:12-13 Ag 7 '87

Don't believe all the epitaphs. M. Greenfield. il *Newsweek* 110:124 N 16 '87

The follies of 1987 [special section] il *World Press Rev* 34:32-4 Jl '87

Grave new world. M. Jacobson. il *Esquire* 108:65+ S '87

Greed that starts at the top. A. Fotheringham. il *Macleans* 100:52 Mr 2 '87

If moral decay is the question, is a feminist ethic the answer? G. Steinem. il *Ms* 16:57-9+ S '87

In defense of our common culture. W. J. Bennett. il por *USA Today (Periodical)* 115:45-7 Mr '87

Integrity and trust [address, January 21, 1987] P. Dawkins. *Vital Speeches Day* 53:344-7 Mr 15 '87

Love or money. L. H. Lapham. *Harpers* 274:10-11 Je '87

Money and the moral vacuum. B. Amiel. il *Macleans* 100:9 N 9 '87

A nation in decline? B. W. Tuchman. il *N Y Times Mag* p52+ S 20 '87

A nation of liars? [special section] M. McLoughlin. il *U S News World Rep* 102:54-61 F 23 '87

The no-fault confession. M. Greenfield. il *Newsweek* 109:80 Je 15 '87

On the springboard of notoriety [J. Hahn, D. Rice and F. Hall] F. Trippett. il pors *Time* 130:64-5 O 12 '87

Policy based on morality. H. Saltz. il *World Press Rev* 34:14 S '87

Sliding into paganism. T. C. Muck. il *Christ Today* 31:14-15 N 6 '87

What's wrong [hypocrisy, betrayal and greed; cover story; special section] il *Time* 129:14-23+ My 25 '87

Will seat-of-the-pants morality ever wear thin? R. E. Burns. *U S Cathol* 52:2 O '87

The world crisis and American responsibility [address, March 26, 1987] E. W. Lefever. *Vital Speeches Day* 53:518-20 Je 15 '87

Anecdotes, facetiae, satire, etc.

Naughty, naughty. A. P. Weisman. *New Repub* 196:43 F 2 '87

You can have it all! [ads promoting the seven deadly sins] il *Harpers* 275:43-50 N '87

Morale, National

See Morale, National

National parks and reserves

See National parks and reserves

Nationalism

The religious character of American patriotism. F. Edwords. il por *Humanist* 47:20-4+ N/D '87

Photographs and photography

A day in the life of America. J. Augustine. il *Petersens Photogr Mag* 15:4 F '87

A day in the life of America [excerpts] il *Read Dig* 130:26-32 F '87

In search of America. J. Sternfeld. il *N Y Times Mag* p32-5 Mr 15 '87

Lovelorn tracts, minced wilderness [work of J. Sternfeld] R. Lacayo. il *Time* 129:84 Ap 20 '87

Portrait of a golden day [amateur contest sponsored by Popular photography in coordination with the Day in the life of America book project] il *Pop Photogr* 94:36-51 Ja '87

Politics and government

See also

Black suffrage

Blacks—Political activities

Bureaucracy

Business—Political aspects

Campaign issues

Caucuses

Committee on the Constitutional System (U.S.)

Communist Party (U.S.)

Conservatism

Democratic Party (U.S.)

Elections

Federal and state relations

Green Party (U.S.)

Legislation

Liberalism

Lobbyists and lobbying

Political attitudes

Political campaigns

Political candidates

Political forecasting

Populism

Presidential campaigns

Presidential candidates

Presidential primaries

Presidents

Republican Party (U.S.)

Socialism—United States

State governments

Trade unions—Political activities

United States. Congress

Videotapes—Government use

Women—Political activities

And now for Ronald Reagan's finale. R. Darman. il *U S News World Rep* 103:31 D 28 '87-Ja 4 '88

Beltway bandits. D. Corn and J. Morley. See issues of The Nation beginning July 18-25, 1987

Bombshells. F. Barnes. *New Repub* 197:10+ D 14 '87

Brain dead [Reagan administration agenda for 1987] F. Barnes. *New Repub* 196:10-11 Ja 19 '87

The case against glee [R. Reagan's decline] M. Kondracke. *New Repub* 196:16-17 Ja 26 '87

A change in the weather [Reagan era comes to a close; cover story] L. Morrow. il *Time* 129:28-34+ Mr 30 '87

United States—Politics and government—*cont.*
A chat with the commander in chief [interview with R. Reagan] por *U S News World Rep* 103:22-3 S 21 '87
[Column] M. Greenfield. See occasional issues of Newsweek
[Column] G. F. Will. See occasional issues of Newsweek
Crise du jour. *Natl Rev* 39:19-20 My 8 '87
Darkness on the edge of the shining city [B. Springsteen and the end of Reaganism] J. Morley. il *New Repub* 196:20-3 Mr 23 '87
Dead duck [R. Reagan] F. Barnes. *New Repub* 197:16-17 N 9 '87
Edward Kennedy [interview] W. Greider. il por *Roll Stone* p99-100 N 5-D 10 '87
The Ford years [Reagan as compared to G. Ford] F. Barnes. *New Repub* 196:7-9 My 25 '87
Four presidents challenge America [special section] il *Life* 10:24-31 O '87
Fraternalist manifesto [excerpt from address, November 1986] C. Lasch. *Harpers* 274:17-20 Ap '87
From Washington straight. J. McLaughlin. See issues of National Review
George McGovern [interview] W. Greider. il por *Roll Stone* p103-4+ N 5-D 10 '87
'I had a plan . . . to deal from strength' [interview with R. Reagan] D. Frost. il pors *U S News World Rep* 103:31-2 D 7 '87
The last battles [R. Reagan's struggle to reassert leadership] G. J. Church. il por *Time* 129:16-18 Ja 12 '87
Let's get to work, Mr. President. M. B. Zuckerman. il *U S News World Rep* 102:80 F 9 '87
Letter from Washington. E. Drew. *New Yorker* 63:140-6+ My 4 '87
Letter from Washington. E. Drew. *New Yorker* 63:150-4+ N 2 '87
Letter from Washington. Cato. See issues of National Review
Life after death [President Reagan] F. Barnes. *New Repub* 197:12-13 Ag 10-17 '87
National affairs. W. Greider. See issues of Rolling Stone
The national interest. M. Kramer. See issues of New York through March 30, 1987
The new shape of American politics. W. Schneider. il *Atlantic* 259:39-48+ Ja '87
Notebook. See issues of The New Republic
Often, momentum can lead to a bad arms treaty [interview with G. R. Ford] D. Frost. por *U S News World Rep* 103:33 D 7 '87
Peephole on the presidency [excerpt from Behind the scenes] M. K. Deaver. il pors *Life* 10:49-50+ D '87
The presidency. H. Sidey. See issues of Time
Putting the presidency back to work. J. F. Stacks. il por *Time* 130:20 N 23 '87
Reagan: 'an old lion in winter' [presidential leadership vacuum] M. McLoughlin. il por *U S News World Rep* 103:16-18 N 30 '87
Reagan at ground zero. K. T. Walsh. il por *U S News World Rep* 102:20-2 Ja 12 '87
Reagan: what has gone wrong? *Natl Rev* 39:17 S 25 '87
Ronald Reagan. H. Sidey. il pors *People Wkly* 28:28-31 D 28 '87-Ja 4 '88
The Schlesinger thesis [A. M. Schlesinger's The cycles of American history] K. S. Lynn. *Commentary* 83:46-52 Mr '87
TRB from Washington. M. Kinsley. See issues of The New Republic beginning April 25, 1983
Trying to put it all behind him [R. Reagan] G. Borger and K. T. Walsh. il por *U S News World Rep* 103:20-1 Ag 24 '87
Two more years [Reagan presidency] *Nation* 244:3-4 Ja 10 '87
Wake-up call [views of R. Reagan] F. Barnes. *New Repub* 197:10-11 O 26 '87
Washington confidential: an interview with Tip O'Neill. C. Hunter-Gault. por *Vogue* 177:756-7+ S '87
Washington outlook. See issues of Business Week
Washington whispers. See issues of U.S. News & World Report
What Washington should worry about. J. M. Fallows. il *U S News World Rep* 102:37 Ja 12 '87
Anecdotes, facetiae, satire, etc.
My and Ed's peace proposals. V. Geng. *New Yorker* 63:74 S 7 '87

History
See United States—History
Popular culture
The avant-garde: moving into middle America. M. Horn. il *U S News World Rep* 102:68-9 My 18 '87

Chic speak. See issues of Seventeen beginning July 1986 through July 1987
Creeping commercialism [Monroe Friedman's study of brand names used in novels, plays, and song lyrics] P. McCarthy. *Psychol Today* 21:16 Ag '87
Hot [cover story; special issue] il *Roll Stone* p29-31+ My 21 '87
Showing our true colors: trends covered the spectrum—and then some. D. C. Craig. il *Life* 10:104-5+ Ja '87
U.S. culture, worldwide fans. S. Flack. il *Sch Update* 120:37 O 2 '87
Word up! See issues of Seventeen beginning August 1987

Population
See also
Baby boom generation
Baby bust generation
Immigrants
Immigration and emigration
Migration, Internal
Minorities
United States—Census
Public opinion
See Public opinion
Race relations
See also
Church and race relations
Attitudes in black and white [results of Time poll] il *Time* 129:21 F 2 '87
Beyond tolerance to equal rights. J. M. Wall. *Christ Century* 104:395-6 Ap 29 '87
Black leaders in uproar over new surge of racism. il *Jet* 71:6-8 Ja 26 '87
Black psychiatrists tell how racism hurts whites, too. il *Jet* 72:16-17 Jl 20 '87
A cause for alarm. *Commonweal* 114:5-6 Ja 16 '87
A conversation with . . . Dr. Frances Cress Welsing about her theory of skin color and oppression. K. J. Halliburton. pors *Essence* 18:32 My '87
Dexter King says 'tone' promotes racist actions. por *Jet* 72:33 Je 1 '87
Do conservatives discriminate against blacks? *Society* 25:4+ N/D '87
The empty shoes of a native son [J. Baldwin] F. Bruning. por *Macleans* 100:13 D 21 '87
Growing up with privilege and prejudice [cover story] K. K. Russell. il pors *N Y Times Mag* p22-8 Je 14 '87
Is an ugly past returning to haunt America? T. Gest. il *U S News World Rep* 102:12 F 2 '87
Is Jesse the great white hope? [cover story] A. Kopkind. il *Nation* 245:773+ D 26 '87-Ja 2 '88
Isiah & Bernhard. J. Morley. *Nation* 245:4-5 Jl 4-11 '87
'It's not easy being green' [difficulties of being biracial] L. Mahdesian. por *U S News World Rep* 103:8 N 23 '87
The King to come [adaptation of address, January 19, 1987] B. Rustin. *New Repub* 196:19-21 Mr 9 '87
Majority of blacks have been insulted due to race [telephone poll] *Jet* 71:31 F 23 '87
Mean streets in Howard Beach [overt racism once again a national problem] T. E. Johnson. il *Newsweek* 109:24-5 Ja 5 '87
My gloves are off, sisters [women's movement and racism] M. A. Gillespie. por *Ms* 15:19-20 Ap '87
New alarm over rising racial violence. B. Levin. il *Macleans* 100:56-7 F 2 '87
A new racism. *Nation* 244:1 Ja 10 '87
Prejudice against Asians: anxiety and acceptance. K. Zinsmeister. *Current* 297:37-40 N '87
Racism, depression peril black America, Jacob says [J. E. Jacob of National Urban League] por *Jet* 71:4 F 2 '87
Racism on the rise. O. Friedrich. il *Time* 129:18-21 F 2 '87
The 'racism' racket. *Natl Rev* 39:18-19 Mr 13 '87
Reagan flays racism during King observance. il por *Jet* 71:6 F 2 '87
The resegregation of America. J. Sleeper. il *Commonweal* 114:619-23 N 6 '87
Rethinking race. *New Repub* 196:7-10 F 9 '87
A society that is just and fair [address, July 19, 1987] J. E. Jacob. *Vital Speeches Day* 53:733-6 S 15 '87
Stemming the tide of racial violence. E. G. Graves. il *Black Enterp* 17:9 Ap '87
To make a nation whole [14th Amendment and racial reform] D. A. Bell. il *N Y Times Mag* p42-4+ S 13 '87

United States—Race relations—*cont.*

The unending nightmare of racism. L. Wainwright. il *Life* 10:13 F '87

V.P. Bush tells Dillard grads racism's 'ugly head' always will be chopped off. il pors *Jet* 72:29 Je 8 '87

What's behind the resurgence of racism in America? W. Leavy. il *Ebony* 42:132-3+ Ap '87

Regulatory agencies

See Regulatory agencies

Religious institutions and affairs

See also

African Methodist Episcopal Church

Amish

Assemblies of God

Baptists—United States

Catholic Church—United States

Christian Church (Disciples of Christ)

Church and state

Church of Christ, Scientist

Church Universal and Triumphant

Episcopal Church—United States

Evangelical Orthodox Church

Evangelicalism

Hinduism—United States

Jehovah's Witnesses

John Paul II, Pope, 1920——Visit to the United States, 1987

Lutheran Church—United States

Mennonites

Missions—United States

Mormons and Mormonism

Orthodox Eastern Church—United States

Presbyterian Church—United States

Protestant churches—United States

Puritans and puritanism

Reformed Church in America

Shakers

Unification Church

Unitarian Universalist Association

United Church of Christ

United Methodist Church

Universal Fellowship of Metropolitan Community Churches

Religious ignorance. D. R. Carlin, Jr. *Commonweal* 114:7-8 Ja 16 '87

Secular and religious America. E. C. Ladd. *Society* 24:63-8 Mr/Ap '87

History

Another look at colonial religion [P. Bonomi's Under the cope of heaven] M. E. Marty. *Christ Century* 104:314-15 Ap 1 '87

The Constitution and the congregation: time to celebrate. M. E. Marty. il *Christ Century* 104:523-5 Je 3-10 '87

The Constitution at 200 [cover story; special section] il *Christ Today* 31:18-30 Jl 10 '87

Irony of ironies: evaluating the moderns [M. E. Marty's Modern American religion] G. M. Marsden. *Christ Century* 104:359-61 Ap 15 '87

Neutrality and religious freedom [Northwest Ordinance of 1787] M. E. Marty. *Christ Century* 104:580-1 Jl 1-8 '87

We, the theologians [views of T. Jefferson and J. Madison] L. W. Gibbs. pors *Christ Today* 31:29-31 D 11 '87

Science policy

See Science and state

Secretaries of State

See Secretaries of State (U.S.)

Social conditions

See also

Blacks

Child welfare

Children

Crime and criminals

Divorce

Family

Homeless

Labor

Morale, National

Poor

Recreation

Social change

Social forecasting

United States—Moral conditions

Violence

Youth

The death of social conscience. B. G. Harrison. *Mademoiselle* 93:124 D '87

The Disposable Society. J. S. Lang. il *U S News World Rep* 102:68 Je 1 '87

What's next? G. F. Kreyche. *USA Today (Periodical)* 115:98 Mr '87

History

See United States—Social history

Social history

See also

Business depression, 1929-1939

Slavery

Women—History

High hats & coronets: nothing succeeds like excess. J. Etra. il *Harpers Bazaar* 121:70+ D '87

Social life and customs

See also

Family reunions

Social change

Suburban life

Thanksgiving Day

Corporate etiquette. L. H. Lapham. *Harpers* 275:7-8 Ag '87

You call this a party? [L. Baldrige's Complete guide to a great social life] J. Adler. il por *Newsweek* 110:90 O 5 '87

Colonial period, ca. 1600-1775

See also

Old Sturbridge Village

Williamsburg (Va.)

Anecdotes, facetiae, satire, etc.

Life in these United States. See issues of Reader's Digest

Social policy

See also

Aged

Child welfare

Civil rights

Day care—Federal aid

Economic assistance, Domestic

Family

Medical policy

Poor

Public welfare

United States—Urban policy

Women

Youth

America's underclass: what can be done? M. Magnet. *Current* 295:17-24 S '87

America's underclass: what to do? M. Magnet. il *Fortune* 115:130-4+ My 11 '87

Blacks and poverty. J. E. Jacob. *Cent Mag* 20:55-6 Ja/F '87

Carterized [Reagan administration domestic legislative proposals floundering in wake of Iran arms scandal] F. Barnes. *New Repub* 196:14-15 Mr 16 '87

Inequality in America: where do we stand? G. T. Burtless. il *Current* 297:4-10 N '87

Making business pay for welfare [mandated benefits bills] B. Cohn and J. Schwartz. il por *Newsweek* 109:49 Je 15 '87

Malthus then and now. J. L. Hess. il *Nation* 244:496-500 Ap 18 '87

The not-so-great society. *America* 156:165 F 28 '87

Put up the price of beans [mandated benefits policy] J. Novack and H. Banks. il *Forbes* 139:32-5 Ap 6 '87

Re-examining America's underclass [views of W. J. Wilson] J. E. White. il por *Time* 129:28 My 11 '87

Reaganomics with a human face [neoliberalism; excerpt from Visions and nightmares] R. Lekachman. *Harpers* 274:24+ Mr '87

Should business be forced to help bring up baby? [battle over 'mandated benefits'] M. E. Recio. il *Bus Week* p39-40 Ap 6 '87

We need to rethink the "unthinkable". R. D. Lamm. il *USA Today (Periodical)* 116:20-1 S '87

Where's that Great Society? B. Buchanan. por *U S News World Rep* 102:6 F 23 '87

Will the underclass always be with us? R. P. Nathan. il *Society* 24:57-62 Mr/Ap '87

Statistics

See also

Economic indicators

Economic statistics

United States—Census

Every day in America . . . [condensed from In one day] T. Parker. il *Read Dig* 131:85 S '87

Playing the numbers game [Statistical abstract of the United States] R. J. Samuelson. il *Newsweek* 109:49 Je 1 '87

Quality [excerpts from address, March 30, 1987] J. L. Norwood. *Mon Labor Rev* 110:2 Ap '87

Study and teaching

See American studies; United States—History—Study and teaching

United States—*cont.*

Territories and possessions
See also
Marshall Islands
Micronesia (Federated States)
Pacific Islands (Trust territory)
Palau
Developing islands. il *Futurist* 21:51-2 Jl/Ag '87

Trade policy
See United States—Commercial policy

Treaties
See also
United States—Commercial treaties and agreements
Amend the Constitution's treaty clause [outmoded requirement that treaties be ratified by a two-thirds vote of the Senate] B. S. Loeb. bibl f il *Bull At Sci* 43:38-41 O '87
Promises, promises [international treaties and Christian morality] T. C. Muck. il *Christ Today* 31:18-19 Ja 16 '87
Treaties: current actions. See issues of Department of State Bulletin

Netherlands Antilles
A Eurobond bombshell [U.S. ends tax treaty] R. Brady and V. English. *Bus Week* p100 Jl 13 '87
The sun isn't setting on this tax haven. G. DeGeorge. il *Bus Week* p57-8 Ag 31 '87
A tempest hits the Treasury [cancels Antilles tax treaty] D. Zigas and V. English. il *Bus Week* p124 Jl 20 '87

Panama
See also
Panama Canal Treaties (1977)

Soviet Union
See also
Strategic Arms Limitation Talks

Taiwan
Does the U.S. president have the right to cancel a treaty? [mutual defense treaty with Taiwan] T. Fung. il *Sch Update* 120:40 S 18 '87

Urban policy
See also
United States. Dept. of Housing and Urban Development
Planning, American style. G. Sternlieb. *Society* 25:21-3 N/D '87
Rescuing the urban poor. T. H. Kean. il *USA Today (Periodical)* 116:72-5 N '87

Vital statistics
See also
Mortality
United States—Census

United States. Administration on Aging
Commissioner's corner. C. F. Fisk. il *Aging* no355:inside cover '87
Life planning for old age, focus of AoA projects. J. H. Wehling. *Aging* no356:37-8 '87
Seniors meet child care and youth needs in AoA, foundation projects. C. Schreter. il *Aging* no356:35-7 '87

United States. Agency for International Development
Abortion more precious than $20 mil. grant: Wattleton [Planned Parenthood grant] *Jet* 72:36 My 11 '87
Diplomat wins $150,000 for job discrimination [C. A. Sadler] *Jet* 72:16 Jl 6 '87
Food aid to Lebanon [State Dept. statement, July 10, 1987] *Dep State Bull* 87:47 S '87
In the shadow of Uncle Sam [effect on Bangladesh of USAID cutoff of funds to Family Planning International Assistance] A. Boggan. il *Ms* 16:69 N '87
Mike Benge and his marvelous tree [leucaena used to halt deforestation] J. G. Hubbell. il por *Read Dig* 131:103-7 Ag '87
Secretary praises AID and comments on Iran [remarks, November 25, 1986] G. P. Shultz. *Dep State Bull* 87:23 Ja '87
U.S. antiabortion policy may increase abortions. C. Holden. *Science* 238:1222 N 27 '87
U.S. development strategy for Sub-Saharan Africa [statement, February 26, 1987] M. P. McPherson. *Dep State Bull* 87:56-8 My '87
U.S. food aid program for Lebanon [State Dept. statement, April 28, 1987] il *Dep State Bull* 87:61 Jl '87
Wattleton raps Reagan's cut of overseas abortion funds. por *Jet* 72:9 Ag 17 '87
Why foreign aid? il *Dep State Bull* 87:1-22 Ja '87

United States. Agricultural Stabilization and Conservation Service
Grain pools help beat red tape. G. Johnston. *Success Farm* 85:5 Ag '87

Proposed changes threaten big farms [$50,000 payment rules] D. Allen and P. Smith. il *Success Farm* 85:42-4 Ag '87

United States. Air Force
Forecast 2 programs may revolutionize USAF command, control technology. K. J. Stein. il *Aviat Week Space Technol* 126:68-9+ Mr 23 '87
France, USAF discuss joint efforts on Project Forecast 2 technologies. *Aviat Week Space Technol* 126:78-9 Je 1 '87
Race into space: the Pentagon overtakes NASA by a missile length [expendable launcher] S. Budiansky. il *U S News World Rep* 103:10 Ag 17 '87

Appropriations and expenditures
Air Force altering budget priorities for Project Forecast 2. J. D. Morrocco. il *Aviat Week Space Technol* 126:22-3 Ap 13 '87
Air Force seeks funding for new STOL transports. *Aviat Week Space Technol* 126:24 Ja 19 '87
Battle brews over follow-on close air support aircraft [successor to A-10 Thunderbolt] *Aviat Week Space Technol* 126:19 F 2 '87
Black holes in the budget [line item requests for research and development programs that are classified] D. C. Morrison. il *Harpers* 274:50-1 Ja '87
Congress approves additional ALS funds [advanced launch system] *Aviat Week Space Technol* 127:21 Jl 13 '87
Defense Dept. unveils $1.2-billion ASAT restructuring plan. *Aviat Week Space Technol* 126:19-21 Mr 16 '87
USAF revises goal of acquiring 40 fighter wings by early 1990s. *Aviat Week Space Technol* 126:24-5 Ja 12 '87
USAF seeks initial funding for new multiengine trainer. P. Proctor. il *Aviat Week Space Technol* 127:142+ O 12 '87

Blacks
Air Force's Randolph is tabbed for 4-star general. por *Jet* 72:22 My 11 '87
Bernard P. Randolph: the armed forces' only black four-star general. D. M. Cheers. il pors *Ebony* 43:154+ N '87
Randolph is the top black U.S. gen.; gets 4th star [B. P. Randolph] il por *Jet* 72:6 Ag 17 '87

Education
See also
Air Force Survival School (U.S.)
United States Air Force Academy

Forces in Germany (West)
First F110-powered F-16Cs join wing at Ramstein Air Base. il *Aviat Week Space Technol* 126:212-13 Je 15 '87

Forces in Spain
The message from Madrid [U.S. asked to remove F-16s from Torrejón Air Base] H. Anderson. il *Newsweek* 110:83 N 16 '87
Washington could get burned by putting the heat on Madrid. J. Patterson and others. il *Bus Week* p58 N 23 '87
When the stepping stones of world power are rocky bases [Spain-U.S. dispute over Torrejón Air Base] J. Wallace. il *U S News World Rep* 103:30-1 N 23 '87

Forces in the Philippines
The day of the sparrow [U.S. airmen murdered near Clark Air Base] H. Anderson. il *Newsweek* 110:54 N 9 '87

Maneuvers
See Military maneuvers

Procurement
The $40 billion dogfight [Advanced Tactical Fighter] H. Banks. il *Forbes* 139:35-8 My 4 '87
Aerojet completes tests of engine for adaptable space propulsion system [Transtar] R. G. O'Lone. il *Aviat Week Space Technol* 127:130-1 Ag 10 '87
Air Force crews cite progress of B-1B in initial operations. C. A. Shifrin. il *Aviat Week Space Technol* 126:21-3 Mr 30 '87
Air Force defends MX management as Northrop is charged with fraud. M. Mecham. *Aviat Week Space Technol* 127:16-18 Ag 31 '87
Air Force exploits speed, range of Gulfstream C-20 in VIP role. P. Proctor. il *Aviat Week Space Technol* 126:74-5 Je 8 '87
Air Force institutes plan to reduce and streamline competition advocate program. *Aviat Week Space Technol* 126:81 Mr 16 '87
Air Force issues RFPs for Chinese F-8-2 avionic upgrade kits. *Aviat Week Space Technol* 126:19 Mr 23 '87

United States. Air Force—Procurement—*cont.*

Air Force refers Northrop investigation to U.S. Attorney; Late IMUs delay scheduled MX deployment [inertial measurement units] B. A. Smith. *Aviat Week Space Technol* 126:72 Je 15 '87

Air Force reorganizes procurement hierarchy. *Aviat Week Space Technol* 126:22-3 Mr 2 '87

Air Force RFP opens bidding on aircraft to calibrate navigation, approach aids [business jets] *Aviat Week Space Technol* 126:150 Ap 27 '87

Army/USAF use diverse technologies to validate Joint STARS concepts. il *Aviat Week Space Technol* 126:84-5+ Mr 2 '87

B-1B: a timely lesson in risk management. L. A. Skantze. *Aviat Week Space Technol* 126:11 Mr 23 '87

B-1B bomber inquiry triggers Aspin probes of Stealth weapons [House Armed Services Committee] P. Mann. *Aviat Week Space Technol* 126:18-20 Mr 23 '87

The B-1B: haste is making waste. D. Griffiths. *Bus Week* p29 F 9 '87

Boeing wins contract to design MX rail-garrison basing system. B. A. Smith. *Aviat Week Space Technol* 127:21 S 21 '87

The case against the Air Force [developing planes designed to deliver smart bombs behind enemy lines at the expense of providing close air support] R. Coram. il *Wash Mon* 19:17-24 Jl/Ag '87

Congress questions cost of B-1B recovery program. *Aviat Week Space Technol* 126:28-9 Mr 2 '87

Congressional pressure prompts order to revive anti-radar drone [Seek Spinner program] J. D. Morrocco. il *Aviat Week Space Technol* 127:84-5 Ag 3 '87

Defense Dept. asks USAF to broaden design options for new CAS aircraft [close air support] il *Aviat Week Space Technol* 127:28-9 N 23 '87

Defense keeps tightening the screws on contractors [Lockheed reduces price of Air Force C-5B] D. Griffiths. il *Bus Week* p34 F 2 '87

Digital protests terms of Air Force call for computer bids. *Aviat Week Space Technol* 127:157 O 12 '87

ELV manufacturers charge USAF with decision delays [expendable launch facilities] *Aviat Week Space Technol* 126:27 My 11 '87

Europeans will enter ATR42 in U.S. STOL competition [military cargo version] il *Aviat Week Space Technol* 126:28-9 F 23 '87

F-16 wing buckles in static test, forcing USAF to restrict training. M. Mecham. *Aviat Week Space Technol* 127:32-3 N 9 '87

First production GPS receiver delivered ahead of schedule [Global Positioning System/Navstar] P. J. Klass. il *Aviat Week Space Technol* 127:93+ S 21 '87

Flight International will provide USAF electronic warfare training [use of corporate jets] *Aviat Week Space Technol* 126:101 Je 1 '87

Forum stresses Air Force's dependence on computers [conference with vendors] D. Hughes. *Aviat Week Space Technol* 127:85+ N 2 '87

Guidance unit shortage keeps 8 MXs off alert [Northrop contract] M. Mecham. *Aviat Week Space Technol* 127:22-3 Jl 6 '87

House panel warns of future risks in B-1B program costs and schedule [Armed Services Committee] *Aviat Week Space Technol* 126:20-1 Ap 6 '87

Inadequate procurement rates threaten Air Guard capability. B. M. Greeley, Jr. *Aviat Week Space Technol* 127:24 Jl 6 '87

Industry group criticizes Air Force draft agreement on ELVs [expendable launch vehicles and commercial launch industry] *Aviat Week Space Technol* 126:23 F 16 '87

Launcher companies sign first commercialization agreements. *Aviat Week Space Technol* 127:26-7 Ag 10 '87

Litton, Loral to deliver F-16 warning systems. *Aviat Week Space Technol* 126:104 F 9 '87

Lockheed trims $273-million from C-5B price. *Aviat Week Space Technol* 126:30 Ja 26 '87

Logistics procurement legislation fosters increasing competition. il *Aviat Week Space Technol* 126:93 F 9 '87

LTV receives Air Force contract to modernize, reengine A-7Ds. C. A. Shifrin. il *Aviat Week Space Technol* 126:85+ Je 1 '87

Martin converts USAF Titan 2 to launch vehicle for placing defense payloads into polar orbit. il *Aviat Week Space Technol* 127:18-19 Ag 10 '87

NASA may be forced to take minor role in heavy launcher. T. M. Foley. *Aviat Week Space Technol* 126:56-7 Mr 23 '87

Navy, Air Force plan HARM upgrade to extend missile life through 1990s. il *Aviat Week Space Technol* 126:101+ F 9 '87

New infrared line scanner to enter Air Force service [Honeywell AN/AAD-5B] il *Aviat Week Space Technol* 127:108 S 7 '87

Northrop boosts IMU deliveries, expects to meet schedule in March [inertial measurement units for MX intercontinental ballistic missile] B. A. Smith. il *Aviat Week Space Technol* 127:31-2 S 7 '87

Old Crows cite contractor optimism, program instability for EW problems. *Aviat Week Space Technol* 126:107-8 F 9 '87

Pratt & Whitney captures lead in USAF fighter engine competition. *Aviat Week Space Technol* 126:30 F 9 '87

Rockwell sneaks up on the Stealth bomber [challenging Northrop] D. Griffiths. il *Bus Week* p96 Je 29 '87

Science board seeks new MX test procedures, affirms IMU reliability. M. Mecham. *Aviat Week Space Technol* 127:32-3 N 2 '87

T-46 requiem. D. E. Fink. *Aviat Week Space Technol* 127:9 Ag 31 '87

T-46 termination will force closure of Fairchild facility on Long Island. *Aviat Week Space Technol* 126:27 Mr 23 '87

Three international teams compete for USAF contract to provide flight inspection aircraft. *Aviat Week Space Technol* 127:25 Ag 17 '87

U.S. to bolster its capability in small space launch vehicles. C. Covault. il *Aviat Week Space Technol* 127:73+ D 7 '87

USAF, Aerojet revive concept of integrated rocket stages. R. G. O'Lone. il *Aviat Week Space Technol* 126:37-8 Ap 27 '87

USAF, Army grapple with key issues of close air support mission. B. M. Greeley, Jr. *Aviat Week Space Technol* 126:50-1+ Mr 23 '87

USAF awards McDonnell Douglas contract to build, operate MLVs [medium launch vehicles] B. A. Smith. *Aviat Week Space Technol* 126:20-1 Ja 26 '87

USAF, Defense Dept. reach compromise on new CAS aircraft [close air support] *Aviat Week Space Technol* 127:33 D 7 '87

USAF expects fully operational B-1B by 1988 within spending limits. il *Aviat Week Space Technol* 126:24-5 Ja 26 '87

USAF initiatives promote automation of weapon subcontractors' shops. E. H. Phillips. *Aviat Week Space Technol* 127:89 D 7 '87

USAF may develop Agile Falcon without allied participation. J. D. Morrocco. *Aviat Week Space Technol* 127:23-4 O 26 '87

USAF plans to introduce A-10s into forward air control fleet. J. D. Morrocco. *Aviat Week Space Technol* 126:23 F 9 '87

USAF probes Northrop's MX program purchases. *Aviat Week Space Technol* 126:27 Je 1 '87

USAF pursues standardized allied reconnaissance data. *Aviat Week Space Technol* 127:25 S 21 '87

USAF, Rockwell strengthen B-1B against bird strikes. D. M. North. *Aviat Week Space Technol* 127:30 D 21 '87

USAF seeks designs for close air support successor to A-10. *Aviat Week Space Technol* 126:37 Je 22 '87

USAF seeks industry responses for advanced launch system. *Aviat Week Space Technol* 126:26 My 11 '87

USAF seeks new RPVs by 1993 [remotely piloted vehicles] J. D. Morrocco. *Aviat Week Space Technol* 126:17-18 F 16 '87

USAF seeks technology to cut heavy-lift launch costs; USAF prepares program to procure heavy-lift vehicles. *Aviat Week Space Technol* 126:24-5 Ja 26 '87

USAF suspends AIL from new contracts pending billing inquiry. *Aviat Week Space Technol* 127:30 N 16 '87

USAF withholds MX progress payments from Northrop. *Aviat Week Space Technol* 126:23 Ap 13 '87

Uniforms

Ordering a surgical fashion strike, the Air Force reclaims its legacy in leather—the bomber jacket. il *People Wkly* 28:47 S 28 '87

United States. Air Force. Alaskan Air Command

Alaskan air defense network [special section] il map *Aviat Week Space Technol* 126:64-5+ My 25 '87

United States. Air Force. Avionics Laboratory *See* Air Force Avionics Laboratory (U.S.)

United States. Air Force. Civil Reserve Air Fleet *See* United States. Civil Reserve Air Fleet

United States. Air Force. Eastern Test Range
USAF modernizes Eastern Test Range for high shuttle, ELV launch pace. E. H. Kolcum. il *Aviat Week Space Technol* 126:69-72 F 2 '87

United States. Air Force. Flight Dynamics Laboratory *See* Air Force Flight Dynamics Laboratory (U.S.)

United States. Air Force. Flight Test Center *See* Air Force Flight Test Center (U.S.)

United States. Air Force. Military Airlift Command
Douglas stresses reliability early in C-17 development. B. A. Smith. il *Aviat Week Space Technol* 127:61-2 Jl 20 '87

Four teams will study system to track USAF airlift missions. D. Hughes. *Aviat Week Space Technol* 127:85+ D 7 '87

Military Airlift Command will transition to C-130 flight crew training system. K. J. Stein. il *Aviat Week Space Technol* 127:109-10 Jl 6 '87

United conducts total training of MAC C-5 crews. il *Aviat Week Space Technol* 127:112 Jl 6 '87

USAF weighs methods to boost strategic cargo airlift capacity [Civil Reserve Air Fleet] *Aviat Week Space Technol* 127:49+ S 7 '87

United States. Air Force. Space Command
The challenge of space surveillance. J. A. Howell. il *Sky Telesc* 73:584-6+ Je '87

NORAD, Space Command request system for surveillance of Soviet weapons. C. Covault. *Aviat Week Space Technol* 126:73+ Ap 6 '87

Space Command completes acquisition of Pave Paws warning radar installations. *Aviat Week Space Technol* 126:128-9 My 18 '87

United States. Air Force. Space Command. Space Defense Operations Center
New Space Operations Center will improve threat assessment. C. Covault. il *Aviat Week Space Technol* 126:50+ My 25 '87

United States. Air Force. Space Division
Air Force awards contracts for Phase 1 ALS studies [advanced launch system] M. A. Dornheim. il *Aviat Week Space Technol* 127:25 Jl 20 '87

Easing of shuttle weight limits key to new USAF upper stage [Adaptable Space Propulsion System] B. A. Smith. *Aviat Week Space Technol* 126:25 Ja 19 '87

USAF narrows contractors for new upper stage. *Aviat Week Space Technol* 126:25 My 4 '87

United States. Air Force. Space Technology Center *See* Air Force Space Technology Center (U.S.)

United States. Air Force. Strategic Air Command
New automated testing system aids SAC FB-111 maintenance. K. J. Stein. il *Aviat Week Space Technol* 126:91+ Mr 2 '87

SAC sergeant says no to spy flights [D. Cobos objects to espionage missions over Nicaragua] B. E. Johansen. il por *Progressive* 51:12 O '87

SAC stresses air crew training to defeat Soviet defenses. B. M. Greeley, Jr. il *Aviat Week Space Technol* 126:72-3+ F 9 '87

Strategic Air Command bombs out [Minnesota residents block low-altitude bomber training flights] M. Helmberger. il *Progressive* 51:11-12 Ag '87

United States. Air Force. Thunderbirds
America the beautiful's team. F. Deford. il *Sports Illus* 67:66-72+ Ag 3 '87

United States. Air Force Logistics Command
Air Force Division oversees EW modifications, upgrades. *Aviat Week Space Technol* 126:97 F 9 '87

Logistics procurement legislation fosters increasing competition. il *Aviat Week Space Technol* 126:93 F 9 '87

United States. Air Force Survival School *See* Air Force Survival School (U.S.)

United States. Air Force Systems Command
Aero-Space Plane project chief named [R. R. Barthelemy] *Aviat Week Space Technol* 127:28 O 5 '87

Air Force defines milestones for Project Forecast 2 initiatives. J. D. Morrocco. *Aviat Week Space Technol* 126:139+ My 11 '87

Bernard P. Randolph: the armed forces' only black four-star general. D. M. Cheers. il pors *Ebony* 43:154+ N '87

Randolph is the top black U.S. gen.; gets 4th star [B. P. Randolph] il por *Jet* 72:6 Ag 17 '87

United States. Air National Guard
Inadequate procurement rates threaten Air Guard capability. B. M. Greeley, Jr. *Aviat Week Space Technol* 127:24 Jl 6 '87

United States. Animal and Plant Health Inspection Service
A close watch on U.S. borders to keep the world's bugs out. E. Larson. bibl (p154) *Smithsonian* 18:106-8+ Je '87; il

United States. Armed Forces Radio and Television Service
Military personnel get a taste of the blues. *Jet* 72:62 Ag 31 '87

United States. Arms Control and Disarmament Agency
Arms Control Agency challenges Nunn's contention on legality of testing kinetic systems [ABM Treaty restrictions] *Aviat Week Space Technol* 126:29 Mr 23 '87

Compromise candidate [R. Lehman proposed as new director] por *Newsweek* 110:4 S 14 '87

United States. Army
Academy helps Army be all that it can be [report on human performance enhancement] C. Holden. *Science* 238:1501-2 D 11 '87

Doing the nerve gas shuffle. S. Zakin. il *Sierra* 72:26+ Jl/Ag '87

Expanded night-fighting capability shapes Army flight training needs [helicopters] il *Aviat Week Space Technol* 126:115+ Ja 19 '87

Appropriations and expenditures
The Army loses a battle: cutting ground forces to pay SDI and Stealth. T. Monmaney. il *Newsweek* 109:20-1 Ja 19 '87

Army modernization slows; aircraft programs hardest hit. *Aviat Week Space Technol* 126:29-30 Ja 12 '87

Army seeks additional AH-64, UH-60 helicopters. il *Aviat Week Space Technol* 126:27 Mr 16 '87

Senators urge Army to keep helicopter production lines open. *Aviat Week Space Technol* 126:23 Mr 23 '87

Blacks
AIDS more prevalent in black military recruits. *Jet* 72:37 Ag 3 '87

Army Gen. Colin Powell is picked for NSC's no. 2 spot. il por *Jet* 71:24 Ja 12 '87

Fred Gorden first black commandant at West Point Academy. por *Jet* 72:4 Ag 31 '87

Education
See also
United States Military Academy

Forces in Germany (West)
Back to the front [Certain Strike maneuvers in West Germany] A. T. Hadley. *New Repub* 197:16-18 N 16 '87

The battle for Berlin. G. Martin. il *Esquire* 108:204-13 N '87

See the world—and pinch pfennigs [effect of weak dollar on American G.I.s] J. D. Reed. il *Time* 130:24 D 28 '87

Helicopters
See Helicopters—Military use

Management
Army, Navy Secretaries initiate major changes in staff structure. J. D. Morrocco. il *Aviat Week Space Technol* 126:79-81 Mr 16 '87

Pay, allowances, etc.
Army families face financial hardships [study by Robert J. Thoresen] il *USA Today (Periodical)* 116:4-5 D '87

Procurement
After Divad, an $11-billion plan. S. Budiansky. il *Science* 236:137-40 Ap 10 '87

Army/USAF use diverse technologies to validate Joint STARS concepts. il *Aviat Week Space Technol* 126:84-5+ Mr 2 '87

Army again changes LHX acquisition plan. *Aviat Week Space Technol* 126:24-5 Ap 20 '87

Army air combat [special section] il *Aviat Week Space Technol* 127:18-22 O 19 '87

Army analysis of LHX program cites strengths of tilt-rotor. B. M. Greeley, Jr. *Aviat Week Space Technol* 126:22-3 Mr 23 '87

Army developing helicopter derivatives for special operations missions. S. W. Kandebo. il *Aviat Week Space Technol* 127:47+ D 14 '87

Army limits pedestal-mounted Stinger competition to two rivals. *Aviat Week Space Technol* 126:30 My 4 '87

Army may reengine UH-1H if LHX is delayed further. B. M. Greeley, Jr. *Aviat Week Space Technol* 127:32 S 14 '87

Army modifies UH-60s to cut electromagnetic interference in controls. *Aviat Week Space Technol* 127:27-8 N 16 '87

Army proposes changing strategy to acquire new air defense system. *Aviat Week Space Technol* 126:22 Mr 2 '87

Army tests line-of-sight air defense systems [forward area air defense system] C. A. Shifrin. *Aviat Week Space Technol* 126:20-2 Jl 6 '87

Army will begin ADATS field testing in 1989. *Aviat Week Space Technol* 127:24 D 21 '87

United States. Army—Procurement—cont.

Army will shield UH-60 hydraulics against EMI [electromagnetic interference] *Aviat Week Space Technol* 127:29 N 23 '87

Army's analysis of LHX helicopters will omit close air support issue. *Aviat Week Space Technol* 126:18 F 16 '87

Beggs and General Dynamics cleared of fraud [Divad gun case] I. Goodwin. *Phys Today* 40 pt1:53 Ag '87

Bell/McDonnell team reviews design of Army LHX entry. *Aviat Week Space Technol* 126:85-6 Ja 19 '87

Boeing Aerospace wins contract to provide LOS-R Stinger system [line of sight-rear component of the Army's forward area air defense system] C. A. Shifrin. il *Aviat Week Space Technol* 127:25-6 Ag 31 '87

Defense Board to review LHX prior to full-scale development. B. M. Greeley, Jr. *Aviat Week Space Technol* 126:22-3 F 9 '87

The first Chrysler bail-out: the M-1 tank. R. A. Mendel. il *Wash Mon* 19:17-23 F '87

GE cannot meet Army air defense test deadline [forward-area air defense system] *Aviat Week Space Technol* 126:30 Ja 19 '87

General Dynamics, Beggs cleared of fraud charges. *Aviat Week Space Technol* 126:25-6 Je 29 '87

Indictment of Beggs dropped [General Dynamics Divad gun fraud case] E. Marshall. *Science* 237:21 Jl 3 '87

Joint venture to bid on LOS-F-H portion of FAADs [line of sight-forward heavy portion of the Army's forward area air defense system] *Aviat Week Space Technol* 126:29 Ap 20 '87

Justice Dept.'s broadax [dismissal of indictment against General Dynamics in Divad gun case] D. E. Fink. *Aviat Week Space Technol* 127:9 Jl 13 '87

Let the Army fly its own close air support. B. M. Greeley, Jr. *Aviat Week Space Technol* 126:11 F 9 '87

Martin Marietta ADATS wins Army air defense competition [Anti-Tank Air Defense System] J. D. Morrocco. il *Aviat Week Space Technol* 127:26-7 D 7 '87

Martin Marietta selected to design potential nuclear SDI systems [nuclear-powered X-ray laser platform and nuclear hypervelocity pellet system] T. M. Foley. *Aviat Week Space Technol* 127:113-14 Ag 10 '87

Salvaging the LHX. D. E. Fink. *Aviat Week Space Technol* 126:11 Mr 30 '87

SDI budget constraints likely to foil new Army contract awards. *Aviat Week Space Technol* 127:22 N 2 '87

Short Brothers pushes Starstreak for U.S. Army air defense. D. A. Brown. il *Aviat Week Space Technol* 126:68-9 Ap 6 '87

Slow progress may delay decision on antitactical missile. J. D. Morrocco. *Aviat Week Space Technol* 127:26-7 N 23 '87

Tadiran-General Dynamics team will compete as second-source for Army Sincgars radios. *Aviat Week Space Technol* 127:28 Jl 13 '87

USAF, Army grapple with key issues of close air support mission. B. M. Greeley, Jr. *Aviat Week Space Technol* 126:50-1+ Mr 23 '87

Who's counting? [Justice Dept. abandons Divad gun fraud case against General Dynamics] W. Biddle. *Nation* 245:148-9 Ag 29 '87

Recruiting, enlistment, etc.

An ad agency's war with the Army [N. W. Ayer] P. Dwyer. *Bus Week* p102+ Ap 13 '87

Uncle Sam wants you . . . and just about anybody [recruiting scandals] *Newsweek* 109:29 Ja 26 '87

Women

See Servicewomen

United States. Army. Camel Corps

The short, unhappy life of the U.S. Camel Cavalry. A. S. Kramer. il *Am Hist Illus* 22:52-7 Mr '87

United States. Army. Corps of Engineers

The Army's giant swampbuster [proposed draining of Yazoo Backwater Swamp, Miss.] J. McCafferty. il *Sierra* 72:84-5 Jl/Ag '87

Atchafalaya [Old River Control operation] J. A. McPhee. *New Yorker* 63:39-44+ F 23 '87

Defending our shores. R. Thompson. il *Oceans* 20:34-41 Mr/Ap '87

An end to ecstasy. D. E. Worster. il *Wilderness* 51:18-21+ Fall '87

The "sewer ditch" undone [dismantling the Kissimmee River channel] F. Graham. il maps *Audubon* 89:114-15 Mr '87

Standoff at Oregon Inlet [Army Corps of Engineers proposal to build jetties at Cape Hatteras, N.C.] L. S. Bates. il *Oceans* 20:5-6 Mr/Ap '87

United States. Army. Counter Intelligence Corps

The Barbie file [cover story] T. Morgan. il pors *N Y Times Mag* p18-24+ My 10 '87

United States. Army. Special Forces

The secret Army. G. J. Church. il *Time* 130:12-14 Ag 31 '87

United States. Army. Special Operations Division

Who's in charge here? [covert Army unit] S. M. Hersh. il por *N Y Times Mag* p34-5+ N 22 '87

United States. Army Air Forces

Postcard from Framlingham [English WWII airfield used by American bombers] L. Morgan. il *Flying* 114:10-11 Ja '87

United States. Army Aviation Systems Command

Army's R&D plan stresses development of passive interferometry detectors. *Aviat Week Space Technol* 126:113 F 9 '87

United States. Army Reserve

Crimes and misdemeanors

'The Second Beast of Revelation' [M. A. Aquino accused of child molestation at the day care center at Presidio Army Base, Calif.] J. Adler. il por *Newsweek* 110:73 N 16 '87

United States. Attorney General's Commission on Pornography

Another kind of censorship [reluctance of publishers and booksellers to deal with report] M. J. McManus. por *Publ Wkly* 231:70 Ja 23 '87

LC provides legal guidelines for Meese Commission proposals. H. Fields. *Publ Wkly* 231:20 F 20 '87

The Meese Commission: sex, violence, and censorship. C. Hefner. il por *Humanist* 47:25-9+ Ja/F '87

Of many things [U.S. Catholic Conference's synopsis of the findings] G. W. Hunt. *America* 156:inside cover Ja 3-10 '87

Pornography [discussion of August 1987 article, The pornography report that never was] T. Teachout. *Commentary* 84:14-15+ N '87

Pornography and its discontents [special section] bibl *Society* 24:6-32 Jl/Ag '87

The pornography report that never was. T. Teachout. *Commentary* 84:51-7 Ag '87

United States. Biotechnology Science Coordinating Council *See* Biotechnology Science Coordinating Council (U.S.)

United States. Bureau of Labor Statistics

BLS prepares to broaden scope of its white-collar pay survey. J. D. Morton. bibl f il *Mon Labor Rev* 110:3-7 Mr '87

United States. Bureau of Land Management

An about-face for the BLM [planting sagebrush in Idaho] G. Oakley. il *Sierra* 72:13-14 Ja/F '87

Preserving old-growth forests. D. B. Edelson. bibl f il *Environment* 29:3-5 O '87

United States. Bureau of Mines

Dismantling the helium empire. M. Crawford. il *Science* 237:238-40 Jl 17 '87

United States. Bureau of Reclamation

BuRec gives up plan to mine in Grand Teton [reconstruction of the Jackson Lake Dam] il *Natl Parks* 61:35 Jl/Ag '87

Dryland farmers say no to water [Colorado farmers sue over Dolores River Project] J. Price. il *Progressive* 51:11 Jl '87

An end to ecstasy. D. E. Worster. il *Wilderness* 51:18-21+ Fall '87

United States. Cabinet

See also

Secretaries of State (U.S.)

Executive suite [Reagan Cabinet] il por *Life* 10:100-1 Fall '87

United States. Centers for Disease Control *See* Centers for Disease Control (U.S.)

United States. Central Intelligence Agency

Ace reporter Bob Woodward lifts the Veil on the secrets of CIA chief William Casey. M. Green. il pors *People Wkly* 28:40-1 O 12 '87

Amy Carter and Abbie Hoffman win acquittal, but they want to keep the C.I.A. on trial. F. A. Bernstein. il pors *People Wkly* 27:57-8+ My 4 '87

Amy's day [A. Carter acquitted in protest against CIA campus recruiting] J. Nocera. *New Repub* 196:11-13 My 11 '87

Bob Gates will have to bring the CIA in from the cold. E. Clark. por *Bus Week* p43 F 16 '87

Books [B. Woodward's book on W. Casey and the CIA] L. Hirschberg. il por *N Y* 20:110-11 S 21 '87

The C.I.A. goes back to college. J. Wiener. il *Nation* 245:719-20 D 12 '87

The C.I.A.'s war in Costa Rica. T. Avirgan and M. Honey. *Nation* 244:105-7 Ja 31 '87

United States. Central Intelligence Agency—*cont.*
Casey and Woodward: who used whom? M. Kempton. il *N Y Rev Books* 34:61 N 5 '87
Casey's boys [advisers to contras] M. Kondracke. *New Repub* 197:42 Ag 24 '87
Casey's secret [B. Woodward's reporting in Veil] *Nation* 245:363-4 O 10 '87
Casey's well-groomed successor [R. Gates] N. Traver. il por *Time* 129:22-3 F 16 '87
The Central Intelligence Agency [address, August 8, 1987] W. H. Webster. *Vital Speeches Day* 53:738-40 O 1 '87
The CIA & the legacy of William Casey. J. B. Judis. il *Commonweal* 114:752-6 D 18 '87
The CIA: a straight arrow for director [W. H. Webster] T. Morganthau. il por *Newsweek* 109:24-5 Mr 16 '87
The CIA and American foreign policy. R. M. Gates. bibl f *Foreign Aff* 66:215-30 Wint '87/'88
CIA, DIA at odds over Soviet threat. M. Krepon. *Bull At Sci* 43:6-7 My '87
The CIA-Harvard controversy over secrecy. T. A. Idinopulos. il *USA Today (Periodical)* 115:38-40 My '87
CIA scrapbook in Serbo-Croatian [publication of photographic history] il *U S News World Rep* 102:26 Ja 26 '87
The CIA sizes up the Mexican domino. *Harpers* 274:21 My '87
The CIA's 'cowboys': out of control? [disclosures by G. P. Shultz] L. Martz. il por *Newsweek* 109:22-4 F 2 '87
Cleaning up the mess [cover story; special section] il pors *Newsweek* 110:24-30+ O 12 '87
Closing argument [protest against CIA campus recruitment; closing remarks to jury, April 15, 1987] A. Hoffman. *Nation* 244:562-3 My 2 '87
Covert aid and the Church [aid to Cardinal Obando y Bravo of Nicaragua] R. Parry and T. Jacoby. il por *Newsweek* 109:27-8 Je 15 '87
Covert no more? [CIA and Iran-contra] J. McLaughlin. *Natl Rev* 39:22 Ag 28 '87
A cult of 'covert ops'. T. Jacoby. il *Newsweek* 110:22+ Jl 20 '87
Did a dead man tell no tales? [furor over allegations in B. Woodward's Veil] R. Zoglin. il pors *Time* 130:28+ O 12 '87
Did Woodward get it right? [book on CIA and W. Casey] G. Witkin. il por *U S News World Rep* 103:23 O 12 '87
Double-dealing over Iran [relationship of arms dealer M. Ghorbanifar to the CIA] E. Magnuson. il por *Time* 129:22+ F 2 '87
Factoid time? [B. Woodward's book on W. J. Casey and the CIA] *Natl Rev* 39:19 O 23 '87
A fedora full of secrets [death of agent J. Angleton] J. L. Galloway. il *U S News World Rep* 102:16 My 25 '87
Former British P.M. Harold Wilson is unimpressed by claims that the CIA sought his downfall. F. Hauptfuhrer. il pors *People Wkly* 28:91-2+ D 21 '87
The future is yours (still) [closing remarks to jury, April 15, 1987] A. Hoffman. *Harpers* 275:21+ Jl '87
G-man among the spooks [W. Webster nominated to head the CIA] E. Shannon. il por *Time* 129:28 Mr 16 '87
Hard times once again in the spookhouse. W. L. Chaze. il por *U S News World Rep* 102:22-3+ Ja 26 '87
How the CIA went wrong [Iran-contra scandal] R. Parry. il *Newsweek* 109:26 Mr 2 '87
Knock on Woodward [B. Woodward's Veil] F. Barnes. il *New Repub* 197:11-13 O 26 '87
Letter from Washington [successor to William Casey] Cato. *Natl Rev* 39:14 F 13 '87
The life and death of an intelligence man [R. Krobock killed in El Salvador helicopter crash] M. Healy. il pors *U S News World Rep* 102:22-3 My 11 '87
Lifting the Veil on the CIA's secrets [B. Woodward's book] M. Elfin. il pors *U S News World Rep* 103:26-7 O 5 '87
'Little worm' or big fish? [Sandinista R. Miranda defects to the U.S.] N. Cooper. por *Newsweek* 110:80 N 16 '87
Lost in Afghanistan. D. Corn and J. Morley. *Nation* 245:43 Jl 18-25 '87
The man who wasn't there [B. Woodward's book on W. J. Casey] D. M. Alpern. il por *Newsweek* 110:44-5 O 5 '87
The Marine's private army [Oliver North's use of former CIA agents and military officers in his covert operations] J. F. Stacks. il *Time* 130:32 Jl 13 '87

Minority report [evidence of C.I.A.-contra-narcotics connection] C. Hitchens. *Nation* 244:531 Ap 25 '87
New look at an old failure [views of ex-CIA historian J. Pfeiffer on the Bay of Pigs] J. Peterzell. il por *Time* 129:29 Je 1 '87
Nominating a hero for 1987 [J. Rauh's suit against CIA mind control experiments performed on Canadians] A. Fotheringham. il *Macleans* 100:64 Ja 19 '87
Not guilty by necessity [A. Carter acquitted in protest against CIA recruiting on campus] por *Time* 129:71 Ap 27 '87
On trial: cheers and jeers for Amy Carter. por *Newsweek* 109:33 Ap 20 '87
Out in the cold [covert operations directed by W. J. Casey] *Time* 130:20 S 7 '87
Reagan's secret wars and missed opportunities [revelations from B. Woodward's Veil] J. M. Wall. *Christ Century* 104:907-8 O 21 '87
Reforming U.S. intelligence. A. E. Goodman. bibl f *Foreign Policy* 67:121-36 Summ '87
The secret wars of the CIA [excerpts from Veil] B. Woodward. il *Newsweek* 110:46-8+ O 5 '87
The selling of the F.D.N. [CIA-backed contra propaganda operations] P. Kornbluh. il *Nation* 244:40-4 Ja 17 '87
Silent witness: William Casey, Iranscam's mystery man, will tell no tales. E. Barnes and M. Dubrow. il pors *Life* 10:28-31 S '87
The spectator in solitary [former CIA agent E. P. Wilson convicted of selling guns to Libyan terrorists] F. Trippett. il por *Time* 129:19 Je 15 '87
Spies out in the cold [appointment of R. M. Gates] J. McLaughlin. *Natl Rev* 39:24 Mr 13 '87
A spy, and his secrets, are buried [death of W. Casey] C. Fenyvesi. il *U S News World Rep* 102:29 My 18 '87
Spy master revelations [B. Woodward's account of W. J. Casey's CIA] M. McDonald. il pors *Macleans* 100:30-1 O 12 '87
A spy's secret dies with him [W. J. Casey] M. Healy. por *U S News World Rep* 103:25 Jl 20 '87
Story of a consummate bureaucrat [cover story] J. Morley. *Nation* 245:737+ D 19 '87
Truth and reason upside down [CIA employees accused of selling rare postage stamps that were government property] J. V. Lamar, Jr. il *Time* 130:32 S 14 '87
Webster's third? [director-designate W. H. Webster] *Nation* 244:347-8 Mr 21 '87
What Yevgeny knew [Y. Yevtushenko's claim that the CIA helped the Soviets muzzle the writers A. Sinyavsky and I. Daniel] D. Jameson. *New Repub* 196:39-41 Je 22 '87
Who's in charge here? [covert Army unit] S. M. Hersh. il por *N Y Times Mag* p34-5+ N 22 '87
William Casey. por *People Wkly* 28:84-5 D 28 '87-Ja 4 '88
William Casey: silent witness. T. Jacoby. il *Newsweek* 109:46 My 18 '87
With Casey out, who will fill the CIA's top job? *Newsweek* 109:21 Ja 12 '87
Woodward on Casey. T. H. Stahel. *America* 157:236-7 O 17 '87
Would you believe . . . Iranian moderates? [politicization of intelligence; cover story] M. McDonald. *Wash Mon* 19:39-45+ Mr '87

United States. Children's Bureau
Children's Bureau 75th anniversary: 1912-1987. C. Reece. il por *Child Today* 16:4-7 S/O '87
Preventing out-of-home placement of children: the first step to permanency planning. C. Sudia. il *Child Today* 15:4-5 N/D '86

United States. Civil Reserve Air Fleet
USAF weighs methods to boost strategic cargo airlift capacity. *Aviat Week Space Technol* 127:49+ S 7 '87

United States. Civil Rights Commission *See* United States Commission on Civil Rights

United States. Coast Guard
Bill Bolling: boarded, bothered and busted [arrested for interfering with Coast Guardsmen trying to board boat] P. Whittell. il pors *Mot Boat Sail* 159:66-9+ F '87
Boarding—with dignity [change in Coast Guard policy] P. A. Janssen. il *Mot Boat Sail* 159:11 My '87
Flying with the Coasties. S. Wilkinson. il *Oceans* 20:12-19 N/D '87
Night patrol in the drug war [patrol in the Gulf Stream off Miami] C. Davis. il *Mot Boat Sail* 159:46-9+ Mr '87

Appropriations and expenditures
Coast Guard 1988 budget declines. *Aviat Week Space Technol* 126:24 Ja 19 '87

United States. Coast Guard—*cont.*

Boats

Power prop [new design] D. H. Van Liew. il *Pop Sci* 231:80-1+ O '87

Education

They learn to work calmly while instinct warns they're about to die [Coast Guard Motor Life Boat School] M. Parfit. il *Smithsonian* 18:98-102+ My '87

United States. Commodity Futures Trading Commission

The chickens guarding the chicken coop. S. Waldman. *Wash Mon* 19:27-9 Mr '87

A giant trader under fire [Philipp Brothers] D. Pauly and B. Powell. il *Newsweek* 109:36-40 Ja 19 '87

United States. Congress

See also
> Lobbyists and lobbying
> Pork barrel legislation

Recent action in the Congress:
> Bilingual education. *Congr Dig* 66:74-5+ Mr '87
> Drug testing. *Congr Dig* 66:137+ My '87

The view from the 100th Congress [congressional history; special section] il *People Wkly* 27:26-33 Mr 23 '87

Committees

Seniority system

Jess and Les [J. Helms and L. Aspin reappointed committee chairmen] por *Time* 129:25 F 2 '87

Powers and duties

See also
> War and emergency powers

Call five cases that shaped Congress. D. Pawelek. il *Sch Update* 119:12-14 Ja 12 '87

The chains of liberty [address, September 17, 1987] E. S. Muskie. *Vital Speeches Day* 54:4-7 O 15 '87

Disease of distrust [presidential and congressional duties in foreign policy] D. Gergen. il *U S News World Rep* 103:64 Jl 27 '87

Foreign affairs and the Constitution. L. Henkin. bibl f *Foreign Aff* 66:284-310 Wint '87/'88

Global intervention and a new imperial presidency. T. G. Carpenter. il *USA Today (Periodical)* 115:10-18 Mr '87

The imperial Congress. G. Szamuely. *Commentary* 84:27-32 S '87

The nation's town meeting. il *Life* 10:96-9 Fall '87

Who's in charge here? [Congress's role in foreign policy] T. Jacoby. il *Newsweek* 110:18 Jl 27 '87

Voting

65 mph: America steps on the gas [Congress votes to change rural speed limit] il *U S News World Rep* 102:12 Mr 30 '87

Step on it [Congress votes to increase the speed limit on rural interstate highways] *Time* 129:26 Mr 30 '87

United States. Congress (1st: 1789-1790)

When Congress made up the nation's rules. S. Kane. il *Sch Update* 119:15 Ja 12 '87

United States. Congress (99th: 1985-1986)

The 99th Congress: action on the environment. R. Livernash. *Environment* 28:5+ D '86

Recent action in the Congress:
> Federal minimum wage. *Congr Dig* 66:198-9+ Ag/S '87
> Product liability legislation. *Congr Dig* 66:6-7 Ja '87

Scorecard [record on environmental issues] *Sierra* 72:16-17 Ja/F '87

Wins outweigh losses in 99th Congress [parks bills] *Natl Parks* 61:39-40 Ja/F '87

United States. Congress (99th, 2nd session: 1986)

The month in Congress. *Congr Dig* 66:1-2 Ja '87

Recent action in the Congress:
> Political action committees. *Congr Dig* 66:39+ F '87

United States. Congress (100th, 1st session: 1987)

See also
> Iran-contra affair—Congressional hearings

The 100th Congress [address, October 5, 1987] W. L. Renfro. *Vital Speeches Day* 54:95-6 N 15 '87

The 100th Congress: the Democrats take charge [special issue] il maps *Sch Update* 119:2-24 Ja 12 '87

AIDS commission bills proliferate. D. M. Barnes. *Science* 235:1136 Mr 6 '87

Arms control in the new Congress. J. D. Isaacs. il *Bull At Sci* 43:4-5 Ja/F '87

At long last, coming to grips with the deficit. G. Borger. il *U S News World Rep* 102:20-1 Ap 6 '87

Bicentenary resolutions. *Nation* 244:33 Ja 17 '87

Black reps cheered as they take on 100th U.S. Congress. il *Jet* 71:4-5 Ja 26 '87

Bob and Jim play a duet [R. Byrd and J. Wright] G. Hackett. il pors *Newsweek* 109:29 F 9 '87

Catastrophic health care may be flat on its back. S. B. Garland. *Bus Week* p45 Jl 13 '87

Clean Water bill sent back to Reagan. J. Raloff. *Sci News* 131:71 Ja 31 '87

Congress and arms control. D. B. Fascell. bibl f *Foreign Aff* 65:730-49 Spr '87

Congress considers global climate change. N. Bell. *BioScience* 37:258 Ap '87

Congress considers species legislation. A. L. Spitler. *BioScience* 37:383 Je '87

Congress is lusting after higher excise taxes. D. Harbrecht. il *Bus Week* p26 Je 29 '87

Congress is uninterested in examining industry consolidation. H. Fields. *Publ Wkly* 231:26 Je 12 '87

Congress tries again on arms control. J. D. Isaacs. il *Bull At Sci* 43:3-4 Je '87

Corporate angst on Capitol Hill [opposition to pro-labor bills by business lobby] G. Bock. il *Time* 129:48 Je 22 '87

Dealing with Congress [protectionist sentiment clouds U.S.-Canada free trade accord] I. Austen. il *Macleans* 100:17 Ap 6 '87

Democratic jubilation has given way to sober reality. il *Nations Bus* 75:87 D '87

The Democrats are getting to work on welfare reform. S. B. Garland. il *Bus Week* p39 Ag 3 '87

The Democrats go home licking their wounds. D. Harbrecht. il por *Bus Week* p72 D 28 '87-Ja 4 '88

The Democrats: no more cover. G. Borger. il *U S News World Rep* 102:18-19 Mr 23 '87

Gearing up for the 100th Congress. A. L. Spitler. il *BioScience* 37:107 F '87

Getting a trade bill is going to take a lot of trading. D. Harbrecht and B. Javetski. il por *Bus Week* p34 S 28 '87

Legislative alert: what we want from the 100th Congress. J. E. Grenier. il *Ms* 15:24 Ap '87

The month in Congress. *Congr Dig* 66:129-30 My '87

The month in Congress. *Congr Dig* 66:225-6 O '87

The month in Congress. *Congr Dig* 66:161-2 Je/Jl '87

No issues? The new Congress could be one of the most exciting in a long time. il *Nations Bus* 75:72 Ja '87

Recent action in the Congress:
> The ABM Treaty. *Congr Dig* 66:263+ N '87
> Broadcasting Fairness Doctrine. *Congr Dig* 66:232-3 O '87
> Catastrophic health insurance. *Congr Dig* 66:102-3 Ap '87
> Foreign trade policy. *Congr Dig* 66:168-9+ Je/Jl '87
> War Powers Act. *Congr Dig* 66:294+ D '87

Slower than a Refrigerator? A. Holzinger. il *Nations Bus* 75:12 F '87

Small business and Congress [lobbying priorities] R. Thompson. il *Nations Bus* 75:9+ Mr '87

So many issues, so little time. D. Harbrecht. il *Bus Week* p32-3 S 14 '87

What Congress is pushing now [business legislation] A. C. Isgrò. il *Fortune* 115:99+ My 11 '87

Year of the donkey. J. McLaughlin. *Natl Rev* 39:28 Ja 30 '87

United States. Congress. House

See also
> Gerrymander

Letter from Washington [Texas delegation] Cato. *Natl Rev* 39:14 Jl 17 '87

Speakers

The new Speaker is stepping on everyone's toes [J. Wright] D. Harbrecht and H. Gleckman. *Bus Week* p55 Ja 12 '87

The outspoken Speaker has Democrats in a cold sweat [tax hike pronouncements by J. Wright] D. Harbrecht and R. Fly. por *Bus Week* p49 Mr 23 '87

Surprise! It's the Wright stuff. A. Plattner. il pors *U S News World Rep* 103:18-19 S 7 '87

Texan Jim Wright is the new king of the Hill as Congress opens its historic 100th session. W. Plummer. il por *People Wkly* 27:78-9 Ja 12 '87

A Texan's tough road ahead [J. Wright] A. Plattner. il por *U S News World Rep* 102:20-1 Ap 6 '87

Voting

Congress shows its impatience [House votes for moratorium on aid to contras] R. Stengel. il *Time* 129:16+ Mr 23 '87

The protectionists may have spent their fury [vote on Gephardt Amendment] D. Harbrecht and H. Gleckman. il *Bus Week* p44 My 11 '87

United States. Congress. House. Committee on Appropriations

House weighs major cuts for combat aircraft, missiles. *Aviat Week Space Technol* 127:32-3 O 19 '87

United States. Congress. House. Committee on Appropriations—*cont.*

Panel votes $279 billion for 1988 defense spending. *Aviat Week Space Technol* 127:34 N 2 '87

Science budgets fare well in House action. M. Crawford. *Science* 237:22 Jl 3 '87

United States. Congress. House. Committee on Appropriations. Subcommittee on HUD-Independent Agencies

House subcommittee trims funding for space station by $50 million. T. M. Foley. *Aviat Week Space Technol* 126:35 Je 22 '87

United States. Congress. House. Committee on Armed Services

Aspin's scalp [chairman L. Aspin deposed] *New Repub* 196:7 F 2 '87

B-1B bomber inquiry triggers Aspin probes of Stealth weapons. P. Mann. *Aviat Week Space Technol* 126:18-20 Mr 23 '87

The fall and rise of Les Aspin. J. D. Isaacs. il por *Bull At Sci* 43:4-5 Ap '87

House Armed Services forced to rewrite defense budget; House Armed Services Committee reports $306-billion defense authorization for fiscal 1988. M. Mecham. *Aviat Week Space Technol* 126:26-8 Ap 20 '87

House committee faults tactics instead of equipment in Stark attack. M. Mecham. *Aviat Week Space Technol* 126:32-3 Je 22 '87

House Committee reduces defense budget further. *Aviat Week Space Technol* 126:28-9 My 4 '87

House panel warns of future risks in B-1B program costs and schedule. *Aviat Week Space Technol* 126:20-1 Ap 6 '87

In the House, an abrasive defender of defense [L. Aspin] D. Griffiths. por *Bus Week* p53 Ag 24 '87

'Never double-cross your friends' [chairman L. Aspin handed no confidence vote] G. Borger. il por *U S News World Rep* 102:21 Ja 19 '87

The Old Breed strikes back [backlash against L. Aspin] C. J. Matthews. il *New Repub* 196:21-3 Mr 2 '87

United States. Congress. House. Committee on Energy and Commerce

Corporate watchdog [J. Dingell] T. Noah. il por *Newsweek* 109:50-1 Ap 20 '87

Detroit powerhouse. J. McLaughlin. *Natl Rev* 39:24 F 27 '87

United States. Congress. House. Committee on Energy and Commerce. Subcommittee on Oversight and Investigations

Atomic gaffe [study of security at nuclear weapons manufacturing plants] *Nation* 244:349 Mr 21 '87

United States. Congress. House. Committee on Energy and Commerce. Subcommittee on Telecommunications and Finance

Capitol spat over TV news. il *U S News World Rep* 102:10 My 11 '87

Markey see, Markey do. M. Brown. por *Channels* 7:26 My '87

No more malarkey from Edward Markey? F. Seghers and V. Cahan. por *Bus Week* p71 N 2 '87

United States. Congress. House. Committee on Foreign Affairs. Subcommittee on Western Hemisphere Affairs

Crockett and the patriots [pro-Communist views of Congressman G. Crockett] *Natl Rev* 39:18-19 Ag 14 '87

United States. Congress. House. Committee on Public Works and Transportation. Subcommittee on Aviation

Delays, service problems prompt strong congressional reaction [airlines] J. Ott. *Aviat Week Space Technol* 127:33-5 Ag 10 '87

House panel considers reregulation of airlines. C. Preble. *Aviat Week Space Technol* 126:74-5 Je 15 '87

United States. Congress. House. Committee on Public Works and Transportation. Subcommittee on Economic Development

Rep. Savage heads group to examine industrial policy of United States. por *Jet* 71:32 F 2 '87

United States. Congress. House. Committee on Science, Space, and Technology

New look for House committee. C. Norman. *Science* 235:629 F 6 '87

Science committee okays Supercollider. M. Crawford. *Science* 238:477 O 23 '87

United States. Congress. House. Committee on the Budget

Bill Gray can't lose in the budget battle. D. Harbrecht. il por *Bus Week* p25-6 S 7 '87

Congressman Gray puts together first trillion dollar budget in history of U.S. S. Booker. il pors *Jet* 72:12-13 Jl 13 '87

Gray works to save fed. programs cut by Reagan [Rep. W. Gray] *Jet* 71:4 Mr 9 '87

United States. Congress. House. Committee on Un-American Activities

Memories of HUAC. P. Bosworth. *Nation* 245:436-7 O 24 '87

Notes on the . . . blacklist [Hollywood blacklisting period; special section] il *Film Comment* 23:37-9+ N/D '87

The odyssey of Daniel Boorstin [legacy of HUAC testimony; cover story] J. Wiener. il *Nation* 245:289+ S 26 '87

United States. Congress. House. Committee on Ways and Means

House unit urges textbook costs be deducted as they are incurred. H. Fields. *Publ Wkly* 232:15 Ag 21 '87

It worked with the tax bill—and it just might work with trade [role of D. Rostenkowski] H. Gleckman and D. Harbrecht. il por *Bus Week* p42 Mr 9 '87

Washington's odd couple shakes up taxes [B. Packwood and D. Rostenkowski] A. R. Dowd. il pors *Fortune* 115:40-1 Ja 5 '87

United States. Congress. House. Democratic Caucus *See* House Democratic Caucus (U.S.)

United States. Congress. House. Office of Legislative Operations

John Jenkins is new House bill operations chief. il por *Jet* 72:4 Ag 3 '87

United States. Congress. House. Select Committee on Aging. Subcommittee on Health and Long-Term Care

Lobbies rock the retirement boat [American Assoc. of Retired Persons vs. C. Pepper] C. Murphy. il *50 Plus* 27:13-14 Ja '87

United States. Congress. House. Select Committee on Intelligence

Rep. Stokes heads House Intelligence Committee. por *Jet* 71:7 Ja 12 '87

United States. Congress. House. Select Committee on Narcotics Abuse and Control

Drugs and contras. *Nation* 244:786-7 Je 13 '87

United States. Congress. Senate

The hearings ahead [INF Treaty] W. F. Buckley. *Natl Rev* 39:54 D 31 '87

How to wreck the treaty [possible Senate amendments to the INF Treaty] J. V. Lamar, Jr. il *Time* 130:26 D 21 '87

The new Senate Democrats: no bunch of rookies. D. Harbrecht. il *Bus Week* p74-5 Ja 26 '87

Nice guys do finish first—just ask Al Simpson [minority whip] D. Harbrecht. por *Bus Week* p94 N 9 '87

No more Mr. Nice guys [Senate Republicans] H. Klingeman. *Natl Rev* 39:40-1 Jl 17 '87

Senate infighting on treaty [INF] J. D. Isaacs. il *Bull At Sci* 43:3-4 N '87

Senate minority could imperil treaty [arms control] J. D. Isaacs. il *Bull At Sci* 43:5-6 S '87

Senators will load the trade bill with goodies. D. Harbrecht. *Bus Week* p58 My 25 '87

To ratify or not to ratify? [outlook for Senate ratification of proposed arms control deal with the Soviets] J. McLaughlin. *Natl Rev* 39:28 S 25 '87

Turning the trade bill into a 'Christmas tree'. D. Harbrecht. il *Bus Week* p70 Jl 20 '87

Will the Senate kill the treaty? [INF Treaty] T. Morganthau. il *Newsweek* 110:29 D 21 '87

Powers and duties

Amend the Constitution's treaty clause [outmoded requirement that treaties be ratified by a two-thirds vote] B. S. Loeb. bibl f il *Bull At Sci* 43:38-41 O '87

Foundermania breaks out in the Senate. J. Weisberg. il *Newsweek* 110:14 Ag 24 '87

Voting

Congress is closing in on a plant-closing law. S. B. Garland. il *Bus Week* p35 Jl 27 '87

A 'devil in the detail' [Senate passes sweeping protectionist trade bill] I. Austen. il *Macleans* 100:30-1 Ag 3 '87

Senate passes $15.6-billion Trust Fund spending bill [Aviation Trust Fund] *Aviat Week Space Technol* 127:44 N 2 '87

Senate votes financial aid to semiconductor consortium. *Aviat Week Space Technol* 127:155 O 12 '87

'Sleazy' is the word for it [Senate votes against immediate cut-off of aid to Nicaraguan resistance] *America* 156:266 Ap 4 '87

Trade bill addresses 'dumping' and Canada's bar to investment. H. Fields. *Publ Wkly* 232:19 Ag 14 '87

United States. Congress. Senate. Committee on Appropriations

Senate committee drops small ICBM in favor of railgarrison MX. *Aviat Week Space Technol* 127:26 D 7 '87

United States. Congress. Senate. Committee on Armed Services

Sam Nunn is sticking to his guns. D. Griffiths. il por *Bus Week* p52-3 Ag 24 '87

Senate Committee boosts conventional forces, limits ABM reinterpretation. M. Mecham. *Aviat Week Space Technol* 126:28-9 My 11 '87

United States. Congress. Senate. Committee on Banking, Housing and Urban Affairs

. . . and Proxmire takes aim at takeover abuses. V. Cahan. *Bus Week* p35 Ap 20 '87

Banking on deregulation. J. McLaughlin. *Natl Rev* 39:24 O 23 '87

Suddenly, Proxmire the gadfly looks more like a godsend [retirement] V. Cahan. *Bus Week* p47 S 14 '87

United States. Congress. Senate. Committee on Commerce, Science, and Transportation

Senate panel approves bill requiring airlines to reveal on-time data. *Aviat Week Space Technol* 127:34 Jl 20 '87

United States. Congress. Senate. Committee on Finance

Washington's odd couple shakes up taxes [B. Packwood and D. Rostenkowski] A. R. Dowd. il pors *Fortune* 115:40-1 Ja 5 '87

United States. Congress. Senate. Committee on Foreign Relations

Coming soon: the odd couple [Senators C. Pell and J. Helms] T. Noah and E. Clift. il pors *Newsweek* 109:28 F 2 '87

Senate Foreign Relations: facing gridlock. D. Harbrecht. *Bus Week* p41 F 2 '87

United States. Congress. Senate. Committee on Labor and Human Resources

Labor Committee's left turn. il *Nations Bus* 75:10+ Ja '87

United States. Congress. Senate. Committee on the Budget

Will a new chairman polarize the Senate Budget Committee? [retirement of L. Chiles] D. Harbrecht. *Bus Week* p49 D 21 '87

United States. Congress. Senate. Committee on the Judiciary

All eyes on the undecideds [Senate Judiciary Committee hearings on Supreme Court nominee R. Bork] T. Jacoby. il por *Newsweek* 110:30 O 5 '87

The battle against Bork will be long, bitter—and likely to fail. P. Dwyer and D. Harbrecht. por *Bus Week* p45 Jl 13 '87

Believing in Judge Bork [Supreme Court nominee's hearings] T. Gest. il *U S News World Rep* 103:29 S 28 '87

Biden Star Chamber? [creation of all-Democratic screening panel for Reagan judicial nominees] M. Fumento. *Natl Rev* 39:30 Mr 13 '87

Bidenquiddick [J. Biden's about-face on the R. H. Bork nomination] *Natl Rev* 39:15+ Ag 28 '87

Biden's main chance [R. H. Bork hearings] T. Morganthau. il por *Newsweek* 110:35-6 S 21 '87

A Bork without the bite [Supreme Court nominee's hearings] J. V. Lamar, Jr. il por *Time* 130:18-19 S 28 '87

Democratic majority [vote against nomination of R. Bork] *Nation* 245:397 O 17 '87

A fight for one man, one vote [hearings on Supreme Court nominee R. Bork] J. V. Lamar, Jr. il *Time* 130:25 O 5 '87

The grilling of Judge Bork. A. Press. il por *Newsweek* 110:27+ S 28 '87

'The hottest fight in a decade' [J. Biden vs. R. Bork's nomination to Supreme Court] N. Cooper. il pors *Newsweek* 110:30 Jl 20 '87

In the pit [excerpt from remarks] A. K. Simpson. *Natl Rev* 39:30 Ap 10 '87

Judging Robert Bork. M. McDonald. il por *Macleans* 100:26 S 28 '87

Letter from Washington [hearings on R. H. Bork's Supreme Court nomination] E. Drew. *New Yorker* 63:150-4+ N 2 '87

The old frontier [E. Kennedy's opposition to R. H. Bork] J. Klein. il por *N Y* 20:26+ O 19 '87

On trial: character [R. Bork's Supreme Court confirmation hearings] G. Borger. il pors *U S News World Rep* 103:26-7 S 28 '87

Shifting odds in the fight over Bork [Supreme Court nominee's hearings] T. Gest. il por *U S News World Rep* 103:25 O 5 '87

A 'tempest in a teapot' (pace Cicero) [R. Bork's Supreme Court confirmation hearings] M. Kramer. il *U S News World Rep* 103:20 S 28 '87

United States. Congress. Senate. Special Committee to Investigate Organized Crime in Interstate Commerce

Capone to Kefauver: organised crime in America. M. Woodiwiss. bibl il *Hist Today* 37:8-15 Je '87

United States. Constitution

200 and going strong. il *Nations Bus* 75:49-50 Jl '87

1787 [views of T. Jefferson] *Am Herit* 38:30 D '87

America—200 years on. E. Wright. il *Hist Today* 37:7-10 S '87

America's sacred text. E. L. Doctorow. *Current* 294:8-15 Jl/Ag '87

Celebrating the real Constitution. *America* 157:3-4 Jl 4-11 '87

A citizen reads the Constitution [adaptation of address, September 1986] E. L. Doctorow. il *Nation* 244:208-9+ F 21 '87

The Constitution [cover story; special issue] il *Life* 10:6-15+ Fall '87

The Constitution [discussion of May 1987 article, Why blacks, women & Jews are not mentioned in the Constitution] R. A. Goldwin. *Commentary* 84:2+ O '87

The Constitution and the consumer: discovering the connections. W. F. Janssen. il *FDA Consum* 21:8-11 S '87

The Constitution and the people left out: a study in original intent. R. A. Goldwin. *Current* 295:4-10 S '87

The Constitution at 200 [cover story; special section] il *Christ Today* 31:18-30 Jl 10 '87

The Constitution at 200 [special issue] il *Time* 130:20-30+ Jl 6 '87

Does the Constitution need reform? H. Evans. il *U S News World Rep* 102:34 Ap 27 '87

Editorial. W. Garrett. il *Antiques* 132:513 S '87

First word [approaching constitutional storm] A. M. Dershowitz. il *Omni* 9:6 S '87

Foreign affairs and the Constitution. L. Henkin. bibl f *Foreign Aff* 66:284-310 Wint '87/'88

The great voyage: two hundred years of the Constitution [cover story; special issue] il *N Y Times Mag* p14+ S 13 '87

In God we trust [seminars conducted by W. C. Skousen] il por *Time* 129:26 F 9 '87

In order to [address, August 10, 1987] L. A. Iacocca. *Vital Speeches Day* 53:745-8 O 1 '87

Justice Thurgood Marshall on the living Constitution [excerpt from address; May 6, 1987] T. Marshall. *Ms* 16:111 S '87

A more perfect union. N. G. Thomas. il *USA Today (Periodical)* 116:16-19 S '87

Notes and comment [war powers aspect of the Constitution and aid to the contras] *New Yorker* 63:23-4 Je 1 '87

On Constitution's bicentennial, OTA examines effects of science [report entitled Science, technology and the Constitution] I. Goodwin. il *Phys Today* 40:43-5 N '87

Ordered liberty [address, July 29, 1987] C. Mathias. *Vital Speeches Day* 53:706-10 S 15 '87

Our Constitution: after 200 years, the great experiment continues [cover story; special issue] il maps *Sch Update* 120:4-26 S 4 '87

Our flawed and glorious Constitution. C. Kocol. por *Humanist* 47:37-8 My/Je '87

Our secular Constitution. E. Doerr. *Humanist* 47:43-4 Mr/Ap '87

Psychology and the Constitution [impact on Supreme Court decisions] A. J. Tomkins. bibl (p58) *Psychol Today* 21:48-50 S '87

Reasons and arguments in the Constitution [views expressed in The founders' Constitution] M. A. Noll. il *Christ Century* 104:499-500+ My 20-27 '87

Saving the Constitution [cover story; special section] il *Natl Rev* 39:30-7+ Jl 17 '87

Some truths are not self-evident. H. Zinn. *Nation* 245:87-8 Ag 1-8 '87

Take our Constitution quiz. M. O'Koon. *Good Housekeep* 205:267 S '87

To form a more perfect union [black America and the Constitution; cover story; special section; with editorial comment by Earl G. Graves] il *Black Enterp* 17:11, 51+ Jl '87

To form a more perfect union [with editorial comment] Publius. *New Leader* 70:2, 11-12 Jl 13-27 '87

The United States Constitution today [views of the American Assembly] *Cent Mag* 20:60-1+ S/O '87

Unraveling the Constitution. S. D. Pollack. bibl *Society* 24:56-9 Ja/F '87

Unraveling the Constitution: a rule of law. S. D. Pollack. *Current* 297:18-21 N '87

We hold these truths [excerpts; with editorial comment by Bruce M. Smith] M. J. Adler. il *Phi Delta Kappan* 69:250, 269-74 D '87

United States. Constitution—*cont.*
We the people [cover story; special issue; with editorial comment by Ed Holm] B. McGinty. il *Am Hist Illus* 22:4, 10-48+ Summ '87
We, the theologians [views of T. Jefferson and J. Madison] L. W. Gibbs. pors *Christ Today* 31:29-31 D 11 '87
What the spirit of the people provides [address, September 1987] R. Carlson. *Vital Speeches Day* 54:104-5 D 1 '87
Why blacks, women & Jews are not mentioned in the Constitution. R. A. Goldwin. *Commentary* 83:28-33 My '87
A word from the right on rights [controversial textbook The making of America] A. T. Podesta. il por *Progressive* 51:13-14 Jl '87

Amendments
See also
United States. Constitution. Equal Rights Amendment (Proposed)
Amend the Constitution's treaty clause [outmoded requirement that treaties be ratified by a two-thirds vote of the Senate] B. S. Loeb. bibl f il *Bull At Sci* 43:38-41 O '87
Amendment addendum [last 10 amendments] R. Baker. il *N Y Times Mag* p28 S 13 '87
Balance the budget—but not with an amendment. A. S. Blinder. il *Bus Week* p16 Jl 27 '87
The battle over preserving the English language [English Language Amendment] G. Imhoff and G. Bikales. il *USA Today (Periodical)* 115:63-5 Ja '87
The Constitution and the 14th Amendment [with discussion] W. F. Murphy. il por *Cent Mag* 20:9-30 Jl/Ag '87
Equality before the law: the Civil War amendments [cover story; with discussion] H. Belz. il por *Cent Mag* 20:4-19 N/D '87
Four views of the Constitution [First, Sixth and Fourteenth amendments and black civil rights] il *Black Enterp* 17:59-60+ Jl '87
How hard it is to change. M. F. Berry. il *N Y Times Mag* p93-4+ S 13 '87
Is it broke? Should we fix it? Changing the Constitution is not easy, but plenty of people keep trying. R. Lacayo. il map *Time* 130:54-5 Jl 6 '87
Let's get representative [proposed constitutional amendment calling for national proportional representation] H. Hertzberg. *New Repub* 196:15-18 Je 29 '87
Letting 'We the people' speak [fear of a runaway constitutional convention; cover story] R. S. Kay. il *New Leader* 70:8-10 Jl 13-27 '87
The lost amendment [congressional pay amendment] R. Zagarri. *New Repub* 196:13 F 2 '87
Modern dilemmas: the three most cited amendments today. R. Robotham. il *Life* 10:121-4 Fall '87
Move over, James Madison [suggestions for amendments; cover story] *New Repub* 196:19-21 Je 29 '87
Quirks & quacks: in trivial pursuit of constitutional oddities. il *Life* 10:90 Fall '87
To make a nation whole [14th Amendment and racial reform] D. A. Bell. il *N Y Times Mag* p42-4+ S 13 '87
"We the people . . . " [proposed Environmental Quality Amendment; excerpts from address, March 1987] J. D. Hair. il *Natl Wildl* 25:25-6 Je/Jl '87

Anecdotes, facetiae, satire, etc.
The phantom amendment & the Duchess of Baltimore [E. P. Bonaparte] W. H. Earle. il pors *Am Hist Illus* 22:32-9 N '87

Anecdotes, facetiae, satire, etc.
Up the rebels! M. Ivins. il *Progressive* 51:28 N '87

Bibliography
Bicentennial samplings. il *Time* 130:78-9 Jl 6 '87
A Constitution reader. *Am Hist Illus* 22:6+ Summ '87
Constitutional update. *Publ Wkly* 231:62 F 13 '87
Popular fiction. E. S. Morgan. il *New Repub* 196:25-32+ Je 29 '87

Centennial celebrations, etc.
200th anniversary of the signing of the Constitution [address, September 17, 1987] R. Reagan. *Vital Speeches Day* 54:2-3 O 15 '87
ACT promotes TV-smart viewing, bicentennial participation. il *Child Today* 16:4-5 Mr/Ap '87
Around the Mall and beyond. E. Park. il *Smithsonian* 18:24+ Ag '87
A bicentennial botch-up [Philadelphia] P. McKillop and J. Schwartz. il *Newsweek* 109:62 My 18 '87
Bicentennial events. D. Kalb. bibl il *U S News World Rep* 102:32-3 Ap 27 '87
Bill Moyers on our U.S. Constitution [interview] L. Kravitz. por *Sch Update* 119:29 My 18 '87
Birthday bash. il *Newsweek* 110:83 S 28 '87

Celebrate the bicentennial: create a Constitution garden. A. Reilly. il *Flower Gard* 31:80-1 Ap/My '87
Celebrating the Constitution. R. Deigh. il *Saturday Evening Post* 259:54-6+ My/Je '87
Celebrating the Constitution. R. Goldsborough. il *Americana* 15:70+ My/Je '87
Celebrating the Constitution: a dissent [excerpt from address, May 6, 1987] T. Marshall. *Harpers* 275:17-19 Jl '87
Congress goes home again [Philadelphia ceremonies] F. Trippett. il *Time* 130:26 Jl 27 '87
The Constitution [excerpt from address, May 6, 1987] T. Marshall. por *Essence* 18:166 S '87
The Constitution 1787-1987 [special section; with editorial comment by Byron Dobell] il *Am Herit* 38:7, 30-51+ My/Je '87
The Constitution across the nation. J. Long. il *Am Herit* 38:132+ My/Je '87
The Constitution and the congregation: time to celebrate. M. E. Marty. il *Christ Century* 104:523-5 Je 3-10 '87
Constitution bicentennial activities. *Am Hist Illus* 22:50 Summ '87
Constitution gardening. W. Shipman. il *Ctry J* 14:14 Ap '87
A Constitutional celebration. J. Adler. il *Newsweek* 109:21-2 Ja 19 '87
Federal judge Damon Keith hosts bicentennial banquet for nation's Constitution. il pors *Jet* 71:32-3 Mr 2 '87
Garden gate [gardening projects] S. O. Daniels. il *Rodale's Org Gard* 34:6 Mr '87
Happy 200th to the Constitution. M. Engel. *Glamour* 85:48+ Jl '87
Happy Juneteenth! It's time to celebrate [blacks and the bicentennial] E. Walton. por *U S News World Rep* 102:9 My 25 '87
Justice Marshall's minority report [asserting that the Constitution helped entrench slavery] T. Gest. il por *U S News World Rep* 102:12-13 My 18 '87
Low-key bicentennial. il *World Press Rev* 34:41 Ag '87
Marshall cites faults of Constitution at 200th year. por *Jet* 72:12 My 25 '87
A new "Federalist" [replica of the 1788 Federalist] il *Am Hist Illus* 22:38 S '87
Paper party [Philadelphia celebration] il *Time* 130:24 S 28 '87
Parading the Constitution ["We the People 200" parade in Philadelphia] B. Weber. il *N Y Times Mag* p162 S 13 '87
Parks and the Constitution: celebrating on common soil [cover story; special section; with editorial comment by Paul C. Pritchard] il *Natl Parks* 61:5, 12-29+ Mr/Ap '87
Philadelphia, 1987 [celebration marking bicentennial] il *Am Hist Illus* 22:26-33 My '87
The Philadelphia story [commemorating 200th birthday of U.S. Constitution] G. Bain. il *Travel Holiday* 167:44-8 Ap '87
Public backs Marshall in his views on Constitution [Supreme Court Justice T. Marshall] por *Jet* 72:32 Je 1 '87
The pursuit of tackiness. A. Wilentz. il *Time* 129:26 F 9 '87
'Reagan people only' [protestors banned from Philadelphia ceremonies] K. Kilimnik. *Progressive* 51:11 S '87
The real meaning of the Constitution bicentennial [address, May 6, 1987] T. Marshall. il pors *Ebony* 42:62+ S '87
Reliving the Constitution [Colonial Williamsburg] il *Parents* 62:15 S '87
A republic, if you can keep it [cover story; special section] il map *Newsweek* 109:44-52+ My 25 '87
The selling of the Constitution. il *U S News World Rep* 102:9 F 23 '87
Tale of two cities: did party poopers prevail? [Philadelphia's plans for celebration] W. L. Chaze. il *U S News World Rep* 102:26 My 4 '87
There's a big party on! G. Clarke. il *Time* 130:62-4 Jl 6 '87

Collectibles
Praise Madison and pass the ammunition [limited edition pistol to commemorate the 200th anniversary of the U.S. Constitution] il *Harpers* 275:21+ N '87

Exhibitions
Bicentennial of the Constitution—Chicago [We the people: creating a new nation, 1765-1820 at the Chicago Historical Society] S. B. Sherrill. il *Antiques* 132:420+ S '87

United States. Constitution—Exhibitions—_cont._
Bicentennial of the Constitution—New York City [Government by choice: inventing the United States Constitution at the New York Historical Society] S. B. Sherrill. il *Antiques* 132:410+ S '87
Roads to Liberty exhibit. *Am Hist Illus* 22:14 S '87
Why it happened [Are we to be a nation? exhibit at the New York Public Library] B. A. Weisberger. il *Americana* 15:24-6+ My/Je '87

Pictorial works
Picturing the Constitution. H. Holzer and M. E. Neely, Jr. il *Am Hist Illus* 22:30-5 S '87

Study and teaching
Five teachers who breathe life into our national charter ['Constitution in the Classroom' Bicentennial Awards'] E. Dzik. il *Sch Update* 120:24-5 S 4 '87

Terminology
The incongruous 'We' [use in Preamble] R. Blount. il *N Y Times Mag* p14+ S 13 '87

United States. Constitution. 1st-10th amendments
See also
Freedom of speech
Advertising pleads the First. M. L. Wulf. *Commonweal* 114:75-9 F 13 '87
Bill of Rights draft found [R. Sherman draft] *Am Hist Illus* 22:12 O '87
Connecticut Yankee Roger Sherman's draft of the Bill of Rights makes a surprise appearance in Washington. il por *People Wkly* 28:71 Ag 17 '87
The Fifth freedom. *Progressive* 51:10-11 F '87
Is First Amendment in trouble? [views of Gary Colboth and George Heneghan] il *USA Today (Periodical)* 116:10 Ag '87
Power to the people [9th and 10th Amendments] W. B. Reynolds. il *N Y Times Mag* p116-18+ S 13 '87
Rights show their roots [discovery of R. Sherman's handwritten Bill of Rights draft] por *Time* 130:25 Ag 10 '87
The wall that never was [First Amendment] T. C. Muck. il *Christ Today* 31:16-17 Jl 10 '87

United States. Constitution. Equal Rights Amendment (Proposed)
The ERA renewal drive. R. T. Eisler. *Humanist* 47:35-6 Ja/F '87
The ERA: should we eat our words? E. Smeal. *Ms* 16:170+ Jl/Ag '87
Not NOW [renewed campaign for the ERA] J. J. Mansbridge. *Nation* 244:5 Ja 10 '87
Those 24 words are back: ERA surfaces once more amid doubts about its urgency. J. Smolowe. il *Time* 130:91 Jl 6 '87

United States. Constitutional Convention (1787)
Birth of a true nation. W. E. Burger. il *Read Dig* 131:33-5 S '87
The Constitution 1787-1987 [special section; with editorial comment by Byron Dobell] il *Am Herit* 38:7, 30-51+ My/Je '87
Constitution-making weather: Philadelphia, 1787. D. M. Ludlum. *Ctry J* 14:70 Jl '87
The Constitutional Convention and the framers. il *Sch Update* 120:15 S 4 '87
Constitutional Convention, Philadelphia, 1787. E. Bowen. bibl (p146) il map *Smithsonian* 18:32-43 Jl '87
Countdown to a miracle: the making of our Constitution. T. J. Fleming. il *Read Dig* 131:132-40+ S '87
Creating a more perfect union. W. E. Burger. il *Natl Parks* 61:12-14 Mr/Ap '87
Designing a ship of state [special section] il *Life* 10:19-24+ Fall '87
'The great compromise' drafting the American Constitution, 1787 [cover story] J. N. Rakove. bibl il *Hist Today* 37:19-25 S '87
How the deed was done: when 55 men spent a hot summer arguing their way to greatness. O. Friedrich. il *Time* 130:58-61 Jl 6 '87
James Madison: architect of the Constitution. A. J. Hall. il pors supp (folded map) map *Natl Geogr* 172:340-69 S '87
The miracle at Philadelphia [cover story] M. McLoughlin. bibl il *U S News World Rep* 102:24-7 Ap 27 '87
A more perfect union. N. G. Thomas. il *USA Today (Periodical)* 116:16-19 S '87
The non-signers [E. Randolph, G. Mason and E. Gerry] C. L. Mee. pors *Am Herit* 38:78-9 S/O '87
Philadelphia, 1787. H. Holzer. il *Am Hist Illus* 22:20-5 My '87
Philadelphia: the city that gave us a nation. A. Green. il *Natl Parks* 61:24-9 Mr/Ap '87
A republic, if you can keep it [cover story; special section] il map *Newsweek* 109:44-52+ My 25 '87

The story of the Constitution: conflict and compromise. C. McHugh. il *Sch Update* 120:8-11 S 4 '87
We the people [cover story; special issue; with editorial comment by Ed Holm] B. McGinty. il *Am Hist Illus* 22:4, 10-48+ Summ '87
Why it happened [Are we to be a nation? exhibit at the New York Public Library] B. A. Weisberger. il *Americana* 15:24-6+ My/Je '87

Anecdotes, facetiae, satire, etc.
What if TV had been there? Imagining how the framers might fare in the media age. W. Shapiro. il *Time* 130:62-3 Jl 6 '87

United States. Consumer Product Safety Commission *See* U.S. Consumer Product Safety Commission
United States. Council of Economic Advisers *See* Council of Economic Advisers (U.S.)
United States. Court of Appeals (District of Columbia Circuit)
One rung below. *U S News World Rep* 103:29 Jl 13 '87
United States. Customs Service *See* U.S. Customs Service
United States. Declaration of Independence
John Pierce proved that the writing on the wall was a relic [print made in 1776 in Rhode Island by Solomon Southwick] il por *People Wkly* 27:51 F 16 '87
The pursuit of happiness. Publius. il *New Leader* 70:12-13 O 5 '87
We, the theologians [views of T. Jefferson and J. Madison] L. W. Gibbs. pors *Christ Today* 31:29-31 D 11 '87
United States. Defense Advanced Research Projects Agency
DARPA will team with services to develop prototype weapons. P. J. Klass. *Aviat Week Space Technol* 126:97+ My 4 '87
Program delays spur NASA, DARPA to restructure X-wing flight tests. *Aviat Week Space Technol* 127:23-4 Ag 31 '87
Some researchers concerned with Defense funding of AI projects [Strategic Computing Initiative] *Byte* 12:40 O '87
Technological problems, rising costs force X-wing program to scale down. *Aviat Week Space Technol* 127:23 O 19 '87
Tight government budgets threaten Lightsat program. M. A. Dornheim. *Aviat Week Space Technol* 127:28 O 19 '87
U.S. planning new emphasis on lightweight satellite systems. R. G. O'Lone. il *Aviat Week Space Technol* 127:22-3 Ag 10 '87
"Unmanned" warfare due in the future? il *Radio-Electron* 58:4 Ap '87
United States. Defense Intelligence Agency
CIA, DIA at odds over Soviet threat. M. Krepon. *Bull At Sci* 43:6-7 My '87
United States. Defense Science Board
Defense Science Board urges semiconductor consortium. B. D. Nordwall. *Aviat Week Space Technol* 126:94 Mr 2 '87
DOD is asked to aid semiconductor firms. J. Raloff. *Sci News* 131:117 F 21 '87
DOD Science Board finds SDI Phase I reasonable but 'sketchy'. I. Goodwin. il *Phys Today* 40:54-6 S '87
Weinberger cites need to boost chip industry. *Aviat Week Space Technol* 126:24 My 18 '87
United States. Dept. of Agriculture
Black appointed to USDA office; fourth director. *Jet* 72:22 Je 15 '87
Can you believe the pig report? G. Johnston. il *Success Farm* 85 no6:18T Mr '87
Farm women sue USDA [farm program payment discrimination] C. Tevis. il *Success Farm* 85:24 S '87
Gene-altered hog vaccine causes stir for USDA [Omnivac pseudorabies vaccine] *Success Farm* 85 no6:18AZ Mr '87
Reverse discrimination on the Street [decision to distribute Rural Housing Senior Mortgage passthroughs by minority firms] D. Seligman. il *Fortune* 116:142 O 26 '87
United States. Dept. of Agriculture. Animal and Plant Health Inspection Service *See* United States. Animal and Plant Health Inspection Service
United States. Dept. of Agriculture. Animal Parasitology Institute *See* Animal Parasitology Institute (U.S.)
United States. Dept. of Agriculture. Conservation Reserve Program
Across the editor's desk. R. Krumme. il *Success Farm* 85:3 O '87
The call of the wild [wildlife habitat funding] J. Walter. il *Success Farm* 85:62-3 N '87
Keeping soil down on the farm. W. Sinclair. il *Sierra* 72:26-9 My/Je '87

United States. Dept. of Agriculture. Conservation Reserve Program—*cont.*

Your cost to comply with new conservation rules. J. Walter. il *Success Farm* 85 no6:8-9 Mr '87

United States. Dept. of Agriculture. Extension Service *See* United States. Extension Service

United States. Dept. of Agriculture. Farmers Home Administration *See* United States. Farmers Home Administration

United States. Dept. of Agriculture. Forest Service *See* United States. Forest Service

United States. Dept. of Agriculture. Soil Conservation Service *See* United States. Soil Conservation Service

United States. Dept. of Commerce

Broader R&D role sought for Commerce. M. Crawford. il *Science* 237:19 Jl 3 '87

Can Verity pick up where Baldrige left off? S. J. Dryden and M. Schroeder. por *Bus Week* p30 Ag 24 '87

Commerce lost Baldrige just when it needed him most. S. J. Dryden. *Bus Week* p35 Ag 10 '87

Defense, Commerce Departments clash again over export controls. *Aviat Week Space Technol* 126:28-9 F 16 '87

A letter to Mr. Verity. *Natl Rev* 39:19-20 S 11 '87

Science panel urges lead export role for Commerce [study by National Academy of Sciences] P. Mann. *Aviat Week Space Technol* 126:20 Ja 19 '87

Space censors? [satellite photos] A. A. Lappen. il *Forbes* 140:12 S 7 '87

Appropriations and expenditures

Commerce urged to divert weather satellite funding to save Landsat. *Aviat Week Space Technol* 126:62-3 Mr 23 '87

United States. Dept. of Commerce. National Technical Information Service *See* United States. National Technical Information Service

United States. Dept. of Defense

Biological warfare research under fire [DOD held accountable for environmental impact] D. D. Edwards. *Sci News* 131:132 F 28 '87

Cap on top [C. Weinberger] F. Barnes. il *New Repub* 196:13-15 Ap 20 '87

Changing of the guards [C. Weinberger replaced by F. Carlucci] G. J. Church. il por *Time* 130:21-2 N 16 '87

Defense, Commerce Departments clash again over export controls. *Aviat Week Space Technol* 126:28-9 F 16 '87

Defense Dept. plans to study earth-penetrating nuclear weapons. J. D. Morrocco. *Aviat Week Space Technol* 126:28-9 Je 8 '87

DOD revises its space policy. *Sci News* 131:189 Mr 21 '87

DOD to reassess bioweapons' risks. M. Crawford. *Science* 235:968 F 27 '87

Farewell, Dark Prince [resignation of R. Perle] il por *Time* 129:14 Mr 23 '87

The flawed legacy of 'Cap the Knife'. il por *Macleans* 100:23 N 16 '87

Forbidden facts. P. Bagne. il *Omni* 9:18+ F '87

Hard choices, less money [resignation of C. W. Weinberger] T. Morganthau. il *Newsweek* 110:60-1+ N 16 '87

In the wake of 'Cap the Shovel' [resignation of C. Weinberger] P. R. Range. il por *U S News World Rep* 103:16-17 N 16 '87

Name, rank and computer log-on [Ada computer language foul-ups] K. Healy. il *Forbes* 139:87+ Ap 20 '87

The national guards. D. Goldberg. il *Omni* 9:44-6+ My '87

A new hot seat for the cool Frank Carlucci. B. Javetski. por *Bus Week* p70 N 16 '87

Pentagon forms unit to coordinate arms projects with allies [Defense Cooperation Working Group] *Aviat Week Space Technol* 126:21 Ja 26 '87

Pentagon, State Dept. granted veto over U.S. remote sensing satellites. T. M. Foley. *Aviat Week Space Technol* 127:20-1 Jl 20 '87

Pentagon task force to develop model for radar technology transfer. J. D. Morrocco. *Aviat Week Space Technol* 127:30 Ag 24 '87

The 'Prince of Darkness' calls it quits [R. Perle leaves] T. Jacoby. il por *Newsweek* 109:27 Mr 23 '87

Richard Perle did his best. *Natl Rev* 39:21 Ap 10 '87

Story of a consummate bureaucrat [cover story] J. Morley. *Nation* 245:737+ D 19 '87

Weinberger's legacy: a stronger nation and a management mess. D. Griffiths. por *Bus Week* p71 N 16 '87

Appropriations and expenditures

Biological research and military funding. S. Shulman. il *Technol Rev* 90:13-14 Ap '87

Budget jeopardizes SDI timetable; research efforts scaled back. T. M. Foley. *Aviat Week Space Technol* 127:25-6 N 9 '87

Budget slashing would kill A-6F, small ICBM and Aquila. B. M. Greeley, Jr. *Aviat Week Space Technol* 127:31 D 21 '87

Carlucci is teaching the Pentagon a new word—'cutback'. D. Griffiths. *Bus Week* p49 D 21 '87

Congress approves air show deductions, cuts Exim funding. *Aviat Week Space Technol* 127:23 Jl 13 '87

Congress balks at proposal to speed space-based antimissile defense. P. Mann. *Aviat Week Space Technol* 126:22-4 Ja 26 '87

Congress reluctant to cut defense for third consecutive year. P. Mann. il *Aviat Week Space Technol* 126:67+ Mr 9 '87

The dark secret of the black budget. T. Weiner. *Wash Mon* 19:31-5 My '87

Declining U.S. defense budget held hostage by economic summit [stock market crash aftermath] P. Mann. *Aviat Week Space Technol* 127:22-4 N 2 '87

The defense buildup, 1977-85: effects on production and employment. D. K. Henry and R. P. Oliver. bibl f il *Mon Labor Rev* 110:3-11 Ag '87

Defense Dept. cancels shuttle planning complex. *Aviat Week Space Technol* 126:29 F 9 '87

Defense Dept. seeks funds to continue P-3C production. J. D. Morrocco. *Aviat Week Space Technol* 127:26 Ag 31 '87

Defense Dept. seeks launcher for SDI in supplemental budget. *Aviat Week Space Technol* 126:21 Ja 5 '87

Defense Dept. will seek funds to expand Navstar constellation. P. J. Klass. map *Aviat Week Space Technol* 127:30-2 O 5 '87

Defense spending's role in the economy. M. Christopher. map *Sch Update* 119:17 F 23 '87

Deficit cuts impact defense, NASA budgets. *Aviat Week Space Technol* 127:29 O 19 '87

Electronics will gain larger share of budget. B. D. Nordwall. il *Aviat Week Space Technol* 126:227+ Mr 9 '87

The end of an era for U.S. global power? W. J. Holstein. il *Bus Week* p170+ N 16 '87

Farmers plow up Pentagon's budget [movement to transfer funding from the military budget to Iowa's FmHA program] M. Helmreich. *Progressive* 51:15-16 Mr '87

Fiscal 1988 budgets [special section] il *Aviat Week Space Technol* 126:18-32 Ja 12 '87

A frightening new numbers game. R. J. Shapiro. il *U S News World Rep* 103:32-3 S 28 '87

Geographical limit on research funds in bill seen as swipe at peer review [University Research Initiative program] J. Walsh. *Science* 238:1506 D 11 '87

Gramm-Rudman revision threatens defense cuts of $19-30 billion. P. Mann. *Aviat Week Space Technol* 127:24-5 O 5 '87

Gramm-Rudman threatens to disrupt defense contracts, research programs. P. Mann. *Aviat Week Space Technol* 127:22-4 N 9 '87

Health care bites the bullet [health care competes with military budget] H. H. Hiatt. *Bull At Sci* 43:7-8 Je '87

A hidden cost of military research: less national security. D. S. Greenberg. il *Discover* 8:94+ Ja '87

High cost of aircraft avionics threatens U.S. defense capability. B. D. Nordwall. *Aviat Week Space Technol* 126:79+ Je 8 '87

House Armed Services forced to rewrite defense budget; House Armed Services Committee reports $306-billion defense authorization for fiscal 1988. M. Mecham. *Aviat Week Space Technol* 126:26-8 Ap 20 '87

House Committee reduces defense budget further. *Aviat Week Space Technol* 126:28-9 My 4 '87

It's time for 'Cap the Knife' to cut a deal with Congress. D. Griffiths. il por *Bus Week* p62 F 16 '87

Less bang may mean more bucks for growth. K. Pennar. il *Bus Week* p128 O 19 '87

Make 'em pay [getting America's allies to shoulder more of the burden for their own defense] M. Kondracke. *New Repub* 197:15-17 O 12 '87

Military funding: does it add up? [support for math research] I. Peterson. *Sci News* 131:71 Ja 31 '87

NATO allies narrow gap in defense spending as U.S. outlays decline. *Aviat Week Space Technol* 126:20-1 My 18 '87

New space systems test facilities to cost $7 billion [Strategic Defense Initiative and National Aerospace Plane] il *Aviat Week Space Technol* 126:85 Ap 27 '87

NSF lends a hand with DOD award [Sematech project] J. Walsh. il *Science* 238:748 N 6 '87

United States. Dept. of Defense—Appropriations and expenditures—*cont.*

Nuts, bolts, & death [budget cuts undermine readiness] H. G. Summers. *Wash Mon* 18:51-2 Ja '87

Outline of a defense budget. C. Norman. *Science* 238:1225 N 27 '87

Overall budget reductions force cut in Conventional Defense Initiative. B. M. Greeley, Jr. *Aviat Week Space Technol* 126:30-1 My 4 '87

Panel finds defense policies erode U.S. technology base [Senate Armed Services Committee report] M. Mecham. *Aviat Week Space Technol* 126:21-2 My 18 '87

Panel votes $279 billion for 1988 defense spending [House Appropriations Committee] *Aviat Week Space Technol* 127:34 N 2 '87

Pentagon boosts research spending to develop practical superconductors. D. Hughes. il *Aviat Week Space Technol* 127:57-9 N 16 '87

The Pentagon budget: cuts are certain, but where? D. Griffiths. il *Bus Week* p177 N 16 '87

Poisons from the Pentagon [increase in funding for biological warfare research; cover story] S. Shulman. il *Progressive* 51:16-19 N '87

Pro-SDI panel forecasts $121-billion antimissile costs, excluding research. *Aviat Week Space Technol* 126:133 F 9 '87

Push for early SDI deployment could spur Air Defense Initiative. J. D. Morrocco. *Aviat Week Space Technol* 126:18-20 F 2 '87

Reagan's 1988 military budget. S. A. Cain and G. Adams. il *Bull At Sci* 43:50-2 Mr '87

Reagan's funding of C^3 program yields hardware, systems. P. J. Klass. *Aviat Week Space Technol* 126:231+ Mr 9 '87

Reduced tactical weapons budget cuts purchases, dampens new starts. M. A. Dornheim. il *Aviat Week Space Technol* 126:237-8+ Mr 9 '87

Report finds R&D budget growth could limit readiness funds. *Aviat Week Space Technol* 127:111 Jl 13 '87

SDI: losing momentum over what is affordable and possible. I. Goodwin. il *Phys Today* 40:47-51 Ja '87

SDI programs face delays due to fiscal 1988 cutbacks. T. M. Foley. *Aviat Week Space Technol* 127:28 Ag 17 '87

Senate Committee boosts conventional forces, limits ABM reinterpretation [Armed Services] M. Mecham. *Aviat Week Space Technol* 126:28-9 My 11 '87

Shortfall in estimated budget slows conventional force buildup. D. M. North. il *Aviat Week Space Technol* 126:45+ Mr 9 '87

Shrinking defense budget [special section] *Aviat Week Space Technol* 127:22-6 N 23 '87

Study calls for matching budget reviews to program milestones. *Aviat Week Space Technol* 127:26 Ag 3 '87

Taft memos order budget cuts, emphasize weapons terminations [William H. Taft] P. Mann. il *Aviat Week Space Technol* 127:24-6 D 7 '87

Trouble for the triad. J. Barry. il *Newsweek* 110:17-18 S 7 '87

Two in Congress debate U.S. defense [interview with P. Schroeder and D. Hunter] J. Martin. pors *Sch Update* 119:22 F 23 '87

U.S. Congress and Pentagon gird for weapon cancellations in 1989. P. Mann. *Aviat Week Space Technol* 127:26-7 N 30 '87

U.S. deficit law threatens major strategic weapons. P. Mann. il *Aviat Week Space Technol* 126:20-1 F 9 '87

What's behind the high cost of defense. M. Christopher. il *Sch Update* 119:15-16 F 23 '87

Where did it all go? *New Repub* 196:7-9 Ap 20 '87

Which weapons will work? B. Duffy. il *U S News World Rep* 102:18-20 Ja 19 '87

Why defense spending is likely to fall. H. Banks. il *Forbes* 139:27 My 4 '87

Procurement

See also

Project on Military Procurement

United States. President's Commission on Defense Management

Abrahamson asks contractors to gear up for mass production of SDI components. T. M. Foley. *Aviat Week Space Technol* 126:22-3 Ja 26 '87

Acquisition Board endorses low-rate AMRAAM production [advanced medium-range air-to-air missile] *Aviat Week Space Technol* 126:24 Je 8 '87

Acquisition chief's successor named [R. B. Costello] *Aviat Week Space Technol* 127:30-1 S 28 '87

Acquisition czar dethroned [resignation of R. Godwin] D. E. Fink. *Aviat Week Space Technol* 127:11 S 21 '87

Avco pleads guilty to $1.5-million overcharge. *Aviat Week Space Technol* 126:21 Je 29 '87

CBO claims most weapons systems fail to meet return on investment [Congressional Budget Office study] il *Aviat Week Space Technol* 126:77-8 Mr 30 '87

Contractor expands inventory for airborne threat training [Flight International] B. M. Greeley, Jr. il *Aviat Week Space Technol* 127:139+ O 12 '87

Defense Dept. acknowledges weak quality control. *Aviat Week Space Technol* 126:23 Ja 19 '87

Defense Dept. analyzes problems in strengthening industrial base. P. Mann. *Aviat Week Space Technol* 127:21-2 Jl 13 '87

Defense Dept. developing range of launch vehicle concepts. B. A. Smith. il *Aviat Week Space Technol* 126:115+ Mr 9 '87

Defense Dept. moving toward achieving EW commonality. il *Aviat Week Space Technol* 126:50-1+ F 9 '87

Defense faces a slowdown—sort of. S. Toy. il *Bus Week* p69-70 Ja 12 '87

Defense procurement controversy. B. D. Nordwall. *Aviat Week Space Technol* 127:11 Ag 17 '87

Desperately seeking defense contracts [black businesses] D. C. Ruffin. il *Black Enterp* 18:43 D '87

GAO renews criticism of services for lack of radar warning receiver commonality. *Aviat Week Space Technol* 127:93 Ag 24 '87

GAO tells House Security Subcommittee Defense Dept. fails to follow guideline on common radar warning receiver. B. D. Nordwall. *Aviat Week Space Technol* 126:33 My 11 '87

Godwin decides to resign as Defense acquisition chief. J. D. Morrocco. *Aviat Week Space Technol* 127:33 S 14 '87

Gramm-Rudman threatens to disrupt defense contracts, research programs. P. Mann. *Aviat Week Space Technol* 127:22-4 N 9 '87

Industry grapples with challenges posed by contract compliance. W. H. Gregory. *Aviat Week Space Technol* 126:84-5+ F 2 '87

Industry presses congressional review of marketing cost ban. M. Mecham. *Aviat Week Space Technol* 127:77 N 2 '87

International firms to compete for procurement of 800 engines. il *Aviat Week Space Technol* 126:74-5 Ja 19 '87

Major defense program costs remain stable in first quarter. *Aviat Week Space Technol* 127:114+ Jl 13 '87

Martin, Lockheed, TRW win work on SDI Zenith Star laser. T. M. Foley. *Aviat Week Space Technol* 127:32-3 O 12 '87

Military aircraft: how much high tech is enough? D. Griffiths. il *Bus Week* p76+ My 11 '87

Overpricing continues in noncompetitive defense procurement. *Aviat Week Space Technol* 126:87 Mr 9 '87

Pentagon Council to review new munitions master plan. J. D. Morrocco. *Aviat Week Space Technol* 127:23-4 Jl 13 '87

Pentagon formalizes charter for Defense Acquisition Office. *Aviat Week Space Technol* 126:29 F 16 '87

Pentagon initiative triggers new interest in joint ventures [aircraft upgrade projects] *Aviat Week Space Technol* 127:23 Ag 3 '87

Pentagon lists top 100 companies according to prime contracts. il *Aviat Week Space Technol* 126:50-1 Mr 23 '87

Pentagon reviews trade pacts to standardize joint projects. J. D. Morrocco. il *Aviat Week Space Technol* 127:45+ O 19 '87

The political economy of military waste. J. B. Anderson and D. R. Lee. il *USA Today (Periodical)* 115:30-3 My '87

Procurement reform [special section] *Aviat Week Space Technol* 126:98-9+ Ap 13 '87

Sack Weinberger, bankrupt General Dynamics, and other procurement reforms. G. Easterbrook. il *Wash Mon* 18:33-8+ Ja '87

Science Board urges major changes in Pentagon software purchasing. B. D. Nordwall. *Aviat Week Space Technol* 127:72-3 D 21 '87

Scientists find corporate support building for deployment of SDI. J. D. Morrocco. il *Aviat Week Space Technol* 126:81 Ap 27 '87

Six SDI programs win approval of Defense Acquisition Board. T. M. Foley. *Aviat Week Space Technol* 127:28-9 Ag 10 '87

United States. Dept. of Defense—Procurement—*cont.*
Star Wars fell on Alabama [Huntsville profits from Strategic Defense Initiative] D. Charles. il *Nation* 245:748-50 D 19 '87
Weapons buying: did anyone really want reform? [departure of R. Godwin] D. Griffiths. il por *Bus Week* p33 S 28 '87
Why defense spending is likely to fall. H. Banks. il *Forbes* 139:27 My 4 '87
Why the Pentagon's waste-watcher can't trim the fat [R. P. Godwin] D. Griffiths. *Bus Week* p49 Je 8 '87

United States. Dept. of Defense. Defense Advanced Research Projects Agency *See* United States. Defense Advanced Research Projects Agency

United States. Dept. of Defense. Joint Requirements & Management Board
Defense Board to review LHX prior to full-scale development. B. M. Greeley, Jr. *Aviat Week Space Technol* 126:22-3 F 9 '87

United States. Dept. of Defense. Operational Test and Evaluation
It's hard to flunk a weapons test. T. Noah. il *Newsweek* 110:18 S 7 '87

United States. Dept. of Education
Beryl Dorsett lauded in new education post with a $5.4 billion budget. il pors *Jet* 73:22+ N 23 '87
Better grades for Bill Bennett. E. Bowen. il por *Time* 129:60-1 Ja 19 '87
Bill Bennett's dilemma. D. Wagner. il *Natl Rev* 39:28-31+ Je 19 '87
Blacks slated for key posts in U.S. Dept. of Education. il *Jet* 72:27 Je 1 '87
Education Dept. warns student loan defaulters. *Jet* 72:23 Ag 3 '87
Get involved—write a letter! [restoration of Title IX to original strength to aid women's sports] *Women's Sports Fitness* 9:64 Je '87
Japanese versus U.S. texts: Dept. of Ed. assessment. H. Fields. *Publ Wkly* 231:21 F 6 '87
Mister Ed [W. J. Bennett] J. B. Judis. *New Repub* 196:16-19 Ap 27 '87
Mister Ed: William Bennett. J. B. Judis. *Educ Dig* 53:36-8 D '87
What's in the future for women's sports? [demise of gymnastics at Southwest Texas State University as an example of effects of weakened Title IX regulations] C. L. Hogan. il *Women's Sports Fitness* 9:42-7 Je '87

United States. Dept. of Education. Office for Civil Rights
Running the rights scam at DOE. L. A. Uzzell. *Natl Rev* 39:39-40+ Mr 13 '87

United States. Dept. of Education. Office of Vocational and Adult Education *See* United States. Office of Vocational and Adult Education

United States. Dept. of Energy
Chalk one up for the permanent government [oil overcharge cases] R. Jaroslovsky. *Wash Mon* 19:33-7 O '87
Delaying DOE's radwaste program. *Sci News* 131:106 F 14 '87
DOE undermines own nonproliferation effort [plans for a reactor that will use highly enriched uranium] D. Charles. *Science* 238:1224 N 27 '87
Energy Department blurs line between civilian, military reactors [plan to convert Unit One of the Washington Public Power Supply System to weapons purposes] M. M. Hoenig. bibl f *Bull At Sci* 43:25-7 Je '87
The greening of DOE [hazardous waste] E. Marshall. *Science* 235:1315 Mr 13 '87
Hunter and Nelson named to DOE posts. I. Goodwin. *Phys Today* 40 pt1:53 Ag '87
Massie, Davenport get high level Energy Dept. posts. *Jet* 72:22 Je 15 '87
Report on reports: Energy security: a report to the president of the United States. J. Darmstadter. bibl f il *Environment* 29:25-7 Jl/Ag '87
Safety of DOE reactors questioned [National Research Council report] E. Marshall. *Science* 238:741 N 6 '87
Uncle Sam's risky bomb plants. S. Budiansky. il map *U S News World Rep* 102:75-6 My 25 '87
Why is D.O.E. for food irradiation? [justifying the extraction of plutonium from commercial nuclear wastes for use in nuclear weapons] K. Terry. il *Nation* 244:142+ F 7 '87

Appropriations and expenditures
DOE submits 36 SSC site bids while House seeks to micro-manage project. I. Goodwin. map *Phys Today* 40:45-6 N '87

Pork barrel unbound? [funds for the Center for Molecular Medicine and Immunology in N.J.] J. Walsh. *Science* 237:352 Jl 24 '87
Race for the ring: DOE reacts to Congress's anxieties on SSC. I. Goodwin. il *Phys Today* 40 pt1:47-50 Ag '87

United States. Dept. of Health and Human Services
The future of federal family-planning programs [interview with N. Cabaniss] il por *Christ Today* 31:42-3 O 16 '87
One step forward . . . [enforcing a 1970 law that prohibits organizations that promote abortions from receiving federal funds] M. Gallagher. *Natl Rev* 39:29-30 Mr 13 '87

United States. Dept. of Health and Human Services. Office of Human Development Services *See* United States. Office of Human Development Services

United States. Dept. of Housing and Urban Development
Bernice Williams will lead trade group to China. por *Jet* 72:37 S 7 '87
HUD escalates building-renovation efforts as policy. J. Trewhitt. *Archit Rec* 175:35+ Jl '87
HUD grants $4.3 billion to black business under Pierce. il por *Jet* 72:12 Ap 20 '87

United States. Dept. of Justice
Beggs and General Dynamics cleared of fraud [Divad gun case] I. Goodwin. *Phys Today* 40 pt1:53 Ag '87
Behind the lines in the information war [former Justice Dept. attorney Q. Shea's work with Freedom of Information Act appeals] D. A. Demac. il *Progressive* 51:32 My '87
Black politicos condemn U.S. probe of Marion Barry. *Jet* 72:31 Jl 27 '87
Challenging the special prosecutors [Justice Dept. takes a stand against independent investigations] D. Baer and G. Borger. il *U S News World Rep* 102:24 Mr 9 '87
D.C. mayor Barry sues U.S. Atty. over 'leak a week'. *Jet* 72:5 Jl 13 '87
A defense case may break [witnesses get immunity in General Dynamics ship probe] S. Payne. *Bus Week* p40+ Mr 23 '87
Did the good guys go too far? [crackdown on political corruption hamstrung by Supreme Court ruling on mail fraud] P. Dwyer. il *Bus Week* p29 Ag 31 '87
The General Dynamics case sets a bad precedent [decision not to seek indictment] P. Dwyer and S. Payne. il *Bus Week* p41 Je 8 '87
History deleted [attempt to win R. M. Nixon the right to keep secret thousands of historically significant documents] *Nation* 244:669-70 My 23 '87
Indictment of Beggs dropped [General Dynamics Divad gun fraud case] E. Marshall. *Science* 237:21 Jl 3 '87
The InJustice of it all [Dept. of Justice found guilty of stealing computer program from Inslaw] il *Time* 130:52 O 12 '87
Justice Dept.'s broadax [dismissal of indictment against General Dynamics in Divad gun case] D. E. Fink. *Aviat Week Space Technol* 127:9 Jl 13 '87
Letter from Washington [case against Teamster boss J. Presser] Cato. *Natl Rev* 39:13 Jl 31 '87
Meese's legal troubles have him hog-tied at Justice. P. Dwyer. por *Bus Week* p39 Je 29 '87
Probe scuttled [drops inquiry of General Dynamics] *Time* 129:51 Je 1 '87
The return of the blacklist [use of suspension orders against government contractors] D. Fanning. il *Forbes* 139:84 Ap 6 '87
Who's counting? [Justice Dept. abandons Divad gun fraud case against General Dynamics] W. Biddle. *Nation* 245:148-9 Ag 29 '87

United States. Dept. of Justice. Antitrust Division
Pulling the plug on antitrust law [role of E. Meese] J. S. Cohen and J. W. Cuneo. il *Nation* 245:296-7 S 26 '87

United States. Dept. of Justice. Civil Rights Division
Cicero case prompts bias charges against Detroit suburbs: Justice Dept. *Jet* 71:7 Ja 19 '87

United States. Dept. of Justice. Drug Enforcement Administration *See* United States. Drug Enforcement Administration

United States. Dept. of Justice. Federal Bureau of Investigation *See* United States. Federal Bureau of Investigation

United States. Dept. of Justice. Immigration and Naturalization Service *See* United States. Immigration and Naturalization Service

United States. Dept. of Justice. Marshals Service *See* United States. Marshals Service

United States. Dept. of Justice. Office of the Solicitor General
The tenth justice (I). L. Caplan. *New Yorker* 63:29-32+ Ag 10 '87
The tenth justice (II). L. Caplan. *New Yorker* 63:30-2+ Ag 17 '87
United States. Dept. of Justice. Witness Security Program
Once a hit man, now a stoolie, Jimmy 'the Weasel' Fratianno says the feds owe him a living [interview] J. Wadler. il pors *People Wkly* 28:38-40 D 21 '87
United States. Dept. of Labor
Bill Brock's balancing act. M. E. Recio. il por *Bus Week* p146-7 F 23 '87
Reagan picks a 'good soldier' [A. D. McLaughlin nominated as secretary] S. B. Garland and H. Bradford. *Bus Week* p71 N 16 '87
Seventy-fifth anniversary year of the Department of Labor [proclamation, April 23, 1987] R. Reagan. *Mon Labor Rev* 110:2 Je '87
United States. Dept. of Labor. Bureau of Labor Statistics *See* United States. Bureau of Labor Statistics
United States. Dept. of Labor. Employment Service *See* United States Employment Service
United States. Dept. of Labor. Occupational Safety and Health Administration *See* United States. Occupational Safety and Health Administration
United States. Dept. of State
See also
Secretaries of State (U.S.)
State Dept. Building (Washington, D.C.)
Alan Keyes resigns State Dept. post; charges racism. por *Jet* 73:4 O 5 '87
By a thread [future of E. Abrams] F. Barnes. *New Repub* 197:11-13 Jl 13-20 '87
Elliott Abrams: the teflon Assistant Secretary. E. Alterman. por *Wash Mon* 19:19-22+ My '87
Foggy Bottom's feeble fight [security lapses at the State Dept.] C. Fenyvesi and G. Borger. il *U S News World Rep* 102:16 My 11 '87
George Shultz's feisty lawyer [A. Sofaer, State Dept. legal adviser] B. Van Voorst. por *Time* 129:31 Ap 6 '87
Minority report [State Dept. orders closing of Washington information office of the PLO] C. Hitchens. *Nation* 245:366 O 10 '87
Minority report [views of legal adviser A. D. Sofaer] C. Hitchens. *Nation* 244:103 Ja 31 '87
Pentagon, State Dept. granted veto over U.S. remote sensing satellites. T. M. Foley. *Aviat Week Space Technol* 127:20-1 Jl 20 '87
Publications. See issues of Department of State Bulletin
Shultz's way. R. Steel. il pors *N Y Times Mag* p14-21+ Ja 11 '87
State Dept. denies license to export U.S. satellites to the Soviet Union [use of Proton] *Aviat Week Space Technol* 127:59 Jl 27 '87
Testing time for Shultz. H. Trewhitt. il por *U S News World Rep* 102:14-16 My 11 '87
Trying to undo the damage [State Dept. admits role in embassy security lapses] M. Santini. il *U S News World Rep* 102:23 My 25 '87
U.S. orders closure of Palestine Information Office [State Dept. statement, September 15, 1987] *Dep State Bull* 87:43 N '87
U.S.-Soviet agreement on embassy construction in Washington [statement, May 19, 1987] R. I. Spiers. *Dep State Bull* 87:34-5 Jl '87
Why State can't lead. D. L. Clarke. bibl f *Foreign Policy* 66:128-42 Spr '87

Appropriations and expenditures
Budgetary resources and foreign policy [statement, March 19, 1987] E. J. Derwinski. *Dep State Bull* 87:84-7 Je '87
Challenges facing the Foreign Service [address, May 1, 1987] R. I. Spiers. *Dep State Bull* 87:30-4 Jl '87
Correspondence from the Secretary of State. G. P. Shultz. *Foreign Aff* 66:426-8 Wint '87/'88
The fiscal threat to U.S. foreign policy [address, October 15, 1986] R. I. Spiers. *Dep State Bull* 86:47-50 D '86
The foreign affairs budget crisis: a threat to our vital interests [statement, January 23, 1987] G. P. Shultz. il *Dep State Bull* 87:7-14 Mr '87
Maintaining the momentum in U.S. foreign policy [address, February 25, 1987] J. C. Whitehead. *Dep State Bull* 87:35-6 Ap '87
Restoring the foreign affairs budget [address, November 3, 1986] G. P. Shultz. *Dep State Bull* 87:24-6 Ja '87

Underfunding and undermining our foreign policy infrastructure [statements, February 26 and March 4, 1987] R. I. Spiers. *Dep State Bull* 87:23-7 My '87
United States. Dept. of State. Foreign Buildings Office *See* United States. Foreign Buildings Office
United States. Dept. of State. Foreign Service
Challenges facing the Foreign Service [address, May 1, 1987] R. I. Spiers. *Dep State Bull* 87:30-4 Jl '87
Crockett heads committee exposing racism within the U.S. Foreign Service. il por *Jet* 72:5 Ag 17 '87
"Do you want any more secret documents put in the safe, Mr. Ambassador?" "No, Ivan, that's all for tonight" [hiring foreign service nationals for American embassies] P. Witt. *Wash Mon* 19:17-18+ Ap '87
Managing diplomacy: problems and issues [statement, August 6, 1987] R. I. Spiers. *Dep State Bull* 87:20-3 O '87
Toward a more representative Foreign Service [recruiting blacks; address, October 3, 1986] R. I. Spiers. *Dep State Bull* 86:50-1 D '86
Why our embassies are nests for spies [hiring foreign service nationals for American embassies] P. Witt. il *Read Dig* 131:111-14 O '87
United States. Dept. of State. Office of Munitions Control *See* United States. Office of Munitions Control
United States. Dept. of State. Policy Planning Staff
Those who thought ahead [reunion of former directors] D. Aikman. il *Time* 129:41 My 25 '87
United States. Dept. of the Interior
Shale shock on the western slope. S. M. Voynick. il *Sierra* 72:29-31 My/Je '87
The twilight ozone [D. Hodel's alleged remarks concerning the international protocol on ozone] H. Klingeman. *Natl Rev* 39:40-1 Ag 14 '87
Undamming Hetch Hetchy [proposal by D. P. Hodel] C. Pope. il *Sierra* 72:34-8 N/D '87
Worse than Watt [D. P. Hodel] *New Repub* 197:7-9 Jl 6 '87
United States. Dept. of the Interior. Bureau of Land Management *See* United States. Bureau of Land Management
United States. Dept. of the Interior. Bureau of Mines *See* United States. Bureau of Mines
United States. Dept. of the Interior. Fish and Wildlife Service *See* U.S. Fish and Wildlife Service
United States. Dept. of the Interior. Geological Survey *See* Geological Survey (U.S.)
United States. Dept. of the Interior. National Park Service *See* United States. National Park Service
United States. Dept. of the Interior. Office of Royalty Management *See* United States. Office of Royalty Management
United States. Dept. of the Interior. Office of Surface Mining, Reclamation, and Enforcement *See* United States. Office of Surface Mining, Reclamation, and Enforcement
United States. Dept. of the Treasury
Challenge for a great persuader [Secretary J. A. Baker] J. Castro. il por *Time* 129:61 Je 8 '87
Dick Darman calls it quits [deputy secretary] E. Thomas. il por *Newsweek* 109:27 Ap 13 '87
The president's budget battler [J. A. Baker] L. Smith. il por *Fortune* 116:58 N 23 '87
Richard Darman: why he's joining the 'corpocracy' [interview] L. Walczak. il por *Bus Week* p36-7 Ap 13 '87
A tempest hits the Treasury [cancels Antilles tax treaty] D. Zigas and V. English. il *Bus Week* p124 Jl 20 '87
United States. Dept. of the Treasury. Customs Service *See* U.S. Customs Service
United States. Dept. of Transportation
Airline officials split on usefulness of expanded consumer reports. J. Ott. il *Aviat Week Space Technol* 127:31+ N 16 '87
Airlines view flight adjustments as trend toward reregulation. J. Ott. *Aviat Week Space Technol* 126:32-4 F 9 '87
Carriers discuss schedule changes in response to Transportation order. il *Aviat Week Space Technol* 126:33 Mr 23 '87
Charming her way to the White House [E. H. Dole; cover story] P. Weiss. *Wash Mon* 19:29+ S '87
Dole proposes upgrade of nine radar service areas to TCA status [airport terminal control areas] *Aviat Week Space Technol* 127:33 Ag 31 '87
Dole resigns, raising concerns about Department's leadership. *Aviat Week Space Technol* 127:34 S 21 '87
How not to eliminate flight delays. J. Ott. *Aviat Week Space Technol* 126:11 Ap 6 '87

United States. Dept. of Transportation—*cont.*
Is this any way to sell a railroad? [Conrail's public offering] L. Smith. il *Fortune* 115:91-2+ My 25 '87
Policing air delays. *Newsweek* 110:57 S 14 '87
Slow role [rescue the FAA from the DOT] R. L. Collins. *Flying* 114:32 Je '87
Transportation Dept. approves proposed USAir/Piedmont merger. J. Ott. *Aviat Week Space Technol* 127:44 N 9 '87
Transportation Dept. imposes standards for on-time performance [airlines] J. Ott. *Aviat Week Space Technol* 127:36-7 S 7 '87
Transportation Dept. to study need for airline smoking ban. *Aviat Week Space Technol* 127:39 O 12 '87

United States. Dept. of Transportation. National Highway Traffic Safety Administration See United States. National Highway Traffic Safety Administration

United States. Dept. of Transportation. National Transportation Safety Board See United States. National Transportation Safety Board

United States. Dept. of Veterans Affairs
Why Reagan's gift to the veterans was such a shocker. R. Fly. il *Bus Week* p69 D 7 '87

United States. Drug Enforcement Administration
Breaking a drug lord [cocaine dealer C. E. Lehder Rivas] K. Scanlon. por *Macleans* 100:45 F 23 '87
Caught: cocaine's 'Mr. Big' [C. Lehder Rivas] M. Satchell. il por *U S News World Rep* 102:12 F 16 '87
Crazy Charlie [arrest of C. Lehder Rivas] *Nation* 244:203-5 F 21 '87
A desperate quest in Beirut [search for W. Buckley] G. Shamis. por *U S News World Rep* 102:22 Je 29 '87
The fall of a cocaine kingpin [capture of Colombian C. Lehder Rivas] J. Smolowe. il por *Time* 129:37 F 16 '87
How the drug czar got away [botches case against Colombian J. L. Ochoa Vasquez] M. A. Lee. il *Nation* 245:189-92 S 5 '87
"Operation Rx" sting [D. Hall helps break pharmacists' prescription drug scam in Los Angeles] J. Fincher. il *Read Dig* 131:36-41 S '87
Snaring the king of coke [capture of C. Lehder Rivas] R. Nordland. il por *Newsweek* 109:16-18 F 16 '87

United States. Employment Service See United States Employment Service

United States. Environmental Protection Agency
Another antismog device? [controlling ozone by trapping vapors from gasoline refueling] il *U S News World Rep* 103:8 Ag 3 '87
Biotech tests given go-ahead, look-see. *Sci News* 131:122 F 21 '87
BioTechnica tests EPA review process [field test of Rhizobium bacteria] M. Crawford. *Science* 235:840 F 20 '87
Chemical cleanup [EPA cleanup at closed facilities of Arkansas Chemical Co. in Newark, N.J.] B. Weber. il *N Y Times Mag* p42 D 27 '87
Chlordane sales halted. *Sci News* 132:102 Ag 15 '87
Costly cleanups at the gas pump [storage tank rules] T. Smart. *Bus Week* p28-9 Ap 20 '87
EPA attacks vapor villain [reducing ozone pollution by trapping gasoline vapors emitted during refueling] *Mot Trend* 39:44 N '87
EPA indicts formaldehyde, 7 years later. E. Marshall. *Science* 236:381 Ap 24 '87
The EPA may just be blowing smoke on Clean Air. T. Smart. *Bus Week* p49 Je 8 '87
EPA rule change threatens black contractors' jobs. *Jet* 72:5 Ag 31 '87
EPA to cut U.S. CFC production to protect ozone in stratosphere. M. Crawford. il *Science* 238:1505 D 11 '87
EPA's predicament over regulating pesticides. M. Sun. il *Science* 238:20-1 O 2 '87
Getting the lead out [regulations concerning lead in the water supply] *Sci News* 132:269 O 24 '87
Hazardous waste: where to put it? M. Crawford. il *Science* 235:156-7 Ja 9 '87
How safe are the pesticides on food? [testing process] P. Durner. il *Rodale's Org Gard* 34:69-76 Je '87
L.A. to E.P.A.: don't hold your breath. M. Cone. il *Sierra* 72:27+ N/D '87
Last stage of Love Canal cleanup. *Sci News* 132:319 N 14 '87
Love Canal: a new cleanup plan stirs old fears. T. Smart. il *Bus Week* p30 Ag 31 '87
The new debate over Superfund: how clean is clean enough? T. Smart. il *Bus Week* p34 Jl 13 '87
No time for termites [EPA forces end to production of Termide] *Time* 130:46 Ag 24 '87

Nowhere to run from radon. M. Galen. il *Nation* 244:180-2 F 14 '87
Once more, with compliance [Clean Air Act] C. Pope. il *Sierra* 72:34+ S/O '87
Proposed EPA rules on petroleum storage may boost fuel costs [underground fuel tanks] *Aviat Week Space Technol* 127:33 Jl 6 '87
R&D eroding at EPA. M. Crawford. il *Science* 236:904-5 My 22 '87
Radon: EPA's biggest air pollutant . . . and its leading water pollutant. *Sci News* 132:105 Ag 15 '87
Regulating pesticides: the "Delaney paradox". C. Norman. il *Science* 236:1054-5 My 29 '87
Risk assessment in environmental policy-making. M. Russell and M. Gruber. bibl f *Science* 236:286-90 Ap 17 '87
See no evil [approval of Sonar herbicide based on incomplete data] T. Turner. *Mother Earth News* 106:114-15 Jl/Ag '87
Smog-ozone policy shift. J. Raloff. *Sci News* 131:244 Ap 18 '87
Smog, the EPA, and cans of paint yanked off the shelf. *Sunset* 179:86 S '87
A smogbound quest for Clean Air [EPA delays penalties for noncompliance] il *U S News World Rep* 103:10 N 30 '87
Turf battle over federal responsibility for groundwater. A. L. Spitler. *BioScience* 37:317 My '87

United States. Equal Employment Opportunity Commission
Black colleges get EEOC settlement of $3.6 million. il *Jet* 71:4 Mr 23 '87
A case goes unheard at the EEOC [Navy waitress M. Farrell] F. Greve. il por *50 Plus* 27:16+ N '87
Courts v. EEOC on over-65 pension rights. A. J. Sheinman. *50 Plus* 27:19-20 Je '87
EEOC defines "age harassment". A. J. Sheinman. *50 Plus* 27:14+ Ag '87
EEOC's Thomas wants blacks in high-paying fed. jobs. por *Jet* 73:38 O 12 '87
A question of fairness [chairman C. Thomas] J. Williams. il pors *Atlantic* 259:70-5+ F '87
Women's history and EEOC v. Sears [sex discrimination case; special section] *Society* 24:4-16 S/O '87

United States. Export-Import Bank See Export-Import Bank of the United States

United States. Extension Service
Friend and advisor to western gardeners . . . the county agent. il *Sunset* 179:240 O '87
Whither the Cooperative Extension Service? J. Cook. *Ctry J* 14:41 Jl '87

United States. Farmers Home Administration
Farmers plow up Pentagon's budget [movement to transfer funding from the military budget to Iowa's FmHA program] M. Helmberger. *Progressive* 51:15-16 Mr '87

United States. Federal Aviation Administration
Agency suspends Omniflight scheduled services in New York. *Aviat Week Space Technol* 126:37 Je 8 '87
Air traffic controllers sue to block FAA drug testing. C. Preble. *Aviat Week Space Technol* 126:32-3 Mr 2 '87
The answer to intolerable congestion at America's airports [getting the FAA out of air traffic control] M. S. Forbes, Jr. il *Forbes* 140:29 Jl 27 '87
ATA proposes easing rules on foreign repair stations. *Aviat Week Space Technol* 126:53 Ja 26 '87
Bum rap. R. L. Collins. *Flying* 114:28 N '87
Carriers, FAA continue talks on Atlanta Hartsfield schedule. *Aviat Week Space Technol* 126:36 Ap 20 '87
Carriers question U.S. timetable for mandatory T/CAS operation. P. J. Klass. *Aviat Week Space Technol* 127:42+ D 21 '87
Computer and software advances will boost controller productivity. W. B. Scott. il *Aviat Week Space Technol* 127:95+ N 9 '87
Easing airport congestion. M. S. Forbes, Jr. il *Forbes* 139:25 Ja 26 '87
East Side story [FAA's East Coast Plan] R. L. Collins. il *Flying* 114:14 Je '87
Eastern Airlines agrees to pay fine of $9.5 million for safety violations. *Aviat Week Space Technol* 126:34 F 16 '87
Engen warns against local challenges to national airspace system. *Aviat Week Space Technol* 126:50 Ap 13 '87
Engine shutdown prompts FAA directive [accidental shutdown caused by hitting fuel control switches] *Aviat Week Space Technol* 127:36 Jl 6 '87
Executives debate new structure for FAA. *Aviat Week Space Technol* 126:40 Ja 26 '87

United States. Federal Aviation Administration—*cont.*

FAA adopting new certification strategies for foreign aircraft, parts [airworthiness bilaterals] J. Ott. il *Aviat Week Space Technol* 126:307-8+ Je 15 '87

FAA assessing impact of regulation setting airline noise budget at Denver's Stapleton Airport. *Aviat Week Space Technol* 126:33 Mr 30 '87

FAA defends domestic airport security measures. C. Preble. *Aviat Week Space Technol* 126:36 Je 29 '87

FAA developing new policy for pilot type ratings. J. Ott. *Aviat Week Space Technol* 126:30-1 Mr 30 '87

FAA disputes recommendations for summer traffic reductions. *Aviat Week Space Technol* 126:36 Je 1 '87

FAA faults Eastern's maintenance procedures; airline disputes findings. P. Proctor. *Aviat Week Space Technol* 127:34 D 7 '87

FAA investigation focuses on Delta operations, training. C. Preble. il *Aviat Week Space Technol* 127:31 Jl 27 '87

FAA investigators seek pattern in near-midair collisions. P. Proctor. il *Aviat Week Space Technol* 126:63-4 Ap 27 '87

FAA officials visit MD-82 facilities in China [inspect controls and procedures for coproduction of MD-82 transports in Shanghai] *Aviat Week Space Technol* 126:42 Ap 6 '87

FAA orders expansion of Los Angeles TCA [terminal control area serving Los Angeles International Airport] map *Aviat Week Space Technol* 127:23-4 Ag 24 '87

FAA plans MLS installation at major New York airports [microwave landing systems] K. J. Stein. *Aviat Week Space Technol* 127:65+ Jl 27 '87

FAA prepares for second phase of expanded East Coast Plan. K. J. Stein. *Aviat Week Space Technol* 127:115+ Jl 6 '87

FAA receives general support for plan to mandate T/CAS [traffic alert/collision avoidance system] P. J. Klass. *Aviat Week Space Technol* 127:14 S 14 '87

FAA solicits information on en route noise levels. *Aviat Week Space Technol* 126:40 Mr 23 '87

FAA uncovers additional PA-28s with cracked wing spars. *Aviat Week Space Technol* 127:53 Ag 10 '87

FAA urges China to clear path to bilateral airworthiness pact. *Aviat Week Space Technol* 127:38-9 Ag 17 '87

FAA urges use of standard procedures, more discipline in Delta cockpits. E. H. Phillips. *Aviat Week Space Technol* 127:44 S 28 '87

FAA will ease regulations on foreign repair stations. C. Preble. *Aviat Week Space Technol* 126:34 Ap 20 '87

Full circle [new union, the National Air Traffic Controllers Association] A. A. Lappen. il *Forbes* 140:12 Jl 13 '87

Hang 'em High [new stance on TCA airspace] J. M. McClellan. *Flying* 114:28-9 F '87

How to end airport gridlock. T. Jacoby. il *Newsweek* 109:28 My 11 '87

Improved weather alerts offset by poor delivery to cockpit. J. Ott. *Aviat Week Space Technol* 127:33-4 O 5 '87

Industry group urges Stage 2 phase-out, halt to noise limits. C. Preble. *Aviat Week Space Technol* 127:30-1 Jl 13 '87

Israelis petition FAA for repair station rule exemption. *Aviat Week Space Technol* 126:31 Mr 30 '87

Kind words for Continental [FAA accused of suppressing critical report] J. S. DeMott. il *Time* 129:30 Ja 12 '87

McArtor cites quality control in call for inspection program. E. H. Phillips. *Aviat Week Space Technol* 127:41 O 5 '87

McArtor orders industry-wide assessment of pilot training. *Aviat Week Space Technol* 127:20-1 Ag 24 '87

McArtor presses for safety gains, airport construction in 1988 plan. P. Proctor. *Aviat Week Space Technol* 127:36 S 21 '87

The new FAA chief flies into a storm of flak [T. A. McArtor] S. Payne. por *Bus Week* p33 Ag 24 '87

New FAA chief will require airline safety audit. *Aviat Week Space Technol* 127:38 Ag 3 '87

No more Mister Nice Guy [enforcement policy] S. Hamilton. il *Flying* 114:93 Ag '87

NOAA, FAA consider volcano monitoring system. il *Aviat Week Space Technol* 127:30-1 Jl 6 '87

Nominee for FAA administrator cites safety, improved ATC as priorities [T. A. McArtor] P. Proctor. *Aviat Week Space Technol* 127:32 Jl 13 '87

Pacific growth could lead to expanded FAA safety duties. J. Ott. *Aviat Week Space Technol* 126:40+ Ap 6 '87

'Playing chicken' aloft. J. B. Copeland. il *Newsweek* 109:54 Je 8 '87

Proposed rulemaking sets mandatory T/CAS timetable [airborne traffic alert/collision avoidance system] P. J. Klass. *Aviat Week Space Technol* 127:145+ Ag 10 '87

Red for La Guardia, brown for J.F.K. [new air traffic control computer system] P. Elmer-Dewitt. il *Time* 129:60-1 Je 1 '87

Rough chop ahead for the FAA. P. Cary. il *U S News World Rep* 103:62-3+ Jl 6 '87

Safe air and hot air [need to improve air traffic control system] M. B. Zuckerman. il *U S News World Rep* 103:84 S 21 '87

Slow role [rescue the FAA from the DOT] R. L. Collins. *Flying* 114:32 Je '87

Talking union [National Air Traffic Controllers Association] J. Merwin. il *Forbes* 139:35-6 Ap 6 '87

TCA trauma [cover story; special section] il *Flying* 114:28-34+ D '87

Traffic reduction plan results in hundreds of airline delays. J. Ott. *Aviat Week Space Technol* 126:79 Je 15 '87

Appropriations and expenditures

Budget cuts could cause shortages in air traffic system personnel. *Aviat Week Space Technol* 127:45 D 14 '87

FAA budget would increase critical safety staffing levels. J. Ott. il *Aviat Week Space Technol* 126:34 Ja 12 '87

Reagan submits legislation to improve airports, airways. *Aviat Week Space Technol* 126:33 F 23 '87

Flight service stations

IBM Host computer system operational at Boston center [FAA air traffic control system] *Aviat Week Space Technol* 127:56 O 26 '87

Speed briefs [automated flight service station at Millville, N.J.] P. Scott. il por *Flying* 114:70-2+ O '87

Procurement

FAA initiates two-phase effort to speed acceptance of MLS [microwave landing systems] K. J. Stein. *Aviat Week Space Technol* 126:36+ Mr 23 '87

FAA plans Inmarsat satellite surveillance of oceanic routes. P. J. Klass. *Aviat Week Space Technol* 127:47+ D 7 '87

New policy backs acquisition, use of traditional ILSs [instrument landing system] *Aviat Week Space Technol* 126:36 Mr 23 '87

Production of ATC modernization equipment moves into high gear [National Airspace System Plan] J. Ott. *Aviat Week Space Technol* 126:31-2 Mr 23 '87

United States. Federal Bureau of Investigation

All mixed up on Martin Luther King. W. F. Buckley. *Natl Rev* 39:62 F 27 '87

And what about those red hills she painted? [investigation of G. O'Keeffe at height of McCarthyism] J. Herzfeld. il *Art News* 86:198 Ap '87

Black FBI agent sues bureau for harassment; white wife threatened [D. Rochon] il por *Jet* 73:16 N 23 '87

Charges of break-ins and infiltration [FBI investigation of the sanctuary movement] J.-M. Andriote. il *Christ Today* 31:44-5 Ap 17 '87

Conyers hits plan to open the FBI's arrest records [impact on black employment] *Jet* 73:12 N 9 '87

The death squads hit home: which side is the FBI on? [attacks against Salvadoran exiles in the U.S.] V. Bielski and others. il *Progressive* 51:15-19 O '87

The defiling of writers [FBI files on American authors; cover story] N. S. Robins. il *Nation* 245:367-70+ O 10 '87

Faces of middle class America: Bonnie Jenkins is single and living in Washington D.C. [translator] il pors *Ebony* 42:146+ Ag '87

The FBI gets its man [W. S. Sessions appointed chief] M. Kaus. il por *Newsweek* 110:20 Ag 3 '87

FBI investigating fraud charges against Morton Thiokol in manufacture of shuttle solid rocket motors. *Aviat Week Space Technol* 126:41-2 Ap 27 '87

Has the F.B.I. really changed? *Nation* 245:399-400 O 17 '87

How the FBI fights top crime threats. L. Eskin. il *Sch Update* 120:18-19 D 4 '87

The intelligence community [address, December 8, 1986] W. H. Webster. *Vital Speeches Day* 53:324-7 Mr 15 '87

Name black to head FBI, president Reagan urged. il *Jet* 71:5 Mr 23 '87

Next chief of the FBI: a tall Texan [W. S. Sessions] il por *U S News World Rep* 103:7 Ag 3 '87

Once a G-man, now a pacifist [J. C. Ryan] T. E. Johnson. il por *Newsweek* 110:24 N 23 '87

Policing America's writers [FBI files on great American writers] H. Mitgang. *New Yorker* 63:47-8+ O 5 '87

United States. Federal Bureau of Investigation—*cont.*
Rooting out organized crime [address, November 17, 1986] W. H. Webster. *Vital Speeches Day* 53:262-5 F 15 '87
Scoundrel time again. E. Knoll. *Progressive* 51:4 D '87
Secord agent [use of FBI to investigate journalists suing Gen. Secord] *Nation* 245:40-1 Jl 18-25 '87
The Sunday school fascist [R. G. Powers' biography of J. E. Hoover] T. Branch. *Wash Mon* 19:46-8 Ap '87
That old, rugged cross [book by D. Garrow details FBI harassment of M. L. King] J. E. White. il por *Time* 129:24 Ja 19 '87
Three lives [discussion of October 10, 1987 article, The defiling of writers] N. S. Robins. *Nation* 245:666 D 5 '87
Tough Texan [W. Sessions nominated as director] por *Time* 130:18 Ag 3 '87
Two writers probe FBI surveillance of American authors [H. Mitgang and N. S. Robins] W. Goldstein. *Publ Wkly* 232:38 O 30 '87
Varelli: in from the cold [involvement in FBI spying on Committee in Solidarity with the People of El Salvador] D. R. Gordon. *Nation* 244:273+ Mr 7 '87
Appropriations and expenditures
The high cost of the FBI's high-tech crime wars. P. Cary. il *U S News World Rep* 103:22-3 N 30 '87
United States. Federal Bureau of Investigation. National Stolen Art File
FBI computer tracks purloined Picassos. A. Thorson. il *Art News* 86:54+ Ja '87
United States. Federal Communications Commission
Affirmative action, FCC-style [preference policies for minorities and women in broadcasting] N. Gunther. *Channels* 7:12 My '87
Are the feds hobbling AT&T's rivals? [rate cut] F. Seghers. *Bus Week* p33-4 Ja 19 '87
Black media in danger. K. Jackson. *Black Enterp* 18:20 Ag '87
Blue boys of the airwaves [FCC broadens definition of indecency] R. H. Bork, Jr. il *U S News World Rep* 102:16-17 Ap 27 '87
Bradley Holmes is slated for FCC seat by Reagan. por *Jet* 73:10 D 7 '87
The broadcasting Fairness Doctrine. *Congr Dig* 66:227-56 O '87
A compromise that could clear the static over the airwaves. F. Seghers. il *Bus Week* p28 Jl 6 '87
Data companies are mad as hell at the FCC. F. Seghers. il *Bus Week* p60+ O 19 '87
Edging the government out of TV [dropping the Fairness Doctrine] O. Friedrich. il *Time* 130:58 Ag 17 '87
The F.C.C. cleans up the airways. R. Corn. il *Nation* 245:679-81 D 5 '87
F.C.C. launches inquiry into policies preferential to minorities and women. *Jet* 71:16 Ja 12 '87
FCC doublespeak [indecency standard] L. P. Sheinfeld. il *Film Comment* 23:87-90 S/O '87
FCC faces records meltdown. R. O'Brien. il *Channels* 7:11 Ja '87
FCC permits broadcast satellite operators to broaden services. *Aviat Week Space Technol* 126:149 F 9 '87
FCC proposes plan to offer competitive air-to-ground links. *Aviat Week Space Technol* 126:36 My 4 '87
FCC rejects Arinc proposal to form global aviation satellite system. P. J. Klass. *Aviat Week Space Technol* 127:27 S 21 '87
FCC shuts hatch on pirate station [Radio New York International] R. Tannenbaum. il *Roll Stone* p32+ S 24 '87
The FCC's new chief will keep dialing deregulation. F. Seghers. il por *Bus Week* p156 Mr 23 '87
Groups seek FCC approval for mobile satellite systems. *Aviat Week Space Technol* 127:136 Ag 10 '87
An indecent proposal [new definition of indecency] J. Saltzman. il *USA Today (Periodical)* 116:95 Jl '87
The invincible voice of Cape Ann [FCC's attempt to revoke license of WVCA, S. Geller's classical music station] R. J. Bidinotto. il por *Read Dig* 131:201-2+ O '87
Is the FCC backing away from women? [preference policy] M. Engel. il *Glamour* 85:76+ Ap '87
Kid gloves, same punch [commissioner to be D. R. Patrick] F. Seghers. *Bus Week* p37 F 2 '87
Life after Fowler. J. L. Swerdlow. il *Channels* 7:14 Mr '87
Midnight blue [FCC guidelines on "indecent" programming] *Time* 130:61 D 7 '87
Phone rates: cheaper calls for the new year. il *Newsweek* 109:42 Ja 12 '87

Radio daze [FCC issues warnings to radio stations for broadcasting obscene material] R. Stengel. il por *Time* 129:32 Ap 27 '87
Raunch 'n' roll radio is here to stay. J. Reed. il *U S News World Rep* 102:52 My 4 '87
Seven companies seek FCC approval for new communications satellites. *Aviat Week Space Technol* 127:48 O 5 '87
Suffer the little children: the FCC does it again. R. L. Fischer. il *USA Today (Periodical)* 115:84-6 Ja '87
A telephonic Tower of Babel. J. Andresky. il *Forbes* 139:92 Ap 6 '87
To be or not to be commercial?—That is the question [public broadcasting] R. L. Fischer. *USA Today (Periodical)* 116:89-91 S '87
Turning off RKO's licenses. *Time* 130:42 Ag 24 '87
Two mobile satellite groups compete for FCC monopoly. il *Aviat Week Space Technol* 127:47 O 5 '87
Unfair air? [abolishing the Fairness Doctrine] R. Coorsh. il *Consum Res Mag* 70:4 S '87
Why the FCC wants to cap rates instead of profits [overhauling AT&T price regulations] F. Seghers. il *Bus Week* p88 Ag 17 '87
Will GenCorp bow out of broadcasting—or be pushed? [decision threatens RKO's licenses] D. Lieberman and others. il *Bus Week* p25 Ag 24 '87
United States. Federal Deposit Insurance Corporation *See* Federal Deposit Insurance Corporation
United States. Federal Election Commission
The Federal Election Commission. *Congr Dig* 66:35+ F '87
United States. Federal Emergency Management Agency
County blocks bomb exercise [Clatsop County, Or., self-declared nuclear free zone, subjected to mock nuclear attack] D. Friedrich. *Progressive* 51:16 My '87
Patting the missile: making nuclear war less threatening. il *Discover* 8:6 Ag '87
United States. Federal Energy Regulatory Commission
Public sector pragmatist [chairman M. O. Hesse] L. M. Keefe. il por *Forbes* 139:283+ Ja 12 '87
United States. Federal Home Loan Bank Board
A chance for a fresh start at the Home Loan Bank Board. V. Cahan. il *Bus Week* p29 Ap 20 '87
Danny Wall dives right into the swamp [new chairman] V. Cahan. il por *Bus Week* p28 Ag 31 '87
Git along, little thrifts [plan for rounding up Texas' ailing S&Ls by M. H. Meyerson and R. E. Rainwater] T. Mason. il por *Bus Week* p33 O 26 '87
Going once, going twice . . . [W. Popejoy's plan for Financial Corp. of America] T. Carson. il por *Bus Week* p102 O 5 '87
Oil Patch thrifts are deep in gloom [guidelines for revaluing assets] T. Vogel. il *Bus Week* p47-8 F 23 '87
One deal away from being Mr. Megathrift [A. M. Frank of First Nationwide wants Financial Corp. of America] J. B. Levine. il por *Bus Week* p103-4 O 26 '87
Psst! Wanna buy the big daddy of thrifts? [looking for a buyer of Financial Corp. of America] T. Carson. *Bus Week* p36 Mr 30 '87
An S&L whodunit where everyone's a suspect [Independent American Savings & Loan] J. Weber, Jr. il por *Bus Week* p96-8 Jl 13 '87
S&Ls in Wright country [Texas thrifts and House Speaker J. Wright] *Natl Rev* 39:19-20 Ag 28 '87
There may be a buyer for FCA [Financial Corp. of America] T. Carson. *Bus Week* p38-9 Je 8 '87
"We're the lifeblood" [regulators turn to money brokers for help with weak thrifts] M. Schifrin. il *Forbes* 140:43-4 Jl 27 '87
White knights or black hats? J. Heins. il *Forbes* 140:386+ Jl 13 '87
United States. Federal Housing Administration
FHA mortgages: pros and cons. T. Tilling. *Parents* 62:47-8 My '87
Insurance refund packaged in red tape [FHA mortgage insurance] H. Porter. il *Fam Handyman* 37:12 S '87
United States. Federal National Mortgage Association *See* Federal National Mortgage Association
United States. Federal Railroad Administration
A matter of rail safety. S. Shane. *Travel Holiday* 168:6 S '87
United States. Federal Reserve System *See* Federal Reserve System (U.S.)
United States. Federal Savings and Loan Insurance Corporation *See* Federal Savings and Loan Insurance Corporation

United States. Federal Trade Commission

Imagine a cutthroat CPA. G. Weiss. il *Bus Week* p96 S 28 '87

Thunder from the right at the Federal Trade Commission [chairman D. Oliver] P. Dwyer. il por *Bus Week* p139-40 Ja 12 '87

Zuckerman bound [J. Zuckerman] G. Slutsker. il por *Forbes* 139:123 F 9 '87

United States. Financing Corporation *See* Financing Corporation (U.S.)

United States. Fish and Wildlife Service *See* U.S. Fish and Wildlife Service

United States. Food and Drug Administration

After the battle, tPA declared a winner. D. D. Edwards. *Sci News* 132:325 N 21 '87

AIDS vaccine: a sliver of hope? [MicroGeneSys to begin tests] R. Rhein, Jr. *Bus Week* p30-1 Ag 31 '87

Alzheimer's drug trial put on hold. J. L. Marx. il *Science* 238:1041-2 N 20 '87

Benefit vs. risk: how FDA approves new drugs. D. Farley. il *FDA Consum* 21:6-18 D '87/Ja '88

Birth of a blockbuster: how Genentech delivered the goods [FDA approves TPA] J. O. Hamilton. il *Bus Week* p138-40+ N 30 '87

Breaking the F.D.A. drugjam [AIDS drugs] A.-C. D'Adesky. il *Nation* 245:405-6+ O 17 '87

Compassion vs. control: FDA investigational drug regulation. D. H. Gieringer. il *USA Today (Periodical)* 115:69-73 Mr '87

A 'complaint department' for medical devices [Device Experience Network] R. C. Thompson. il *FDA Consum* 21:10-13 Mr '87

The Constitution and the consumer: discovering the connections. W. F. Janssen. il *FDA Consum* 21:8-11 S '87

Dying for drugs. R. Bazell. *New Repub* 197:17-19 N 9 '87

Experimental drugs for the desperately ill. F. E. Young. il *FDA Consum* 21:2-3 Je '87

Experimental drugs for the desperately ill. F. E. Young. il *Consum Res Mag* 70:34-5 Ag '87

An experimental wonder drug awaits approval [TPA] J. P. Shapiro. il *U S News World Rep* 103:68 S 21 '87

FDA puts new heart drug on hold. M. Sun. il *Science* 237:16-18 Jl 3 '87

Gender kits—caveat emptor [FDA censures Gender Choice kit manufacturer] il *U S News World Rep* 102:12 F 9 '87

Genentech sues FDA on growth hormone. M. Crawford. il *Science* 235:1454-5 Mr 20 '87

Genentech takes a tumble [adverse ruling on TPA] D. Pauly. il *Newsweek* 109:48 Je 15 '87

Go-ahead for a wonder drug [approval of TPA] il *Time* 130:68 N 23 '87

The government bends to AIDS victims' pleas [approval of AZT] D. S. Greenberg. il *U S News World Rep* 102:76 Mr 23 '87

Harvesting the fruits of biotechnology. F. E. Young. il *FDA Consum* 21:2-3 S '87

Investigators' reports. See issues of FDA Consumer

Looking for trouble in medical devices [Mechanics and Materials Laboratory] D. W. Stearman. il *FDA Consum* 21:18-23 S '87

A nasty shock for Genentech [rejects TPA] J. O. Hamilton and R. Rhein, Jr. *Bus Week* p37 Je 15 '87

New data clinch heart drug approval. M. Sun. il *Science* 238:1031 N 20 '87

The notebook. See issues of FDA Consumer

Picking up the pieces at Genentech [denies marketing approval for TPA] G. Bylinsky. il *Fortune* 116:60-1 Jl 6 '87

A prescription for cutting the red tape. J. Seligmann. il *Newsweek* 109:52-3 Je 1 '87

The public health payoffs of FDA research. F. E. Young. il *FDA Consum* 21:4-5 D '87/Ja '88

Rushing drugs to market. T. Kiely. il *Technol Rev* 90:12-13 Ag/S '87

THA trials suspended, research probed. R. Weiss. *Sci News* 132:292 N 7 '87

TPA and PDQ. D. E. Koshland, Jr. *Science* 237:341 Jl 24 '87

Updates. See issues of FDA Consumer

United States. Foreign Buildings Office

Our new Moscow embassy—bungled and bugged [failure of Foreign Buildings Office to get properly built embassies] J. Barron. *Read Dig* 130:100-4 Je '87

United States. Forest Service

Congress should investigate Forest Service violations [with editorial comment by George T. Frampton] il *Wilderness* 50:2-3 Summ '87

Curbing abuses in computer modeling [FORPLAN] B. R. Herrick. il *Technol Rev* 90:24-5 O '87

The degradation factor [timber management and watershed protection in western national forests] M. Anderson and C. Gehrke. il *Wilderness* 51:38-40 Fall '87

The Forest Service's road to nowhere [timber contracts and roadbuilding projects threaten Tongass National Forest] K. E. Franklin. il *Progressive* 51:12 Je '87

The lifeblood of wilderness [enforcement of federal reserved water rights in Colorado wilderness areas] D. Drabelle. il *Wilderness* 51:36-8 Fall '87

The lopsided ledger [management of the national forests] L. Williamson. il *Outdoor Life* 179:18+ Ja '87

Preserving old-growth forests. D. B. Edelson. bibl f il *Environment* 29:3-5 O '87

A winner in the White Mountains [appeal of Forest Service plan] *Wilderness* 51:3 Wint '87

United States. General Services Administration

A loss for Serra [R. Serra loses court fight to save Tilted arc from being removed from Federal Plaza in Manhattan] G. Danto. il *Art News* 86:61 O '87

Serra goes to court [R. Serra's battle over Tilted arc] A. Decker. *Art News* 86:29 Ap '87

Tilted arc goes to court [R. Serra files suit] *Art Am* 75:168 F '87

United States. Geological Survey *See* Geological Survey (U.S.)

United States. Government Printing Office

Bias suit wins $2.4 mil. for 362 black GPO workers. *Jet* 72:17 S 7 '87

Black GPO workers awarded $2.4 million in bias case. *Jet* 72:22 Je 8 '87

United States. Human Nutrition Research Center *See* Human Nutrition Research Center (U.S.)

United States. Immigration and Naturalization Service

Casa Romero closes: where do they go from here? [INS closes Catholic Church-run shelter for Central American refugees in Brownsville, Tex.] C. McElroy. il map *Focus* 37:28-9 Spr '87

Doors and walls [rules for processing applications for amnesty for aliens] *America* 156:294 Ap 11 '87

El Norte's sheltering arms [Supreme Court ruling on asylum cases] il *U S News World Rep* 102:13 Mr 23 '87

End of the road for littlest illegals. P. Dworkin. il *U S News World Rep* 102:23 Ap 13 '87

Excludable from justice [Cuban detainees at U.S. penitentiary in Atlanta] G. Galbaugh. *America* 156:315-16 Ap 18 '87

Gimme shelter [Supreme Court requires INS to use more lenient standards in asylum cases] R. Lacayo. il *Time* 129:70 Mr 23 '87

Imprisoned in limbo [Cubans in U.S. jails] K. S. Smith. *Commonweal* 114:552-3 O 9 '87

New workers: your papers, please. il *U S News World Rep* 102:12 F 2 '87

A question of fees [fees on international airline tickets to cover the rising costs of inspections] S. Shane. *Travel Holiday* 167:39 F '87

Stricter visa rules could keep new acts out of U.S. [foreign rock bands] M. Goldberg. *Roll Stone* p25+ F 26 '87

The untouchables [harassment of Arab Americans] *Nation* 244:348-9 Mr 21 '87

United States. Information Agency

Glasnost [address, March 13, 1987] C. Z. Wick. *Vital Speeches Day* 53:418-20 My 1 '87

How the U.S. fights to win the world's hearts and minds. D. O. Relin. il *Sch Update* 120:33-4 O 2 '87

United States. Information Agency. Artistic Ambassador Program *See* Artistic Ambassador Program (U.S.)

United States. Internal Revenue Service

00501 [Holtsville, N.Y. service center] *New Yorker* 62:27-8 F 2 '87

Congress wants a fierce IRS the public will love [Taxpayers' Bill of Rights] C. Yang. il *Bus Week* p35 O 26 '87

Does Guess have a friend in the IRS? [Guess vs. Jordache] R. Behar. il map *Forbes* 140:146-50+ N 16 '87

Getting ahead in government [B. Crawford, IRS employee] L. Gite. il por *Black Enterp* 17:93-4+ F '87

How to take the IRS to court—and make it pay. L. Wiener. il *U S News World Rep* 102:52-3 Je 22 '87

The IRS mess [corruption charges surrounding Guess, Inc. feud with Jordache] R. Behar. il *Forbes* 140:8 N 30 '87

Making the IRS accountable [Taxpayers' Bill of Rights] A. Holzinger. il *Nations Bus* 75:38-9 D '87

United States. Internal Revenue Service—*cont.*
The new chief of the IRS discusses how it, too, needs reform [interview with L. B. Gibbs] W. L. Updegrave. il por *Money* 16:128 F '87
Reining in the tax man [proposed Omnibus Taxpayer Bill of Rights Act] S. Dentzer. il *Newsweek* 110:41 Jl 13 '87
Restraining overeager IRS agents. L. Wiener. il *U S News World Rep* 102:62 My 25 '87
The scariest dunner [Taxpayers' Bill of Rights] L. Saunders. il *Forbes* 140:76+ N 2 '87
Squeal [tax informers] L. Saunders. il *Forbes* 139:62-3 My 4 '87
Suing the IRS—and winning. G. W. Padwe. *Nations Bus* 75:70 Jl '87
Taxing matters. See issues of Forbes
The taxman goes on-line [electronic filing] H. Fersko-Weiss. il *Pers Comput* 11:82-3 Ap '87
Unsure about a deduction? Run it by the IRS. S. Woolley. il *Bus Week* p117 S 7 '87
Why we need to enact a Taxpayers' Bill of Rights. il *Nations Bus* 75:71 Je '87

United States. International Trade Administration
Commerce Dept. black cites job bias and is demoted [R. Nichols] por *Jet* 73:17 N 30 '87

United States. Joint Chiefs of Staff
The wary warlords [views on Euromissile treaty] D. Gates. il *Newsweek* 109:5 My 11 '87

United States. Library of Congress See Library of Congress

United States. Marine Corps
"And to keep our honor clean". W. Shapiro. il *Time* 129:20-1 Ap 20 '87
The littlest Marine [honorary Marine J. Zimmerman] J. Stuller. il pors *Read Dig* 131:123-7 Jl '87
Marine Corps: is shape-up time at hand? M. Satchell. il *U S News World Rep* 102:10 Je 29 '87
The Marine Corps says goodbye to Charles Russell, its last active-duty WW II combat vet. R. Arias. il pors *People Wkly* 28:159-60 N 23 '87
When looking good is not enough. J. W. Kent. por *U S News World Rep* 102:5 My 11 '87

Airplanes
See Airplanes, Military

Appropriations and expenditures
Funding cut would halt AV-8B attack squadron upgrade. il *Aviat Week Space Technol* 127:25-6 Jl 6 '87

Blacks
Navy commissions 1st war ship named for a black medal of honor winner [R. M. Davis] il por *Jet* 72:38 Je 1 '87

Forces in the Soviet Union
The battle of the bugs [Soviet and American embassies; special section] il map *Newsweek* 109:18-22 Ap 20 '87
Black Marine's parents cry their son is a 'scapegoat' in sex for secrets case [A. Bracy's family] il por *Jet* 72:5 Ap 20 '87
Booze, brawls and skirt chasing [U.S. Marine guard spy scandal at Moscow embassy] E. Magnuson. il *Time* 129:20+ Ap 13 '87
The case of espionage in the embassy. B. Duffy. il *U S News World Rep* 102:18-20 Ap 13 '87
Charges of espionage and seduction [Marine guards in the Soviet Union] il *Macleans* 100:20 Ap 20 '87
Crawling with bugs [Moscow embassy spy scandal; cover story; special section] il *Time* 129:14-18+ Ap 20 '87
Fallout from the scandal [Marine guard spy case] il *Time* 129:22-3 Ap 27 '87
The fiasco in Moscow [security breach at U.S. embassy] L. Martz. il *Newsweek* 109:20-2 Ap 13 '87
From Russia with love and espionage [charges against C. Lonetree and A. Bracy, Marine guards at U.S. embassy in Moscow] il pors *Macleans* 100:18-19 Ap 13 '87
Holes in a spy scandal [Moscow embassy case] S. W. Cloud. il por *Time* 130:31 Jl 20 '87
The honey-trap spy case widens [charges against C. Lonetree and A. Bracy, Marine guards at the U.S. Embassy in Moscow] il pors *U S News World Rep* 102:12 Ap 6 '87
How to protect U.S. embassies. W. L. Chaze. il *U S News World Rep* 102:18-20 Ap 20 '87
Innocent man [charges against A. Bracy dropped] por *Time* 129:23 Je 22 '87
Is the Marine spy case unraveling? G. Witkin. il *U S News World Rep* 102:14 My 4 '87
A Marine and his "swallow" [security guard at U.S. Embassy in Moscow accused of spying] B. Duffy. il por *U S News World Rep* 102:25 Ja 26 '87

The Marine case falls apart [charges dropped against A. Bracy] M. Kaus. il por *Newsweek* 109:23 Je 22 '87
The Marine spy scandal: "It's a biggie" [Moscow embassy guards C. Lonetree and A. Bracy] A. Wilentz. il pors *Time* 129:21-2 Ap 6 '87
The Marine traitors. *Natl Rev* 39:18 Ap 24 '87
Military justice comes to attention [Marine guard spy case] R. Lacayo. il por *Time* 129:62 My 18 '87
Moonlighting in Moscow? [Marine guards C. Lonetree and A. Bracy charged with espionage] R. Watson. il pors *Newsweek* 109:32-3 Ap 6 '87
No entry [C. Lonetree denies allowing Soviets into Moscow embassy] il por *Time* 130:22 N 23 '87
Semper fie [Marine security guard C. Lonetree arrested for spying] por *Time* 129:19 Ja 26 '87
Spy charges against black Marine dropped [case of A. Bracy] por *Jet* 72:9 Je 29 '87
Spy woes [testimony retracted in Marine guard spy case] *Time* 129:22 My 11 '87
Why Moscow is winning [with interview with A. Hartman] W. L. Chaze. il *U S News World Rep* 102:36-8 Ap 27 '87

History
Ollie and Old Gimlet Eye [S. D. Butler] G. C. Ward. il *Am Herit* 38:14+ N '87

Procurement
Marines would swap A-6Es for all-weather F/A-18Ds. il *Aviat Week Space Technol* 127:21-2 O 26 '87

Training camps
See Military training camps

Women
See Servicewomen

United States. Marshals Service
Taking a byte out of crime [Scorecard program used to track federal fugitives] E. Shannon. il *Time* 129:63 My 25 '87

United States. Merchant Marine Academy
Wharton by the sea [federal government spends millions to train shipping executives] S. Feinberg. il *Wash Mon* 19:29-30+ O '87

United States. Minority Business Development Agency
Mfume, Flake, Lewis team to save Minority Agency. *Jet* 72:12 Ap 20 '87
NBL, Black Caucus at odds over status of the MBDA. *Jet* 72:30 My 4 '87

United States. National Academy of Sciences See National Academy of Sciences (U.S.)

United States. National Aeronautics and Space Administration
All in the name of science, Houston's Richard Fitzpatrick goes flat out for NASA—in bed [researching connection between weightlessness and bone loss] B. Stewart. il pors *People Wkly* 28:59-60 D 21 '87
America grounded [cover story; special section] il *Newsweek* 110:34-7+ Ag 17 '87
America in space: where next? [cover story] L. David. il *Sky Telesc* 74:23-9 Jl '87
The anti-space act of 1986 [restricting access to NASA tech briefs] J. Rhea. il *Space World* X-7-283:3 Jl '87
Beggs and General Dynamics cleared of fraud [Divad gun case] I. Goodwin. *Phys Today* 40 pt1:53 Ag '87
Beyond the Challenger era [proposed space program from the astronauts] R. Wolkomir. il *Omni* 9:62-4+ Mr '87
Boland, NASA at odds over launch of Mars Observer. M. M. Waldrop. por *Science* 235:743 F 13 '87
The broken promise of commercial space. T. M. Foley. *Aviat Week Space Technol* 127:15 S 14 '87
Crippled birds in search of wings. O. Friedrich. il *Time* 130:72-3 O 5 '87
The devastating delay [postponement of the Mars Observer] T. J. Frieling. il *Space World* X-7-283:27-30 Jl '87
Disaster and indecision could cost U.S. entire generation of space scientists. il *USA Today (Periodical)* 115:1-2 Je '87
E.T., phone NASA [SETI project] S. Vogel. il *Discover* 8:78-9 O '87
First word. K. Keeton. por *Omni* 10:6 O '87
General Dynamics, Beggs cleared of fraud charges. *Aviat Week Space Technol* 126:25-6 Je 29 '87
Getting NASA back on track [report by S. Ride] A. Toufexis. il *Time* 130:56 Ag 31 '87
Hacking through NASA [penetration of Space Physics Analysis Network] W. D. Marbach. il *Newsweek* 110:38 S 28 '87
How to get America back into space. W. Schirra. il *Pop Mech* 164:76-8+ Mr '87

United States. National Aeronautics and Space Administration—*cont.*

Ike's nightmare is upon us [views of K. Glennan] H. Sidey. il por *Time* 130:24 S 14 '87

Indictment of Beggs dropped [General Dynamics Divad gun fraud case] E. Marshall. *Science* 237:21 Jl 3 '87

Interview [J. Fletcher] A. R. Oberg. il por *Omni* 10:120-2+ D '87

Launchlog '87: inching back into space. J. Eberhart. *Sci News* 131:22 Ja 10 '87

Lights! Camera! NASA! L. Suid. il *Space World* X-6-282:16-20 Je '87

Limited occupancy [two phase space station plan] *Sci Am* 256:25 Je '87

Mars-struck [Mars Observer] il *Sci Am* 256:63+ Ap '87

Microgravity Task Force recommends sweeping changes to NASA program. T. M. Foley. il *Aviat Week Space Technol* 127:50-1 Jl 20 '87

Mission gap. T. Reichhardt. il *Space World* X-3-279:3 Mr '87

Musical chairs at NASA and Smithsonian. I. Goodwin. *Phys Today* 40:66 O '87

NASA announces a plan to reform management practices. M. M. Waldrop. *Science* 235:275-6 Ja 16 '87

NASA begins work on Mars mission to rejuvenate U.S. space program. C. Covault. il *Aviat Week Space Technol* 126:24-6 Mr 16 '87

NASA changes management structure. *Aviat Week Space Technol* 126:74-5 Ja 26 '87

NASA deputy endorses heavy-lift launch vehicle [views of Dale Myers] E. H. Kolcum. il *Aviat Week Space Technol* 126:60-1 Mr 23 '87

NASA forms office to study manned lunar base, Mars missions. il *Aviat Week Space Technol* 126:22-3 Je 8 '87

NASA initiates flights to obtain supernova data. *Aviat Week Space Technol* 127:28 N 9 '87

NASA issues five directives on commercial space policy. *Aviat Week Space Technol* 127:52-4 Jl 20 '87

NASA managers fear loss of space program leadership. C. Covault. *Aviat Week Space Technol* 126:21-2 F 2 '87

NASA may be forced to take minor role in heavy launcher. T. M. Foley. *Aviat Week Space Technol* 126:56-7 Mr 23 '87

NASA: no flight plan. il *Sci Am* 256:58+ F '87

NASA panel urges U.S. control of space station operations. T. M. Foley. *Aviat Week Space Technol* 126:341-2+ Je 15 '87

NASA panel would withhold accident witness accounts [Space Flight Safety Panel] il *Aviat Week Space Technol* 127:128-9 S 7 '87

NASA plans other baskets for its eggs [expendable launch vehicles] J. Eberhart. *Sci News* 131:341 My 30 '87

NASA plans to fight threats to its role in space program. C. Covault. il *Aviat Week Space Technol* 127:61-2 O 26 '87

NASA reaffirms strong support for space commercialization. C. Covault. *Aviat Week Space Technol* 127:31 O 5 '87

NASA seeks major role in developing heavy launcher. T. M. Foley. *Aviat Week Space Technol* 126:25-6 Ap 6 '87

NASA to decide between two options for 1989 new-start science project. *Aviat Week Space Technol* 127:138 Jl 13 '87

NASA under siege. D. E. Fink. *Aviat Week Space Technol* 126:11 F 2 '87

NASA: what's needed to put it on its feet? W. Biddle. il *Discover* 8:30-4+ Ja '87

NASA's Nazis. L. Hunt. *Nation* 244:671 My 23 '87

NASA's next stop in space [space station] W. D. Marbach. il *Newsweek* 109:52-3 Ja 19 '87

Picking up the space banner. D. E. Fink. *Aviat Week Space Technol* 127:11 O 19 '87

President's message. B. Bova. il *Space World* X-2-278:40 F '87

Program delays spur NASA, DARPA to restructure X-wing flight tests. *Aviat Week Space Technol* 127:23-4 Ag 31 '87

Race into space: the Pentagon overtakes NASA by a missile length. S. Budiansky. il *U S News World Rep* 103:10 Ag 17 '87

Review team urges close scrutiny of critical shuttle components. *Aviat Week Space Technol* 126:75 Ja 26 '87

Ride panel calls for aggressive action to assert U.S. leadership in space [with editorial comment by Donald E. Fink] C. Covault. il *Aviat Week Space Technol* 127:11, 26-7 Ag 24 '87

Ride panel will urge lunar base, earth science as new space goals. C. Covault. il *Aviat Week Space Technol* 127:16-18 Jl 13 '87

Ride report: charting the nation's future course in space. I. Goodwin. por *Phys Today* 40:64-6 O '87

Ride report: the going, not the goal. J. Eberhart. *Sci News* 132:117 Ag 22 '87

Sally Ride on America's future in space. S. K. Ride. *Space World* X-9-285:25 S '87

Sally Ride to leave NASA orbit; exodus at NSF. I. Goodwin. *Phys Today* 40:45 Jl '87

Science and the space station. E. Marshall. il *Science* 236:1176-9 Je 5 '87

Space [address, October 12, 1987] J. C. Fletcher. *Vital Speeches Day* 54:66-8 N 15 '87

Space 101: NASA hits the classroom. S. E. Sutphin. il *Space World* X-12-288:27-34 D '87

Space leadership void. D. E. Fink. *Aviat Week Space Technol* 127:9 Jl 27 '87

Space program said to lack direction [report by S. Ride] C. Norman. il por *Science* 237:965 Ag 28 '87

Space scuttle [need for coherent policy] R. Bazell. *New Repub* 197:11-12 O 12 '87

Space, the political imperative. C. Covault. *Aviat Week Space Technol* 127:9 N 30 '87

Spacebound again: the mixing of the fleet [cover story] J. Eberhart. il *Sci News* 132:330-1 N 21 '87

Two steps forward . . . T. Beardsley. *Sci Am* 257:18 S '87

U.S. must renew commitment to planetary exploration. D. Morrison. por *Aviat Week Space Technol* 127:143 Ag 10 '87

U.S. space program: struggling to recover [special section; with editorial comment by Donald E. Fink] il *Aviat Week Space Technol* 127:11, 18-27 Ag 10 '87

United States space program [address, June 24, 1987] J. C. Fletcher. *Vital Speeches Day* 53:642-4 Ag 15 '87

What color is your spacecraft? [getting a job with NASA; cover story] M. J. Dyson. il *Space World* X-12-288:9-11 D '87

What's wrong with America's space program. S. Budiansky. il *U S News World Rep* 103:32-4 D 28 '87-Ja 4 '88

Who will lead the world's next age of discovery? T. O. Paine. por *Aviat Week Space Technol* 127:43+ S 21 '87

A year later, a space agency still racked. S. N. Wellborn. il *U S News World Rep* 102:64-5 F 2 '87

Appropriations and expenditures

Alms for an orbiter [budget authority to fund construction of a replacement orbiter] T. J. Frieling. il *Space World* X-2-278:29-31 F '87

Committee cuts NSF, NASA funds. M. Crawford. *Science* 236:1517 Je 19 '87

Congress approves additional ALS funds [advanced launch system] *Aviat Week Space Technol* 127:21 Jl 13 '87

Congress to postpone station funding if NASA constrains materials science. *Aviat Week Space Technol* 127:29 O 12 '87

Congressmen support man-tended station [William Proxmire and Ed Boland] *Aviat Week Space Technol* 126:85 Mr 30 '87

A crisis in space research. M. M. Waldrop. il *Science* 235:426-9 Ja 23 '87

Deficit cuts impact defense, NASA budgets. *Aviat Week Space Technol* 127:29 O 19 '87

Fiscal 1988 station funding faces battle in Senate. *Aviat Week Space Technol* 127:21-2 Ag 31 '87

The flying I-beam [space station; cover story; with editorial comment by Tony Reichhardt] J. Rhea. il *Space World* X-5-281:3, 9-11 My '87

Gentlemen, start your rockets. J. Rhea. il *Space World* X-2-278:3 F '87

House subcommittee trims funding for space station by $50 million. T. M. Foley. *Aviat Week Space Technol* 126:35 Je 22 '87

Larceny at the launch pad. G. Easterbrook. il *Read Dig* 131:209-16 D '87

NASA: $13 billion in 1989? L. Garver. il *Space World* X-10-286:4 O '87

NASA apologizes for illegal lobbying to preserve budget, space station. T. M. Foley. *Aviat Week Space Technol* 127:20-1 Ag 31 '87

NASA budget needs exceed CBO spending levels by $14 billion. *Aviat Week Space Technol* 126:25 Ap 6 '87

NASA: budgeting back from Challenger. J. Eberhart. *Sci News* 131:85 F 7 '87

United States. National Aeronautics and Space Administration—Appropriations and expenditures—*cont.*

NASA may need $350-million fund boost to restore shuttle to safe flight status. *Aviat Week Space Technol* 126:28-9 Ap 13 '87

NASA, NSF await the ax. M. Crawford. *Science* 237:717 Ag 14 '87

NASA request includes increase to revitalize space programs. C. Covault. *Aviat Week Space Technol* 126:30-2 Ja 12 '87

NASA seeks to block massive reductions in station budget. *Aviat Week Space Technol* 127:29 D 14 '87

NASA to seek OMB approval for $12 billion 1989 budget. *Aviat Week Space Technol* 127:29 Jl 27 '87

NASA will begin $1.7-billion program to revitalize space technology base. il *Aviat Week Space Technol* 127:28-9 N 9 '87

NASA will proceed with scaled-back space station. T. M. Foley. il *Aviat Week Space Technol* 126:26-7 Mr 30 '87

OMB says budget cuts will postpone station. *Aviat Week Space Technol* 127:32 O 26 '87

Orbital Sciences, Space Agency disagree on cost of using transfer orbit stage as upper stage for the Mars Observer. *Aviat Week Space Technol* 126:27 My 11 '87

Panel doubts NASA can hold to space station R&D budget [National Research Council team] T. M. Foley. *Aviat Week Space Technol* 127:18-20 Jl 13 '87

President's message. B. Bova. il *Space World* X-9-285 Space Advocate:6 S '87

President's message [cutbacks in space station program] B. Bova. il *Space World* X-1-277:40 Ja '87

Reagan to consider additional funding for station program. C. Covault. *Aviat Week Space Technol* 126:260-1 Mr 9 '87

Rep. Nelson criticizes administration space station funding estimate. T. M. Foley. *Aviat Week Space Technol* 126:27-8 Ap 13 '87

The satellite the White House hates [Advanced Communications Technology Satellite; cover story] J. Rhea. il *Space World* X-8-284:21-3 Ag '87

Science funding steady despite limited flights. il *Aviat Week Space Technol* 126:118-19+ Mr 9 '87

Severe budget cuts affect space station project. *Aviat Week Space Technol* 127:23 D 21 '87

Space station faces possible two-year deployment delay. T. M. Foley. *Aviat Week Space Technol* 126:28-30 F 9 '87

A strategic initiative for NASA's future [Civil Space Technology Initiative] J. Rhea. il *Space World* X-3-279:30-2 Mr '87

We shouldn't build the space station now. A. Roland. il *Technol Rev* 90:22-3 Jl '87

White House delays action on new station cost estimates. T. M. Foley. *Aviat Week Space Technol* 126:26-7 Mr 2 '87

Winning the battle of the space budget. M. Sickler. il *Astronomy* 15:26+ Ag '87

Procurement

Committee identifies shuttle contract issues [processing contract with Lockheed analyzed by Estess Committee] *Aviat Week Space Technol* 126:89 Mr 30 '87

Congress, booster manufacturers criticize joint redesign program [Thiokol design for shuttle booster] C. Covault. il *Aviat Week Space Technol* 126:116-17 F 9 '87

NASA agreement with 3M sets precedent for large commercial space commitments [shuttle research] T. M. Foley. *Aviat Week Space Technol* 126:102-3 Ja 12 '87

NASA briefs contractors on Mars rover/sample return mission. M. A. Dornheim. il *Aviat Week Space Technol* 126:22-3 Ap 6 '87

NASA cites strengths, weaknesses of space station contract bids. *Aviat Week Space Technol* 127:23-4 D 21 '87

NASA delays space station contracts as industrial research interest grows. C. Covault. il *Aviat Week Space Technol* 127:30-1 N 9 '87

NASA denies shuttle launch to commercial space firm [Spacehab, Inc.] T. M. Foley. *Aviat Week Space Technol* 127:26-8 S 7 '87

NASA evaluates transportation of large space station payloads [C-5A modifications] B. A. Smith. il *Aviat Week Space Technol* 127:47+ Ag 10 '87

NASA, industry managers assess rise in station cost estimates. T. M. Foley. *Aviat Week Space Technol* 126:28-9 Ja 19 '87

NASA issues station RFPs after agreeing to changes mandated by Congress [requests for proposals for space station hardware] *Aviat Week Space Technol* 126:26 My 4 '87

NASA may seek proposals for shuttle-derived booster. T. M. Foley. *Aviat Week Space Technol* 126:24-5 Je 29 '87

NASA nears decision to end Atlas Centaur program. *Aviat Week Space Technol* 127:21 Ag 31 '87

NASA revamps commercial policies, lifts ban on industry agreements. T. M. Foley. *Aviat Week Space Technol* 127:28-9 N 2 '87

NASA selects seven new Centers for Commercial Development of Space. *Aviat Week Space Technol* 127:31 Ag 3 '87

NASA to seek design concepts for station crew escape vehicle. C. Covault. il *Aviat Week Space Technol* 127:30 Ag 17 '87

NASA will consider use of commercial space facility [Space Industries' Industrial Space Facility] *Aviat Week Space Technol* 127:55 N 2 '87

Quality gains new emphasis after shuttle processing review. E. H. Kolcum. *Aviat Week Space Technol* 126:85+ Mr 30 '87

Selling to NASA. *Space World* X-12-288:13-14 D '87

Shuttle payload policy counters effort to attract private station suppliers. *Aviat Week Space Technol* 127:62 S 7 '87

Six aerospace firms compete to build space station hardware. T. M. Foley. il *Aviat Week Space Technol* 127:26-7 Jl 27 '87

Space station contracts [special section; with editorial comment by Donald E. Fink] il *Aviat Week Space Technol* 127:11, 18-23 D 7 '87

The space station launching a thousand contracts. S. Payne. il *Bus Week* p126-7+ N 23 '87

Suddenly last spring [space station contracts] L. Garver and P. Chien. *Space World* X-6-282:5 Je '87

U.S. to bolster its capability in small space launch vehicles. C. Covault. il *Aviat Week Space Technol* 127:73+ D 7 '87

United States. National Aeronautics and Space Administration. Ames Research Center *See* Ames Research Center

United States. National Aeronautics and Space Administration. George C. Marshall Space Flight Center *See* George C. Marshall Space Flight Center

United States. National Aeronautics and Space Administration. Hugh L. Dryden Flight Research Center *See* Hugh L. Dryden Flight Research Center

United States. National Aeronautics and Space Administration. Jet Propulsion Laboratory *See* Jet Propulsion Laboratory (U.S.)

United States. National Aeronautics and Space Administration. John F. Kennedy Space Center *See* John F. Kennedy Space Center

United States. National Aeronautics and Space Administration. Langley Research Center *See* Langley Research Center (U.S.)

United States. National Aeronautics and Space Administration. Lewis Research Center *See* Lewis Research Center (U.S.)

United States. National Aeronautics and Space Administration. Lyndon B. Johnson Space Center *See* Lyndon B. Johnson Space Center

United States. National Aeronautics and Space Administration. National Scientific Balloon Facility *See* National Scientific Balloon Facility

United States. National Archives and Records Administration

For the record [preservation of documents] *Sci Am* 256:59-60 Ja '87

Keeping the dreams of a nation. K. Lingo. il *South Living* 22:40+ My '87

A pilgrimage to the Archives. *Saturday Evening Post* 259:56 My/Je '87

A visible legacy [U.S. Constitution on display] il *Life* 10:62-3 Fall '87

United States. National Cancer Institute *See* National Cancer Institute (U.S.)

United States. National Commission on Space *See* National Commission on Space (U.S.)

United States. National Gallery of Art *See* National Gallery of Art (U.S.)

United States. National Geodetic Survey *See* National Geodetic Survey (U.S.)

United States. National Guard

See also

National Committee for Employer Support of the Guard and Reserve (U.S.)

United States. National Highway Traffic Safety Administration

The controversy over rear-seat lap belts. J. Tomerlin. il *Road Track* 38:63-4+ Ja '87

Sudden acceleration stumps NHTSA [Audi 5000S] T. Orme. *Mot Trend* 39:48+ Je '87

United States. National Hurricane Center *See* National Hurricane Center

United States. National Institute of Arthritis, Musculoskeletal, and Skin Diseases *See* National Institute of Arthritis, Musculoskeletal, and Skin Diseases (U.S.)

United States. National Institute of Mental Health *See* National Institute of Mental Health (U.S.)

United States. National Institutes of Health *See* National Institutes of Health (U.S.)

United States. National Labor Relations Board
Dotson's exit: a lot more than politics. A. Bernstein and S. B. Garland. por *Bus Week* p114 N 9 '87

United States. National Library of Medicine *See* National Library of Medicine (U.S.)

United States. National Marine Fisheries Service
Not the best way to save turtles [proposed experiment to study the impact of underwater explosions on endangered sea turtles] il *Oceans* 20:69 N/D '87

United States. National Mediation Board
Federal mediator joins American, pilot talks. *Aviat Week Space Technol* 126:31 F 16 '87

United States. National Museum of American Art *See* National Museum of American Art (U.S.)

United States. National Museum of American History *See* National Museum of American History (U.S.)

United States. National Museum of Natural History *See* National Museum of Natural History (U.S.)

United States. National Oceanic and Atmospheric Administration
NOAA, FAA consider volcano monitoring system. il *Aviat Week Space Technol* 127:30-1 Jl 6 '87

Appropriations and expenditures
The budget and the environment [funding the Coastal Zone Management Program] il *Oceans* 20:65 Mr/Ap '87

Commerce Dept. will buy ELVs from private sector. *Aviat Week Space Technol* 126:24-5 Mr 23 '87

NOAA to hold competition to buy GOES launchers [Geostationary Operational Environmental Satellites] *Aviat Week Space Technol* 126:24 Ja 19 '87

Unisys wins $60-million contract for Nexrad Doppler weather radar. *Aviat Week Space Technol* 127:35 D 7 '87

United States. National Oceanic and Atmospheric Administration. National Weather Service *See* United States. National Weather Service

United States. National Oceanic and Atmospheric Administration. Office of Sea Grant Programs
Building on success. *Oceans* 20:5 Jl/Ag '87

United States. National Oceans Policy Commission *See* National Oceans Policy Commission (U.S.)

United States. National Park Service
Disputed territory. R. Cahn and P. Cahn. il *Natl Parks* 61:28-33 My/Je '87

Horace M. Albright: in memoriam [excerpt from The National Park Service] H. M. Albright. il *Natl Parks* 61:46-7 Jl/Ag '87

How to save our national parks [cover story] A. Chase. il *Atlantic* 260:35-44 Jl '87

National Park Service Handbooks [with editorial comment by Ed Holm] il *Am Hist Illus* 22:4, 10-11 O '87

The national park system: looking back and moving ahead. W. P. Mott, Jr. il *USA Today (Periodical)* 115:18-28 My '87

NPCA report. See issues of National Parks

Patrolling the park beat [National Park Service rangers] L. Peach. il *Natl Parks* 61:24-9 N/D '87

Risky business [national park rangers] J. Heinrichs. il *Natl Wildl* 25:12-15 Je/Jl '87

Smokey would never believe this [views of D. Hummel] A. Chase. *Wash Mon* 19:45-6+ N '87

Takeover at the Park Service [dispute between W. P. Mott and W. P. Horn] R. Cahn. *Natl Parks* 61:53 Mr/Ap '87

Taking a count of threats [natural resource inventories and monitoring] R. Cahn. il *Natl Parks* 61:33-4 Jl/Ag '87

Appropriations and expenditures
NPS gets needed funds from Congress for FY 87. *Natl Parks* 61:36-7 Ja/F '87

United States. National Science Foundation *See* National Science Foundation (U.S.)

United States. National Security Council
Army Gen. Colin Powell is picked for NSC's no. 2 spot. il por *Jet* 71:24 Ja 12 '87

Break point [Iran-contra case; special section] il *Newsweek* 109:18-25 F 23 '87

Carlucci and the N.S.C. J. Bamford. il *N Y Times Mag* p16-19+ Ja 18 '87

Carlucci cleans up the act at the NSC. H. Anderson. il por *Newsweek* 109:19-20 Ja 19 '87

Gen. Colin Powell steps in as National Security chief. il por *Jet* 73:10 N 23 '87

The general takes command [C. Powell] J. V. Lamar, Jr. il por *Time* 130:22 N 16 '87

How a Macy's engineer and his pals became rogue American agents [K. Kattke] N. M. Renfrew and P. Blauner. il pors *N Y* 20:102-4+ D 7 '87

The I.S.A. behind the N.S.C. [Intelligence Support Activity] M. Perry. il *Nation* 244:33+ Ja 17 '87

Inside Ollie's mind [O. L. North] E. Alterman. il *New Repub* 196:12-15 F 16 '87

McFarlane's folly. D. Schorr. *New Leader* 70:3-4 F 9-23 '87

A memo to Reagan [alleged harassment of contra critic J. Terrell by O. North and staff] il pors *Newsweek* 110:7 S 21 '87

A mini-C.I.A. M. Ratner and D. Lerner. *Nation* 245:113+ Ag 15-22 '87

NSC and Ocean Drilling [Soviet participation] J. A. Knauss. *Environment* 29:2-3 Jl/Ag '87

The NSC's midlife crisis. Z. Brzezinski. *Foreign Policy* 69:80-99 Wint '87/'88

Oliver North's strange recruits. P. Maas. il *N Y Times Mag* p20-2+ Ja 18 '87

Ollie's shadow operators [O. North and Iran-contra scandal] N. Cooper. il por *Newsweek* 109:24-6 Mr 2 '87

Out of the basement. M. Kondracke. *New Repub* 196:10+ Ja 5-12 '87

The phantom interview [R. Reagan interview on Radio Marti staged by the National Security Council] A. Lopez-Muñoz. *New Repub* 196:11 Je 29 '87

Security Council blocks NSF grant to IIASA. C. Norman. il *Science* 236:514-15 My 1 '87

The story of Fawn Hall, all-American secretary. J. Adler. il pors *Newsweek* 109:36-7 Mr 9 '87

Taming the NSC [L. B. Johnson] J. P. Roche. *Natl Rev* 39:40-2 Mr 27 '87

'The ultimate no. 2' for NSC [C. Powell] T. M. DeFrank. il por *Newsweek* 110:63 N 16 '87

The White House tapes, again. A. Nairn. il *Progressive* 51:20-3 Ap '87

Anecdotes, facetiae, satire, etc.
Reflagging: the secret NSC agenda. D. Halberstein. il *New Repub* 197:11 Ag 24 '87

United States. National Severe Storms Forecast Center
Oklahoma keeps an eye on the storms [work of research meteorologist D. Burgess] D. Young. il por *South Living* 22:134+ My '87

United States. National Space Technology Laboratories *See* National Space Technology Laboratories (U.S.)

United States. National Technical Information Service
Privatizing tech info. R. Chalk. il *Technol Rev* 90:8+ F/Mr '87

Will NTIS go private? M. Crawford. *Science* 236:140 Ap 10 '87

United States. National Transportation Safety Board
The controversy over rear-seat lap belts. J. Tomerlin. il *Road Track* 38:63-4+ Ja '87

The docket. P. Bradley. See issues of Flying beginning July 1986 through August 1987

FAA disputes recommendations for summer traffic reductions. *Aviat Week Space Technol* 126:36 Je 1 '87

NTSB analyzes factors leading to California midair collision of DC-9, Piper aircraft. *Aviat Week Space Technol* 127:59-60+ N 30 '87

NTSB blames ATC system for midair crash [Aug. 31, 1986 collision of Aeromexico DC-9-30 and Piper PA-28-181] *Aviat Week Space Technol* 127:34 Jl 13 '87

NTSB determines probable causes of Delta accident [Dallas/Ft. Worth Delta airline crash, August 2, 1985] *Aviat Week Space Technol* 126:95+ Ja 26 '87

NTSB evaluates factors in Detroit MD-82 crash [Northwest Airlines crash] il *Aviat Week Space Technol* 127:18-20 Ag 24 '87

NTSB focuses on cockpit communication, inspection methods in Milwaukee crash [September 1985 crash of a Midwest Express DC-9] P. Proctor. *Aviat Week Space Technol* 126:41 F 16 '87

NTSB recommends limits to ease summer air traffic congestion. C. Preble. il *Aviat Week Space Technol* 126:32-3 My 4 '87

NTSB recommends upgraded training, reporting to avoid wind shear [August 2, 1985 Delta Flight 191 crash at Dallas/Ft. Worth] *Aviat Week Space Technol* 126:93+ F 2 '87

NTSB urges traffic reductions in congested control zones. *Aviat Week Space Technol* 126:31 My 18 '87

Safety Board cites 1986 as one of safest years ever. *Aviat Week Space Technol* 126:36 Ja 19 '87

United States. National Transportation Safety Board—
cont.
Safety Board cites limitations of airport weather surveillance [August 2, 1985 Delta Flight 191 crash at Dallas/ Ft. Worth] *Aviat Week Space Technol* 126:113-14+ Ja 12 '87
Safety Board urges mandatory use of FDR/CVRs in commuter transports [flight data and cockpit voice recorders] E. H. Phillips. il *Aviat Week Space Technol* 127:73-5 Ag 31 '87

United States. National Weather Service
Old problems; new answers. il *Earth Sci* 40:17-18 Spr '87

United States. Naval Air Reserve
Naval Air Reserve will add A-6Es as part of modernization effort. D. M. North. il *Aviat Week Space Technol* 126:64-5+ Mr 2 '87

United States. Naval Air Systems Command
Streamlining the U.S. acquisition system. E. A. Pyatt. por *Aviat Week Space Technol* 127:123 O 19 '87

United States. Naval Air Test Center *See* Naval Air Test Center (U.S.)

United States. Naval Security and Investigative Command
A lawyer's touch [appointment of J. E. Gordon] L. Howard. il *Newsweek* 110:6 N 16 '87

United States. Naval War College *See* Naval War College (U.S.)

United States. Navy
See also
Navy yards and naval stations
Walker family espionage case
Anchors aweigh: help for Navy families [stress of separations] H. Hall. il *Psychol Today* 21:16 Ap '87
Anchors aweigh: the United States Navy story [videotape] *Am Hist Illus* 22:16 S '87
EMP: fallout over a naval EMPRESS [Navy proposal for electromagnetic pulse simulator] J. Raloff. *Sci News* 131:182 Mr 21 '87
In harm's way [strategy for global conventional war; cover story] J. Beatty. il map *Atlantic* 259:37-46+ My '87
Naval strategy: America rules the waves? D. Charles. *Science* 236:24 Ap 3 '87
The Navy after Lehman: rough sailing ahead? D. Charles. il por *Science* 236:22-5 Ap 3 '87
Navy master plan emphasizes airborne ASW systems. J. D. Morrocco. *Aviat Week Space Technol* 127:111-12+ Jl 13 '87
The Navy sails on rough seas. J. Barry. il *Newsweek* 109:23-6 Je 1 '87
Navy's new leatherneck Secretary [J. Webb] M. Doan and J. M. Hildreth. il por *U S News World Rep* 102:16 Mr 2 '87
New Navy boss: poet and warrior [J. H. Webb] E. Thomas. il pors *Newsweek* 109:6 My 4 '87
Seapower [address, October 28, 1987] J. H. Webb. *Vital Speeches Day* 54:98-100 D 1 '87
Superpower arms race at sea [cover story; special section] bibl f il *Bull At Sci* 43:13-28+ S '87
'You buy carriers to protect everything else' [interview with J. F. Lehman] por *U S News World Rep* 102:28 Je 15 '87

Appropriations and expenditures
Navy opts for aircraft carriers over modifications, weapons. D. M. North. *Aviat Week Space Technol* 126:27-8 Ja 12 '87
Navy's emphasis on ATA threatens A-6F funding. D. M. North. *Aviat Week Space Technol* 127:20-1 O 26 '87
Shipbuilders: caught in the wake of Navy cutbacks. S. Payne. *Bus Week* p70 Ja 12 '87
Sneak attack [C. Weinberger requests funding for aircraft carriers] por *Time* 129:32 Ap 27 '87

Blacks
Blacks among 37 sailors killed in attack on Stark. il *Jet* 72:14 Je 8 '87
Cmdr. Dew is first black to head Seabee battalion. por *Jet* 72:6 Ag 17 '87
Ebony update: Lt. Robert O. Goodman. il pors *Ebony* 42:124+ My '87
Navy tackles McCallum, and checks Robinson [N. McCallum and D. Robinson] pors *Jet* 72:50 My 11 '87

Boats
See also
Hydrofoils
Minesweepers
Submarines
Warships
Stealth outboard [military amphibious reconnaissance system outboard motors] B. McKeown. il *Pop Sci* 230:75 Je '87

Civilian employees
A case goes unheard at the EEOC [Navy waitress M. Farrell] F. Greve. il por *50 Plus* 27:16+ N '87

Forces in Japan
Jets to invade a national park [Fuji-Hakone-Izu National Park] J. Hamilton. il *Sierra* 72:132-3 Ja/F '87

Forces in Lebanon
Ebony update: Lt. Robert O. Goodman. il pors *Ebony* 42:124+ My '87

Forces in the Persian Gulf region
See also
Stark (Warship)—Iraqi missile attack, 1987
Administration cancels missile sale; Congress critical of Middle East policy. M. Mecham. *Aviat Week Space Technol* 126:70-1 Je 15 '87
Administration to cite Saudi involvement in Gulf as justification for arms sale. M. Mecham. *Aviat Week Space Technol* 127:31 Ag 24 '87
AH-1T Cobra attack helicopters deploy with Persian Gulf force. il *Aviat Week Space Technol* 127:42-3 O 19 '87
American hubris: from Truman to the Persian Gulf. T. Draper. bibl f il *N Y Rev Books* 34:40-8 Jl 16 '87
America's Gulf minuet [protection of shipping lanes] W. L. Chaze. il *U S News World Rep* 102:18-19 Je 8 '87
America's nemesis. R. Watson. il *Newsweek* 110:28-31 Ag 17 '87
Assistant Secretary Murphy's interview on "Meet the press" [transcript of program, August 23, 1987] R. W. Murphy. *Dep State Bull* 87:44-8 O '87
An attack in the Gulf [attack on Iranian ship laying mines] M. Nichols. il map *Macleans* 100:26-8 O 5 '87
A balance sheet in the Gulf. N. Cooper. il *Newsweek* 110:59 N 9 '87
Ballots and bloodshed [debate over whether Congress should invoke the War Powers Act over events in the Persian Gulf] *New Repub* 197:4+ O 19 '87
A battle for sea lanes [renewed attacks on shipping] R. Laver. il *Macleans* 100:20 S 14 '87
The broader picture. B. Crozier. *Natl Rev* 39:28+ N 6 '87
Buildup in the Gulf [U.S. commitment to keep shipping lanes open; special section] il map *Newsweek* 109:32-5 Je 8 '87
Can't anybody here play this game? [U.S. unpreparedness in Persian Gulf] M. Kramer. il *U S News World Rep* 103:11 Ag 10 '87
Caught in the act [U.S. captures Iranians laying mines] E. Magnuson. il map *Time* 130:20-3 O 5 '87
A chain of violence. il *Macleans* 100:17 Ag 10 '87
Chin to chin in a sea of trouble [Iranian missiles hit Kuwaiti tanker sailing under U.S. flag] B. Duffy. il map *U S News World Rep* 103:25 O 26 '87
Collision course? [U.S. flags to protect Kuwaiti oil tankers in Persian Gulf] L. Howard. il *Newsweek* 109:5 My 25 '87
Combined U.S. forces defeat Iranian mine-laying mission. B. M. Greeley, Jr. il map *Aviat Week Space Technol* 127:32-3 S 28 '87
Convoy to a minefield [mine blast hits Kuwaiti tanker under American escort] B. Levin. il *Macleans* 100:20-1 Ag 3 '87
Coping with the unfathomable. J. V. Lamar, Jr. il *Time* 130:39 Ag 17 '87
Credibility Gulf. L. Ackland. *Bull At Sci* 43:2 Jl/Ag '87
Crisis in the Gulf: waiting for the other shoe to drop. J. L. Galloway. il *U S News World Rep* 103:38 Jl 13 '87
The dangers deepen, and so do the doubts [special section] il map *U S News World Rep* 103:18-23 Ag 17 '87
The dangers of taking sides. L. C. Wilson. *USA Today (Periodical)* 116:47 N '87
Democrats cite risk in Kuwaiti reflagging [report by Democratic Study Group] P. Mann. *Aviat Week Space Technol* 126:33 Je 22 '87
A direct hit in reply [U.S. warships destroy Iranian oil installation] A. Bilski. il *Macleans* 100:25 N 2 '87
Does the United States have any interests? [views of Democratic presidential candidates] *Natl Rev* 39:17-18 N 20 '87
Drowning in the Gulf. B. Rubin. *Foreign Policy* 69:120-34 Wint '87/'88
Engulfed. *Commonweal* 114:467-8 S 11 '87
Escort service for the Gulf [U.S. plans to keep shipping lanes open] J. V. Lamar, Jr. il *Time* 129:23 Je 8 '87

United States. Navy—Forces in the Persian Gulf region—*cont.*

F-14 crew fires at Iranian jet to defend Navy Gulf patrol. B. M. Greeley, Jr. il *Aviat Week Space Technol* 127:22-3 Ag 17 '87

The gang that can shoot straight. M. Kramer. il *U S News World Rep* 103:17 N 23 '87

Go it alone in the Gulf [U.S. protection of shipping lanes] M. Kramer. il *U S News World Rep* 102:20 Je 8 '87

The good life in the Persian Gulf. D. Kirk. il *New Leader* 70:3-5 S 7 '87

Gorbachev's Gulf game. M. Whitaker. il por *Newsweek* 110:32-3 Jl 20 '87

The Gulf. il *World Press Rev* 34:6-7 D '87

The Gulf [cover story; special section] il *World Press Rev* 34:13-16+ O '87

The Gulf: an important success [trapping Iran in minelaying operations] *Natl Rev* 39:20 O 23 '87

The Gulf war—among friends [United States protects shipping lanes] J. L. Galloway. il map *U S News World Rep* 102:26-8 Je 15 '87

Gulf—or abyss? I. F. Stone. *Nation* 244:838-9 Je 20 '87

Here a mine, there a mine. J. Greenwald. il *Time* 130:24-7 Ag 24 '87

High drama in the Persian Gulf. R. Evans and R. D. Novak. il map *Read Dig* 131:133-6 D '87

How to defend the Gulf [U.S. to protect neutral shipping] *New Repub* 196:7-9 Je 22 '87

If necessary, a superpower acts alone [U.S. decision to protect shipping lanes] C. Krauthammer. il map *Time* 129:83-4 Je 22 '87

In deeper in the Gulf [special section] il *Newsweek* 110:14-17 Ag 31 '87

Into rough water [U.S./Kuwaiti tankers encounter mines in the Persian Gulf] W. Isaacson. il *Time* 130:8-10 Ag 10 '87

Just war in the Gulf. *New Repub* 197:10-11 N 9 '87

Losing patience with Iran. *Natl Rev* 39:18 S 11 '87

Lost empires. *Nation* 245:111-12 Ag 15-22 '87

The military underpinnings of diplomacy [address, September 21, 1987] C. W. Weinberger. *Vital Speeches Day* 54:34-7 N 1 '87

The mines of August. R. Watson. il map *Newsweek* 110:22-4 Ag 24 '87

The mining episode . . . and more to come? [U.S.-flagged tanker Bridgeton hits mine in Persian Gulf] il maps *U S News World Rep* 103:26-7 Ag 3 '87

Missile attack, Kuwaiti pact could draw U.S. into Gulf war. J. D. Morrocco. il map *Aviat Week Space Technol* 126:23-5 My 25 '87

Missing mine sweepers. H. Evans. il *U S News World Rep* 103:68 Ag 24 '87

More blood in the Gulf [U.S. helicopters shoot it out with Iranian gunboats] R. Watson. il map *Newsweek* 110:44-5 O 19 '87

Navy deploys helicopters to counter Gulf mine threat [Sikorsky RH-53D Sea Stallion] M. Mecham. *Aviat Week Space Technol* 127:25-6 Ag 3 '87

News conference of August 6, 1987. G. P. Shultz. *Dep State Bull* 87:11-14 O '87

'No reason ever to withdraw' [interview with F. Carlucci] por *U S News World Rep* 103:28 Ag 24 '87

An offer spurned [U.S. turns down offer of offshore naval facility inside Kuwait's waters] L. Howard. il *Newsweek* 110:7 D 7 '87

Oil, the Gulf and the Iranians. D. Hiro. *Nation* 245:261-3 S 19 '87

On the battle fronts [Central America and the Persian Gulf] D. Schorr. *New Leader* 70:6 O 19 '87

Patrolling the Gulf. *Natl Rev* 39:15+ Jl 17 '87

Perseverance pays [reflagging and escort operation] M. Kondracke. *New Repub* 197:13-14+ S 14-21 '87

The Persian Gulf. il *World Press Rev* 34:8-9 S '87

Persian Gulf [remarks, May 29, 1987] R. Reagan. *Dep State Bull* 87:81-2 Ag '87

The Persian Gulf: where U.S. policy is adrift. D. Griffiths. il *Bus Week* p41 Je 15 '87

Piloting the camel [U.S. reflagging commitment to Kuwait] M. B. Zuckerman. il *U S News World Rep* 103:76 Jl 6 '87

Pitfalls and promises in the Persian Gulf powder keg. J. L. Galloway. il *U S News World Rep* 102:18-19 Je 29 '87

Policy at sea. *Time* 129:25 Je 15 '87

Powder-keg politics. R. Laver. il map *Macleans* 100:14-15 Ag 31 '87

Pressing the attack [U.S. presses Iran] K. Scanlon. il *Macleans* 100:31-2 O 19 '87

Pressure yes, retreat no. W. F. Buckley. *Natl Rev* 39:72 S 11 '87

Prevailing in the Gulf [US forces as sign of power] D. Gergen. il *U S News World Rep* 103:84 S 14 '87

Pseudo-crisis in the Persian Gulf [U.S. to defend free shipping] *Natl Rev* 39:20-1 Jl 3 '87

Punch, counterpunch [U.S. attacks Iranian oil-loading platforms] M. S. Serrill. il *Time* 130:62-4 N 2 '87

Questions from the Persian Gulf. *America* 157:316 N 7 '87

Reflagging folly [U.S. plan to flag Kuwaiti ships and reinforce American military presence] N. Safran. *New Repub* 197:10-11 Ag 3 '87

Rough seas and new names [Kuwaiti tankers flying under American flag] J. V. Lamar, Jr. il map *Time* 129:13 Je 29 '87

Running the gauntlet [U.S.-flagged Kuwaiti tanker hits Iranian mine in the Persian Gulf] W. E. Smith. il map *Time* 130:24-7 Ag 3 '87

A salvo for Teheran [U.S. destroyers fire on Iranian oil rig] A. Deming. il map *Newsweek* 110:63+ N 2 '87

Settling in for a long stay. H. Anderson. il *Newsweek* 110:34 S 28 '87

Shoot-out in the Gulf, echoes on Capitol Hill [American helicopter gunships vs. Iranian gunboats] J. L. Galloway. il *U S News World Rep* 103:8 O 19 '87

Showing the flag in the Gulf is already showing results. J. P. Tarpey and others. il *Bus Week* p49 S 21 '87

Shunning Uncle Sam in the Gulf. W. L. Chaze. il *U S News World Rep* 103:39-40 N 2 '87

Silkworm's sting [Iranian missile attack on Kuwaiti tanker sailing under American flag] M. S. Serrill. il map *Time* 130:42-3 O 26 '87

Simmering about the Saudis [U.S. wants support in the Persian Gulf] H. Anderson. il *Newsweek* 109:40 Je 15 '87

A sting in the Gulf [mine blast hits Kuwaiti tanker under American escort] H. Anderson. il map *Newsweek* 110:24-6 Ag 3 '87

A study in contrast: Central America & the Persian Gulf [competing Soviet and U.S. interests] J. B. Hehir. il *Commonweal* 114:439 Ag 14 '87

Superpowers in the Gulf. S. Pope. il *World Press Rev* 34:39 Ag '87

Supersap [U.S. effort to protect access to Persian Gulf oil results in price rise] *New Repub* 197:4 Ag 31 '87

Swept up in the tides of the Gulf. H. Anderson. il *Newsweek* 110:40-2 Ag 10 '87

Time bombs in the ocean [mines] A. Bilski. il *Macleans* 100:24 Ag 24 '87

Time for sweeping gestures [mines in the Persian Gulf] M. S. Serrill. *Time* 130:26 Ag 31 '87

Tonkin Gulf redux. *Nation* 245:541 N 14 '87

Top secret [War Powers Act and U.S. presence in the Persian Gulf] W. F. Buckley. *Natl Rev* 39:64 S 25 '87

A U.S. ambush in the Gulf [trapping Iran in the act of laying mines] R. Watson. il map *Newsweek* 110:24-7 O 5 '87

U.S. destroyers bombard Iranian oil platform. *Aviat Week Space Technol* 127:34 O 26 '87

The U.S. may face a long war of nerves. D. F. Graham and J. P. Tarpey. il *Bus Week* p34 Ag 17 '87

U.S. policy in the Persian Gulf and Kuwaiti reflagging [statement, June 16, 1987] M. H. Armacost. *Dep State Bull* 87:78-81 Ag '87

U.S. takes defensive action in Persian Gulf [statement, September 24, 1987] R. Reagan. *Dep State Bull* 87:43-4 N '87

U.S. will attack Iranian missile sites if hostile intent is evident. P. Mann. *Aviat Week Space Technol* 127:29-30 Jl 20 '87

Under Secretary Armacost's interview on "Meet the press" [transcript of program, August 30, 1987] *Dep State Bull* 87:32-4 O '87

Undertow from the Gulf. W. Glasgall. il *Bus Week* p32-4 Ag 17 '87

Up Shiites creek. W. Greider. il *Roll Stone* p32+ O 22 '87

Waiting for Iran [U.S. capture of Iranian mine laying vessels; with editorial comment by Mortimer B. Zuckerman] W. L. Chaze. il map *U S News World Rep* 103:22-4, 88 O 5 '87

War games in the Gulf. A. Wilson-Smith. il map *Macleans* 100:16-17 Ag 17 '87

War Powers Act and the Persian Gulf. il *Congr Dig* 66:289-314 D '87

War Powers inaction [congressional inaction in face of U.S. commitment in the Persian Gulf] T. Noah. *New Repub* 197:11-12 Jl 6 '87

United States. Navy—Forces in the Persian Gulf region—*cont.*
Washington is protecting much more than Kuwaiti tankers. B. Javetski and others. il *Bus Week* p89 Jl 20 '87

"We engaged" [Iranians shoot at U.S. helicopters] E. Magnuson. il map *Time* 130:12-14 O 19 '87

Weinberger's war. I. F. Stone. *Nation* 245:364-5 O 10 '87

Where are U.S. minesweepers? Out of service and out-of-date, says arms expert William Lind [interview] M. Wilhelm. il por *People Wkly* 28:30-1 Ag 24 '87

Why Reagan pulled his punch in the Persian Gulf [retaliating against Iran for missile attack on a U.S.-flagged tanker] B. Javetski and D. Griffiths. il *Bus Week* p161 N 2 '87

Why we are uneasy. *America* 156:473 Je 13 '87

Will Reagan hit back at Iran? [retaliation for missile strike against U.S.-flagged tanker] N. Cooper. il *Newsweek* 110:42-3 O 26 '87

Anecdotes, facetiae, satire, etc.

Reflagging: the secret NSC agenda. D. Halberstein. il *New Repub* 197:11 Ag 24 '87

True North. T. Southern. *Nation* 245:41-2 Jl 18-25 '87

Management

Army, Navy Secretaries initiate major changes in staff structure. J. D. Morrocco. il *Aviat Week Space Technol* 126:79-81 Mr 16 '87

Procurement

Airship's fortunes are suddenly afloat. M. Maremont. il *Bus Week* p52 Je 22 '87

Boeing selected over Lockheed for P-3 avionics update award. B. M. Greeley, Jr. *Aviat Week Space Technol* 127:22-3 Jl 20 '87

Boeing withdraws from bidding to replace Navy ASW aircraft. *Aviat Week Space Technol* 127:25 N 16 '87

The case for the $435 hammer. J. Fairhall. *Wash Mon* 18:47-8+ Ja '87

A case of rank vs. privilege [Senator A. Specter's attempt to get Navy to reimburse Dravo Corp. for plant construction cost overruns] T. Gup. il *Time* 130:29 S 14 '87

Congressional, Navy leaders back Grumman A-6F at roll-out. il *Aviat Week Space Technol* 127:31 Ag 10 '87

A defense case may break [witnesses get immunity in General Dynamics ship probe] S. Payne. *Bus Week* p40+ Mr 23 '87

Four contenders vie for Navy maritime patrol aircraft contract [P-3 successor] P. Proctor. il *Aviat Week Space Technol* 127:24-5 Jl 27 '87

GAO warns Congress of flaws that may cause missiles to fail. *Aviat Week Space Technol* 127:34-5 S 28 '87

The General Dynamics case sets a bad precedent [Justice Dept. decides not to seek indictment] P. Dwyer and S. Payne. il *Bus Week* p41 Je 8 '87

Grumman gets a slap in the face from the Navy [F-14 contract] D. Griffiths. *Bus Week* p45 Ap 13 '87

House, Senate panels support Navy plan to replace carriers. B. M. Greeley, Jr. il *Aviat Week Space Technol* 126:127+ My 11 '87

The little airplane that could [Navy Pioneer mini-RPV based on Israel's Mastiff] P. Hellman. il *Discover* 8:78-87 F '87

Manufacturer investigating modified Gulfstream 4s as Navy P-3 follow-on. P. Proctor. il *Aviat Week Space Technol* 126:94-5 Ap 13 '87

Navy, Air Force plan HARM upgrade to extend missile life through 1990s. il *Aviat Week Space Technol* 126:101+ F 9 '87

Navy evaluates Israeli R&D programs for use on U.S. weapon systems. M. Mecham. *Aviat Week Space Technol* 126:20-1 Je 1 '87

Navy expanding competition for follow-on patrol aircraft [P-3C successor] D. M. North. il *Aviat Week Space Technol* 126:21-2 Mr 23 '87

Navy may buy larger airship as surveillance platform. *Aviat Week Space Technol* 126:28 Je 29 '87

Navy opts to cut F-14D buy, will compete F-14A update. D. M. North. *Aviat Week Space Technol* 126:18-20 Mr 30 '87

Navy restricts Sikorsky helicopter flights [defect in the transmission gear] *Aviat Week Space Technol* 126:27 F 23 '87

Navy seeks 125 maritime patrol aircraft. *Aviat Week Space Technol* 126:19 F 23 '87

Navy solicits proposals for P-3C ASW successor [antisubmarine warfare aircraft] B. D. Nordwall. *Aviat Week Space Technol* 127:30-2 S 28 '87

Navy to exploit V-22's VTOL, range in hunting Arctic subs. B. M. Greeley, Jr. *Aviat Week Space Technol* 126:30-1 Je 8 '87

Navy will request information on ATF concepts this spring [advanced tactical fighter] *Aviat Week Space Technol* 126:20 Ap 6 '87

Navy will request proposals for advanced interdiction weapon. J. D. Morrocco. *Aviat Week Space Technol* 126:71-2 My 4 '87

Probe scuttled [Justice Dept. drops inquiry of General Dynamics] *Time* 129:51 Je 1 '87

Raytheon wins contract to design new version of Standard Missile. D. Hughes. il *Aviat Week Space Technol* 127:24-5 Ag 17 '87

Sikorsky/Navy program to prolong service life of SH-3 helicopter. il *Aviat Week Space Technol* 126:100-1 My 18 '87

SimuFlite wins bid to train Navy aircrews. *Aviat Week Space Technol* 127:29 N 2 '87

Streamlining the U.S. acquisition system. E. A. Pyatt. por *Aviat Week Space Technol* 127:123 O 19 '87

T-45A trainer will be built, tested at Palmdale. *Aviat Week Space Technol* 127:136 O 12 '87

Westinghouse-Airship joint venture wins Navy aerial surveillance contract. *Aviat Week Space Technol* 126:69 Je 15 '87

Women

See Servicewomen

United States. Navy. Reserve Officers' Training Corps
Savannah State faces loss of NROTC program. *Jet* 73:36 N 2 '87

United States. Nuclear Regulatory Commission *See* U.S. Nuclear Regulatory Commission

United States. Occupational Safety and Health Administration
Blood, sweat and fears. G. Bock. il *Time* 130:50-1 S 28 '87

OSHA awakens from its six-year slumber. H. Bradford. il *Bus Week* p27 Ag 10 '87

United States. Office of Economic Opportunity. Project Head Start *See* Project Head Start (U.S.)

United States. Office of Human Development Services

Appropriations and expenditures

Report blasts Human Development Office [report by the House Committee on Government Operations] C. Holden. *Science* 236:386-7 Ap 24 '87

United States. Office of Management and Budget
Census a public burden? C. Holden. *Science* 237:839 Ag 21 '87

The OMB is digging in its heels on the budget. H. Gleckman. por *Bus Week* p41 F 9 '87

OMB stalks the "burgeoning growth of biomedicine". E. Marshall. *Science* 237:847-8 Ag 21 '87

Sparks are already flying over the 1990 census. S. B. Garland. *Bus Week* p47 S 14 '87

United States. Office of Munitions Control
State Dept. faulted for poor control of munitions exports. *Aviat Week Space Technol* 127:30 S 21 '87

United States. Office of Personnel Management. Combined Federal Campaign *See* Combined Federal Campaign (U.S.)

United States. Office of Policy Development
The mouse that roars [G. L. Bauer] J. B. Judis. *New Repub* 197:23-5 Ag 3 '87

United States. Office of Royalty Management
You think the NSC is screwed up? Take a look at Washington's worst run program. J. Eisendrath. il *Wash Mon* 19:13-16 Ap '87

United States. Office of Surface Mining, Reclamation, and Enforcement
Can strip mining clean up its act? [failure to enforce Surface Mining Control and Reclamation Act] W. Marx. il *Read Dig* 130:121-5 Mr '87

United States. Office of the U.S. Trade Representative
Clayton Yeutter speaks softly and carries a big agenda. S. J. Dryden. il por *Bus Week* p30-1 F 2 '87

United States. Office of Vocational and Adult Education
From welfare roll to White House payroll [assistant secretary B. Guiton] R. L. Haywood. il pors *Jet* 72:6-8 Ag 31 '87

United States. Park Police
The last working horses [use by U.S. Park Police and park rangers] C. Carnie. il *Natl Parks* 61:30-5 Mr/Ap '87

United States. Patent and Trademark Office
Back at the Patent Office . . . G. Bronson. *Forbes* 139:145 My 4 '87

United States. Peace Corps *See* Peace Corps (U.S.)

United States. Pension Benefit Guaranty Corporation *See* Pension Benefit Guaranty Corporation

United States. Postal Service *See* United States Postal Service

United States. Presidential Commission on AIDS

An admiral in command [J. D. Watkins named chairman] *Newsweek* 110:10 O 19 '87

AIDS panel gets Reagan's approval. D. M. Barnes. *Science* 236:771-2 My 15 '87

AIDS panel politics. il *Time* 130:58 Ag 3 '87

Fresh troops for president's AIDS panel. W. Booth. pors *Science* 238:1034 N 20 '87

Presidential AIDS panel named. D. M. Barnes. *Science* 237:481 Jl 31 '87

President's AIDS panel in disarray. W. Booth. il *Science* 238:262-3 O 16 '87

Reagan names black MD to AIDS Commission [W. A. Myers] il por *Jet* 72:6 Ag 10 '87

Ronald Reagan's AIDS panel: more gray than gay. G. Witkin. il *U S News World Rep* 103:8 Ag 3 '87

Step in the right direction [first report] C. Gorman. il *Time* 130:75 D 14 '87

Trouble on the AIDS panel. D. Gates. il *Newsweek* 110:10 O 5 '87

United States. President's Commission on Americans Outdoors

Americans and the great outdoors. C. Elfring. il *BioScience* 37:778-80 D '87

Americans outdoors. P. C. Pritchard. il *Natl Parks* 61:12-13 My/Je '87

Greenways: keeping the outdoors great. il *Futurist* 21:51 Jl/Ag '87

A network of green corridors, threading its way through city and countryside, is proposed by a presidential commission. J. P. Wiley, Jr. il *Smithsonian* 18:26+ Jl '87

Outdoor recreation for the year 2000 . . . and beyond. il *Sunset* 178:272 Ap '87

Recreation report held up by lawsuit. il *Natl Parks* 61:48-9 Mr/Ap '87

Tract to the future. L. Williamson. il *Outdoor Life* 179:16-17 My '87

Will an orphan recreation report spark a prairie fire? C. Wille. il *Audubon* 89:102-5 Jl '87

United States. President's Commission on Defense Management

Packard Commission faults changes in weapons acquisition policy. *Aviat Week Space Technol* 127:29 Jl 20 '87

Packard Commission set to reconvene. B. D. Nordwall. *Aviat Week Space Technol* 126:80+ Mr 30 '87

Sack Weinberger, bankrupt General Dynamics, and other procurement reforms. G. Easterbrook. il *Wash Mon* 18:33-8+ Ja '87

United States. President's Foreign Intelligence Advisory Board

President meets with Foreign Intelligence Advisory Board [White House statement, July 14, 1987] *Dep State Bull* 87:31 S '87

United States. Public Health Service

PHS revitalization plan stirs up NIH [views of C. E. Koop] G. Kolata. il por *Science* 236:1055-6 My 29 '87

United States. Public Health Service. Centers for Disease Control *See* Centers for Disease Control (U.S.)

United States. Rapid Deployment Force

Study finds Rapid Deployment Force could thwart Soviet attack on Iran [study by Joshua M. Epstein of the Brookings Institution] P. Mann. il map *Aviat Week Space Technol* 126:85+ Ja 12 '87

United States. Readiness Command

General Nutting and the invaders. W. M. Arkin. *Bull At Sci* 43:6-7 Ja/F '87

United States. Securities and Exchange Commission

Blind 'em and rob 'em [investigation of Blinder, Robinson & Co.] M. Schifrin. il por *Forbes* 140:8 N 2 '87

Crime wave [securities crime; cover story] R. L. Stern and M. Schifrin. il *Forbes* 139:67-70 Je 29 '87

Drexel in the cross hairs. B. Powell and C. Friday. il *Newsweek* 109:48 F 16 '87

Drexel sweats the SEC probe. S. P. Sherman. il *Fortune* 115:38-42 Mr 16 '87

Haste makes waste [Edgar computer system] G. Slutsker and J. Novack. il *Forbes* 140:94+ Ag 24 '87

How Ruder will steer the SEC. V. Cahan. *Bus Week* p29 Je 29 '87

Icahn's juggle: TWA, USX, SEC. C. J. Loomis. il por *Fortune* 115:81-2 My 11 '87

Mr. Malec versus the bureaucrats [SEC's involvement in Central & South West Corp's factoring operations] E. A. Finn, Jr. il por *Forbes* 140:44 D 28 '87

Now Drexel Burnham is fighting on two fronts. C. Welles. il por *Bus Week* p90-3+ F 16 '87

Protecting your securities investment. *Consum Res Mag* 70:33-5 O '87

The SEC isn't clearing up anything [insider trading] G. Weiss. il *Bus Week* p22 Ag 24 '87

The SEC rattles its saber: trying to give small stockholders a break. C. Yang. *Bus Week* p96 S 28 '87

The SEC report: program trading gets off easy. J. N. Frank and S. Zucker. il *Bus Week* p38 Ap 6 '87

The SEC's busy crimebuster [G. Lynch] F. Rice. il por *Fortune* 115:51 Ja 5 '87

The SEC's Kathryn McGrath keeps mutual funds in line. L. N. Vreeland. il por *Money* 16:160 Jl '87

The SEC's new boss [D. S. Ruder] *Newsweek* 109:47 Je 29 '87

Stale dope [insider trades reported late] J. Novack. *Forbes* 140:180 N 2 '87

A top law firm feels the heat [Sullivan & Cromwell's G. C. Kern charged by SEC with violating disclosure rules during Campeau's bid on Allied Stores] C. Friday. *Newsweek* 110:40-1 Jl 13 '87

Two guardians of the nation's economy. il *Sch Update* 120:13 D 18 '87

A way to stop a stock-market 'meltdown'? [chairman D. Ruder's proposals for curbing program trading] por *Newsweek* 110:60 O 19 '87

Were Drexel and Boesky in cahoots? J. Egan and D. Baer. il por *U S News World Rep* 102:45 F 16 '87

When companies talk turkey, investors should be told [charges against G. C. Kern and Allied Stores over inadequate disclosure in Campeau hostile takeover] V. Cahan. il *Bus Week* p100 Jl 13 '87

WHOOPS haunts the Street. C. Farrell. *Bus Week* p122 Mr 16 '87

Wrangling over the booty from insider trading. C. Yang. il *Bus Week* p158+ O 12 '87

United States. Small Business Administration

Neal stays as lone black SBA policymaker in D.C. [E. C. Neal] *Jet* 72:12 Ag 24 '87

'A political snake pit' comes under the spotlight [Wedtech scandal] P. Cary. il *U S News World Rep* 102:22-4 Je 15 '87

United States. Soil Conservation Service

Agriculture Dept. terminals demonstrate reliability of meteor-burst communications. map *Aviat Week Space Technol* 126:81 Ja 26 '87

Oak Ridge Boys help out USDA [Take Pride in America campaign] P. Smith. il *Success Farm* 85:24 N '87

United States. Superintendent of Documents

See also

United States. Government Printing Office

United States. Supreme Court

286 editors sign letter against Bork nomination. *Publ Wkly* 232:13 O 16 '87

1787 and all that [nomination of R. Bork] *Nation* 245:37 Jl 18-25 '87

Abortion law complications [parental notification argument] *Christ Today* 31:47+ D 11 '87

Advise and dissent [nomination of R. Bork; cover story; special section] il pors *Time* 130:12-18+ S 21 '87

All eyes on the undecideds [Senate Judiciary Committee hearings on nominee R. Bork] T. Jacoby. il por *Newsweek* 110:30 O 5 '87

Area Man [rivalry between national and local newspapers as demonstrated by R. Bork nomination coverage] M. McGough. *New Repub* 197:17 S 14-21 '87

Author and publisher groups make filings in two Supreme Court cases [libel suit brought against Hustler magazine by J. Falwell and challenge to a Virginia law on how certain books may be displayed] H. Fields. *Publ Wkly* 232:12 S 4 '87

The ball's in Reagan's court [resignation of L. F. Powell] T. Gest. il por *U S News World Rep* 103:20-1 Jl 6 '87

The battle against Bork will be long, bitter—and likely to fail. P. Dwyer and D. Harbrecht. por *Bus Week* p45 Jl 13 '87

The battle begins [nomination of R. Bork] R. Lacayo. il por *Time* 130:10-12 Jl 13 '87

The battle of Bork. M. Laurino. il por *Ms* 16:111-12 S '87

The battle of Judge Bork. M. McDonald. il por *Macleans* 100:30-1 O 19 '87

Battle of the Bork. *Commonweal* 114:547-8 O 9 '87

The battle over Bork. L. Martz. il por *Newsweek* 110:12-14 Ag 24 '87

Believing in Judge Bork [nominee's hearings] T. Gest. il *U S News World Rep* 103:29 S 28 '87

Betrayal. H. S. Scott. *New Repub* 197:12-13 D 14 '87

Bidenquiddick [J. Biden's about-face on the R. H. Bork nomination] *Natl Rev* 39:15+ Ag 28 '87

Biden's main chance [R. H. Bork hearings] T. Morganthau. il por *Newsweek* 110:35-6 S 21 '87

United States. Supreme Court—*cont.*

The bitter legacy of the battle over Bork. P. Dwyer. por *Bus Week* p67 O 19 '87

Black thought, black talk [E. M. Kennedy's attack on R. H. Bork] W. F. Buckley. *Natl Rev* 39:54-5 Ag 14 '87

Blacks get group of state legislators to dump Bork. *Jet* 72:29 S 21 '87

Bork and Bird [pro-Bork campaign contrasted with pro-Bird campaign in California] H. Meyerson. *New Repub* 197:21+ S 14-21 '87

The Bork appointment. *Natl Rev* 39:14-15 Jl 31 '87

Bork bashers beware. M. S. Forbes, Jr. il *Forbes* 140:25 Ag 10 '87

The Bork battle. *Natl Rev* 39:17-18 S 11 '87

The Bork battle [cover story; special section] il pors *Newsweek* 110:22-6+ S 14 '87

The Bork disaster. *Natl Rev* 39:16 N 6 '87

The Bork fight. *Natl Rev* 39:17-18 O 9 '87

Bork in the balance. A. Press. il por *Newsweek* 110:38+ O 12 '87

The Bork nomination. *America* 157:99-100 Ag 29-S 5 '87

The Bork nomination. R. M. Dworkin. bibl f il *N Y Rev Books* 34:3+ Ag 13 '87

'The Bork nomination': an exchange [discussion of August 13, 1987 article] R. M. Dworkin. il *N Y Rev Books* 34:59-61 O 8 '87

The Bork nomination and the political game. J. M. Wall. *Christ Century* 104:707-8 Ag 26-S 2 '87

Bork nomination threatens basic liberties. E. Doerr. il *Humanist* 47:41 S/O '87

Bork of the month. J. Klein. il *N Y* 20:28+ S 21 '87

The Bork screw. A. Sullivan. *New Repub* 197:14+ O 19 '87

Bork talk. F. Barnes. *New Repub* 197:9-11 S 7 '87

Bork v. Senate. *Natl Rev* 39:16-18 O 23 '87

Bork v. the First. J. Kalven. *Nation* 245:269-70 S 19 '87

A Bork without the bite [nominee's hearings] J. V. Lamar, Jr. il por *Time* 130:18-19 S 28 '87

Bork's bite. *New Repub* 197:7-9 Jl 27 '87

Bork's last stand. A. Press. il por *Newsweek* 110:26-7 O 19 '87

Bork's progress. M. Lerner. *New Repub* 197:18+ S 14-21 '87

Bound by the Constitution [R. H. Bork] D. A. Degnan. *Commonweal* 114:481-3 S 11 '87

A brief against Bork. il *Progressive* 51:7-8 S '87

The brief on Judge Bork [cover story] M. Kramer. il pors *U S News World Rep* 103:18-24 S 14 '87

Business can't bank on Judge Kennedy's vote. P. Dwyer. il por *Bus Week* p33 N 30 '87

Can a state require public schools to allow a moment of silence? [New Jersey statute] H. Hagerman; R. L. Maddox. il *Christ Today* 31:52 N 20 '87

Can Christians hand out gospel tracts in airports? [Supreme Court case involving Jews for Jesus at Los Angeles International Airport] B. Spring. il *Christ Today* 31:43-4 Ap 3 '87

Can states restrict a minor's access to abortion? [upcoming decision] *Christ Today* 31:44+ Ap 3 '87

The case against Bork. *New Repub* 197:7-10 O 5 '87

A civics lesson at Hazelwood East [principal of Missouri high school censors student newspaper] S. Visser. il *Nation* 245:441-2 O 24 '87

Civil rights supporters plea for defeat of Bork. il *Jet* 73:8 O 12 '87

The Constitution, the courts, and judicial competence. M. Cuomo. por *USA Today (Periodical)* 116:34-6 Jl '87

Constitutional wrongs [upcoming Supreme Court case challenging Congress' attempt to overrule and impose estate taxes retroactively] L. Saunders. il *Forbes* 140:154 S 21 '87

Coup at the Court [R. Bork's writings and W. Rehnquist's book The Supreme Court: how it was, how it is] R. Adler. il *New Repub* 197:37+ S 14-21 '87

The Court's pivot man [resignation of L. Powell] G. J. Church. il por *Time* 130:10-11 Jl 6 '87

The creation-science case: is it science or religion? [Louisiana case] E. J. Larson. *Christ Today* 31:50-1 Ja 16 '87

Creationism case argued before Supreme Court [Louisiana case] R. Lewin. *Science* 235:22-3 Ja 2 '87

Damage control [to decide on damages awarded in suit against Bankers Life] D. Fanning. il *Forbes* 139:84 Je 29 '87

Deadlock at the Court [business cases] P. Dwyer. il *Bus Week* p36-7 O 12 '87

Death row clerk [death penalty work] C. Sloan. *New Repub* 196:18+ F 16 '87

Defining the real Robert Bork. J. V. Lamar, Jr. il por *Time* 130:16 Ag 24 '87

Democratic majority [Senate Judiciary Committee vote against nomination of R. Bork] *Nation* 245:397 O 17 '87

The Democrats' glass chin [opposition to R. Bork nomination] G. F. Will. il *Newsweek* 110:66 Jl 20 '87

The effort to intimidate Reagan [L. Tribe on R. H. Bork nomination] W. F. Buckley. *Natl Rev* 39:57 Jl 31 '87

'Emotional distress' briefs to High Court [Hustler vs. J. Falwell] il *Publ Wkly* 232:13 Jl 17 '87

Exit the smoking judge [D. Ginsburg] I. Austen. il por *Macleans* 100:32 N 16 '87

Far more judicious [nominee A. M. Kennedy] G. J. Church. il por *Time* 130:16-18 N 23 '87

A fight for one man, one vote [Senate Judiciary Committee hearings on nominee R. Bork] J. V. Lamar, Jr. il *Time* 130:25 O 5 '87

For all the marbles [confirmation process for nominee R. Bork] G. Borger. il por *U S News World Rep* 103:20-3 S 21 '87

For want of a nail [losing the Bork fight] M. Gallagher. il *Natl Rev* 39:32+ N 20 '87

The frantic reflagging of Bork [cover story] H. Schwartz. il *Nation* 245:253+ S 19 '87

From Bork to Kennedy. R. M. Dworkin. bibl f il *N Y Rev Books* 34:36+ D 17 '87

From Hazelwood to the High Court [principal of Missouri high school deletes articles from school newspaper] M. A. Uhlig. il *N Y Times Mag* p100-7 S 13 '87

The Ginsburg test: bad logic. C. Krauthammer. il *Time* 130:102 N 23 '87

Going . . . going . . . [R. Reagan fails to win support for nominee R. Bork] G. Borger. il pors *U S News World Rep* 103:20-2 O 12 '87

Gone with the wind [R. Reagan's failure to win support for nominee R. Bork] J. V. Lamar, Jr. il por *Time* 130:18-20 O 12 '87

The great debate inside Robert Bork [business rulings and writings] P. Dwyer. il por *Bus Week* p34-5 S 14 '87

The grilling of Judge Bork. A. Press. il por *Newsweek* 110:27+ S 28 '87

Here comes the judge. M. Gallagher. *Natl Rev* 39:33+ D 18 '87

Hey, look Kennedy over [A. Kennedy nomination] *Nation* 245:773 D 26 '87-Ja 2 '88

High Court asked to rule on RICO bookstore case [adult bookstore in Indiana] *Publ Wkly* 232:10 N 13 '87

High Court queries leave outcome of 'Hustler'-Falwell case uncertain. H. Fields. *Publ Wkly* 232:15 D 18 '87

High Court to review Va. minors access law. M. Yen. *Publ Wkly* 231:30 Mr 6 '87

The High Court's unofficial arbiters [lawyers L. Tribe and W. B. Reynolds consulted on nominee matters] D. Baer. il pors *U S News World Rep* 103:23-4 N 23 '87

The high hurdles between Ginsburg and the High Court. P. Dwyer. il *Bus Week* p77 N 16 '87

The higher law: Bork, Burke, & moral relativism. D. R. Carlin, Jr. *Commonweal* 114:729-30 D 18 '87

'The hottest fight in a decade' [J. Biden vs. R. Bork's nomination] N. Cooper. il pors *Newsweek* 110:30 Jl 20 '87

If at first you don't succeed . . . [nomination of D. Ginsburg] J. V. Lamar, Jr. il por *Time* 130:52 N 9 '87

Into the trenches over Bork. T. Gest. il por *U S News World Rep* 103:39 Ag 17 '87

Is alcoholism a disease? [case of Eugene Traynor and James P. McKelvey vs. the Veterans Administration] C. Holden. *Science* 238:1647 D 18 '87

Is eight enough? [cases scheduled for shorthanded Court] R. Lacayo. il *Time* 130:20 O 12 '87

Jerry Falwell vs. Larry Flynt [emotional distress suit] A. Press. il pors *Newsweek* 110:76 D 14 '87

The Judge Bork blues. il *Commonweal* 114:579-80 O 23 '87

Judging Ginsburg. *Nation* 245:543-4 N 14 '87

Judging Robert Bork. M. McDonald. il por *Macleans* 100:26 S 28 '87

Judging the judges: High Court confirmations: a history. T. Gest. il *U S News World Rep* 103:22-3 S 14 '87

A judicial shift to the right [R. H. Bork nomination] por *Macleans* 100:18 Jl 13 '87

United States. Supreme Court—*cont.*

Justice revealed. D. E. Haupt. il *Life* 10:105-12 Fall '87

The justice-to-be whom nobody really knows [nominee A. M. Kennedy] T. Gest. il por *U S News World Rep* 103:48 D 14 '87

Kennedy for the Court. A. Press. il por *Newsweek* 110:21 N 23 '87

The last hurrahs [Reagan administration moves on contra aid, arms control and R. Bork nomination] *Nation* 245:291-2 S 26 '87

Legal attack by bishops [National Conference of Catholic Bishops has asked the Supreme Court to overturn an order demanding that the bishops relinquish church files to critics of their stand on abortion] *Christ Century* 104:881-2 O 14 '87

Letter from Washington [role of H. Baker in R. H. Bork confirmation debacle] Cato. *Natl Rev* 39:14 N 6 '87

Letter from Washington [Senate hearings on R. H. Bork's nomination] E. Drew. *New Yorker* 63:150-4+ N 2 '87

The line on Bork. D. Seligman. *Fortune* 116:96 Ag 17 '87

A look at the issues in Blatty's appeal to the Supreme Court [best seller list dispute with N.Y. times] C. E. Rinzler. *Publ Wkly* 232:16-17 Ag 28 '87

Marshall will outlive 'those bastards' who want his resignation. por *Jet* 73:18 N 2 '87

Marshall's ex-clerk tabbed for U.S. Supreme Court seat [D. Ginsburg] *Jet* 73:5 N 16 '87

NAACP, NEA opposing Reagan's pick for Court [R. Bork nomination] il *Jet* 72:8 Jl 20 '87

NBA pres. urges High Court to uphold affirm. action [views of T. J. Broome] por *Jet* 71:26 Ja 12 '87

The new case of Douglas Ginsburg: a 'baby Bork'? [nomination to Supreme Court] T. Gest. il por *U S News World Rep* 103:15 N 9 '87

A new majority moves to the right [nomination of R. H. Bork] T. Gest. il por *U S News World Rep* 103:28-9 Jl 13 '87

Nice try; If you have tears . . . W. F. Buckley. *Natl Rev* 39:70-1 O 23 '87

Notes and comment [nomination of R. H. Bork] *New Yorker* 63:17-20 Ag 3 '87

Obscenity test challenged in U.S. Supreme Court [intent of Miller test questioned in Pope v. Illinois] H. Fields. *Publ Wkly* 231:10 Mr 13 '87

The old frontier [E. Kennedy's opposition to R. H. Bork] J. Klein. il por *N Y* 20:26+ O 19 '87

On the Bork front. D. Schorr. *New Leader* 70:5-6 O 19 '87

On trial: character [R. Bork's confirmation hearings] G. Borger. il pors *U S News World Rep* 103:26-7 S 28 '87

Open and shut [nomination of R. Bork] *New Repub* 197:4 Ag 24 '87

The other Kennedy [A. M. Kennedy] *Natl Rev* 39:13-14 D 31 '87

A piece of the action [Agent Orange litigation and lawyer compensation] D. Fanning. il *Forbes* 140:68 O 19 '87

Pot & politics [D. H. Ginsburg's nomination; cover story] A. Press. il pors *Newsweek* 110:46-52 N 16 '87

A record that speaks for itself [R. H. Bork] F. J. Flaherty. il *Commonweal* 114:477-80 S 11 '87

Religion cases declined. *Christ Century* 104:961 N 4 '87

The road to Bork's last stand. J. V. Lamar, Jr. il por *Time* 130:15-16 O 19 '87

Ronald Reagan and the Supremes. V. S. Navasky. il *Esquire* 107:77-80+ Ap '87

Round II [R. Reagan's selection of D. Ginsburg as nominee] F. Barnes. *New Repub* 197:9-11 N 23 '87

Rules of the game [nomination of D. Ginsburg] *New Repub* 197:4+ N 23 '87

Second thoughts on Bork. *Natl Rev* 39:18-19 S 25 '87

Shifting odds in the fight over Bork [nominee's Senate Judiciary Committee hearings] T. Gest. il por *U S News World Rep* 103:25 O 5 '87

Should a Mormon-owned corporation be able to fire a Mormon who does not tithe? [discrimination case of F. Mayson] R. F. Drinan. il *America* 156:375-6 My 9 '87

Simmons, Jones mastermind move to dump Robert Bork. pors *Jet* 73:12 O 26 '87

Sins of the past [drug use by D. Ginsburg derails nomination] M. Hornblower. por *Time* 130:18-20 N 16 '87

The skirmishing begins again [Reagan nominees] A. Press. por *Newsweek* 110:32 O 26 '87

Spoiling for a second round [nomination of D. H. Ginsburg; special section] il pors *Newsweek* 110:42-3+ N 9 '87

The struggle for the uncommitted [fight over R. Bork's confirmation] T. Gest. il *U S News World Rep* 103:24 Ag 24 '87

Sue your stockbroker? You can't, you know. S. Weiss. il *Bus Week* p75-6 Mr 2 '87

Supreme Court considers a second moment-of-silence law [New Jersey statute] *Christ Today* 31:56 N 6 '87

Supreme Court hears arguments on teaching 'creation science' [Louisiana case] I. Goodwin. il *Phys Today* 40:64-6 F '87

Supreme Court hears challenge to church hiring policies [discrimination case filed by F. Mayson against the Mormon church] E. J. Larson. *Christ Today* 31:49-50 My 15 '87

Supreme Court justices quiz both sides in Virginia minors access law. H. Fields. *Publ Wkly* 232:16 N 20 '87

Supreme Court weighs liability in military contractor suit [Boyle vs. Sikorsky over helicopter crash] M. Mecham. il *Aviat Week Space Technol* 127:81-2 O 26 '87

Supreme Court will rule on moment-of-silence law [New Jersey statute] B. Spring. il *Christ Today* 31:56+ Mr 20 '87

The Supreme Court with a smile [first 100 days of the Rehnquist Court] T. Gest. il por *U S News World Rep* 102:23 Ja 12 '87

A 'tempest in a teapot' (pace Cicero) [R. Bork's confirmation hearings] M. Kramer. il *U S News World Rep* 103:20 S 28 '87

Texaco vs. Pennzoil: next stop, Washington [Texas Supreme Court refuses to review judgment won by Pennzoil] T. Vogel. il *Bus Week* p68 N 16 '87

A time for panic [nomination of A. M. Kennedy] *Natl Rev* 39:17-18 D 4 '87

To the bitter end [R. Bork's decision to keep fighting; with interview with E. Meese] G. Borger. il por *U S News World Rep* 103:18-20 O 19 '87

Trying to leave a conservative legacy [nomination of R. Bork] A. Press. il por *Newsweek* 110:22-3 Jl 13 '87

Up in smoke: the undoing of a High Court nominee [D. Ginsburg] B. Duffy and D. Baer. il por *U S News World Rep* 103:24-6 N 16 '87

Waiting in the wings [potential nominees if R. Bork is rejected] il *U S News World Rep* 103:22 O 12 '87

Watching a changing Court: will the center hold? [education cases] D. G. Savage. *Phi Delta Kappan* 69:135-7 O '87

Who's afraid of Robert Bork? [cover story] R. Vigilante. il *Natl Rev* 39:25-30 Ag 28 '87

Why roast Bork? C. W. Colson. il *Christ Today* 31:80 O 2 '87

Will a new justice tip the Court's delicate balance? [nomination of R. H. Bork] L. Kravitz. por *Sch Update* 120:13 S 4 '87

Will counterrevolution continue? [criminal procedure and the Rehnquist Court; views of Charles Whitebread] il *USA Today (Periodical)* 116:11 Ag '87

Will the Court turn right? [L. Powell's departure] A. Press. il por *Newsweek* 110:16-18 Jl 6 '87

Winning one from the Gipper [People for the American Way campaign against R. H. Bork] A. R. Dowd. il pors *Fortune* 116:125+ N 9 '87

With Bork out, Reagan starts over. A. Press. il por *Newsweek* 110:56 N 2 '87

Anecdotes, facetiae, satire, etc.

Cool with Coolidge [R. H. Bork] M. Meltsner. *Nation* 245:365 O 10 '87

Just say no comment [D. Ginsburg nomination] A. Z. Posner. *New Repub* 197:10 N 30 '87

Uncivil liberties. C. Trillin. il *Nation* 245:510 N 7 '87

Decisions

See also

Dred Scott case

Affirmative action: after the debate, opportunity [Santa Clara case] P. Dwyer. il *Bus Week* p37 Ap 13 '87

AIDS & the law [discussion of October 1986 article, Sodomy and the Supreme Court] D. Robinson. *Commentary* 83:2+ F '87

AIDS: a job-rights victory. G. Witkin. il *U S News World Rep* 102:10-11 Mr 16 '87

The appointment of death [rejects view that death penalty is racially biased] M. Kempton. il *N Y Rev Books* 34:40 My 28 '87

United States. Supreme Court—Decisions—*cont.*

Baker, banker, clergyman, thief. il *Life* 10:84-5+ Fall '87

Balancing act [expands affirmative action in Santa Clara County, Calif. case] R. Stengel. il *Time* 129:18-20 Ap 6 '87

Battling your broker gets harder [arbitration upheld] D. P. Wiener. il *U S News World Rep* 102:51 Je 22 '87

The bench and the chair [ruling that death penalty doesn't discriminate against blacks] *Natl Rev* 39:15 My 22 '87

The Betamax case (II). J. Lardner. *New Yorker* 63:60-81 Ap 13 '87

The bicentennial and church-related schools. T. A. Rayer. *America* 157:427-9+ D 5 '87

Black TB victim in Fla. wins fight for her job [G. Arline case] *Jet* 72:39 Mr 30 '87

Black woman's 'murder wish' for Reagan is free speech, Supreme Court says [case of A. M. Jackson] il por *Jet* 72:30 Jl 13 '87

Brennanism [decision in Santa Clara, Calif. affirmative action case] D. Seligman. *Fortune* 115:283+ Ap 27 '87

The Burger Court: bad, but not that bad. D. Farber. *Wash Mon* 19:52-4 My '87

Business and pregnancy: good will is no longer good enough. A. Bernstein. il *Bus Week* p37 F 2 '87

Call five cases that shaped Congress. D. Pawelek. il *Sch Update* 119:12-14 Ja 12 '87

Can the Court be swayed? [amicus briefs; study by Karen O'Connor] *USA Today (Periodical)* 116:11-12 Ag '87

Can't sue your broker? It's no big loss [upholds arbitration] D. Zigas. il *Bus Week* p128 Je 22 '87

The case of common sense vs. Miranda. E. H. Methvin. il *Read Dig* 131:96-100 Aug '87

Clearing a path to the chair [rejects argument that the death penalty discriminates against blacks] R. Lacayo. il *Time* 129:80 My 4 '87

The Constitution and the Court: could Meese be right? S. Levinson. *Current* 292:32-5 My '87

Court rules for women [maternity leaves] J. C. Baker. *Black Enterp* 17:20 Ap '87

Court ruling affirmative [Santa Clara affirmative action case] J. C. Baker. *Black Enterp* 17:20 Jl '87

Court upholds racial quota [blacks in the Alabama state trooper force] D. Camper. il *Black Enterp* 17:15 My '87

David Boies: the ace litigator playing Texaco's hand. L. J. Tell. il por *Bus Week* p79 Ap 20 '87

Debunking the 'reasonable man' rule [ruling on obscenity] C. Rembar. por *Publ Wkly* 231:16 Je 26 '87

Decide seven Court cases that test teenagers' rights. M. Christopher. il *Sch Update* 120:16-18+ S 4 '87

Did the good guys go too far? [crackdown on political corruption hamstrung by ruling on mail fraud] P. Dwyer. il *Bus Week* p29 Ag 31 '87

Earth diary: Justice Rehnquist and the land. T. Turner. il *Mother Earth News* 103:112+ Ja/F '87

El Norte's sheltering arms [asylum cases] il *U S News World Rep* 102:13 Mr 23 '87

Ending sexual harassment [M. Vinson case] C. E. Simmons. *Vogue* 177:70 S '87

The family way [rulings on maternity leaves by Supreme Court] *Commonweal* 114:67-9 F 13 '87

The final say. L. H. Tribe. il *N Y Times Mag* p68-70+ S 13 '87

First jail, then a trial [upholds preventive detention] il *Newsweek* 109:19 Je 8 '87

First the sentence, then the trial [ruling on preventive detention] R. Lacayo. il *Time* 129:69 Je 8 '87

Garland's bouquet [ruling supports pregnancy leave] A. Wilentz. il por *Time* 129:14-15 Ja 26 '87

Gender-based hiring and promotions approved [decision in Santa Clara County, Calif. affirmative action case] *Mon Labor Rev* 110:41-2 My '87

Gimme shelter [Supreme Court requires INS to use more lenient standards in asylum cases] R. Lacayo. il *Time* 129:70 Mr 23 '87

Government by lawyers & judges. W. Berns. *Commentary* 83:17-24 Je '87

Gridlock on death row [rejects view that death penalty is racist] A. Press. il *Newsweek* 109:60-1 My 4 '87

Handicap rights [Supreme Court extends rights to those with contagious diseases] R. Lacayo. il *Time* 129:66 Mr 16 '87

Handicapped thinkers. D. Seligman. *Fortune* 115:110 Ap 13 '87

The heirs of Oliver Brown: in Topeka, a landmark equality case is still before the courts [Brown v. Board of Education] J. E. White. il por *Time* 130:88-9 Jl 6 '87

High Court backs jailing without bail; Justice Thurgood Marshall dissents. por *Jet* 72:4 Je 15 '87

High Court rejects creationism law [Louisiana case] J. Raloff. *Sci News* 131:404 Je 27 '87

High Court splits on search of public employee's office [O'Connor v. Ortega] T. J. Flygare. *Phi Delta Kappan* 68:792-4 Je '87

High Court: the day God and Darwin collided [teaching of creationism in Louisiana ruled unconstitutional] T. Gest and L. Solórzano. il *U S News World Rep* 102:12 Je 29 '87

Insider trading: the High Court hasn't ended the confusion. C. Yang. il por *Bus Week* p34 N 30 '87

John Marshall and the evolution of judicial review. D. G. Stephenson, Jr. il por *USA Today (Periodical)* 116:37-9 Jl '87

A judge's breach of confidence [former law clerk P. Elman's revelations about F. Frankfurter and Brown v. Board of Education] R. Lacayo. il pors *Time* 129:71 Ap 6 '87

Judicial review [discussion of June 1987 article, Government by lawyers & judges] W. Berns. *Commentary* 84:6+ N '87

Justice Scalia's misunderstanding [dissenting opinion on Louisiana creationism case] S. J. Gould. il *Nat Hist* 96:14+ O '87

Keeping God out of the classroom [ruling on Louisiana creation science law] L. Martz. il *Newsweek* 109:23-4 Je 29 '87

Keeping the word [rules that 3 Canadian films are propaganda] *Time* 129:49 My 11 '87

Ladies' day [ruling in Santa Clara affirmative action case] *New Repub* 196:4+ Ap 20 '87

A look at Robert Bork and rulings affecting the church. K. A. Lawton. il por *Christ Today* 31:42-3 Ag 7 '87

The Meese lie [effort to overturn Miranda decision] S. Gillers. *Nation* 244:205 F 21 '87

Meet Larry Tribe, Pennzoil's hole card [bested Texaco in Supreme Court] L. Helm and P. Dwyer. il por *Bus Week* p78-9 Ap 20 '87

Memories of the monkey trial [rules against creationism law in Louisiana] A. L. Sanders. il *Time* 129:54 Je 29 '87

A new family issue [maternity leave decision] A. Press. il por *Newsweek* 109:22-4 Ja 26 '87

No bail for the baddest. T. Gest. il *U S News World Rep* 102:12 Je 8 '87

No taking without paying [compensation for confiscated land] A. L. Sanders. il *Time* 129:64-5 Je 22 '87

Of loose lips and stock tips [upholds conviction of R. F. Winans for insider trading] J. Castro. il por *Time* 130:63 N 30 '87

An old anti-bias law's widened bite [rulings on 1866 statute] T. Gest. il *U S News World Rep* 102:10-11 Je 1 '87

On unwarranted fears [confers privileged victim status on individuals with contagious diseases] *America* 156:266-7 Ap 4 '87

One case: a step-by-step account of its progress through the Supreme Court [Louisiana creationism case] il *Life* 10:114-15 Fall '87

A one-white, one-black quota for promotions [Alabama state trooper case] T. Gest. il *U S News World Rep* 102:8 Mr 9 '87

Open door to the execution chamber? [ruling that death penalty does not discriminate against blacks] T. Gest. il *U S News World Rep* 102:25 My 4 '87

Pregnancy job protection upheld by Supreme Court. il *Jet* 71:5 F 2 '87

Psychology and the Constitution. A. J. Tomkins. bibl (p58) *Psychol Today* 21:48-50 S '87

A racial quota for Alabama [state trooper hirings] A. Press. il *Newsweek* 109:55 Mr 9 '87

Replying in the affirmative [approves promotion quotas for black state troopers in Alabama] R. Lacayo. il *Time* 129:66 Mr 9 '87

Rotary action [ruling on admission of women] *Time* 129:62 My 18 '87

Rotary: women's turn comes round. *U S News World Rep* 102:14 My 18 '87

Ruckus over Rotary women. J. Seligmann. il *Newsweek* 109:47 My 18 '87

Saving the Constitution [cover story; special section] il *Natl Rev* 39:30-7+ Jl 17 '87

Saying "yes" to affirmative action [ruling in Santa Clara case] M. Takas. *Vogue* 177:58 N '87

United States. Supreme Court—Decisions—*cont.*

Schools can not require religious and scientific evolution teachings: Court. *Jet* 72:17 Jl 6 '87

Science, 7; creationism, 2 [ruling on Louisiana statute] *Sci Am* 257:14 Ag '87

A shared fate [ruling that death penalty is not racially biased] M. O. Finkelstein. *Nation* 244:599 My 9 '87

The Supreme Court [barriers to hostile takeover bids upheld] M. S. Forbes, Jr. il *Forbes* 139:33 My 18 '87

Supreme Court abolishes Louisiana creationism law. H. Fields. *Publ Wkly* 232:13 Jl 3 '87

Supreme Court approves quotas for promotions [Alabama state troopers case] *Jet* 71:8 Mr 16 '87

Supreme Court bars creationism in schools [Louisiana law] I. Goodwin. *Phys Today* 40:56-7 S '87

Supreme Court eases rules on political asylum. R. Frame. *Christ Today* 31:45 Ap 17 '87

Supreme Court extends affirmative action goals for women, minorities. *Jet* 72:5 Ap 13 '87

Supreme Court extends limits on suits by military personnel. M. Mecham. *Aviat Week Space Technol* 126:26 My 25 '87

Supreme Court fine-tunes third part of 'Miller' test [Pope v. Illinois] *Publ Wkly* 231:20 My 22 '87

Supreme Court gives motherhood its legal due [L. Garland's maternity leave case] B. Brophy. il por *U S News World Rep* 102:12 Ja 26 '87

Supreme Court holds that contagious diseases are handicaps. T. J. Flygare. *Phi Delta Kappan* 68:705-6 My '87

Supreme Court on 'flat souls' [ruling on Louisiana law ordering equal treatment of creationism with evolution] J. M. Wall. *Christ Century* 104:579 Jl 1-8 '87

Supreme Court overturns injunction blocking Delta-Western merger. C. Preble. map *Aviat Week Space Technol* 126:32-3 Ap 6 '87

The Supreme Court puts the mike in Diane Joyce's hands, giving feminists a major victory [Santa Clara County, Calif. affirmative action case] W. Plummer. il pors *People Wkly* 27:49-50+ Ap 13 '87

Supreme Court rule may give new trials to blacks [blacks convicted by all white juries] *Jet* 71:6 F 2 '87

Supreme Court strikes down "creation science" law as promotion of religion [Louisiana case] C. Norman. *Science* 236:1620 Je 26 '87

Supreme Court strikes down Louisiana creationism act. T. J. Flygare. il *Phi Delta Kappan* 69:77-9 S '87

Supreme Court upholds promotion quotas [Alabama state troopers case] *Mon Labor Rev* 110:41 My '87

Takeover artists take a direct hit [upholds states' power to restrict hostile bids] P. Dwyer. il *Bus Week* p35 My 4 '87

Takeover hurdle [decision allows state regulation of corporate takeovers] *Time* 129:74 My 4 '87

Texaco takes a knockdown punch [sends Pennzoil case back to Texas] T. Thompson. il *Bus Week* p27 Ap 20 '87

Thinking about the death penalty [rules death penalty not racially biased] *America* 156:393 My 16 '87

Tillich in an Alice-in-Wonderland world [court decisions pertaining to school textbooks and secular humanism] J. McBride. *Christ Century* 104:519-20 Je 3-10 '87

Tribal justice [opinion upholding the legality of Santa Clara, Calif. affirmative action plan] *Natl Rev* 39:17-18 Ap 24 '87

Unemployment pay may be denied jobless new moms [women on maternity leave who don't return] *Jet* 71:25 Mr 23 '87

The verdict on creationism [ruling on Louisiana law] S. J. Gould. il *N Y Times Mag* p32+ Jl 19 '87

A victory for AIDS victims. A. Press. il *Newsweek* 109:33 Mr 16 '87

Viva Miranda [Justice Dept. offensive against Miranda decision] J. Toobin. *New Repub* 196:11-12 F 16 '87

What am I? A potted plant? [strict constructionism] R. A. Posner. *New Repub* 197:23-5 S 28 '87

What they say it is: the justices' words instruct the nation, and often address history. il *Time* 130:44+ Jl 6 '87

Why stockbrokers sleep at night [binding arbitration upheld] M. Meyer. il *Money* 16:105-8+ Jl 7 '87

A woman's day in court [Santa Clara County, Calif. affirmative action case] A. Press. il *Newsweek* 109:58-9 Ap 6 '87

The women win—again [Santa Clara County, Calif. affirmative action case] T. Gest. il *U S News World Rep* 102:18-19 Ap 6 '87

Your Constitution. See issues of Scholastic Update (Teachers' edition) beginning September 22, 1986

Abortion decisions

Abortion: the battle heats up again [nomination of R. H. Bork] M. Engel. il por *Glamour* 85:192+ O '87

A world without Roe? M. Kaus. map *Newsweek* 110:33 S 14 '87

Would Roe go? [position of R. H. Bork] R. Stengel. il *Time* 130:14-15 S 21 '87

United States. Surgeon-General's Office

Disowning the Surgeon General. P. Schlafly and P. Weyrich. *Harpers* 275:16-17 Ag '87

A fall from grace on the right [views of C. E. Koop] D. deF. Whitman. il por *U S News World Rep* 102:27-8 My 25 '87

Koop makes waves in his war on AIDS. C. O'Connor. por *Newsweek* 109:31 Mr 2 '87

The missionary doctor [C. E. Koop] il por *Time* 129:22 Je 8 '87

Warning: the Surgeon General may be good for your health [C. E. Koop] P. Glastris. por *Wash Mon* 19:13-16+ Mr '87

United States. Unified Space Command

U.S. Space Command focuses on strategic control in wartime. C. Covault. il *Aviat Week Space Technol* 126:83-4 Mr 30 '87

United States. Veterans Administration

Is alcoholism a disease? [case of Eugene Traynor and James P. McKelvey vs. the Veterans Administration] C. Holden. *Science* 238:1647 D 18 '87

Putting vets in the shredder [suit brought by National Association of Radiation Survivors] M. Perry. il *Nation* 245:554-6 N 14 '87

Hospitals

Conditions less than honorable. M. Perry. il *Progressive* 51:24-7 My '87

It's closing time. J. Stein. il *Progressive* 51:28 My '87

Onwards and downwards with the VA. M. Engel. il *50 Plus* 27:14-15 Je '87

Report from the front [AIDS] P. Morrisroe. il *N Y* 20:58-70 N 30 '87

United States. Volunteers in Service to America

Hands reach out to a hungry heartland. C. Tevis. il *Success Farm* 85 no3:M1 F '87

United States. Women's Bureau

Shirley Dennis hailed as new Women's Bureau boss. il por *Jet* 71:4 Mr 23 '87

United States Air Force Academy

Twelve years out of Vietnam, Air Force cadet Hoang Nhu Tran discovers the sky's the limit [top academic graduate] R. Arias. il pors *People Wkly* 27:45-6 Je 15 '87

United States and Cameroon *See* Cameroon and the United States

United States and Canada *See* Canada and the United States

United States and China *See* China and the United States

United States and Japan *See* Japan and the United States

United States and Latin America *See* Latin America and the United States

United States and Libya *See* Libya and the United States

United States and Nicaragua *See* Nicaragua and the United States

United States and the Soviet Union *See* Soviet Union and the United States

United States-Australia air agreements *See* Aviation—International aspects

United States Catholic Conference

See also

Catholic Church. National Conference of Catholic Bishops

AIDS education: the moral substance. D. Hollenbach. *America* 157:493-4 D 26 '87

America's bishops rule on condoms. *Newsweek* 110:57 D 21 '87

The bishops' split on AIDS [controversy over condoms divides the Catholic hierarchy] R. N. Ostling. il *Time* 130:64 D 28 '87

The bishops' statement on AIDS. *America* 157:491-2 D 26 '87

Catholics, AIDS and condoms [statement by bishops] *Time* 130:60 D 21 '87

Of many things [synopsis of the findings of the Attorney General's Commission on Pornography] G. W. Hunt. *America* 156:inside cover Ja 3-10 '87

United States Catholic Conference. Campaign for Human Development *See* Campaign for Human Development

United States Chamber of Commerce *See* Chamber of Commerce of the United States of America

United States-China air agreements *See* Aviation—International aspects

United States Commission on Civil Rights
A farewell to civil rights. J. Nuechterlein. *Commentary* 84:25-36 Ag '87
Mary Frances Berry. J. Barthel. por *Ms* 15:68-70+ Ja '87
Study of race violence a 'ploy,' Berry says. por *Jet* 71:31 F 23 '87
United States embassy buildings *See* Embassies (Buildings)
United States Employment Service
Normal nonsense [reverse discrimination seen in rankings of General Aptitude Test Battery scores] D. Seligman. il *Fortune* 116:165-6 N 9 '87
United States Film Festival *See* Motion picture festivals—Utah
United States Football League
Ex-Bears' QB Evans sues USFL for $1.3 million pay. por *Jet* 71:49 F 2 '87
USFL Blitz ordered to pay QB Evans $1.6 million [V. Evans] por *Jet* 72:50 Ap 27 '87
United States-Great Britain air agreements *See* Aviation—International aspects
United States Gypsum Co.
See also
USG Corporation
United States in literature
Literature lost in the thickets. F. Turner. il *N Y Times Book Rev* 92:1+ F 15 '87
United States Information Agency *See* United States. Information Agency
United States Institute for Theatre Technology
1987 conference celebrates "A theatrical heritage" [special section] M. LaRue. il *Theatre Crafts* 21:18-24+ Ap '87
United States Institute for Theatre Technology. Control Communications Standard Committee
Entertainment industry standards. S. Terry. *Theatre Crafts* 21:22-3 O '87
United States Institute of Peace
Former diplomat becomes head of U.S. Institute of Peace [S. W. Lewis] il por *Christ Today* 31:44-5+ D 11 '87
Hawks nest on Peace Board. A. Simmons. *Progressive* 51:16 Mr '87
United States Lines, Inc.
Will USL join Davy Jones? S. Payne. *Bus Week* p30-1 Mr 30 '87
United States Military Academy
Fred Gorden first black commandant at West Point Academy. por *Jet* 72:4 Ag 31 '87
HM spends $600G for book on West Pt. Class of '66 [R. Atkinson's The long gray line] *Publ Wkly* 231:37 My 8 '87
Reagan: a valedictory for an old soldier? T. M. DeFrank. il por *Newsweek* 110:26-7 N 9 '87
U.S. Military Academy seeks minority candidates. *Jet* 71:22 F 23 '87
West Pointers flip and fall for Marian Rockwell. L. Rozen. il pors *People Wkly* 27:65-7 Mr 23 '87
United States-Netherlands air agreements *See* Aviation—International aspects
United States Olympic Committee
Notes and comment [T. Waddell v. USOC over restrictions on use of term Olympics] *New Yorker* 63:19-20 Ag 24 '87
United States Postal Service
See also
Chicago (Ill.). Post Office
Collective labor agreements—Postal service
New York (N.Y.). Post Office
Postal rates
Can Bob Tisch get the mail moving? F. Seghers. il *Bus Week* p29 Ag 3 '87
Postal Service contract. il *Mon Labor Rev* 110:47 O '87
The postman cometh with a lot of new construction. P. Hoffmann. il *Archit Rec* 175:35 S '87
Reinstates San Francisco postmaster 'forced' to quit [case of J. Wilson] *Jet* 73:35 N 30 '87
The twenty-five cent stamp: why it's here and why it shouldn't be. M. Szegedy-Maszak. il *Wash Mon* 19:39-42 N '87
Why your mail is so slow [New York City; cover story] J. Blyskal and M. Hodge. il *N Y* 20:42-52+ N 9 '87
United States Postal Service. Postal Inspection Service
A friend on their side [work of K. R. McClelland as consumer protection specialist] E. J. Kahn. *New Yorker* 62:72-7 Ja 19 '87
This is the Post Office. Come out with your hands up. C. Farrell. il *Bus Week* p32 Mr 2 '87

United States-Saudi Arabia Joint Economic Commission
Joan Wallace probes Saudi problems in agriculture. por *Jet* 71:6 Mr 2 '87
United States Steel Corp.
See also
USX Corporation
United States Steel Corp. USS Chemicals Division
See also
Aristech Chemical Corporation
United States-Switzerland air agreements *See* Aviation—International aspects
United States Tennis Association
Arthur Ashe seeks cure for U.S. tennis malaise [development of black players] por *Jet* 72:49 Ag 31 '87
The future is wow! [views of president G. D. Jorgensen] N. Amdur. por *World Tennis* 34:6 Mr '87
A master plan for American tennis [proposals for changes in the structure of junior tennis] S. Flink. il *World Tennis* 35:16-17 N '87
Pro tennis seeks black players for USA's future. *Jet* 72:48 Ap 13 '87
United States-Western Europe air agreements *See* Aviation—International aspects
United Steelworkers of America
It's a no-win situation for both sides at USX [strike] M. Rothman and G. L. Miles. il *Bus Week* p55-6 Ja 19 '87
A retirement offer they couldn't refuse [employees] il *Newsweek* 109:44 Je 22 '87
Steel workers on the line [strike against Brenner Tank Company] M. Wettstein, Jr. and J. Gormican. *Progressive* 51:15-16 Ja '87
Steelmakers want to make teamwork an institution. A. Bernstein and M. Rothman. il *Bus Week* p84 My 11 '87
USX contract ends 6-month strike. *Mon Labor Rev* 110:55-6 Ap '87
United Technologies Corp.
"Achieve or leave". H. Banks. por *Forbes* 140:344-5 Jl 13 '87
As UTC gets its act together, its stock gets active. G. G. Marcial. il *Bus Week* p73 Ag 24 '87
Finally, some new blood at the top [R. F. Daniell] C. Leinster. il por *Fortune* 116:56 Ag 3 '87
UTC's diet hasn't been much help—yet. R. Mitchell. il por *Bus Week* p53 My 18 '87
United Technologies Corp. Hamilton Standard Division
Flight test validations near for Hamilton Standard propfans. il *Aviat Week Space Technol* 126:78-9 Ap 13 '87
United Technologies Corp. Pratt & Whitney Aircraft Group *See* Pratt & Whitney Aircraft Group
United Way of America
Fund raising in trying times [work of chairman J. D. Robinson] A. Gabor. il por *U S News World Rep* 102:53 My 4 '87
Unitedbank-Houston
"Nobody thought it would be us" [FDIC liquidates Unitedbank-Houston] R. Woodbury. il *Time* 129:53 My 11 '87
Unitel Video, Inc.
What do Live from the Met and Family ties have in common? il pors *Bus Week* p71 Ag 31 '87
Universal Fellowship of Metropolitan Community Churches
A gay witness to Pope John Paul II. N. L. Wilson. *Christ Century* 104:845-6 O 7 '87
Universal language
Toward a universal language. E. A. Imbert. *Américas* 39:54-5 Jl/Ag '87
Universal life insurance *See* Insurance, Life
Universal Life Insurance Company
Universal Life's policy for growth. N. McCall. il por *Black Enterp* 17:232-4+ Je '87
Universal Negro Improvement Association
November issue of Ebony remembers Marcus Garvey. il por *Jet* 73:37 N 16 '87
Universal Pictures
Kong is back . . . [construction of mechanical King Kong for Universal Studios tour] il *Natl Geogr World* 137:9-15 Ja '87
Universal Postal Union
The Universal Postal Union. H. Herst, Jr. il *Antiques Collect Hobbies* 92:86-7 O '87
Universal Television
Universal changing the rules. J. Von Herrmann. por *Channels* 7:12 My '87
Universalism (Theology)
Universalism: will everyone be saved? [special section] il *Christ Today* 31:31-45 Mr 20 '87

Universe

See also

Anthropocentrism
Astronomy
Cosmic strings
Creation
Dark matter (Astronomy)
Galaxies
Hubble constant
Superstring theories (Physics)

Before the Big Bang: the big foam [excerpt from Thursday's universe] M. Bartusiak. il *Discover* 8:76-83 S '87

Big-Bang bashers. J. Horgan. il *Sci Am* 257:22+ S '87

Cosmic clock dates the universe [rhenium-osmium isotopes] R. Layne. *Pop Sci* 230:53 Mr '87

Do-it-yourself universes [research by Alan H. Guth and others] M. M. Waldrop. *Science* 235:845-6 F 20 '87

End of the world: you won't feel a thing. D. E. Thomsen. *Sci News* 131:391 Je 20 '87

The expanding universe. il *Astronomy* 15:16 O '87

Exploring the Lyman-alpha forest [work of Wallace L. W. Sargent] M. M. Waldrop. *Science* 235:284 Ja 16 '87

Goodbye Olbers' paradox! [work of Paul S. Wesson and others] il *Sky Telesc* 74:458 N '87

Has cosmology become metaphysical? T. Rothman and G. Ellis. il *Astronomy* 15:6-22 F '87

In the beginning was quantum mechanics [cover story] D. E. Thomsen. *Sci News* 131:346-7 My 30 '87

Interview [D. Bohm] J. Briggs and F. D. Peat. por *Omni* 9:68-70+ Ja '87

Is that all there is? [edge of the visible universe; research by J. Anthony Tyson and Patrick Seitzer] il *Discover* 8:10+ S '87

The large-scale structure of the universe gets larger—maybe [research by R. Brent Tully] M. M. Waldrop. il *Science* 238:894 N 13 '87

Large-scale structure, streaming and galaxy formation. P. H. Andersen. bibl il *Phys Today* 40:19-21 O '87

Light from the depths of time. R. Kippenhahn. il *Sky Telesc* 73:140-2 F '87

Particle physics and inflationary cosmology. A. Linde. bibl f il *Phys Today* 40:61-8 S '87

Probing the early universe with quasar light [Lyman alpha forest] B. M. Schwarzschild. bibl f il *Phys Today* 40:17-20 N '87

Revising the Copernican revolution. K. Kolenda. por *Humanist* 47:41-2 Mr/Ap '87

Science & the ways to God [views of S. L. Jaki] H. Rolston. *Commonweal* 114:313-16 My 22 '87

Starlight reflected in a diamond. D. Lago. il *Astronomy* 15:28+ My '87

This is the way the world ends [cover story] T. Rothman. il *Discover* 8:82-4+ Jl '87

To the Big Bang and beyond. S. Odenwald. il *Astronomy* 15:90-5 My '87

True ZITs: can such things be? [anisotropies] D. E. Thomsen. *Sci News* 131:4-5 Ja 3 '87

Where are we going? T. Ferris. il *Sky Telesc* 73:486-90 My '87

White dwarfs and the age of the universe [research by Donald E. Winget and others] il *Sky Telesc* 74:347-8 O '87

A younger universe is seen in the stars [thorium dating; work of Harvey R. Butcher] M. M. Waldrop. il *Science* 237:361-2 Jl 24 '87

Universidad Autónoma de Guadalajara

Neo-Nazi U [stronghold of secret society Los Tecos] C. Pyes. il *New Repub* 196:17-18+ Ja 19 '87

Universidad Centroamericana

The university and revolution. K. M. Cahill. *America* 157:77-8 Ag 15-22 '87

Universidad de Chile

Uncertainties over University of Chile. J. Walsh. *Science* 238:1037 N 20 '87

Universities See Colleges and universities

University education See College education

University extension

Face-to-face or not to face [discussion of September 1986 article, College credits through telecommunication] P. Lemmons. il *Byte* 12:186-8+ F '87

The quiet revolution [electronic university] B. N. Meeks. *Byte* 12:183-4+ F '87

University Glee Club of New York City

A joyful noise. H. B. Noble. il *N Y Times Mag* p31 D 27 '87

University Hospital Center at Sart Tilman (Liège, Belgium) See Centre Hospitalier Universitaire au Sart Tilman (Liège, Belgium)

University libraries See College libraries

University of Alabama

They stood guard in Tuscaloosa [Jasons' Shrine] il *South Living* 22:53 S '87

University of Arizona

Culture on campus. K. Dahood. il *Horizon* 30:43 My '87

University of Arizona Press

Two press profiles. C. B. Grannis. il *Publ Wkly* 231:35-7 Je 5 '87

University of Arkansas, Fayetteville. University Museum

Treasures of an Arkansas museum. il *South Living* 22:55 Ap '87

University of Bombay

Politics and the university [examination fixing scandal] P. G. Altbach. il *Change* 19:56-9 Jl/Ag '87

University of California. Lawrence Berkeley Laboratory See Lawrence Berkeley Laboratory

University of California, Berkeley

Berkeley changes tack on reactor [decision to shut down reactor use for military-related research] J. Walsh. *Science* 235:273 Ja 16 '87

A physicist objects [C. Schwartz stops teaching classes in higher physics at Berkeley] J. J. Neuburger. il por *Progressive* 51:12-13 Jl '87

Research reactor closed at Berkeley for mixed reasons. W. Sweet. *Phys Today* 40:56 Je '87

Use of Berkeley reactor questioned on military-related research [views of Charles Schwartz] J. Walsh. *Science* 235:23 Ja 2 '87

University of California, Berkeley. Los Alamos Scientific Laboratory See Los Alamos Scientific Laboratory

University of California, Los Angeles

Jews for Jesus ministers settle out of court [suit against UCLA for prohibiting distribution of religious literature on campus] B. Bird. il *Christ Today* 31:46 Mr 6 '87

More help for UCLA visitors. il *Sunset* 178:32 Ja '87

University of California, Riverside. California Museum of Photography See California Museum of Photography

University of California, Santa Barbara

The C.I.A. goes back to college. J. Wiener. il *Nation* 245:719-20 D 12 '87

University of California, Santa Cruz

Fight, fight, fight, fight, banana slugs, banana slugs [mascot] J. Stuller. il *Audubon* 89:128-30+ Mr '87

New images of chaos that are stirring a science revolution. J. Gleick. bibl (p205) il *Smithsonian* 18:122-4+ D '87

Touring the campus or hiking the forests at UC Santa Cruz. il *Sunset* 179:37-8 Ag '87

University of California (System)

Clark Kerr: the masterbuilder at 75 [cover story] A. Levine. il pors *Change* 19:12-27+ Mr/Ap '87

UC told to review impact of research [ruling primarily benefits small farmers] M. Sun. *Science* 238:1221 N 27 '87

University of California (System). Bodega Marine Laboratory See Bodega Marine Laboratory

University of California Press

Book series on King's life slated for 1990: Mrs. King. *Jet* 72:22 Ap 27 '87

'Public publishing': a new approach by a scholarly press [efforts to build an endowment for publication of humanities books] L. See. *Publ Wkly* 232:41 O 30 '87

UC Press to publish King papers. *Publ Wkly* 231:38 My 8 '87

University of Chicago. Center for Decision Research

The wisdom of Solomon. J. McCormick. il *Newsweek* 110:62-3 Ag 17 '87

University of Chicago. Divinity School

Anecdotes, facetiae, satire, etc.

We were number one [1905 beauty contest winner Della Carson] M. E. Marty. il *Christ Century* 104:151 F 4-11 '87

University of Chicago. Graduate School of Business. Center for Decision Research See University of Chicago. Center for Decision Research

University of Chicago. Law School

Reagan's Chicago farm team [law and economics training] J. McCormick. il *Newsweek* 110:46 N 9 '87

University of Chile See Universidad de Chile

University of Colorado at Boulder

Bullish on space. E. Truitt. il *Space World* X-1-277:24 Ja '87

University of Dakar

CSU's Thomas visits Senegal and forms socio-economic tie. il por *Jet* 71:21 Mr 2 '87

University of Georgia
Jan Kemp [professor's stand against college athletes' low academic standards] C. Reece. il por *Ms* 15:44+ Ja '87

University of Georgia. School of Pharmacy
Black student 'outraged' after she is fired from white pharmacy in Georgia [T. F. Bateman] il por *Jet* 72:30 Ag 31 '87

University of Idaho. Lionel Hampton School of Music
The Univ. of Idaho honors Hampton with Music School. por *Jet* 71:22 F 23 '87

University of Illinois at Urbana-Champaign. Krannert Center for the Performing Arts *See* Krannert Center for the Performing Arts

University of Iowa. College of Law
Uncommon law [circular building] G. Anderson. il *Archit Rec* 175:106-13 Ag '87

University of Iowa. Iowa Center for the Book
The Iowa Center for the Book. W. T. Taylor. il *Am Craft* 47:26-33 Je/Jl '87

University of Kansas
A dynamic relationship between the university and the community nurtures art and culture. G. D. Boone and M. Wade. il *Horizon* 30:17-18 S '87

University of Khartoum
Building the Sudan. B. Wallach. il map *Focus* 37:12-15 Fall '87

University of Manitoba
Over-achiever [Wallace Building] P. M. Sachner. il *Archit Rec* 175:130-3 My '87

University of Maryland, College Park
Musical events:
Performance of Handel's opera Tolomeo. A. Porter. *New Yorker* 63:134+ My 4 '87

University of Maryland at Baltimore
Md. group awards money to UMAB grad students [Lois Young-Thomas Scholarship] *Jet* 72:22 S 21 '87

University of Massachusetts at Amherst. Fine Arts Center
Arts American-style. K. Simmons. il *Horizon* 30:44 N '87

University of Miami
Time to play Foote ball? [president Tad Foote striving for excellence in academics at football power Miami] R. Sullivan. il *Sports Illus* 67:58-60+ D 21 '87

University of Miami. Comprehensive Pain Center
Hubert Rosomoff only hurts the back-pain patients he loves. D. Van Biema. il pors *People Wkly* 27:73-4+ My 18 '87

University of Miami. School of Architecture
Aldo Rossi makes his American debut [design of new architecture school] K. D. Stein. il por *Archit Rec* 175:67 My '87

University of Michigan
Racial jokes bring end of campus radio station. *Jet* 71:33 Mr 23 '87
The real 'Big chill' in Michigan [reunion of 1960s Ann Arbor activists] E. Frank. il *Nation* 245:480-2 O 31 '87
University of Michigan agrees to blacks' demands; Jesse Jackson assists. *Jet* 72:5 Ap 13 '87
What I learned in school today [sitting in on a class taken by football players] S. Shuger. il *Sport Mag* 78:60-1 O '87

University of Michigan. Law School
Trial by fire [law student J. Picozzi accused of arson] T. Senger. il *Roll Stone* p111-12+ S 24 '87

University of Minnesota. Institute for Theoretical Physics *See* Institute for Theoretical Physics (Minn.)

University of Minnesota, Duluth
The artistic riches at the University of Minnesota reach far beyond the campus. E. Beck. il *Horizon* 30:13-15 Ap '87

University of Minnesota, Duluth. Tweed Museum of Art *See* Tweed Museum of Art (Duluth, Minn.)

University of Mississippi
Finding the "Ole" in Ole Miss [early campus buildings] il *South Living* 22:20 Mr '87
Phi Beta Sigma 1st blacks on U. of Miss. frat row. *Jet* 72:24 Ag 31 '87

University of Missouri—Rolla
Stonehenge in Missouri [half-scale model] il *Sky Telesc* 74:83 Jl '87

University of Nebraska Press
U. of Nebraska Press extols the joys of series publishing. *Publ Wkly* 231:35-6 Je 26 '87

University of North Dakota. Aerospace Training and Research Center
Training firm, university plan ab initio program. il *Aviat Week Space Technol* 127:96-7 O 5 '87

University of North Dakota. Energy Research Center
Citizens douse a hazardous burn [plan to incinerate PCBs] J. Hamilton. il *Sierra* 72:88-9 N/D '87

University of Notre Dame
Father Hesburgh retires. *America* 156:433 My 30 '87
George Gipp: "One for the Gipper!". J. Gustaitis. por *Am Hist Illus* 22:40-1 N '87
His trumpet was never uncertain [retirement of president T. Hesburgh] E. Bowen. il por *Time* 129:68+ My 18 '87
Notre Dame's 'Father Ted' bids farewell [T. Hesburgh retires] K. L. Woodward. por *Newsweek* 109:75+ My 11 '87
Of many things [T. M. Hesburgh] G. W. Hunt. *America* 156:inside cover My 30 '87

University of Ottawa. Heart Institute Research Centre *See* Heart Institute Research Centre

University of Oxford
The last diploma he got was in high school, but Ed Gorman, 69, is setting his cap on a masters from Oxford [American student] il por *People Wkly* 27:58 Ap 20 '87
Oxford election draws clergy interest [chancellorship] K. Slack. *Christ Century* 104:303 Ap 1 '87
There'll always be an England [contest for chancellor] W. F. Buckley. *Natl Rev* 39:63 Mr 27 '87

University of Oxford. Pitt Rivers Museum *See* Pitt Rivers Museum (Oxford, England)

University of Pennsylvania
Angry and stupid. H. Klingeman. *Natl Rev* 39:41-2 O 9 '87
'Silent man' gets master's; more studies at U. of Pa. [J. Francis] *Jet* 71:24 Ja 26 '87

University of Pennsylvania. Hospital
Hospital architecture [Founders Pavilion] M. Gaskie. il *Archit Rec* 175:108-11 O '87

University of Pennsylvania. Wharton School of Finance and Commerce *See* Wharton School

University of Pittsburgh
The nationality rooms [Cathedral of Learning] M. A. Zimmermann. il *Focus* 36:34-5 Wint '86

University of Rochester. Libraries
See also
Rush Rhees Library

University of Southern California. Entrepreneurship Program
A better way to communicate [audio cassettes] S. Nelton. il *Nations Bus* 75:68 Jl '87

University of Southern California. Ethel Percy Andrus Gerontology Center *See* Ethel Percy Andrus Gerontology Center

University of Stellenbosch
Rocking the cradle of the *volk*. B. W. Nelan. il *Time* 129:38 My 4 '87

University of Tennessee, Knoxville
Trouble in Tennessee [football program violations; with editorial comment by Neil Cohen] J. D. Miller and D. Whitford. il *Sport Mag* 78:6, 68-73+ N '87

University of Texas (System)
Campbell back in school; assists student-athletes. *Jet* 71:49 Ja 26 '87
CORE's Farmer gives his personal papers to Univ. of Texas [J. Farmer] *Jet* 72:22 S 21 '87
Earl Campbell finds fame is fleeting on UT campus. por *Jet* 72:48 Ap 20 '87
Longhorns 8, Crimson 4 [endowments] W. P. Barrett. il *Forbes* 140:116+ O 19 '87

University of Texas at Austin
UT-Austin names campus to honor black student [H. Sweatt] por *Jet* 72:38 S 14 '87

University of the District of Columbia
Cortada faces myriad of problems as new UDC chief. *Jet* 72:16 Ag 24 '87

University of Virginia
Blacks protest at Univ. of Virginia on race bias. *Jet* 73:6 N 9 '87

University of Wisconsin Press
Two press profiles. C. B. Grannis. il *Publ Wkly* 231:35-7 Je 5 '87

University of Wisconsin—Madison
The University of Wisconsin hatches toxins [biological warfare research] R. Jannaccio. il *Progressive* 51:20 N '87

University of Wisconsin—Milwaukee. Dept. of Architecture
Integration of law and practice into the curriculum. B. Greenstreet. il por *Archit Rec* 175:43 Mr '87

University presidents *See* College presidents

University presses
See also
Association of American University Presses
University of Arizona Press
University of California Press

University presses—See also—*cont.*
   University of Nebraska Press
   University of Wisconsin Press
25 years of university press best sellers. *N Y Times Book Rev* 92:58 O 11 '87
The day New York became harmless [titles of academic books] A. Broyard. il *N Y Times Book Rev* 92:11 O 4 '87
University press publishing: a special report. il *Publ Wkly* 231:19-24+ Je 5 '87
Who needs a blockbuster? Another way of publishing. C. Sternhell. il *N Y Times Book Rev* 92:40 O 11 '87

Finance
'Public publishing': a new approach by a scholarly press [University of California Press' efforts to build an endowment for publication of humanities books] L. See. *Publ Wkly* 232:41 O 30 '87

Great Britain
   See also
   Oxford University Press

University research *See* Colleges and universities—Research
University students *See* College students
University teachers *See* College teachers
Univox California, Inc.
   Black businessman charges conspiracy behind losses [J. N. Grayson] il por *Jet* 71:15 Mr 23 '87
UniWorld Group
   Avon picks UniWorld. K. Smikle. il *Black Enterp* 17:24 F '87
Unix operating system *See* Computers—Operating systems
UNK (Accelerator) *See* Accelerators (Electrons, etc.)
Unklesbay, A. G.
   Midwest earthquakes. il map *Earth Sci* 40:11-13 Wint '87
Unmarried couples
   Breaking up with my out-laws. L. Mosedale. il *Glamour* 85:324 N '87
   Couples: getting together, staying together, making it work [special section] il *Vogue* 177:384-93+ F '87
   Headed for a painful breakup? Sociologist Diane Vaughan discusses the warning signs [inteview] M. Wilhelm. il pors *People Wkly* 27:97-8+ Mr 2 '87
   Houston Catholics must refrain from sex to have gala church wedding. *Jet* 73:33 N 16 '87
   The incredible shrinking couple! Therapy for the commitment-shy [use of marriage counseling by unmarried couples] D. Kent. il *Mademoiselle* 93:302-3+ S '87
   The long goodbye [failing relationships; cover story] D. Vaughan. il *Psychol Today* 21:36-8+ Jl '87
   "Meet my (uh) friend": how to identify your guy. B. G. Harrison. *Mademoiselle* 93:206 Mr '87
   More couples live together; fear catching AIDS. *Jet* 72:37 S 14 '87
   A plan for Catholic marriages [penalty for cohabitation in Houston] K. L. Woodward. il *Newsweek* 110:73 D 14 '87
   The pregnancy test—how to get positive results [effect of unplanned pregnancy on relationship to the baby's father] C. Rickey. *Mademoiselle* 93:100 F '87
   Public pillow talk [secret codes used by lovers; study by Robert A. Bell] C. Simon. il *Psychol Today* 21:18 O '87
   An unmarried couple. R. Ragaini. il *50 Plus* 27:55-7 N '87

Legal status, laws, etc.
   See also
   Palimony
Unmarried men *See* Single men
Unmarried people *See* Single people
Unmarried women *See* Single women
Unowsky, R. David
   about
   A literary repast for a Hungry Mind. S. Little. il por *Publ Wkly* 232:41-3 N 13 '87
UNRWA *See* United Nations Relief and Works Agency for Palestine Refugees in the Near East
Unseld, Wes
   about
   Wes Unseld, Bullets VP, to add coaching duties. por *Jet* 72:48 Ag 31 '87
Unselfishness *See* Altruism
Unser, Al, 1939-
   about
   Have helmet, will travel. S. Moses. il por *Sports Illus* 66:30-3 Je 1 '87
Unsworth, Tim
   American Catholics: what's happened to your Church in the last 25 years? [with readers' comments] il *U S Cathol* 52:6-11 Je '87

Let's take the must out of Sunday Mass [with readers' comments] *U S Cathol* 52:14-20 Ja '87
Parish finances: are Catholics reluctant to pay their own way? [with editorial comment by Robert E. Burns] il *U S Cathol* 52:2, 32-8 S '87
A second collection on Catholic giving [discussion of September 1987 article, Parish finances] *U S Cathol* 52:46-7 D '87
Son, behold your mother. *U S Cathol* 52:28-30 Jl '87
Truth or consequences: what U.S. Catholic readers admit about their everyday honesty. il *U S Cathol* 52:6-17 Mr '87
Untidiness *See* Messiness
The Untouchables [film] *See* Motion picture reviews—Single works
UNU *See* United Nations University
Unwed mothers *See* Single mothers
Updike, John
   Bech in Czech [story] *New Yorker* 63:32-42+ Ap 20 '87
   Brother grasshopper [story] *New Yorker* 63:40-6 D 14 '87
   The burglar alarm [story] *New Yorker* 63:30-1 Mr 9 '87
   Conjunction [story] *New Yorker* 63:29-32 Jl 27 '87
   December [poem] il *Ladies Home J* 104:137 D '87
   Five days in Finland at the age of fifty-five. *New Yorker* 63:86-8+ S 28 '87
   Goodbye, Göteborg [poem] *New Yorker* 63:42 O 26 '87
   Heavily hyped Helga. *New Repub* 197:27-30 D 7 '87
   Howells as anti-novelist. *New Yorker* 63:78-88 Jl 13 '87
   Radio romance. il *Esquire* 107:117-18 Je '87
   Returning native [poem] *New Repub* 197:33 Ag 3 '87
   Switzerland [poem] *Nation* 244:740 My 30 '87
   Tuning out the inner critic [remarks, May 1987] *N Y Times Book Rev* 92:29 Je 21 '87
   Wildlife [story] il *Esquire* 108:62-4+ Ag '87
   about
   The downward trajectory of John Updike. D. Mehl. *Natl Rev* 39:53-4+ F 13 '87

Anecdotes, facetiae, satire, etc.
   Reading Updike. E. Abbey. *Nation* 244:409-10 Mr 28 '87
Upholstery
   Look what new fabric can do. C. Engle. il *South Living* 22:148+ My '87
   Reupholster or slipcover a sofa. il *Glamour* 85:310 My '87
   The springs of comfort. M. Hampton. il *House Gard* 159:46+ O '87

Care
   See also
   Antimacassars
Upper atmosphere *See* Atmosphere, Upper
Upper classes
   See also
   Elite (Social sciences)
   Rich
High hats & coronets: nothing succeeds like excess. J. Etra. il *Harpers Bazaar* 121:70+ D '87

Language
Locust Valley lockjaw. W. Safire. il *N Y Times Mag* p8+ Ja 18 '87
Upper Midwest Booksellers Association
   UMBA show reaches new high. S. Little. il *Publ Wkly* 232:32-4 O 23 '87
Upper Volta *See* Burkina Faso
Upper West Side (New York, N.Y.)
   One block: a tale of two cities on West 80th Street. D. Blum. il *N Y* 20:24-32 F 9 '87
   A walker in the city—again. A. Kazin. il *N Y* 20:32-5 Ja 19 '87
Upperline (New Orleans, La.: Restaurant) *See* New Orleans (La.)—Restaurants, nightclubs, bars, etc.
Upshaw, Dawn
   about
   Musical events. A. Porter. *New Yorker* 62:97-8 Ja 12 '87
Upshaw, Gene
   about
   The guard who would be quarterback. F. Deford. il pors *Sports Illus* 67:64-9+ S 14 '87
   Upshaw claims racism influences NFL strike. por *Jet* 73:49 O 19 '87

Upside-down cake See Cake
Upton, Joe
The round haul [excerpt from Amaretto] il *Oceans* 20:8-17 Ja/F '87
Uranium
DOE undermines own nonproliferation effort [plans for a reactor that will use highly enriched uranium] D. Charles. *Science* 238:1224 N 27 '87
Uranium enrichment See Uranium metallurgy
Uranium industry
    See also
      UNC Inc.
        Environmental aspects
Colorado: the legacy of uranium mining [radon] A. J. Hazle. il *Environment* 29:13+ Ja/F '87
Uranium metallurgy
Pakistan's bomb-making capacity [gas centrifuge enrichment plant at Kahuta] D. Albright. bibl f il *Bull At Sci* 43:30-3 Je '87
Uranium enrichment: heading for a cliff? C. Norman. il *Science* 236:906-8 My 22 '87
Uranium mines and mining
        Environmental aspects
    See Uranium industry—Environmental aspects
        Colorado
Colorado: the legacy of uranium mining [radon] A. J. Hazle. il *Environment* 29:13+ Ja/F '87
Uranus (Planet)
    See also
      Space flight—Voyager flights
        Atmosphere
Uranus' methane cloud [work of Gunnar F. Lindal and others] il *Sky Telesc* 73:273 Mr '87
        Magnetic properties
Electroglow explained [Uranus glows in ultraviolet light] *Sky Telesc* 73:274 Mr '87
        Ring system
The rings of Uranus [Voyager 2 findings] J. N. Cuzzi and L. W. Esposito. bibl (p116) il *Sci Am* 257:52-4+ Jl '87
        Satellites
The moons of Uranus. T. V. Johnson and others. il *Sci Am* 256:48-60 Ap '87
        Geology
The mystery of the tumbling moon [Miranda] *Newsweek* 110:62 Ag 3 '87
Urban, Dean L., and others
Landscape ecology. bibl f il *BioScience* 37:119-27 F '87
Urban archeology
    See also
      London (England)—Antiquities
Urban design See City planning
Urban Earth (Musical group)
Harvie Swartz's Urban Earth. F. Bouchard. il por *Down Beat* 54:56 Je '87
Urban ecology
The urban maze. il *Courier* 40:8-11 O '87
Urban economics
    See also
      Grants-in-aid
Main Street feels the pinch [plant closings] J. Castro. il *Time* 129:47 F 16 '87
World urban areas: the anatomy of cities. il *Current* 293:28-35 Je '87
Urban education See Education, Urban
Urban flora
As cities crumble, plants may be at the root of it; ed. by Sylvia E. Merschel. D. R. Perry. il *Smithsonian* 17:72-9 Ja '87
Plants that eat cities; ed. by Sylvia E. Merschel. D. R. Perry. il *Read Dig* 131:126-8 O '87
Urban growth See Cities and towns—Growth
Urban Institute
A Washington wallflower starts to bloom. H. Gleckman. il *Bus Week* p112+ Mr 9 '87
Urban life See City and town life
Urban planning See City planning
Urban policy (U.S.) See United States—Urban. policy
Urban poor See Poor
Urban renewal
    See also
      ACORN (Organization)
      Business districts
      Gentrification
      United States. Dept. of Housing and Urban Development
Urban services See Municipal services
Urban transportation
    See also
      Cable railroads
      Local transit

Urbanization See Cities and towns—Growth
Urbanized areas See Metropolitan areas
Urbanska, Wanda
Danny De Vito & Rhea Perlman. il pors *McCalls* 145:36+ Mr '87
They used to say don't trust anyone over the age of 30. Now everyone is suspicious of those of us under 30. il *Glamour* 85:68 F '87
Urchins, Sea See Sea urchins
Urdang, Constance
Robert's friends [poem] *New Repub* 196:33 Ap 27 '87
Urethanes
Water, water everywhere, but . . . [alcoholic beverage contamination] S. Weiss. *Sci News* 132:390-1 D 19-26 '87
Urinary calculi See Bladder stones; Kidney stones
Urinary organs
    See also
      Bladder
      Kidneys
Urinary thermometers See Thermometers, Clinical
Urine
Your bladder: use it or lose it? [dangers of postponing urination] *Sci News* 131:200 Mr 28 '87
        Analysis
    See also
      Drug abuse—Testing
Pregnancy hypertension marker found. *Sci News* 131:344 My 30 '87
        Incontinence
Incontinence comes out of the closet. D. Farley. il *FDA Consum* 21:4-9 Mr '87
        Proteins
Identification of human uromodulin as the Tamm-Horsfall urinary glycoprotein. D. Pennica and others. bibl f il *Science* 236:83-8 Ap 3 '87
Uris, Leon, 1924-
        about
'Exodus' in samizdat: still popular and still subversive. E. McDowell. il *N Y Times Book Rev* 92:13 Ap 26 '87
Uromodulin
Identification of human uromodulin as the Tamm-Horsfall urinary glycoprotein. D. Pennica and others. bibl f il *Science* 236:83-8 Ap 3 '87
Uromodulin (Tamm-Horsfall glycoprotein): a renal ligand for lymphokines. C. Hession and others. bibl f il *Science* 237:1479-84 S 18 '87
Urquhart, Brian E.
The last disaster of the war. il *N Y Rev Books* 34:27-30 S 24 '87
Urriolagoitia V., Gastón
Saving cultural assets. il *Américas* 39:56 Ja/F '87
Urrutia, Roberto
        about
Once a Cuban hero, Roberto Urrutia aims to give the U.S. a boost—and Castro a lesson—in the Pan American Games. P. Jordan. il pors *People Wkly* 28:105-6+ Ag 10 '87
Uruguay
        Politics and government
Closing the book. *Nation* 244:239-40 F 28 '87
Us (Periodical)
Now star-studded Us has more ad pages, too. D. Lieberman. il por *Bus Week* p83+ Je 8 '87
US Air, Inc.
Carl Icahn is at it again [bid for USAir] C. Hawkins. *Bus Week* p42+ Mr 16 '87
For Carl Icahn, the flight path never ends [takeover bid for USAir] por *Newsweek* 109:50 Mr 16 '87
How USAir cut Icahn out [plan to buy Piedmont] S. Payne. il por *Bus Week* p35 Mr 23 '87
Law judge rejects USAir/Piedmont merger on regional antitrust grounds. M. Mecham. *Aviat Week Space Technol* 127:41+ S 28 '87
Teamsters' vote clears path for USAir's acquisition of PSA. C. Preble. il *Aviat Week Space Technol* 126:41 My 25 '87
Transportation Dept. approves proposed USAir/Piedmont merger. J. Ott. *Aviat Week Space Technol* 127:44 N 9 '87
USAir, Piedmont ask administration to overturn decision against merger. *Aviat Week Space Technol* 127:44 O 12 '87
USAir-Piedmont merger pending government, shareholder approval. C. Preble. map *Aviat Week Space Technol* 126:34-6 Mr 16 '87
What's standing between USAir and Piedmont. S. Payne. il *Bus Week* p40 O 5 '87

US Sprint Communications Inc.
AT&T is eating 'em alive. J. J. Keller. il *Bus Week* p28-9 F 16 '87
Sprint's chance to gallop [contract to supply network services to GM] J. J. Keller. il *Bus Week* p33 Je 15 '87
Sprint's new chief has a lot of wires to untangle [R. H. Snedaker vs. C. M. Skibo] M. Ivey. il por *Bus Week* p29 Jl 27 '87

USA *See* United Scenic Artists

USA for Africa
USA for Africa moves to close books. F. Goodman. *Roll Stone* p23 O 8 '87
'We are the world' tune, Hands Across America net $82.5 million for needy. *Jet* 72:58 Ap 13 '87

USA today (Newspaper)
Allen H. Neuharth. P. Jordan. il pors *People Wkly* 28:65+ S 28 '87
Good news is no news. D. Remnick. il pors *Esquire* 108:156-8+ O '87
The king of the road [A. Neuharth's USA today bus tour] J. Alter. il por *Newsweek* 109:66-7 My 4 '87
Never forget the egomania [founder A. Neuharth] R. J. Samuelson. il *Newsweek* 110:65 S 21 '87
Progress report on three picked as winners. M. S. Forbes. il *Forbes* 139:24 Ja 12 '87
USA today [5th anniversary] L. Zuckerman. il *Time* 130:63 O 12 '87

USA today (Periodical)
USA today wins peace award [Olive Branch Award] *USA Today (Periodical)* 116:4 Ag '87

USAF *See* United States. Air Force
USAir, Inc. *See* US Air, Inc.
USDA *See* United States. Dept. of Agriculture
Used airplanes *See* Airplanes, Used
Used automobiles *See* Automobiles, Used
Used boats *See* Boats, Used
Used cameras *See* Cameras, Used
Used sporting goods *See* Sporting goods, Used
User fees
See also
Airports—Fees
Aviation—Fees
Hunting—Fees
National parks and reserves—Fees

USES *See* United States Employment Service
USFL *See* United States Football League
USG Corporation
Are USG's walls crumbling? [Desert Partners bid] J. E. Ellis. il *Bus Week* p59 O 19 '87
Cold turkey [USG forbids employees to smoke at work or at home] *Time* 129:32 F 2 '87

Ushenko, Audrey Andreyevna, 1945-
about
Audrey Ushenko. E. Agar. il *Am Artist* 51:42-5+ Mr '87

USIA *See* United States. Information Agency
USITT *See* United States Institute for Theatre Technology
USOC *See* United States Olympic Committee
USSR (Union of Soviet Socialist Republics) *See* Soviet Union
USTA *See* United States Tennis Association
USTR *See* United States. Office of the U.S. Trade Representative
USW *See* United Steelworkers of America
USX Corporation
The battle for USX: Icahn retreats for now. *Newsweek* 109:42 Ja 19 '87
A CEO as tough as steel [D. M. Roderick] B. Saporito. il por *Fortune* 116:64 Ag 3 '87
Icahn's juggle: TWA, USX, SEC. C. J. Loomis. il por *Fortune* 115:81-2 My 11 '87
It's a no-win situation for both sides at USX [strike] M. Rothman and G. L. Miles. il *Bus Week* p55-6 Ja 19 '87
Not in the next 30 days. J. Merwin. il por *Forbes* 140:72-5+ Jl 13 '87
The raiders may be sniffing 'round USX again. G. G. Marcial. il *Bus Week* p74 Mr 30 '87
Roderick's plan for an encore will not wow the Street [restructuring] G. L. Miles. il por *Bus Week* p32 F 2 '87
USX contract ends 6-month strike. *Mon Labor Rev* 110:55-6 Ap '87
The USX restructuring takes a bloody turn [$1 billion in write-downs] G. L. Miles. *Bus Week* p35-6 F 16 '87
Waterloo at USX [chairman D. Roderick fends off takeover attempt by C. Icahn] J. Castro. il por *Time* 129:51 Ja 19 '87

Utagawa, Hiroshige *See* Hiroshige (Andō Hiroshige), 1797-1858

Utah
See also
Bryce Canyon National Park (Utah)
Child welfare—Utah
Colorado Plateau
Colorado River (Colo.-Mexico)
Dolores River (Colo. and Utah)
Floods—Utah
Great Salt Lake (Utah)
Hunting—Utah
Lake Powell (Utah and Ariz.)
Motion picture festivals—Utah
Radioactive pollution—Utah
Resorts—Utah
Skis and skiing—Utah

Description and travel
See also
Cruising—Utah
Amazing canyon country. G. S. Bush. il map *Better Homes Gard* 65:128+ Je '87
In Utah's northeastern corner, a hidden, hay-scented valley. il map *Sunset* 179:10-11+ Jl '87

Religious institutions and affairs
See also
Mormons and Mormonism

Ute Indians
Helicopters at Mesa Verde cause run-in with Utes. il *Natl Parks* 61:8 N/D '87

Uterus
See also
Cervix
Placenta

Surgery
See also
Hysterectomy

UtiliCorp United Inc.
Building a powerhouse, one utility at a time [UtiliCorp's acquisitions] M. Ivey. il por *Bus Week* p81 F 2 '87

Utilities, Public *See* Public utilities
Utilities (Computer programs) *See* Computer programming
Utility carts *See* Carts
Utility knives *See* Knives
Utility rates *See* Public utilities—Rates
Utility tables *See* Tables
Utilization of land *See* Land utilization
UTL Corp.
UTL is ready to equip those AWACS. G. G. Marcial. *Bus Week* p130 My 25 '87

Utopias
America as utopia: the city upon a hill. R. A. Nisbet. *Current* 293:4-8 Je '87
Keep your compassion, give me your madness [life of C. Fourier] A. Broyard. il *N Y Times Book Rev* 92:12 Je 21 '87
Stalled thinkers. T. Todorov. *New Repub* 196:26-7 Ap 13 '87

Utopias in literature
Looking back at Edward Bellamy. por *Futurist* 21:52 N/D '87

Utroska, Daniel
Holes in the U.S. nuclear safety net. bibl f il *Bull At Sci* 43:36-40 Jl/Ag '87

Utset, Manuel F., and others
Region-specific expression of two mouse homeo box genes. bibl f il *Science* 235:1379-82 Mr 13 '87

Utt, Ronald
about
Selling Uncle Sam's assets: why Reagan has a real shot now. P. Magnusson. il por *Bus Week* p41 S 28 '87

Utz, Peter
Pan & zoom. il *Pop Photogr* 94:68-9 Ja '87

Uzbekistan (Soviet Union)
Politics and government
Where old ways die hard. S. Strasser. *Newsweek* 109:39 Je 22 '87

Uzzell, Lawrence A.
Neocentralists vs. neopluralists: the battle over educational reform. il *USA Today (Periodical)* 115:70-3 Ja '87
Running the rights scam at DOE. *Natl Rev* 39:39-40+ Mr 13 '87

V

V-tails *See* Airplanes, Light—Tails
VA *See* United States. Veterans Administration
Vacation condominiums *See* Condominiums
Vacation houses
> *See also*
> Beach architecture
> House decoration
> Lakeside architecture

An Appalachian labor of love [150 year old log cabin forms nucleus of weekend retreat] C. Engle. il *South Living* 22:74-5 O '87
Architectural digest visits: Paul Simon [Long Island summer home designed by Paul Krause] J. Thurman. il *por Archit Dig* 44:108-115 S '87
Build-it-yourself! The big-savings way into your own vacation home [special section] P. S. Gelfman. il *Fam Handyman* 37:42+ Ja '87
Buy the beloved country: finding an affordable retreat [within striking distance of New York City] M. W. Robbins. il *N Y* 20:48-56+ My 25 '87
In search of the perfect getaway. P. Dworkin. il *U S News World Rep* 103:59-60 Ag 10 '87
Magnificent obsession: a house in the country [cover story] E. Abeel. il *N Y Times Mag* p20-6+ Ap 19 '87
Maine light: the summer house of Mr. and Mrs. Douglas Auchincloss. S. M. Alsop. il *Archit Dig* 44:188-95 Je '87
A mix of two country styles. L. Joyner. il *South Living* 22:112-13 Jl '87
Notes and comment [summer cottage on Maine coast] *New Yorker* 63:15-16 Ag 10 '87
Of the past, of the place [Seaside, Useppa Island, and Sea Oaks resorts] L. Joyner. il *South Living* 22:120-3 My '87
A place in the sun. C. Luckey. *Changing Times* 41:14 Ap '87
Simplicity was the goal for this vacation house. il *Sunset* 178:158 My '87
The sticks [Pardo weekend house in East Hampton, N.Y.] D. Brenner. il *Archit Rec* 175:134-9 mid-Ap '87
Sunspots [Caribbean] L. J. Gallagher. il *Esquire* 107:36 F '87
Vacation homes: how to cope with the new tax rules. M. Schiffres. il *Changing Times* 41:35-6+ Je '87
Venturing into the country. L. J. Gallagher. il *Esquire* 107:61 Mr '87
The villa transformer [Schwartz/Fiekowsky weekend house, West Stockbridge, Mass.] C. K. Gandee. il *Archit Rec* 175:114-21 mid-Ap '87

Leasing and renting
> *See also*
> Vacation Properties Network

Beating winter in a home away from home [villa and private home rentals in the Caribbean] B. Bauer. il *U S News World Rep* 102:58-9 F 9 '87
Groupies are not necessarily rock fans [finding and sharing a ski house] D. B. Witchel. il *Skiing* 40:151-2+ O '87
Our Regency rental [summer house in Ireland] A. Emmet. il *House Gard* 159:52+ Jl '87
Playing house in the Caribbean. il *Esquire* 108:148-55 O '87
Vacation homes may cut your taxes. H. Porter. *Fam Handyman* 37:12+ Ja '87
What a difference a day makes [tax angles on vacation homes] L. Saunders. il *Forbes* 139:221-2 My 18 '87

Timesharing ownership
See Timesharing (Real estate)
Vacation houses, Condominium *See* Condominiums
Vacation Properties Network
They've got one-stop shopping for vacation homes. P. Houston. il *pors Bus Week* p75 Ag 10 '87
Vacation villages
> *See also*
> Club Méditerranée SA
Vacations
> *See also*
> Camping
> Cruising
> Resorts
> Travel

5 great getaways for fall. il *Harpers Bazaar* 120:156+ O '87
7 great family vacations. C. Kitch. il *Good Housekeep* 204:202 Mr '87

10 retreats for the restless. L. J. Gallagher and W. Lowe. il *Esquire* 107 Summ Traveler:T30-T37 Ap '87
Alaskan adventure [Christmas vacation with the Eskimos] E. Murphy. map *Seventeen* 46:90+ D '87
The art of vacationing. S. A. Franzmeier. il *Nations Bus* 75:83+ My '87
The business of selling adventure. S. Ocko. il *Technol Rev* 90:64-9+ F/Mr '87
Buying adventure—with or without frills. B. Bauer. il *U S News World Rep* 102:52-3 Ja 12 '87
Dream vacations you can afford. il *Glamour* 85:218+ Ag '87
Family adventure vacations. il *Better Homes Gard* 65:183-4+ Ap '87
Focus on spring! [special section] il *Seventeen* 46:142-3 Ap '87
Fun family getaways. E. C. Ray. il *Essence* 18:20+ Jl '87
A gardener's vacation plan. K. Martin. il *Rodale's Org Gard* 34:53-7 Jl '87
Great family vacations. P. Plawin. il *Changing Times* 41:35-9 Jl '87
Heartbreak hotel [Debora Phillips' learning vacations to deal with problems of love] D. Zevin. il *Health* 19:18 Ja '87
Hi-trek holidays [adventure vacations for women] G. Wiltsie. il *Harpers Bazaar* 120:174+ My '87
How to stretch your vacation dollar. il *Good Housekeep* 204:276-7 My '87
Into the outdoors. M. Ingebretsen. il *Better Homes Gard* 65:195-6 O '87
Learn-something-new vacations! il *Better Homes Gard* 65:57-8 Mr '87
Mystery weekend vacations. il *Glamour* 85:86 O '87
On the grapefruit circuit [visiting baseball spring training camps] J. Rachlin. il *U S News World Rep* 102:48 Mr 9 '87
The perfect vacation: a first-class beauty and fashion guide. L. J. Johnson. il *Ladies Home J* 104:110-17 Jl '87
Summer adventures—under $500! N. K. Crowell. il *Women's Sports Fitness* 9:49-51 My '87
Summer school: for singles, couples and families [learning vacations at colleges] G. Hechinger. il *Glamour* 85:364+ Ap '87
Time enough to learn [measurement of summer learning gains; work of Maxine Wintre] P. Chance. *Psychol Today* 21:14 Ap '87
Up, up, and away [weekend outdoor adventure vacations close to New York City] J. Seabury. il *N Y* 20:36-42 Ag 3 '87
Vacationer's atlas. See issues of Travel Holiday beginning March 1984
Weekend getaways. L. Schnurnberger. il *Parents* 62:227-9+ O '87
Weekends European-style. N. Berkowitz. il *Harpers Bazaar* 120:42+ Je '87
What TV stars are doing on their vacations. il *Jet* 72:58-9 Je 8 '87
Whatever happened to the lazy weekend at home? C. P. Work. il *U S News World Rep* 102:65-6 Mr 16 '87
Where seldom is heard a stock ticker [adventure vacations] I. Pave. il *Bus Week* p236-7 N 16 '87
Why solo vacations are my secret salvation. C. Bickley. il *Glamour* 85:28+ Ag '87
A working vacation [instructional workshops that teach rural skills] il *Ctry J* 14:57-60 Ja '87
Your 1987 vacation planner. S. Birnbaum. il *Good Housekeep* 204:54+ Ja '87

Anecdotes, facetiae, satire, etc.
My hotel weekend. E. Berg. il *Parents* 62:48+ F '87
The Type A vacation (or The case for staying home). K. Fury. il *Work Woman* 12:104 Jl '87
What is a perfect vacation? B. Adler. il *Good Housekeep* 205:44 Ag '87

Psychological aspects
Buying a wonderful time (wish you were here!). L. Stains. il *Prevention* 39:68-9 Mr '87
Take a real vacation! B. A. Baldwin. il *Read Dig* 130:89-91 Ap '87
A vacation for the hidden you. M. Golin. il *Prevention* 39:65-7 Mr '87

Vacca, John R.
Restoring America's space treasures. il *Space World* X-8-284:10-13 Ag '87
Vaccines, Anti-pregnancy *See* Contraceptives
Vaccines and vaccination
> *See also*
> AIDS (Disease)—Vaccines and vaccination
> Cats—Diseases and pests—Vaccines and vaccination

Vaccines and vaccination—See also—*cont.*

    Cattle—Diseases and pests—Vaccines and vaccination

    Chicken pox—Vaccines and vaccination

    Children—Diseases—Vaccines and vaccination

    Cytomegalovirus—Vaccines and vaccination

    Dental caries—Vaccines and vaccination

    Dogs—Diseases and pests—Vaccines and vaccination

    Hepatitis—Vaccines and vaccination

    Hib infections—Vaccines and vaccination

    Influenza—Vaccines and vaccination

    Leprosy—Vaccines and vaccination

    Malaria—Vaccines and vaccination

    Measles—Vaccines and vaccination

    Meningitis—Vaccines and vaccination

    Parasitic diseases—Vaccines and vaccination

    Rabies—Vaccines and vaccination

    Rocky Mountain spotted fever—Vaccines and vaccination

    Schistosomiasis—Vaccines and vaccination

    Smallpox—Vaccines and vaccination

    Swine—Diseases and pests—Vaccines and vaccination

    Tuberculosis—Vaccines and vaccination

    Typhoid fever—Vaccines and vaccination

Big shots [adult immunizations] P. Spencer. *Health* 19:73-4+ N '87

A catalogue for the cold chain. il *World Health* p30 Ja/F '87

The cold chain. il *World Health* p13 Ja/F '87

'Cold chain' has meant business for developed world. il *World Health* p30-1 Mr '87

Indo-U.S. vaccine pact disputed. J. Walsh. *Science* 238:19 O 2 '87

New roles for an old-trouper vaccine? [bacillus Calmette-Guérin mycobacteria used as a multipurpose vaccine] *Sci News* 131:396 Je 20 '87

Supervaccines. J. M. Toal. il *Omni* 9:20+ Jl '87

Vaccines for adult diseases. T. Monmaney. il *Newsweek* 110:92-3 O 12 '87

Vaccinia virus *See* Pox viruses

Vachss, Andrew H.

    about

The last angry man: lawyer Andrew Vachss takes to novels to fight child abuse. E. Pooley. il por *N Y* 20:42-4+ My 25 '87

Vacuum

    See also

    American Vacuum Society

Vacuum physics. il *Phys Today* 40:S66-S69 Ja '87

Vacuum cleaner industry

    See also

    Regina Co.

        Advertising

CU wins a round in fight to stay out of advertising [use of Consumers Union ratings in Regina vacuum cleaner commercials] *Consum Rep* 52:526 S '87

Vacuum cleaners

Car vacuum cleaners. M. Thompson. il *Fam Handyman* 37:64-6 D '87

Hand-held cordless vacuum cleaners. il *Consum Rep* 52:260-2 D '87

Vacuum cleaners. il *Consum Rep* 52:254-60 D '87

Vacuum pumps

700 hours of vacuum power [Sigma Tek Gold Label pump] J. M. McClellan. *Flying* 114:104 Jl '87

        Failure

Spiral dive [airplanes] R. L. Collins. il *Flying* 114:12+ D '87

Vacuum failure [causes near crash of Mooney 201] J. Apfelbaum. il *Flying* 114:112 N '87

Vacuum tubes

    See also

    Radio tubes

Seduced by the pure music of Virgin Commies. W. Biddle. il *Discover* 8:68-75 My '87

Vader, J. E.

Big plus for females. por *Sports Illus* 67:100 N 23 '87

Vaessen, Ruud T. M. J., and others

Post-transcriptional control of class I MHC mRNA expression in adenovirus 12-transformed cells. bibl f il *Science* 235:1486-8 Mr 20 '87

Vagelos, P. Roy

    about

The miracle company [cover story] J. A. Byrne. il pors *Bus Week* p84-8+ O 19 '87

Vagina

Woman awarded $6 million after doctor/husband sewed her vagina shut [D. Crandall-Millar] *Jet* 73:12 N 23 '87

Vaginal ring (Contraceptive) *See* Contraceptives

Vagrancy

    See also

    Homeless children

Vagus nerve

Eat to remember [research by James F. Flood and others] S. Weisburd. *Sci News* 131:327 My 23 '87

Modulation of memory processing by cholecystokinin: dependence on the vagus nerve. J. F. Flood and others. bibl f il *Science* 236:832-4 My 15 '87

Vainu Bappu Observatory *See* Astronomical observatories—India

Vakarelis, Janis

    about

Liszt and Prokofiev. R. Freed. il por *Stereo Rev* 52:127 O '87

Vaky, Viron P.

Positive containment in Nicaragua. *Foreign Policy* 68:42-58 Fall '87

Val d'Isère (France)

On skis in L'espace Killy. A. H. Greenberg. il *Skiing* 40:61-5+ D '87

Valaitis, Joseph

    about

A doctor's prize catch. P. Skalka. il *Read Dig* 130:128-32 Mr '87

Valdez, Luis

    about

La bamba [film] Reviews

    Glamour 85:200 Ag '87

    Macleans il 100:47 Jl 27 '87. N. Jennings

    New Yorker 63:71-2 Ag 10 '87. P. Kael

    Roll Stone il p13 Ag 13 '87. A. DeCurtis

    Time il 130:62 Ag 17 '87. R. Corliss

    U S News World Rep il 103:48-9 Ag 10 '87. J. Podhoretz

Putting the border onstage. G. C. Lubenow. il por *Newsweek* 109:79 My 4 '87

Valdivieso, Rafael

A "culture of concern" for at-risk students. *Educ Dig* 52:29-31 Ja '87

Vale, Juliet, and Vale, Malcolm

Knightly codes and piety. bibl il *Hist Today* 37:12-17 N '87

Vale, Malcolm

(jt. auth) See Vale, Juliet, and Vale, Malcolm

Valence (Chemistry)

    See also

    Chemical bonds

Valens, Ritchie, 1941-1959

      Anecdotes, facetiae, satire, etc.

La Bamba Hot Line. B. A. Mason. *New Yorker* 63:27 S 7 '87

Valentine, Bobby

    about

Beers with [interview] B. Shapiro. il por *Sport Mag* 78:23-4 Ag '87

Valentine, Lanci, and Little, Nina Fletcher

Rufus Hathaway, artist and physician. bibl f il *Antiques* 131:628-41 Mr '87

Valentine, Laura

    about

Great looks: a day in the life of a model. il pors *Harpers Bazaar* 120:278-83 Mr '87

Valentine, Michael J.

Spelling for dollars. *Phi Delta Kappan* 69:312-13 D '87

Valentine, Phillip A.

    about

Metaphysical healing [interview] K. J. Halliburton. il por *Essence* 18:20 S '87

Valentine, Scott

    about

Making the big screen scene. il pors *Teen* 31:77 Ag '87

Valentines

      Collectors and collecting

Dating antique valentines. J. C. Schweitzer. il *Antiques Collect Hobbies* 91:42-6 F '87

Valentine postcards were right from the heart. S. S. Carver. il *Antiques Collect Hobbies* 91:76-9 F '87

Valentine's Day

Heartsick. G. Waggoner. il *Esquire* 107:26 F '87

Put your heart into Valentine's Day. *Teen* 31:24 F '87

Where to find that perfect Valentine's feast. T. Segal. il *Bus Week* p89 F 2 '87

Valentine's Day cake *See* Cake
Valentine's Day candy *See* Candy
Valentine's Day cookies *See* Cookies
Valentine's Day desserts *See* Desserts
Valentine's Day dinners *See* Dinners and dining
Valentine's Day gifts *See* Gifts
Valentine's Day wreaths *See* Wreaths
Valentino
about
In Rome: the eternal romance . . . of Valentino. il *Vogue* 177:300-3 My '87
Valentino (Santa Monica, Calif.: Restaurant) *See* Santa Monica (Calif.)—Restaurants, nightclubs, bars, etc.
Valenzeno, Dennis Paul, and Pooler, John P.
Photodynamic action. bibl f il *BioScience* 37:270-6 Ap '87
Valenzuela, Luisa, 1938-
The new Argentina. il *Vogue* 177:248+ Ap '87
Valhi Inc.
Harold Simmons is set to roll another seven [proposal to merge with NL Industries] G. G. Marcial. il por *Bus Week* p106 O 5 '87
Valiunas, Algis
In the capital of modern cruelty. *Commentary* 83:45-56 Ja '87
Valladares, Armando
Against all hope: the prison memoirs of Armando Valladares [condensation] il *Read Dig* 131:172-6+ Jl '87
about
Twenty-two years in Castro's prisons. D. Peerman. il por *Christ Century* 104:1029-33 N 18 '87
Vallance, Jim
about
At work with a wizard of song. N. Jennings. il por *Macleans* 100:38 Jl 6 '87
Valle de las Leñas (Argentina: Resort) *See* Resorts—Argentina
Valle Grande Mountains (N.M.) *See* Jemez Mountains (N.M.)
Valley, Paul
Lessons for UNICEF. il por *World Press Rev* 34:53-4 Mr '87
Valley arts (Periodical)
California's Valley arts. il *Horizon* 30:31-2 Ja/F '87
Valley Forge National Historical Park (Pa.)
They didn't carry out the trash [use of remote sensing to locate hut remains; work of Jay Parrish] R. Monastersky. *Sci News* 132:319 N 14 '87
Valley Mills (Tex.)
Description
We passed this way again [visits 12 years apart] A. Fichter. il *South Living* 22:76 Ag '87
Valli, Frankie
about
A handshake for all seasons. C. P. Alexander. il pors *Time* 129:54 My 11 '87
Valls-Russell, Janice
Donkey business and asinine journalism. il *New Leader* 70:5-7 Ap 6 '87
The future of cohabitation in France. il *New Leader* 70:3-4 Mr 9 '87
The next time you see Paris. il *New Leader* 70:7-8 Jl 1-15 '87
Offering retirement to the ETA. il *New Leader* 70:9-10 N 30 '87
The summer of French discontent. il *New Leader* 70:8-9 S 21 '87
Valonia *See* Algae
Valproic acid
Cytochrome P-450-catalyzed formation of Δ^4-VPA, a toxic metabolite of valproic acid. A. E. Rettie and others. bibl f il *Science* 235:890-3 F 20 '87
Valsan Inc.
Valsan reengining 727-200s to meet noise regulations. *Aviat Week Space Technol* 126:121 F 16 '87
Valsan's 727-200 reengining program enters final design engineering phase [cockpit, fuselage and engine modifications] S. W. Kandebo. il *Aviat Week Space Technol* 127:137+ S 7 '87
Valse fantaisie [ballet] *See* Ballet reviews—Single works
Valsecchi, Pier Fausto Bagatti *See* Bagatti Valsecchi, Pier Fausto, baron
Valsella Meccanotecnica (Firm)
'Irangate' unfolds in Italy [arms smuggling charges against F. Borletti] W. C. Symonds. *Bus Week* p46 S 21 '87
Valuation
See also
Antiques—Valuation
Appraisers
Corporations—Valuation

Real property—Valuation
Value added tax
Politics v. economics. W. F. Buckley. *Natl Rev* 39:62-3 Je 19 '87
Replace social security with a stable, permanent retirement system. N. Gingrich. il *USA Today (Periodical)* 116:22-3 Jl '87
VAT is a bad idea. R. S. McIntyre. il *Atlantic* 259:26-8+ Ja '87
Western Europe
Europe without borders. A. Vernholes. *World Press Rev* 34:56 O '87
Value analysis
See also
Cost effectiveness
Value Line convertibles (Newsletter) *See* Investment newsletters
Value Line Inc.
Mr. Convertibles [A. S. Lyons of Value Line convertibles] P. Brimelow. por *Forbes* 139:109 My 18 '87
Paying the piper [investment formula] W. Baldwin. il *Forbes* 140:208+ O 19 '87
Value of education *See* College education, Value of
Value of life *See* Man—Economic value
Values
How deep are your convictions? [address, March 17, 1987] S. G. Jones. *Vital Speeches Day* 53:492-4 Je 1 '87
Humanists and traditional moral values. L. Hyman. por *Humanist* 47:29+ Mr/Ap '87
Looking to its roots [reestablishing American values] E. Bowen. il *Time* 129:26-9 My 25 '87
Victorian values (I) [cover story; special section] bibl il *Hist Today* 37:14-28 Mr '87
Victorian values (II) [special section] bibl il *Hist Today* 37:27-39 Ap '87
Victorian values (III) [special section] bibl il *Hist Today* 37:30-43 My '87
Victorian values (IV) [special section] bibl il *Hist Today* 37:24-37 Je '87
Victorian values (V) [special section] bibl il *Hist Today* 37:32-45 Jl '87
Victorian values (VI) [special section] bibl il *Hist Today* 37:11-22 Ag '87
Victorian values (VII) [special section] bibl il *Hist Today* 37:33-46 S '87
Study and teaching
See Moral education
Valvano, Jim
about
Beers with . . . [interview] B. Jacobs. il por *Sport Mag* 78:25-6 Ap '87
Valverde, Robert
about
In San Francisco, teacher Robert Valverde fights teen pregnancy with flour power. D. Gorgan. il por *People Wkly* 27:34-5 Ap 27 '87
Valves
See also
Automobile engines—Valves
Motorcycle engines—Valves
Vampires
Count Malabar [J. B. Crutchley kidnaps a woman and drinks one third of her blood] S. Baker. il por *Omni* 9:84 Ja '87
Van, Barbara
about
Career makeover: from bank officer to restaurant V.P. il por *Glamour* 85:170 Ap '87
Van Allen, James Alfred, 1914-
about
Van Allen visits. S. Jochums. *Space World* X-8-284 Space Advocate:3-4 Ag '87
Van Ballenberghe, Victor
Giants of the wilderness: Alaskan moose. il map *Natl Geogr* 172:260-80 Ag '87
Van Beek, Gus W.
Arches and vaults in the ancient Near East [cover story] il map *Sci Am* 257:96-103 Jl '87
Van Berg, Jack, 1936-
about
The home stretch. J. Rolfe. il pors *Sport Mag* 78:49-50+ D '87
Triple Crown showdown. P. Axthelm. il pors *Newsweek* 109:86+ Je 8 '87
Van Bruggen, Coosje *See* Bruggen, Coosje van
Van Buren, Abigail, 1918-
Guest columnist: Dear Abby. por *Teen* 31:12 D '87
Van Cleve, Jane
Golden service: Portland's Contemporary Crafts Gallery marks its 50th year. il *Am Craft* 47:38-41 O/N '87

Van de Stadt, C. Dominique
People. See issues of World Press Review beginning October 1986
Van den Bergh, Sidney, 1929-
Century 21: the age of space junk? il *Sky Telesc* 74:4 Jl '87
Van den Heuvel, Cor, 1931-
Concision, perception, awareness—haiku. il *N Y Times Book Rev* 92:1+ Mr 29 '87
Van der Klugt, Cornelius *See* Klugt, Cornelius van der
Van der Meer, Antonia
How to live with a difficult man. *Redbook* 169:104-5+ My '87
Van Dover, Cindy Lee
ArgoRise: outline of an oceanographic expedition. il *Sea Front* 33:186-94 My/Je '87
Van Eyck, Hubert *See* Eyck, Hubert van, ca. 1366-1426
Van Eyck, Jan *See* Eyck, Jan van, ca. 1390-1441
Van Gelder, Lindsy
AIDS. il *Ms* 15:64+ Ap '87
Alice Miller: the cost of parental tyranny. il por *Ms* 16:82+ O '87
Cross-addiction: surprising results of the Ms. survey. il *Ms* 15:44-7+ F '87
Dependencies of independent women. il *Ms* 15:36-9+ F '87
Enjoying the brave new world of computer music. il *Ms* 16:42+ O '87
Gay gothic. il *Ms* 16:146-7+ Jl/Ag '87
Mad about duck. il *Ms* 16:44+ S '87
Margaret Atwood. il por *Ms* 15:48-50+ Ja '87
Personal politics: a lesson in straight talk. il *Ms* 16:95 N '87
Van Gelder, Lindsy, and Brandt, Pam
Beyond sex ed: school clinics tackle the teen-pregnancy epidemic. il *McCalls* 114:89+ My '87
Van Gelder, Pat
Representing realist artists. il *Am Artist* 51:64-9+ My '87
Van Gogh, Vincent *See* Gogh, Vincent van, 1853-1890
Van Halen, Eddie
about
"He is my life". N. Gittelson. il pors *McCalls* 114:14-15+ F '87
Van Horn, Dana
about
Dana Van Horn. J. Tully. il por *Am Artist* 51:42-7+ F '87
Van Horn, Royal
Laser videodiscs in education: endless possibilities. il *Phi Delta Kappan* 68:696-700 My '87
Van Horn, Welby
The U.S. talent drought: it's elementary. *World Tennis* 34:64 Ja '87
Van Lancker, Diana
Old familiar voices. il *Psychol Today* 21:12-13 N '87 (jt. auth) See Kempler, Daniel, and Van Lancker, Diana
Van Lier, Norm
about
Wrong chemistry brings end for coach Van Lier. por *Jet* 71:46 F 16 '87
Van Lith, Curt
about
A tale of two bucks. J. Murray and M. Pearce. il pors *Outdoor Life* 180:68-9+ Jl '87
Van Ness, Daniel W., 1949-
Punishable by death. il por *Christ Today* 31:24-7 Jl 10 '87
Van Peebles, Mario
about
Eastwood asked Van Peebles to play role in new flick. por *Jet* 71:57 Ja 19 '87
Introducing: Mario Van Peebles. F. White, III. il pors *Ebony* 42:80+ My '87
Mario Van Peebles makes it big in 'Jaws the revenge' [cover story] A. Collier. il pors *Jet* 72:28-30 Jl 27 '87
You've met dad Van Peebles, now here's the son. J. Stark. il pors *People Wkly* 27:91+ Mr 2 '87
Van Peebles, Melvin, 1932-
about
Van Peebles makes most of stock market crash. il por *Jet* 73:6 N 9 '87
Van Pier, Andre
about
Andre Van Pier's bras of gold and crystal inspire a boom at the top. il por *People Wkly* 28:92-3 Jl 13 '87

Van Tieghem, David
about
David Van Tieghem. B. Milkowski. por *Down Beat* 54:15 S '87
Van Tilburg, Johannes
about
Architecture: Johannes Van Tilburg. J. Giovannini. il *Archit Dig* 44:136-42 F '87
Van Vliet, Claire, 1933-
about
Claire Van Vliet's Janus Press. W. T. Taylor. il por *Am Craft* 47:52-9+ F/Mr '87
Van Wachem, L. C.
about
Management by committee—it works. R. I. Kirkland, Jr. por *Fortune* 116:28 Ag 3 '87
Van Zandt, Steve
about
Little Steven lets 'Freedom' ring. A. DeCurtis. por *Roll Stone* p19 My 21 '87
"That road is all mine". J. Cocks. il por *Time* 129:89 My 11 '87
Vanaik, Achin
A White House divided. *World Press Rev* 34:11-12 F '87
VanCaspel, Venita, 1922-
About investing. il *Saturday Evening Post* 259:30+ My/Je '87
About investing. il *Saturday Evening Post* 259:112 Mr '87
Answering your financial questions. il *Saturday Evening Post* 259:16+ D '87
Answering your financial questions. il *Saturday Evening Post* 259:12+ S '87
Making your money grow. *Saturday Evening Post* 259:34+ N '87
about
Helping dollars make sense. H. G. Miller. il pors *Saturday Evening Post* 259:46-7+ Mr '87
Vance, Bob
about
Trouble on three wheels. W. Plummer. il pors *People Wkly* 27:30-3 F 23 '87
Vance, Courtney B.
about
'Hamburger Hill' star says filming was hell. il pors *Jet* 72:56 S 21 '87
Vance, Mary Ann
about
Florida woman wins suit against Southern Bell, who must pay $3.5 million. *Jet* 72:29 My 4 '87
Vancouver (B.C.)
Banks
A bid for major-league banking. P. C. Newman. il por *Macleans* 100:33 F 16 '87
Crime
Epidemic of murder [murders thought to be linked to Washington State serial murderer] J. O'Hara. *Macleans* 100:12 Jl 20 '87
Young and merciless [Chinese gangs] J. O'Hara. il *Macleans* 100:59 O 26 '87
Description
Vancouver a year later. il map *Sunset* 179:32+ S '87
Gardens and gardening
Gardens: levels of beauty [home of Joseph and Rosalie Segal] J. Chatfield-Taylor. il *Archit Dig* 44:152-7 D '87
Hotels, motels, etc.
A slice of history [addition to Sylvia Hotel] P. M. Sachner. il *Archit Rec* 175:108-11 N '87
Music festivals
See Music festivals—British Columbia
Street traffic
Trouble in paradise [skateboarders] J. O'Hara. il *Macleans* 100:48 Ap 6 '87
Vancouver (B.C.). Expo 86 *See* Expo 86 (Vancouver, B.C.)
Vancouver (Wash.)
Education
Inside a school of choice [Alternative Learning Center] R. L. Fizzell. il *Phi Delta Kappan* 68:758-60 Je '87
Vancouver Island (B.C.)
Description and travel
Vancouver Island. A. Furst. il *50 Plus* 27:52-5 Ap '87
Vancouver Island's undersea kaleidoscope: a diver's paradise. L. Wood. il *Sea Front* 33:97-104 Mr/Ap '87
Vancouver Stock Exchange *See* Stock exchanges—Vancouver exchange
Vandalia Gathering (Charleston, W. Va.) *See* Music festivals—West Virginia

Vandalism
See also
Art—Mutilation, defacement, etc.
Graffiti
An echo of past battles [Quebec Court of Appeal decision declaring mandatory French-only signs illegal sparks vandalism] B. Wallace. il *Macleans* 100:14 Ja 12 '87
Just for kicks [vandalism by youths] J. Brondfield. il *Read Dig* 131:33-7 Ag '87

Vanden Heuvel, Katrina
Yevtushenko feels a fresh wind blowing [cover story; interview] il pors *Progressive* 51:24-31 Ap '87

VanDenBerg, John, and Minton, Barbara A.
Alaska native youth: a new approach to serving emotionally disturbed children and youth. il *Child Today* 16:15-18 S/O '87

Vandenberg Air Force Base (Calif.) *See* Air bases

Vandenhove, Charles
about
That Palladian feeling. C. Jencks. il *House Gard* 159:160-5+ Je '87
An unexpected surprise. G. Bekaert. il *Archit Rec* 175:126-35 Jl '87

Vander Zalm, William
about
Revolution on the right. J. Pifer. il por *Macleans* 100:28 Ag 31 '87
Vander Zalm's bold plans. J. O'Hara. il por *Macleans* 100:14-16 N 2 '87

Vanderbilt, Cornelius, 1794-1877
about
My Vanderbilt movie. P. Baida. il *Am Herit* 38:20+ N '87

Vanderbilt, Gloria, 1924-
about
Women facing women. il pors *Vogue* 177:54 Ag '87

Vanderbilt University
Vanderbilt orders frats to integrate or close. *Jet* 71:21 F 23 '87

Vanderbyl, Michael
about
Nouvelle cuisine for the eyes. K. Andersen. il pors *Time* 129:88-9 Je 8 '87

Vanderkooi, Jane M., and others
On the prevalence of room-temperature protein phosphorescence. bibl f il *Science* 236:568-9 My 1 '87

Vandertuin, Jan
Vegetables for all. il *Rodale's Org Gard* 34:72+ S '87

Vanderwerff, Joyce E.
(jt. auth) See Anderson, Roland C., and Vanderwerff, Joyce E.

Vandeweghe, Kiki
about
More than meets the eye. J. McCallum. il por *Sports Illus* 66:162+ F 9 '87

Vandross, Luther
about
Luther Vandross' drummer killed in 17-story leap. il por *Jet* 72:53 Je 29 '87
Vandross buys Rona Barrett Calif. estate for $6 million. il por *Jet* 71:23 F 9 '87
Vandross cancels Phoenix concerts to protest Ariz. snubbing of King holiday. por *Jet* 72:53 Je 15 '87

Vanguard Group Inc.
These funds want to tie the averages [new Bond Market Fund and Quantitative Portfolios] C. S. Eklund. il por *Bus Week* p80 Ja 19 '87
Watching the pennies. J. Clements. *Forbes* 140:164 S 7 '87

Vanguard satellites *See* Artificial satellites—History

Vanguard World-U.S. Growth Fund
Vanguard fires a skipper [Wellington Management Co. ousted] *Money* 16:35 O '87

Vanhecke, Charles
Stroessner still rules as an almost forgotten dictator. *World Press Rev* 34:26 D '87

Vanilla
Versatile vanilla. *Good Housekeep* 205:232 S '87

Vanities (Furniture)
Powder room pair. D. Stover. il *Pop Sci* 231:70-1 Ag '87
Wall-hung vanity. N. Roberts. il *Workbench* 43:71+ My/Je '87

Vanity
about
Prince's intriguing women [cover story] L. Norment. il pors *Ebony* 43:162-3+ N '87

Vanity
Vanity is good for you [views of J. Brothers] por *USA Today (Periodical)* 116:11 Ag '87

Vanity fair (Periodical)
Progress report on three picked as winners. M. S. Forbes. il *Forbes* 139:24 Ja 12 '87

Vanity license plates *See* Automobiles—License plates

Vannevar Bush Award *See* Science—Awards

Vans
Chevy Astro and Ford Aerostar [owners report] M. Lamm. il *Pop Mech* 164:90-2+ D '87
Fleur de Lys Newark [replica vans made in England] D. Nye. il *Road Track* 38:71+ Mr '87
Unique concept [Execucoach, a limousine service using elegant vans] *New Yorker* 63:19-21 Jl 13 '87
Design
Concept Voyager. D. McCosh. il *Pop Sci* 230:18 Ap '87
Ford gets Aerostar in Ghia. P. Lienert. il *Road Track* 39:92+ S '87
Testing
Another small van [Mitsubishi] J. Koblenz. il *Home Mech* 83:79 Jl '87
Chrysler stretches its minivans. M. Ferrara. il *Home Mech* 83:108 N '87
Eddie Bauer Aerostar. D. Fuller. il *Mot Trend* 39 no12 Sp Issue:74-7 '87
High-performance family vans [Chevy Astro/GMC Safari, Dodge Caravan/Plymouth Voyager, Ford Aerostar] D. C. Ross. il *Mot Trend* 39:70-6 Je '87
Living with the Mercedes, the Taurus, the Astro Van. il *Consum Rep* 52:194 Ap '87
Mass transit [family vans] il *Pop Mech* 164:71-5 N '87
The maxi challenge: stretched Voyager tackles Astro and Aerostar. T. Wilkinson. il *Pop Sci* 231:24-6+ O '87
Maxi mini-van [Plymouth Grand Voyager and Dodge Grand Caravan vans] R. Stepler. il *Pop Sci* 231:75 Ag '87
Mini-van challenge [Mitsubishi Wagon LS, Nissan Van GXE, and Toyota Van LE] J. Keebler. il *Pop Sci* 231:90-3 N '87
Mini-vans: maxi versatility [Toyota, Nissan, and Mitsubishi] G. Brown. il *Mot Trend* 39:86-91+ Jl '87
Mitsubishi vans. M. Allen. il *Pop Mech* 164:158+ Ap '87
Mitsubishi Wagon LS. D. Sherman. il *Car Driv* 32:93+ Mr '87
Nissan Van GXE. P. Lyons. il *Car Driv* 33:123-5 Ag '87
Plymouth Grand Voyager LE. T. Assenza. il *Car Driv* 33:75-7+ Jl '87
Plymouth's great Grand Voyager. M. Thompson. il *Fam Handyman* 37:94+ S '87
Versatile van from Japan [Mitsubishi Wagon] H. Shuldiner. il *Pop Sci* 230:33 My '87
Volkswagen Vanagon Syncro. W. Hampton. il *Ctry J* 14:67-8 My '87
Volkswagen Vanagon Wolfsburg Edition. J. R. Nerad. il *Mot Trend* 39:94-5 Jl '87

Vans, Remodeled
Van conversion. R. Mateer. il *Workbench* 43:50+ Mr/Ap '87
Testing
Building a sporting van [Chevrolet Astro] M. Anson. il *Mot Trend* 39:78-9 Je '87

Vanunu, Mordechai
about
A case of treason. A. Bilski. il por *Macleans* 100:25 S 14 '87
Minority report. C. Hitchens. *Nation* 244:387 Mr 28 '87
A right to disobedience? S. Seibert. il por *Newsweek* 110:41 S 7 '87

Vapors
See also
Fumes

Vara, Jon
The housesmith. See issues of Country Journal beginning October 1986

Varelli, Frank
about
Varelli: in from the cold. D. R. Gordon. *Nation* 244:273+ Mr 7 '87

Varga, Bálint András
Liszt galore. il *High Fidel* 37:61 Mr '87
The phenomenon Kocsis. il pors *High Fidel* 37:71-2 Ja '87

Vargas, Pat
Dieter's delight. il *Flower Gard* 31:8+ Je/Jl '87

Vargas, Virgilio Barco *See* Barco Vargas, Virgilio
Vargas Llosa, Mario, 1936-
In defense of the black market; tr. by Alfred J. MacAdam. il *N Y Times Mag* p28-31+ F 22 '87
To nurture Latin democracy [excerpt from address, March 1987] *Harpers* 274:15-18 Je '87

about

The bankers' hero. A. Cockburn. *Nation* 245:402 O 17 '87
Mario meets Crazy Horse. H. G. Chua-Eoan. il *Time* 130:30 S 7 '87
Vargas Llosa's 'demon'. A. D'Orrico. il por *World Press Rev* 34:61 Ag '87
Variable life insurance *See* Insurance, Life
Variable stars *See* Stars, Variable
Variation (Biology)

See also

Mosaics (Biology)
Mutation
Asymmetry of lineages and the direction of evolutionary time. S. J. Gould and others. il *Science* 236:1437-41 Je 12 '87
Biodiversity and the public lands [cover story; special section; with editorial comment by T. H. Watkins] il maps *Wilderness* 50:10-38+ Spr '87
Biological diversity and public policy [Office of Technology Assessment report] S. Shen. il *BioScience* 37:709-12 N '87
Can only evapotranspiration make a tree? [variation in biodiversity by locale; research by David J. Currie and Viviane Paquin] map *Sci News* 132:215 O 3 '87
Community diversity: relative roles of local and regional processes. R. E. Ricklefs. bibl f il *Science* 235:167-71 Ja 9 '87
Deep questions about shallow seas [diversity of species in the waters around the Hawaiian Islands] K. E. F. Watt. il *Nat Hist* 96:60-5 Jl '87
Dual infection of the central nervous system by AIDS viruses with distinct cellular tropisms. Y. Koyanagi and others. bibl f il *Science* 236:819-22 My 15 '87
Genetic analysis of the human malaria parasite Plasmodium falciparum. D. Walliker and others. bibl f il *Science* 236:1661-6 Je 26 '87
Identification and isolation of a variant surface glycoprotein from Trypanosoma vivax. P. R. Gardiner and others. bibl f il *Science* 235:774-7 F 13 '87
Interocean differences in size and nutrition of coral reef sponge populations [cover story] C. R. Wilkinson. il *Science* 236:1654-7 Je 26 '87
Molecular diversity of the human T-gamma constant region genes. P. G. Pelicci and others. bibl f il *Science* 237:1051-5 Ag 28 '87
Report urges funds for conservation biology [report by the Office of Technology Assessment] R. Lewin. il *Science* 236:257-9 Ap 17 '87
Species richness: a geographic approach to protecting future biological diversity [cover story] J. M. Scott and others. bibl f il map *BioScience* 37:782-8 D '87
Suburban "hotbeds of sexual diversity" [New England reptile microhabitat study by M. Klemens] B. D. Stutz. il *Nat Hist* 96:80-3 S '87
The surprising genetics of bottlenecked flies [research by Edwin Bryant and others] R. Lewin. *Science* 235:1325-7 Mr 13 '87
Two bottlenecks for cheetahs? *Sci News* 131:88 F 7 '87
U.S. should take lead in preserving biological diversity. R. C. Cowen. il *Technol Rev* 90:25+ Ag/S '87
Variations pour une porte et un soupir [ballet] *See* Ballet reviews—Single works
Varig SA Viação Aérea Rio-Grandense
Brazil's Varig foresees steady growth in domestic, international air traffic. E. H. Kolcum. il *Aviat Week Space Technol* 127:40-1+ Ag 31 '87
Varig, Cruzeiro share directors, facilities. *Aviat Week Space Technol* 127:44 Ag 31 '87
Varig upgrades computerized passenger information system. *Aviat Week Space Technol* 127:45 Ag 31 '87
Varki, Ajit P.
(jt. auth) *See* Muchmore, Elaine A., and Varki, Ajit P.
Varmus, Harold E.
Oncogenes and transcriptional control. bibl f *Science* 238:1337-9 D 4 '87
Reverse transcription. bibl (p120) il *Sci Am* 257:56-9+ S '87
Varnedoe, Kirk, 1946-
Views of Edo: high and low. il *Art Am* 75:98-105 Jl '87

Varney, Carleton
A visit to the Carters' home in Plains, Georgia. il pors *Good Housekeep* 204:110-13+ Je '87
Varnish and varnishing

See also

Lacquer and lacquering
Varnish removers *See* Paint and varnish removers
Varrelman, Shawn

about

Remembering a special student. J. Fincher. il por *Read Dig* 131:149-54 O '87
Vartanian, Hasmig

about

Hasmig Vartanian at Simonne Stern. M. E. Vetrocq. il *Art Am* 75:185 S '87
Varzi, Achille, 1904-1948

about

Varzi's honor. L. S. Riggs. il pors *Car Driv* 32:143-4+ Mr '87
Vasa (Warship)
A new home for the Wasa. J. Richards-Williams. il *Hist Today* 37:2-3 Ja '87
Vasari
The Vasari diary. See issues of Art News
Vasconcellos, John

about

Okay, we make fun of California; now the state is putting money where its mouth is. Yikes! N. Faber. il por *People Wkly* 27:32+ Mr 2 '87
Vasconcelos, Nana

about

Nana Vasconcelos. G. Santoro. il por *Down Beat* 54:14 Ag '87
Vascular surgery *See* Blood vessels—Surgery
Vascular system *See* Blood vessels; Cardiovascular system
Vases

See also

Tussie mussies
Antiques: companions for flowers. J. Gruen. il *Archit Dig* 44:186-91 Ap '87
The flowers are the show [use of clear vases] L. C. Askey. il *South Living* 22:60-1 N '87
Vases, Roman

See also

Amphoras
Vasilyev, A.
Rx: a conference. *World Press Rev* 34:13-14 Jl '87
Vasinsky, Aleksandr
Democracy is not easy. *World Press Rev* 34:18-19 Ap '87
Vaskevitch, Nahum

about

The British connection. A. Miller. il por *Newsweek* 109:39 Mr 23 '87
The insider scandal travels abroad. S. Koepp. il por *Time* 129:51 Mr 23 '87
Vasoactive intestinal polypeptide
Identification of nuclear receptors for VIP on a human colonic adenocarcinoma cell line. M. B. Omary and M. F. Kagnoff. bibl f il *Science* 238:1578-81 D 11 '87
Vasoconstrictors

See also

Serotonin
Vasodilators
Atherosclerosis KOs anti-spasm fighter [endothelium-derived relaxing factor; research by Donald D. Heistad and others] D. D. Edwards. *Sci News* 132:342 N 28 '87
Vasopressin
Absence of significant cellular dilution during ADH-stimulated water reabsorption. K. Strange and K. R. Spring. bibl f il *Science* 235:1068-70 F 27 '87
Arginine vasopressin as a thyrotropin-releasing hormone. M. D. Lumpkin and others. bibl f il *Science* 235:1070-3 F 27 '87
VASP *See* Viacao Aerea Sao Paolo SA
Vasquez, Andres

about

First Andres Vasquez learned about pain, suffering and patience; then he became a doctor. J. Calio. il pors *People Wkly* 28:73-4 Ag 17 '87
Vasquez, Jorge Luis Ochoa *See* Ochoa Vasquez, Jorge Luis
Vassart, Gilbert, and others
A sequence in M13 phage detects hypervariable minisatellites in human and animal DNA. bibl f il *Science* 235:683-4 F 6 '87

Vasyutin, Vladimir
about
Case history: Vladimir Vasyutin. L. Dorr. il por *Space World* X-3-279:36 Mr '87
VAT *See* Value added tax
Vatican. Biblioteca Apostolica *See* Biblioteca Apostolica Vaticana
Vatican. Cappella Sistina
Art historian James Beck urges the Vatican to clean up its act, not Michelangelo's frescoes [interview] H. Shapiro. il por *People Wkly* 27:69+ Mr 30 '87
Controversy over the Sistine ceiling. J. Dillenberger. *Christ Century* 104:708-9 Ag 26-S 2 '87
Crown moves up Sistine Chapel video [documentary on restoration of Michelangelo's frescoes] il *Publ Wkly* 231:32 Mr 27 '87
Dispelling clouds [restoration of Sistine Chapel frescoes] J. Gardner. *Commonweal* 114:599-601 O 23 '87
He didn't paint by the numbers, but he's getting digitized now [restoration of Michelangelo's frescoes] il *Discover* 8:8 My '87
Michelangelo rediscovered [restoration; cover story] M. K. Talley, Jr. il *Art News* 86:159-70 Summ '87
Out of grime, a domain of light [restoration of frescoes in the Sistine Chapel] R. Hughes. il *Time* 129:86-7 Ap 27 '87
Recovering Michelangelo's true colors. J. Arias. *World Press Rev* 34:60 Ap '87
Storm over the Sistine ceiling. J. Pope-Hennessy. il *N Y Rev Books* 34:16+ O 8 '87
Vatican. Library *See* Biblioteca Apostolica Vaticana
Vatican City
Finance
Did corruption soil Vatican's inner sanctum? [Banco Ambrosiano scandal] J. P. Shapiro. il por *U S News World Rep* 102:10 Mr 9 '87
Following the money [Banco Ambrosiano scandal aftermath] J. Howse. il por *Macleans* 100:11 Jl 27 '87
Hiding behind the walls [arrest warrant issued for P. Marcinkus] S. Allis. il por *Time* 129:54 Mr 9 '87
Spoons & just deserts. *Commonweal* 114:373 Je 19 '87
Vatican bank scandal. *Christ Century* 104:265 Mr 18-25 '87
Vatican horror: a banking scandal widens. por *Newsweek* 109:48 Mr 9 '87
The Vatican's finances [cover story] S. Tully. il *Fortune* 116:28-35+ D 21 '87
The Vatican's money troubles. J.-P. Clerc. *World Press Rev* 34:46 S '87
Why the Vatican needs money. il *Fortune* 115:6 Ap 27 '87
Vatican Council (2nd: 1962-1965)
American Catholics: what's happened to your Church in the last 25 years? [cover story; special issue; with editorial comment by Robert E. Burns] il *U S Cathol* 52:2, 6-61+ Je '87
Vatz, Richard E., and Weinberg, Lee S.
The politics of psychiatry. il *USA Today (Periodical)* 116:71-3 Jl '87
Vaucouleurs, Antoinette de
Obituary
Sky Telesc il por 74:598 D '87. L. J. Robinson
Vaucouleurs, Gerard Henri de
Discovering M31's spiral shape. il por *Sky Telesc* 74:595-8 D '87
Vaudeville
America's 'new vaudevillians'. M. Horn. il *U S News World Rep* 103:64-5 S 14 '87
Vaughan, Chris
Bill Kreutzmann/Mickey Hart: Rhythm Devils. il pors *Down Beat* 11:23-5 N '87
Vaughan, Christopher
Second wind for second-messenger research: how do G proteins and external signals influence intracellular activity? il *BioScience* 37:642-6 O '87
Vaughan, Diane
The long goodbye [cover story] il *Psychol Today* 21:36-8+ Jl '87
about
Headed for a painful breakup? Sociologist Diane Vaughan discusses the warning signs [interview] M. Wilhelm. il pors *People Wkly* 27:97-8+ Mr 2 '87
Vaughan, Richard, 1927-
Chasing a sphinx: Charles the Bold's Burgundy [cover story] bibl il pors map *Hist Today* 37:24-9 My '87
Vaughn, Victoria
My very own write-in campaign. por *Publ Wkly* 232:66 N 27 '87

Vaults (Architecture)
Arches and vaults in the ancient Near East [cover story] G. W. Van Beek. il map *Sci Am* 257:96-103 Jl '87
Vause, Chester A.
(jt. auth) *See* Walker, James S., and Vause, Chester A.
Väyrynen, Raimo
Minimum deterrence, mutual security. *Bull At Sci* 43:45-7 Mr '87
VCRs (Video cassette recorders) *See* Videotape recorders and recording
VD *See* Venereal diseases
VDTs (Video display terminals) *See* Information display systems
Veal
See also
Cooking—Meat
Veblen, Thomas T.
Trees of the trembling earth. il *Nat Hist* 96:42-7 S '87
Vecsey, Christopher
Sun dances, corn pollen, & the cross. il *Commonweal* 114:345-51 Je 5 '87
Vecsey, David
Old at seventeen. il *N Y Times Mag* p50 D 20 '87
Vecsey, Peter
Beers with . . . [interview with L. Bird] por *Sport Mag* 78:19-20 Mr '87
Vedeckis, Wayne V.
(jt. auth) *See* Ali, Masarrat, and Vedeckis, Wayne V.
Vedral, Joyce
"I'm sorry!". il *Parents* 62:91-4 Ap '87
Vega, Suzanne
about
Suzanne Vega. E. Costello. il pors *Stereo Rev* 52:127-9 N '87
Suzanne Vega, ethereal girl. C. McGuigan. il por *Newsweek* 110:69 Ag 3 '87
Suzanne Vega: "Part of my appeal is that I'm not a big sex thing". J. Powell. il por *Glamour* 85:162 D '87
Vega's good 'Standing'. D. Browne. il por *Roll Stone* p81-3 Je 18 '87
Vega's "Solitude standing". M. Peel. por *Stereo Rev* 52:73 Ag '87
Village voice. E. Pooley. il pors *N Y* 20:52-5 Ap 27 '87
Viva la Vega. S. Pond. por *Roll Stone* p24-6 Je 4 '87
When Suzanne Vega peeled away her folkie label, fans found a pop-rock star. K. Hubbard. il pors *People Wkly* 27:71-2 Je 8 '87
Vegetable appetizers *See* Appetizers
Vegetable diet *See* Vegetarianism
Vegetable gardens and gardening
See also
Cold frames
Companion crops
Mulching
Plants—Protection
Rotation of crops
Truck farming
The believe-it-or-not one-day vegetable garden. il *Sunset* 178:88-91 Mr '87
Fall gardening: how to grow a second harvest of vegetables. D. A. Jimerson. il *Better Homes Gard* 65:82-5 Ag '87
A gardener's vacation plan. K. Martin. il *Rodale's Org Gard* 34:53-7 Jl '87
Get a jump on spring. T. Steadman. il *South Living* 22:70-1 Ja '87
Making space matter [customized plant spacing] K. Martin. il *Rodale's Org Gard* 34:68-73 F '87
Planning a medium-sized garden. N. Bubel. il *Ctry J* 14:38-44 Ap '87
Putting your beds to bed. W. Chandoha. il *Ctry J* 14:64-7 O '87
A small garden with high yield. il *South Living* 22:96 Mr '87
The vegetable garden. N. Bubel. See issues of Country Journal beginning October 1986
Insect control
See Insect control
Arizona
How zucchini won 5th-grade hearts [cover story] D. Cavaliere. il *Child Today* 16:18-21 My/Je '87
Colorado
How three bountiful Colorado gardens solved mountain problems. il *Sunset* 178:264-5 My '87

Vegetable gardens and gardening—*cont.*
Connecticut
Self-reliance grows in their garden [C. and P. Bjorke] J. Ruttle. il por *Rodale's Org Gard* 34:66-8 Je '87
Missouri
First comes soil [methods of R. and S. Carpenter] M. Kane. il pors *Rodale's Org Gard* 34:60-3+ Je '87
North Dakota
Deep mulch on the High Plains [Podoll family garden] J. Ruttle. il *Rodale's Org Gard* 34:42-4+ Mr '87
South Carolina
A lesson from a country gardener. il *South Living* 22:94-5 My '87
Southern States
Beat the southern broccoli blues. B. Pleasant. il map *Rodale's Org Gard* 34:80+ N '87
Vermont
A garden gone wild [Vermont forager B. Mraz] J. Burnett. il por *Rodale's Org Gard* 34:84-6 N '87
Vegetable sauces *See* Sauces
Vegetable soups *See* Soups
Vegetable stock *See* Stocks (Cooking)
Vegetables
See also
Cooking—Vegetables
Greens, Edible
Vegetable gardens and gardening
Vegetarianism
See also names of vegetables
The beauty of vegetables. S. O. Daniels. por *Rodale's Org Gard* 34:7-8 D '87
Better veggies ahead. L. Shapiro. il *Newsweek* 110:87-8 O 5 '87
Get fresh! [choosing ripe produce] A. Arnott. il *McCalls* 114:132+ Ag '87
A taste of the Orient. D. S. Wechsler. il *Rodale's Org Gard* 34:28-30 D '87
Drying
See also
Tomatoes—Drying
Hanging the harvest. B. R. Rogers. il *Ctry J* 14:73-5 O '87
Home food drying. N. Bubel. bibl il *Ctry J* 14:50-5 Ag '87
Seed
Heirloom vegetables [seed savers and swappers] W. B. Logan. il *House Gard* 159:62+ My '87
Varieties
Do your own variety trials. D. S. Wechsler. il por *Rodale's Org Gard* 34:61-4 F '87
General Kline's secret army [Cornell's Extension agent R. A. Kline] J. Cook. il pors *Ctry J* 14:36-41 Jl '87
Growing food with that ol' time flavor. S. D. Atchison. il *Bus Week* p106 Mr 2 '87
New plants. il *Flower Gard* 32:21-8+ D '87/Ja '88
New varieties for your garden. il *Rodale's Org Gard* 34:34-7+ Ja '87
Pick of the crop [cover story] B. Elswick. il *Mother Earth News* 104:26-33 Mr/Ap '87
Raising short-season varieties. M. J. Caduto. il *Rodale's Org Gard* 34:98-101 D '87
Special vegetables. R. A. Kline. il *Ctry J* 14:28-32 Ap '87
Ted Torrey interview. J. Lowe. il por *Flower Gard* 32:48+ D '87/Ja '88
Vegetable growing 1987 [cover story] il *Sunset* 178:112-17 Ap '87
Vegetables for a traditional Thanksgiving. N. Bubel. il *Ctry J* 14:64-6 N '87
Vegetarianism
Beyond meat and potatoes [M. Hart's diet] L. Kleinmann. por *Health* 19:40 Jl '87
Does meatless equal painless for arthritics? [work of Lars Sköldstam] *Prevention* 39:100 Ap '87
No fat advantage in meatless meals? [research by Bonnie Worthington-Roberts] il *Prevention* 39:8 N '87
She found a career when she lost 80 pounds; ed. by Maria Mihalik. S. Fraleigh. il por *Prevention* 39:60-2+ N '87
The vegetarian good life [cover story] M. R. Shulman. il *Health* 19:36-9+ Jl '87
Your diet: meatless meals. J. S. Stern. *Vogue* 177:238 Ja '87
Vegetation maps
Detection of Rift Valley fever viral activity in Kenya by satellite remote sensing imagery [vegetation measurement linked to flood conditions that produce mosquitoes] K. J. Linthicum and others. bibl f il maps *Science* 235:1656-9 Mr 27 '87

Rift Valley fever: long-distance diagnosis [vegetation measurement linked to floods and mosquitoes; study by Kenneth J. Linthicum and others] J. Silberner. *Sci News* 131:199 Mr 28 '87
Vehicles
See also
Human powered vehicles
Lunar vehicles
Magnetic levitation vehicles
Motor vehicles
Scooters
Veins
See also
Spider veins
Vela, Rosie
about
Jeans! Rosie Vela model-turned-singer lives in them. J. Powell. il pors *Glamour* 85:244-9 F '87
Sexy looks: celebrity secrets. il pors *Harpers Bazaar* 120:146-57 My '87
Special appearance. pors *Vogue* 177:320-1 Ap '87
Vela (Constellation) *See* Constellations
Velásquez, William C.
about
'All these guys owe Willie'. D. Pedersen. il por *Newsweek* 109:30+ Mr 16 '87
Velázquez, Fidel
about
Death watch in Mexico. T. Rosenberg. il *Nation* 244:500-2+ Ap 18 '87
Velella *See* By-the-wind sailor (Hydrozoa)
Velez, Lisa *See* Lisa Lisa
Veliotes, Nicholas A.
about
A new broom at the AAP. T. Weyr. il pors *Publ Wkly* 232:16-20 N 6 '87
Veljkovic, Morag
Vassili Sulich's desert song. il pors *Dance Mag* 61:66-9 Ja '87
Vellutino, Frank R.
Dyslexia [cover story] bibl (p128) il *Sci Am* 256:34-41 Mr '87
Velu, Thierry J., and others
Epidermal growth factor-dependent transformation by a human EGF receptor proto-oncogene. bibl f il *Science* 238:1408-10 D 4 '87
Venango River Corporation
Rolling right along. A. A. Lappen. il *Forbes* 140:8 D 28 '87
Vendettas *See* Feuds
Vending machines
See also
Triangle Industries, Inc.
Vendors, Street *See* Street trades
Veneers and veneering
Fancy veneer gives new life to cast-off relic [writing desk] B. Gould. il *Workbench* 43:10+ Ja/F '87
Venereal diseases
See also
AIDS (Disease)
Gonorrhea
Herpesviruses
Human papilloma virus
Syphilis
The silent epidemic behind the AIDS epidemic. R. T. Francoeur. *Humanist* 47:25+ Jl/Ag '87
Society still at sexual risk. il *USA Today (Periodical)* 116:8-9 Jl '87
Prevention
Condoms to the rescue: New Zealand's Ettie Rout "made vice safe" in World War I. J. Tolerton. il pors *Ms* 15:28-30 My '87
Contraception fights STD's [sexually transmitted diseases] M. Adero and M. Whigham. il *Essence* 17:13+ F '87
Safe sex 1987: how to make love this year. E. Kunes. il *Mademoiselle* 93:106+ Ag '87
Spermicides for safer sex? M. Karpen. *Health* 19:25 Ag '87
'Two birds, one stone' birth control? *Sci News* 131:296 My 9 '87
Venezia, Mike
about
Muddy track, hopeless long shots . . . it's a living. J. Rolfe. il *Sport Mag* 78:98 Mr '87
Venezolana Internacional de Aviacion SA
VIASA revamps fleet, routes to advance financial recovery. il *Aviat Week Space Technol* 127:58-9 Ag 31 '87

Venezuela
See also
Airplane service stations—Venezuela
Caracas (Venezuela)
Fishing—Venezuela
Industry and state—Venezuela
Investments, American—Venezuela
Natural history—Venezuela
Rain forests—Venezuela
Air Force
F-16s give Venezuelan Air Force realistic combat capability. il *Aviat Week Space Technol* 127:67-8 Ag 24 '87
Antiquities
Points of order: excavations in Venezuela and Colombia put the Ice Age hunters of North America in a new perspective. A. L. Bryan. maps *Nat Hist* 96:6+ Je '87
Defenses
See also
Airplanes, Military—Venezuela
Venezuela—Air Force
Discovery and exploration
The earthly paradise [Orinoco River as Eden; excerpt from The four voyages of Christopher Columbus] C. Columbus. il *Courier* 40:8-9 Ap '87
Industries
See also
Aerovias Venezolanas SA
Petroleum industry—Venezuela
Venezolana Internacional de Aviacion SA
Navy
Venezuelan Navy role expands to meet new border threats. *Aviat Week Space Technol* 127:68 Ag 24 '87
Vengeance *See* Revenge
Venice (Calif.)
Architecture
Her life for art [Bjornson House/Studio] C. K. Gandee. il *Archit Rec* 175:140-7 mid-Ap '87
Galleries and museums
Santa Monica & Venice: a guide to the galleries. map *Art Am* 75:90-1 My '87
Restaurants, nightclubs, bars, etc.
For stars (and crocodiles, too) Rebecca's is the hot new hangout [owners R. and B. Marder] M. Neill. il pors *People Wkly* 28:148-9 S 7 '87
Spécialités de la maison:
72 Market St. Oyster Bar & Grill. C. Bates. il *Gourmet* 47:42+ D '87
Rebecca's. C. Bates. il *Gourmet* 47:42+ Ag '87
Röckenwagner. C. Bates. il *Gourmet* 47:36+ F '87
Venice (Italy)
City planning
Venice is shrinking. M. Rossi. *World Press Rev* 34:58 Ja '87
Description
After April in Paris, try May in Venice. W. C. Symonds. il *Bus Week* p132 Ap 27 '87
'Delicious! Ah! What else is like the gondola?'. D. J. Hamblin. bibl (p147) il *Smithsonian* 18:96-105 Jl '87
Education
Together in Venice [Mauri Booksellers School] H. R. Lottman. il *Publ Wkly* 231:25-7 My 1 '87
Festivals
See also
Carnival (Pre-Lenten festival)—Italy
Historic houses, sites, etc.
See also
Save Venice Inc.
History
Bibliography
Venetian secrets. F. Gilbert. il *N Y Rev Books* 34:37-9 Jl 16 '87
Hotels, motels, etc.
The Cipriani life. B. Kafka. il *Vogue* 177:556+ S '87
Social life and customs
Saving la dolce Venice. G. D. Garcia. il *Time* 130:72-3 S 14 '87
Venice Film Festival *See* Motion picture festivals—Italy
Venice summit, 1987 *See* Economic conferences
Venison
See also
Cooking—Game
Venkataswamy, G.
Cataract in India. il *World Health* p25-6 My '87
Venom
See also
Snake venom

Venrick, E. L., and others
Climate and chlorophyll a: long-term trends in the central North Pacific Ocean. bibl f il maps *Science* 238:70-2 O 2 '87
Ventilation
See also
Air conditioning
Ventilators
Let your house breathe. P. V. Fossel. il *Ctry J* 14:35-9 N '87
Ventilation (Physiology) *See* Respiration
Ventilators
Cool your attic with the sun [attic ventilator that runs on solar power] M. Fillon. il *Workbench* 43:60-1 My/Je '87
Even with air conditioning you need a whole-house fan. P. McCafferty. il *Pop Sci* 230:76+ Ap '87
How to install a bathroom ventilator. P. Barrett. il *Pop Mech* 164:117-20 S '87
The pollution within [use of heat recovery ventilator] P. V. Fossel. il *Ctry J* 14:44-9 S '87
Vents (Hydrothermal) *See* Hot springs
Ventura, Susana *See* Arcade, Penny
Venture (Periodical)
Venture magazine [article submission policy] J. Mandelker. il *Writer* 100:27 S '87
Venture capital
Here come the venture capitalists—again. A. Gabor. il *U S News World Rep* 102:52+ My 18 '87
Venture capital companies
See also
Adler & Company
Bain Capital Fund Limited Partners
D. H. Blair & Co., Inc.
Gabelli Value Partners
Hambrecht & Quist Incorporated
KBA Partners
Maine Capital Corporation
MarketCorp Venture Associates
TA Associates of Boston
Every man a venture capitalist [limited partnership] A. E. Serwer. il *Fortune* 116:107-8 Jl 20 '87
Finding capital in the tax reform era. M. King. il *Black Enterp* 17:60-5 Ap '87
The grass looks greener [venture capitalists going into leveraged buyouts] J. Heins. il *Forbes* 139:50-1 Ja 26 '87
Looking for an angel? *Nations Bus* 75:18 N '87
Silicon Valley phoenixes. C. Barron. il *Fortune* 116:128-9+ N 23 '87
Venture capital: how old dogs learn new tricks. il *Bus Week* p86 N 2 '87
Venture capital is changing course [health care] il *Bus Week* p71 Ag 31 '87
Venture capital's new gold rush [superconductors] J. B. Levine. *Bus Week* p66+ O 5 '87
Wildcatters in the laboratory [medical technology ventures in Houston] T. Mack. il *Forbes* 140:258+ N 16 '87
International aspects
See also
Advent International
Taxation
Raising venture capital now. J. C. Szabo. il *Nations Bus* 75:31-4 F '87
Canada
A strange way to run a company [questionable practices by Technigen Platinum Corp.] D. Francis. il *Macleans* 100:11 S 28 '87
Switzerland
Swiss risk [views of B. Weiss] R. Morais. il por *Forbes* 139:49 Je 1 '87
Ventures, Joint *See* Joint ventures
Venturi, Robert
about
The shape of ourselves—Robert Venturi's chairs. V. J. Scully. il *Archit Dig* 44:62+ Ap '87
Venturino, Janet
When is a cocktail a mocktail? il *Women's Sports Fitness* 9:8-9 Ag '87
Venus (Planet)
See also
Space flight to Venus
April's occultation of Venus. D. Di Cicco. il *Sky Telesc* 74:214-16 Ag '87
A beautiful occultation of Venus. S. J. O'Meara. il *Sky Telesc* 73:412 Ap '87
Atmosphere
Laying bare Venus' dark secrets [infrared observations with the Anglo-Australian Telescope] D. A. Allen. il *Sky Telesc* 74:350-3 O '87

Venus (Planet)—*cont.*

Geology

Evidence for divergent plate-boundary characteristics and crustal spreading on Venus. J. Head and L. S. Crumpler. bibl f il maps *Science* 238:1380-5 D 4 '87

Surface

Fractured Aphrodite [plate tectonics; research by James W. Head and Larry S. Crumpler] *Sci Am* 257:19 Jl '87

Was Venus wet? Deuterium reconsidered. D. H. Grinspoon. bibl f il *Science* 238:1702-4 D 18 '87

Vera, Billy

about

Billy Vera's big moment. M. Goldberg. il por *Roll Stone* p28 F 26 '87

You won't catch pop veteran Billy Vera sneering at a hit song—at least not At this moment. R. Wolmuth. il pors *People Wkly* 27:52-3 Mr 16 '87

Veracruz (Mexico: State)

Description and travel

The road to Veracruz. M. Richie. il *Américas* 39:22-5+ Mr/Ap '87

Verapamil

Drug resistance: malaria-cancer similarity? J. Silberner. *Sci News* 131:148 Mr 7 '87

Reversal of chloroquine resistance in Plasmodium falciparum by verapamil. S. K. Martin and others. bibl f il *Science* 235:899-901 F 20 '87

Verba, Sidney

(jt. auth) See Schlozman, Kay L., and Verba, Sidney

Verbal insults *See* Invective

Verbo Church *See* Pentecostal churches—Guatemala

Verde River (Ariz.)

The House abandons a desert dam [compromise on Cliff Dam on Verde River and Central Arizona Project] D. Dagget. il *Sierra* 72:84+ N/D '87

Verdecchia, Enrico

It could be your office that is 'sick'. *World Press Rev* 34:50 My '87

Verderber, Gustav W.

Botanical close encounters. il *Conservationist* 42:40-3 N/D '87

Verdi, Giuseppe, 1813-1901

about

Aida [opera] Reviews
   Time il 129:87 My 18 '87
Un ballo in maschera [opera] Reviews
   Opera News il 52:33 D 19 '87
Nabucco [opera] Reviews
   New Yorker 62:76+ Ja 26 '87. A. Porter
Rigoletto [opera] Reviews
   Opera News il 51:26-9 Ja 3 '87
La traviata [opera] Reviews
   Opera News il 52:28-30, 32 D 19 '87
Il Trovatore [opera] Reviews
   N Y 20:83-5 N 30 '87. P. G. Davis
   New Yorker 63:129-30 N 30 '87. A. Porter
   Newsweek il 110:86 N 23 '87. L. Shapiro
   Opera News il 52:14-17+ D 19 '87. M. O. Lee
   Opera News il 52:22-3, 26 D 19 '87

Verdiglione, Armando

about

Letter from Europe. J. Kramer. *New Yorker* 63:88+ Je 8 '87

Verdin, Eric M., and others

Visualization of viral clearance in the living animal. bibl f il *Science* 236:439-42 Ap 24 '87

Verdoorn, Todd A., and others

Rat brain N-methyl-D-aspartate receptors expressed in Xenopus oocytes. bibl f il *Science* 238:1114-16 N 20 '87

Vereen, Ben

about

Ben Vereen's daughter killed in car accident. il pors *Jet* 73:28 D 21 '87

Vereen, Naja, d. 1987

about

Ben Vereen's daughter killed in car accident. il pors *Jet* 73:28 D 21 '87

Veres, Gabor, and others

The molecular basis of the sparse fur mouse mutation. bibl f il *Science* 237:415-17 Jl 24 '87

Vergès, Jacques

about

In France, when a terrorist needs a lawyer, Jacques Vergès usually gets the call. P. Andriotakis. il pors *People Wkly* 27:109-10 Mr 9 '87

Letter from Europe. J. Kramer. *New Yorker* 63:130-6+ O 12 '87

Standing up for Barbie. M. McIver. il por *Macleans* 100:41 My 25 '87

Verheylewegen, Jamy

about

He's unknown now, but the world's top underwater artist is waiting for his reputation to surface. il pors *People Wkly* 28:147 N 30 '87

Verhoeven, Paul

about

RoboCop [film] Reviews
   Macleans 100:47 Jl 27 '87. L. O'Toole
   N Y il 20:58+ Jl 27 '87. D. Denby
   New Yorker 63:72-3 Ag 10 '87. P. Kael
   Newsweek il 110:58-9 Jl 20 '87. D. Ansen
   People Wkly il 28:12 Jl 27 '87. S. Haller
   Time il 130:75 Jl 27 '87. R. Corliss

Verification of disarmament compliance *See* Disarmament—Inspection; Nuclear weapons—Testing—Detection

Verification of nuclear test ban compliance *See* Nuclear weapons—Testing—Detection

Verissimo, Luiz Fernando

Millions of Brazilians—all unreasonable. *World Press Rev* 34:34 O '87

Verity, Calvin William

about

Can Verity pick up where Baldrige left off? S. J. Dryden and M. Schroeder. por *Bus Week* p30 Ag 24 '87

A letter to Mr. Verity. *Natl Rev* 39:19-20 S 11 '87

Verlaine, Tom

about

The cult of Verlaine. K. Dieckmann. por *N Y* 20:22 Ag 10 '87

Tom Verlaine. G. Santoro. il por *Down Beat* 54:14 D '87

Vermont

See also
Architecture, Domestic—Vermont
Blacks—Vermont
Courts—Vermont
Hunting—Vermont
Jazz music—Vermont
Rural planning—Vermont
Vegetable gardens and gardening—Vermont

Description and travel

See also
Cycling—Vermont

Vermont in art

Gary Milek [egg tempera paintings] E. Feit. il *Am Artist* 51:64-9+ O '87

Vermonters

Anecdotes, facetiae, satire, etc.

Last laugh. il *Mother Earth News* 105:128 My/Je '87

Last laugh. il *Mother Earth News* 104:132 Mr/Ap '87

Vernal equinox

An ancient shell game: balancing eggs to celebrate the spring. S. Morris. il *Omni* 9:114-15 Mr '87

Vernholes, Alain

Europe without borders. *World Press Rev* 34:56 O '87

Vernon, Adele

No room for a hermit. il *Int Wildl* 17:22-4 N/D '87

Vernon, Raymond, 1913-

Ethics of transnationalism. *Society* 24:53-6 Mr/Ap '87

Vernon, Russ

about

Groceries with glamour. J. C. Snow. il por *Nations Bus* 75:57-8 Mr '87

Vernon (Lillian) Corporation *See* Lillian Vernon Corporation

Verona (Italy)

Music

See also
Opera—Italy

Verona International Jazz Festival *See* Music festivals—Italy

Veronica Ristorante Italiano (New York, N.Y.) *See* New York (N.Y.)—Restaurants, nightclubs, bars, etc.

Versatile Corp.

Seeking new salvation [seeks Canadian government contract to build Polar 8 icebreaker] J. O'Hara. il *Macleans* 100:36 Mr 16 '87

Verschuur, Gerrit L., 1937-

Something passing in the night. il *Astronomy* 15:26-31 D '87

Verticillium wilt *See* Wilt diseases

Vertigo *See* Dizziness

Vertol Company *See* Boeing Co. Boeing Vertol Company (Div.)

Veruschka *See* Lehndorff, Vera

Very high-frequency omnirange receivers *See* Radio in aviation

Very high speed integrated circuits *See* Integrated circuits
Very Large Array radio telescope *See* Radio telescopes
Very large scale integrated circuits *See* Integrated circuits
Very Long Baseline Array network of radio telescopes
　See Radio telescopes
Very long baseline interferometry *See* Interferometers and
　interferometry
Veselka, Vanessa
　(jt. auth) See Ellerbee, Linda, and Veselka, Vanessa
Vesilind, Prit J.
　Antarctica. il map *Natl Geogr* 171:556-60 Ap '87
　Brazil: moment of promise & pain. il maps *Natl Geogr*
　171:348-85 Mr '87
Vespa (Motor scooter) *See* Motor scooters
Vespers (Music)
　See also
　　Tape recordings—Vespers (Music)
Vesta (Asteroid) *See* Asteroids
Vesteq Financial Corporation
　The once and future fat cat [workout specialist C. Hall]
　L. M. Keefe. por *Forbes* 139:106 Je 29 '87
Vestron Inc.
　Fancy dancing. G. Morgenson. il por *Forbes* 140:194
　S 21 '87
　A jungle war over the 'Platoon' video. il *Newsweek*
　110:56 N 23 '87
　Lights, camera, lawyers! [battle over video rights to
　Platoon] W. Harris. il *Forbes* 140:33 Ag 10 '87
　The rise and stall of Vestron Inc. M. Frankel. il *Channels*
　7:57-9 O '87
Vests
　Rekindling a vested interest [men's vests] R. La Ferla.
　il *N Y Times Mag* p46 Ag 16 '87
Veterans
　See also
　　Black veterans
　　United States. Veterans Administration
　　Vietnam Veterans Memorial (Washington, D.C.)
　　Welcome Home concert, 1987
　　Women veterans
　Oliver Stone's Platoon buddies recall the war 20 years
　later. il por *People Wkly* 27:81-4+ My 11 '87
　Return to Wake [World War II veterans] R. Wilkerson.
　il *Am Hist Illus* 22:46-8 D '87
Benefits
　Caught in the VA-Medicaid trap [veterans needing nursing
　home care] S. Nohlgren. *50 Plus* 27:23 O '87
Employment
　The 9 to 5 Garage [Bronx Volvo garage owned by
　Vietnam veterans] W. Weith. il *Car Driv* 32:25-6 Mr
　'87
　Do you discriminate against Vietnam vets? L. Washer.
　Work Woman 12:21-2 Mr '87
　Labor force status of Vietnam-era veterans. S. R. Cohany.
　bibl f il *Mon Labor Rev* 110:11-17 F '87
Health and hygiene
　See also
　　AIDS (Disease) and veterans
　　United States. Veterans Administration—Hospitals
　Agent Orange study hits brick wall [Vietnam veterans]
　W. Booth. il *Science* 237:1285-6 S 11 '87
　Answers at last? [Agent Orange research] J. Gardner.
　il *Nation* 244:460-2 Ap 11 '87
　Caught in the VA-Medicaid trap [veterans needing nursing
　home care] S. Nohlgren. *50 Plus* 27:23 O '87
　Is alcoholism a disease? [case of Eugene Traynor and
　James P. McKelvey vs. the Veterans Administration]
　C. Holden. *Science* 238:1647 D 18 '87
　A piece of the action [Agent Orange litigation and lawyer
　compensation] D. Fanning. il *Forbes* 140:68 O 19
　'87
　A war with hope [Vietnam vet's battle with Agent
　Orange-induced cancer]; ed. by John Grossmann. E.
　Zumwalt, III. il por *Health* 19:86+ Je '87
Mortality
　Deadly aftermath for Vietnam veterans [study by the
　Centers for Disease Control] B. Bower. *Sci News* 131:117
　F 21 '87
Political activities
　The hunger artists [fast by veterans protesting U.S. policy
　in Nicaragua] W. F. Schulz, Jr. il *Progressive* 51:14-15
　Je '87
　A VFW post with a spiritual vision [Bill Motto Post
　5888] C. W. Bare. *Christ Century* 104:193-4 F 25
　'87
Psychology
　Lifting the Vietnam stigma. M. Stout. por *U S News
　World Rep* 103:10 N 16 '87
Veterans Administration *See* United States. Veterans
　Administration

Veterans Affairs Dept. (U.S.) *See* United States. Dept.
　of Veterans Affairs
Veterans' memorials *See* War memorials
Veterans of Foreign Wars of the U.S.A.
　A VFW post with a spiritual vision [Bill Motto Post
　5888] C. W. Bare. *Christ Century* 104:193-4 F 25
　'87
Veterans' organizations
　See also
　　Royal Canadian Legion
　　Veterans of Foreign Wars of the U.S.A.
Veterinary drugs
　See also
　　Ivermectin
　You can mix probiotics with certain antibiotics. *Success
　Farm* 85:58 S '87
Labeling
　Kitty odor product seized [Scent-free product mislabeled
　as drug] D. Farley. il *FDA Consum* 21:37-8 Je '87
Veterinary hospitals
Great Britain
　Driver, spare that hedgehog [St. Tiggywinkle's clinic in
　Aylesbury] il *Time* 130:38 N 23 '87
Veterinary medicine
　See also
　　First aid for animals
　　Pets—Care
　　Veterinary hospitals
　Chiropractic for animals? R. H. Pitcairn. il *Prevention*
　39:81-4 Ja '87
　His life is a zoo [Baltimore Zoo head veterinarian M.
　Cranfield] D. Young. il por *South Living* 22:145 Mr
　'87
　Something about Nancy Belser rubs animals the right
　way. il por *People Wkly* 27:121 My 18 '87
Africa
　War on cattle disease divides the troops [rinderpest]
　J. Walsh. il map *Science* 237:1289-91 S 11 '87
Veterinary surgery
　See also
　　Elephants—Care
Veto
　Congress smells blood after Reagan's highway-bill defeat
　. . . R. Fly and D. Harbrecht. *Bus Week* p35 Ap
　20 '87
　Despite a college try, the Gipper loses one [congressional
　override of highway bill veto] il *Newsweek* 109:23
　Ap 13 '87
　The Gipper goes down [Congress overrides R. Reagan's
　highway legislation veto] A. Plattner. il *U S News
　World Rep* 102:22 Ap 13 '87
　Just saying no [Reagan veto strategy] F. Barnes. *New
　Repub* 196:8+ My 11 '87
　Road warriors [Congress overrides R. Reagan's veto
　of highway bill] W. Shapiro. il por map *Time* 129:16-19
　Ap 13 '87
　Whose credibility? [congressional override of R. Reagan's
　veto of highway bill] W. F. Buckley. *Natl Rev* 39:61
　My 8 '87
VF Corp.
　Back to basic blues [women's jeans] M. Morris. il *Work
　Woman* 12:55-6 Je '87
VFR (Visual flight rules) *See* Airplanes—Piloting
VFW *See* Veterans of Foreign Wars of the U.S.A.
VHF radiotelephone on ships, boats, etc. *See* Radiotelephone
　on ships, boats, etc.
VHSIC (Very high speed integrated circuits) *See* Integrated
　circuits
Viação Aérea Rio-Grandense *See* Varig SA Viação Aérea
　Rio-Grandense
Viacao Aerea Sao Paolo SA
　VASP plans to trim workforce, improve operations in
　quest for profitability. il *Aviat Week Space Technol*
　127:47-8 Ag 31 '87
Viacom International Inc.
　Home rule comes to a former O&O [KMOV, St. Louis]
　R. Buck. il *Channels* 7:14 Jl/Ag '87
　Now Redstone is a media giant [S. Redstone wins Viacom]
　D. Lieberman and L. Therrien. il por *Bus Week* p42
　Mr 16 '87
Il viaggio a Reims [opera] See Rossini, Gioacchino,
　1792-1868
VIASA *See* Venezolana Internacional de Aviacion SA
Vibration
　See also
　　Motorcycles—Vibration
　　Oscillations
　Sensory tuning of lateral line receptors in Antarctic fish
　to the movements of planktonic prey [teleosts] J. C.
　Montgomery and J. A. Macdonald. bibl f il *Science*
　235:195-6 Ja 9 '87

Vibration Society (Musical group)
The Vibration Society. M. Bourne. il *Down Beat* 54:14-15 Mr '87
Vice
See also
Pornography
Prostitution
Vice-Presidents
Religion
See also
Bush, George, 1924——Religion
Vichy government *See* France—History—German occupation, 1940-1945
Vickery, Ann M., and Melosh, H. J.
The large crater origin of SNC meteorites. bibl f il *Science* 237:738-43 Ag 14 '87
Vickery, Jim Dale
The land is alive with wolves . . . il *Audubon* 89:52-61 Ja '87
Vicksburg (Miss.)
Galleries and museums
See also
Old Court House Museum-Eva Whitaker Davis Memorial
Toys and Soldiers Museum (Vicksburg, Miss.)
Vico (New York, N.Y.: Restaurant) *See* New York (N.Y.)—Restaurants, nightclubs, bars, etc.
Victims of crime
See also
Asian Americans—Crimes against
Black women—Crimes against
Blacks—Crimes against
Children—Crimes against
Hostages
Parents of murdered children
Salvadorans—United States—Crimes against
Son of Sam laws
Women—Crimes against
Crime and punishment (U.S.A.). il *Read Dig* 131:54-8 Jl '87
The dynamics of blame. A. Gross. *Vogue* 177:783+ S '87
Houston man waits in dark, kills assailant [B. Gibson slays man who had robbed him of his social security money] *Jet* 72:12 Ag 24 '87
How many times does a victim have to pay? A. Smith. il *Esquire* 108:83-4 N '87
Incident in the park [mugging and theft of bicycle in Central Park] D. Galef. il *N Y Times Mag* p56 F 8 '87
Let's be careful out there [self blame] R. C. Davis. *Psychol Today* 21:10 Ag '87
Redress for victims of crime [Canada] M. Rose. *Macleans* 100:21 N 16 '87
Washington watch [extending the Victims of Crime Assistance Act] S. Goen. il *Ms* 16:75 D '87
Whose trial is it anyway? [defense lawyers attacking victims and prosecutors in court] R. Lacayo. il *Time* 129:62 My 25 '87
Victoria, Queen of Great Britain, 1819-1901
about
Victorian in name only, the queen was amused in the bedroom and elsewhere [interview with S. Weintraub] L. Rozen. il pors *People Wkly* 27:58+ Je 22 '87
Victoria (B.C.)
Transit systems
This summer, one more way to get to Victoria by water. il *Sunset* 179:34-5 Ag '87
Victorian architecture *See* Architecture, Victorian
Victorian art *See* Art, Victorian
Victorian Christmas decorations *See* Christmas decorations
Victorian house decoration *See* House decoration, Victorian
Victorian painting *See* Painting, Victorian
Victorian period
Adventurous Victorians [women] L. Siemers. il *Travel Holiday* 167:92 My '87
Classes and the masses in Victorian England. G. Crossick. bibl il *Hist Today* 37:29-35 Mr '87
Victorian values (I) [cover story; special section] bibl il *Hist Today* 37:14-28 Mr '87
Victorian values (II) [special section] bibl il *Hist Today* 37:27-39 Ap '87
Victorian values (III) [special section] bibl il *Hist Today* 37:30-43 My '87
Victorian values (IV) [special section] bibl il *Hist Today* 37:24-37 Je '87
Victorian values (V) [special section] bibl il *Hist Today* 37:32-45 Jl '87
Victorian values (VI) [special section] bibl il *Hist Today* 37:11-22 Ag '87

Victorian values (VII) [special section] bibl il *Hist Today* 37:33-46 S '87
Bibliography
Paperback history. P. Adelman. *Hist Today* 37:57 Ja '87
Victorville (Calif.)
Education
A teen fights for frog rights, and bio may never be the same [J. Graham refuses to dissect frog in biology class] il por *People Wkly* 27:109 My 25 '87
Victory City
The world according to Orville [O. Simpson] A. Fadiman. il por *Life* 10:15-16+ S '87
Victory Hotel (Stockholm, Sweden) *See* Stockholm (Sweden)—Hotels, motels, etc.
Vicunas
Gathering the golden fleece. P. E. Rogers. il *Américas* 39:34-9 S/O '87
My two decades with America's camels [llamas, alpacas, guanacos and vicunas; cover story] W. L. Franklin. il *Int Wildl* 17:34-43 S/O '87
Vidal, Gore, 1925-
The con-man as Peck's bad boy. il *Newsweek* 110:20 Jl 13 '87
Dawn Powell, the American writer. il *N Y Rev Books* 34:52-60 N 5 '87
The making of the president [fiction] il *Harpers* 274:31-4 My '87
about
Anti-Semitism, left & right [discussion of November 1986 article, The hate that dare not speak its name] N. Podhoretz. *Commentary* 83:2+ Mr '87
Making McKinley sexy. S. Waldman. *Wash Mon* 19:45-6+ S '87
The rise and fall of the American empire [interview] A. P. Sanoff. por *U S News World Rep* 103:62 Jl 13 '87
The white peril. J. M. Fallows. il *Atlantic* 259:18+ My '87
Vidal-Hall, Judith
The new battle for Lebanon. il *World Press Rev* 34:28-9 Je '87
Vidal Rucabado, Luis
Argentina's Switzerland. il *World Press Rev* 34:62 Ag '87
Vidalia onions *See* Onions
Vida's Vintage Vehicles Antique Car Museum
A showroom of classics. il *South Living* 22:27 Mr '87
Video art
Avant-garde art for videophiles. T. Carson. il *Bus Week* p120 Je 1 '87
Exhibitions
Nam June Paik at Holly Solomon. W. Robinson. il *Art Am* 75:157 Je '87
Where we are now [Homo video at the New Museum in New York] M. Gever. il *Art Am* 75:43-9 Jl '87
Wolfgang Staehle at Daniel Newburg. P. McGrath. il *Art Am* 75:125-6 Jl '87
Video broadcasting *See* Television broadcasting
Video camera shutters
Super slo-mo at home [high speed shutters] J. B. Meigs. il *Pop Mech* 164:38 Ag '87
Video cameras
8mm crystal ball. J. B. Meigs. il *Pop Mech* 164:61-2 Ap '87
8mm vs. VHS [camcorders] S. Sweetow. il *Petersens Photogr Mag* 15:54-5+ Ja '87
All about camcorders. M. J. Ficeto. il *Good Housekeep* 205:100 S '87
Aspects of camcorder choice. D. Ranada. il *High Fidel* 37:20 F '87
Electronic still cameras [PMA Show] G. Schaub. il *Pop Photogr* 94:69-70 My '87
Electronic still cameras hit the marketplace. G. Schaub. il *Pop Photogr* 94:70-1 S '87
Electronics roundup [camcorders at the Summer Consumer Electronics Show] P. Sealfon. il *Petersens Photogr Mag* 16:12+ S '87
ESP: image of the future [electronic still photography] S. A. Booth. il *Pop Mech* 164:16+ F '87
Family fun for summer: camcorders, VCRs are all the rage. il *Ebony* 42:29-30+ Je '87
Filmless photos. J. Free. il *Pop Sci* 231:54-5 N '87
Format furor. P. Hoban. il *N Y* 20:14-15 F 16 '87
Format wars [VHS vs. 8mm] J. B. Meigs. il *Roll Stone* p43-4 Ja 15 '87
The important things about photography will not change [video still cameras] N. Rothschild. il *Pop Photogr* 94:10 Ja '87
Kodak electronic photos [still video systems] S. A. Booth. il *Pop Mech* 164:40 O '87

Video cameras—*cont.*

Kodak launches a new still video system. N. Goldberg. il *Pop Photogr* 94:68-70 S '87

Korea ups the ante [4mm format] S. A. Booth. il *Pop Mech* 164:57 My '87

Let's go to the videotape. M. Grimm and T. Grimm. il *Travel Holiday* 168:16-17+ Jl '87

Making movies [camcorders] J. B. Meigs. il *Pop Mech* 164:88-90+ Ja '87

New camcorders bring pro features home. E. Stecker. il *Pop Photogr* 94:72-3 S '87

Poor man's storage scope. D. Bernard. il *Radio-Electron* 58:113-14 N '87

Solid pictures, or gathering MOS. D. Ranada. il *High Fidel* 37:16 O '87

Taking the fifth [camcorders at the Winter Consumer Electronics Show] G. Schaub and E. Stecker. il *Pop Photogr* 94:74-5 Ap '87

Video [PMA Show] E. Stecker. il *Pop Photogr* 94:69 My '87

Video wars: the camcorder revolution. M. C. Lehrer. il *USA Today (Periodical)* 115:66-8 Ja '87

Why 8mm? D. Ranada. il *High Fidel* 37:47-8+ F '87

Care

See Video cameras—Maintenance and repair

Maintenance and repair

Clean machines. C. Gromer. il *Pop Mech* 164:111-13 Ja '87

Testing

Autumn and Super VHS [camcorders by JVC] il *High Fidel* 37:8+ N '87

A buyer's guide to camcorders. F. Vizard. il *Radio-Electron* 58:47-51 Mr '87

Canovision VM-E2 [camcorder] S. Sweetow. il *Petersens Photogr Mag* 16:60-1 Ag '87

Creative camcorder [Minolta 3300] E. Stecker. il *Pop Photogr* 94:98+ N '87

A handier Handycam. A. Goldsmith. il *Pop Photogr* 94:54-5 Jl '87

Instant replay [camcorders] J. B. Meigs. il *Pop Mech* 164:74-7+ F '87

Kidcorder [Fisher-Price camcorder] W. J. Hawkins. il *Pop Sci* 231:59 Ag '87

Lensmanship [Minolta C-3300 VHS C camcorder] il *High Fidel* 37:12 My '87

Minolta C3300 VHS-C camcorder. M. Stensvold. il *Petersens Photogr Mag* 16:12 Jl '87

Minolta: hands on [Master C-3300 camcorder] J. B. Meigs. il *Pop Mech* 164:37+ D '87

Minolta Master C-3300 VHS-C camcorder. S. Sweetow. il *Petersens Photogr Mag* 16:58-9 S '87

The new home movies [camcorders] il *Consum Rep* 52:656-61 N '87

The new video camcorders. C. Begole. il *Better Homes Gard* 65:200+ N '87

Olympus Movie 8 [camcorder] S. Sweetow. il *Petersens Photogr Mag* 15:45-6 Mr '87

Palm-sized camcorder—smallest unit yet is a complete VCR, too [Samsung 4mm unit] W. J. Hawkins. il *Pop Sci* 230:47+ My '87

Panasonic 5000 digital video camera. D. Brooks. il *Petersens Photogr Mag* 16:66-9 My '87

Pentax Movie 8 [mini-camcorder] S. Sweetow. il *Petersens Photogr Mag* 16:51-2 Je '87

Play it again, camcorders. B. Young. il *Roll Stone* p81+ O 22 '87

Sony CCD-V110 camcorder. S. Sweetow. il *Petersens Photogr Mag* 16:46-7 Jl '87

Two Minolta camcorders. S. Sweetow. il *Petersens Photogr Mag* 15:52-4 Ap '87

Vivitar Magic 8 camcorder. S. Sweetow. il *Petersens Photogr Mag* 16:52+ N '87

Video cassette recorders *See* Videotape recorders and recording

Video cassettes *See* Videotapes

Video conferencing *See* Teleconferencing

Video dating *See* Videotapes—Social aspects

Video discs *See* Videodiscs

Video display terminals *See* Information display systems

Video editors (Videotapes) *See* Videotape recorders and recording—Equipment

Video equipment

See also

Television projection

Television receivers

Television stations—Equipment

Videotape recorders and recording

Communications in 2001—the third age of video. C. N. Judice. il *Radio-Electron* 58:102-5 My '87

Home video. J. B. Meigs. See issues of Popular Mechanics beginning January 1986

Video and the digital revolution. G. Brockhouse. il *High Fidel* 37:51+ N '87

Video news. D. Lachenbruch. See issues of Radio-Electronics

Video's new image. R. Jaccoma. il *Stereo Rev* 52:70-3 O '87

Exhibitions

Berlin International Audio and Video Fair. M. Smolen. il *Stereo Rev* 52:99-103 D '87

Video games

See also

Bally Manufacturing Corp.

Computer novels

Electronic Arts Inc.

Interactive computer periodicals

Sex in video games

"After MAD": a computer game of nuclear strategy that ends in a Prisoner's Dilemma. A. K. Dewdney. il *Sci Am* 257:174-7 O '87

Enter the 'silent service' [submarine simulation video games] *U S News World Rep* 102:42 Je 15 '87

Games that grownups play [designed for business computers] P. Elmer-Dewitt. il map *Time* 130:68 Jl 27 '87

Here come the Super Mario Bros. N. Gross. il *Bus Week* p138 N 9 '87

A program called MICE nibbles its way to victory at the first Core War tournament. A. K. Dewdney. il *Sci Am* 256:14-16+ Ja '87

VCR games for grownups. T. Segal. il *Bus Week* p239 N 16 '87

Video games make a Christmas comeback. il *Fortune* 116:8 D 7 '87

Design

An adventure authoring system [using AdvSys for writing text adventure games] D. Betz. il *Byte* 12:125-6+ My '87

Exhibitions

Games bounce back [Consumer's Electronics Show] J. B. Meigs. il *Pop Mech* 164:28+ O '87

Psychological use

Psychic log on [biofeedback videos by Bodylog, Inc.] D. Groves. il *Health* 19:18 Ja '87

A quicker response [improving response time in the elderly; research by Jane E. Clark] P. McCarthy. *Psychol Today* 21:23 O '87

Testing

Computer congressmen [National Association of Manufacturers video game, Congressional Insight] T. Noah. *New Repub* 196:10-12 Ap 6 '87

A computerized gridiron guide. R. Lockwood. il *Pers Comput* 11:91-3 S '87

Hardguy software [Balance of Power strategic computer game designed by C. Crawford] J. Ledbetter. *Nation* 244:150-3 F 7 '87

The next small step [T. L. Keller's Space M*A*X space station construction simulation program] S. Ditlea. il *Omni* 10:22 D '87

Profits into orbit [Space M*A*X and EOS: earth orbit station system] J. L. Wilson. *Space World* X-6-282:21 Je '87

VCR games for kids. il *Parents* 62:24 Ag '87

What's new in entertainment software. D. Caruso. il *Pers Comput* 11:127-31+ Jl '87

Video games and youth

VCR games for kids. il *Parents* 62:24 Ag '87

Video kiosks (Retail trade) *See* Electronic shopping

Video monitors

Across the lines [resolution of video monitors] C. Sarver. il *High Fidel* 37:55+ D '87

Do you need a monitor/receiver? W. Wolfe. il *Stereo Rev* 52:16 My '87

Screen gems. J. B. Meigs. il *Roll Stone* p83+ O 22 '87

Testing

Flat and white [Amdek 410 monitor] C. O'Malley. il *Pers Comput* 11:172 Jl '87

In sync with the times [Ultrasync monitor] C. O'Malley. il *Pers Comput* 11:252 N '87

The long view [Genius monochrome monitor] M. Antonoff. il *Pers Comput* 11:278 N '87

Nanao 8060S spans generations. S. R. Reed. il *Pers Comput* 11:142 Ag '87

Proton VT-210 monitor/receiver. il *High Fidel* 37:35-7 Jl '87

A razor-sharp full-page screen [LM-300 monochrome monitor] P. Honan. il *Pers Comput* 11:272 N '87

A sight for sore eyes [Thomson EGA monitor, Model 4350] C. Spencer. il *Pers Comput* 11:194 Ap '87

Sony's Multiscan serves many needs [CPD-1302 color monitor] M. Antonoff. il *Pers Comput* 11:52 Ja '87

Video monitors—Testing—*cont.*

A versatile monitor [Thomson 4375M UltraScan] A. C. Hixson. il *Pers Comput* 11:206 My '87

What's new in high-resolution monitors. P. Honan. il *Pers Comput* 11:149-51+ S '87

Video records *See* Videodiscs

Video Software Dealers Association

Sales hold the key to video business future. *Publ Wkly* 232:56-8 S 11 '87

Video stores

See also

Blockbuster Entertainment Corp.

Video Software Dealers Association

There's many a way to get that $2.25 a night. I. Mayer and P. Sweeting. il *Channels* 7 Sp Issue:128 D '87

Video telephone *See* Picturephones

Video transfer system *See* Film-to-video transfer system

Video yearbooks

Lights! Camera! Graduation! R. Zoglin. il *Time* 129:77 Je 15 '87

Videodisc players

See also

Compact disc video

Videodisc reviews

Single works

:

Break every rule, starring Tina Turner

High Fidel 37:94 D '87. J. Bessman

Davies, Ray: Return to Waterloo

Stereo Rev il 52:94 Ag '87. L. Meredith

Help!

Stereo Rev il 52:205 N '87. L. Meredith

Videodiscs

See also

Compact disc video

Computer novels

Interactive video

Art

A brand-new way to organize fine art [J. Creiger's Omnivex, Inc. computerized videodisc art catalog] A. Oshins. il por *Work Woman* 12:66+ My '87

Clever, and it's art [Omnivex Network] il *Pers Comput* 11:257 Jl '87

Aviation use

Jeppesen charts by laser [Lasertrak FP100] J. M. McClellan. il *Flying* 114:107 N '87

Educational use

Laser videodiscs in education: endless possibilities. R. Van Horn. il *Phi Delta Kappan* 68:696-700 My '87

Rock music

Ray Davies on film [Return to Waterloo] L. Meredith. por *Stereo Rev* 52:94 Ag '87

Turner, Tina: Break every rule, starring Tina Turner. J. Bessman. *High Fidel* 37:94 D '87

Videophones *See* Picturephones

Videotape, Magnetic *See* Tape, Magnetic

Videotape recorders and recording

See also

Film-to-video transfer system

Interactive video

A checklist for the first-time VCR buyer. W. Wolfe. il *Stereo Rev* 52:22+ Mr '87

Family fun for summer: camcorders, VCRs are all the rage. il *Ebony* 42:29-30+ Je '87

Focus [special section] il *Pop Mech* 164:79-82+ Ja '87

Format wars [VHS vs. 8mm] J. B. Meigs. il *Roll Stone* p43-4 Ja 15 '87

Get ready for S-VHS. J. B. Meigs. *Pop Mech* 164:21 Je '87

Improving your image [Super VHS] P. Hoban. il *N Y* 20:12-13 Ag 3 '87

In case you tuned in late [new features] P. Elmer-Dewitt. il *Time* 130:59 D 21 '87

Movies on the go. W. J. Hawkins. il *Pop Sci* 231:22 S '87

New video. E. B. Meyer. il *High Fidel* 37:53-4 S '87

One-inch wonder: minimizing the visual shortcomings of video [shooting of television program First frontier] B. Kuerten. il *Theatre Crafts* 21:103-5 My '87

Pan & zoom. P. Utz. il *Pop Photogr* 94:68-9 Ja '87

Poor man's storage scope. D. Bernard. il *Radio-Electron* 58:113-14 N '87

Seeing the future. D. Ranada. il *High Fidel* 37:22 Ag '87

Sharp and super: a new VCR's got the picture. D. Lachenbruch. il *Channels* 7 Sp Issue:124-5 D '87

Sight and sound: a hopeless wodge: unscrambling the international TV picture. C. Fuselli. *Opera News* 52:36+ Ag '87

Stacking the decks [latest technology] P. Hoban. il *N Y* 20:14 F 16 '87

Super formats sharpen the video picture [Super VHS] E. Stecker. il *Pop Photogr* 94:71-2 S '87

Super VHS. D. Lachenbruch. il *Pop Sci* 231:65+ Jl '87

Super VHS, finally! D. Ranada. il *High Fidel* 37:21 Ap '87

Tape at 11:00 [when you encounter a news event, keep the camcorder running] E. Stecker. il *Pop Photogr* 94:98-9 D '87

Tape tracks. R. Long. See issues of High Fidelity (New York, N.Y.) beginning May 1986

To video or not to video . . . [results of reader survey] J. Augustine. il *Petersens Photogr Mag* 15:4 Ja '87

Toshiba non-interlaced TV and digital VCR [CZ2697 and DX-900] D. O'Neill. il *Petersens Photogr Mag* 16:9 Ag '87

TV's for ears as well as eyes. il *U S News World Rep* 103:93-4+ N 9 '87

Vain attempts? [Sony's ED Beta system and Philips CD-V format] D. Ranada. il *High Fidel* 37:19 Je '87

Video and the digital revolution. G. Brockhouse. il *High Fidel* 37:51+ N '87

Video magic [digital VCRs] G. McComb. il *Pop Sci* 231:71-4 S '87

Video to go. W. J. Hawkins. il *Pop Sci* 231:40-2 N '87

Videotaping: how to get the most out of a VCR. W. Wolfe. il *Stereo Rev* 52:50-3 Ap '87

What's hot: watching! il *Ladies Home J* 104:74+ Ap '87

Why 8mm? D. Ranada. il *High Fidel* 37:47-8+ F '87

The year the feds stole Christmas [unavailability of dual deck videocassette recorders and digital audio tape technology] Z. Lazarević. il *Forbes* 140:286 N 16 '87

You say you want resolution? Super VHS is now the best home-video format. B. Young. il *Roll Stone* p75-6 S 10 '87

Cameras

See Video cameras

Cold weather conditions

Winter shooting. J. Bishop. il *Pop Photogr* 94:60-1 F '87

Equipment

See also

Desktop video

Home videotape editing system [Videonics system] C. J. Esse. il *High Fidel* 37:12+ Mr '87

Hot box [Videonics processor] J. B. Meigs. il *Pop Mech* 164:46 F '87

Macrovision stabilizer [cover story] D. Dupre. il *Radio-Electron* 58:49-54 D '87

Exhibitions

CES picks and pans [Super VHS] M. Riggs. il *High Fidel* 37:3 S '87

Heads

Putting heads together. J. B. Meigs. il *Pop Mech* 164:16 Je '87

Maintenance and repair

Is your VCR in the shop? You are not alone. D. Pauly. il *Newsweek* 110:62-3 O 19 '87

Replace a VCR belt. C. Grover. il *Workbench* 43:66 S/O '87

Manufacture

See Television equipment industry

Noise

Top NEC digital VCR [digital noise reduction system] il *High Fidel* 37:15 Jl '87

Prices

Low-cost VCRs—what do you get for your money? G. McComb. il *Pop Sci* 230:78-9 Ja '87

Sound quality

Akai VS-525U VHS hi-fi VCR. il *High Fidel* 37:25+ My '87

Akai VS-565U VHS hi-fi VCR. J. D. Hirsch. il *Stereo Rev* 52:27-8+ Ap '87

A digital alternative [Toshiba DX-900 video recorder with built-in PCM adapter] C. J. Esse. il *High Fidel* 37:11 Ag '87

Hi-fi VCR's [with manufacturers directory] W. Wolfe. il *Stereo Rev* 52:73-6+ Ap '87

JVC HR-S7000U super VHS hi-fi VCR. il *High Fidel* 37:27+ O '87

NEC DX-2000U VHS hi-fi VCR. il *High Fidel* 37:39+ Ap '87

NEC DX-5000U VHS hi-fi VCR. il *High Fidel* 37:43+ D '87

Surround-sound attractions. R. B. Schulein. il *High Fidel* 37:49+ Je '87

Special effects

See also

Desktop video

Videotape recorders and recording — Special effects — *cont.*

Video effects generator (I) [cover story] R. F. Graf and W. Sheets. il *Radio-Electron* 58:41-5+ S '87

Video effects generator (II). R. F. Graf and W. Sheets. il *Radio-Electron* 58:48-52+ O '87

Storage

Where to put the VCR? il *Glamour* 85:306-8 O '87

Terminology

A crash course in VCR lingo. S. Woolley. *Bus Week* p163 Je 22 '87

Testing

Akai VS-525U VHS hi-fi VCR. il *High Fidel* 37:25+ My '87

Akai VS-565U VHS hi-fi VCR. J. D. Hirsch. il *Stereo Rev* 52:27-8+ Ap '87

JVC HR-S7000U super VHS hi-fi VCR. il *High Fidel* 37:27+ O '87

NEC DX-2000U VHS hi-fi VCR. il *High Fidel* 37:39+ Ap '87

NEC DX-5000U VHS hi-fi VCR. il *High Fidel* 37:43+ D '87

VCRs. il *Consum Rep* 52:17-26 Ja '87

Video cassette recorders. il *Consum Rep* 52:319-26 D '87

Videotape reviews

Scanning the electronic library. B. D. Johnson. il *Macleans* 100:37 Je 1 '87

V.C.R. (video cassette report). il *Teen* 31:59 O '87

Single works

Anchors aweigh: the United States Navy story
    Am Hist Illus 22:16 S '87

Baryshnikov: the dancer and the dance
    Dance Mag il 61:74 Ja '87. J. Gruen

Conquest
    Am Hist Illus 22:6 My '87

Earth scientists at work
    Earth Sci 40:29-30 Fall '87

Fighter aces of WWII
    Am Hist Illus 22:6 My '87

Future flight
    Space World X-8-284:36 Ag '87. K. McMains

A hard day's night
    High Fidel il 37:79-80 Je '87. D. Browne

Help!
    High Fidel il 37:79-80 Je '87. D. Browne

How to beat a speeding ticket
    Cycle il 38:56 Ap '87

Jackson, Michael: Bad
    Nation 245:728-9 D 12 '87. D. Wolff

Jarrett, Keith/Peacock, Gary/DeJohnette, Jack: Standards
    Stereo Rev il 52:93 Ag '87. C. Albertson

Jones, Bobby: How I play golf
    Sports Illus 67:101 D 21 '87. I. Maisel

Louis Armstrong and his orchestra 1942-1965
    Stereo Rev 52:111-12 Mr '87. C. Albertson

Napoleon
    Stereo Rev il 52:111 Mr '87. S. Simels

Piano legends
    High Fidel 37:79 Ag '87. R. C. Walls

Return to glory: Michelangelo revealed
    Publ Wkly il 231:32 Mr 27 '87

Streisand, Barbra: Color me Barbra
    Stereo Rev il 52:121 My '87. C. Albertson

Streisand, Barbra: My name is Barbra
    Stereo Rev il 52:121 My '87. C. Albertson

Vietnam: a television history
    Am Herit 38:14 Jl/Ag '87. G. C. Ward

Videotapes

See also
    Advertising mediums—Videotapes
    Blacks in videotapes
    Booksellers and bookselling—Videotapes
    CBS-Fox Video, Inc.
    Crown Video (Firm)
    Film-to-video transfer system
    Infants in videotapes
    Interactive video
    J2 Communications (Firm)
    Kartes Video Communications, Inc.
    Lorimar-Telepictures Corporation
    New World Video (Firm)
    Pets in videotapes
    Simon & Schuster Inc. Video Publishing Division
    Vestron Inc.
    Video art
    Video stores
    Women in videotapes
    World War, 1939-1945, in videotapes

Audio/video plus. T. Spain. See issues of Publishers Weekly beginning May 9, 1986

Fall video cassettes. J. Zinsser and T. Spain. il *Publ Wkly* 232:45-53 Ag 28 '87

Spring videocassettes. J. Zinsser and T. Spain. il *Publ Wkly* 231:40+ Mr 13 '87

Video S.I.P. [special interest programming] M. Mancini. il *Film Comment* 23:44-9 Ja/F '87

Amateur recordings

Rock-video boutiques can make you a star. M. Rogers. il *Newsweek* 110:60-1 Ag 10 '87

Animated films

See also
    Western Publishing Co.

Kartes licenses Peanuts from sister company [arrangement with United Media for home video rights] il *Publ Wkly* 231:50+ Ap 24 '87

Somebody say hallelujah! [J. Barbera's animated Bible stories] G. Buchalter. il por *Forbes* 139:160 Mr 23 '87

Art use

Crown moves up Sistine Chapel video [documentary on restoration of Michelangelo's frescoes] il *Publ Wkly* 231:32 Mr 27 '87

How artists use videocassettes. C. J. Goodman. il *Am Artist* 51:58-61 Jl '87

Videocassette tapes: a source directory [instructional] K. J. Thomas. *Am Artist* 51:62+ Jl '87

Arts

See also
    Kultur International Films Ltd.

Aviation use

New videos from ATC [Aviation Training Center] J. M. McClellan. *Flying* 114:99-100 Ag '87

Updater videos from King. J. M. McClellan. *Flying* 114:95 D '87

Ballet

Baryshnikov: the dancer and the dance. J. Gruen. il *Dance Mag* 61:74 Ja '87

Bible stories

Somebody say hallelujah! [J. Barbera's animated Bible stories] G. Buchalter. il por *Forbes* 139:160 Mr 23 '87

Bird study

Audubon Society's video guide to the birds of North America. H. W. Trimm. il *Conservationist* 42:53 S/O '87

Bookselling use

Author video in the bookstore: will it turn viewers into buyers? A. Symons. il *Publ Wkly* 231:43 Ap 3 '87

Seen any good books lately? K. Hannon. il *Forbes* 140:180-1 S 21 '87

Business use

Howdy Letzring can make your company meetings immortal. M. Frons. il por *Bus Week* p103 Ja 26 '87

Monday morning at the movies. A. E. LaForge. il *Work Woman* 12:50+ Je '87

Children's use

See also
    Family Home Entertainment (Firm)
    Scholastic Lorimar (Firm)
    Western Publishing Co.

Ms. pix kids vids. B. Cornfeld. il *Ms* 16:81-2 D '87

Toy Fair report: children's video seeks broader market. T. Spain. il *Publ Wkly* 231:92-4 Mr 6 '87

College catalogs

Princeton—the video. B. Kallen. il *Forbes* 140:114+ S 7 '87

Comedy

Kodak hopes Cosby video will boost market share. il por *Jet* 72:16 S 14 '87

Dance

Dancevideo. D. Towers. See issues of Dance Magazine beginning November 1984

Spotlight on video [special section] il *Dance Mag* 61:40-50 Mr '87

Do-it-yourself work

Do-it-yourselfer's videos. See issues of Workbench beginning May/June 1987

Video review [tapes from The do-it-yourself show] R. N. Hoffman. il *Workbench* 43:11 Mr/Ap '87

Earth sciences use

Earth scientists at work. *Earth Sci* 40:29-30 Fall '87

Editing

See also
    Desktop video

Editing. D. Towers. il *Dance Mag* 61:62 D '87

Help [grants offered to artists for the use of video facilities] D. Towers. *Dance Mag* 61:56 Jl '87

Home videotape editing system [Videonics system] C. J. Esse. il *High Fidel* 37:12+ Mr '87

Videotapes—Editing—*cont.*

Hot box [Videonics processor] J. B. Meigs. il *Pop Mech* 164:46 F '87

Non-linear nuances: Ediflex is cutting up Hollywood [television editing] C. Eller. il *Theatre Crafts* 21:89-90+ O '87

Educational use

Editors' choice: 9 how-to videos. L. J. Brown. il *Good Housekeep* 205:206 Jl '87

An enthusiasm to learn through video [Santo Domingo Indian children] B. Atencio. *Phi Delta Kappan* 68:632-3 Ap '87

Instructional video [photography tutorials] L. Nielsen. il *Petersens Photogr Mag* 16:57-9 Ag '87

Instructional video directory [dance use] D. Towers. il *Dance Mag* 61:44-50 Mr '87

Ortho plans fall introduction for how-to video series. il *Publ Wkly* 231:69-70 Ap 10 '87

Videos that teach computer basics. J. Koblenz. *Black Enterp* 17:24 Ja '87

What can tapes teach you? More than just leg lifts. G. Hechinger. il *Glamour* 85:328-9 O '87

Electronic music

The secrets of analog and digital synthesis. J. Balleras. *Down Beat* 54:53 My '87

Employment use

Job hunting? Let's go to the videotape. T. Segal. il *Bus Week* p114 Je 15 '87

Estate planning use

Lights, camera, action! [videotaping your will] D. Fanning. il *Forbes* 139:72 F 9 '87

Exercise use

Aerobics videos: the top 30. K. Allard. il *Women's Sports Fitness* 9:30-3 D '87

Is there too much sex in aerobics? K. Andes. il *Women's Sports Fitness* 9:60 Ja '87

News in video fitness. S. Connelly. *Ms* 15:37 Ap '87

Running in place—your own place. M. Leepson. il *Nations Bus* 75:64 F '87

Video fitness. il *Seventeen* 46:16 F '87

Video madness. D. Schefer. il *Vogue* 177:417+ N '87

Video shopping. il *Women's Sports Fitness* 9:94 Mr '87

Videos you won't find in stores. il *Women's Sports Fitness* 9:66 F '87

Exhibitions

Around the booths: audio and video [American Booksellers convention] il *Publ Wkly* 231:225+ My 15 '87

CES report: video moves further into mainstream markets. *Publ Wkly* 231:358+ Ja 30 '87

Looking ahead to ABA: no video ghetto in D.C. il *Publ Wkly* 231:49-50 Mr 20 '87

Toy Fair report: children's video seeks broader market. T. Spain. il *Publ Wkly* 231:92-4 Mr 6 '87

Video sales market continues to expand [Summer Consumer Electronics Show] il *Publ Wkly* 231:39-40 Je 26 '87

Gardening use

You get what you see. A. Davis. il *Home Mech* 83:12 My '87

Government use

Letter from Washington [Congressman C. Hecht's video newsletter] Cato. *Natl Rev* 39:15 O 23 '87

Guitar music

Guitar 101 [guitar instructional videos] B. Milkowski. *Down Beat* 54:57 O '87

Household inventory use

See Household records

Jazz music

Coltrane, John: Coltrane legacy. J. Blum. *High Fidel* 37:74-5 Jl '87

Keith Jarrett/Gary Peacock/Jack DeJohnette: Standards. il *Stereo Rev* 52:93 Ag '87

Live on-screen. K. Lynch. il *Down Beat* 54:48 Je '87

Louis Armstrong and his orchestra 1942-1965. C. Albertson. *Stereo Rev* 52:111-12 Mr '87

Piano legends. R. C. Walls. *High Fidel* 37:79 Ag '87

Putting jazz back into the picture [tapes from Rhapsody Films] F. Davis. il *High Fidel* 37:71-2 Jl '87

Trumpet kings. M. Ullman. il *High Fidel* 37:74 Jl '87

Leasing and renting

Video victims. R. Rosenbaum. il *Mademoiselle* 93:69+ F '87

Marketing

Without a studio partner, a hit is hard to find. P. Sweeting and I. Mayer. il *Channels* 7 Sp Issue:127 D '87

Meteorological use

Audio visuals about the weather. E. Brotak. il *Weatherwise* 40:107 Ap '87

Audio visuals about the weather. E. Brotak. *Weatherwise* 40:159 Je '87

Moral and religious aspects

See also
Sex in videotapes
Violence in videotapes

Motion pictures

At war with the pirates. D. Bollier. il *Channels* 7:28-31+ Mr '87

The battle for Platoon [video rights] J. Vitale. il *Channels* 7:59 O '87

Child's play [children renting violent movies] il *Time* 129:31 Je 1 '87

History for rent [fiction films with historical settings] G. C. Ward. il *Am Herit* 38:16+ Ap '87

Hollywood's video boom is stuck on pause. R. Grover. il *Bus Week* p56 Je 29 '87

Home movies: sports films to go. A. Mancuso. il *Sport Mag* 78:88 N '87

A jungle war over the 'Platoon' video. il *Newsweek* 110:56 N 23 '87

Killer bimbos & galactic gigolos star in video's grade Z future [low budget exploitation movies] D. Hutchings and D. Lindeman. il *People Wkly* 28:159-60+ S 7 '87

Lights, camera, lawyers! [battle over video rights to Platoon] W. Harris. il *Forbes* 140:33 Ag 10 '87

Movie price promotions focus on genres, stars. *Publ Wkly* 231:52 Ap 24 '87

Movies for Christmas. il *Publ Wkly* 232:37-8 Ag 21 '87

New Year's Eve in Hollywood. J. Farber. il *Seventeen* 46:64 D '87

One, two, three, four! [Beatles on CD and video] il *High Fidel* 37:70-2+ Je '87

A scourge of video pirates. D. Pauly. il *Newsweek* 110:40-1 Jl 27 '87

Video news and notes. T. Seideman. See issues of Rolling Stone beginning September 12, 1985

Video victims. R. Rosenbaum. il *Mademoiselle* 93:69+ F '87

New Age movement

New Age on tape. il *Publ Wkly* 232:65+ S 25 '87

New media for a New Age. il *Publ Wkly* 232:60-1 S 25 '87

Opera

Great expectations. *Opera News* 52:24-5 Ag '87

Videocassettes. T. Eckert, Jr. See occasional issues of Opera News beginning January 17, 1987

Piano music

Piano legends. R. C. Walls. *High Fidel* 37:79 Ag '87

Vlad tidings from Milan [V. Horowitz recording sessions of Mozart's Piano concerto in A] E. Greenfield. il pors *High Fidel* 37:58-9 S '87

Popular music

Editor on the loose! K. Richardson. il *High Fidel* 37:75+ S '87

In short order. See issues of High Fidelity (New York, N.Y.)

Mini-a-tour. il *High Fidel* 37:70-2+ My '87

The Streisand specials. C. Albertson. por *Stereo Rev* 52:121 My '87

Prices

Movie price promotions focus on genres, stars. *Publ Wkly* 231:52 Ap 24 '87

Movies for Christmas. il *Publ Wkly* 232:37-8 Ag 21 '87

Religious use

Christian film and video: hard questions and entertaining answers. il *Christ Today* 31:57+ S 18 '87

In the one Spirit [video of John Paul II's visit to Taizé] *America* 156:453 Je 6 '87

Of many things [video entitled March 25: a day in the life of Catholic laity in America to be shown to the Pope] J. W. Donohue. *America* 157:122 S 12-19 '87

Rock music

See also
MTV Networks Inc.
MTV Video Music Awards

Michael Jackson: Bad; Prince: Sign o' the times. D. Wolff. *Nation* 245:728-9 D 12 '87

Mick meets HDTV [recording M. Jagger's Let's work] P. Hoban. il pors *N Y* 20:31 Ag 24 '87

No home-video release likely for Springsteen footage. A. DeCurtis. *Roll Stone* p34 Mr 26 '87

Rock-video boutiques can make you a star. M. Rogers. il *Newsweek* 110:60-1 Ag 10 '87

Video news and notes. T. Seideman. See issues of Rolling Stone beginning September 12, 1985

Videotapes—Rock music—*cont.*

Video vérité: Jackson Browne makes his point about U.S. policy in Central America. A. DeCurtis. il por *Roll Stone* p12 Ja 29 '87

Women in rock. K. Walter. il *High Fidel* 37:79 Jl '87

Self help use

See also

Positive Communications Inc.

Anecdotes, facetiae, satire, etc.

Whose brain is it anyway? J. Gorman. il *Discover* 8:38+ N '87

Social aspects

The high-tech date [video dating] J. Giese. il *Ms* 16:25-7+ N '87

Stars until the tape runs out [sports fans and other spectators viewing themselves on videotape] C. Gordon. il *Macleans* 100:37 My 18 '87

Video rites of the new Saturday night. J. Vitale. il *Channels* 7:62-4 Ja '87

Space sciences use

Conquest. *Am Hist Illus* 22:6 My '87

Film and game [Future flight] K. McMains. *Space World* X-8-284:36 Ag '87

Sports

1986 GP season [Powersports Video Grand Prix tapes] C. Hodenfield. il *Cycle* 38:17+ Ag '87

Bank shot [CBS-Fox Video's line of NBA basketball tapes] A. D. Frank. il *Forbes* 139:252+ Je 15 '87

Bobby Jones shows you how to hit 'em [How I play golf video] I. Maisel. *Sports Illus* 67:101 D 21 '87

Mad Max, video recruiter [M. Emfinger offers video analysis of Texas high school football prospects] D. Whitford. il por *Sport Mag* 78:19 Ag '87

Taped crusaders [instructional tennis videos] P. Stites. il *World Tennis* 35:12-13 D '87

Two American heroes [videotapes by E. Knievel and Freddie Spencer] C. Hodenfield. il *Cycle* 38:14 F '87

What's on the tube? Videos to go. D. Garr. il *Sport Mag* 78:91+ Mr '87

Tax return use

The book is better than the movie [Touche Ross video tax guide 1987] il *Consum Rep* 52:133 Mr '87

Television programs

The Streisand specials. C. Albertson. por *Stereo Rev* 52:121 My '87

Trumpet music

Trumpet kings. M. Ullman. il *High Fidel* 37:74 Jl '87

Unauthorized use

At war with the pirates. D. Bollier. il *Channels* 7:28-31+ Mr '87

The Betamax case (I). J. Lardner. *New Yorker* 63:45-8+ Ap 6 '87

The Betamax case (II). J. Lardner. *New Yorker* 63:60-81 Ap 13 '87

Macrovision stabilizer [cover story] D. Dupre. il *Radio-Electron* 58:49-54 D '87

A scourge of video pirates. D. Pauly. il *Newsweek* 110:40-1 Jl 27 '87

The year the feds stole Christmas [unavailability of dual deck videocassette recorders and digital audio tape technology] Z. Lazarević. il *Forbes* 140:286 N 16 '87

Weddings

Videotaping weddings. S. Sweetow. il *Petersens Photogr Mag* 16:68-70 O '87

Canada

A nation's home movies [video program of National Film Board] B. D. Johnson. il *Macleans* 100:46 Jl 27 '87

Eastern Europe

Torn curtain. D. Graff. il *Channels* 7:68-9 Jl/Ag '87

Soviet Union

Kremlinologists play a video game [tape of R. Gorbachev] N. Cooper. il por *Newsweek* 109:35 Ap 13 '87

Videotapes and youth

Child's play [children renting violent movies] il *Time* 129:31 Je 1 '87

Video rites of the new Saturday night. J. Vitale. il *Channels* 7:62-4 Ja '87

Videotapes as gifts

Christmas book roundup and video cassettes too [woodworking] R. N. Hoffman. il *Workbench* 43:26 N/D '87

Video gifts for that special couch potato on your Xmas list. D. Towers. il *Dance Mag* 61:67 N '87

Videotex systems *See* Information storage and retrieval systems

La vie est à nous [film] *See* Motion picture reviews—Single works

Vienna (Austria)

Galleries and museums

See also

Kunsthistorisches Museum (Vienna, Austria)

Hotels, motels, etc.

Four historic Viennese hotels. L. Langseth-Christensen. il *Gourmet* 47:64-9+ Mr '87

Music

See also

Opera—Austria

Social life and customs

A design for living [excerpt] L. Langseth-Christensen. il *Gourmet* 47:66+ Ag '87

Vienna Convention for the Protection of the Ozone Layer (1985). Montreal Protocol (1987)

A breath of fresh air. G. Garelik. il *Time* 130:35 S 28 '87

Equity and ozone protection. J. T. B. Tripp and others. bibl f *Environment* 29:43-5 Jl/Ag '87

An exemplary ozone agreement. S. Begley. il *Newsweek* 110:8 S 28 '87

Fresh hope in the sky. L. Van Dusen. il *Macleans* 100:56-7 S 28 '87

A global pact to patch the roof. il *U S News World Rep* 103:12 S 21 '87

Global pact to protect ozone is just a first step. il *Earth Sci* 40:7-8 Wint '87

Holes in the ozone accord. D. Israelson. *World Press Rev* 34:54 N '87

Is the pact too little, too late? J. Gliedman. il *Nation* 245:376-80 O 10 '87

Landmark ozone treaty negotiated. M. Crawford. il *Science* 237:1557 S 25 '87

Ozone accord draws praise and concern. R. Monastersky. *Sci News* 132:196-7 S 26 '87

Ozone and global warming: what to do? S. Weisburd. *Sci News* 131:86 F 7 '87

Ozone plan splits administration. M. Crawford. il *Science* 236:1052-3 My 29 '87

Ozone plan: tough bargaining ahead. M. Crawford. *Science* 237:1099 S 4 '87

Protecting the ozone layer. J. Negroponte. *Dep State Bull* 87:58-60 Je '87

The twilight ozone [D. Hodel's alleged remarks] H. Klingeman. *Natl Rev* 39:40-1 Ag 14 '87

Worldwide progress in ozone talks. S. Weisburd. *Sci News* 131:295 My 9 '87

Vienna Philharmonic

Age of gold [concerts conducted by L. Bernstein at Carnegie Hall and Avery Fisher Hall] P. G. Davis. il *N Y* 20:80+ O 12 '87

Musical events:

Leonard Bernstein conducting at Carnegie Hall. A. Porter. *New Yorker* 63:122-3 O 12 '87

Small world [six concert Beethoven cycle at Carnegie Hall] P. G. Davis. il *N Y* 20:92+ Mr 23 '87

The 'tramp of a giant' [Beethoven tribute at Carnegie Hall] A. Rich. il *Newsweek* 109:69 Mr 9 '87

The Vienna Philharmonic: the complete Beethoven symphonies and concertos [Carnegie Hall performances] E. W. Said. *Nation* 244:619-20+ My 9 '87

Vienna State Opera Ballet *See* Ballet—Austria

Vieques Island (Puerto Rico)

See also

Puerto Mosquito (Vieques Island, Puerto Rico)

Vietmeyer, Noel, 1940-

The captivating kiwifruit. il *Natl Geogr* 171:682-8 My '87

Dazzling! il *Int Wildl* 17:30-5 Jl/Ag '87

How a bug made the world see red. il *Int Wildl* 17:42-7 Mr/Ap '87

They created the Jet Age. il *Read Dig* 130:162-6 My '87

Vietnam

See also

Americans—Vietnam

Vietnamese

Defenses

See also

Soviet Union—Armed Forces—Forces in Vietnam

Economic policy

The choice: 'reform or perish'. N. Cooper. il *Newsweek* 110:32 Jl 13 '87

Glasnost takes a slow boat to Vietnam. C. Debes and others. il *Bus Week* p51 S 28 '87

Vietnam has a new agenda. S. Butler. *World Press Rev* 34:39 Je '87

With new energy, Vietnam gets down to business. L. M. Simons. il *Smithsonian* 18:62-6+ Ap '87

Vietnam—*cont.*

Foreign relations
China
See China—Foreign relations—Vietnam
Kampuchea
See Kampuchea—Foreign relations—Vietnam
Thailand
See Thailand—Foreign relations—Vietnam
United States
See United States—Foreign relations—Vietnam
Native peoples
See also
Montagnards (Vietnamese people)
Photographs and photography
At home in Vietnam. G. C. Clifford. il *Life* 10:58-61+
D '87
Politics and government
See also
Communist Party (Vietnam)
An interview with Viet Nam's Nguyen Van Linh. D.
Brelis. il por *Time* 130:40 S 21 '87
Vietnam moves toward pragmatism. W. J. Duiker. bibl
f *Curr Hist* 86:148-51+ Ap '87
Vietnam: time to change course. T. J. S. George. il
World Press Rev 34:29+ F '87
Social conditions
Vietnam: time to change course. T. J. S. George. il
World Press Rev 34:29+ F '87
Vietnam veterans *See* Veterans; Women veterans
Vietnam Veterans Memorial (Washington, D.C.)
The unsung heroines of Vietnam [recognition of women
veterans at the Vietnam Veterans Memorial] J. McRob-
bie. il pors *McCalls* 114:159 My '87
The wall that heals. W. Broyles. il *Read Dig* 130:70-6
My '87
Photographs and photography
Heroes, past and present [cover story; special section]
il *Newsweek* 110:52-6+ Jl 6 '87
Reflections on 'the wall'. C. Bond. il *Smithsonian* 17:149
F '87
Vietnamese

United States
Christianity today talks to Steve Standiford [adopting
refugee children] *Christ Today* 31:35 F 20 '87
Twelve years out of Vietnam, Air Force cadet Hoang
Nhu Tran discovers the sky's the limit [top academic
graduate] R. Arias. il pors *People Wkly* 27:45-6 Je
15 '87
Warm welcomes for forgotten allies [Montagnard refugees
resettled in North Carolina] J. Bennett. il *Macleans*
100:5+ Mr 23 '87
Vietnamese cooking *See* Cooking, Vietnamese
Vietnamese refugees *See* Refugees, Vietnamese
Vietnamese War, 1957-1975
See also
Vietnam Veterans Memorial (Washington, D.C.)
American participation
Oliver Stone's Platoon buddies recall the war 20 years
later. il por *People Wkly* 27:81-4+ My 11 '87
Remembering Vietnam. H. J. Kaplan. *Commentary*
84:13-29 D '87
Art and the war
Cynthia Carlson: McIntosh/Drysdale. A. Thorson. il *Art
News* 86:164 D '87
Blacks
An angry Vietnam war correspondent charges that black
combat soldiers are Platoon's M.I.A.s [interview with
W. Terry] M. Wilhelm. il pors *People Wkly* 27:101-2+
Ap 20 '87
Casualties
See also
Vietnamese War, 1957-1975—Missing in action
Children
No greater love [willingness of Vietnamese boy to give
up his life for another during wartime] J. W. Mansur.
il *Read Dig* 131:49-50 Ag '87
Conscientious objectors
Your Constitution: can non-believers be CO's? D.
Pawelek. *Sch Update* 119:8 My 4 '87
Memorials and monuments
See War memorials
Missing in action
Looking for the mysterious 'Mr. Roly' [possible identifica-
tion of MIA C. S. Rowley] il pors *Life* 10:119-20+
N '87
Missing [cover story] M. C. Hickey and others. il *Life*
10:110-14+ N '87
Resolving the POW/MIA issue [address, July 18, 1987]
G. P. Shultz. *Dep State Bull* 87:18-19 S '87

U.S.-Lao POW/MIA consultations held in Vientiane [joint
statement, August 12, 1987] *Dep State Bull* 87:23
O '87
Moral and religious aspects
American churches and Vietnam [address, October 18,
1986] E. W. Lefever. *Vital Speeches Day* 53:327-30
Mr 15 '87
Easter on Hill 17 [chaplain in Vietnam] G. H. Meyer.
il por *Christ Today* 31:18-22 Ap 17 '87
Prisoners and prisons
Resolving the POW/MIA issue [address, July 18, 1987]
G. P. Shultz. *Dep State Bull* 87:18-19 S '87
U.S.-Lao POW/MIA consultations held in Vientiane [joint
statement, August 12, 1987] *Dep State Bull* 87:23
O '87
Psychological aspects
See also
Veterans—Psychology
From Platoon to Pan Am [views on morale by J. W.
Gibson] R. McGough. il por *Forbes* 139:105 Ap 20
'87
Reporters and reporting
Hard looks at hidden history [Vietnam: a television
history available on videotape] G. C. Ward. il *Am
Herit* 38:12+ Jl/Ag '87
Westy's revenge [controversy over Gen. Westmoreland's
libel suit against CBS leads to current network crisis;
cover story] F. Barnes. *New Repub* 196:21+ Ap 6
'87
Study and teaching
Vietnam comes of age. A. P. Sanoff. il *U S News World
Rep* 102:58-9 F 2 '87
Veterans
See Veterans; Women veterans
Vietnamese War, 1957-1975, in motion pictures
The American film industry & Vietnam [cover story]
M. Paris. bibl il *Hist Today* 37:19-26 Ap '87
The ballad of a haunted soldier [O. Stone's Platoon]
G. Peary. il por *Macleans* 100:61-2 Mr 30 '87
A battalion of films follows 'Platoon'. *World Press Rev*
34:59 My '87
A celluloid war of credibility [Platoon and Amerika]
F. Bruning. por *Macleans* 100:7 Mr 16 '87
Missing from the action. S. Ulstein. il *Christ Today*
31:70+ O 2 '87
Platoon. R. Corliss. il pors *Time* 129:54-61 Ja 26 '87
'Platoon' and Iranamok. *New Repub* 196:4+ Mr 9 '87
Semper fi [making of Full metal jacket] R. Lacayo.
il por *Film Comment* 23:11-14 S/O '87
Soldier's story [O. Stone's Platoon] F. Schruers. il por
Roll Stone p23-4+ Ja 29 '87
View from the trenches. il *U S News World Rep* 102:59
F 2 '87
Vietnamese War, 1957-1975, in television
Prime time for Vietnam. H. F. Waters. il *Newsweek*
110:68-9 Ag 31 '87
View cameras *See* Cameras
View-Master Ideal Group Inc.
A way to play Michael [M. Jackson's Bad on reel]
T. Jaffe. por *Forbes* 140:221 S 21 '87
Viewpoint (Fiction) *See* Fiction—Narration
Views (Scenery)
Scenic sites under siege [air pollution in national parks]
C. Peterson. il *Natl Wildl* 25:44-5 Je/Jl '87
Vigeland, Tone, 1938-
about
Tone Vigeland. J. Evans. il por *Am Craft* 47:24-31 Ap/My
'87
Vigilante, Richard
Who's afraid of Robert Bork? [cover story] il *Natl Rev*
39:25-30 Ag 28 '87
Vikhlyayev, Nikolai
A Soviet expert discusses Chernobyl [interview with V.
Legasov] il por *Bull At Sci* 43:32-4 Jl/Ag '87
Viking flights *See* Space flight to Mars
Viking Penguin Inc.
British official suggests ousting Viking board to stop
'Spycatcher' [effort to prevent U.S. publication of book
by P. Wright] V. Menkes. *Publ Wkly* 232:311 Ag
7 '87
Vila, Bob
Old house restoration. See issues of Popular Mechanics
beginning May 1986
Vila Verde (Portugal) *See* Country estates—Portugal
Vilchis, Ricardo Legorreta *See* Legorreta Vilchis, Ricardo,
1931-
Vilenkin, Alexander
Cosmic strings. bibl (p158) il *Sci Am* 257:94-8+ D '87
Villa d'Este (Como, Italy: Hotel) *See* Como (Italy)—Hotels,
motels, etc.

Villa-Lobos, Heitor
about
Magdalena [musical] Reviews
New Yorker 63:163-4 D 7 '87. A. Porter
Musical events:
Centenary concerts. A. Porter. New Yorker 63:109-10
Mr 30 '87
Villa Melzi (Bellagio, Italy) See Country estates—Italy
Villa Nicola (Firm)
Pooling the Iacocca talent, Lee makes Lia head of his
winery. il pors People Wkly 28:85 S 14 '87
Villa Polissena (Italy) See Country estates—Italy
Villa Savoye (Poissy, France) See Poissy (France)—Historic
houses, sites, etc.
Villa Vera Hotel & Racquet Club (Acapulco, Mexico) See
Resorts—Mexico
Village life
The hamlet handicap [effect of village life on talented
youth] K. Seelinger. por Newsweek 109:10-11 My 18
'87
Village Vanguard (New York, N.Y.: Nightclub) See New
York (N.Y.)—Restaurants, nightclubs, bars, etc.
Villages
See also
Village life
France
See also
Saint-Paul-de-Vence (France)
Great Britain
English village names. B. Bryson. il Travel Holiday 168:94
S '87
Nepal
See also
Phalabang (Nepal)
Villages, Restored
See also
Henry Ford Museum and Greenfield Village
Historic Deerfield, Inc.
Mystic Seaport Museum
Old Salem, Inc.
Old Sturbridge Village
Shaker Village of Pleasant Hill (Harrodsburg, Ky.)
Williamsburg (Va.)
Take a fascinating trip back in time. S. Birnbaum. il
por Good Housekeep 204:134+ My '87
Villages, Underwater See Underwater villages
Villar Perosa (Italy: Country estate) See Country estates—
Italy
Villard Books
A hot property [story behind Are you lonesome tonight?]
L. Fleischer. Publ Wkly 231:69 Mr 13 '87
Villarosa, Linda
The great sports debate. il Health 19:27-30+ Jl '87
Working out at work. il Essence 17:106+ Mr '87
Villarosa, Linda, and Roberts, Joan
Nobody's safe. Essence 18:73-4+ Je '87
Villas See Country estates
Ville de Goyet, Claude de
Disaster preparedness in the Americas. il World Health
p20-2 O '87
Villedieu, Yanick
Tomorrow's medicine. il Courier 40:28-33 Ag '87
La Villette (Paris, France)
France's crystal ball. D. D. Meehan. Travel Holiday
168:82 Jl '87
Vimy Ridge, Battle of, 1917
Remembering Vimy Ridge [Canadian vets return to
France for 70th anniversary of battle] il Macleans
100:10-11 Ap 20 '87
Vin Santo (Wine) See Wine
Vinculin
The cytoskeletal protein vinculin contains transformation-
sensitive, covalently bound lipid. P. Burn and M.
M. Burger. bibl f il Science 235:476-9 Ja 23 '87
Vine, Barbara
See also
Rendell, Ruth, 1930-
Vinegar
Herb vinegars. B. O. Neher. il Ctry J 14:26-9 Jl '87
Vinen, W. F.
(jt. auth) See Dahm, Arnold J., and Vinen, W. F.
Vines See Climbing plants
Vineyard, George H.
about
Obituary
Phys Today por 40:146+ O '87. M. Blume
Vineyard Opera (New York, N.Y.)
Musical events:
G. Sarti's I due litiganti. A. Porter. New Yorker
63:100-1 Ap 6 '87

N. Piccinni's La buona figliuola. A. Porter. New
Yorker 63:146+ N 9 '87
Ringing in the new [production of N. Piccinni's La
buona figliuola] P. G. Davis. N Y 20:113 O 26 '87
Vineyards See Viticulture
Vinson, Mechelle
about
Ending sexual harassment. C. E. Simmons. Vogue 177:70
S '87
Vinson, Ronald W.
Insuring a growing country. il Nations Bus 75:89+ S
'87
Vinson family
about
Faces of middle class America: the Vinsons of Stamford
take time out for a baby. il Ebony 42:156+ Ag '87
Vintage automobile racing See Automobile racing
Vintage automobile shows See Automobiles—Exhibitions
Vintage motorcycle racing See Motorcycle racing
Vintners International Company
Paul Schlem uncorks a turnaround plan. J. O. Hamilton.
il por Bus Week p102 S 28 '87
Vinton, Will
about
Filmmaker Will Vinton and his feats of clay are giving
animation a new raisin d'être. D. Van Biema. il pors
People Wkly 27:76+ Mr 9 '87
Raisins. New Yorker 63:29 My 4 '87
Vinton (Will) Productions Inc. See Will Vinton Productions
Inc.
Vinyl flooring See Flooring, Plastic
Vinyl wall coverings See Wall coverings
Viola, Frank, 1960-
about
Concerto for Viola & Twins. P. Gammons. il por Sports
Illus 67:32-3 N 2 '87
Viola, Victor E., and Mathews, Grant J.
The cosmic synthesis of lithium, beryllium and boron.
il Sci Am 256:38-45 My '87
Violence
See also
Assault and battery
Family violence
Riots
School violence
Terrorism
Wife abuse
Advances reported in predicting violence [study by An-
tonio Convit and others] J. Greenberg. Sci News
131:324-5 My 23 '87
Murder in mind [views of homicide authority D. Archer]
J. Wilkes. il pors Psychol Today 21:26-8+ Je '87
On cooling a beef [recommendation that pro athletes
use the body punch in arguments during games] P.
Berger. il Sport Mag 78:79-80 S '87
Stemming the tide of racial violence. E. G. Graves.
il Black Enterp 17:9 Ap '87
U.S. youth and violent death. G. W. Carey and others.
il maps Focus 37:30-2 Spr '87
Violence in motion pictures
See also
Motion pictures—Horror films
North, Goetz, and the American audience. J. Saltzman.
USA Today (Periodical) 116:55 N '87
Violence in sports
See also
Baseball, Professional—Ethical aspects
Hockey—Ethical aspects
Hockey, Professional—Ethical aspects
Soccer, Professional—Ethical aspects
Good old violence. C. Kirkpatrick. por Sports Illus 66:66
Ja 5 '87
Violence in television
How on-screen violence hurts your kids. B. Spock. il
Redbook 170:26+ N '87
This is what you thought: 88% say TV violence makes
kids violent [results of survey] Glamour 85:89 F '87
Violent family hour. Society 24:2 Ja/F '87
What TV does to kids. N. S. Schwartzberg. il Parents
62:100-4 Je '87
Violence in videotapes
Child's play [children renting violent movies] il Time
129:31 Je 1 '87
A new twist to video violence. F. Bruning. por Macleans
100:9 Je 8 '87
Violin
Fiddling with the future [work of C. M. Hutchins] T.
Rothman and A. Mereson. il pors Discover 8:58-64+
S '87

Violin—*cont.*

Study and teaching

The genius of teaching geniuses [interview with D. DeLay] M. Horn. il por *U S News World Rep* 103:59 Jl 27 '87

Theft

A violinist's deathbed confession solves the 51-year riddle of a stolen Stradivarius. R. Arias. il pors *People Wkly* 27:36-8 Je 1 '87

Violin music

See also

    Compact discs—Violin music
    Phonograph records—Violin music
    Tape recordings—Violin music

Violinists

See also

    Altman, Julius
    Cerovsek, Corey
    Fiddlers
    Kennedy, Nigel
    Menuhin, Yehudi, 1916-
    Midori, 1971-
    Milenkovic, Stefan, 1977-
    Salerno-Sonnenberg, Nadja
    Schulte, Rolf, 1949-
    Sitkovetsky, Dmitry

Viollet-Le-Duc, Eugène Emmanuel, 1814-1879

about

Eugene Viollet-le-Duc: restorer of France's architectural legacy. C. Styles-McLeod. il por *Archit Dig* 44:172+ Ag '87

Vionnet, Madeleine, 1876-1975

about

Designing women. D. Drier. il pors *Art Am* 75:21-3 My '87

In fashion. *New Yorker* 63:29-30 Mr 16 '87

Viorst, Judith

Between us. See issues of Redbook

Viorst, Milton

Ending the 20-year war. il *Newsweek* 109:10 Je 15 '87

The Kissinger covenant and other reasons Israel is in trouble [excerpt from Sands of sorrow; cover story] por map *Wash Mon* 19:23-9+ Je '87

The view from the Mustansiriyah. map *New Yorker* 63:92+ O 12 '87

The view from the Mustansiriyah. map *New Yorker* 63:76-96 O 19 '87

VIP Scandinavia

A couple of Norwegian dogs. T. Jaffe. il *Forbes* 139:109 My 4 '87

Virago Press Ltd.

Virago Press completes buyout from Random House's CBC Group. il *Publ Wkly* 232:310 Ag 7 '87

Virago quits Chatto consortium as Graham Greene enters fray [management buyout] V. Menkes. *Publ Wkly* 231:20 Ap 17 '87

Viral mutation *See* Mutation—Viruses

Virgin Gorda (British Virgin Islands)

Description

Bliss on the rocks. D. Messinesi. il *Vogue* 177:145 Jl '87

Virgin Islands of the United States

See also

    Historic houses, sites, etc.—Virgin Islands of the United States
    Investments, American—Virgin Islands of the United States
    Saint Thomas (Virgin Islands of the U.S.)
    Salt River Bay (Virgin Islands of the U.S.)

Description and travel

The U.S. Virgin Islands: another reason. J. Colihan. il *Am Herit* 38:20+ Jl/Ag '87

Virgin Mary *See* Mary, Blessed Virgin, Saint

Virgin Records America

Virgin's odd couple [executives J. Ayeroff and J. Harris] S. Pond. pors *Roll Stone* p22+ Ap 9 '87

Virginia

See also

    Appomattox Court House National Historical Park (Va.)
    Architecture, Domestic—Virginia
    Assateague Island National Seashore (Md. and Va.)
    Birth control clinics—Virginia
    Booksellers and bookselling—Virginia
    Chesapeake Bay (Md. and Va.)
    Courts—Virginia
    Criminal justice, Administration of—Virginia
    Educational laws and regulations—Virginia
    Fairfax County (Va.)
    Festivals—Virginia
    Gardens and gardening—Virginia

    George Washington National Forest (Va. and W. Va.)
    Historic houses, sites, etc.—Virginia
    Law—Virginia
    Music festivals—Virginia
    New River (N.C.-W. Va.)
    Patrick County (Va.)
    Plantations—Virginia
    Prisons—Virginia
    Shenandoah National Park (Va.)
    Wildlife sanctuaries—Virginia
    Wolf Trap Farm Park for the Performing Arts

History

"I'll call this land Virginia" [portfolio of paintings] O. De Mejo. il *Am Herit* 38:49-57 F/Mr '87

A stately duel in Virginia [homes of the participants and excerpts from the constitutional ratification debate of 1788] D. G. Kinney. il *Life* 10:66-74 Fall '87

Race relations

Blacks want new lyrics for 'racist' Va. state song [Carry me back to old Virginia] *Jet* 73:7 N 30 '87

Virginia Beach (Va.)

Architecture

Family business [Salasky/Sedel two family house] K. D. Stein. il *Archit Rec* 175:86-93 mid-Ap '87

Virginia cooking *See* Cooking, American

Virginia in art

"I'll call this land Virginia". O. De Mejo. il *Am Herit* 38:49-57 F/Mr '87

Virginia Museum of Fine Arts

Art has a place in the South. il *South Living* 22:62-7 F '87

Sidney and Frances Lewis—the quest for the best in art. J. Tully. il pors *Smithsonian* 18:84-8+ N '87

Virginia quilts *See* Quilts and quilting

Virginity

Crossing the border [loss of virginity] J. Heifetz. *Glamour* 85:174+ Ap '87

The virgin. B. Greene. il *Esquire* 108:47-8 N '87

Virginity regained [excerpt from Sex respect] C. K. Mast. *Harpers* 274:20-2 Ap '87

Virgo Cluster (Galaxies) *See* Galaxies

Virnig, David

about

Maimed in a terrible accident, Minnesota farm boy David Virnig boldly faces life without arms. D. Chu. il pors *People Wkly* 28:67-8 O 19 '87

Viroids

The curse of cadang-cadang [Philippine coconut palm disease] K. Maramorosch. il *Nat Hist* 96:20-2 Jl '87

Virshup, Amy

The $2 million man. il por *Art News* 86:112-14 S '87

BAM goes boom [cover story] il *N Y* 20:38-47 O 12 '87

The East Village: rebels and immigrants in the land of the Stuyvesants. il map *N Y* 20:54-6 My 4 '87

The fun's over: the East Village scene gets burned by success. il *N Y* 20:48-50+ Je 22 '87

Movin' uptown. il pors *N Y* 20:46-9 Mr 30 '87

Perfect people? [cover story] il *N Y* 20:26-34 Jl 27 '87

La virtù de' strali d'Amore [opera] *See* Cavalli, Pier Francesco, 1602-1676

Virtual computer systems

A shared network spreadsheet [virtual memory routines] P. R. Horton and M. D. Morris. *Byte* 12:185-6+ Jl '87

Virtual Prototypes, Inc.

Virtual Prototyping System speeds evaluation of cockpit configurations. il *Aviat Week Space Technol* 127:81+ D 7 '87

Virtue

See also

    Character

Josef Pieper and the pursuit of virtue. D. Heim. *Christ Century* 104:1076-7 D 2 '87

Virus diseases

See also

    Cold (Disease)

Virus diseases in animals

See also

    Rabies

Visualization of viral clearance in the living animal. E. M. Verdin and others. bibl f il *Science* 236:439-42 Ap 24 '87

Viruses

See also

    Arboviruses
    Bacteriophages
    Bunyaviruses
    Cytomegalovirus

Viruses—See also—*cont.*
    Epstein-Barr virus
    Hepatitis viruses
    Herpesviruses
    HIV viruses
    HTLV viruses
    Human papilloma virus
    Influenza viruses
    Leukemia viruses
    Mutation—Viruses
    Oncogenic viruses
    Papilloma viruses
    Poliomyelitis virus
    Pox viruses
    Retroviruses
    Rotaviruses
    Simian viruses
    Viroids
Activation of adenovirus promoters by the adenovirus E1A protein in cell-free extracts. R. Spangler and others. bibl f il *Science* 237:1044-6 Ag 28 '87
The adenovirus major late transcription factor activates the rat γ-fibrinogen promoter. L. A. Chodosh and others. bibl f il *Science* 238:684-8 O 30 '87
The atomic structure of Mengo virus at 3.0 Å resolution. M. Luo and others. bibl f il *Science* 235:182-91 Ja 9 '87
Viruses emerge as a new key for unlocking life's mysteries [cover story] F. Hapgood. bibl (p270) il *Smithsonian* 18:116-27 N '87
Viruses in search of 'compatible' diseases. D. D. Edwards. *Sci News* 132:246 O 17 '87

Inactivation
    See also
    Interferon
    Ribavirin
Antiviral therapy. M. S. Hirsch and J. C. Kaplan. il *Sci Am* 256:76-85 Ap '87

Reproduction
Cytokines alter AIDS virus production [research by Anthony Fauci and Thomas Folks] D. M. Barnes. il *Science* 236:1627 Je 26 '87
U3 sequences from HTLV-I and -II LTRs confer p*x* protein response to a murine leukemia virus LTR. H. Kitado and others. bibl f il *Science* 235:901-4 F 20 '87

Viruses, Computer *See* Computer viruses
Viruses, Insect
Insect viruses invade biotechnology [baculoviruses] B. R. Jasny. il *Science* 238:1653 D 18 '87
Viruses, Plant
The 30-kilodalton gene product of tobacco mosaic virus potentiates virus movement. C. M. Deom and others. bibl f il *Science* 237:389-94 Jl 24 '87
Duplication of CaMV 35S promoter sequences creates a strong enhancer for plant genes [cauliflower mosaic virus] R. Kay and others. bibl f il *Science* 236:1299-302 Je 5 '87
In vivo uncoating and efficient expression of foreign mRNAs packaged in TMV-like particles [tobacco mosaic virus] D. R. Gallie and others. bibl f il *Science* 236:1122-4 My 29 '87
RNA satellites confer viral resistance [work of Bryan D. Harrison and others] R. Weiss. *Sci News* 132:133 Ag 29 '87

Visa International Inc.
Visa's back-office strategy in the credit-card wars [cutting the cost of electronic transactions] J. B. Levine. il *Bus Week* p75 Ap 20 '87
Visas *See* Passports
Viscachas
At home up high. il map *Natl Geogr World* 137:24-5 Ja '87
Viscosity
F-actin and microtubule suspensions as indeterminate fluids. R. E. Buxbaum and others. bibl f il *Science* 235:1511-14 Mr 20 '87
Viscott, David S., 1938-
Putting the romance back into sex [excerpt from I love you] il *Good Housekeep* 205:148-9+ O '87
Why can't we be closer? [excerpt from I love you] il *Health* 19:44-6+ O '87
Vises
Sighting in made easy [adjusting the scope by holding rifle in a vise] T. Clauss. il *Outdoor Life* 179:112 Ja '87
Vision
    See also
    Blindness
    Color blindness
    Color vision

    Contact lenses
    Eye
    Eyeglasses
    Visual perception
Focus! [development of eye-tracking skills in athletes] S. Schneider. il *Women's Sports Fitness* 9:18 Je '87
Focusing on 'vision therapy'. S. Findlay. *U S News World Rep* 103:78 O 12 '87
Open your eyes to vision training [improving athletes' vision; views of Harvey Ratner] L. N. DeLuca. il *World Tennis* 35:16-17 Ag '87
What deer? [deer hunters] G. Clancy. il *Outdoor Life* 179:59+ Mr '87

Animals
Gone in a flash [game spooked by reflective hunting gear] B. McRae. il *Field Stream* 92:68-9+ Jl '87

Arachnids
How ticks tick [work of John F. Carroll and Lawrence G. Pickens] il *Ctry J* 14:12 Jl '87

Fish
Color vision and the retinex theory [discussion of February 8, 1985 article, The goldfish as a retinex animal] D. J. Ingle. il *Science* 238:1731-2 D 18 '87

Testing
    See Eye—Examination
Vision systems (Machines)
    See also
    Robots
"Unmanned" warfare due in the future? il *Radio-Electron* 58:4 Ap '87
Visitation rights *See* Parent and child (Law)
Visitor centers
    See also
    Smithsonian Institution. Information Center
A Hallmark expression [Hallmark Visitors Center in Kansas City] F. Warnecke. *Travel Holiday* 168:16-17 D '87
More help for UCLA visitors. il *Sunset* 178:32 Ja '87

Architecture
A colossus remodeled [visitor facilities at the Statue of Liberty] G. Anderson. il *Archit Rec* 175:98-103 Ap '87
Visitors *See* Guests
Visitors, Hospital *See* Hospitals—Visitors
Visitors, Nursing home *See* Nursing homes—Visitors
Visser, Steve
A civics lesson at Hazelwood East. il *Nation* 245:441-2 O 24 '87
VISTA (U.S.) *See* United States. Volunteers in Service to America
Vista Chemical Company
Buried treasure. J. Willoughby. il *Forbes* 139:201 My 18 '87
Visual cells *See* Rods and cones
Visual flight rules *See* Airplanes—Piloting
Visual illusions *See* Optical illusions
Visual images *See* Visualization
Visual perception
    See also
    Color vision
    Motion perception
    Optical illusions
    Optical pattern recognition
    Space perception
Conduction velocity variations minimize conduction time differences among retinal ganglion cell axons. L. R. Stanford. bibl f il *Science* 238:358-60 O 16 '87
Dynamics of automatic and controlled visual attention. E. Weichselgartner and G. Sperling. bibl f il *Science* 238:778-80 N 6 '87
Dyslexia: reading both ends against the middle [study by Gad Geiger and Jerome Lettvin] C. Greene. *Psychol Today* 21:18 N '87
Here's not looking at U [skewed peripheral masking in dyslexics; work of Gad Geiger and Jerome Lettvin] *Discover* 8:10-11 O '87
The inversion of sensory processing by feedback pathways: a model of visual cognitive functions. E. Harth and others. bibl f il *Science* 237:184-7 Jl 10 '87
Probing the mind's eye [visual sensation induced by electronic stimulation of the brain] *Sci Am* 256:85 F '87
Ties that bind [tight neckwear affects perceptual skills; report by Leonora M. Langan and Susan M. Watkins] B. L. Benderly. il *Psychol Today* 21:16 O '87
Tight collars put a squeeze on vision [research by Susan Watkins] *Prevention* 39:10+ N '87
Visual pigments
    See also
    Visual purple

Visual purple
Intracellular topography of rhodopsin bleaching [toads] C. L. Makino and others. bibl f il *Science* 238:1716-17 D 18 '87
Receptor gene family is growing. J. L. Marx. il *Science* 238:615-16 O 30 '87
The visual cycle operates via an isomerase acting on all-trans retinol in the pigment epithelium. C. D. Bridges and R. A. Alvarez. bibl f il *Science* 236:1678-80 Je 26 '87

Visualization
Mind control [visuo-motor behavior rehearsal technique of R. M. Suinn] M. Teich and G. Dodeles. il *Omni* 10:53-60 O '87
Who will stop the pain [overcoming injuries through positive imagery] K. Porter and J. Foster. il *World Tennis* 35:28-30 Jl '87

Visually handicapped
See also
Blind

Education
Breaking down the barriers for visually handicapped children [Portugal] M. A. M. de M. Alves. il *Courier* 40:30-2 Jl '87

Equipment
New help for low vision. C. Schaeffer. *Changing Times* 41:18+ Je '87

Vital statistics
See also
Birth rate
Children—Mortality
Infant mortality
Mortality

Vitale, Alberto
about
Bantam's Vitale to head Doubleday-Dell trade group. *Publ Wkly* 231:24 Ja 9 '87
Playing marriage counselor to Doubleday and Bantam. C. Power. il por *Bus Week* p73 Ag 10 '87

Vitale, Dick
about
Unlike his hairline, Dick Vitale's persona has never sounded retreat. R. Novak. il pors *People Wkly* 27:104-6 Mr 16 '87

Vitality
Body management: weight loss/energy gain [special section] il *Work Woman* 12:85-6+ F '87
Energy to burn: 12 ways to light your fire. E. Wilson. il *Mademoiselle* 93:90+ D '87
Future youth: how to regenerate your energy [excerpt; with editorial comment by Mark Bricklin] C. Keough. il *Prevention* 39:57, 102+ Jl '87
The great energy game. il *Seventeen* 46:260-1 Mr '87
How to eat for more energy. N. Stedman. il *Read Dig* 130:112-15 F '87
Secrets of vitality. K. Hepburn. por *Saturday Evening Post* 259:26 S '87

Vitamin receptors *See* Chemoreceptors

Vitamins
See also
United Sciences of America Inc.
The A's and C's of vitamins. T. Mendoza. il *Curr Health 2* 14:18-21 D '87
Color is the key to vitamins [cooking tips] B. E. Templeton. il *South Living* 22:174+ S '87
The elusive vitamin requirement. H. Fisher. il *Prevention* 39:108+ F '87
The perils of megavitamin therapy. il *Consum Res Mag* 70:16 Jl '87
Smart shopping for vitamins. T. Ratto. il *Women's Sports Fitness* 9:16 Ja '87
Vitamin and mineral supplements: do you need them? il *Glamour* 85:238 Je '87
Vitamin or drug? A clarification. H. Fisher. *Prevention* 39:121-4+ My '87
Vitamin supplements often wasteful [views of William Evers] *USA Today (Periodical)* 115:14 F '87
Vitamin update. il *Better Homes Gard* 65:68-9 F '87
Vitamins for your inner youth. H. Rodale. *Prevention* 39:27-31 Ap '87

Vitamin A
See also
Carotene
Blinding malnutrition. A. Sommer. il *World Health* p20-2 My '87
New benefits seen in vitamin A therapy. J. Raloff. *Sci News* 131:325 My 23 '87
A three-pronged programme [fighting Vitamin A deficiency] E. M. DeMaeyer. il *World Health* p22 My '87

The visual cycle operates via an isomerase acting on all-trans retinol in the pigment epithelium. C. D. Bridges and R. A. Alvarez. bibl f il *Science* 236:1678-80 Je 26 '87
Why vitamin A may fight infections [research by Susan Smith and Colleen Hayes] *Sci News* 132:46 Jl 18 '87

Vitamin A acid
See Retinoic acid

Vitamin B complex
See also
Folic acid
Niacin
Nicotinamide

Vitamin B₆
B₆: a solution to a painful problem [carpal tunnel syndrome] H. Fisher. il *Prevention* 39:56-8 Ja '87
Vitamin B₆ may put more fight in immune system. *Prevention* 39:113-14 S '87
A walking example of B₆ deficiency [ataxia; research by Monica C. Schaeffer] *Prevention* 39:104-5 Ag '87

Vitamin B₁₂
New nostril nostrum [Ener-B intranasal gel] *Time* 129:74 Mr 30 '87
A new way to take vitamins [Ener-B nasal gel] il *Newsweek* 110:48 Jl 20 '87
Snow job or nose job, California's new health craze is snorting vitamin B₁₂. il *People Wkly* 27:57 F 23 '87

Vitamin Bₜ
See Carnitine

Vitamin C
Diabetics need vitamin C for healthy skin. *Prevention* 39:124 Ja '87
Get 'hip' with vitamin C [avoiding hip fractures] *Prevention* 39:8 Jl '87
Make mine OJ [alcohol consumption and vitamin C; research by Vincent G. Zannoni and Robert Susick] il *Prevention* 39:10 D '87
Promising sulfite alternatives [research by Gerald M. Sapers] *Sci News* 132:63 Jl 25 '87
Super-C for hunters and dogs [preventing muscle soreness] L. Mueller. il *Outdoor Life* 180:76+ S '87
Vitamin C goes with the flow. *Prevention* 39:8 Mr '87
Vitamin C helps keep gums healthy; Folate may help, too. *Prevention* 39:79 F '87
Vitamin C KO's cholesterol. *Prevention* 39:67 N '87
Vitamins patrol artery walls. *Prevention* 39:54 O '87
Youth in a bottle [Avon's Collagen Booster Line Controlling Lotion] M. Fox. il *Health* 19:18 My '87

Vitamin D
Molecular cloning of complementary DNA encoding the avian receptor for vitamin D. D. P. McDonnell and others. bibl f il *Science* 235:1214-17 Mr 6 '87
Vitamin D for psoriasis? *Prevention* 39:14 S '87

Vitamin E
Bypass heart damage with vitamin E [free radical formation; research by Nicholas Cavarocchi] *Prevention* 39:11 O '87
Drug trial for Parkinson's [Deprenyl/tocopherol] R. Lewin. *Science* 236:1420 Je 12 '87
Firms, officials indicted over unsafe infants' drug [premature babies given vitamin E supplement E-Ferol] *FDA Consum* 21:4 O '87
Parkinson's treatment to be tested [Deprenyl/tocopherol; research by Ira Shoulson] *Prevention* 39:78 N '87
PMS eased by vitamin E [study by Robert London] il *Prevention* 39:14+ D '87
Smoke screened by vitamin E. *Prevention* 39:14 F '87
Vitamin E: a new weapon against cancer. H. Rodale. *Prevention* 39:17-19 F '87
Vitamins patrol artery walls. *Prevention* 39:54 O '87

Viterito, Arthur
The Koeppen climate classification system. il *Weatherwise* 40:160-1 Je '87

Vitetta, Ellen S., and others
Redesigning nature's poisons to create anti-tumor reagents. bibl f il *Science* 238:1098-104 N 20 '87

Vitex *See* Chaste tree

Viticulture
See also
Wine making
The hybrids [wine grapes] J. L. Newman. *Focus* 36:36 Wint '86

Vitousek, Peter M., and others
Biological invasion by Myrica faya alters ecosystem development in Hawaii. bibl f il *Science* 238:802-4 N 6 '87

Vitrification
Beyond the cutting edge of cold [vitrification of organs; cover story] S. Weisburd. il *Sci News* 132:138-41 Ag 29 '87

Vitz, Paul C., 1935-
Paul Vitz on censorship [excerpts from Censorship: evidence of bias in our children's textbooks] *Phi Delta Kappan* 68:453 F '87

Vivacqua, Eduardo
Ancient Lisbon—at old-time prices. il *World Press Rev* 34:62 Je '87

Vivaldi, Antonio, 1678-1741
about
Giustino [opera] Reviews
New Yorker 63:141-5 N 2 '87. A. Porter

Vivar, Rodrigo Díaz de *See* Cid, ca. 1043-1099

Viveros, Joy
Untitled [poem] *Essence* 18:122 Ag '87

Vivian, C. T.
about
C.T. Vivian faces threat of losing right to vote. *Jet* 72:23 Je 22 '87

Vivian, John
Taking on livestock (I). il *Mother Earth News* 104:56-61 Mr/Ap '87
Taking on livestock (II). il *Mother Earth News* 105:80-4+ My/Je '87

Vivier, Roger
about
In Vivier's shoes. P. McColl. il *N Y Times Mag* p36 D 27 '87
Once upon a shoe . . . a maker of magic: Roger Vivier. J. J. Buck. il por *Vogue* 177:292-7+ D '87

Viviparity
Bringing up baby [live birth for Brontosaurs; work of Robert T. Bakker] *Sci Am* 256:68+ Mr '87

Vivisection *See* Animal experimentation

Vizard, Frank
Audio. See issues of Popular Mechanics beginning October 1986
Auto sound [cover story; special section] il *Radio-Electron* 58:31-3+ Jl '87
A buyer's guide to camcorders. il *Radio-Electron* 58:47-51 Mr '87

Vizcachas *See* Viscachas

Vizcaya Museum and Gardens
The residence of James Deering's winters. il *South Living* 22:38 N '87

VLA (Very Large Array) radio telescope *See* Radio telescopes

VLBI (Very long baseline interferometry) *See* Interferometers and interferometry

VLI Corporation
Frozen out [B. Vorhauer shoved aside] J. Merwin. il por *Forbes* 140:100+ Jl 27 '87

VLSI (Very large scale integrated) circuits *See* Integrated circuits

Vobejda, Barbara
Why censor religion? Faiths and the textbooks. *Current* 296:30-2 O '87

Vocabulary
Context clues and word meaning: you takes your chances [conflicting research of William Nagy and Elinore Schatz and R. Scott Baldwin] G. W. Bracey. il *Phi Delta Kappan* 68:702-3 My '87
How children learn words. G. A. Miller and P. M. Gildea. il *Sci Am* 257:94-9 S '87
Words, quoted in context [increasing students' vocabularies] G. W. Bracey. *Phi Delta Kappan* 68:548-9 Mr '87

Vocabulary tests
It pays to enrich your word power. P. Funk. See issues of Reader's Digest

Vocal music
See also
Embellishment (Music)
Phonograph records—Vocal music
Singing
Musical events:
Voice and ensemble music. A. Porter. *New Yorker* 63:122-3 D 14 '87

Vocal organs *See* Voice

Vocal training *See* Singing—Study and teaching

Vocation in religion
God isn't finished with me yet. R. Brickley. *Commonweal* 114:410-11 Jl 17 '87
Ministry and vocations: going back to the drawing board. A. F. Deck. *America* 156:212-13+ Mr 14 '87
A royal priesthood. M. K. Hellwig. *America* 156:inside back cover My 9 '87

Vocations and the laicization of religious life. A. DiIanni. *America* 156:207-11 Mr 14 '87

Vocational aptitude tests *See* Aptitude tests

Vocational counseling *See* Vocational guidance

Vocational education *See* Vocational-technical education

Vocational guidance
See also
Mentors in business
Occupations
Outplacement consultant services
Career strategies: women at work [special section] il *Black Enterp* 17:99-100+ F '87
Dear Betty Harragan. B. L. Harragan. See issues of Working Woman
Educate, preach and pray [executives' children] D. Machan. il *Forbes* 139:146+ Mr 9 '87

Vocational-technical education
See also
Business and education
Business education
Business schools and colleges
Minorities—Vocational-technical education
Proprietary schools
Retraining, Occupational
Rutledge Education System
Single mothers—Vocational-technical education
United States. Office of Vocational and Adult Education
The last day of school is usually a zoo, but for 11 Ohio kids it was meant to be [Cincinnati's Zoo School] il *People Wkly* 27:60 Je 15 '87
Rethinking the role of vocational education. D. S. Spence. *Educ Dig* 52:48-51 F '87
States share successful strategies for increasing voc ed enrollment. *Phi Delta Kappan* 68:483-4 F '87
Statistics
Career schools: an overview. il *Change* 19:29-34 Ja/F '87

Canada
Building blocks for a new era. D. Cohen. por *Macleans* 100:7 F 2 '87

Vocations *See* Occupations

Vock, Jeffrey
Snow job. il *Skiing* 40:197-202 N '87

Vocoders
Resounding sensation [Tacticon 1600 invented by Frank Saunders] J. R. Goldberg. il *Health* 19:18 Ap '87

Vodka
Unlimited additions [flavored vodkas] E. Fried. il *Black Enterp* 17:148 F '87
Vodka: that old white magic. A. Fraser. il *Vogue* 177:328 Mr '87

Voell, Richard A.
Unbinding Gulliver [address, April 9, 1987] *Vital Speeches Day* 53:661-5 Ag 15 '87

Vogel, Carol
The Aulenti uproar. il por *N Y Times Mag* p26-32+ N 22 '87
Clustered for leisure: the changing home [cover story] il *N Y Times Mag* p12-17+ Je 28 '87

Vogel, Carole Garbuny
(jt. auth) See Goldner, Kathryn Allen, and Vogel, Carole Garbuny

Vogel, Dory Street
about
A woman's place. il por *Mot Boat Sail* 159:61 F '87

Vogel, Marta
Help for slow-growing children. il *FDA Consum* 21:14-17 Mr '87
What pregnant dreams mean. il *Parents* 62:120-2+ My '87

Vogel, Steven, 1940-
Mythology in introductory biology. bibl *BioScience* 37:611-14 S '87

Vogt, Markus W., and others
Ribavirin antagonizes the effect of azidothymidine on HIV replication. bibl f il *Science* 235:1376-9 Mr 13 '87

Vogt, Thomas F., and others
Raf, a trans-acting locus, regulates the α-fetoprotein gene in a cell-autonomous manner. bibl f il *Science* 236:301-3 Ap 17 '87

Voice
See also
Larynx
Singing
Speech
Speech processing systems
Is your voice holding you back? il *Glamour* 85:142 My '87

Voice—*cont.*

The sounds of success. J. Sherman. *Work Woman* 12:72 D '87

Voice coders *See* Vocoders

Voice culture *See* Singing—Study and teaching

Voice mail systems

The Complete Answering Machine. N. Baran. il *Byte* 12:100-1 D '87

Voice for sale. J. Jainschigg. il *Work Woman* 12:60 Ap '87

Voice messaging systems *See* Voice mail systems

Voice of America (Radio program)

Inciting the Libyans [editorials aired during the bombing of Tripoli and Benghazi] L. Alexandre. *Nation* 244:850 Je 20 '87

VOA-Europe: message radio. N. Martin. *Nation* 244:848-52 Je 20 '87

Voice of the Evil Empire [Radio Moscow can now be heard on AM radios throughout southern Florida] B. R. Johnson. *Natl Rev* 39:41 Ag 14 '87

Voice recognition (Psychology) *See* Recognition (Psychology)

Voice teachers *See* Singing teachers

Voiceovers (Advertising)

Anecdotes, facetiae, satire, etc.

My brilliant career. D. K. Mano. *Natl Rev* 39:60 Jl 31 '87

Voigt, Ellen Bryant, 1943-

Frog [poem] *Atlantic* 259:40 My '87

Voiku, Daniel

about

White professor wins reverse bias law suit against black college. *Jet* 72:32 Ap 20 '87

Voinovich, Vladimir, 1932-, and Zalygin, Sergei

Where *glasnost* has its limits; tr. by John Glad and Marie Arana-Ward. por *N Y Times Mag* p30-1 Jl 19 '87

Volcanic activity prediction

Correlation of volcanic activity with sulfur oxyanion speciation in a crater lake [cover story] B. Takano. bibl f il map *Science* 235:1633-5 Mr 27 '87

Raising the stakes at Mount St. Helens. R. A. Kerr. il *Science* 236:254-5 Ap 17 '87

Volcanic aerosols *See* Aerosols

Volcanic ash, tuff, etc.

See also

Aviation—Volcano hazards

San Salvador: small quake, big problems [volcanic ash amplifies earthquake] J. Silberner. *Sci News* 131:212 Ap 4 '87

Volcanic craters *See* Craters

Volcanic rocks *See* Rocks, Igneous

Volcanoes

See also

Aviation—Volcano hazards

Lava

Surtsey (Iceland)

Volcanic activity prediction

Volcanic ash, tuff, etc.

Collapsing volcanoes. P. Francis and S. Self. bibl (p136) il *Sci Am* 256:90-7 Je '87

Earthly belches perturb the weather. I. Teinowitz. il map *U S News World Rep* 103:65+ D 7 '87

Frozen fire [study of volcanic aerosols in Greenland ice cores] il *Earth Sci* 40:14-16 Spr '87

Geologic events. See issues of Earth Science

Recent mafic volcanism on Mars. B. K. Lucchitta. bibl f il maps *Science* 235:565-7 Ja 30 '87

Recent Martian volcanism indicated by new study [work of Baerbel Lucchitta] *Astronomy* 15:74-5 Je '87

Release of juvenile water on Mars: estimated amounts and timing associated with volcanism. R. Greeley. bibl f il *Science* 236:1653-4 Je 26 '87

Seamount serendipity in the South Pacific [eruption of MacDonald Seamount] R. Monastersky. *Sci News* 132:262 O 24 '87

Watering Mars with volcanism [research by Ronald Greeley] *Sci News* 132:9 Jl 4 '87

Alaska

See also

Augustine Volcano (Augustine Island, Alaska)

Aleutian Islands (Alaska)

Volcanic history in the Aleutian arc [research by Thomas P. Miller and Robert L. Smith] R. Monastersky. il *Sci News* 131:357 Je 6 '87

Central America

Nature's red-hot caldrons. J. Incer. il *Américas* 39:18-25 Ja/F '87

Colombia

See also

Nevado del Ruiz (Colombia)

Greece

See also

Thera (Greece: Island)

Hawaii

See also

Kilauea (Hawaii)

Loihi (Hawaii)

India

Volcanoes and extinctions: round two [theory of Vincent E. Courtillot and Stanley Cisowski] S. Weisburd. il map *Sci News* 131:248-50 Ap 18 '87

Japan

Correlation of volcanic activity with sulfur oxyanion speciation in a crater lake [cover story] B. Takano. bibl f il map *Science* 235:1633-5 Mr 27 '87

Martinique

See also

Mount Pelée (Martinique)

Mexico

See also

El Chichón (Mexico)

Sicily

See also

Mount Etna (Sicily)

Washington (State)

See also

Mount Saint Helens (Wash.)

Mount Saint Helens National Volcanic Monument (Wash.)

Volcanoes in art

Roden's eye [J. Turrell's Roden Crater] F. Hapgood. il por *Atlantic* 260:46-52 Ag '87

Exhibitions

Dream space [J. Turrell's new site installation at P.S. 1 and observatory at Roden Crater] S. Gablik. il *Art Am* 75:132-3+ Mr '87

Volchok, Susan M.

I've spent years listening to men talk about their interests. When will they ask me about mine? il *Glamour* 85:19 Ja '87

Volcker, Paul A.

about

Are we ready for life after Volcker? B. Riemer. il *Bus Week* p41 Ja 26 '87

Exit Volcker, enter Greenspan. *Natl Rev* 39:17+ Jl 3 '87

Greenspan isn't a Volcker clone. L. Smith. il pors *Fortune* 116:34-6 Jl 6 '87

How Volcker sabotaged the president's agenda. P. C. Roberts. il *Bus Week* p18 Je 15 '87

An inflation fighter steps down. I. Austen. il pors *Macleans* 100:34-5 Je 15 '87

A model of discretion. por *U S News World Rep* 103:28 N 9 '87

The new Mr. Dollar [cover story; special section] il pors *Time* 129:46-53 Je 15 '87

Nice work if you can get it. il por *Newsweek* 110:10 O 19 '87

Paul Volcker seems a bit lost. M. McNamee. il por *Bus Week* p93 S 28 '87

Paul Volcker was the Babe Ruth of central banking. A. S. Blinder. il *Bus Week* p12 Je 29 '87

The price of money (I). W. Greider. *New Yorker* 63:54-6+ N 9 '87

The price of money (III). W. Greider. *New Yorker* 63:49-50+ N 23 '87

Reagan's man at the Fed [special section] il pors *Newsweek* 109:16-20+ Je 15 '87

The rising risk of recession. J. Egan. il pors *U S News World Rep* 102:47+ Je 15 '87

Vale, Volcker [cover story] G. P. Brockway. il *New Leader* 70:9-11 Jl 1-15 '87

Volcker on the crash. L. S. Silk. il por *N Y Times Mag* p40+ N 8 '87

Volcker: the absent 'icon'. R. Thomas. por *Newsweek* 110:39 N 9 '87

Volcker tries wrestling a bear called bank reform. B. Riemer and V. Cahan. por *Bus Week* p51 Mr 16 '87

Volcker: will he stay? [cover story] B. Riemer. il pors *Bus Week* p76-80+ Mr 30 '87

Weaving a dollar crisis out of whole cloth. P. C. Roberts. il *Bus Week* p31 F 23 '87

What's in store at the Fed [cover story; special section] il pors *Bus Week* p26-30 Je 15 '87

The world after Volcker. C. Smallwood and J. Cassidy. il *World Press Rev* 34:44-5 Ag '87

Anecdotes, facetiae, satire, etc.

And now, the Fed letters. pors *U S News World Rep* 103:43 Jl 27 '87

Vold, Mona
This land is their land. il *Ms* 16:76+ N '87
Volel, Yves, d. 1987

about

Obituary
Nation 245:473 O 31 '87. P. G. Meyer
Völgyes, Iván, 1936-
Hungary: before the storm breaks. *Curr Hist* 86:373-6+ N '87
Volhard, Christiane Nüsslein- *See* Nüsslein-Volhard, Christiane
Volk, Patricia
A family of firsts. il *N Y Times Mag* p70-1 O 4 '87
A word from our sponsor. il *N Y Times Mag* p12+ Ag 23 '87
Volkart, Bill
Do your homework before you buy. il *Astronomy* 15:48-53 O '87
Volkswagen (Automobile) *See* Automobiles, Foreign
Volkswagen AG
Can Volkswagen pull itself out of the mud? [currency fraud charges] R. Ingersoll. il por *Bus Week* p60-1 Je 22 '87
Computer fraud at VW [foreign-exchange fraud] P. Lewis. il *Macleans* 100:32 Mr 30 '87
A currency scandal adds to VW's woes. J. E. Pluenneke. *Bus Week* p54+ Mr 23 '87
How the shocker at VW could undo a buddy system [banks go public with criticism of management] J. E. Pluenneke. il *Bus Week* p61 Je 22 '87
A speed demon hits a slippery patch [C. H. Hahn] L. S. Richman. il por *Fortune* 116:41 Ag 3 '87
What ended VW's American dream. J. Templeman. il *Bus Week* p63 D 7 '87
Volkswagen de Mexico SA de CV
Mexican auto workers resist cuts [strike] J. Slaughter. *Progressive* 51:12-13 O '87
Volkswagen of America Inc.
What ended VW's American dream [closing plant in Westmoreland County, Pa.] J. Templeman. il *Bus Week* p63 D 7 '87
A 'wise' decision backfires on Volkswagen [closing plant in New Stanton, Pa.] il *Newsweek* 110:62 D 7 '87
Voll, Daniel
The dark playground. il *N Y Times Mag* p86 O 4 '87
Vollers, Maryanne
The rhino wars. il *Sports Illus* 66:60-8+ Mr 2 '87
Volleyball
A juggling act [N. Matthies, beach volleyball player] P. Freeman. il pors *Women's Sports Fitness* 9:39-42 Ag '87
Our women in Havana [U.S. team finishes second in NORCECA Zone Championships] D. Stathoplos. il *Sports Illus* 66:46-7 Je 29 '87
The sultan of spike [K. Kiraly] P. Richmond. il pors *Roll Stone* p87+ Jl 16-30 '87
Volleyball, College

Tournaments

West versus the rest [dispute over selection process for women's NCAA championships] il *Women's Sports Fitness* 9:17 Mr '87
With Ozzie, it was easy [UCLA defeats USC for NCAA title] B. Anderson. il por *Sports Illus* 66:87+ My 11 '87
Volleyball, Professional
Black star leads women's volleyball team to title [R. Crockett] *Jet* 72:48 Je 15 '87
For outdoor volleyball ace Sinjin Smith, going to work is a day at the beach. K. Hubbard. il pors *People Wkly* 28:39-40 Ag 31 '87
Vollmer Associates
It takes a 'sixth sense' to operate underneath the streets of New York. D. D. Jackson. il *Smithsonian* 18:38-47 Ag '87
Vollum Institute for Advanced Biomedical Research
Minds over matter. D. Brenner. il *Archit Rec* 175:102-11 S '87
Volpi, Nathalie

about

Villa Rocca nel Circeo: Nathalie Volpi's creation on the Tyrrhenian Sea. C. Aillaud. il *Archit Dig* 44:116-25 Ja '87
Volsky, George
In Castro's gulag. il pors *N Y Times Mag* p80-2+ O 18 '87
Volstad, Ozzie

about

With Ozzie, it was easy. B. Anderson. il por *Sports Illus* 66:87+ My 11 '87

Voltage regulators
Computer-assisted regulator design. J. Cunkelman. il *Radio-Electron* 58 ComputerDigest:110-11 F '87
Regulating the voltage of a DC motor [astrophotography; with comments by Roger W. Sinnott] A. Kremers. il *Sky Telesc* 74:198-201 Ag '87
Transformerless 5-volt regulator. R. F. Scott. il *Radio-Electron* 58:92-3+ F '87
Voltmeters

See also

Voltohmmeters
Voltohmmeters
How to use an ohmmeter [VOM] M. J. Schultz. il *Pop Mech* 164:103-4 O '87
Volume control (Audio systems) *See* Audio systems—Volume control
Volunteer fire departments *See* Fire departments
Volunteer service

See also

Dorcas Place Parent Literacy Center
Helping Hands (Organization)
Literacy Volunteers of America
National service
Science museums—Volunteer workers
Senior Companion Program (U.S.)
Service Credit Volunteer Program
Tennis—Tournaments—Volunteer workers
United States. Volunteers in Service to America
Volunteer workers in education
AIDS volunteers. J. Stone. il *Glamour* 85:288-9+ Mr '87
Finding a satisfying volunteer job. il *Glamour* 85:98-9 S '87
I'm just a girl who can't say no. E. F. Belitsky. il *Ms* 15:48+ F '87
Involving children and youth in community projects [New Mexico] N. Kalishman and others. bibl f il *Child Today* 16:23-6 Mr/Ap '87
Learning to serve: high school service programs. A. C. Lewis. *Educ Dig* 53:50-1 N '87
'A little lower than the angels' [athletes who help others; cover story; special section; with introd. by Frank Deford] il *Sports Illus* 67:12-31 D 21 '87
Silver bullets for the needy [college students] A. Toufexis. il *Time* 129:72-3 Mr 16 '87
Students in public service: honoring those who care [interview with winners of Robinson Student Humanitarian Achievement Award] F. Newman. il *Change* 19:19-27 Jl/Ag '87
Their hearts are as important as their heads [youth volunteer service] A. C. Lewis. *Phi Delta Kappan* 68:572-3 Ap '87
With our own hands [excerpt from Everything to gain] J. Carter and R. Carter. il pors *McCalls* 114:44+ Jl '87
Youth participation [address, July 20, 1987] J. C. Cutler. *Vital Speeches Day* 54:11-13 O 15 '87
Volunteer service, International

See also

Operation Raleigh
Overseas Development Network
Peace Corps (U.S.)
Volunteer workers *See* Volunteer service
Volunteer workers in education
Helping kids: the ripple effect [elderly volunteers in Monroe, Mich.] il *Aging* no355:28 '87
Special "cooking friends" add spice to Head Start nutrition programs [American Home Economics Association's Volunteer Nutrition Consultant Project] S. A. Koblinsky and M. G. Phillips. il *Child Today* 16:26-9 Jl/Ag '87
Volunteering at school. F. Roberts. *Parents* 62:58+ F '87
Volunteers of Legal Service
The Dean of pro bono law. A. Prud'homme. il por *N Y* 20:36 N 9 '87
Volvo (Automobile) *See* Automobiles, Foreign
VOM *See* Voltohmmeters
Von Braun, Wernher, 1912-1977

about

Starman. G. Williams. il *Omni* 9:86-93 Jl '87
Von Briel, Rudi
Urban majesty. il *Petersens Photogr Mag* 16:42-3 Jl '87
Von Buchau, Stephanie
Barbary Coast bonanza. il *Opera News* 52:18+ S '87
Funding opera: an endearing attitude. il por *Opera News* 51:14+ Je '87
Not just an entertainment. il *Opera News* 52:24+ O '87

Von Bulow, Claus
about
Dark and dangerous men. B. G. Harrison. *Mademoiselle* 93:114 Je '87
Von Dreele, W. H.
[Poems] See issues of National Review
Von Germeten, James N.
about
High-octane banking. J. Willoughby. il por *Forbes* 140:58+ S 21 '87
Von Hippel, Frank
A U.S. scientist addresses Gorbachev [address, February 16, 1987] *Bull At Sci* 43:12-13 My '87
Von Hoffman, Nicholas
Should the press play vice cop? [cover story] *Nation* 244:835+ Je 20 '87
Von Hofmannsthal, Hugo See Hofmannsthal, Hugo von, 1874-1929
Von Kuehnelt-Leddihn, Erik See Kuehnelt-Leddihn, Erik von
Von Nostitz, Pamela
The healthy parent. See issues of Parents beginning January 1987 through September 1987
Von Ohain, Hans See Ohain, Hans von
Von Puttkamer, Peter
about
New options (positive) for the troubled Doubleday clubs [interview] R. A. Roel. il pors *Publ Wkly* 232:21-3 O 23 '87
Von Ranke, Leopold See Ranke, Leopold von, 1795-1886
Von Rezzori, Beatrice See Rezzori, Beatrice von
Von Rezzori, Gregor See Rezzori, Gregor von
Von Stroheim, Erich, 1885-1957
about
First encounters. E. Sorel and N. C. Sorel. il *Atlantic* 260:73 S '87
Von Tiesenhausen, Georg See Tiesenhausen, Georg von, 1914-
Von Trotta, Margarethe See Trotta, Margarethe von
Vonnegut, Kurt, 1922-
Skyscraper National Park. il por *Archit Dig* 44:76+ N '87
Vons Grocery Co.
Food as fashion. S. B. Weiner and E. Paris. il *Forbes* 140:106-7 S 7 '87
Voodoo lilies
Salicylic acid: a natural inducer of heat production in Arum lilies. I. Raskin and others. bibl f il *Science* 237:1601-2 S 25 '87
Voodooism
'Root doctor' held in murder of his former wife [T. L. Berry of Blakely, Ga.] *Jet* 72:29 Je 1 '87
Brazil
Brazil's black magic [Macumba] H. J. Maier, Jr. il *Travel Holiday* 167:100 Mr '87
Voodooism in motion pictures
Black magic. P. Aufderheide. il *Progressive* 51:26-7 S '87
Voorhees, Eugenie
about
Pure Nantucket. J. Chancellor. il *House Gard* 159:78-85+ Ag '87
VOR (Very high-frequency omnirange receivers) See Radio in aviation
Vorbeck, Jill
about
Quest for flavor. J. Ruttle. il *Rodale's Org Gard* 34:42-4+ D '87
Vorbeck, Tom
about
Quest for flavor. J. Ruttle. il *Rodale's Org Gard* 34:42-4+ D '87
Vorhauer, Bruce
about
Frozen out. J. Merwin. il por *Forbes* 140:100+ Jl 27 '87
Vortex foils (Hydraulic engineering) See Hydraulic engineering
Vortex generators
Low-profile vortex generators provide aerodynamic improvements through boundary layer control. il *Aviat Week Space Technol* 126:88+ Je 1 '87
Wing-tip dynamos spin out extra power. D. Stover. il *Pop Sci* 231:65+ S '87
Vortex motion
Ames-Dryden to study airflow around fighter aircraft at high angles of attack. *Aviat Week Space Technol* 126:20 Mr 30 '87
F-106 aids vortex flow study to improve fighter performance [advanced-technology fighters] E. H. Phillips. il *Aviat Week Space Technol* 127:51-2 S 21 '87

Langley develops new airflow visualization system [analysis and evaluation of vortex flap effectiveness] *Aviat Week Space Technol* 127:76-7 N 16 '87
Quantized vortices in superfluid helium-4. W. I. Glaberson and K. W. Schwarz. bibl f il *Phys Today* 40:54-60 F '87
Vortices in rotating superfluid He^3. P. Hakonen and O. V. Lounasmaa. bibl f il *Phys Today* 40:70-8 F '87
Vorwärts (Newspaper) See Jewish daily forward
Vos Savant, Marilyn Mach
about
There's nothing artificial about the way Robert Jarvik's heart beats for his brainy bride-to-be. K. McMurran. il pors *People Wkly* 28:46-50 Jl 27 '87
Voskhod flights See Space flight—Voskhod flights
Voss, Gilbert L.
Crow's nest. See issues of Sea Frontiers beginning November/December 1986
Voter registration
See also
National Coalition of Black Voter Participation
Southwest Voter Registration Education Project
Honor King's birthday with vote drive, says Chicago commissioner [views of J. H. Stroger] il por *Jet* 71:14 Ja 26 '87
Voting
See also
Black suffrage
Presidents—Election
Proportional representation
Referendum
Television broadcasting—Election results
United States. Congress—Voting
United States. Congress. House—Voting
United States. Congress. Senate—Voting
Voter registration
Woman suffrage
Blacks win major offices; black voters show power. il *Jet* 73:4+ N 23 '87
Kirk's cant [P. Kirk's proposal to arrest the decline of voter participation in elections] T. Ferguson. *Nation* 244:385 Mr 28 '87
The least you can do is vote [with readers' comments] M. O'Connell. *U S Cathol* 52:14-20 My '87
Why Americans don't vote. R. Kuttner. *New Repub* 197:19-21 S 7 '87
Psychological aspects
Sending messages, getting replies. K. L. Schlozman and S. Verba. *Society* 24:48-55 My/Je '87
Voting Rights Act See Election laws
Voucher plan in education
A key to school reform. *America* 156:118 F 14 '87
Public choice, yes; vouchers, no! M. A. Raywid. bibl f il *Phi Delta Kappan* 68:762-9 Je '87
Should government help kids attend private schools? J. H. DeDakis. il *Christ Today* 31:52-3 My 15 '87
Vouchers, Housing See Housing vouchers
Voyager (Airplane)
Around-the-world flight [special section; with editorial comment by Donald E. Fink] il *Aviat Week Space Technol* 126:13, 22-7 Ja 5 '87
Around the world on a tank of gas. I. Peterson. il *Sci News* 131:5 Ja 3 '87
Gallant victory for an odd bird. S. Moses. il pors *Sports Illus* 66:36-9 Ja 5 '87
A magical world flight. il *Macleans* 100:23 Ja 5 '87
New horizons. N. Moll. il *Flying* 114:138-40 S '87
Now, Voyager [paper model] il *Omni* 9 Omni Exper:14-16 Ap '87
The R&T/Voyager connection. P. Egan. il *Road Track* 38:50-5 My '87
Sketchy details [evolution of design] P. Garrison. il *Flying* 114:20-2 Jl '87
Tailwinds, thunderstorms and turbulence: the weather story of the Voyager flight [cover story] P. Mueller and L. Burch. il map *Weatherwise* 40:240-7 O '87
Voyager: flight fantastic [with editorial comment by Richard L. Collins] P. Garrison. il *Flying* 114:24, 28-32+ Mr '87
Voyager is home for a while in Mojave's Hangar 77. il *Sunset* 178:18 My '87
With a few gallons to spare. W. D. Marbach. il *Newsweek* 109:28 Ja 5 '87
Photographs and photography
Fantastic! Voyager. il *Life* 10:6-11 F '87
Voyager flights See Space flight—Voyager flights
Voyages
See also
Antarctic exploration
Arctic exploration

Voyages—See also—*cont.*
> Cruising
> Ocean liners
> Seafaring life
> Shipwrecks

In Florida: everyman's dream [Couvreux family] G. Jaynes. il *Time* 129:16-17 Mr 9 '87

Land creatures [E. Gillet kayaks across Pacific Ocean] *New Yorker* 63:30-1 S 21 '87

On eye opening [blind sailor J. Dickson attempts to sail across the Atlantic alone] W. F. Buckley. *Natl Rev* 39:73 S 11 '87

Passage at Cape Horn [D. and D. Hays sail 25 foot cutter around Cape Horn and back to Connecticut] A. Smith. il pors *Esquire* 107:88-90+ Mr '87

Racing through paradise (I) [Honolulu to New Guinea] W. F. Buckley. *New Yorker* 62:40-4+ F 9 '87

Racing through paradise (II) [Honolulu to New Guinea] W. F. Buckley. *New Yorker* 62:71-88 F 16 '87

History

A boy at sea [memories of life aboard a Pacific lumber schooner in 1915] R. B. Hope. il por *Am Hist Illus* 21:14-18 Ja '87

"Captain" Mary Patten [1854-55 voyage from New York to San Francisco via Cape Horn] P. L. Brosnan. il por *Oceans* 20:36-9 S/O '87

Travellers' tales [cover story; special issue; with editorial comment by Edouard Glissant] bibl il *Courier* 40:3-38 Ap '87

Voyages around the world

Around the world in 29 months, Tania Aebi blows into New York with a record Guinness may not validate [sailing trip] T. Cunneff. il pors *People Wkly* 28:128-9 N 23 '87

Around the world in 80 days [attempt to break powerboat record in boat built by Certified Marine] B. Duke and S. Duke. il map *Mot Boat Sail* 159:48-51+ Ap '87

Hal Roth: on to Bali [tenth leg of circumnavigation] H. Roth. *Mot Boat Sail* 159:170+ Ja '87

Hal Roth: sailing to the Seychelles [eleventh leg of circumnavigation] H. Roth. *Mot Boat Sail* 159:158+ F '87

On board with Philippe Monnet [holds record for around-the-world solo sailing] M. Pennybaker. il por *Mot Boat Sail* 160:54-5+ N '87

History

Nellie Bly. C. Bergman and M. Nussbaum. il pors *Am Hist Illus* 22:22-6+ Mr '87

Voyageur Wilderness Books (Firm)

Voyageur Press of Minnesota launches Wilderness imprint. *Publ Wkly* 232:64 O 9 '87

Voynick, Stephen M.

Shale shock on the western slope. il *Sierra* 72:29-31 My/Je '87

Voznesenskiĭ, Andreĭ, 1933-

A poet's view of *glasnost*; tr. by Antonina W. Bouis. *Nation* 244:810-12 Je 13 '87

about

A Soviet poet's praise for freedom. W. French. il *World Press Rev* 34:61 Je '87

Vradenburg, Trish

Happily ever after, indeed! il *Read Dig* 131:177-8 D '87

Vreeland, Nancy *See* Dalva, Nancy Vreeland

V'Soske, Inc.

Fancy footwork. D. Brenner. il *Archit Rec* 175:152-5 mid-S '87

Vuitton (Louis) (Firm) *See* Louis Vuitton (Firm)

Vultures

See also
> Condors
> Turkey vultures

Riddle of Gettysburg's vultures. E. Daniels. il *Audubon* 89:82-4+ Ja '87

VW (Automobile) *See* Automobiles, Foreign

Vychodil, Ladislav

about

Svoboda & Vychodil: Czechoslovakia's two master scenographers. J. M. Burian. il *Theatre Crafts* 21:34-7+ O '87

W

W (Periodical)

Of power, glory and the rich and famous [influence of J. Fairchild] A. Gabor. il por *U S News World Rep* 103:55 Ag 24 '87

W. A. Baxter & Sons Ltd. *See* Baxters of Speyside Ltd.

W. A. Krueger Co.

Krueger buys Nelson's Interstate Book Mfrs. *Publ Wkly* 231:54 Je 19 '87

Krueger signs intent to buy 50% of Koon Wah. *Publ Wkly* 232:44 Jl 3 '87

W. R. Berkley Corp.

Earnings from insuring against a big fish. il *Money* 16:8 Mr '87

Waack, William

Eight questions for higher education. *Des Arts Educ* 88:32-5 Ja/F '87

Wachner, Linda Joy, 1946-

about

Linda Wachner. C. Donahue. il por *Ms* 15:78+ Ja '87

New outfit for a queen of beauty. A. L. Taylor, III. il por *Fortune* 115:56 Ja 5 '87

Turning trials into triumph. R. B. Tooley. il por *Work Woman* 12:66-8+ Ja '87

Wachsman, William, and others

HTLV *x* gene mutants exhibit novel transcriptional regulatory phenotypes. bibl f il *Science* 235:674-7 F 6 '87

Wachtel, Howard M.

The global funny money game. il *Nation* 245:784-6+ D 26 '87-Ja 2 '88

Wachtel, Paul Spencer

Return of the bloodsucker. il *Int Wildl* 17:44-6 S/O '87

Wachtel, Ruth E.

Personal bibliographic databases. bibl f il *Science* 235:1093-6 F 27 '87

Wacker, Grant, 1945-

America's Pentecostals: who they are. il por *Christ Today* 31:16-21 O 16 '87

Wacker, Jeanne

Radical, teacher, technician. *Natl Rev* 39:33-4 S 11 '87

Wackler, Rebecca

about

Tent meeting [drama] Reviews
  N Y 20:70-1 Ap 20 '87. J. Simon
  Nation 244:585-6 My 2 '87. T. M. Disch

Wacoal Corp.

Western wear. H. Katayama. il por *Forbes* 140:305 N 16 '87

Waddell, Charles L.

(jt. auth) See Hanzek, Michael J., and Waddell, Charles L.

Waddell, Tom, 1937-1987

about

Notes and comment. *New Yorker* 63:19-20 Ag 24 '87

Obituary

Sports Illus il pors 67:26-8+ Jl 27 '87. D. Schaap

Waddenzee (Netherlands)

See also
> Marine pollution—Waddenzee (Netherlands)

Waddick, James W.

Dwarf bamboo for ground cover that's different. il *Flower Gard* 31:34+ F/Mr '87

Wade, Danny

about

Daredevil: the man who fell to earth. C. Hodenfield. il pors *Cycle* 38:29-34 N '87

Wade, Donald C.

about

Stand up to AIDS. M. G. Stoddard. il pors *Saturday Evening Post* 259:54-5 S '87

Wade, Marcia

Art times two. il *Horizon* 30:58-61 My '87

Red Grooms. il por *Horizon* 30:12-16 Jl/Ag '87

Utopia revisited. il *Horizon* 30:13-16 Je '87

Wade, Paul J.

Cycling in Suffolk. il maps *Gourmet* 48:54-9+ Je '87

Gourmet holidays: cross-country skiing from Baden-Baden. il map *Gourmet* 47:48-53+ F '87

Gourmet holidays: trout fishing in New Zealand. il maps *Gourmet* 47:54-9+ Ap '87

Wading

Tips for safer wading. T. Thomas. *Field Stream* 92:96 Je '87

Wading birds *See* Shore birds
Wadsley, Pat
 Mini masterpieces: teasers, trailers and spots before your eyes. il *Theatre Crafts* 21:69-72 Ja '87
Wadsworth, Jack
 about
 Although lacking a movie deal, the Wadsworths (He- and She-) find they still have the power. D. Van Biema. il pors *People Wkly* 27:87+ My 4 '87
Wadsworth, Leslie
 about
 Although lacking a movie deal, the Wadsworths (He- and She-) find they still have the power. D. Van Biema. il pors *People Wkly* 27:87+ My 4 '87
Wadsworth Atheneum
 The Austin phenomenon. R. Lynes. il pors *Archit Dig* 44:51+ O '87
 European decorative arts [exhibition entitled J. Pierpont Morgan, collector: European decorative arts from the Wadsworth Atheneum] S. B. Sherrill. il *Antiques* 131:48+ Ja '87
 Tycoon taste [exhibition entitled J. Pierpont Morgan, collector: European decorative arts from the Wadsworth Atheneum] J. Strouse. il por *House Gard* 159:94+ My '87
Wafer scale integrated circuits *See* Integrated circuits
Wage agreements *See* Collective labor agreements
Wage bargaining *See* Collective bargaining
Wage differentials
 See also
 Equal pay for equal work
 The debate over new jobs is turning into mudslinging. R. Kuttner. il *Bus Week* p22 Ap 13 '87
 The myth of 'McJobs'. *Natl Rev* 39:19-20 Ap 10 '87
 The wages of discrimination: comparing salaries. W. R. Beer. *Current* 297:33-6 N '87
 Why two-tier wage scales are starting to self-destruct. A. Bernstein. il *Bus Week* p41 Mr 16 '87
 Women's pay: the catch-up game quickens. B. Brophy. *U S News World Rep* 103:10 S 14 '87
Wage-price policy
   Yugoslavia
 Striking at the system. il *Macleans* 100:21 Ap 13 '87
Wageman, Tom
 about
 Getting savers to take a shine to Sunbelt. J. Weber, Jr. il pors *Bus Week* p74+ N 9 '87
Wager, George
 about
 Have your kids been tagged? il *Read Dig* 131:11-12 N '87
Wages and salaries
 See also
 Bonus system
 Collective labor agreements
 Cost and standard of living
 Equal pay for equal work
 Income
 Minimum wage
 Overtime
 Profit sharing
 Severance pay
 Skill-based pay
 Tipping
  See also subhead Salaries, pensions, etc. under classes of persons
 Are you underpaid? V. Consoli. il *McCalls* 114:63 Je '87
 Bigger pay for better work [results of survey] J. C. Horn. il *Psychol Today* 21:54-7 Jl '87
 The bustling economy won't add heft to paychecks [views of Robert J. Barbera] G. Koretz. il *Bus Week* p22 S 21 '87
 The eighth annual Working woman salary survey. H. McCrum and H. Rubin. il *Work Woman* 12:53-5+ Ja '87
 Five ways to a fatter paycheck. L. Sorenson. *Work Woman* 12:102-3 Je '87
 Higher learning means higher earnings, study. *Jet* 73:12 N 16 '87
 How to ask for a raise—and get it! A 7-point plan for talking to the boss. T. Fischer. *McCalls* 114:122 Ja '87
 How to get the salary you deserve [women] il *Glamour* 85:162 O '87
 If you're so smart . . . how come you're working for that salary? A. Gates. il *Mademoiselle* 93:238-9+ Ag '87
 A lament: all work and less pay [rise in productivity as wages are cut] S. Koepp. il *Time* 130:48 Jl 13 '87

 Money issues on the job [excerpt from Everything college didn't teach you about money] B. Brophy. il *Essence* 18:122+ S '87
 Pay expectations: the spouse factor [study by John Mirowsky] J. Meer. *Psychol Today* 21:11 Ap '87
 Real wages are headed for a fall. H. Banks. *Forbes* 139:27 F 23 '87
 Salary roundup: who earns what [black professionals] il *Black Enterp* 17:71-2 F '87
 Test your money smarts [excerpt from Money talks] R. Skolnik. *Good Housekeep* 204:204 F '87
 'Thanks for the bonus, but where's my raise?'. B. Brophy and M. Walsh. il *U S News World Rep* 103:43-4 Jl 20 '87
 Underpaid? Check our salary list. R. Colletti and others. il *Good Housekeep* 204:80+ Je '87
 When a pay cut may be your best bet. L. Bethel. il *Black Enterp* 18:76-8 S '87
 Women's pay: the catch-up game quickens. B. Brophy. *U S News World Rep* 103:10 S 14 '87
 You can get that raise. A. M. Scheele. *Read Dig* 131:55-6+ N '87
   Anecdotes, facetiae, satire, etc.
 A heap of trouble. R. Baker. il *N Y Times Mag* p12 F 1 '87
   Laws and regulations
 See also
 Wage-price policy
 What price peace? [upcoming decision on whether lump-sum payments should be computed as overtime] D. Fanning. il *Forbes* 140:56 D 28 '87
   Statistics
 Analyzing employers' costs for wages, salaries, and benefits. F. Nathan. bibl f il *Mon Labor Rev* 110:3-11 O '87
 Employment and wage changes of families from CE Survey data [Consumer Expenditure Survey] M. F. Kokoski. bibl f il *Mon Labor Rev* 110:31-3 F '87
 Employment, hours, and earnings data from establishment surveys. See issues of Monthly Labor Review
 State and local government pay increases outpace five-year rise in private industry. R. Schumann. il *Mon Labor Rev* 110:18-20 F '87
 Wage and compensation data. See issues of Monthly Labor Review
 Weekly earnings in 1986: a look at more than 200 occupations. E. F. Mellor. bibl f il *Mon Labor Rev* 110:41-6 Je '87
 Workers at the minimum wage or less: who they are and the jobs they hold. E. F. Mellor. bibl f il *Mon Labor Rev* 110:34-8 Jl '87
   Taxation
 See also
 Social security—Taxation
 Withholding tax
   Korea (South)
 An Asian Norma Rae [fighting for better wages] J. Gittelsohn. il *U S News World Rep* 103:52 S 14 '87
Waggoner, Glen
 Heartsick. il *Esquire* 107:26 F '87
 How to break a date. *Esquire* 107:24 Ja '87
 Now the bell for round two. il *Esquire* 108:30 Ag '87
 School for swingers. il *Esquire* 108:31-2 N '87
 The swing's the thing. il *Esquire* 107:25-6 My '87
 Three mean punches. il *Esquire* 107:24+ Ja '87
 Wellness for the well-heeled. il *Esquire* 107:55 Je '87
Wagner, A. James
 Northern Hemisphere steering currents. il *Weatherwise* 40:17-20 F '87
Wagner, C. Peter
 America's Pentecostals: see how they grow. il *Christ Today* 31:28-9 O 16 '87
Wagner, David
 Bill Bennett's dilemma. il *Natl Rev* 39:28-31+ Je 19 '87
Wagner, Geoffrey
 Some fell slow and some fell fast. *Natl Rev* 39:32-3 Je 5 '87
Wagner, Jon
 Teaching and research as student responsibilities: integrating community and academic work. il *Change* 19:26-31+ S/O '87
Wagner, Leila
 about
 Lady in a fast lane. G. Maranto. il pors *Sports Illus* 67:44-7 S 28 '87
 Woman to watch: Leila Wagner. B. Cooper. il por *Women's Sports Fitness* 9:62 N '87

Wagner, Martha
Super books for healthy cooks. il *Women's Sports Fitness* 9:62-3 Je '87
Wagner, Melissa J.
(jt. auth) See Stigler, Stephen M., and Wagner, Melissa J.
Wagner, Richard, 1813-1883
about
Full cycle. D. Harris. il *Opera News* 51:12-14+ F 28 '87
Most happy cello. P. G. Davis. il por *N Y* 20:108-9 Mr 9 '87
Parsifal [opera] Reviews
Opera News il 51:16-18 Ap 11 '87. M. O. Lee
Opera News il 51:22-4 Ap 11 '87
Das Rheingold [opera] Reviews
N Y il 20:112-13 O 26 '87. P. G. Davis
New Yorker 63:136+ O 26 '87. A. Porter
Opera News il 51:40+ Mr 28 '87. S. Modi
'Ring' of magic. P. G. Davis. il *N Y* 20:116-17 Ag 24 '87
Seattle. D. Harris. il *Opera News* 52:36 D 19 '87
Tannhäuser [opera] Reviews
Opera News il 51:26-9 Ja 17 '87
Opera News il 51:30-3+ Ja 17 '87. J. Potter
Tristan und Isolde [opera] Reviews
Newsweek il 110:73 D 21 '87. J. Huck
Wagner as anti-Semite. S. Lipman. *Commentary* 83:57-60 Ja '87
Wagner's "Ring" cycle on CD. W. Livingstone. il *Stereo Rev* 52:156-7 D '87
Die Walküre [opera] Reviews
Opera News il 51:28-31 F 28 '87
Wagner, Robert
about
Architectural digest visits: Robert Wagner. J. Allen. il pors *Archit Dig* 44:124-31+ My '87
Robert Wagner: Hollywood's incurable romantic. D. De Dubovay. il pors *McCalls* 145:158+ Mr '87
Wagner, Rudolf
(jt. auth) See Goldman, Merle, and Wagner, Rudolf
Wagner, William E., Jr.
(jt. auth) See Ryan, Michael J. (Michael Joseph), 1953-, and Wagner, William E., Jr.
Wagner & Brown
GenCorp feels the pincers [Wagner & Brown-AFG team] T. Carson and Z. Schiller. *Bus Week* p33-4 Mr 30 '87
Wagon trains
Pioneer [E. Bessette's covered wagon trip across America] *New Yorker* 63:27-8 F 23 '87
Wagons
See also
Gypsy wagons
Wagstaff, Sam
about
Silver futures. N. F. Weber. il *House Gard* 159:42+ Mr '87
Wahat al-Salam (Israel) See Neve Shalom (Israel)
Wahl, Gabriel
Analyzing China. *World Press Rev* 34:55 N '87
Waidhofer, Linde
about
Linde Waidhofer [interview] M. Corbett. il por *Natl Parks* 61:32-3 Ja/F '87
Waikiki Aquarium
Fish's-eye views of Hawaii at Waikiki and Sea Life Park. il *Sunset* 179:82-3 N '87
Waikiki Beach (Honolulu, Hawaii)
Stores
She sells springboks by the seashore [A. De Geer's shop, Africa in Hawaii] T. Ryan. il por *Sierra* 72:17 Ja/F '87
Wailers (Musical group)
Bob Marley and The Wailers: The Roxy, Los Angeles, May 26th, 1976. D. Fricke. il pors *Roll Stone* p93-4 Je 4 '87
Wainright, Sam C.
Stimulation of heterotrophic microplankton production by resuspended marine sediments. bibl f il *Science* 238:1710-12 D 18 '87
Wainwright, Loudon
The view from here. See issues of Life
Waist exercises See Exercise
Wait time See Reaction time
Waite, Terry
about
Hostages in danger. B. Levin. il por *Macleans* 100:18-19 F 16 '87

Terry Waite, a symbol of hope for hostages in the Mideast, vanishes on a mercy mission. L. Aitken. il por *People Wkly* 27:109 F 23 '87
Waiters and waitresses
A case goes unheard at the EEOC [Navy waitress M. Farrell] F. Greve. il por *50 Plus* 27:16+ N '87
Waiting
Waiting is a power game [cover story] R. Levine. il *Psychol Today* 21:24-6+ Ap '87
Waiting for Lefty [drama] See Odets, Clifford, 1906-1963
Waiting for the moon [film] See Motion picture reviews—Single works
Waiting for the moon [television program] See Television program reviews—Single works
Waiting lines See Queues (Waiting lines)
Waitley, Denis, and Tucker, Robert B.
How to think like an innovator. il *Futurist* 21:9-15 My/Je '87
Waits, Tom, 1949-
about
Tom Waits [New York City concert] D. Handelman. il por *Roll Stone* p24 D 3 '87
Wake, David B., and Larson, Allan
Multidimensional analysis of an evolving lineage. bibl f il *Science* 238:42-8 O 2 '87
Wake Island, Battle of, 1941
The defense of Wake. P. Andrews. bibl il map *Am Herit* 38:65-80 Jl/Ag '87
Return to Wake [World War II veterans] R. Wilkerson. il *Am Hist Illus* 22:46-8 D '87
Wake's forgotten survivors [civilian construction workers] R. Wilkerson. il por map *Am Hist Illus* 22:40-5 D '87
Wakefield, Celia
Specifics in nonfiction writing. *Writer* 100:23-4 Mr '87
Wakefield, Dan
My six years on the couch [excerpt from Returning] il *N Y Times Mag* p32-3+ D 20 '87
Wakefield, Elizabeth
The road visitor. il *South Living* 22:94 O '87
Wakening from sleep
Rise and shine! G. Williams. il *Read Dig* 131:167-9 O '87
Wakerman, Elyce
The legacy of father-loss: "men that I love will leave me". *Glamour* 85:132+ My '87
Wal-Mart Stores, Inc.
Censorship or sales marketing? [Wal-Mart stops selling rock magazines] K. Henderson. *Seventeen* 46:86 Ja '87
Down-home dynasty. T. Fennell. il por *Macleans* 100:32+ D 7 '87
Make that sale, Mr. Sam. S. Koepp. il por *Time* 129:54-5 My 18 '87
Play it again, Sam. H. Rudnitsky. il por *Forbes* 140:48 Ag 10 '87
Walberg, David
Before the roar [photographs] il *Sport Mag* 78:62-5+ O '87
Walbot, Virginia
about
Virginia Walbot. B. Lawren. *Omni* 9:40+ S '87
Walcott, Derek
Summer elegy [poem] *New Repub* 196:40 Ja 19 '87
Summer elegy II [poem] *New Repub* 196:40 Ja 19 '87
Sunday in the old republic [poem] *Atlantic* 259:43 Ja '87
Sundays [poem] *New Yorker* 62:37 Ja 19 '87
Wald, Richard
about
Friends in high places. B. Yagoda. il pors *Channels* 7:54-61 Ja '87
Walde, William L.
about
The better idea. M. Schifrin. il *Forbes* 140:57-8 O 5 '87
Walden, Narada Michael
about
Introducing: producer/songwriter Narada Michael Walden. il pors *Ebony* 43:68+ D '87
Walden, William
The lobber baron. il *World Tennis* 34:18-19 Mr '87
Walden Pond (Mass.)
Keep Walden Pond open: Thoreau's watering hole should remain a public domain. R. Sullivan. por *Sports Illus* 67:86 Ag 17 '87
Waldenbooks
Crown and Walden to launch mass market category line. il *Publ Wkly* 232:16 Jl 31 '87

Waldenbooks—*cont.*
Walden, WPS just say 'no' to condoms [refusal to carry cassette packaged with condoms] il *Publ Wkly* 232:48 O 30 '87
Waldenbooks intends to resign from ABA. A. Symons. *Publ Wkly* 231:12 Mr 27 '87
Waldenbooks officially withdraws from Booksellers Association. il *Publ Wkly* 231:10 Ap 3 '87
Waldenbooks promotes plans to capture new markets. A. Symons. il *Publ Wkly* 231:44-5 Mr 20 '87

Waldenkids (Firm)
Waldenbooks tries hooking young bookworms. R. Mitchell. il *Bus Week* p48 My 11 '87
Waldenkids stores will stress learning and continuity. il *Publ Wkly* 231:41 My 29 '87

Waldheim, Kurt
about
The case against Kurt Waldheim. B. Amiel. il *Macleans* 100:7 Jl 20 '87
The case against Waldheim. N. Cooper. il pors *Newsweek* 109:40 My 11 '87
Haunted by ghosts of a Nazi past. S. Masterman. il por *Macleans* 100:36 My 11 '87
The invitation. *Newsweek* 109:43 Je 29 '87
Jews dismayed by Pope. *Christ Century* 104:586 Jl 1-8 '87
Kurt Waldheim: persona non grata. M. Doan and C. Fenyvesi. il por *U S News World Rep* 102:8-9 My 11 '87
Kurt Waldheim's Roman holiday. il pors *U S News World Rep* 103:14 Jl 6 '87
Mr. Waldheim visits the Vatican. *America* 157:27 Jl 18-25 '87
One must bear witness. M. B. Zuckerman. il *U S News World Rep* 103:66 Jl 13 '87
The pariah and the Pope. pors *Time* 130:16 Jl 6 '87
The Pope and the pariah. K. L. Woodward. pors *Newsweek* 110:45 Jl 6 '87
The Pope's letter. W. F. Buckley. *Natl Rev* 39:64-5 S 25 '87
The Pope's precedent. S. Masterman. pors *Macleans* 100:29 Je 29 '87
A reception and a snub. A. Bilski. *Macleans* 100:20 Jl 6 '87
Removing the welcome mat. W. R. Doerner. il por *Time* 129:38-9 My 11 '87
Seeing Waldheim. *Commonweal* 114:405-6 Jl 17 '87
The Waldheim case limps on. E. von Kuehnelt-Leddihn. *Natl Rev* 39:46 Je 19 '87
Waldheim must resign. L.-M. Delloff. *Christ Century* 104:1167-8 D 23-30 '87
Waldheim's end game? F. Willey. il por *Newsweek* 110:29 D 28 '87

Bibliography
Waldheim's Austria [discussion of October 9, 1986 article, The Waldheim file] G. A. Craig. *N Y Rev Books* 34:44 F 26 '87

Waldman, Bernard, 1913-1986
about
Obituary
Phys Today 40:108 D '87. C. P. Brown

Waldman, Debby
The town that remembers Christa. il *Ladies Home J* 104:76+ F '87

Waldman, Steven
The best & the worst of American unions [cover story] il *Wash Mon* 19:28-32+ Jl/Ag '87
Futures shock. il *Wash Mon* 19:25-9+ Mr '87
Making McKinley sexy. *Wash Mon* 19:45-6+ S '87

Waldman, Susan
The diet that nurtures your nature. il *Mademoiselle* 93:167-9+ F '87

Waldron, Hicks Benjamin
about
Anyhow, it was nice while it lasted. G. Morgenson. il por *Forbes* 139:50+ Ja 12 '87

Waldrop, Charles P.
The conquest of Sam Houston. il pors *Am Hist Illus* 21:36-43 Ja '87

Waldrop, Heidi
How to manage a growing company. il *Work Woman* 12:39-42 Ap '87

Waldrop, Howard
Night of the cooters [fiction] il *Omni* 9:92-4+ Ap '87

Waldrop, M. Mitchell
The mirror maker. il pors *Discover* 8:78-84+ D '87

Wales
See also
Cardiff (Wales)
Christmas—Wales

Gold mines and mining—Wales
Historic houses, sites, etc.—Wales
Wye River (Wales and England)

Antiquities
See also
Arthur, King—Tomb

History
Bibliography
Modern Wales. G. H. Jenkins. il *Hist Today* 37:49-53 F '87

Wałęsa, Lech, 1943-
about
Fayard and Holt settle dispute over world rights to Walesa autobio. W. Goldstein. il pors *Publ Wkly* 232:23-4 Jl 31 '87
Lech's secret project. L. Howard. il por *Newsweek* 109:6 Ap 27 '87
Lunch with Lech. N. Bethell. *New Repub* 197:13-14 N 2 '87
A worker's tale. W. Svoboda. il por *Time* 129:70 My 4 '87

WALHI *See* Indonesian Environmental Forum
A walk in the woods [drama] *See* Blessing, Lee
Walk of Fame (Hollywood, Calif.)
Rock 'n' roller Berry gets Hollywood star. *Jet* 73:53 O 26 '87

Walk of Fame (Philadelphia, Pa.)
'Dizzy', 'Chubby' enshrined on music 'Walk of Fame'. il *Jet* 72:55 My 11 '87

Walker, A. Maceo, Sr.
about
Universal Life's policy for growth. N. McCall. il por *Black Enterp* 17:232-4+ Je '87

Walker, Alice, 1944-
about
Black victims, black villains. D. Pinckney. bibl f il *N Y Rev Books* 34:17-20 Ja 29 '87

Walker, Arthur J.
See also
Walker family espionage case

Walker, Beverly
Anjelica [interview with A. Huston] il por *Film Comment* 23:24-6 S/O '87
Limbo land. il *Film Comment* 23:34-8+ Ja/F '87
Midnacht at the oasis. il por *Film Comment* 23:4+ Jl/Ag '87

Walker, Bill
Oslo: a taste of things to come. il map *Travel Holiday* 167:62-7+ Je '87

Walker, Bree
Born with deformed hands and feet, an anchorwoman overcomes TV's obsession with perfect looks; ed. by Kristin McMurran. il pors *People Wkly* 28:117-18+ N 30 '87

Walker, Bryce S.
Tales of sunken gold and hunters of the depths. bibl (p132) il map *Smithsonian* 17:96-102+ Ja '87

Walker, Chet
about
The making of a movie mogul. il por *Sports Illus* 66:16 Mr 9 '87

Walker, Chuck, 1952-
about
Chuck Walker. S. Taylor. il *Art News* 86:31-2 F '87

Walker, Daniel A., and others
Cumulative impacts of oil fields on northern Alaskan landscapes. bibl f il map *Science* 238:757-61 N 6 '87

Walker, Doris
about
Along with crippling retardation, Doris Walker finds in her students a baffling paradox—genius. M. Neill. il pors *People Wkly* 28:159-61 D 14 '87
They all have high hopes. E. M. Reingold. il por *Time* 129:61 Mr 2 '87

Walker, Emilie
Collecting for fun, education, and the Arizona Kidney Foundation. *Phi Delta Kappan* 68:402-3 Ja '87

Walker, George, 1873-1911
about
Williams & Walker: showmen extraordinaire. B. Ault. il pors *Antiques Collect Hobbies* 92:48-51 Ap '87

Walker, George F.
about
Beautiful city [drama] Reviews
Macleans il 100:70 O 19 '87. J. Bemrose
Zastrozzi [drama] Reviews
Macleans il 100:55 My 25 '87. J. Bemrose

Walker, Giles
about
Films: brief encounters. P. Hluchy. il por *Macleans* 100:60 O 19 '87
The last straw [film] Reviews
Macleans il 100:60 O 19 '87. B. D. Johnson
Walker, Henry A., Jr.
about
A boardroom drama as time ran out for Amfac's CEO. J. B. Levine. il pors *Bus Week* p59 D 7 '87
Walker, James S., and Vause, Chester A.
Reappearing phases. bibl (p128) il *Sci Am* 256:98-105 My '87
Walker, Jearl, 1945-
The amateur scientist. See issues of Scientific American
Walker, Jerry Jeff, 1942-
about
Roped in by a hard-swearing wife named Sue, Jerry Jeff Walker, the outlaw, hollers but walks the line. D. Grogan. il pors *People Wkly* 28:81+ Ag 31 '87
Walker, Jimmie
about
J.J. Walker to return to tube in new role. por *Jet* 71:57 Ja 19 '87
Jimmie Walker, Vonetta McGee star in TV's 'Bustin loose' [cover story] il pors *Jet* 73:58-60 N 2 '87
Walker, John Anthony
See also
Walker family espionage case
Walker, John E.
Local opinion polling for educators. *Educ Dig* 53:26-9 D '87
Walker, Katherine Forestier- *See* Forestier-Walker, Katherine
Walker, Lisa
From 100 Elvis stories. *New Yorker* 63:38-9 N 2 '87
Walker, Liz
about
Black Boston TV anchor goes public on pregnancy. por *Jet* 72:32 Jl 6 '87
Walker, Lou Ann
The empty crib. il por *Ladies Home J* 104:76+ Mr '87
What comforts AIDS families [cover story] il *N Y Times Mag* p16-22+ Je 21 '87
(jt. auth) See Kyle, Cynthia, and Walker, Lou Ann
Walker, Martin, 1947-
Strains in the welfare state. il *World Press Rev* 34:24-6 O '87
Walker, Michael Lance
See also
Walker family espionage case
about
The spy who came in from the mall. H. Blum. il pors *Roll Stone* p71-2+ O 8 '87
Walker, Nathaniel
about
Innocent man's eight-year prison ordeal. W. Leavy. il pors *Ebony* 42:86+ Mr '87
Walker, Newman
about
The human dimension of data-based decision making [interview] D. B. Strother. il por *Phi Delta Kappan* 68:470-3 F '87
Walker, Nora Sue
It can happen to you! il *Mother Earth News* 103:88+ Ja/F '87
Walker, Patric
about
Star man. E. Newhall. il por *N Y* 20:20 F 23 '87
Walker, Richard W.
The Saatchi factor. il por *Art News* 86:117-21 Ja '87
Turn of the century: America's imperial collectors. il *Art News* 86:157-9 N '87
Walker, Sue
about
Roped in by a hard-swearing wife named Sue, Jerry Jeff Walker, the outlaw, hollers but walks the line. D. Grogan. il pors *People Wkly* 28:81+ Ag 31 '87
Walker, Tom, 1945-
Otter delight [photograph] il *Nat Hist* 96:80-1 My '87
Walker, William
about
Should the contras get more U.S. aid? [interview] S. Manning. pors *Sch Update* 119:10 Mr 9 '87
Walker, William, 1824-1860
about
Contra-courant. G. Fuller. il *Film Comment* 23:50-1 Jl/Ag '87
Nicaragua: radical flick. R. Nordland. il por *Newsweek* 109:44 Ap 20 '87

Rebel rouser. F. Schruers. il por *Roll Stone* p29+ S 10 '87
Walker [film] See Motion picture reviews—Single works
Walker Books Ltd.
Julia MacRae moves to Walker U.K. J. Taylor. *Publ Wkly* 232:48 N 27 '87
Walker family espionage case
The spy family that imperiled America [condensed from Breaking the ring] J. Barron. il *Read Dig* 130:62-70+ Ap '87
The spy who came in from the mall [M. L. Walker] H. Blum. il pors *Roll Stone* p71-2+ O 8 '87
Walking
See also
Backpacks and backpacking
Hiking
Race walking
WalkWays Center (Organization)
A celebration of walking—and life [cardiac rehabilitation program at Duke University] T. Shealey. il *Prevention* 39:102-4 Ap '87
The death of jogging: how to walk (not run) into shape. S. Levin. il *Mademoiselle* 93:60 Jl '87
First you put your right foot . . . S. Blotnick. il *Forbes* 139:190 Ap 6 '87
Five great American walking weekends. map *Prevention* 39:60-1+ S '87
Four legs bad, two legs good [bipedal locomotion] R. Lewin. bibl *Science* 235:969-71 F 27 '87
Grand walking at the Grand Canyon. S. Zarrow. il *Prevention* 39:44-6+ My '87
Night walking. J. Harrison. il *Roll Stone* p91+ Mr 26 '87
Rambling through the English countryside. S. F. Godbey. il *Prevention* 39:60-2+ Je '87
A skeptic's guide to walking. S. Levin. il *Health* 19:30-2+ Ap '87
The tao of walking. J. Poppy. il *Esquire* 107:31-2 F '87
There's fitness afoot [cover story] H. Higdon. il *50 Plus* 27:26-30 Mr '87
Walk on! C. Adams. il *Essence* 18:116 Jl '87
Walk-shape yourself. S. Kiesling. il *Good Housekeep* 204:100 My '87
Walk your way to super health and slimmer hips [cover story] T. Shealey. il *Prevention* 39:66-8+ Ap '87
Walk your way to weight loss. L. Vaughn. il *Prevention* 39:44+ S '87
A walker in the city [95 yr. old G. Clark of New York City] B. Kevles. il por *N Y* 20:32 S 28 '87
A walker slips through the barriers of automobile-age conformity and finds it is the best way to see the real world. J. P. Wiley, Jr. *Smithsonian* 18:36+ S '87
Walker's world. See issues of Prevention (Emmaus, Pa.) beginning January 1987
Walking: a ten-page fitness/health special [special section] il *Vogue* 177:240-9+ Je '87
Walking up your HDL [study of mailmen by Timothy Cook] il *Prevention* 39:6 My '87
Well-known walkers. D. Groves. il *Good Housekeep* 205:118 O '87
What's hot: walking! il *Ladies Home J* 104:72+ Ap '87
World-girdler Steve Newman sets a record by walking in a very, very big circle [solo walk around the world] R. Wolmuth. il pors *People Wkly* 27:38-40 Mr 30 '87

Psychological aspects
A happy pace [study by Sara Snodgrass] S. Vandershaf. il *Psychol Today* 21:68 Ja '87
The joy of walking. P. Steinhart. il *Audubon* 89:8+ S '87
Step away from stress. M. Spilner. il *Prevention* 39:54+ N '87
Tired? Take a walk [study by Robert E. Thayer] H. Hall. *Psychol Today* 21:18 My '87
Storm hazards
Walking in the rain. il *Prevention* 39:72-3+ Ap '87
Walking clubs See Sports clubs
Walking dolls See Dolls
Walking of dogs See Dogs—Care
Walking shoes
All about walking shoes. D. Longstreet. *Good Housekeep* 205:80+ O '87
The all-star review of high-tech walking shoes. L. Vaughn. il *Prevention* 39:52-3+ S '87
Comfort your sole. T. Brunick. il *Women's Sports Fitness* 9:55-8 N '87
Fit feet. J. Schmid. il *Vogue* 177:246-7+ Je '87

Walking shoes—*cont.*
The right shoe for stepping out in style. H. Higdon. il *50 Plus* 27:78-80+ Ap '87
Shoes for serious walkers. S. Woolley. il *Bus Week* p83 Ag 10 '87
Sneaker alternatives: walk to work in comfort and style. il *Glamour* 85:88 Mr '87
Step into walking shoes? C. Schaeffer. il *Changing Times* 41:98 Ap '87
Walk before you run [Kangaroos' walking and running shoe designs] T. H. Cole. il *Pop Mech* 164:48 Mr '87
Walking [Reebok introduces new line] *New Yorker* 62:27-9 F 16 '87
We test-walk the new shoes. T. Shealey. il *Prevention* 39:74+ Ap '87

Walkom, Thomas
Korea's endless surprises. il *World Press Rev* 34:20-2 Ag '87

Walks (Paths)
Cutting a corner to update the entry. il *South Living* 22:60 D '87
Design and lay a flagstone walk. P. V. Fossel. il *Americana* 15:63-5 My/Je '87
Pavers and plants add a soft touch. il *South Living* 22:70-1 N '87
A walk with a different approach [entry walk] il *South Living* 22:61 O '87

Die Walküre [opera] *See* Wagner, Richard, 1813-1883

WalkWays Center (Organization)
Bringing walkways to your doorstep. C. Evans. il *Prevention* 39:90+ S '87

Wall, Carol F.
Thirty-fourth winter. il *South Living* 22:80 Ja '87

Wall, James A.
Management among thieves [interview with armed robber; excerpt from Bosses] *Harpers* 274:23-4 F '87

Wall, James M.
Authority meets mystery. *America* 157:403-5 N 28 '87
'Moments' in movies: Montreal's World Film Festival. il *Christ Century* 104:787-90 S 23 '87

Wall, M. Danny
about
Danny Wall dives right into the swamp. V. Cahan. il por *Bus Week* p28 Ag 31 '87

Wall board *See* Wallboard
Wall cabinets *See* Cabinets (Furniture)
Wall coverings
See also
Wallpaper and wallpapering
Alarming wallpaper [fire sensing vinyl wall coverings introduced by B. F. Goodrich] il *Prevention* 39:14 Mr '87
Make old walls look new. G. Branson. il *Fam Handyman* 37:80+ S '87

Wall decoration *See* Mural painting and decoration
Wall fasteners *See* Fasteners
Wall gardens and gardening *See* Garden walls
Wall hangings
You make this three-dimensional fabric wall hanging without touching a needle and thread. il *Sunset* 179:98+ D '87

Wall paper *See* Wallpaper and wallpapering
Wall patching materials *See* Patching materials
Wall plaques *See* Plaques and plaquettes
Wall shelves *See* Shelves and racks
Wall-Smith, Stephen B.
José María Arguedas: godfather of liberationism. *Christ Century* 104:1034-9 N 18 '87

Wall Street (New York, N.Y.)
Reflections on Wall Street. L. Auchincloss. il por *Archit Dig* 44:254+ N '87
The Street [historical tour] M. Gelfand. il map *Am Herit* 38:53-6+ N '87

Wall Street [film] *See* Motion picture reviews—Single works
Wall Street crash, 1929 *See* Business depression, 1929-1939
Wall Street crash, 1987 *See* Stock market crash, 1987
Wall Street journal
How now, Dow Jones? E. Diamond. il *N Y* 20:26-8 N 30 '87
Of loose lips and stock tips [Supreme Court upholds conviction of R. F. Winans for insider trading] J. Castro. il por *Time* 130:63 N 30 '87
Offsetting true believers [news pages vs. editorial pages] T. Griffith. il *Time* 130:76 O 5 '87

Wallace, Carol McD., 1955-
Poor little rich girls. il *Forbes* 140 Sp Issue:62+ O 26 '87

Wallace, David Rains, 1945-
A naturalist's guide to prime time [excerpt from The untamed garden and other personal essays] *Harpers* 274:32-4 Ap '87
Reflections from a dragonfly's wing [excerpt from Life in the balance] *Wilderness* 51:51-2+ Fall '87
Sand County's conservation prophet. il pors *Sierra* 72:62-7 N/D '87

Wallace, De Witt, 1889-1981
about
Unforgettable DeWitt Wallace. C. W. Ferguson. il pors *Read Dig* 130:177-80+ F '87

Wallace, G. David
Enterprise. See issues of Business Week beginning July 27, 1987

Wallace, George M.
about
He's been working on the railroad in Denver. S. D. Atchison. il por *Bus Week* p42 Je 8 '87

Wallace, Joan
about
Joan Wallace probes Saudi problems in agriculture. por *Jet* 71:6 Mr 2 '87

Wallace, Joaquin
about
Black youth from ghetto to Giants' front office. *Jet* 72:46 Ag 31 '87

Wallace, John
Music to their ears. il *Publ Wkly* 231:140+ F 27 '87
Office in a box. *Work Woman* 12:60+ Ap '87

Wallace, Lila Acheson, 1889-1984
about
One woman's gift to the 20th century. P. B. Osborne. il por *Read Dig* 131:274-81 N '87

Wallace, Michele
Baby Faith. il por *Ms* 16:154+ Jl/Ag '87

Wallace, Mike, 1918-
about
Newsman Mike Wallace apologizes at UM for past racist remark. *Jet* 72:31 My 25 '87

Wallace, Robert Glenn
The great oil giveaway [address, September 4, 1987] *Vital Speeches Day* 54:17-20 O 15 '87

Wallace, Ronald, 1945-
Breakdown [poem] il *Atlantic* 260:45 Ag '87

Wallace, Ruth
about
A no-nonsense nanny strolls into Charles and Di's nursery. il pors *People Wkly* 27:45 Mr 30 '87

Wallace (Lila Acheson) Garden (Williamsburg, Va.) *See* Williamsburg (Va.)—Gardens and gardening
Wallace (Lila Acheson) Wing *See* Metropolitan Museum of Art (New York, N.Y.). Lila Acheson Wallace Wing
Wallace H. Campbell & Company
Rose finally unpacked her belongings [Wallace H. Campbell & Co. and Jewish Family Services team up to run high-rise apartment for the elderly in Baltimore, Md.] J. B. Kurland and G. E. J. Lipsitz. il *Aging* no355:6-9 '87

Wallach, Bret
Building the Sudan. il map *Focus* 37:12-15 Fall '87
Cranbrook. il *Focus* 37:16-19 Spr '87
Parkmerced. il *Focus* 36:12-15 Wint '86
The simplest of counties. il *Focus* 37:18-21 Summ '87

Wallach, Janet, 1942-
about
Folk tales: of baseballs and weathervanes in Washington, D.C. C. T. Buckley. il pors *Archit Dig* 44:62-7+ Jl '87

Wallach, John P.
about
Folk tales: of baseballs and weathervanes in Washington, D.C. C. T. Buckley. il pors *Archit Dig* 44:62-7+ Jl '87

Wallboard
How to install trouble-free wallboard. G. Branson. il *Fam Handyman* 37:40+ Jl/Ag '87
Popped drywall nails. B. Duggan. il *Home Mech* 83:30 F '87
The walls around us. D. Owen. il *Atlantic* 259:71-9 My '87

Wallenberg, Peter
about
Peter Wallenberg is rebuilding a dynasty. J. Kapstein. il pors *Bus Week* p158-9 N 2 '87

Wallenberg Group
A financial gambler tries to trump the Wallenbergs again [E. Penser's moves on Swedish Match] J. Kapstein. *Bus Week* p50+ Ja 19 '87
Peter Wallenberg is rebuilding a dynasty. J. Kapstein. il pors *Bus Week* p158-9 N 2 '87

Wallenmeyer, William A.

about

SURA gets new president from DOE: NSF loses two computer chiefs. I. Goodwin. *Phys Today* 40:60-1 D '87

Waller, Douglas C., and Bruce, James T.

Holes in the impenetrable shield. *Bull At Sci* 43:5-6 O '87

Waller, Harold M.

Canada's sober socialists. il *New Leader* 70:10-11 O 5 '87

Waller, J. Michael, and Sobran, Joseph

Congress's Red Army [cover story] il *Natl Rev* 39:25-8 Jl 31 '87

Waller, P. J. (Philip J.)

Robert Ensor, Edwardian rationalist. bibl f il por *Hist Today* 37:49-54 Ja '87

Waller, Philip J. *See* Waller, P. J. (Philip J.)

Wallets

Theft

Help! My wallet's gone! [minimizing damage from loss of credit and ID cards] H. R. Kennedy. *U S News World Rep* 103:77 N 23 '87

Walleye fishing

Are walleyes better than bass? J. Murray. il *Outdoor Life* 179:60-1+ Ap '87

Big river walleyes [Columbia River] J. Gibbs. il *Outdoor Life* 179:100-1+ My '87

Current tactics for river walleyes. T. Huggler. il *Outdoor Life* 179:50-1+ F '87

The day of the walleyes [Minnesota] P. Kaminsky. il *Field Stream* 91:68-9+ Mr '87

Manitoba river walleyes. K. Schultz. il map *Field Stream* 92:49+ O '87

Nail 'em in neutral [neutrally buoyant crankbaits] J. Murray. il *Outdoor Life* 180:62-3+ Ag '87

No-faze spring walleyes. J. Murray. il *Outdoor Life* 179:70-1+ Mr '87

Summer walleyes: weeds and walls. J. Gibbs. il *Outdoor Life* 180:46+ Ag '87

Wrong-way walleyes. D. Sternberg. il *Outdoor Life* 180:82-3+ Jl '87

Competitions

See Fishing—Competitions

Walliker, David, and others

Genetic analysis of the human malaria parasite Plasmodium falciparum. bibl f il *Science* 236:1661-6 Je 26 '87

Wallinga, Charlotte, and others

When a brother or sister is ill. *Psychol Today* 21:42-3 Ag '87

Wallinger, Karl

about

The Party of the year. D. Wild. il por *Roll Stone* p18 Ja 29 '87

Wallis, W. Allen

International protection of U.S. copyrights [statement, July 23, 1987] *Dep State Bull* 87:26-8 O '87

Structural adjustment, dialogue, and U.S.-Japan economic relations [address, February 16, 1987] *Dep State Bull* 87:36-40 My '87

U.S.-EC relations and the international trading system [address, October 8, 1986] *Dep State Bull* 87:43-7 Ja '87

U.S.-Japan subcabinet meets [statement, October 31, 1986] *Dep State Bull* 87:42-3 Ja '87

U.S.-Japan trade relations [address, April 13, 1987] *Dep State Bull* 87:54-8 Je '87

Wallman, Josh, and others

Local retinal regions control local eye growth and myopia [cover story] bibl f il *Science* 237:73-7 Jl 3 '87

Wallop, Malcolm

Offense-defense strategic balance in the 1990s [address, May 6, 1987] *Vital Speeches Day* 53:610-13 Ag 1 '87

Wallpaper and wallpapering

Hanging wallpaper: when to hire a pro [interview with S. Warshaw] N. Cooper. il por *Home Mech* 83:28+ My '87

Paper medallion. N. Cooper. il *Home Mech* 83:51 D '87

Restoration wallpaper. B. Vila. il *Pop Mech* 164:24+ N '87

TFH wallpaper clinic. K. Childers. il *Fam Handyman* 37:54+ S '87

A wallpaper primer. T. Snider. il *Ctry J* 14:46-51 Mr '87

Collectors and collecting

Collectors' finds in Paris: discoveries in painting, wallpaper and posters [papier peint wallpapers and art deco advertising posters] J. A. Cuadrado. il *Archit Dig* 44:210+ D '87

Wallraff, Barbara

1-800 . . . il *Atlantic* 260:18+ O '87

Walls, Michael

about

In Paris: designing men. C. Mongo. il pors *Essence* 18:43 O '87

Walls, Nancy

Three generations of love. il *Aging* no355:2-5 '87

Walls

See also

Garden walls

Mural painting and decoration

Paneling

Partitions

Pass-throughs (Architecture)

Retaining walls

Storage walls

Bringing down the walls. il *Mother Earth News* 108:102+ N/D '87

Heat-storing walls [Heat Soak] N. J. Freundlich. il *Pop Sci* 231:98 S '87

Out of the commonplace [display system of mutable floating walls for Museum of the Borough of Brooklyn] M. Gaskie. il *Archit Rec* 175:162-5 mid-S '87

The walls around us. D. Owen. il *Atlantic* 259:71-9 My '87

Walls, Concrete

A plasterlike finish for basement walls. R. Barnhart. il *Home Mech* 83:132+ O '87

Wally the Beerman *See* McNeil, Wally

Walruses

Tough, tusky giants [cover story] il *Natl Geogr World* 141:3-6 My '87

Food and feeding

Whales and walruses as tillers of the sea floor [side-scan sonar studies of the Bering Sea] C. H. Nelson and K. R. Johnson. il maps *Sci Am* 256:112-17 F '87

Walsers

The Walser. P. Zinsli. il *Courier* 40:14-15 F '87

Walsh, Christopher

(jt. auth) See O'Halloran, Thomas, and Walsh, Christopher

Walsh, Jill Paton *See* Paton Walsh, Jill, 1937-

Walsh, Joan

Enterprising women. il *Ms* 15:69-72 My '87

Is "homework" the answer? il *Ms* 16:124-5+ Jl/Ag '87

Walsh, Judith C.

(jt. auth) See Strickler, Susan E., and Walsh, Judith C.

Walsh, Julia

about

How to get on a board. il por *Nations Bus* 75:57 N '87

Walsh, Lawrence E.

about

And now for the hard part. D. Baer. il por *U S News World Rep* 103:35 Ag 17 '87

'Big shoe' delayed. il por *Newsweek* 110:6 Ag 31 '87

Have brief, will travel. S. Lichtman. il *New Repub* 197:14-16 Ag 24 '87

One deliberate step at a time, a prosecutor builds his case. J. Friedman. il por *People Wkly* 28:58-9 D 7 '87

A passel of new trouble from a posse of lawyers. D. Baer and M. Healy. il por *U S News World Rep* 102:19-20 Je 15 '87

Prosecutor in a cocoon. il por *Newsweek* 110:17 Jl 27 '87

Timing tiff. *Time* 129:26 Mr 23 '87

Walsh makes his move. P. Shenon. il por *N Y Times Mag* p46-7+ O 25 '87

Walsh vs. Congress. T. Morganthau. il pors *Newsweek* 109:24+ Mr 23 '87

What will they say—and when? M. Healy. il pors *U S News World Rep* 102:20 Mr 23 '87

Walsh, Michael

Sounds of silents. il *Film Comment* 23:66-9 Jl/Ag '87

Walt, Stephen M.

Politicians and professors: a double standard. il *Bull At Sci* 43:3-4 Jl/Ag '87

Walt Disney Company

See also

Euro Disneyland

Behind the scenes at the Magic Kingdom [the management seminar business] R. Simon. il *Forbes* 140:427+ Jl 13 '87

Walt Disney Company—*cont.*

Can Disney's magic work on network television? S. Behrens. il *Channels* 7:36-9+ N '87

Disney's magic. R. Grover. il por *Bus Week* p62-5+ Mr 9 '87

It's King Kong vs. the 'ravenous rat' [MCA and Disney compete for theme park market in Europe] K. Kelly. il *Bus Week* p54 O 5 '87

Most improved. il *Forbes* 139:158 Ja 12 '87

Ordeal by Disney [writing the script for The magnificent rebel in 1958 post-blacklist period] J. Scott. il pors *Film Comment* 23:52-4+ N/D '87

Pluto's paymaster [G. L. Wilson] P. E. Bauer. por *Channels* 7:54 Je '87

Putting magic back in the Magic Kingdom [M. Eisner] M. Magnet. il por *Fortune* 115:65 Ja 5 '87

Theme parks: this slugfest is no fantasy [Disney vs. MCA] R. Grover. il *Bus Week* p38 Mr 23 '87

Walt Disney Productions
See also
Walt Disney Company

Walt Disney World (Fla.)
See also
EPCOT (Fla.)

Disney: coast to coast [historical reconstruction] R. F. Snow. il *Am Herit* 38:22+ F/Mr '87

Fort Wilderness: Disney World's "Hinterland". M. T. O'Keefe. il *Saturday Evening Post* 259:92-4+ Ja/F '87

A vacation to remember. il *Ebony* 42:136+ Ag '87
Gardens and gardening

Disney World: the magic behind the plants [cover story] L. B. Trigg. il *South Living* 22:72-9 Je '87

Walter, Claire
How to enjoy skiing with your kids. il *Skiing* 39:93-4+ Ja '87

Walter, John
The great outdoors. See issues of Successful Farming beginning February 1987

Walter, Richard C., Jr.
What time is it? il *Astronomy* 15:38-40 F '87

Walter (Jim) Corp. See Jim Walter Corp.

Walters, Barbara, and Glass, Ellen
Eight great anger-busters. il *Seventeen* 46:80+ Mr '87

Walters, John
A love affair. il *N Y Times Mag* p76 N 22 '87

Walters, Judith R., and others
D$_1$ dopamine receptor activation required for postsynaptic expression of D$_2$ agonist effects. bibl f il *Science* 236:719-22 My 8 '87

Walters, Mark J.
An autumn apparition. il *Read Dig* 131:71-4+ O '87
The soul of a prodigy. il por *Read Dig* 130:84-8 Mr '87

Walters, Norby
about
Agents of turmoil. C. Neff. il pors *Sports Illus* 67:34-40+ Ag 3 '87
Agents of violence? B. Selcraig. il por *Sports Illus* 66:25 Ap 6 '87

Walters, Peter I.
about
A policeman's son enjoys tough calls. R. I. Kirkland, Jr. il por *Fortune* 116:30 Ag 3 '87

Walters, Vernon A.
Human rights in Cuba [statement, March 5, 1987] *Dep State Bull* 87:71-4 My '87
Situation in Cambodia [statement, October 20, 1986; with text of General Assembly resolution] *Dep State Bull* 87:80-2 Ja '87
UN administration and finances [statement, October 15, 1986] *Dep State Bull* 87:77-8 F '87

Walters family
about
"Where are my children?" [Walters family of Marshall County, Ky. reunited after fifty years] S. Kelly. il *Read Dig* 130:151-2+ Je '87

Walterspiel, Alfred
about
A meister chef's legacy. L. Langseth-Christensen. il por *Gourmet* 47:80-1+ O '87

Walthamstow (England)
History
'Picture shows': the early British film industry in Walthamstow. M. O'Brien and J. Holland. bibl il *Hist Today* 37:9-15 F '87

Waltner, Elma, 1912-
How to propagate baby's-tears. il *Flower Gard* 31:60 Ap/My '87

Walton, Clyde
about
The flack who came in from the cold. L. Minard. il por *Forbes* 140:120+ D 28 '87

Walton, Eugene
Happy Juneteenth! It's time to celebrate. por *U S News World Rep* 102:9 My 25 '87

Walton, Sam M.
about
Down-home dynasty. T. Fennell. il por *Macleans* 100:32+ D 7 '87
Make that sale, Mr. Sam. S. Koepp. il por *Time* 129:54-5 My 18 '87
Play it again, Sam. H. Rudnitsky. il por *Forbes* 140:48 Ag 10 '87

Walton, Tony
about
Tony Walton at the Beaumont [cover story] G. Stern. il por *Theatre Crafts* 21:16-21+ Mr '87

Walton, William, 1909-
Mango Bay: Pamela Harriman's residence on Barbados. il por *Archit Dig* 44:84-9 Ja '87
Pavilions in the sun. il *House Gard* 159:118-25 D '87
A weekend with Claudette. il *House Gard* 159:156-9+ Je '87

Walton sextuplets See Sextuplets

Waltzes
See also
Compact discs—Waltzes

Walwyn Inc.
Bay Street bickering [Wood Gundy sues employees hired away by Walwyn Inc.] P. Best. il *Macleans* 100:30 S 28 '87

Walz, Barbara
Why do I love you? il *Ladies Home J* 104:83+ Ap '87

Walzer, Michael
Israel's great victory [cover story] il *New Repub* 196:22-3+ Je 8 '87
about
Prophets with tenure. R. J. Neuhaus. *Commentary* 84:49-52 Jl '87

Wamsley, James S.
Antiques: toys in transit. il *Archit Dig* 44:168-73 D '87
Blue Ridge variation: augmenting a house in the Virginia horse country. il *Archit Dig* 44:176-9 Ap '87
Jamaican cadence: Rose Marie Bogley's cottage above Montego Bay. il *Archit Dig* 44:202-7 My '87

Wan Qinghua
Low-cost irrigation project interests other developing countries. il *UN Chron* 24:65 Ag '87

Wanakee
about
Eye on beauty [interview] M. Garth-Taylor. pors *Essence* 17:30+ Ja '87

Waney, Arjun C.
about
Keeping teens decked out in whatever's hot. il por *Bus Week* p88 My 25 '87

Wang, An
about
A $150 million paper loss. il pors *U S News World Rep* 103:59 Jl 6 '87
An Wang: getting to the essentials. K. Berney. il pors *Nations Bus* 75:85-6 D '87

Wang, Frederick A., 1950-
about
A $150 million paper loss. il pors *U S News World Rep* 103:59 Jl 6 '87
Frederick Wang. A. Beam. il por *Bus Week* Sp Issue:244 Ap 17 '87
Strong medicine from the son of Doctor Wang. A. Beam. il *Bus Week* p33 Ja 19 '87

Wang, Josephine J.
Should Congress enact the Quayle amendments to the Bilingual Education Act? [excerpts from testimony, June 5, 1986] *Congr Dig* 66:92+ Mr '87

Wang, Kan, and others
Site-specific nick in the T-DNA border sequence as a result of Agrobacterium vir gene expression. bibl f il *Science* 235:587-91 Ja 30 '87

Wang, Lulu
about
Growth stocks prosper in the new year [interview] A. E. Serwer. il por *Fortune* 115:114 F 2 '87

Wang, Thomas
about
An old-fashioned preacher [interview] por *Christ Today* 31:52 Mr 6 '87

Wang, Wayne, 1949?-
about
Slam dance [film] Reviews
  Vogue il 177:154 S '87. M. Haskell
Wang, Zhen-Ru
Two gamma-ray sources and ancient guest stars. bibl
  f il *Science* 235:1485-6 Mr 20 '87
Wang Chung (Musical group)
Twin ads: a case of mistaken identity [Michelob and
  ABC Sports run commercials using song Everybody
  have fun tonight] *Newsweek* 110:37 Ag 24 '87
Wang Chung. E. Miller. il *Seventeen* 46:95-6+ N '87
Wang Laboratories Inc.
A $150 million paper loss [computer makers A. and
  F. Wang] il pors *U S News World Rep* 103:59 Jl
  6 '87
Frederick Wang. A. Beam. il por *Bus Week* Sp Issue:244
  Ap 17 '87
Mr. Outside [I. Diery] G. Slutsker. il por *Forbes* 140:194+
  S 21 '87
New sales tool: computer lingo. il *Newsweek* 109:47
  Ap 6 '87
Strong medicine from the son of Doctor Wang. A. Beam.
  il *Bus Week* p33 Ja 19 '87
An Wang: getting to the essentials. K. Berney. il pors
  Nations Bus 75:85-6 D '87
Wang Lan
about
Woodcuts by Wang Lan; Sketches by Xu Donglin. il
  World Press Rev 34:58-9 Je '87
Wang Meng
about
Writing in China. M. Hopkins. il *New Leader* 70:27-8
  My 4-18 '87
Wangerin, Walter
Ashes, ashes [poem] *Christ Today* 31:53 F 6 '87
Gentle into that good night. il por *Christ Today* 31:23-5
  N 6 '87
A matter of being, and a matter of being right. il *Christ
  Century* 104:591-3 Jl 1-8 '87
about
PW interviews. W. Griffin. por *Publ Wkly* 231:95-6
  Mr 6 '87
Sonnets on the sly. D. Neff. *Christ Today* 31:53 F
  6 '87
Wankel engines *See* Rotary engines
Wann, David
Environmental crime: putting offenders behind bars. bibl
  f il *Environment* 29:5+ O '87
Wanner (Johann) (Firm) *See* Johann Wanner (Firm)
Wanniski, Jude, 1936-
Can Kemp do it? il *Natl Rev* 39:28-31 Ag 14 '87
The Wannsee Conference [film] *See* Motion picture
  reviews—Single works
Want ads *See* Advertising, Classified
Wanted dead or alive [film] *See* Motion picture
  reviews—Single works
Wants *See* Desire
Wanttaja, Ronald
Tiny bubbles. il *Flying* 114:100 My '87
Wapner, Joseph A.
Judge Wapner's favorite cases [excerpt from A view
  from the bench] il pors *Good Housekeep* 205:50+ O
  '87
about
Judge Wapner appeals. R. Schoenstein. il por *50 Plus*
  27:94+ F '87
War
See also
  Anti-submarine warfare
  Children and war
  Iranian-Iraqi War, 1980-
  Israel-Arab Wars, 1967-
  Korean War, 1950-1953
  Militarism
  Military art and science
  Naval warfare
  Nuclear warfare
  Pacifism
  Peace
  Punic Wars
  Space warfare
  Submarine warfare
  Vietnamese War, 1957-1975
  War games
  Women and war
  World War, 1914-1918
  World War, 1939-1945
  World War III

Computer combat [technological revolution in conven-
  tional warfare; cover story] E. A. Cohen. *New Repub*
  196:15-17 Ap 20 '87
The world at war: why armed conflict plagues more
  than 30 nations [cover story; special issue] il map
  Sch Update 119:1-15 My 4 '87
Causes
Wars aren't 'accidental'. G. F. Will. il *Newsweek* 110:104
  O 26 '87
Why fighting rages: a survey of five wars. P. M. Jones.
  il *Sch Update* 119:9-10 My 4 '87
Moral aspects
See War and morals
Prevention
U.S. presidents on war and peace. O. Berger. il *Saturday
  Evening Post* 259:36+ Ja/F '87
Religious aspects
See War and religion
War and emergency powers
See also
  War Powers Resolution
Bring back war [formal declaration of war not discussed
  by Iran-contra dealmakers] H. Fairlie. *New Repub*
  197:16-17 Ag 10-17 '87
Commagate [Roosevelt's illegal sale of destroyers to Great
  Britain in 1940 compared to Iran-contra scandal] D.
  Seligman. *Fortune* 116:217+ O 12 '87
Minority report [views of State Dept. legal adviser A.
  D. Sofaer] C. Hitchens. *Nation* 244:103 Ja 31 '87
Notes and comment [war powers aspect of the Constitu-
  tion and aid to the contras] *New Yorker* 63:23-4 Je
  1 '87
The politics of empire [Reagan presidency] N. Birnbaum.
  il *Nation* 244:9-12 Ja 10 '87
Reagan's junta. T. Draper. bibl f il *N Y Rev Books*
  34:5+ Ja 29 '87
Reagan's junta [discussion of January 29, 1987 article]
  T. Draper. *N Y Rev Books* 34:47-8 Ap 23 '87
To provide for the common defense. Publius. *New Leader*
  70:12-14 N 16 '87
Tug-of-war. W. Safire. il *N Y Times Mag* p61-2+ S
  13 '87
War is declared. il *Progressive* 51:7-8 N '87
Wars without declarations: Congress struggles to reclaim
  its constitutional authority. G. J. Church. il *Time*
  130:38 Jl 6 '87
War and literature
Fighting words: the myth of the 'hereditary enemy'.
  J. Blot. il *Courier* 40:25-8 Jl '87
War and morals
See also
  El Salvador—Civil War, 1980- —Moral and religious
    aspects
  Iranian-Iraqi War, 1980- —Moral and religious
    aspects
  Nuclear warfare and religion
  Nuclear winter and religion
  Vietnamese War, 1957-1975—Moral and religious
    aspects
  War and religion
  World War, 1939-1945—Moral and religious aspects
Reflections on war. A. E. Hartle. por *Humanist* 47:41-2
  Ja/F '87
War and religion
See also
  El Salvador—Civil War, 1980- —Moral and religious
    aspects
  Iranian-Iraqi War, 1980- —Moral and religious
    aspects
  Just war doctrine
  Nuclear warfare and religion
  Nuclear winter and religion
  Vietnamese War, 1957-1975—Moral and religious
    aspects
  World War, 1939-1945—Catholic Church
  World War, 1939-1945—Moral and religious aspects
Catholic thought on war & peace [discussion of September
  11 and September 25, 1987 articles, The heritage
  abandoned?] P. Steinfels. *Commonweal* 114:690+ D
  4 '87
The heritage abandoned? (I) [G. Weigel's critique of
  the Catholic position on war and peace, Tranquillitas
  ordinis] P. Steinfels. *Commonweal* 114:487-92 S 11
  '87
The heritage abandoned? (II) [G. Weigel's critique of
  the Catholic position on war and peace, Tranquillitas
  ordinis] P. Steinfels. il *Commonweal* 114:530-3 S 25
  '87
Our great blind spot [Catholics] C. Derrick. *America*
  156:437-9+ My 30 '87

War and religion—*cont.*

Reclaiming the Catholic heritage [G. Weigel's Tranquillitas ordinis and M. Novak's Will it liberate?] A. R. Muggeridge. *Commentary* 84:39-44 S '87

Return of the big stick. T. C. Muck. il *Christ Today* 31:18-19 S 4 '87

Bibliography

'Eternal peace lasts only until the next war'. R. J. Grecco. *America* 156:509-11 Je 20-27 '87

War and science

Facing reality: computer scientists aid war efforts. J. Weizenbaum. il *Technol Rev* 90:22-3 Ja '87

A physicist objects [C. Schwartz stops teaching classes in higher physics at Berkeley] J. J. Neuburger. il por *Progressive* 51:12-13 Jl '87

War crime trials

France

Barbie and the children [roundup of the children of Izieu] *Newsweek* 109:44 Je 15 '87

The Barbie file [cover story] T. Morgan. il pors *N Y Times Mag* p18-24+ My 10 '87

Barbie on trial. M. Ophuls. *Nation* 244:634-5 My 16 '87

The Barbie trial: J'accuse [witness L. Lesèvre] F. Coleman. il pors *Newsweek* 109:41 My 11 '87

Barbie's mockery of justice [refusal to appear at his trial] M. S. Serrill. il por *Time* 129:51 My 25 '87

Breaking the silence [K. Barbie and role of the Catholic Church] K. McCaffrey. il *Commonweal* 114:418-20 Jl 17 '87

The "Butcher of Lyons" in the dock [K. Barbie] W. R. Doerner. il por *Time* 129:49 My 18 '87

Europe faces its Nazi past [K. Barbie trial] S. Sullivan. il pors *Newsweek* 109:34-6 Ap 20 '87

Final verdict for the Butcher of Lyons [conviction of K. Barbie] P. Lewis. il por *Macleans* 100:20 Jl 13 '87

France brings Barbie—and itself—to trial [with interview with B. Klarsfeld] R. Z. Chesnoff. il pors *U S News World Rep* 102:35-6 My 18 '87

Judgment at Lyons: the prisoner is guilty [K. Barbie trial] F. Coleman. il pors *Newsweek* 110:29 Jl 13 '87

Klaus Barbie's circus of evil. M. Ophuls. il *Nation* 244:884-7 Je 27 '87

Letter from Europe [K. Barbie trial] J. Kramer. *New Yorker* 63:130-6+ O 12 '87

The Nazi hunt [cover story; special section] il pors *Macleans* 100:34-41 My 25 '87

Remembering Liane, age six [L. Krochmal, victim of K. Barbie] G. F. Will. il por *Newsweek* 109:80 My 25 '87

A rush from judgment [K. Barbie boycotts trial] F. Coleman. il por *Newsweek* 109:28 My 25 '87

The threat of Klaus Barbie. H. Evans. il *U S News World Rep* 102:74 Ap 13 '87

A verdict on the Butcher [conviction of K. Barbie] F. Painton. il por *Time* 130:40 Jl 13 '87

Voices from the Barbie trial [cover story] T. Morgan. il pors *N Y Times Mag* p20-5+ Ag 2 '87

Was he normal? Human? Poor humanity [K. Barbie] E. Wiesel. il pors *Time* 129:93-4 My 11 '87

Israel

Demjanjuk in Jerusalem. L. Wieseltier. *New Repub* 196:15-16 Mr 30 '87

Eerie echoes of the Nazi death camps [trial of J. Demjanjuk] M. McIver. por *Macleans* 100:42 Ag 17 '87

The hell of Treblinka [trial of J. Demjanjuk] K. Scanlon. il por *Macleans* 100:23 Mr 23 '87

"I can't even kill a chicken" [trial of J. Demjanjuk] M. S. Serrill. il por *Time* 130:23 Ag 10 '87

Ivan the Terrible? [J. Demjanjuk] *Natl Rev* 39:18-19 Mr 27 '87

'Like long-gone history' [J. Demjanjuk's trial] N. Cooper. il por *Newsweek* 109:36 Mr 2 '87

'A trial against forgetting' [alleged Nazi war criminal J. Demjanjuk] R. Rosenberg. il por *U S News World Rep* 102:36 Mr 9 '87

Trial by bitter recollection [alleged Nazi war criminal J. Demjanjuk] W. E. Smith. il por *Time* 129:31 Mr 2 '87

Trials of an expert witness [conflict arising from being asked to testify in defense of accused war criminal J. Demjanjuk] E. F. Loftus. por *Newsweek* 109:10-11 Je 29 '87

War crimes

See also

War crime trials

War criminals *See* World War, 1939-1945—War criminals

War games

See also

Military maneuvers

"After MAD": a computer game of nuclear strategy that ends in a Prisoner's Dilemma. A. K. Dewdney. il *Sci Am* 257:174-7 O '87

The battle for Berlin. G. Martin. il *Esquire* 108:204-13 N '87

Enter the 'silent service' [submarine simulation video games] *U S News World Rep* 102:42 Je 15 '87

The game of chicken may lead to nuclear war [views of Steven Brams and Marc Kilgour] il *Discover* 8:10 Ap '87

Hardguy software [Balance of Power strategic computer game designed by C. Crawford] J. Ledbetter. *Nation* 244:150-3 F 7 '87

Your move, General Lee. D. R. Smith. il *Americana* 14:66-9 Ja/F '87

War in art

See also

Vietnamese War, 1957-1975—Art and the war

War in literature

See also

Spain—History—Civil War, 1936-1939—Literature and the war

United States—History—Civil War, 1861-1865—Fiction

United States—History—Civil War, 1861-1865—Literature and the war

World War, 1939-1945—Fiction

World War, 1939-1945, in literature

War memorials

See also

Stone Mountain Memorial (Ga.)

Vietnam Veterans Memorial (Washington, D.C.)

Dutch tribute to gay pride [Amsterdam monument to homosexuals killed during Nazi regime] K. Golden. *Ms* 15:32 Je '87

Old castles and Old Glory: Luxembourg pays tribute to America. C. Males. il map *Travel Holiday* 168:34-41 D '87

Raleigh honors Vietnam vets. il *South Living* 22:53 O '87

Requiem for a fiasco [Englishman K. Small's crusade to honor Americans killed in World War II landing maneuvers at Slapton Sands] M. Brower. il pors *People Wkly* 28:60-5 N 30 '87

War news

See also

United States—History—Civil War, 1861-1865—Reporters and reporting

Greece—History—Civil War, 1944-1949—Reporters and reporting

Holocaust, Jewish (1939-1945)—Reporters and reporting

Iranian-Iraqi War, 1980- —Reporters and reporting

Israel-Arab Wars, 1967- —Reporters and reporting

Vietnamese War, 1957-1975—Reporters and reporting

World War, 1939-1945—Reporters and reporting

War novels (Civil War) *See* United States—History—Civil War, 1861-1865—Fiction

War objectors *See* Conscientious objectors

War of 1812 *See* United States—History—War of 1812

War powers *See* War and emergency powers

War Powers Resolution

Ballots and bloodshed [debate over Congress' position in Persian Gulf events] *New Repub* 197:4+ O 19 '87

The president's military power under the Constitution. J. F. Lea. il *USA Today (Periodical)* 116:12-15 S '87

Tonkin Gulf redux [U.S. in the Persian Gulf] *Nation* 245:541 N 14 '87

Top secret [U.S. presence in the Persian Gulf] W. F. Buckley. *Natl Rev* 39:64 S 25 '87

War Powers Act and the Persian Gulf. il *Congr Dig* 66:289-314 D '87

War Powers inaction [congressional inaction in face of U.S. commitment in the Persian Gulf] T. Noah. *New Repub* 197:11-12 Jl 6 '87

Warburg (E.M.), Pincus & Co., Inc. *See* E.M. Warburg, Pincus & Co., Inc.

Warburg (S.G.) Group plc *See* S.G. Warburg Group plc

Warburton, Andrew, d. 1986

about

Terror in the forest. il *Macleans* 100:45 Ap 20 '87

WARC *See* World Administrative Radio Conference

Ward, Alex

The Magic touch. il pors *N Y Times Mag* p66-8+ D 6 '87

Ward, Ashley
about
Ashley Ward. J. Meyer. il *Art News* 86:37 Mr '87
Ward, Benjamin
about
Charges prisons ruled by 'institutional racism'. por *Jet* 73:22 N 16 '87
'Sorry' for comment to white woman: Ward. por *Jet* 72:28 Ag 24 '87
Ward, Doris M.
about
Calif. educator makes bid for congressional seat. por *Jet* 72:9 Mr 30 '87
Ward, Douglas Turner, 1930-
about
20 years of theatrical excellence. R. Howell. il pors *Ebony* 42:92+ Mr '87
Ward, Fred, 1935-
Jade: stone of heaven [cover story] il map *Natl Geogr* 172:282-315 S '87
Ward, Geoffrey C.
The house at Hyde Park. il pors *Am Herit* 38:41-6+ Ap '87
India's intensifying dilemma: can tigers and people coexist? bibl (p269) il *Smithsonian* 18:52-62+ N '87
Jim Corbett: the reluctant executioner. il por maps *Audubon* 89:44-9+ Jl '87
Presidents, imperial and otherwise. il *Am Herit* 38:18+ My/Je '87
Seeing Murrow now. il *Am Herit* 38:16+ F/Mr '87
Ward, John L., and Sorenson, Laurel
A family needs a mission statement. il *Nations Bus* 75:45+ O '87
Ward, Olivia
The women of Greenham Common. il *World Press Rev* 34:32-4 Ap '87
Ward, Thomas J.
about
The questions surrounding Guinness' U.S. connection. P. Dwyer and M. Maremont. il por *Bus Week* p36-7 Ap 27 '87
Ward, W. Dixon
about
Ward is president-elect of Acoustical Society of America. *Phys Today* 40:75-6 S '87
Wardair Inc.
Midair clashes. D. Jenish. il *Macleans* 100:26-7 N 23 '87
Wardair flies high. A. Faujas. *World Press Rev* 34:48 D '87
Warde, John
Preparing radiators for winter. il *Consum Res Mag* 70:22-3 D '87
Wardens, Game *See* Game wardens
Wardle, Francis
Outdoor play . . . one Head Start program's approach [cover story] il *Child Today* 16:16-19 Mr/Ap '87
Wardrobes (Furniture) *See* Armoires
Wards *See* Guardian and ward
Ware, Carl
about
These guys don't blink. A. Edmond, Jr. il pors *Black Enterp* 17:310-12+ Je '87
Ware, Jane
Cutouts of fashion. il por *Americana* 15:41-5 Jl/Ag '87
Ware, Rochelle
about
High school dropout strikes it rich in Calif. lottery. *Jet* 71:23 Ja 12 '87
Warehouse clubs
See also
Price Co.
Warehouse clubs: an expanding market [books] J. Crichton. il *Publ Wkly* 231:56-8+ F 13 '87
Warehouses
See also
Self storage warehouses
Warfield, Paul
about
Ex-football star quits Browns' front office job. por *Jet* 71:46 Nr 23 '87
Warfield, Wallis *See* Windsor, Wallis Warfield, Duchess of, 1896-1986
Warga, Claire
Pain's gatekeeper. bibl (p67) il pors *Psychol Today* 21:50-6 Ag '87
Warhol, Andy, 1928?-1987
about
Andy Warhol at Dia Art Foundation and Larry Gagosian. D. Bourdon. il *Art Am* 75:213-14 Ap '87

A hospital stands accused. C. Wallis. il por *Time* 129:64 Ap 27 '87
Modern times. J. Perl. il *Vogue* 177:90+ Ag '87
Monograph and bio on Andy Warhol are due. *Publ Wkly* 231:36 Ap 3 '87
New York Hospital on the spot: three baffling deaths jolt a proud institution. M. Stone. il pors *N Y* 20:40-7 Je 22 '87
Obituary
Art Am il pors 75:137-43 My '87
Art Am 75:254 Ap '87
Art News il pors 86:128-32 My '87. A. C. Danto
Macleans il por 100:58 Mr 9 '87. G. MacKay
N Y il pors 20:38-45+ Mr 9 '87. J. Kornbluth
New Repub 196:25-8 My 18 '87. M. Stevens
New Yorker 63:27-8 Ap 27 '87
Newsweek il pors 109:64-6 Mr 9 '87. J. Kroll
People Wkly il pors 27:32-5 Mr 9 '87. M. Small
Roll Stone il pors p31-3+ Ap 9 '87. K. Loder
Time il por 129:90 Mr 9 '87. R. Hughes
U S News World Rep por 102:56-7 Mr 9 '87
Possession obsession. S. M. L. Aronson. il por *House Gard* 159:186-96 D '87
Saturday disasters: trace and reference in early Warhol [cover story] T. E. Crow. bibl f il por *Art Am* 75:128-36 My '87
Ultra Violet on Andy [excerpt from Ultra Violet remembers Andy Warhol] Ultra Violet. il pors *N Y* 20:46-7 Mr 9 '87
Waring, Richard H.
Characteristics of trees predisposed to die. bibl il *BioScience* 37:569-74 S '87
Wark, John, and Marx, Gary
Faith, hope, and chicanery. il *Wash Mon* 18:25-31 Ja '87
Warm Springs (Ga.)
Historic houses, sites, etc.
See also
Little White House Historic Site (Warm Springs, Ga.)
Warnaco Inc.
Linda Wachner. C. Donahue. il por *Ms* 15:78+ Ja '87
New outfit for a queen of beauty [L. Wachner] A. L. Taylor, III. il por *Fortune* 115:56 Ja 5 '87
Turning trials into triumph [L. Wachner] R. B. Tooley. il por *Work Woman* 12:66-8+ Ja '87
Warne, Colston E., 1900-1987
about
Obituary
Consum Rep il pors 52:405 Jl '87
Consum Rep 52:403 Jl '87. R. H. Karpatkin
Warne (Frederick) & Co. Ltd. *See* Frederick Warne & Co. Ltd.
Warnecke, Floyd
A Hallmark expression. *Travel Holiday* 168:16-17 D '87
Warner, Chris
Great expectations. il pors *Sport Mag* 78:70-2+ Mr '87
Warner, Gale
At the summit meeting. il map *Sierra* 72:57-60 Jl/Ag '87
Warner, Jack
Slouching toward Bethlehem. il *America* 157:472-4 D 19 '87
Warner, John W.
Should Congress move to invoke the War Powers Resolution? [excerpts from debates, October 1 and 20, 1987] *Congr Dig* 66:297+ D '87
Should the Levin-Nunn Amendment be approved? [excerpts from address, May 13, 1987] *Congr Dig* 66:265+ N '87
Warner, Malcolm-Jamal
about
Getting to know Malcolm-Jamal Warner. por *Teen* 31:76 Ag '87
Hunks & heartthrobs. pors *Teen* 31:54 Mr '87
Warner, Patricia
International style: Oriental touch for Mexico City. il *Archit Dig* 44:84-91 Jl '87
Venice-on-the-Hudson. il *Archit Dig* 44:140-7+ N '87
Warner Amex Cable Communications Inc.
Sweet year for a barn cleaner [D. Lewis] P. Nulty. il por *Fortune* 115:82-3 Ja 5 '87
Warner Audio Publishing
Random House buys Warner Audio for second audio line. il *Publ Wkly* 231:56-7 My 22 '87
Warner Books Inc.
Lawyer's first novel goes to Warner for $750,000 floor [G. Bernau's Promises to keep] W. Goldstein. *Publ Wkly* 232:78 Ag 14 '87

Warner Bros. Inc.
Warner Bros. reactivates Reprise. F. Goodman. *Roll Stone* p33 S 24 '87
Warner Communications Inc.
The feud at Warner just keeps getting hotter [H. J. Siegel vs S. J. Ross] S. Benway. il pors *Bus Week* p76-8+ Je 29 '87
Ross gets a few dollars more [S. Ross] B. Dumaine. il pors *Fortune* 115:57-8+ Ap 13 '87
The Warner war: why Steve Ross and Herb Siegel can't get along [cover story] J. Taylor. il pors *N Y* 20:34-42 Jl 13 '87
Warner-Lambert Company
A powerful tonic for Warner-Lambert [anticholesterol drug Lopid] L. Baum. il por *Bus Week* p144+ N 30 '87
Six months and half a million dollars, all for 15 seconds [Young & Rubicam does a television commercial for Warner-Lambert's Rolaids] J. E. Pfeiffer. il *Smithsonian* 18:134-8+ O '87
Warner Publishers Services, Inc.
Berkley makes a move [distribution deal with Warner Publisher Services] A. Symons. il *Publ Wkly* 231:50-2 My 8 '87
Walden, WPS just say 'no' to condoms [refusal to carry cassette packaged with condoms] il *Publ Wkly* 232:48 O 30 '87
Warnes, Jennifer, 1947-
about
Jennifer Warnes sings songs of Leonard Cohen. A. Nash. il pors *Stereo Rev* 52:78+ My '87
Jenny sings Lenny. S. Pond. pors *Roll Stone* p16 Mr 12 '87
Warnke, Paul C., 1920-
about
Star Wars: does it help or hurt arms-control efforts? [interview] J. Scarlott. il por *Sch Update* 120:20-1 N 20 '87
Warnock, John E.
about
How two pioneers brought publishing to the desktop. K. M. Hafner. il pors *Bus Week* p61-2 O 5 '87
Warrants, Currency exchange *See* Currency exchange warrants
Warrants, Stock purchase *See* Stock purchase warrants
Warranty
See also
American Warranty Company
Absolutely guaranteed [warranty offered by A. Burger's exterminating service] J. Livingston. il por *Nations Bus* 75:51-2 N '87
Car warranties: the (deceptively) long and (too) short of Detroit's new promises. J. Reid. il *Money* 16:181-2 S '87
Chrysler/AMC warranties. M. J. Schultz. *Pop Mech* 164:22 O '87
Extended warranties: marketing gimmick or real benefit? [automobiles] M. Keller. il *Mot Trend* 39:130 Jl '87
Ford's warranty commitment. M. J. Schultz. *Pop Mech* 164:24+ S '87
Home warranties: insurance for faulty construction work? T. Tilling. il *Parents* 62:49-50 N '87
Understanding warranties [cars] il *Mother Earth News* 108:123-4+ N/D '87
Understanding warranties proves vital to your protection. H. Porter. *Fam Handyman* 37:24 Mr '87
Warranties: circa 1987 [General Motors] M. J. Schultz. il *Pop Mech* 164:24+ Ag '87
Warranty review. P. L. Spencer. *Consum Res Mag* 70:2 Je '87
Warranty warfare [automobiles] B. Bauer. il *U S News World Rep* 102:46 F 16 '87
Warranty wars [automobiles] E. Henry. il *Changing Times* 41:101-3 My '87
Warren, Andrew C., and others
Evidence for reduced recombination on the nondisjoined chromosomes 21 in Down syndrome. bibl f il *Science* 237:652-4 Ag 7 '87
Warren, Elizabeth V.
Amish quilts in the Museum of American Folk Art. bibl f il *Antiques* 132:514-23 S '87
Warren, Henry C.
Olympic National Park [excerpt from Olympic] il *Natl Parks* 61:46-7 My/Je '87
Warren, Jerry
The secret to long, strong turns. il *Skiing* 39:98-100 Spr '87
Warren, Richard
Wine, words, & song. il *High Fidel* 37:53-5 Mr '87

Warren, Robert Penn, 1905-
about
The Nobel Prize deferred again. P. H. Samway. *America* 157:359+ N 14 '87
Robert Penn Warren. J. Parini. por *Horizon* 30:36-7 Je '87
Warren, Stephen T., and others
The fragile X site in somatic cell hybrids: an approach for molecular cloning of fragile sites [cover story] bibl f il *Science* 237:420-3 Jl 24 '87
Warren (Mich.)
Race relations
Mich. mom flees crime, is stopped by racism [C. Hawk] *Jet* 72:16 Ag 3 '87
Warren (S. D.) Co. *See* S. D. Warren Co.
Warrior (Battleship)
H.M.S. Warrior. W. Brownlee. il *Sci Am* 257:130-6 D '87
Wars *See* War
Wars of the Roses, 1455-1485 *See* Great Britain—History— Wars of the Roses, 1455-1485
Warsaw (Poland)
History
Uprising of 1943
The curious case of Marek Edelman [last leader of the Warsaw Ghetto uprising remaining in Poland] L. S. Dawidowicz. *Commentary* 83:66-9 Mr '87
Poles and Jews [discussion of March 1987 article, The curious case of Marek Edelman] L. S. Dawidowicz. *Commentary* 84:2-4+ Ag '87
Warsaw Ballet
U.S. tour is among Warsaw Ballet's current plans. P. Chynowski. *Dance Mag* 61:99 Ap '87
Warsaw ghetto uprising, 1943 *See* Warsaw (Poland)— History—Uprising of 1943
Warsaw Pact Organization *See* Warsaw Treaty Organization
Warsaw Treaty Organization
Battle of the bean counters [effect of zero option proposal on NATO and Warsaw Pact forces] C. Redman. il map *Time* 129:33-4 Je 15 '87
Conventional forces in Europe [special section] bibl f il *Bull At Sci* 43:9-20 D '87
Military security in Europe. J. Dean. *Foreign Aff* 66:22-40 Fall '87
NATO's war-game guests [Soviet bloc military observers] K. Scanlon. il *Macleans* 100:20-1 S 28 '87
The Warsaw Treaty Organization. R. F. Staar. bibl f il *Curr Hist* 86:357-60+ N '87
Warshaw, David M., and others
Corkscrew-like shortening in single smooth muscle cells. bibl f il *Science* 236:1457-9 Je 12 '87
Warshaw, Stan
about
Hanging wallpaper: when to hire a pro [interview] N. Cooper. il por *Home Mech* 83:28+ My '87
Warshawski, Evy
Video résumés: sharpening the competitive edge. il *Dance Mag* 61:40-1 Mr '87
Warships
See also
Aircraft carriers
Constitution (Frigate)
Monitor (Ironclad)
Rodney M. Davis (Warship)
Stark (Warship)
Submarines
Triremes
Armaments
See also
Guided missiles—Launching from ships
When attackers become targets [U.S. Navy] R. Hornik. il *Time* 129:23 Je 1 '87
Identification
Inverse synthetic aperture technology aids radar identification of ships. P. J. Klass. il *Aviat Week Space Technol* 127:88-9 S 7 '87
Great Britain
See also
Mary Rose (Ship)
Warrior (Battleship)
Poland
They couldn't hit a . . . oops! [Polish ship accidentally fires at West German ship in the Baltic Sea] il *Time* 129:39 Je 29 '87
Sweden
See also
Vasa (Warship)

Warships—*cont.*

United States
See Warships

Warshofsky, Fred
A cure for doctors who are hazardous to health. il *Read Dig* 130:70-4 Ja '87

Wartik, Nancy
Out on a ledge. il *Ms* 15:34 My '87

Warts
Worried about warts? V. DeBenedette. *McCalls* 114:150 S '87

Warwick, Dionne
about
Dionne Warwick organizing AIDS fund-raiser in D.C.; cited by Reagan and Barry. il pors *Jet* 73:22+ O 12 '87
Warwick 'cries to bank' over luck with her songs. por *Jet* 71:16 Mr 2 '87
Warwick wows Reagan, French premier, and others at White House. il por *Jet* 72:6 Ap 20 '87

Wasa (Warship) *See* Vasa (Warship)

Washburn, Chris
about
Will the sleeping giant ever awake? R. Wiley. il pors *Sports Illus* 66:42-4+ F 2 '87

Washers, Pressure *See* Pressure washers

Washing machines
Maintenance and repair
Self-reliance [repairing Sears Kenmore machine] C. Maxwell. il *Fam Handyman* 37:72 N '87

Washing of clothes *See* Laundry

Washington, Alicia
Kidnapping
Concern erases risk as Leonard helps rescue tot. por *Jet* 72:46 Je 22 '87

Washington, Denzel
about
Becoming Biko. E. Mitchell. il por *Roll Stone* p32 D 3 '87
Movies. D. Denby. il por *N Y* 20:54-5 S 21 '87

Washington, George, 1732-1799
about
George and Martha in Alabama. il pors *South Living* 22:51 N '87
George Washington's Patowmack Canal. W. E. Garrett. il maps *Natl Geogr* 171:716-53 Je '87
The legacy of two leaders. J. T. Ellis. *America* 157:149-50 S 26 '87
Patowmack Canal connection. B. Culhane. il *Natl Parks* 61:16-17 Mr/Ap '87
Anecdotes, facetiae, satire, etc.
Uncivil liberties. C. Trillin. *Nation* 244:242 F 28 '87
Assassination plot, 1776
The plot to kill Washington. B. C. Fenwick. il por *Am Hist Illus* 21:8-12 F '87
Homes
Washington and Lincoln slept here. C. B. Hayes. il maps *Travel Holiday* 167:46-50 F '87
Statues, portraits, etc.
Scenes from the life of Washington [portfolio of paintings by J.L.G. Ferris] J. L. G. Ferris. il *Am Hist Illus* 21:22-31 F '87
Washington didn't sleep in Richmond. il *Am Herit* 38:82-3 D '87

Washington, Harold
about
Big shoulders on the lakefront. il por *U S News World Rep* 102:9 Mr 9 '87
Black beauty industry fetes Chicago's Mayor Washington. il *Jet* 71:12 Mr 2 '87
Chicago: as durable as Daley? J. McCormick. il por *Newsweek* 109:10 Ap 20 '87
Chicago city college renamed to honor late mayor Harold Washington. il por *Jet* 73:32 D 21 '87
Chicago's two solitudes. I. Austen. il pors *Macleans* 100:16 Mr 2 '87
Eugene Sawyer vows to continue reforms of Mayor Washington. R. E. Johnson. il pors *Jet* 73:4-6+ D 21 '87
Harold Washington: Chicago mayor charts new direction for next four years [cover story] R. E. Johnson. il pors *Jet* 72:4-6 My 4 '87
In Chicago a machine dies. G. Rivlin. il *Nation* 244:424-6 Ap 4 '87
The mayor everybody knows. C. Whitaker. il pors *Ebony* 43:78-80+ D '87
Mayor Washington wins historic second term. il pors *Jet* 72:4+ Ap 27 '87
Obituary
Christ Century 104:1131-2 D 16 '87. J. M. Wall
Jet il pors 73:4-6+ D 14 '87

Newsweek il por 110:45 D 7 '87. J. McCormick
Time por 130:27 D 7 '87. J. E. White
A rematch in the Windy City. M. Bosc. il pors *U S News World Rep* 102:20 F 23 '87
Spoils and spoilers. C. Page. *New Repub* 196:13-15 Mr 2 '87

Washington, J. Leon
about
Black admissions director hired at Oberlin College. *Jet* 73:22 S 28 '87

Washington, Kermit
about
Another return engagement. J. McCallum. il *Sports Illus* 67:42 N 16 '87

Washington, Martha, 1731-1802
about
George and Martha in Alabama. il pors *South Living* 22:51 N '87

Washington, Otis
about
Ex-Southern grid coach gets $50,000 settlement. *Jet* 72:46 Ap 6 '87

Washington, William A.
My family, my team. il *World Tennis* 35:18+ O '87

Washington (D.C.)
See also
Booksellers and bookselling—Washington (D.C.)
Music festivals—Washington (D.C.)
Airports
United Airlines increases flights at Washington Dulles. *Aviat Week Space Technol* 126:49 Ja 26 '87
Blacks
Washington, D.C.: a thriving center of power and culture. D. C. Ruffin. il *Black Enterp* 17:75-6+ My '87
History
Interior Dept. opens black history trail in District. *Jet* 72:22 Ap 20 '87
Buildings
See also
Washington Harbour (Washington, D.C.)
Churches (Buildings)
Church files $40 million damage suit; A.M.E. bishops announce their support [Metropolitan A.M.E. Church] *Jet* 72:29 Ap 20 '87
Historic D.C. church closed; blame nearby construction [Metropolitan African Methodist Episcopal Church] il *Jet* 71:37-8 Ja 26 '87
City planning
See also
Washington Harbour (Washington, D.C.)
Pennsylvania Ave: making an American place. P. Morris. il map *South Living* 22:66-71 S '87
Climate
Man and machine forecast big snow. R. A. Kerr. il *Science* 235:1460-1 Mr 20 '87
Courts
See also
United States. Court of Appeals (District of Columbia Circuit)
D.C. judge assailed for remark to black prosecutor [Frederick Weisberg's comments to R. Dixon] *Jet* 72:17 Jl 20 '87
Crime
See also
Reagan, Ronald, 1911———Assassination attempt, March 30, 1981
Washington, Alicia—Kidnapping
Criminal justice, Administration of
Ex-teacher in D.C. gets 52-155 yrs. for sex abuse [J. B. Crawford] *Jet* 72:36 Jl 27 '87
Description
Adventures: kids in the capital. A. K. Horowitz. il *Publ Wkly* 231:144-5 My 15 '87
D.C. guide. maps *Publ Wkly* 231:146-8 My 15 '87
My New York, my New York [comparison with New York City] R. Brookhiser. *Natl Rev* 39:37-9 F 13 '87
A walk through history. C. T. Rowan and D. M. Mazie. il *Read Dig* 131:20-5 O '87
Walking the federal triangle. R. G. Kennedy. il *Good Housekeep* 205:108-9 O '87
Washington: a city of letters . . . [favorite places of writers living in the capital; symposium] il *Publ Wkly* 231:140-2 My 15 '87
A Washington portrait. D. Graff. il *Travel Holiday* 168:51-5 O '87
Education
Inner-city students are bullish on investing. P. Rowe. il *Child Today* 16:22-6 My/Je '87

Washington (D.C.)—Education—*cont.*
Keeping youth in school: a public-private collaboration [peer mentor program for high school students sponsored by Catholic University and Marriott; with reports by J. Payne and J. Smith] S. Lee and others. il *Child Today* 16:15-21 Jl/Ag '87

Galleries and museums
See also
Anacostia Neighborhood Museum (Washington, D.C.)
Arthur M. Sackler Gallery (Washington, D.C.)
National Gallery of Art (U.S.)
National Museum of American History (U.S.)
National Museum of Natural History (U.S.)
National Museum of Women in the Arts (U.S.)
Renwick Gallery
Smithsonian Institution
Textile Museum (Washington, D.C.)
U.S. Holocaust Memorial Museum
Museum buys in D.C. [museum shops] D. P. Marshall. *Travel Holiday* 167:66-8 Ja '87

Gardens and gardening
See also
Enid A. Haupt Garden (Washington, D.C.)
National Arboretum (U.S.)

Historic houses, sites, etc.
See also
Dumbarton Oaks
White House (Washington, D.C.)
Social graces in Georgetown: Polly and Clayton Fritchey's Victorian enclave. S. M. Alsop. il pors *Archit Dig* 44:188-91 O '87

Hospitals, Psychiatric
See Hospitals, Psychiatric—Washington (D.C.)

Hotels, motels, etc.
A stately Willard proudly receives guests once more. D. A. Marks. il *Smithsonian* 17:78-82+ F '87

Housing
How the homeless bought a Rolls for Cornelius Pitts [running a welfare hotel] M. Szegedy-Maszak. il por *Wash Mon* 19:11-15 Jl/Ag '87

Justice, Administration of
See also
Washington (D.C.)—Criminal justice, Administration of

Libraries
See also
Folger Shakespeare Library

Monuments, statues, etc.
See also
Lincoln Memorial (Washington, D.C.)
Vietnam Veterans Memorial (Washington, D.C.)
Alphas move to erect King memorial in D.C. [Alpha Phi Alpha] *Jet* 71:28 F 9 '87

Music
See also
National Symphony Orchestra
Washington Opera
Music, military style [outdoor concerts] K. Lingo. il *South Living* 22:10-12 Jl '87

Newspapers
See also
Washington post
Washington times

Politics and government
Barry promises youth jobs, training at start of term 3. il por *Jet* 71:9 Ja 26 '87
Black politicos condemn U.S. probe of Marion Barry. *Jet* 72:31 Jl 27 '87
D.C. mayor Barry sues U.S. Atty. over 'leak a week'. *Jet* 72:5 Jl 13 '87
D.C. mayor Marion Barry denies cocaine usage. il por *Jet* 72:4 Jl 6 '87
Fauntroy renews bid to gain statehood for D.C. *Jet* 71:5 Mr 23 '87
The imperial mayor [M. Barry] J. Williams. *New Repub* 197:21-3 O 26 '87
The trials of Marion Barry. G. Hackett. il por *Newsweek* 110:21 Ag 31 '87
Walter Fauntroy closer to gaining statehood for D.C. *Jet* 72:4 Je 22 '87
Whistle stop campaigning for D.C. statehood drive. il *Jet* 72:6 Ag 3 '87

Poor
Black solons camp out in D.C. streets for needy. il *Jet* 71:32 Mr 23 '87
A homeless Vietnam veteran's unhappy story of high hopes and misfortune [Jesse Moses] L. Cohler. *Sch Update* 119:8-9 Mr 23 '87
Poor in Washington. A. Evans-Pritchard. il *World Press Rev* 34:64 N '87

Posing as a bag lady, housewife Beulah Lund finds fear and love in the homeless netherworld. R. Arias. il pors *People Wkly* 27:32-4+ F 16 '87

Protests, demonstrations, etc.
As it never was [Mobilization for Justice and Peace in Central America and Southern Africa] *Nation* 244:597-8 My 9 '87
For a new coalition [National March for Lesbian and Gay Rights] *Nation* 245:433 O 24 '87
Friends and enemies [march for Soviet Jewish emigration] M. Walzer. *New Repub* 197:13-14 D 28 '87
A new activism in the streets [Mobilization for Justice and Peace in Central America and Southern Africa] F. Bruning. por *Macleans* 100:7 My 11 '87
On the march [Mobilization for Justice and Peace in Central America and Southern Africa, April 25, 1987] *Nation* 244:529 Ap 25 '87
Red in the rainbow [J. Jackson's participation in Peace and Justice in Central America and South Africa march] *Natl Rev* 39:17-18 My 22 '87
Rites of passage [Mobilization for Justice and Peace in Central America and Southern Africa; April 25, 1987 protest march] *Nation* 244:491-2 Ap 18 '87
Rustin, organizer of 1963 march on Washington, dies [B. Rustin] il *Jet* 72:54 S 7 '87
Stealing a march [Mobilization for Justice and Peace] M. Kondracke. *New Repub* 196:10+ My 4 '87
Those were the gays [March on Washington for Gay and Lesbian Rights] R. Blow. *New Repub* 197:14-16 N 2 '87

Public buildings
See also
State Dept. Building (Washington, D.C.)

Public welfare
D.C. welfare mother gets house she asked of mayor [J. Williams] il por *Jet* 72:12 Ag 31 '87

Race relations
D.C. judge assailed for remark to black prosecutor [Frederick Weisberg's comments to R. Dixon] *Jet* 72:17 Jl 20 '87

Religious institutions and affairs
Osei 1st black to head UCC conference in D.C. *Jet* 72:38 Jl 27 '87
Vice President Bush worships at black church, boosts families [Shiloh Baptist Church] il pors *Jet* 71:24-5 Ja 19 '87

Restaurants, nightclubs, bars, etc.
Fine dining: guide to the great restaurants of Washington, DC. il *Publ Wkly* 231:121-2+ My 15 '87
Potomac: food and fantasy in Washington, D.C. K. Merlino. il *USA Today (Periodical)* 116:38-43 S '87

Social life and customs
Banning the free lunch [executive branch officials prohibited from accepting free lunches] E. Clift. il *Newsweek* 110:19 D 28 '87
The banquet beat. M. Aronson. *New Repub* 196:11-12 Je 22 '87
Games people play. F. Reed. *Harpers* 275:72-4 Jl '87
The lady has a Midas touch [Democratic fund raising dinners hosted by P. Harriman] E. Thomas. il pors *Newsweek* 109:32-3 Je 15 '87
Mr. Peepers's nights: Mrs. Huffington entertains. il *N Y* 20:37-8 Ap 27 '87
Washington, D.C.: great jobs in the fast lane [special section] *Harpers Bazaar* 121:46+ N '87

Anecdotes, facetiae, satire, etc.
Miss Manners' convention etiquette [guidelines for American Booksellers convention] J. Martin. il por *Publ Wkly* 231:143 My 15 '87

Stores
Yetta Galiber: Christmas every day of the year [special store for disabled] il pors *Ebony* 43:27-30 D '87

Streets
See also
Pennsylvania Avenue (Washington, D.C.)

Theater
The eyes and ears have it in DC [Audio Description narration service] S. Green. il *Theatre Crafts* 21:41+ Ap '87

Georgetown
See Georgetown (Washington, D.C.)

Theodore Roosevelt Island
See Theodore Roosevelt Island (Washington, D.C.)

Washington (D.C.). Dumbarton Oaks *See* Dumbarton Oaks
Washington (D.C.). Folger Shakespeare Library *See* Folger Shakespeare Library
Washington (D.C.). Urban Institute *See* Urban Institute
Washington (George) Bridge (N.Y. and N.J.) *See* George Washington Bridge (N.Y. and N.J.)

Washington (George) National Forest (Va. and W. Va.)
See George Washington National Forest (Va. and W. Va.)
Washington (Harold) College *See* Harold Washington College
Washington (State)
See also
Architecture, Domestic—Washington (State)
Booksellers and bookselling—Washington (State)
Columbia River
Crime and criminals—Washington (State)
Earthquakes—Washington (State)
Environment—Washington (State)
Fishing—Washington (State)
Historic houses, sites, etc.—Washington (State)
Mount Rainier National Park (Wash.)
Mount Saint Helens (Wash.)
Mount Saint Helens National Volcanic Monument (Wash.)
Olympic National Park (Wash.)
Organic farming—Washington (State)
Padilla Bay (Wash.)
Prisons—Washington (State)
Public welfare—Washington (State)
Puget Sound (Wash.)
Radioactive waste disposal—Washington (State)
Capitol
Politics outlives art [controversy surrounding murals by A. Mason and M. Spafford for the state capitol in Olympia] L. Smallwood. il *Art News* 86:28 D '87
Description and travel
A coast of many moods. A. Furst. il map *50 Plus* 27:78-82 O '87
Industries
See also
Washington Public Power Supply System
Wine industry
Washington Ballet
First decade for Washington Ballet: the company that just happened. A. Tomalonis. il *Dance Mag* 61:64-5 Ap '87
Washington Harbour (Washington, D.C.)
Cooking with history [complex designed by A. C. Moore; with editorial comment by Mildred F. Schmertz] D. Dietsch. il *Archit Rec* 175:9, 84-93 Ja '87
Washington Opera
Edward Rothstein on music [G. C. Menotti's Goya] E. Rothstein. *New Repub* 196:27-9 Ja 26 '87
Washington, D.C. C. Jahant. il *Opera News* 51:36 F 14 '87
Washington, D.C. D. P. Stearns. il *Opera News* 51:38 Mr 14 '87
Washington post
Beat the devil [pro contra reporting by W. Branigin] A. Cockburn. *Nation* 244:790-1 Je 13 '87
"Equally bizarre, but somewhat different" [further notes on how the Washington post was scooped on Truman's letter to music critic P. Hume] M. S. Forbes. *Forbes* 140:18-19 Ag 10 '87
Here's how the Washington post was scooped on Truman's letter [letter to music critic P. Hume over review of daughter Margaret's singing] M. S. Forbes. il *Forbes* 139:18 Je 29 '87
How Advo is moving in on Washington post territory. il *Bus Week* p127 N 2 '87
Pulling punches [coverage of blacks] C. Coulson. *New Repub* 196:10-12 My 25 '87
Triple reverse [appeals court reverses decision in W. Tavoulareas' libel suit] por *Time* 129:70 Mr 23 '87
Washington press corps *See* Presidents—Press relations
Reagan, Ronald, 1911——Press relations
Washington Public Power Supply System
Energy Department blurs line between civilian, military reactors [plan to convert Unit One to weapons purposes] M. M. Hoenig. bibl f *Bull At Sci* 43:25-7 Je '87
The jury's still out on 'WHOOPS'—way out. H. Gleckman. il *Bus Week* p168 N 2 '87
The safe Whoopses [projects 1, 2 and 3] B. Weberman. il *Forbes* 139:297 Ja 12 '87
WHOOPS haunts the Street [SEC investigation] C. Farrell. *Bus Week* p122 Mr 16 '87
Wonders never cease [comeback in bonds] B. Weberman. il *Forbes* 140:213 O 19 '87
Washington times
Moonie journalism. T. McNichol. *Wash Mon* 19:23-8 O '87
Morrow to sue 'Washington times' over excerpts from Deaver book. H. Fields. *Publ Wkly* 232:19 D 25 '87
Notes & asides [editorial controversy] W. F. Buckley. il *Natl Rev* 39:20+ My 22 '87

Underdog to an 800-pound gorilla. L. Zuckerman. il por *Time* 129:64-5 Je 15 '87
War of independence [charges of editorial interference by Unification Church] *Newsweek* 109:63 Ap 27 '87
Washstands (Cabinets) *See* Cabinets (Furniture)
Wasik, Vince
about
First, kick the tires. S. B. Weiner. il por *Forbes* 140:50+ O 5 '87
Wasps
Another way to get rid of houseflies? It's biological [use of parasitic wasps] il *Sunset* 178:204-5 Je '87
Parasitic wasps keep on ticking [research by Jonathan M. Schmidt and J. J. B. Smith] R. Weiss. *Sci News* 132:134 Ag 29 '87
Short interval time measurement by a parasitoid wasp. J. M. Schmidt and J. J. B. Smith. bibl f il *Science* 237:903-5 Ag 21 '87
Wasps! T. Krautwurst. il *Mother Earth News* 106:60-3 Jl/Ag '87
Photographs and photography
Wasp pickup [thynnine wasp mating] B. A. Wells and A. G. Wells. il *Nat Hist* 96:84-5 Ap '87
Reproduction
See Insects—Reproduction
Sexual behavior
See Sexual behavior—Insects
Wassarman, Paul M.
The biology and chemistry of fertilization. bibl f il *Science* 235:553-60 Ja 30 '87
Wassef, Habiba H.
Women—the managers of food. il *World Health* p18-19 Mr '87
Wasserman, Fred William, 1939-
about
Corporate partners in a maxi-marriage. C. Hutton. il pors *Fortune* 115:46 Ja 5 '87
'A time bomb is ticking at Maxicare'. J. Flynn. *Bus Week* p116 Jl 20 '87
Wasserman, Harvey
Summer of our discontent. *Nation* 245:233-4 S 12 '87
Wasserman, Louis R.
about
A Hollywood thriller: MCA vs. the sharks. J. Egan. il por *U S News World Rep* 103:44-5 S 7 '87
Wasserman, Robert
(jt. auth) See Sacks, Oliver W., and Wasserman, Robert
Wasserman, Steve
about
Wasserman named publisher of Noonday Press, Hill and Wang. por *Publ Wkly* 232:12 S 11 '87
Wassermann, Selma
Teaching for thinking: Louis E. Raths revisited. bibl f il *Phi Delta Kappan* 68:460-6 F '87
Waste, Industrial *See* Trade waste
Waste as fuel *See* Refuse as fuel
Waste disposal *See* Hazardous substances—Disposal; Medical waste disposal; Radioactive waste disposal; Refuse and refuse disposal; Trade waste—Disposal
Waste disposal in the ocean
OTA issues warning. *Oceans* 20:5 Jl/Ag '87
OTA warning on wastes in coastal waters. S. Weisburd. *Sci News* 131:309 My 16 '87
Troubled waters [cover story] il map *Bus Week* p88-91+ O 12 '87
Waste disposers *See* Refuse disposers
Waste in government spending (U.S.) *See* United States—Appropriations and expenditures
Waste Management, Inc.
Of dumps, Chicago politics & herons [environmentalists fight to save wetlands threatened by landfill] J. Sullivan. il *Audubon* 89:122-6 Mr '87
Waste products
See also
Trade waste
Waste products as fuel *See* Refuse as fuel
Waste recycling *See* Recycling (Waste, etc.)
Waste water reclamation *See* Water reuse
Wat Phou *See* Temples—Laos
Watanabe, Sadao
about
Sadao Watanabe's bop/pop chops. G. Kalbacher. il pors *Down Beat* 54:19-21 Ja '87
Watch industry
Marketing
See also
Gruen Marketing Corporation
Abe Breguet, meet Christian Dior. R. Morais. il *Forbes* 140:92+ D 14 '87

Watch industry—*cont.*

Japan
See also
Hattori Seiko Co. Ltd.

Switzerland
Abe Breguet, meet Christian Dior. R. Morais. il *Forbes* 140:92+ D 14 '87

Watches
Clip-on clocks are clicking. il *Time* 130:51 Ag 17 '87
The essence of time. il *Black Enterp* 18:78 Ag '87
Organize your time. il *Harpers Bazaar* 120:38 Mr '87
Timeworn tickers add class to any wrist. T. Segal. il *Bus Week* p141 N 9 '87
Wristful thinking. il *Esquire* 107:105 My '87

Anecdotes, facetiae, satire, etc.
A time for watches. C. Schine. il *N Y Times Mag* p14 F 15 '87

Prices
Abe Breguet, meet Christian Dior. R. Morais. il *Forbes* 140:92+ D 14 '87

Watches, Electronic
Best of times [sport-tech designs] J. Skorupa. il *Pop Mech* 164:64-6+ S '87

Photographs and photography
Macro dimensional view. W. J. Watt. il *Petersens Photogr Mag* 16:52-3 Ag '87
Time on time. D. Collins. il *Petersens Photogr Mag* 15:26-7 F '87

Prices
A tough sell? K. Murray. il *Forbes* 139:137-8 Mr 9 '87

Water
See also
Dew
Drinking water
Drops
Ice
Lakes
Plants—Water requirements
Ponds
Rivers
Runoff
Sea water
Springs
Waves
Reflections from a water surface display some curious properties. J. Walker. il *Sci Am* 256:120-4+ Ja '87

Analysis
Household hazards. G. Reiger. *Field Stream* 92:12+ Je '87
Is your well well? [testing for contaminants] C. Tevis. il *Success Farm* 85 no1:32-3 Ja '87
Testing water. A. Davis. il *Home Mech* 83:82 F '87
Well water: how to be sure it's pure. S. Woolley. il *Bus Week* p84 Ag 10 '87

Microbiology
Little drop of horrors [life in a drop of pond water; work of A. Rakosy] H. Wouk. il *Omni* 10:84-9 N '87

Nitrogen content
Hope for blighted bays: the reduction of nitrogen inflow may benefit coastal waters. T. Beardsley. *Sci Am* 257:26-7+ N '87

Photographs and photography
Fountainheads. il *Wilderness* 51:22-31 Fall '87

Physiological effects
See Water in the body

Rates
See Water rates

Temperature
See also
Lakes—Temperature
Ocean temperature

Water, Bottled *See* Bottled water
Water, Distilled
See also
Distillation equipment

Water, Fear of *See* Aquaphobia
Water, Underground
See also
Hot springs
Ogallala Aquifer

Pollution
See Water pollution

Water bars
A Beverly Hills bar has water, water from everywhere, and that's all there is to drink [Ixi:z owned by S. Mills] il *People Wkly* 27:109-10 F 9 '87

Water beds *See* Waterbeds
Water bird shooting
Getting the lead out [waterfowl poisoning from lead shot] M. Rosenthal. il *Ctry J* 14:10-11 O '87
Steeling ourselves for the future (I) [steel shot for waterfowl] B. Brister. il *Field Stream* 92:66+ Ag '87
Steeling ourselves for the future (II) [steel shot for waterfowl] B. Brister. il *Field Stream* 92:129-30+ S '87
Why I'm out there. G. Hill. il *Field Stream* 92:13+ N '87

Water birds
See also
Ducks, Wild
Flamingos
Geese, Wild
Pelicans
Sea birds
Shore birds
Storks
Swans

Migration
DEC's 1987 migratory waterfowl print and stamp. il *Conservationist* 42:54 Jl/Ag '87
Empty the skies [loss of wetland habitat for migrating water birds] P. Steinhart. il maps *Audubon* 89:70-97 N '87
The wings of spring [return of migrating ducks; cover story] G. Lemmo. il *Conservationist* 41:26-31 Mr/Ap '87

Photographs and photography
Beating wings. J. A. Barrie. il *Audubon* 89:62-9 N '87

Water bloom
See also
Red tide
Scallops transplanted to algae-damaged beds [Long Island] J. C. Rose. il *Oceans* 20:6 Ja/F '87

Water color painting *See* Watercolor painting
Water conservation
See also
Terraces (Agriculture)
Water reuse
How much water does your lawn really need? il *Sunset* 178:213-19 Je '87
Water efficiency in the house. il *Sunset* 179:154+ S '87

Water coolers
Poison in the plumbing? [lead and water coolers] T. Monmaney. il *Newsweek* 110:56 D 21 '87
Water, water everywhere, but . . . [lead in drinking fountains] S. Weiss. *Sci News* 132:390-1 D 19-26 '87

Water drops *See* Drops
Water exercises
Get wet, get fit: shaping up with water exercises. il *Better Homes Gard* 65:59-61+ Ag '87
Water workout: cool in the pool. K. Allard. bibl il *Women's Sports Fitness* 9:43 Ag '87
A water workout that works! S. McCoy. il *Teen* 31:90-1 Je '87

Water filters and filtration
Under-sink water filters—two install-it-yourself kits. T. O. Bakke. il *Pop Sci* 230:104-5 F '87
Water filter system you install [Sears equipment] H. Wicks. il *Home Mech* 83:84 O '87
Water filters for your home. *Better Homes Gard* 65:80 Mr '87

Water fowl *See* Water birds
Water fronts *See* Waterfronts
Water Gardens (Fort Worth, Tex.)
Fort Worth's water wonderworld. il *South Living* 22:18 N '87

Water gardens and gardening
See also
Hydroponics
Water Gardens (Fort Worth, Tex.)

Water hammer
Stopping water hammer. G. Branson. il *Fam Handyman* 37:88-9 My/Je '87

Water heaters
Connect plastic pipe to your water heater? R. Day. il *Pop Sci* 231:81 S '87
The everything box [Therma-Vent HPV-80 heat-pump water heater] S. Clarke. il *Pop Sci* 231:76 Ag '87
Installing a water heater. il *Home Mech* 83:42 Ja '87
When your furnace or central air conditioner or water heater needs replacement. L. Green. il *Good Housekeep* 204:218+ Ap '87

Water hyacinths
Sludge busters [San Diego's water hyacinth sewage treatment system] R. Stayton. il *Pop Sci* 230:43-4 F '87

Water in literature
Anecdotes, facetiae, satire, etc.
Total immersion: Henry James and mineral waters [effect of new Paris water bar on French literature] A. Broyard. il *N Y Times Book Rev* 92:10 Ja 4 '87
Water in the Bible
Water of life. M. K. Hellwig. *America* 156:inside back cover Mr 14 '87
Water in the body
See also
　Osmoregulation
Allure of the sea: spa secrets. il *Harpers Bazaar* 120:224-7+ O '87
Exercise and fluid replacement: your body's balancing act. T. Osborne. il *Curr Health 2* 14:16-17 N '87
Liquid assets. A. Barr. il *Good Housekeep* 204:124-5 My '87
The surprising beauty and health benefits of water. il *Glamour* 85:326-9 Ap '87
Water, the neglected nutrient. H. Fisher. *Prevention* 39:112+ Ag '87
Why does your body bloat? A. Spence. il *Redbook* 170:114-15+ N '87
Your diet: water works. J. S. Stern. *Vogue* 177:262 Je '87
Water insects *See* Insects, Aquatic
Water on Mars *See* Mars (Planet)—Surface
Water on Venus *See* Venus (Planet)—Surface
Water pipes
See also
　Water hammer
Freezing
First, do no harm. J. Vara. *Ctry J* 14:16-19 D '87
Maintenance and repair
Patching plastic pipe. R. Day. il *Pop Sci* 230:91 Mr '87
Water pipes, Plastic
Connect plastic pipe to your water heater? R. Day. il *Pop Sci* 231:81 S '87
Patching plastic pipe. R. Day. il *Pop Sci* 230:91 Mr '87
Water pollution
See also
　Acid rain
　Fish contamination
　Marine pollution
　Oil pollution
　Water bloom
Heavy metal on tap [lead in drinking water] M. Kantor. il *Sierra* 72:18-20 N/D '87
Household hazards. G. Reiger. *Field Stream* 92:12+ Je '87
Is our drinking water safe? J. Schmid. il *Vogue* 177:406-7+ O '87
Is your well well? [testing for contaminants] C. Tevis. il *Success Farm* 85 no1:32-3 Ja '87
Lead in your drinking water? H. Manley. il map *Good Housekeep* 204:199-200 Mr '87
Poison in the plumbing? [lead and water coolers] T. Monmaney. il *Newsweek* 110:56 D 21 '87
Potential risk of ag chemicals in well water. *Success Farm* 85:66F S '87
Shower shudders [breathing toxins; research by Julian Andelman] G. Woolley. il *Sierra* 72:13-14 Jl/Ag '87
Using tires to track pollution. R. Monastersky. *Sci News* 132:6 Jl 4 '87
Water, water everywhere, but . . . [lead in drinking fountains] S. Weiss. *Sci News* 132:390-1 D 19-26 '87
Well water: how to be sure it's pure. S. Woolley. il *Bus Week* p84 Ag 10 '87
You can help turn the toxic tide (II) [groundwater pollution] R. Rodale. il *Rodale's Org Gard* 34:18-20 Ag '87
Control
See also
　Cleaning of lakes, rivers, etc.
The poisoned well [groundwater] F. Powledge. il *Wilderness* 51:40-3 Fall '87
Water [Environmental Quality Index] il *Natl Wildl* 25:36 F/Mr '87
Laws and regulations
See also
　Clean Water Act
　Safe Drinking Water Act
Clean legislation. *Wilderness* 51:41 Fall '87
Clean water: adding up the balance sheet. R. A. Taylor. il *U S News World Rep* 102:22-3 F 16 '87
Costly cleanups at the gas pump [EPA storage tank rules] T. Smart. *Bus Week* p28-9 Ap 20 '87
Groundwater: invisible, but not clean. J. D. Hair. il *Natl Wildl* 25:26 Ag/S '87

Report on reports: Ground water quality protection: state and local strategies [U.S. National Research Council report] S. Keith. *Environment* 29:25-7 My '87
Turf battle over federal responsibility for groundwater. A. L. Spitler. *BioScience* 37:317 My '87
Monitoring
U.S. river quality: not all signs are good. J. Raloff. *Sci News* 131:214 Ap 4 '87
Water-quality trends in the nation's rivers. R. A. Smith and others. bibl f il maps *Science* 235:1607-15 Mr 27 '87
Alaska
Of gold fever and brown rivers. T. Turner. il *Sierra* 72:30-3 Jl/Ag '87
California
The case of the poisoned wildlife refuge [J. Claus discovers selenium at Kesterson National Wildlife Refuge] R. Fitzgerald. il por *Read Dig* 131:133-7 O '87
Dead cats, toxins and typhoid [New River] M. Riley. il *Time* 129:68-9 Ap 20 '87
Fowl play [selenium pollution at Kesterson National Wildlife Refuge] C. Caufield. il *Omni* 9:22+ Je '87
Fungi: California's answer to selenium? [Kesterson National Wildlife Refuge] *Sci News* 132:8 Jl 4 '87
Kesterson: an unsolvable problem? [environmental impact of drainage from federally serviced irrigation districts] K. E. Claus. bibl f *Environment* 29:4-5 Jl/Ag '87
Colorado
Decontaminating federal facilities: the case of the Rocky Mountain Arsenal [with editorial comment by Wallace N. Quintrell] K. B. Wiley and S. L. Rhodes. bibl f il maps *Environment* 29:2-3, 16-20+ Ap '87
Georgia
See also
　Plains (Ga.)—Water pollution
Great Lakes
The great & fragile lakes [cover story] W. Ashworth. il *Sierra* 72:42-50 N/D '87
The Great Lakes pact: a model, a hope. J. D. Hair. il *Int Wildl* 17:26 Jl/Ag '87
The Great Lakes' troubled waters. C. E. Cobb. il supp (folded map) maps *Natl Geogr* 172:2-31 Jl '87
Showdown over pollution [Kimberly-Clark paper mill on Lake Superior ordered to install pollution controls] S. Aikenhead. il *Macleans* 100:81 F 2 '87
Toxics in a great river—putting the pieces together [pollution flowing from Niagara River into Lake Ontario] M. Kadlecek. il *Conservationist* 42:34-9 N/D '87
Massachusetts
See also
　Boston (Mass.)—Water pollution
Sunken PCBs taint the Housatonic. J. Fahys. il *Sierra* 72:85 Jl/Ag '87
Mexico
Dead cats, toxins and typhoid [New River] M. Riley. il *Time* 129:68-9 Ap 20 '87
New York (State)
Cleaner waters pay off in better fishing. L. Smith and E. Stegemann. il *Conservationist* 41:6-15 Mr/Ap '87
The riverkeeper [J. Cronin, monitor of the Hudson] A. Wilkinson. il *New Yorker* 63:49-50+ My 11 '87
Save the queen! [Lake George] C. C. Morrison. il *Conservationist* 42:6-11 Jl/Ag '87
Ontario
See also
　Hamilton (Ont.)—Water pollution
Siberia (Soviet Union)
Scientist Vladimir Fialkov focuses on the future of a unique natural wonder: crystalline Lake Baikal. S. K. Reed. il pors *People Wkly* 27:121+ Ap 6 '87
Soviet Union
Glasnost and the Soviet environment. D. Dickson. *Science* 236:1180 Je 5 '87
Western Europe
See also
　Rhine River chemical spills, 1986
Western States
The degradation factor [timber management and watershed protection in western national forests] M. Anderson and C. Gehrke. il *Wilderness* 51:38-40 Fall '87
Wisconsin
See also
　Green Bay (Wis.)—Water pollution
How they protect their groundwater [farmers] B. Freese. il *Success Farm* 85:12-13 S '87
Water power
See also
　Dams
　Hydroelectric power

Water power—See also—*cont.*
    Tide power
    Wave power
Water power electric plants *See* Hydroelectric plants
Water projects *See* Water resources development
Water pumping stations *See* Pumping stations
Water pumps
    A global search yields affordable water. D. Kinley. il
    UN Chron 24:71-2 Ag '87
Water purification
    See also
        Hot tubs—Sanitation
        Swimming pools—Sanitation
        Water filters and filtration
        Water reuse
    Home water treatment. M. Cala. il *Home Mech* 83:66
    F '87
    Is your well well? [testing for contaminants] C. Tevis.
    il *Success Farm* 85 no1:32-3 Ja '87
Water rates
    Just add water marketing. J. R. Udall. *Sierra* 72:37-8+
    Mr/Ap '87
Water reclamation *See* Water reuse
Water resources development
    See also
        Central Arizona Project
        Dams
        Hetch Hetchy Water Supply Project
        International Drinking Water Supply and Sanitation
        Decade, 1981-1990
        Irrigation
    Report on reports: Currents of change: final report,
    Inquiry on Federal Water Policy, Canada. H. P. Caul-
    field, Jr. *Environment* 28:25-7 D '86
    Water and the dimensions of crisis [cover story; special
    issue; with editorial comment by T. H. Watkins] il
    map *Wilderness* 51:12-50 Fall '87
Water reuse
    The marsh that Arcata built. J. W. Price. il *Sierra*
    72:51-3 My/Je '87
    Recycled waste water: Denver's scheme [Potable Water
    Reuse Demonstration Plant] R. A. Marcus. il *Pop
    Sci* 231:44 S '87
    Sludge busters [San Diego's water hyacinth sewage treat-
    ment system] R. Stayton. il *Pop Sci* 230:43-4 F '87
Water rights
    See also
        Indians of North America—Water rights
    The lifeblood of wilderness [enforcement of federal reser-
    ved water rights in Colorado wilderness areas] D.
    Drabelle. il *Wilderness* 51:36-8 Fall '87
    This land is my land [posting of private land] B. Trebil-
    cock. il *Ctry J* 14:50-5 S '87
Water safety *See* Boats and boating—Safety devices and
    measures; Drowning—Prevention
Water skis and skiing
    See also
        Jet skis and skiing
    California screamin' [waterskiers racing from Long Beach
    to Catalina] D. Wallace. il *Mot Boat Sail* 160:50-3+
    N '87
    No one beats slalom champ Camille Duvall at making
    waves where the buoys are. M. Neill. il pors *People
    Wkly* 28:58-60 Jl 13 '87
    A two-time national barefoot water ski champion at
    11 [A. Wilson] H. Brown. il *Ebony* 42:61-2+ Je '87
    Wild West water skiing [Lake Powell] C. Davis. il *Mot
    Boat Sail* 159:52-7+ F '87
Water slides
    Their 100-foot water slide. il *Sunset* 178:164 My '87
Water speed records *See* Boat speed records
Water sports *See* Aquatic sports
Water sprinklers *See* Sprinklers
Water supply
    See also
        Boats and boating—Water supply
        Dams
        Droughts
        Irrigation
        Pumping stations
        Water conservation
        Water purification
        Water reuse
        Watersheds
        Waterworks
    Water and the dimensions of crisis [cover story; special
    issue; with editorial comment by T. H. Watkins] il
    map *Wilderness* 51:12-50 Fall '87

International aspects
    See also
    International Drinking Water Supply and Sanitation
    Decade, 1981-1990
Pollution
    See Water pollution
Arizona
    See also
    Central Arizona Project
California
    See also
    Hetch Hetchy Water Supply Project
    Los Angeles (Calif.)—Water supply
    Palm Springs (Calif.)—Water supply
    California: wet years on the Colorado may have provided
    a reprieve, but there are dry times—and tough deci-
    sions—ahead. *Sunset* 178:94 Mr '87
Canada
    Report on reports: Currents of change: final report,
    Inquiry on Federal Water Policy, Canada. H. P. Caul-
    field, Jr. *Environment* 28:25-7 D '86
Colorado
    See also
    Denver (Colo.)—Water supply
Developing countries
    See also
    International Drinking Water Supply and Sanitation
    Decade, 1981-1990
    A global search yields affordable water. D. Kinley. il
    UN Chron 24:71-2 Ag '87
Great Plains
    See also
    Ogallala Aquifer
Latin America
    Water, source of life. H. Otterstetter and A. Flores.
    il *World Health* p11-13 O '87
Pennsylvania
    See also
    Pittsburgh (Pa.)—Water supply
Southwestern States
    Drink and be merry. E. Paris. il *Forbes* 140:42+ Ag
    10 '87
Texas
    See also
    El Paso (Tex.)—Water supply
Western States
    Drink and be merry. E. Paris. il *Forbes* 140:42+ Ag
    10 '87
    The function of aridity. W. E. Stegner. il *Wilderness*
    51:14-18 Fall '87
    Just add water marketing. J. R. Udall. *Sierra* 72:37-8+
    Mr/Ap '87
    The West's water future. map *Sunset* 178:92-4 Mr '87
Water supply, Rural
    Understanding rural water systems. il *Mother Earth News*
    107:76-9 S/O '87
Water supply engineering
    See also
    Dams
Water tanks
    Throw water weight around with caddies. D. Mowitz.
    il *Success Farm* 85:18T-18U Ap '87
Water utilities *See* Waterworks
Water works *See* Waterworks
Waterbeds
    Oh, wow, water beds are back. A. Toufexis. il *Time*
    130:57 Jl 13 '87
Waterborne infection
    See also
    Giardiasis
    Schistosomiasis
    Are there bugs in the tub? J. Venturino. il *Women's
    Sports Fitness* 9:17 D '87
    Little tub of horrors: pools and hot tubs can make
    you sick. J. C. Johnson. il *Mademoiselle* 93:74 Je
    '87
Watercolor painting
    Art: European watercolors: luminous washes by
    nineteenth-century painters. C. Finch. il *Archit Dig*
    44:140-5 S '87
    The California school of watercolor. J. Lovoos. il por
    Am Artist 51:62-9+ Ap '87
    Catherine Burchfield Parker. M. C. Nelson. il por *Am
    Artist* 51:58-61+ D '87
    Eileen Monaghan Whitaker: painting from the heart.
    J. Lovoos. il por *Am Artist* 51:36-41 Mr '87
    Kay Polk: combining pastels and watercolors to paint
    portraits. B. D. Stroud. il *Am Artist* 51:60-3 O '87
    Painting atmospheric effects in watercolor. J. DeVore.
    il *Am Artist* 51:58-61 Ap '87

Watercolor painting—*cont.*

Reeve Schley III. M. Mathews-Berenson. il *Am Artist* 51:70-3+ N '87

Technical page [technique of C. Demuth] J. R. Doyle. il *Am Artist* 51:32+ S '87

Tom Lynch: Paris sketchbook. V. R. Rivers. il por *Am Artist* 51:S7-S10 N '87

The watercolor page. See issues of American Artist

The watercolors of John La Farge. B. D. Gallati. bibl f il *Antiques* 132:1290-301 D '87

Exhibitions

Artsmart [American traditions in watercolor from Worcester Art Museum] il *Harpers Bazaar* 120:190 Mr '87

British marine painting [Masters of the sea: British marine watercolors, 1650-1930 at the Yale Center for British Art] S. B. Sherrill. il *Antiques* 131:1182 Je '87

The late watercolor/pastels of Maurice Prendergast [exhibition at the Coe Kerr Gallery in New York City; cover story] C. Langdale. bibl f il *Antiques* 132:1084-95 N '87

Technique in American watercolors from the Worcester Art Museum, Worcester, Massachusetts. S. E. Strickler and J. C. Walsh. bibl f il *Antiques* 131:412-25 F '87

The watercolor page [American Artist Golden Anniversary National Art Competition] il *Am Artist* 51:56-61 Je '87

The watercolors from Worcester [American traditions in watercolor] K. M. Burke. il *Smithsonian* 18:192 S '87

Study and teaching

A feather on the wind [watercolorist Lei Yu] D. Frankel. il por *N Y* 20:21 F 9 '87

Waterfalls

See also
　Kaaterskill Falls (N.Y.)
　Niagara Falls (N.Y. and Ont.)

Photographs and photography

Waterfalls in black and white. P. Craig. il *Petersens Photogr Mag* 15:16-18 Mr '87

Waterford (Va.)

Architecture

Equine expectations [broodmare barn and turnout ring at Catoctin Stud] M. Gaskie. il *Archit Rec* 175:122-5 My '87

Waterford Glass Group plc

Table for two [Waterford-Wedgwood merger] A. A. Lappen. il *Forbes* 140:8 D 28 '87

Waterfowl *See* Water birds

Waterfowl Festival (Easton, Md.) *See* Easton (Md.)—Festivals

Waterfowl shooting *See* Water bird shooting

Waterfronts

See also
　Boston (Mass.)—Harbor
　Jacksonville (Fla.)—Waterfront
　New Orleans (La.)—Waterfront
　Norfolk (Va.)—Waterfront
　San Francisco (Calif.)—Harbor

The best waterfront restaurants. J. F. Mariani. il *Mot Boat Sail* 159:32 My '87

Canada

See also
　Toronto (Ont.)—Waterfront

Watergate case

Déjà vu all over again [contragate and Watergate] *Nation* 245:665 D 5 '87

The guns of Watergate. L. Garment. *Commentary* 83:15-23 Ap '87

Iranian arms and contra aid [address, March 6, 1987] A. Cox. *Vital Speeches Day* 53:531-3 Je 15 '87

John Dean on Ollie: the ugly road ahead. J. W. Dean. il por *Newsweek* 110:28-9 Jl 20 '87

Special prosecutor

This smoking gun won't shoot [R. Bork's firing of A. Cox] M. Kramer. il por *U S News World Rep* 103:16 S 21 '87

Watering of gardens, lawns, etc.

See also
　Garden hose
　Sprinklers

Changing from sprinklers to drip. il *Sunset* 179:148-9 Ag '87

The drip difference. M. Kane. il *Rodale's Org Gard* 34:58-61 O '87

Drip irrigation. D. Dale. il *Ctry J* 14:42-7 Jl '87

How much water does your lawn really need? il *Sunset* 178:213-19 Je '87

Irrigation innovations. il *Flower Gard* 31:48-50 Je/Jl '87

Low-cost irrigation project interests other developing countries [drip irrigation] Wan Qinghua. il *UN Chron* 24:65 Ag '87

When the gardener's away [automatic water timers] J. Ruttle. il *Rodale's Org Gard* 34:50-2+ My '87

Waterloo, Battle of, 1815

The ghosts of Waterloo. J. Keegan. il *World Press Rev* 34:29-31 Ag '87

Waterman, Robert H., Jr.

The renewal factor [excerpt] il *Bus Week* p100-1+ S 14 '87

Strategy in a more volatile world. il por *Fortune* 116:181-2 D 21 '87

about

How the best get better. J. A. Byrne. il por *Bus Week* p98-9 S 14 '87

Waterproof clothing *See* Clothing, Waterproof

Waterproof fabrics *See* Textile fabrics, Waterproof

Waterproofing

See also
　Automobiles—Leakage

Critical steps to a leak-proof roof (I) [flashing] G. Branson and C. J. De Groote. il *Fam Handyman* 37:98+ My/Je '87

Critical steps to a leak-proof roof (II) [flashing] G. Branson and C. J. De Groote. il *Fam Handyman* 37:34+ D '87

Cures for wet basements. K. McCormally. *Changing Times* 41:22-3 O '87

Dry goods: protective gear can keep your equipment safe from the perils of water and sand [photography] E. Stecker. il *Pop Photogr* 94:78-81 Jl '87

Keeping dry. B. Vila. il *Pop Mech* 164:40+ F '87

Product reports 1988. il *Archit Rec* 175:51-3+ D '87

Trouble in the underworld [excess moisture can cause rot] R. McCarthy. il *Ctry J* 14:18-21 S '87

Waters, Bob

about

The battle of his life. R. Fimrite. il pors *Sports Illus* 67:72-80 Ag 24 '87

An incurable killer strikes three ex-49ers, and an anguished victim doubts it's a coincidence. D. Grogan. il por *People Wkly* 27:94-5 F 9 '87

Waters, Enoch P., 1909-1987

about

Obituary
　Jet por 72:7 Je 29 '87

Waters, Maxine

about

Maxine Waters blocks controversial text in California legislature. *Jet* 72:5 Ap 6 '87

Waters, Roger

about

Roger Waters [Madison Square Garden concert] D. Fricke. il por *Roll Stone* p21 O 22 '87

Roger Waters's new LP. M. Kaplan. *Roll Stone* p29 Je 4 '87

Watersheds

Water and the dimensions of crisis [cover story; special issue; with editorial comment by T. H. Watkins] il map *Wilderness* 51:12-50 Fall '87

Ethiopia

Ethiopian landscapes. D. Stevens. il *Commonweal* 114:652-4 N 20 '87

Waterspouts

Waterspouts. A. Everling. il *Weatherwise* 40:206-8 Jl/Ag '87

Waterton-Glacier International Peace Park (Alta. and Mont.)

Just between friends. J. E. Bahls. il *Sierra* 72:16 My/Je '87

Pride of two nations. D. S. Boyer. il maps *Natl Geogr* 171:796-823 Je '87

Waterton Lakes National Park (Alta.)

See also
　Waterton-Glacier International Peace Park (Alta. and Mont.)

Waterways

See also
　Great Lakes
　Intracoastal Waterway
　Mississippi River
　Rivers
　Tennessee-Tombigbee Waterway

India

India's backwater highways [Malabar Coast] K. Brueckmann and D. Brueckmann. il map *Oceans* 20:24-9 Ja/F '87

Waterways—*cont.*
United States
See Waterways
Waterworks
See also
Dams
Hetch Hetchy Water Supply Project
Rates
See Water rates
Securities
Ring of bright water. T. Jaffe. *Forbes* 140:247 N 2
'87
Watkins, Charles, d. 1973
about
What Charles knew: homage to an English teacher [excerpt
from An apple for my teacher] H. A. Baker. pors
N Y Times Book Rev 92:3+ Mr 22 '87
Watkins, Hays T.
about
If it isn't profitable, don't do it. J. Cook. il por *Forbes*
140:54+ N 30 '87
Watkins, James D.
about
Microwave popcorn: the heat is on. M. J. Pitzer. il
por *Bus Week* p52 Jl 6 '87
Watkins, James D.
about
An admiral in command. *Newsweek* 110:10 O 19 '87
Watkins, Mary M.
about
Make believers. R. Katz. il *Omni* 10:126-8+ N '87
Watkins, Sallie A.
about
Watkins starts work as AIP senior education fellow.
por *Phys Today* 40:85 N '87
Watkins, T. H. (Tom H.), 1936-
Typewritten on both sides: the conservation career of
Wallace Stegner. il por *Audubon* 89:88-90+ S '87
Watkins, Tom H. *See* Watkins, T. H. (Tom H.), 1936-
Watkins Glen Grand Prix Course *See* Speedways
Watley, Jody
about
Jody Watley: singer is sexy on stage, concerned mom
at home [cover story] C. Waldron. il pors *Jet* 72:56-8
Je 22 '87
Jody Watley's 'New love'. A. DeCurtis. il por *Roll Stone*
p23 Je 18 '87
A star is engineered. R. O'Connor. por *Vogue* 177:174
S '87
Watlington, Jeri
Using your vacation for article ideas. *Writer* 100:19-21
Ag '87
Watson, Doc, 1923-
about
After years of hard traveling, mountain maestro Doc
Watson looks to find some easy pickin' at last. R.
Wolmuth. il pors *People Wkly* 28:57-8+ Ag 10 '87
Watson, Don
about
Life on the Mississippi . . . P. Whittell. il pors *Mot
Boat Sail* 159:78-81+ F '87
Watson, Francis John Bagott, 1907-
Mounted oriental porcelain [cover story] il *Antiques*
131:812-23 Ap '87
Watson, Georgette
about
1987 Essence Awards. A. Edwards. pors *Essence* 18:121+
My '87
Watson, Marlene
about
Family business: murder would settle it, and Debra
Banister knew who to ask. J. Wadler. il pors *People
Wkly* 28:57-8+ Jl 6 '87
Watson, Richard A.
(jt. auth) *See* Brucker, Roger, and Watson, Richard A.
Watson, Ross
about
Rescuer of the lost files. S. Ditlea. il por *Pers Comput*
11:67 Ja '87
Watson, Ruth M.
Celtuce . . . where has it been all your life? il *Flower
Gard* 31:80-1 F/Mr '87
Why didn't my bulbs bloom? *Flower Gard* 31:42-3 Ap/My
'87
Watson, Shirley
about
Life on the Mississippi . . . P. Whittell. il pors *Mot
Boat Sail* 159:78-81+ F '87
Watson, Thomas J., Jr.
The greatest capitalist in history [cover story] il pors
Fortune 116:24-32+ Ag 31 '87

about
From Moscow to the Bering Sea. S. Talbott. il pors
Time 130:34 Ag 3 '87
Watson, Tom, 1949-
about
At last Tom has a fling. J. Diaz. il por *Sports Illus*
67:44-5 N 9 '87
An Open and shut case [cover story] R. Reilly. il pors
Sports Illus 66:20-7 Je 29 '87
Watson, Wendy M., 1948-
(jt. auth) *See* Staiti, Paul J., and Watson, Wendy M.,
1948-
Watsonville Canning and Frozen Food Company
Victory on Cannery Row [settlement of strike] R. Erlich.
il *Progressive* 51:26-7 Jl '87
Watt, Kenneth E. F., 1929-
Deep questions about shallow seas. il *Nat Hist* 96:60-5
Jl '87
Watt, Walter W.
Can your car go the distance? il *Consum Res Mag*
70:25-8 Je '87
Prepping your car for winter. il *Consum Res Mag* 70:25-8
D '87
Watt, William J.
Macro dimensional view. il *Petersens Photogr Mag* 16:52-3
Ag '87
Wattenberg, Ben J.
The birth dearth: dangers ahead? [excerpts; cover story]
il por *U S News World Rep* 102:56-62+ Je 22 '87
about
Battling over birth policy. E. Bowen. il *Time* 130:58
Ag 24 '87
The birth dearth debate. A. Levine. il *U S News World
Rep* 102:64-5 Je 22 '87
Watters, Wendell W.
Christianity & mental health [cover story; with reply
by P. R. Breggin] il *Humanist* 47:5-13+ N/D '87
Watterson, William Collins
Nightscape with doves [poem] *New Yorker* 62:77
F 9 '87
Wattleton, Faye
about
Abortion more precious than $20 mil. grant: Wattleton.
Jet 72:36 My 11 '87
Faye Wattleton. C. Green. *Black Enterp* 17:42+ Ap '87
Wattleton raps Reagan's cut of overseas abortion funds.
por *Jet* 72:9 Ag 17 '87
Watts, André, 1946-
about
André Watts: classical music prodigy turns 40. il pors
Ebony 42:44-6+ Ap '87
Watts, Charlie
about
The Charlie Watts interview. B. Beuttler. il pors *Down
Beat* 54:16-19+ F '87
Charlie Watts's jazz dream. D. Fricke. il por *Roll Stone*
p35 F 26 '87
Watts, David
Insecurely secure. *World Press Rev* 34:17-18 Ag '87
Watts, Grady
Caribbean charters: luxury yachting in the British Virgin
Islands. il *Archit Dig* 44 Archit Dig Travels:4+ O
'87
Watts, Jeff
about
Blindfold test. M. Bourne. il por *Down Beat* 54:46 F
'87
Watts (Charlie) Orchestra *See* Charlie Watts Orchestra
Watts (Los Angeles, Calif.)
Close to home [telecommuting program for blacks] J.
Koblenz. il *Black Enterp* 17:22 F '87
Wauer, Roland H.
Caribbean landing point. il *Natl Parks* 61:20-1 Ja/F
'87
Waugh, Auberon
about
Villains, and victims of AIDS. G. Bain. il *Macleans*
100:44 Ap 20 '87
Waugh, Denis
about
Echoes. J. Furth. il *Life* 10:56-60 O '87
Wave mechanics
See also
Tunneling (Physics)
Wave power
Coastal wave energy [cover story] M. J. Changery and
R. G. Quayle. bibl il map *Sea Front* 33:259-62 Jl/Ag
'87
Here's to wave power. J. Page. il *Oceans* 20:10 S/O
'87

Wave power—*cont.*
Norway
Wave-driven air turbine. D. Scott. il *Pop Sci* 231:96-7 N '87
Waveform analysis
How to analyze waveforms. G. D. Carey. il *Radio-Electron* 58:59-60+ D '87
Waves
> *See also*
> Alfvén waves
> Electromagnetic waves
> Seismic waves
> Shock waves
> Sound waves
> Tidal waves
> Turbulence
> Ultrasonic waves

Energy for life among the waves [research by Egbert G. Leigh, Jr. and others] I. Peterson. *Sci News* 131:183 Mr 21 '87
Life thrives under breaking ocean waves [research by Egbert Leigh and others] R. Lewin. il *Science* 235:1465-6 Mr 20 '87
The onshore transport of an oil spill by internal waves. A. L. Shanks. bibl f il map *Science* 235:1198-200 Mr 6 '87
Wax, Barry
> *about*
Someone's in the kitchen with Barry. F. Odabas-Geldiay. il por *Nations Bus* 75:48 Ap '87
Wax, Jack
Criminal treatment: the jails become holding tanks for the mentally ill. il *Progressive* 51:26-7 O '87
Wax plants
Big promise from the wee hoyas. C. M. Burton. il *Flower Gard* 31:74-7 F/Mr '87
Waxes
> *See also*
> S. C. Johnson & Son, Inc.
> Turtle Wax (Firm)
Waxman, Armond, 1938-
> *about*
Back from the brink. G. Morgenson. il pors *Forbes* 139:109-10 Je 15 '87
Waxman, Melvin, 1934-
> *about*
Back from the brink. G. Morgenson. il pors *Forbes* 139:109-10 Je 15 '87
Waxman Industries, Inc.
Back from the brink. G. Morgenson. il pors *Forbes* 139:109-10 Je 15 '87
Wayang
Shadow world of the Javanese [wayang performances] W. Keeler. il *Nat Hist* 96:68-72+ N '87
Wayne, Jane O.
Waiting [poem] *Am Sch* 56:342 Summ '87
Wayne, Michael
> *about*
No longer just hitching a ride on pickups. J. B. Treece. il por *Bus Week* p85-6 My 25 '87
Wayne County (Mich.)
Criminal justice, Administration of
Dispensing forgiveness and justice in equal measure, Father Mike Callahan is a man of the cloth and the law. S. K. Reed. il pors *People Wkly* 28:143-4+ D 7 '87
Politics and government
Charles Diggs defeated in race for Wayne County board of commissioners. *Jet* 73:25 O 12 '87
Ex-rep. Diggs enters Wayne County commission race. *Jet* 72:29 Ag 3 '87
Wayne's (Dennis) Dancers *See* Dennis Wayne's Dancers
Ways and Means Committee *See* United States. Congress. House. Committee on Ways and Means
WBBM (Chicago, Ill.: Television station) *See* Television stations
WCC *See* World Council of Churches
We are the children [television program] *See* Television program reviews—Single works
Weak interactions (Nuclear physics) *See* Nuclear reactions
Weakfish
Squeteague: New York's saltwater trout. A. M. Weber. il *Conservationist* 42:20-3 S/O '87
Weakland, Rembert G., 1927-
> *about*
Of many things. G. W. Hunt. *America* 157:258 O 24 '87
Weakly interacting massive particles *See* Particles (Nuclear physics)

Wealth
> *See also*
> Billionaires
> Cost and standard of living
> Income
> Millionaires
> Rich

Building family wealth [cover story; special section] il *Money* 16:52-6+ O '87
Finding a prescription for black wealth [Black enterprise Board of Economists] D. T. Dingle. il *Black Enterp* 17:38-40+ Ja '87
How the bull market has enriched the economy. J. Berger and N. Jonas. il *Bus Week* p54-5 Ag 10 '87
How the other haves live [world's richest countries] R. H. Bork, Jr. il *U S News World Rep* 102:47 Je 22 '87
The skewing of America: disparities in wealth and income. R. D. Pasquariello. il *Christ Century* 104:164-6 F 18 '87
The wealth of nations: the world is getting richer. L. Smith. il *Fortune* 116:35 S 14 '87
What scared the markets? [anti-wealth policies] A. Reynolds. il *Natl Rev* 39:47-9 N 20 '87
Weapons
> *See also*
> Airplanes, Military—Armaments
> Anti-helicopter weapons
> Anti-satellite weapons
> Anti-tank weapons
> Bayonets
> Chemical and biological weapons
> Electromagnetic weapons
> Firearms
> Guided missiles
> Kinetic kill vehicles
> Lasers—Military use
> Nuclear weapons
> Particle beam weapons
> Rockets
> Soft kill weapons
> Space warfare
> Stone implements and weapons

Bag 'em with the Un-Gun [less-lethal beanbag weapons] T. Dworetzky. il *Discover* 8:26-7 N '87
Bringing SDI down to earth [development of smart conventional weapons] D. Charles. il *Science* 237:713-15 Ag 14 '87
Cautious optimism on high-tech weapons for NATO forces [report by the Office of Technology Assessment] D. Charles. *Science* 236:1622 Je 26 '87
One shot, one kill: a new era of 'smart' weapons [offsetting Soviet Union's edge in conventional firepower; special section] il *U S News World Rep* 102:28-35 Mr 16 '87
Soviet strategic force upgrade paces U.S. modernization effort. J. D. Morrocco. il *Aviat Week Space Technol* 126:31-3+ Mr 9 '87
Spoils of the Saharan sands [weapons left behind by Libyans] J. Greenwald. il *Time* 129:42 Ap 27 '87
Costs
> *See also*
> Project on Military Procurement

Budget slashing would kill A-6F, small ICBM and Aquila. B. M. Greeley, Jr. *Aviat Week Space Technol* 127:31 D 21 '87
CBO claims most weapons systems fail to meet return on investment [Congressional Budget Office study] il *Aviat Week Space Technol* 126:77-8 Mr 30 '87
The dark secret of the black budget. T. Weiner. *Wash Mon* 19:31-5 My '87
Fiscal 1988 major weapon system spending detailed by military services. *Aviat Week Space Technol* 126:22-3 Ja 12 '87
Overall budget reductions force cut in Conventional Defense Initiative. B. M. Greeley, Jr. *Aviat Week Space Technol* 126:30-1 My 4 '87
Shortfall in estimated budget slows conventional force buildup. D. M. North. il *Aviat Week Space Technol* 126:45+ Mr 9 '87
U.S. Congress and Pentagon gird for weapon cancellations in 1989. P. Mann. *Aviat Week Space Technol* 127:26-7 N 30 '87
Testing
> *See also*
> Proving grounds
> United States. Dept. of Defense. Operational Test and Evaluation

Pentagon weighs plan to expand testing schedule of weapon systems. *Aviat Week Space Technol* 126:264-5 Mr 9 '87

Weapons control *See* Disarmament
Weapons smuggling *See* Smuggling
Weapons trade *See* Munitions—Export-import trade
Wearable art
Here's a real coat of paint for those who want to wear
their art on their sleeve—and chest and back. L.
Aitken. il *People Wkly* 27:69-70+ Mr 2 '87
Wearable art. P. Berman. il *Forbes* 140:102-4 O 19
'87
Weasels
See also
Ferrets
Weather
See also
Atmospheric pressure
Climate
Clouds
Droughts
Fronts (Meteorology)
Hot weather
Meteorological equipment
Meteorology
Rain and rainfall
Snow
Storms
Sun and meteorology
Winds
See also subhead Climate under names of conti-
nents, countries, states, cities, etc.
Almanac. D. M. Ludlum. See issues of Country Journal
beginning October 1986
A weather eye. P. Stark. il *Read Dig* 130:118-20 Mr
'87
The weather of 1986 [cover story; special issue] il
Weatherwise 40:8-44 F '87
Weatherwatch. D. M. Ludlum. See issues of Weatherwise
History
President's weather. D. M. Ludlum. *Ctry J* 14:76-7 Mr
'87
Mental and physiological effects
See also
Crime and weather
Hot weather—Mental and physiological effects
The body barometer. L. Garvey. il *Health* 19:80-2+ Je
'87
Research
See Meteorology
Weather, Prehistoric *See* Paleoclimatology
Weather and crime *See* Crime and weather
Weather and health *See* Weather—Mental and physiological
effects
Weather and industry *See* Industry and weather
Weather and plants *See* Plants, Effect of climate on
Weather Channel
Anecdotes, facetiae, satire, etc.
Will the Weather Channel save America? J. Gorman.
il *Discover* 8:30+ D '87
Weather charts *See* Meteorology—Charts, diagrams, etc.
Weather equipment *See* Meteorological equipment
Weather forecasting
See also
Airplanes in meteorology
Artificial satellites—Meteorological use
Computers—Meteorological use
Information storage and retrieval systems—
Meteorological use
Television broadcasting—Weather forecasts
United States. National Severe Storms Forecast Cen-
ter
United States. National Weather Service
Weather lore
World Meteorological Organization
El Niño and winter weather. R. A. Kerr. map *Science*
238:1508 D 11 '87
Forecasting for the frigid desert of Antarctica [cover
story] D. P. Mullen. il map *Weatherwise* 40:304-11
D '87
Scientific basis of modern weather prediction. J. J. Tribbia
and R. A. Anthes. bibl f il map *Science* 237:493-9
Jl 31 '87
Spring and clearer predictions ahead [Canada] J. Barber.
il *Macleans* 100:44-5 Mr 16 '87
Vacationer's atlas. See issues of Travel Holiday beginning
March 1984
Weather regimes: the challenge in extended-range
forecasting. B. Reinhold. bibl f il maps *Science*
235:437-41 Ja 23 '87
Weather in art
Painting atmospheric effects in watercolor. J. DeVore.
il *Am Artist* 51:58-61 Ap '87

Weather insurance *See* Insurance, Weather
Weather lore
The climythology of America. D. M. Ludlum. il map
Weatherwise 40:255-9 O '87
Weather photography *See* Meteorological photography
Weather predictions *See* Weather forecasting
Weather radar *See* Radar meteorology
Weather records
The nation's hottest temperature. D. H. Hickcox. *Focus*
37:31 Summ '87
Temperature extremes [1866] D. H. Hickcox. il
Weatherwise 40:38-40 F '87
Weather research *See* Meteorology
Weather satellites *See* Artificial satellites—Meteorological
use
Weather Underground (Organization)
The Weathermen, twenty years on. P. Marin. il *Harpers*
275:26-8 D '87
Weathering
See also
Erosion
Herbivory in rocks and the weathering of a desert [impact
of lichen feeding by snails] M. Shachak and others.
bibl f il *Science* 236:1098-9 My 29 '87
Microbial trace-fossil formation, biogenous, and abiotic
weathering in the Antarctic cold desert. E. I. Friedmann
and R. Weed. bibl f il *Science* 236:703-5 My 8 '87
Snails dine at desert dust depot [research by Clive G.
Jones and others] K. Hartley. il *Sci News* 131:373
Je 13 '87
Weatherproofing
See also
Waterproofing
First, do no harm. J. Vara. *Ctry J* 14:16-19 D '87
Weatherstrip garage door. G. Branson. il *Fam Handyman*
37:54 F '87
Weatherstripping *See* Weatherproofing
Weatherwise Photography Contest *See* Photography—Com-
petitions
Weaver, Carolyn
Sally Cooper. por *Ms* 16:112+ Jl/Ag '87
Weaver, Jerry
Making American industry competitive again [address,
April 16, 1987] *Vital Speeches Day* 53:560-2 Jl 1
'87
Weaver, Lelland A. C.
Factories in space: the role of robots [cover story] il
por *Futurist* 21:29-34 My/Je '87
Weaver, Matthew
about
Matthew Weaver: helping the down-and-out in L.A. C.
Lapin. por *Seventeen* 46:111 O '87
Weaver, R. Kent, 1953-
The politics of blame: public policy and avoidance
behavior. *Current* 296:11-15 O '87
Weaver, Richard L., 1941-
Second wind: capitalizing on your full creative potential
[address, December 7, 1986] *Vital Speeches Day*
53:235-7 F 1 '87
Weaver, Susan
Athens on these shores. il *Americana* 15:22-5 Jl/Ag '87
Roving the Italian Riviera. il *Prevention* 39:114-16+ F
'87
Weaver, Susan, 1959-
Women on wheels: a buyer's guide to bicycles, clothing,
and accessories. il *Women's Sports Fitness* 9:33+ F
'87
Weaver, William, 1923-
Decoration for a dynasty. il *House Gard* 159:100-11+
F '87
A drama of Rome. il *Opera News* 52:24-5 D 5 '87
Weaver family
about
Weavers of boxing dreams. F. Lidz. il *Sports Illus* 67:83
Ag 3 '87
Weaving
See also
Cane weaving
Indian blankets, rugs, etc. (American)
Tapestry
Loom rooms with a view. il *Sunset* 179:124 N '87
Navajo weaving: centuries of change. K. P. Kent. bibl
il *Am Craft* 47:34-8+ Ag/S '87
Woven in Oaxaca [Zapotec industry] R. C. Toll and
M.-P. Toll. il *House Gard* 159:102+ My '87
Exhibitions
Interlacing: the elemental fabric [exhibit at the American
Craft Museum] B. Freudenheim. il *Am Craft* 47:42-9
Ap/My '87
Tradition updated [Navaho weaving] F. J. Dockstader.
il *Am Craft* 47:39-45 Ag/S '87

Webb, Beatrice Potter, 1858-1943
about
The Webbs: working on trade union history. C. Wrigley. bibl il pors *Hist Today* 37:51-5 My '87
Webb, Bill
about
Oyster lovers, rejoice! Summer is no longer your off-season. il *People Wkly* 28:57 Ag 31 '87
Webb, Francis T. G.
The Chinese experience. il *World Health* p22-3 N '87
Webb, James H.
Seapower [address, October 28, 1987] *Vital Speeches Day* 54:98-100 D 1 '87
about
Navy's new leatherneck Secretary. M. Doan and J. M. Hildreth. il por *U S News World Rep* 102:16 Mr 2 '87
New Navy boss: poet and warrior. E. Thomas. il pors *Newsweek* 109:6 My 4 '87
Webb, Lillian Frier
Sexual health. See issues of Essence
Webb, Marilyn
Best in bloom. il *Harpers Bazaar* 121:56+ D '87
Webb, Michael, 1937-
Historic houses: Cecil B. De Mille: family scenario for a Hollywood legend. il por *Archit Dig* 44:144-53+ Mr '87
Hollywood: legend and reality. il *USA Today (Periodical)* 116:44-59 Jl '87
A man who made architecture an art of the unexpected. bibl (p162) il por *Smithsonian* 18:48-54+ Ap '87
Rancho La Vista: western themes in California's Ojai Valley. il pors *Archit Dig* 44:112-19 D '87
Webb, Sidney, 1859-1947
about
The Webbs: working on trade union history. C. Wrigley. bibl il pors *Hist Today* 37:51-5 My '87
Webb, Spud
about
Basketball's biggest little man: Spud Webb. il pors *Ebony* 42:46-8+ F '87
Webb, Wellington E.
about
Webb wins, becomes 1st black auditor of Denver. por *Jet* 72:38 Ag 10 '87
Webb (Del E.) Corp. *See* Del E. Webb Corp.
Webb-Mitchell, Brett
Formation and transformation at Camp Ahus. *Christ Century* 104:531-2 Je 3-10 '87
Webber, Andrew Lloyd *See* Lloyd Webber, Andrew, 1948-
Webber, Robert
Who are the evangelicals? il *USA Today (Periodical)* 115:88-9 My '87
Webber, Russell
Jerusalem-cherries for holiday color; grow your own. il *Flower Gard* 31:28 O/N '87
Weber, Alice M.
Squeteague: New York's saltwater trout. il *Conservationist* 42:20-3 S/O '87
Weber, Bruce
Alone together: the unromantic generation [cover story] il *N Y Times Mag* p22-6+ Ap 5 '87
Cher's next act. il pors *N Y Times Mag* p42-4+ O 18 '87
His. See issues of Mademoiselle beginning October 1986
Weber, Bruce
Intensely Isabella [photographs] il pors *Vogue* 177:180-7 Je '87
about
Taking direct action. D. Hershkovits. pors *Harpers Bazaar* 121:144-5 N '87
Weber, Bruce, 1951-
A sense of light and air in landscapes. bibl f il *Am Artist* 51:40-7+ Ap '87
Weber, George B.
The Red Cross [address, February 19, 1987] *Vital Speeches Day* 53:461-3 My 15 '87
Weber, Ken
Slower learners need a slower and steady pace. *Educ Dig* 52:51-3 Mr '87
Weber, Lena
Sister Gertrude and the children of Karachi. il *Christ Century* 104:887-9 O 14 '87
Weber, Melva
Health. See issues of Vogue
Weber, Michael
American themes at the Richard York Gallery. il por *Archit Dig* 44:162+ F '87
Metropolitan life. il *Archit Dig* 44:100-7 Mr '87

Weber, Michael John
We celebrate our wedding anniversaries apart. il *Glamour* 85:282 Ag '87
Weber, Nicholas Fox, 1947-
Biedermeier keepsakes. il *House Gard* 159:120-3+ Ag '87
An everyday luxury. il *House Gard* 159:76+ F '87
Silver futures. il *House Gard* 159:42+ Mr '87
Weber, Pete
about
Thank you, Pete Weber. D. S. Looney. il pors *Sports Illus* 66:26-7 My 4 '87
Weber, Peter
Scenes from the squatting life. il *Natl Rev* 39:28-32 F 27 '87
The streets were paved with gold diggers [cover story] il *Natl Rev* 39:24-7 Je 5 '87
Weber, Peter C., and others
Rapid identification of nonessential genes of herpes simplex virus type 1 by Tn5 mutagenesis. bibl f il *Science* 236:576-9 My 1 '87
Weberman, Ben
Capital markets. See issues of Forbes
Webs, Spider *See* Spider webs
Webster, Arthur Gordon, 1863-1923
about
Arthur Gordon Webster, founder of the APS. M. Phillips. il pors *Phys Today* 40:48-52 Je '87
Webster, Bruce F.
According to Webster. See issues of Byte beginning July 1985 through June 1987
Webster, James C.
Agriculture on the high seas. il *Nations Bus* 75:49-50 D '87
Webster, Judith A.
(jt. auth) See Moss, Vicki A., and Webster, Judith A.
Webster, Sally
Pattern & decoration in the public eye. il *Art Am* 75:118-25 F '87
Webster, William H.
The Central Intelligence Agency [address, August 8, 1987] *Vital Speeches Day* 53:738-40 O 1 '87
The intelligence community [address, December 8, 1986] *Vital Speeches Day* 53:324-7 Mr 15 '87
Rooting out organized crime [address, November 17, 1986] *Vital Speeches Day* 53:262-5 F 15 '87
about
The CIA: a straight arrow for director. T. Morganthau. il por *Newsweek* 109:24-5 Mr 16 '87
Cleaning up the mess [cover story; special section] il pors *Newsweek* 110:24-30+ O 12 '87
G-man among the spooks. E. Shannon. il por *Time* 129:28 Mr 16 '87
Webster's third? *Nation* 244:347-8 Mr 21 '87
Wechsler, Bert
Home-grown labels from Scandinavia. il *High Fidel* 37:76-7 Ja '87
Wechsler, Deborah S.
Do your own variety trials. il por *Rodale's Org Gard* 34:61-4 F '87
A taste of the Orient. il *Rodale's Org Gard* 34:28-30 D '87
Wechsler, Gil
about
Light show. C. Mobley. il pors *Opera News* 51:14-16+ Mr 14 '87
Wechsler, Jill
Don't leave home to buy it! Catalog shopping is the working woman's answer. *Work Woman* 12:91-3 Mr '87
Real-estate management made easy. il por *Work Woman* 12:70+ My '87
Weck, Egon
New hope for those with diverticular disease. il *FDA Consum* 21:23-5 Jl/Ag '87
Taking a look at eye exams. il *FDA Consum* 21:14-17 My '87
Weckl, Dave
about
Dave Weckl: new drumslinger in town [cover story] B. Beuttler. il por *Down Beat* 54:16-18 D '87
Weddell seals *See* Seals (Animals)
Wedding anniversaries
We celebrate our wedding anniversaries apart. M. J. Weber. il *Glamour* 85:282 Ag '87
Wedding chapels
Japan
An exchange of vows [Mt. Rokko, Kobe] il *Archit Rec* 175:104-9 F '87

Wedding clothes

Bridal elegance. E. W. Johnson. il *Ebony* 42:100-2+ Je '87

Brides: on the aisle. il *Harpers Bazaar* 120:72 Je '87

Moments in time: for the mother of the bride. il *50 Plus* 27:34-7 Ag '87

Spider-man bride wears Willi Smith's last design. il *Jet* 72:53 Je 22 '87

Wed & wacky. il *Life* 10:86-7 Je '87

Wedding gifts

The box [lost wedding gifts returned to owner after 50 years] R. H. Kelly. il *South Living* 22:82 D '87

Gourmet's wedding gifts. il *Gourmet* 48:66-72 Je '87

Unique wedding gifts. H. Cole and C. Cherry. il *Essence* 17:89-90 F '87

When newlyweds spurn toasters [luxury gifts] J. A. Tooley. il *U S News World Rep* 102:54 Je 22 '87

Wedding meals

Anecdotes, facetiae, satire, etc.

The bride wore oven mitts. A. Ronning. il *Gourmet* 48:80+ Je '87

Wedding receptions

Vanessa Williams and husband Ramon Hervey hold L.A. reception. il pors *Jet* 71:57 Mr 16 '87

A wedding party. J. Williams and J. Severson. il *Better Homes Gard* 65:70-3+ Je '87

Wedding rings

Not strictly all business [retired wedding ring salesman B. Schifrin] *New Yorker* 63:27-9 My 25 '87

Wedding supplies and services industry

Consultants who help you tie the knot. J. Flynn. il *Bus Week* p182 My 25 '87

Wedding fair at Bookworks [Albuquerque retailers hold promotion featuring author M. Stewart] B. List. il *Publ Wkly* 232:45-6 Ag 21 '87

Weddings

See also

Videotapes—Weddings

Atlanta mayor's daughter weds before 500 guests [L. and D. Alston] il pors *Jet* 72:33 Jl 27 '87

Attention, shoppers: check out the wedding special in aisle 2! [D. Francis and V. Radeka marry at Florida supermarket where they met] L. Tielis. il pors *People Wkly* 28:143-5 O 26 '87

Catch-2: author Joe Heller remarries; this time it's the nurse who brought him back to health. K. Gross. il pors *People Wkly* 27:42+ Ap 27 '87

Cybill marries her other Bruce. L. Armstrong and others. il pors *People Wkly* 27:98-9+ Mr 16 '87

Diahann Carroll and Vanessa Williams take the bridal path, as Lee Iacocca and Leonard Nimoy trot off alone. M. Neill. il *People Wkly* 27:32-4 Ja 19 '87

Diahann Carroll and Vic Damone marry at Golden Nugget Casino. il pors *Jet* 71:12-14 Ja 19 '87

Eartha Kitt's daughter weds attorney in N.Y. il pors *Jet* 72:60-1 Jl 6 '87

EEOC chair weds labor lawyer in D.C. ceremony [C. Thomas weds V. Lamp] il pors *Jet* 72:30 Je 29 '87

Ex-Miss America Vanessa Williams weds her publicist. pors *Jet* 71:14 Ja 19 '87

Father of the bride [D. Fox's relationship with his daughter] J. Adler. il pors *Esquire* 107:170-2+ Je '87

From L.A. to Russia with love: promoter Joanna Stingray says 'Da' to her Soviet rocker [Y. Kasparyan] il pors *People Wkly* 28:68-70 N 30 '87

In a Nevada chapel, under a veil of secrecy, Tom Selleck marries his kitten from Cats [J. Mack] il pors *People Wkly* 28:34-5 S 21 '87

Iowans have a Grandy Old Party as their G.O.P. Gopher takes a bride in a blizzard. il por *People Wkly* 27:99 Ap 13 '87

June madness [stress of weddings] G. Witkin-Lanoil. il *Health* 19:90 Je '87

Mark Thatcher bridles [marriage to D. Burgdorf] il pors *People Wkly* 27:26-7 Mr 2 '87

Marriage Vegas-style [B. Midler and H. Kipper] D. Worrell. il por *Time* 129:69 Mr 2 '87

Now married to Mimi Rogers, Tom's Cruising days are over. pors *People Wkly* 27:83 My 25 '87

Now the bell for round two [second weddings] G. Waggoner. il *Esquire* 108:30 Ag '87

One weekend in June. il *People Wkly* 27:30-40 Je 29 '87

Pendergrass marries in ceremony at his home. il por *Jet* 72:64 Jl 6 '87

Vanessa Williams and Ramon Hervey take marriage vows. A. Collier. il pors *Jet* 71:54-7 F 2 '87

Wedding day beauty blunders. il *Essence* 17:62-6+ F '87

Wondrous weddings [special section] il *Essence* 17:81-4+ F '87

Economic aspects

Weddings: for richer or poorer, till debt do us part. il *Money* 16:28 My '87

Photographs and photography

Abigail Heyman reaps the rewards of being a stay-at-home [Dreams and schemes: love and marriage in modern times] H. Chapnick. il por *Pop Photogr* 94:32 Ag '87

A guest at the wedding. G. Schaub. il *Pop Photogr* 94:40-7 Je '87

I do. I do. And they did. And did [celebrity weddings of 1986] il *Life* 10:72-4+ Ja '87

Wedgwood plc

Table for two [Waterford-Wedgwood merger] A. A. Lappen. il *Forbes* 140:8 D 28 '87

Wedtech Corporation

$4 billion worth of temptation. W. Shapiro. il *Time* 129:20 Je 15 '87

A Bronx scandal tars Meese. C. O'Connor. il por *Newsweek* 109:20 My 25 '87

Charges of bribery [M. Biaggi indicted] B. Levin. il por *Macleans* 100:30 Je 15 '87

Edwin Meese and the Wedtech web. D. Baer. il por *U S News World Rep* 102:14 My 18 '87

Edwin Meese's quiet year turns unquiet. D. Baer and P. Cary. il por *U S News World Rep* 102:14-15 My 25 '87

The Meese mess gets muddier. P. Dwyer. por *Bus Week* p68 D 28 '87-Ja 4 '88

Meese's troubles go way beyond Wedtech. P. Dwyer and H. Collingwood. il por *Bus Week* p26-7 Jl 27 '87

Mitchell sons indicted in a federal bribery case. *Jet* 72:14 Ap 20 '87

The new questions about Ed Meese's finances. P. Dwyer. il por *Bus Week* p46-7 My 11 '87

'A political snake pit' comes under the spotlight. P. Cary. il *U S News World Rep* 102:22-4 Je 15 '87

Resign, Ed Meese. il *New Repub* 197:7-9 N 9 '87

A tale of urban greed. R. Stengel. il *Time* 129:30+ Ap 20 '87

Wedtech: the bombshells keep dropping. P. Dwyer and H. Collingwood. il *Bus Week* p45-6 Je 22 '87

Wedtech: where fingers are pointing now [accountants, lawyers, and bankers] P. Dwyer. il *Bus Week* p34+ O 5 '87

Wedtech—and the web it wove. *U S News World Rep* 102:12 F 16 '87

Wee Scots (Organization)

Buddies [founder D. Newton and annual convention in Indiana] J. Stern and M. Stern. *New Yorker* 63:78+ S 21 '87

Weed, Rebecca

(jt. auth) See Friedmann, E. Imre, and Weed, Rebecca

Weed control

See also

Aquatic weed control

Herbicides

Knapweed—Control

Leafy spurge—Control

Mulching

Poison ivy—Control

Beans in wheat . . . and weeds in both [relay intercropping] D. Ohrtman. il *Success Farm* 85 no4:18AH F '87

Ground ivy: one mean weed. L. C. Askey. il *South Living* 22:56 O '87

Weed & insect control issue [special section] il *Success Farm* 85 no1:19-26+ Ja '87

Weed control in lawns and other turf. il *Consum Res Mag* 70:16-18+ Ap '87

Weeds

See also

Aquatic weeds

Grasses

Thistles

Witchweed

Good weeds. S. Sides. il *Mother Earth News* 106:70-1 Jl/Ag '87

Weird weeds [conservation tillage] B. Freese. il *Success Farm* 85:18U My '87

Control

See Weed control

Weeds [film] See Motion picture reviews—Single works

Weekend activities *See* Leisure

Weekend houses *See* Vacation houses

Weekend vacations *See* Vacations

Weekes, Trevor C.

(jt. auth) See Lamb, R. C., and Weekes, Trevor C.

Weekley, Carolyn J.

Joshua Johnson. bibl f il *Antiques* 132:524-37 S '87

Weeks, Terry
Garden Week in Charlottesville. il *Gourmet* 47:66-71 Ap '87
Gourmet holidays: Christmas in Nantucket. il map *Gourmet* 47:66-71+ D '87

Weems, Renita
This mother's daughter. il *Essence* 18:75-6+ My '87
Whispering hope. il *Ms* 16:40-1 D '87

Weeping *See* Crying

Weevils
Clean up a thistle patch with a $200 sack of bugs [musk thistle weevil] *Success Farm* 85 no1:26 Ja '87

Wegman, William
about
William Wegman: the artist and his dog. A. Hempel. il pors *N Y Times Mag* p40-2+ N 29 '87

Wegner, Wayne
Filling the bill [photograph] il *Nat Hist* 96:76-7 Je '87

Wehle, Michael
Costs of a flimsy card. il *Progressive* 51:50 Ap '87

Wei, Lilly
Talking abstract (I) [cover story] il *Art Am* 75:80-97 Jl '87
Talking abstract (II) [cover story; interviews with nine American painters] il *Art Am* 75:112-29+ D '87

Weichselgartner, Erich, and Sperling, George
Dynamics of automatic and controlled visual attention. bibl f il *Science* 238:778-80 N 6 '87

Weicker, Lowell P., Jr.
Should Congress move to invoke the War Powers Resolution? [excerpts from debate, October 20, 1987] *Congr Dig* 66:296+ D '87
about
Excavating the Titanic. W. F. Buckley. *Natl Rev* 39:65 S 25 '87

Weidenbaum, Murray L.
The pedagogy of competition. *Society* 25:46-54 N/D '87
Responding to corporate takeovers. *Society* 24:26-9 S/O '87

Weidenfeld & Nicolson (New York, N.Y.)
Weidenfeld and Grove: a flying start. C. T. Anthony. il *Publ Wkly* 232:15-18 S 4 '87

Weider, Joe
about
Marketing muscle. L. Gubernick. il por *Forbes* 140:270+ N 16 '87

Weider Health & Fitness Corporation
Marketing muscle. L. Gubernick. il por *Forbes* 140:270+ N 16 '87

Weidman, Jerome, 1913-
The Garment Center. il *N Y* 20:90 D 21-28 '87

Weigel, George
about
Catholic thought on war & peace [discussion of September 11 and September 25, 1987 articles, The heritage abandoned?] P. Steinfels. *Commonweal* 114:690+ D 4 '87
The heritage abandoned? (I). P. Steinfels. *Commonweal* 114:487-92 S 11 '87
The heritage abandoned? (II). P. Steinfels. il *Commonweal* 114:530-3 S 25 '87
Reclaiming the Catholic heritage. A. R. Muggeridge. *Commentary* 84:39-44 S '87

Weigensberg, Emmanuel
about
The Canada connection; Threats behind the disclosure. M. McDonald. il por *Macleans* 100:22-5 Ag 3 '87

Weight (Physiology)
See also
Anorexia nervosa
Birth weight
Bulimia
Diet
Exercise
Obesity
Weight reducing preparations
Fat or fantasy? P. Von Nostitz. il *Parents* 62:200+ Mr '87
How fat is too fat? P. Gadsby. il *Good Housekeep* 204:205 Mr '87
How to quit without gaining weight [smoking; views of John B. Morrison] il *USA Today (Periodical)* 115:13-14 Ap '87
'Middle aged' spread tied to lack of exercise. *Jet* 73:28 S 28 '87
Overweight or underconfident? Coming to terms with your body. K. McCoy. *Seventeen* 46:32+ F '87
Wanted: weight. A. S. Brodoff. *Vogue* 177:248 Ja '87
Weight control: what works. *Vogue* 177:258 Jl '87

When thin isn't in (reaching the right weight doesn't always mean dieting). L. Manske. il *Mademoiselle* 93:114 O '87
Anecdotes, facetiae, satire, etc.
Oh yes you can (be too rich or too thin). K. Fury. il *Work Woman* 12:114 F '87

Weight and size regulations for trucks *See* Trucks—Laws and regulations

Weight lifting
See also
Body building
Accentuate the negative [lowering weights instead of raising them] M. Brzycki. il *Women's Sports Fitness* 9:62 My '87
Add a power surge [weight training] J. Torrey. il *Women's Sports Fitness* 9:34-7 O '87
Being strong takes more than muscles [women competitors] R. Silverman. il por *Women's Sports Fitness* 9:60 O '87
Build a better body—with weights! [women] il *McCalls* 114:42 My '87
Gaining good weight [athletes and weight training] C. Pesmen. il *Sport Mag* 78:87-8 Mr '87
The great weight-machine workout. B. Kevles. il *Mademoiselle* 93:110 O '87
Lining up for FIRM form [aerobic workout with weights] G. Bakoulis. il *Health* 19:62-4 Je '87
Once a Cuban hero, Roberto Urrutia aims to give the U.S. a boost—and Castro a lesson—in the Pan American Games. P. Jordan. il pors *People Wkly* 28:105-6+ Ag 10 '87
The purpose of lifting. L. Kriegel. il *N Y Times Mag* p50 Ap 12 '87
Upper-body work out. S. Festa. il *Women's Sports Fitness* 9:22-6 Jl '87
Terminology
Come to terms. il *Women's Sports Fitness* 9:22 S '87

Weight loss resorts *See* Health resorts, watering places, etc.

Weight reducing equipment *See* Exercising equipment

Weight reducing preparations
See also
Dinitrophenol
Redotex (Drug)
730-lb. man trying Dick Gregory's formula to aid in weight loss [S. Smith] il pors *Jet* 72:52 My 4 '87
Dick Gregory launches new enterprise with Slim-Safe Bahamian Diet. il por *Jet* 72:16 Mr 30 '87
Dick Gregory starts workshops, seminars to market formulas. por *Jet* 72:16 Ap 6 '87
Dick Gregory thrilled with response to new company, diet formulas. por *Jet* 72:16 Ap 13 '87
New sugar may help fat, thin alike [research by Michael DiNovi and Robert Rafka] J. Raloff. *Sci News* 131:251 Ap 18 '87
Sugar alternatives for weight control. B. T. Hunter. il *Consum Res Mag* 70:8-9 Ag '87

Weight training *See* Weight lifting

Weight Watchers diet *See* Diet

Weightlessness
See also
Seeds, Effect of weightlessness on
All in the name of science, Houston's Richard Fitzpatrick goes flat out for NASA—in bed [researching connection between weightlessness and bone loss] B. Stewart. il pors *People Wkly* 28:59-60 D 21 '87
Europe seeks additional opportunities for microgravity space experiments. J. M. Lenorovitz. il *Aviat Week Space Technol* 127:133-5 Jl 13 '87
Fanning flames in space [research by Felix J. Weinberg and F. B. Carleton] I. Peterson. *Sci News* 132:389 D 19-26 '87
Fitness at zero-G [exercise program for astronauts] E. Smith. il *Women's Sports Fitness* 9:86 Mr '87
Inner ears and outer space [work of M. D. Ross on utricular macula cell morphology] R. Spangenburg and D. Moser. il por *Space World* X-9-285:17-20 S '87
Project Bluestar [zero gravity think tank space station] il *Futurist* 21:29-32 Ja/F '87
A question of gravity. R. Spangenburg and D. Moser. il *Space World* X-2-278:8-11 F '87
The sixth mission: a space station diary. N. McAleer. il *Space World* X-5-281:12-19 My '87
Soviets to extend duration of manned missions. il *Aviat Week Space Technol* 127:116 O 19 '87
Travelling light: coping with weightlessness in space. O. G. Gazenko. il *Courier* 40:12-13 Je '87
Weightless; tr. by Piers Spence. P. Levi. *Harpers* 275:38 O '87

Weightlessness simulators
KC-135 provides microgravity testbed. il *Aviat Week Space Technol* 126:61 F 23 '87
Weightlifting *See* Weight lifting
Weightman, John
Summing up Sartre. il *N Y Rev Books* 34:42-6 Ag 13 '87
Weights (Exercising equipment) *See* Exercising equipment
Weights and measures
See also
Measurement
Metric system
Weijer, Jan
about
Hell no, it won't grow! Canada's Dr. Jan Weijer has a lawn you'll have to mow only once a year. il por *People Wkly* 28:39 Ag 10 '87
Weilbaecher, Sharon
The watercolor page. il por *Am Artist* 51:56-7 Je '87
Weiley, Susan
Newman's people. il por *Art News* 86:128-34 D '87
Weill, Jean-Claude, and Reynaud, Claude-Agnès
The chicken B cell compartment. bibl f il *Science* 238:1094-8 N 20 '87
Weill, Kurt, 1900-1950
about
Kurt Weill's deadly sin. E. Rothstein. *New Repub* 197:25+ N 23 '87
Musical events. A. Porter. *New Yorker* 63:99-100+ O 19 '87
Weill, Sanford I.
about
Sandy Weill is doing just fine on Main Street, thank you. S. Bartlett. il *Bus Week* p96-7+ S 21 '87
Sanford Weill. C. S. Eklund. il por *Bus Week* Sp Issue:230 Ap 17 '87
Will Sandy Weill snare Hutton? G. G. Marcial. il *Bus Week* p73 Ag 24 '87
Weimer, Maryellen Gleason
(jt. auth) *See* McMullen-Pastrick, Miriam, and Weimer, Maryellen Gleason
Wein, Betty
Pornography on the march. il *Read Dig* 131:153-8 N '87
Wein, Bibi
Rivalry: the two-career clash. *Harpers Bazaar* 120:299+ Mr '87
The special stresses of second marriages. *Redbook* 169:100-1+ Je '87
Weinberg, John L.
about
John Weinberg. A. Bianco. por *Bus Week* Sp Issue:224 Ap 17 '87
Weinberg, Lee S.
(jt. auth) *See* Vatz, Richard E., and Weinberg, Lee S.
Weinberg, Steven
Holes and loose ends in particle physics [adaptation of address, July 1986] por *Phys Today* 40:7+ Ja '87
Weinberger, Barbara
Keeping the peace? Policing strikes 1906-26. bibl il *Hist Today* 37:29-35 D '87
Weinberger, Caspar W.
The military underpinnings of diplomacy [address, September 21, 1987] *Vital Speeches Day* 54:34-7 N 1 '87
Why offense needs defense. *Foreign Policy* 68:3-18 Fall '87
about
Cap on top. F. Barnes. il *New Repub* 196:13-15 Ap 20 '87
Changing of the guards. G. J. Church. il por *Time* 130:21-2 N 16 '87
The flawed legacy of 'Cap the Knife'. il por *Macleans* 100:23 N 16 '87
Hard choices, less money. T. Morganthau. il *Newsweek* 110:60-1+ N 16 '87
In the wake of 'Cap the Shovel'. P. R. Range. il por *U S News World Rep* 103:16-17 N 16 '87
It's time for 'Cap the Knife' to cut a deal with Congress. D. Griffiths. il por *Bus Week* p62 F 16 '87
Sack Weinberger, bankrupt General Dynamics, and other procurement reforms. G. Easterbrook. il *Wash Mon* 18:33-8+ Ja '87
A shield against arms control. S. Talbott. il por *Time* 129:25 F 2 '87
Sneak attack. por *Time* 129:32 Ap 27 '87
Space race. F. Barnes. *New Repub* 196:10-12 F 23 '87
Uncapping Star Wars. *Nation* 244:201 F 21 '87
Weinberger cites need to boost chip industry. *Aviat Week Space Technol* 126:24 My 18 '87

Weinberger endorses phased deployment of SDI. *Aviat Week Space Technol* 126:22-3 Ja 19 '87
Weinberger firm on military uses for space station. *Aviat Week Space Technol* 127:32 S 21 '87
Weinberger foresees no technical blocks to first-phase SDI deployment. R. G. O'Lone. *Aviat Week Space Technol* 126:103 My 11 '87
Weinberger objects to bill limiting military station use. T. M. Foley. *Aviat Week Space Technol* 126:27-8 My 18 '87
Weinberger's legacy: a stronger nation and a management mess. D. Griffiths. por *Bus Week* p71 N 16 '87
Weinberger's war. I. F. Stone. *Nation* 245:364-5 O 10 '87
Weinberger, Eliot
(tr) *See* Paz, Octavio, 1914-. Food of the gods
Weiner, Elliot
Gifts: you're a wonderful giver. How well do you receive? il *Glamour* 85:20+ D '87
Weiner, Ellis
A good woman is hard to find: the sad saga of an eligible man. il *Mademoiselle* 93:122-3+ Jl '87
It's hip to be: (a) square, (b) cool, (c) hot. *Mademoiselle* 93:146-7+ D '87
The young and the sex less: a yuppie love story. il *Mademoiselle* 93:110-11+ Ja '87
Weiner, Henry L., and others
Tissue distribution and developmental expression of the messenger RNA encoding angiogenin. bibl f il *Science* 237:280-2 Jl 17 '87
Weiner, Joshua
Casting back [poem] *Am Sch* 56:248-9 Spr '87
Weiner, Tim
The dark secret of the black budget. *Wash Mon* 19:31-5 My '87
Weingarten, Robert I., 1941-
about
Instant tycoon. J. Heins. il por *Forbes* 139:38+ Mr 23 '87
Weingarten Equity Fund, Inc.
A patient card player's picks [interview with H. Hutzler] J. P. Newport, Jr. il por *Fortune* 116:176 N 9 '87
Weingarten Realty, Inc.
Real estate profits in Houston? Yes, in Houston [CEO S. J. Alexander] J. E. Davis. il por *Bus Week* p178 D 28 '87-Ja 4 '88
Weinhouse, Beth
Medinews. *See* issues of Ladies' Home Journal
Summer first-aid guide [excerpt from The healthy traveler] *Ladies Home J* 104:34+ Je '87
Weinhouse, Beth, and Feldinger, Frank
The miracle baby. il *Ladies Home J* 104:104+ Ap '87
Weinstein, Bernard L., and Gross, Harold T.
National change and the regional conundrum. *Society* 25:55-61 N/D '87
Weinstein, David
about
CP Shades's David Weinstein is cashing in on color and comfort—no haute couture need apply. B. Johnson. il por *People Wkly* 28:106-7 O 19 '87
Weinstein, Grace W.
Your money. *See* issues of Good Housekeeping
Weinstein, Michael
about
"This was a business of old men". B. Leonard. il por *Forbes* 139:120+ Mr 9 '87
Weinstein, Norman
Reggae or not: jazz goes dread? il *Down Beat* 54:63 Mr '87
Weinstein, Robert A.
Puget Sound: the maritime world of Wilhelm Hester. il *Am Hist Illus* 21:20-35 Ja '87
Weinstein, Robert V.
How to get along with a difficult co-worker. il *McCalls* 114:129 S '87
Weinstock, Cheryl Platzman
Cosmic tech. il *Omni* 9:32+ My '87
Medicines from the body. il *FDA Consum* 21:6-10 Ap '87
Weinstock, Lotus
about
Lili and Lotus. il pors *Teen* 31:60 D '87
Weintraub, Jerry
about
Coke's latest movie deal could be boffo. R. Grover. il por *Bus Week* p44 F 23 '87
Weintraub, Stanley, 1929-
about
Victorian in name only, the queen was amused in the bedroom and elsewhere [interview] L. Rozen. il pors *People Wkly* 27:58+ Je 22 '87

Weintraub, William
Teaching computer ethics in the schools. *Educ Dig* 52:34-5 F '87

Weintraub Entertainment Group Inc.
Coke's latest movie deal could be boffo [backing J. Weintraub] R. Grover. il por *Bus Week* p44 F 23 '87

Weir, Benjamin
about
Weir urges direct negotiations. C. W. Richard. *Christ Century* 104:324-5 Ap 8 '87
Kidnapping
Hostage in Lebanon. J. V. Loudon. pors *Publ Wkly* 231:38-40 Mr 6 '87

Weir, Carol
about
Hostage in Lebanon. J. V. Loudon. pors *Publ Wkly* 231:38-40 Mr 6 '87

Weir, David, 1947-
The Bhopal syndrome [excerpt] il *Omni* 10:38+ N '87
(jt. auth) See Porterfield, Andrew, and Weir, David, 1947-

Weir, Patricia A.
Can't is a coward too lazy to try [address, July 14, 1987] *Vital Speeches Day* 54:26-9 O 15 '87

Weir, Peter, 1944-
about
The Mosquito Coast [film] Reviews
Glamour il 85:132 Ja '87. J. G. Boyum
Theatre Crafts il 21:71-2 F '87. S. Gowin
USA Today (Periodical) il 115:95-6 Mr '87. K. R. Hey
The special chemistry of Harrison Ford and Peter Weir. J. Powell. il por *Glamour* 85:132 Ja '87

Weirton Steel Corporation
Class consciousness raising. S. W. Angrist. il *Forbes* 140:77-8 N 30 '87
How workers saved their steel mill. P. Gaynor. il *Sch Update* 119:9 Ja 26 '87

Weis, Judith S.
(jt. auth) See Mitteldorf, Arthur J., and Weis, Judith S.

Weisang, Myriam
Aiming for the mind's eye: Sha Sha Higby's costume sculptures. il *Theatre Crafts* 21:42-3+ Ap '87
Masters of the universe. il *Theatre Crafts* 21:28-9+ Ja '87

Weisberg, Jacob
The Mafia and the melting pot [cover story] il *New Repub* 197:33-4+ O 12 '87
Sex and drugs and Heidegger. *Wash Mon* 19:49-53 S '87

Weisberg, Ruth
about
The Scroll. *New Yorker* 63:36-7 N 23 '87

Weisberger, Bernard A., 1922-
American history is falling down. il *Am Herit* 38:26-32 F/Mr '87
The forgotten four hundred: Chicago's first millionaires. il *Am Herit* 38:34-45 N '87
The (non) teaching of American history: U.S. history is falling down. *Current* 293:20-7 Je '87
Why it happened. il *Americana* 15:24-6+ My/Je '87

Weisberger, Eleanor
The parent as an effective and loving manager [excerpt from When your child needs you] *Work Woman* 12:176+ N '87

Weisenberg, Richard C., and others
Microtubule gelation-contraction: essential components and relation to slow axonal transport. bibl f il *Science* 238:1119-22 N 20 '87

Weisenfeld, Paulette
about
Affordable luxury. R. Koselka. il por *Forbes* 139:164 My 4 '87

Weisfelner, Marion
"A notorious killer car". *Car Driv* 32:53 Je '87

Weisman, Alan
Up in arms in Arizona. il por *N Y Times Mag* p50-1+ N 1 '87

Weisman, Steven R.
Doing the needful. il *N Y Times Mag* p6+ Jl 12 '87
The great game. *New Repub* 197:20-3 Ag 10-17 '87
Sri Lanka: a nation disintegrates [cover story] il map *N Y Times Mag* p34-8+ D 13 '87

Weisman (Frederick R.) Museum *See* Frederick R. Weisman Museum

Weiss, Barry D.
(jt. auth) See Lurie, Paul M., and Weiss, Barry D.

Weiss, Branco
about
Swiss risk. R. Morais. il por *Forbes* 139:49 Je 1 '87

Weiss, Carol Hirschon
Evaluating social programs: what have we learned? *Society* 25:40-5 N/D '87

Weiss, David, 1946-
about
Masters of the glum "eureka!". C. Ratcliff. il *Art Am* 75:98-101 Ja '87

Weiss, Farley
Qualifiers deserve a break. il *World Tennis* 35:80 N '87

Weiss, James N., and Lamp, Scott T.
Glycolysis preferentially inhibits ATP-sensitive K+ channels in isolated guinea pig cardiac myocytes. bibl f il *Science* 238:67-9 O 2 '87

Weiss, Jerome
about
Researcher disqualified. *FDA Consum* 21:30 Jl/Ag '87

Weiss, Julian M.
Jamaica's new agriculture. il *Américas* 39:52-3 Mr/Ap '87

Weiss, Margie
Don't feel sorry for my kids. il *Women's Sports Fitness* 9:78 F '87

Weiss, Michael
about
Michael Weiss: real bop is back. C. Albertson. il por *Stereo Rev* 52:90+ O '87

Weiss, Michael J.
Nancy Reagan gets tough. por *Ladies Home J* 104:64+ Ag '87

Weiss, Mike
Black Botham. il pors *Esquire* 107:82-6 Ja '87

Weiss, Miles
Solar power satellites: still in the dark. il *Space World* X-11-287:21-5 N '87

Weiss, Philip
Charming her way to the White House [cover story] *Wash Mon* 19:29+ S '87
Invasion of the Gannettoids. il *New Repub* 196:18-20+ F 2 '87

Weiss, Robert
about
Winter dreams [ballet] Reviews
Dance Mag 61:28-9 N '87. C. Hardy

Weissbourd, Bernice
As they grow/2-year-olds. See issues of Parents

Weisser, Graziella
The emergence of African voices. *World Press Rev* 34:62 Mr '87

Weisskopf, Michael
Lead astray: the poisoning of America. il *Discover* 8:68-74 D '87

Weisskopf, Victor Frederick
The task for a new peace movement. il *Bull At Sci* 43:26-32 Ja/F '87

Weissler, Paul
Auto Q&A. See issues of Home Mechanix beginning January 1985
Car repair. See issues of Home Mechanix beginning January 1985

Weissman, Bernard E., and others
Introduction of a normal human chromosome 11 into a Wilms' tumor cell line controls its tumorigenic expression. bibl f il *Science* 236:175-80 Ap 10 '87

Weissman, Michaele
At home with Tira. il por *Ms* 16:36+ S '87

Weissman, Paul R.
Realm of the comets. il *Sky Telesc* 73:238-41 Mr '87

Weissman, Susan
(jt. auth) See Miller, Jo Ann, and Weissman, Susan

Weitzenhoffer, Kenneth
The education of Mary Somerville. por *Sky Telesc* 73:138-9 F '87

Weizenbaum, Joseph
Facing reality: computer scientists aid war efforts. il *Technol Rev* 90:22-3 Ja '87

Weizmann, Chaim, 1874-1952
about
Israel's providential men. P. Johnson. *Commentary* 84:60-3 O '87

Welbilt Corp.
Rise and fall and rise. B. Leonard. il por *Forbes* 139:98-9 F 9 '87

Welbilt Electronic Die Corporation *See* Wedtech Corporation

Welch, John F., Jr.
about
General Electric is stalking big game again. J. R. Norman. il por *Bus Week* p112-13 Mr 16 '87
Jack Welch: how good a manager? [cover story] R. Mitchell. il pors *Bus Week* p92-6+ D 14 '87
John Welch. R. W. King. il por *Bus Week* Sp Issue:240 Ap 17 '87
Jumping Jack strikes again. P. Elmer-Dewitt. il *Time* 130:44 Ag 3 '87
The man who brought GE to life. P. Petre. por *Fortune* 115:76-7 Ja 5 '87
Turning on the juice. P. Petre. il por *Fortune* 116:31 Ag 3 '87

Welch, Kim
Orion, the hunter. il *Flying* 114:102-4 O '87

Welch, Priscilla
about
New look in the long run. C. Neff. il pors *Sports Illus* 67:24-5 N 9 '87
Woman to watch: Priscilla Welch. M. Goldberg. il por *Women's Sports Fitness* 9:18 Mr '87

Welch, William John, and others
Star formation in W49A: gravitational collapse of the molecular cloud core toward a ring of massive stars. bibl f il *Science* 238:1550-5 D 11 '87

Welcome Back to Brooklyn Festival *See* Brooklyn (New York, N.Y.)—Festivals

Welcome Home concert, 1987
Fogerty plays Creedence songs at vets benefit. A. DeCurtis. il por *Roll Stone* p14 Ag 13 '87

Welebit, Diane
The art that is life. il *Americana* 14:32-4 Ja/F '87
The simple life [with editorial comment by Sandra Wilmot] il *Americana* 15:3, 37-9 S/O '87

Welfare *See* Public welfare

Welfare funds (Trade unions) *See* Trade unions—Benefit funds

Welfare hotels
Against all odds [Jackson children living at Brooklyn Arms welfare hotel] B. Campbell. il *N Y* 20:68-74+ N 16 '87
How the homeless bought a Rolls for Cornelius Pitts [running a welfare hotel] M. Szegedy-Maszak. il por *Wash Mon* 19:11-15 Jl/Ag '87
Manhattan's Martinique [hotel for homeless families] R. Hirschfeld. *Commonweal* 114:71-2 F 13 '87
The Martinique Hotel: housing the homeless. R. Hirschfield. *America* 156:90-1 F 7 '87
Where Christmas never comes [children in New York shelters and hotels] M. Small. il *People Wkly* 28:50-60 D 14 '87

Well rescues *See* Rescue work

Wellbutrin
Sensuous side effect [antidepressant increases sexual desire] *Time* 129:86 My 4 '87

Wellcome Foundation Ltd.
Companies vie over new heart drug [Genentech vs. Wellcome] M. Sun. il *Science* 237:120-2 Jl 10 '87

Wellemeyer, Marilyn
On your own time. See alternate issues of Fortune

Weller, Gunter, and others
Laboratory Antarctica: research contributions to global problems. bibl f il maps *Science* 238:1361-8 D 4 '87

Weller, Michael
about
Moonchildren [drama] Reviews
New Yorker 63:106-7 D 21 '87. M. Kramer

Weller, Samuel, 1851-1925
about
Samuel Weller: illustrious citizen of Zanesville. A. G. McDonald. il *Antiques Collect Hobbies* 92:32-5 Ap '87

Weller, Sheila
A story about professionalism, attachment and women's hearts. *Glamour* 85:134+ Mr '87
Today's man: the doubled-edged charm of Bryant Gumbel. il pors *McCalls* 114:69-71+ Je '87

Weller Pottery Company
Samuel Weller: illustrious citizen of Zanesville. A. G. McDonald. il *Antiques Collect Hobbies* 92:32-5 Ap '87

Wellesley College
A picture of health [Sports Center] D. Dietsch. il *Archit Rec* 175:90-5 Ag '87

Wellesley College. Stone Center for Developmental Services and Studies
Campus report: is there a drinker in the house? [Alcohol Informational Theater] K. FitzGerald. il *Ms* 15:30 F '87

Wellington Management Company
Vanguard fires a skipper [ousted by Vanguard World-U.S. Growth Fund] *Money* 16:35 O '87

Welliver, Neil
about
Neil Welliver. G. Henry. il *Art News* 86:150+ My '87

Wells, A. G.
(jt. auth) See Wells, B. A., and Wells, A. G.

Wells, B. A., and Wells, A. G.
Wasp pickup. il *Nat Hist* 96:84-5 Ap '87

Wells, Bruce, 1950-
about
Tales of Hans Christian Andersen [ballet] Reviews
Dance Mag il 61:52-4 N '87. I. M. Fanger

Wells, David F.
Everlasting punishment. il por *Christ Today* 31:41-2 Mr 20 '87

Wells, James A.
(jt. auth) See Carter, Paul, and Wells, James A.

Wells, Lawrence
Down in the wiregrass. il *South Living* 22:108 Jl '87

Wells, Linda
Big man in the kitchen. il pors *N Y Times Mag* p40-1+ D 13 '87

Wells, Patricia
After quiche. il *N Y Times Mag* p61-2 O 4 '87
When things go right. il *N Y Times Mag* p123-4+ S 13 '87

Wells, Rosemary, 1943-
Words & pictures: the right order [adaptation of address] por *Publ Wkly* 231:146 F 27 '87

Wells, Sherrill Brown
Long-time friends: early U.S.-Moroccan relations, 1777-87. bibl f il *Dep State Bull* 87:1-15 S '87

Wells, Ted
about
Black lawyer keys Donovan's trial win. il pors *Jet* 72:6 Je 22 '87

Wells, Terrie, 1983-
about
$4.5 mil. lawsuit won in Mississippi medical case. *Jet* 72:14 Jl 20 '87

Wells, Tracy
about
Star gazing: Tracy Wells. il pors *Teen* 31:62-3 Ja '87

Wells
Pollution
See Water pollution

Wells Fargo & Co.
Most improved. il *Forbes* 139:75 Ja 12 '87

Wells Fargo Bank, National Association
Constitutional wrongs [upcoming Supreme Court case challenging Congress' attempt to overrule and impose estate taxes retroactively] L. Saunders. il *Forbes* 140:154 S 21 '87
Fighting to stave off foreclosure, farmer Garth Conlan ends up taking his bank to the cleaners. D. Grogan. il por *People Wkly* 28:50-2 Ag 10 '87
Guard hailed by police fired by bank; gets a better job and pay raise [J. Massey] *Jet* 72:12 Mr 30 '87

Wellstood, Dick, 1927-1987
about
Obituary
Natl Rev il por 39:20-2+ S 25 '87. W. F. Buckley
New Yorker 63:90-2 Ag 31 '87. W. Balliett

Welsh, Christopher Norton- *See* Norton-Welsh, Christopher

Welsh, Jerry C.
about
Welsh: making his firm a better listener. M. N. Vamos. il por *Bus Week* p94 N 23 '87

Welsh, Patrick
Teachers fight for control of their own profession. *Educ Dig* 53:18-21 S '87
What education reform? *Educ Dig* 52:6-9 F '87

Welsh, Carson, Anderson & Stowe
Infomaniac [R. Carson manages leveraged buyouts of information companies] L. Jereski. il por *Forbes* 140:224+ O 5 '87

Welsing, Frances Cress
about
A conversation with . . . Dr. Frances Cress Welsing about her theory of skin color and oppression. K. J. Halliburton. pors *Essence* 18:32 My '87

Welter, Cole H.
Discipline-based art education: not if, but where? bibl f *Des Arts Educ* 89:22-8 N/D '87

Welter, John
My store of grievances. il *Atlantic* 260:26 Ag '87

Weltner, Linda, 1938-
Every 27 minutes . . . il *Read Dig* 130:136-8 F '87

Welty, Eudora, 1909-
about
Eudora Welty's eye for the story [cover story] P. H. Samway. il *America* 156:417-20 My 23 '87
Wen Ruitang
Treasures from an ancient Chinese tomb. il *Courier* 40:32-3 Ja '87
Wendoloski, J. J., and others
Molecular dynamics of a cytochrome c-cytochrome b₅ electron transfer complex. bibl f il *Science* 238:794-7 N 6 '87
Wendt, Henry
about
SmithKline: sprinting just to stay in place. S. Benway. il por *Bus Week* p74+ Ag 31 '87
Wendy's International Inc.
Coke may be going where the beef is [merger with Wendy's] G. G. Marcial. *Bus Week* p74 Mr 30 '87
Wendy's tries warming up the basic burger. D. Cook. il *Bus Week* p51 My 18 '87
Wener, Richard, and others
Building better jails. bibl (p56) il *Psychol Today* 21:40-4+ Je '87
Weneser, Joseph
(jt. auth) See Friedlander, Gerhart, and Weneser, Joseph
Weneser, Joseph, and Friedlander, Gerhart
Solar neutrinos: questions and hypotheses. bibl f il *Science* 235:755-9 F 13 '87
Wenner, Gene C.
Why would anyone with money want to give it to arts education? *Des Arts Educ* 88:28-9 Mr/Ap '87
Wenner, Jann S.
about
Now star-studded Us has more ad pages, too. D. Lieberman. il por *Bus Week* p83+ Je 8 '87
Werlich, David P.
Debt, democracy and terrorism in Peru. bibl f *Curr Hist* 86:29-32+ Ja '87
Werner, Dagmar
about
Nights—and days—of the iguana. J. P. Cohn. il por *Américas* 39:34-9 Jl/Ag '87
Werner, Laurie
A holiday survival-manual [special section] il *Ladies Home J* 104:70+ D '87
My husband is irresponsible. il *Ladies Home J* 104:12+ N '87
Werner, Louis
North to Cairo along the scorching Way of the Forty. il map *Smithsonian* 17:120-4+ Mr '87
Werner, Peter
about
No man's land [film] Reviews
People Wkly il 28:14 N 16 '87. R. Novak
Werner, Robert J.
A case history of one foundation's philanthropy. *Des Arts Educ* 88:19-22 Mr/Ap '87
Wernick, Robert
Jacob Lawrence: art as seen through a people's history. bibl (p153) il por *Smithsonian* 18:56-64+ Je '87
Philip II's grand design for the glory of God and empire. bibl (p205) il pors *Smithsonian* 18:152-6+ D '87
A riddle within a mystery inside an enigma: Klee. bibl (p144) il *Smithsonian* 17:64-6+ F '87
Where there's fire there is smoke—and usually a 'chimney'. bibl (p187) il *Smithsonian* 18:140-4+ S '87
Werran, Holly
Onomatopoeias: the wily photo pun strikes again! il *Petersens Photogr Mag* 16:40-2 N '87
Werren, John H.
Labile sex ratios in wasps and bees. bibl f il *BioScience* 37:498-506 Jl/Ag '87
Wertmüller, Lina
about
Dancing with Carmen. K. Kertess. il pors *Art Am* 75:180-5+ Ap '87
Summer night [film] Reviews
New Repub 197:27-8 Jl 6 '87. S. Kauffmann
Weschler, Lawrence
A miracle, a universe (I). *New Yorker* 63:69-84+ My 25 '87
A miracle, a universe (II). *New Yorker* 63:72-80+ Je 1 '87
Outside history. *Harpers* 274:16-18 Ja '87
Stella's flying ships [cover story] il por *Art News* 86:92-9 S '87
Wesley, Charles Harris, 1891-1987
about
CSU celebrates 100th year, pays tribute to Dr. Charles H. Wesley. *Jet* 72:10 Ap 27 '87

Obituary
Jet por 72:53 S 7 '87
Wesley Theological Seminary. Center for the Arts and Religion
A seminary's artist in residence: Cathy Kapikian's fabric of faith. L.-M. Delloff. il *Christ Century* 104:267-71 Mr 18-25 '87
Wesleyan University (Middletown, Conn.)
Cosby to speak at Wesleyan for daughter's graduation. *Jet* 72:58 My 18 '87
Wesray Capital Corporation
Sans Simon, Wesray cleans up on Avis. il *Fortune* 116:8-9 O 26 '87
When you own the company, you try harder [employee buyout at Avis] E. Spragins. *Bus Week* p32-3 S 28 '87
Wessler, Susan R., and others
The maize transposable element Ds is spliced from RNA. bibl f il *Science* 237:916-18 Ag 21 '87
Wessner, Kenneth T., 1922-
about
ServiceMaster: looking for new worlds to clean. M. D. Oneal. il pors *Bus Week* p60-1 Ja 19 '87
West, Gordon
Electronics Q&A. See issues of Motor Boating & Sailing
West, Linda
about
Miss. kids finding homes thanks to preacher's wife. il por *Jet* 71:32 Ja 19 '87
West, Paul, 1930-
Ode to corn [excerpt from A rocking horse on Mars] il *Harpers* 275:30-1 S '87
West, Susan
Christmas takes the cake. il *Ladies Home J* 104:138-41+ D '87
West, Ted
Going West. See issues of Road & Track beginning June 1985
West, William D.
Summer night's dream. il *Opera News* 51:34-5 Je '87
West (John Howe) Inc. See John Howe West Inc.
West (U.S.) See Western States
West Africa
　See also
　　British—West Africa
　　Burkina Faso
　　Cameroon
　　Ghana
　　Liberia
　　Mali
　　Nigeria
　　Public health—West Africa
　　Scots—West Africa
　　United Nations—West Africa
　　　Exploring expeditions
Long nose, white skin and 'honey mouth' [visit to the king; excerpt from Travels into the interior of Africa] M. Park. por *Courier* 40:18+ Ap '87
West Africa's Mary Kingsley. D. Birkett. bibl il pors *Hist Today* 37:10-16 My '87
　　　Native peoples
　　See also
　　Yorubas
West and East See East and West
West Bank Palestinian Arab students See Palestinian Arab students
West Bank territorial question See Israel-Arab Wars, 1967- —Territorial questions
West Berlin See Berlin (Germany: West)
West Chester (Pa.)
　　　Advertising
The case of the kidnapped couple [practice of stopping cars from out of town to show off as part of Boost Pennsylvania Week] B. Greene. il *Esquire* 107:45-6 Mr '87
　　　Politics and government
Crusader Charles Melton gets last wish; new vote system for Westchester, Pa. il por *Jet* 73:6-7 S 28 '87
West Co., Inc.
Shot in the arm [stock price] T. Jaffe. il *Forbes* 140:218 O 19 '87
West Germany See Germany (West)
West Indian cooking See Cooking, West Indian
West Indies
　　See also
　　Anguilla
　　Bahamas
　　Barbados
　　Cayman Islands
　　Dominica
　　Haiti

West Indies—See also—*cont.*
Jamaica
Saint Barthélemy (Guadeloupe)
Saint Martin
Turks and Caicos Islands
Native peoples
See Indians of the West Indies
West Islip (N.Y.)
Hospitals
Long Island's 'angel of death' [male nurse R. Angelo charged with murder of patients at Good Samaritan Hospital] D. Gates. il por *Newsweek* 110:35 N 30 '87
West Memphis (Ark.)
Crime
West Memphis youth shot by friend watching gun commercial on television [Andre McGee shot] *Jet* 73:46 N 2 '87
West Orange (N.J.)
Historic houses, sites, etc.
See also
Edison National Historic Site
West Penn Hospital *See* Pittsburgh (Pa.)—Hospitals
West Point (N.Y.). Military Academy *See* United States Military Academy
West Point Market
Groceries with glamour. J. C. Snow. il por *Nations Bus* 75:57-8 Mr '87
West Stockbridge (Mass.)
Architecture
The villa transformer [Schwartz/Fiekowsky weekend house] C. K. Gandee. il *Archit Rec* 175:114-21 mid-Ap '87
West Valley nuclear reprocessing plant (N.Y.) *See* Nuclear facilities
West Virginia
See also
Coal mines and mining—West Virginia
Colleges and universities—West Virginia
Finance—West Virginia
Fortification—West Virginia
George Washington National Forest (Va. and W. Va.)
Music festivals—West Virginia
New River (N.C.-W. Va.)
Politics and government
Economic paralysis could stop Arch Moore cold [gubernatorial race] M. Rothman. il por *Bus Week* p86+ N 30 '87
West Virginia State Museum
A salute to the simple times. il *South Living* 22:42 Mr '87
West Virginia University
Homecoming [Erickson Alumni Center] il *Archit Rec* 175:96-9 Mr '87
W. Va. Univ. elects first black homecoming queen [T. L. Cunningham] *Jet* 71:27 Ja 19 '87
West Week
New products: West Week. il *Archit Rec* 175:158-9+ My '87
Westchester County (N.Y.)
Crime
Incident at Exit 20 [A. Salomon shoots G. Cotugno on the Hutchinson River Parkway] M. Stone. il pors *N Y* 20:50-4+ O 5 '87
Westcott Bay Sea Farms
Oyster lovers, rejoice! Summer is no longer your off-season. il *People Wkly* 28:57 Ag 31 '87
Westen, Robin
Childhood memories we can't erase. il *Glamour* 85:168+ O '87
Masturbation: who, what, where, when and why. *Glamour* 85:156+ My '87
Westerfield, Nancy G.
Amortization [poem] *Commonweal* 114:618 N 6 '87
Smoke [poem] *Commonweal* 114:19 Ja 16 '87
Westergaard, Fred
Thoroughbred compost you can bet on. il por *Rodale's Org Gard* 34:77-80 F '87
Western, John
Closely observed trains [cover story] il *Focus* 37:10-17 Summ '87
Western Air Lines, Inc.
Supreme Court overturns injunction blocking Delta-Western merger. C. Preble. map *Aviat Week Space Technol* 126:32-3 Ap 6 '87

Western and country music *See* Country music
Western civilization *See* Civilization
Western cooking *See* Cooking, American
Western Desert (Egypt)
Exploring deserts [Viking images of Mars compared to the Western Desert of Egypt] T. A. Maxwell. il *Earth Sci* 39:12-14 Wint '86
Western Digital Corp.
One-stop shopping for IBM copycats. J. Flynn. il por *Bus Week* p76+ Ag 24 '87
Western Diversification Office (Canada) *See* Canada. Western Diversification Office
Western Europe
See also
Air freight service—Routes—Western Europe
Air traffic control—Western Europe
Americans—Western Europe
Amusement parks—Western Europe
Anti-nuclear movement—Western Europe
Automobile racing—Western Europe
Aviation and state—Western Europe
Birds—Western Europe
Business management—Western Europe
Canadians—Western Europe
Civil service—Western Europe
Colleges and universities—Western Europe
Credit cards—Western Europe
Direct broadcast satellite services—Western Europe
Economic assistance, European
Education—Western Europe
Electronics research—Western Europe
Employment—Western Europe
Genetic research—Western Europe
Hotels, motels, etc.—Western Europe
Immigration and emigration—Western Europe
Investments, European
Investments, Italian—Western Europe
Military research—Western Europe
Motorcycle racing—Western Europe
Nuclear research—Western Europe
Obscenity (Law)—Western Europe
Opera—Western Europe
Passports—Western Europe
Poor—Western Europe
Privatization—Western Europe
Public welfare—Western Europe
Radio broadcasting—Western Europe
Radioactive waste disposal—Western Europe
Railroads—Western Europe
Resorts—Western Europe
Rhine River
Science—Western Europe
Securities—Western Europe
Skis and skiing—Western Europe
Space research—Western Europe
Stone Age—Western Europe
Taxation—Western Europe
Technology—Western Europe
Television broadcasting—Western Europe
Terrorism—Western Europe
Unemployment—Western Europe
Value added tax—Western Europe
Civilization
Vive la différence! [comparison of Chinese and Western civilizations in the 1880s; excerpt from Nouvelles lettres édifiantes et curieuses d'Extrême-Occident par des voyageurs lettrés chinois à la Belle Epoque] T.-C. Yuan. il *Courier* 40:28-9 Ap '87
Climate
On the continent, growth is in the deep freeze. J. Templeman. il *Bus Week* p46 F 2 '87
Commerce
See also
Coordinating Committee on Multilateral Export Controls
European Economic Community
Basking in Europhoria. C. Redman. il *Time* 130:48 O 19 '87
Iran
See Iran—Commerce—Western Europe
Japan
See Japan—Commerce—Western Europe
Persian Gulf region
Protecting allied security [European ships] il *Macleans* 100:27 O 5 '87
Troubled waters [European and Japanese dependence on oil from the Persian Gulf] il *Time* 129:22 Je 1 '87
Why Europe and Japan won't help. F. Willey. il *Newsweek* 109:35 Je 8 '87

Western Europe—Commerce—*cont.*
United States
See United States—Commerce—Western Europe
Commercial policy
See also
European Economic Community
Defenses
See also
Airplanes, Military—Western Europe
Airplanes, Military transport—Western Europe
Aviation, Military—Western Europe
Guided missiles, European
North Atlantic Treaty Organization
Remotely piloted vehicles—Western Europe
United States—Armed Forces—Forces in Europe
Big idea, little future: Europe eyes own defenses. H. Trewhitt. il *U S News World Rep* 103:36 Jl 20 '87
Defence of a continent. P. Lewis. il *Macleans* 100:28-9 O 5 '87
Entering the postnuclear age. E. N. Luttwak. il *N Y Times Mag* p49+ Ap 5 '87
Europe at 30. R. J. Gwyn. il *World Press Rev* 34:21-3 My '87
Europe should begin to assert itself. H. Schmidt. il *World Press Rev* 34:21-3 F '87
A European strategy for peace. E. Rothschild. il *N Y Times Mag* p48-9 Ap 5 '87
Finlandizing Europe. J. McLaughlin. *Natl Rev* 39:20 D 31 '87
Other items on the agenda. *World Press Rev* 34:17-18 N '87
Description and travel
See also
Automobile driving—Western Europe
Automobile touring—Western Europe
Europe countdown '87. il *Glamour* 85:246-8+ Mr '87
It's not too late to go to Europe. B. Bauer. il *U S News World Rep* 103:46-7 Jl 27 '87
See Europe by train [Eurailpass] il *Glamour* 85:170+ Je '87
Too expensive now to go to Europe? Guess again. B. Bauer. il *U S News World Rep* 102:48-9 Ap 6 '87
Tours d'argent. B. Kallen. il *Forbes* 139:150 My 4 '87
Economic conditions
Europe can't move any faster than Germany. J. Templeman. il *Bus Week* p50-1 Ap 6 '87
Europe's quiet revolution [interview with R. Prodi] S. Solomon. il por *Forbes* 140:52+ D 14 '87
Europe's recovery keeps rolling [views of Time's European Board of Economists] C. Redman. il *Time* 129:50-1 F 9 '87
Has Europe's growth peaked? [views of Time's European Board of Economists] C. Redman. il *Time* 130:34 Ag 10 '87
On the continent, growth is in the deep freeze. J. Templeman. il *Bus Week* p46 F 2 '87
Stagnation in Europe. R. J. Samuelson. il *Newsweek* 110:66 O 19 '87
Economic relations
Germany (West)
See Germany (West)—Economic relations—Western Europe
Foreign relations
See also
North Atlantic Treaty Organization
Soviet Union
See Soviet Union—Foreign relations—Western Europe
Turkey
See Turkey—Foreign relations—Western Europe
United States
See United States—Foreign relations—Western Europe
Industries
See also
Aerospace industries—Western Europe
Airbus Industrie
Airlines—Acquisitions and mergers—Western Europe
Airlines—Western Europe
Airplane industry—Western Europe
Arianespace
Audio equipment industry—Western Europe
Automobile industry—Acquisitions and mergers—Western Europe
Automobile industry—Western Europe
Clothing industry—Western Europe
Corporations—Acquisitions and mergers—Western Europe
Electric industries—Acquisitions and mergers—Western Europe

Electronic industries—Acquisitions and mergers—Western Europe
Guided missile industries—Western Europe
Helicopter industry—Western Europe
Investment banking—Acquisitions and mergers—Western Europe
Munitions—Western Europe
Panavia Aircraft GmbH
Small business—Western Europe
Telephone companies—Western Europe
Television industry—Western Europe
Tourist trade—Western Europe
Trading companies—Western Europe
Turbo-Union, Ltd.
Basking in Europhoria. C. Redman. il *Time* 130:48 O 19 '87
Politics and government
See also
Conservatism—Western Europe
Elections—Western Europe
Green Party (Western Europe)
Politics, Corruption in—Western Europe
Socialism—Western Europe
Western Europe—Royal families
Europe should begin to assert itself. H. Schmidt. il *World Press Rev* 34:21-3 F '87
The lessons of defeat. D. Singer. *Nation* 245:81-4 Ag 1-8 '87
Population
See also
Immigrants—Western Europe
Race relations
No foreigners needed here. X. Mellish. *Progressive* 51:14-15 My '87
Religious institutions and affairs
See also
Church and state—Western Europe
Sanctuary movement (Refugee aid)—Western Europe
Royal families
Europe's other royals. P. Lewis. il *Macleans* 100:34 Jl 27 '87
Western Europe-United States air agreements *See* Aviation—International aspects
Western films *See* Motion pictures—Westerns
Western Hemisphere *See* America
Western Hemisphere Affairs Subcommittee *See* United States. Congress. House. Committee on Foreign Affairs. Subcommittee on Western Hemisphere Affairs
Western Home Awards
Western Home Awards 1987-1988 [cover story] il *Sunset* 179:71-89 O '87
Western Home Awards are coming up. Meet our distinguished jury. il *Sunset* 178:284 My '87
Western Publishing Co.
Western: marketing on a massive scale. T. Unsworth. *Publ Wkly* 232:53 S 11 '87
Western Sahara
See also
United Nations—Western Sahara
Western Sahara conflict, 1975-
Endless desert war. B. Shelby. *World Press Rev* 34:40 Ag '87
Secretary-General discusses Western Sahara with King Hassan of Morocco. *UN Chron* 23:76 N '86
Western States
See also
Air pollution—Western States
Architecture, Domestic—Western States
Birds—Western States
Camping—Western States
Colleges and universities—Western States
Cowboys
Cycling—Western States
Fishing—Western States
Gardens and gardening—Western States
Gold mines and mining—Western States
Hunting—Western States
Irrigation—Western States
Lakes—Western States
Music festivals—Western States
National forests—Western States
National parks and reserves—Western States
Paleontology—Western States
Public lands—Western States
Resorts—Western States
Restaurants—Western States
Skis and skiing—Western States
Water pollution—Western States
Water supply—Western States
Westerners
Wildlife management—Western States

Western States—See also—cont.
Yellowstone National Park

Description and travel

[Month] travel in the West. See issues of Sunset (Central edition)

Of prairie dogs, VCR's and Indian scouts [retracing Lewis and Clark; interview with D. Duncan] A. P. Sanoff. il por map *U S News World Rep* 103:72 Jl 6 '87

Reach for your road map, pardner—and head west. S. D. Atchison. il *Bus Week* p111 Je 15 '87

Forest fires

See Forest fires

History

See also

Frontier and pioneer life—Western States
Lewis and Clark Expedition

Who are the Westerners? W. E. Stegner. il *Am Herit* 38:34-41 D '87

Western States in art

Charles Deas. C. Clark. il por *Am Hist Illus* 22:18-33 Ap '87

Painting the American frontier [excerpt from American frontier life] P. H. Hassrick. il *Nat Hist* 96:36-41 My '87

Rancho La Vista: western themes in California's Ojai Valley [western art collector V. Milner] M. Webb. il pors *Archit Dig* 44:112-19 D '87

Exhibitions

Frontier life: portrayals of the American West [American frontier life: early western painting and prints] L. Ayres. il *USA Today (Periodical)* 116:76-83 N '87

Western States in literature

See also

Cowboy poetry
Western stories

Western stories

Anecdotes, facetiae, satire, etc.

Your book saved my life, Mister. G. Keillor. *New Yorker* 63:40-1 D 28 '87

Authorship

PW interviews [I. Doig] W. Smith. por *Publ Wkly* 232:156-7 S 18 '87

Writing realistic Western fiction. E. Kelton. il *Writer* 100:11-13 My '87

Western Union Corporation

The Drexel connection [potential partners in Western Union takeover offer scared off by Pacific Asset's dealings with Drexel] J. Crudele. *N Y* 20:24 Ap 20 '87

Drexel's heavy hand [bid to restructure Western Union] C. Friday. il *Newsweek* 110:53+ N 23 '87

The sad saga of Western Union's decline. A. Bianco. il pors *Bus Week* p108-10+ D 14 '87

Western wear

A cowboy Christmas. il *Sunset* 179:88-90 D '87

Hats, boots, chaps, neckerchiefs, dusters, and more: western wear by mail. *Sunset* 179:62-3 D '87

Westerners

Who are the Westerners? W. E. Stegner. il *Am Herit* 38:34-41 D '87

Photographs and photography

Through Eastern eyes [R. Avedon's In the American West] M. Kozloff. il *Art Am* 75:90-7 Ja '87

Westfall, Stephen

Melancholy mapping. il *Art Am* 75:104-9 F '87

Westfield Group

"You keep your eyes and ears open" [Westfield Group media buys] T. Jaffe. por *Forbes* 139:36 Ap 6 '87

Westheimer, Frank H.

Are our universities rotten at the "core"? [adaptation of address, February 23, 1987] bibl f *Science* 236:1165-6 Je 5 '87

The core curriculum [discussion of June 5, 1987 article, Are our universities rotten at the core?] *Science* 237:474-5 Jl 31 '87

Why nature chose phosphates. bibl f il *Science* 235:1173-8 Mr 6 '87

Westheimer, Ruth

Dr. Ruth says: oh, grow up! il por *Redbook* 169:106-7+ My '87

about

Over the Alps and through the shops with Dr. Ruth. G. Jaynes. il pors *Life* 10:127-8+ N '87

Westies (Gang)

The lords of Hell's Kitchen. J. Traub. il pors *N Y Times Mag* p38+ Ap 5 '87

Westinghouse Electric Corp.

Danforth picks his heirs [J. C. Marous and P. E. Lego] G. L. Miles and M. Rothman. *Bus Week* p26-7 Ag 10 '87

Most improved. il *Forbes* 139:116 Ja 12 '87

The toxic waste battle is boiling over [court fight with insurers] M. Schroeder. il *Bus Week* p73-4 Ag 3 '87

Westinghouse-Airship joint venture wins Navy aerial surveillance contract. *Aviat Week Space Technol* 126:69 Je 15 '87

Westinghouse seeks top position as supplier of airborne EW systems [electronic warfare] il *Aviat Week Space Technol* 126:76-8 F 16 '87

Westinghouse unit prepared to buy space module hardware [Industrial Space Facility] *Aviat Week Space Technol* 127:28-9 S 7 '87

Westinghouse Science Talent Search *See* Science Talent Search

Westlake, Melvyn

Trouble in the third world's environment. *World Press Rev* 34:53 Jl '87

Westland plc

British research funding method hampers rotary-wing developments. il *Aviat Week Space Technol* 126:105-7+ Ja 19 '87

Westminster Kennel Club show *See* Dog shows

Westmoreland, William C.

about

The press on trial. R. M. Dworkin. bibl f il *N Y Rev Books* 34:27-37 F 26 '87

Westy's revenge [cover story] F. Barnes. *New Repub* 196:21+ Ap 6 '87

Westoff, Leslie Aldridge

A Faulkner flirtation. il por *N Y Times Mag* p69+ My 10 '87

Weston, Carol

10 ways to keep your marriage strong [excerpt from How to honeymoon] il *Essence* 18:65-6+ N '87

Weston, Edward, 1886-1958

about

Edward Weston. G. Morris. il *Art News* 86:37 Ap '87

Supreme instants: photography of Edward Weston. T. Pitts and N. Solomon. il por *USA Today (Periodical)* 116:56-65 N '87

Weston, Randy

about

Randy Weston. F. Bouchard. il por *Down Beat* 54:13 Ag '87

Weston, Susan B.

How do you tell a good science fiction story? *Writer* 100:18-20 S '87

Westport Ballet Theater

Small is beautiful for Kansas City's "other" ballet. J. Williams. il *Dance Mag* 61:18 My '87

Westwood, Vivienne

about

For Britain's Vivienne Westwood, the mother of punk, it's the prophet motive that counts. B. Johnson. il pors *People Wkly* 27:66-8 My 4 '87

Westwood (Los Angeles, Calif.) *See* Los Angeles (Calif.)

Westwood One, Inc.

Jumping Jack strikes again [J. Welch sells NBC Radio Network] P. Elmer-Dewitt. il *Time* 130:44 Ag 3 '87

The Norman conquest [N. Pattiz] C. Capuzzi. il pors *Channels* 7:28-31+ Ap '87

Radio days. M. Beauchamp. il *Forbes* 140:200+ N 30 '87

Radio's new golden age. A. Miller. il *Newsweek* 110:41 Ag 3 '87

Wet flies *See* Fishing lures, flies, etc.

Wet nurses

Wet-nursing boom in England explored [research by Valerie Fildes] G. Kolata. il *Science* 235:745-7 F 13 '87

Wetlands

See also

Estuarine area conservation
Marshes

Coastal wetland management: the advance designation approach. R. H. Platt. bibl f il maps *Environment* 29:16-20+ N '87

The swampbusters. L. Williamson. il *Outdoor Life* 179:42-3 F '87

US forested wetlands: 1940-1980 [Forest Service surveys] Y. Abernethy and R. E. Turner. bibl il maps *BioScience* 37:721-7 N '87

Wetlands: fortifying federal and regional cooperation. M. F. Baldwin. bibl f il *Environment* 29:16-20+ S '87

California

Empty the skies [loss of wetland habitat for migrating water birds] P. Steinhart. il maps *Audubon* 89:70-97 N '87

A salt marsh in L.A.(!) and other good news. R. L. Di Silvestro. il *Audubon* 89:98-9 N '87

Wetlands—*cont.*

Canada

Biogenic sulfur and the acidity of rainfall in remote areas of Canada. J. O. Nriagu and others. bibl f il *Science* 237:1189-92 S 4 '87

Sulfur that doesn't stay put [study by Jerome O. Nriagu and others] *Sci News* 132:204 S 26 '87

Connecticut

". . . and then I heard the chain saws". C. N. Barnard. il *Natl Wildl* 26:46-9 D '87/Ja '88

Florida

See also

Everglades (Fla.)

Illinois

Of dumps, Chicago politics & herons [environmentalists fight to save wetlands threatened by landfill] J. Sullivan. il *Audubon* 89:122-6 Mr '87

Louisiana

See also

Bayous

Louisiana's bayou blues. F. Gibney. il map *Newsweek* 109:54-5 Je 22 '87

Mississippi

The Army's giant swampbuster [proposed draining of Yazoo Backwater Swamp] J. McCafferty. il *Sierra* 72:84-5 Jl/Ag '87

Missouri

Swamps, towns, and football downs [proposed St. Louis Cardinals stadium in the Missouri Bottoms] R. R. Pryor. il *Sierra* 72:136-7 Ja/F '87

Wetmore family

about

The golden age of Newport. A. Pryce-Jones. il *House Gard* 159:190-7+ Je '87

Wetterau Incorporated

Wetterau: fat and sassy from food wholesaling. il *Money* 16:8 F '87

Wettstein, Mike, Jr., and Gormican, John

Steel workers on the line. *Progressive* 51:15-16 Ja '87

Wetzel, Heinz

A historic German visit. il *Macleans* 100:19 S 14 '87

Wetzsteon, Ross

A double fault for U.S. tennis. il *Sport Mag* 78:64-7 Ja '87

Hot commodities: will the man shortage spoil men? *Mademoiselle* 93:184-5+ F '87

Lone star. il pors *N Y* 20:92-4+ D 7 '87

Unglaublich! il pors *Sport Mag* 78:35-40 D '87

What's eating Jim Rice? il pors *Sport Mag* 78:40-1+ Je '87

Wexford Festival *See* Music festivals—Great Britain

Wexler, Anne

about

The powers that shouldn't be: five Washington insiders the next Democratic president shouldn't hire [cover story] P. Glastris. pors *Wash Mon* 19:39-46+ O '87

Wexner, Leslie H.

about

The battle of Bendel's. J. Kornbluth. il pors *N Y* 20:26-33 F 23 '87

The Unlimited? [cover story] S. B. Weiner. il *Forbes* 139:76-80 Ap 6 '87

Weyland, Jack

about

Physics, Hollywood style. B. Lawren. *Omni* 9:35 Je '87

Weymouth, George A.

about

George A. Weymouth. M. S. Doherty. il pors *Am Artist* 51:32-7+ Ja '87

Weymouth, Lally

Black Monday and beyond: a talk with Bill Bradley. il pors *N Y* 20:56-9 D 14 '87

From Nixon to Lincoln. il pors *N Y* 20:42-7 Ag 31 '87

Weyr, Thomas

A new broom at the AAP. il pors *Publ Wkly* 232:16-20 N 6 '87

UPs and the trade book. *Publ Wkly* 231:23-4 Je 5 '87

Weyrich, Paul

(jt. auth) See Schlafly, Phyllis, and Weyrich, Paul

WFAN (New York, N.Y.: Radio station) *See* Radio stations

WFFA (Dallas, Tex.: Television station) *See* Television stations

WGN (Chicago, Ill.: Television station) *See* Television stations

WGPR (Detroit, Mich.: Television station) *See* Television stations, Black

Whalen, D. H., and Liberman, Alvin M.

Speech perception takes precedence over nonspeech perception. bibl f il *Science* 237:169-71 Jl 10 '87

Whales

See also

International Whaling Commission

Whaling

Boning up on bowhead habitats [work of Donald M. Schell and others] S. Weisburd. *Sci News* 131:6-7 Ja 3 '87

Born free—home free [New England Aquarium saves pilot whales] M. Starr. il *Newsweek* 110:56 Jl 13 '87

Cape Cod diarist [whale watching] H. Hertzberg. *New Repub* 197:42 S 7 '87

A fluke to call your very own [whale adoption programs] M. Gaines. il *Sierra* 72:13 N/D '87

Gray whales at play in Baja's San Ignacio Lagoon. S. L. Swartz and M. L. Jones. il maps *Natl Geogr* 171:754-71 Je '87

Of whales and weather [biotelemetry tracking of whales in deep water; work of Bruce Mate] S. Strauss. il *Technol Rev* 90:11 Jl '87

Stranded whales [discussion of June 1987 article, Why do whales strand?] R. Ellis. *Oceans* 20:3+ Jl/Ag '87

Tails of whales and fins, too. P. F. Major. il *Sea Front* 33:90-6 Mr/Ap '87

Updates. G. Reiger. *Field Stream* 91:15-16+ F '87

Watching the whales [cover story] E. Kenney. il *Conservationist* 42:24-31 S/O '87

Whale encounter during a yacht race [California gray whale off Rosarito Beach, Mexico] il *Sea Front* 33:61-2 Ja/F '87

Whale tracking is all up in the air [work of Bruce R. Mate] K. Hartley. il *Sci News* 132:118 Ag 22 '87

Whales' new lease on life [pilot whales saved by New England Aquarium] M. B. Simpson. il *Oceans* 20:57-8 S/O '87

Why do whales strand? R. Ellis. il *Oceans* 20:24-9+ My/Je '87

Food and feeding

Sonic punch: dolphins and whales generate "bangs" that may stun prey [research by Kenneth Marten and Kenneth S. Norris] T. Beardsley. *Sci Am* 257:36 O '87

Whales and walruses as tillers of the sea floor [side-scan sonar studies of the Bering Sea] C. H. Nelson and K. R. Johnson. il maps *Sci Am* 256:112-17 F '87

Whales, Fossil

Whale of a discovery [Seymour Island] *Sea Front* 33:303 Jl/Ag '87

Whales, Killer *See* Killer whales

The whales of August [film] *See* Motion picture reviews—Single works

Whaling

See also

International Whaling Commission

History

Captain Scammon: the whaler who turned naturalist. D. Rutherford. il pors map *Sea Front* 33:18-26 Ja/F '87

Editorial. W. Garrett. il *Antiques* 132:1278-9 D '87

Azores

Whaling in the Azores [reenactment during Sea Week] R. B. Silverman. il *Sea Front* 33:174-82 My/Je '87

Faroe Islands

Whales off the Faeroe Islands. L. Lockett. por *Newsweek* 110:11 N 23 '87

Iceland

Research whaling on the table. J. Walsh. *Science* 237:481 Jl 31 '87

Japan

Deadly experiments [government sponsored whale hunt called a scientific study] B. Wallace. il *Macleans* 100:53 S 7 '87

Whalum, Wendell, 1931-1987

about

Obituary

Jet il por 72:7 Je 29 '87

Wharncliffe, Richard Wortley, 5th Earl of

about

Richard Wortley, a Yankee from Maine, joins Britain's ruling class as the new Earl of Wharncliffe. W. Plummer. il por *People Wkly* 27:94-5 Je 29 '87

Wharton, Clifton R.

"Demanding families" and black student achievement. *Educ Dig* 52:18-20 My '87

about

Clifton R. Wharton Jr.: the nation's highest-paid black executive. il pors *Ebony* 42:29-30+ S '87

Wharton to head fund. P. A. Jones. por *Black Enterp* 17:16 Ja '87

Wharton, Donald
Caulked boots and white water. il *Conservationist* 41:38-43 Mr/Ap '87
Wharton, Edith, 1862-1937
about
Edith Wharton: on her 125th anniversary. A. Berman. il por *Archit Dig* 44:310+ N '87
Wharton, William
about
Who is William Wharton? E. V. Nagel. il *Horizon* 30:33-5 My '87
Wharton School
Their eyes are on the main chance. R. Greene. il *Forbes* 139:69-72 Mr 9 '87
WHCLIS *See* White House Conference on Library and Information Services
Whealy, Kent
about
Kent Whealy's seedy operation provides garden variety veggies from centuries past. N. Geeslin. il por *People Wkly* 27:91-2 My 11 '87
Wheat
Monitoring biosynthesis of wheat cell-wall phenyl-propanoids in situ. N. G. Lewis and others. bibl f il *Science* 237:1344-6 S 11 '87
Cultivation
Beans in wheat . . . and weeds in both [relay intercropping] D. Ohrtman. il *Success Farm* 85 no4:18AH F '87
Hybrids
Hybrid wheat bulls pull in their horns. *Success Farm* 85:56L N '87
Prices
See also
Agricultural administration
Seeding
Anhydrous on drill, but seed feels no pain [no-till wheat] M. Holmberg. il *Success Farm* 85 no1:30 Ja '87
Wheat trade
One good subsidy merits another [U.S. subsidizes wheat sale to Soviet Union] *Newsweek* 109:61 My 11 '87
Seeds of discontent [Prairie Provinces, Canada] A. Walmsley. il *Macleans* 100:30-1 Ap 6 '87
Wheatland Conference on Literature *See* Authors' conferences
Wheaton, Wil
about
Hunks & heartthrobs. pors *Teen* 31:54 Mr '87
Young Wil Wheaton. D. Scheuer. por *Sch Update* 119:28 Mr 9 '87
Wheaton (Md.)
Galleries and museums
See also
National Capital Trolley Museum
Wheaton College (Norton, Mass.)
A sisterhood under siege [Wheaton to go coed] E. Salholz. il *Newsweek* 109:77 Mr 30 '87
Wheel balancing *See* Motorcycles—Wheels
Wheel of fortune [television program] *See* Television program reviews—Single works
Wheelbarrows, Toy *See* Toys
Wheelchair athletics *See* Handicapped—Sports
Wheelchairs
See also
Everest & Jennings International
Stair-climbing wheelchair [Rollsteiger] B. Most. il *Pop Sci* 230:108 Ap '87
Wheeler, Anne
about
The stepfather [film] Reviews
Vogue il 177:34 Je '87. M. Haskell
Wheeler, David
about
One of each, please. B. Barol. il pors *Newsweek* 109:54-5 Ap 6 '87
Wheeler, Gerald F.
about
AAPT elects Wheeler to be its new president in 1988. por *Phys Today* 40:72 Ap '87
Wheeler, J. Craig, and Harkness, Robert P.
Helium-rich supernovas. bibl (p150) il *Sci Am* 257:50-8 N '87
Wheeler, Lonnie
Tailgating: nobody does it better than seniors! il *50 Plus* 27:68-70 S '87
Wheelock, William Efner
about
The William Efner Wheelock Collection at the East Hampton Historical Society. J. A. Graybeal and P. M. Kenny. bibl f il *Antiques* 132:328-39 Ag '87

Wheels
See also
Automobiles—Wheels
Motorcycles—Wheels
Wheels, Toy *See* Toys
Wheetley, Kim Alan
Drama/theatre education: what K-12 teachers need to know and be able to do. bibl f *Des Arts Educ* 89:36-40 S/O '87
Whelan, Clémentine
Learning democracy's ways. il *Américas* 39:50-2 S/O '87
Whelan, Elizabeth M.
AIDS: everything you must know [special issue] bibl il por map *USA Today (Periodical)* 116:1-16 O '87
Health hoax and a health scare [address, September 22, 1987] il *Vital Speeches Day* 54:57-61 N 1 '87
The truth about Americans' health [cover story] il *USA Today (Periodical)* 115:54-8 My '87
Whelan, Elizabeth M., and Olsen, Robert E.
U.S. cholesterol guidelines are off-target. il *Consum Res Mag* 70:36-7 D '87
Whelan, Jack
Letter from Seattle. *America* 156:463-5+ Je 6 '87
Where the Wild Things are [opera] *See* Knussen, Oliver, 1952-
Whetstine, Roy
about
The kindest cut of all turns stone-broke Roy Whetstine's $10 buy into a million-buck rock of ages. K. Demaret. il pors *People Wkly* 27:79+ F 16 '87
Whey
Wrong whey [false claims for Rockland Corporation beverage mix] il *FDA Consum* 21:38 D '87/Ja '88
Whidah (Ship)
The truth about pirates. B. Lawren. il *Omni* 9:30+ Je '87
Whidden, Tom
How we won the Cup. il por *Mot Boat Sail* 159:30+ Ap '87
Whiddon, Jim
about
Jim Whiddon. G. Parrill. il por *Road Track* 38:198 Je '87
Whimbey, Arthur
A 15th-grade reading level for high school seniors? il *Phi Delta Kappan* 69:207 N '87
Whining
Winning against whining. T. F. Murphy. il *Parents* 62:110-12 Ag '87
Whipple, Fred Lawrence, 1906-
The black heart of Comet Halley. il *Sky Telesc* 73:242-5 Mr '87
Whipple House (Ipswich, Mass.) *See* Ipswich (Mass.)—Historic houses, sites, etc.
Whiptail lizard sexual behavior *See* Sexual behavior—Reptiles
Whirlwinds
UFO update [circles of flattened grain in southern England fields possibly a hoax; research by Paul Fuller and Terence Meaden] J. Randles. il *Omni* 10:141 O '87
Whiskers *See* Beards
Whiskey
The scotch for purists: single-malt. T. Segal. il *Bus Week* p124 Mr 9 '87
Single-malt scotch—an acquired taste. E. Fried. il *Black Enterp* 17:70 Ap '87
The whistle blower [film] *See* Motion picture reviews—Single works
Whistle blowing (Public interest)
Think before you blow the whistle. J. A. Byrne. il *Bus Week* p161 My 18 '87
A whistle-blower. D. Rosendale. il *N Y Times Mag* p56 Je 7 '87
Laws and regulations
A good deed that pays. *Consum Rep* 52:329 Je '87
Revisions to fraud statute aid suit against Raytheon. *Aviat Week Space Technol* 127:27 N 9 '87
Whistler (B.C.: Resort) *See* Resorts—British Columbia
Whiston, William, 1667-1752
about
The godfather of disaster. S. J. Gould. il *Nat Hist* 96:20+ S '87
Whitaker, Charles
TV's new daytime darling [cover story] il pors *Saturday Evening Post* 259:42-5 Jl/Ag '87
Whitaker, Eileen Monaghan, 1911-
about
Eileen Monaghan Whitaker: painting from the heart. J. Lovoos. il por *Am Artist* 51:36-41 Mr '87

Whitaker, James, 1931-
 A triumphant transformation: Fergie's first year. il pors *McCalls* 114:32-4+ Je '87
White, Armond
 The 16th New Directors/New Films Series. il *Film Comment* 23:64+ My/Je '87
 Amour fools. il *Film Comment* 23:26-31 Ja/F '87
 Apartheid chic. il *Film Comment* 23:11-12+ N/D '87
 Class clowns. il *Film Comment* 23:11-14 Mr/Ap '87
 Margaret Mead Film Festival. *Nation* 245:353-4 O 3 '87
 Running on recall. il *Film Comment* 23:72+ Jl/Ag '87
White, Betty
 "Let's get personal" [excerpt from Betty White in person] il pors *Redbook* 169:138-41+ O '87
White, Christopher
 Our classroom is the whole outdoors. il *Conservationist* 41:42-7 My/Je '87
White, Claire Nicolas
 A rain of paper confetti. il *Commonweal* 114:134-5 Mr 13 '87
White, Constance C. R.
 The new racists. il *Ms* 16:68 O '87
White, Dana
 Glasses for sport. il *Skiing* 39:53-7 Spr '87
White, David
 Growing unrest. il *World Press Rev* 34:29-30 Ap '87
White, David Cowden
 Methodists involved in Fiji coup. *Christ Century* 104:548-9 Je 17-24 '87
White, David R.
			about
 Dance Magazine Awards 1987. il pors *Dance Mag* 61:44-6 F '87
 Sixties in the eighties: programming the revolution. J. R. Acocella. il pors *Dance Mag* 61:70-3 F '87
White, Devon
			about
 Devon White. M. Toll. por *Sports Illus* 67:44+ Jl 13 '87
White, Frank, III
 Avery Brooks: a.k.a. Hawk. il pors *Ebony* 42:62+ Ap '87
 Full speed ahead at 94. il pors *Ebony* 42:52-4+ Je '87
 Introducing: Mario Van Peebles. il pors *Ebony* 42:80+ My '87
 Janet Norfleet: in charge of the world's largest post office. il pors *Ebony* 42:80+ Jl '87
 June and Judy Thaxton: twins in engineering. il pors *Ebony* 42:116+ Mr '87
 A star is reborn. il pors *Ebony* 42:104+ F '87
White, Gary L.
			about
 Gary White leads biggest U.S. minority trucking firm. *Jet* 72:36 S 7 '87
White, Sir Gordon
			about
 Beware the Romeo raider. C. Knowlton. il por *Fortune* 115:42 Ja 5 '87
White, Jackie
			about
 Trotters quietly sign their 2nd woman player. il por *Jet* 71:48 Ja 19 '87
White, James F.
 Moving Christian worship toward social justice. il *Christ Century* 104:558-60 Je 17-24 '87
White, Joyce
 What's new about wines? They blush! il *Essence* 18:112 My '87
White, Juanita Mitchell
			about
 S.C. rep. Juanita White elected to committee post. por *Jet* 72:24 Ag 24 '87
White, Lorenzo
			about
 Lorenzo White. M. Bishop. il por *Sports Illus* 67:83 Ag 31 '87
White, Merry I.
			about
 A society where students are no. 1 [interview] il por *U S News World Rep* 102:65 Ja 19 '87
 Zen and the art of cultural misappropriation. J. Rowe. *Wash Mon* 19:49-52 My '87
White, Michael
 Neil in the 'lion's den'. il *World Press Rev* 34:13-14 My '87
White, Nancy J.
 My husband is cheating on me. il *Ladies Home J* 104:14+ Ap '87
White, Nicholas E.
 New-wave pulsars. il *Sky Telesc* 73:22-4 Ja '87

White, Peter T.
 Laos. il maps *Natl Geogr* 171:772-95 Je '87
White, Philip M.
 Transplanting trees and shrubs in the fall. il *Ctry J* 14:32-4 N '87
White, Phyllis L.
 Evaluating elementary principals. il *Phi Delta Kappan* 69:143-4 O '87
White, Robert H.
			about
 From working stiff to political hero. E. B. Terry. il por *Bus Week* p60-1 Mr 30 '87
 White knight on a crusade. M. McIver. il por *Macleans* 100:34 Jl 13 '87
White, Robert J.
			about
 Unorthodox behavior. G. Emerson. il *Macleans* 100:17 Je 8 '87
White, Robert J.
 Bioethical shock. il *America* 156:174-6 F 28 '87
White, Robert M.
 The challenge to U.S. competitiveness. *Science* 236:1041 My 29 '87
 Magnetic engineering. *Phys Today* 40:89 N '87
White, Roger J.
			about
 A Christmas dinner "for sale". J. Siroto. il por *McCalls* 114:63-5 Ja '87
White, Ryan
			about
 AIDS: a diary of the plague in America [cover story] J. Friedman and D. Van Biema. il pors *People Wkly* 28:61-4+ Ag 3 '87
 An AIDS patient's fight for life. M. Nichols. il por *Sch Update* 119:4 Ap 20 '87
 Diver Greg Louganis returns to dancing, his first love, before the eyes of his pal Ryan White. W. Plummer. il pors *People Wkly* 28:44-5 N 9 '87
White, Stephen W.
 Whither education reform? *Humanist* 47:24-6+ My/Je '87
White, Timothy
 Rebel with a cause. il pors *N Y Times Mag* p40-1+ S 27 '87
White, Vanna
 Vanna speaks [excerpt]; ed. by Patricia Romanowski. il pors *Ladies Home J* 104:94-5+ My '87
 The world of Vanna [excerpt from Vanna speaks]; ed. by Patricia Romanowski. il por *Ladies Home J* 104:40+ Je '87
			about
 The celebrity wheel of fortune. J. Saltzman. *USA Today (Periodical)* 115:41 My '87
 Her f ce is f mili r. R. Jackson. il por *Sports Illus* 66:24 Je 1 '87
 The millionaire who made Vanna White a star. V. Scott. il pors *Good Housekeep* 204:66+ My '87
 Oh, Vanna! [cover story] T. Klein. il pors *Saturday Evening Post* 259:42-3+ My/Je '87
 Pat Sajak: Vanna White and me. V. Scott. il pors *Good Housekeep* 205:34+ N '87
 Vanna squeaks. B. G. Harrison. *Mademoiselle* 93:148 O '87
 What a deal! H. F. Waters. il pors *Newsweek* 109:62-8 F 9 '87
White, Wallace, 1930-
 The Big Singing. il *New Yorker* 62:78-84+ Ja 19 '87
White, Wendy
 Envy: the enemy you should befriend. il *Teen* 31:62+ My '87
 Keep living: dealing with death. il *Teen* 31:52+ O '87
 Putting the brakes on drunk driving. il *Teen* 31:22+ Mr '87
White, William
 Three great meals. *New Yorker* 63:28-9 Je 1 '87
White
 The quality of white [decorative effects] M. Hampton. il *House Gard* 159:44+ Jl '87
 The versatility of white. il *Glamour* 85:182-4 Jl '87
White blood cells *See* Leukocytes
White chocolate desserts *See* Desserts
White collar crimes *See* Commercial crimes
White collar workers
 Is America over-managed? [dismal white collar productivity] il *World Press Rev* 34:55 F '87
			Salaries, pensions, etc.
 BLS prepares to broaden scope of its white-collar pay survey. J. D. Morton. bibl f il *Mon Labor Rev* 110:3-7 Mr '87
 Survey planning [Bureau of Labor Statistics] *Mon Labor Rev* 110:2 S '87

White collar workers—Salaries, pensions, etc.—*cont.*
White-collar salaries. il *Mon Labor Rev* 110:2 Ag '87
White-collar salaries vary widely in the service industries.
C. J. Cooper, Jr. il *Mon Labor Rev* 110:21-3 N '87
White-crowned pigeons *See* Pigeons
White dwarf stars *See* Stars, Dwarf
White flies
Control
What's the diagnosis? W. S. Moore. il *Flower Gard* 31:15 Ag/S '87
White House (Washington, D.C.)
Eighteen acres of harmony [trees on the grounds] H. Sidey. il *Time* 130:25 S 28 '87
Painting tips from the White House. B. Kneemiller. il *Workbench* 43:88-90 Mr/Ap '87
Presidents, imperial and otherwise. G. C. Ward. il *Am Herit* 38:18+ My/Je '87
Employees
Executive toque [chef J. Hill] por *Time* 130:64 Ag 31 '87
White House (Washington, D.C.). Lincoln Bedroom
Maureen Reagan meets Lincoln's ghost. il *Newsweek* 109:29 F 2 '87
White House Conference on Library and Information Services
White House library conference to emphasize literary services [proposed for 1989] H. Fields. *Publ Wkly* 231:15 Ap 24 '87
White House entertaining *See* Government entertaining
White House press corps *See* Presidents—Press relations
Reagan, Ronald, 1911-—Press relations
White House staff *See* Presidents—Staff White House (Washington, D.C.)—Employees
White lies *See* Lying
White Mountain National Forest (N.H. and Me.)
Devils Hopyard, New Hampshire. R. H. Mohlenbrock. il map *Nat Hist* 96:38-40+ O '87
A winner in the White Mountains [appeal of Forest Service plan] *Wilderness* 51:3 Wint '87
White Night Cafe (New York, N.Y.) *See* New York (N.Y.)—Restaurants, nightclubs, bars, etc.
White Sands Missile Range (N.M.)
Star Wars in Orogrande [laser testing site] F. Gibney. il map *Newsweek* 110:42 O 19 '87
White sharks *See* Sharks
White water boating *See* Running rapids
White wines *See* Wine
Whiteflies *See* White flies
Whitehead, John C.
African development: an administration perspective [address, May 7, 1987] *Dep State Bull* 87:15-17 Jl '87
Maintaining the momentum in U.S. foreign policy [address, February 25, 1987] *Dep State Bull* 87:35-6 Ap '87
Terrorism: the challenge and the response [address, December 10, 1986] *Dep State Bull* 87:70-3 F '87
U.S.-Soviet relations [address, March 5, 1987] *Dep State Bull* 87:43-5 My '87
Whitehead, Kenneth D.
Religiously affiliated colleges and American freedom. *America* 156:96-8+ F 7 '87
Whitehead, Kevin
The many sides of Branford Marsalis. il pors *Down Beat* 54:16-19 Mr '87
Steve Lacy [interview] il pors *Down Beat* 54:24-6+ D '87
String Trio of New York: a decade of perseverance. il *Down Beat* 11:26-8 N '87
Tim Berne: beyond the five-year plan. il pors *Down Beat* 54:23-5 Jl '87
Whitehead, Mary Beth
See also
Baby M case
Whitehead, William Grant, d. 1987
about
Obituary
Publ Wkly por 232:20-1 D 18 '87
Whiteley, H. Ellen
Vets on pets. See issues of The Saturday Evening Post beginning January/February 1984
Whiteman, Paul, 1890-1967
about
"The birth of Rhapsody in blue". E. Salzman. il *Stereo Rev* 52:110 Ap '87
Whitemore, Hugh
about
Breaking the code [drama] Reviews
N Y il 20:86-7 N 30 '87. J. Simon
New Yorker 63:121 N 30 '87. E. Oliver
Newsweek il 110:85 N 23 '87. J. Kroll
Time il 130:101 N 23 '87. W. A. Henry

Whiteside, Katherine
Early American pleasures. il *House Gard* 159:110-19+ Jl '87
Gathering moss. il *House Gard* 159:144-9+ My '87
Reshaping a corner of Connecticut. il *House Gard* 159:152-5+ Jl '87
Wing Haven. il *House Gard* 159:166-73+ Je '87
Whiteside, Thomas
C.E.O., TV. *New Yorker* 63:39-40+ Jl 6 '87
Whitesnake (Musical group)
Critics hiss and fans cheer as David Coverdale's Whitesnake slithers up the charts. S. Dougherty. il pors *People Wkly* 28:85-6 O 5 '87
Whitetailed deer *See* Deer
Whitetailed deer hunting *See* Deer hunting
Whitewing dove shooting *See* Pigeon shooting
Whitford, David
(jt. auth) *See* Miller, J. David (Joseph David), 1964-, and Whitford, David
Whitford, Deborah
(ed) *See* Clark, Georgie. Tales from a river woman
Whitford, Genevieve Smith
For you, my children [poem] il *Redbook* 169:31-2 My '87
Whithorn (Scotland)
Antiquities
Scotland's earliest town uncovered? il *Hist Today* 37:3 Ja '87
Whiting, Margaret
about
After three marriages crooner Margaret Whiting lands her ideal in X-rated star Jack Wrangler. J. Stark. il pors *People Wkly* 27:120-1+ My 4 '87
Whitley, Andrew
Peres' big mistake. *World Press Rev* 34:15 Jl '87
Torn between two chariots. *World Press Rev* 34:11 Jl '87
Whitley (William) House State Historic Site *See* Stanford (Ky.)—Historic houses, sites, etc.
Whitman, Bob
about
Running to extremes. M.-C. Wrenn. il pors *Life* 10:46-8+ F '87
Whitman, David
The key to welfare reform. il *Atlantic* 259:22-5 Je '87
Whitman, Martin
about
Who says utilities can't be raider bait? C. Brown. il por *Bus Week* p112 N 23 '87
Whitman, Ruth, 1922-
(tr) *See* Cassian, Nina. September
Whitman, Walt, 1819-1892
about
Editorial. W. Garrett. il *Antiques* 132:288-9 Ag '87
Oscar meets Walt. R. Ellmann. bibl f il *N Y Rev Books* 34:43-4 D 3 '87
Whitmire, Kathryn J.
about
Kathy Whitmire. M. Ivins. il pors *Work Woman* 12:120-2+ Mr '87
Whitmore, Arnold P.
about
Flying high with Church's Chicken. il pors *Ebony* 42:72+ Jl '87
Whitmore, Wanda
Breaking stride in the corporate marathon. il *Black Enterp* 17:56-8+ Mr '87
Whitney, Eli, 1765-1825
about
Eli Whitney's other talent. P. Baida. il *Am Herit* 38:22-3 My/Je '87
Whitney, Phyllis A., 1903-
A matter of life or death: finding a dynamic problem for your story. il *Writer* 100:7-9+ Jl '87
Whitney Biennial *See* Whitney Museum of American Art. Biennial Exhibition
Whitney Museum of American Art
A far, far better thing: the Guggenheim and Whitney redesign their expansion schemes. il *Archit Rec* 175:45+ Ap '87
Growing pains [new expansion plans] M. Filler. il *Art Am* 75:14-19 Jl '87
Heir heads [proposed additions] K. Larson. il *N Y* 20:94-5 Mr 30 '87
Whitney Museum of American Art. Biennial Exhibition
Art. A. C. Danto. *Nation* 244:659-62 My 16 '87
Art smart. il *Harpers Bazaar* 120:150 Ap '87
Artburn. J. Perl. il *Vogue* 177:308-11+ My '87
Good neighbors. K. Larson. il *N Y* 20:122+ Ap 27 '87

Whitney Museum of American Art. Biennial Exhibition
—*cont.*

Navigating a cultural trough. R. Hughes. il *Time* 129:81-2 My 11 '87

A pleasant walk through. J. Gardner. il *Commonweal* 114:356+ Je 5 '87

Two years on. R. Atkins. il *Horizon* 30:29-32 Ap '87

The Whitney's dancing dog. H. Cotter. il *Art News* 86:137 S '87

Whitney Museum of American Art. Independent Study Program

Teaching tomorrow's avant-garde. C. Bromberg. il *Art News* 86:100-3 S '87

Whittaker, Bob

about

With repossession you get egg rolls. P. M. Fielding. il pors *Nations Bus* 75:60 Mr '87

Whittaker, Louis

about

With repossession you get egg rolls. P. M. Fielding. il pors *Nations Bus* 75:60 Mr '87

Whittelsey, Harry

about

A personal best. W. Hoffer. il pors *Nations Bus* 75:93-4 My '87

Whittemore, Meg

Franchising: T-shirt on your back. il *Nations Bus* 75:58-9 My '87

Narrowing the field. il *Nations Bus* 75:34-6 O '87

Whitten, Lisa

On the network. *Essence* 18:114 Jl '87

Whittier, Charles H.

about

The questions lawmakers ask about religion. *Christ Today* 31:66 O 2 '87

Whittington, Jim

about

High-speed heaven. P. A. Janssen. il pors *Mot Boat Sail* 160:32-7+ Jl '87

Whittle, Frank, 1907-

about

The inventions that change our lives often meet with indifference, even active resistance—as did the jet engine. R. M. Adams. *Smithsonian* 18:12 Jl '87

Jet engine milestone. *Aviat Week Space Technol* 126:15 Ap 13 '87

They created the Jet Age. N. Vietmeyer. il *Read Dig* 130:162-6 My '87

Whittlesey, Faith Ryan

about

Keeping Faith. M. Schapiro and E. Burnand. *Nation* 244:42 Ja 17 '87

The petty inquisitors. M. Charen. il *Natl Rev* 39:36+ D 18 '87

Whitton, Margaret

about

After snacking on boyish Michael J. Fox, the sexy Margaret Whitton beefs up for a go at Jack Nicholson. J. Stark. il pors *People Wkly* 27:92-4 Je 1 '87

Whitworth, Jerry A.

See also

Walker family espionage case

WHO *See* World Health Organization

Who (Musical group)

Pete Townshend [interview] D. Fricke. il pors *Roll Stone* p179-80+ N 5-D 10 '87

The Who: the Metropolitan Opera House, New York City, June 7th, 1970. D. Fricke. il *Roll Stone* p74-5 Je 4 '87

Whole-house ventilators *See* Ventilators

Whole wheat bread *See* Bread

Wholesalers, Book *See* Book wholesalers and distributors

Whooping cough

Vaccines and vaccination

See also

DPT vaccine

Whooping cranes *See* Cranes (Birds)

Who's that girl [film] *See* Motion picture reviews—Single works

Who's who in America

Bio-tech [lapses in fact checking] J. Queenan. il *New Repub* 197:12-14 O 12 '87

Whyte, William Hollingsworth

about

Bureaucracy as life. R. J. Samuelson. il *Newsweek* 109:43 Ja 12 '87

Wiarda, Howard J., 1939-

Ethnocentrism and third world development. bibl *Society* 24:55-64 S/O '87

Letters [discussion of Winter 1986-1987 article, Misreading Latin America—again] *Foreign Policy* 67:177-80 Summ '87

United States relations with South America. *Curr Hist* 86:1-4+ Ja '87

WIBC *See* World Institute of Black Communications

Wichita Mountains National Wildlife Refuge (Okla.) *See* Wildlife sanctuaries—Oklahoma

Wick, Charles Z.

Glasnost [address, March 13, 1987] *Vital Speeches Day* 53:418-20 My 1 '87

Wicker, John

about

Interracial couple in Richmond, Va. fight to overcome racism. il pors *Jet* 73:52-5 D 28 '87-Ja 4 '88

Wicker, Marion

about

Interracial couple in Richmond, Va. fight to overcome racism. il pors *Jet* 73:52-5 D 28 '87-Ja 4 '88

Wicker furniture

A darker look for wicker. D. Hastings. il *South Living* 22:152+ S '87

Collectors and collecting

Why wicker? F. Donegan. il *Americana* 15:18-20 S/O '87

Maintenance and repair

Repairing wicker. R. Saunders. il *Home Mech* 83:30 Je '87

Wickers, Brian

A seashell from the Seychelles [poem] *Atlantic* 260:66 Ag '87

Wickes Companies, Inc.

The fix-up artist goes on the attack [S. C. Sigoloff] B. O'Reilly. il pors *Fortune* 115:105 Ja 5 '87

Sanford Sigoloff. S. Toy. il por *Bus Week* Sp Issue:214 Ap 17 '87

Wickett, John F.

Getting your money's worth. il *World Health* p24-5 Ag/S '87

Smallpox showed the world the way. il *World Health* p26-7 Ja/F '87

Wickham, DeWayne

Network to network. il *Black Enterp* 17:123-4+ F '87

Power. bibl il *Black Enterp* 17:52-4+ Ap '87

Wickham, Trevor

WALHI: the Indonesian Environmental Forum. *Environment* 29:2-4 S '87

Wickner, William T.

(jt. auth) See Dalbey, Ross E., and Wickner, William T.

Wicks, Sue

about

Heiress apparent. A. Wolff. il por *Sports Illus* 66:54 F 2 '87

Widdicombe, Judith

about

Domestic terrorism: on the front line at an abortion clinic. M. Kort. il por *Ms* 15:48-51+ My '87

Widdrington, Peter

about

Canada's Labatt has just one way to grow: south. E. B. Terry. il por *Bus Week* p70 N 9 '87

Wide-angle lenses *See* Lenses, Photographic

Wide screen motion pictures *See* Motion pictures—Wide screen films

Widmann, Carlos

The present and the apocalypse. *World Press Rev* 34:51 Mr '87

Widoff, Joyce E.

Blockheads: how to make dimensional photographic caricatures. il *Petersens Photogr Mag* 16:80-1+ D '87

The Widow Claire [drama] *See* Foote, Horton

Widow sacrifice *See* Suttee

Widows

See also

Association of Sicilian Women Against the Mafia

April is a woman. B. Lindeman. il *50 Plus* 27:4-5 Ap '87

Coping with widowhood: 'who am I without my mate?' [excerpt from To live again] G. D. Ginsburg. il por *50 Plus* 27:44-5+ Je '87

Jacqueline Picasso and me: the widow-of-the-great-man syndrome. J. T. Steichen. il por *Ms* 15:76 Mr '87

A second life [excerpt from Getting better all the time] L. Carpenter. il pors *McCalls* 114:142+ Ag '87

To live again: coping with widowhood [excerpt] G. D. Ginsburg. il pors *50 Plus* 27:52+ My '87

What not to say to a widow. L. Becker. il *U S Cathol* 52:28-30 F '87

When I lost my husband. M. Dickens. *Read Dig* 130:114-17 Mr '87

Widows—*cont.*

Economic conditions

With large tuition bills ahead, a widow plans a flexible portfolio of income investments [Joanne Venutolo] B. Hager. il *Money* 16:61 Je '87

Employment

Taking over: how to decide, what to do [woman who inherits a family-owned company when her husband dies] L. Sorenson. *Work Woman* 12:40 Jl '87

Housing

Reflections on a venerable British tradition [dower houses] Lady C. Hesketh. il por *Archit Dig* 44:98+ Je '87

Political activities

Putting the arm on rich, right-wing widows [C. Channell's fund raising activities for the contras] G. Hackett. il por *Newsweek* 109:30 Ap 20 '87

Wiedemann, Carl

New York's famous and historic trees. il *Conservationist* 41:32-7 Mr/Ap '87

Wiedemann, Erich

Is saving the seals killing the Eskimos? il *World Press Rev* 34:35-7 Jl '87

Wieland, Joyce, 1931-

about

The protean vision of Joyce Wieland. G. James. il por *Macleans* 100:53-4 Ap 27 '87

Wiener, Alan D.

The first wave. il *Am Herit* 38:136-8 My/Je '87

Wiener, David

about

Inspiration for would-be designers. J. R. Provey. il por *Home Mech* 83:86-8 O '87

Wiener, Jon

Beatles buy-out. *New Repub* 196:13-14 My 11 '87

The C.I.A. goes back to college. il *Nation* 245:719-20 D 12 '87

Not necessarily the First Lady. *Nation* 245:337 O 3 '87

The odyssey of Daniel Boorstin [cover story] il *Nation* 245:289+ S 26 '87

When historians judge their own. il *Nation* 245:584-6+ N 21 '87

Wiener, Nina

about

Fierce attachments [dance] Reviews

N Y il 20:81 N 30 '87. T. Tobias

Wiener (Nina) and Dancers *See* Nina Wiener and Dancers

Wier, W. G., and others

Cellular and subcellular heterogeneity of [Ca^{2+}]$_i$ in single heart cells revealed by fura-2. bibl f il *Science* 235:325-8 Ja 16 '87

Wiersma, D. A., and Duppen, K.

Picosecond holographic-grating spectroscopy. bibl f il *Science* 237:1147-54 S 4 '87

Wiesel, Elie, 1928-

Was he normal? Human? Poor humanity. il pors *Time* 129:93-4 My 11 '87

about

Broken continuities: Night and White crucifixion [cover story] K. A. Plank. il por *Christ Century* 104:963-6 N 4 '87

Light, darkness and bridges in Norway. R. M. Brown. *Christ Century* 104:5-6 Ja 7-14 '87

Wieseltier, Leon

Democracy and Colonel North. *New Repub* 196:22-5 Ja 26 '87

Wiesenthal, Simon

about

A career of Nazi hunting. M. Gray. il por *Macleans* 100:40 My 25 '87

Wiester, John

Should public schools teach creation science? por *Christ Today* 31:50 S 18 '87

Wiewandt, Thomas A.

Buried alive! il *Natl Wildl* 25:18-19 F/Mr '87

Wife abuse

Battered justice. J. Meier. *Wash Mon* 19:37-45 My '87

Battered wife's dilemma. L. F. Webb. il *Essence* 18:14 N '87

Battered women. F. M. Eckman. *McCalls* 115:157+ N '87

A beaut of a shiner [black eye assumed to be result of beating] J. Slaughter. il *Progressive* 51:50 My '87

Can you beat this? [ruling that J. Fedders is to receive share of profits from abused wife's book] L. Fleischer. *Publ Wkly* 232:56 N 13 '87

Home is where the hurt is [upper middle class battered wives] A. Toufexis. il *Time* 130:68 D 21 '87

I was a battered wife. il *Good Housekeep* 205:22+ S '87

New York woman acquitted of killing her husband [battered woman, K. Straw] *Jet* 73:46 N 2 '87

Not without my daughter [escape of American woman trapped by husband in Iran; excerpt]; ed. by William Hoffer. B. Mahmoody. il por *Ladies Home J* 104:20+ Ag '87

Spouse beaters—the handcuff cure. *U S News World Rep* 102:12 Mr 2 '87

Survivor of a violent marriage, a former Washington official's wife recalls years of abuse; ed. by Jane Sims Podesta. C. O. Fedders. il pors *People Wkly* 28:113-14+ D 14 '87

Wife and husband quarrels *See* Quarrels

Wiggins, Marianne

Kafkas [story] *Harpers* 275:32+ S '87

Wiggins, Mitchell

about

Rockets' pair bombed out of NBA for cocaine use. pors *Jet* 71:50 F 2 '87

Wight, James Alfred *See* Herriot, James

Wigner Medal *See* Physics—Awards

Wigs

See also

Aderans Corporation of America

Big wig [theatrical hairstylist P. Della Illien] J. Roberts. il por *N Y* 20:16 Ja 12 '87

Faux hair coming on strong! il *Essence* 18:47 Je '87

Wil Swanson and Dancers

Reviews:

Performances at the Bessie Schönberg Theater, New York City. L. Garafola. *Dance Mag* 61:37-8 Ja '87

Wilbur, Amy E.

Women's contraceptives: technologies of the future. il *McCalls* 114:88 Ag '87

Wilbur, Richard, 1921-

about

Richard Wilbur. D. Van Biema. il pors *People Wkly* 28:91-2+ O 5 '87

Wilby, Sorrel

Nomads' land: a journey through Tibet. il pors map *Natl Geogr* 172:764-85 D '87

Wilcox, Brent

The Kronos Quartet. il *Down Beat* 54:55-7 Ap '87

Wilcox, Celeste, and others

Acylation of proteins with myristic acid occurs cotranslationally. bibl f il *Science* 238:1275-8 N 27 '87

Wilcox, J. Ross

(jt. auth) See Reynolds, John E., III, and Wilcox, J. Ross

Wilcox, Marie

about

Marie Wilcox, 65. M. Kort. il por *Women's Sports Fitness* 9:18 O '87

Wild, David

The oeuvre de Woody (a short, uptight quiz). il pors *Esquire* 107:91 Ap '87

Wild, Russell

The turtles of Mona Island. il *Wash Mon* 19:35-8 Mr '87

Wild, Walter J.

A gamma-ray pinhole camera. il *Sky Telesc* 74:126-7 Ag '87

Wild and scenic rivers

See also

Dolores River (Colo. and Utah)

Friends of the River (Organization)

North Saint Vrain Creek (Colo.)

West Virginia rivers bill adds to the park system. il *Natl Parks* 61:15 N/D '87

Wild animals *See* Wildlife

Wild blue [drama] *See* Pintauro, Joseph

Wild children

Uganda's wild child. R. Poole. il *Sierra* 72:14+ Ja/F '87

Wild ducks *See* Ducks, Wild

Wild flowers *See* Wildflowers

Wild geese *See* Geese, Wild

Wild goats *See* Goats, Wild

Wild honey [drama] *See* Frayn, Michael

Wild horses *See* Horses, Wild

Wild mushrooms *See* Mushrooms

The wild one [film] *See* Motion picture reviews—Single works

Wild rivers *See* Wild and scenic rivers

Wild sheep *See* Mountain sheep

Wild turkeys *See* Turkeys, Wild

Wildavsky, Aaron B.

President Reagan as political strategist. *Society* 24:56-62 My/Je '87

Wilde, Jennifer
The slipper [fiction] il *Good Housekeep* 205:173-88+ Jl '87
Wilde, Kim
about
New star style! il pors *Harpers Bazaar* 121:178-97 N '87
Rock's supergirl stars. pors *Teen* 31:58 O '87
Wilde, Oscar, 1854-1900
about
The importance of being earnest [drama] Reviews *New Yorker* 63:70-1 Jl 13 '87. M. Kramer
Oscar meets Walt. R. Ellmann. bibl f il *N Y Rev Books* 34:43-4 D 3 '87
Oscar Wilde: comedy as tragedy. P. Ackroyd. il *N Y Times Book Rev* 92:14 N 1 '87
Wilde in New York: beauty packed them in. R. Ellmann. il por *N Y Times Book Rev* 92:15-16 N 1 '87
Wildebeest
Migration
Despite long odds, mighty herds still plunge across the Serengeti. J. H. Heminway. bibl (p143) il *Smithsonian* 17:50-6+ F '87
Wilderness areas
See also
Greenbelts
Wild and scenic rivers
Wildlife sanctuaries
Preserving wildness. W. Berry. il *Wilderness* 50:39-40+ Spr '87
Some additional unfinished business . . . [proposed wilderness areas] il *Wilderness* 50:25-7 Summ '87
Treasured places [favorite wilderness areas of 8 American writers; cover story] il *Life* 10:35-42+ Jl '87
Roads
Where the roads ought to stop [Temagami Wilderness, Ont.] B. A. Back. il *Sierra* 72:76-7 S/O '87
Wilderness worth more than gold [Arc Dome roadless area] T. Turner. il *Sierra* 72:86-8 N/D '87
Arizona
Sycamore Canyon, Arizona. R. H. Mohlenbrock. il map *Nat Hist* 96:16-18 S '87
California
Alpine scenery and solitude early in the season . . . Yolla Bolly. il map *Sunset* 178:42+ Je '87
Ishi's rugged wilderness. il map *Sunset* 178:88-90 Ap '87
A worldly wilderness: California Desert. B. H. Lopez. il map *Natl Geogr* 171:42-77 Ja '87
Colorado
The lifeblood of wilderness [enforcement of federal reserved water rights] D. Drabelle. il *Wilderness* 51:36-8 Fall '87
Idaho
The unfinished wilderness [northern Rockies] D. Zaslowsky. il map *Wilderness* 50:10-24 Summ '87
Maine
True grit [Outward Bound program for sedentary women over 30] I. Borger. il *Vogue* 177:356-7+ Ag '87
Montana
The unfinished wilderness [northern Rockies] D. Zaslowsky. il map *Wilderness* 50:10-24 Summ '87
Nevada
Wilderness worth more than gold [Arc Dome roadless area] T. Turner. il *Sierra* 72:86-8 N/D '87
Ontario
Where the roads ought to stop [Temagami Wilderness] B. A. Back. il *Sierra* 72:76-7 S/O '87
Oregon
Unprotected wilderness along the route of the New Oregon Trail. map *Sierra* 72:58-9 My/Je '87
Pacific Northwest
Where the grizzlies go. L. S. Brady. il *Esquire* 107:33-4 Mr '87
Wilderness conservation *See* Wilderness areas
Wilderness guides *See* Guides
Wilderness Society
Butler new Conservation head [S. J. Butler] por *Wilderness* 51:3 Fall '87
Conservation up front. G. Frampton. *Wilderness* 50:2 Spr '87
Conservation up front. G. Frampton. *Wilderness* 51:2 Fall '87
Field notes: reports from the regional offices. *Wilderness* 50:8-9+ Spr '87
Field notes: reports from the regional offices. *Wilderness* 51:9-10+ Wint '87
Field notes: reports from the regional offices. *Wilderness* 51:55-7+ Fall '87
Field notes: reports from the regional offices. il *Wilderness* 50:49-52 Summ '87

The Wilderness connection [Greater Yellowstone Ecosystem] P. Byrnes. il *Wilderness* 51:55 Wint '87
The Wilderness Society annual report 1986. il *Wilderness* 50 Ann Rep:1-8 Spr '87
The Wilderness Society's plan of action, 1988-1991. il *Wilderness* 51:13-15 Wint '87
Wilderness watch. See issues of Wilderness
Wilderness survival
See also
Air Force Survival School (U.S.)
Outward Bound Inc.
Reevis Mountain School of Self-Reliance
Danger in the wilderness [programs for executives] il *Fortune* 116:6 S 14 '87
Does survival training make better managers? P. Plawin. il *Changing Times* 41:78 Ag '87
Lost! (but not for long) [survival instruction course at Big Thicket National Preserve] M. W. Perin. il *Parents* 62:92-4+ Jl '87
Terror in the forest [failure to find missing boy, A. Warburton, spurs efforts to teach wilderness survival in Canada] il *Macleans* 100:45 Ap 20 '87
What to do when you're lost. il *Natl Wildl* 25:23 F/Mr '87
Wilderness vacations *See* Vacations
Wildflower gardens and gardening
A bit · of wilderness in your own backyard [planting a meadow] L. C. Martin. il por *Natl Wildl* 25:22-8 Ap/My '87
Flowers wild and red. L. C. Askey. il *South Living* 22:98+ My '87
We're on the right track in saving wildflowers. P. F. Frese. il *Flower Gard* 31:40-3+ Ag/S '87
Wildflowers. N. Bubel. il *Ctry J* 14:36-42 My '87
Wildflowers for a sunny border. H. R. Phillips. il *Rodale's Org Gard* 34:72-7+ My '87
Wildflowers
See also
Jack-in-the-pulpits
National Wildflower Research Center
Shooting stars (Flowers)
Wild things. J. Walter. il *Success Farm* 85:44 Je '87
Wildflower preservation. N. Bubel. il *Ctry J* 14:11-12 Ag '87
New York (State)
Rare and protected [cover story] F. Knight. bibl il *Conservationist* 41:2-9 My/Je '87
Wildflowers in art
Natural wonders: the lampwork of Paul J. Stankard. P. Hollister. il *Am Craft* 47:36-43 F/Mr '87
Wilding, Michael, 1953-
about
Don't call him junior and don't dare call him Elizabeth Taylor's kid—he's actor Michael Wilding. J. Stark. il pors *People Wkly* 28:85-6+ O 19 '87
Wilding, Suzanne
Critical care nurses. il *Good Housekeep* 204:136+ My '87
Heidelberg. il *Gourmet* 47:48-53+ Ja '87
Isabel O'Neil and the Art of the Painted Finish. il *Gourmet* 47:76-9+ My '87
The Royal Windsor Horse Show. il *Gourmet* 47:60-5+ Ap '87
Wildlife
See also
Cave fauna
Forest fauna
Pesticides and wildlife
Sketches from nature. P. Schullery. See issues of Country Journal beginning December 1986
Anecdotes, facetiae, satire, etc.
Little-known facts about wildlife. E. Zern. il *Field Stream* 92:184 S '87
Photographs and photography
Camera safari. C. Caiati. il *Pop Mech* 164:68-70 Mr '87
The nature of wildlife photography. A. Carey. il pors *Mother Earth News* 105:60-3+ My/Je '87
Patience makes perfect: waiting for better light. J. Shaw. il *Pop Photogr* 94:32-3 Je '87
Shooting from a mobile blind. D. Spier. il *Conservationist* 41:44-7 Mr/Ap '87
Spring's renewal: a small portfolio of new life. il *Conservationist* 41:29-32 My/Je '87
Wild about wildlife. P. Hermann and L. Hermann. il *Petersens Photogr Mag* 15:28-31 Ap '87
Africa
See also
Elephants
African safari guide from new Florida publisher [work of M. Nolting] por *Publ Wkly* 231:60 Je 12 '87

Wildlife—Africa—_cont._

Africa's threatened wildlife. il _Futurist_ 21:45-6 Mr/Ap '87

Alaska

How to be safe in bear country [survival course taught by B. Brown] M. Reiss. il _Outdoor Life_ 179:50-1+ Ja '87

Last stronghold of the grizzly. J. W. Schoen and others. il map _Nat Hist_ 96:50-61 Ja '87

Strange encounter on Coho Creek [timber wolves] M. H. Erwin. il _Read Dig_ 130:11-16 My '87

Antarctic regions

Encounter under the ice [crabeater seals meet humans off coast of Antarctica] D. Allan. il _Int Wildl_ 17:48-51 Mr/Ap '87

Arctic regions

See also
Polar bears
Walruses

Snow place to hide. il _Natl Geogr World_ 148:24-5+ D '87

Arizona

Prisoner of geography [Kaibab squirrels] G. Turbak. il _Natl Wildl_ 25:14-17 F/Mr '87

Baja California (Mexico: Peninsula)

Gray whales at play in Baja's San Ignacio Lagoon. S. L. Swartz and M. L. Jones. il maps _Natl Geogr_ 171:754-71 Je '87

Borneo

Interview [B. Galdikas] D. Lessem. por _Omni_ 9:76-8+ Jl '87

Botswana

Botswana: beauty and the beasts [Okavango delta] A. Faujas. il _World Press Rev_ 34:62 Ap '87

Brazil

C. subspinosus, I presume? [thin-spined porcupine] il _Sci News_ 131:88 F 7 '87

Grass roots of the maned wolf. J. J. Dietz. il _Nat Hist_ 96:52-9 Mr '87

Mild and woolly monkeys [male bonding and female dispersal in muriquis; research by Karen B. Strier] _Sci News_ 132:334 N 21 '87

These are real swinging primates [muriqui monkeys] S. Brownlee. il map _Discover_ 8:66-8+ Ap '87

California

Living is tough for the desert fox [San Joaquin kit fox] D. Holing. il _Natl Wildl_ 25:14-17 Ap/My '87

Christmas Island (Indian Ocean)

Red crabs on the march on Christmas Island. J. W. Hicks. il map _Natl Geogr_ 172:822-31 D '87

East Africa

Africa. L. Morrow. il _Time_ 129:44-8+ F 23 '87

What are friends for? [East African olive baboons] B. Smuts. il _Nat Hist_ 96:36-45 F '87

Photographs and photography

An African journey. N. Leifer. il _Time_ 129:34-43 F 23 '87

Mystery, immensity and solitude. R. Künkel. il _Int Wildl_ 17:44-51 Jl/Ag '87

Ellesmere Island (N.W.T.)

At home with the Arctic wolf. L. D. Mech. il map _Natl Geogr_ 171:562-93 My '87

Ethiopia

Changing of the guard [aging gelada baboon loses his harem to a younger male] R. I. M. Dunbar. il _Int Wildl_ 17:30-3 Ja/F '87

Galapagos Islands

In the society of lions [Galapagos sea lions] T. De Roy. il _Int Wildl_ 17:30-5 N/D '87

Seals under the sun [Galapagos fur seals] F. Trillmich. il _Nat Hist_ 96:42-9 O '87

When aliens take over [feral animals] T. De Roy. il _Int Wildl_ 17:34-7 Ja/F '87

Photographs and photography

Following Darwin's footsteps in the Galápagos Islands. C. Purcell and A. Purcell. il _Pop Photogr_ 94:32+ D '87

India

Photographs and photography

Rajesh Bedi's indelible India. D. Alexander. il por _Int Wildl_ 17:52-9 Mr/Ap '87

Isle of Rum (Scotland)

Getting the author's goat [discussion of November 1986 article, Rhum deal for goats] R. I. M. Dunbar. il _Nat Hist_ 96:2+ Mr '87

Japan

Japan's monkey treasures [macaques; cover story] il map _Natl Geogr World_ 147:4-9 N '87

Latin America

See also
Viscachas

Minnesota

The land is alive with wolves . . . J. D. Vickery. il _Audubon_ 89:52-61 Ja '87

Nepal

My close call with a rhino. F. Sunquist. il _Int Wildl_ 17:16-17 Jl/Ag '87

New England

Suburban "hotbeds of sexual diversity" [New England reptile microhabitat study by M. Klemens] B. D. Stutz. il _Nat Hist_ 96:80-3 S '87

New York (State)

Young wildlife: look—don't touch! S. H. Clarke. il _Conservationist_ 41:26-8 My/Je '87

Northwest Territories

Photographs and photography

Warming to an Arctic spring. B. Milne. il _Int Wildl_ 17:30-4 My/Je '87

Oregon

Ancient ram's death foreshadows disaster [decimation of Oregon bighorn herd] il _Audubon_ 89:18 N '87

Puerto Rico

Fatherhood in frogdom [coqui forest frogs] D. S. Townsend. il _Nat Hist_ 96:28-35 My '87

Saskatchewan

What it means to be a fox [red foxes] J. D. Henry. il _Int Wildl_ 17:12-16 N/D '87

Shetland (Scotland)

Outermost otters. H. Kruuk. il _Nat Hist_ 96:34-41 Jl '87

Tanzania

Game watching in Tanzania [Lake Manyara National Park] B. McBride. il _Travel Holiday_ 168:22+ Jl '87

Wildlife, Attracting of

Planting for wildlife [backyard habitat; work of Michael and Carol Gunther] R. Haskell. il _Flower Gard_ 31:48-50 Ag/S '87

Wildlife and pesticides _See_ Pesticides and wildlife

Wildlife baits and repellents

See also
Bear baits and repellents
Deer baits and repellents

Wildlife conservation

See also
Bird sanctuaries
Fish protection
Game preserves
Marine parks and reserves
National Wildlife Federation
Pesticides and wildlife
Rare animals
U.S. Fish and Wildlife Service
Wetlands
Wilderness areas
Wildlife, Attracting of
Wildlife management
Wildlife sanctuaries

Biological diversity and public policy [Office of Technology Assessment report] S. Shen. il _BioScience_ 37:709-12 N '87

Nature stories. R. L. Di Silvestro. See issues of Audubon beginning July 1987

People who make a difference. il _Natl Wildl_ 25:4-13 Ap/My '87

Readers share conservation ideas. _Success Farm_ 85:25 My '87

Report urges funds for conservation biology [report by the Office of Technology Assessment] R. Lewin. il _Science_ 236:257-9 Ap 17 '87

U.S. should take lead in preserving biological diversity. R. C. Cowen. il _Technol Rev_ 90:25+ Ag/S '87

The ultimate wildlife threat [human population expansion] L. Williamson. il _Outdoor Life_ 180:28+ D '87

Wildlife [Environmental Quality Index] il _Natl Wildl_ 25:34 F/Mr '87

Finance

The continuing success of Return a Gift to Wildlife [tax checkoff in New York State] S. Keeler. il _Conservationist_ 41:2-5 Mr/Ap '87

Many happy returns for wildlife [state income tax checkoffs] S. Q. Stranahan. il _Natl Wildl_ 25:50-1 Ap/My '87

International aspects

See also
Bat Conservation International
International Wildlife Coalition
World Wildlife Fund

For those biologists who want to save life as well as study it, a sense of hope is the most important equipment. J. P. Wiley, Jr. _Smithsonian_ 18:30+ Ag '87

Wildlife conservation—International aspects—*cont.*

Trying to save the animals. il *U S News World Rep* 102:63 My 4 '87

U.S. role in wildlife conservation [remarks, May 18, 1987] J. Negroponte. *Dep State Bull* 87:34-5 S '87

Wildlife au naturel [expeditions sponsored by zoos] D. G. Gordon. *Travel Holiday* 168:30-1 Jl '87

Laws and regulations

See also

Fishery laws and regulations
Game laws
Game wardens
Marine mammals—Laws and regulations

The call of the wild [wildlife habitat funding through the Conservation Reserve Program] J. Walter. il *Success Farm* 85:62-3 N '87

Dogs and deer [dogs as deer killers] B. Shipman. il *Ctry J* 14:17-20 Ap '87

Restoring New York's wildlife [Pittman-Robertson program] L. DeGraff and J. Dell. il *Conservationist* 42:2-11+ N/D '87

Belize

Jaguars: why protect a killer? [work of A. Rabinowitz; cover story] J. T. Bohlen. il map *Int Wildl* 17:4-11 Mr/Ap '87

Brazil

Rescuing Brazil's muriqui: monkey in peril. R. Mittermeier. il map *Natl Geogr* 171:386-95 Mr '87

California

Mass meeting on the Coast [monarch butterflies] D. Ackerman. il *Life* 10:21+ My '87

Canada

See also

Delta Waterfowl and Wetlands Research Station (Man.)

China

Charting conservation's future in China. il *Natl Wildl* 25:32 O/N '87

New plan drafted to save the panda. J. Raloff. *Sci News* 131:168 Mr 14 '87

Costa Rica

Egg thieves of Playa Grande [leatherback turtle eggs] R. Hamm. il map *Sea Front* 33:27-33 Ja/F '87

Florida

Debate around the collar [collaring Florida panthers] B. Latoof. il *Sierra* 72:18+ Mr/Ap '87

People, power plants, and manatees. J. E. Reynolds, III and J. R. Wilcox. il map *Sea Front* 33:263-9 Jl/Ag '87

Recovery plan focuses on panther survival [Florida panther] il *Natl Parks* 61:45 Mr/Ap '87

USAF to the rescue [Atlantic loggerhead turtle nest sites at Eglin Air Force Base] *Oceans* 20:4-5 N/D '87

Florida Keys (Fla.)

Trouble in paradise [Key deer] J. Carey. il map *Natl Wildl* 25:42-5 O/N '87

France

Guiding toads to safe sex can cause a case of tunnel vision. il *People Wkly* 27:154-5 Ap 13 '87

Ghana

Return to Ghana. B. Jamieson. il *Int Wildl* 17:38-41 N/D '87

Great Britain

Britain goes batty over bats. H. Gibson. il *Int Wildl* 17:42-4 N/D '87

Guiding toads to safe sex can cause a case of tunnel vision. il *People Wkly* 27:154-5 Ap 13 '87

Toads [tunnels built to protect road-crossing toads] *New Yorker* 63:16-18 Ag 17 '87

India

India's intensifying dilemma: can tigers and people coexist? G. C. Ward. bibl (p269) il *Smithsonian* 18:52-62+ N '87

Japan

Why the Japanese will save cranes but not their habitat. R. L. Di Silvestro. il *Audubon* 89:16 N '87

Latin America

Encouraging conservation [World Wildlife Fund] J. P. Cohn. *Américas* 39:58-9 My/Je '87

Mexico

Guarding the monarch's kingdom [plan to protect butterfly's wintering grounds; cover story] S. Sullivan. il map *Int Wildl* 17:4-11 N/D '87

Mona Island (Puerto Rico)

The turtles of Mona Island [shipwrecked ferry imperils turtles] R. Wild. il *Wash Mon* 19:35-8 Mr '87

New York (State)

See also

New York (State). Dept. of Environmental Conservation

Restoring New York's wildlife [Pittman-Robertson program] L. DeGraff and J. Dell. il *Conservationist* 42:2-11+ N/D '87

Peru

Gathering the golden fleece [vicunas] P. E. Rogers. il *Américas* 39:34-9 S/O '87

Serengeti Plain (Tanzania)

Despite long odds, mighty herds still plunge across the Serengeti. J. H. Heminway. bibl (p143) il *Smithsonian* 17:50-6+ F '87

South America

Much ado about pudu [work of M. MacNamara] J. P. Cohn. il *Int Wildl* 17:38 Ja/F '87

Tropics

We're killing our world [address, February 14, 1987] P. H. Raven. *Vital Speeches Day* 53:472-8 My 15 '87

Wyoming

Fertile ferret? [capture of last known black-footed ferret living in the wild] il *Nat Hist* 96:6-7 My '87

Anecdotes, facetiae, satire, etc.

Yet another true study of mankind [black-footed ferrets] R. Blount. il *Atlantic* 259:34 Ap '87

Zimbabwe

The rhino wars [battling black rhino poachers] M. Vollers. il *Sports Illus* 66:60-8+ Mr 2 '87

A war to save the black rhino [battle against poachers] M. Vollers. il *Time* 130:62-3 S 7 '87

Wildlife in art *See* Animals in art

Wildlife introduction *See* Animal introduction

Wildlife Legislative Fund of America

The battle for hunting rights. D. L. Johnson. il *Outdoor Life* 179:78-80+ Mr '87

Editorial [Protect What's Right campaign] D. E. Petzal. *Field Stream* 92:7 O '87

Wildlife management

See also

Bird control
Wildlife Legislative Fund of America

How many creatures? [discussion of October 1986 article, Cultural carrying capacity: a biological approach to human problems] G. J. Hardin. *BioScience* 37:246-7 Ap '87

Recall of the wild wolf [controversial recovery plans to reestablish wolf packs in the wild] D. D. Edwards. il map *Sci News* 131:378-9 Je 13 '87

Too many cooks. G. Reiger. il *Field Stream* 92:15-16+ N '87

Study and teaching

Around the Mall and beyond [Smithsonian's Conservation and Research Center Wildlife Conservation and Management Training Program] E. Park. *Smithsonian* 18:26+ O '87

Canada

See also

Delta Waterfowl and Wetlands Research Station (Man.)

Great Britain

Public vs. private hunting. G. Reiger. *Field Stream* 91:38+ Mr '87

Kenya

The "Gang" moves to a strange new land [Pumphouse Gang of olive baboons translocated to new habitat] S. Strum. il por map *Natl Geogr* 172:676-90 N '87

Montana

The grizzly attacked! [attack on Louis Kis] R. P. Smith. il *Outdoor Life* 180:82-4 O '87

Return of the western wolf. il *Nat Hist* 96:4 O '87

New York (State)

See also

New York (State). Dept. of Environmental Conservation

Pennsylvania

A bear of America [Pocono Mountain black bears; work of G. Alt] C. Fergus. il *Ctry J* 14:43-7+ O '87

Rocky Mountains region

Should we cry wolf? [recovery plan to repopulate Rocky Mountain areas] J. Zumbo. il *Outdoor Life* 180:50-1+ D '87

United States

See Wildlife management

Western States

The final roundup for America's wild horses? M. Satchell. il *U S News World Rep* 102:68-9 Mr 2 '87

High noon at western haystacks [conflicts between ranchers and wild animals] S. Robertson. *Sierra* 72:28-9+ Ja/F '87

Tracking down mustangs. il map *Sunset* 178:46+ F '87

Wildlife management—*cont.*

Wyoming

What price, hunting? [privatization of wildlife and public lands access] L. Williamson. il *Outdoor Life* 180:38+ Ag '87

Wildlife management areas *See* Wildlife sanctuaries
Wildlife on postage stamps *See* Postage stamps
Wildlife poaching *See* Poaching
Wildlife population control *See* Wildlife management
Wildlife print fabrics *See* Textile fabrics
Wildlife refuges *See* Wildlife sanctuaries
Wildlife sanctuaries
　　See also
　　Bird sanctuaries

America's unknown wildlands [National Wildlife Refuge System; cover story] L. Rice. il *Sierra* 72:44-53 Mr/Ap '87

Refuge hunting: perverse use or logical harvest? M. Satchell. il *U S News World Rep* 102:26 Ja 12 '87

A shelter for refuges [National Wildlife Refuge System] W. C. Reffalt. *Wilderness* 50:60 Summ '87

Alaska

The Alaska lands debate, part two [opening Arctic National Wildlife Refuge to oil and gas exploration] J. D. Hair. il *Int Wildl* 17:26 Ja/F '87

All caribou are not the same [petroleum development threatens Arctic National Wildlife Refuge] L. Minard. il maps *Forbes* 139:43-5 Mr 9 '87

Arctic National Wildlife Refuge. L. Rice. il *Sierra* 72:52-3 Mr/Ap '87

Arctic National Wildlife Refuge: oil field or wilderness? A. L. Spitler. *BioScience* 37:714 N '87

Arctic schemes [proposed oil exploration in the Arctic National Wildlife Refuge] M. K. Udall. *Wilderness* 50:60 Spr '87

A compromise the caribou will like [oil exploration in Arctic National Wildlife Refuge] il *Fortune* 115:9 My 25 '87

Cumulative impacts of oil fields on northern Alaskan landscapes [Arctic National Wildlife Refuge] D. A. Walker and others. bibl f il map *Science* 238:757-61 N 6 '87

Edge of the Arctic [Arctic National Wildlife Refuge; cover story] D. Frazier. il *Natl Parks* 61:18-23 N/D '87

Fighting a new threat to the North [proposed oil development in the Arctic National Wildlife Refuge] I. Austen. il map *Macleans* 100:12 My 4 '87

First word [proposed oil exploration of the Arctic National Wildlife Refuge] G. Nelson. por *Omni* 10:8 N '87

Fuel for an Arctic controversy [opening Arctic National Wildlife Refuge to oil and gas exploration] L. Williamson. il *Outdoor Life* 179:42+ Mr '87

High stakes in a land of plenty [Arctic National Wildlife Refuge; cover story; with editorial comment by Jay D. Hair] T. A. Lewis. il map *Natl Wildl* 25:4-11, 28 Je/Jl '87

Into the second century [Arctic National Wildlife Refuge in Alaska] P. A. A. Berle. *Audubon* 89:4 Mr '87

NPCA opposes damage to Arctic Wildlife Refuge [proposed oil and gas exploration] il *Natl Parks* 61:36 My/Je '87

Polar opposites [oil development versus wilderness in the Arctic National Wildlife Refuge] J. R. Udall. il map *Sierra* 72:40-8 S/O '87

Preserving Alaska's wildlife [Arctic National Wildlife Refuge] L. Williamson. il *Outdoor Life* 180:40+ O '87

Staking out the last frontier [Arctic National Wildlife Refuge] M. K. Udall. il por *Natl Parks* 61:16-17 N/D '87

Threats to the North [U.S. threat to Canadian sovereignty in the Arctic and dispute over Arctic National Wildlife Refuge] M. Janigan. il map *Macleans* 100:10-11 Ja 26 '87

Arizona

Cabeza Prieta National Wildlife Refuge. L. Rice. il *Sierra* 72:49-50 Mr/Ap '87

California

The case of the poisoned wildlife refuge [J. Claus discovers selenium at Kesterson National Wildlife Refuge] R. Fitzgerald. il por *Read Dig* 131:133-7 O '87

Fowl play [selenium pollution at Kesterson National Wildlife Refuge] C. Caufield. il *Omni* 9:22+ Je '87

Fungi: California's answer to selenium? [Kesterson National Wildlife Refuge] *Sci News* 132:8 Jl 4 '87

Kesterson: an unsolvable problem? [environmental impact of drainage from federally serviced irrigation districts] K. E. Claus. bibl f *Environment* 29:4-5 Jl/Ag '87

Kesterson Wildlife Refuge. B. G. Norton. il map *Wilderness* 50:32-3 Spr '87

Lizard and the links [Coachella Valley fringe-toed lizard] D. Holing. il map *Audubon* 89:38-42+ N '87

The marsh that Arcata built. J. W. Price. il *Sierra* 72:51-3 My/Je '87

Take binoculars to Ash Creek. *Sunset* 178:54 Mr '87

China

Panda outposts [Wolong Natural Reserve] G. E. Machlis and K. Johnson. il map *Natl Parks* 61:14-16 S/O '87

Florida

A warden's story [Audubon warden R. Chandler of Kissimmee Prairie Sanctuary] F. Graham. il pors *Audubon* 89:105-21 Mr '87

Kauai (Hawaii)

Suburbs close in on a seabird colony [proposed expansion of Kilauea National Wildlife Refuge] J. Yoshimoto and C. Proczka. il *Sierra* 72:69-70 My/Je '87

Mexico

Flight of the butterflies [monarch butterfly sanctuary in El Rosario, is open to visitors] P. Primack. il *Travel Holiday* 168:96 N '87

Mississippi
Anecdotes, facetiae, satire, etc.

The Place. D. G. Schueler. il *Audubon* 89:110-14+ My '87

Montana

Charles M. Russell National Wildlife Refuge. L. Rice. il *Sierra* 72:51-2 Mr/Ap '87

Nepal

New ZIP codes for resident rhinos in Nepal [restocking Bardia Wildlife Reserve with rhinos captured from Royal Chitawan National Park] H. R. Mishra and E. Dinerstein. il *Smithsonian* 18:66-73 S '87

Nevada

Ash Meadows National Wildlife Refuge. B. G. Norton. il map *Wilderness* 50:21-3 Spr '87

Man-made dangers invade wildlife refuges [Stillwater National Wildlife Management Area] il *Newsweek* 109:33 Mr 16 '87

Sheldon-Hart Mountain National Antelope refuges; Desert National Wildlife Range. L. Rice. il *Sierra* 72:47-8 Mr/Ap '87

New Mexico

El Jefe is building a desert 'ark' to keep zebras and other equids afloat [Canyon Colorado Equid Sanctuary] J. Fincher. bibl (p184) il pors *Smithsonian* 18:138-42+ My '87

Oklahoma

Wichita Mountains National Wildlife Refuge. L. Rice. il *Sierra* 72:48-9 Mr/Ap '87

Oregon

Sheldon-Hart Mountain National Antelope refuges; Desert National Wildlife Range. L. Rice. il *Sierra* 72:47-8 Mr/Ap '87

Peru

A jungle haven in Peru [Tambopata Wildlife Reserve] M. Bonta. il *Américas* 39:8-13 Ja/F '87

Virginia

Short-term thinking at Chincoteague. *Wilderness* 51:6-7 Wint '87

Wildlife telemetry *See* Biotelemetry
Wilds, Mary Catherine
　Hiram's ghost [story] il *Teen* 31:28+ N '87
　Hiram's ghost [story] il *Teen* 31:42+ O '87
Wilentz, Amy
　The priest who fights the regime [cover story] *Nation* 245:217+ S 12 '87
Wiles, Q. T. (Quentin T.)
　　about
　A high-tech repairman who 'can fix anything'. il por *Bus Week* p111 S 21 '87
Wiles, Quentin T. *See* Wiles, Q. T. (Quentin T.)
Wiley, John P., Jr.
　Phenomena, comment and notes. See issues of Smithsonian
Wiley, Karen B., and Rhodes, Steven L.
　Decontaminating federal facilities: the case of the Rocky Mountain Arsenal [with editorial comment by Wallace N. Quintrell] bibl f il maps *Environment* 29:2-3, 16-20+ Ap '87
Wiley, Kim Wright
　After miscarriage: healing the hurt. il *Health* 19:80-5 My '87
　The hurricane hour. il *Health* 19:54-8 Ag '87
　Indulge. il pors *Health* 19:37-48+ D '87
Wiley, Ralph
　And . . . it's super sub! il pors *Sports Illus* 66:50-2+ My 11 '87
　Bittersweet twilight for Sugar. il pors *Sports Illus* 67:68-72+ Jl 13 '87

Wiley, Ralph—*cont.*
By divine Providence. il *Sports Illus* 66:16-17 Mr 30 '87
Fourth title for Thomas. il pors *Sports Illus* 67:34-6 N 9 '87
Full steam ahead. il *Sports Illus* 67:18-21 Ag 17 '87
How the Tide has turned. il *Sports Illus* 66:32-4 F 2 '87
Iron Mike passes a test. il pors *Sports Illus* 66:26-7 Je 8 '87
Jack the Ripper. il pors *Sports Illus* 67:38-41 Jl 20 '87
Like father, like son. il pors *Sports Illus* 67:74-6+ O 12 '87
A man of bars and measures. il pors *Sports Illus* 66:50+ Je 15 '87
Pouring on the orange crush. il *Sports Illus* 67:30-3 S 28 '87
A real nobody did it better. il pors *Sports Illus* 66:32-4+ Ja 12 '87
Reggie to the rescue. il pors *Sports Illus* 66:34-8 F 23 '87
Rice is a breed apart. il pors *Sports Illus* 67:40-3 S 28 '87
These are Red letter days [cover story] il pors *Sports Illus* 66:36-8+ My 25 '87
USC rose to the occasion. il *Sports Illus* 67:28-30+ N 30 '87
Which way will you go, Bo? [cover story] il pors *Sports Illus* 67:24-6+ D 14 '87
Will the sleeping giant ever awake? il pors *Sports Illus* 66:42-4+ F 2 '87
You're barely better in '87. il *Sports Illus* 67:36-8+ D 7 '87

Wiley, William
about
William T. Wiley at Allan Frumkim. R. G. Edelman. *Art Am* 75:133 Ja '87

Wilhelm II, German Emperor *See* William II, German Emperor, 1859-1941

Wilhelm, Dave
Fireworks! il *Petersens Photogr Mag* 16:22-3 Jl '87

Wilhelm, Kate
Forever yours, Anna [fiction] il *Omni* 9:58-60+ Jl '87

Wilhelm-Lehmbruck-Museum der Stadt Duisburg
Buchheim vs. Duisburg: another round. J. Dornberg. il por *Art News* 86:45+ N '87

Wilhite, Don
Take the 'A' strain: a hearing test. il *Down Beat* 54:60-1 Je '87

Wilkerson, Earl
about
Wake's forgotten survivors. R. Wilkerson. il por map *Am Hist Illus* 22:40-5 D '87

Wilkerson, Isabel
Essence brides: one staff, six styles. il *Essence* 17:82-4+ F '87

Wilkerson, Margaret B.
about
Work in progress: the definitive Lorraine Hansberry. R. L. Bray. pors *Ms* 15:31 F '87

Wilkerson, Reba
Return to Wake. il *Am Hist Illus* 22:46-8 D '87
Wake's forgotten survivors. il por map *Am Hist Illus* 22:40-5 D '87

Wilkerson, Willie
about
Aretha Franklin finds happiness with new love in her life [cover story] T. S. Moore. il pors *Jet* 72:30-2 Ap 27 '87

Wilkes, H. G.
Plant genetic resources: why privatize a public good? bibl f *BioScience* 37:215-17 Mr '87

Wilkes, John
Murder in mind. il pors *Psychol Today* 21:26-8+ Je '87

Wilkes, Paul, 1938-
Truths my father never told me. *America* 156:497-8 Je 20-27 '87

Wilkie, Angus
Biedermeier chairs. il *Antiques* 132:798-807 O '87
about
Gemütlich grandeur. M. Boodro. il por *House Gard* 159:20+ F '87

Wilkie, Jane
Just Say No. il *Good Housekeep* 204:64+ Ja '87

Wilkie (Angus) Antiques (Firm) *See* Angus Wilkie Antiques (Firm)

Wilkins, Mike
Last word. il *Omni* 9:134 Je '87

A visit to 'The Home Shopping Club'. il *Film Comment* 23:70-2+ Mr/Ap '87
(jt. auth) *See* Barth, Jack, and Wilkins, Mike

Wilkins, Mike, and Barth, Jack
A salute to Klassik Klassix year-and-a-half anniversary: eighteen months of quality entertainment. il *Film Comment* 23:63-7 Ja/F '87

Wilkinson, Alec, 1952-
The riverkeeper. il *New Yorker* 63:49-50+ My 11 '87

Wilkinson, Clive R.
Interocean differences in size and nutrition of coral reef sponge populations [cover story] il *Science* 236:1654-7 Je 26 '87

Wilkinson, Colm
about
Irish tenor Colm Wilkinson gives glorious voice to a French classic in Broadway's Les misérables. A. Chambers. il pors *People Wkly* 27:53-4 Mr 30 '87

Wilkinson, Mary Louise
Panama's moving murals. il *Américas* 39:44-7 Mr/Ap '87
Quito: a sense of history. il *Américas* 39:42-7 Ja/F '87

Wilkinson, Peter
What is DAT, and why are the record companies trying to keep it away from you? il *Roll Stone* p69-70+ S 10 '87

Wilkinson, Signe
Soft covers for children. *N Y Times Book Rev* 92:47 My 3 '87

Wilkinson, Stephan
Flying with the Coasties. il *Oceans* 20:12-19 N/D '87
The heroine of homegrown manufacturing. il pors *Work Woman* 12:108-9+ N '87
The keeper (and stoker) of the company flame. il pors *Work Woman* 12:70-1+ O '87

Wilks, Mike
The Omni alphabestiary. il *Omni* 9:75-9 Ag '87

Will, George F.
[Column] *See* occasional issues of Newsweek
Why the Democrats lose elections [cover story] il *Natl Rev* 39:28-9+ D 18 '87
about
George Will among the polysyllables. W. A. Henry. il por *Esquire* 107:87-92 Ja '87
George Will overboard. W. F. Buckley. *Natl Rev* 39:62-3 F 27 '87
The lightweight philosopher. S. Blumenthal. *Wash Mon* 19:53-7 O '87
Minority report. C. Hitchens. *Nation* 244:170 F 14 '87
Pinch-hitting for Harry. W. Taaffe. il por *Sports Illus* 66:117 Ap 20 '87

Will, Rosalyn B., and Lydenberg, Steven D.
20 corporations that listen to women [results of survey] il *Ms* 16:45-52 N '87

Will
See also
Brainwashing

Will Rogers Memorial
At home with Will Rogers. J. S. Lewis. il *Travel Holiday* 168:32+ Jl '87

Will Vinton Productions Inc.
Filmmaker Will Vinton and his feats of clay are giving animation a new raisin d'être. D. Van Biema. il pors *People Wkly* 27:76+ Mr 9 '87
Raisins [use of popular commercial to celebrate Festival of Claymation at the Metro Cinema in Manhattan] *New Yorker* 63:29 My 4 '87
What's to become of me? Claymation! [cover story] il *Natl Geogr World* 148:3-7 D '87

Willard, Mary Joan
about
Monkeys with helping hands. J. T. MacFadyen. il por *Read Dig* 131:38-43 Ag '87

Willard, Nancy
Aquarium [poem] *New Yorker* 63:108 S 21 '87
Little elegy with books and beasts [poem] *New Yorker* 63:28 Ag 24 '87
The potato picker [poem] *New Yorker* 63:48 D 14 '87

Willard, Richard K.
Is the administration approach to federal employee drug testing sound? [excerpts from testimony, September 25, 1986] *Congr Dig* 66:148+ My '87
The time has come for tort reform. il *USA Today (Periodical)* 115:48-9 Mr '87

Willard Hotel (Washington, D.C.) *See* Washington (D.C.)—Hotels, motels, etc.

Willard Psychiatric Center (Ithaca, N.Y.) *See* Hospitals, Psychiatric—New York (State)

Willcox & Gibbs Inc.
Back from the brink. A. A. Lappen. por *Forbes* 140:8
O 19 '87
Wille, Chris
Will an orphan recreation report spark a prairie fire?
il *Audubon* 89:102-5 Jl '87
Willeford, Charles Ray, 1919-1988
about
PW interviews. S. S. Steinberg. por *Publ Wkly* 231:78-9
F 6 '87
Willens, Michele
Career on hold: the big stall. il *Harpers Bazaar* 120:160+
O '87
Divide & conquer: an interview with divorce lawyer
Raoul Felder. *Harpers Bazaar* 120:141+ Ag '87
William II, German Emperor, 1859-1941
about
J. P. Morgan and Kaiser Wilhelm II. E. Sorel and
N. C. Sorel. il *Atlantic* 259:67 Mr '87
William, Prince of Great Britain, 1982-
about
Di's bad boy. J. Robinson. il pors *Redbook* 169:88-9+
Je '87
His brat attacks behind him, Britain's Prince William
turns 5, almost old enought for long pants. L. Rozen.
il pors *People Wkly* 27:124-5 Je 15 '87
William B. Hartsfield-Atlanta International Airport *See*
Atlanta (Ga.)—Airports
William Collins plc
Collins in profile. il *Publ Wkly* 231:21 My 29 '87
Murdoch to sell half of Harper & Row to Collins,
to become co-chairman. J. Mutter and V. Menkes.
Publ Wkly 232:70 S 18 '87
William Esty Company
Desperately seeking survival. B. Kanner. il *N Y* 20:20+
Je 15 '87
How to survive in advertising [R. Joseph] D. Machan.
il por *Forbes* 140:446+ Jl 13 '87
The incredible shrinking William Esty. A. Dunkin. por
Bus Week p54 My 18 '87
William Morrow & Co., Inc.
Arbor House to become imprint of Morrow. *Publ Wkly*
231:16 Je 19 '87
But does God get 15%? [E. Koch and J. J. O'Connor
to collaborate on a book] L. Fleischer. *Publ Wkly*
232:48 S 4 '87
Morrow pays $155,000 for first novel by 23-year-old
author [M. Chabon's The mysteries of Pittsburgh] W.
Goldstein. por *Publ Wkly* 231:73-4 Ap 10 '87
Morrow to sue 'Washington times' over excerpts from
Deaver book. H. Fields. *Publ Wkly* 232:19 D 25
'87
William O'Neil & Co., Inc.
A brash young investing champ gets rich by defying
old rules [D. Ryan] G. Anrig, Jr. il por *Money* 16:140
Ag '87
William Whitley House State Historic Site *See* Stanford
(Ky.)—Historic houses, sites, etc.
Williams, A. R.
Bridgetown: sights of the Caribbean. il *Américas* 39:18-23+
N/D '87
Eighty years of elegance and excellence. il *Américas*
39:14-19 S/O '87
The lavish tropics in tandem. il *Américas* 39:14-21 Mr/Ap
'87
San Miguel de Allende's special appeal. il *Américas*
39:42-8 My/Je '87
Williams, Andy
about
Architectural digest visits: Andy Williams [cover story]
C. Ratcliff. il por *Archit Dig* 44:40-7+ Jl '87
The stars who make Christmas special. L. Feldman.
il pors *McCalls* 115:90+ D '87
Williams, B. David, and Cunningham, Doug
Embattled Aquino gets a new mandate. *Christ Century*
104:157-8 F 18 '87
Williams, Barbara
about
Air pair. il pors *Ebony* 42:36+ Ap '87
Williams, Barbara
about
Williams 1st woman on UAW Local 249 exec. bd.
Jet 72:30 Ag 24 '87
Williams, Bernice
about
Bernice Williams will lead trade group to China. por
Jet 72:37 S 7 '87
Williams, Bert, 1875-1922
about
Williams & Walker: showmen extraordinaire. B. Ault.
il pors *Antiques Collect Hobbies* 92:48-51 Ap '87

Williams, Billy
about
Billy Williams joins his friends in baseball hall. il pors
Jet 71:46-7 F 2 '87
Billy Williams' speech fans Hall of Fame fires. il por
Jet 72:51+ Ag 10 '87
Black managers far off, say Williams, Roseboro. il por
Jet 73:46 O 19 '87
Williams, C. K. (Charles Kenneth), 1936-
Alzheimer's [poem] *Atlantic* 259:55 Ap '87
Williams, Charles
about
Half the man he used to be: Rev. Charles Williams
loses 188 pounds. il pors *Ebony* 42:86+ O '87
Williams, Charles
about
Two Georgia commissioners indicted for extortion. *Jet*
73:12 N 2 '87
Williams, Charles Kenneth *See* Williams, C. K. (Charles
Kenneth), 1936-
Williams, Clayton Wheat, Jr.
about
There's still money to be made in oil—but not as much.
P. Nulty. il por *Fortune* 115:53 Mr 16 '87
Williams, David
In praise of the potato [poem] *Atlantic* 259:74 Mr
'87
Williams, David A., and others
Regional changes in calcium underlying contraction of
single smooth muscle cells. bibl f il *Science* 235:1644-8
Mr 27 '87
Williams, Debbie
about
Rescue in midair! P. O. D'Aulaire and E. D'Aulaire.
il *Read Dig* 131:100-5 N '87
Williams, Dennis A.
Black family adoption: making homes for our own. il
Essence 18:87+ My '87
Making the system work [interview] por *Essence* 18:80+
S '87
Williams, Dorothy
Should sex education teach more than abstinence? [inter-
view] il por *Christ Today* 31:40 Ap 17 '87
Williams, Doug
about
Black QBs' face-off: first in NFL in 5 years. por *Jet*
73:46 O 5 '87
Williams, Edy
about
Famous for her nude romps in the world's pools, Edy
Williams tries to make one more Hollywood splash.
J. Stark. il pors *People Wkly* 27:88-91 Je 29 '87
Williams, Ellen P.
Picture this! The most beautiful books of the year. il
Vogue 177:186+ D '87
Williams, Francis M.
about
Demolition demon. B. Leonard. il por *Forbes* 139:61-2
Ap 20 '87
Williams, Frank J.
Lincolniana in 1986. bibl il pors *Antiques Collect Hobbies*
91:68-73 F '87
Williams, Genie
about
An angel from Tennessee. J. L. McCoy. il pors *McCalls*
114:132-4 Je '87
Williams, Greg, and Williams, Pat
The seasons of the garden. See issues of The Mother
Earth News beginning July/August 1985
Williams, Gurney, 1941-
A chirping 'bird' helps rescuers find planes that vanish.
bibl (p183) il map *Smithsonian* 17:136-40+ Mr '87
Dimensions. il *Omni* 9:52-4+ My '87
Into the night. il *Omni* 9:36-8+ Jl '87
Medical disputes you should know about. *Ladies Home
J* 104:56+ Mr '87
A new program offers important advice to couples just
thinking of having a baby. *McCalls* 115:62-3 O '87
Rise and shine! il *Read Dig* 131:167-9 O '87
Starman. il *Omni* 9:86-93 Jl '87
Williams, Gurney, 1941-, and Williams, Linda
Eating for two. il *Health* 19:47-9+ F '87
Williams, Harold M.
The role of the private foundation. *Des Arts Educ* 88:12-14
Mr/Ap '87
Williams, Helen
about
Model firsts: pioneers in black beauty. B. Summers.
il pors *Essence* 17:38-42+ Ja '87

Williams, Howard
about
Air pair. il pors *Ebony* 42:36+ Ap '87
Williams, Hugh Aldersey- *See* Aldersey-Williams, Hugh
Williams, Jacqueline
about
D.C. welfare mother gets house she asked of mayor. il por *Jet* 72:12 Ag 31 '87
Williams, Jimmy
about
Linebacker music. R. Telander. il pors *Sports Illus* 67 Sp Issue:64+ S 9 '87
Williams, John Alfred, 1925-
Jacob's ladder [fiction] il *Essence* 18:62-4+ Jl '87
about
John A. Williams talks about Jacob's ladder. C. Y. Greene. por *Essence* 18:64+ Jl '87
Archives
John A. Williams Archive established at university. por *Jet* 71:24 Ja 26 '87
Williams, John Hoyt
Paraguay's Stroessner: losing control? bibl f *Curr Hist* 86:25-8+ Ja '87
Williams, Joseph Dalton, 1926-
about
A powerful tonic for Warner-Lambert. L. Baum. il por *Bus Week* p144+ N 30 '87
Williams, Juan
The imperial mayor. *New Repub* 197:21-3 O 26 '87
A question of fairness. il pors *Atlantic* 259:70-5+ F '87
Williams, Keith
about
Paradise found. N. Rabinowitz. il pors *Mot Boat Sail* 160:54-7+ D '87
Williams, Linda
(jt. auth) See Williams, Gurney, 1941-, and Williams, Linda
Williams, Marcus D.
about
Fairfax County, Va. gets its first black judge. *Jet* 72:36 Ag 17 '87
Williams, Marion
about
Mamas and papas. M. Jefferson. il pors *Vogue* 177:100 O '87
Williams, Maureen Smith
Is your child fit? il *McCalls* 114:57 Ag '87
Williams, Neil, 1934-1988
about
Neil Williams at the Clocktower. C. Ratcliff. il *Art Am* 75:187-8 My '87
Williams, Pat
(jt. auth) See Williams, Greg, and Williams, Pat
Williams, Quentin, and others
The melting curve of iron to 250 gigapascals: a constraint on the temperature at earth's center. bibl f il *Science* 236:181-2 Ap 10 '87
Williams, Raymond B.
Hinduism in America. *Christ Century* 104:247-9 Mr 11 '87
Williams, Reba White
Searching for serigraphs. il *Am Artist* 51:68-71 S '87
Williams, Reggie
about
Reggie to the rescue. R. Wiley. il pors *Sports Illus* 66:34-8 F 23 '87
Williams, Reggie
about
He knows whereof he speaks. S. Ballard. il pors *Sports Illus* 67:30-1 D 21 '87
Williams, Richard
What your windshield shows about the clouds. il *Weatherwise* 40:260-1 O '87
Williams, Robin, 1952-
about
Playtime for Gonzo. R. Corliss. il pors *Time* 130:75 D 28 '87
Williams, Robin M., Jr.
(jt. auth) See Jaynes, Gerald David, and Williams, Robin M., Jr.
Williams, Roger
about
Rep photographer makes camera his marketing tool. B. List. il *Publ Wkly* 231:53-4 My 29 '87
Williams, Roger
The decline of the British science empire. il *Bull At Sci* 43:45-8 O '87
Williams, Rosalie
Please don't hurt me! il por *Ladies Home J* 104:18+ S '87

Williams, Samm-Art
about
In a shocker show, Cagney & Lacey tests limits with the most vicious racial slurs ever heard on TV. J. Hall. il por *People Wkly* 28:62-4 O 5 '87
Williams, Stanley
about
Stanley Williams. *New Yorker* 63:26-7 My 4 '87
Williams, Steve
Hard rain [poem] *Essence* 18:139 N '87
Williams, Sylvia
about
Sylvia Williams: equal time. A. Thorson. il por *Art News* 86:91-2 O '87
Williams, T. Franklin
about
One hundred candles [interview] E. Kiester. il *50 Plus* 27:28-30 Je '87
Williams, Ted
Frankenstein's fish. il *Audubon* 89:74-7 S '87
On the reservation: America's apartheid [cover story] il *Natl Rev* 39:28-30 My 8 '87
Williams, Tennessee, 1911-1983
about
The milk train doesn't stop here anymore [drama] Reviews
New Yorker 63:165-6+ D 7 '87. M. Kramer
Williams, Thelma
about
Thelma Williams' daredevil nose probes the pungent secrets of America's toes. R. Arias. il por *People Wkly* 28:164-5 S 7 '87
Williams, Thomas Lanier *See* Williams, Tennessee, 1911-1983
Williams, Tod
The house that turns to the sun. il *House Gard* 159:150-7+ F '87
Williams, Vanessa
about
Ex-Miss America Vanessa Williams weds her publicist. pors *Jet* 71:14 Ja 19 '87
Miss America Jr. il por *Life* 10:71 O '87
A new life for Vanessa. C. Whitaker. il por *Ebony* 42:115-16+ Ap '87
Vanessa Williams and hubby have baby girl. il pors *Jet* 72:28 Jl 20 '87
Vanessa Williams and husband Ramon Hervey hold L.A. reception. il pors *Jet* 71:57 Mr 16 '87
Vanessa Williams and Ramon Hervey take marriage vows. A. Collier. il pors *Jet* 71:54-7 F 2 '87
Vanessa Williams: now that the storm is over [cover story] L. B. Randolph. il pors *Essence* 18:87-9+ Jl '87
Vanessa Williams tells how she combines motherhood and career [cover story] il pors *Jet* 73:54-6 S 28 '87
Williams, Walter
about
Walking the Cyclone. *New Yorker* 63:28-9 S 14 '87
Williams, Walter Fred, 1929-
about
Walter Williams. G. L. Miles. il por *Bus Week* Sp Issue:250 Ap 17 '87
Williams, William G.
(jt. auth) See Mitchell, Bruce M., and Williams, William G.
Williams, William L., 1937-1986
about
Obituary
Phys Today por 40:90+ Jl '87. R. R. Lewis
Williams (Dr. Lacey Kirk) Educational Trust *See* Dr. Lacey Kirk Williams Educational Trust
Williams (Shelby) Industries, Inc. *See* Shelby Williams Industries, Inc.
Williams-Bryant, Cecelia
about
This far by faith. H. Cole and A. Edwards. il pors *Essence* 18:107-8+ S '87
Williams College. Museum of Art
Charles Moore at Williams. V. J. Scully. il por *Archit Dig* 44:66+ D '87
Good neighbors [architect C. Moore] K. Norment and C. Giuliano. il *Art News* 86:51-2 Ja '87
Williams College coup [G. Panza di Biumo Collection to be housed in North Adams, Mass.] C. Giuliano. *Art News* 86:58+ Summ '87
Williams International
P&W, Williams joint venture for helicopter engine work. il *Aviat Week Space Technol* 127:33 N 2 '87
Williamsburg (Va.)
Reliving the Constitution. il *Parents* 62:15 S '87

Williamsburg (Va.)—*cont.*
Gardens and gardening
Note from the editor [Lila Acheson Wallace Garden]
S. Wilmot. il *Americana* 14:4 Ja/F '87
Williamson, Barbara Fisher
Kudos for Emma, thumbs down on Becky. por *Publ Wkly* 232:159 Jl 24 '87
Williamson, Chilton
The right books. See issues of National Review
Williamson, Denise J.
Apple picking time. il *Americana* 15:54-7+ S/O '87
Williamson, John, 1937-
The search for a new exchange-rate regime. bibl f il *Science* 237:489-93 Jl 31 '87
Williamson, Larry
about
If you're 20 fathoms down and out of oxygen, the answer is Larry Williamson's Spare Air. il por *People Wkly* 27:65 My 18 '87
Williamson, Lonnie
Taking aim. See issues of Outdoor Life
Williamson, Philemona
about
Painter Philemona Williamson. C. James. il por *Essence* 18:91-2 Ag '87
Williamson, Verna
about
Verna Williamson. R. Brown. il por *Ms* 16:102+ Jl/Ag '87
Williamson (W. Va.)
Public health
AIDS: when fear takes charge [victim driven out of Williamson, W. Va.; cover story] L. Rosellini and E. E. Goode. il map *U S News World Rep* 103:62-5+ O 12 '87
Williamstown (Mass.)
Description
Williamstown: culture in the country. G. Trotta. il *Gourmet* 47:56-9+ Ag '87
Galleries and museums
See also
Sterling and Francine Clark Art Institute
Williams College. Museum of Art
Willie, Charles Vert, 1927-
Appearances and sensitivities. bibl *Society* 24:19-22 Ja/F '87
Willimon, William H.
Answering Pilate: truth and the postliberal church. *Christ Century* 104:82-5 Ja 28 '87
The chains of religious freedom. il por *Christ Today* 31:28-30 S 18 '87
A challenge to Willimon's postliberalism [discussion of January 28, 1987 article, Answering Pilate: truth and the postliberal church] *Christ Century* 104:306-10 Ap 1 '87
Willis, Bob
Can't anyone out there repair this phone? por *U S News World Rep* 103:12 N 9 '87
Willis, Bruce
about
Behind the scenes at Moonlighting. E. Sherman. pors *Ladies Home J* 104:34+ Mr '87
Bruce Willis. K. Loder. il por *Roll Stone* p26 F 26 '87
Bruce Willis goes Moonlighting. S. Dupler. il por *Pop Mech* 164:80-1 N '87
For Bruce Willis and Mr. T, the good-neighbor policy has just been canceled. N. Geeslin. il pors *People Wkly* 27:34-5 Je 15 '87
Gambling that their love is here to stay, Bruce Willis and Demi Moore hit Vegas to get seriously married. il pors *People Wkly* 28:71 D 7 '87
Here comes '87. il pors *People Wkly* 27:44-5 Ja 5 '87
Riding for a fall? S. Peters. il pors *Life* 10:100-2 N '87
Willis, Carol
The Machine Age in America, 1918-1941. il *Archit Rec* 175:77+ F '87
Willis, Connie
Lord of hosts [fiction] *Omni* 9:110 Je '87
Willis, Ellen
Teen lust. il *Ms* 16:68-70+ Jl/Ag '87
Willis, Judith
'The pill' may not mix well with other drugs. il *FDA Consum* 21:26-8 Mr '87
Why women don't get mammograms (And why they should). il *FDA Consum* 21:5-7 My '87
Willis, Margaret E.
Back from the USSR: Bolshoi blockbuster [cover story] il *Dance Mag* 61:34-8 Jl '87

The Bolshoi's big news: Irek Mukhamedov, superstar. il pors *Dance Mag* 61:58-63 Ap '87
Catá and his Ballet du Nord: France's northern lights. il *Dance Mag* 61:50-3 O '87
Extracts from a Bolshoi diary: on the road again. il *Dance Mag* 61:39-44 Jl '87
Farther from Denmark: the two sides of Peter Schaufuss. il pors *Dance Mag* 61:56-9 D '87
A night at the Opéra: Cinderella in Tinseltown. il *Dance Mag* 61:58-63 F '87
Williston Lake (B.C.)
Rocky Mountain high. D. Fales. il *Mot Boat Sail* 160:38-41+ N '87
WilliWear (Firm)
WilliWear partner talks about future of WilliWear [L. Mallet] por *Jet* 72:52 My 25 '87
Willmot, Eric
about
Interview. K. Keeton. il por *Omni* 9:80-2+ Je '87
Willow ptarmigans *See* Ptarmigans
Willows, A. O. Dennis
(jt. auth) See Lohmann, Kenneth J., and Willows, A. O. Dennis
Wills, Garry, 1934-
Hart's guilt trick. il *Newsweek* 110:17-18 D 28 '87
Interview with a founding father. il por *Am Herit* 38:82-6+ My/Je '87
What happened? il *Time* 129:40-1 Mr 9 '87
Wills, Maury
about
Maury Wills favors drug testing for all players. il por *Jet* 71:46 Mr 2 '87
Wills
See also
Executors and administrators
Living wills
Probate law and practice
The $70 million battle over Georgia O'Keeffe's will. S. D. Atchison. il pors *Bus Week* p44 Ja 26 '87
The battle over Georgia O'Keeffe's multimillion-dollar legacy. A. Decker. il pors *Art News* 86:120-7 Ap '87
Beckmann will challenged [estate of painter M. Beckmann] A. Decker. *Art News* 86:21 Mr '87
A dignified settlement [G. O'Keeffe's will] A. Decker. *Art News* 86:57+ O '87
Last will and testament: how to do God's will with your own. J. Deedy. il *U S Cathol* 52:32-7 Mr '87
Lights, camera, action! [videotaping your will] D. Fanning. il *Forbes* 139:72 F 9 '87
Miami judge nixes will awarding $1.5 mil. real estate to black gardener [L. Newkirk's will] *Jet* 72:24 Jl 13 '87
Three-decades-long Texas estate feud being chronicled in Norton book [S. K. East case in Final wishes by G. Getschow] M. J. O'Brien. *Publ Wkly* 232:29 O 23 '87
Will power. S. A. Newman. il *N Y* 20:75+ Mr 23 '87
Willson, Brian
about
Body on the line. B. Kessler. *Nation* 245:329 O 3 '87
Willson, Matthew F.
Tips for shooting clusters and nebulae. il *Astronomy* 15:56-9 Ag '87
Wilmerding, John, 1938-
The national image: American paintings in the State Department. il *Antiques* 132:146-59 Jl '87
Wilmette (Ill.)
Architecture
A comfortable house [Hansen House] P. M. Sachner. il *Archit Rec* 175:104-7 mid-Ap '87
Wilmington (Del.)
Historic houses, sites, etc.
Living with antiques:
Mount Cuba in Delaware. M. H. Heckscher. il *Antiques* 131:1078-87 My '87
Wilmore, Jack H., 1938-
Women and exercise. *Vogue* 177:90 Ja '87
Wilms, Wellford W.
Proprietary schools. il *Change* 19:10-22 Ja/F '87
Wilms' tumor *See* Kidneys—Cancer
Wilsey, Dede
about
In the light of the Bay. L. H. Bucklin. il por *House Gard* 159:124-33+ S '87
Wilson, A. N., 1950-
about
PW interviews. M. Field. il por *Publ Wkly* 231:262-3 My 15 '87

Wilson, Alicia
about
A two-time national barefoot water ski champion at 11. H. Brown. il *Ebony* 42:61-2+ Je '87
Wilson, August
Fences [excerpt from text of drama] il *Sport Mag* 78:62-3 Jl '87
about
August Wilson. B. Staples. por *Essence* 18:50-1+ Ag '87
August Wilson: hottest new playwright. A. Poinsett. il pors *Ebony* 43:68+ N '87
Blacks win Pulitzer prizes in drama, poetry categories. pors *Jet* 72:9 My 4 '87
Fences [drama] Reviews
    America 156:508 Je 20-27 '87. G. G. Seibert
    Commonweal 114:320-1 My 22 '87. G. Weales
    Jet 11:72:54 Je 22 '87
    N Y il 20:92+ Ap 6 '87. J. Simon
    Nation 244:518 Ap 18 '87. T. M. Disch
    New Leader il 70:20-1 Ap 6 '87. L. Sauvage
    New Yorker 63:81 Ap 6 '87. E. Oliver
    Newsweek il 109:70 Ap 6 '87. J. Kroll
    Time il 129:81 Ap 6 '87. W. A. Henry
    Vogue 177:70 Jl '87. S. Bolotin
    Vogue il 177:118 O '87. L. Garchik
Joe Turner's come and gone [drama] Reviews
    Nation 245:726 D 12 '87. T. M. Disch
Playwright August Wilson working on next drama. *Jet* 72:57 S 21 '87
A voice from the streets. S. G. Freedman. il pors *N Y Times Mag* p36+ Mr 15 '87
Wilson, Brian
about
Brian Wilson [interview] S. Pond. il por *Roll Stone* p174-6 N 5-D 10 '87
Wilson, Bruce L.
(jt. auth) See Corcoran, Thomas B., and Wilson, Bruce L.
Wilson, Charles Reagan
about
Pink flamingos & Presleyana: the strange obsessions of Ole Miss Prof. Charles Wilson. K. Hubbard. il pors *People Wkly* 28:107-8+ D 14 '87
Wilson, Donald Roller, 1940?-
about
Donald Roller Wilson at Coe Kerr. C. Little. il *Art Am* 75:154-5 Je '87
Wilson, Edmund, 1895-1972
about
Edmund Wilson among the 'despicable English'. Sir I. Berlin. il por *N Y Times Book Rev* 92:1+ Ap 12 '87
Wilson, Edwin P.
about
The old boys' role in the Iran-contra affair. P. Cary. il pors *U S News World Rep* 103:16-17 Ag 10 '87
The spectator in solitary. F. Trippett. il por *Time* 129:19 Je 15 '87
Wilson, Elizabeth
Energy to burn: 12 ways to light your fire. il *Mademoiselle* 93:90+ D '87
Wilson, Gary Lee, 1940-
about
Pluto's paymaster. P. E. Bauer. por *Channels* 7:54 Je '87
Wilson, Glen P.
Space politics forum. See issues of Space World beginning December 1987
Wilson, Grady, 1919-1987
about
Obituary
    Christ Today il por 31:38 D 11 '87
Wilson, Sir Harold, 1916-
about
Former British P.M. Harold Wilson is unimpressed by claims that the CIA sought his downfall. F. Hauptfuhrer. il pors *People Wkly* 28:91-2+ D 21 '87
The 'Spycatcher' secrets. P. Wright. il por *Macleans* 100:38-40 Ag 3 '87
Wilson, Helen Miranda
about
Places for the hungry heart. M. Moorman. il por *Art News* 86:71-2 F '87
Wilson, Hugh
about
Burglar [film] Reviews
    Macleans 100:55 Ap 6 '87. L. O'Toole
    People Wkly il 27:12 Ap 13 '87. R. Novak
    Time il 129:78 Ap 13 '87. R. Schickel

Wilson, J. Graydon
about
Gardening saved his life. P. H. Johnson. il por *Rodale's Org Gard* 34:60-4 My '87
Wilson, Jackie
about
Jackie Wilson oldie hits again in London. por *Jet* 71:59 F 2 '87
Remove Jackie Wilson from unmarked grave; fans buy a mausoleum. il pors *Jet* 72:22-3 Je 29 '87
Wilson, James, 1742-1798
about
Interview with a founding father. G. Wills. il por *Am Herit* 38:82-6+ My/Je '87
Wilson, Janet
Baubling along . . . rage for rocks. il *Harpers Bazaar* 120:142+ O '87
Wilson, Jeanie
How to stay thin after 25. il *Read Dig* 130:41-2+ My '87
Sexual chemistry. il *Ladies Home J* 104:40+ Ag '87
Wilson, Jefferson
about
Reinstates San Francisco postmaster 'forced' to quit. *Jet* 73:35 N 30 '87
Wilson, Jerry W.
More precious than gold. il *Progressive* 51:11 N '87
The Sioux reject nuclear waste. *Progressive* 51:11-12 S '87
Wilson, Sir John, 1919-
Vaccines versus disability. il *World Health* p14-15 Ja/F '87
Wilson, John Anthony Burgess See Burgess, Anthony, 1917-
Wilson, Johnny L.
Profits into orbit. *Space World* X-6-282:21 Je '87
Wilson, Josleen
Choosing parenthood: help for couples who can't decide [excerpt from The pre-pregnancy planner] il *Glamour* 85:128 Ja '87
The gentlest cut of all. *Health* 19:57-8+ O '87
Wilson, Julie
about
Profiles. W. Balliett. pors *New Yorker* 63:72-4+ Ap 6 '87
Wilson, Kathryn M.
Body donation: an enigmatic subject. *Humanist* 47:30+ Mr/Ap '87
Wilson, Kim
The hottest houseplants. il *Rodale's Org Gard* 34:68+ D '87
Wilson, Lanford, 1938-
about
Burn this [drama] Reviews
    Commonweal 114:749-50 D 18 '87. G. Weales
    N Y il 20:168-9 O 26 '87. J. Simon
    Nation 245:569-70 N 14 '87. T. M. Disch
    New Leader 70:21-2 N 16 '87. L. Sauvage
    New Yorker 63:130 O 26 '87. E. Oliver
    Newsweek il 110:88-9 O 26 '87. J. Kroll
    Time il 130:136 O 26 '87. W. A. Henry
Wilson, Larman C.
The dangers of taking sides. *USA Today (Periodical)* 116:47 N '87
Wilson, Mary, 1944-
about
Ex-Supreme Mary Wilson enjoys family-career mix. *Jet* 71:18 Mr 16 '87
Judge OKs Mary Wilson's use of the name 'Supremes'. por *Jet* 71:56 Ja 26 '87
Wilson, Mary C.
Jordan's malaise. bibl f *Curr Hist* 86:73-6+ F '87
Wilson, Michael
about
Tigers hire black exec, answer civil rights call. *Jet* 72:52 Je 22 '87
Wilson, Michael H.
about
'Trying to pull it all together' [interview] M. Drohan. il por *Macleans* 100:24 Mr 2 '87
Waiting for tax reform. M. Drohan. il por *Macleans* 100:8-9 Mr 2 '87
Wilson, Nancy
about
Nancy Wilson celebrates 50th birthday; puts final touches on upcoming LP. il pors *Jet* 71:16 Mr 16 '87
Nancy Wilson: home on the range. L. Robinson. il pors *Ebony* 43:116-18+ N '87
Wilson, Nancy L.
A gay witness to Pope John Paul II. *Christ Century* 104:845-6 O 7 '87

Wilson, Pete
Should the Levin-Nunn Amendment be approved? [excerpts from address, May 14, 1987] *Congr Dig* 66:281+ N '87

about
Can Pete Wilson keep his 'jinxed' Senate seat? R. Grover. il por *Bus Week* p70-2 D 14 '87

Wilson, R. J. A.
Roman Britain. il *Hist Today* 37:47-51 Ag '87

Wilson, R. L. (Robert Lawrence), 1939-, and Ricciuti, Edward R.
A canvas of steel. il *Audubon* 89:100-9 N '87

Wilson, Rand
(jt. auth) See Early, Steve, and Wilson, Rand

Wilson, Richard, 1926-
Chernobyl public health effects [discussion of June 26, 1987 article, A visit to Chernobyl] *Science* 238:10-11 O 2 '87
A visit to Chernobyl. bibl f *Science* 236:1636-40 Je 26 '87

Wilson, Richard, 1926-, and Crouch, Edmund A. C.
Risk assessment and comparisons: an introduction. bibl f il *Science* 236:267-70 Ap 17 '87

Wilson, Robert, 1941-
about
The CIVIL warS [drama] Reviews
Dance Mag il 61:20+ Ap '87. C. Hardy
Unfinished symphonies. C. Clay. il pors *Esquire* 107:106-9 My '87

Wilson, Robert
The great Christmas ham: a report from Southside Virginia. il *Ctry J* 14:33-8 Ja '87

Wilson, Robert J.
about
Md. fire chief reprimanded for telling a racist joke. *Jet* 71:5 Ja 19 '87

Wilson, Robert Lawrence See Wilson, R. L. (Robert Lawrence), 1939-

Wilson, Robert N. (Robert Neal), 1924-
Green and other colors. *Society* 24:21-3 My/Je '87

Wilson, Ronald G.
Meeting at the McLean House. il pors *Am Hist Illus* 22:46-9 S '87

Wilson, Sheree J.
about
Sheree J. Wilson brings new plot twists—and some heavy petting—to Dallas. J. Grant. il pors *People Wkly* 27:91-2 Ap 13 '87

Wilson, Teddy, 1912-1986
about
35th annual International Critics Poll [with editorial comment by Art Lange] J. McDonough. il pors *Down Beat* 54:5, 20-4 Ag '87

Wilson, Wayne
about
The couple with the hippest greeting cards in town. P. Finch. il pors *Bus Week* p80 Je 8 '87
Their season to be jolly. M. Barrier. il pors *Nations Bus* 75:75 D '87

Wilson, William Julius
about
Re-examining America's underclass. J. E. White. il por *Time* 129:28 My 11 '87

Wilson (Comet) See Comets

Wilson Sporting Goods Co.
Jordan's Wilson deal nets him $1 million [M. Jordan] por *Jet* 73:50 O 26 '87
Racket man [J. Kramer signature tennis rackets] B. Greene. il por *Esquire* 108:35-7 Ag '87

Wilt diseases
Induced resistance and interspecific competition between spider mites and a vascular wilt fungus [verticillium wilt] R. Karban and others. bibl f il *Science* 235:678-80 F 6 '87
Mite and fungus: foe and friend? [spider mites and verticillium wilt; research by Richard Karban and others] D. D. Edwards. *Sci News* 131:101 F 14 '87

Wiltsie, Gordon
Hi-trek holidays. il *Harpers Bazaar* 120:174+ Mr '87

Wilvert, Calvin
California escargot. il *Focus* 37:28-30 Summ '87

Wimmer, John R., 1956-
'Messy Christmas'. *Christ Century* 104:1132-3 D 16 '87

Wimpey, Chris
British survivors in America. il *Cycle* 38:78-82 My '87

WIMPs (Weakly interacting massive particles) See Particles (Nuclear physics)

Winans, R. Foster
about
Insider trading: the High Court hasn't ended the confusion. C. Yang. il por *Bus Week* p34 N 30 '87

Of loose lips and stock tips. J. Castro. il por *Time* 130:63 N 30 '87

Winbergh, Gösta, 1943-
about
Lyric taste. C. Norton-Welsh. por *Opera News* 52:42+ D 5 '87

Winchester, Sarah
about
Mystery mansion. J. Ashbery. il por *House Gard* 159:148-53+ Mr '87

Winchester (N.H.)
Education
Fighting over a principal [movement to fire principal D. Littky] S. Doherty. il por *Newsweek* 109:76 My 25 '87

Winckler, Suzanne
High style in the heartland. il *House Gard* 159:98+ Ap '87

Wind, Herbert Warren, 1918-
The Haig and some recent Masters. *New Yorker* 63:89-100+ My 18 '87
The Olympic Club and the Open. *New Yorker* 63:47-8+ Jl 27 '87

Wind See Winds
Wind, Solar See Solar wind
Wind Cave National Park (S.D.)
A prairie dog companion [work of J. Hoogland] J. Grossmann. il pors *Audubon* 89:52-4+ Mr '87

Wind instruments
See also
Alpenhorn
Bagpipe

Wind mills See Windmills
Wind pollination See Fertilization of plants
Wind power
See also
Windmills

Wind pressure
Billow clouds, wind pressure. T. Schlatter. il *Weatherwise* 40:156-8 Je '87

Wind quintets
See also
Tape recordings—Wind quintets

Wind shear
Descent into disaster [SimuFlite's microburst simulator profile] J. M. McClellan. *Flying* 114:100-1 Ag '87
The devil and Delta 191 [microburst in August 2, 1985 Dallas/Ft. Worth crash] J. M. McClellan. *Flying* 114:18+ Ja '87
Mastering the microburst [cover story] R. Monastersky. il *Sci News* 131:185-7 Mr 21 '87
New factors cited in Challenger accident [undetected wind shear and a weakened attach ring that holds boosters to external tank] C. Covault. il *Aviat Week Space Technol* 126:21-2 F 23 '87
NTSB recommends upgraded training, reporting to avoid wind shear [August 2, 1985 Delta Flight 191 crash at Dallas/Ft. Worth] *Aviat Week Space Technol* 126:93+ F 2 '87
Safety Board cites limitations of airport weather surveillance [August 2, 1985 Delta Flight 191 crash at Dallas/Ft. Worth] *Aviat Week Space Technol* 126:113-14+ Ja 12 '87
Wind shear [microbursts] R. Gannon. il *Pop Sci* 230:66-70+ Mr '87
Wind shear and airplane crashes [microbursts; research by T. T. Fujita] il *USA Today (Periodical)* 115:5 Je '87

Wind shear detectors
Flight Dynamics prepares to test wind shear guidance with HUD [holographic head-up display] il *Aviat Week Space Technol* 126:107+ Ja 12 '87
Pilots glean shear information from operational LLWAS tests [low-level wind shear alert system at Denver's Stapleton International Airport] *Aviat Week Space Technol* 127:25 Ag 24 '87
Wind shear systems provide recovery guidance cues. W. B. Scott. il *Aviat Week Space Technol* 126:347+ Je 15 '87

Wind Star (Ship)
Whiz ship. D. Stover. il *Pop Sci* 231:59+ Jl '87

Wind tunnels
Ames wind tunnel to reopen after seven-year shutdown. R. G. O'Lone. il *Aviat Week Space Technol* 126:26-7 Je 29 '87
Crest seat tested in wind tunnel up to Mach 3. *Aviat Week Space Technol* 127:34 N 9 '87
Wind tunnel measures drift [dry granule agricultural chemicals displaced by wind] R. Fee. il *Success Farm* 85 no5:26AN Mr '87

Wind tunnels—*cont.*
X-31A highly maneuverable fighter design tested in wind tunnel. il *Aviat Week Space Technol* 126:18-19 Mr 30 '87
Windbreaks
Instant living snow fence. J. Walter. il *Success Farm* 85 no4:8 F '87
Windbreaks you can grow. N. Bubel. il *Ctry J* 14:13-16 Mr '87
Windchill index
Windchill. D. M. Driscoll. bibl il *Weatherwise* 40:321-6 D '87
Windham, Kathryn Tucker
Tombstone in the kitchen. il *Mother Earth News* 107:72-5 S/O '87
Windmills
Transforming the sea wind. R. J. Hutchinson. il *Oceans* 20:12-19 S/O '87
Windom, Robert E.
Testing for AIDS [address, June 26, 1987] *Vital Speeches Day* 53:676-9 S 1 '87
Window blinds *See* Blinds
Window boxes *See* Flower boxes, planters, etc.
Window curtains and draperies *See* Curtains and draperies
Window displays *See* Show windows
Window frames *See* Windows
Window gardens and gardening
See also
Flower boxes, planters, etc.
Herbs with a view. T. James. il *50 Plus* 27:38-40+ Ag '87
Windowbox gardens. J. Glattstein. il *Home Mech* 83:46-8 Je '87
Window greenhouses *See* Greenhouses
Window shades
A little fabric makes a big impact [balloon shades] il *South Living* 22:165 Mr '87
Window coverings to seal the cold out. J. Seisler. il *Consum Res Mag* 70:14-16 D '87
Window shutters *See* Shutters
Windows
See also
Airplanes, Jet—Windows
Automobiles—Windows
Garage doors—Windows
Glazes and glazing (Glass)
Skylights
Bay is handsome addition. il *South Living* 22:114-15 D '87
Bringing in light, underfoot and overhead [light well] il *Sunset* 178:123 Mr '87
"Corral windows". il *Sunset* 178:156-7 Ap '87
How to install a bay window. D. A. Warren. il *Fam Handyman* 37:32 F '87
How to trim windows. G. Branson. il *Fam Handyman* 37:38-9 Ja '87
Product reports 1988. il *Archit Rec* 175:79-83+ D '87
Replacement windows [low-emissivity glass] M. Brett. il *Pop Sci* 230:60-2 My '87
Shelter with a storm. il *Mother Earth News* 107:88+ S/O '87
Smart windows [electrochromic glass] B. Moore. il *Pop Sci* 231:68-70 D '87
Understanding low-E glass. J. Vara. il *Ctry J* 14:32-3 Mr '87
What can a window do for a garden wall? il *Sunset* 179:76-7 Jl '87
What you should know about replacing windows [interview with J. M. Motsenbocker] L. Stains. il por *Home Mech* 83:28+ Mr '87
Why wood windows? il *Sunset* 179:70-2+ Ag '87
Window buying guide. il *Workbench* 43:64-9 My/Je '87
Window insulation kit with double-stick tape [3M kit] J. Wicks. il *Workbench* 43:48 S/O '87
Window literally brings a garden bed indoors. il *Sunset* 178:157 Je '87
Window watching [dew on windows] C. F. Bohren. il *Weatherwise* 40:150-3 Je '87
Window with a view to the future. J. Hayes. il *Saturday Evening Post* 259:28+ O '87
Windows: techniques for restoration and replacement. W. Haynes. il *Archit Rec* 175:150-65 Je '87
Maintenance and repair
Care and repair of jalousie windows. M. Thompson. il *Fam Handyman* 37:106 My/Je '87
New windows, new look. J. A. Hufnagel. il *Better Homes Gard* 65:50 Ag '87
Replacing glass. G. Branson. il *Fam Handyman* 37:80 My/Je '87

Windows, Stained glass *See* Glass painting and staining
Windows (Computer programs)
Managing windows. il *Byte* 12:137 Ag '87
Spying on Windows. M. Geary. il *Byte* 12 no12 Sp Issue:97-8+ '87
Windows dressing. S. R. Reed. il *Pers Comput* 11:35 D '87
Windows for Basic. J. W. Ross. il *Byte* 12 no12 Sp Issue:201-4+ '87
Testing
Comparison of window systems [Macintosh Toolbox, Microsoft Windows X Window System, and NeWS] H. L. Stern. bibl il *Byte* 12:265-6+ N '87
DESQview 2.00. J. McCormick. *Byte* 12:281-3 S '87
DESQview yet again. J. Pournelle. *Byte* 12:290+ S '87
Microsoft Windows Software Development Kit. D. Hart and L. Hart. il *Byte* 12:250-2+ Je '87
A new window on computing [Desqview] J. Blackford. il *Pers Comput* 11:49-50 Ja '87
Three C language screen-utility packages for PCs [Windows for Data, C-Worthy, and Vitamin C.] J. Robie. il *Byte* 12:223-4+ O '87
Windows shopping. R. Lockwood. il *Pers Comput* 11:140-1 O '87
Windows in art
Exhibitions
The looking glass [The window in twentieth-century art, at Houston's Contemporary Arts Museum] E. P. Williams. il *Vogue* 177:82 Ap '87
Winds
See also
Aviation—Storm hazards
Cyclones
Hurricanes
Jet stream
Plants, Effect of wind on
Tornadoes
Whirlwinds
Windchill index
Bedform alignment in directionally varying flows [cover story] D. M. Rubin and R. E. Hunter. bibl f il *Science* 237:276-8 Jl 17 '87
Confronting the warm winds of winter [chinook winds in Calgary] H. Quinn. il *Macleans* 100:58 D 7 '87
Northern Hemisphere steering currents [700 mb circulation during 1986] A. J. Wagner. il *Weatherwise* 40:17-20 F '87
Sea surface temperature, surface wind divergence, and convection over tropical oceans. N. E. Graham and T. P. Barnett. bibl f il *Science* 238:657-9 O 30 '87
Variations on a Pacific theme [wind patterns] *Sci News* 131:377 Je 13 '87
The wayward wind [ballistics discussion] J. Carmichel. il *Outdoor Life* 179:18-19+ F '87
Wind hurts pattern, but not control [insecticide application] R. Fee. il *Success Farm* 85 no1:20-1 Ja '87
Wind speed and mortality rate of a marine fish, the northern anchovy (Engraulis mordax). R. M. Peterman and M. J. Bradford. bibl f il *Science* 235:354-6 Ja 16 '87
Winds, pollutants drive ozone hole. R. A. Kerr. il map *Science* 238:156-8 O 9 '87
Winds, Stellar *See* Stellar winds
Winds Bar and Grill (Lenexa, Kan.) *See* Lenexa (Kan.)—Restaurants, nightclubs, bars, etc.
Windshear *See* Wind shear
Windshear detectors *See* Wind shear detectors
Windshield defrosters *See* Automobiles—Windshield defrosters
Windshield wipers *See* Automobiles—Windshield wipers
Windshields (Automobiles) *See* Automobiles—Windshields
Windships
See also
Wind Star (Ship)
Windsor, Edward, Duke of, 1894-1972
about
Jewels of Windsor. C. Vogel. il pors *N Y Times Mag* p34-6+ F 8 '87
Mr. Peepers: more and more and more—the Windsor jewels. il pors *N Y* 20:27-8 Mr 30 '87
A multifaceted, rock-solid romance. il por *Newsweek* 109:83 Mr 30 '87
Of Vincent and Eanum Pig. R. Hughes. il *Time* 129:80-1 Ap 13 '87
Windsor, Wallis Warfield, Duchess of, 1896-1986
about
Everything the Duchess of Windsor touched has turned to gold (plated), thanks to Carolee Friedlander. il por *People Wkly* 27:137 My 11 '87

Windsor, Wallis Warfield, Duchess of, 1896-1986 —
about—*cont.*

Jewels of Windsor. C. Vogel. il pors *N Y Times Mag* p34-6+ F 8 '87

Knocking off a royal jewel collection. il *Newsweek* 110:59 S 14 '87

Mr. Peepers: more and more and more—the Windsor jewels. il pors *N Y* 20:27-8 Mr 30 '87

A multifaceted, rock-solid romance. il por *Newsweek* 109:83 Mr 30 '87

Of Vincent and Eanum Pig. R. Hughes. il *Time* 129:80-1 Ap 13 '87

Queen of diamonds. B. Darrach. il pors *People Wkly* 27:28-33 Ap 27 '87

Windsor Fund

An encouraging word from Windsor's John Neff [interview] L. N. Vreeland. il por *Money* 16:130 D '87

The manager his peers admire most [portfolio manager J. B. Neff] L. N. Vreeland. il por *Money* Sp Issue:66-7 Fall '87

Windsurfing *See* Boardsailing

Wine, Barry
about

A Passover seder. J. Nathan. il *N Y Times Mag* p63-4 Ap 5 '87

Wine
See also
Champagne
Cooking—Wine
Viticulture

Bargains from Spain. F. J. Prial. il *N Y Times Mag* p48 Ag 16 '87

Bi-coastal distinctions [New York and Oregon wines] A. Bespaloff. il *N Y* 20:60-1 Jl 13 '87

California beauties. A. Bespaloff. il *N Y* 20:95-6 Ap 13 '87

California, here I come [dinner with 26 vintage California wines] F. J. Prial. il *N Y Times Mag* p66 Mr 29 '87

Calling on the reserves. A. Richman. il *Esquire* 107:22+ F '87

Choosing wines. C. Meherani. il *Ms* 15:12+ Ja '87

The connoisseur's coolers [German wines] E. Fried. il *Harpers Bazaar* 120:108+ My '87

Cookies and wine [Biscotti di Prato and Vin Santo] C. Kummer. il *Atlantic* 259:71-3 Je '87

The dating game. A. Bespaloff. il *N Y* 20:108-9 O 5 '87

Everything's coming up rosés. J. F. Mariani. il *Mot Boat Sail* 159:30 Je '87

Family ties [Cabernet Sauvignon] A. Bespaloff. il *N Y* 20:77-8 Mr 16 '87

The final course [port] M. Gersh. *Vogue* 177:298 O '87

Foods and finos of Spain [sherry of Jerez] T. Lydecker. il *Travel Holiday* 167:16+ F '87

The golden age of Chianti Riservas. M. Gersh. *Vogue* 177:220 Ap '87

The hybrids [wine grapes] J. L. Newman. *Focus* 36:36 Wint '86

In with the new. A. Bespaloff. il *N Y* 20:93-4 D 14 '87

The last word on the 1982 Bordeaux: the stuff of legend—or fatally flawed? M. Gersh. *Vogue* 177:284+ F '87

Learning to love Sauternes. J. Cooperman. il *Esquire* 108:34+ N '87

Life beyond Chardonnay [white wines] A. Bespaloff. il *N Y* 20:108-9 Ag 24 '87

Muscat ramble. W. Grimes. il *Esquire* 107:34 My '87

A musty myth [reverence for old wines] F. J. Prial. il *N Y Times Mag* p78 Ja 18 '87

Our Christmas Madeira. N. R. Campion. il *Gourmet* 47:100+ D '87

Port salute [vintage port] A. Bespaloff. il *N Y* 20:125-6 F 23 '87

Quality tells. F. J. Prial. il *N Y Times Mag* p130 D 6 '87

Red, white & American. H. Minetree. il *Harpers Bazaar* 120:108+ O '87

Return of the big whites. M. Gersh. *Vogue* 177:126 Jl '87

Sailing into port. L. Gruson. il *N Y Times Mag* p50 S 27 '87

Simply reds. M. Gersh. *Vogue* 177:214+ My '87

Slow fizz [crémant] W. Grimes. il *Esquire* 108:44+ D '87

Splendor in the glass [California Zinfandel and Australian Shiraz] A. Bespaloff. il *N Y* 20:90-1 O 26 '87

Stonegate Winery's spectacular wines: slow aging and intimations of greatness. M. Gersh. *Vogue* 177:110 Ja '87

A symphony in every bottle [wines from Iron Horse Vineyards, Sonoma County, Calif.] M. Gersh. *Vogue* 177:204 Ag '87

A trip beyond the 'B' wines. M. Wechsler. il *U S News World Rep* 103:46 Jl 20 '87

True confession [white wines] F. J. Prial. il *N Y Times Mag* p82 Je 7 '87

The veritas about vino. J. Friedrich. il *Mademoiselle* 93:264 Ap '87

Vintage buys. D. P. Marshall. il *Travel Holiday* 167:31-5 My '87

What's in the glass of wine you're drinking. il *Glamour* 85:334 N '87

What's new about wines? They blush! J. White. il *Essence* 18:112 My '87

Wine. A. Bespaloff. il *N Y* 20:64+ My 18 '87

Wine. E. Fried. See issues of Black Enterprise

Wine and food. G. Asher. il *Gourmet* 47:36+ D '87

Anecdotes, facetiae, satire, etc.

Winter racing. P. Egan. il *Road Track* 38:16 Mr '87

Collectors and collecting

See Wine as an investment

Equipment

The one-man wine bar [dispensers] W. Grimes. il *Esquire* 107:34 Mr '87

Labeling

What's in a name? [second labels of California's wineries] E. Fried. il *Black Enterp* 18:86 Ag '87

Names

The name is the game. F. J. Prial. il *N Y Times Mag* p30 Jl 5 '87

Prices

Fair-weather friends [Chardonnays and red Bordeaux under $10] A. Bespaloff. il *N Y* 20:75-7 Je 8 '87

For a few dollars less [California négociant labels] A. Bespaloff. il *N Y* 20:50-1 Ag 10 '87

Looking for bargains in Bordeaux. R. Z. Chesnoff. il *U S News World Rep* 103:45-6 Jl 20 '87

Something for everyone [less than $10] A. Bespaloff. il *N Y* 20:59-60 Ja 12 '87

Spanish wines can be upscale, too. L. Walczak. il *Bus Week* p158 My 18 '87

What price Bordeaux? F. J. Prial. il *N Y Times Mag* p156 S 13 '87

What price glory? F. J. Prial. il *N Y Times Mag* p73 Ap 12 '87

Storage

See also
Wine cellars

Taste testing

See Wine tasting

Terminology

Wine, words, & song [wine and audiophile jargon] R. Warren. il *High Fidel* 37:53-5 Mr '87

Words, words, words. F. J. Prial. il *N Y Times Mag* p52 Mr 1 '87

Transportation

Night without end [racing across France to bring Beaujolais nouveau back to England] P. Bingham. il *Mot Trend* 39:55-6+ My '87

Wine, Nonalcoholic

Calories and alcohol in wine and beer coolers. il *Consum Res Mag* 70:30-2 Mr '87

Liquor without the alcohol kicker. A. Robbins. il *Mademoiselle* 93:332 S '87

When is a cocktail a mocktail? J. Venturino. il *Women's Sports Fitness* 9:8-9 Ag '87

Wine as an investment

Buy now, sip much later: these are wines to wait for [Mondavi wine futures] *Money* 16:13 My '87

Buying wine before its time [views of newsletter publisher O. Ashenfelter] S. W. Angrist. il por *Forbes* 140:222+ N 30 '87

Can you bank on Bordeaux? D. R. Katz. il *Esquire* 107:61-2 My '87

Investment-grade wines. E. McCoy and J. F. Walker. il *Forbes* 139:84-5 Ja 26 '87

Liquidity of investment. F. J. Prial. il *N Y Times Mag* p44 My 24 '87

Vintage investments. G. Thomas. bibl il *Changing Times* 41:72-6+ Jl '87

Vintage memories. J. Plumb. il por *House Gard* 159:30+ Ag '87

Vintage years and wine futures. H. J. De Blij. *Focus* 37:36 Summ '87

Wine cellars

A cellar performance. R. Sennett. il *Vogue* 177:248+ N '87

Wine cellars—*cont.*
Out of the cellar [A. Stillman of Smith & Wollensky buys M. Tucci's cellar from Oscar's Delmonico's restaurant] F. J. Prial. il por *N Y Times Mag* p56 N 29 '87

Wine consultants
Select company. L. Gruson. il *N Y Times Mag* p46 F 1 '87

Wine coolers
Are wine coolers leading kids to drink? E. Ehrlich. il *Bus Week* p38 O 26 '87
Calories and alcohol in wine and beer coolers. il *Consum Res Mag* 70:30-2 Mr '87
Italian coolers . . . they're sparkling fruit fizzes. il *Sunset* 179:128-9 Ag '87
Miller jumps into a cooler cooler market. M. D. Oneal. il *Bus Week* p36+ O 26 '87

Wine critics and criticism
See also
Parker, Robert M., Jr.

Wine dispensers *See* Wine—Equipment

Wine industry
See also
Bonny Doon Vineyard
Clos Pegase Winery
E. & J. Gallo Winery
Robert Mondavi Winery
Schramsberg Vineyards Co.
Simi (Firm)
Stonegate Winery
Villa Nicola (Firm)
Vintners International Company
Women in the wine industry
Bi-coastal distinctions [New York and Oregon wines] A. Bespaloff. il *N Y* 20:60-1 Jl 13 '87
Biking the quieter wine valleys . . . Alexander and Dry Creek [California] il map *Sunset* 178:12-14 Ap '87
Blending arts with wine [Monterey County, Calif.] M. Wade. il *Horizon* 30:60-1 Jl/Ag '87
Maturity with taste: a visit to northern California wine country in a Mitsubishi Galant. il *Mot Trend* 39:101+ Jl '87
Stop and smell the rosé [northern California wine tasting vacation; cover story] B. St. Pierre. il map *50 Plus* 27:31-8 Je '87
Where the tasting never stops [Sonoma Valley wineries] J. Hooper. il *Esquire* 108:51+ S '87
Wine journal [complaint that California has too many wines; comparison with France] G. Asher. il *Gourmet* 47:44+ O '87
Wine journal [Sonoma Valley wineries] G. Asher. il *Gourmet* 48:26+ Je '87
Wine journal [Washington State wines] G. Asher. il *Gourmet* 47:48+ Ap '87
Wines of the Southeast. H. J. De Blij. *Focus* 37:36 Spr '87

Acquisitions and mergers
The ferment in California winemaking. J. O. Hamilton. il *Bus Week* p86-7 F 2 '87

Advertising
Brut force [champagne and sparkling wine markets] B. Kanner. il *N Y* 20:9-10 Ja 19 '87
Some vintage advertising [use of Bartles and Jaymes takeoffs to promote Iowa State football program] il *Sports Illus* 67:18 O 12 '87

Export-import trade
Counting the cost of protectionism [GATT ruling against Canadian beer and wine tariffs] M. Janigan. il *Macleans* 100:14 N 23 '87
Potential victims of a trade pact [protectionist sentiment in Canada] M. Drohan. il *Macleans* 100:22-3 Ag 10 '87

International aspects
Champagne's California twist [French wine makers in the Napa Valley] G. C. Lubenow and A. Miller. il *Newsweek* 110:40 Ag 24 '87

Marketing
The hyping of Napa Valley. P. Abramson and A. Miller. il *Newsweek* 110:51 Ag 10 '87
Paul Schlem uncorks a turnaround plan. J. O. Hamilton. il por *Bus Week* p102 S 28 '87
Quality tells. F. J. Prial. il *N Y Times Mag* p130 D 6 '87

Photographs and photography
The spirit of photography [exhibit The story of a winery] M. Wade. il *Horizon* 30:61 Jl/Ag '87

Africa
African wine frontiers. H. J. De Blij. il *Focus* 37:37 Fall '87

Australia
Hard work, vintage rewards [Hunter Valley wineries] M. C. Kestigian. il *Travel Holiday* 167:24-7 F '87
Wine journal. G. Asher. il *Gourmet* 47:16+ Ag '87

Canada
Potential victims of a trade pact [protectionist sentiment] M. Drohan. il *Macleans* 100:22-3 Ag 10 '87

France
See also
Château Haut-Brion (Firm)
Moët Hennessy
A delightful tour of Bordeaux and Cognac. F. E. Ruffin. il *Black Enterp* 18:109-10 O '87
In possession of his fortune [A. Lichine] F. J. Prial. il por *N Y Times Mag* p58 Je 21 '87
A reporter's reporter [P.-M. Doutrelant] F. J. Prial. il por *N Y Times Mag* p96 N 8 '87
Stealing from thieves [use of copper sulfate in Bordeaux vineyards] F. J. Prial. il *N Y Times Mag* p74 Mr 15 '87
Wine journal [complaint that California has too many wines; comparison with France] G. Asher. il *Gourmet* 47:44+ O '87

Germany (West)
See also
German Wine Academy

Hungary
Getting there is half the fun [Tokay caves] F. J. Prial. il *N Y Times Mag* p52 D 20 '87

New Zealand
Architecture: Ian Athfield: a residence for vintners in Hawkes Bay, New Zealand. F. FitzGerald. il por *Archit Dig* 44:78-83 Ja '87

United States
See Wine industry

Wine journalism
A reporter's reporter [P.-M. Doutrelant] F. J. Prial. il por *N Y Times Mag* p96 N 8 '87

Wine lists
Bistro's best. F. J. Prial. il *N Y Times Mag* p48 My 10 '87
Demystifying the wine list. il *Glamour* 85:350 Ap '87
Vintage prose [list at Anotherthyme Restaurant and Bar in Durham, N.C.] *Harpers* 274:30 Je '87
Wining and dining out [New York City restaurants] A. Bespaloff. il *N Y* 20:105-8 N 16 '87

Wine making
Wines and sulfites: a necessary marriage. *Sci News* 131:409 Je 27 '87

Wine newsletters
Buying wine before its time [views of newsletter publisher O. Ashenfelter] S. W. Angrist. il por *Forbes* 140:222+ N 30 '87
Learning about wine. H. R. Kennedy. bibl *U S News World Rep* 103:81 S 14 '87

Wine service
The returns are in [sending back a bad bottle of wine] F. J. Prial. il *N Y Times Mag* p64 Ap 26 '87
Sending back wine. J. MacQuitty. *World Press Rev* 34:60 Ag '87

Wine societies
See also
German Wine Academy
A gourmet at large [investiture into L'Ordre des Coteaux de Champagne] F. Ferretti. il *Gourmet* 47:34+ Ja '87

Wine tasting
California, here I come [dinner with 26 vintage California wines] F. J. Prial. il *N Y Times Mag* p66 Mr 29 '87
Icebreakers and tastemakers. N. Hazelton. *Natl Rev* 39:49-50 Je 5 '87
The man with a paragon palate [R. M. Parker] J. Elson. il por *Time* 130:89 D 14 '87
The merciless man of wine [R. M. Parker] J. Adler. il por *Newsweek* 110:77 D 14 '87
Stop and smell the rosé [northern California wine tasting vacation; cover story] B. St. Pierre. il map *50 Plus* 27:31-8 Je '87
Taking a wine class in the Bay Area and Napa Valley. il *Sunset* 179:66+ O '87
Toss a wine tasting. J. Friedrich. il *Mademoiselle* 93:196 F '87
Where the tasting never stops [Sonoma Valley wineries] J. Hooper. il *Esquire* 108:51+ S '87

Wineburg, Samuel S.
When good intentions aren't enough. il *Phi Delta Kappan* 68:544-5 Mr '87

Wineland, David J., and Itano, Wayne M.
Laser cooling [cover story] bibl f il *Phys Today* 40:34-40 Je '87

Wineland, Judi
about
The company's bigger, but is it better? W. Lowe. il pors *Work Woman* 12:45-8 Je '87
Winer, Deborah Grace, and McGovern, Dennis
Arias alfresco. il *Opera News* 51:24+ Je '87
Winer, Lucy
about
Rate it X [film] Reviews
Christ Today il pors 31:64 Mr 6 '87. S. Ulstein
Wineries *See* Wine industry
Winfield, Dave, 1951-
about
Reggie picks Winfield to go to bat for blacks. pors *Jet* 72:50 Je 15 '87
Winfield gets divorce suit from his child's mother. il por *Jet* 73:48 D 21 '87
Winfield joins Morehouse School of Medicine board. por *Jet* 72:26 Je 1 '87
Winfrey, Oprah
about
1987 Essence Awards. A. Edwards. pors *Essence* 18:121+ My '87
An intimate talk with Oprah. S. L. Taylor. il pors *Essence* 18:57-8+ Ag '87
Oprah. A. Richman. il pors *People Wkly* 27:48-50+ Ja 12 '87
Oprah [excerpt from Everybody loves Oprah!] N. King. il pors *Good Housekeep* 205:107+ Ag '87
Oprah, ABC execs discuss new sitcom for fall lineup. *Jet* 72:58 Mr 30 '87
Oprah! Thriving on faith. L. Rubinstein. il pors *McCalls* 114:136-8+ Ag '87
Oprah Winfrey. il por *People Wkly* 28:74 D 28 '87-Ja 4 '88
Oprah Winfrey sweeps daytime Emmy Awards. il por *Jet* 72:22 Jl 20 '87
Oprah Winfrey: the most talked-about TV talk show host. C. Whitaker. il pors *Ebony* 42:38-40+ Mr '87
Oprah Winfrey to earn top salary in show biz. por *Jet* 71:26 Ja 26 '87
Oprah Winfrey's success story. E. Sherman. il pors *Ladies Home J* 104:64+ Mr '87
TV's new daytime darling [cover story] C. Whitaker. il pors *Saturday Evening Post* 259:42-5 Jl/Ag '87
'Winfrey' knocks 'Donahue' out of no. 1 spot; Oprah plans TV sitcom and movie. por *Jet* 72:24 My 18 '87
Winged peas
An oddity with taste—asparagus pea. D. E. Reinhardt. il *Flower Gard* 31:95 F/Mr '87
Winget, Donald E.
(jt. auth) *See* Kawaler, Steven D., and Winget, Donald E.
Wingo, Nancie
about
U.S. policy, not militia gunfire, drives missionary teacher Nancie Wingo out of Lebanon. M. Avrech. il pors *People Wkly* 27:32-4+ Mr 16 '87
Wingo, Walter S.
The American way today. il *Nations Bus* 75:54+ S '87
The proper business look. il *Nations Bus* 75:42-3 Mr '87
The tiny starts of titans. il *Nations Bus* 75:38-9 Ja '87
What's ahead for tomorrow. il *Nations Bus* 75:68+ S '87
Wings West Airlines
Wings West commuter orders 10 British Advanced Turboprops. *Aviat Week Space Technol* 127:37 S 28 '87
Wings West orders 15 Jetstream 31 commuters. *Aviat Week Space Technol* 127:36 O 19 '87
Winick, Herman
Synchrotron radiation. il *Sci Am* 257:88-93+ N '87
Winkel, Gabrielle
Adobe blowup. il *House Gard* 159:122-5 Ja '87
Luminous close-ups. il *House Gard* 159:210-17 Ap '87
Winkler, K.-H. A. (Karl-Heinz A.), 1948-, and others
A numerical laboratory. bibl f il *Phys Today* 40:28-37 O '87
Winkler, Karl-Heinz A. *See* Winkler, K.-H. A. (Karl-Heinz A.), 1948-
Winn, Marie
The Czechs' defiant playwright. il por *N Y Times Mag* p78-82+ O 25 '87
about
Marie Winn and Penguin designate November 'No TV Month'. *Publ Wkly* 231:49-50 Je 5 '87

Winnerman, Robert H.
about
Looking to build an empire—again. S. Benway. il por *Bus Week* p114 Jl 20 '87
Winnie the Pooh (Fictional character)
Illustrator Boris Diodorov gives a winning Russian accent to a bear called 'Vinni-Pukh'. J. W. Seymore. il por *People Wkly* 27:52-4 Ap 6 '87
In which Pooh finds a home. il *Newsweek* 110:73 S 28 '87
Winning *See* Success
Winsberg, Morton D.
The changing Florida orange industry. map *Focus* 36:30-1 Wint '86
The Corn Belt: waning in importance? il *Focus* 37:32 Summ '87
Winslow, George
(jt. auth) *See* Cooney, John, and Winslow, George
Winston, Barry
Why I defend guilty clients. il *Read Dig* 130:81-4 My '87
Winston, Kate
The AIDS virus: "Does my husband have it? . . . If yes, do I, too? . . . I had to know". il *Glamour* 85:292-3+ O '87
Winston, William
about
Bloody house puzzles Atlanta couple, cops. il por *Jet* 73:29 O 12 '87
Winston-Salem (N.C.)
Historic houses, sites, etc.
See also
Old Salem, Inc.
Industries
A sudden exodus leaves Winston-Salem eating dust [RJR Nabisco] S. Ticer. *Bus Week* p69 S 7 '87
Stores
Welcome to a Carolina cotton mill [Brookstown Mill] il *South Living* 22:24-5 Ja '87
Winter, Marsha Terry
Write of passage. il *Writer* 100:5-6 D '87
Winter, Roger, 1934-
about
Roger Winter. B. D. Stroud. il *Am Artist* 51:52-5 Jl '87
Winter, Ruth, 1930-
The "lite rite" diet. il *Harpers Bazaar* 120:166-7+ Ap '87
Winter
See also
December
February
January
Snow
Snowstorms
El Niño and winter weather. R. A. Kerr. map *Science* 238:1508 D 11 '87
Extreme fluctuations characterize recent winters. D. H. Hickcox. *Focus* 36:31-2 Wint '86
How we earn our place in the sun [enduring Canadian winters] C. Gordon. por *Macleans* 100:7 F 9 '87
Waiting out the big chill [Europe] T. A. Sancton. il *Time* 129:34-5 Ja 26 '87
Winter's bitter changes [Europe] A. Steacy. il *Macleans* 100:42-3 Ja 26 '87
Photographs and photography
Snowballs, toboggans, red cheeks—. C. Begole. il *Glamour* 85:194 F '87
The white stuff. B. Hagin. il *Pop Photogr* 94:88-91 D '87
Winter Antiques Show *See* Antiques—Exhibitions
Winter carnivals *See* Carnivals
Winter cities
Designing the livable winter city. M. F. Schmertz. *Archit Rec* 175:9 F '87
Winter clothing *See* Clothing, Cold weather
Winter cycling *See* Motorcycling—Winter cycling
Winter depression *See* Seasonal affective disorder
Winter dreams [ballet] *See* Ballet reviews—Single works
Winter driving *See* Automobile driving—Winter driving
Winter festivals *See* Festivals
Winter fishing *See* Fishing, Winter
Winter flying *See* Aviation—Winter flying
Winter maintenance of automobiles *See* Automobiles—Maintenance and repair
Winter Park (Colo.: Resort) *See* Resorts—Colorado
Winter Park (Fla.)
Architecture
Cottage charm in Florida. il *South Living* 22:112 Je '87
Same house, new face. il *South Living* 22:208-9 N '87

Winter protection of plants *See* Plants—Protection
Winter resorts *See* Resorts
Winter sleep *See* Hibernation
Winter sports
> *See also*
> Curling (Sport)
> Hockey
> Ice skating
> Ice surfing
> Ski racing
> Skis and skiing
> Sleds and sledding
> Snowboarding
> Snowmobiles and snowmobiling
> Snowshoes and snowshoeing

In the tracks of the Olympians. il map *Sunset* 179:50+ D '87
Winter vegetables *See* Vegetables
Winterberry *See* Holly
Winters, Catherine
Fit and fun: fitness strategies for kids and their parents. il *Work Woman* 12:159+ S '87
The lowdown on low-impact exercise. il *Work Woman* 12:151+ N '87
Winters, Patricia
> *about*
Tricks of the trade. B. Kanner. il por *N Y* 20:18+ N 2 '87
Winterson, Jeanette
Stories and histories [fiction] *Harpers* 275:22-3 S '87
Winwood, Steve
> *about*
Steve Winwood's higher style. L. Robinson. por *Vogue* 177:58 Jl '87
Steve Winwood's solo on Empty pages—an electric piano transcription. J. T. Cohen. il *Down Beat* 54:60-1 Ag '87
Wion, Karen L., and others
Human lipoprotein lipase complementary DNA sequence. bibl f il *Science* 235:1638-41 Mr 27 '87
WiP (Organization) *See* Freedom and Peace (Organization)
Wire
> *See also*
> Electric wire and wiring
Phosphorus in antique iron music wire. M. Goodway. bibl f il *Science* 236:927-32 My 22 '87
The well-tempered clavier [use of phosphorus alloy in harpsichord strings; research by Martha Goodway] il *Sci Am* 257:20+ Ag '87
Wire industry
> *See also*
> Seymour Specialty Wire Company
Wire Train (Musical group)
Wire Train's hippie conductor [K. Hunter] M. Goldberg. il por *Roll Stone* p38 Mr 26 '87
Wireless cable television *See* Multichannel multipoint distribution service
Wireless telephone *See* Radiotelephone
Wiretapping
> *See also*
> Iran-contra affair—Wiretaps
> Watergate case
How the Soviets are bugging America. D. P. Moynihan. il map *Pop Mech* 164:102-5 Ap '87
Spies under fire [Canadian Security Intelligence Service] H. Mackenzie. il *Macleans* 100:12-14 S 28 '87
Tommy the Cork: the secret world of Washington's first modern lobbyist [T. Corcoran] A. J. Lichtman. il por *Wash Mon* 19:41-9 F '87
Wiring, Electric *See* Electric wire and wiring
Wirth, David A.
The World Bank and the environment. bibl *Environment* 28:33-4 D '86
Wirth, Mary G.
Benefits of a writers' conference [with list of 1987 conferences] il *Writer* 100:23-33 My '87
Wischmann, Lesley
Tibetan Buddhism survives nightmare of repression. il *Christ Century* 104:529-31 Je 3-10 '87
Turmoil in Tibet. il map *Christ Century* 104:1118-19 D 9 '87
Wisconsin
> *See also*
> Agriculture—Wisconsin
> Child welfare—Wisconsin
> Crime and criminals—Wisconsin
> Fox River (Wis.)
> Irrigation—Wisconsin
> Labor laws and regulations—Wisconsin
> Opera—Wisconsin

> Roads—Wisconsin
> Water pollution—Wisconsin
Wisdom
30 wise men: eleven literary lights reveal their modern Magi. il *Esquire* 108:291 D '87
A word to the wise. G. G. Seibert. *America* 157:47 Jl 18-25 '87
Wisdom [film] *See* Motion picture reviews—Single works
Wise, Arthur E., and others
Effective teacher selection. *Educ Dig* 53:14-18 N '87
Wise, Christy
Grass roots partnerships for development. *Américas* 39:52-3 S/O '87
The story of the century. il *Space World* X-4-280:22-5 Ap '87
Wise, William
No sign of Santa [poem] il *McCalls* 115:13-16 D '87
Wisecarver, Sonny
> *about*
He's no longer In the mood, but Ellsworth "Woo Woo" Wisecarver was a real play boy in the 1940s. T. Allis. il por *People Wkly* 28:169-70+ N 16 '87
'The Woo Woo Kid'. M. Reese. il por *Newsweek* 110:77 S 28 '87
Wiseman, Carter
Cityscape. *See* occasional issues of New York
Penn Station. il *N Y* 20:84-5 D 21-28 '87
A vision with a message. il *Archit Rec* 175:112-21 Mr '87
Wiseman, Peter
Julius Caesar and the Hereford world map. bibl il maps *Hist Today* 37:53-7 N '87
Wisenberg, S. L.
Vacation at Club Dead. il *Progressive* 51:34 Jl '87
Wish you were here [film] *See* Motion picture reviews—Single works
Wishard, William Van Dusen
The 21st century economy. il por *Futurist* 21:23-8 My/Je '87
Challenges for the twenty-first century. *Futurist* 21:60 S/O '87
Wishinsky, Frieda
A new era in Canadian children's books. *Publ Wkly* 231:36 Mr 20 '87
Wishnia, Steven
Rockin' with the First Amendment. il *Nation* 245:444-6 O 24 '87
Wishnow, Jerry
> *about*
Hype in a good cause. L. Brown. il por *Channels* 7:26 Jl/Ag '87
Wisse, Ruth R.
Israel: a house divided? *Commentary* 84:33-8 S '87
Letter to a new Israeli. *Commentary* 83:44-9 Je '87
A light unto the nations? *Commentary* 84:30-5 D '87
The New York (Jewish) intellectuals. *Commentary* 84:28-38 N '87
Poland's Jewish ghosts. *Commentary* 83:25-33 Ja '87
Poles and Jews [discussion of January 1987 article, Poland's Jewish ghosts] *Commentary* 83:2+ My '87
Wistow, Graeme, and Piatigorsky, Joram
Recruitment of enzymes as lens structural proteins. bibl f il *Science* 236:1554-6 Je 19 '87
Wit and humor *See* Humor
Witch doctors *See* Medicine men
Witchcraft
> *See also*
> Medicine men
> Voodooism
A mini-primer on witchcraft. C. Kocol. il *Humanist* 47:37 S/O '87
Salem's official witch, Laurie Cabot, finds grave errors in Eastwick. C. Neuhaus. il por *People Wkly* 27:52-3 Je 29 '87

> **Europe**
Witch hunts: the sex factor. A. Barstow. il *Ms* 16:85 N '87
The witches of Eastwick [film] *See* Motion picture reviews—Single works
Witchweed
A predator plant's chemical radar [research by David Lynn and others] S. Weisburd. *Sci News* 132:190 S 19 '87
Witherell, Harvey J.
> *about*
The last brickmaker in America. C. Kuralt. il *Read Dig* 130:53-6 My '87

Witherspoon, Tim

about

Fighters sue Don King for $35 million in damages. *Jet* 72:40 Je 1 '87

New champs' date with destiny promises action; Loss least of woes for Tim Witherspoon. il pors *Jet* 71:48 Ja 12 '87

Withholding tax

Curing your W-4 blues. *Money* 16:14 Mr '87

Don't let that *&¢! W-4 get you down. G. Weiss. il *Bus Week* p149 F 23 '87

Going over like a lead zeppelin [tax reform in West Germany] J. Templeman. il *Bus Week* p47 O 26 '87

Meet the new, slimmed-down W-4. L. Wiener. il *U S News World Rep* 102:67 Mr 16 '87

Paychecks are fatter—but maybe not for long. J. Berger. il *Bus Week* p28 F 9 '87

Those W-4s: help, Henry! B. Powell. il *Newsweek* 109:49 F 16 '87

Timely answers to taxing questions. K. McCormally. il *Changing Times* 41:35-6+ Mr '87

Who's afraid of the big bad W-4? *Changing Times* 41:8 Je '87

Withholding taxes: new forms, new rules, new strategies. M. Daly. il *Better Homes Gard* 65:20 Je '87

Anecdotes, facetiae, satire, etc.

Alice in W-4 land. J. Keefauver. *Natl Rev* 39:30 Je 5 '87

Withnail and I [film] *See* Motion picture reviews—Single works

Withrow, Greg

about

Greg Withrow's neo-Nazi past returns to inflict the ultimate scourge: crucifixion. M. Green. il pors *People Wkly* 28:41-2+ S 21 '87

Witkin, Joel-Peter, 1939-

about

The wizard of id. M. Kozloff. il por *Vogue* 177:120 Ap '87

Witkin-Lanoil, Georgia

Emotional best. See occasional issues of Health (New York, N.Y.) beginning July 1985

Witkowski, Bob

Boxers, Leicas, and available light. il *Petersens Photogr Mag* 16:50-3 D '87

Witness Security Program (Dept. of Justice) *See* United States. Dept. of Justice. Witness Security Program

Witnesses

A questionable witness to abuse [Canadian bill would eliminate need for corroboration of unsworn testimony of a child in sexual abuse cases] B. Amiel. il *Macleans* 100:9 Ja 26 '87

UFO update [evidence from responsible witnesses] H. E. Goldfluss. il *Omni* 9:95 Je '87

'We just want the truth' [child witnesses and sex abuse cases in Montreal] L. Van Dusen. il *Macleans* 100:56+ N 2 '87

Witnesses, Expert *See* Evidence, Expert

Witsell, Rebecca

about

Arkansas stencilers. T. Kazas. il pors *Americana* 15:35-9 My/Je '87

Witt, Katarina

about

Fire on ice. E. Greenspan. il pors *Women's Sports Fitness* 9:22-5+ Mr '87

Thou swell, thou Witt-y. E. M. Swift. il pors *Sports Illus* 66:20-3 Mr 23 '87

Witt, Priscilla

"Do you want any more secret documents put in the safe, Mr. Ambassador?" "No, Ivan, that's all for tonight". *Wash Mon* 19:17-18+ Ap '87

Why our embassies are nests for spies. il *Read Dig* 131:111-14 O '87

Witten, E.

about

A theory of everything [cover story] K. C. Cole. il pors *N Y Times Mag* p20-6+ O 18 '87

Wittkopf, Eugene R., 1943-

(jt. auth) See Kegley, Charles W., and Wittkopf, Eugene R., 1943-

Wittkowski, Michael

No longer the biggest lottery winner ever, a Chicagoan reclaims a different prize: his privacy; ed. by Civia Tamarkin. il pors *People Wkly* 28:117-18+ N 23 '87

Wittman, S. A.

Voyage of a peace activist. il por *Progressive* 51:16 F '87

Wittwer, Sylvan Harold, 1917-

about

Setting a full table. G. Garelik. il *Time* 130:55 O 12 '87

Wives

See also
Adultery
Baseball players' wives
Congressmen's wives
Dictators' wives
Divorce
Farm women
Heads of state—Wives
Homemakers
Husbands
Marriage
Married couples
Married women
Politicians' wives
Presidential candidates—Wives
Presidents—Wives
Separation (Law)
Widows
Wife abuse

WJZ (Baltimore, Md.: Television station) *See* Television stations

Wodarski, John S., and Lockhart, Lettie L.

Teenage parents on welfare. bibl f *Society* 24:48-52 Mr/Ap '87

Woddis, Roger

Jaws 4 [poem] *World Press Rev* 34:16 F '87

Wodiczko, Krzysztof

about

Urban disturbances. E. Lajer-Burcharth. bibl f il *Art Am* 75:146-53+ N '87

Woditsch, Gary A., and others

The skillful baccalaureate. il *Change* 19:48-57 N/D '87

Wofford, Dan

about

Dan Wofford at Twining. T. Towle. il *Art Am* 75:153-4 Je '87

Woiwode, Larry

Alpha [story] *New Yorker* 63:34-44+ O 26 '87

Wojciechowska, Maia, 1927-

What I teach in creative writing classes. *Writer* 100:5-6 Jl '87

Wojnarowicz, David, 1955-

about

David Wojnarowicz at Ground Zero. P. Smith. il *Art Am* 75:182-3 S '87

Wojtyła, Karol *See* John Paul II, Pope, 1920-

Wok cooking

A country wok; ed. by Margaret Tong. G. W. Albee. il *Ctry J* 14:26-31 F '87

Wolf, Edward C.

Grains of hope. il *Courier* 40:22-4 Mr '87

Growing a forest from scratch. il por *Futurist* 21:41-2 Jl/Ag '87

Wolf, James L.

Alliance to Save Energy. *Environment* 29:3-4 Ap '87

Wolf, Jeanne

The many faces of Cher. pors *Ladies Home J* 104:36+ Ag '87

Wolf, Paul G., and others

Electrophoretic evidence for genetic diploidy in the bracken fern (Pteridium aquilinum). bibl f il *Science* 236:947-9 My 22 '87

Wolf, Reinhart, 1930-

about

Good enough to eat. R. Sokolov. il *Nat Hist* 96:58-64 S '87

Wolf, Stephen M.

about

Tiger by the tail. M. Beauchamp. il por *Forbes* 139:124-5 My 4 '87

United names Wolf, shares CRS codes with British Airways. *Aviat Week Space Technol* 127:35 D 14 '87

Wolf at the door [film] *See* Motion picture reviews—Single works

Wolf family

about

Down and out and no place to go [Newark, N.J.] T. McCarroll. il *Time* 130:20-1 Ag 24 '87

Wolf prizes

Wolf Foundation honors six with 1987 awards. il *Phys Today* 40 pt1:81-2 Ag '87

Wolf Trap Farm Park for the Performing Arts

Arts park for a nation. M. Wade. il *Horizon* 30:19-20 Jl/Ag '87

Wolfe, Art

Food for the brood. il *Nat Hist* 96:92-3 F '87

Wolfe, George C.
The last mama-on-a-couch play [excerpt from The colored museum] *Harpers* 274:31-3 F '87
about
The colored museum [drama] Reviews
  Commonweal 114:321 My 22 '87. G. Weales
Showstopper. H. Als. il *Essence* 17:26 Mr '87
Wolfe, James H.
Reluctant reform in the Communist world. *USA Today (Periodical)* 115:29 My '87
Southern attitudes and world affairs. *USA Today (Periodical)* 115:9 Ja '87
Treaties of guarantee. il *USA Today (Periodical)* 116:63 Jl '87
The truth about sanctions. *USA Today (Periodical)* 115:9 Mr '87
Yugoslavia's national question. il *USA Today (Periodical)* 116:51 S '87
Wolfe, Linda
The new sexual realism. il *Ladies Home J* 104:58+ Ap '87
The people versus Robert Chambers. il pors *N Y* 20:92-9+ O 26 '87
Think of wives in old China [story] il *Ladies Home J* 104:84+ Mr '87
Wolfe, Linda, and Cecil, Jennifer
Island travel. il *N Y* 20:64-6+ N 9 '87
Wolfe, Lisa
The Palestinian campus. il *N Y Times Mag* p67-8+ Ap 19 '87
Wolfe, Louis
about
Wolfe and Fine form mass market company. pors *Publ Wkly* 231:20 My 22 '87
Wolfe, Thomas, 1900-1938
about
Big bad Wolfe? M. K. Spears. il *N Y Rev Books* 34:34-7 S 24 '87
PW interviews [biographer D. H. Donald] S. Staggs. por *Publ Wkly* 231:366-7 Ja 30 '87
Wolfe in love. D. H. Donald. il por *N Y Times Book Rev* 92:1+ Ja 11 '87
Wolfe, Tom
about
Tom Wolfe [interview] B. Mewborn. il por *Roll Stone* p214-19 N 5-D 10 '87
Tom Wolfe's walk on the wild side [interview] A. P. Sanoff. il pors *U S News World Rep* 103:57-8 N 23 '87
An unleashed Wolfe. D. Lehman. il pors *Newsweek* 110:84-5 O 26 '87
Wolfe, Traci
about
Making a splash with Traci Wolfe. S. Orlean. il pors *Seventeen* 46:112-13+ F '87
Wolfe, William
Video basics. See alternate issues of Stereo Review beginning January 1987
Wolfe (Thomas) Society *See* Thomas Wolfe Society
Wolfer, Barbara
Five poems that spelled danger. il *Commonweal* 114:107-11 F 27 '87
Wolff, Al
The last Untouchable; ed. by Civia Tamarkin. il pors *People Wkly* 28:53-4+ Jl 13 '87
Wolff, Alexander
Bright wheels rolling. il *Sports Illus* 67:54-5 Jl 20 '87
The fall roundup. il *Sports Illus* 67:46-50+ Ag 31 '87
Flood Tide in the SEC. il *Sports Illus* 66:18-19 Mr 16 '87
Good show, comrades. il *Sports Illus* 66:79-80 Je 1 '87
A graceful descent. il *Sports Illus* 66:82 My 4 '87
The hot way to turn up the heat. il *Sports Illus* 67 Sp Issue:46-50 N 18 '87
How 'bout those Expos? il *Sports Illus* 67:28-9 O 5 '87
The juco express. il *Sports Illus* 67 Sp Issue:6-13 N 18 '87
Las Vegas hit the jackpot. il *Sports Illus* 66:22-3 Mr 30 '87
A new kind of Orient Express. il por *Sports Illus* 66:28-9 My 18 '87
Oh, what a sorry state. il *Sports Illus* 66:44-5 Mr 2 '87
Playing by her own rules. il por *Sports Illus* 67:38-9 Jl 6 '87
Score a big one for the Irish. il por *Sports Illus* 67:22-3 Ag 3 '87
A strange new tennis racket. il *Sports Illus* 67:24-7 D 7 '87

Strutting their stuff. il *Sports Illus* 66:26-30+ Mr 23 '87
That championship touch. il pors *Sports Illus* 66:36-8 Ap 13 '87
Tiger of another stripe. il pors *Sports Illus* 66:76-81 Ja 12 '87
A time for heeling. il *Sports Illus* 67:50-1+ N 30 '87
A wheeler, but no dealer. il pors *Sports Illus* 66:58+ Je 29 '87
(jt. auth) See Keteyian, Armen, and Wolff, Alexander
Wolff, Anita
about
Anita Wolff's portraits and landscapes in pastel. M. S. Schulzke. il por *Am Artist* 51:60-3+ S '87
Wolff, Bobby
about
Making it in big-time bridge. T. Buckley. il pors *N Y Times Mag* p22-5+ Jl 26 '87
Wolff, Charles L., and Hickey, John R.
Solar irradiance change and special longitudes due to r-modes. bibl f il *Science* 235:1631-3 Mr 27 '87
Wolff, Craig
First love. il pors *Sport Mag* 78:51-5 Je '87
Wolff, Daniel
Music. *Nation* 245:137-9 Ag 15-22 '87
Wolff, Geoffrey, 1937-
A day at the beach. il *Esquire* 108:254-6+ D '87
Wolff, Hugh
about
Between a rock (New York) and another hard place (Philadelphia), Hugh Wolff conducts a revival. V. Burns. il por *People Wkly* 28:87-8 Ag 31 '87
Wolff, Jackie
about
At home with Tira. M. Weissman. il por *Ms* 16:36+ S '87
Wolff, Janet, and Arscott, Caroline
'Cultivated capital'. bibl il *Hist Today* 37:22-8 Mr '87
Wolff, Tobias, 1945-
Smorgasbord [story] il *Esquire* 108:236-8+ S '87
Wolfman, Ira
Insecurities about security: face to face with the building-protection crisis. il *Archit Rec* 175:126-31 Ag '87
It's still full speed ahead for Ralph Nader. il por *50 Plus* 27:24-7 N '87
Wolgemuth and Hyatt
'Wainscoting & Hairshirt'. W. Griffin. il *Publ Wkly* 232:42-3 O 9 '87
Woliner, Ellen
about
The art of the cold call. D. Shilling. il pors *Work Woman* 12:50-3 D '87
Woliver, Robbie
about
The sound of success. S. Mieses. il por *N Y* 20:22 Ap 6 '87
Wolkenberg, Frank
Out of a darkness. il *N Y Times Mag* p62+ O 11 '87
Wolkomir, Joyce
(jt. auth) See Wolkomir, Richard, and Wolkomir, Joyce
Wolkomir, Richard
Alien worlds: the search heats up [cover story; with editorial comment by Paul Hoffman] il *Discover* 8:4, 66-8+ O '87
Astrocrops. il *Omni* 9:16+ Jl '87
Beyond the Challenger era. il *Omni* 9:62-4+ Mr '87
It is easy to get bushed when you're threading a maze. il *Smithsonian* 18:108-12+ D '87
Roxie Laybourne: feather detective. il pors *Natl Wildl* 26:20-5 D '87/Ja '88
Sculpture in the subways? Is there a better place for it? il *Smithsonian* 18:114-18+ Ap '87
Shapeful islands for a 'tied up' businessman. il *Smithsonian* 17:192 Mr '87
She's an artist whose explosives make a lasting impression. il pors *Smithsonian* 18:166-8+ D '87
'Wafted to Mars, he fights four-armed green Tharks'. il *Smithsonian* 18:192 My '87
With tabloids, 'Zip! You're in another world!'. il *Smithsonian* 18:240 O '87
Wolkomir, Richard, and Wolkomir, Joyce
Between a rock and a cold place. il *Natl Wildl* 25:46-51 Je/Jl '87
Clairvoyant crime busters. il por *McCalls* 115:162-4+ O '87
When adventure is a snow job. il *Natl Wildl* 25:50-1 F/Mr '87
Woll, Josephine
Moscow revisited. il *New Leader* 70:7-9 F 9-23 '87

Wollett, Bill
(jt. auth) See Wollett, Mary, and Wollett, Bill
Wollett, Mary, and Wollett, Bill
American historical glass. See issues of Antiques & Collecting Hobbies beginning March 1985
American historical glass. See issues of Hobbies through February 1985
Wolman, Clive
A study in disinvestment. *World Press Rev* 34:54 O '87
Wolong Natural Reserve (China) *See* Wildlife sanctuaries—China
Wolpe, Howard
Should Congress adopt the House-passed "Gephardt Amendment"? [excerpts from debate, April 29, 1987] *Congr Dig* 66:190 Je/Jl '87
Wolterstorff, Nicholas
about
The tears of God. M. E. Marty. *Christ Century* 104:607 Jl 1-8 '87
Wolverine (Aircraft carrier)
The side-wheel carriers. G. C. Long. il *Am Herit* 38:104-7 F/Mr '87
Wolverine Exploration Company
Once more to the well [W. T. Smith] J. Willoughby. il por *Forbes* 140:194 S 21 '87
Wolverine World Wide Inc.
Why Hush Puppies need some fancy footwork. W. Zellner. il *Bus Week* p64 Ag 3 '87
Wolves
See also
Coyotes
At home with the Arctic wolf. L. D. Mech. il map *Natl Geogr* 171:562-93 My '87
Grass roots of the maned wolf [Brazil] J. J. Dietz. il *Nat Hist* 96:52-9 Mr '87
His howl is a lot worse than his bite [research by Fred Harrington] il *Discover* 8:10+ Jl '87
The land is alive with wolves . . . J. D. Vickery. il *Audubon* 89:52-61 Ja '87
The man who cries wolf. F. H. Harrington. il *Nat Hist* 96:22+ F '87
Recall of the wild wolf [controversial recovery plans to reestablish wolf packs in the wild] D. D. Edwards. il map *Sci News* 131:378-9 Je 13 '87
Red wolf in the wilderness [captive breeding program] J. P. Cohn. il *BioScience* 37:313-16 My '87
Return of the western wolf. il *Nat Hist* 96:4 O '87
The return of the wolf people [Yellowstone] T. H. Watkins. il *Wilderness* 51:46-7 Wint '87
Running with the pack. il *Natl Geogr World* 138:4-9 F '87
Should we cry wolf? [recovery plan to repopulate Rocky Mountain areas] J. Zumbo. il *Outdoor Life* 180:50-1+ D '87
Strange encounter on Coho Creek [timber wolves in Alaska] M. H. Erwin. il *Read Dig* 130:11-16 My '87
Who's afraid of the big bad wolf? J. Carey. il *Natl Wildl* 25:4-11 Ag/S '87
Wolves in religion, folklore, etc.
Who's afraid of the big bad wolf? J. Carey. il *Natl Wildl* 25:4-11 Ag/S '87
Wolynes, Peter G.
(jt. auth) See Kuki, Atsuo, and Wolynes, Peter G.
Woman *See* Women
Woman suffrage
Exhibitions
Political quilts [De Anza College in Cupertino, Calif.] il *Sunset* 178:40-1 Mr '87
Womanizer (Term)
Vamping till ready. W. Safire. il *N Y Times Mag* p14+ My 3 '87
Woman's day (Periodical)
Woman's day [manuscript submission policy] R. Greer. il *Writer* 100:31 Ap '87
Women
See also
Alcohol and women
Beauty, Personal
Black women
Christmas gifts for women
Drugs and women
Farm women
Feminism
Heroes and heroines
Homeless women
Indians of North America—Women
Jewish women
—Married women
Music and women
—Sex differences

—Single women
Smoking and women
Widows
Young women
Alice Walker, Coretta King most outstanding: poll [World almanac poll] il *Jet* 71:27 Ja 19 '87
America's 10 most beautiful women [cover story] il *Harpers Bazaar* 120:340-71+ S '87
America's 10 most beautiful women reveal their beauty secrets [special section] il *Harpers Bazaar* 120:30+ S '87
Between us. L. Davis. See issues of Vogue
Class makes a comeback: the return of the lady. K. Heller. il *Mademoiselle* 93:214-15+ My '87
Heroic proportions [most admired men and women polls; study by Tom W. Smith] A. H. Rosenfeld. il *Psychol Today* 21:15 Jl '87
The highs, the lows: lasting memories of 1986. K. Burkett and M. McNamara. il *Ms* 15:19-21+ Ja '87
Lessons we learned from the women of '87. il *Glamour* 85:62 D '87
Look who won our most admired women and men polls. il *Good Housekeep* 204:48 Ja '87
News from all over. See issues of Ms. beginning January 1986
Over-40 & young! [special section] il *Harpers Bazaar* 120:124-37+ Ag '87
What the U.S. has to learn . . . [lack of centralized social policy] G. Steinem. il *Ms* 16:162 Jl/Ag '87
Winnie one of world's 'most important women' [W. Mandela cited by Ladies' home journal] il por *Jet* 73:38 O 26 '87
A woman today. See issues of Ladies' Home Journal beginning July 1983
Women right now. L. Mosedale. See issues of Glamour
The world's most controversial women [special section] il *Ladies Home J* 104:121-4+ Mr '87
The world's ten most important women. il *Ladies Home J* 104:133-5+ N '87
Anatomy and physiology
See also
Breast
Menstruation
Vagina
Listening to your body. J. Kaplan. *Vogue* 177:366+ Ap '87
Attitudes
Back off, buddy [Women and love report by S. Hite; cover story] C. Wallis. il *Time* 130:68-73 O 12 '87
Bedroom eyes: erotic movies come home. E. Abeel. il *Mademoiselle* 93:194-5+ O '87
Cross-addiction: surprising results of the Ms. survey. L. Van Gelder. il *Ms* 15:44-7+ F '87
How optimistic are American women? [results of poll] il *Ms* 16:172-4+ Jl/Ag '87
How women's minds have changed in the last five years [Glamour survey] il *Glamour* 85:214-3a '87
Men aren't her only problem [S. Hite] B. Barol. il por *Newsweek* 110:76 N 23 '87
The private life of the American woman [results of survey] C. Enos and S. F. Enos. il *Ladies Home J* 104:98+ Ap '87
Special survey results: 26,000 women reveal the secrets of intimacy. C. Rubenstein and C. Tavris. il *Redbook* 169:147-9+ S '87
The subject is you: Vogue's twelfth annual American Woman symposium; ed. by Lorraine Davis. il *Vogue* 177:172-9+ Je '87
Tapping a mine of female discontent [Women and love report by S. Hite] M. McIver. il por *Macleans* 100:44-5 O 19 '87
Awards
Women of the Year: the 1986 awards [special section] il *Ms* 15:39-41+ Ja '87
Bibliography
Books. See issues of Ms.
Clothing and dress
See Clothing and dress
Crime
Women: the new white-collar criminals. C. Kirschenbaum. *Glamour* 85:306-7+ Mr '87
Crimes against
See also
Rape
Self defense for women
Fears of a serial killer [Edmonton, Alta.] *Macleans* 100:14 Ap 13 '87
Male guilt [men perceived as criminals by women] P. Mehlman. il *Glamour* 85:332 Ap '87

Women—Crimes against—*cont.*

Violence on the Island [P. Pope resigns from Prince Edward Island legislature after admitting to beating a woman] M. Gee. por *Macleans* 100:12 Ja 19 '87

Washington watch [extending the Victims of Crime Assistance Act] S. Goen. il *Ms* 16:75 D '87

Women right to kill men who brutalize them: group [Committee on Domestic Violence and Incarcerated Women] *Jet* 72:28 Jl 13 '87

Diseases

See also

　AIDS (Disease) and women
　Anorexia nervosa
　Breast—Cancer
　Bulimia
　Endometriosis
　Gynecology
　Menstruation—Disorders
　Osteoporosis
　Pelvic inflammatory disease
　Premenstrual syndrome
　Reproductive organs—Diseases

Diseases women get: what you need to know. *McCalls* 145:77+ Mr '87

The female heart [difference in numbers of men and women referred for catheterization] il *U S News World Rep* 103:6 Ag 3 '87

Science discovers women [overlooked in medical research] R. Wolkomir and J. Wolkomir. *Omni* 10:37 O '87

Those lips, those eyes . . . what your looks reveal about your health. K. P. Behan. il *Mademoiselle* 93:76+ Ja '87

Economic conditions

See also

　Black women—Economic conditions
　Wages and salaries

10 good money resolutions to make for 1988. C. B. Steger. il *Work Woman* 12:84-5+ D '87

The bottom line for women. E. Card. il *Ms* 16:48+ Jl/Ag '87

Dollars & sense. C. E. Rinzler. See isssues of Mademoiselle

Enterprising women [improving economic conditions] J. Walsh. il *Ms* 15:69-72 My '87

How to be successful with money [results of survey] B. Siverd and M. Morris. il *Work Woman* 12:121-5+ N '87

How to live rich on your salary. L. Savan. il *Mademoiselle* 93:222-3+ My '87

Letter to the past [imaginary letter to S. B. Anthony detailing current economic status of women] C. McHugh. il por *Sch Update* 119:12-14 My 18 '87

Managing your money. See issues of Vogue beginning June 1984

Money. See issues of Working Woman

More for your money. B. G. Quint. See issues of Glamour

Rich for life [special section] il *Work Woman* 12:31-4+ F '87

A step back to the workhouse? [workfare's effect] B. Ehrenreich. il por *Ms* 16:40-2 N '87

A surge in inequality [international competition and the feminization of poverty are distorting the distribution of income] L. C. Thurow. bibl (p128) il *Sci Am* 256:30-7 My '87

Ten painless ways to get more money out of your paycheck. G. Worth. *Work Woman* 12:72-3 Jl '87

Why women are afraid of money [excerpt from Unbalanced accounts] A. R. Lieberman and V. Lindner. il *Glamour* 85:318-19+ Ap '87

Education

See also

　Colleges for women
　Dorcas Place Parent Literacy Center
　Sex discrimination in education
　Women college students

Back to school full-time: should you go for it? G. Hechinger. *Glamour* 85:248+ Je '87

Education. G. Hechinger. See issues of Glamour

I thought I was a terrific teacher until one day . . . [dealing with older women returning to college] M. Yudkin. il *Ms* 16:66-7 O '87

No boys allowed: a smart solution? [girls attending single-sex Catholic high schools do better academically; research by Valerie E. Lee and Anthony S. Bryk] S. Vandershaf. il *Psychol Today* 21:68 F '87

Who needs women? K. C. Cole. *Omni* 9:35 My '87

Anecdotes, facetiae, satire, etc.

I'm counting up good news (on my fingers). K. Fury. il *Work Woman* 12:152 Je '87

Employment

See also

　Black women—Employment
　Businesswomen
　—Equal pay for equal work
　Married women—Employment
　Maternity leaves
　Mothers—Employment
　Single mothers—Employment
　United States. Women's Bureau
　Widows—Employment
　—Women—Occupations

20 corporations that listen to women [results of survey] R. B. Will and S. D. Lydenberg. il *Ms* 16:45-52 N '87

Affirmative action: after the debate, opportunity [Supreme Court decision in Santa Clara case] P. Dwyer. il *Bus Week* p37 Ap 13 '87

Assignment: sports [discrimination against women sportswriters in the men's locker rooms] J. Lannin. il *Women's Sports Fitness* 9:77-9+ Mr '87

Balancing act [Supreme Court expands affirmative action in Santa Clara County, Calif. case] R. Stengel. il *Time* 129:18-20 Ap 6 '87

Big bucks, baby—get wise to the ways to rise. A. Gates. *Mademoiselle* 93:154-5 F '87

Brennanism [Supreme Court decision in Santa Clara, Calif. affirmative action case] D. Seligman. *Fortune* 115:283+ Ap 27 '87

Catch-28 [young women disillusioned in work could endanger future job opportunities for women] L. J. Nonkin. il *Work Woman* 12:118-20+ My '87

Court ruling affirmative [Supreme Court decides Santa Clara affirmative action case] J. C. Baker. *Black Enterp* 17:20 Jl '87

Dear Betty Harragan. B. L. Harragan. See issues of Working Woman

Dear Betty Harragan [task force assignments reflect sex discrimination] B. L. Harragan. il *Work Woman* 12:26+ F '87

Determination in the workplace. A. Steacy. il *Macleans* 100:48-9 N 16 '87

An excuse for workplace hazard [fetal protection policies discriminate against women] C. Marshall. il *Nation* 244:532-4 Ap 25 '87

Farm women sue USDA [farm program payment discrimination] C. Tevis. il *Success Farm* 85:24 S '87

Gender-based hiring and promotions approved [Supreme Court decision in Santa Clara County, Calif. affirmative action case] *Mon Labor Rev* 110:41-2 My '87

Healthsmart. C. Schrader. *Harpers Bazaar* 121:94+ N '87

How and why I sued my boss for sex discrimination. K. Stone. *Glamour* 85:228-9+ Je '87

How do demographic changes affect labor force participation of women? D. T. Lichter and J. A. Costanzo. bibl f il *Mon Labor Rev* 110:23-5 N '87

"I don't want to work anymore": the new career dropouts. L. R. Gallese. il *Mademoiselle* 93:268-9+ Mr '87

Is your work harmful to your unborn baby? C. Loomis. il *Parents* 62:13 Jl '87

Job strategies. M. M. Kennedy. See issues of Glamour

Ladies' day [Supreme Court ruling in Santa Clara affirmative action case] *New Repub* 196:4+ Ap 20 '87

Letter to the past [imaginary letter to S. B. Anthony detailing current economic status of women] C. McHugh. il por *Sch Update* 119:12-14 My 18 '87

The next wave [feminism and working class women] B. Ehrenreich. il *Ms* 16:166-8+ Jl/Ag '87

Pay discrimination against women settled [San Francisco, Tennessee Valley Authority and Sumitomo Corp. of America cases] *Mon Labor Rev* 110:56 Je '87

Productivity is the best affirmative action plan. G. S. Becker. il *Bus Week* p18 Ap 27 '87

Quick quiz: what qualifies as sex discrimination? *Glamour* 85:89 Mr '87

Saying "yes" to affirmative action [Supreme Court ruling in Santa Clara case] M. Takas. *Vogue* 177:58 N '87

Sex bias costly to companies [bias against women in performance evaluations; views of Gregory Dobbins] il *USA Today (Periodical)* 115:4 Ap '87

Status of working women exaggerated on TV, study. *Jet* 71:32 F 2 '87

Supreme Court extends affirmative action goals for women, minorities. *Jet* 72:5 Ap 13 '87

The Supreme Court puts the mike in Diane Joyce's hands, giving feminists a major victory [Santa Clara County, Calif. affirmative action case] W. Plummer. il pors *People Wkly* 27:49-50+ Ap 13 '87

Women—Employment—*cont.*

Those wild tuna guys [objections by crew to placing women observers aboard tuna fishing boats] *Harpers* 274:19-20 Je '87

Tribal justice [Supreme Court majority opinion upholding the legality of Santa Clara, Calif. affirmative action plan] *Natl Rev* 39:17-18 Ap 24 '87

Understanding women [excerpt from Ortho Pharmaceuticals recruiting memo] *Harpers* 274:23-4 Ap '87

Warning: men at work may be hazardous to your career [subtle sexism] P. Schmidt. il *Mademoiselle* 93:178-9+ D '87

A woman's day in court [Supreme Court decision in Santa Clara County, Calif. affirmative action case] A. Press. il *Newsweek* 109:58-9 Ap 6 '87

Women at war with each other [views of T. R. Madden] S. Nelton. il por *Nations Bus* 75:58 N '87

Women at work [charts] il *Sch Update* 119:4 My 18 '87

The women win—again [Supreme Court decision in Santa Clara County, Calif. affirmative action case] T. Gest. il *U S News World Rep* 102:18-19 Ap 6 '87

Women's work plans: contrasting expectations and actual work experience. L. B. Shaw and D. Shapiro. bibl f il *Mon Labor Rev* 110:7-13 N '87

Work wise. B. L. Harragan. See issues of Mademoiselle

You get ahead, he gets mad . . . will success spoil your romance? M. F. Coburn. *Mademoiselle* 93:186-7+ O '87

Your brilliant career. R. Sharp. See issues of Mademoiselle beginning May 1987

Your career crossroads [special section] *Harpers Bazaar* 120:298-9+ Mr '87

History

Businesswomen: equal but different. W. Hoffer. il *Nations Bus* 75:46-7 Ag '87

Women's history and EEOC v. Sears [sex discrimination case; special section] *Society* 24:4-16 S/O '87

Psychological aspects

See Psychology, Industrial

Equal rights

See also

Equal pay for equal work

National Organization for Women

Sex discrimination

United Nations. Commission on the Status of Women

United Nations. Committee on the Elimination of Discrimination against Women

United States. Constitution. Equal Rights Amendment (Proposed)

Woman suffrage

Women—Employment

Assembly calls for priority measures to improve status of women. *UN Chron* 24:118 F '87

The Constitution [discussion of May 1987 article, Why blacks, women & Jews are not mentioned in the Constitution] R. A. Goldwin. *Commentary* 84:2+ O '87

The Constitution and the people left out: a study in original intent. R. A. Goldwin. *Current* 295:4-10 S '87

Measures to implement women's 'forward-looking strategies' called for in Third Committee. il *UN Chron* 23:70-1 Ja '86

Measuring the equality gap [University of New Hampshire study] il *USA Today (Periodical)* 115:4-5 Ap '87

Our flawed and glorious Constitution. C. Kocol. por *Humanist* 47:37-8 My/Je '87

Why blacks, women & Jews are not mentioned in the Constitution. R. A. Goldwin. *Commentary* 83:28-33 My '87

Women in America: how equal today? [cover story; special issue] il map *Sch Update* 119:3-14+ My 18 '87

Health and hygiene

See also

Beauty, Personal

Black women—Health and hygiene

Feminine hygiene products

Gynecologic examinations

Gynecologists and patients

Menopause

Menstruation

Physical fitness

Pregnancy

Young women—Health and hygiene

Beauty & health report. S. Young. See issues of Glamour

Body management: leveling off at terrific [special section] il *Work Woman* 12:117-18+ Je '87

Can you be fit without being healthy? D. Pine. il *Women's Sports Fitness* 9:34-7 Je '87

Feel & look your best! C. Schrader. il *Harpers Bazaar* 120:130-1+ Ja '87

Feeling good. See issues of Mademoiselle

Health style. See issues of Vogue

Healthsmart. C. Schrader. *Harpers Bazaar* 120:68+ Ag '87

How old is your body? Beat-the-clock strategies. J. Kaplan. il *Mademoiselle* 93:92+ Je '87

Natural beauty [special section] il *Harpers Bazaar* 120:210-27+ O '87

New mind/body basics [special section] il *Vogue* 177:354-73+ Ap '87

Our bodies, our world: how the environment affects health [special section] il *Vogue* 177:402-7+ O '87

Pressure points . . . active answers [special section] il *Vogue* 177:352-9+ Ag '87

Quick health tips for women only [excerpt from Listen to your body] E. Michaud and L. Anastas. *Prevention* 39:89 D '87

Sex & health. S. Zussman. See issues of Glamour beginning November 1986

Shape-up. L. Gordon. See issues of Glamour

Wake up and be healthy [cover story; special section] il *Ms* 15:39-56+ Ap '87

Women's health handbook [special section] il *McCalls* 145:77+ Mr '87

Women's symptoms not to ignore. G. J. Subak-Sharpe. *Ladies Home J* 104:31-2 Ap '87

Work up a beauty sweat. il *Mademoiselle* 93:154-9 Ja '87

Health insurance

See Insurance, Health

Height

See Stature

History

Jessie Benton Frémont [with editorial comment by Ed Holm] P. Herr. il pors *Am Hist Illus* 22:18, 20-9+ S '87

Poor little rich girls [19th century American heiresses who married British nobility] C. M. Wallace. il *Forbes* 140 Sp Issue:62+ O 26 '87

Women in their time [special section; with editorial comment by Byron Dobell] il *Am Herit* 38:5, 44-63+ S/O '87

Bibliography

Book notes [women homesteaders] J. Long. *Nation* 244:371-4 Mr 21 '87

Historiography

Without a history . . . [excerpt from address] A. Kessler-Harris. *Ms* 16:84-5 N '87

International aspects

See also

United Nations. Commission on the Status of Women

United Nations. Committee on the Elimination of Discrimination against Women

Assembly calls for priority measures to improve status of women. *UN Chron* 24:118 F '87

Measures to implement women's 'forward-looking strategies' called for in Third Committee. il *UN Chron* 23:70-1 Ja '86

Women around the world [chart] il *Sch Update* 119:26 My 18 '87

Legal status, laws, etc.

See also

Divorce

Woman suffrage

15 milestones. M. McNamara; G. Jacobs. il *Ms* 16:90 Jl/Ag '87

Eat right, stay off your feet—or go to jail [proposed measures protecting fetal rights at the expense of the mother] M. Takas. *Vogue* 177:148 My '87

How state laws affect women. D. O. Relin. il map *Sch Update* 119:22-3 My 18 '87

Legislative alert: what we want from the 100th Congress. J. E. Grenier. il *Ms* 15:24 Ap '87

A matter of neglect [fetal rights vs. maternal rights] J. Bermel. il *Parents* 62:335-6+ N '87

Newslines from Washington. M. Engel. See issues of Glamour

The ordeal of Pamela Rae Stewart [charged with irresponsible prenatal care] A. Bonavoglia. il pors *Ms* 16:92-5+ Jl/Ag '87

Policing pregnancy [views on forced obstetrical procedures] *Sci Am* 257:26+ Ag '87

Reproductive rights for today. L. Gordon. il *Nation* 245:230-2 S 12 '87

Nutrition

See also

Pregnancy—Nutritional aspects

Women—Nutrition—See also—*cont.*
  Premenstrual syndrome—Nutritional aspects
For nutrition research, women in Grand Forks, North Dakota are licking their plates clean. J. Friedman. il *People Wkly* 27:109-10+ Ap 20 '87
Get smart! Foods and workouts that sharpen your outlook. L. Manske. il *Mademoiselle* 93:182 S '87
The good-nutrition guide [special section] il *Mademoiselle* 93:136+ Ap '87
Is your diet sabotaging your looks? il *Glamour* 85:280-3 Mr '87
Nutrition: for women only. *McCalls* 145:86 Mr '87
Nutrition know-how. J. Schmid. il *Vogue* 177:359+ Ag '87
The truth about lunch. S. M. Sims. il *Vogue* 177:449-51+ Mr '87
A week of healthy eating. N. Clark. il *Women's Sports Fitness* 9:41-4 S '87
Why smart women don't diet anymore. il *Glamour* 85:306-11 N '87
Your diet. J. S. Stern. See issues of Vogue beginning October 1984

Occupations
  See also
  Black women—Occupations
  Businesswomen
  Equal pay for equal work
The 25 hottest careers of 1987 [cover story] W. Konrad and J. Tedeschi. il *Work Woman* 12:57-62+ Jl '87
All the right moves . . . work/love [career changes by women] il *Vogue* 177:300-4+ Ag '87
The eighth annual Working woman salary survey. H. McCrum and H. Rubin. il *Work Woman* 12:53-5+ Ja '87
How internships help with career choices [Women's Sports Foundation program] il *Women's Sports Fitness* 9:78-9 N '87
If you're so smart . . . how come you're working for that salary? A. Gates. il *Mademoiselle* 93:238-9+ Ag '87
Meet ten outstanding young working women for 1987. il *Glamour* 85:217+ F '87
Modern-day mentors: five lessons in success [role models] L. Rosch. il *Work Woman* 12:55-9 Ag '87
Washington, D.C.: great jobs in the fast lane [special section] *Harpers Bazaar* 121:46+ N '87
Where women are succeeding. A. B. Fisher. il *Fortune* 116:78-80+ Ag 3 '87

Photographs and photography
  See also
  Black women—Photographs and photography
Some of her parts. A. MacWeeney. il *Esquire* 107:200-3 Je '87

Physical fitness
  See Physical fitness

Political activities
  See also
  Black women—Political activities
  National Women's Political Caucus
  Woman suffrage
  Women political candidates
  Women public officers
A global click! J. O'Reilly. il *Ms* 16:60-1+ Jl/Ag '87
Iceland's feminists: power at the top of the world [Kvennalistinn Party] J. Edgar. il *Ms* 16:30+ D '87
Newslines from Washington. M. Engel. See issues of Glamour
On political courage [excerpt from address] M. Kunin. por *Ms* 16:84 N '87
Washington, D.C.: great jobs in the fast lane [special section] *Harpers Bazaar* 121:46+ N '87
Women: a new politics. T. Jacoby. il *Newsweek* 110:20-1 S 7 '87
Women of the people. il *Life* 10:122-7 Ja '87

Psychiatric care
In search of self [E. Cacho, psychotherapist to Mexican American women] M. Rochlin. il pors *Ms* 16:58-60 N '87

Psychology
  See also
  Abortion—Psychological aspects
  Beauty, Personal—Psychological aspects
  Black women—Psychology
  Body image
  Femininity (Psychology)
  Pregnancy—Psychological aspects
Are you too hard to please? [excerpt from Women men love/women men leave] C. Cowan and M. Kinder. *Redbook* 169:96-7+ Jl '87
Are you too tough on yourself? When to lighten up, when to tighten up. J. Stone. *Glamour* 85:88 D '87

The baby bandwagon. S. Jacoby. il *Glamour* 85:388-9+ S '87
Brokenhearted me. E. Pell. il *Ms* 15:80 Je '87
Competitive women risk heart attacks [findings of Carl Thoresen] il *USA Today (Periodical)* 116:8 S '87
Dance with an intimate stranger [interview with H. G. Lerner] C. Tavris. *Vogue* 177:44 D '87
Dr. Joyce Brothers answers your questions. J. Brothers. See issues of Good Housekeeping
Fear of intimacy: not for men only [excerpt from Women men love/women men leave] C. Cowan and M. Kinder. il *Glamour* 85:96+ O '87
Hard choices: the tough decisions women must make today [roundtable discussion] S. S. Stautberg. il *Ladies Home J* 104:96-7+ Ja '87
How to get what you want—nicely. A. Gottlieb. *McCalls* 114:54-5 Ja '87
"I don't want to work anymore": the new career dropouts. L. R. Gallese. il *Mademoiselle* 93:268-9+ Mr '87
Is there life after being a good girl? E. Jong. *Glamour* 85:268-9+ Ag '87
The legacy of father-loss: "men that I love will leave me". E. Wakerman. *Glamour* 85:132+ My '87
Living with trouble that won't go away and learning how to keep it from dominating your life [chronic stress caused by illness or other problems] S. Jacoby. il *Glamour* 85:266-7+ My '87
Loving too much [R. Norwood's Women who love too much] C. Leerhsen. il por *Newsweek* 109:52-3 Mr 9 '87
Lucky, plucky Becky Sinkler. D. Hurford. il por *50 Plus* 27:50+ Ag '87
Mind health. C. Tavris. See issues of Vogue
The parable of the cheek-turners and the cheek-smiters [feminist opposition to proposed revision of the Diagnostic and statistical manual of mental disorders] S. Boxer. il *Discover* 8:80-3 Ag '87
Patterns of addiction [cover story; special section; with list of treatment resources] il *Ms* 15:35-9+, 63-6 F '87
The politics of masochism [feminists challenge proposed revisions to Diagnostic and statistical manual of mental disorders] D. Franklin. il *Psychol Today* 21:52-7 Ja '87
Psychologist's journal. S. Friedman. See issues of Ladies' Home Journal beginning September 1983
The road well-taken: why you rely on past tactics to confront the present. B. L. Stern. *Vogue* 177:444 F '87
Smart women, foolish books: can your love life be saved in ten chapters or less? A. Landi. *Mademoiselle* 93:180-1+ O '87
Stress, pressure, and peak performance [cover story; special section] il *Ms* 15:37-9+ My '87
Turning 30 and going nowhere? [special section] il *Harpers Bazaar* 120:160+ O '87
Who is the right man for a woman like you? [excerpt from The Type E woman] H. B. Braiker. il *Work Woman* 12:72-4+ Ja '87
Why is all the relationship-repair advice aimed at women? il *Glamour* 85:64 F '87
Why women cheat. P. Grant. il *Glamour* 85:148-9+ Jl '87
Why women lie about their age. M. Hodge. il *50 Plus* 27:40-2 F '87
Why would a woman peel off her clothes and pose nude for Playboy? Three women tell their stories. S. Helgesen. il *Glamour* 85:218-19+ Je '87
Women and the new midlife crisis. R. Grant. il *Ladies Home J* 104:87-9+ Ag '87
Women at war with each other [views of T. R. Madden] S. Nelton. il por *Nations Bus* 75:58 N '87
  Bibliography
Addicted to love. J. Maynard. il *Mademoiselle* 93:90+ Ag '87
Women who read too much [self-help books] S. Bolotin. il *Vogue* 177:246+ F '87

Reading
Women who read too much [self-help books] S. Bolotin. il *Vogue* 177:246+ F '87

Religious life
  See also
  Ordination of women
  Women clergy
The new victims of cults [middle aged and aged women] D. Salvatore. *Ladies Home J* 104:46+ Ag '87
Shake the universe [spirituality of women] M. L'Engle. il *Ms* 16:182-4+ Jl/Ag '87

Women—*cont.*

Salaries

See Wages and salaries

Scholarships and fellowships

See Scholarships and fellowships

Self defense

See Self defense for women

Sexual behavior

See Sexual behavior

Social conditions

See also

Divorce
Misogyny
Prostitution

America's women: meeting the challenges of today. M. Christopher. il *Sch Update* 119:5-7 My 18 '87

Calling all cousins—who connects the family [role of women] C. Tavris. *Vogue* 177:122 My '87

Readers & writers: reflecting the demands upon women. A. McCarthy. *Commonweal* 114:6-7 Ja 16 '87

There will always be a Texas. M. Ivins. il *Ms* 16:82-4 Jl/Ag '87

Women: where we are today [special section] il *Ladies Home J* 104:93-5+ Mr '87

Women—the managers of food. H. H. Wassef. il *World Health* p18-19 Mr '87

Sports

See also

Baseball, Professional
Basketball, College
Basketball, High school
Basketball, Professional
Bicycle racing
Billiards
Bowling
Coed sports
Cycling
Fencing
Gliding and soaring
Golf
Gymnastics
Heptathlon
Kayaks and kayaking
Marathon running
Mountaineering
National Women in Sports Day
Rowing
Rowing, Indoor
Running
Ski racing
Skin diving
Skis and skiing
Soccer, College
Softball
Squash (Sport)
Surfing
Swimming
Tennis
Track and field athletics
Triathlon
Volleyball
Volleyball, College
Volleyball, Professional
Water skis and skiing
Weight lifting
Women's Sports Foundation

Aging gracefully. N. Kuscsik. il *Women's Sports Fitness* 9:16-21 O '87

Be an Olympian [women in the Senior Olympics] il *Women's Sports Fitness* 9:56 Je '87

Big plus for females [sports interest and math skills] J. E. Vader. por *Sports Illus* 67:100 N 23 '87

Dating games [tennis, racquetball, badminton and volleyball] il *Mademoiselle* 93:200-3 Ag '87

Fast breaks [1986 in review] M. B. Nelson. il *Women's Sports Fitness* 9:17-20 Ja '87

Fear-free! S. Cummings. il *Health* 19:44-6+ N '87

Get involved—write a letter! [restoration of Title IX to original strength] *Women's Sports Fitness* 9:64 Je '87

Getting high on danger. J. Laughridge. *Harpers Bazaar* 120:89-90+ Jl '87

Great places to live: the ten best cities for active women. C. Abbott and J. Starker. il map *Women's Sports Fitness* 9:42-6 My '87

The many shapes of sport [women's bodies] K. Delhagen. il *Women's Sports Fitness* 9:28-31 F '87

Poster girls [ads celebrating benefits of women's participation in sports] *Women's Sports Fitness* 9:62 Ag '87

Splash! The fitness plunge. il *Harpers Bazaar* 120:136-9+ My '87

Sports: much more than "just fun". B. Phillips. il *Sch Update* 120:2-3 S 18 '87

Summer champions. C. Davis. il *Mot Boat Sail* 159:52-7+ Je '87

What turns girls on to sports? F. E. Halpert. il *Women's Sports Fitness* 9:98-9 S '87

What's in the future for women's sports? [demise of gymnastics at Southwest Texas State University as an example of effects of weakened Title IX regulations] C. L. Hogan. il *Women's Sports Fitness* 9:42-7 Je '87

Which sport will you excel in? [clues from body shapes] J. Mattera. il *Glamour* 85:122+ O '87

Win a few, lose a few [review of events of 1987] il *Women's Sports Fitness* 9:74 D '87

Winning at beauty [teenage athletes L. Harwood, L. Blasko, I. Rubinshtein, and S. Rehe] il pors *Teen* 31:74-7 Jl '87

You and sports: finding the right fit. M. Curren. il *McCalls* 114:39+ My '87

Bibliography

Mixed media. See occasional issues of Women's Sports & Fitness

Information services

Call 1-800-227-3988 [toll-free number for Women's Sports Foundation service] il *Women's Sports Fitness* 9:52 Ja '87

Scholarships and fellowships

See Scholarships and fellowships

Statistics

. . about women. K. Berry. il *Ms* 16:164-5 Jl/Ag '87

Taxation

You and your 1040: how women fare under the new tax law. E. Card. il *Ms* 15:68+ F '87

Travel

Adventurous Victorians. L. Siemers. il *Travel Holiday* 167:92 My '87

Hi-trek holidays [adventure vacations for women] G. Wiltsie. il *Harpers Bazaar* 120:174+ Mr '87

Volunteer service

See Volunteer service

Wages

See Wages and salaries

Argentina

See also

Grandmothers of the Plaza de Mayo (Organization)

Canada

No to sexual harassment [Canadian Supreme Court rules that employers under federal jurisdiction are responsible for acts of harassment their employees commit] M. Clark. il por *Macleans* 100:44 Ag 10 '87

Trudeau's star turn [criticism of the constitutional accord] M. Janigan. il por *Macleans* 100:14-16+ S 7 '87

What women want now [cover story; special section; with editorial comment by Kevin Doyle] il *Macleans* 100:2, 42-4+ N 16 '87

China

Holding up the sky. C. Kocol. por *Humanist* 47:37-8 Mr/Ap '87

Look, Mao—no pajamas! [female body builders in China permitted to compete in bikinis] O. Schell. il *Women's Sports Fitness* 9:68+ Ag '87

Developing countries

Where women face age-old prejudices. P. M. Jones. il *Sch Update* 119:24-5 My 18 '87

Women on the sidelines. A. M. Diop. bibl f il *Courier* 40:20-2 Ja '87

East Asia

The slow march of Asian women. F. Fearon. *World Press Rev* 34:56 Ag '87

Egypt

Bedouin blues [Bedouin poetry] L. Abu-Lughod. il *Nat Hist* 96:24-33 Jl '87

Great Britain

History

Adventurous Victorians. L. Siemers. il *Travel Holiday* 167:92 My '87

Greece

Margarita Papandreou [interview] C. Dreifus. il *Progressive* 51:21-4 D '87

Iceland

Iceland's feminists: power at the top of the world [Kvennalistinn Party] J. Edgar. il *Ms* 16:30+ D '87

Latin America

History

Devoted wives, determined rebels. E. M. Cherpak. il *Américas* 39:32-7 Mr/Ap '87

Mexico

Little progress for Mexico's women. S. Hall. *World Press Rev* 34:53-4 My '87

Women—*cont.*

Namibia
See also

International Day of Solidarity with the Struggle of Women of South Africa and Namibia

Southern African women caught in the middle. M. McNamara. il *Ms* 15:23 Mr '87

Portugal
In the absence of men [male emigration] C. B. Brettell. il *Nat Hist* 96:52-61 F '87

Saudi Arabia
Women of Saudi Arabia [cover story] M. Alireza. il *Natl Geogr* 172:422-53 O '87

Siberia (Soviet Union)
Siberia's new women. S. K. Reed. il *People Wkly* 27:69-70+ Ap 6 '87

South Africa
See also

International Day of Solidarity with the Struggle of Women of South Africa and Namibia

Southern Africa
Women battling apartheid [black women on lecture tour of U.S.] M. Oshin. il *Essence* 17:24 Ja '87

Soviet Union
The burden of caring [women and Russian literature] B. Heldt. *Nation* 244:820-4 Je 13 '87

Gorbo's other woman [role of Soviet leader's wife] G. Freidin. *New Repub* 197:15-16 D 28 '87

The horrors of war behind her, Galina Fedyanina emerges as a triumph of socialist labor. J. W. Seymore. il pors *People Wkly* 27:88+ Ap 6 '87

Male chauvinism, Soviet style. J. L. Galloway. il *U S News World Rep* 103:10-11 D 14 '87

Wanted: a nude *glasnost* [women's magazines in the Soviet Union] S. Drakulich. il *Nation* 244:846-8 Je 20 '87

Trinidad and Tobago
Working women on the move. M. James-Bryant and H. Cole. il *Essence* 17:86-8+ Ap '87

United States
See Black women; Women

Women, Aged *See* Aged

Women, Black *See* Black women

Women & Children First (Chicago, Ill.: Bookstore) *See* Booksellers and bookselling—Illinois

Women air pilots
See also

Earhart, Amelia, 1898-1937

Flying the safer skies [research by Gayle Vail] K. Burkett. il *Ms* 15:33 Je '87

Women and drugs *See* Drugs and women

Women and men
See also

Adultery
Courtship
Dating (Social customs)
Flirting
Interpersonal attraction
Love
Misogyny
Romance
Sex differences
Sex role

3 secrets about men that women won't keep. il *Jet* 73:34 N 16 '87

10 'perfect 10' men. L. Hirschberg. il *Harpers Bazaar* 120:64+ My '87

25 ways to find a good man. il *Ebony* 42:146+ Mr '87

All eyes on her [younger woman-older man] E. Harper. il *N Y Times Mag* p40 My 24 '87

Alone together: the unromantic generation [cover story] B. Weber. il *N Y Times Mag* p22-6+ Ap 5 '87

Anxiety busters: when you run into an ex. il *Glamour* 85:98 Ap '87

Are his friends crowding you out? C. Elflein. il *Seventeen* 46:240-1+ Mr '87

Are you losing each other? [quiz; excerpt from How to make love all the time] B. De Angelis. *McCalls* 114:88 F '87

Are you the one for me? [excerpt] J. James and I. Schlesinger. il *Glamour* 85:378-9+ S '87

Are you too hard to please? [excerpt from Women men love/women men leave] C. Cowan and M. Kinder. *Redbook* 169:96-7+ Jl '87

Are you turning men off? [special section] il *Harpers Bazaar* 120:300+ S '87

Back off, buddy [Women and love report by S. Hite; cover story] C. Wallis. il *Time* 130:68-73 O 12 '87

Body and soul. M.-B. Rosenbaum. See issues of *Mademoiselle*

A boy's-eye view. G. Schwartz. See issues of *Seventeen* through July 1987

Breaking the age taboo [loving a man younger than you] B. M. Campbell. il *Essence* 17:50-2+ F '87

Breaking up: how to know when you should. A. Bell. il *Teen* 31:22+ Jl '87

Changing to please a man: how much is too much? J. Stone. *Glamour* 85:44 O '87

Dark and dangerous men. B. G. Harrison. *Mademoiselle* 93:114 Je '87

Dating games you can't win. D. Raffel. il *Seventeen* 46:72+ Ja '87

The end of the man shortage (and about time, too). P. Longman. il *Mademoiselle* 93:180-1+ D '87

Fear of intimacy: not for men only [excerpt from Women men love/women men leave] C. Cowan and M. Kinder. il *Glamour* 85:96+ O '87

Fitness times two. H. Platt. *Harpers Bazaar* 120:132+ Ja '87

Getting over the breakup blues. K. McCoy. *Seventeen* 46:34+ Mr '87

A good woman is hard to find: the sad saga of an eligible man. E. Weiner. il *Mademoiselle* 93:122-3+ Jl '87

Grandpa and the kid [trout fishing with girls] D. Sisson. il *Field Stream* 92:61+ Jl '87

Has the black male shortage spoiled black men? il *Ebony* 42:116+ My '87

Him. G. Schwartz. See issues of *Seventeen* beginning August 1987

His. B. Weber. See issues of *Mademoiselle* beginning October 1986

His 'n hers fantasies [excerpt from Sexual static] M. H. Shaevitz. il *Health* 19:74-6+ Ap '87

Hot commodities: will the man shortage spoil men? R. Wetzsteon. *Mademoiselle* 93:184-5+ F '87

How to catch a star [meeting and marrying a celebrity] C. Kramer. il *McCalls* 114:85-7 F '87

How to handle a picky boyfriend. S. Squire. il *Seventeen* 46:206-7+ S '87

How to keep your love alive: playing for keeps [excerpts from Intimate play] W. Betcher. il *Glamour* 85:250-2+ F '87

How to live with a moody man. L. Lague. il *Glamour* 85:74+ Jl '87

How to meet a man/how to meet a woman. L. Dormen and M. Zussman. il *Glamour* 85:288-9+ My '87

How to talk to a boy. D. Seeley. il *Seventeen* 46:306-7+ Ag '87

How working with women has made my life better [lone male teacher] H. S. Karlitz. il por *Work Woman* 12:100-1+ Jl '87

In search of the rare redhead. P. Mehlman. *Harpers Bazaar* 120:111+ Jl '87

The intelligent woman's guide to sex. D. Heyn. See issues of *Mademoiselle* beginning December 1986

Intimacy: how to get it; how to give it. R. Masello. *Glamour* 85:158-9+ Ja '87

Is there a man in your man's life? What every girl should know about the bisexual guy. A. C. Heller. *Mademoiselle* 93:134-5+ Jl '87

It's 1987. Do you know where your love life is? [M. Cohen's course All about men and women] D. Kent. *Mademoiselle* 93:138-9+ F '87

It's about your heart [teenage boy and older woman] B. Greene. il *Esquire* 108:59-60+ S '87

I've learned from my female boss; ed. by Julie Chenault. D. Davis. il por *Essence* 18:111 N '87

I've spent years listening to men talk about their interests. When will they ask me about mine? S. M. Volchok. il *Glamour* 85:19 Ja '87

Jake: a man's opinion. See issues of *Glamour*

Kiss kiss/pow pow! The love/hate rhythms of a romance. A. Kagle. il *Mademoiselle* 93:202-3+ My '87

The legacy of father-loss: "men that I love will leave me". E. Wakerman. *Glamour* 85:132+ My '87

Let's hear it from the boys ['Teen's survey] M. L. Baer. il *Teen* 31:30+ Ap '87

Living with a friend's love swings. C. Rickey. *Mademoiselle* 93:94 Ja '87

The loneliness of the long-distance lover. C. Jakobson. il *Mademoiselle* 93:178-9 F '87

The long and bumpy road from lovers to just friends. S. Nelson and S. Simels. il *Glamour* 85:194-5+ Je '87

Looking for the "perfect" man. P. R. Satran. il *Glamour* 85:216-17+ D '87

A love affair. J. Walters. il *N Y Times Mag* p76 N 22 '87

Love life fix-ups: readers tell how they rescued a problem relationship. il *Glamour* 85:298-301 Mr '87

Women and men—*cont.*

A love story, sort of. J. Gonick. il *Glamour* 85:204+ My '87

Loving a coke addict. C. Jacobs. il *Glamour* 85:298-9+ My '87

Making men comfortable [women executives] S. Nelton. il *Nations Bus* 75:4 My '87

Making peace with your—and his—romantic past. C. L. Mithers. *Glamour* 85:284 Ag '87

Man traps are tacky. G. Blair. *Mademoiselle* 93:122 D '87

Mastery: taking it home [life skills] G. B. Leonard. il *Esquire* 107:149-52 My '87

Men aren't her only problem [S. Hite] B. Barol. il por *Newsweek* 110:76 N 23 '87

My shoplifter [girlfriend] M. S. Zurita. il *Glamour* 85:126+ Je '87

A new light on love [interview with Z. Adams] J. Simmons. il por *Essence* 18:83-4+ My '87

A new way to love [black women and men] J. A. Ladner. por *Essence* 18:140 D '87

The other sex [adolescents] J. P. Comer. il *Parents* 62:212 S '87

Perfumed girls . . . how scents keep a man spellbound. D. Seeley. il *Mademoiselle* 93:150-1+ Je '87

Phone frictions: how to understand the pitfalls of sharing a phone with a man. B.-J. Raphael. *Glamour* 85:26 Mr '87

The return of hard to get (smart cookies don't phone first). C. Jakobson. il *Mademoiselle* 93:220-1+ Mr '87

Rewriting your romantic résumé. L. Dormen. il *Glamour* 85:316-17+ N '87

Romancing the phone. A. L. Ball. il *Mademoiselle* 93:132-3+ Je '87

Say, brother [change in economic status affects relationships with women] R. Clements. por *Essence* 18:6 O '87

Say, brother [relationship with older woman] L. Smith. por *Essence* 18:10+ Jl '87

Second-hand woes. When you wallow in his worries, are you hiding from your own? J. Stone. *Glamour* 85:259 Mr '87

She says monogamy, he says monotony: closing the guy/girl gap. W. D. Leight. *Mademoiselle* 93:220-1+ Ap '87

A short (guy) love story. H. Dlugozima. il *Seventeen* 46:134 My '87

Sick of love? 4 cures for cynics. C. Rickey. *Mademoiselle* 93:170 My '87

Skiing with the guys. C. Ettlinger. il *Work Woman* 12:76-9 F '87

Smart women, foolish books: can your love life be saved in ten chapters or less? A. Landi. *Mademoiselle* 93:180-1+ O '87

Something in the way he works . . . why we have an eye for the driven guy. B. G. Harrison. il *Mademoiselle* 93:262-3+ S '87

Tapping a mine of female discontent [Women and love report by S. Hite] M. McIver. il por *Macleans* 100:44-5 O 19 '87

Things his mother taught him [impact on relationships with other women] R. Wetzsteon. *Mademoiselle* 93:110+ S '87

Three [relations between police partners of opposite sexes] *New Yorker* 63:38-9 O 12 '87

Today's troubled men. H. J. Freudenberger. bibl (p63) il *Psychol Today* 21:46-7 D '87

The truth is not simple. R. Ragaini. il *N Y Times Mag* p38 Ja 11 '87

Type A: affairs of the heart [research by Michael J. Strube] J. Goetz. *Psychol Today* 21:20 My '87

What are the limits of love? J. Glass. il *Glamour* 85:198 S '87

What you don't know about men [special section] il *Health* 19:31-6+ N '87

What's a nice couple like you doing in a fight like this? Why guys and girls can't talk. C. Jakobson. il *Mademoiselle* 93:190+ N '87

When his old flame reappeared: how I put out the fire. S. A. Sage. il *Glamour* 85:222+ Ap '87

When women fight for equality, says Warren Farrell, fairness to men may be one of the casualties [interview] L. Powell. il pors *People Wkly* 27:49-50+ Je 15 '87

Who is the right man for a woman like you? [excerpt from The Type E woman] H. B. Braiker. il *Work Woman* 12:72-4+ Ja '87

Why can't we be closer? [excerpt from I love you] D. S. Viscott. il *Health* 19:44-6+ O '87

Why is all the relationship-repair advice aimed at women? il *Glamour* 85:64 F '87

Why men confuse the women they love [condensed from Sexual static] M. H. Shaevitz. il *Read Dig* 131:65-6+ N '87

Why smart men still want dumb women. R. Grant. il *Ladies Home J* 104:78+ S '87

The women we love: a definitive selection [symposium] il *Esquire* 107:154-68 Je '87

Would you spy on your man? Meet 8 women who did. J. Ralston. il *Glamour* 85:266+ S '87

You & your guy: rate your relationship [quiz] il *Teen* 31:78-9 O '87

You get ahead, he gets mad . . . will success spoil your romance? M. F. Coburn. *Mademoiselle* 93:186-7+ O '87

Anecdotes, facetiae, satire, etc.

12 things no woman has the right to ask her man to give up. P. Richmond. il *Glamour* 85:44+ Je '87

Be your own woman (even if you're somebody's girl). S. Brush. il *Mademoiselle* 93:106-7+ Jl '87

Boy talk [excerpt from The 100th boyfriend] B. Daly and J. Skeels. *Harpers* 275:31-2 S '87

Breaking up without falling apart. B. Feirstein. *Harpers Bazaar* 120:80-1+ Ja '87

Cracking the manspeak code. P. Mehlman. *Mademoiselle* 93:138-9+ Ja '87

Envy (Freud had it all wrong). K. Fury. il *Work Woman* 12:160 Mr '87

Let's bring back the bad old rules of love. S. P. Haven. il *Glamour* 85:206 Mr '87

Top 10 turnoffs. B. Feirstein. *Harpers Bazaar* 120:306+ S '87

The world's worst-matched couples. B.-J. Raphael. *Glamour* 85:104 D '87

The young and the sex less: a yuppie love story. E. Weiner. il *Mademoiselle* 93:110-11+ Ja '87

Bibliography

Addicted to love. J. Maynard. il *Mademoiselle* 93:90+ Ag '87

Advice givers strike gold. L. Shapiro. il *Newsweek* 109:64-5 Je 1 '87

Women and men in literature

Sex wars: not the fun kind. S. M. Gilbert and S. Gubar. il *N Y Times Book Rev* 92:1+ D 27 '87

Women and music *See* Music and women

Women and peace

Anecdotes, facetiae, satire, etc.

The great baby sit-in for peace [world leaders babysit during imagined summit conference] M. K. Blakely. il por *Ms* 16:83-5 D '87

Women and politics *See* Women—Political activities

Women and religion

See also

Evangelical Women's Caucus

Men, Women and God: Christians for Biblical Equality (Organization)

Nuns

Ordination of women

Women—Religious life

Women clergy

Women in the Bible

The battle of the lexicons [meeting of the Evangelical Theological Society titled Male and female in biblical and theological perspective] D. Neff. il *Christ Today* 31:44+ Ja 16 '87

'Claiming our power' [Women-Church conference in Cincinnati] K. S. Smith. il *Commonweal* 114:613-15 N 6 '87

Don't call us, we'll call you: what the synod said to women. A. McCarthy. il *Commonweal* 114:695-6 D 4 '87

Ear of the beholder [Just as the women said, Catholic pastoral letter] *Commonweal* 114:548-9 O 9 '87

Female and Catholic: please don't bring me flowers anymore [interview with M. L. Tobin] il *U S Cathol* 52:20-6 Ap '87

Gettin' over [feminism and religion] il *Ms* 16:44 D '87

The impact of the women's movement(s) on the family: a father's perspective. E. Marciniak. *America* 156:194-6 Mr 7 '87

Is feminism God's gift to the Catholic Church? M. O'Connell. il *U S Cathol* 52:12-19 Je '87

A mini-primer on witchcraft. C. Kocol. il *Humanist* 47:37 S/O '87

Of many things [views of R. G. Weakland on women and the Catholic Church] G. W. Hunt. *America* 157:258 O 24 '87

Sailing to the edge of the world [role of women in the Church of England] S. Fletcher. il *Hist Today* 37:10-11 S '87

Women and religion—*cont.*

Trinity and unity [discussion of April 15, 1987 article, The Trinity and women's experience] B. Brown Zikmund. *Christ Century* 104:534-6 Je 3-10 '87

The Trinity and women's experience. B. Brown Zikmund. *Christ Century* 104:354-6 Ap 15 '87

Was this trip necessary? [vague statement on the status of women by the Synod of Bishops] R. N. Ostling. il *Time* 130:89 N 9 '87

Women explore formation of alternative feminist group [Christian feminists investigate need for an alternative to the Evangelical Women's Caucus] D. Neff. il *Christ Today* 31:45-6 Ap 17 '87

Women in the church: a token of our affliction. R. E. Burns. *U S Cathol* 52:2 N '87

The women's challenge [Catholic Church and feminism] G. G. Higgins. *America* 156:3-6 Ja 3-10 '87

Bibliography

Women, religion, & utopia. M. Gerhart. *Commonweal* 114:682-3 N 20 '87

Women and the church *See* Women and religion

Women and the environment

See also

Ecofeminism

Women and war

Do women really love peace? C. Tavris. *Vogue* 177:122 My '87

Of arms and the woman. M. Piercy. *Harpers* 274:30+ Je '87

Women anthropologists

See also

Fossey, Dian

Mead, Margaret, 1901-1978

Thomas, Elizabeth Marshall, 1931-

Anecdotes, facetiae, satire, etc.

Last word. T. Runté. il *Omni* 9:142 Ap '87

Women architects

See also

Aulenti, Gae

Fisher, Ronne

Gray, Eileen, 1879-1976

Hadid, Zaha M., 1951?-

Hann, Marlys

Morgan, Julia

Puppo, Ethel

Spear, Laurinda

Women artists

See also

Abakanowicz, Magdalena

Arias, Susana

Asher, Elise

Bach, Elvira

Barron, Slater

Bartlett, Jennifer, 1941-

Bourgeois, Louise

Canright, Sarah, 1941-

Carlson, Cynthia

Coe, Sue, 1951-

Coffey, Susanna

Davis, Debby

Daw, Leila

Driscoll, Ellen

Estes, Merion

Frey, Jane

Gechtoff, Sonia, 1926-

Goldin, Nan

Goodwin, Betty

Graves, Nancy, 1940-

Grossen, Françoise, 1943-

Hughes, Holly, 1951-

Iglesias, Cristina, 1956-

Kaplowitz, Jane

Klein, Pat

Klement, Vera, 1929-

Kligman, Ruth

Kozloff, Joyce

Krasner, Lee, 1908-1984

Kruger, Barbara

Layton, Elizabeth

Lemieux, Suzanne

Loe, Kathleen, 1953-

MacQueen, Elizabeth

Martin, Agnes, 1912-

McKiernan, Janet

Morisot, Berthe, 1841-1895

Muldavin, Phyllis Smirle

Münter, Gabriele, 1877-1962

Murray, Elizabeth

National Museum of Women in the Arts (U.S.)

Nazor, Maria

Noah, Barbara

O'Keeffe, Georgia, 1887-1986

Olsen, Barbara

Pacheco, Maria Luisa

Page, Ann Takayoshi

Parker, Catherine Burchfield

Pepper, Beverly, 1924-

Poirier, Anne

Polk, Kay

Porter, Katherine, 1941-

Preston, Astrid

Rankin, Aimee

Ringgold, Faith

Rockburne, Dorothea, 1934-

Rohan-Chabot, Joy de

Rosenberg, Evelyn

Rothenberg, Susan

Schön, Nancy

Sheehan, Maura

Slavick, Susanne

Slavit, Ann

Small, Deborah

Snyder, Joan, 1940-

Solano, Susana, 1946-

Steir, Pat, 1940-

Stuart, Michelle

Tanning, Dorothea, 1913-

Truitt, Anne, 1921-

Ushenko, Audrey Andreyevna, 1945-

Weisberg, Ruth

Whitaker, Eileen Monaghan, 1911-

Wieland, Joyce, 1931-

Williamson, Philemona

Wilson, Helen Miranda

Wolff, Anita

Women's Caucus for Art

American women artists, 1830-1930 [exhibition at National Museum of Women in the Arts] M. Moorman. il *Art News* 86:57-8 Summ '87

Art: schoolgirl paintings: nineteenth-century works by American amateur artists. J. R. Mellow. il *Archit Dig* 44:140-5+ D '87

How wide is the gender gap? E. Heartney. il *Art News* 86:139-45 Summ '87

Sculptors strengthen ties at landmark conference [National Sculpture Conference: Works by Women] F. Grossen. *Am Craft* 47:13 O/N '87

A woman's place [American women artists, 1830-1930 exhibit at the National Museum of Women in the Arts] A. Schwartz. il *Americana* 15:30-2+ Mr/Ap '87

Women astronauts

See also

Jemison, Mae C.

McAuliffe, Christa

Ride, Sally K.

Women astronomers

See also

Vaucouleurs, Antoinette de

Women athletes

See also

Sex discrimination in sports

Tennis players

Women—Sports

Women's Sports Foundation

Women's Sports Hall of Fame

See also names of women athletes

Fast breaks [preview of events in Pan Am Games] M. Kort. il *Women's Sports Fitness* 9:47-8+ Ag '87

Is she or isn't she? [growing movement to end gender testing in the Olympics] L. Fink. il *Women's Sports Fitness* 9:71 D '87

Sports: new path to college for women [black women] il *Ebony* 42:27-8+ Ap '87

Winning at life. L. T. Bessone. il *Women's Sports Fitness* 9:46-50 S '87

Attitudes

Fantasies of the stars. il *Women's Sports Fitness* 9:18-19 Mr '87

Ethics

See Sports—Ethical aspects

Health and hygiene

No periods? New clues. E. T. Becker. *Women's Sports Fitness* 9:57 F '87

Nutrition

Anemia—are you at risk? [iron deficiency anemia] E. Coleman. il *Women's Sports Fitness* 9:12 Mr '87

How to make every bite count. C. Harvey. il *Women's Sports Fitness* 9:12 My '87

It's not how far you go [low calorie intake may contribute to amenorrhea] J. Venturino. il *Women's Sports Fitness* 9:20 S '87

Women athletes—*cont.*

Photographs and photography

Women in motion [excerpts from Athletes: photographs 1860-1986]; ed. by Ruth Silverman. il *Women's Sports Fitness* 9:38-9 D '87

Salaries, pensions, etc.

The good life of the new amateurs. M. Kort. il *Women's Sports Fitness* 9:23-6+ Ja '87

The money game. G. Bakoulis. il *Women's Sports Fitness* 9:28-9 Ja '87

Training

Coming back after pregnancy. S. Festa. il *Women's Sports Fitness* 9:32 Ap '87

Muscle balance. S. Zakin. il *Women's Sports Fitness* 9:38-41 My '87

Women authors

See also

Atwood, Margaret, 1939-
Auel, Jean M.
Austen, Jane, 1775-1817
Austin, Doris Jean
Beattie, Ann
Beauman, Sally
Bradley, Marion Zimmer
Brown, Margaret Wise, 1910-1952
Brown, Mary Ward
Collins, Jackie
Didion, Joan
Dillard, Annie
Drabble, Margaret, 1939-
Eisenstadt, Jill
Gibbons, Kaye, 1960-
Gordimer, Nadine, 1923-
Gordon, Mary, 1949-
Green, Judith H.
Grimes, Martha
Hearon, Shelby, 1931-
Hellman, Lillian, 1906-1984
Holley, Marietta, 1836-1926
Howatch, Susan
Humphreys, Josephine
Isaacs, Susan, 1943-
Janowitz, Tama
Jhabvala, Ruth Prawer
Kingsley, Mary Henrietta, 1862-1900
Kleypas, Lisa
Koen, Karleen
Lawrence, Rae
McCarthy, Mary, 1912-
Montgomery, L. M. (Lucy Maud), 1874-1942
Morrison, Toni, 1931-
Nasrallah, Emily
Nuns as authors
O'Connor, Flannery
O'Marie, Carol Anne
Ortese, Anna Maria
Ozick, Cynthia
Piercy, Marge
Potter, Beatrix, 1866-1943
Powell, Dawn
Raskin, Barbara
Rendell, Ruth, 1930-
Simpson, Mona
Thomas, Elizabeth Marshall, 1931-
Walker, Alice, 1944-
Welty, Eudora, 1909-
Wharton, Edith, 1862-1937

The burden of caring [women and Russian literature] B. Heldt. *Nation* 244:820-4 Je 13 '87

The case of the missing woman [mystery writers] C. G. Heilbrun. il *Ms* 16:76+ O '87

Great unexpectations [tribulations of being a woman author] M. Atwood. il *Ms* 16:78-9+ Jl/Ag '87

Oxford to publish 19th century black women writers series. B. Levine. il *Publ Wkly* 231:48-9 Je 5 '87

Women automobile drivers

Autohypochondria. W. Shipman. il *Ctry J* 14:10 N '87

Women automobile industry workers

Sexual harassment at Smyrna [Nissan plant] J. Junkerman. il *Progressive* 51:19 Je '87

Women bankers

Career makeover: from secretary to assistant vice president [S. Coe's career with First National Bank of Chicago] il por *Glamour* 85:84+ Ja '87

Dressing in the rich tradition [E. Patterson] W. Konrad. il pors *Work Woman* 12:83-4+ Jl '87

From teaching nun to bank president [R. Greco] M. Rowland. il por *Work Woman* 12:60 D '87

Peripatetic banker [K. Horn] D. Machan. il por *Forbes* 139:170+ Je 1 '87

Susan Harman: an instinct for high-tech success [investment banker at Robertson, Colman & Stephens] P. Finch. por *Bus Week* p81 F 9 '87

Two very different first ladies of finance [K. Horn and C. Gargalli] N. J. Perry. il pors *Fortune* 116:191 O 12 '87

Women basketball coaches *See* Basketball coaches

Women bishops

Episcopal 'gentlemen's club' now open? J. C. Lyles. *Christ Century* 104:909-10 O 21 '87

Women body builders *See* Body building

Women brokers

Big fish, nice pond [broker E. DeVries' office] F. Greenberg. il por *Work Woman* 12:54-5 Jl '87

Investing in a confident style [broker K. Reiman] J. Giambanco. il pors *Work Woman* 12:103-4+ D '87

Women cartoonists

See also

Barry, Lynda
Chast, Roz

Women chemists

See also

Blum, Arlene, 1945-

Dear Betty Harragan [short woman having problems supervising fellow chemists] B. L. Harragan. il *Work Woman* 12:46+ N '87

Women clergy

See also

Ordination of women
Women deacons
Women missionaries

This far by faith [C. Williams-Bryant, black woman minister at Bethel AME Church, Baltimore] H. Cole and A. Edwards. il pors *Essence* 18:107-8+ S '87

Women of faith. D. Salvatore. il *Ladies Home J* 104:91-2+ D '87

Women coaches *See* Coaches (Athletics)

Women college deans

See also

Black, Barbara Aronstein

Women college graduates

See also

Business schools and colleges—Graduates

100 outstanding women college graduates. il *Good Housekeep* 205:78+ Jl '87

Employment

Post-grad campus to career. il *Harpers Bazaar* 120:104-5+ Je '87

Post-grad job-smart dressing. il *Harpers Bazaar* 120:100-3 Je '87

Women college presidents

See also

Cole, Johnnetta B.
Kappner, Augusta Souza
Sudarkasa, Niara

Women college students

See also

College sororities
Sex discrimination in education

Campus queens at black colleges. il *Ebony* 42:70-2+ Ap '87

The fall roundup [persuasive hostesses help recruit top football prospects] A. Wolff. il *Sports Illus* 67:46-50+ Ag 31 '87

Top ten college women '87. il *Glamour* 85:258-60+ Ag '87

W. Va. Univ. elects first black homecoming queen [T. L. Cunningham] *Jet* 71:27 Ja 19 '87

Women college teachers *See* College teachers

Women comedians

See also

Barr, Roseanne
Boosler, Elayne, 1952?-
Dunn, Nora
Haydn, Lili
Jackson, Victoria
Jones, Cathy
Just June
Mabley, Moms, 1897-1975
Rivers, Joan, 1937-
Stickney, Phyllis
Tenuta, Judy
Weinstock, Lotus

Women composers

See also

Dean, Laura
Gillon, Iris E.

Women conductors (Music)

See also

Worby, Rachael

Women consumers

Back to natural fibers. M. Rowland. il *Work Woman* 12:101+ N '87

The books women buy [Gallup survey] L. A. Wood. *Publ Wkly* 231:27 My 22 '87

Cars women want: a driving force. M. Knepper. *Harpers Bazaar* 120:174+ S '87

The dawn of supermilks. A. Stern. il *Work Woman* 12:43+ Jl '87

Ford chasing women. il *Mot Trend* 39:38 Ag '87

Hey, big spender [selling furs to women] K. Haynes. il *Work Woman* 12:48 Ja '87

Jewelers woo the working woman. S. Caminiti. il *Fortune* 115:71-2 Je 8 '87

Making millions on women over 30 [Noxell] F. Rice. il *Fortune* 115:75+ My 25 '87

A new way to reach America's good ol' girls [corporate sponsors trying to attract women stock car fans] B. Bauer. il *U S News World Rep* 102:41 Je 29 '87

Shaking up the spice industry. D. Tuller. il *Work Woman* 12:78+ O '87

Soft sell [women car buyers] E. Henry. il *Changing Times* 41:82 Jl '87

Sushi and an oil change [auto repair malls] J. Parr. il *Forbes* 140:93-4 Ag 24 '87

Women and cars. L. J. Nonkin. See issues of Vogue beginning January 1986

Women contractors
See also
Directions Metropolitan (Firm)

Women cooks
See also
Massia, Christiane
Stewart, Martha

A cook's fantasy comes true. A. L. Ball. il *Work Woman* 12:164 N '87

Simply delicious la belle cuisine [women chefs in France] A. Stone-Sweet. il por *Harpers Bazaar* 120:292+ S '87

Women corporation directors See Corporations—Directors
Women deacons

Bring back women deacons [Catholic Church] A. Swidler. *U S Cathol* 52:30-1 Ag '87

Women detectives

The girl with the silver gun [D. Lonigro] C. Siebert. il pors *Mademoiselle* 93:247-9+ Mr '87

Women doctors See Women physicians
Women dramatists
See also
Norman, Marsha

Women editors
See also
Amsterdam, Jane
Futter, Deborah
Kenison, Katrina
Rock, Victoria

Dear Betty Harragan [sex discrimination] B. L. Harragan. *Work Woman* 12:28+ S '87

Women educators
See also
Women school superintendents and principals

Women electronics workers
Health and hygiene

Childbearing: the dangers of high tech [AT&T policy regarding pregnant semiconductor workers] il *U S News World Rep* 102:12 Ja 26 '87

Clean-room controversy [study by Digital Equipment Corp. on toxic hazards that affect a worker's ability to have children] R. Wilson. il *Technol Rev* 90:10+ Ag/S '87

Danger in the clean room [semiconductor workers have increased risk of miscarriage at AT&T] il *Time* 129:48 Ja 26 '87

Moms-to-be banned from 'chip room' [AT&T policy] *Sci News* 131:73 Ja 31 '87

Women engineers

June and Judy Thaxton: twins in engineering. F. White, III. il pors *Ebony* 42:116+ Mr '87

Women in science and engineering is focus of conferences. *Science* 238:86 O 2 '87

Women entrepreneurs
See also
American Woman's Economic Development Corporation

Building an empire [black woman contractor J. Bradley] P. F. Stewart. il por *Ladies Home J* 104:158 O '87

Businesswomen: equal but different. W. Hoffer. il *Nations Bus* 75:46-7 Ag '87

Carving out success in homespun niches [special section] J. Ciabattari. il *Work Woman* 12:134-8 N '87

The dream job you create for yourself. D. E. Gumpert. il *Work Woman* 12:39-41 O '87

Enterprise. See issues of Working Woman beginning September 1983

From rags to riches [special section] P. F. Stewart. il *Ladies Home J* 104:148+ O '87

How to reduce your risk as an entrepreneur [views of Mary Del Brady] H. Rubin. il *Work Woman* 12:62 Ja '87

Leaving the corporate nest. J. Coleman. il *Work Woman* 12:42 O '87

The new entrepreneurs: women who've made it in high tech [special section] il *Work Woman* 12:61+ My '87

Starting their own. S. Nelton and K. Berney. il *Nations Bus* 75:23 My '87

What it takes to be an entrepreneur. E. Prescott. *Work Woman* 12:34 Ag '87

Anecdotes, facetiae, satire, etc.

Snow White & Seven Dwarfs, Inc. (or Even a princess has to work). J. Viorst. il *Redbook* 170:36+ N '87

Awards

1987 Harriet Alger Award. il *Work Woman* 12:53-7 N '87

Bibliography

Starting out: where to get good advice. H. McCrum. *Work Woman* 12:33 Ag '87

Women executives
See also
Clothing and dress—Businesswomen
Corporations—Directors
Women entrepreneurs

Assertiveness breeds contempt [male vs. female evaluations of assertive female managers; study by David L. Mathison] V. Bozzi. *Psychol Today* 21:15 S '87

Can't is a coward too lazy to try [address, July 14, 1987] P. A. Weir. *Vital Speeches Day* 54:26-9 O 15 '87

Career workshop [special section] il *Work Woman* 12:79-82+ Je '87

Corporate women [cover story; special section] il *Bus Week* p72-8+ Je 22 '87

Dear Betty Harragan. B. L. Harragan. See issues of Working Woman

The executive woman's guide to headhunters. B. G. Kempton. il *Work Woman* 12:110-12+ Ap '87

The fine art of asking smart questions [excerpt from Smart questions] D. Leeds. il *Work Woman* 12:132-3+ N '87

I've learned from my female boss; ed. by Julie Chenault. D. Davis. il por *Essence* 18:111 N '87

Like father, like daughter [father-daughter corporations] R. Rooney. il *Good Housekeep* 204:108-9+ Je '87

The managerial mother [special section] il *Work Woman* 12:117-18+ D '87

Managing maternity. D. L. Gittens. il *Essence* 18:106+ Je '87

Smart questions to ask to get ahead in your job [excerpts from Smart questions] D. Leeds. il *Glamour* 85:116+ My '87

A view from the top [black women executives; cover story] il *Black Enterp* 17:40-2+ Ap '87

When it's your turn to be the boss. J. Ciabattari. il *Work Woman* 12:109-12+ Mr '87

Where women are succeeding. A. B. Fisher. il *Fortune* 116:78-80+ Ag 3 '87

Women: the second wave [cover story] S. Nelton and K. Berney. il *Nations Bus* 75:18-20+ My '87

Attitudes

Managing nine critical career turning points [results of survey] J. Ciabattari. il *Work Woman* 12:87-90+ O '87

Awards

The 1987 Working Woman Hall of Fame. il *Work Woman* 12:107-9+ N '87

Dismissal

Dear Betty Harragan [anti-nepotism policy instituted after corporate merger] B. L. Harragan. il *Work Woman* 12:38+ D '87

Health and hygiene

The career woman's guide to lifelong good health [special section] il *Work Woman* 12:127+ O '87

The workaholic's guide to staying on your feet [special section] H. Twidale. il *Work Woman* 12:139-40+ Ap '87

Promotion

The art of getting what you want. J. Etra. *Harpers Bazaar* 120:298+ Mr '87

Career on hold: the big stall. M. Willens. il *Harpers Bazaar* 120:160+ O '87

Don't write women off as leaders. F. N. Schwartz. il por *Fortune* 115:185+ Je 8 '87

Women executives—Promotion—*cont.*

The making of a top manager. B. Insel. il *Work Woman* 12:105-8+ My '87

Managing nine critical career turning points [results of survey] J. Ciabattari. il *Work Woman* 12:87-90+ O '87

Women with promise: who succeeds, who fails? [excerpt from Breaking the glass ceiling] A. M. Morrison and others. il *Work Woman* 12:79-82+ Je '87

You won't get ahead without a mentor (and other executive phony tales). P. McBroom. il *Mademoiselle* 93:238-9+ Ap '87

Psychology

Bitches in business. S. Dooley. il *Harpers Bazaar* 120:308+ S '87

Creating solutions, not showdowns. M. J. Parson. il *Work Woman* 12:127-9 My '87

Crossover dreams [black women in a white corporate world] A. Edwards. *Essence* 17:45+ Mr '87

Executive women: substance plus style. A. M. Morrison and others. il *Psychol Today* 21:18-21+ Ag '87

Fear of speaking. L. J. Nonkin. il *Vogue* 177:161+ My '87

The feminine art of management. K. V. Brailsford. il *Black Enterp* 17:102+ F '87

How to spot the leaders on your staff. B. Serlen. *Work Woman* 12:18 Mr '87

It's your move! [black women executives] S. Chassler. *Essence* 17:47+ Mr '87

The kind of stress managers know best. J. Ciabattari. il *Work Woman* 12:125-8+ S '87

Making changes: how to budge the office mule. M. J. Parson. il *Work Woman* 12:139-41 S '87

Making men comfortable. S. Nelton. il *Nations Bus* 75:4 My '87

Managing sideways. R. E. Lefton. il *Work Woman* 12:34+ O '87

Objets d'office: executive security blankets. B. Andrews. il *Work Woman* 12:121 S '87

Short power. P. R. Satran. il *Work Woman* 12:98-100 Je '87

When change is in the wind . . . heads up! J. Ciabattari. il *Work Woman* 12:63-6+ F '87

Why depression is different for high-achieving women. H. B. Braiker. il *Work Woman* 12:79-83 D '87

Rating

Sex bias costly to companies [bias against women in performance evaluations; views of Gregory Dobbins] il *USA Today (Periodical)* 115:4 Ap '87

Salaries, pensions, etc.

Beyond salary: bargaining for benefits. W. Kalbacker. *Work Woman* 12:112 Ap '87

Selection and appointment

How to groom a great successor. K. Berman. *Work Woman* 12:28 My '87

Sexual behavior

Making time for love. C. Rubenstein. il *Work Woman* 12:154+ O '87

Taxation

The executive who tried all the (tax) angles. B. Siverd. *Work Woman* 12:116-17+ Mr '87

Training

Executive education programs: who goes? Can you? G. Hechinger. il *Glamour* 85:333+ My '87

The making of a manager [Executive Women Project Workshop at the Center for Creative Leadership] E. Stark. il *Psychol Today* 21:28-32 Ag '87

Transfer

Five career ruts you can't afford. E. LaPlante. *Work Woman* 12:59 N '87

Hidden costs of job hopping. S. Rose. *Work Woman* 12:21 F '87

Travel

See Business travel

Women executives in motion pictures

Working women of the silver screen: do you know these celluloid executives? [quiz] K. Scott. il *Work Woman* 12:66-7 Ag '87

Women explorers

Fearless spirits: tales of women explorers. L. Shapiro. il *Newsweek* 110:65 Ag 3 '87

Women fashion designers *See* Fashion designers

Women for Sobriety

Finding A.A. too male-oriented, Jean Kirkpatrick heads a movement to aid women alcoholics. S. K. Reed. il por *People Wkly* 27:101-3 Je 29 '87

Women geologists

Adventure in Manitoba. S. M. Marcus. il *Earth Sci* 40:21-3 Summ '87

Women in advertising

Advertising success in Minneapolis [M. Betsch at Campbell-Mithun] J. Giambanco. il pors *Work Woman* 12:117-18+ O '87

Adwoman of the mountain [Grey Advertising account executive and professional ski racer L. Feinberg] J. Seabury. il por *N Y* 20:22 Mr 16 '87

Barbara Rudd Gross, Ebony account exec, new advertising group prexy. por *Jet* 72:30 Je 15 '87

Career makeover: from ticket agent to advertising director [L. Lockman-Brooks] il por *Glamour* 85:134 Ag '87

Jane Brite: riding the Madison Avenue express. P. Finch. il por *Bus Week* p146 D 7 '87

No comment. See occasional issues of Ms.

The power of positive stress [S. Minard] K. Brady. il pors *Work Woman* 12:74-7 Jl '87

A thinly disguised message [link between image of women in advertisements and anorexia nervosa] D. Marquardt. il *Ms* 15:33 My '87

Women in agriculture *See* Farm women

Women in art

The greatest moments in a girl's life [postcards by H. Fisher] C. E. Rinzler. il *Am Herit* 38:34-5 F/Mr '87

Wyeth's world: how a woman named Helga came to haunt the art of America's foremost realist. R. Meryman. il pors *Life* 10:72-6+ Je '87

Exhibitions

Elvira Bach. N. Grimes. il *Art News* 86:148 S '87

Heavily hyped Helga [exhibit of A. Wyeth's paintings] J. Updike. *New Repub* 197:27-30 D 7 '87

The Helga pictures [National Gallery of Art exhibit] A. Thorson. il *Art News* 86:193 O '87

Helgamania goes on the road [A. Wyeth exhibit] pors *U S News World Rep* 102:13 Je 1 '87

Mystery lady [J. Trumbull's wife Sarah appears in painting The resignation of General Washington in Capitol Rotunda] I. B. Jaffe. il pors *Art News* 86:34-5 Mr '87

Too much of a medium-good thing [exhibit of A. Wyeth's Helga paintings] R. Hughes. il *Time* 129:77 Je 1 '87

Wyeth paintings and the Helga controversy [cover story] M. S. Doherty. il pors *Am Artist* 51:10-11 My '87

Anecdotes, facetiae, satire, etc.

Vickie Lou's letters from Long Island [exhibit of A. Wyeth's Helga paintings] il *Am Artist* 51:18+ S '87

Women in business *See* Businesswomen

Women in cable television

Broadcasting exec gets apology from organization following racial insult [X. Clayton snubbed by Rome, Ga. affiliate of National Federation of Business and Professional Women's Clubs] il por *Jet* 72:32 My 18 '87

Guess what they watch in China on Sunday nights? [Y.-S. Kan's One world series] D. J. Yang. il por *Bus Week* p91 Ja 19 '87

Helping East meet West via TV, America's Yue-Sai Kan has become the most famous woman in China. S. K. Reed. il pors *People Wkly* 27:123-4 My 18 '87

Southern exposure [X. Clayton of WTBS, Atlanta] M. Scott. il pors *Essence* 17:97-8+ Mr '87

Women in fast food restaurant management

McQueen of the Golden Arches [black franchisee L. Heard] L. Gite. il pors *Black Enterp* 18:64-6+ S '87

Women in fishing

The fine art of fly fishing. R. L. Graham. il *Women's Sports Fitness* 9:52-4+ My '87

Grandpa and the kid [trout fishing with girls] D. Sisson. il *Field Stream* 92:61+ Jl '87

Those wild tuna guys [objections by crew to placing women observers aboard tuna fishing boats] *Harpers* 274:19-20 Je '87

Women in hotel management

A hotel of one's own [Y. Lembi-Detert partnered with father in the Hotel Group of America] M. Dowie. il por *Ms* 16:38-9 D '87

Success in the sun [N. Symonette, black woman owner of Casuarinas Hotel in Nassau, the Bahamas] J. C. McAdams and J. Simmons. il pors *Essence* 17:101-2+ Ap '87

Women in investment banking

Investment banking's top rank: no longer 'gentlemen only'. A. Bianco. il *Bus Week* p113 F 23 '87

Money, honey! The six-figure kids of Wall Street. A. L. Ball. il *Mademoiselle* 93:236-7+ Ag '87

The wonder woman of muni bonds [C. A. Fitts of Dillon, Read] A. Bianco. il por *Bus Week* p112-13 F 23 '87

Women in literature

See also

Camille (Fictional character)

Women in literature—See also—*cont.*
    Pollyanna (Fictional character)
    Samantha (Fictional character)
    Women—Bibliography
The burden of caring [women and Russian literature] B. Heldt. *Nation* 244:820-4 Je 13 '87
Little shop of horrors [discussion of July 17, 1987 article] M. Z. Stange. *Commonweal* 114:546+ O 9 '87
Little shop of horrors [women in the fiction of A. Greeley; cover story] M. Z. Stange. il por *Commonweal* 114:412-17 Jl 17 '87
Narratives: the Doris Lessing standard. L. Stone. il *Ms* 16:29-30+ Jl/Ag '87

Women in motion pictures
    See also
    Women in the motion picture industry
Is Hollywood rejecting today's new women? il *Glamour* 85:100 Ap '87
The tyranny of the tight butt [depiction of over-30 women in films] R. Rosenbaum. il *Mademoiselle* 93:102 Mr '87

Women in mythology
The heroic women of Greek epic. M. R. Lefkowitz. *Am Sch* 56:503-18 Aut '87

Women in newspaper publishing
After a woman is scorned, a publishing family cashes out [S. Bingham] J. Nielsen. il por *Fortune* 115:93 Ja 5 '87
Dayton Newspapers Inc. names asst. business mgr. [K. G. Milton] por *Jet* 73:25 O 5 '87

Women in opera
    See also
    Femmes fatales in opera
Women in politics *See* Women—Political activities
Women in public relations
At-home professionalism [P. Tagliarino's office] P. Kripke. il por *Work Woman* 12:106-7 Mr '87
Exercising options in Florida [Y. Rubio, public relations director of Safety Harbor Spa] J. Giambanco. il pors *Work Woman* 12:105-6+ Je '87

Women in publishing
    See also
    Women editors
    Women in newspaper publishing
Book-smart style [office of S. Petersen, president of Ballantine Books] P. Kripke. il por *Work Woman* 12:118-19 N '87
The keeper (and stoker) of the company flame [G. Crain] S. Wilkinson. il pors *Work Woman* 12:70-1+ O '87
Staying power in publishing [black woman M. Brown] J. Simmons. il por *Essence* 18:135-6 My '87
Women at the top. M. Charnizon. il *Publ Wkly* 231:27-31 Ja 23 '87

Women in religion *See* Women and religion
Women in restaurant management
Career makeover: from bank officer to restaurant V.P. [B. Van of the Peasant Restaurant chain] il por *Glamour* 85:170 Ap '87
Specialties of the house [black women restaurant owners] J. Nash. il *Essence* 18:97-100+ My '87

Women in sailing
Close encounter at sea [Canadian ships introduce women crew members] C. Wood. il *Macleans* 100:45 Je 1 '87
Crow's nest. G. L. Voss. *Sea Front* 33:242-3 Jl/Ag '87
Sail for your supper [working as crew member] J. Cohen. il *Women's Sports Fitness* 9:16 Je '87
Summer champions. C. Davis. il *Mot Boat Sail* 159:52-7+ Je '87

Women in sales *See* Sales personnel
Women in sports *See* Women athletes
Women in television
    See also
    Women in the television industry
    Women lawyers in television
The dream girls. D. Seligman. *Fortune* 115:119+ Mr 2 '87
Even career girls get the blues [The days and nights of Molly Dodd] M. Christensen. il *Roll Stone* p63+ My 21 '87
Sharon Gless & Tyne Daly [portrayals of women's friendship on Cagney & Lacey] M. Gordon. il pors *Ms* 15:40-1+ Ja '87
Status of working women exaggerated on TV, study. *Jet* 71:32 F 2 '87
TV's race with reality. S. B. Levine. *Ms* 15:37 Je '87
Why do we love the queens of evil? J. Collins. il por *Redbook* 168:62+ F '87

Women in the anti-nuclear movement *See* Anti-nuclear movement

Women in the Armed Forces *See* Servicewomen
Women in the Bible
Biblical traditions and women's experience. P. Perkins. il *America* 157:294-6 O 31 '87
God as woman. G. G. Seibert. *America* 157:311 O 31 '87
Hagar & her sisters: precedent for conduct [surrogate motherhood in the Bible] J. Gaffney. il *Commonweal* 114:240-2 Ap 24 '87
Hanged on his own gallows [views of H. Hamann in Women, authority and the Bible] M. E. Marty. *Christ Century* 104:1127 D 9 '87

Women in the candy industry
Katherine Prescott: a chat with a candy maker. il por *McCalls* 114:110-11 Ag '87

Women in the computer industry
Apple Computer's Debi Coleman. M. Dowie. il por *Ms* 15:60-2+ My '87
Good, better, best [D. Coleman of Apple] F. M. Henley. il pors *Work Woman* 12:86-9 D '87

Women in the computer service industries
All-around achiever [IBM executive J. Donald's commitment to helping young people] J. Sands. il por *Essence* 18:102+ Je '87
The new entrepreneurs: women who've made it in high tech [special section] il *Work Woman* 12:61+ My '87
Susan Catalano: software keeps her on her toes. P. Finch. il por *Bus Week* p58 Ap 27 '87

Women in the food industry
Foods with flair: Sarabeth's Kitchen [S. Levine] J. Ciabattari. il por *Work Woman* 12:134-6 N '87

Women in the mass media industry
Affirmative action, FCC-style [preference policies for minorities and women in broadcasting] N. Gunther. *Channels* 7:12 My '87
F.C.C. launches inquiry into policies preferential to minorities and women. *Jet* 71:16 Ja 12 '87
Is the FCC backing away from women? [preference policy] M. Engel. il *Glamour* 85:76+ Ap '87

Women in the medical equipment industry
Career makeover: from aerobics instructor to high-tech medical equipment sales [K. Clark] il por *Glamour* 85:68 Jl '87
From nurse to medical-supply executive [K. Parker] J. Giambanco. il pors *Work Woman* 12:77-8+ Ag '87

Women in the motion picture industry
L.A.'s eclectic entertainment executive [B. Mutchnick] J. Giambanco. il pors *Work Woman* 12:128+ Ap '87
The lady moguls. A. Thompson. il *Ms* 16:18+ N '87
Romantic porn in the boudoir [influence of women filmmakers] J. Leo. il *Time* 129:63+ Mr 30 '87

Women in the petroleum industry
Staying up when your industry's down [A. L. Holland of Mayco Petroluem] D. Holder. il pors *Work Woman* 12:45-6 My '87

Women in the radio industry
Dear Betty Harragan [burnout experienced by woman radio station manager] B. L. Harragan. il *Work Woman* 12:24+ Ag '87
Dorothy Brunson. K. Smikle. *Black Enterp* 17:45-6 Ap '87
Footloose or screw loose? Sondra Lowell gives listeners all the news that's fit to tap. il por *People Wkly* 27:102-3 Ja 19 '87
Topping the charts [V. Green, general manager of Detroit radio station WJLB-FM] J. Chenault. il *Essence* 17:90+ Ja '87

Women in the television industry
    See also
    Women in cable television
17 hours with Mariette Hartley. L. Eisenberg. il pors *Good Housekeep* 204:180-1+ My '87
Black Boston TV anchor goes public on pregnancy [L. Walker] por *Jet* 72:32 Jl 6 '87
Born with deformed hands and feet, an anchorwoman overcomes TV's obsession with perfect looks; ed. by Kristin McMurran. B. Walker. il pors *People Wkly* 28:117-18+ N 30 '87
The business of show biz [M. A. Thomas, black executive with Carson Productions] S. Herbert. il por *Essence* 18:116+ S '87
Chat show host Emma Freud, Sigmund's great-granddaughter, gets the lowdown by lying down [host of British show Pillow talk] M. Neill. il pors *People Wkly* 28:155-6 D 7 '87
Connecticut's on-air authority [anchorwoman J. Peckinpaugh] J. Giambanco. il pors *Work Woman* 12:91-2+ Ja '87
How and why I sued my boss for sex discrimination. K. Stone. *Glamour* 85:228-9+ Je '87

Women in the television industry—*cont.*

An intimate talk with Oprah. S. L. Taylor. il pors *Essence* 18:57-8+ Ag '87

Jane Pauley's charmed life. J. Stone. il por *McCalls* 114:152+ Ap '87

Joan Lunden: now she's got it all! J. Rovin. il pors *Ladies Home J* 104:62+ Ap '87

Langhart is fired after refusing TV lottery job [J. Langhart] por *Jet* 72:40 Jl 13 '87

NBC's crack (of dawn) news anchor, Deborah Norville, shoots for a spot as the next morning star. J. Hall. il pors *People Wkly* 28:79-80 Jl 27 '87

Oprah. A. Richman. il pors *People Wkly* 27:48-50+ Ja 12 '87

Oprah [excerpt from Everybody loves Oprah!] N. King. il pors *Good Housekeep* 205:107+ Ag '87

Oprah! Thriving on faith. L. Rubinstein. il pors *McCalls* 114:136-8+ Ag '87

Oprah Winfrey. il por *People Wkly* 28:74 D 28 '87-Ja 4 '88

Oprah Winfrey sweeps daytime Emmy Awards. il por *Jet* 72:22 Jl 20 '87

Oprah Winfrey: the most talked-about TV talk show host. C. Whitaker. il pors *Ebony* 42:38-40+ Mr '87

Oprah Winfrey to earn top salary in show biz. por *Jet* 71:26 Ja 26 '87

Oprah Winfrey's success story. E. Sherman. il pors *Ladies Home J* 104:64+ Mr '87

Pam Zekman [head of WBBM-TV's investigative unit] J. Vitale. il pors *Channels* 7:31-2 O '87

The Sawyer exception [D. Sawyer's new CBS contract] por *Newsweek* 109:41 Ja 12 '87

Scoop du jour [interview with N. Collins] L. Smith. il por *Vogue* 177:352-3+ Ap '87

Terry Louise Fisher: how she dreamed up the women of "L.A. law". M. Kort. por *Ms* 15:38-9+ Je '87

Texas TV pioneer: Clara McLaughlin is first black woman to own stations. M. Marshall. il pors *Ebony* 42:78+ Mr '87

TV's new daytime darling [O. Winfrey; cover story] C. Whitaker. il pors *Saturday Evening Post* 259:42-5 Jl/Ag '87

Weighed as a future anchor, Diane Sawyer joins TV's million-dollar men's club. J. Hall. il por *People Wkly* 27:30-1 Ja 19 '87

'Winfrey' knocks 'Donahue' out of no. 1 spot; Oprah plans TV sitcom and movie. por *Jet* 72:24 My 18 '87

Women in the theater

Mending Fences [producer C. Shorenstein Hays] L. Garchik. por *Vogue* 177:118 O '87

Women in the wine industry

Pooling the Iacocca talent, Lee makes Lia head of his winery. il pors *People Wkly* 28:85 S 14 '87

Zelma of Simi [Z. Long] N. Hazelton. *Natl Rev* 39:57-8 F 13 '87

Women in trade unions *See* Trade unions—Women

Women in videotapes

Essence woman [views of TV producer J. Brown on black women in video] L. B. Randolph. il por *Essence* 17:24 Ja '87

Women investment advisers

Helping dollars make sense [V. VanCaspel] H. G. Miller. il pors *Saturday Evening Post* 259:46-7+ Mr '87

Laura Scher: doing good business helps good causes. M. Mallory. il por *Bus Week* p76 O 26 '87

Women journalists

See also

Cochrane, Elizabeth, 1867-1922

Hunter-Gault, Charlayne

Women judges

See also

Bird, Rose Elizabeth

Thomas, Maxine F.

Women lawyers

See also

Bernstein, Madeline

Ciani, Judithe

Fairstein, Linda

Girton, Brenda M.

Handler, Sharon J.

Joyner, Gail Tusan

Simmons, Althea

When doctors refuse to treat lawyers [obstetricians vs. women lawyers in Brunswick, Ga.] P. Cooke. il *Read Dig* 131:100-4 O '87

Women and the law: will real life catch up to TV? H.-J. P. Mullins. il *Ms* 15:64-5 Je '87

Women lawyers in television

The women of "L.A. law". M. Kort. il *Ms* 15:43 Je '87

Women legislators

Black woman speaker pro tempore of Michigan House [T. P. Hunter] por *Jet* 71:22 Ja 12 '87

S.C. rep. Juanita White elected to committee post. por *Jet* 72:24 Ag 24 '87

Women lighthouse tenders *See* Lighthouse tenders

Women lobbyists and lobbying

Lawyer in the lobby [black woman lawyer B. M. Girton of Washington, D.C. corporate governmental affairs office of Sears, Roebuck] N. A. Williams. il por *Essence* 18:113+ Jl '87

Women marketing managers

Career makeover: from secretary to assistant vice president [S. Coe's career with First National Bank of Chicago] il por *Glamour* 85:84+ Ja '87

Women mayors

See also

Feinstein, Dianne

Perkins, Helen

Shackelford, Lottie

Sigmund, Barbara

Whitmire, Kathryn J.

Women medical students

Anatomy and destiny [feminism] P. Klass. *Ms* 16:66+ Jl/Ag '87

Women missionaries

On the land for good [Navajo missionary A. Garber] R. Wilkins. il pors *Christ Today* 31:12-13 Je 12 '87

Women motion picture characters *See* Women in motion pictures

Women motion picture directors

See also

Barrett, Lezli-An

Bemberg, Maria Luisa

Hoffs, Tamar

Keaton, Diane

Kurys, Diane

Rozema, Patricia

Women motion picture producers

See also

Silver, Diane

Steel, Dawn

Women municipal employees

Dear Betty Harragan [on the job corruption and discrimination] B. L. Harragan. il *Work Woman* 12:30+ O '87

Women municipal officers

Sharon Gist Gilliam: the woman in charge of Chicago's $3.8 billion budget. il pors *Ebony* 42:31-2+ Mr '87

Women musicians

See also

Women rock musicians

Women naturalists

See also

Rothschild, Miriam

Women newscasters *See* Television broadcasting—News

Women newspaper publishers *See* Women in newspaper publishing

Women of the Calabash (Musical group)

Showing off with Women of the Calabash. J. Gruber. il *Essence* 18:36 Je '87

Women photo stylists *See* Photo stylists

Women photographers

See also

Austen, Alice

Bloom, Barbara

Carey, Ellen

Gilpin, Laura

Goldin, Nan

Heyman, Abigail

Hofer, Evelyn

Kasten, Barbara

Kruger, Barbara

Mann, Sally, 1951-

Mark, Mary Ellen, 1940-

Moutoussamy-Ashe, Jeanne, 1951-

Noah, Barbara

Sherman, Cindy

Skoglund, Sandy, 1946-

Tomlin, Elaine

Women physicians

See also

Ascher, Nancy

Jones, Edith Irby

Koblenzer, Caroline

Nuns as physicians

Donald Thornton's magnificent dream [black man's wish to see all his daughters become doctors] J. Coudert. il por *Read Dig* 130:121-5 F '87

Women physicians—*cont.*

Full moons and white men [woman physician attempts to dispel bias that favors white males] S. P. Harwood. il *Ms* 16:103 O '87

Women physicians and drugs *See* Drugs and physicians

Women physicists

See also

Watkins, Sallie A.

Women poets

See also

Agustini, Delmira, 1886-1914
Brooks, Gwendolyn
Dickinson, Emily, 1830-1886
Dove, Rita
Gallagher, Tess
Jacobsen, Josephine
Kelly, Brigit Pegeen, 1951-
Moore, Marianne, 1887-1972
Plath, Sylvia
Ratushinskaya, Irina
TSvetaeva, Marina Ivanovna, 1892-1941

Women political candidates

A new battlefield for NOW's fearless leader [efforts of E. Smeal] por *Newsweek* 110:30-1 Jl 20 '87

Women postal employees

Religious life

I can no longer remain a bystander. R. M. Hart. il *Commonweal* 114:556-7 O 9 '87

Women priests

See also

Ordination of women

Women prison officials and employees *See* Prisons—Officials and employees

Women prisoners

Among sisters of crime [J. Kastner's documentary Prison mother, prison daughter] P. Hluchy. il por *Macleans* 100:54-5 Ja 12 '87

When mothers serve time. M. Christopher. il *Sch Update* 119:8 F 9 '87

Women behind bars [separation from children] N. Rubin. il *McCalls* 114:36+ Ag '87

Health and hygiene

A tough assignment—working out inside [J. Prinzmetal runs exercise program at California Institution for Women] M. Kort. il por *Ms* 16:32 O '87

Monitoring

Michigan woman jailed; can't serve time at home [case of C. Doa] *Jet* 72:25 My 18 '87

Treatment

Follow-up [Female High Security Unit in Lexington, Ky. to close] *Nation* 245:436 O 24 '87

Pregnant woman found hanged in N.Y. jail cell; angry blacks ask probe [case of S. A. Harris-Smith] *Jet* 72:8 Jl 13 '87

The women of Lexington Prison [S. L. Rosenberg and A. Torres charge they are victims of brainwashing] W. A. Reuben and C. Norman. il *Nation* 244:881-4 Je 27 '87

Women psychologists

See also

Maccoby, Eleanor E., 1917-

Women public officers

Women who won. L. Edmunds. il *Ms* 15:29+ Ja '87

Women real estate agents

From Alabama fields to Holmby Hills [E. McClaney, black woman realtor] P. F. Stewart. il por *Ladies Home J* 104:154 O '87

Women rock musicians

Glitter girls. il *Teen* 31:52-3 F '87

Ladies pay their dues. T. Young. il *Vogue* 177:54 Je '87

Women in rock [videotape] K. Walter. il *High Fidel* 37:79 Jl '87

Women sailors *See* Women in sailing

Women school administrators

Do women in education need mentors? J. Dodgson. *Educ Dig* 52:26-8 Ja '87

Women school superintendents and principals

White woman jailed for hitting black principal who paddled her son [incident in Moody, Ala.] il por *Jet* 73:6-7 N 30 '87

A woman at old Exeter [principal K. S. O'Donnell] F. Schumer. il pors *N Y Times Mag* p98-101 O 11 '87

Women scientists

Letters [discussion of February 1987 article, Marriage, motherhood and research performance in science] J. R. Cole and H. Zuckerman. *Sci Am* 257:4+ Ag '87

Marriage, motherhood and research performance in science. J. R. Cole and H. Zuckerman. il *Sci Am* 256:119-25 F '87

Motherhood and science do mix [study by Jonathan R. Cole and Harriet Zuckerman] E. Stark. il *Psychol Today* 21:14 Je '87

Who needs women? K. C. Cole. *Omni* 9:35 My '87

Women in science and engineering is focus of conferences. *Science* 238:86 O 2 '87

Women singers

Big mamas who made the most of the blues [reissued blues recordings compiled by Rosetta Reitz] C. Brown. il *Essence* 18:28 Jl '87

New sirens of song: note worthy. J. Farber. il *Harpers Bazaar* 120:234+ S '87

Women social workers *See* Social workers

Women sports journalists *See* Sports journalism

Women telephone workers *See* Telephone workers

Women television characters *See* Women in television

Women television producers

See also

Cerre, Gina
Cooney, Joan Ganz
Kan, Yue-Sai
Mandabach, Caryn
Schuyler, Linda

Women tennis players *See* Tennis players

Women veterans

The unsung heroines of Vietnam [recognition of women veterans at the Vietnam Veterans Memorial] J. McRobbie. il pors *McCalls* 114:159 My '87

Women warriors, Mythical *See* Amazons

Women's Caucus for Art

Now you see us. E. Heartney. il *Art News* 86:10+ F '87

Women honor women. C. Giuliano. il *Art News* 86:18 My '87

Women's colleges *See* Colleges for women

Women's exercises *See* Exercise

Women's friendships *See* Friendship

Women's gymnasiums *See* Gymnasiums

Women's health clinics *See* Health facilities

Women's liberation movement *See* Feminism

Women's organizations

See also

Black Women's Agenda
Concerned Women for America
Displaced Homemakers Network
National Council of Jewish Women
National Council of Negro Women
National Organization for Women
Society of Woman Geographers

Canada

See also

Mothers Are Women (Organization)
REAL Women (Organization)

Women's periodicals *See* Periodicals for women

Women's prisons *See* Prisons

Women's shoes *See* Footwear

Women's sports *See* Women—Sports

Women's Sports Foundation

Strides. See issues of Women's Sports & Fitness

Women's Sports Hall of Fame

1987 Hall of Fame: the winners' circle. il *Women's Sports Fitness* 9:58-9 O '87

Madeline Manning-Mims elected to Sports Hall. *Jet* 73:48 S 28 '87

Women's wear daily

Of power, glory and the rich and famous [influence of J. Fairchild] A. Gabor. il por *U S News World Rep* 103:55 Ag 24 '87

Wonder, Stevie

about

Ariz. gov. nixes King Day; Wonder snubs the state. *Jet* 71:60 F 9 '87

Blind piano player, 3, visits Stevie Wonder. il pors *Jet* 72:18 Je 22 '87

CSU honors Stevie Wonder for role in national King holiday. il por *Jet* 71:12-13 F 9 '87

Dr. Gloster weeps as he awards Wonder last degree as president of Morehouse. il pors *Jet* 72:24 Je 8 '87

Stevie Wonder [interview] M. Goldberg. por *Roll Stone* p153-4 N 5-D 10 '87

Stevie Wonder, Nile Rodgers produce disc from 2 coasts. il pors *Jet* 71:56 Mr 23 '87

Stevie Wonder releases 'Characters'. J. Ressner. *Roll Stone* p15 N 19 '87

Wonder to undergo surgery for growth on his finger. por *Jet* 72:19 Ag 31 '87

Wonders *See* Curiosities and wonders

Wong, Carey

Build scale models. il *Theatre Crafts* 21:90+ Ap '87

Wong, Gerard C. H.
about
Wong and Yeh win 1987 Apker Award for achievements as undergraduates. *Phys Today* 40:103 D '87
Wong, Gordon G., and others
Human CSF-1: molecular cloning and expression of 4-kb cDNA encoding the human urinary protein. bibl f il *Science* 235:1504-8 Mr 20 '87
Wong, May
The difficulty of moonlight in the 6th arrondissement [poem] *New Yorker* 63:36 Jl 6 '87
Wonner, Paul, 1920-
about
Paul Wonner at Hirschl & Adler Modern. J. Weinberg. il *Art Am* 75:161 D '87
Wood, Abigail
Relating. See issues of Seventeen
Wood, Christopher
The beat of Brazil. il *World Press Rev* 34:24-6 Mr '87
Irving's taxing battle. il por *Macleans* 100:34 Ag 3 '87
Wood, Clinton M.
Strain-gage transducers. il *Radio-Electron* 58:61-3+ D '87
Wood, Clive
The character of personality. il *Psychol Today* 21:8+ Mr '87
Wood, Grant, 1892-1942
about
An Iowa town debates the fate of Grant Wood's gothic backdrop. il *People Wkly* 28:111 S 7 '87
Wood, James, 1930-
about
Just how good is the Great A&P? B. Saporito. il por *Fortune* 115:92-3 Mr 16 '87
Wood, Larry
Vancouver Island's undersea kaleidoscope: a diver's paradise. il *Sea Front* 33:97-104 Mr/Ap '87
Wood, Leonard A.
The Gallup survey. See occasional issues of Publishers Weekly
Wood, Lowell
about
A star warrior aims at the moon. R. Spangenburg and D. Moser. il por *Space World* X-4-280:30-2 Ap '87
Wood, Peter D. (Peter Douglas), 1929-
about
The running debate. J. Poppy. il *Esquire* 107:49-50 Mr '87
Wood, Phyllis J.
A checklist for instructional supervision. *Educ Dig* 52:46-7 Ap '87
Wood, Ralph C.
The Thanatos syndrome: exciting, horrifying, disappointing. il por *Christ Century* 104:857-8 O 7 '87
Wood, Robert Chapman
Japan's economic masochism. il *Forbes* 140:138+ S 21 '87
Wood, Sid
Decorating. See issues of McCall's beginning May 1986
Wood, William J.
Teach the children well. il *America* 156:397-400 My 16 '87
Wood
See also
Lignin
Lumber
Plywood
Deterioration
A new repair system stops wood rot [Minwax High Performance Wood Hardener and Filler] R. N. Hoffman. il *Workbench* 43:65 Jl/Ag '87
Diseases and pests
See also
Termites
Dryers and drying
Solar kiln [solar heated lumber drying kiln] R. W. Rice. il *Workbench* 43:6+ Ja/F '87
Finishes and finishing
See also
Furniture—Finishes and finishing
Stains and staining
Clear wood finishes. il *Consum Rep* 52:497-501 Ag '87
Clear wood finishes. il *Consum Rep* 52:225-9 D '87
Color washing technique. il *Fam Handyman* 37:54-5 My/Je '87
Wood revival [use of Dekswood and Aquatrol] R. Barnhart. il *Home Mech* 83:12 Jl '87
Preservation and preservatives
See also
Wood—Dryers and drying

Guide to preservative treated wood. K. Childers. il *Fam Handyman* 37:94+ My/Je '87
A new repair system stops wood rot [Minwax High Performance Wood Hardener and Filler] R. N. Hoffman. il *Workbench* 43:65 Jl/Ag '87
Staining
See Stains and staining
Storage
See also
Woodbins, racks, etc.
Wood appliqué *See* Appliqué work
Wood as fuel
See also
Wood stoves
Burning sensations [product picks from the Wood Heating Alliance Show] S. Maviglio. il *Home Mech* 83:56-9 S '87
Firewood gathering hits a snag [endangering bird habitats in national forests] M. Kantor. il *Sierra* 72:24+ Mr/Ap '87
My life as a woodburner. D. D. Sleeper. il *Ctry J* 14:11-13 S '87
Wood-burning almanac [cover story] il *Mother Earth News* 107:42-9 S/O '87
Wood block prints *See* Wood engraving
Wood carving
See also
Carvers and Gilders (Firm)
Cigar store Indians
Fake masks [African art market] N. Lemann. il *Atlantic* 260:24+ N '87
Homage to Grinling Gibbons [limewood carving] D. Esterly. il por *House Gard* 159:18+ Ja '87
Little big top [work of A. Kveck] J. Colihan. il *Am Herit* 38:42-7 D '87
Philadelphia carving shops: Hercules Courtenay and his school. L. Beckerdite. bibl f il *Antiques* 131:1044-63 My '87
Pipe dreams [free-form custom-carved pipes] C. Caiati. il *Pop Mech* 164:72-3+ Ja '87
Santos by Roybal. N. C. Benson. il por *Americana* 15:45-8 Mr/Ap '87
Wood construction
See also
Plywood construction
American Wood Council 1986 Remodeling Awards. il *Archit Rec* 175:56-7 Ap '87
Idea house '87 [joint Home mechanix/American Wood Council venture] H. Wicks. il *Home Mech* 83:40-3+ F '87
Wood cuts *See* Wood engraving
Wood cutting
The esoteric art of splitting (and fitting) wood shingles. D. Petersen. il *Mother Earth News* 105:56-9 My/Je '87
In Missouri: outdoor work, very heavy lifting [woodcutter R. Tune] S. Hubbell. il por *Time* 130:12+ Ag 24 '87
Wood-burning almanac [cover story] il *Mother Earth News* 107:42-9 S/O '87
Wood cutting equipment
Cutting brush [cover story] D. Thomas. il *Ctry J* 14:58-63 My '87
Wood engraving
Techniques for making white-line woodblock prints. R. Hogan. il *Am Artist* 51:62-5 D '87
Wood epoxy compounds
Wood-epoxy construction makes a featherweight camper cap. P. Butler and M. Butler. il *Pop Sci* 231:86-8 O '87
Wood family
about
A Wood Family Toby jug. S. Bagdade and A. Bagdade. il *Antiques Collect Hobbies* 92:37 Je '87
Wood fillers *See* Filling materials
Wood finishing *See* Wood—Finishes and finishing
Wood flooring *See* Flooring
Wood floors *See* Floors
Wood furniture *See* Furniture
Wood graining *See* Graining
Wood Gundy Incorporated
Bay Street bickering [sues employees hired away by Walwyn Inc.] P. Best. il *Macleans* 100:30 S 28 '87
A megamerger in the works [Wood Gundy and Royal Bank of Canada] P. C. Newman. il *Macleans* 100:46 My 4 '87
A pair of prescient winners [T. Tugman of Wood Gundy wins Fortune's investment challenge] P. Nulty. il pors *Fortune* 116 Sp Issue:176-9 Fall '87

Wood Gundy Incorporated—*cont.*
Reckoning for a broker [First National Bank of Chicago considers purchasing stake in Wood Gundy] T. Tedesco. il *Macleans* 100:37 D 7 '87

Wood houses
Tree house retreat: a designer's Fire Island aerie [M. Dwork's house] P. Carlsen. il *Archit Dig* 44:60-5 Ag '87

Wood Memorial (Race) *See* Horse racing
Wood paneling *See* Paneling
Wood poles
The art of poling. B. Stearns. il *Field Stream* 92:69-70 D '87

Wood posts
Maintenance and repair
Posthaste post repair. J. R. Provey. il *Home Mech* 83:26+ O '87

Wood pulp industry
What's tall, tough and read all over? [use of kenaf as a pulp supply] *Sci News* 132:72 Ag 1 '87
Brazil
Two giant U.S. business efforts that failed in Brazil [H. Ford's Fordlandia and D. Ludwig's Jari Project] M. S. Forbes. il *Forbes* 140:18-19 O 19 '87
Siberia (Soviet Union)
Power's new Siberian connection [pulp operation to be constructed by Power Corp. of Canada] P. C. Newman. il por *Macleans* 100:44 Je 1 '87

Wood sculpting *See* Wood carving
Wood siding (Building) *See* Siding (Building)
Wood sorrel *See* Oxalis
Wood stove cooking
Woodstove cooking: beyond soups and stews. B. Marcks. *Ctry J* 14:42 O '87

Wood stoves
Burning sensations [product picks from the Wood Heating Alliance Show] S. Maviglio. il *Home Mech* 83:56-9 S '87
Central heating from a wood stove. R. Barnhart. il *Home Mech* 83:34 O '87
Clean heating with wood stoves. J. Perry. il *Consum Res Mag* 70:10-13 D '87
Computerized pellet stove [New Buck Peltron] J. T. Black. il *Pop Sci* 230:77 Mr '87
Home on the solid-fuel range: an introduction to wood and coal cookstoves. J. Schneider. il *Ctry J* 14:36-41 O '87
Homemade brick hearth for a wood stove. J. Collins. il *Workbench* 43:56-9 N/D '87
Keep the home fires burning. il *Esquire* 108:226-7 D '87
My life as a woodburner. D. D. Sleeper. il *Ctry J* 14:11-13 S '87
New national woodstove emissions standards. W. Shipman. il *Ctry J* 14:10-13 Je '87
Up in smoke. L. Green. il *Pop Mech* 164:116+ Ja '87
Wood stoves must clean up their act [new emission standards] C. M. Fiorillo. il *Pop Sci* 231:46 D '87
Safety devices and measures
The dangers of wood stoves. il *Parents* 62:26 Ja '87
How to use your fireplace and woodburning stove—safely. A. Arnott. il *McCalls* 114:103 F '87

Wood turning *See* Turning (Machine work)
Wood type *See* Type and typefounding
Wood working *See* Woodworking
Woodard, Alfre
about
Playing South African activist Winnie Mandela, Alfre Woodward captures the soul of a nation. M. Dougherty. il pors *People Wkly* 28:103-4+ S 28 '87

Woodard, Josef
Don Preston: synthesizer from Apocalypse now to Zappa. il por *Down Beat* 54:25-7 Ag '87

Woodard, Lynette
about
1st female Globetrotter quits in contract flap. il pors *Jet* 73:48 N 16 '87

Woodbins, racks, etc.
Firewood bin loads from outside. il *Sunset* 178:106 Mr '87

Woodcarving *See* Wood carving
Woodchucks
Me and that groundhog [reprint from May 1969 issue] C. E. Gillham. il *Audubon* 89:72-5 Jl '87

Woodcock, George, 1912-
Riding the Silk Road in China [cover story] il *New Leader* 70:10-15 S 21 '87

Woodcock, Gordon
Mars next? por *Space World* X-10-286:36 O '87
Who are we? por *Space World* X-6-282:36 Je '87

Woodcock shooting
A bird in the bush. G. Hill. il *Field Stream* 91:27-8 Ap '87
Route to woodcock. T. Huggler. il *Outdoor Life* 180:100-1+ S '87

Woodcuts *See* Wood engraving
Woodcutting *See* Wood cutting
Wooden boats *See* Boats and boating—Materials
Wooden ceilings *See* Ceilings
Wooden houses *See* Wood houses
Wooden motor boats *See* Motor boats—Materials
Wooden poles *See* Wood poles
Wooden toys *See* Toys
Woodentops (Musical group)
The Woodentops. M. Kaplan. il *Roll Stone* p20+ Ja 15 '87

Woodenware
See also
Bowls

Woodham, Joyce
about
Jamaicans fuel a skyrocketing market. A. McKenzie. il por map *Black Enterp* 18:93-4+ D '87

Woodhouse, John H.
(jt. auth) See Dziewonski, Adam M., and Woodhouse, John H.

Woodier, Olwen, 1942-
Marmalade [cover story] il *Americana* 14:46-9+ Ja/F '87
Sweet taste of summer. il *Americana* 15:46-50 Jl/Ag '87

Woodin, Nick
A simpler way with seedlings. il *Rodale's Org Gard* 34:74-9 Mr '87

Woodiwiss, Michael
Capone to Kefauver: organised crime in America. bibl il *Hist Today* 37:8-15 Je '87

Woodlots
Farming your woodlands for profit. il *Success Farm* 85 no4:21 F '87
Is woodland management for you? [home study course] D. J. Decker. il *Conservationist* 41:38-41 Ja/F '87
My 40 years in a woodlot. H. S. Kernan. il *Conservationist* 42:36-41 S/O '87
Woodlot wherefores. *Ctry J* 14:12 Jl '87

Woodman, Josef
Tips for DTP users. *Publ Wkly* 232:28 N 13 '87

Woodmere (N.Y.)
Crime
Blood and money: the unsolved murder of a Long Island woman leads to a novel suit against her husband [case of M. S. Schwartz] M. Ryan. il pors *N Y* 20:38-44 Je 8 '87

Woodner, Ian
about
The old master. P. Gardner. il por *Art News* 86:120-3 S '87

Woodpeckers
Endangered species? Load the shotgun! [K. Ghumman accused of shooting red cockaded woodpeckers in Florida] R. L. Di Silvestro. il *Audubon* 89:12 S '87
"I saw it!" [ivory-billed woodpecker in Cuba] L. L. Short and J. F. M. Horne. il *Int Wildl* 17:22-3 Mr/Ap '87

Woodpiles
Winning woodpiles. il *Mother Earth News* 107:48-9 S/O '87

Woodring, Paul, 1907-
Too bright to be a teacher? il *Phi Delta Kappan* 68:617-18 Ap '87

Woodrow, Bill
about
Clashing furniture and whatnot. W. Feaver. il por *Art News* 86:38+ F '87

Woodruff, Elvira
Santa knows [story] il *Parents* 62:129-32+ D '87

Woodruff, R. C., and others
Hybrid dysgenesis in D. melanogaster is not a general release mechanism for DNA transpositions. bibl f il *Science* 237:1206-8 S 4 '87

Woods, Donald, 1933-
about
Donald and Wendy Woods talk about the real-life drama behind Cry freedom [interview] C. Krupp. il pors *Glamour* 85:166+ D '87
Newsman Donald Woods still seeks justice for Stephen Biko in the film Cry freedom. W. Plummer. il pors *People Wkly* 28:64+ N 23 '87
What's wrong with this picture? E. Mitchell. il *Roll Stone* p31-2 D 3 '87

Woods, Donald, 1933----about—cont.
"You already did Gandhi, I said. Let's do Biko."—Donald Woods [interview] A. White. il por *Film Comment* 23:13 N/D '87
Woods, Frank W.
The acid rain question. il por *Futurist* 21:34-7 Ja/F '87
Woods, James
Shark Bay. il map *Sea Front* 33:324-33 S/O '87
Woods, Thomas B.
Simulating clusters on your computer. il *Astronomy* 15:63-7 S '87
Woods, Wendy
about
Donald and Wendy Woods talk about the real-life drama behind Cry freedom [interview] C. Krupp. il pors *Glamour* 85:166+ D '87
Woods Hole Laboratories *See* Marine Biological Laboratory (Woods Hole, Mass.)
Woods-Jones, Dezie
about
Keeper of the faith. M. Marshall. il pors *Ebony* 42:92+ Ag '87
Woodson, Jacqueline
Untitled [poem] *Essence* 18:137 D '87
Woodward, Ann
about
Could they get away with murder? B. Darrach. il pors *People Wkly* 27:52-4+ F 16 '87
Woodward, Billy
about
Could they get away with murder? B. Darrach. il pors *People Wkly* 27:52-4+ F 16 '87
Woodward, Bob, 1943-
The secret wars of the CIA [excerpts from Veil] il *Newsweek* 110:46-8+ O 5 '87
about
Ace reporter Bob Woodward lifts the Veil on the secrets of CIA chief William Casey. M. Green. il pors *People Wkly* 28:40-1 O 12 '87
Bob Woodward and Bill Casey: the odd couple. J. Alter. il *Newsweek* 110:26-7 O 12 '87
Books. L. Hirschberg. il por *N Y* 20:110-11 S 21 '87
Casey and Woodward: who used whom? M. Kempton. il *N Y Rev Books* 34:61 N 5 '87
Casey's secret. *Nation* 245:363-4 O 10 '87
Did a dead man tell no tales? R. Zoglin. il pors *Time* 130:28+ O 12 '87
Did Woodward get it right? G. Witkin. il por *U S News World Rep* 103:23 O 12 '87
Factoid time? *Natl Rev* 39:19 O 23 '87
Knock on Woodward. F. Barnes. il *New Repub* 197:11-13 O 26 '87
Lifting the Veil on the CIA's secrets. M. Elfin. il pors *U S News World Rep* 103:26-7 O 5 '87
The man who wasn't there. D. M. Alpern. il por *Newsweek* 110:44-5 O 5 '87
Reagan's secret wars and missed opportunities. J. M. Wall. *Christ Century* 104:907-8 O 21 '87
Spy master revelations. M. McDonald. il pors *Macleans* 100:30-1 O 12 '87
Woodward on Casey. T. H. Stahel. *America* 157:236-7 O 17 '87
Woodward, C. Vann (Comer Vann), 1908-
The black and the red. por *New Repub* 196:32-6 Mr 16 '87
The dreams of Martin Luther King. bibl f il pors *N Y Rev Books* 33:3+ Ja 15 '87
Woodward, Comer Vann *See* Woodward, C. Vann (Comer Vann), 1908-
Woodward, Elsie
about
Could they get away with murder? B. Darrach. il pors *People Wkly* 27:52-4+ F 16 '87
Woodward, Joanne, 1930-
about
Joanne Woodward: a class act. M. Cantwell. il por *Vogue* 177:390-1+ N '87
Woodward, Richard B.
Four saxmen, one great voice. il *N Y Times Mag* p46-7+ Ap 12 '87
Nobody's fools. il pors *Art News* 86:172-8 N '87
Woodwind music
See also
New York Woodwind Quintet
Woodworkers
See also
Stocksdale, Bob, 1913-
Woodworking
See also
Dowels

Joints (Carpentry)
Miter boxes, gages, etc.
Planes and planing
Sanding and sanding equipment
Saws and sawing
Turning (Machine work)
Veneers and veneering
Wood carving
Whirligigs and whimsies: enchanting folk art you can build. J. Williams and J. Severson. il *Better Homes Gard* 65:102-4+ My '87
Woodworking guide [special section] il *Pop Mech* 164:93+ N '87
Workshop minicourse. R. Capotosto. See issues of Popular Mechanics beginning January 1986
Bibliography
Christmas book roundup and video cassettes too. R. N. Hoffman. il *Workbench* 43:26 N/D '87
Designs and plans
How to enlarge drawings; Draw an ellipse without math, strings or tacks. W. J. Larsen. il *Workbench* 43:104 S/O '87
Projects
See also
Plywood construction
See also names of projects
11 summer projects [cover story; special section] il *Workbench* 43:31-61 Jl/Ag '87
Shopwork guide [special section] R. Capotosto. il *Pop Mech* 164:115-22+ Jl '87
Woodworks. See issues of The Family Handyman beginning October 1986
Caricatures and cartoons
Wordless workshop. R. Doty. See issues of Popular Science
Woody plants
See also
Shrubs
Wool
The evolution of the fleece. M. L. Ryder. il *Sci Am* 256:112-19 Ja '87
Wool industry
Peru
Gathering the golden fleece [vicunas] P. E. Rogers. il *Américas* 39:34-9 S/O '87
Wooldridge, Raymond A.
about
Prefab pokeys: when prison space is tight. D. Foust. il por *Bus Week* p86 N 2 '87
Wooldridge, Wilfred E.
Better asparagus . . . is on the way. il *Flower Gard* 31:38-9 Ap/My '87
For scrumptious salads, blend your lettuces. il *Flower Gard* 31:79-80 F/Mr '87
It's time for pickling. il *Flower Gard* 31:50 O/N '87
Let's have high tea! il *Flower Gard* 32:79 D '87/Ja '88
Try marrow . . . if you're tired of zucchini. il *Flower Gard* 31:26 Je/Jl '87
Woolf, Robert Gary, 1928-
about
Bob Woolf: the man behind the $8 million man. L. Therrien. il por *Bus Week* p125-6 Ap 27 '87
Woolworth (F. W.) Co. *See* F. W. Woolworth Co.
Woolworth Holdings plc
"You can't market variety". J. A. Trachtenberg. il *Forbes* 140:82-3 Jl 27 '87
Wooster, Martin, and Fund, John
Up from public housing. il *Read Dig* 131:139-43 Jl '87
Wooster, Warren S.
Immiscible investigators: oceanographers, meteorologists, and fishery scientists. *BioScience* 37:728-30 N '87
Wooster Group
Radical cheek to cheek [E. LeCompte and W. Dafoe] L. Liebmann. pors *Vogue* 177:90 Ap '87
Worby, Rachael
about
Have baton, will travel. S. Mieses. il por *N Y* 20:25 F 16 '87
Worcester (Mass.)
Arts
See also
Mechanics Hall (Worcester, Mass.)
Festivals
Cultural countdown [First Night] K. Milam. il *Horizon* 30:22-3 My '87
Galleries and museums
See also
Worcester Art Museum

Worcester (Mass.)—*cont.*
Religious institutions and affairs
An heiress vs. a pastor [E. Dovydenas vs. C. Stevens and his Bible Speaks church] G. Hackett. por *Newsweek* 109:33 Ap 20 '87

Worcester Art Museum
Artsmart [American traditions in watercolor] il *Harpers Bazaar* 120:190 Mr '87
Technique in American watercolors from the Worcester Art Museum, Worcester, Massachusetts. S. E. Strickler and J. C. Walsh. bibl f il *Antiques* 131:412-25 F '87
The watercolors from Worcester [American traditions in watercolor] K. M. Burke. il *Smithsonian* 18:192 S '87

Worcester County (Mass.)
Arts
Worcester County [special section] il *Horizon* 30:17-30+ My '87
Description and travel
Worcester County [special section] il *Horizon* 30:17-30+ My '87

Word games
See also
Scrabble (Game)
Shades of summer. L. Philipson. il *Seventeen* 46:92 Ag '87
Word ladders and a Tower of Babel lead to computational heights defying assault. A. K. Dewdney. il *Sci Am* 257:108-11 Ag '87

Word Handler (Word processor program) *See* Word processors and processing—Programming

Word Inc.
The problems at the 'big three'. D. D. Buss. il *Christ Today* 31:60-1 Mr 6 '87
Word How-To Library offers spiritual perspective. il *Publ Wkly* 232:40 N 20 '87

Word of God (Theology)
Oases of faith. G. G. Seibert. *America* 157:23 Jl 4-11 '87

Word-of-mouth advertising
The best kind of advertising [word of mouth makes M. S. Peck's The road less traveled into best seller] J. A. Trachtenberg. il por *Forbes* 139:91-2 Ap 20 '87

Word processor industry
See also
Harris Corp.
Wang Laboratories Inc.

Word processors and processing
See also
Text processing (Computer science)
Its master's voice [R. Kurzweil's Voice works] D. Lander. il por *Pop Mech* 164:69-71 O '87
Talk may be cheap, but Ray Kurzweil stands to make millions by yakking to his voice computer. L. Rozen. il pors *People Wkly* 27:113-14 Mr 9 '87
Word processing. See issues of Personal Computing beginning May 1987
A wordsmith pure and simple [personal writers] T. McCarroll. il *Time* 129:50 Mr 2 '87
Authors' use
The curse of Chaos Manor [deadlines, equipment problems and Comdex] J. Pournelle. *Byte* 12:251-2+ Mr '87
Release [blind author R. Russell and his talking word processor] *New Yorker* 63:28-32 S 28 '87
Business use
Word-processing primer for the hunt-and-peck manager. H. McCandless. *Work Woman* 12:65 D '87
Programming
See also
Hypertext
The best get better. C. O'Malley. il *Pers Comput* 11:88-91+ O '87
Dark horse applications [MyWord! and Write Now [Airus version]] E. Shapiro. il *Byte* 12 Sp Issue:33-5 Summ '87
Data structures in a bit-mapped text editor: how Carnegie-Mellon University displays text on the IBM RT PC. W. J. Hansen. il *Byte* 12:183-4+ Ja '87
Developing good form [customized form letters] C. O'Malley. il *Pers Comput* 11:99-102+ My '87
Full featured but friendly [OfficeWriter] S. Makrias. il *Pers Comput* 11:192-3 Ap '87
Getting in your two cents' worth [For Comment] S. R. Reed. il *Pers Comput* 11:54 F '87
Holiday cheer [MacCalligraphy, Spellin!, spelling checker, and FastTRAP trackball device] E. Shapiro. il *Byte* 12:215-16+ D '87

How many ways can you say thesaurus? S. Ditlea. il *Pers Comput* 11:107-9+ My '87
How well do you spell? [spelling checkers] S. Ditlea. il *Pers Comput* 11:91-3+ Mr '87
IBM rethinks word processing [DisplayWrite 4] R. Lockwood. il *Pers Comput* 11:238 Je '87
An inexpensive word processor [Celebrity] S. Makrias. il *Pers Comput* 11:174 Jl '87
The Intelligent Assistant [Q&A's natural-language interface] G. G. Hendrix and B. A. Walter. il *Byte* 12:251-2+ D '87
An "intuitive" word processor [Write Now [Airus version]] S. R. Reed. il *Pers Comput* 11:196+ Ap '87
Key to perfect spelling [spelling checker programs] N. Henderson. *Changing Times* 41:104 My '87
Laser Author. M. O'Neil. il *Byte* 12:344-5 Ja '87
Let's hear it for CAW [computer aided writing] R. Nelson. il *Pers Comput* 11:49-50+ Ag '87
A look at the upgrade [WordStar 4.0] M. Antonoff. il *Pers Comput* 11:68-9 F '87
Lyrix. G. R. Allen. *Byte* 12:251-3 My '87
A more complete XyWrite processor. S. Quigley. il *Pers Comput* 11:262+ N '87
A more flexible MultiMate edition [Advantage II] M. Antonoff. il *Pers Comput* 11:140+ Ag '87
Outlining with InLine. S. Quigley. il *Pers Comput* 11:210 My '87
Q&A. J. Pournelle. *Byte* 12:294-6+ S '87
Q&A 2.0. P. R. Robinson. *Byte* 12:249-51 My '87
Q&A Write: spinoff software. S. R. Reed. il *Pers Comput* 11:256-7 N '87
The rebirth of a classic [WordStar] C. Spencer. il *Pers Comput* 11:62-5+ F '87
Scribble! W. Block. il *Byte* 12:342-4 Ja '87
Something special [Microsoft Word 3.0] E. Shapiro. il *Byte* 12:395-6+ Ja '87
Souped-up software for writers [XyWrite III Plus] O. Port. il *Bus Week* p122 Ag 17 '87
Split decisions [WordStar Professional 4.1 and WordPerfect Executive] E. Shapiro. *Byte* 12:241-2+ N '87
Spreadsheet and text processing [Words & Figures] H.-J. Taferner. il *Pers Comput* 11:56 F '87
Trading up is hard to do. R. Nelson. il *Pers Comput* 11:65 Je '87
Under a spell [Thunder spelling checker] J. Bell. il *Pers Comput* 11:150 Mr '87
Useful stuff: a speller for Works and a duo of telecommunications packages for MCI Mail. E. Shapiro. *Byte* 12:283-4+ Jl '87
Webster's new On-Line Thesaurus . . . il *Radio-Electron* 58 ComputerDigest:5 Ja '87
A weighty word processor [Lotus Manuscript] M. Antonoff. il *Pers Comput* 11:56 Ap '87
What's new in low-priced word processors. S. Makrias. il *Pers Comput* 11:97+ Ag '87
Word for the Mac: the next level [Word 3.0] J. Bell. il *Pers Comput* 11:179-80 Ap '87
Word Handler. M. O'Neil. il *Byte* 12:257-8+ Ap '87
Word processing file conversion [Word for Word] B. Sillery. il *Pers Comput* 11:156 Mr '87
Word processing made easy [Bank Street Writer Plus and PC-Write] N. Henderson. il *Changing Times* 41:104+ My '87
Word processors. P. R. Robinson. il *Byte* 12 Sp Issue:55-64+ Summ '87
Word wrapping in Lotus 1-2-3 [4Word] M. Antonoff. il *Pers Comput* 11:232 Je '87
WordPerfect. J. Pournelle. *Byte* 12:272+ F '87
WordStar enters the modern world [WordStar Professional] M. Antonoff. il *Pers Comput* 11:192+ My '87
The write dilemma. J. Pournelle. *Byte* 12:258+ O '87
WriteNow for the Macintosh [T/Maker version] M. O'Neil. il *Byte* 12:237-8 Mr '87
Writing in a spreadsheet. M. Antonoff. il *Pers Comput* 11:51-2+ Jl '87
XyWrite III Plus. E. White. *Byte* 12:97-8 N '87
Testing
The Magnavox Videowriter. il *Consum Rep* 52:493-4 Ag '87
The Magnavox Videowriter. *Consum Rep* 52:306-7 D '87
A spiritual heir to the Macintosh [Canon Cat] E. Shapiro. il *Byte* 12:121-3 O '87
Typewriter or computer? [Smith Corona PWP14] il *Consum Rep* 52:685 N '87
Translating use
See Machine translating

Word tests *See* Vocabulary; Vocabulary tests
Worden, Simon P.
Why astronomers should love SDI. *Sky Telesc* 74:340 O '87

WordPerfect (Word processor program) *See* Word processors and processing—Programming

Words

See also

English language—Etymology
English language—Terms and phrases
Spelling
Vocabulary

Psychology

See Psycholinguistics

Words, New

Word watch. A. H. Soukhanov. See issues of The Atlantic beginning January 1987

Words, Obscene

Four-letter words. E. Knoll. *Progressive* 51:4 F '87

Words in art

Diversionary (syn)tactics [work of B. Kruger] C. Squiers. il por *Art News* 86:76-85 F '87

WordStar (Word processor program) *See* Word processors and processing—Programming

Wordsworth, William, 1770-1850

about

Sharing the poet's obsession. R. Hughes. il *Time* 130:95 D 14 '87

Words' worth. K. Larson. il *N Y* 20:140+ D 7 '87

WordsWorth (Cambridge, Mass.: Bookstore) *See* Booksellers and bookselling—Massachusetts

Work

See also

Absenteeism
Hours of labor
Job satisfaction
Labor
Occupational health and safety
Skilled labor
Telecommuting
Workaholics

Back-of-the-envelope philosopher [L. Solomon] D. Machan. il por *Forbes* 140:106-7 Ag 24 '87

Beyond "trendy" forecasts: the next 10 years for work. S. A. Levitan. il por *Futurist* 21:28-32 N/D '87

The menace of high-tech employment [office of the future] J. H. Foegen. il por *Futurist* 21:38-40 S/O '87

Rethinking how we work: the office of the future. S. E. Bleecker. il por *Futurist* 21:15-21 Jl/Ag '87

The work ethic lives! G. J. Church. il *Time* 130:40-2 S 7 '87

Anecdotes, facetiae, satire, etc.

All in a day's work. See issues of Reader's Digest

Work accidents *See* Industrial accidents

Work benches *See* Workbenches

Work boats

See also

Barges

Work ethic *See* Work

Work for hire book contracts *See* Authors and publishers

Work force *See* Labor supply

Work gloves *See* Gloves

Work performance standards *See* Performance standards

Work relief *See* Unemployment—Relief measures

Work satisfaction *See* Job satisfaction

Work stress *See* Job stress

Work-study programs *See* Business and education

Work tables *See* Tables

Work therapy *See* Occupational therapy

Work training *See* Employees—Training

Workaholics

The workaholic's guide to staying on your feet [special section] H. Twidale. il *Work Woman* 12:139-40+ Ap '87

You're probably working too hard. F. S. Worthy. il *Fortune* 115:133+ Ap 27 '87

Workbench (Periodical)

Editor's column. J. W. Hedden. il por *Workbench* 43:4 Ja/F '87

Letter from the editor. R. N. Hoffman. il *Workbench* 43:6 My/Je '87

Letter from the editor. R. N. Hoffman. il *Workbench* 43:6 Mr/Ap '87

Workbenches

Benchmark. R. Capotosto. il *Pop Mech* 164:116-22 Jl '87

Superbench [cover story] P. McCafferty. il *Pop Sci* 231:76-80+ S '87

Worker leasing *See* Employee leasing

Worker safety *See* Occupational health and safety

Workers' compensation *See* Insurance, Workers' compensation

Workers for Freedom (Firm)

An overnight sensation in London. il *Newsweek* 109:61 Mr 30 '87

Workfare

Back on the chain gang. il *Progressive* 51:7-8 Ag '87

Caging the welfare monster. R. B. Carleson. il *Read Dig* 131:86-90 S '87

California: an ambitious effort to give welfare recipients education and job skills. S. LaFee. il *Sch Update* 119:25 Mr 23 '87

Have we seen the future? [M. Dukakis' program in Massachusetts; cover story] A. Kopkind. il *Nation* 244:631+ My 16 '87

Is the time ripe for welfare reform? C. Holden. il *Science* 238:607-9 O 30 '87

The key to welfare reform. D. Whitman. il *Atlantic* 259:22-5 Je '87

Massachusetts's ET program: workfare that stresses choices and child care. J. Krasner. *Sch Update* 119:24-5 Mr 23 '87

Public policies that perform [Massachusetts] il *U S News World Rep* 103:18-19 Ag 10 '87

Should the poor earn their keep? [Christian values and welfare policy] S. V. Monsma. il por *Christ Today* 31:28-31 Je 12 '87

A step back to the workhouse? [effect on women] B. Ehrenreich. il por *Ms* 16:40-2 N '87

Welfare: a new drive to clean up the mess. T. Morganthau. il *Newsweek* 109:24-5 F 2 '87

Welfare-plus in Washington [Family Independence Program] H. G. Chua-Eoan. il *Time* 129:23 Ja 19 '87

Welfare reform may finally be in the works. S. B. Garland. il *Bus Week* p108-9+ N 2 '87

When did I welcome you, Lord? *America* 156:314 Ap 18 '87

Workfare [California program; cover story] L. Udesky. il *Progressive* 51:14-17 D '87

Workfare that works. il *New Repub* 197:7-9 Ag 24 '87

Workhorses (Wood supports) *See* Sawhorses

Working Assets Funding Service

Laura Scher: doing good business helps good causes. M. Mallory. il por *Bus Week* p76 O 26 '87

Working classes *See* Labor

Working girls [film] *See* Motion picture reviews—Single works

Working mothers *See* Mothers—Employment

Working woman (Periodical)

The 1987 Working Woman Hall of Fame. il *Work Woman* 12:107-9+ N '87

Working women *See* Women—Employment

Workmen's compensation *See* Insurance, Workers' compensation

Workout investments

Boom in the bust market [R. D. Smith & Co.] E. Linden. il *Time* 130:52 O 12 '87

The green berets of corporate management [turnaround specialists] G. L. Miles and M. Rothman. il *Bus Week* p110-12+ S 21 '87

Make-over fever. J. Crudele. il *N Y* 20:14+ Ag 17 '87

The once and future fat cat [workout specialist C. Hall] L. M. Keefe. por *Forbes* 139:106 Je 29 '87

Paul Bunyan in pinstripes [B. Engel of WTD Industries] J. Willoughby. il por *Forbes* 139:118+ Ap 6 '87

A 'rescue finance' team takes on banking [Hallwood Group takes on BancTexas Group] D. Cook. il por *Bus Week* p120 Mr 16 '87

Who says utilities can't be raider bait? [M. J. Whitman's play for Public Service of N.H. includes debt by Seabrook nuclear plant] C. Brown. il por *Bus Week* p112 N 23 '87

Works of art, Taxation of *See* Taxation of works of art

Workshops

See also

Artists' studios

Build a dream workshop. K. Schweikhart. il *Workbench* 43:48-51 My/Je '87

Shop and shed. A. Gutierrez and G. Campbell. il *Home Mech* 83:62-6 Je '87

Equipment

See also

Tools

Home & shop improvements. M. Thompson. See issues of The Family Handyman beginning September 1986

New/workshop. See issues of Popular Mechanics through October 1987

New products for the workshop. See issues of Workbench beginning January/February 1986

Scrap-heap engineering creates handier tools for farm shops. il *Success Farm* 85 no3:18Y F '87

Shop improvements [farm shops] D. Mowitz and C. Finck. il *Success Farm* 85 no2:20-1 Ja '87

Shop stuff. il *Pop Mech* 164:85-6+ O '87

Workshops—Equipment—*cont.*

Shopsmith Dust Collector. K. Collier. il *Fam Handyman* 37:48-9 D '87

Shopwork guide [special section] R. Capotosto. il *Pop Mech* 164:115-22+ Jl '87

These shop hoists roost in the rafters [farm shops] C. Finck. il *Success Farm* 85 no6:18AJ Mr '87

Workshops, Photographic *See* Photography—Study and teaching

Workstations

See also

Sun Microsystems Inc.

Computer graphics are animating another market [industrial design] K. M. Hafner. il *Bus Week* p88+ Mr 16 '87

'Diskless' computing. M. Liskin. il *Pers Comput* 11:59-60+ Jl '87

Evolving toward workstations. R. A. Shaffer. il *Pers Comput* 11:37 My '87

Low-cost image processing [workstation built around the Amiga] C. McManis. il *Byte* 12:191-5 Mr '87

Workstation technology [special section] il *Byte* 12:249-54+ N '87

Workstations: a hands-on evaluation of three IBM PC-compatible models offers a tantalizing glimpse of where personal computers are going. C. D. Weston and G. A. Stewart. il *Byte* 12:85-6+ F '87

Workstations blaze the trail for PCs. W. Joy. por *Pers Comput* 11:234 O '87

Worktables *See* Tables

World, End of the *See* End of the world

World Administrative Radio Conference

World Radio Conference concludes. *Dep State Bull* 87:74-5 Jl '87

World Airways, Inc.

The prodigy who came to World's rescue [T. C. Andrews] P. Finch. il por *Bus Week* p58 Ap 27 '87

World Bank

Africa's population growth erodes living standards, World Bank study says. *UN Chron* 23:107 N '86

Changes underway at the World Bank [environmental policies] L. Hannah. *BioScience* 37:186 Mr '87

Conable's year of living dangerously at the World Bank. B. Javetski. il por *Bus Week* p118-19 Jl 20 '87

Debt and the dollar: the markets are making all the rules. W. Glasgall and M. McNamee. il *Bus Week* p57 O 12 '87

The dollar gets no respect [meeting of the World Bank and the International Monetary Fund] A. Zagorin. il *Time* 129:53 Ap 20 '87

'Integrated plan of action' outlined at World Bank meeting in Seoul. *UN Chron* 22:103 N/D '85

A new international lending environment [adoption of environmental guidelines] il *Discover* 8:10+ F '87

A new road in the Philippines spurs development [project supported by World Bank loan] L. V. Coronel. il *UN Chron* 24:66-7 Ag '87

Policy reforms, freer trade, new approaches to agriculture essential for sustained global economic growth, World Bank reports. *UN Chron* 23:104-5 N '86

The third world debt crisis [address, October 29, 1986] J. J. LaFalce. *Vital Speeches Day* 53:162-6 Ja 1 '87

Tightening up on third world loans [tying loans to environmental policy] J. De Onis. il *U S News World Rep* 103:41 O 5 '87

A turning point for environmentally sound development. L. Hannah. *BioScience* 37:464 Jl/Ag '87

The World Bank and the environment. D. A. Wirth. bibl *Environment* 28:33-4 D '86

World Bank launches new environment policy. C. Holden. il *Science* 236:769 My 15 '87

World Bank on track. A. Brummer. *World Press Rev* 34:48 N '87

The World Bank's portfolio of sorrow [environmental consequences of development] il *Sierra* 72:46-9 Ja/F '87

The World Bank's turn [debt quagmire] J. Egan. il *U S News World Rep* 103:54 O 12 '87

World Commission on Environment and Development

Report on reports: Our common future. I. Burton. bibl f *Environment* 29:25-9 Je '87

Trouble in the third world's environment. M. Westlake. *World Press Rev* 34:53 Jl '87

World Conference on Church, Community, and State (1937)

John Bennett on Oxford '37. D. McCreary. il por *Christ Century* 104:942-4 O 28 '87

World Congress on Copyright Teaching and Information

A World Congress on Copyright Teaching. Y. Gaubiac. il *Courier* 40:34 Jl '87

World cooperation *See* International cooperation

World Council of Churches

WCC antiracism grants. *Christ Century* 104:1137 D 16 '87

World Court *See* International Court of Justice

World cruises *See* Voyages around the world

World Cup (Ski racing) *See* Ski racing

World economic herald

China's trumpet of reform [interview with Qin Ben Li] D. R. Shanor. il por *World Press Rev* 34:38 O '87

World economic policy *See* Economic policy

World economics *See* Economic conditions

World education *See* International education

World Environment Day

World Environment Day observed by 10,000 at headquarters. il *UN Chron* 24:59 Ag '87

World Festival of Games, Sports and Traditions

Games, sports and traditions. il *Courier* 40:30-1 Ja '87

World flights *See* Aviation—World flights

World Food Council

World Food Council pledges to eliminate 'scourge of hunger' forever. il *UN Chron* 24:68 Ag '87

World Food Day

World Food Day, 1986. R. Reagan. *Dep State Bull* 86:66 D '86

World Food Prize *See* General Foods World Food Prize

World food supply *See* Food supply—International aspects

World Future Society

Really planning for the future: joining WFS for a lifetime. T. Willard. *Futurist* 21:7 Mr/Ap '87

World Game

The World Game at 20. M. Gabel. il por *Futurist* 21:20-3 S/O '87

World government *See* International organization

World Health Assembly

Paying for HFA [Health for all by the year 2000] il *World Health* p27 Mr '87

World Health Organization

And now, a worldwide war against AIDS. J. Carey. il map *U S News World Rep* 102:13 Ap 6 '87

Ottawa charter for health promotion [charter for action to achieve Health for all by the year 2000 and beyond] il *World Health* p16-17 My '87

Smallpox: never again! [cover story; special issue] il *World Health* p1-25 Ag/S '87

Smoking ban at WHO HQ. il *World Health* p30 My '87

WHO Executive Board agrees on $633 million budget. *UN Chron* 24:76 My '87

WHO launches world-wide AIDS 'awareness' campaign. il *UN Chron* 24:74 Ag '87

Wide spectrum of health issues addressed by WHO at fortieth session. il *UN Chron* 24:73 Ag '87

World Health Organization. World Health Assembly *See* World Health Assembly

World Heritage Convention

Nature and culture. il *Courier* 40:16-17 O '87

World history *See* History

World Institute of Black Communications

Ed Bradley, Mike Tyson among World Institute of Communications honorees. *Jet* 72:18 Ap 20 '87

World International Growth Portfolio

His time horizon is long [interview with R. Foulkes] M. McFadden. il por *Fortune* 115:20 Ja 5 '87

World law *See* International law

World leaders *See* Heads of state

World maps

Scholastic world atlas 1987-88. il maps *Sch Update* 120:19-26 O 2 '87

The World [shower curtain with world map] *New Yorker* 63:24-5 Je 22 '87

World Meteorological Organization

African drought subject of regional seminar. *UN Chron* 23:60 Ja '86

World military expenditures *See* Armed Forces—Appropriations and expenditures

World news *See* Foreign news

World Party (Musical group)

The Party of the year. D. Wild. il por *Roll Stone* p18 Ja 29 '87

World peace *See* Peace

World Peace Run, 1987

Carl Lewis, two musicians kick off World Peace Run. *Jet* 71:29 F 23 '87

World politics

See also

Balance of power

Current events

Geopolitics

International relations

United Nations

World politics—See also—*cont.*
War
Above the battle, democracy gains. H. Trewhitt. il *U S News World Rep* 103:26-7 Jl 27 '87
Abroad. See alternate issues of National Review
America's vision of the future [address, September 21, 1987] R. Reagan. *Dep State Bull* 87:1-4 N '87
From World War to cold war. T. Garton Ash. bibl f il *N Y Rev Books* 34:44-50 Je 11 '87
The protracted conflict. B. Crozier. See issues of National Review
The world affairs annual 1987-88 [cover story; special issue] il *Sch Update* 120:4-10+ O 2 '87
World beat. J. R. Moskin. See issues of World Press Review through April 1987
The world looks at. See issues of World Press Review
Worldgram: newsletter. See issues of U.S. News & World Report

World population *See* Population

World press review
From the editors [translators for World press review] il *World Press Rev* 34:4 N '87
From the editors. il *World Press Rev* 34:4 Ag '87

World records
See also
Airplane speed records
Automobile speed records
Aviation records
Boat speed records
Motorcycle speed records
Sports records
World-girdler Steve Newman sets a record by walking in a very, very big circle [solo walk around the world] R. Wolmuth. il pors *People Wkly* 27:38-40 Mr 30 '87

World Saxophone Quartet
Four saxmen, one great voice. R. B. Woodward. il *N Y Times Mag* p46-7+ Ap 12 '87

World Series (Baseball) *See* Baseball, Professional—World Series

World Sports & Entertainment, Inc.
Agents of turmoil [N. Walters and L. Bloom accused of wooing blue chip college athletes with cash] C. Neff. il pors *Sports Illus* 67:34-40+ Ag 3 '87
Agents of violence? [dealings of N. Walters and L. Bloom] B. Selcraig. il por *Sports Illus* 66:25 Ap 6 '87

World tennis (Periodical)
Editor's page. N. Amdur. See issues of World Tennis beginning June 1984

World terrorism *See* Terrorism—International aspects

World Trade Center (Baltimore, Md.)
Baltimore from the top [Top of the World observation deck] il *South Living* 22:33 Je '87

World Trade Center (New York, N.Y.)
Photographs and photography
Urban majesty. R. Von Briel. il *Petersens Photogr Mag* 16:42-3 Jl '87

World Trade Week
World Trade Week, 1987 [proclamation, May 15, 1987] R. Reagan. *Dep State Bull* 87:45 Jl '87

World Vision (Organization)
Afghan refugees find help at the border [World Vision outreach program in Pakistan] il *Christ Today* 31:40-1 Ap 3 '87

World War, 1914-1918
Campaigns and battles
France
See also
Somme, Battle of the, 1916
Vimy Ridge, Battle of, 1917
Causes
Preventing World War III [discussion of March 1987 article, World War I, World War II, World War III] D. Kagan. *Commentary* 83:2+ Je '87
World War I, World War II, World War III. D. Kagan. *Commentary* 83:21-40 Mr '87
Communications
The telegraph and WWI. R. D. Fitch. il *Radio-Electron* 58:88-91 F '87
Conscientious objectors
The longest war [H. W. Moore] R. F. Sayre. *Nation* 244:133 F 7 '87
Medical and sanitary affairs
Condoms to the rescue: New Zealand's Ettie Rout "made vice safe" in World War I. J. Tolerton. il pors *Ms* 15:28-30 My '87
Propaganda
Ernst Lissauer and the Hymn of hate [WWI anti-English propaganda poem by German-Jewish poet] C. C. Aronsfeld. bibl il por *Hist Today* 37:48-50 D '87

Canada
Echoes and voices summoned from a half-hour in hell [Royal Newfoundland Regiment casualties at the Battle of the Somme] J. D. Atwater. bibl (p271) il map *Smithsonian* 18:196-200+ N '87
Remembering Vimy Ridge [Canadian vets return to France for 70th anniversary of battle] il *Macleans* 100:10-11 Ap 20 '87

World War, 1939-1945
Aerial operations
See also
Hiroshima (Japan)—Bombardment, 1945
Nagasaki (Japan)—Bombardment, 1945
From Moscow to the Bering Sea [T. Watson retraces WWII flights] S. Talbott. il pors *Time* 130:34 Ag 3 '87
A gathering of legends [students in Ames, Iowa arrange reunion of Eddie Rickenbacker's WW2 flight crew] J. Fincher. il *Read Dig* 131:49-53 Jl '87
Lieutenant Holguin's final mission [return to New Guinea to recover bodies of crew mates killed in 1943 B-17 crash] J. P. Blank. il *Read Dig* 130:83-8 Ap '87
Postcard from Framlingham [English WWII airfield used by American bombers] L. Morgan. il *Flying* 114:10-11 Ja '87
Where is Bill? [air pilots] L. Morgan. il *Flying* 114:10+ Je '87

Airplanes, Military
See Airplanes, Military—History
Airplanes, Military transport
See Airplanes, Military transport—History
Art and the war
See also
National socialism and art
Atrocities
See also
Holocaust, Jewish (1939-1945)
Campaigns and battles
See also
World War, 1939-1945—Aerial operations
World War, 1939-1945—Naval operations
Europe
See World War, 1939-1945—Campaigns and battles—Western
France
See also
Ardennes, Battle of the, 1944-1945
D-Day Invasion, 1944
Dieppe Raid, 1942
Great Britain
Requiem for a fiasco [Englishman K. Small's crusade to honor Americans killed in landing maneuvers at Slapton Sands] M. Brower. il pors *People Wkly* 28:60-5 N 30 '87
Italy
Monte Cassino: a story of death and resurrection. O. Friedrich. bibl (p163) il map *Smithsonian* 18:128-32+ Ap '87
Netherlands
See also
Arnhem, Battle of, 1944
The last disaster of the war [Operation Market Garden] B. E. Urquhart. il *N Y Rev Books* 34:27-30 S 24 '87
Pacific
See also
Okinawa, Battle of, 1945
Tarawa, Battle of, 1943
Wake Island, Battle of, 1941
Western
Unforgettable Omar Bradley. C. B. Hansen. il por *Read Dig* 131:118-24 Ag '87
Casualties
See also
World War, 1939-1945—Missing in action
Catholic Church
Breaking the silence [K. Barbie and role of the Catholic Church] K. McCaffrey. il *Commonweal* 114:418-20 Jl 17 '87
Shameful silence [myth of silence of Pius XII] *Natl Rev* 39:17 F 13 '87
The 'silence' of Pius XII: again. J. Gallagher. il *America* 156:279-81 Ap 4 '87
Causes
Preventing World War III [discussion of March 1987 article, World War I, World War II, World War III] D. Kagan. *Commentary* 83:2+ Je '87
World War I, World War II, World War III. D. Kagan. *Commentary* 83:21-40 Mr '87

World War, 1939-1945—*cont.*

Children

"I am Bryan, your brother" [Australian son fathered by an American serviceman is united with his sisters in the U.S.] J. L. Block. il por *Good Housekeep* 204:82+ Mr '87

Desertions

The example of Private Slovik [soldier executed for desertion] B. B. Kimmelman. il pors *Am Herit* 38:97-104 S/O '87

Diplomatic history

See also
Yalta Conference (1945)

Economic aspects

See also
Lend-lease operations, 1941-1945

Fiction

Of arms and the woman. M. Piercy. *Harpers* 274:30+ Je '87

Jews

See also
Warsaw (Poland)—History—Uprising of 1943
Holocaust, Jewish (1939-1945)

Memorials and monuments

See War memorials

Meteorological aspects

Escapers' weather. R. S. Cerveny and B. R. Skeeter. bibl il *Weatherwise* 40:248-54 O '87

Missing in action

Lieutenant Holguin's final mission [return to New Guinea to recover bodies of crew mates killed in 1943 B-17 crash] J. P. Blank. il *Read Dig* 130:83-8 Ap '87

Moral and religious aspects

See also
World War, 1939-1945—Catholic Church
Worship in wartime. W. J. Leonard. *America* 157:58-60 Ag 1-8 '87

Naval operations

See also
Dieppe Raid, 1942
Sable (Aircraft carrier)
Shinano (Aircraft carrier)
Wolverine (Aircraft carrier)
World War, 1939-1945—Submarine operations
British author 'vindicated' by new edition of '67 book [D. Irving's The destruction of Convoy PQ. 17] *Publ Wkly* 232:24-5 S 4 '87

Peace

From World War to cold war. T. Garton Ash. bibl f il *N Y Rev Books* 34:44-50 Je 11 '87

Personal narratives

1944: a soldier's Christmas in Wales. H. H. Broun. il por *50 Plus* 27:35-42 D '87
The last disaster of the war [Operation Market Garden] B. E. Urquhart. il *N Y Rev Books* 34:27-30 S 24 '87

Prisoners and prisons

Escapers' weather. R. S. Cerveny and B. R. Skeeter. bibl il *Weatherwise* 40:248-54 O '87
Wake's forgotten survivors [civilian construction workers] R. Wilkerson. il por map *Am Hist Illus* 22:40-5 D '87

Refugees

Hope and despair through refugees' eyes [Bitter hope: from Holocaust to haven; exhibit at the New York State Museum] il *USA Today (Periodical)* 115:50-9 Ja '87

Reporters and reporting

The big leak [U.S. war plans against Germany in 1941] T. J. Fleming. il por *Am Herit* 38:64-71 D '87

Secret service

The spy wore red [excerpt] Aline, Countess of Romanones. il pors *Saturday Evening Post* 259:46-9 N '87

Strategy

Churchill at war. E. A. Cohen. *Commentary* 83:40-9 My '87

Submarine operations

The sinking of a supercarrier [American submarine attack on Japanese aircraft carrier Shinano] J. F. Enright and J. W. Ryan. il *Wash Mon* 19:13-18 My '87

Veterans

See Veterans

War criminals

See also
War crime trials
Accusations of war crimes [I. Finta captured in Canada] M. Gray. *Macleans* 100:31 D 21 '87
Accused: 28 years a U.S. citizen, Bohdan Koziy is suspected of killing Jews in World War II [Ukrainian living in Costa Rica] E. Barnes. il pors *Life* 10:54-5+ My '87

The case against Kurt Waldheim. B. Amiel. il *Macleans* 100:7 Jl 20 '87
The case against Waldheim [Justice Dept. denies entry to the U.S.] N. Cooper. il pors *Newsweek* 109:40 My 11 '87
Haunted by ghosts of a Nazi past [K. Waldheim barred from entering U.S.] S. Masterman. il por *Macleans* 100:36 My 11 '87
The invitation [Pope John Paul to meet with K. Waldheim] *Newsweek* 109:43 Je 29 '87
Jews dismayed by Pope [meeting with K. Waldheim] *Christ Century* 104:586 Jl 1-8 '87
Kurt Waldheim: persona non grata [Justice Dept. report leads to denial of entry into the U.S.] M. Doan and C. Fenyvesi. il por *U S News World Rep* 102:8-9 My 11 '87
Kurt Waldheim's Roman holiday [visit with Pope John Paul II] il pors *U S News World Rep* 103:14 Jl 6 '87
Linnas and the long war [deportation to the Soviet Union] *Natl Rev* 39:19-20 My 22 '87
The Linnas case: was justice done? [deportation to Soviet Union of Estonian war criminal] N. Cooper. il por *Newsweek* 109:33-4 My 4 '87
Mr. Waldheim visits the Vatican. *America* 157:27 Jl 18-25 '87
NASA's Nazis. L. Hunt. *Nation* 244:671 My 23 '87
The Nazi hunt [cover story; special section] il pors *Macleans* 100:34-41 My 25 '87
Nazi hunt goes on. il *U S News World Rep* 103:16 Jl 13 '87
Nazi trail [UN opens War Crimes Commission files] il *Time* 130:36 D 7 '87
Nazis and Communists [case of K. Linnas] *New Repub* 196:4+ My 11 '87
No place to hide [K. Linnas deported to the Soviet Union] il por *Time* 129:70 My 4 '87
One must bear witness [K. Waldheim's visit to John Paul II] M. B. Zuckerman. il *U S News World Rep* 103:66 Jl 13 '87
The pariah and the Pope [K. Waldheim visits the Vatican] pors *Time* 130:16 Jl 6 '87
The Pope and the pariah [visit with K. Waldheim] K. L. Woodward. pors *Newsweek* 110:45 Jl 6 '87
The Pope's letter [Holocaust letter marred by recent meeting with K. Waldheim] W. F. Buckley. *Natl Rev* 39:64-5 S 25 '87
The Pope's precedent [K. Waldheim invited to the Vatican] S. Masterman. pors *Macleans* 100:29 Je 29 '87
Problems of crime and punishment [ethics of U.S. use of Soviet evidence against Nazi war criminal K. Linnas] R. Lacayo. il *Time* 129:60 Ap 20 '87
Questions about the Nazi chase. *America* 156:394-5 My 16 '87
A reception and a snub [Pope John Paul meets with K. Waldheim] A. Bilski. *Macleans* 100:20 Jl 6 '87
Removing the welcome mat [K. Waldheim barred from the U.S.] W. R. Doerner. il por *Time* 129:38-9 My 11 '87
A safe haven no longer [Canadian government agrees to track down and prosecute Nazi war criminals] M. Drohan. il *Macleans* 100:14-15 Mr 23 '87
Seeing Waldheim [visit to the Vatican] *Commonweal* 114:405-6 Jl 17 '87
Shame and punishment [M. Ophuls' documentary on K. Barbie] J. J. Buck. il pors *Vogue* 177:392-3+ N '87
Soviet firing squad awaits [U.S. deportation of suspected Estonian war criminal K. Linnas] por *U S News World Rep* 102:14 Ap 13 '87
The Waldheim case limps on. E. von Kuehnelt-Leddihn. *Natl Rev* 39:46 Je 19 '87
Waldheim must resign. L.-M. Delloff. *Christ Century* 104:1167-8 D 23-30 '87
Waldheim's end game? [problems of a Nazi past] F. Willey. il por *Newsweek* 110:29 D 28 '87

Bibliography

Waldheim's Austria [discussion of October 9, 1986 article, The Waldheim file] G. A. Craig. *N Y Rev Books* 34:44 F 26 '87

Canada

Honoring the Dieppe dead [Canadian participation] D. Eisler. il *Macleans* 100:11-12 Ag 31 '87

France

See also
France—History—German occupation, 1940-1945

Great Britain

See also
World War, 1939-1945—Aerial operations

World War, 1939-1945—Great Britain—*cont.*
Churchill at war. E. A. Cohen. *Commentary* 83:40-9 My '87
Churchill's anthrax bombs: a debate [discussion of January/February 1987 article, Churchill's secret biological weapons] B. J. Bernstein. *Bull At Sci* 43:42-5 N '87
Churchill's secret biological weapons [British plans to use biological warfare] B. J. Bernstein. bibl f *Bull At Sci* 43:46-50 Ja/F '87
The Roosevelt precedent [decision to provide Britain with destroyers in 1940] por *Time* 129:26 Je 1 '87

Japan
See also
Hiroshima (Japan)—Bombardment, 1945
Nagasaki (Japan)—Bombardment, 1945

New Guinea
See also
World War, 1939-1945—Aerial operations
Worship in wartime. W. J. Leonard. *America* 157:58-60 Ag 1-8 '87

Soviet Union
Myth and memory in Soviet society. N. Tumarkin. *Society* 24:69-72 S/O '87

United States
See also
Japanese Americans—Evacuation and relocation, 1942-1945
The birth of the U.S. biological-warfare program. B. J. Bernstein. bibl (p136) il *Sci Am* 25.116-21 Je '87
Of many things [E. Larrabee's book Commander in chief] G. W. Hunt. *America* 157:74 Ag 15-22 '87

World War, 1939-1945, in literature
Books on World War II. W. J. Bosch. *America* 156:256-8+ Mr 28 '87

World War, 1939-1945, in videotapes
Fighter aces of WWII. *Am Hist Illus* 22:6 My '87

World War III
Preventing World War III [discussion of March 1987 article, World War I, World War II, World War III] D. Kagan. *Commentary* 83:2+ Je '87
Spoils of war. L. H. Lapham. *Harpers* 275:11-13 D '87
Wind of war out of Washington [Defense Dept. scenario] D. Goldberg. *Harpers* 274:56-7 Je '87
World War I, World War II, World War III. D. Kagan. *Commentary* 83:21-40 Mr '87

World Wildlife Fund
Brother sun, sister moon [25th anniversary celebration at Assisi] L. Harris. *New Yorker* 63:80-92+ Ap 27 '87
Encouraging conservation. J. P. Cohn. *Américas* 39:58-9 My/Je '87

World's Columbian Exposition (1893: Chicago, Ill.)
Collectibles
Administration Building powder jar. M. Wollett and B. Wollett. il *Antiques Collect Hobbies* 92:30 Je '87
Columbian Exposition paperweight. M. Wollett and B. Wollett. il *Antiques Collect Hobbies* 92:21 D '87
Columbian Exposition satchel [glass replica of bag carried by Nellie Bly] M. Wollett and B. Wollett. il *Antiques Collect Hobbies* 92:39 Ag '87
Columbus paperweight. M. Wollett and B. Wollett. il *Antiques Collect Hobbies* 92:29 My '87
Santa Maria boat [glass souvenir] M. Wollett and B. Wollett. il *Antiques Collect Hobbies* 92:42 Ap '87

World's Fair (1986: Vancouver, B.C.) *See* Expo 86 (Vancouver, B.C.)

World's Fair (1988: Brisbane, Australia) *See* Expo 88 (Brisbane, Australia)

World's fairs
See also
Expo 86 (Vancouver, B.C.)
Expo 88 (Brisbane, Australia)
World's Columbian Exposition (1893: Chicago, Ill.)
Anecdotes, facetiae, satire, etc.
World Expo Larry 'n' Dot '87: an appraisal. B. McCall. il *New Yorker* 63:32-3 F 23 '87

Worlds of Curls (Firm)
Worlds of Curls present college scholarship awards. il *Jet* 72:13 Ag 31 '87

Worlds of Wonder Inc.
Teddy Ruxpin stumbles. H. Rudnitsky. il *Forbes* 140:35 Ag 24 '87
Top gun in the toy business [D. Kingsborough] A. Ramirez. il pors *Fortune* 115:88-90+ Mr 2 '87

Worley, Joyce
Affordable personal computers. il *Essence* 18:114+ My '87

Worley, William H.
about
Demand-side journalism. R. McGough. il pors *Forbes* 139:68+ F 23 '87
What's black and white—and in the red? M. Ivey. il pors *Bus Week* p60 F 16 '87

Worms
See also
Annelids
Earthworms
Nematodes
Trematodes

Worms, Computer *See* Computer viruses
Worms, Plastic *See* Fishing lures, flies, etc.

Wormser, Baron
Dropping acid at Aunt Bea's [poem] *Harpers* 275:31 Ag '87

Worrall-Thompson, Antony
about
A menagerie of delights. C. Claiborne and P. Franey. il *N Y Times Mag* p41-2 Ja 11 '87

Worry
An eye on the cradle. C. F. H. Henry. il por *Christ Today* 31:26-7 N 6 '87
The fine art of worrying. D. Heyn. *Seventeen* 46:158+ S '87
Worrying: how much is too much and who can help you stop? il *Better Homes Gard* 65:44-6+ S '87

Worsaae, Jens-Jacob
about
Jens-Jacob Worsaae sets a sparkling stage: designing the light fantastic. M. Hunt. il por *Dance Mag* 61:48-52 Ap '87

Worship
See also
Church attendance
Prayer
Creativity and the challenge of worship [Languages of Worship Workshop at Boston U. School of Theology] P. P. Allen. il *Christ Century* 104:756-8 S 9-16 '87
Lutherans and liturgy [discussion of July 29-August 5, 1987 article, Making a real return to church possible] P. G. Johnson. *Christ Century* 104:794-6 S 23 '87
Making a real return to church possible [Lutherans] P. G. Johnson. il *Christ Century* 104:656-9 Jl 29-Ag 5 '87
Moving Christian worship toward social justice. J. F. White. il *Christ Century* 104:558-60 Je 17-24 '87
Worship's focus: seeking the face of God. M. Horst. *Christ Century* 104:991-2 N 11 '87

Worsley Alumina Trust
Reynolds hits pay dirt Down Under [gold] G. L. Miles. il *Bus Week* p99 Jl 13 '87

Worster, Donald E., 1941-
An end to ecstasy. il *Wilderness* 51:18-21+ Fall '87

Worth, Gretchen
Ten painless ways to get more money out of your paycheck. *Work Woman* 12:72-3 Jl '87

Wortham Theater Center
Can do [home of the Houston Grand Opera; special section] G. Schmidgall. il *Opera News* 52:12-16+ O '87
Houston greets advanced opera house. E. Elam. il *Dance Mag* 61:7 Ag '87
Musical events:
Premiere performances. A. Porter. *New Yorker* 63:156+ D 7 '87
Wortham opens in a big way. M. Sommers. il *Theatre Crafts* 21:20 My '87
Wortham Theater Center. M. Loeffler. il *Theatre Crafts* 21:42-3+ D '87

Worthington, Christa
Aesthetics in fashion. il *Harpers Bazaar* 120:88+ Ag '87
Le Maître: Yves Saint Laurent. il *Harpers Bazaar* 120:188-91+ My '87
The new créateurs. il *Harpers Bazaar* 120:246+ S '87
Paris in the pink. il *Harpers Bazaar* 120:40+ Je '87
Le snob appeal. il *Harpers Bazaar* 120:172+ O '87

Worthington, Phillip, b. 1986
Kidnapping
Kidnapped! E. Fein. il pors *Ladies Home J* 104:46+ Je '87

Wortley, Richard *See* Wharncliffe, Richard Wortley, 5th Earl of

Wouk, Henry
Little drop of horrors. il *Omni* 10:84-9 N '87

Wound healing
Accelerated healing of incisional wounds in rats induced by transforming growth factor-β. T. A. Mustoe and others. bibl f il *Science* 237:1333-6 S 11 '87

Wound healing—_cont._

Beyond the Band-Aid [epidermal growth factors] G. Bronson. il *Forbes* 139:160-1 Je 1 '87

Epithelial wound healing enhanced by transforming growth factor-α and vaccinia growth factor. G. S. Schultz and others. bibl f il *Science* 235:350-2 Ja 16 '87

Heat up to heal faster [use of hot packs to heal stubborn wounds] *Prevention* 39:9 Jl '87

How skin heals. il *FDA Consum* 21:29-30 Je '87

Stimulating recovery [use of growth regulators] T. Beardsley. *Sci Am* 257:30+ N '87

Wounds

See also

Bites, Human

Traumatism

Therapy

See Wound healing

Wozzeck [opera] *See* Gurlitt, Manfred, 1890-1973

WPP Group plc

And Madison Avenue thought, 'it can't happen here' [J. Walter Thompson gets bid from WPP Group] M. N. Vamos and R. A. Melcher. il *Bus Week* p48 Je 22 '87

Hang on, Madison Avenue, Martin Sorrell isn't finished [acquires J. Walter Thompson] R. A. Melcher and M. N. Vamos. il por *Bus Week* p80-1 Jl 13 '87

WPWR (Chicago, Ill.: Television station) *See* Television stations

Wrangell Island (Alaska)

Description and travel

Alaska in the rough: the frontier spirit of Wrangell. S. Eppenbach. il maps *Travel Holiday* 167:40-5+ Je '87

Wrangler, Jack

about

After three marriages crooner Margaret Whiting lands her ideal in X-rated star Jack Wrangler. J. Stark. il pors *People Wkly* 27:120-1+ My 4 '87

Wrapping materials

See also

Food wraps

Wrapping of packages

All wrapped up! Great looks for gifts [Christmas packages] il *McCalls* 115:52 D '87

Dazzling gift wraps [Christmas gifts] S. Wood. il *McCalls* 114:33-4 Ja '87

Grand openings [Christmas wrappings] il *Seventeen* 46:120-1 D '87

Special occasion gift wraps. S. Wood and E. Young. il *McCalls* 114:18+ My '87

Wrasses

Female fish fond of male's fiefdom [bluehead wrasse] S. Weisburd. *Sci News* 132:295 N 7 '87

Wrath of God *See* God—Wrath

Wray (Colo.)

Buildings

A scholastic prairie village [Wray School] H. L. Smith, Jr. il *Archit Rec* 175:94-7 S '87

Wreaths

See also

Christmas wreaths

Have a heart: valentine wreaths to make. il *McCalls* 114:176 F '87

Wreaths [herbs and flowers] B. R. Rogers. il *Ctry J* 14:50-4 Ja '87

Wrecking

See also

Kimmins Industrial Services Corp.

Oil well drilling rigs—Wrecking

When buildings needn't be preserved. S. C. Florman. il *Technol Rev* 90:19+ Ap '87

Wrecks, Ship *See* Shipwrecks

Wren, Christopher Sale

Climb and tell: or, It's a long way from Annapurna. il *N Y Times Book Rev* 92:7 F 15 '87

Wrenches

Oil-filter wrenches. il *Consum Rep* 52:99-101 F '87

Oil-filter wrenches. il *Consum Rep* 52:90-4 D '87

Pliers & wrenches. H. Wicks. il *Home Mech* 83:20 Jl '87

Quick-wrist ratchet wrenches. R. Capotosto. il *Pop Mech* 164:40 N '87

Socket to 'em. H. Wicks. il *Home Mech* 83:8 Jl '87

Wrenn, Bill

Canoeing Saskatchewan: Canada's watery highways. il *Travel Holiday* 168:22+ S '87

Paraguay's mission towns. il *Travel Holiday* 168:8+ O '87

Wrestling

See also

Arm wrestling

National Wrestling Hall of Fame

Talk about slimy deals! Peanut butter wrestling is now in the mainstream! [promoter B. Rosenbaum] A. Fine. il por *People Wkly* 28:99-100 N 9 '87

Wrestling, College

Grand grapple in the Midwest [Iowa defeats Iowa State] A. Murphy. il *Sports Illus* 66:20-1 Mr 2 '87

Tournaments

Stopped short of the magic X [Iowa State defeats Iowa for NCAA championship] D. S. Looney. il *Sports Illus* 66:36-7 Mr 30 '87

Wrestling, Professional

Photographs and photography

On location: a day at the Monster Factory. S. Griswold, Jr. il *Petersens Photogr Mag* 15:32-5 Ap '87

Mexico

A ring and a prayer [Mexican priest S. Gutierrez wrestles to earn money for orphanage] R. Reilly. il pors *Sports Illus* 67:88-92+ D 21 '87

Wrestling in motion pictures

Slugfests del sur [Mexican wrestling films] A. Coe. il *Film Comment* 23:27-8+ Jl/Ag '87

Wright, Asa, d. 1971

about

Asa Wright and her tropical forest ark. F. Graham. il maps *Audubon* 89:82-95 My '87

Wright, Charles, 1935-

From a journal of the Year of the Ox [poem] *New Yorker* 62:26-7 Ja 5 '87

Visiting Emily Dickinson [poem] *New Yorker* 63:36 Ap 27 '87

Wright, Deborah

Starting at the finish line. il por *Work Woman* 12:132 Je '87

Wright, Dee

about

The Wrights and their robot 'kids'. il pors *Ebony* 42:72+ Mr '87

Wright, Esmond

America—200 years on. il *Hist Today* 37:7-10 S '87

Wright, Frank Lloyd, 1867-1959

about

Frank Lloyd Wright. S. B. Sherrill. il *Antiques* 131:950+ My '87

The sky line. B. Gill. *New Yorker* 63:49-50+ Je 8 '87

Somewhere, Wright is smiling. M. Stevens. il *Art News* 86:238 N '87

The Wright people. S. Staggs. il *Art News* 86:9-10 Ja '87

Wright's furnishings. F. Donegan. il *Americana* 15:16+ My/Je '87

Wright, Jaime

about

A miracle, a universe (I). L. Weschler. *New Yorker* 63:69-84+ My 25 '87

A miracle, a universe (II). L. Weschler. *New Yorker* 63:72-80+ Je 1 '87

Wright, James Arlington, 1927-1980

about

In Ohio: a town and the bard who left it. B. Morgan. il por *Time* 130:9-10 O 19 '87

Wright, James Claude *See* Wright, Jim, 1922-

Wright, Jim, 1922-

about

Bob and Jim play a duet. G. Hackett. il pors *Newsweek* 109:29 F 9 '87

The Democrats go home licking their wounds. D. Harbrecht. il por *Bus Week* p72 D 28 '87-Ja 4 '88

Jim Wright makes it the old-fashioned way [cover story] R. C. Kirkwood. il por *Natl Rev* 39:36-7+ O 23 '87

Jim Wright: pork-barrel politician as statesman. M. Miller and R. Thomas. il pors *Newsweek* 110:26-7 N 30 '87

The Jim Wright shuffle. J. Morley. *Nation* 245:185+ S 5 '87

Live opposition. J. S. DeMott. il por *Time* 129:18 F 9 '87

New House Speaker Wright's awfully wrong turn. M. S. Forbes. *Forbes* 139:17 Ja 26 '87

The new Speaker is stepping on everyone's toes. D. Harbrecht and H. Gleckman. *Bus Week* p55 Ja 12 '87

Ortega gets the Wright stuff. C. A. Robbins. il por *U S News World Rep* 103:35 N 23 '87

The outspoken Speaker has Democrats in a cold sweat. D. Harbrecht and R. Fly. por *Bus Week* p49 Mr 23 '87

Wrongful life—*cont.*
Compassion as contempt. D. Neff. *Christ Today* 31:15 O 16 '87
New form of medical malpractice [views of Robert L. Rabin] il *USA Today (Periodical)* 116:3-4 Ag '87

WSGP International (Firm)
An empire rising in the West [work of W. E. Simon] T. McCarroll. il por *Time* 130:42 S 7 '87

WSMV (Nashville, Tenn.: Television station) *See* Television stations

WTD Industries, Inc.
Paul Bunyan in pinstripes [B. Engel] J. Willoughby. il por *Forbes* 139:118+ Ap 6 '87

WTZA (N.Y.: Television station) *See* Television stations

Wu, Carl, and others
Purification and properties of Drosophila heat shock activator protein. bibl f il *Science* 238:1247-53 N 27 '87

Wu, Gordon
about
The man who envisions a New Jersey Turnpike in China. L. Kraar. il por *Fortune* 116:89 Jl 6 '87

Wuensch, Walter
about
Wimps. *New Yorker* 63:18-19 Jl 13 '87

Wulf, Melvin L.
Advertising pleads the First. *Commonweal* 114:75-9 F 13 '87

Wulf, Steve
Angling to win the Rat race. il pors *Sports Illus* 67:72+ Jl 6 '87
A crash landing for an ace. il pors *Sports Illus* 66:32-4 Ap 13 '87
An error for baseball: why aren't Leo Durocher and Roger Maris in the Hall? il por *Sports Illus* 67:92 Ag 10 '87
Heading for a photo finish. il *Sports Illus* 67:34-6+ S 14 '87
Humm-dinger of a playoff. il *Sports Illus* 67:30-4+ O 19 '87
Jim Bunning (R., Ky.). il pors *Sports Illus* 66:64-8 F 23 '87
Moments of pure delight. il por *Sports Illus* 67:104 D 21 '87
More bang for more bucks. il pors *Sports Illus* 66:32-3 My 11 '87
Standing tall at short. il *Sports Illus* 66:132-5+ F 9 '87
Take that! il *Sports Illus* 67:18-21 S 21 '87
Taking the rap. il pors *Sports Illus* 67:20-3 Jl 13 '87
about
From the publisher. D. J. Barr. il por *Sports Illus* 67:4 Ag 24 '87

Wulff, Kurt
about
Who's afraid of the new Kurt Wulff? J. R. Norman. il por *Bus Week* p74 Je 15 '87

Wuliger, Ernest M.
about
Mattress wars. J. Andresky. il por *Forbes* 139:41 Je 15 '87

Wurlitzer, Rudolph
about
Frontiersman [interview] M. Golden. il por *Film Comment* 23:40-4 Jl/Ag '87

Wurtman, Judith J.
Mood foods to raise your energy or lower your stress [excerpt from Managing your mind and mood through food]; ed. by Margaret Danbrot. il *Redbook* 168:106-9+ F '87

Wustman, John
about
Sharing the music [interview] J. W. Freeman. il pors *Opera News* 52:16-18+ Jl '87

WVCA (Gloucester, Mass.: Radio station) *See* Radio stations
WWF *See* World Wildlife Fund

Wyatt, Oscar Sherman, Jr.
about
Jack Stanley's 30-year oil feud is sizzling. J. R. Norman. il *Bus Week* p58-9 Ap 13 '87

Wyatt, Walter, Jr.
about
Alone in the shark-filled sea. P. Michelmore. il *Read Dig* 131:116-21 O '87

Wycliffe, John, d. 1384
about
Dissidents in an age of faith? Wyclif and the Lollards. J. Catto. bibl il *Hist Today* 37:46-52 N '87

Wycliffites *See* Lollards

Wyden, Peter
The blockbustering of Lee Iacocca. il *N Y Times Book Rev* 92:1+ S 13 '87

Wydler-Roth, Irene
Stirring up Swan Lake in Basel. il *Dance Mag* 61:74-5 Mr '87

Wye River (Wales and England)
River adventure [canoeing and kayaking with PGL Young Adventure] il map *Natl Geogr World* 142:24-9 Je '87

Wyeth, Andrew, 1917-
N.C. [excerpt from An American vision] il pors *Am Herit* 38:106-15 My/Je '87
about
Heavily hyped Helga. J. Updike. *New Repub* 197:27-30 D 7 '87
The Helga pictures. A. Thorson. il *Art News* 86:193 O '87
Helgamania goes on the road. pors *U S News World Rep* 102:13 Je 1 '87
Too much of a medium-good thing. R. Hughes. il *Time* 129:77 Je 1 '87
The Wyeth legacy. M. Wade. il pors *Horizon* 30:52-7 Ap '87
Wyeth paintings and the Helga controversy [cover story] M. S. Doherty. il pors *Am Artist* 51:10-11 My '87
Wyeth's world: how a woman named Helga came to haunt the art of America's foremost realist. R. Meryman. il pors *Life* 10:72-6+ Je '87
Anecdotes, facetiae, satire, etc.
Vickie Lou's letters from Long Island [exhibit of A. Wyeth's Helga paintings] il *Am Artist* 51:18+ S '87

Wyeth, Jamie, 1946-
about
The Wyeth legacy. M. Wade. il pors *Horizon* 30:52-7 Ap '87

Wyeth, N. C. (Newell Convers), 1882-1945
about
N.C. [excerpt from An American vision] A. Wyeth. il pors *Am Herit* 38:106-15 My/Je '87
The Wyeth legacy. M. Wade. il pors *Horizon* 30:52-7 Ap '87

Wyeth, Newell Convers *See* Wyeth, N. C. (Newell Convers), 1882-1945

Wyeth family
about
A family vision: the Wyeth legacy. il *Read Dig* 131:25-31 S '87

Wyles, John
Craxi leaves behind 'a new Italy'. *World Press Rev* 34:37 Ap '87

Wylie, Peter
about
Problem bosses: they come in all sizes, shapes and styles—and everybody thinks that he's got one [interview] T. Cunneff. il pors *People Wkly* 27:95-6+ Je 8 '87

Wyly, Sam E.
about
Sam Wyly: will the hunter become the hunted? T. Mason. il pors *Bus Week* p110 Jl 13 '87

Wyly Corp.
See also
Uccel Corporation

Wyman, Thomas
about
The golden parachutes open on media row. por *Newsweek* 109:55 Ap 20 '87

Wyndham, George O'Brien *See* Egremont, Sir George O'Brien Wyndham, 3rd Earl of, 1751-1837

Wyngaarden, James B.
The National Institutes of Health in its centennial year. bibl f il *Science* 237:869-74 Ag 21 '87
about
Wyngaarden to chair Biotech Council. M. Crawford. *Science* 238:1504-5 D 11 '87

Wynia, Gary W., 1942-
Readjusting to democracy in Argentina. bibl f *Curr Hist* 86:5-8+ Ja '87

Wynn, Elisa Sisti
Inside NSS. See issues of Space World beginning June 1987
The making of Mir Watch. il *Space World* X-10-286:31-2 O '87

Wynn, Malcolm
about
First black police chief hired in Greenville, Miss. por *Jet* 72:10 Ag 31 '87

Wynn, Ned
You're handsomer than Jimmy Stewart, and you will always live in Beverly Hills. il pors *Roll Stone* p79+ O 8 '87
Wynn, Stephen A.
about
Steve Wynn on high rollers. D. Seligman. il pors *Fortune* 115:116 Mr 2 '87
Trump vs. Wynn: 'giant egos on the line'. R. Grover. il por *Bus Week* p31-2 Jl 27 '87
Zero-sum game. R. Phalon. il pors *Forbes* 139:110-12 Mr 23 '87
Wynne, Elaine
Storytelling in therapy and counseling. bibl f il *Child Today* 16:11-15 Mr/Ap '87
Wyoming
See also
Black Hills (S.D. and Wyo.)
Crime and criminals—Wyoming
Grand Teton National Park (Wyo.)
Hunting—Wyoming
Paleontology—Wyoming
Prisons—Wyoming
Public lands—Wyoming
Ranches—Wyoming
Resorts—Wyoming
Skis and skiing—Wyoming
Wildlife conservation—Wyoming
Wildlife management—Wyoming
Description and travel
Wyoming's Greater Yellowstone ecosystem [northwest Wyoming] il map *Mother Earth News* 106:38-44 Jl/Ag '87
Wyoming Women's Center (Lusk, Wyo.: Prison) *See* Prisons—Wyoming
Wypijewski, JoAnn
Was the U.S. behind it? il *Nation* 245:117-18+ Ag 15-22 '87
What's it all about, AAFLI? [discussion of August 15-22, 1987 article, Was the U.S. behind it?] *Nation* 245:666+ D 5 '87
Wyse, Lois
The finer points of power building [excerpt from Company manners] il *Work Woman* 12:78-80+ Ja '87
The way we are. See issues of Good Housekeeping
Wyse Technology
And the last shall be first. K. K. Wiegner. il por *Forbes* 140:100+ N 16 '87
Wysocki, Charles J.
(jt. auth) See Gilbert, Avery N., and Wysocki, Charles J.

X

X [opera] *See* Davis, Anthony
X-29 airplanes *See* Airplanes, Military
X-31A airplanes *See* Airplanes, Military
X chromosomes *See* Chromosomes
X ray astronomy
From Aerobee to AXAF. D. H. Smith. il *Sky Telesc* 73:606-7 Je '87
Keeping up with Cygnus X-3. il *Sky Telesc* 73:272 Mr '87
New-wave pulsars. N. E. White. il *Sky Telesc* 73:22-4 Ja '87
Observing the energetic universe. D. H. Smith. il *Technol Rev* 90:66-73 My/Je '87
Results from X-ray satellites [Japanese satellites] *Sky Telesc* 73:11 Ja '87
Supernova X-rays: too little too soon [1987A] D. E. Thomsen. *Sci News* 132:263 O 24 '87
What do we learn from space? Space science in Japan. M. Oda. bibl il *Phys Today* 40:26-33 D '87
Why do stars emit X rays? E. N. Parker. bibl f il *Phys Today* 40:36-42 Jl '87
X-ray photographs of a solar active region with a multilayer telescope at normal incidence. J. H. Underwood and others. bibl f il *Science* 238:61-4 O 2 '87
X ray crystallography *See* Crystallography
X ray equipment
A most powerful X-ray machine [Saturn X-ray simulator] D. E. Thomsen. il *Sci News* 132:276 O 31 '87
Travel-protect your film [getting film through airport security] W. Hampton. il *Petersens Photogr Mag* 16:24+ O '87
Defects
Off the track. il *FDA Consum* 21:36 N '87

X ray lasers *See* Lasers
X ray microscopes and microscopy
See also
Microtomography
Great X-pectations. *Sci Am* 256:72-3 Ap '87
Hologram: new dimension for X-rays. S. Weisburd. *Sci News* 132:279 O 31 '87
Imaging unaltered cell structures with X-rays [scanning microscope] A. L. Robinson. il *Science* 237:723-4 Ag 14 '87
X-ray holograms at improved resolution: a study of zymogen granules. M. Howells and others. bibl f il *Science* 238:514-17 O 23 '87
X ray photography *See* Radiography
X ray spectroscopy *See* Spectrum analysis
X rays
See also
Radiography
Diffraction
See also
Crystallography
First X-ray pattern of hydrogen solid [work of Russell Hemley and others] *Sci News* 131:201 Mr 28 '87
Laser-stimulated luminescence used to measure X-ray diffraction of a contracting striated muscle. Y. Amemiya and others. bibl f il *Science* 237:164-8 Jl 10 '87
Time-resolved X-ray diffraction of biological materials. S. M. Gruner. bibl f il *Science* 238:305-12 O 16 '87
Use of X-ray methods for the study of chemical composition. R. Jenkins. *Science* 235 pt2:G169+ F 27 '87
Medical use
See Radiography, Medical
X-wing aircraft *See* Rotor aircraft
Xenix operating systems *See* Computers—Operating systems
Xenografts
Heart to heart: can a chimp transplant save human life? [research conducted at Columbia Presbyterian Medical Center, N.Y.] N. Taylor. il *N Y* 20:44-8 Jl 13 '87
Xerophthalmia
Nutritional aspects
Blinding malnutrition. A. Sommer. il *World Health* p20-2 My '87
New benefits seen in vitamin A therapy. J. Raloff. *Sci News* 131:325 My 23 '87
Xerox Corp.
Can this man keep Team Xerox no. 1? [A. B. Rand] A. Edmond, Jr. il *Black Enterp* 18:58-60+ Ag '87
Copying the success of its once nifty past. il *Money* 16:8 My '87
Culture shock at Xerox. J. A. Byrne. il por *Bus Week* p106+ Je 22 '87
World's largest up & comer [acquisition of Crum & Forster] H. Rudnitsky. il *Forbes* 139:78+ My 18 '87
Xerox moves Rand to top [A. B. Rand] M. A. Fortune. por *Black Enterp* 17:17 My '87
Xian Aircraft Corp.
Plant expansions underscore China's aviation commitment. R. G. O'Lone. il *Aviat Week Space Technol* 127:54-5+ D 21 '87
Xi'an Incident, 1936 *See* China—History—Xi'an Incident, 1936
Xilitla (Mexico)
Architecture
The surreal life of Edward James. A. Cockburn. il por *House Gard* 159:198-206+ Je '87
Ximenez-Fatio House (Saint Augustine, Fla.) *See* Saint Augustine (Fla.)—Historic houses, sites, etc.
Xing Sishao
Plant therapy in the fight against cancer. il *Courier* 40:20 Ag '87
XTC (Musical group)
Rock's lost God [Dear God] P. Crescenti. il *Christ Today* 31:64 D 11 '87
Xu Donglin
about
Woodcuts by Wang Lan; Sketches by Xu Donglin. il *World Press Rev* 34:58-9 Je '87
Xuan Tong *See* Pu Yi, 1906-1967
Xuanzang *See* Hsüan-tsang, ca. 596-664
Xylitol
Chewing away cavities [use of xylitol gum; research by Kauko Makinen] *Prevention* 39:15 S '87
Making weight loss even sweeter. *Prevention* 39:52 O '87
XyWrite (Word processor program) *See* Word processors and processing—Programming

Y

Ya'ari, Ehud
Behind the terror. il *Atlantic* 259:18-22 Je '87
Yaari, Yoel, and others
Development of two types of calcium channels in cultured mammalian hippocampal neurons. bibl f il *Science* 235:680-2 F 6 '87
Yacht clubs
Blueblood boating [Far Hills Yacht Club regatta for yacht models] D. Wallace. il *Mot Boat Sail* 160:42-5+ Ag '87
Yacht decoration *See* Boat decoration
Yacht models *See* Ship and boat models
Yacht racing
    See also
    America's Cup races
King of the seven seas [P. Jeantot's victory in BOC Challenge] E. M. Swift. il por *Sports Illus* 66:74-5 My 18 '87
Marathon man [P. Jeantot beats his own record to win BOC race] P. Whittell. il pors *Mot Boat Sail* 160:56-9+ Jl '87
My brilliant career [Celebrity race of New York's Liberty Cup] R. Marshall. il *Mot Boat Sail* 160:10 D '87
Tompkins's big chance [Melbourne to Osaka race] J. Lowenstein. il *Oceans* 20:72 S/O '87
Voyage around the Horn [BOC Challenge competitor J. Hughes] il por *Macleans* 100:27 Ap 13 '87
    Accidents and injuries
BOC update: dismasted in the Tasman Sea. W. Luhrs. il *Mot Boat Sail* 159:57-9+ Mr '87
A slice of humble pie [running aground during race from Falmouth Foreside to Southwest Harbor, Maine] H. Halsted. il *Mot Boat Sail* 160:22 D '87
Whale encounter during a yacht race [California gray whale off Rosarito Beach, Mexico] il *Sea Front* 33:61-2 Ja/F '87
    Rules
The twelve-meter rule. P. Lyons. *Car Driv* 32:106 F '87
    Television broadcasting
    See Television broadcasting—Sports
Yachts and yachting
    See also
    Cruisers (Pleasure boats)
    Seamanship
    Women in sailing
    Yacht racing
Confessions: what yacht captains really think of owners. C. Davis. il *Mot Boat Sail* 160:48-9+ N '87
Down to the sea in dreams. J. A. Trachtenberg. il *Forbes* 140 Sp Issue:362-4 O 26 '87
High life afloat: superduper yachts. M. Smilgis. il *Time* 130:70-1 S 7 '87
High-seas paradise. P. Lemos. il *Harpers Bazaar* 120:134+ F '87
New American super yachts. J. A. Fishman. il *Mot Boat Sail* 160:42-7+ N '87
New boat 1987 directory [special section] T. Bottomley. *Mot Boat Sail* 159:79-118 Ja '87
Trends '88 [cover story; special section] il *Mot Boat Sail* 160:42-55 S '87
    Chartering
    See Yachts and yachting—Leasing and renting
    Design
The America's Cup: may the best technology win. O. Port. il *Bus Week* p74-5 F 2 '87
The America's Cup yacht of the future [work of Francis Clauser] T. Dworetzky. il *Discover* 8:16 Ap '87
A better 12-meter [work of F. H. Clauser] P. A. Janssen. il por *Mot Boat Sail* 159:64-5 F '87
Cup tech continued. il *Pop Mech* 164:68 Je '87
Design board. See issues of Motor Boating & Sailing
The holy war [Golden Gate Challenge syndicate's USA in America's Cup challenge races] P. Lyons. il *Car Driv* 32:102-4+ F '87
Light as a feather [Sarissa ultralight motor yacht designed by G. Griffith] D. Wallace. il por *Mot Boat Sail* 159:54-6+ Mr '87
Sailing back to the future [New Zealand challenge to race supermaxis in America's Cup competition] S. Ballard. il *Sports Illus* 67:28-30+ D 7 '87
Sails & science [America's Cup] T. H. Cole. il *Pop Mech* 164:67-70 F '87
Stars & Stripes [cover story] J. S. Letcher, Jr. and others. il *Sci Am* 257:34-40+ Ag '87
Techno-yachts [America's Cup] H. Aldersey-Williams. il *Pop Sci* 230:84-7+ F '87

Water wings [work of Cornelis P. van Dam] il *Sci Am* 256:74 Ap '87
    Leasing and renting
Blazing the charter trail in Baja. B. Duke and S. Duke. il *Mot Boat Sail* 160:56-9+ Ag '87
Caribbean charters: luxury yachting in the British Virgin Islands. G. Watts. il *Archit Dig* 44 Archit Dig Travels:4+ O '87
Charter tips [bareboat charters] J. Gould. il *Mot Boat Sail* 160:64-5+ Ag '87
Commodore for a night. W. G. Flanagan. il *Forbes* 140:112+ S 7 '87
Monkey Business Inc. [Turnberry Isle resort is home port to yacht made famous in G. Hart scandal] il *Newsweek* 109:48 Je 29 '87
Yachting for the not-so-rich [Caribbean charters] B. Bauer. il *U S News World Rep* 103:87 N 16 '87
    Directories
Worldwide power & sail charter directory. il *Mot Boat Sail* 160:69-80 Ag '87
    Testing
Southern comfort [visiting Charleston, S.C. via the Intracoastal Waterway in a Grand Banks 42 motor yacht] J. Clemans. il *Mot Boat Sail* 159:42-5+ Mr '87
Taming the Amazon [cruise on 148-ft. yacht Calliope] P. Whittell. il *Mot Boat Sail* 159:36-43+ My '87
Yaffe, Michael
Equality for the arts in the media. *Des Arts Educ* 88:17-19 Jl/Ag '87
Yager, Robert E.
STS science teaching emphasizes problem solving. *Educ Dig* 53:39-41 S '87
Yagoda, Ben
At home with Julie and David (I). il pors *Saturday Evening Post* 259:64-7+ Ja/F '87
At home with Julie and David (II). il pors *Saturday Evening Post* 259:68-70+ Mr '87
Friends in high places. il pors *Channels* 7:54-61 Ja '87
Making a new Merv. il pors *Channels* 7:46-50 F '87
Yakima Indians
Of salmon and sovereignty [trial of Yakima leader D. Sohappy for illegally selling fish] J. Rosenberg. *Christ Century* 104:428-9 My 6 '87
Yakovlev, Aleksander
    about
Not just another pretty face. J. O. Jackson. por *Time* 130:39 Jl 13 '87
A split in the party? 'Nothing like that' [interview] M. B. Zuckerman. por *U S News World Rep* 103:52 N 16 '87
'We shall again astonish you in the West' [interview] por *U S News World Rep* 102:38 Je 1 '87
Yaks
A beast for all seasons [photographs] B. Alexander. il map *Int Wildl* 17:44-51 My/Je '87
Yale daily news
Passion among Ivypersons [avoidance of sexist language] W. F. Buckley. *Natl Rev* 39:63 Ap 24 '87
Yale Jazz Festival *See* Music festivals—Connecticut
Yale University
Have gays taken over Yale? J. Adler. il *Newsweek* 110:96 O 12 '87
Is Yale now colored mauve? [gay and lesbian presence] J. Hart. *Natl Rev* 39:30 O 9 '87
Show opening in New Haven [homosexuality] J. Hart. *Natl Rev* 39:26 N 20 '87
Yale anti-apartheid protest. il *Jet* 72:15 Je 15 '87
Yale University. School of Drama
Leaving his imprint on Broadway [L. Richards] S. G. Freedman. il pors *N Y Times Mag* p38+ N 22 '87
Yale University. School of Medicine
Yale takes action against psychiatrists for financial improprieties. C. Holden. *Science* 238:745 N 6 '87
Yale University. School of Organization and Management
Yale B-School struggles to make the grade. J. R. Norman. il *Bus Week* p86+ N 23 '87
Yallop, Richard
Australia had the Pat hand. il por *Sports Illus* 66:26-7 Ja 5 '87
Still upbeat Down Under. il por *Sports Illus* 66:90 F 16 '87
Yalta Conference (1945)
Yalta II [implications of Soviet Union's zero option INF proposal] J. Morley. *New Repub* 196:14-15 Mr 30 '87
Yamaguchi, Jack K.
Letter from Japan. See issues of Road & Track through December 1987
Yamaha Motor Co. Ltd.
Create or die. A. Tanzer. il *Forbes* 139:52+ Ap 6 '87

Yamaha Motor Co. Ltd.—*cont.*
Yamaha to build Ford V6. D. McCosh. il *Pop Sci* 231:14 S '87
YB4 and 5: the Yamaha connection [motorcycle engines used by Bimota] B. De Prato. il *Cycle* 38:87-8 Jl '87
Yamamoto, Masashi, 1956-
about
Robinson's garden [film] Reviews
Film Comment il 23:6+ My/Je '87. A. Vogel
Yamamoto, Yohji
about
'The monk' and 'the nun'. J. Conant. il pors *Newsweek* 109:80 F 2 '87
Yams
Do you really want twins? Try yams [stimulates release of the follicle-stimulating hormone in the Yoruba tribe] il *Newsweek* 110:62 N 23 '87
Yancy Minerals Inc.
Minority firm awarded $3-million coal pact. *Jet* 72:55 S 7 '87
Yang, Pei
(jt. auth) See Huang, H. T., and Yang, Pei
Yangtao cooking See Cooking—Fruit
Yankee (Periodical)
Unforgettable Uncle Robb [condensed from The education of a Yankee] J. D. Hale. il por *Read Dig* 131:87-8+ N '87
Yankelovich Clancy Shulman (Firm)
A case of malpractice—in market research? [Beecham sues Yankelovich over research on new detergent] M. Rothman. *Bus Week* p28-9 Ag 10 '87
Yanoama Indians
An Amazon love story [marriage of anthropologist K. Good to Yanomamo Indian Yarima] R. Arias. il pors *People Wkly* 27:24-9 Ja 19 '87
An imperilled people [endangered by Amazonian development] B. Levin. il map *Macleans* 100:26-7 Je 29 '87
Yanofsky, Joel
Breaking into print with book reviews. *Writer* 100:28-9 Ja '87
Yanomamo Indians See Yanoama Indians
Yanow, Scott
Free Flight. il *Down Beat* 54:20-2 My '87
The Yellowjackets' new attitude. il *Down Beat* 54:23-5 F '87
Yard, Molly
about
Septuagenarian Molly Yard may not be unsinkable, but she's just the thing for NOW. K. McMurran. il pors *People Wkly* 28:38-9 O 12 '87
Yard lighting See Lighting, Outdoor
Yard tools See Lawn equipment
Yard tractors See Tractors
Yardley, Jonathan
TV: show business or education? *Des Arts Educ* 88:46-7 Jl/Ag '87
Yards See Home grounds
Yarima
about
An Amazon love story. R. Arias. il pors *People Wkly* 27:24-9 Ja 19 '87
Yarrow, Andrew
Canada's Jasper National Park. il *Travel Holiday* 167:24+ My '87
Yarrow, Leah
"They'll outgrow it" and other myths about children [excerpt] il *Parents* 62:78-80+ Ja '87
Yarus, Michael
(jt. auth) See Curran, James F., and Yarus, Michael
Yasmin Aga Khan See Khan, Yasmin
Yasuda, Ginji
about
Bucking odds in Vegas. L. Brody. *Fortune* 116:84 D 7 '87
Yasuda Fire & Marine Insurance Co. Ltd.
Conspicuous consumer [Y. Goto buys van Gogh's Sunflowers] H. Katayama. il por *Forbes* 139:252 Je 15 '87
Yasuda Mutual Life Insurance Company
PaineWebber gets a little insurance from Japan [18% stake] C. Farrell. il *Bus Week* p118 D 14 '87
Yatani, Atsuko, and others
Direct activation of mammalian atrial muscarinic potassium channels by GTP regulatory protein G_k. bibl f il *Science* 235:207-11 Ja 9 '87
A G protein directly regulates mammalian cardiac calcium channels. bibl f il *Science* 238:1288-92 N 27 '87
Yates, Brock W.
[Column] See issues of Car and Driver

Yates, Clarence
about
100 deer with a bow. J. E. Phillips. il *Outdoor Life* 179:52-3+ F '87
Yates, Jerome
about
Shot by a cop. D. O. Relin. il por *Sch Update* 120:7 D 4 '87
Yates, John W., II
What would ALF say? por *Christ Today* 31:33 S 4 '87
Yates, Nigel
Pugin & the medieval dream. bibl il *Hist Today* 37:33-40 S '87
Yates, Peter
about
Suspect [film] Reviews
Macleans 100:71 N 16 '87. L. O'Toole
N Y il 20:94-5 N 2 '87. D. Denby
New Yorker 63:145-6 N 16 '87. P. Kael
Newsweek il 110:86 O 26 '87. D. Ansen
People Wkly il 28:14 N 9 '87. R. Novak
Yavapai County (Ariz.)
Description and travel
Arizona's Yavapai County. S. Pacher. il map *Mother Earth News* 103:56-64 Ja/F '87
Yaw, Yvonne
Penny Royal [story] il por *McCalls* 114:63-6 My '87
Yawning
Are we boring you? [research by Robert R. Provine and others] R. Weiss. *Sci News* 132:360 D 5 '87
Yawning to breathe free? [research by Robert Provine] P. McCarthy. il *Psychol Today* 21:9-10 F '87
Yazoo River (Miss.)
Delta
The Army's giant swampbuster [proposed draining of Yazoo Backwater Swamp] J. McCafferty. il *Sierra* 72:84-5 Jl/Ag '87
Yazov, Dmitry
about
Marching orders. R. Watson. il pors *Newsweek* 109:34-6 Je 15 '87
Yeager, Chuck, 1923-
Breaking the sound barrier. il pors *Pop Mech* 164:90-2+ N '87
about
Chuck Yeager sees changes in the air. por *Newsweek* 110:26 Jl 27 '87
Fishing with the right stuff. J. Zumbo. il por *Outdoor Life* 179:64-5+ Ap '87
Yeager, Jeana
about
Gallant victory for an odd bird. S. Moses. il pors *Sports Illus* 66:36-9 Ja 5 '87
Yeager, Kurt E.
(jt. auth) See Balzhiser, Richard E., and Yeager, Kurt E.
A year in the life [television program] See Television program reviews—Single works
Year of the Reader, 1987
Chas. Levy employees describe 'books that made a difference' [contest] il *Publ Wkly* 232:12+ O 30 '87
What everyone should know about 'The Year of the Reader'. P. Holt. il *Publ Wkly* 231:36-7 My 29 '87
Yearbooks, High school See High school yearbooks
Yearbooks, Video See Video yearbooks
Yeast bread See Bread
Yeast enzymes See Enzymes, Fungal
Yeast infections See Candidiasis
Yeasts
The bun also rises with freeze-hearty yeast. S. Weisburd. *Sci News* 132:9 Jl 4 '87
CDC25: a component of the RAS-adenylate cyclase pathway in Saccharomyces cerevisiae. L. C. Robinson and others. bibl f il *Science* 235:1218-21 Mr 6 '87
Clathrin requirement for normal growth of yeast. S. K. Lemmon and E. W. Jones. bibl f il *Science* 238:504-9 O 23 '87
Cloning of large segments of exogenous DNA into yeast by means of artificial chromosome vectors. D. T. Burke and others. bibl f il *Science* 236:806-12 My 15 '87
Growth switch [cell division gene of yeast; work of Melanie G. Lee and Paul Nurse] *Sci Am* 257:23 Jl '87
Homeo domain of the yeast repressor α2 is a sequence-specific DNA-binding domain but is not sufficient for repression. M. N. Hall and A. D. Johnson. bibl f il *Science* 237:1007-12 Ag 28 '87

Yeasts—cont.

Meiotic recombination in yeast: alteration by multiple heterozygosities. R. H. Borts and J. E. Haber. bibl f il *Science* 237:1459-65 S 18 '87

The mitochondrial genotype can influence nuclear gene expression in yeast. V. S. Parikh and others. bibl f il *Science* 235:576-80 Ja 30 '87

Multiple global regulators control HIS4 transcription in yeast. K. T. Arndt and others. bibl f il *Science* 237:874-80 Ag 21 '87

"No—Bug Lite" [BioTechnica's high tech beer made with recombinant yeast] *Sci Am* 256:89 F '87

Phagocytosis of Candida albicans enhances malignant behavior of murine tumor cells. I. Ginsburg and others. bibl f il *Science* 238:1573-5 D 11 '87

Saccharomyces cerevisiae has a U1-like small nuclear RNA with unexpected properties. P. G. Siliciano and others. bibl f il *Science* 237:1484-7 S 18 '87

The structure of sister minichromosome DNA before anaphase in Saccharomyces cerevisiae. D. Koshland and L. H. Hartwell. bibl f il *Science* 238:1713-16 D 18 '87

A subset of yeast snRNA's contains functional binding sites for the highly conserved Sm antigen. N. Riedel and others. bibl f il *Science* 235:328-31 Ja 16 '87

"Switching" in yeast and slime molds [research by David Soll and others] il *Science* 236:30 Ap 3 '87

Transcriptional regulation in the yeast life cycle. K. Nasmyth and D. Shore. bibl f il *Science* 237:1162-70 S 4 '87

Mutation
See Mutation—Fungi

Yeh, C. James
about
Wong and Yeh win 1987 Apker Award for achievements as undergraduates. *Phys Today* 40:103 D '87

Yeh, Susan Fillin- *See* Fillin-Yeh, Susan

Yellin, Linda Nell
A date with fate [story] il *Redbook* 168:38+ Ja '87

What are friends for [story] il *Redbook* 169:74+ S '87

Yellow
Let the sun shine in [yellow in house decoration] M. D. Glass. il *Ladies Home J* 104:96-101 Je '87

Yellow-eyed penguins *See* Penguins

Yellow pages *See* Telephone directories

Yellow rain *See* Chemical and biological weapons

Yellow Stone (Steamboat)
The short, dramatic life of the steamboat Yellow Stone. D. D. Jackson. il map *Am Herit* 38:121-8 My/Je '87

Yellowjackets (Musical group)
The Yellowjackets' new attitude. S. Yanow. il *Down Beat* 54:23-5 F '87

Yellowstone National Park
Burdensome bison. J. Robbins. il *Audubon* 89:24+ Ja '87

Cult builds complex at Yellowstone borders [Church Universal and Triumphant] *Natl Parks* 61:36-7 My/Je '87

The gift of a Yellowstone Christmas. R. S. Fuller. il *Natl Wildl* 26:4-11 D '87/Ja '88

Making bad bears into good bears could spare bears [retraining bad bears; work of C. Jonkel] G. Laycock. il *Audubon* 89:22-4+ Mr '87

The photographer who got too close [W. J. Tesinsky killed by grizzly bear] J. G. Mitchell. il *Audubon* 89:28+ Mr '87

Threatening the Yellowstone Complex. *Wilderness* 50:3 Spr '87

The Yellowstone Complex. B. G. Norton. il map *Wilderness* 50:26-30 Spr '87

Yellowstone National Park region
The challenge of Greater Yellowstone [cover story; with editorial comment by T. H. Watkins] C. E. Little. il map *Wilderness* 51:16-56 Wint '87

Wyoming's Greater Yellowstone ecosystem. il map *Mother Earth News* 106:38-44 Jl/Ag '87

Yeltsin, Boris
about
Downfall of a folk hero. C. Redden. il por *Macleans* 100:21 N 23 '87

Gorbachev's disillusioned intellectuals. F. Coleman. il por *Newsweek* 110:37 N 30 '87

"I am very guilty". W. R. Doerner. il pors *Time* 130:34 N 23 '87

Moscow politics percolates in public. J. Trimble. il por *U S News World Rep* 103:10-11 N 30 '87

Rehab job. *Time* 130:37 N 30 '87

Round 2: Gorbachev vs. the hard-liners. J. Trimble and D. Stanglin. il por *U S News World Rep* 102:29-30 Je 29 '87

The Yeltsin affair. *Natl Rev* 39:17 D 18 '87

Yeltsin walks the plank. R. Watson. por *Newsweek* 110:37 N 23 '87

Yemelyanov, Vasily S.
The making of the Soviet bomb [excerpt from How it began]; tr. by John Crowfoot. *Bull At Sci* 43:39-41 D '87

Yen, Marianne
(jt. auth) *See* Reuter, Madalynne, and Yen, Marianne

Yen, Y. C. James, 1893-
about
Jimmy Yen: crusader for mankind. J. Hersey. il por *Read Dig* 131:138-45+ O '87

Yerkovich, Anthony
about
Cops and rockers. M. Christensen. il por *Roll Stone* p41-2 S 24 '87

Television. J. Leonard. il *N Y* 20:60-1 S 21 '87

Yersinia
Protein plays Trojan horse [invasin] *Sci News* 132:204 S 26 '87

Yes Fund
Now you see it, now you don't. A. Sloan. il *Forbes* 140:136-7 S 7 '87

Yeutter, Clayton K.
Protectionism [address, January 29, 1987] *Vital Speeches Day* 53:290-3 Mr 1 '87

U.S. trade policy and the trade deficit [statement, February 10, 1987] il *Dep State Bull* 87:22-30 Ap '87

about
Clayton Yeutter speaks softly and carries a big agenda. S. J. Dryden. il por *Bus Week* p30-1 F 2 '87

Fighting words on trade. M. Gee. *Macleans* 100:16 F 16 '87

Yevsyukov family
about
The Yevsyukovs: a test of the new line. il por *Newsweek* 109:22-3 Ja 5 '87

Yevtushenko, Yevgeny Aleksandrovich, 1933-
First word; tr. by Antonina W. Bouis. il *Omni* 9:6 Ag '87

A poet's view of glasnost. il *Time* 129:32-3 F 9 '87

A rebirth of Soviet arts. il por *World Press Rev* 34:26-8 F '87

A verse from 'Fuku' [poem] *Progressive* 51:26-7 Ap '87

about
A visit with Yevtushenko. W. H. Gass. *Harpers* 274:36+ Ja '87

What Yevgeny knew. D. Jameson. *New Repub* 196:39-41 Je 22 '87

Yevtushenko. D. K. Mano. *Natl Rev* 39:53-5 Jl 17 '87

Yevtushenko feels a fresh wind blowing [cover story; interview] K. Vanden Heuvel. il pors *Progressive* 51:24-31 Ap '87

Yews
Useless yew aids cancer fight [drug from Pacific yew bark] il *Audubon* 89:14 S '87

Yglesias, Helen
Invoking America: a Gitche Gumee memoir [adaptation of address] il *N Y Times Book Rev* 92:1+ Jl 5 '87

Ying, Mildred
Food editor's tips. *See* issues of Good Housekeeping

Yip, Brandon, and others
Time-resolved three-dimensional concentration measurements in a gas jet. bibl f il *Science* 235:1209-11 Mr 6 '87

YMCA
Jimmy Yen: crusader for mankind. J. Hersey. il por *Read Dig* 131:138-45+ O '87

Southern comfort [facility in Birmingham, Ala.] D. Dietsch. il *Archit Rec* 175:96-9 Ag '87

Yo-yos
Quest for the perfect yo-yo [research by Tom Kuhn] E. Zuckerman. il *Read Dig* 130:189-92 Je '87

Yoakam, Dwight
about
Dwight Yoakam. A. Nash. por *Stereo Rev* 52:87 Jl '87

Yodeling
Song without words. M. Müller. il *Courier* 40:31 F '87

Yoder, John Howard
Books on religion and politics. *America* 157:89-90 Ag 15-22 '87

Yoder family
>   *about*

Everybody in this picture is named Miller or Yoder except for one poor guy [postmaster T. Hagedorn's problem with family names in town of Kalona, Iowa] D. Van Biema. il por *People Wkly* 27:46-8 Mr 30 '87

Yoga

Fitness now [classes in Hollywood] I. Borger. il *Vogue* 177:302+ S '87

The low stress, high energy workout [yogaerobics] il *Mademoiselle* 93:280-3 Mr '87

Yogurt

It's yogurt—not ice cream. il *South Living* 22:138-9 Je '87

Yogurt stores
>   *See also*

Zack's Famous Frozen Yogurt, Inc.

Yolen, Jane

Happy anniversary, writers! *Writer* 100:7-8 Ja '87

Yolla Bolly-Middle Eel Wilderness Area (Calif.) *See* Wilderness areas—California

Yonas, Gerold

SDI: a progress report [with discussion] il por *Cent Mag* 20:5-14 My/Je '87
>   *about*

Former SDI scientist believes gains in defensive capabilities could achieve limited nuclear attack protection. *Aviat Week Space Technol* 126:20 F 2 '87

Yonath, A., and others

A tunnel in the large ribosomal subunit revealed by three-dimensional image reconstruction. bibl f il *Science* 236:813-16 My 15 '87

Yopo P., Boris

The elusive 'opening'. il *World Press Rev* 34:27 D '87

Yorba Linda (Calif.)
>   **Historic houses, sites, etc.**

A small town fights for native son Nixon. S. Angel. il *50 Plus* 27:14+ Ja '87

York, Donald
>   *about*

Taylor and York to show a decade's collaboration. S. Reiter. por *Dance Mag* 61:6 Ap '87

York, Richard
>   *about*

American themes at the Richard York Gallery. M. Weber. il por *Archit Dig* 44:162+ F '87

York, Rowland, d. 1588
>   *about*

A patriot for whom? Stanley, York and Elizabeth's Catholics. S. Adams. bibl il *Hist Today* 37:46-50 Jl '87

York, Sarah Mountbatten-Windsor, Duchess of *See* Sarah, Duchess of York, 1959-

York (Richard) Gallery *See* Richard York Gallery

York Minster (England)
>   **Fire, 1829**

Arsonist immortalized on transfer-printed mug. S. Bagdade and A. Bagdade. il *Antiques Collect Hobbies* 92:46 Mr '87

Yorke, Rowland *See* York, Rowland, d. 1588

Yorkshire, Heidi

Pam Dawber: what, a producer too? il pors *McCalls* 114:83-4+ Je '87

A table for one, please. il *Work Woman* 12:132-4 S '87

Those remarkable Designing women. il pors *McCalls* 115:78-9+ N '87

Yorubas

Do you really want twins? Try yams [stimulates release of the follicle-stimulating hormone] il *Newsweek* 110:62 N 23 '87

Yosemite National Park (Calif.)
>   *See also*

Hetch Hetchy Water Supply Project

Get back to your manzanita berries! [new black bear policies] il *Sunset* 179:42 Ag '87

Patrolling the park beat [National Park Service rangers] L. Peach. il *Natl Parks* 61:24-9 N/D '87

Rafting, hiking, fishing in and around Yosemite's river . . . the Merced. il map *Sunset* 178:14-16 My '87

Too late to book into Yosemite? *Sunset* 178:39 Je '87

Yoshimura, Fumio, 1926-
>   *about*

Comment. A. Palinkas. il *Am Craft* 47:20+ D '87/Ja '88

Yoshiya Company Ltd.

America's challenge [M. Kobayashi] H. Katayama. il por *Forbes* 140:452+ Jl 13 '87

Yost, Barbara

(ed) See Jorgensen, Bernadette. "I'm allergic to my family"

Yost, David S. (David Scott), 1948-

Soviet aims in Europe. *Society* 24:72-9 Jl/Ag '87

Youmans, Floyd
>   *about*

Expos' Youmans enters drug treatment clinic. *Jet* 73:50 N 2 '87

Young, A. S.

40th anniversary: biggest breakthrough in sports [excerpt from Negro firsts in sports] il pors *Ebony* 42:66-8+ My '87

Young, Alice
>   *about*

A gale of fresh air at Milbank Tweed. L. J. Tell. il pors *Bus Week* p102-4 Jl 20 '87

Young, Andrew, 1932-
>   *about*

Andrew Young's ill-timed call. il por *Time* 129:34 My 25 '87

Atlanta mayor testifies in drug probe; says his family shaken by slurs. il pors *Jet* 72:4 Je 1 '87

Atlanta mayor wears disguise and feels hurt of the homeless. T. S. Moore. il pors *Jet* 71:22-4 Mr 16 '87

Atlanta mayor Young to testify before grand jury in city's drug scandal. por *Jet* 72:4 My 25 '87

Black mayors of Atlanta, New Orleans will host 1988 political conventions. il pors *Jet* 71:5 Mr 2 '87

Julian Bond denies using cocaine and lashes media; Mayor Young implicated. pors *Jet* 72:8 My 4 '87

A scandal scars Atlanta. T. E. Johnson. il pors *Newsweek* 109:28 Je 1 '87

Young clear in drug probe, fellow Democrats cheer; ponders bid for governor. il pors *Jet* 72:24 Jl 6 '87

Young, Bob

You say you want resolution? Super VHS is now the best home-video format. il *Roll Stone* p75-6 S 10 '87

Young, Bobby Joe
>   *about*

Sunset in Sunrise for the Hawk. P. Putnam. il por *Sports Illus* 67:16 Ag 17 '87

Young, Coleman
>   *about*

Black press is vital, says Detroit mayor Young. por *Jet* 72:40 Jl 13 '87

Young, D. J.

Another (easier) way with leeks. il *Flower Gard* 31:26-7 F/Mr '87

Stretch your harvest. il *Flower Gard* 31:71 Je/Jl '87

Young, David
>   *about*

Fire [drama] Reviews

Macleans il 100:55 Ja 26 '87. M. Abley

Young, Dick
>   *about*

Obituary

Natl Rev 39:19-20 S 25 '87

Young, Frank E.

Experimental drugs for the desperately ill. il *Consum Res Mag* 70:34-5 Ag '87

Experimental drugs for the desperately ill. il *FDA Consum* 21:2-3 Je '87

Harvesting the fruits of biotechnology. il *FDA Consum* 21:2-3 S '87

The public health payoffs of FDA research. il *FDA Consum* 21:4-5 D '87/Ja '88

Questions about your medicine? Go ahead—ask. il *FDA Consum* 21:2-3 O '87

The reality behind the headlines. il *FDA Consum* 21:4-5 N '87

Young, Frank E., and Skinner, Karen J.

Summer food safety tips. il *FDA Consum* 21:16-19 Je '87

Young, Ivy

Sweet Honey in the Rock. il *Essence* 18:92-4+ My '87

Young, James, 1916-

(jt. auth) See Hope, Marjorie, and Young, James, 1916-

Young, La Monte, 1935-
>   *about*

La Monte Young's minimalist marathon. A. Rich. *Newsweek* 110:58 Jl 27 '87

The well-tuned piano. B. Wentz. *Down Beat* 54:34 Ag '87

Young, Lisa *See* Alston, Lisa Young

Young, Michael, 1952-
>   *about*

Michael Young at MOMA "Projects". H. Cotter. il *Art Am* 75:176 N '87

Young, Neil
about
Neil Young and Crazy Horse: U.S. tour, September-October 1978. D. Fricke. il pors *Roll Stone* p99-100 Je 4 '87
Young rejoins CSN. M. Goldberg. *Roll Stone* p29+ Mr 26 '87
Young, Purvis
about
Purvis Young: Greene. E. Turner. il *Art News* 86:168 D '87
Young, Robert
about
And they called it puppy love. D. Hurley. *50 Plus* 27:18+ F '87
Young, Robert, 1907-
about
'I was full of terror and fright'. L. Marx. il pors *People Wkly* 27:35-6 Ja 12 '87
Young, Robert M.
Herbert Spencer and 'inevitable' progress. bibl il por *Hist Today* 37:18-22 Ag '87
Young, Roger
about
The squeeze [film] Reviews
Macleans il 100:46 Jl 20 '87. L. O'Toole
People Wkly il 28:12 Jl 27 '87. R. Novak
Young, Sean
about
Sean Young. D. Keeps. pors *Harpers Bazaar* 120:176, 352-3 S '87
Sean Young says she only did a nude scene because her role left her No way out—your votes please. M. Dougherty. il pors *People Wkly* 28:61-2 S 7 '87
Young, Stephanie
Beauty & health report. See issues of Glamour
Young, Steven H., and Chow, Ida
Quantal release of transmitter is not associated with channel opening on the neuronal membrane. bibl f il *Science* 238:1712-13 D 18 '87
Young, Susan
about
Scenes and stitches. A. B. Carter. il por *Americana* 15:33-6 S/O '87
Young (Arthur) & Company *See* Arthur Young & Company
Young (Chas. P.) Co. *See* Chas. P. Young Co.
Young (Neil) and Crazy Horse (Musical group) *See* Neil Young and Crazy Horse (Musical group)
Young & Rubicam Inc.
Jane Brite: riding the Madison Avenue express. P. Finch. il por *Bus Week* p146 D 7 '87
Six months and half a million dollars, all for 15 seconds [television commercial for Warner-Lambert's Rolaids] J. E. Pfeiffer. il *Smithsonian* 18:134-8+ O '87
Young adults *See* Youth
Young adults' literature
See also
Young adults' reading
The YA cover story [book covers] D. Evans. il *Publ Wkly* 232:112-15 Jl 24 '87
Authorship
Creating suspense in the young mystery. J. L. Nixon. *Writer* 100:19-21+ O '87
Bibliography
10 great books for teens [novels] C. Weston. il *Redbook* 169:84+ S '87
15 great books for the teenagers in the family. N. Klein. *Ms* 16:160 Jl/Ag '87
Four novel ideas for spring. il *Seventeen* 46:76-7 Mr '87
Have you read . . . ? il *Teen* 31:59 My '87
Have you read . . . ? il *Teen* 31:69 O '87
Have you read . . . ? il *Teen* 31:68 S '87
Have you read . . . ? il *Teen* 31:51 Ag '87
Have you read . . . ? il *Teen* 31:36+ Je '87
Themes
Teaching about teen suicide using young-adult novels. P. S. Berger. *Educ Dig* 52:48-9 Ap '87
Young adults' reading
Crackin' the books: page-turning tips. K. Silverman. bibl il *Teen* 31:42 Ag '87
Young Astronaut Council
I was a teen-age cosmonaut [Young Astronauts-Young Cosmonauts exchange] K. McMains. il *Space World* X-2-278:32-3+ F '87
Young Harry Houdini [television program] See Television program reviews—Single works
Young-Johnson, Connie
Artists, persevere! por *Essence* 17:140 Ap '87

Young men
See also
Youth
Attitudes
A boy's-eye view. G. Schwartz. See issues of Seventeen through July 1987
Boys' eye view of beauty. il *Teen* 31:76-7 Ap '87
Him. G. Schwartz. See issues of Seventeen beginning August 1987
Let's hear it from the boys ['Teen's survey] M. L. Baer. il *Teen* 31:30+ Ap '87
Sexual behavior
See Youth—Sexual behavior
Young men and young women *See* Women and men
Young Men's and Young Women's Hebrew Association. 92nd Street Y *See* 92nd Street Y (New York, N.Y.)
Young Men's Christian Associations *See* YMCA
Young Playwrights Festival *See* Drama festivals—New York (State)
Young-Thomas (Lois) Scholarship and Leadership Guild *See* Lois Young-Thomas Scholarship and Leadership Guild
Young urban professionals *See* Yuppies
Young women
See also
Women college students
Youth
Women's work plans: contrasting expectations and actual work experience. L. B. Shaw and D. Shapiro. bibl f il *Mon Labor Rev* 110:7-13 N '87
Diseases
See also
Anorexia nervosa
Bulimia
Group homes
See Group homes for children
Health and hygiene
Body basics. See issues of 'Teen beginning November 1987
Dear doctor. R. Rosen. See issues of 'Teen beginning June 1984
Teen-agers and the calcium crisis. P. Mann. il *Saturday Evening Post* 259:68-71 Ap '87
What kind of shape are you in? [quiz] il *Teen* 31:30 S '87
Psychology
Catch-28 [young women disillusioned in work could endanger future job opportunities for women] L. J. Nonkin. il *Work Woman* 12:118-20+ My '87
Future phobia: take charge of your tomorrow. S. Glass. il *Teen* 31:58+ Jl '87
Life after high school. P. S. Rix. il *Teen* 31:24+ S '87
Too hard on yourself? [excerpt from Perfectionism] M. Adderholdt-Elliott. *Teen* 31:40+ S '87
The unmaking of a southern belle. R. F. Dew. il pors *Ms* 16:92+ O '87
Young women and young men *See* Women and men
Youngerman, Jack, 1926-
about
The geometry of nature and the nature of geometry. J. Gruen. il pors *Art News* 86:86-92 F '87
Youngren, William H.
American soundings. il *Atlantic* 259:83-5 Mr '87
Monteverdi's modernity. il *Atlantic* 259:82-5 Ap '87
The symphonic Furtwängler. il *Atlantic* 259:77-80 Ja '87
Your show of shows [television program] See Television program reviews—Single works
Yousoufian, Richard
about
An eye for making money. R. Cullen. il por *Pers Comput* 11:95 Ap '87
Youth
See also
Adolescence
Alcohol and youth
Black youth
College students
Computers and youth
Dating (Social customs)
Dropouts
Drugs and youth
High school graduates
High school students
Mass media and youth
Problem children
Smoking and youth
Social work with youth
Socially handicapped children
Students

Youth—*cont.*
Unemployment
See Unemployment
Volunteer service
See Volunteer service
California
Skinheads on the rampage [neo-Nazi youths in California] G. Hackett. il *Newsweek* 110:22 S 7 '87
Canada
Growing pains [cover story; special section; with editorial comment by Kevin Doyle] il *Macleans* 100:2, 36-9+ S 7 '87
China
See also
Beijing (China)—Youth
Two young Chinese who enjoy their nation's new freedoms [Liu Fang and Le Geng] J. Florcruz. il pors *Sch Update* 120:8-9 S 18 '87
Germany (East)
See also
Berlin (Germany: East)—Youth
Great Britain
See also
Newcastle Upon Tyne (England)—Youth
Sloane Rangers
Hong Kong
Freda Dan: an open style in Hong Kong. J. O'Connor. por *Sch Update* 119:5 Ap 6 '87
Israel
Victory's children. B. Levin. il *Macleans* 100:30-4 Je 1 '87
Japan
I love New York, L.A., Hawaii . . . [young Japanese tourists in the U.S.] B. Buell. il *Bus Week* p54 Mr 23 '87
Ikuko's bout with 'exam hell'. M. Lord. il *U S News World Rep* 102:63 Ja 19 '87
Junko Katohda: mixing East and West in Japan. J. O'Connor. il por *Sch Update* 119:4 Ap 6 '87
Nevada
See also
Las Vegas (Nev.)—Youth
New Jersey
See also
Bergenfield (N.J.)—Youth
New York (State)
Make strides to help minority youths: N.Y. gov. [views of M. Cuomo] *Jet* 72:30 My 25 '87
Nicaragua
A young Sandinista's effort to serve her nation [M. Arguello] J. Lantigua. il por *Sch Update* 119:17 Mr 9 '87
Singapore
Victor Chua: studying hard for Singapore. J. O'Connor. por *Sch Update* 119:4-5 Ap 6 '87
South Africa
Gray calls on Reagan to help S. African detainees. por *Jet* 72:12 Ag 31 '87
South Africa's war on children. R. A. Falk. il *Nation* 245:516-17 N 7 '87
Stop the torture! B. F. Chavis. por *Essence* 18:146 O '87
T shirts that shout [worn by black South Africans] il *Time* 129:48 Ja 12 '87
Soviet Union
Back in the U.S.S.R. M. R. Benson. *Nation* 244:824-6 Je 13 '87
Rebels without a cause. J. Alter. il *Newsweek* 110:39+ D 14 '87
Russia's restless youth [cover story] B. Keller. il *N Y Times Mag* p14-19+ Jl 26 '87
What's God got to do with it? R. E. Burns. *U S Cathol* 52:2 My '87
United States
See Youth
Youth 2000 (Program)
The role of intergenerational programs in: the "Youth 2000" campaign. J. K. Elder. il *Aging* no356:17-19 '87
Youth 2000. J. K. Elder. por *Child Today* 16:32-3 Mr/Ap '87
Youth-adult relationship
See also
Generation gap
Parent-child relationship
Eugene Cain: black men must help black youth. *Jet* 73:24 O 26 '87
On becoming a writer [teenager attends workshop with adults] J. Buxton. il *Seventeen* 46:89+ N '87

The role of intergenerational programs in: the "Youth 2000" campaign. J. K. Elder. il *Aging* no356:17-19 '87
Seniors meet child care and youth needs in AoA, foundation projects. C. Schreter. il *Aging* no356:35-7 '87
Youth and alcohol *See* Alcohol and youth
Youth and business
See also
Junior Achievement
Youth market
Bizkids. B. Leonard. il *Forbes* 139 Ann Directory:59-60 Ap 27 '87
Denny Daughters, teenage shopkeeper, is a soft touch when it comes to helping blind customers [proprietor of Please Touch in Castro Valley, Calif.] il por *People Wkly* 28:120 O 12 '87
Giving kids the business. R. Thompson. il *Nations Bus* 75:43-4 Ag '87
Greed on Sesame Street? A. Miller. il *Newsweek* 110:38-40 Jl 20 '87
Making money is kid stuff for new breed tyke-oons who are striking it rich in their teens. M. Small. il *People Wkly* 28:163-4+ N 30 '87
Teen tycoons. M. L. Baer. il *Teen* 31:60-1 Mr '87
Awards
Fostering young entrepreneurs [Careers Magazine Leadership Awards] N. L. Croft. il *Nations Bus* 75:55-6 My '87
Youth and death
Keep living: dealing with death. W. White. il *Teen* 31:52+ O '87
Youth and drugs *See* Drugs and youth
Youth and telephone *See* Telephone and youth
Youth and television *See* Television and youth
Youth and videotapes *See* Videotapes and youth
Youth as actors and actresses
Canada's rising 'Brat Pack'. B. D. Johnson. il *Macleans* 100:52-3 D 7 '87
From 'Teen to the screen [models become actresses] il *Teen* 31:50 Ap '87
A new look at the Brat Pack. il *Teen* 31:56-8 Je '87
Star beauty attractions [Hollywood's hottest stars] il *Teen* 31:98-9 O '87
Star search. il *Seventeen* 46:103-7 Jl '87
Tube talk. il *Teen* 31:55 F '87
Young Hollywood. P. Sinclaire and L. J. Nonkin. il *Vogue* 177:322-7+ D '87
Youth as archeologists
Digging for the past [excavations at Cahawba, Ala.] il map *Natl Geogr World* 144:19-23 Ag '87
Youth as authors
The word's out: put your feelings on paper. il *Teen* 31:88 My '87
Youth as consumers *See* Youth market
Youth counseling *See* Peer counseling
Youth for Christ (Organization)
The Insane Dragons meet the Unknown Vice Lords [work with gangs in Chicago] G. Lewis. il *Christ Today* 31:10+ N 20 '87
Youth gangs *See* Gangs
Youth in television
Singing the puberty blues [Canadian producers L. Schuyler and K. Hood's series Degrassi Junior High] P. Hluchy. il *Macleans* 100:54 Ja 19 '87
Youth market
Addressing the student market [M. Lerner of American List Corp.] M. Gill. il por *Esquire* 108:76 D '87
Getting a good rep [student field representatives in the record industry] M. Kaplan. il *Roll Stone* p115-16+ Mr 26 '87
The spoils of success. D. Menaker. il *N Y Times Mag* p24-5+ Ag 9 '87
Toddlers in $90 suits? You gotta be kidding. J. B. Levine and A. Dunkin. il *Bus Week* p52+ S 21 '87
Turning off youthful readers [high prices, shoddy production, and poor editorial quality of books] C. R. Larson. por *Publ Wkly* 232:49 N 20 '87
Japan
Japan's prodigal young are dippy about imports. F. H. Katayama. il *Fortune* 115:118 My 11 '87
Mickey Mouse, meet Hello Kitty. M. Beauchamp and H. Katayama. il por *Forbes* 139:68+ My 18 '87
Youth movement
United States
See Youth movement
Yugoslavia
Yugoslav youth stir it up. S. Drakulich. il *Nation* 244:601-3 My 9 '87

Youth Symphony Orchestra of New York
Musical events:
First music series. A. Porter. *New Yorker* 63:87
Je 8 '87
Youvan, Douglas C., and Marrs, Barry L.
Molecular mechanisms of photosynthesis. bibl (p136)
il *Sci Am* 256:42-8 Je '87
Ypsilanti (Mich.)
Education
Preventive preschool programming that works. J. A.
Harper. il *Phi Delta Kappan* 69:81-2 S '87
Ytterbium
Yb or not Yb? That is the question [mistake in element
listing in publishing of Paul Chu's ceramic oxide
superconducting formula] G. Kolata. il *Science*
236:663-4 My 8 '87
Yttrium
Yb or not Yb? That is the question [mistake in element
listing in publishing of Paul Chu's ceramic oxide
superconducting formula] G. Kolata. il *Science*
236:663-4 My 8 '87
Yuan, Tsu-chi, 1827-1898
Vive la différence! [excerpt from Nouvelles lettres édifian-
tes et curieuses d'Extrême-Occident par des voyageurs
lettrés chinois à la Belle Epoque] il *Courier* 40:28-9
Ap '87
Yuan Zuzhi *See* Yuan, Tsu-chi, 1827-1898
Yuba Natural Resources, Inc.
Glitter and dirt. A. A. Lappen. il *Forbes* 140:8 N 30
'87
Yucatan (Mexico: State)
Antiquities
See also
Chichén Itzá (Mexico)
Satellites help in study of ancient civilization [Mayan
civilization] *Astronomy* 15:64 Ag '87
Yucca Mountain (Nev.)
The politics and promises of nuclear waste disposal:
the view from Nevada. R. H. Bryan. bibl f il maps
Environment 29:14-17+ O '87
Siting the nuclear waste repository: last stand at Yucca
Mountain. L. J. Carter. bibl f il map *Environment*
29:8-13+ O '87
Yuccas
Walk on the dry side [coastal areas of New York and
southern New England] J. E. Connolly. il
Conservationist 42:26-7 Jl/Ag '87
Yucky (Term)
Weather report: yucky. W. Safire. il *N Y Times Mag*
p8+ My 24 '87
Yudkin, Marcia
I thought I was a terrific teacher until one day . .
. il *Ms* 16:66-7 O '87
Yugo (Automobile) *See* Automobiles, Foreign
Yugo America Inc.
Almost Japanese. M. Kuntz. il por *Forbes* 139:179 Je
1 '87
Yugoslavia
See also
Adriatic Sea region
Albanians—Yugoslavia
Anti-nuclear movement—Yugoslavia
Ballet—Yugoslavia
Kosovo (Yugoslavia)
Medjugorje (Yugoslavia)
Military service, Compulsory—Yugoslavia
Monasteries—Yugoslavia
Paleontology—Yugoslavia
Politics, Corruption in—Yugoslavia
Radioactive pollution—Yugoslavia
Slovenia (Yugoslavia)
Strikes—Yugoslavia
Wage-price policy—Yugoslavia
Youth movement—Yugoslavia
Zagreb (Yugoslavia)
Description and travel
See also
Automobile touring—Yugoslavia
Cruising—Yugoslavia
Economic conditions
Teetering on the brink. J. Greenwald. il *Time* 130:32
N 30 '87
Economic policy
Corruption and scandal [F. Abdic scandal's effect on
Yugoslavia's economic system] T. Fennell. il por
Macleans 100:38 S 21 '87
Industries
See also
Agrokomerc (Firm)

Nationalism
Nation versus class in Yugoslavia. R. A. Remington.
bibl f *Curr Hist* 86:365-8+ N '87
Yugoslavia's national question. J. H. Wolfe. il *USA
Today (Periodical)* 116:51 S '87
Politics and government
Nation versus class in Yugoslavia. R. A. Remington.
bibl f *Curr Hist* 86:365-8+ N '87
Teetering on the brink. J. Greenwald. il *Time* 130:32
N 30 '87
Where Balkanizing got its name and still deserves it.
D. Stanglin. il map *U S News World Rep* 103:47+
D 28 '87-Ja 4 '88
Religious institutions and affairs
See also
Catholic Church—Yugoslavia
Yukichi, Fukuzawa
Diplomats under surveillance [excerpt from
Autobiography] il *Courier* 40:27-8 Ap '87
Yukon Territory
Antiquities
New dates from old bones [Old Crow site] W. N. Irving.
map *Nat Hist* 96:8+ F '87
Industries
See also
Gold mines and mining—Yukon Territory
Politics and government
'Yukon Erik' steps down [Tory MP E. Nielsen] C. Barrett.
il por *Macleans* 100:26 F 2 '87
Yuli, Itzhak, and Oplatka, Avraham
Cytosolic acidification as an early transductory signal
of human neutrophil chemotaxis. bibl f il *Science*
235:340-2 Ja 16 '87
Yulsman, Tom
(jt. auth) See Fibich, Sylvia, and Yulsman, Tom
Yunick, Smokey
Say, Smokey. See issues of Popular Science
Yunis, Adel A.
(jt. auth) See Jimenez, Joaquin J., and Yunis, Adel
A.
Yunis, Fawaz
about
A sting on the Mediterranean. S. Seibert. il por *Newsweek*
110:36 S 28 '87
Yupik Eskimos *See* Eskimos
Yuppies
See also
Dinks
Are you raising a yuppie-puppy? B. M. Katz. il *Parents*
62:74-6 Ja '87
Gazing into Bergdorf's window. P. Freundlich. *Harpers*
275:73-6 D '87
It's time people stopped putting down yuppies. J. Harayda.
il *Glamour* 85:40 O '87
Making the scene [advertising in avant garde magazines
to reach yuppie market] B. Kallen. il *Forbes* 140:230
D 14 '87
Maxwell House serves up a yuppie brew [Private Collec-
tion gourmet line] A. Dunkin. il *Bus Week* p62 Mr
2 '87
Snapped by their own suspenders [effect of stock market
crash] M. Hornblower. il *Time* 130:53 N 2 '87
There goes the neighborhood: gangs of yuppies move
onto the turf of New York's Hells Angels [East Village]
J. S. Kunen. il *People Wkly* 28:119-20+ S 7 '87
They used to say don't trust anyone over the age of
30. Now everyone is suspicious of those of us under
30. W. Urbanska. il *Glamour* 85:68 F '87
'Two-computer yuppies' fuel a new boom. G. Lewis.
il *Bus Week* p130+ N 9 '87
We're black yuppies. Which world do we belong in?
C. King. il *Glamour* 85:78 My '87
What's so bad about being a yuppie? D. Curran. *U
S Cathol* 52:31-3 F '87
Yuppie be, yuppie buy [study by John J. Burnett and
Alan J. Bush] A. H. Rosenfeld. *Psychol Today* 21:16
Ja '87
Anecdotes, facetiae, satire, etc.
After the hippies and the yuppies . . . [dumpies] G.
Phillips. *World Press Rev* 34:34 Je '87
Puppy-Aid. J. Queenan. *New Repub* 197:18 D 7 '87
The young and the sex less: a yuppie love story. E.
Weiner. il *Mademoiselle* 93:110-11+ Ja '87
Political activities
Onward and yupward [study by M. Kent Jennings and
Gregory B. Markus] *Sci Am* 256:62-3 Ap '87
Yuppies, politics, and elections [views of M. Kent Jen-
nings and Gregory B. Markus] *USA Today (Periodical)*
116:6-7 Ag '87

Yuppies—cont.

Sports

A clean, well-lighted alley [bowling and yuppies] B. Barol. il *Newsweek* 109:63 Mr 2 '87

Japan

The rise and rise of the Japanese yuppie. L. Armstrong and B. Buell. il *Bus Week* p54+ F 16 '87

Yuppies in television

Yup, yup and away! R. Zoglin. il *Time* 130:89-90 O 5 '87

Yuppievision [thirtysomething and A year in the life] T. Minsky. il *Roll Stone* p41-2 D 3 '87

Yurchenko, Marina

Sisters of the mists [photographs] il *Life* 10:134-5+ N '87

Yurts

Yurts! [ski camping shelters] E. Hermann. il *Sierra* 72:51-4 N/D '87

Yusuf Khan

about

A patriot for whom? Yusuf Khan: conflicts of loyalty in eighteenth-century India. A. Bakshian. il map *Hist Today* 37:40-4 Ap '87

Yvonne

Receive this white garment [poem] il *Ms* 16:52 Jl/Ag '87

Z

Zaadi dolls *See* Dolls
Zabaglione *See* Custards

Zabar, Abbie

Easter in a Loire Valley château. il *Gourmet* 47:72-3+ Ap '87

Zable, Walter Joseph, 1915-

about

How Walter Zable missed his wake-up call. M. Beauchamp. il por *Forbes* 140:72-3 D 28 '87

Zaccaro, Dolores

about

The shopper. B. Kanner. il por *N Y* 20:21-3 Je 22 '87

Zaccaro, John

about

'Dallas' on the Hudson. il pors *Newsweek* 110:10 O 26 '87

Zacharias, Jerrold R., 1905-1986

about

Obituary
Phys Today por 40:85-6 Jl '87. H. Feshbach

Zack's Famous Frozen Yogurt, Inc.

A yogurt named Zack's. D. Marth. il por *Nations Bus* 75:52 Ag '87

Zadeh, Mousalreza Ibrahim

about

The contra con. J. S. DeMott. por *Time* 129:16+ My 11 '87

Zagarri, Rosemarie

The lost amendment. *New Repub* 196:13 F 2 '87

Zagat, Nina

about

Getting rich on dinner. L. Shapiro. il pors *Newsweek* 110:60 D 21 '87

In the world according to the Zagats, everyone's a critic. K. Johnson. il pors *People Wkly* 28:52-4 Jl 6 '87

Zagat, Tim

about

Getting rich on dinner. L. Shapiro. il pors *Newsweek* 110:60 D 21 '87

In the world according to the Zagats, everyone's a critic. K. Johnson. il pors *People Wkly* 28:52-4 Jl 6 '87

Zagato (Firm)

The Spydermaker. A. St. Antoine. *Car Driv* 33:53 S '87

Zagreb (Yugoslavia)

Galleries and museums

Real and fake in the 'Zagreb Louvre' [A. T. Mimara Collection] A. Decker. il pors *Art News* 86:151-8 Summ '87

Zagury, Daniel

about

AIDS: the search for a vaccine. M. Clark. il por *Newsweek* 109:79 Mr 30 '87

Taking his own medicine. E. Magnuson. il por *Time* 129:25 Mr 30 '87

Zaharias, Babe Didrikson, 1911-1956

about

Babe Didrikson: America's greatest athlete? J. Gustaitis. il por *Am Hist Illus* 22:34-5 Ap '87

Zahir Shah *See* Mohammed Zahir Shah, King of Afghanistan, 1914-

Zahn, Kenneth, and Blattner, Frederick R.

Direct evidence for DNA bending at the lambda replication origin. bibl f il *Science* 236:416-22 Ap 24 '87

Zaire

Description and travel

Where jungle meets river [Congo River] D. Jacobs. il *World Press Rev* 34:62 O '87

Zaitsev, Vyacheslav

A fashion designer recommends . . . il por *World Press Rev* 34:58 My '87

about

'Eefningwear' for America. A. Miller. il por *Newsweek* 110:64 O 19 '87

Fashion designer Slava Zaitsev works to convince a reluctant public that style is for the masses. S. K. Reed. il por *People Wkly* 27:133-5 Ap 6 '87

The House of Zaitsev. *New Yorker* 63:36-7 N 16 '87

Red Square chic. G. Perrelli and E. Regazzoni. il *World Press Rev* 34:19-20 Ap '87

Zak, Victoria, and others

The fat to muscle diet [excerpt] il *Ladies Home J* 104:70+ Je '87

Zakariya, Sally Banks

Improving relations between schools and the press. *Educ Dig* 53:8-11 N '87

Zakharov, Gennadi

See also

Daniloff-Zakharov espionage case, 1986

Zakin, Susan

Doing the nerve gas shuffle. il *Sierra* 72:26+ Jl/Ag '87

Muscle balance. il *Women's Sports Fitness* 9:38-41 My '87

Žaknić, Ivan

(tr) See Le Corbusier, 1887-1965. The Parthenon at dusk

Zakroff, Zanne Early

A cooking school in Chianti. il pors *Gourmet* 47:70-5+ My '87

Zalaf, Mahmud Abu *See* Abu Zalaf, Mahmud

Zaleski, Carol Goldsmith

about

Is there life after life? A scholar goes out on a limb. J. Cott. il *Vogue* 177:312+ My '87

Zalm, William Vander *See* Vander Zalm, William

Zalygin, Sergei

(jt. auth) See Voïnovich, Vladimir, 1932-, and Zalygin, Sergei

Zamba, Frieda

about

Queen of the surf. D. Geringer. il pors *Sports Illus* 67:60-3 Jl 27 '87

Zambia

See also

AIDS (Disease)—Zambia
Hunting—Zambia
Loans, Foreign—Zambia

Foreign relations

South Africa

See South Africa—Foreign relations—Zambia

Religious institutions and affairs

See also
Church and social problems—Zambia

Zamboni, Frank J.

about

You're an old smoothie. L. Montville. il pors *Sports Illus* 66:38-40+ Mr 30 '87

Zamboni machines *See* Ice skating rinks—Equipment

Zambrano, David

about

Reviews:
S. Forti and D. Zambrano at the Ethnic Folk Arts Center, New York City. C. Hardy. *Dance Mag* 61:40-1 Ap '87

Zamora, Rubén

about

El Salvador: heading home. C. Lane. il por *Newsweek* 110:50 S 21 '87

Ruben Zamora: politics & belief [interview] G. Palumbo. il *Commonweal* 114:733-5 D 18 '87

Zamula, Evelyn

Rheumatic fever: down but not out. il *FDA Consum* 21:26-8 Jl/Ag '87

Stomach 'bubble': diet device not without risks. il *FDA Consum* 21:28-31 Ap '87

Travelers' advisory: malaria still threatens much of globe. il *FDA Consum* 21:8-13 My '87

Zamula, Evelyn—*cont.*
When it comes to stylish sushi, it's safer to be square. il *FDA Consum* 21:18-21 F '87
Zander, Richard H.
TAXACOM, an online service for systematic botany. il *BioScience* 37:616-18 S '87
Zane, Arnie
about
The animal trilogy [dance] Reviews
Dance Mag 61:23-4 Jl '87. C. Hardy
N Y il 20:47 Ja 5 '87. T. Tobias
Zangezi [drama] *See* Khlebnikov, Velimir, 1885-1922
Zanzibar
See also
Slave trade—Zanzibar
Zapol, Warren M., 1942-
Diving adaptations of the Weddell seal. bibl (p136) il *Sci Am* 256:100-5 Je '87
Zapotec Indians
A blue future for Mexican indigo. G. N. Ross. il *Américas* 39:40-6 Jl/Ag '87
Zapotec weaving *See* Weaving
Zappa, Dweezil
about
Leave it to Dweezil. D. De Nicolo. il por *Vogue* 177:44 Jl '87
Zappa, Frank
about
Frank Zappa. R. C. Walls. *High Fidel* 37:74-5 Ap '87
Zappa. M. Smolen. il pors *Stereo Rev* 52:93-5 Je '87
Zappa, Toussa
Sponge divers of Kalymnos. *World Press Rev* 34:57-8 Ja '87
Zappe, Ronald
about
Ron Zappe's Cajun potato chips are really hot in Louisiana, and he'd like to run them bayou too. il por *People Wkly* 27:81 Ja 19 '87
Zaragoza, Federico Mayor *See* Mayor, Federico
Zardari, Asif Ali
about
Getting to know you. il pors *Time* 130:23 Ag 10 '87
A match made in Pakistan. R. Nordland. il pors *Newsweek* 110:47 Ag 10 '87
Something old, something new. il pors *Newsweek* 110:31 D 28 '87
Zarela (New York, N.Y.: Restaurant) *See* New York (N.Y.)—Restaurants, nightclubs, bars, etc.
Zarin, Cynthia
Wildlife [poem] *New Yorker* 63:74 Mr 9 '87
Zarins, Juris, 1945-
about
Has the Garden of Eden been located at last? D. J. Hamblin. bibl (p184) il map *Smithsonian* 18:127-35 My '87
Zasloff, Michael
about
The case of the frog that healed leads Dr. Michael Zasloff to a medical leap ahead. M. Brower. il por *People Wkly* 28:34-5 Ag 17 '87
Zaslow, Jeffrey
about
Defeating 12,000, odd couple Diane Crowley and Jeff Zaslow win Ann Landers' old job. M. Vespa. il pors *People Wkly* 27:49-50 Je 22 '87
Mr. and Ms. Lonelyhearts. M. Bosc. il pors *U S News World Rep* 102:12 Je 15 '87
Zaslowsky, Dyan
The unfinished wilderness. il map *Wilderness* 50:10-24 Summ '87
Zastrozzi [drama] *See* Walker, George F.
Zatuchni, Gerald I., 1933-
about
Gerald Zatuchni plays midwife to innovations in birth control [interview] G. Breu. il pors *People Wkly* 27:101-2+ F 9 '87
Die Zauberflöte [opera] *See* Mozart, Wolfgang Amadeus, 1756-1791
Zavaleta, Tomás
about
Death and resurrection in Matiguás. E. Rivera. *America* 157:261-2 O 24 '87
Zavrian, Suzanne Ostro
The way we were. por *Publ Wkly* 231:41 Ap 24 '87
Zayka, Gail
about
Helping children cope. il *Ms* 16:28 D '87
Playing doctor with Gail Zayka's lifelike dolls helps kids facing surgery get over their fears. B. Taubman. il pors *People Wkly* 28:57-8 S 14 '87

Zayre Corp.
At Zayre, the skies were just starting to clear [takeover threat by E. J. De Bartolo] C. Brown. *Bus Week* p59-60 O 19 '87
Zea, Leopoldo, 1912-
'A new form of self-expression'. il *Courier* 40:34-5 S '87
Zea mays *See* Corn
Zeal
Zeal without understanding: reflections on Rambo and Oliver North. R. Jewett. il *Christ Century* 104:753-6 S 9-16 '87
Zeani, Virginia, 1928-
about
Keepers of the flame. C. Battaglia. il pors *Opera News* 52:28-30+ N '87
Zebra Books
The second time around [forthcoming biography of R. Reagan by son M. Reagan] L. Fleischer. il *Publ Wkly* 231:375 Ja 30 '87
Zeffirelli, Franco
about
Chinese junk. P. G. Davis. il *N Y* 20:62+ Mr 30 '87
Viewpoint. J. W. Freeman. *Opera News* 51:4 Je '87
Zegura, Stephen L.
Blood test. il *Nat Hist* 96:8+ Jl '87
Zehme, Bill
Foxy lady. il por *Roll Stone* p39-41+ Ag 27 '87
Taken for Granted. il pors *Roll Stone* p33-5 Je 18 '87
Zeidner, Lisa
Child's moon [poem] *New Repub* 196:40 Ap 6 '87
Zeiger, Martin
The generic drug industry: an overview [address, October 8, 1987] *Vital Speeches Day* 54:142-7 D 15 '87
Zeigler, Kenneth
about
The pride of Globe, Arizona. J. K. Beatty. il por *Sky Telesc* 74:192-3 Ag '87
Zeisel, Eva, 1906-
about
Profiles. S. Lessard. il *New Yorker* 63:36-40+ Ap 13 '87
Zekman, Pam
about
Pam Zekman. J. Vitale. il pors *Channels* 7:31-2 O '87
Zelazny, Roger
Quest's end [fiction] *Omni* 9:60-1+ Je '87
Zeleny, Lawrence
about
A bird in the helping hand. D. Young. il por *South Living* 22:136+ My '87
Zelinsky, Hollis
Bullish on calves and sheep. il por *Ms* 15:23 Ap '87
Zell, Samuel
about
Booby trap. R. King, Jr. *Forbes* 140:48 N 30 '87
Zellers Inc.
All in the family [D. K. R. Thomson named president] T. Tedesco. il por *Macleans* 100:35 Je 15 '87
Zeloznicki, Susan
(jt. auth) *See* Sarde, Cliff, and Zeloznicki, Susan
Zemke, Ron
Making your investment pay off. il *Work Woman* 12:49+ S '87
Zemor, Olivia
More prevention, less treatment. il *World Health* p11 Ap '87
Zen, Ron
Personal posterization. il *Petersens Photogr Mag* 16:64-6 D '87
Zencey, Eric
The two-person career on college campuses. *Educ Dig* 53:56-8 O '87
Zenith, Richard
(tr) *See* Melo Neto, João Cabral de, 1920-. The voice of the canefield
Zenith Electronics Corp.
Zenith is sticking its neck out in a cutthroat market [TV] L. Therrien. il *Bus Week* p72-3 Ag 17 '87
Zenith Laboratories, Inc.
Trouble for the shorts in Zenith Labs? G. G. Marcial. il *Bus Week* p72 Ap 6 '87
Zenith Radio Corp.
See also
Zenith Electronics Corp.
Zenith Star (Satellite) *See* Artificial satellites—Military use
Zern, Ed
Exit laughing. See issues of Field & Stream

Zerner, Henri
(jt. auth) See Rosen, Charles, 1927-, and Zerner, Henri
Zero coupon bonds
Costly zeros [life insurance wrapped around Treasury zeros] B. Weberman. il *Forbes* 140:131 D 28 '87
Zero coupon bombs. B. Weberman. il *Forbes* 139:103 Ja 26 '87
Zero gravity See Weightlessness
Zero knowledge proofs
Zero-knowledge proofs [data encryption] P. Wayner. il *Byte* 12:149-52 O '87
Zero option disarmament See Disarmament
Zevon, Warren
about
Warren Zevon's new LP: a star-studded comeback. A. DeCurtis. por *Roll Stone* p19 Je 18 '87
Zhang Xinxin
Beijing's popcorn entrepreneur [excerpt from Chinese lives] *Harpers* 275:35-6+ N '87
Zhang Zhian
(jt. auth) See Swanson, Austin D., and Zhang Zhian
Zhao Ziyang
about
China passes the torch. M. Hopkins. por *New Leader* 70:5-6 N 30 '87
China takes the reformist road. A. Joyce. il *Nation* 245:752-4 D 19 '87
China's changing of the guard. F. Willey. il por *Newsweek* 110:78 N 16 '87
China's heir apparent. D. Elliott. il por *Newsweek* 110:69 N 2 '87
The Moscow/Peking dilemma. B. Crozier. *Natl Rev* 39:26 D 18 '87
Three for tomorrow. R. Thomson. il por *World Press Rev* 34:23 D '87
Zhao gives China a swift kick toward a free market. M. Shao. il por *Bus Week* p89 N 16 '87
Zia-ul-Haq, Mohammad
about
Knocking at the nuclear door [interview] W. R. Doerner. il por *Time* 129:42-3 Mr 30 '87
The perils of Pakistan. M. Ispahani. *New Repub* 196:19-21+ Mr 16 '87
Zia's Afghan dilemma. N. Cooper. il por *Newsweek* 109:42 F 16 '87
Zidovudine See Azidothymidine
Ziegel, Vic
Eddie Condon's. il por *N Y* 20:70-1 D 21-28 '87
Ziegler, Charles E.
The bear's view: Soviet environmentalism. il *Technol Rev* 90:44-51 Ap '87
Ziegler, Edward
My father, Mr. Lincoln and me. il *Read Dig* 130:35-40 F '87
The railing on the stairs. il *Read Dig* 131:97-9 N '87
What's behind our UFO mania? *Read Dig* 131:113-17 Ag '87
Ziegler, John A., Jr.
about
John Ziegler's spectacular save: the NHL. B. Welling. il por *Bus Week* p110 My 18 '87
Ziegler, John K.
about
Back from the brink. A. A. Lappen. por *Forbes* 140:8 O 19 '87
Zietz, Stephen J.
Botanical illustration. il *Antiques* 131:600-13 Mr '87
Ziff-Davis Publishing Co.
"We'll get back to you on that" [how Ziff-Davis magazines are faring at CBS and Murdoch group] R. Behar. il *Forbes* 139:42+ Ap 6 '87
Zigler, Edward Frank, 1930-
about
Project Day-care. R. J. Trotter. bibl (p63) il pors *Psychol Today* 21:32-8 D '87
Zigman, Laura
The one-minute publicist. por *Publ Wkly* 232:57 S 25 '87
Zihuatanejo (Mexico)
Architecture
Mexican open house [LoGiudice-Rivers house] M. Ennis. il *House Gard* 159:130-5+ F '87
Zikmund, Barbara Brown See Brown Zikmund, Barbara
Zilbergeld, Bernie
Notes from the overblown. il *Psychol Today* 21:10-12 My '87
Zimbabwe
See also
Civil rights—Zimbabwe
Droughts—Zimbabwe
Massacres—Zimbabwe

National parks and reserves—Zimbabwe
Public health—Zimbabwe
Wildlife conservation—Zimbabwe
Description and travel
Naipaulia. M. Elliott. *New Repub* 197:12+ N 16 '87
Economic policy
Poised on the brink. J. Shepherd. il *Atlantic* 260:26-31 Jl '87
Native peoples
Zimbabwe's 'situation' and prayers for unity. E. Jorstad. *Christ Century* 104:710-11 Ag 26-S 2 '87
Politics and government
Poised on the brink. J. Shepherd. il *Atlantic* 260:26-31 Jl '87
Watching Zimbabwe [white political privilege to end] N. Cooper. il *Newsweek* 109:47 Ap 27 '87
Zimbabwe solons says no to white privilege. *Jet* 72:14 S 14 '87
Zimbabwe's 'situation' and prayers for unity. E. Jorstad. *Christ Century* 104:710-11 Ag 26-S 2 '87
Zimbabwe's tortured path. B. Berkeley. *New Repub* 196:21-3 F 16 '87
Race relations
Watching Zimbabwe [white political privilege to end] N. Cooper. il *Newsweek* 109:47 Ap 27 '87
Zimbabwe solons says no to white privilege. *Jet* 72:14 S 14 '87
Religious institutions and affairs
See also
Church and social problems—Zimbabwe
Missions—Zimbabwe
Zimbabwean sculpture See Sculpture, Zimbabwean
Zimmer, Dieter E.
The light: fantastic! *World Press Rev* 34:55 Ap '87
Zimmer, Elizabeth
After postmodernism: waiting for the end of the world. il *Dance Mag* 61:64-9 F '87
Paul Taylor, pace maker: those who can, do. il *Dance Mag* 61:36-40 S '87
Zimmer Corp.
Zimmer QuickSilver [cover story] P. Bedard. il *Car Driv* 32:36-40 Ap '87
Zimmer nuclear power plant (Ohio) See Nuclear power plants
Zimmerman, James M.
Schools are my business. por *Newsweek* 109:6-7 My 11 '87
Zimmerman, John, d. 1985
about
The littlest Marine. J. Stuller. il pors *Read Dig* 131:123-7 Jl '87
Zimmerman, Lisa Horton
The youngest old lady in the world [story] *Redbook* 168:70+ Mr '87
Zimmerman, Michael
Keep guard up after evolution victory. *BioScience* 37:636 O '87
Zimmerman, Patrick
about
The termite connection. D. M. Schwartz. il por *Int Wildl* 17:38-42 Jl/Ag '87
Zimmerman, Paul
Assault on Mount Landry. il por *Sports Illus* 67:40-3 D 21 '87
Brutal face-off. il *Sports Illus* 67 Sp Issue:32-41 S 9 '87
Charge! il pors *Sports Illus* 67:14-19 N 23 '87
The chase is on. il *Sports Illus* 67 Sp Issue:14-17 S 9 '87
Closing in on the big one. il *Sports Illus* 66:22-6+ Ja 26 '87
Deep-sixing the Niners. il *Sports Illus* 66:22-4 Ja 12 '87
Dr. Z charts the '87 draft. il *Sports Illus* 66:56-7 Ap 27 '87
Grin and bear it, Giants. il *Sports Illus* 67:34-6+ S 21 '87
Hey, it's heavenly. il *Sports Illus* 67:20-3 D 7 '87
'I can catch the rock'. il pors *Sports Illus* 67:74-8+ Ag 10 '87
Just a breeze for the Giants. il *Sports Illus* 66:21-4+ Ja 19 '87
Killer Giants. il *Sports Illus* 66:14-22+ F 2 '87
Left with an empty feeling. il *Sports Illus* 67:38-40+ O 12 '87
Legend in the making [cover story] il pors *Sports Illus* 67 Sp Issue:50-4+ S 9 '87
Meeting of minds in Maui. il *Sports Illus* 66:51-2 Mr 30 '87
Miracles of the Midway. il *Sports Illus* 67:28-30+ N 16 '87

Zimmerman, Paul—*cont.*
On the outside looking in. il *Sports Illus* 67:54-6+ O 26 '87
The secondary is primary in K.C. il *Sports Illus* 67 Sp Issue:118-22 S 9 '87
Wake-up call for the Jets. il *Sports Illus* 66:12-15 Ja 5 '87
Welcome back to the NFL. il *Sports Illus* 67:62-3 O 26 '87
When push came to shove. il *Sports Illus* 67:38-41 O 5 '87
Zimmerman, Paul D.
But will he, she or it play in Peoria? il *U S News World Rep* 103:22 Jl 27 '87
Zimmerman, R. D.
My say. por *Publ Wkly* 231:39 Je 19 '87
Zimmerman, Raymond
about
Catalog of woes. M. Kuntz. il por *Forbes* 139:75+ My 4 '87
Zimmerman, Robert Allen See Dylan, Bob, 1941-
Zimmerman, William
about
No customers, no profits. D. Henry. il *Forbes* 139:52+ F 23 '87
Zimmermann, Bernd Alois, 1918-1970
about
Die Soldaten [opera] Reviews
Opera News 52:62 N '87. H. Koegler
Zimmermann, Karl
Ding, ding, ding. il *Americana* 15:58-60+ Mr/Ap '87
Zimmermann, Marge Tardy
What happened to my daughter? il por *Good Housekeep* 204:82+ Ap '87
Zimmermann, Mary Ann
The nationality rooms. il *Focus* 36:34-5 Wint '86
Zimmermann, Warren
The evolving Soviet approach to human rights [addresses, January 27 and February 20, 1987] *Dep State Bull* 87:67-9 Je '87
Zimring, Franklin E.
Hot boxes for ex-smokers. por *Newsweek* 109:12 Ap 20 '87
Zinc in the body
Does fetal zinc affect later immunity? [research by Pamela Fraker and others] J. Raloff. *Sci News* 131:375 Je 13 '87
Get a zing out of zinc. *Prevention* 39:8 D '87
Zinc: a key element for growth. *Prevention* 39:17 D '87
Zinc: moderator in brain cell chatter? [research by D. Choi and others] *Sci News* 131:313 My 16 '87
Zinc selectively blocks the action of N-methyl-D-aspartate on cortical neurons. S. Peters and others. bibl f il *Science* 236:589-93 My 1 '87
Zinc mines and mining
Alaska
An ambitious venture in Alaska [Teck Corp. to develop reserves at the Red Dog Mine] P. C. Newman. il por *Macleans* 100:34 Ag 24 '87
Zinfandel wines See Wine
Zingales, Rosi
about
Rosi Zingales, costume draper. T. Hardin. il por *Seventeen* 46:233 Ag '87
Zingl, Harald, 1927-1987
about
Obituary
Phys Today por 40:92 Jl '87. M. J. Moravcsik
Zinn, E. Z.
about
The net drops on Crazy Eddie. T. Vogel. il *Bus Week* p62 N 2 '87
Zinn, Elias See Zinn, E. Z.
Zinn, Howard, 1922-
Some truths are not self-evident. *Nation* 245:87-8 Ag 1-8 '87
Zinnias
At ease with zinnias. il *South Living* 22:102-3 Ap '87
Zinno (New York, N.Y.: Restaurant) See New York (N.Y.)— Restaurants, nightclubs, bars, etc.
Zinser, Adolfo Aguilar See Aguilar Zinser, Adolfo
Zinsli, Paul
The Walser. il *Courier* 40:14-15 F '87
Zinsmeister, Karl
The American dream: the family's tie. *Current* 290:9-13 F '87
Prejudice against Asians: anxiety and acceptance. *Current* 297:37-40 N '87

Zinsser, John
Music to buy books by. il *Publ Wkly* 231:40+ Ap 17 '87
Stress-management tapes. il *Publ Wkly* 232:413-17 Ag 7 '87
Word-for-word. il *Publ Wkly* 231:52+ F 20 '87
Zinsser, John S., Jr.
about
After 36 years at Condensed Books, Zinsser looks back— and forward. C. T. Anthony. il por *Publ Wkly* 232:16 Ag 14 '87
Zion, Libby
about
New York Hospital on the spot: three baffling deaths jolt a proud institution. M. Stone. il pors *N Y* 20:40-7 Je 22 '87
Zionism
Among the anti-Semites: memoirs of a British Zionist. H. Fairlie. *New Repub* 196:24 Je 8 '87
Is messianism good for the Jews? J. Katz. *Commentary* 83:31-6 Ap '87
Israel: a house divided? R. R. Wisse. *Commentary* 84:33-8 S '87
Israel's dangerous fundamentalists [Gush Emunim] I. S. Lustick. bibl f *Foreign Policy* 68:118-39 Fall '87
Israel's providential men. P. Johnson. *Commentary* 84:60-3 O '87
Letter to a new Israeli. R. R. Wisse. *Commentary* 83:44-9 Je '87
A light unto the nations? R. R. Wisse. *Commentary* 84:30-5 D '87
Zionism in drama
British traditions [controversy surrounding J. Allen's play Perdition] A. Cockburn. *Nation* 245:187 S 5 '87
Foul play [controversy surrounding J. Allen's Perdition] D. Pryce-Jones. *New Repub* 196:15-17 Mr 2 '87
Zipes, Jack David
Kissing off Snow White. *N Y Times Book Rev* 92:32 Mr 22 '87
Zipkin, Jerome
about
Man about town at home. C. T. Buckley. il por *House Gard* 159:190-3+ O '87
Zippers
Zipper man [H. Stiefel] *New Yorker* 63:34-6 D 14 '87
Zipprodt, Patricia
about
The gift of garb. B. Weber. il por *N Y Times Mag* p94 N 1 '87
Zircon
Alpha-decay-induced fracturing in zircon: the transition from the crystalline to the metamict state [cover story] B. C. Chakoumakos and others. bibl f il *Science* 236:1556-9 Je 19 '87
Zirkel, Perry A.
The Full Employment for Attorneys Act. bibl f il *Phi Delta Kappan* 69:165-6 O '87
The textbook cases: secularism on appeal. bibl f *Phi Delta Kappan* 69:308-10 D '87
Zirkel, Perry A., and Reichner, Henry F.
Is in loco parentis dead? bibl f il *Phi Delta Kappan* 68:466-9 F '87
Zisson, Harry
about
Thomson McKinnon [interview] il por *Fortune* 116 Sp Issue:188-9 Fall '87
Znaimer, Moses
about
The little TV station that grew. P. C. Newman. il por *Macleans* 100:32 Ap 20 '87
Zoback, Mark D., and others
New evidence on the state of stress of the San Andreas fault system. bibl f il maps *Science* 238:1105-11 N 20 '87
Zodiac
Zodiacal signs vs. constellations. G. Lovi. il *Sky Telesc* 74:506-8 N '87
Zodiacal light
Seeing the zodiacal light. R. Burnham. il *Astronomy* 15:54-5 S '87
Zoffany, Johann, 1733?-1810
about
Johan Zoffany and the eighteenth-century interior [cover story] G. Jackson-Stops. bibl f il *Antiques* 131:1264-79 Je '87
Zolensky, Michael E.
Refractory interplanetary dust particles. bibl f il *Science* 237:1466-8 S 18 '87
Zolotow, Maurice, 1913-
Unforgettable Fred Allen. il *Read Dig* 131:55-6+ O '87

Zolotow, Maurice, 1913——*cont.*
Why I believe in Santa Claus. il *McCalls* 115:138-40 D '87
Zolp, Marshall
about
The big chill. J. Crudele. il *N Y* 20:19+ Ag 24 '87
Zondervan Corp.
The problems at the 'big three'. D. D. Buss. il *Christ Today* 31:60-1 Mr 6 '87
Zone system (Photography) *See* Photography—Exposure
Zoning
New York (State)
See also
New York (N.Y.)—Zoning
Zoo animal breeding *See* Breeding
Zoo animals *See* Zoos
Un zoo, la nuit [film] *See* Motion picture reviews—Single works
Zoological exhibits
See also
Larson Company
Zoological gardens *See* Zoos
Zoological specimens
Photographs and photography
History in bits and pieces: body snatcher [interview with R. W. Purcell] D. Lessem. il *Omni* 10:82-9 D '87
Zoology
See also
Dissection
Natural history
Psychology, Comparative
Ecology
See Animal ecology
Zoology, Economic
See also
Animal introduction
Wildlife conservation—Finance
Zoom lenses *See* Lenses, Photographic
Zoomracks (Data base management system) *See* Information storage and retrieval systems—Management
Zoonoses *See* Animals as carriers of infection
Zoos
Phenomena, comment and notes [how zoo visitors perceive animals] M. Robinson. il *Smithsonian* 17:30+ F '87
What's new at the zoo? D. M. Kennedy. il *Technol Rev* 90:66-73 Ap '87
Wildlife au naturel [expeditions sponsored by zoos] D. G. Gordon. *Travel Holiday* 168:30-1 Jl '87
Breeding programs
See Breeding
Buildings
See also
Larson Company
Animal house [World of Primates at the Philadelphia Zoo] K. D. Stein. il *Archit Rec* 175:120-5 F '87
Design
No rms, jungle vu. M. F. Greene. il *Atlantic* 260:62-8+ D '87
Australia
See also
Taronga Zoo
California
See also
San Diego Wild Animal Park (Escondido, Calif.)
Great Britain
Wild gaming [private zoo at Howletts, country home of J. Aspinall] B. Masters. il por *House Gard* 159:222-5+ N '87
Louisiana
See also
Audubon Park and Zoological Garden (New Orleans, La.)
Maryland
See also
Baltimore Zoo
New York (State)
See also
Bronx Zoo
Central Park Zoo
Prospect Park Zoo (New York, N.Y.)
Ohio
See also
Cincinnati Zoological Garden
Oklahoma
See also
Oklahoma City Zoo
Pennsylvania
See also
Philadelphia Zoological Garden

South Carolina
See also
Riverbanks Zoological Park (Columbia, S.C.)
Zoro
about
Zoro makes his mark [interview] por *Teen* 31:57 My '87
Zotti, Ed
about
He's the wisest of wise guys. E. Dolnick. il por *Discover* 8:82-4+ Ja '87
Is a yawn really contagious? E. Dolnick. il *Read Dig* 131:99-102 Jl '87
Zraket, Charles A.
Uncertainties in building a strategic defense. bibl f *Science* 235:1600-6 Mr 27 '87
Zubaidi, Hassan
about
The Assad connection. R. Morais. il *Forbes* 139:32-3 Je 15 '87
Zubenko, George S., and others
Family study of platelet membrane fluidity in Alzheimer's disease. bibl f il *Science* 238:539-42 O 23 '87
Zuber, Paul B., 1926-1987
about
Obituary
Jet por 72:13 Mr 30 '87
Zucchini *See* Squashes
Zucchini cooking *See* Cooking—Vegetables
Zucchini relish *See* Pickles and relishes
Zucker, Eric
about
Assets that dollars can't buy. J. Fierman. il por *Fortune* 115:28 Ap 13 '87
Zucker, Stefan
Changing your tune. il *Opera News* 51:32-4+ Ja 3 '87
Zuckerman, Edward
Does malpractice make perfect? *Vogue* 177:176+ My '87
How now to sell a cow? il *N Y Times Mag* p68-70+ N 29 '87
Quest for the perfect yo-yo. il *Read Dig* 130:189-92 Je '87
Zuckerman, Frederick William, 1934-
about
Why Chrysler's cash handles like a dream. S. Weiss. il por *Bus Week* p116 Je 8 '87
Zuckerman, Harriet
(jt. auth) *See* Cole, Jonathan R., and Zuckerman, Harriet
Zuckerman, Jeffrey
about
Zuckerman bound. G. Slutsker. il por *Forbes* 139:123 F 9 '87
Zuckerman, Jim
Golden light. il *Petersens Photogr Mag* 16:52-5 O '87
Reflections: where you want them. il *Petersens Photogr Mag* 15:50-1+ Ap '87
Zuckerman, Mortimer B.
about
Sic transit Gloria mundi. N. J. Perry. *Fortune* 116:92 Ag 31 '87
Zuckerman, Seth
Living there. il *Sierra* 72:61-6 Mr/Ap '87
Zuckerman, Sir Solly, 1904-
The nuclear opening. bibl f il *N Y Rev Books* 34:42-6 My 7 '87
Reagan's highest folly. bibl f il *N Y Rev Books* 34:35-41 Ap 9 '87
What price Star Wars? bibl f il *N Y Rev Books* 34:8+ Ap 23 '87
Zulu language
Useful Zulu phrases [managing servants in South Africa] L. Freed. il *Harpers* 274:26-8 My '87
Zulus
The chief [G. Buthelezi] M. Massing. bibl f il por *N Y Rev Books* 34:15-22 F 12 '87
A search for harmony [Zulu leaders propose new province of KwaNatal] il *U S News World Rep* 102:30 My 11 '87
South Africa's Zulu chief [G. Buthelezi] G. Behrens. il pors *World Press Rev* 34:34-5 Ja '87
Won't someone listen? [G. Buthelezi's views] *Natl Rev* 39:22 Ja 30 '87
Zumino, Bruno
about
Bruno Zumino and Bryce Dewitt receive Dirac medals. pors *Phys Today* 40:111 N '87
Zumwalt, Elmo, III
A war with hope; ed. by John Grossmann. il por *Health* 19:86+ Je '87

Zuni Café & Grill (San Francisco, Calif.) *See* San Francisco (Calif.)—Restaurants, nightclubs, bars, etc.

Zuñi Indians
Gardening the Zuni way [waffle gardens help beat the heat] C. A. Doherty. il *Rodale's Org Gard* 34:62-4 Ag '87

Zur Loye, Hans-Conrad, and others
Oxygen isotope effect in high-temperature oxide superconductors. bibl f il *Science* 238:1558-60 D 11 '87

Zurbarán, Francisco de, 1598-1664
about
The art world. S. Schwartz. *New Yorker* 63:151-4 D 7 '87
From the dark heart of Spain. R. Hughes. il *Time* 130:78-9 O 5 '87
The glory of Zurbarán. B. Rose. il *Vogue* 177:264-5 D '87
The Metropolitan Museum of Art. il *Antiques Collect Hobbies* 92:54-5 Ag '87
Spanish inquisition. K. Larson. il *N Y* 20:96-7 O 12 '87
A Spanish old master. M. Stevens. il *Newsweek* 110:76 N 30 '87
The visions of others. J. Gardner. il *Commonweal* 114:750-2 D 18 '87
Zurbaran's theater of martyrs. C. Fuentes. il *Art News* 86:116-19 O '87

Zurbriggen, Pirmin
about
On the edge of greatness: Olympian Pirmin Zurbriggen [cover story] T. Gabriel. il pors *N Y Times Mag* p10-13+ D 27 '87
Z-man is a real he-man. W. O. Johnson. il pors *Sports Illus* 66:42-3 Mr 23 '87

Zurich (Switzerland)
Monuments, statues, etc.
Burghers block the box [rejection of S. Lewitt's sculpture The cube] E. Beck. il *Art News* 86:57 S '87

Zurich Ballet
Reviews:
Performances of works by U. Scholz. H. Koegler. *Dance Mag* 61:27-8 F '87

Zurick, David
A question of balance. il *Sierra* 72:46-50 Jl/Ag '87

Zurita, Michael S.
My shoplifter. il *Glamour* 85:126+ Je '87

Zussman, Mark
(jt. auth) See Dormen, Lesley, and Zussman, Mark

Zussman, Shirley
Sex & health. See issues of Glamour beginning November 1986

Zusy, Catherine
Stained glass for the home. bibl f il *Antiques* 131:848-57 Ap '87

Zwack, Anne Marshall
Artisans of Florence. il *Gourmet* 47:50-5+ Jl '87
Shopping in Milan. il *Gourmet* 47:86-91+ N '87
Siena. il *Gourmet* 47:54-9+ F '87

Zweig, Connie
The big thrill. il *Omni* 9:26+ Ap '87

Zweig, Martin
about
Famous artists. R. Phalon. il pors *Forbes* 139:102+ Je 1 '87

Zweig Fund
Famous artists [C. Allmon, M. Gabelli and M. Zweig] R. Phalon. il pors *Forbes* 139:102+ Je 1 '87

Zweigbaum, Steven
about
Steven Zweigbaum minds Me and my girl. A. M. Hale. il por *Theatre Crafts* 21:88+ N '87

Zweigenhaft, Burton
about
What's not in the prospectus. G. Morgenson. il *Forbes* 140:61-2 Jl 27 '87

Zwinger, Susan
Adobes of God. il map *Americana* 15:65-9 N/D '87

Zwingle, Erla
"Doc" Edgerton: the man who made time stand still. il pors *Natl Geogr* 172:464-83 O '87

Zwonitzer, Mark
Cut, cut, snip, snip. The Turk comes a-calling. il *Sport Mag* 78:92 N '87

Zydeco music
See also
Phonograph records—Zydeco music
Allons danser. B. Sandmel. il *Atlantic* 260:88+ Jl '87
Buckwheat Zydeco makes music accordion to bayou tradition, and who can say him neigh? A. Abrahams. il pors *People Wkly* 28:151-2 D 7 '87

Zymogens See Proteases

Zysman, John
(jt. auth) See Cohen, Stephen S., and Zysman, John

ZZZZ Best Company
Wall-to-wall trouble for the carpet-cleaning king [B. Minkow] K. Kelly. il por *Bus Week* p83 Jl 13 '87
A whiz kid goes wrong [B. Minkow] J. B. Copeland. il por *Newsweek* 110:40 Jl 20 '87
ZZZZ Best may be ZZZZ worst. P. Elmer-Dewitt. por *Time* 130:56 Jl 20 '87

BOOK REVIEWS

8 }. 1987
New Repub 197:26-7 Ag 31 '87. S. Kauffmann
'86 massive neutrinos in astrophysics and in particle physics.
1986
Science 236:341-2 Ap 17 '87. L. Wolfenstein
The 1987 MediaGuide. 1987
N Y Times Book Rev 92:15 Jl 12 '87. J. D. Atwater

A

Aaron, H. J. and Schwartz, W. B. The painful prescription.
1984
Mon Labor Rev 110:46 My '87. G. F. Rohrlich
Abbott, L. K. Strangers in paradise. 1986
N Y Times Book Rev 92:12 F 8 '87. W. Ferguson
Abel, L. Important nonsense. 1987
N Y Times Book Rev 92:27 Mr 1 '87. R. Rosenthal
Abell, G. O. and others. Exploration of the universe. 5th
ed. 1987
Astronomy 15:39-40 Jl '87. R. Burnham
Abortion, medicine, and the law. 3rd ed. 1986
America 156:447-8 My 30 '87. L. S. Cahill
About men. 1987
Vogue 177:188 My '87. L. A. Schreiber
Abraham, D. The collapse of the Weimar Republic. 1986
N Y Times Book Rev 92:12-13 Ag 2 '87. V. R. Berghahn
Abraham, R. Alexander Kerensky. 1987
N Y Times Book Rev 92:29 Jl 19 '87. W. C. Fuller
Abramson, H. S. National geographic. 1987
Wash Mon 19:58 Je '87. T. Simonelli
Abu-Lughod, L. Veiled sentiments. 1986
N Y Times Book Rev 92:24 F 15 '87. I. Bushnaq
Acker, K. Don Quixote. 1986
New Repub 196:38-41 My 4 '87. D. Van Leer
Ackerley, J. R. My dog Tulip. 1987
N Y Times Book Rev 92:9+ F 8 '87. E. Hawes
Ackermann, R. J. Religion as critique. 1985
Society 24:96 Mr/Ap '87. J. R. Kelly
Acton, E. Russia. 1986
Hist Today 37:53-4 F '87. M. Raeff
Adams, J. The financing of terror. 1986
Commentary 83:76-8 Ja '87. W. McGurn
Adams, P. Moon, Mars, and meteorites. 1986
Earth Sci 39:32-3 Wint '86
Adams, W. and Brock, J. W. The bigness complex. 1986
Bus Week p14-15 Ja 19 '87. H. Gleckman
Cent Mag 20:37-8 Jl/Ag '87. D. McDonald
N Y Times Book Rev 92:10 Ja 11 '87. R. Lekachman
Nation 244:512+ Ap 18 '87. M. Waldman
Technol Rev 90:75-6 Jl '87. J. P. Lewis
Adamson, G. My pride and joy. 1986
N Y Times Book Rev 92:27 Ag 30 '87. B. Webster
Adcock, F. The incident book. 1986
N Y Times Book Rev 92:46 O 18 '87. S. Dobyns
Adler, J. The Jews of Paris and the final solution. 1987
N Y Times Book Rev 92:24 S 20 '87. H. R. Lottman
Adler, K. Manet. 1986
America 157:196-7 O 3 '87. A. Hilton
Adler, M. J. We hold these truths. 1987
Cent Mag 20:40-1 Mr/Ap '87. D. McDonald
Adler, R. Reckless disregard. 1986
Cent Mag 20:36-8 Mr/Ap '87. D. McDonald
Commentary 83:70-4 Mr '87. J. Q. Wilson
N Y Rev Books 34:27-37 F 26 '87. R. M. Dworkin
Natl Rev 39:48-50 Ap 10 '87. C. T. Buckley
Advanced telescope making techniques. 2v 1986
Sky Telesc 73:619-20+ Je '87. E. J. Hysom
Advances in animal conservation. 1985
BioScience 37:735 N '87. N. Myers
Africa and the Second World War. 1986
Hist Today 37:58 Mr '87. J. D. Hargreaves
African pygmies. 1986
Science 235:600 Ja 30 '87. P. T. Ellison
Agadati. 1986
Dance Mag 61:72-3 O '87. A. Barzel
Agee, P. On the run. 1987
N Y Times Book Rev 92:7 Ag 2 '87. T. Powers
Aho, C. M. and Aronson, J. D. Trade talks. 1985
Mon Labor Rev 110:45-6 Mr '87. R. M. Devens,
Jr.
AIDS and the education of our children.

Natl Rev 39:50-1 D 18 '87. W. Lutton
Air pollution and plant life. 1984
BioScience 37:138-9 F '87. R. Kohut
Aksenov, V. P. In search of melancholy baby. 1987
N Y Times Book Rev 92:5-6 Jl 19 '87. R. R. Lingeman
New Repub 197:36-8 S 7 '87. S. Barańczak
Time 130:62 Ag 31 '87. D. Morrison
Al-Hassan, A. Y. and Hill, D. R. Islamic technology.
1986
Hist Today 37:56-7 O '87. F. Robinson
Alaskan missionary spirituality. 1987
Christ Century 104:1006 N 11 '87. J. Gros
Albrecht, D. Designing dreams. 1986
Archit Rec 175:89 Je '87. R. Lavenstein
Albright, D. Tennyson. 1986
N Y Rev Books 34:17-19 O 22 '87. R. B. Martin
Alcorn, G. D. Owls. 1986
Conservationist 42:50-1 Jl/Ag '87. P. L. Nelson
Alcott, L. M. The selected letters of Louisa May Alcott.
1987
N Y Times Book Rev 92:45 O 25 '87. B. L. Packer
Aldo Leopold. 1987
Wilderness 51:66-7 Wint '87. C. E. Little
Alexander, L. The El Dorado adventure. 1987
N Y Times Book Rev 92:29 Je 7 '87. S. Isaacs
Ali, M. A. and Klyne, M. A. Vision in vertebrates. 1985
BioScience 37:430-1 Je '87. M. Wilson
Alic, M. Hypatia's heritage. 1986
Science 235:1092 F 27 '87. A. H. Koblitz
Aliki. How a book is made. 1986
N Y Times Book Rev 92:26 F 8 '87. U. Shulevitz
Aline, Countess of Romanones. The spy wore red. 1987
N Y Times Book Rev 92:10 Je 21 '87. M. Gross
Allard, A. Turbocharging & supercharging. 1986
Previous ed.: 1982
Road Track 38:34 Jl '87. J. S. McKibben
Allen, J. Designer's guide to color 3. 1986
Am Artist 51:93 D '87. D. C. Hines
Allen, J. Perdition. 1987
New Repub 197:33-4+ N 2 '87. W. Laqueur
Allen, T. B. and Polmar, N. Ship of gold. 1987
Oceans 20:62 N/D '87. P. Kopper
Allende, I. Of love and shadows. 1987
Commonweal 114:460-2 Ag 14 '87. S. Gernes
N Y Times Book Rev 92:23 Jl 12 '87. G. H. Bell-Villada
New Yorker 63:84-5 Ag 24 '87. J. Updike
Allman, T. D. Miami, city of the future. 1987
N Y Times Book Rev 92:12-13 My 10 '87. J. A.
Lukas
Natl Rev 39:54+ N 20 '87. J. C. Cohen
Alloula, M. The colonial harem. 1986
N Y Times Book Rev 92:24 Ja 11 '87. C. Shloss
Allport, S. Explorers of the black box. 1986
BioScience 37:731-2 N '87. K. Lukowiak
Psychol Today 21:80 Ap '87. W. Herbert
Alpern, S. Freda Kirchwey, a woman of the Nation. 1987
N Y Times Book Rev 92:14 Ag 9 '87. R. G. Davis
Nation 245:238-40 S 12 '87. E. Showalter
New Repub 197:38-41 S 7 '87. D. Wrong
Alpert, H. Fellini, a life. 1986
America 157:90 Ag 15-22 '87. J. Cunneen
Altick, R. D. Deadly encounters. 1986
Smithsonian 17:175-7 Mr '87. A. Ryan
Altick, R. D. Paintings from books. 1985
Hist Today 37:60-1 Ja '87. M. Pointon
N Y Rev Books 34:29-30 F 12 '87. R. B. Martin
Altman, L. K. Who goes first? 1985
N Y Times Book Rev 92:9 Je 28 '87. F. Mullan
Altruism and aggression. 1986
Science 236:728 My 8 '87. N. Eisenberg
Alvarez, L. W. Alvarez. 1987
N Y Times Book Rev 92:14 Je 7 '87. J. S. Trefil
Phys Today 40:83-4 D '87. R. Garwin
Ambrose, S. E. Nixon. 1987
Commentary 84:78-80 Ag '87. R. J. Neuhaus
N Y Rev Books 34:10-13 Jl 16 '87. A. Brinkley
N Y Times Book Rev 92:3+ Ap 26 '87. R. Steel
New Leader 70:23-5 My 4-18 '87. H. S. Parmet
New Repub 197:30-4 Jl 6 '87. S. Blumenthal
Newsweek 109:74+ Ap 27 '87. J. Miller
Time 129:101 My 4 '87. P. Gray

America: art and the West. 1987
 Americana 15:12-13 My/Je '87. M. Durham
American architecture. 1986
 Archit Rec 175:75 F '87. J. V. Iovine
American frontier life. 1987
 Americana 15:20 N/D '87. J. Neary
American society. 1986
 Commentary 84:70-2 S '87. L. Lenkowsky
American Yiddish poetry. 1986
 New Repub 197:44-7 O 12 '87. H. Halkin
Amis, K. The old devils. 1987
 N Y Rev Books 34:15-17 Mr 26 '87. D. Lodge
 N Y Times Book Rev 92:14 Mr 22 '87. W. H. Pritchard
 Natl Rev 39:52 My 8 '87. J. Meyers
 New Repub 196:33-5 Mr 30 '87. J. Wolcott
 New Yorker 63:102-4 Ap 27 '87. V. S. Pritchett
 Time 129:77 Mr 9 '87. P. Gray
Amis, M. Einstein's monsters. 1987
 N Y Times Book Rev 92:28 My 17 '87. C. See
 Natl Rev 39:60-1 N 20 '87. D. Lipsky
Amis, M. The moronic inferno. 1987
 New Leader 70:12-13 Mr 23 '87. B. Gewen
 New Repub 196:36-8 Ja 26 '87. S. Birkerts
 Smithsonian 17:172 Mr '87. B. Schiff
 Vogue 177:94+ Ja '87. E. White
Amis, M. Success. 1987
 N Y Times Book Rev 92:8 S 6 '87. J. Parini
And the laugh shall be first; a treasury of religious humor.
 1986
 Christ Today 31:64-5 Ja 16 '87. D. Neff
Andersen, C. P. The serpent's tooth. 1987
 N Y Times Book Rev 92:28 S 13 '87. M. Jones
Anderson, A. B. and Pickering, G. W. Confronting the
 color line. 1986
 Christ Century 104:974-5 N 4 '87. S. Shoemaker
Anderson, J. The American Dance Festival. 1987
 N Y Times Book Rev 92:16-17 Je 21 '87. H. Saal
Anderson, J. Stories from the warm zone and Sydney
 stories. 1987
 N Y Times Book Rev 92:7 N 29 '87. H. Pakula
Anderson, J. and Hevenor, H. Burning down the house.
 1987
 New Leader 70:18-20 S 21 '87. R. Leiter
Anderson, J. D. Introduction to flight. 2nd ed. 1985
 Phys Today 40:125-6 O '87. L. Hunter
Anderson, W. T. To govern evolution. 1987
 Futurist 21:34-5 N/D '87. R. L. Olson
 Sierra 72:89-91 S/O '87. J. Hart
Andrade, C. D. de. Travelling in the family. 1986
 N Y Times Book Rev 92:32-3 D 13 '87. D. H. Rosenthal
Andreyev, L. Visions. 1987
 N Y Times Book Rev 92:8-9 D 27 '87. D. Fanger
Anglesey, G. C. H. V. P. A history of the British cavalry,
 1816 to 1919; v4, 1899-1913. 1973
 Hist Today 37:58-9 Ag '87. B. H. Reid
Animal cell biotechnology. 2v 1985
 BioScience 37:738 N '87. J. M. Robl
Animal extinctions. 1985
 BioScience 37:426-8 Je '87. F. J. Ayala
Anson, R. S. Best intentions. 1987
 N Y Rev Books 34:20-1 Jl 16 '87. N. Lemann
 N Y Times Book Rev 92:3+ My 17 '87. R. Coles
 Newsweek 109:66 Je 1 '87. D. Gates
 Time 130:64 Ag 17 '87. R. Stengel
Antarctic treaty system. 1986
 Sea Front 33:75 Ja/F '87. G. L. Voss
Antler, J. Lucy Sprague Mitchell. 1986
 Child Today 16:34-5 S/O '87. M. Lewis
 N Y Times Book Rev 92:39 Mr 22 '87. E. Chesler
 Nation 244:690-2 My 23 '87. B. M. Solomon
Antonio, G. The AIDS cover-up? 1986
 Christ Today 31:36-7 S 4 '87. W. W. Hoffman
Appelfeld, A. To the land of the cattails. 1986
 N Y Rev Books 33:40-1 Ja 15 '87. D. J. Enright
Apple, M. Propheteers. 1987
 N Y Times Book Rev 92:13-14 Mr 15 '87. C. McFadden
 Newsweek 109:77 F 23 '87. P. S. Prescott
Apple, R. W. Apple's Europe, an uncommon guide. 1986
 Atlantic 259:88-9 Ja '87. C. Michener
An Apple for my teacher. 1986
 N Y Times Book Rev 92:34 My 3 '87. W. Lesser
Appleman, R. E. East of Chosin. 1987
 N Y Times Book Rev 92:13 Ap 19 '87. B. E. Trainor
Arad, Y. Belzec, Sobibor, Treblinka. 1987
 N Y Times Book Rev 92:15 Je 28 '87. M. R. Marrus
The Arcimboldo effect. 1987
 N Y Rev Books 34:41-4 S 24 '87. C. Hope
Are Australian ecosystems different?
 Science 235:226-7 Ja 9 '87. G. H. Orians
Arendell, T. Mothers and divorce. 1986
 Psychol Today 21:78 Ja '87. E. Stark

Argentina. Comisión Nacional sobre la Desaparición de
 Personas. Nunca más. 1986
 Nation 244:88-90 Ja 24 '87. J. Polk
Argueta, M. Cuzcatlán. 1987
 N Y Times Book Rev 92:8 Jl 26 '87. A. J. MacAdam
Arizona: the land and the people. 1986
 Earth Sci 40:28 Fall '87
Arkes, H. First things. 1986
 Natl Rev 39:51-2 My 8 '87. J. Sobran
Arlacchi, P. Mafia business. 1986
 New Repub 197:33-4+ O 12 '87. J. Weisberg
The Armchair angler. 1986
 Conservationist 41:52-3 Ja/F '87. J. Rowen
Armitage, S. John Held, Jr., illustrator of the jazz age.
 1987
 N Y Times Book Rev 92:14 D 6 '87. A. Hirschfeld
Arms control verification. 1986
 Commonweal 114:90-1 F 13 '87. J. Richelson
 Science 235:1090-1 F 27 '87. B. E. Fridling
Arnold, J. Baby Houston. 1987
 N Y Times Book Rev 92:10 Jl 26 '87. E. O. Stone
Arnold, L. A very special relationship. 1987
 Science 238:409 O 16 '87. T. Findlay
Aronson, T. Crowns in conflict. 1986
 Hist Today 37:59-60 My '87. J. Terraine
Art, H. W. A garden of wildflowers. 1986
 Americana 15:51 Jl/Ag '87. P. Hagan
Artists' pigments; v1. 1986
 Sci Am 257:118 S '87. P. Morrison
Aschan, U. The man whom women loved. 1987
 N Y Times Book Rev 92:1+ Ag 23 '87. D. Ackerman
Ashbery, J. April galleons. 1987
 New Leader 70:17-18 N 30 '87. P. Pettingell
Ashby, T., Jr. The bear in the back yard. 1987
 Natl Rev 39:51 Je 5 '87. C. Williamson
Ashworth, W. The late, Great Lakes. 1986
 Earth Sci 40:30-1 Spr '87
Astell, M. The first English feminist. 1986
 Hist Today 37:56 My '87. I. Roots
Astley, T. It's raining in Mango. 1987
 N Y Times Book Rev 92:14 N 22 '87. R. Brown
Athearn, R. G. The mythic West in twentieth-century
 America. 1986
 Smithsonian 18:141-3 Ag '87. G. Weales
 USA Today (Periodical) 115:92-3 Mr '87. G. F. Kreyche
Atreya, S. K. Atmospheres and ionospheres of the outer
 planets and their satellites. 1986
 Science 236:729-30 My 8 '87. J. H. Waite, Jr.
Attali, J. A man of influence. 1987
 Bus Week p14+ S 28 '87. C. Farrell
 N Y Times Book Rev 92:9 S 6 '87. J. E. Garten
Attwood, W. The twilight struggle. 1987
 Bus Week p12 Jl 27 '87. M. A. Reichek
 N Y Times Book Rev 92:12 Ag 30 '87. L. Garrison
Atwood, M. Bluebeard's egg, and other stories. 1986
 New Leader 70:18-19 Mr 9 '87. A. Neufeld
 Time 129:74 Ja 12 '87. P. Blake
Atwood, M. The handmaid's tale. 1986
 Christ Century 104:496-8 My 20-27 '87. J. K. Larson
Atwood, W. G. Fryderyk Chopin. 1987
 N Y Rev Books 34:9-11 My 28 '87. C. Rosen
 N Y Times Book Rev 92:28 Ap 26 '87. J. Machlis
Auchincloss, L. Diary of a yuppie. 1986
 Commonweal 114:119 F 27 '87. D. Morrissey
Auchincloss, L. Skinny island. 1987
 N Y Times Book Rev 92:5 My 24 '87. P. Cameron
 Time 129:85 My 11 '87. P. Gray
Auerbach, N. Ellen Terry, player in her time. 1987
 N Y Times Book Rev 92:11-12 Jl 26 '87. M. Peters
 Nation 245:170-2 Ag 29 '87. C. McGee
 New Repub 197:42-4 O 12 '87. R. Jenkyns
Augsburger, M. S. and Curry, D. C. Nuclear arms. 1987
 Christ Today 31:35-6 Je 12 '87. B. Connell-Bishop
Ausmus, H. J. Will Herberg, from right to right. 1987
 N Y Times Book Rev 92:15-16 Ag 30 '87. R. W.
 Fox
 Natl Rev 39:44-6 D 31 '87. P. Gottfried
Auster, P. In the country of last things. 1987
 N Y Times Book Rev 92:11-12 My 17 '87. P. Powell
Auster, P. The locked room. 1986
 N Y Times Book Rev 92:14 Ja 4 '87. S. Schiff
Austin, D. J. After the garden. 1987
 N Y Times Book Rev 92:20 Ag 16 '87. R. G. O'Meally
Avedon, R. In the American West. 1985
 Art Am 75:90-7 Ja '87. M. Kozloff
Ayer, A. J. Voltaire. 1986
 New Repub 196:36-40 Mr 2 '87. J. N. Shklar

B

Baars, B. J. The cognitive revolution in psychology. 1986

Science 236:1683-4 Je 26 '87. H. Levin
Babbitt, N. The Devil's other storybook. 1987
N Y Times Book Rev 92:36 N 1 '87. L. Graeber
Bach, M. J. The design of the UNIX operating system. 1986
Byte 12:68+ Ap '87. T. M. Houser
Bachmann, I. The thirtieth year. 1987
N Y Times Book Rev 92:14-15 N 29 '87. M. Gordon
Backstory. 1986
N Y Times Book Rev 92:37 Ja 18 '87. G. Mast
Bacon, M. H. Mothers of feminism. 1986
N Y Times Book Rev 92:28 F 1 '87. E. Griffith
Progressive 51:44-5 My '87. A. M. Davidon
Bacteria in nature; v1, Bacterial activities in perspective. 1985
BioScience 37:686+ O '87. J. T. Staley
Bacterial adhesion. 1985
BioScience 37:357-8 My '87. K. H. Baker
Badcock, C. R. The problem of altruism. 1986
Christ Century 104:446 My 6 '87. P. Heinegg
Baer, K. E. von. Autobiography of Dr. Karl Ernst von Baer. 1986
Science 236:472 Ap 24 '87. T. J. Horder
Baez, J. And a voice to sing with. 1987
N Y Times Book Rev 92:30 Je 21 '87. B. Goldsmith
Newsweek 110:63 Jl 20 '87. C. McGuigan
Vogue 177:110 Jl '87. M. Jefferson
Bailey, A. Major André. 1987
N Y Times Book Rev 92:10 Jl 5 '87. E. Wright
Bailey, P. Gabriel's lament. 1987
N Y Times Book Rev 92:34 O 18 '87. J. Johnston
Bailyn, B. The peopling of British North America. 1986
N Y Rev Books 34:27-9 Ja 29 '87. T. H. Breen
Nation 244:188-90 F 14 '87. D. Levin
Bailyn, B. Voyagers to the West. 1986
Hist Today 37:56-7 Ag '87. E. Countryman
N Y Rev Books 34:27-9 Ja 29 '87. T. H. Breen
Nation 244:188-90 F 14 '87. D. Levin
New Yorker 63:133-5 F 23 '87. N. Bliven
Baker, J. H. Mary Todd Lincoln. 1987
Am Herit 38:34+ S/O '87
N Y Times Book Rev 92:38 S 13 '87. P. Longsworth
Bakhtin, M. M. Speech genres and other late essays. 1986
N Y Times Book Rev 92:31 Mr 22 '87. S. Stewart
Ball, H. Justice downwind. 1986
Science 235:227 Ja 9 '87. R. A. Divine
Balliett, W. American musicians. 1986
Down Beat 54:48 My '87. J. McDonough
New Leader 70:15-16 F 9-23 '87. B. Cook
Balthasar, H. U. von. The glory of the Lord; v3, Studies in theological style: lay style. 1986
America 156:488+ Je 13 '87. E. T. Oakes
Baly, M. E. Florence Nightingale and the nursing legacy. 1986
Hist Today 37:58-9 F '87. F. M. L. Thompson
Banerji, S. Cobwebwalking. 1987
N Y Times Book Rev 92:26 O 18 '87. R. F. Dew
Bangs, L. Psychotic reactions and carburetor dung. 1987
N Y Times Book Rev 92:15 N 22 '87. K. Tucker
Roll Stone p25 N 19 '87. K. Loder
Banham, R. A concrete Atlantis. 1986
Art Am 75:13-14 Ja '87. J. Masheck
Technol Rev 90:76-8 F/Mr '87. T. Frick
Banta, M. Imaging American women. 1987
N Y Times Book Rev 92:18 Ag 30 '87. J. P. Tompkins
Banville, J. The Newton letter. 1987
N Y Times Book Rev 92:19 Jl 19 '87. M. Hite
Baraka, I. A. and Baraka, A. The music. 1987
Down Beat 54:56 Ag '87. K. Whitehead
Barbera, J. and McBrien, W. Stevie, biography of Stevie Smith. 1987
N Y Rev Books 34:27-8 Je 25 '87. R. Dinnage
N Y Times Book Rev 92:24 My 10 '87. K. Pollitt
Nation 244:580-2+ My 2 '87. A. Bernard
New Yorker 63:94-6 S 28 '87. C. James
Barfoot, J. Duet for three. 1986
Ms 15:19 F '87. J. Gies
N Y Times Book Rev 92:19 Ap 5 '87. R. F. Dew
Barich, B. Hard to be good. 1987
N Y 20:79-80 N 30 '87. R. Koenig
N Y Times Book Rev 92:7 D 13 '87. R. Banks
Barker, D. A life in jazz. 1986
Smithsonian 18:174-5 My '87. D. Lancashire
Barker, J. R. V. The tournament in England, 1100-1400. 1986
Hist Today 37:59-61 S '87. C. T. Allmand
Barlow, F. Thomas Becket. 1986
America 157:307-8 O 31 '87. L. B. Pascoe
Barnard, M. Time and the white tigress. 1986
N Y Times Book Rev 92:22+ Ja 4 '87. E. Grosholz
Barnes, J. Metroland. 1987

N Y Times Book Rev 92:26 My 3 '87. J. Parini
Barnes, J. Staring at the sun. 1986
Macleans 100:49 Je 22 '87. M. McDonald
N Y Rev Books 34:21 My 7 '87. D. Lodge
N Y Times Book Rev 92:3+ Ap 12 '87. C. Fuentes
New Repub 196:37-9 My 11 '87. A. Hulbert
Barnett, C. The pride and the fall. 1987
Bus Week p14 Jl 13 '87. R. A. Melcher
N Y Times Book Rev 92:35 Jl 12 '87. C. P. Kindleberger
Natl Rev 39:51-2 D 18 '87. W. R. Hawkins
Barnett, D. F. and Crandall, R. W. Up from the ashes. 1986
Mon Labor Rev 110:59 Je '87. R. M. Devens, Jr.
Barnett, J. The elusive city. 1986
Archit Rec 175:75 F '87. J. V. Iovine
Barnhart, J. E. The Southern Baptist holy war. 1986
Christ Century 104:412+ Ap 29 '87. A. L. Pratt
N Y Times Book Rev 92:16 F 1 '87. K. Northcott
Barr, A. H. Defining modern art. 1986
Art News 86:27-8 Mr '87. B. B. Stretch
Barrell, J. The political theory of painting from Reynolds to Hazlitt. 1986
New Repub 197:39-42 Ag 10-17 '87. R. Paulson
Barrett, W. Death of the soul. 1986
Christ Today 31:31 Ap 3 '87. B. Durbin, Jr.
Barrientos, J. J. Borges y la imaginación. 1986
Américas 39:54-5 N/D '87. M. de S. Donahue
Barron, J. Breaking the ring. 1987
Natl Rev 39:46-8 Jl 31 '87. W. Murchison
Barrow, J. D. and Silk, J. The left hand of creation. 1983
Sky Telesc 74:611-12 D '87. D. Lindley
Barrow, J. D. and Tipler, F. J. The anthropic cosmological principle. 1986
Phys Today 40:84+ S '87. J. L. Anderson
Sky Telesc 73:156-7 F '87. J. N. Islam
Barth, J. The Tidewater tales. 1987
N Y Times Book Rev 92:7 Je 28 '87. W. H. Pritchard
New Repub 197:35-7 Ag 10-17 '87. S. Birkerts
Barthelme, D. Forty stories. 1987
N Y Times Book Rev 92:14-15 O 25 '87. C. James
Barthelme, F. Chroma. 1987
N Y Times Book Rev 92:12 My 3 '87. B. Pesetsky
Barthelme, S. And he tells the little horse the whole story. 1987
N Y Times Book Rev 92:8 D 20 '87. T. LeClair
Bartlett, R. Trial by fire and water. 1986
Hist Today 37:58-9 Je '87. P. Hyams
Barton, B. J. Gardening by mail. 1986
Flower Gard 31:40+ F/Mr '87. J. Anderson
Bartram, M. The Pre-Raphaelite camera. 1985
Art Am 75:21+ Jl '87. C. Bedient
Bartusiak, M. Thursday's universe. 1986
Astronomy 15:36+ Jl '87. R. Burnham
Sky Telesc 74:261-2 S '87. D. E. Thomsen
Base, G. Animalia.
N Y Times Book Rev 92:54 N 8 '87. G. Wilson
Bates, R. L. Stone, clay, glass. 1987
Earth Sci 40:36-7 Fall '87
Bateson, G. and Bateson, M. C. Angels fear. 1987
N Y Times Book Rev 92:48 N 15 '87. D. L. Miller
Batra, R. N. The great depression of 1990. 1987
N Y Times Book Rev 92:11-12 Jl 12 '87. E. Janeway
The Battered child. 4th ed. 1987
Child Today 16:35-6 S/O '87. C. Sudia
Baum, J. The calculating passion of Ada Byron. 1986
Technol Rev 90:75-6 My/Je '87. F. C. Kirwan
Baumbach, J. The life and times of Major Fiction. 1986
N Y Times Book Rev 92:22 Je 7 '87. E. Toynton
Bausch, R. Spirits and other stories. 1987
Commonweal 114:568-9 O 9 '87. T. Cahill
N Y Times Book Rev 92:16 Je 14 '87. M. S. Bell
Bawer, B. The middle generation. 1986
Natl Rev 39:56-7 Mr 27 '87. J. Meyers
Baxter, C. First light. 1987
N Y Times Book Rev 92:18 O 4 '87. M. Mifflin
Time 130:81+ S 14 '87. P. Gray
Bayer, C. H. A guide to liberation theology for middle-class congregations. 1986
Christ Century 104:697 Ag 12-19 '87. R. M. Brown
Beach, E. L. The United States Navy. 1986
America 156:470-1 Je 6 '87. D. Tomlinson
Sea Front 33:72-3 Ja/F '87
Beales, D. E. D. Joseph II; v1, In the shadow of Maria Theresa, 1741-1780. 1987
Hist Today 37:53 S '87. J. Black
Beato, F. and others. Once upon a time. 1986
Nat Hist 96:72+ Jl '87. E. O. Reischauer
Beaton, Sir C. Beaton in Vogue. 1986
Art Am 75:15-17+ Ja '87. D. Bourdon
Beattie, A. Where you'll find me, and other stories. 1986

America 156:141 F 14 '87. R. Wendling
Beauchemin, Y. The alley cat. 1986
  N Y Times Book Rev 92:14 Ja 11 '87. B. Coleman
Becher, P. and others. Gauge theories of strong and electroweak interactions. 1983
  Phys Today 40:86+ D '87. P. H. Frampton
Becker, C. The invisible drama. 1987
  Psychol Today 21:71 Je '87. P. J. Black
Becker, E. When the war was over. 1986
  Natl Rev 39:50-2 F 27 '87. F. B. Randall
  New Leader 69:26-7 D 1-15 '86. D. Kirk
Beckett, J. C. A short history of Ireland. 6th ed. 1986
  Hist Today 37:53-4 Ap '87. J. Biggs-Davison
Beckwith, R. T. The Old Testament canon of the New Testament Church and its background in early Judaism. 1985
  Christ Century 104:560+ Je 17-24 '87. J. D. Kingsbury
Beecher, J. Charles Fourier. 1987
  N Y Times Book Rev 92:22 My 17 '87. E. J. Weber
Beerbohm, M. The illustrated Zuleika Dobson. 1985
  Orig. pub.: 1911
  N Y Rev Books 34:3 N 5 '87. V. S. Pritchett
Beerbohm, M. Rossetti and his circle. 1987
  N Y Rev Books 34:3 N 5 '87. V. S. Pritchett
Behavioral biology of killer whales. 1986
  Science 237:204 Jl 10 '87. P. O. Thomas
Beit-Hallahmi, B. The Israeli connection. 1987
  N Y Rev Books 34:8-10+ O 8 '87. S. Hoffmann
Belfrage, S. Living with war. 1987
  N Y Times Book Rev 92:15 S 20 '87. J. Thomas
Bell, D. A. And we are not saved. 1987
  N Y Times Book Rev 92:7+ O 11 '87. V. Harding
  New Repub 197:36-9 N 16 '87. J. Rieder
Bell, M. S. The year of silence. 1987
  N Y Times Book Rev 92:15-16 N 15 '87. R. Silman
Bell, M. S. Zero db, and other stories. 1987
  N Y Times Book Rev 92:15 F 15 '87. A. Bernays
Bell, R. M. Holy anorexia. 1985
  New Repub 197:36-8 Ag 24 '87. J. Boswell
Bellow, S. More die of heartbreak. 1987
  Macleans 100:50 Je 22 '87. G. James
  N Y 20:72 Je 8 '87. R. Koenig
  N Y Rev Books 34:3-4 Jl 16 '87. A. Kazin
  N Y Times Book Rev 92:1+ My 24 '87. W. Gaddis
  Natl Rev 39:49-50 Jl 17 '87. J. Meyers
  New Repub 197:36-8 Ag 31 '87. L. Wieseltier
  New Yorker 63:89-91 Jl 20 '87. T. Rafferty
  Newsweek 109:79+ Je 8 '87. W. Clemons
  Progressive 51:30 N '87. G. Bluestein
  Time 129:71 Je 15 '87. P. Gray
  U S Cathol 52:48-51 N '87. G. M. Costello
Bely, A. The dramatic symphony; and, The forms of art. 1987
  N Y Times Book Rev 92:22 O 4 '87. A. Woronzoff
Ben Jelloun, T. The sand child. 1987
  N Y Times Book Rev 92:49 O 25 '87. B. Harlow
Bender, T. New York intellect. 1987
  N Y Times Book Rev 92:18-19 Jl 26 '87. R. Boyers
  Natl Rev 39:47-8 Jl 17 '87. D. Brooks
Benderly, B. L. The myth of two minds. 1987
  Psychol Today 21:66+ N '87. D. Cole
Benedict, P. Town smokes. 1987
  N Y Times Book Rev 92:13-14 Jl 12 '87. D. McWhorter
Beniger, J. R. The control revolution. 1986
  Science 236:970-2 My 22 '87. G. Porter
Benison, S. and others. Walter B. Cannon. 1987
  Science 237:542-3 Jl 31 '87. J. H. Warner
Bennett, G. Crimewarps. 1987
  Psychol Today 21:68 Je '87. M. Wells
Benoit, J. Running tide. 1987
  N Y Times Book Rev 92:28 N 1 '87. J. D. Cain
Bensman, D. and Lynch, R. Rusted dreams. 1987
  Commonweal 114:628-30 N 6 '87. E. Janeway
Bentley, E. Thinking about the playwright. 1987
  N Y Times Book Rev 92:21 Jl 5 '87. R. Bryden
Berg, A. and Schoenberg, A. The Berg-Schoenberg correspondence. 1986
  N Y Rev Books 34:30-3 N 5 '87. R. Craft
Berg, H. C. Random walks in biology. 1984
  Phys Today 40:73-4 Mr '87. F. J. Dyson
Berger, J. Once in Europa. 1987
  N Y Times Book Rev 92:9-10 Ap 5 '87. R. Critchfield
Berger, P. L. The capitalist revolution. 1986
  Christ Today 31:56 Jl 10 '87. D. Bandow
  Commentary 83:70-3 Ja '87. M. J. Ulmer
  Society 25:111-12 N/D '87. W. M. McCord
Berger, R. Federalism. 1987
  America 157:225-6 O 10 '87. O. Root
  Natl Rev 39:45-6 Ag 28 '87. G. W. Carey
  Wash Mon 19:59 S '87. D. Farber
Berger, T. Being invisible. 1987

N Y Times Book Rev 92:9 Ap 12 '87. F. Prose
Time 129:80+ Ap 27 '87. C. Porterfield
Bergmann, B. R. The economic emergence of women. 1986
  Fortune 115:135-6 Mr 2 '87. D. R. Henderson
Berkowitz, W. R. Local heroes. 1987
  Psychol Today 21:73+ N '87. E. Stark
Berman, M. Time capsule. 1987
  N Y Times Book Rev 92:38 Mr 22 '87. F. Howe
Bernard, K. The Maldive chronicles.
  N Y Times Book Rev 92:43 N 15 '87. L. G. Gordon
Bernstein, J. The life it brings. 1987
  N Y Times Book Rev 92:20 Ap 5 '87. D. G. Stork
Bernstein, M. H. Art and design at Alfred. 1986
  Am Craft 47:22-3 O/N '87. R. Barnard
Bernstein, R. B. and Rice, K. S. Are we to be a nation? 1987
  Cent Mag 20:39 Jl/Ag '87. D. McDonald
  N Y Times Book Rev 92:26 My 3 '87. M. Cunliffe
Bernstein, T. William Meyerowitz, the artist speaks. 1986
  Am Artist 51:91-2 D '87. C. Movalli
Berrigan, D. The Mission. 1986
  Christ Century 104:361-2 Ap 15 '87. D. J. Snider
Berry, C. Chuck Berry. 1987
  N Y Times Book Rev 92:13 O 18 '87. D. McLeese
Berry, M. F. Why ERA failed. 1986
  Nation 244:692+ My 23 '87. M. J. Collins
Berry, W. Home economics. 1987
  N Y Times Book Rev 92:30 S 27 '87. L. Hyde
  Wilderness 51:62-3 Fall '87. K. E. Franklin
Berryman, P. Liberation theology. 1987
  America 156:411-12 My 16 '87. A. T. Hennelly
  Christ Century 104:1040-1 N 18 '87. J. Leonard
  N Y Times Book Rev 92:15 Je 14 '87. A. Riding
  New Repub 196:31-6 My 4 '87. C. Coulson
Bertell, R. No immediate danger. 1985
  Technol Rev 90:75-6 Ap '87. B. Jacobs
Bertier de Sauvigny, G. de. Metternich. 1986
  Hist Today 37:57-8 Je '87. R. Elvin
Bettelheim, B. A good enough parent. 1987
  N Y Times Book Rev 92:3+ My 24 '87. B. Ehrenreich
  Psychol Today 21:66-7 D '87. D. Elkind
A Better start. 1986
  N Y Times Book Rev 92:31 Ja 25 '87. S. Mernit
Betts, R. K. Nuclear blackmail and nuclear balance. 1987
  Science 238:1447 D 4 '87. W. H. Donnelly
Bialer, S. The Soviet paradox. 1986
  Cent Mag 20:42-3 Mr/Ap '87. D. McDonald
  Commentary 83:17-27 My '87. N. Eberstadt
  Progressive 51:42-3 F '87. H. Fireside
  Society 24:82-4 S/O '87. V. Tismaneanu
Bickley, R. B. Joel Chandler Harris. 1987
  Nation 244:614+ My 9 '87. J. A. Miller
Bieder, R. E. Science encounters the Indian, 1820-1880. 1986
  Science 235:1409-10 Mr 13 '87. W. N. Fenton
Bienek, H. September light. 1987
  N Y Times Book Rev 92:35 F 22 '87. J. A. Snead
Bierhorst, J. Doctor Coyote. 1987
  N Y Times Book Rev 92:44 N 22 '87. G. B. Smith
Biermans, J. T. The odyssey of new religious movements. 1986
  Christ Century 104:862 O 7 '87. R. P. Scharlemann
"Binghamton" Geomorphology Symposium (17th: State University of New York at Binghamton). Aeolian geomorphology. 1986
  Science 236:1126-7 My 29 '87. N. Lancaster
Binkin, M. Military technology and defense manpower. 1986
  Technol Rev 90:76-7 Ap '87. W. Rosenau
Biography as high adventure. 1986
  USA Today (Periodical) 115:94 Ja '87. S. G. Kellman
Biology of fertilization; v1, Model systems and oogenesis. 1985
  BioScience 37:745 N '87. R. A. Wallace
Biology of fertilization; v3, The fertilization response of the egg. 1985
  BioScience 37:745-6 N '87. N. H. Hart
The Biology of marine fungi. 1986
  Science 237:543-4 Jl 31 '87. I. K. Ross
The Biology of the actinomycetes. 1984
  BioScience 37:78-9 Ja '87. B. Mullin
Biotechnology. 1985
  BioScience 37:289 Ap '87. K. Sauber
Birch, D. L. Job creation in America. 1987
  Fortune 116:177-8 D 21 '87. R. I. Kirkland, Jr.
Birkerts, S. An artificial wilderness. 1987
  N Y Times Book Rev 92:16 N 8 '87. D. Hall
Birmingham, S. America's secret aristocracy. 1987
  N Y Times Book Rev 92:24 S 27 '87. E. D. Baltzell

Birnbaum, J. H. and Murray, A. S. Showdown at Gucci Gulch. 1987
  Bus Week p14-15 Jl 6 '87. H. Gleckman
  Commentary 84:76-8 O '87. R. Brookhiser
  Fortune 116:116-18 Jl 20 '87. I. Ross
  N Y Times Book Rev 92:9 Jl 5 '87. R. Lekachman
  Wash Mon 19:52-6 Je '87. P. Glastris
Bishop, J. Joyce's book of the dark, Finnegans wake. 1986
  N Y Times Book Rev 92:14-15 Ja 18 '87. R. M. Adams
Bitburg and beyond. 1987
  Christ Century 104:1008-9 N 11 '87. A. R. Eckardt
Bitov, A. Pushkin house. 1987
  N Y Rev Books 34:9-10 O 22 '87. J. Bayley
  New Leader 70:6-7 D 14 '87. J. Woll
Black, E. and Black, M. Politics and society in the South. 1987
  N Y Rev Books 34:7-9 Je 11 '87. C. V. Woodward
Blackmur, R. P. Selected essays of R.P. Blackmur. 1986
  N Y Rev Books 34:28-30 My 7 '87. M. Wood
Blainey, G. Surrender Australia?
  Hist Today 37:58-9 Ja '87. G. Bolton
Blais, M. C. Deaf to the city. 1987
  N Y Times Book Rev 92:12-13 S 20 '87. P. West
Blinder, A. S. Hard heads, soft hearts. 1987
  Fortune 116:185+ N 9 '87. D. R. Henderson
  N Y Times Book Rev 92:30 O 25 '87. R. Lekachman
Bliss, M. Northern enterprise. 1987
  Macleans 100:49-50 My 25 '87. P. Best
Blitzer, W. Between Washington and Jerusalem. 1985
  America 156:59 Ja 24 '87. C. M. Kulwin
Bloch, E. Natural law and human dignity. 1986
  Cent Mag 20:38-9 Mr/Ap '87. D. McDonald
Bloch, E. The principle of hope. 3v 1986
  Christ Century 104:416-18 Ap 29 '87. T. Peters
  New Repub 196:38-42 Mr 9 '87. J. P. Stern
Bloch, E. M. The paintings of George Caleb Bingham. 1986
  Am Artist 51:24+ N '87. M. C. Nelson
Bloom, A. Prodigal sons. 1986
  Society 25:105-7 N/D '87. D. Wrong
Bloom, A. D. The closing of the American mind. 1987
  Christ Today 31:67-8 N 20 '87. G. N. Schram
  Commonweal 114:422-3 Jl 17 '87. D. O'Brien
  Humanist 47:44 N/D '87. M. Hillar
  Macleans 100:45 Jl 27 '87. T. Manson
  N Y Rev Books 34:20-6 N 5 '87. M. C. Nussbaum
  N Y Times Book Rev 92:7 Ap 5 '87. R. Kimball
  Nation 244:710-16+ My 30 '87. R. Pattison
  Natl Rev 39:34-8 O 9 '87
  Natl Rev 39:51-3 Ap 24 '87. J. Sobran
  New Leader 70:17-18 Je 29 '87. R. G. Davis
  New Repub 196:38-41 My 25 '87. L. Menand
  Psychol Today 21:70-1 Ag '87. A. Kohn
  Read Dig 131:81-4 O '87. R. K. Bennett
  Society 25:98-101 N/D '87. H. J. Graff
  Wash Mon 19:49-53 S '87. J. Weisberg
Blotnick, S. Ambitious men. 1987
  Psychol Today 21:70 Je '87. D. Heller
Blueschists and eclogites. 1986
  Science 235:491-2 Ja 23 '87. W. G. Ernst
Blum, C. Rousseau and the republic of virtue. 1986
  New Repub 196:36-40 Mr 2 '87. J. N. Shklar
Blum, H. I pledge allegiance. 1987
  N Y 20:106 O 19 '87. R. Koenig
  N Y Rev Books 34:24 N 19 '87. M. Kempton
  N Y Times Book Rev 92:11 O 11 '87. J. A. Lukas
Blume, J. Just as long as we're together. 1987
  N Y Times Book Rev 92:33 N 8 '87. J. Humphreys
Blumenthal, S. The rise of the counter-establishment. 1986
  Bull At Sci 43:45-7 Ap '87. S. W. Van Evera
  Commonweal 114:113-16 F 27 '87. F. F. Siegel
  New Leader 69:19-20 D 1-15 '86. D. M. Oshinsky
Bobrick, B. Fearful majesty. 1987
  N Y Times Book Rev 92:60 N 8 '87. A. J. Rieber
Bock, R. D. and Moore, E. G. J. Advantage and disadvantage. 1986
  Science 236:204-5 Ap 10 '87. J. Catterall
Bockstoce, J. R. Whales, ice, and men. 1986
  Oceans 20:58-60 Ja/F '87. R. Ellis
  Sea Front 33:234-5 My/Je '87. G. L. Voss
Boesak, A. A. Comfort and protest. 1987
  Christ Century 104:1006-7 N 11 '87. P. Nelson
Boesche, R. The strange liberalism of Alexis de Tocqueville. 1987
  Atlantic 260:80-3 Ag '87. S. Wolin
Boff, L. The maternal face of God. 1987
  Christ Century 104:560 Je 17-24 '87. A. Carr
Bok, D. C. Higher learning. 1986
  America 157:42-3 Jl 18-25 '87. G. C. Hentschke

Change 19:50-2 Ja/F '87. W. J. McKeachie
Boland, E. The journey and other poems. 1987
  N Y Times Book Rev 92:23 Mr 22 '87. A. Libby
Böll, H. The casualty. 1987
  N Y Times Book Rev 92:29 Ag 23 '87. R. A. Berman
Bolt, B. A. Earthquakes. 1987
  Earth Sci 40:30-1 Wint '87
Bombeck, E. Family. 1987
  N Y Times Book Rev 92:7 S 20 '87. J. Viorst
Bongie, L. L. The love of a prince. 1986
  Hist Today 37:59-60 Jl '87. A. I. Macinnes
Bonin, B. Ring complex granites and anorogenic magmatism. 1986
  Science 235:1091 F 27 '87. J. Gittins
Bonner, A. Among the Afghans. 1987
  N Y Times Book Rev 92:17 N 8 '87. D. Manuel
Bonner, E. Alone together. 1986
  New Repub 196:33-7 F 16 '87. P. Reddaway
  New Yorker 62:88-91 Ja 19 '87. J. Updike
Bonner, R. Waltzing with a dictator. 1987
  Bus Week p10-11 Ag 10 '87. G. G. Marcial
  Commentary 84:68+ O '87. G. Russell
  N Y Rev Books 34:24-7 Ag 13 '87. I. Buruma
  N Y Times Book Rev 92:1+ My 17 '87. R. H. Ullman
  Nation 245:22-4 Jl 4-11 '87. J. Conason
  Newsweek 109:82 Je 8 '87. T. Jacoby
  Wash Mon 19:53-6 S '87. J. M. Fallows
Bonomi, P. U. Under the cope of heaven. 1986
  Christ Century 104:314-15 Ap 1 '87. M. E. Marty
  New Repub 197:39-41 Ag 3 '87. J. P. Diggins
Bookchin, M. The rise of urbanization and the decline of citizenship. 1987
  N Y Times Book Rev 92:18 N 8 '87. R. Bender
Bookplates in the news, 1970-1985. 1986
  Am Artist 51:42 N '87. F. Johnson
Booth, A. The roads to Sata. 1986
  Smithsonian 18:224-6 O '87. J. D. Kirwan
Bordering on trouble. 1986
  Sierra 72:103-6 N/D '87. J. Karliner
Bordin, R. Frances Willard. 1986
  Christ Century 104:860 O 7 '87. A.-C. Carls
Bordman, G. M. American musical theatre. 1986
  Smithsonian 18:143-5 Jl '87. D. Drabelle
Borgeson, G. Errett Lobban Cord. 1984
  Mot Trend 39:38 S '87
Boris, E. Art and labor. 1986
  Am Craft 47:14+ F/Mr '87. C. Lynn
Borodin, L. Partings. 1987
  N Y Rev Books 34:9-10 O 22 '87. J. Bayley
  N Y Times Book Rev 92:30 O 4 '87. D. M. Thomas
Borsi, F. and Godoli, E. Vienna 1900. 1986
  Archit Rec 175:75+ Mr '87. S. Gutterman
Borysenko, J. Minding the body, mending the mind. 1987
  Psychol Today 21:68 D '87. L. Miller
Bosker, G. and Lencek, L. Frozen music. 1985
  Archit Rec 175:59 Ap '87. D. Gantenbein
Boskin, J. Sambo. 1986
  N Y Times Book Rev 92:8 Ja 4 '87. R. G. O'Meally
Boswell, J. Boswell, the English experiment, 1785-1789. 1986
  Smithsonian 18:172+ My '87. M. Dirda
Boswell, R. Crooked hearts. 1987
  N Y Times Book Rev 92:12 Jl 5 '87. S. S. Stark
  New Yorker 63:71-2 Ag 17 '87. W. Balliett
Bottigheimer, R. B. Grimms' bad girls & bold boys. 1987
  N Y Rev Books 34:22-4 D 3 '87. J. A. Smith
Bottles, S. L. Los Angeles and the automobile. 1987
  Wash Mon 19:57-8 N '87. T. Noah
Boudriot, J. The seventy-four gun ship. 2v 1986
  Oceans 20:60-1 Jl/Ag '87. B. N. Powell
Bourjaily, V. N. The great fake book. 1986
  N Y Times Book Rev 92:35 Ja 18 '87. R. P. Brickner
Bourne, J. M. Patronage and society in nineteenth-century England. 1986
  Hist Today 37:56-7 F '87. G. Finlayson
Bourne, P. G. Fidel. 1986
  Commentary 83:69-71 F '87. L. E. Aguilar
  Natl Rev 39:48-50 F 13 '87. T. Bethell
  Progressive 51:38-40 Ja '87. S. Landau
Bouvier, N. The scorpion-fish. 1987
  N Y Times Book Rev 92:18 S 27 '87. S. Vogan
Bowden, C. Frog Mountain blues. 1987
  Wilderness 50:58 Summ '87. D. Drabelle
Bowen, H. R. and Schuster, J. H. American professors. 1986
  America 157:43-5 Jl 18-25 '87. A. J. Hamilton
Bowman, A. K. Egypt after the pharaohs. 1986
  Hist Today 37:55 S '87. S. Price
Boyd, J. M. Fraser Darling's islands. 1986
  Science 236:1360 Je 5 '87. P. Marler
Boyer, E. L. College. 1987

N Y Times Book Rev 92:26-7 Mr 8 '87. P. Brooks
USA Today (Periodical) 116:96 Jl '87. F. Cordasco
Boyer, P. S. By the bomb's early light. 1987
Natl Rev 39:54-5 Mr 27 '87. T. Doherty
Phys Today 40:123-4 O '87. P. L. Cantelon
Boyle, T. C. World's end. 1987
N Y Times Book Rev 92:1+ S 27 '87. B. DeMott
Bozell, L. B. Mustard seeds.
Natl Rev 39:45-6 Je 5 '87. K. Lynch
Brackman, A. C. The other Nuremberg. 1987
N Y Times Book Rev 92:12 Ap 5 '87. G. Smith
Bradbury, M. Cuts. 1987
N Y Times Book Rev 92:9 O 18 '87. L. Moore
New Repub 197:38+ D 14 '87. A. Hulbert
Bradley, G. Terms to be met. 1986
N Y Times Book Rev 92:26 Mr 1 '87. J. Ash
Bradley, M. Z. The firebrand. 1987
N Y Times Book Rev 92:27 N 29 '87. M. R. Lefkowitz
Brainerd, J. W. The nature observer's handbook. 1986
Conservationist 41:52 My/Je '87. F. Knight
Brand, S. The Media Lab. 1987
N Y Times Book Rev 92:38 S 27 '87. L. Hunter
Brandt, W. Arms and hunger. 1986
Bull At Sci 43:54-6 Mr '87. K. Braden
Cent Mag 20:31-2 Ja/F '87. D. McDonald
Branley, F. M. Star guide. 1987
Earth Sci 40:35-6 Fall '87
Brans, J. Mother, I have something to tell you. 1987
Child Today 16:32-inside back cover My/Je '87. F. V. Mannino
N Y Times Book Rev 92:29 Ja 25 '87. C. Carmichael
Psychol Today 21:68-9 Je '87. P. Hersch
Bratko, I. Prolog programming for artificial intelligence. 1986
Byte 12:81-2+ Ag '87. A. Lane
Braudy, L. The frenzy of renown. 1987
Harpers 274:72+ Je '87. C. Romano
Breckenridge, J. Civil blood. 1986
N Y Times Book Rev 92:22+ Ja 4 '87. E. Grosholz
Brent, R. Liberal Anglican politics. 1987
Hist Today 37:56 O '87. E. Norman
Breslin, C. First ladies. 1987
Ms 16:32+ Jl/Ag '87. J. Mann
N Y Times Book Rev 92:12 Je 14 '87. A. McCarthy
Brett, G. Through our own eyes. 1986
Art Am 75:25+ O '87. Y.-A. Bois
Nation 244:184-6 F 14 '87. F. Pfeil
Brewin, B. and Shaw, S. Vietnam on trial. 1987
N Y Times Book Rev 92:13 Ap 5 '87. K. Evans
Breytenbach, B. End papers. 1986
Natl Rev 39:60-1 Ap 24 '87. J. Hart
Brians, P. Nuclear holocausts. 1986
Bull At Sci 43:45-6 D '87. R. Hostetter
Bridgers, S. E. Permanent connections. 1987
N Y Times Book Rev 92:21 Jl 26 '87. H. Rochman
Brimblecombe, P. The big smoke. 1987
Sci Am 257:112 Ag '87. P. Morrison
Brimelow, P. The patriot game. 1987
Fortune 116:217+ N 23 '87. D. R. Henderson
British Society for Developmental Biology. Symposium (8th: 1983: Nottingham, England). A history of embryology. 1986
Science 236:1475 Je 12 '87. K. R. Benson
Britton, J. A. Carleton Beals. 1987
Nation 245:759-61 D 19 '87. G. Black
Broch, H. The spell. 1986
N Y Times Book Rev 92:31 Ja 25 '87. E. Heller
Broder, D. S. Behind the front page. 1987
N Y Times Book Rev 92:14 Ap 26 '87. T. Griffith
Natl Rev 39:42-3 Je 5 '87. J. Sobran
New Repub 196:41-2 Je 29 '87. J. Weisberg
Brodrick, J. The progress of the Jesuits (1556-79). 1986
Christ Century 104:1152 D 16 '87. J. Hitchcock
Brodsky, J. Less than one. 1986
Am Sch 56:298-301 Spr '87. G. S. Morson
Brodsky, M. Xman. 1987
N Y Times Book Rev 92:31 N 15 '87. H. Marten
Broido, V. Lenin and the Mensheviks. 1987
Hist Today 37:58-9 O '87. W. V. Wallace
Brolin, B. C. Flight of fancy. 1985
Am Craft 47:18 Je/Jl '87. R. Jensen
Brook, P. The shifting point—1946-1987. 1987
N Y Times Book Rev 92:15 O 18 '87. F. H. King
New Leader 70:11-12 D 14 '87. J. Simon
Brookner, A. The misalliance. 1987
N Y Times Book Rev 92:10 Mr 29 '87. F. Eberstadt
Vogue 177:322+ Mr '87. M. Cantwell
Brooks, B. Midnight hour encores. 1986
N Y Times Book Rev 92:33 Ja 4 '87. K. Rile
Brooks, C. The language of the American South. 1985
N Y Rev Books 34:38-41 My 7 '87. M. K. Spears

Brooks, C. W. Pettyfoggers and vipers of the Commonwealth. 1986
Hist Today 37:57-8 Ap '87. R. O'Day
Brooks, J. The takeover game. 1987
Bus Week p17-18 S 21 '87. A. Bianco
N Y Times Book Rev 92:28 O 25 '87. S. B. Shepard
Brown, D. A. Conspiracy of knaves. 1987
N Y Times Book Rev 92:12-13 Ja 11 '87. T. J. Fleming
Brown, D. W. Biblical pacifism. 1986
Christ Century 104:386-7 Ap 22 '87. A. Geyer
Brown, G. M. A time to keep, and other stories. 1987
N Y Times Book Rev 92:9 Mr 22 '87. S. Gordon
Brown, J. Velazquez, painter and courtier. 1986
America 157:308-10 O 31 '87. E. Van Schaack
Brown, J. L. Helping and communal breeding in birds. 1987
Science 238:697-8 O 30 '87. P. W. Ewald
Brown, J. L. and Pizer, H. Living hungry in America. 1987
N Y Times Book Rev 92:20 N 15 '87. T. Clarke
Brown, L. R. State of the world, 1987. 1987
Sierra 72:92-4 Mr/Ap '87. M. Philips
Brown, R. The mariner's trivia book. 1986
Sea Front 33:152 Mr/Ap '87. F. G. W. Smith
Brown, R. E. Biblical exegesis and church doctrine. 1985
Commonweal 114:22-3 Ja 16 '87. P. Perkins
Browne, A. When battered women kill. 1987
Psychol Today 21:78 Ag '87. P. J. Black
Browning, D. S. Religious thought and the modern psychologies. 1987
America 157:141 S 12-19 '87. E. F. Block, Jr.
Commonweal 114:505-6 S 11 '87. E. Fontinell
Bruce, R. V. The launching of modern American science, 1846-1876. 1987
N Y Rev Books 34:17-20 N 19 '87. D. Joravsky
N Y Times Book Rev 92:26-7 My 17 '87. R. Williams
Science 237:1515-16 S 18 '87. L. D. Stephens
Brucker, G. A. Giovanni and Lusanna. 1986
N Y Times Book Rev 92:7 F 1 '87. A. B. Giamatti
Brucker, R. W. and Watson, R. A. The longest cave. 1987
Earth Sci 40:34-6 Summ '87
Bruckner, P. The tears of the white man. 1986
Commentary 83:70-1 Ap '87. S. McConnell
Commonweal 114:533-6 S 25 '87. S. Englund
Brunette, P. Roberto Rossellini. 1987
N Y Times Book Rev 92:42 S 13 '87. M. D'Amico
Bruns, R. The damndest radical. 1987
N Y Times Book Rev 92:17 F 1 '87. P. Clinton
Progressive 51:30 S '87. A. Weinberg
Brush, S. G. and Landsberg, H. E. The history of geophysics and meteorology. 1985
Phys Today 40:109 F '87. W. K. Wootters
Bryan, T. S. The geysers of Yellowstone. 1986
Sci Am 257:148 D '87. P. Morrison and P. Morrison
Bryson, J. Evil angels. 1987
N Y Times Book Rev 92:43 Mr 22 '87. L. Wolfe
Buch, H. C. The wedding at Port-au-Prince. 1987
New Leader 70:14-15 F 9-23 '87. S. Rodman
Buchanan, E. The corpse had a familiar face. 1987
N Y Times Book Rev 92:23 D 13 '87. A. Rice
Buchanan, R. and McCauley, J. R. Roadside Kansas. 1987
Earth Sci 40:34-5 Fall '87
Buck, J. J. Daughter of the swan. 1987
N Y Times Book Rev 92:14 O 4 '87. W. J. Harding
Vogue 177:470 S '87. E. R. Lipson
Buckley, W. F. Racing through paradise. 1987
N Y Times Book Rev 92:34 My 31 '87. T. Foote
Natl Rev 39:44+ Jl 31 '87. H. Kenner
Time 129:72 Je 15 '87. R. Z. Sheppard
Buechner, F. Brendan. 1987
N Y Times Book Rev 92:15 Ag 9 '87. J. O'Faolain
Buell, L. New England literary culture. 1986
Hist Today 37:52 Ag '87. M. Cunliffe
Buhle, P. Marxism in the United States. 1987
Nation 244:894-7 Je 27 '87. N. Xenos
Bui, D. In the jaws of history. 1987
N Y Times Book Rev 92:16 S 13 '87. A. Tonelson
The Building systems integration handbook. 1986
Archit Rec 175:73+ F '87. A. Fisher
Bullock, D. K. Marine gamefish of the middle Atlantic. 1986
Sea Front 33:233-4 My/Je '87. D. P. De Sylva
Bunting, E. Ghost's hour, spook's hour. 1987
N Y Times Book Rev 92:36 N 15 '87. A. Banks
Burdon, J. J. Diseases and plant population biology. 1987
Science 238:221 O 9 '87. A. H. Purcell and S. E. Lindow
Burg, S. L. Conflict and cohesion in socialist Yugoslavia. 1983
Society 24:95-6 Ja/F '87. S. Zukin

The Burger years. 1987
 N Y Times Book Rev 92:18-19 Je 21 '87. R. A.
 Smolla
 Wash Mon 19:52-4 My '87. D. Farber
Burgess, A. Little Wilson and big God. 1986
 America 157:20-1 Jl 4-11 '87. I. C. Todd
 N Y Rev Books 34:3+ My 7 '87. G. Vidal
 N Y Times Book Rev 92:9 F 22 '87. R. Davies
 Time 129:70 F 16 '87. P. Gray
Burke, J. G. Cosmic debris. 1986
 Sci Am 256:24-5 My '87. P. Morrison
 Science 235:1681 Mr 27 '87. U. B. Marvin
 Sky Telesc 73:618-19 Je '87. D. W. Hughes
Burnett, C. One more time. 1986
 N Y Rev Books 33:37-9 Ja 15 '87. M. Haskell
Burnshaw, S. Robert Frost himself. 1986
 Natl Rev 39:56-7 Ap 24 '87. T. P. McDonnell
Burrows, W. E. Deep black. 1986
 Commentary 83:77-80 My '87. A. M. Codevilla
 N Y Times Book Rev 92:14-15 F 15 '87. J. Newhouse
 Sci Am 256:22-3 My '87. P. Morrison
Burton, R. and others. Eggs. 1987
 Sci Am 257:155-6 D '87. P. Morrison and P. Morrison
Busch, A. The photography of architecture. 1987
 Archit Rec 175:77 Ag '87. S. Gutterman
Bush, G. Looking forward. 1987
 Wash Mon 19:57 N '87. W. Shapiro
Butcher, L. Accidental millionaire. 1987
 N Y Times Book Rev 92:32-3 O 25 '87. J. Taylor
Buttenwieser, P. Their pride and joy. 1987
 N Y Times Book Rev 92:9+ O 4 '87. J. Conarroe
Butzel, H. M. Genetics in the courts. 1987
 Science 238:969 N 13 '87. S. L. Carter
By no extraordinary means. 1986
 Christ Century 104:447-8 My 6 '87. D. J. Snyder
Byatt, A. S. Sugar and other stories. 1987
 N Y Times Book Rev 92:5 Jl 19 '87. L. S. Schwartz
Bynum, C. W. Holy feast and holy fast. 1986
 Christ Century 104:507 My 20-27 '87. W. T. Foley
 N Y Rev Books 34:42-4 O 8 '87. M. H. Keen
 N Y Times Book Rev 92:26 Ap 5 '87. J. Freccero
 New Repub 197:36-8 Ag 24 '87. J. Boswell

C

Cadbury, W. H. Arthur Fitzwilliam Tait. 1986
 Am Artist 51:36+ Ap '87. M. C. Nelson
Cadogan, P. H. From quark to quasar. 1985
 Astronomy 15:44-6 Mr '87. G. O. Clark
Cady, S. and others. Sophia. 1986
 Christ Century 104:889 O 14 '87. D. W. Ferm
Cain, B. E. and others. The personal vote. 1986
 Wash Mon 19:57-8 Jl/Ag '87. D. R. Mayhew
Calcium in biological systems. 1985
 BioScience 37:523-4 Jl/Ag '87. D. J. Triggle
Caldwell, E. With all my might. 1987
 N Y Times Book Rev 92:18 My 10 '87. D. Kaufman
Caldwell, F. E. Land of the ocean mists. 1986
 Oceans 20:58 Ja/F '87. B. Matsen
A Calendar of the correspondence of Charles Darwin,
 1821-1882. 1983
 New Yorker 63:171-2+ D 7 '87. D. J. Kevles
Calisher, H. Age. 1987
 N Y Times Book Rev 92:14 O 18 '87. T. Mallon
Callahan, D. Setting limits. 1987
 N Y Times Book Rev 92:7 S 27 '87. E. E. Shelp
 New Leader 70:17 N 16 '87. B. Gewen
Calleo, D. P. Beyond American hegemony. 1987
 N Y Times Book Rev 92:11 N 1 '87. P. M. Kennedy
Calvin, W. H. The river that flows uphill. 1986
 Smithsonian 17:128-9 Ja '87. D. Lessem
 Wilderness 50:57 Spr '87. C. E. Little
Camazine, S. The naturalist's year. 1987
 Sci Am 257:156-7 D '87. P. Morrison and P. Morrison
The Cambridge history of Africa; v7, From 1905 to 1940.
 1986
 Hist Today 37:58 Mr '87. J. D. Hargreaves
Campbell, B. M. Successful women, angry men. 1987
 U S Cathol 52:48-9 S '87. G. M. Costello
Campbell, C. Managing the presidency. 1986
 America 156:467-8 Je 6 '87. J. P. Burke
Campbell, J. Winston Churchill's afternoon nap. 1986
 N Y Times Book Rev 92:14-15 Mr 8 '87. F. Gonzalez-
 Crussi
Campbell, J. Aneurin Bevan and the mirage of British
 socialism. 1987
 N Y Times Book Rev 92:22 S 13 '87. K. Harris
Campbell, S. Widower. 1987
 Psychol Today 21:72-3 O '87. D. Cole
Campbell, W. D. Forty acres and a goat. 1986
 Christ Century 104:89-90 Ja 28 '87. M. A. Marty

Progressive 51:30-1 Ag '87. F. Gaillard
Campolo, A. Who switched the price tags? 1986
 Christ Today 31:38-9 F 20 '87. L. Sibley
Cancer in atomic bomb survivors. 1986
 Science 236:99 Ap 3 '87. J. W. Hollingsworth
Canemaker, J. Winsor McCay, his life and art. 1987
 Am Herit 38:34 S/O '87
 N Y Times Book Rev 92:16 D 6 '87. L. Maltin
 Smithsonian 18:262-4 N '87. G. Weales
Cantor, N. L. Legal frontiers of death and dying. 1987
 America 157:362-4 N 14 '87. M. B. Mahowald
Capitel, A. and Solà-Morales Rubió, I. Contemporary
 Spanish architecture. 1986
 Archit Rec 175:75 Mr '87. D. N. Cohn
Caplan, L. The tenth justice. 1987
 N Y Times Book Rev 92:13 O 25 '87. M. E. Price
Capote, T. Answered prayers. 1986
 N Y Rev Books 34:3+ D 17 '87. J. Richardson
 N Y Times Book Rev 92:13 S 13 '87. T. Brown
 New Repub 197:30-3 D 21 '87. R. Poirier
 New Yorker 63:113-16+ S 21 '87. T. Rafferty
 Time 130:65-6 S 7 '87. R. Z. Sheppard
Capote, T. A Capote reader. 1986
 N Y Rev Books 34:3+ D 17 '87. J. Richardson
 New Repub 197:30-3 D 21 '87. R. Poirier
 Time 130:65-6 S 7 '87. R. Z. Sheppard
Caputo, P. Indian country. 1987
 N Y Times Book Rev 92:7 My 17 '87. F. Conroy
Caring and curing. 1986
 Christ Century 104:864 O 7 '87. W. A. Johnson
Carmen, I. H. Cloning and the Constitution. 1985
 BioScience 37:285-6 Ap '87. F. E. Sharples
Carnegie, T. Indy 500. 1986
 Mot Trend 39:52 Je '87. T. C. Browne
Carney, R. American vision. 1986
 America 157:117 Ag 29-S 5 '87. N. P. Hurley
Caroe, G. M. The Royal Institution. 1985
 Phys Today 40:69-70 Jl '87. L. Badash
Caroli, B. B. First ladies. 1987
 Wash Mon 19:59-60 O '87. S. Fields
Carosso, V. P. Morgans. 1987
 N Y Times Book Rev 92:18 Ap 5 '87. M. Mayer
Carpenter, L. Getting better all the time. 1987
 N Y Times Book Rev 92:10 Ag 2 '87. J. O'Reilly
Carpini, M. X. D. Stability and change in American politics.
 1986
 America 156:387-8 My 9 '87. R. McAulay
Carrière, J.-C. The Mahabharata. 1987
 New Leader 70:11-12 D 14 '87. J. Simon
Carroll, J. Forced entries. 1987
 N Y Times Book Rev 92:8 Ag 2 '87. M. Stevens
 Vogue 177:110 Jl '87. M. Jefferson
Carroll, J. Supply of heroes. 1986
 U S Cathol 52:48-51 Ag '87. G. M. Costello
Carroll, M. P. The cult of the Virgin Mary. 1986
 Commonweal 114:569-70 O 9 '87. L. S. Cunningham
 New Repub 196:37-9 Je 15 '87. J. Boswell
Carruth, H. Sitting in. 1986
 Down Beat 54:59 My '87. W. Corbett
Carse, J. P. Finite and infinite games. 1986
 N Y Times Book Rev 92:32 Ap 12 '87. F. Kane
Carter, A. Saints and strangers. 1986
 N Y Rev Books 34:15-16 F 26 '87. D. J. Enright
Carter, D. S. His majesty, Queen Hatshepsut. 1987
 N Y Times Book Rev 92:20 D 20 '87. J. A. West
Carter, G. and Hough, J. T. A dream season. 1987
 N Y Times Book Rev 92:14 My 3 '87. J. Oppenheimer
Carter, J. and Carter, R. Everything to gain. 1987
 N Y Times Book Rev 92:16+ My 31 '87. L. C. Pogrebin
 U S Cathol 52:48-51 O '87. G. M. Costello
Cartiér, X. W. Be-bop, re-bop.
 N Y Times Book Rev 92:12 D 13 '87. V. Smith
Carver, R. Ultramarine. 1987
 N Y Times Book Rev 92:15 Je 7 '87. P. Hampl
Cash, A. H. Laurence Sterne, the later years. 1986
 N Y Rev Books 34:29-31 Mr 26 '87. J. Bayley
 N Y Times Book Rev 92:13 Ja 11 '87. M. Byrd
Cassedy, J. H. Medicine and American growth, 1800-1860.
 1986
 Science 236:981-2 My 22 '87. A. E. Cowdrey
Cassini, O. In my own fashion. 1987
 N Y Times Book Rev 92:5-6 S 6 '87. M. Haskell
Castro, F. and Betto, Frei. Fidel and religion. 1987
 N Y Times Book Rev 92:15 Je 14 '87. A. Riding
 Natl Rev 39:48-9 Jl 3 '87. J. Sobran
 New Repub 196:31-6 My 4 '87. C. Coulson
Cateura, L. Growing up Italian. 1987
 N Y Times Book Rev 92:30 Mr 1 '87. R. D. Heffner
Cather, W. Early novels and stories. 1987
 New Repub 197:38-41 Ag 24 '87. P. K. Bell
 Smithsonian 18:146+ Je '87. B. Allen

The Catholic challenge to the American economy. 1987
 Christ Century 104:562 Je 17-24 '87. J. P. Wogaman
Cattermole, M. J. G. and Wolfe, A. F. Horace Darwin's
 shop. 1987
 Science 237:783 Ag 14 '87. D. B. Wilson
Caught looking. 1988
 Nation 244:153 F 7 '87. M. Margaronis
Cave Brown, A. "C". 1987
 N Y Times Book Rev 92:5-6 D 27 '87. K. Follett
CD ROM; v2, Optical publishing. 1987
 Byte 12:81-2+ S '87. P. Hoffman
Cecil Beaton, a retrospective. 1986
 Art Am 75:15-17+ Ja '87. D. Bourdon
**Cell culture and somatic cell genetics of plants; v1,
 Laboratory procedures and their applications.** 1984
 BioScience 37:78 Ja '87. J. L. Caruso
Central America and the Reagan doctrine. 1987
 Natl Rev 39:68 S 11 '87. C. Williamson
The Central American crisis reader. 1987
 Nation 244:855-7 Je 20 '87. P. Anderson
**Cetus-UCLA Symposium on Yeast Cell Biology (1985:
 Keystone, Colo.).** Yeast cell biology. 1986
 Science 235:374 Ja 16 '87. R. C. Dickson
Chadwick, O. Britain and the Vatican during the Second
 World War. 1986
 America 157:276-7 O 24 '87. R. E. Sullivan
 Natl Rev 39:48-9 Je 19 '87. J. Sobran
Chafuen, A. A. Christians for freedom. 1986
 Natl Rev 39:47-8 Ag 28 '87. T. Bethell
Chance, P. Thinking in the classroom. 1986
 Phi Delta Kappan 68:403-4 Ja '87. B. B. Hudgins
**Changes in eukaryotic gene expression in response to
 environmental stress.** 1985
 BioScience 37:75 Ja '87. P. E. Barker
The Changing Samoans. 1986
 Science 237:87-8 Jl 3 '87. P. J. Byard
Chaplin, P. Albany Park. 1987
 N Y Times Book Rev 92:18 Ag 2 '87. I. Kurtz
Chapman, A. B. Man sharing. 1986
 Psychol Today 21:75 Mr '87. P. Knight
Chapman, G. C. Facing the nuclear heresy. 1986
 Christ Century 104:415-16 Ap 29 '87. M. D. Wilde
Chapman, W. Inside the Philippine revolution. 1987
 N Y Times Book Rev 92:7 O 4 '87. P. H. Kreisberg
 Wash Mon 19:53-6 S '87. J. M. Fallows
Chappell, F. The Fred Chappell reader. 1987
 Natl Rev 39:61-3 N 20 '87. J. O. Tate
Charters, S. B. Louisiana black. 1986
 N Y Times Book Rev 92:22 Ja 11 '87. W. R. Ferris
Charyn, J. Paradise man. 1987
 N Y Times Book Rev 92:11 Mr 29 '87. R. D. Rosen
Chase, A. Playing God in Yellowstone. 1986
 BioScience 37:133-4 F '87. D. T. Patten
Chatwin, B. The songlines. 1987
 Commonweal 114:684+ N 20 '87. M. Wimsatt
 N Y 20:46 Jl 20 '87. R. Koenig
 N Y Times Book Rev 92:1+ Ag 2 '87. A. Harvey
 New Repub 197:36-9 N 30 '87. D. Rieff
 Time 130:59+ Ag 24 '87. R. Z. Sheppard
Cheever, S. Doctors & women. 1987
 N Y Times Book Rev 92:16 Je 28 '87. S. Kenney
Chelminski, R. Superwreck. 1987
 N Y Times Book Rev 92:27 Mr 29 '87. J. Maxtone-
 Graham
Cheney, D. P. and Mumford, T. F. Shellfish & seaweed
 harvests of Puget Sound. 1986
 Sea Front 33:315 Jl/Ag '87. E. S. Iversen
Cheng, N. Life and death in Shanghai. 1987
 Ms 15:22+ Je '87. M. B. Young
 N Y Rev Books 34:5-6+ Jl 16 '87. J. Shapiro
 N Y Times Book Rev 92:9+ My 31 '87. J. M. Coetzee
 New Repub 197:37-8 Ag 10-17 '87. M. Goldman
 Vogue 177:114+ Je '87. M. Cantwell
Cheo, P. K. Fiber optics. 1985
 Phys Today 40 pt1:72 Ag '87. A. H. Cherin
Cherniak, C. Minimal rationality. 1986
 Technol Rev 90:75-6 N/D '87. J. Rubin
Chernobyl: the end of the nuclear dream. 1987
 Cent Mag 20:36 Jl/Ag '87. D. McDonald
 Humanist 47:46 My/Je '87. M. Irwin
Chess, S. and Thomas, A. Know your child. 1987
 Psychol Today 21:66-7 D '87. D. Elkind
Chesterton, G. K. Daylight and nightmare. 1986
 Natl Rev 39:53 Ag 14 '87. J. E. Person, Jr.
Chief of staff. 1986
 Commonweal 114:394 Je 19 '87. F. Rotondaro
**Chilam Balam de Chumayel (Manuscript). English &
 Mayan.** Heaven born Merida and its destiny. 1986
 Science 236:1004-5 My 22 '87. D. A. Freidel
Child development and education in Japan. 1986
 Science 236:205-6 Ap 10 '87. T. S. Lebra

Chisman, F. P. and Pifer, A. J. Government for the
 people. 1987
 N Y Times Book Rev 92:48 O 25 '87. C. R. Morris
Choate, P. and Linger, J. K. The high-flex society. 1986
 New Repub 196:39-40+ Ap 13 '87. R. Kuttner
Chomsky, N. Knowledge of language. 1985
 New Repub 196:34+ Mr 23 '87. E. Gellner
Chopin. 1987
 N Y Rev Books 34:9-11 My 28 '87. C. Rosen
Chopp, R. S. The praxis of suffering. 1986
 Christ Century 104:61-2 Ja 21 '87. G. E. Paul
Christianity and the world religions. 1986
 Christ Century 104:137-9 F 4-11 '87. N. Smart
Christiansen, F. B. and Feldman, M. W. Population genetics.
 1986
 BioScience 37:518-19 Jl/Ag '87. R. Borowsky
Chronic, H. Pages of stone; v2, Sierra Nevada, Cascades,
 & Pacific Coast. 1986
 Earth Sci 40:32 Spr '87
Church, F. F. The Devil & Dr. Church. 1986
 Christ Century 104:895-6 O 14 '87. P. R. Powell,
 Jr.
The Church and culture since Vatican II. 1985
 America 156:108 F 7 '87. T. L. Schubeck
Churches on the wrong road. 1986
 Christ Today 31:49-50 F 6 '87. D. Bandow
Churchland, P. S. Neurophilosophy. 1986
 Science 236:990-2 My 22 '87. G. S. Stent
Churchmen and the western Indians, 1820-1920. 1985
 America 156:431 My 23 '87. M. D. Green
Citati, P. Tolstoy. 1986
 Natl Rev 39:49-50 Jl 31 '87. J. Meyers
Clampitt, A. Archaic figure. 1987
 N Y Times Book Rev 92:12 D 20 '87. M. Rudman
Clancy, T. Patriot games. 1987
 N Y Times Book Rev 92:11 Ag 2 '87. R. Thomas
 Newsweek 110:68 Ag 17 '87. D. Lehman
Clancy, W. Time's covenant. 1987
 Commonweal 114:334-5 My 22 '87. J. Finn
Clark, D. H. The quest for SS433. 1986
 Sky Telesc 73:45-6 Ja '87. J. C. Kemp
Clark, J. C. D. Revolution and rebellion. 1986
 Hist Today 37:54-5 Mr '87. R. Hutton
Clark, J. G. Energy and the federal government. 1987
 Science 236:978 My 22 '87. D. Greenberg
Clark, R. B. Marine pollution. 1986
 Oceans 20:60 Ja/F '87. D. L. Taylor
Clark, T. The exile of Celine. 1987
 N Y Times Book Rev 92:28 F 8 '87. F. Sauzey
Clarke, L. J. Surface crystallography: an introduction to
 low energy electron diffraction. 1985
 Phys Today 40:83-4 Ap '87. P. M. Marcus
Clary, D. A. Timber and the Forest Service. 1986
 Wilderness 50:57-8 Summ '87. D. Drabelle
Classical Mediterranean spirituality. 1986
 Christ Century 104:506-7 My 20-27 '87. I. Anders
Clayton, B. Buck Clayton's jazz world. 1987
 Down Beat 54:63 S '87. J. Sohmer
Clayton, D. D. The Joshua factor. 1986
 Sky Telesc 74:44 Jl '87. D. H. Smith
Cleverley, J. F. and Phillips, D. C. Visions of childhood.
 1986
 Child Today 16:32-3 Ja/F '87. M. H. Lystad
Climate impact assessment. 1985
 Environment 29:28-9 Mr '87. T. R. Carter
Close, F. E. and others. The particle explosion. 1987
 Sky Telesc 74:609-10 D '87. P. C. W. Davies
Clough, A. H. Selected poems. 1987
 New Leader 70:18 N 30 '87. P. Pettingell
Coastal waders and wildfowl in winter. 1984
 BioScience 37:812 D '87. P. A. Buckley
Coates, J. Armed and dangerous. 1987
 N Y Times Book Rev 92:22 N 29 '87. W. King
 Psychol Today 21:76 O '87. P. Chance
Cobb, T. Crazy heart. 1987
 N Y Times Book Rev 92:27 O 11 '87. R. Hogan
Cobb, V. Skyscraper going up! 1987
 N Y Times Book Rev 92:33 N 8 '87. P. Goldberger
Cockburn, A. Corruptions of empire. 1987
 New Leader 70:15-16 D 14 '87. S. Kanfer
 New Repub 197:27-30+ D 28 '87. H. Fairlie
Cocteau, J. Past tense; v1, 1951-1952. 1987
 N Y Times Book Rev 92:18-19 Mr 8 '87. F. Brown
 New Repub 197:36-9 Ag 3 '87. M. Gallant
Codrescu, A. Comrade Past & Mister Present. 1986
 N Y Times Book Rev 92:15 Ja 25 '87. B. Shlain
Coe, C. I look divine. 1987
 N Y Times Book Rev 92:11 Ag 30 '87. R. Burgin
Coetzee, J. M. Foe. 1986
 N Y 20:91-2 F 9 '87. R. Koenig
 N Y Rev Books 34:18-20 My 28 '87. D. J. Enright

N Y Times Book Rev 92:1+ F 22 '87. D. Donoghue
Nation 244:402-5 Mr 28 '87. G. Packer
New Repub 196:36-8 Mr 9 '87. N. Auerbach
Newsweek 109:77 F 23 '87. P. S. Prescott
Time 129:84 Mr 23 '87. S. Kanfer
Coevolution and systematics. 1986
Science 237:441-2 Jl 24 '87. D. J. Futuyma and J. Kim
Cohen, A. Artists & enemies. 1987
Art Am 75:27 Jl '87. P. Plagens
N Y Times Book Rev 92:20 Ap 12 '87. M. H. Philipson
Cohen, B. J. In whose interest? 1986
New Leader 69:15-16 D 29 '86. M. Levinson
Cohen, F. G. Treaties on trial. 1986
Sea Front 33:314-15 Jl/Ag '87. S. K. Meltzoff
Cohen, I. B. The birth of a new physics. 1985
Sci Am 257:178+ O '87. P. Morrison
Cohen, J. L. The new Chinese painting, 1949-1986. 1987
Art News 86:74 N '87. R. Bass
Cohen, R. I. The burden of conscience. 1987
N Y Times Book Rev 92:7 My 24 '87. B. Wasserstein
Cohen, S. S. and Zysman, J. Manufacturing matters. 1987
Bus Week p16+ Je 22 '87. N. Jonas
Commonweal 114:628-30 N 6 '87. E. Janeway
Fortune 115:135-6 My 25 '87. D. Seligman
N Y Times Book Rev 92:36 Jl 12 '87. R. M. Solow
Cohen, T. Remaking Japan. 1987
N Y Times Book Rev 92:12 Ag 9 '87. C. Johnson
Cohen-Solal, A. Sartre. 1987
N Y Times Book Rev 92:3+ Jl 26 '87. S. Hoffmann
New Repub 196:36-9 Je 29 '87. D. Hollier
Newsweek 109:76+ Je 22 '87. S. Sullivan
Colbert, E. H. Wandering lands and animals. 1985
Earth Sci 40:36-7 Spr '87
Cole, B. The goats.
N Y Times Book Rev 92:31 N 8 '87. R. Hansen
Cole, H. The marble queen. 1986
N Y Times Book Rev 92:20 Ap 19 '87. L. McMahon
Coleman, J. S. and Hoffer, T. Public and private high schools. 1987
Christ Century 104:945-6 O 28 '87. M. A. Marty
Christ Today 31:60 N 6 '87. D. B. Lockerbie
Commonweal 114:216-18 Ap 10 '87. J. Ratté
Science 237:1357-8 S 11 '87. L. B. Otto
Coleman, L. and others. Unattended children.
Child Today 16:36 Jl/Ag '87. C. Sudia
Coleman, S. Aspects of symmetry. 1985
Phys Today 40:63-4 Je '87. S. B. Treiman
Coleman, W. Yellow fever in the North. 1987
Science 237:543 Jl 31 '87. C. Hannaway
Colen, B. D. Hard choices. 1986
Commonweal 114:249+ Ap 24 '87. T. P. Hill
Technol Rev 90:72-3 N/D '87. A. L. Caplan
Coles, R. Dorothy Day, a radical devotion. 1987
N Y Times Book Rev 92:10 S 6 '87. K. L. Woodward
Coles, R. The moral life of children. 1987
Phi Delta Kappan 68:404-5 Ja '87. N. J. Anastasiow
Coles, R. The political life of children. 1986
Phi Delta Kappan 68:404-5 Ja '87. N. J. Anastasiow
Coles, R. Simone Weil, a modern pilgrimage. 1987
Commonweal 114:638-9 N 6 '87. E. O. Springsted
N Y Times Book Rev 92:10 S 6 '87. K. L. Woodward
Colet, L. Lui, a view of him. 1986
N Y Times Book Rev 92:3 Ap 5 '87. E. O'Brien
New Repub 196:54-6 Je 8 '87. M. Wood
Coll, S. The deal of the century. 1986
Bus Week p21+ F 23 '87. J. J. Keller
New Leader 69:18-19 D 1-15 '86. R. Lekachman
Technol Rev 90:76-8 O '87. P. Aufderheide
Coll, S. The taking of Getty Oil. 1987
New Leader 70:19-20 N 16 '87. M. Levinson
Collier, J. L. Duke Ellington. 1987
N Y Rev Books 34:3-4+ N 19 '87. E. J. Hobsbawm
N Y Times Book Rev 92:22 N 22 '87. D. Morgenstern
Nation 245:692-4 D 5 '87. G. Santoro
New Yorker 63:90-1 D 28 '87. W. Balliett
Newsweek 110:85+ O 12 '87. J. Miller
Collier, P. and Horowitz, D. The Fords. 1987
Bus Week p16+ D 7 '87. W. J. Hampton
N Y 20:106-7 O 19 '87. R. Koenig
N Y Times Book Rev 92:35 O 25 '87. J. Nocera
Collington, P. The angel and the soldier boy. 1987
N Y Times Book Rev 92:32 My 17 '87. J. Trelease
Collins, J. Trust your heart. 1987
N Y Times Book Rev 92:17 N 29 '87. D. Mason
Comini, A. The changing image of Beethoven. 1987
N Y Times Book Rev 92:44 S 13 '87. M. Kimmelman
Companion to A sand county almanac. 1987
Wilderness 51:66-7 Wint '87. C. E. Little
Comyns, B. Sisters by a river. 1987
Copyright 1947

N Y Times Book Rev 92:22 Mr 22 '87. L. A. Walker
Comyns, B. The skin chairs. 1986
Copyright 1962
N Y Times Book Rev 92:22 Mr 22 '87. L. A. Walker
Conaway, J. The kingdom in the country. 1987
Wilderness 51:67-8 Wint '87. C. E. Little
Condé, M. Segu. 1987
N Y Times Book Rev 92:47 My 31 '87. C. R. Larson
Conference on Megakaryocyte Development and Function (1985: Woods Hole, Mass.). Megakaryocyte development and function. 1986
Science 235:96 Ja 2 '87. D. G. Nathan
Conference on Soviet Strategic Deception (1985: Naval Postgraduate School). Soviet strategic deception. 1987
Natl Rev 39:65 O 9 '87. C. Williamson
Congregation. 1987
N Y Times Book Rev 92:1+ D 20 '87. E. Hirsch
Connell, J. The new Maginot line. 1986
Bull At Sci 43:48+ Je '87. G. Adams
Conner, D. Comeback. 1987
N Y Times Book Rev 92:32 My 31 '87. B. Lloyd
Connolly, B. and Anderson, R. First contact. 1987
Sci Am 257:180-2 O '87. P. Morrison
Conover, C. The adventures of Simple Simon. 1987
N Y Times Book Rev 92:28-9 N 29 '87. P. Neumeyer
Conover, T. Coyote. 1987
N Y Times Book Rev 92:7 S 13 '87. T. D. Allman
Conquest, R. The harvest of sorrow. 1986
Commentary 83:74-7 Je '87. A. Puddington
N Y Rev Books 34:43-5 Mr 26 '87. P. J. de la F. Wiles
Natl Rev 39:48-50 F 27 '87. E. H. Methvin
Wash Mon 19:59 F '87. D. K. Shipler
Conrad, J. The collected letters of Joseph Conrad; v2, 1898-1902. 1986
N Y Times Book Rev 92:16 Ja 25 '87. L. Menand
Natl Rev 39:51-2 Ap 10 '87. J. Meyers
Conrad, P. A song of love and death. 1987
N Y Times Book Rev 92:15 N 8 '87. E. Downes
Conroy, J. Belfast diary. 1987
N Y Times Book Rev 92:14 D 20 '87. M. F. Nolan
Constantine, M. and Larsen, J. L. Beyond craft. 1986
Am Craft 47:14+ Ap/My '87. G. Moss
Consuming fears. 1986
Technol Rev 90:74 F/Mr '87. G. K. Wilson
Contemporary Jewish religious thought. 1986
N Y Times Book Rev 92:30-1 Mr 29 '87. A. Gottschalk
Contopoulos, G. and Kotsakis, D. Cosmology. 1987
Sky Telesc 74:260-1 S '87. V. Trimble
Cook, G. The expectation of the poor. 1985
America 156:108-9 F 7 '87. T. L. Schubeck
Cooper, E. The sexual perspective. 1986
Art Am 75:23+ O '87. J. Weinberg
Cooper, J. C. Some soul to keep. 1987
N Y Times Book Rev 92:23 N 8 '87. T. McMillan
Cooper, W. F. Claude McKay. 1987
N Y Rev Books 34:15-16+ D 17 '87. D. Pinckney
N Y Times Book Rev 92:21 S 20 '87. A. A. Bontemps
Coover, R. A night at the movies. 1987
Film Comment 23:78 My/Je '87. L. O'Toole
N Y Times Book Rev 92:15 F 1 '87. E. White
Coover, R. Whatever happened to Gloomy Gus of the Chicago Bears? 1987
N Y Times Book Rev 92:9 S 27 '87. R. Kelly
Cope, E. S. Politics without parliaments, 1629-1640. 1987
Hist Today 37:58 S '87. J. P. Sommerville
Copernicus, N. Complete works; v3, Minor works. 1985
Sky Telesc 73:281 Mr '87. O. Gingerich
Corbin, A. The foul and the fragrant. 1986
New Leader 69:12-13 D 29 '86. B. Gewen
New Repub 196:27-31 F 23 '87. S. Schama
Cordingly, D. Nicholas Pocock, 1740-1821. 1986
Sea Front 33:313-14 Jl/Ag '87. G. L. Voss
Corish, P. J. The Irish Catholic experience. 1985
America 156:331 Ap 18 '87. E. Grace
Corman, A. 50. 1987
N Y Times Book Rev 92:9 Ag 23 '87. L. J. Davis
Cornell, J. World cruising routes. 1987
Oceans 20:59-60 S/O '87. M. M. Drake
Cosby, B. Time flies. 1987
N Y Times Book Rev 92:7 S 20 '87. J. Viorst
Newsweek 110:78-9 S 14 '87. H. F. Waters
Cott, J. The search for Omm Sety. 1987
N Y Times Book Rev 92:7-8 Jl 26 '87. J. A. West
Cott, N. F. The grounding of modern feminism. 1987
Ms 16:80 O '87. J. W. Scott
Cotten, J. Vanity will get you somewhere. 1987
N Y Times Book Rev 92:47 S 13 '87. B. Stein
Countryman, E. The American Revolution. 1985

Hist Today 37:53 Je '87. H. Brogan
The Countryside in the age of capitalist transformation.
1985
  N Y Rev Books 34:37-9 Ap 23 '87. G. M. Fredrickson
Cousins, N. Albert Schweitzer's mission. 1985
  America 156:17-20 Ja 3-10 '87. N. J. Paulhus
Cox, A. The court and the Constitution. 1987
  N Y Times Book Rev 92:3+ S 20 '87. L. M. Friedman
  Natl Rev 39:46-7 Ag 28 '87. J. Sobran
Crace, J. Continent. 1987
  N Y Times Book Rev 92:30 Je 28 '87. R. O. Butler
Craik, A. D. D. Wave interactions and fluid flows. 1985
  Science 235:1522-3 Mr 20 '87. T. R. Akylas
Crandall, R. J. Shaking your family tree. 1986
  Americana 15:14 My/Je '87. M. Durham
Crane, H. The poems of Hart Crane. 1986
  New Repub 196:36-8 Je 22 '87. A. Corn
Cranston, M. Philosophers and pamphleteers. 1986
  Hist Today 37:61 S '87. P. Burley
Crassweller, R. D. Perón and the enigmas of Argentina.
1986
  N Y Times Book Rev 92:22 Ja 18 '87. M. Falcoff
  New Leader 70:17-18 Ap 6 '87. A. M. Shapiro
Craven, W. Colonial American portraiture. 1986
  Antiques 132:262+ Ag '87. R. G. Stewart
Crawford, A. C.R. Ashbee. 1985
  Am Craft 47:14+ F/Mr '87. C. Lynn
Crawford, C. and Shannon, D. Balance of power. 1986
  Byte 12:76+ My '87. R. Grehan
  Nation 244:150-3 F 7 '87. J. Ledbetter
Crease, R. P. and Mann, C. C. The second creation.
1986
  Phys Today 40:92-3 N '87. D. Park
Creasy, R. The gardener's handbook of edible plants. 1986
  Conservationist 41:50 Mr/Ap '87. S. A. Schwartz
Creationism, science, and the law. 1983
  BioScience 37:70+ Ja '87. L. V. Giddings
Crevel, R. Difficult death.
  N Y Times Book Rev 92:14 Ja 4 '87. H. Davies
Crews, H. All we need of hell. 1987
  N Y Times Book Rev 92:9+ F 1 '87. R. Banks
Crichton, M. Sphere. 1987
  N Y Times Book Rev 92:18 Jl 12 '87. R. McKinley
Crippa, M. A. Carlo Scarpa. 1986
  Archit Rec 175:87 O '87. S. Holt
Criticism in society. 1987
  New Leader 70:17 S 21 '87. P. Pettingell
Crombac, G. Colin Chapman. 1986
  Road Track 38:132 Ap '87. I. Ireland
Crompton, J. The snake. 1987
  N Y Times Book Rev 92:53 My 17 '87. B. B. Gordon
Crompton, J. The spider. 1987
  N Y Times Book Rev 92:53 My 17 '87. B. B. Gordon
Crone, H. D. Chemicals & society. 1986
  Environment 29:29 S '87. D. E. Burmaster
Crowe, F. E. Old things and new. 1985
  America 157:45 Jl 18-25 '87. A. J. Hamilton
Crowe, M. J. The extraterrestrial life debate, 1750-1900.
1986
  Sky Telesc 73:40-1 Ja '87. E. R. Paul
Crowley, J. Aegypt. 1987
  N Y Times Book Rev 92:9+ My 3 '87. J. Clute
Cruse, H. Plural but equal. 1987
  Natl Rev 39:64-5 S 11 '87. J. Sobran
Crustacean and mollusk aquaculture in the United States.
1985
  BioScience 37:356 My '87. M. Landau
Culbertson, J. and Randall, T. Permanent New Yorkers.
1987
  Am Herit 38:110 D '87
Cullen, E. J. Our war and how we won it. 1987
  N Y Times Book Rev 92:38 Je 21 '87. M. Chernoff
Cultures in contention. 1985
  Nation 244:184-6 F 14 '87. F. Pfeil
Curley, D. Mummy. 1987
  N Y Times Book Rev 92:11 Ap 26 '87. R. Plunket
Curran, C. E. Faithful dissent. 1986
  Christ Century 104:200-1 F 25 '87. R. M. Brown
  Commonweal 114:537-9 S 25 '87. R. G. Hoyt
Curran, C. E. Toward an American Catholic moral theology.
1987
  America 157:114 Ag 29-S 5 '87. E. C. Vacek
  Christ Century 104:796+ S 23 '87. R. H. King
Curran, D. In advance of the landing. 1985
  Astronomy 15:64-5 F '87. R. Burnham
Current perspectives in primate social dynamics. 1986
  BioScience 37:516-17 Jl/Ag '87. J. Robinson
Currie, E. Confronting crime. 1985
  N Y Rev Books 34:33-41 F 12 '87. C. Jencks
Curtis, M. K. No state shall abridge. 1986
  Commonweal 114:391-2 Je 19 '87. H. N. Meyer

Humanist 47:45 N/D '87. T. T. Lewis
Cutler, A. H. and Cutler, H. E. The Jew as ally of the
Muslim. 1986
  Commentary 83:74-6 Mr '87. D. Pipes

D

Da Cruz, F. Kermit, a file transfer protocol. 1987
  Byte 12:68+ My '87. J. W. West
Daalder, I. H. The SDI challenge to Europe. 1987
  Bull At Sci 43:49-50 N '87. S. J. Breyman
  Science 237:1625-6 S 25 '87. D. Hafner
Dadié, B. B. The black cloth. 1987
  N Y Times Book Rev 92:9+ Je 28 '87. R. F. Thompson
Dahl, R. Going solo. 1986
  Smithsonian 17:134-5 F '87. J. Parton
Daiber, F. C. Conservation of tidal marshes. 1986
  BioScience 37:222+ Mr '87. C. T. Hackney
Dale, S. Frederick Hurten Rhead.
  Am Craft 47:14+ F/Mr '87. C. Lynn
Daley, S. High cotton. 1987
  N Y Times Book Rev 92:8 Jl 5 '87. S. Bolotin
Dalton, R. Miguel Mármol. 1987
  Nation 245:240-2 S 12 '87. F. Pfeil
Dalzell, R. F. Enterprising elite. 1987
  N Y Times Book Rev 92:42 O 25 '87. N. W. Aldrich,
  Jr.
Dan, U. Blood libel. 1987
  N Y Times Book Rev 92:13 Ap 5 '87. K. Evans
Danilova, A. Choura. 1986
  Dance Mag 61:70-1 O '87. J. R. Acocella
  N Y Times Book Rev 92:13 Ja 4 '87. J. Dunning
  New Yorker 63:94-5 Ap 13 '87. A. Croce
Danto, A. C. The philosophical disenfranchisement of art.
1986
  Art News 86:71 N '87. B. Schwabsky
  N Y Times Book Rev 92:23 F 1 '87. P. Guyer
  New Repub 196:26-30 My 25 '87. R. E. Krauss
Danto, A. C. The state of the art. 1987
  Art News 86:71 N '87. B. Schwabsky
  N Y Times Book Rev 92:21 Ap 5 '87. F. Schier
  New Repub 196:27-30 My 25 '87. R. E. Krauss
Danto, A. C. The transfiguration of the commonplace.
1981
  New Repub 196:27-30 My 25 '87. R. E. Krauss
A Dark science. 1986
  Ms 15:17+ F '87. J. Johnston
  New Repub 196:38-41 Mr 16 '87. E. Showalter
  Psychol Today 21:66-7 Je '87. C. Fortune
Darlington, D. In condor country. 1987
  Sierra 72:71-2 Jl/Ag '87. T. Turner
  Wilderness 51:61-2 Fall '87. K. E. Franklin
Darwin, C. The correspondence of Charles Darwin; v1,
1821-1836. 1985
  New Yorker 63:171-2+ D 7 '87. D. J. Kevles
Darwin, C. The correspondence of Charles Darwin; v2,
1837-1843. 1985
  New Yorker 63:171-2+ D 7 '87. D. J. Kevles
  Science 236:988-9 My 22 '87. P. Corsi
The Darwinian heritage. 1985
  Science 235:224-5 Ja 9 '87. A. Desmond
Daugherty, T. Desire provoked. 1986
  N Y Times Book Rev 92:24 F 1 '87. R. Loewinsohn
Davenport, G. Every force evolves a form. 1987
  Natl Rev 39:57-8 Ap 24 '87. D. Hall
David, S. R. Third World coups d'état and international
security. 1987
  Bull At Sci 43:47-9 N '87. S. Hune
Davidson, C. N. Revolution and the word. 1986
  Nation 244:226-8 F 21 '87. S. Watts
Davidson, E. H. Gene activity in early development. 3rd
ed. 1986
  Science 235:695 F 6 '87. I. B. Dawid
Davidson, N. The failure of feminism. 1987
  Natl Rev 39:54 D 18 '87. J. Sobran
Davie, D. Czesław Miłosz and the insufficiency of lyric.
1986
  New Repub 197:40-2 Jl 13-20 '87. S. Barańczak
Davies, H. M. and Yard, S. Francis Bacon. 1986
  Art Am 75:25+ Je '87. P. Plagens
Davies, J. K. Cosmic impact. 1986
  Sky Telesc 73:393 Ap '87. J. K. Beatty
Davies, P. The last election. 1987
  N Y Times Book Rev 92:21 Mr 22 '87. P. McGrath
Davis, B. This 'n that. 1987
  N Y Times Book Rev 92:16 Ap 26 '87. H. Rubin
  Newsweek 109:69 Mr 30 '87. C. McGuigan
Davis, C. What is living, what is dead in Christianity
today? 1986
  Christ Century 104:227-8 Mr 4 '87. L. E. Snook
Davis, F. In the moment. 1986

Eberle, P. and Eberle, S. The politics of child abuse. 1986
   Psychol Today 21:70-1 S '87. C. Fortune
Echenoz, J. Cherokee. 1987
   N Y Times Book Rev 92:31 S 20 '87. C. McGee
Eckalbar, J. Flying the Beech Bonanza. 1986
   Flying 114:87 O '87. J. M. McClellan
Eckardt, A. R. Jews and Christians, the contemporary meeting. 1986
   America 156:428 My 23 '87. M. B. McGarry
Eco, U. Travels in hyper reality. 1986
   Am Sch 56:594-600 Aut '87. J. Simon
Ecological aspects of social evolution. 1986
   Science 236:470 Ap 24 '87. S. N. Austad
Ecological theory and integrated pest management practice. 1986
   Science 238:410-11 O 16 '87. R. J. Prokopy
The Ecology and biology of mammal-like reptiles. 1986
   Science 236:862-3 My 15 '87. T. S. Kemp
Ecology of biological invasions. 1986
   Science 236:1000-2 My 22 '87. T. J. Case
Ecology of biological invasions of North America and Hawaii. 1986
   Science 236:1000-2 My 22 '87. T. J. Case
The Ecology of natural disturbance and patch dynamics. 1985
   BioScience 37:138 F '87. B. C. Bennett
The Ecology of woodland rodents. 1985
   Science 237:305-6 Jl 17 '87. W. Z. Lidicker
An Ecosystem approach to aquatic ecology. 1985
   BioScience 37:226 Mr '87. G. R. Marzolf
Edds, M. Free at last. 1987
   N Y Times Book Rev 92:38 O 4 '87. T. Chaffin
Edelman, M. W. Families in peril. 1987
   Christ Century 104:862-3 O 7 '87. S. B. Thistlethwaite
   N Y Times Book Rev 92:12 Je 7 '87. D. Wycliff
Edgerton, C. Walking across Egypt. 1987
   N Y Times Book Rev 92:17 Mr 29 '87. K. Morton
Edmond, M. Rare Sir William Davenant. 1987
   Hist Today 37:55+ D '87. G. E. Aylmer
Edsall, N. C. Richard Cobden, independent radical. 1986
   Hist Today 37:55-6 S '87. G. Watson
Edwards, A. Early Reagan. 1987
   N Y Times Book Rev 92:7 Jl 26 '87. R. Sklar
Edwards, R. D. Victor Gollancz. 1987
   Hist Today 37:52-3 Ap '87. B. Crick
Edwards, T. Fight the wild island. 1987
   Smithsonian 18:182+ S '87. A. Ryan
The Effects of SO$_2$ on a grassland. 1984
   BioScience 37:138-9 F '87. R. Kohut
Egerton, R. F. Electron energy-loss spectroscopy in the electron microscope. 1986
   Phys Today 40:94-5 N '87. D. E. Newbury
Ehrenreich, B. and others. Re-making love. 1986
   Nation 244:266-7 F 28 '87. J. Abraham
Ehrensaft, D. Parenting together. 1987
   Psychol Today 21:68 S '87. J. Goetz
Eikelberner, G. and Agadjanian, S. The compleat American glass candy containers handbook. 1986
   Antiques Collect Hobbies 91:76 Ja '87
Einstein, A. The collected papers of Albert Einstein; v1, The early years, 1879-1902. 1987
   N Y Times Book Rev 92:33 S 27 '87. R. McCormmach
   New Yorker 63:77-80 Jl 6 '87. J. Bernstein
   Sci Am 257:117-18 S '87. P. Morrison
Eiseley, L. C. The lost notebooks of Loren Eiseley. 1987
   N Y Times Book Rev 92:14-15 S 20 '87. R. Finch
Eisenberg, E. The recording angel. 1987
   Nation 245:96-7 Ag 1-8 '87. D. Hamilton
Eisenhower, D. Eisenhower: at war, 1943-1945. 1986
   Commentary 83:62+ F '87. E. N. Luttwak
   Natl Rev 39:58 Ja 30 '87. F. McDonald
Eisenstein, S. The inner garden.
   N Y Times Book Rev 92:43 My 3 '87. S. Vogan
Eisler, R. T. The chalice and the blade. 1987
   N Y Times Book Rev 92:32 O 4 '87. E. Fox-Genovese
Eldredge, N. Time frames. 1985
   Humanist 47:45 Mr/Ap '87. J. R. Cole
Elegant, R. S. From a far land. 1987
   N Y Times Book Rev 92:39 S 20 '87. J. Fast
Elkin, S. The rabbi of Lud. 1987
   N Y Times Book Rev 92:12 N 8 '87. W. H. Pritchard
Elkington, J. The gene factory. 1985
   BioScience 37:284-5 Ap '87. H. Strauss
Eller, V. Christian anarchy. 1987
   Christ Today 31:34-5 Je 12 '87. R. Clapp
Ellerbee, L. "And so it goes". 1986
   New Repub 196:35-7 Mr 30 '87. D. Owen
Elliot, E. A chance to die. 1987
   Christ Today 31:61 N 6 '87. K. Andraski
Elliott, J. H. The Count-Duke of Olivares. 1986

   New Yorker 63:95-7 Ag 31 '87. N. Bliven
Elliott, S. L. Waiting for childhood. 1987
   N Y Times Book Rev 92:5 S 6 '87. A. R. Gurney
Elliott, S. R. Physics of amorphous materials. 1984
   Phys Today 40 pt1:69-70 Ag '87. K. Moorjani
Ellis, A. T. Unexplained laughter. 1987
   N Y Times Book Rev 92:22 O 18 '87. W. Gimbel
Ellis, B. E. The rules of attraction. 1987
   N Y Times Book Rev 92:14-15 S 13 '87. S. Spencer
   New Yorker 63:142-6 O 26 '87. T. Rafferty
   Newsweek 110:72 S 7 '87. D. Lehman
Ellis, J. The social history of the machine gun. 1986
   Repr. Orig. pub.: N.Y.: Pantheon Bks., c1975
   Technol Rev 90:74-5 Ja '87. W. Rosenau
Ellis, M. H. Toward a Jewish theology of liberation. 1987
   Christ Century 104:975-6 N 4 '87. D. H. Compier
Ellmann, R. Oscar Wilde. 1987
   Macleans 100:58 D 21 '87. G. James
Ellsberg, M. R. Created to praise. 1986
   America 157:389 N 21 '87. R. F. Morneau
Ellul, J. The subversion of Christianity. 1986
   Christ Century 104:892 O 14 '87. D. B. Clendenin
Elshtain, J. B. Women and war. 1987
   Progressive 51:29-30 Jl '87. A. M. Davidon
Elton, G. R. The Parliament of England, 1559-1581. 1986
   Hist Today 37:53 F '87. P. Collinson
Emerson, L. J. The selected letters of Lidian Jackson Emerson. 1987
   N Y Times Book Rev 92:24 N 29 '87. M. Walker
Emmons, N. Manson in his own words. 1986
   Vogue 177:96+ Ja '87. E. White
Empty promise. 1986
   Commonweal 114:392-3 Je 19 '87. P. Wild
   N Y Rev Books 34:35-41 Ap 9 '87. Sir S. Zuckerman
   Space World X-5-281:20 My '87. J. Rhea
The Encyclopedia of climatology. 1987
   Environment 29:28 N '87. K. H. Cook
Encyclopedia of materials science and engineering. 8v 1986
   Phys Today 40:71-2 Mr '87. C. B. Duke
The Encyclopedia of religion. 16v 1986
   Christ Today 31:33 O 16 '87. T. C. Muck
Encyclopedia of the American Constitution. 1986
   Cent Mag 20:35-6 Jl/Ag '87. D. McDonald
Energy conservation. 1986
   Mon Labor Rev 110:46 Mr '87. E. A. Schroeder, IV
Enriching professional skills through general semantics. 1986
   Humanist 47:45 Mr/Ap '87. S. Fogel
Enrico, R. and Kornbluth, J. The other guy blinked. 1986
   Fortune 115:123-5 F 16 '87. I. Ross
Epstein, C. J. The consequences of chromosome imbalance. 1986
   Science 235:916 F 20 '87. R. S. Sparkes
Epstein, J. Once more around the block. 1987
   N Y Times Book Rev 92:13 Je 7 '87. J. Conarroe
   New Repub 196:45-8 Je 8 '87. D. Bromwich
Epstein, L. D. Political parties in the American mold. 1986
   N Y Rev Books 34:8-10+ Mr 26 '87. T. B. Edsall
Erdman, P. E. The panic of '89. 1987
   Bus Week p16-17+ Mr 9 '87. C. Welles
   Macleans 100:64 Mr 23 '87. T. Kierans
   N Y Times Book Rev 92:9 Ja 11 '87. J. E. Garten
   Time 129:70 F 2 '87. R. Z. Sheppard
Erdrich, L. The beet queen. 1986
   N Y Rev Books 33:14-15 Ja 15 '87. J. Rubins
Erikson, E. H. A way of looking at things. 1987
   N Y Rev Books 34:8+ D 3 '87. J. S. Bruner
   N Y Times Book Rev 92:36-7 Ap 5 '87. S. Turkle
   Psychol Today 21:67-8 O '87. R. Atkinson
Erim, K. T. Aphrodisias. 1986
   N Y Times Book Rev 92:24 Mr 1 '87. R. J. A. Wilson
Estes, J. W. and Goodman, D. M. The changing humors of Portsmouth. 1986
   Science 237:924-5 Ag 21 '87. J. W. Leavitt
Estrich, S. Real rape. 1987
   Ms 16:32+ S '87. R. Warshaw
   Wash Mon 19:57 Jl/Ag '87. P. M. Barrett
Ettinger, E. Rosa Luxemburg. 1986
   N Y Rev Books 34:3+ Mr 26 '87. J. Joll
   N Y Times Book Rev 92:13-14 Je 14 '87. E. Kamenka
   Nation 244:546-9 Ap 25 '87. D. Egger
   Progressive 51:30-1 O '87. A. Weinberg
Evans, A. F. and others. Pedagogies for the non-poor. 1986
   Christ Century 104:1043-4 N 18 '87. M. D. Wilde
Evans, D. S. and Mulholland, J. D. Big and bright. 1986
   Astronomy 15:72-4 Ap '87. R. Burnham
   Sky Telesc 73:389-90 Ap '87. R. A. Schorn
Evans, G. R. and others. The science of theology. 1986
   Christ Century 104:974 N 4 '87. J. D. Godsey

Evans, S. M. and Boyte, H. C. Free spaces. 1986
　America 156:38-9 Ja 17 '87. D. Shelton
The Evolution of human behavior. 1987
　Science 236:1125 My 29 '87. R. S. O. Harding
The Evolution of primate behavior. 2d ed. 1985
　BioScience 37:230-1 Mr '87. J. M. Whitehead
Evolution versus Creationism. 1983
　BioScience 37:70+ Ja '87. L. V. Giddings
Ewart, G. The Gavin Ewart Show. 1986
　N Y Rev Books 34:35-6 Ja 29 '87. L. Kirstein
Ewart, G. The young Pobble's guide to his toes. 1985
　N Y Rev Books 34:35-6 Ja 29 '87. L. Kirstein
Ewing, C. P. Battered women who kill. 1987
　Psychol Today 21:78 Ag '87. P. J. Black
Ewing, W. A. The photographic art of Hoyningen-Huene.
　1986
　Art Am 75:15-17+ Ja '87. D. Bourdon
Excitatory amino acid transmission. 1987
　Science 237:1517-18 S 18 '87. A. MacDermott
Experimental approaches to mammalian embryonic develop-
　ment. 1986
　Science 238:970 N 13 '87. J. J. Eppig
Explosive remnants of war. 1985
　BioScience 37:358 My '87. H. D. Grover
Extrachromosomal elements in lower eukaryotes. 1986
　Science 237:307 Jl 17 '87. E. H. Blackburn
Eyes, D. and Lichty, R. Programming the 65816. 1986
　Byte 12:68+ Ja '87. J. D. Sheinwald

F

Faber, R. Young England. 1987
　Hist Today 37:56 O '87. E. Norman
The Faber book of contemporary Irish poetry. 1986
　N Y Rev Books 34:25-6 F 26 '87. D. Donoghue
Faden, R. R. and others. A history and theory of informed
　consent. 1986
　America 156:109-11 F 7 '87. M. L. Stackhouse
Fagan, B. M. The great journey.
　N Y Times Book Rev 92:46 D 6 '87. J. Hemming
Fairbank, J. K. China watch. 1987
　Bus Week p19-20 N 30 '87. D. J. Yang
Faldbakken, K. The honeymoon. 1987
　N Y Times Book Rev 92:38 Je 21 '87. I. Kapp
Falk, D. S. and others. Seeing the light. 1985
　Phys Today 40:66 Je '87. D. R. Overheim
Falwell, J. Strength for the journey. 1987
　N Y Times Book Rev 92:6 D 27 '87. R. Reed
Family. 1987
　Psychol Today 21:72-3 N '87. S. Pollak
Faragher, J. M. Sugar Creek. 1986
　N Y Rev Books 34:37-9 Ap 23 '87. G. M. Fredrickson
Farah, N. Maps. 1986
　N Y Times Book Rev 92:40 N 15 '87. C. Hope
Farber, B. Making people talk. 1987
　N Y Times Book Rev 92:22 N 1 '87. J. Jarvis
Farley, M. A. Personal commitments. 1986
　Christ Century 104:201-2 F 25 '87. D. E. Messer
Farley, M. B. and Farley, L. K. Diver's guide to underwater
　Mexico. 1986
　Oceans 20:60-1 Ja/F '87. C. Pyle
Farm work and fieldwork. 1987
　Science 236:982-3 My 22 '87. R. H. Halperin
Farmer, R. Universal essence. 1986
　Humanist 47:44 S/O '87. C. Lamont
Farrell, W. Why men are the way they are. 1986
　Psychol Today 21:73+ Jl '87. H. Hall
Farwell, B. The Great War in Africa, 1914-1918. 1986
　Natl Rev 39:49 Ag 28 '87. J. Meyers
Faur, J. Golden doves with silver dots. 1985
　New Repub 196:27-33 Ja 5-12 '87. R. Alter
Favorite folktales from around the world. 1986
　N Y Times Book Rev 92:12 Ja 25 '87. B. L. Clark
Faw, B. and Skelton, N. Thunder in America. 1986
　Christ Century 104:798+ S 23 '87. C. Fager
　Wash Mon 19:56-8 F '87. T. Branch
Feather, L. The jazz years. 1986
　Down Beat 54:54-5 Ag '87. J. McDonough
Fedders, C. O. and Elliott, L. Shattered dreams. 1987
　Wash Mon 19:58-9 D '87. A. E. Schwartz
Fein, R. Medical care, medical costs. 1986
　Cent Mag 20:41 Mr/Ap '87. D. McDonald
Feinstein, E. A captive lion. 1987
　N Y Rev Books 34:20+ O 8 '87. J. Bayley
　N Y Times Book Rev 92:22-3 S 27 '87. E. Proffer
Feldman, D. H. and Goldsmith, L. T. Nature's gambit.
　1986
　Psychol Today 21:72-4 Ap '87. P. Chance
　Smithsonian 18:150+ Je '87. C. Eron
Fenn, R. K. The spirit of revolt. 1986
　Christ Century 104:831-2 S 30 '87. M. L. Stackhouse

Fenstermacher, G. D. and Soltis, J. F. Approaches to
　teaching. 1986
　Phi Delta Kappan 68:479 F '87. A. Berger
Ferguson, A. That new pet! 1986
　N Y Times Book Rev 92:28 Ja 18 '87. N. B. Cardozo
Ferguson, J. H. Mammalian physiology. 1985
　BioScience 37:748 N '87. K. B. Armitage
Ferguson, R. Enigma. 1987
　N Y Times Book Rev 92:28 Je 7 '87. T. Clark
　New Leader 70:20-1 S 21 '87. L. Kahn
Ferguson, T. and Rogers, J. Right turn. 1986
　Commonweal 114:113-16 F 27 '87. F. F. Siegel
Ferm, D. W. Third World liberation theologies: an
　introductory survey. 1985
　America 156:107-8 F 7 '87. T. L. Schubeck
　Christ Century 104:167 F 18 '87. J. Stanley
Fermor, P. L. Between the woods and the water. 1986
　N Y Times Book Rev 92:30-1 F 8 '87. G. Gibson
　New Repub 196:36-8 Ja 19 '87. V. Klinkenborg
Fermor, P. L. A time of gifts. 1983
　New Repub 196:36-8 Ja 19 '87. V. Klinkenborg
Fernow, R. C. Introduction to experimental particle physics.
　1986
　Science 235:1091-2 F 27 '87. C. Blocker
Ferrill, A. The fall of the Roman Empire. 1986
　Natl Rev 39:52-4 Je 19 '87. H. W. Crocker, III
Ferriss, H. The metropolis of tomorrow. 1986
　Archit Rec 175:55 Ja '87. S. Gutterman
Fertilizer technology and use. 3rd ed. 1985
　Sci Am 256:22-3 Ja '87. P. Morrison
Festinger, T. Necessary risk. 1986
　Child Today 16:31-2 Ja/F '87. E. J. Schwartz
Feuer, L. S. Imperialism and the anti-imperialist mind.
　1986
　Commentary 83:68+ Ap '87. S. McConnell
Ffinch, M. G.K. Chesterton. 1986
　N Y Times Book Rev 92:18 F 22 '87. H. Kenner
　Natl Rev 39:58-60 Ja 30 '87. J. P. McCarthy
Field, A. VN, the life and art of Vladimir Nabokov.
　3rd ed. 1986
　Smithsonian 17:174-5 Mr '87. M. Dirda
The Field & stream treasury of trout fishing. 1986
　Conservationist 41:52-3 My/Je '87. J. Rowen
Fifty years of neutron diffraction. 1987
　Science 238:221 O 9 '87. J. D. Axe
Figes, E. Little Eden. 1987
　N Y Times Book Rev 92:14 Ag 16 '87. L. G. Segal
Figes, E. The seven ages. 1986
　Commonweal 114:248-9 Ap 24 '87. R. E. Hosmer,
　Jr.
　Ms 15:14 Mr '87. K. FitzGerald
　N Y Times Book Rev 92:7 F 22 '87. A. Goreau
Fildes, V. A. Breasts, bottles and babies. 1986
　Hist Today 37:60 Ja '87. N. Tucker
　Sci Am 257:114-114A Ag '87. P. Morrison
Finch, C. American watercolors. 1986
　Am Artist 51:12+ Je '87. M. C. Nelson
　Americana 14:79-80 Ja/F '87. M. Durham
Finch, R. Outlands. 1986
　Oceans 20:62-3 Jl/Ag '87. M. Leffler
Fine, A. The shaky game. 1986
　Science 238:409-10 O 16 '87. D. Howard
Fine, R. A. Escape of the guilty. 1986
　Wash Mon 19:59-60 Mr '87. T. Bethell
Fink, I. A scrap of time and other stories. 1987
　N Y Times Book Rev 92:7+ Jl 12 '87. J. Kaplan
Finlayson, I. The sixth continent. 1986
　New Leader 69:15 D 1-15 '86. P. Pettingell
Finlayson-Pitts, B. J. and Pitts, J. N. Atmospheric
　chemistry. 1986
　Science 235:1263-4 Mr 6 '87. G. E. Gordon
Finn, J. The bluesman. 1986
　Down Beat 54:48+ My '87. L. Birnbaum
Finnegan, W. Crossing the line. 1986
　U S Cathol 52:48-51 Jl '87. G. M. Costello
Finney, E. J. Birds landing. 1986
　America 156:111-12 F 7 '87. R. S. Phillips
Finnis, J. and others. Nuclear deterrence, morality, and
　realism. 1987
　N Y Rev Books 34:38-43 N 5 '87. J. M. Cameron
Fire ants and leaf-cutting ants. 1986
　Science 235:1682-3 Mr 27 '87. N. F. Carlin
Fischer, M. 65816/65802 assembly language programming.
　1986
　Byte 12:68+ Ja '87. J. D. Sheinwald
Fischhoff, A. Birth to Three. 1986
　Child Today 16:34-5 Mr/Ap '87. S. Wieder
Fischler, M. A. and Firschein, O. Intelligence. 1987
　Byte 12:90+ Ag '87. G. Beinhorn
Fischnaller, S. Northwest shore dives. 1986
　Oceans 20:63-4 N/D '87. D. G. Gordon

The Fish book.
Success Farm 85:24 My '87. J. Walter
Fisher, B. and Ross, B. The America's Cup, 1987. 1987
N Y Times Book Rev 92:32 My 31 '87. B. Lloyd
Fisher, C. Postcards from the edge. 1987
Mademoiselle 93:158+ S '87. J. Maynard
Vogue 177:186+ Ag '87. E. G. Carter
Fisher, D. E. The birth of the earth. 1987
Sky Telesc 74:373 O '87. T. Page
Fisher, J. The Lindbergh case. 1987
N Y Rev Books 34:4+ N 5 '87. F. Russell
N Y Times Book Rev 92:48 O 11 '87. J. Katzenbach
Fisher, P. Los Alamos experience. 1985
Phys Today 40 pt1:72-3 Ag '87. J. S. Wilson
Fishman, R. Bourgeois utopias. 1987
New Leader 70:3-4 D 14 '87. B. Gewen
Wash Mon 19:56 D '87. N. Lemann
FitzGerald, F. Cities on a hill. 1986
Christ Century 104:30-1 Ja 7-14 '87. W. M. Goering
Christ Today 31:29-31 Ap 3 '87. P. Yancey
Commonweal 114:117-18 F 27 '87. R. W. Fox
N Y Rev Books 34:3-4 Ja 29 '87. D. Johnson
Fitzgerald, P. Charlotte Mew and her friends. 1984
N Y Rev Books 33:25-6+ Ja 15 '87. B. Leithauser
Fitzgerald, P. Offshore. 1987
N Y Times Book Rev 92:51 S 13 '87. B. F. Williamson
Fjermedal, G. The tomorrow makers. 1986
Space World X-9-285:36 S '87. J. D. Kirwan
Flagg, F. Fried green tomatoes at the Whistle-Stop Cafe. 1987
N Y Times Book Rev 92:14 O 18 '87. J. Butler
Flake, C. Tarnished crown. 1987
N Y Times Book Rev 92:26 Ap 26 '87. W. Tower
Flam, J. D. Matisse, the man and his art, 1869-1918. 1986
Art Am 75:13+ Ap '87. J. Elderfield
Art News 86:71-2 D '87. M. Phillips
Natl Rev 39:63-4 N 20 '87. J. Meyers
Flapan, S. The birth of Israel. 1987
New Repub 197:32-4+ D 7 '87. M. Syrkin
Fleischman, S. The whipping boy. 1986
N Y Times Book Rev 92:23 F 22 '87. M. Saxton
Fleming, T. J. Time and tide. 1987
N Y Times Book Rev 92:7+ S 13 '87. W. Lord
Flora of the Great Plains. 1986
Science 235:800-1 F 13 '87. N. R. Morin
Florence, G. Kitchen glassware of the Depression years. 1987
Antiques Collect Hobbies 92:71 My '87
Florence, G. Pocket guide to Depression glass. 1987
Antiques Collect Hobbies 92:70-1 My '87
Floridi, A. U. Moscow and the Vatican. 1986
America 156:13-15 Ja 3-10 '87. R. E. Sullivan
Florman, S. C. The civilized engineer. 1987
Commonweal 114:758 D 18 '87. C. Mitcham
Flower, J. E. Literature and the left in France. 1985
America 157:115-16 Ag 29-S 5 '87. M. Lavallée-Williams
Flynn, R. Wanderer Springs. 1987
N Y Times Book Rev 92:55 O 11 '87. D. McWhorter
Flynt, C. Mother love. 1987
N Y Times Book Rev 92:13 Je 28 '87. J. Markus
Folk artists biographical index. 1986
Antiques 132:482 S '87. F. J. Miele
Folktales of India. 1987
Sci Am 257:153 D '87. P. Morrison and P. Morrison
For Nelson Mandela. 1987
N Y Times Book Rev 92:35 N 1 '87. S. R. Cudjoe
Ford, B. Betty, a glad awakening. 1987
N Y Times Book Rev 92:9 Mr 1 '87. M. Sandmaier
Ford, H. D. Four lives in Paris.
N Y Times Book Rev 92:16 F 15 '87. H. Goldgar
Ford, R. Rock Springs. 1987
N Y Rev Books 34:12 N 5 '87. A. Kazin
N Y Times Book Rev 92:1+ S 20 '87. J. E. Wideman
Natl Rev 39:55-6 D 4 '87. D. Klinghoffer
Time 130:88-9 N 16 '87. P. Gray
Fore, W. F. Television and religion. 1987
Christ Century 104:945 O 28 '87. A. P. Klausler
Forer, L. G. A chilling effect. 1987
N Y Times Book Rev 92:12 Je 14 '87. H. Simons
Forest, J. H. Love is the measure. 1986
Christ Century 104:508-9 My 20-27 '87. P. Kountz
Forester, T. High-tech society. 1987
N Y Times Book Rev 92:43 S 27 '87. R. Kling
Forman, R. T. T. and Godron, M. Landscape ecology. 1986
BioScience 37:734-5 N '87. J. A. Wiens
Forsyth, M. Buildings for music. 1985
Technol Rev 90:75-6 Ja '87. N. C. Pickering

Fortescue, S. The Communist Party and Soviet science. 1986
Science 236:861 My 15 '87. P. Josephson
Fossil invertebrates. 1987
Science 238:1153 N 20 '87. D. Jablonski
Foster, J. R. Adirondack portraits. 1986
Conservationist 41:51 Mr/Ap '87. T. L. Cobb
Foucault, M. The history of sexuality; v3, The care of the self. 1986
Commentary 84:63-4 Jl '87. R. T. Marin
N Y Times Book Rev 92:31 Ja 18 '87. J. Boswell
Psychol Today 21:68-9 O '87. M. S. Kimmel
Foucault. 1986
Commentary 84:64-5 Jl '87. R. T. Marin
N Y Times Book Rev 92:31 Ja 18 '87. J. Boswell
The Founders' Constitution. 5v 1987
Christ Century 104:499-500+ My 20-27 '87. M. A. Noll
N Y Times Book Rev 92:3+ Mr 15 '87. P. A. Freund
Fowler, P. B. Abortion. 1987
Christ Today 31:37-8 S 4 '87. M. J. Gorman
Fox, A. and Guy, J. Reassessing the Henrician Age. 1986
Hist Today 37:60 Jl '87. J. Loach
Fox, C. Londoners. 1987
Hist Today 37:57-8 O '87. F. Barker
Fox, M. W. Agricide. 1986
Environment 29:28 N '87. J. H. Perkins
Sierra 72:153-4 Ja/F '87. M. James
Francis, C. and Gontier, F. Simone de Beauvoir. 1987
Natl Rev 39:58-9 S 25 '87. M. Liccione
Francis, D. Bolt. 1987
New Leader 70:17-18 Jl 1-15 '87. H. H. Davis
Franco, J. Hoffa's man. 1987
Fortune 116:225 N 23 '87. M. Brody
Frank, D. Less than conquerors. 1986
Christ Century 104:830-1 S 30 '87. M. E. Marty
Christ Today 31:33-4 Je 12 '87. T. Stafford
Frank, J. Dostoevsky; v3, The stir of liberation, 1860-1865. 1986
New Repub 196:40-2 Ap 27 '87. D. Fanger
Frank, P. and McKenzie, M. New, used, and improved. 1987
Art Am 75:35 D '87. P. Plagens
Art News 86:72 D '87. J. Sturman
Frankl, R. Televangelism. 1987
Christ Today 31:51-2 Ag 7 '87. Q. J. Schultze
Frankland, M. The sixth continent. 1987
N Y Times Book Rev 92:18 N 22 '87. C. R. Whitney
Franklin, J. Molecules of the mind. 1987
N Y Times Book Rev 92:15 F 8 '87. B. L. Jacobs
Psychol Today 21:72-3 Jl '87. J. Alper
Frantz, D. Levine & Co. 1987
Bus Week p20-2 S 14 '87. G. Weiss
Fortune 116:195+ S 28 '87. T. Teachout
N Y Times Book Rev 92:36 O 25 '87. P. O'Toole
Frantzen, A. J. King Alfred. 1986
Hist Today 37:61 Jl '87. S. Keynes
Fraser, F. Emma, Lady Hamilton. 1987
N Y Times Book Rev 92:9+ Je 14 '87. V. Tiger
Vogue 177:212 Ap '87. E. Jenkins
Fraser, K. Scenes from the fashionable world. 1987
Mademoiselle 93:48+ Jl '87. J. Maynard
N Y Times Book Rev 92:40 S 13 '87. A. T. Wallach
Frazier, I. Nobody better, better than nobody. 1987
N Y Times Book Rev 92:9 My 3 '87. R. R. Harris
Time 129:67 My 25 '87. P. Gray
Freed, L. Home ground. 1986
Seventeen 46:78 F '87. R. Schwartz
Freedman, L. The price of peace. 1986
Bull At Sci 43:56 Ja/F '87. P. F. Walker
N Y Times Book Rev 92:33 Ja 25 '87. S. W. Van Evera
Freedman, R. Indian chiefs. 1987
N Y Times Book Rev 92:44 N 22 '87. G. B. Smith
Freeman, D. S. Lee's lieutenants. 3v 1942
Copyright 1970, 1971, 1972 respectively
Am Herit 38:36-7 S/O '87
Freeman, L. and others. Belle. 1986
Progressive 51:29 S '87. D. Thelen
French, M. Her mother's daughter. 1987
N Y 20:88 O 12 '87. R. Koenig
N Y Times Book Rev 92:7 O 25 '87. A. Hoffman
Fresh produce. 1987
Sunset 178:168-9 Mr '87
Frewin, L. R. The late Mrs. Dorothy Parker. 1986
New Repub 196:37-9 Je 1 '87. F. Rich
Time 129:72 Je 15 '87. W. A. Henry
Fried, M. Realism, writing, disfiguration. 1987
New Yorker 63:121-6 O 5 '87. J. Malcolm
Friedman, H. Sun and Earth. 1985
Astronomy 15:68 Ja '87. D. Jourdan

Friedman, I. S. Toward world prosperity. 1987
  N Y Times Book Rev 92:53 My 3 '87. M. Kahler
Friedman, J.-A. Home health care. 1986
  Aging no355:33 '87
Friedman, R. E. Who wrote the Bible? 1987
  N Y Times Book Rev 92:9 Ag 9 '87. R. Davidson
Friedrich, O. City of nets. 1986
  America 157:90 Ag 15-22 '87. J. Cunneen
  N Y Rev Books 33:23-4 Ja 15 '87. N. Lemann
Friend, D. Family laundry. 1986
  N Y Times Book Rev 92:10 Ja 18 '87. R. Robinson
Fuller, J. Selected poems, 1954 to 1982. 1985
  N Y Times Book Rev 92:25-6 N 29 '87. R. Richman
Fuller, J. G. Tornado watch #211. 1987
  N Y Times Book Rev 92:40 S 27 '87. S. Blakeslee
Fuller, R. C. Americans and the unconscious. 1986
  Christ Century 104:249 Mr 11 '87. W. C. Gilpin
  Psychol Today 21:70-1 Jl '87. L. Miller
Fundamentals of aquatic toxicology. 1985
  BioScience 37:742 N '87. R. Eisler
Fundamentals of insect physiology. 1985
  BioScience 37:752 N '87. T. A. Miller
Furguson, E. B. Hard right. 1986
  N Y Rev Books 34:31-5 My 7 '87. G. Epps
  Wash Mon 19:56-8 F '87. T. Branch
Furlong, M. Zen effects. 1986
  Christ Century 104:602-3 Jl 1-8 '87. R. Kaftan
Furman, L. Tuxedo park. 1986
  New Repub 196:41-2 Ja 5-12 '87. L. E. Obolensky
Fye, B. The development of American physiology. 1987
  Science 237:665-6 Ag 7 '87. P. J. Pauly

G

Gabbard, A. Vintage & historic racing cars.
  Mot Trend 39:48 N '87. T. C. Browne
Gabriel, R. A. No more heroes. 1987
  Psychol Today 21:72-3+ S '87. P. J. Black
Gaddis, J. L. The long peace. 1987
  N Y Times Book Rev 92:15 N 15 '87. C. S. Maier
Gado, F. The passion of Ingmar Bergman. 1986
  America 157:90+ Ag 15-22 '87. J. Cunneen
Gage, J. J.M.W. Turner. 1987
  New Repub 197:47-9 O 12 '87. E. V. Thaw
The Galaxy and the solar system. 1986
  Science 236:619 My 1 '87. M. E. Bailey
Galbraith, J. K. Economics in perspective. 1987
  Bus Week p18-19+ N 2 '87. N. Jonas
  N Y Rev Books 34:44-6 N 5 '87. R. L. Heilbroner
  N Y Times Book Rev 92:27+ O 25 '87. L. S. Silk
Galeano, E. H. Memory of fire; pt1, Genesis. 1985
  Nation 244:183-4 F 14 '87. J. Franco
Galeano, E. H. Memory of fire; pt2, Faces and masks. 1987
  Nation 244:183-4 F 14 '87. J. Franco
Galeener-Moore, L. Collecting dead relatives. 1987
  Antiques Collect Hobbies 92:68-71 S '87. C. E. Kraft
Galileo Galilei. 1987
  America 157:507-9 D 26 '87. M. R. O'Connell
Gallagher, T. The lover of horses. 1986
  America 156:111-12 F 7 '87. R. S. Phillips
Gallant, M. Overhead in a balloon. 1987
  N Y Times Book Rev 92:7-8 Mr 15 '87. P. Rose
Galloway, B. The union of England and Scotland, 1603-1608. 1986
  Hist Today 37:59-60 Ja '87. G. E. Aylmer
Gallup, G. and Castelli, J. The American Catholic people. 1987
  America 156:104-7 F 7 '87. A. M. Greeley
Gann, L. H. and Duignan, P. The Hispanics in the United States. 1986
  Natl Rev 39:56+ O 9 '87. D. L. Huddle
Gao, Y. Born red. 1987
  N Y Times Book Rev 92:34 My 3 '87. T. Tung
  New Repub 197:37-8 Ag 10-17 '87. M. Goldman
García Márquez, G. Clandestine in Chile. 1987
  Christ Century 104:1042-3 N 18 '87. D. Strieter
  N Y Times Book Rev 92:10 Ag 9 '87. M. Wood
  New Yorker 63:85-6 Ag 24 '87. J. Updike
The Garden seed inventory. 1985
  Sunset 178:191 F '87
The Gardener's palette. 1987
  Rodale's Org Gard 34:16 Jl '87
Gardner, H. The mind's new science. 1985
  BioScience 37:520-1 Jl/Ag '87. N. Greenberg
Gardner, M. Keeping warm. 1987
  Mademoiselle 93:70+ Ja '87. L. Darling
  N Y Times Book Rev 92:8 Ja 18 '87. C. Goodrich
Garfield, J. The life of a real girl. 1986
  Psychol Today 21:77-8 Jl '87. R. J. Moss
Garnett, H. Family skeletons. 1987

N Y Times Book Rev 92:32 Je 14 '87. N. Auerbach
Garraty, J. A. The Great Depression. 1986
  Natl Rev 39:66 D 4 '87. J. C. Chalberg
Garro, E. Recollections of things to come.
  Ms 15:32+ Ap '87. B. G. Chevigny
Garrow, D. J. Bearing the cross. 1986
  America 157:18+ Jl 4-11 '87. J. P. Hanigan
  Black Enterp 17:13 Ap '87. T. Bolden Davis
  Christ Century 104:197-200 F 25 '87. P. N. Williams
  N Y Rev Books 33:3+ Ja 15 '87. C. V. Woodward
  Nation 244:221-4 F 21 '87. W. H. Chafe
  Natl Rev 39:48-9 My 8 '87. J. Chamberlain
  New Repub 196:34+ Ja 5-12 '87. D. B. Davis
  New Yorker 63:102+ Ap 6 '87. B. McKibben
  Progressive 51:40-2 Ap '87. F. Powledge
Gasser, R. P. H. An introduction to chemisorption and catalysis by metals. 1984
  Phys Today 40:128-9 O '87. G. Ehrlich
Gati, C. Hungary and the Soviet bloc. 1986
  Commonweal 114:509-11 S 11 '87. I. Sanders
Gauch, P. L. Christina Katerina and the time she quit the family. 1987
  N Y Times Book Rev 92:51 N 8 '87. E. Schecter
Gay, P. The bourgeois experience; v2, The tender passion.
  Hist Today 37:55-6 Ja '87. M. Brock
Gay, P. A Godless Jew. 1987
  N Y Times Book Rev 92:39+ O 11 '87. J. C. Marshall
Gaylin, W. Rediscovering love. 1986
  Psychol Today 21:74-5 Mr '87. D. Heller
Gaynor, J. and Hatcher, C. The psychology of child firesetting. 1987
  Child Today 16:35 Jl/Ag '87. M. Baizerman and B. Emshoff
Geffré, C. The risk of interpretation. 1987
  Christ Century 104:1007-8 N 11 '87. D. Pellauer
Geiger, R. L. To advance knowledge. 1986
  Change 19:60-3 Jl/Ag '87. C. N. Breiseth
  Science 236:983-4 My 22 '87. A. Thackray
Gelb, N. The Berlin wall. 1987
  N Y Times Book Rev 92:21 F 8 '87. J. M. Markham
Gene banks and the world's food. 1987
  Science 236:617-18 My 1 '87. W. L. Brown
General circulation of the ocean. 1987
  Science 238:92-3 O 2 '87. P. Rhines
Genetic flux in plants. 1985
  BioScience 37:289-90 Ap '87. B. L. Wanner
Genetic variation and its maintenance. 1986
  Science 236:1475-6 Je 12 '87. J. F. Crow
Genovesi, V. J. In pursuit of love. 1987
  America 157:113 Ag 29-S 5 '87. E. C. Vacek
Geology: the active earth. 1987
  Earth Sci 40:33 Summ '87
Geomorphology from space. 1986
  Science 238:1298 N 27 '87. L. H. Lattman
George, J. C. One day in the prairie. 1986
  Conservationist 42:51 Jl/Ag '87. N. M. Payne
  Earth Sci 40:31-2 Spr '87
George, J. C. Water sky. 1987
  N Y Times Book Rev 92:26 My 10 '87. B. L. Clark
Gerber, A. Rumor of an elephant. 1987
  N Y Times Book Rev 92:24 Ag 30 '87. W. Cloonan
Gerstein, M. The mountains of Tibet. 1987
  N Y Times Book Rev 92:44 N 8 '87. J. Bierhorst
Gervasi, T. The myth of Soviet military supremacy. 1986
  Bull At Sci 43:51-2 Je '87. D. R. Jones
Gesensway, D. and Roseman, M. Beyond words. 1987
  N Y Times Book Rev 92:9-10 Jl 19 '87. F. Kometani
  New Leader 70:18-20 Ag 10-24 '87. C. Kaplan
Geyer, D. The Russian Revolution. 1987
  Hist Today 37:58-9 O '87. W. V. Wallace
Giardina, D. Storming heaven. 1987
  N Y Times Book Rev 92:39 S 20 '87. D. Bauer
Gibbons, K. Ellen Foster. 1987
  N Y Times Book Rev 92:13 My 31 '87. A. Hoffman
Gibbs, H. M. Optical bistability. 1985
  Phys Today 40 pt1:71-2 Ag '87. D. Sarid
Giddins, G. Rhythm-a-ning. 1985
  Am Sch 56:296-8 Spr '87. P. Schwendener
Gies, M. and Gold, A. L. Anne Frank remembered. 1987
  N Y Times Book Rev 92:7 My 10 '87. T. Des Pres
Gilbert, J. B. A cycle of outrage. 1986
  America 156:386-7 My 9 '87. R. McAulay
Gilbert, M. Winston S. Churchill; v7, Road to victory, 1941-1945. 1986
  N Y Rev Books 34:22-7 My 7 '87. T. Garton Ash
  Natl Rev 39:47-8 Ag 14 '87. J. Mysak
  New Repub 196:38-40 F 16 '87. P. M. Kennedy
Gilbert, S. F. Developmental biology. 1985
  BioScience 37:430 Je '87. I. Brick
Gilder, G. F. Men and marriage. 1986
  Christ Today 31:35-7 Mr 6 '87. J. P. Dennis

Commentary 83:76-8 Ap '87. T. Teachout
Natl Rev 39:52 F 27 '87. M. D. Aeschliman
Society 25:108-9 N/D '87. M. S. Kimmel
Gildner, G. The second bridge. 1987
  N Y Times Book Rev 92:18 Ap 26 '87. R. Goodman
Gildner, G. A week in South Dakota. 1987
  N Y Times Book Rev 92:18 Ap 26 '87. R. Goodman
Gill, B. Many masks. 1987
  N Y Times Book Rev 92:15 D 13 '87. M. Filler
Gill, B. M. Nursery crimes. 1987
  New Leader 70:18-19 Jl 1-15 '87. H. H. Davis
Gillon, S. M. Politics and vision. 1987
  New Leader 70:17 O 5 '87. B. Gewen
Gilman, R. Faith, sex, mystery. 1986
  Commonweal 114:85-6+ F 13 '87. P. Baumann
  N Y Times Book Rev 92:1+ Ja 18 '87. M. Gordon
  New Leader 69:11-12 D 1-15 '86. R. G. Davis
  New Repub 196:37-8 F 16 '87. A. Sullivan
  Vogue 177:100 Ja '87. F. Prose
Gilmore, D. D. Aggression and community. 1987
  N Y Rev Books 34:41-2 My 28 '87. R. Carr
Gilpin, R. and Gilpin, J. M. The political economy of
  international relations. 1987
  N Y Times Book Rev 92:22 Ag 16 '87. R. N. Rosecrance
Gingher, M. Bobby Rex's greatest hit. 1986
  Mademoiselle 93:68+ Ja '87. L. Darling
Ginsberg, A. Howl. 1986
  New Leader 70:15-16 Mr 9 '87. P. Pettingell
Ginsberg, A. White shroud. 1986
  New Leader 70:16 Mr 9 '87. P. Pettingell
Ginsberg, B. The captive public. 1986
  N Y Times Book Rev 92:32 F 8 '87. M. C. Miller
Ginzburg, N. The city and the house. 1987
  N Y Times Book Rev 92:30 S 13 '87. A. Cornelisen
  Nation 245:686-8 D 5 '87. D. Harris
Ginzburg, N. The Manzoni family. 1987
  Nation 245:686-8 D 5 '87. D. Harris
Gish, L. An actor's life for me. 1987
  N Y Times Book Rev 92:31 N 8 '87. J. Rothman
Gitlin, T. The sixties. 1987
  N Y Times Book Rev 92:13-14 N 8 '87. J. Miller
Gjertsen, D. The Newton handbook. 1986
  Sci Am 257:178+ O '87. P. Morrison
Glazebrook, P. Captain Vinegar's commission. 1987
  N Y Times Book Rev 92:11-12 N 15 '87. E. C. Munro
Glees, A. The secrets of the service. 1987
  N Y Rev Books 34:47-53 S 24 '87. N. G. A. Annan,
  Baron
  N Y Times Book Rev 92:9+ D 13 '87. Z. S. Steiner
Gleick, J. Chaos. 1987
  N Y Times Book Rev 92:11 O 25 '87. J. R. Maddox
  Nation 245:721-2 D 12 '87. D. Park
Glendinning, V. Rebecca West. 1987
  N Y Times Book Rev 92:3 O 18 '87. J. Kaplan
  New Leader 70:21 N 30 '87. C. Cleaver
  New Repub 197:46-9 O 19 '87. S. L. Hynes
  New Yorker 63:132-4 D 21 '87. V. S. Pritchett
  Vogue 177:276+ O '87. M. Jefferson
Glendon, M. A. Abortion and divorce in Western law.
  1987
  Wash Mon 19:58-9 N '87. C. B. Palese
Glickman, G. Years from now. 1987
  N Y Times Book Rev 92:20 O 18 '87. R. Houston
Glimpses of the Harvard past. 1986
  Am Sch 56:431-5 Summ '87. J. Wauck
Gloag, J. Only yesterday. 1987
  N Y Times Book Rev 92:17 F 22 '87. C. Gaiser
Global geocancerology. 1986
  Sci Am 256:27+ F '87. P. Morrison
Global resources and international conflict. 1986
  Bull At Sci 43:52-3 My '87. N. Myers
Glossbrenner, A. How to look it up online. 1987
  Byte 12:90+ Jl '87. B. N. Meeks
Glover, W. B. Biblical origins of modern secular culture.
  1984
  Natl Rev 39:50 D 31 '87. C. Williamson
Goble, P. Death of the iron horse. 1986
  N Y Times Book Rev 92:44 N 22 '87. G. B. Smith
God and nature. 1986
  Christ Century 104:891-2 O 14 '87. P. Hefner
  Christ Today 31:32 Ap 3 '87. C. E. Hummel
  Commonweal 114:298-300 My 8 '87. J. F. McCue
Godwin, G. A southern family. 1987
  N Y Times Book Rev 92:1+ O 11 '87. B. Lowry
  Time 130:82 O 5 '87. P. Gray
Goebbels, J. Michael. 1987
  New Repub 197:43-5 O 19 '87. J. Joll
Goetzmann, W. H. New lands, new men. 1986
  N Y Times Book Rev 92:22 Ja 11 '87. W. Kittredge
  Science 236:987-8 My 22 '87. W. Stanton
  Sierra 72:80-1+ My/Je '87. V. A. Walsh

Goffen, R. Piety and patronage in Renaissance Venice.
  1986
  N Y Rev Books 34:37-9 Jl 16 '87. F. Gilbert
Goffstein, M. B. An actor. 1987
  N Y Times Book Rev 92:31 N 8 '87. J. Rothman
Gold, T. Power from the earth. 1987
  Sci Am 257:147-8 N '87. P. Morrison
Goldbarth, A. Arts & sciences. 1986
  N Y Times Book Rev 92:22+ Ja 4 '87. E. Grosholz
Goldberg, L. In Siberia it is very cold. 1987
  N Y Times Book Rev 92:13 Ag 2 '87. O. Conant
Goldberg, V. Margaret Bourke-White. 1986
  America 156:161-3 F 21 '87. A. J. Lane
Golden, R. and McConnell, M. Sanctuary. 1985
  Progressive 51:40-1 Mr '87. S. Landau
Goldin, N. The ballad of sexual dependency. 1986
  New Repub 197:31-3 Ag 24 '87. A. Bernard
Golding, W. Close quarters. 1987
  N Y Times Book Rev 92:44 My 31 '87. R. M. Adams
  Time 129:80+ Je 8 '87. P. Gray
Goldman, L. The part of fortune. 1987
  N Y Times Book Rev 92:10-11 Ja 25 '87. C. Pelletier
Goldman, M. I. Gorbachev's challenge. 1987
  N Y Times Book Rev 92:9 Je 21 '87. W. W. Leontief
  New Repub 197:29-34+ Ag 3 '87. R. B. Reich
Goldman, W. Brothers. 1987
  N Y Times Book Rev 92:18 F 15 '87. S. Dobyns
Goldsmith, B. Johnson v. Johnson. 1987
  N Y 20:129-30 F 23 '87. R. Koenig
  N Y Times Book Rev 92:15 N 8 '87. J. Allen
Gombrich, E. H. Aby Warburg. 2nd ed. 1986
  New Repub 196:38-41 Mr 23 '87. F. Kermode
  New Yorker 62:95-8 F 2 '87. G. Steiner
Goncharov, I. A. The frigate Pallada. 1987
  N Y Times Book Rev 92:9 S 20 '87. A. Tyler
González, J. L. Ballard of another time.
  Nation 245:688-90 D 5 '87. S. Klawans
Goodall, J. The chimpanzees of Gombe. 1986
  BioScience 37:732-3 N '87. R. H. Wiley
  N Y Rev Books 34:20-5 Je 25 '87. S. J. Gould
  Science 235:694-5 F 6 '87. J. Altmann
Goodall, J. S. The story of a main street. 1987
  N Y Times Book Rev 92:33 N 8 '87. P. Goldberger
Goodman, C. Hans Hofmann. 1986
  Art Am 75:25 Je '87. P. Plagens
Goodwin, D. K. The Fitzgeralds and the Kennedys. 1986
  Commentary 83:68-72 Je '87. K. S. Lynn
  N Y Rev Books 34:3-4+ Ap 23 '87. F. Russell
  N Y Times Book Rev 92:11-12 F 15 '87. G. C. Ward
  New Leader 70:14-15 Jl 1-15 '87. B. Gewen
  New Repub 196:36-8 Mr 16 '87. G. Wills
  Newsweek 109:72 F 9 '87. J. Miller
  Time 129:69 F 16 '87. R. Z. Sheppard
  Vogue 177:256+ F '87. D. Berg
  Wash Mon 19:47-9 My '87. C. Peters
Gooneratne, Y. Relative merits. 1986
  New Repub 196:33-8 F 23 '87. D. L. Horowitz
Gorbachev, M. Perestroika. 1987
  N Y Times Book Rev 92:3+ D 13 '87. R. Legvold
  New Leader 70:5-6 D 14 '87. R. C. Tucker
Gordimer, N. A sport of nature. 1987
  Macleans 100:50 Je 1 '87. G. MacKay
  N Y Rev Books 34:8-9 Jl 16 '87. D. Johnson
  N Y Times Book Rev 92:1+ My 3 '87. M. Howard
  Nation 244:731-3 My 30 '87. A. B. Snitow
  New Leader 70:18-19 Ap 20 '87. O. Conant
  New Repub 196:33-6 My 18 '87. J. Krauss
  New Yorker 63:87-90 Je 29 '87. J. Thurman
  Time 129:76 Ap 6 '87. P. Gray
Gordimer, N. and Goldblatt, D. Lifetimes: under apartheid.
  1986
  Nation 244:578-80 My 2 '87. R. Nixon
Gordis, R. Judaic ethics for a lawless world. 1986
  Christ Century 104:1180-1 D 23-30 '87. N. P. Kollar
Gordon, J. S. The golden guru. 1987
  N Y Times Book Rev 92:15 S 13 '87. M. E. Marty
Gordon, M. Temporary shelter. 1987
  N Y Times Book Rev 92:8 Ap 19 '87. R. Billington
  Time 129:74 Ap 20 '87. P. Gray
Gordon, S. Waiting for the rain. 1987
  N Y Times Book Rev 92:21 D 20 '87. L. Freed
Gordon, S. and Gordon, J. Raising a child conservatively
  in a sexually permissive world. 1986
  Humanist 47:37 Ja/F '87. A. M. Jackson
Gordon Smith, R. Travels in the land of the gods
  (1898-1907). 1986
  Smithsonian 18:224-6 O '87. J. D. Kirwan
Gore, T. Raising PG kids in an X-rated society. 1987
  Nation 245:61-3 Jl 18-25 '87. M. Landsberg
  Psychol Today 21:80 S '87. P. Hersch
Gorn, E. J. The manly art. 1986

N Y Times Book Rev 92:8 Ja 11 '87. D. Kelly
Nation 244:262-3 F 28 '87. D. Nasaw
Gornick, V. Fierce attachments. 1987
N Y Times Book Rev 92:7 Ap 26 '87. M. Simpson
Nation 244:549-50 Ap 25 '87. W. Gimbel
Smithsonian 18:266-8 N '87. B. Hall
Gossage, H. L. Is there any hope for advertising? 1986
Cent Mag 20:40 My/Je '87. D. McDonald
Gottfried, K. and Weisskopf, V. F. Concepts of particle physics. v2 1984
Phys Today 40:84+ D '87. T. D. Sanders
Gottfried, P. The search for historical meaning. 1986
Natl Rev 39:44-6 My 22 '87. R. A. Nisbet
Gottlieb, A. Do you believe in magic? 1987
Commentary 83:74-7 My '87. T. Lindberg
N Y Times Book Rev 92:14 Ap 5 '87. L. Shapiro
Psychol Today 21:78 Ap '87. D. Drabelle
Gould, S. J. Time's arrow, time's cycle. 1987
Earth Sci 40:37 Fall '87
N Y Rev Books 34:37-40 My 28 '87. F. J. Sulloway
N Y Times Book Rev 92:35 Je 14 '87. D. R. Wallace
New Yorker 63:105-8 S 7 '87. J. Updike
Goytisolo, J. Landscapes after the battle. 1987
N Y Times Book Rev 92:7 Je 14 '87. R. Kiely
Graber, R. Doc. 1986
N Y Times Book Rev 92:29 Mr 15 '87. P. Campbell
Grade, C. My mother's Sabbath days. 1986
Christ Century 104:969-70 N 4 '87. S. N. Rosenbaum
Graff, H. J. The legacies of literacy. 1986
Commentary 84:47-8 Jl '87. J. W. Tuttleton
New Repub 196:47-9 Ap 20 '87. A. P. Weisman
Grafton, D. Red, hot and rich! 1987
N Y Times Book Rev 92:14-15 Je 21 '87. S. McCauley
Graham, J. The end of beauty. 1987
N Y Times Book Rev 92:9 Jl 26 '87. J. D. McClatchy
Nation 245:206-8 S 5 '87. J. Greenbaum
New Yorker 63:74-7 Jl 27 '87. H. H. Vendler
Graham, L. R. Science, philosophy, and human behavior in the Soviet Union. 1987
N Y Times Book Rev 92:34 S 27 '87. C. Sagan
Graham, M. B. W. RCA and the VideoDisc. 1986
Science 236:1358-9 Je 5 '87. E. A. Blackstone
Graham, W. A green flash. 1987
N Y Times Book Rev 92:20 O 25 '87. S. Offit
Granfield, P. The limits of the papacy. 1987
America 157:460-2 D 12 '87. K. L. M. Orsy
Commonweal 114:633-4 N 6 '87. P. Chirico
Granger, L. and Granger, B. The magic feather. 1986
Nation 244:228-9 F 21 '87. J. Wolfe
Psychol Today 21:76-8 Ap '87. P. Chance
Grant, G. P. Technology and justice. 1986
Macleans 100:57 Mr 30 '87. J. Bemrose
Grant, P. R. Ecology and evolution of Darwin's finches. 1986
Science 236:1002-3 My 22 '87. R. T. Holmes
Grant, V. The evolutionary process. 1985
BioScience 37:739-40 N '87. S. B. McDowell
Grant, Z. Over the beach. 1987
N Y Times Book Rev 92:25 Ja 11 '87. R. Witkin
Grass, G. The rat. 1987
N Y Rev Books 34:45-6 S 24 '87. D. J. Enright
N Y Times Book Rev 92:6 Jl 5 '87. J. T. Hospital
New Repub 197:29-32 Jl 13-20 '87. J. Anders
Time 130:73 Jl 20 '87. P. Gray
Graves, R. P. Robert Graves, the assault heroic, 1895-1926. 1987
N Y Rev Books 34:8-11 Je 25 '87. J. Wain
Natl Rev 39:48-9 My 22 '87. J. Meyers
New Repub 196:37-9 Mr 30 '87. S. L. Hynes
Smithsonian 18:138-9 Ag '87. M. Dirda
Gray, A. The fall of Kelvin Walker. 1985
N Y Rev Books 34:15-16 F 26 '87. D. J. Enright
Gray, F. du P. Adam & Eve and the city. 1987
N Y Times Book Rev 92:13 Ag 30 '87. J. Alter
Gray, R. Cardinal Manning. 1985
Natl Rev 39:54+ Ag 28 '87. R. P. Rooney
Greek literature. 1985
N Y Rev Books 33:44-5 Ja 15 '87. O. Taplin
Greek tragedy and political theory. 1986
Cent Mag 20:41-2 My/Je '87. D. McDonald
Greeley, A. M. American Catholics since the Council. 1985
Natl Rev 39:53 Je 5 '87. P. Stravinskas
Greeley, A. M. Patience of a saint. 1987
N Y Times Book Rev 92:31 F 8 '87. J. Sullivan
Greeley, R. Planetary landscapes. 1985
Astronomy 15:44-5 Mr '87. D. F. Robertson
Green, M. B. and others. Superstring theory. 2v 1987
Phys Today 40:91-2 N '87. P. H. Frampton
Science 238:94-5 O 2 '87. D. Z. Freedman

Green, R. The "sissy boy syndrome" and the development of homosexuality. 1986
Child Today 16:34-5 Jl/Ag '87. M. F. Shore
Vogue 177:316+ Mr '87. E. Gregersen
Greenberg, C. The collected essays and criticism. 2v 1986
Am Sch 56:535-45 Aut '87. S. Schwartz
Art Am 75:122-7+ My '87. S. Tillim
Commentary 84:78-80 D '87. R. Kimball
New Repub 196:26-8+ Mr 2 '87. J. Perl
Greenberg, J. Age of consent. 1986
N Y Times Book Rev 92:11 D 27 '87. M. J. Gerber
Greenfeld, H. The devil and Dr. Barnes. 1987
N Y Times Book Rev 92:13-14 N 22 '87. A. C. Danto
Greenfeld, J. A client called Noah. 1987
N Y Times Book Rev 92:1+ F 15 '87. S. Kenney
Greenly, M. Chronicle. 1986
Futurist 21:16 Mr/Ap '87. E. S. Cornish
Greenstein, G. Frozen star. 1985
Harpers 274:75-6 Ja '87. L. A. Marschall
Greenya, J. Blood relations. 1987
N Y Times Book Rev 92:28 S 13 '87. M. Jones
Greer, G. The madwoman's underclothes. 1987
N Y Times Book Rev 92:14 O 11 '87. L. Blandford
Nation 245:690-2 D 5 '87. C. Sternhell
Gregory, T. B. and Smith, G. R. High schools as communities: the small school reconsidered. 1987
Phi Delta Kappan 68:556-7 Mr '87. M. A. Raywid
Grekova, I. The ship of widows. 1985
N Y Times Book Rev 92:35 F 8 '87. P. Meyer
Grenville, K. Dreamhouse. 1987
N Y Times Book Rev 92:24 N 22 '87. M. Peacock
Griffin, W. Clive Staples Lewis. 1986
America 156:57-8 Ja 24 '87. J. B. Breslin
Christ Today 31:61-2 Ja 16 '87. L. W. Dorsett
Natl Rev 39:57-8 D 18 '87. J. T. Como
Grimes, M. The five bells and bladebone. 1987
N Y Times Book Rev 92:53 S 13 '87. E. Jolley
Grin, A. Selected short stories. 1987
N Y Times Book Rev 92:10 D 20 '87. H. Robinson
Groce, N. Everyone here spoke sign language. 1985
Sci Am 256:27-9 Mr '87. P. Morrison
Gross, M. G. Oceanography, a view of the earth. 4th ed. 1987
Sea Front 33:473-4 N/D '87. K. M. Sullivan
Gross, M. L. The Red President. 1987
Natl Rev 39:50-1 Mr 13 '87. J. Sobran
Grove, A. S. One-on-one with Andy Grove. 1987
Fortune 115:184 Je 22 '87. A. Kupfer
The Growth and form of modular organisms. 1986
Science 237:1626-7 S 25 '87. L. W. Buss
Grumbach, D. The magician's girl. 1987
N Y Times Book Rev 92:22 F 1 '87. P. Deitz
Grünbaum, B. and Shephard, G. C. Tilings and patterns. 1986
Science 236:996-7 My 22 '87. J. Malkevitch
Grunfeld, F. V. Rodin. 1987
N Y Times Book Rev 92:1+ D 13 '87. B. Read
Grushkin, P. The art of rock. 1987
N Y Times Book Rev 92:13-14 D 13 '87. E. Sanders
Gübelin, E. J. and Koivula, J. I. Photoatlas of inclusions in gemstones.
Sci Am 256:26 Ja '87. P. Morrison
Gumpert, G. Talking tombstones and other tales of the media age. 1987
N Y Times Book Rev 92:23 Mr 8 '87. N. Postman
Psychol Today 21:64 S '87. P. Hersch
Gundlach, J. K. My mother before me. 1986
Psychol Today 21:78-9 S '87. D. Dowling
Gunn, G. The culture of criticism and the criticism of culture. 1987
America 157:140 S 12-19 '87. E. F. Block, Jr.
Christ Century 104:600-1 Jl 1-8 '87. W. A. Kort
N Y Times Book Rev 92:14 My 10 '87. C. Ricks
Guralnick, P. Sweet soul music. 1986
Down Beat 54:55 Mr '87. G. Santoro
Gurewich, D. Travels with Dubinsky and Clive. 1987
N Y Times Book Rev 92:24 O 25 '87. J. Greenfeld
Gustafson, R. F. Leo Tolstoy, resident and stranger. 1986
Natl Rev 39:49-50 Jl 31 '87. J. Meyers
Gutiérrez, G. On Job. 1987
Christ Century 104:1039-40 N 18 '87. P. LeMasters
Gutmann, A. Democratic education. 1987
New Repub 197:36-8 O 26 '87. B. R. Barber
Gwynne, S. C. Selling money. 1986
Wash Mon 18:55-7 Ja '87. C. Lane

H

Hacker, B. C. The dragon's tail. 1987
Bull At Sci 43:46+ D '87. R. Alvarez

Headley, G. and Meulenkamp, W. Follies. 1986
Hist Today 37:55-6 Ap '87. S. Jones
Heaney, S. The haw lantern. 1987
N Y Times Book Rev 92:12 D 20 '87. M. Rudman
New Repub 197:36-9 D 21 '87. J. D. McClatchy
Hearn, M. P. The porcelain cat. 1987
N Y Times Book Rev 92:50 N 8 '87. P. MacLachlan
Hearne, B. G. Eli's ghost. 1987
N Y Times Book Rev 92:33 Mr 22 '87. D. Felder
Hearne, V. Adam's task. 1986
N Y Rev Books 34:20-5 Je 25 '87. S. J. Gould
Psychol Today 21:70-1+ F '87. H. Ritvo
Hearnshaw, J. B. The analysis of starlight. 1987
Science 237:783-4 Ag 14 '87. D. H. DeVorkin
Hearon, S. Five hundred scorpions. 1987
N Y Times Book Rev 92:7 My 10 '87. L. Pei
Heatley, C. J., III. The cutting edge. 1986
Oceans 20:60 Jl/Ag '87. S. Wilkinson
Hebblethwaite, P. In the Vatican. 1986
America 156:84-5 Ja 31 '87. T. J. Gumbleton
Christ Century 104:91 Ja 28 '87. K. B. Cully
Hebert, E. The passion of Estelle Jordan. 1987
N Y Times Book Rev 92:30 Mr 1 '87. D. Smith
Hecht, J. The laser guidebook. 1986
Phys Today 40:96 My '87. D. C. Peckham
Hedderwick, M. Katie Morag and the tiresome Ted. 1986
N Y Times Book Rev 92:41 F 15 '87. B. Mason
Hedderwick, M. Katie Morag and the two grandmothers. 1986
N Y Times Book Rev 92:41 F 15 '87. B. Mason
Hedeen, R. A. The oyster. 1986
Sea Front 33:471-2 N/D '87. E. S. Iversen
Heinemann, L. Close quarters. 1986
New Yorker 63:111-12 My 11 '87. V. Geng
Heinemann, L. Paco's story. 1987
N Y Times Book Rev 92:19 N 8 '87. C. E. G. Benfey
New Yorker 63:112-14 My 11 '87. V. Geng
Heller, D. The children's God. 1986
Child Today 16:32 Ja/F '87. M. H. Lystad
Heller, M. and Nekrich, A. M. Utopia in power. 1986
Commentary 83:76-8 Mr '87. M. Friedberg
Commonweal 114:297-8 My 8 '87. L. Menashe
Helminiak, D. A. The same Jesus. 1986
America 157:338-40 N 7 '87. R. A. Krieg
Helwig, D. The bishop. 1986
N Y Times Book Rev 92:23 Ja 11 '87. J. Leggett
Hemming, R. The melody lingers on. 1986
Smithsonian 18:143-5 Jl '87. D. Drabelle
Hemocytic and humoral immunity in arthropods. 1986
Science 236:1684-5 Je 26 '87. T. C. Cheng
Hendershot, J. In coal country. 1987
N Y Times Book Rev 92:33 My 17 '87. L. Smith
Henderson, M. C. Theater in America. 1986
Americana 15:20-1 N/D '87. M. Durham
Henry, C. F. H. Confessions of a theologian. 1986
Christ Today 31:35+ F 20 '87. B. L. Shelley
Henry, J. D. Red fox. 1986
Conservationist 41:52 Ja/F '87. H. W. Trimm
Hepburn, K. The making of The African queen. 1987
New Yorker 63:107-8 S 21 '87. P. Kael
Herbers, J. The new heartland. 1986
Sierra 72:147-8 Ja/F '87. S. Zuckerman
Herken, G. Counsels of war. 1985
Society 24:85-8 My/Je '87. J. F. Pilat
Hermann Weyl, 1885-1985. 1986
Science 236:998-9 My 22 '87. L. Michel
Herodotus. The history. 1987
N Y Rev Books 34:11-12+ Ap 9 '87. J. Griffin
N Y Times Book Rev 92:13-14 Je 28 '87. P. Levi
Herr, P. Jessie Benton Fremont. 1987
Am Hist Illus 22:8 My '87
Hersey, J. Blues. 1987
N Y Times Book Rev 92:12 My 31 '87. V. Klinkenborg
Time 129:66-7 My 25 '87. S. Kanfer
Hersh, S. M. "The target is destroyed". 1986
Natl Rev 39:52-4 Mr 27 '87. J. E. Oberg
Hertz, R. More equal than others. 1986
Psychol Today 21:65+ S '87. J. Goetz
Herzog, A. Vesco. 1987
N Y Times Book Rev 92:37 O 25 '87. R. Rosenbaum
Hewett, J. On camera. 1987
N Y Times Book Rev 92:31 N 8 '87. J. Rothman
Hewett, J. Rosalie. 1987
N Y Times Book Rev 92:40-1 My 17 '87. A. M. Bregman
Hey, A. J. G. and Walters, P. The quantum universe. 1987
Science 238:558 O 23 '87. O. W. Greenberg
Heyen, W. The chestnut rain.
N Y Times Book Rev 92:42 F 15 '87. R. Von Hallberg
Hibbert, C. The English. 1986

Hist Today 37:54-5 Jl '87. J. Critchley
N Y Times Book Rev 92:11-12 Ap 12 '87. M. Quilligan
A Hierarchical concept of ecosystems. 1986
Science 236:206-7 Ap 10 '87. R. E. Ricklefs
Higgins, G. V. Outlaws. 1987
Time 130:79+ S 14 '87. R. Z. Sheppard
Higgins, J. Night of the fox. 1986
N Y Times Book Rev 92:15 Ja 18 '87. R. Lourie
Higgins, T. The perfect failure. 1987
N Y Times Book Rev 92:3 N 29 '87. S. Hoffmann
Higgs, R. Crisis and leviathan. 1987
Fortune 116:101-2 Ag 31 '87. D. R. Henderson
Higher plant cell respiration. 1985
BioScience 37:742-3 N '87. C. C. Black
Hill, C. The collected essays of Christopher Hill; v3, People and ideas in 17th century England. 1986
Hist Today 37:55 Jl '87. R. C. Richardson
Hill, E. My daughter Beatrice. 1986
Phys Today 40:74-5 Jl '87. M. Phillips
Science 235:915-16 F 20 '87. G. R. Knapp
Sky Telesc 74:261 S '87. L. Y. Schweizer
Hillesum, E. Letters from Westerbork. 1986
Christ Today 31:32 O 16 '87. P. W. Nisly
N Y Rev Books 34:29-34 My 28 '87. N. Ascherson
Smithsonian 17:177-9 Mr '87. L. Simon
Hills, P. John Singer Sargent. 1986
Antiques 131:144+ Ja '87. M. Lovell
Himmelfarb, G. Marriage and morals among the Victorians. 1986
N Y Rev Books 34:26-8 My 28 '87. K. V. Thomas
Himmelfarb, G. The new history and the old. 1987
N Y Rev Books 34:59-62 D 17 '87. L. Stone
Time 130:122+ O 26 '87. O. Friedrich
Hinde, W. Richard Cobden. 1987
Hist Today 37:55-6 S '87. G. Watson
New Repub 196:34-6 Je 22 '87. D. Cannadine
Hindle, B. and Lubar, S. D. Engines of change. 1986
Science 236:972-3 My 22 '87. C. Pursell
Hine, T. Populuxe. 1986
Archit Rec 175:73+ Ag '87. D. Gantenbein
The Hippocampus; v3-4. 1986
Science 235:1682 Mr 27 '87. L. Nadel
Hiroshige. One hundred famous views of Edo. 1986
Art Am 75:98-105 Jl '87. K. Varnedoe
Hirsch, E. D. Cultural literacy. 1987
Commentary 84:45-7 Jl '87. J. W. Tuttleton
Commonweal 114:542-3 S 25 '87. T. O'Brien
N Y Times Book Rev 92:36 Ap 26 '87. R. B. Stevens
Nation 244:710-16+ My 30 '87. R. Pattison
New Yorker 63:106-10 Je 1 '87. G. Steiner
Science 236:973 My 22 '87. L. A. Coser
Time 130:72-3 Jl 20 '87. S. Kanfer
Hirschman, A. O. Rival views of market society and other recent essays. 1986
New Repub 197:46-9 N 23 '87. R. Kuttner
The History of cartography; v1, Cartography in prehistoric, ancient, and medieval Europe and the Mediterranean. 1987
N Y Times Book Rev 92:13 S 20 '87. J. N. Wilford
A History of private life; v1, From pagan Rome to Byzantium. 1987
Atlantic 259:90-2 My '87. B. M. W. Knox
Hist Today 37:54-5 S '87. N. Tucker
N Y Times Book Rev 92:14-15 My 3 '87. H. Chadwick
New Repub 196:39-41 Je 29 '87. G. W. Bowersock
The History of the University of Oxford; v5, The eighteenth century. 1986
Hist Today 37:56 Ja '87. J. C. D. Clark
Hite, S. Women and love. 1987
Ms 16:90+ D '87. L. Duggan
N Y Times Book Rev 92:3+ N 15 '87. A. R. Hochschild
Newsweek 110:86 O 19 '87. L. Shapiro
Hoagland, E. Seven rivers west. 1986
New Yorker 63:120-2 Mr 30 '87. J. Updike
Hoban, R. The Medusa frequency. 1987
N Y Times Book Rev 92:11 N 8 '87. S. Erickson
Hochachka, P. W. and Guppy, M. Metabolic arrest and the control of biological time. 1987
Science 236:1003 My 22 '87. A. F. Bennett
Hodges, D. C. Intellectual foundations of the Nicaraguan revolution. 1986
New Repub 197:26-8+ N 16 '87. A. Cruz, Jr.
Hodges, T. Western Sahara. 1983
Society 24:95 Mr/Ap '87. I. W. Zartman
Hoel, M. L. Land's edge. 1986
Oceans 20:60-1 Mr/Ap '87. P. Kopper
Hoffman, A. Illumination night. 1987
Glamour 85:202 Ag '87. L. Mathews
N Y Times Book Rev 92:7+ Ag 9 '87. G. Cravens
Hoffmann, S. Janus and Minerva. 1987
Commentary 84:70-2 Jl '87. D. Gress

Ignatius, D. Agents of innocence. 1987
   Time 130:91 N 2 '87. P. Gray
Ignatow, D. New and collected poems, 1970-1985. 1986
   N Y Times Book Rev 92:30 Ja 11 '87. P. Stitt
Immaculate & powerful. 1985
   America 157:412-13 N 28 '87. S. R. Hiatt
In the field of fire. 1987
   N Y Times Book Rev 92:25+ My 3 '87. D. Bradley
Ingalls, R. I see a long journey. 1985
   New Repub 196:48-9 F 9 '87. K. Kearns
Ingalls, R. The pearlkillers. 1986
   N Y Times Book Rev 92:24 N 15 '87. U. K. Le
   Guin
Ingham, K. Jan Christian Smuts. 1986
   Hist Today 37:54 Ap '87. R. Turrell
   N Y Times Book Rev 92:15 Mr 15 '87. J. F. Burns
The INGRES papers. 1986
   Byte 12:90 Je '87. H. Kilov
Inman, R. Home fires burning. 1986
   N Y Times Book Rev 92:17 Ja 25 '87. T. Wicker
Inner space/outer space. 1986
   Science 235:372-3 Ja 16 '87. P. J. E. Peebles
Inoué, S. Video microscopy. 1986
   Science 235:1263 Mr 6 '87. J. Capowski
Insect flight. 1986
   Science 236:618-19 My 1 '87. D. Roff
International Astronomical Union. Symposium (117th: 1985: Princeton, N.J.). Dark matter in the universe. 1987
   Science 237:86-7 Jl 3 '87. J. S. Gallagher
International Astronomical Union. Symposium (112th: 1984: Boston University). The search for extraterrestrial life—recent developments. 1985
   Phys Today 40:92 D '87. F. J. Tipler
International car collectors' yearbook.
   Mot Trend 39:32 Mr '87. T. C. Browne
International School of Radiation Damage and Protection (5th: 1983: Erice, Sicily). Biological effects and dosimetry of static and ELF electromagnetic fields. 1985
   BioScience 37:740-1 N '87. A. Sheppard
International Symposium on Immunogenetics (1983: Tokyo, Japan). Immunogenetics. 1984
   BioScience 37:228-9 Mr '87. I. Magrath
International Symposium on Synergetics (1985: Schloss Elmau, Bavaria). Complex systems, operational approaches in neurobiology, physics, and computers. 1985
   Phys Today 40:74-6 Mr '87. F. Varela
International Symposium on Synergetics (1983: Berlin, Germany). Synergetics, from microscopic to macroscopic order. 1984
   Phys Today 40:76-7 Mr '87. J.-P. Dupuy
International Task Force on Prevention of Nuclear Terrorism. Preventing nuclear terrorism. 1987
   Science 236:977-8 My 22 '87. R. J. Rydell
Invented lives. 1987
   N Y Times Book Rev 92:3+ O 4 '87. H. L. Gates
IRAS Conference (1st: 1985: Noordwijk, Netherlands). Light on dark matter. 1986
   Science 235:695-6 F 6 '87. T. Herter
Irvine, L. Runaway. 1987
   Vogue 177:314+ Mr '87. F. Prose
Irwin, R. The Arabian nightmare. 1987
   N Y Times Book Rev 92:14 N 15 '87. J. Crowley
Isaacson, W. and Thomas, E. The wise men. 1986
   Commentary 83:37-48 Ap '87. H. J. Kaplan
   Natl Rev 39:50-2 F 13 '87. A. Beichman
   New Repub 196:40-4 F 9 '87. G. Hodgson
   Wash Mon 19:57-8 Ap '87. H. McPherson
Isserman, M. If I had a hammer—. 1987
   N Y Rev Books 34:10+ O 22 '87. A. Brinkley
   N Y Times Book Rev 92:15 S 27 '87. G. Tyler
   Nation 245:565-8 N 14 '87. S. Wilentz
   Wash Mon 19:60 N '87. J. Miller
Itō, T. Tsujigahana, the flower of Japanese textile art. 1985
   Am Craft 47:14 Ap/My '87. G. Moss
Itzkoff, S. W. Why humans vary in intelligence. 1987
   Fortune 116:228 O 12 '87. D. Seligman
Ives, E. W. Anne Boleyn. 1986
   N Y Rev Books 34:40-3 Je 11 '87. J. H. Elliott
Ivimey, J. W. The complete story of the three blind mice. 1987
   N Y Times Book Rev 92:28-9 N 29 '87. P. Neumeyer
Iwagō, M. Serengeti, natural order on the African plain. 1987
   Nat Hist 96:74-7 Jl '87. R. D. Estes

J

Jablonski, E. Gershwin. 1987
   Commentary 84:69-70+ D '87. W. H. Youngren
   N Y Times Book Rev 92:14 S 27 '87. F. Davis

   Time 130:76 S 21 '87. S. Kanfer
Jackson, D. D. Voyages of the steamboat Yellow Stone. 1987
   USA Today (Periodical) 116:96-7 S '87. G. F. Kreyche
Jackson, J. Straight from the heart. 1987
   Black Enterp 18:17 N '87. T. Bolden Davis
Jackson, P. W. The practice of teaching. 1986
   Phi Delta Kappan 68:710-11 My '87. E. L. Ihle
Jackson, S. W. Melancholia and depression. 1986
   N Y Rev Books 34:5-6+ F 12 '87. M. Critchley
   N Y Times Book Rev 92:32 Ap 5 '87. R. M. A.
   Hirschfeld
Jackson, W. Altars of unhewn stone. 1987
   N Y Times Book Rev 92:30 S 27 '87. L. Hyde
   Wilderness 51:66 Wint '87. C. E. Little
Jacobs, D. The brutality of nations. 1987
   N Y Times Book Rev 92:15-16 Mr 29 '87. C. Campbell
   New Repub 196:32-4 Je 15 '87. R. Morris
   Wash Mon 19:58 S '87. R. D. Kaplan
Jacobs, H. A. Incidents in the life of a slave girl. 1987
   Am Herit 38:108-9 D '87
   N Y Times Book Rev 92:12 N 22 '87. H. L. Gates
   Nation 245:242 S 12 '87. W. L. Aponte
Jacobs, R. Slow burn, a photodocument of Centralia, Pennsylvania. 1986
   N Y Times Book Rev 92:16 Ja 4 '87. B. A. Franklin
Jacobsen, J. Adios, Mr. Moxley. 1986
   Nation 245:644-6 N 28 '87. M. Hacker
Jacobsen, J. The sisters. 1987
   Nation 245:644-6 N 28 '87. M. Hacker
Jacoby, R. The last intellectuals. 1987
   Atlantic 260:104-6 O '87. M. C. Miller
   N Y Times Book Rev 92:44 O 25 '87. M. Krupnick
   Nation 245:493-5 O 31 '87. C. Blake
   Natl Rev 39:53-4 D 4 '87. J. Sobran
   New Leader 70:19-20 N 2 '87. W. L. O'Neill
   New Repub 197:33-4+ N 9 '87. L. Menand
Jacques, B. Redwall. 1986
   N Y Times Book Rev 92:27 Ag 23 '87. S. G. Lanes
Jaffe, E. B. and Jaffe, H. W. Geology of the Adirondack high peaks region. 1986
   Earth Sci 40:32-3 Wint '87
Jagger, J. Solar-UV actions on living cells. 1985
   BioScience 37:737 N '87. A. D. Woodhead
Jaki, S. L. Chesterton, a seer of science. 1986
   Natl Rev 39:46-7 Je 5 '87. P. E. Hodgson
James, H. The complete notebooks of Henry James. 1987
   N Y Rev Books 34:49-51 N 5 '87. M. Bell
   New Yorker 63:101-4 Mr 9 '87. H. Moss
James, M. Society, politics, and culture. 1986
   Hist Today 37:58 My '87. C. Cross
James, T. Exile within. 1987
   Wash Mon 19:60 O '87. J. Zimmerman
Jamieson, P. F. Adirondack pilgrimage. 1986
   Conservationist 42:52 S/O '87. T. L. Cobb
Jane Freilicher—paintings. 1986
   Am Artist 51:86-7 S '87. M. C. Nelson
Janeway, E. Improper behavior. 1987
   N Y Times Book Rev 92:13 Jl 5 '87. D. English
Janovy, J. Fields of friendly strife. 1987
   N Y Times Book Rev 92:11 Je 14 '87. K. Stabiner
   Psychol Today 21:72 Je '87. E. Stark
Janowitz, T. A cannibal in Manhattan. 1987
   N Y Times Book Rev 92:12 O 4 '87. F. Prose
   New Yorker 63:142-6 O 26 '87. T. Rafferty
   Newsweek 110:72 S 7 '87. D. Lehman
Japanese tales. 1987
   N Y Times Book Rev 92:14 Je 28 '87. M. Ury
Jay, M. Permanent exiles. 1985
   Society 24:91-2 Jl/Ag '87. L. A. Coser
Jefferies, R. P. S. The ancestry of the vertebrates. 1986
   Science 236:1476 Je 12 '87. J. Sprinkle
Jehlen, M. American incarnation. 1986
   Cent Mag 20:40-1 My/Je '87. D. McDonald
Jenkins, B. Sir William Gregory of Coole. 1986
   Hist Today 37:55 Mr '87. C. Townshend
Jenkinson, D. Maserati 3011.
   Road Track 38:132 Ag '87. G. Borgeson
Jerusalem Winter School for Theoretical Physics (1st: 1983-1984: Jerusalem). Intersection between elementary particle physics and cosmology. 1986
   Science 236:999-1000 My 22 '87. F. Wilczek
Jerusalem Winter School for Theoretical Physics (2nd: 1984-1985: Institute for Advanced Study of the Hebrew University). Physics in higher dimensions. 1986
   Science 236:999-1000 My 22 '87. F. Wilczek
Jesus in history and myth. 1986
   America 157:338-40 N 7 '87. R. A. Krieg
Jhabvala, R. P. Three continents. 1987
   N Y Rev Books 34:45-6 O 8 '87. R. Towers
   N Y Times Book Rev 92:3+ Ag 23 '87. P. Ackroyd

Joan, P. Preventing teenage suicide. 1986
   Child Today 16:30 Ja/F '87. M. Burnison
Johannsen, R. W. To the halls of the Montezumas. 1985
   Hist Today 37:53 Ap '87. H. Brogan
Johansson, C. M. Music and ministry.
   Christ Today 31:63 My 15 '87. C. Kroeker
John Paul II, Pope. The collected plays and writings on theater. 1987
   New Repub 197:47-8 D 14 '87. S. Barańczak
Johnson, B. The four days of courage. 1987
   Macleans 100:54 My 18 '87. M. Gee
   N Y Times Book Rev 92:9 Je 14 '87. D. H. Bain
Johnson, B. E. How to make up to $20,000 a year in antiques and collectibles without leaving your job. 1986
   Antiques Collect Hobbies 92:55 Je '87
Johnson, D. Persian nights. 1987
   Commonweal 114:358-60 Je 5 '87. R. Jones
   N Y Rev Books 34:14 Ap 23 '87. R. Dinnage
   N Y Times Book Rev 92:8 Ap 5 '87. J. A. Phillips
   New Repub 196:45-7 Ap 20 '87. D. Wickenden
   Time 129:83 Mr 23 '87. P. Gray
   Vogue 177:314 Mr '87. F. Prose
Johnson, D. The veil. 1987
   N Y Times Book Rev 92:46 O 18 '87. S. Dobyns
Johnson, G. Machinery of the mind. 1986
   Psychol Today 21:102-3 My '87. J. Meer
Johnson, L. T. The writings of the New Testament. 1986
   Christ Century 104:503-5 My 20-27 '87. M. T. Norwood, Jr.
Johnson, P. A history of the Jews. 1987
   Christ Century 104:1149-50 D 16 '87. W. Weinberg
   Commentary 83:64+ Je '87. M. Gilbert
   N Y Rev Books 34:7 O 8 '87. A. Momigliano
   N Y Times Book Rev 92:11-12 Ap 19 '87. A. Hertzberg
   Natl Rev 39:45-6 Ag 14 '87. J. Neusner
   Time 129:84-5 My 11 '87. R. Z. Sheppard
   U S Cathol 52:48-51 D '87. G. M. Costello
Johnson, R. W. Shootdown. 1986
   Natl Rev 39:52-4 Mr 27 '87. J. E. Oberg
Johnson, U. Anniversaries II. 1987
   N Y Times Book Rev 92:61 N 8 '87. T. Ziolkowski
Jolley, E. The newspaper of Claremont Street. 1987
   Time 130:87 D 7 '87. P. Gray
Jolley, E. Palomino. 1987
   N Y Times Book Rev 92:11 Jl 19 '87. J. Hendin
Jolley, E. The well. 1986
   New Repub 196:38-41 F 23 '87. W. H. Pritchard
Jones, E. Gentlemen and Jesuits. 1986
   Hist Today 37:54 Mr '87. K. R. Andrews
Jones, H. Mutiny on the Amistad. 1986
   N Y Rev Books 34:34-7 N 5 '87. D. B. Davis
   N Y Times Book Rev 92:9-10 Ja 18 '87. W. S. McFeely
   Natl Rev 39:49-50 Jl 3 '87. R. H. Ferrell
Jones, J. and Wilson, W. An incomplete education. 1987
   Esquire 108:54+ S '87
Jones, J. T. Wayward skeptic. 1986
   N Y Rev Books 34:28-30 My 7 '87. M. Wood
Jones, M. Getting it on. 1987
   N Y Times Book Rev 92:13-14 D 13 '87. E. Sanders
Jones, R. Julia Paradise. 1987
   N Y Times Book Rev 92:12 O 11 '87. W. Herbert
Jones, S. It all began with Daisy. 1987
   N Y Times Book Rev 92:33 Je 21 '87. B. Coleman
Jones, V. C. Manhattan, the Army and the atomic bomb. 1985
   Phys Today 40:72+ Jl '87. J. S. Walker
Jones-Jackson, P. When roots die. 1987
   Nat Hist 96:66+ S '87. T. Rosengarten
Jong, E. Serenissima. 1987
   N Y Times Book Rev 92:12 Ap 19 '87. M. Malone
   USA Today (Periodical) 116:96 S '87. S. G. Kellman
Jordan, C. F. Nutrient cycling in tropical forest ecosystems. 1985
   BioScience 37:220+ Mr '87. P. M. Vitousek
Jordan, C. J. What to save from the '80s. 1986
   Antiques Collect Hobbies 92:70 My '87
Joseph, H. Side by side. 1987
   N Y Times Book Rev 92:37 Ag 30 '87. S. Mufson
Joyce, B. R. Improving America's schools. 1986
   Phi Delta Kappan 68:634-5 Ap '87. A. J. Pautler
Judt, T. Marxism and the French Left. 1986
   America 157:114-15 Ag 29-S 5 '87. M. Lavallée-Williams
Jüngel, E. Karl Barth, a theological legacy. 1986
   Christ Century 104:920 O 21 '87. P. E. Stroble
Just, W. S. The American ambassador. 1987
   N Y Times Book Rev 92:1+ Mr 15 '87. R. Stone
Justice, D. R. The sunset maker. 1987
   N Y Times Book Rev 92:20 Ag 23 '87. E. Hirsch

K

Kadare, I. Chronicle in stone. 1987
   Nation 245:652-5 N 28 '87. E. Eisenberg
Kadimakara. 1985
   Science 235:1408-9 Mr 13 '87. S. D. Webb
Kagan, D. The fall of the Athenian Empire. 1987
   Atlantic 260:119-21 N '87. B. M. W. Knox
Kahan, A. M. Acid rain. 1986
   Environment 29:28-9 N '87. H. E. Wright
Kahan, S. The wolf of the Kremlin. 1987
   New Leader 70:18-19 N 16 '87. G. Sosin
Kahn, A. My life as a gal. 1987
   Vogue 177:188+ My '87. L. A. Schreiber
Kahn, R. Joe & Marilyn. 1986
   Mademoiselle 93:76+ F '87. L. Moore
   Natl Rev 39:66-7 Ja 30 '87. M. Shannon
Kahne, H. Reconceiving part-time work. 1985
   Mon Labor Rev 110:58 Ag '87. T. J. Nardone
Kamerman, S. B. and Kahn, A. J. The responsive workplace. 1987
   Mon Labor Rev 110:75 S '87. H. Hayghe
Kammen, M. G. A machine that would go of itself. 1986
   America 157:224-5 O 10 '87. O. Root
   Cent Mag 20:29-30 Ja/F '87. D. McDonald
   Commentary 83:67-9 F '87. W. Berns
Kanatchikov, S. A radical worker in Tsarist Russia. 1986
   Hist Today 37:54-5 Je '87. C. Read
Kane, D. N. Environmental hazards to young children. 1985
   Environment 29:30 Ja/F '87. A. U. White
Kantrow, A. M. The constraints of corporate tradition. 1987
   N Y Times Book Rev 92:36 O 25 '87. H. Goodman
Kanturková, E. My companions in the bleak house. 1987
   N Y Times Book Rev 92:30 D 13 '87. F. P. Brent
Kaplan, D. M. Comfort. 1987
   N Y Times Book Rev 92:41 Je 14 '87. S. Wood
Kaplan, L. Working with multiproblem families. 1986
   Child Today 15:33-4 N/D '86. M. Allen and W. Deutelbaum
Kaplan, L. S. Entangling alliances with none. 1987
   N Y Times Book Rev 92:30-1 Je 14 '87. D. M. Kennedy
Kaplan, S. A. and Barsness, K. J. Raven's journey. 1986
   Science 236:1005-6 My 22 '87. M. B. Blackman
Kaplan, S. R. The encyclopedia of tarot; v2. 1986
   Antiques Collect Hobbies 92:54 Ap '87
Kapuściński, R. Another day of life. 1986
   N Y Times Book Rev 92:12-13 F 15 '87. W. Boyd
   New Leader 70:18-19 Ap 6 '87. R. Wright
   Newsweek 109:68 F 2 '87. P. S. Prescott
Karlinsky, S. Marina Tsvetaeva. 1986
   N Y Rev Books 34:20+ O 8 '87. J. Bayley
Kastner, J. A world of watchers. 1986
   Audubon 89:118-20 My '87. F. Graham
   N Y Times Book Rev 92:19 F 22 '87. E. J. Fisk
   Nat Hist 96:72+ F '87. M. Harwood
Katchen, C. Painting faces and figures. 1986
   Am Artist 51:18+ Jl '87. D. C. Hines
Katrovas, R. Snug Harbor. 1986
   N Y Times Book Rev 92:68 N 8 '87. S. Santos
Katz, D. R. The big store. 1987
   Atlantic 260:100+ O '87. N. Lemann
   Bus Week p20-1 O 26 '87. J. E. Ellis
   Fortune 116:225-6+ O 12 '87. B. Saporito
   N Y Times Book Rev 92:34 O 25 '87. K. W. Arenson
Katz, J. The darker side of genius. 1986
   Commentary 83:57-60 Ja '87. S. Lipman
Katz, M. B. In the shadow of the poorhouse. 1986
   Cent Mag 20:39-40 My/Je '87. D. McDonald
   USA Today (Periodical) 115:93 Ja '87. F. Cordasco
Katz, S. Florry of Washington Heights.
   N Y Times Book Rev 92:6 Jl 19 '87. R. P. Brickner
Katzenbach, J. The traveler. 1987
   N Y Times Book Rev 92:10 Mr 15 '87. P. Anderson
Kaufman, C. and Kaufman, G. Hotel boy. 1987
   N Y Times Book Rev 92:26 Je 14 '87. S. Roberts
Kaufman, S. R. The ageless self. 1986
   N Y Times Book Rev 92:1+ F 15 '87. P. West
Kaufmann, E. Fallingwater, a Frank Lloyd Wright country house. 1986
   Americana 15:80 Mr/Ap '87. M. Durham
Kawabata, Y. The old capital. 1987
   N Y Times Book Rev 92:10-11 Ag 2 '87. M. J. Salter
Kay, G. G. The darkest road. 1986
   Macleans 100:66-7 Mr 23 '87. P. Giffen
Kazin, M. Barons of labor. 1987
   Nation 244:550+ Ap 25 '87. J. B. Freeman
Keegan, J. The mask of command. 1987
   Nation 245:722-5 D 12 '87. G. G. Field
   New Repub 197:32-4+ N 30 '87. E. N. Luttwak

Newsweek 110:83-4 D 14 '87. J. Miller
Time 130:105 N 9 '87. O. Friedrich
Keen, S. Faces of the enemy. 1986
Christ Century 104:536 Je 3-10 '87. J. J. Farrell
Keillor, G. Leaving home. 1987
Mademoiselle 93:92+ O '87. J. Maynard
N Y Times Book Rev 92:9 O 4 '87. S. Gray
Newsweek 110:82-3 O 5 '87. B. Barol
Time 130:118 O 26 '87. R. Schickel
Kelder, D. The great book of post-impressionism. 1986
Am Artist 51:24 N '87. C. Movalli
Keller, G. Green Henry.
N Y Rev Books 34:39-40 Je 25 '87. G. A. Craig
Keller, H. Goodbye, Max. 1987
N Y Times Book Rev 92:40-1 My 17 '87. A. M. Bregman
Kelley, C. M. and Davis, J. K. Kelley. 1987
N Y Times Book Rev 92:12-13 S 13 '87. R. Sherrill
Kelly, J. The all-seasons garden. 1987
Americana 15:51-2 Jl/Ag '87. P. Hagan
Kelly, J. N. D. The Oxford dictionary of Popes. 1986
Am Sch 56:445-8 Summ '87. H. R. Kuehn
Kelman, M. A guide to critical legal studies. 1987
New Leader 70:22-3 D 14 '87. C. Dalton
Kelman, S. Making public policy. 1987
Christ Century 104:1179-80 D 23-30 '87. I. Nerken
N Y Times Book Rev 92:23 Je 7 '87. M. Tolchin
New Leader 70:11-13 My 4-18 '87. R. Lekachman
New Repub 197:33-5 Ag 24 '87. J. Rieder
Kelsey, M. and Kelsey, B. Sacrament of sexuality.
America 156:447 My 30 '87. L. S. Cahill
Kelso, L. O. and Kelso, P. H. Democracy and economic power. 1986
Futurist 21:45 Jl/Ag '87. A. Brown
Kemp, P. K. and Ormond, R. The great age of sail. 1986
Oceans 20:63 N/D '87. B. N. Powell
Sea Front 33:473 N/D '87. G. L. Voss
Kendrick, W. M. The secret museum. 1987
N Y Times Book Rev 92:3+ My 3 '87. L. Stone
New Leader 70:15-16 Jl 13-27 '87. B. Gewen
New Repub 196:28-32 Je 15 '87. S. Marcus
Keneally, T. The playmaker. 1987
N Y Times Book Rev 92:7+ S 20 '87. J. Atlas
Kenner, H. The mechanic muse. 1987
Natl Rev 39:48-9 Ag 14 '87. J. Sobran
Kennett, L. B. G.I. 1987
Bus Week p14+ Ap 27 '87. M. A. Reichek
Wash Mon 19:59-60 Je '87. P. L. Savage
Kenney, M. Biotechnology. 1986
N Y Times Book Rev 92:32-3 F 15 '87. R. Novick
Technol Rev 90:75-6 O '87. R. A. Weinberg
Kenyon, J. The boat of quiet hours.
N Y Times Book Rev 92:13 Je 21 '87. C. Muske
Kerman, C. E. and Eldridge, R. The lives of Jean Toomer. 1987
N Y Times Book Rev 92:7+ Ag 30 '87. A. Rampersad
Kershaw, K. A. Physiological ecology of lichens. 1985
BioScience 37:227-8 Mr '87. B. N. Smith
Kesden, B. Sex, drugs & AIDS. 1987
N Y Times Book Rev 92:26 S 27 '87. P. Theroux
Keuls, Y. The mother of David S. 1986
Psychol Today 21:78-9 F '87. R. J. Moss
Kevles, D. J. In the name of eugenics. 1985
Commonweal 114:120-1 F 27 '87. T. A. Shannon
Khalaf, S. Lebanon's predicament. 1987
N Y Times Book Rev 92:12 F 8 '87. T. L. Friedman
Khalsa, D. K. I want a dog. 1987
N Y Times Book Rev 92:32 N 8 '87. R. Chast
Khan-Magomedov, S. O. Rodchenko. 1986
N Y Times Book Rev 92:13-14 My 17 '87. S. F. Starr
Kibbey, A. The interpretation of material shapes in Puritanism. 1986
Christ Century 104:63 Ja 21 '87. S. M. Promey
Kidd, C. Debrett goes to Hollywood. 1987
Vogue 177:121 Je '87. J. Robinson-Shaw
Kiernan, T. Citizen Murdoch. 1986
Bus Week p14 Mr 16 '87. M. N. Vamos
Christ Century 104:801-2 S 23 '87. B. Daily
Macleans 100:49 Ja 26 '87. P. Roberts
Kim, D. J. Prison writings. 1986
Christ Century 104:1095-6 D 2 '87. M. G. Cartwright
Commentary 84:78-80 N '87. W. McGurn
N Y Rev Books 34:21-6 Ja 29 '87. I. Buruma
N Y Times Book Rev 92:13 Jl 5 '87. C. Haberman
New Repub 197:34+ S 28 '87. A. Mendelsohn
Kin recognition in animals. 1987
Science 238:1592-3 D 11 '87. G. J. Gamboa
Kiner, R. Kiner's korner. 1987
N Y Times Book Rev 92:14 My 3 '87. J. Oppenheimer
King, M. Freedom song. 1987

N Y Times Book Rev 92:12-13 Ag 30 '87. S. Brownmiller
King, M. L. A testament of hope. 1986
New Yorker 63:107-12 Ap 6 '87. B. McKibben
King, M. L. Venetian humanism in an age of patrician dominance. 1986
N Y Rev Books 34:37-9 Jl 16 '87. F. Gilbert
King, S. The eyes of the dragon. 1987
N Y Times Book Rev 92:12-13 F 22 '87. B. Tritel
King, S. Misery. 1987
N Y Times Book Rev 92:20 My 31 '87. J. Katzenbach
King, S. The Tommyknockers. 1987
N Y Times Book Rev 92:8 D 20 '87. N. Auerbach
King-Smith, D. Harry's mad. 1987
N Y Times Book Rev 92:38 My 17 '87. K. Kuskin
Kingery, W. D. and Vandiver, P. B. Ceramic masterpieces. 1986
Sci Am 256:23-4+ Ap '87. P. Morrison
Kingsland, S. E. Modeling nature. 1985
BioScience 37:431-2 Je '87. M. Levandowsky
Kinsley, M. Curse of the giant muffins, and other Washington maladies. 1987
Commentary 84:77-8 N '87. T. Teachout
Fortune 116:178 D 21 '87. D. Seligman
Natl Rev 39:52-3 D 4 '87. R. Brookhiser
Wash Mon 19:51-3 D '87. J. Rowe
Kipling, R. Gunga Din. 1987
N Y Times Book Rev 92:52-3 N 8 '87. J. Cott
Kipling, R. The jungle book. 1987
N Y Times Book Rev 92:52-3 N 8 '87. J. Cott
Kipling, R. Just so stories. 1987
N Y Times Book Rev 92:52-3 N 8 '87. J. Cott
Kippenhahn, R. Light from the depths of time. 1987
Sky Telesc 74:262 S '87. E. R. Harrison
Kirkland, G. Dancing on my grave. 1986
New Yorker 63:94-5 Ap 13 '87. A. Croce
Kiselev, V. F. and Krylov, O. V. Adsorption processes on semiconductor and dielectric surfaces. 1985
Phys Today 40:82-3 Ap '87. J. T. Yates, Jr.
Kishlansky, M. A. Parliamentary selection. 1986
Hist Today 37:53 Ag '87. K. Sharpe
Kitchen, M. British policy towards the Soviet Union during the Second World War. 1986
N Y Rev Books 34:44-50 Je 11 '87. T. Garton Ash
Kitson, N. Where sixpence lives. 1987
N Y Times Book Rev 92:46 N 22 '87. J. D. Battersby
Kittelson, J. M. Luther the reformer. 1986
Christ Century 104:921-2 O 21 '87. M. L. Wagner
Kizer, C. The nearness of you. 1986
N Y Times Book Rev 92:23 Mr 22 '87. A. Libby
Klein, H. S. African slavery in Latin America and the Caribbean. 1986
N Y Rev Books 34:34-7 N 5 '87. D. B. Davis
Klein, N. Going backwards. 1986
N Y Times Book Rev 92:29 Mr 15 '87. P. Campbell
Kleinman, R. Anne of Austria. 1985
N Y Rev Books 34:40-3 Je 11 '87. J. H. Elliott
Klitgaard, R. E. Choosing elites. 1985
Am Sch 56:439-43 Summ '87. A. Stark
Society 24:80-1 S/O '87. S. I. Keller
Kluger, R. and Kluger, P. The paper. 1986
Natl Rev 39:53-4 F 27 '87. J. Mysak
Wash Mon 19:58-9 Ap '87. D. Kiker
Knight, D. The age of science. 1986
Hist Today 37:55-6 Mr '87. M. Crosland
Knightley, P. The second oldest profession. 1987
Bus Week p16 F 2 '87. E. Clark
Macleans 100:56 Mr 9 '87. R. Miller
N Y Times Book Rev 92:12 F 1 '87. Z. S. Steiner
Nation 244:436-8 Ap 4 '87. R. W. Winks
New Leader 70:15-16 My 4-18 '87. R. Alan
Newsweek 109:66 Ja 12 '87. D. Gates
Time 129:74 Ja 12 '87. R. Z. Sheppard
Knightley, P. and Kennedy, C. An affair of state. 1987
N Y 20:64+ Ag 31 '87. R. Koenig
N Y Times Book Rev 92:11 S 20 '87. A. Howard
Knuth, D. E. Computers & typesetting. 5v 1986
Byte 12:67-8+ Mr '87. A. Hoenig
Koch, S. The bachelors' bride. 1986
Art Am 75:17 Mr '87. D. V. Gast
Kochan, T. A. and others. The transformation of American industrial relations. 1986
Mon Labor Rev 110:42 F '87. K. McLennan
Koenig, W. D. and Mumme, R. L. Population ecology of the cooperatively breeding acorn woodpecker. 1987
Science 238:1590-1 D 11 '87. C. R. Brown
Kogan, J. Nothing but the best. 1987
N Y Times Book Rev 92:31 O 4 '87. K. Gann
Kohlmaier, G. and Sartory, B. von. Houses of glass. 1986
Sci Am 256:31-2+ F '87. P. Morrison
Kohn, A. No contest. 1986
Christ Century 104:448-9 My 6 '87. I. Nerken

Science 238:695-6 O 30 '87. H. Etzkowitz
Lattimore, D. N. The flame of peace. 1987
N Y Times Book Rev 92:44 N 8 '87. J. Bierhorst
Lauda, N. Niki Lauda, meine story. 1986
Car Driv 32:34 My '87. T. Swan
Road Track 38:146 My '87. B. S. Narkiewicz
Laustsen, S. and others. Exploring the southern sky. 1987
Sky Telesc 74:608-9 D '87. C. Raymo
Lavallée, D. and others. Telarmachay. 2v 1985
Science 236:1685-6 Je 26 '87. J. W. Rick
Lawner, L. Lives of the courtesans. 1987
N Y Rev Books 34:35-7 My 28 '87. C. Hope
Lawrence, E. Gardening for love. 1987
N Y Times Book Rev 92:53-4 O 11 '87. S. Kunitz
Laxalt, R. Sweet promised land. 1986
Natl Rev 39:70 S 11 '87. N. B. Williamson
Layzer, D. Constructing the universe. 1984
Phys Today 40:95 My '87. J. S. Trefil
Le Corbusier. Journey to the East. 1987
N Y Times Book Rev 92:14 Jl 12 '87. M. Grant
Le Roy Ladurie, E. The French peasantry, 1450-1660. 1986
New Repub 197:38-41 Jl 27 '87. E. J. Weber
Leaders in the study of animal behavior. 1985
Science 235:598-9 Ja 30 '87. H. Markl
Leaf, M. The eyes of the dragon. 1987
N Y Times Book Rev 92:18 Jl 19 '87. C. Brightman
Leahy, J. A. Eagle's chase. 1986
Phi Delta Kappan 69:168-70 O '87. C. Eisele
Learning and literature in Anglo-Saxon England. 1985
Hist Today 37:57-8 F '87. M. Budny
Leavey, J. P. Glassary. 1986
N Y Times Book Rev 92:3 S 13 '87. J. Sturrock
Leavitt, J. W. Brought to bed. 1986
New Repub 196:38-9+ Ja 19 '87. C. N. Degler
Science 238:556 O 23 '87. S. Reverby
Lebow, R. N. Nuclear crisis management. 1987
Bull At Sci 43:55-6 S '87. B. M. Blechman
Science 236:1359-60 Je 5 '87. J. Richelson
Lee, D. R. Regulating government. 1987
Fortune 115:141-2+ Ja 19 '87. D. R. Henderson
Lee, L.-Y. Rose.
N Y Times Book Rev 92:24 O 4 '87. M. Flamm
Lee, S. Spike Lee's gotta have it. 1987
N Y Times Book Rev 92:14 D 13 '87. S. S. Martin
Lee, S. Susan Lee's ABZs of economics. 1987
N Y Times Book Rev 92:23 Ap 5 '87. P. O'Toole
Lees, G. Singers and the song. 1987
N Y Times Book Rev 92:1+ N 15 '87. P. Conrad
Lehman, D. An alternative to speech. 1986
N Y Times Book Rev 92:26 Mr 1 '87. J. Ash
Leighton, F. S. The search for the real Nancy Reagan. 1987
Ms 16:32+ Jl/Ag '87. J. Mann
Vogue 177:110+ Je '87. B. Ehrenreich and J. O'Reilly
Leiser, E. The Metz book of hackle. 1987
Conservationist 42:50 N/D '87. J. Rowen
Lekachman, R. Visions and nightmares. 1987
Bus Week p17 Mr 30 '87. H. Gleckman
N Y Times Book Rev 92:14 Mr 29 '87. M. Janeway
Natl Rev 39:41-2 My 22 '87. J. Sobran
New Repub 197:32+ Jl 13-20 '87. P. Starr
Lem, S. Fiasco. 1987
N Y Times Book Rev 92:1+ Je 7 '87. P. Delany
Time 129:70 Je 1 '87. P. Gray
Léon-Dufour, X. Life and death in the New Testament. 1986
America 156:201-3 Mr 7 '87. P. Perkins
Leonard, E. Bandits. 1987
Macleans 100:61 Ja 19 '87. R. Miller
N Y Rev Books 34:50-1 Ag 13 '87. T. R. Edwards
N Y Times Book Rev 92:7 Ja 4 '87. W. Percy
Newsweek 109:58 Ja 5 '87. P. S. Prescott
Time 129:72 Ja 12 '87. P. Gray
Leonard, L. S. On the way to the wedding. 1986
Psychol Today 21:76 Ap '87. D. Heller
Leopold, A. K. Victorian splendor. 1986
Americana 14:80-1 Ja/F '87. G. Schelling
Leschak, P. M. Letters from Side Lake. 1987
N Y Times Book Rev 92:15 Je 28 '87. J. Tallmadge
Lesser, W. The life below the ground. 1987
N Y Times Book Rev 92:26 N 22 '87. E. Toynton
Lester, J. The tales of Uncle Remus. 1987
N Y Times Book Rev 92:32 My 17 '87. J. Jordan
Lesy, M. The forbidden zone. 1987
N Y Times Book Rev 92:10 Jl 19 '87. L. Harris
Psychol Today 21:71-2 Jl '87. D. Cole
Vogue 177:200 Ag '87. M. Cantwell
Leung, Y. C. Physics of dense matter. 1985
Phys Today 40:86 S '87. J. W. Negele

Levack, B. P. The witch-hunt in early modern Europe. 1987
Hist Today 37:54 S '87. H. Kamen
Levey, Sir M. Giambattista Tiepolo. 1986
Art Am 75:31+ D '87. J. Gash
N Y Times Book Rev 92:34 Je 14 '87. D. Posner
Lévi, J. The Chinese emperor. 1987
N Y Times Book Rev 92:1+ O 4 '87. J. D. Spence
Levi, P. The drowned and the saved. 1988
Time 130:65 D 28 '87. R. Z. Sheppard
Levi, P. The monkey's wrench. 1986
N Y Rev Books 33:40-1 Ja 15 '87. D. J. Enright
Levin, H. Playboys and killjoys. 1987
N Y Times Book Rev 92:25 Mr 8 '87. T. Tanner
Levin, J. Shimoni's lover. 1987
N Y Times Book Rev 92:19 N 29 '87. J. Silber
Levin, M. G. The Socratic method. 1987
N Y Times Book Rev 92:9 D 27 '87. S. Turow
Levin, P. L. Abigail Adams. 1987
N Y Times Book Rev 92:16 Je 7 '87. J. Fritz
Levin, T. Backtracking. 1987
Ctry J 14:11 O '87. W. Shipman
Levine, D. O. The American college and the culture of aspiration, 1915-1940. 1986
Science 235:798-9 F 13 '87. D. Karen
Levine, H. Life choices. 1987
Commonweal 114:249+ Ap 24 '87. T. P. Hill
Technol Rev 90:72-3 N/D '87. A. L. Caplan
Levinson, R. DinnieAbbieSister-r-r! 1986
N Y Times Book Rev 92:26 Mr 29 '87. B. A. Porte
Levitin, S. The return. 1987
N Y Times Book Rev 92:36 My 17 '87. S. S. Klass
Lewis, A. R. and Runyan, T. J. European naval and maritime history, 300-1500. 1985
Sea Front 33:73 Ja/F '87. F. G. W. Smith
Lewis, B. Semites and anti-Semites. 1986
Commentary 83:65-7 F '87. R. S. Wistrich
Lewis, C. S. Present concerns. 1986
Christ Today 31:62 My 15 '87. L. Billingsley
Lewis, F. Europe. 1987
N Y Times Book Rev 92:11 N 22 '87. S. R. Graubard
Lewis, J. S. and Lewis, R. A. Space resources. 1987
Science 238:1447-8 D 4 '87. T. B. McCord
Leyton, E. Compulsive killers. 1986
Psychol Today 21:70-1 Je '87. M. Wells
Liberal Protestantism. 1986
America 157:67-9 Ag 1-8 '87. J. Gros
Lichter, S. R. and others. The media elite. 1986
Commentary 83:78-80 Ja '87. T. Teachout
Natl Rev 39:49-50 Mr 13 '87. W. Murchison
New Leader 69:7-8 D 1-15 '86. D. Schorr
Lieberman, M. Beyond public education. 1986
Phi Delta Kappan 68:555-6 Mr '87. B. Brodinsky
Lieberson, S. Making it count. 1985
Society 24:87-8 Ja/F '87. H. S. Becker
A Life distilled. 1987
Nation 245:308-12 S 26 '87. C. C. Park
LIFE, the first fifty years, 1936-1986. 1986
New Repub 196:36-40 F 9 '87. J. K. Glassman
Lifton, R. J. The future of immortality and other essays for a nuclear age. 1987
Psychol Today 21:71-3 Ag '87. P. R. Loeb
Lifton, R. J. The Nazi doctors. 1986
Cent Mag 20:26-8 Ja/F '87. D. McDonald
N Y Rev Books 34:29-34 My 28 '87. N. Ascherson
New Leader 69:3-4 D 1-15 '86. B. Gewen
Lillie, D. W. Our radiant world. 1986
Natl Rev 39:58-9 D 18 '87. K. Smith
Limerick, P. N. The legacy of conquest. 1987
N Y Times Book Rev 92:15 Ag 2 '87. A. Kolodny
Limnology in Australia. 1986
Science 236:1579-81 Je 19 '87. S. MacIntyre
Limonov, Éduard. His butler's story. 1987
N Y Times Book Rev 92:2 Jl 5 '87. M. Paley
Nation 245:313-14 S 26 '87. E. J. Brown
Lincoln, W. B. Passage through Armageddon. 1986
Macleans 100:54 F 16 '87. J. Keep
Linderman, G. F. Embattled courage. 1987
N Y Times Book Rev 92:11-12 Jl 5 '87. S. W. Sears
Lindner, R. M. The fifty-minute hour. 1982
Repr. Orig. pub.: NY: Rinehart 1955
Psychol Today 21:104 My '87. S. Pollak
Lindquist, M. Sad movies. 1987
N Y Times Book Rev 92:12 D 13 '87. S. Schiff
Lingeman, R. R. Theodore Dreiser; v1, At the gates of the city, 1871-1907. 1986
Natl Rev 39:50-1 Ap 10 '87. J. W. Tuttleton
New Repub 196:31-3 F 23 '87. A. Kazin
Smithsonian 18:178+ My '87. G. Weales
Linn's U.S. stamp yearbook 1986. 1987
Antiques Collect Hobbies 92:71+ Je '87. H. Herst, Jr.

Linsky, M. Impact. 1986
New Leader 69:7-8 D 1-15 '86. D. Schorr
Wash Mon 19:56-7 Ap '87. J. Alter
Lipman, J. and others. Young America. 1986
N Y Times Book Rev 92:15-16 F 22 '87. C. Cerny
Lipton, E. Looking into Degas. 1987
Art News 86:78 Ap '87. J. H. Levi
Lisle, J. T. The great Dimpole oak. 1987
N Y Times Book Rev 92:36 D 13 '87. J. O'Reilly
Listfield, E. Variations in the night. 1987
N Y Times Book Rev 92:12 S 6 '87. R. D. Rosen
The Literary guide to the Bible. 1987
N Y Times Book Rev 92:1+ D 20 '87. E. S. Malbon
New Repub 197:28-30+ O 26 '87. D. Davie
Littwin, S. The postponed generation. 1986
Change 19:52-3 Mr/Ap '87. T. W. Hartle
Christ Century 104:665-6 Jl 29-Ag 5 '87. W. H. Willimon
Litwak, M. Reel power. 1986
Wash Mon 18:60 Ja '87. T. Noah
Living invertebrates. 1987
Sci Am 257:182-3 O '87. P. Morrison
Lloyd, D. The ridiculous story of Gammer Gurton's needle. 1987
N Y Times Book Rev 92:44 My 17 '87. A. Goreau
Lock, S. A difficult balance. 1985
BioScience 37:291-3 Ap '87. S. Jasanoff
Lockhart, R. B. Halfway to heaven. 1986
N Y Times Book Rev 92:28 F 8 '87. P. Zaleski
Loeb, G. E. and Gans, C. Electromyography for experimentalists. 1986
Science 236:470-1 Ap 24 '87. G. E. Goslow, Jr.
Loeb, P. R. Hope in hard times. 1986
Psychol Today 21:70-1 Mr '87. S. Haas
Loeb, P. R. Nuclear culture. 1982
Psychol Today 21:70 Mr '87. S. Haas
Loewenich, W. von. Martin Luther. 1986
Christ Century 104:922 O 21 '87. T. Tredway
Christ Today 31:47-8 Ap 17 '87. H. A. Oberman
Loewinsohn, R. Where all the ladders start. 1987
N Y Times Book Rev 92:14 Jl 19 '87. S. Braudy
Logue, J. Boats against the current. 1987
N Y Times Book Rev 92:31 Ap 26 '87. H. Mayer
Lohse, B. Martin Luther. 1986
Christ Today 31:47-8 Ap 17 '87. H. A. Oberman
Long, C. H. Significations. 1986
Christ Century 104:412 Ap 29 '87. T. Moore
Longman, P. Born to pay. 1987
New Leader 70:18-20 O 5 '87. R. Lekachman
Lopate, P. The rug merchant. 1987
N Y Rev Books 34:45-6 Je 25 '87. R. Towers
N Y Times Book Rev 92:12 Mr 8 '87. J. Charyn
Lopes, H. The laughing cry. 1987
N Y Times Book Rev 92:32 My 3 '87. D. E. Westlake
Lorenz, K. The waning of humaneness. 1987
N Y Times Book Rev 92:30 Jl 12 '87. M. Konner
Loughlin, J. Gladstone, home rule, and the Ulster question, 1882-93. 1987
Hist Today 37:60 Je '87. N. Yates
Lourie, R. Zero gravity. 1987
N Y Times Book Rev 92:12 O 18 '87. C. T. Buckley
Lovell, M. S. Straight on till morning. 1987
N Y Times Book Rev 92:1+ Ag 23 '87. D. Ackerman
Nation 245:600-2 N 21 '87. D. Ketcham
Time 130:83-4 O 5 '87. J. Skow
Lowell, R. Collected prose. 1987
N Y Times Book Rev 92:22-3 Jl 12 '87. D. Davie
Nation 244:475-6+ Ap 11 '87. D. Bogen
Natl Rev 39:49-51 Ag 14 '87. J. Meyers
New Repub 196:30-3 Mr 30 '87. H. H. Vendler
Lowenthal, A. F. Partners in conflict. 1987
N Y Times Book Rev 92:34 S 20 '87. J. Rohwer
Lowenthal, D. The past is a foreign country. 1985
Harpers 274:72+ Je '87. C. Romano
Lowry, B. The perfect Sonya. 1987
N Y Times Book Rev 92:10 Jl 26 '87. L. Freed
Lowry, L. Rabble Starkey. 1987
N Y Times Book Rev 92:33 My 17 '87. L. A. Walker
Luce, R. D. Response times. 1986
Science 237:1060 Ag 28 '87. J.-C. Falmagne
Lucet, J.-P. The mystery of the charity of Joan of Arc. 1986
Commonweal 114:88-9 F 13 '87. R. Gilman
Ludmerer, K. M. Learning to heal. 1985
BioScience 37:358-9 My '87. B. Gastel
Lukas, J. A. Common ground. 1985
Society 24:82-4 My/Je '87. G. C. Homans
Lunden, J. Good morning, I'm Joan Lunden. 1986
New Repub 196:35-7 Mr 30 '87. D. Owen
Lustiger, J.-M. Dare to believe. 1986
Christ Century 104:202 F 25 '87. J. T. Pawlikowski

Luttwak, E. N. On the meaning of victory. 1986
America 156:329-31 Ap 18 '87. W. T. Perkins
Luttwak, E. N. Strategy. 1987
Commentary 84:56+ Jl '87. E. A. Cohen
N Y Times Book Rev 92:22 Ag 30 '87. H. G. Summers
Natl Rev 39:44-5 Jl 3 '87. B. Bruce-Briggs
New Repub 196:30-4 My 11 '87. P. Paret
Lux, T. Half promised land. 1986
N Y Times Book Rev 92:20 Ap 19 '87. L. McMahon
A Lycanthropy reader. 1986
N Y Times Book Rev 92:33 Ap 5 '87. A. Rice
Lydenberg, S. D. and others. Rating America's corporate conscience. 1986
N Y Rev Books 34:37 F 26 '87. M. Kempton
N Y Times Book Rev 92:29 Ja 18 '87. R. L. Heilbroner
Lynch, T. Skating with Heather Grace. 1986
Commonweal 114:507-8 S 11 '87. W. Koestenbaum
N Y Times Book Rev 92:24 O 4 '87. M. Flamm
Lynn, J. and Jay, A. The complete Yes minister. 1986
Commentary 84:72-4 S '87. N. W. Polsby
N Y Times Book Rev 92:11 Je 21 '87. C. T. Buckley
Lynn, K. S. Hemingway. 1987
Atlantic 260:91-2 Jl '87. B. DeMott
Commentary 84:66+ O '87. J. Hart
N Y Rev Books 34:30-7 Ag 13 '87. F. C. Crews
N Y Times Book Rev 92:3+ Jl 19 '87. D. Johnson
Natl Rev 39:57 S 25 '87. J. Meyers
New Repub 197:27-9 Jl 13-20 '87. A. Kazin
Lynton, E. A. and Elman, S. E. New priorities for the university. 1987
Change 19:60-3 Jl/Ag '87. C. N. Breiseth

M

MaAleer, N. The Omni space almanac.
Space World X-7-283:8 Jl '87. J. Rhea
Mabey, R. The Frampton flora. 1986
Smithsonian 17:132-3 F '87. B. Hall
MacCulloch, D. Suffolk and the Tudors. 1986
Hist Today 37:59 Jl '87. P. Slack
MacDonald, C. A. Korea, the war before Vietnam. 1987
Bus Week p16-18 My 25 '87. W. J. Holstein
Macdonald, N. Homage to the Spanish exiles. 1987
N Y Rev Books 34:30-2 F 12 '87. M. McCarthy
New Leader 70:17-18 Mr 9 '87. G. Woodcock
MacEóin, G. Memoirs & memories. 1986
Christ Century 104:697-8 Ag 12-19 '87. G. Bergman
Commonweal 114:362-3 Je 5 '87. J. Cunneen
MacFarlane, S. N. Superpower rivalry & 3rd World radicalism. 1985
Society 24:94 My/Je '87. J. M. Scolnick, Jr.
Machlis, G. E. and Tichnell, D. L. The state of the world's parks. 1985
BioScience 37:134+ F '87. A. Mathews
Mack, M. Alexander Pope. 1986
Am Sch 56:435-9 Summ '87. L. Lipking
Mackey, S. The Saudis. 1987
N Y Times Book Rev 92:13 Jl 12 '87. E. Sciolino
MacKinnon, C. A. Feminism unmodified. 1987
N Y Times Book Rev 92:3+ My 3 '87. A. M. Jaggar
Nation 244:720+ My 30 '87. M. Mullarkey
Psychol Today 21:68-9 S '87. J. B. Ciulla
MacKinnon, J. R. and MacKinnon, S. R. Agnes Smedley. 1988
N Y Times Book Rev 92:22 D 13 '87. J. P. Diggins
Nation 245:761-3 D 19 '87. O. Schell
MacKinnon, S. R. and Friesen, O. China reporting. 1987
N Y Times Book Rev 92:52 O 11 '87. S. F. Fishkin
MacLaine, S. Dancing in the light. 1985
N Y Rev Books 34:16-19 Ap 9 '87. M. Gardner
MacLaine, S. Out on a limb. 1983
N Y Rev Books 34:16-19 Ap 9 '87. M. Gardner
Macquarrie, J. Theology, church, and ministry. 1986
Christ Century 104:249-51 Mr 11 '87. D. W. Musser
Macrorie, K. Twenty teachers. 1984
Cent Mag 20:36-7 Jl/Ag '87. D. McDonald
Madden, T. R. Women vs. women. 1987
Fortune 116:195+ O 26 '87. F. S. Chapman
Madrick, J. G. Taking America. 1987
Bus Week p10+ Ap 20 '87. J. H. Dobrzynski
N Y Times Book Rev 92:31 My 10 '87. M. Kandel
Madsen, A. Cousteau. 1986
N Y Times Book Rev 92:16-17 Mr 8 '87. L. Wylie
Magmatic processes. 1987
Science 237:925 Ag 21 '87. R. Jeanloz
Magubane, P. Soweto. 1986
Nation 244:578-80 My 2 '87. R. Nixon
Maguire, D. C. The moral revolution. 1986
Repr. art. orig. pub. 1968-1984. With corrections
Christ Century 104:890 O 14 '87. S. E. Henking
Mahedy, W. P. Out of the night. 1986

Christ Today 31:31 O 16 '87. G. H. Meyer
Commonweal 114:604-5 O 23 '87. B. J. Verkamp
Mahmoody, B. Not without my daughter. 1987
N Y Times Book Rev 92:12 D 27 '87. M. Golden
Mahony, P. Freud and the Rat Man. 1986
Psychol Today 21:77 Ag '87. S. Pollak
Mahy, M. 17 kings and 42 elephants. 1987
N Y Times Book Rev 92:40 N 8 '87. A. Yorinks
Mahy, M. The tricksters. 1986
N Y Times Book Rev 92:31+ My 17 '87. R. McKinley
Major, C. My amputations. 1986
Nation 244:90-2 Ja 24 '87. S. Klawans
Major, C. Such was the season. 1987
N Y Times Book Rev 92:19 D 13 '87. A. Young
Makers of modern strategy. 1986
Hist Today 37:56-7 S '87. A. Sked
Malabre, A. L. Beyond our means. 1987
Fortune 115:189+ My 11 '87. D. R. Henderson
N Y Times Book Rev 92:7 Ap 12 '87. A. Smith
Nation 244:584-5 My 2 '87. S. L. Malcomson
New Leader 70:18-19 My 4-18 '87. P. Davidson
Malcolm, A. H. This far and no more. 1987
N Y Times Book Rev 92:15 Ap 26 '87. G. Hochman
Psychol Today 21:71-2 O '87. R. J. Moss
Malinowski, Rivers, Benedict, and others. 1986
Science 236:1579 Je 19 '87. V. Crapanzano
Malkin, L. The national debt. 1987
N Y Times Book Rev 92:11 My 3 '87. A. Balk
Maluccio, A. N. and others. Permanency planning for children. 1986
Child Today 16:36 Mr/Ap '87. J. DiLeonardi
Mamet, D. Writing in restaurants. 1986
USA Today (Periodical) 115:96-7 My '87. L. Carper
Managing nuclear operations. 1987
Bull At Sci 43:43-5 D '87. D. F. Ford
Science 236:1359-60 Je 5 '87. J. Richelson
Mandel, D. Uncommon eloquence. 1986
Dance Mag 61:71 O '87. I. M. Fanger
Mandelbaum, M. and Talbott, S. Reagan and Gorbachev. 1986
N Y Times Book Rev 92:7 Ja 25 '87. M. I. Goldman
Maneli, M. Freedom and tolerance. 1984
Humanist 47:45 My/Je '87. K. Kolenda
Mangan, S. Blackness of a white night. 1986
Nation 244:898-9 Je 27 '87. S. Klawans
Mann, T. Pro and contra Wagner. 1985
Orig. German ed. pub. 1963
Opera News 52:51 Jl '87. G. Schmidgall
Mannheim, K. Conservatism. 1986
Society 25:102-4 N/D '87. R. A. Nisbet
Manns, W. Painted ponies. 1986
Am Herit 38:112 N '87
Mansbridge, J. J. Why we lost the ERA. 1986
Nation 244:692+ My 23 '87. M. J. Collins
Manushkin, F. Little Rabbit's baby brother. 1986
N Y Times Book Rev 92:28 Ja 18 '87. N. B. Cardozo
Maor, E. To infinity and beyond. 1987
N Y Rev Books 34:34-6 D 3 '87. M. Gardner
Science 237:666-7 Ag 7 '87. J. Callahan
Mapp, A. J. Thomas Jefferson. 1987
N Y Times Book Rev 92:11 Jl 5 '87. J. Lewis
Maravall, J. A. Culture of the baroque. 1986
N Y Rev Books 34:26-9 Ap 9 '87. J. H. Elliott
Marcotty, M. and Ledgard, H. F. The world of programming languages. 1987
Byte 12:84+ Je '87. J. W. West
Marcus, C. Prolog programming. 1986
Byte 12:52+ D '87. A. Lane
Marek, E. The children at Santa Clara. 1987
N Y Times Book Rev 92:26 Ap 5 '87. R. Brown
Psychol Today 21:72 Jl '87. R. J. Moss
Marek, R. Works of genius. 1987
N Y Times Book Rev 92:14 Ag 30 '87. H. F. Mosher
Margulis, L. and Sagan, D. Microcosmos. 1986
BioScience 37:682-3 O '87. M. L. Sogin
Maria Moors Cabot Symposium (6th: 1983: Harvard Forest). On the economy of plant form and function. 1986
Science 235:1523 Mr 20 '87. J. A. Teeri
Markham, B. The splendid outcast. 1987
N Y Times Book Rev 92:1+ Ag 23 '87. D. Ackerman
Markova, Dame A. Markova remembers. 1986
Dance Mag 61:70-1 O '87. J. R. Acocella
Marks, P. Skullduggery. 1987
N Y Times Book Rev 92:11 Ag 23 '87. P. McGrath
Marples, D. R. Chernobyl and nuclear power in the USSR. 1986
N Y Times Book Rev 92:31 F 1 '87. R. Wilson
Marrus, M. R. The Holocaust in history. 1987
N Y Times Book Rev 92:38-9 N 22 '87. D. S. Wyman
Marsh, D. Glory days. 1986
N Y Times Book Rev 92:7 Jl 5 '87. P. Watrous

Newsweek 109:74-5 Ap 13 '87. J. Miller
Roll Stone p18+ Je 4 '87. A. DeCurtis
Marsh, P. E. and Collett, P. Driving passion. 1986
Car Driv 33:34 Jl '87. D. Abrahamson
Marshall, F. R. Unheard voices. 1987
Mon Labor Rev 110:50 O '87. S. Deutsch
Marshall, J. and others. The Iran-Contra connection. 1987
Nation 245:172-3 Ag 29 '87. L. Bensky
Marshall, K. In the combat zone. 1987
Nation 245:27-8 Jl 4-11 '87. C. L. Mithers
Martel, G. Imperial diplomacy. 1986
Hist Today 37:56-7 Je '87. I. R. Smith
Martin, C. R. Endocrine physiology. 1984
BioScience 37:747-8 N '87. R. R. Novales
Martin, D. Fly-tying methods. 1987
Conservationist 42:50 N/D '87. J. Rowen
Martin, E. O. St. EOM in the land of Pasaquan.
N Y Times Book Rev 92:18 D 13 '87. P. Schjeldahl
Martin, M. The Jesuits. 1987
America 156:229-31+ Mr 21 '87. G. G. Higgins
Christ Century 104:601-2 Jl 1-8 '87. J. M. McShane
Commonweal 114:219-21 Ap 10 '87. F. X. Murphy
Macleans 100:46 Ag 17 '87. P. Russell
N Y Rev Books 34:34 Je 25 '87. J. M. Cameron
N Y Times Book Rev 92:15 Ap 5 '87. P. Hofmann
Natl Rev 39:54-6 Ap 24 '87. M. Liccione
Martin, V. A recent martyr. 1987
N Y Times Book Rev 92:37 Je 7 '87. C. Banks
Marty, M. E. Modern American religion; v1, The irony of it all, 1893-1919. 1986
America 156:286 Ap 4 '87. L. G. Patterson
Christ Century 104:359-61 Ap 15 '87. G. M. Marsden
Christ Today 31:48-9 Ap 17 '87. M. A. Noll
N Y Times Book Rev 92:13 Ja 4 '87. J. M. Cooper
Marty, M. E. Religion and republic. 1987
America 157:227-9 O 10 '87. M. Massa
Marvick, E. W. Louis XIII. 1986
N Y Rev Books 34:40-3 Je 11 '87. J. H. Elliott
Marx, S. A gaudy spree. 1987
N Y Times Book Rev 92:43 My 31 '87. R. Dooley
Masaoka, M. M. They call me Moses Masaoka. 1987
N Y Times Book Rev 92:31 N 29 '87. D. MacEachron
Maslow, J. E. Bird of life, bird of death. 1986
Environment 29:28 Ap '87. A. H. Westing
Masson, R. The charmed circle. 1987
Commonweal 114:687 N 20 '87. M. D. Lowery
Masters, W. H. and others. Masters and Johnson on sex and human loving. 1986
America 156:446-7 My 30 '87. L. S. Cahill
Psychol Today 21:76 Ja '87. M. S. Kimmel
Matheopoulos, H. Divo. 1986
N Y Times Book Rev 92:15 Ja 11 '87. B. Holland
Mathews, H. Cigarettes. 1987
N Y Times Book Rev 92:23 N 29 '87. L. Zeidner
Mathews, N. M. Mary Cassatt. 1987
Antiques 132:1027+ N '87. D. M. Sokol
Matsumoto, K. Jōdai-gire. 1984
Am Craft 47:14 Ap/My '87. G. Moss
Matsunaga, S. M. The Mars project. 1986
Space World X-3-279:25-6 Mr '87. S. F. Singer
Matter, H. and Matter, M. Alberto Giacometti. 1987
Vogue 177:108+ O '87. J. Perl
Matthee, D. Fiela's child. 1986
America 156:86-7 Ja 31 '87. E. Spangler
Matthew, H. C. G. Gladstone, 1809-1874. 1986
Hist Today 37:59-60 Je '87. N. Yates
Matthews, G. G. Cellular physiology of nerve & muscle. 1986
BioScience 37:619 S '87. N. A. Ingoglia
Matthews, W. Foreseeable futures. 1987
N Y Times Book Rev 92:9 Jl 26 '87. J. D. McClatchy
Matthiasdottir, L. Louisa Matthiasdottir, small paintings. 1986
Am Artist 51:24+ D '87. F. Johnson
Matty, A. J. Fish endocrinology. 1985
BioScience 37:432 Je '87. M. Schreibman
May, R. and others. Politics and innocence. 1986
Psychol Today 21:99-100 My '87. A. Kohn
Mayer, M. Making news. 1987
N Y Times Book Rev 92:22 My 3 '87. J. H. Jaffe
Mayer, M. The Pied Piper of Hamelin. 1987
N Y Times Book Rev 92:28-9 N 29 '87. P. Neumeyer
Maynard, J. Domestic affairs. 1987
New Repub 197:31-3 Ag 24 '87. A. Bernard
Maynard, J. New house. 1987
N Y Times Book Rev 92:50 O 25 '87. C. Dragonwagon
McAleer, N. The mind-boggling universe. 1986
Sky Telesc 74:262-3 S '87. C. Raymo
McBeth, L. The Baptist heritage. 1987
Christ Century 104:832 S 30 '87. W. B. Shurden
McBrien, R. P. Caesar's coin. 1987

Sky Telesc 73:503+ My '87. A. MacRobert
Merkin, D. Enchantment. 1986
Vogue 177:98+ Ja '87. G. L. Buckley
Merser, C. "Grown-ups". 1987
N Y Times Book Rev 92:11 O 18 '87. F. Klagsbrun
Mesmerized by the bear. 1987
Natl Rev 39:53 Ag 28 '87. C. Williamson
Mewshaw, M. Money to burn. 1987
N Y Times Book Rev 92:28 S 13 '87. M. Jones
Meyer, D. B. Sex and power. 1987
N Y Times Book Rev 92:23 O 11 '87. K. M. Offen
Meyers, J. Manic power. 1987
Natl Rev 39:46-7 D 31 '87. H. Kenner
Time 130:90+ N 23 '87. S. Kanfer
Meyrowitz, J. No sense of place. 1985
Cent Mag 20:44 Mr/Ap '87. D. McDonald
Michaud, M. A. G. Reaching for the high frontier. 1986
Sky Telesc 73:507-8 My '87. B. Bova
Space World X-4-280:20 Ap '87. J. Rhea
Michelet, J. Michelet. 1987
New Repub 197:33-4+ O 26 '87. J. Clive
Michener, J. A. The legacy. 1987
N Y Times Book Rev 92:6 S 6 '87. J. Martin
Michnik, A. Letters from prison and other essays. 1985
Commentary 83:71-2 F '87. M. Friedberg
Middlemas, K. Power, competition and the state; v1, Britain in search of balance, 1940-61. 1986
Hist Today 37:55 My '87. K. O. Morgan
Middleton, C. Two horse wagon going by. 1986
N Y Times Book Rev 92:32-3 N 15 '87. A. Corn
Midrash and literature. 1986
Commentary 84:76-8 Ag '87. B. Hochman
New Repub 196:27-33 Ja 5-12 '87. R. Alter
Mikheev, D. The Soviet perspective on the Strategic Defense Initiative. 1987
Natl Rev 39:60 S 25 '87. C. Williamson
Milkman, H. B. and Sunderwirth, S. G. Craving for ecstasy. 1987
Psychol Today 21:78 S '87. P. J. Black
Milkman, R. Gender at work. 1986
Nation 244:550 Ap 25 '87. J. B. Freeman
Miller, A. Timebends. 1987
N Y 20:106+ N 9 '87. R. Koenig
N Y Times Book Rev 92:1+ N 8 '87. R. Shattuck
Nation 245:632-4+ N 28 '87. J. Lardner
New Leader 70:15-16 D 28 '87. S. Rodman
New Yorker 63:150-4 D 14 '87. A. Kazin
Newsweek 110:110+ N 16 '87. P. S. Prescott
Time 130:88 N 23 '87. W. A. Henry
Vogue 177:266-7 N '87. E. White
Miller, H. Henry VIII and the English nobility. 1986
Hist Today 37:56+ Ja '87. J. Loach
Miller, J. Bourbon and Stuart. 1987
Hist Today 37:53-4 S '87. K. H. D. Haley
Miller, J. "Democracy is in the streets". 1987
Cent Mag 20:39-40 S/O '87. D. McDonald
N Y Rev Books 34:10+ O 22 '87. A. Brinkley
N Y Times Book Rev 92:1+ Je 21 '87. H. Hertzberg
Nation 245:58-61 Jl 18-25 '87. N. Xenos
New Leader 70:16-17 O 5 '87. B. Gewen
New Repub 197:28-35 Ag 10-17 '87. P. Berman
Newsweek 110:64 Jl 13 '87. D. Lehman
Progressive 51:29-30 N '87. B. Blum
Wash Mon 19:60 S '87. N. Lemann
Miller, J. Subsequent performances. 1986
New Yorker 62:83-5 Ja 26 '87. V. Geng
Opera News 51:41 Ja 31 '87. K. Mauney
Miller, J. B. Toward a new psychology of women. 2nd ed. 1986
Psychol Today 21:100-2 My '87. P. J. Caplan
Miller, J. M. and Hayes, J. H. A history of ancient Israel and Judah. 1986
America 157:306-7 O 31 '87. J. J. M. Roberts
Miller, M. Ike the soldier. 1987
N Y Times Book Rev 92:10-11 D 20 '87. R. F. Weigley
Miller, M. E. The murals of Bonampak. 1986
Sci Am 256:26-7 F '87. P. Morrison
Science 235:1522 Mr 20 '87. C. Coggins
Miller, R. L. Under the cloud. 1986
Science 235:227 Ja 9 '87. R. A. Divine
Miller, S. Inventing the Abbotts, and other stories. 1987
N Y Times Book Rev 92:5 My 24 '87. P. Lively
Miller, S. Painted in blood. 1987
Bus Week p16 Je 15 '87. R. E. Farrell
Miller, T. The Panama hat trail. 1986
Américas 39:60-1 Jl/Ag '87. C. Healy
Miller, W. D. All is grace. 1987
Christ Century 104:1092-3 D 2 '87. J. Carlson Brown
Natl Rev 39:58 Ap 10 '87. T. P. McDonnell
Miller, W. L. The first liberty. 1986
Christ Today 31:56 S 18 '87. J. W. Skillen

Commonweal 114:23+ Ja 16 '87. R. L. Spaeth
Mills, E. S. The burden of government. 1986
Natl Rev 39:58 Mr 27 '87. C. Williamson
Mills, J. The underground empire. 1986
New Repub 197:33-4+ O 12 '87. J. Weisberg
Milne, H. Bhagwan. 1987
Newsweek 109:78 Ja 26 '87. D. Gates
Mind and brain. 1986
Science 235:373-4 Ja 16 '87. B. Bridgeman
Minear, P. S. Death set to music. 1987
Christ Century 104:1152-3 D 16 '87. P. Westermeyer
Ministry and the miraculous. 1987
Christ Today 31:54-5 S 18 '87. T. Stafford
Minsky, M. L. The society of mind. 1986
Byte 12:84+ O '87. D. Kirkpatrick
Discover 8:84+ S '87. P. Hoffman
N Y Rev Books 34:33-5 Je 11 '87. B. A. O. Williams
N Y Times Book Rev 92:10 F 22 '87. J. W. Lance
New Repub 196:42-5 Ap 20 '87. I. Hacking
The Missing dimension. 1985
Society 24:95-6 My/Je '87. J. B. Keely
Mitchell, A. W. The enchanted canopy. 1986
Sci Am 256:32-3 Mr '87. P. Morrison
Mitchell, R. H. Kimberlites. 1986
Science 236:729 My 8 '87. D. J. Schulze
Mitsch, W. J. and Gosselink, J. G. Wetlands. 1986
BioScience 37:735-6 N '87. J. P. Stout
Mo, T. An insular possession. 1987
N Y Times Book Rev 92:2 Ap 19 '87. R. W. Winks
New Repub 196:39-41 My 11 '87. I. Buruma
Modular organisms: case studies. 1986
Science 237:1626-7 S 25 '87. L. W. Buss
Moggach, D. To have and to hold. 1987
N Y Times Book Rev 92:19 Mr 29 '87. E. Villars
Mojtabai, A. G. Blessed assurance. 1986
Bull At Sci 43:47-8 Ap '87. C. J. Greenhouse
Molander, R. C. and Nichols, R. Who will stop the bomb? 1985
Futurist 21:33 Ja/F '87. F. S. Hopkins
Moldea, D. E. Dark victory. 1986
N Y Rev Books 33:23-4 Ja 15 '87. N. Lemann
Molecular bases of neural development. 1985
BioScience 37:748-9 N '87. G. M. Jonakait
Molecular biology and human disease. 1984
BioScience 37:291 Ap '87. G. D. Frenkel
The Molecular biology of ciliated protozoa. 1986
Science 237:306 Jl 17 '87. V. A. Zakian
Molecular evolutionary genetics. 1985
Science 235:599 Ja 30 '87. M. T. Clegg
Molecular immunology. 1984
BioScience 37:75-6 Ja '87. J. E. Nagel
Mollat, M. The poor in the Middle Ages. 1986
N Y Rev Books 33:42-3 Ja 15 '87. M. H. Keen
Molnar, T. S. The pagan temptation. 1987
Natl Rev 39:48-9 Jl 31 '87. R. Martin
Moltmann, J. God in creation. 1985
Christ Today 31:66 Mr 20 '87. S. Grenz
Moltmann-Wendel, E. A land flowing with milk and honey. 1986
Christ Century 104:890-1 O 14 '87. N. A. Hardesty
Mondrian, P. The new art, the new life. 1986
Art News 86:71-2 N '87. Y.-A. Bois
N Y Times Book Rev 92:13-14 Mr 1 '87. P. Gay
Monitoring neurotransmitter release during behaviour. 1986
Science 238:1448-9 D 4 '87. R. W. Keller, Jr. and M. J. Zigmond
Monkhouse, C. P. and Michie, T. S. American furniture in Pendleton House.
Antiques 131:986-7 My '87. M. Kaye
Monninger, J. Second season. 1987
N Y Times Book Rev 92:29 N 1 '87. L. Rosenberg
Monroe, J. G. and Williamson, R. A. They dance in the sky. 1987
N Y Times Book Rev 92:44 N 22 '87. G. B. Smith
Monsoons. 1987
Science 237:1236-7 S 4 '87. H. Riehl
Montgomery, D. The fall of the house of labor. 1987
Atlantic 260:100-2 S '87. B. Ehrenreich
N Y Times Book Rev 92:30 N 29 '87. N. Lichtenstein
Nation 245:201-4 S 5 '87. M. Kazin
Wash Mon 19:59-60 N '87. C. Euchner
Montgomery Ward & Co. Fall & winter 1894-95.
Antiques Collect Hobbies 92:55 Je '87
Moody, J. and Boyes, R. The priest and the policeman. 1987
N Y Times Book Rev 92:9 Mr 15 '87. N. Davies
Moore, A. and Gibbons, D. Watchmen.
Nation 245:386-7 O 10 '87. F. P. Smoler
Moore, B. The color of blood. 1987
America 157:460 D 12 '87. K. Reed
Commonweal 114:634-6 N 6 '87. J. V. Long

N Y Rev Books 34:44+ D 17 '87. N. Ascherson
N Y Times Book Rev 92:11 S 27 '87. C. Sigal
Nation 245:345-6 O 3 '87. T. Flanagan
New Repub 197:47-8 N 2 '87. S. Kanfer
Time 130:84 O 5 '87. P. Iyer
Moore, G. E. G.E. Moore. 1986
N Y Rev Books 34:37-9 Mr 26 '87. S. Hampshire
Moore, G. S. The banker's life. 1987
Fortune 116:119 Jl 20 '87. D. Seligman
Moore, J. N. The secret war in Central America. 1987
Natl Rev 39:68 S 11 '87. C. Williamson
Moore, M. The complete prose of Marianne Moore. 1986
Commonweal 114:186-7 Mr 27 '87. W. Koestenbaum
New Yorker 63:94-6 Mr 16 '87. H. H. Vendler
Moore, M. The state and peasant politics in Sri Lanka. 1985
New Repub 196:33-8 F 23 '87. D. L. Horowitz
Moore, P. Exploring the night sky with binoculars. 1986
Astronomy 15:85-6 N '87. G. O. Clark
Sky Telesc 73:503+ My '87. A. MacRobert
Moore, S. The immortal 2.9.
Road Track 39:70 N '87. L. Paddock
Moorehead, C. Troublesome people. 1987
Atlantic 260:78-80 Ag '87. T. Powers
Moorjani, K. and Coey, J. M. D. Magnetic glasses. 1984
Phys Today 40:77 Ja '87. J. W. Lynn
Moos, S. von. Venturi, Rauch & Scott Brown. 1987
Art Am 75:23+ N '87. J. Merkel
Moosa, M. The Maronites in history. 1986
America 156:286-8 Ap 4 '87. W. P. Tayah
Morales, R. J. The amateur astronomer's catalog of 500 deep-sky objects. v1
Sky Telesc 73:281-2 Mr '87. P. Harrington
Moravcsik, M. J. Musical sound. 1987
Sci Am 257:149-50 D '87. P. Morrison and P. Morrison
Moravia, A. The voyeur. 1987
N Y Times Book Rev 92:15 Mr 29 '87. L. Re
Morgan, R. Dry your smile. 1987
N Y Times Book Rev 92:16 S 27 '87. A. Becker
Morita, A. Made in Japan. 1986
N Y Rev Books 34:16-18 Mr 12 '87. I. Buruma
Morland, A. Lamborghini. 1985
Mot Trend 39:42 D '87. T. C. Browne
Morley, J. D. The case of Thomas N. 1987
N Y Times Book Rev 92:26 S 13 '87. A. Hulbert
Morley, S. Spread a little happiness. 1987
N Y Times Book Rev 92:22 N 15 '87. J. Gerard
Mormino, G. R. and Pozzetta, G. E. The immigrant world of Ybor City. 1987
USA Today (Periodical) 116:97 Jl '87. F. Cordasco
Morone, J. G. and Woodhouse, E. J. Averting catastrophe. 1986
Bull At Sci 43:48-50 Ap '87. C. Perrow
Morris, G. W. The kids next door. 1985
Psychol Today 21:74 Ap '87. J. Meer
Morris, J. Manhattan '45. 1987
N Y Times Book Rev 92:8 Ap 19 '87. R. Starr
Time 129:74 Ap 20 '87. M. Walsh
Vogue 177:211-12 Ap '87. R. Sennett
Morris, J. N. A schedule of benefits. 1987
New Leader 70:13-14 D 14 '87. P. Pettingell
Morris, R. B. The forging of the Union, 1781-1789. 1987
N Y Times Book Rev 92:24 Je 14 '87. M. G. Kammen
Morrison, T. Beloved. 1987
Commonweal 114:631-3 N 6 '87. K. Baker-Fletcher
Ms 16:66+ N '87. M. A. Gillespie
N Y Rev Books 34:18-19 N 5 '87. T. R. Edwards
N Y Times Book Rev 92:1+ S 13 '87. M. Atwood
Nation 245:418-21 O 17 '87. R. Brown
Natl Rev 39:54-5 D 4 '87. D. K. Mano
New Leader 70:20-1 N 2 '87. H. H. Davis
New Repub 197:38-43 O 19 '87. S. Crouch
New Yorker 63:175-80 N 2 '87. J. Thurman
Newsweek 110:74-5 S 28 '87. W. Clemons
Time 130:75 S 21 '87. P. Gray
Mortenson, J. Whale songs and wasp maps. 1986
Psychol Today 21:79 Jl '87. H. Hall
Mortimer, J. C. Charade. 1986
First pub.: Bodley Head, 1947
N Y Times Book Rev 92:24 Mr 8 '87. M. Stasio
Morton, F. The crosstown sabbath. 1987
N Y Times Book Rev 92:18 S 13 '87. P. Lopate
Moss, H. Minor mounuments. 1986
New Repub 196:30-3 Mr 30 '87. H. H. Vendler
Moss, N. Klaus Fuchs. 1987
N Y Rev Books 34:54-60 N 19 '87. S. E. Toulmin
N Y Times Book Rev 92:9+ D 13 '87. Z. S. Steiner
Science 238:831 N 6 '87. R. Bothwell
Mosse, G. L. German Jews beyond Judaism. 1985
Am Sch 56:290+ Spr '87. R. Gay
Motion, A. The Lamberts. 1987

N Y Times Book Rev 92:21 Ag 2 '87. J. Rockwell
Mountain people. 1986
Sierra 72:148-50 Ja/F '87. K. Ohnuma
Mowat, F. Woman in the mists. 1987
Glamour 85:252 N '87. L. Mathews
N Y Rev Books 92:15-16+ O 25 '87. E. Linden
Time 130:122 O 26 '87. S. Kanfer
Vogue 177:252+ N '87. T. Young
Mowsesian, R. Golden goals, rusted realities. 1986
Bus Week p18-19 Ag 17 '87. W. E. Kennedy
Muggeridge, A. R. The desolate city.
Commonweal 114:58-9 Ja 30 '87. L. S. Cunningham
Muir, J. Muir among the animals. 1986
N Y Rev Books 34:20-5 Je 25 '87. S. J. Gould
Muirhead, J. Those who fall. 1986
N Y Times Book Rev 92:30 F 15 '87. T. Ferrell
Munro, E. C. On glory roads. 1987
N Y Times Book Rev 92:9+ Ap 26 '87. R. Blythe
Munson, G. B. The awakening Twenties. 1985
Am Sch 56:427-31 Summ '87. D. Clayton
Muravchik, J. The uncertain crusade. 1986
New Repub 196:38-41 F 2 '87. C. Layne
Murdoch, I. Acastos. 1987
New Yorker 63:113-15 My 18 '87. J. Updike
Murphy, N. T. P. In search of Blandings. 1986
Natl Rev 39:50-1 Ag 28 '87. H. Bering-Jensen
Murphy, R. F. The body silent. 1987
Commonweal 114:324+ My 22 '87. R. Jackall
Murphy, W. F. Upon this rock. 1987
N Y Times Book Rev 92:26+ D 6 '87. J. Koenig
Murray, J. C. We hold these truths.
New Repub 196:30-4 Je 1 '87. A. Sullivan
Murray, P. Song in a weary throat. 1986
Christ Century 104:828+ S 30 '87. N. S. Montgomery
Ms 15:14+ My '87. S. McHenry
N Y Times Book Rev 92:12 Mr 29 '87. P. J. Williams
Nation 244:689-90 My 23 '87. P. Giddings
Murray, W. When the fat man sings. 1987
N Y Times Book Rev 92:22 N 8 '87. T. Hillerman
Murray, W. H. and Pappas, C. H. 80386/80286 assembly language programming. 1986
Byte 12:76+ Ja '87. J. Unger
Murray, W. J., III. Nicaragua.
Natl Rev 39:58 N 6 '87. C. Williamson
Myers, J. E. As long as you're happy.
N Y Times Book Rev 92:15 Ja 25 '87. B. Shlain
Myers, W. D. Crystal. 1987
N Y Times Book Rev 92:48 S 13 '87. J. Betancourt
Myres, J. N. L. The English settlements. 1986
Hist Today 37:56-8 Mr '87. T. M. Charles-Edwards

N

Nabokov, V. V. The enchanter. 1986
N Y Rev Books 34:9 Mr 12 '87. V. S. Pritchett
Nader, R. and Taylor, W. The big boys. 1986
Car Driv 32:36-7 Mr '87. D. Abrahamson
Nadolny, S. The discovery of slowness. 1987
N Y Times Book Rev 92:15 D 20 '87. S. Blackburn
New Repub 197:39-41 D 7 '87. V. Klinkenborg
Nagel, P. C. The Adams women. 1987
Am Herit 38:113 N '87
N Y Times Book Rev 92:23 O 25 '87. J. Lewis
Nagel, T. The view from nowhere. 1986
N Y Rev Books 34:31-4 Ap 9 '87. J. Glover
Naipaul, S. An unfinished journey. 1987
N Y Times Book Rev 92:26 Mr 22 '87. J. F. Avedon
New Repub 196:26-30 My 11 '87. G. Wheatcroft
Naipaul, V. S. The enigma of arrival. 1987
Macleans 100:55 My 18 '87. G. James
N Y 20:80 Mr 16 '87. R. Koenig
N Y Rev Books 34:3-4 Ap 9 '87. J. Bayley
N Y Times Book Rev 92:11-12 Mr 22 '87. F. Kermode
Natl Rev 39:49-50 Ag 28 '87. R. Royal
New Repub 196:27-31 Ap 13 '87. D. Walcott
Time 129:75 Mr 2 '87. P. Gray
Napier, J. R. and Napier, P. H. The natural history of the primates. 1985
BioScience 37:733-4 N '87. A. A. Eudey
Narayan, R. K. Talkative man. 1987
N Y Rev Books 34:45-6 O 8 '87. R. Towers
Natl Rev 39:50-1 Jl 17 '87. A. Bakshian
Nash, R. H. Evangelicals in America. 1987
Christ Today 31:68 O 2 '87. B. L. Shelley
Nash, R. H. Poverty and wealth. 1986
Christ Today 31:56 Jl 10 '87. D. Bandow
Nathan, R. S. The white tiger. 1987
N Y Times Book Rev 92:9-10 S 6 '87. J. A. Cohen
National Research Council (U.S.). Panel on Adolescent Pregnancy and Childbearing. Risking the future. v1 1987
Commentary 83:71-4 My '87. A. Ryerson

Native American mathematics. 1986
Science 236:1006-7 My 22 '87. C. G. Moore
Native American parent aide training curriculum. 2v
Child Today 16:inside back cover My/Je '87. C. Sudia
NATO Advanced Study Institute: "On Growth and Form"
(1985: Cargèse, Corsica). On growth and form. 1986
Sci Am 256:26-7 Ja '87. P. Morrison
NATO Advanced Study Institute on High Energy
Phenomena around Collapsed Stars (1985: Cargèse,
Corsica). High energy phenomena around collapsed stars.
1987
Science 238:970 N 13 '87. F. Melia
The Nature of the lower continental crust. 1986
Science 236:861-2 My 15 '87. A. W. Bally
The Nature of time. 1986
N Y Times Book Rev 92:16 My 3 '87. M. Talbot
Navacelle, T. de. Woody Allen on location. 1987
N Y Times Book Rev 92:16 Ap 12 '87. E. Weiner
Navarre, Y. Cronus' children. 1986
N Y Times Book Rev 92:18 My 3 '87. A. E. Johnson
Navarre, Y. Our share of time.
N Y Times Book Rev 92:18 My 3 '87. A. E. Johnson
Nay, C. The black and the red. 1987
Commentary 84:77-80 S '87. R. Kaplan
N Y Times Book Rev 92:18 Je 28 '87. R. O. Paxton
Natl Rev 39:45-7 Jl 3 '87. F. M. Oppenheimer
New Leader 70:29-30 My 4-18 '87. M. Kesselman
Naylor, R. T. Hot money and the politics of debt. 1987
N Y Times Book Rev 92:45 Ap 26 '87. P. O'Toole
Wash Mon 19:51-2 O '87. S. C. Gwynne
Neal, E. G. The natural history of badgers. 1986
Science 238:970-1 N 13 '87. M. Hancox
Needham, J. Science and civilisation in China; v5 pt7,
Chemistry and chemical technology. 1986
Sci Am 257:114-15 Jl '87. P. Morrison
Needham, J. Science and civilisation in China; v6 pt1,
Biology and biological technology. 1986
Science 236:728-9 My 8 '87. P. S. Ashton
Ne'eman, Y. and Kirsh, Y. The particle hunters. 1986
Phys Today 40:86 D '87. M. L. Perl
Science 236:999 My 22 '87. J. D. Bjorken
Nei, M. Molecular evolutionary genetics. 1987
Science 237:782 Ag 14 '87. D. L. Hartl
Nelkin, D. The creation controversy. 1984
BioScience 37:70+ Ja '87. L. V. Giddings
Nelkin, D. Selling science. 1987
Science 236:973-4 My 22 '87. S. Panem
Nelson, B. A. Assimilation.
Natl Rev 39:56 My 8 '87. C. Williamson
Nelson, G. M. To dance with God. 1986
Commonweal 114:508-9 S 11 '87. F. Howe
Nelson, K. Event knowledge. 1986
Science 236:471-2 Ap 24 '87. C. E. Snow
Nelson, K. A. On the frontier of adoption. 1985
Child Today 16:30-1 Ja/F '87. E. J. Schwartz
Neotropical ornithology. 1985
BioScience 37:622-3 S '87. D. Siegel-Causey
Neuman, W. R. The paradox of mass politics. 1986
N Y Rev Books 34:8-10+ Mr 26 '87. T. B. Edsall
Neural transplantation and regeneration. 1986
BioScience 37:750-1 N '87. R. D. Lund
Neurobiology of taste and smell. 1987
Science 237:203 Jl 10 '87. J. G. Hildebrand
Neurochemical analysis of the conscious brain. 1986
Science 238:1448-9 D 4 '87. R. W. Keller, Jr. and
M. J. Zigmond
Neuromodulation. 1987
Science 236:863 My 15 '87. I. Kupfermann
Neusner, J. Death and birth of Judaism. 1987
Christ Century 104:666-7 Jl 29-Ag 5 '87. A. R. Eckardt
Neusner, J. Self-fulfilling prophecy. 1987
Christ Century 104:946 O 28 '87. M. A. Sweeney
Neustadt, R. E. and May, E. R. Thinking in time. 1986
Am Sch 56:591-4 Aut '87. H. Orlans
The New book of Christian prayers. 1986
Christ Century 104:26+ Ja 7-14 '87. T. E. Moody
The New Oxford book of Irish verse. 1986
N Y Rev Books 34:25-6 F 26 '87. D. Donoghue
Newbigin, L. Foolishness to the Greeks. 1986
Christ Century 104:864-5 O 7 '87. D. Heim
Newman, P. C. Caesars of the wilderness. 1987
N Y Times Book Rev 92:9 D 20 '87. J. Barfoot
Newmeyer, F. J. The politics of linguistics. 1986
New Repub 196:34+ Mr 23 '87. E. Gellner
Nguyen, G. T. H. and Schecter, J. L. The palace file.
1986
N Y Times Book Rev 92:11 Ja 18 '87. G. M. Kahin
New Repub 196:34-6 Mr 9 '87. R. Holbrooke
Niblack, W. An introduction to digital image processing.
1986
Byte 12:78 F '87. J. V. Olson

Nicolson, N. and Nicolson, A. Two roads to Dodge City.
1987
N Y Times Book Rev 92:47 Ap 12 '87. K. A. Marling
Time 129:103 My 4 '87. P. Iyer
Nin, A. Henry and June. 1986
Mademoiselle 93:74+ F '87. L. Moore
Nixon, C. Racing the silver arrows. 1986
Mot Trend 39:44 Jl '87
Nobel Conference (1980: Gustavus Adolphus College). The
aesthetic dimension of science. 1982
Phys Today 40:68 Je '87. O. Gingerich
Noll, M. A. Between faith and criticism. 1986
Christ Century 104:1004-5 N 11 '87. I. J. Hesselink
Christ Today 31:50-1 F 6 '87. D. K. McKim
The Nonprofit sector. 1987
Science 236:984-5 My 22 '87. B. D. Karl
Nooteboom, C. In the Dutch mountains. 1987
N Y Times Book Rev 92:42 O 11 '87. M. Malone
Norman, D. Encounters. 1987
Art Am 75:27+ O '87. C. Little
N Y Times Book Rev 92:19 Je 28 '87. A. Anderson
Norman, M. The fortune teller. 1987
N Y Times Book Rev 92:10 My 24 '87. A. Hempel
Vogue 177:199 My '87. M. Kramer
Norse, E. A. and others. Conserving biological diversity
in our national forests. 1986
BioScience 37:425-6 Je '87. F. W. Stearns and G.
Guntenspergen
North Atlantic palaeoceanography. 1986
Science 236:619-20 My 1 '87. W. A. Berggren
Norwood, R. Women who love too much. 1986
Newsweek 109:52-3 Mr 9 '87. C. Leerhsen
Nossiter, B. D. The global struggle for more. 1987
N Y Times Book Rev 92:53 My 3 '87. M. Kahler
New Leader 70:17-18 My 4-18 '87. J. N. Bhagwati
Novak, B. Alice's neck. 1987
Vogue 177:280 O '87. M. Jefferson
Novak, B. The Thyssen-Bornemisza Collection.
Antiques 132:1034+ N '87. L. Ayres
Novak, M. Will it liberate? 1986
America 156:410-11 My 16 '87. A. T. Hennelly
Christ Century 104:1042 N 18 '87. R. O. Hathaway
Christ Today 31:54+ Jl 10 '87. C. H. Pinnock
Commentary 84:42-3 S '87. A. R. Muggeridge
Commonweal 114:185-6 Mr 27 '87. P. E. Sigmund
Natl Rev 39:46 Ag 14 '87. R. Royal
New Repub 196:31-6 My 4 '87. C. Coulson
Nuclear energy. 1985
Phys Today 40:70 Jl '87. D. Bodansky
Numerical recipes. 1986
Byte 12:65-6+ Ja '87. J. Alper and M. Bridger
Phys Today 40:120+ O '87. P. B. Kramer
Nunn, K. Unassigned territory. 1987
N Y Times Book Rev 92:7-8 Jl 5 '87. E. Tallent
Nurses in Vietnam. 1987
Nation 245:27-8 Jl 4-11 '87. C. L. Mithers
Nutritional biochemistry and metabolism. 1985
BioScience 37:620+ S '87. M. W. Hamm
Nye, D. The autocourse history of the grand prix car
1966-1985. 1986
Mot Trend 39:42 Ag '87
Nye, J. S., Jr. Nuclear ethics. 1986
America 156:85-6 Ja 31 '87. J. J. Langan
Bull At Sci 43:53-4 Ja/F '87. S. Nathanson
Nye, M. J. Science in the provinces. 1986
Science 235:1408 Mr 13 '87. R. S. Turner
Nyiszli, M. Auschwitz. 1986
Copyright 1960
N Y Rev Books 34:29-34 My 28 '87. N. Ascherson

O

Oates, J. C. On boxing. 1987
N Y Times Book Rev 92:8 Mr 15 '87. A. Broyard
Newsweek 109:68 Mr 9 '87. D. Lehman
Oates, J. C. You must remember this. 1987
America 157:360+ N 14 '87. R. S. Phillips
N Y Times Book Rev 92:3 Ag 16 '87. S. Birkerts
New Yorker 63:119-23 D 28 '87. J. Updike
Time 130:62 Ag 31 '87. R. Z. Sheppard
Oates, S. B. William Faulkner, the man and the artist.
1987
Atlantic 260:91-2 Jl '87. B. DeMott
N Y Times Book Rev 92:18 S 20 '87. L. D. Rubin
Natl Rev 39:58-60 O 23 '87. C. Williamson
Oates, W. E. The presence of God in pastoral counseling.
1986
Christ Century 104:505-6 My 20-27 '87. F. L. Fowler,
III
Ober, W. B. Bottoms up! 1988
N Y Times Book Rev 92:13 N 29 '87. R. Selzer

Hist Today 37:60-1 N '87. B. H. Reid
Parker, R. B. Pale kings and princes. 1987
   N Y Times Book Rev 92:26 My 31 '87. T. Weesner
Parkin, F. The mind and body shop. 1987
   N Y Times Book Rev 92:9 Ag 16 '87. E. Hawes
Parks, T. Tongues of flame. 1986
   Mademoiselle 93:96+ Mr '87. L. Moore
   N Y Times Book Rev 92:9-10 Ja 4 '87. M. Wolitzer
Parks, V. D. and Jones, M. Jump! 1986
   N Y Times Book Rev 92:29 F 1 '87. P. Neumeyer
Parry, J. P. Democracy and religion. 1986
   Hist Today 37:60 Je '87. N. Yates
Pasternak, B. L. The voice of prose; v1, Early prose and autobiography. 1986
   New Repub 197:37-9 Jl 6 '87. T. Venclova
Pastor, R. A. Condemned to repetition. 1987
   N Y Times Book Rev 92:56 N 8 '87. S. K. Purcell
Patterson, J. T. The dread disease. 1987
   N Y Times Book Rev 92:43 S 27 '87. A. Fels
   New Leader 70:16-17 N 16 '87. B. Gewen
   Science 238:1589 D 11 '87. C. G. Lasby
Pattison, R. The triumph of vulgarity. 1987
   N Y Times Book Rev 92:7-8 Ja 25 '87. L. Moore
   Nation 244:405-7 Mr 28 '87. S. Frith
   Natl Rev 39:51-2 Ag 14 '87. J. Wooten
   New Repub 196:41-2 Mr 23 '87. L. Menand
Patton, P. Open road. 1986
   Car Driv 33:36 D '87. T. Assenza
Paul, H. W. From knowledge to power. 1985
   Science 235:1408 Mr 13 '87. R. S. Turner
Paul, R. The Bond Street burlesque. 1987
   N Y Times Book Rev 92:19 Mr 15 '87. J. Fast
Paulson, A. B. Watchman tell us of the night. 1987
   N Y Times Book Rev 92:33 Ag 9 '87. A. Barnet
Pauly, P. J. Controlling life. 1987
   N Y Rev Books 34:17-20 N 19 '87. D. Joravsky
   Science 237:305 Jl 17 '87. J. W. Servos
Payne, S. G. The Franco regime, 1936-1975. 1987
   N Y Times Book Rev 92:16 D 27 '87. P. Preston
PC LAN primer. 1987
   Byte 12:86+ Jl '87. D. Kirkpatrick
Peace in a nuclear age. 1986
   Commonweal 114:425-6 Jl 17 '87. E. W. Doherty
Pearson, T. R. The last of how it was. 1987
   N Y Times Book Rev 92:13 N 1 '87. P. Henley
Pechenik, J. A. Biology of the invertebrates. 1985
   BioScience 37:356-7 My '87. F. H. Barnwell
Peck, M. S. The different drum. 1987
   N Y Times Book Rev 92:11 Je 28 '87. L. B. Rubin
Pedraza-Bailey, S. Political and economic migrants in America. 1985
   Society 24:95-6 Jl/Ag '87. L. Perez
Pedrosa, C. N. Imelda Marcos. 1987
   N Y Rev Books 34:10+ Je 11 '87. I. Buruma
Peitgen, H.-O. and Richter, P. H. The beauty of fractals. 1986
   Byte 12:67-8 My '87. E. A. Bobinsky
Pelikan, J. J. Bach among the theologians. 1986
   Christ Century 104:362-3 Ap 15 '87. P. Westermeyer
Pelta, K. Bridging the Golden Gate. 1987
   Sci Am 257:152 D '87. P. Morrison and P. Morrison
The Penguin book of modern Yiddish verse. 1987
   New Repub 197:34-8 D 14 '87. D. Donoghue
Penrose, B. and Freeman, S. Conspiracy of silence. 1987
   N Y Rev Books 34:3-4+ O 22 '87. N. G. A. Annan, Baron
   N Y Times Book Rev 92:11-12 Ag 16 '87. S. Koch
   Time 130:51 Ag 10 '87. P. Gray
Percy, W. The thanatos syndrome. 1987
   America 156:308-9+ Ap 11 '87. P. H. Samway
   Atlantic 259:86+ Ap '87. D. Bauer
   Christ Century 104:857-8 O 7 '87. R. C. Wood
   Christ Today 31:50-1 Ag 7 '87. R. Coles
   Commonweal 114:540-1 S 25 '87. J. B. Breslin
   N Y Rev Books 34:45-6 Je 25 '87. R. Towers
   N Y Times Book Rev 92:1+ Ap 5 '87. G. Godwin
   Natl Rev 39:50-2 My 22 '87. R. Royal
   New Repub 196:31-3 Ap 13 '87. S. Birkerts
   New Yorker 63:91-2 Je 15 '87. T. Rafferty
   Time 129:71 Mr 30 '87. P. Gray
Pérec, G. Life, a user's manual. 1987
   N Y Times Book Rev 92:7 N 15 '87. P. Auster
   Time 130:89-90 N 23 '87. P. Gray
Perelman, S. J. Don't tread on me. 1987
   N Y 20:46-7 Jl 20 '87. R. Koenig
   N Y Times Book Rev 92:1+ Ag 9 '87. M. Richler
   Nation 245:129-30 Ag 15-22 '87. J. Rubins
   New Leader 70:190-21 S 7 '87. H. H. Davis
   Smithsonian 18:196+ D '87. D. Drabelle
   Time 130:52 Ag 10 '87. S. Kanfer
Perera, V. Rites. 1986

Christ Century 104:1041-2 N 18 '87. L. B. Barr
Peřina, J. Quantum statistics of linear and nonlinear optical phenomena. 1984
   Phys Today 40:109-10 F '87. N. B. Abraham
Perlmutter, A. The life and times of Menachem Begin. 1987
   N Y Times Book Rev 92:3+ Je 21 '87. G. Gottlieb
   New Repub 196:48-53 Je 8 '87. S. Avineri
Perloff, M. The futurist moment. 1986
   Commonweal 114:459-60 Ag 14 '87. T. Materer
   New Repub 197:30-1 Jl 27 '87. R. Shattuck
Perry, D. R. Life above the jungle floor. 1986
   Sci Am 256:32-3 Mr '87. P. Morrison
Peruvian prehistory. 1987
   Nat Hist 96:26-8 Ap '87. J. R. Alden
Peshkin, A. God's choice. 1986
   Christ Century 104:167-8 F 18 '87. R. V. Pierard
Pessoa, F. The keeper of sheep. 1986
   N Y Times Book Rev 92:32-3 D 13 '87. D. H. Rosenthal
   New Repub 197:33-6 S 7 '87. J. Hollander
   Vogue 177:96 Ja '87. E. White
Pessoa, F. The poems of Fernando Pessoa. 1986
   N Y Times Book Rev 92:32-3 D 13 '87. D. H. Rosenthal
   New Repub 197:33-6 S 7 '87. J. Hollander
Peter, J. Vladimir's carrot. 1987
   N Y Times Book Rev 92:30 N 22 '87. R. Gilman
Peters, R. Practical intelligence. 1987
   Fortune 115:183-4 Je 22 '87. R. J. Herrnstein
Peters, T. J. Thriving on chaos. 1987
   Bus Week p19+ D 21 '87. J. H. Dobrzynski
   N Y Times Book Rev 92:30 O 25 '87. R. Krulwich
Peters, W. A more perfect union. 1987
   N Y Times Book Rev 92:3+ N 15 '87. J. N. Rakove
Peterson, M. D. The great triumvirate. 1987
   N Y Times Book Rev 92:65 N 8 '87. D. B. Cole
   New Yorker 63:151-4 N 9 '87. N. Bliven
Petit, M. Variable stars. 1987
   Sky Telesc 74:374 O '87. M. L. Hazen
Petzinger, T. Oil & honor. 1987
   Bus Week p25+ Je 1 '87. J. R. Norman
   N Y Times Book Rev 92:11-12 Je 21 '87. E. Bailey
Peukert, D. J. K. Inside Nazi Germany. 1987
   N Y Times Book Rev 92:27 Ag 9 '87. M. Nolan
Peyser, J. Bernstein. 1987
   Commentary 84:66+ Ag '87. W. H. Youngren
   N Y 20:93-4 Je 1 '87. P. G. Davis
   N Y Times Book Rev 92:3+ My 10 '87. L. Botstein
   New Repub 196:27-9 Je 22 '87. E. Rothstein
Pfanz, H. W. Gettysburg—the second day. 1987
   Atlantic 260:108-9 D '87. T. Wicker
Pfeffer, S. B. The year without Michael. 1987
   N Y Times Book Rev 92:38 N 8 '87. E. Lenz
Philadelphia Museum of Art. British painting in the Philadelphia Museum of Art. 1986
   Antiques 131:1190+ Je '87. M. Cormack
Philipson, M. H. Somebody else's life. 1987
   N Y Times Book Rev 92:31 F 15 '87. B. DeMott
Phillips, C. The European tribe. 1987
   N Y Times Book Rev 92:7 Ag 9 '87. A. Lee
Phillips, C. R. Six galleons for the king of Spain. 1986
   Oceans 20:60 My/Je '87. B. C. Busch
Phillips, D. L. Toward a just social order. 1986
   Cent Mag 20:38-9 My/Je '87. D. McDonald
Phillips, J. A. Fast lanes. 1987
   N Y Times Book Rev 92:7 My 3 '87. J. McInerney
   Time 129:70 Je 1 '87. P. Iyer
Phillips, J. G. and others. Physiological strategies in avian biology. 1985
   BioScience 37:686 O '87. C. F. Leck
Phosphate deposits of the world; v1, Proterozoic and Cambrian phosphorites. 1986
   Science 236:1125-6 My 29 '87. P. Cloud
Photosynthesis during leaf development. 1985
   BioScience 37:743-4 N '87. K. E. Pallett
Photosynthesis in relation to plant production in terrestrial environments. 1985
   BioScience 37:744 N '87. S. A. Sovonick-Dunford
Physics in medicine & biology encyclopedia. 2v 1986
   Phys Today 40:88-9 S '87. J. R. Cameron
Physics of the sun. 3v 1986
   Phys Today 40:79-80 Ap '87. J. V. Hollweg
Physiological ecology of North American plant communities. 1984
   BioScience 37:226-7 Mr '87. B. C. Bennett
The Physiological properties of plant protoplasts. 1985
   BioScience 37:743 N '87. R. F. Davis
Pianka, E. R. Ecology and natural history of desert lizards. 1986
   Science 235:492-3 Ja 23 '87. J. Travis
Picasso, P. Picasso, peintre-graveur; v3, Catalogue raisonné de l'oeuvre grave et des monotypes, 1935-45. 1987

Art News 86:34 O '87. S. G. Calassi
Pickens, T. B., Jr. Boone. 1987
 Bus Week p16 Mr 2 '87. J. R. Norman
 N Y Times Book Rev 92:18 Mr 22 '87. E. Prescott
A Piece of my heart. 1986
 Nation 245:27-8 Jl 4-11 '87. C. L. Mithers
Pierce, C. When things get back to normal and other stories. 1987
 N Y Times Book Rev 92:33 My 3 '87. J. Humphreys
Piercy, M. Gone to soldiers. 1987
 N Y Times Book Rev 92:11 My 10 '87. H. Wolitzer
 Nation 245:24-7 Jl 4-11 '87. A. F. Loewenstein
 New Leader 70:19-20 Jl 13-27 '87. H. H. Davis
Piety and politics. 1987
 Natl Rev 39:58 D 4 '87. C. Williamson
Pileggi, N. Wiseguy. 1985
 New Repub 197:33-4+ O 12 '87. J. Weisberg
Pin Yathay. Stay alive, my son. 1987
 Natl Rev 39:54+ O 23 '87. J. Sobran
Pinch, T. J. Confronting nature. 1986
 Science 235:225-6 Ja 9 '87. Y. Gingras
Pinget, R. The apocrypha. 1986
 New Yorker 63:110+ My 18 '87. J. Updike
Pinson, L. J. Electro-optics. 1985
 Phys Today 40:70-1 Jl '87. P. K. Cheo
Piper, J. Desiring God. 1986
 Christ Today 31:67-8 O 2 '87. J. Hoover
Pires, J. C. Ballad of Dogs' Beach. 1986
 N Y Times Book Rev 92:13 My 3 '87. A. Hyde
Planas, R. Liberation theology. 1986
 America 156:409-10 My 16 '87. A. T. Hennelly
 Christ Century 104:726 Ag 26-S 2 '87. H. Clark
The Planets. 1985
 Astronomy 15:64 F '87. R. Burnham
Plant, R. The pink triangle. 1986
 Nation 244:123 Ja 31 '87. G. De Stefano
Plant ecology. 1986
 Science 238:556-7 O 23 '87. R. B. Primack
Plant virus epidemics. 1986
 Science 236:340-1 Ap 17 '87. A. H. Purcell
Plasmids in bacteria. 1985
 BioScience 37:288-9 Ap '87. R. Condit
Plé, A. Duty or pleasure? 1987
 America 157:113-14 Ag 29-S 5 '87. E. C. Vacek
Pleck, E. H. Domestic tyranny. 1987
 Psychol Today 21:71-2 S '87. J. Meer
Plimpton, G. The curious case of Sidd Finch. 1987
 N Y Times Book Rev 92:2 Jl 5 '87. A. B. Giamatti
Pogue, F. C. George C. Marshall. 1987
 Atlantic 259:78-80 Je '87. J. L. Gaddis
 N Y Rev Books 34:11-13 Ag 13 '87. G. A. Craig
 N Y Times Book Rev 92:3 Je 28 '87. P. M. Kennedy
 Wash Mon 19:54-5 Jl/Ag '87. E. Thomas
Poincelot, R. P. Toward a more sustainable agriculture. 1986
 Environment 29:29 Mr '87. J. H. Perkins
Poirier, R. The renewal of literature. 1987
 N Y Rev Books 34:50-2 Je 25 '87. D. Donoghue
 N Y Times Book Rev 92:37 Mr 22 '87. N. Baym
 Nation 244:766-70 Je 6 '87. D. Crase
 New Repub 196:28-32 Ap 27 '87. A. Delbanco
Poizner, H. and others. What the hands reveal about the brain. 1987
 Science 238:833 N 6 '87. P. Menyuk
Polin. v1 1986
 Hist Today 37:58 Ag '87. W. J. Fishman
Political culture in modern Britain. 1987
 Hist Today 37:53-4 Je '87. R. Waller
Pollard, J. F. The Vatican and Italian fascism, 1929-32. 1985
 America 156:13-15 Ja 3-10 '87. R. E. Sullivan
Pollen and spores. 1986
 Science 238:557-8 O 23 '87. J. A. Doyle
Pollutants in a multimedia environment. 1986
 Environment 29:28-9 S '87. J. W. Farrington
Polster, E. Every person's life is worth a novel. 1987
 N Y Times Book Rev 92:32 N 1 '87. S. Schneiderman
Poole, L. Lon Poole's Mac insights. 1986
 Byte 12:72+ My '87. B. L. Walker
Poole, M. Industrial relations. 1986
 Mon Labor Rev 110:47 Jl '87. H. M. Douty
Population biology and evolution of clonal organisms. 1986
 Science 235:1264 Mr 6 '87. R. R. Vance
Population genetics & fishery management. 1986
 Science 237:1236 S 4 '87. D. Hedgecock
Population growth in Latin America and U.S. national security. 1986
 Bull At Sci 43:52-3 My '87. N. Myers
 Natl Rev 39:54 Jl 31 '87. C. Williamson
Porazińska, J. The enchanted book. 1987
 N Y Times Book Rev 92:32 S 20 '87. J. Yolen

Pornography. 1986
 U S Cathol 52:48-51 Ap '87. G. M. Costello
Porsche. 1985
 Mot Trend 39:26 Ja '87. T. C. Browne
Porter, E. Eliot Porter. 1987
 Nat Hist 96:24-9 D '87. M. Harwood
Porter, E. and Auerbach, E. Mexican churches. 1987
 N Y Times Book Rev 92:3+ D 20 '87. O. Paz
Porter, T. M. The rise of statistical thinking, 1820-1900. 1986
 Science 235:1262-3 Mr 6 '87. M. Stone
Posner, G. and Ware, J. Mengele: the complete story. 1986
 N Y Rev Books 34:29-34 My 28 '87. N. Ascherson
Potter, N. A. J. Legacies. 1987
 N Y Times Book Rev 92:22 Jl 19 '87. R. Atwan
Potts, M. and Behr, P. The leading edge. 1987
 Bus Week p17 Mr 23 '87
Powe, B. W. The solitary outlaw.
 Macleans 100:47 Je 15 '87. P. Roberts
Powe, L. A., Jr. American broadcasting and the First Amendment. 1987
 N Y Times Book Rev 92:19 Ap 19 '87. H. Dorfman
Powell, C. Turner in the South. 1987
 New Repub 197:47-9 O 12 '87. E. V. Thaw
Powell, J. M. Anatomy of a crusade, 1213-1221. 1986
 Hist Today 37:54-5 D '87. N. Housley
Powell, M. A life in movies. 1987
 N Y Rev Books 34:14-16 Ag 13 '87. G. O'Brien
 New Repub 196:24-6 My 11 '87. S. Kauffmann
Powell, P. A woman named Drown. 1987
 N Y Times Book Rev 92:9 Je 7 '87. T. C. Boyle
 Time 129:79 My 18 '87. P. Gray
Powers, R. G. Secrecy and power. 1986
 N Y Rev Books 34:15-18 Ap 23 '87. A. Brinkley
 N Y Times Book Rev 92:1+ Mr 8 '87. N. Morris
 Nation 244:365-8 Mr 21 '87
 New Leader 70:13-14 My 4-18 '87. D. M. Oshinsky
 Newsweek 109:74 F 16 '87. J. Miller
 Progressive 51:29-30 Ag '87. R. J. Goldstein
 Wash Mon 19:46-8 Ap '87. T. Branch
Prager, E. Clea & Zeus divorce. 1987
 N Y Times Book Rev 92:9 N 22 '87. R. Plunket
 Newsweek 110:89 O 19 '87. C. Leerhsen
Prat Garcia, J. Medio milenio del Nuevo Mundo. 1985
 Américas 39:62-3 Mr/Ap '87. P. Sáenz
Pratt, C. W. In the orchard. 1986
 Commonweal 114:122-3 F 27 '87. J. Fandel
Pratt-Johnson, B. 141 dives in the protected waters of Washington and British Columbia. 1985
 Oceans 20:63-4 N/D '87. D. G. Gordon
Predation. 1987
 Science 238:93-4 O 2 '87. J. D. Allan
Prehistoric hunter-gatherers in Japan. 1986
 Science 235:916-17 F 20 '87. D. K. Charles
Prescott-Allen, C. and Prescott-Allen, R. The first resource. 1986
 Nat Hist 96:64-5 Je '87. B. G. Norton
Prest, W. R. The rise of the barristers. 1986
 Hist Today 37:58 N '87. A. Fletcher
Primate evolution and human origins. 1985
 BioScience 37:517-18 Jl/Ag '87. J. Moore
Pringle, L. P. Throwing things away. 1986
 Conservationist 41:52 My/Je '87. N. M. Payne
 Earth Sci 40:34-5 Spr '87
Pritchard, M. Spirit seizures. 1987
 Ms 16:93-4 D '87. D. Leimbach
 N Y Times Book Rev 92:11 N 22 '87. E. Tallent
Proteins of excitable membranes. 1987
 Science 237:443-4 Jl 24 '87. C. Miller
Proust, M. On reading Ruskin. 1987
 N Y Rev Books 34:24-7 O 22 '87. T. Hilton
 New Repub 197:42+ N 2 '87. F. Brown
Proven profits from pollution prevention: case studies in resource conservation and waste reduction. 1986
 Environment 29:30 Je '87. D. E. Burmaster
Provensen, A. and Provensen, M. Shaker lane. 1987
 N Y Times Book Rev 92:33 N 8 '87. P. Goldberger
Provine, W. B. Sewall Wright and evolutionary biology. 1986
 BioScience 37:812-14 D '87. D. L. Hartl
Pruett, K. D. The nurturing father. 1986
 N Y Times Book Rev 92:24 Mr 8 '87. A. L. Goldman
 U S Cathol 52:50-1 S '87. G. M. Costello
Pryce-Jones, D. The afternoon sun. 1986
 N Y Rev Books 34:28-9 Je 11 '87. G. Annan
 New Repub 197:39-41 Jl 6 '87. M. Syrkin
Pryor, B. The house on Maple Street. 1987
 N Y Times Book Rev 92:21 Ap 19 '87. J. Prindle
Pryor, E. B. Clara Barton. 1987
 N Y Times Book Rev 92:46 O 11 '87. S. Reverby

Psychological testing and American society, 1890-1930. 1987
Science 237:1358-9 S 11 '87. H. Kuklick
The Public face of architecture. 1987
New Leader 70:17-18 O 19 '87. B. Gewen
Puig, M. Pubis angelical. 1986
Nation 244:510-12 Ap 18 '87. J. Franco
Purcell, R. W. and Gould, S. J. Illuminations. 1986
Humanist 47:37-8 Ja/F '87. L. R. Godfrey
Sci Am 256:34+ F '87. P. Morrison
Purdy, C. Least of all. 1987
N Y Times Book Rev 92:32 S 20 '87. J. Yolen
Purdy, J. The candles of your eyes, and thirteen other
stories. 1987
N Y Times Book Rev 92:23 S 6 '87. E. Munk
Purdy, K. The kings of the road. 1949
Road Track 38:34+ Jl '87. R. Busenkell
The Pushcart Prize XII.
N Y Times Book Rev 92:29 O 11 '87. G. Johnson
Puttfarken, T. Roger de Piles' theory of art. 1986
Art Am 75:29 F '87. J. Masheck
Pyenson, L. The young Einstein. 1985
Phys Today 40:74 Jl '87. J. Bernstein
Pyle, R. M. Wintergreen. 1986
Sierra 72:83-4+ My/Je '87. C. Camuto
Pyne, S. J. The ice. 1986
N Y Times Book Rev 92:11-12 Ja 11 '87. R. Kirk
Sci Am 256:23-4 My '87. P. Morrison

Q

Quaife, G. R. Godly zeal and furious rage. 1987
Hist Today 37:54 S '87. H. Kamen
Quammen, D. Natural acts. 1985
Commonweal 114:364 Je 5 '87. T. O'Brien
Quammen, D. The soul of Viktor Tronko. 1987
N Y Times Book Rev 92:12 Jl 12 '87. W. Hood
Quandt, W. B. Camp David. 1986
America 156:329 Ap 18 '87. W. T. Perkins
Quantitative aspects of the ecology of biological invasions.
1987
Science 236:1000-2 My 22 '87. T. J. Case
Quaternary glaciations in the Northern Hemisphere. 1986
Science 236:1581-2 Je 19 '87. H. E. Wright
Queller, D. E. The Venetian patriciate. 1986
N Y Rev Books 34:37-9 Jl 16 '87. F. Gilbert
Quinn, S. A mind of her own. 1987
N Y Rev Books 34:14-17 N 5 '87. P. Grosskurth
N Y Times Book Rev 92:10-11 N 29 '87. R. Dinnage
Psychol Today 21:70-2 N '87. L. Simon
Vogue 177:262 N '87. L. J. Kaplan

R

Raban, J. Coasting. 1987
N Y Rev Books 34:39-41 O 22 '87. M. Wood
N Y Times Book Rev 92:14 F 1 '87. J. Krich
New Repub 197:36-8 Jl 27 '87. V. Klinkenborg
Rabinowitz, A. Jaguar. 1986
Audubon 89:132-4 N '87
"Race," writing, and difference. 1986
Cent Mag 20:40-1 S/O '87. D. McDonald
Radvanyi, M. K. The politics of reform in the Soviet
Union.
Natl Rev 39:50 Ag 14 '87. C. Williamson
Rakosi, C. The collected poems of Carl Rakosi.
N Y Times Book Rev 92:22 Mr 8 '87. M. Heller
Ramana Murthy, P. V. and Wolfendale, A. W. Gamma-ray
astronomy. 1986
Science 237:442 Jl 24 '87. F. W. Stecker
Ramazani, R. K. Revolutionary Iran. 1986
N Y Rev Books 33:10-13 Ja 15 '87. S. Bakhash
Ramdin, R. The making of the black working class in
Britain. 1987
Hist Today 37:55-6 Jl '87. Z. Layton-Henry
Ramet, P. Nationalism and federalism in Yugoslavia,
1963-1983. 1984
Society 24:95-6 Ja/F '87. S. Zukin
Ramos-Horta, J. Funu. 1987
N Y Times Book Rev 92:26 Ja 11 '87. H. Kamm
Progressive 51:42 Mr '87. B. D. Nossiter
Rampersad, A. The life of Langston Hughes. 1986
New Leader 70:16 Ja 12-26 '87. P. Pettingell
Ramsey, B. and others. The quilts of Tennessee. 1986
Americana 15:78 Mr/Ap '87. M. Durham
Ramsey, D. K. The corporate warriors. 1987
N Y Times Book Rev 92:30 Ap 12 '87. A. Feinberg
Ramtha. Ramtha. 1986
N Y Rev Books 34:16-19 Ap 9 '87. M. Gardner
Randall, J. E. Microcomputers and physiological simulation.
2nd ed. 1986
Byte 12:52+ N '87. K. S. Wittman

Rangel, C. Third World ideology and Western reality.
1986
Natl Rev 39:64 O 23 '87. W. Lutton
Rape. 1986
N Y Times Book Rev 92:11 Ja 4 '87. E. Showalter
Rappaport, D. Trouble at the mines. 1986
N Y Times Book Rev 92:33 My 17 '87. L. Smith
Rapping, E. The looking glass world of nonfiction TV.
1987
Progressive 51:42-3 My '87. E. S. Herman
Raskin, B. Hot flashes. 1987
N Y Times Book Rev 92:13 S 27 '87. J. Rascoe
Raskin, M. G. The common good. 1986
Christ Century 104:1067-8 N 25 '87. C. E. Brewster
Rasputin, V. G. You live and love and other stories.
1986
N Y Times Book Rev 92:22 My 10 '87. J. H. Billington
Ratushinskaya, I. Beyond the limit. 1987
N Y Times Book Rev 92:12 Je 28 '87. M. Carlson
Ratzinger, J., Cardinal. Principles of Catholic theology.
America 157:483-5 D 19 '87. J. B. Benestad
Christ Century 104:970 N 4 '87. K. B. Osborne
Raup, D. M. The nemesis affair. 1986
Sky Telesc 73:39-40 Ja '87. P. R. Weissman
Society 24:89-90 S/O '87. P. Shaw
Raven, P. H. and Johnson, G. B. Biology. 1986
BioScience 37:428 Je '87. J. M. Maiello
Ray, S. The unicorn expedition, and other fantastic tales
of India. 1987
N Y Rev Books 34:12+ N 19 '87. I. Buruma
N Y Times Book Rev 92:25 S 20 '87. G. Wilson
Raymo, C. The soul of the night. 1985
Harpers 274:75-6 Ja '87. L. A. Marschall
Rayner, M. Mrs. Pig gets cross and other stories. 1987
N Y Times Book Rev 92:34 My 17 '87. M. Rosenberg
Rayner, R. The winning moment. 1986
Oceans 20:61 S/O '87. J. B. Hightower
Raz, J. The morality of freedom. 1986
New Repub 197:30-2 D 7 '87. M. Walzer
Read, P. P. The free Frenchman. 1986
N Y Times Book Rev 92:15 Ap 12 '87. T. J. Fleming
Reading the news. 1987
Progressive 51:42+ Mr '87. B. Bagdikian
Reams, B. D. University-industry research partnerships.
1986
BioScience 37:287-8 Ap '87. L. Gilbert
Redondi, P. Galileo heretic (Galileo eretico). 1987
America 157:507-9 D 26 '87. M. R. O'Connell
N Y Rev Books 34:13-14 O 8 '87. I. Calvino
N Y Times Book Rev 92:13-14 N 15 '87. P. Corsi
Science 237:1059-60 Ag 28 '87. R. S. Westfall
Reduced instruction set computers. 1986
Byte 12:65-6+ Ap '87. P. R. Robinson
Reed, I. Reckless eyeballing. 1986
N Y Rev Books 34:17-20 Ja 29 '87. D. Pinckney
Reed, K. Catholic girls. 1987
America 157:509 D 26 '87. J. C. Hawley
Reedy, G. E. The U.S. Senate. 1986
Wash Mon 19:59-60 Ap '87. T. Noah
Reef diagenesis. 1986
Science 236:1684 Je 26 '87. J. L. Wilson
Reese, W. J. Power and the promise of school reform.
1986
Phi Delta Kappan 69:314-15 D '87. J. Wrigley
Regan, T. Bloomsbury's prophet. 1986
N Y Rev Books 34:37-9 Mr 26 '87. S. Hampshire
Regis, E. Who got Einstein's office? 1987
N Y Times Book Rev 92:39-40 S 27 '87. J. Weiner
Register, C. Living with chronic illness. 1987
N Y Times Book Rev 92:12 O 4 '87. N. Mairs
Psychol Today 21:72 S '87. J. Fischman
Rehnquist, W. H. The Supreme Court. 1987
N Y Times Book Rev 92:3+ S 20 '87. P. B. Kurland
Natl Rev 39:56-7 S 25 '87. J. Sobran
New Repub 197:44-6+ S 14-21 '87. R. Adler
Reich, L. S. The making of American industrial research.
1985
Phys Today 40:124-5 O '87. S. Goldberg
Reich, R. B. Tales of a new America. 1987
Bus Week p16-18 Ap 13 '87. N. Jonas
Cent Mag 20:37-8 My/Je '87. D. McDonald
Commonweal 114:326+ My 22 '87. J. Clark
N Y Times Book Rev 92:7+ Mr 22 '87. N. Lemann
Natl Rev 39:49-51 Ap 24 '87. D. Brooks
New Leader 70:11-13 My 4-18 '87. R. Lekachman
Wash Mon 19:51-6 Mr '87. T. J. Peters
Reid, J. and Donaldson, M. Teacher's book 3. 1985
Hist Today 37:58-9 F '87. F. M. L. Thompson
Reid, R. G. B. Evolutionary theory. 1985
BioScience 37:683-4 O '87. D. Simberloff
Reidinger, P. The best man. 1986

Natl Rev 39:48-9 Je 5 '87. J. Mysak
Rossiter, S. Beyond this bitter air. 1987
N Y Times Book Rev 92:15 Ag 9 '87. E. Spencer
Roth, J. Hotel Savoy. 1986
N Y Times Book Rev 92:30 F 8 '87. H. Gold
Roth, J. Tarabas, a guest on earth. 1987
New Yorker 63:154-60 N 23 '87. S. Lardner
Roth, P. The counterlife. 1986
Atlantic 259:89-91 F '87. M. Amis
Commentary 84:54-5 Jl '87. R. Alter
Macleans 100:53 Ja 26 '87. N. Levine
N Y 20:67 Ja 26 '87. R. Koenig
N Y Rev Books 34:40-2 Mr 26 '87. J. Rubins
N Y Times Book Rev 92:1+ Ja 4 '87. W. H. Gass
New Leader 70:5-6 My 4-18 '87. M. Apple
New Repub 196:36-8 F 2 '87. R. Alter
New Yorker 63:107-9 Mr 2 '87. J. Updike
Newsweek 109:69 Ja 12 '87. P. S. Prescott
Vogue 177:94 Ja '87. E. White
Rothschild, S. Rothschild on antiques & collectibles. 1986
Antiques Collect Hobbies 92:70 Jl '87
Rouse, I. Migrations in prehistory. 1986
Sci Am 256:28-9 Ap '87. P. Morrison
Rowan, D. and MacDonald, J. D. A friendship. 1986
Time 129:71 F 16 '87. C. Porterfield
Roxburgh, A. Pravda. 1987
N Y Times Book Rev 92:18 O 18 '87. A. Austin
Wash Mon 19:59 N '87. J. Frankel
Rubens, B. Our Father. 1987
N Y Times Book Rev 92:11 D 27 '87. M. Paley
Rubenstein, R. E. Alchemists of revolution. 1987
N Y Times Book Rev 92:22 Je 28 '87. D. Fromkin
Wash Mon 19:55-6 Ap '87. D. Ignatius
Rubin, B. M. Modern dictators. 1987
N Y Times Book Rev 92:17 Ap 5 '87. B. D. Nossiter
Natl Rev 39:52-3 S 25 '87. S. T. Francis
Rubin, D. After the Raj. 1986
N Y Times Book Rev 92:14 Mr 15 '87. L. Graver
Rubin, L. B. Quiet rage. 1986
N Y Rev Books 34:22-4+ Ap 23 '87. G. P. Fletcher
Psychol Today 21:80 Ja '87. W. Herbert
Rubinstein, D. Before the suffragettes. 1986
Hist Today 37:54 Ag '87. L. Davidoff
Rubinstein, R. L. Singular paths. 1986
Society 24:87-8 S/O '87. H. Z. Lopata
Rucker, R. von B. Mind tools. 1987
N Y Rev Books 34:34-6 D 3 '87. M. Gardner
Rüegg, J. C. Calcium in muscle activation. 1986
Science 238:223 O 9 '87. A. G. Szent-Györgyi
Rule, A. Small sacrifices. 1987
N Y Times Book Rev 92:32 Je 14 '87. A. Jones
Rumelhart, D. E. and McClelland, J. L. Parallel distributed processing. 2v 1986
N Y Times Book Rev 92:28 Ja 4 '87. J. G. Greeno
Science 236:992-6 My 22 '87. K. J. Holyoak
Runte, A. National parks. 1987
Wilderness 50:57 Summ '87. D. Drabelle
Rupp, L. J. and Taylor, V. Survival in the doldrums. *America* 157:412-13 N 28 '87. S. R. Hiatt
Rushdie, S. The jaguar smile. 1987
Commentary 83:74-6 Ap '87. G. Russell
N Y Times Book Rev 92:14 Mr 8 '87. J. LeMoyne
New Leader 70:16 Mr 23 '87. A. Husarska
New Repub 196:30-4 Ap 20 '87. X. Arguello
Time 129:78 Ap 6 '87. P. Iyer
Wash Mon 19:48-51 Je '87. C. Lane
Rusher, W. A. A short course on South Africa.
Natl Rev 39:62 N 20 '87. C. Williamson
Ruspoli, M. The cave of Lascaux. 1987
Nat Hist 96:84+ O '87. J. E. Pfeiffer
Sci Am 257:148-9 N '87. P. Morrison
Russell, C. 100 predictions for the baby boom. 1987
Vogue 177:192 My '87. L. A. Schreiber
Russell, D. W. B. R., Countess. The Dora Russell reader. 1983
Humanist 47:45 My/Je '87. B. Earles
Russell, F. The knave of Boston. 1987
Natl Rev 39:53-4 N 6 '87. M. Mirsky
Russell, J. B. Mephistopheles. 1986
Atlantic 259:84+ Ja '87. A. Burgess
Commonweal 114:56-8 Ja 30 '87. F. Oakley
N Y Times Book Rev 92:28 Mr 8 '87. R. Coles
Natl Rev 39:52-3 Jl 17 '87. M. D. Aeschliman
Russell, L. B. Is prevention better than cure? 1986
Mon Labor Rev 110:45 My '87. E. Steinberg
Russian jazz. 1985
Down Beat 54:55-6 Ag '87. B. Shoemaker
Rustow, D. A. Turkey, America's forgotten ally. 1987
N Y Times Book Rev 92:26 O 18 '87. A. Cowell
Ruta, S. Stalin in the Bronx, and other stories. 1987
N Y Times Book Rev 92:10 N 29 '87. E. Pall

Rutan, D. and Yeager, J. Voyager. 1987
N Y Times Book Rev 92:10 D 27 '87. M. Collins
Rutherfurd, E. Sarum. 1987
N Y Times Book Rev 92:14 S 13 '87. M. Quilligan
Ruthven, M. Traveller through time. 1986
Smithsonian 17:129-30 Ja '87. D. Drabelle
Rutland, R. A. James Madison. 1987
N Y Times Book Rev 92:20 O 4 '87. A. Todd
Rutler, G. W. The four last things. 1986
Natl Rev 39:60-1 Ja 30 '87. M. Liccione
Ruttenbaum, S. Mansions in the clouds. 1986
Archit Rec 175:77 Ag '87. S. Gutterman
Ryan, M. J. The túngara frog. 1985
BioScience 37:230 Mr '87. C. A. Loffredo
Ryder, L. H. Quantum field theory. 1985
Phys Today 40:86+ D '87. P. H. Frampton
Ryken, L. Windows to the world. 1985
Christ Today 31:63-4 Ja 16 '87. B. Matthews
Rylant, C. Henry and Mudge. 1987
N Y Times Book Rev 92:49 O 4 '87. J. V. Leeuwen
Rylant, C. Henry and Mudge in puddle trouble. 1987
N Y Times Book Rev 92:49 O 4 '87. J. V. Leeuwen

S

Sachar, H. M. A history of Israel; v2, From the aftermath of the Yom Kippur War. 1976
N Y Times Book Rev 92:13 Jl 26 '87. W. Reich
Sack, H. and Wilk, M. American treasure hunt. 1986
Antiques 131:987 My '87. J. A. H. Sweeney
Sādāt, J. A woman of Egypt. 1987
N Y Times Book Rev 92:15 Ag 30 '87. B. Slavin
Safire, W. Freedom. 1987
N Y Rev Books 34:23-6 S 24 '87. C. V. Woodward
N Y Times Book Rev 92:6-7 Ag 23 '87. W. S. McFeely
Natl Rev 39:49-50 D 18 '87. J. Mysak
Newsweek 110:57 Ag 31 '87. D. Lehman
Time 130:61 Ag 31 '87. P. Gray
Sagan, L. A. The health of nations. 1987
N Y Times Book Rev 92:9 N 29 '87. L. Margulis
Sage, B. The arctic & its wildlife. 1986
Sea Front 33:472 N/D '87. O. T. Owre
Sahlins, M. Islands of history. 1985
Society 24:93-4 Ja/F '87. S. W. Foster
Said, E. W. and Mohr, J. After the last sky. 1986
Nation 244:21-2 Ja 10 '87. L. Hazleton
Saint, H. F. Memoirs of an invisible man. 1987
N Y Times Book Rev 92:15 My 10 '87. D. Finkle
Time 129:80+ Ap 27 '87. C. Porterfield
Saint-Phalle, N. de. AIDS.
Psychol Today 21:76 D '87. H. Hall
Salzman, M. Iron and silk. 1986
N Y Times Book Rev 92:9 F 1 '87. R. Selzer
Smithsonian 18:142-3 Jl '87. W. Dieter
Time 129:76 Mr 2 '87. D. Morrison
Sampson, A. Black and gold. 1987
Bus Week p23+ My 11 '87. S. Mufson
Macleans 100:47 Ag 17 '87. N. Hirst
N Y Times Book Rev 92:11 My 24 '87. A. Cowell
Sams, F. The widow's mite.
N Y Times Book Rev 92:7 D 13 '87. S. Hearon
Samuels, E. and Samuels, J. Bernard Berenson, the making of a legend. 1987
N Y Rev Books 34:3+ O 8 '87. R. Dinnage
N Y Times Book Rev 92:1+ Mr 29 '87. J. Updike
New Repub 197:35-40 Jl 13-20 '87. D. Rosand
Time 129:77-8 Ap 6 '87. R. Z. Sheppard
Sanday, P. R. Divine hunger. 1986
N Y Times Book Rev 92:39 My 3 '87. D. B. Gewertz
Sanders, J. A. From sacred story to sacred text. 1987
Christ Century 104:1122 D 9 '87. A. B. Cook
Sanger, C. Ordering the oceans. 1987
Oceans 20:62-3 N/D '87. D. K. Conner
Santayana, G. Persons and places; v1. 1986
N Y Times Book Rev 92:27-8 Ap 26 '87. B. Kuklick
New Repub 196:28-33 My 18 '87. D. Aaron
Saramago, J. Baltasar and Blimunda. 1987
N Y Times Book Rev 92:7+ N 1 '87. I. Howe
Sartre, J. P. The family idiot; v2. 1987
New Repub 196:54-6 Je 8 '87. M. Wood
New Yorker 63:94-6 Je 22 '87. N. Bliven
Sartre, J. P. The Freud scenario. 1986
Psychol Today 21:67-8 Je '87. J. Meer
Saslow, J. M. Ganymede in the Renaissance. 1986
Art Am 75:23+ O '87. J. Weinberg
Satellites. 1986
Science 237:1517 S 18 '87. J. S. Lewis
Satta, S. The day of judgement. 1987
N Y Times Book Rev 92:13-14 O 4 '87. J. Barnes
New Yorker 63:115-19 O 19 '87. G. Steiner
Saul, N. Scenes from provincial life. 1986

Seiberling, G. Amateurs, photography, and the mid-Victorian imagination. 1986
  Art Am 75:21+ Jl '87. C. Bedient
Seidler, T. A rat's tale. 1986
  N Y Times Book Rev 92:23 Ja 25 '87. K. C. Davis
Seidler, T. The tar pit. 1987
  N Y Times Book Rev 92:38 O 18 '87. F. Prose
Seinfeld, J. H. Atmospheric chemistry and physics of air pollution. 1986
  Science 235:1263-4 Mr 6 '87. G. E. Gordon
Sekler, E. F. Josef Hoffmann. 1985
  Archit Rec 175:77 S '87. B. Bergdoll
Seldes, G. Witness to a century. 1987
  N Y Times Book Rev 92:18 Ag 16 '87. S. I. Toll
  Nation 245:97-8 Ag 1-8 '87. P. Schrag
Semenov, IÙ. S. TASS is authorized to announce—. 1987
  Macleans 100:63 O 12 '87. A. Wilson-Smith
Sen, A. K. Choice, welfare and measurement. 1982
  N Y Rev Books 34:41-4 O 22 '87. A. B. Atkinson
Sen, A. K. Resources, values, and development. 1984
  N Y Rev Books 34:41-4 O 22 '87. A. B. Atkinson
Senghaas, D. Die Zukunft Europas. 1986
  Bull At Sci 43:50-2 My '87. T. Risse-Kappen
Senior, J. M. Optical fiber communications. 1984
  Phys Today 40:128 O '87. L. Kazovsky
Sennett, R. Palais-Royal. 1986
  N Y Rev Books 34:23-5 Ap 9 '87. D. J. Enright
  N Y Times Book Rev 92:14 F 8 '87. R. Holmes
Serpell, J. In the company of animals. 1986
  BioScience 37:811-12 D '87. M. Robinson
  N Y Rev Books 34:20-5 Je 25 '87. S. J. Gould
Setright, L. J. K. and others. With flying colours. 1987
  Mot Trend 39:34 O '87. T. C. Browne
Sexton, R. American style. 1987
  Americana 15:18+ N/D '87. J. Neary
Seymour, G. A song in the morning. 1987
  New Leader 70:19 Ap 6 '87. R. Lekachman
Shabtai, Y. Past perfect. 1987
  N Y Times Book Rev 92:11 Ag 9 '87. R. Alter
Shadbolt, M. Season of the Jew. 1987
  N Y Times Book Rev 92:9 Ag 2 '87. C. C. O'Brien
Shaefer, A. T. and Brittain, J. L. The AutoCAD productivity book. 1986
  Byte 12:81-2 Je '87. S. H. Rogers
Shafer, I. H. Eros and the womanliness of God. 1986
  Christ Century 104:1095-6 D 2 '87. M. G. Cartwright
Shakespeare, W. Shakespeare's lost play, Edmund Ironside. 1985
  N Y Rev Books 34:23-6 F 12 '87. E. A. J. Honigmann
Shane, H. G. Teaching and learning in a microelectronic age. 1987
  Phi Delta Kappan 68:633-4 Ap '87. R. G. Stakenas
Shanin, T. The roots of otherness: Russia's turn of century; v2, Russia, 1905-07: revolution as a moment of truth. 1986
  Hist Today 37:54-5 Je '87. C. Read
Shannon, T. A. What are they saying about genetic engineering? 1985
  Christ Today 31:50-1 F 6 '87. D. B. Fletcher
Shapiro, A. Happy hour. 1987
  N Y Times Book Rev 92:9 Jl 26 '87. J. D. McClatchy
Shapiro, G. A skeleton in the darkroom. 1986
  Sci Am 257:149 D '87. P. Morrison and P. Morrison
Shaplen, R. Bitter victory. 1986
  New Leader 69:26-7 D 1-15 '86. D. Kirk
  Progressive 51:42-4 Ap '87. W. Steif
Sharp, G. Making Europe unconquerable. 1986
  Bull At Sci 43:54-6 Ja/F '87. T. B. Taylor
Shaw, A. The Jazz Age. 1987
  N Y Times Book Rev 92:57 O 25 '87. P. Keepnews
Shaw, R. W. Abbott and Avery. 1987
  N Y Times Book Rev 92:19 O 4 '87. D. R. Slavitt
Sheard, S. Almost Japanese. 1987
  N Y Times Book Rev 92:23 Ag 16 '87. K. Jones
Shearer, M. Balletmaster. 1987
  Dance Mag 61:71-2 O '87. J. R. Acocella
  New Yorker 63:99 Ap 13 '87. A. Croce
Shechner, M. After the revolution. 1987
  Christ Century 104:920-1 O 21 '87. M. Krupnick
  N Y Times Book Rev 92:14-15 My 10 '87. E. Rothstein
Sheed, W. The boys of winter. 1987
  N Y 20:65 Ag 17 '87. R. Koenig
  N Y Times Book Rev 92:3+ Ag 2 '87. H. Gold
  Time 130:64 Ag 3 '87. P. Gray
Sheehan, S. A missing plane. 1986
  Cent Mag 20:30 Ja/F '87. D. McDonald
Sheehan, T. The first coming. 1986
  Christ Century 104:28-30 Ja 7-14 '87. P. L. Maier
  Commonweal 114:60-3 Ja 30 '87. W. M. Thompson
Shelley, M. W. The journals of Mary Shelley. 2v
  N Y Rev Books 34:35-8 N 19 '87. C. Tomalin

Shepherds speak. 1986
  Christ Today 31:49-50 F 6 '87. D. Bandow
Sheridan, C. Count Basie. 1986
  Down Beat 54:61 My '87. J. McDonough
Sherlock, R. Preserving life. 1987
  America 157:362-4 N 14 '87. M. B. Mahowald
Sherry, M. S. The rise of American air power. 1987
  Bull At Sci 43:51-2 O '87. R. Jervis
  Sci Am 257:116-17 S '87. P. Morrison
Shiga, N. The paper door.
  N Y Times Book Rev 92:16 Ap 5 '87. H. Sato
Shilts, R. And the band played on. 1987
  Bus Week p18+ N 9 '87. J. O. Hamilton
  N Y Times Book Rev 92:9 N 8 '87. H. J. Geiger
  Nation 245:526-8 N 7 '87. D. S. Greenberg
  Natl Rev 39:50-2 D 4 '87. H. Klingeman
  Newsweek 110:91+ O 19 '87. J. Miller
Shimazaki, T. Before the dawn. 1987
  N Y Times Book Rev 92:44-5 O 18 '87. E. McClellan
  New Yorker 63:72-6 Ag 3 '87. B. Leithauser
Shipler, D. K. Arab and Jew. 1986
  Christ Century 104:800-1 S 23 '87. C. A. Kimball
  Commentary 83:66+ Ja '87. E. Alexander
  New Leader 69:24-6 D 1-15 '86. H. M. Waller
Sholem Aleichem. Tevye the dairyman and The railroad stories. 1987
  Commentary 84:70-3 N '87. R. Alter
  New Repub 197:38-41 N 9 '87. D. G. Roskies
Shreve, A. Remaking motherhood. 1987
  Psychol Today 21:69-70 O '87. B. L. Benderly
Shreve, S. R. Queen of hearts. 1986
  N Y Times Book Rev 92:10 Ja 11 '87. A. McDermott
Shrivastava, P. Bhopal. 1987
  Science 236:979 My 22 '87. R. P. Gephart, Jr.
Shriver, G. H. Philip Schaff. 1987
  Christ Century 104:863-4 O 7 '87. J. A. Patterson
Shriver, L. The female of the species. 1987
  N Y 20:98 Mr 30 '87. R. Koenig
  N Y Times Book Rev 92:13 Jl 19 '87. K. Bouton
Shuckburgh, E. Descent to Suez. 1987
  Commentary 84:65-8 Jl '87. D. Pryce-Jones
Shulman, A. K. In every woman's life—. 1987
  N Y Times Book Rev 92:56 My 31 '87. M. S. Willis
Siegman, A. E. Lasers. 1986
  Phys Today 40:89-90 D '87. M. O. Scully
Signoret, S. Adieu, Volodya. 1986
  New Yorker 62:100-1 Ja 12 '87. S. Lardner
Silber, J. In the city. 1987
  Ms 15:17-18+ My '87. R. Brown
  N Y Times Book Rev 92:8-9 Mr 29 '87. J. Johnson
Sills, B. and Linderman, L. Beverly. 1987
  N Y 20:94 Je 1 '87. P. G. Davis
  N Y Times Book Rev 92:28 My 31 '87. D. Harris
Silman, R. The dream dredger. 1986
  N Y Times Book Rev 92:12 Ja 4 '87. D. Guy
Silverman, D. Selling culture. 1986
  Art Am 75:15-17+ F '87. R. Storr
  N Y Times Book Rev 92:34 Ja 4 '87. M. Kozloff
  Progressive 51:41-2 My '87. M. A. Rosenberg
Simic, C. Unending blues. 1986
  N Y Times Book Rev 92:46 O 18 '87. S. Dobyns
Simmons, C. The Belles lettres papers. 1987
  N Y Times Book Rev 92:10 My 24 '87. S. Schiff
  Newsweek 109:81 My 18 '87. W. Clemons
  Time 129:80 My 18 '87. R. Z. Sheppard
Simon, M. The enchanted room. 1986
  N Y Times Book Rev 92:20 Ap 19 '87. L. McMahon
Simon, P. Let's put America back to work. 1987
  Christ Century 104:860-2 O 7 '87. R. Luecke
  Nation 244:584-5 My 2 '87. S. L. Malcomson
  Wash Mon 19:58-9 Mr '87. M. Kaus
Simon, R. The portrait in Britain and America. 1987
  Antiques 132:1026-7 N '87. B. D. Gallati
Simons, L. M. Worth dying for. 1987
  N Y Times Book Rev 92:8 S 6 '87. R. J. Kessler
Simpson, C. Artful partners. 1986
  N Y Rev Books 34:19-20 Mr 12 '87. J. Pope-Hennessy
  N Y Times Book Rev 92:1+ Mr 29 '87. J. Updike
  Time 129:77-8 Ap 6 '87. R. Z. Sheppard
Simpson, E. B. Orphans. 1987
  N Y Times Book Rev 92:1+ Jl 19 '87. S. Ballantyne
  Psychol Today 21:80 O '87. R. J. Moss
  Time 130:52 Ag 10 '87. O. Friedrich
  Vogue 177:112 Jl '87. B. K. Rothman
Simpson, M. Anywhere but here. 1986
  N Y Times Book Rev 92:7 Ja 11 '87. L. A. Schreiber
  Newsweek 109:69 F 2 '87. L. Shapiro
  Vogue 177:98+ Ja '87. G. L. Buckley
Sinclair, A. The red and the blue. 1986
  Atlantic 259:92-4 My '87. A. Burgess
  N Y Times Book Rev 92:12-13 Mr 8 '87. S. Koch

Natl Rev 39:47-8 My 22 '87. H. Bering-Jensen
New Leader 70:16 My 4-18 '87
Singer, B. C. J. Society, theory, and the French Revolution. 1986
    Hist Today 37:54-5 Ag '87. P. Burley
Singer, I. The nature of love. v3 1984
    N Y Times Book Rev 92:1-2+ D 27 '87. M. V. Miller
Singular, S. Talked to death. 1987
    N Y Times Book Rev 92:24 Mr 29 '87. C. Leppek
Sis, P. Rainbow Rhino. 1987
    N Y Times Book Rev 92:42 N 8 '87. J. Van de Wetering
The Sistine Chapel. 1st American ed. 1986
    N Y Rev Books 34:16+ O 8 '87. J. Pope-Hennessy
Sitton, T. and Rowold, M. C. Ringing the children in. 1987
    Smithsonian 18:180-2 S '87. D. D. Jackson
Skármeta, A. Burning patience. 1987
    N Y Times Book Rev 92:36 My 3 '87. W. S. Merwin
Skehan, J. W. Modern science and the book of Genesis. 1986
    Earth Sci 40:34-5 Wint '87
Skutch, A. F. Helpers at birds' nests. 1986
    Audubon 89:130+ N '87
Škvorecký, J. Dvorak in love. 1986
    N Y 20:91-2 F 9 '87. R. Koenig
    N Y Times Book Rev 92:11 F 22 '87. E. Hoffman
    New Repub 196:27-30 Je 1 '87. E. Rothstein
Slote, B. Willa Cather.
    Americana 14:79 Ja/F '87. A. Stern
Slusser, G. H. From Jung to Jesus. 1986
    America 156:139-40 F 14 '87. H. C. Kee
Small, D. The river in winter. 1987
    N Y Times Book Rev 92:8 Ja 25 '87. L. Zeidner
Smedes, L. B. Choices. 1986
    Christ Century 104:31 Ja 7-14 '87. R. Webber
Smedinghoff, T. J. The legal guide to developing, protecting, and marketing software. 1986
    Byte 12:76 F '87. D. A. Price
Smedley, A. Daughter of earth. 1987
    N Y Times Book Rev 92:14 Ag 23 '87. M. Jehlen
Smiley, J. The age of grief. 1987
    N Y Times Book Rev 92:12 S 6 '87. A. Bernays
Smith, B. Imagine the sound. 1985
    Down Beat 54:56+ Mr '87. K. Whitehead
Smith, D. T. and Tomerlin, J. Beating the radar rap. 1986
    Car Driv 33:36 Ag '87. T. Swan
Smith, J. A. Printers and press freedom. 1988
    N Y Times Book Rev 92:30 N 1 '87. F. Abrams
Smith, J. A. Schoenberg and his circle. 1986
    N Y Rev Books 34:30-3 N 5 '87. R. Craft
Smith, L. B. Treason in Tudor England. 1986
    N Y Rev Books 34:36-8 My 7 '87. C. Hill
Smith, R. N. The Harvard century. 1986
    Change 19:60-3 Jl/Ag '87. C. N. Breiseth
Smith, T. Thinking like a Communist. 1987
    N Y Times Book Rev 92:9 Ag 23 '87. W. G. Hyland
    Natl Rev 39:54 Jl 17 '87. C. Williamson
Smith, W. S. The closest of enemies. 1987
    Atlantic 259:92-4 Mr '87. W. LaFeber
    Commentary 83:77-80 Je '87. M. Falcoff
    N Y Times Book Rev 92:18 Mr 1 '87. J. Castañeda
    Nation 244:298-302 Mr 7 '87. T. G. Paterson
Smullyan, R. M. Forever undecided. 1987
    N Y Times Book Rev 92:35 Je 21 '87. G. Johnson
Smuts, R. M. Court culture and the origins of a royalist tradition in early Stuart England. 1987
    Hist Today 37:55+ D '87. G. E. Aylmer
Smyth, W. H. The Bedford Catalogue. 1986
    Astronomy 15:68-9 Ja '87. R. Burnham
Snider, D. and Bashe, P. Dee Snider's Teenage survival guide. 1987
    Roll Stone p20 O 8 '87. R. Tannenbaum
Snodgrass, W. D. Selected poems, 1957-1987. 1987
    N Y Times Book Rev 92:52 S 13 '87. G. Ewart
Snook, L. E. The anonymous Christ. 1986
    Christ Century 104:538-9 Je 3-10 '87. R. Booth
Snyder, H. A. and Runyon, D. V. The divided flame. 1986
    Christ Today 31:37-8 Mr 6 '87. K. G. Wolfe
Snyder, T. and Palmer, J. In search of the most amazing thing. 1986
    Byte 12:67-8+ F '87. K. S. Wittman
Snyder, Z. K. And condors danced. 1987
    N Y Times Book Rev 92:17 D 27 '87. W. Martin
Sobel, M. I. Light. 1987
    N Y Times Book Rev 92:32 S 27 '87. J. Cornell
Sobel, R. and Sicilia, D. B. The entrepreneurs. 1986
    Americana 15:12 My/Je '87. M. Durham
The Social construction of technological systems. 1987

Science 238:1152-3 N 20 '87. C. S. Fischer
Society for General Microbiology. Symposium (37th: 1985: University of Warwick). Viruses and cancer. 1985
    BioScience 37:522-3 Jl/Ag '87. D. Kabat
    BioScience 37:750 N '87. D. Kabat
Sohmer, S. Favorite son. 1987
    Nation 245:424-5 O 17 '87. S. Klawans
Solar radiophysics. 1985
    Science 235:800 F 13 '87. R. G. Stone
Solomon, D. Jackson Pollock. 1987
    Art Am 75:23 N '87. P. Plagens
    N Y Times Book Rev 92:24 O 18 '87. M. Brenson
Soloveitchik, J. D. The Halakhic mind. 1986
    Commentary 83:73-6 Ja '87. D. Singer
Someth May. Cambodian witness. 1987
    Progressive 51:30-1 Je '87. W. Steif
    Time 129:64-5 F 9 '87. P. Iyer
Sometimes when it rains. 1987
    Nation 245:456-7 O 24 '87. S. Sonnenberg
Sordi, M. The Christians and the Roman Empire. 1986
    Hist Today 37:61 Jl '87. R. A. Markus
Soros, G. The alchemy of finance. 1987
    New Repub 197:40-1 O 5 '87. J. N. Bhagwati
Souers, P. C. Hydrogen properties for fusion energy. 1986
    Sci Am 256:23-4+ Ja '87. P. Morrison
Southern, D. W. Gunnar Myrdal and Black-white relations. 1987
    Atlantic 259:86-9 My '87. D. M. Kennedy
Southern, R. W. Robert Grosseteste. 1986
    Hist Today 37:56 F '87. C. N. L. Brooke
Sowell, T. Compassion versus guilt, and other essays. 1987
    Natl Rev 39:60-1 O 9 '87. J. Sobran
Sowell, T. A conflict of visions. 1987
    Commentary 83:78-80 Mr '87. L. D. Nachman
    Fortune 115:124+ Mr 16 '87. D. Seligman
    N Y Times Book Rev 92:14 Ja 25 '87. F. Barnes
    Natl Rev 39:52-3 F 13 '87. J. Sobran
    New Repub 196:46-8 F 9 '87. D. Wrong
    Time 129:79-80 Mr 16 '87. O. Friedrich
Sowell, T. Education: assumptions versus history. 1985
    Phi Delta Kappan 69:83-4 S '87. P. Nesselrodt
Space weapons and international security. 1986
    N Y Rev Books 34:35-41 Ap 9 '87. Sir S. Zuckerman
Spada, J. Grace. 1987
    Macleans 100:45 Jl 27 '87. Y. Cox
Spanier, S. W. Kay Boyle, artist and activist. 1986
    Progressive 51:44-5 F '87. A. M. Davidon
Spark, M. Mary Shelley. 1987
    N Y Rev Books 34:35-8 N 19 '87. C. Tomalin
    N Y Times Book Rev 92:7 S 6 '87. S. Gubar
Spasowski, R. The liberation of one. 1986
    Christ Today 31:54 S 18 '87. D. Knippers
The 'Special relationship'. 1986
    Commentary 84:74-6 Ag '87. G. Szamuely
Spector, L. S. Going nuclear. 1987
    Sierra 72:72+ Jl/Ag '87. E. Winchester
Spence, J. Putting myself in the picture. 1986
    Art Am 75:23+ Jl '87. A. Solomon-Godeau
Spencer, J. P. S., Earl. The Red Earl; 2v. 1981
    Hist Today 37:59 S '87. D. Judd
Spender, S. Oedipus trilogy. 1985
    New Repub 196:36-8 My 4 '87. B. M. W. Knox
Sperber, A. M. Murrow, his life and times. 1986
    USA Today (Periodical) 115:92 Mr '87. R. L. Fischer
Speriglio, M. The Marilyn conspiracy. 1986
    Society 24:85-6 S/O '87. G. McCann
Špidlík, T. The spirituality of the Christian East. 1986
    America 156:369 My 2 '87. J. F. Baldovin
Spiegelman, A. Maus. 1986
    Nation 244:23-4 Ja 10 '87. R. Grossman
    New Repub 196:29-34 Je 22 '87. A. Gopnik
Spiel, H. Vienna's golden autumn, 1866-1938. 1987
    Hist Today 37:58 D '87. R. Grunberger
Spiers, E. M. Chemical warfare. 1986
    Environment 29:28 S '87. A. H. Westing
Sprigg, J. Shaker design. 1986
    Antiques 131:780 Ap '87. K. L. Ames
Sprigg, J. Shaker: life, work, and art. 1987
    Americana 15:18 N/D '87. M. Durham
Spring, J. H. The American school, 1642-1985. 1986
    Phi Delta Kappan 68:709-10 My '87. F. Parker
Springhall, J. Coming of age. 1986
    Hist Today 37:59 Ap '87. N. Tucker
Squire, L. R. Memory and brain. 1987
    Science 238:697 O 30 '87. M. Gallagher
Stackhouse, M. L. Public theology and political economy. 1987
    Christ Century 104:1093-4 D 2 '87. G. E. Paul
Stake, R. E. Quieting reform. 1986
    Child Today 16:33-4 S/O '87. M. Baizerman
Standiford, D. and Standiford, S. Sudden family. 1986

Christ Today 31:34-5 F 20 '87. R. Winter
Stanley, S. M. Extinction. 1987
Earth Sci 40:31-2 Wint '87
Stannard, M. Evelyn Waugh; v1, The early years 1903-1939. 1987
Commonweal 114:602-3 O 23 '87. N. Braybrooke
N Y Times Book Rev 92:1+ Ag 30 '87. E. Morris
Stansell, C. City of women. 1986
Nation 244:257-8 F 28 '87. A. Kessler-Harris
Stanwood, D. A. The seventh Royale. 1987
Mot Trend 39:26 Ap '87. T. C. Browne
Stares, P. B. The militarization of space. 1985
Society 24:88-90 Mr/Ap '87. W. A. McDougall
Stares, P. B. Space and national security. 1987
New Repub 197:40-2 S 28 '87. B. M. Blechman
Science 238:1589-90 D 11 '87. G. L. Epstein
Stark, S. S. A wrestling season. 1987
N Y Times Book Rev 92:15 Mr 1 '87. J. Daynard
Starobinski, J. Montaigne in motion. 1985
N Y Rev Books 34:50-3 N 19 '87. N. Z. Davis
Starr, C. G. Individual and community. 1986
Hist Today 37:58-9 N '87. P. Cartledge
Starr, K. Inventing the dream. 1985
Hist Today 37:58-9 My '87. J. Richards
Statistics and the law. 1986
Science 236:980-1 My 22 '87. M. J. Saks
Stauffer, D. Introduction to percolation theory. 1985
Phys Today 40:122-3 O '87. A. Bunde
Steele, I. K. The English Atlantic, 1675-1740. 1986
Hist Today 37:57 Ag '87. E. Countryman
Steele, P. Expatriates. 1985
America 157:92-3 Ag 15-22 '87. M. Wimsatt
Steele, T. Sapphics against anger, and other poems. 1986
N Y Times Book Rev 92:13-14 Ja 18 '87. W. Logan
Steering the elephant. 1986
Natl Rev 39:45-6 Jl 17 '87. J. Sobran
Stegner, W. E. Crossing to safety. 1987
Commonweal 114:630-1 N 6 '87. B. A. Bannon
N Y Times Book Rev 92:14 S 20 '87. D. Grumbach
Steig, W. The Zabajaba Jungle. 1987
N Y Times Book Rev 92:37 N 8 '87. J. Yolen
Stein, E. and others. Life in a Jewish family. 1986
America 156:7-9+ Ja 3-10 '87. J. W. Donohue
Stein, G. Operas & plays. 1987
N Y Times Book Rev 92:9 My 24 '87. R. Howard
Stein, G. Picasso. 1985
Art News 86:76 N '87. M. Rudman
Stein, G. and Van Vechten, C. The letters of Gertrude Stein and Carl Van Vechten, 1913-1946. 2v 1986
America 156:288-91 Ap 4 '87. R. Bridgman
Steinhart, P. Tracks in the sky. 1987
Nat Hist 96:80-2 N '87. K. R. Margolis
Stella, F. Working space. 1986
Art News 86:27 Mr '87. E. Heartney
Stellar Populations Meeting (1986: Baltimore, Md.). Stellar populations. 1986
Science 237:1626 S 25 '87. J. G. Cohen
Stephens, D. W. and Krebs, J. R. Foraging theory. 1986
Science 238:831-3 N 6 '87. G. H. Pyke
Steptoe, J. Mufaro's beautiful daughters. 1987
N Y Times Book Rev 92:27 Je 28 '87. P. C. White
Sterling, L. and Shapiro, E. Y. The art of Prolog. 1986
Byte 12:76+ Ap '87. S. H. Rogers
Stern, F. R. Dreams and delusions. 1987
N Y Times Book Rev 92:7+ O 25 '87. W. J. Mommsen
Stern, R. A. M. and others. New York, 1930. 1987
N Y Times Book Rev 92:3 My 31 '87. P. Goldberger
Stern, S. Lazar Malkin enters heaven. 1987
N Y Times Book Rev 92:11 Mr 1 '87. M. Dickstein
Sternberg, R. J. Intelligence applied. 1986
Phi Delta Kappan 69:315-16 D '87. K. Carlson
Stevens, J. Storming heaven. 1987
Commonweal 114:605-6 O 23 '87. D. Toolan
Newsweek 110:63 Ag 24 '87. J. Miller
Stevens, M. Power of attorney. 1986
Wash Mon 19:59-60 F '87. P. Barrett
Stevens, W. and Rodríguez Feo, J. Secretaries of the moon. 1986
N Y Times Book Rev 92:33 F 8 '87. H. Padilla
Stevenson, A. Selected poems, 1956-1986. 1987
N Y Times Book Rev 92:32-3 N 15 '87. A. Corn
Stevenson, J. Higher on the door. 1987
N Y Times Book Rev 92:33 S 20 '87. J. G. Dunne
Stewart, J. B. The prosecutors. 1987
N Y Times Book Rev 92:20 S 27 '87. S. Wishman
Stigler, S. M. The history of statistics. 1986
Science 235:1262-3 Mr 6 '87. M. Stone
Stocking, G. W. Victorian anthropology. 1987
N Y Times Book Rev 92:22+ Mr 1 '87. G. Levine
Science 237:1516-17 S 18 '87. J. A. Boon

Stokes, D. W. and Stokes, L. Q. A guide to animal tracking and behavior. 1986
Conservationist 42:51 Jl/Ag '87. H. W. Trimm
Stoler, P. The war against the press. 1986
N Y Times Book Rev 92:12 Ja 18 '87. T. Winship
Stomatal function. 1987
Science 238:1297-8 N 27 '87. A. H. Markhart, III
Stommel, H. M. A view of the sea. 1987
Science 238:696-7 O 30 '87. R. Hide
Stone, C. D. Earth and other ethics. 1987
Nat Hist 96:60-1 Ag '87. J. L. Sax
Stone, M. A. Contemporary American woodworkers. 1986
Americana 15:21-2 S/O '87. M. Durham
Storace, P. Heredity. 1987
N Y Times Book Rev 92:68 N 8 '87. S. Santos
Storr, R. Philip Guston. 1986
Art Am 75:27+ Je '87. B. Berkson
Stott, J. R. W. The cross of Christ. 1986
Christ Today 31:35-6 S 4 '87. J. I. Packer
Stout, H. S. The New England soul. 1986
Christ Century 104:64 Ja 21 '87. J. Corrigan
Stoutenburg, A. Land of superior mirages. 1986
N Y Times Book Rev 92:42 F 15 '87. R. Von Hallberg
Stowe, K. S. Essentials of ocean science. 1987
Sea Front 33:392-3 S/O '87. K. M. Sullivan
Strasberg, L. A dream of passion. 1987
N Y Times Book Rev 92:13-14 N 29 '87. S. Aaron
New Repub 197:37-9 D 7 '87. D. Van Leer
Strategic defenses and Soviet-American relations. 1987
Science 237:1625-6 S 25 '87. D. Hafner
Straus, D. The birthmark. 1987
N Y Times Book Rev 92:11 Ap 12 '87. D. Grumbach
Street-Porter, T. Freestyle, the new architecture and interior design from Los Angeles. 1986
Archit Rec 175:71 Jl '87. S. Gutterman
Strem, G. G. Agnosticism is also faith. 1987
Humanist 47:46 N/D '87. C. L. Wiles
Strieber, W. Communion. 1987
Commonweal 114:426-8 Jl 17 '87. M. Zeik
N Y Times Book Rev 92:15 Mr 15 '87. G. Benford
Nation 244:328-34+ Mr 14 '87. T. M. Disch
Stroud, C. Close pursuit. 1987
Macleans 100:49 Mr 2 '87. D. Cumming
N Y Times Book Rev 92:28 Ap 12 '87. D. Uhnak
Stubbing, R. A. The defense game. 1986
Bull At Sci 43:48+ Je '87. G. Adams
Stuckey, S. Slave culture. 1987
Nation 245:390-2 O 10 '87. W. E. Martin
New Repub 197:39-41 O 12 '87. E. D. Genovese
The Study of variable stars using small telescopes. 1986
Sky Telesc 74:374 O '87. M. L. Hazen
The Substance of thing hoped for. 1987
Commonweal 114:300 My 8 '87. D. Toolan
Subtelny, O. Domination of Eastern Europe. 1986
Hist Today 37:56 Je '87. J. Black
Sukenick, R. Down and in. 1987
N Y Times Book Rev 92:3+ N 1 '87. L. Rivers
Nation 245:276-8 S 19 '87. S. Klawans
Sulfur dioxide and vegetation. 1985
BioScience 37:139-40 F '87. R. Alscher
Sullivan, N. J. The Dodgers move west. 1987
Natl Rev 39:53 D 31 '87. J. Mysak
Sulzberger, C. L. The world and Richard Nixon. 1987
N Y Times Book Rev 92:18 Ag 2 '87. S. Neal
Wash Mon 19:58-9 Je '87. M. A. Fernandez
Sundquist, J. L. Constitutional reform and effective government. 1986
America 156:38-9 Ja 17 '87. D. Shelton
Supercomputers in theoretical and experimental science. 1985
Phys Today 40:81-2 Ap '87. D. W. Duke
Superstrings. 2v 1985
Phys Today 40:124 O '87. P. Ramond
Süskind, P. Perfume: the story of a murderer. 1986
New Repub 196:27-31 F 23 '87. S. Schama
Sword, W. President Washington's Indian War. 1985
America 156:429-31 My 23 '87. M. D. Green
Symmetry. 1986
Sci Am 256:22-3 Ap '87. P. Morrison
Systematics of the green algae. 1984
BioScience 37:738-9 N '87. D. B. Czarnecki
Syvitski, J. P. M. and others. Fjords. 1987
Science 236:1126 My 29 '87. B. Molnia
Szasz, T. S. Insanity. 1987
Christ Century 104:507-8 My 20-27 '87. D. L. Heetland
Humanist 47:45-6 N/D '87. W. R. McKee
N Y Times Book Rev 92:22 Mr 15 '87. D. Sobel
Szulc, T. Fidel. 1986
Christ Century 104:338 Ap 8 '87. P. F. McCleary
Commentary 83:69-71 F '87. L. E. Aguilar
Macleans 100:52 F 9 '87. G. Allen

Nation 244:85-8 Ja 24 '87. G. Black
Natl Rev 39:48-50 F 13 '87. T. Bethell
New Leader 70:17-19 Ja 12-26 '87. A. de la Carrera
New Repub 196:28-30+ Ja 19 '87. K. S. Karol

T

Takhtadzhiān, A. L. Floristic regions of the world. 1986
Science 236:100 Ap 3 '87. R. F. Thorne
Talbot, M. Beyond the quantum. 1986
N Y Times Book Rev 92:11 Ja 25 '87. L. B. Young
Tallent, E. Time with children. 1987
N Y Times Book Rev 92:11 N 15 '87. C. See
Tamari, M. With all your possessions. 1987
Commentary 84:73-6 O '87. E. Isaac
Tambiah, S. J. Sri Lanka. 1986
New Repub 196:33-8 F 23 '87. D. L. Horowitz
Tanner, T. Jane Austen. 1986
New Repub 196:36+ My 18 '87. D. Bromwich
Tarbell, D. S. and Tarbell, A. T. Essays on the history of organic chemistry in the United States, 1875-1955. 1986
Science 236:1476-7 Je 12 '87. L. Gortler
Tarkovsky, A. Sculpting in time. 1987
N Y Times Book Rev 92:20 S 20 '87. A. Insdorf
Tatar, M. M. The hard facts of the Grimms' fairy tales. 1987
N Y Rev Books 34:22-4 D 3 '87. J. A. Smith
N Y Times Book Rev 92:28 N 15 '87. H. Carpenter
Tate, J. Reckoner. 1986
Commonweal 114:506-7 S 11 '87. W. Koestenbaum
N Y Times Book Rev 92:26 Mr 1 '87. J. Ash
Tatsuno, S. The technopolis strategy. 1986
Technol Rev 90:75 F/Mr '87. J. D. Kirwan
Tauber, M. J. and others. Seasonal adaptations of insects. 1986
BioScience 37:751-2 N '87. W. J. Bell
Taubes, G. Nobel dreams. 1986
N Y Times Book Rev 92:11 Ja 25 '87. L. B. Young
Phys Today 40:64-6 Je '87. A. Firestone
Taylor, D. The myth of certainty. 1986
Christ Today 31:67-8 Mr 20 '87. J. Crosby
Taylor, J. Storming the Magic Kingdom. 1987
Bus Week p26-7 My 18 '87. R. Grover
Film Comment 23:78-9 Jl/Ag '87. R. Natale
N Y Times Book Rev 92:1+ My 10 '87. D. McClintick
Taylor, M. D. The gold Cadillac. 1987
N Y Times Book Rev 92:37 N 15 '87. V. W. Wesley
Taylor, P. Private domain. 1987
Dance Mag 61:40-2 S '87. O. Stuart
N Y Rev Books 34:30-2 Je 11 '87. L. Kirstein
N Y Times Book Rev 92:9 My 17 '87. A. Kisselgoff
Time 129:83-4 My 11 '87. M. Duffy
The Teaching of writing. 1986
Phi Delta Kappan 68:799-800 Je '87. E. J. Farrell
Technology and global industry. 1987
Science 238:92 O 2 '87. R. E. Litan
Tectonostratigraphic terranes of the circum-Pacific region. 1985
Science 237:88-9 Jl 3 '87. M. Cloos
Teeda Butt Mam and Criddle, J. To destroy you is no loss. 1987
N Y Times Book Rev 92:8-9 Ag 2 '87. B. Crossette
Teichman, J. Pacifism and the just war. 1986
Humanist 47:42 Jl/Ag '87. A. E. Hartle
N Y Times Book Rev 92:30-1 Ap 26 '87. J. P. Dolan
Tejima, K. Fox's dream. 1987
N Y Times Book Rev 92:49 N 8 '87. J. Cech
Temko, N. To win or to die. 1987
N Y Times Book Rev 92:23 Ag 16 '87. H. D. S. Greenway
Temple, R. K. G. The genius of China. 1986
Sci Am 257:151-2 D '87. P. Morrison and P. Morrison
Tennyson, A. T. , Baron. The letters of Alfred Lord Tennyson; v2, 1851-1870. 1987
N Y Rev Books 34:17-19 O 22 '87. R. B. Martin
Terich, T. Living with the shore of Puget Sound and the Georgia Strait. 1987
Oceans 20:60-1 S/O '87. D. G. Gordon
Terrell, J. Prehistory of the Pacific Islands. 1986
Science 235:1683-4 Mr 27 '87. R. L. Kirk
Terrill, R. The Australians. 1987
N Y Times Book Rev 92:16 S 20 '87. J. Perlez
Teveth, S. Ben-Gurion. 1987
N Y Times Book Rev 92:3+ Je 21 '87. M. Gilbert
New Repub 196:48-53 Je 8 '87. S. Avineri
TEX for scientific documentation. 1986
Byte 12:58+ N '87. A. Hoenig
Texier, C. Love me tender. 1987
N Y Times Book Rev 92:13-14 Je 7 '87. E. Prager
Thackray, J. The age of earth. 1986

Earth Sci 39:30-1 Wint '86
The Federalist. The Federalist. 1977
Time 130:78-80 Jl 6 '87. E. Bowen
Theatre for youth. 1986
Child Today 16:35 S/O '87. C. E. Guiles
Thernstrom, A. M. Whose votes count? 1987
N Y Times Book Rev 92:40 O 18 '87. A. Clymer
New Repub 197:39-41 N 30 '87. H. W. Stanley
Wash Mon 19:51-5 N '87. P. H. Schuck
Theroux, A. An adultery. 1987
N Y Times Book Rev 92:11 O 18 '87. R. Hansen
Theroux, P. Night lights. 1987
N Y Times Book Rev 92:13 Mr 15 '87. N. Mairs
Theroux, P. O-Zone. 1986
New Yorker 62:108-9 F 16 '87. S. Lardner
Theweleit, K. Male fantasies; v1, Women, floods, bodies, history. 1985
N Y Times Book Rev 92:14 Je 21 '87. P. A. Robinson
Nation 245:64-5 Jl 18-25 '87. M. P. Rogin
The Third generation. 1987
Natl Rev 39:46+ My 8 '87. P. Weyrich
Wash Mon 19:58-9 O '87. M. Gladwell
Third World liberation theologies. 1986
Christ Century 104:167 F 18 '87. J. Stanley
Thomas, D. M. Sphinx. 1987
N Y Rev Books 34:23-5 Ap 9 '87. D. J. Enright
N Y Times Book Rev 92:6 Ja 18 '87. G. Stade
Thomas, E. M. Reindeer Moon. 1987
New Yorker 63:122-4 Mr 30 '87. J. Updike
Thomas, H. Armed truce. 1987
Bus Week p19-21 My 4 '87. S. J. Dryden
Commentary 83:72-4 Je '87. D. Kagan
N Y Rev Books 34:44-50 Je 11 '87. T. Garton Ash
N Y Times Book Rev 92:1+ Mr 1 '87. M. D. Shulman
Natl Rev 39:42+ My 22 '87. S. T. Francis
Thomas, M. Antonia saw the oryx first. 1987
N Y Times Book Rev 92:12 Je 7 '87. M. Gorra
Thomas, M. Come to Africa and save your marriage, and other stories. 1987
N Y Times Book Rev 92:11-12 O 11 '87. B. Thompson
Thomas, M. and others. Textile art. 1985
Am Craft 47:14+ Ap/My '87. G. Moss
Thomas, M. M. The ropespinner conspiracy. 1987
N Y Times Book Rev 92:9 Ja 11 '87. V. Patrick
Thomas, R. Out on the rim. 1987
Newsweek 110:89 O 19 '87. D. Lehman
Thomas, S. D. The last navigator. 1987
Sci Am 257:112-14 Ag '87. P. Morrison
Thompson, E. A. Who was St. Patrick? 1986
America 156:331 Ap 18 '87. E. Grace
Thompson, E. B. American daughter. 1986
Nation 244:899-900 Je 27 '87. J. Long
Thomson, D. Warren Beatty and Desert Eyes. 1987
Macleans 100:50-1 Jl 13 '87. G. Peary
Newsweek 109:78 My 18 '87. D. Ansen
Thoreau, H. D. A week on the Concord and Merrimack rivers. 1985
N Y Rev Books 33:46-51 Ja 15 '87. G. O'Brien
Thoreau, H. D. The winged life. 1986
N Y Rev Books 33:46-51 Ja 15 '87. G. O'Brien
Thornton, L. Imagining Argentina. 1987
N Y Times Book Rev 92:11-12 S 20 '87. L. Hafrey
Thornton, T. P. The challenge to U.S. policy in the Third World. 1986
Bull At Sci 43:47-9 N '87. S. Hune
Thurm, M. Walking distance. 1987
N Y Times Book Rev 92:9 My 10 '87. D. Mason
Thurston, A. F. Enemies of the people. 1987
N Y Times Book Rev 92:3+ F 22 '87. M. Goldman
Thurston, C. The romance revolution. 1987
Psychol Today 21:66 O '87. K. Ellis
Tichi, C. Shifting gears. 1987
N Y Times Book Rev 92:9-10 Ap 19 '87. A. Nehamas
Tiffany and Company. The new Tiffany table settings. 1981
Antiques Collect Hobbies 92:54-5 Ap '87
Tiger, L. The manufacture of evil. 1987
N Y Times Book Rev 92:10 Ag 23 '87. L. Marx
Tilly, C. The contentious French. 1986
Am Sch 56:443-5 Summ '87. M. Burns
Tiner, R. W., Jr. A field guide to coastal wetland plants of the northeastern United States. 1987
Sea Front 33:390-1 S/O '87. G. L. Voss
Tintner, A. R. The museum world of Henry James. 1986
N Y Rev Books 34:29-30 Ap 9 '87. L. Auchincloss
Titus, A. C. Bombs in the backyard. 1986
Environment 29:29 N '87. R. Ferm
Tivnan, E. The Lobby. 1987
Commentary 84:58+ Jl '87. J. Muravchik
N Y Rev Books 34:8-10+ O 8 '87. S. Hoffmann
N Y Times Book Rev 92:24 My 17 '87. B. Gwertzman

Nation 244:770-3 Je 6 '87. R. I. Friedman
Tokyo, form and spirit. 1986
New Repub 196:40-2 F 16 '87. N. Palevsky
Topitsch, E. Stalin's war. 1987
N Y Times Book Rev 92:35 N 15 '87. A. Dallin
Torańska, T. "Them". 1987
Commentary 84:73-6 N '87. A. Puddington
N Y Times Book Rev 92:15-16+ My 17 '87. A. Walicki
Nation 245:131-3 Ag 15-22 '87. D. Singer
Tournier, M. The golden droplet. 1987
N Y Times Book Rev 92:37 N 1 '87. R. Sieburth
Toynbee, A. J. and Cary-Elwes, C. An historian's conscience. 1986
America 156:160-1 F 21 '87. T. G. Kardong
Christ Today 31:69 O 2 '87. C. T. McIntire
Trachtenberg, M. and Hyman, I. Architecture, from prehistory to post-modernism. 1986
Archit Rec 175:77 Ag '87. S. Gutterman
Art Am 75:13+ Mr '87. J. Merkel
Trager, P. and Scully, V. J. The villas of Palladio. 1986
Antiques 132:698 O '87. H. S. Bryant, Jr.
Train, J. The Midas touch. 1987
N Y Times Book Rev 92:57 My 31 '87. J. Grigsby
Transport processes, iono- and osmoregulation. 1985
BioScience 37:746-7 N '87. L. H. Mantel
Trebach, A. S. The great drug war. 1987
Fortune 116:141-2+ S 14 '87. A. Hacker
The Tree of liberty. 1986
Cent Mag 20:28-9 Ja/F '87. D. McDonald
Trees I. 1986
BioScience 37:287 Ap '87. E. G. Kirby, III
Trefil, J. S. Meditations at sunset. 1987
N Y Times Book Rev 92:7 Jl 12 '87. J. Weiner
Tremblay, B. Duhamel.
N Y Times Book Rev 92:15 Ja 25 '87. B. Shlain
Trento, J. J. Prescription for disaster. 1987
Space World X-2-278:36 F '87. J. Rhea
Technol Rev 90:78 Ag/S '87. R. G. Nichols
Wash Mon 19:48-54 Ap '87. G. Easterbrook
Trevelyan, R. The golden oriole. 1987
N Y Times Book Rev 92:3+ N 22 '87. J. Morris
New Leader 70:21-2 O 19 '87. G. Woodcock
Treverton, G. F. Covert action. 1987
Commonweal 114:752-6 D 18 '87. J. B. Judis
N Y Times Book Rev 92:3 N 29 '87. S. Hoffmann
New Repub 197:33-4+ D 21 '87. F. Fukuyama
Trevor, W. The news from Ireland & other stories. 1986
America 156:371 My 2 '87. T. P. Hill
Trillin, C. If you can't say something nice. 1987
N Y Times Book Rev 92:11 N 8 '87. M. Russell
Troyat, H. Peter the Great. 1987
N Y Times Book Rev 92:62 S 13 '87. F. D. Reeve
Truitt, A. Turn. 1987
Am Artist 51:36+ N '87. D. C. Hines
Trump, D. J. Trump. 1988
Bus Week p26-7+ D 28 '87-Ja 4 '88. J. R. Norman
N Y Times Book Rev 92:7 D 20 '87. T. Morgan
Tsvetaeva, M. I. Selected poems of Marina Tsvetayeva. 1987
N Y Rev Books 34:20+ O 8 '87. J. Bayley
N Y Times Book Rev 92:22-3 S 27 '87. E. Proffer
Turner, A. W. Nettie's trip South. 1987
N Y Times Book Rev 92:19 Ag 16 '87. G. Overholser
Turner, B. S. The body and society. 1986
Society 24:94 Mr/Ap '87. E. Shorter
Turner, E. L. B. The spirit and the drum. 1987
Christ Century 104:1005-6 N 11 '87. S. M. Talarico
Turner, H. A. The two Germanies since 1945. 1987
N Y Times Book Rev 92:19 D 20 '87. W. E. Griffith
Turner, J. Without God, without creed. 1985
Natl Rev 39:51-2 Je 19 '87. C. R. Schmahl
Turner, R. H. and others. Waiting for disaster. 1986
Science 235:94-6 Ja 2 '87. C. Perrow
Turow, S. Presumed innocent. 1987
Mademoiselle 93:116+ N '87. J. Maynard
N Y Rev Books 34:21-2 N 19 '87. R. Towers
N Y Times Book Rev 92:1+ Je 28 '87. A. Rice
Newsweek 109:70 Je 29 '87. W. Clemons
Time 130:71 Jl 20 '87. P. Gray
Tuttle, R. Apes of the world. 1986
Science 236:1004 My 22 '87. R. W. Wrangham
Twenty years of Jewish-Catholic relations. 1986
America 156:429 My 23 '87. M. B. McGarry
Twitchell, J. B. Forbidden partners. 1986
N Y Times Book Rev 92:7-8 Ja 18 '87. M. V. Miller
Tyacke, N. Anti-Calvinists. 1986
Hist Today 37:58 S '87. J. P. Sommerville
Tyler, P. Running critical. 1986
New Repub 196:36-40 Ap 27 '87. R. English
Tynan, K. The life of Kenneth Tynan. 1987
N Y 20:108+ N 9 '87. D. Hare

N Y Rev Books 34:5-7 D 3 '87. J. Osborne
New Repub 197:23-5 N 16 '87. R. Brustein
Time 130:85+ D 7 '87. R. Schickel
Tyson, J. L. Prophets or useful idiots. 1986
Natl Rev 39:55 F 27 '87. C. Williamson
Tysse, G. J. The 1986 Immigration Act. 1987
Mon Labor Rev 110:58 Ap '87. E. Sehgal

U

Uncivil religion. 1987
Christ Century 104:892+ O 14 '87. R. E. Wentz
Underhill, R. The woodwright's workbook. 1986
Workbench 43:47 My/Je '87. R. N. Hoffman
Unger, R. M. Passion. 1986
Society 24:89-90 Ja/F '87. J. B. Elshtain
Unions in transition. 1986
Mon Labor Rev 110:46-7 Jl '87. H. P. Cohany
United States. Attorney General's Commission on Pornography. Final report of the Attorney General's Commission on Pornography. 1986
Christ Today 31:62 Ja 16 '87. T. Minnery
Commentary 84:51-7 Ag '87. T. Teachout
United States. Constitutional Convention (1787). Notes of debates in the Federal Convention of 1787. 1987
Time 130:78-80 Jl 6 '87. E. Bowen
Updike, J. Roger's version. 1986
Natl Rev 39:53-4+ F 13 '87. D. Mehl
New Repub 196:41-2 F 2 '87. D. J. Enright
Radio-Electron 58 ComputerDigest:137 My '87
Updike, J. Trust me. 1987
N Y Times Book Rev 92:1+ Ap 26 '87. M. Robinson
Newsweek 109:82 My 18 '87. D. Lehman
Time 129:103 My 4 '87. R. Z. Sheppard
Urquhart, B. E. A life in peace and war. 1987
N Y Rev Books 34:27-9 N 5 '87. A. Hertzberg
N Y Times Book Rev 92:14-15 S 27 '87. C. W. Maynes
Time 130:88 N 16 '87. G. Russell
Useem, E. L. Low tech education in a high tech world. 1986
Science 235:799 F 13 '87. H. M. Levin
Uys, E. L. Brazil. 1986
Commonweal 114:121-2 F 27 '87. J. A. Page

V

Václav Havel, or, Living in truth. 1987
N Y Times Book Rev 92:12 Jl 19 '87. T. Venclova
Valladares, A. Against all hope. 1986
Natl Rev 39:48-50 F 13 '87. T. Bethell
Van Allsburg, C. The Z was zapped. 1987
N Y Times Book Rev 92:54 N 8 '87. G. Wilson
Van den Haag, E. and Conrad, J. P. The U.N., in or out? 1987
N Y Times Book Rev 92:33 O 4 '87. E. W. Foell
Natl Rev 39:53-4 S 25 '87. J. G. Pilon
Van Doren, M. The selected letters of Mark Van Doren. 1987
Commentary 84:68-70 Jl '87. J. Hart
Van Rose, S. Earthquakes. 1983
Earth Sci 40:30-1 Fall '87
Van Rose, S. and Mercer, I. Volcanoes. 1986
Earth Sci 40:36 Spr '87
Vanderbilt, G. Black knight, white knight. 1987
N Y 20:81-2 Ap 20 '87. R. Koenig
N Y Times Book Rev 92:22+ My 31 '87. N. Johnson
Vargas Llosa, M. The perpetual orgy. 1986
N Y Rev Books 34:35-6 Jl 16 '87. R. Shattuck
New Leader 70:13 D 1-15 '86. G. Woodcock
New Repub 196:54-6 Je 8 '87. M. Wood
Vargas Llosa, M. Who killed Palomino Molero? 1987
N Y Times Book Rev 92:13 My 31 '87. R. Lourie
New Yorker 63:83-4 Ag 24 '87. J. Updike
World Press Rev 34:61 Ag '87. A. D'Orrico
Varnedoe, K. Vienna 1900. 1986
Archit Rec 175:75+ Mr '87. S. Gutterman
Varotsos, P. A. and Alexopoulos, K. D. Thermodynamics of point defects and their relation with bulk properties. 1986
Phys Today 40:95-6 N '87. R. O. Simmons
Vassiltchikov, M. Berlin diaries, 1940-1945. 1987
N Y Rev Books 34:7-8+ Ap 9 '87. G. Annan
N Y Times Book Rev 92:6-7 Ap 5 '87. G. A. Craig
Natl Rev 39:49-50+ Mr 27 '87. A. Horne
New Leader 70:19 Jl 1-15 '87. S. Rodman
New Yorker 63:113-20 My 25 '87. W. Maxwell
Time 129:75-6 Ap 13 '87. R. Z. Sheppard
Vaughan, D. Uncoupling. 1986
Psychol Today 21:78-9 Mr '87. D. Dowling
Veatch, H. B. Human rights. 1985
America 156:109-11 F 7 '87. M. L. Stackhouse

Veatch, R. M. The patient as partner. 1987
  America 157:362-4 N 14 '87. M. B. Mahowald
Vellay, M. and Frampton, K. Pierre Chareau. 1985
  Archit Rec 175:75 F '87. J. V. Iovine
Venturi, R. and Scott Brown, D. A view from the
  Campidoglio. 1984
  Art Am 75:23+ N '87. J. Merkel
Vermeij, G. J. Evolution and escalation. 1987
  Science 237:1235-6 S 4 '87. A. J. Kohn
Vernon, F. Privileged children. 1987
  N Y Times Book Rev 92:25 Ag 9 '87. F. Simon
Verschuur, G. L. The invisible universe revealed. 1987
  Astronomy 15:84-5 N '87. R. Burnham
  Sky Telesc 73:500-1 My '87. K. I. Kellermann
The Vertebrate neuromuscular junction. 1987
  Science 237:202-3 Jl 10 '87. S. Schuetze
Vickers, H. Cecil Beaton. 1986
  Art Am 75:15-17+ Ja '87. D. Bourdon
Vidal, G. Empire. 1987
  N Y 20:72-3 Je 8 '87. R. Koenig
  N Y Rev Books 34:31-3 S 24 '87. R. Poirier
  N Y Times Book Rev 92:1+ Je 14 '87. J. Kaplan
  New Repub 197:49-50+ S 14-21 '87. A. Delbanco
  Newsweek 109:70 Je 15 '87. D. Gates
  Time 129:73-4 Je 22 '87. P. Gray
  USA Today (Periodical) 116:94-5 N '87. S. G. Kellman
  Wash Mon 19:45-6+ S '87. S. Waldman
Viereck, P. R. E. Archer in the marrow. 1987
  New Leader 70:16-17 Ag 10-24 '87. P. Pettingell
Villoldo, A. and Krippner, S. Healing states. 1987
  Psychol Today 21:78-9 Ag '87. D. Dowling
Violence in the home. 1986
  Child Today 16:35-6 Mr/Ap '87. H. M. Hughes
Viorst, M. Sands of sorrow. 1987
  Commentary 84:78-80 O '87. D. Bar-Illan
Visser, M. Much depends on dinner. 1987
  Macleans 100:58 Ja 19 '87. R. Manson
Visual neuroscience. 1987
  Science 237:544-5 Jl 31 '87. R. M. Shapley
Vitz, P. C. Censorship.
  Natl Rev 39:64 Ja 30 '87. C. Williamson
Vogan, S. Scenes from the homefront. 1987
  N Y Times Book Rev 92:20 Ag 2 '87. M. Peacock
Voigt, E. B. The lotus flowers. 1987
  N Y Times Book Rev 92:20 Ag 23 '87. E. Hirsch
Voinovich, V. Moscow 2042. 1987
  N Y Times Book Rev 92:1+ Je 7 '87. M. Bradbury
  New Leader 70:30-1 My 4-18 '87. G. Gibian
Vollmann, W. T. You bright and risen angels. 1987
  N Y Times Book Rev 92:10 Je 21 '87. G. Pool
Von Hoelle, J. J. Thimble collector's encyclopedia. 3rd
  ed. 1986
  Antiques Collect Hobbies 92:66 Ag '87
Von Tscharner, R. and Fleming, R. L. New Providence.
  1987
  N Y Times Book Rev 92:33 N 8 '87. P. Goldberger
Vonnegut, K. Bluebeard. 1987
  N Y Times Book Rev 92:12 O 18 '87. J. Moynahan
Vorob'ev, N. A. and others. The history and art of the
  Russian icon from the X to the XX centuries. 1986
  Antiques Collect Hobbies 92:47 Mr '87
Voznesenskiĭ, A. An arrow in the wall. 1987
  N Y Rev Books 34:36-7 D 3 '87. E. Feinstein
  N Y Times Book Rev 92:7 Mr 29 '87. J. Bayley

W

Wade, N. A world beyond healing. 1987
  N Y Times Book Rev 92:11 Jl 19 '87. R. P. Gale
Wade, W. C. The fiery cross. 1987
  Commonweal 114:361-2 Je 5 '87. K. S. Smith
  N Y Times Book Rev 92:32-3 Ap 26 '87. T. Rosengarten
Waggoner, G. and others. Baseball by the rules. 1987
  Esquire 107:32 Ap '87
Wagner-Martin, L. Sylvia Plath. 1987
  N Y Times Book Rev 92:12-13 O 25 '87. I. Hamilton
  Nation 245:656+ N 28 '87. D. W. Middlebrook
  New Leader 70:18 N 2 '87. P. Pettingell
Wahlgren, E. The Vikings and America. 1986
  Oceans 20:61-2 Jl/Ag '87. B. C. Busch
Wainwright, L. The great American magazine. 1986
  New Repub 196:36-40 F 9 '87. J. K. Glassman
Walcott, D. The Arkansas testament. 1987
  N Y Times Book Rev 92:12 D 20 '87. M. Rudman
  New Repub 197:46-7 N 2 '87. D. J. Enright
Walcott, D. Collected poems, 1948-1984. 1986
  Américas 39:60-2 Mr/Ap '87. D. Lyon
Wald, A. M. The New York intellectuals. 1987
  N Y Times Book Rev 92:24 Je 7 '87. D. M. Oshinsky
  Nation 245:94-6 Ag 1-8 '87. E. Schrecker
  New Leader 70:3-4 My 4-18 '87. B. Gewen

Wald, R. M. General relativity. 1984
  Phys Today 40:94-5 My '87. J. W. York, Jr.
Waldron, A. Close connections. 1987
  N Y Times Book Rev 92:18 N 15 '87. D. Betts
Waldrop, R. The hanky of Pippin's daughter. 1986
  N Y Times Book Rev 92:12 Mr 1 '87. R. Weinreich
Wałęsa, L. A way of hope. 1987
  N Y Times Book Rev 92:3+ D 13 '87. L. Kołakowski
Walker, A. The color purple. 1985
  N Y Rev Books 34:17-20 Ja 29 '87. D. Pinckney
Walker, G. Solomon's children. 1986
  Psychol Today 21:71+ Mr '87. D. Dowling
Walker, G. A. H. Astronomical observations. 1987
  Sky Telesc 74:610-11 D '87. J. Huchra
Walkey, D. G. A. Applied plant virology. 1985
  BioScience 37:619-20 S '87. K. Maramorosch
Wall, J. A. Bosses. 1986
  Psychol Today 21:79 Mr '87. R. J. Moss
Wallace, A. F. C. St. Clair. 1987
  N Y Times Book Rev 92:15-16 O 18 '87. R. Rosenzweig
Wallace, D. F. The broom of the system. 1987
  N Y Times Book Rev 92:22 Mr 1 '87. C. James
Wallace, R. K. Emily Brontë and Beethoven. 1986
  Natl Rev 39:54-5 Je 19 '87. J. O. Tate
Wallop, M. and Codevilla, A. M. The arms control delusion.
  1987
  Natl Rev 39:56 D 18 '87. C. Williamson
Walser, M. Breakers. 1987
  N Y Times Book Rev 92:43 N 1 '87. S. Ruta
  New Repub 197:40-2 D 28 '87. S. Birkerts
Walsh, K. and King, A. Handbook of international
  manpower market comparisons. 1986
  Mon Labor Rev 110:36-7 N '87. C. Sorrentino
Walsh, M. J. The triumph of the meek. 1986
  Christ Century 104:509-10 My 20-27 '87. J. T. Fitzgerald
Walton, J. K. Lancashire. 1987
  Hist Today 37:59 Je '87. G. Marsden
Walzer, M. Interpretation and social criticism. 1987
  Commentary 84:49-52 Jl '87. R. J. Neuhaus
  N Y Times Book Rev 92:11-12 Mr 15 '87. J. P.
  Diggins
  Natl Rev 39:46-7 Jl 17 '87. W. McGurn
Wambaugh, J. Echoes in the darkness. 1987
  N Y Times Book Rev 92:12 Mr 1 '87. L. Franks
  Time 129:75+ F 23 '87. R. Z. Sheppard
Wapner, J. A. A view from the bench. 1987
  N Y Times Book Rev 92:19 D 13 '87. M. E. Gale
Wareham, J. Wareham's basic business types. 1987
  Fortune 115:174 Je 8 '87. W. Kiechel, III
Waring, R. H. and Schlesinger, W. H. Forest ecosystems.
  1985
  BioScience 37:222 Mr '87. B. C. Bennett
Warner, J. H. The therapeutic perspective. 1986
  Science 235:1521-2 Mr 20 '87. M. S. Pernick
Warner, S. The wide, wide world. 1987
  Orig. pub.: N.Y.: Putnam, 1850
  N Y Times Book Rev 92:16 My 10 '87. S. Mitchell
Warner, W. E. The woman evangelist. 1986
  Christ Today 31:60 My 15 '87. G. Wacker
Warnock, M. A question of life. 1985
  BioScience 37:519-20 Jl/Ag '87. S. C. Poland and G.
  D. Hodgen
Warship; v9. 1985
  Sea Front 33:235-6 My/Je '87. D. S. Schwartz
Washburn, P. S. A question of sedition. 1986
  Progressive 51:43-4 My '87. G. Robinson
Watching television. 1987
  N Y Times Book Rev 92:7 F 8 '87. B. Staples
  Psychol Today 21:64-5 S '87. P. Hersch
Watkin, D. A history of Western architecture. 1986
  Art Am 75:13+ Mr '87. J. Merkel
Watkins, P. Story of the W and Z. 1986
  Phys Today 40 pt1:72 Ag '87. A. Firestone
Watson, L. The dreams of dragons. 1987
  N Y Times Book Rev 92:28 My 10 '87. R. Lewis
Watson-Jones, V. Contemporary American women
  sculptors. 1986
  Am Artist 51:91 D '87. V. R. Rivers
Wattenberg, B. J. The birth dearth. 1987
  Fortune 116:113+ Jl 6 '87. F. S. Chapman
  N Y Times Book Rev 92:9 Jl 12 '87. T. Jacoby
  Natl Rev 39:58-60 O 9 '87. W. Lutton
Wayne, R. P. Chemistry of atmospheres. 1984
  Phys Today 40:77-8 Ja '87. R. J. Cicerone
Weaponry in space. 1987
  Bull At Sci 43:54-5 S '87. J. Boutwell
Weapons in space. 1986
  N Y Rev Books 34:35-41 Ap 9 '87. Sir S. Zuckerman
**Webb Society deep-sky observer's handbook; v6-7,
  Anonymous galaxies; The southern sky.**
  Sky Telesc 74:375-6 O '87. R. O. Evans

Weber, N. F. Leland Bell. 1986
　Am Artist 51:89-91 D '87. F. Johnson
Wedel, W. R. Central Plains prehistory. 1986
　Science 236:339-40 Ap 17 '87. R. A. Krause
Weedman, D. W. Quasar astronomy. 1986
　Sky Telesc 74:151-2 Ag '87. H. J. Smith
Weesner, T. The true detective. 1986
　N Y Times Book Rev 92:20 Ap 26 '87. J. Coleman
Weigel, G. Tranquillitas ordinis. 1987
　Commentary 84:40-2 S '87. A. R. Muggeridge
　Commonweal 114:530-3 S 25 '87. P. Steinfels
　Commonweal 114:488-92 S 11 '87. P. Steinfels
　N Y Times Book Rev 92:30-1 Ap 26 '87. J. P. Dolan
　Natl Rev 39:46-7 Ag 14 '87. R. Royal
　New Repub 196:30-4 Je 1 '87. A. Sullivan
Weil, S. Formative writings, 1929-1941. 1986
　America 157:139 S 12-19 '87. G. L. Farre
　Commonweal 114:638-9 N 6 '87. E. O. Springsted
　N Y Times Book Rev 92:19 Ag 2 '87. E. Young-Bruehl
　New Leader 70:18-19 Je 29 '87. G. Woodcock
Weintraub, S. Victoria. 1987
　Hist Today 37:61 S '87. T. Fisher
　N Y 20:79-80 Mr 16 '87. R. Koenig
　N Y Rev Books 34:30-1 Ap 23 '87. D. Cannadine
　N Y Times Book Rev 92:16 Mr 22 '87. R. B. Henkle
　Smithsonian 18:222-4 O '87. G. Foty
Weir, B. and Weir, C. Hostage bound, hostage free. 1987
　N Y Times Book Rev 92:18 Je 14 '87. L. Kennedy
Weir, D. The Bhopal syndrome. 1987
　N Y Times Book Rev 92:16 N 29 '87. J. R. Luoma
Weiss, T. R. From Princeton one autumn afternoon. 1987
　New Leader 70:13-14 D 14 '87. P. Pettingell
Weissmann, G. They all laughed at Christopher Columbus. 1987
　N Y Times Book Rev 92:39 Ap 5 '87. M. W. Lear
　Smithsonian 18:194+ D '87. C. Eron
Weitzenhoffer, F. The Havemeyers. 1986
　Art News 86:77-8 Ap '87. A. Berman
　New Repub 196:39-41 Je 15 '87. E. V. Thaw
Weitzman, L. J. The divorce revolution. 1985
　Society 24:93-4 Jl/Ag '87. J. Blake
Weldon, F. The Shrapnel Academy. 1987
　Ms 15:34-5 Ap '87. A. Blue
　N Y Times Book Rev 92:14 Ap 26 '87. C. Sigal
　Vogue 177:208+ Ap '87. J. Forrest
Wellek, R. A history of modern criticism: 1750-1950; v5-6, English criticism, 1900-1950; American criticism, 1900-1950. 1986
　Am Sch 56:286+ Spr '87. E. R. Marks
Wellershoff, D. Winner takes all. 1986
　N Y Times Book Rev 92:20 Ja 4 '87. J. Brooks
Wells-Gosling, N. Flying squirrels. 1985
　Conservationist 41:50 Mr/Ap '87. G. Cook
Welty. 1988
　N Y Times Book Rev 92:63 O 11 '87. C. Cook
Wenk, E., Jr. Tradeoffs. 1986
　Technol Rev 90:73-4 N/D '87. D. Grossman
Wensberg, P. C. Land's Polaroid. 1987
　Bus Week p16-17+ O 12 '87. K. H. Hammonds
Werner, H. and Schmeidler, F. Synopsis of the nomenclature of the fixed stars. 1986
　Sky Telesc 73:391-3 Ap '87. G. Lovi
West, P. C. Introduction to supersymmetry and supergravity. 1986
　Phys Today 40:92 N '87. S. J. Gates
West, Dame R. Sunflower. 1987
　N Y Times Book Rev 92:26 F 15 '87. T. Mallon
　Nation 244:438-41 Ap 4 '87. J. Marcus
West, T. Horace Plunkett. 1986
　Hist Today 37:55 Mr '87. C. Townshend
Wharton, W. Tidings. 1987
　N Y Times Book Rev 92:18 D 6 '87. S. Kenney
What a morning! 1987
　N Y Times Book Rev 92:80-1 D 6 '87. R. L. Bray
What is feminism? 1986
　Nation 244:149-50 F 7 '87. C. R. Stimpson
Wheat, E. H. Jacob Lawrence, American painter. 1986
　Am Artist 51:28+ S '87. F. Johnson
Wheatcroft, L. The courtship narrative of Leonard Wheatcroft. 1986
　Hist Today 37:51+ D '87. M. Chaytor
Whipple, A. B. C. The Challenge. 1987
　N Y Times Book Rev 92:6 Jl 26 '87. T. Gibbs
Whitaker, E. M. Eileen Monaghan Whitaker paints San Diego. 1986
　Am Artist 51:18 Jl '87. D. C. Hines
White, F. The overview effect. 1987
　Space World X-12-288:35 D '87. K. McMains
White, M. I. The Japanese educational challenge. 1987
　N Y Times Book Rev 92:12 F 22 '87. E. B. Fiske
　Psychol Today 21:80 Jl '87. P. Chance

Wash Mon 19:49-52 My '87. J. Rowe
White, R. Dark caves, bright visions. 1986
　Sci Am 256:26-7 Mr '87. P. Morrison
White, V. Vanna speaks. 1987
　New Repub 196:40-1 My 18 '87. M. Howard
Whitehead, J. W. The freedom of religious expression in the public high schools. 1983
　Natl Rev 39:56 Ap 10 '87. C. Williamson
Whitlock, B. W. Educational myths I have known and loved. 1986
　Phi Delta Kappan 68:478 F '87. M. K. Pollok
Whitlock, S. L. Donovan scares the monsters. 1987
　N Y Times Book Rev 92:48 O 4 '87. A. Fels
Whitmer, P. O. and VanWyngarden, B. Aquarius revisited. 1987
　Nation 245:276-8 S 19 '87. S. Klawans
Whittemore, E. Jericho mosaic. 1987
　N Y Times Book Rev 92:18 Mr 29 '87. R. S. Elegant
Whittington, H. B. The Burgess Shale. 1985
　Science 235:94 Ja 2 '87. M. E. Taylor
Whittock, M. The origins of England, 410-600. 1987
　Hist Today 37:60-1 Jl '87. S. Keynes
Wicomb, Z. You can't get lost in Cape Town. 1987
　N Y Times Book Rev 92:7-8 My 24 '87. B. Mukherjee
Wideman, J. E. Reuben. 1987
　N Y Times Book Rev 92:3 N 8 '87. W. Kendrick
Wiersbe, W. W. Real worship. 1986
　Christ Today 31:37-8 F 20 '87. C. Miller
Wiggins, M. Herself in love, and other stories. 1987
　N Y Times Book Rev 92:32 O 18 '87. J. Penner
Wigoder, D. Images of destruction. 1987
　N Y Times Book Rev 92:9 N 1 '87. A. A. Stone
　Psychol Today 21:74-5 D '87. C. Simon
Wilcox, J. Miss Undine's living room. 1987
　N Y Times Book Rev 92:53 O 18 '87. R. Daniell
Wilde, O. More letters of Oscar Wilde. 1985
　Commonweal 114:20-1 Ja 16 '87. W. Dunlea
Wilke, R. B. And are we yet alive? 1986
　Christ Century 104:62-3 Ja 21 '87. J. A. Patterson
Will, C. M. Was Einstein right? 1986
　Phys Today 40:93-4 My '87. B. F. Schutz
　Sci Am 256:29-32 Mr '87. P. Morrison
　Sky Telesc 73:501+ My '87. B. F. Schutz
Will, G. F. The new season. 1987
　Natl Rev 39:41-2 D 31 '87. T. Teachout
　New Leader 70:21-2 D 14 '87. R. Lekachman
　New Repub 197:39-41 D 21 '87. W. Schneider
　Wash Mon 19:53-7 O '87. S. Blumenthal
Willard, N. The mountains of Quilt. 1987
　N Y Times Book Rev 92:50 N 8 '87. P. MacLachlan
Willard, N. The voyage of the Ludgate Hill. 1986
　N Y Times Book Rev 92:31 Jl 12 '87. A. Yorinks
Williams, C. K. Flesh and blood. 1987
　N Y Times Book Rev 92:20 Ag 23 '87. E. Hirsch
　Nation 244:734-6 My 30 '87. D. Bogen
Williams, R. C. Klaus Fuchs, atom spy. 1987
　N Y Rev Books 34:54-60 N 19 '87. S. E. Toulmin
　N Y Times Book Rev 92:9+ D 13 '87. Z. S. Steiner
　Science 238:831 N 6 '87. R. Bothwell
Williams, R. C. The other Bolsheviks. 1986
　Hist Today 37:58-9 O '87. W. V. Wallace
Williams, T. I. The history of invention. 1987
　Sci Am 257:151-2 D '87. P. Morrison and P. Morrison
Williams, W. C. The collected poems of William Carlos Williams; v1, 1909-1939. 1986
　N Y Times Book Rev 92:3+ Ja 4 '87. R. Pinsky
　New Repub 196:34-9 Ap 20 '87. D. Davie
Williams, W. L. The spirit and the flesh. 1986
　N Y Times Book Rev 92:10 Mr 29 '87. E. Gregersen
　Nation 244:123-4 Ja 31 '87. G. De Stefano
　Psychol Today 21:74-5 Ap '87. B. L. Benderly
Williamson, C. Desert light. 1987
　Natl Rev 39:61-2 O 9 '87. M. E. Bradford
Willis, J. The monster bed. 1987
　N Y Times Book Rev 92:48 O 4 '87. A. Fels
Wills, G. Reagan's America. 1987
　Atlantic 259:90-2 Mr '87. J. Beatty
　Bus Week p16 F 16 '87. S. H. Wildstrom
　Commentary 83:64+ My '87. S. Garment
　Commonweal 114:681-2+ N 20 '87. W. V. Shannon
　Macleans 100:68 Mr 23 '87. T. S. Axworthy
　N Y Rev Books 34:3-4+ My 28 '87. S. Hoffmann
　N Y Times Book Rev 92:1+ Ja 11 '87. C. V. Woodward
　Nation 244:52-4 Ja 17 '87. R. Lekachman
　Natl Rev 39:47-8 F 27 '87. J. Sobran
　Time 129:76 Ja 26 '87. S. Kanfer
　Vogue 177:244 F '87. C. Hitchens
　Wash Mon 19:56 Ap '87. N. Lemann
Wilson, A. N. Love unknown. 1987
　N Y Times Book Rev 92:14 Je 14 '87. W. Schott
Wilson, E. The fifties. 1986

America 156:468-70 Je 6 '87. R. E. Long
New Yorker 62:83-5 Ja 5 '87. V. S. Pritchett
Progressive 51:45-6 F '87. W. McCann
USA Today (Periodical) 115:93-4 Mr '87. F. Kernowski
Wilson, G. Eddy Deco's last caper. 1987
  N Y Times Book Rev 92:9 D 20 '87. B. Coleman
Wilson, G. C. Supercarrier. 1986
  Oceans 20:60-1 My/Je '87. M. Leffler
Wilson, I. The mysterious shroud. 1986
  Natl Rev 39:66 Ja 30 '87. J. Hart
Wilson, J. Q. and Herrnstein, R. J. Crime and human nature. 1985
  N Y Rev Books 34:33-41 F 12 '87. C. Jencks
  Society 24:92-3 My/Je '87. D. C. Gibbons
Wilson, R. The red truck. 1987
  N Y Times Book Rev 92:62 S 13 '87. J. L. Sensibal
Wilson, W. J. The truly disadvantaged. 1987
  N Y Times Book Rev 92:1+ O 25 '87. R. Greenstein
  New Leader 70:19-20 O 19 '87. S. Kelman
Wilton, A. Turner in his time. 1987
  New Repub 197:47-9 O 12 '87. E. V. Thaw
Wimber, J. Power healing. 1987
  Christ Today 31:55 S 18 '87. T. Stafford
Winchester, S. The sun never sets. 1985
  Smithsonian 18:156+ Ap '87. D. Lancashire
Windsor, W. W., Duchess of and Windsor, E., Duke of. Wallis and Edward. 1986
  New Leader 69:16-17 D 1-15 '86. R. Alan
Wine, women, & death. 1986
  Commentary 83:68+ My '87. R. Alter
Wines, R. A. Fertilizer in America. 1985
  Sci Am 256:22-3 Ja '87. P. Morrison
Winfree, A. T. When time breaks down. 1986
  Science 237:1360 S 11 '87. S. Kauffman
Winks, R. W. Cloak & gown. 1987
  N Y Times Book Rev 92:7+ Ag 16 '87. G. Hodgson
  Nation 245:204-6 S 5 '87. J. Wiener
  New Leader 70:19 N 30 '87. J. P. Roche
Winn, J. A. John Dryden and his world. 1987
  Atlantic 260:116+ N '87. A. Burgess
  New Repub 197:32-6 D 28 '87. L. Lipking
Winner, L. The whale and the reactor. 1986
  Bull At Sci 43:57-8 Mr '87. M. O'Connell
Winnicott, D. W. Holding and interpretation. 1986
  N Y Times Book Rev 92:3+ My 24 '87. O. W. Sacks
Winnicott, D. W. Home is where we start from. 1986
  Psychol Today 21:78-9 Ap '87. S. Pollak
Winnicott, D. W. The spontaneous gesture. 1987
  N Y Times Book Rev 92:3+ My 24 '87. O. W. Sacks
Winquist, C. E. Epiphanies of darkness. 1986
  Christ Century 104:475 My 13 '87. G. N. Boyd
Winston, B. Misunderstanding media. 1986
  Science 235:490-1 Ja 23 '87. G. Wise
Winston, M. L. The biology of the honey bee. 1987
  Science 238:1591-2 D 11 '87. J. B. Free
Winternitz, H. East along the equator. 1987
  N Y Times Book Rev 92:30 S 20 '87. G. Overholser
Winthrop, E. Maggie and the monster. 1987
  N Y Times Book Rev 92:48 O 4 '87. A. Fels
The Wisdom of the saints. 1987
  Christ Century 104:447 My 6 '87. E. G. Hinson
Wit, B. de and Smith, J. Field theory in particle physics. v1 1986
  Phys Today 40:96+ D '87. P. H. Frampton
Witzenburg, G. Fiero. 1986
  Mot Trend 39:34 My '87. T. C. Browne
Wolfe, T. The bonfire of the vanities. 1987
  Atlantic 260:104+ D '87. N. Lemann
  Bus Week p18-19 N 23 '87. A. Bianco
  N Y 20:96+ N 2 '87. R. Koenig
  N Y Times Book Rev 92:1+ N 1 '87. F. Conroy
  Nation 245:636-40+ N 28 '87. J. Leonard
  Natl Rev 39:46+ D 18 '87. R. Vigilante
  New Repub 197:42+ N 23 '87. F. Rich
  Newsweek 110:84-5 O 26 '87. D. Lehman
  Time 130:101+ N 9 '87. R. Z. Sheppard
Wolfe, T. The complete short stories of Thomas Wolfe. 1987
  N Y Rev Books 34:34-7 S 24 '87. M. K. Spears
Wolff, C. G. Emily Dickinson. 1986
  N Y Rev Books 34:46-9 Mr 26 '87. C. E. G. Benfey
  Nation 244:117-20 Ja 31 '87. C. C. Park
  Natl Rev 39:51-2 Jl 17 '87. T. P. McDonnell
  New Leader 69:14-15 D 1-15 '86. P. Pettingell
  New Repub 196:40-1 Mr 2 '87. M. J. Salter
Wollheim, R. Painting as an art. 1987
  New Leader 70:16-17 D 28 '87. D. Carrier
Wolterstorff, N. Lament for a son. 1987
  Christ Century 104:607 Jl 1-8 '87. M. E. Marty
  Christ Today 31:60-1 D 11 '87. P. W. Nisly
Womack, J. Ambient. 1987

  N Y Times Book Rev 92:49 S 27 '87. S. Dobyns
  New Repub 197:41-2 Ag 3 '87. D. Max
Women in science. 1984
  BioScience 37:515-16 Jl/Ag '87. A. P. Woodhull-McNeal
Women of mathematics. 1987
  Science 238:1153-4 N 20 '87. R. E. Rider
Women, state and revolution. 1987
  Hist Today 37:59 Ag '87. J. F. McMillan
Women's ways of knowing. 1986
  Commonweal 114:423-4 Jl 17 '87. J.-A. Mort
Wongar, B. Gabo Djara. 1987
  N Y Times Book Rev 92:27 S 6 '87. M. Gorra
Woocher, J. S. Sacred survival. 1986
  Christ Century 104:832-3 S 30 '87. I. Nerken
  Commentary 84:74-6 D '87. J. D. Sarna
Wood, A. Heckedy Peg. 1987
  N Y Times Book Rev 92:50 N 8 '87. P. MacLachlan
Wood, F. J. Tidal dynamics. 1986
  Sea Front 33:393-4 S/O '87. H. B. Stewart
Wood, G. The myth of neurosis. 1986
  Christ Today 31:68 Mr 20 '87. H. N. Malony
Woodress, J. L. Willa Cather. 1987
  N Y Times Book Rev 92:44 O 11 '87. D. S. Reynolds
Woodward, B. Veil. 1987
  Bus Week p12-14 O 19 '87. E. Clark
  Commentary 84:65-6+ D '87. M. Ledeen
  Commonweal 114:752-6 D 18 '87. J. B. Judis
  N Y Rev Books 34:8-11 N 19 '87. T. Powers
  N Y Times Book Rev 92:1+ O 18 '87. D. C. Martin
  Nation 245:562-4 N 14 '87. J. Morley
  Natl Rev 39:48+ D 4 '87. V. Gold
  Progressive 51:30-1 D '87. S. Landau
  Wash Mon 19:56-8 D '87. G. Easterbrook
Woolf, V. The essays of Virginia Woolf; v1, 1904-1912. 1987
  New Yorker 63:100-3 Ap 13 '87. W. Maxwell
Work, health, and income among the elderly. 1987
  Wash Mon 19:58-9 My '87. M. Cooper
A World unsuspected. 1987
  N Y Times Book Rev 92:41 O 11 '87. W. Percy
Worth, P. W. and Cartwright, J. John McCormack. 1986
  Opera News 51:45 Ja 3 '87. C. J. Luten
Worthy, J. C. William C. Norris. 1987
  Bus Week p10-12 Ag 3 '87. P. Houston
Wresch, W. A practical guide to computer uses in the English/language arts classroom. 1987
  Byte 12:70+ F '87. K. S. Wittman
Wright, F. L. Frank Lloyd Wright letters trilogy. 3v
  N Y Times Book Rev 92:3+ F 15 '87. A. L. Huxtable
Wright, H. James Lick's monument. 1987
  Science 236:986-7 My 22 '87. M. Rothenberg
  Sky Telesc 74:373-4 O '87. A. A. Hoag
Wright, P. Spycatcher. 1987
  N Y Rev Books 34:47-53 S 24 '87. N. G. A. Annan, Baron
  N Y Times Book Rev 92:13 Ag 16 '87. C. M. Andrew
  New Leader 70:20-1 O 19 '87. J. P. Roche
  Time 130:51 Ag 10 '87. P. Gray
Wright, S. American racer, 1940-1980. 1986
  Cycle 38:9 My '87. P. Schilling
Wright, W. Lillian Hellman. 1986
  Natl Rev 39:46-7 Ap 10 '87. D. Evanier
  New Repub 196:39-41 Mr 30 '87. E. Breindel
  USA Today (Periodical) 115:96 My '87. M. Smelstor
Writers at work. 1986
  Smithsonian 17:141-2 F '87. W. Claire
Wyclif in his times. 1986
  Hist Today 37:56 F '87. C. N. L. Brooke
Wyden, P. The unknown Iacocca. 1987
  Bus Week p20-1+ N 16 '87. W. J. Hampton
  Fortune 116:188+ N 9 '87. J. Nocera

Y

Yamamoto, A. Organotransition metal chemistry. 1986
  Science 235:1410-11 Mr 13 '87. J. Schwartz
Yaniv, A. Dilemmas of security. 1987
  N Y Times Book Rev 92:40 O 4 '87. M. Widlanski
Yarborough, C. Cale. 1986
  Car Driv 33:36 N '87. T. Swan
Yardley, M. T.E. Lawrence. 1987
  Natl Rev 39:47-9 D 31 '87. A. Bakshian
Yarmolinsky, J. V. Angels without wings. 1987
  N Y Times Book Rev 92:14 O 25 '87. G. Wolff
The Year left 2. 1987
  Nation 244:739-40 My 30 '87. A. Kopkind
Yeats, W. B. The collected letters of W.B. Yeats; v1, 1865-1895. 1986
  New Yorker 63:96+ Mr 16 '87. H. H. Vendler
Yevtushenko, Y. A. Almost at the end. 1987
  N Y Times Book Rev 92:12 Je 28 '87. M. Carlson

Time 129:65 My 25 '87. R. Z. Sheppard
Yglesias, H. The saviors. 1987
    N Y Times Book Rev 92:14-15 Ag 16 '87. T. Talbot
    Vogue 177:194+ Ag '87. F. Prose
Yglesias, J. Home again. 1987
    N Y Times Book Rev 92:28 N 1 '87. C. Reynolds
Yorinks, A. Hey, Al. 1986
    N Y Times Book Rev 92:38 Ja 11 '87. J. Viorst
York, H. F. Making weapons, talking peace. 1987
    Science 238:1446 D 4 '87. C. Kaysen
Yost, G. Spy-tech. 1985
    Space World X-7-283:8 Jl '87. J. Rhea
Young, A. R. Tudor and Jacobean tournaments. 1987
    Hist Today 37:59-61 S '87. C. T. Allmand
Young, S. D. The rule of experts. 1987
    Wash Mon 19:59 Jl/Ag '87. J. K. Lieberman
Younger, G. D. From new creation to urban crisis. 1987
    Christ Century 104:726+ Ag 26-S 2 '87. C. E. Kramer
Your future in space. 1986
    Sky Telesc 74:153-4 Ag '87. C. C. Petersen
Yourcenar, M. Two lives and a dream. 1987
    N Y Times Book Rev 92:18 Ap 19 '87. J. Sturrock
Yourgrau, B. Wearing dad's head. 1987
    N Y Times Book Rev 92:7 N 8 '87. K. Acker
Yule, Sir H. and Burnell, A. C. Hobson-Jobson.
    N Y Rev Books 34:44-5 N 19 '87. J. Suraiya

Z

Zaleski, C. Otherworld journeys. 1987
    Atlantic 260:96-7 Jl '87. N. Lemann
    N Y Times Book Rev 92:3+ Je 14 '87. R. A. Shweder
Zallen, R. The physics of amorphous solids. 1983
    Phys Today 40 pt1:69-70 Ag '87. K. Moorjani
Zee, A. Fearful symmetry. 1986
    N Y Times Book Rev 92:18 F 8 '87. R. N. Kahn
Zeitlin, I. M. Ancient Judaism. 1984
    Society 24:91-3 Mr/Ap '87. G. Shafir
Zeman, Z. Heckling Hitler. 2nd ed. 1987
    N Y Times Book Rev 92:60 O 11 '87. E. Sorel
Zhang, X. and Sang, Y. Chinese lives. 1987
    N Y Times Book Rev 92:7 O 18 '87. J. Shapiro
Zhang Jie. Love must not be forgotten. 1986
    N Y Times Book Rev 92:36 Ja 18 '87. L. O.-F. Lee
Ziefert, H. I won't go to bed! 1987
    N Y Times Book Rev 92:36 N 15 '87. A. Banks
Zimmermann, M. Wilhelm Marr. 1986
    Commentary 83:71-4 Ap '87. R. S. Levy
Ziomek, L. J. Underwater acoustics. 1985
    Phys Today 40:91-2 D '87. S. Chamberlain
Zuccotti, S. The Italians and the Holocaust. 1987
    Atlantic 260:93-6 Jl '87. A. Stille
    N Y Times Book Rev 92:22+ Ap 12 '87. R. Trevelyan
    New Leader 70:16-17 Jl 1-15 '87. S. F. Senigallia
Zug, C. G. Turners & burners. 1986
    Am Craft 47:22-3 O/N '87. R. Barnard
Zumwalt, E. R. and Zumwalt, E., III. My father, my son. 1986
    U S Cathol 52:48-51 F '87. G. M. Costello

SEP 27 '88

SEP 27 '88 T